D1796692

THE DICTIONARY OF CLASSICAL HEBREW

Volume V

נ—מ

The Dictionary of Classical Hebrew

David J.A. Clines
Editor

Philip R. Davies   J. Cheryl Exum   John W. Rogerson
Consulting Editors

Volume V

מ—נ

David Stec,
with
John Elwolde, Siam Bhayro
Research Associates

Published under the auspices of
The Society for Old Testament Study

The Dictionary of Classical Hebrew

David J.A. Clines
Editor

Volume V

נ—מ

Sheffield
Sheffield Academic Press

2001

Published by
Sheffield Academic Press Ltd.
Mansion House
19 Kingfield Road
Sheffield S11 9AS
England
www.SheffieldAcademicPress.com

Printed on acid-free paper in Great Britain by
Bookcraft Ltd, Midsomer Norton, Bath.

British Library Cataloguing-in-Publication Data

Dictionary of Classical Hebrew. – Vol. 5: Mem–Nun
I. Clines, David J.A.
492.43

ISBN 1 84127 217 5

CONTENTS

Preface 7

Introduction 11

The Sources 14

Words Beginning with Mem and Nun in Order of Frequency 32

Abbreviations and Signs 93

מ Mem 96

נ Nun 576

Bibliography 820

English–Hebrew Index 923

PREFACE

In the period since the previous volume of the Dictionary was published, in August 1998, the project to produce the Dictionary has faced serious difficulties, which have now been happily resolved. The publishers of the Dictionary, Sheffield Academic Press, who had supported the research for the Dictionary most generously, were unable to continue that support, and for a time the future of the Dictionary was in question. However, applications for funding from the newly constituted Arts and Humanities Research Board proved successful, and grants amounting to almost £200,000 were awarded to meet the cost of two Research Associates to prepare the present volume. In 2000, we learned of a further grant from the AHRB, of over £500,000, which will ensure the support of the Dictionary until its completion, now envisaged by the end of the year 2005. The rights to the Dictionary have been acquired by a new company, The Dictionary of Classical Hebrew Ltd, which holds the copyright to the work, while Sheffield Academic Press remains the publisher and distributor.

The last three years have also seen important changes in the staffing of the Dictionary: John Elwolde, who had been one of the Dictionary team since its inception in 1988 and had served as Executive Editor from 1993 to 1998, left for another post. The term of Frank Gosling, who joined the project as Research Associate in June 1994, came to an end in July 1998, and we thank both for the important contributions they made to the Dictionary. Fortunately, David Stec, who has been with the project since 1992, remains as its mainstay, and Siam Bhayro joined us in November 2000. With these two researchers in place, and our funding assured to the completion of the project with Volume 8, we have nothing to distract us from the main business of delivering the remaining volumes in timely fashion.

In the Preface to Volume 4, I gave a sketch of the method of working we employ in the composition of the articles of the Dictionary. In this Preface,

I will present an outline of the way in which the Bibliography has been compiled.

The Bibliography to Mem and Nun (containing over 3500 items) has been created, as a full-time task occupying the Editor for the first six months of 2001, from a number of sources such as the *Elenchus Bibliographicus Biblicus*, the 'Bibliographische Dokumentation' in *Zeitschrift für Althebraistik*, and the *Hebräisches und aramäisches Lexikon zum Alten Testament* of Ludwig Koehler and Walter Baumgartner (*HALAT*) and its translation into English by M.E.J. Richardson (*HALOT*), as well as a personal perusal of all the works of G.R. Driver and Mitchell Dahood (insofar as they were accessible to me). The bibliography has been weighted toward more recent works, and on the whole has not included literature that does not propound a new view but merely supports the view of another scholar.

Once the Bibliography had been compiled from its sources, I created what I called my Library Search Database and uploaded into it the bibliographical data for all the references I had not already read in my study and would need to visit a library to read. For each item in a journal, I had three fields: (1) Hebrew word, (2) journal name, volume and year, (3) author, article title, with journal and page references. From the database I could then print out a list of all the items arranged by journal and volume number, so that in the library I could easily pull from the shelves all the volumes I needed of *Biblische Zeitschrift* or *Vetus Testamentum* or whatever, load them on my library trolley, and take them to my desk to look up each item in turn. The checklist told me exactly which items I needed to consult, what the page reference was, and what the Hebrew word was I was looking for on that page—as well as distinguishing items already checked from those that were yet to be checked.

Once I had a given article open before me, my first task was to check the author's name (I believe in citing authors by the name they use of themselves), the title of the article (more than half the items I had derived from my bibliographical sources either did not mention the title or else quoted it incorrectly) and the reference, with correct page numbers for the entire article and specific page numbers in brackets where appropriate (another fertile source of errors). My second task was to read as much of the article as I needed in order to discover the author's view, usually the proposal of a new sense for an already known word or of a new word altogether, or of an emendation that we would not otherwise have known about. I would then check the proof of our own article on the word in question to see how we were handling it, and, in the light both of the journal article and of our own Dictionary article, I would write a note of a few lines in my Additions file for my Dictionary associates, spelling out the changes that would be necessary. The Research Associates were in the best position to make changes to the articles they themselves had drafted, taking care of insertions and corrections and formatting and cross-referencing.

For books and articles in books such as Festschriften, the procedure was slightly different. For these, my file for uploading to the database had just two fields for each item: (1) Hebrew word and (2) all the rest of the bibliographical information. Once the data were loaded, it was time to find out where I could read the books I had in the Bibliography. Quite recently, the electronic union catalogue known as COPAC has reached the zenith of its development, and I could now access from my home computer the catalogues of the twenty members of the Consortium of University Research Libraries (CURL), the largest university libraries in the United Kingdom. I needed to enter on the search screen no more, usually, than the author's surname and one word of the book title to find which British libraries held it, what its shelfmark was in each library, and whether it was at that moment in the library or out. In the database, I entered the shelfmark (classmark) of every title I needed in Sheffield, or, failing that, in Manchester, or failing that, in Leeds, or, failing that, in Cambridge. I was also able to fill out all the bibliographical details and make the Bibliography for this volume reasonably complete before visiting a library and checking the book itself. In my printout of books to be checked, the database arranged the items by library and by shelfmark, so that I knew which books I would need to see in which of my library visits, and was able to move around the various libraries in a sedate and efficient manner. Once I actually had the book in my hands, I worked just as I did with the articles. Not surprisingly, working though the literature uncovered new items that needed to be examined; by entering them then and there into the database, they appeared in my checklist at the right place.

Preparing a bibliography, and ensuring it is correct, may seem a mechanical task; my experience for this Dictionary has been that the mechanical aspects are the least of it, and that the better part of the work has been a rewarding, even exciting, intellectual task. The result is, I believe, an unrivalled resource, an index (necessarily far from exhaustive) of scholarly work on Hebrew words during the twentieth century. (More about the principles of the Bibliography may be found in the Introduction to this volume.)

This is the moment to express my appreciation to Milton Eng, Victor Avigdor Hurowitz and Gary Rendsburg, who contributed information for the Bibliography. A note of thanks is in order here also to the firm of Linguists' Software, and especially to its founder and guide, Philip Payne, for creating type faces for biblical scholars working on the Macintosh, enabling them to reproduce every feature of the Masoretic text and type all the diacritics for the Semitic languages in transliteration. We have continued to prepare the Dictionary in Microsoft Word 5.1, having found later versions of the programme too unstable and unreliable.

I should finally mention how the work of preparing this Volume has been divided up. David Stec was responsible for writing the greater part of it, as well as for preparing the revisions to the List of Sources. John Elwolde wrote the drafts of certain words beginning Mem Aleph and of most words beginning Mem Yod, Mem Samek, Mem Ayin, Mem Sin and Mem Shin (to מִשְׁעֶנֶת *support*), as well as the article מָה *what*, while Siam Bhayro drafted the remainder of the words beginning Mem Shin and the article מֹשֶׁה *Moses*. Everything else was written by David Stec. Togther, David Stec and Siam Bhayro wrote articles for all the 'new' words and amended the original drafts in accordance with the data of the Bibliography. Rosemarie Kossov contributed the entries from *TDOT* and *TLOT* to the Bibliography, and prepared the English–Hebrew Index. David Clines edited and proofread the entire volume in its three sets of proofs, and prepared the Bibliography.

DJAC
Sheffield
June 30, 2001

Introduction

The principles and procedures followed in the previous volumes of the Dictionary have been continued here without any substantive changes; in only one respect has there been a revision of earlier practice, as noted below.

1. *'New' Words and Bibliography*

In all the volumes of the Dictionary, 'new' words have been included that have been recognized or proposed (rightly or wrongly) in the scholarly literature of recent decades. Such words, which we have previously defined as not having entered the mainstream of the lexicographic tradition, have been prefixed by an asterisk referring to a supportive entry in the Bibliography (though not in Volume 1).

From this volume onward, we are adopting a closer definition of a 'new' word: it is, simply, a word that did not appear in the Brown–Driver–Briggs lexicon of 1907. The asterisk before an entry is now applied to all words, including proper names, that are not to be found in that lexicon, whether the word occurs first in Ben Sirach or in the Dead Sea Scrolls or in Hebrew inscriptions, or whether the word has been identified or suggested by a scholar since that date. Some of these words have of course found their way into Koehler's *Lexicon* or the Koehler and Baumgartner *Hebräisches und aramäisches Lexikon zum Alten Testament* (Leiden: E.J. Brill, 1967–94), translated as *The Hebrew and Aramaic Lexicon of the Old Testament*, or into the *Lexicon Hebraicum* of Franz Zorell. In such cases, the Bibliography notes the fact. In the majority of cases, however, this Dictionary is the first to cite such 'new' words. In principle, each asterisk refers to an item in the Bibliography; in a number of cases, however, with words occurring first in Ben Sira or in Qumran texts, no substantive discussion of the word in the scholarly literature has been identified, and the asterisk simply records that the word is 'new', without any corresponding entry in the Bibliography.

Readers may be interested to know that in this Volume, devoted to words beginning with Mem or Nun, some 720 words are registered as 'new' words not occurring in BDB; this figure may be compared with the c. 1400 words recognized by that lexicon. The meaning of many of these 'new' words is inferred from our existing knowledge of the Hebrew language, as when, for example, a noun occurring for the first time in a Qumran manuscript can be easily identified as a formation from a well-known Hebrew verb. The meaning, and indeed the very existence, of many others depend upon an association with a word in another Semitic language. In almost all cases, key evidence for the existence of a 'new' word is noted, in the format מִסְעָד II *step* (cf. Arab. ṣa'ida *go up*) or מִנְהָרָה II *signal station* (cf. נהר II *shine*); the meaning of the word compared is not however stated if it is the same as that of the Hebrew lemma. The citation of cognates in other languages is not intended to be exhaustive, and such citation does not indicate that we agree that the comparison with the apparently cognate word is valid (or even that we accept the genuine existence of the word in question in the other language). The notation merely indicates the ground that the scholar cited has put forward in support of the proposal.

It should be stressed that the inclusion of a word in this Dictionary does not carry with it any assurance that its existence is established. Many of the proposals are in fact mutually exclusive. Nevertheless, we have come to the view that it is the proper business of a dictionary of the classical Hebrew language at this juncture to record, as far as is feasible, the very many proposals that have been made in the twentieth century for the refinement and expansion of our knowledge of the Hebrew vocabulary.

The system of arrangement in the Bibliography is as follows. Within each of its paragraphs, items are usually arranged by date order; it may be assumed that authors mentioned are in favour of the meaning given, but occasionally an author provides a critique or reviews a proposal without making a decision for or against (in such cases, the entry is usually preceded by 'cf.'). Different senses given to a word each form a separate paragraph and are arranged alphabetically. Phrases in which the word occurs follow senses in which the word itself is used. Bibliography relating to an individual occurrence of the word in question, such as proposals for the emendation of the Masoretic text, come last, and are prefixed by the verse reference. Readers may refer to the Bibliography on נֶפֶשׁ *soul* or נשׂא *lift up* for examples of how the system of notation works.

2. *Exhaustive Treatment*

In this volume every word beginning with Mem or Nun has been treated exhaustively, with only one exception: the preposition *min*, which occurs more than 9000 times in the corpus of Classical Hebrew. For all other words, every place they occur in Classical Hebrew has been cited, and every occurrence has been analysed according to the principles of the Dictionary.

THE SOURCES

a. *Qumran and Related Texts*

The following list and bibliography replaces those of Volume 1, pp. 34-45, 51-54, Volume 2, pp. 15-31, Volume 3, pp. 11-27, and Volume 4, pp. 14-29. The second list of Dead Sea Scrolls published in Volume 1 (pp. 45-51), which correlates the sigla used in the Dictionary with numbers assigned to documents, will be replaced in the final volume of the Dictionary.

For this Volume, we have adopted the text of the Qumran Secular Manuscripts module (ed. Martin Abegg) in the Accordance program as our standard text for certain documents, such as the Temple Scroll (11QT). Such cases are noted in the fourth column of the following list. In the case of the Thanksgiving Hymns (1QH), we have used the edition of Licht for words beginning with Mem, and the Accordance text for words beginning with Nun. Readers should note that these two texts use different systems of numbering.

QUMRAN AND RELATED NON-BIBLICAL TEXTS IN CAVE AND NUMBER ORDER

In this list, which is intended to include all known non-biblical texts in Hebrew, published and unpublished, from Qumran and related sites, there appear, in the five columns, the following:

(1) The number by which the texts are known (in the case of four major Qumran texts from Cave 1 and several minor Cave 4 texts, no number is assigned).

(2) The abbreviated title used in the Dictionary.

(3) Short title or description of the text (titles are capitalized, whereas mere descriptions, such as 'sapiential', are shown in lower case).

(4) A reference to the edition of the text that has been the standard for this Dictionary.

(5) A reference to the page numbers of the translation of the text (or part of it) by F. García Martínez; but occasionally the reference is to another English translation, notably that of

M. Wise, M. Abegg, and E. Cook ([WAC]). For the third column in particular, we have also made use of the latest translation of the Dead Sea Scrolls by G. Vermes.

As far as we can tell, all published texts—that is, texts that have been printed in transcription, with or without translation and technical notes—have been read for the Dictionary and incorporated in it. As further texts are published, information relating to them will be included in updated lists in future volumes of the Dictionary.

No.	Siglum	Name / Description	Edition	Translation
Cave 1				
	1QH	Thanksgiving Hymns (*Hodayot*)	Licht (מ) Accordance 4.1 (נ)	317-61
	1QM	War Scroll (includes 1Q33: two fragments of 1QM, col. 19)	Accordance 4.1	
	1QpHab	Habakkuk *pesher*	Accordance 4.1	
	1QS	Community Rule	Accordance 4.1	
1Q14	1QpMic	Micah *pesher*	DJD, I, 77-80	193-94
1Q15	1QpZeph	Zephaniah *pesher*	DJD, I, 80	202
1Q16	1QpPs	Psalms *pesher*	DJD, I, 81-82	206
1Q17	$1QJub^{a}$	Jubilees	DJD, I, 82-83	245
1Q18	$1QJub^{b}$	Jubilees	DJD, I, 83-84	245
1Q19	1QNoah	Book of Noah	DJD, I, 84-86, 152	263
1Q22	1QDM	Words of Moses/*Dibre Mosheh*	DJD, I, 91-97	276-77
1Q25		prophetic	DJD, I, 100-101	
1Q26		sapiential	DJD, I, 101-102	388[WAC]
1Q27	1QMyst	wisdom text mentioning *razim*	DJD, I, 102-107	399-400
1Q28a	1QSa	Community Rule	Accordance 4.1	
1Q28b	1QSb	Community Rule	Accordance 4.1	
1Q29		Liturgy of the Three Tongues of Fire	DJD, I, 130-32	277-78
1Q30		liturgical	DJD, I, 132-33	438
1Q31		liturgical	DJD, I, 133-34	438
1Q34	1QLitPr	Festival Prayers	DJD, I, 152-55	411
1Q35	$1QH^{b}$	two fragments of 1QH	DJD, I, 136-38	361-62
1Q36		Hymns	DJD, I, 138-41	
1Q37-40		hymnic	DJD, I, 141-43	438
1Q41-50		unidentified	DJD, I, 144-45	
1Q51		Eternal Fragment	DSS, II, 216	
1Q52-62		unidentified	DJD, I, 146-47	
1Q69		unidentified	DJD, I, 148	

Cave 2

2Q19	2QJub[a]	Jubilees	DJD, III, 77-78	244
2Q20	2QJub[b]	Jubilees	DJD, III, 78-79	245
2Q21	2QapMoses	perh. Moses Apocryphon	DJD, III, 79-81	281
2Q22	2QapDavid	perh. David Apocryphon	DJD, III, 81-82	224
2Q23	2QapProph	Apocryphal prophecy	DJD, III, 82-84	
2Q25	2QJuridical	juridical	DSS, II, 218	86
2Q27		unidentified	DJD, III, 91	
2Q28	2QVerdict	Verdict Fragment	DSS, II, 223	
2Q29–33		unidentified	DJD, III, 92-93	

Cave 3

3Q4	3QpIsa	Isaiah *pesher*	DJD, III, 95-96	185
3Q5	3QJub	Jubilees	DJD, III, 96-98	244
3Q6	3QHymn	Hymn	DJD, III, 98	401
3Q7	3QTJud	Testament of Judah	DJD, III, 99	265
3Q8		Angel of Peace	DJD, III, 100	
3Q9		perh. sectarian	DJD, III, 100-101	
3Q10-11		unidentified	DJD, III, 101-102	
3Q15	3QTr	Copper Scroll	DJD, III, 284-302	461-63

Cave 4

4Q88	4QPs[f]	apocryphal compositions	DSS, IVA, 202-211	
4Q158	4QBibPar	Biblical Paraphrase	DJD, V, 1-6	219-22
4Q159	4QOrd[a]	Ordinances	DSS, I, 150-57	86-87
4Q160	4QVisSam	Vision of Samuel	DJD, V, 9-11	284
4Q161	4QpIsa[a]	Isaiah *pesher*	DJD, V, 11-15	185-86
4Q162	4QpIsa[b]	Isaiah *pesher*	DJD, V, 15-17	186-87
4Q163	4QpIsa[c]	Isaiah *pesher*	DJD, V, 17-27	187-90
4Q164	4QpIsa[d]	Isaiah *pesher*	DJD, V, 27-28	190-91
4Q165	4QpIsa[e]	Isaiah *pesher*	DJD, V, 28-30	191
4Q166	4QpHos[a]	Hosea *pesher*	DJD, V, 31-32	191-92
4Q167	4QpHos[b]	Hosea *pesher*	DJD, V, 32-36	192-93
4Q168	4QpMic	Micah *pesher*	DJD, V, 36	194-95
4Q169	4QpNah	Nahum *pesher*	DJD, V, 37-42	195-97
4Q170	4QpZeph	Zephaniah *pesher*	DJD, V, 42	203
4Q171	4QpPs[a]	Psalms *pesher*	DJD, V, 42-50	203-206
4Q172	4QpUnid	unidentified *pesher*	DJD, V, 50-51	
4Q173	4QpPs[b]	Psalms *pesher*	DJD, V, 51-53	206-207
4Q174	4QMidrEschat[a]	eschatological	Steudel, 23-29	136-37
4Q175	4QTestim	Testimonia	DJD, V, 57-60	137-38
4Q176	4QTanḥ	Consolations	DJD, V, 60-67	208-209
4Q176a	4QJub[i]	Jubilees 23 (=4Q176 fr. 19-21)	Kister, *RQ* 12 (1987)	244

4Q177	4QMidrEschat^{b}	eschatological	Steudel, 71-76	209-11
4Q178		unidentified	DJD, V, 74-75	
4Q179	4QapLam^{a}	Lamentation on Jerusalem	DJD, V, 75-77	401-402
4Q180	4QAges^{a}	Ages of Creation/ Wicked and Holy	DSS, II, 206-10	211-12
4Q181	4QAges^{b}	Ages of Creation/ Wicked and Holy	DSS, II, 208-12	212-13
4Q182	4QCat	Catena	DJD, V, 80-81	213
4Q183		historical	DJD, V, 81-82	213
4Q184	4QWiles	Wiles of the Wicked Woman	DJD, V, 82-85	379-80
4Q185		Eulogy on Wisdom	DJD, V, 85-87	380-82
4Q186	4QCrypt	horoscopes	DJD, V, 88-91	456
4Q200	4QTobit^{e}	Tobit	DJD, XIX, 63-76	297-99
4Q215	4QTNaph	Testament of Naphtali	DJD, XXII, 78-81	270-71
4Q215a	4QTime	Time of Righteousness	WA, III, 7-8	271
4Q216	4QJub^{a}	Jubilees 1-2	DJD, XIII, 5-22	238-40
4Q217	4QJub^{b}	Jubilees (perh. 1-2)	DJD, XIII, 24-33	
4Q218	4QJub^{c}	Jubilees 2	DJD, XIII, 37-38	242
4Q219	4QJub^{d}	Jubilees 21-22	DJD, XIII, 42-53	242-43
4Q220	4QJub^{e}	Jubilees 21	DJD, XIII, 57-61	
4Q221	4QJub^{f}	Jubilees 21-23, 33, 37-39	DJD, XIII, 66-85	243-44 (fr. 1)
4Q222	4QJub^{g}	Jubilees 25, 27, 48	DJD, XIII, 89-94	
4Q223-24	4QJub^{h}	Jubilees 32, 34-40	DJD, XIII, 101-40	
4Q225	4QpsJub^{a}	Pseudo-Jubilees / Genesis and Exodus Paraphrase	DJD, XIII, 143-55	262-63^{WAC}
4Q226	4QpsJub^{b}	Pseudo-Jubilees	DJD, XIII, 159-69	263-64^{WAC}
4Q227	4QpsJub^{c}	Pseudo-Jubilees / Enoch and the Watchers	DJD, XIII, 172-75	245 (fr. 2)
4Q228	4QCitJub	Text with a Citation of Jubilees	DJD, XIII, 178-85	
4Q229		pseudepigraphon in Mishnaic Hebrew		
4Q230		Catalogue of Spirits		
4Q231		Catalogue of Spirits		
4Q232		perh. New Jerusalem		
4Q233		place names		
4Q234		exercise on Genesis 27.20-21		
4Q239		*pesher* on the true Israel		
4Q240		perh. commentary on Song of Songs		
4Q241		fragments citing Lamentations		
4Q247	4QApocWeeks	*pesher* on Apocalypse of Weeks	Milik, *Enoch*, 256	
4Q248	4QActs	Acts of a Greek King	WA, III, 33	271^{WAC}
4Q249-50	4QMSM	*Midrash Sepher Mosheh*		
4Q251	4QHalakhah^{a}	halakhic	WA, III, 34-40	272-74^{WAC}
4Q252	4QCommGenA	Commentary on Genesis	DJD, XXII, 193-207	212-15

4Q253	4QCommGenB	Commentary on Genesis	DJD, XXII, 210-12	215
4Q253a	4QCommMal	Commentary on Malachi	DJD, XXII, 214-15	215
4Q254	4QCommGenC	Commentary on Genesis	DJD, XXII, 220-36	215-16
4Q254a	4QCommGenD	Commentary on Genesis	DJD, XXII, 234-36	216
4Q255	4QS^{a}	Community Rule	DJD, XXVI, 27-38	20
4Q256	4QS^{b}	Community Rule	DJD, XXVI, 39-64	21 (fr. 5)
4Q257	4QS^{c}	Community Rule	DJD, XXVI, 65-82	21-22 (fr. 1)
4Q258	4QS^{d}	Community Rule	DJD, XXVI, 83-128	22 (fr. 1.1)
4Q259	4QS^{e}	Community Rule	DJD, XXVI, 129-52	26-27
4Q260	4QS^{f}	Community Rule	DJD, XXVI, 153-67	29-30
4Q261	4QS^{g}	Community Rule	DJD, XXVI, 169-87	30-31
4Q262	4QS^{h}	Community Rule	DJD, XXVI, 189-95	31
4Q263	4QS^{i}	Community Rule	DJD, XXVI, 197-200	31
4Q264	4QS^{j}	Community Rule	DJD, XXVI, 201-206	31-32
4Q265	4QSD	Community Rule and Damascus Document	WA, III, 72-78	279-81^{WAC}
4Q266	4QD^{a}	Damascus Document	DJD, XVIII, 31-93	48-57
4Q267	4QD^{b}	Damascus Document	DJD, XVIII, 96-113	60-62
4Q268	4QD^{c}	Damascus Document	DJD, XVIII, 119-21	47-48
4Q269	4QD^{d}	Damascus Document	DJD, XVIII, 125-36	67-69
4Q270	4QD^{e}	Damascus Document	DJD, XVIII, 141-68	62-67
4Q271	4QD^{f}	Damascus Document	DJD, XVIII, 173-83	57-60
4Q272	4QD^{g}	Damascus Document	DJD, XVIII, 188-91	69-70
4Q273	4QD^{h}	Damascus Document	DJD, XVIII, 194-98	70
4Q274	4QTohA	Purification Rules	WA, III, 79-82	88-89
4Q275	4QTohB^{a}	Purification/Initiation Rules	DJD, XXVI, 209-216	89
4Q276	4QTohB^{b}	Purification Rules	WA, III, 85	89
4Q277	4QTohB^{c}	Purification Rules	WA, III, 86-87	89-90
4Q278	4QTohC	Purification Rules	WA, III, 88	90
4Q279	4QTohD	Purification Rules	DJD, XXVI, 217-223	286^{WAC}
4Q280	4QBer^{f}	Curse on Melchiresha	WA, III, 91	434
4Q281-83		Purification Rules		
4Q284	4QNidd	Menstrual Impurity	WA, III, 92-95	290^{WAC}
4Q284a	4QLeqeṭ	Gleaning	WA, III, 96	90
4Q285	4QM^{g}	perh. War Scroll (fr. 1=11QM)	WA, II, 223-27	292-94^{WAC}
4Q286	4QBer^{a}	Blessings and Curses	DJD, XI, 12-44	434-35
4Q287	4QBer^{b}	Blessings	DJD, XI, 50-60	435-36
4Q288	4QBer^{c}	Blessings and Curses	DJD, XI, 62-65	289^{WAC}
4Q289	4QBer^{d}	Blessings and Curses	DJD, XI, 68-71	289^{WAC}
4Q290	4QBer^{e}	Blessings and Curses	DJD, XI, 73-74	
4Q291	4QPrayers^{a}		WA, III, 115-16	
4Q292	4QPrayers^{b}		WA, III, 117	
4Q293	4QPrayers^{c}		WA, III, 118	

4Q294–97		rules and prayers		
4Q298	4QCryptA	Words of the *Maskil*	DJD, XX, 19-30	382
4Q299	4QMyst[a]	wisdom text mentioning *razim*	DJD, XX, 34-97	400 (fr. 3a2-b)
4Q300	4QMyst[b]	wisdom text mentioning *razim*	DJD, XX, 100-112	400-401
4Q301	4QMyst[c]	perh. related to foregoing	DJD, XX, 114-23	401
4Q302	4QAdmonPar	Admonitory Parable	DJD, XX, 129-49	296[WAC] (fr. 2.2; 3.2)
4Q303	4QCreatA	Meditation on Creation	DJD, XX, 152-53	
4Q304	4QCreatB	Meditation on Creation	DJD, XX, 155	
4Q305	4QCreatC	Meditation on Creation	DJD, XX, 157-58	
4Q306	4QErr	Men of People who Err	WA, III, 122-23	
4Q307		sapiential		
4Q308		sapiential		
4Q311		unidentified		
4Q312		Hebrew text in cursive Phoenician		
4Q313		unidentified, cryptic		
4Q316		unidentified		
4Q317	4QAstrCrypt	Phases of Moon (cryptic)	Milik, *Enoch*, 68-69	302-303[WAC]
4Q319	4QOtot	Heavenly Concordances	WA, I, 96-101	27-29
4Q320	4QMishA	Priestly Calendar	WA, I, 60-67	452-54
4Q321	4QMishB[a]	Priestly Calendar	WA, I, 68-73	454-55
4Q321a	4QMishB[b]	Priestly Calendar	WA, I, 74-76	312[WAC]
4Q322	4QMishC[a]	Priestly Calendar	WA, I, 77-78	314[WAC]
4Q323	4QMishC[b]	Priestly Calendar	WA, I, 79-81	315[WAC]
4Q324	4QMishC[c]	Priestly Calendar	WA, I, 81-82	315[WAC]
4Q324a	4QMishC[d]	Priestly Calendar	WA, I, 82-84	316[WAC]
4Q324b	4QMishC[e]	Priestly Calendar	WA, I, 84-85	316[WAC]
4Q324c	4QMishC[f]	Priestly Calendar		
4Q325	4QMishD	Priestly Calendar	WA, I, 86-87	317-18[WAC]
4Q326	4QMishE[a]	Priestly Calendar	WA, I, 88	318[WAC]
4Q327	4QMishE[b]	Priestly Calendar	WA, I, 89-91	455
4Q328	4QMishF[a]	Priestly Calendar	WA, I, 92	320[WAC]
4Q329	4QMishF[b]	Priestly Calendar	WA, I, 93-95	321[WAC]
4Q329a	4QMishG	Priestly Calendar	WA, I, 94	322[WAC]
4Q330	4QMishH	Priestly Calendar	WA, I, 95	322[WAC]
4Q331		historical		
4Q332		historical		
4Q333		historical		
4Q334	4QOrdo	Liturgical Calendar	WA, III, 124-25	323[WAC]
4Q335–336		astronomical		
4Q337		calendar		
4Q338		genealogical		

4Q340	4QNetin	List of Nethinim	DJD, XIX, 82	
4Q341	4QNames	List of Proper Names	Naveh, *IEJ* 36 (1986)	
4Q344		Debt Acknowledgment		
4Q348		act regarding ownership	DJD XXVII, 300-303	
4Q349		sale of property		
4Q356		account of money		
4Q360		writing exercise		
4Q362		cryptic		
4Q363		cryptic		
4Q363a		cryptic		
4Q364	4QRP[b]	Reworked Pentateuch	DJD, XIII, 205-54	325-26[WAC]
4Q365	4QRP[c]	Reworked Pentateuch	DJD, XIII, 263-318	222-23
4Q365a		perh. shorter version of Temple Scroll	DJD, XIII, 322-33	223-24 (fr. 2)
4Q366	4QRP[d]	Reworked Pentateuch	DJD, XIII, 337-43	
4Q367	4QRP[e]	Reworked Pentateuch	DJD, XIII, 347-51	
4Q368	4QapPent	Pentateuch Apocryphon	WA, III, 135-39	
4Q369	4QPrEnosh	perh. Prayers of Enosh and Enoch	DJD, XIII, 354-62	329-30[WAC]
4Q370	4QAdmon	Admonition on the Flood	DJD, XIX, 90-97	224-25
4Q371	4QapJoseph[a]	Joseph Apocryphon	WA, III, 140-44	
4Q372	4QapJoseph[b]	Joseph Apocryphon	WA, III, 145-53	225-26
4Q373	4QapJoseph[c]	Joseph Apocryphon	WA, III, 154	226
4Q374	4QDiscourse	Discourse on the Exodus / Conquest Tradition	DJD, XIX, 100-110	278 (Col.2.2)
4Q375	4QapMos[a]	Moses Apocryphon	DJD, XIX, 113-18	278
4Q376	4QapMos[b]	Moses Apocryphon (1.1-2 = 1Q29 1)	DJD, XIX, 123-29	279
4Q377	4QapMos[c]	Moses Apocryphon	WA, III, 164-66	338[WAC]
4Q378	4QapJoshua[a]	Joshua Apocryphon	DJD, XXII, 242-37	282, 340-41[WAC]
4Q379	4QapJoshua[b]	Joshua Apocryphon	DJD, XXII, 264-88	283
4Q380	4QapPs[a]	Non-Canonical Psalms	DJD, XI, 78-85	311-12
4Q381	4QapPs[b]	Non-Canonical Psalms	DJD, XI, 92-172	312-16
4Q382	4QparaKings	Elijah Apocryphon	DJD, XIII, 364-416	348[WAC] (fr. 1, 2, 9, 31, 104)
4Q383	4QapJerA	Jeremiah Apocryphon		
4Q384	4QapJerB	perh. Jeremiah Apocryphon	DJD, XIX, 140-52	350[WAC] (fr. 7, 9)
4Q385	4QpsEzek[a]	Pseudo-Ezekiel, Pseudo-Moses, Apocryphal Jeremiah	WA, III, 228-44	350-52[WAC]
4Q386	4QpsEzek[b]	Pseudo-Ezekiel	WA, III, 245-47	287

4Q387	4QpsEzek[c]	Pseudo-Ezekiel	WA, III, 248-51	353-54[WAC]
4Q388	4QpsEzek[d]	Pseudo-Ezekiel, Pseudo-Moses	WA, III, 252-58	
4Q389	4QpsMos[d]	Pseudo-Ezekiel, Pseudo-Moses, Apocryphal Jeremiah	WA, III, 259-63	354-55[WAC]
4Q390	4QpsMos[e]	Pseudo-Moses	WA, III, 264-66	280-81
4Q391	4QpsEzek[e]	Pseudo-Ezekiel	DJD, XIX, 156-93	
4Q392		liturgical	WA, II, 38-39	438
4Q393	4QConfess	Communal Confession	WA, III, 267-70	357[WAC]
4Q394-99	4QMMT	Halakhic Composition	DJD, X, 44-63	77-85
4Q400	4QShirShabb[a]	Songs of the Sabbath Sacrifice	DJD, XI, 176-96	419-20
4Q401	4QShirShabb[b]	Songs of the Sabbath Sacrifice	DJD, XI, 199-219	420
4Q402	4QShirShabb[c]	Songs of the Sabbath Sacrifice	DJD, XI, 223-37	420-21
4Q403	4QShirShabb[d]	Songs of the Sabbath Sacrifice	DJD, XI, 256-92	421-24
4Q404	4QShirShabb[e]	Songs of the Sabbath Sacrifice	DJD, XI, 294-305	424-25
4Q405	4QShirShabb[f]	Songs of the Sabbath Sacrifice	DJD, XI, 316-93	426-30
4Q406	4QShirShabb[g]	Songs of the Sabbath Sacrifice	DJD, XI, 395-98	
4Q407	4QShirShabb[h]	Songs of the Sabbath Sacrifice	400-401	
4Q408		sapiential	WA, II, 240-43	377[WAC]
4Q409	4QLiturgy	liturgical	WA, III, 297-98	402
4Q410		sapiential	WA, II, 40	380[WAC]
4Q411	4QsapHymn	Sapiential Hymn	DJD, XX, 160-62	
4Q412	4QsapDidA	Sapiential-Didactic Work	DJD, XX, 164-67	379[WAC] (fr. 1)
4Q413	4QdivProv	On Divine Providence	DJD, XX, 169-71	382-83
4Q414	4QBapt	Baptismal Hymn	WA, III, 299-307	439
4Q415		sapiential	WA, II, 44-53	380-82WAC (fr. 6, 9)
4Q416		sapiential/Children of Salvation	WA, II, 54-62	383-85
4Q417		sapiential	WA, II, 63-76	385-87
4Q418		sapiential/Children of Salvation	WA, II, 77-154	388-93
4Q419		sapiential	WA, II, 155-58	393
4Q420	4QWays[a]	Ways of Righteousness	DJD, XX, 174-82	390[WAC] (fr. 1a2-b)
4Q421	4QWays[b]	Ways of Righteousness	DJD, XX, 185-201	390[WAC] (fr. 1a2-b)
4Q422	4QParGenEx	Paraphrase of Genesis and Exodus	DJD, XIII, 421-41	391-93[WAC]
4Q423		sapiential	WA, II, 166-73	388[WAC]
4Q423a		sapiential	WA, II, 166	
4Q424		sapiential/Sons of Righteousness	WA, II, 174-76	393-94
4Q425	4QsapDidB	Sapiential-Didactic Work	DJD, XX, 204-10	
4Q426	4QsapHymnA	Sapiential Hymnic Work	DJD XX, 212-24	
4Q427	4QHod[a]	*Hodayot*/Hymns	WA, II, 254-61	362-66

4Q428	4QHod[b]	*Hodayot*/Hymns	WA, II, 262-74	367
4Q429	4QHod[c]	*Hodayot*/Hymns	WA, II, 275-78	367-69
4Q430	4QHod[d]	*Hodayot*/Hymns	WA, II, 279	369
4Q431	4QHod[e]	*Hodayot*/Hymns	WA, II, 280	369
4Q432	4QHod[f]	*Hodayot*/Hymns	WA, II, 281-84	
4Q433	4QpsHod[a]	*Hodayot*-like	WA, III, 308	
4Q434	4QBark[a]	Bless, my soul	WA, III, 309-313	436, 439
4Q435	4QBark[b]	Bless, my soul	WA, III, 314-15	
4Q436	4QBark[c]	Bless, my soul	WA, III, 316-17	437
4Q437	4QBark[d]	Bless, my soul	WA, III, 318-22	396-97[WAC]
4Q438	4QBark[e]	Bless, my soul	WA, III, 323-25	
4Q439	4QBark[f]	perh. Bless, my soul	WA, III, 327-28	397[WAC]
4Q440	4QpsHod[b]	*Hodayot*-like	WA, III, 329-30	
4Q441		prayer/hymn		
4Q442	4QPrayer[b]	prayer/hymn	WA, III, 331	
4Q443	4QPrayer[c]	prayer/hymn	WA, III, 332-34	398[WAC]
4Q444	4QPrayer[d]	prayer/Meditation of Sage	WA, III, 335-36	398-99[WAC]
4Q445		poetic fragments		
4Q446	4QPoet[b]	poetic fragments	WA, III, 337	
4Q447		poetic fragments		
4Q448	4QJonathan	Paean for King Jonathan, Psalms 135, 154	DJD, XI, 416-25	399-400[WAC]
4Q449	4QPrayer[e]	prayer/hymn	WA, III, 338	
4Q450		prayer/hymn		
4Q451	4QPrayer[g]	prayer/hymn	WA, III, 339	
4Q452		prayer/hymn		
4Q453	4QPrayer[i]	prayer/hymn	WA, III, 340	
4Q454-56		prayers/hymns		
4Q457	4QPrayer[m]	prayer/hymn	WA, III, 341-42	
4Q458	4QNarrA	Tree of Evil	WA, II, 287-91	228
4Q459	4QPseud[a]	pseudepigraphic	WA, III, 343	
4Q460	4QPseud[b]	pseudepigraphic	WA, III, 344-47	
4Q461	4QNarrB	narrative	WA, III, 348-49	
4Q462	4QNarrC	Return from Exile and Restoration of Jerusalem	DJD, XIX, 198-209	226-27 (fr. 1)
4Q463	4QNarrD	Israel's Restoration	DJD, XIX, 211-14	
4Q464	4QPatr	Exposition on the Patriarchs	DJD, XIX, 217-30	402[WAC]
4Q464[a]	4QNarrE	perh. Interpretation of Exodus	DJD, XIX, 231-32	
4Q464[b]		unidentified	DJD, XIX, 233-34	
4Q465		unidentified		
4Q466-68		apocryphon		
4Q469		apocryphon	WA, III, 359-60	
4Q470	4QZedek	Michael and Zedekiah	DJD, XIX, 237-43	403[WAC]

4Q471	$4QM^{h}$	Texts perhaps related to War or Temple Scroll, prayer of Michael, polemical text	WA, II, 294-96	404-405[WAC]
4Q472		sapiential		
4Q473	4QTwoWays	Deuteronomic admonitions	DJD, XXII, 291-94	405[WAC]
4Q474		sapiential	WA, III, 362	
4Q475		sapiential		
4Q476		sapiential	WA, II, 297-98	
4Q477	4QRebukes	offences and punishments	WA, III, 363-64	90-91
4Q478	4QFest	Fragment Mentioning Festivals	DJD, XXII, 295-96	
4Q479	4QDescDavid	David's Descendants	DJD, XXII, 297-99	
4Q480	4QNarrF	fragment mentioning God's miracles	DJD, XXII, 301-302	
4Q481	4QMixedKinds	Text Mentioning Mixed Kinds	DJD, XXII, 303-304	
4Q481a	4QapElisée	Elisha Apocryphon	DJD, XXII, 306-309	
4Q481b	4QNarrG	Restoration of Israel	DJD, XXII, 311-12	
4Q481c	4QPrMercy	Prayer for Mercy	DJD, XXII, 313-14	
4Q481d	4QRedInk	includes words in red ink	DJD, XXII, 315-19	
4Q481e	4QNarrH	perh. consequences of failure to attend to words of God	DJD, XXII, 321-22	
4Q482		perh. Jubilees	DJD, VII, 1-2	
4Q483		perh. Jubilees	DJD, VII, 2	
4Q484	4QTJud	Testament of Judah	DJD, VII, 3	
4Q485	4QProph	prophetic or sapiential	DJD, VII, 4	
4Q486	$4QSap^{a}$	sapiential	DJD, VII, 4-5	
4Q487	$4QSap^{b}$	sapiential	DJD, VII, 5-10	
4Q491	$4QM^{a}$	War Scroll	DSS, II, 142-66	115-19
4Q492	$4QM^{b}$	War Scroll	DSS, II, 168-70	120
4Q493	$4QM^{c}$	War Scroll	DSS, II, 172	120-21
4Q494	$4QM^{d}$	War Scroll	DSS, II, 174	121
4Q495	$4QM^{e}$	War Scroll	DSS, II, 176	121
4Q496	$4QM^{f}$	War Scroll	DSS, II, 178-96	121-23
4Q497	$4QM^{g}$	War Scroll	DSS, II, 198-202	
4Q498	4QHymnSap	hymnic or sapiential	DJD, VII, 73-74	
4Q499	4QHymnPr	hymns and prayers	DJD, VII, 74-79	
4Q500	4QBen	Benediction	DJD, VII, 78-79	402
4Q501	$4QapLam^{b}$	Lamentation	DJD, VII, 79-80	403
4Q502	4QRitMar	Marriage Rite	DJD, VII, 81-105	440-41
4Q503	4QPrQuot	Daily Prayers	DJD, VII, 105-36	407-10
4Q504	$4QDibHam^{a}$	Words of the Luminaries	DJD, VII, 137-68	414-17
4Q505	$4QDibHam^{b}$	Words of the Luminaries	DJD, VII, 168-70	418
4Q506	$4QDibHam^{c}$	Words of the Luminaries	DJD, VII, 170-75	418
4Q507	$4QPrFêtes^{a}$	Festival Prayers	DJD, VII, 175-77	411-12

4Q508	4QPrFêtes[b]	Festival Prayers	DJD, VII, 177-84	412
4Q509	4QPrFêtes[c]	Festival Prayers	DJD, VII, 184-215	412-13
4Q510	4QShir[a]	Songs of the Sage	DJD, VII, 215-19	371
4Q511	4QShir[b]	Songs of the Sage	DJD, VII, 219-62	371-76
4Q512	4QRitPur	Ritual of Purification	DJD, VII, 262-86	441-42
4Q513	4QOrd[b]	Ordinances	DSS, I, 158-75	91
4Q514	4QOrd[c]	Ordinances	DSS, I, 178-79	91-92
4Q515–520		unidentified	DJD, VII, 299-312	
4Q521	4QapMes	Messianic Apocalypse	DJD, XXV, 1-38	394-95
4Q522	4QSela	perh. Joshua Apocryphon/ Rock of Zion	DJD, XXV, 39-74	227-28
4Q523		Hebrew fragment B	DJD, XXV, 75-83	
4Q524	4QT	Temple Scroll	DJD, XXV, 85-114	
4Q525	4QBéat	Beatitudes	DJD, XXV, 115-178	395
4Q526		Hebrew fragment C	DJD, XXV, 179-81	
4Q527		Hebrew fragment D	DJD, XXV, 183-85	
4Q528		Hebrew fragment E	DJD, XXV, 187-90	
	4QAcademyFr	Academy Fragments	AHL, 368	
	4QpsHod[c]	*Hodayot*-like	WA, III, 369-70	446-47[WAC]
	4QpsHistA	pseudo-historical	WA, III, 371	
	4QpsHistB	pseudo-historical	WA, III, 372	
	4QHymnA	hymnic	WA, III, 373	
	4QSl*	perh. apocryphon	WA, III, 374	
	4QS[z]	Community Rule	WA, III, 375-76	
	4QUnidA	unidentified	WA, III, 377	
	4QUnidC	unidentified	WA, III, 378	
	4QUnidD	unidentified	WA, III, 379	
	4QUnidE	unidentified	WA, III, 380	
	4QUnidF	unidentified	WA, III, 381	
4Q577	4QDéluge	memtioning the Flood	DJD, XXV, 195-203	
4Q578	4QHistB	historical	DJD, XXV, 205-208	
5Q579	4QHymnB	hymnic	DJD, XXV, 209-211	

Cave 5

5Q9	5QTopon	toponyms	DJD, III, 179-80	
5Q10	5QapMal	Malachi *pesher* or apocryphon	DJD, III, 180	203
5Q11	5QS	Community Rule	DSS, I, 106-107	32
5Q12	5QD	Damascus Document	DJD, III, 181	70-71
5Q13	5QRègle	similar to Community Rule and Damascus Document	DSS, I, 134-43	73
5Q14		liturgical curses	DJD, III, 183-84	403
5Q16-25		unidentified	DJD, III, 193-97	

Cave 6				
6Q9	6QapSamKgs	Samuel and Kings Apocryphon	DJD, III, 119-23	284
6Q10	6QProph	prophetic	DJD, III, 123-25	
6Q11	6QAllegory	Allegory of the Vine	DJD, III, 125-26	403
6Q12	6QapProph	apocryphal prophecy	DJD, III, 126	
6Q13	6QPriestProph	priestly prophecy	DJD, III, 126-27	
6Q15	6QD	Damascus Document	DJD, III, 128-31	71
6Q16	6QBen	blessings	DJD, III, 131-32	437
6Q17	6QCal	calendar	DJD, III, 132-33	
6Q18	6QHymn	Hymn	DJD, III, 133-36	403
6Q20	6QDeut	perh. Deuteronomy-related	DJD, III, 136-37	228
6Q21	6QfrProph	unidentified	DJD, III, 137	
6Q22		unidentified	DJD, III, 137	
6Q24–25		unidentified	DJD, III, 138	
6Q26		account or contract	DJD, III, 139	
6Q27–31		unidentified	DJD, III, 139-41	
6QX1–2		unidentified		
Cave 8				
8Q3	8QPhyl	phylactery	DJD, III, 149-57	
8Q5	8QHymn	liturgical poem	DJD, III, 161-63	404
Cave 9				
9Q1		unidentified	DJD, III, 163	
Cave 10				
10Q1		ostracon	DJD, III, 164	
Cave 11				
11Q5	11QPs[a]	apocryphal compositions (Cols. 18-19, 22, 24, 26-28)	DJD, IV, 39-40, 43, 45, 47-49, 53-93	304-10
11Q6	11QPs[b]	apocryphal compositions (frags 4-5, 6)	DJD, XXIII, 42-45	
11Q11	11QPsAp[a]	Apocryphal Psalms	DJD, XXIII, 185-205	376
11Q12	11QJub	Jubilees; fragments of Temple Scroll, MS A	DJD, XXIII, 209--20	241-42
11Q13	11QMelch	Melchizedek	DJD, XXIII, 224-41	
11Q14	11QM	perh. War Scroll (= 4Q285, fr. 1)	DJD, XXIII, 245-51	124
11Q15	11QHymn[a]	*Hodayot*-like	DJD, XXIII, 253-56	404
11Q16	11QHymn[b]	*Hodayot*-like	DJD, XXIII, 257-58	
11Q17	11QShirShabb	Songs of the Sabbath Sacrifice	DJD, XXIII, 267-304	430-31
11Q19	11QT	Temple Scroll, MS A	Accordance 4.1	
11Q20	11QT[b]	Temple Scroll MS B	Accordance 4.1	

11Q21	$11QT^{c}$	Temple Scroll, MS C?	DJD, XXIII, 411-14	
11Q22-23		unidentified	DJD, XXIII, 415-20	
11Q25-27		unidentified	DJD, XXIII, 423-30	
11Q29		related to Community rule	DJD, XXIII, 433-34	
11Q30		unclassified fragments	DJD, XXIII, 435-44	
Masada				
MasShirShabb		Songs of the Sabbath Sacrifice	DJD, XI, 240-48	
MasJub		Jubilees fragment mentioning Mastemah	Talmon, 171-72	
MasUnid1		unidentified	Talmon, 173-76	
MasUnid2		unidentified	Talmon, 176-77	
Murabba'at				
Mur 6		hymn	DJD, II, 86	
Mur 7		contract	DJD, II, 86	
Mur 22		deed of sale	DJD, II, 118-19	
Mur 24		farming contracts	DJD, II, 122-34	
Mur 29		deed of sale	DJD, II, 140-44	
Mur 30		deed of sale	DJD, II, 144-48	
Mur 42	MurEpBeth-Mashiko	Bar-Kokhba correspondence	DJD, II, 155-59	Pardee, 124
Mur 43	$MurEpBarC^{a}$	Bar-Kokhba correspondence	DJD, II, 159-61	Pardee, 130
Mur 44	$MurEpBarC^{b}$	Bar-Kokhba correspondence	DJD, II, 161-63	Pardee, 132
Mur 45		Bar-Kokhba correspondence	DJD, II, 163-64	Pardee, 134
Mur 46	MurEpJon-athan	Bar-Kokhba correspondence	DJD, II, 164-66	Pardee, 136
Mur 47		Bar-Kokhba correspondence	DJD, II, 166-67	Pardee, 137
Mur 48		Bar-Kokhba correspondence	DJD, II, 167-68	Pardee, 138
Naḥal Ḥever				
5/6 ḤevBA 44		deed of sale	Nebe, 156	
5/6 ḤevBA 45		contract	AHL, 407	Yadin, 178
5/6 ḤevBA 45 fr. 1–2			AHL, 407	Yadin, 178
5/6 ḤevBA 46		contract	AHL, 410	Yadin, 180
5/6 ḤevEp 1		Bar-Kokhba correspondence	AHL, 420	
5/6 ḤevEp 5		Bar-Kokhba correspondence	AHL, 421	
5/6 ḤevEp 12		Bar-Kokhba correspondence	AHL, 422	
5/6 ḤevEp 12 fr.		Bar-Kokhba correspondence	AHL, 422	
XḤev/Se 8		deed of sale	DJD, XXVII, 26-33	
XḤev/Se 30		Bar-Kokhba correspondence	DJD, XXVII, 103-104	
XḤev/Se 49		Pomisory note	DJD, XXVII, 121-122	

Cairo Genizah

CD	Damascus Document	Accordance 4.1
GnzPs	apocryphal psalms	AHL, 54-57

Bibliography

Academy of the Hebrew Language (The Historical Dictionary of the Hebrew Language), *Materials for the Dictionary. Series I. 200 B.C.E.—300 C.E.* (Jerusalem: The Academy of the Hebrew Language, 1988).

Accordance 4.1 (Oaktree Software; Altamonte Springs, FL, 1999) [Qumran Secular Manuscripts module edited by Martin Abegg].

AHL, *see* Academy of the Hebrew Language.

Alexander, Philip S. and Geza Vermes, *Qumran Cave 4*. XXVI. *Serakh Ha-Yaḥad abd Two Related Texts* (Discoveries in the Judaean Desert, 26; Oxford: Clarendon Press, 1998).

Allegro, John M., with the collaboration of Arnold A. Anderson, *Qumrân Cave 4, I (4Q158–4Q186)* (Discoveries in the Judaean Desert of Jordan, 5; Oxford: Clarendon Press, 1968).

Attridge, Harold, Torleif Elgvin, Jozef Milik, Saul Olyan, John Strugnell, Emanuel Tov, James VanderKam and Sidnie White, in consultation with James VanderKam, *Qumran Cave 4; VIII: Parabiblical Texts, Part 1* (Discoveries in the Judaean Desert, 13; Oxford: Clarendon Press, 1994).

Baillet, M., *Qumrân Grotte 4 (4Q482–4Q520)* (Discoveries in the Judaean Desert, 7; Oxford: Clarendon Press, 1982).

—, J.T. Milik and R. de Vaux, *Les 'petites grottes' de Qumrân* (Discoveries in the Judaean Desert of Jordan, 3; Oxford: Clarendon Press, 1962).

Barthélemy, D. and J.T. Milik, with contributions by R. de Vaux, G.M. Crowfoot, H.J. Plenderleith and G.L. Harding, *Qumran Cave I* (Discoveries in the Judaean Desert, 1; Oxford: Clarendon Press, 1955).

Baumgarten, Joseph, on the basis of transcriptions by Józef T. Milik, with contributions by Stephen Pfann and Ada Yardeni, *Qumran Cave 4*. XIII. *The Damascus Document (4Q266–273)* (Discoveries in the Judaean Desert, 18; Oxford: Clarendon Press, 1996).

Benoit, P., J.T. Milik and R. de Vaux, with contributions by G.M. Crowfoot, E. Crowfoot and A. Grohmann, *Les grottes de Murabba'ât* (Discoveries in the Judaean Desert, II; Oxford: Clarendon Press, 1961).

Brooke, George, John Collins, Torleif Elgvin, Peter Flint, Jonas Greenfield, Erik Larson, Carol Newsom, Émile Puech, Lawrence H. Schiffman, Michael Stone, and Julio Trebolle Barrera, in consultation with James VanderKam, *Qumran Cave 4*. XVII. *Parabiblical Texts, Part 3* (Discoveries in the Judaean Desert, 22; Oxford: Clarendon Press, 1996).

Broshi, Magen, Esther Eshel, Joseph Fitzmyer, Erik Larson, Carol Newsom, Lawrence Schiffman, Mark Smith, Michael Stone, John Strugnell and Ada Yardeni, in consultation with James VanderKam, *Qumran Cave 4*. XIV. *Parabiblical Texts, Part 2* (Discoveries in the Judaean Desert, 19; Oxford: Clarendon Press, 1995).

Charlesworth, James H. (ed.), *Rule of the Community and Related Documents* (The Dead Sea Scrolls: Hebrew, Aramaic, and Greek Texts with English Translations, 1; Tübingen/Louisville: J.C.B. Mohr [Paul Siebeck]/Westminster John Knox Press, 1994).

—*Damascus Document, War Scroll, and Related Documents* (The Dead Sea Scrolls: Hebrew, Aramaic, and Greek Texts with English Translations, 2; Tübingen/Louisville: J.C.B. Mohr [Paul Siebeck]/Westminster John Knox Press, 1995).

—*Pseudepigraphic and Non-Masoretic Psalms and Prayers* (The Dead Sea Scrolls: Hebrew, Aramaic, and Greek Texts with English Translations, 4A; Tübingen/Louisville: J.C.B. Mohr [Paul Siebeck]/Westminster John Knox Press, 1997).

Cotton, Hannah M. and Ada Yardeni, *Aramaic, Hebrew and Greek Documentary Texts from Naḥal Ḥever and Other Sites* (Discoveries in the Judaean Desert, XXVII; Oxford: Clarendon Press, 1977).

DJD, I, *see* Barthélemy, D. and J.T. Milik.

DJD, II, *see* Benoit, P., J.T. Milik and R. de Vaux.

DJD, III, *see* Baillet, M., J.T. Milik and R. de Vaux.

DJD, IV, *see* Sanders, J.A.

DJD, V, *see* Allegro, J.M.

DJD, VII, *see* Baillet, M.

DJD, X, *see* Qimron, Elisha and John Strugnell.

DJD XI, *see* Eshel, Esther, Hanan Eshel, Carol Newsom, *et al.*

DJD, XIII, *see* Attridge, Harold, Torleif Elgvin, Jozéf Milik, *et al.*

DJD, XVIII, *see* Baumgarten, Joseph M. (1996).

DJD, XIX, *see* Broshi, Magen, Esther Eshel, Joseph Fitzmyer, *et al.*

DJD, XX, *see* Elgvin, Torleif, Menachem Kister, Timothy Lim, *et al.*

DJD, XXII, *see* Brooke, George, John Collins, Torleif Elgvin, *et al.*

DJD XXIII, *see* García Martínez, Florentino, Eibert J.C. Tigchelaar, *et al.*

DJD XXV, *see* Puech, Émile.

DJD XXVI, *see* Alexander, Philip S. and Geza Vermes.

DJD, XXVII, *see* Cotton, Hannah M. and Ada Yardeni.

DSS, I, *see* Charlesworth, James H. (1994).

DSS, II, *see* Charlesworth, James H. (1995).

DSS, IVA, *see* Charlesworth, James H. (1997).

Eisenman, Robert H. and Michael Wise, *The Dead Sea Scrolls Uncovered* (Shaftesbury, Dorset: Element, 1992).

Elgvin, Torleif, Menachem Kister, Timothy Lim, Bilhah Nitzan, Stephen Pfann, Elisha Qimron, Lawrence H. Schiffman, and Annette Steudel, in consultation with Joseph A. Fitzmyer, *Qumran Cave 4*. XV. *Sapiential Texts, Part 1* (Discoveries in the Judaean Desert, 20; Oxford: Clarendon Press, 1977).

Eshel, Esther and Hanan Eshel and Ada Yardeni, 'A Qumran Composition Containing Part of Ps 154 and a Prayer for the Welfare of King Jonathan and his Kingdom', *IEJ* 42 (1992), pp. 199-229.

Eshel, Esther, Hanan Eshel, Carol Newsom, Bilhah Nitzan, Eileen Schuller, and Ada Yardeni, in consultation with James Vanderkam and Monica Brady, *Qumran Cave 4* VI. *Poetical and*

Liturgical Texts, Part I (Discoveries in the Judaean Desert, XI: Oxford: Clarendon Press, 1990).

EW, *see* Eisenman, Robert H. and Michael Wise.

García Martínez, Florentino, *The Dead Sea Scrolls Translated: The Qumran Texts in English* (tr. Wilfred G.E. Watson; Leiden: E.J. Brill, 1994).

García Martínez, Florentino, Eibert J.C. Tigchelaar, and Adam S. van der Woude, incorporating earlier editions by J.P.M. van der Ploeg, O.P., with a contribution by Edward Herbert, *Qumran Cave 11* II. *11Q2-18, 11Q20-31* (Discoveries in the Judaean Desert, XXIII; Oxford: Clarendon Press, 1998).

Horgan, Maurya P., *Pesharim: Qumran Interpretations of Biblical Books* (The Catholic Biblical Quarterly Monograph Series, 8; Washington, DC: The Catholic Biblical Association of America, 1979).

Kister, M., 'Newly Identified Fragments of the Book of Jubilees: Jub. 23:21-23, 30-31', *Revue de Qumran* 12 (1985–87), pp. 529-36.

Licht, J., *The Thanksgiving Scroll* (Jerusalem: The Bialik Institute, 1957).

Milik, Józef T., 'A propos de 11QJub', *Biblica* 54 (1973), pp. 77-78.

—with the collaboration of Matthew Black, *The Books of Enoch: Aramaic Fragments of Qumrân Cave 4* (Oxford: Clarendon Press, 1976).

Naveh, Joseph, 'A Medical Document or a Writing Exercise? The So-called 4Q Therapeia', *Israel Exploration Journal* 36 (1986), pp. 52-55.

Nebe, G.W., 'Die hebräische Sprache der Naḥal Ḥever Dokumente 5/6Ḥev 44–46', in *The Hebrew of the Dead Sea Scrolls and Ben Sira: Proceedings of a Symposium held at Leiden University, 11–14 December 1995* (ed. T. Muraoka and J.F. Elwolde; Studies on the Texts of the Desert of Judah, 26; Leiden: E.J. Brill, 1997), pp. 150–57.

Newsom, Carol, *Songs of the Sabbath Sacrifice: A Critical Edition* (Harvard Semitic Studies, 27; Atlanta, GA: Scholars Press, 1985).

Pardee, Dennis, *Handbook of Ancient Hebrew Letters: A Study Edition* (SBL Sources for Biblical Study, 15; Chico, CA: Scholars Press, 1982) .

Ploeg, J. van der, 'Les manuscrits de la grotte XI de Qumran', *Revue de Qumran* 12 (1985), pp. 3-15.

Puech, Émile, 'Notes sur le manuscrit de 11QMelkîsédeq', *Revue de Qumran* 12 (1987), pp. 483-513.

—'*11QPsAp*ᵃ: Un rituel d'exorcismes. Essai de reconstruction', *Revue de Qumran* 14 (1990), pp. 377-408.

—'Un apocalypse messianique (4Q521)', *Revue de Qumran* 15 (1992), pp. 475-519 .

—'La pierre de Sion et l'autel des holocaustes d'après un manuscrit hébreu de la grotte 4', *Revue Biblique* 99 (1992), pp. 676-96.

—*Qumrân Grotte 4*. XVIII. *Textes Hébreux (4Q521-4Q528, 4Q576-4Q579)* (Discoveries in the Judaean Desert, 25; Oxford: Clarendon Press, 1998).

Qimron, Elisha, 'The Text of CDC', in *The Damascus Document Reconsidered* (ed. Magen Broshi; Jerusalem: The Israel Exploration Society/The Shrine of the Book, Israel Museum, 1992), pp. 9-49.

—and John Strugnell, in consultation with Y. Sussmann and with contributions by Y. Sussmann and A. Yardeni, *Qumran Cave 4. V. Miqṣat Ma'aśe ha-Torah* (Discoveries in the Judaean Desert, 10; Oxford: Clarendon Press, 1994).

—*The Temple Scroll: A Critical Edition with Extensive Reconstructions* (Bibliography by Florentino García Martínez; Judean Desert Studies; Beer Sheva: Ben Gurion University of the Negev Press/Israel Exploration Society, 1996).

Richter, Hans-Peter, 'A Preliminary Concordance to the Hebrew and Aramaic Fragments from Qumrân Caves II–X' (5 vols., unpublished, printed in Göttingen, 1988, and distributed by Hartmut Stegemann on behalf of John Strugnell).

Sanders, J.A., *The Psalms Scroll of Qumrân Cave 11* (Discoveries in the Judaean Desert of Jordan, 4; Oxford: Clarendon Press, 1965).

Schuller, Eileen, *Non-Canonical Psalms from Qumran: A Pseudepigraphic Collection* (Harvard Semitic Studies, 28; Atlanta: Scholars Press, 1986).

Steudel, Annette, *Der Midrasch zur Eschatologie aus der Qumrangemeinde (4QMidrEschat$^{a.b}$): Materielle Rekonstruktion, Textbestand, Gattung und traditionsgeschichtliche Einordnung des durch 4Q174 ('Florilegium') und 4Q177 ('Catena A') repräsenterten Werkes aus den Qumranfunden* (Studies on the Texts of the Desert of Judah, 13; Leiden: E.J. Brill, 1994).

Talmon, Shemaryahu, 'Hebrew Written Fragments from Masada', *Dead Sea Discoveries* 3 (1996), pp. 168-77.

Vermes, Geza, *The Complete Dead Sea Scrolls in English* (London: Allen Lane/Penguin, 1997).

WA, *see* Wacholder, Ben Zion and Martin G. Abegg.

WAC, *see* Wise, Michael, Martin G. Abegg and Edward Cook.

Wacholder, Ben Zion and Martin G. Abegg (and, for Fascicle 4, James Bowley), *A Preliminary Edition of the Unpublished Dead Sea Scrolls: The Hebrew and Aramaic Texts from Cave Four Based on a Reconstruction of the Original Transcriptions of Jozef T. Milik, John Strugnell and Jean Starcky*, Fascicles 1–4 (Washington, DC: Biblical Archaeology Society, 1991–96).

Wise, Michael, Martin G. Abegg and Edward Cook, *The Dead Sea Scrolls: A New Translation* (London: HarperCollins, 1996).

Woude, Adam van der, 'Ein neuer Segensspruch aus Qumran (11QBer)', in *Bibel und Qumran: Beiträge zur Erforschung der Beziehungen zwischen Bibel- und Qumranwissenschaft: Hans Bardtke zum 22.8.1966* (ed. S. Wagner; Berlin: Evangelische Haupt-Bibelgesellschaft, 1968).

—'Fragmente des Buches Jubiläen aus Qumran Höhle XI (11QJub)', in *Tradition und Glaube: Das frühe Christentum in seiner Umwelt: Festgabe für Karl Georg Kuhn zum 65. Geburtstag* (ed. Gert Jeremias, Heinz-Wolfgang Kuhn, and Hartmut Stegemann; Göttingen: Vandenhoeck & Ruprecht, 1971), pp. 140-46.

Yadin, Yigael, *Bar-Kokhba: The Rediscovery of the Legendary Hero of the Last Jewish Revolt against Imperial Rome* (London: Weidenfeld and Nicolson, 1971).

b. *Inscriptions*

The following texts are supplementary to those listed in Volume 1, pp. 55-66, Volume 3, pp. 28-32, and Volume 4, p. 29.

DH (before Bulla or Ostracon number)
Robert Deutsch and Michael Heltzer, *New Epigfraphic Evidence from the Biblical Period* (Tel Aviv–Jaffa: Archaeological Center Publications, 1995).
D (before Bulla or Ostracon number)
Robert Deutsch, *Messages from the Past: Hebrew Bullae from the Time of Isaiah through the Destruction of the First Temple* (Tel Aviv: Archaeological Center Publications, 1999).

WORDS BEGINNING WITH MEM AND NUN IN ORDER OF FREQUENCY

In these tables are listed all the words beginning with Mem and Nun, in descending order of their frequency of occurrence in the corpus of classical Hebrew. Including proper names, there are 1428 words beginning with Mem, and 596 with Nun, 2024 in all. Words that are conjectured, and for which therefore no occurrence statistics are noted in the Dictionary, are of course absent from this list. Words for which the lemma form is reconstructed (for example, when only plural forms are attested and the presumed singular form is therefore shown within square brackets) are included, without their square brackets.

In the first column, a number ranks the words in order of frequency. Following the Hebrew word itself, and (in the case of homonyms) a roman numeral to distinguish one word from another spelled alike, five columns of figures follow. They record in turn the number of occurrences of the word in the four corpora of texts that comprise Classical Hebrew—the Masoretic text of the Hebrew Bible (MT), Ben Sira (Si), the Dead Sea Scrolls (Qumran and related texts) (Q) and the Hebrew inscriptions (Inscr)—and the total number of occurrences. It is this total that determines a word's position in the table. In the next column the part of speech is noted, and a simple gloss follows, to identify the word in question.

מ

Rank	Lemma		MT	Si	Q	Inscr	Total	Type	Gloss
1	מִן		7717	55	1300	106	9178	prep	*from*
2	מֶלֶךְ	I	2518	16	130	70	2734	nm	*king*
3	מות		842	10	75	1	928	vb	*die*
4	מִשְׁפָּט		421	20	420		861	nm	*judgment*
5	מֹשֶׁה		762	4	75		841	prnm	*Moses*
6	מַיִם		580	9	168	3	760	nm	*water(s)*
7	מִצְרַיִם	I	674	0	34	2	710	prnm	*Egypt*
8	מָה	I	492	46	122		660	pron	*what?*
9	מֵאָה	I	579	3	63	3	648	nm&f	*hundred*
10	מַעֲשֶׂה	I	243	40	293		576	nm	*deed*
11	מצא	I	457	32	66		555	vb	*find*
12	מִי		423	28	81	3	535	pron	*who?*
13	מָקוֹם		401	10	65	4	480	nm&f	*place*
14	מִלְחָמָה	I	318	4	147		469	nf	*war*
15	מִזְבֵּחַ		400	3	46		449	nm	*altar*
16	מוֹעֵד	I	223	6	140		369	nm	*appointment*
17	מלך	I	347	1	8	1	357	vb	*be king*
18	מְאֹד	I	299	10	30	1	340	adv	*very*
19	מִשְׁפָּחָה		304	2	22		328	nf	*clan*
20	מלא		250	8	46	2	306	vb	*be full*
21	מַלְאָךְ		213	1	81		295	nm	*messenger*
22	מִדְבָּר	I	271	2	16		289	nm	*steppe*
23	מַטֶּה	I	252	4	19	2	277	nm	*staff, tribe*
24	מַחֲנֶה		215	1	58		274	nm&f	*camp*
25	מִנְחָה		211	1	38		250	nf	*offering*
26	מִצְוָה		181	9	45		235	nf	*commandment*
27	מָוֶת		155	22	30		207	nm	*death*
28	מְלָאכָה		166	7	19	1	193	nf	*work*
29	מוֹאָב		178	1	4	1	184	prnmf	*Moab*
30	מַעַל	II	141	2	32		175	n[m]	*height*
31	משל	I	81	14	71		166	vb	*rule*

Rank	Lemma		MT	Si	Q	Inscr	Total	Type	Gloss
32	מִסְפָּר	I	133	11	20		164	nm	*number*
33	מִקְדָּשׁ		74	5	81		160	nm	*sanctuary*
34	מְנַשֶּׁה		146		9	4	159	prnm	*Manasseh*
35	מַמְלָכָה		117	3	26		146	nf	*kingdom*
36	מִשְׁכָּן		139		6		145	nm	*tabernacle*
37	מַלְכוּת		91	2	47		140	nf	*kingdom*
38	מַחֲשָׁבָה		56	4	73		133	nm	*thought*
39	מַרְאֶה		103	6	22		131	nm	*sight*
40	מְעַט		101	11	12		124	n[m]	*few*
41	מאס	I	74	10	33		117	vb	*reject*
42	מִגְרָשׁ	I	114				114	nm	*land outside city*
43	מלט	I	95	4	10		109	vb	*escape*
44	מִזְרָח		74		29		103	n[m]	*sunrise, east*
45	מכר	I	80	1	22		103	vb	*deliver (over)*
46	מָרוֹם		54	10	30		94	nm	*height*
47	מִשְׁמֶרֶת		78	1	9		88	nf	*watch*
48	מֶמְשָׁלָה		17	6	64		87	nf	*dominion*
49	מַעֲרָכָה		20	2	63		85	nf	*array*
50	מהר	I	67	5	11		83	vb	*hasten*
51	מוֹשָׁב		44	2	36		82	nm	*seat*
52	מִקְנֶה		76		6		82	nm	*cattle*
53	מִדָּה	I	54		27		81	nf	*measure*
54	מָלֵא		64	6	10		80	adj	*full*
55	משׁח	I	71	3	6		80	vb	*anoint*
56	מָגֵן	I	60	1	14		75	nm&f	*shield*
57	מַדּוּעַ		72	2	1		75	adv	*why?*
58	מוּסָר		50	13	11		74	nm	*discipline*
59	מִשְׁקָל		49	3	17		69	nm	*weight*
60	מַכָּה		48	4	15		67	nf	*stroke*
61	מַעַל	I	29	3	32		64	n[m]	*sin*
62	מִזְמוֹר		57	5	1		63	n[m]	*psalm*
63	מרה	I	45	5	13		63	vb	*be rebellious*
64	מָשִׁיחַ		39	1	23		63	nm	*anointed one*
65	מדד		53		9		62	vb	*measure*

Words Beginning with Mem

Rank	Lemma		MT	Si	Q	Inscr	Total	Type	Gloss
66	מִדְיָן	I	59		3		62	prnm	*Midian*
67	מִגְדָּל	I	48		13		61	nm	*tower*
68	מָרְדֳּכַי		60				60	prnm	*Mordecai*
69	מָקוֹר	I	18	2	39		59	nm	*source*
70	מִשְׁכָּב		46	3	9		58	nm	*bed*
71	מָחָר		52	2	1	2	57	n[m]	*morrow*
72	מַצָּה	I	53		4		57	nf	*unleavened bread*
73	מוט		37	8	11		56	vb	*totter*
74	מֶרְכָּבָה		44	1	11		56	nf	*chariot*
75	מַשָּׂא	I	37	4	14	1	56	nm	*burden*
76	מָתְנַיִם		47	3	6		56	nmdu	*loins*
77	מְדִינָה	I	54		1		55	nf	*province*
78	מַעֲלָה	I	47		8		55	nf	*step*
79	מַחֲלֹקֶת	I	43	2	9		54	nf	*division*
80	מוֹפֵת		36	2	14		52	nm	*wonder*
81	מַעֲמָד		5	1	46		52	n[m]	*place*
82	מִשְׁתֶּה		46	5			51	nm	*feast*
83	מוֹצָא	I	27	3	19	1	50	nm	*going out*
84	מָעוֹן	I	19	1	29		49	n[m]	*dwelling place*
85	מאן		46	1	1		48	vb	*refuse*
86	מִרְמָה	I	39	1	8		48	nf	*deceit*
87	מָתַי		43	1	3		47	adv	*when?*
88	מַלְכִּיָּה		16		13	17	46	prnm	*Malchi(j)ah*
89	מָשָׁל	I	39	5	2		46	nm	*proverb*
90	מחה	I	34	4	5	2	45	vb	*wipe*
91	מְלֹא		38		6	1	45	nm	*fullness*
92	מִלָּה		38		7		45	nf	*word*
93	מעל		35		10		45	vb	*sin*
94	מַעֲלָל		41		4		45	nm	*deed*
95	מִשְׁנֶה	I	35		10		45	n[m]	*second*
96	מַאֲכָל		30	6	8		44	nm	*food*
97	מָטָר		38	2	4		44	nm	*rain*
98	מְנוֹרָה		42	1	1		44	nf	*lampstand*
99	מָעוֹז	I	34	1	9		44	nm	*refuge*

Rank	Lemma		MT	Si	Q	Inscr	Total	Type	Gloss
100	מְעָרָה	I	40		4		44	nf	*cave*
101	משך	I	36	2	6		44	vb	*pull*
102	מִין		31	4	8		43	nm	*kind*
103	מַעֲשֵׂר		32	1	10		43	nm	*tenth*
104	מָבוֹא		25	2	15		42	nm	*entrance*
105	מִבְצָר	I	37	1	4		42	nm&f	*fortification*
106	מַצֵּבָה		38		4		42	nf	*pillar*
107	מַר	I	38	3	1		42	adj	*bitter*
108	מְשֻׁלָּם	I	25			17	42	prnm	*Meshullam*
109	מֵעֶה		34	3	3	1	41	nm	*belly*
110	מְרָרִי	I	39		2		41	prnm	*Merari*
111	מסס		23	1	15	1	40	vb	*melt*
112	מִצְפָּה		40				40	pln	*Mizpah*
113	מָאוֹר		19	1	19		39	nm	*luminary*
114	מנע		29	8	2		39	vb	*withhold*
115	מַעְיָן		23	1	15		39	n[m]	*spring*
116	מול	I	30		8		38	vb	*circumcise*
117	מוּל	I	36		1		37	n[m]	*front*
118	מְזִמָּה		19	2	16		37	nf	*plan*
119	מִזְרָק		32		5		37	nm	*basin*
120	מנה		28	3	4	2	37	vb	*count*
121	מעט	I	23	4	10		37	vb	*be few*
122	מִקְרָא		23		14		37	nm	*convocation*
123	מוֹקֵשׁ	I	27	3	6		36	nm	*snare*
124	מוש	I	20	3	13		36	vb	*depart*
125	מַחְסוֹר		13	1	22		36	n[m]	*lack*
126	מָחֳרָת		32		4		36	nf	*morrow*
127	מִיכָיְהוּ		21			15	36	prnm	*Micaiah*
128	מַלְכָּה		35		1		36	nf	*queen*
129	מִיכָה		33			2	35	prnm	*Micah*
130	מֶלַח	I	28	3	4		35	nm	*salt*
131	מָעוֹז	II	24	1	9		34	nm	*strength*
132	מַשָּׂא	II	29	1	4		34	nm	*utterance*
133	מוּם		21	4	7		32	nm	*blemish*

Words Beginning with Mem

Rank	Lemma		MT	Si	Q	Inscr	Total	Type	Gloss
134	מְנַחֵם	I	8		1	23	32	prnm	*Menahem*
135	מְסִלָּה	I	27		5		32	nf	*road*
136	מְעִיל		28	2	1		31	nm	*robe*
137	מרד		25	2	4		31	vb	*rebel*
138	מַגֵּפָה		26	1	3		30	nf	*plague*
139	מְחִיר	I	15	4	11		30	nm	*price*
140	מַחֲצִית		16		14		30	nf	*half*
141	מִטָּה		29	1			30	nf	*bed*
142	מָכוֹן		17	2	11		30	nm	*place*
143	מִצְרִי	I	30				30	gent	*Egyptian*
144	מִשְׁמָר	I	22	1	6	1	30	nm	*watch*
145	מְכוֹנָה		25	2	2		29	nf	*base*
146	מְנוּחָה		21	1	7		29	nf	*resting place*
147	מַעֲרָב	I	14		15		29	n[m]	*west*
148	מִכְשׁוֹל		14	2	12		28	nm	*stumbling block*
149	מְלוּכָה	I	24		4		28	nf	*kingship*
150	מִישֹׁר		23	1	3		27	nm	*plain*
151	מַס	I	23		3	1	27	nm	*levy*
152	מָדוֹן	I	20		6		26	nm	*strife*
153	מוֹסָד	I	13		13		26	nm	*foundation*
154	מָסָךְ		25		1		26	n[m]	*screen*
155	מַרְפֵּא	I	15	2	9		26	nm	*healing*
156	מַת	I	22	2	2		26	nm	*man*
157	מוג	I	17	1	7		25	vb	*melt*
158	מוג	II	17	1	7		25	vb	*wave, waver*
159	מור	I	16	1	8		25	vb	*change*
160	מַסֵּכָה	I	25				25	nf	*image*
161	מַחְתָּה		22		2		24	nf	*firepan*
162	מַכְאוֹב		16	3	5		24	nm	*pain*
163	מִשְׁחָה	I	23		1		24	nf	*anointing*
164	מַחְסֶה		20		3		23	nm	*shelter*
165	מַטָּה		19		4		23	adv	*downwards*
166	מָכִיר		22			1	23	prnm	*Machir*
167	מִקְצֹעַ		12		11		23	nm	*corner*

Rank	Lemma		MT	Si	Q	Inscr	Total	Type	Gloss
168	מְרִי		23				23	n[m]	*rebellion*
169	מַתָּנָה	I	17	3	3		23	nf	*gift*
170	מְהֵרָה		20			2	22	nf	*haste*
171	מוֹלֶדֶת		22				22	nf	*birth, kindred*
172	מִיָּמִן		4		18		22	prnm	*Mijamin*
173	מֹאזְנַיִם		15	1	5		21	n[m]du	*balances*
174	מַבּוּל		13	1	7		21	nm	*flood*
175	מְגִלָּה		21				21	nf	*scroll*
176	מַעֲלֶה		19	1	1		21	nm	*ascent*
177	מָצוֹר	I	20		1		21	n[m]	*siege*
178	מִקְוֶה	II	7	5	9		21	nm	*collection*
179	מִקְלָט		20		1		21	n[m]	*refuge*
180	מֶרְחָק		19		2		21	nm	*distance*
181	מַתָּן	II	2			19	21	prnm	*Mattan*
182	מְזוּזָה		19		1		20	nf	*doorpost*
183	מֵלִיץ	I	5	1	14		20	nm	*interpreter*
184	מֵלִיץ	II	5	1	14		20	nm	*one who speaks freely*
185	מָנוֹחַ	II	18			2	20	prnm	*Manoah*
186	מִסְפֵּד		16	1	3		20	nm	*mourning*
187	מְצוּלָה		12		8		20	nf	*depth*
188	משׁל	II	18	2			20	vb	*be like*
189	מִבְטָח		16		3		19	nm	*trust*
190	מְהוּמָה		12	1	6		19	nf	*discomfiture*
191	מַחְמָד		13	4	2		19	nm	*desirable thing*
192	מחץ	I	15	1	2	1	19	vb	*strike through*
193	מַעֲשֵׂיָה		17			2	19	prnm	*Maaseiah*
194	מְצוּדָה	II	17		2		19	nf	*stronghold*
195	מִשְׂגָּב	I	17		2		19	nf	*stronghold*
196	מַהֵר		14		4		18	adv	*quickly*
197	מוֹאָבִי		16		2		18	gent	*Moabite*
198	מטר		17		1		18	vb	*rain*
199	מִיכַל		18				18	prnf	*Michal*
200	מָנָה	I	12	2	4		18	nf	*portion*
201	מָנוֹחַ	I	7	2	9		18	nm	*resting place*

Rank	Lemma		MT	Si	Q	Inscr	Total	Type	Gloss
202	מַעֲכָה	I	18				18	prnmf	*Maacah*
203	מַקֵּל		18				18	nmf	*rod*
204	מַרְאָה		12		6		18	nf	*vision*
205	מרר	I	16	2			18	vb	*be bitter*
206	מִשְׁעֶנֶת		11		7		18	nf	*support*
207	מַתַּנְיָהוּ		3			15	18	prnm	*Mattaniah*
208	מִיכָאֵל		13		4		17	prnm	*Michael*
209	מֵישָׁרִים	I	16		1		17	nmpl	*righteousness*
210	מִכְסֶה		16		1		17	nm	*covering*
211	מַעֲנֶה	I	7	3	7		17	nm	*answer*
212	מְפִיבֹשֶׁת		15		2		17	prnm	*Mephibosheth*
213	מָשׂוֹשׂ	I	17				17	nm	*joy*
214	מַשְׁקֶה	II	6	1	10		17	nm	*drink*
215	מוֹרָא	I	12	1	3		16	nm	*fear*
216	מַטָּרָה		16				16	nf	*guard, target*
217	מִלֻּא		15		1		16	nm	*consecration*
218	מַסַּע	I	12		4		16	n[m]	*journey*
219	מַעֲלָה	II	15		1		16	nf	*extolment*
220	מַצְרֵף		2		14		16	n[m]	*crucible*
221	מִקְנָה		15	1			16	nf	*purchase*
222	מִרְיָם	II	15		1		16	prnf	*Miriam*
223	מַשְׂטֵמָה	I	2		14		16	nf	*hostility*
224	מָגוֹר	I	11	1	3		15	n[m]	*sojourning*
225	מָדַי		15				15	prnm	*Madai, Media*
226	מָה	II	15				15	part	*not*
227	מהה		9	3	3		15	vb	*delay*
228	מִמְשָׁל		3		12		15	nm	*dominion*
229	מָן	I	14		1		15	nm	*manna*
230	מֵצַח		13	1	1		15	nm	*forehead*
231	מַרְעִית		10	1	4		15	nf	*pasturing*
232	מַשְׂאֵת	I	12	2	1		15	nf	*gift*
233	מָתוֹק		12		3		15	adj	*sweet*
234	מִבְחָר	I	14				14	nm	*choice*
235	מַטְעָם		8	6			14	n[m]	*delicacy*

Rank	Lemma		MT	Si	Q	Inscr	Total	Type	Gloss
236	מִסְגֶּרֶת	I	14				14	nf	*panel*
237	מַעֲשֵׂיָהוּ		7			7	14	prnm	*Maaseiah*
238	מְצוּקָה		7	2	5		14	nf	*distress*
239	מִצְנֶפֶת		12	1	1		14	nf	*turban*
240	מרט		14				14	vb	*make smooth*
241	מָרֹר		3		11		14	nm	*bitter thing*
242	מַשְׂכִּיל	I	14				14	n[m]	*maskil*
243	מַשְׂכִּיל	II	14				14	n[m]	*responsive song*
244	מַשְׂכִּיל	III	14				14	n[m]	*instructive song*
245	מְשׁוּבָה	I	12	2			14	nf	*going back*
246	מַתַּנְיָה		13			1	14	prnm	*Mattaniah*
247	מַדָּע	I	6	2	5		13	nm	*knowledge*
248	מִחְיָה		8	3	2		13	nf	*life*
249	מַחֲנַיִם	I	13				13	pln	*Mahanaim*
250	מִמְכָּר		10	2	1		13	nm	*mortgaged property*
251	מְעוֹנָה		9	4			13	nf	*dwelling place*
252	מְצִלְתַּיִם		13				13	nfdu	*cymbals*
253	מִרְעֶה		13				13	nm	*pasture*
254	מִשְׁבָּר	I	5		8		13	n[m]	*breaker*
255	מַשְׁקֶה	I	13				13	nm	*cup-bearer*
256	מְגִדּוֹ		12				12	pln	*Megiddo*
257	מוֹטָה		12				12	nf	*bar*
258	מַחְבֶּרֶת		10		2		12	nf	*join*
259	מַחְלִי	I	12				12	prnm	*Mahli*
260	מַחְסֵיָה		2			10	12	prnm	*Mahseiah*
261	מְחִתָּה		11		1		12	nf	*terror*
262	מֶכֶר		3		9		12	nm	*value*
263	מלח	I	5	1	6		12	vb	*salt*
264	מַלְקוֹשׁ		8		4		12	nm	*latter rain*
265	מָנוֹס		8		4		12	nm	*flight*
266	מְצָד		11		1		12	nf	*stronghold*
267	מִצְעָד		3		9		12	n[m]	*step*
268	מִקְרֶה		10		2		12	nm	*accident*
269	מֹר	I	12				12	nm	*myrrh*

Words Beginning with Mem

Rank	Lemma		MT	Si	Q	Inscr	Total	Type	Gloss
270	מַשְׁחִית	I	10		2		12	n[m]	*destruction*
271	מַתָּן	I	5	7			12	nm	*gift*
272	מַאֲמָר		3	2	6		11	nm	*word*
273	מַבְנִית	I			11		11	nf	*structure*
274	מוֹלָד				11		11	n[m]	*birth*
275	מַחְשָׁךְ		7		4		11	nm	*dark place*
276	מַטָּע		6		5		11	nm	*planting*
277	מִכְמָס		11				11	pln	*Michmas*
278	מִלְכָּה		11				11	prnf	*Milcah*
279	מַמְזֵר		2		9		11	nm	*bastard*
280	מְנָת		9		2		11	nf	*portion*
281	מִסְתָּר		10	1			11	n[m]	*hiding place*
282	מַעְגָּל	I	11				11	nm	*track*
283	מַצָּב		10		1		11	nm	*standing place*
284	מִקְוֶה	I	5		6		11	nm	*hope*
285	מְרִיבָה	II	11				11	pln	*Meribah*
286	מָשׁוֹב				11		11	n[m]	*going back*
287	מתק	I	5	5	1		11	vb	*be sweet*
288	מָגוֹר	II	9		1		10	nm	*fear*
289	מִדְיָן	II	10				10	nm	*strife*
290	מִדְרָשׁ		2	1	7		10	n[m]	*study*
291	מַטַּעַת				10		10	nf	*planting*
292	מֶכֶס		6		3	1	10	nm	*tribute*
293	מִכְתָּב		9			1	10	nm	*writing*
294	מַמְלְכוּת		9		1		10	nf	*kingdom*
295	מַמְרֵא	I	9		1		10	pln	*Mamre*
296	מָנֶה	I	5		5		10	nm	*mina*
297	מַקֵּדָה		9			1	10	pln	*Makkedah*
298	מקק		10				10	vb	*rot*
299	מִקְשָׁה	I	9	1			10	nf	*hammered work*
300	מְרַאֲשׁוֹת		10				10	n[f]pl	*place of head*
301	מִשְׁבְּצָה		9		1		10	nf	*(ornamental) setting*
302	מִשְׁלָח		7		3		10	n[m]	*extending*
303	משׁשׁ	I	10				10	vb	*feel*

Rank	Lemma		MT	Si	Q	Inscr	Total	Type	Gloss
304	מַד	I	9				9	nm	*garment*
305	מוֹרָשָׁה		9				9	nf	*possession*
306	מַחֲשָׁב	I			9		9	nm	*design*
307	מִיאָמֵן					9	9	prnm	*Miamun*
308	מֵיתָר		9				9	n[m]	*cord*
309	מִלּוֹא	I	7		2		9	n[m]	*citadel*
310	מָלוֹן		8		1		9	nm	*lodging place*
311	מַעֲרָב	II	9				9	nm	*merchandise*
312	מַעֲרֶכֶת		9				9	nf	*array*
313	מִפְלָג				9		9	n[m]	*division*
314	מַפֶּלֶת		8	1			9	nf	*downfall*
315	מֹץ		8		1		9	nm	*chaff*
316	מִצְעָר	I	5	2	2		9	nm	*small thing*
317	מַר	II	9				9	adj	*strong*
318	מֶרְחָב		6		3		9	n[m]	*broad place*
319	מָרִיא		8		1		9	n[m]	*fatling*
320	מֵרֵעַ		9				9	nm	*friend*
321	מֶשֶׁךְ	IV	9				9	pln	*Meshech*
322	מִשְׁעָן	I	4	3	2		9	n[m]	*support*
323	מַשְׁקוֹף		3		6		9	n[m]	*lintel*
324	מַתַּת		6	3			9	nf	*gift*
325	מַתִּתְיָה		4		2	3	9	prnm	*Mattithiah*
326	מאר		4		4		8	vb	*be painful*
327	מֶגֶד		8				8	nm	*choice produce*
328	מִדְיָנִי		8				8	gent	*Midianite*
329	מַהֲלַלְאֵל		7		1		8	prnm	*Mahalalel*
330	מוֹסֵרָה	I	8				8	nf	*bond*
331	מוּשִׁי	I	8				8	prnm	*Mushi*
332	מְחֹלָה		8				8	nf	*dance*
333	מַלְבּוּשׁ		8				8	nm	*garment*
334	מֹלֶךְ	I	8				8	prn[m]	*Molech*
335	מַנְעוּל		6		2		8	n[m]	*bolt*
336	מַעְבָּרָה		8				8	nf	*pass*
337	מָעוּזְיָה				8		8	prnm	*Mauzzijah*

Rank	Lemma	MT	Si	Q	Inscr	Total	Type	Gloss
338	מַעֲכָתִי	8				8	gent	*Maacathite*
339	מַעֲמָק	5		3		8	n[m]	*depth*
340	מִפְקָד	5	2		1	8	n[m]	*muster*
341	מִפְתָּן	8				8	n[m]	*threshold*
342	מָצוֹר II	6		2		8	n[m]	*fortification*
343	מְצוּרָה I	8				8	nf	*fortification*
344	מִקְנֵיָהוּ	2			6	8	prnm	*Mikneiah*
345	מְרֵמוֹת	6			2	8	prnm	*Meremoth*
346	מִרְמָס	7		1		8	n[m]	*trampling place*
347	מַשְׂכִּית I	6		2		8	nf	*image*
348	מִשְׁלֹחַ	3		5		8	n[m]	*extending*
349	מְשַׁמָּה I	7		1		8	nf	*devastation*
350	מַאְרָב	5		2		7	nm	*ambush*
351	מוֹעֵצָה I	7				7	nf	*counsel*
352	מִזָּל			7		7	n[m]	*flow*
353	מִזְעָר I	4	3			7	n[m]	*a little, a few*
354	מַחֲלָה	4	3			7	nf	*sickness, disease*
355	מָחֲלַת II	7				7	prnf	*Mahalath*
356	מִישָׁאֵל	7				7	prnm	*Mishael*
357	מִכְבָּר	6		1		7	nm	*grating*
358	מִכְוָה	7				7	nf	*(scar of a) burn*
359	מִכְנָסַיִם	5	1	1		7	nmdu	*breeches*
360	מִלּוֹא II	7				7	pln	*Millo*
361	מלל I	6		1		7	vb	*wither*
362	מַלְקוֹחַ	7				7	nm	*spoil*
363	מֶלְקָחַיִם	6		1		7	n[m]du	*tongs*
364	מִסְכְּנוֹת I	7				7	nf	*supplies*
365	מעד	7				7	vb	*shake*
366	מצה	7				7	vb	*drain*
367	מָצוֹק	6	1			7	n[m]	*distress*
368	מִצְפֶּה II	6		1		7	pln	*Mizpeh*
369	מִצְרַיִם II	7				7	pln	*Mizraim*
370	מְרָיוֹת	7				7	prnm	*Meraioth*
371	מִשְׂרָה	2		5		7	nf	*government*

Rank	Lemma		MT	Si	Q	Inscr	Total	Type	Gloss
372	מְשֹׁאָה		3	1	3		7	nf	*devastation*
373	מַשְׁבֵּר		1		6		7	n[m]	*mouth of cervix*
374	משך	II	7				7	vb	*seize*
375	מְתוּשֶׁלַח		6		1		7	prnm	*Methuselah*
376	מַבּוּעַ		3		3		6	n[m]	*spring*
377	מִגְדֹּל		6				6	pln	*Migdol*
378	מָגוֹג		4		2		6	prnm	*Magog*
379	מָגֵן	V				6	6	prnm	*Magen*
380	מַהֲלָךְ		5	1			6	nm	*journey*
381	מַהְפֵּכָה		6				6	nf	*overthrow*
382	מוֹ		6				6	n[m]	*water*
383	מוך		5	1			6	vb	*be low*
384	מוֹרָד	I	5		1		6	n[m]	*descent*
385	מִזְלָגָה		5		1		6	nf	*fork*
386	מָחוֹל	I	6				6	nm	*dance*
387	מַחֲלֶה		2		4		6	nm	*sickness*
388	מַטְמוֹן	I	5	1			6	n[m]	*treasure*
389	מֵיטָב		6				6	n[m]	*best*
390	מָכִי		1			5	6	prnm	*Machi*
391	מַכְפֵּלָה		6				6	pln	*Machpelah*
392	מִכְתָּם	I	6				6	n[m]	*Miktam*
393	מִכְתָּם	II	6				6	n[m]	*secret prayer*
394	מִכְתָּם	III	6				6	n[m]	*inscription*
395	מִכְתָּם	IV	6				6	n[m]	*gold inscription*
396	מִכְתָּם	V	6				6	n[m]	*song*
397	מְלֵאָה		3		3		6	nf	*full produce*
398	מַלּוּךְ		6				6	prnm	*Malluch*
399	מַלָּח		4		2		6	nm	*mariner*
400	מלל	II	4	1	1		6	vb	*speak*
401	מְנַקִּית		4		2		6	nf	*bowl*
402	מסך	I	5		1		6	vb	*mix (wine)*
403	מִסְכֵּן		4	2			6	adj	*poor*
404	מַסְמֵר		5		1		6	nm	*nail*
405	מִסְפּוֹא		5	1			6	nm	*fodder*

Words Beginning with Mem

Rank	Lemma		MT	Si	Q	Inscr	Total	Type	Gloss
406	מְצוֹדָה	I	2	1	3		6	nf	*net*
407	מרץ	I	4		2		6	vb	*be sick*
408	מרר	III	5	1			6	vb	*be strong*
409	מָרֵשָׁה	I	6				6	pln	*Mareshah*
410	מְשׂוּרָה		4		2		6	nf	*measure*
411	מַשְׂכֹּרֶת		4		2		6	nf	*recompense*
412	מִשְׁמָן		6				6	nm	*fat*
413	מְשִׁסָּה		6				6	nf	*plunder*
414	מַתְכֹּנֶת		5	1			6	nf	*measurement*
415	מאס	II	5				5	vb	*flow*
416	מְאֵרָה	I	5				5	nf	*curse*
417	מִגְבָּעָה	I	4		1		5	nf	*headdress*
418	מָדוֹר				5		5	n[m]	*dwelling place*
419	מוֹלָדָה		4			1	5	pln	*Moladah*
420	מוֹסֵר		3		2		5	nm	*bond*
421	מוֹצָא	II	5				5	prnm	*Moza*
422	מְזַמֶּרֶת	I	5				5	nf	*snuffer*
423	מְזַמֶּרֶת	II	5				5	nf	*musical instrument*
424	מִזְרָחִי				5		5	adj	*eastern*
425	מַחֲבַת		5				5	nf	*griddle*
426	מַחְלָה		5				5	prnf	*Mahlah*
427	מֵידְבָא		5				5	pln	*Medeba*
428	מִכְמֹרֶת		3		2		5	nf	*net*
429	מַלְכִּי־צֶדֶק		2		3		5	prnm	*Melchizedek*
430	מַלְכִּי־שׁוּעַ		5				5	prnm	*Malchishua*
431	מְלֶכֶת		5				5	nf	*queen*
432	מָמוֹן			1	4		5	n[m]	*wealth*
433	מֶמְשָׁת					5	5	pln	*Memshath*
434	מֵסַב		4		1		5	n[m]	*couch*
435	מַסָּה	II	5				5	pln	*Massah*
436	מִסְכְּנוֹת	II	5				5	nf	*forced labour*
437	מִסְפָּר	II	3		2		5	n[m]	*account*
438	מַעֲדָן	I	4		1		5	n[m]	*delicacy*
439	מָעוֹן	IV	5				5	pln	*Maon*

Rank	Lemma		MT	Si	Q	Inscr	Total	Type	Gloss
440	מעך		3		2		5	vb	*press*
441	מַעֲרָבִי				5		5	adj	*western*
442	מִפְעָל		3	2			5	n[m]	*deed*
443	מצא	II	5				5	vb	*suffice*
444	מָצוֹר	IV	5				5	pln	*Egypt*
445	מֵצַר		3		2		5	n[m]	*distress*
446	מִקְרָה				5		5	nf	*beam-work*
447	מֵרַב		4			1	5	prnf	*Merab*
448	מַרְבִּית		5				5	nf	*increase*
449	מַרְבֵּק		4	1			5	n[m]	*stall*
450	מַרְגְּלוֹת		5				5	n[f]pl	*place of feet*
451	מָרָה	II	5				5	pln	*Marah*
452	מְרִיב בַּעַל		4			1	5	prnm	*Merib-baal*
453	מָרִים	I	5				5	nm	*blessing*
454	מרק	I	4		1		5	vb	*rub*
455	מִשְׁמָע	I	1		4		5	n[m]	*hearing*
456	מַתִּתְיָהוּ		4			1	5	prnm	*Mattithiah*
457	מַאֲכֶלֶת		4				4	nf	*knife*
458	מִבְנֶה		1		3		4	nm	*structure*
459	מִגְבָּל				4		4	n[m]	*kneading*
460	מִגְדָּנוֹת		4				4	nfpl	*precious things*
461	מגן	I	3		1		4	vb	*deliver up*
462	מָגֵן	III	4				4	adj	*insolent*
463	מַגָּע				4		4	nm	*contact*
464	מגר		2		2		4	vb	*throw*
465	מְגֵרָה		4				4	nf	*saw*
466	מַד	II	3		1		4	n[m]	*measure*
467	מַדְהֵבָה	I	1		3		4	nf	*distress, calamity*
468	מַדְהֵבָה	II	1		3		4	nf	*rout, defeat*
469	מֹדָע		2		2		4	nm	*relative*
470	מָהִיר	II	4				4	adj	*skilled*
471	מַהְפֶּכֶת		4				4	nf	*stocks*
472	מהר	II	3		1		4	vb	*acquire*
473	מוֹט	II	4				4	n[m]	*pole*

Rank	Lemma		MT	Si	Q	Inscr	Total	Type	Gloss
474	מוֹסָר	II	4				4	n[m]	*heart*
475	מושׁ	II	3		1		4	vb	*feel*
476	מוֹתָר		3		1		4	nm	*abundance*
477	מַזְדַּי					4	4	prnm	*Mazdaeus*
478	מָזוֹר	I	3		1		4	n[m]	*wound*
479	מָזוֹר	II	3		1		4	n[m]	*sore*
480	מָזוֹר	III	3		1		4	n[m]	*running sore*
481	מַזְמֵרָה		4				4	nf	*pruning knife*
482	מַחֲזֶה		4				4	n[m]	*vision*
483	מֶחֱזָה		4				4	nf	*window*
484	מַחְלוֹן		4				4	prnm	*Mahlon*
485	מִיכָא		4				4	prnm	*Mica*
486	מִיכָיָה		4				4	prnm	*Micaiah*
487	מְכַסֶּה		4				4	nm	*covering*
488	מכר	II	3	1			4	vb	*practise deceit*
489	מִלֻּאָה		3	1			4	nf	*setting*
490	מְלוּכָה	II	4				4	nf	*king*
491	מְלֵחָה		3		1		4	nf	*salt land*
492	מלל	IV	4				4	vb	*cut off*
493	מָנוֹר		4				4	n[m]	*weaver's beam*
494	מְנַשִּׁי		4				4	gent	*Manassite*
495	מְסִבָּה		1		3		4	nf	*circle*
496	מַסְגֵּר	I	4				4	n[m]	*smith*
497	מַסְגֵּר	II	3			1	4	n[m]	*prison*
498	מסה		4				4	vb	*melt*
499	מַסָּה	I	4				4	nf	*trial*
500	מְעוּנִי		4				4	gent	*Maonite*
501	מִפְלֶצֶת		4				4	nf	*horrible image*
502	מִפְרָשׂ		2		2		4	n[m]	*spreading*
503	מַפְתֵּחַ		3	1			4	nm	*key*
504	מֹצָה		1			3	4	pln	*Moza*
505	מָצוֹד	II	3		1		4	n[m]	*stronghold*
506	מְצוּדָה	I	4				4	nf	*net*
507	מָצוֹר	V	4				4	nm	*whey*

Rank	Lemma		MT	Si	Q	Inscr	Total	Type	Gloss
508	מַקֶּבֶת	I	4				4	nf	*hammer*
509	מִקְטֶרֶת		2		2		4	nf	*censer*
510	מִקְלוֹת		4				4	prnm	*Mikloth*
511	מִקְלַעַת		4				4	nf	*carving*
512	מִרְדֹּף				4		4	n[m]	*puruit*
513	מָרוּד		3	1			4	n[m]	*wandering*
514	מְרוּצָה	I	4				4	nf	*running*
515	מַרְפֵּא	II	3	1			4	nm	*calmness*
516	מַרְפֶּה		3		1		4	nm	*relaxation*
517	מרץ	II	4				4	vb	*be forceful*
518	מָרַק		3		1		4	n[m]	*broth*
519	מִרְקַחַת		3	1			4	nf	*ointment mixture*
520	מְרֹרָה	I	4				4	nf	*bitter thing*
521	מַשְׂאֵת	III	3			1	4	nf	*beacon*
522	מִשְׂרָפָה		4				4	nf	*burning*
523	מִשְׁאֶרֶת		4				4	nf	*kneading trough*
524	מֹשֶׁל	I	2	2			4	n[m]	*rule*
525	מִשְׁמָע	II	4				4	prnm	*Mishma*
526	מִשְׁמַעַת		4				4	nf	*hearing*
527	מִשְׁקֶלֶת		2		2		4	nf	*levelling implement*
528	מֶתֶג		4				4	nm	*bridle*
529	מְתַלְּעָה		3		1		4	nf	*tooth*
530	מְאוּם	I	1		2		3	pron	*anything*
531	מַאֲסָף				3		3	n[m]	*gathering*
532	מְבוּסָה		3				3	nf	*trampling*
533	מַבָּט		3				3	nm	*hope*
534	מִבְטַחְיָהוּ					3	3	prnm	*Mibtahiah*
535	מִבְשָׂם		3				3	prnm	*Mibsam*
536	מְגוֹרָה		3				3	nf	*fear*
537	מְהֵיטַבְאֵל		3				3	prnmf	*Mehetabel*
538	מֹהַר		3				3	n[m]	*bride-gift*
539	מַהֲרַי		3				3	prnm	*Maharai*
540	מוֹט	I	3				3	n[m]	*shaking, slipping*
541	מול	II	3				3	vb	*fend off*

Words Beginning with Mem

Rank	Lemma		MT	Si	Q	Inscr	Total	Type	Gloss
542	מוֹעֵצָה	II	3				3	nf	*disobedience*
543	מוּצָק	I	2	1			3	nm	*casting*
544	מוּצָק	II	3				3	n[m]	*constraint, distress*
545	מוֹרַג		3				3	nm	*threshing sledge*
546	מוֹרָה	I	3				3	nm	*razor*
547	מוֹרֶה	I	3				3	n[m]	*early rain*
548	מוֹרֶה	II	3				3	pln	*Moreh*
549	מִזָּה		3				3	prnm	*Mizzah*
550	מָזוֹן		2		1		3	n[m]	*food*
551	מַזָּלוֹת		1		2		3	n[f]pl	*planets*
552	מחא	I	3				3	vb	*clap*
553	מַחְצֵב		3				3	n[m]	*hewing*
554	מַחַת		3				3	prnm	*Mahath*
555	מיל		3				3	vb	*ward off*
556	מֵיפַּעַת		3				3	pln	*Mephaath*
557	מִיץ	I	3				3	nm	*pressure*
558	מִיץ	II	3				3	nm	*churning*
559	מֵישָׁרִים	II	3				3	nmpl	*wine*
560	מְכוּרָה		3				3	nf	*origin*
561	מכך		3				3	vb	*be brought low*
562	מִכְלָא		3				3	n[m]	*fold*
563	מִכְלוֹל		2		1		3	n[m]	*perfection*
564	מִכְסָה		2		1		3	nf	*number*
565	מַלְבֵּן		3				3	n[m]	*brickmould*
566	מלה				3		3	vb	*be full*
567	מְלִיצָה	I	2	1			3	nf	*mocking poem*
568	מְלִיצָה	II	2	1			3	nf	*allusive saying*
569	מְלִיצָה	III	2	1			3	nf	*sharp saying*
570	מְלִיצָה	IV	2	1			3	nf	*sweet saying*
571	מְלִיצָה	V	2	1			3	nf	*trope*
572	מַלְכִּיאֵל		3				3	prnm	*Malchiel*
573	מַלְכִּירָם		1			2	3	prnm	*Malchiram*
574	מִלְכֹּם		3				3	prn[m]	*Milcom*
575	מְמוּכָן		3				3	prnm	*Memucan*

Rank	Lemma		MT	Si	Q	Inscr	Total	Type	Gloss
576	מִמְכֶּרֶת		1		2		3	nf	*sale*
577	מֵן	I	2	1			3	n[m]	*string*
578	מִנְהָג		2		1		3	n[m]	*driving*
579	מִנְיָמִין		3				3	prnm	*Miniamin*
580	מִסְגֶּרֶת	II	3				3	nf	*stronghold*
581	מַסְוֶה		3				3	n[m]	*veil*
582	מְסִלָּה	III	3				3	nf	*gatehouse*
583	מַסַּע	II	1		2		3	n[m]	*breaking of camp*
584	מִסְפַּחַת		3				3	nf	*scab*
585	מָסֹרֶת	IV			3		3	nf	*division*
586	מַעֲבָר	I	3				3	n[m]	*pass*
587	מַעְגָּל	II	3				3	nm	*encampment*
588	מָעָה	I	1		2		3	nf	*particle*
589	מָעוֹן	II	3				3	n[m]	*help*
590	מָעוֹן	V	3				3	prnm	*Maon*
591	מַעֲכָה	II	3				3	pln	*Maacah*
592	מַעֲנֶה	II	1	2			3	n[m]	*purpose*
593	מַעֲרֹם		1	2			3	n[m]	*nakedness*
594	מֹף		1		2		3	pln	*Memphis*
595	מַפָּלָה		3				3	nf	*ruin*
596	מַפָּץ		1		2		3	n[m]	*shattering*
597	מַצָּה	II	3				3	nf	*strife*
598	מָצוֹד	I	3				3	n[m]	*net*
599	מָצוּק		2	1			3	n[m]	*pillar*
600	מִצְפֶּה	I	2	1			3	nm	*watchtower*
601	מַרְבֵּץ		2		1		3	n[m]	*resting place*
602	מְרִירִי	I	2	1			3	adj	*bitter*
603	מֶרְכָּב		3				3	nm	*saddle*
604	מַשָּׁא		3				3	nm	*debt*
605	מִשְׁאָלָה		2		1		3	nf	*request*
606	מִשְׁגָּה				3		3	nf	*error*
607	מִשְׁגֶּה		1		2		3	nm	*mistake*
608	משה		3				3	vb	*pull*
609	מִשְׁחָה	II	2		1		3	nf	*measurement*

Rank	Lemma		MT	Si	Q	Inscr	Total	Type	Gloss
610	מִשְׁחָה	III	2		1		3	nf	*consecrated portion*
611	מְשֵׁיזַבְאֵל		3				3	prnm	*Meshezabel*
612	מֹשֶׁל	II	2	1			3	n[m]	*likeness*
613	מִשְׁלַחַת		2		1		3	nf	*undertaking*
614	מְשֶׁלֶמְיָהוּ		3				3	prnm	*Meshelemiah*
615	מְשֻׁלֶּמֶת		1			2	3	prnf	*Meshullemeth*
616	מִשְׁנֶה	II	3				3	n[m]	*equivalent*
617	מְתֹם		3				3	n[m]	*well-being*
618	מַתְּנַי		3				3	prnm	*Mattenai*
619	מֶתֶק		2		1		3	nm	*sweetness*
620	מֵאָה	II	2				2	pln	*Tower of Hundred*
621	מַאֲכֹלֶת		2				2	nf	*fuel*
622	מאס	V	2				2	vb	*err, transgress*
623	מַאֹשׁ					2	2	prnm	*Maash*
624	מְבוּכָה		2				2	nf	*confusion*
625	מִבְחוֹר		2				2	n[m]	*choice*
626	מִבְטָא		2				2	n[m]	*impetuous utterance*
627	מְבִינָה				2		2	nf	*understanding*
628	מַבָּע				2		2	n[m]	*flow*
629	מִבְצָר	II	2				2	prnm	*Mibzar*
630	מַגְדִּיאֵל		2				2	prnm	*Magdiel*
631	מִגְדַּל־עֵדֶר		2				2	pln	*Migdal-eder*
632	מְגוּרָה	II	2				2	nf	*furrow*
633	מַגָּל		2				2	n[m]	*sickle*
634	מִגְרוֹן	I	2				2	pln	*Migron*
635	מִדָּה	II	1		1		2	nf	*garment*
636	מִדָּה	III	1		1		2	nf	*tribute*
637	מַדְהֹב	I			2		2	n[m]	*distress*
638	מַדְהֹב	II			2		2	n[m]	*driven out person*
639	מַדּוּ		2				2	nm	*garment*
640	מַדְוֶה		2				2	nm	*disease*
641	מָדוֹן	III	2				2	pln	*Madon*
642	מְדוּרָה		2				2	nf	*pile*
643	מְדִינָה	II	2				2	nf	*place of judgment*

Rank	Lemma		MT	Si	Q	Inscr	Total	Type	Gloss
644	מְדֹכָה		1		1		2	nf	*mortar*
645	מַדְמַנָּה		2				2	pln	*Madmannah*
646	מְדָן		2				2	prnm	*Medan*
647	מַדְרֵגָה		2				2	nf	*steep place*
648	מִדְרָךְ		1		1		2	n[m]	*treading place*
649	מַהֲלֻמוֹת		2				2	nfpl	*beatings*
650	מַהֲמֹרָה		1	1			2	nf	*pit*
651	מֹהֵר		2				2	n[m]	*warrior*
652	מָהֵר שָׁלָל חָשׁ בַּז		2				2	prnm	*Mahershalalhashbaz*
653	מַהֲתַלָּה		1		1		2	nf	*deception*
654	מוֹבָא		2				2	n[m]	*entrance*
655	מוֹט	III	2				2	n[m]	*Quagmire*
656	מוֹסָד	II			2		2	n[m]	*council*
657	מוּסָד		2				2	nm	*foundation*
658	מוֹסָדָה		2				2	nf	*foundation*
659	מוֹצָאָה		2				2	nf	*origin, latrine*
660	מוּצֶקֶת	I	2				2	nf	*casting, pipe*
661	מוֹקֵד		2				2	nm	*hearth*
662	מוֹרִיָּה		2				2	pln	*Moriah*
663	מוֹרָשׁ	I	2				2	n[m]	*possession*
664	מוֹרַשְׁתִּי		2				2	gent	*Morashtite*
665	מוּשִׁי	II	2				2	gent	*Mushite*
666	מְז					2	2	n[m]	*extract*
667	מזז				2		2	vb	*join*
668	מַזְלֵג		2				2	nm	*fork*
669	מִזְקָה				2		2	nf	*canal*
670	מִזְרֶה		2				2	n[m]	*pitchfork*
671	מֵחַ		2				2	n[m]	*fatling*
672	מְחַבְּרָה		2				2	nf	*beam*
673	מָחוֹז		1		1		2	n[m]	*harbour*
674	מְחוּיָאֵל		2				2	prnm	*Mehujael*
675	מַחֲזִיאוֹת		2				2	prnm	*Mahazioth*
676	מְחִידָא		2				2	prnm	*Mehida*
677	מְחִלָּה		1		1		2	nf	*hole*

Rank	Lemma		MT	Si	Q	Inscr	Total	Type	Gloss
678	מַחְלִי	II	2				2	gent	*Mahlite*
679	מַחֲלָפָה	I	2				2	nf	*plait*
680	מַחֲלָפָה	II	2				2	nf	*copious hair*
681	מַחֲלָצָה	I	2				2	nf	*festive robe*
682	מַחֲלָצָה	II	2				2	nf	*white garments*
683	מָחֲלַת	I	2				2	n[f]	*Mahalath*
684	מְחֹלָתִי		2				2	gent	*Meholathite*
685	מַחְמֹד		2				2	n[m]	*precious thing*
686	מַחְמֶצֶת		2				2	nf	*leavened thing*
687	מַחֲנֵה־דָן		2				2	pln	*Mahaneh-dan*
688	מַחֲנַיִם	II			2		2	prnm	*Mahanaim*
689	מַחַץ		1		1		2	n[m]	*wound*
690	מֶחֱצָה		2				2	nf	*half*
691	מֶחְקָר		1		1		2	n[m]	*searching*
692	מַחֲרֵשָׁה		2				2	nf	*ploughshare*
693	מַחְשֹׂף		1		1		2	n[m]	*stripping*
694	מַחְתֶּרֶת		2				2	nf	*breaking in, burglary*
695	מַטֶּה	II	2				2	n[m]pl	*mace*
696	מֻטֶּה		1		1		2	n[m]	*injustice*
697	מָטוּ		2				2	n[m]	*war, company*
698	מִטָּל		2				2	n[m]	*dew*
699	מִטְפַּחַת		2				2	nf	*cloak*
700	מַטְרֵד		2				2	prnf	*Matred*
701	מֵידָד		2				2	prnm	*Medad*
702	מֵי זָהָב	I	2				2	prn	*Me-zahab*
703	מֵי זָהָב	II	2				2	pln	*Me-zahab*
704	מִיכָיָהוּ		2				2	prnmf	*Micaiah*
705	מֵישָׁרִים	III	2				2	nmpl	*smoothness*
706	מֵישָׁרִים	IV	2				2	nmpl	*gullet*
707	מַכָּא					2	2	prnm	*Makka*
708	מִכְמָר		2				2	n[m]	*net*
709	מִכְמְתָת		2				2	pln	*Michmethath*
710	מַכָּר	I	2				2	n[m]	*business assessor*
711	מַכָּר	II	2				2	n[m]	*acquaintance*

Rank	Lemma		MT	Si	Q	Inscr	Total	Type	Gloss
712	מַכָּר	III	2				2	n[m]	*sale*
713	מַכְשֵׁלָה		2				2	nf	*ruin*
714	מַכְתֵּשׁ	I	2				2	nm	*mortar*
715	מַלְאָכִי		1			1	2	prnm	*Malachi*
716	מְלוּנָה		2				2	nf	*hut*
717	מַלּוֹתִי		2				2	prnm	*Mallothi*
718	מלח	II	1		1		2	vb	*dissipate*
719	מֶלַח	II	2				2	n[m]	*frayed clothing*
720	מַלְיָהוּ					2	2	prn[m]	*Maliah*
721	מְלִילָה		1		1		2	nf	*ear of corn*
722	מלך	II	2				2	vb	*counsel*
723	מֶלֶךְ	II	2				2	prnm	*Melech*
724	מַלְמָד		1	1			2	n[m]	*goad*
725	מלץ		2				2	vb	*be smooth*
726	מֶלְצַר		2				2	nm	*guardian*
727	מלק		2				2	vb	*pinch off*
728	מָלָשׁ					2	2	prn[m]	*Malash*
729	מָמוֹת		2				2	n[m]	*death*
730	מִמְסָךְ	I	2				2	n[m]	*(bowl of) mixed wine*
731	מַמְרֵא	II	2				2	prnm	*Mamre*
732	מַמְתַקִּים		2				2	n[m]pl	*sweetness*
733	מֹנֶה		2				2	n[m]	*time*
734	מָנוֹן	I	1	1			2	adj	*insolent*
735	מְנוּסָה		2				2	nf	*flight*
736	מָנַחַת	I	2				2	prnm	*Manahath*
737	מִנִּית	I	2				2	pln	*Minnith*
738	מָס		1		1		2	adj	*melting*
739	מִסְחָר		1		1		2	n[m]	*goods*
740	מסך	II	2				2	vb	*draw*
741	מַסֵּכָה	II	2				2	nf	*covering*
742	מַסֶּכֶת		2				2	nf	*web*
743	מִסְפָּחָה		2				2	nf	*veil*
744	מִסְפָּר	IV	1			1	2	prnm	*Mispar*
745	מסר	II			2		2	vb	*hand over*

Words Beginning with Mem

Rank	Lemma		MT	Si	Q	Inscr	Total	Type	Gloss
746	מסר	III	2				2	vb	*deliver up*
747	מַסֹּרֶת	I	1		1		2	nf	*collecting point*
748	מָסֹרֶת	I	1		1		2	nf	*bond*
749	מָסֹרֶת	II	1		1		2	nf	*tradition*
750	מֹסֵרֹת		2				2	pln	*Moseroth*
751	מַעְבָּד	I	1	1			2	n[m]	*deed*
752	מַעֲבֶה		1		1		2	n[m]	*thickness*
753	מַעְגָּל	III	2				2	nm	*pasture*
754	מַעַדְיָה		2				2	prnm	*Maadiah*
755	מַעֲדָן	II	2				2	n[f]	*bond*
756	מִעוּט			1	1		2	n[m]	*small thing*
757	מְעִינִי		2				2	gent	*perh Minaean*
758	מַעֲנָה		2				2	nf	*furrow*
759	מַעֲצָד		2				2	n[m]	*axe*
760	מַעֲצוֹר		1	1			2	n[m]	*stopping*
761	מַעֲקֶה		1		1		2	n[m]	*parapet*
762	מַעֲקָשׁ		1		1		2	n[m]	*rough place*
763	מַעַר		2				2	n[m]	*nakedness*
764	מַעֲשֶׂה	II	2				2	nm	*covering*
765	מַעֲשַׁקָּה		2				2	nf	*extortion*
766	מַפָּח		1	1			2	nm	*expiring*
767	מַפָּל		2				2	nm	*refuse, fold (of flesh)*
768	מִפְלַגָּה		1		1		2	nf	*division*
769	מַפֵּץ		1		1		2	n[m]	*club*
770	מִפְתָּח		1		1		2	n[m]	*opening*
771	מִצְהָלָה		2				2	nf	*neighing*
772	מָצוֹר	III			2		2	n[m]	*creature*
773	מַצּוּת		1	1			2	nf	*strife*
774	מְצִירוֹק				2		2	nm	*emission of spittle*
775	מִצְרִי	II				2	2	prnm	*Mizri*
776	מַק		2				2	nm	*rottenness*
777	מִקְדֵּשׁ		2				2	n[m]	*holiest part*
778	מַקְהֵל		2				2	n[m]	*assembly*
779	מַקְהֵלֹת		2				2	pln	*Makheloth*

Rank	Lemma		MT	Si	Q	Inscr	Total	Type	Gloss
780	מִקְוֶה	III	2				2	nm	*abode*
781	מָקוֹר	II	2				2	n[m]	*convocation*
782	מִקָּח		1		1		2	n[m]	*taking*
783	מִקְנֵמֶלֶךְ					2	2	prnm	*Miknemelech*
784	מִקְסָם		2				2	n[m]	*divination*
785	מְקֵרָה		2				2	nf	*coolness*
786	מִקְשָׁה	II	2				2	nf	*cucumber field*
787	מַר	V	2				2	n[m]	*abortion*
788	מרא	I	1		1		2	vb	*be rebellious*
789	מֻרְאָה		2				2	nf	*crissum*
790	מַרְבַּד		2				2	n[m]	*cover*
791	מַרְבֶּה		2				2	n[m]	*abundance*
792	מֶרֶד	I	1		1		2	n[m]	*rebellion*
793	מֶרֶד	II	2				2	prnm	*Mered*
794	מַרְדּוּת	II		2			2	nf	*chastisement*
795	מְרֹדַךְ בַּלְאֲדָן		2				2	prnm	*Merodach-baladan*
796	מֹרָה		2				2	nf	*bitterness*
797	מֵרוֹם		2				2	pln	*Merom*
798	מְרוּקִים		1		1		2	n[m]pl	*cosmetic treatment*
799	מַרְזֵחַ		2				2	nm	*feasting*
800	מַרְחֶשְׁוָן				2		2	prn[m]	*Marcheshvan*
801	מַרְחֶשֶׁת		2				2	nf	*pan*
802	מְרִיבָה	I	2				2	nf	*strife*
803	מְרִירִי	II	2				2	nm	*demon*
804	מְרֹנֹתִי		2				2	gent	*Meronothite*
805	מרץ	III	2				2	vb	*be victorious*
806	מַרְצֵעַ		2				2	n[m]	*awl*
807	מרק	II			2		2	vb	*complete*
808	מֶרְקָחָה		2				2	nf	*pot of ointment*
809	מָרֵשָׁה	II	2				2	prnm	*Mareshah*
810	מַשָּׂא	IV	2				2	prnm	*Massa*
811	מַשְׂאֵת	II	1			1	2	nf	*utterance*
812	מְשׂוֹרָה				2		2	nf	*government*
813	מַשְׂטֵמָה	II	2				2	nf	*snare*

Rank	Lemma		MT	Si	Q	Inscr	Total	Type	Gloss
814	מַשְׂכִּית	II	2				2	nf	*desire*
815	מִשְׂרְפוֹת מַיִם		2				2	pln	*Misrephoth-maim*
816	מַשְׂרֵקָה		2				2	pln	*Masrekah*
817	מַשְׂרֵת		1		1		2	nf	*pan*
818	מַשׁ	I	2				2	prnm	*Mash*
819	מֵשָׁא	II	1		1		2	prnm	*Mesha*
820	מַשָּׁאָה		2				2	nf	*debt*
821	מַשֻּׁאָה		2				2	nf	*deception*
822	מִשְׁאָל		2				2	pln	*Mishal*
823	מַשֶּׁה		1		1		2	nm	*debt*
824	מְשׁוּכִים				2		2	pln	*Meshuchim*
825	מְשׁוּסָּה		1		1		2	nf	*plunder*
826	משׁח	III			2		2	vb	*measure*
827	מֶשַׁח				2		2	n[m]	*distance*
828	מָשְׁחָה	I	2				2	nf	*anointment*
829	מָשְׁחָת		2				2	n[m]	*blemish*
830	מִשְׁטָח		2				2	n[m]	*spreading place*
831	מֶשִׁי		2				2	n[m]	*fine cloth*
832	מְשִׁיחָה				2		2	nf	*anointing*
833	מֶשֶׁךְ	I	2				2	n[m]	*trail; acquisition*
834	מֶשֶׁךְ	II	2				2	n[m]	*(leather) pouch*
835	מְשִׁלֵּמוֹת		2				2	prn[m]	*Meshillemoth*
836	מִשְׁפְּתַיִם	I	2				2	n[m]du	*fire-places*
837	מִשְׁפְּתַיִם	II	2				2	n[m]du	*saddle-bags*
838	מִשְׁפְּתַיִם	III	2				2	n[m]du	*divided sheepfolds*
839	מִשְׁפְּתַיִם	IV	2				2	n[m]du	*double wall*
840	מִשְׁפְּתַיִם	V	2				2	n[m]du	*grazing places*
841	משׁשׁ	II	1	1			2	vb	*arrive*
842	מְתוּשָׁאֵל		2				2	prnm	*Methushael*
843	מַתָּנָה	III	2				2	pln	*Mattanah*
844	מִתְקָה		2				2	pln	*Mithkah*
845	מִתְרְדָת		2				2	prnm	*Mithredath*
846	מַאֲבוּס		1				1	n[m]	*granary*
847	מַאֲבָן				1		1	n[m]	*ballista*

Rank	Lemma		MT	Si	Q	Inscr	Total	Type	Gloss
848	מְאֹד	II	1				1	n[m]	*burden*
849	מַאֲוַי		1				1	n[m]	*desire*
850	מָאוֹס		1				1	n[m]	*refuse*
851	מְאוּרָה	I	1				1	nf	*light-hole*
852	מְאוּרָה	II	1				1	nf	*den*
853	מְאוּרָה	III	1				1	nf	*fiery coals*
854	מְאוּרָה	IV	1				1	nf	*eye*
855	מְאוּרָה	V	1				1	nf	*young*
856	מַאֲמָץ		1				1	n[m]	*exertion*
857	מאס	III	1				1	vb	*discharge pus*
858	מאס	IV	1				1	vb	*gape open*
859	מַאַס					1	1	prn[m]	*Maas*
860	מַאֲפֶה		1				1	n[m]	*baked food*
861	מַאֲפֵל		1				1	n[m]	*darkness*
862	מַאְפֵלָה				1		1	nf	*darkness*
863	מַאְפֵלְיָה		1				1	nf	*deep darkness*
864	מְאֵרָה	II	1				1	nf	*starvation*
865	מְאֵרָה	III	1				1	nf	*twitching (of limbs)*
866	מִבְדָּלָה		1				1	nf	*enclave*
867	מְבוּקָה		1				1	nf	*void*
868	מְבוּשִׁים		1				1	n[m]pl	*genitals*
869	מִבְחָר	II	1				1	prnm	*Mibhar*
870	מִבְטָחָה				1		1	nf	*confidence*
871	מַבְלָגָה				1		1	nf	*cunning simile*
872	מַבְלִיגִית		1				1	nf	*cheerfulness*
873	מָבָן					1	1	prn[m]	*Maban*
874	מְבֻנַּי		1				1	prnm	*Mebunnai*
875	מִבְרָח	I	1				1	nm	*fugitive*
876	מִבְרָח	II	1				1	nm	*hero*
877	מִבְרָח	III	1				1	nm	*picked men*
878	מִבְקָע				1		1	n[m]	*cleavage*
879	מְבַשְּׁלוֹת		1				1	nfpl	*hearths*
880	מַגְבִּישׁ	I	1				1	prnm	*Magbish*
881	מַגְבִּישׁ	II	1				1	pln	*Magbish*

Rank	Lemma	MT	Si	Q	Inscr	Total	Type	Gloss
882	מְגֻבָּלֹת	1				1	nfpl	*forged work*
883	מגד I			1		1	vb	*give*
884	מְגַדֵּפָה			1		1	nf	*blasphemy*
885	מִגְדּוֹל I	1				1	n[m]	*tower*
886	מִגְדָּל II			1		1	n[m]	*magnification*
887	מִגְדַּל־אֵל	1				1	pln	*Migdal-el*
888	מִגְדַּל־גָּד	1				1	pln	*Migdal-gad*
889	מָגוֹר III	1				1	n[m]	*storage pit*
890	מָגוֹר IV	1				1	n[m]	*throat*
891	מְגוּרָה I	1				1	nf	*granary*
892	מְגָזָה			1		1	nf	*ford*
893	מַגְזֵרָה	1				1	nf	*axe*
894	מְגַמָּה	1				1	nf	*multitude*
895	מָגֵן II			1		1	n[m]	*protection*
896	מֶגֶן	1				1	n[m]	*gift*
897	מְגִנָּה I	1				1	nf	*covering*
898	מְגִנָּה II	1				1	nf	*shamelessness*
899	מִגְעֶרֶת I	1				1	nf	*rebuke*
900	מִגְעֶרֶת II	1				1	nf	*dysentery*
901	מַגְנֵס			1		1	prn[m]	*Magnus*
902	מַגְפִּיעָשׁ	1				1	prnm	*Magpiash*
903	מִגְרוֹן II	1				1	n[m]	*threshing floor*
904	מִגְרָן			1		1	n[m]	*destruction*
905	מִגְרָעָה	1				1	nf	*recess*
906	מֶגְרָפָה I	1				1	nf	*shovel*
907	מֶגְרָפָה II	1				1	nf	*floodwater*
908	מֶגְרָפָה III	1				1	nf	*dyke*
909	מִגְרָשׁ II	1				1	nm	*driven waves*
910	מִדְבָּר II	1				1	nm	*mouth*
911	מַדּוּחִים I	1				1	n[m]pl	*enticement*
912	מַדּוּחִים II	1				1	n[m]pl	*false claims*
913	מַדּוּחִים III	1				1	n[m]pl	*folly*
914	מָדוֹן II	1				1	n[m]	*(object of) contempt*
915	מִדְחֶה	1				1	nm	*downfall, ruin*

Rank	Lemma		MT	Si	Q	Inscr	Total	Type	Gloss
916	מַדְחֵפָה		1				1	nf	*thrust*
917	מָדִי		1				1	gent	*Mede*
918	מִדִּין		1				1	pln	*Middin*
919	מְדִינָה	III	1				1	nf	*prefect*
920	מַדְמֵן		1				1	pln	*Madmen*
921	מַדְמֵנָה	I	1				1	nf	*dung-pit*
922	מַדְמֵנָה	II	1				1	pln	*Madmena*
923	מַדָּע	II	1				1	n[m]	*repose*
924	מַדָּע	III	1				1	n[m]	*friend*
925	מַדָּע	IV	1				1	n[m]	*kinsman*
926	מַדָּע	V	1				1	n[m]	*messenger*
927	מֹדַעַת		1				1	nf	*relative*
928	מֶדֶף	I			1		1	n[m]	*trap*
929	מֶדֶף	II			1		1	n[m]	*uncleanness*
930	מַדְקָרָה		1				1	nf	*piercing*
931	מִדְרוֹךְ				1		1	n[m]	*treading place*
932	מִדְרָס				1		1	n[m]	*floor*
933	מְדֻשָׁה		1				1	nf	*threshing*
934	מְהוּמָן		1				1	prnm	*Mehuman*
935	מְהוּתָלָה				1		1	nf	*praise*
936	מָהִיר	I	1				1	adj	*quick*
937	מהל	I	1				1	vb	*dilute*
938	מהל	II			1		1	vb	*circumcise*
939	מהל	III	1				1	vb	*weaken*
940	מַהֲלֶכֶת			1			1	nf	*gait*
941	מַהֲלָל		1				1	n[m]	*praise*
942	מהם	I		1			1	vb	*melt*
943	מהם	II		1			1	vb	*be pleasant*
944	מַהְפָּךְ				1		1	nf	*turning*
945	מְהֻקְצָעוֹת		1				1	nfpl	*corner rooms*
946	מהר	III	1				1	vb	*serve*
947	מהר	IV	1				1	vb	*sell, betray*
948	מוד	II			1		1	n[m]	*love*
949	מוֹדָה					1	1	nf	*measure*

Words Beginning with Mem

Rank	Lemma		MT	Si	Q	Inscr	Total	Type	Gloss
950	מוֹכֵן				1		1	n[m]	*locust*
951	מוּלָה		1				1	nf	*circumcision*
952	מוֹלִיד		1				1	prnm	*Molid*
953	מוּסָב		1				1	n[m]	*enclosure*
954	מוּסָךְ	I	1				1	n[m]	*covered way*
955	מוּסָךְ	II	1				1	n[m]	*fence*
956	מוּסָךְ	III	1				1	n[m]	*bench*
957	מוֹסָר	I	1				1	n[m]	*bond*
958	מוֹסֵרָה	II	1				1	pln	*Moserah*
959	מוּעָד	I	1				1	n[m]	*place of assembly*
960	מוּעָד	II	1				1	n[m]	*horde*
961	מוֹעֵד	II		1			1	adj	*fresh, tender*
962	מוּעָדָה		1				1	nf	*appointment*
963	מוֹעַדְיָה		1				1	prnm	*Moadiah*
964	מוּעָף	I	1				1	n[m]	*darkness*
965	מוּעָף	II	1				1	n[m]	*gleam, lustre*
966	מוּעָף	III	1				1	n[m]	*flight, escape*
967	מוּעָקָה	I	1				1	nf	*affliction*
968	מוּעָקָה	II	1				1	nf	*ulcer*
969	מוֹצָא	III	1				1	n[m]	*star, sparkler*
970	מוֹצָא	IV	1				1	n[m]	*smelter*
971	מוּצָק	III	1				1	n[m]	*outpouring*
972	מוּצֶקֶת	II	1				1	nf	*cast metal*
973	מוק		1				1	vb	*mock*
974	מוֹקְדָה		1				1	nf	*hearth*
975	מוֹקִר					1	1	prn[m]	*Mokir*
976	מוֹקֵשׁ	II	1				1	n[m]	*boomerang*
977	מוֹרָד	II	1				1	n[m]	*watering-place*
978	מוֹרָד	III	1				1	n[m]	*rivulet*
979	מוֹרָה	III	1				1	nf	*muzzle*
980	מוֹרָשׁ	II	1				1	n[m]	*desire*
981	מוֹרָשׁ	III	1				1	n[m]	*string*
982	מוֹרֶשֶׁת־גַּת		1				1	pln	*Moresheth-gath*
983	מוֹשֶׁבֶת				1		1	nf	*dwelling*

Rank	Lemma		MT	Si	Q	Inscr	Total	Type	Gloss
984	מוֹשָׁעָה		1				1	nf	*salvation*
985	מֶזֶג		1				1	nm	*mixed wine*
986	מָזֶה	I	1				1	adj	*emaciated*
987	מָזֶה	II	1				1	adj	*thin*
988	מִזֶּה		1				1	prnm	*spurt*
989	מָזוּ		1				1	nm	*storehouse*
990	מָזוֹר	IV	1				1	n[m]	*trap, net, noose*
991	מַזּוֹרוֹת	I			1		1	n[f]pl	*rotten eggs*
992	מַזּוֹרוֹת	II			1		1	n[f]pl	*catapults*
993	מַזּוֹרוֹת	III			1		1	n[f]pl	*constellations*
994	מֵזַח	I	1				1	n[m]	*shipyard*
995	מֵזַח	II	1				1	nm	*girdle*
996	מְזִיחַ		1				1	n[m]	*girdle*
997	מְזַעְזֵעַ	I	1				1	nm	*one who reminds*
998	מַזָּרוֹת		1				1	prnm	*Mazzaroth*
999	מְזָרִים	I	1				1	n[m]pl	*press*
1000	מִזְרָע		1				1	nm	*place of sowing*
1001	מֹחַ		1				1	nm	*marrow*
1002	מחא	II			1		1	vb	*refuse*
1003	מַחֲבֵא		1				1	n[m]	*hiding place*
1004	מַחֲבֹא		1				1	n[m]	*hiding place*
1005	מִחְבָּן		1				1	n[m]	*fertile land*
1006	מַחֲגֹרֶת		1				1	nf	*robe*
1007	מחה	II	1				1	vb	*strike*
1008	מחה	III	1				1	vb	*be full of marrow*
1009	מָחָה		1				1	nf	*female prophet*
1010	מְחוּגָה		1				1	nf	*compass*
1011	מָחוֹל	II	1				1	prnm	*Mahol*
1012	מְחוֹלְלָה				1		1	nf	*dance*
1013	מָחוֹת		1				1	nfpl	*full measure*
1014	מְחִי		1				1	n[m]	*thrust*
1015	מְחִיר	II	1				1	prnm	*Mehir*
1016	מחל				1		1	vb	*forgive*
1017	מַחֲלֻיִים		1				1	n[m]pl	*sickness, suffering*

Words Beginning with Mem

Rank	Lemma		MT	Si	Q	Inscr	Total	Type	Gloss
1018	מַחֲלָף	I	1				1	nm	*knife*
1019	מַחֲלָף	II	1				1	nm	*censer*
1020	מַחֲלֻקוֹת			1			1	nf	*distribution*
1021	מַחֲלֹקֶת	II	1				1	nf	*smoothness*
1022	מַחְמָאֹת		1				1	nf	*curd-like things*
1023	מַחְמַד		1				1	pln	*Machomades*
1024	מַחְמָל		1				1	n[m]	*compassion*
1025	מַחְמָם					1	1	prn[m]	*Mahmam*
1026	מַחֲנָה		1				1	nf	*mantlet*
1027	מַחְמָם					1	1	prn[m]	*Mahmam*
1028	מַחֲנָק		1				1	n[m]	*strangling*
1029	מַחְסוֹם		1				1	n[m]	*muzzle*
1030	מחץ	II	1				1	vb	*drip*
1031	מחץ	III	1				1	vb	*run*
1032	מחק		1				1	vb	*crush*
1033	מַחֲקֹרֶת			1			1	nf	*searching out*
1034	מַחֲרָאָה		1				1	nf	*latrine*
1035	מַחֲרָשׁ				1		1	n[m]	*scheming*
1036	מַחֲרֵשָׁה		1				1	nf	*goad*
1037	מַחְשָׁב	II			1		1	nm	*fissure*
1038	מַחְתּוֹשׁ				1		1	prn[m]	*Mahtosh*
1039	מַטְאֲטֵא	I	1				1	n[m]	*broom*
1040	מַטְאֲטֵא	II	1				1	n[m]	*means of destruction*
1041	מַטְבֵּחַ		1				1	n[m]	*slaughter*
1042	מָטֶה		1				1	adj	*reaching*
1043	מֻטָּה		1				1	nf	*outspreading*
1044	מַטְוֶה		1				1	n[m]	*yarn*
1045	מָטוֹן				1		1	n[m]	*hiding place*
1046	מְטִיל	I	1				1	n[m]	*rod*
1047	מְטִיל	II	1				1	adj	*strong*
1048	מַטְמֹנֶת			1			1	nf	*treasure*
1049	מַטְרִי		1				1	gent	*Matrite*
1050	מיד		1				1	vb	*shake*
1051	מִיכָהוּ		1				1	prnm	*Micah*

Rank	Lemma		MT	Si	Q	Inscr	Total	Type	Gloss
1052	מִיכָל	I	1				1	n[m]	*pool*
1053	מִיכָל	II	1				1	n[m]	*collection*
1054	מִיץ	I	1				1	vb	*press*
1055	מִיץ	II	1				1	vb	*churn (milk)*
1056	מֵיץ		1				1	nm	*extortioner*
1057	מִיר		1				1	vb	*procure*
1058	מֵישָׁא		1				1	prnm	*Mesha*
1059	מֵישַׁךְ		1				1	prnm	*Meshach*
1060	מֵישַׁע		1				1	prnm	*Mesha*
1061	מֵישָׁע		1				1	prnm	*Mesha*
1062	מַכְבֵּנָה	I	1				1	prn[m]	*Machbenah*
1063	מַכְבֵּנָה	II	1				1	pln	*Machbenah*
1064	מַכְבַּנַּי		1				1	prnm	*Machbannai*
1065	מַכְבֵּר		1				1	n[m]	*cover*
1066	מָכִירִי		1				1	gent	*Machirite*
1067	מִכְלוֹת		1				1	nfpl	*perfection*
1068	מַכְלֻל		1				1	n[m]	*ornate robe*
1069	מִכְלָל		1				1	n[m]	*perfection*
1070	מַכֹּלֶת		1				1	nf	*food*
1071	מִכְמָן		1				1	n[m]	*treasure*
1072	מַכְנַדְבַי		1				1	prnm	*Machnadebai*
1073	מְכֹנָה		1				1	pln	*Meconah*
1074	מִכְרֶה	I	1				1	nm	*pit*
1075	מִכְרֶה	II	1				1	nm	*heap*
1076	מְכֵרָה	I	1				1	nf	*counsel*
1077	מְכֵרָה	II	1				1	nf	*weapon*
1078	מְכֵרָה	III	1				1	nf	*staff*
1079	מְכֵרָה	IV	1				1	nf	*beguilement*
1080	מִכְרִי		1				1	prnm	*Michri*
1081	מַכְרֵת		1				1	nf	*circumcision blade*
1082	מְכֵרָתִי		1				1	gent	*Mecherathite*
1083	מְכִתָּה		1				1	nf	*fragment*
1084	מַכְתֵּשׁ	II	1				1	pln	*Machtesh*
1085	מַלְאָכוּת		1				1	nf	*message*

Rank	Lemma		MT	Si	Q	Inscr	Total	Type	Gloss
1086	מִלֵּאת	I	1				1	nf	*setting*
1087	מִלֵּאת	II	1				1	nf	*waterhole*
1088	מִלֵּאת	III	1				1	nf	*stream*
1089	מִלֵּאת	IV	1				1	nf	*pool*
1090	מִלֵּאת	V	1				1	nf	*fullness*
1091	מַלּוּחַ		1				1	n[m]	*saltwort*
1092	מַלּוּכִי		1				1	prnm	*Malluchi*
1093	מָלוֹשׁ				1		1	n[m]	*kneeding trough*
1094	מלח	III	1				1	vb	*be dark*
1095	מִלְחָמָה	II	1				1	nf	*sistrum*
1096	מלט	II	1				1	vb	*be bald*
1097	מלט	III	1				1	vb	*bite*
1098	מלט	IV	1				1	vb	*cleave*
1099	מֶלֶט		1				1	n[m]	*mortar*
1100	מְלַטְיָה		1				1	prnm	*Melatiah*
1101	מלך	III	1				1	vb	*tear away*
1102	מֶלֶךְ	III	1				1	n[m]	*counsel*
1103	מֹלֶךְ	II	1				1	nm	*kingdom*
1104	מְלֹךְ		1				1	nm	*counsel*
1105	מַלְכֹּדֶת		1				1	nf	*snare*
1106	מַלְכִּי					1	1	prnm	*Malchi*
1107	מַלְכִּיאֵלִי		1				1	gent	*Malchielite*
1108	מַלְכִּי־רֶשַׁע				1		1	prnm	*Melchiresha*
1109	מַלְכָּם		1				1	prnm	*Malcam*
1110	מַלְכִּנֵר					1	1	prn[m]	*Malchiner*
1111	מְלֶכֶת		1				1	nf	*sororach*
1112	מלל	III	1				1	vb	*scrape*
1113	מִלֲלַי		1				1	prnm	*Milalai*
1114	מַלְקוֹחַיִם		1				1	n[m]du	*jaws*
1115	מֶלְתָּחָה		1				1	nf	*clothes store*
1116	מַלְתָּעוֹת		1				1	nfpl	*jawbone*
1117	מַמְּגוּרָה		1				1	nf	*granary*
1118	מֵמַד		1				1	n[m]	*measurement*
1119	מִמְסָךְ	II	1				1	n[m]	*bowl*

Rank	Lemma		MT	Si	Q	Inscr	Total	Type	Gloss
1120	מֶמֶר		1				1	n[m]	*bitterness*
1121	מַמְרֹרִים		1				1	n[m]pl	*bitterness*
1122	מִמְשַׁח	I	1				1	n[m]	*anointing*
1123	מִמְשַׁח	II	1				1	n[m]	*extension*
1124	מִמְשַׁח	III	1				1	n[m]	*sparkling*
1125	מִמְשָׁק	I	1				1	n[m]	*ground*
1126	מִמְשָׁק	II	1				1	n[m]	*place of possession*
1127	מָן	II	1				1	pron	*what?*
1128	מֵן	II	1				1	n[m]	*portion*
1129	מַנְגִּינָה		1				1	nf	*mocking song*
1130	מָנָה	III			1		1	nf	*fate*
1131	מָנֶה	II			1		1	n[m]	*portion*
1132	מִנְהָרָה	I	1				1	nf	*perh hollow place*
1133	מִנְהָרָה	II	1				1	nf	*signal station*
1134	מָנוֹ				1		1	plnm	*Mano*
1135	מָנוֹד		1				1	n[m]	*shaking*
1136	מָנוֹן	II	1				1	adj	*weak*
1137	מָנוֹן	III	1				1	adj	*pained*
1138	מִנְּזָר	I	1				1	n[m]	*consecrated one*
1139	מִנְּזָר	II	1				1	n[m]	*guard*
1140	מִנְּזָר	III	1				1	n[m]	*courtier*
1141	מִנְּזָר	IV	1				1	n[m]	*exorcist*
1142	מָנַחַת	II	1				1	pln	*Manahath*
1143	מָנַחְתִּי		1				1	gent	*Manahathite*
1144	מְנִי		1				1	n[m]	*fate*
1145	מִנִּי	I	1				1	pln	*Minni*
1146	מִנְיָן				1		1	n[m]	*number*
1147	מָנֵיס				1		1	prn[m]	*Manes*
1148	מִנִּית	II	1				1	n[m]	*rice*
1149	מִנְלֶה		1				1	n[m]	*acquisition(s)*
1150	מָנֹס				1		1	pln	*Manos*
1151	מִנְעָל		1				1	n[m]	*bolt*
1152	מַנְעַמִּים		1				1	n[m]pl	*delicacies*
1153	מְנַעַנְעִים		1				1	n[m]pl	*sistrum*

Rank	Lemma		MT	Si	Q	Inscr	Total	Type	Gloss
1154	מָנֹר					1	1	prn[m]	*Manor*
1155	מַס	II	1				1	n[m]	*melting*
1156	מַסְבָּלָא				1		1	prnm	*Masbala*
1157	מַסְגֵּר	III	1				1	n[m]	*women of the harem*
1158	מַסָּד		1				1	n[m]	*foundation*
1159	מִסְדְּרוֹן		1				1	n[m]	*porch*
1160	מַסָּה	III	1				1	nf	*despair*
1161	מִסָּה		1				1	nf	*perh sufficiency*
1162	מְסוּכָה	I	1				1	nf	*hedge*
1163	מְסוּכָה	II	1				1	nf	*covering*
1164	מְסוֹלָל				1		1	n[m]	*road*
1165	מַסָּח	I	1				1	adv	*by turns*
1166	מַסָּח	II	1				1	n[m]	*detachment*
1167	מֶסֶךְ	I	1				1	n[m]	*mixed wine*
1168	מֶסֶךְ	II	1				1	n[m]	*bowl*
1169	מַסֵּכָה	III	1				1	nf	*libation*
1170	מַסֵּכָה	IV	1				1	nf	*scheme*
1171	מְסָכָה				1		1	nf	*screen*
1172	מִסְכֵּן	I	1				1	n[m]	*poor one*
1173	מִסְכֵּן	II	1				1	n[m]	*mulberry tree*
1174	מְסֻכָּן	III	1				1	n[m]	*sisu tree*
1175	מִסְכְּנוֹת	III	1				1	nf	*threshing place*
1176	מִסְכֵּנֻת		1				1	nf	*poverty*
1177	מְסַכְסְכָה				1		1	nf	*covering*
1178	מְסִלָּה	II	1				1	nf	*high praise*
1179	מַסְלוּל		1				1	nm	*road*
1180	מִסְלָע		1				1	n[m]	*rocky place*
1181	מְסַמָּא				1		1	nf	*sealing stone*
1182	מַסָּע	I	1				1	n[m]	*quarry*
1183	מַסָּע	II	1				1	n[m]	*missile*
1184	מִסְעָד	I	1				1	n[m]	*table*
1185	מִסְעָד	II	1				1	n[m]	*step*
1186	מִסְעָר			1			1	nf	*storm*
1187	מִסְפָּר	III	1				1	n[m]	*border*

Rank	Lemma	MT	Si	Q	Inscr	Total	Type	Gloss
1188	מִסְפֶּרֶת I	1				1	prn	*Mispereth*
1189	מִסְפֶּרֶת II		1			1	nf	*scholarship*
1190	מסר I	1				1	vb	*count*
1191	מסר IV	1				1	vb	*select*
1192	מֹסָר	1				1	n[m]	*discipline*
1193	מְסָרֵף I	1				1	nm	*maternal uncle*
1194	מְסָרֵף II	1				1	nm	*incense burner*
1195	מָסֹרֶת III	1				1	nf	*number*
1196	מָסֹרֶת V			1		1	nf	*command post*
1197	מִסְתּוֹר	1				1	n[m]	*shelter*
1198	מַסְתֵּר	1				1	n[m]	*hiding*
1199	מַעְבָּד II	1				1	n[m]	*path*
1200	מַעֲבַדְיָה				1	1	prn[m]	*Maabadiah*
1201	מַעֲבָר II	1				1	n[m]	*burning*
1202	מַעְגָּל IV	1				1	nm	*cart*
1203	מַעֲדַי	1				1	prnm	*Maadai*
1204	מַעֲדָן III	1				1	n[f]	*faltering*
1205	מַעֲדָן IV	1				1	n[f]	*reluctant*
1206	מְעֻדָּנָה				1	1	prnf	*Meuddanah*
1207	מַעֲדֶנֶת	1				1	n[f]	*company*
1208	מַעְדֵּר	1				1	n[m]	*hoe*
1209	מָעָה II	1				1	nf	*multitude*
1210	מָעוֹג I	1				1	n[m]	*circle*
1211	מָעוֹג II	1				1	n[m]	*provisions*
1212	מָעוֹג III	1				1	n[m]	*round silo*
1213	מָעוֹג IV	1				1	n[m]	*store*
1214	מָעוֹג V	1				1	n[m]	*lame person*
1215	מָעוּז		1			1	nm	*arrogance*
1216	מָעוֹזֶן	1				1	n[m]	*refuge*
1217	מָעוֹךְ	1				1	prnm	*Maoch*
1218	מָעוֹן III	1				1	n[m]	*reminder of sin*
1219	מְעוֹנֹתַי	1				1	prnm	*Meonothai*
1220	מָעוּף	1				1	n[m]	*darkness*
1221	מָעוֹר	1				1	n[m]	*nakedness*

Rank	Lemma		MT	Si	Q	Inscr	Total	Type	Gloss
1222	מַעֲזְיָה		1				1	prnm	*Maaziah*
1223	מַעַזְיָהוּ		1				1	prnm	*Maaziah*
1224	מַעֲזֵן		1				1	n[m]	*mart*
1225	מעט	II	1				1	vb	*draw*
1226	מָעֹט		1				1	adj	*small*
1227	מַעֲטֶה		1				1	n[m]	*garment*
1228	מַעֲטֶפֶת		1				1	nf	*garment*
1229	מָעַי		1				1	prnm	*Maai*
1230	מְעִי	I	1				1	n[m]	*ruin*
1231	מַעֲכָת		1				1	prnm	*Maacath*
1232	מֹעַל	I	1				1	n[m]	*raising*
1233	מַעֲלִיל		1				1	n[m]	*deed*
1234	מָעֳמָד		1				1	n[m]	*standing ground*
1235	מַעֲמָסָה		1				1	nf	*burden*
1236	מַעֲנִית		1				1	nf	*furrow*
1237	מַעַץ		1				1	prnm	*Maaz*
1238	מַעֲצֵבָה		1				1	nf	*pain*
1239	מַעֲצָר		1				1	n[m]	*stopping*
1240	מַעֲרָבָה		1				1	nf	*west*
1241	מַעֲרֶה	I	1				1	n[m]	*empty place*
1242	מַעֲרֶה	II	1				1	n[m]	*approaches*
1243	מְעָרָה	II	1				1	nf	*empty place*
1244	מְעָרָה	III	1				1	pln	*Mearah*
1245	מַעֲרָךְ		1				1	n[m]	*disposition*
1246	מַעֲרָף			1			1	n[m]	*drop (of rain)*
1247	מַעֲרָצָה		1				1	nf	*terror*
1248	מַעֲרָת		1				1	pln	*Maarath*
1249	מַעֲשֶׂה	III	1				1	nm	*evening*
1250	מַעֲשֶׂה	IV	1				1	nm	*storehouse*
1251	מַעֲשַׂי		1				1	prnm	*Maasai*
1252	מִפְאָר				1		1	nm	*beauty*
1253	מִפְגָּע		1				1	n[m]	*target*
1254	מַפֻּחַ		1				1	nm	*bellows*
1255	מֻפִּים	I	1				1	prnm	*Muppim*

Rank	Lemma		MT	Si	Q	Inscr	Total	Type	Gloss
1256	מֵפִּים	II	1				1	n[m]pl	*defects*
1257	מֵפִיץ	I	1				1	n[m]	*scatterer*
1258	מֵפִיץ	II	1				1	n[m]	*club*
1259	מִפְלָאָה		1				1	nf	*wondrous work*
1260	מִפְלָט		1				1	n[m]	*refuge*
1261	מִפְלָשׂ		1				1	n[m]	*poising*
1262	מִפְרָץ	I	1				1	n[m]	*landing place*
1263	מִפְרָץ	II	1				1	n[m]	*wadi*
1264	מַפְרֶקֶת		1				1	nf	*neck*
1265	מִפְשָׂע				1		1	n[m]	*marching*
1266	מִפְשָׂעָה		1				1	nf	*buttocks*
1267	מֻצָּב	I	1				1	n[m]	*siege mound*
1268	מַצָּבָה		1				1	nf	*guard*
1269	מְצֹבָיָה		1				1	gent	*Mezobaite*
1270	מְצוֹדָה	II	1				1	nf	*stronghold*
1271	מְצוּדָה	III	1				1	nf	*steppe*
1272	מִצְחָה		1				1	nf	*greaves*
1273	מְצִלָּה		1				1	nf	*bell*
1274	מִצְלַחַת			1			1	nf	*success*
1275	מַצָּע		1				1	nm	*couch*
1276	מִצְעָר	II	1				1	pln	*Mizar*
1277	מַצְפּוֹן		1				1	n[m]	*hidden treasure*
1278	מצץ		1				1	vb	*suck*
1279	מֶצֶר					1	1	prnm	*Mezer*
1280	מַקֶּבֶת	II	1				1	nf	*excavation*
1281	מִקְוָה		1				1	nf	*reservoir*
1282	מַקָּחָה		1				1	nf	*ware*
1283	מִקְטָר		1				1	n[m]	*place of burning*
1284	מֻקְטָר		1				1	nm	*incense*
1285	מְקַטֶּרֶת		1				1	nf	*incense altar*
1286	מַקְלִיַח				1		1	prn[m]	*Makliah*
1287	מְקִמְיָהוּ					1	1	prnm	*Mekimiah*
1288	מֵקֵן					1	1	prn[m]	*Meken*
1289	מָקַץ		1				1	pln	*Makaz*

Words Beginning with Mem

Rank	Lemma		MT	Si	Q	Inscr	Total	Type	Gloss
1290	מַקְצֻעָה	I	1				1	nf	*knife*
1291	מַקְצֻעָה	II	1				1	nf	*square*
1292	מְקָרֶה		1				1	nm	*beam-work*
1293	מְקַרְקַר		1				1	n[m]	*echoing shout*
1294	מִקְשֶׁה		1				1	n[m]	*locks of hair*
1295	מַר	III	1				1	n[m]	*drop*
1296	מַר	IV	1				1	n[m]	*dust*
1297	מרא	II	1				1	vb	*beat*
1298	מרא	IV	1				1	vb	*act the man*
1299	מָרָא		1				1	prnf	*Mara*
1300	מִרְבָּה		1				1	nf	*much*
1301	מַרְגּוֹעַ		1				1	n[m]	*(place of) rest*
1302	מַרְגָּלִית				1		1	nf	*jewel*
1303	מַרְגֵּמָה	I	1				1	nf	*sling*
1304	מַרְגֵּמָה	II	1				1	nf	*heap of stones*
1305	מַרְגֵּעָה		1				1	nf	*(place of) rest*
1306	מַרְדּוּת	I	1				1	nf	*rebelliousness*
1307	מְרֹדַךְ		1				1	prnm	*Merodach*
1308	מֻרְדָּף		1				1	n[m]	*persecution*
1309	מרה	II			1		1	vb	*change*
1310	מרה	IV	1				1	vb	*be strong*
1311	מָרָה	I	1				1	n[f]	*instruction*
1312	מָרֶה		1				1	nm	*disputed matter*
1313	מַרְהֵבָה				1		1	nf	*raging*
1314	מְרוֹ		1				1	n[m]	*violent man*
1315	מְרוֹגֶלֶת				1		1	nf	*clothing for legs*
1316	מֵרוֹז		1				1	pln	*Meroz*
1317	מָרוֹחַ		1				1	n[m]	*crushing*
1318	מֵרוֹץ		1				1	n[m]	*race*
1319	מְרוּצָה	II	1				1	nf	*extortion*
1320	מָרוֹת		1				1	pln	*Maroth*
1321	מרח		1				1	vb	*rub*
1322	מְרָיָה		1				1	prnm	*Meraiah*
1323	מְרִירוּת		1				1	nf	*bitterness*

Rank	Lemma		MT	Si	Q	Inscr	Total	Type	Gloss
1324	מְרִירִי	III	1				1	adj	*mighty*
1325	מֹרֶךְ		1				1	n[m]	*faintness*
1326	מַרְכֹּלֶת		1				1	nf	*market place*
1327	מִרְמָה	II	1				1	prnm	*Mirmah*
1328	מִרְמָשׂ				1		1	n[m]	*reptile*
1329	מֶרֶס		1				1	prnm	*Meres*
1330	מַרְסְנָא		1				1	prnm	*Marsena*
1331	מַרְעֶה		1				1	nm	*pasturage supervisor*
1332	מַרְעֲלָה		1				1	pln	*Maralah*
1333	מִרְפָּשׂ		1				1	n[m]	*muddied waterhole*
1334	מֶרֶץ				1		1	n[m]	*agony*
1335	מַרְצֶפֶת		1				1	nf	*pavement*
1336	מֶרְקָח		1				1	n[m]	*perfume*
1337	מרר	II	1				1	vb	*flow*
1338	מְרֵרָה		1				1	nf	*gall*
1339	מְרֹרָה	II	1				1	nf	*strong thing*
1340	מְרָרִי	II	1				1	gent	*Merarite*
1341	מִרְשַׁעַת		1				1	nf	*wickedness*
1342	מְרָתַיִם		1				1	pln	*Merathaim*
1343	מַשָּׂא	III	1				1	n[m]	*tribute*
1344	מַשָּׂאָה		1				1	nf	*burden*
1345	מִשְׂגָּב	II	1				1	pln	*Misgab*
1346	מִשֶּׂה		1				1	nm	*sheep eating place*
1347	מְשׂוּכָה		1				1	nf	*hedge*
1348	מְשׂוּכָּה		1				1	nf	*hedge*
1349	מָשׂוֹר				1		1	n[m]	*measure*
1350	מַשּׂוֹר		1				1	nm	*saw*
1351	מָשׂוֹשׂ	II	1				1	nm	*rottenness*
1352	מִשְׂחָק		1				1	n[m]	*(object of) laughter*
1353	מִשְׂטָם				1		1	n[m]	*hostility*
1354	מֵשִׂים		1				1	n[m]	*attention*
1355	מִשְׂמָחָה			1			1	nf	*celebration*
1356	מִשְׂפָּח	I	1				1	n[m]	*bloodshed*
1357	מִשְׂפָּח	II	1				1	n[m]	*legal infringement*

Words Beginning with Mem

Rank	Lemma		MT	Si	Q	Inscr	Total	Type	Gloss
1358	מֹשֹׁשׁ		1				1	vb	*melt*
1359	מַשׁ	III	1				1	nm	*statue*
1360	מֵישָׁא	I	1				1	pln	*Mesha*
1361	מַשְׁאָב		1				1	n[m]	*watering hole*
1362	מַשָּׁאוֹן		1				1	n[m]	*deception*
1363	מִשְׁבָּת	I	1				1	n[m]	*cessation*
1364	מִשְׁבָּת	II	1				1	n[m]	*shattering*
1365	מְשׁוֹבָב		1				1	prnm	*Meshobab*
1366	מְשׁוּבָה	II	1				1	nf	*idleness*
1367	מְשׁוּגָה		1				1	nf	*mistake*
1368	מָשׁוֹט		1				1	n[m]	*oar*
1369	מִשּׁוֹט		1				1	n[m]	*oar*
1370	מְשׁוּלֶּמֶת					1	1	prnf	*Meshullemeth*
1371	משׁח	II			1		1	vb	*mar*
1372	מָשְׁחָה	II	1				1	nf	*prescribed portion*
1373	מִשְׁחָר	I	1				1	n[m]	*dawn*
1374	מִשְׁחָר	II	1				1	n[m]	*radiance*
1375	מַשְׁחֵת		1				1	n[m]	*destruction*
1376	מִשְׁחַת		1				1	nf	*disfigurement*
1377	מִשְׁטוֹחַ		1				1	n[m]	*spreading place*
1378	מִשְׁטָר		1				1	n[m]	*writing*
1379	מְשִׁיכָה				1		1	nf	*drawing (of water)*
1380	משׁך	III	1				1	vb	*scent*
1381	מֶשֶׁךְ	III	1				1	n[m]	*price*
1382	מֹשֶׁכֶת		1				1	nf	*belt*
1383	מָשָׁל	II	1				1	pln	*Mashal*
1384	מְשֶׁלֶמְיָה		1				1	prnm	*Meshelemiah*
1385	מְשִׁלֵּמִית		1				1	prnm	*Meshillemith*
1386	מְשֻׁלָּשׁ		1				1	n[m]	*triad*
1387	מֵשַׁם				1		1	n[m]	*desolation*
1388	מַשְׁמָן		1				1	n[m]	*rich food*
1389	מִשְׁמַנָּה		1				1	prnm	*Mishmannah*
1390	מִשְׁמַנָּה		1				1	prnm	*Mashmannah*
1391	מִשְׁמָר	II	1				1	nm	*muzzle*

Rank	Lemma		MT	Si	Q	Inscr	Total	Type	Gloss
1392	מִשְׁמָר	III	1				1	nm	*wakefulness*
1393	מִשְׁמָרָה				1		1	nf	*guardhouse*
1394	מְשַׁמֵּשׁ					1	1	prnm	*Meshammesh*
1395	מִשְׁנֶה	III	1				1	n[m]	*the best*
1396	מִשְׁעוֹל		1				1	n[m]	*pathway*
1397	מִשְׁעִי	I	1				1	n[f]	*cleansing*
1398	מִשְׁעִי	II	1				1	n[f]	*rubbing*
1399	מִשְׁעִי	III	1				1	n[f]	*midwife*
1400	מִשְׁעִי	IV	1				1	n[f]	*smoothness*
1401	מִשְׁעָם		1				1	prnm	*Misham*
1402	מַשְׁעֵן		1				1	n[m]	*support*
1403	מִשְׁעָן	II				1	1	prnm	*Mishan*
1404	מַשְׁעֵנָה		1				1	nf	*support*
1405	מֶשֶׁק	I	1				1	n[m]	*acquisition*
1406	מֶשֶׁק	II	1				1	n[m]	*libation*
1407	מֶשֶׁק	III	1				1	prnf	*Meshek*
1408	מַשָּׁק	I	1				1	n[m]	*rushing about*
1409	מִשָּׁק	II	1				1	n[m]	*swarm*
1410	מִשְׁקוֹל		1				1	n[m]	*weight*
1411	מִשְׁקָע		1				1	n[m]	*what is settled*
1412	מִשְׁרָה		1				1	nf	*juice*
1413	מִשְׁרָעִי		1				1	gent	*Mishraite*
1414	מֹת		1				1	nm	*louse*
1415	מַתְבֵּן		1				1	n[m]	*heap of straw*
1416	מֶתֶג הָאַמָּה		1				1	pln	*Metheg-ammah*
1417	מָתוֹר				1		1	n[m]	*following after*
1418	מתח		1				1	vb	*spread out*
1419	מַתָּךְ				1		1	n[m]	*outpouring*
1420	מַתְּלָאָה		1				1	interj	*what a weariness!*
1421	מְתִלָּה				1		1	nf	*deception*
1422	מַתָּנָה	II	1				1	nf	*violence*
1423	מִתְנִי		1				1	gent	*Mithnite*
1424	מתק	II	1				1	vb	*suck*
1425	מָתָק		1				1	nm	*sweetness*

Words Beginning with Mem

Rank	Lemma		MT	Si	Q	Inscr	Total	Type	Gloss
1426	מֹתֶק		1				1	n[m]	*sweetness*
1427	מִתְקָל				1		1	nm	*offence*
1428	מַתַּתָּה		1				1	prnm	*Mattathah*

נ

Rank	Lemma		MT	Si	Q	Inscr	Total	Type	Gloss
1	נתן		2015	62	228	26	2331	vb	*give*
2	נֶפֶשׁ	I	754	64	197	2	1017	nf	*soul*
3	נשׂא	I	659	27	68		754	vb	*lift*
4	נכה		502	3	23	1	529	vb	*strike*
5	נפל	I	434	13	73		520	vb	*fall*
6	נָא	I	405	4	10	3	422	part	*pray*
7	נגד		371	7	32	1	411	vb	*tell*
8	נְאֻם		376		1		377	nm	*utterance*
9	נָבִיא		325	5	44	2	376	nm	*prophet*
10	נַחֲלָה	I	222	12	77		311	nf	*inheritance*
11	נַעַר		240	4	11	9	264	nn	*lad*
12	נצל		213	7	34		254	vb	*deliver*
13	נטה		216	16	20	1	253	vb	*stretch out*
14	נגע	I	150	11	65		226	vb	*touch*
15	נֶגֶד	I	151	8	44		203	prep	*in front of*
16	נָשִׂיא	I	130	1	45	1	177	nm	*prince*
17	נוח	I	142	15	14	1	172	vb	*rest*
18	נוס	I	158	2	3		163	vb	*flee*
19	נגשׁ		125	4	31		160	vb	*draw near*
20	נַחַל	I	139	3	17		159	nm	*wadi*
21	נְחֹשֶׁת	I	140	2	10		152	nm&f	*copper*
22	נסע	II	141		2		143	vb	*travel*
23	נָהָר	I	119	2	11		132	nm	*river*
24	נֶגַע		78	2	49		129	nm	*stroke*

Rank	Lemma		MT	Si	Q	Inscr	Total	Type	Gloss
25	נחם		108	3	18		129	vb	*regret*
26	נבא		115		9		124	vb	*prophesy*
27	נֶגֶב	I	112		3		115	nm	*south*
28	נבט		69	17	26		112	vb	*look*
29	נחל	I	59	7	34		100	vb	*inherit*
30	נִדָּה	I	29		68		97	nf	*impurity*
31	נִדָּה	II	29		68		97	nf	*flow*
32	נֶסֶךְ	I	58		29	1	88	nm	*libation*
33	נֵצַח	I	41	3	39	1	84	nm	*endurance*
34	נצב	I	75		7		82	vb	*stand*
35	נשׂג		49	10	16		75	vb	*reach*
36	נדח	I	55	3	15		73	vb	*thrust*
37	נֶדֶר		60		12		72	nm	*vow*
38	נצח	I	64		8		72	vb	*oversee*
39	נצר	I	63	2	5		70	vb	*keep*
40	נטע		58	2	8		68	vb	*plant*
41	נִיחֹחַ		43	1	20		64	n[m]	*soothing*
42	נַעֲרָה	I	63				63	nf	*young woman*
43	נגף		49		13		62	vb	*strike*
44	נֵרִיָּה		10		1	51	62	prnm	*Neriah*
45	נְבוּכַדְרֶאצַּר		60		1		61	*prn[m]*	*Nebuchadrezzar*
46	נֹחַ		46	1	14		61	prnm	*Noah*
47	נכר	I	40	4	16		60	vb	*recognize*
48	נְעוּרִים		46	7	6		59	nfpl	*youth*
49	נקה		44	6	8	1	59	vb	*be clean*
50	נַפְתָּלִי		51		7		58	prnm	*Naphtali*
51	נְבֵלָה		48		7		55	nf	*corpse*
52	נקם		35	1	18		54	vb	*avenge*
53	נָכְרִי		45	2	4		51	adj	*foreign*
54	נָקִי		43		7		50	adj	*clean*
55	נוף	I	35	7	6	1	49	vb	*wave*
56	נוף	V	35	7	6	1	49	vb	*raise*
57	נֵכָר		36	1	12		49	n[m]	*foreignness*
58	נֵר	I	44	3	2		49	nm	*lamp*

Words Beginning with Nun

Rank	Lemma		MT	Si	Q	Inscr	Total	Type	Gloss
59	נָתָן		42	1		6	49	prnm	*Nathan*
60	נָגִיד		44	2	2		48	nm	*leader*
61	נוע	I	41	3	3		47	vb	*tremble*
62	נטשׁ	I	40	4	3		47	vb	*leave*
63	נָדִיב		27	5	13		45	adj	*willing, noble*
64	נתץ		42	1	1		44	vb	*pull down*
65	נסה	I	36	1	4	1	42	vb	*test*
66	נדר		31		10		41	vb	*vow*
67	נזה	I	24		17		41	vb	*sprinkle*
68	נחה	I	39		1		40	vb	*lead*
69	נְדָבָה		26		13		39	nf	*freewill*
70	נאץ		24	1	13		38	vb	*have contempt*
71	נָקָם		17	5	16		38	nm	*vengeance*
72	נְקָמָה		27	1	10		38	nf	*vengeance*
73	נהג	I	30	4	3		37	vb	*drive*
74	נֵבֶל	I	11	1		22	34	nm	*jar*
75	נדד	I	28	1	5		34	vb	*flee*
76	נֵבֶל	II	27	3	3		33	nm	*harp*
77	נָוֶה		32	1			33	nm	*habitation*
78	נֹכַח		25	5	3		33	n[m]	*front*
79	נדב		17	1	14		32	vb	*impel*
80	נוּן		30	1	1		32	prnm	*Nun*
81	נְשָׁמָה		24	2	5	1	32	nf	*breath*
82	נאף		31				31	vb	*commit adultery*
83	נָחָשׁ	I	31				31	nm	*serpent*
84	נצת		29	2			31	vb	*kindle*
85	נשׁק	I	31				31	vb	*kiss*
86	נְתִיבָה	I	21		10		31	nf	*path*
87	נֶשֶׁר		26		4		30	nm	*eagle*
88	נתק		27		3		30	vb	*tear away*
89	נְקֵבָה		22		7		29	nf	*female*
90	נֵזֶר	I	25		3		28	nm	*consecration*
91	נסך	I	26		2		28	vb	*pour out*
92	נְבָט		25	1	1		27	prnm	*Nebat*

Rank	Lemma		MT	Si	Q	Inscr	Total	Type	Gloss
93	נוד	I	24	2	1		27	vb	*move to and fro*
94	נַחוּם	1				27	27	prnm	*Nahum*
95	נְתַנְיָה		20			7	27	prnm	*Nethaniah*
96	נֹגַהּ	I	19		7		26	nf	*brightness*
97	נטף		18		8		26	vb	*drip*
98	נָבָל	II	18	4	3		25	adj	*outcast, sacrilegious*
99	נָבָל	IV	18	4	3		25	adj	*low-class*
100	נגשׂ		23		2		25	vb	*press*
101	נתשׁ		21	3	1		25	vb	*pluck up*
102	נָבָל	I	18	4	2		24	adj	*foolish*
103	נֵס	I	21		3		24	n[m]	*standard*
104	נתך		21		3		24	vb	*pour out*
105	נבל	I	20	1	2		23	vb	*wither*
106	נבע	I	10	6	7		23	vb	*gush*
107	נְחֶמְיָה		8	1		14	23	prnm	*Nehemiah*
108	נָבוֹת		22				22	prnm	*Naboth*
109	נַעַל		22				22	nf	*sandal*
110	נקף	II	18	3	1		22	vb	*go around*
111	נוף	IV	20		1		21	vb	*declare superfluous*
112	נָעֳמִי		21				21	prnf	*Naomi*
113	נָדָב		20				20	prnm	*Nadab*
114	נטר	II	5		15		20	vb	*be angry*
115	נפח	I	13	1	5		19	vb	*blow*
116	נקב	I	19				19	vb	*pierce*
117	נְגִינָה		14	1	3		18	nf	*music*
118	נזל		16	1	1		18	vb	*flow*
119	נָחוֹר		18				18	prnm	*Nahor*
120	נפץ	I	18				18	vb	*shatter*
121	נשׁה	I	13		5		18	vb	*lend*
122	נֵתַח		14	1	3		18	nm	*piece*
123	נֶתֶק		14		4		18	nm	*scall*
124	נגן		15	1	1		17	vb	*play music*
125	נָזִיר	I	16	1			17	nm	*consecrated one*
126	נֶזֶם		17				17	nm	*ring*

Words Beginning with Nun

Rank	Lemma		MT	Si	Q	Inscr	Total	Type	Gloss
127	נזר	I	10		7		17	vb	*consecrate*
128	נִינְוֵה		17				17	pln	*Nineveh*
129	נָתִין		17				17	nm	*temple servant*
130	נְבוּזַרְאֲדָן		15		1		16	*prnm*	*Nebuzaradan*
131	נוא		8		8		16	vb	*restrain*
132	נַעֲמָן		16				16	prnm	*Naaman*
133	נְצִיב	I	14	1	1		16	nm	*pillar*
134	נֵר	III	16				16	prnm	*Ner*
135	נָאוֶה		11	4			15	adj	*comely, fitting*
136	נגח		11		3		14	vb	*gore*
137	נָוָה		14				14	nf	*pasture*
138	נָעִים	I	13		1		14	adj	*pleasant*
139	נִשְׁכָּה		3		11		14	nf	*chamber*
140	נֶשֶׁף	I	12	1	1		14	n[m]	*twilight*
141	נְתַנְאֵל		14				14	prnm	*Nethanel*
142	נְבוֹ	I	12		1		13	pln	*Nebo*
143	נְבָלָה		13				13	nf	*sacrilege*
144	נגר	I	10		3		13	vb	*pour*
145	נדף	I	9	1	3		13	vb	*drive*
146	נְחוּשָׁה	I	10		3		13	nf	*copper*
147	נהל		10		2		12	vb	*lead*
148	נחשׁ	I	11		1		12	vb	*practise divination*
149	נָכֹחַ		8	2	2		12	adj	*straight*
150	נעם	I	8	4			12	vb	*be pleasant*
151	נער	II	11	1			12	vb	*shake*
152	נער	III	11	1			12	vb	*strip*
153	נשׁא	II	11	1			12	vb	*deceive*
154	נשׁך	I	11	1			12	vb	*bite*
155	נֶשֶׁךְ		12				12	n[m]	*interest*
156	נום	I	6	1	4		11	vb	*be drowsy*
157	נַחַת	II	7	4			11	n[f]	*quietness*
158	נֶטַע	I	4	4	3		11	n[m]	*plant*
159	נְטֹפָתִי		11				11	gent	*Netophathite*
160	נֵצֶר		4	1	6		11	nm	*shoot*

Rank	Lemma		MT	Si	Q	Inscr	Total	Type	Gloss
161	נֶגֶף		7	1	2		10	nm	*striking*
162	נֵזֶר	II	9		1		10	nm	*flower*
163	נַחְשׁוֹן		10				10	prnm	*Nahshon*
164	נכר	II	7	2	1		10	vb	*be foreign*
165	נצה	I	8	2			10	vb	*fight*
166	נֶשֶׁק		10				10	n[m]	*weapons*
167	נתח		9		1		10	vb	*cut into pieces*
168	נְבוּאָה		3	4	2		9	nf	*prophecy*
169	נוב		4		5		9	vb	*flow*
170	נָחָשׁ	II	9				9	prnm	*Nahash*
171	נָקֹד		9				9	adj	*speckled*
172	נתר	I	5		4		9	vb	*be loose*
173	נגהּ		6	2			8	vb	*shine*
174	נְהִי		7	1			8	n[m]	*lamentation*
175	נחת	I	8				8	vb	*go down*
176	נְכֹה		8				8	prnm	*Neco*
177	נֶכֶס		5	1	2		8	nm	*wealth*
178	נֹעַם		7	1			8	nm	*pleasantness*
179	נשׁה	II	7		1		8	vb	*forget*
180	נֹב		7				7	pln	*Nob*
181	נְבִיאָה		6		1		7	nf	*prophet* (fem)
182	נבל	II	5	1	1		7	vb	*be foolish*
183	נבל	III	5	1	1		7	vb	*be sacrilegious*
184	נבל	IV	5	1	1		7	vb	*act ignominiously*
185	נֵד	I	6		1		7	nm	*heap*
186	נהר	III	6		1		7	vb	*be noisily excited*
187	נוף	II	2	1	4		7	vb	*sprinkle*
188	נַחְנוּ		6			1	7	pron	*we*
189	נִיר	II	7				7	n[m]	*untilled ground*
190	נסח		4	2		1	7	vb	*tear away*
191	נֹף		7				7	pln	*Memphis*
192	נֹפֶת		6		1		7	nm	*flowing honey*
193	נשׁל		7				7	vb	*slip off*
194	נֹאד		6				6	nm	*skin bottle*

Rank	Lemma		MT	Si	Q	Inscr	Total	Type	Gloss
195	נגר	II	3		3		6	vb	*smite*
196	נָזִיד		6				6	n[m]	*pottage*
197	נָיוֹת		6				6	pln	*Naioth*
198	נָכֵא		3		3		6	adj	*stricken*
199	נָמֵר		6				6	nm	*leopard*
200	נִסּוּי			2	4		6	n[m]	*trial*
201	נעל	I	6				6	vb	*lock*
202	נצח	II	0	3	3		6	vb	*shine*
203	נֵצַח	II	5		1		6	nm	*glory*
204	נצץ	I	4		2		6	vb	*sparkle*
205	נקר		6				6	vb	*bore*
206	נקשׁ	II	5	1			6	vb	*ensnare*
207	נשׁא	I	5		1		6	vb	*lend*
208	נָתִיב		5		1		6	nm	*path*
209	נֹא		5				5	pln	*No, Thebes*
210	נאה		3	1	1		5	vb	*be fitting*
211	נֶאָצָה		3		2		5	nf	*reviling*
212	נְבָיוֹת		5				5	prnm	*Nebaioth*
213	נהם	I	5				5	vb	*growl*
214	נוּמָה		1	4			5	nf	*drowsiness, slumber*
215	נַחַת	IV	5				5	prnm	*Nahath*
216	נטר	I	4		1		5	vb	*keep*
217	נִין		3	2			5	nm	*offspring*
218	נִיר	I	5				5	n[m]	*lamp*
219	נֶכֶד		3	2			5	nm	*progeny*
220	נִמְשִׁי		5				5	prnm	*Nimshi*
221	נָסִיךְ	III	4	1			5	nm	*prince*
222	נסע	I	5				5	vb	*pull up*
223	נַעֲוִיָה				5		5	nf	*perversity*
224	נֹפֶךְ		4	1			5	n[m]	*turquoise*
225	נפץ	II	4		1		5	vb	*scatter*
226	נצה	II	5				5	vb	*go to ruin*
227	נִקָּיוֹן		5				5	n[m]	*cleanness*
228	נָשִׂיא	II	4		1		5	n[m]	*mist*

Rank	Lemma		MT	Si	Q	Inscr	Total	Type	Gloss
229	נשׁב		3	1	1		5	vb	*blow*
230	נשׁך	II	5				5	vb	*pay interest*
231	נְאָקָה		4				4	nf	*groaning*
232	נבב		4				4	vb	*hollow out*
233	נדה	I	2	1	1		4	vb	*thrust aside*
234	נהה	I	3	1			4	vb	*lament*
235	נהר	II	3		1		4	vb	*shine*
236	נוע	III	4				4	vb	*be rootless*
237	נוֹצָה		4				4	nf	*plumage*
238	נחל	II	4				4	vb	*sift*
239	נִחֻמִים		3		1		4	n[m]pl	*comfort*
240	נטל		4				4	vb	*lift*
241	נָכֶה		3		1		4	adj	*stricken*
242	נכל		4				4	vb	*be deceitful*
243	נִמְרֹד		4				4	prnm	*Nimrod*
244	נֶסֶךְ	II	4				4	nm	*molten image*
245	נסס	III	4				4	vb	*sway*
246	נֹעָה	I	4				4	prnf	*Noah*
247	נַעֲמָה	I	4				4	prnf	*Naamah*
248	נַעֲמָתִי		4				4	gent	*Naamathite*
249	נֹעַר		4				4	n[m]	*(time of) youth*
250	נֶפֶג		4				4	prnm	*Nepheg*
251	נָפָה	III	4				4	nf	*yoke, bridle; district*
252	נְפִלִים		3		1		4	nmpl	*giants*
253	נֵץ	I	1	2	1		4	nf	*blossom*
254	נצר	II	4				4	vb	*murmur*
255	נְקוֹדָא		4				4	prnm	*Nekoda*
256	נתר	II	3		1		4	vb	*spring*
257	נָאֶה			2	1		3	adj	*fitting*
258	נֶאֱמָנוּת				3		3	nf	*trustworthiness*
259	נָבִי					3	3	prn[m]	*Nabi*
260	נַגָּח		2		1		3	adj	*prone to gore*
261	נְדַבְיָה		1			2	3	prnm	*Nedabiah*
262	נדד	III	3				3	vb	*bow down*

Rank	Lemma		MT	Si	Q	Inscr	Total	Type	Gloss
263	נדח	II	3				3	vb	*impel, wield*
264	נְדִיבָה		3				3	nf	*nobility*
265	נדף	II	3				3	vb	*dry up*
266	נְהָמָה	I	2		1		3	nf	*growling*
267	נהר	I	3				3	vb	*flow*
268	נֹוב		1	2			3	n[m]	*what flows*
269	נֹוחַ		1		2		3	n[m]	*rest*
270	נוע	II	3				3	vb	*dominate*
271	נֶחֱלָמִי		3				3	gent	*Nehelamite*
272	נַחְשִׁיר	I			3		3	nm	*carnage*
273	נְטִישָׁה		3				3	nf	*tendril*
274	נטשׁ	II	3				3	vb	*dash to the ground*
275	נִיב	I	2	1			3	n[m]	*fruit*
276	נִיצֹוץ		1	2			3	n[m]	*spark*
277	ניר	I	3				3	vb	*break up*
278	נִיר	V	3				3	n[m]	*dominion*
279	נְמוּאֵל		3				3	prnm	*Nemuel*
280	נֶמֶשׁ					3	3	prnm	*Nemesh*
281	נִמְשָׁר					3	3	prnm	*Nimshar*
282	נִסָּיֹון			3			3	n[m]	*test*
283	נַעֲלָם	II	1	1	1		3	n[m]	*bribe*
284	נַעֲרָה	II	3				3	prnf	*Naarah*
285	נַעֲרוּת			3			3	nf	*youth*
286	נְעַרְיָה		3				3	prnm	*Neariah*
287	נָפָה	II	3				3	nf	*height*
288	נָפִישׁ		3				3	prnm	*Naphish*
289	נֵפֶל		3				3	nm	*miscarriage*
290	נפשׁ		3				3	vb	*breathe*
291	נֵץ	II	3				3	nm	*hawk*
292	נְצִיב	II	1			2	3	pln	*Nezib*
293	נקב	II	3				3	vb	*slander*
294	נְקָבָה					3	3	nf	*boring through*
295	נִקּוּד		3				3	n[m]	*crumb*
296	נָקִיק		3				3	n[m]	*cleft*

Rank	Lemma		MT	Si	Q	Inscr	Total	Type	Gloss
297	נקע		3				3	vb	*recoil*
298	נקף	I	2		1		3	vb	*strike off*
299	נֹקֶף		2		1		3	n[m]	*striking* (off)
300	נְקָרָה		2		1		3	nf	*crevice*
301	נֵרְדְּ		3				3	nm	*nard*
302	נשק	II	3				3	vb	*be equipped (with)*
303	נשק	III	2		1		3	vb	*be in order*
304	נשק	IV	3				3	vb	*seal*
305	נשת		3				3	vb	*be dry*
306	נאו		2				2	vb	*praise*
307	נִאוּפִים		2				2	n[m]pl	*adultery*
308	נְאָצָה		2				2	nf	*disgrace*
309	נאק		2				2	vb	*groan*
310	נאר	I	2				2	vb	*repudiate*
311	נאר	II	2				2	vb	*curse*
312	נֹבַח	II	2				2	pln	*Nobah*
313	נַבְלוּת	I	1		1		2	nf	*lewdness*
314	נֶגֶב	II	2				2	n[m]	*provision*
315	נֶגֶב	III				2	2	prn[m]	*Negeb*
316	נֹגַהּ	II	2				2	prnm	*Nogah*
317	נֵד	III	2				2	nm	*mud-bank*
318	נדה	II	2				2	vb	*throw*
319	נדה	III	2				2	vb	*be impure*
320	נְהִיָה	I	1		1		2	nf	*lamentation*
321	נַהֲלָל		2				2	pln	*Nahalal*
322	נַהַם		2				2	n[m]	*growling*
323	נהק		2				2	vb	*bray*
324	נְהָרָה		1	1			2	nf	*light*
325	נוה	I	2				2	vb	*dwell*
326	נוה	II	1	1			2	vb	*glorify*
327	נוה	III	2				2	vb	*aim at*
328	נוֹעַדְיָה		2				2	prnmf	*Noadiah*
329	נָזִיר	II	2				2	n[m]	*accursed one*
330	נחה	IV	2				2	vb	*aim at*

Words Beginning with Nun

Rank	Lemma	MT	Si	Q	Inscr	Total	Type	Gloss
331	נַחַל II	2				2	n[m]	*date palm*
332	נַחַל III	2				2	n[m]	*tomb*
333	נַחֲלָה IV	2				2	pln	*Nahalah*
334	נַחֲלִיאֵל	2				2	*pln*	*Nahaliel*
335	נֶחָמָה	2				2	nf	*comfort*
336	נחר I	2				2	vb	*snort*
337	נַחְרַי	2				2	prnm	*Naharai*
338	נַחַשׁ	2				2	n[m]	*divination*
339	נחת II	2				2	vb	*be strong*
340	נחת IV	2				2	vb	*fashion*
341	נְטִיפָה	2				2	nf	*pendant*
342	נְטֹפָה	2				2	pln	*Netophah*
343	נטשׁ III	2				2	vb	*sharpen*
344	נִיסָן	2				2	prn[m]	*Nisan*
345	נכא I	1		1		2	vb	*strike*
346	נְכֹאת	2				2	nf	*ladanum*
347	נֵכֶל	1		1		2	n[m]	*deceitfulness*
348	נכר III	2				2	vb	*acquire*
349	נכר IV	2				2	vb	*acquire, sell*
350	נכר V	2				2	vb	*remove, repudiate*
351	נְכֹת	2				2	n[f]	*treasure*
352	נְמָלָה	2				2	nf	*ant*
353	נִמְרִים	2				2	pln	*Nimrim*
354	נסך II	2				2	vb	*weave*
355	נִסְרֹךְ	2				2	prnm	*Nisroch*
356	נֹעָה II				2	2	pln	*Noah*
357	נָעִים II	2				2	adj	*musical*
358	נעל II	2				2	vb	*provide with sandals*
359	נַעֲצוּץ	2				2	n[m]	*thornbush*
360	נְעֹרֶת	2				2	nf	*tow*
361	נֶפֶץ	1		1		2	n[m]	*cloudburst*
362	נֶפְתּוֹחַ	2				2	pln	*Nephtoah*
363	נַפְתֻּחִי	2				2	gent	*Naphtuhite*
364	נִצָּה	2				2	nf	*blossom*

Rank	Lemma		MT	Si	Q	Inscr	Total	Type	Gloss
365	נצח	IV			2		2	vb	*conquer*
366	נֵצַח	III			2		2	nm	*victory*
367	נֵצַח	IV	2				2	nm	*juice*
368	נְצִיחַ		2				2	prnm	*Neziah*
369	נִצָּן		1		1		2	n[m]	*blossom*
370	נֶצֶף					2	2	n[m]	*nezeph*
371	נֹקֵד	I	2				2	nm	*sheep breeder*
372	נֹקֵד	II	2				2	nm	*soothsayer*
373	נֹקֵד	III	2				2	nm	*cultic official*
374	נקשׁ	I	1	1			2	vb	*strike*
375	נֵרְגַל שַׂר־אֶצֶר		2				2	*prnm*	*Nergal-sharezer*
376	נשׂא	II	2				2	vb	*utter*
377	נְשִׁיקָה		2				2	nf	*kiss*
378	נשׁף		2				2	vb	*blow*
379	נֵשֶׁק	I	2				2	n[m]	*perfume*
380	נִשְׁתְּוָן		2				2	n[m]	*letter*
381	נְתַן־מֶלֶךְ		1			1	2	*prnm*	*Nathan-melech*
382	נתע	I	1	1			2	vb	*break*
383	נֶתֶר	I	2				2	n[m]	*natron*
384	נָא	II	1				1	adj	*raw*
385	נָאָה		1				1	nf	*oasis*
386	נָאהֲבַת					1	1	prnf	*Nahabath*
387	נָאוֹר		1				1	n[m]	*Shining One*
388	נאם		1				1	vb	*utter oracle*
389	נַאֲפוּפִים		1				1	*n[n]pl*	*adultery*
390	נְבוֹ	I	1				1	prnm	*Nebo*
391	נְבוֹךְ				1		1	n[m]	*spring*
392	נְבוּשַׁזְבָּן		1				1	*prnm*	*Nebushazban*
393	נבח		1				1	vb	*bark*
394	נֹבַח	I	1				1	prnm	*Nobah*
395	נִבְחַז		1				1	prn[m]	*Nibhaz*
396	נֵבֶךְ	I	1				1	n[m]	*spring*
397	נֵבֶךְ	II	1				1	n[m]	*sandy depths*
398	נָבָל	III	1				1	adj	*noble*

Words Beginning with Nun

Rank	Lemma		MT	Si	Q	Inscr	Total	Type	Gloss
399	נָבָל	V	1				1	prnm	*Nabal*
400	נַבְלוּת	II	1				1	nf	*ruin*
401	נְבַלָּט		1				1	pln	*Neballat*
402	נֹבֶלֶת	I	1				1	nf	*unripe figs*
403	נבע	II	1				1	vb	*ferment*
404	נבק		1				1	vb	*pour*
405	נֶבֶשׁ					1	1	n[f]	*soul*
406	נִבְשָׁן		1				1	pln	*Nibshan*
407	נֶגְבִּי					1	1	prnm	*Negbi*
408	נֶגֶד	II	1				1	n[m]	*blow*
409	נְגֹהָה		1				1	nf	*brightness*
410	נגע	II	1				1	vb	*rest*
411	נֵד	II	1				1	n[m]	*mist*
412	נֹד	I	1				1	n[m]	*wandering*
413	נֹד	II	1				1	n[m]	*grief, lament*
414	נדא		1				1	vb	*drive away*
415	נדד	II	1				1	vb	*be burned up*
416	נְדֻדִים		1				1	n[m]pl	*restlessness*
417	נֵדֶה		1				1	nm	*gift*
418	נדח	III	1				1	vb	*widen*
419	נָדָן	I	1				1	n[m]	*sheath*
420	נָדָן	II	1				1	n[m]	*gift*
421	נֹהַּ		1				1	n[m]	*pre-eminence*
422	נהג	II	1				1	vb	*lament*
423	נהה	II	1				1	vb	*follow*
424	נהה	III	1				1	vb	*turn away*
425	נַהַל					1	1	prn[m]	*Nahal*
426	נַהֲלֹל	I	1				1	n[m]	*watering place*
427	נַהֲלֹל	III	1				1	pln	*Nahalol*
428	נהם	III	1				1	vb	*sleep*
429	נוד	II	1				1	vb	*grieve, lament*
430	נוֹד		1				1	pln	*Nod*
431	נוֹדָב		1				1	prnm	*Nodab*
432	נוח	II	1				1	vb	*sigh*

Rank	Lemma		MT	Si	Q	Inscr	Total	Type	Gloss
433	נֹוחָה	II	1				1	prnm	*Nohah*
434	נֹוחָה	III	1				1	pln	*Nohah*
435	נוּחָה	II		1			1	nf	*respite*
436	נוט		1				1	vb	*shake*
437	נָוִי					1	1	prnm	*Navi*
438	נֹויָה					1	1	prnf	*Noijah*
439	נוס	II	1				1	vb	*tremble*
440	נוס	III	1				1	vb	*dry up*
441	נוס	IV	1				1	vb	*swing*
442	נוף	VI	1				1	vb	*deliver in large*
443	נֹוף	I	1				1	n[m]	*height*
444	נֹוף	II	1				1	pln	*Memphis*
445	נוץ	I	1				1	vb	*flee*
446	נוץ	II	1				1	vb	*sparkle*
447	נוּר			1			1	n[m]	*fire*
448	נוש	I	1				1	vb	*be sick*
449	נוש	II	1				1	vb	*tremble*
450	נֹותֹוס				1		1	prnm	*Nothos*
451	נזה	II	1				1	vb	*leap*
452	נזף			1			1	vb	*reprove*
453	נֵזֶק		1				1	n[m]	*injury*
454	נזר	II	1				1	vb	*guard against*
455	נַחְבִּי		1				1	prnm	*Nahbi*
456	נחה	II	1				1	vb	*turn to*
457	נחה	III	1				1	vb	*support*
458	נחה	V	1				1	vb	*ally oneself*
459	נְחוּם		1				1	prnm	*Nehum*
460	נָחוּשׁ		1				1	n[m]	*bronze*
461	נְחוּשָׁה	II	1				1	nf	*enchantment*
462	נְחִילֹות	I	1				1	nfpl	*flutes, flute playing*
463	נָחִיר		1				1	n[m]	*nostril*
464	נַחַל	IV	1				1	n[m]	*(mine) shaft*
465	נַחַל	V	1				1	n[m]	*dust*
466	נַחַל	VI	1				1	n[m]	*excavation*

Words Beginning with Nun

Rank	Lemma		MT	Si	Q	Inscr	Total	Type	Gloss
467	נַחֲלָה	II	1				1	nf	*destruction*
468	נַחֲלָה	III	1				1	nf	*wasting disease*
469	נַחַם		1				1	prnm	*Naham*
470	נֹחַם		1				1	nm	*compassion*
471	נַחֲמָנִי		1				1	prnm	*Nahamani*
472	נחן		1				1	vb	*groan*
473	נחץ	I	1				1	vb	*urge*
474	נחץ	II	1				1	vb	*be private*
475	נחר	II	1				1	vb	*be parched*
476	נַחַר		1				1	n[m]	*snorting*
477	נַחֲרָה		1				1	nf	*snorting*
478	נחשׁ	II	1				1	vb	*become rich*
479	נַחְשׁוֹל				1		1	n[m]	*gale*
480	נַחְשִׁיר	II			1		1	nm	*hunting*
481	נַחְשִׁיר	III			1		1	nm	*fear*
482	נְחֹשֶׁת	II	1				1	n[f]	*indecency*
483	נְחֻשְׁתָּא		1				1	prnf	*Nehushta*
484	נְחֻשְׁתָּן		1				1	prnm	*Nehushtan*
485	נחת	III	1				1	vb	*deport*
486	נַחַת	I	1				1	n[m]	*descent*
487	נַחַת	III	1				1	n[m]	*strength*
488	נָחֵת		1				1	adj	*descending*
489	נטב		1				1	vb	*drop*
490	נָטִיל		1				1	adj	*laden*
491	נָטִיעַ		1				1	n[m]	*plant*
492	נֵטֶל		1				1	n[m]	*weight*
493	נְטָעִים		1				1	pln	*Netaim*
494	נָטָף		1				1	n[m]	*incense*
495	נָטֹף				1		1	pln	*Natoph*
496	נֵטֶף		1				1	n[m]	*drop*
497	נִי		1				1	n[m]	*wailing*
498	נִיב	II	1				1	n[m]	*speech*
499	נֵיבָי		1				1	prnm	*Nebai*
500	נִיד		1				1	nm	*shaking*

Rank	Lemma		MT	Si	Q	Inscr	Total	Type	Gloss
501	נִידָה	I	1				1	nf	*impurity*
502	נִידָה	II	1				1	nf	*shaking of head*
503	נִין		1				1	vb	*increase*
504	נִיס		1				1	nm	*fugitive*
505	נִיר	III	1				1	n[m]	*sign of power*
506	נִיר	IV	1				1	n[m]	*mark*
507	נִיר	VI	1				1	n[m]	*new break*
508	נכא	II	1				1	vb	*be low*
509	נכא	III	1				1	vb	*put to flight*
510	נָכָא		1				1	adj	*stricken*
511	נֵכֶה		1				1	adj	*stricken*
512	נָכוֹן	I	1				1	n[m]	*blow*
513	נָכוֹן	II	1				1	prnm	*Nacon*
514	נְכָנְיָהוּ					1	1	prn[m]	*Neconiah*
515	נכר	VI	1				1	vb	*disapprove* of
516	נֵכֶר		1				1	n[m]	*misfortune*
517	נֹכֶר		1				1	n[m]	*misfortune*
518	נלה	I	1				1	vb	*finish*
519	נְמוּאֵלִי		1				1	gent	*Nemuelite*
520	נִמְטָר					1	1	prn[m]	*Nimtar*
521	נִמְרָה		1				1	pln	*Nimrah*
522	נֵס	II	1				1	n[m]	*trembling*
523	נֵס	III	1				1	n[m]	*(means of) flight*
524	נְסִבָּה		1				1	nf	*turn of affairs*
525	נסג		1				1	vb	*forge*
526	נָסִיךְ	I	1				1	n[m]	*libation*
527	נָסִיךְ	II	1				1	n[m]	*molten image*
528	נסס	I	1				1	vb	*be sick*
529	נסס	II	1				1	vb	*sparkle*
530	נסס	IV	1				1	vb	*suffer convulsions*
531	נסס	V	1				1	vb	*rally to the banner*
532	נֵעָה		1				1	pln	*Neah*
533	נְעִיאֵל		1				1	pln	*Neiel*
534	נְעִימָה			1			1	nf	*melody*

Words Beginning with Nun

Rank	Lemma		MT	Si	Q	Inscr	Total	Type	Gloss
535	נעם	II		1			1	vb	*sing*
536	נַעַם		1				1	prnm	*Naam*
537	נְעַמְאֵל					1	1	prn[m]	*Neamel*
538	נַעֲמָה		1				1	pln	*Naamah*
539	נַעֲמִי		1				1	gent	*Naamite*
540	נַעֲמָנִים		1				1	n[m]pl	*pleasantness*
541	נער	I	1				1	vb	*growl*
542	נער	V	1				1	vb	*be parched*
543	נער	VII	1				1	vb	*be a youth*
544	נַעֲרָה	II	1				1	nf	*sparrow*
545	נַעֲרָה	IV	1				1	pln	*Naarah*
546	נְעֻרוֹת		1				1	nfpl	*youth*
547	נַעֲרַי		1				1	prnm	*Naarai*
548	נַעֲרָן		1				1	pln	*Naaran*
549	נָפָה	I	1				1	nf	*sieve*
550	נְפוּשְׁסִים		1				1	prnm	*Nephushesim*
551	נפח	II	1				1	vb	*beat, afflict*
552	נֹפַח		1				1	pln	*Nophah*
553	נְפִיסִים		1				1	prnm	*Nephisim*
554	נפל	II	1				1	vb	*wither*
555	נֶפֶת		1				1	nf	*height*
556	נַפְתּוּלִים		1				1	n[m]pl	*wrestlings*
557	נצא		1				1	vb	*fly*
558	נצב	II	1				1	vb	*be weak*
559	נצב	III	1				1	vb	*vanish*
560	נִצָּב	II	1				1	n[m]	*image*
561	נצה	III	1				1	vb	*fly*
562	נצה	IV	1				1	vb	*hasten*
563	נֹצָה	II	1				1	nf	*hawk*
564	נָצוּר	I	1				1	n[m]	*secret place*
565	נָצוּר	II	1				1	n[m]	*mountain*
566	נצח	III	1				1	vb	*endure*
567	נָצִיר	I	1				1	adj	*preserved*
568	נִצְפָּה				1		1	nf	*caper bush*

Rank	Lemma		MT	Si	Q	Inscr	Total	Type	Gloss
569	נצץ	II	1				1	vb	*become dry*
570	נֶקֶב	I	1				1	n[m]	*engraving*
571	נֶקֶב	II	1				1	n[m]	*pipe*
572	נֶקֶב	III	1				1	n[m]	*mine*
573	נְקֻדָּה		1				1	nf	*bead*
574	נִקּוּף				1		1	n[m]	*gleaning*
575	נִקְלָה				1		1	prnm	*Niklah*
576	נִקָנֹר					1	1	prnm	*Nicanor*
577	נִקְפָּה		1				1	nf	*rope*
578	נֵר	II	1				1	n[m]	*mark*
579	נֵרְגַל		1				1	prnm	*Nergal*
580	נְשׂוּאָה		1				1	nf	*thing carried*
581	נָשִׂיא	III	1				1	n[m]	*one brought*
582	נשׁה	III	1				1	vb	*give up*
583	נָשֶׁה		1				1	n[m]	*sciatic* nerve
584	נְשִׁי		1				1	n[m]	*debt*
585	נְשִׁיָּה		1				1	nf	*forgetfulness*
586	נשׁם		1				1	vb	*pant*
587	נֶשֶׁף	II	1				1	n[m]	*trace*
588	נשׁק	V	1				1	vb	*acquiesce*
589	נְתִבְיָהוּ					1	1	prnm	*Nethibiah*
590	נְתִיבָה	II	1				1	nf	*ruin*
591	נתס	I	1				1	vb	*break up*
592	נתס	II	1				1	vb	*place thorns (in)*
593	נתע	II	1				1	vb	*cease*
594	נתע	III	1				1	vb	*pull out*
595	נתר	III	1				1	vb	*tear*
596	נֶתֶר	II	1				1	n[m]	*wound*

ABBREVIATIONS AND SIGNS

TEXTS

Gn Ex Lv Nm Dt Jos Jg 1 S 2 S 1 K 2 K Is Jr Ezk Ho Jl Am Ob Jon Mc Na Hb Zp Hg Zc Ml Ps Jb Pr Ru Ca Ec Lm Est Dn Ezr Ne 1 C 2 C

Si $Si_{(M)}$ (Sirach from Masada)

SIGNS

+ = the following is used in association with the preceding

:: = the following is used in contrast or opposition to the preceding

|| = the following is used in parallel to the preceding, or, the following text is parallel to the preceding

§ = section

† = not all these occurrences are listed in this article

* (at the beginning of an article) = see the Bibliography for discussion of the existence of this word

* (elsewhere in an article) = see the Bibliography for further semantic studies

⇨ = the following are related words

ABBREVIATIONS

abs. = absolute

accus. = accusative

acc. to =according to

add. = additional (inscription)

adj. = adjective

adv. = adverb

AHL = Academy of the Hebrew Language

Akk. = Akkadian

alw. = always

anat. = anatomical

aph.= aphel

app. = apposition

appar. = apparently

Arab. = Arabic

Aram. = Aramaic

architect. = architectural

assoc. = associated, association

BCE = before the Common Era

BHS = *Biblia hebraica stuttgartensia*

CE = Common Era

cent. = century

cit = quotation in rabbinic literature

coll. = miscellaneous collocations

conj. = conjunction

consec. = consecutive

corrupt. = corruption

cpl = common plural

cs = common singular

cstr. = construct

del. = delete

denom. = denominative

der. = derivands, derivatives, i.e. morphologically related forms
descr. = describing, description
design. = designation, designating
du. = dual
em., *see* if em., or em.
emph. = emphatic
encl. = enclitic
erased = erased reading
esp. = especially
Eth. = Ethiopic
EW = Eisenman and Wise
f., fem. = feminine
fpl = feminine plural
fr. = fragment
freq. = frequently
fs = feminine singular
gen. =genitive
gent. = gentilic
Gnz = Genizah fragment, manuscript
graf. = graffito
Heb. = Hebrew
hi. = hiphil
HN = Horbury and Noy
ho. = hophal
hothp. = hothpael
htp. = hithpael
htpal. = hithpalel
htpalp. = hithpalpel
htpo. = hithpoel
htpol. = hithpolal, hithpolel
I = inscription
ident. = to be identified
if em. = the foregoing results from an emendation
impf. = imperfect
impv. = imperative
inf. = infinitive
ins. = insert
inscr. = inscription
intens. = intensive
interj. = interjection
intrans. = intransitive
interrog. = interrogative
Kh. = Khirbet
Kt = ketiv
L = Codex Leningradensis B19 A, text of *BHS*
lit. = literally
m., masc. = masculine
mg = marginal, sublinear, supralinear reading
MH = Mishnaic Hebrew
mod. = modern
mpl = masculine plural
ms = manuscript; (in morphology) masculine singular
MT = Masoretic Text
n. = noun
ni. = niphal
nom. cl. = noun clause
ntp. = nithpael
nu. = nuphal (ni. mixed with pu.)
obj. = object
oft. = often
or em. = the foregoing will not be the case if the following emendation is accepted
orig. = originally
OSA = Old South Arabic
ost. = ostracon
pal. = palel
part. = particle
pass. = passive
PC = Preliminary Concordance (Richter)
perh. = perhaps
pf. = perfect
Phoen. = Phoenician
pi. = piel

pilp. = pilpel
pl., plur. = plural
pl.n. = place name
po. = poel, poal,
pol. = polal, polel
polp. = polpal
prep. = preposition
pr.n. = personal name
prob. = probably
pron. = pronoun
pronom. = pronominal
ptc. = participle
pu. = pual
pulp. = pulpal
Q = Qumran
Qr = qere
ref. = reference
Sam = Samaritan
Seb = Sebir (supposed reading)
sf. = suffix
sg. = singular
Si = Ben Sira
sim. = similar, similarly
sing. = singular
specif. = specifially
subj. = subject
suff. = suffix
syn. = synonym
Syr. = Syriac
T. = Tel, Tell
t = times
TiqSof = tiqqun soferim
trans. = transitive
Ug. = Ugaritic
usu. = usually
var. = variant
vb. = verb
voc. = vocative
W. = Wadi
WA = Wacholder and Abegg
Y. = Yhwh

OTHER ABBREVIATIONS

Other abbreviations will be found in The Sources and in the Bibliography

מ

*ם־ (enclitic mem)—particle, attached to the end of a word, without meaning; prob. vocalized *-ma* or *-mi* after a consonant, and *-m* after a vowel; it is not recognized by the MT, but vocalized as, e.g., a pl. ending or suffix; most identified occurrences are in poetry; numbers in square brackets at the end of an example refer to the item in the Bibliography with the same number; the following list is by no means exhaustive.

1. after a construct noun, Gn 1_{9} יִקָּווּ הַמַּיִם מִתַּחַת הַשָּׁמַיִם אֶל־מָקוֹם אֶחָד *let the waters under heaven be gathered into a single pool* (if em. מִקְוֵ[ה]־ם אֶחָד) [21, 23; cf. 73], Gn 14_{6} וְאֶת־הַחֹרִי בְּהַרְרָם שֵׂעִיר *and the Horites in the mountains of Seir* (if em. בְּהַרְרֵי־ם שֵׂעִיר) [10, 12, 21; cf. 73], Nm 21_{14} וְאֶת־הַנְּחָלִים אַרְנוֹן *and the wadis* (if em. נַחֲלֵי־ם) *of the Arnon* [21; cf. 73], Nm 24_{8} יֹאכַל גּוֹיִם צָרָיו *he devours the bodies of* (if em. גְּוֵי־ם) *his enemies* [31, 38], Nm 24_{17} כּוֹכָב מִיַּעֲקֹב וְקָם שֵׁבֶט מִיִּשְׂרָאֵל *stars of Jacob* (if em. כּוֹכְבֵ־ם יַעֲקֹב) *and tribes of Israel* (if em. שִׁבְטֵי־ם יִשְׂרָאֵל) *will rise* [3b, 6, 21, 53; cf. 73], Dt 32_{43} הַרְנִינוּ גוֹיִם עַמּוֹ כִּי דַם־עֲבָדָיו יִקּוֹם *rejoice, O corpses of* (if em. גְּוֵי־ם) *his people, for he will avenge the blood of his servants* [38], Dt 33_{11} מְחַץ מָתְנַיִם קָמָיו *crush the loins of* (if em. מָתְנֵי־ם) *his enemies* [3b, 5, 15, 21, 25, 27, 53, 64; cf. 73], Jg 5_{13} אָז יְרַד שָׂרִיד לְאַדִּירִים עָם *then down marched the remnant of the leaders of the people* (if em. לְאַדִּירֵי־ם) [60], 1 K 22_{27} מַיִם לַחַץ *water, oppression,* i.e. water of oppression (if em. מֵי־ם לַחַץ *water of oppression* [1QIsa 30_{20} מי לחץ]) [45, 63].

Is 10_{1} וּמְכַתְּבִים עָמָל כִּתֵּבוּ *and writings of oppression* (if em. וּמִכְתְּבֵי־ם) *they have written* [2, 21, 63; cf. 73], Is 17_{9} עָרֵי מָעֻזּוֹ *his strong cities* (if em. עָרֵי־ם עֻזּוֹ) [21], Is 18_{2} הַשֹּׁלֵחַ בַּיָּם צִירִים וּבִכְלֵי־גֹמֶא עַל־פְּנֵי־מַיִם *that sends ambassadors on the Nile, in vessels of papyrus upon the face of the Nile* (if em. פְּנֵי־ם יָם) [72], Is 19_{6} חָרְבוּ יְאֹרֵי מָצוֹר *the streams of the mountains will dry up* (if em. יְאֹרֵי־ם צוֹר) [28], Is 19_{9} וְאֹרְגִים חוֹרָי *and weavers of* (if em. וְאֹרְגֵי־ם) *white cloth,* Is 24_{18} אֲרֻבּוֹת מִמָּרוֹם נִפְתָּחוּ *the windows of heaven* (if em. אֲרֻבּוֹת־ם מָרוֹם) *are opened* [21], Is 28_{1} עַל־רֹאשׁ גֵּיא־שְׁמָנִים הֲלוּמֵי יָיִן *on the head of the rich valley of* (if em. גֵּיא־שַׁמְנֵי־ם) *those overcome by wine* [21; cf. 73], Is 28_{9} גְּמוּלֵי מֵחָלָב עַתִּיקֵי מִשָּׁדָיִם *those weaned from milk* (if em. גְּמוּלֵי־ם חָלָב), *those taken from the breast* (if em. עַתִּיקֵי־ם שָׁדָיִם) [21; cf. 73], Is 29_{4} וְהָיָה כְּאוֹב מֵאֶרֶץ קוֹלֵךְ *and your voice will be like a ghost of the underworld* (if em. כְּאוֹב־ם אֶרֶץ) [21], Is 30_{20} מַיִם לַחַץ *water, oppression,* i.e. water of oppression (if em. מֵי־ם לַחַץ *water of oppression* (1QIsa מי לחץ) [45], Is 37_{25} וְאַחְרִב בְּכַף־פְּעָמַי כֹּל יְאֹרֵי מָצוֹר *and I dried with my foot all the streams of the mountain* (if em. יְאֹרֵי־ם צוֹר) [28].

Jr 10_{10} וַיי׳ אֱלֹהִים אֱמֶת הוּא־אֱלֹהִים חַיִּים *and Y. is a God of* (if em. אֱלֹהֵי־ם) *truth, he is a God of* (if em. אֱלֹהֵי־ם) *life* [21], Ezk 26_{12} וַאֲבָנַיִךְ וְעֵצַיִךְ וַעֲפָרֵךְ בְּתוֹךְ מַיִם יָשִׂימוּ *and your stones and your beams and your dust they shall put into the midst of the sea* (if em. בְּתוֹךְ־ם יָם) [31, 54], Ezk 26_{20} וְהוֹשַׁבְתִּי בְּאֶרֶץ תַּחְתִּיּוֹת כָּחֳרָבוֹת מֵעוֹלָם *and I will make you dwell in the underworld, with the eternal ruins* (if em. כְּחָרְבוֹת־ם עוֹלָם) [54], Ezk 27_{34} עֵת נִשְׁבֶּרֶת מִיַּמִּים בְּמַעֲמַקֵּי־מָיִם *now you are shattered by the sea* (if em. עַתָּ[ה] נִשְׁבַּרְתְּ יָם־ם) *in the depths of the sea* (if em. בְּמַעֲמַקֵּי־ם־יָם) [54].

Ho 5_{7} בָּנִים זָרִים יָלָדוּ *they have engendered children of foreign fathers,* i.e. gods (if em. בְּנֵי־ם זָרִים) [66], Ho 7_{5} הֶחֱלוּ שָׂרִים חֲמַת מִיָּיִן *the princes became sick from the heat of wine,* i.e. perh. poisoned wine (if em. חֲמַת־ם יַיִן) [21, 66], Ho 7_{16} יִפְּלוּ בַחֶרֶב שָׂרֵיהֶם מִזַּעַם לְשׁוֹנָם זוֹ לַעְגָּם *their princes fell by the sword—out of the rage of the One who mocked them* (if em. לְשׁוֹן־ם זוֹ לַעֲגָם) [66], Ho 13_{2} אֹמְרִים זֹבְחֵי *sacrificial lambs* (if em. אִמְרֵי־ם זֶבַח) [61, 63, 66], Ho 14_{3} וּנְשַׁלְּמָה פָרִים שְׂפָתֵינוּ *and we will pay the fruit of our lips* (if em. פָּרֵי־ם שְׂפָתֵינוּ or פְּרִי־ם *the bullocks of our pens*) [15,

61, 66], Jon 2_9 מְשַׁמְּרִים הַבְלֵי־שָׁוְא *those who pay regard to* (if em. מְשַׁמְּרֵי־ם) *vain images* [21], Mc 7_{12} יָבוֹא לְמִנִּי אַשּׁוּר וְעָרֵי מָצוֹר וּלְמִנִּי מָצוֹר וְעַד־נָהָר *and they will come from Assyria and the city of the rock* (if em. וְעִר־ם צוּר), i.e. Sela, *and from Tyre* (if em. וּלְמִנִּי־ם צוּר) *to the River (Nile)* [28].

Ps 18_{16} אֲפִיקֵי מַיִם *channels of the waters* (if em. אֲפִיקֵי־ם יָם *channels of the sea*, as אֲפִקֵי יָם in par. 2 S 22_{16}) [4, 14a, 14b, 15, 21, 25, 45, 53, 63; cf. 73], Ps 18_{28} עֵינַיִם רָמוֹת תַּשְׁפִּיל *the haughty-eyed* (if em. עֵינֵי־ם רָמוֹת) *you humble* [14c, 21, 53; cf. 73], Ps 59_6 י״־אֱלֹהִים צְבָאוֹת *Y., God of Hosts* (if em. אֱלֹהֵי־ם) [21; cf. 73], Ps 60_{11} מִי יֹבִלֵנִי עִיר מָצוֹר *who will bring me to Rock City?* (if em. עִיר־ם צוּר) [21], Ps 68_{17} לָמָּה תְּרַצְּדוּן הָרִים גַּבְנֻנִּים *why do you look with envy, O mountains of* (if em. הָרֵי־ם) *peaks*, i.e. domed mountains [3b, 4, 5, 11, 15, 21, 53; cf. 73], Ps 74_{12} וֵאלֹהִים מַלְכִּי מִקֶּדֶם *and God, Ancient King* (if em. מֶלֶךְ־ם קֶדֶם) [21], Ps 77_6 חִשַּׁבְתִּי יָמִים מִקֶּדֶם *I consider the days of old* (if em. יְמֵי־ם קֶדֶם) [21], Ps 77_{18} זֹרְמוּ מַיִם עָבוֹת *the waters of the clouds pour down* (if em. מֵי־ם עָבוֹת) [15, 21; cf. 73], Ps 80_5 י״ אֱלֹהִים צְבָאוֹת *Y., God of Hosts* (if em. אֱלֹהֵי־ם) [21].

Ps 80_8 אֱלֹהִים צְבָאוֹת הֲשִׁיבֵנוּ *restore us, God of Hosts* (if em. אֱלֹהֵי־ם) [21], Ps 80_{15} אֱלֹהִים צְבָאוֹת שׁוּב־נָא *turn again, O God of Hosts* (if em. אֱלֹהֵי־ם) [21], Ps 84_9 י״ אֱלֹהִים צְבָאוֹת שִׁמְעָה תְפִלָּתִי *O Y., God of Hosts, hear my prayer* (if em. אֱלֹהֵי־ם) [21], Ps 88_7 בְּמַחֲשַׁכִּים בִּמְצֹלוֹת *in the darkness of the depths* (if em. בְּמַחֲשַׁכֵּי־ם מְצֹלוֹת) [21], Ps 89_{51} שְׂאֵתִי בְחֵיקִי כָּל־רַבִּים עַמִּים remember *my bearing in my bosom all the disputes of* (if em. רִבֵי־ם) *the peoples* [21; cf. 73], Ps 110_3 מֵרֶחֶם מִשְׁחָר לְךָ טַל יַלְדֻתֶיךָ *from the womb of morning* (if em. מֵרֶחֶם־ם שַׁחַר) *your dew will come to you* [21; cf. 73], Ps 141_4 אֶת־אִישִׁים פֹּעֲלֵי־אָוֶן *with a man of* (if em. אִישׁ־ם) *of the workers of iniquity* [4, 21; cf. 73].

Jb 5_{15} וַיֹּשַׁע מֵחֶרֶב מִפִּיהֶם (if em. מֵחֶרֶב־ם פִּיהֶם) *and he delivers* the needy *from the sword of their mouth* [17, 44, 69], Jb 11_8 עֲמֻקָּה מִשְּׁאוֹל מַה־תֵּדָע *the depth of Sheol! what can you know?* (if em. עֲמֻקָּה־ם שְׁאוֹל) [39, 69], Pr 22_{21} אֲמָרִים אֱמֶת *words of truth* (if em. אִמְרֵי־ם אֱמֶת, cf. אִמְרֵי אֱמֶת, v. 21a) [36, 57, 63], Ec 4_6 טוֹב מְלֹא כַף נָחַת מִמְּלֹא חָפְנַיִם עָמָל *better a handful of peace* (i.e. נַחַת II) *than handfuls of trouble* (if em. חָפְנֵי־ם עָמָל) [33].

2. after a noun or particle with pronominal suffix, Dt 33_2 וְאָתָה מֵרִבְבֹת קֹדֶשׁ *and with him were myriads of holy ones* (if em. וְאִתֹּה־ם רִבְבֹת) [7, 21, 53], Dt 33_3 אַף חֹבֵב עַמִּים *indeed, he loves his people* (if em. עַמּוֹ־ם) [21; cf. 73], Is 3_{12} עַמִּי נֹגְשָׂיו מְעוֹלֵל *my people are oppressors of children* (if em. נֹגְשֵׂי־ם עוֹלֵל) [21; cf. 73], Is 3_{13} וְעֹמֵד לָדִין עַמִּים *and he stands to judge his people* (if em. עַמּוֹ־ם) [21; cf. 73], Is 10_5 וּמַטֶּה־הוּא בְיָדָם זַעְמִי *and a staff is he in the hand of my rage* (if em. בְּיַד־ם) [2, 8, 21, 34; cf. 73], Is 30_{27} בֹּעֵר אַפּוֹ וְכֹבֶד מַשָּׂאָה *burning with fire and his liver raging* (if em. וְכַבְדוֹ־ם שֹׂאָה) [21; cf. 73], Is 40_{12} מִי־מָדַד בְּשָׁעֳלוֹ מַיִם *who has measured in his hand the sea* (if em. בְּשָׁעֳלוֹ־ם יָם; 1QIsa בשעלו מי ים) [41, 45], Is 40_{17} כָּל־הַגּוֹיִם כְּאַיִן נֶגְדּוֹ מֵאֶפֶס וָתֹהוּ נֶחְשְׁבוּ־לוֹ *all the nations are as nothing before him; vanity* (if em. נֶגְדּוֹ־ם אֶפֶס; cf. 1QIsa נגדו וכאפס) *and emptiness they are accounted by him* [21, 45], Is 63_3 מֵעַמִּים אֵין־אִישׁ אִתִּי *from my people no one was with me* (if em. מֵעַמִּי־ם, cf. 1QIsa מעמי) [45], Ho 9_1 אַל־תִּשְׂמַח יִשְׂרָאֵל אֶל־גִּיל כָּעַמִּים *do not rejoice, O Israel; do not be glad, my people* (if em. אַל גִּילְךָ עַמִּי־ם) [61], Zp 2_8 וַיַּגְדִּילוּ עַל־גְּבוּלָם *and they boasted* (גדל II) *against my mountain* (if em. גְּבוּלִ־ם, from גְּבוּל II) [59], Zp 3_9 אֶהְפֹּךְ אֶל־עַמִּים שָׂפָה *I will change the speech of my people* (if em. עַמִּי־ם) [59].

Ps 4_8 נָתַתָּה שִׂמְחָה בְלִבִּי מֵעֵת *you have put happiness in my heart; now …* (if em. בְּלִבִּי־ם עַתָּ[ה]) [46], Ps 5_{10} קִרְבָּם הַוּוֹת *his belly* (if em. קִרְבּוֹ־ם, ‖ פִּיהוּ *his mouth*) *is destruction* [46], Ps 10_{17} תָּכִין לִבָּם תַּקְשִׁיב אָזְנֶךָ *you will strengthen your attention* (if em. לֵב־ם), *you will incline your ear* [46], Ps 21_2 וּבִישׁוּעָתְךָ מַה־יָּגֶיל מְאֹד *and in your salvation he greatly rejoices* (if em. וּבִישׁוּעָתְךָ־ם יָגִיל) [21, 46], Ps 22_{16} וּלְשׁוֹנִי מֻדְבָּק מַלְקוֹחָי *and my tongue clings to* (if em. וּלְשׁוֹנִי־ם דֹּבֵק) *my palate* [21], Ps 31_{12} מִכָּל־צֹרְרַי הָיִיתִי חֶרְפָּה וְלִשְׁכֵנַי מְאֹד *I was a reproach among all my enemies and calamity to my neighbours* (if em. וְלִשְׁכֵנַי־ם אֵיד) [21, 46; cf. 73], Ps 38_{20} וְאֹיְבַי חַיִּים עָצֵמוּ *and the enemies of my life* (if em. וְאֹיְבַי חַיַּי־ם) *are mighty* [21], Ps 49_9 וְיֵקַר פִּדְיוֹן נַפְשָׁם *and costly is the ransom of his soul* (if em. נַפְשׁוֹ־ם) [21, 46; cf. 73].

Ps 54_{5} לֹא שָׂמוּ אֱלֹהִים לְנֶגְדָּם *they did not regard God as my Leader* (if em. לְנְגִידִי־ם) [48], Ps 55_{19} פָּדָה בְשָׁלוֹם נַפְשִׁי מִקְּרָב־לִי *he ransomed my life into safety; he drew near to me* (if em. נַפְשִׁי־ם קָרַב) [48], Ps 68_{23} אָמַר אֲדֹנָי מִבָּשָׁן אָשִׁיב *My Lord said* (if em. אֲדֹנָי־ם בָּשָׁן), *I have smashed* (if em. אָשֹׁב, from שׁבב) *the serpent* [26, 48, 53], Ps 68_{24} לְשׁוֹן כְּלָבֶיךָ מֵאֹיְבִים מִנֵּהוּ *the tongues of your dogs—(your) foes were their portion* (if em. כְּלָבֶיךָ־ם אֹיְבִים) [48], Ps 69_{8} כִּסְּתָה כְלִמָּה פָנָי: מוּזָר *shame has covered my face. A stranger* (if em. פָּנָי־ם: זָר) [48].

Ps 81_{13} וָאֲשַׁלְּחֵהוּ בִּשְׁרִירוּת לִבָּם *so I repudiated him for the hardness of his heart* (if em. לִבּוֹ־ם) [48], Ps 84_{6} מְסִלּוֹת בִּלְבָבָם *(your) extolments are in his heart* (if em. בִּלְבָבוֹ־ם) [48], Ps 86_{14} וְלֹא שָׂמוּךָ לְנֶגְדָּם *they do not regard you as my Leader* (if em. לְנְגִידִי־ם) [48], Ps 95_{4} בְּיָדוֹ מֶחְקְרֵי־אָרֶץ *in his hand are the recesses of the netherworld* (if em. בְּיָדוֹ־ם חִקְרֵי) [48, 69], Ps 102_{18} וְלֹא־בָזָה אֶת־תְּפִלָּתָם *and he will not despise his prayer* (if em. תְּפִלָּתוֹ־ם) [21; cf. 73], Ps 109_{13} בְּדוֹר אַחֵר יִמַּח שְׁמָם *may his name* (if em. שְׁמוֹ־ם, || אַחֲרִיתוֹ *his end*) *be wiped out from the age to come* [58], Ps 109_{15} וְיַכְרֵת מֵאֶרֶץ זִכְרָם *let his memory* (if em. זִכְרוֹ־ם) *be cut off from the earth* [21], Ps 119_{15} וְיַכְרֵת מֵאֶרֶץ זִכְרָם *and let him cut off his memory* (if em. זִכְרוֹ־ם) *from the earth* [58], Ps 139_{16} גָּלְמִי רָאוּ עֵינֶיךָ *your eyes saw my life-stages* (if em. גְּלַי־ם) [24, 58], Ps 144_{10} הַנּוֹתֵן תְּשׁוּעָה לַמְּלָכִים *who gives victory to his king* (if em. לְמַלְכִּי־ם, 3ms sf.) [54, 58].

Jb 13_{10} אִם־בַּסֵּתֶר פָּנִים תִּשָּׂאוּן *if in secret you lift up his face,* i.e. show partiality to him (if em. פָּנָי־ם, 3 ms sf.) [49, 69], Jb 15_{18} וְלֹא כִחֲדוּ מֵאֲבוֹתָם *and their fathers did not hide it* (if em. כִחֲדוּ־ם אֲבוֹתָם) [17, 39, 44, 54], Jb 15_{29} וְלֹא־יִטֶּה לָאָרֶץ מִנְלָם *and he shall not bring down* (if em. יַטֶּה) *to the netherworld his possessions* (if em. מִנְלָ[וֹ]־ם) [39, 54], Jb 17_{6} וְהִצִּגַנִי לִמְשֹׁל עַמִּים *and he has made me a byword for my people* (if em. עַמִּי־ם) [54], Jb 18_{3} נִטְמִינוּ בְּעֵינֵיכֶם *we hide* (if em. נִטְמַנּוּ, from טמן ni.) *from your sight* (if em. בְּעֵינֶיךָ־ם) [54], Jb 33_{17} וְגֵוָה מִגֶּבֶר יְכַסֶּה *and he reveals his word* (if em. וְגֵהוֹ־ם, from גה *voice*, with 3ms sf.) *before a man* [61].

Pr 3_{18} עֵץ־חַיִּים הִיא לַמַּחֲזִיקִים בָּהּ וְתֹמְכֶיהָ מְאֻשָּׁר *she is a tree of life to those who grasp her, a cedar (to) those who lay hold of her* (if em. וְתֹמְכֶיהָ־ם אַשֻּׁר, from אַשֻּׁר II *cedar*) [cf. 57], Pr 4_{1} שִׁמְעוּ בָנִים מוּסַר אָב *listen, my son, to the instruction of a father* (if em. שְׁמַע בְּנִי־ם) [57], Pr 5_{7} וְעַתָּה בָנִים שִׁמְעוּ־לִי וְאַל־תָּסוּרוּ מֵאִמְרֵי־פִי *and now, my son* (if em. בְּנִי־ם), *listen* (if em. שְׁמַע) *to me and do not depart* (if em. תָּסוּר) *from the words of my mouth* [36, 61], Pr 11_{7} וְתוֹחֶלֶת אוֹנִים אָבָדָה *and the expectation of his wealth* (if em. אוֹנִי־ם, with 3 ms sf.) *perishes* [57], Lm 4_{6} וְלֹא־חָלוּ בָהּ יָדָיִם *and my hands were not laid on it* (if em. יָדַי־ם) [50].

3. other uses with nouns and adjectives, Gn 1_{10} וּלְמִקְוֵה הַמַּיִם קָרָא יַמִּים *and the pool of the waters* (if em. מִקְוֵ[ה]־ם אֶחָד) *he called Sea* (if em. יָם־ם) [54], Nm 21_{18} בִּמְחֹקֵק בְּמִשְׁעֲנֹתָם *with a rod, with a staff* (if em. בְּמִשְׁעֶנֶת־ם) [21], Nm 23_{10} תָּמֹת נַפְשִׁי מוֹת יְשָׁרִים *let me die the death of the righteous* (if em. יָשָׁר־ם) [3d, 25, 53], Nm 23_{22} אֵל מוֹצִיאָם מִמִּצְרָיִם *God brought (them)* (if em. אֵל־ם הוצאה) out of Egypt [3a, 21, 53; cf. 73], Nm 24_{8} אֵל מוֹצִיאוֹ מִמִּצְרַיִם *God brought (them)* (if em. אֵל־ם הוצאה) out of Egypt [3a, 21], 1 S 1_{1} וַיְהִי אִישׁ אֶחָד מִן־הָרָמָתַיִם צוֹפִים *and there was a man from Ramathaim, a Zuphite* (if em. צוֹפִי־ם) [22].

Is 1_{18} יִהְיוּ חֲטָאֵיכֶם כַּשָּׁנִים כַּשֶּׁלֶג יַלְבִּינוּ *your sins like scarlet* (if em. כַּשָּׁנִי־ם; 1QIsa שני) *shall become white like snow* [22, 45, 63], Is 5_{23} וְצִדְקַת צַדִּיקִים יָסִירוּ *and the deliverance of the righteous one* (if em. צַדִּיק־ם) *they turn aside* [8, 21, 22,, 61; cf. 73], Is 5_{26} וְנָשָׂא־נֵס לַגּוֹיִם מֵרָחוֹק *and he will raise a signal for a nation afar off* (if em. לַגּוֹי־ם or לְגוֹי־ם with genitive ending) [59], Is 17_{10} תִּטְּעִי נִטְעֵי נַעֲמָנִים *you plant plants of pleasantness* (if em. נַעֲמָן־ם) [22], Is 19_{4} בְּיַד אֲדֹנִים קָשֶׁה *in the hand of a hard master* (if em. אָדוֹן־ם, not intensive pl.) [21], Is 24_{22} וְסֻגְּרוּ עַל־מַסְגֵּר וּמֵרֹב יָמִים יִפָּקֵדוּ *and they will be shut up in a prison; for many days they will be punished* (if em. מַסְגֵּר־ם רֹב) [21], Is 33_{2} הֱיֵה זְרֹעָם לַבְּקָרִים *be (our) arm* (if em. זְרֹעַ־ם) *in the mornings* [8, 21; cf. 73], Is 33_{17} תִּרְאֶינָה אֶרֶץ מַרְחַקִּים *they will behold a distant land* (if em. אֶרֶץ מֶרְחָק־ם) [21], Is 33_{21} מְקוֹם־נְהָרִים יְאֹרִים *a gathering of* (if em. מִקְוֵ[ה]־ם) *rivers (and) streams* [21], Is 33_{23} בַּל־יְחַזְּקוּ כֵן־תָּרְנָם *it does not hold the mast firm* (if em. תֹּרֶן־ם) [21], Is 47_{14} אֵין־גַּחֶלֶת לַחְמָם *there is no coal for warmth* (if em. לְחֹם־ם) [21; cf. 73], Is 53_3 נִבְזֶה וַחֲדַל אִישִׁים *despised and rejected by men* (if em. אִישׁ־ם) [21; cf. 73].

Jr 3_{23} אָכֵן לַשֶּׁקֶר מִגְּבָעוֹת *truly vain are the hills* (if em. לַשֶּׁקֶר־ם גְּבָעוֹת) [21; cf. 73], Jr 6_{26} אֵבֶל יָחִיד עֲשִׂי לָךְ מִסְפַּד תַּמְרוּרִים *make mourning bitterly* (if em. תַּמְרוּר־ם, as adv.), *as for an only son* [21], Jr 8_{19} מֵאֶרֶץ מַרְחַקִּים *from a distant land* (if em. מֵאֶרֶץ מֶרְחָק־ם) [21], Jr 13_{19} הָגְלָת שְׁלוֹמִים *it is exiled utterly* (if em. שָׁלוֹם־ם, adv. accus.) [21], Jr 22_6 אֲשִׁיתְךָ מִדְבָּר עָרִים לֹא נוֹשָׁבָה *I will make you a desert, a city* (if em. עִר־ם) *uninhabited*, Jr 31_{15} קוֹל בְּרָמָה נִשְׁמָע נְהִי בְּכִי תַמְרוּרִים *a voice is heard in Ramah, lamentation and weeping bitterly* (if em. תַּמְרוּר־ם, as adv.) [21].

Ezk 8_{17} וְהִנָּם שֹׁלְחִים אֶת־הַזְּמוֹרָה אֶל־אַפָּם *see, they are thrusting (their) branch under (my) nose* (if em. אַף־ם) [54], Ezk 26_{10} מִשִּׁפְעַת סוּסָיו יְכַסֵּךְ אֲבָקָם *through the surge of his horses he will cover you with dust* (if em. אָבָק־ם) [54], Ezk 26_{17} אֵיךְ אָבַדְתְּ נוֹשֶׁבֶת מִיַּמִּים *how have you perished, O one shattered by the sea* (if em. נִשְׁבַּת יָם־ם) [54], Ezk 27_4 בְּלֵב יַמִּים גְּבוּלָיִךְ *your borders are the midst of the sea* (if em. יָם־ם) [54], Ezk 27_{25} וַתִּכְבְּדִי מְאֹד בְּלֵב יַמִּים *and you were heavily laden in the midst of the sea* (if em. יָם־ם) [54], Ezk 27_{26} אֹתָךְ רוּחַ הַקָּדִים שְׁבָרֵךְ בְּלֵב יַמִּים *the east wind has wrecked you in the heart of the sea* (if em. יָם־ם) [54], Ezk 27_{27} יִפְּלוּ בְּלֵב יַמִּים בְּיוֹם מַפַּלְתֵּךְ *and they will sink into the heart of the sea* (if em. יָם־ם) *on the day of your ruin* [54], Ezk 27_{33} בְּצֵאת עִזְבוֹנַיִךְ מִיַּמִּים *through the export of your merchandise by sea* (if em. מִיָּם־ם) [54], Ezk 27_{34} עֵת נִשְׁבֶּרֶת מִיַּמִּים בְּמַעֲמַקֵּי־מָיִם *now you are shattered by the sea* (if em. עַתָּ[ה] נִשְׁבַּרְתְּ יָם־ם) *in the depths of the sea* (if em. בְּמַעֲמַקֵּי־ם־יָם) [54], Ezk 28_2 יָשַׁבְתִּי בְּלֵב יַמִּים *I dwell in the heart of the sea* (if em. יָם־ם) [54] , Ezk 28_8 וָמַתָּה מְמוֹתֵי חָלָל בְּלֵב יַמִּים *and you will die the death of the slain in the heart of the sea* (if em. יָם־ם) [54].

Ho 12_{15} הִכְעִיס אֶפְרַיִם תַּמְרוּרִים *Ephraim has provoked bitterly* (if em. תַּמְרוּר־ם, as adv.) [21], Ob $_{13}$ אַל־תָּבוֹא בְשַׁעַר־עַמִּי בְּיוֹם אֵידָם *you should not have entered the gate of my city* (from עַם *fortress, town*) on the day of (its) calamity (if em. אֵיד־ם) [54], Jon 2_3 וַתַּשְׁלִיכֵנִי מְצוּלָה בִּלְבַב יַמִּים *and you cast me into the deep, into the heart of the sea* (if em. יָם־ם) [54], Mc 7_{19} וְתַשְׁלִיךְ בִּמְצֻלוֹת יָם כָּל־חַטֹּאותָם *and you will cast all (our) sins* (if em. חַטֹּאות־ם) *into the depths of the sea* [21; cf. 73], Na 3_8 אֲשֶׁר־חֵיל יָם מִיָּם חוֹמָתָהּ *whose rampart was the sea, and the sea her wall* (if em. יָם־ם יָם) [54], Hb 3_8 הֲבִנְהָרִים חָרָה י׳ אִם בַּנְּהָרִים אַפֶּךָ *was your wrath against the River* (if em. הֲבַנָּהָר־ם), *O Y., was your anger against the River* (if em. בַּנָּהָר־ם)? [21, 53; cf. 73].

Ps 7_7 וְעוּרָה אֵלַי מִשְׁפָּט צִוִּיתָ *and awake, O God, command, O Ruler* (if em. אֵלִי־ם שֹׁפֵט צַוֵּה) [21; cf. 73], Ps 8_8 וּדְגֵי הַיָּם עֹבֵר אָרְחוֹת יַמִּים *and the fish of the sea, who pass along the paths of the sea* (if em. יָם־ם) [54], Ps 29_1 הָבוּ לַיהוָה בְּנֵי אֵלִים *ascribe to Y., O sons of El* (if em. אֵל־ם) [21, 25], Ps 38_4 אֵין־מְתֹם בִּבְשָׂרִי *there is no soundness* (if em. אֵין־ם תֹּם, with enclitic mem) *in my flesh* [21, 46], Ps 46_3 וּבְמוֹט הָרִים בְּלֵב יַמִּים *and though the mountains shake in the heart of the sea* (if em. יָם־ם) [54], Ps 49_{15} שְׁאוֹל מִזְּבֻל לוֹ *and Sheol is a dwelling for him* (if em. שְׁאוֹל־ם זְבֻל) [21; cf. 73], Ps 56_3 רַבִּים לֹחֲמִים לִי מָרוֹם *many are fighting against me bitterly* (if em. מַר־ם) [21; cf. 73], Ps 58_2 מֵישָׁרִים תִּשְׁפְּטוּ בְּנֵי אָדָם *do you judge upright(ly)* (if em. מֵישָׁר־ם), *you humans?* [21].

Ps 61_5 אָגוּרָה בְאָהָלְךָ עוֹלָמִים *let me dwell in your tent for ever* (if em. עוֹלָם־ם) (and perh. 10 other occurrences of עוֹלָמִים) [21], Ps 65_6 מִבְטָח כָּל־קַצְוֵי־אֶרֶץ וְיָם רְחֹקִים *the hope of the ends of the earth and of the distant sea* (if em. וְיָם רְחֹקִי־ם) [48], Ps 65_{10} תָּכִין דְּגָנָם *you provide grain* (if em. דָּגָן־ם) [21, 48], Ps 78_{15} יְבַקַּע צֻרִים בַּמִּדְבָּר *he split the rock* (if em. צֻר־ם) *in the steppe* [48], Ps 99_4 וְעֹז מֶלֶךְ *and strength is yours* (if em. וְעֹז־ם לָךְ) [21; cf. 73], Ps 104_{29} תֹּסֵף רוּחָם יִגְוָעוּן *you take back (your) spirit* (if em. רוּחַ־ם, || פָּנֶיךָ *your face*) *and they die* [58], Ps 106_7 וַיַּמְרוּ עַל־יָם *and they defied the Most High* (if em. אֱלִי־ם) [58], Ps 111_{10} שֵׂכֶל טוֹב לְכָל־עֹשֵׂיהֶם *a good understanding (belongs to) all those who acquire it (wisdom)* (if em. עֹשֶׂיהָ־ם) [58], Ps 130_6 נַפְשִׁי לַאדֹנָי מִשֹּׁמְרִים לַבֹּקֶר *my soul is toward the Lord, through the watches* (if em. לַאדֹנָי־ם שֹׁמְרִים) *to the morning* [58].

Jb 3_{19} קָטֹן וְגָדוֹל שָׁם הוּא וְעֶבֶד חָפְשִׁי מֵאֲדֹנָיו *the small and the great are there, slave, freedman and master* (if em. חָפְשִׁי־ם אֲדֹנָיו) [54, 69], Jb 4_{20} מִבְּלִי מֵשִׂים לָנֶצַח יֹאבֵדוּ *without a name* (if em. מִבְּלִי־ם שֵׁם) *they perish for ever* [54], Jb 7_{15} וַתִּבְחַר מַחֲנָק נַפְשִׁי מָוֶת מֵעַצְמוֹתָי (if em. מָוֶת־ם עַצְמוֹתָי) *and my life chooses strangling, and my bones death* [17, 39, 44, 54, 69], Jb 8_{8} וְכוֹנֵן לְחֵקֶר אֲבוֹתָם *and consider the discovery of the fathers* (if em. אָבוֹת־ם) [17, 43, 54, 69], Jb 14_{12} וְלֹא־יֵעֹרוּ מִשְּׁנָתָם *and he is not aroused* (sg. ending *-u*) *from (his) sleep* (if em. מִשֵּׁנָת־ם, fem. abs. ending *-t*, or מִשְּׁנָתוֹ־ם *his sleep*) [54, 69], Jb 18_{5} אוֹר רְשָׁעִים יִדְעָךְ *the light of the wicked* (if em. רָשָׁע ,רְשָׁעִי־ם with gen. *-î*) *is put out* [54], Jb 20_{3} וְרוּחַ מִבִּינָתִי יַעֲנֵנִי *and the spirit within me gives answer* (if em. וְרוּחַ־ם בֵּינֹתַי) [20], Jb 21_{22} וְהוּא רָמִים יִשְׁפּוֹט *and will he judge the Most High* (if em. רָם־ם or רֹם־ם *the Exalted One*) [20], Jb 31_{11} וְהִיא עָוֹן פְּלִילִים *and that would be a criminal iniquity* (if em. פְּלִילִי־ם) [65].

Pr 1_{18} יִצְפְּנוּ לְנַפְשֹׁתָם *they set an ambush for (their) life* (if em. לְנַפְשֹׁת־ם) [cf. 57], Pr 4_{23} מִכָּל־מִשְׁמָר נְצֹר לִבֶּךָ *more than all one guards, keep your heart* (if em. מִכָּל־ם שָׁמַר) [cf. 57], Pr 16_{12} תּוֹעֲבַת מְלָכִים עֲשׂוֹת רֶשַׁע *wrongdoing is an abomination to a king* (if em. מַלְכִי־ם, with gen. ending) [54], Pr 16_{13} רְצוֹן מְלָכִים שִׂפְתֵי־צֶדֶק *righteous lips are the delight of a king* (if em. מֶלֶךְ־ם) [57], Pr 28_{1} וְצַדִּיקִים כִּכְפִיר יִבְטָח *and the righteous one is as bold as a lion* (if em. וְצַדִּיק־ם) [21; cf. 57], Pr 30_{13} דּוֹר מָה־רָמוּ עֵינָיו *there is a generation whose eyes are lofty* (if em. דּוֹר־ם רָמוּ) [21; cf. 57], Ec 10_{15} עֲמַל הַכְּסִילִים תְּיַגְּעֶנּוּ *the labour of a fool* (if em. הַכְּסִיל־ם) *wearies him* [13, 21; cf. 73], Ec 10_{18} בַּעֲצַלְתַּיִם יִמַּךְ הַמְּקָרֶה *through indolence* (if em. בְּעַצְלֻת־ם) *the roof sags* [13, 21, 57; cf. 73].

4. after a verb, Gn 6_{13} וְהִנְנִי מַשְׁחִיתָם אֶת־הָאָרֶץ *and behold I am destroying the earth* (if em. מַשְׁחִית־ם) [66], Ex 15_{9} תִּמְלָאֵמוֹ נַפְשִׁי אָרִיק חַרְבִּי תּוֹרִישֵׁמוֹ יָדִי *my desire will have its fill* (if em. תִּמְלָא־ם), *I will draw my sword, my hand shall dispossess* (if em. תּוֹרִישׁ־ם) [16, 21, 25, 53; cf. 73], Ex 15_{15} יֹאחֲזֵמוֹ רָעַד *they are seized by trembling* (if em. יֶאֱחֲזוּ־ם רָעַד) [16. 53], Ex 15_{16} בִּגְדֹל זְרוֹעֲךָ יִדְּמוּ כָּאָבֶן *by your powerful arm they are hurled* (if em. יֻדּוּ־ם, qal pass.) *like a stone* [29], Nm 24_{19} וְיֵרְדְּ מִיַּעֲקֹב *and Jacob went down* (if em. וַיֵּרֶד־ם יַעֲקֹב) [3c, 21; cf. 73], Dt 33_{3} יִשָּׂא מִדַּבְּרֹתֶיךָ *that they may receive your utterances* or *carry out your decisions* (if em. יִשְׂאֻ־ם דַּבְּרֹתֶיךָ) [6, 7, 21; cf. 73], Dt 33_{22} יְזַנֵּק מִן־הַבָּשָׁן *which attacks a viper* (if em. יְזַנֵּק־ם בָּשָׁן) [11, 53], 1 S 9_{19} וַאֲכַלְתֶּם עִמִּי הַיּוֹם *and you (sg.) shall eat with me today* (if em. וַאֲכַלְתָּ־ם) [22], 1 K 20_{28} וִידַעְתֶּם כִּי־אֲנִי י׳ *and you (sg.) will know* (if em. וְיָדַעְתָּ־ם) *that I am Y.* [22].

Is 1_{29} כִּי יֵבֹשׁוּ מֵאֵילִים אֲשֶׁר חֲמַדְתֶּם *for the oaks in which you delighted shall dry up* (if em. יָבְשׁוּ־ם אֵילִים) [34], Is 9_{18} נֶעְתַּם אָרֶץ *the earth reeled* (if em. נָעָת־ם, from נוע *tremble*) [10, 21, 34; cf. 73], Is 10_{2} לְהַטּוֹת מִדִּין דַּלִּים *to pervert the cause of* (if em. לְהַטּוֹת־ם דִּין) *the poor* [8, 21; cf. 73], Is 11_{15} וְהֵנִיף יָדוֹ עַל־הַנָּהָר בַּעְיָם *and he will wave* (נוף I) or *lift up* (נוף V) *his hand over the River when it boils up* (בע[ה]־ם, inf. cstr. of בעה I *boil*) [21; cf. 73], Is 17_{13} וְנָס מִמֶּרְחָק *and it will flee far away* (if em. וְנָס־ם מֶרְחָק) [21], Is 25_{2} שַׂמְתָּ מֵעִיר לַגָּל *you have made a city* (if em. שַׂמְתָּ־ם עִיר) *into a heap* [21; cf. 73], Is 25_{10} כְּהִדּוּשׁ מַתְבֵּן *like the trampling of straw* (if em. כְּהִדּוּשׁ־ם תֶּבֶן) [21; cf. 73], Is 62_{10} סַקְּלוּ מֵאֶבֶן *clear away stones* (if em. סַקְּלוּ־ם אֶבֶן) [21], Is 65_{20} לֹא־יִהְיֶה מִשָּׁם עוֹד עוּל יָמִים *there will not again be* (יִהְיֶ[ה]־ם שָׁם) *there a suckling of days* [21].

Jr 10_{4} בְּמַסְמְרוֹת וּבְמַקָּבוֹת יְחַזְּקוּם *with nails and with hammers they fasten it* (if em. יְחַזְּקֻהוּ־ם) [21], Jr 18_{14} הֲיַעֲזֹב מִצּוּר שָׂדַי *do flints leave the field* (if em. הֲיַעֲזֹב־ם צוּר) [30], Jr 18_{15} וַיַּכְשִׁלוּם בְּדַרְכֵיהֶם *and they have stumbled in their ways* (if em. וַיִּכָּשְׁלוּ־ם ni.) [21; cf. 73], Jr 46_{5} וְגִבּוֹרֵיהֶם יֻכַּתּוּ וּמָנוֹס נָסוּ *and their heroes have been beaten down and have utterly fled* (if em. יֻכַּתּוּ־ם נוֹס נָסוּ, נוֹס as inf. abs.) [21], Jr 50_{26} פִּתְחוּ מַאֲבֻסֶיהָ *open its granaries* (if em. פִּתְחוּ־ם אֵבֻסֶיהָ, from אֵבוּס) [18, 21], Ho 5_{7} עַתָּה יֹאכְלֵם חֹדֶשׁ אֶת־חֶלְקֵיהֶם *now he will devour their property at the new moon* (if em. יֹאכַל־ם) [66; cf. 61], Ho 11_{7} וְעַמִּי תְלוּאִים לִמְשׁוּבָתִי *and my people make themselves strong in their falling away* (if em. תִלָּאוּ־ם, impf. ni. of לאה *be strong*) [61], Jl 1_{17} נֶהֶרְסוּ מַמְּגֻרוֹת *the barns are overturned* (if em. נֶהֶרְסוּ־ם מְגֻרוֹת) [6, 21; cf. 73], Zp 3_{19} וְשַׂמְתִּים לִתְהִלָּה וּלְשֵׁם בְּכָל־הָאָרֶץ בָּשְׁתָּם *and I will change* (if em. וְשַׂמְתִּי־ם) *their shame into praise and fame* [59].

Ps 12$_{8}$ אַתָּה־י׳ תִּשְׁמְרֵם תִּצְּרֶנּוּ *O Y., you will protect (us)* (if em. תִּשְׁמְר־ם) *and keep us* [21, 46; cf. 73], Ps 18$_{22}$ וְלֹא־רָשַׁעְתִּי מֵאֱלֹהָי *and I have not been guilty, O my God* (if em. רָשַׁעְתִּי־ם אֱלֹהָי) [46], Ps 18$_{41}$ וּמְשַׂנְאַי אַצְמִיתֵם *and my enemies I exterminated* (if em. אַצְמִית־ם) [46], Ps 18$_{46}$ וְיַחְרְגוּ מִמִּסְגְּרוֹתֵיהֶם *and their hearts are seized with anguish* (if em. וְיַחְרְגוּ־ם מִסְגְּרוֹתֵיהֶם) [46], Ps 22$_{2}$ רָחוֹק מִישׁוּעָתִי *dismissing my plea* (if em. רָחוֹק־ם שַׁוְעָתִי) [46], Ps 26$_{8}$ אָהַבְתִּי מְעוֹן בֵּיתֶךָ *I love to dwell* (if em. אָהַבְתִּי־ם עוֹן) *in your house* [46], Ps 29$_{6}$ וַיַּרְקִידֵם כְּמוֹ־עֵגֶל לְבָנוֹן *he makes Lebanon skip* (if em. וַיַּרְקִיד־ם) *like a calf* [1, 2, 4, 6, 21, 46, 60, 64; cf. 73], Ps 30$_{4}$ חִיִּיתַנִי מִיּוֹרְדֵי־בוֹר *you restored me to life* (if em. חִיִּיתַנִי־ם יָרְדִי) *after I had gone down to the Pit* [46], Ps 31$_{11}$ וַעֲצָמַי עָשֵׁשׁוּ׃ מִכָּל־צֹרְרַי *and my bones are wasted away. All my enemies* (if em. עָשְׁשׁוּ־ם׃ כָּל־צֹרְרַי) [46], Ps 38$_{9}$ שָׁאַגְתִּי מִנַּהֲמַת לִבִּי *I sigh and groan (in) my heart* (if em. שָׁאַגְתִּי־ם נָהַמְתִּ[י]) [46].

Ps 42$_{5}$ אֶדַּדֵּם עַד־בֵּית אֱלֹהִים *I went* (if em. אדד־ם) *to the temple* [6, 21; cf. 73], or, *I prostrated myself* (if em. אֶדַּדֶּ־ם) *toward the temple* [46], Ps 46$_{9}$ לְכוּ־חֲזוּ מִפְעֲלוֹת י׳ *come, see the works of Y.* (if em. חֲזוּ־ם פְּעָלוֹת) [21, 46; cf. 73], Ps 55$_{20}$ יִשְׁמַע אֵל וְיַעֲנֵם *God will give ear and will answer* (if em. וְיַעַן־ם) [48], Ps 58$_{12}$ יֵשׁ־אֱלֹהִים שֹׁפְטִים בָּאָרֶץ *surely there is a God who judges* (if em. שֹׁפֵט־ם) *on earth* [21], Ps 66$_{5}$ לְכוּ וּרְאוּ מִפְעֲלוֹת אֱלֹהִים *come and see the works of God* (if em. וּרְאוּ־ם פְּעָלוֹת) [48], Ps 67$_{5}$ וּלְאֻמִּים בָּאָרֶץ תַּנְחֵם *and peoples into the land you will lead* (if em. תַּנְחֶ[ה]־ם) [48], Ps 68$_{28}$ שָׁם בִּנְיָמִן צָעִיר רֹדֵם (if em. רד־ם) *there is little Benjamin going out to battle* [56, 61], Ps 72$_{16}$ כַּלְּבָנוֹן פִּרְיוֹ וְיָצִיצוּ מֵעִיר כְּעֵשֶׂב הָאָרֶץ *let his fruit flourish* (if em. וְיָצִיצוּ־ם) *like Lebanon, flourishing* (if em. עָרֹ[ה], inf. abs. of ערה *flourish*) *like the grass of the earth* [48], Ps 73$_{10}$ יָשִׁיב עַמּוֹ *they gorged themselves* (if em. יִשְׂבְּעוּ־ם) [48], Ps 78$_{3}$ אֲשֶׁר שָׁמַעְנוּ וַנֵּדָעֵם *which we have known and heard* (if em. וַנֵּדַע־ם) [21].

Ps 80$_{6}$ הֶאֱכַלְתָּם לֶחֶם דִּמְעָה *you have fed (us) with tears for food* (if em. הֶאֱכַלְתָּ־ם || וַתַּשְׁקֵמוֹ *and you have made us drink*) [48], Ps 81$_{7}$ הֲסִירוֹתִי מִסֵּבֶל שִׁכְמוֹ *I removed the burden of his shoulder* (if em. הֲסִירוֹתִי־ם סֵבֶל) [48], Ps 83$_{12}$ שִׁיתֵמוֹ נְדִיבֵמוֹ כְּעֹרֵב וְכִזְאֵב *make* (if em. שִׁית־ם) *their nobles like Oreb and Zeeb* [4, 21, 48; cf. 73], Ps 85$_{4}$ הֱשִׁיבוֹתָ מֵחֲרוֹן אַפֶּךָ *you withdrew the anger of* (if em. הֱשִׁיבוֹתָ־ם חֲרוֹן) *your wrath* [21, 26, 48, 60; cf. 73], Ps 88$_{16}$ וְגֹוֵעַ מִנֹּעַר *and groaning I die* (if em. וְגֹוֵעַ־ם נֹעַר) [48], Ps 89$_{10}$ בְּשׂוֹא גַלָּיו אַתָּה תְשַׁבְּחֵם *when its waves rise, you still (them)* (if em. תְשַׁבֵּחַ־ם) [21], Ps 107$_{39}$ וַיִּמְעֲטוּ וַיָּשֹׁחוּ מֵעֹצֶר רָעָה וְיָגוֹן *and they are brought low by* (if em. וַיָּשֹׁחוּ־ם עֹצֶר, i.e. all three nouns are adv. accus.) *oppression, evil and sorrow* [21], Ps 119$_{152}$ יָדַעְתִּי מֵעֵדֹתֶיךָ *I have acknowledged your stipulations* (if em. יָדַעְתִּי־ם עֵדֹתֶיךָ) [58], Ps 125$_{1}$ הַבֹּטְחִים בַּי׳ כְּהַר־צִיּוֹן *the one who trusts* (if em. הַבֹּטֵחַ־ם) *in Y. is like Mount Zion* [15, 21; cf. 73], Ps 147$_{20}$ וּמִשְׁפָּטִים בַּל־יְדָעוּם *and his ordinances they do not know* (if em. יְדָעוּ־ם) [21].

Jb 4$_{19}$ יְדַכְּאוּם לִפְנֵי־עָשׁ *they are pure* (if em. יִדְכְּאוּ־ם, from דכא = זכה *be pure*) *before their Maker* (עֹשֶׂ[ה]) [54, 69], Jb 8$_{18}$ אִם־יְבַלְּעֶנּוּ מִמְּקוֹמוֹ *if his place devours him* (if em. יְבַלְּעֶנּוּ־ם מְקוֹמוֹ) [17, 69], Jb 9$_{18}$ יַשְׂבִּעַנִי מַמְּרֹרִים *he fills me with bitterness* (if em. יַשְׂבִּעַנִי־ם מְרֹרִים) [47, 54, 69], Jb 12$_{25}$ וַיַּתְעֵם כַּשִּׁכּוֹר *and they wander about* (if em. וַיִּתְעוּ־ם) *like a drunken man* [39, 54, 69], Jb 15$_{18}$ וְלֹא כִחֲדוּ מֵאֲבוֹתָם *and their fathers did not hide it* (if em. כִּחֲדוּ־ם אֲבוֹתָם) [17, 39, 44, 54], Jb 17$_{7}$ וִיצֻרַי כַּצֵּל כֻּלָּם *and my limbs fail like a shadow* (if em. כָּלוּ־ם) [17, 54], Jb 26$_{5}$ הָרְפָאִים יְחוֹלָלוּ מִתַּחַת מַיִם וְשֹׁכְנֵיהֶם *the Shades writhe in pain, the waters and their inhabitants are crushed* (if em. יְחוֹלָלוּ־ם תֻּחַת, תֻּחַת 3 fs חתת ni. *crush*) [54], Jb 28$_{9}$ הָפַךְ מִשֹּׁרֶשׁ הָרִים *he overturned the root of mountains* (if em. הָפַךְ־ם שֹׁרֶשׁ) [21, 54], Jb 31$_{14}$ וּמָה אֶעֱשֶׂה כִּי־יָקוּם אֵל *and what shall I do if God calls me to account?* (if em. יְקַוֶּ־ם, from קוי *call*) [46, 54], Jb 36$_{7}$ וְאֶת־מְלָכִים לַכִּסֵּא וַיֹּשִׁיבֵם *and with kings on the throne he seats him* (if em. וַיֹּשִׁיב־ם, with emphatic waw) [54].

Pr 15$_{30}$ וּתְפִלַּת צַדִּיקִים יִשְׁמָע׃ מְאוֹר־עֵינַיִם יְשַׂמַּח־לֵב *but he hears the prayer of the wicked. The light of the eyes rejoices the heart* (if em. יִשְׁמַע־ם׃ אוֹר) [57], Pr 20$_{4}$ וְכָל־אֱוִיל יִתְגַּלָּע׃ מֵחֹרֶף עָצֵל לֹא־יַחֲרֹשׁ *but every fool will be quarrelling. In the autumn the sluggard does not plough* (if em. יִתְגַּלַּע־ם חֹרֶף, חֹרֶף being accus. of time) [57], Lm 3$_{17}$ וַתִּזְנַח מִשָּׁלוֹם נַפְשִׁי *and my soul rejected* (if em. (וַתִּזְנַח־ם שָׁלוֹם) *peace* [21, 50; cf. 73], Lm 3_{26} טוֹב וְיָחִיל וְדוּמָם *it is good to wait quietly* (if em. וְדוּם־ם, i.e. qal inf., unless דּוֹמֵם pol. inf.) [50].

5. after conjunctive waw (perh. as emphasizing or explicative), Gn 41_{32} וּמְמַהֵר הָאֱלֹהִים לַעֲשֹׂתוֹ *and God will hasten to do it* (if em. וּ־ם מַהֵר) [55, 70], Nm 23_{10} מִי מָנָה עֲפַר יַעֲקֹב וּמִסְפָּר אֶת־רֹבַע יִשְׂרָאֵל *who can count the dust of Jacob or number* (if em. וּ־מ־סְפַר) *the fourth part of Israel?* [70], Jg 13_{19} וַיַּעַל עַל־הַצּוּר לַי׳ וּמַפְלִא לַעֲשׂוֹת *and he offered it on the rock to Y., (even) to him who works wonders* (if em. וּ־מ־פלא) [55; cf. 70], 2 S 16_{5} יָצֹא יָצוֹא וּמְקַלֵּל *he went, going and cursing* (if em. וּ־מ־קַלֵּל, inf. abs.) [55, 70], 1 K 14_{14} יַכְרִית אֶת־בֵּית יָרָבְעָם זֶה הַיּוֹם וּמֶה גַּם־עָתָּה *he will cut off the house of Jeroboam today, even now* (if em. וּ־מ־גַּם־עַתָּה) [70].

Ezk 48_{16} וּמִפְּאַת קָדִים חֲמֵשׁ מֵאוֹת וְאַרְבַּעַת אֲלָפִים *and the east side* (if em. וּ־מ־פְּאַת) *four thousand five hundred (cubits)* [70], Ezk 48_{22} וּמֵאֲחֻזַּת הַלְוִיִּם וּמֵאֲחֻזַּת הָעִיר בְּתוֹךְ אֲשֶׁר לַנָּשִׂיא יִהְיֶה *and the property of* (if em. וּ־מ־אֲחֻזַּת) *the Levites and the property of* (if em. וּ־מ־אֲחֻזַּת) *the city shall be in the midst of what belongs to the prince* [70], Am 6_{10} וּנְשָׂאוֹ דּוֹדוֹ וּמְסָרְפוֹ *and a man's kinsman will take him up and he will burn him* (if em. וּ־ם סְרָפוֹ, perf. with sf.) [55, 68, 70], Na 2_{13} וּמְחַנֵּק לְלִבְאֹתָיו *and he strangles (prey) for his female lions* (if em. וּ־מ־חַנֵּק) [70].

Ps 147_{3} וּמְחַבֵּשׁ לְעַצְּבוֹתָם *and he binds up,* or *searches, their wounds* (if em. וּ־מ־חִבֵּשׁ) [70], Jb 6_{22} וּמִכֹּחֲכֶם שִׁחֲדוּ בַעֲדִי *and offer your wealth as a bribe for me* (if em. וּ־מ־כֹּחֲכֶם) [55, 70], Jb 7_{14} וּמֵחֶזְיֹנוֹת תְּבַעֲתַנִּי *and you terrify me (with) visions* (if em. וּ־מ־חֶזְיֹנוֹת) [55, 70], Jb 10_{14} וּמֵעֲוֹנִי לֹא תְנַקֵּנִי *and you do not clear my iniquity* (if em. וּ־מ־עֲוֹנִי) [55, 70], Jb 19_{26} וּמִבְּשָׂרִי אֶחֱזֶה אֱלוֹהַּ *and (in) my flesh I shall see God* (if em. וּ־מ־בְּשָׂרִי) [55, 70], Jb 21_{20} וּמֵחֲמַת שַׁדַּי יִשְׁתֶּה *and let him drink the wrath of the Almighty* (if em. וּ־מ־חֲמַת) [55, 70], Ru 4_{5} וּמֵאֵת רוּת you are buying *also Ruth* (if em. וּ־ם אֵת) [55, 62, 67, 68, 70, 71], Ne 5_{11} הָשִׁיבוּ נָא לָהֶם כְּהַיּוֹם שְׂדֹתֵיהֶם ... וּמְאַת הַכֶּסֶף *return to them today their fields ... and the money* (if em. וּ־מ־אֵת) [70, 71, 72].

6. after another preposition or particle, Nm 24_{22} עַד־מָה אַשּׁוּר *while I gaze* (if em. עַד־ם אֲשׁוּר) [3, 53], 1 S 10_{2} וְדָאַג לָכֶם לֵאמֹר מָה אֶעֱשֶׂה לִבְנִי *and he is anxious about you (sg.)* (if em. לְךָ־ם), *saying, What shall I do about my son?*[22], Is 1_{6} אֵין־בּוֹ מְתֹם *there is no soundness in it* (if em. אֵין־בּוֹ־ם תֹּם) [21], Is 19_{12} אַיָּם אֵפוֹא חֲכָמֶיךָ *where then are your wise men?* (if em. אַיֵּ[ה]־ם) [21], Jr 48_{32} עַד יָם יַעְזֵר נָגָעוּ *they have reached as far as* (if em. עֲדֵי־ם) *Jazer* [21; cf. 73], Ho 4_{4} וְעַמְּךָ כִּמְרִיבֵי כֹהֵן *and your people are assuredly my foes, O priest* (if em. כִּ־ם רִיבַי, asseverative kaph) [61, 66], Ho 8_{6} כִּי מִיִּשְׂרָאֵל *surely Israel* (if em. כִּ־ם יִשְׂרָאֵל, asseverative kaph) [66], Ps 68_{29} זוּ פָּעַלְתָּ לָּנוּ: מֵהֵיכָלֶךָ *what you have done for us. Your temple* (if em. לָנוּ־ם: הֵיכָלֶךָ) [48], Ps 72_{15} וִיחִי וְיִתֶּן־לוֹ מִזְּהַב שְׁבָא *may he live and may gold of Sheba be given to him* (if em. וְיִתֶּן־לוֹ־ם זְהַב) [21], Ps 137_{3} שִׁירוּ לָנוּ מִשִּׁיר צִיּוֹן *sing us a song of Zion* (if em. לָנוּ־ם שִׁיר) [21; cf. 73], Ps 147_{15} עַד־מְהֵרָה יָרוּץ דְּבָרוֹ *to the mountain his thunder speeds* (if em. עַד־ם הָרָה) [58].

7. after a pronoun, Is 42_{17} הָאֹמְרִים לְמַסֵּכָה אַתֶּם אֱלֹהֵינוּ *who say to an image, You* (if em. אַתָּ־ם) *are our god* [20], Ps 92_{9} וְאַתָּה מָרוֹם לְעֹלָם י׳ *but you are the Exalted for ever, O Y.* (if em. וְאַתָּ־ם רוֹם) [20], Lm 3_{63} אֲנִי מַנְגִּינָתָם *I am the burden of their mocking songs* (if em. אֲנִי־ם נְגִינָתָם) [32, 38a]

8. internal enclitic mem, Gn 5_{29} יְנַחֲמֵנוּ *he will give us rest* (if em. to יְנַחֲ־מ־נוּ, from נוח *rest*) [46], Gn 10_{28} אֲבִימָאֵל *Abiel* (if em. אֲבִי־מ־אֵל) [60], Jr 11_{19} נַשְׁחִיתָה עֵץ בְּלַחְמוֹ *let us destroy the tree in its vigour* (if em. בְּלֵחַ־מ־וֹ) [31], Zp 1_{17} וְשֻׁפַּךְ דָּמָם כֶּעָפָר וּלְחֻמָם כַּגְּלָלִים *their blood shall be poured out like dust and their vigour* (if em. לֵחָ־מ־ם) *like dung* [59], Ps 23_{4} יְנַחֲמֻנִי *let them lead me* (if em. to יְנַחֲ־מ־נִי, from נחה *lead*) [46], 1 C 1_{22} אֲבִימָאֵל *Abiel* (if em. אֲבִי־מ־אֵל) [60].

[מֹאָב], see מוֹאָב *Moab*.

[מַאֲבוּס] 1 n.[m.] **granary** or **cattle-pen**—pl. sf. מַאֲבֻסֶיהָ—<OBJ> פתח *open* Jr 50_{26} (or em. פִּתְחוּ מַאֲבֻסֶיהָ *open its granaries* to פִּתְחוּ־ם אֲבֻסֶיהָ *open its granaries*, from אֵבוּס *granary*).*

⇒ אבס *fatten*.

*[מַאֲבָן] 0.0.1 n.[m.] **ballista, catapult,** <CSTR> ... יַד הַמאבן *hand,* i.e. side, *of ... the ballista* 4QM^{c} 1$_{5}$ (|| חֵרֶף *catapult*).

<SYN> חֵרֶף *catapult.*

⇒ אֶבֶן *stone.*

*[מָאֵד] I n.m. **Grand One, Almighty,** divine name —perh. vocalized מְאֹד—<SUBJ> מצא ni. *be found (to be)* Ps 46$_{2}$ (if em. מְאֹד *very* to מָאֵד; עֶזְרָה בְצָרוֹת נִמְצָא מְאֹד *the Grand One has been found (to be) a help in trouble*), הלל pu. *be praiseworthy* Ps 48$_{2}$||96$_{4}$||145$_{3}$||1 C 16$_{25}$ (all four if em. מְאֹד *very* to מָאֵד; גָּדוֹל י׳ וּמְהֻלָּל מְאֹד *Y. is great and the Grand One is praiseworthy*), שׂגה hi. *prosper* Jb 8$_{7}$ (if em. אַחֲרִיתְךָ יִשְׂגֶּה מְאֹד *your future shall be very great* to אַחֲרִיתְךָ יַשְׂגֵּה מָאֵד *the Grand One will prosper your future*), פרה hi. *make fruitful* Ps 105$_{24}$, עצם hi. *make mighty* Ps 105$_{24}$ (both if em. מְאֹד *very* to מָאֵד; וַיֶּפֶר אֶת־עַמּוֹ מְאֹד וַיַּעֲצִמֵהוּ מִצָּרָיו *and the Grand One has made his people fruitful and he has made them mightier than his enemies*), מאס *reject* Ps 78$_{59}$ (if em. מְאֹד *very* to מָאֵד; וַיִּמְאַס מְאֹד בְּיִשְׂרָאֵל *and the Almighty rejected Israel*).

<NOM CL> עַל־כָּל־הָאָרֶץ מְאֹד *the Grand One is over all the earth* Ps 97$_{9}$ (if em. מְאֹד *very* to מָאֵד).

<APP> י׳ *Y.* Ps 92$_{6}$ 109$_{30}$, עַד *perpetuity* Ps 119$_{8.43.51}$ Lm 5$_{22}$.

<COLL> vocative, *O Grand One* (if em. מְאֹד *very* to מָאֵד) Ps 21$_{2}$ (וּבִישׁוּעָתְךָ מַה־יָּגֶיל מְאֹד *and in your victory how he exults, O Grand One!*) 92$_{6}$ (מַה־גָּדְלוּ מַעֲשֶׂיךָ י׳ מְאֹד *how great are your works, O Y., the Grand One!*) 119$_{96}$ (רְחָבָה מִצְוָתְךָ מְאֹד *your commandment is broad, O Grand One!*) 119$_{138}$ (צִוִּיתָ צֶדֶק עֵדֹתֶיךָ וֶאֱמוּנָה מְאֹד *you righteously imposed your stipulations and fidelity, O Grand One!*) 119$_{140}$ (צְרוּפָה אִמְרָתְךָ מְאֹד *your word is tested, O Grand One!*) 142$_{7}$ (דַלּוֹתִי מְאֹד *I am brought low, O Grand One*).

מָאֵד || י׳ *Y.* Ps 48$_{2}$||96$_{4}$||145$_{3}$||1 C 16$_{25}$.

⇒ cf. מְאֹד *very.*

*[מָאֵד] II n.f. **calamity; terror**—perh. vocalized מְאֹד —**1. calamity,** perh. as a name for Sheol, all if em. מְאֹד *very* to מָאֵד, <SUBJ> שׂער ni. *be stormy* Ps 50$_{3}$ (וּסְבִיבָיו נִשְׂעֲרָה מְאֹד *and around him calamity blusters*). <PREP> עַד *unto,* + עוה ni. *be twisted* Ps 38$_{7}$, ענה ni. *be afflicted* Ps 119$_{107}$, שׁחח *bow down* Ps 38$_{7}$; without prep. *(by) calamity,* + בהל ni. *be dismayed* Ps 6$_{4.11}$, דלל *be brought low* Ps 79$_{8}$, ענה *be afflicted* Ps 116$_{10}$.

2. (object of) terror, הָיִיתִי חֶרְפָּה וְלִשְׁכֵנַי מְאֹד וּפַחַד לִמְיֻדָּעָי *I have become an object of reproach, and to my neighbours an object of terror, and to my acquaintances an object of fear* Ps 31$_{12}$ (or em. מָנוֹד *object of shaking [of head]* or מָגוֹר or מֹרָא *object of fear* or מָדוֹן *object of contention* or וְלַשְּׁכֵנִים/וְלִשְׁכֵנַי־ם אֵד *and to the/my neighbours a calamity,* unless מְאֹד II *burden*).

⇒ cf. אֵיד *disaster.*

*[מָאֹד] I n.[m.] **burden,** הָיִיתִי ... לִשְׁכֵנַי מְאֹד *I have become ... to my neighbours a burden* Ps 31$_{12}$ (if em. מְאֹד *very* to מָאֹד).

⇒ cf. אֵיד *disaster,* מְאֹד II *disaster.*

*[מָאֹד] II n.[m.] **nightfall,** תֵּרֵד מְאֹד *you shall go down (at) nightfall* 1 S 20$_{19}$ (if em. מְאֹד *very* to מָאֹד).

מְאֹד I 299.10.30.1 adv. **very**—Q מאוד, מאדה, מואדה, מאודה, מודה; sf. Q מודי, מְאֹדֶךָ (Si מאודך), Q מ[מ]אודם.*

1. as adverb
   - **a.** modifying verb, p. 103b
   - **b.** modifying predicative adjective, p. 105b
   - **c.** modifying attributive adjective, p. 106a
   - **d.** modifying adverb, p. 106b
2. as adjective, p. 106b
3. as noun
   - **a.** **strength,** p. 106b
   - **b.** עַד־לִמְאֹד/עַד־מְאֹד/בִּמְאֹד, p. 107a
   - **c.** **property,** p. 107a

1. as adverb, **very, very much, greatly,** also, in context, **dearly** (1 S 16$_{21}$ 19$_{1}$ Ps 119$_{167}$), **well** (Ps. 139$_{14}$ [or em.]), **(for) a long way** (1 S 20$_{19}$ [or em.] Jr 49$_{30}$), perh. **easily** (Ps 46$_{2}$ [or em.]), sometimes perh. **completely, utterly** (e.g. Ps 78$_{59}$ 1QS 4$_{1}$ [if em.]), etc.

a. modifying verb, כון ni. *be established* 1 K 2$_{12}$, אמן ni. *be reliable* Ps 93$_{5}$ (or em. מְאֹד to מֵאָז *of old**), טוב *be good* Gn 1$_{31}$ Jg 18$_{9}$, נעם *be pleasing* 2 S 1$_{26}$, יפה

be beautiful Ezk 16$_{13}$ (בִּמְאֹד), יקר *be precious* 1 S 18$_{30}$, אדר ni. *be majestic* Si 43$_{11(B)}$ (Bmg, M הדר ni. *be majestic*), חכם *be wise* Zc 9$_{2}$, רהב hi. *be arrogant* Si 13$_{8}$, רעע *be evil* Gn 21$_{11}$ Ne 13$_{8}$.

גבה *be high* Is 52$_{13}$ perh. 4QTime 1.2$_{10}$ (ומודה גבה השכל) *and very high has become intelligence*, unless *and knowledge* [מוֹדַע] *has become high, intelligence* or *and strength* [מְאֹד, §3a] *has become high, intelligence*), hi. *make* wall *high* 2 C 33$_{14}$, עלה ni. *be raised*, i.e. exalted Ps 47$_{10}$, עמק *be deep* Ps 92$_{6}$, דלל *be low* Jg 6$_{6}$ Ps 79$_{8}$ (or em. מְאֹד *very* to מָאֵד *calamity*) 142$_{7}$ (or em. מְאֹד *very* to מָאֵד *Grand One*).

גדל *be great* Gn 26$_{13}$ Jb 2$_{13}$ Si 47$_{24}$, hi. *become great* Dn 8$_{8}$ (עַד־מְאֹד), שׂגה *be great* Jb 8$_{7}$ (or em. אַחֲרִיתְךָ יִשְׂגֶּה מְאֹד *your future shall be very great* to אַחֲרִיתְךָ יַשְׂגֶּה מָאֵד *the Grand One will prosper your future*), רבה *be great* Gn 7$_{18}$ 47$_{27}$ Ps 107$_{38}$ 4Q416 2.2$_{16}$ (=4Q417 1.2$_{21}$ [מ]אדה]), hi. *increase* Gn 15$_{1(Sam)}$ (MT הַרְבֵּה מְאֹד *very great*) 17$_{2.20}$ (both בִּמְאֹד) 34$_{12}$ Dt 17$_{17}$=11QT 66$_{19}$ 4Q418 81$_{5}$ appar. 4Q418 137$_{4}$, כבד *be great* Gn 18$_{20}$, *be oppressive* 1 S 5$_{11}$, *be heavy-laden* Ezk 27$_{25}$, hi. *honour* Nm 22$_{17}$, *make* yoke *heavy* Is 47$_{6}$.

גבר *be strong* Gn 7$_{19}$, hi. *act mightily* 1QH 11$_{3}$, חזק *be strong* Ex 19$_{19}$ 23$_{6}$, אמץ *be strong* Jos 1$_{7}$, pi. *strengthen* Na 2$_{2}$, עצם *be powerful* Gn 26$_{16}$ Ex 1$_{7.20}$ (both בִּמְאֹד) Is 31$_{1}$, מהר pi. *be rapid* Jr 48$_{16}$.

שׂער ni. *be stormy* Ps 50$_{3}$ (mss סער ni. in same sense; or em. מְאֹד *very* to מָאֵד *calamity*), חרה *be inflamed* (of anger) Gn 4$_{5}$ 34$_{7}$ Nm 11$_{10}$ 16$_{15}$ 1 S 11$_{6}$ 18$_{8}$ 2 S 3$_{8}$ 12$_{5}$ 13$_{21}$ Ne 4$_{1}$ 5$_{6}$ 2 C 25$_{10}$, אנף htp. *become angry* Dt 9$_{20}$ 2 K 17$_{18}$, קצף *be angry* Is 64$_{8}$ Lm 5$_{22}$ (both עַד־מְאֹד) Est 1$_{12}$, מרר *be bitter* Ru 1$_{13}$, hi. *embitter* Ru 1$_{20}$.

ענה *be afflicted* Ps 116$_{10}$, ni. *be afflicted* Ps 119$_{107}$ (or em. מְאֹד *very* to מָאֵד *calamity*), pi. *humiliate* Is 64$_{11}$ (עַד־מְאֹד), קלה ni. *be dishonoured* Si 11$_{6}$, בושׁ *be ashamed* Jr 9$_{18}$ 20$_{11}$ 50$_{12}$, כלם ni. *be shamed* 2 S 10$_{5}$|| 1 C 19$_{5}$, כנע ni. *be humbled* 2 C 33$_{12}$, חיל htpalp. *be distressed* Est 4$_{4}$, צרר *be in distress* Jg 2$_{15}$ 10$_{9}$ 1 S 30$_{6}$, חרב *be desolate* Jr 2$_{12}$, חיל *be in pain* 1 S 31$_{3}$ (or em. וַיָּחֶל *and he was in pain* to וַיֵּחַל *and he was pierced*, i.e. חלל ni.) Zc 9$_{5}$, חלה ho. *be wounded* 2 C 35$_{23}$, דכה ni. *be crushed* Ps 38$_{9}$ (mss דכא ni. *be crushed*; עַד־מְאֹד), עיף *be weary* 1 S 14$_{31}$, צמא *be thirsty* Jg 15$_{18}$, שׂבע *be satisfied* Ps 78$_{29}$.

ירא *fear* Gn 20$_{8}$ 32$_{8}$ Ex 14$_{10}$ Jos 9$_{24}$ 10$_{2}$ 1 S 12$_{18}$ 17$_{11.24}$ 21$_{13}$ 28$_{20}$ 31$_{4}$||1 C 10$_{4}$ 1 K 18$_{3}$ (הָיָה יָרֵא אֶת־יי *was* very *fearful of* Y.) 2 K 10$_{4}$ Arad ost. 111$_{3}$ ([י]רא מאד]), גור *fear* Nm 22$_{3}$, חרד *tremble* Ex 19$_{18}$ 1 S 28$_{5}$, בהל ni. *feel panic* 1 S 28$_{21}$ Ps 6$_{4.11}$ (both or em. מְאֹד *very* to מָאֵד *calamity*), אבל htp. *mourn* Nm 14$_{39}$.

אהב *love* 1 S 16$_{21}$ Ps 119$_{167}$, חפץ *love* 1 S 19$_{1}$ Ps 112$_{1}$, שׂמח *rejoice* 1 S 11$_{15}$ 1 K 5$_{21}$ 1QM 12$_{13}$=19$_{5}$=4QM^{b} 1$_{5}$, גיל *rejoice* Zc 9$_{9}$ Ps 21$_{2}$ (or em. מְאֹד *very* to מָאֵד *Grand One*), מאס *reject* Ps 78$_{59}$ (or em. מְאֹד *very* to מָאֵד *Grand One*), תעב pi. *abominate* 1QS 4$_{1}$ (if em. אחת תעב סודה *one, he abominates its counsel* to מודה abominates *utterly*),* hi. *behave abominably* 1 K 21$_{26}$, ידע *know* Ps 139$_{14}$ (or em. מֵאָד/מֵאָז *from of old**; read יֹדַעַת as יָדַעְתָּ), בין htpol. *examine* Jr 2$_{10}$ 4Q415 11$_{11}$ 4Q417 3$_{3}$ ([התבונן]) 4Q418 81$_{17}$, ברך pi. *bless* Gn 24$_{35}$, הלל pi. *praise* 2 S 14$_{25}$ 4Q416 3$_{5}$, pu. *be praised* Ps 48$_{2}$=96$_{4}$=145$_{3}$=1 C 16$_{25}$ (or em. מְאֹד *very* to מָאֵד *Grand One*), פצר *insist* Gn 19$_{3.9}$ 30$_{43}$, ליץ hi. *mock* Ps 119$_{51}$ (עַד־מְאֹד), ידה hi. *thank* Ps 109$_{30}$ (or em. מְאֹד to מָאֵד *Grand One*).

אזל *go* Jr 2$_{36}$ (or em. תֵּזְלִי how very [far] *you go* to תָּזֵלִּי how very *lightly you regard*, i.e. זלל hi.), ירד *go down* 1 S 20$_{19}$ (or em. תֵּרֵד מְאֹד appar. *you will go down a great distance* to תִּפָּקֵד מְאֹד *you will be greatly missed*, or em. מְאֹד to מָאֵד *(at) nightfall*), i.e. be over (of day) Jg 19$_{11}$, נפל *fall* Ne 6$_{16}$, שׁחח *bow down* Ps 38$_{7}$ (עַד־מְאֹד; or em. מְאֹד *very* to מָאֵד *calamity*), שׁפל hi. *make* pride *low* Si 7$_{17}$, נדד *flee* Jr 49$_{30}$, נצל hi. *allow to escape* Ps 119$_{43}$ (עַד־מְאֹד), עזב *leave* Ps 119$_{8}$ (עַד־מְאֹד), רחק hi. *distance oneself* Jos 8$_{4}$.

מצא *find* grace 1 K 11$_{19}$, ni. *be found* Ps 46$_{2}$ (or em. מֵאָד/מֵאָז *from of old** or מָאֵד *Grand One*), שׁמר *keep*, i.e. look after (soul) Dt 4$_{9}$, observe (instruction) Dt 24$_{8}$ Jos 22$_{5}$ Ps 119$_{4}$, ni. *be cautious* Dt 2$_{4}$ 4$_{15}$ Jos 23$_{11}$ 1Q DM 2$_{9}$ (השׁ]מרו מא[דה]) 4QBéat 14.2$_{26}$ 4Q418 123.2$_{7}$ 177$_{7}$ ([מאו]ד), פרה hi. *make fruitful* Gn 17$_{6}$ Ps 105$_{24}$ (or em. מְאֹד *very* to מָאֵד *Grand One*).

פלא hi. *act wonderfully* 1QH 9$_{38(AHL)}$ (בהפלא

(מאד[ה]) fr. $10_{9(AHL)}$ ([ה]פלא מאדה) 1QS 10_{16}=4QS^{b} 9_{3}=4QS^{f} 1.4_{2}, עשׂה *do* horrible thing Jr 18_{13}, חטא *sin* 2 S 24_{10}||1 C 21_{8}, חלל pi. *profane* Ezk 20_{13}.

<COLL> מְאֹד immediately follows verb it modifies, Gn 13_{1} $7_{18.19}$ 18_{20} 26_{13} 47_{27} Ex $1_{7.20}$ (both בִּמְאֹד) 14_{10} 19_{19} Nm 22_{17} Dt 2_{4} 4_{15} 24_{8} Jos 1_{7} 9_{24} 10_{2} 22_{5} $23_{6.11}$ Jg 15_{18} 18_{9} 19_{11} 1 S 5_{11} 16_{21} $17_{11.24}$ 20_{19} 21_{13} $28_{20.21}$ 31_{3} 31_{4}|| 1 C 10_{4} 1 S 31_{4} 2 S 10_{5}||1 C 19_{5} 2 S 24_{10}||1 C 21_{8} 1 K 2_{12} 5_{21} 21_{26} 2 K 10_{4} Is 31_{1} 52_{13} 64_{11} (עַד־מְאֹד) Jr $2_{10.12.36}$ 9_{18} 18_{13} 20_{11} 48_{16} 49_{30} Ezk 16_{13} (בִּמְאֹד) 20_{13} 27_{25} Zc $9_{2.5.9}$ Ps $6_{4.11}$ (both or em. מְאֹד *very* to מָאֵד *calamity*) 21_{2} 38_{7} (or em. מְאֹד *very* to מָאֵד *calamity*) 38_{9} (both עַד־מְאֹד) 46_{2} (or em. מֵאָז/מֵאֵד *from of old*) 48_{2}=96_{4}=145_{3}=1 C 16_{25} (or em. מְאֹד *very* to מָאֵד *Grand One*) Ps 50_{3} (or em. מְאֹד *very* to מָאֵד *calamity*) $78_{29.5}$ 79_{8} (or em. מְאֹד *very* to מָאֵד *calamity*) 93_{5} 112_{1} 116_{10} $119_{4.8.51.107}$ (all three עַד־מְאֹד) 119_{167} 139_{14} (or em. מֵאֵד/מֵאָז *from of old*) 142_{7} (or em. מְאֹד *very* to מָאֵד *Grand One*) Jb 8_{7} Dn 8_{8} (עַד־מְאֹד) Ne 6_{16} 2 C $33_{12.14}$ 35_{23} Si 11_{6} 13_{8} 1QH $9_{38(AHL)}$ (בהפלא מאד[ה]) 11_{3} fr. $10_{9(AHL)}$ ([ה]פלא מאדה) 1QS 10_{16}=4QS^{b} 9_{3}=4QS^{f} 1.4_{2} 1QM 12_{13}=19_{5}=4QM^{b} 1_{5} 1QDM 2_{9} (השׁ]מרו מא[דה) 4Q415 11_{11} 4Q416 2.2_{16} (=4Q417 1.2_{21} [מ]אדה) 3_{5} 4Q417 3_{3} 4Q418 $81_{5.17}$ 123.2_{7} 137_{4} 177_{7} ([מאו]ד) 4QBéat 14.2_{26} Arad ost. 111_{3} (י]רא] מאד).

מְאֹד precedes verb, Ps 47_{10} (מְאֹד נַעֲלָה *he is very exalted*) 92_{6} (מְאֹד עָמְקוּ מַחְשְׁבֹתֶיךָ *very deep are your thoughts*; or em. מְאֹד *very* to מָאֵד *Grand One*) 104_{1} (מְאֹד נַעֲלֵיתָ *greatly are you exalted* over all the gods) 107_{38} Si 7_{17} (מאד מאד השׁפיל גאוה *make [your] pride extremely low*) 43_{11} (B כי מאד נארדה [בכ]בוד *for it is very majestic in [its] glory*) perh. 4QTime 1.2_{10}.

וְהַמַּיִם גָּבְרוּ מְאֹד מְאֹד *extremely* Gn 7_{19} (unless מְאֹד מְאֹד = *and the waters became very strong everywhere*, i.e. more distributive than emphatic) Gn $17_{2.6.20}$ (all three + בִּמְאֹד מְאֹד) 30_{43} Ex 1_{7} (בִּמְאֹד מְאֹד) 2 K 10_{4} Ezk 16_{13} (בִּמְאֹד מְאֹד) Si 7_{17} 1QH $11_{3(mg)}$ (מודה מודה).

מְאֹד might modify two or more conjoined verbs, Gn 47_{27} (וַיִּפְרוּ וַיִּרְבּוּ מְאֹד perh. *and they became very fruitful and numerous*) Ex 1_{7} (וַיִּרְבּוּ וַיַּעַצְמוּ בִּמְאֹד perh. *and they became very numerous and powerful*) Jos 1_{7} (רַק חֲזַק וֶאֱמַץ מְאֹד perh. *but be very strong and insistent*) 1 S 28_{5} (וַיִּרָא וַיֶּחֱרַד לִבּוֹ מְאֹד perh. *and his heart was very fearful and trembling*) Is 52_{13} (יָרוּם וְנִשָּׂא וְגָבַהּ מְאֹד perh. *he will be very high and raised up and exalted*) Jr 49_{30} (נֻסוּ נֻּדוּ מְאֹד *flee [and] take flight [for] a long way*) Ezk 27_{25} (וַתִּמָּלְאִי וַתִּכְבְּדִי מְאֹד perh. *and you were very full and heavy-laden*) Ps $6_{4.11}$ (יֵבֹשׁוּ וְיִבָּהֲלוּ מְאֹד perh. my enemies *will be very ashamed and in panic*; both or em. מְאֹד *very* to מָאֵד *calamity*) 38_{7} (נַעֲוֵיתִי שַׁחֹתִי עַד־מְאֹד perh. *I was very humbled and bowed down*; or em. מְאֹד *very* to מָאֵד *calamity*) 38_{9} (נְפוּגוֹתִי וְנִדְכֵּיתִי עַד־מְאֹד perh. *I was very numb and crushed*) 48_{2}=96_{4}=145_{3}=1 C 16_{25} (גָּדוֹל י׳ וּמְהֻלָּל מְאֹד perh. *for very great and praiseworthy is Y.*; or em. מְאֹד *very* to מָאֵד *Grand One*); וַיְהִי קוֹל הַשּׁוֹפָר הוֹלֵךְ וְחָזֵק מְאֹד perh. *and the sound of the trumpet started to be very strong* Ex 19_{19}.

b. modifying adjective used predicatively, after היה *be* or in nom. cl., e.g. כִּי־יָפָה הִיא מְאֹד *for she was very beautiful* Gn $12_{14(Qr)}$, וְאַבְרָם כָּבֵד מְאֹד *and Abram was very wealthy* Gn 13_{2} (but sometimes forms can also be regarded as stative verbs, as §1a), גָּדוֹל *great* Ex 11_{3} Nm 13_{28} 1 S 2_{17} 4_{10} Ezk 9_{9} (בִּמְאֹד), *rich* 1 S 25_{2} 2 S 19_{33}, רַב *great* Ezk $47_{9.10}$ Jl 2_{11}, הַרְבֵּה *great* Gn 15_{1} (Sam אַרְבֶּה your reward *I shall increase* exceedingly), *many* Dt 3_{5}, עֲצוּם *numerous* Nm 32_{1}.

רָחָב *wide* Ps 119_{96} (or em. מְאֹד *very* to מָאֵד *Grand One*), קָרוֹב *near* Dt 30_{14}, רָחוֹק *distant* Jos 9_{22}, מַהֵר *fast-approaching* Zp 1_{14}, יָבֵשׁ *dry* Ezk 37_{2}, צָמֵא *thirsty* Si 51_{24}, שִׁכֹּר *drunk* 1 S 25_{36} (עַד־מְאֹד), זָקֵן *old* 1 S 2_{22} 1 K 1_{15}.

טוֹב *good* Gn 24_{16} (טֹבַת מַרְאֶה *good of appearance*) Nm 14_{7} 1 S 19_{4} 2 S 11_{2} (טוֹבַת מַרְאֶה) 1 K 1_{6} (טוֹב־תֹּאַר *good of appearance*) Jr 24_{3}, *well-behaved* 1 S 25_{15}, צָרוּף *pure* Ps 119_{140} (or em. מְאֹד to מָאֵד *Grand One*), יָפֶה *fair* Gn 12_{14} 1 K 1_{4} (עַד־מְאֹד).

כָּבֵד *rich* Gn 13_{2}, *severe* Gn 41_{31} 47_{13}, *numerous* Gn 50_{9}, חָזָק *severe* 1 K 17_{17}, קָשֶׁה *fierce* 2 S 2_{17} (עַד־מְאֹד), נוֹרָא *awe-inspiring* Jl 2_{11} Si $43_{29(Segal)}$ (נורא ... מ[אד]), חַטָּא *sinful* Gn 13_{13}, רַע *bad* Gn 41_{19} (רָעוֹת תֹּאַר *displeasing of appearance*) Jr 24_{3}, גֵּא *proud* Is 16_{6}, גֵּאֶה *proud* Is $16_{6(mss)}$=Jr 48_{29}, עָנָו *humble* Nm $12_{3(Qr)}$ (עָנָיו), בָּזוּי *despised* Ob 2 (בָּזוּי אַתָּה מְאֹד *you are very much de-*

spised; or em. to בָּזוּי בָּאָדָם I have made you *despised by humankind* ||Jr 49$_{15}$).

<COLL> מְאֹד modifies adjective in construct chain, Gn 13$_{2}$ 15$_{1}$ 24$_{16}$ (טֹובַת מַרְאֶה מְאֹד *very good of appearance*) 41$_{19}$ (רָעוֹת תֹּאַר מְאֹד *very bad of appearance*) 50$_{9}$ Ex 11$_{3}$ Nm 12$_{3}$ 13$_{28}$ 32$_{1}$ Dt 3$_{5}$ 1 S 2$_{17.22}$ 4$_{10}$ 25$_{2.36}$ 2 S 2$_{17}$ (both עַד־מְאֹד) 11$_{4}$ (טֹובַת מַרְאֶה מְאֹד) 1 K 1$_{4}$ (עַד־מְאֹד) 1$_{6}$ (טוֹב־תֹּאַר מְאֹד *very handsome*) 1$_{15}$ 17$_{17}$ Is 16$_{6}$=Jr 48$_{29}$ Jr 24$_{3.3}$ Ezk 9$_{9}$ (בִּמְאֹד בִּמְאֹד) 37$_{2}$ 47$_{9.10}$ Jl 2$_{11.11}$ Zp 1$_{14}$ Si 51$_{24}$.

מְאֹד מְאֹד *exceptionally* Nm 14$_{7}$ Ezk 9$_{9}$ (בִּמְאֹד מְאֹד) Si 43$_{29}$ ([מ]אד מאד).

מְאֹד might modify two conjoined adjectives or participles, Gn 13$_{13}$ (רָעִים חַטָּאִים לַי׳ מְאֹד perh. and the people of Sodom were *very evil and guilty before Y.*) Jl 2$_{11}$ (גָּדוֹל יוֹם־י׳ וְנוֹרָא מְאֹד perh. *very great and awe inspiring is the day of Y.*) Zp 1$_{14}$ (גָּדוֹל וּמַהֵר מְאֹד perh. *very great and fast-approaching*).

c. modifying adjective (or form functioning as adjective) used attributively, רַב *great* Nm 11$_{33}$ Ezk 47$_{7}$ Ezr 10$_{1}$ 1 C 18$_{8}$ 2 C 32$_{29}$ 11QapPs 4$_{9}$ ([ר]בה מואדה), *many* Jos 11$_{4}$ 22$_{8}$ Ezk 37$_{2}$ Jb 1$_{3}$, הַרְבֵּה *much* Gn 41$_{49}$ (וַיִּצְבֹּר יוֹסֵף בָּר כְּחוֹל הַיָּם הַרְבֵּה מְאֹד *and Joseph amassed very much grain, like the sand of the sea*) 2 S 8$_{8}$ 1 K 5$_{9}$ 2 K 21$_{16}$ 2 C 14$_{12}$ 32$_{27}$ perh. 4Q418 137$_{4}$ ([ה]רבה מא[וד]), *many* Jos 22$_{8}$ 2 S 12$_{2}$ 1 K 10$_{10.11}$ Jr 40$_{12}$, גָּדוֹל *great* Gn 27$_{33.34}$ (both גְּדֹלָה עַד־מְאֹד *exceedingly great*) Jos 10$_{20}$ Jg 11$_{33}$ 1 S 5$_{9}$ 14$_{20}$ 2 S 13$_{15.36}$ 18$_{17}$ Ezk 37$_{10}$ Zc 14$_{4}$ Ne 8$_{17}$ 2 C 7$_{8}$ 16$_{14}$ (עַד־לְמְאֹד), עָצוּם *powerful* Dn 11$_{25}$, כָּבֵד *heavy* Ex 9$_{18.24}$, *profound* Gn 50$_{10}$, *severe* Ex 9$_{3}$, *numerous* Ex 12$_{38}$ 1 K 10$_{2}$||2 C 9$_{1}$, חָזָק *strong* Ex 10$_{19}$ 19$_{16}$, רָחוֹק *distant* Dt 20$_{15}$=11QT 62$_{12}$ Jos 9$_{9}$, טוֹב *good* Jr 24$_{2}$, רַע *bad* Jr 24$_{2}$, נוֹרָא *awe-inspiring* Jg 13$_{6}$, גְּבֹהָה *high* Ezk 40$_{2}$, עָנֹג *pampered* Dt 28$_{54}$, נַחְלָה *painful* Jr 14$_{17}$, בָּרִיא *fat* Jg 3$_{17}$, מַשְׂכִּיל *successful* 1 S 18$_{15}$, חָכָם *wise* 2 S 13$_{3}$, מֹרֶה appar. *refractory* oppression 2 K 14$_{26}$ (or em. הַמַּר *the* very *bitter* oppression).

<COLL> מְאֹד immediately follows modified adj., Gn 27$_{33.34}$ (both עַד־מְאֹד) 41$_{49}$ Ex 9$_{3.18.24}$ 10$_{19}$ 12$_{38}$ 19$_{16}$ Nm 11$_{33}$ 28$_{54}$ Jos 9$_{9}$ 10$_{20}$ 11$_{4}$ 22$_{8.8}$ Jg 3$_{17}$ 11$_{33}$ 13$_{6}$ 1 S 5$_{9}$ 14$_{20}$ 18$_{15}$ 2 S 8$_{8}$ 12$_{2}$ 13$_{3.15.36}$ 18$_{17}$ 1 K 5$_{9}$ 10$_{2}$||2 C 9$_{1}$ 1 K 10$_{10.11}$ 2 K 14$_{26}$ 21$_{16}$ Jr 14$_{17}$ 24$_{2.2}$ 40$_{12}$ Ezk 37$_{2.10}$ 40$_{2}$ 47$_{7}$ Zc 14$_{4}$ Jb 1$_{3}$ Dn 11$_{25}$ (עַד־מְאֹד) Ezr 10$_{1}$ Ne 8$_{17}$ 1 C 18$_{8}$ 2 C 16$_{14}$ (עַד־לְמְאֹד) 32$_{27.29}$ 4Q418 137$_{4}$ (מא[וד]) 11QapPs 4$_{9}$ ([ר]בה מואדה).

מְאֹד מְאֹד *extremely* Ezk 37$_{10}$.

מְאֹד might modify two conjoined adjectives, Gn 50$_{10}$ (מִסְפֵּד גָּדוֹל וְכָבֵד מְאֹד perh. *very great and profound mourning*) Dn 11$_{25}$ (בְּחַיִל־גָּדוֹל וְעָצוּם עַד־מְאֹד perh. *with a very great and powerful force*).

d. modifying adjective or noun used adverbially, + כָּבֵד *in great numbers* Ex 10$_{14}$, הַרְחֵק *at a distance* Jos 3$_{16}$, הַרְבֵּה *largely* Jos 13$_{1}$, *greatly* 1 S 26$_{21}$ Ne 2$_{2}$ 2 C 11$_{12}$, *in great quantity* 2 S 12$_{30}$||1 C 20$_{2}$ 2 C 16$_{8}$, יֶתֶר *exceedingly* Is 56$_{12}$ (גָּדוֹל יֶתֶר מְאֹד *[very] exceedingly great*). <COLL> מְאֹד immediately follows modified adj. or noun, Ex 10$_{14}$ Jos 3$_{16}$ 13$_{1}$ 1 S 26$_{21}$ 2 S 12$_{30}$||1 C 20$_{2}$ Is 56$_{12}$ Ne 2$_{2}$ 2 C 11$_{12}$ 16$_{8}$.

2. as adjective (modifying noun), **very great,** + רֹב *abundance* of way, i.e. very great distance Jos 9$_{13}$ (unless מְאֹד modifies וּנְעָלֵינוּ בָּלוּ *and our sandals are* very *worn out*, as §1a), of vessels 1 K 7$_{47}$||2 C 4$_{18}$, of spices 2 C 9$_{9}$, of plunder Zc 14$_{14}$, of army 2 C 24$_{24}$, of congregation 2 C 30$_{13}$, עָצְמָה *power* of spells Is 47$_{9}$, רִיב *struggle* Jg 12$_{2}$ (or ins. ענה pi. *oppress* greatly, as §1a), צַר *distress* 1 S 28$_{15}$ 2 S 24$_{14}$||1 C 21$_{13}$ (all three צַר־לִי מְאֹד *I have* [i.e. am in] *very great distress*), אֱמוּנָה *faithfulness* Ps 119$_{138}$ (unless צִוִּיתָ צֶדֶק עֵדֹתֶיךָ וֶאֱמוּנָה מְאֹד = *you have righteousness as your decrees and faithfulness as strength*, as §3a; or em. מְאֹד *very* to מָאֵד *Grand One*), פַּשׁ appar. *folly* Jb 35$_{15}$ (or em. פֶּשַׁע *sin*). <COLL> מְאֹד מְאֹד *extremely great* 1 K 7$_{47}$.

3. as noun, **a. strength,** <CSTR> [כול] מואדה with *all strength* 4QBéat 14.2$_{24(EW)}$, כָּל־מְאֹדֶךָ with *all your strength* Dt 6$_{5}$ Si 7$_{30(A)}$ (מאודך), כָּל־מְאֹדוֹ with *all his strength* 2 K 23$_{25}$, כול מודי with *all my strength* 11QPs^{a} 22$_{1}$ (unless מוֹד II *love*), [כול מ]אודם with *all their strength* 4QShir^{b} 15$_{3}$. <PREP> בְּ of instrument, *by (means of), with*, + אהב *love* Y. Dt 6$_{5}$ Si 7$_{30}$ 4QShir^{b} 15$_{3}$ ([בכול מ]אודם) 11QPs^{a} 22$_{1}$, שׁוּב *go back* to Y. 2 K 23$_{25}$, pol. *reply* 4QBéat 14.2$_{24(EW)}$ ([ואל תשובב בכול] מואדה *and do not reply with all strength*). <COLL> מְאֹד || נֶפֶשׁ *soul* Dt 6$_{5}$ 2 K 23$_{25}$, לֵבָב *heart* Dt 6$_{5}$ 2 K 23$_{25}$ Si 7$_{30}$ (לֵב).

b. preceded by בְּ or עַד, forming an adverb equivalent to (or perh. more emphatic than) מְאֹד on its own, **(1)** בִּמְאֹד מְאֹד perh. lit. *in the quality of greatness exceedingly*, i.e. very greatly, exceptionally, Gn $17_{2.20}$ (both + רבה hi. *increase*) 17_6 (+ פרה hi. *make fruitful*) Ex 1_7 (+ עצם *be powerful*) Ezk 9_9 (+ גָּדוֹל *great*) 16_{13} (+ יפה *be beautiful*).

(2) עַד־מְאֹד *unto greatness*, i.e. exceedingly, completely Gn $27_{33.34}$ (both + גָּדוֹל *great*) 1 S 11_{15} (+ שׂמח *rejoice*) 25_{36} (+ שִׁכֹּר *drunk*) 2 S 2_{17} (+ קָשֶׁה *fierce*) 1 K 1_4 (+ יָפֶה *beautiful*) Is 64_8 (+ קצף *be angry*) 64_{11} (+ ענה pi. *humiliate*) Ps 38_7 (+ שׁחח *bow down*; or em. מְאֹד *very* to מָאֵד *calamity*) 38_9 (+ דכה ni. *be crushed*) 119_8 (+ עזב *leave*) 119_{43} (+ נצל hi. *allow to escape*) 119_{51} (+ ליץ hi. *mock*) 119_{107} (+ ענה ni. *be afflicted*; or em. מְאֹד *very* to מָאֵד *calamity*) Lm 5_{22} (+ קצף *be angry*) Dn 8_8 (+ גדל hi. *become great*) 11_{25} (+ עָצוּם *powerful*). <COLL> אַל ... עַד־מְאֹד *not ... completely* Is 64_8 (+ אַל־לָעַד *not for ever*).

(3) עַד־לִמְאֹד *exceedingly* 2 C 16_{14} (+ גָּדוֹל *great*).

c. appar. **property**, ולא נודע מי גנבו ממאד המחנה *and it is not known who stole it from the property of the camp* CD 9_{11} (unless ממאד המחנה = who *of the strength of the camp*, i.e. which person in the camp, stole it?, as §3a), ומגרונו ומגתו אל ימכר להם בכל מאדו *and from his threshing floor and from his olive press he is not to sell to them any of his property* CD 12_{10} (unless בכל מאדו = he is not to sell, i.e. he is to refuse to sell, *with all his strength*, as §3a), perh. ידרוש מודו *he will seek his property* 4QD[a] 7.3_3(WA) (Baumgarten מידו seek *from his hand*).

Also 1QDM 43_2 (מ[א]דה) 1Q51_2 ([מ]אוד) 4QMyst[a] 6.2_{15} 4QparaKings 25_6(WA) (מואדה; Olyan בוגדה *treacherous*) 4Q474 1_5 4QDibHam[a] 25_3 4QPrFêtes[c] 8_6 ([מ]אוד).*

⇒ cf. מָאֵד *Grand One*.

*מְאֹד II 1 n.[m.] **burden, object of distress**, הָיִיתִי חֶרְפָּה וְלִשְׁכֵנַי מְאֹד וּפַחַד לִמְיֻדָּעָי *I have become an object of reproach, (and) to my neighbours a burden, and to my acquaintances an object of fear* Ps 31_{12} (or em. מָנוֹד *object of shaking [of head]* or מָגוֹר or מֹרָא *object of fear* or מָדוֹן *object of contention* or וְלִשְׁכֵנִים/וְלִשְׁכֵנַי־ם אֵד *and to the/my neighbours a calamity*).

⇒ אֵיד *disaster*.

מְאֹד III *Grand One*, see מָאֵד I *Grand One*.

*מאה vb. **Pi. repeat a hundred times**, <SUBJ> worshipper Ps 22_{26} (if em. מֵאִתְּךָ *from you* to מְאֵיתִיךָ *I will repeat to you a hundred times*) 66_{20} (if em. מֵאִתִּי *from me* to מְאֵיתִי *I will repeat a hundred times*), פְּעֻלָּה *recompense* Ps 109_{20} (if em. מֵאֵת *from* to מְאֵיתָה *it repeats a hundred times*). <OBJ> תְּהִלָּה *song of praise* Ps 22_{26} (if em.; see Subj.), חֶסֶד *kindness* Ps 66_{20} (if em.; see Subj.) 4QTanḥ 2.8_{12} (MT מֵאִתְּךָ *from you*). <PREP> בְּ of place, *in, within*, + קָהָל *congregation* Ps 22_{26} (if em.; see Subj.).

⇒ מֵאָה *hundred*, מֵאַת *a hundred times*.

מֵאָה I 579.3.63.3 n.m.&f. **hundred**—appar. מְאַת (Ec 8_{12}); cstr. מְאַת; pl. מֵאוֹת (מְאֹת; Kt/Q מאיות, Q מיואת); sf. Q מאיותיו; du. מָאתַיִם (מָאתַיִם, Q מאתין)—appar. no distinction between use of absolute and construct.*

1. time
- years, p. 108a
- days, p. 109a
- others, p. 109a

2. measurement
- cubits, p. 109a
- rods, p. 109b

3. money (unit or material not alw. explicit)
- silver shekels, p. 109b
- gold shekels, p. 110a
- bronze, iron shekels, p. 110a
- silver talents, p. 110a
- gold talents, p. 110a
- iron talents, p. 110a
- silver minas, p. 110a
- kesitahs, p. 110a
- measures, p. 110b

4. persons
- souls, p. 110b
- males, p. 110b

brothers, p. 110b
sons (returning exiles), p. 111a
men (returning exiles), p. 111b
men (oft. warriors), p. 111b
youths (warriors), p. 112a
mustered men, p. 112a
people on foot, p. 112b
warriors (various), p. 112b
riders, p. 113a
dead, slain, p. 113a
priests, Levites, prophets, p. 113a
adminstrators (various), p. 113a
servants (various), p. 113b
women (various), p. 113b
others, p. 113b

5. beasts (various), p. 113b

6. equipment
chariots, p. 114a
shields, p. 114a
cultic, p. 114a

7. songs, psalms, p. 114b

8. foreskins, p. 114b

Collocations
1. as military unit or unit of population, p. 114b
2. without unit of measurement specified, p. 114b

(throughout article, items are listed in ascending order within each paragraph)

1. 100 years מְאַת שָׁנָה Gn 11_{10} (Shem) 21_{5} (Abraham), מֵאָה־שָׁנָה Gn 17_{17} (Abraham) Is $65_{20.20}$ (both of lifespan in new Jerusalem) Si $18_{7(Segal)}$ מאה ... שנים ([מאה שנה]), Si $41_{4(M)}$ (לעשר מאה ו[אל]ף שנים *be it ten, a hundred, or a thousand years;* B לאלף שנים מאה ועשר *be it a thousand years, a hundred, or ten*; human lifespan).

105 years חָמֵשׁ שָׁנִים וּמְאַת שָׁנָה Gn 5_{6} (Seth), 110 years מֵאָה וָעֶשֶׂר שָׁנִים Gn $50_{22.26}$ (both Joseph) Jos 24_{49} Jg 2_{8} (both Joshua) 2QJub[b] 46_{3} (וימות יוסף]בן[ ]מאה ו[עשר] שנים *and Joseph died [as] a son of 110 years*), 119 years תְּשַׁע־עֶשְׂרֵה שָׁנָה וּמְאַת שָׁנָה (Nahor), 120 years מֵאָה וְעֶשְׂרִים שָׁנָה Gn 6_{3} (lifespan before Flood) Dt 31_{2} 34_{7} (both Moses) 4QCommGenA 1_{2} (longest lifespan), 123 years שָׁלֹשׁ וְעֶשְׂרִים וּמְאַת שָׁנָה Nm 33_{39} (Aaron), 127 years מֵאָה שָׁנָה וְעֶשְׂרִים שָׁנָה וְשֶׁבַע שָׁנִים Gn 23_{1} (Sarah), 130 years שְׁלֹשִׁים וּמְאַת שָׁנָה Gn 5_{3} (Adam) 47_{9} (Jacob), מֵאָה וּשְׁלֹשִׁים שָׁנָה 2 C 24_{15} (Jehoiada), 133 years שָׁלֹשׁ וּשְׁלֹשִׁים וּמְאַת שָׁנָה Ex 6_{18} (Kohath), 137 years מְאַת שָׁנָה שֶׁבַע וּשְׁלֹשִׁים שָׁנָה וְשֶׁבַע שָׁנִים וּשְׁלֹשִׁים Gn 25_{17} (Ishmael), מֵאָה וּמְאַת שָׁנָה Ex 6_{16} (Levi) 6_{20} (Amram), 140 years וְאַרְבָּעִים שָׁנָה Jb 42_{16} (Job), 147 years שֶׁבַע שָׁנִים וְאַרְבָּעִים וּמְאַת שָׁנָה Gn 47_{28} (Jacob), 162 years שְׁתַּיִם וְשִׁשִּׁים שָׁנָה וּמְאַת שָׁנָה Gn 5_{18} (Jared), 175 years מְאַת שָׁנָה וְשִׁבְעִים שָׁנָה וְחָמֵשׁ שָׁנִים Gn 25_{7} (Abraham), 180 years מְאַת שָׁנָה וּשְׁמֹנִים שָׁנָה Gn 35_{28} (Isaac), 182 years שְׁתַּיִם וּשְׁמֹנִים שָׁנָה וּמְאַת שָׁנָה Gn 5_{28} (Lamech), 187 years שֶׁבַע וּשְׁמֹנִים שָׁנָה וּמְאַת שָׁנָה Gn 5_{25} (Methuselah).

200 years מָאתַיִם שָׁנָה Gn 11_{23} (Serug), 205 years חָמֵשׁ שָׁנִים וּמָאתַיִם שָׁנָה Gn 11_{32} (Terah), 207 years שֶׁבַע שָׁנִים וּמָאתַיִם שָׁנָה Gn 11_{21} (Reu), 209 years תֵּשַׁע שָׁנִים וּמָאתַיִם שָׁנָה Gn 11_{19} (Peleg), 300 years שְׁלֹשׁ מֵאוֹת שָׁנָה Gn 5_{22} (Enoch) Jg 11_{26} (occupation by Israel), 350 years שְׁלֹשׁ מֵאוֹת שָׁנָה וַחֲמִשִּׁים שָׁנָה Gn 9_{28} (Noah), 365 years חָמֵשׁ וְשִׁשִּׁים שָׁנָה וּשְׁלֹשׁ מֵאוֹת שָׁנָה Gn 5_{23} (Enoch), 390 years שנים שלוש מאות ותשעים CD 1_{5}=4QD[c] 1_{13} (ש[נים]; exile), 400 years אַרְבַּע מֵאוֹת שָׁנָה Gn 15_{13} (oppression in Egypt), 403 years שָׁלֹשׁ שָׁנִים וְאַרְבַּע מֵאוֹת שָׁנָה Gn 11_{13} (Arpachshad) 11_{15} (Shelah), 430 years שְׁלֹשִׁים שָׁנָה וְאַרְבַּע מֵאוֹת שָׁנָה Gn 11_{17} (Eber) Ex $12_{40.41}$ (both Israel in Egypt), ארבע מאות שלו[שים שנה] 4QApocWeeks 1_{3}, 440 years מאה וארו[ב]עים שנה 4QCommGenA 2_{8} (Terah), 480 years שְׁמוֹנִים שָׁנָה וְאַרְבַּע מֵאוֹת שָׁנָה 1 Kgs 6_{1} (since exodus), 480th year בשנת ארבע מאות ושמונים 4QCommGenA 1_{1} (Noah), 500 years חֲמֵשׁ מֵאוֹת שָׁנָה Gn 5_{32} (Noah) 11_{11} (Shem), 595 years חָמֵשׁ וְתִשְׁעִים שָׁנָה וַחֲמֵשׁ מֵאוֹת שָׁנָה Gn 5_{30} (Lamech).

600 years שֵׁשׁ מֵאוֹת שָׁנָה Gn $7_{6.11}$ (שֵׁשׁ־; both Noah), 600th year בשנת שש מאות שנה 4QCommGenA 1_{3} (Noah), 601 years אַחַת וְשֵׁשׁ־מֵאוֹת שָׁנָה Gn 8_{13} (Noah) 4QCommGenA 2_{1} (Noah), 777 years שֶׁבַע וְשִׁבְעִים שָׁנָה וּשְׁבַע מֵאוֹת שָׁנָה Gn 5_{31} (Lamech), 782 years שְׁתַּיִם וּשְׁמוֹנִים שָׁנָה וּשְׁבַע מֵאוֹת שָׁנָה Gn 5_{26} (Methuselah), 800 years שְׁמֹנֶה מֵאֹת שָׁנָה Gn 5_{4} (Adam) 5_{19} (Jared), 805 years חָמֵשׁ שָׁנִים וּשְׁמֹנֶה מֵאוֹת שָׁנָה Gn 5_{7} (Seth), 815 years חֲמֵשׁ עֶשְׂרֵה שָׁנָה וּשְׁמֹנֶה מֵאוֹת שָׁנָה Gn 5_{10} (Enosh), 830 years שְׁלֹשִׁים שָׁנָה

וּשְׁמֹנֶה מֵאוֹת שָׁנָה Gn 5_{16} (Mahalel), 840 years אַרְבָּעִים שָׁנָה וּשְׁמֹנֶה מֵאוֹת שָׁנָה Gn 5_{13} (Kenan), 895 years חָמֵשׁ וְתִשְׁעִים שָׁנָה וּשְׁמֹנֶה מֵאוֹת שָׁנָה Gn 5_{17} (Mahalel), 905 years חָמֵשׁ שָׁנִים וּתְשַׁע מֵאוֹת שָׁנָה Gn 5_{11} (Enosh), 910 years עֶשֶׂר שָׁנִים וּתְשַׁע מֵאוֹת שָׁנָה Gn 5_{14} (Kenan), 912 years שְׁתֵּים עֶשְׂרֵה שָׁנָה וּתְשַׁע מֵאוֹת שָׁנָה Gn 5_8 (Seth), 930 years תְּשַׁע מֵאוֹת שָׁנָה וּשְׁלֹשִׁים שָׁנָה Gn 5_5 (Adam), 950 years תְּשַׁע מֵאוֹת שָׁנָה וַחֲמִשִּׁים שָׁנָה Gn 9_{29} (Noah), 962 years שְׁתַּיִם וְשִׁשִּׁים שָׁנָה וּתְשַׁע מֵאוֹת שָׁנָה Gn 5_{20} (Jared), 969 years תֵּשַׁע וְשִׁשִּׁים שָׁנָה וּתְשַׁע מֵאוֹת שָׁנָה Gn 5_{27} (Methuselah).

100 days מאה יום 4QDa 10.2_1 (punishment), 150 days חֲמִשִּׁים וּמְאַת יוֹם Gn 7_{24} 8_3 4QCommGenA $1_{7.9}$ (all four flood), 200 days [מאת]ים ימים 4QDa 10.2_1 (punishment), 364 days of the year כול ימי השנה ארבעה וששים ושלוש מאות 11QPsa 27_7, שנה תמימה לימים שלוש מאות ששים וארבאה 4QCommGenA 2_3, ושלמה השנה שלוש מאת ש[שים וארבאה] יום 4QMMT A_{20}, 390 days שְׁלֹשׁ־מֵאוֹת וְתִשְׁעִים יוֹם Ezk $4_{5.9}$ (both Ezekiel's lying down), 1,290 days יָמִים אֶלֶף מָאתַיִם וְתִשְׁעִים Dn 12_{11} (after erection of abomination), 1,335 days יָמִים אֶלֶף שְׁלֹשׁ מֵאוֹת שְׁלֹשִׁים וַחֲמִשָּׁה Dn 12_{12} (after erection of abomination), 5,000 days חמשים מאות יום 4QCommGenA $1_{7(WA)}$ (flood).

100 times מֵאָה פְּעָמִים 2 S 24_3||1 C 21_3, 2,300 evenings and mornings עֶרֶב בֹּקֶר אַלְפַּיִם וּשְׁלֹשׁ מֵאוֹת Dn 8_{14} (suspension of sacrifice).

2. 100 cubits מֵאָה בָּאַמָּה Ex $27_{9.11}$||$38_{9.11}$ (at 27_{11} MT lacks בָּאַמָּה; both hangings of court of tabernacle) 27_{18} (court of tabernacle) 11QT 38_{12} (court of temple) 46_9 (moat around temple), מֵאָה אַמָּה 1 K 7_2 (house of forest of Lebanon) Ezk $40_{19.23.47.47}$ (all four temple court) 41_{13} (temple) 41_{13} (vacant space to east of temple) 41_{14} (front of temple) 41_{15} (structure facing vacant space) 42_8 (temple chambers), מֵאָה אַמּוֹת Ezk 40_{27} (temple court), אַמּוֹת הַמֵּאָה Ezk 42_2 (or em. אֶל־פְּנֵי־אֹרֶךְ אַמּוֹת הַמֵּאָה פֶּתַח הַצָּפוֹן appar. *in front of the length of a hundred cubits was the north entrance* to אָרְכָּה מֵאָה אַמּוֹת פְּאַת הַצָּפוֹן *its*, i.e. chamber's, *length was a hundred cubits in the north corner*), מ[א]ת אמה Siloam tunnel inscr.$_5$ (height of tunnel).

120 cubits [עשרים ומאה באמה] 11QT 36_4 ([עשרים ומאה באמה]) 36_{13} (both of distance to corner of temple gate).

300 cubits שְׁלֹשׁ מֵאוֹת אַמָּה Gn 6_{15} (Noah's ark), 360 cubits שלוש מאות וששים באמה 11QT 40_{13} 41_2 ([שלוש מאות וששים באמה]) 41_3 ([שלוש מאות וששים ב]אמה) 41_6 + 4Q 365a 2.2_2 11QT 41_8 + 4Q365a 2.2_2 11QT 46_{10} + 4Q365a 2.2_3 11QT 46_{11} + 4Q365a 2.2_4 (all seven distance between gates), ששים ושלוש מאות באמה 11QT 40_{14} 41_4 + 4Q 356a 2.2_1 ([ששים ושלוש] מאות באמה) 11QT 41_5 + 4Q365a 2.2_1 (ששי]ם ו[שלוש) 11QT 41_9 + 4Q365a 2.2_3 (all four distance between gates).

400 cubits אַרְבַּע מֵאוֹת אַמָּה 2 K 14_{13}||2 C 25_{23} (wall of Jerusalem), 480 cubits שמונים וארבע מאות באמה 11QT $38_{13(mg)}$ (outer court), 1200 cubits מאתי[ם ו]אלף אמה Siloam tunnel inscr.$_5$ (water flow in tunnel); also 4Q 365a 2.2_1 (מאות באמה).

500 rods חֲמֵשׁ־מֵאוֹת קָנִים Ezk $42_{16(Qr)}$ (Kt חֲמֵשׁ־אמות קָנִים *five cubits [namely] rods*) $42_{17.18.19}$ (all four temple court).

3. 100 silver (shekels) מֵאָה כֶסֶף Dt 22_{19}=11QT 55_{14} (slandering husband's fine), 100 (pieces) of silver מְאַת הַכֶּסֶף Ne 5_{11} (debt to be cancelled; or em. מְאַת to מַשָּׁאת *debt*), מאת ככר 4QOrda 1.2_8 (redemption fee), 150 silver (shekels) כֶּסֶף ... חֲמִשִּׁים וּמֵאָה 1 K 10_{29}||2 C 1_{17} (cost of horse), 200 silver shekels מָאתַיִם שְׁקָלִים כֶּסֶף Jos 7_{21} (Achan), 200 (silver) shekels מָאתַיִם שְׁקָלִים 2 S 14_{26} (Absalom's hair), 300 silver (shekels) שְׁלֹשׁ מֵאוֹת כֶּסֶף Gn 45_{22} (Joseph), 400 silver shekels אַרְבַּע מֵאֹת שֶׁקֶל־כֶּסֶף Gn $23_{15.16}$ (מֵאוֹת שֶׁקֶל כֶּסֶף; both Abraham), 600 silver (shekels) שֵׁשׁ מֵאוֹת כֶּסֶף 1 K 10_{29}||2 C 1_{17} (cost of chariot).

1,100 silver (shekels) אֶלֶף וּמֵאָה כֶּסֶף Jg 16_5 (Delilah) Jg 17_2 (הַכֶּסֶף) 17_3 (אֶלֶף־וּמֵאָה הַכֶּסֶף; both Micah), 1,365 (silver) shekels (donation to sanctuary), חֲמִשָּׁה וְשִׁשִּׁים וּשְׁלֹשׁ מֵאוֹת וָאֶלֶף בְּשֶׁקֶל Nm 3_{50}, 1,775 (silver) shekels אֶלֶף וּשְׁבַע מֵאוֹת וַחֲמִשָּׁה וְשִׁבְעִים שֶׁקֶל Ex $38_{25.28}$ (הָאֶלֶף וּשְׁבַע הַמֵּאוֹת וַחֲמִשָּׁה וְשִׁבְעִים *the 1,775 [shekels]*; both donation to sanctuary), 2,400 silver shekels כֶּסֶף ... אַלְפַּיִם וְאַרְבַּע־מֵאוֹת בְּשֶׁקֶל Nm 7_{85} (sanctuary plates and ladles).

250 (silver) shekels-worth of fragrant cinnamon קִנְּמָן־בֶּשֶׂם ... חֲמִשִּׁים וּמָאתָיִם Ex 30_{23}, 250 (silver) shekels-worth of fragrant cane קְנֵה־בֹשֶׂם חֲמִשִּׁים וּמָאתָיִם Ex 30_{23}, 500 (silver) shekels-worth of flowing myrrh מָר־דְּרוֹר חֲמֵשׁ מֵאוֹת Ex 30_{23}, 500 (silver) shekels-worth of cassia קִדָּה חֲמֵשׁ מֵאוֹת Ex 30_{24}.

120 gold shekels זָהָב ... עֶשְׂרִים וּמֵאָה Nm 7_{86} (sanctuary ladles), 300 gold (shekels) שְׁלֹשׁ מֵאוֹת זָהָב 2 C 9_{16} (Solomon's bucklers), 600 gold (shekels) שֵׁשׁ מֵאוֹת זָהָב 1 K 10_{16}||2 C 9_{15} (Solomon's shields), 600 gold shekels שִׁקְלֵי זָהָב ... שֵׁשׁ מֵאוֹת 1 C 21_{25} (David), 730 (gold) shekels שְׁבַע מֵאוֹת וּשְׁלֹשִׁים שֶׁקֶל Ex 38_{24} (donation to sanctuary), 1,700 gold (shekels) אֶלֶף וּשְׁבַע־מֵאוֹת זָהָב Jg 8_{26} (Kedemite booty), 16,750 (gold) shekels שִׁשָּׁה עָשָׂר אֶלֶף שְׁבַע־מֵאוֹת וַחֲמִשִּׁים שָׁקֶל Nm 31_{52} (booty given to Y.).

2,400 (bronze) shekels אַלְפַּיִם וְאַרְבַּע־מֵאוֹת שָׁקֶל Ex 38_{29} (donation to sanctuary), 600 iron shekels שֵׁשׁ־מֵאוֹת שְׁקָלִים בַּרְזֶל 1 S 17_7 (Goliath's spearhead).

100 silver talents מְאַת כִּכַּר הַכֶּסֶף Ex 38_{27} (for pedestals of sanctuary), מְאַת הַכִּכָּר Ex 38_{27} (for pedestals of sanctuary) 2 C 25_9 (Amaziah), מֵאָה כִכַּר־כֶּסֶף 2 K 23_{33}|| 2 C 36_3 (Neco) 2 C 25_6 (Amaziah) 27_5 (Jotham), 200 silver talents כסף ככ מאתין 3QTr 4_{10}, 300 silver talents שְׁלֹשׁ מֵאוֹת כִּכַּר־כֶּסֶף 2 K 18_{14} (Hezekiah), 400 talents (perh. gold, not silver) ככרין ארבע מאות 3QTr 7_7, 600 silver talents 3QTr 12_7 וכסף הכל ככרין שש מאות, 650 silver talents כֶּסֶף כִּכָּרִים שֵׁשׁ מֵאוֹת וַחֲמִשִּׁים Ezr 8_{26} (for new temple), 900 silver talents [כסף ככ] תשע מואת 3QTr 11_{17}.

100 gold talents זָהָב מֵאָה כִכָּר Ezr 8_{26} (for new temple), 120 gold talents מֵאָה וְעֶשְׂרִים כִּכַּר זָהָב 1 K 9_{14} (Hiram) 10_{10}||2 C 9_9 (Queen of Sheba), 300 gold talents ככרין שלש מאות זהב 3QTr 10_{10}, 420 gold talents זָהָב אַרְבַּע־מֵאוֹת וְעֶשְׂרִים כִּכָּר 1 K 9_{28} (Ophir), 450 gold talents אַרְבַּע־מֵאוֹת חֲמִשִּׁים כִּכַּר זָהָב 2 C 8_{18} (Ophir), 600 gold talents זָהָב ... לְכִכָּרִים שֵׁשׁ מֵאוֹת 2 C 3_8 (covering holy of holies), 666 gold talents שֵׁשׁ מֵאוֹת שִׁשִּׁים וָשֵׁשׁ כִּכַּר זָהָב 1 K 10_{14}||2 C 9_{13} (וְשִׁשִּׁים וָשֵׁשׁ כִּכְּרֵי; Solomon), 900 talents (perh. of silver, not gold) ככרין תשע מאת 3QTr 1_8, 100,000 gold talents זָהָב כִּכָּרִים מֵאָה־אֶלֶף 1 C 22_{14} (David's contribution to temple).

100,000 iron talents וּבַרְזֶל מֵאָה־אֶלֶף כִּכָּרִים 1 C 29_7 (contribution to temple).

500 silver minas וְכֶסֶף מָנִים חֲמֵשׁ מֵאוֹת Ne 7_{69} (if em. וַחֲמֵשׁ מֵאוֹת *five hundred and* thirty priestly tunics), 2,200 silver minas וְכֶסֶף מָנִים אַלְפַּיִם וּמָאתָיִם Ne 7_{70}.

100 kesitahs (or perh. lambs) מֵאָה קְשִׂיטָה Gn 33_{19} Jos 24_{32} (both Jacob).

100 measures, i.e. a hundredfold, מֵאָה שְׁעָרִים Gn 26_{12} (Isaac).

100 pomegranates רִמּוֹנִים מֵאָה 2 C 3_{16} (on temple capitals), 100 raisin cakes מֵאָה צִמֻּקִים 1 S 25_{18} (Abigail) 2 S 16_1 (or em. אֵיפַת *an ephah of*; Ziba), 100 summer fruits מֵאָה קַיִץ 2 S 16_1 (or em. אֵיפַת *an ephah of*; Ziba), 200 fig cakes מָאתַיִם דְּבֵלִים 1 S 25_{18} (Abigail), 200 loaves מָאתַיִם לֶחֶם 1 S 25_{18} (Abigail) 2 S 16_1 (Ziba), [לח]ם [מא]תים Arad ost. 10_3 (others אמתים perh. *two hundred* or [ל]כתים bread *for the Kittim* or [ולח]ם א[ר]בעת ים *and bread for four days*, אל בתים bread *for households* or [לצ]מא [ה]בתים *for the thirst of the households* or [ו]מ[ל]א [ה]בתים *and fill the baths*), 400 pomegranates וְאֶת־הָרִמֹּנִים אַרְבַּע מֵאוֹת 1 K 7_{42}||2 C 4_{13} (הָרִמּוֹנִים; on temple capitals), 1,100 (jars) of oil אל[ף] שמן ומאה T. Qasile ost. 2_2.

4. 745 souls נֶפֶשׁ שְׁבַע מֵאוֹת אַרְבָּעִים וַחֲמִשָּׁה Jr 52_{30} (Judahite exiles), 832 souls נֶפֶשׁ שְׁמֹנֶה מֵאוֹת שְׁלֹשִׁים וּשְׁנָיִם Jr 52_{29} (Jerusalemite exiles), there were 4,600 souls כָּל־נֶפֶשׁ אַרְבַּעַת אֲלָפִים וְשֵׁשׁ מֵאוֹת Jr 52_{30} (total exiled).

110 males מֵאָה וַעֲשָׂרָה הַזְּכָרִים Ezr 8_{12} (Johanan), 150 males זְכָרִים מֵאָה וַחֲמִשִּׁים Ezr 8_3 (Zechariah), 160 males מֵאָה וְשִׁשִּׁים הַזְּכָרִים Ezr 8_{10} (Shelomith), 200 males מָאתַיִם הַזְּכָרִים Ezr 8_4 (Eliehoenai), 218 males מָאתַיִם וּשְׁמֹנָה עָשָׂר הַזְּכָרִים Ezr 8_9 (Obadiah), 300 males שְׁלֹשׁ מֵאוֹת הַזְּכָרִים Ezr 8_5 (Shecaniah), 8,300 males (Kohathites) זָכָר ... שְׁמֹנַת אֲלָפִים וְשֵׁשׁ מֵאוֹת Nm 3_{28}.

112 brothers וְאֶחָיו מֵאָה וּשְׁנֵים עָשָׂר 1 C 15_{10} (Amminadab), 120 brothers וְאֶחָיו מֵאָה וְעֶשְׂרִים 1 C 15_5 (Kohathites) 15_6 (Merarites), 128 brothers וַאֲחֵיהֶם ... מֵאָה עֶשְׂרִים וּשְׁמֹנָה Ne 11_{14} (Adaiah and Amashsai), 130 brothers וְאֶחָיו מֵאָה וּשְׁלֹשִׁים 1 C 15_7 (Gershonites), 200 brothers וְאֶחָיו מָאתָיִם 1 C 15_8 (Shemaiah), 242 brothers וְאֶחָיו ... מָאתַיִם אַרְבָּעִים וּשְׁנָיִם Ne 11_{13} (Adaiah), 690 brothers וַאֲחֵיהֶם שֵׁשׁ־מֵאוֹת וְתִשְׁעִים 1 C 9_6 (Zerahites), 822 brothers וַאֲחֵיהֶם ... שְׁמֹנֶה מֵאוֹת עֶשְׂרִים Ne 11_{12} (Jedaiah, Jachin, and Seraiah), 928 brothers וְאֶחָיו ... תְּשַׁע מֵאוֹת עֶשְׂרִים וּשְׁמֹנָה Ne 11_8 (if em. וְאַחֲרָיו גַּבַּי סַלָּי *and after him were Gabbai, Sallai* [and] 928 [helpers] to אֶחָיו גִּבֹּרֵי־חָיִל *and his brothers, men of valour*, were 928; Sallu), 956 brothers וַאֲחֵיהֶם ... תְּשַׁע מֵאוֹת וַחֲמִשִּׁים וְשִׁשָּׁה 1 C 9_9 (Benjamites), 1,700 brothers וְאֶחָיו ... אֶלֶף

וּשְׁבַע־מֵאוֹת 1 C 26$_{30}$ (Hebronites), 1,760 brothers וַאֲחֵיהֶם ... אֶלֶף וּשְׁבַע מֵאוֹת וְשִׁשִּׁים 1 C 9$_{13}$ (priests), 2,700 brothers וְאֶחָיו ... אַלְפַּיִם וּשְׁבַע מֵאוֹת 1 C 26$_{32}$ (Hebronites).

112 sons of Jorah בְּנֵי יוֹרָה מֵאָה וּשְׁנֵים עָשָׂר Ezr 2$_{18}$, 112 sons of Hariph בְּנֵי חָרִיף מֵאָה שְׁנֵים עָשָׂר Ne 7$_{24}$, 123 sons of Bethlehem בְּנֵי בֵית־לָחֶם מֵאָה עֶשְׂרִים וּשְׁלֹשָׁה Ezr 2$_{21}$, 128 sons of Asaph בְּנֵי אָסָף מֵאָה עֶשְׂרִים וּשְׁמֹנָה Ezr 2$_{41}$, 139 sons of gatekeepers בְּנֵי הַשֹּׁעֲרִים ... מֵאָה שְׁלֹשִׁים וְתִשְׁעָה Ezr 2$_{42}$, 148 sons of Asaph בְּנֵי אָסָף מֵאָה אַרְבָּעִים וּשְׁמֹנָה Ne 7$_{44}$, 150 sons of Ulam בָּנִים ... מֵאָה וַחֲמִשִּׁים 1 C 8$_{40}$, 156 sons of Magbish בְּנֵי מַגְבִּישׁ מֵאָה חֲמִשִּׁים וְשִׁשָּׁה Ezr 2$_{30}$, 223 sons of Hashum בְּנֵי חָשֻׁם מָאתַיִם עֶשְׂרִים וּשְׁלֹשָׁה Ezr 2$_{19}$, 320 sons of Harim בְּנֵי חָרִם שְׁלֹשׁ מֵאוֹת וְעֶשְׂרִים Ezr 2$_{32}$||Ne 7$_{35}$, 323 sons of Bezai בְּנֵי בֵצָי שְׁלֹשׁ מֵאוֹת עֶשְׂרִים וּשְׁלֹשָׁה Ezr 2$_{17}$, 324 sons of Bezai בְּנֵי בֵצָי שְׁלֹשׁ מֵאוֹת עֶשְׂרִים וְאַרְבָּעָה Ne 7$_{23}$, 328 sons of Hashum בְּנֵי חָשֻׁם שְׁלֹשׁ מֵאוֹת עֶשְׂרִים וּשְׁמֹנָה Ne 7$_{22}$, 345 sons of Jericho בְּנֵי יְרֵחוֹ שְׁלֹשׁ מֵאוֹת אַרְבָּעִים וַחֲמִשָּׁה Ezr 2$_{34}$||Ne 7$_{36}$, 372 sons of Shephatiah בְּנֵי שְׁפַטְיָה שְׁלֹשׁ מֵאוֹת שִׁבְעִים וּשְׁנָיִם Ezr 2$_{4}$||Ne 7$_{9}$, 452 sons of Adin בְּנֵי עָדִין אַרְבַּע מֵאוֹת חֲמִשִּׁים וּשְׁנָיִם Ezr 2$_{15}$.

621 sons of Ramah and Geba בְּנֵי הָרָמָה וָגָבַע שֵׁשׁ מֵאוֹת עֶשְׂרִים וְאֶחָד Ezr 2$_{26}$ (||Ne 7$_{30}$ אַנְשֵׁי *men of*), 623 sons of Bebai בְּנֵי בֵבָי שֵׁשׁ מֵאוֹת עֶשְׂרִים וּשְׁלֹשָׁה Ezr 2$_{11}$, 628 sons of Bebai בְּנֵי בֵבָי שֵׁשׁ מֵאוֹת עֶשְׂרִים וּשְׁמֹנָה Ne 7$_{16}$, 642 sons of Bani בְּנֵי בָנִי שֵׁשׁ מֵאוֹת אַרְבָּעִים וּשְׁנָיִם Ezr 2$_{10}$, 642 sons of Delaiah, Tobiah, and Nekoda בְּנֵי־דְלָיָה בְנֵי־טוֹבִיָּה בְּנֵי נְקוֹדָא שֵׁשׁ מֵאוֹת וְאַרְבָּעִים וּשְׁנָיִם Ne 7$_{62}$, 648 sons of Binnui בְּנֵי בִנּוּי שֵׁשׁ מֵאוֹת אַרְבָּעִים וּשְׁמֹנָה Ne 7$_{15}$, 652 sons of Arah בְּנֵי אָרַח שֵׁשׁ מֵאוֹת חֲמִשִּׁים וּשְׁנָיִם Ne 7$_{10}$, 652 sons of Delaiah, Tobiah, and Nekoda בְּנֵי־דְלָיָה בְנֵי־טוֹבִיָּה בְּנֵי נְקוֹדָא שֵׁשׁ מֵאוֹת חֲמִשִּׁים וּשְׁנָיִם Ezr 2$_{60}$, 655 sons of Adin בְּנֵי עָדִין שֵׁשׁ מֵאוֹת חֲמִשִּׁים וַחֲמִשָּׁה Ne 7$_{20}$, 666 sons of Adonikam בְּנֵי אֲדֹנִיקָם שֵׁשׁ מֵאוֹת שִׁשִּׁים וְשִׁשָּׁה Ezr 2$_{13}$, 667 sons of Adonikam בְּנֵי אֲדֹנִיקָם שֵׁשׁ מֵאוֹת שִׁשִּׁים וְשִׁבְעָה Ne 7$_{18}$.

721 sons of Lod, Hadid, and Ono בְּנֵי־לֹד חָדִיד וְאֹנוֹ שְׁבַע מֵאוֹת וְעֶשְׂרִים וְאֶחָד Ne 7$_{37}$, 725 sons of Lod, Hadid, and Ono בְּנֵי־לֹד חָדִיד וְאוֹנוֹ שְׁבַע מֵאוֹת עֶשְׂרִים וַחֲמִשָּׁה Ezr 2$_{33}$, 743 sons of Kiriath-arim, Chephirah, and Beeroth בְּנֵי קִרְיַת עָרִים כְּפִירָה וּבְאֵרוֹת שְׁבַע מֵאוֹת וְאַרְבָּעִים וּשְׁלֹשָׁה Ezr 2$_{25}$ (||Ne 7$_{29}$ אַנְשֵׁי קִרְיַת יְעָרִים *men of Kiriath-jearim*), 760 sons of Zaccai בְּנֵי זַכָּי שְׁבַע מֵאוֹת וְשִׁשִּׁים Ezr 2$_{9}$||Ne 7$_{14}$, 775 sons of Arah בְּנֵי אָרַח שְׁבַע מֵאוֹת חֲמִשָּׁה וְשִׁבְעִים Ezr 2$_{5}$, 845 sons of Zattu בְּנֵי זַתּוּא שְׁמֹנֶה מֵאוֹת וְאַרְבָּעִים וַחֲמִשָּׁה Ne 7$_{13}$, 945 sons of Zattu בְּנֵי זַתּוּא תְּשַׁע מֵאוֹת וְאַרְבָּעִים וַחֲמִשָּׁה Ezr 2$_{8}$, 973 sons of Jedaiah בְּנֵי יְדַעְיָה ... תְּשַׁע מֵאוֹת שִׁבְעִים וּשְׁלֹשָׁה Ezr 2$_{36}$||Ne 7$_{39}$.

1,222 sons of Azgad בְּנֵי עַזְגָּד אֶלֶף מָאתַיִם עֶשְׂרִים וּשְׁנָיִם Ezr 2$_{12}$, 1,247 sons of Pashhur בְּנֵי פַשְׁחוּר אֶלֶף מָאתַיִם אַרְבָּעִים וְשִׁבְעָה Ezr 2$_{38}$||Ne 7$_{41}$, 1,254 sons of Elam בְּנֵי עֵילָם (...) אֶלֶף מָאתַיִם חֲמִשִּׁים וְאַרְבָּעָה Ezr 2$_{7.31}$||Ne 7$_{12.34}$, 2,172 sons of Parosh בְּנֵי פַרְעֹשׁ אַלְפַּיִם מֵאָה שִׁבְעִים וּשְׁנָיִם Ezr 2$_{3}$ (||Ne 7$_{8}$ וְשִׁבְעִים), 2,322 sons of Azgad בְּנֵי עַזְגָּד אַלְפַּיִם שְׁלֹשׁ מֵאוֹת עֶשְׂרִים וּשְׁנָיִם Ne 7$_{17}$, 2,812 sons of Pahath-moab בְּנֵי־פַחַת מוֹאָב ... אַלְפַּיִם שְׁמֹנֶה מֵאוֹת וּשְׁנֵים עָשָׂר Ezr 2$_{6}$, 2,818 sons of Pahath-moab בְּנֵי־פַחַת מוֹאָב ... אַלְפַּיִם וּשְׁמֹנֶה מֵאוֹת שְׁמֹנָה עָשָׂר Ne 7$_{11}$, 3,630 sons of Senaah בְּנֵי סְנָעָה שְׁלֹשֶׁת אֲלָפִים וְשֵׁשׁ מֵאוֹת וּשְׁלֹשִׁים Ezr 2$_{35}$, 3,930 sons of Senaah בְּנֵי סְנָעָה שְׁלֹשֶׁת אֲלָפִים תְּשַׁע מֵאוֹת וּשְׁלֹשִׁים Ne 7$_{38}$.

122 men of Michmas אַנְשֵׁי מִכְמָס מֵאָה עֶשְׂרִים וּשְׁנָיִם Ezr 2$_{27}$ (||Ne 7$_{31}$ וְעֶשְׂרִים), 123 men of Bethel and Ai אַנְשֵׁי בֵית־אֵל וְהָעָי מֵאָה עֶשְׂרִים וּשְׁלֹשָׁה Ne 7$_{32}$, 128 men of Anathoth אַנְשֵׁי עֲנָתוֹת מֵאָה עֶשְׂרִים וּשְׁמֹנָה Ezr 2$_{23}$||Ne 7$_{27}$, 188 men of Bethlehem and Netophah אַנְשֵׁי בֵית־לֶחֶם וּנְטֹפָה מֵאָה שְׁמֹנִים וּשְׁמֹנָה Ne 7$_{26}$, 223 men of Bethel and Ai אַנְשֵׁי בֵית־אֵל וְהָעָי מָאתַיִם עֶשְׂרִים וּשְׁלֹשָׁה Ezr 2$_{28}$.

100 men מֵאָה־אִישׁ Jg 7$_{19}$ (or em. הָאִישׁ; Gideon) 1 K 18$_{13}$ (Obadiah) 2 K 4$_{43}$ (מֵאָה אִישׁ; Elisha), 150 men מֵאָה וַחֲמִשִּׁים אִישׁ Ne 5$_{17}$ (Nehemiah), 200 men מָאתַיִם אִישׁ 1 S 18$_{27}$ (slain Philistines) 30$_{10}$ (David) 2 S 15$_{11}$ (Absalom), מָאתַיִם הָאֲנָשִׁים 1 S 30$_{21}$, 250 men אֲנָשִׁים ... חֲמִשִּׁים וּמָאתָיִם Nm 16$_{2}$ (Israelite worthies), אִישׁ ... חֲמִשִּׁים וּמָאתַיִם Nm 16$_{17}$ (Korah's followers), הַחֲמִשִּׁים וּמָאתַיִם אִישׁ Nm 16$_{35}$ 26$_{10}$ (אֵת חֲמִשִּׁים; both Korah's followers), 300 men שְׁלֹשׁ מֵאוֹת אִישׁ Jg 7$_{6.7}$ (הָאִישׁ) 7$_{8.16}$ 8$_{4}$ (all three שְׁלֹשׁ־מֵאוֹת הָאִישׁ; all five Gideon), 360 men שְׁלֹשׁ־מֵאוֹת וְשִׁשִּׁים אִישׁ 2 S 2$_{31}$ (Abner), 400 men אַרְבַּע־מֵאוֹת אִישׁ Gn 32$_{7}$ 33$_{1}$ (both Esau) 1 S 22$_{2}$ 25$_{13}$ (all three אַרְבַּע מֵאוֹת) 30$_{10}$ (all three David) 30$_{17}$ (אַרְבַּע מֵאוֹת; Amalekites), 468 men of wealth אַרְבַּע מֵאוֹת שִׁשִּׁים וּשְׁמֹנָה אַנְשֵׁי־חָיִל Ne 11$_{6}$ (sons of Perez).

500 men אֲנָשִׁים חֲמֵשׁ מֵאוֹת 1 C 4$_{42}$ (Simeonites), 600

men שֵׁשׁ־מֵאוֹת אִישׁ Jg 3_{31} (Shamgar's slain) $18_{11.16}$ (both Danites) 20_{47} (Benjaminites) 1 S 13_{15} 14_{2} (both שֵׁשׁ מֵאוֹת; both Saul) 23_{13} 27_{2} 30_{9} (all three David) 2 S 15_{18} (Gittites), 700 men שְׁבַע מֵאוֹת אִישׁ Jg 20_{16} (Benjaminites) 2 K 3_{26} (שְׁבַע־; Mesha), 25,100 men עֶשְׂרִים וַחֲמִשָּׁה אֶלֶף וּמֵאָה אִישׁ Jg 20_{35} (Benjaminites), 120,000 men מֵאָה וְעֶשְׂרִים אֶלֶף אִישׁ Jg 8_{10} (Kedemites), 400,000 men אַרְבַּע מֵאוֹת אֶלֶף אִישׁ Jg $20_{2.17}$ (both Israelites) 2 C 13_{3} (אַרְבַּע־מֵאוֹת; Abijah), 470,000 men אַרְבַּע מֵאוֹת וְשִׁבְעִים אֶלֶף אִישׁ 1 C 21_{5} (Judahites), 500,000 men חֲמֵשׁ־מֵאוֹת אֶלֶף אִישׁ 2 S 24_{9} (Judahites) 2 C 13_{17} (Jeroboam's slain), 800,000 men שְׁמֹנֶה מֵאוֹת אֶלֶף אִישׁ 2 S 24_{9} (Israelites) 2 C 13_{3} (שְׁמוֹנֶה; Jeroboam), 1,100,000 men אֶלֶף אֲלָפִים וּמֵאָה אֶלֶף אִישׁ 1 C 21_{5} (Israelites).

180,000 youths מֵאָה וּשְׁמֹנִים אֶלֶף בָּחוּר 1 K 12_{21}||2 C 11_{1} (Rehoboam), 300,000 youths שְׁלֹשׁ־מֵאוֹת אֶלֶף בָּחוּר 2 C 25_{5} (Amaziah).

2,630 mustered (Gershonites) פְּקֻדֵיהֶם ... אַלְפַּיִם וְשֵׁשׁ מֵאוֹת וּשְׁלֹשִׁים Nm 4_{40}, 2,750 mustered (Kohathites) פְּקֻדֵיהֶם ... אַלְפַּיִם שְׁבַע מֵאוֹת וַחֲמִשִּׁים Nm 4_{36}, 3,200 mustered (Merarites) פְּקֻדֵיהֶם ... שְׁלֹשֶׁת אֲלָפִים וּמָאתָיִם Nm 4_{44}, 6,200 mustered (Merarites) וּפְקֻדֵיהֶם ... שֵׁשֶׁת אֲלָפִים וּמָאתָיִם Nm 3_{34}, 7,500 mustered (Gershonites) פְּקֻדֵיהֶם שִׁבְעַת אֲלָפִים וַחֲמֵשׁ מֵאוֹת Nm 3_{22}, 8,580 mustered (Levites) פְּקֻדֵיהֶם שְׁמֹנַת אֲלָפִים וַחֲמֵשׁ מֵאוֹת וּשְׁמֹנִים Nm 4_{48}.

22,200 mustered Simeonites פְּקֻדֵיהֶם שְׁנַיִם וְעֶשְׂרִים אֶלֶף וּמָאתָיִם Nm 26_{14} (if ins. לִפְקֻדֵיהֶם), 32,200 mustered (Manassites) פְּקֻדֵיהֶם ... שְׁנַיִם וּשְׁלֹשִׁים אֶלֶף וּמָאתָיִם Nm 1_{35} 2_{21}, 32,500 mustered (Ephraimites) פְּקֻדֵיהֶם שְׁנַיִם וּשְׁלֹשִׁים אֶלֶף וַחֲמֵשׁ מֵאוֹת Nm 26_{37}, 35,400 mustered (Benjaminites) פְּקֻדֵיהֶם ... חֲמִשָּׁה וּשְׁלֹשִׁים אֶלֶף וְאַרְבַּע מֵאוֹת Nm 1_{37} 2_{23}, 40,500 mustered (Ephraimites, Gadites) פְּקֻדֵיהֶם ... אַרְבָּעִים אֶלֶף וַחֲמֵשׁ מֵאוֹת Nm 1_{33} 2_{19} 26_{18}, 41,500 mustered (Asherites) פְּקֻדֵיהֶם ... אֶחָד וְאַרְבָּעִים אֶלֶף וַחֲמֵשׁ מֵאוֹת Nm 1_{41} 2_{28}, 43,730 mustered (Reubenites) פְּקֻדֵיהֶם שְׁלֹשָׁה וְאַרְבָּעִים אֶלֶף וּשְׁבַע מֵאוֹת וּשְׁלֹשִׁים Nm 26_{7}, 45,400 mustered (Naphtalites) פְּקֻדֵיהֶם חֲמִשָּׁה וְאַרְבָּעִים אֶלֶף וְאַרְבַּע מֵאוֹת Nm 26_{50}.

45,600 mustered (Benjamites) פְּקֻדֵיהֶם חֲמִשָּׁה וְאַרְבָּעִים אֶלֶף וְשֵׁשׁ מֵאוֹת Nm 26_{41}, 45,650 mustered (Gadites) פְּקֻדֵיהֶם ... חֲמִשָּׁה וְאַרְבָּעִים אֶלֶף וְשֵׁשׁ מֵאוֹת וַחֲמִשִּׁים Nm 1_{25} 2_{15} (פְּקֻדָיו), 46,500 mustered (Reubenites) פְּקֻדֵיהֶם ... שִׁשָּׁה וְאַרְבָּעִים אֶלֶף וַחֲמֵשׁ מֵאוֹת Nm 1_{21} 2_{11} (פְּקֻדָיו), 52,700 mustered (Manassites) פְּקֻדֵיהֶם שְׁנַיִם וַחֲמִשִּׁים אֶלֶף וּשְׁבַע מֵאוֹת Nm 26_{34}, 53,400 mustered (Naphtalites, Asherites) פְּקֻדֵיהֶם ... שְׁלֹשָׁה וַחֲמִשִּׁים אֶלֶף וְאַרְבַּע מֵאוֹת Nm 1_{43} 2_{30} 26_{47}, 54,400 mustered (Issacharites) פְּקֻדֵיהֶם ... אַרְבָּעָה וַחֲמִשִּׁים אֶלֶף וְאַרְבַּע מֵאוֹת Nm 1_{29} 2_{6} (פְּקֻדָיו), 57,400 mustered (Zebulunites) פְּקֻדֵיהֶם ... שִׁבְעָה וַחֲמִשִּׁים אֶלֶף וְאַרְבַּע מֵאוֹת Nm 1_{31} 2_{8} (פְּקֻדָיו), 59,300 mustered (Simeonites) פְּקֻדֵיהֶם ... תִּשְׁעָה וַחֲמִשִּׁים אֶלֶף וּשְׁלֹשׁ מֵאוֹת Nm 1_{23} 2_{13} (פְּקֻדָיו).

60,500 mustered (Zebulunites) פְּקֻדֵיהֶם שִׁשִּׁים אֶלֶף וַחֲמֵשׁ מֵאוֹת Nm 26_{27}, 62,700 mustered (Danites) פְּקֻדֵיהֶם ... שְׁנַיִם וְשִׁשִּׁים אֶלֶף וּשְׁבַע מֵאוֹת Nm 1_{39} 2_{26}, 64,300 mustered (Issacharites) פְּקֻדֵיהֶם אַרְבָּעָה וְשִׁשִּׁים אֶלֶף וּשְׁלֹשׁ מֵאוֹת Nm 26_{25}, 64,400 mustered (Danites) פְּקֻדֵיהֶם אַרְבָּעָה וְשִׁשִּׁים אֶלֶף וְאַרְבַּע מֵאוֹת Nm 26_{43}, 74,600 mustered (Judahites) פְּקֻדֵיהֶם ... אַרְבָּעָה וְשִׁבְעִים אֶלֶף וְשֵׁשׁ מֵאוֹת Nm 1_{27} 2_{4}, 76,500 mustered (Judahites) פְּקֻדֵיחֶם שִׁשָּׁה וְשִׁבְעִים אֶלֶף וַחֲמֵשׁ מֵאוֹת Nm 26_{22}.

108,100 mustered (Ephraimites) כָּל־הַפְּקֻדִים ... מְאַת אֶלֶף וּשְׁמֹנַת־אֲלָפִים וּמֵאָה Nm 2_{24}, 151,450 mustered (Reubenites) כָּל־הַפְּקֻדִים ... מְאַת אֶלֶף וְאֶחָד וַחֲמִשִּׁים אֶלֶף וְאַרְבַּע־מֵאוֹת וַחֲמִשִּׁים Nm 2_{16}, 157,600 mustered (Danites) כָּל־הַפְּקֻדִים ... מְאַת אֶלֶף וְשִׁבְעָה וַחֲמִשִּׁים אֶלֶף וְשֵׁשׁ מֵאוֹת Nm 2_{31}, 186,400 mustered (Judahites) כָּל־הַפְּקֻדִים ... מְאַת אֶלֶף וּשְׁמֹנִים אֶלֶף וְשֵׁשֶׁת־אֲלָפִים וְאַרְבַּע־מֵאוֹת Nm 2_{9}.

601,730 mustered in total פְּקוּדֵי ... שֵׁשׁ־מֵאוֹת אֶלֶף וָאָלֶף שְׁבַע מֵאוֹת וּשְׁלֹשִׁים Nm 26_{51}, 603,550 mustered in total כָּל־הַפְּקֻדִים שֵׁשׁ־מֵאוֹת אֶלֶף וּשְׁלֹשֶׁת אֲלָפִים וַחֲמֵשׁ מֵאוֹת וַחֲמִשִּׁים Nm 1_{46} 2_{32} (כָּל־פְּקוּדֵי־).

100,000 on foot מֵאָה־אֶלֶף רַגְלִי 1 K 20_{29} (Aram), 200,000 on foot מָאתַיִם אֶלֶף רַגְלִי 1 S 15_{4} (Saul), 600,000 on foot שֵׁשׁ־מֵאוֹת אֶלֶף רַגְלִי Ex 12_{37} (exodus) Nm 11_{21} Si 16_{10} 46_{8} (all three complaining Israelites) 4QOrd[a] 1.2_{8} (לשש מא[ו]ת האלף *for the 600,000*).

20,800 warriors עֶשְׂרִים אֶלֶף וּשְׁמוֹנֶה מֵאוֹת גִּבּוֹרֵי חַיִל 1 C 12_{31} (Ephraimites), 100,000 warriors מֵאָה אֶלֶף גִּבּוֹר חַיִל 2 C 25_{6} (Amaziah), 200,000 warriors מָאתַיִם אֶלֶף גִּבּוֹר חָיִל 2 C 17_{16} (Amasiah), 300,000 warriors גִּבּוֹרֵי חַיִל שְׁלֹשׁ מֵאוֹת אָלֶף 2 C 17_{14} (Adnah).

200,000 men armed with bow and shield נֹשְׁקֵי־קֶשֶׁת

וּמָגֵן מָאתַיִם אֶלֶף 2 C 17_{17} (Benjamin), 280,000 men with shields and archers נֹשְׂאֵי מָגֵן וְדֹרְכֵי קֶשֶׁת מָאתַיִם וּשְׁמוֹנִים אָלֶף 2 C 14_{7} (Benjamin).

17,200 battle-ready troops שִׁבְעָה־עָשָׂר אֶלֶף וּמָאתַיִם יֹצְאֵי צָבָא 1 C 7_{11} (sons of Jediael), 44,760 battle-ready troops אַרְבָּעִים וְאַרְבָּעָה אֶלֶף וּשְׁבַע־מֵאוֹת וְשִׁשִּׁים יֹצְאֵי צָבָא 1 C 5_{18} (Reubenites, Gadites, and Manassites).

6,800 armed troops שֵׁשֶׁת אֲלָפִים וּשְׁמֹנֶה מֵאוֹת חֲלוּצֵי צָבָא 1 C 12_{25} (Judahites), 180,000 armed troops מֵאָה־וּשְׁמוֹנִים אֶלֶף חֲלוּצֵי צָבָא 2 C 17_{18} (Jozabad).

4,600 battle warriors גִּבּוֹרֵי חַיִל לַצָּבָא ... אַרְבַּעַת אֲלָפִים וְשֵׁשׁ מֵאוֹת 1 C 12_{27} (Levites), 7,100 battle warriors גִּבּוֹרֵי חַיִל לַצָּבָא שִׁבְעַת אֲלָפִים וּמֵאָה 1 C 12_{26} (Simeonites).

28,600 warriors arrayed for battle עֹרְכֵי מִלְחָמָה עֶשְׂרִים־וּשְׁמוֹנָה אֶלֶף וְשֵׁשׁ מֵאוֹת 1 C 12_{36} (Danites), 307,500 troops שְׁלֹשׁ מֵאוֹת אֶלֶף וְשִׁבְעַת אֲלָפִים וַחֲמֵשׁ מֵאוֹת עוֹשֵׂי מִלְחָמָה 2 C 26_{13} (Uzziah).

200 riders מאתים פרשים 1QM 6_{9}, 700 riders שבע מאות פרשים 1QM 6_{8}, שבע מאות ... פרשים 1QM 6_{9}, 1,700 riders אֶלֶף וּשְׁבַע־מֵאוֹת פָּרָשִׁים 2 S 8_{4} (Hadadezer), 6,500 riders ששת אלפים חמש מאות ... הפרשים 1QM 6_{11} (sons of light).

300 slain שְׁלֹשׁ מֵאוֹת חָלָל 2 S 23_{18}||1 C 11_{20} (Abishai) 1 C 11_{11} (שְׁלֹשׁ־מֵאוֹת; Ishbaal), 800 slain שְׁמֹנֶה מֵאוֹת חָלָל 2 S 23_{8} (Ishbaal), 14,700 dead הַמֵּתִים ... אַרְבָּעָה עָשָׂר אֶלֶף וּשְׁבַע מֵאוֹת Nm 17_{14} (Korah's plague).

120 priests כֹּהֲנִים לְמֵאָה וְעֶשְׂרִים 2 C 5_{12}, 284 Levites כָּל־הַלְוִיִּם ... מָאתַיִם שְׁמֹנִים וְאַרְבָּעָה Ne 11_{18}.

100 prophets מֵאָה נְבִאִים 1 K 18_{4} (Obadiah), (about) 400 prophets הַנְּבִיאִים כְּאַרְבַּע מֵאוֹת אִישׁ 1 K 22_{6}||2 C 18_{5} (lacks כְּ; הַנְּבִאִים; Ahab), 400 prophets of Asherah נְבִיאֵי הָאֲשֵׁרָה אַרְבַּע מֵאוֹת 1 K 18_{19}, 450 prophets of Baal נְבִיאֵי הַבַּעַל אַרְבַּע מֵאוֹת וַחֲמִשִּׁים 1 K $18_{19.22}$ (אַרְבַּע־מֵאוֹת וַחֲמִשִּׁים אִישׁ).

250 overseers שָׂרֵי הַנִּצָּבִים ... חֲמִשִּׁים וּמָאתָיִם 2 C 8_{10}, 550 overseers שָׂרֵי הַנִּצָּבִים ... חֲמִשִּׁים וַחֲמֵשׁ מֵאוֹת 1 K 9_{23} (Solomon), 3,300 overseers שָׂרֵי הַנִּצָּבִים ... שְׁלֹשֶׁת אֲלָפִים וּשְׁלֹשׁ מֵאוֹת 1 K 5_{30} (Solomon), 3,600 overseers מְנַצְּחִים ... שְׁלֹשֶׁת אֲלָפִים וְשֵׁשׁ מֵאוֹת 2 C 2_{1} (Solomon), שְׁלֹשֶׁת אֲלָפִים וְשֵׁשׁ מֵאוֹת מְנַצְּחִים 2 C 2_{17} (Solomon).

232 local administrators נַעֲרֵי שָׂרֵי הַמְּדִינוֹת ... מָאתַיִם שְׁנַיִם וּשְׁלֹשִׁים 1 K 20_{15} (Ahab).

138 gatekeepers הַשֹּׁעֲרִים ... מֵאָה שְׁלֹשִׁים וּשְׁמֹנָה Ne 7_{45}, 172 gatekeepers וְהַשּׁוֹעֲרִים ... מֵאָה שִׁבְעִים וּשְׁנָיִם Ne 11_{19}, 212 gatekeepers שֹׁעֲרִים ... מָאתַיִם וּשְׁנֵים עָשָׂר 1 C 9_{22}.

220 Nethinim נְתִינִים מָאתַיִם וְעֶשְׂרִים Ezr 8_{20}, 392 Nethinim כָּל־הַנְּתִינִים ... שְׁלֹשׁ מֵאוֹת תִּשְׁעִים וּשְׁנָיִם Ezr 2_{58}||Ne 7_{60}.

7,337 servants עַבְדֵיהֶם ... שִׁבְעַת אֲלָפִים שְׁלֹשׁ מֵאוֹת שְׁלֹשִׁים וְשִׁבְעָה Ezr 2_{65}||Ne 7_{67}.

318 retainers חֲנִיכָיו ... שְׁמֹנָה עָשָׂר וּשְׁלֹשׁ מֵאוֹת Gn 14_{14} (Abram).

200 singers מְשֹׁרְרִים ... מָאתָיִם Ezr 2_{65}, 245 singers מְשֹׁרְרִים ... מָאתַיִם וְאַרְבָּעִים וַחֲמִשָּׁה Ne 7_{67}, 288 skilled (singers) כָּל־הַמֵּבִין מָאתַיִם שְׁמוֹנִים וּשְׁמוֹנָה 1 C 25_{7}.

200 chiefs רָאשֵׁיהֶם מָאתַיִם 1 C 12_{33} (Issacharites), the 273 additional (firstborn Israelites) הַשְּׁלֹשָׁה וְהַשִּׁבְעִים וְהַמָּאתָיִם הָעֹדְפִים Nm 3_{46}, 22,200 heads of ancestral houses רָאשֵׁי בֵּית אֲבוֹתָם ... עֶשְׂרִים אֶלֶף וּמָאתָיִם 1 C 7_{9} (Bichrites), 22,273 mustered (firstborn males) לִפְקֻדֵיהֶם שְׁנַיִם וְעֶשְׂרִים אֶלֶף שְׁלֹשָׁה וְשִׁבְעִים וּמָאתָיִם Nm 3_{43}, 300,000 Israelites בְּנֵי־יִשְׂרָאֵל שְׁלֹשׁ מֵאוֹת אֶלֶף 1 S 11_{8}, 603,550 persons passing (into registered group) לְכֹל הָעֹבֵר ... שֵׁשׁ־מֵאוֹת אֶלֶף וּשְׁלֹשֶׁת אֲלָפִים וַחֲמֵשׁ מֵאוֹת וַחֲמִשִּׁים Ex 38_{26}.

300 secondary wives פִּלַגְשִׁים שְׁלֹשׁ מֵאוֹת 1 K 11_{3} (Solomon), 400 girls אַרְבַּע מֵאוֹת נַעֲרָה Jg 21_{12}, 700 wives נָשִׁים ... שְׁבַע מֵאוֹת 1 K 11_{3} (Solomon), 200,000 women מָאתַיִם אֶלֶף נָשִׁים 2 C 28_{8} (captured Judahites).

5. 100 sheep מֵאָה צֹאן 1 K 5_{3} (Solomon) 4QPatr 7_{6} (Jacob), 100 rams אֵילִים מֵאָה 2 C 29_{32} (Hezekiah's sacrifice), 1/100 birds, beast, and fish לעוף ולחיה ולדגים אחד מן המאה 11QT 60_{8}, 1/100 doves אחד מן המאה מן בני היונה 11QT 60_{10}, 200 goats עִזִּים מָאתַיִם Gn 32_{15} (Jacob), 200 lambs כְּבָשִׂים מָאתָיִם 2 C 29_{32} (Hezekiah's sacrifice), 200 ewes רְחֵלִים מָאתַיִם Gn 32_{15} (Jacob), 245 mules פִּרְדֵיהֶם מָאתַיִם אַרְבָּעִים וַחֲמִשָּׁה Ezr 2_{66} (returning exiles), 300 oxen בָּקָר שְׁלֹשׁ מֵאוֹת 2 C 35_{8} (Josiah's passover), 300 foxes שְׁלֹשׁ־מֵאוֹת שׁוּעָלִים Jg 15_{4} (Samson), 435 camels גְּמַלֵּיהֶם אַרְבַּע מֵאוֹת שְׁלֹשִׁים וַחֲמִשָּׁה Ezr 2_{67}||Ne 7_{68} (returning exiles), 500 oxen בָּקָר חֲמֵשׁ מֵאוֹת 2 C 35_{9} (Josiah's passover), 500 yoke of oxen חֲמֵשׁ מֵאוֹת צֶמֶד־בָּקָר Jb 1_{3} (Job), 500 she-asses חֲמֵשׁ מֵאוֹת אֲתוֹנוֹת Jb 1_{3} (Job), 600 oxen בָּקָר שֵׁשׁ מֵאוֹת 2 C 29_{33} (Hezekiah's sacrifice), 675 sheep הַצֹּאן שֵׁשׁ מֵאוֹת חָמֵשׁ וְשִׁבְעִים

Nm 31_{37} (as tax), 700 oxen בָּקָר שְׁבַע מֵאוֹת 2 C 15_{11} (sacrificed at Asa's covenant renewal ceremony), 736 horses סוּסֵיהֶם שְׁבַע מֵאוֹת שְׁלֹשִׁים וְשִׁשָּׁה Ezr 2_{66} (returning exiles).

6,720 donkeys חֲמֹרִים שֵׁשֶׁת אֲלָפִים שְׁבַע מֵאוֹת וְעֶשְׂרִים Ezr 2_{67}||Ne 7_{68} (returning exiles), 7,700 rams אֵילִים שִׁבְעַת אֲלָפִים וּשְׁבַע מֵאוֹת 2 C 17_{11} (Jehoshaphat), 7,700 he-goats תְּיָשִׁים שִׁבְעַת אֲלָפִים וּשְׁבַע מֵאוֹת 2 C 17_{11} (Jehoshaphat), 30,500 donkeys חֲמֹרִים שְׁלֹשִׁים אֶלֶף וַחֲמֵשׁ מֵאוֹת Nm 31_{39} (total plundered) 31_{45} (given to community), 100,000 lambs מֵאָה־אֶלֶף כָּרִים 2 K 3_{4} (Mesha), 100,000 rams מֵאָה אֶלֶף אֵילִים 2 K 3_{4} (Mesha), 120,000 sheep צֹאן מֵאָה וְעֶשְׂרִים אֶלֶף 1 K 8_{63}||2 C 7_{5} (Solomon's sacrifice), 250,000 sheep צֹאן מָאתַיִם וַחֲמִשִּׁים אֶלֶף 1 C 5_{21} (Hagrites), 337,500 sheep הַצֹּאן שְׁלֹשׁ־מֵאוֹת אֶלֶף וּשְׁלֹשִׁים אֶלֶף וְשִׁבְעַת אֲלָפִים וַחֲמֵשׁ מֵאוֹת Nm 31_{36} (retained as booty) 31_{43} (אֶלֶף שִׁבְעַת; given to community), 675,000 sheep צֹאן שֵׁשׁ־מֵאוֹת אֶלֶף וְשִׁבְעִים אֶלֶף וַחֲמֵשֶׁת־אֲלָפִים Nm 31_{32} (total plundered).

6. 100 chariots מֵאָה רָכֶב 2 S 8_{4}||1 C 18_{4} (Hadadezer), 300 chariots מַרְכָּבוֹת שְׁלֹשׁ מֵאוֹת 2 C 14_{8} (Zerah), 600 chariots שֵׁשׁ־מֵאוֹת רֶכֶב Ex 14_{7} (Pharaoh), 700 chariot(eer)s שְׁבַע מֵאוֹת רֶכֶב 2 S 10_{18} (Shobach), 900 chariots תְּשַׁע מֵאוֹת רֶכֶב Jg $4_{3.13}$ (both Sisera), 1,200 chariots אֶלֶף וּמָאתַיִם רֶכֶב 2 C 12_{3} (Shishak), 1,400 chariots אֶלֶף וְאַרְבַּע־מֵאוֹת רֶכֶב 1 K 10_{26}||2 C 1_{14} (Solomon) 1QM 6_{10} (sons of light).

100 bucklers on each side מאה מגן מאה 1QM 9_{13} (sons of light), 200 shields מָאתַיִם צִנָּה 1 K 10_{16}||2 C 9_{15} (Solomon), 300 bucklers שְׁלֹשׁ־מֵאוֹת מָגִנִּים 1 K 10_{17}||2 C 9_{16} (Solomon), מגנים שלוש מאות 1QM 9_{14} (sons of light).

100 pedestals מְאַת אֲדָנִים Ex 38_{27} (of sanctuary), 100 gold bowls מִזְרְקֵי זָהָב מֵאָה 2 C 4_{8}, 100 talents-worth of silver vessels וּכְלֵי־כֶסֶף מֵאָה לְכִכָּרִים Ezr 8_{26} (for new temple), 400 silver bowls כְּפוֹרֵי כֶסֶף ... אַרְבַּע מֵאוֹת וַעֲשָׂרָה Ezr 1_{10} (returned by Cyrus), 5,400 vessels ... כֵּלִים חֲמֵשֶׁת אֲלָפִים וְאַרְבַּע מֵאוֹת Ezr 1_{11} (returned by Cyrus).

108 (priestly) chambers שמונה ומאה נשכה 11QT 44_{6}.

100 priestly tunics כָּתְנֹת כֹּהֲנִים מֵאָה Ezr 2_{69}, 530 priestly tunics כָּתְנוֹת כֹּהֲנִים שְׁלֹשִׁים וַחֲמֵשׁ מֵאוֹת Ne 7_{69} (or em. וְכֶסֶף מָנִים חֲמֵשׁ מֵאוֹת to וַחֲמֵשׁ מֵאוֹת thirty tunics *and silver: 500 minas*).

7. 3,600 psalms תהלים שלושת אלפים ושש מאות 11QPs[a] 27_{5}, 4,446 songs כול השיר ... ששה וארבעים וארבע מאות 11QPs[a] 27_{9}.

8. 100 foreskins מֵאָה עָרְלוֹת 1 S 18_{25} 2 S 3_{14}.

<COLL> **1.** מֵאָה **hundred,** as military unit or unit of population, שָׂרֵי מֵאוֹת *princes of hundreds* Ex $18_{21.25}$ Dt 1_{15} 1 S 8_{12} (if em. חֲמִשִּׁים *of fifties*) 22_{7} 2 S 18_{1} 11QT 57_{4} (פמאיות), שָׂרֵי הַמֵּאוֹת *the princes of hundreds* Nm $31_{14.48.52}$ 2 K $11_{4(Qr)}$||2 C 23_{1} 2 K $11_{9(Qr)}$ 2 K $11_{10(Qr).15(Qr).19}$||2 C $23_{9.14.20}$ 1 C 28_{1} 2 C 25_{5} 4QapJoshua[a] 3.27 שָׂרֵי (המיאות), 11QT 42_{15} (המאיות) 58_{4} ([שרי] המאיות) הָאֲלָפִים וְהַמֵּאוֹת *princes of the thousands and the hundreds* 1 C 13_{1} 26_{26} 27_{1} 29_{6} 2 C 1_{2}, שמות שרי מאיותיו *the names of the princes of his hundreds* 1QM 4_{2}.

אות המאה *the standard of the hundred* 1QM 4_{2}, וְסַרְנֵי פְלִשְׁתִּים עֹבְרִים לְמֵאוֹת *and the Philistine commanders passed in hundreds* and in thousands 1 S 29_{2}, וְכָל־הָעָם יָצְאוּ לְמֵאוֹת *and all the people went out by hundreds* and by thousands 2 S 18_{4}, אֶפֶס מֵאוֹתִי *his centuries will be naught* Is 54_{15} (if em. מֵאוֹתִי to (מְאוֹתֵי)*, רָאשֵׁי הַצָּבָא אֶחָד לְמֵאָה הַקָּטָן *chiefs of the army: the lesser (commander) was one to,* i.e. in charge of, *a hundred,* and the greater, a thousand 1 C 12_{15}, ... ועברו לאלפים ולמאיות ולחמשים לעוש[ר]ות *and they will pass ... by thousands and by hundreds and by fifties and by tens* 4QM[a] 1_{10}; also 1QM 3_{17} (מאיותיו)

2. מֵאָה used without unit of measurement specified, ונתנו ... ללויים אחד מן המאה *and they will give ... to the Levites one (part of the booty) out of a hundred* 11QT 58_{13}, להרים לשה [אח]ד מן המאה *to offer as a sheep one out of a hundred* 4QD[f] 2_{3}, וְרָדְפוּ מִכֶּם חֲמִשָּׁה מֵאָה וּמֵאָה מִכֶּם רְבָבָה יִרְדֹּפוּ *and five of you will chase a hundred and a hundred of you will chase ten thousand* Lv 26_{8}, הָעִיר הַיֹּצֵאת אֶלֶף תַּשְׁאִיר מֵאָה וְהַיּוֹצֵאת מֵאָה תַּשְׁאִיר עֲשָׂרָה *the city that goes out as a thousand is left a hundred and the one that goes out a hundred is left ten* Am 5_{3}, וְלָקַחְנוּ עֲשָׂרָה אֲנָשִׁים לַמֵּאָה ... וּמֵאָה לָאֶלֶף *and we took ten men per hundred ... and a hundred per thousand* Jg 20_{10}, כָּל־הָרִמּוֹנִים מֵאָה *there were a hundred pomegranates in total* Jr 52_{23}.

תֵּחַת גְּעָרָה בְמֵבִין מֵהַכּוֹת כְּסִיל מֵאָה *a reproach sinks into an understanding one more (easily) than strik-*

ing a fool a hundred (times) Pr 17_{10} (or em. תָּחֵת a reproach *shatters* or אַחַת *one* reproach to an understanding one is better than; and/or לֵב נָבוֹן *an intelligent heart/the heart of an intelligent one*).

אִם יוֹלִיד אִישׁ מֵאָה *if a man begets a hundred (children)* Ec 6_3, חֹטֶא עֹשֶׂה רָע מְאַת וּמַאֲרִיךְ לוֹ *a sinner does evil a hundred (times)* (unless רָע מְאַת = does *a hundred evils*)* *and extends (his life) for himself* Ec 8_{12} (or em. מְאַת וּמַאֲרִיךְ to וְאֶת־יָמָיו מַאֲרִיךְ *and extends his days* or מֵאָז וּמַאֲרִיךְ *from of old and extends* or מֵת וּמַאֲרִיךְ does evil, *dies, and extends*; or מֵאֹת וּמַאֲרִיךְ *hundreds [of times] and extends* or רַע מֵאֹת וּמַאֲרִיךְ does *the evil of hundreds and extends*).*

קַעֲרַת־כֶּסֶף אַחַת שְׁלֹשִׁים וּמֵאָה מִשְׁקָלָהּ *one plate of silver; its weight was 130 (shekels)* Nm 7_{13+11t}, שְׁלֹשִׁים וּמֵאָה הַקְּעָרָה הָאַחַת *the one plate*, i.e. each plate, *was 130 (silver shekels in weight)* Nm 7_{85}.

וְהָרִמּוֹנִים מָאתַיִם *there were two hundred pomegranates* 1 K 7_{20}, הָאֶלֶף לְךָ שְׁלֹמֹה וּמָאתַיִם לְנֹטְרִים אֶת־פִּרְיוֹ *the thousand are for you, O Solomon, and two hundred for ones who guard its fruit* Ca 8_{12} (Gnz לַנֹּטְרִים *for those who guard*), וְשֶׂה־אַחַת מִן־הַצֹּאן מִן־הַמָּאתַיִם *and one sheep of the flock from every two hundred* Ezk 45_{15}, וּמָאתַיִם יָשְׁבוּ עַל־הַכֵּלִים *and two hundred sat on the baggage* 1 S 25_{13}, צָפוֹנָה חֲמִשִּׁים וּמָאתַיִם and the pasture land will extend *250 (cubits) to the north* Ezk 48_{17}, sim. $48_{17.17.17}$, וַיִּתְקְעוּ שְׁלֹשׁ־מֵאוֹת הַשּׁוֹפָרוֹת *and three hundred blew the trumpets* Jg 7_{22} (or em. הַמֵּאוֹת *the* three *hundred*), וּמִשְׁקַל קֵינוֹ שְׁלֹשׁ מֵאוֹת מִשְׁקַל נְחֹשֶׁת *and the weight of his spear was three hundred (shekels) in weight of copper* 2 S 21_{16} (or em. קוֹבָעוֹ *his helmet*).

אֶחָד נֶפֶשׁ מֵחֲמֵשׁ הַמֵּאוֹת *one person out of 500 (warriors)* Nm 31_{28}, אֹרֶךְ חֲמֵשׁ מֵאוֹת וְרֹחַב חֲמֵשׁ מֵאוֹת *(the) length was 500 (rods) and (the) width was 500 (rods)* Ezk 42_{20}, יִהְיֶה מִזֶּה אֶל־הַקֹּדֶשׁ חֲמֵשׁ מֵאוֹת בַּחֲמֵשׁ מֵאוֹת מְרֻבָּע סָבִיב *of this there belongs to the sanctuary 500 (cubits) by 500 (cubits) square all around* Ezk 45_2.

כל שש מאות ותשעה *(the) total is 609 (vessels)* 3QTr 3_4, וְאַחֲרָיו גַּבַּי סַלָּי תְּשַׁע מֵאוֹת עֶשְׂרִים וּשְׁמֹנָה *and after him were Gabbai, Sallai (and) 928 (helpers)* Ne 11_8 (or em. וְאֶחָיו גִּבֹּרֵי־חָיִל *and his brothers, men of valour*, were 928).

כֹּל מִסְפַּר רָאשֵׁי הָאָבוֹת ... אַלְפַּיִם וְשֵׁשׁ מֵאוֹת *the total number of the ancestral heads ... was 2,600* 2 C 26_{12}, נָתְנוּ לַפְּסָחִים אַלְפַּיִם וְשֵׁשׁ מֵאוֹת *they gave as the passover victims 2,600 (beasts)* 2 C 35_8, וְעִמּוֹ שְׁלֹשֶׁת אֲלָפִים וּשְׁבַע מֵאוֹת *and with him were 3,700 (troops)* 1 C 12_{28}, פְּאַת צָפוֹן חֲמֵשׁ מֵאוֹת וְאַרְבַּעַת אֲלָפִים *(the) north corner is 4,500 (cubits)* Ezk 48_{16}, sim. $48_{16(Qr)+6t}$, הכול שש מאות וארבעת אלפים *the total is 4,600* 1QM 6_{10}.

מִסְפָּרָם ... עֶשְׂרִים־וּשְׁנַיִם אֶלֶף וְשֵׁשׁ מֵאוֹת *their number ... was 22,600* 1 C 7_2, כָּל־הַקָּהָל כְּאֶחָד אַרְבַּע רִבּוֹא אַלְפַּיִם שְׁלֹשׁ־מֵאוֹת שִׁשִּׁים *all the assembly united was 42,360 (people)* Ezr 2_{64} (||Ne 7_{66} וְשִׁשִּׁים).

מִן־הָראוּבֵנִי ... מֵאָה וְעֶשְׂרִים אֶלֶף *of the Reubenites ... there were 120,000* 1 C 12_{38}, וַיַּהֲרֹג פֶּקַח ... בִּיהוּדָה מֵאָה וְעֶשְׂרִים אֶלֶף *and Pekah killed ... 120,000 (people) in Judah* 2 C 28_6, וַיִּמָּצְאוּ מֵאָה וַחֲמִשִּׁים אֶלֶף וּשְׁלֹשֶׁת אֲלָפִים וְשֵׁשׁ מֵאוֹת *and there were found (to be) 153,600 (Israelites)* 2 C 2_{16}, וַיַּךְ בְּמַחֲנֵה אַשּׁוּר מֵאָה שְׁמֹנִים וַחֲמִשָּׁה אָלֶף *and he struck in the camp of Asshur 185,000 (men)* 2 K 19_{35}||Is 37_{36} (וַיַּכֶּה ... וּשְׁמֹנִים וַחֲמִשָּׁה), וְעִמּוֹ מָאתַיִם וּשְׁמוֹנִים אָלֶף *and with him were 280,000 (warriors)* 2 C 17_{15}, חַיִל ... שְׁלֹשׁ מֵאוֹת אֶלֶף *an army ... (consisting of) 300,000 (men)* 2 C 14_7.

Also 11QT 7_4 (מאה ועשר *110*; others אמה ועשר *a cubit and ten*) $7_{7(Yadin)}$ (מאה) $36_{2(Yadin)}$ (ומאה *and 100*) 11Q Melch 3_{16} (מאתים).*

⇒ מאה pi. *repeat a hundred times.*

מֵאָה II $_2$ pl.n. of tower in Jerusalem, מִגְדַּל הַמֵּאָה *the Tower of the Hundred* Ne 3_1 12_{39}.

⇒ מאה pi. *repeat a hundred times.*

מְאַהֵב *lover*, see אהב Pi. *love*.

[מַאֲוַי] $_1$ n.[m.] **desire**—pl. cstr. מַאֲוַיֵּי—<OBJ> נתן *give* Ps 140_9 (+ זָמָם *plan*). <CSTR> מַאֲוַיֵּי רָשָׁע *desires of the wicked* Ps 140_9.

⇒ אוה I *desire*.

מְאוּם I $_{1.0.2}$ indefinite pron. **anything, nothing,** אל ידור איש למזבח מאום אנוס *let no man vow to the altar anything forced*, i.e. taken by force CD 16_{13}, לוא ידבק

בידכה מאום מן החרם *nothing from the devoted objects shall cling to your hand* 11QT 55$_{11}$ (=Dt 13$_{18}$ מְאוּמָה *nothing*), perh. אִם ... בְּכַפַּי דָּבַק מְאוּם *if ... anything has clung to my hands* Jb 31$_{7(mss)}$ (unless from מוּם *blemish*; L מְאוּם).

⇒ cf. מְאוּמָה *anything*.

מְאוּם II, see מוּם *blemish*.

מְאוּמָה 32.2.1.1 indefinite pron. **anything**—L מְאוּמָה—**1. anything, nothing, a.** in negative sentence with (1) לֹא *not*, e.g. לֹא־תִתֶּן־לִי מְאוּמָה *you shall not give me anything* Gn 30$_{31}$, לֹא־נִפְקַד לָהֶם מְאוּמָה *there was nothing missing to them* 1 S 25$_{7}$, Gn 39$_{6.9}$ 40$_{15}$ Dt 13$_{18}$ 1 S 12$_{4.5}$ 20$_{26.39}$ 25$_{15.21}$ 29$_{3}$ 1 K 10$_{21}$ Ec 5$_{14}$ 7$_{14}$ 1QS 5$_{15}$.

(2) אַל *not*, e.g. אַל־תַּעַשׂ לוֹ מְאוּמָה *do not do anything to him* Gn 22$_{12(mss)}$ (L מְאוּמָּה), 1 S 21$_{3}$ (§3) Jr 39$_{12}$ Jon 3$_{7}$.

(3) אַיִן *not*, e.g. הַמֵּתִים אֵינָם יוֹדְעִים מְאוּמָה *the dead do not know anything* Ec 9$_{5}$, מְאוּמָה אֵין בְּיָדוֹ *there was nothing in his hand* Jg 14$_{6}$, [מא]ומה אין בכיס *there was nothing in the purse* 4QBéat 25$_{4}$, Gn 39$_{23}$ 1 K 18$_{43}$ Jr 39$_{10.12}$ Ec 5$_{13}$ 2 C 9$_{20}$ Si 14$_{10}$ (if em.; see Nom. Cl.) 18$_{33}$ (מאומ[ה]).

b. in interrogative sentence with (1) הֲ *is?*, הֲיָכוֹל אוּכַל דַּבֵּר מְאוּמָה *am I not indeed able to say anything?* Nm 22$_{38}$.

(2) מָה *what?*, מה יעשה לי מאומה *what will he do to me? Anything?* Si 5$_{4(A)}$.

2. anything, something, in affirmative sentence, **a.** statement, וַיִּפָּלֵא בְּעֵינֵי אַמְנוֹן לַעֲשׂוֹת לָהּ מְאוּמָה *it was impossible in the sight of Amnon to do anything to her* 2 S 13$_{2}$, בַּעֲבוּר מְאוּמָה תְּחַבֵּל *on account of anything you take a pledge* Mc 2$_{10}$ (if em. טֻמְאָה *impurity*).

b. oath, אִם ... אֶטְעַם־לֶחֶם אוֹ כָל־מְאוּמָה may God do so to me and more, *if ... I taste bread or anything (else) at all* 2 S 3$_{35}$, חַי י׳ כִּי אִם־רַצְתִּי אַחֲרָיו וְלָקַחְתִּי מֵאִתּוֹ מְאוּמָה *as Y. lives, I will run after him, and take something from him* 2 K 5$_{20}$.

c. as *nomen rectum*, מַשַּׁאת מְאוּמָה *loan of anything* Dt 24$_{10}$, מְעַט מְאוּמָה *a little of something*, i.e. something small Mc 2$_{10}$ (if em. טֻמְאָה *impurity*).

3. used adverbially, **in anything, at all,** אִישׁ אַל־יֵדַע מְאוּמָה אֶת־הַדָּבָר *let no one know in anything*, i.e. anything about, *the matter* 1 S 21$_{3}$, [ל]א אתן בה וכל מאומ[ה] *I will not pay any attention to it at all* Lachish ost. 3$_{13}$ (others אתננהו אל מאומ[ה] *I can repeat it [with respect] to anything*, i.e. in the smallest detail).

<SUBJ> דבק *cling* Dt 13$_{18}$, פקד ni. *be missing* 1 S 25$_{7.21}$.

<NOM CL> אֵין מְאוּמָה *there is nothing* 1 K 18$_{43}$, vars. Jg 14$_{6}$ Jr 39$_{10}$ Ec 5$_{13}$ Si 18$_{33}$ (מאומ[ה]), מאומה אין על שלחנו *there is nothing on his table* Si 14$_{10}$ (if em. מהומה *discomfiture* is upon his table).

<OBJ> עשׂה *do* Gn 22$_{12}$ 40$_{15}$ 2 S 13$_{2}$ Si 5$_{4}$, נתן *give* Gn 30$_{31}$, לקח *take* 1 S 12$_{4}$ 2 K 5$_{20}$ 1QS 5$_{16}$, נשׂא *bear* Ec 5$_{14}$, חשׂך *withhold* Gn 39$_{9}$, מצא *find* 1 S 12$_{5}$ 29$_{3}$ Ec 7$_{14}$, פקד *miss* 1 S 25$_{15}$, דבר pi. *speak* Nm 22$_{38}$ 1 S 20$_{26}$, ידע *know* Gn 39$_{6}$ 1 S 20$_{39}$ 21$_{3}$ Ec 9$_{5}$, טעם *taste* Jon 3$_{7}$ 2 S 3$_{35}$.

<CSTR> מַשַּׁאת מְאוּמָה *loan of anything* Dt 24$_{10}$, מְעַט מְאוּמָה *a little of something*, i.e. something small Mc 2$_{10}$ (if em. טֻמְאָה *impurity*), כָּל־מְאוּמָה *any thing at all* Gn 39$_{23}$ 2 S 3$_{35}$ 1QS 5$_{16}$ (כול) Lachish ost. 3$_{13}$ (כל מאומ[ה]; others אל מאומ[ה] *[with respect] to*).

<APP> רַע *evil* Jr 39$_{12}$ (מְאוּמָה רָע *anything, harm*, i.e. anything harmful).

<PREP> לְ *as*, + חשׁב ni. *be reckoned* 1 K 10$_{21}$||2 C 9$_{20}$; אֶל *(with respect) to*, + תנן *repeat* Lachish ost. 3$_{13}$ (אל מאומ[ה]; others כל מאומ[ה] *[in] anything at all*); בַּעֲבוּר *on account of*, + חבל pi. *take in pledge* Mc 2$_{10}$ (if em. טֻמְאָה *impurity*).

<COLL> מְאוּמָה מִן־הַחֵרֶם *nothing from the devoted objects* Dt 13$_{18}$, מִכָּל־אֲשֶׁר־לוֹ מְאוּמָה *nothing of all that was his* 1 S 25$_{21}$.*

⇒ cf. מְאוּם *anything*.

מָאוֹס 1 n.[m.] **refuse,** <OBJ> שׂים *place*, i.e. make into Lm 3$_{45}$ (|| סְחִי *offscouring*).

<SYN> סְחִי *offscouring*.

⇒ מאס *reject*.

מָאוֹר 19.1.19 n.m. **luminary**—מָאֹר; cstr. מְאוֹר; pl. מְאֹרֹת (מְאוֹרֹת, Q מאורות), Q מאורים; cstr. Q מאורות, מְאוֹרֵי)—**1. luminary,** sun and moon (Gn 1$_{14.15.16.16.16}$ Ezk 32$_{8}$ Ps 136$_{7[11QPs^a]}$ [MT אוֹר *light*] Si 43$_{4}$ 1QH 12$_{5}$ 1QS 10$_{3}$

4QShir^b 2.1$_8$), perh. specifically moon as distinct from sun (Ps 74$_{16}$), stars (1QH 1$_{11}$ 1QM 10$_{11}$ 4QMyst^a 5$_1$ [מאור[ות]]).

2. light, in general (1QH 9$_{26}$ 1QM 13$_{10}$), of lamp (Ex 25$_6$||35$_8$ 27$_{20}$ 35$_{14.14.28}$ 39$_{37}$ Lv 24$_2$ Nm 4$_{9.19}$), of countenance (Ps 90$_8$ 1QH 5$_{32}$), of the eyes (Pr 15$_{30}$ Ca 4$_9$ [if em.; see Prep.]); Y. as a light (1QH 7$_{25}$).

<SUBJ> היה *be* Gn 1$_{14}$, בדל hi. *separate* Gn 1$_{14}$, אור hi. *give light* Gn 1$_{15}$, יפע hi. *shine out* 1QS 10$_3$, יצא *go out* 4QPrQuot 215$_6$ (ב[צא]ת), חשך *be dark* 1QH 5$_{32}$, משל *rule* Gn 1$_{16.16}$, שמח pi. *make glad* Pr 15$_{30}$.

<OBJ> עשה *make* Gn 1$_{16.16}$ Ps 136$_7$(11QPs^a), כון *establish* Ps 74$_{16}$, אור *cause to shine* 1QH 9$_{26}$, קדר hi. *darken* Ezk 32$_8$, גלה *reveal* 1QH fr. 2$_{12}$, פתח *open* 4QpsHod^b 1$_1$.

<CSTR> מאור פני *light of my countenance* 1QH 5$_{32}$, מְאוֹר פָּנֶיךָ *light of your countenance* Ps 90$_8$ (or em. לְמוֹ אוֹר פָּנֶיךָ *before the light of your countenance*)*, ־עֵינַיִם *of the eyes* Pr 15$_{30}$, מאור [עו]לם *light of everlastingness*, i.e. everlasting light 1QH 7$_{25}$, מ[א]ור ברכה *light of blessing* 4QHod^a 3.1$_{13}$, מאור [היומם] *luminary of the daytime* 4QPrQuot 215$_6$, מְאוֹרֵי אוֹר *luminaries of light* Ezk 32$_8$, [מאור]ות כוכבים *luminaries of the stars* 4QMyst^a 5$_1$, מאורי פלא *luminaries of wonder* 4QBer^a 1.2$_3$, מאורות כבודו *luminaries of his glory* 4QShir^b 2.1$_8$.

לשון מאור *tongue*, i.e. ray, *of the luminary* Si 43$_4$(Bmg, M) (B לשאון appar. *at the roar of*), חוקות מאור *fixed times of the luminary* 1QH 12$_5$, פני אור ומא[ור] *presence of light and the luminary* 1QMyst^c 2b$_4$, צבא מאורות *host of luminaries* 1QM 10$_{11}$, מלא[כי] מאורות *angels of the luminaries of* 4QShir^b 2.1$_8$, שר מאור *prince of light* 1QM 13$_{10}$, מְנֹרַת הַמָּאוֹר *lampstand of*, i.e. for, *the light* Ex 35$_{14}$ Nm 4$_9$, שֶׁמֶן *oil of*, i.e. for Ex 35$_{14}$ 39$_{37}$ Nm 4$_{16}$, כָּל־מְאוֹרֵי *all luminaries of* Ezk 32$_8$.

<APP> רוּחַ *spirit* 1QH 1$_{11}$, שֶׁמֶשׁ *sun* Ps 136$_7$(11QPs^a), יָרֵחַ *moon* Ps 136$_7$(11QPs^a), כּוֹכָב *star* Ps 136$_7$(11QPs^a) 1QH 1$_{11}$.

<ADJ> גָּדוֹל *great* Gn 1$_{16.16}$ Ps 136$_7$(11QPs^a) 1QH 12$_5$ 1QLitPr 3.2$_1$ ([גדו]ל) 4QpsHod^b 1$_1$, קָטֹן *small* Gn 1$_{16}$.

<PREP> לְ *as* or introducing predicate 1QH 7$_{25}$, + היה *be* Gn 1$_{15}$ 1QH 1$_{11}$ ([והיו]), שִׂים *place*, i.e. make 1QSb 4$_{27}$; of benefit, *for*, + לקח *take* oil Ex 25$_6$ 27$_{20}$ Lv 24$_2$, בוא hi. *bring* oil Ex 35$_{8.28}$; *before*, + שִׁית *place* Ps 90$_8$ (or em.; see below).

בְּ of instrument, *by (means of), with*, + לבב pi. *seduce* Ca 4$_9$ (if em. בְּאַחַד *with one (glance)* to בְּמָאוֹר *with the light* from your eyes).

לְמוֹ *before*, + שִׁית *place* Ps 90$_8$ (if em. לִמְאוֹר to לְמוֹ אוֹר)*.

<COLL> מָאוֹר || שֶׁמֶשׁ *sun* Ps 74$_{16}$ (מָאוֹר וָשֶׁמֶשׁ); + כּוֹכָב *star* Gn 1$_{16}$, נֵר *lamp* Ex 27$_{20}$ Lv 24$_2$ Nm 4$_9$, הוֹד *splendour* 1QH 5$_{32}$, זֹהַר *brightness* 4QBer^a 1.2$_3$, שָׁבִיב *flame* 4QBer^a 1.2$_3$, שְׁמוּעָה good *report* Pr 15$_{30}$.

שְׁנֵי הַמְּאֹרֹת *the two luminaries* Gn 1$_{16}$; מאורות לרזיהם *luminaries according to their mysteries* 1QH 1$_{11}$.

Also 4QBer^b 1$_1$ 4QShirShabb^c 12$_2$ 4Q418 1$_5$ perh. 4QPrQuot 18$_3$ ([מ]אור).

<SYN> שֶׁמֶשׁ *sun*.*

⇨ אור *be light*.

[מְאוּרָה] I $_1$ n.f. **light-hole**—cstr. מְאוּרַת; pl. cstr. Q מאורות—appar. **light-hole,** entrance to a den of a snake, <CSTR> מְאוּרַת צִפְעוֹנִי *light-hole of the snake* Is 11$_8$ (1QIsa^a מאורות *light-holes of*; or em. מְעָרַת *hole of*, or מְעוֹנַת *dwelling place of*; || חֻר *hole*). <PREP> עַל *over*, + שעע pilp. *play* Is 11$_8$ (or em.; see Cstr.).

<SYN> חֹר *hole*.

⇨ אור *be light*.

*[מְאוּרָה] II $_1$ n.f. **den**—cstr. מְאוּרַת; pl. cstr. Q מאורות —**den** of snake, <CSTR> מְאוּרַת צִפְעוֹנִי *den of the snake* Is 11$_8$ (1QIsa^a מאורות *dens of*; or em. מְעָרַת *hole of*, or מְעוֹנַת *dwelling place of*; || חֻר *hole*). <PREP> עַל *over*, + שעע pilp. *play* Is 11$_8$ (or em.; see Cstr.).

<SYN> חֹר *hole*.

*[מְאוּרָה] III $_1$ n.f. **fiery coals (?)**—cstr. מְאוּרַת; pl. cstr. Q מאורות—<CSTR> מְאוּרַת צִפְעוֹנִי perh. *fiery coals of the snake* Is 11$_8$ (1QIsa^a מאורות; or em. מְעָרַת *hole of*, or מְעוֹנַת *dwelling place of*; || חֻר *hole*). <PREP> עַל *over*, + שעע pilp. *play* Is 11$_8$ (or em.; see Cstr.).

<SYN> חֹר *hole*.

⇨ (?) אור *be light*.

*[מְאוּרָה] IV $_1$ n.f. **eye**—cstr. מְאוּרַת; pl. cstr. Q

מאורות—appar. **light-hole**, entrance to a den of a snake, <CSTR> מְאוּרַת צִפְעוֹנִי *eye of the snake* Is 11$_8$ (1QIsa^a מאורות *eyes of*; or em. מְעָרַת *hole of*, or מְעוֹנַת *dwelling place of*; || חֹר *hole*). <PREP> עַל *over*, + שׁעע pilp. *play* Is 11$_8$ (or em.; see Cstr.).

<SYN> חֹר *hole*.

⇒ אור *be light*.

*[מְאוּרָה] V $_1$ n.f. **young**—cstr. מְאוּרַת; pl. cstr. Q מאורות—**young**, of a snake, <CSTR> מְאוּרַת צִפְעוֹנִי *young of the snake* Is 11$_8$ (1QIsa^a מאורות *young ones of*; or em. מְעָרַת *hole of*, or מְעוֹנַת *dwelling place of*; || חֹר *hole*). <PREP> עַל *over*, + שׁעע pilp. *play* Is 11$_8$ (or em.; see Cstr.).

<SYN> חֹר *hole*.

מֹאזְנַיִם 15.1.5 n.[m.]du. **balances**—מֹאזְנַיִם (Q מוזנים, Si, Q מזנים); cstr. מֹאזְנֵי (Q מוזני)—**balances, scales,** for weighing money (Jr 32$_{10}$), hills (Is 40$_{12}$=4QShir^b 30$_5$ [[מוזנ]ים]), humans (Ps 62$_{10}$ Jb 31$_6$), <SUBJ> היה *be* Lv 19$_{36}$ Ezk 45$_{10}$.

<NOM CL> בְּיָדוֹ מֹאזְנֵי מִרְמָה *in his hand are deceptive balances* Ho 12$_8$, מֹאזְנֵי מִרְמָה תּוֹעֲבַת י׳ *deceptive balances are an abomination of*, i.e. to, *Y.* Pr 11$_1$, מֹאזְנֵי מִרְמָה לֹא־טוֹב *deceptive balances are not good* Pr 20$_{23}$, מֹאזְנֵי מִשְׁפָּט לַי׳ *just balances are*, i.e. belong, *to Y.* Pr 16$_{11}$ (or em. מֹאזְנַיִם לַי׳ *balances are to Y.*, or מֹאזְנַיִם מִפְעַל י׳ *balances are the work of Y.*).

<OBJ> לקח *take* Ezk 5$_1$, עות pi. *make crooked*, i.e. falsify Am 8$_5$.

<CSTR> מֹאזְנֵי רֶשַׁע *balances of wickedness*, i.e. wicked balances Mc 6$_{11}$, מִרְמָה *of deceit*, i.e. deceptive balances Ho 12$_8$ Am 8$_5$ Pr 11$_1$ 20$_{23}$, צֶדֶק *of righteousness*, i.e. right balances Lv 19$_{36}$ Jb 31$_6$ 4Q418 127$_6$ (מוזני) 167$_2$ (מוזני צדו[ק]), מִשְׁפָּט *of justice*, i.e. just balances Pr 16$_{11}$ (or em.; see Nom Cl.), מִשְׁקָל *of*, i.e. for, *weighing* Ezk 5$_1$; שַׁחַק מֹאזְנַיִם *dust of*, i.e. on, *the balances* Is 40$_{15}$ (or em. מֹזְנַיִם rags of *clouds*; 1QIsa^a מוזנים) Si 42$_{4(B)}$ (M שחקי מזנים).

<PREP> בְּ of place, *in* perh. 4Q418 207$_4$, + עלה *go up* Ps 62$_{10}$, נשׂא *lift* Jb 6$_2$; of instrument, *by (means of), with*, + שׁקל *weigh* Is 40$_{12}$=4QShir^b 30$_5$ ([במוזנ]ים) Jr 32$_{10}$ Jb 31$_6$ 4Q418 127$_6$; of accompaniment, *with, in (the presence of)*, + זכה *be pure* Mc 6$_{11}$ (or em. זכה pi. *acquit*).

כְּ *as* 4Q415 9$_{12}$ 4Q418 167$_2$.

<COLL> פֶּלֶס || מֹאזְנַיִם *scale* Is 40$_{12}$=4QShir^b 30$_5$ ([מוזנ]ים) Pr 16$_{11}$ Si 42$_4$, אֵיפָה *ephah* Lv 19$_{36}$ Ezk 45$_{10}$, הִין *hin* Lv 19$_{36}$, בַּת *bath* Ezk 45$_{10}$, שֶׁקֶל *shekel* Am 8$_5$ (+), אֶבֶן *stone*, i.e. weight Lv 19$_{36}$ Pr 11$_1$ (+) 16$_{11}$ (+) 20$_{23}$ (+), כִּיס *bag* of weights Mc 6$_{11}$ Pr 16$_{11}$ (+), דְּלִי *bucket* Is 40$_{15}$ (+).

<SYN> פֶּלֶס *scale*, אֵיפָה *ephah*, הִין *hin*, בַּת *bath*, אֶבֶן *stone*, i.e. weight, כִּיס *bag* of weights.*

⇒ אזן II *weigh*.

מֵאיוֹת, see מֵאָה *hundred*.

מַאֲכָל 30.6.8 n.m. **food**—cstr. מַאֲכַל; sf. מַאֲכָלְךָ, מַאֲכָלוֹ, מַאֲכָלָהּ, מַאֲכָלְכֶם; pl. sf. Q מאכליהם—**food, nourishment**, in ref. to produce of trees (Gn 2$_9$ 3$_6$ Lv 19$_{23}$ Dt 20$_{20}$ Ezk 47$_{12.12}$ Ne 9$_{25}$ 4QMMT B$_{62}$), honey (Jg 14$_{14}$), grain (Is 62$_8$), baked food (Gn 40$_{17}$), meat (Ps 44$_{12}$), food of ant (Pr 6$_8$), human corpse as food for birds and animals (Dt 28$_{26}$ Jr 7$_{33}$ 16$_4$ 19$_7$ 34$_{20}$ Ps 79$_2$), wild asses as prey of lion (Si 13$_{19}$).

<SUBJ> היה *be* Gn 6$_{21}$, אכל ni. *be eaten* Gn 6$_{21}$, קדשׁ *be holy* Hg 2$_{12}$, נעם *be pleasant* appar. Si 36$_{23(Bmg)}$, יצא *go out* Jg 14$_{14}$, עלה *go up* Si 33$_{13}$.

<NOM CL> יש מאכל *there is food* Si 36$_{23(Bmg)}$, מַאֲכָלְךָ ... בְּמִשְׁקוֹל עֶשְׂרִים שֶׁקֶל לַיּוֹם *your food shall be ... by weight twenty shekels per day* Ezk 4$_{10}$, מַאֲכָלוֹ בְּרָאָה *his food is fat* Hb 1$_{16}$ (or em. בְּרָאָה to בָּרִיא *fat*), מאכל ארי פראי מדבר *the wild asses of the steppe are the food of the lion* Si 13$_{19}$.

<OBJ> אכל *eat* Gn 40$_{17}$ Ezk 4$_{10}$ Si 36$_{23}$, ראה *see* 1 K 10$_5$||2 C 9$_4$, אגר *gather* Pr 6$_8$, אסף *gather* Gn 6$_{21}$, מנה pi. *appoint* Dn 1$_{10}$, בוא hi. *bring* 1 C 12$_{41}$, יצא hi. *take out* 4QSD 7.1$_5$ ([יו]ציא] ... מאכו[ל]), נתן *give* Ezr 3$_7$, חלק pi *divide* 1QpHab 6$_7$, קדשׁ pi. *sanctify* CD 16$_{14}$, זהם pi. *abhor* Jb 33$_{20}$.

<CSTR> מַאֲכַל פַּרְעֹה *food of Pharaoh* Gn 40$_{17}$, שֻׁלְחָנוֹ *of his* (Solomon's) *table* 1 K 10$_5$||2 C 9$_4$, תַּאֲוָה *of desire*, i.e. desirable food Jb 33$_{20}$, מאכל תענוג *food of delight*, i.e. delightful food Si 37$_{20}$, פיהו *of his mouth* CD16$_{14}$,

שֵׁן *of a tooth,* i.e. for eating 4Q418 127$_{3}$, ארי *of the lion* Si 13$_{19}$; צֹאן מַאֲכָל *sheep of,* i.e. for, food Ps 44$_{12}$, עֵץ *tree of,* i.e. for Lv 19$_{23}$ Dt 20$_{20}$ Ezk 47$_{12}$ Ne 9$_{25}$, עצי המאכל *trees of,* i.e. for, food 4QD[a] 6.4$_{2}$ ([המ]אכל) 4QMMT B$_{62}$, אֹצְרוֹת מַאֲכָל *stores of food* 2 C 11$_{11}$, כָּל־מַאֲכָל *every (kind of) food* Gn 6$_{21}$ 40$_{17}$ (כֹּל) Hg 2$_{12}$ Si 36$_{23}$ 37$_{20}$ (כֹּל).

<APP> מַעֲשֵׂה *work* of baker Gn 40$_{17}$, לֶחֶם *bread* 1 C 12$_{41}$ (Gnz לָהֶם *to them*), קֶמַח *flour* 1 C 12$_{41}$, דְּבֵלָה *fig* 1 C 12$_{41}$, צִמּוּק *raisin* 1 C 12$_{41}$, יַיִן *wine* 1 C 12$_{41}$, שֶׁמֶן *oil* 1 C 12$_{41}$, בָּקָר *oxen* 1 C 12$_{41}$, צֹאן *sheep* 1 C 12$_{41}$, עֹל *yoke* 1QpHab 6$_{7}$, מַס *forced labour* 1QpHab 6$_{7}$.

<PREP> לְ *as, for (the purpose of)* Gn 2$_{9}$ 3$_{6}$, + היה *be* Dt 28$_{26}$ Jr 7$_{33}$ 16$_{4}$ 34$_{20}$ Ezk 47$_{12}$ 4QJub[h] 40$_{4}$ (וי[ה'] [למ]אכל) 4Q418 127$_{3}$, נתן *give* Jr 19$_{7}$.

מִן of direction, *from* perh. 4QNidd 2.2$_{3}$, + בצר ni. *be cut off* Si 37$_{20}$; partitive, *(some) of* Gn 40$_{17}$, + לקח *take* Gn 6$_{21}$; comparative, *(more) than,* + נעם *be pleasant* Si 36$_{23(Bmg)}$.

אֶל *to,* + נגע *reach,* i.e. touch Hg 2$_{12}$.

<COLL> מַאֲכָל || מִשְׁתֶּה *drink* Dn 1$_{10}$ Ezr 3$_{7}$, לֶחֶם *bread* Hg 2$_{12}$ Jb 33$_{20}$ Pr 6$_{8}$, נָזִיד *pottage* Hg 2$_{12}$, יַיִן *wine* Hg 2$_{12}$ 2 C 11$_{11}$, שֶׁמֶן *oil* Hg 2$_{12}$ Ezr 3$_{7}$ 2 C 11$_{11}$, תְּרוּפָה *healing* Ezk 47$_{12}$.

+ אֹכֶל *food* Si 36$_{23(B)}$, מַטְעַם *delicacy* Si 33$_{13}$, מָתוֹק *sweet thing* Jg 14$_{14}$, מַרְעִית *pasturage* Si 13$_{19}$.

מַאֲכָל used adverbially, *as food,* + נתן *give* Is 62$_{8}$ Ps 74$_{14}$ 79$_{2}$.

Also perh. 4QDibHam[a] 16$_{2}$ ([מ]אכל) 4QPrFêtes[c] 184.1$_{12}$ 4QOrd[b] 2.2$_{5}$.

<SYN> מִשְׁתֶּה *drink,* לֶחֶם *bread,* נָזִיד *pottage,* יַיִן *wine,* שֶׁמֶן *oil,* תְּרוּפָה *healing.**

⇒ אכל *eat.*

מַאֲכֶלֶת 4 n.f. **knife**—pl. מַאֲכָלוֹת—<NOM CL> מַאֲכָלוֹת מְתַלְּעֹתָיו *his teeth are knives* Pr 30$_{14}$ (|| חֶרֶב *sword*). <OBJ> לקח *take* Gn 22$_{6}$ (+ אֵשׁ *fire*) 22$_{10}$ Jg 19$_{29}$.

<SYN> חֶרֶב *sword.*

⇒ אכל *eat.*

[מַאֲכֹלֶת] 2 n.f. **fuel,** perh. also **food** (as byform of מַאֲכָל *food*)—cstr. מַאֲכֹלֶת—<CSTR> מַאֲכֹלֶת אֵשׁ *fuel of,* i.e. for, the fire Is 9$_{4.18}$ (or em.; see Prep.). <APP> שְׂרֵפָה *burning* Is 9$_{4}$. <PREP> לְ *as* or introducing predicate, + היה *be* Is 9$_{4}$; כְּ *as,* + היה *be* Is 9$_{18}$ (or em. כְּמַאֲכֹלֶת אֵשׁ *as fuel for the fire* to כְּמוֹ אֹכֶלֶת/אֹכְלֵי אִשׁ *as one who devours/ones who devour men*).*

⇒ אכל *eat.*

מאמן, see מִיאָמִן *Miamun.*

[מַאֲמָץ] 1 n.[m.] **exertion, power;** or **wealth, expense**—pl. cstr. מַאֲמַצֵּי—<SUBJ> ערך *arrange* Jb 36$_{19}$ (or em. יַעֲרֹךְ *will it arrange* to הַיְעִרְךָ *will it rouse you?*). <CSTR> כֹּל מַאֲמַצֵּי־כֹחַ *all exertions,* or *wealth, of strength* Jb 36$_{19}$.*

⇒ אמץ *be strong.*

[מַאֲמָר] 3.2.6 n.m. **word, command**—cstr. מַאֲמַר; sf. Q מאמרו, Q מאמרה (Q ממרה)—**word** (Si 3$_{8}$ 37$_{16}$), **command** (Est 1$_{15}$ [= פִּתְגָם *command* 1$_{20}$] 2$_{20}$ 9$_{32}$ 4QD[f] 3$_{14}$), of Y. (4QTobit[e] 2$_{4}$), in legal document, next to signature of the party on whose authority it was drawn up (Mur 24 C$_{20}$ 5/6ḤevBA 44$_{28.29.30}$), <SUBJ> קום pi. *establish* Est 9$_{32}$, כתב ni. *be written* Est 9$_{32}$. <NOM CL> ראש כל מעשה מאמר *a word is the source of any deed* Si 37$_{16(Bmg, D)}$ (B דָּבָר *word;* || מַחֲשֶׁבֶת *thought*). <OBJ> עשה *do* Est 1$_{15}$ 2$_{20}$, כתב *write* 5/6ḤevBA 44$_{28.29.30}$. <CSTR> מַאֲמַר אֶסְתֵּר *command of Esther* Est 9$_{32}$, מָרְדֳּכַי *of Mordecai* Est 2$_{20}$, הַמֶּלֶךְ אֲחַשְׁוֵרוֹשׁ *of King Ahasuerus* Est 1$_{15}$ (+ בְּיַד הַסָּרִיסִים *by the hand of the eunuchs*), מאמר המבקר *command of the overseer* 4QD[f] 3$_{14}$. <PREP> בְּ of instrument, *by (means of), with,* + כבד pi. *honour* Si 3$_{8}$ (|| מַעֲשֶׂה *deed*); מִן *on account of, through* Mur 24 C$_{20}$ ([מן]), + ברר pass. *be chosen* 4QD[f] 3$_{14}$.

<SYN> מַעֲשֶׂה *deed,* מַחֲשֶׁבֶת *thought.*

⇒ אמר *say.*

מאן 46.1.1 vb. **refuse**—**Pi.** 46 Pf. מֵאֵן (מֵאִין), מֵאֲנָה, מֵאַנְתָּ, מֵאַנְתֶּם, מֵאֲנוּ, מֵאַנְתְּ; impf. יְמָאֵן, 2ms Si תמאן, יְמָאֲנוּ, וַתְּמָאֲנוּ; + waw וַיְמָאֵן, 3fs וַתְּמָאֵן, 2ms וַתְּמָאֵן, וַיְמָאֲנוּ, וַתְּמָאֲנוּ; ptc. מָאֵן, מֵאֲנִים; inf. abs. מָאֵן—**refuse,** usu. followed by inf. (see Coll.); used absolutely (Gn 39$_{8}$ 48$_{19}$ 1 S 28$_{23}$ 2 K 5$_{16}$ Is 1$_{20}$ Pr 1$_{24}$), **act defiantly** (Si 4$_{27}$).

<SUBJ> Y. Nm 22$_{13}$ Ml 2$_{13}$ (if em. מֵאֵין *because there*

is not to מֵאֵן י׳ *Y. has refused*), Israel(ites) Ex 16$_{28}$ Is 1$_{20}$ Jr 3$_{3}$ 5$_{3.3}$ Ho 11$_{5}$ Zc 7$_{11}$ Ps 78$_{10}$ Ne 9$_{17}$, Jerusalem Jr 8$_{5}$ (unless del. יְרוּשָׁלַםִ *Jerusalem*), Edom Nm 33$_{13}$, עַם *people* 1 S 8$_{19}$ Jr 8$_{5}$ 13$_{10}$, גּוֹי *nation* Jr 25$_{28}$, יִזְרְעֵאלִי *Jezreelite* 1 K 21$_{15}$, Amnon 2 S 13$_{9}$, Asahel 2 S 2$_{23}$, Balaam Nm 22$_{14}$, David 1 S 24$_{11}$ (if em. וְאָמַר *and he said* to וָאֲמָאֵן *and I refused*), Elisha 2 K 5$_{16}$, Jacob Gn 37$_{35}$, Joseph Gn 39$_{8}$, Naboth 1 K 21$_{15}$, Rachel Jr 31$_{15}$, Saul 1 S 28$_{23}$, Sihon Jg 11$_{20}$ (if em. וְלֹא־הֶאֱמִין *and he would not trust* to וַיְמָאֵן *and he refused*), Vashti Est 1$_{12}$, Zedekiah Jr 38$_{21}$, אִישׁ *man* 1 K 20$_{35}$ Jr 9$_{5}$, אָב *father* Gn 49$_{19}$ Ex 22$_{16}$ Jr 11$_{10}$, בֵּן *son* Si 4$_{27}$, יָבָם *husband's brother* Dt 25$_{7}$, מֶלֶךְ *king* Jr 38$_{21}$, מַלְכָּה *queen* Est 1$_{12}$, פַּרְעֹה *Pharaoh* Ex 4$_{23}$ 7$_{14.27}$ 9$_{2}$ 10$_{3.4}$, שֹׁבֶה *captor* Jr 50$_{33}$, פֶּתִי *simple one* Pr 1$_{24}$, לֵץ *scorner* Pr 1$_{24}$, כְּסִיל *fool* Pr 1$_{24}$, רָשָׁע *wicked one* Pr 21$_{7}$, שׁוב ptc. *one who goes back* 4QpPs[a] 1.2$_{3}$, יָד *hand* Pr 21$_{25}$, נֶפֶשׁ *soul* Ps 77$_{3}$ Jb 6$_{7}$, מַכָּה *wound* Jr 15$_{18}$.

<PREP> לִפְנֵי *before*, + מֹשֵׁל *ruler* Si 4$_{27}$.

<COLL> מאן pi. followed by infinitive of שׁמע *listen* 1 S 8$_{19}$ Jr 11$_{10}$ 13$_{10}$ Ne 9$_{17}$, קשׁב hi. *pay attention* Zc 7$_{11}$, ידע *know* Jr 8$_{5}$, אכל *eat* 2 S 13$_{9}$, הלך *go* Nm 22$_{14}$ Ps 78$_{10}$, בוא *come* Est 1$_{12}$, יצא *go out* Jr 38$_{21}$, סור *turn aside* intrans. 2 S 2$_{23}$, שׁוב *go back* Jr 5$_{3}$ 8$_{5}$ Ho 11$_{5}$ 4QpPs[a] 1.2$_{3}$, פנה *turn* Ml 2$_{13}$ (if em.; see Subj.), שׁלח pi. *let go* Ex 4$_{23}$ 7$_{14.27}$ 9$_{2}$ 10$_{4}$ Jr 50$_{33}$, קום hi. *raise up* Dt 25$_{7}$, שׁמר *keep* Ex 16$_{28}$, עשׂה *do* Pr 21$_{7.25}$, נתן *give* Ex 22$_{16}$ Nm 20$_{21}$ 22$_{13}$ 1 K 21$_{15}$, לקח *take* Jr 5$_{3}$ 25$_{28}$, נכה hi. *strike* 1 K 20$_{35}$, הרג *kill* 1 S 24$_{11}$ (if em.; see Subj.), ענה ni. *humble oneself* Ex 10$_{3}$, כלם ni. *be ashamed* Jr 3$_{3}$, נחם ni. *be comforted* Jr 31$_{15}$ Ps 77$_{3}$, htp. *be comforted* Gn 37$_{35}$, רפא ni. *be healed* Jr 15$_{18}$, נגע *touch* Jb 6$_{7}$.

:: אבה *be willing* Dt 25$_{7}$ Is 1$_{20}$, קשׁב hi. *pay attention* Pr 1$_{24}$; + מרה *rebel* Is 1$_{20}$.

+ adverb, עַד־מָתַי *how long?* Ex 10$_{3}$, עַד־אָנָה *how long?* Ex 16$_{28}$; inf. abs. used with finite verb, Ex 22$_{16}$.

Also perh. 4QHymnPr 6$_{2}$ perh. 4QPrFêtes[c] 201$_{2}$.

<ANT> אבה *be willing*, קשׁב hi. *pay attention*.*

מאס I $_{74.10.33}$ vb. **reject—Qal** $_{71.4.31}$ Pf. מָאַס (מְאָסָם), מָאַסְתָּ (מְאַסְתָּה, מְאַסְתָּנוּ), מָאַסְתִּי (מְאַסְתִּיךָ, מְאַסְתִּיו, מְאַסְתִּים, מְאַסְתִּיהוּ), מָאֲסוּ, מָאֲסוּ (מָאֲסוּ, Q מאשו), מְאַסְתֶּם, Q מאסנו; impf. יִמְאַס (יִמְאָסֵם, יִמְאָסֶם), 2ms תִּמְאַס (תִּמְאָס), אֶמְאַס (mss אֶמְאָסְךָ, L אֶמְאָסְאךָ [Ho 4$_{6}$]), תִּמְאָסוּ, יִמְאָסוּן; + waw וּמָאַסְתִּי; וַיִּמְאַס (וַיִּמְאָסֵם, וַיִּמְאָסְךָ), 2ms וַתִּמְאַס, וַיִּמְאֲסוּ; ptc. מֹאֵס (מוֹאֵס), מֹאֶסֶת, Q מואסי, Q מואסיהם; pass. Q מאוסי; inf. abs. מָאוֹס (מָאֹס); inf. cstr. Q מאס (מָאֳסָם, מָאָסְכֶם).

1. reject, spurn, despise, oft. in religious contexts, of Y. rejecting or being rejected; without object, perh. **feel loathing, contempt, revulsion*** (Ps 89$_{39}$ Jb 34$_{33}$ 36$_{5}$ 42$_{6}$), or **despise** (life) (Jb 7$_{16}$), **reject** (commandments) (CD 20$_{8}$); followed by infinitive, **refuse (to do something)** (Jb 30$_{1}$ 1QS 2$_{25}$ 4QBer[f] 1$_{7}$).

<SUBJ> Y. Lv 26$_{44}$ 1 S 15$_{23.26}$ 16$_{1.7}$ 2 K 17$_{20}$ 23$_{27}$ Is 41$_{9}$ Jr 2$_{37}$ 6$_{30}$ 7$_{29}$ 14$_{19.19}$ 31$_{37}$ 33$_{24.26}$ Ho 4$_{6}$ 9$_{17}$ Am 5$_{21}$ Ps 53$_{6}$ 78$_{59.67}$ 89$_{39}$ Jb 8$_{20}$ 10$_{3}$ 36$_{5}$ (unless מאס II *cower*) Lm 5$_{22.22}$ 1QS 1$_{4}$ 1QLitPr 3.2$_{4}$ 4QDibHam[a] 1.5$_{6}$ GnzPs 1$_{3}$, Israel(ites) Lv 26$_{16.43}$ Is 30$_{12}$ Is 5$_{24}$ 41$_{9}$ Ezk 5$_{6}$ 21$_{15}$ (if em. מֹאֶסֶת *it despises* to מָאַסְתָּ) Ps 106$_{24}$, Judah Am 2$_{4}$, עַם *people* Nm 11$_{20}$ 1 S 8$_{7.7}$ Is 8$_{6}$ Jr 6$_{19}$, בַּיִת *house* of Israel Ezk 20$_{13.16}$, Gaal Jg 9$_{38}$, Immanuel Is 7$_{15}$, Job Jb 5$_{17}$ 7$_{16}$ (unless מאס II *waste away*) 9$_{21}$ 30$_{1}$ 31$_{13}$ 34$_{33}$ 42$_{6}$ (unless מאס II *waste away*), Saul 1 S 15$_{23.26}$.

אִישׁ *man* Is 31$_{6}$ 1QpHab 5$_{11}$, גֶּבֶר *man* Si 38$_{4}$, בֵּן *son* Pr 3$_{11}$ Si 7$_{19}$ 8$_{9}$ 41$_{4}$ 4QD[e] 7.1$_{11}$ CD 2$_{15}$, of Israel Nm 14$_{31}$ 1 S 10$_{19}$ 2 K 17$_{15}$ 4QpsMos[d] 1.2$_{4}$, נַעַר *lad* Is 7$_{16}$, עֲוִיל *child* Jb 19$_{18}$, עֶבֶד *servant* 1QH 17$_{24}$, כֹּהֵן *priest* Ho 4$_{6}$, worshipper 4QDibHam[a] 1.6$_{6}$, תָּמִים *perfect one* 1QH 13$_{7}$, פרע ptc. *one who lets go* Pr 15$_{32}$, רָשָׁע *wicked one* Ps 36$_{5}$ 1QH 15$_{18}$, שֹׁדֵד *destroyer* Is 33$_{8}$, בֹּגֵד *treacherous one* Is 33$_{8}$, מֵרֵעַ *friend* Jb 6$_{14}$ (if em. לַמָּס מֵרֵעֵהוּ *to the despairing one from his friend* to לֹא מָאַס מֵרֵעַ *a friend does not refuse*), עֹגֵב *lover* Jr 4$_{30}$, בֹּנֶה *builder* Ps 118$_{22}$ GnzPs 1$_{18}$, חָכָם *wise one* Jr 8$_{9}$, appar. חֶרֶב *sword* Ezk 21$_{15}$ (or em.; see above) 21$_{18}$, כֹּל *everyone* 1QS 2$_{25}$ 3$_{5}$; subj. not specified, Is 33$_{15}$ 4QD[a] 11$_{5}$ CD 3$_{17}$ 7$_{9}$=19$_{5}$ 8$_{19}$=19$_{32}$ 20$_{8.11}$.

<OBJ> Y. Nm 11$_{20}$ 1 S 8$_{7}$ 10$_{19}$, אֱלִיל *idol* Is 31$_{6}$, Israel(ites) Lv 26$_{44}$ Lm 5$_{22}$, Judah Jr 14$_{19.19}$, Ephraim Ho 9$_{17}$, Jerusalem 2 K 23$_{2}$, עִיר *city* 2 K 23$_{27}$ Is 33$_{8}$ (1QIsa[a] עֵד *testimony*), בַּיִת *house* 2 K 23$_{2}$, מִשְׁפָּחָה *clan* Jr 33$_{24}$, זֶרַע *seed* Jr 33$_{26}$, דּוֹר *generation* Jr 7$_{29}$, Eliab 1 S 16$_{7}$, Samuel 1 S 8$_{7}$, Saul 1 S 15$_{23.26}$ 16$_{1}$, אִשָּׁה *wife* Si 7$_{19}$, אָב *father* Jb 30$_{1}$, בֵּן *son* of man Ps 53$_{6}$, כֹּהֵן *priest* Ho 4$_{6}$,

עֶבֶד *servant* Is 41$_{9}$, תָּם *blameless one* Jb 8$_{20}$, נֶפֶשׁ *soul,* i.e. self Pr 15$_{32}$, מַיִם *water* Is 8$_{6}$ CD 3$_{17}$, שֵׁבֶט *rod* Ezk 21$_{15.18}$, עֵץ *wood* Ezk 21$_{15}$ (or em. עֵץ to עֵצָה *counsel*), אֶבֶן *stone* Ps 118$_{22}$, פִּנָּה *corner(-stone)* GnzPs 1$_{18}$, דָּבָר *word* of Y. 1 S 15$_{23.26}$, תּוֹרָה *law* Is 5$_{24}$ Am 2$_{4}$ 4QpIsa^{c} 23.2$_{14a}$ 1QpHab 5$_{11}$, חֹק *statute* 2 K 17$_{15}$, חֻקָּה *statute* Ezk 20$_{24}$ 4QpsMos^{d} 1.2$_{4}$, מִשְׁפָּט *ordinance* Ezk 20$_{13}$ 4QD^{e} 7.1$_{11}$, *cause* Jb 31$_{13}$, בְּרִית *covenant* 2 K 17$_{15}$, עֵדוּת *testimony* 2 K 17$_{15}$, דַּעַת *knowledge* Ho 4$_{6}$, מוּסָר *discipline* Jb 5$_{17}$ Pr 3$_{11}$, רַע *evil* Ps 36$_{5}$, חֶסֶד *loyalty* Jb 6$_{14}$ (if em.; see Subj.), חַיִּים *life* Jb 9$_{21}$, יְגִיעַ *product* Jb 10$_{3}$, חַג *festival* Am 5$_{21}$.

<PREP> בְּ introducing object, + Israel Ps 78$_{59}$, עַם *people* Jg 9$_{38}$ Jr 6$_{30}$, Job Jb 19$_{19}$, זֶרַע *seed* 2 K 17$_{20}$ Jr 31$_{37}$ 1QLitPr 3.2$_{4}$ 4QDibHam^{a} 1.5$_{6}$, שׁדד ptc. pass. *devastated one* Jr 4$_{30}$, אֹהֶל *tent* of Joseph Ps 78$_{67}$, דָּבָר *word* Is 30$_{12}$ Jr 8$_{9}$, תּוֹרָה *law* Jr 6$_{19}$ Si 41$_{4}$ 1QpHab 1$_{11}$ 4QD^{a} 7.3$_{5}$ (המוא]ס בת[ותה), חֹק *statute* CD 19$_{5}$, חֻקָּה *statute* Lv 26$_{15}$, מִשְׁפָּט *ordinance* Lv 26$_{43}$ Ezk 5$_{6}$ 20$_{16}$ 1QH 13$_{7}$ ([ב]כול משפט) 1QS 3$_{5}$ 4QD^{a} 11$_{5}$, מִצְוָה *commandment* CD 19$_{5}$ 8$_{19}$=19$_{32}$, עֵדוּת *testimony* 4QBer^{b} 9$_{3}$ ([מאו]ס), יִסּוּר *precept* 4QBéat 5$_{11}$, בְּרִית *covenant* 1QH 15$_{18}$ ([בבריכ]ה) CD 20$_{11}$, אֲמָנָה *agreement* CD 20$_{11}$, תּוֹכֵחָה *rebuke* 4QBéat 5$_{10}$, אֶרֶץ *land* Nm 14$_{31}$ Ps 106$_{24}$, רַע *evil* Is 7$_{15.16}$, עָוֶל *injustice* GnzPs 1$_{3}$ (בעיול), בֶּצַע *gain* Is 33$_{15}$, מִבְטָח *confidence* Jr 2$_{37}$, שְׁמִיעָה *(oral) tradition* Si 8$_{9}$, נִסּוּי *trial* 4QDibHam^{a} 1.6$_{6}$, תְּרוּפָה *healing (plant)* Si 38$_{4(B)}$, סַם *spice* Si 38$_{4(Bmg)}$ (שמים), אֲשֶׁר *that which* CD 2$_{15}$ (if em. כאשר *as* to באשר), כֹּל *everything* 1QH 17$_{24}$.

עַל *on account of*, + אֲשֶׁר *that which* Jr 31$_{37}$.

בְּתוֹךְ *within*, עֵצָה *council* 1QpHab 5$_{11}$.

<COLL> מאס || געל *abhor* Lv 26$_{15.43.44}$ Jr 14$_{19}$ 4QpsMos^{d} 1.2$_{4}$ 4QDibHam^{a} 1.6$_{6}$, קוץ *loathe* Pr 3$_{11}$, זנח *reject* Ps 89$_{39}$, נאץ pi. *despise* Is 5$_{24}$, נטשׁ *forsake* Jr 7$_{29}$, שׂנא *hate* Am 5$_{21}$, פרר hi. *break* covenant Is 33$_{8}$, נחם ni. *repent* Jb 42$_{6}$.

+ סור hi. *remove* 2 K 23$_{2}$, ענה pi. *afflict* 2 K 17$_{20}$, עבר htp. *be angry* Ps 89$_{39}$.

:: בחר *choose* Is 7$_{15.16}$ 41$_{9}$ Jr 33$_{24}$ Ps 78$_{67}$ 1QS 1$_{4}$ CD 2$_{15}$, הלך *walk* in statutes, etc. Ezk 5$_{6}$ 20$_{13.16}$, עשׂה *do* ordinances Ezk 20$_{24}$, שׁמר *keep* statutes Am 2$_{4}$, חפץ *delight in* GnzPs 1$_{3}$, ריח hi. *smell*, i.e. take delight in Am 5$_{21}$.

מאס followed by inf. cstr. with privative מִן, *reject from (being, doing), so as not (to be, do)*, + היה *be* king 1 S 15$_{26}$, מלך *be king* 1 S 8$_{7}$ 15$_{23(Gnz)}$ (L מִמֶּלֶךְ *from [being] king*) 16$_{1}$, כהן pi. *be priest* Ho 4$_{6}$, לקח *take* Jr 33$_{26}$; inf. cstr. with לְ *refuse to*, + שׁית *place* Jb 30$_{1}$, בוא *enter* 1QS 2$_{25}$ 4QBer^{f} 1$_{7}$.

מאס with adverb, מָה *why?* Si 41$_{4}$.

Inf. abs. used with finite verb, Jr 14$_{19}$ Lm 5$_{22.22}$.

2. pass. **be rejected,** הם מאוסי אלוהי[ם] *they are rejected of*, i.e. by, *God* 4Q 476 1$_{5}$.

Also 4QD^{b} 8$_{6}$ ([המו]אס) 4QapPs^{a} 4$_{2}$ 4Q418 148.2$_{3}$ 4Q 423 13$_{3}$ 4QM^{h} 1$_{4}$.

<SYN> געל *abhor*, קוץ *loathe*, זנח *reject*, נאץ pi. *despise*, נטשׁ *forsake*, שׂנא *hate*, פרר hi. *break* covenant, נחם ni. *repent*.

<ANT> בחר *choose*, הלך *walk* in statutes, etc., עשׂה *do* ordinances, שׁמר *keep* statutes, חפץ *delight in*, ריח hi. *smell*, i.e. take delight in.

Ni. 3.6.1 Pf. Q נמאסתי; impf. Si ימאס, 3fs תִּמָּאֵס, 2ms Si תמאס; ptc. נִמְאָס—**be rejected, be despised, be reprobate,** <SUBJ> אִשָּׁה *wife* Is 54$_{6}$, נִין *offspring* Si 41$_{5(B, M)}$, בֵּן *son* Si 34$_{16.17}$ 41$_{5(Bmg)}$ (if em.; see below), בַּת *daughter* Si 42$_{9(M)}$ ([ת]מאס), חָכָם *wise one* Si 37$_{20}$, בזה ni. ptc. *contemptible one* Ps 15$_{4}$, כֶּסֶף *silver* Jr 6$_{30}$, appar. דִּבָּה *gossip* Si 41$_{5(Bmg)}$ (כן נמאס דבת ערים *so is the gossip of cities despised*; or em. כן to בן *son*), appar. worshipper 1QH 4$_{8}$ (נמאסתי; or em. נמאסו, with מַעֲשֶׂה *deed* as subj.); subj. not specified, Si 20$_{5}$. <PREP> לְ of agent, *by*, + עַם *people* 1QH 4$_{8}$; בְּ of place, *in*, + עַיִן *eye*, i.e. sight Ps 15$_{4}$; of accompaniment, *with, in*, + רִיב *strife* Si 20$_{5}$. <COLL> מאס ni. with adverb, כֵּן *so* Si 41$_{5}$ (Bmg) (or em.; see Subj.).

***Pi. accept, prefer** (i.e. privative pi.), מָאַסְתִּי מָוֶת מֵעַצְמוֹתָי *I prefer the death of my bones* Jb 7$_{16}$, אֶמְאַס וְנִחַמְתִּי עַל־עָפָר וָאֵפֶר *I accept and repent upon dust and ashes* Jb 42$_{6}$.

Pu. 0.0.1 Ptc. Q ממואסה—**be rejected,** <SUBJ> פִּנָּה *corner(-stone)* GnzPs 1$_{18}$.*

⇒ מָאוֹס *refuse*.

מאס II 5 vb. **flow, waste away,** perh. cower—**Qal** 3 Pf.

מָאַסְתִּי—**waste away,** perh. **cower,** <SUBJ> Y. Jb 36$_{5}$ (אֵל כַּבִּיר וְלֹא יִמְאָס *God is mighty and he does not cower;* unless מאס I *feel loathing*), Job Jb 7$_{16}$ (unless מאס I *despise life*) 42$_{6}$ (עַל־כֵּן אֶמְאַס *therefore I am wasting away;* unless מאס I *feel loathing*).

Ni. 2 Impf. יִמָּאֲסוּ; + waw וַיִּמָּאֵס—**flow (away), run,** <SUBJ> רָשָׁע *wicked one* Ps 58$_{8}$ (+ הלך htp. *go*), עוֹר *skin* Jb 7$_{5}$ (i.e. *discharge, fester;* or em. וַיִּמָּאֵס to וַיִּמַּס *and it melts;* + רגע *harden*). <PREP> כְּ *as,* + מַיִם *water* Ps 58$_{8}$.

⇒ cf. מסס *melt,* מסה *melt.*

*מאס III 1 vb. **discharge pus; fester,** <SUBJ> עוֹר *skin* Jb 7$_{5}$ (or em. וַיִּמָּאֵס to וַיִּמַּס *and it melts*).

*מאס IV 1 vb. **gape open,** <SUBJ> עוֹר *skin* Jb 7$_{5}$ (or em. וַיִּמָּאֵס to וַיִּמַּס *and it melts*).

*מאס V 2 vb. **err, transgress,** <SUBJ> Job Jb 7$_{16}$, רָשָׁע *wicked one* Ps 58$_{8}$ (unless מאס II *flow;* or em. וַיִּמַּס *and it melts*). <PREP> כְּ *as,* + מַיִם *water* Ps 58$_{8}$.

*[מַ֫אַס] 0.0.0.1 pr.n.[m.] **Maas, 1.** father of Hilkiah, <CSTR> בן מאס *son of Maas* Seal 150 (others מאפס *Meappes;* Lachish, 8th/7th cent.).

2. appar. father of Nathan, Seal 765 (7th cent.).

*[מַאֲסָף] 0.0.3 n.[m.] **gathering, 1. gathering** of troops in battle (1QM 3$_{2}$ 7$_{13}$ 1QM^{a} 1$_{14}$). **2. swarm,** as gathering, of locusts (Is 33$_{4}$ [if em.; see Prep.]). **3.** perh. **withdrawal** of troops from battle (cf. אסף §2 *remove;** 1QM 7$_{13}$). <CSTR> מַאֲסַף הֶחָסִיל *swarm of locusts* Is 33$_{4}$ (if em.; see Prep.); חצוצרות המאסף *trumpets of the gathering* (or *withdrawal*) 1QM 3$_{2}$ 7$_{13}$. <PREP> כְּ *as,* + אסף pu. *be gathered* Is 33$_{4}$ (if em. שְׁלַלְכֶם אֹסֶף *your booty, a swarm of* to שְׁלָל כְּמַאֲסַף *booty as a swarm of*). <COLL> המאסף מימין ומשמאול ובא[חור ובפנים] *the gathering on the right and on the left, and in the rear and in front* 1QM^{a} 1$_{14}$.

Also 4QM^{c} 1$_{12}$ ([המא]סף).

⇒ אסף *gather.*

מְאַסֵּף *rearguard,* see אסף *gather,* Pi. §3b.

[מַאֲפֶה] 1 n.[m.] **baked food**—cstr. מַאֲפֵה—<CSTR> מַאֲפֵה תַּנּוּר *something baked of,* i.e. in, *the oven* Lv 2$_{4}$. <APP> מִנְחָה *cereal offering* Lv 2$_{4}$.

⇒ אפה *bake.*

*[מַאֲפִילָה] adj. **waterless, becoming parched late in the season;** a land **late in bearing produce,** used attributively of אֶרֶץ *land* Jr 2$_{31}$ (if em. מַאְפֵּלְיָה *deep darkness*).

מַאֲפֵל 1 n.[m.] **darkness,** between Israelites and Egyptians, <OBJ> שׂים *place* Jos 24$_{7}$ (or em. אֹפֶל *darkness*).

⇒ cf. אֹפֶל *darkness,* מַאְפֵּלְיָה *deep darkness.*

*[מַאְפֵּלָה] 0.0.1 n.f. **darkness,** <OBJ> כון hi. *prepare* 4QJub^{a} 2$_{2}$ ([הכי]ן; + שַׁחַר *dawn*).

⇒ cf. אֹפֶל *darkness.*

מַאְפֵּלְיָה 1 n.f. **deep darkness,** <CSTR> אֶרֶץ מַאְפֵּלְיָה *land of deep darkness* Jr 2$_{31}$ (or em. מַאְפֵּלְיָה *darkness;* + מִדְבָּר *steppe*).*

⇒ מַאֲפֵל *darkness* + יָהּ *Yah.*

[מַאְפֵּלְיָה], see מַאְפֵּלְיָה *deep darkness.*

מְאַפֵּס *Meappes,** see מַאַס *Maas.*

מאר 4.0.4 vb. **be painful—Qal feel hatred,** <SUBJ> אוֹיֵב *enemy* Ps 71$_{10}$ (if em. אָמְרוּ *they say* to מָאֲרוּ);* subj. not specified, Ps 4$_{5}$ (if em. אִמְרוּ *say* to מְאָרוּ).* <PREP> לְ of direction, *to, towards* Ps 71$_{10}$ (if em.; see Subj.); בְּ of place, *in, within,* + לֵבָב *heart* Ps 4$_{5}$ (if em.; see Subj.).

Ni. 0.0.3 Ptc. Q נאמר, נאמרים—**be painful, be malignant,** <SUBJ> נֶגַע *plague* 1QH 5$_{28}$ (‖ אנשׁ pass. *be incurable*).

Also 4QsapHymnA 9$_{1}$ 4QHod^{b} 16$_{4}$.

<SYN> אנשׁ pass. *be incurable.*

Hi. 4.0.1 Ptc. מַמְאֶרֶת, מַמְאִיר—**1. cause pain,** <SUBJ> סִלּוֹן *brier* Ezk 28$_{24}$ (‖ כאב hi. *hurt*).

2. be malignant, <SUBJ> צָרַעַת *leprosy* Lv 13$_{51.52}$ 14$_{44}$ (all three Sam ממארת *obstinate,* i.e. מרא hi.) 4QD^{a}

6.15 (ה[צ]רעת]).

<SYN> §1 כאב hi. *hurt*.*

מַאְרָב 5.0.2 n.m. **ambush**—cstr. מַאְרַב—**1. (place of) ambush, lying in wait** (Jos 8:9 Jg 9:35 Ps 10:8). **2. (people waiting in) ambush, lying in wait** (2 C 13:13.13). **3. (act of) ambush, lying in wait** (1QM 3:2.8).

<SUBJ> בוא *come* 2 C 13:13. <NOM CL> הַמַּאְרָב מֵאַחֲרֵיהֶם *the ambush was behind them* 2 C 13:13. <OBJ> נתן *set* 2 C 20:22 (if em. מְאָרְבִים *those lying in wait* to מַאְרָבִים *ambushes*, i.e. distractions),* סבב hi. *turn round* 2 C 13:13. <CSTR> מַאְרַב הַחֲצֵרִים *ambush of*, i.e. in, *the villages* Ps 10:8 (or em. הַחֲצֵרִים to חֲצִרִים *of*, i.e. among, *the reeds*; + מִסְתָּר *hiding place*); חצוצרות המארב *trumpets of the ambush* 1QM 3:2.8. <PREP> בְּ of place, *in*, + ישׁב *sit* Ps 10:8; אֶל *to*, + הלך *go* Jos 8:9; מִן of direction, *from*, + קום *rise* Jg 9:35.*

⇨ ארב I *wait in ambush*.

מְאָרֵב, *one lying in wait*, see ערב Pi. *lie in wait*.

מְאֵרָה I 5 n.f. **curse**—cstr. מְאֵרַת; pl. מְאֵרוֹת—<NOM CL> מְאֵרַת י׳ בְּבֵית רָשָׁע *the curse of Y. is on the house of the wicked* Pr 3:33. <OBJ> שׁלח pi. *send* Dt 28:20 (unless מְאֵרָה II *starvation* or III *twitching (of limbs)*; || מְהוּמָה *discomfiture*, מִגְעֶרֶת *rebuke*) Ml 2:2. <CSTR> מְאֵרַת י׳ *curse of*, i.e. from, *Y.* Pr 3:33; רַב מְאֵרוֹת *(one) abounding of*, i.e. in, *curses* Pr 28:27 (Gnz רֹב *abundance of*). <PREP> בְּ of instrument, *by (means of), with*, + ארר ni. *be cursed* Ml 3:9.

<SYN> מְהוּמָה *discomfiture*, מִגְעֶרֶת *rebuke*.

⇨ ארר *curse*.

***מְאֵרָה** II 1 n.f. **starvation**, <OBJ> שׁלח pi. *send* Dt 28:20 (unless מְאֵרָה I *curse*; || מְהוּמָה *discomfiture*, מִגְעֶרֶת *rebuke*).

***מְאֵרָה** III 1 n.f. **twitching (of limbs)**, <OBJ> שׁלח pi. *send* Dt 28:20 (unless מְאֵרָה I *curse*; || מְהוּמָה *discomfiture*, מִגְעֶרֶת *rebuke*).

[מַאשׁ], see מאס I *reject*.

*** [מַאשׁ]** 0.0.0.2 pr.n.m. **Maash, 1.** Seal 279 (4th/3rd cent.). **2.** son of Manoah, scribe, <APP> בֵּן *son* Seal 345 (7th cent.), סֹפֵר *scribe* Seal 345 (7th cent.). <PREP> לְ of possession, *(belonging) to, of* Seal 345 (7th cent.).

*** [מְאַשֵּׁר]** n.[m.] **evergreen tree, cedar,** <NOM CL> וְתֹמְכֶיהָ מְאֻשָּׁר *and (she is) a cedar (to) those who hold her fast* Pr 3:18 (if em. מְאֻשָּׁר *one who is pronounced happy* to מְאַשֵּׁר).

⇨ cf. תְּאַשּׁוּר *box-tree*.

מְאֻשָּׁר, *one who is led*, see אשׁר pu. *go forward*.

*** [מַאֲשֶׁר]** n.m. **that which,** <SUBJ> בוא *come* Is 47:13 (if em. מֵאֲשֶׁר *from which* to מַאֲשֶׁר).

⇨ אֲשֶׁר *which*.

*** [מְאַת]** adv. **a hundred times,** with preceding verb שׁאל *ask* Ps 27:4 (if em. מֵאֵת *from* to מְאַת).

⇨ מאה pi. *repeat a hundred times*.

מֵאֵת, see מִן *from*, אֵת *with*.

מבא, see מָבוֹא entrance.

[מִבְדָּלָה] 1 n.f. **enclave**—pl. מִבְדָּלוֹת—<APP> עִיר *city* Jos 16:9 (or em. הַמֻּבְדָּלוֹת or הַמְּבְדָּלוֹת *separated*, i.e. ho. ptc.; or em. הַנִּבְדָּלוֹת, i.e. ni. ptc., in same sense).

⇨ בדל *be separate*.

מָבוֹא 25.2.15 n.m. **entrance**—Q מבואי; cstr. מְבוֹא (Q מבא); sf. Kt מבואך, מְבוֹאוֹ (מְבֹאוֹ); pl. cstr. מְבוֹאֵי, מְבוֹאֹת; sf. mss מְבוֹאָיו, Si, Q מבואיה, מבואיהם—**1. entrance, entryway** of city (Jg 1:24.25 Pr 8:3 1 C 4:39), of building (2 K 11:16||2 C 23:15 2 K 16:18 Jr 38:14 Ezk 42:9 43:11[mss[46:19 1 C 9:19 2 C 23:13 Si 42:11 3QTr 11:16), of the sea, i.e. harbour (Ezk 27:3), of wisdom (Si 14:22 11QPs[a] 18:6), <NOM CL> מָבוֹא הַשְּׁלִישִׁי אֲשֶׁר בְּבֵית י׳ *the third entrance that is in the house of Y.* Jr 38:14, בַּמָּבוֹא אֲשֶׁר עַל־כֶּתֶף הַשַּׁעַר *through the entrance that was at the side of the gate* Ezk 46:19, המבוא מֵהַקָּדִים *the entrance was from the east* Ezk 42:9(Kt) (Qr הַמֵּבִיא *the one bringing in*). <OBJ> ראה

hi. *show* Jg $1_{24.25}$, ידע hi. *make known* Ezk $43_{11(mss)}$ (L מוֹבָא *entrance*; :: מוֹצָא *exit*), רצד pi. *watch* Si 14_{22}, נבט hi. *overlook* Si 42_{11}, סבב hi. *turn round* 2 K 16_{18}.

<CSTR> מבא די[רת] *entrance of the lodge of* 3QTr 11_{16}, מְבוֹא הָעִיר *entrance of the city* Jg $1_{24.25}$, גְּדֹר *of Gedor* 1 C 4_{39}, פְּתָחִים *of the portals* Pr 8_3 (+ שַׁעַר *gate*), הַמֶּלֶךְ *of*, i.e. for, *the king* 2 K 11_{16}, הַסּוּסִים *of the horses* 2 K 11_{16}||2 C 23_{15}, מְבוֹאֹת יָם *entrance(s) of*, i.e. to, *the sea* Ezk 27_3; שֹׁמְרֵי הַמָּבוֹא *keepers of the entrance* 1 C 9_{19}, דֶּרֶךְ־מְבוֹא *way of the entrance of* 2 K 11_{16}||2 C 23_{15}, אולמי מבואיהם *vestibules of their entrances* 4QShirShab^{f} 14.1_4, כל מבואיה *all her* (wisdom's) *entrances* Si 14_{22}. <ADJ> חִיצוֹן *outer* 2 K 11_{16}, שְׁלִישִׁי *third* Jr 38_{14}. <PREP> לְ of direction, *to*, + הלך *go* 1 C 4_{39}; בְּ of place, *in, at, through* 3QTr 11_{16} perh. 4Q525 15_5, + עמד *stand* 2 C 23_{13}, בוא hi. *bring* Ezk 46_{19}; מִן of direction, *from*, + נדח ni. *wander* 11QPs^{a} 18_6 (|| פֶּתַח *portal*); אֶל *to*, + בוא *go in* 2 C 23_{15}, לקח *take* Jr 38_{14}; עַל *at*, + ישׁב *dwell* Ezk 27_3; מָבוֹא without preposition, *at the entrance*, + רנן *shout* Pr 8_3.

2. entering, (act of) entry, sometimes perh. **those who enter,** temple (Ezk 44_5), city by force (Ezk 26_{10} 1QH 6_{28}); entry of gods (4QShirShab^{f} 23.$1_{8.9.10}$), king (4QShirShab^{f} 14.1_5), **coming in** (in phrase 'going out and coming in', referring to one's activity as a whole 2 S $3_{25[Kt]}$), **coming (together)** of people (Ezk 33_{31}), **coming, arrival** of light (1QH 12_4), day (1QH 12_7), day and night (1QM 14_{13} [מ[בו]א] 1QS 10_{10}), seasons (1QS 10_3), years (4Q418 123.2_2).

<NOM CL> אין מבוא *there is no entry* 1QH 6_{28}. <OBJ> ידע *know* 2 S $3_{25(Kt)}$ (Qr מוֹבָא *coming in*; :: מוֹצָא *going out*). <CSTR> מבואי אלי *entry of the gods of* 4QShirShab^{f} 23.1_8, מלך *of the king* 4QShirShab^{f} 14.1_5, מְבוֹא־עָם *coming of people* Ezk 33_{31}, מְבוֹא הַבַּיִת *entering of*, i.e. into, *the house* Ezk 44_5 (+ מוֹצָא *going out*), מְבוֹאֵי עִיר *entering of*, i.e. into, breached *city* Ezk 26_{10} (or em. מְבוֹא sing.), מבוא אור *arrival of light* 1QH 12_4 (:: מוֹצָא), יומם *of day* 1QH 12_7 (:: מוֹצָא), יומם ולילה *of day and night* 1QM 14_{13} (מ[בו]א), יום ולילה *of day and night* 1QS 10_{10} (:: מוֹצָא), מועדים *of the seasons* 1QS 10_3, שנים *of years* 4Q418 123.2_2 (:: מוֹצָא); אולמי מבואי *vestibules of the entry of* 4QShirShab^{f} 14.1_5 11QShirShab 4_4 (מבו[אי]), פתחי מבואי *portals of entry* 4QShirShab^{f} 23.1_9 (:: מוֹצָא) 11QShirShab 10_7.

<PREP> לְ *at* 4Q418 123.2_2, + אסף ni. *be brought in* 1QH 12_7; בְּ of time, *in, at, during* perh 4QShirShab^{c} 1_1 (במבו[או]) 4QShirShab^{f} 23.1_8 (:: מוֹצָא *going out*), + אסף ni. *be brought in* 1QS 10_3, הלל pi. *praise* 23.1_{10} (:: מוֹצָא); כְּ *as*, + בוא *go in* Ezk 26_{10} 33_{31}; עִם *with*, i.e. at 1QM 14_{13} (מ[בו]א), + בוא *come* 1QS 10_{10}, חנן htp. *make supplication* 1QH 12_4.

3. as cstr. with שֶׁמֶשׁ or with sf. in ref. to שֶׁמֶשׁ, **going in, setting** of sun, **the west,** <OBJ> ידע *know* Ps 104_{19}. <CSTR> מְבוֹא הַשֶּׁמֶשׁ *setting of the sun* Dt 11_{30} Jos 1_4 (הַשָּׁמֶשׁ) 23_4 Zc 8_7 (both הַשֶּׁמֶשׁ); דֶּרֶךְ מְבוֹא *way of the setting of* Dt 11_{30}, אֶרֶץ *land of* Zc 8_7 (+ מִזְרָח *east*). <PREP> עַד *to* Ml 1_{11} Ps 50_1, הלל pu. *be praised* Ps 113_3; מְבוֹא הַשֶּׁמֶשׁ, etc. without preposition, *to the setting of the sun, in the west* Jos 1_4 23_4. <COLL> מִמִּזְרַח־שֶׁמֶשׁ (וְ)עַד־מְבוֹאוֹ *from the rising of the sun to its setting* Ml 1_{11} Ps 50_1 113_3.

<SYN> §1 פֶּתַח *portal*.

<ANT> §1, 2 מוֹצָא *exit, going out*.

⇒ בוא *come*.

מְבוּכָה 2 n.f. **confusion**—sf. מְבוּכָתָם—<SUBJ> היה *be* Mc 7_4. <CSTR> יוֹם מְהוּמָה וּמְבוּסָה וּמְבוּכָה *day of discomfiture and trampling and confusion* Is 22_5 (מְבוּכָה lacking in mss).

<SYN> מְהוּמָה *discomfiture*, מְבוּסָה *trampling*.

⇒ בוך *be disturbed*.

מַבּוּל 13.1.7 n.m. **flood,** in time of Noah; heavenly **flood,** i.e. water above the firmament (Ps 29_{10}); **flood** of fire* (Jb 18_{15}; if em.; see Subj.); **flood** of anger (Jb 20_{23}; if em.; see Obj.), <SUBJ> היה *be* Gn $7_{6.17}$ 9_{11} 4QParGenEx 2_{11}, שׁכן *dwell* Jb 18_{15} (if em. מִבְּלִי־לוֹ *without to him* to מַבּוּל), שׁחת pi. *destroy* Gn 6_{17} $9_{11.15}$ 4QParGenEx 2_{11}, חדל *cease* Si 44_{17}. <OBJ> בוא hi. *bring* Gn 6_{17}, מטר hi. *cause to rain* Jb 20_{23} (if em. עָלֵימוֹ בִּלְחוּמוֹ *upon him, on his flesh* to עָלָיו מַבּוּל חֲמָתוֹ *upon him the flood of his anger*). <CSTR> מַבּוּל חֲמָתוֹ *flood of his anger* Jb 20_{23} (if em.; see Obj.); מֵי הַמַּבּוּל *waters of the flood* Gn $7_{7.10}$ 9_{11} 4QCommGenA $1_{3.3}$ (both מבול) 4QAdmon 1_8 4Q

ParGenEx 2₄. <APP> מַיִם *water* Gn 6₁₇. <PREP> לְ introducing predicate, + היה *be* Gn 9₁₅; *upon, over,* + ישׁב *sit* Ps 29₁₀ (perh. *from before*); * בְּ of instrument, *by (means of), with,* + אבד pi. *destroy* 4QAdmon 1₅; אַחַר *after,* + חיה *live* Gn 9₂₈, ילד ni. *be born* Gn 10₁, hi. *beget* Gn 11₁₀, פרד ni. *be separated* Gn 10₃₂.

Also 4QDéluge 4₁.*

⇒ יָבָל *stream, flood.*

מְבוֹנִים, see בין *understand,* Hi.

מְבוּסָה ₃ n.f. **trampling, subjugation,** <CSTR> יוֹם מְהוּמָה וּמְבוּסָה וּמְבוּכָה *day of discomfiture and trampling and confusion* Is 22₅, גּוֹי קַו־קָו וּמְבוּסָה *nation of line (upon) line,* or *of kav-kav,* perh. idle chatter, *and of subjugation* Is 18₂.₇.

<SYN> מְהוּמָה *discomfiture,* מְבוּכָה *confusion,* קַו־קָו *line upon line.*

⇒ בוס *trample.*

מַבּוּעַ ₃.₀.₃ n.[m.] **spring**—pl. cstr. מַבּוּעֵי—**spring, (public) fountain,** <OBJ> שׂים *place* 1QH 8₁₆ (+ גֶּשֶׁם *rain*). <CSTR> מבוע מים *spring of water* 1QH 8₄ (|| מָקוֹר *source*) 8₁₆ (מים חיים *of living water*), מַבּוּעֵי מַיִם *springs of water* Is 35₇ (מַיִם; || אֲגַם *pool;* :: צִמָּאוֹן *thirsty ground*) 49₁₀; פי המבוע *mouth of the spring* 3QTr 12₆. <PREP> לְ as or introducing predicate, + היה *be* Is 35₇; בְּ of place, *at, by,* + נתן *give,* i.e. place 1QH 8₄; עַל *beside,* + נהל pi. *lead* Is 49₁₀, שׁבר ni. *be broken* Ec 12₆ (|| בּוֹר *cistern*). <COLL> מבוע מים בארץ ציה *a spring of water in a dry land* 1QH 8₄, המבוע של בית שם *the spring of Beth-sham* 3QTr 12₆.

<SYN> מָקוֹר *source,* אֲגַם *pool,* בּוֹר *cistern.*

<ANT> צִמָּאוֹן *thirsty ground.*

⇒ נבע I *gush.*

מְבוּקָה ₁ n.f. **void, devastation,** <COLL> בּוּקָה מְבוּקָה וּמְבֻלָּקָה *(there will be only) emptiness, void, and devastation* Na 2₁₁.

<SYN> בּוּקָה *emptiness,* בלק pu. ptc. *devastation.*

⇒ cf. בּוּקָה *emptiness.*

[מְבוּשִׁים] ₁ n.[m.]pl. **genitals**—sf. מְבֻשָׁיו—of a man, <PREP> בְּ introducing object, + חזק hi. *take hold of* Dt 25₁₁ (Sam בִּבְשָׂרוֹ *his flesh,* i.e. genitals).

⇒ בושׁ I *be ashamed.*

מִבְחוֹר ₂ n.m. **choice**—cstr. מִבְחוֹר—**choice, choicest (one),** <OBJ> כרת *cut down* 2 K 19₂₃. <CSTR> מִבְחוֹר בְּרֹשָׁיו *choicest of his junipers* 2 K 19₂₃ (mss and ||Is 37₂₄ מִבְחַר *choicest of*); עִיר מִבְחוֹר *city of choice,* i.e. choice city 2 K 3₁₉ (lacking in ms; + עִיר מִבְצָר *fortified city*). <APP> קוֹמָה *height,* i.e. highest 2 K 19₂₃.

⇒ בחר I *choose.*

[מִבְחָר] I ₁₄ n.m. **choice**—cstr. מִבְחַר; pl. sf. מִבְחָרָיו—**choice, choicest (one[s]),** <SUBJ> היה *be* Is 22₇, מלא *be full* Is 22₇, נחם ni. *be comforted* Ezk 31₁₆, ירד *go down* Jr 48₁₅, טבע pu. *be drowned* Ex 15₄, נפל *fall* Ezk 17₂₁₍ₘₛₛ₎. <NOM CL> מִבְחַר בְּנֵי אַשּׁוּר כֻּלָּם *all of them were choicest of the Assyrians* Ezk 23₇. <OBJ> כרת *cut down* 2 K 19₂₃₍ₘₛₛ₎||Is 37₁₄ Jr 22₇, מלא pi. *fill with* Ezk 24₄, בוא hi. *bring* Dt 12₁₁, לקח *take* Ezk 24₅ (or em. מִבְחַר to מִמִּבְחַר *some of the choicest of*).

<CSTR> מִבְחַר בְּנֵי אַשּׁוּר *choicest of the Assyrians* Ezk 23₇, שָׁלִשָׁיו *of his officers* Ex 15₄, בַּחוּרָיו *of his young men* Jr 48₁₅, עֲצָמִים *of the bones* Ezk 24₄, הַצֹּאן *of the flock* Ezk 24₅, אֲרָזֶיךָ *of your cedars* Jr 22₇, בְּרֹשָׁיו *of his junipers* 2 K 19₂₃₍ₘₛₛ₎||Is 37₂₄ (2 K 19₂₃ L מִבְחוֹר *choicest of*), עֲמָקַיִךְ־ *of your valleys* Is 22₇, קְבָרֵינוּ *of our sepulchres* Gn 23₆, נִדְרֵיכֶם *of your votive offerings* Dt 12₁₁, מִבְחַר וְטוֹב־לְבָנוֹן *the choicest and best of the Lebanon* Ezk 31₁₆; עַם מִבְחָרָיו *people of his choice ones,* i.e. his choice people (troops) Dn 11₁₅ (or em. בַּחֻרָיו *his young men*), כֹּל מִבְחַר *all the choicest ones of* Dt 12₁₁, כָּל־מִבְחָרָיו *all his choice ones* (troops) Ezk 17₂₁₍ₘₛₛ₎ (L [Qr] מִבְרָחָיו *his fugitives*). <APP> קוֹמָה *height,* i.e. highest 2 K 19₂₃₍ₘₛₛ₎||Is 37₁₄, עֵץ *tree* Ezk 31₁₆. <PREP> בְּ of place, *in,* + קבר *bury* Gn 23₆; מִן partitive, *(some) of, from (among),* + לקח *take* Ezk 24₅ (if em.; see Obj.). <COLL> מִבְחַר || טוֹב *good,* i.e. best (one) Ezk 31₁₆; + טוֹב *good* Ezk 24₅.

<SYN> טוֹב *good,* i.e. best (one).

⇒ בחר I *choose.*

מִבְחָר II 1 pr.n.m. **Mibhar,** one of David's warriors, son of Hagri, <NOM CL> גִּבּוֹרֵי הַחֲיָלִים ... מִבְחָר *the mighty ones of the armies were ... Mibhar* 1 C 11_{38}. <APP> בֶּן *son* 1 C 11_{38}.

⇨ בחר I *choose.*

[מַבָּט] 3 n.m. **hope**—sf. מַבָּטָם, מַבָּטֵנוּ, מֶבָּטָהּ—**(object of) hope, expectation,** of Ethiopia as hope of Judah (Is $20_{5.6}$), of Tyre as hope of Ekron (Zc 9_5), as hope of ships of Tarshish (Is 23_1 [if em.; see Subj.]), <SUBJ> בוש hi. *be put to shame* Zc 9_5 (or em. מִבְטָחָהּ *her confidence*), שׁדד pu. *be devastated* Is 23_1 (if em. מִבַּיִת *without a house* to מַבַּטְכֶם *your hope*). <NOM CL> כֹּה מַבָּטֵנוּ אֲשֶׁר־נַסְנוּ שָׁם לְעֶזְרָה *thus is our hope to which we fled for help* Is 20_6. <APP> כּוּשׁ *Ethiopia* Is 20_5 (1QIsa[a] מבטחם *their confidence;* || תִּפְאָרָה *glorying*). <PREP> מִן of cause, *on account of,* + בוש *be ashamed* Is 20_5.

<SYN> תִּפְאָרָה *glorying.**

⇨ נבט *look.*

[מִבְטָא] 2 n.[m.] **impetuous utterance**—cstr. מִבְטָא —<NOM CL> עָלֶיהָ ... מִבְטָא שְׂפָתֶיהָ *upon her is ... the impetuous utterance of her lips* Nm 30_7. <OBJ> אסר *bind,* i.e. vow Nm $30_{7.9}$ (both + נֶדֶר *vow*), פרר hi. *annul* Nm 30_9. <CSTR> מִבְטָא שְׂפָתֶיהָ *impetuous utterance of her lips* Nm $30_{7.9}$.

⇨ בטא *speak impetuously.*

מִבְטָח 16.0.3 n.m. **trust**—cstr. מִבְטַח (מִבְטָח); sf. מִבְטַחִי, מִבְטָחֵךְ, מִבְטַחוֹ (mss מִבְטָחוֹ), מִבְטֶחָהּ (Gnz מִבְטָחָהּ), מִבְטֶחָם; pl. מִבְטַחִים; sf. מִבְטָחַיִךְ—**trust, confidence, security,** usu. of object of trust; also of placing of trust (Pr 21_{22} 22_{19} 25_{19} 11QPs[a] 24_{14}), <SUBJ> היה *be* Jr 17_7 Pr 22_{19}, ענה *answer* Ps 65_6. <NOM CL> בֵּית עַכָּבִישׁ מִבְטַחוֹ *his trust is a spider's web* Jb 8_{14} (+ כֶּסֶל *confidence*), אַתָּה ... מִבְטַחִי מִנְּעוּרָי *you are ... my trust from my youth* Ps 71_5, שֵׁן רֹעָה וְרֶגֶל מוּעֶדֶת מִבְטָח בּוֹגֵד *(as) a broken tooth or a foot that slips is trust in a traitor* Pr 25_{19} (or del.), בְּיִרְאַת י׳ מִבְטַח־עֹז *in the fear of Y. is confidence of strength,* i.e. strong confidence Pr 14_{26} (+ מַחְסֶה *refuge*), מבטחי י׳ לפנ[י]כה *my trust, O Y., is before you* 11QPs[a] 24_{14}, [אלוהי] מבטח [אבטח] בו *my God is the security in which I trust* 11QPsAp[a] 6_4. <OBJ> שׂים *place Y. as* Ps 40_5.

<CSTR> מִבְטַח בּוֹגֵד *trust of,* i.e. in, *a treacherous one* Pr 25_{19} (or del.), מִבְטַח־עֹז *confidence of strength,* i.e. strong confidence Pr 14_{26} (or em. עֹז to עַז *of a strong one*), מִבְטָח כָּל־קַצְוֵי־אֶרֶץ וְיָם *trust of all the ends of the earth and of the sea* Ps 65_6 (or em. וְיָם to וְאִיִּם *and of the isles*); עֹז מִבְטֶחָהּ *strength of its trust,* i.e. in which it (city) trusts Pr 21_{22} (Gnz מִבְטָחָהּ), מִשְׁכְּנוֹת מִבְטַחִים *dwellings of security,* i.e. secure dwellings Is 32_{18} (|| שָׁלוֹם *peace,* + שַׁאֲנָן *at ease*). <APP> אֱלֹהִים *God* Ps 65_6, בֵּית אֵל *Bethel* Jr 48_{13}, כּוּשׁ *Ethiopia* Is 20_5(1QIsa[a]) (MT מַבָּטָם *their hope*), אֹהֶל *tent* Jb 18_{14}, תִּקְוָה *hope* Ps 71_5. <PREP> לְ *as* or introducing predicate, + היה *be* Ezk 29_{16}; בְּ *in,* + בטח *trust* 11QPsAp[a] 6_4 ([אבטח]); introducing object, + מאס *reject* Jr 2_{37}; מִן of direction. *from,* + נתק ni. *be torn* Jb 18_{14}; of cause, *on account of,* + בוש *be ashamed* Is 20_5(1QIsa[a]) Jr 48_{13}, ישׁב *dwell* (corrected to שׁכב *lie down*) 4QapPs[b] 48_5. <COLL> לַכֶּתֶם אָמַרְתִּי מִבְטַחִי *I said to gold, (You are) my trust* Jb 31_{24} (|| כֶּסֶל *confidence*).

<SYN> שָׁלוֹם *peace,* כֶּסֶל *confidence.*

⇨ בטח I *trust;* cf. מִבְטַחְיָהוּ *Mibtahiah.*

***[מִבְטָחָה]** 0.0.1 n.f. **confidence**—pl. Q מבטחות— <ADJ> גָּדוֹל *great* GnzPs 4_2. <PREP> לְ *into,* + *turn* trembling and shaking GnzPs 4_2.

⇨ בטח I *trust.*

***[מִבְטַחְיָהוּ]** 0.0.0.3 pr.n.m. **Mibtahiah, 1.** son of Jeremiah, <APP> בֶּן *son* Lachish ost. 14.

2. royal official, <APP> עֶבֶד *servant* of the king Bulla 924, אֲשֶׁר *who is* over the house Bulla D 6. <PREP> לְ of possession, *of, (belonging) to* Bulla 924.

⇨ מִבְטָח *trust* + י׳ *Y.*

מֵבִין *one who understands, expert,* see בין Hi. *understand.*

***[מְבִינָה]** 0.2 n.f. **understanding**—sf. Q מבינתו; pl. Q מבינות—<CSTR> [יצר] מבינתו *inclination of his understanding* 4Q417 2.1_{11}, כושר מבינות *propriety of understanding* 4Q417 2.1_{11}. <PREP> לְ introducing object, + פרשׂ *spread* 4Q417 2.1_{10} ([פ]רשׂ למ[ב]ינתם).

Also 4Q417 29.1$_7$.
⇒ בין *understand*.

*[מַבָּךְ] n.[m.] **source (of waters), fountain,** <OBJ> חבשׁ pi. *bind* Jb 28$_{11}$ (if em.; see Cstr.), בכה *weep* Is 16$_9$ Jr 48$_{32}$ (both if em.; see Cstr.). <CSTR> מַבְּכֵי נְהָרוֹת *sources of the rivers* Jb 28$_{11}$ (if em. מִבְּכִי *without trickling*), מַבְּכֵי יַעְזֵר *fountains of Jazer* Is 16$_9$ (if em. בִּבְכִי יַעְזֵר *with the weeping of Jazer*; or em. עַל־כֵּן אֶבְכֶּה מַבַּךְ יַעְזֵר *therefore I weep, O fountain of Jazer*) Jr 48$_{32}$ (if em. מִבְּכִי יַעְזֵר *(more) than the weeping of Jazer*).
⇒ cf. נֵבֶךְ *spring*; נְבוֹךְ *spring*.

*[מָבָל] pr.n.[m.] **Mabal,** Lachish ost. 19 (others מכל *Michal* or עמדל *Amdal*).

*[מַבֵּל] n.f. **fire,** <SUBJ> שׁכן *dwell* Jb 18$_{15}$ (if em. מִבְּלִי־לוֹ *without to him* to גָּפְרִית||מַבֵּל *brimstone*; perh. em. תִּשְׁכּוֹן to תָּשְׁכַּן pu. *be set*). <OBJ> מטר hi. *cause to rain* Jb 20$_{23}$ (if em. עָלֵימוֹ בִּלְחוּמוֹ *upon him, on his flesh* to עָלָיו מַבֵּל חֲמָתוֹ *upon him the fire of his anger*).* <CSTR> מַבֵּל חֲמָתוֹ *fire of his anger* Jb 20$_{23}$ (if em.; see Obj.).

*[מַבְלָגָה] 0.0.1 n.f. **cunning simile**—pl. Q מבלגות—**cunning simile,** <OBJ> חתף *snatch away* 4QHod[c] 1.3$_{10}$. <CSTR> מבלגות פתנים *cunning similes of serpents* 4QHod[c] 1.3$_{10}$.
⇒ (?) בלג I *shine*.

[מַבְלִיגִית] 1 n.f. **cheerfulness**—sf. מַבְלִיגִיתִי—<NOM CL> מַבְלִיגִיתִי עָלַי יָגוֹן appar. *my cheerfulness is upon grief* Jr 8$_{18}$ (or em. מִבְּלִי גְהֹת עָלָה יָגוֹן *grief without healing has gone up*).
⇒ בלג I *shine*.

*[מַבְלֵל] n.f. **mixed herbs** for use in exorcism, <SUBJ> שׁכן *abide* Jb 18$_{15}$ (if em. מִבְּלִי־לוֹ *without to him* to גָּפְרִית||מַבְלֵל *brimstone*; or מַבְלִיל or מַבְלוֹל or מַבְלוּל).
⇒ בלל *mix*.

מְבַלֵּעַ *devourer*, see בלע I Pi. *swallow*.

מְבֻלָּקָה *devastation*, see בלק *devastate*.

*[מָבָן] 0.0.0.1 pr.n.[m.] **Maban,** <PREP> לְ of possession, *of, (belonging) to* Seal 206 (Shechem, 7th cent.).

[מִבְנֶה] 1.0.3 n.m. **structure**—cstr. מִבְנֵה (Q מבני)—<NOM CL> אני ... מבנה החטאה *I am ... a structure of sin* 1QH 1$_{22}$ (|| כּוּר *smelting pot*, + מְגֻבָּל *thing kneaded*, יֵצֶר *formation*, סוד *foundation*, מָקוֹר *source*), הוא מבנה עפר *he is a structure of dust* 1QS 13$_{15}$ (|| מְגֻבָּל). <CSTR> מִבְנֵה־עִיר *structure of a city* Ezk 40$_2$, מבנה החטאה *structure of sin* 1QH 1$_{22}$, עפר *of dust* 1QS 13$_{15}$, מבני צדק *structure(s) of righteousness* 4QBer[a] 1.2$_7$ (|| מָכוֹן *established place*). <PREP> כְּ *as* Ezk 40$_2$.
<SYN> כּוּר *smelting pot*, מְגֻבָּל *thing kneaded*, מָכוֹן *established place*.
⇒ בנה I *build*.

מְבֻנַּי 1 pr.n.m. **Mebunnai,** one of David's warriors, <APP> חֻשָׁתִי *Hushathite* 2 S 23$_{27}$ (or em. סִבְּכַי *Sibbecai* with ||1 C 11$_{29}$).

*[מַבְנִית] I 0.0.11 n.f. **structure**—cstr. Q מבנית; sf. Q מבניתי, Q מבניתו, Q מבניתה, Q מבניתם; pl. cstr. Q מבניתי—**structure, building** of the earth (4QBer[a] 5$_4$), heavenly sanctuary (4QShirShabb[d] 1.14$_1$ 4QShirShabb[f] 14.1$_6$ 11QShirShabb 10$_8$), community (1QS 11$_8$), person, i.e. **body** (Jb 20$_3$ [if em.; see Cstr.] 1QH 7$_{4.9}$), <NOM CL> מעפר מבניתם *their structure is of dust* 4QMyst[a] 6.1$_{13}$. <OBJ> כון hi. *establish* 1QH 7$_9$ (+ אֹשׁ *foundation*), ידה hi. *praise* 4QShirShabb[d] 1.14$_4$ (להוד[ות] ... כו[ו]ל [מבנ]יתו).
<CSTR> מבנית קודש *structure of holiness* 1QS 11$_8$, [מקדש] *of the sanctuary of* holiness 4QShirShabb[f] 14.1$_6$, מבניתי חוק *structures of statute* 4QPrayer[d] 1.1$_2$; סוד מבנית *foundation of a structure of* 1QS 11$_8$, רוּחַ מַבְנִיתִי *spirit of my body* Jb 20$_3$ (if em. מִבִּינָתִי *from my understanding*), אושי מבניתי *foundations of my structure* 1QH 7$_4$, מבניתה *of its structure* 4QBer[a] 5$_4$, פנות מבניתו *corners of its structure* 4QShirShabb[d] 1.14$_1$ 11Q ShirShabb 10$_8$ ([פנ]ות), כו[ו]ל [מבנ]יתו *all its structure* 4QShirShabb[d] 1.14$_4$. <PREP> בְּ perh. of instrument, *by*

(*means of*), *with* 4QPrayer[d] 1.1$_{2}$; כְּ *as* 1QH fr. 47$_{5}$. Also 4QShir[b] 111$_{8}$ 11QShirShabb 1$_{5}$ ([מבני[ת).
⇒ בנה I *build*.

*[מַבְנִית] II n.f. **likeness**, <CSTR> מַבְנִית עֲצַבִּים *likeness of idols* Ho 13$_{2}$ (if em.; see Prep.). <PREP> כְּ *according to*, + עשׂה *make* Ho 13$_{2}$ (if em. כִּתְבוּנָם *according to their understanding* to כְּמַבְנִית *according to the likeness*).

*[מַבָּע] 0.0.2 n.[m.] **flow**—cstr. Q מבע; pl. cstr. Q מבעי—**flow** of breath, **utterance**, <OBJ> שׂים *place* 1QH 1$_{29}$ (+ דָּבָר *word*), יצא hi. *bring out* 1QH 1$_{29}$ (+ קַו perh. *sound*). <CSTR> מבע רוח *flow of breath of* lips 1QH 1$_{29}$, מבעי רוחות *flows of breath*, or perh. *utterances of the spirits* 1QH 1$_{29}$.
⇒ נבע *flow*.

*[מַבְעֵרָה] n.[f.] **burning**, <PREP> לְ of purpose, *for (the purpose of)*, + נתן *give* Jr 8$_{13}$ (if em. וָאֶתֵּן לָהֶם יַעַבְרוּם *and I gave them (permission) to pass them* to וְאֶתְּנֵם לְמַבְעֵרָה).
⇒ בער *burn*.

מִבְצָר I 37.1.4 n.m.&f. **fortification**—cstr. מִבְצַר; pl. מִבְצָרִים, מִבְצָרוֹת; cstr. מִבְצְרֵי; sf. מִבְצָרֶיךָ, מִבְצָרַיִךְ, מִבְצְרֵיהֶם, מִבְצָרֶיהָ, מִבְצָרָיו, (מִבְצָרֵיִךְ)—**fortification, fortress, stronghold**, <SUBJ> שׁבת ni. *cease* Is 17$_{3}$, שׁדד ho. *be devastated* Ho 10$_{14}$.

<NOM CL> כָּל־מִבְצָרַיִךְ תְּאֵנִים עִם־בִּכּוּרִים *all your fortresses are fig trees with first fruits* Na 3$_{12}$.

<OBJ> נתן *give*, i.e. make into Jr 6$_{27}$ (or em.; see App.), שׂים *place*, i.e. make, (into) a ruin Ps 89$_{41}$, חזק pi. *strengthen* Na 3$_{14}$, לכד *capture* Hb 1$_{10}$, שׁלח pi. *send*, i.e. set, on fire 2 K 8$_{12}$, שׁחח hi. *lay low* Is 25$_{12}$ (or del.), נפל hi. *cause to fall* Is 25$_{12}$ (or del.), נגע hi. *cause to reach* the ground Is 25$_{12}$ (or del.) Lm 2$_{2}$, הרס *tear down* Mc 5$_{10}$ Lm 2$_{2}$, שׁחת pi. *destroy* Jr 48$_{18}$ Lm 2$_{5}$, קנה *acquire* Si 36$_{29(B)}$.

<CSTR> מִבְצַר־צֹר *fortification of Tyre* Jos 19$_{29}$ 2 S 24$_{7}$, מִבְצַר מִשְׂגַּב *fortification of the refuge of* your walls Is 25$_{12}$ (or del. מִבְצַר), מִבְצְרֵי מָעֻזִּים *strongholds of fortification*, i.e. fortified strongholds Dn 11$_{39}$, בַּת *of the daughter of* Judah Lm 2$_{2}$, מבצרי העמים *fortifications of the peoples* 1QpHab 4$_{6}$.

עִיר מִבְצָר *city of fortification*, i.e. fortified city 1 S 6$_{18}$ 2 K 3$_{19}$ 10$_{2}$ 17$_{9}$ 18$_{8}$ Jr 1$_{18}$ Ps 108$_{11}$ (mss מָצוֹר *of fortification*) Si 36$_{29(Bmg, C, D)}$ 1QH 3$_{7}$, עָרֵי *cities of* Nm 32$_{17}$ (הַמִּבְצָר) 32$_{36}$ Jos 10$_{20}$ 19$_{35}$ 2 K 10$_{2(mss)}$ Jr 4$_{5}$ 8$_{14}$ (both הַמִּבְצָר) 34$_{7}$ 2 C 17$_{19}$ (הַמִּבְצָר), מִבְצָרֶיךָ *of your fortifications*, i.e. your fortified cities Jr 5$_{17}$, עִיר מִבְצַר *city of the fortification of*, i.e. fortified city of Jos 19$_{29}$, עִיר מִבְצָרוֹת *city of fortifications*, i.e. well-fortified city Dn 11$_{15}$, ערי מבצרים *cities of fortifications*, i.e. well-fortified cities 2QapDavid 1.1$_{3}$, כָּל־מִבְצָר *every fortress* Hb 1$_{10}$, כָּל־מִבְצָרֶיךָ *all your fortresses* Ho 10$_{14}$ Mc 5$_{10}$, כָּל־מִבְצָרַיִךְ *all your* (fem.) *fortresses* Na 3$_{12}$.

<APP> בָּחוֹן *assayer* or *watchtower* Jr 6$_{27}$ (or em. מִבְצָר to מְבַצֵּר *assayer* or מִבְצָרוֹ *its testing*, i.e. inf. of בצר II *test* or del.), אִשָּׁה *wife* Si 36$_{29(B)}$, רֵאשִׁית *first (one)* Si 36$_{29(B)}$.

<PREP> לְ *at*, + שׂחק *laugh* Hb 1$_{10}$; *against*, + עשׂה *act* Dn 11$_{39}$.

בְּ of place, *in(to)* Is 34$_{13}$, + ישׁב *dwell* Nm 13$_{19}$, בוא *come* 1QH 6$_{35}$.

עַל *against*, + בוא *come* Am 5$_{9}$ (or em. מְבַצֵּר *Vindemiator* ['the grape harvester']),* חשׁב pi. *devise* Dn 11$_{24}$; introducing object, + בזה *despise* 1QpHab 4$_{6}$.

מִבְצָר without preposition, *to the fortress*, + בוא *come* 2 S 24$_{7}$.

<COLL> מִבְצָר || אַרְמוֹן *fortress* Is 34$_{13}$ (+) Lm 2$_{5}$, מַמְלָכָה *kingdom* Is 17$_{3}$ Lm 2$_{2}$ (+); :: מַחֲנֶה *camp* Nm 13$_{19}$; + עִיר *city* Nm 13$_{19}$ 2 S 24$_{7}$ Mc 5$_{10}$, גְּדֵרָה *wall* Ps 89$_{41}$, עַמּוּד *pillar* Si 36$_{29(B)}$, נָוֶה *habitation* Lm 2$_{2}$, עֵזֶר *help* Si 36$_{29(B)}$.

עִיר מִבְצָר *fortified city* + כֹּפֶר הַפְּרָזִי *unwalled village* 1 S 6$_{18}$, עִיר מִבְחוֹר *choice city* 2 K 3$_{19}$, מִגְדַּל נוֹצְרִים *tower of the sentries* 2 K 17$_{9}$ 18$_{8}$, עַמּוּד בַּרְזֶל *pillar of iron* Jr 1$_{18}$, חֹמוֹת נְחֹשֶׁת *walls of bronze* Jr 1$_{18}$.

<SYN> אַרְמוֹן *fortress*, מַמְלָכָה *kingdom*.*
⇒ בצר I *cut*.

מִבְצָר II 2 pr.n.m. **Mibzar**, Edomite tribal chief, <SUBJ> היה *be* 1 C 1$_{53}$. <NOM CL> אֵלֶּה שְׁמוֹת אַלּוּפֵי עֵשָׂו ... מִבְצָר *these are the names of the chiefs of Esau*

… *Mibzar* Gn 36$_{42}$. <APP> אַלּוּף *chief* Gn 36$_{42}$||1 C 1$_{53}$.

*[מִבַצֵּר] n.[m.] **the Vintager,** a star, also known as **Vendemiator,** <PREP> עַל *upon,* + בוא *come* Am 5$_9$ (הַמַּבְלִיג שֹׁד עַל־עָז וְשֹׁד עַל־מִבְצָר יָבוֹא) *who makes the Bull to rise hard upon (the rising of) the She-goat and the Bull comes upon (the rising of) the Vintager;* if em. מִבְצָר *fortification* to מִבַצֵּר and שֹׁד *ruin* to שׁוֹר *bull* and עָז *strong* to עֵז *she-goat).*
⇒ בצר *cut off.*

*[מִבְקָע] 0.0.1 n.[m.] **cleavage**—cstr. Q מבקע—**cleavage, rift,** <CSTR> מבקע תהומות *cleavage of the deeps* 1QM 10$_{13}$.
⇒ בקע I *split.*

מְבַקֵּר, *inspector, overseer,** see בקר I *seek.*

[מִבְרָח] I 1 n.m. **fugitive**—sf. Kt מבחרו; pl. sf. Qr מִבְרָחָיו—<SUBJ> נפל *fall* Ezk 17$_{21}$ (unless מִבְרָח II *hero* or מִבְרָח III *picked men*). <CSTR> כָּל־מִבְרָחָיו *all his fugitives* Ezk 17$_{21(Qr)}$ (Kt מבחרו; mss מִבְחָרָיו *his choice ones*). <COLL> כָּל־מִבְרָחָיו בְּכָל־אֲגַפָּיו *all his refugees among all his troops* Ezk 17$_{21(Qr)}$ (or em. בְּכָל to וְכָל *and all*).
⇒ ברח I *flee.**

*[מִבְרָח] II 1 n.m. **hero, commander, court** or **military staff**—sf. Kt מבחרו; pl. sf. Qr מִבְרָחָיו—<SUBJ> נפל *fall* Ezk 17$_{21}$ (unless מִבְרָח I *fugitive* or מִבְרָח III *picked men*). <CSTR> כָּל־מִבְרָחָיו *all his heroes* Ezk 17$_{21(Qr)}$ (Kt מבחרו; mss מִבְחָרָיו *his choice ones*). <COLL> כָּל־מִבְרָחָיו בְּכָל־אֲגַפָּיו *all his heroes among all his troops* Ezk 17$_{21(Qr)}$ (or em. בְּכָל to וְכָל *and all*).
⇒ ברח I *flee.*

*[מִבְרָח] III 1 n.m. **picked men**—sf. Kt מבחרו; pl. sf. Qr מִבְרָחָיו—<SUBJ> נפל *fall* Ezk 17$_{21}$ (unless מִבְרָח I *fugitive* or מִבְרָח II *hero*). <CSTR> כָּל־מִבְרָחָיו *all his picked men* Ezk 17$_{21(Qr)}$ (Kt מבחרו; mss מִבְחָרָיו *his choice ones*). <COLL> כָּל־מִבְרָחָיו בְּכָל־אֲגַפָּיו *all his picked men among all his troops* Ezk 17$_{21(Qr)}$ (or em. בְּכָל to וְכָל *and all*).
⇒ ברח I *flee.*

מִבְשָׂם 3 pr.n.m. **Mibsam, 1.** son of Ishmael, <NOM CL> אֵלֶּה שְׁמוֹת בְּנֵי יִשְׁמָעֵאל ... מִבְשָׂם *these are the names of the sons of Ishmael … Mibsam* Gn 25$_{13}$, אֵלֶּה תֹּלְדוֹתָם ... מִבְשָׂם *these are their genealogies … Mibsam* 1 C 1$_{29}$.

2. Simeonite, son of Shallum, <NOM CL> בְּנֵי שִׁמְעוֹן ... מִבְשָׂם *the sons of Simeon were … Mibsam* 1 C 4$_{25}$. <APP> בֵּן *son* 1 C 4$_{25}$.
⇒ בֶּשֶׂם *balsam.*

מְבַשֵּׂר I *messenger,* see בשׂר I *give news.*

מְבַשֵּׂר II *refuter, defending counsel,* see בשׂר II Pi. *refute.**

מְבַשְּׁלוֹת 1 n.f.pl. **hearths,** for boiling sacrificial offerings, <SUBJ> עשׂה pass. *be made* Ez 46$_{23}$.
⇒ בשׁל *boil.*

מָג, see רַב־מָג *Rabmag.*

מַגְבִּישׁ I 1 pr.n.m. **Magbish,** ancestor of returning exiles, perh. ident. with Magpiash at Ne 10$_{21}$ (unless מַגְבִּישׁ II), <CSTR> בְּנֵי מַגְבִּישׁ *sons of Magbish* Ezr 2$_{30}$.

מַגְבִּישׁ II 1 pl.n. **Magbish,** village in Judah inhabited by returning exiles, Kh. el-Makhbiyeh or Kh. Qanan Mugheimis, c. 20 km SW of Jerusalem (unless מַגְבִּישׁ I), <CSTR> בְּנֵי מַגְבִּישׁ *sons,* i.e. inhabitants, *ofMagbish* Ezr 2$_{30}$.*

*[מִגְבָּל] 0.0.4 n.[m.] **kneading**—cstr. Q מגבל; sf. Q מגבלו—**kneading, thing kneaded,** unless ptc. pu. of גבל *forge,* i.e. knead; alw. of human being, <NOM CL> אני ... מגבל המים *I am … a thing kneaded with water* 1QH 1$_{21}$ (||יֵצֶר *creature* of clay) 1, + הוא מגב *he is a thing kneaded with water* 1QH 13$_{15}$ (||מִבְנֶה *structure* of dust), מעפר מגבלו *his kneading is from dust* 1QS 11$_{21}$ (+ מָדוֹר *dwelling*), מחושך מגב[לי] *my kneading was from the*

darkness 4QShir^b 28$_4$. <CSTR> מגבל המים *thing kneaded of,* i.e. with, *water* 1QH 1$_{21}$ 12$_{25}$ (מגבו]ל המים]) 13$_{15}$ (מים). <COLL> מגבל במים *thing kneaded with water* 1QH 3$_{24}$.

<SYN> יֵצֶר *creature,* מִבְנֶה *structure.*

⇒ (?) גבל II *forge.*

מִגְבָּלֹת 1 n.f.pl. **forged work,** making braided chains, <OBJ> עשׂה *make* Ex 28$_{14}$ (מִגְבָּלֹת תַּעֲשֶׂה אֹתָם *you shall make them* [chains] *forged work*; or em. מְגֻבָּלֹת *forged,* i.e. גבל pu.). <APP> מַעֲשֵׂה עֲבֹת *work of,* i.e. like, *cord* Ex 28$_{14}$.

⇒ גבל II *forge.*

[מִגְבָּעָה] I 4.0.1 n.f. **headdress**—pl. מִגְבָּעוֹת (מִגְבָּעֹת) —**headdress, turban, headband** of priest, <NOM CL> לַשֶּׁקֶר מִגְבָּעוֹת *the headdresses are a delusion* Jr 3$_{23}$ (if em. מִגְּבָעוֹת *from the hills*).* <OBJ> עשׂה *make* Ex 28$_{40}$ (+ אַבְנֵט *girdle,* כֻּתֹּנֶת *tunic*), חבשׁ *bind* Ex 29$_9$ (+ אַבְנֵט) Lv 8$_{13}$ (+ כֻּתֹּנֶת, אַבְנֵט). <CSTR> פַּאֲרֵי הַמִּגְבָּעֹת *headdresses (consisting) of the turbans* Ex 29$_{28}$ (+ מִצְנֶפֶת *turban,* מִכְנָסַיִם *breeches*) 1QM 7$_{11}$ (פרי מגבעות).*

⇒ cf. גִּבְעָה *hill.*

*__[מִגְבָּעָה]__ II n.f. **hilly place,** if em. מִגְּבָעוֹת *from the hills,** unless מִגְבָּעָה I *headdress,* <NOM CL> לַשֶּׁקֶר מִגְבָּעוֹת *the hilly places are a delusion* Jr 3$_{23}$.

⇒ cf. גִּבְעָה *hill.*

*__מגד__ I 0.0.1 vb. **give—Qal** 0.0.1 + waw Q ותמגדנו—**give,** <SUBJ> Y. Is 64$_6$(1QIsa^a) (MT וַתְּמוּגֵנוּ appar. *and you have caused us to melt*). <OBJ> Israelites Is 64$_6$(1QIsa^a). <PREP> בְּ of place, *into,* + יָד *hand* Gn 14$_{20}$ Is 64$_6$(1QIsa^a).

*__[מגד]__ II vb. **be excellent, Pi. make excellent, make abundant,** <SUBJ> subj. not specified, Am 4$_{13}$ (if em. מַגִּיד לְאָדָם מַה־שֵּׂחוֹ *declaring to humans what is his thought* to מְמַגֵּד לְאֲדָמָה שִׂיחָהּ *making abundant its plants for the earth*). <OBJ> שִׂיחַ *plant* Am 4$_{13}$ (if em.; see Subj.). <PREP> לְ of benefit, *for,* + אֲדָמָה *earth* Am 4$_{13}$ (if em.; see Subj.).

⇒ מֶגֶד *choice produce,* מִגְדָּנוֹת *precious things.*

[מֶגֶד] 8 n.m. **choice produce**—cstr. מֶגֶד; pl. מְגָדִים; sf. מְגָדָיו—**excellence,** i.e. **choice produce,** fed by dew (Dt 33$_{13}$) and ripened by the sun (Dt 33$_{14}$), found in a garden (Ca 4$_{16}$), eaten fresh or kept stored (Ca 7$_{14}$), or perh. **excellence, bounty** as an abstr., <NOM CL> עַל־פְּתָחֵינוּ כָּל־מְגָדִים *at our doors are all choice fruits* Ca 7$_{14}$ (+ דּוּדָאִים *mandrakes*). <OBJ> ספר *count* Is 33$_{18}$ (if em. הַמִּגְדָּלִים *the towers* to הַמְּגָדִים).

<CSTR> מֶגֶד שָׁמַיִם *excellence of heaven* Dt 33$_{13}$ (or em.; see Prep.), תְּבוּאֹת *of produce of* the sun Dt 33$_{14}$ (or em.; see Prep.), גֶּרֶשׁ *of yield of* months Dt 33$_{14}$ (or em.; see Prep.), גִּבְעוֹת *of hills of* eternity Dt 33$_{15}$ (or em.; see Prep.), הַרְרֵי *of the hills of* old Dt 33$_{15}$ (if em.; see Prep.), אֶרֶץ וּמְלֹאָהּ *of the earth and its fullness* Dt 33$_{16}$ (or em.; see Prep.); פְּרִי מְגָדִים *fruit of excellence* Ca 4$_{13}$, מְגָדָיו *of its excellence* Ca 4$_{16}$, כָּל־מְגָדִים *all choice fruits* Ca 7$_{14}$. <PREP> מִן of cause, *because of,* + ברך pu. *be blessed* Dt 33$_{13.14.14}$ (or em. all three מִנֶּגֶד *from before*) 33$_{15}$ (if em. מֵרֹאשׁ *because of the head* to מִמֶּגֶד) 33$_{15.16}$ (or em. both מִנֶּגֶד *from before*); עִם *with* Ca 4$_{13}$ (+ נֵרְדְּ *nard*).*

⇒ מגד *be excellent;* מַגְדִּיאֵל *Magdiel;* cf. מִגְדָּנוֹת *precious things.*

מְגִדּוֹ 12 pl.n. **Megiddo**—מְגִדּוֹן—Canaanite and then Israelite city in valley of Jezreel, allotted to Manasseh, T. el-Mutesellim 35 km N of Samaria, <NOM CL> אֲחֻזָּתָם וּמֹשְׁבֹתָם ... מְגִדּוֹ *their possessions and settlements were ... Megiddo* 1 C 7$_{29}$. <OBJ> בנה *build* 1 K 9$_{15}$. <CSTR> מֶלֶךְ מְגִדּוֹ *king of Megiddo* Jos 12$_{21}$, יֹשְׁבֵי *inhabitants of* Jos 17$_{11}$ Jg 1$_{27}$ (יוֹשְׁבֵי), בִּקְעַת *plain of* Zc 12$_{11}$ (מְגִדּוֹן) 2 C 35$_{22}$, מֵי *waters of* Jg 5$_{19}$. <PREP> בְּ of place, *in,* + מות hi. *kill* 2 K 23$_{29}$; מִן of direction, *from,* + רכב hi. *cause to ride* 2 K 23$_{30}$; מְגִדּוֹ without preposition, *in Megiddo* 1 K 4$_{12}$; *to Megiddo,* + נוס *flee* 2 K 9$_{27}$. <COLL> מְגִדּוֹ וּבְנֹתֶיהָ *Megiddo and its villages* Jos 17$_{11}$ 1 C 7$_{29}$, var. Jg 1$_{27}$, תַּעְנַךְ עַל־מֵי מְגִדּוֹ *Taanach by the waters of Megiddo* Jg 5$_{19}$.

[מִגְדּוֹל] I 1 n.[m.] **tower**—cstr. Qr מִגְדּוֹל—1 S 22$_{51}$(Qr) (Kt מגדיל *makes great,* i.e. גדל hi.); ||Ps 18$_{51}$ Kt מגדל (from מִגְדָּל *tower*), Qr מַגְדִּיל (i.e. גדל hi.), <NOM CL>

מִגְדּוֹל יְשׁוּעוֹת מַלְכּוֹ *his king is a tower of salvation* 1 S 22$_{51(Qr)}$. <CSTR> מִגְדּוֹל יְשׁוּעוֹת *tower of salvation* 1 S 22$_{51(Qr)}$.

⇒ גדל *be great*.

מִגְדּוֹל II, see מִגְדֹּל *Migdol*.

מְגִדּוֹן, see מְגִדּוֹ *Megiddo*.

מַגְדִּיאֵל 2 pr.n.m. **Magdiel,** Edomite tribal chief, <SUBJ> היה *be* 1 C 1$_{54}$. <NOM CL> אֵלֶּה שְׁמוֹת אַלּוּפֵי עֵשָׂו ... מַגְדִּיאֵל *these are the names of the chiefs of Esau ... Magdiel* Gn 36$_{43}$. <APP> אַלּוּף *chief* Gn 36$_{43}$|| 1 C 1$_{54}$.

⇒ מֶגֶד *excellence* + אֵל *God*.

מִגְדָּל I 48.0.13 n.m. **tower**—cstr. מִגְדַּל; pl. מִגְדָּלִים, מִגְדָּלוֹת; pl. cstr. מִגְדְּלוֹת; sf. מִגְדָּלֶיהָ, (מִגְדְּלוֹתַיִךְ) מִגְדְּלוֹתַיִךְ —1. **tower,** along city wall (e.g. Jr 31$_{38}$ Ne 3$_{1}$ 12$_{38}$ 2 C 14$_{6}$ 32$_{5}$ 1QSb 5$_{23}$), as stronghold within city (e.g. Jg 9$_{51}$), watchtower (2 K 17$_{9}$ 18$_{8}$), in vineyard (Is 5$_{2}$), for storage (1 C 27$_{25}$), <SUBJ> היה *be* Jg 9$_{51}$ Ps 61$_{4}$, בנה pass. *be built* Ca 4$_{4}$, יסד pu. *be founded* Ca 7$_{5}$ (if ins. מְיֻסָּד עַל אַדְנֵי־בַהַט *founded on bases of porphyry*), נפל *fall* Is 30$_{25}$ (unless §6) Ezk 38$_{20}$ (if em. הַמַּדְרֵגוֹת *the steep places* to הַמִּגְדָּלוֹת), יצא *go out*, i.e. protrude Ne 3$_{25.26.27}$, צפה *watch over* Ca 7$_{5}$.

<NOM CL> מִגְדַּל־עֹז שֵׁם י׳ *the name of Y. is a tower of strength* Pr 18$_{10}$, מגדל יְשׁוּעוֹת מַלְכּוֹ *his king is a tower of salvation* Ps 18$_{51(Kt)}$ (Qr מַגְדִּיל *makes* salvation great, i.e. גדל hi.).

<OBJ> בנה *build* Gn 11$_{4.5}$ (both || עִיר *city*) Is 5$_{2}$ (+ יֶקֶב *wine vat*) 2 C 26$_{9.10}$ 27$_{4}$ (|| בִּירָה *fortress*, + עִיר), נצב hi. *establish* 4QTestim$_{26}$=4QapJosh^{b} 22.2$_{12}$ (|| חוֹמָה *wall*), חזק pi. *strengthen* 2 C 26$_{9}$, hi. *repair* Ne 3$_{11}$, עלה hi. *raise* 2 C 32$_{5}$ (if em. עַל־הַמִּגְדָּלוֹת *upon the towers* to עָלֶיהָ מִגְדָּלוֹת *towers upon it*), הרס *tear down* Ezk 26$_{4}$ (+ חוֹמָה *wall*), נתץ *break down* Jg 8$_{9.17}$ Ezk 26$_{9}$ (+ חוֹמָה), שׂרף *burn* Jg 9$_{52}$, ראה *see* Gn 11$_{5}$, ספר *count* Is 33$_{18}$ (unless §4; or em. הַמְּגָדִים *the excellence*) Ps 48$_{13}$; סבב מִגְדָּלִים hi. *surround with towers* 2 C 14$_{6}$ (|| חוֹמָה *wall*, דֶּלֶת *door*, בְּרִיחַ *bar*).

<CSTR> מִגְדַּל דָּוִיד *tower of David* Ca 4$_{4}$, חֲנַנְאֵל *of Hananel* Jr 31$_{38}$ Zc 14$_{10}$ Ne 3$_{1}$ 12$_{39}$, פְּנוּאֵל *of Penuel* Jg 8$_{17}$, הַלְּבָנוֹן *of the Lebanon* Ca 7$_{5}$, ־שְׁכֶם *of Shechem* Jg 9$_{46.47.49}$, הַמֵּאָה *of the Hundred* Ne 3$_{1}$ 12$_{39}$, הַתַּנּוּרִים *of the ovens* Ne 3$_{11}$ 12$_{38}$, יְשׁוּעוֹת *of salvation* Ps 18$_{51(Kt)}$ (Qr מַגְדִּיל *makes great*, i.e. גדל hi.), ־עֹז *of strength*, i.e. strong tower, perh. towered fortress* Jg 9$_{51}$ Ps 61$_{4}$ Pr 18$_{10}$ 1QH 7$_{8}$ (|| חוֹמָה) 1QSb 5$_{23}$ (both עוז), הַשֵּׁן *of ivory* Ca 7$_{5}$, נוֹצְרִים *of the watchers*, i.e. watchtower 2 K 17$_{9}$ 18$_{8}$; אַנְשֵׁי מִגְדַּל *men of the tower of* Jg 9$_{49}$, בַּעֲלֵי *lords of* Jg 9$_{46.47}$, פֶּתַח הַמִּגְדָּל *entrance of the tower* Jg 9$_{52}$, גַּג *roof of* Jg 9$_{51}$, כָּל־מִגְדָּל *every tower* Is 2$_{15}$ (|| חוֹמָה *wall*).

<APP> מַחְסֶה *refuge* Ps 61$_{4}$, נָטִיעַ *pavilion* Ps 144$_{12}$ (if em.; see Prep.).

<ADJ> גָּבֹהַּ *high* Is 2$_{15}$, גָּדוֹל *great* Ne 3$_{27}$, זֶה *this* Jg 8$_{9}$.

<PREP> בְּ of place, *in* 1 C 27$_{25}$ (|| עִיר *city*, כָּפָר *village*), + היה *be* Ezk 27$_{11}$ (+ חוֹמָה *wall*); *against*, + לחם ni. *fight* Jg 9$_{52}$; כְּ *as* Ps 144$_{12}$ (if em. כִּנְטִעִים מְגֻדָּלִים *as plants full grown* to כִּנְטָעִים מִגְדָּלִים *as pavilions (or as) towers*) Ca 4$_{4}$ 7$_{5.5}$ 8$_{10}$ (+ חוֹמָה) 1QSb 5$_{23}$ 4QapJoseph^{c} 1$_{4}$ (מגן כמגדל *a shield like a tower*), + שׂים *place*, i.e. make 1QH 7$_{8}$; מִן *from* 2 K 17$_{9}$ 18$_{8}$ (both מִמִּגְדַּל נוֹצְרִים עַד־עִיר מִבְצָר *from watchtower to fortified city*, i.e. both ... and) Zc 14$_{10(mss, Gnz)}$, + בנה ni. *be built* Jr 31$_{38}$, חזק hi. *repair* Ne 3$_{25}$; עַל *upon, above* Ne 12$_{39.39}$, + היה *above* 2 C 26$_{15}$ (|| פִּנָּה *corner*), עמד *stand* 2 K 9$_{17}$, תלה pass. *be hung* Ca 4$_{4}$, עלה hi. *raise* 2 C 32$_{5}$ (unless em.; see Obj.); *against* Is 2$_{15}$; מֵעַל *from above* Ne 12$_{38}$; עַד *to, as far as* Ne 12$_{39(Seb).39(Seb)}$, + בוא *come* Jg 9$_{52}$, קדשׁ pi. *consecrate* Ne 3$_{1.1}$; נֶגֶד *opposite*, + ישׁב *dwell* Ne 3$_{26}$; מִנֶּגֶד *from opposite*, + חזק hi. *repair* Ne 3$_{37}$.

<COLL> הַמִּגְדָּל בְּיִזְרְעֶאל *the tower in Jezreel* 2 K 9$_{17}$.

2. raised platform, pulpit, <OBJ> עשׂה *make* Ne 8$_{4}$. <CSTR> מִגְדַּל־עֵץ *raised platform of wood* Ne 8$_{4}$. <PREP> עַל *upon*, + עמד *stand* Ne 8$_{4}$.

3. raised bed* of garden, **bank,** <CSTR> מִגְדְּלוֹת מֶרְקָחִים *raised beds of perfume* Ca 5$_{13}$ (unless §4 or 5; or em. מִגְדָּנוֹת *precious things of*, or מְגַדְּלוֹת *yielding* perfume, i.e. גדל pi.). <APP> עֲרוּגָה *garden bed* Ca 5$_{13}$ (unless §4 or 5; or em.; see Cstr.). <PREP> כְּ *as* Ca 5$_{13}$ (unless §4 or 5; or em.; see Cstr.).

4. heap, pile (of coins),* <OBJ> ספר *count* Is 33$_{18}$

(unless §1). <CSTR> מִגְדְּלוֹת מֶרְקָחִים *heaps of perfume* Ca 5_{13} (unless §3). <APP> עֲרוּגָה *garden bed* Ca 5_{13} (unless §3). <PREP> כְּ *as* Ca 5_{13} (unless §3).

5. chest, box,* <CSTR> מִגְדְּלוֹת מֶרְקָחִים *boxes of perfume* Ca 5_{13} (unless §3 or 4). <APP> עֲרוּגָה *garden bed* Ca 5_{13} (unless §3 or 4). <PREP> כְּ *as* Ca 5_{13} (unless §3 or 4).

6. high-ranking officer,* <SUBJ> נפל *fall* Is 30_{25} (unless §1).

7. tower, as name of a particular battle formation, <SUBJ> יצא *go out* 1QM 9_{12} (המג[ד]לות). <OBJ> סבב *surround* 1QM 9_{13} (י]סבו]). <CSTR> פני המגדל *face,* i.e. side, *of the tower* 1QM 9_{13}, מגני המגדלות *shields of the towers* 1QM $9_{12.14}$. <PREP> לְ of possession, *(belonging) to, of* 1QM 9_{14} (שערים שנים למגדל *there shall be two gates to the tower*). <COLL> גליל כפים ומגדלות *a folding of hands,* i.e. pincer movement, *and towers* 1QM 9_{10}, קשת ומגדלות *a bow and towers* 1QM 9_{11}, מאה מגן ומאה פני המגדל *there shall be a hundred shields to each side of the tower* 1QM 9_{13}.

<SYN> §1 בִּירָה *fortress,* עִיר *city,* כָּפָר *village,* חוֹמָה *wall,* פִּנָּה *corner,* דֶּלֶת *door,* בְּרִיחַ *bar.**

⇨ גדל *be great,* מִגְדַּל־אֵל *Migdal-el,* מִגְדַּל־גָּד *Migdal-gad,* מִגְדַּל־עֵדֶר *Migdal-eder,* מִגְדּוֹל *tower.*

מִגְדָּל II 0.0.1 n.[m.] **magnification,** <CSTR> מגדל [א]ל[הי] *magnification of the God of* 4QShirShabb[d] 1.2_{25} (+ תשבחות רומם *praises of exaltation*).

⇨ גדל *be great.*

מִגְדֹּל 6 pl.n. **Migdol**—מִגְדּוֹל—city (or perh. cities) in Egypt, location unknown, near Pi-ha-hiroth and Baal-zephon (Ex 14_2 Nm 33_7); mentioned with Memphis and Tahpanhes as dwelling place of Jews (Jr 44_1 46_{14}); with Syene, a geographical extreme of Egypt (Ezk 29_{10} 30_6), <PREP> בְּ of place, *in,* + ישב *dwell* Jr 44_1, שמע hi. *proclaim* Jr 46_{14}; מִן of direction, *from* Ezk 29_{10} 30_6; בֵּין *between,* + חנה *encamp* Ex 14_2; לִפְנֵי *before,* + חנה *encamp* Nm 33_7.*

מִגְדַּל־אֵל 1 pl.n. **Migdal-el,** town in Naphtali, perh. Kh. el-Meğdel, 33 km ESE of Tyre, <NOM CL> הַמִּבְצָר ... מִגְדַּל־אֵל *the fortified cities are ... Migdal-el* Jos 19_{38}. <APP> עִיר *city* Jos 19_{38}.

⇨ מִגְדָּל *tower* + אֵל *God.*

מִגְדַּל־גָּד 1 pl.n. **Migdal-gad,** town in Judah, perh. Kh. el-Meğdele, 20 km W of Hebron, <NOM CL> בַּשְּׁפֵלָה אֶשְׁתָּאוֹל ... וּמִגְדַּל־גָּד *in the lowland were Eshtaol ... and Migdal-gad* Jos 15_{37}. <APP> עִיר *city.*

⇨ מִגְדָּל *tower* + גָּד *Gad.*

מִגְדַּל־עֵדֶר 2 pl.n. **Migdal-eder,** town near Bethlehem, unless 'tower of the flock', as name of tower, <APP> עֹפֶל *mound* of daughter of Zion Mc 4_8. <PREP> לְ מֵהָלְאָה *beyond,* + נטה *pitch* tent Gn 35_{21}; עַד *to,* + אתה *come* Mc 4_8. <COLL> מִגְדַּל־עֵדֶר as vocative Mc 4_8.

⇨ מִגְדָּל *tower* + עֵדֶר *flock.*

מִגְדָּנוֹת 4 n.f.pl. **precious things**—מִגְדָּנֹת—<OBJ> נתן *give* Gn 24_{53} (+ בֶּגֶד *garment,* כְּלִי *jewellery*), בוא hi. *bring* 2 C 32_{23} (|| מִנְחָה *gift*). <CSTR> מִגְדָּנוֹת מֶרְקָחִים *precious things of perfumes,* i.e. precious perfumes Ca 5_{13} (if em. מִגְדְּלוֹת *raised beds of*). <APP> בֹּשֶׂם *spice* Ca 5_{13} (if em.; see Cstr.). <PREP> לְ of benefit. *to, for,* + עשׂה *make* treasuries 2 C 32_{27} (if em. לְמָגִנִּים *for shields*); *(consisting) of* 2 C 21_3 (|| זָהָב *gold,* כֶּסֶף *silver*); בְּ of instrument, *by (means of), with (the help of),* + חזק pi. *encourage* Ezr 1_6 (|| רְכוּשׁ *goods,* בְּהֵמָה *beast,* זָהָב, + כְּלִי *vessel* of silver).

<SYN> מִנְחָה *gift,* רְכוּשׁ *goods,* בְּהֵמָה *beast,* זָהָב *gold,* כֶּסֶף *silver.*

⇨ מגד *be excellent.*

*[מְגַדְּפָה] 0.0.1 n.f. **blasphemy**—pl. sf. Q מגדפותם—<PREP> מִן of cause, *on account of,* + חתת ni. *be terrified* Is 51_7(1QIsa[a]) (ממגדפותם corrected from מגדפותם; MT מִגִּדֻּפֹתָם from גִּדּוּף).

⇨ גדף *revile.*

מָגוֹג 4.0.2 pr.n.m. **Magog, 1.** son of Japheth, <NOM CL> בְּנֵי יֶפֶת ... וּמָגוֹג *the sons of Japheth were ... and Magog* Gn 10_2||1 C 1_5.

2. nation in the north, otherwise unidentified, appar.

regarded as descended from §1, <CSTR> אֶרֶץ הַמָּגוֹג *land of Magog* Ezk 38$_{2}$ (or em. אַרְצָה מָגוֹג *to the land of Magog*; or del.). <PREP> בְּ *against*, + שׁלח pi. *send* fire Ezk 39$_{6}$. <COLL> גוג ומגוג *Gog and Magog* 4Q523 1$_{5}$.
Also 4QpIsa[a] 8$_{20}$.

[מָגוֹר] I 11.1.3 n.[m.] **sojourning**—sf. מְגוּרָם; cstr. מְגוּרֵי; sf. מְגוּרַי (מְגוּרֶי), מְגֻרֶיךָ, מְגוּרָיו, מְגוּרֵיהֶם (מְגֻרֵיהֶם)—(pl. except Ps 55$_{16}$ 1QH 5$_{8}$), **1. sojourning, dwelling,** <CSTR> מְגוּרֵי אָבִיו *sojourning of his father* Gn 37$_{1}$; ארץ מגורים *land of sojourning* 4QD[a] 6.4$_{3}$, אֶרֶץ מְגוּרֵי *land of the sojourning of* Gn 37$_{1}$, מְגֻרֶיךָ *your sojourning* Gn 17$_{8}$ 28$_{4}$, מְגוּרֵיהֶם *of their sojourning* Gn 36$_{8}$ Ex 6$_{4}$ (מְגֻרֵיהֶם) Ezk 20$_{38}$, בֵּית מְגוּרָי *house of my sojourning* Ps 119$_{54}$, שְׁנֵי מְגוּרַי *years of my sojourning* Gn 47$_{9}$, יוֹם מְגֻרֶיךָ *day of your sojourning* Zc 9$_{12}$ (if em. הַיּוֹם מַגִּיד *today [I] declare*), יְמֵי מְגוּרֵיהֶם *days of their sojourning* Gn 47$_{9}$ (+ חַיִּים *life*).

2. sojourning place, dwelling place, <CSTR> [מגו]רי דמשק *dwelling places of*, i.e. in, *Damascus* 4QD[b] 2$_{12}$, מגורי לוט *dwelling places of Lot* Si 16$_{8}$; כל מגוריהם *all their dwelling places* 1QS 6$_{2}$. <PREP> בְּ of place, *in* Ps 55$_{16}$ (unless מָגוֹר III *heart* or מְגוּרָה II *furrow*; + בְּקִרְבָּם *among them*) Jb 18$_{19}$, + גור *sojourn* 4QD[b] 2$_{12}$ (וי[גורו במגו]ר), שִׂים *place* 1QH 5$_{8}$ (unless מָגוֹר II *fear*), הלך htp. *walk* 1QS 6$_{2}$; עַל *upon*, + חמל *have compassion* Si 16$_{8}$.
⇒ גור I *sojourn*.

מָגוֹר II 9.0.1 n.m. **fear**—pl. sf. מְגוּרַי—**(object of) fear, terror,** <SUBJ> היה *be* Ps 31$_{12}$ (if em. מְאֹד *very*). <OBJ> קרא *call*, i.e. summon Lm 2$_{22}$ (or em.; see Coll.), i.e. name Jr 20$_{3}$. <PREP> לְ *as*, + נתן *give*, i.e. make into Jr 20$_{4}$; בְּ of place, *in*, + שִׂים *place* 1QH 5$_{8}$ (unless מָגוֹר I *sojourning*); מִן of cause, *on account of*, + עבר *pass away* Is 31$_{9}$. <COLL> מָגוֹר מִסָּבִיב *terror all around*, as exclamation Jr 6$_{25}$ 20$_{10}$ 46$_{5}$ 49$_{29}$ Ps 31$_{14}$, as name for Passhur Jr 20$_{3}$, מְגוּרַי מִסָּבִיב *my terrors all round* Lm 2$_{22}$ (or em. מְגוֹרְרַי *those who frighten me*, i.e. גור III pol.), מָגוֹר לְךָ וּלְכָל־אֹהֲבֶיךָ *a terror to you and all your friends* Jr 20$_{4}$.
⇒ גור III *fear*.

*[מָגוֹר] III n.[m.] **storage pit** (unless מָגוֹר I *sojourning* or IV *throat* or מְגוּרָה II *furrow*)—sf. מְגוּרָם—**storage pit,** i.e. heart, mind, <PREP> בְּ of place, *in* Ps 55$_{16}$ (|| קֶרֶב *inner part*).
<SYN> קֶרֶב *inner part*.
⇒ cf. מְגוּרָה I *granary*.

*[מָגוֹר] IV n.[m.] **throat** (unless מָגוֹר I *sojourning* or III *storage pit*)—sf. מְגוּרָם—<PREP> בְּ of place, *in* Ps 55$_{16}$ (|| קֶרֶב *inner part*).
<SYN> קֶרֶב *inner part*.
⇒ cf. גָּרוֹן *neck, throat*.

[מְגוֹרָה] 3 n.f. **fear**—cstr. מְגוֹרַת; pl. sf. מְגוּרוֹתַי, מְגוּרוֹתָם—**(object of) fear, dread,** <SUBJ> בוא *come* Pr 10$_{24}$. <OBJ> בוא hi. *bring* Is 66$_{4}$ (+ תַּעֲלוּלִים *wantonness*). <CSTR> מְגוֹרַת רָשָׁע *dread of*, i.e. thing dreaded by, *the wicked* Pr 10$_{24}$, כָּל־מְגוּרוֹתַי *all my fears* Ps 34$_{5}$. <PREP> מִן *from*, + נצל hi. *deliver* Ps 34$_{5}$.
⇒ גור III *fear*.

מְגוּרָה I 1 n.f. **granary,** or **grain pit, bin,** <SUBJ> הרס ni. *be torn down* Jl 1$_{17}$ (if em. מַמְּגֻרוֹת *granaries* to מְגֻרוֹת). <PREP> בְּ of place, *in*, + גרע ni. (of seed) *be diminished* Hg 2$_{19}$ (if ins. נִגְרַע; unless מְגוּרָה II *furrow*); מִן of direction, *from* or partitive, *some of*, + הרס ni. *be torn down* Jl 1$_{17}$ (if em. מַמְּגֻרוֹת *granaries* to מִמְּגֻרוֹת).*
⇒ אגר *gather*.

*מְגוּרָה II 2 n.f. **furrow**—sf. מְגוּרָם—<PREP> בְּ of place, *in* Ps 55$_{16}$ (|| קֶרֶב *inner part*; unless מָגוֹר I *sojourning* or III *heart* or IV *storage pit*), + גרע ni. (of seed) *be diminished* Hg 2$_{19}$ (if ins. נִגְרַע; unless מְגוּרָה I *granary*).

*[מְגוּרָה] III n.f. **pool,** unless מְגוּרָה I *granary*, <SUBJ> הרס ni. *be broken* Jl 1$_{17}$ (if em. מַמְּגֻרוֹת *granaries* to מְגֻרוֹת).

*[מְגָזָה] 0.0.1 n.f. **ford**—cstr. Q מגזת—<CSTR> מגזת הכוהן הגדול *ford of the high priest* 3QTr 6$_{14}$. <PREP> בְּ of place, *in*, + חפר *dig* 3QTr 6$_{14}$.

[מַגְזֵרָה] 1 n.f. **axe**—pl. cstr. מַגְזְרֹת—<CSTR> מַגְזְרֹת הַבַּרְזֶל *axes of iron* 2 S 12$_{31}$ (lacking in mss; || חָרִיץ *pickaxe*, מְגֵרָה *saw*). <PREP> בְּ of accompaniment, *with*, + שׂים *place*, i.e. set to work 2 S 12$_{31}$||1 C 20$_{3}$ (1 C if em. וַיָּשַׂר ... בַּמְּגֵרוֹת *and he sawed them ... with saws* to וַיָּשֶׂם ... בַּמַּגְזֵרוֹת *and he set them to work ... with axes*).
<SYN> חָרִיץ *pickaxe*, מְגֵרָה *saw*.
⇒ גזר *cut*.

מַגִּיד, *messenger*, see נגד Hi. *tell*.

מַגָּל 2 n.[m.] **sickle**, <OBJ> שׁלח *send*, i.e. put to the harvest Jl 4$_{13}$, תפשׂ *hold* Jr 50$_{16}$ (תֹּפֵשׂ מַגָּל בְּעֵת קָצִיר *the one who holds the axe in the time of harvest*).*

מְגִלָּה 21 n.f. **scroll**—cstr. מְגִלַּת—**scroll**, on which to write, <SUBJ> היה *be* Ezk 3$_{3}$, כתב pass. *be written* Ezk 2$_{9}$, עוף *fly* Zc 5$_{1.2}$, תמם *be consumed* Jr 36$_{23}$. <NOM CL> הִנֵּה מְגִלָּה *behold, there was a scroll* Zc 5$_{1}$, בּוֹ מְגִלַּת סֵפֶר *in it was a scroll of writing* Ezk 2$_{9}$. <OBJ> ראה *see* Zc 5$_{2}$, לקח *take* Jr 36$_{2+5t}$, נתן *give* Jr 36$_{32}$ Ezk 3$_{3}$, כתב *write* Jr 36$_{6}$, קרא *read* Jr 36$_{21}$ 4QWays^{b} 8$_{2}$ ([מג]לת), פרשׂ *spread* Ezk 2$_{9}$, פקד hi. *deposit* Jr 36$_{20}$, אכל *eat* Ezk 3$_{1.3}$, hi. *feed* Ezk 3$_{2}$, מלא pi. *fill with* Ezk 3$_{3}$, שׂרף *burn* Jr 36$_{25.27.28.29}$. <CSTR> מְגִלַּת־סֵפֶר *scroll of writing* Jr 36$_{2.4}$ Ezk 2$_{9}$ Ps 40$_{8}$ 4QWays^{b} 8$_{2}$ ([מג]לת); כָּל־הַמְּגִלָּה *all the scroll* Jr 36$_{23}$. <ADJ> רִאשׁוֹן *first* Jr 36$_{28}$, אַחֵר *another* Jr 36$_{28.32}$, זאת *this* Jr 36$_{29}$ Ezk 3$_{1.2.3}$. <PREP> בְּ of place, *in*, i.e. from, + קרא *read* Jr 36$_{6.14}$, כתב pass. *be written* Ps 40$_{8}$; אֶל *upon*, + כתב *write* Jr 36$_{2}$, pass. *be written* Ezk 2$_{9}$; עַל *upon*, + היה *be* Jr 36$_{28}$, כתב *write* Jr 36$_{4.28.29.32}$.
⇒ גלל I *roll*.

[מְגַמָּה] 1 n.f. **multitude**—cstr. מְגַמַּת—perh. **multitude, totality, massing**, <NOM CL> מְגַמַּת פְּנֵיהֶם קָדִימָה perh. *the multitude of their faces is (directed) forwards* Hb 1$_{9}$. <CSTR> מְגַמַּת פְּנֵיהֶם *multitude of their faces* Hb 1$_{9}$.

*__מגן__ I 3.0.1 vb. **deliver up**—**Pi.** 3.0.1 Pf. מִגֵּן, Q מגנתה; impf. 3fs תְּמַגְּנֶךָּ, אֲמַגֶּנְךָ—**1. deliver up, surrender,** <SUBJ> Y. Ho 11$_{8}$ (|| נתן *give*) Is 64$_{6}$ (if em. וַתְּמוּגֵנוּ *and you have melted us* to וַתְּמַגְּנֵנוּ *and you have delivered us up*) 1QM 18$_{13}$, אֵל עֶלְיוֹן *God Most High* Gn 14$_{20}$. <OBJ> Israel(ites) Ho 11$_{8}$ Is 64$_{6}$ (if em.; see Subj.), צַר *enemy* Gn 14$_{20}$, לֵב *heart* 1QM 18$_{13}$. <PREP> בְּ of place, *into*, + יָד *hand* Gn 14$_{20}$ Is 64$_{6}$ (if em.; see Subj.). <COLL> מגן + לאין מעמד *so that there is no standing*, i.e. so that none could stand 1QM 18$_{13}$.
2. bestow upon or **shield**,* <SUBJ> חָכְמָה *wisdom* Pr 4$_{9}$ (|| נתן *give*), בִּינָה *understanding* Pr 4$_{9}$. <OBJ> 1. gift, עֲטֶרֶת *crown* Pr 4$_{9}$; 2. recipient, בֵּן *son* Pr 4$_{9}$.
<SYN> §§ 1, 2 נתן *give*.*
⇒ מֶגֶן *gift*.

*__מגן__ II vb. **beseech**, ptc. as noun, **beggar**, <APP> אִישׁ *man* Pr 6$_{11}$=24$_{34}$ (if em. כְּאִישׁ מָגֵן *as a man of a shield* to כְּאִישׁ מֹגֵן *as a beggar*; or em. מַגָּן *beggar*). <PREP> כְּ *as*, + בוא *come* Pr 6$_{11}$=24$_{34}$ (if em.; see Subj.).
⇒ מַגָּן *beggar*.

*__[מָגֵן]__ 18 n.m. **benefactor** (vocalization perh. מָגֵן or מֹגֵן; unless מָגֵן I *shield*)—cstr. מָגֵן; sf. מָגִנֵּנוּ, מָגִנִּי; pl. cstr. מָגִנֵּי—**benefactor, suzerain, general,** <SUBJ> ירד hi. *bring down* Ps 59$_{12}$, אדם pu. *be made red* Na 2$_{4}$. <NOM CL> אָנֹכִי מָגֵן לָךְ *I am a benefactor for you* Gn 15$_{1}$, אַתָּה ... מָגֵן *you are ... a benefactor* Ps 3$_{4}$, var. Ps 119$_{114}$, מָגֵן הוּא *he is the Suzerain* 2 S 22$_{31}$||Ps 18$_{31}$ Pr 30$_{5}$, var. Ps 115$_{9}$, מָגִנִּי *(he is) my suzerain* Ps 144$_{2}$, מָגֵן לְהֹלְכֵי תֹם *(he is) a benefactor to those who walk in integrity* Pr 2$_{7}$, מָגִנִּי עַל־אֱלֹהִים *my shield is the Most High God* Ps 7$_{11}$, שֶׁמֶשׁ וּמָגֵן י׳ *Sovereign* (lit. *Sun*) *and Suzerain is Y.* Ps 84$_{12}$, כִּי לֵאלֹהִים מָגִנֵּי־אֶרֶץ *truly God is the Suzerain of the earth* Ps 47$_{10}$, כִּי לַי׳ מָגִנֵּנוּ *truly Y. is our Suzerain* Ps 89$_{19}$. <OBJ> ראה *see* Ps 84$_{10}$. <CSTR> מָגֵן שָׁאוּל *the general of Saul* 2 S 1$_{21}$, גִּבּוֹרִים *of the warriors* 2 S 1$_{21}$, גִּבֹּרֵיהוּ *of his mighty men* Na 2$_{4}$. <APP> אֲדֹנָי *Adonai* Ps 59$_{12}$.

*__[מַגָּן]__ n.m. **beggar**, <APP> אִישׁ *man* Pr 6$_{11}$=24$_{34}$ (if em. כְּאִישׁ מָגֵן *as a man of a shield* to כְּאִישׁ מַגָּן *as a beggar*; or em. מֹגֵן, i.e. מגן II ptc.). <PREP> כְּ *as*, + בוא *come* Pr 6$_{11}$=24$_{34}$ (if em.; see Subj.).
⇒ מגן II *beseech*.

מָגֵן I $_{60.1.14}$ n.m.&f. **shield**—cstr. מָגֵן; sf. מָגִנֵּי, מָגִנֵּנוּ, מָגִנָּם; pl. מָגִנִּים, מָגִנּוֹת; cstr. מָגִנֵּי; sf. מָגִנָּיו—**1. shield, buckler,** **a.** used by warrior, Jg 5$_{8}$ 2 S 1$_{21}$ 2 K 19$_{32}$||Is 37$_{33}$ Is 21$_{5}$ 22$_{6}$ Jr 46$_{3.9}$ Ezk 23$_{24}$ 27$_{10}$ 38$_{4.5}$ 39$_{9}$ Na 2$_{4}$ Ps 76$_{4}$ Jb 15$_{26}$ Ne 4$_{10.17}$ (if em.; see Obj.) 1 C 5$_{18}$ 2 C 14$_{7}$ 17$_{17}$ 23$_{9}$ 26$_{14}$ 32$_{5}$ 1QM 5$_{4.5.6}$ 6$_{5.5.15}$ 7$_{15}$ 9$_{12.13.14.14}$ 4QapJoseph^{c} 1$_{4}$.

b. as ornament in palace, 1 K 10$_{17.17}$||2 C 9$_{16.16}$ 1 K 14$_{26.27}$||2 C 12$_{9.10}$; adorning a tower, Ca 4$_{4}$; part of royal treasure, 2 C 32$_{27}$.

c. Y. as shield (some refs. perh. מָגֵן IV *benefactor*), Gn 15$_{1}$ Dt 33$_{29}$ 2 S 22$_{3.31}$||Ps 18$_{3.31}$ Ps 3$_{4}$ 28$_{7}$ 33$_{20}$ 59$_{12}$ (or em.; see App.) 84$_{10}$ (or the king as shield) 84$_{12}$ 115$_{9.10.11}$ 119$_{114}$ 144$_{2}$ Pr 2$_{7}$ 30$_{5}$ Si 51$_{12}$, providing a shield for protection, 2 S 22$_{36}$||Ps 18$_{36}$ 7$_{11}$ 35$_{2}$ 89$_{19}$ 4QShirShabb^{d} 1.1$_{25}$.

d. human ruler as shield, Ps 47$_{10}$ perh. 84$_{10}$.

2. shield, i.e. **scale,** of Leviathan, Jb 41$_{7}$.

<SUBJ> היה *be* 1QM 9$_{12}$, ראה *see* Ps 84$_{10}$ (unless מָגִנֵּנוּ is obj.), ni. *be seen* Jg 5$_{8}$, נבט hi. *look* Ps 84$_{10}$, ברך pu. *be blessed* Ps 144$_{2}$, געל ni. *be abhorred* 2 S 1$_{21}$, משח pass. *be anointed* 2 S 1$_{21(\text{mss})}$ (L מָשִׁיחַ *anointed*), אדם pu. *be made red* Na 2$_{4}$, הרג *kill* Ps 59$_{12}$ (or em.; see App.), נוע hi. *cause to totter* Ps 59$_{12}$ (or em.; see App.), ירד hi. *bring down* Ps 59$_{12}$ (or em.; see App.), תלה pass. *be hung* Ca 4$_{4}$, סבב ho. *be surrounded,* i.e. bordered 1QM 5$_{5}$.

<NOM CL> מָגִנִּי ... ′י *Y. is ... my shield* 2 S 22$_{3}$||Ps 18$_{3}$ Ps 28$_{7}$, var. Ps 84$_{12}$, אָנֹכִי מָגֵן לָךְ *I am a shield for you* Gn 15$_{1}$, מָגֵן הוּא *he is a shield* 2 S 22$_{31}$||Ps 18$_{31}$ Pr 30$_{5}$, vars. Ps 33$_{20}$ 115$_{9.10.11}$, מָגֵן ... אַתָּה *you are ... a shield* Ps 3$_{4}$, var. Ps 119$_{114}$, מָגִנּוֹ עֶזְרֶךָ *his shield is your help* Dt 33$_{29}$ (if em. מָגֵן *shield of* your help), מָגֵן לְהֹלְכֵי תֹם *(he is) a shield to those who walk in integrity* Pr 2$_{7}$, לַי′ מָגִנֵּנוּ *our shield is,* i.e. belongs, *to Y.* Ps 89$_{19}$, לֵאלֹהִים מָגִנֵּי־אֶרֶץ *the shields of the earth are,* i.e. belong, *to God* Ps 47$_{10}$ (unless מָגֵן III *mighty ones*; or em.; see Cstr.), ... הַמָּגִנּוֹת אֲשֶׁר לַמֶּלֶךְ דָּוִיד *the shields ... that were,* i.e. belonged, *to King David* 2 C 23$_{9}$, מָגִנִּי עַל־אֱלֹהִים *my shield is upon God* Ps 7$_{11}$ (or em. עַל to עָלַי my shield *over me* is God), מָגֵן שָׁאוּל בְּלִי מָשִׁיחַ *the shield of Saul was not anointed* 2 S 1$_{21}$ (mss מָשׁוּחַ *anointed*), מאה מגן ומאה פני המגדל *each side of the tower shall be a hundred shields* 1QM 9$_{13}$.

<OBJ> עשה *make* 1 K 10$_{17}$||2 C 9$_{16}$ 1 K 14$_{26.27}$||2 C 12$_{9}$. $_{10}$ 2 C 32$_{5}$, נתן *give, place* 2 S 22$_{36}$||Ps 18$_{36}$ 1 K 10$_{17}$||2 C 9$_{16}$ 2 C 23$_{9}$, שׂים *place* Ezk 23$_{24}$, לקח *take* 1 K 14$_{26}$||2 C 12$_{9}$, פקד hi. *entrust* 1 K 14$_{27}$||2 C 12$_{10}$, ערה pi. *uncover* Is 22$_{6}$, ראה *see* perh. Ps 84$_{10}$ (but prob. מָגִנֵּנוּ is subj.), משח *anoint* Is 21$_{5}$, כון hi. *prepare* 2 C 26$_{14}$, ערך *arrange* Jr 46$_{3}$, חזק hi. *hold* Ps 35$_{2}$ Ne 4$_{10}$ 1QM 5$_{4}$ 6$_{5.5}$ (מחזיקי מגן *ones who hold a shield*) 6$_{15}$, תפשׂ *hold* Jr 46$_{9}$ (תֹּפְשֵׂי מָגֵן *ones who hold a shield*), נשׂא *carry* 1 C 5$_{18}$ 2 C 14$_{7}$ (both נֹשְׂאֵי מָגֵן *ones who carry a shield*), נשק *be armed with* 2 C 17$_{17}$ (נֹשְׁקֵי ... מָגֵן *ones armed ... with a shield*), פשׁט *take off* Ne 4$_{17}$ (if em. הַמַּיִם to וּמָגִנּוֹ *and his shield*), תלה pi. *hang* Ezk 27$_{10}$, שׁבר pi. *break* Ps 76$_{4}$.

<CSTR> מגן אברהם *shield of Abraham* Si 51$_{12}$, מָגֵן שָׁאוּל *shield of Saul* 2 S 1$_{21}$, גִּבּוֹרִים *of the warriors* 2 S 1$_{21}$, גִּבֹּרֵיהוּ *of his warriors* Na 2$_{4}$, עֶזְרֶךָ *of your help* Dt 33$_{29}$ (or em. מָגִנּוֹ *his shield* is your help), מָגֵן יִשְׁעֶךָ *shield of your salvation* 2 S 22$_{36}$||Ps 18$_{36}$, מגני עוז *shields of strength,* i.e. strong shields 4QShirShabb^{d} 1.1$_{25}$, עזי *of my strength,* i.e. my strong shield 4QPrayer^{e} 2$_{2}$, עגלה *of roundness,* i.e. round shields 1QM 6$_{15}$, מָגִנֵּי הַזָּהָב *shields of gold* 1 K 14$_{26}$||2 C 12$_{9}$, נְחֹשֶׁת *of bronze* 1 K 14$_{27}$||2 C 12$_{10}$ 1QM 5$_{4}$ (נחושת), ־אֶרֶץ *of the earth* Ps 47$_{10}$ (unless מָגֵן III *mighty one*; or em. מָגִנֵּי to סִגְנֵי *rulers of*), מגני המגדלות *shields of the towers* 1QM 9$_{12.14}$.

Perh. אִישׁ מָגֵן *man of a shield,* i.e. armed man Pr 6$_{11}$= 24$_{34}$ (perh. *insolent man,* i.e. מָגֵן III; or em. מְגַן *beggar* or מֹגֵן man *of gifts,* i.e. beggar), מחזיקי מגן *ones who hold a shield* 1QM 6$_{5}$, תֹּפְשֵׂי מָגֵן *ones who hold a shield* Jr 46$_{9}$, נֹשְׂאֵי מָגֵן *ones who carry a shield* 1 C 5$_{18}$ 2 C 14$_{7}$, נֹשְׁקֵי ... מָגֵן *ones armed ... with a shield* 17$_{17}$, אורך המגן *length of the shield* 1QM 5$_{6}$, גַּבֵּי מָגִנָּיו *bosses of his shield(s)* Jb 15$_{26}$, אֲפִיקֵי מָגִנִּים *furrows of shields* Jb 41$_{7}$, כָּל־מָגִנֵּי *all the shields of* 1 K 14$_{26}$ 1QM 9$_{14}$ (כול).

<APP> ′י Y. Dt 33$_{29}$ Ps 144$_{2}$, אֲדֹנָי *Adonai* Ps 59$_{12}$ (or em. מָגִנֵּנוּ to מְנָעֵמוֹ *hold them back*), אֱלֹהִים *God* perh. Ps 84$_{10}$, זָהָב *gold* 1 K 10$_{17}$||2 C 9$_{16}$.

<ADJ> אֶחָד *one* 1 K 10$_{17}$||2 C 9$_{16}$.

<PREP> לְ of benefit, *to, for,* + עשׂה *make* 2 C 32$_{27}$; of direction, *to,* + ידה hi. *give thanks* Si 51$_{12}$; *as* 4QShir Shabb^{d} 1.1$_{25}$; בְּ of agent, *by, through,* + ישׁע ni. *be saved* Dt 33$_{29}$; introducing object, + בער pi. *burn* Ezk 39$_{9}$, שׂלק hi. *burn* Ezk 39$_{9}$; עַל *upon* 1QM 7$_{15}$, + עלה *go up,* i.e.

go into 1 K 10_{17}||2 C 9_{16}, כתב *write* 1QM 9_{14}; תַּחַת *instead of*, + עשׂה *make* 1 K 14_{26}||2 C 12_{9}.

<COLL> מָגֵן || צִנָּה *(large) shield* 1 K 10_{17}||2 C 9_{16} (+) Jr 46_{3} Ezk 23_{24} 38_{4} 39_{9} Ps 35_{2} 2 C 14_{7} (+), שֶׁלֶט *shield* 2 C 23_{9} Ca 4_{4} (+), חֶרֶב *sword* Dt 33_{29} (+) Ps 76_{4} 1 C 5_{18}, כִּידוֹן *(Spanish) sword* 1QM 6_{5}, חֵץ *arrow* 2 K 19_{32}||Is 37_{33} (+) Ezk 39_{9}, קֶשֶׁת *bow* Jr 46_{9} Ezk 39_{9} Ps 76_{4} (all three +) Ne 4_{10} 1 C 5_{18} 2 C 14_{7} (both +) 17_{17} 26_{14}, רֹמַח *spear* Jg 5_{8} Ezk 39_{9} Ne 4_{10} 2 C 14_{7} (+) 26_{14} 1QM 6_{15} 9_{12} (+), חֲנִית *spear* 2 C 23_{9} 1QM 6_{5}, מַקֵּל *staff* Ezk 39_{9}, נֶשֶׁק *weapons* Ezk 39_{9}, שֶׁלַח *weapons* 2 C 32_{5}, כּוֹבַע *helmet* Ezk 27_{10} 38_{5} 2 C 26_{14}, קוֹבַע *helmet* Ezk 23_{24}, שִׁרְיוֹן *body armour* Ne 4_{10} 2 C 26_{14}, עֵזֶר *help* Ps $115_{9.10.11}$, סֵתֶר *hiding place* 119_{114}, עֹז *strength* Ps 28_{7}, מִלְחָמָה *war* Ps 76_{4}, שֶׁמֶשׁ *sun* Ps 84_{12}.

+ אַשְׁפָּה *quiver* Is 22_{6}, אֶבֶן *stone* 2 C 26_{14} (weapon) 2 C 32_{27} (precious), כְּלִי *vessel* 2 C 32_{27}, בֹּשֶׂם *spice* 2 C 32_{27}, זָהָב *gold* 2 C 32_{27}, כֶּסֶף *silver* 2 C 32_{27}, קֶרֶן *horn* of salvation 2 S 22_{3}||Ps 18_{3}, סֹלְלָה *siege mound* 2 K 19_{32}|| Is 37_{33}, מִשְׂגָּב *stronghold* 2 S 22_{3}||Ps 18_{3} Ps 144_{2}, מְצוּדָה *fortress* Ps 144_{2}, מָנוֹס *refuge* 2 S 22_{3}, חֶסֶד *loyalty* Ps 144_{2}, מְפַלֵּט *deliverer* Ps 144_{2}.

חמשים מגן *fifty shields* 1QM 7_{15}, מאה מגן *a hundred shields* 1QM 9_{13}, מגנים שלוש מאות *three hundred shields* 1QM 9_{14}, שְׁלֹשׁ־מְאוֹת מָגִנִּים *three hundred shields* 1 K 10_{17}||2 C 9_{16}, אֶלֶף הַמָּגֵן *a thousand shields* Ca 4_{4}.

לֹא־יְקַדְּמֶנָּה מָגֵן *he will not come against it (with) a shield* 2 K 19_{32}||Is 37_{33}, קָהָל רַב ... מָגֵן *a great company ... (with) a shield* Ezk 38_{4}, כֻּלָּם מָגֵן *all of them (with) a shield* Ezk 38_{5}, מגן כמגדל *a shield like a tower* 4QapJoseph[c] 1_{4}.

<SYN> צִנָּה *(large) shield*, שֶׁלֶט *shield*, חֶרֶב *sword*, כִּידוֹן *(Spanish) sword*, חֵץ *arrow*, קֶשֶׁת *bow*, רֹמַח *spear*, חֲנִית *spear*, מַקֵּל *staff*, נֶשֶׁק *weapons*, שֶׁלַח *weapons*, כּוֹבַע *helmet*, קוֹבַע *helmet*, שִׁרְיוֹן *body armour*, עֵזֶר *help*, סֵתֶר *hiding place*, עֹז *strength*, מִלְחָמָה *war*, שֶׁמֶשׁ *sun*.*

⇒ גנן *cover*.

*[מָגֵן] II $_{0.0.1}$ n.[m.] **protection,** <CSTR> דלתי מגן *doors of protection*, i.e. protecting doors 1QH 6_{27} (+ לאין מבוא *without entry*, i.e. so that none can enter) 4QSapDidA 1_{5} (מ[גן]).

⇒ גנן *cover*.

*מָגֵן III $_{4}$ adj. **insolent**—pl. cstr. מָגִנֵּי; sf. מָגִנֶּיהָ—**1.** attributively of אִישׁ *man* Pr 6_{11}=24_{34} (unless אִישׁ מָגֵן *man of a shield*, i.e. מָגֵן I).

2. as noun, **insolent one, bold one, mighty one,** <SUBJ> אהב *love* Ho 4_{18} (unless מָגִנֶּיהָ is from מֶגֶן *gift*). <NOM CL> לֵאלֹהִים מָגִנֵּי־אֶרֶץ *the mighty ones of the earth are*, i.e. belong, *to God* Ps 47_{10} (unless מָגֵן I *shield*). <CSTR> מָגִנֵּי־אֶרֶץ *mighty ones of the earth* Ps 47_{10} (unless מָגֵן I *shield*).

⇒ מְגִנָּה II *shamelessness*.

מָגֵן IV *benefactor, suzerain*,* see מָגָן *benefactor, suzerain*.

[מָגֵן] V $_{0.0.0.6}$ pr.n.m. **Magen, 1.** appar. father of Geber, T. ʿIra jar inscr. 1.

2. appar. father of Tanhum, Jar Stamp 192 (Gibeon, 8th cent.) 404 (others מתן *Mattan*; Lachish, 8th cent.) 493 (others מתן; Ramat Raḥel, 8th cent.) 791 (Lachish, 8th cent.) 952 953 (both T. Beit Mirsim?, 8th cent.).

3. father of Gemariah, <CSTR> בן גמריה *son of Gemariah* Seal 819 (City of David, 7th/6th cent.).

*[מֶ֫גֶן] $_{1}$ n.[m.] **gift** (or perh. מָגָן)—pl. sf. מָגִנֶּ֫יהָ—**gift, reward,** for drunkenness or prostitution, <NOM CL> קָלוֹן מָגִנֶּיהָ *shame is its gift* Ho 4_{18} (or em. מִגְּאוֹנָם they love shame *more than magnificence*, or קְלוֹן גַּגֵּיהֶם *the shame of their roofs*). <CSTR> אִישׁ מֶגֶן *man of a gifts*, i.e. beggar Pr 6_{11}=24_{34} (if em. מָגֵן *of a shield*).*

⇒ מגן I *deliver up*.

[מֹגֵן] I *benefactor, suzerain*, see מָגָן *benefactor, suzerain*.

[מֹגֵן] II *beggar*, see מגן *beseech*.

[מְגִנָּה] I $_{1}$ n.f. **covering** (unless מְגִנָּה I *shamelessness*) —cstr. מְגִנַּת—<OBJ> נתן *give* Lm 3_{65}. <CSTR> מְגִנַּת־לֵב *covering of the heart* Lm 3_{65}.

⇒ גנן *cover*.

*[מְגִנָּה] II $_{1}$ n.f. **shamelessness** (unless מְגִנָּה I *covering*)—cstr. מְגִנַּת—<OBJ> נתן *give* Lm 3$_{65}$. <CSTR> מְגִנַּת־לֵב *shamelessness of heart* Lm 3$_{65}$.
⇒ cf. מָגַן III *insolent*.

*[מַגְנֵס] $_{0.0.1}$ pr.n.[m.] **Magnus,** name in writing exercise, 4QNames$_{4}$.

*[מַגָּע] $_{0.0.4}$ n.m. **contact**—cstr. Q מגע; sf. Q מגעו—**contact, one who has contact,** with person who has a discharge, <CSTR> מגע טמאת *contact of,* i.e. with, *the uncleanness of* one who touches 4QTohB^{c} 1.1$_{12}$. <PREP> כְּ *as* 4QD^{g} 1.2$_{5}$ 4QTohB^{c} 1.1$_{12}$. <COLL> אם תצ[א ממנו] שכבת הזרע מגעו וטמא ה[ו]א *if there went out from him an emission of semen, (any)one who has contact with him will be unclean* 4QTohA 1.1$_{8}$.
Also 4QD^{g} 1.2$_{5}$.
⇒ נגע *touch*.

מִגְעֶרֶת I $_{1}$ n.f. **rebuke,** perh. **threat,** <OBJ> שׁלח pi. *send* Dt 28$_{20}$ (unless מִגְעֶרֶת II *dysentery;* || מְאֵרָה *curse,* מְהוּמָה *discomfiture*).
<SYN> מְאֵרָה *curse,* מְהוּמָה *discomfiture.*
⇒ גער *rebuke.*

*מִגְעֶרֶת II $_{1}$ n.f. **dysentery,** <OBJ> שׁלח pi. *send* Dt 28$_{20}$ (|| מְאֵרָה *curse,* מְהוּמָה *discomfiture*).
<SYN> מְאֵרָה *curse,* מְהוּמָה *discomfiture.*

מגפא, see מַגֵּפָה *plague.*

מַגֵּפָה $_{26.1.3}$ n.f. **plague**—Q מגפא; cstr. מַגֵּפַת; pl. sf. מַגֵּפֹתַי—**1. plague, pestilence, stroke** (Ezk 24$_{16}$), sent by Y., <SUBJ> היה *be* Nm 31$_{16}$ Zc 14$_{12.15.18}$, פרץ *break out* Ps 106$_{29}$, עצר ni. *be restrained* Nm 17$_{13.15}$ 25$_{8}$ 2 S 24$_{21}$|| 1 C 21$_{22}$ 1 S 24$_{25}$ Ps 106$_{30}$. <NOM CL> מַגֵּפָה אַחַת לְכֻלָּם וּלְסַרְנֵיכֶם *one plague,* i.e. the same plague, *was upon all of them and your lords* 1 S 6$_{4}$ (mss לְכֻלְּכֶם *upon all of you*). <OBJ> שׁלח *send* Ex 9$_{14}$, נגף *strike with* Zc 14$_{12.18}$ 2 C 21$_{14}$ 4QpsHistB 1$_{2}$. <CSTR> מַגֵּפַת הַסּוּס הַפֶּרֶד הַגָּמָל וְהַחֲמוֹר וְכָל־הַבְּהֵמָה *plague of,* i.e. upon, *the horses, the mules, the camels, the asses and all the beasts* Zc 14$_{15}$; יוֹם הַמַּגֵּפָה *day of the plague* Nm 25$_{18}$, כָּל־מַגֵּפֹתַי *all my plagues* Ex 9$_{14}$. <ADJ> אֶחָד *one* 1 S 6$_{4}$, גָּדוֹל *great* 2 C 21$_{14}$, רַב *great* 4QpsHistB 1$_{2}$, זֹאת *this* Zc 14$_{15}$.
<PREP> לְ *for,* i.e. in order to cause, + היה *be* 1 C 21$_{17}$ (or em. בְּעַמְּךָ לֹא לְמַגֵּפָה *against your people not for a plague* to בָּעָם כַּלֵּא לַמַּגֵּפָה *among the people withhold the plague*); בְּ of instrument, *by (means of), through,* + מות *die* Nm 14$_{37}$ 17$_{14}$ 25$_{9}$, לקח *take* Ezk 24$_{16}$, המם *discomfit* Si 48$_{21}$; כְּ *as,* + היה *be* Zc 14$_{15}$; אַחֲרֵי *after,* + היה *be* Nm 25$_{19}$.
2. slaughter, defeat in battle, <SUBJ> היה *be* 1 S 4$_{17}$ 2 S 17$_{9}$ 18$_{7}$. <CSTR> מגפת עולמים *slaughter of everlastingness,* i.e. everlasting slaughter 1QM 18$_{1}$, כלה *of destruction,* i.e. destructive slaughter 1QM 18$_{12}$ (מגפה; appar. error for מגפת). <ADJ> גָּדוֹל *great* 1S 4$_{17}$. <PREP> לְ of benefit, *for* 1QM 18$_{12}$ (למגפה; appar. error for למגפת); בְּ of accompaniment, *with, in,* + נשׂא ni. (of hand) *be raised* 1QM 18$_{1}$ (בהנ[ש]א).*
⇒ נגף *strike.*

מגפה, see מַגֵּפָה *plague.*

מַגְפִּיעָשׁ $_{1}$ pr.n.m. **Magpiash,** family head, co-signatory with Nehemiah, perh. ident. with Magbish at Ezr 2$_{30}$, <NOM CL> רָאשֵׁי הָעָם ... מַגְפִּיעָשׁ *the heads of the people were ... Magpiash* Ne 10$_{21}$.

מגר $_{2.0.2}$ vb. **throw—Qal** $_{1.1}$ Ptc. pass. Q מגור, מְגוּרֵי—pass. **be thrown, be delivered up,** to the sword (Ezk 21$_{17}$), **be cast down,** by sickness (1QH 8$_{26}$), <SUBJ> נָשִׂיא *prince* Ezk 21$_{17}$ (or em.; see Prep.), worshipper 1QH 8$_{26}$. <PREP> אֶל *to,* + חֶרֶב *sword* Ezk 21$_{17}$ (or em. מְגוּרֵי to מֻגָּרֵי *they are poured out,* i.e. נגר ho.); אֵת *with,* + עַם *people* Ezk 21$_{17}$ (or em.); עִם *with,* i.e. because of, + חֳלִי *sickness* 1QH 8$_{26}$.
Pi. $_{1.1}$ Pf. מִגַּרְתָּה; impf. 2ms Q תמגרה—**throw down,** <SUBJ> Y. Ps 89$_{45}$ 11QPs^{a} 24$_{5}$ (:: בנה *build*). <OBJ> נֶפֶשׁ *soul* 11QPs^{a} 24$_{5}$, כִּסֵּא *throne* Ps 89$_{45}$. <PREP> לְ of direction, *to,* + אֶרֶץ *ground* Ps 89$_{45}$.
<ANT> בנה *build.*

מְגֵרָה $_{4}$ n.f. **saw**—pl. מְגֵרוֹת—<PREP> בְּ accompaniment, *with*, + שִׂים *place*, i.e. set to work 2 S 12$_{31}$||1 C 20$_{3}$ (1 C if em. וַיָּשַׂר *and he sawed them* to וַיָּשֶׂם *and he set them to work*; || חָרִיץ *pickaxe*, מַגְזֵרָה *axe*) 1 C 20$_{3}$ (or em. בְּמַגְזֵרוֹת *with axes*); of instrument, *by (means of)*, *with*, + גרר po. *be sawn* 1 K 7$_{9}$.

<SYN> חָרִיץ *pickaxe*, מַגְזֵרָה *axe*.

⇒ גרר *drag*.

מִגְרוֹן I $_{2}$ pl.n. **Migron,** prob. the Wadi es-Swenit, a canyon descending from the central highlands to the Jordan valley near Jericho,* or else a town or district in Benjamin, near Gibeah (1 S 14$_{2}$) and Michmash (Is 10$_{28}$), <PREP> בְּ of place, *in*, *through* 1 S 14$_{2}$ (unless מִגְרוֹן II *threshing floor*), + עבר *pass* Is 10$_{28}$.*

*מִגְרוֹן II $_{1}$ n.[m.] **threshing floor** (unless מִגְרוֹן I *Migron*), <PREP> בְּ of place, *in*, *through* 1 S 14$_{2}$.

⇒ cf. גֹּרֶן *threshing floor*.

*[מִגְרָן] $_{0.0.1}$ n.[m.] perh. **destruction, threshing,** <PREP> כְּ *as* 4QpsHod^{a} 1$_{3}$ (+ עִיר perh. *agitation*).

⇒ cf. גֹּרֶן *threshing floor*.

[מִגְרָע], see מִגְרָעָה *recess*.

[מִגְרָעָה] $_{1}$ n.f. **recess**—pl. מִגְרָעוֹת—**recess, rebatement,** in wall, <OBJ> נתן *give*, i.e. place 1 K 6$_{6}$.

⇒ גרע *diminish*.

*[מִגְרָף] n.m. **shovel**—<OBJ> נשׂא *lift* Am 6$_{10}$ (if em. וּמְסָרְפוֹ *and the one who burns him* to מִגְרָפוֹ *his spade*).

⇒ גרף *sweep away*.

[מֶגְרָפָה] I $_{1}$ n.f. **shovel**—pl. sf. מֶגְרְפֹתֵיהֶם—**shovel, spade,** <PREP> תַּחַת *under*, + עבשׁ *shrivel* Jl 1$_{17}$ (or em. תַּחַת to חתת their floodwaters [מֶגְרָפָה II] *fail*; or em. תַּחַת מֶגְרְפֹתֵיהֶם to חַתּוּ גָּרְנֹתֵיהֶם *their threshing floors are dismayed*, i.e. חתת).

⇒ גרף *sweep away*.

*[מֶגְרָפָה] II $_{1}$ n.f. **floodwater, alluvial soil**—pl. sf. מֶגְרְפֹתֵיהֶם—<SUBJ> חתת *be dry* Jl 1$_{17}$ (if em. תַּחַת *under* to חתת).

⇒ גרף *sweep away*.

*[מֶגְרָפָה] III $_{1}$ n.f. **dyke**—pl. sf. מֶגְרְפֹתֵיהֶם—<SUBJ> חתת *be dry* Jl 1$_{17}$ (if em. תַּחַת *under* to חתת).

מִגְרָשׁ I $_{114}$ n.m. **land outside city walls**—cstr. מִגְרַשׁ; מִגְרָשָׁהּ; pl. מִגְרֹשׁוֹת; cstr. מִגְרְשֵׁי; sf. מִגְרָשֶׁיהָ, מִגְרְשֵׁיהֶם, מִגְרְשֵׁיהֶן—**land outside city walls,** whether as claimed territory of a city, exclusion zone to which others had no right, or as sacral zone; often used as pasture land (Nm 35$_{3}$ Jos 14$_{4}$ 21$_{2}$), though the term prob. does not mean that, and for villages (1 C 5$_{16}$); surrounding Levitical city (Lv 25$_{34}$ Nm 35$_{3.2.4.5.7}$ Jos 14$_{4}$ 21$_{2+56t}$ 1 C 6$_{40+41t}$ 13$_{2}$ 2 C 11$_{14}$ 31$_{19}$), surrounding Jerusalem (Ezk 45$_{4}$ [if em.; see Subj.] 48$_{15.17}$), surrounding temple (Ezk 45$_{2}$).

<SUBJ> היה *be* Nm 35$_{3.5}$ Jos 21$_{42}$ Ezk 45$_{4}$ (if em. וּמִקְדָּשׁ *and a sacred place* to וּמִגְרָשׁ *and pasture land*) 48$_{17}$, רעשׁ *shake* Ezk 27$_{28}$ (unless מִגְרָשׁ II *driven wave*). <NOM CL> מִגְרְשֵׁי הֶעָרִים ... מִקִּיר הָעִיר וָחוּצָה אֶלֶף אַמָּה סָבִיב *the pasture lands of the cities shall be ... from the wall of the city and outward, a thousand cubits all round* Nm 35$_{4}$, כָּל־הֶעָרִים עֶשֶׂר וּמִגְרְשֵׁיהֶן *all the cities and their pasture lands were ten* Jos 21$_{26}$, sim. Jos 21$_{19.33.41}$, חֲמִשִּׁים אַמָּה מִגְרָשׁ לוֹ סָבִיב *there shall be to it an open space of fifty cubits all round* Ezk 45$_{2}$. <OBJ> נתן *give* Nm 35$_{2.7}$ Jos 14$_{4}$ 21$_{2+51t}$ 1 C 6$_{40+41t}$, עזב *leave* 2 C 11$_{14}$.

<CSTR> מִגְרְשֵׁי הֶעָרִים *pasture lands of the cities* Nm 35$_{4.5}$, מִגְרַשׁ עָרֵיהֶם *pasture land of their cities* Lv 25$_{34}$ 2 C 31$_{19}$, מִגְרְשֵׁי שָׁרוֹן *pasture lands of Sharon* 1 C 5$_{16}$; עָרֵי מִגְרְשֵׁיהֶם *cities of their pasture lands* 1 C 13$_{2}$, שְׂדֵה מִגְרַשׁ *fields of the pasture land of* Lv 25$_{34}$ 2 C 31$_{19}$ (שְׂדֵי), כָּל־מִגְרְשֵׁי *all the pasture lands of* 1 C 5$_{16}$. <PREP> לְ of benefit, *to*, *for* Ezk 48$_{15}$; בְּ of place, *in*, + ישׁב *dwell* 1 C 5$_{16}$. <COLL> מִגְרָשׁ || מוֹשָׁב *dwelling place* Ezk 48$_{15}$, אֲחֻזָּה *possession* 2 C 11$_{14}$; + עִיר *city* Nm 35$_{2.3.7}$ Jos 14$_{4}$ 21$_{2+7t}$ Ezk 48$_{17}$ 1 C 6$_{49}$, + named city Jos 21$_{11+48t}$ 1 C 6$_{40+40t}$.

<SYN> מוֹשָׁב *dwelling place*, אֲחֻזָּה *possession*.

⇒ גרשׁ *expel*.

*[מִגְרָשׁ] II $_1$ n.m. **driven wave**—pl. מִגְרָשׁוֹת—<SUBJ> רעשׁ *shake* Ezk 27_{28}.

⇨ גרשׁ *expel.*

*[מַגָּשׁ] n.m. **offering,** <SUBJ> קטר ho. *be burned* Ml 1_{11} (if em. מֻגָּשׁ *brought near,* i.e. נגשׁ ho.).

⇨ נגשׁ *approach.*

[מַד] I $_9$ n.m. **garment**—sf. מִדּוֹ (מַדּוֹ); pl. מַדִּין; sf. מַדָּיו (perh. מַדּוֹ*)—**1. (outer) garment, clothing** (Jg 3_{16} 1 S 4_{12} Ps 109_{18}), of priest (Lv 6_3), of warrior, perh. **undergarment** (2 S 10_4 = 1 C 19_4); perh. **armour** (1 S $17_{38.39}$ 18_4 2 S 20_8). **2. cloth, rug,** perh. as saddle (Jg 5_{10}).

<NOM CL> מַדָּם קָלוֹן *their garment is shame* Pr 3_{35} (if em. מֵרִים appar. *raises* to מַדָּם). <OBJ> לבשׁ *put on* Lv 6_3 (+ מִכְנָסַיִם *breeches*), hi. *dress with* 1 S 17_{38} (+ קוֹבַע *helmet*, שִׁרְיוֹן *body armour*), נתן *give* 1 S 18_4 (+ מְעִיל *robe*, חֶרֶב *sword*, קֶשֶׁת *bow*, חֲגוֹר *belt*), קרע pass. *be torn* 1 S 4_{12}. <CSTR> מַדֵּי בַד *garments of linen* Lv 6_3 (if em.; see App.). <APP> בַּד *linen* Lv 6_3 (or em. מִדּוֹ בַד *his garment, linen* to מַדֵּי בַד *garments of linen*; or מִדּוֹ =pl.),* לְבוּשׁ *clothing* 2 S 20_8. <PREP> כְּ *as (though it were)*, + לבשׁ *dress oneself* Ps 109_{18}; עַל *upon, over* 2 S 20_8, + ישׁב *sit* Jg 5_{10}; מֵעַל לְ *over*, + חגר *gird oneself with* 1 S 17_{39}; מִתַּחַת לְ *underneath*, + חגר *gird oneself with* Jg 3_{16}. <COLL> יוֹאָב חָגוּר מִדּוֹ *Joab was girded with his garment* 2 S 20_8.*

⇨ cf. מִדָּה II *garment*, מָדוּ *garment*.

[מַד] II $_{3.0.1}$ n.[m.] **measure**—sf. Q מידו, מִדָּהּ; pl. Kt מדין; sf. מַדַּיִךְ—**measure(ment), (great) stature,** <NOM CL> אֲרֻכָּה מֵאֶרֶץ מִדָּה *its measure is longer than the earth* Jb 11_9 (or em. מִדָּתָהּ *its measure* [from מִדָּה], or מִדָּה *[in] measure* it is longer). <CSTR> אִישׁ מדין *man of (great) stature* 1 S $21_{20(Kt)}$ (Qr מָדוֹן *of strife*; or em. מִדָּה *of [great] stature*, as at ||1 C 20_6), מְנָת־מִדַּיִךְ *the portion of your measure*, i.e. measured out to you Jr 13_{25} (or em. מֶרְיֵךְ *of your rebellion*; + גּוֹרָל *lot*), כול מידו *all its measure* 4QTohA 2.2_9. <PREP> בְּ *in* 4QTohA 2.2_9.*

⇨ מדד *measure.*

מִדְבָּר I $_{271.2.16}$ n.m. **steppe**—+ ה- of direction, מִדְבָּרָה; sf. מִדְבָּרָהּ; cstr. מִדְבַּר; + ה- of direction מִדְבָּרָה; pl. cstr. Q מדברי—**steppe, wilderness, desert,** as **a.** place for pasturing flocks and herds (Gn 36_{24} Ex 3_1 1 S 17_{28}).

b. place of wild animals and birds (Jr 2_{24} Ml 1_3 Ps 102_7 Jb 24_5 Lm $4_{3[Qr]}$ Si 13_{19}).

c. desolate (Is 64_9 Jr 12_2 Jl 2_3 4_{19} Ps 102_7 perh. 4QBer^a 5_3), uncultivated (Jr 2_2).

d. largely uninhabited (Jr 17_6 22_6 Jb 38_{26} Ps 107_4), though having cities (Jos 15_{61} Is 42_{11} 2 C 8_4).

e. dry and thirsty (Is 41_{18} Ezk 19_{13} Ho 2_5 13_5 Zp 2_{13} Ps $107_{33.35}$), salty (Jr 17_6).

f. southern border of land settled by Israelites (Ex 23_{31} Nm 34_3 Dt 11_{24} Jos 1_4), eastern border beyond Jordan (Jg 11_{22}).

g. perh. to express superlative (נְאוֹת מִדְבָּר *boundless meadows* Ps 65_{13}).*

<SUBJ> היה *be* Is 32_{15} $64_{9.9}$ Jr 2_{31}, יצא *go out* Nm 21_{13}, סגר *close in* Ex 14_3, שׂושׂ *rejoice* Is 35_1, נשׂא *lift* Is 42_{11}.

<NOM CL> הַכַּרְמֶל הַמִּדְבָּר *the orchard was a steppe* Jr 4_{26}, הִנֵּה ... מִדְבָּר *behold ... a steppe* Jr 50_{12}, אַחֲרָיו מִדְבַּר שְׁמָמָה *after him is a desolate wilderness* Jl 2_3, מִדְבַּר סִין אֲשֶׁר בֵּין־אֵילִם וּבֵין סִינָי *the steppe of Sin which is between Elim and Sinai* Ex 16_1, בַּמִּדְבָּר אֲשֶׁר עַל־פְּנֵי מוֹאָב *in the steppe which is opposite Moab* Nm 21_{11}, מִדְבַּר יְהוּדָה אֲשֶׁר בְּנֶגֶב עֲרָד *the steppe of Judah which is in the Negeb of Arad* Jg 1_{16}.

<OBJ> הלך *go through* Dt 1_{19} 2_7, עבר *pass through* appar. 2 S 15_{23}, שׂים *place*, i.e. make Is 50_2 Is 41_{18} 51_3 Ps 107_{35}, שׁית *place*, i.e. make Jr 22_6, נתן *give*, i.e. make Ml 1_3 (if em.; see Cstr.), ראה *see* Dt 1_{19}, חיל hi. *cause writhing* Ps $29_{8.8}$.

<CSTR> מִדְבַּר אֱדוֹם *of Edom* 2 K 3_8, אֵתָם *of Etham* Nm 33_8, בְּאֵר שָׁבַע *of Beer-sheba* Gn 21_{14}, בֵּית אָוֶן *of Beth-aven* Jos 18_{12} (מִדְבַּרָה), גִּבְעוֹן *Gibeon* 2 S 2_{24}, דִּבְלָתָה *of Diblah* Ezk 6_{14} (or em. מִמִּדְבַּר דִּבְלָתָה to מֵהַמִּדְבָּר רִבְלָתָה *from the steppe to Riblah*), דַּמֶּשֶׂק *of Damascus* 1 K 19_{15} (מִדְבַּרָה), זִיף־ *Zip* 1 S $23_{14.15}$ $26_{2.2}$, יְהוּדָה *of Judah* Jg 1_{16} Ps 63_1, יְרוּאֵל *of Jeruel* 2 C 20_{16}, ירושלים *of Jerusalem* 1QM 1_3, מוֹאָב *of Moab* Dt 2_8, מָעוֹן *of Maon* 1 S $23_{24.25.25}$, סִין *of Sin* Ex 16_1 17_1 Nm $33_{11.12}$, סִינַי *of Sinai* Ex 19_1 (סִינָי) 19_2 Lv 7_{38} (סִינָי) Nm $1_{1.9}$

(סִינַי) 34$_{4.14}$ 9$_{1.5}$ 10$_{12}$ (both סִינַי) 26$_{64}$ 33$_{15}$ (both סִינַי) 33$_{16}$ (סִינַי), עֵין גֶּדִי *of En-gedi* 1 S 24$_{2}$, פָּארָן *of Paran* Gn 21$_{21}$ Nm 10$_{12}$ 12$_{16}$ 13$_{3.26}$ (all four Sam פראן) 1 S 25$_{1}$, ־צִן *of Zin* Nm 13$_{21}$ 20$_{1}$ 27$_{14.14}$ 33$_{36}$ 34$_{3}$ Dt 32$_{51}$ Jos 15$_{1}$, קְדֵמוֹת *of Kedemoth* Dt 2$_{26}$, קָדֵשׁ *of Kadesh* Ps 29$_{8}$, שׁוּר *of Shur* Ex 15$_{22}$, תְּקוֹעַ *of Tekoa* 2 C 20$_{20}$.

מדברי חור[ב] *steppes of Horeb*, or perh. *of desolation* 4QBer^{a} 5$_{3}$, מִדְבַּר אֶרֶץ *steppe of the land of* Egypt Ezk 20$_{36}$, הָרִים appar. *of the mountains* Ps 75$_{7}$ (or em. מִמִּדְבָּר *from the steppe* is lifting up), ־יָם *of the sea* Is 21$_{1}$ (or em. מִדְבַּר־יָם to מִדְבָּר), שְׁמָמָה *of desolation*, i.e. desolate steppe Jr 12$_{10}$ Jl 2$_{3}$ 4$_{19}$, הָעַמִּים *of the peoples* Ezk 20$_{35}$ 1QM 1$_{3}$ 4QpIsa^{a} 5$_{2}$ (הע[מ]ים).

אֶרֶץ מִדְבָּר *land of steppe* Dt 32$_{10}$ (Sam הַמִּדְבָּר) Pr 21$_{19}$, דֶּרֶךְ הַמִּדְבָּר *way of the steppe* Ex 13$_{18}$ Jos 8$_{15}$ Jg 20$_{42}$ (mss הַמִּדְבָּרָה), דֶּרֶךְ מִדְבַּר *way of the steppe of* Dt 2$_{8}$ 2 S 2$_{24}$ 2 K 3$_{8}$, קְצֵה הַמִּדְבָּר *edge of the steppe* Ex 13$_{20}$ Nm 33$_{6}$, פְּנֵי *face of* Ex 16$_{14}$ 2 C 20$_{16}$ (or em. פְּנֵי to לִפְנֵי *before*), עברות *fords of* 2 S 15$_{28(Kt)}$ 17$_{16(mss)}$, עַרְבוֹת *plains of* 2 S 15$_{28(Qr)}$ 17$_{16}$, נְאוֹת מִדְבַּר *pastures of the steppe* Jr 9$_{9}$ 23$_{10}$ Jl 1$_{19.20}$ (הַמִּדְבָּר) 1$_{22}$ Ml 1$_{3}$ (if em.; see below) Ps 65$_{13}$, תַּנּוֹת *jackals of* Ml 3 (or em. תַּנּוֹת to נְוֹת *pastures of*, or נָתַתִּי *I have given*, i.e. made into, desert), קְאַת *pelican of* Ps 102$_{7}$, פראי מדבר *wild asses of the steppe* Si 13$_{1}$, קוֹצֵי הַמִּדְבָּר *thorns of the steppe* Jg 8$_{7.16}$, חֶרֶב *sword of* Lm 5$_{9}$, רוּחַ *wind of* Jr 13$_{24}$ (מִדְבָּר), מַשָּׂא מִדְבַּר *oracle of the steppe of* Is 21$_{1}$ (or em. מִדְבָּר *of the steppe*), גולת המדבר *exiles of the steppe* 1QM 1$_{2}$, שבי *penitents of* 4QpPs^{a} 1.3$_{1}$, לִמֻּד מִדְבָּר *one used to the steppe* Jr 2$_{24}$, כָּל־הַמִּדְבָּר *all the steppe* Dt 1$_{19}$, כול מדברי *all the steppes of* 4QBer^{a} 5$_{3}$.

<APP> עֲרָבָה *desert-plain* Jr 50$_{12}$, צִיָּה *dry land* Jr 50$_{12}$, אַחֲרִית *last* of the nations Jr 50$_{12}$, אֶרֶץ *land* Jr 2$_{2}$ 17$_{6}$ Ezk 19$_{13}$ Ho 13$_{5}$ Jb 38$_{26}$, עִיר *city* Jr 22$_{6}$.

<ADJ> גָּדוֹל *great* Dt 1$_{19}$ 2$_{7}$ 8$_{15}$ 1QM 2$_{12}$, נוֹרָא *dreadful* Dt 1$_{19}$ 8$_{15}$, זֶה *this* Nm 14$_{2.29.32.35}$ 20$_{4}$ Dt 2$_{7}$ 4QpsJub^{b} 3$_{3}$ ([ה]מדבר ה[זה]).

<PREP> לְ introducing predicate, + היה *be* Jl 4$_{19}$; *as*, *into*, + נתן *give*, i.e. make Jr 12$_{10}$, שׂים *place*, i.e. make Ps 107$_{33}$, ברא *create* 1QM 10$_{13}$; of direction, *(in)to*, *towards* 2 C 20$_{24}$ 1QS 9$_{20}$, + הלך *go* 1QS 8$_{13}$, יצא *go out* 2 C 20$_{20}$.

בְּ of place, *in(to)* Gn 16$_{7}$ 37$_{22}$ Nm 21$_{13}$ Dt 4$_{43}$ Jos 5$_{5}$ 12$_{8}$ 15$_{61}$ 20$_{8}$ 1 S 23$_{15.24}$ 24$_{2}$ 2 S 16$_{2}$ 17$_{29}$ 1 K 2$_{34}$ Jr 3$_{2}$ 4$_{11}$ (or em. בַּמִּדְבָּר to בָּא מִמִּדְבָּר *it has come from the steppe*) 12$_{12}$ 48$_{6}$ Ho 9$_{10}$ Ps 95$_{8}$ Jb 24$_{5}$ 38$_{26}$ 1 C 6$_{63}$ 2 C 24$_{9}$ 4QapJoshua^{a} 19.2$_{6}$, + היה *be* Nm 15$_{32}$ Ps 63$_{1}$, ישׁב *dwell* Gn 21$_{20.21}$ 1 S 23$_{14.14.25}$ 26$_{3}$ Jr 9$_{25}$ Ezk 34$_{25}$, שׁכן *dwell* Nm 10$_{12}$ Is 32$_{16}$ Jr 17$_{6}$ 25$_{24}$, לין *lodge* Ps 55$_{8}$, חנה *encamp* Ex 19$_{2}$ Nm 10$_{31}$ 12$_{16}$ 21$_{11}$ 33$_{11.15.36}$ 1QM 1$_{3}$.

הלך *go* Ex 3$_{18}$ 5$_{3}$ 8$_{23}$ 15$_{22}$ Nm 33$_{8}$ Jos 5$_{6}$ 14$_{10}$ Jg 11$_{16.18}$ 1 K 19$_{4}$ Jr 2$_{2}$, hi. *lead* Dt 8$_{2.15}$ 29$_{4}$ Is 63$_{13}$ (or em. כַּמִּדְבָּר) Jr 2$_{6}$ Am 2$_{10}$ Ps 106$_{9(mss)}$ Ps 136$_{16}$, נהג pi. *lead* Ps 78$_{52}$, תעה *wander* Gn 21$_{14}$ Nm 14$_{33}$ (if em.; see below) Ps 107$_{4}$, נוע *wander* Nm 14$_{33}$ (if em.; see below), hi. *cause to wander* Nm 32$_{13}$, שׁלח pi. *send* Lv 16$_{22}$, רדף *pursue* Jos 8$_{24}$ 1 S 23$_{25(mss)}$, בקשׁ pi. *seek* 1 S 26$_{2}$, ארב *wait in ambush* Lm 4$_{19}$, מצא *find* Gn 36$_{24}$ Jr 31$_{2}$ (if em.; see below), עזב *leave* Ne 9$_{19}$, נטשׁ *leave* 1 S 17$_{28}$, רעה *pasture* Nm 14$_{33}$ (unless em. רֹעִים *pasturing* to תֹּעִים *wandering*, or נָעִים *wandering*) Ho 13$_{5}$ (if em. יְדַעְתִּיךָ *I knew you* to רְעִיתִיךָ *I pastured you*), נוח hi. *leave* Nm 32$_{15}$, בקע ni. *break out* Is 35$_{6}$, pi. *split* Ps 78$_{15}$.

חגג *celebrate festival* Ex 5$_{1}$, זבח *sacrifice* Ex 8$_{24}$, קרב hi. *bring near*, i.e. offer Lv 7$_{38}$ Nm 3$_{4}$, נגשׁ hi. *bring near*, i.e. offer Am 5$_{25}$, עבד *serve* Ex 7$_{16}$, עשׂה *do, make* Nm 9$_{5}$ 14$_{22}$ Dt 1$_{31}$ 11$_{5}$ Ezk 20$_{17}$ 1 C 21$_{29}$ 2 C 1$_{3}$, שׁמר *keep* 1 S 25$_{21}$, פנה pi. *prepare* Is 40$_{3}$=1QS 8$_{14}$, ערך *arrange*, i.e. spread, table Ps 78$_{19}$, בנה *build* 1 K 9$_{18}$||2 C 8$_{4}$ 2 C 26$_{10}$, נתן *give* Jr 9$_{1}$, i.e. place Is 41$_{19}$ 43$_{20}$, שׂים *place* Is 43$_{19}$ Ps 105$_{27}$ (if em. בָּם דִּבְרֵי *among them words of* to בַּמִּדְבָּר), נשׂא *lift* hand, i.e. swear Ezk 20$_{15.23}$, שׁתל pass. *be transplanted* Ezk 19$_{13}$, כול pilp. *sustain* Ne 9$_{21}$, אכל hi. *feed* Ex 16$_{32}$ Dt 8$_{16}$.

ידע *know* Ho 13$_{5}$ (or em.; see above), שׁמע *hear* 1 S 25$_{4}$, אמר *say* Ezk 20$_{18}$, דבר pi. *speak* Nm 1$_{1}$ 3$_{14}$ 9$_{1}$ Dt 1$_{1}$, לין ni. *murmur* Ex 16$_{2(Qr)}$, מרה *rebel* Nm 27$_{14}$, hi. Ezk 20$_{13}$ Ps 78$_{40}$, קצף hi. *anger* Dt 9$_{7}$, אוה htp. *desire* Ps 106$_{14}$, קנא pi. *be jealous* Si 45$_{18}$, פקד *number* Nm 1$_{19}$ 26$_{64}$, נפל *fall* Nm 14$_{29.32}$, hi. *cause to fall* Ps 106$_{26}$, שׁפך *pour* wrath Ezk 20$_{13}$, כלה pi. *accomplish* anger Ezk 20$_{21}$, שׁפט ni. *enter into judgment* Ezk 20$_{36}$, כרת ni. *be cut off* CD 3$_{7}$, נכה hi. *strike* 1 S 4$_{8}$, שׁחט *slay* Nm 14$_{16}$, מות *die* Ex 14$_{11.12}$ Nm 14$_{2}$ 21$_{5}$ 26$_{65}$ 27$_{3}$ Jos 5$_{4}$, hi. *kill* Nm 16$_{13}$ Dt

9_{28}, ho. *be killed* Nm $26_{65(\text{mss, Sam}^{\text{mss}})}$, הרג *kill* Jos 8_{24}, תמם *come to an end* Nm $14_{33.35}$.

כְּ *as* Zp 2_{13} 4QNarrG 1_4, + היה *be* 4QapLam^a 1.1_{12}, שׂים *place*, i.e. make Is 14_{17} Ho 2_5, עזב ni. *be forsaken* Is 21_{10}; *as in*, + הלך hi. *lead* Is 63_{13} (if em. כַּסּוּס בַּמִּדְבָּר *like a horse in the steppe* to כַּמִּדְבָּר כַּסּוּס *as in the steppe; like a horse*) Ps 106_9, מצא Jr 31_2 (if em. בַּמִּדְבָּר *in the steppe*).

מִן of direction, *from* Nm 21_{18} Ezk 6_{14} Ps 75_7 4Qps Ezek^a 5_3 ([מן המדבנ]ר) 4QBark^a 3.2_2 ([ממדבנ]ר), + היה *be* Nm 34_3 Dt 11_{24} Jos 1_4, בוא *come* Is 21_1 Jr 4_{11} (if em.; see above), ho. *be brought* Ezk 23_{42} (or em. ho. to qal), עלה *go up* Ho 13_{15} Ca 3_6 8_5, נסע *journey* Ex 17_1 Nm 10_{12} $33_{12.15}$, שׁלח *send* Nm 13_3 Dt 2_{26} 1 S 25_{14}, שׁוב *go back* 1QM 1_3 4QpIsa^a 5_2, תור *spy out* Nm 13_{21}, שׁית *place* border Ex 23_{31}, ירשׁ *possess* Jg 11_{22}.

אֶל *(in)to, towards*, + הלך *go* 1 S $25_{1(\text{mss})}$ 26_2, בוא *come* Ex 16_1 18_5 Nm 13_{26}, hi. *bring* Nm 20_4 Ezk $20_{10.35}$, יצא *go out* Ex 15_{22}, hi. *bring out* Ex 16_3, ירד 1 S 25_1 26_2, עבר *pass* 2 S $15_{23(\text{mss})}$, פנה *turn* Ex 16_{10}, נוס *flee* Jos $8_{20(\text{mss})}$, שׁית *set* face Nm 24_1.

עַל *upon, in* Gn 14_6 Nm $21_{13(\text{Sam})}$, + מטר hi. *rain* Jb 38_{26}.

עַד *as far as*, + לחם ni. *fight* 1QM 2_{12}.

לִפְנֵי *before* 2 C 20_{16} (if em.; see Cstr.).

מֵעֵבֶר *from across*, + בוא *come* Jb 1_{19}.

אַחַר *behind*, + נהג *drive* Ex 3_1.

ה- of direction, *in(to), towards* 1 C 12_9, + היה *be* Jos 18_{12}, בוא *come* 1 S 26_3 1 C 5_9, נסע *journey* Nm $14_{25(\text{mss, Sam})}$ Dt 1_{40} 2_1, עבר *pass* Nm 33_8, שׁוב *go back* 1 K 19_{15}, נוס *flee* Jg $20_{45.47}$, שׁלח *send* Is 16_1, pi. Lv $16_{10.21}$, קרא *meet* Ex 4_{27} Nm 21_{23}, שׁקף ni. *look down* 1 S 13_{18}, נטשׁ *leave* Ezk 29_5.

מִדְבָּר (without ה- of direction) *in(to), towards the steppe* Nm 27_{14} Dt 32_{51}, + היה *be* Jos 15_1, הלך hi. *lead* Ho 2_{16}, בוא *come* Ex $19_{1.2}$ Nm 20_1, יצא *go out* Jos 16_1, עלה *go up* Jg 1_{16}, ירד *go down* 1 S $25_{1(\text{mss})}$, נסע *journey* Nm 14_{25} (mss, Sam + ה- of direction), תעה *wander* Is 16_8, נוס *flee* Jos 8_{20} (mss אֶל *to*), רדף *pursue* 1 S 23_{25}, שׁלח *send* 11QT 26_{13}.

<COLL> מִדְבָּר || עֲרָבָה *steppe, Arabah* Dt 1_1 Jos 12_8 1 S 23_{24} (+) Is $35_{1.6}$ 40_3 41_{19} 51_3 Jr 2_6 (+) 17_6 (+) 1QM 10_{13} (+), יְשִׁימוֹן *desert, Jeshimon* Dt 32_{10} (+) 1 S 23_{24} (+) Is $43_{19.20}$ Ps 78_{40} 106_{14} 107_4, שְׁמָמָה *desolation* Is 64_9 Jl 4_{19} (+) Zp 2_{13} (+) Ml 1_3 (+), חָרְבָּה *waste* Ps 102_7, צִמָּאוֹן *thirsty ground* Ps 107_{33}, צִיָּה *dryness* Is 35_1 Is 41_{18} (+) Ezk 19_{13} (+) Ho 2_5 (+) Zp 2_{13} (+) Ps 107_{35} (+) 4QapJoshua^a 19.2_6 (+), נֶגֶב *Negeb* Jos 12_8, כַּרְמֶל *orchard* Is $32_{15.16}$, אֲשֵׁדָה *slope* Jos 12_8, הַר *mountain* Jos 12_8 Jr 9_9 (+) Lm 4_{19}, שְׁפֵלָה *lowland* Jos 12_8.

+ תֹּהוּ *emptiness* Dt 32_{10}, מִישׁוֹר *plain* Dt 4_{43} Jos 20_8, גִּבְעָה *hill* Ps 65_{13}, יַעַר *forest* Ezk 34_{25} 4QBer^a 5_3, שָׂדֶה *field* Jl 1_{19}, לְבָנוֹן *Lebanon* Dt 11_{24} Jos 1_4, צָמָא *thirst* Ezk 19_{13}, תַּלְאֻבָה *drought* Ho 13_5, שׁוּחָה *pit* Jr 2_6, מַאְפֵּלְיָה *darkness* Jr 2_{31}.

:: גַּן *garden* Jl 2_3 5_{13}, כַּרְמֶל *orchard* Is 32_{15}, אֲגַם *pool* Is 41_{18} Ps 107_{35}.

הַמִּדְבָּר אֲשֶׁר־הוּא חֹנֶה שָׁם *the steppe where he was camping* Ex 18_5, מִדְבָּר לֹא־אָדָם בּוֹ *a steppe in which there is no human* Jb 38_{26}.

Also perh. 4QCitJub 2_3 4QDibHam^a 1.1_{10} ([מ]דבר) 7_{14} ([מד]בר).

<SYN> עֲרָבָה *steppe, Arabah*, יְשִׁימוֹן *desert, Jeshimon*, שְׁמָמָה *desolation*, חָרְבָּה *waste*, צִמָּאוֹן *thirsty ground*, צִיָּה *dryness*, אֲשֵׁדָה *slope*, נֶגֶב *Negeb*, כַּרְמֶל *orchard*, הַר *hill*, שְׁפֵלָה *lowland*.

<ANT> גַּן *garden*, כַּרְמֶל *orchard*, אֲגַם *pool*.*

[מִדְבָּר] II 1 n.m. **mouth**—sf. מִדְבָּרֵיךְ (Kt^mss, Gnz מִדְבָּרַיִךְ; Qr^mss מִדְבָּרֵךְ)—as organ of speech, <NOM CL> מִדְבָּרֵיךְ נָאוֶה *your mouth is beautiful* Ca 4_3 (+ שָׂפָה *lip*).*

⇨ דבר I *speak*.

מדד 53.0.9 vb. **measure—Qal** 43.0.7 Pf. מָדַד (מָדָד, מָדְדוּ); impf. Q מדה, 2ms תָּמֹד, תְּמֹדּוּ; + waw וּמַדֹּתִי, וּמָדְדוּ, וּמַדֹּתֶם; וַיָּמֹד (Q וימוד), וַיָּמֹדּוּ; ptc. Q מודד; inf. מֹד—**1. measure**, usu. length, distance; also capacity (Ex 16_{18} Is 40_{12} Ru 3_{15} Mur 24 A_{16} C_{17} E_{11} F_{15}). **2. measure out (recompense)** deeds, **reward** (Is 65_7 4Q185 1.2_{10}).

<SUBJ> Y. Is 65_7 4Q185 1.2_{10} 4QCryptA 3.1_6, Israel(ites) Ezk 45_3 47_{18} (or em. תָּמֹדּוּ *you shall measure* to תָּמָרָה *to Tamar*), Boaz Ru 3_{15}, Hillel Mur 24 C_{17}, Judah Mur 24 E_{11} (י[ה]ודה), אִישׁ *man* Ezk 40_{5+15t} 41_{1+6t} 42_{15+5t}

47$_{3.4.4.5}$ Zc 2$_{6}$, בֵּן *son* Mur 24 E$_{11}$, of Israel Ex 16$_{18}$ Nm 35$_{5}$, זָקֵן *elder* Dt 21$_{2}$, שֹׁפֵט *judge* Dt 21$_{2}$, שֹׁטֵר *official* Dt 21$_{2(Sam)}$, בַּיִת *house* of Israel Ezk 43$_{10}$, מִי *who?* Is 40$_{12}$ (|| תכן pi. *measure*); subj. not specified, appar. Is 14$_{31}$ (1QIsa^{a}) (MT בדד *be alone*).

<OBJ> Jerusalem Zc 2$_{6}$, אֹרֶךְ *length* Ezk 40$_{20}$ 41$_{2.4.15}$ 45$_{3}$, רֹחַב *width* Ezk 40$_{5.11.19.20}$ 41$_{2.3}$ (or em. רֹחַב *width of* to כִּתְפוֹת *sides of*) 41$_{4.5}$ 45$_{3}$, קוֹמָה *height* Ezk 40$_{5}$, פֵּאָה *side* Nm 35$_{5}$, רוּחַ *side* Ezk 42$_{16.17.18}$, קִיר *wall* Ezk 41$_{5.13}$, סַף *threshold* Ezk 40$_{6}$, פֶּתַח *entrance* Ezk 41$_{3}$, שַׁעַר *gate* Ezk 40$_{13.28.32}$, אוּלָם *porch* Ezk 40$_{8.9.24}$, אַיִל *pillar* Ezk 40$_{9.24.48}$ 41$_{1.3}$, אַתִּיק *ledge* Ezk 41$_{15}$, חָצֵר *court* Ezk 40$_{47}$, בַּיִת *house* Ezk 41$_{13}$ 42$_{20}$, בִּנְיָה *building* Ezk 41$_{13}$, גִּזְרָה *space* Ezk 41$_{13}$, מַיִם *water* Is 40$_{12}$ (or em. מַיִם to מֵי יַמִּים *seas*), חִטָּה *barley* Mur 24 E$_{11}$, שְׂעֹרָה *(measure of) barley* Ru 3$_{15}$, תֹּכֶן *measure* 4QCryptA 3.1$_{6}$, תָּכְנִית *pattern* Ezk 43$_{10}$ (or em. תָּכְנִית to תְּכֻנָתוֹ *its arrangement*), פְּעֻלָּה *deed* Is 65$_{7}$, אֵלֶּה *these* Mur 24 C$_{17}$.

<PREP> לְ of direction, *to*, + גַּג *roof* Ezk 40$_{13}$ (or em לְגַגּוֹ to לְגַוּוֹ *to its back*); *on*, + רוּחַ *side* Ezk 42$_{20}$.

בְּ of place, *in*, + הֵרוֹדִיס *Herodium* Mur 24 E$_{11}$, שֹׁעַל *hollow of hand* Is 40$_{12}$; *upon*, + רֹאשׁ *head* Is 65$_{7}$ (וּמַדֹּתִי פְּעֻלָּתָם בְּרֹאשָׁם *and I will measure out [punishment for] their deeds upon their own heads*; if em. רִאשֹׁנָה *former* deeds); *in* (specifying unit of measurement), + אַמָּה *cubit* Nm 35$_{5}$ Ezk 47$_{3}$; of instrument, *in, by (means of), with*, + קָנֶה *reed* Ezk 42$_{16}$, עֹמֶר *omer* Ex 16$_{18}$; of benefit, *to, for*, + Hillel Mur 24 E$_{11}$, בֵּן *son* Mur 24 E$_{11}$; *against* appar. Is 14$_{31(1QIsa^{a})}$ (MT בדד *be alone*).

כְּ *according to*, + מִדָּה *measure* Ezk 40$_{24.28.32.35}$.

מִן of direction, *from*, + גַּג *roof* Ezk 40$_{13}$ (or em. מִגַּג to מִגַּוּ *from the back*), בַּיִת *house* Ezk 40$_{8}$, שַׁעַר *gate* Ezk 40$_{23.28}$, גְּבוּל *border* Ezk 47$_{18}$ (or em.; see Subj.); *from (out of)*, + מִדָּה *measure* 4Q185 1.2$_{10}$ ([ממד[ת), *measured section* Ezk 45$_{3}$.

אֶל *(the distance) to*, + עִיר *city* Dt 21$_{2}$, שַׁעַר *gate* Ezk 40$_{23.28}$; *into*, + חֵיק *bosom* Is 65$_{7(Qr)}$ (unless insert וְשִׁלַּמְתִּי *and I will repay*).

עַל *(the distance) to*, + עִיר *city* Dt 21$_{2(Sam)}$, יָם *sea* Ezk 47$_{18}$ (or em.; see Subj.); *upon*, + גַּג *roof* Mur 24 A$_{16}$ ([על]) [גג] C$_{17}$ F$_{15}$ ([ג]ג); *into* perh. 4QConfess 1.2$_{8}$, + חֵיק *bosom* Is 65$_{7(Kt)}$ (unless insert וְשִׁלַּמְתִּי *and I will repay*).

מִלִּפְנֵי *from before*, + שַׁעַר *gate* Ezk 40$_{19}$.

מִחוּץ לְ *outside*, + עִיר *city* Nm 35$_{5}$.

<COLL> מְדָדוֹ סָבִיב סָבִיב *he measured it all round* Ezk 42$_{15}$, וַיָּמָד ... דֶּרֶךְ הַדָּרוֹם *and he measured ... towards the south* Ezk 40$_{27}$, וּמַדֹּתֶם ... אַלְפַּיִם בָּאַמָּה *and you shall measure ... two thousand in cubits*, i.e. a length of two thousand cubits Nm 35$_{5}$, sim. Ezk 47$_{3}$, וַיָּמָד אֶלֶף *and he measured (a length of) a thousand (cubits)* Ezk 47$_{4.4.5}$; measurement given in following nom. cl., e.g. וַיָּמָד אֶת־הֶחָצֵר אֹרֶךְ מֵאָה אַמָּה *and he measured the court; the length was a hundred cubits* Ezk 40$_{47}$, וַיָּמָד אֶת־רֹחַב הַבִּנְיָן קָנֶה אֶחָד *and he measured the width of the structure; (it was) one reed* Ezk 40$_{5}$, Ezk 40$_{6+6t}$ 41$_{1+6t}$ 42$_{16.17.18.19}$ 45$_{3}$.

<SYN> תכן pi. *measure*.

Ni. 3.0.1 Impf. יִמַּד, יִמַּדּוּ—**be measured,** <SUBJ> שָׁמַיִם *heaven* Jr 31$_{37}$ (|| חקר ni. *be searched out*), חוֹל *sand* Jr 33$_{22}$ Ho 2$_{1}$ (both || ספר ni. *be counted*), מַיִם *water* 4QShir^{b} 30$_{4}$, חֵלֶק *portion* Mc 2$_{4}$ (if em.; see Prep.). <PREP> בְּ of place, *in*, + שֹׁעַל *hollow of hand* 4QShir^{b} 30$_{4}$; of instrument, *by (means of), with*, + חֶבֶל *line* Mc 2$_{4}$ (if em. יָמִיר *he changes* to יִמַּד בַּחֶבֶל *it will be measured with a line*).

<SYN> ספר ni. *be counted*, חקר ni. *be searched out*.

Pi. 5 Pf. מִדֵּד; impf. אֲמַדֵּד; + waw וַיְמַדֵּד (וַיְמַדְּדֵם)—**1. measure,** <SUBJ> אֱלֹהִים *God* Ps 60$_{8}$||108$_{8}$ (|| חלק pi. *measure*), David 2 S 8$_{2.2}$. <OBJ> Moab 2 S 8$_{2}$, עֵמֶק *valley* of Succoth Ps 60$_{8}$||108$_{8}$, חֶבֶל *line* 2 S 8$_{2}$, מְלֹא *fullness* of line, i.e. full line 2 S 8$_{2}$. <PREP> בְּ of instrument, *by (means of), with*, + חֶבֶל *line* 2 S 8$_{2}$.

2. extend, continue, <SUBJ> עֶרֶב *evening* Jb 7$_{4}$ (or em. מִדַּד to מִדֵּי *as often as* evening [comes], or מִדַּד is *from the breast of* evening, i.e. from early evening).*

<SYN> §1 חלק pi. *measure*.

Poel 1 + waw וַיְמֹדֶד—**measure,** unless מוד pol. *cause to shudder*, <SUBJ> אֱלוֹהַּ *God* Hb 3$_{6}$ (unless מיד *shake*). <OBJ> אֶרֶץ *earth* Hb 3$_{6}$.

Htpo. 1 וַיִּתְמֹדֵד—**stretch oneself out,** <SUBJ> Elijah 1 K 17$_{21}$. <PREP> עַל *upon*, + יֶלֶד *child* 1 K 17$_{21}$. <COLL> וַיִּתְמֹדֵד ... שָׁלֹשׁ פְּעָמִים *and he stretched himself out ... three times* 1 K 17$_{21}$.

⇒ מַד *measure*, מִדָּה *measure*, מֵמַד *measurement*.

מִדָּה I $_{54.0.27}$ n.f. **measure**—Q מידה; cstr. מִדַּת; sf. Q מדתם; pl. מִדּוֹת (מִדֹּת); cstr. מִדּוֹת; sf. Q מִדּוֹתֶיהָ, מדותיו—

1. measure, measuring of length, distance Lv 19_{35} (|| מִשְׁקָל *weight*, מְשׂוּרָה *capacity*, + מִשְׁפָּט *justice*) Jr 31_{39} Ezk $40_{3.5}$ 41_{17} (or del.) $42_{15.16}$ (or del.) $42_{16.17.18.19}$ Zc 2_5 1 C 23_{29} (|| מְשׂוּרָה) 2 C 3_3, liquid Jb 28_{25} (+ מִשְׁקָל), truth 1QS 8_4 (|| תֹּכֶן *measure*), goodness 4Q185 1.2_{10} ([מד]ת), breath 1QH 1_9 4QBark[a] 1.2_{10} (|| מִשְׁקָל), glory 1QH 5_{21} 4Q418 159.2_6, majesty 4QBéat 11_2, wisdom 1QH 9_{17} 4Q185 1.2_{10}.

2. measurement, size, extent, of ark 4QComm GenD 1_4, curtains of tabernacle Ex $26_{2.8}$||$36_{9.15}$, temple furnishings 1 K 6_{25} 7_{37} Ezk 43_{13}, temple buildings and area Ezk 40_{10+9t} 46_{22} 2 C 3_3 (if em.; see Coll.) 11QT $33_{8.10}$ 36_5 ([מ]ד[ה]) 36_{13} 39_{14} $40_{8.13}$ ([מדה]) $40_{15.15}$ 42_{10}, stones for building 1 K $7_{9.11}$, area of city Ezk $48_{16.30.33}$, space between people and ark Jos 3_4, space between pure and impure persons 4QTohA 1.1_2, time Ps 39_5 (+ קֵץ *end*).

3. (great) size, (great) stature, Nm 13_{32} 2 S 21_{20} 23_{21} (both, if em.; see Cstr.) Is 45_{14} Jr 22_{14} 1 C 11_{23} 20_6.

4. (measured) section, portion, of temple area Ezk 45_3, wall Ne 3_{11+6t}, knowledge 4QsapHymnA1.1_1.

5. in prohibition, בכול מידה **in any measure,** i.e. **in no way, not at all,** בכול מידה [א]ל תתערב *in no way may she mingle* 4QTohA 1.1_5.

<SUBJ> היה *be* 11QT 12_8 36_{13}.

<NOM CL> אֵלֶּה מִדּוֹת הַמִּזְבֵּחַ בָּאַמּוֹת *these are the measurements of the altar in cubits* Ezk 43_{13}, sim. 48_{16}, פְּאַת־נֶגְבָּה חֲמֵשׁ מֵאוֹת וְאַרְבַּעַת אֲלָפִים מִדָּה *the south side (which is) four thousand five hundred (cubits in) measurement* Ezk 48_{33}, sim. 48_{30} 2 C 3_3 (if em.; see Coll.), בין שער לשער מדה ... תשע ותשעים באמה *between one gate and the other the measurement is ... ninety-nine cubits* 11QT 39_{14}, sim. 40_{13} ([מדה]), מִדָּה אַחַת לְכָל־הַיְרִיעֹת *there was one measure to all the curtains,* i.e. they were all the same size Ex 26_2||36_9, sim. 26_8||36_{15} 1 K 6_{25} 7_{37} Ezk $40_{10.10}$ 46_{22}, ... אֶל־כָּל־הַקִּיר סָבִיב סָבִיב מִדּוֹת appar. *on all the walls round about were ... measures* Ezk 41_{17} (or del.), כבודכה לאין מדה *your glory is without measure,* i.e. it cannot be measured 1QH 5_{21}, לחכמתכה אין מדה *there is no measure to your wisdom* 1QH 9_{17}.

<OBJ> כלה pi. *finish* Ezk 42_{15}, חזק pi. *repair* Ne 3_{19}, hi. Ne 3_{11+5t}, ידע hi. *make known* Ps 39_5, יסף hi. *add* 4QWays[a] 2_3 (ל[הו]סיף]; unless מִדָּה III *tribute*), יסד pi. *establish* 2 C 3_3 (if em. אֵלֶּה הוּסַד appar. *these are what* Solomon *established* to אֵלֶּה הַמִּדּוֹת אֲשֶׁר יִסַּד *these are the measurements that* Solomon *established*).

<CSTR> מדת התבה *measurement of the ark* 4Q CommGenD 1_4, מִדּוֹת גָּזִית *measurements of hewn stone* 1 K 7_9 (מִדֹּת) 7_{11}, הַמִּזְבֵּחַ *of the altar* Ezk 43_{13}, מִדַּת הַשַּׁעַר *measurement of the gate* Ezk $40_{21.22}$, מדת שער *measurement of the gate of* 11QT 33_{10}, כול השערים *of all the gates* 11QT 36_{13}, התחתונות *of the lower (floors)* 11 QT 42_{10}, מִדּוֹת הַבַּיִת *measuring of the house* Ezk 42_{15}, מדת [ב]ית הכיור *measurement of the house of the laver* 11QT 33_8, מִדַּת יָמַי *measurement of my days* Ps 39_5, מדת דעת *measured portion of knowledge* 4Qsap HymnA1.1_1, מדת האמת *measure of truth* 1QS 8_4, כבודכה *of your glory* 4Q418 159.2_6, הדר *of majesty* 4QBéat 11_2, מד[ת ט]ב *measure of goodness,* i.e. good measure 4Q 185 1.2_{10}.

קַו הַמִּדָּה *line of,* i.e. for, *measuring* Jr $31_{39(Qr)}$ (Kt קוה), חֶבֶל *line of,* i.e. for Zc 2_5 (מִדָּה), קְנֵה *reed of,* i.e. for Ezk $40_{3.5}$ 42_{16} (or del.) $42_{16.17.18.19}$, אִישׁ מִדָּה *man of (great) stature* 2 S 21_{20} (if em. מדין *of [great] stature*) $23_{21(Qr)}$ (if em. מַרְאֶה *of appearance*) 1 C 11_{23} 20_6, אַנְשֵׁי *men of* Is 45_{14}, אַנְשֵׁי מִדּוֹת *men of (great) stature* Nm 13_{32}, בֵּית מִדּוֹת *house of (great) size* Jr 22_{14}, משפלת מדה *lowness of measure* 1QH 17_1, כָּל־ ... מִדָּה *every ... measure* 1 C 23_{29} 4QTohA 1.1_5 (כול מידה).

<ADJ> רִאשׁוֹן *former* 2 C 3_3, אֶחָד *one* Ex $26_{2.8}$||$36_{9.15}$ 1 K 6_{25} 7_{37} Ezk $40_{10.10}$ 46_{22}, שֵׁנִי *second* Ne 3_{11+6t}, זאת *this* 4QTohA 1.1_2 11QT 36_5 ([כמ]דה הזואת]) $40_{8.15.15}$, אֵלֶּה *these* Ezk 40_{24+5t}.

<PREP> לְ of benefit, *to, for* 1 C 23_{29}.

בְּ of instrument, *by (means of), with,* + תכן pi. *measure* Jb 28_{25}, עשׂה *do* wrong Lv 19_{35}; *in, according to* Jos 3_4 2 C 3_3 1QH 1_9 4QMyst[a] 29_3, + נתן *give* 4QBark[a] 1.2_{10} ([נתן]), הלך htp. *walk* 1QS 8_4, ערב htp. *mingle* 4QTohA 1.1_5.

כְּ *according to* 1 K $7_{9.11}$ 4QD[a] 13_2 11QT 5_4 33_{10} 36_5 ([כמ]ד[ה]) $40_{8.15.15}$ 42_{10}, + היה *be* Ezk $40_{21.22}$, עשׂה *make*

11QT 33$_8$, מדד *measure* Ezk 40$_{24.28.32.35}$, ישב *dwell* 4Q TohA 1.1$_2$.

מִן *from (out of)*, + מדד *measure* Ezk 45$_3$ 4Q185 1.2$_{10}$ ([ממדו]ת).

עִם *with* 4QBéat 11$_2$ ([עם]).

Also perh. 1QH fr. 11$_2$ 4Q418 77$_4$.

<SYN> §1 תֹּכֶן *measure*, מִשְׁקָל *weight*, מְשׂוּרָה *capacity*.*

⇒ מדד *measure*.

*[**מִדָּה**] II 1.0.1 n.f. **garment**—cstr. Q מדת; pl. sf. מִדּוֹתָיו—**garment, robe,** of Aaron (Ps 133$_2$), of those who walk in the truth (1QS 4$_8$), <CSTR> מדת הדר *garment of splendour* 1QS 4$_4$ (+ כְּלִיל *crown*); פִּי מִדּוֹתָיו *mouth,* i.e. collar, *of his robes* Ps 133$_2$ (or del.). <PREP> עִם *with* 1QS 4$_8$.

⇒ cf. מַד I *garment,* מָדוּ *garment.*

[**מִדָּה**] III 1.0.1 n.f. **tribute**—cstr. מִדַּת—**tribute, tax,** <OBJ> יסף hi. *add* 4QWays^a 2$_3$ (להו[סיף]; unless מִדָּה I). <CSTR> מִדַּת הַמֶּלֶךְ *tribute of the king* Ne 5$_4$. <PREP> לְ *for (the purpose of),* + לוה *borrow* Ne 5$_4$.*

*[**מַדְהֵב**] I 0.0.2 n.[m.] **distress**—sf. Q מדהבכם, Q מדהובם—<CSTR> כל מדהובם *all their distress* CD 13$_9$. <PREP> לְ *for,* + שׁקד *be concerned* CD 13$_9$; מִן of cause, *on account of,* + שׁקד *be concerned* 4Q416 2.2$_{14}$.

⇒ cf. דוב *pine away;* מַדְהֵבָה I *distress.*

*[**מַדְהֵב**] II 0.0.2 n.[m.] **driven out person**—sf. Q מדהבכם, Q מדהובם—<CSTR> כל מדהובם *all those driven out* CD 13$_9$. <PREP> לְ *for,* + שׁקד *be concerned* CD 13$_9$; מִן of cause, *on account of,* + שׁקד *be concerned* 4Q416 2.2$_{14}$.

⇒ cf. מַדְהֵבָה II *rout.*

***מַדְהֵבָה** I 1.0.3 n.f. perh. **distress, calamity,** unless error for מַרְהֵבָה *raging,* <SUBJ> היה *be* 1QH 3$_{25}$ (והוות מדהבה עם מצעדי *and distress was with my steps;* + מְהוּמָה *discomfiture*) 4Q418 176$_3$, שׁבת *cease* Is 14$_4$ (1QIsa^a מרהבה *raging;* + נֹגֵשׂ *oppressor*). <NOM CL> [א]ין עוד מדהבה *there shall no longer be distress* 1QH 12$_{18}$.

⇒ cf. דוב *pine away;* מַדְהֵב I *distress.*

***מַדְהֵבָה** II 1.0.3 n.f. **rout, defeat,** unless error for מַרְהֵבָה *raging,* <SUBJ> היה *be* 1QH 3$_{25}$ (והוות מדהבה עם מצעדי *and disasters of a rout were with my steps;* + מְהוּמָה *discomfiture*) 4Q418 176$_3$, שׁבת *cease* Is 14$_4$ (1QIsa^a מרהבה *raging;* + נֹגֵשׂ *oppressor*). <NOM CL> [א]ין עוד מדהבה *there shall no longer be defeat* 1QH 12$_{18}$.

⇒ cf. מַדְהֵב II *driven out person.*

[**מָדוּ**] 2 n.m. **garment**—pl. sf. מַדְוֵיהֶם—of David's servants, <OBJ> כרת *cut* 2 S 10$_4$||1 C 19$_4$.*

⇒ cf. מַד I *garment,* מִדָּה II *garment.*

[**מַדְוֶה**] 2 n.m. **disease**—cstr. מַדְוֵה; pl. cstr. מַדְוֵי—**disease, plague,** <SUBJ> דבק *cling* Dt 28$_{60}$ (+ חֳלִי *sickness,* מַכָּה *affliction*). <OBJ> שׁוב hi. *bring back* Dt 28$_{60}$, סור hi. *remove* Dt 7$_{15}$ (+ חֳלִי *sickness*), ידע *know* Dt 7$_{15}$, שׂים *place* Dt 7$_{15}$, נתן *give,* i.e. place Dt 7$_{15}$. <CSTR> מַדְוֵה מִצְרַיִם *disease of Egypt* Dt 7$_{15(mss)}$ 28$_{60}$, מַדְוֵי *diseases of* Dt 7$_{15}$ 28$_{60(mss)}$, כָּל־מַדְוֵה *every disease of* Dt 7$_{15(mss)}$ 28$_{60}$, כָּל־מַדְוֵי *all the diseases of* Dt 7$_{15}$ 28$_{60(mss)}$. <ADJ> רַע *bad* Dt 7$_{15}$. <PREP> מִפְּנֵי *on account of,* + יגר *fear* Dt 28$_{60}$.

⇒ דוה *be faint.*

מַדּוּחִים I 1 n.[m.]pl. **enticement** (unless מַדּוּחִים II *false claims* or III *folly*), <OBJ> חזה *see* Lm 2$_{14}$ (if em.; see App.). <CSTR> מַשְׂאוֹת שָׁוְא וּמַדּוּחִים *oracles of vanity and enticement,* i.e. vain and enticing oracles Lm 2$_{14}$ (or em.; see App.). <APP> מַשְׂאֵת *oracle* Lm 2$_{14}$ (if em. מַשְׂאוֹת *oracles of* to מַשָּׂאוֹת *oracles*).*

⇒ נדח I *thrust.*

***מַדּוּחִים** II 1 n.[m.]pl. **false claims** (unless מַדּוּחִים I *enticement* or III *folly*), <OBJ> חזה *see* Lm 2$_{14}$ (if em.; see App.). <CSTR> מַשְׂאוֹת שָׁוְא וּמַדּוּחִים *oracles of vanity and false claims* Lm 2$_{14}$ (or em.; see App.). <APP> מַשְׂאֵת *oracle* Lm 2$_{14}$ (if em. מַשְׂאוֹת *oracles of* to מַשָּׂאוֹת *oracles*).

⇒ נדח I *thrust.*

***מַדּוּחִים** III 1 n.[m.]pl. **folly** (unless מַדּוּחִים I *enticement* or II *false claims*), <OBJ> חזה *see* Lm 2$_{14}$ (if em.; see App.). <CSTR> מַשְׂאוֹת שָׁוְא וּמַדּוּחִים *oracles of vanity and folly* Lm 2$_{14}$ (or em.; see App.). <APP> מַשְׂאֵת *oracle* Lm 2$_{14}$ (if em. מַשְׂאוֹת *oracles of* to מַשָּׂאוֹת *oracles*).

מדוכה, see מְדֹכָה *mortar.*

מָדוֹן I 20.0.6 n.m. **strife**—pl. מְדָנִים (Kt מדונים)—**1.** usu. **strife, contention, quarrelling.**

2. (object of) strife (Ps 80$_6$).

<SUBJ> היה *be* Ps 31$_{12}$ (if em. מְאֹד *very*), יצא *go out* Pr 22$_{10}$ (|| דִּין *strife*, קָלוֹן *dishonour*), שׁתק *be quiet* Pr 26$_{20}$ (+ אֵשׁ *fire*). <NOM CL> מדונים כִּבְרִיחַ אַרְמוֹן *strife is like the bars of a fortress* Pr 18$_{19}$(Kt) (Qr מִדְיָנִים *strife*, from מִדְיָן; or em. מְיֻדָּע *intimate friend*), לְמִי מדונים *to whom is there strife?* Pr 23$_{29}$(Kt) (Qr מִדְיָנִים; || שִׂיחַ *complaint*). <OBJ> שִׂים *place*, i.e. make into Ps 80$_7$ (unless מָדוֹן II *[object of] contempt*; or em. מָנוֹד *shaking of the head*), נשׂא *raise* Hb 1$_3$ (+ רִיב *strife*), שׁלח pi. *send* Pr 6$_{14}$(Kt) (Qr מִדְיָנִים *strife*, from מִדְיָן) 6$_{19}$ 16$_{28}$ 4QsapDidA 2$_4$ (מ[ו]שלח), גרה pi. *provoke* Pr 15$_{18}$ (+ רִיב) 28$_{25}$ 29$_{22}$, עיר pol. *stir up* Pr 10$_{12}$.

<CSTR> אִישׁ מָדוֹן *man of strife* Jr 15$_{10}$ (|| רִיב *strife*) 2 S 21$_{20}$(Qr) (Kt מדין *of [great] stature* [from מַד II *measure*]; || 1 C 20$_6$ מִדָּה *of [great] stature*), איש מדונים *man of strife* Pr 26$_{21}$(Kt) (Qr מִדְיָנִים *of strife*, from מִדְיָן; + רִיב), אֵשֶׁת *woman of* Pr 21$_{19}$(Kt) (|| כַּעַס *vexation*) 25$_{24}$(Kt) 27$_{15}$(Kt) (all three Qr מִדְיָנִים), בעל מדנים *owner of*, i.e. one who causes, *strife* 1QH 5$_{35}$ (+ רִיב), רֵאשִׁית מָדוֹן *beginning of strife of* Pr 17$_{14}$ (+ רִיב), קנאת מדנים *jealousy of strife* 4QMyst[b] 2.2$_3$. <PREP> לְ as or introducing predicate, + היה *be* 1QH 5$_{23}$ (|| רִיב *strife*). <COLL> מָדוֹן לִשְׁכֵנֵינוּ *(an object of) strife to our neighbours* Ps 80$_6$.

Also MasJub 2$_4$.

<SYN> רִיב *strife*, דִּין *strife*, כַּעַס *vexation*, שִׂיחַ *complaint*, קָלוֹן *dishonour*.

⇒ דִּין *judge.*

***מָדוֹן** II 1 n.[m] **(object of) contempt** (unless מָדוֹן I *[object of] strife*), <OBJ> שִׂים *place*, i.e. make into Ps 80$_7$.

מָדוֹן III 2 pl.n. **Madon,** Canaanite city in Galilee, perh. Kh. Madīn, 17 km NW of Mount Tabor, <CSTR> מֶלֶךְ מָדוֹן *king of Madon* Jos 11$_1$ 12$_{19}$.

מַדּוּעַ 72.2.1 interrog. adv. **why?**—מַדֻּעַ—**why?** either not distinct semantically from לָמָּה *why?*, or esp. with ref. to past events or present situations (לָמָּה being used esp. with ref. to future events or intentions), or else esp. with factual questions (לָמָּה being used esp. for reproach or complaint).*

1a. in direct question, with following (first) verb, היה *be* Jr 2$_{14}$, קרא *befall* Jr 13$_{22}$, חיה *live* Jb 21$_7$, הלך *go* 2 K 4$_{23}$, בוא *come* Gn 26$_{27}$ Jg 11$_7$ 1 S 20$_{27}$ 2 S 3$_7$ 24$_{21}$ 2 K 9$_{11}$ Is 50$_2$, עלה *go up* Jr 8$_{22}$, ירד *go down* 2 S 11$_{10}$, נגשׁ ni. *draw near* 2 S 11$_{20}$, קדם pi. *meet* Jb 3$_{12}$, עבר *cross* Jg 12$_1$, *transgress* Est 3$_3$, שׁוב pol. *turn away* Jr 8$_5$, נוס *flee* Jr 46$_{15}$ (if em. נִסְחַף why *is he prostrated?* to נָס חַף why *has Apis fled?*), מהר pi. *hasten* Ex 2$_{18}$, אחר pi. *be delayed* Jg 5$_{28}$, בושׁ pol. *be delayed* Jg 5$_{28}$, קוה pi. *wait* Is 5$_4$, קצר (of spirit) *be short*, i.e. impatient Jb 21$_4$, מצא *find* Ru 2$_{10}$, עזב ni. *be forsaken* Ne 13$_{11}$, ישׁב *sit* Ex 18$_{14}$, לין *lodge* Ne 12$_{21}$

ראה *see* Jr 30$_6$ 46$_5$, נבט hi. *look* Si 37$_4$(Bmg), אכל *eat* Lv 10$_{17}$, ירא *fear* Nm 12$_8$, בכה *weep* 2 K 8$_{12}$, כתב *write* Jr 36$_{29}$, חשׁב ni. *be reckoned* Jb 18$_3$, עשׂה *do* Ex 1$_{18}$ 2 S 16$_{10}$ 1 K 1$_6$, כלה pi. *complete* Ex 5$_{14}$, חזק pi. *repair* 2 K 12$_8$, יצר ni. *be formed* Si 37$_3$, נתן *give* Jos 17$_{14}$, ירשׁ *possess* Jr 49$_1$, שׁמר *keep* 1 K 2$_{43}$, עבד *serve* Jg 9$_{28}$, אמר *say* Jr 2$_{31}$, נבא ni. *prophesy* Jr 26$_9$ 32$_3$, דרשׁ *require* 2 C 24$_6$, כעס hi. *provoke* Jr 8$_{19}$, ריב *strive* Jb 33$_{13}$, נשׂא *bear* Ezk 18$_{19}$, htp. *exalt oneself* Nm 16$_3$, מלך *reign* 1 K 1$_{13}$, צלח *prosper* Jr 12$_1$, נצל hi. *deliver* Jg 11$_{26}$, צפן ni. *be hidden* Jb 24$_1$, סתר hi. *hide* 1 S 20$_2$, בזה *despise* 2 S 12$_9$, קלל hi. *despise* 2 S 19$_{44}$, בגד *betray* Ml 2$_{10}$ 4QSD 4$_2$ (מד[ו]ע), גנב *steal* 2 S 19$_{42}$, נכה hi. *strike* 2 S 18$_{11}$ Jr 14$_{19}$, טול ho. *be thrown down* Jr 22$_{28}$, המה *be in uproar* 1 K 14$_1$, רעע *be bad*, i.e. sad Ne 2$_3$.

1b. in indirect question, with following verb, בער *burn* Ex 3$_3$.

2. in nom. cl. מַדּוּעַ פְּנֵיכֶם רָעִים *why are your faces bad*, i.e. sad? Gn 40$_7$, var. Ne 2$_2$, מַדּוּעַ אַתָּה לְבַדֶּךָ *why are you alone?* 1 S 21$_2$, מַדּוּעַ אַתָּה כָּכָה דַּל *why are you so* dejected? 2 S 13_4, מַדּוּעַ אָדֹם לִלְבוּשֶׁךָ *why is your clothing red?* Is 63_2.

<COLL> מַדּוּעַ with other interrogatives: הֲ ... אִם ... מַדּוּעַ, e.g. הַעֶבֶד יִשְׂרָאֵל אִם־יְלִיד בַּיִת הוּא מַדּוּעַ הָיָה לָבַז *is Israel a slave? Is he one born at home? Why then has he become a prey?* Jr 2_{14}, Jr $8_{5.22}$ 14_{19} 22_{28} 49_1; הֲ ... מַדּוּעַ, e.g. הֲלֹא אַתֶּם שְׂנֵאתֶם אוֹתִי ... וּמַדּוּעַ בָּאתֶם אֵלַי *do you not hate me? ... why then have you come to me?* Jg 11_7, Jg 9_{28} 2 S 11_{10} 1 K 1_{13} Ml 2_{10}; לָמָּה, לָמָּה ... מַדּוּעַ; לֹא מֵרֶחֶם אָמוּת ... מַדּוּעַ קִדְּמוּנִי בִרְכָּיִם *why did I not die from the womb? ... why did the knees meet me?* Jb 3_{12}; הֲ ... מַדּוּעַ, e.g. מַדּוּעַ אַתָּה כָּכָה דַּל ... הֲלוֹא תַּגִּיד לִי *why are you so downcast? ... will you not tell me?* 2 S 13_4, 2 S 11_{20} Is 50_2; מַדּוּעַ ... וּמַה, מַדּוּעַ קִדְּמוּנִי בִרְכַּיִם וּמַה־שָּׁדַיִם *why did the knees meet me? Or why the breasts?* Jb 3_{12}; הֶ ... וְאִם־מַדּוּעַ, הֶאָנֹכִי לְאָדָם שִׂיחִי וְאִם־מַדּוּעַ לֹא־תִקְצַר רוּחִי *is my complaint against humans? Or why should I be impatient?* Jb 21_4.*

⇒ ידע *know*.

*[**מָדוֹר**] 0.0.5 n.[m.] **dwelling place**—cstr. Q מדור; sf. Q מדורו—**dwelling place, station, turning point** (Hb 3_{10}; if em.; see Obj.), <NOM CL> לחם רמה מדורו perh. *his dwelling place is the food of maggots* 1QS 11_{21} (+ מְגִבָּל *kneading*), בשמים מדורו[ו] *his dwelling place is in heaven* 4QMyst[a] 53_9. <OBJ> נשה *forget* Hb 3_{10} (if em. רוֹם יָדֵיהוּ נָשָׂא. שֶׁמֶשׁ *it lifted its hand on high. The sun* to מְדוֹרֵיהוּ נָשָׂא שֶׁמֶשׁ *the sun forgot its turning points*). <CSTR> מדור חושך *dwelling place of darkness* 1QH 12_{25}, מדור שדיך perh. *dwelling place of your fields* 4QpsEzek[b] 1.3_4 (unless *from the generation of your devastation*). <COLL> מדור לרשעי גוים *a dwelling place for the wicked ones of the nations* 1QpNah 3.1_1.

⇒ דור I *dwell*.

מְדוּרָה 2 n.f. **pile**—מְדֻרָתָהּ—**pile** of wood, **pyre,** <NOM CL> מְדֻרָתָהּ אֵשׁ וְעֵצִים הַרְבֵּה *its pyre is fire and much wood* Is 30_{33}. <OBJ> גדל hi. *make great* Ezk 24_9.

⇒ דור II *heap up*.

מִדְחֶה 1 n.m. **downfall, ruin,** caused by flattering speech, <OBJ> עשׂה *make* Pr 26_{28}.

⇒ דחה *push*.

[**מַדְחֵפָה**] 1 n.f. **thrust**—pl. מַדְחֵפֹת—**thrust, blow,** or perh. **haste,** or perh. **exile,** as a name for the underworld,* <PREP> לְ צוד *hunt with* Ps 140_{12} (לְמַדְחֵפֹת *with thrust upon thrust*, or *blow upon blow*, or *with haste*; or *into exile*, or em. לְמוֹ פַּחַת *him [with] a pit*; or del.).*

⇒ דחף *drive, hasten*.

מָדַי 15 pr.n.m. **Madai, Media**—מָדָי—**1. Madai,** son of Japheth, <NOM CL> בְּנֵי יֶפֶת ... וּמָדַי *the sons of Japheth were ... and Madai* Gn 10_2||1 C 1_5.

2. Media, ancient kingdom in present NW Iran, its inhabitants appar. regarded as descended from §1, <CSTR> עָרֵי מָדָי *cities of Media* 2 K 17_6 18_{11} 1 C 5_{26} (if ins.), מַלְכֵי מָדַי *kings of Media* Jr 25_{25} (מָדָי; + עֵילָם *Elam*) $51_{11.28}$ Est 10_2 (מָדַי וּפָרָס *of Media and Persia*), שָׂרֵי פָּרַס וּמָדַי *princes of Persia and Media* Est 1_{14}, שָׂרוֹת *ladies of* Est 1_{18}, חֵיל *army of* Est 1_3, דָּתֵי *laws of* Est 1_{19}.

3. Medes, inhabitants of Media, distinction between §§2, 3 not alw. clear, <SUBJ> חשׁב *value* Is 13_{17}, חפץ *desire* Is 13_{17}, רחם pi. *have compassion* Is 13_{17}, צור *besiege* Is 21_2 (+ עֵילָם *Elam*). <OBJ> עור hi. *stir up* Is 13_{17}. <CSTR> זֶרַע מָדָי *offspring of the Medes* Dn 9_1.*

⇒ מָדִי *Mede*.

מָדִי 1 gent. **Mede,** <APP> דָּרְיָוֶשׁ הַמָּדִי *Darius the Mede* Dn 11_1. <PREP> לְ of possession, *(belonging) to, of* Dn 11_1.

⇒ מָדַי *Madai, Media*.

מַדַּי, see דַּי *sufficiency*, §1, Coll.

מִדֵּי, see דַּי *sufficiency*, §2c.

מִדִּין 1 pl.n. **Middin,** town in the wilderness of Judah, <NOM CL> בַּמִּדְבָּר ... מִדִּין *in the desert was ... Middin* Jos 15_{61}.

מִדְיָן I 59.0.3 pr.n.m. **Midian, 1.** son of Abraham and Keturah, <OBJ> ילד *give birth to* Gn 25_2||1 C 1_{32}, <CSTR> בְּנֵי מִדְיָן *sons of Midian* Gn 25_4||1 C 1_{33}.

2. Arabian tribe living in the N Hejaz, east of the Gulf of Aqaba, regarded as descended from §1, and its territory (e.g. Ex 4$_{19}$ Nm 25$_{15}$ 1 K 11$_{18}$); sometimes as collective noun, **Midianites** (e.g. Jg 6$_{3}$ 7$_{24}$).

<SUBJ> עלה *go up* Jg 6$_{3}$, בוא *come* Jg 6$_{3}$, עבר *pass* Jg 6$_{33}$, אסף ni. *be gathered,* חנה *encamp* Jg 6$_{3.33}$, נפל *fall,* i.e. lie Jg 7$_{12}$, שׁחת pi. *destroy* Jg 6$_{3}$, hi. Jg 6$_{3}$, כנע ni. *be subdued* Jg 8$_{28}$, שׁאר hi. *leave* Jg 6$_{3}$. <OBJ> נכה hi. *strike* Gn 36$_{35}$ Jg 6$_{16}$ 1 C 1$_{46}$, נתן *give* Jg 7$_{2.7.14}$, רדף *pursue* Jg 7$_{25}$ (if em.; see Prep.), קרא *meet* Jg 7$_{24}$. <CSTR> נְשֵׁי מִדְיָן *women of Midian* Nm 31$_{9}$, מַלְכֵי *kings of* Nm 31$_{8.8}$ Jg 8$_{5.12.26}$ 4QapJoseph[b] 3$_{12}$ GnzPs 1$_{24}$, נְשִׂיא *prince of* Nm 25$_{18}$, נְשִׂיאֵי *princes of* Jos 13$_{21}$, שָׂרֵי *princes of* Jg 7$_{25}$ 8$_{3}$, כֹּהֵן *priest of* Ex 2$_{16}$ 3$_{1}$ 18$_{1}$, זִקְנֵי *elders of* Nm 22$_{4.7}$, יַד *hand of* Jg 6$_{1.2}$ 8$_{22}$ 9$_{17}$, כַּף *hand of* Jg 6$_{13.14}$, בִּכְרֵי *young camels of* Is 60$_{6}$, אֶרֶץ *land of* Ex 2$_{15}$ Hb 3$_{7}$ (or del. אֶרֶץ), יְרִיעוֹת *curtains of* Hb 3$_{7}$ (if del. אֶרֶץ *land of*), מַחֲנֵה *camp of* Jg 7$_{1.8.13.15}$, מַכַּת *defeat of* Is 10$_{26}$, יוֹם *day of* Is 9$_{3}$, כָּל־מִדְיָן *all (the) Midian(ites)* Jg 6$_{33}$.

<PREP> לְ of benefit, *to, for,* + עשׂה *do* 4QapJoseph[b] 3$_{11}$; *against,* + לכד *seize* water Jg 7$_{24}$; בְּ of place, *in* Nm 25$_{15}$, + אמר *say* Ex 4$_{19}$; *against,* + לחם ni. *fight* Jg 8$_{1}$, נתן *give* vengeance Nm 31$_{3}$; כְּ *as* Ps 83$_{10}$ (or del.); מִן of direction, *from,* + קום *rise* 1 K 11$_{18}$; אֶל *to,* + רדף *pursue* Jg 7$_{25}$ (or em. אֶל to אֶת object marker); עַל *against,* + היה *be* Nm 31$_{3}$ (or em. וְיִהְיוּ *and they shall be* to לַי׳ *for Y.*), צבא *wage war* Nm 31$_{7}$; מִפְּנֵי *on account of* Jg 6$_{2}$, + דלל *be low* Jg 6$_{6}$, עשׂה *make* dens Jg 6$_{2}$; *from (before),* + נוס hi. *hide* Jg 6$_{11}$; עַל אֹדוֹת *on account of,* + זעק *cry* Jg 6$_{7}$; אַחֲרֵי *after,* + רדף *pursue* Jg 7$_{23}$. <COLL> מִדְיָן עֲמָלֵק וּבְנֵי־קֶדֶם *the Midianites, the Amalekites and the sons of the east* Jg 6$_{3.33}$, var. 7$_{12}$.

⇒ מִדְיָנִי *Midianite.*

[מִדְיָן] II $_{10}$ n.m. **strife**—pl. מִדְיָנִים; cstr. מִדְיְנֵי—**strife, contention, quarrelling,** <NOM CL> דֶּלֶף טֹרֵד מִדְיְנֵי אִשָּׁה *the quarrelling of a wife is a continuous dripping* Pr 19$_{13}$, מִדְיָנִים כִּבְרִיחַ אַרְמוֹן *strife is like the bars of a fortress* Pr 18$_{19(Qr)}$ (Kt מדונים *quarrelling,* from מָדוֹן; or em. מְיֻדָּע *intimate friend*), לְמִי מִדְיָנִים *to whom is there strife?* Pr 23$_{29(Qr)}$ (Kt מדונים; || שִׂיחַ *complaint*). <OBJ> שׁלח pi. *send* Pr 6$_{14(Qr)}$ (Kt מדנים *strife,* from מָדוֹן), שׁבת hi. *cause to cease* Pr 18$_{18}$. <CSTR> מִדְיְנֵי אִשָּׁה *quarrelling of a wife* Pr 19$_{13}$; אִישׁ מִדְיָנִים *man of strife* Pr 26$_{21(Qr)}$ (Kt מדונים *of strife,* from מָדוֹן; + רִיב *strife*), אֵשֶׁת *woman of* Pr 21$_{9.19(Qr)}$ (|| כַּעַס *vexation*) 25$_{24(Qr)}$ 27$_{15(Qr)}$ (all three Kt מדונים).

<SYN> כַּעַס *vexation,* שִׂיחַ *complaint.*

⇒ דין *judge.*

מְדִינָה I $_{54.0.1}$ n.f. **province**—pl. מְדִינוֹת—**province, district,** or perh. sometimes **town,*** of Israel (1 K 20$_{14.15.17.19}$), of Babylonian empire (Ezk 19$_{8}$ [or em.; see Prep.] Lm 1$_{1}$ Dn 8$_{2}$), of Persian empire (Est 1$_{1+5t}$ 2$_{3.18}$ 3$_{8+7t}$ 4$_{3.3.11}$ 8$_{5+10t}$ 9$_{2+8t}$), in general (Ec 2$_{8}$ 5$_{7}$ Dn 11$_{24}$ 4Q418 1$_{2}$), <NOM CL> הַמְּדִינוֹת אֲשֶׁר מֵהֹדּוּ וְעַד־כּוּשׁ *the provinces that were from Ethiopia to India* Est 8$_{9}$.

<OBJ> מלך *reign over* Est 1$_{1}$.

<CSTR> מְדִינוֹת הַמֶּלֶךְ *provinces of the king* Est 1$_{16.22}$ 3$_{13}$ 4$_{11}$ 8$_{5.12}$ 9$_{2.12.16.20}$, מַלְכוּתוֹ *of his kingdom* Est 2$_{3}$, מַלְכוּתֶךָ *of your kingdom* Est 3$_{8}$; בְּנֵי הַמְּדִינָה *sons,* i.e. people, *of the province* Ezr 2$_{1}$||Ne 7$_{6}$, שָׂרֵי הַמְּדִינוֹת *governors of the provinces* 1 K 20$_{14.15.17.19}$ Ec 2$_{8}$ (if em.; see below) Est 1$_{3}$ 8$_{9}$ 9$_{3}$, רָאשֵׁי הַמְּדִינָה *chiefs of the province* Ne 11$_{3}$, מִשְׁמַנֵּי מְדִינָה *fat ones,* i.e. perh. richest parts, *of the province* Dn 11$_{24}$, סְגֻלַּת מְלָכִים וְהַמְּדִינוֹת *treasure of kings and provinces* Ec 2$_{8}$ (unless מְדִינָה II *place of judgment* or III *prefect;* or em. וְהַמְּדִינוֹת to וְשָׂרֵי הַמְּדִינוֹת *and the governors of the provinces*), חֵיל ... מְדִינָה *army of ... a province* Ezr 8$_{11}$, שְׁאָר מְדִינוֹת *remainder of the provinces of* Est 9$_{12}$, כָּל־מְדִינָה וּמְדִינָה *every province* Est 3$_{14}$ 4$_{3}$ 8$_{13.17}$, כָּל־הַמְּדִינוֹת *all the provinces* Est 9$_{4}$, כָּל־מְדִינוֹת *all the provinces of* Est 1$_{16.22}$ 2$_{3}$ 3$_{8.13}$ 4$_{11}$ 8$_{5.12}$ 9$_{2.16(mss).20}$.

<APP> עֵילָם *Elam* Dn 8$_{2}$, מָקוֹם *place* Est 4$_{3}$.

<PREP> לְ of benefit, *to, for,* + עשׂה *make* Est 2$_{18}$; בְּ of place, *in, throughout* Lm 1$_{1}$ Est 1$_{16}$ 3$_{8}$ 4$_{3}$ 8$_{5.17}$ 9$_{16.20}$ Dn 8$_{2}$, + הלך *go* Est 9$_{4}$, קהל ni. *be gathered* Est 9$_{2}$, שׁאר ni. *remain* Ne 1$_{3}$, ראה *see* Ec 5$_{7}$ (unless מְדִינָה II *place of judgement*), נתן ni. *be given* Est 3$_{14}$ 8$_{13}$, בזז *plunder* Est 8$_{12}$, פקד hi. *appoint* Est 2$_{3}$, עשׂה ni. *be done,* i.e. observed Est 9$_{28}$; מִן of direction, *from* Ezk 19$_{8}$ (or em. מְצוּדוֹת *nets*); אֶל *to,* + שׁלח *send* Est 1$_{22.22.22}$ 9$_{30}$, ni. *be sent* Est 3$_{13}$; עַל *over, in charge of* Est 3$_{12}$.

<COLL> מְדִינָה || עַם *people* Est 1$_{22.22}$ 3$_{12.12.14}$ (+) 8$_{9.9.11.13}$ (+), עִיר *city* Est 8$_{17.28.28}$ 9$_{2}$ (+), דּוֹר *generation* Est 9$_{28}$, מִשְׁפָּחָה *clan* Est 9$_{28}$; מְדִינָה וּמְדִינָה *province and province*, i.e. every province Est 1$_{22}$ 3$_{12.12.14}$ 4$_{3}$ 8$_{9.13.17}$ 9$_{28}$, שֶׁבַע וְעֶשְׂרִים וּמֵאָה מְדִינָה *a hundred and twenty-seven provinces* Est 1$_{1}$ 8$_{9}$ 9$_{30}$, מדינה לאיש ואיש perh. *the province of every man* 4Q418 1$_{2}$.

<SYN> עַם *people*, עִיר *city*, דּוֹר *generation*, מִשְׁפָּחָה *clan*.*

⇒ דין *judge*.

*מְדִינָה II $_{2}$ n.f. **place of judgment**, <CSTR> סְגֻלַּת מְלָכִים וְהַמְּדִינוֹת *the treasure of kings and places of judgment* Ec 2$_{8}$ (unless מְדִינָה I *province* or III *prefect*). <PREP> ראה *see* Ec 5$_{7}$ (unless מְדִינָה I *province*).

⇒ דין *judge*.

*[מְדִינָה] III $_{1}$ n.f. **prefect** (unless מְדִינָה I *province* or II *place of judgment*)—pl. מְדִינוֹת—<CSTR> סְגֻלַּת מְלָכִים וְהַמְּדִינוֹת *the treasure of kings and prefects* Ec 2$_{8}$.

⇒ דין *judge*.

מִדְיָנִי $_{8}$ gent. **Midianite**—fem. מִדְיָנִית; pl. מִדְיָנִים (מְדָנִים) —**1.** attributive adj., **Midianite,** + אִישׁ *man* Gn 37$_{28}$, אִשָּׁה *woman* Nm 25$_{15}$.

2. as sing. noun, a particular **Midianite, a.** masc., <APP> רְעוּאֵל הַמִּדְיָנִי חֹתֵן מֹשֶׁה *Reuel the Midianite, the father-in-law of Moses* Nm 10$_{29}$ (or [if em. חֹתֵן to חֲתַן *son-in-law*] הַמִּדְיָנִי refers to חֹבָב בֶּן־ *Hobab the son of* Reuel).

b. fem., <OBJ> קרב hi. *bring near* Nm 25$_{6}$. <PREP> אֵת *with*, + נכה ho. *be killed* Nm 25$_{14}$.

3. as plural noun, **Midianites,** <SUBJ> מכר *sell* Gn 37$_{36}$ (מְדָנִים; or em. מִדְיָנִים), צרר *show hostility toward* Nm 25$_{17}$, נכל pi. *deceive* Nm 25$_{17}$. <OBJ> צרר *show hostility toward* Nm 25$_{17}$, נכה hi. *strike* Nm 25$_{17}$. <PREP> מֵאֵת *from*, i.e. upon, + נקם *avenge* Nm 31$_{2}$.

⇒ מִדְיָן I *Midian*.

*[מָדָךְ] pr.n.[m.] **Madach,** <CSTR> בן מדך *son of Madach* Frey 1285$_{9}$ (others סדן *Sadan*; others מדר *Madar*).

מְדֹכָה $_{1.0.1}$ n.f. **mortar**—Q מדוכה—<OBJ> טהר pi. *purify* 11QT 49$_{14}$ (|| רֵחַיִם *mill*, + כְּלִי *vessel*). <PREP> בְּ of place, + דוך *crush* Nm 11$_{8}$ (|| רֵחַיִם *mill*, פָּרוּר *pot*). <APP> כְּלִי *vessel* 11QT 49$_{14}$.

<SYN> רֵחַיִם *mill*, פָּרוּר *pot*.

⇒ דוך *crush*.

*[מְדָל] I n.m. **cloud,** <SUBJ> נזל *pour out* Nm 24$_{7}$ (if em. מִדָּלְיָו *from his buckets* to מְדָלָיו). <CSTR> מַר מְדָל *drop of*, i.e. from., *a cloud* Is 40$_{15}$ (if em. מִדְּלִי *from a bucket*).

*[מְדָל] II n.m. **thunderbolt,** <SUBJ> נזל *pour out* Nm 24$_{7}$ (if em. מִדָּלְיָו *from his buckets* to מְדָלָיו). <CSTR> מַר מְדָל *drop of*, i.e. from., *a thunderbolt* Is 40$_{15}$ (if em. מִדְּלִי *from a bucket*).

*[מַדְלֵי] n.[m.] **scales,** גּוֹיִם כְּמַר מִדְּלִי *the nations are like the fine dust of the scales* Is 40$_{15}$ (if em. מִדְּלִי *from a bucket*; || מֹאזְנַיִם *scales*).

מַדְמֵן $_{1}$ pl.n. **Madmen,** town in central Moab, perh. Kh. Dimneh, c. 5 km NW of Rabbah, <SUBJ> דמם *be silent* Jr 48$_{2}$. <PREP> אַחֲרֵי *after*, + הלך *go* Jr 48$_{2}$.

⇒ דֹּמֶן *dung*.

מַדְמַנָּה $_{2}$ pl.n. **Madmannah,** town in S Judah, perh. Kh. Umm Demineh or Kh. Tarit, c. 20 km NE of Beer-sheba, perh. ident. with Meconah at Ne 11$_{28}$, <SUBJ> היה *be* Jos 15$_{31}$. <CSTR> אֲבִי מַדְמַנָּה *(founding) father of Madmannah* 1 C 2$_{49}$.

⇒ דֹּמֶן *dung*.

מַדְמֵנָה I $_{1}$ n.f. **dung-pit,** <CSTR> מֵי מַדְמֵנָה *water of a dung pit* Is 25$_{10(Kt)}$. <PREP> בְּמוֹ *in*, + דוש ni. *be trampled* Is 25$_{10(Qr)}$.

⇒ דֹּמֶן *dung*.

מַדְמֵנָה II $_{1}$ pl.n. **Madmenah,** town c. 3 km N of Jerusalem, btw. Nob and Anathoth, <SUBJ> נדד *flee* Is 10$_{31}$.

מְדָן 2 pr.n.m. **Medan,** son of Abraham and Keturah, <OBJ> ילד *give birth to* Gn 25_2||1 C 1_{32}.

מְדָנִים, see מִדְיָן I *Midian,* and II *strife.*

מַדָּע I 6.2.5 n.m. **knowledge**—Si מַדַּע; cstr. Q מדע; sf. מַדָּעֲךָ, Q מדעו—**1. knowledge, understanding, intelligence,** <SUBJ> נתן pass. *be given* 2 C 1_{12}. <NOM CL> עמך ... מדע תורה *with you is ... knowledge of the law* 4QMMT C_{28}. <OBJ> בין hi. *understand* Dn 1_4, שׁאל *ask for* 2 C 1_{11}, נתן *give* Dn 1_{17} 2 C 1_{10}, שׁוב hi. *bring* 1QS 6_9. <CSTR> מדע תורה *knowledge of the law* 4QMMT C_{28}; מְבִינֵי מַדָּע *ones understanding of,* i.e. who possess, *knowledge* Dn 1_4, חֲסֵירֵי מַדָּע *ones lacking of,* i.e. in, *knowledge* Si 13_8. <PREP> בְּ of accompaniment, *with, in,* i.e. knowingly, + כחשׁ pi. *lie* 4QSD 1.1_9 ([במ]דעו). <COLL> מַדָּע || דַּעַת *knowledge* Dn 1_4, חָכְמָה *wisdom* Dn 1_4 2 C $1_{10.11.12}$, + עָרְמָה *wisdom.*

2. (place of) carnal knowledge, i.e. bedroom* (unless §1 *knowledge,* i.e. thought, or מַדָּע II *repose* or III *friend* or IV *kinsman* or V *messenger*), <PREP> בְּ of place, *in,* + קלל pi. *curse* Ec 10_{20}.

3. mind, thought, <SUBJ> חסר *fail* Si 3_{13}. <PREP> בְּ of place, *in,* + קלל pi. *curse* Ec 10_{20} (unless מַדָּע II *repose;* or em. בְּמַצָּעֲךָ *on your couch*). <PREP> בְּ of accompaniment, *with, in,* + כחס pi. *lie* 1QS 7_3,* עשׂה *practise* deceit 1QS 7_5.* <COLL> מַדָּע + חַדְרֵי מִשְׁכָּבְךָ *chambers of your bed* Ec 10_{20}.

Also 4QapPs^b 15_8 ([מד]עך) 4QparaKings 127_3.

<SYN> §1 דַּעַת *knowledge,* חָכְמָה *wisdom.*

⇒ ידע I *know.*

*[מַדָּע] II 1 n.[m.] **repose** (unless מַדָּע I *knowledge*) —sf. מַדָּעֲךָ—<PREP> בְּ of place, *in,* + קלל pi. *curse* Ec 10_{20}. <COLL> מַדָּע + חַדְרֵי מִשְׁכָּבְךָ *chambers of your bed* Ec 10_{20}.

⇒ ידע II *be quiet.*

*[מַדָּע] III 1 n.[m.] **friend** (unless מַדָּע I *knowledge*) —sf. מַדָּעֲךָ—<PREP> בְּ *to,* + קלל pi. *curse* Ec 10_{20}.

*[מַדָּע] IV 1 n.[m.] **kinsman** (unless מַדָּע I *knowledge*) —sf. מַדָּעֲךָ—<PREP> בְּ *among,* + קלל pi. *curse* Ec 10_{20}.

⇒ ידע I *know.*

*[מַדָּע] V 1 n.[m.] **messenger** (unless מַדָּע I *knowledge*) —sf. מַדָּעֲךָ—<PREP> בְּ *among,* + קלל pi. *curse* Ec 10_{20}.

מוֹדַע 2.0.2 n.m. **relative**—מוֹדָע; pl. sf. Q מודעי, Q מודעיו—**relative, kinsman,** perh. **acquaintance** (1QH 4_9), <SUBJ> נדח ni. *be banished* 1QH 4_9 (|| רֵעַ *friend*). <NOM CL> לְנָעֳמִי מֹדַע לְאִישָׁהּ *(belonging) to Naomi there was a relative of her husband's* Ru 2_1(Qr) (Kt מידע, i.e. ידע pu. ptc.). <OBJ> קרא *call,* i.e. name Pr 7_4 (+ אָחוֹת *sister*). <APP> מֹדַע ... אִישׁ גִּבּוֹר חַיִל *a relative ... a man, a mighty one of valour* Ru 2_1(Qr). <PREP> בְּ *against,* + מדד *measure* appar. Is 14_{31}(1QIsa^a) (MT אֵין בּוֹדֵד בְּמוֹעָדָיו *none is alone in his ranks*).

<SYN> רֵעַ *friend.*

⇒ ידע I *know.*

[מוֹדַעַת] 1 n.f. **relative**—sf. מֹדַעְתָּנוּ—**relative, kin, acquaintance,** <NOM CL> הֲלֹא בֹעַז מֹדַעְתָּנוּ *is not Boaz our relative?* Ru 3_2. <CSTR> מוֹדַעַת מְזִמּוֹת *acquaintance of discretion* Pr 8_{12} (if em. דַּעַת מְזִמּוֹת אֶמְצָא *I find knowledge [and] discretion* to מוֹדַעַת מְזִמּוֹת אִמָּצֵא *I am found as the acquaintance of discretion*).

⇒ ידע I *know.*

*[מַדֵּף] I 0.0.1 n.[m.] **trap, stone sealing a tomb,** concealing treasure, <PREP> תַּחַת *under* 3QTr 3_{12}.

*[מַדֵּף] II 0.0.1 n.[m.] **uncleanness,** concealing treasure, <PREP> תַּחַת *under* 3QTr 3_{12}.

[מַדְקָרָה] 1 n.f. **piercing**—pl. cstr. מַדְקְרוֹת—**piercing, stab,** <CSTR> מַדְקְרוֹת חָרֶב *piercings of the sword* Pr 12_{18}. <PREP> כְּ *as* Pr 12_{18}.

⇒ דקר *pierce.*

*[מָדָר] pr.n.[m.] **Madar,** <CSTR> בן מדר *son of Madar* Frey 1285_9 (others סדן *Sadan;* others מדך *Madach*).

*[מֶדֶר] n.[m.] **wet clay,** <OBJ> שׁקט hi. *let fall* Jb 37_{17} (if em. מִדָּרוֹם *on account of the south wind* to מְדָרֶם

their wet clay).

מַדְרֵגָה 2 n.f. **steep place**—pl. מַדְרֵגוֹת—**steep place, cliff,** <SUBJ> נפל *fall* Ezk 38_{20} (or em. הַמִּגְדָּלוֹת *the towers*; || הַר *mountain*, + חוֹמָה *wall*). <CSTR> סֵתֶר הַמַּדְרֵגָה *hidden place of the cliff* Ca 2_{14} (|| סֶלַע *rock*).
<SYN> הַר *mountain*, סֶלַע *rock*.

*[**מִדְרוֹךְ**] 0.0.1 n.[m.] **treading place**—cstr. Q מדרוך—<CSTR> כול מדרוך כף [רגל] *every treading place of a sole of a foot of* human beings 4QJub^{h} 32_{18}. <PREP> בְּ *over*, + משל *rule* 4QJub^{h} 32_{18} (וימש[לו]).
⇒ דרך *tread*.

[**מִדְרָךְ**] 1.0.1 n.[m.] **treading place**—cstr. מִדְרַךְ—<CSTR> מִדְרַךְ כַּף־רָגֶל *treading place of the sole of a foot* Dt 2_{5}, מדרו[ך] קודשכה *treading place of your holiness* 4QBer^{a} 1.2_{1}. <PREP> עַד *as much as*, + נתן *give* Dt 2_{5}.
⇒ דרך *tread*.

*[**מִדְרָס**] 0.0.1 n.[m.] **floor**—cstr. Q מדרס—**floor, treading place,** <CSTR> מדרס דבירי פלא *floor of the inner sanctuaries of wonder* 4QShirShabb^{f} 19_{2}.

[**מִדְרָשׁ**] 2.1.7 n.[m.] **study**—cstr. מִדְרַשׁ; sf. Si מדרשי—**study, inquiry, interpretation, midrash** (4QMidr Eschat^{a} 3_{14}), **(written) discourse** (2 C 13_{22} 24_{27} 4QS^{d} 1_{1}), perh. **explanation, development** of existing data,* <NOM CL> היאה מדרש התורה *it is the study of the law* 1QS 8_{15}. <OBJ> עשה *do* 1QS 8_{15}. <CSTR> מִדְרַשׁ הַנָּבִיא *discourse of the prophet* Iddo 2 C 13_{22}, סֵפֶר הַמְּלָכִים *of the book of the kings* 2 C 24_{27}, מדרש היחד *inquiry of the community* 1QS 6_{24}, מדרש התורה *study of the law* 1QS 8_{15} 4QD^{e} 7.2_{15} ([ה]תורה) CD 20_{6}, מדרש אשרי [ה]איש *midrash of 'Happy is the man'* 4QMidr Eschat^{a} 3_{14}; בית מדרשי *house of my study*, i.e. my academy Si 51_{23}. <ADJ> אַחֲרוֹן *final* 4QD^{e} 7.2_{15}.

<PREP> בְּ of place, time, *in, during* 1QS 8_{26} (|| מוֹשָׁב *session*, עֵצָה *council*), + כתב pass. *be written* 2 C 13_{22}, שפט *judge* 1QS 6_{24}; of accompaniment, *with, in*, + הלך htp. *walk* CD 20_{6}; עַל *upon, in*, + כתב pass. *be written* 2 C 24_{27}; עַל *in accordance with*, + כתב pass. *be written* 4QD^{e} 7.2_{15} ([כ]תוב); כְּפִי *in accordance with*, + יפע hi. *display* deeds CD 20_{6}. <COLL> מדרש למשכיל על אנשי התורה *a discourse for the master concerning the men of the law* 4QS^{d} 1_{1}.
Also perh. 4QTohD 2_{2} (המ[דרש]).
<SYN> מוֹשָׁב *session*, עֵצָה *council*.*
⇒ דרשׁ *seek*.

[**מְדֻשָׁה**] 1 n.f. **threshing**—sf. מְדֻשָׁתִי—**threshing,** i.e. that which is threshed, <COLL> מְדֻשָׁה as vocative Is 21_{10} (+ בֶּן־גָּרְנִי *son*, i.e. product, *of my threshing floor*).
⇒ דושׁ *thresh*.

מָה I 492.46.122 pronoun **what?**—**1.** usu. מַה־, with dagesh in following consonant; **2.** with א, ר, or in pause, מָה[־]; **3.** with ע, מֶה[־], except מָה עִמָּדִי (Gn 31_{32}) and מָה עַבְדְּךָ (2 K 8_{13}); **4.** with ה, מַה[־], except מָה[־]הֵמָּה, מָה הֵנָּה, מָה־הוֹעִיל (Hb 2_{18}), מֶה[־]הָיָה; **5.** with article alw. מָה[־] except מֶה הָאָדָם (Ec 2_{12}); **6.** with ח, מַה[־] or מֶה[־] (alw. מֶה[־] חָ/חֱ); **7.** מֶה sometimes before letters other than ח or ע (perh. dialectal):* e.g. מֶה בַּר (Pr 31_{2}), מֶה כְבוֹדִי (Ps 4_{3}), מֶה נִּאֵץ (Ps 10_{13}), מֶה לֹא (Jb 7_{21}), מֶה מִשְׁפַּט (2 K 1_{7}), מֶה נְאֻם (Hg 1_{9}), מֶה תַּכּוּ (Is 1_{5}), מֶה קוֹל (1 S $4_{6.14}$ 15_{14}); **8.** מַה־ without following dagesh: e.g. L מַה־מִנִּי (mss מַה־מִּנִּי Jb 16_{6}), מַה־יָּדַעְתָּ (mss מַה־יָּדַעְתָּ Jb 34_{33}); **9.** variant orthographies: Q מא (4QapPs^{b} $13_{1.1}$), מהו (= מָה הוּא MurEp Jonathan$_{9}$), מהיא (= מָה הִיא 4QMyst^{a} 6.2_{8}); Kt מהם (Qr מָה הֵם Ezk 8_{6}), מזה (Qr מַה־זֶּה Ex 4_{2}), מלכם (Qr מַה־לָּכֶם Is 3_{15}); **10.** prefixed forms: בַּמֶּה (20 times), before א or ה (but not ע [2 C 7_{21}]) or in pause (1 K 22_{21}|| 2 C 18_{20}) בַּמָּה (9 times); כַּמָּה (10 times), כַּמֶּה (3 times).

1. interrogative, **what?, how?, why?**
   - **a.** + perfect, p. 151b
   - **b.** + imperfect, p. 152a
   - **c.** + infinitive, p. 153a
   - **d.-e.** + participle, p. 153a
   - **f.** + adjective, p. 153b
   - **g.** + pronoun, p. 153b
   - **h.** + noun, p. 153b

   Collocations

   (1) word separates מָה from noun, p. 155a

(2) מה א׳ לְב׳, p. 155a
(3)-(4) followed by relative clause, p. 155b
i. + preposition
(1) לְ *to, for,* p. 156a
(2) other prepositions, p. 157a
j. + adverb, p. 157a
k. as open question, p. 157a
Collocations (all of §1)
(1) word-order irregularities, p. 157a
(2) מָה ... כִּי *what (is) ... that?,* p. 157a
(3) in subordinate clause, p. 157b
(4) first element in direct speech, p. 158a
(5) מָה ... מָה ... מָה, p. 158a
2. as exclamation, **how (much)!**, p. 158a
3. what is there?, what happens?, p. 159b
4. what if?, p. 159b
5. what ails?, what need is there?, p. 159b
6. how much?, p. 159b
7a. as indefinite pronoun, **anything**, p. 159b
7b. בְּלִי־מָה **void**, p. 159b
8. as relative, **what(ever)**, p. 159b
9. מַה־שֶּׁ- **what(ever)**, p. 160b
10. מָה אֲשֶׁר **what(ever)**, p. 160b
11. בַּמָּה, p. 160b
12. כַּמָּה, p. 161a
13. עַד־כַּמֶּה, p. 161a
14. לָמָּה
a. why?, p. 161a
b. lest, p. 161a
15. שֶׁמָּה **lest**, p. 161b
16. יַעַן מֶה **on account of what?**, p. 161b
17. עַד־מָה **how long?**, p. 161b
18. עַל־מָה **why?**, p. 162a
19. תַּחַת מָה **why?**, p. 162a

1. (in all senses listed, מָה oft. introduces a rhetorical question) **what?** (in nom. cl., **what is/are?**, etc.); if ref. is to animate beings, perh. **who?** (e.g. כיא מה צעיר מרש *for who/what is lowlier than a pauper?*); esp. in disjunctions, **which (is/are)?** (e.g. Jg 9_{2}); **of what value/importance is** a mere human, etc.? (e.g. Gn 21_{29} 23_{15} $16_{7.8}$ 2 S 9_{8} Ec 2_{2} Ezk 17_{12} Ps 8_{5} 144_{3} Jb 3_{12} 7_{17} Si 16_{17} 1QH 4QShirShabb[a] $2_{6.7}$); in the construction מה א׳ לְב׳ **what is the significance of** A for B?, **what does** A **mean** to B? (§1h, Coll., 2); **how?**, i.e. **in which way?** (with חטא *sin,* שׁגה *err,* יטב *be good,* צדק *be righteous,* htp. *justify oneself,* עבד *serve,* לאה hi. *weary*); **how is it possible to?** (with ישׁב *dwell,* יצב htp. *take one's stand;* חזק htp. *strengthen oneself,* עזר *help,* גאה *be proud,* חכם htp. *display wisdom,* חבר htp. *ally oneself,* אפק htp. *restrain oneself,* קבב *curse,* זעם *curse,* ישׁע hi. *save*).

With other verbs **how?** may also sometimes be the more appropriate sense, depending on context (e.g. with דבר pi. *speak,* אנח ni. *groan,* בין *understand,* htp. *look closely,* נשׂא *raise,* נתן *give,* שׁפך *pour,* יעל hi. *profit,* שׁוב hi. *repay*), or, in nom. cl., **what is/are ... like?, what kind of?** (e.g. Nm $13_{18.19.19.20}$ Jg 18_{8} 1 K 9_{13} Hg 2_{3} Ca $5_{9.9}$); perh. **why?** (e.g. Gn 31_{26} Ex 14_{15} $17_{2.2}$ 2 S 16_{2} 2 K 7_{3} Is $45_{10.10}$ Jr 30_{15} 49_{4} Na 1_{9} Ps 39_{8} $42_{6=12}$=43_{5} 52_{3} Jb 7_{21} Ca 7_{1} $8_{4.4}$ [unless in both מָה II *not*] Ec 7_{10} Lm 3_{39} Si 13_{2} 32_{22} 41_{4}); perh. **what is/are ... doing?, why is/are ... here?** (e.g. 1 S 29_{3}); in subordinate clauses, following verbs of informing and perceiving, מָה oft. equivalent to [אֶת־]אֲשֶׁר **that which** (but distinction between §1, final Coll., [3], and §8, oft. uncertain).

a. + perfect of היה *be* 1 S 4_{16} 2 S 1_{4} Ec 7_{10}, *occur* Ex $32_{1=23}$ Lm 5_{1}, ni. *occur* Jr 48_{19}, יכל *be able* Jg 8_{3}, נדד *flee* 4QsapDidB 4.2_{1}, אמר *say* 1 S 10_{15} 2 K 8_{14} 20_{14}||Is 39_{3} (+ מֵאַיִן *whence?*), דבר pi. *speak* Nm 23_{17} Jr $23_{35.37}$ 33_{24} $38_{25.25}$, ni. *say to one another* Ml 3_{13}, ענה *answer* Jr $23_{35.37}$, יעץ *counsel* Is 19_{12} Mc 6_{5} Jb 26_{3}, ידע *know* Jb 15_{9} 22_{13} (+ -הֲ interrogative) 34_{33}, ראה *see* Gn 20_{10} 1 S 28_{13} 2 K 20_{15}||Is 39_{4}, בעל *despise* 4QapPs[b] 13_{1}, נאץ pi. *despise* 4QapPs[b] 13_{1}, לאה hi. *weary* Mc 6_{3}, מצא *find* Gn 31_{37} 1 S 29_{8} Jr 2_{5} (מַה־מָּצְאוּ אֲבוֹתֵיכֶם בִּי עָוֶל *what was [the] iniquity that your ancestors found in me?*), קוה pi. *await* Ps 39_{8} (or em. מַה־קִּוִּיתִי *what/why do I await* to מַה־תִּקְוָתִי *what is my hope*), חטא *sin* Gn 20_{9} 1 K 18_{9} Jr 37_{18}, שׁגה *err* Jb 6_{24}, עשׂה *do* Gn 4_{10} 20_{9} (both [־]מֶה עָשִׂית) 31_{26} Ex 32_{21} Nm 22_{28} 23_{11} Jos 7_{19} Jg 8_{2} 1 S 13_{11} 14_{43} 17_{29} $20_{1.32}$ 26_{18} 29_{8} 2 S 3_{24} 24_{17}||1 C 21_{17} 1 K 19_{20} Jr 2_{23} 8_{6} Mc 6_{3} Est 9_{12} 2 C 32_{13}, פעל *do* Ps 11_{3} (or em.

impf.).

<COLL> מָה separated from verb cited above by subject noun Jr 33_{24}.

b. + imperfect of היה *be* Gn 37_{20} Jg 13_{12} 1 K 14_{3} Jon 4_{5} Ec 6_{12} 11_{2} (מַה־יִּהְיֶה רָעָה *what evil will there be?*) Si $5_{4(C)}$ $11_{19(Segal)}$ ([ומה יה[יה]) perh. 4QHodª 7.2_{14} ([]ומה יה), צדק *be righteous* Jb 9_{2} (unless מָה II *not*) 25_{4}, htp. *justify oneself* Gn 44_{16}, זכה *be pure* Jb 25_{4}, יטב *be good* Si $30_{19(Segal)}$ (מה יט]ב לאלי[לי הגוים *how can it be good for the idols of the nations?*), גאה *be proud* Si 10_{9}, שׁחח htpo. *be made low* Ps $42_{6=12}$=43_{5}, אפק htp. *restrain oneself* Si $32_{22(mg)}$ (main text לֹא does *not* restrain himself) $33_{22(mg)}$, חזק htp. *strengthen oneself* 1QH 10_{6} fr. 3_{12}, חבר htp. *ally oneself* Si $13_{2.2(mg).2(mg)}$, pu. *be allied* Si 13_{17}.

דמה *be compared* 4QShirShabb 2_{6} (וק]ודשנו מה ידמה לקודש] קודשי[הם *and as for our holiness, how can it be compared with their supreme holiness?*), pi. *compare* Lm 2_{13}, ערך *compare* Lm 2_{13} (if em. אֲעִידֵךְ what *can I call to witness for you?* to אֶעֱרָךְ what *can I compare?*), שׁוה hi. *compare* Lm 2_{13} (or em. מָה־אַשְׁוֶה *what can I compare?* to מִי יוֹשִׁיעַ *who will save?*).

הלך *go* Jb 16_{6} (unless מָה II *not*), עזב *leave* Si 11_{23} (unless ni. *be left*), יצב htp. *take one's stand* 1QH 12_{28}, עבר hi. *remove* Jb 7_{21}, perh. מושׁ hi. *remove* 4QapPsª 5_{3}, בוא hi. *bring* 1 S 9_{7}, נשׂא *raise* Si $13_{2(mg)}$, *forgive* Jb 7_{21}, יסף hi. *add* 2 S 7_{20}||1 C 17_{18} Ps 120_{3} (ms ho. *be added*) 11QPsaª 24_{15}, נתן *give* Gn 15_{2} 30_{31} 38_{16} 1 K 3_{5}|| 2 C 1_{7} 2 K 4_{43} Ho 9_{14} Ps 120_{3} (or em. ho. *be given*) Jb 35_{7}, לקח *take* perh. Jb 15_{12} (מַה־יִּקָּחֲךָ לִבֶּךָ appar. *what has taken from you your mind?* unless *why has your heart emboldened you?*, i.e. יקח pi.*) 35_{7}.

אמר *say* Gn 44_{16} Ex 3_{13}* Jos 7_{8} Jr 13_{21} Jb 23_{5} 37_{19} Pr 31_{2} (if em. מַה־בְּרִי *what, O my son?* to מַה־לְּמוּאֵל בְּכֹרִי אֹמַר אֵלֶיךָ *what, O Lemuel my firstborn, shall I say to you?*), דבר pi. *speak* Gn 44_{16} Jg 7_{11} Hb 2_{1} Is 38_{15} Jr 5_{15} Hb 2_{1} Ps 85_{9} 1QH 12_{3} 10_{7} $12_{32.32}$ 4QShir^{b} 126_{2}, נגד hi. *tell* Ca 5_{8} (unless מָה II *not*), ספר pi. *relate* 1QH 12_{5}, ענה *answer* Is 14_{32}, שׁוב hi. *reply* 2 S 24_{13}||1 C 21_{12} (מָה־אָשִׁיב [אֶת־]שֹׁלְחִי דָּבָר *what word shall I return the one who sent me?*) Hb 2_{1} Jb 31_{14} 40_{4} 1QS 11_{22}=4QSj$_{10}$ (מה] [ישיב) 1QH 12_{6} 12_{27} fr. 10_{2}, *repay* Ps 116_{12}, צוה pi. *command* Nm 9_{8}, קרא *call* Gn 2_{19} Is 40_{6} 4QapJoshua^{b} $5_{2(WA)}$, עוד hi. *call to witness* Lm 2_{13} (or em. אֲעִידֵךְ what *can I call to witness for you?* to אֶעֱרָךְ what *can I compare?*), צעק *cry out* Ex 14_{15}, זעק *cry out* Jr 30_{15}, קבב *curse* Nm 23_{8}, זעם *curse* Nm 23_{8}, יכח hi. *reprove* Jb 6_{25}, *argue* 1QH 1_{25}, אנח ni. *groan* 4Q418 69.2_{5}, אנן htpo. *complain* Lm 3_{39}, המה *make a noise* Ps $42_{6=12}$=43_{5}.

חזה *see* Ca 7_{1}, נבט hi. *look* 1QH 18_{19} (ה[מ]), יחל hi. *hope* 2 K 6_{33}, בקשׁ pi. *seek* Gn 37_{15}, נסה pi. *test* Ex 17_{2}, בין hi. *understand* Pr 20_{24} (or em. מַה־יָּבִין *how can he understand?* to מַה־יָּכִין *how can he establish?*) 1QS 11_{22}=4QSj$_{10}$, appar. hi. *teach* Si 38_{36} (משל בינה ... ראה מה יבין ושריהו *a saying of wisdom ..., see what it teaches and hurry to pursue it;* or em. מִי see *who* is intelligent and hurry to pursue him), htpol. *look closely* Jb 31_{1} (unless מָה II *not;* or em. מָה אֶתְבּוֹנֵן *how could I look closely?* to מֵהִתְבּוֹנֵן *not to look closely*) 4QMystª $8_{5(mg)}$, חכם htp. *display wisdom* Si 35_{4} 38_{25}, חשׁב *reckon* Na 1_{9}, htp. *be accounted* 1QH 10_{5} 4QShirShabbª 2_{6}, זמם *think* 1QH 10_{5}, ידע *know* Jb 11_{8}, מאס *despise* Si $41_{4(B)}$, הלל htp. *glory* Jr 49_{4} Ps 52_{3}.

עשׂה *do* Gn 27_{37} 31_{43} Ex 17_{4} 33_{5} Jos 7_{9} Jg 13_{8} 18_{14} $21_{7.16}$ 1 S 5_{8} 6_{2} 10_{2} 22_{3} 25_{17} 28_{15} 2 S 16_{20} 21_{3} 2 K 2_{9} 4_{2} Is 10_{3} 45_{9} Jr 4_{30} 5_{31} Ho $6_{4.4}$ 9_{5} 10_{3} Ps $56_{5.12}$ 118_{6} Jb 9_{12} 31_{14} 35_{6} Pr 25_{8} Ca 8_{8} Ec 8_{4} 1 C 12_{33} 2 C 20_{12} Si $5_{4(A)}$ (unless ni. what can *be done?*) 33_{10} 4QapPs^{b} 31_{6} (ומה יעשה אנוש *and what can a mortal do?*, unless *and what can be done?; weak* am I, i.e. עשׂה ni.), ni. *be done* Ex 2_{4} Nm 15_{34} 1 S 17_{26} Est 2_{11} 6_{3}, פעל *do* Ps 11_{3} (if em. pf.) Jb 7_{20} 11_{8} 22_{17} 35_{6} Si $33_{10(mg)}$.

ישׁב *dwell* 1QS 11_{21}, עור hi. *rouse* love Ca 8_{4} (unless מָה II *not;* or em. אִם *if*), htpol. *rouse* love Ca 8_{4} (unless מָה II; or em. אִם), ילד *give birth* Pr 27_{1} Si 8_{18}, hi. *beget* Is 45_{10}, חיל *give birth* Is 45_{10}, אכל *eat* Lv 25_{20}, שׁתה *drink* Ex 15_{24} (unless מָה II *not*), שׁפך *pour* Si 35_{4}, רזם perh. *flash* Jb 15_{12} (mss רמז *intimate;* or em. רום *be high*), עבד *serve* Ex 10_{26}, עזר *help* Jb 26_{2}.

יעל hi. *profit* Hb 2_{18} Jb 21_{15} 35_{3} Si 38_{21}, סכן *benefit* Jb 35_{3}, ישׁע hi. *save* 1 S 10_{27} Jb 26_{2}, ריב *strive* Ex 17_{2}, מרץ hi. *distress* Jb 16_{3} (mss מִי *who?*).

Also 1QH 12_{33} ([]ומה א *and what can I?*).

<COLL> מָה separated from verb cited above by

subject noun Jr 33_{24} Jb 16_6.

... בלוא ... מה *what/how could I ... unless you had ...?*, e.g. [מ]ה אביט בלוא גליתה עיני *how could I look unless you had uncovered my eye?* 1QH 18_{19}, also Si 35_4 (ובלא מזמר מה תשפך שיח *and without a psalm how can you pour out feeling?*) 1QH $10_{5.6.7}$ 12_{33} 4QShir^b 75_2 ([בלוא פתח]תה פי מה [אדבר] *had you not opened my mouth, how could I speak?*) 4QMyst^a $8_{5(mg)}$ (ומה יתבונן גב[ו]ר בלוא ידע ולוא שמע *and what could a mortal examine unless he had first known and heard*); sim. Si 35_4 (ובל עת מה תתחכם *and without the appropriate time, how can you display wisdom?*) 1QH 1_{23} (מה אדבר בלא נודע perh. *how can I speak without it being known?*) 10_5 (ומה אתחשב באין רצונכה *and what am I accounted without your will*, i.e. unless you will it?) 12_{32} (ומה אדבר כיא אם פתחתה פי *and how could I speak unless you had opened my mouth?*) 4QMyst^a 3_{34} ([מה גבורה [בלוא] perh. *what is might without?*), מָה אֶקֹּב לֹא קַבֹּה אֵל וּמָה אֶזְעֹם לֹא זָעַם י׳ *how could I curse what God has not cursed and how could I curse what Y. has not cursed?* Nm 23_8.

c. + infinitive of עשה *do* 2 K $4_{13.14}$ (both מָה לַעֲשׂוֹת *what is to do*, i.e. to be done?) Is 5_4 (+ מַדּוּעַ *why?*) Est 1_{15} 6_6 2 C 25_9 (all four מַה־לַּעֲשׂוֹת).

d. + participle (without subject), of קרא ni. *be called* 4QMyst^a 3a 2_2 (מה נקרא ה[] *what is the ... called?*, unless *what shall we call the ...?*; =4QMyst^b 5_3 lacks ה[]) 4QMyst^b 5_4 (ומה נקרא לאדם *and what is a* good and righteous *person called?*; =4QMyst^a 3a 2_3 [ומה] נקרא [לאד]ם).

e. + participle with subject, מָה אַתָּה עֹשֶׂה *what are you doing?* Ezk 12_9, וּמָה־אַתָּה עֹשֶׂה בָזֶה *and what are you doing here?* Jg 18_3 (+ מִי *who* brought you hither?), מָה אַתֶּם עֹשִׂים *what are you doing?* Jg 18_{18} 2 C 19_6 (מָה־אַתֶּם), מָה הֵמָּה עֹשִׂים *what are they doing?* Jr 7_{17} Ezk $8_{6(Qr)}$ (מָה הֵם), מַה־זֹּה עֹשָׂה *what does this do?* Ec 2_2, מָה אֲנִי עֹשֶׂה *what am I doing?* Ne 2_{16} (+ אָנָה *whither?*), מָה הַיְּהוּדִים הָאֲמֵלָלִים עֹשִׂים *what are the wretched Jews doing?* Ne 3_{34} (+ -הֲ interrogative).

מָה אַתָּה רֹאֶה *what are you seeing?* Jr $1_{11.13}$ 24_3 Am 7_8 8_2 (both מָה־) Zc 4_2 5_2, וּמָה אַתֶּם רֹאִים אֹתוֹ עַתָּה *and how do you see it now?* Hg 2_3, מָה י׳ אֱלֹהֶיךָ שֹׁאֵל מֵעִמָּךְ *what does Y. your God ask of you?* Dt 10_{12}, מָה־י׳ דּוֹרֵשׁ מִמְּךָ he has told you *what Y. is seeking from you* Mc 6_8, וּמָה הָאֶחָד מְבַקֵּשׁ *and what is the One seeking* Ml 2_{15}.

מָה אֲדֹנִי מְדַבֵּר אֶל־עַבְדּוֹ *what is my lord saying to his servant?* Jos 5_{14}, מָה־אַתָּה חָסֵר עִמִּי *what are you lacking with me?* 1 K 11_{22}, מָה אַתֶּם נוֹעָצִים *what are you planning?* 1 K 12_9||2 C 10_9, מָה אֲנַחְנוּ יֹשְׁבִים פֹּה *why are we sitting here?* 2 K 7_3, מָה אֱלֹהַי נֹתֵן אֶל־לִבִּי *what is my God placing in my heart?* Ne 2_{12}, מָה אֵלֶּה בָאִים לַעֲשׂוֹת *what are these coming to do?* Zc 2_4, מַה־הֹוֶה לָאָדָם *what (benefit) is to humankind?* Ec 2_{22}.

f. + adjective, רָם *high* 4QMyst^b 7_1, רַע *evil* Si $37_{27(D)}$ 4QMyst^b 7_1 10_2 4Q410 1_6, טוֹב *good* Jg 9_2 Mc 6_8 Jb 34_4 Ec 6_{12} 4Q410 1_6, מָתוֹק *sweet* Jg 14_{18}, 4Q416 2.3_{15}=4Q418 9_{16}, מַר *bitter* 4Q416 2.3_{15}=4Q418 9_{16} ([מה מר]), עַז *strong* Jg 14_{18}, צָעִיר *small* 4Q417 1.1_{10}.

g. + pronoun (see also מַה־זֶּה at §5), אֲנִי *I* 1QH 3_{24} (+ ואני מגבל מים what am I, *one kneaded of water?*) 11_3 (ואני מה כיא appar. *and what am I, that?*) fr. 2_4 (ואני מה כיא *and what am I, for* I was taken from dust), הוּא *it* Ex 16_{15} 4QMyst^a 3a 2_7, *he* Nm 16_{11} (וְאַהֲרֹן מַה־הוּא *and Aaron, of what importance is he?*) Est 8_1, הִיא *it* Gn $23_{15(Qr)}$ Nm $13_{18(Qr)}$ Zc 5_6 Ps 39_5 (וּמִדַּת יָמַי מַה־הִיא *and the measure of my days, what is it?*) 4QMyst^a 6.2_8, נַחְנוּ *we* Ex $16_{7.8}$ (both וְנַחְנוּ מָה *and of what importance are we?*), אַתֶּם *you* Jg 18_8 (or em. מָה אַתֶּם appar. *how have you fared?* to מִי אַתֶּם *who are you?*) Jl 4_4, הֵמָּה *they* Zc 1_9 4_5 (both מָה הֵמָּה אֵלֶּה *what are these?*), הֵנָּה *they* Is 41_{22} (הָרִאשֹׁנוֹת מָה הֵנָּה *the first things, what are they?*), זֶה *this* Gn 27_{20} Ex 4_2 Jg 18_{24} Est 4_5, זֹאת *this* Gn 3_{13} 12_{18} 26_{10} 29_{25} 42_{28} Ex 13_{14} $14_{5.11}$ Jg 2_2 15_{11} Jon 1_{10} Si 39_{34} (זה רע מה זה *this is evil; what is this?*; mg מזה this is *more* evil *than this*), אֵלֶּה *these* 2 S 16_2 Ezk 17_{12} 24_{19} 37_{18} Zc 1_9 (מָה הֵמָּה אֵלֶּה *what are these?*) 2_2 $4_{4.5}$ (מָה הֵמָּה אֵלֶּה) 4_{13} 6_4.

h. + noun, שַׁדַּי *Shaddai* Jb 21_{15}, אָדָם *human being* Ps 144_3 1QH 10_3, אֱנוֹשׁ *human being* Ps 8_5 Jb 7_{17} 15_{14}, אִישׁ *man* 1QH 7_{32}, בָּשָׂר *flesh* 1QH 15_{21} 18_{21} fr. 7_{10}=4QHod^a 7.2_{14} 4QMyst^c 5_3 ([מ]ה), שָׁב *one who goes back* to dust 1QH 10_{12} 12_{31}, יָלוּד *one born* of woman 1QH 13_{14}, אָב *father* 4QMyst^a 6.2_5, בֵּן *son* Ps 8_5 144_3 1QS 11_{20}, זֶרַע *offspring* Si 10_{19}, דּוֹד *beloved* Ca $5_{9.9}$, יוֹעֵץ *counsellor* Si

$37_{8(mg)}$ (מה יועץ שמור נפשך *what [good] is a counsellor?; guard your soul*; main text מיועץ guard your soul *from a counsellor*), עֶבֶד *servant* 2 S 9_{8} 2 K 8_{13}, עִבְרִי *Hebrew* 1 S 29_{3}, עַם *people* 4QMyst^{a} 3a 2_{16} ([ומה]עמים כ[י] בראם *and of what value are peoples, that he created them?*).

כִּבְשָׂה *ewe* Gn 21_{29}, אֶרֶץ *land* Nm 13_{18} (הָאָרֶץ מַה־הִיא *the land, what is it like*, i.e. what is the land like?) $13_{19.20}$, זַיִת *olive tree* Zc 4_{11} (מַה־שְּׁנֵי הַזֵּיתִים הָאֵלֶּה *what do these two olive trees mean?*), שִׁבֹּלֶת *ear* Zc 4_{12} (מַה־שְּׁתֵּי שִׁבֲּלֵי הַזֵּיתִים *what do the two ears of the olive trees mean?*), נֶפֶשׁ *soul* Si 16_{17}, שַׁד *breast* Jb 3_{12} (+ מַדּוּעַ *why?*), עִיר *city* Nm 13_{19} 1 K 9_{13}, בָּמָה *high place* Ezk 20_{29}, אֶבֶן *stone* Jos $4_{6.21}$, אֵפֶר *ash* 4QMyst^{c} 4_{3}, עָפָר *dust* 1QH fr. 2_{7} 4QMyst^{c} 4_{3} (ומה אפר [ועפר] *and what is mere ash and dust?*).

רָעָה *evil* Jg 20_{12} 1 S 26_{18} (וּמַה־בְּיָדִי רָעָה *and what evil is in my hand?*) Ec 11_{2} (מַה־יִּהְיֶה רָעָה *what evil will there be?*), חַטָּאת *sin* Gn 31_{36} 1 S 20_{1} Jr 16_{10}, פֶּשַׁע *sin* Gn 31_{36}, מַעַל *transgression* Jos 22_{16}, עָוֶל *iniquity* Jr 2_{5} (מַה־מָּצְאוּ אֲבוֹתֵיכֶם בִּי עָוֶל *what was [the] iniquity that your ancestors found in me?*), עָוֹן *iniquity* 1 S 20_{1} Jr 16_{10}, אָשָׁם *guilt offering* 1 S 6_{4}.

כֹּחַ *strength* Jb 6_{11} 1QH 3_{24} (מה כוח לי *what is my strength?* or *what strength do I have?*), perh. גְּבוּרָה *might* 4QMyst^{a} 33_{4} ([]מה גבורה), בִּטָּחוֹן *security* 2 K 18_{19}||Is 36_{4}, כִּשְׁרוֹן *success* Ec 5_{10}, בֶּצַע *gain* Gn 37_{26} Ml 3_{14} Ps 30_{10}, יוֹתֵר *advantage* Ec $6_{8.11}$ (or em. יִתְרוֹן *profit* in both) 1QMyst 1.2_{3}, יִתְרוֹן *profit* Ec 1_{3} 3_{9} 5_{15} $6_{8.11}$ (if em. in both), תּוֹעֵלָה *profit* Si 41_{14}, perh. טוּב *goodness* 4Q418 69.2_{4}, חָכְמָה *wisdom* Jr 8_{9} (or em. וְחָכְמַת־מֶה לָהֶם *and the wisdom of what*, i.e. what wisdom, *do they have?* to וְחָכְמָתָם מֶה לָהֶם *as for their wisdom, what is [left] to them?*) 4QMyst^{b} 1a2-b_{3} (מ[ה]; =4QMyst^{a} $3c_{3}$ [חכמה]), צֶדֶק *righteousness* Si $16_{22(erased)}$ (mg מַעֲשֵׂה *deed of* righteousness), צְדָקָה *righteousness* 2 S 19_{29} (וּמַה־יֶּשׁ־לִי עוֹד צְדָקָה *and what righteousness is left to me?*).

דָּבָר *thing* Ex 18_{14} (+ מַדּוּעַ *why?*) Jg 8_{1} 2 S 12_{21} Ne 2_{19} 13_{17}, *word* 1 S 3_{17} 2 S 24_{13}||1 C 21_{12} (מָה־אָשִׁיב שֹׁלְחִי דָּבָר *what word shall I return the one who sent me?*) Ezk 33_{30}, מַעֲשֶׂה *deed* Gn 44_{15} 46_{33} 47_{3} 4QMyst^{b} 6_{2} (מע[שה]), פְּעֻלָּה *deed* or *recompense* Si 15_{11}, אוֹת *sign* 2 K 20_{8}||Is 38_{22} 1Q52 1_{1}, צִיּוּן *sign* 2 K 23_{17}, שֵׂחַ *thought* Am 4_{13}, חֲלוֹם *dream* Gn 37_{10}, חִידָה *riddle* 4QMyst^{c} $2b_{1}$, perh. רָז *secret* 4QMyst^{b} 8_{7}, מָשָׁל *proverb* Ezk 12_{22}, בַּקָּשָׁה *request* Est $5_{3.6}$ 7_{2} 9_{12}, שְׁאֵלָה *request* Est 5_{6} 7_{2} 9_{12}, שֵׁם *name* Gn 32_{28} Ex 3_{13} Pr $30_{4.4}$ (+ מִי *who?*) 4QRP^{b} 5b 2_{12}, קוֹל *voice* 1 S $4_{6.14}$ $15_{14.14}$, שֵׁמֶץ perh. *whisper* Jb 26_{14} (+ מִי),* perh. מִצְוָה *commandment* 4QMyst^{a} 32_{2} (המצו[ה]), חֹק *statute* Dt 6_{20}, עֵדָה *testimony* Dt 6_{20}, מִשְׁפָּט *judgment* Dt 6_{20} 4Q418 69.2_{5}, *nature* 2 K 1_{7}, תֹּאַר *form* 1 S 28_{14}, דְּמוּת *likeness* Is 40_{18}.

חַיִּים *life* Si $34_{27.27}$, דֶּרֶךְ *way* Ec 11_{5}, חֶלֶד *duration* Ps 89_{48} (or em. זְכָר־אֲנִי מֶה־חָלֶד *remember, as for me, what is [my] duration?* to זְכֹר מֶה־חָדֵל אֲנִי עוֹלָם *remember how lacking I am eternally*), מִדָּה *measure* Ps 39_{5} (וּמִדַּת יָמַי מַה־הִיא *and the measure of my days, what is it?*), יוֹם *day* Si 9_{11}, אַחֲרִית *future* Dt 32_{20}, אָחוֹר *future* 4QMyst^{b} 8_{2}, קֵץ *end* Jb 6_{11}, קֶדֶם *past* 4QMyst^{b} 8_{2}, רִאשֹׁנָה *first thing* Is 41_{22} (הָרִאשֹׁנוֹת מָה הֵנָּה *the first things, what are they?*).

כְּהֻנָּה *priesthood* 4QShirShabb^{a} 2_{6} (וכוהנתנו מה במעוניהם *and what is our priesthood in their dwelling places?*), עֲבֹדָה *service* Ex 12_{26}, perh. מֶמְשָׁלָה *government* 4Q417 2.1_{9} ([]מה יצרה וממשלת מעשיה perh. *what is its inclination and the government of its deeds?*), מְלָאכָה *mission* Jon 1_{8} (+ לְמִי *of whom?*, מֵאַיִן *whence?*, אֵי־מִזֶּה *from which?*).

מַשְׂכֹּרֶת *salary* Gn 29_{15}, תְּרוּמָה *contribution* 4QShirShabb^{a} 2_{7} ([מה] תרומת לשון עפרנו בדעת אל[ים] *what is the contribution of our tongue of dust compared with the knowledge of angels?*), עֵרָבוֹן *pledge* Gn 38_{18}, נַחֲלָה *inheritance* Jb 31_{2}, חֵלֶק *portion* 1 K 12_{16}||2 C 10_{16} (מָה־לָּנוּ חֵלֶק בְּדָוִ[י]ד *what is our portion in David?*; unless מָה I *not*) Jb 31_{2}.

שָׁלוֹם *peace* 2 K 9_{22}, שֶׁקֶט *silence* 4Q418 69.2_{5} ([מה]), חֵפֶץ *desire* Jb 21_{21}, תִּקְוָה *hope* Ps 39_{8} (if em. מַה־קִּוִּיתִי *what/why do I await* to מַה־תִּקְוָתִי *what is my hope*) Jb 27_{8} Si 16_{22}, פַּחַד *fear* 4QMyst^{b} 2.2_{2}, צֹרֶךְ *need* Si 37_{8},

מַשָּׂא *burden* Jr $23_{33.33}$ (or em. וְאָמַרְתָּ אֲלֵיהֶם אֶת־מַה־מַשָּׂא appar. *and you are to say to them, What is the burden?* to אַתֶּם הַמַּשָּׂא say to them, *You are the burden*), מַכָּה *blow* Zc 13_{6}, חֳרִי *burning* Dt 29_{23}, יֵצֶר *creation* 1QH

4_{29}, perh. *inclination* 4Q417 2.1$_{9}$ (מה יצרה[] perh. *what is its inclination?*), יצא ptc. *one that goes out* Zc 5_{5} (or em. מָה הַיּוֹצֵאת הַזֹּאת *what is this thing coming out?* to הָאֵיפָה הַיּוֹצֵאת הַזֹּאת see *this ephah that is coming out*).

<COLL> **(1)** word or words separates מָה from noun cited in main section Gn 21_{29} (and in the two following two paragraphs).

מה הוא היותר *what is the advantage?* 1QMyst 1.2$_{3}$, ומה הוא איש תהו *and what is a man of emptiness?* 1QH 7_{32}, מה הוא המצו[ה] *what is the commandment,* or, *one who commands?* 4QMyst^{a} 32$_{2}$, כי מ[ה] היא חכמה נכחדת *for what value is hidden wisdom?* 4QMyst^{b} 1a2-b$_{3}$ (=4Q Myst^{a} 3c$_{3}$ introduces this sequence by שמעו *hear;* Myst^{b}, by שמו *his name*), ומה אפהו אדם *and what indeed is a human being?* 10_{3}, ומה אף הואה בן האדם *and what indeed is a human being?* 1QS 11_{20}, ומה אף הוא בשר *and what indeed is flesh?* 1QH 15_{21}, ומה אפהוא שב לעפרו *and what indeed is one who returns to his dust?* 1QH 10_{12}, ומה אפהו שב אל עפרו *and what indeed is one who returns to his dust?* 1QH 12_{31}, ומה אפה[ו] *and what indeed is he?* 1QH fr. 4_{10}, ומה אפוא *and what therefore* [אֵפוֹא], or, *indeed is he* [אַפּוּא]? 4Q423 6_{2}.

מָה הָעֵדֹת וְהַחֻקִּים וְהַמִּשְׁפָּטִים *what are the testimonies and the statutes and the judgments?* Dt 6_{20}, וּמֶה קוֹל־הַצֹּאן הַזֶּה ... וְקוֹל הַבָּקָר *and what is this sound of sheep ... and sound of cattle?* 1 S 15_{14}, וּמֶה חֵלֶק אֱלוֹהַּ ... וְנַחֲלַת שַׁדַּי *and what is the portion of God ... or the inheritance of Shaddai?* Jb 31_{2}, מָה אֱנוֹשׁ ... וּבֶן־אָדָם *what is a person ... or a human being?* Ps 8_{5} (sim. 144_{3}), מַה־תִּשְׁתּוֹחֲחִי נַפְשִׁי וַתֶּהֱמִי עָלָי *why are you made low, my soul, and make a noise against me?* Ps 42_{6} (=42_{12}=43_{5} וּמַה־ *and why* do you make a noise?), וּמֶה לֹא־תִשָּׂא פִשְׁעִי וְתַעֲבִיר אֶת־עֲוֹנִי *and why do you not forgive my sin or remove my iniquity?* Jb 7_{21}, מֶה־עָזַרְתָּ ... הוֹשַׁעְתָּ *how have you been able to help ... been able to save?* Jb 26_{2}, מַה־טֹּבוּ דֹדַיִךְ מִיַּיִן וְרֵיחַ שְׁמָנַיִךְ מִכָּל־בְּשָׂמִים *how much better than wine is your lovemaking and the fragrance of your oils than all spices* Ca 4_{10} (or em. דַּדַּיִךְ *your breasts* and/or וְשַׂלְמֹתַיִךְ *your garments*).

(2) מה א׳ לְב׳ usu. *what is the significance of* A for B?, *what does* A *mean* to B?, מה אב לבנים *what is (the significance of) a father for children?* 4QMyst^{a} 6.2$_{3}$, מה פחד [לאדם] *what does fear mean to a person?* 4Q Myst^{b} 2.2$_{2}$, ומה החידה לכמה חונ[ק]רי בשורשי בינה *and what does the riddle mean to you, O investigators of the roots of understanding?* 4QMyst^{c} 2b$_{1}$, [מה] השקט ללוא היה perh. *what does silence mean for one that has not yet come into being?* 4Q418 69.2$_{5}$, ועתה אוילי לב מה טוב ללוא perh. *and now, O foolish of mind, what is goodness for one that has not?* 4Q418 69.2$_{4}$, ומה משפט ללוא נוסד *and what does judgment mean for that which has not yet been established?* 4Q418 69.2$_{5}$, מָה הָעֲבֹדָה הַזֹּאת לָכֶם *what does this service mean for you?* Ex 12_{26}, מָה הָאֲבָנִים הָאֵלֶּה לָכֶם *what do these stones mean for you?* Jos 4_{6}, מָה־אֵלֶּה לָּךְ perh. *why do you have these?* 2 S 16_{2}, מַה־לִּי דוּדָיִךְ *what do your baskets mean to me?* Jr 11_{15} (if em. מָה לִידִידִי *why is my beloved,* or, *what is the point of my beloved being,* in my house?).

מָה הַמָּשָׁל הַזֶּה לָכֶם perh. *what does this proverb mean to you (all)?* Ezk 12_{22} (unless *what is this proverb of yours?*), מָה־אֵלֶּה לָּךְ perh. *what do these things mean to you?* Ezk 37_{18} (unless *what are these things of yours?*), מַה־לָּכֶם הַמָּשָׁל הַזֶּה *what does this proverb mean to you (all)?* Ezk 18_{2} (if del. intervening אַתֶּם מֹשְׁלִים אֶת־ what does it mean to you?; *you recite* this proverb), מַה־לִּי בְּרִית לְבִתֵּךְ *what does your daughter's covenant mean to me?* Ezk 16_{30} (if em. מָה אֲמֻלָה לִבָּתֵךְ *how enfeebled is your spirit?*), מָה־אֵלֶּה לָּנוּ *what do these things mean for us?* Ezk 24_{19}, מַה־יִּתְרוֹן לוֹ perh. *what does profit mean to him?* Ec 5_{15} (unless *what is his profit?*), מַה־יִּתְרוֹן לָאָדָם perh. *what does profit mean to humankind?* Ec 1_{3} 6_{11} (if em. יֹתֵר *advantage;* unless in both *what is humankind's profit?*), מַה־כִּשְׁרוֹן לִבְעָלֶיהָ *what does success mean to those who possess it?* Ec 5_{15} (unless *what is the success of its owners?*), כִּי מַה־יּוֹתֵר לֶחָכָם *for what advantage does the sage have?* Ec 6_{8} (4QQoh^{a} כַּמָּה *how much?* for כִּי מַה־; or em. יִתְרוֹן *profit*), מַה־טּוֹב לָאָדָם *what is good for humankind?* Ec 6_{12}, מַה הוּא־לָהּ *what is his relationship to her?* Est 8_{1}.

(3) (§§g, h) מָה + (pro)noun + verb (but without relative particle), מַה־זֹּאת עָשִׂיתָ *what is this that you have done?* Gn 3_{13} (עָשִׂית) 12_{18} 26_{10} 29_{25} Ex 14_{11} Jg 15_{11} Jon 1_{10} (sim. Gn 42_{28} Ex 14_{5} Jg 2_{2}), מַה־זֶּה מִהַרְתָּ לִמְצֹא *what is* *this that you have hurried to find?* Gn 27$_{20}$, וּמַה־זֶּה תֹּאמְרוּ אֵלַי *and what is this that,* i.e. how on earth can, *you say to me?* Jg 18$_{24}$, מַה־זֶּה הָיָה לְבֶן־קִישׁ *what is this that has happened to the son of Kish?* 1 S 10$_{11}$; מָה־הַדָּבָר הַזֶּה עָשִׂיתָ *what is this thing that you have done?* Jg 8$_{1}$, וּמַה־דְּמוּת תַּעַרְכוּ לוֹ *and what is the likeness that you should set against him?* Is 40$_{18}$, מַה־מָּצְאוּ אֲבוֹתֵיכֶם בִּי עָוֶל *what was (the) iniquity that your ancestors found in me?* Jr 2$_{5}$.

(4) (§§g, h) מָה ... אֲשֶׁר *what is (the) ... that?* Gn 37$_{10}$ 38$_{18}$ 44$_{15}$ Ex 18$_{14}$ Nm 13$_{18.19}$ Dt 6$_{20}$ Jos 22$_{16}$ Jg 20$_{12}$ 1 S 3$_{17}$ 6$_{4}$ 15$_{14}$ 2 S 12$_{21}$ 2 K 1$_{7}$ 18$_{19}$||Is 36$_{4}$ 2 K 23$_{17}$ Jr 16$_{10}$ Ezk 20$_{29}$ Zc 4$_{12}$ Ne 2$_{19}$ 13$_{17}$, ומה והוא אשר יעשה ג[בר] *and what indeed is it that a mortal can do?* 4QMyst^{a} 3a 2$_{7}$, מהיא אשר *what is it that?* 4QMyst^{a} 6.2$_{8}$, מה יגאה עפר ואפר אשר בחייו יורם גויו *how can dust and ash be proud, whose body is being removed during its very lifetime?* Si 10$_{9}$, מָה הַדָּבָר הַיּוֹצֵא *what is the word that comes out?* Ezk 33$_{30}$.

i. + preposition, **(1)** לְ *to, for* (also, at 2 S 19$_{29}$ 2 K 4$_{2}$, מַה־יֵּשׁ לְ *what is there to/for?*), מַה־לִּי עוֹד *what else is (left) to me?* Jg 18$_{24}$, מַה־לָּךְ הָגָר *what is to you, O Hagar?*, perh. why are you preoccupied, or what concerns you? Gn 21$_{17}$ (+ אַל־תִּירְאִי *do not be afraid*), sim. Jos 15$_{18}$=Jg 1$_{14}$ (Achsah) 18$_{23.24}$ (Micah) 2 S 14$_{5}$ (woman of Tekoa) 1 K 1$_{16}$ (Bathsheba) 2 K 6$_{28}$ (bereaved prostitute) Ps 114$_{5}$ (subdued sea) perh. Est 5$_{3}$ (Esther), מַה־לָּעָם כִּי יִבְכּוּ *what is to,* i.e., what concerns, *the people that they weep?* 1 S 11$_{5}$, מַה־לְּךָ וּלְשָׁלוֹם *what is to you and to peace?*, perh. *what concern of yours is peace?* 2 K 9$_{18.19}$ (Joram's horsemen), מַה־לָּכֶם וְלַי׳ *what is to you and to Y.*, appar. what relationship do you have to Y? Jos 22$_{24}$, מַה־לִּי וָלָךְ *what is to you and to me?*, appar. what relationship do we (Elisha and Jehoram) have? 2 K 3$_{13}$.

מַה־לִּי וְלִבְרִיתֵךְ *what is to me and to your covenant?*, i.e. what do I have to do with your covenant? Ezk 16$_{30}$ (if em. מָה אֲמֻלָה לִבָּתֵךְ *how enfeebled is your spirit*), מַה־לִּי עוֹד לָעֲצַבִּים *what more is to me to idols*, appar. what further relationship shall I have will idols? Ho 14$_{9}$ (or em. לוֹ *to him*), מַה־לַתֶּבֶן אֶת־הַבָּר *what is to straw with grain*, i.e. what relationship do they have?, how can they be compared? Jr 22$_{28}$, מַה־לְּךָ פֹה *what is to you here?*, perh. why are you here? Jg 18$_{3}$ (Micah's Levite) 1 K 19$_{9.13}$ (Elijah), appar. what is there for you (Shebna) here? Is 22$_{16}$ (+ וּמִי לְךָ פֹה *and whom do you have here?*), מַה־לָּךְ אֵפוֹא *what is to you therefore?*, perh. what has befallen you? Is 22$_{1}$ (defeated Jerusalemites), מַה־לְּךָ נִרְדָּם *what is to you fast asleep?*, perh. why are you (Jonah) still fast asleep Jon 1$_{6}$.

מַה־לָּךְ לְדֶרֶךְ מִצְרַיִם/אַשּׁוּר perh. *what is it to you concerning the way of Egypt/Assyria*, perh. why do you (fleeing Israelites) go, or what is the point of your going, to Egypt/Assyria? Jr 2$_{18}$, מַה־לְּךָ לְסַפֵּר חֻקָּי *what is it to you to relate my statutes?*, perh. why do you (wicked) relate, or, what is the point of your relating, my statutes? Ps 50$_{16}$, מֶה לִידִידִי בְּבֵיתִי *what is it to my beloved in my house?*, perh. why is my beloved, or, what is the point of my beloved being, in my house? Jr 11$_{15}$ (or em. מַה־לִּי דּוּדַיִךְ *what do your baskets mean to me?*), מַה־לִּי וָלָךְ *what is to me and to you*, perh. what harm have I done you (Ammonites) (that you have come to fight)? Jg 11$_{12}$ (Jephthah and Ammonites) 2 C 35$_{21}$ (Neco and Josiah), מַה־לִּי וְלָכֶם *what is to me and to you*, perh. what harm have I (David) done you (sons of Zeruiah) (that you curse)? 2 S 16$_{10}$ (sim. 19$_{23}$), מַה־לִּי וָלָךְ *what is to me and to you*, perh. what harm have I (widow) done you (Elijah)? 1 K 17$_{18}$, מָה־אַתֶּם לִי צֹר וְצִידוֹן *what are you to me, O Tyre and Sidon*, perh. what harm are you doing to me? Jl 4$_{4}$.

מַה־לָּכֶם תְּדַכְּאוּ עַמִּי *what is it to you*, perh. what gain do you (elders) have, *that you crush my people?* Is 3$_{15}$(Qr), מַה־לָּכֶם אַתֶּם מֹשְׁלִים אֶת־הַמָּשָׁל הַזֶּה appar. *what is it to you?; you recite*, perh. why do you recite, or, what does it mean to you to recite, *this proverb?* Ezk 18$_{2}$ (or del. אַתֶּם מֹשְׁלִים אֶת־, leaving מַה־לָּכֶם הַמָּשָׁל הַזֶּה *what does this proverb mean to you [all]?*), מה לעבדך *what is to your servant?*, i.e. what is he to do? Lachish ost. 5$_{9}$ (others ים האל עבדך *today; will he* bring *to your servant?*), וּמַה־יֶּשׁ־לִי עוֹד צְדָקָה *and what righteousness is left to me?* 2 S 19$_{29}$, מַה־יֶּשׁ־לָךְ בַּבָּיִת *what do you have in the house?* 2 K 4$_{2}$, מַה־לָּנוּ חֵלֶק בְּדָוִ[י]ד *what is our portion in David?* 1 K 12$_{16}$||2 C 10$_{16}$ (unless מָה II *not*), וְעַתָּה מַה־לִּי־פֹה *and now, what do I have here,* for my people have been taken Is 52$_{5}$(Qr) (Kt מִי *who?*), וְחָכְמָתָם,

מֶה לָהֶם *as for their wisdom, what is [left] to them?* Jr 8$_{9}$ (if em. וְחָכְמַת־מֶה לָהֶם *and the wisdom of what,* i.e. what wisdom, *do they have?*)

(2) other prepositions, בְּ *in,* מַה־בַּבָּיִת know *what is in the house?* Gn 39$_{8}$ (Sam מְאוּמָה בְבֵיתוֹ *anything in his house*), וּמַה־בְּיָדִי רָעָה *and what evil is in my hand?* 1 S 26$_{18}$; מִן *from,* שֹׁמֵר מַה־מִלַּיְלָה שֹׁמֵר מַה־מִלֵּיל *look-out, what is from,* i.e. what happened during, or, what is left of, *(the) night?; look-out, what is from (the) night?* Is 21$_{11}$; עִם *with,* מָה עִמָּדִי see *what is with me,* i.e. see what I have Gn 31$_{32}$; אֵת *with,* מָה אִתָּנוּ *what is with us?,* i.e. what do we have? 1 S 9$_{7}$; מַה־יֵּשׁ תַּחַת *what is there below?* 1 S 21$_{4}$ (ms הֲיֵשׁ *is there?* or em. אִם־יֵשׁ *if there is;* + יָדְךָ below *your hand*), מַה־בְּפִיו hear *what is in his mouth?* 2 S 17$_{5}$.

j. + adverb, זֶה הַיּוֹם וּמֶה גַם־עָתָּה appar. he will cut off the house of Jeroboam *this very day, and what also is now?*, perh. but what does, Now, mean? 1 K 14$_{14}$ (or em. בַּיּוֹם הַהוּא וְגַם מֵעַתָּה יַכֶּה will cut off *on that day but even from now he will strike [the house of Jeroboam]).**

k. appar. as open question or exclamation, מַה־בְּרִי וּמַה־בַּר־בִּטְנִי וּמֶה בַּר־נְדָרָי *what, O my son, indeed what, O son of my womb, and what, O son of my vows?* Pr 31$_{2}$ (or em. מַה־בְּרִי to מַה־לְמוּאֵל בְּכֹרִי אֹמַר אֵלֶיךָ *what, O Lemuel my firstborn, shall I say to you?*).

<COLL> (all of §1) **(1)** irregularities in word order, צַדִּיק מַה־פָּעָל *a righteous one, what did he do?* Ps 11$_{3}$ (or em. יִפְעָל what *could he do?*), וּמִדַּת יָמַי מַה־הִיא *and the measure of my days, what is it?* Ps 39$_{5}$, זרע נכבד מה זרע לאנוש *what are honourable offspring?: the offspring of a person* Si 10$_{19(A)}$ (B נקלה *despicable*), כבד ממך מה תשא ואל עשיר ממך מה תתחבר *what is too heavy for you, how can you lift, and to one that is richer than you, how can you ally yourself?* Si 13$_{2}$ (מה in mg), ותקות מה כי *and what is the hope that?* Si 16$_{22}$, חיי מה לחסר תירוש *what life is there to one who lacks new wine?* Si 34$_{27}$, עֲמֻקָּה מִשְּׁאוֹל מַה־תֵּדָע *it is deeper than Sheol—what do you know?* Jb 11$_{8}$, גָּבְהֵי שָׁמַיִם מַה־תִּפְעָל *it is higher than heaven—what can you do?* Jb 11$_{8}$ (if em. גָּבְהֵי שָׁמַיִם *the heights of heaven*).

(2) כִּי ... מָה *what (is) ... that?* Gn 20$_{9.10}$ 37$_{26}$ 38$_{16}$ Ex 16$_{7}$ Nm 16$_{11}$ Dt 10$_{12}$ (כִּי אִם *except*) Jg 18$_{23}$ 2 K 8$_{13}$ 1 S 11$_{5}$ 20$_{1}$ 25$_{17}$ 2 S 9$_{8}$ 16$_{10(Kt)}$ 19$_{23}$ 2 K 20$_{8}$||Is 38$_{22}$ Is 22$_{1.16}$ Jr 4$_{30}$ 13$_{21}$ (כִּי = *when*) Ezk 24$_{19}$ Hb 2$_{18}$ Ml 3$_{14}$ Ps 8$_{5}$ 114$_{5}$ Jb 3$_{12}$ 6$_{11.11}$ 7$_{17.21}$ 15$_{14}$ 16$_{3}$ 21$_{15.15}$ 27$_{8}$ 31$_{14.14}$ (מָה ... כִּי; כִּי = *when* in both) Pr 30$_{4}$ Ec 5$_{10}$ (כִּי אִם *except*) 7$_{10}$ Lm 2$_{13}$ (כִּי = *for* in both) Si 16$_{22}$ 4QMyst[a] 3a 2$_{16}$; י׳ מָה־אָדָם וַתֵּדָעֵהוּ *Y., of what significance is a human being that you know him?* Ps 144$_{3}$, מָה־אֶשְׁוֶה־לָּךְ וַאֲנַחֲמֵךְ *what can I compare with you that I might console you?* Lm 2$_{13}$ (or em. מִי יוֹשִׁיעַ לָךְ וְנִחֲמֵךְ *who will save you and console you?*), מַה־דּוֹדֵךְ מִדּוֹד שֶׁכָּכָה הִשְׁבַּעְתָּנוּ *in what way is your beloved better than (another) beloved, that thus you* (masc.) *have adjured us?* Ca 5$_{9}$ (or em. הִשְׁבַּעְתִּנוּ you [fem.] have adjured us), וּמַה־יִּתְרוֹן לוֹ שֶׁיַּעֲמֹל לָרוּחַ *and what is his profit that he toils for the wind?* Ec 5$_{15}$, מַה־לָּכֶם תְּדַכְּאוּ עַמִּי *what is it to you,* perh. what gain do you have, *that you crush my people?* Is 3$_{15(Qr)}$.

(3) מָה as first part of subordinate clause (but distinction from §8 oft. uncertain) introduced by לְ + infinitive of ראה *see* Gn 2$_{19}$ Hb 2$_{1}$ Si 38$_{36}$, ידע *know* Ex 2$_{4}$ Est 2$_{11}$ 4$_{5}$ 1 C 12$_{33}$, hi. *inform* 1 S 28$_{15}$.

+ imperative of בין hi. *teach* Jb 6$_{24}$ (וּמַה־שָּׁגִיתִי הָבִינוּ *and how have I erred, teach me?*), נגד hi. *tell* Gn 29$_{15}$ Jos 7$_{19}$ 1 S 10$_{15}$ 14$_{43}$ 2 S 1$_{4}$ (מֶה־הָיָה הַדָּבָר הַגֶּד־נָא לִי *what was the word, tell me, please?*) 2 K 4$_{2}$ Is 41$_{22}$ (הָרִאשֹׁנוֹת מָה הֵנָּה הַגִּידוּ *the first things, what are they, tell [us]?*) Jr 38$_{25}$ Jon 1$_{8}$ 4QRP[b] 5b 2$_{12}$ (הגידה נא]לי מה[שמכה *tell me, please, what is your name?*; =Gn 32$_{30}$ הַגִּידָה־נָּא שְׁמֶךָ *tell me, please, your name*), דבר pi. *speak* Jb 34$_{33}$ (וּמַה־יָּדַעְתָּ דַבֵּר *and what you know, speak*), שׁאל *ask* 1 K 3$_{5}$||2 C 1$_{7}$ 2 K 2$_{9}$, ידע *know* Ex 33$_{5}$ 1 S 25$_{17}$ Jg 18$_{14}$ Jr 2$_{23}$ Si 37$_{8}$, hi. *inform* Ps 39$_{5}$ Jb 37$_{19}$, זכר *remember* Mc 6$_{5}$ Lm 5$_{1}$, ראה *see* 1 S 25$_{17}$ 2 S 24$_{13}$||1 C 21$_{12}$ Jr 33$_{24}$ Zc 5$_{5}$ (or em. מָה הַיּוֹצֵאת הַזֹּאת see *what is this thing coming out?* to הָאֵיפָה הַיּוֹצֵאת הַזֹּאת see *this ephah that is coming out*) 2 C 19$_{6}$ Si 37$_{27(D)}$, שׁמע *hear* Ezk 33$_{30}$, נכר hi. *look* Gn 31$_{32}$.

+ imperfect (including waw cons. + imperfect) of נגד hi. *tell* 1 K 14$_{3}$ Ezk 24$_{19}$ Ec 6$_{12}$, ידע *know* Ex 10$_{26}$ 32$_{1=23}$ 1 S 22$_{3}$ Is 19$_{12}$ Jb 34$_{4}$ Ec 11$_{2}$ 2 C 20$_{12}$ 32$_{13}$ Si 8$_{18}$ 9$_{11}$ 11$_{19}$ 4Q416 2.3$_{15}$ Pr 27$_{1}$, בין hi. *understand* Jb 23$_{5}$, ראה *see* Gn 37$_{20}$ Dt 32$_{20}$ Jon 4$_{5}$, hi. *show* Zc 1$_{9}$, ירה hi. *instruct* Jg 13$_{8}$, שׁמע *hear* Nm 9$_{8}$ 2 S 17$_{5}$ Jr 5$_{15}$ Ps 85$_{9}$, ירא *fear*

Ps 118$_{6}$.

+ perfect (including waw cons. + perfect) of נגד hi. *tell* Mc 6$_{8}$ Est 8$_{1}$ Ne 2$_{12}$, ידע *know* Gn 39$_{8}$ (Sam מְאוּמָה *anything*) Ex 16$_{15}$ 2 S 18$_{29}$ (unless §3, *what was taking place*, or §7a, *anything*) Ezk 17$_{12}$ Zc 4$_{5.13}$ Ne 2$_{16}$, ראה *see* Nm 13$_{18}$, שׁמע *hear* Jg 7$_{11}$, פרשׁ pu. *be explained* Nm 15$_{34}$, perh. pi. *explain* 4Q417 2.1$_{9}$ (פרש ... []מה יצרה perh. *he explained ...what its inclination is*).

+ participle of ראה *see* Jr 7$_{17}$ Ezk 8$_{6(Qr)}$, נגד *tell* Am 4$_{13}$, ידע *know* Ec 6$_{12}$ 11$_{5}$.

(4) מָה as first element in direct speech (or following introductory vocative) preceded by אמר *say* Gn 3$_{13}$ 4$_{10}$ 12$_{18}$ 15$_{2}$ 20$_{9.10}$ 21$_{17.29}$ 27$_{20}$ 30$_{31}$ 31$_{26.36}$ 32$_{28}$ 37$_{10.15.26}$ 38$_{16.18.29}$ 44$_{15.16}$ 46$_{33}$ 47$_{3}$ Ex 3$_{13}$ 4$_{2}$ 12$_{26}$ 13$_{14}$ 14$_{15}$ 15$_{24}$ 17$_{2}$ 18$_{14}$ 32$_{21}$ Lv 25$_{20}$ Nm 22$_{28}$ 23$_{11.17}$ Dt 6$_{20}$ 29$_{23}$ Jos 4$_{6.21}$ 5$_{14}$ 7$_{25}$ 15$_{18}$=Jg 1$_{14}$ Jos 22$_{16.24}$ Jg 8$_{1.2}$ 11$_{12}$ 14$_{18}$ 18$_{3.8.18.23.24}$ 20$_{12}$ 21$_{16}$ 1 S 3$_{17}$ 4$_{6.14.16}$ 5$_{8}$ 6$_{2.4}$ 9$_{7}$ 10$_{2.11.27}$ 11$_{5}$ 13$_{11}$ 15$_{14}$ 17$_{26.29}$ 20$_{1.32}$ 28$_{14}$ 29$_{4.8}$ (וַיֹּאמֶר ... כִּי מֶה עָשִׂיתִי perh. *and he said ..., What I have done?*, i.e. כִּי introduces speech) 2 S 1$_{4}$ 3$_{24}$ 6$_{20}$ 9$_{8}$ 12$_{21}$ 14$_{5}$ 16$_{2.10}$ 19$_{23}$ 21$_{3.4}$ 1 K 1$_{16}$ 9$_{13}$ 11$_{22}$ (with כִּי) 12$_{9.16}$||2 C 10$_{9.16}$ 1 K 17$_{18}$ 18$_{9}$ 19$_{9.13}$ 2 K 1$_{5.7}$ 3$_{13}$ 4$_{2.14.43}$ 6$_{28}$ 7$_{3}$ 8$_{13}$ (with כִּי) 8$_{14}$ 9$_{18.19.22}$ 18$_{19}$||Is 36$_{4}$ 2 K 20$_{8}$|| Is 38$_{22}$ 2 K 20$_{14.15}$||Is 39$_{3.4}$ 2 K 23$_{17}$ Is 40$_{16}$ 45$_{9.10}$ Jr 1$_{11.13}$ 2$_{5}$ 8$_{6}$ 16$_{10}$ 23$_{33.35.37}$ 24$_{3}$ 37$_{18}$ 48$_{19}$ Ezk 12$_{9}$ 19$_{2}$ 20$_{29}$ Am 7$_{8}$ 8$_{2}$ Jon 1$_{6.10}$ Zc 2$_{2.4}$ 4$_{2.4.11.12}$ 5$_{2.6}$ 6$_{4}$ 13$_{6}$ Ml 3$_{13}$ Ps 50$_{16}$ 66$_{3}$ Jb 9$_{12}$ 19$_{28}$ 22$_{13.17}$ 35$_{3}$ Ec 2$_{2}$ 7$_{10}$ 8$_{4}$ Est 5$_{3.6}$ 6$_{3.6}$ 7$_{2}$ Ne 2$_{19}$ 3$_{34}$ 13$_{17}$ 35$_{21}$ Si 15$_{11}$ 33$_{10}$ 4QRP[b] 5b 2$_{12}$ ([ויואמר]), דבר pi. *say* Jg 9$_{2}$ 1 K 21$_{5}$, קרא *call* Is 21$_{11}$, ענה *answer* Mc 6$_{3}$ (עַמִּי מֶה־עָשִׂיתִי לְךָ וּמָה הֶלְאֵתִיךָ עֲנֵה בִי *my people, what have I done to you and in what way have I wearied you? Answer me*).

(5) מָה ... מָה ... מָה *what ? ... what? ... what?* Gn 44$_{16}$ Jg 18$_{24}$ 1 S 1$_{8}$ (לָמֶה ... לָמֶה ... לָמֶה *why? ... why? ... why?*) 20$_{1}$ 26$_{18}$ (לָמָּה ... מָה ... מָה *why? ... what? ...what?*) Jr 16$_{10}$ (עַל־מֶה ... מֶה ... מֶה *why? ... what? ...what?*) Pr 31$_{2}$ Lm 2$_{13}$ (+ מִי *who?*) Est 9$_{12}$ 4Q418 69.2$_{4}$ (מה ... [מה] ... ומה ... ומה) 4Q418 43$_{2}$ ([למה ... ומה ... במ[ה) 43$_{3}$ (... [למ[ה ... ולמה ... במה) 4QBéat 35$_{2}$.

2. as exclamation, **how (much, great, greatly, etc.)!**, ומה רבו פצעי רוכל *and how many are the blows of a slanderer* Si 11$_{29}$, מה ירבו פשעי בוצע *how great are the sins of an extortioner*, or, *slanderer* Si 11$_{29}$, מָה רַב־טוּבְךָ *how great is your bounty* Ps 31$_{20}$, מָה־רַבּוּ צָרָי *how many are my enemies* Ps 3$_{2}$, מָה־רַבּוּ מַעֲשֶׂיךָ *how many are your deeds* Ps 104$_{24}$, מַה־גָּדְלוּ מַעֲשֶׂיךָ *how great are your deeds* Ps 92$_{6}$, [מה נגד]ל [את זרבבל] *how greatly we should extol Zerubbabel* Si 49$_{11(Segal)}$.

מַה־נּוֹרָא הַמָּקוֹם הַזֶּה *how fearful is this place* Gn 28$_{17}$, מה נורא אתה אליהו *how fearful are you, O Elijah* Si 48$_{4}$, מַה־נּוֹרָא מַעֲשֶׂיךָ *how fearful are your deeds* Ps 66$_{3}$, מה נורא מעשי י׳ *how fearful are the deeds of Y.* Si 43$_{2(B)}$ (M כלי נורא מעשי [ע]ליון *an awe-inspiring mechanism, an act of the Most High*), מה נורא בהשתנותו *how fearful when it changes* Si 43$_{8(B)}$ (mg בתשובתו *when it turns*).

מַה־נִּכְבַּד הַיּוֹם מֶלֶךְ יִשְׂרָאֵל *how honoured is Israel's king today* 2 S 6$_{20}$, מה נכבד לבב והוא ממש[ל] *how honoured is a mind when it rules* 4QMyst[c] 2a$_{2}$, [ו]הם על משכבו ומה יתנדב ואתם perh. *when they are upon his bed, how ennobled he feels, but you* 4QapPent 10.1$_{6}$, מָה־אַדִּיר שִׁמְךָ *how majestic is your name* Ps 8$_{2.10}$, מה אדיר לכם *how majestic for you* 4QMyst[c] 2b$_{2}$, מה נהדר בנטותו יד *how majestic when he extends his hand* Si 46$_{2}$, מה נהדר בהשגיחו מאהל *how majestic when he looked out from the tent* Si 50$_{5}$, מַה־יָּקָר חַסְדְּךָ *how precious is your loyalty* Ps 36$_{8}$, מַה־יָּקְרוּ רֵעֶיךָ אֵל מֶה עָצְמוּ רָאשֵׁיהֶם perh. *how precious are your companions, O God, how strong their heads* Ps 139$_{17}$ (mss וּמֶה *and how* strong).

מה טוב *how good* Si 41$_{2(M)}$, מַה־טֹּבוּ אֹהָלֶיךָ יַעֲקֹב *how good are your tents, O Jacob* Nm 24$_{5}$, הִנֵּה מַה־טּוֹב וּמַה־נָּעִים שֶׁבֶת אַחִים גַּם־יָחַד *behold, how good and how pleasant for brothers also to dwell together* Ps 133$_{1}$, דָּבָר בְּעִתּוֹ מַה־טּוֹב *a word in its proper time, how good* Pr 15$_{23}$, קְנֹה־חָכְמָה מַה־טּוֹב מֵחָרוּץ *to acquire wisdom, how much better than gold* Pr 16$_{16}$ (mss קְנֵה *acquire*; or em. קֹנֶה *one who acquires* and/or del. מָה), מַה־טֹּבוּ דֹדַיִךְ מִיַּיִן וְרֵיחַ שְׁמָנַיִךְ מִכָּל־בְּשָׂמִים *how much better than wine is your lovemaking and the fragrance of your oils than all spices* Ca 4$_{10}$ (or em. דַּדַּיִךְ *your breasts* and/or וְשַׂלְמֹתַיִךְ *your garments*), מַה־יָּפוּ דֹדַיִךְ *how fair is your lovemaking* Ca 4$_{10}$ (or em. דַּדַּיִךְ), מַה־יָּפוּ פְעָמַיִךְ *how fair are your steps* Ca 7$_{2}$, מַה־יָּפִית וּמַה־נָּעַמְתְּ *how fair you are and how pleasant you are* Ca 7$_{7}$, מַה־נָּאווּ ... רַגְלֵי מְבַשֵּׂר *how fair ... are the feet of a mes-*

senger Is 52_{7}, מַה־נִּמְלְצוּ לְחִכִּי אִמְרָתֶךָ מַה־דָּבְשׁוּ לְפִי *how tasty to my palate are your words, how sweet to my mouth** Ps 119_{103} (if em. מִדְּבַשׁ *than honey* to מַה־דָּבְשׁוּ *how sweet*).

מַה־טּוּבוֹ וּמַה־יָּפְיוֹ *how great is his prosperity and how great is his beauty* Zc 9_{17}, מָה־אָהַבְתִּי תוֹרָתֶךָ *how I have loved your law* Ps 119_{97}, מַה־יְּדִידוֹת מִשְׁכְּנוֹתֶיךָ *how beloved are your dwelling places* Ps 84_{2}, מה חכמת בנעריך *how wise you were in your youth* Si 47_{14}, מַה־תֵּיטִבִי דַּרְכֵּךְ *how well you have made your way* Jr 2_{33}, מַה־נֵּחַנְתְּ *how graced you were* Jr 22_{23} (or em. נֶאֱנַחְתְּ/נֵנַחְתְּ how *you groaned*), מַה־נֶּאֶנְחָה בְהֵמָה נָבֹכוּ עֶדְרֵי בָקָר *how much beasts groan, how confused are the herds of cattle* Jl 1_{18}.

כיא מה הוא יחיד בכול מעשה perh. *for how unique he is in every deed*, or, *among every creation* 4Q417 1.1_{6}, מָה אִמְּךָ לְבִיָּא *how great a lioness was your mother* Ezk 19_{2}, [מה עמוק לא[יש perh. *how deep for a man* 4QMyst[b] 6_{6}, מה יוחן חובר נשוך *how pitiable is a snake-charmer when bitten* Si 12_{13}(erased) (mg מי *who* is to be pitied?: a snake-charmer), חיים למות מה [מ]ר יברך perh. *(from) death to life, how bitterly does it give blessing* Si 41_{1}(B) (mg הוי *alas*, O death; M [ז]כרך how bitter is *your mention*).

מה מתבהלת היאה בתי *how anxious*, or, *hurried*, *is my daughter* 4QTNaph 1_{5}, מַה־תֵּזְלִי מְאֹד לְשַׁנּוֹת אֶת־דַּרְכֵּךְ *how very far you go to change your direction* Jr 2_{36} (or em. תָּזֹלִּי how very *lightly you regard* changing your direction), מַה־פָּרַצְתָּ עָלֶיךָ פָּרֶץ *how great a breach you have made around yourself* Gn 38_{29}, מֶה עֲכַרְתָּנוּ *how greatly you have troubled us* Jos 7_{25}, מַה־יִּהְיֶה עֵץ־הַגֶּפֶן מִכָּל־עֵץ *how (better) is the wood of the vine than any (other) wood* Ezk 15_{2}, מָה אֲמֻלָה לִבָּתֵךְ *how enfeebled is your spirit* Ezk 16_{30} (or em. אֶמָּלֵא/אִמָּלֵא how *I am filled* with anger against you, or מַה־לִּי וְלִבְרִיתֵךְ *what do I have to do with your covenant?*, or מַה־לִּי בְּרִית לְבִתֵּךְ *what is your daughter's covenant to me?*).

מַה־יָּגֶל מְאֹד *how very much he should rejoice* Ps 21_{2} (Kt יָגִיל *he rejoices*; or del. מָה), מַה־נִּמְלְצוּ לְחִכִּי אִמְרָתֶךָ מִדְּבַשׁ לְפִי *how much smoother to my palate is your word than honey is to my mouth* Ps 119_{103} (mss אִמְרָתֶיךָ are *your words*), מַה־נִּמְרְצוּ אִמְרֵי־יֹשֶׁר *how distressing are words of uprightness* Jb 6_{25} (ms מַה־נִּמְלְצוּ *how smooth*), מַה־נִּרְדָּף־לוֹ *how we shall pursue him* Jb 19_{28}, דּוֹר מָה־רָמוּ עֵינָיו וְעַפְעַפָּיו יִנָּשֵׂאוּ perh. *a generation whose eyes are so haughty that their eyelids have moved up* Pr 30_{13}.

3. as combined existential and interrogative particle, **what is there?, what is taking place?, what happens?**, ומה אשר יפצה מידו *and what is there that can deliver*, or, *be delivered, from his hand?* 4QTobit[e] 6_{7}, וְלֹא יָדַעְתִּי מָה *but I did not know what (was taking place)* 2 S 18_{29} (unless §7a, *anything*), וּבַל־יָדְעָה מָּה *and she does not know what (is going on)* Pr 9_{13} (unless §7a, *anything*; or em. כְּלִמָּה *shame*); וּמָה אִם־גַּם־שֵׁבֶט מֹאֶסֶת appar. *and what (happens) if it even despises a staff?* Ezk 21_{18}.

4. appar. as combined interrogative and conditional particle, **what if?**, מִי יַגִּיד לִי אוֹ מַה־יַּעַנְךָ אָבִיךָ קָשָׁה *who will tell me?, or what if your father gives you a harsh response?* 1 S 20_{10} (or em. אוֹ מַה־ to אִם [misunderstood as abbreviation] tell me *if* your father).

5. what ails?, what need is there?, מַה־בְּרִי וּמַה־בַּר־בִּטְנִי וּמֶה בַּר־נְדָרָי *what ails my son? what ails the son of my womb? what ails the son of my vows?* Pr 31_{2}, מַה־שַּׁדַּי כִּי־נַעַבְדֶנּוּ *what need has the Almighty that we should serve him?* Jb 21_{15}.

6. how much?, מַה־מִּלַּיְלָה *how much of the night?* Is 21_{11}, מַה־מִּנִּי יַהֲלֹךְ *how much of it will go away?* Jb 16_{6}.

7a. as indefinite pronoun, **anything, something,** וּבַל־יָדְעָה מָּה *and she does not know anything* Pr 9_{13} (unless §3, *what is going on*; or em. כְּלִמָּה *shame*), וְלֹא יָדַעְתִּי מָה *but I did not know anything* 2 S 18_{29} (unless §3, *what was taking place*),

b. בְּלִי־מָה appar. **not anything**, i.e. **nothing(ness), void,** נֹטֶה צָפוֹן עַל־תֹּהוּ תֹּלֶה אֶרֶץ עַל־בְּלִי־מָה *extending Zaphon over emptiness, suspending earth over a void* Jb 26_{7} (mss בְּלִימָה).*

8. appar. as combined relative particle and antecedent (but distinction from §1, final Coll., §3, oft. uncertain), **what(ever).**

a. + imperfect of אמר *say* 1 S 20_{4} (מַה־תֹּאמַר נַפְשְׁךָ וְאֶעֱשֶׂה־לָּךְ *whatever your soul says I shall do for you*), בוא *come* CD 2_{10} (וידע ... לכל הוי עולמים ונהיית עד מה

יבוא בקציהם *and he knew … in accordance with all that exist through eternity, or that will exist, including whatever might come [about], in their [appointed] times*; =4QD^{a} 2.2$_{10}$ only preserves עד מה) 4QD^{c} 1$_{8}$ (ויבינו בכול נהיות עד מה יבוא במה *and that they might understand all that are to be, up to whatever might come [about] at whatever [time],* or *come upon them*), היה *be* 2 S 18$_{22}$ (וִיהִי מָה אָרֻצָה־נָּא *and whatever occurs, let me run, please*) 18$_{23}$ (וִיהִי־מָה אָרוּץ *and whatever occurs, I shall run*) 4Q418 123.2$_{3}$ (כול הנהיה בו ומה היה ומה יהיה perh. *every event in it, both what has been and what will be*).

זמם *consider* MasShirShabb 1$_{6}$ (לא ישכילו כול [עושי] צד]ק מה יזום *none of the doers of righteousness can understand what he plans*), עבר *pass* Jb 13$_{13}$ (וְיַעֲבֹר עָלַי מָה *whatever passes over me,* i.e. come what may), ראה *see* Nm 23$_{3}$ (וּדְבַר מַה־יַּרְאֵנִי וְהִגַּדְתִּי לָךְ *and whatever word he shows me I shall tell you*), שׁוה *resemble* 4Q416 2.2$_{14}$ (א]ל]תבטח למה תשוה perh. *do not trust in whatever you [yourself] resemble*; or em. תשנא/תשגה lest you *err/be hated* [לָמָּה תִשְׁגֶּה/תִשָּׂנֵא]) 4Q418 172$_{12}$.

b. + perfect of היה *be* 4Q418 123.2$_{3}$, ni. *occur* 4Q418 43$_{2.2}$ (קדם למה נהיה ומה נהיה במ[ה]) perh. *prior to,* or, *he preceded, whatever has occurred, and whatever has occurred is with whatever*) 43$_{3}$ (ולמ[ה] נהיה במה *and [to] whatever has occurred with whatever*), perh. חיה *live* 4Q418 79$_{3}$ (ולמה חי[]) perh. *and to whatever has lived*), נגע hi. *reach* Est 9$_{26}$ (עַל־כָּל־דִּבְרֵי הָאִגֶּרֶת הַזֹּאת … וּמָה הִגִּיעַ אֲלֵיהֶם *on account of all the words of this letter … and [of] what had befallen them*), פעל *do* Nm 23$_{23}$ (כָּעֵת יֵאָמֵר … מַה־פָּעַל אֵל *immediately it is said … what God has done*), ראה *see* Jg 9$_{48}$ (מָה רְאִיתֶם עָשִׂיתִי מַהֲרוּ עֲשׂוּ כָמוֹנִי *what you have seen that I did, hurry, do like me*) 1 S 19$_{3}$ (וְרָאִיתִי מָה וְהִגַּדְתִּי לָךְ *and whatever I see I shall tell you*) Est 9$_{26}$ (עַל־כָּל־דִּבְרֵי הָאִגֶּרֶת הַזֹּאת וּמָה־רָאוּ *on account of all the words of this letter and [of] what they had seen*), רצה *desire* 4QShir^{b} 63.2$_{2}$ (ובכול מה רצ[]) *and in everything that [you] have desired*), perh. שׁנה pi. *change* 4Q418 172$_{11}$.

c. + participle of אמר *say* 2 S 21$_{4}$ (מָה־אַתֶּם אֹמְרִים אֶעֱשֶׂה לָכֶם *and whatever you say, I shall do for you*), היה *be* 4Q418 43$_{3}$ (למה הויא *[to] whatever is*); also 4Q418 43$_{2}$ (במ[ה]) 43$_{3}$ (במה) 106$_{2}$ (ולמה) 122.1$_{6}$ (או למה עוד[] perh. *or to whatever else*).

d. + adjective, רַע *evil* Si 37$_{27(B)}$ (וראה מה רע לה אל תתן לה *and see [that] whatever is bad for it do not give to it*).

9. -מַה־שֶּׁ 8.1 **what(ever),*** + perfect of היה *be* Ec 1$_{9}$ 3$_{15}$ (+ וַאֲשֶׁר לִהְיוֹת *and whatever is to be*) 6$_{10}$ 7$_{24}$ (רָחוֹק מַה־שֶּׁהָיָה *whatever has been is far away*), ירשׁ ho. *be endowed* Si 3$_{22(B)}$ (במה שהורשית התבונן *reflect upon whatever has been endowed to you*; C בַּאֲשֶׁר in same sense), עשׂה ni. *be done* Ec 1$_{9}$; + imperfect of היה *be* Ec 3$_{22}$ (לִרְאוֹת בְּמֶה שֶׁיִּהְיֶה אַחֲרָיו *to look upon what will be after him*) 8$_{7}$ (כִּי־אֵינֶנּוּ יֹדֵעַ מַה־שֶּׁיִּהְיֶה *for he cannot know what will be*) 10$_{14}$ (+ וַאֲשֶׁר יִהְיֶה *and whatever will be*).

Also perh. 4Q417 26$_{2}$ ([]משמיע מה ש[] perh. *proclaiming whatever*).

10. מָה אֲשֶׁר **what(ever),** + imperfect of בוא *come* 1QMyst 1.1$_{4}$ (ולוא ידעו מה אשר יבוא עליהמה *and they did not know what was coming against them*).

11. בַּמָּה (29.0.1) **by what (means)?, how?;** also **with what** (Ex 22$_{26}$ 1 S 29$_{4}$ Mc 6$_{6}$ and perh. elsewhere, but distinction from preceding sense oft. uncertain), **in what (part)?, where?** (Jg 16$_{5.6.15}$), **against what?** (Pr 4$_{19}$), **why?** (2 C 7$_{21}$).

a. + perfect of היה *be* 1 S 14$_{38}$ (בַּמָּה הָיְתָה הַחַטָּאת הַזֹּאת הַיּוֹם see *how this sin occurred today*; or em. בְּמִי *by whom?*), אהב *love* Ml 1$_{2}$, בזה *despise* Ml 1$_{6}$, גאל pi. *defile* Ml 1$_{7}$, יגע hi. *weary* Ml 2$_{17}$, קבע *cheat* Ml 3$_{8}$, עשׂה *do* 2 C 7$_{21}$.

b. + imperfect of יכל *be able* Jg 16$_{5}$, אסר ni. *be bound* Jg 16$_{6.10.13}$, כשׁל ni. *stumble* Pr 4$_{19}$, שׁכב *lie down* Ex 22$_{26}$, שׁלח pi. *send away* 1 S 6$_{2}$, קדם pi. *approach* Mc 6$_{6}$, שׁוב *go back* Ml 3$_{7}$, ידע *know* Gn 15$_{8}$, ni. *be known* Ex 33$_{16}$, רצה htp. *ingratiate oneself* 1 S 29$_{4}$, כפר pi. *atone* 2 S 21$_{3}$, זכה pi. *purify* Ps 119$_{9}$, ישׁע hi. *save* Jg 6$_{15}$.

c. + participle (+ noun) of חשׁב ni. *be accounted* Is 2$_{22}$ 1QS 5$_{17}$.

d. + noun, כֹּחַ *strength* Jg 16$_{5.6.15}$.

e. without following verb, etc., but in ref. to earlier statement, 1 K 22$_{21}$||2 C 18$_{20}$ (וַיֹּאמֶר אֲנִי אֲפַתֶּנּוּ וַיֹּאמֶר י׳ אֵלָיו בַּמָּה *and he said, I shall deceive him; and Y. said, How?*).

<COLL> בַּמָּה as first part of subordinate clause introduced by imperative of נגד hi. *tell* Jg $16_{6.10.13}$, ידע *know* 1 S 14_{38} (or em. בְּמִי *by whom?*), hi. *inform* 1 S 6_2, ראה *see* Jg 16_5 1 S 14_{38} (or em.); by perfect of נגד hi. *tell* Jg 16_{15}, ידע *know* Pr 4_{19}; בַּמָּה as first element in direct speech, preceded by אמר *say* Gn 15_8 Jg 6_{15} 1 S 21_3 1 K 22_{21}||2 C 18_{20} Ml $1_{2.6.7}$ 2_{17} $3_{7.8}$ 2 C 7_{21}.

Also 4QCryptA 3.1_2.

12. כַּמָּה 11.0.1 **a. how many?,** + שָׁנָה *year* Gn 47_8 Ps 119_{84} (+ מָתַי *when?*), יוֹם *day* 2 S 19_{35}, עָוֹן *iniquity* Jb 13_{23}, חַטָּאת *sin* Jb 13_{23}.

Also 4Q418 148.1_5.

b. how much?, how great?, + אֹרֶךְ *length* Zc 2_6, רֹחַב *width* Zc 2_4, יוֹתֵר *advantage* 4QQoh^a 6_8 (MT כִּי־מַה *for what?*). <COLL> כַּמָּה as first part of subordinate clause introduced by לְ + infinitive of ראה *see* Zc 2_6.

c. how long?, אֲדֹנָי כַּמָּה תִּרְאֶה *my Lord, how long will you watch?* Ps 35_{17}.

d. how long until?, when?, כַּמָּה לֹא־תִשְׁעֶה *how long will you not watch?* Jb 7_{19}.

e. how often?, כַּמָּה נֵר־רְשָׁעִים יִדְעָךְ וְיָבֹא עָלֵימוֹ אֵידָם *how often does the lamp of evildoers go out or their calamity come upon them?* Jb 21_{17}.

f. as exclamation, **how often!,** כַּמָּה יַמְרוּהוּ בַמִּדְבָּר יַעֲצִיבוּהוּ בִּישִׁימוֹן *how often they would rebel against him in the steppe, cause him pain in the wilderness* Ps 78_{40} (or em. הֵמָּה *they* would rebel).

g. as adjective, **several,** + שָׁנָה *year* Zc 7_3 (זֶה כַּמֶּה שָׁנִים *these several years*).

13. עַד־כַּמֶּה **(unto) how many?,** + פַּעַם *time* 1 K 22_{16}||2 C 18_{15}. <COLL> עַד־כַּמֶּה as first element in direct speech preceded by אמר *say* 1 K 22_{16}||2 C 18_{15}.

14. לָמָּה **a. why?,** see *DCH*, IV, pp. 551a-52b.

b. lest, + imperfect of שׁגג *err* 4QD^a 5.2_3 + 4QD^b 5.3_5 (לא יקרא בספר התורה למה ישוג בדבר מות *he is not to read from the Torah scroll lest he errs in a capital matter*), פתה htp. *prove oneself naïve* 4QD^a 8.1_2 ([ואל] יודיעהו איש ... למה [יתפ]תה בה בדרשה אותו *and let no one inform him ... lest he prove himself naïve in it during his examination* [=CD 15_{11} [בו בדרשו]), בוא hi. *bring* 4QD^f 3_8 (את כול מומיה יספר לו למה יביא עליו את [הארור] משפט *all her blemishes he is to tell him lest he bring upon himself the judgment of the curse*), שׁגה *err* 4Q416 2.2_{14} (if em. א[ל]תבטח למה תשוה perh. *do not trust in whatever you [yourself] resemble* [לָמָּה תִּשְׁוֶה] to תשגה lest *you err*), שׂנא ni. *be hated* 4Q416 2. 2_{14} (if em. תִּשְׁוֶה whatever *you resemble* to תִּשָּׂנֵא lest *you be hated*), נשׂא *bear* iniquity 4Q417 1.1_{23} (אל תכזבן [לי למה תשה עון *do not lie to me lest you bear iniquity*), perh. ערב *become guarantor* or *mix* 4Q418 88_3 (השמר לכה למה תערב perh. *guard yourself lest you become a guarantor*), היה *be* 4Q418 103.2_7 (אל תערוב ... למה יהיה כלאים *do not mix ... lest it become hybrid*).

15. שֶׁמָּה **lest,** + imperfect of פתה htp. *prove oneself naïve* CD 15_{11} (ואל יודיעהו איש ... שמה יתפתה בו בדרשו אתו *and let no one inform him ... lest he prove himself naïve when he examines him*; =4QD^a 8.1_2 לָמָּה *lest*; see above, §14b).

16. יַעַן מֶה **on account of what?, why?,** יַעַן מֶה נְאֻם י׳ צְבָאוֹת יַעַן בֵּיתִי *on account of what?, saying of Y. of hosts; on account of my house* Hg 1_9.

17. עַד־מָה **a.** as interrogative, **until what (time?), how long?,** עַד־מֶה כְבוֹדִי לִכְלִמָּה תֶּאֱהָבוּן רִיק *how long will my glory be as a reproach, will you love vanity?* Ps 4_3 (or em. כְּבוֹדִי to נִכְבָּדַי *my honoured ones* or כִּבְדֵי לֵב to לִכְלִמָּה how long [will you be] *heavy of heart?*, i.e. dull-witted; and/or ins. לָמָּה *why* do you love?), אֵין־עוֹד נָבִיא וְלֹא־אִתָּנוּ יֹדֵעַ עַד־מָה *there is no longer a prophet and there is not with us one who knows how long* Ps 74_9, עַד־מָה י׳ תֶּאֱנַף לָנֶצַח תִּבְעַר כְּמוֹ־אֵשׁ קִנְאָתֶךָ *how long, O Y., will you be utterly angry, will your jealousy burn like fire?* Ps 79_5, עַד־מָה י׳ תִּסָּתֵר לָנֶצַח תִּבְעַר כְּמוֹ־אֵשׁ חֲמָתֶךָ *how long, O Y., will you be utterly hidden, will your anger burn like fire?* Ps 89_{47} (or em. תִּקְצֹף *will you be angry*).

b. perh. as conjunction, **until (the time that),** יִהְיֶה לְבָעֵר קָיִן עַד־מָה אַשּׁוּר תִּשְׁבֶּךָ *Kain will be for destruction until Assyria takes you captive* Nm 24_{22} (Sam עד מֵאַשּׁוּר תּוֹשָׁבֵךְ appar. *until from Assyria is your restoration*; or em. לִבְעֹר קֵן עָרְמָה though there be *to Beor a nest of prudence*, Assyria will take you captive; or עֲרֵמָה וְאַשְׁפֹּת מֹשָׁבֵךְ *your dwelling place will be a heap and a midden*; and/or del. קַיִן).

18. עַל־מָה on account of what?, why?.

a. + perfect of אבד *die* Jr 9_{11}, טבע ho. *be sunk* Jb 38_6, עָשָׂה *do* Dt 29_{23} 1 K 9_8 Jr 22_8, ברא *create* Ps 89_{48} (or em. עַל־מַה־שָּׁוְא בָּרָאתָ *why have you created* all human beings *as futility?* or *on account of what futility have you created* all human beings? to עוֹלָם הֲשָׁוְא בָּרָאתָ the duration of *eternity; have you created* all human beings *as futility?*), נכה hi. *strike* Nm 22_{32}, ho. *be struck* Is 1_5, דבר pi. *speak* Jr 16_{10}, נאץ pi. *despise* Ps 10_{13}. <COLL> after עַל־מָה subj. (or obj.) precedes verb, Jb 38_6.

b. + imperfect of ריב *contend* Jb 10_2, נשׂא *raise* Jb 13_{14} (or del. עַל־מָה).

c. + pronoun + participle of ישׁב *sit* Jr 8_{14} 2 C 32_{10}, אנח ni. *groan* Ezk 21_{12}, בקשׁ pi. *seek* Ne 2_4 (עַל־מַה־זֶּה אַתָּה מְבַקֵּשׁ lit. *why is this?; you are seeking*), בטח *trust* 2 C 32_{10}.

d. + pronoun (as sole predicate) זֶה *this* Est 4_5 Ne 2_4 (see above).

e. without following verb, etc., but in ref. to earlier statement, Ml 2_{14} (וַאֲמַרְתֶּם עַל־מָה עַל כִּי־י׳ הֵעִיד *and you said, Why?; because Y. has testified*).

<COLL> עַל־מָה as first part of subordinate clause introduced by infinitive of ידע *know* Est 4_5, hi. *inform* Jb 10_2; by imperfect of נגד hi. *tell* Jr 9_{11}; עַל־מָה as first element in direct speech, preceded by אמר *say* Jos 7_{19} 1 K 9_8 Jr 22_8 Nm 22_{32} Jr 16_{10} Ezk 21_{12} Ml 2_{14}.

19. תַּחַת מָה on account of what?, why?, + perfect of עָשָׂה *do* Jr 5_{19}. <COLL> תַּחַת־מָה as first element in direct speech, preceded by אמר *say* Jr 5_{19}.

Also 1QH fr. 4_{11} 13_5 1QMyst 1.2_7 10_2 4QapPs^a 5_3 4QapPs^b 19.2_5 33_8 4QMyst^a 2_3 3a 2_{15} 6.2_{14} 27_3 4QMyst^b 12_1 4QparaKings 46_1; perh. 4QD^a 16a$_1$ (כמה[]) 4QD^c 1_3 (אשר יבוא במה כי perh. *which comes with whatever, for,* unless *which comes upon them, for*) 1_8 (יבוא במה perh. *might come at whatever [time],* unless *might come upon them*) 4QD^d 7_1 (מה היא[] perh. *whatever it is*) 4QBer^a 20_2(WA) (Nitzan כמצות[מה יוכיחנו] *according to their commandments one will reprove him*) 4Q Myst^a 3a 1_5 (מה[]) 4QMyst^c $2b_2$ (מה[]) 4Q417 2.1_9 (מה[]) MurEpJonathan$_9$ (מהו *what is it?*).

מָה II $_{15}$ negative part. **not, a.** הִשְׁבַּעְתִּי אֶתְכֶם ... מַה־תָּעִירוּ וּמַה־תְּעֹרְרוּ אֶת־הָאַהֲבָה *I adjure you ... that you do not awaken and do not arouse love* Ca 8_4 (unless מָה I *why* should you awaken/arouse love?; or em. אִם *if*), הִשְׁבַּעְתִּי אֶתְכֶם ... אִם־תִּמְצְאוּ אֶת־דּוֹדִי מַה־תַּגִּידוּ לוֹ *I adjure you ..., if you find my beloved, do not tell him* Ca 5_8 (unless מָה I *what* will you tell him?), בְּרִית כָּרַתִּי לְעֵינָי וּמָה אֶתְבּוֹנֵן עַל־בְּתוּלָה *a covenant I made with my eyes indeed not to look closely at a young woman* Jb 31_1 (unless מָה I *how* could I look?; or em. מֵהִתְבּוֹנֵן *not to look closely*), אָמְנָם יָדַעְתִּי כִי־כֵן וּמַה־יִּצְדַּק אֱנוֹשׁ עִם־אֵל *indeed I know that this is so and a person cannot be righteous compared with God* Jb 9_2 (unless מָה I *how* can a person?).

אִם־אֲדַבְּרָה לֹא־יֵחָשֵׂךְ כְּאֵבִי וְאַחְדְּלָה מַה־מִּנִּי יַהֲלֹךְ *if I speak my pain is not withheld and (if) I cease it does not go from me* Jb 16_6 (unless מָה I *what* will, or, *how* will it, go from me?; mss מֵה־מִּנִּי), מַה־נִּשְׁתֶּה *we cannot drink* the waters of Meribah Ex 15_{24} (unless מָה I *what* shall we drink?), מַה־לָּנוּ חֵלֶק בְּדָוִד וְלֹא־נַחֲלָה בְּבֶן־יִשַׁי *we have no portion in David and no inheritance in the son of Jesse* 1 K 12_{16}||2 C 10_{16} (בְּדָוִיד ,בְּבֶן־; unless מָה I *what is* our portion?), מָה אֶקֹּב לֹא קַבֹּה אֵל וּמָה אֶזְעֹם לֹא זָעַם י׳ *I shall not curse whom God has not cursed, and I shall not denounce whom Y. has not denounced* Nm 23_8; Jr 8_9 Ho 10_3 Jb 11_8 22_{17} Ps 11_3.*

b. if em. מִי *who* to מָה, מִי־גוֹי גָּדוֹל *there is no great people* Dt $4_{7.8}$, מִי הָאִישׁ אֲשֶׁר יָחֵל לְהִלָּחֵם *there is no man who will begin to fight* Jg 10_{18}, וּמִי בְּכָל־עֲבָדֶיךָ כְּדָוִד נֶאֱמָן *and there is none faithful among all your servants like David* 1 S 22_{14}, מִי־גֶבֶר כְּאִיּוֹב *there is no man like Job* Jb 34_7, וּמִי כְעַמְּךָ כְּיִשְׂרָאֵל גּוֹי אֶחָד בָּאָרֶץ *there is no other nation on earth like Israel* 2 S 7_{23}|| 1 C 17_{21}, מִי עִוֵּר *there is none blind* Is $42_{19.19}$, מִי חָכָם *there is none wise* Ho 14_{10}, מִי שֹׁמֵעַ *there is none hearing* Ps 59_8, מִי־אֵל בַּשָּׁמַיִם וּבָאָרֶץ *there is no God in the heavens or on the earth* Dt 3_{24}, מִי בְּכָל־אֱלֹהֵי הָאֲרָצוֹת *there is none among all the gods of the lands* 2 K 18_{35}|| Is 36_{20}||2 C 32_{14}, מִי־אֵל מִבַּלְעֲדֵי י׳ *there is no God beside Y.* 2 S 22_{32} Ps 18_{32}, מִי־אֵל כָּמוֹךָ *there is no God like you* Mc 7_{18}, מִי כָמוֹךָ *there is none like you* Ex 15_{11} (מִי־כָמֹכָה) 15_{11} (כָּמֹכָה) Ps 35_{10} 71_{19} 89_9, מִי־כָמוֹנִי *there is none like me* Is 44_7, מִי כָמוֹךָ בְּיִשְׂרָאֵל *there is none like you in*

Israel 1 S 26$_{15}$, מִי־אֵל גָּדוֹל כֵּאלֹהִים *there is no god as great as God* Ps 77$_{14}$.

2. perh. in compound double negatives, **a.** מָאַיִן *none*, וּמֵעַמִּי מָאַיִן אֵין־אִישׁ אִתִּי *and of my people not a man was with me* Is 63$_{3}$ (if em. וּמֵעַמִּים אֵין *of the peoples there was not*; 1QIsa[a] ומעמי).

b. מָאֶפֶס *nothing*, מֵאֶפֶס וָתֹהוּ נֶחְשְׁבוּ־לוֹ *absolute naught and void they are reckoned by him* Is 40$_{17}$ (if em. מֵאֶפֶס).

c. בְּלִי־מָה *absolute void*, תֹּלֶה אֶרֶץ עַל־בְּלִי־מָה *he hangs the earth on absolute void* Jb 26$_{7}$.

מהה 9.3.3 vb. **delay** (intrans.)—**Palp.** perh. 1QM 11$_{18}$ (unless למהמה is from מְהוּמָה *discomfiture*).

Htpalp. 9.3.3 Pf. הִתְמַהְמָהְתִּי ,הִתְמַהְמָהוּ ,הִתְמַהְמָהְנוּ; impf. יִתְמַהְמָהּ, Q תתמהמה, Q יתמהמהו; + waw וַיִּתְמַהְמָהּ; impv. הִתְמַהְמָהוּ; ptc. מִתְמַהְמֵהַּ; inf. הִתְמַהְמֵהַּ (התמהמהם)—**delay** (intrans.), **linger, wait,** <SUBJ> Y. Si 32$_{22}$ (|| אפק htp. *restrain oneself*), Israelites Is 29$_{9}$ (or em. הִתַּמְּהוּ or הִתְמַהְמְהוּ *be astounded* [i.e. תמה htpalp. or htp.]), Lot Gn 19$_{16}$, אִישׁ *man* Jg 19$_{8}$, בֵּן *son* of Israel Ex 12$_{39}$, brothers of Joseph Gn 43$_{10}$, מֶלֶךְ *king* 2 S 15$_{28}$, עֶבֶד *servant* Jg 3$_{26}$, צַר *enemy* Si 12$_{16}$, worshipper Ps 119$_{60}$ (:: חושׁ *hasten*), רוּחַ *spirit* 4QShirShabb[f] 23.1$_{11}$ (+ רוץ *run*), חָזוֹן *vision* Hb 2$_{3}$ (+ אחר pi. *delay* intrans.), יוֹם *day* Ezk 7$_{7}$ (if em. מְהוּמָה וְלֹא־הֵד הָרִים *discomfiture, and not (joyful) shouting (upon) the mountains* to לֹא מִתְמַהְמֵהַּ וְלֹא מְאַחֵר *it shall not linger or delay*), מָוֶת *death* Si 14$_{12}$. <PREP> בְּ of place, *in, at*, + עֲבָרָה *ford* 2 S 15$_{28(Kt)}$ (Qr עֲרָבָה *steppe*); of instrument, *by (means of), with*, + שָׂפָה *lip* Si 12$_{16}$; מִן of direction, *(away) from*, + גְּבוּל *border* 4QShirShabb[f] 23.1$_{11}$. <COLL> מהה htpalp. followed by inf. of שׁמר *keep* commandments Ps 119$_{60}$.

<SYN> אפק *restrain oneself.*

<ANT> חושׁ *hasten.*

Also 4Q415 9$_{2}$ 11QShirShabb 7$_{3}$.

מְהוּמָה 12.1.6 n.f. **discomfiture**—cstr. מְהוּמַת; pl. מְהוּמוֹת (מְהוּמֹת)—**discomfiture, uproar, panic, disturbance,** <SUBJ> היה *be* 1 S 5$_{11}$ Zc 14$_{13}$ 1QM 1$_{5}$.

<NOM CL> מְהוּמָה בוֹ *discomfiture is in it* (treasure) Pr 15$_{16}$, מְהוּמֹת רַבּוֹת עַל כָּל־יוֹשְׁבֵי הָאֲרָצוֹת *great disturbances were upon all the inhabitants of the lands* 2 C 15$_{5}$, מהומה על שלחנו *discomfiture is upon his table* Si 14$_{10}$ (or em. מאומה אין *there is nothing* upon his table).

<OBJ> שׁלח pi. *send* Dt 28$_{20}$ (|| מְאֵרָה *curse*, מִגְעֶרֶת *rebuke*), ראה *see* Am 3$_{9}$ (|| עֲשׁוּקִים *oppression*).

<CSTR> מְהוּמַת־י׳ *discomfiture of Y.* Zc 14$_{13}$, מהומת אל *discomfiture of God* 1QM 4$_{7}$, מְהוּמַת־מָוֶת *discomfiture of death*, i.e. extreme discomfiture 1 S 5$_{11}$; יוֹם מְהוּמָה *day of discomfiture* Is 22$_{5}$ (|| מְבוּכָה *confusion*, מְבוּסָה *trampling*), רַבַּת הַמְּהוּמָה *one great* (fem.) *of discomfiture* Ezk 22$_{5}$, הוות מהומה *destruction of discomfiture* 1QH 3$_{38}$, כול מהומות *all disturbances* 4QPseud[b] 1$_{6}$.

<ADJ> גָּדוֹל *great* Dt 7$_{23}$ 1 S 5$_{9}$ 14$_{20}$, רַב *great* Am 3$_{9}$ Zc 14$_{13}$ 2 C 15$_{5}$ 1QH 3$_{25}$ (מהומות רבה).

<PREP> לְ *as* perh. 1QM 11$_{18}$ (unless למהמה is palp. of מהה *delay*) 4QPseud[b] 5.1$_{2}$; מִן *on account of*, + דאג *be anxious* 4QPseud[b] 1$_{6}$; עַל *upon* 3QJub 1$_{2}$ ([על מהומה]); עִם *with*, + גור *sojourn* 1QH 3$_{25}$.

<COLL> וְהָמָם מְהוּמָה גְדֹלָה *and he will discomfit them with a great discomfiture* Dt 7$_{23}$, וַתְּהִי יַד־י׳ בָּעִיר מְהוּמָה גְּדוֹלָה מְאֹד *and the hand of Y. was against the city (causing) a very great discomfiture* 1 S 5$_{9}$, הָיְתָה חֶרֶב אִישׁ בְּרֵעֵהוּ מְהוּמָה גְּדוֹלָה מְאֹד *the sword of each man was against his fellow, a very great discomfiture* 1 S 14$_{20}$, קָרוֹב הַיּוֹם מְהוּמָה וְלֹא־הֵד הָרִים *the day is near, (it is one of) discomfiture, and not (joyful) shouting (upon) the mountains* Ezk 7$_{7}$ (or em. לֹא מִתְמַהְמֵהַּ וְלֹא מְאַחֵר *it shall not linger or delay*), מהו[מה על מהומה] *discomfiture upon discomfiture* 3QJub 1$_{2}$.

<SYN> מְאֵרָה *curse*, מִגְעֶרֶת *rebuke*, עֲשׁוּקִים *oppression*, מְבוּכָה *confusion*, מְבוּסָה *trampling.*

⇒ הום *discomfit.*

מְהוּמָן 1 pr.n.m. **Mehuman,** eunuch at the court of Ahasuerus, <SUBJ> בוא hi. *bring* Est 1$_{10}$, שׁרת pi. *minister* 1$_{10}$. <APP> סָרִיס *eunuch* Est 1$_{10}$.

*[**מְהוֹתָלָה**] 0.0.1 n.f. perh. **praise**—pl. Q מהותלות—<PREP> בְּ perh. of accompaniment, *with* 4QBark[e] 12$_{2}$.

מְהֵיטַבְאֵל 3 pr.n.m.&f. **Mehetabel, 1.** daughter of

Matred, wife of Hadar the king of Edom, <NOM CL> שֵׁם אִשְׁתּוֹ מְהֵיטַבְאֵל *the name of his wife was Mehetabel* Gn 36$_{39}$||1 C 1$_{50}$. <APP> בַּת *daughter* Gn 36$_{39}$||1 C 1$_{50}$.

2. father of Delaiah and grandfather of the prophet Shemaiah, <CSTR> בֶּן־מְהֵיטַבְאֵל *son of Mehetabel* Ne 6$_{10}$.

⇒ יטב *be good* + אֵל *God*.

מָהִיר I 1 adj. **quick**—cstr. מְהִר—as noun, **quick one,** <SUBJ> ישׁב *sit* Is 16$_{5}$. <CSTR> מְהִר צֶדֶק *one quick of,* i.e. zealous for, *righteousness* Is 16$_{5}$ (unless מָהִיר II *one skilled of,* i.e. in, *justice;* + דרשׁ ptc. *one who seeks* justice).

⇒ מהר I *hasten.*

מָהִיר II 4 adj. **skilled**—cstr. מְהִר—**skilled, expert, 1.** used attributively of אִישׁ *man* Pr 22$_{29}$, סֹפֵר *scribe* Ps 45$_{2}$ Ezr 7$_{6}$. <COLL> מָהִיר בְּתוֹרַת מֹשֶׁה *skilled in the law of Moses* Ezr 7$_{6}$, מָהִיר בִּמְלַאכְתּוֹ *skilled in his work* Pr 22$_{29}$.

2. as noun, <CSTR> מְהִר צֶדֶק *one skilled of,* i.e. in, justice Is 16$_{5}$ (unless מָהִיר I *one quick of,* i.e. zealous for, *righteousness;* + דרשׁ ptc. *one who seeks* justice).

3. as divine title, **Scribe,*** <SUBJ> זכר *remember,* i.e. record, iniquities Ps 79$_{8}$ (if em. מַהֵר *quickly*).

מהל I 1 vb. **dilute** (unless מהל III *weaken*)—**Qal** 1 Ptc. pass. מָהוּל—pass. **be diluted,** <SUBJ> סֹבֶא *liquor* Is 1$_{22}$ (or em. מוֹהַל *juice*). <PREP> בְּ of instrument, *by (means of), with,* + מַיִם *water* Is 1$_{22}$ (or בְּ comparative, *[more] than* [סָבְאֵךְ מָהוּל בַּמָּיִם *your drink weaker than water*];* or em.; see Subj.).

***מהל II** 0.0.1 vb. **circumcise—Qal** 0.0.1 Ptc. מוהלת—<SUBJ> רוּחַ *spirit* 4QBéat 6.2$_{3}$.

⇒ see also מול *circumcise.*

***מהל III** 1 vb. **weaken** (unless מהל I *dilute*)—**Qal** 1 Ptc. pass. מָהוּל—pass. **be weakened,** <SUBJ> סֹבֶא *liquor* Is 1$_{22}$ (or em. מוֹהַל *juice*). <PREP> בְּ of instrument, *by (means of), with,* + מַיִם *water* Is 1$_{22}$ (or בְּ comparative, *[more] than* [סָבְאֵךְ מָהוּל בַּמָּיִם *your drink weaker than water*];* or em.; see Subj.).

[מַהֲלָךְ] 5.1 n.m. **journey**—cstr. מַהֲלַךְ; sf. מַהֲלָכְךָ; pl. מַהְלְכִים—**1. journey** (Ne 2$_{6}$), of specified time as measurement of distance (Jon 3$_{3.4}$), one's life-journey (Si 11$_{12}$). **2. passage** in temple buildings (Ezk 42$_{4}$), of way through desert (Is 35$_{8}$ [if em.; see Nom. Cl.]). **3.** pl. **(right of) access**(Zc 3$_{7}$).

<SUBJ> היה *be* Jon 3$_{3}$. <NOM CL> לִפְנֵי הַלְּשָׁכוֹת מַהֲלַךְ עֶשֶׂר אַמּוֹת רֹחַב *before the chambers was a passage of ten cubits width* Ezk 42$_{4}$, עַד־מָתַי יִהְיֶה מַהֲלָכְךָ *how long will your journey be?* Ne 2$_{6}$, הוּא מַהֲלַךְ דֶּרֶךְ *it is a passage of a way,* i.e. a way for passage Is 35$_{8}$ (if em. לָמוֹ הֹלֵךְ *for them one going* to מַהֲלַךְ).* <OBJ> נתן *give* Zc 3$_{7}$. <CSTR> מַהֲלַךְ יוֹם אֶחָד *a journey of one day* Jon 3$_{4}$, מַהֲלַךְ שְׁלֹשֶׁת יָמִים *of three days* Jon 3$_{3}$, מַהֲלַךְ עֶשֶׂר אַמּוֹת רֹחַב *a passage of ten cubits width* Ezk 42$_{4}$, מַהֲלַךְ דֶּרֶךְ *a passage of a way,* i.e. a way for passage Is 35$_{8}$ (if em.; see Nom. Cl.); רשׁ ואבד מהלך *(one) poor and perishing (in respect) of his (life-)journey* Si 11$_{12}$. <APP> עִיר *city* Jon 3$_{3}$. <COLL> וַיָּחֶל יוֹנָה לָבוֹא בָעִיר מַהֲלַךְ יוֹם אֶחָד *and Jonah began to go into the city, (going) a journey of one day* Jon 3$_{4}$, מַהְלְכִים בֵּין הָעֹמְדִים הָאֵלֶּה *access among these standing (here)* Zc 3$_{7}$ (or em. מַהֲלָכִים with same meaning).

⇒ הלך *go.*

***[מַהֲלֹכֶת]** 0.1 n.f. **gait,** unless הלך pi. ptc. *walking,* <COLL> עבד רע צלע מהלמת *a bad servant who limps in his gait* Si 42$_{5(M)}$ (or read מהלכת *because of beatings*).

⇒ הלך *go.*

[מַהֲלָל] 1 n.[m.] **praise**—sf. מַהֲלָלוֹ—**praise, reputation,** <PREP> לְפִי *according to* Pr 27$_{21}$ (אִישׁ לְפִי מַהֲלָלוֹ *a man is according to his praise,* i.e. as others praise him; or em. מְהַלְלָיו *those who praise him* or מְהֻלָּלוֹ *that which is praised by him* or מַעֲלָלָיו *his deeds*).

⇒ הלל I *praise.*

מְהֻלָּל *praiseworthy,* see הלל pu. *praise.*

מַהֲלַלְאֵל 7.0.1 pr.n.m. **Mahalalel, 1.** son of Kenan,

<SUBJ> חיה *live* Gn $5_{15.16}$, ילד hi. *beget* Gn $5_{15.16}$, מות *die* Gn 5_{17}. <NOM CL> מהללאל דור חמישי *Mahalalel was a fifth generation* 4QPrEnosh 1.1_{9}, [מהללאל בנו] *Mahalalel was his son* 4QPrEnosh 1.1_{9}. <OBJ> ילד hi. *beget* Gn $5_{12.13}$. <CSTR> יְמֵי מַהֲלַלְאֵל *days of Mehalalel* Gn 5_{17}. <COLL> קֵינָן מַהֲלַלְאֵל יָרֶד *Kenan, Mahalalel, Jared* 1 C 1_{2}.

2. Judahite, descendant of Perez, <CSTR> בֶּן־מַהֲלַלְאֵל *son of Mahalalel* Ne 11_{4}.

⇒ הלל I *praise* + אֵל *God*.

מַהֲלֻמוֹת 2 n.f.pl. **beatings,** <NOM CL> מַהֲלֻמוֹת לְגֵו כְּסִילִים *beatings are for the back of fools* Pr 19_{29} (+ שֶׁפֶט *judgment*). <PREP> לְ *for*, + קרא *call* Pr 18_{6}. <COLL> עבד רע צלע מהלמת perh. *a bad servant who limps because of beatings* Si $42_{5(M)}$ (or read מהלכת *of gait*, i.e. מַהֲלֶכֶת, or *walking*, i.e. הלך pi.).

⇒ הלם *hammer*.

*מהם I 0.1 vb. **melt** (unless מהם *from them*)—**Qal** 0.1 Pf. מהם—**melt,** <SUBJ> כּוּר *furnace* Si $43_{4(B)}$. <OBJ> מָצוּק *solid casting* Si $43_{4(B)}$.

*מהם II 0.1 vb. **be pleasant** (unless מהה htpalp. *delay*) —**Htp.** 0.1 Impf. יתמהמה—**make oneself pleasant,** <SUBJ> צַר *enemy* Si 12_{16}. <PREP> בְּ of instrument, *by (means of), with,* + שָׂפָה *lip* Si 12_{16}.

מָהֵם, see מָה *what?*, הֵם *they*.

[מַהֲמֹרָה] 1.1 n.f. **pit**—pl. מַהֲמֹרוֹת—**pit,** perh. as filled with water, or as name for the underworld, or perh. **effusion,*** <OBJ> חשב *plan* Si 12_{16}. <ADJ> עָמֹק *deep* Si 12_{16}. <PREP> בְּ of place, *in(to)*, + נפל hi. *cause to fall* Ps 140_{11} (or em. qal *fall*).

*[מַהְפָּךְ] 0.0.1 n.[m.] **turning**—Q מהפכיהם—of gates or spirits, <CSTR> כול מהפכיהם *all their turnings* 4Q ShirShabb[d] 1.1_{4}. <PREP> בְּ of place, *in* 4QShirShabb[d] 1.1_{4}.

⇒ הפך *turn*.

[מַהְפֵּכָה] 6 n.f. **overthrow**—cstr. מַהְפֵּכַת—sometimes as verbal noun with object (see Coll.), <CSTR> מַהְפֵּכַת אֱלֹהִים *overthrow of,* i.e. by, *God* Is 13_{19} Jr 50_{40} Am 4_{11}, זָרִים *of,* i.e. by, *strangers* Is 1_{7} (or em. זָרִים to סְדֹם *of Sodom*), מַהְפֵּכַת סְדֹם *overthrow of Sodom* Dt 29_{22} Is 1_{7} (if em.; see above), סְדֹם וַעֲמֹרָה וּשְׁכֵנֶיהָ *of Sodom and Gomorrah and its neighbours* Jr 49_{18}. <PREP> כְּ *as* Dt 29_{22} Is 1_{7} 13_{19} Jr 49_{18} 50_{40} Am 4_{11}. <COLL> כְּמַהְפֵּכַת אֱלֹהִים אֶת־סְדֹם וְאֶת־עֲמֹרָה *as when God overthrew Sodom and Gomorrah* Is 13_{19} Jr 50_{40} (+ וְאֶת־שְׁכֵנֶיהָ *and its neighbours*) Am 4_{11}.

⇒ הפך *turn*.

מַהְפֶּכֶת 4 n.f. **stocks**—מַהְפָּכֶת—**stocks,** or similar apparatus for punishment, <NOM CL> הַמַּהְפֶּכֶת אֲשֶׁר בְּשַׁעַר בִּנְיָמִן הָעֶלְיוֹן *the stocks that were in the upper gate of Benjamin* Jr 20_{2}. <CSTR> בֵּית הַמַּהְפֶּכֶת *house of the stocks* 2 C 16_{10}. <PREP> מִן of direction, *from*, + יצא hi. *bring out* Jr 20_{3}; אֶל *(in)to*, + נתן *give*, i.e. place Jr 29_{26} (|| צִינֹק *iron collar*); עַל *upon, (in)to*, + נתן *give*, i.e. place Jr 20_{2}.

<SYN> צִינֹק *iron collar*.

⇒ הפך *turn*.

מְהֻקְצָעוֹת 1 perh. n.f.pl. **corner rooms,** <NOM CL> לְאַרְבַּעְתָּם מְהֻקְצָעוֹת *to the four of them were corner rooms* Ezk 46_{22} (but prob. קצע ho. ptc. *be made for corners*).

⇒ קצע *be made for corners*.

מהר I 67.5.11 vb. **hasten**—**Ni.** 4.1.6 Pf. נִמְהָרָה, Si נמהרו; ptc. נִמְהָר, נִמְהָרִים, נִמְהֲרֵי—**1. act quickly** (Si 50_{17}); **be hurried (to destruction)** (Jb 5_{13}), <SUBJ> עֵצָה *counsel* of the wily Jb 5_{13} (unless מהר IV *sell, betray*), בָּשָׂר *flesh* Si 50_{17}. <COLL> נמהרו ונפלו *they acted quickly and fell down*, i.e. fell down quickly Si 50_{17}.

2a. ptc. as adj. **hasty, impetuous,** used attributively of גּוֹי *nation* Hb 1_{6} (+ מַר *bitter*).

b. ptc. as noun, **hasty one,** as rash (Is 32_{4}), anxious (Is 35_{4} 1QH 13_{5} 2_{9} 1QS 10_{26}), eager (1QH 5_{21} 4QShir Shabb[d] 1.1_{20} 4QShirShabb[f] 3.2_{10}), <SUBJ> היה *be* 1QH 13_{5}, חזק *be strong* Is 35_{4}, ירא *fear* Is 35_{4}. <OBJ> ישע hi.

save Is 35$_{4}$. <CSTR> נִמְהֲרֵי־לֵב *ones hasty of mind,* i.e. anxious Is 35$_{4}$ 1QH 2$_{9}$, נמהרי צדק *ones hasty of,* i.e. eager for, *righteousness* 1QH 5$_{21}$, רצונו *of,* i.e. eager for, *his good favour* 4QShirShabb^{d} 1.1$_{20}$ 4QShirShabb^{f} 3.2$_{10}$; לְבַב נִמְהָרִים *mind of the hasty* Is 32$_{4}$ (|| עִלֵּג *stammerer*), כול נמהרי *all hasty ones of* 1QH 2$_{9}$ 4QShir Shabb^{d} 1.1$_{20}$. <PREP> לְ of direction, *to,* + אמר *say* Is 35$_{4}$; of benefit, *to, for,* + היה *be* 1QH 2$_{9}$; of possession, *of, (belonging) to* 1QS 10$_{26}$ ([לנמהר]ים); introducing object, + ברך pi. *bless* 4QShirShabb^{d} 1.1$_{20}$ ([וברכו]); עִם *with* 1QH 5$_{21}$.

<SYN> §2b עִלֵּג *stammerer.*

Pi. 63.3.5 Pf. מִהַר, מִהֲרָה, מִהַרְתָּ, מִהַרְתְּ, מִהֲרוּ, מִהַרְתֶּן; impf. יְמַהֵר, 3fs תְּמַהֵר, 2ms Si תמהר, יְמַהֲרוּ, 3fpl תְּמַהֵרְנָה, תְּמַהֲרוּ; + waw וַיְמַהֵר, 3fs וַתְּמַהֵר, וַיְמַהֲרוּ; וּמִהַרְתֶּם; impv. מַהֵר (מַהֲרָה), מַהֲרִי, מַהֲרוּ; ptc. מְמַהֵר (מַהֵר), Q ממהרים, מְמַהֲרוֹת; inf. מַהֵר.

1. hasten, come quickly, go quickly, <SUBJ> Y. Is 5$_{19}$ (+ חוּשׁ hi. *make to hasten*), Abraham Gn 18$_{6}$, Joseph Gn 43$_{30}$, Saul 1 S 9$_{12}$ (or em. הָרֹאֶה *the seer;* lacking in ms), אִישׁ *man* 1 C 12$_{9}$, בֵּן *son* Is 49$_{17}$, בֹּנֶה *builder* Is 49$_{17}$(1QIsa^{a}), עֹרֵךְ *one who arranges* 1 C 12$_{9}$, גִּבּוֹר *warrior* 1 C 12$_{9}$, רָשָׁע *wicked one* 1QH 5$_{17}$, the wicked Is 59$_{7}$, חַטָּא *sinner* Pr 1$_{16}$, אַדִּיר *majestic one* Na 2$_{6}$, צִפּוֹר *bird* Pr 7$_{23}$, רָעָה *misfortune* Jr 48$_{16}$ (+ קָרוֹב *near*), יוֹם *day* Zp 1$_{14}$ (+ קָרוֹב) 4QpsEzek^{a} 3$_{3}$. <PREP> בְּ of accompaniment, *with,* + מְצוּקָה *affliction* 1QH 5$_{17}$; כְּ *as,* + צְבִי *gazelle* 1 C 12$_{9}$; מִן *at, on account of,* + קוֹל *sound* 4QShirShabb^{f} 18$_{4}$; of comparison, *(more) than,* + הרס ptc. *one who tears down* Is 49$_{17}$ (if em. מְהָרְסַיִךְ *those who tear you down* [pi.] to מֵהֹרְסַיִךְ *than those who tear you down* [qal]); אֶל *to,* + Sarah Gn 18$_{6}$, פַּח *trap* Pr 7$_{23}$; ה- of direction, + אֹהֶל *tent* Gn 18$_{6}$, חוֹמָה *wall* Na 2$_{6}$ (if em. חוֹמָתָהּ *[to] its wall* to חוֹמָתָה *to the wall*). <COLL> מהר pi. + infinitive of purpose, שׁפך *shed* blood Is 59$_{7}$ Pr 1$_{16}$; + adverb, מְאֹד *much* Jr 48$_{16}$ Zp 1$_{14}$.

2. hasten, act quickly, a. as auxiliary with another verb, e.g. go, come **hastily, quickly,** <SUBJ> Y. Gn 41$_{32}$ Ps 69$_{18}$ 102$_{3}$ 143$_{7}$ (unless in all three מַהֵר inf. as adv. *quickly*), Benjaminite 2 S 19$_{17}$, Egyptians Ex 12$_{33}$, עַם *people* Jos 4$_{10}$ Jg 8$_{48}$, Abigail 1 S 25$_{18.23.34.42}$, Absalom 2 S 15$_{14}$, David 1 S 17$_{48}$, Haman Est 6$_{10}$, Lot Gn 19$_{22}$, Moses Ex 34$_{8}$, Rebekah Gn 24$_{18.20.46}$, Saul 1 S 23$_{27}$ 28$_{20}$, Shimei 2 S 19$_{17}$, אִישׁ *man* Gn 44$_{11}$ Jos 8$_{14}$ 1 S 4$_{14}$ 1 K 20$_{33.41}$ 2 K 1$_{11}$ (if em. מְהֵרָה *quickly*) 9$_{13}$, אִשָּׁה *woman* Jg 13$_{10}$ 1 S 28$_{24}$, אָב *father* Ps 106$_{13}$, בֵּן *son* Gn 27$_{20}$ 2 S 19$_{17}$ Si 5$_{11}$ 6$_{7}$, בַּת *daughter* Ex 2$_{18}$, אָח *brother* Gn 45$_{9.13}$, פַּרְעֹה *Pharaoh* Ex 10$_{16}$, נַעַר *lad* Gn 18$_{7}$, עֶבֶד *servant* 2 S 15$_{14}$, צעה ptc. *one who crouches* Is 51$_{14}$, קין pol. ptc. fem. *mourning woman* Jr 9$_{17}$, אֹרֵב *ambush* Jos 8$_{19}$, לָשׁוֹן *tongue* Is 32$_{4}$, רֶגֶל *foot* Pr 6$_{18}$, לֵב *heart* Ec 5$_{1}$ (+ בהל pi. *be in haste*), כֹּל *anyone* 4QD^{b} 5.3$_{3}$ ([כול]); subj. not specified, 4Q417 2.2$_{5}$ (unless מַהֵר adv.).

<COLL> (1) with infinitive of הלך *go* 2 S 15$_{14}$, בוא *come* Ex 2$_{18}$ (+ מַדּוּעַ *why?*), יצא hi. *bring out,* i.e. utter, word Ec 5$_{1}$, רוץ *run* Pr 6$_{18}$, אזן hi. *hear* Si 5$_{11}$, דבר pi. *speak* Is 32$_{4}$, קרא *call* Ex 10$_{16}$, שׁלח pi. *send* Ex 12$_{33}$, בין hi. *understand* 4QD^{b} 5.3$_{3}$ ([להב]ין), בטח *trust* Si 6$_{7}$, עשׂה *do* Gn 18$_{7}$ 41$_{32}$, מצא *find* Gn 27$_{20}$, פתח ni. *be released* Is 51$_{14}$.

(2) with finite form (usu. with waw consecutive) of ירד *go down* 1 S 25$_{23}$ 2 S 19$_{17}$, hi. *bring down* Gn 24$_{18.20(Sam).46}$ 44$_{11}$ 45$_{13}$, בוא *come* 1 S 4$_{14}$ 25$_{34}$, יצא *go out* Jos 8$_{14}$, עבר *pass* Jos 4$_{10}$, רוץ *run* Jg 13$_{10}$ 1 S 17$_{48}$, נשׂג hi. *overtake* 2 S 15$_{14}$, קום *rise* 1 S 25$_{42}$, שׁכם hi. *rise early* Jos 8$_{14}$, נפל *fall* 1 S 28$_{20}$, ערה pi. *empty* Gn 24$_{20}$, קדד *bow down* Ex 34$_{8}$, יצת hi. *set fire to* Jos 8$_{19}$, לקח *take* 1 S 25$_{18}$ 2 K 9$_{13}$, חלט *accept* 1 K 20$_{33}$, סור hi. *remove* 1 K 20$_{41}$, זבח *sacrifice* 1 S 28$_{24}$, שׁכח *forget* Ps 106$_{13}$, נשׂא *raise* lamentation Jr 9$_{17}$

(3) with imperative of הלך *go* 1 S 23$_{27}$, עלה *go up* Gn 45$_{9}$, רדה *go down* 2 K 1$_{11}$ (if em. מְהֵרָה *quickly*), מלט ni. *escape* Gn 19$_{22}$, עשׂה *do* Jg 9$_{48}$, ענה *answer* Ps 69$_{18}$ 102$_{3}$ 143$_{7}$ (unless all three מַהֵר inf. as adv. *quickly*), לקח *take* Est 6$_{10}$, נתן *give* 4Q417 2.2$_{5}$ (unless מַהֵר inf. as adv.).

2b. מהר alone, <SUBJ> כֹּהֵן *priest* 2 C 24$_{5}$, לֵוִי *Levite* 2 C 24$_{5.5}$. <PREP> לְ *with respect to, in,* + דָּבָר *matter* 2 C 24$_{5}$.

3. trans. **hasten,** i.e. prepare quickly (Gn 18$_{6}$), bring quickly (1 K 22$_{9}$||2 C 18$_{8}$ Est 5$_{5}$ Si 45$_{3}$), <SUBJ> Y. Si 45$_{3}$, Sarah Gn 18$_{6}$, סָרִיס *eunuch* 1 K 22$_{9}$||2 C 18$_{8}$; subj. not specified, Est 5$_{5}$. <OBJ> Haman Est 5$_{5}$, Micaiah 1 K 22$_{9}$|| 2 C 18$_{8}$, בֵּן *son* 1 K 22$_{9}$||2 C 18$_{8}$, אוֹת *sign* Si 45$_{3}$(Segal) ([אותות]), סְאָה *seah* Gn 18$_{6}$ (שְׁלֹשׁ סְאִים קֶמַח סֹלֶת *three* *seahs of fine flour).* <PREP> בְּ of instrument, *by (means of), with,* + דָּבָר *word* Si 45$_{3(Segal)}$ (בד[בריו]).

4. ptc. as adj., **swift, keen,** used attributively of עֵד *witness* Ml 3$_{5}$.

Also perh. 4Q418 160$_{2}$.

Hi. $_{0.1}$ Ptc. Si ממהיר—**hasten, make haste,** אל תבוש ... על ממהיר [מ]מכר תגר perh. *do not be ashamed of ... (being) one who hastens (after) the wares of a merchant* Si 42$_{5(B)}$ (M ממחיר *bargaining*).

⇒ מָהִיר *quick,* מַהֵר *quickly,* מְהֵרָה *haste,* מַהֵר שָׁלָל חָשׁ בַּז *Maher-shalal-hash-baz.*

מהר II $_{3.0.1}$ vb. **acquire—Qal** $_{3}$ Pf. מָהֲרוּ; impf. יִמְהָרֶנָּה; ptc. Q מוהר; inf. abs. מָהֹר—**1. acquire** as wife, **acquire with bride-gift** (Ex 22$_{15.15}$), perh. **acquire** another god (Ps 16$_{4}$ [unlesss מהר III *serve;* or em.; see Obj.]), <SUBJ> אִישׁ *man* Ex 22$_{15}$; subj. not specified, Ps 16$_{4}$ (unless מהר III *serve;* or em.; see Obj.). <OBJ> בְּתוּלָה *young woman* Ex 22$_{15}$, אַחֵר *another one* Ps 16$_{4}$ (unless מהר III *serve;* or em. אַחֵר מָהָרוּ to אֲחֵרִים יִירָאוּ *they fear others* or אָרְחָם הֵרֵעוּ *they make evil their way* or אָרְחָם הֵמִירוּ *they change their way).* <PREP> לְ *as,* + אִשָּׁה *wife* Ex 22$_{15}$.

2. ptc. as noun, **merchant,** <PREP> כְּ *as,* + perh. ענה *answer* 4QBéat 14.2$_{22}$.

⇒ מֹהַר *bride-gift.*

***מהר** III vb. **serve** (unless מהר II *purchase*)—**Qal** $_{1}$ Pf. מָהָרוּ—**serve,** <SUBJ> subj. not specified, Ps 16$_{4}$. <OBJ> אַחֵר *another one* Ps 16$_{4}$.

***מהר** IV vb. **sell, betray** (unless מהר I *hasten*)—**Ni.** $_{1}$ Pf. נִמְהָרָה—**be betrayed,** <SUBJ> עֵצָה *counsel* of the wily Jb 5$_{13}$.

מַהֵר $_{14.0.4}$ adv. **quickly,** pi. inf. abs. of מהר *hasten,* **1.** with preceding verb סור *turn aside* Ex 32$_{8}$ Dt 9$_{12.16}$ (lacking in mss Sam^{mss}) Jg 2$_{17}$, הלך *go* Nm 17$_{11(Sam)}$, ירד *go down* Dt 9$_{12}$, יצא *go out* Pr 25$_{8}$ (if em. לָרִב *to strive* to לָרֹב *to the multitude),* רדף *pursue* Jos 2$_{5}$, בהל htp. *hasten* 4QpsEzek^{a} 3$_{2}$, אבד *perish* Dt 4$_{26}$ 11$_{17(Sam)}$ 28$_{20}$ (or del.), hi. *destroy* Dt 9$_{3}$, שׁמד hi. *destroy* Dt 7$_{4}$, כלה pi. *destroy* Dt 7$_{22}$, ירשׁ hi. *drive out* Jg 2$_{23}$, ריב *strive* Pr 25$_{8}$ (or em.; see above), ספר *reckon* 4Q417 1.1$_{4}$, שׁלם pi. *pay* 4Q417 1.2$_{6}$.

2. with following verb קדם pi. *meet* Ps 79$_{8}$ (or em. מָהִיר *Scribe),* perh. ענה *answer* Ps 69$_{18}$ 102$_{3}$ 143$_{7}$ (but all three prob. מהר pi. impv.), נתן *give* 4Q417 2.2$_{5}$ (but prob. מַהֵר impv.), מלל *fade* 1QM 15$_{11}$.

⇒ מהר I *hasten.*

מֹהַר $_{3}$ n.[m.] **bride-gift**—cstr. מֹהַר—<OBJ> רבה hi. *increase* Gn 34$_{12}$ (|| מַתָּן *gift).* <CSTR> מֹהַר הַבְּתוּלֹת *bride-gift of the young women* Ex 22$_{16}$. <PREP> בְּ *for* 1 S 18$_{25}$ (אֵין־חֵפֶץ לַמֶּלֶךְ בְּמֹהַר *the king has no desire for any bride-gift* except a hundred Philistine foreskins); כְּ *according to,* + שׁקל *weigh* silver Ex 22$_{16}$.

<SYN> מַתָּן *gift.*

⇒ מהר II *acquire.*

***[מֹהֵר]** $_{2}$ n.[m.] **warrior,** in name *Maher-shalal-hash-baz* Is 8$_{1.3}$.

מְהֵרָה $_{20.0.0.2}$ n.f. **haste, 1.** as noun, **haste, speed,** <PREP> בְּ of accompaniment, *with, in,* + נתק ni. *be torn apart* Ec 4$_{12}$; עַד *unto,* + רוץ *run* Ps 147$_{15}$ (or em. עַד to עַל *according to).*

2. as adverb, **hastily, quickly, soon, a.** with preceding verb הלך *go* 2 S 17$_{18}$, hi. *take* Nm 17$_{11}$, עלה *go up* Jos 10$_{6}$, קום *rise* Jos 8$_{19}$, עבר *pass over* 2 S 17$_{21}$, שׁלח *send* 2 S 17$_{16}$ Arad ost. 17$_{5}$, שׁוב ho. *be brought back* Jr 27$_{16}$, אבד *perish* Dt 11$_{17}$ Jos 23$_{16}$, קרא *call* Jg 9$_{54}$, נתן *give* Arad ost. 12$_{3}$, עשׂה ni. *be done* Ec 8$_{11}$.

b. with following verb חושׁ *hasten* 1 S 20$_{38}$, בוא *come* Is 5$_{26}$ (|| קַל *swiftly),* ירד *go down* 2 K 1$_{11}$ (or em. מְהֵרָה *hasten,* i.e. מהר pi. impv.), שׁוב hi. *bring back* Jl 4$_{4}$ (|| קַל), נצל hi. *deliver* Ps 31$_{3}$, צמח *spring up* Is 58$_{8}$, מלל *fade* Ps 37$_{2}$.

<SYN> קַל *swiftly.*

⇒ מהר I *hasten.*

מַהֲרַי $_{3}$ pr.n.m. **Maharai,** warrior and official of David, <NOM CL> הָעֲשִׂירִי ... מַהְרַי *the tenth was ... Maharai* 1 C 27$_{13}$. <APP> נְטֹפָתִי *Netophathite* 2 S 23$_{28}$||1 C 11$_{30}$

1 C 27_{13}.

מַהֵר שָׁלָל חָשׁ בַּז 2 pr.n.m. **Maher-shalal-hash-baz,** 'the spoil speeds, the prey hastens', name given to son of Isaiah, <OBJ> קרא *call* name Is 8_3. <PREP> לְ of possession, *of, (belonging) to* Is 8_1.

⇒ מהר I *hasten* + שָׁלָל *spoil* + חוש I *hasten* + בַּז *prey.*

[מַהֲתַלָּה] 1.0.1 n.f. **deception**—pl. מַהֲתַלּוֹת—<OBJ> חזה *see* Is 30_{10} (or em. מְהַתְּלוֹת, from תלל *mock, deceive,* as 1QIsa[a]; || חָלָק *smooth thing,* i.e. flattery). <PREP> בְּ introducing object, + בחר *choose* CD 1_{18} (|| חָלָק *smooth thing,* i.e. flattery).

<SYN> חָלָק *smooth thing.*

⇒ התל *mock.*

*מוֹ 6 n.[m.] **water**—cstr. מוֹ—<SUBJ> בקע *split* Ps 141_7, פלח *cleave* Ps 141_7, כסה *cover* Ps 140_{10} (if em.; see Cstr.). <CSTR> מוֹ־שָׁלֶג *water of snow,* i.e. snow-water Jb 9_{30}, מוֹ־נָחַל *water of a wadi* Jb 6_{15}, מוֹ יָם *water of the sea* Ps 140_{10} (if em. יְכַסּוּמוֹ: יָמִיטוּ *they will cover them, they will dislodge* to יְכַסּוּ מוֹ יָם *the water of the sea will cover*). <ADJ> אַכְזָב *deceptive* Jr 15_{18}, רָם *high* Ps 78_{69}. <PREP> לְ of direction, *to* Is 53_8 (נֶגַע לָמוֹ *a blow to the Waters (of death),* i.e. he was stricken to death; unless לָמוֹ *=to them*), + קרב *draw near* Jb 33_{22} (if em. לַמְמִתִים *to those who cause death* to לְמוֹ מֵתִים *to the waters of the dead*); בְּ of instrument, *with,* + רחץ htp. *wash oneself* Jb 9_{30} (unless בְּמוֹ = *with*); כְּ *like* Ps 141_7 (unless כְּמוֹ = *as*), + היה *be* Jr 15_{18} (unless כְּמוֹ = *as*), בנה *build* Ps 78_{69} (unless כְּמוֹ = *as*), בגד *betray* Jb 6_{15} (unless כְּמוֹ = *as*). <COLL> מוֹ || מַיִם *waters* Jr 15_{18}.

<SYN> מַיִם *water.*

מוֹאָב 178.1.4.1 pr.n.m. (sometimes f.) **Moab**—I מאב—**1.** son of Lot, eponymous ancestor of Moabites, <OBJ> קרא *call* name Gn 19_{37}.

2a. Moab, territory and kingdom E of Dead Sea. **b.** as collective noun, **Moabites** (distinction not alw. clear), e.g. Gn 19_{37} Nm $22_{3.3.4}$ 25_1 Dt 2_9 Jg 3_{28} 10_6 2 S 8_2|| 1 C 18_2 1 K $11_{7.33}$ 2 K $3_{10.13.21}$ 13_{20} 23_{13}.

<SUBJ> היה *be* 2 S 8_2||1 C 18_2 Jr $48_{26.39}$ Zp 2_9, גור *fear* Nm 22_3, בושׁ *be ashamed* Jr $48_{13.39}$, hi. Jr 48_{20}, חתת *be dismayed* Jr 48_{20}, קוץ *feel loathing* Nm 22_3, חרף pi. *reproach* Zp 2_8, ילל hi. *wail* Is 15_2 16_7, לאה ni. *weary oneself* Is 16_{12}, שׁקט *be quiet* Jr 48_{11}, יעץ ni. *take counsel* Ps 83_7, שׁאן palel *be at ease* Jr 48_{11}, יכל *be able* Is 16_{12}, כרת *cut,* i.e. make, covenant Ps 83_7, שׁמע *hear* 2 K 3_{21}, ראה *see* 2 K 3_{22}, ni. *appear* Is 16_{12} (or del. נִרְאָה), אמר *say* Nm 22_4 2 K 3_{22} Ezk 25_8 Si 33_{12}(B, פלל htp. *pray* Is 16_{12}, ידע *know* Ezk 25_{11}, הלך *go* Jr 48_{11}, בוא *come* Is 16_{12}, שׁכם hi. *rise early* 2 K 3_{22}, עמד *stand* 2 C 20_{23}, פנה hi. *turn* Jr 48_{39}, נוס *flee* 2 K 3_{24}, מלט ni. *escape* Dn 11_{41}, נצא *fly* Jr 48_9, פשׁע *rebel* 2 K 1_1, גדל hi. *magnify oneself* Jr $48_{26.42}$ Zp 2_8, ספק *slap,* i.e. splash, into vomit Jr 48_{26}, כלה pi. *make an end of* 2 C 20_{23}, חרם hi. *destroy* 2 C 20_{23}, שׁמד hi. *destroy* 2 C 20_{23}, ni. *be destroyed* Jr 48_{42}, דמה ni. *be destroyed* Is 15_1, שׁדד pu. *be despoiled* Jr 48_{15} (or em.; see Prep.) 48_{20}, שׁבר ni. *be broken* Jr 48_4, כנע ni. *be subdued* Jg 3_{30}, דושׁ ni. *be trampled down* Is 25_{10}, ריק ho. *be emptied* Jr 48_{11}, מות *die* Am 2_2.

<NOM CL> מוֹאָב סִיר רַחְצִי *Moab is my washbasin* Ps 60_{10}||108_{10}, אֱדוֹם ... מִשְׁלוֹחַ יָדָם *Moab ... is (the object of) the outstretching of their hand* Is 11_{14}(L) (mss מִשְׁלוֹחַ).

<OBJ> צרר hi. *harass* Dt 2_9, שׁבר *break* Jr 48_{38}, נכה hi. *strike* Jg 3_{29} 2 S 8_2||1 C 18_2 2 K $3_{24.24}$, שׁכב hi. *cause to lie down* 2 S 8_2, בזז *plunder* Zp 2_9, נחל *possess* Zp 2_9, נתן *give* Jg 3_{28} 2 K 3_{18} Jr 25_{21}, מדד *measure* 2 S 8_2, צעה pi. *tilt* Jr 48_{11}, שׁכר hi. *make drunk* Jr 48_{26}.

<CSTR> אֱלֹהֵי מוֹאָב *god(s) of Moab* Jg 10_6 1 K 11_{33}, שִׁקֻּץ *abomination of* 1 K 11_7 2 K 23_{13}, תּוֹעֲבַת *abomination of* 1 K 11_{33}, אֲבִי־ *father of* Gn 19_{37}, בְּנֵי *sons of* 2 C $20_{1.22}$ (... בְּנֵי), בְּנוֹת *daughters of* Nm 25_1 Is 16_2, מֶלֶךְ *king of* Nm 21_{26} 22_{10} 23_7 Jos 24_9 Jg $3_{12.14.15.17}$ $11_{17.25}$ 1 S 12_9 $22_{3.4}$ 2 K $3_{4.5.7.26}$ Jr 27_3 Mc 6_5 6QapSamKings 33_3 Lachish ost. 8_3 ([מ]לך מאב), שָׂרֵי *princes of* Nm $22_{8.14.21}$ $23_{6.17}$, אֵילֵי *leaders of* Ex 15_{15}, זִקְנֵי *elders of* Nm 22_7, אֲרִאֵל *Ariel of* 2 S 23_{20}||1 C 11_{22} (or em. אַרְאֵלֵי *heroes of* or אֲ[רוֹ]ן אֵלֵי *priests of*), גִּבּוֹרֵי *warriors of* Jr 48_{41}, חֲלֻצֵי *armed men of* Is 15_4 (or em. חַלְצֵי *loins of*), גדוד ... מואב *troop of ... Moab* 1QM 1_1, גְּדוּדֵי מוֹאָב *troops of Moab* 2 K 13_{20} (ms גְּדוּד) 24_2 4QJub[f] 38_6 ([גד]ודי מוא[ב]), פְּלֵיטַת *fugitives of* Is 15_9, יוֹשֵׁב *inhabitant of* Jr 48_{43}, יֹשְׁבֵי *inhabitants of* Jr 48_{28}, נִדְּחֵי *outcasts of* Is 16_4(mss), שֹׁדֵד *despoil-*

er of Jr 48_{15} (if em.; see Prep.) 48_{19}, ־יַד *hand of* 2 K $3_{10.13}$, חַלְצֵי *loins of* Is 15_4 (if em.; see above), פְּאַת *corner*, i.e. temple of head, *of* Jr 48_{45}, פַּאֲתֵי *corners*, i.e. temples of head, *of* Nm 24_{17}=1QM 11_6 Si $33_{12(B)}$ (Bmg אויב *of the enemy*), קֶרֶן *horn of* Jr 48_{25}.

אֶרֶץ מוֹאָב *land of Moab* Dt 1_5 28_{69} 32_{49} $34_{5.6}$ Jg $11_{15.18.18}$ Jr $48_{24.33}$, גְּבוּל *border of* Nm $21_{13.15}$ 33_{44} Dt 2_{18} Jg $11_{18.18}$ Is 15_8, שְׂדֵה *countryside of* Gn 36_{35}||1 C 1_{46} Nm 21_{20} Ru $1_{1.2.6}$ (all three שְׂדֵי) Ru $1_{6.22}$ (שְׂדֵי) 2_6 4_3 1 C 8_8, מִדְבַּר *steppe of* Dt 2_8, עַרְבֹת *plains of* Nm 22_1 (עַרְבוֹת) $26_{3.63}$ 31_{12} $33_{48.49.50}$ 35_1 36_{13} Dt $34_{1.8}$ Jos 13_{32} (עַרְבוֹת), כֶּתֶף *slope of* Ezk 25_9, עִיר *city of* Nm 22_{36} (or em.; see below), עָרֵי *cities of* Nm 21_{28} (or em.; see below), גַּגּוֹת *roofs of* Jr 48_{38}, עָר *Ar of* Nm 21_{28} (or em. עָרֵי *cities of*) 22_{36} (if em. עִיר *city of*), קִיר *Kir of* Am 2_2 (if em.; see Prep.), מַשָּׂא *oracle of*, i.e. concerning Is 15_1, ־גְּאוֹן *pride of* Is 16_6 Jr 48_{29}, כְּבוֹד *glory of* Is 16_{14}, תְּהִלַּת *praise of* Jr 48_2, ־אֵיד *disaster of* Jr 48_{16}, שְׁבוּת *turning*, i.e. fortunes, *of* Jr 48_{47}, מִשְׁפַּט *judgment of*, i.e. against Jr 48_{47}, פִּשְׁעֵי *transgressions of* Am 2_1, חֶרְפַּת *reproach of* Zp 2_8, ־כָּל מוֹאָב *all Moab* 2 K 3_{21}.

<APP> אוֹיֵב *enemy* Jg 3_{28} 1 S 14_{47}, נִדָּח *outcast* Is 16_4 (mss נִדְּחֵי *outcasts of* Moab), גּוֹי *nation* 2 S 8_{12}||1 C 18_{11}.

<PREP> לְ of possession, *of, (belonging) to* Nm 21_{29} 22_4 Jr 48_{46}; of direction, *to*, + שׁלח pi. *send* Jr 48_{11}, נתן *give* Jr 48_9; *concerning*, or of cause, *on account of*, + אמר *say* Jr 48_1, זעק *cry out* Is 15_5 Jr 48_{31}, המה *moan* Jr 16_{11} 48_{36}, ילל hi. *wail* Is 16_7 (or del.); *against*, + לכד *capture* Jg 3_{28}; *at, in*, + שׁבת hi. *cause to cease* Jr 48_{35}; בעל לְ *marry into*, or *rule over* 1 C 4_{22}

בְּ of place, *in, among* Jr 40_{11}, + בוא *come* 2 C 20_{10}; *against*, + לחם ni. *fight* 1 S 14_{47} 2 K 3_{21}, גרה htp. *fight* Dt 2_9, שׁלח pi. *send* fire Am 2_2 (or em. בְּמוֹאָב to בְּקִיר מוֹאָב *against Kir of Moab*), עשׂה *do* Ezk 25_{11}.

מִן of place, *from*, + קדשׁ hi. *consecrate* 2 S 8_{12}||1 C 18_{11}.

אֶל *to*, + הלך *go* 2 K 3_7; *concerning*, + דבר pi. *speak* Is 16_{13}; *against*, + בוא hi. *bring* Jr 48_{44}, פרשׂ *spread* wings Jr 48_{40}.

עַל *on account of, for*, + ילל hi. *wail* Jr 48_{31}; *against*, + עלה *go up* Jr 48_{15} (if em. שֻׁדַּד מוֹאָב וְעָרֶיהָ עָלָה *Moab is destroyed and her cities have gone up* to שֹׁדֵד מוֹאָב עָלָיו עָלָה *the despoiler of Moab has gone up against him*); introducing object, + פקד *punish* Jr 9_{25}.

עַד *unto*, + אכל *devour* Nm $21_{28(mss)}$.

עַל־פְּנֵי *opposite* Nm 21_{11}.

בֵּין *between* Nm 21_{13} (+ הָאֱמֹרִי *the Amorites*).

תַּחַת *under*, i.e. in place of, + דושׁ ni. *be trampled down* Is 25_{10}.

אַחֲרֵי *after*, + ירד *go down* Jg 3_{28}.

<COLL> מוֹאָב as vocative, Nm 21_{29} 2 K 3_{23} Jr 48_{46}.

בְּנֵי־עַמּוֹן + מוֹאָב *sons of Ammon* Jg 10_6 1 S 14_{47} 2 S 8_{12}|| 1 C 18_{11} 1 K 11_{33} 23_{13} 2 K 24_2 Is 11_{14} Jr 9_{25} 25_{21} 40_{11} Zp $2_{8.9}$ Ps 83_7 (עַמּוֹן *Ammon*) Dn 11_{41} 2 C $20_{1.10.22.23}$ 1QM 1_1, עַמּוֹנִים *Ammonites* 2 C 20_1, אֱדוֹם *Edom* Ex 15_{15} Jg $11_{18.17}$ 1 S 14_{47} 2 S $8_{12(mss)}$||1 C 18_{11} 2 K 3_{26} Is 11_{14} Jr 9_{25} 25_{21} 27_3 40_{11} Ps 60_{10}||108_{10} 83_7 Dn 11_{41} 1QM 1_1 4QBark[a] 3.2_3, שֵׂעִיר *Seir* Ezk 25_8 2 C $20_{10.22}$ (both הַר־שֵׂעִיר *Mount Seir*), אֲרָם *Aram* Jg 10_6 2 K 24_2 2 S 8_{12}, פְּלִשְׁתִּים *Philistines* Jg 10_6 1 S 14_{47} 2 S 8_{12}||1 C 18_{11}, פְּלֶשֶׁת *Philistia* Ps 60_{10}||108_{10} 83_7 1QM 1_1, עֲמָלֵק *Amalek* 2 S 8_{12}||1 C 18_{11} Ps 83_7, מִצְרַיִם *Egypt* Jr 9_{25}, מִדְיָן *Midian* Nm 22_7, כְּנַעַן *Canaan* Ex 15_{15}, אֱמֹרִי *Amorites* Nm 21_{13}, צוֹר *Tyre* Ps 83_7, צִידוֹן *Sidon* Jg 10_6 1 K 11_{33} 2 K 23_{13}, צוֹבָה *Zobah* 1 S 14_{47}, כַּשְׂדִּים *Chaldaeans* 2 K 24_2, אַשּׁוּר *Assyria* Ps 83_7 1QM 1_1, כִּתִּים *Kittim* 1QM 1_1, גְּבָל *Gebal* Ps 83_7, יִשְׁמְעֵאלִים *Ishmaelites* Ps 83_7, הַגְרִים *Hagrites* Ps 83_7, בְּנֵי־שֵׁת *sons of Sheth* Nm 24_{17}=1QM 11_6, עַם כְּמוֹשׁ *people of Chemosh* Nm 21_{29} Jr 48_{46}.

⇨ מוֹאָבִי *Moabite*, פַּחַת מוֹאָב *Pahath-moab*.

מוֹאָבִי 16.0.2 gent. **Moabite**—מֹאָבִי; fem. מוֹאֲבִיָּה (מֹאֲבִיָּה), מוֹאָבִית; plur. מוֹאָבִים (מֹאָבִים); fem. מוֹאֲבִיּוֹת (מֹאֲבִיּוֹת)—**1.** as plur. noun, **Moabites, a.** masc., <SUBJ> ישׁב *dwell* Dt 2_{29}, קרא *call*, i.e. name Dt 2_{11}, עשׂה *do* Dt 2_{29}. <COLL> בְּנֵי עֵשָׂו + הַמּוֹאָבִים *sons of Esau* Dt 2_{29}.

b. fem., <OBJ> אהב *love* 1 K 11_1. <APP> אִשָּׁה *woman* 1 K 11_1. <COLL> מוֹאֲבִיּוֹת עַמֳּנִיּוֹת אֲדֹמִיֹּת צֵדְנִיֹּת חִתִּיֹּת *Moabite, Ammonite, Edomite, Sidonian (and) Hittite women* 1 K 11_1.

2. as collective sing. noun, **Moabites,** <PREP> לְ of possession, *of, (belonging) to* Ezr 9_1. <COLL> לַכְּנַעֲנִי הַפְּרִזִּי הַיְבוּסִי הָעַמֹּנִי הַמֹּאָבִי הַמִּצְרִי הָאֱמֹרִי *of the Canaanite, the Perizzite, the Jebusite, the Ammonite, the Mo-*

abite, the Egyptian (and) the Amorite Ezr 9_{1}.

3. as sing. noun, a particular **Moabite, a.** masc., <SUBJ> בוא *come* Dt 23_{4} Ne 13_{1} 4QMidrEschat[a] 1_{4}, קדם pi. *meet* Dt 23_{4}, שׂכר *hire* Dt 23_{4}. <NOM CL> גִּבּוֹרֵי הַחֲיָלִים ... הַמּוֹאָבִי *the mighty men of the armies were ... the Moabite* 1 C 11_{46}. <APP> Ithmah 1 C 11_{46}. <PREP> לְ of possession, *of, (belonging) to* Dt 23_{4}; עַל *concerning* 4QMMT B39 ([על]). <COLL> עַמּוֹנִי + מוֹאָבִי *Ammonite* Dt 23_{4} Ne 13_{1} 4QMidrEschat[a] 1_{4}.

b. fem., <SUBJ> שׁוב *go back* Ru 1_{22} 2_{6}, אמר *say* Ru $2_{2.21}$. <OBJ> קנה *purchase* Ru 4_{5} (if em.; see Prep.) 4_{10}. <CSTR> בֶּן־ ... הַמּוֹאָבִית *son of ... the Moabite woman* 2 C 24_{26}. <APP> Ruth Ru 1_{22} $2_{2.21}$ $4_{5.10}$, Shimrith 2 C 24_{26}, אִשָּׁה *wife* Ru $4_{5.10}$, כַּלָּה *daughter-in-law* Ru 1_{22}, נַעֲרָה *young woman* Ru 2_{6}. <PREP> מֵאֵת *from*, + קנה *purchase* Ru 4_{5} (or em. מֵאֵת to גַּם אֶת־ *also*).

4. Moabite, as attributive adj. of אִשָּׁה *woman* Ru 1_{4} Ne 13_{23}. <COLL> נָשִׁים אַשְׁדֳּודִיּוֹת עַמֳּנִיּוֹת מוֹאֲבִיּוֹת *Ashdodite, Ammonite and Moabite women* Ne $13_{23(Qr)}$.

⇒ מוֹאָב *Moab*.

מוֹאל, see מוּל *front*.

מוֹבָא 2 n.[m.] **entrance**—sf. Qr מוֹבָאֶךָ; pl. sf. מוֹבָאָיו—**1. entrance** of temple, <OBJ> ידע hi. *make known* Ezk 43_{11} (mss מָבוֹא *entrance*; :: מוֹצָא *exit*).

2. coming in (in phrase מוֹצָאָיו וּמוֹבָאָיו *its going out and its coming in*, referring to one's activity as a whole), <OBJ> ידע *know* 2 S $3_{25(Qr)}$ (Kt מבואו *coming in*; :: מוֹצָא *going out*).

<ANT> מוֹצָא *exit, going out*.

⇒ בוא *come*.

מוג I 17.1.7 vb. **melt—Qal** 4 Impf. 3fs תָּמוּג; + waw 3fs וַתָּמוֹג, 2ms וַתְּמוּגֵנוּ; inf. מוּג—**1.** intrans. **melt, faint,** <SUBJ> לֵב *heart* Ezk 21_{20} (Gnz נמוג [ni.]; or em. הִמּוֹג [ni.]), אֶרֶץ *earth* Am 9_{5} Ps 46_{7}.

2. (cause to) melt, <SUBJ> Y. Is 64_{6} (1QIsa[a] ותמגדנו *and you have given us*; or em. וַתְּמַגְּנֵנוּ *and you have delivered us up*). <OBJ> Israelites Is 64_{6} (or em.; see Subj.). <PREP> בְּ of place. *into*, + יָד *hand* Is 64_{6} (or em.; see Subj.).

Ni. 8.1.2 Pf. נָמוֹג, נָמֹגוּ; ptc. נְמוֹגִים, Q נמוגי—**1. melt away, faint, tremble,** perh. **fluctuate** (1 S 14_{16}), <SUBJ> Arpad Jr 49_{23} (or em.; see below), Hamath Jr 49_{23} (or em.; see below), Philistia Is 14_{31}, אִישׁ *man* 4QapPs[b] 48_{9} ([אנשי]), יֹשֵׁב *inhabitant* Ex 15_{15} Jos $2_{9.24}$ Ps 75_{4}, הָמוֹן *multitude* 1 S 14_{16}, לֵב *heart* Jr 49_{23} (if em. נָמֹגוּ בַּיָּם דְּאָגָה *they melt; in the sea there is anxiety* to נָמוֹג לִבָּם מִדְּאָגָה *their heart melts on account of anxiety*; or em. נָמֹגוּ כַּיָּם *they surge like the sea*) Ezk $21_{20(Gnz)}$ Si 48_{19} ([נ]מוגו), הֵיכָל *palace* Na 2_{7}, אֶרֶץ *earth* Ps 46_{3} (if em. בְּהָמִיר *when it changes* to בְּהִמּוֹג *when it melts away*) 75_{4}. <PREP> בְּ perh. *despite*, + גָּאוֹן *pride* Si 48_{19} ([נ]מוגו); מִן of cause, *on account of*, + דְּאָגָה *anxiety* Jr 49_{23} (if em.; see Subj.); מִפְּנֵי *(from) before, on account of*, + Israelites Jos $2_{9.24}$.

2. ptc. as noun, **trembling one,** <CSTR> נמוגי ברכים *trembling ones of*, i.e. ones who tremble in, *the knees* 1QM 14_{6}=4QM[a] 8_{4} (נמוגי בורכים [corrected from מוגי]). <PREP> לְ of direction, *to*, + נתן *give* 1QM 14_{6}; introducing object, + למד pi. *teach* 4QM[a] 8_{4}.

Pol. 2 2ms תְּמֹגְגֵנִי (תְּמֹגְגֶנָּה)—**dissipate, soften,** <SUBJ> Y. Ps 65_{11} Jb 30_{22}. <OBJ> Job Jb 30_{22}, אֶרֶץ *earth* Ps 65_{11}. <PREP> בְּ of instrument, *by (means of), with*, + רְבִיבִים *showers* Ps 65_{11}. <COLL> תְּמֹגְגֵנִי תֻּשִׁיָּה *you dissipate me in the storm* Jb 30_{22}.

Htpol. 3.0.5 Pf. הִתְמוֹגָגוּ; impf. 3fs תִּתְמוֹגָג, 3fpl תִּתְמוֹגַגְנָה; + waw Q ויתמוגגו—**melt away, dissolve,** <SUBJ> perh. Israelites 4QDiscourse 2.2_{7} ([י]תמוגגו) 2.2_{9} (+ חגג *stagger*; both + נוע htpol. *tremble*), נֶפֶשׁ *soul* Ps 107_{26}, גִּבְעָה *hill* Am 9_{13} (+ נטף hi. *drip*) Na 1_{5} (+ רעשׁ *shake*), אֹשׁ *foundation* 1QH 3_{35}, כֹּל *everyone* 1QH 3_{34}. <PREP> בְּ *on account of*, + רָעָה *trouble* Ps 107_{26}, הַוָּה *destruction* 1QH 3_{34}.

Also 4QShir[b] 20.2_{4} (יתמוגג[ו]).

***מוג II** 17.1.7 vb. **wave, waver—Qal** 4 Impf. 3fs תָּמוּג; + waw 3fs וַתָּמוֹג, 2ms וַתְּמוּגֵנוּ; inf. מוּג—**1.** intrans. **waver,** <SUBJ> לֵב *heart* Ezk 21_{20} (Gnz נמוג [ni.]; or em. הִמּוֹג [ni.]), אֶרֶץ *earth* Am 9_{5} Ps 46_{7}.

2. (cause to) waver (unless §3), <SUBJ> Y. Is 64_{6}. <OBJ> Israelites Is 64_{6}. <PREP> בְּיַד *on account of*, + עָוֹן *iniquity* Is 64_{6}.

3. perh. **turn away, depart,** וַתְּמוּגֵנוּ בְּיַד־עֲוֺנֵנוּ *and you have withdrawn from us because of our iniquities* Is 64$_{6}$ (unless §2).*

Ni. 8.1.2 Pf. נָמֹגוּ, נָמוֹג; ptc. נְמוֹגִים, Q נמוגי—**1. waver,** <SUBJ> Arpad Jr 49$_{23}$ (or em.; see below), Hamath Jr 49$_{23}$ (or em.; see below), Philistia Is 14$_{31}$, אִישׁ *man* 4QapPs^{b} 48$_{9}$ ([אנשי]), יֹשֵׁב *inhabitant* Ex 15$_{15}$ Jos 2$_{9.24}$ Ps 75$_{4}$, הָמוֹן *multitude* 1 S 14$_{16}$, לֵב *heart* Jr 49$_{23}$ (if em. נָמֹגוּ בַּיָּם דְּאָגָה *they waver; in the sea there is anxiety* to נָמוֹג לִבָּם מִדְּאָגָה *their heart wavers on account of anxiety*; or em. נָמֹגוּ כַּיָּם *they surge like the sea*) Ezk 21$_{20(Gnz)}$ Si 48$_{19}$ ([נ]מוגו), הֵיכָל *palace* Na 2$_{7}$, אֶרֶץ *earth* Ps 46$_{3}$ (if em. בְּהָמִיר *when it changes* to בְּהִמּוֹג *when it wavers*) 75$_{4}$. <PREP> בְּ perh. *despite,* + גָּאוֹן *pride* Si 48$_{19}$ ([נ]מוגו); מִן of cause, *on account of,* + דְּאָגָה *anxiety* Jr 49$_{23}$ (if em.; see Subj.); מִפְּנֵי *(from) before, on account of,* + Israelites Jos 2$_{9.24}$.

2. ptc. as noun, **wavering one,** <CSTR> נמוגי ברכים *wavering ones of,* i.e. ones who waver in, *the knees* 1QM 14$_{6}$=4QM^{a} 8$_{4}$ (נמוגי בורכים [corrected from מוגי]). <PREP> לְ of direction, *to,* + נתן *give* 1QM 14$_{6}$; introducing object, + למד pi. *teach* 4QM^{a} 8$_{4}$.

Pol. 2 2ms תְּמֹגְגֶנָּה (תְּמֹגְגֵנִי)—**cause to waver,** <SUBJ> Y. Ps 65$_{11}$ Jb 30$_{22}$. <OBJ> Job Jb 30$_{22}$, אֶרֶץ *earth* Ps 65$_{11}$. <PREP> בְּ of instrument, *by (means of), with,* + רְבִיבִים *showers* Ps 65$_{11}$. <COLL> תְּמֹגְגֵנִי תֻּשִׁיָּה *you dissipate me in the storm* Jb 30$_{22}$.

Htpol. 3.0.5 Pf. הִתְמֹגָגוּ; impf. 3fs תִּתְמוֹגָג, 3fpl תִּתְמוֹגַגְנָה; + waw Q ויתמוגגו—**waver,** <SUBJ> perh. Israelites 4QDiscourse 2.2$_{7}$ (תמוגגו[י]) 2.2$_{9}$ (+ חגג *stagger*; both + נוע htpol. *tremble*), נֶפֶשׁ *soul* Ps 107$_{26}$, גִּבְעָה *hill* Am 9$_{13}$ (+ נטף hi. *drip*) Na 1$_{5}$ (+ רעשׁ *shake*), אֹשׁ *foundation* 1QH 3$_{35}$, כֹּל *everyone* 1QH 3$_{34}$. <PREP> בְּ *on account of,* + רָעָה *trouble* Ps 107$_{26}$, הַוָּה *destruction* 1QH 3$_{34}$.

Also 4QShir^{b} 20.2$_{4}$ (יתמוגג[ו]).

מוּד, see מיד *shake, convulse.*

מוֹד I *strength,* see מְאֹד *strength.*

*[מוֹד] II 0.0.1 n.[m.] **love**—sf. Q מודי—<PREP> בְּ of accompaniment, *with,* + אהב *love* 11QPs^{a} 22$_{1}$ (unless from מְאֹד *strength*).

*[מוֹדָה] 0.0.0.1 n.f. perh. **measure,** Ost. DH76 בשנה השׁשׁת בשׁבעי מודה סלת 50 *in the sixth year, in the seventh (month), measure (?), 50 (seahs of) fine flour.*

[מוֹהֵר] *merchant,* see מהר II *purchase.*

מוט 37.8.11 vb. **totter**—**Qal.** 12.2.3 Pf. מָטָה, מָטוּ; impf. 3fs תָּמוּט, Q אמוט, 3fpl תְּמוּטֶינָה; + waw וּמָטָה; ptc. מָטִים; ptc. pass. Si מוט; inf. abs. מוֹט; cstr. מוֹט (Q מוטך, Si מוטו)—**1. totter, shake, slip,** sometimes perh. fatally, **die** (Ps 55$_{23}$),* <SUBJ> צַדִּיק *righteous one* Pr 25$_{26}$, פעל ptc. *one who does* good Si 3$_{31}$, מַשְׂכִּיל *instructor* 1QS 11$_{12}$, perh. wise one 4QBéat 14.2$_{7}$, יָד *hand* Lv 25$_{35}$, רֶגֶל *foot* Dt 32$_{35}$ Ps 38$_{17}$ 66$_{9}$ (if em. לַמּוֹט *to slipping* to לָמוּט *to slip*) 94$_{18}$ 121$_{3}$ (if em. לַמּוֹט to לָמוּט) GnzPs 1$_{26}$, אֶרֶץ *earth* Is 24$_{19}$ Ps 60$_{4}$ (+ רעשׁ hi. *cause to shake*), הַר *mountain* Ps 46$_{3}$ (|| מור hi. *change*), גִּבְעָה *hill* Is 54$_{10}$ (|| מושׁ *depart*), מַמְלָכָה *kingdom* Ps 46$_{7}$ (|| המה *make a noise*), בְּרִית *covenant* Is 54$_{10}$ (|| מושׁ); subj. not specified, Pr 24$_{11}$ (unless מָטִים is from מָטֶה *reaching*; or em.; see Prep.).

<PREP> לְ of direction, *to,* + הֶרֶג *slaughter* Pr 24$_{11}$ (unless מָטִים is from מָטֶה *reaching*; or em. מֻטִּים *those being led away* [נטה ho.] or מַטִּים *rods* [from מַטֶּה]); בְּ of place, *in(to),* + לֵב *heart* of sea Ps 46$_{3}$; עִם *with,* + Israelites Lv 25$_{35}$; לִפְנֵי *before,* + רָשָׁע *wicked one* Pr 25$_{26}$. <COLL> עֵת תָּמוּט רַגְלָם *the time when their foot shall slip* Dt 32$_{35}$, עת מוטו *the time when he slips* Si 3$_{31}$, var. 4QBéat 14.2$_{7}$; inf. abs. qal + finite form htpol. Is 24$_{19}$ (מוֹט הִתְמוֹטְטָה).

2. pass. **be made to slip,** <SUBJ> עָשִׁיר *rich one* Si 13$_{21}$. <PREP> בְּ of instrument, *by (means of), with,* + סֶמֶךְ *support* of friend appar. Si 13$_{21}$ (but prob. בסמך is error for נסמך *he is supported* by a friend).

<SYN> מושׁ *depart,* מור hi. *change,* המה *make a noise.*

Ni. 23.5.3 Pf. נָמֹטּוּ; impf. יִמּוֹט, 3fs תִּמּוֹט, אֶמּוֹט, יִמֹּטוּ; ptc. Si נמוט—**1. be shaken, moved, made to slip, made to drop** (Ps 140$_{11[Qr]}$; or em.; see Subj.); **stumble,** <SUBJ> אֱלֹהִים *God* 4QShirShabb^{f} 23.1$_{4}$, אִישׁ *man* Ps 112$_{6}$, בֵּן *son* Si 12$_{15}$ (+ נפל *fall*), מֶלֶךְ *king* Ps 21$_{8}$, צַדִּיק *righteous one* Pr 10$_{30}$, רָשָׁע *wicked one* Ps 10$_{6}$, worshipper Ps 13$_{5}$ 16$_{8}$ 30$_{7}$ 62$_{3.7}$ 1QH 7$_{7}$, ירא ptc. *one who fears* Y. Si 15$_{4}$ (|| בוש *be put to shame*), עשׂה ptc. *one who does* Ps 15$_{5}$, בוא ptc. *one who comes* 1QH 6$_{27}$, דַּל *poor one* Si 13$_{21.22}$, מַפָּל pl. *hanging parts* of crocodile's flesh Jb 41$_{15}$, פַּעַם *footstep* Ps 17$_{5}$, שֹׁרֶשׁ *root* of the righteous Pr 12$_{3}$, אֶרֶץ *earth* Ps 104$_{5}$, תֵּבֵל *world* Ps 93$_{1}$ (:: כון ni. *be established*) 96$_{10}$||1 C 16$_{30}$ (or del.; :: כון ni.), עִיר *city* Ps 46$_{6}$, הַר *mountain* Ps 125$_{1}$ (+ לְעוֹלָם יֵשֵׁב *it remains for ever*), מוֹסָד *foundation* Ps 82$_{5}$, גַּחֶלֶת *coal* Ps 140$_{11(Qr)}$ (or em. מטר ni. *be rained*), חֶסֶד *loyalty* Si 40$_{17(B)}$ (:: כון ni.).

<PREP> לְ *unto, throughout,* + דּוֹר *generation* Ps 10$_{6}$, עוֹלָם *everlastingness* Ps 15$_{5}$ 30$_{7}$ 104$_{5(mss)}$ 112$_{6}$ Pr 10$_{30}$ Si 40$_{17(B)}$ 4QShirShabb^{f} 23.1$_{4}$; בְּ of instrument, *by (means of), through, with,* + חֶסֶד *loyalty* Ps 21$_{8}$; עַל *upon,* + סבב hi. ptc. *one who surrounds* Ps 140$_{11(Qr)}$ (or em.; see Subj.). <COLL> מוט ni. + noun used adverbially, רַבָּה *greatly* Ps 62$_{3}$ (ms lacks רַבָּה), עוֹלָם וָעֶד *for ever and ever* Ps 104$_{5}$.

2. move, <SUBJ> פֶּסֶל *idol* Is 40$_{20}$ perh. 41$_{7}$.

<SYN> §1 בוש *be put to shame.*

<ANT> §1 כון ni. *be established.*

Hi. 2.0.1 Impf. יָמִיטוּ; ptc. Q ממיטה—**1. let fall, drop,** perh. **dislodge** (Ps 55$_{4}$ 140$_{11}$),* <SUBJ> אוֹיֵב *enemy* Ps 55$_{4}$ (or em. עיט hi. *cry* or מטר hi. *rain*), רָשָׁע *wicked one* Ps 55$_{4}$ (or em.; see above); subj. not specified, Ps 140$_{11(Kt)}$ (or em. מטר hi. *rain;* + נפל hi. *cause to fall*). <OBJ> אָוֶן *trouble* Ps 55$_{4}$ (or em.; see Subj.), גַּחֶלֶת *coal* Ps 140$_{11(Kt)}$ (or em.; see Subj.). <PREP> עַל *upon,* + worshipper Ps 55$_{4}$ (or em.; see Subj.), סבב hi. ptc. *one who surrounds* Ps 140$_{11(Kt)}$ (or em.; see Subj.).

2. shake, tremble, <SUBJ> תְּהוֹם *abyss* 4QHymnB 1$_{4}$.

Pol. 0.0.1 Q Ptc. מוטטי—**totter, slip,** <COLL> כול מוטטי רגל *all the tottering ones of feet,* i.e. whose feet totter, slip 11QPs^{a} 19$_{2}$.

Htpol. 1.1.3 Pf. הִתְמוֹטְטָה, impf. 2ms Q תתמוטט; + waw Q ויתמוטטו; ptc. Si מתמוטט—**1. be shaken** (Is 24$_{19}$ 4QBéat 14.2$_{6}$), **be tossed about** (Si 36$_{2}$), **stagger** (1QH 6$_{21}$), <SUBJ> צמד ni. ptc. *adherent* 1QH 6$_{21}$, perh. wise one 4QBéat 14.2$_{6}$, appar. אֹזֶן *ear* Si 36$_{2(E)}$ (or em. אזנו *his ear* to אוני *ship*), אֶרֶץ *earth* Is 24$_{19}$ (|| רעע htpo. *be broken,* פרר htpo. *be split*). <PREP> כְּ *as (in),* + מִסְעָר *storm* Si 36$_{2(E)}$; מִן of direction, *from,* + דֶּרֶךְ *way* 1QH 6$_{21}$. <COLL> מוט הִתְמוֹטְטָה *it shall be greatly shaken* Is 24$_{19}$.

2. ptc. as noun, **totterer,** perh. **capricious one,** <SUBJ> נתך ni. *be melted* 4Q424 1$_{4}$ (מתמ[ו]טט), עמד *stand* 4Q424 1$_{4}$ (מתמ[ו]טט). <PREP> עִם *with,* + בוא *come* 4Q424 1$_{4}$ (מתמ[ו]טט).

<SYN> §1 רעע htpo. *be broken,* פרר htpo. *be split.*

⇒ מוֹט I *shaking.*

מוֹט I 3 n.[m.] **shaking, slipping,** <OBJ> נתן *give* Ps 55$_{23}$. <PREP> נתן לְ *give* feet *to,* i.e. allow feet to slip Ps 66$_{9}$ 121$_{3}$ (unless both מוֹט III *quagmire;* or em. לָמוּט *to slip*).

⇒ מוט *totter.*

מוֹט II 4 n.[m.] **pole**—sf. מֹטֵהוּ—**pole,** for carrying cluster of grapes (Nm 13$_{23}$), **frame,** for carrying cultic objects (Nm 4$_{10.12}$), **bar** of yoke (Na 1$_{13}$), <OBJ> שׁבר *break* Na 1$_{13}$ (or em. מֹטָה *yoke,* or מַטֵּהוּ *his staff;* + מוֹסֵר *bond*). <PREP> בְּ of instrument, *by (means of), with,* + נשׂא *carry* Nm 13$_{23}$; עַל *upon,* + נתן *give,* i.e. place Nm 4$_{10.12}$.

***מוֹט III** 2 n.[m.] **Quagmire,** as name for the underworld (unless מוֹט I *shaking*), <PREP> לְ *in,* + נתן *give* i.e. place, feet Ps 66$_{9}$ 121$_{3}$.

מוֹטָה 12 n.f. **bar**—pl. מֹטוֹת (מֹטֹת); cstr. מֹטוֹת (מֹטֹת, מוֹטֹת)—**1. bar** of yoke, **yoke,** <OBJ> עשׂה *make* Jr 27$_{2}$ (|| מוֹסֵר *bond*) 28$_{13}$, נתן *give,* i.e. place Jr 27$_{2}$, לקח *take* Jr 28$_{10}$, שׁבר *break* Lv 26$_{13}$ Jr 28$_{10.12.13}$ Ezk 30$_{18}$ (or em; see Cstr.) 34$_{27}$ Na 1$_{13}$ (if em. מֹטֵהוּ *his bar* to מֹטָה), נתק pi. *break* Is 58$_{6}$, סור hi. *remove* Is 58$_{9}$ (or em. מֻטֶּה *injustice*). <CSTR> מֹטֹת עֻלְּכֶם *bars of your yoke* Lv 26$_{13}$, עֻלָּם *of their yoke* Ezk 34$_{27}$ (מֹטוֹת), בַּרְזֶל *of iron* Jr 28$_{13}$, עֵץ *of wood* Jr 28$_{13}$ (מֹטֹת), מִצְרַיִם *of Egypt* Ezk 30$_{18}$ (מֹטוֹת; or em. מַטּוֹת *staffs of*); אֲגֻדּוֹת מוֹטָה *bonds of,* i.e. tying one to, *the bar* Is 58$_{6}$ (+ חַרְצֻבָּה *fetter*), כָּל־מוֹטָה *every bar* Is 58$_{6}$. <PREP> תַּחַת *instead of,* + עשׂה *make* Jr 28$_{13}$.

2. pole, for carrying ark, <PREP> בְּ of instrument, *by (means of), with,* + נשׂא *carry* 1 C 15$_{15}$.

<SYN> §1 מוֹסֵר *bond.*

*[מוֹטָח] n.[m.] **club,** <NOM CL> מֹטְחוֹת זְרֹעֹת עוֹלָם *clubs are the arms of the Eternal* Dt 33_{27} (if em. מִתַּחַת *underneath*). <COLL> מֹטָח תַּשִּׁים י׳ *with a club you annihilate them, O Y.* Lm 3_{66} (if em. מִתַּחַת שְׁמֵי י׳ *from under the heavens of Y.*).*

מוך $_{5.1}$ vb. **be low—Qal** $_{5.1}$ Impf. יָמוּךְ; + waw וּמָךְ; ptc. מָךְ —**1. become poor,** <SUBJ> אִישׁ *man* Lv 27_8, אָח *brother* Lv $25_{25.35.39.47}$. <PREP> מִן of comparison, *too much for*, i.e. too poor to pay, + עֵרֶךְ *valuation* Lv 27_8.

2. ptc. as noun, **poor one, downtrodden one,** <OBJ> יקר hi. *honour* Si 12_5 (unless הקיר is from קרר hi. *make cool*, i.e. refresh; :: זֵד *presumptuous one*).

<ANT> §2 :: זֵד *presumptuous one.*

⇒ see also מכך *be low.*

*[מוֹכֵן] $_{0.0.1}$ n.[m.] **locust,** used collectively, <PREP> כְּ *as*, + מות *die* Is $51_{6(1QIsa^b)}$ (MT כְּמוֹ־כֵן *like gnats*, or *like thus*, i.e. likewise).

מוֹכֵר *trader*, see מכר *deliver (over).*

מול I $_{30.0.8}$ vb. **circumcise—Qal** $_{12.0.7}$ Pf. מָלוּ, מָל; + waw וּמַל, וּמַלְתָּה, וּמַלְתֶּם, וְנִמַּל; וַיָּמָל (Q וימול); impv. Q מול; pass. ptc. מוּל, מֻלִים; inf. Q מול, Q מולה—**1. circumcise,** <SUBJ> Y. Dt 30_6 1QH 11_5 4QBark[a] 1.24 4QDibHam[a] 4_{11}, Israel(ites) Ex 12_{44} Dt 10_{16} Jos $5_{5.7}$, Abraham Gn 17_{23} 21_4, Joshua Jos $5_{3.4.5.7}$ 4QpsJub[a] 1_4, אִישׁ *man* 1QS 5_5, כֹּהֵן *priest* 1QpHab 11_{13}. <OBJ> עַם *people* Jos 5_5 (or em. וְכָל־הָעָם ... לֹא־מִילוּ *and all the people ... were not circumcised*, i.e. qal pass.),* Isaac Gn 21_4, בֵּן *son* Gn 21_4 Jos $5_{7.7}$, of Israel Jos 5_3, עֶבֶד *servant* Ex 12_{44}, עָרְלָה *foreskin* Dt 10_{16} 1QpHab 11_{13} 1QS 5_5 4QBark[a] 1.24 4Q DibHam[a] 4_{11} 4QPrFêtes[c] 287 ([ע]ורלת), בָּשָׂר *flesh* of foreskin Gn 17_{23}, לֵבָב *heart* Dt 30_6, שָׂפָה *lip* 1QH 11_5, מִקְנָה *purchase*, i.e. one purchased Ex 12_{44}. <PREP> בְּ of place, *in*, + דֶּרֶךְ *way* Jos 5_7, יַחַד *community* 1QS 5_5; *into*, i.e. so as to be, + מָכוֹן *place* of rejoicing 1QH 11_5; of time, *on*, + עֶצֶם *self* Gn 17_{23} (בְּעֶצֶם הַיּוֹם הַזֶּה *on that selfsame day*); אֶל *at*, + Gibeath-haaraloth Jos 5_3.

2. pass. **a. be circumcised,** <SUBJ> עַם *people* Jos 5_5; subj. not specified, Jr 9_{24}. <PREP> בְּ of place, *in*, + עָרְלָה *foreskin* Jr 9_{24}.

b. ptc. as noun, (1) **circumcised one,** <PREP> לְ of possession, *of, (belonging) to* Ex 4_{26} (if em. לַמּוּלֹת *because of the circumcision* to לַמּוּלִים).

(2) **circumcision,** <OBJ> נתן *give*, i.e. make 1QH 11_5 (others מזל *utterance of*). <CSTR> מול שפתי *circumcision of my lips* 1QH 11_5 (others מזל *utterance of*).

Ni. $_{18.0.1}$ Pf. נִמּוֹל (Q נימול), נִמֹּלוּ; impf. יִמּוֹל; ptc. נִמֹּלִים; inf. abs. הִמּוֹל, cstr. הִמּוֹל (הִמֹּל, הִמֹּלוֹ)—**be circumcised,** <SUBJ> גּוֹי *nation* Jos 5_8, Abraham Gn $17_{24.26}$ CD 16_6, Hamor Gn 34_{17}, Ishmael Gn $17_{25.26}$, Shechem Gn 34_{17}, זָכָר *male* Gn $17_{10.12.14}$ $34_{15.22.24}$ Ex 12_{48}, אִישׁ *man* Gn 17_{27} 34_{22} Jr 4_4, אָב *father* Gn 34_{17}, בֵּן *son* Gn $17_{12.25.26}$, יָלִיד *one born* Gn $17_{12.13.13.27}$, מִקְנָה *purchase*, i.e. one purchased Gn $17_{12.13.13.27}$, עָרֵל *uncircumcised one* Gn 17_{14} בָּשָׂר *flesh* Lv 12_3, יצא ptc. *one who goes out* Gn 34_{24}. <PREP> לְ of benefit, *to, for* or perh. *by* (לְ of agent),* + Y. Jr 4_4; *(of those belonging) to*, + Abram and descendants Gn $17_{10.12}$, Hamor and family Gn $34_{15.22}$; בְּ of time, *on*, + יוֹם *day* CD 16_6, עֶצֶם *self* Gn 17_{26} (בְּעֶצֶם הַיּוֹם הַזֶּה *on that selfsame day*); אֵת *with*, + Abraham Gn 17_{27}. <COLL> inf. abs. + finite form of מול ni. Gn 17_{13}; עָרֵל זָכָר אֲשֶׁר לֹא יִמּוֹל אֶת־בְּשַׂר עָרְלָתוֹ *an uncircumcised male who is not circumcised in respect of the flesh of his foreskin* Gn 17_{14}, sim. Gn $17_{24.25}$.

⇒ מוּלָה *circumcision*; cf. מלל IV *circumcise.*

מול II $_3$ vb. **fend off** (unless מיל in same sense)—**Hi.** $_3$ Impf. אֲמִילַם (mss אֲמִלַם)—**fend off, drive away,** <SUBJ> worshipper Ps $118_{10.11.12}$ (or em. all three אַפִּילֵם *I caused them to fall*, or אִמָּלֵט *I was delivered*). <OBJ> גּוֹי *nation* Ps $118_{10.11.12}$ (or em. all three; see Subj.). <PREP> בְּ of accompaniment, *in, with*, + שֵׁם *name* Ps $118_{10.11.12}$ (or em. all three; see Subj.).

מול I $_{36.0.1}$ n.[m.] **front**—מוּל (מוֹאל); cstr. מוּל; sf. מֻלַי— **1.** as noun, **front** (1 K 7_5; or del.), **opposite** (or em.; see Prep.), <NOM CL> מוּל מֶחֱזָה אֶל־מֶחֱזָה *the front of a window was towards a window* 1 K 7_5 (or del.). <CSTR> מוּל מֶחֱזָה *front of window* 1 K 7_5 (or del.). <PREP> לְ of direction, *to*, + הלך *go* Ne 12_{38} (לְמוֹאל; mss לְמוּל; or em. לִשְׂמֹאל *to the left*).

2. as prep., **a.** מול alone, **in front of, before, opposite,** followed by noun, אֱלֹהִים *God* Ex 18$_{19}$, אִישׁ *man* 4QMyst^{a} 7$_{4}$, בֵּן *son* Dt 2$_{19}$, the Arabah Jos 18$_{18}$ (or em. מוּל־הָעֲרָבָה to בֵּית־עֲרָבָה *Beth-arabah*), Beth-peor Dt 3$_{29}$ 4$_{46}$ 34$_{6}$, Geba 1 S 14$_{5}$, Gilgal Dt 11$_{30}$, Joppa Jos 19$_{46}$, Michmash 1 S 14$_{5}$, Suph Dt 1$_{1}$ (מוֹל).

With verb, היה *be* Ex 18$_{19}$, ישׁב *remain* Dt 4$_{29}$, קרב *draw near* Dt 2$_{19}$.

b. אֶל־מוּל **in front of, before,** followed by noun, הַר *mountain* Ex 34$_{3}$ Jos 8$_{33.33}$, אֶרֶץ *land* Jos 22$_{11}$, Lebanon Jos 9$_{1}$, אַחֵר *another* 1 S 17$_{30}$.

With verb, סבב *turn* 1 S 17$_{30}$, רעה *pasture* Ex 34$_{3}$, בנה *build* Jos 22$_{11}$.

c. אֶל־מוּל פְּנֵי **in front of, at the front of,** followed by noun or suffix in ref. to noun, אֹהֶל *tent* Ex 26$_{9}$, אֵפֹד *ephod* Ex 28$_{25}$||39$_{18}$, מִצְנֶפֶת *turban* Ex 28$_{37}$ appar. Lv 8$_{9}$, מְנוֹרָה *lampstand* Nm 8$_{2.3}$, מִלְחָמָה *battle* 2 S 11$_{15}$ (mss אֶל־פְּנֵי).

With verb, היה *be* Ex 28$_{37}$, כפל *double (over)* Ex 26$_{9}$, שׂים *place* Lv 8$_{9}$, נתן *give*, i.e. place Ex 28$_{25}$||39$_{18}$ Lv 8$_{9}$ (Sam), יהב *give*, i.e. place 2 S 11$_{15}$ (or em. הָבוּ to הָבֵא *bring*, i.e. בוא hi.; mss אֶל־פְּנֵי), אור hi. *give light* Nm 8$_{2}$, עלה hi. *set up* Nm 8$_{3}$.

d. מִמּוּל **from the front of, from before, at the front of, (from) opposite,** followed by noun or suffix in ref. to noun, Balak Nm 22$_{5}$, בֵּן *son* Nm 22$_{5}$, מֶלֶךְ *king* Nm 22$_{5}$, עֹרֶף *neck* Lv 5$_{8}$, perh. רוּחַ *breath* 4QBéat 10$_{2}$ (others ממזל *by the utterance of*), בָּכָא *balsam* 2 S 5$_{23}$|| 1 C 14$_{14}$, נֶגֶב *south* 1 K 7$_{39}$||2 C 4$_{10}$ (קֵדְמָה מִמּוּל נֶגֶב *eastwards opposite the south*, i.e. in the south-east), שַׂלְמָה *garment* Mc 2$_{8}$ (or em. מֵעַל שַׂלְמִים/שְׁלֵמִים *from upon the peaceful*).

With verb, ישׁב *dwell* Nm 22$_{5}$, בוא *come* 2 S 5$_{23}$||1 C 14$_{14}$, נתן *give*, i.e. place 1 K 7$_{39}$||2 C 4$_{10}$, מלק *wring* Lv 5$_{8}$, פשׁט *strip* Mc 2$_{8}$ (or em.; see above).

e. מִמּוּל פְּנֵי **from the front of,** followed by suffix in ref. to אֵפֹד *ephod* Ex 28$_{27}$||39$_{20}$; with verb נתן *give*, i.e. place Ex 28$_{27}$||39$_{20}$.

מוּל II *circumcised one*, see מול *circumcise*.

*[מוֹלָד] 0.0.11 n.[m.] **birth**—pl. Q מולדים; cstr. Q מולדי; sf. Q מולדיו, מולדיהם—**birth, origin, source;** perh. also **ones born, offspring** (e.g. 1QMyst 1.1$_{5}$ 4Q416 2.3$_{20}$ 4Q417 1.1$_{11}$). <SUBJ> סגר ni. *be shut up* 1QMyst 1.1$_{5}$. <OBJ> דרשׁ *seek* 4Q416 2.3$_{9}$, לקח *take* 4Q416 2.3$_{20}$ 4Q417 1.1$_{11}$. <CSTR> מולדי עת *births of time*, i.e. moments when a period of time begins 1QH 12$_{8}$ (|| יְסוֹד *foundation*, תְּקוּפָה *circuit*), מולדי עולה *sources/offspring of injustice* 1QMyst 1.1$_{5}$, ישׁע *of salvation* 4Q417 1.1$_{11}$; בית מולדים perh. *house*, i.e. time, *of birth* 4Q Myst^{a} 1$_{4}$ 3a.2$_{13}$ 5$_{5}$ 4Q415 2.2$_{9}$, כול מולדי *all the births of* 1QH 12$_{8}$. <PREP> בְּ of time, *in* 1QH 3$_{11}$, הפך ni. *turn* 1QH 3$_{11}$.

<SYN> יְסוֹד *foundation*, תְּקוּפָה *circuit*.

⇒ ילד *give birth*.

מוֹלָדָה 4.0.0.1 pl.n. **Moladah**—I מלדה—town in Simeon, perh. Kh. el-Waṭen, 13 km ENE of Beer-sheba, <SUBJ> היה *be* Jos 15$_{26}$ 19$_{2}$. <PREP> בְּ of place, *in*, + ישׁב *dwell* Ne 11$_{26}$ 1 C 4$_{28}$; מִן of direction, *from* Ḥorvat ʿUza ost 1$_{2}$.

⇒ ילד *give birth*.

[מוֹלֶדֶת] 22 n.f. **birth; kindred**—cstr. מוֹלֶדֶת; sf. מוֹלַדְתִּי, מוֹלַדְתֵּנוּ, מוֹלַדְתָּהּ, מוֹלַדְתּוֹ, מוֹלַדְתֵּךְ, (מוֹלְדֹתֵךְ) מוֹלַדְתֵּךְ, מוֹלַדְתָּם; pl. sf. מוֹלְדוֹתַיִךְ (מוֹלְדֹתַיִךְ)—**1. birth,** or perh. better **birthplace,*** <NOM CL> מוֹלְדֹתַיִךְ מֵאֶרֶץ הַכְּנַעֲנִי *your birth was from the land of the Canaanites* Ezk 16$_{3}$. <CSTR> אֶרֶץ מוֹלַדְתִּי *land of my birth* Gn 24$_{7}$, מוֹלַדְתֶּךָ *of your birth* Gn 31$_{13}$, מוֹלַדְתֵּךְ *of your* (fem.) *birth* Ru 2$_{11}$, מוֹלַדְתּוֹ *of his birth* Gn 11$_{28}$ Jr 22$_{10}$, מוֹלַדְתֵּנוּ *of our birth* Jr 46$_{16}$, מוֹלַדְתָּם *of their birth* Ezk 23$_{15}$. <COLL> מוֹלֶדֶת || מְכֹרָה *origin* Ezk 16$_{3}$; + עַם *people* Jr 46$_{16}$, אָב *father* Ru 2$_{11}$, אֵם *mother* Ru 2$_{11}$, בַּיִת *house* of father Gn 24$_{7}$; וּמוֹלְדוֹתַיִךְ ... לֹא־כָרַּת שָׁרֵּךְ *and as for your birth ... your navel was not cut* Ezk 16$_{4}$.

2. kindred, <OBJ> נגד hi. *tell of* Est 2$_{10.20}$. <CSTR> אָבְדַן מוֹלַדְתִּי *destruction of my kindred* Est 8$_{6}$. <PREP> לְ of direction, *to*, + שׁוּב *go back* Gn 31$_{3}$ 32$_{10}$; *concerning*, + שׁאל *ask* Gn 43$_{7}$; מִן of direction, *from*, + הלך *go* Gn 12$_{1}$; אֶל *to*, + הלך *go* Gn 24$_{4}$ Nm 10$_{30}$. <COLL> מוֹלֶדֶת || עַם *people* Est 2$_{10.20}$, אֶרֶץ *land* Gn 12$_{1}$ 24$_{4}$ 31$_{3}$ (+) 32$_{10}$ Nm 10$_{8}$; + בַּיִת *house* of father Gn 12$_{1}$.

3. **one born, offspring,** <SUBJ> היה *be* Gn 48$_{6}$. <OBJ> ילד hi. *beget* Gn 48$_{6}$. <CSTR> מוֹלֶדֶת אָבִיךָ *one born of your father* Lv 18$_{11}$, בַּיִת *of the house(hold)* Lv 18$_{9}$, חוּץ *of the outside*, i.e. not of the household Lv 18$_{9}$. <APP> בַּת *daughter* Lv 18$_{9.9.11}$, אָחוֹת *sister* Lv 18$_{9.9}$.

<SYN> §1 מְכֹרָה *origin*; §2 עַם *people*, אֶרֶץ *land*.

⇒ ילד *give birth*.

[מוּלָה] 1 n.f. **circumcision**—pl. מוּלֹת—<PREP> לְ *because of, with respect to* Ex 4$_{26}$ (חֲתַן־דָּמִים לַמּוּלֹת *a bridegroom of blood because of the circumcision(s)*; or em. לַמּוּלִים *belonging to the circumcised*, i.e. מול pass.).

⇒ מול I *circumcise*.

מוֹלִיד 1 pr.n.m. **Molid,** Judahite, son of Abishur and Abihail, <OBJ> ילד *bear* 1 C 2$_{29}$.

⇒ ילד *give birth*.

מוּם 21.4.7 n.m. **blemish**—מְאוּם (mss מְאוּם); cstr. Si, Q מוּם; sf. מוּמוֹ, מוּמָם; pl. sf. Q מומיה—**blemish, defect, disfigurement, a.** physical, (1) in human (2 S 14$_{25}$ perh. Pr 9$_{7}$* Ca 4$_{7}$ Dn 1$_{4}$ 4QD^{f} 3$_{8}$), resulting from injury (Lv 24$_{19.20}$); as disqualifying from priestly service (Lv 21$_{17.18.21.21.23}$ 22$_{20.21.25}$), military service (1QM 7$_{4}$), participation in assembly (1QSa 2$_{6}$).

(2) in animal, rendering it unsuitable for sacrifice (Nm 19$_{2}$ Dt 17$_{1}$ 15$_{21.21}$ 11QT 52$_{4.10.10}$), though it may be eaten at a suitable distance from the temple (11QT 52$_{17}$).

b. moral, Dt 32$_{5}$ Jb 11$_{15}$ 31$_{7}$ Pr 9$_{7}$ (or em.; see Obj.) Si 11$_{33}$ 30$_{31}$ 44$_{19(B)}$ 47$_{20}$.

<SUBJ> היה *be* Lv 21$_{17}$ 22$_{21}$ Dt 17$_{1}$ 15$_{21.21}$ 2 S 14$_{25}$ 11QT 52$_{4.10.10}$, דבק *cling* Jb 31$_{7}$ (מְאוּם; mss מְאוּם; perh. מְאוּם I *anything*), נתן ni. *be given* Si 44$_{19(B)}$ (Bmg דֹּפִי *blemish*).

<NOM CL> בּוֹ מוּם *in him there is a blemish* Lv 21$_{18.21}$ 22$_{20}$, vars. Lv 21$_{21.23}$ 22$_{25}$ (|| מָשְׁחָת *corruption*), אֵין־בָּהּ מוּם *there is no blemish in it* Nm 19$_{2}$, vars. Ca 4$_{7}$ Dn 1$_{4}$ (+ טוֹבֵי מַרְאֶה *of good appearance*), יש בה מום *there is a blemish in it* 11QT 52$_{17}$, מום עולם בבשרו *there is a permanent blemish in his flesh* 1QM 7$_{4}$.

<OBJ> נתן *give*, i.e. cause Lv 24$_{19.20}$ Si 30$_{31}$ 47$_{20}$ (ת[תן]), נשׂא *lift*, i.e. incur Si 11$_{33}$, לקח *receive* Pr 9$_{7}$ (or em. כְּלִמָּה *shame*, or חֶרְפָּה *reproach*), ספר pi. *disclose* 4QD^{f} 3$_{8}$.

<CSTR> מום עולם *blemish of everlastingness*, i.e. permanent blemish Si 11$_{33}$ 1QM 7$_{4}$; בני מום *sons of a blemish*, i.e. blemished sons Dt 32$_{5(Sam)}$, כָּל־מוּם *any blemish* Lv 22$_{21}$ Dt 15$_{21}$ (כֹּל) Dn 1$_{4(Qr)}$ (Kt מאום) 11QT 52$_{4.10}$ (both כול), כול מומיה *all her blemishes* 4QD^{f} 3$_{8}$.

<APP> כֹּל דָּבָר רָע *any bad thing* Dt 17$_{1}$.

<ADJ> רַע *bad* Dt 15$_{21}$ 11QT 52$_{4.10}$.

<PREP> מִן privative, *without*, + נשׂא *lift* face Jb 11$_{15}$.

<COLL> מום מנוגע בבשרו לראות עינים *one who is stricken with a blemish in his flesh visible to the eyes* 1QSa 2$_{6}$, לֹא בָּנָיו מוּמָם appar. *they are not his sons (because of) their blemish* Dt 32$_{5}$ (Sam בני מום *sons of a blemish*).

Also perh. 4QNidd 2.1$_{2}$ (במומו; others בימי *in the days of*) perh. 4Q415 11$_{5}$ (מומיה; others מימיה *her waters*).

<SYN> מָשְׁחָת *corruption*.

מומכן, see מְמוּכָן *Memucan*.

[מוֹנֶה] *merchant*, see מנה *count*.

[מוּסָב] 1 n.[m.] **enclosure**—cstr. מוּסַב—<NOM CL> מוּסַב־הַבַּיִת לְמַעְלָה לְמַעְלָה *enclosure of the house was upwards and upwards* Ezk 41$_{7}$ (or em. מוּסָב the house *was surrounded*, i.e. סבב ho.). <CSTR> מוּסַב־הַבַּיִת *enclosure of the house* Ezk 41$_{7}$ (or em.; see Nom. Cl.).

⇒ סבב *surround*.

[מוֹסָד] I 13.0.13 n.m. **foundation**—Q מוסד; cstr. Q מוסד; pl. Q מוסדים, מוֹסָדוֹת; cstr. מוֹסְדוֹת (מֹסְדוֹת), מוֹסְדֵי (מֹסְדֵי)—**foundation, ruins, remains** (Is 58$_{12}$), <SUBJ> שמע *hear* Mc 6$_{2}$, רוע hi. *shout* 4Q418 69.2$_{9}$, מוט ni. *be shaken* Ps 82$_{5}$, רגז *quake* 2 S 22$_{8}$, רעשׁ *tremble* Is 24$_{18}$, נוע *tremble* 4QAdmon 1$_{4}$ (ו[י]נעו), גלה ni. *be revealed* 2 S 22$_{16}$||Ps 18$_{16}$, חקר ni. *be searched out* Jr 31$_{37}$, שׂרף ni. *be burned* 1QH 17$_{13}$ ([בהשרף]).

<OBJ> להט pi. *set ablaze* Dt 32$_{22}$, בין hi. *understand* Is 40$_{21}$ (or em.; see Cstr.), יסד pi. *establish* 1QS 5$_{5}$, קום pol. *raise up* Is 58$_{12}$, חקק *decree* Pr 8$_{29}$ (unless חוק

gather; or em. חזק pi. *strengthen*).

<CSTR> מוסד אמת *foundation of truth* 1QS 5_{5}, מוֹסְדֵי אֶרֶץ *foundations of the earth* Mc 6_{2} (מֹסְדֵי) Is 24_{18} (אָרֶץ) 40_{21} (מוֹסְדוֹת הָאָרֶץ, perh. *laws of nature;** or em. מִיסֻּדַת *from the foundation of* [from יְסוּדָה]) Jr 31_{37} Ps 82_{6} Pr 8_{29} (perh. *the laws of nature;** both אֶרֶץ) 4QAdmon 1_{4} ([ארו]ץ) 4QShir^{b} 10_{12} 42_{6} (הארץ), מוֹסְדֵי הָרִים *foundations of the mountains* Dt 32_{22} Ps 18_{8} (mss מוֹסְדוֹת) 1QH 17_{13}, מוֹסְדוֹת תֵּבֵל *foundations of the world* 2 S 22_{16}||Ps 18_{16} (2 S מֹסְדוֹת) 4QNarrB 1_{7} ([מ]וסדות), הַשָּׁמַיִם *of the heavens* 2 S 22_{8} (mss הָרִים as ||Ps 18_{8}), הרקיע *of the firmament* 4Q418 69.2_{9}, רקיע *of the firmament of* wonder 11QShirShabb 8_{5}, עפרו *of his dust* 4QShir^{b} 16_{3}, אש *of fire* 4QBer^{a} 1.2_{3}, פלא *of wonder*, i.e. wonderful foundations 11QShirShabb 8_{7}, מוֹסְדֵי דוֹר־וָדוֹר *remains of many generations* Is 58_{12}; כָּל־מוֹסְדֵי *all the foundations of* Ps 82_{5} 4QAdmon 1_{4} 4QShir^{b} 10_{12} (כול).

<APP> אֵיתָן *reliable one* Mc 6_{2}.

<PREP> לְ *as, for (the purpose of)* perh. 11QShirShabb 8_{7}, + לקח *take* Jr 51_{26} (|| פִּנָּה *corner[stone]*); בְּ of place, *in* 4QShir^{b} 10_{12}, + אכל *devour* 4QShir^{b} 16_{3}; אֶל *to* 4QShir^{b} 42_{6}; לְעֻמַּת *alongside*, + עשׂה ni. *be made* 11QT 40_{10} ([ע]שוים).

<COLL> מוֹסָד || פִּנָּה *corner(stone)* Jr 51_{26}, אָפִיק *channel* 2 S 22_{16}||Ps 18_{16}, חָרְבָּה *ruin* Is 58_{12}; + שָׁמַיִם *heaven* Jr 31_{37}, אֶרֶץ *earth* Dt 32_{22}, יָם *sea* Pr 8_{29}.

ארבעת מוסדי *four foundations of* 11QShirShabb 8_{5}.

Also 4Q417 2.1_{26} ([מ]וסודו) 4QNarrB 2_{2} (מוסדו[ת]) 11QShirShabb 5_{10}.

<SYN> פִּנָּה *corner(stone)*, אָפִיק *channel*, חָרְבָּה *ruin*.

⇒ יסד I *establish*.

*[מוֹסָד] II $_{0.0.2}$ n.[m.] **council**—pl. cstr. Q מוסדי— <CSTR> מוסדי אנשים *councils of men* 4QShirShabb^{a} 2_{2} (+מַחֲנֶה *camp*); משמע ... מוסדי *hearing of ... the councils of* 4QShirShabb^{d} 1.2_{12}. <PREP> לְ of agent, *by*, + ירא ni. *be revered* 4QShirShabb^{a} 2_{2}.

⇒ cf. סוֹד *council*.

מוּסָד $_{2}$ n.m. **foundation**—cstr. מוּסַד—**foundation** (Is 28_{16} Pr 15_{33} [if em.; see Nom. Cl.]), **founding, laying of foundation** (2 C 8_{16}), **base** (2 K 16_{18} [if em.; see Cstr.]), <SUBJ> יסד ho. *be established* Is 28_{16} (מוּסָד lacking in mss). <NOM CL> יִרְאַת י׳ מוּסַד חָכְמָה *the fear of Y. is a foundation of wisdom* Pr 15_{33} (if em. מוּסַר *discipline of*). <OBJ> בנה *build* 2 K 16_{18} (if em.; see Cstr.), סבב hi. *turn*, i.e. remove 2 K 16_{18} (if em.; see Cstr.). <CSTR> מוּסַד בֵּית־י׳ *founding of the house of Y.* 2 C 8_{16}, מוּסַד חָכְמָה *foundation of wisdom* Pr 15_{33} (if em.; see Nom. Cl.), מוּסַד הַשֶּׁבֶת *base of the seat* 2 K 16_{18} (if em. מוּסַךְ הַשַּׁבָּת [Qr] perh. *covered way of the sabbath*); פִּנַּת יִקְרַת מוּסָד *a precious cornerstone of a foundation* Is 28_{16}, יוֹם מוּסַד *day of the founding of* 2 C 8_{16}.

⇒ יסד I *establish*.

מוּסָדָה $_{2}$ n.f. **foundation, appointment**—pl. cstr. Qr מוּסְדוֹת—**1. foundation,** <NOM CL> מוּסְדוֹת הַצְּלָעוֹת מְלוֹ הַקָּנֶה *foundations of the side chambers were*, i.e. measured, *a full reed* Ezk $41_{8(Qr)}$. <CSTR> מוּסְדוֹת הַצְּלָעוֹת *foundations of the side chambers* Ezk $41_{8(Qr)}$ (Kt מיסדות *foundations of*, i.e. יסד pu. ptc.).

2. appointment, <CSTR> מַטֵּה מוּסָדָה *staff of appointment*, i.e. appointed staff Is 30_{32} (or em. מוּסָרֹה *of his discipline*).

⇒ יסד I *establish*.

מוּסָדוֹת, see מוֹסָד I *foundation*.

[מוּסָךְ] I $_{1}$ n.[m.] **covered way** (unless מוּסָךְ II *fence* or III *bench*)—cstr. Qr מוּסַךְ (Kt מיסך)—appar. **covered way,** in Ahab's palace, <OBJ> בנה *build* 2 K $16_{18(Qr)}$, סבב hi. *turn*, perh. remove 2 K $16_{18(Qr)}$. <CSTR> מוּסַךְ הַשַּׁבָּת *covered way of the sabbath* 2 K $16_{18(Qr)}$ (or em. מוּסַד הַשֶּׁבֶת *base of the seat*).

⇒ סכך *cover*.

*[מוּסָךְ] II $_{1}$ n.[m.] **fence** (unless מוּסָךְ I *covered way* or III *bench*)—cstr. Qr מוּסַךְ (Kt מיסך)—**fence, rampart,** at Ahab's palace, <OBJ> שׁבת hi. *remove* 2 K 16_{18} (Qr) (if em. מוּסַךְ הַשַּׁבָּת appar. *rampart of the sabbath* to מוּסַךְ הִשְׁבִּת *he removed the rampart*).

*[מוּסָךְ] III $_{1}$ n.[m.] **bench** (unless מוּסָךְ I *covered*

way or II *fence*)—cstr. Qr מוּסַךְ (Kt מיסך)—**bench, divan,** in Ahab's palace, <OBJ> בנה *build* 2 K 16$_{18(Qr)}$, סבב hi. *turn*, perh. remove 2 K 16$_{18(Qr)}$. <CSTR> מוּסַךְ הַשַּׁבָּת *bench of the sabbath* 2 K 16$_{18(Qr)}$.

*[מוֹסָר] I $_1$ n.[m.] **bond**—sf. מֹסָרָם—(unless מוֹסָר II *heart* or from מוּסָר *discipline* or מוֹסֵר *bond*), <PREP> בְּ *from*, + חתה *snatch* Jb 33$_{16}$ (if em. יַחְתֹּם appar. *he seals* to יַחְתֹּם).

*[מוֹסָר] II $_4$ n.[m.] **heart**—cstr. מוּסַר; sf. מֹסָרָם—**heart, basis, essence** (unless from מוּסָר *discipline*), <NOM CL> יִרְאַת י׳ מוּסַר חָכְמָה *the fear of Y. is the essence of wisdom* Pr 15$_{33}$, מוּסַר הֲבָלִים עֵץ הוּא *the heart of idols is wood* Jr 10$_8$. <CSTR> מוּסַר הֲבָלִים *heart of idols* Jr 10$_8$, אֱוִיל *of a fool* Pr 7$_{22}$, חָכְמָה *of wisdom* Pr 15$_{33}$. <PREP> בְּ of place, *in(to), on*, + בוא *come* Pr 7$_{22}$, חתם *seal* Jb 33$_{16}$ (unless מוֹסָר I *bond*).

[מוֹסֵר] $_{3.0.2}$ n.m. **bond**—pl. cstr. מוֹסְרֵי; sf. מוֹסְרַי, מוֹסְרֵיכֶם—**bond, fetter; trap** for deer (Pr 7$_{22}$ if em.; see Prep.), <SUBJ> חזק *be strong* Is 28$_{22}$. <NOM CL> אֲנִי מוֹסֵר לְכֻלָּם *I am a bond for all of them* Ho 5$_2$ (if em. מוּסָר *chastisement*). <OBJ> פתח pi. *loosen* Jb 12$_{18}$ (if em.; see Cstr.), htp. *loosen* Is 52$_2$ (or em.; see Prep.), שׂים *place* 4QSapDidA 1$_5$ ([שׂ]ים). <CSTR> מוֹסֵר מְלָכִים *bond of kings* Jb 12$_{18}$ (if em. מוּסַר *discipline of*), מוֹסְרֵי צַוָּארֵךְ *bonds of your neck* Is 52$_2$. <PREP> לְ introducing object, + פתח pi. *loosen* Ps 116$_{16}$; בְּ introducing object, + חתם *seal* perh. Jb 33$_{16}$ (but prob. מֹסָרָם is from מוּסָר *discipline*); מִן of direction, *from*, + פתח htp. *loosen oneself* Is 52$_2$ (if em. מוֹסְרֵי to מִמּוֹסְרֵי *from the bonds of*); אֶל *to*, + בוא *come* Pr 7$_{22}$ (if em. מוּסַר *chastisement of*).

Also 4QBark^e 3$_3$.

⇒ אסר *bind*.

מוּסָר $_{50.13.11}$ n.m. **discipline**—cstr. מוּסַר; sf. מוּסָרִי, מוּסָרְךָ (Q מוסרכה), מֻסָרָם—**1. discipline,** as **instruction, training,** Dt 11$_2$ Jr 10$_8$ (unless from מוֹסָר II *heart*) 17$_{23}$ 35$_{13}$ Ps 50$_{17}$ (+ דָּבָר *word*) Jb 20$_3$ Pr 1$_2$ (|| חָכְמָה *wisdom*, + אִמְרֵי בִינָה *words of understanding*) 1$_3$ (+ צֶדֶק *righteousness*, מִשְׁפָּט *justice*, מֵישָׁר *uprightness*) 1$_7$ (|| חָכְמָה, + דַּעַת *knowledge*) 1$_8$ (|| תּוֹרָה *teaching*) 3$_{11}$ (+ תּוֹכַחַת *reproof*) 4$_1$ (+ בִּינָה *understanding*) 4$_{13}$ 5$_{12}$ (+ תּוֹכַחַת) 5$_{23}$ 6$_{23}$ 8$_{10}$ (+ דַּעַת; :: כֶּסֶף *silver*) 8$_{33}$ 10$_{17}$ (+ תּוֹכַחַת) 12$_1$ (|| דַּעַת; + תּוֹכַחַת) 13$_1$ (or em.; see Cstr.) 13$_{18}$ 15$_{5.32}$ (all three + תּוֹכַחַת) 15$_{33}$ (unless from מוֹסָר II *heart*; or em.; see Cstr.) 16$_{22}$ 19$_{20}$ (|| עֵצָה *counsel*) 19$_{27}$ (+ אִמְרֵי־דָעַת *words of knowledge*) 23$_{12}$ (+ אִמְרֵי־דָעַת) 23$_{23}$ (|| חָכְמָה, בִּינָה) 24$_{32}$ Si 6$_{22}$ 34$_{12.17.22}$ 35$_{2.14}$ (|| מַעֲנֶה *answer*) 37$_{31}$ 41$_{14(B).14}$ 47$_{14}$ 50$_{27}$ (|| מָשָׁל *proverb*) 1QH 2$_{14}$ (+ אֱמֶת *truth*) 1QS 6$_{14}$ 4Q416 2.3$_{13}$ 4QBéat 1$_2$ (מו[סר]).

2. discipline, as **correction, chastisement** (distinction from §1 not alw. clear), Is 26$_{16}$ 30$_{32}$ (if em.; see Cstr.) 53$_5$ (+ חַבּוּרָה *blow*) Jr 2$_{30}$ 5$_3$ 7$_{28}$ 30$_{14}$ 32$_{33}$ Ho 5$_2$ (or em.; see Nom. Cl.) Zp 3$_{2.7}$ Jb 5$_{17}$ appar. 12$_{18}$ (or em.; see Cstr.) Pr 7$_{22}$ (unless from מוֹסָר II *heart*; or em.; see Cstr.) 13$_{24}$ 15$_{10}$ (or em.; see Nom. Cl.) 22$_{15}$ 23$_{13}$ Si 42$_{5(Bmg).8(B)}$ 1QH 6$_4$ (מו[סר]) 4QDibHam^a 1.5$_{17}$.

3. warning, Ezk 5$_{15}$ (|| מְשַׁמָּה *horror*, + חֶרְפָּה *reproach*, גְּדוּפָה *reproach*) Jb 36$_{10}$.

<SUBJ> היה *be* Ezk 5$_{15}$.

<NOM CL> בֵּן חָכָם מוּסַר אָב appar. *a wise son is the discipline of his father* Pr 13$_1$ (or em.; see Cstr.), יִרְאַת י׳ מוּסַר חָכְמָה *the fear of Y. is the discipline of wisdom* Pr 15$_{33}$ (unless from מוֹסָר II *heart*; or em.; see Cstr.), מוּסַר אֱוִלִים אִוֶּלֶת *the discipline of fools is folly* Pr 16$_{22}$, מוּסַר הֲבָלִים עֵץ הוּא *the instruction of images is wood* Jr 2$_8$ (or em. עֵץ to מֵעֵצָה *without counsel*), אֲנִי מוּסָר לְכֻלָּם *I am a chastisement for all of them* Ho 5$_2$ (or em. מְיַסֵּר לָכֶם *the one who chastises you*, or מוֹסֵר *a bond*), מוּסָרְךָ לָמוֹ *your chastisement was to them* Is 26$_{16}$, מוּסַר שְׁלוֹמֵנוּ עָלָיו *the chastisement of*, i.e. that brings, *our wholeness was upon him* Is 53$_5$, מוּסָר רָע לְעֹזֵב אֹרַח *there is severe discipline for the one who abandons the path* Pr 15$_{10}$ (or em. אֹרַח רָע לְעֹזֵב מוּסָר *there is an evil path for the one who abandons discipline*), המוסר כשמה כן הוא *discipline is like her* (wisdom's) *name* Si 6$_{22}$.

<OBJ> שׁמע *hear* Jb 20$_3$ Pr 1$_8$ 4$_1$ 8$_{10}$ 19$_{27}$ (or em. לִשְׁמֹעַ to לִשְׁמֹר *to keep*) Si 41$_{14}$, ראה *see* Dt 11$_2$, ידע *know* Dt 11$_2$ Pr 1$_2$ 4QBéat 1$_2$ (מו[סר ... לדע]ת), לקח *take* Jr 2$_{30}$ 5$_3$ 7$_{28}$ 17$_{23}$ 32$_{33}$ Zp 3$_{2.7}$ Pr 1$_3$ 8$_{10}$ 24$_{32}$ Si 34$_{22}$ 35$_{14}$ 4Q469 2$_2$, קבל pi. *accept* Pr 19$_{20}$, שׁמר *keep* Pr 10$_{17}$ 19$_{27}$ (if em.;

see above), קנה *buy* Pr 23_{23}, נשׂג hi. *attain to* 1QS 6_{14}, צוף hi. *overflow with* Si 47_{14}, נכה hi. *strike with* Jr 30_{14}, שׁחר pi. *seek with* Pr 13_{24}, אהב *love* Pr 12_1 13_1 (if em.; see Cstr.) 1QH 2_{14}, אוב *love* Pr 13_1 (if em.; see Cstr.), שׂנא *hate* Ps 50_{17} Pr 5_{12}, בוז *despise* Pr 1_7, נאץ *spurn* Pr 15_5, מאס *reject* Jb 5_{17} Pr 3_{11}, עזב *forsake* Pr 15_{10} (if em.; see Nom. Cl.), פרע *let go of* Pr 13_{18} 15_{32}, מנע *withhold* Pr 23_{13}, פתח pi. *loosen* Jb 12_{18} (or em.; see Cstr.).

<CSTR> מוּסַר י׳ *discipline of Y.* Dt 11_2 Pr 3_{11}, שַׁדַּי *of the Almighty* Jb 5_{17}, אָב *of a father* Pr 4_1 13_1 (or em. מוּסָר אֹהֵב *loves discipline*, or מוּסָר אָב *loves discipline*, i.e. אָב is אוב ptc.;* ms יִשְׁמַע אָב *he hears his father*), אָבִיךָ *of your father* Pr 1_8, אָבִיו *of his father* Pr 15_5, מְלָכִים *of kings* Jb 12_{18} (or em. מוֹסֵר *bond of*), אֱוִלִים *of fools* Pr 16_{22}, חָכְמָה *of wisdom* Pr 15_{33} (unless from מוּסָר II *heart*; or em. מוּסַד *foundation of*), הַשְׂכֵּל *of prudence* Pr 1_3, מוּסַר הֲבָלִים *instruction of images* (or worthless instruction) Jr 10_8 (unless from מוּסָר II *heart*), מוסר לחם ויין *instruction of*, i.e. concerning, *food and wine* Si 34_{12}, בשת *of*, i.e. concerning, *shame* Si $41_{14(B).14}$, שכל *of wisdom* Si 50_{27}.

מו[ו]סר מוכיחי *correction of those who rebuke of*, i.e. with, righteousness 1QH 6_4, מוּסַר אַכְזָרִי *chastisement of a cruel one* Jr 30_{14} (or em. מוּסָר cruel *chastisement*), אֱוִיל *of a fool* Pr 7_{22} (unless from מוּסָר II *heart*; or em. מוּסֵר אַיָּל *a deer* enters *a trap*), מוסר פותה וכסיל *chastisement of the simple one and the fool* Si $42_{8(B)}$ (Bmg מרדות *chastisement of*), מוּסַר שְׁלוֹמֵנוּ *chastisement of*, i.e. that brings, *our wholeness* Is 53_5, כְּלִמָּתִי *of my disgrace*, i.e. that dishonours me Jb 20_3 (or em. כִּלְיוֹתַי *of my heart*).

אוהבי מוסר *ones who love discipline* 1QH 2_{14}, תּוֹכְחוֹת מוּסָר *reproofs of discipline* Pr 6_{23} (ms תּוֹכַחַת *reproof of*), צקון מוסרכה perh. *distress of your chastisement* 4QDibHam^a 1.5_{17}, שֵׁבֶט מוּסָר *rod of chastisement* Pr 22_{15}, מַטֵּה מוּסָרֹה *staff of his chastisement* Is 30_{32} (if em. מוּסָדָה *of appointment*), כל מוסר *all discipline* 4Q 416 2.3_{13}.

<APP> מַכָּה *blow* Jr 30_{14}.

<ADJ> אַכְזָרִי *cruel* Jr 30_{14} (if em.; see Cstr.).

<PREP> לְ of direction, *to*, + בוא hi. *bring* Pr 23_{12}, גלה *uncover* ear Jb 36_{10} 1QH 6_4 (ל[מו]סר); בְּ of instrument, *by (means of), with*, + חתם *seal* Jb 33_{16} (unless מֹסָרָם is from מוֹסֵר *bond* or מוּסָר I *bond* or II *heart*; or em. יַחְתֹּם to יְחָתֵּם for their instruction *he descends to them* [from נחת]; or em. בְּמֹסָרָם יַחְתֹּם to בְּמוֹרָאִים יְחִתֵּם *he terrifies them with fearful things*); of place, *into*, + בוא hi. *bring* 4Q416 2.3_{13}; introducing object, + חזק hi. *grasp* Pr 4_{13}; אֶל *to* Pr 7_{22} (unless from מוּסָר II *heart*; or em.; see Cstr.); עַל *on account of*, + נשׂא *bear* favour Si 35_2, בושׁ *be ashamed* Si $42_{5Bmg).8(B)}$; בַּעֲבוּר *for the sake of*, + חדל *cease* Si 34_{17}.

<COLL> הוּא יָמוּת בְּאֵין מוּסָר *he dies through lack of discipline* Pr 5_{23}, בלא מוסר רבים יגועו *for lack of discipline many die* Si 37_{31}, מוסר שכל ... לשמעון *instruction of wisdom ... of Simeon* son of Jeshua, son of Eleazar, son of Sira Si 50_{27}.

Also 4QMyst^a 30_4 4QsapDidB 1_1 4Q418 169_3 257_1 4QBark^c 1.1_8 4QBark^f 1.14.

<SYN> §1 חָכְמָה *wisdom*, בִּינָה *understanding*, תּוֹרָה *teaching*, דַּעַת *knowledge*, עֵצָה *counsel*, מַעֲנֶה *answer*, מָשָׁל *proverb*; §3 מְשַׁמָּה *horror*.

<ANT> כֶּסֶף *silver*.

⇒ יסר I *discipline*.

[מוֹסֵרָה] I $_8$ n.f. **bond**—pl. מוֹסֵרוֹת; cstr. מֹסְרוֹת; מוֹסְרוֹתֵיהֶם, מוֹסְרוֹתֵימוֹ, מוֹסְרוֹתַיִךְ, מוֹסְרוֹתֶיךָ—**bond, fetter, thong** of yoke (Jr 27_2), <OBJ> נתק pi. *tear apart* Jr 2_{20} 5_5 30_8 Na 1_{13} Ps 2_3 107_{14}, פתח pi. *loosen* Jb 39_5, עשׂה *make* Jr 27_2. <CSTR> מֹסְרוֹת עָרוֹד *bonds of the wild ass* Jb 39_5. <COLL> מוֹסֵרָה || עֹל *yoke* Jr 2_{20} 5_5 30_8 (+), מוֹט *bar (of yoke)* Jr 27_2 Na 1_{13} (+), עֲבֹות *cord* Ps 2_3.

<SYN> עֹל *yoke*, מוֹט *bar (of yoke)*, עֲבֹות *cord*.

⇒ אסר *bind*.

מוֹסֵרָה II $_1$ pl.n. **Moserah,** station of the Exodus, where Aaron died, location unknown, ident. with מֹסֵרוֹת *Moseroth* at Nm $33_{30.31}$, <COLL> בְּנֵי יִשְׂרָאֵל נָסְעוּ ... מוֹסֵרָה *the Israelites journeyed ... (to) Moserah* Dt 10_6 (Sam מִמֹּסֵרוֹת *from Moseroth*).

⇒ מֹסֵרוֹת *Moseroth*.

[מוֹעָד] I $_1$ n.[m.] **place of assembly** (unless מוֹעָד II *hoarde*)—pl. sf. מוֹעָדָיו—in army, <PREP> בְּ of place, *in, among*, + בדד *be alone* Is 14$_{31}$ (or em. בְּמוֹ־עֲדָיו *in his haste*, or מִבַּעֲרוֹ *from his burning*; 1QIsa^{a} אין מודד במודעיו appar. *none measures against his acquaintances*).

⇒ יעד *appoint*.

*[מוֹעָד] II $_{1}$ n.[m.] **horde** (unless מוֹעֵד I *place of assembly*)—pl. sf. מוֹעָדָיו—<PREP> בְּ *from*, + בדד *withdraw*, i.e. escape Is 14$_{31}$.

מוֹעֵד I $_{223.6.140}$ n.m. **appointment, meeting**—מֹעֵד; cstr. מוֹעֵד (מֹעֵד); sf. מוֹעֲדוֹ (מֹעֲדוֹ), מוֹעֲדָהּ, מוֹעֲדֵךְ, מוֹעֲדֵנוּ, מוֹעֲדָם; pl. מוֹעֲדִים, מוֹעֲדוֹת; cstr. מוֹעֲדֵי (מֹעֲדֵי); sf. מוֹעֲדַי (מֹעֲדַי), Sam מוֹעֲדָיו, מוֹעֲדֶיהָ, mss מוֹעֲדֵינוּ, מוֹעֲדֵיכֶם (מֹעֲדֵיכֶם), Q מועדיהם (Q מועדיהמה).

1a. meeting, assembly, <SUBJ> שׁמע *hear* Mc 6$_{9}$ (if em. מוֹעֵד: מִי יְעָדָהּ *who has appointed it. Yet to* מוֹעֵד הָעִיר *assembly of the city*). <OBJ> קרא *call*, i.e. summon Lm 1$_{15}$. <CSTR> מוֹעֵד הָעִיר *assembly of the city* Mc 6$_{9}$ (if em.; see Subj.); קְרָאֵי מוֹעֵד *summoned ones*, i.e. members, *of the assembly* Nm 16$_{2}$, קוראי מועד *summoned ones*, i.e. members, *of the assembly* 1QM 2$_{7}$ 1QSa 2$_{2.11.13}$ (both [קורא]י), בֵּית מוֹעֵד *house of meeting* Jb 30$_{23}$ 1QM 3$_{4}$ 4QM^{a} 1$_{9}$ ([מו]עד), הַר־ *mountain of* Is 14$_{13}$. <COLL> מוֹעֵד || עֵדָה *congregation* Nm 16$_{2}$; בֵּית מוֹעֵד לְכָל־חָי *house of meeting for all living* Jb 30$_{23}$.

1b. אֹהֶל מוֹעֵד **tent of meeting,** <CSTR> אֹהֶל מוֹעֵד *tent of meeting* Ex 27$_{21}$ 28$_{43}$ 29$_{4+6t}$ 30$_{16.18.20.26.36}$ 31$_{7}$ 33$_{7.7}$ 35$_{21}$ 38$_{8.30}$ 39$_{32}$ 39$_{40}$ 40$_{2+11t}$ Lv 1$_{1.3.5}$ 3$_{2.8.13}$ 4$_{4+7t}$ 6$_{9.19.23}$ 8$_{3.4.31.33.35}$ 9$_{5.23}$ 10$_{7.9}$ 12$_{6}$ 14$_{11.23}$ 15$_{14.29}$ 16$_{7+5t}$ 17$_{4.5.6.9}$ 19$_{21}$ 24$_{3}$ Nm 1$_{1}$ 2$_{2.17}$ 3$_{7.8.25.25.38}$ 4$_{3+15t}$ 6$_{10.13.18}$ 7$_{5.89}$ 8$_{9+5t}$ 10$_{3}$ 11$_{16}$ 12$_{4}$ 14$_{10}$ 16$_{18.19}$ 17$_{7.8.15.19}$ 18$_{4+5t}$ 19$_{4}$ 20$_{6}$ 25$_{6}$ 27$_{2}$ 31$_{54}$ Dt 31$_{14.14}$ Jos 18$_{1}$ 19$_{51}$ 1 S 2$_{22}$ 1 K 8$_{4}$||2 C 5$_{5}$ 1 C 6$_{17}$ 9$_{21}$ 23$_{32}$ 2 C 1$_{3.6.13}$ 4QTohB^{b} 1$_{5}$ (א[ו]הל) 4QSela 9.2$_{2}$ ([מו]עד) 9.2$_{12.13}$ (both א]הל מו[עד).

2. meeting place, appointed place, <OBJ> שׂרף *burn* Ps 74$_{8}$, שׁחת pi. *destroy* Lm 2$_{6}$. <CSTR> כָּל־מוֹעֲדֵי־אֵל *all the meeting places of God* Ps 74$_{8}$. <PREP> לְ *at*, + קרא *meet* Jos 8$_{14}$ (or em. לַמּוֹרָד *at the descent*); בְּקֶרֶב *within*, + שׁאג *roar* Ps 74$_{4}$.

3. appointed time, due season; oft. in general, **time, season,** <SUBJ> בוא *come* Ps 102$_{14}$ (or del.), תמם *come to an end* 1QH 12$_{17}$ (יתמו כול מו[עדי]).

<NOM CL> מועד מלחמה היום הזה *today is the appointed time of war* 1QM 15$_{12}$ (יום *day of* corrected to מועד), היום מועדו להכניע ולהשפיל *today is his appointed time to humble and to bring low* 1QM 17$_{5}$, הלא די אנוש נכון מועד *is not the appointed time sufficient for a well-established person?* Si 34$_{19(Bmg)}$ (B מִזְעָר *a little*), מועדי צרותם בממשלת משטמתו *the appointed times of their distress are because of the dominion of his hostility* 1QS 3$_{23}$.

<OBJ> דבר pi. *speak of* Gn 21$_{2}$ 2 K 4$_{17}$, אמר *speak of* 1 S 13$_{8(mss)}$, ידע *know* Jr 8$_{7}$, שׂים *set* Ex 9$_{5}$ Jb 34$_{34}$ (if em. עוֹד *yet*), לקח *take*, i.e. set Ps 75$_{3}$, קבל pi. *accept* 4QpPs^{a} 1.2$_{9}$, יעד *appoint* 2 S 20$_{5}$, פקד *appoint* Si 33$_{10(B)}$ (Bmg מִצְעָר *a little while*), קום pol. *establish* 4QPrFêtes^{b} 2$_{3}$, עבר hi. *cause to pass* Jr 46$_{17}$.

<CSTR> מועד אל *appointed time of God* 1QM 1$_{8}$ 3$_{7}$ 4$_{7}$, מוֹעֵד דָּוִד *of*, i.e. time agreed by, *David* 1 S 20$_{35}$, מוֹעֵד צֵאתְךָ *time of your going out* Dt 16$_{6}$, [מו]עד צרכך *time of your need* Si 10$_{26}$, מוֹעֵד הַיָּמִים *appointed time of the days* 1 S 13$_{11}$, [מו]עדי השנה *appointed times of the year* 4QNidd 1.1$_{4}$, מֹעֵד שְׁנַת *appointed time of the year of* Dt 31$_{10}$ 1QM 2$_{6}$ (מועד), מועד לילה *appointed time of the night* 1QH 12$_{6}$, מועד[י] לילה *appointed times of the night* 4QPrQuot 33.10$_{21}$ 41.2$_{10}$ ([מ]ועדי לילה) 51$_{10}$, [מו]עדי יום ולילה *appointed times of day and night* 4QParGenEx 2$_{12}$, מוֹעֵד קֵץ *appointed time of the end* Dn 8$_{19}$, מועדי תעודותי *appointed times of my fixed times* 4QShir^{b} 63.2$_{2}$, תעודותיו *of his fixed times* 1QS 3$_{10}$, תעודותם *of their fixed times* 1QS 1$_{9}$, תעודות *of the fixed times of* 1QM 14$_{13}$.

מועד פקודה *appointed time of visitation* 1QS 4$_{18}$ 4QD^{a} 1$_{2}$, פקודתו *of his visitation* 1QS 3$_{18}$, משפט *of judgment* 1QS 4$_{20}$, נקם *of vengeance* 1QM 15$_{6}$, מלחמה *of war* 1QM 15$_{5}$ ([המלח]מה) 15$_{12}$ (יום *day of* corrected to מועד), התעות *of error* 4QpPs^{a} 1.2$_{9}$ 1.3$_{3}$ (ה[תע]ות), דרור *of liberty* 1QS 10$_{8}$, [מו]עדי דרו[ר] *appointed times of liberty* 4QBer^{a} 1.2$_{11}$, מועד רצון *appointed time of goodwill* 1QH 15$_{15}$, רחמיך *of your compassion* 4QPrFêtes^{b} 2$_{2}$, מועדי בריתי *appointed times of my covenant* 4QpsEzek^{a} 45$_{6}$, מועד שלומנו *appointed time of our peace* 1QLitPr 1$_{1}$ (שלומ[נו]) 4QPrFêtes^{c} 3$_{2}$, [מ]ועדי של[ום] *ap-*

pointed times of peace 4QRitPur 17_{2}, מועד מנוח *appointed time of rest* 4QPrQuot 24.7_{5} ([מו]עד]), תענית *of fasting* 4QPrFêtes^{b} 2_{3}.

מועדי צרות *appointed times of distress* 4QShir^{b} 11_{2} ([מו]עדי), צרותם *of their distress* 1QS 3_{23}, חושך *of darkness* 1QM 1_{8}, שממה *of desolation* 1QH 12_{17} ([מו]עדי]), קודש *of holiness* 1QM 10_{15} 4QRitMar 76_{2} ([ק]ודש]), טוהר *of purification* 4QBapt 10_{6}, עולם *of eternity* 1QH 13_{20} ([מו]עדי עולם]) 4QPrQuot 29.8_{21} (מועד[י עו]ל[ם]), עולמים *of eternity* 1QM 12_{3} 13_{8} (מוע[ד]י) 4QM^{a} 8.1_{16} 4QPrQuot 64_{8} (מ[ו]ע[ד]י) 4QShir^{b} 35_{8} ([מ]ועדי [עולמים]).

מועד קציר *appointed time of harvest* 1QS 10_{7} 4QRitPur 33.4_{3} (ק[צ]יר), זרע *of sowing* 1QS 10_{7}, דשא *of grass* 1QS 10_{7}, מועדי דשא *appointed times of grass* 4QPrFêtes^{c} 3_{7}, חום *of heat* 4QMyst^{a} 5_{3}, שנים *of the years* 1QS 10_{7}, עתיה *of her times*, i.e. her menstrual periods 4QNidd 3_{1}.

טהורי מועדי *pure ones of the appointed times of* 4QBapt 2.1_{2}, תפלת מועד *prayer of the appointed time of* war 1QM 15_{5}, מבוא מועדים *arrival of the appointed times* 1QS 10_{3}, תקופת מועדים *coming round of the appointed times* 1QH 12_{8}, מועדיהם *of their appointed times* 1QS 10_{6} (=4QS^{b} 19_{5} [תקופו]ת מועדים]), ראשי מועדים *beginnings of the appointed times* 1QS 10_{5}, תום מועד *completion of the appointed time of* 4QD^{a} 1_{2}, תום ... מועדי *completion of ... the appointed times of* 1QM 1_{8}, כול מועדי *all the appointed times of* 1QH 12_{17} ([כול] מו[עדי]) 1QM 1_{8} 12_{3} 4QBer^{b} 1_{3} 2_{7} (מועד[י]) 4QM^{a} 8.1_{16} 11.2_{18} 4QPrQuot 29.8_{21} ([מו]עדי]) 33.10_{21} (מועד[י]) 41.2_{10} ([מ]ועדי]) 51_{10} ([כול]) 64_{8} ([כול] מ[ו]ע[ד]י) 4QShir^{b} 35_{8} ([כול מ]ועדי), כול מועדיהם *all their appointed times* 1QH 1_{24}, כול מועדיה *all her appointed times* 4Q418 118_{3}.

<APP> חֹדֶשׁ *month* Ex 23_{15} 34_{18}, עֶרֶב *evening* Dt 16_{6}, קֵץ *end time* 1QH 13_{20} (מועד[י]).

<ADJ> זֶה *this* Gn 17_{21} 2 K $4_{16.17}$ 1QLitPr 2_{3} (במוע[ד] [הזה]).

<PREP> לְ of time, *at, throughout* Dn 11_{27} 1QH 12_{6} 4QCommGenA 2_{4} perh. 4Q418 118_{3} perh. 4QPrQuot 24.7_{5} ([מו]עד]), + בוא *come* 1 S 13_{11}, יצא *go out* 1 S 20_{35} 4QCommGenD 3_{2}, שׁוב *go back* Gn 18_{14} Dn 11_{29}, ילד *bear* Gn 17_{21} 21_{2} 2 K 4_{17}, אכל *eat* Ex 23_{15} 34_{18}, שׁמר *keep* Ex 13_{10}, קום hi. *establish* 1QM 13_{8} (למוע[ד]י), עשׂה *make* MasShirShabb 1_{4}, חבק *embrace* 2 K 4_{16}, גלה ni. *be revealed* 1QS 1_{9}, פלג pi. *apportion* judgment 1QH 1_{17}.

לְ *to, until* Hb 2_{3} Dn 11_{35} 12_{7} perh. 4QHod^{a} 3.1_{3} 1QS $10_{7.8}$ perh. 4QShir^{b} 35_{8} ([לכול מ]ועדי), + שׁמר pass. *be kept* 1 S 9_{24}, חבא pi. *hide* 1QH 9_{24} ([ל]מועדו).

לְ of benefit, *to, for*, + עשׂה Ps 104_{19}, חרץ pass. *be destined* 1QM 15_{6}, כון hi. *establish* 1QH 15_{15}; of possession, *of, (belonging) to* 4QMyst^{a} 53_{4} ([למוע]ד]); *according to*, + יחל pi. *wait* 1 S 13_{8}; *concerning* Dn 8_{19}, + צוה pi. *command* 1QS 3_{10}; *as* or introducing predicate perh. 1QLitPr 3.2_{1}, + היה *be* Gn 1_{14}; introducing object, + ידע *know* 1QM 18_{10}.

בְּ of time, *in, at* Si 10_{26} ([במו]עד]) 1QH 1_{24} 1QM 3_{7} 1QS 10_{5} 1QLitPr 2_{3} (במוע[ד]) 4QBer^{a} 6_{2} 4QBer^{b} 1_{3} 2_{7} 4QBapt 10_{6} 4QM^{a} 8.1_{16} 11.2_{18} 4QPrQuot 33.10_{21} 41.2_{1} ([בכול מ]ועדי]) perh. 45_{2} 51_{10} ([בכול]) perh. 64_{4} (במוע[ד]) 4QPrFêtes^{c} 3_{7} 11QMelch 7_{4}, + חיה pi. *keep alive* 4QpPs^{a} 1.3_{3}, עמד *stand* 4QRitPur 29.7_{6} ([עומד] ... במוע[ד]), קרא *proclaim* Lv 23_{4}, *read* Dt 31_{10}, ספר pi. *recount* 4QShir^{b} 63.2_{2}, אור hi. *shine* 1QM 1_{8}, ברך pass. *be blessed* 4QPrQuot 64_{8} ([ברוך ... בכול] מ[ו]ע[ד]י), עשׂה *do*, i.e. keep Nm $9_{2.3}$, קרב hi. *bring near*, i.e. offer Nm $9_{7.13}$ 28_{2}, זבח *sacrifice* Dt 16_{6}, סרך *arrange* 1QM 2_{6}, מלך *reign* perh. 1QM 12_{3}, לקח *take* Ho 2_{11}, שׁמד hi. *destroy* 1QS 4_{18}.

מִן *from, beyond*, + אחר hi. *delay* intrans. 2 S 20_{5} 4QD^{a} 2.1_{2}.

עַד *until*, + הלך htp. *walk* 1QS 3_{18}, גלל htpo. *pollute oneself* 1QS 4_{20}, כלה pi. *destroy* flesh 1QH 8_{31}.

<COLL> מוֹעֵד || עֵת *time* Ho 2_{11} 1QH 12_{8}, + עֵת Gn 18_{14} 2 K $4_{16.17}$ Jr 8_{7} Ps 102_{14} (or del.) Dn 11_{35} 1QM 14_{13} 4QPrFêtes^{b} 2_{2}; || קֵץ *end* Si $33_{10(B)}$ 1QH 8_{31} 12_{8}, + קֵץ Hb 2_{3} Dn $11_{27.35}$; || אוֹת *sign* Gn 1_{14}; + יוֹם *day* Gn 1_{14}, שָׁנָה *year* Gn 1_{14}.

מוֹעֵד מוֹעֲדִים וָחֵצִי *appointed time, appointed times and a half* Dn 12_{7}, מועדים לימי חודש *the appointed time for the days of the new moon* 1QS 10_{3}, מועדים לרצונכה *the appointed times of your good pleasure* 1QM 18_{14}, מועד למועד perh. *(from) appointed time to appointed time* 4QHod^{a} 3.1_{3}.

4. festival, (time of) appointed feast, of national festivals (not usu. including sabbath and new moon), sometimes used collectively; perh. specif. one of the four seasons of the year (1QS 10_3),* <SUBJ> היה *be* Is 1_{14}, קדשׁ pu. *be sanctified* Ezr 3_5.

<NOM CL> מועדיה *its festivals are* (followed by calendar of festivals) 4QMishA $4.3_{1.11}$ 4.4_6 4.5_9 4.6_4 4QMishG 1_2 (מ[ועד]יה) $1_{3.4.5}$, אֵלֶּה מוֹעֲדֵי י׳ *these are the festivals of Y.* Lv $23_{4.37}$ 11QT 29_2 ([מועדי י׳]), אֵלֶּה הֵם מוֹעֲדָי *these are my festivals* Lv 23_2, הו[א] מועד הבכורים *it is the festival of the firstfruits* 4QJub^d 22_1, אחר השבת מ[וע]ד השמן *after the sabbath is the festival of the (new) oil* 4QMishE^b 2.2_8, יש מהם מועדים *there are among them festivals* Si 36_8, בם מועד *by means of them are the festivals* Si $43_{7(B)}$ (Bmg בו *by means of it*; M לו מו[ע]ד *according to it are the festivals*), בעשרים ושנים בו מועד השמן *on the twenty-second of it is the festival of the (new) oil* 4QMishE^b 1.2_6 4QMMT Av$_4$, sim. 4QMishE^a 1_4.

<OBJ> שׁמר *keep* CD 6_{18}, קרא *proclaim* Lv $23_{2.4.37}$, דבר pi. *speak of* Lv 23_{44}, גלה pi. *reveal* CD 3_{14}, זכר *remember* 4QPrFêtes^c 131.2_5, תכן pi. *regulate* 4QShir^b 2.1_9, נתן *give* 4QRitMar 9_8 ([נתן ... מ[ועד]), פקד *appoint* 4Q423 5_6, שׁכח *forget* 4QpsMos^e 1_7, pi. *cause to forget* Lm 2_6, אכל *eat* 2 C 30_{22} (or em. וַיֹּאכְלוּ *and they ate* to וַיְכַלּוּ *and they spent*, i.e. כלה pi.), שׂנא *hate* Is 1_{14}, שׁבת hi. *cause to cease* Ho 2_{13}, חלל pi. *profane* 4QpsMos^e 2.1_9 ([ויחללו ... המו[עדים]) CD 12_4.

<CSTR> מוֹעֲדֵי י׳ *festivals of Y.* Lv $23_{2.4.37.44}$ Ezr 3_5 2 C 2_3, בֵּית *of the house of* Israel Ezk 45_{17}, מועדי הגואים *festivals of the nations* 4QpHos^a 2_{16}, כבוד *of glory*, i.e. glorious festivals 4QBer^a 1.2_{10} 4QPrQuot 1.3_{13} ([כ]בוד) 1.3_{15} ([כבו]ד) 4QPrFêtes^b 13_2, כבודו *of his glory*, i.e. his glorious festivals CD 3_{14}, [שמ]חתנו *of our joy*, i.e. our joyful festivals 4QPrQuot 48_5 ([מו]עדי]), שׁנה *of the year* 4QShir^b 2.1_9.

מועד שבת *festival of the sabbath* 4QRitPur 33.4_1, התירושׁ *of the new wine* 11QT $43_{8.8}$, היצהר *of the new oil* 4QRP^c 23_9 ([מ]ועד]), השמן *of the (new) oil* 11QT 11_{12}, 4QMishE^b 1.2_6 2.2_8 ([מ]וע]ד השמ[ן]) 4QMMT Av$_4$, [השׂ]עורים *of the barley* 4QMishE^a 1_4, [הבכורים] *of the firstfruits* 4QJub^d 22_1 ([מועד]), מועדי הקיץ *festivals of the summer* 4Q423 5_6.

בָּאֵי מוֹעֵד *ones who come to the festivals* Lm 1_4 4QapLam^a 1.1_{11}, עולת המועד *burnt offering of the festival* 11QT 42_{16}, יוֹם מוֹעֵד *day of the festival* Ho 9_5 Zp 3_{18} (if em. נוּגֵי מִמּוֹעֵד appar. *ones grieved because of a festival*) Lm $2_{7.22}$, יום מועד *day of the festival of* 11QT $43_{8.8}$, מועדו *of its festival* 11QT 43_9, יְמֵי מוֹעֵד *days of the festival* Ho 12_{10} Si $50_{6.8}$ (unless מוֹעֵד II *fresh figs*), ימי המועדים *days of the festivals* 11QT 43_{15} 11QPs^a 27_8 (המועדות), קֵץ מועד *end of the festival* 1QpHab 11_6, קצי מ[ועד] *times of festivals* 4QBer^a 7.1_4, קִרְיַת מוֹעֲדֵנוּ *city of our festival* Is 33_{20} (1QIsa^a mss מוֹעֲדֵינוּ), כָּל־מוֹעֲדֵי *all the festivals of* Ezk 45_{17} Ezr 3_5 perh 4QRitMar 24_1 (כול), כָּל־מוֹעֲדָהּ *all her festivals* Ho 2_{13}, כול מועדיהם *all their festivals* 1QS 1_{15} 4QPrEnosh 1.1_4 (מו[עדי]הם).

<APP> יוֹם *day* 11QT 43_8, מִקְרָא *convocation* Lv $23_{2.4.37}$, סתר ni. ptc. *hidden thing* CD 3_{14}.

<ADJ> טוֹב *good* Zc 8_{29}.

<PREP> לְ *as* or introducing predicate, + היה *be* Zc 8_{19}; of time, *at* Ezr 3_5 2 C 2_3 31_3 4QapPs^b 1_8 (למועד במועד *at a festival in a festival*, i.e. festival after festival) perh. 4QHymnPr 8_3 perh. 4QRitMar 103_1 ([למוע[ד]) perh. 4QRitPur 33.4_1 11QT 43_{10}, + עלה hi. *cause to go up*, i.e. offer 1 C 23_{31} 2 C 8_{13}, יצב htp. *stand* 1QM 2_4; of benefit, *to, for* perh. 4QPrFêtes^c 10.2_8, + נתן *give* Ne 10_{34}.

בְּ of time, *in, at* Ezk 36_{38} 1QSb 3_2 ([במו[עדי]) 4QapPs^b 1_8 4Q416 1_3 4QPrQuot 48_5 ([במו[עדי]) 4QPrFêtes^b 13_2 perh. 30_2 perh. 4QPrFêtes^c 32_3 11QT 11_{12}, + היה *be* Ezk 45_{17} 46_{11}, בוא *come* Ezk 46_9, תקע *sound* trumpet Nm 10_{10}, עשׂה *do*, i.e. offer Nm 15_3 29_{39}, שׁמר *keep* Ezk 44_{24}, הלל htpo. *act like a mad one* 1QH 4_{12}; *according to*, + הלך hi. *bring* 4QpHos^a 2_{16}.

מִן *from*, + יתר ni. *remain* 11QT 43_{11}; partitive, *(some) of*, + אחר htp. *delay* 1QS 1_{15}; of cause, *on acount of*, + יגה ni. *be grieved* Zp 3_{18} (or em.; see Cstr.).

<COLL> מוֹעֵד || חַג *feast* Ezk 46_{11} Ho 9_5, + חַג Ezk 45_{17} 2 C 8_{13}; || שַׁבָּת *sabbath* Lm 2_6 1 C 23_{31} 2 C 2_3 8_{13} 31_3 1QM 2_4 4QpsMos^e 1_7 CD 3_{14} 12_4, + שַׁבָּת Ho 2_{13} Ezk 45_{17} Ne 10_{34} CD 6_{18}; || חֹדֶשׁ *new moon, month* Is 1_{14} 1 C 23_{31} 2 C 2_3 8_{13} 31_3 1QM 2_4, + חֹדֶשׁ Nm 10_{10} Ezk 45_{17} Ho 2_{13} Ezr 3_5 Ne 10_{34} 11QPs^a 27_8; || יוֹם *day* 4QapPs^b 1_8,

בְּרִית *covenant* 4QpsMos[e] 1$_7$, חֹק *statute* 4QpsMos[e] 1$_7$; + שִׂמְחָה *joy* Nm 10$_{10}$ Zc 8$_{19}$, מָשׂוֹשׂ *joy* Ho 2$_{13}$, זמני חוק *times of statute,* i.e. prescribed times Si 43$_{7(B)}$, יום התענית *day of fasting* CD 6$_{18}$.

גרתי עמו מועדי *I sojourned with him (for) my festivals* 4QVisSam 7$_2$, כול מו[עדי]הם בקציהם *all their festivals in their periods* 4QPrEnosh 1.1$_4$, מועדי כבוד [בתעודות]מה *glorious festivals in their fixed times* 4QBer[a] 1.2$_{10}$, מועד במועד *festival in festival,* i.e. festival after festival 4Q416 1$_3$.

5. agreement, appointment, perh. **appointed signal,** <SUBJ> היה *be* Jg 20$_{38}$. <CSTR> עֵת מוֹעֵד *time of the appointment* 2 S 24$_{15}$.

Also 4QPrEnosh 4$_5$ 4QShirShabb[b] 9$_3$ 4Q418 286$_3$ 4QFest$_4$ 4QHymnPr 8$_3$ 23$_2$ 4QRitMar 183$_2$ 192$_2$ ([מ]ועד) 4QPrQuot 33.10$_4$ 56.1$_3$ 69$_3$ 70$_3$ 93$_2$ (מו[עדי]) 4QPrFêtes[c] 104$_1$ 143$_1$ 220$_1$ 4QRitPur 33.4$_2$ (מוע[ד]) 4Q519 1$_3$ ([מ]ועדיהם).

<SYN> §1a עֵדָה *congregation;* §3 עֵת *time,* קֵץ *end,* אוֹת *sign;* §4 חַג *feast,* שַׁבָּת *sabbath,* חֹדֶשׁ *new moon, month,* יוֹם *day,* בְּרִית *covenant,* חֹק *statute.*

⇨ יעד *appoint.*

*[מוֹעֵד] II 0.1 adj. **fresh, tender, 1.** used attributively of תְּאֵנָה *fig* Jr 24$_1$ (if em. מוּעָדִים *place* [יעד ho.] to מוֹעֲדִים).

2. as noun, **fresh figs,** <CSTR> ימי מועד *days of fresh figs* Si 50$_8$ (unless מוֹעֵד I *festival*).

מוּעָדָה 1 n.f. **appointment,** <CSTR> עָרֵי הַמּוּעָדָה *cities of the appointment,* i.e. the cities appointed (for refuge) Jos 20$_9$.

⇨ יעד *appoint.*

מוֹעַדְיָה 1 pr.n.m. **Moadiah,** ancestor of priestly family, perh. ident. with Maadiah at Ne 12$_5$, <PREP> לְ of possession, *of, (belonging) to,* + היה *be* Ne 12$_{17}$ (mss לְמַעַדְיָה *of Maadiah*).

⇨ (?) יעד *appoint* + ־יָ *Y.*

מוּעָף I 1 n.[m.] **darkness,** <NOM CL> לֹא מוּעָף לַאֲשֶׁר מוּצָק לָהּ *there is no darkness to her that was in distress* Is 8$_{23}$ (or em. לֹא and לָהּ to לוֹ *to him*).

*מוּעָף II 1 n.[m.] **gleam, lustre,** <NOM CL> לֹא מוּעָף לַאֲשֶׁר מוּצָק לָהּ *there is no gleam for her that was in distress* Is 8$_{23}$ (or em. לֹא and לָהּ to לוֹ *to him*).

*מוּעָף III 1 n.[m.] **flight, escape,** <NOM CL> לֹא מוּעָף לַאֲשֶׁר מוּצָק לָהּ *there is no escape for her that was in distress* Is 8$_{23}$ (or em. לֹא and לָהּ to לוֹ *to him*).

[מוֹעֵצָה] I 7 n.f. **counsel**—pl. מֹעֵצוֹת; sf. mss מוֹעֲצֹתַי, מֹעֲצוֹתֵיהֶם (מוֹעֲצוֹתֵיהֶם)—**counsel, plan; evidence** (Is 41$_{21}$ [if em.; see Obj.]), <OBJ> נגשׁ hi. *bring near* Is 41$_{21}$ (if em. עֲצֻמוֹתֵיכֶם *your defence* to מֹעֲצוֹתֵיכֶם *your evidence*). <PREP> לְ *before,* + דמם *be silent* Jb 29$_{21(mss)}$ (L לְמוֹ עֲצָתִי); בְּ of accompaniment, *with, in,* + הלך *go* Jr 7$_{24}$ (unless מוֹעֵצָה II *disobedience*) Mc 6$_{16}$ Ps 81$_{13}$ (unless מוֹעֵצָה II; both + שְׁרִירוּת *stubbornness*); *concerning, on account of,* + כתב *write* Pr 22$_{20}$ (or em. בָּם עֵצוֹת *in them is counsel;* || דַּעַת *knowledge*); מִן of cause, *on account of,* or of instrument, *by (means of), with,* + אכל *devour* Ho 11$_6$ (or em. בְּמְצוּדוֹתָיו *in his fortresses*), נפל *fall* Ps 5$_{11}$ (unless מוֹעֵצָה II *disobedience*), שׂבע *be satisfied* Pr 1$_{31}$ (+ פְּרִי *fruit* of their way).

<SYN> דַּעַת *knowledge.*

⇨ יעץ *advise.*

*[מוֹעֵצָה] II 3 n.f. **disobedience** (unless מוֹעֵצָה I *counsel;* or em. all as from מַעֲצָה *disobedience*)—pl. מֹעֵצוֹת; sf. מֹעֲצוֹתֵיהֶם (מוֹעֲצוֹתֵיהֶם)—<PREP> בְּ of accompaniment, *with, in,* + הלך *go* Jr 7$_{24}$ Ps 81$_{13}$ (+ שְׁרִירוּת *stubbornness*); מִן of cause, *on account of,* נפל *fall* Ps 5$_{11}$.

מוּעָקָה I 1 n.f. **affliction, distress** (unless מוּעָקָה II *ulcer*), <OBJ> שׂים *place* in loins Ps 66$_{11}$ (or em. מְצוּקָה *distress*).

⇨ עוק *press.*

*מוּעָקָה II 1 n.f. **ulcer** (unless מוּעָקָה I *affliction*), <OBJ> שׂים *place* on loins Ps 66$_{11}$.

מופעת, see מֵיפַעַת *Mephaath.*

מוֹפֵת $_{36.2.14}$ n.m. **wonder**—sf. מוֹפֶתְכֶם; pl. מֹפְתִים (מוֹפְתִים); cstr. Q מופתי; sf. מוֹפְתַי, Q מופתיכה, מֹפְתָיו (מוֹפְתָיו), Q מופתיהמה—**1. wonder, sign, portent, miracle,** of Y. (Ex 7$_{3}$ 11$_{9}$ Dt 4$_{34}$ 6$_{22}$ 7$_{19}$ 26$_{8}$ 29$_{2}$ Jr 32$_{20.21}$ Jl 3$_{3}$ Ps 78$_{43}$ 105$_{5}$||1 C 16$_{12}$ Ps 135$_{9}$ Ne 9$_{10}$ Si 33$_{6[B]}$ 4QParGenEx 3$_{5.11}$ 11QPsAp^{a} 3$_{3}$ [[המופ]תים]]), through agency of Moses (Ex 4$_{21}$ 34$_{11}$), Moses and Aaron (Ex 7$_{9}$ 11$_{10}$ Ps 105$_{27}$); of humans (4QShir^{b} 48.2$_{5}$); as token of future event, given by Y. (2 C 32$_{24.31}$), prophet (Dt 13$_{2.3}$=11QT 64$_{9}$ 1 K 13$_{3.5}$ Si 48$_{12}$); sign, portent, consisting of person (Is 8$_{18}$ Ezk 12$_{6.11}$ 24$_{24.27}$ Zc 3$_{8}$ Ps 71$_{7}$ [unless §2] 1QH 7$_{21}$ 13$_{16}$ 15$_{20}$ [[מו]פת]]), symbolic act (Is 20$_{3}$), the effects of curses (Dt 28$_{46}$).

<SUBJ> היה *be* 2 C 32$_{31}$, בוא *come to pass* Dt 13$_{3}$=11QT 64$_{9}$, רבה hi. *be multiplied* Ex 11$_{9}$.

<NOM CL> זֶה הַמּוֹפֵת *this is the sign* 1 K 13$_{3}$, אֲנִי מוֹפֶתְכֶם *I am your sign* Ezk 12$_{11}$.

<OBJ> זכר *remember* Dt 7$_{19}$ Ps 105$_{5}$||1 C 16$_{12}$, ראה *see* Dt 29$_{2}$, דבר pi. *speak* Dt 13$_{3}$=11QT 64$_{9}$ 1 K 13$_{3}$, דרשׁ *inquire about* 2 C 32$_{31}$, נתן *give* Ex 7$_{9}$ Dt 6$_{22}$ 13$_{2}$=11QT 64$_{9}$ 1 K 13$_{3.5}$ Ezk 12$_{6}$ Jl 3$_{3}$ Ne 9$_{10}$ 2 C 32$_{24}$, שׂים *place* Ex 4$_{21}$ Jr 32$_{20}$ Ps 78$_{43}$ 105$_{27}$, שׁלח *send* Ps 135$_{9}$, עשׂה *do* Ex 4$_{21}$ 11$_{10}$ Dt 34$_{11}$ 11QPsAp^{a} 3$_{3}$ ([ע]שה ... המופ[תים]), רבה hi. *multiply* Ex 7$_{3}$ Si 48$_{12}$ 4QParGenEx 3$_{11}$, חדשׁ pi. *renew* Si 33$_{6(B)}$.

<CSTR> מופתי גבר *wonders of a man* 4QShir^{b} 48.2$_{5}$; אַנְשֵׁי מוֹפֵת *men of,* i.e. as, *a sign* Zc 3$_{8}$ 1QH 7$_{21}$ 4QBark^{b} 4$_{2}$ ([אנשי]), מופת דורות *wonder of,* i.e. for, *the generations* 1QH 13$_{16}$, כָּל־הַמֹּפְתִים *all the wonders* Ex 4$_{21}$ 11$_{10}$, כול מופתי *all the wonders of* 4QShir^{b} 48.2$_{5}$.

<ADJ> גָּדוֹל *great* Dt 6$_{22}$ 29$_{2}$ 4QapJoshua^{a} 26$_{5}$, רַע *bad* Dt 6$_{22}$, אֵלֶּה *these* Ex 11$_{10}$, הֵם *those* Dt 29$_{2}$.

<PREP> לְ *as* Is 8$_{18}$ perh. 4Q416$_{8}$, + היה *be* Dt 28$_{46}$ Ezk 24$_{24.27}$ 1QH 13$_{16}$ (ומופת ... [לאות]) 15$_{20}$ ([לאות ומו]פת).

בְּ of instrument, *by (means of), with* 4Q392 2$_{2}$ 4QParGenEx 3$_{5}$ 4QPrayers^{g} 1$_{3}$, + יצא hi. *bring out* Dt 26$_{8}$ Jr 32$_{21}$, לקח *take* Dt 4$_{34}$.

כְּ *as,* + היה *be* Ps 71$_{7}$ (unless §2); *according to,* + שׁפך ni. *be poured out* 1 K 13$_{5}$, קרע ni. *be torn down* 1 K 13$_{5}$.

עַל *above,* + יעל hi. *profit* 4QShir^{b} 48.2$_{5}$ ([ואוע]ל).

<COLL> אוֹת || מוֹפֵת *sign* Ex 7$_{3}$ Dt 4$_{34}$ 6$_{22}$ 7$_{19}$ 13$_{2.3}$=11QT 64$_{9.9}$ Dt 26$_{8}$ 28$_{46}$ 29$_{2}$ 34$_{11}$ Is 8$_{18}$ 20$_{3}$ Jr 32$_{20.21}$ Ps 78$_{43}$ 105$_{27}$ (+) 135$_{9}$ Ne 9$_{10}$ Si 33$_{6(B)}$ 48$_{12}$ 4Q392 2$_{2}$ 4Q416$_{8}$ 4QParGenEx 3$_{5}$, מַסָּה *testing* Dt 4$_{34}$ 7$_{19}$ 29$_{2}$, מִלְחָמָה *war* Dt 4$_{34}$, מוֹרָא *terror* Dt 4$_{34}$ 26$_{8}$ Jr 32$_{21}$, זְרוֹעַ outstretched *arm* Dt 4$_{34}$ 7$_{19}$ 26$_{8}$, אֶזְרוֹעַ *arm* Jr 32$_{21}$, יָד mighty *hand* Dt 4$_{34}$ 7$_{19}$ 26$_{8}$ Jr 32$_{21}$; + פלא ni. ptc. *wonderful deed* Ps 105$_{5}$||1 C 16$_{12}$, מִשְׁפָּט *judgment* Ps 105$_{5}$||1 C 16$_{12}$.

הָלַךְ ... עָרוֹם וְיָחֵף ... מוֹפֵת *he has walked ... naked and barefoot ... as a portent* Is 20$_{3}$, אתות הרבה ומופתים כל מוצא פיהו *he multiplied signs and wonders (with) every utterance of his mouth* Si 48$_{12}$, מפתים לאין מספר *wonders without number* 4Q392 1$_{8}$ (others מתים *dead ones*).

2. target of archers,* <PREP> כְּ *as,* + היה *be* Ps 71$_{7}$.

Also 4QapMos^{c} 2.2$_{1}$ 4QpsEzek^{d} 1.2$_{1}$ (מ[ופ]תים) 4QBark^{d} 8$_{1}$ ([מ]ופת]) 4QShir^{b} 26$_{4}$ ([מ]ופת[יו]).

<SYN> אוֹת *sign,* מַסָּה *testing,* מִלְחָמָה *war,* מוֹרָא *terror,* זְרוֹעַ *arm,* אֶזְרוֹעַ *arm,* יָד *hand.*

מוֹץ, see מֹץ *chaff.*

מוֹצָא I n.m. $_{27.3.19.1}$ **going out**—cstr. מוֹצָא (מֹצָא); sf. מוֹצָאוֹ (מֹצָאוֹ), מוֹצָאֵךְ; pl. cstr. מוֹצָאֵי (מֹצָאֵי); sf. מוֹצָאָיו, מוֹצָאֵיהֶן, מוֹצָאֵיהֶם—**1. place of going out, a. exit, way out** of temple (Ezk 43$_{11}$ 44$_{5}$), of chambers of temple (Ezk 42$_{11}$), heavenly temple (11QShirShabb 5$_{5}$ [[מו]צא]]), **door** of house (4QJub^{h} 39$_{10}$ [[המוצ]א]]).

<NOM CL> כֵּן רָחְבָּן וְכָל מוֹצָאֵיהֶן *so was their breadth and all their exits* Ezk 42$_{11}$ (or em. וּכְרָחְבָּן וּכְמוֹצָאֵיהֶן *and according to their breadth and their exits*). <OBJ> ידע hi. *make known* Ezk 43$_{11}$ (:: מוֹבָא *entrance*), שׁבר pi. *break* 4QJub^{h} 39$_{10}$ ([ויש]ביר את המוצ]א]). <CSTR> מוֹצָאֵי הַמִּקְדָּשׁ *exits of the sanctuary* Ezk 44$_{5}$ (+ מָבוֹא *entry,* i.e. ones who enter), [מו]צא אול[מי] *exit of the vestibules of* 11QShirShabb 5$_{5}$; כֹּל מוֹצָאֵי *all the exits of* Ezk 44$_{5}$ 11QShirShabb 10$_{8}$ (כול), כֹּל מוֹצָאֵיהֶן *all their exits* Ezk 42$_{11}$ (or em.; see Nom. Cl.). <PREP> לְ of direction, *to(wards),* + שׂים *place* heart, i.e. consider Ezk 44$_{5}$ (if em. בְּכָל מוֹצָאֵי *with all the exits of* to לְמוֹצָאֵי *to the exits of*); בְּ of place, *in, at, through* Ezk 44$_{5}$ (or em.; see above) 11QShirShabb 5$_{5}$ ([במו]צא); כְּ *according to* Ezk 42$_{11}$ (if em.; see Nom. Cl.); עִם *with* 11QShirShabb 10$_{8}$.

b. place of going out of sun (Ps 19$_{7}$), of morning

and evening, i.e. the east and west (Ps 65$_9$; unless מוֹצָא III *star*), **the east** (Ps 75$_7$), <NOM CL> מִקְצֵה הַשָּׁמַיִם מוֹצָאוֹ *its place of going out is at the end of the heaven* Ps 19$_7$ (+ תְּקוּפָה *circuit*). <OBJ> רנן hi. *cause to shout for joy* Ps 65$_9$ (unless מוֹצָא III *star*). <CSTR> מוֹצָאֵי־ בֹקֶר וָעֶרֶב *the places where morning and evening go out* Ps 65$_9$ (unless מוֹצָא III *star*). <PREP> מִן of direction, *from* Ps 75$_7$ (:: מַעֲרָב *west*; + מִדְבָּר *steppe*).

c. source, spring, of water, prob. sometimes **canal** (2 K 2$_{21}$ Is 41$_{18}$ Ps 105$_{33.35}$ 2 C 32$_{30}$),* <OBJ> שׂים *place* Ps 107$_{33}$, סתם *stop up* 2 C 32$_{30}$. <CSTR> מוֹצָא מַיִם *the spring of water* 2 K 2$_{21}$ (הַמַּיִם) Is 58$_{11}$ (+ גַּן רָוֶה *watered garden*), מֹצָאֵי *springs of* Ps 107$_{33}$ (|| נָהָר *river*; :: צִמָּאוֹן *thirsty ground*) 107$_{35}$=Is 41$_{18}$ (מָיִם; || אֲגַם *pool*, + אֶרֶץ צִיָּה *dry land*), מוֹצָא מֵימֵי *source of the waters of* Gihon 2 C 32$_{30}$. <PREP> לְ *into*, + שׂים *place*, i.e. turn Ps 107$_{35}$=Is 41$_{18}$; כְּ *as*, + היה *be* Is 58$_{11}$; מִן of direction, *from*, + הלך *go*, i.e. flow Siloam Tunnel inscr.$_5$; אֶל *to*, + יצא *go out* 2 K 2$_{21}$. <COLL> מוֹצָא מַיִם אֲשֶׁר לֹא־יְכַזְּבוּ מֵימָיו *a spring of water, whose waters do not fail* Is 58$_{11}$.

d. mine, <NOM CL> יֵשׁ לַכֶּסֶף מוֹצָא *there is a mine for silver* Jb 28$_1$ (unless מוֹצָא IV *smelter*; || מָקוֹם *place*).

e. growing-place, <OBJ> צמח hi. *cause to sprout* Jb 38$_{27}$ (or em. מִצִּיָּה *from the dry ground*). <CSTR> מֹצָא דֶשֶׁא *growing-place of grass* Jb 38$_{27}$ (unless *crop of*, i.e. §3c; or em.; see Obj.).

f. point of departure, <OBJ> כתב *write* Nm 33$_2$.

2. act of going out, a. going out, exit, departure, of Y. (Ho 6$_3$), angels (4QShirShabb^f 23.1$_8$), David (2 S 3$_{25}$), word (Dn 9$_{25}$), night (1QH 12$_7$ 4QMyst^a 5$_4$), evening and morning (1QM 14$_{14}$ 1QS 10$_{10}$), light (1QH 12$_5$), period (4Q418 123.2$_2$), <SUBJ> כון ni. *be sure* Ho 6$_3$ (or em. כַּשַּׁחַר נָכוֹן מוֹצָאוֹ *his going out is as sure as the dawn* to כְּשַׁחֲרֵנוּ כֵּן נִמְצָאֵנוּ *as we seek [him] so we shall find him*). <OBJ> ידע *know* 2 S 3$_{25}$ (:: מָבוֹא *coming in* [Kt], מוֹבָא *coming in* [Qr]). <CSTR> מוצאי מלאכי *goings out of the angels of* 4QShirShabb^f 23.1$_8$, מֹצָא דָבָר *going out of the word* Dn 9$_{25}$, מוצא אור *going out of light* 1QH 12$_5$ (:: מָבוֹא *coming in*), לילה *of night* 1QH 12$_7$ (:: מָבוֹא) 4QMyst^a 5$_4$, ערב ובוקר *of evening and morning* 1QM 14$_{14}$ (מוצאי *goings out of*) 1QS 10$_{10}$ (:: מָבוֹא), קצים *of the periods* 4Q418 123.2$_2$ (:: מָבוֹא); שערי מוצא *gates of exit* 4QShirShabb^f 23.1$_9$ (:: מָבוֹא *entry*). <PREP> לְ *at* 4Q418 123.2$_2$ + אסף ni. *be brought in* 1QH 12$_7$; בְּ of time, *at* 1QH 12$_5$, + שׁמע hi. *proclaim* 4QShirShabb^f 23.1$_8$; מִן *from* Dn 9$_{25}$; עִם *with*, i.e. at 1QM 14$_{14}$, + אמר *say* 1QS 10$_{10}$.

b. export, <NOM CL> מוֹצָא הַסּוּסִים ... מִמִּצְרָיִם *the export of the horses was from ... Egypt* 1 K 10$_{28}$||2 C 1$_{16}$ (or em. מִמִּצְרַיִם to מִמְּצְרִי *from Muzri*). <CSTR> מוֹצָא הַסּוּסִים *export of the horses* 1 K 10$_{28}$||2 C 1$_{16}$.

c. growth, <CSTR> מוצא זרע *growth of seed* Si 37$_{11}$ (Bmg, D) (Bmg מצא; B מוציא רע *one who brings out evil*).

3. that which goes out, a. utterance, <SUBJ> היה *be* Jr 17$_{16}$, קום *stand* Nm 30$_{13}$. <NOM CL> מוצא פיו אוצרו *the utterance of his mouth is his storehouse* Si 39$_{17}$, כִּי מוֹצָא שָׁלָל רָב *for (your) utterance was (my) great reward* Ps 119$_{162}$ (if em. כְּמוֹצֵא *as one who finds*). <OBJ> ידע *know* Jr 17$_{16}$ (if transfer athnach), שׁמר *keep* Dt 23$_{24}$ 11QT 53$_{13}$, קום hi. *raise up*, i.e. fulfil CD 16$_6$, שׁנה pi. *change* Ps 89$_{35}$ (+ בְּרִית *covenant*). <CSTR> מוֹצָא פִּי *utterance of the mouth of* Dt 8$_3$ (+ לֶחֶם *bread*), מוצא פיו *utterance of his mouth* Si 39$_{17}$ 48$_{12}$ (פיהו), פיכה *of your mouth* 4QparaKings 7$_3$ (מו[צא]) 4QBapt 2.2$_7$ 4Q416 2.4$_9$, מוצא שפתי *utterance of the lips of* 4QShirShabb^b 14.2$_8$, מוֹצָא שְׂפָתַי *utterance of my lips* Jr 17$_{16}$ Ps 89$_{35}$ 1QS 10$_{14}$ 4QCryptA 1.1$_3$ ([מ]וצא שפת[י]) 4QShir^b 18.2$_5$, שְׂפָתֶיךָ *of your lips* Dt 23$_{24}$ 11QT 53$_{13}$ (שפתיכה) CD 16$_6$, שפתיו *of his lips* 4QShirShabb^d 1.1$_{35}$ (|| אֹמֶר *word*), שְׂפָתֶיהָ *of her lips* Nm 30$_{13}$, שפתינו *of our lips* 4QHod^a 7.2$_{20}$; תרומת מוצא *offering of the utterance of* 1QS 10$_{14}$, כָּל־מוֹצָא *every utterance of* Nm 30$_{13}$ Dt 8$_3$ Si 48$_{12}$ 4QCryptA 1.1$_3$ (כול [מ]וצא; + מִלָּה *word*).

<PREP> לְ *at* 4QShirShabb^b 14.2$_8$, + היה *be* 4QShirShabb^d 1.1$_{35}$; of possession, *of, (belonging) to* 4QHod^a 7.2$_{20}$; בְּ of accompaniment, *with, in* 4QCryptA 1.1$_3$ (בכול [מ]וצא) 4QShir^b 18.2$_5$ ([ב]מוצא); מִן of direction, *from*, + פרשׁ ni. *be separated* 4QBapt 2.2$_7$ ([נ]פרשה); עַל *by (means of)*, + חיה *live* Dt 8$_3$; introducing object, + פרר hi. *annul* 4Q416 2.4$_9$. <COLL> כָּל־מוֹצָא שְׂפָתֶיהָ לִנְדָרֶיהָ וּלְאִסַּר נַפְשָׁהּ *every utterance of her lips, whether it be her vows* (under duress) *or a vow made of her own free will* Nm 30$_{13}$, אתות הרבה ומופתים כל מוצא פיהו *he multiplied signs and wonders (with) every utterance*

of his mouth Si 48$_{12}$.

b. one who goes out, <CSTR> מוֹצְאֵי גוֹלָה *ones who go out to exile* Ezk 12$_{4}$. <PREP> כְּ *as,* + יצא *go out* Ezk 12$_{4}$.

c. perh. **crop,** <OBJ> צמח hi. *cause to sprout* Jb 38$_{27}$ (or em. מִצִּיָּה *from the dry ground*). <CSTR> מֹצָא דֶשֶׁא *crop of grass* Jb 38$_{27}$ (but prob. *growing-place of,* i.e. §1e; or em.; see Obj.).

<SYN> §1 נָהָר *river,* אֲגַם *pool,* מָקוֹם *place;* §3 אֹמֶר *word.*

<ANT> §1 מַעֲרָב *west,* מוֹבָא *entrance,* צִמָּאוֹן *thirsty ground;* §2 מָבוֹא *coming in,* מוֹבָא *coming in.*

⇒ יצא *go out.*

מוֹצָא II $_{5}$ pr.n.m. **Moza, 1.** son of Zimri, descendant of Saul, <SUBJ> ילד hi. *beget* 1 C 8$_{37}$ 9$_{43}$. <OBJ> ילד hi. *beget* 1 C 8$_{36}$ 9$_{42}$.

2. son of Caleb and Ephah, <OBJ> ילד *bear* 1 C 2$_{46}$.

*[**מוֹצָא**] III $_{1}$ n.[m.] **star, sparkler**—pl. cstr. מוֹצָאֵי—<OBJ> רנן hi. *cause to shout for joy* Ps 65$_{9}$. <CSTR> מוֹצָאֵי־בֹקֶר וָעֶרֶב *stars of the morning and the evening* Ps 65$_{9}$, מוֹצֵא שָׁלוֹם *star of the evening* Ca 8$_{10}$ (if em. כְּמוֹצְאֵת *as one who finds* peace).

***מוֹצָא** IV $_{1}$ n.[m.] **smelter** (unless מוֹצָא I *mine*), <NOM CL> יֵשׁ לַכֶּסֶף מוֹצָא *there is a smelter for silver* Jb 28$_{1}$ (|| מָקוֹם *place*).

⇒ מָקוֹם *place.*

[**מוֹצָאָה**] $_{2}$ n.f. **origin; latrine**—pl. Qr מוֹצָאוֹת; sf. מוֹצָאֹתָיו—**1. origin,** <NOM CL> מוֹצָאֹתָיו מִקֶּדֶם מִימֵי עוֹלָם *his origin is from of old, from ancient days* Mc 5$_{1}$.

2. latrine, <PREP> לְ *into,* + שִׂים *place,* i.e. make, house of Baal 2 K 10$_{27(Qr)}$ (למחראות; Kt למחראות *latrines*).

⇒ יצא *go out.*

מוּצָק I $_{2.1}$ n.m. **casting** of metal (1 K 7$_{37}$ Si 43$_{4[M]}$), **solid mass** of dust (Jb 38$_{38}$), <NOM CL> ... מוּצָק אֶחָד לְכֻלָּהְנָה *there was one casting ... to all of them,* i.e. all were cast alike 1 K 7$_{37}$ (|| מִדָּה *measure,* קֶצֶב *shape*). <ADJ> אֶחָד *one* 1 K 7$_{37}$. <CSTR> מעשי מוצק (of furnace) *work of casting,* i.e. made of cast metal Si 43$_{4(M)}$ (B מצוק *casting;* Bmg מוצק, i.e. יצק ho. *be cast*). <PREP> לְ of direction *to,* + יצק *pour out* Jb 38$_{38}$ (+ רֶגֶב *clod*).

<SYN> מִדָּה *measure,* קֶצֶב *shape.*

⇒ יצק *pour out.*

מוּצָק II $_{3}$ n.[m.] **constraint, distress, 1. constraint,** <NOM CL> רַחַב לֹא־מוּצָק תַּחְתֶּיהָ *a broad place where there is no constraint* Jb 36$_{16}$. <PREP> בְּ *in* Jb 37$_{10}$ (רֹחַב מַיִם בְּמוּצָק *the expanse of water is in constraint* [through being frozen]; unless מוּצָק III *outpouring*).

2. distress, <NOM CL> מוּצָק לָהּ *distress is to her* Is 8$_{23}$ (or em. לָהּ to לוֹ *to him*).

⇒ צוק *constrain.*

***מוּצָק** III $_{1}$ n.[m.] **outpouring** (unless מוּצָק II *constraint*), <CSTR> מוּצַק אַף *outpouring of (his) nostrils* Jb 37$_{10}$ (if em. מוּצָק : אַף). <PREP> בְּ of instrument, *by (means of), with* Jb 37$_{10}$.

מוּצָק IV *cast object,casting,* see יצק Ho.

[**מוּצֶקֶת**] I $_{2}$ n.f. **casting, pipe**—sf. מֻצַקְתּוֹ; pl. מוּצָקוֹת—**1. casting,** <PREP> בְּ of place, *in,* + יצק pass. *be cast* 2 C 4$_{3}$.

2. pipe, <NOM CL> שִׁבְעָה מוּצָקוֹת לַנֵּרוֹת *seven pipes were to the lamps* Zc 4$_{2}$. <COLL> שִׁבְעָה מוּצָקוֹת *seven pipes* Zc 4$_{2}$.

⇒ יצק *pour out* or צוק *be narrow..*

*[**מוּצֶקֶת**] II $_{1}$ n.f. **cast metal**—pl. שִׁבְעָה—מוּצָקוֹת וְשִׁבְעָה מוּצָקוֹת *all seven were (of) cast metal* Zc 4$_{2}$.

מוק $_{1}$ vb. **mock—Hi.** $_{1}$ Impf. יָמִיקוּ—**mock,** <SUBJ> רָשָׁע *wicked one* Ps 73$_{8}$ (+ יְדַבְּרוּ בְרָע *they speak with malice;* or em. יָמִיקוּ to יַעֲמִיקוּ *they make deep* their malicious speech).

מוֹקֵד $_{2}$ n.m. **hearth**—L (כְּ)מוֹ־קֵד (mss [כְּ]מוֹקֵד); pl. cstr. מוֹקְדֵי—**hearth, burning,** <CSTR> מוֹקְדֵי עוֹלָם *burnings of everlastingness,* i.e. everlasting burnings Is

33_{14} (|| אֵשׁ *fire*). <PREP> כְּ *like*, + חרר ni. *be set aglow* Ps 102_4 (unless כְּמוֹ־קֵד, as L, *like dried meat*;* + עָשָׁן *smoke*); עַל *upon* Lv 6_2 (if em. מוֹקְדָה *the hearth* to מוֹקְדָהּ *its hearth*); מוֹקֵד without prep., *in the burning*, + גור *sojourn* Is 33_{14}.

<SYN> אֵשׁ *fire*.

⇒ יקד *be kindled*.

מוֹקְדָה 1 n.f. **hearth** of altar, <PREP> עַל *upon* Lv 6_2 (or em. מוֹקְדָהּ *its hearth*, from מוֹקֵד).

⇒ יקד *be kindled*.

*[מוֹקִר] 0.0.0.1 pr.n.[m.] **Mokir**, T. 'Ira ost. 1_3.

מוֹקֵשׁ I 27.3.6 n.m. **snare**—cstr. מוֹקֵשׁ; pl. מוֹקְשִׁים (מֹקְשִׁים), Si מוקשת; cstr. מוֹקְשֵׁי (מֹקְשֵׁי), מֹקְשׁוֹת—**snare**, or specif. **striker**, the part of a trap that falls on its victim,* or **bait, decoy,*** placed on path (Si 35_{20}), for bird (Am 3_5), to pierce nose of Behemoth (Jb 40_{24}); Y. as snare to inhabitants of Jerusalem (Is 8_{14}), Moses as a snare to the Egyptians (Ex 10_7), Michal as snare to David (1 S 18_{21}); snare consisting of speech (Pr 12_{13} 18_7 20_{25}), transgression (Pr 29_6), worship of other gods (Ex 23_{33} Dt 7_{16} Jg 2_3 Ps 106_{36} 1QDM 1_8), relations with Canaanites (Ex 34_{12} Jos 23_{13} 4QapPent 2_4 11QT 2_5 [[מו]קש]), ephod made by Gideon (Jg 8_{27}), death, the pit (Ps 18_6|| 2 S 22_6 Pr 13_{14} 14_{27} 1QH 2_{21} 4QCitJub 1.1_8 CD 14_2); wine as snare to the fool (Si $34_{30[B]}$), table of wicked as snare to themselves (Ps 69_{23}); snare set by wicked (Ps 64_6 141_9 Jb 34_{30} Si 51_3), proud (Ps 140_6); caused by fear (Pr 29_{25}), anger (Pr 22_{25}).

<SUBJ> קדם pi. *confront* Ps 18_6||2 S 22_6 (|| חֶבֶל *cord* of Sheol).

<NOM CL> שְׂפָתָיו מוֹקֵשׁ נַפְשׁוֹ *his lips are a snare of*, i.e. to, *himself* Pr 18_7 (+ מְחִתָּה *ruin*), מוֹקֵשׁ הוּא לָךְ *it would be a snare to you* Dt 7_{16}, מוֹקֵשׁ אֵין לָהּ *there is no snare for it* Am 3_5 (unless מוֹקֵשׁ II *boomerang*; + פַּח *trap*), בְּפֶשַׁע שְׂפָתַיִם מוֹקֵשׁ רָע *in the transgression of the lips is a snare of*, i.e. to, *an evil person* Pr 12_{13} (or em. נוֹקַשׁ the evil one *is ensnared*), בְּפֶשַׁע אִישׁ רָע מוֹקֵשׁ *in the transgression of an evil man there is a snare* Pr 29_6 (or em. נוֹקַשׁ *he is ensnared*), לכסיל מוקש *to the fool it is a snare* Si $34_{30(B)}$ (Bmg נוקש *he is ensnared*).

<OBJ> נתן *give*, i.e. place Pr 29_{25}, שׁית *place* Ps 140_6 (+ פַּח *trap*, רֶשֶׁת *net*), טמן *conceal* Ps 64_6, hi. 4QBéat 16_4 (הט]מינו]), לקח *take* Pr 22_{25}.

<CSTR> מוֹקֵשׁ אָדָם *snare of*, i.e. to, *a person* Pr 20_{25}, נַפְשׁוֹ *of*, i.e. for, *himself* Pr 18_7, רָע *of*, i.e. to, *an evil person* Pr 12_{13} (or em.; see Nom. Cl.), מֹקְשֵׁי עָם *snares of*, i.e. to, *the people* Jb 34_{30}, מוקש צופי *snare of those watching* Si 51_3, מֹקְשֵׁי מָוֶת *snares of death* Ps 18_6||2 S 22_6 (Ps מוֹקְשֵׁי) Pr 13_{14} 14_{27} Pr 21_6 (if em.; see Coll.), מוקשי שחת *snares of the pit* 1QH 2_{21} 4QCitJub 1.1_8 (מקשי) CD 14_2, מֹקְשׁוֹת פֹּעֲלֵי אָוֶן *snares of evildoers* Ps 141_9 (or em. מִקֶּשֶׁת *from the bows of*); דרך מוקשת *way of*, i.e. set with, *snares* Si 35_{20}, כול מוקשי *all the snares of* 1QH 2_{21} CD 14_2 (כל).

<PREP> לְ *as* or introducing predicate, + היה *be* Ex 10_7 23_{33} 34_{12} Jos 23_{13} (|| פַּח *trap*) Jg 2_3 8_{27} 1 S 18_{21} Is 8_{14} (if em. לְמִקְדָּשׁ *as a sanctuary*) 8_{14} (|| פַּח, + מִקְדָּשׁ *sanctuary*, אֶבֶן *stone*, צוּר *rock*) Jr 3_3 (if em. וּמַלְקוֹשׁ לוֹא הָיָה *and the latter rain was not* to לָךְ הָיוּ וּלְמוֹקֵשׁ *to you they were and as a snare*) Ezk 11_{16} (if em. לְמִקְדָּשׁ) Ps 69_{23} (|| פַּח) 106_{36} 1QDM 1_8 4QapPent 2_4 11QT 2_5 ([למו]קש]); בְּ of instrument, *by (means of), with*, + נקב *pierce* Jb 40_{24} (or em. בְּקִמּוֹשִׁים *with hooks*);* מִן of direction, *from*, + סור *turn aside* Pr 13_{14} 14_{27}, שׁמר *keep* Ps $141_{9(ms)}$ (or em.; see Cstr.), שׂוך *fence off* 1QH 2_{21}, נצל hi. *deliver* CD 14_2, עזר *help* Si 51_3; privative, *without (there being)* Jb 34_{30}.

<COLL> מוֹקֵשׁ אָדָם יָלַע קֹדֶשׁ *it is a snare for a person rashly to say, It is holy* Pr 20_{25}, הֶבֶל נִדָּף מוֹקְשֵׁי מָוֶת *it is needlessly driven into the snares of death* Pr 21_6 (if em. מְבַקְשֵׁי *ones who seek*).*

<SYN> פַּח *trap*, חֶבֶל *cord*.

⇒ יקשׁ *trap*.

***מוֹקֵשׁ** II 1 n.[m.] **boomerang**, to make bird fall to the ground, <NOM CL> מוֹקֵשׁ אֵין לָהּ *there is no boomerang for it*, i.e. to throw at it Am 3_5 (unless מוֹקֵשׁ I *snare*).

מור I 16.1.8 vb. **change—Qal** 1 Ptc. מֵרִים—**obtain, acquire,*** <SUBJ> כְּסִיל *fool* Pr 3_{35} (or em. מָרִים in same sense; unless מֵרִים is hi. ptc. of רום *raise* or מיר *pro-*

cure; || נחל *inherit*). <OBJ> קָלוֹן *disgrace* Pr 3$_{35}$.

<SYN> נחל *inherit*.

Ni. $_{1}$ Pf. נָמָר—**be changed,** <SUBJ> רֵיחַ *scent* of wine Jr 48$_{11}$ (:: עמד *stand*, i.e. remain).

<ANT> עמד *stand*.

Hi. $_{14.1.8}$ Pf. הֵמִיר (הֵימִיר), Q המירותו; impf. יָמִיר (יָמֵר, יְמִירֶנּוּ, יָמֵר), 2ms Si תמיר, אָמִיר; + waw וַיָּמִירוּ (Q וימירום); inf. abs. הָמֵר; cstr. הָמִיר—**1. change, alter,** <SUBJ> Y. Mc 2$_{4}$ (or em. יָמִיר *he changes* to יִמַּד בַּחֶבֶל *it will be measured with a line*), אִישׁ *man* of deceit 1QH 2$_{18}$, אֶרֶץ *earth* Ps 46$_{3}$ (unless from מרר II *flow*; or em. בְּהִמּוֹר *when it quakes* [i.e. מור II] or בְּהִמּוֹג *when it melts* [מוג ni.] or הֲמָר *throat* of hell; || מוט *shake*); subj. not specified, Ps 15$_{4}$. <OBJ> בין hi. ptc. *one who understands* 1QH 2$_{18}$, חֵלֶק *portion* Mc 2$_{4}$ (or em.; see Subj.), דָּבָר 4QapPs^{b} 69$_{9}$. <PREP> לְ *into*, + עַם *people* 1QH 2$_{18}$; בְּ *at the cost of*, + רַע *harm* Ps 15$_{4}$ (if ins. בְּרֵעַ); of instrument, *by (means of), with*, + עָרוֹל *uncircumcision* of lips 1QH 2$_{18}$.

2. exchange, <SUBJ> Y. Ho 4$_{7}$ (or em.; see below), Israelites Ps 106$_{20}$, גּוֹי *nation* Jr 2$_{11}$, עַם *people* Jr 2$_{11}$ Ho 4$_{7}$ (if em. אָמִיר *I* [Y.] *will exchange* to הֵמִירוּ *they have exchanged*), אִישׁ *man* Lv 27$_{33.33.33}$, אִשָּׁה *woman* 4QD^{a} 6.2$_{13}$, בֵּן *son* Si 7$_{18}$, כֹּהֵן *priest* Ezk 48$_{14}$ (or em. ho.; + מכר *sell*, עבר hi. *transfer*), offerer Lv 27$_{10}$ (|| חלף hi. *replace*) 27$_{10}$, worshipper 1QH 2$_{36}$ 14$_{20}$, כְּסִיל *fool* Pr 3$_{35}$ (if em. מֵרִים appar. *he exalts* to מְמִירִים *they exchange*), עשׂה ptc. *one who does* 4QBer^{a} 7.2$_{12}$ ([עושׂ]ין); subj. not specified, 1QH 4$_{10}$. <OBJ> (what the obj. is exchanged for is shown in brackets) אֱלֹהִים *god* Jr 2$_{11}$, אָח *brother* Si 7$_{18}$ (gold), אֹהֵב *friend* Si 7$_{18}$ (price), בְּהֵמָה *beast* Lv 27$_{10}$ (another beast), שֶׂה *lamb* 4QD^{a} 6.2$_{13}$ (ה[שה]; turtledove, pigeon), טוֹב *good one* Lv 27$_{10}$ (bad one), מַעֲשֵׂר *tithe* Lv 27$_{33.33}$, תּוֹרָה *law* 1QH 4$_{10}$ (smooth thing), מִשְׁפָּט *ordinance* 1QH 14$_{20}$ (bribe) 4QBer^{a} 7.2$_{12}$ (משׁ[פטי]ם), אֱמֶת *truth* 1QH 14$_{20}$ (wealth), כָּבוֹד *glory* Jr 2$_{11}$ Ho 4$_{7}$ (shame) Ps 106$_{20}$ (image), קָלוֹן *shame* Pr 3$_{35}$ (if em.; see Subj.), יֵצֶר *imagination* 1QH 2$_{36}$ (folly).

<PREP> בְּ of price, *(in exchange) for*, + מְחִיר *price* Si 7$_{18}$, שֹׁחַד *bribe* 1QH 14$_{20}$, זָהָב *gold* Si 7$_{18}$, הוֹן *wealth* 1QH 14$_{20}$, בְּהֵמָה *beast* Lv 27$_{10}$, תַּבְנִית *images* of ox Ps 106$_{20}$, רַע *bad one* Lv 27$_{10}$, קָלוֹן *shame* Ho 4$_{7}$, הוֹלֵל *folly* 1QH 2$_{36}$, חָלָק *smooth thing* 1QH 4$_{10}$; בְּלוֹא יוֹעִיל *for that which does not profit* Jr 2$_{11}$. <COLL> inf. abs. + finite form of מור hi., Lv 27$_{33}$.

Also 4QapJoshua^{a} 2$_{2}$.

<SYN> §1 מוט *shake*; §2 חלף hi. *replace*.

Ho. be exchanged, <SUBJ> appar. תְּרוּמָה *portion of land* Ezk 48$_{14}$ (if em. לֹא יָמֵר *he shall not exchange* [i.e. hi.] to לֹא יֻמַר *it shall not be exchanged*).

⇒ תְּמוּרָה *exchange*; cf. מרה II *change*.

[מור] II vb. **quake—Ni. quake, shake,** <SUBJ> אֶרֶץ *earth* Ps 46$_{3}$ (if em. בְּהָמִיר *when it changes* to בְּהִמּוֹר *when it quakes*).

מוֹר, see מֹר *myrrh*.

מוֹרָא I $_{12.1.3}$ n.m. **fear**—מֹרָא (מוֹרָה); cstr. Q מורא; sf. מוֹרָאִי, מוֹרָאוֹ, מוֹרַאֲכֶם, Q מוראם; pl. מוֹרָאִים—**1. fear, dread,** with objective suffix in ref. to Israelites (Dt 11$_{25}$), descendants of Noah (Gn 9$_{2}$), followers of Y. (1QH 4$_{26}$). **2. fear, reverence,** due to Y. (Ml 1$_{6}$), inspired by Y. (4QShirShabb^{f} 23.1$_{13}$). **3. (object of) fear, reverence** (Is 8$_{12.13}$ Ml 2$_{5}$ 1QpHab 6$_{5}$), i.e. the one to be feared (Ps 76$_{12}$ [or em.; see Prep.]), perh. a name for God*. **4. terror, terrible deed, fearful thing,** displaying power of Y. (Dt 4$_{34}$ 26$_{8}$ Jr 32$_{21}$ Ps 9$_{21}$ (unless מוֹרָה III *muzzle*; or em.; see Obj.) Jb 33$_{16}$ [if em.; see Prep.] Si 45$_{2[Bmg]}$), performed by Moses (Dt 34$_{12}$).

<SUBJ> היה *be* Gn 9$_{2}$ Ps 31$_{12}$ (if em. מְאֹד *very*).

<NOM CL> כלי מלחמותם המה מוראם *their weapons of war are their objects of reverence* 1QpHab 6$_{5}$, מורא מלך אלוהים נורא על [כו]ל אלוהים *the fear of the king of the divine beings is fear-inspiring above (that of) all the divine beings* 4QShirShabb^{f} 23.1$_{13}$, הוּא מוֹרַאֲכֶם *he shall be your fear*, i.e. object of fear Is 8$_{13}$, אַיֵּה מוֹרָאִי *where is my fear?*, i.e. reverence due to me Ml 1$_{6}$.

<OBJ> מוֹרָא *fear* Is 8$_{12}$, נתן *give* Dt 11$_{25}$ 1QH 4$_{26}$, שׁית *place* Ps 9$_{21}$ (unless מוֹרָה III *muzzle*; or em. מוֹרֶה *teacher*, i.e. ירה hi. ptc.),* עשׂה *do* Dt 34$_{12}$.

<CSTR> מורא מלך *fear of the king of* the divine beings 4QShirShabb^{f} 23.1$_{13}$; כֹּל הַמּוֹרָא *all the terror* Dt 34$_{12}$.

<ADJ> גָּדוֹל *great* Dt 4$_{34}$ 26$_{8}$ 34$_{12}$ Jr 32$_{21}$.

<PREP> לְ of direction, *to*, + יבל hi. *bring* Ps 76$_{12}$ (or em. לַנּוֹרָא *to the one to be feared*, i.e. ירא ni. ptc.); *with respect to* Dt 34$_{12}$; בְּ of instrument, *by (means of), with*, + יצא hi. *bring out* Dt 26$_{8}$ Jr 32$_{21}$, לקח *take* Dt 4$_{34}$, חתת hi. *terrify* Jb 33$_{16}$ (if em. בְּמֹסָרָם יַחְתֹּם *he seals with their discipline* to יְחִתֵּם בְּמוֹרָאִים *he terrifies them with fearful things*), אמץ pi. *strengthen* Si 45$_{2(Bmg)}$ (B במרומים *in the heights*).

<COLL> מוֹרָא || פַּחַד *dread* Dt 11$_{25}$, חַת *terror* Gn 9$_{2}$, כָּבוֹד *glory* Ml 1$_{6}$, אוֹת *sign* Dt 4$_{34}$ 26$_{8}$ Jr 32$_{21}$, מוֹפֵת *wonder* Dt 4$_{34}$ 26$_{8}$ Jr 32$_{21}$, מַסָּה *testing* Dt 4$_{34}$, מִלְחָמָה *war* Dt 4$_{34}$, יָד mighty *hand* Dt 4$_{34}$ 26$_{8}$ 34$_{12}$ Jr 32$_{21}$, זְרוֹעַ outstretched *arm* Dt 4$_{34}$ 26$_{8}$, אֶזְרוֹעַ outstretched *arm* Jr 32$_{21}$, ערץ hi. ptc. *one who inspires with awe* Is 8$_{13}$.

וָאֶתְּנֵם־לוֹ מוֹרָא *and I gave them to him (for) fear*, i.e. so that he would fear Ml 2$_{5}$.

<SYN> §1 פַּחַד *dread*, חַת *terror*; §2 כָּבוֹד *glory*; §3 ערץ hi. ptc. *one who inspires with awe*; §4 אוֹת *sign*, מוֹפֵת *wonder*, מַסָּה *testing*, מִלְחָמָה *war*, יָד *hand*, זְרוֹעַ *arm*, אֶזְרוֹעַ *arm* .

⇒ ירא I *fear*.

מוֹרָא II, see מוֹרָה I *razor*.

מוֹרַג 3 n.m. **threshing sledge**—mss מוֹרָג; pl. מוֹרִגִּים (מֹרִגִּים)—heavy planks of wood, with stones or iron fitted underneath, and pulled over harvested grain by oxen, <OBJ> ראה *see* 2 S 24$_{22}$ (+ כְּלִי *equipment*), נתן *give* 1 C 21$_{23}$. <APP> חָרוּץ *threshing sledge* Is 41$_{15}$ (unless חָרוּץ adj. *sharp*). <ADJ> perh. מוֹרַג חָרוּץ חָדָשׁ *a sharp new threshing sledge* Is 41$_{15}$ (+ בַּעַל פִּיפִיּוֹת *having teeth*; but prob. חָרוּץ = *threshing sledge*). <PREP> לְ *as*, + שׂים *place* Is 41$_{15}$. <COLL> הַמּוֹרִגִּים ... לָעֵצִים *the threshing sledges ... for wood* 2 S 24$_{22}$||1 C 21$_{23}$.

מוֹרָד I 5.0.1 n.[m.] **descent**—cstr. מוֹרַד—**1. descent, slope,** as geographical term, <CSTR> מוֹרַד בֵּית־חוֹרֹן *descent of Beth-horon* Jos 10$_{11}$, חוֹרֹנַיִם *of Horonaim* Jr 48$_{5}$ (+ מַעֲלֶה *ascent*). <PREP> בְּ of place, *in, at* Jos 10$_{11}$, + נכה hi. *strike* Jos 7$_{5}$, נגר ho. *be poured out* Mc 1$_{4}$ (unless מוֹרָד II *watering-place* or III *rivulet*) 1QH 4$_{34}$, שׁמע *hear* Jr 48$_{5}$.

2. hanging, as style of metal work in bronze stands for temple, <CSTR> מַעֲשֵׂה מוֹרָד *work of hanging*, perh. spiral or pendant work 1 K 7$_{29}$ (unless *plated*, i.e. רדד ho. ptc.).

***מוֹרָד** II 1 n.[m.] **watering-place** (unless מוֹרָד I *descent* or III *rivulet*), <PREP> בְּ of place, *in, at*, + נגר ho. *be poured out* Mc 1$_{4}$.

***מוֹרָד** III 1 n.[m.] **rivulet** (unless מוֹרָד I *descent* or II *watering-place*), <PREP> בְּ of place, *in, at*, + נגר ho. *be poured out* Mc 1$_{4}$.

מוֹרָה I 3 n.m. **razor**—mss מורא—<SUBJ> עלה *go up* on head Jg 13$_{5}$ 16$_{7}$ 1 S 1$_{11}$.

מוֹרָה II, see מוֹרָא *fear*.

***מוֹרָה** III 1 n.f. **muzzle** (unless מוֹרָה II *fear*), <OBJ> שׁית *place* Ps 9$_{21}$.

⇒ ירה III *teach*.

מוֹרֶה I 3 n.[m.] **early rain,** from end of October to beginning of December, <SUBJ> עטה *cover* Ps 84$_{7}$ (or em. יַרְוֶה י׳ *Y. saturates*), עשׂה *make* Ps 84$_{7(mss)}$ (or em.; see above). <OBJ> נתן *give* Jl 2$_{23}$ (or del.), ירד hi. *send down* Jl 2$_{23}$ (|| מַלְקוֹשׁ *latter rain*). <APP> גֶּשֶׁם *rain* Jl 2$_{23}$.

<SYN> מַלְקוֹשׁ *latter rain*.

⇒ ירה II *water*.

מוֹרֶה II 3 pl.n. **Moreh**—מֹרֶה (Sam מורא)—**1.** near Shechem, <CSTR> אֵלוֹן מוֹרֶה *terebinth of Moreh* unless *of (the) teacher* Gn 12$_{6}$ Dt 11$_{30}$ (if em. אֵלוֹנֵי מֹרֶה *terebinths of Moreh*; Sam מורא).

2. appar. in valley of Jezreel, perh. Jebel ed-Daḥi, <CSTR> גִּבְעַת הַמּוֹרֶה *hill of Moreh* unless *of the teacher* or *Gibeath-hammoreh* Jg 7$_{1}$. <PREP> מִן *at, by*, + היה *be* Jg 7$_{1}$.

מוֹרֶה III *teacher*, see ירה III *teach*, Hi. §3.

[מוֹרֶה] IV *archer*, see ירה I *throw*, Hi. §1b.

מוֹרֶה V *rebel*, see מרה *rebel*.

מוֹרִיָּה 2 pl.n. **Moriah**—מֹרִיָּה (Sam מוראה)—**1.** place for sacrifice of Isaac, <CSTR> אֶרֶץ הַמֹּרִיָּה *land of Moriah* Gn 22_2 (Sam המוראה).

2. site of temple, <OBJ> חנן *be gracious to* Kh. Beit Lei graf. 7 (המוריה; others פקד יה *Y. has visited*, or נקה יה *Y. has acquitted*). <CSTR> הַר הַמּוֹרִיָּה *Mount Moriah* 2 C 3_1. <APP> נָוֶה *habitation* of Y. Kh. Beit Lei graf. 7.

[מוֹרָשׁ] I 2 n.[m.] **possession**—cstr. מוֹרַשׁ; pl. sf. מוֹרָשֵׁיהֶם—<OBJ> ירשׁ *take possession of* Ob_{17} (or em. מוֹרִישֵׁיהֶם *those who dispossessed them*, i.e. ירשׁ hi.). <CSTR> מוֹרַשׁ קִפֹּד *possession of the hedgehog* Is 14_{23}. <PREP> לְ *as*, + שׂים *place*, i.e. make Is 14_{23}.

⇒ ירשׁ I *take possession of*.

[מוֹרָשׁ] II 1 n.[m.] **desire**—pl. cstr. מוֹרָשֵׁי—(unless מוֹרָשׁ III *string*), <SUBJ> נתק ni. *be torn apart* Jb 17_{11}. <CSTR> מוֹרָשֵׁי לְבָבִי *desires of my heart* Jb 17_{11}. <APP> זִמָּה *plan* Jb 17_{11} (or em. זִמֹּתַי *my plans* to זַמֹּתִי, from זמם *plan*, appar. *I planned* my days that have passed).

⇒ cf. אֲרֶשֶׁת *desire*.

*[מוֹרָשׁ] III 1 n.[m.] **string**—pl. cstr. מוֹרָשֵׁי—(unless מוֹרָשׁ II *desire*), <SUBJ> נתק ni. *be wrenched out* Jb 17_{11}. <CSTR> מוֹרָשֵׁי לְבָבִי *strings of my heart* Jb 17_{11}. <APP> זִמָּה *cord* Jb 17_{11}.

מוֹרָשָׁה 9 n.f. **possession,** of land (Ex 6_8 Ezk 11_{16} 25_{10} 33_{24} $36_{2.5}$), people (Ezk 25_4 36_3), law (Dt 33_4), <SUBJ> היה *be* Ezk 36_3. <PREP> לְ *as*, + היה *be* Ezk 36_2, נתן *give* Ezk $25_{4.10}$ 36_5, ni. *be given* Ezk 11_{15} 33_{24}. <COLL> וְנָתַתִּי אֹתָהּ לָכֶם מוֹרָשָׁה *and I will give it to you as a possession* Ex 6_8, תּוֹרָה צִוָּה־לָנוּ מֹשֶׁה מוֹרָשָׁה קְהִלַּת יַעֲקֹב *Moses charged us with the law as a possession (for) the assembly of Jacob* Dt 33_4.

⇒ ירשׁ I *take possession of*, מוֹרֶשֶׁת גַּת *Moresheth-gath*.

מוֹרֶשֶׁת גַּת 1 pl.n. **Moresheth-gath,** or Moresheth of Gath, perh. T. ej-Judeideh, 14 km ENE of Gath, <PREP> עַל *to*, + נתן *give* Mc 1_{14}.

⇒ מוֹרָשָׁה *possession* + גַּת II *Gath*.

מוֹרַשְׁתִּי 2 gent. **Morashtite**—מֹרַשְׁתִּי—belonging to Moresheth, as sing. noun, <SUBJ> היה *be* Jr 26_{18}, נבא ni. *prophesy* Jr 26_{18}, אמר *say* Jr 26_{18}, חזה *see* Mc 1_1. <APP> מִיכָה *Micah* Mc 1_1 Jr $26_{18(Qr)}$ (Kt מיכיה *Micaiah*). <PREP> אֶל *to*, + היה *be* Mc 1_1.

⇒ מוֹרֶשֶׁת גַּת *Moresheth-gath*.

מושׁ I, מִישׁ 20.3.13 vb. **depart—Qal** 18.3.13 (some forms perh. Hi.) Pf. מָשׁוּ; impf. יָמִישׁ, יָמוּשׁ (Q ימשׁ), 3fs תָּמוּשׁ, Kt תמישׁ, 2ms תָּמֵשׁ, Q תמישי, אָמִישׁ, יָמוּשׁוּ (יָמֻשׁוּ), Q ימישו; + waw וּמָשׁ, וּמַשְׁתִּי—**1. depart, cease** (e.g. Jr 17_8 Na 3_1 Si 32_{21} 1QH 8_{17}), **be lacking** (1QS $6_{3.6}$ CD 13_2).

<SUBJ> Y. Jg 6_{18}, אֵל *god* Is 46_7 (:: עמד *stand*), Job Jb 23_{12} (unless hi., §2), Joshua Ex 33_{11}, Moses Nm 14_{44}, בֵּן *son* Ex 33_{11}, אִישׁ *man* 1QS $6_{3.6}$ 4QSD 7.2_6 (ימ[וש איש]), CD 13_2, נַעַר *lad* Ex 33_{11}, כֹּהֵן *priest* 1QS 6_3 CD 13_2, רֹפֵא *doctor* Si $38_{12(Segal)}$ ([רופא]), רוּחַ *spirit* Is 59_{21}, זֶרַע *seed* 4Q415 2.1_5, עֵץ *tree* Jr 17_8, שָׁמַיִם *heaven* 1QH 8_{17} (שדים appar. error for שמים), הַר *mountain* Is 54_{10} (|| מוט *shake*), עַמּוּד *pillar* Ex 13_{22}, אֲרוֹן *ark* Nm 14_{44}, דָּבָר *word* Is 59_{21}, סֵפֶר *book* Jos 1_8, שַׁוְעָה *cry for help* Si 32_{21}, טֶרֶף *prey* Na 3_1 1Q55 1_3, חֶרֶב *sword* 4QpNah 3.2_5, יָתֵד *tent peg* Is 22_{25}, חֹק *statute* Jr 31_{36} (+ שׁבת *cease*), חֶסֶד *loyalty* Is 54_{10} (|| מוט), תֹּךְ *oppression* Ps 55_{12}, מִרְמָה *deceit* Ps 55_{12}, רָעָה *evil* Pr 17_{13} appar. Si $40_{10(Bmg)}$ (unless from משׁשׁ II *arrive*; or em. תחוש *it hastens* or תבוא *it comes*), כָּלָה *destruction* appar. Si $40_{10(B)}$ (unless from משׁשׁ II *arrive*; or em.; see above), חֲצִי *half* of mountain Zc 14_4.

<PREP> בְּ of place, *in*, + מָקוֹם *place* 1QS $6_{6.3}$ CD 13_2; perh. of instrument, *by (means of), with*, + לֵבָב *heart* 4Q415 2.2_2; מִן of direction, *from* 1Q55 1_3 4QSD 7.2_6 ([ימ]וש ... מן), + פֶּה *mouth* Jos 1_8 Is 59_{21}, לֵב *heart* 4Q 417 1.1_9, בַּיִת *house* Pr 17_{13}, מִקְדָּשׁ *sanctuary* 11QT 3_{11}, רְחוֹב *square* Ps 55_{12}, מָקוֹם *place* Is 46_7, זֶה *this (place)*, i.e. here Jg 6_{18}; מֵאֵת *from*, + אִישׁ *man* 1QS 6_3; מִתּוֹךְ *from (within)*, + אֹהֶל *tent* Ex 33_{11}; מִקֶּרֶב *from (within)*, + מַחֲנֶה *camp* Nm 14_{44}, עֵדָה *congregation* 4QpNah 3.2_5; לִפְנֵי

(from) before, + עַם people Ex 13_{22}; מִלִּפְנֵי from before, + Y. Jr 31_{36}; מִתַּחַת from under 4QapJoshua[a] 15_3; בַּעֲבוּר on account of, + רָשָׁע wicked one Si $40_{10(Bmg)}$ (unless from מושׁ II arrive); ה- of direction, towards, + צָפוֹן north Zc 14_4, נֶגֶב south Zc 14_4.

<COLL> מִצְוַת שְׂפָתָיו וְלֹא אָמִישׁ as for the commandment of his lips, I have not departed (from it) Jb 23_{12} (unless hi., §2), לֹא יָמִישׁ מֵעֲשׂוֹת פֶּרִי it does not cease from producing fruit Jr 17_8.

2. remove, <SUBJ> Y. Zc 3_9 (or em. וְהֵמַשְׁתִּי, i.e. hi.). <OBJ> עָוֹן guilt Zc 3_9 (or em. see Subj.). <PREP> בְּ of time, in, on, + יוֹם day Zc 3_9 (or em.; see Subj.).

Hi. 3 Impf. יָמִישׁ, אָמִישׁ, תָּמִישׁוּ—**1. remove,** <SUBJ> Y. Mc 2_4 (or em. אֵיךְ יָמִישׁ לִי how he removes [it] from me! to אֵין מֵשִׁיב there is none who restores) Zc 3_9 (if em. וּמַשְׁתִּי and I will remove [qal] to וְהֵמַשְׁתִּי), מִשְׁפָּחָה clan Mc 2_3, אֵלֶּה these Ezr 10_{44} (if em. וַיֵּשׁ מֵהֶם נָשִׁים וַיָּשִׂימוּ בָּנִים appar. and there were of them women and they placed children to וַיָּמִישׁוּ מֵהֶם נָשִׁים וּבָנִים and they removed from among them the women and children). <OBJ> צַוָּאר neck Mc 2_3, עָוֹן guilt Zc 3_9 (if em. see Subj.). <PREP> לְ appar. of direction, from, + wicked Mc 2_4 (or em. see Subj.); בְּ of time, in, on, + יוֹם day Zc 3_9 (if em.; see Subj.); מִן of direction, from, + שָׁם there Mc 2_3. <COLL> מוש + adverb, אֵיךְ how! Mc 2_4 (or em.; see Subj.).

2. dismiss,* <SUBJ> Job Jb 23_{12} (unless אָמִישׁ is qal). <COLL> מִצְוַת שְׂפָתָיו וְלֹא אָמִישׁ as for the commandment of his lips, I have not dismissed (it) Jb 23_{12} (unless qal).

Also 4QapPs[a] 5_3 4QSap[b] 12_2 perh. 4QSela 9.1_{18}.

<SYN> §1 מוט shake.

<ANT> עמד stand.

מוּשׁ II 3.0.1 vb. **feel**—**Qal** 1.0.1 Impf. Q ימושו; + waw וַאֲמֻשְׁךָ—**feel, grope,** <SUBJ> Isaac Gn 27_{21}, יָד hand perh. 4QapLam[a] 1.2_{12}; subj. not specified, Jb 30_3 (if em. אֶמֶשׁ evening to יְמוּשׁוּ they grope). <OBJ> Jacob Gn 27_{21}, תְּכֵלֶת blue (material) perh. 4QapLam[a] 1.2_{12}, שׁוֹאָה destruction Jb 30_3 (if em.; see Subj.), מְשׁוֹאָה devastation Jb 30_3 (if em.; see Subj.).

Hi. 2 + waw יְמִישׁוּן; impv. Qr, mss הֲמִשֵׁנִי (Kt הימשני, i.e. ימשׁ hi.)—**1. feel,** <SUBJ> עָצָב idol Ps 115_7.

2. let feel, let touch, <SUBJ> נַעַר lad Jg $16_{26(Qr, mss)}$. <OBJ> 1. Samson Jg $16_{26(Qr)}$, 2. עַמּוּד pillar Jg $16_{26(Qr, mss)}$.

⇒ cf. also משׁשׁ feel, ימשׁ touch.

מוֹשָׁב 44.2.36 n.m. **seat, dwelling place**—cstr. מוֹשַׁב; sf. מוֹשָׁבִי, מוֹשָׁבֵךְ, מוֹשָׁבוֹ (Q משבו), מוֹשָׁבָם; pl. Q מושבות; cstr. מוֹשְׁבֵי, Q משבות; sf. מוֹשְׁבֹתֵיכֶם (Q מושבותיכמה, מֹשְׁבֹתֵיכֶם), מוֹשְׁבֹתָם, מוֹשְׁבוֹתָם, Q מושבותיהמה, מוֹשְׁבֹתֵיהֶם (מוֹשְׁבוֹתֵיהֶם), מֹשְׁבֹתָם, מֹשְׁבוֹתָם, Q מושבותמה)—**1. seat, place of sitting,** at meal (1 S 20_{18}), in town square (Jb 29_7), as a throne (Ezk 28_2).

<SUBJ> פקד ni. be lacking, i.e. empty 1 S 20_{18}. <OBJ> כון hi. prepare Jb 29_7, בקשׁ pi. seek Si 7_4 (unless §7) 12_{12}. <CSTR> מוֹשַׁב אֱלֹהִים seat of the gods Ezk 28_2 (+ בְּלֵב יַמִּים in the heart of the seas), מוֹשַׁב הַקִּיר seat of, i.e. by, the wall 1 S 20_{25}, מושב כבוד seat of glory, i.e. glorious seat Si 7_4, כבודו of his glory 4QShirShabb[f] 20.2_9, מושבי כבוד seats of glory 4QShirShabb[f] 20.2_4, מושב יקרכה seat of your honour 4QBer[a] 1.2_1 (+ הֲדֹם footstool), אנחה of sighing 4QTohA 1.1_1 (|| מִשְׁכָּב bed); בית מושב house of, i.e. quarters with, seats 11QT 37_8. <PREP> אֶל upon, + ישׁב sit 1 S 20_{25}; עַל upon, + ישׁב sit 1 S 20_{25}; לִפְנֵי before 11QT 37_9; מִתַּחַת (from) beneath 4QShirShabb[f] 20.2_9; מוֹשָׁב without preposition, in the seat, + ישׁב sit Ezk 28_2 4QTohA 1.1_1. <COLL> מושבות לכוהנים seats for the priests 11QT 37_8, מושב ככסא מלכותו a seat like his royal throne 4QShirShabb[f] 20.2_2, מושבי כבוד למרכבו[ת] seats of glory, i.e. glorious seats, of the chariots 4QShirShabb[f] 20.2_4.

2a. (sitting) company, assembly, distinction from §6 not clear at 4QD[a] 5.2_{14} CD $12_{19.22}$ 13_{20} $14_{3.17}$. <OBJ> ראה see 1 K 10_5||2 C 9_4 (|| מַעֲמָד attendance). <NOM CL> זה מושב המחנות this is the assembly of the camps CD 13_{20}. <CSTR> מוֹשַׁב זְקֵנִים company of the elders Ps 107_{32} (|| קְהַל congregation), עֲבָדָיו of his servants 1 K 10_5||2 C 9_4, לֵצִים of scorners Ps 1_1 (|| דֶּרֶךְ way), מושב ערי assembly of (or those who dwell in, i.e. §6) the cities of Israel 4QD[a] 5.2_{14} ([ערי]) CD 12_{19}, המ[חנה] of the camp CD 14_{17}, המחנות of the camps CD 12_{22} (המ[חנו]ת) 13_{20} 14_3 (כל המחנות of all the camps); סרך מושב rule of the *assembly of* 4QD^{a} 5.2$_{14}$ CD 12$_{19.22}$ 14$_{3}$, פרוש *exact statement of* CD 14$_{17}$. <PREP> בְּ of place, *in*, + ישב *sit* Ps 1$_{1}$, הלל pi. *praise* Ps 107$_{32}$.

2b. session, (meeting of) assembly, <NOM CL> [ה]וא [מו]שב אנשי השם *it is the session of the men of repute* 1QSa 2$_{11}$. <CSTR> מושב הרבים *session of the many* 1QS 6$_{8.11}$ 7$_{10.10.13}$ 4QSD 1.2$_{1}$ (אנשי[הרב]ים), *of the men of* repute 1QSa 2$_{11}$ ([מו]שב). <ADJ> אֶחָד *one* 1QS 7$_{11}$. <PREP> לְ of benefit, *for* 1QS 6$_{8}$; בְּ of time, *in, during*, + דבר pi. *speak* 1QS 6$_{11}$, ישׁן *sleep* 1QS 7$_{10}$ 4QSD 1.2$_{1}$ ([ויש]ן), פטר ni. *take leave* 1QS 7$_{10}$ (=4QS^{e} 1$_{7}$ ממוש *from the session of*), תמם *be perfect* appar. 1QS 8$_{26}$ (or em. בם ושב *in them, and he may return*); מִן *from*, + פטר ni. *take leave* 4QS^{e} 1$_{7}$ (= 1QS 7$_{11}$ במושב *in a session of*); עַל *at* 1QS 7$_{11}$; אֶל תּוֹךְ *during* 1QS 7$_{13}$, + רקק *spit* 1QS 7$_{13}$.

3. dwelling place, individual dwelling (e.g. Ex 12$_{20}$ Lv 13$_{46}$), territory, city (e.g. Gn 10$_{30}$ 27$_{39}$ Ezk 6$_{6}$ 1 C 4$_{33}$ 6$_{39}$ 7$_{28}$), Zion as dwelling place of Y. (Ps 132$_{13}$), **inhabited place** (Ezk 34$_{13}$), <SUBJ> היה *be* Gn 27$_{39}$. <NOM CL> מֹשְׁבוֹתָם בֵּית־אֵל וּבְנֹתֶיהָ *their dwelling places were Bethel and its villages* 1 C 7$_{28}$, זֹאת מוֹשְׁבֹתָם *this was their dwelling place* 1 C 4$_{33}$, sim. 6$_{39}$, בשמים משבו *his* (Y.'s) *dwelling place is in heaven* 4QAdmonPar 3.2$_{9}$, מוֹשָׁבָם מִמֵּשָׁא *their dwelling place was from Mesha* Gn 10$_{30}$, מִחוּץ לַמַּחֲנֶה מוֹשָׁבוֹ *his dwelling place shall be outside the camp* Lv 13$_{46}$, אֵיתָן מוֹשָׁבֶךָ *your dwelling place is enduring* Nm 24$_{21}$ (+ קֵן *nest*).

<CSTR> מוֹשְׁבֵי הָאָרֶץ *inhabited places of the land* Ezk 34$_{13}$, מושב הנשי *dwelling place of the men of* injustice 1QS 8$_{13}$ (= 4QS^{e} 3$_{3}$ אנשי; unless §2b), משפחות *of families* 1QM 10$_{14}$, משבות מטות *dwelling places of the tribes of* 11QT 21$_{14}$; כֹּל מוֹשְׁבֵי *all the inhabited places of* Ezk 34$_{13}$, כֹּל מוֹשְׁבֹתֵיכֶם *all your dwelling places* Ex 12$_{20}$ 35$_{3}$ (מֹשְׁבֹתֵיכֶם) Lv 3$_{17}$ 7$_{26}$ 23$_{3.14}$ (מֹשְׁבֹתֵיכֶם) 23$_{21}$ (כָּל־) 23$_{31}$ (מֹשְׁבֹתֵיכֶם) Nm 35$_{29}$ Ezk 6$_{6}$ 11QT 27$_{9}$ (כול מושבותיכמה; corrected from מוֹשְׁבוֹתֵיהֶם,(כול מושבותיכה *their dwelling places* Ezk 6$_{14}$ Ezk 37$_{23}$ (מוֹשְׁבֹתֵיהֶם; or em. מְשׁוּבֹתֵיהֶם *their backslidings*) 11QT 17$_{4}$ (כול מושבותיהמה) 18$_{9}$ ([כול מושבותיה]מה) 21$_{9}$ (מושבותמה) 23$_{01}$ ([כול] מושבותיהמה).

<PREP> לְ *for (the purpose of)* Ezk 48$_{15}$ (|| מִגְרָשׁ *pasture land*), אוה pi. *desire* Ps 132$_{13}$; *according to* Gn 36$_{43}$ (Sam לְמִשְׁפְּחֹתָם *according to their families*).

בְּ of place, *in* Lv 3$_{17}$ 23$_{3.14.21.31}$ Nm 31$_{10}$ 35$_{29}$ 11QT 17$_{4}$ 21$_{9}$ 23$_{01}$ ([בכול] מושותיהמה) 25$_{8}$ ([במושבותיכמה]) 27$_{9}$ 39$_{9}$ 4QM^{f} 13$_{3}$ (במושבותם) 13$_{4}$ ([במושב]ותיהם), + היה *be* Ex 10$_{23}$ 11QT 18$_{9}$ ([בכול מושבותיה]מה), אכל *eat* Ex 12$_{20}$ Lv 7$_{26}$, רעה *pasture* Ezk 34$_{13}$, בער pi. *kindle* Ex 35$_{3}$ (Sam hi.), חרב *be desolate* Ezk 6$_{6}$, נתן *give*, i.e. make, desolate Ezk 6$_{14}$, חלק ni. *be divided* 1QM 2$_{14}$ ([במו]שבותם) 2$_{14}$.

מִן of direction, *from* 11QT 18$_{13}$ 21$_{14}$, + בוא hi. *bring* Lv 23$_{17}$, ישׁע hi. *save* Ezk 37$_{23}$ (or em.; see Cstr.).

מִתּוֹךְ *from (among)*, + בדל ni. *separate oneself* 1QS 8$_{13}$ (unless §2b).

4. dwelling, habitation, <CSTR> מוֹשַׁב עִיר חוֹמָה *dwelling of*, i.e. in, *walled city* Lv 25$_{29}$; עִיר מוֹשָׁב *city of habitation*, i.e. inhabited city Ps 107$_{4.7.36}$, ערי מושב[ותם] *cities of their habitation* 4QRitPur 7.11$_{3}$, אֶרֶץ מוֹשְׁבֹתֵיכֶם *land of your dwelling* Nm 15$_{2}$, בית מושב *house of dwelling* 4QTohA 1.1$_{2}$, בֵּית־מוֹשַׁב *house of dwelling of* Lv 25$_{29}$.

5. (length of) time of dwelling, <NOM CL> מוֹשַׁב בְּנֵי יִשְׂרָאֵל ... שְׁלֹשִׁים שָׁנָה וְאַרְבַּע מֵאוֹת שָׁנָה *the time of the dwelling of the sons of Israel was ... four hundred and thirty years* Ex 12$_{40}$. <CSTR> מוֹשַׁב בְּנֵי יִשְׂרָאֵל *time of dwelling of the sons of Israel* Ex 12$_{40}$ (+ אֲשֶׁר יָשְׁבוּ בְּמִצְרָיִם *which they dwelt in Egypt*).

6. those who dwell, cf. §2a, <NOM CL> כֹּל מוֹשַׁב בֵּית־צִיבָא עֲבָדִים לִמְפִיבֹשֶׁת *all those who dwelt in the house of Ziba were servants of Mephibosheth* 2 S 9$_{12}$. <CSTR> כֹּל מוֹשַׁב בֵּית־צִיבָא *all those who dwelt of*, i.e. in, *the house of Ziba* 2 S 9$_{12}$.

7. situation, position, office, <NOM CL> מוֹשַׁב הָעִיר טוֹב *the situation of the city is good* 2 K 2$_{19}$, שָׁם מוֹשַׁב סֵמֶל הַקִּנְאָה *there was the position of the image of jealousy* Ezk 8$_{3}$. <OBJ> בקשׁ pi. seek Si 7$_{4}$. <CSTR> מוֹשַׁב הָעִיר *situation of the city* 2 K 2$_{19}$, מוֹשַׁב סֵמֶל *position of the image of* jealousy Ezk 8$_{3}$, מושב כבוד *office of honour* Si 7$_{4}$ (unless §1; || מֶמְשָׁלָה *governorship*).

Also 4QD^{a} 5.2$_{16}$ ([מו]שב) 4QTohB^{c} 1$_{12}$ ([מוש]בו) 4Q ShirShabb^{f} 17$_{6}$ 4QRitPur 73$_{3}$.

<SYN> §1 מִשְׁכָּב *bed;* §2a קָהָל *congregation,* מַעֲמָד *attendance,* דֶּרֶךְ *way;* §3 מִגְרָשׁ *pasture land;* §7 מֶמְשָׁלָה *governorship.*
⇒ ישׁב *sit.*

*[מוֹשָׁבָה] n.f. **settlement, transportation,** <PREP> עַל *at, concerning,* + שׂחק *laugh* Lm 1$_{7}$ (if em. מִשְׁבַּתֶּהָ *her inactivity* to מוֹשַׁבְתָּהּ *her transportation*).

*[מוֹשֶׁבֶת] $_{0.0.1}$ n.f. **dwelling,** <CSTR> בית מושבת *house of dwelling* CD 11$_{10}$.
⇒ ישׁב *sit.*

מוּשִׁי I $_{8}$ pr.n.m. **Mushi**—מֻשִׁי—Levite, son of Merari, <NOM CL> בְּנֵי מְרָרִי מַחְלִי וּמוּשִׁי *the sons of Merari were Mahli and Mushi* Ex 6$_{19}$ 1 C 6$_{4}$ (וּמֻשִׁי) 23$_{21}$ 24$_{26}$, var. Nm 3$_{20}$. <CSTR> בֶּן־מוּשִׁי *son of Mushi* 1 C 6$_{32}$, בְּנֵי *sons of* 1 C 23$_{23}$ 24$_{30}$. <APP> בֵּן *son* 1 C 6$_{32}$.
⇒ מוּשִׁי II *Mushite.*

מוּשִׁי II $_{2}$ gent. **Mushite,** descended from Mushi, as collective singular noun, **Mushites,** <CSTR> מִשְׁפַּחַת הַמּוּשִׁי *clan of the Mushites* Nm 3$_{33}$ 26$_{58}$.
⇒ מוּשִׁי I *Mushi.*

מוֹשִׁיַע *saviour, advocate,** see ישׁע *save,* Hi., §1b.

[מוֹשָׁעָה] $_{1}$ n.f. **salvation**—pl. מוֹשָׁעוֹת—<PREP> לְ *of possession, of, (belonging) to* Ps 68$_{21}$ (אֵל לְמוֹשָׁעוֹת *a God of salvation;* + תּוֹצָאָה *escape* from death).
⇒ ישׁע *save.*

מוּת $_{842.10.75.1}$ vb. **die—Qal** $_{628.10.50}$ Pf. מֵת, מֵתָה, מַתְנוּ (מָתְנוּ), מֵתוּ; impf. יָמוּת (יָמֹת), 3fs תָּמוּת (תָּמֹת), 2ms תָּמוּת, תָּמוּתִי, אָמוּת (אָמֻת, אָמוּתָה), יָמוּתוּ (יָמֻתוּ, יְמוּתוּן, יְמֻתוּן), 3fpl תְּמוּתֶינָה, תָּמוּתוּ (תָּמֻתוּ, תְּמוּתוּן, תְּמֻתוּן), נָמוּת; + waw וּמֵת (וָמֵת), וָמֵתָה, וָמַתָּה, וָמַתִּי, וָמַתְנוּ (וָמֵתְנוּ), וּמֵתוּ (וָמֵתוּ); וַיָּמָת (וַיָּמֹת), 3fs וַתָּמָת (וַתָּמֹת), וַיָּמוּתוּ (וַיָּמֻתוּ); impv. מֻת; ptc. מֵת (sf. מֵתִי, מֵתְךָ, מֵתֶךָ, מֵתוֹ), מֵתָה, מֵתִים (Q מיתין, sf. מֵתֶיךָ, Q מתיכמה, Q מתיהמה), מֵתֵי, Q מיתות; inf. abs. מוֹת; cstr. מוּת (מוֹת, מוּתִי, מוֹתִי, Q מותך, מוֹתוֹ, מֹתוֹ, מוּתָהּ, מוּתֵנוּ, מֻתֵנוּ, מֹתָם, Q מותמה, מֻתָן).

1. usu. **die, be dead;** perh. also **become mortal** (Gn 2$_{17}$ 3$_{3.4}$ Ps 82$_{7}$),* **be in danger of death** (1 S 4$_{20}$);* לָמוּת as superlative, **very, exceedingly,** lit. 'to the point of death' (Jg 16$_{16}$ 2 K 20$_{1}$).*

a. of deities (Hb 1$_{12(TiqSof)}$ Ps 82$_{7}$).

b. of humans, including groups of people (e.g. Ex 20$_{19}$ Nm 4$_{19.20}$ 14$_{2.2.35}$ 18$_{3}$ 20$_{4}$ 21$_{5.6}$ 26$_{10}$ Jg 5$_{18}$ 1 S 12$_{49}$ 22$_{16.16}$ 2 S 1$_{4}$ Jr 27$_{13}$ 42$_{16.22}$ Ezk 18$_{31}$ 33$_{11}$ 1 C 10$_{6}$), through natural causes, esp. in old age (e.g. Gn 5$_{5}$ 9$_{29}$ 23$_{2}$ 25$_{8}$ 35$_{29}$ Dt 4$_{22}$ Jg 8$_{32}$ Jb 42$_{17}$ 1 C 29$_{28}$), in childbirth (Gn 35$_{19}$ 1 S 4$_{20}$), as a result of a stroke (1 S 25$_{37}$), disease, pestilence (e.g. 2 K 13$_{14}$ Jr 16$_{4}$ 21$_{6}$ 27$_{13}$ Ezk 5$_{12}$ 6$_{12}$ 33$_{27}$ 2 K 13$_{14}$ 2 C 21$_{19}$), famine (e.g. Gn 43$_{8}$ 1 K 17$_{12}$ 2 K 7$_{4}$ Jr 11$_{22}$ 27$_{13}$ Ezk 6$_{12}$ 2 C 32$_{11}$), warfare (e.g. Dt 20$_{5}$ 1 S 31$_{5}$ 2 S 11$_{15}$), murder (e.g. Ex 21$_{12}$ Nm 35$_{16}$ Dt 19$_{11}$), execution (e.g. Ex 21$_{12}$ 22$_{18}$ 31$_{14}$ Lv 20$_{2}$ 24$_{16}$ Nm 15$_{35}$ Dt 13$_{11}$ 17$_{5}$ 22$_{21}$=11QT 64$_{6}$ 1 K 21$_{13}$ 11QT 64$_{8}$), suicide (e.g. 1 S 31$_{5}$ 2 S 17$_{23}$ 1 K 16$_{18}$), goring by ox (e.g. Ex 21$_{28}$), snake-bite (Nm 21$_{6}$); as punishment, retribution by Y. (e.g. Gn 2$_{17}$ 20$_{3}$ Ex 11$_{5}$ Lv 10$_{2}$ Nm 3$_{4}$ Jos 10$_{11}$ 2 S 6$_{7}$), by relative (e.g. Dt 19$_{12}$ Jos 20$_{9}$ 2 S 3$_{27}$).

c. of animals (e.g. Gn 33$_{13}$ Ex 7$_{18}$ 8$_{9}$ 9$_{6}$ 21$_{35}$ 22$_{9}$ Lv 11$_{39}$ 20$_{16}$ Is 50$_{2}$ 66$_{24}$ 11QT 50$_{21}$).

d. of tree-stump (Jb 14$_{8}$).

e. of abstracts, e.g. land (Gn 47$_{19}$), wisdom (Jb 12$_{2}$), knowledge (Pr 14$_{33}$; if em.; see Subj.), life (Jb 36$_{14}$).

<SUBJ> Y. Hb 1$_{12(TiqSof)}$ (or em.; see below), אֱלֹהִים *god* Ps 82$_{7}$, עַם *people* Ex 20$_{19}$ Nm 14$_{2.2}$ 20$_{4}$ 21$_{5.6}$ Jg 5$_{18}$ 1 S 12$_{49}$ 2 S 1$_{4}$ Jr 27$_{13}$ 42$_{16.22}$, עֵדָה *assembly* Nm 14$_{35}$ 26$_{10}$, שֵׁבֶט *tribe* Nm 4$_{19.20}$ Nm 18$_{3}$, בַּיִת *house* 1 S 22$_{16.16}$ 1 C 10$_{6}$, of Israel Ezk 18$_{31}$ 33$_{11}$.

Amorites Jos 10$_{11}$, Egyptians Gn 47$_{15.19.19}$ Ex 12$_{33}$, Ephraim Ho 13$_{1}$, Israel(ites) Dt 5$_{25.25}$ 18$_{16}$ 2 K 18$_{32}$ Is 22$_{13.14}$ Hb 1$_{12}$ (or em. לֹא נָמוּת *we shall not die* to לְאוֹן מָוֶת *the Victor over Death*)* 2 C 32$_{11}$, Moab Am 2$_{2}$, Reuben Dt 33$_{6}$, Gileadite Jg 12$_{7}$, Hittite 2 S 11$_{17.21.24}$, Pirathonite Jg 12$_{15}$, Zebulunite Jg 12$_{12}$.

Aaron Ex 28$_{35.43}$ 30$_{20.21}$ Lv 8$_{35}$ 10$_{6.7.9}$ 16$_{2.13}$ 22$_{9}$ Nm 18$_{3}$ 20$_{26.28}$ 33$_{38.39}$ Dt 10$_{6}$ 32$_{50}$, Abdon Jg 12$_{15}$, Abihu Lv 10$_{2}$ Nm 3$_{4}$ 26$_{61}$ 1 C 24$_{2}$, Abimelech, king of Gerar Gn 20$_{3.7.7}$, Abimelech, son of Jerubaal Jg 9$_{54.55}$ 2 S 11$_{21}$, Abner 2 S 3$_{27.33}$ 4$_{1}$, Abraham Gn 25$_{8}$ 4QJub^{d} 22$_{1}$, Absalom 2 S 19$_{11}$, Adam Gn 5$_{5}$, Adoni-bezek Jg 1$_{7}$, Adonijah 1 K 1$_{52}$ 2$_{25}$, Adoram 1 K 12$_{18}$, Agur Pr 30$_{7}$, Ahab 2 K 3$_{5}$, Ahaziah, king of Israel 2 K 1$_{4+6t}$, Ahaziah, king of Judah 2 K 9$_{27}$, Ahimelech 1 S 22$_{16.16}$, Ahithophel 2 S 17$_{23}$, Amasa 2 S 20$_{10}$, Amaziah Am 7$_{17}$, Amnon 2 S 13$_{32.33.39}$, Asa 2 C 16$_{13}$, Asahel 2 S 2$_{23.23}$, Azubah 1 C 2$_{19}$, Baal-hanan Gn 36$_{39}$||1 C 1$_{50}$, Barzillai 2 S 19$_{38}$, Bela Gn 36$_{33}$||1 C 1$_{44}$, Ben-hadad 2 K 8$_{10.10.15}$, Chilion Ru 2$_{5}$, Coniah Jr 22$_{26}$, David 1 S 19$_{6(mss)}$ 20$_{2}$ 2 S 12$_{13}$ 1 K 2$_{1}$ 1 C 29$_{28}$, Deborah Gn 35$_{8}$.

Ehud Jg 4$_{1}$, Eleazar, son of Aaron Lv 10$_{6.7}$ Jos 24$_{33}$, Eleazar, son of Mahli 1 C 23$_{22}$, Eli 1 S 4$_{18}$, Elijah 1 K 19$_{4}$, Elimelech Ru 1$_{3}$, Elisha 2 K 13$_{14.20}$, Elon Jg 12$_{12}$, Enosh Gn 5$_{11}$, Er Gn 46$_{12}$ Nm 26$_{19}$, Esau Gn 25$_{32}$, Gedaliah 2 K 25$_{25}$ (lacking in ms), Gideon Jg 6$_{23}$ 8$_{32.33}$, Hadad, son of Bedad Gn 36$_{36}$||1 C 1$_{47}$, Hadad, husband of Mehetebel 1 C 1$_{51}$, Hadoram 2 C 10$_{18}$, Hananiah Jr 28$_{16.17}$, Haran Gn 11$_{28}$, Hazael 2 K 13$_{24}$, Hezekiah 2 K 20$_{1}$||Is 38$_{1}$||2 C 32$_{24}$ 2 K 20$_{1}$||Is 38$_{1}$, Hophni 1 S 4$_{11.17}$, Husham Gn 36$_{35}$||1 C 1$_{46}$, Ibzan Jg 12$_{10}$, Isaac Gn 26$_{9}$ 27$_{4}$ 35$_{29}$ 4QJub^{h} 36$_{18}$ ([וי]מות), Ishmael Gn 25$_{17}$, Ithamar Lv 10$_{6.7}$.

Jacob/Israel Gn 45$_{28}$ 46$_{30}$ 47$_{29}$ 48$_{21}$, Jacob and family Gn 42$_{2}$, Jair Jg 10$_{5}$, Jared Gn 5$_{20}$, Jehoahaz 2 K 23$_{34}$, Jehoiada 2 C 24$_{15}$, Jehoram 2 C 21$_{19}$, Jephthah Jg 12$_{7}$, Jeremiah Jr 11$_{21}$ 26$_{8.8}$ 37$_{20}$ 38$_{9.10.24.26}$, Jeroboam, son of Nebat 2 C 13$_{20}$, Jeroboam, son of Jehoash Am 7$_{11}$, Jether 1 C 2$_{32}$, Joab 1 K 2$_{30}$ 11$_{21}$, Joash 2 K 12$_{22}$ 2 C 24$_{25}$, Job 2$_{9}$ 3$_{11}$ 42$_{17}$, Jobab Gn 36$_{34}$||1 C 1$_{45}$, Johanan Jr 42$_{16.22}$, Jonah Jon 4$_{8}$, Jonathan 1 S 14$_{43.44.44.45.45}$ 20$_{14}$ 2 S 1$_{4.5}$, Joram 1 K 16$_{22}$ (if ins. וְיוֹרָם אָחִיו בָּעֵת הַהִיא *and Joram his brother at that time*), Joseph Gn 50$_{24.26}$ Ex 1$_{6}$, Joshua Jos 24$_{29}$ Jg 2$_{8.21}$, Josiah 2 C 35$_{24}$, Kenan Gn 5$_{14}$, Lamech Gn 5$_{31}$, Lot Gn 19$_{19}$, Mahalalel Gn 5$_{17}$, Mahlon Ru 1$_{5}$, Manoah Jg 13$_{22.22}$, Methuselah Gn 5$_{27}$, Miriam Nm 20$_{1}$, Moses Ex 10$_{28}$ Dt 4$_{22}$ 31$_{14}$ 32$_{50}$ 34$_{5}$ Jos 1$_{2}$.

Nabal 1 S 25$_{38.39}$, Naboth 1 K 21$_{10+5t}$, Nadab Lv 10$_{2}$ Nm 3$_{4}$ 26$_{61}$ 1 C 24$_{2}$, Nahash 1 C 19$_{1}$, Naomi Ru 1$_{17}$, Noah Gn 9$_{29}$, Onan Gn 46$_{12}$ Nm 26$_{19}$, Othniel Jg 3$_{11}$, Pashhur Jr 20$_{6}$, Pelatiah Ezk 11$_{13}$, Phinehas 1 S 4$_{11.17}$, Rachel Gn 30$_{1}$ 35$_{18.19}$ 48$_{7}$, Ruth Ru 1$_{17}$, Samlah Gn 36$_{37}$|| 1 C 1$_{48}$, Samson Jg 15$_{18}$, Samuel 1 S 25$_{1}$ 28$_{3}$, Sarah Gn 23$_{2}$, Saul 1 S 31$_{5.6.7}$||1 C 10$_{5.6.7}$ 2 S 1$_{4.5}$ 2$_{7}$ 4$_{10}$ 1 C 10$_{13}$, Seled 1 C 2$_{30}$, Seth Gn 5$_{8}$, Shallum Jr 22$_{12}$, Shaul Gn 36$_{38}$||1 C 1$_{49}$, Shebna Is 22$_{18}$, Shelah Gn 38$_{11}$, Shimei 2 S 19$_{22(mss).24}$ 1 K 2$_{37.37.42.42.46}$, Shobach 2 S 10$_{18}$, Sisera Jg 4$_{21}$, Terah Gn 11$_{32}$, Tobit 4QTobit^{e} 7.2$_{4}$ (וימ[ו]ת]), Tola Jg 10$_{2}$, Tibni 1 K 16$_{22}$, Uriah 2 S 11$_{15.17.21.24.26}$, Uzzah 2 S 6$_{7}$||1 C 13$_{10}$, Zechariah 2 C 24$_{22}$, Zedekiah Jr 27$_{13}$ 34$_{4.5}$, Zimri 1 K 16$_{18}$.

אָדָם *human being* Gn 2$_{17}$ 3$_{3.4.4}$ Ex 9$_{19}$ Nm 19$_{13.14}$ Jr 21$_{6}$ 4QNidd 4$_{5}$ 4QAdmon 1$_{6}$ (וי[מ]ת) 11QT 49$_{5}$, אֱנוֹשׁ *human being* Is 51$_{12}$, אִישׁ *man, husband* Ex 4$_{19}$ 21$_{12.14}$ 21$_{28}$ Lv 20$_{2.9.15.20.27}$ Nm 14$_{37}$ 15$_{35.36}$ 27$_{8}$ Dt 2$_{16}$ 17$_{5.12}$ 19$_{12}$ 20$_{5.6.7}$ 22$_{22.24.25}$ 24$_{16(Sam)}$ Jos 5$_{4}$ 2$_{14}$ Jg 9$_{49}$ 10$_{2}$ 1 S 4$_{19}$ 5$_{12}$ 31$_{6}$ 2 S 2$_{31}$ 11$_{26}$ 14$_{5}$ 24$_{15}$ 2 K 4$_{1}$ 7$_{3.4.4.4}$ 14$_{6(Kt)}$||2 C 25$_{4}$ Jr 31$_{30}$ 42$_{17}$ Am 6$_{9}$ Ru 1$_{3}$ 4QHalakhah^{a} 3.1$_{3}$ ([איש ... י]מו[ת]) 11QT 35$_{8}$ 64$_{8.11}$, גֶּבֶר *man* Jb 14$_{10.14}$, בַּעַל *husband* Dt 24$_{3(Sam)}$, אִשָּׁה *woman, wife* Gn 3$_{3.4.4}$ 38$_{12}$ Ex 21$_{28}$ Lv 20$_{16.27}$ Dt 13$_{11}$ 17$_{5}$ 22$_{22}$ Jg 13$_{22.22}$ 1 S 4$_{20}$ 2 S 20$_{3}$ 1 K 17$_{12}$ Ezk 24$_{18}$ 11QT 57$_{18}$, פִּלֶגֶשׁ *secondary wife* Jg 20$_{5}$ 2 S 20$_{3}$.

אָב *father* Gn 44$_{22.31}$ 50$_{5.15}$ Nm 6$_{7}$ 27$_{3.3}$ Dt 24$_{16(Sam^{mss})}$, Jr 16$_{4}$ Ezk 18$_{18}$ 2 C 25$_{4}$, חָם *father-in-law* 1 S 4$_{19}$, אֵם *mother* Gn 48$_{7(Sam)}$ Nm 6$_{7}$ Jr 16$_{4}$ 22$_{26}$, בֵּן *son* Gn 36$_{39}$|| 1 C 1$_{50}$ Gn 38$_{11}$ 50$_{26}$ Ex 28$_{43}$ 30$_{20.21}$ Lv 8$_{35}$ 10$_{2.6.7.9}$ 16$_{1}$ 22$_{9}$ Nm 4$_{15}$ 17$_{25}$ 18$_{3}$ 26$_{11}$ Dt 13$_{11}$ 21$_{21}$=11QT 64$_{6}$ Jos 24$_{29.33}$ Jg 2$_{8}$ 3$_{11}$ 6$_{30}$ 8$_{32}$ 10$_{2}$ 12$_{15}$ 1 S 4$_{11.17}$ 31$_{6.7}$||1 C 10$_{6.7}$ 2 S 1$_{4.5}$ 12$_{14.14}$ 13$_{32(mss)33}$ 18$_{20}$ 1 K 3$_{19.21}$ 17$_{12}$ 2 K 8$_{10.10}$ 11$_{1}$||2 C 22$_{10}$ Jr 11$_{22}$ 16$_{4}$ 22$_{12.26}$ 42$_{16.22}$ Ezk 11$_{13}$ 18$_{13.13(mss, Gnz).17}$ Ps 82$_{7}$ Pr 30$_{7}$ 1 C 29$_{28}$ 2 C 25$_{4}$ Si 14$_{13}$ 41$_{9}$, of Israel Ex 14$_{11.12}$ 16$_{3}$ Lv 15$_{31}$ Nm 18$_{22}$, בַּת *daughter* Gn 38$_{12}$ Dt 13$_{11}$ Jr 11$_{22}$ 16$_{4}$, כַּלָּה *daughter-in-law* 1 S 4$_{20}$, אָח *brother* Gn 42$_{38}$ 44$_{20}$ Ex 1$_{6}$ Lv 16$_{2}$ Nm 18$_{3}$ Dt 13$_{11}$ 1 K 16$_{22}$ (if em.; see above), brothers of Joseph Gn 42$_{20}$ 43$_{8}$, אַלְמָנָה *widow* 1 K 17$_{12}$, דּוֹדָה *aunt* Lv 20$_{20}$.

מֶלֶךְ *king* Ex 2$_{23}$ 2 S 10$_{1}$||1 C 19$_{1}$ 2 S 19$_{1}$ 1 K 22$_{35}$||2 C 18$_{34}$ 1 K 22$_{37}$ 2 K 8$_{10.10}$ 13$_{24}$ Jr 22$_{12.26}$ 27$_{13}$ 34$_{4.5}$ Ezk 17$_{16}$, מָשִׁיחַ *anointed one* 1 S 26$_{10}$, נָשִׂיא *prince* Ezk 12$_{13}$, נָגִיד *prince* Ezk 28$_{8.10}$, שַׂר *commander* 2 S 10$_{18}$ 1 K 11$_{21}$ Jr 42$_{16.22}$ Jb 34$_{20}$, שָׁלִישׁ *officer* 2 K 7$_{17.20}$, שׁוֹעַ *noble* Jb 34$_{20}$, אָדוֹן *lord* 2 S 2$_{7}$, עֶבֶד *servant* Gn 44$_{31}$ Ex 21$_{20}$ Dt 34$_{5}$ Jos 1$_{2}$ 24$_{29}$ Jg 2$_{8}$ 2 S 11$_{21.24.24}$ 2 K 4$_{1}$, אָמָה *female servant* Ex 21$_{20}$, וָלָד *foetus* 11QT 50$_{10}$, יֶלֶד *child* 2 S 12$_{18+7t}$ 1 K 14$_{12}$ 2 K 4$_{20}$, נַעַר *lad* 2 S 1$_{15}$ 13$_{32(mss)}$ 1 K 14$_{17}$ Is 65$_{20}$ Jb 1$_{19}$ Pr 23$_{13}$, נַעֲרָה *young woman* Dt 22$_{21.24}$, בָּחוּר *youth* Jr 11$_{22}$,

בְּכוֹר *firstborn* Ex 11$_{5}$, מֵינֶקֶת *(wet) nurse* Gn 35$_{8}$, כֹּהֵן *priest* Nm 33$_{38}$, לֵוִי *Levite* Nm 18$_{32}$, נָבִיא *prophet* Dt 18$_{20}$ 1 K 13$_{31}$ Jr 28$_{17}$ 38$_{10}$, worshipper Ps 41$_{6}$ 118$_{7}$, שֹׁפֵט *judge* Jg 2$_{19}$, זָקֵן *elderly one* Jb 42$_{17}$, חָכָם *wise one* Ps 49$_{11}$ Ec 2$_{16}$, אֱוִיל *fool* Pr 10$_{21}$.

רֵעַ *neighbour* Ex 21$_{18}$ Dt 13$_{11}$ 19$_{5.11}$, אֹהֵב *friend* Jr 20$_{6}$, שׂנא ptc. *one who hates* reproof Pr 15$_{10}$, בזה ptc. *one who despises* Pr 19$_{16(Qr)}$, גִּבּוֹר *mighty one* 1 S 17$_{51}$, גָּדוֹל *great one* Jr 16$_{6}$, קָטָן *small one* Jr 16$_{6}$, רֹצֵחַ *murderer* Nm 35$_{12+5t}$, נכה hi. ptc. *one who strikes* Ex 21$_{12.15}$ Lv 24$_{17}$ Nm 35$_{21}$ Jos 20$_{9}$, נגע ptc. *one who touches* Gn 26$_{11}$ Ex 19$_{2}$, קָרֵב *one who draws near* Nm 17$_{28}$, גנב ptc. *one who steals* Ex 21$_{16}$, גַּנָּב *thief* Ex 22$_{1}$ Dt 24$_{7}$, קלל pi. ptc. *one who curses* Ex 21$_{17}$, נקב ptc. *one who curses* Lv 24$_{16}$, רָכִיל *talebearer* 11QT 64$_{8}$, חלל pi. ptc. *one who profanes* Ex 31$_{14}$, נֹאֵף *adulterer* Lv 20$_{10}$, נֹאֶפֶת *adulterer* (fem.) Lv 20$_{10}$, רָשָׁע *wicked one* Ezk 3$_{18.18.18.19}$ 18$_{21.28}$ 33$_{8+6t}$ Pr 5$_{23}$, חַטָּא *sinner* Am 9$_{10}$, צַדִּיק *righteous one* Ezk 3$_{20.20}$ 18$_{24.26.26}$ 33$_{13.18}$.

עשׂה ptc. *one who does* Ex 31$_{15}$, אכל ptc. *one who eats* Is 59$_{5}$, שָׂבֵעַ *one satisfied*, i.e. full, of days Jb 42$_{17}$ 1 C 29$_{28}$, עשׁר htp. ptc. *rich one* Si 11$_{19}$, שׁכב ptc. *one who lies down* Ex 22$_{18}$, צעה ptc. *one bowed down* Is 51$_{14}$, נשׂא ptc. *one who carries* 1 S 31$_{5}$||1 C 10$_{5}$ 1 S 31$_{6}$, נצר pass. ptc. *protected one* Ezk 6$_{12}$, פקד pass. ptc. *numbered one* Nm 26$_{65.65}$, רָחוֹק *distant one* Ezk 6$_{12}$, יֹשֵׁב *inhabitant* Is 51$_{6}$ Jr 21$_{6.9}$ 38$_{2}$, שָׁכֵן *inhabitant* Jb 4$_{21}$, דּוֹר *generation* Ex 1$_{6}$, שְׁאֵרִית *remnant* Jr 44$_{12}$, חַי *living one* Ec 9$_{5}$, מֵת *dead one* Nm 6$_{9}$ Ec 4$_{2}$ 11QT 49$_{5}$, מֵתָה *dead one* (fem.) Zc 11$_{9}$, חֵרֶם *devoted person* Lv 27$_{29}$, נֶפֶשׁ *soul*, i.e. person Nm 23$_{10}$ 35$_{16+6t}$ Jg 16$_{16.30}$ Ezk 13$_{19}$ 18$_{4.20}$ Jb 36$_{14}$, לֵב *heart* 1 S 25$_{37}$.

בְּהֵמָה *beast* Ex 9$_{19}$ 22$_{9.13}$ Lv 11$_{39}$ 20$_{16}$ Is 50$_{2}$ (if ins. בְּהֵמָה) Jr 21$_{6}$ 4QAdmon 1$_{6}$ ([וי]מ[ות ... ה]בהמה]), בְּעִיר *beast* Nm 20$_{4}$, מִקְנֶה *cattle* Ex 9$_{6.19}$, שׁוֹר *ox* Ex 21$_{35}$ 22$_{9.13}$, שֶׂה *sheep* 22$_{9.13}$, צֹאן *flock* Gn 33$_{13}$, חֲמוֹר *ass* 22$_{9.13}$, צְפַרְדֵּעַ *frog* Ex 8$_{9}$, צָב *lizard* 11QT 50$_{21}$ 51$_{2}$, כֹּחַ *lizard* 11QT 50$_{21}$ 51$_{2}$, חֹמֶט *lizard* 11QT 50$_{21}$ 51$_{2}$, לְטָאָה *lizard* 11QT 50$_{21}$ 51$_{2}$, תִּנְשֶׁמֶת *chameleon* 11QT 50$_{21}$ 51$_{2}$, חֹלֶד *weasel* 11QT 50$_{21}$ 51$_{2}$, עַכְבָּר *mouse* 11QT 50$_{21}$ 51$_{2}$, דָּגָה *fish* Ex 7$_{18.21}$ Is 50$_{2}$ (unless ins. בְּהֵמָה), צִפּוֹר *bird* 4QAdmon 1$_{6}$ ([וי]מ[ת]), כָּנָף *winged creature* 4QAdmon 1$_{6}$ ([וי]מ[ת]), תּוֹלֵעָה *worm* Is 66$_{24}$, שֶׁרֶץ *swarming thing* 11QT 50$_{21}$ 51$_{2}$, גֶּזַע *stump* Jb 14$_{8}$.

אֲדָמָה *land* Gn 47$_{19}$, מַרְבִּית *increase* 1 S 2$_{33}$, חָכְמָה *wisdom* Jb 12$_{2}$, ודע *knowledge* Pr 14$_{33}$ (if em. בְּקֶרֶב כְּסִילִים תִּוָּדֵעַ *inside fools it is known* to בְּקֶרֶב כְּסִיל יָמוּת ודע *inside a fool knowledge dies*),* חַיָּה *life* Jb 36$_{14}$, דָּבָר *thing* Ex 9$_{4}$, רֹב *multitude* 4QM[b] 1$_{10}$ ([מ]תו), חֲצִי *half* 2 S 18$_{3}$, שְׁלִישִׁית *third* Ezk 5$_{12}$, אֶחָד *one* Ex 9$_{6.7}$ Dt 25$_{5}$, שְׁנַיִם *two* Lv 20$_{11.12.13}$ Dt 22$_{22.24}$ 1 S 2$_{34}$ Ru 1$_{5}$, זֶה *this* Jb 21$_{23.25}$, אֵלֶּה *these* Nm 16$_{29}$, אֲשֶׁר *one who* Gn 44$_{9}$ Jos 10$_{11}$ Jg 21$_{5}$ Ezk 7$_{15}$ 33$_{27}$ Si 48$_{11}$, כֹּל *everyone, everything* Gn 7$_{22}$ 20$_{7}$ 4QHalakhah[a] 13$_{6}$, impersonal Nm 35$_{17.18.23}$; subj. not specified, Nm 17$_{14.14}$ 25$_{9}$ 1 S 14$_{39.39}$ 2 S 14$_{14.14}$ 1 K 14$_{11.11}$ 16$_{4.4}$ 21$_{24.24}$ Ec 3$_{2}$ 7$_{17}$ Si 16$_{3}$ 30$_{17.17}$ 4Q416 2.3$_{7}$ CD 15$_{5}$ ([וי]מות]).

<OBJ> מָוֶת *death* Nm 23$_{10}$ Ezk 28$_{10}$, מְמוֹת *death* Jr 16$_{4}$ Ezk 28$_{8}$.

<PREP> לְ *before*, + עַיִן *eye* Gn 47$_{19}$; *at*, + עֵת *time* 2 C 18$_{34}$; *into*, + שַׁחַת *pit* Is 51$_{14}$.

בְּ of time, *in*, + יוֹם *day* Gn 2$_{17}$ Ex 10$_{28}$ 1 S 2$_{34}$ 31$_{6}$, שָׁנָה *year* Nm 33$_{38}$ Jr 28$_{17}$ 2 C 16$_{13}$ 4QJub[d] 22$_{1}$, עֶרֶב *evening* 1 K 22$_{35}$ (lacking in mss) Ezk 24$_{18}$, עֵת *time* 1 K 16$_{22}$ (if em.; see Subj.) Ec 7$_{17}$ (בְּלֹא עִתֶּךָ *when it is not your time*).

בְּ of place, *in*, + אֶרֶץ *land* Gn 11$_{28}$ 46$_{12}$ 48$_{7}$ Ex 16$_{3}$ Nm 14$_{2}$ 26$_{19}$ Dt 4$_{22}$ 34$_{5}$ Jr 16$_{6}$, עִיר *city* 2 S 19$_{38}$ 1 K 14$_{11}$ 16$_{4}$ 21$_{24}$ 11QT 49$_{5}$, Haran Gn 11$_{32}$, Hebron 2 S 4$_{1}$, Hor Nm 33$_{39}$ Dt 32$_{50}$, Jerusalem Jr 34$_{5}$ (if transfer בִּירוּשָׁלִַם from verse 6), Kiriath-arba Gn 23$_{2}$, Thebez 2 S 11$_{21}$, Ur Gn 11$_{28}$, דֶּרֶךְ *way* Gn 48$_{7}$ Jos 5$_{4}$, שָׂדֶה *field* 1 K 14$_{11}$ 16$_{4}$ 21$_{24}$, מִדְבָּר *steppe* Ex 14$_{11.12}$ Nm 14$_{2}$ 21$_{5}$ 26$_{65}$ 27$_{3}$ Jos 5$_{4}$, הַר *mountain* Nm 33$_{39}$ Dt 32$_{50.50}$, ראשׁ *top* of mountain Nm 20$_{28}$, לֵב *heart* of sea Ezk 28$_{8}$, מֵעֶה *womb* 11QT 50$_{10}$, בַּיִת *house* 11QT 49$_{5}$, אֹהֶל *tent* Nm 19$_{14}$ 4QNidd 4$_{5}$ ([ב]אוהל]), עָפָר *dust* Jb 14$_{8}$, מִלְחָמָה *battle* Dt 20$_{5.6.7}$ 2 S 19$_{11}$, אֲשֶׁר *(the place) where* Ru 1$_{17}$, מָקוֹם *place* Jr 22$_{12}$ 42$_{22}$.

בְּ of instrument, *by (means of), with*, + יָד *hand* Ex 16$_{3}$ Jos 20$_{9}$ Jr 11$_{21}$ Ezk 28$_{10}$, אֶבֶן *stone* Nm 35$_{17.23}$, כְּלִי *weapon* Nm 35$_{18}$, חֶרֶב *sword* 1 S 2$_{33(4QSam^{a})}$ Jr 11$_{22}$ 21$_{9}$ 27$_{13}$ 34$_{4}$ 38$_{2}$ 42$_{17.22}$ 44$_{12}$ Ezk 7$_{15}$ Am 7$_{11}$ 9$_{10}$.

בְּ of accompaniment, *with, in*, + שֵׂיבָה *old age* Gn 25$_{8}$ Jg 8$_{32}$ 1 C 29$_{28}$, נֹעַר *youth* Jb 36$_{14}$, פֶּתַע *suddenness* Nm

6$_{9}$, שָׁלוֹם *peace* Jr 34$_{5}$ 4QTobit[e] 7.2$_{4}$ ((וימ]ות]), חָכְמָה *wisdom* Jb 4$_{21}$, עֶצֶם *substance* of prosperity Jb 21$_{23}$, נֶפֶשׁ bitter *soul* Jb 21$_{25}$, שָׁאוֹן *uproar* Am 2$_{2}$, תרוּעָה *shout* Am 2$_{2}$, קוֹל *sound* of trumpet Am 2$_{2}$.

בְּ of cause, *on account of, through,* + טֻמְאָה *impurity* Lv 15$_{31}$ 4QPrFêtes[c] 32$_{2}$ ([בטמא]תם)), חֵטְא *sin* Lv 22$_{9}$ 24$_{16}$ (Sam) Nm 27$_{3}$ 2 K 14$_{6(Kt)}$||2 C 25$_{4}$, חַטָּאת *sin* Ezk 3$_{20}$ 18$_{24}$, עָוֹן *iniquity* Jr 31$_{30}$ Ezk 3$_{18.19}$ 18$_{17.18}$ 33$_{8.9}$, עָוֶל *injustice* Ezk 18$_{26}$ 33$_{13.18}$, מַעַל *treachery* Ezk 18$_{24}$ 1 C 10$_{13}$, צָמָא *thirst* Jg 15$_{18}$ 2 C 32$_{11}$, רָעָב *famine* Jr 11$_{22}$ 21$_{9}$ 27$_{13}$ 38$_{2}$ 42$_{17.22}$ 44$_{12}$ Ezk 6$_{12}$ 2 C 32$_{11}$, דָּם *blood(shed)* 2 S 3$_{27}$, חֳלִי *sickness* 2 K 13$_{14}$, תַּחֲלֻאִים *diseases* 2 C 21$_{19}$, מַגֵּפָה *plague* Nm 17$_{14}$ 25$_{9}$, דֶּבֶר *pestilence* Jr 21$_{6.9}$ 27$_{13}$ 38$_{2}$ 42$_{17.22}$ Ezk 5$_{12}$ 6$_{12}$ 33$_{27}$, חֹסֶר/חֶסֶר *lack* of sense Pr 10$_{21}$ (if em. בַּחֲסַר *as one lacking of*); בְּאֵין מוּסָר *through lack of discipline* Pr 5$_{23}$.

בְּ *as,* + חָסֵר *one lacking* sense Pr 10$_{21}$ (or em.; see above).

כְּ *as,* + אָדָם *human being* Ps 82$_{7}$, אָח *brother* Gn 38$_{11}$, כֵּן *gnat* Is 51$_{6}$ (unless כְּמוֹ־כֵן = *like thus,* i.e. likewise; 1QSb כמוכן perh. *like locusts*); *according to,* + מָוֶת *death* Nm 16$_{29}$ 2 S 3$_{33}$, דָּבָר *word* 2 K 1$_{17}$.

מִן of direction, *from, out of,* + בַּיִת *house* Ex 8$_{9}$, חָצֵר *courtyard* Ex 8$_{9}$, שָׂדֶה *field* Ex 8$_{9}$, רֶחֶם *womb* Jb 3$_{11}$; partitive, *from among,* + עַם *people* 2 S 24$_{15}$.

מִפְּנֵי *on account of,* + רָעָב *hunger* Jr 38$_{9}$.

מִקֶּרֶב *from among,* + עַם *people* Dt 2$_{16}$.

בְּתוֹךְ *within,* + Babylon Ezk 17$_{16}$.

בְּקֶרֶב *within,* + Nabal 1 S 25$_{37}$.

עַל *upon,* + אֲדָמָה *land* Am 7$_{17}$; *upon,* i.e. to the sorrow of, + Jacob Gn 48$_{7}$; *beside,* + אִישׁ *man* Nm 6$_{8}$, אִשָּׁה *woman* Nm 6$_{9}$.

עַל *on account of,* + Rebekah Gn 26$_{9}$, אִשָּׁה *woman, wife* Gn 20$_{3}$ 26$_{9}$, אָב *father* Dt 24$_{16(Sam^{mss})}$ 2 C 25$_{4.4}$, עָוֶל *injustice* Ezk 18$_{26}$, דָּבָר *matter* Nm 17$_{14}$.

עַל־אֹדוֹת *on account of,* + אִשָּׁה *woman* Gn 20$_{3(Sam)}$.

עִם *with, beside,* + Philistines Jg 16$_{30}$, Saul 1 S 31$_{5}$, friends of Job Jb 12$_{2}$, כְּסִיל *fool* Ec 2$_{16}$, אָרוֹן *ark* 2 S 6$_{7}$.

עַל־פְּנֵי *before,* + Terah Gn 11$_{28}$, אָב *father* Gn 11$_{28}$.

לִפְנֵי *before,* + Y. Lv 10$_{2}$ Nm 3$_{4}$ 1 C 13$_{10}$, אָב *father* 1 C 24$_{2}$.

נֶגֶד *before,* + Joseph Gn 47$_{15}$.

תַּחַת *beneath,* + יָד *hand* Ex 21$_{20}$; *in one's place,* + Jeremiah Jr 38$_{9}$.

<COLL> מות || גוע *expire* Gn 25$_{8.17}$ 35$_{29}$ Jb 3$_{11}$ 14$_{10}$, כבה *be extinguished* Is 66$_{24}$, כלה *be consumed* Ezk 5$_{12}$, תמם *be consumed* Jr 44$_{12}$, אבד *perish* Ps 41$_{6}$ (+) 49$_{11}$, כחד ni. *be destroyed* Zc 11$_{9}$, נפל *fall* Jr 44$_{12}$ (+) Ezk 5$_{12}$ 6$_{12}$ Ps 82$_{7}$, זקן hi. *grow old* Jb 14$_{8}$, אסף ni. *be gathered* Gn 25$_{8.17}$ 35$_{29}$ Nm 20$_{26}$ Dt 32$_{50.50}$.

+ יצא (of soul) *depart* Gn 35$_{18}$, שׁכב *lie down* with fathers 2 C 16$_{13}$, חלשׁ *be weak* Jb 14$_{10}$, שׁגה *go astray* Pr 5$_{23}$, קבר *bury* Jos 24$_{29.33}$ 2 K 12$_{22}$ 2 K 13$_{20}$ 2 C 24$_{15.25}$, ni. *be buried* Gn 35$_{8.19}$ Nm 20$_{1}$ Dt 10$_{6}$ Jg 8$_{32}$ 10$_{2.5}$ 12$_{7.10.12.15}$ 2 S 17$_{23}$ Jr 16$_{6}$ 20$_{6}$ Ru 1$_{17}$ 2 C 35$_{24}$.

:: חיה *live* Gn 43$_{8}$ 47$_{19}$ Nm 4$_{19}$ Dt 33$_{6}$ 2 K 8$_{10.10}$ 2 K 18$_{32}$ 20$_{1}$||Is 38$_{1}$ Jr 38$_{2}$ Ezk 13$_{19}$ 18$_{13.17.21.28}$ 33$_{15}$ Ps 118$_{17}$ Jb 14$_{14}$; + חַי *alive* 2 S 12$_{18.21}$ 1 K 21$_{15}$ Ec 4$_{2}$, חַיִּים *life* Si 30$_{17}$; :: ילד *give birth* Ec 3$_{2}$.

מות + adverb or noun used adverbially, בֶּן־ *as a son,* i.e. at the age, *of* Is 65$_{20}$ 2 C 24$_{15}$ 4QJub[h] 36$_{18}$ ((וי]מות בן])), פִּתְאֹם *suddenly* Nm 6$_{9}$, רֶגַע *(in a) moment* Jb 34$_{20}$, הַפַּעַם *now* Gn 46$_{30}$, מָחָר *tomorrow* Is 22$_{13}$, לַיְלָה *(in the) night* 1 K 3$_{19}$, הַשָּׁנָה *this year* Jr 28$_{16}$, לָמָּה *why?* Gn 47$_{15.19}$ Dt 5$_{25}$ Jr 27$_{13}$ Ezk 18$_{31}$ 33$_{11}$ Jb 3$_{11}$ Ec 7$_{17}$, מָתַי *when?* Ps 41$_{6}$, עֲרִירִי *childless* Lv 20$_{20}$ Si 16$_{3}$, לֹא בָנִים *without children* 1 C 2$_{30.32}$, לְבַד *alone* Dt 22$_{25}$ 2 S 13$_{32.33}$, יַחְדָּו *together* 1 S 31$_{6}$||1 C 10$_{6}$, כְּבָר *already* Ec 4$_{2}$, פֹּה *here* 1 K 2$_{3}$, שָׁם *there* Nm 14$_{35}$ 20$_{1.4.26.28}$ 33$_{38}$ Dt 10$_{6}$ 34$_{5}$ Jg 1$_{7}$ 2 S 6$_{7}$||1 C 13$_{10}$ 2 K 7$_{4}$ 9$_{28}$ 23$_{34}$ Is 22$_{15}$ (שָׁמָּה) Jr 20$_{6}$ 22$_{26}$ 37$_{20}$ 38$_{26}$ 42$_{16.17}$ Ezk 12$_{13}$.

מוֹת תָּמוּת *you shall surely die* Gn 2$_{17}$ 20$_{7}$ 1 S 14$_{44}$ 22$_{16.16}$ 1 K 2$_{37.42}$ 2 K 1$_{4.6.16}$ Jr 26$_{8}$ Ezk 3$_{18}$ 33$_{8.13}$, vars. Gn 3$_{4}$ Nm 26$_{65}$ Jg 13$_{22}$ 1 S 14$_{39}$ 2 S 12$_{14}$ 2 S 14$_{14}$ 2 K 8$_{10}$ Ezk 18$_{13(mss, Gnz)}$.

מוֹת יוּמַת and vars., *he shall surely be put to death* Gn 26$_{11}$ Ex 19$_{2}$ 21$_{12.15}$ 21$_{16.17}$ 22$_{18}$ 31$_{14.15}$ Lv 20$_{2+8t}$ 24$_{16.17}$ 27$_{29}$ Nm 15$_{35}$ 35$_{16.17.18.21.31}$ Jg 21$_{5}$ 2 S 12$_{14(4QSam^{a})}$ Ezk 18$_{13}$.

מות used as superlative, חָלָה חִזְקִיָּהוּ לָמוּת *Hezekiah became ill (enough) to die,* or, *became seriously ill* 2 K 20$_{1}$||Is 38$_{1}$||2 C 32$_{24}$ (עַד לָמוּת), וַתִּקְצַר נַפְשׁוֹ לָמוּת *and his soul was vexed (enough) to die,* i.e. exceedingly vexed Jg 16$_{16}$.

הוּא רָשָׁע לָמוּת *he is guilty (and deserves) to die* Nm 35$_{31}$, קָרְבוּ יָמֶיךָ לָמוּת *your time to die has drawn near* Dt 31$_{14}$, var. 1 K 2$_{1}$, וַיִּשְׁאַל אֶת־נַפְשׁוֹ לָמוּת *and he asked for his life, that he might die* 1 K 19$_{4}$ Jon 4$_{8}$, יוֹם מֻתָן *the day when they died* 2 S 20$_{3}$, עֵת לָמוּת *a time to die* Ec 3$_{2}$, הַמֵּת לְיָרָבְעָם *(any)one who dies belonging to Jeroboam* 1 K 14$_{11}$, vars. 1 K 16$_{4.4}$ 21$_{24}$, תמותו לקללה *if you die, (it is) for a curse* Si 41$_{9}$, טוב למות מחיי שוא *it is better to die than (to have) a life of vanity* Si 30$_{17(B)}$, var. 30$_{17}$.

2a. ptc. as noun, (1) **dead (one), one that is to die, about to die** (Dt 17$_{6}$ Zc 11$_{9}$), usu. of humans; of animals (Ex 21$_{34.35}$ Zc 11$_{9}$).

(2) מֵתִים **Death,** i.e. **place of death*** (Ps 88$_{6}$ [or em. בְּמֹתִים *in Death*] Jb 33$_{22}$ [if em.; see Prep.]).

<SUBJ> היה *be* Ex 21$_{34.36}$ Jg 16$_{30}$, חיה *live* Is 26$_{14.19}$, יצא *go out* 11QT 49$_{14}$, ידע *know* Ec 9$_{5}$, הלל pi. *praise* Ps 115$_{17}$, נאק *groan* Jb 24$_{12}$ (if em. מְתִים *men* to מֵתִים), אנח ni. *sigh* 4Q418 69.2$_{5}$, מות *die* Nm 6$_{9}$ Zc 11$_{9}$ 11QT 49$_{5}$, ho. *be put to death* Dt 17$_{6}$, שׁבת *rest* Si 38$_{23(Bmg)}$, ho. *be put to rest* Si 38$_{23(B)}$.

<NOM CL> בְּנֵךְ הַמֵּת *your son is the dead one* 1 K 3$_{22.22.23.23}$, חֲלָלַיִךְ ... לֹא מֵתֵי מִלְחָמָה *your slain ones are ... not the dead of battle* Is 22$_{2}$, אֵין־שָׁם מֵת *there was no one dead there* Ex 12$_{30}$, המת מן [החי] *the dead (skin) is more (extensive) than the living* 4QD^{g} 1.1$_{5}$.

<OBJ> יצא hi. *bring out* 11QT 49$_{11}$, ראה *see* 4QD^{h} 1.1$_{5}$ ([וראה]), קבר *bury* Gn 23$_{4+6t}$ 11QT 48$_{12.13}$, חיה hi. *revive* 2 K 8$_{5}$ 4QapMes 2.2$_{12}$ 5.2$_{6}$, חצה *divide* Ex 21$_{35}$, מות hi. *kill* Jg 16$_{30}$, שׁבח pi. *praise* Ec 4$_{2}$.

<CSTR> מֵת אָדָם *dead of humankind* Ezk 44$_{25}$, מתי עמו *dead of his people* 4QapMes 5.2$_{6}$, מֵתֵי מִלְחָמָה *the dead of*, i.e. in, *battle* Is 22$_{2}$, רָעָב *of,* i.e. through, *hunger* Is 5$_{13}$ (if em. מְתֵי *men of*), עוֹלָם *of eternity* Ps 143$_{3}$ (or em. מְתֵי) Lm 3$_{6}$; אֵשֶׁת־הַמֵּת *wife of the dead* Dt 25$_{5}$ Ru 4$_{5}$, ־שֵׁם *name of* Ru 4$_{5.10.10}$, נֶפֶשׁ מֵת *body of the dead* Nm 6$_{6}$, נַפְשׁוֹת *bodies of* Lv 21$_{11}$, תולעת מתים *worm of the dead* 1QH 6$_{34}$ 11$_{12}$, זִבְחֵי מֵתִים *sacrifices of,* i.e. for, *the dead* Ps 106$_{28}$, מוֹת הַמֵּת *death of the dead* Ezk 18$_{32}$, משפט המת *ordinance of the dead* 4QMMT B$_{74}$, [ת]ערובת *mingling of,* i.e. with 11QT 50$_{2}$, טמאת מת *uncleanness of the dead* 4QTohB^{c} 1$_{2}$.

<APP> נֶפֶשׁ *body* Nm 19$_{13}$.

<PREP> לְ of direction, *to*, + בוא hi. *bring* 1QMyst 13$_{2}$ ([ל]מתים), נתן *give* Dt 26$_{14}$; of benefit, *to, for,* + עשׂה *do* wonders Ps 88$_{11}$; *for, on account of,* + בכה *weep* Jr 22$_{10}$, נוד *lament* Jr 22$_{10}$, שׂים *place* baldness Dt 14$_{1}$ 11QT 48$_{9}$; לְמוֹ *to,* + קרב *draw near* Jb 33$_{22}$ (if em. לַמְמִתִים *to those who cause death* to לְמוֹ מֵתִים *to waters of the dead* or *to Death** or to לִמְקוֹם מֵתִים *to the place of the dead,* abbreviatied as למ׳ מתים).*

בְּ of place, *among* Ps 88$_{6}$ (or em. בְּמֹתִים *in Death*); of cause, *on account of,* + טמא *be unclean* 4QT^{b} 14$_{4}$; introducing object, + נגע *touch* Nm 19$_{11.13.16.18}$ 11QT 50$_{6}$, קבר *bury* MurEpJonathan$_{5}$.

כְּ *as* Is 59$_{10}$ Ps 88$_{6(mss)}$ 143$_{3}$ Lm 3$_{6}$, + היה *be* Nm 12$_{12}$, שׁכח ni. *be forgotten* Ps 31$_{13}$.

מִן of direction, *from,* + מנע *withhold* Si 7$_{33}$, טהר *be purified* 11QT 49$_{21}$.

אֶל *to* Ec 9$_{3}$, + בוא *come* Ezk 44$_{25}$, יסף ni. *be added* 4QD^{a} 6.1$_{11}$; *of,* + דרשׁ *inquire* Dt 18$_{11}$=11QT 60$_{19}$ Is 8$_{19}$.

עַל *for, on account of,* + אבל htp. *mourn* 2 S 14$_{2}$, נחם pi. *comfort* Jr 16$_{7}$, זוב *cause* tears *to flow* Si 38$_{16}$; *to,* + יסף ni. *be added* 4QD^{a} 6.1$_{12}$.

עִם *with,* + היה *be* CD 12$_{4}$, עשׂה *do* Ru 1$_{8}$, חפשׂ ni. *hide oneself* 1QH 8$_{29}$, גלל po. *be defiled* 4QLam^{a} 1.2$_{2}$.

אֵת *with* Ru 2$_{20}$.

מֵעַל פְּנֵי *from before,* + קום *rise* Gn 23$_{3}$.

בֵּין *between,* + עמד *stand* Nm 17$_{13}$.

<COLL> מֵת || רְפָאִים *shades* Is 26$_{14}$ Ps 88$_{11}$ (+), חָלָל *slain one* Nm 19$_{16.18}$ (both +) Is 22$_{2}$ Ps 88$_{6}$ (+) 4QMMT B$_{74}$ 4QapMes 2.2$_{12}$ 11QT 50$_{6}$ (+).

+ נְבֵלָה *corpse* Is 26$_{19}$, שֹׁכֵן *dweller* in dust Is 26$_{19}$, ירד ptc. *one who goes down* Ps 115$_{17}$, עֶצֶם *bone* Nm 19$_{16.18}$ 11QT 50$_{6}$, דָּם *blood* 11QT 50$_{6}$, קֶבֶר *grave* Nm 19$_{16.18}$ 11QT 50$_{6}$.

:: חַי *living (one)* Ex 21$_{35}$ Nm 17$_{13}$ 1 K 3$_{22.22.23.23}$ Is 8$_{19}$ Ru 2$_{20}$ Ec 4$_{2}$ 9$_{5}$ Si 7$_{33}$ 4QD^{a} 6.1$_{11}$.

מֵתִים אֵבֶל לֹא־תַעֲשֶׂה *you shall not make mourning for the dead* Ezk 24$_{17}$, מתים לאין מספר *dead ones without number* 4Q392 1$_{8}$ (others מפתים *wonders*).

2b. ptc. as adj., **dead** (distinction from §1 not alw. clear), used (1) attributively of אָדָם *human being* 11QT 50$_{5.6}$, בֵּן *son* 1 K 3$_{20}$, אָח *brother* Dt 25$_{6}$, פֶּגֶר *body* 2 K 19$_{35}$||Is 37$_{36}$, שַׂעֲרָה *hair* 4QD^{a} 6.1$_{10}$, כֶּלֶב *dog* 1 S 24$_{15}$ 2 S

9_{8} 16_{9}, אַרְיֵה *lion* Ec 9_{4}, זְבוּב *fly* Ec 10_{1} (if em. זְבוּבֵי מָוֶת *flies of death* to זְבוּב מֵת *a dead fly*). <COLL> :: חַי *living* Ec 9_{4} 4QDa 6.1_{10}.

(2) in nom cl., predicatively (distinction between ptc. and pf. [§1] not alw. clear) of נַעַר *lad* 2 K 4_{32}, הוּא *he* (foetus) 11QT 50_{11}, כֹּל *everyone* 2 S 19_{7}. <COLL> :: חַי *alive* 2 S 19_{7}.

(3) adverbially, אֲדֹנֵיהֶם נֹפֵל אַרְצָה מֵת *their lord was lying on the ground dead* Jg 3_{25}, סִיסְרָא נֹפֵל מֵת *Sisera was lying dead* Jg 4_{22}, וַיַּרְכִּבֻהוּ עֲבָדָיו מֵת מִמְּגִדּוֹ *and his servants conveyed him dead from Megiddo* 2 K 23_{30}, וַיַּרְא יִשְׂרָאֵל אֶת־מִצְרַיִם מֵת עַל־שְׂפַת הַיָּם *and Israel saw the Egyptians dead upon the seashore* Ex 14_{30}.

Also 4QOrda 5_{1} 4QDh 3_{1} Ḥorvat 'Uza bowl inscr.$_{12}$.

<SYN> §1 גוע *expire*, כבה *be extinguished*, כלה *be consumed*, תמם *be consumed*, נפל *fall*, כחד ni. *be destroyed*, אבד *perish*, זקן hi. *grow old*, אסף ni. *be gathered*; §2a רְפָאִים *shades*, חָלָל *slain one*.

<ANT> §1 חיה *live*, ילד *give birth*; §2a חַי *living (one)*; §2b חַי *living*.

Polel 9 Pf. מֹתַתִי, מוֹתְתַנִי; impf. 3fs תְּמוֹתֵת; + waw וַאֲמֹתְתֵהוּ, וַיְמֹתְתֵהוּ; impv. מוֹתְתֵנִי (מֹתְתֵנִי); ptc. מְמוֹתֵת; inf. מוֹתֵת—**kill, put to death,** <SUBJ> David 1 S 17_{51}, perh. אִישׁ *man* Jr 20_{17}, נַעַר *lad* Jg 9_{54} 2 S $1_{9.10.16}$, נשׂא ptc. *one who carries* arms Jg 9_{54} 1 S 14_{13}, slanderer Ps 109_{16} (or em. לְמוֹתֵת to לְמוֹתֵת [emphatic lamed] or לַמָּוֶת *to death*), רָעָה *evil* Ps 34_{22}. <OBJ> Philistine 1 S 17_{51}, Abimelech Jg 9_{54}, Jeremiah Jr 20_{17}, Saul 2 S $1_{9.10}$, אִישׁ *man* Ps 109_{16} (or em.; see Subj.), מָשִׁיחַ *anointed one* 2 S 1_{16}, רָשָׁע *wicked one* Ps 34_{22}, כאה ni. ptc. *discouraged one* Ps 109_{16} (or em.; see Subj.). <PREP> מִן *from, since (being in)*, + רֶחֶם *womb* Jr 20_{17}; אַחֲרֵי *after*, + Jonathan 1 S 14_{13}.

Hi. 138.0.10 Pf. הֵמִית, הֱמִיתָם, הֱמִיתָתְהוּ, הֱמִיתוֹ (הֱמִתְהוּ), הֲמִתֶּם; impf. יָמִית (יְמִיתֻנוּ), 3fs תָּמִית (תְּמִיתֵנוּ), 2ms תָּמִית (אֲמִיתֵךְ, אֲמִיתֶךָ, אֲמִיתְךָ) אָמִית, (תְּמִתֵנוּ, תמיתיני Q, תְּמִיתֵנִי), (נְמִיתֵם, נְמִתֵהוּ) נְמִיתֶךָ, (תְּמִיתוּהָ) תְּמִיתֻהוּ, יְמִיתֻנוּ; + waw וַהֲמִיתִיו) וְהֵמַתִּי, וְהֵמַתָּה, וֶהֱמִיתְךָ, וֶהֱמִתָנִי, (והמיתו Q) וְהֵמִית, וַיְמִיתֵם, וַיְמִיתֻהוּ, וַיְמִתֻהוּ) וַיָּמֶת; וַהֲמִתֶן, וַהֲמִתֶּם, (וַהֲמִתִּיהָ, (וַיְמִיתוּהָ, וַיְמִתֻהוּ) וַיָּמִיתוּ, (וַיְמִתֵם); impv. הֲמִיתֵנִי, הָמִיתוּ; ptc. מֵמִית, מְמִיתִים (מְמִתִים); inf. abs. הָמֵת; cstr. (הֲמִתָם, הֲמִיתָם, הֲמִיתֵנוּ, הֲמִתוֹ, הֲמִיתוֹ, הֲמִיתֶךָ, הֲמִיתֵנִי) הָמִית **—put to death, kill, slay, cause death** (1 K 17_{18}), of Y. killing humans (e.g. Gn 18_{25} 38_{7} Ex 4_{24} Nm 14_{15} Dt 9_{28} 32_{39} Jg 13_{23} 1 S 2_{6} 1 K 17_{20} Is 14_{30} 65_{15} Ho 2_{5} 9_{19} 1 C 2_{3} 10_{14} GnzPs 2_{25}); of humans killing in murder, assassination (e.g. Gn 37_{18} 1 S 19_{1} 1 K 16_{10} 2 K 15_{10} Jr 41_{2}), in retribution (e.g. Nm 35_{19} 2 S 14_{7}), in execution (e.g. Lv 20_{4} Dt 13_{10} 17_{7} CD 9_{1}); of Y. killing animals (Ps 105_{29}); of humans killing animals (Ex 17_{3} 1 S 15_{3} 17_{35}); of animal killing humans (Ex 22_{29} 1 K $13_{24.26}$ 2 K 17_{26}).

<SUBJ> Y. Gn 18_{25} $38_{7.10}$ Ex 4_{24} Nm 14_{15} Dt 9_{28} 32_{39} Jg 13_{23} 1 S $2_{6.25}$ 1 K 17_{20} Is 14_{30} 65_{15} Ho 2_{5} 9_{19} Ps 17_{14} (if em. מִמְתִים *from men* to הֲמִיתֵם *slay them* or מְמִיתָם *slay them* [ptc. used as impv.]*) 105_{29} 1 C $2_{3.3}$ (if em.; see Obj.) 10_{14} GnzPs 2_{25}, עַם *people* Lv 20_{4} Jr $26_{15.24}$, מִשְׁפָּחָה *clan* 2 S 14_{7}, Amalekites 1 S 30_{2}, Aramaeans 2 K 7_{4}, Chaldaeans Jr 43_{3}, Edomite 1 S 22_{18}, Gibeonites 2 S 21_{4}, Israel(ites) 11QT 51_{18}, Judah Jr 26_{19}.

Aaron Ex 16_{3} Nm 17_{6} 1 S 11_{12}, Abishai 2 S 21_{17}, Abner 2 S 3_{30}, Absalom 2 S 13_{32}, Ahab 1 K 18_{9}, Amaziah 2 K 14_{6}||2 C 25_{4}, Athaliah 2 C 22_{11}, Baasha 1 K 15_{28}, Benaiah 1 K 2_{34}, David 1 S $17_{35.50}$ 19_{17} 30_{15} 8_{2} 1 K 2_{8} 1 C 19_{18}, Doeg 1 S 22_{18}, Elijah 1 K 17_{18}, Elisha 1 K 19_{17}, Hezekiah Jr 26_{19}, Hoshea 2 K 15_{30}, Ishmael Jr $41_{2.8.8}$, Jehu 1 K 19_{17} 2 C $22_{9(mss)}$ (וַיְמִתֵהוּ *and he put him to death*; L וַיְמִתֻהוּ *and they put him to death*), Joab 2 S 20_{19}, Jonathan 1 S 20_{8}, Joshua Jos 10_{26} 11_{17}, Menahem 2 K 15_{14}, Moses Ex 16_{3} 17_{3} Nm 16_{13} 17_{6}, Neco 2 K 23_{28}, Pekah 2 K 15_{25}, Samson Jg $16_{30.30}$, Saul 1 S 15_{3} $19_{2.5.15}$ 28_{9} 2 S 21_{1}, Shallum 2 K 15_{10}, Solomon 1 K 15_{1} 11_{40}, Zedekiah Jr $38_{15.15.16}$, Zimri 1 K 16_{10}.

אִישׁ *man* Jg 15_{13} 20_{13} 1 K 17_{18} Jr 41_{2}, אָב *father* Gn 42_{37} 1 S $19_{2.5}$ 20_{33}, בֵּן *son* 1 S 19_{1} 2 S 4_{7} 21_{17} 1 K 2_{34} 2 K 14_{6} 2 K $15_{10.14.25.30}$ Jr 41_{2}, בַּת *daughter* Ezk 13_{19}, אָח *brother* Gn 37_{18}, נַעַר *lad* 2 S 13_{28} 18_{15}, מֶלֶךְ *king* 2 S 3_{37} 14_{32} 1 K 15_{1} 22_{6} 2 K 5_{7} 14_{6} 16_{9} 23_{28} 25_{21}||Jr 52_{27} Jr $26_{19.21}$, פַּרְעֹה *Pharaoh* 2 K 23_{28}, נָשִׂיא *prince* 1QSb 5_{25} 4QMg 5_{4}, שַׂר *commander* 2 K $11_{15.20}$||2 C 23_{21} Jr 26_{15} 38_{25} 2 C $23_{14.15}$, עֶבֶד *servant* 1 S 19_{1} 2 K 21_{23}||2 C 33_{24}, מַלְאָךְ *messenger* 1 S 19_{11}, רָץ *guard* 1 S 22_{17}, גֹּאֵל *avenger* Nm $35_{19.19.21}$, כֹּהֵן *priest* 4QpPsa 3.4_{8} ([הכו]הן), מְיַלֶּדֶת *midwife* Ex 1_{16}, נשׂא ptc. *one who carries* arms 2 S 18_{15}, רָשָׁע *wicked one* Ps 37_{32}, נָבָל *fool* 4QpIsae 6_{4} (... נ]בל [להמ]ית), פקד pass. ptc. *appointed one* 2 C $23_{14.15}$, יָד

hand Dt 13$_{10}$=11QT^{b} 16$_{6}$ ([ידכה]) Dt 17$_{7}$.

שׁוֹר *ox* Ex 22$_{29}$, אֲרִי *lion* 2 K 17$_{26}$, אַרְיֵה *lion* 1 K 13$_{24.26}$, נֵצֶר *branch* Is 11$_{4}$, חֹטֶר *shoot* Is 11$_{4}$, אֲרוֹן *ark* 1 S 5$_{10}$ (lacking in mss) 5$_{11}$, קִנְאָה *jealousy* Jb 5$_{2}$, תַּאֲוָה *desire* Pr 21$_{25}$, שׁוֹט *scourge*, i.e. disaster Jb 9$_{23}$, אֶחָד *one* 2 S 14$_{6}$; subj. not specified, 1 K 3$_{26.27}$ 2 K 14$_{19}$||2 C 25$_{27}$ Jr 41$_{4}$ Ps 59$_{1}$ Jb 33$_{22}$ (or em. לַמְמִתִים *to those who cause death* to לְמוֹ מֵתִים *to the waters of the dead** or *to Death** or to לִמְקוֹם מֵתִים *to the place of the dead*, abbreviatied as לִמ׳ מתים)* Pr 19$_{18}$ (or em. הֲמִיתוֹ *putting him to death* to הֶמְיָתוֹ *his moaning*, i.e. המה *make a noise*) Est 4$_{11}$ 2 C 22$_{9}$ CD 9$_{1}$ 4QJub^{f} 33$_{13}$.

<OBJ> עַם *people* Ex 17$_{3}$ Nm 14$_{15}$ 17$_{6}$ Dt 9$_{28}$ 1 S 5$_{11}$ Is 65$_{15}$ Jr 43$_{3}$, גּוֹי *nation* 2 K 17$_{26}$ Is 65$_{15}$, קָהָל *congregation* Ex 16$_{3}$, Benjaminite 1 K 2$_{8}$, Egyptian 1 S 30$_{15}$, Ekronites 1 S 5$_{10}$ (lacking in mss) 5$_{11}$, Gibeonites 2 S 21$_{1}$, Israel(ites) Nm 16$_{13}$, Morashtite Jr 26$_{19}$, Philistine 1 S 17$_{50}$ 2 S 21$_{17}$.

Abiathar 1 K 2$_{26}$, Abner 2 S 3$_{37}$, Absalom 2 S 14$_{32}$ 18$_{15}$, Amaziah 2 K 14$_{19}$||2 C 25$_{27}$, Amnon 2 S 13$_{28}$, Amon 2 K 21$_{23}$||2 C 33$_{24}$, Asahel 2 S 3$_{30}$, Athaliah 2 K 11$_{20}$||2 C 23$_{21}$ 2 C 23$_{14.15}$, David 1 S 19$_{1.2.5.11.15}$ 20$_{8.33}$ Ps 59$_{1}$, Elah 1 K 16$_{10}$, Er Gn 38$_{7}$ 1 C 2$_{3}$, Gedaliah Jr 41$_{2.4}$, Ish-bosheth 2 S 4$_{7}$, Jeremiah Jr 26$_{15.24}$ 38$_{15.16.25}$, Joab 1 K 2$_{34}$, Joash 2 C 22$_{11}$, Joseph Gn 37$_{18}$, Josiah 2 K 23$_{28}$, Manoah Jg 13$_{23}$, Micah Jr 26$_{19}$, Michal 1 S 19$_{17}$, Moses Ex 4$_{24}$, Nadab 1 K 15$_{28}$, Obadiah 1 K 18$_{9}$, Onan Gn 38$_{10}$ 1 C 2$_{3}$ (if ins. וְגַם אוֹנָן מִשְׁנֵהוּ ... וַיְמִיתֵהוּ *and also Onan his second one ... and he slew him*), Pekah 2 K 15$_{30}$, Pekahiah 2 K 15$_{25}$, Rehoboam 1 K 11$_{40}$, Rezin 2 K 16$_{9}$, Samson Jg 15$_{13}$, Saul 1 C 10$_{14}$, Seraiah 2 K 25$_{21}$||Jr 52$_{27}$, Shallum 2 K 15$_{14}$, Shimei 1 K 2$_{8}$, Shophach 1 C 19$_{18}$, Uriah Jr 26$_{21}$, Zechariah 2 K 15$_{10}$, Zephaniah 2 K 25$_{21}$||Jr 52$_{27}$.

אָדָם *human being* CD 9$_{1}$, אִישׁ *man* Ex 22$_{29}$ Lv 20$_{4}$ Dt 17$_{7}$ Jg 20$_{13}$ 1 S 11$_{12}$ 22$_{18}$ 30$_{2.15}$ 2 S 21$_{4}$ 1 K 13$_{24.26}$ 2 K 7$_{4}$ 25$_{21}$||Jr 52$_{27}$ Jr 41$_{8.8}$ Est 4$_{11}$ 4QJub^{f} 33$_{13}$ 4QTohB^{a} 2$_{4}$ 11QT 51$_{18}$, אִשָּׁה *woman, wife* Ex 22$_{29}$ Dt 13$_{10}$ Dt 17$_{7}$ Jg 13$_{23}$ 1 S 28$_{9}$ Est 4$_{11}$, אֵם *mother* Ho 2$_{5}$, בֵּן *son* Gn 42$_{37}$ Ex 1$_{16}$ 17$_{3}$ Dt 13$_{10}$ Jg 20$_{13}$ 1 S 2$_{25}$ 2 S 3$_{37}$ 13$_{32}$ 1 K 2$_{8}$ 15$_{28}$ 16$_{10}$ 17$_{18.20}$ 2 K 14$_{6.19}$||2 C 25$_{4.27}$ 2 K 15$_{10.14.25.30}$ Jr 26$_{21}$ 41$_{2}$ Pr 19$_{18}$ (or em.; see Subj.) 2 C 22$_{11}$, בַּת *daughter* Dt 13$_{10}$, אָח *brother* Dt 13$_{10}$=11QT^{b} 16$_{6}$ 2 S 3$_{30}$, בְּכוֹר *first-born* Gn 38$_{7}$ 1 C 2$_{3}$, יָלוּד *child* 1 K 3$_{26.27}$, יֶלֶד *child* 1 K 3$_{26(mss)}$, נַעַר *lad* 2 S 13$_{32}$, רֵעַ *friend* Dt 13$_{10}$.

מֶלֶךְ *king* Jos 10$_{26}$ 11$_{17}$ 2 K 14$_{19}$ 23$_{28}$, שַׂר *commander* 1 C 19$_{18}$, עֶבֶד *servant* 1 K 1$_{51}$ 18$_{9}$, סָרִיס *eunuch* 2 K 25$_{21}$||Jr 52$_{27}$, סֹפֵר *scribe* 2 K 25$_{21}$||Jr 52$_{27}$, שׁוֹפֵט *judge* CD 10$_{1}$, כֹּהֵן *priest* 1 S 22$_{17}$ 1 K 2$_{26}$ 2 K 25$_{21}$||Jr 52$_{27}$, worshipper GnzPs 2$_{25}$, צַדִּיק *righteous one* Gn 18$_{25}$ Ps 37$_{32}$ 4QpPs^{a} 3.4$_{8}$ ([הצד]יק), רָשָׁע *wicked one* Ps 17$_{14}$ (if em.; see Subj.) Is 11$_{4}$ 1QSb 5$_{25}$ ([רשע]ים), רֹצֵחַ *murderer* Nm 35$_{19.19.21}$, נכה hi. ptc. *one who strikes* 2 S 14$_{7}$, מֵת *dead one* Jg 16$_{30}$, מְצֹרָע *leper* 2 K 7$_{4}$, בוא ptc. *one who comes* 2 K 11$_{15}$, מלט ni. ptc. *one who escapes* 1 K 19$_{17.17}$, שֹׁמֵר *keeper* of threshold 2 K 25$_{21}$||Jr 52$_{27}$, נשׂא ptc. *one who wears* ephod 1 S 22$_{18}$, פֶּתֶה *simple one* Jb 5$_{2}$, עָצֵל *sluggard* Pr 21$_{25}$, נֶפֶשׁ *soul* 4QpIsa^{e} 6$_{4}$ ([להמ]ית נ[פש]), i.e. person Ezk 13$_{19}$.

מִקְנֶה *cattle* Ex 17$_{3}$, אֲרִי *lion* 1 S 17$_{35}$, דֹּב *bear* 1 S 17$_{35}$, דָּגָה *fish* Ps 105$_{29}$, שֹׁרֶשׁ *root* Is 14$_{30}$, עִיר *city* 2 S 20$_{19}$, חֶבֶל *line* of Moabites 2 S 8$_{2}$, מַחְמָד *precious thing* Ho 9$_{16}$, מִשְׁנֶה *second one* 1 C 2$_{3}$ (if em.; see above), אֶחָד *one* 2 S 14$_{6}$.

<PREP> בְּ of place, *in*, + Israel 2 S 21$_{4}$, Megiddo 2 K 23$_{29}$, Riblah 2 K 25$_{21}$||Jr 52$_{27}$, מִדְבָּר *steppe* Nm 16$_{13}$ Dt 9$_{28}$, בַּיִת *house* 2 K 21$_{23}$||2 C 33$_{24}$; of time, *in, at, during*, + יוֹם *day* 1 S 22$_{18}$ 1 K 2$_{26}$, שָׁנָה *year* 1 K 15$_{28}$ 16$_{10}$, בֹּקֶר *morning* 1 S 19$_{11}$, מָוֶת *death* Jg 16$_{30}$, חַיִּים *life* Jg 16$_{30}$.

בְּ of instrument, *by (means of), with*, + חֶרֶב *sword* 1 K 1$_{51}$ 2$_{8}$ 2 K 11$_{15.20}$||2 C 23$_{21}$, רָעָב *hunger* Ex 16$_{3}$ Is 14$_{30}$, צָמָא *thirst* Ex 17$_{3}$ Ho 2$_{5}$, רוּחַ *breath* Is 11$_{4}$; of cause, *on account of*, + נֶפֶשׁ *soul* i.e. life 2 S 14$_{7}$; *according to*, + חֹק *statute* CD 9$_{1}$.

כְּ *according to*, + דָּבָר *word* 1 K 13$_{26}$.

בְּתוֹךְ *among*, + אָח *brother* Jr 41$_{8}$.

עַל *according to, on account of*, + פֶּה *mouth*, i.e. testimony CD 10$_{1}$.

מִן ... עַד *from ... to*, i.e. both ... and, + אִישׁ ... אִשָּׁה *man ... woman* 1 S 15$_{3}$, עֹלֵל ... יוֹנֵק *infant ... suckling child* 1 S 15$_{3}$, שׁוֹר ... שֶׂה *ox ... sheep* 1 S 15$_{3}$, גָּמָל ... חֲמוֹר *camel ... ass* 1 S 15$_{3}$.

עִם *with* Gn 18$_{25}$.

<COLL> מות hi. || הרג *kill* Dt 13$_{10}$ Is 14$_{30}$ (both +) Jb 5$_{2}$, נכה ni. *strike* Jos 10$_{26}$ 11$_{17}$ 1 S 17$_{35.50}$ 2 S 4$_{7}$ 13$_{28}$ 14$_{6}$

18$_{15}$ 21$_{17}$ 1 K 16$_{10}$ 2 K 15$_{10.14.25}$ (all three +) 15$_{30}$ 25$_{21}$ Is 11$_{4}$ Jr 41$_{2}$ (+), מחץ *strike through* Dt 32$_{39}$, שׁבר *break*, i.e. tear 1 K 13$_{26}$.

+ בער pi. *clear* evil Jg 20$_{13}$.

:: חיה pi. *make alive* Dt 32$_{39}$ 1 S 2$_{6}$ 2 K 7$_{4}$ Ezk 13$_{19}$, hi. 2 S 8$_{2}$ 2 K 5$_{7}$; + חיה *live* Ex 1$_{16}$.

+ adverb or noun used adverbially, פִּתְאֹם *suddenly* Jb 9$_{23}$, חִנָּם *for nothing* 1 S 19$_{5}$, לָמָּה *why?* 1 S 19$_{17}$, שָׁם *there* 2 K 14$_{19}$||2 C 25$_{27}$ 2 C 23$_{15}$, בַּיִת *(in the) house* 2 K 11$_{20}$||2 C 23$_{21}$ 2 C 23$_{14}$.

הָמֵת תְּמִיתֵנִי *you will surely kill me* Jr 38$_{15}$, לֹא הָמֵת נְמִיתֶךָ *we will surely not kill you* Jg 15$_{13}$, vars. 1 K 3$_{26.27}$, הֶהָמֵת הֱמִתֻהוּ *did they indeed kill him?* Jr 26$_{19}$.

Also 4QNarrB 1$_{1}$ 4QBéat 16$_{5}$ ([המי]תו).

<SYN> הרג *kill*, נכה ni. *strike*, מחץ *strike through*, שׁבר *break*.

<ANT> חיה pi., hi. *make alive*.

Ho. $_{75.0.15}$ Pf. הֻמְתוּ, הוּמַת; impf. יוּמַת (יוּמָת), 3fs תּוּמַת, יוּמְתוּ (יוּמָתוּ); + waw וְהוּמַת, Q והומתה; 3fs וַתּוּמַת; ptc. מוּמָת, מוּמָתִים—**be put to death, killed, caused to die,** of humans, usu. by execution; also by murder, assassination (1 S 19$_{6.11}$ 20$_{32}$), as a result of conspiracy (2 K 11$_{2[Qr]}$||2 C 22$_{11}$ 2 K 11$_{2.8.15[mss]}$||2 C 23$_{7.14}$ 2 K 11$_{16}$), through illness (Ps 17$_{14}$ [if em.; see Coll.]); of animals (Lv 20$_{16}$ 4QHalakhah^{a} 4$_{3}$).

<SUBJ> Adonijah 1 K 2$_{24}$, Athaliah 2 K 11$_{15.16}$, David 1 S 19$_{6.11}$ 20$_{32}$, Joash 2 K 11$_{2}$, Shimei 2 S 19$_{22}$, אִישׁ *man* Lv 19$_{20}$ 20$_{2.9.10.15.20(Sam).27}$ 24$_{17}$ Nm 15$_{35}$ Dt 19$_{12(Sam)}$ 21$_{22}$ 24$_{16}$ Jos 1$_{18}$ 1 S 11$_{13}$ 2 S 19$_{23}$ 2 K 14$_{6(Qr)}$ Jr 38$_{4}$ 11QT 35$_{5.7}$ 51$_{17}$ 56$_{10}$ 64$_{9}$ 66$_{2.5}$, אִשָּׁה *woman* Lv 19$_{20}$ 20$_{16.27}$, אָב *father* Dt 24$_{16}$ 2 K 14$_{6}$, בֵּן *son* Dt 24$_{16}$ 2 S 21$_{9}$ 2 K 11$_{2(Qr)}$||2 C 22$_{11}$ 2 K 11$_{2}$ 14$_{6}$ Ezk 18$_{13}$, דּוֹדָה *aunt* Lv 20$_{20(Sam)}$, נַעֲרָה *young woman* 11QT 66$_{2}$, בְּתוּלָה *young woman* 4QOrd^{a} 2$_{9}$, נָבִיא *prophet* Dt 13$_{6}$=11QT 54$_{15}$ 4QMos^{a} 1.15$_{6}$ 11QT 61$_{2}$, חֹלֵם *dreamer* Dt 13$_{6}$=11QT 54$_{15}$.

בוא ptc. *one who comes* 2 K 11$_{8.15(mss)}$||2 C 23$_{7.14}$, בזה ptc. *one who despises* Pr 19$_{16(Kt)}$, קָרֵב *one who draws near* Nm 17$_{28(Sam)}$, נגע ptc. *one who touches* Gn 26$_{11}$ Ex 19$_{12}$, נכה hi. ptc. *one who strikes* Ex 21$_{12.15}$ 24$_{21}$ Nm 35$_{21}$, רֹצֵחַ *murderer* Nm 35$_{16.17.18.31}$, גנב ptc. *one who steals* a person Ex 21$_{16}$, קלל pi. ptc. *one who curses* Ex 21$_{17}$, נקב ptc. *one who curses* Lv 24$_{16.16}$, רָכִיל *talebearer* 11QT 64$_{9}$, חלל pi. ptc. *one who profanes* Ex 31$_{14}$, פצע pass. ptc. *wounded one* 4QBéat 15$_{9}$ ([י]ומת[ו]), שֹׁכֵב *one who lies* with beast Ex 22$_{18}$, בַּעַל *owner* Ex 21$_{29}$, זָר *stranger*, i.e. lay Israelite Nm 1$_{51}$ 3$_{10.38}$ 18$_{7}$, חֵרֶם *devoted person* Lv 27$_{29}$, פקד pass. ptc. *numbered one* Nm 26$_{65(mss, Sam^{mss})}$, מֵת *one who is to die* Dt 17$_{6.6}$, עשׂה ptc. *one who does* Ex 31$_{15}$ 35$_{2}$, בְּהֵמָה *beast* Lv 20$_{16}$, שׁוֹר *ox* 4QHalakhah^{a} 4$_{3}$, שְׁנַיִם *two* Lv 20$_{11.12.13}$ 11QT 66$_{2}$ ([שניהמה]), אֲשֶׁר *one who* Gn 44$_{9(Sam)}$ Jg 6$_{31}$ 21$_{5}$ 4QOrd^{a} 2$_{6}$, כֹּל *everyone* 2 C 15$_{13}$ CD 12$_{4}$.

<PREP> בְּ of place, *in*, + יִשְׂרָאֵל *Israel* 2 S 19$_{23}$, מִדְבָּר *steppe* Nm 26$_{65(mss, Sam^{mss})}$; of time, *on, in*, + יוֹם *day* 1 S 11$_{13}$ 2 S 21$_{9}$; of instrument, *by (means of), with*, + חֶרֶב *sword* 2 K 11$_{15(mss)}$||2 C 23$_{14}$; of cause, *on account of*, + חֵטְא *sin* Dt 24$_{16}$ 2 K 14$_{6(Qr)}$.

עַל *on account of*, + אָב *father* Dt 24$_{16}$ 2 K 14$_{6}$, בֵּן *son* Dt 24$_{16}$ 2 K 14$_{6}$, פֶּה *mouth*, i.e. testimony Dt 17$_{6}$ 11QT 64$_{9}$.

עַד *until*, i.e. by (the time of), + בֹּקֶר *morning* Jg 6$_{31}$.

<COLL> מות ho. + סקל *stone* 4QHalakhah^{a} 4$_{3}$, ni. *be stoned* Ex 21$_{29}$, רגם *stone* Lv 20$_{2.27}$ 24$_{16}$ Nm 15$_{35}$, הרג *kill* Lv 20$_{15.16}$.

+ adverb or noun used adverbially, מָחָר *tomorrow* 1 S 19$_{11}$, הַיּוֹם *today* 1 K 2$_{24}$, לָמָּה *why?* 1 S 20$_{32}$, עֲרִירִי *childless* Lv 20$_{20(Sam)}$, שָׁם *there* 2 K 11$_{16}$, בַּיִת *(in the) house* 2 K 11$_{15}$.

מוֹת יוּמַת, and vars. *he shall surely be put to death* Gn 26$_{11}$ Ex 19$_{2}$ 21$_{12.15}$ 21$_{16.17}$ 22$_{18}$ 31$_{14.15}$ Lv 20$_{2+8t}$ 24$_{16.17}$ 27$_{29}$ Nm 15$_{35}$ 35$_{16.17.18.21.31}$ Jg 21$_{5}$ 2 S 12$_{14(4QSam^{a})}$ Ezk 18$_{13}$.

מֻמָתִים מַחֲלָה *caused to die (by) a disease* Ps 17$_{14}$ (if em. מֵחֶלֶד חֶלְקָם *their portion is from the world*).

Ptc. as noun, וְחַיָּתוֹ לַמְמִתִים *and his life to the dead* (if em. לַמֻּמָתִים) Jb 33$_{22}$.*

⇒ מָוֶת *death*, מָמוֹת *death*, תְּמוּתָה *death*, אֲחִימוֹת *Ahimoth*.

מָוֶת $_{155.22.30}$ n.m. **death**—Si מוות; cstr. מוֹת; + ה- of direction מָ֫וְתָה; sf. מוֹתִי, 2ms Q מותך, 2fs Q מותך (Q מותכי), מוֹתוֹ (מֹתוֹ), מוֹתָהּ, מוֹתָם (מֹתָם); pl. cstr. מוֹתֵי; sf. מֹתָיו—**1.** event of death, oft. as marking a point in time, Gn 25$_{11}$ 26$_{18}$ 27$_{2.7.10}$ 50$_{16}$ Lv 16$_{1}$ Nm 35$_{25.28.28.32}$ Dt 31$_{27.29}$ 33$_{1}$

34$_{7}$ Jos 1$_{1}$ 20$_{6}$ Jg 1$_{1}$ 13$_{7}$ 16$_{30}$ (:: חַיִּים *life*) 1 S 15$_{35}$ 20$_{3}$ 2 S 1$_{1.23}$ (::חַיִּים) 6$_{23}$ 1 K 11$_{40}$ 2 K 1$_{1}$ 14$_{17}$||2 C 25$_{25}$ 2 K 15$_{5}$||2 C 26$_{21}$ Is 6$_{1}$ 14$_{28}$ Jr 52$_{11.34}$ Ps 49$_{18}$ 73$_{4}$ (or em.; see Prep.) Pr 11$_{7}$ Ru 2$_{11}$ Ec 3$_{19}$ 7$_{1}$ (:: ילד ni. inf. *being born*) 8$_{8}$ Est 2$_{7}$ 1 C 22$_{4}$ 22$_{5}$ 2 C 22$_{4}$ 24$_{15.17}$ 32$_{33}$ Si 9$_{12}$ 10$_{11}$ (מ[ו]ת) 11$_{28}$ (+ אַחֲרִית *end*) 30$_{32}$ 41$_{3}$ 46$_{20}$ 4QJub^{h} 35$_{8}$ 4Q416 2.3$_{6}$ 4Q 418 127$_{1}$ CD 5$_{3}$; of beasts, Ec 3$_{19}$.

2. state of death, Is 53$_{9}$ (+ קֶבֶר *grave*) Ps 13$_{4}$ Ru 1$_{17}$ Si 48$_{14}$ (:: חַיִּים *life*); of animals, Lv 11$_{31.32}$; of flies, Ec 10$_{1}$ (or em.; see Cstr.).

3. manner of death, 2 S 3$_{33}$ Nm 16$_{29}$ 23$_{10}$ Ezk 28$_{10}$.

4. death as **a.** deserved, Dt 19$_{6}$ 21$_{22}$=11QT 64$_{9}$ Dt 22$_{26}$=11QT 66$_{6}$ Jos 2$_{13}$ 1 S 20$_{31}$ 26$_{16}$ 2 S 12$_{5}$ 19$_{29}$ 1 K 2$_{26}$ Jr 26$_{11.16}$ Ezk 18$_{23.32}$ 33$_{11}$ Pr 11$_{19}$ 14$_{12}$=16$_{25}$ (or §10, if em.; see Cstr.) perh. 14$_{32}$ (or em.; see Prep.) 16$_{14}$ 4QJub^{d} 21$_{22}$ 4QJub^{f} 33$_{13}$ 4QD^{a} 5.2$_{3}$ 6.2$_{10}$ 10.2$_{1}$ 4QapMes 5.2$_{5}$ CD 9$_{6.17}$ 16$_{8.9}$. **b.** undeserved, Jr 18$_{23}$ Pr 24$_{11}$ (+ הֶרֶג *slaughter*).

5a. death as suffering, destruction, Gn 21$_{16}$ 1 S 15$_{32}$ 2 K 2$_{21}$ (|| מְשַׁכֶּלֶת *miscarriage*) 4$_{40}$ Is 25$_{8}$ (+ דִּמְעָה *tears*) Ps 7$_{14}$ (+ חֵץ *arrow*) 56$_{14}$ 116$_{8}$ (|| דִּמְעָה; both || דְּחִי *stumbling*) 116$_{15}$ (or em.; see Prep.) Pr 26$_{18}$ (|| זִק *firebrand*, חֵץ) Ec 7$_{26}$ Si 41$_{1}$ 4Q525 15$_{5}$; **plague,** Ps 78$_{50}$ (+ דֶּבֶר *pestilence*) Jr 15$_{2.2}$ (|| רָעָב *famine*, שְׁבִי *captivity*) 18$_{21}$ (all three || חֶרֶב *sword*) 43$_{11.11}$ (|| שְׁבִי, רָעָב, חֶרֶב) Jb 27$_{15}$ Lm 1$_{20}$ (or em.; see Prep.; + חֶרֶב) Si 40$_{9}$ (|| רָעָה *evil*, + דָּם, שֶׁבֶר *ruin*, שֹׁד *plunder*, חֶרֶב, חַרְחוּר *heated strife*, *blood[shed]*); of destruction caused by locusts, Ex 10$_{17}$.

b. death as danger, premature end of life, Ps 33$_{19}$ 68$_{21}$ 118$_{18}$ Jb 5$_{20}$ (|| חֶרֶב *sword*) Pr 10$_{2}$ Si 9$_{13}$.

6. death as release from suffering, Jb 3$_{21}$ 7$_{15}$ Si 41$_{2}$.

7. death as the opposite of life, Dt 30$_{15}$ (|| רַע *evil*) 30$_{19}$ 2 S 15$_{21}$ Jr 8$_{3}$ 21$_{8}$ Jon 4$_{3.8}$ (all seven :: חַיִּים *life*) Pr 8$_{36}$ 12$_{28}$ (both + חַיִּים) 18$_{21}$ Si 11$_{14}$ (+ רַע *evil*, טוֹב *good*, רִישׁ *poverty*, עֹשֶׁר *wealth*) 15$_{17}$ 36$_{14}$ 37$_{18}$ (B + רָעָה *evil*; Bmg, D + רַע *evil*; all five :: חַיִּים).

8. perh. as superlative,* **a.** in construct phrase, מְהוּמַת־מָוֶת *tumult of death*, i.e. deadly tumult 1 S 5$_{11}$, אֵימוֹת מָוֶת *dread(s) of death*, i.e. frightful dreads Ps 55$_{5}$, var. Si 40$_{5}$, חֶבְלֵי־מָוֶת *pains of death*, i.e. terrible pains Ps 18$_{5}$, מוֹקְשֵׁי מָוֶת *snares of death*, i.e. fearsome snares 2 D 22$_{6}$||Ps 18$_{6}$.

b. with preposition, הֶעֱרָה לַמָּוֶת נַפְשׁוֹ *he poured out his soul to death*, i.e. utterly Is 53$_{12}$, חָרָה־לִי עַד־מָוֶת *I am angry unto death*, i.e. extremely angry Jon 4$_{9}$, עַזָּה כַמָּוֶת אַהֲבָה *love is as strong as death*, i.e. extremely strong Ca 8$_{6}$ (unless §9), עד המות היעצה על צדק *fight for righteousness to the death*, i.e. absolutely Si 4$_{28}$, הלא דין מגיע אל מות *is it not a judgment reaching to death?*, i.e. a very great judgment Si 37$_{2(B)}$ (Bmg עַל *to*, D עַד *unto*; or em. דין to דון *grief*).

c. with definite article, וְיָסֵר מֵעָלַי רַק אֶת־הַמָּוֶת הַזֶּה *that he should but turn aside this death*, i.e. this dreadful thing, *from me* Ex 10$_{17}$.

9. death personified, as deity, **Death, Mot,** 2 S 22$_{5}$|| Ps 18$_{5}$ (|| בְלִיַּעַל *Belial*) 2 S 22$_{6}$||Ps 18$_{6}$ Is 28$_{15.18}$ (all three || שְׁאוֹל *Sheol*) Jr 9$_{20}$ Ho 13$_{14.14}$ (both || שְׁאוֹל) Hb 2$_{5}$ (+ שְׁאוֹל) Ps 49$_{15}$ 55$_{16(Qr)}$ (+ שְׁאוֹל) 116$_{3}$ (|| שְׁאוֹל) Jb 18$_{13}$ 28$_{22}$ (|| אֲבַדּוֹן *Abaddon*) Pr 13$_{14}$ 14$_{27}$ (:: חַיִּים *life*) 21$_{6(mss)}$ Ca 8$_{6}$ (unless 8; || שְׁאוֹל) Lm 1$_{20}$ [if em.; see Prep.] Si 14$_{12}$ (+ שְׁאוֹל) Si 41$_{1}$ (§5a) 41$_{2}$ (§6) 1QH 3$_{8.9.28}$ 9$_{4}$ 11QPs^{a} 19$_{9}$ (both + שְׁאוֹל).

10. place of the dead (distinction from §9 not alw. clear), Is 38$_{18}$ (|| שְׁאוֹל *Sheol*, + בּוֹר *pit*) Ezk 31$_{14}$ (+ אֶרֶץ תַּחְתִּית *lowest land*, i.e. Sheol) Ps 6$_{6}$ (+ שְׁאוֹל) 9$_{14}$ 22$_{16}$ perh. 55$_{16}$ 89$_{49}$ (+ שְׁאוֹל) 107$_{18}$ Jb 30$_{23}$ (+ בֵּית מוֹעֵד לְכָל־חָי *house of meeting for all living*) 38$_{17}$ (|| צַלְמָוֶת *darkness of death*) Pr 2$_{18}$ (|| רְפָאִים *shades*) 5$_{5}$ 7$_{27}$ (both + שְׁאוֹל) 11$_{4}$ 14$_{12}$=16$_{25}$ (if em.; see Cstr.) Si 48$_{5}$ (||שְׁאוֹל) 51$_{2}$ (|| שַׁחַת *pit*) 51$_{6}$ (both || שְׁאוֹל) 1QH 6$_{24}$ 4QWiles 1$_{9.10}$ 4QapPs^{b} 31$_{2}$.

<SUBJ> היה *be* 2 K 2$_{21}$, בוא *come* Jr 9$_{20}$, עלה *go up* Jr 9$_{20}$, מהה htpalp. *delay* intrans. Si 14$_{12}$, אמר *say* Jb 28$_{22}$, הלל pi. *praise* Is 38$_{18}$, רעה *pasture* Ps 49$_{15}$, בחר ni. *be chosen* Jr 8$_{3}$, פרד hi. *separate* Ru 1$_{17}$, כרת hi. *cut off* Jr 9$_{20}$, נשא hi. *be deceitful* Ps 55$_{16(Qr)}$ (Kt ישימות *desolations*).

<NOM CL> דֶּרֶךְ נְתִיבָה אַל־מָוֶת appar. *the way of the path is not death*, or perh. *is immortality* Pr 12$_{28}$ (mss אֶל־ *to* death; perh. em. נְתִיבָה to מְשׁוּבָה *apostasy*, or תּוֹעֵבָה *abomination*), רעה ומות perh. *(there is) evil and death* Si 40$_{9}$ (or em. רעה to רעב *famine*), מָוֶת בַּסִּיר *there is death in the pot* 2 K 4$_{40}$, בַּבַּיִת הַמָּוֶת *death is in the house* Lm 1$_{20}$ (if em.; see Prep.), מָוֶת וְחַיִּים בְּיַד־

לָשׁוֹן *death and life are in the power of the tongue* Pr 18$_{21}$, לפני אדם חיים ומות *before a person are life and death* Si 15$_{17}$, נוכח חיים מות *opposite to life is death* Si 36$_{14}$, חיים ומות ... מי׳ הוא *life and death ... are from Y.* Si 10$_{14}$, כְּמוֹת זֶה כֵּן מוֹת זֶה *as is the death of one so is the death of the other,* i.e. both die Ec 3$_{19}$, טוֹב מוֹתִי מֵחַיָּי *my death is better than my life,* i.e. it is better that I should die than live Jon 4$_{3.8}$.

<OBJ> ראה *see* Ps 89$_{49}$, נתן *give,* i.e. place Dt 30$_{15.19}$ perh. 4Q417 3$_{1}$, פרח hi. *cause to sprout* Si 37$_{18}$, סור hi. *remove* Ex 10$_{17}$, בלע pi. *swallow* Is 25$_{8}$, ירה hi. *throw* Pr 26$_{18}$, אהב *love* Pr 8$_{36}$, חפץ *delight in* Ezk 18$_{23}$, בחר *choose* Jb 7$_{15}$, ירא *fear* Is 44$_{14}$ (if em. מְתֵי *men of* Israel, to מָוֶת or מֹתְיָ [with ָ voc. part.] *death O Israel*),* פחד *dread* Si 41$_{3}$, ישׁן *sleep* Ps 13$_{4}$, מות *die* Nm 16$_{29}$ 23$_{10}$ Ezk 28$_{10}$.

<CSTR> מוֹת אַבְרָהָם *death of Abraham* Gn 25$_{11}$ 26$_{18}$, אַחְאָב *of Ahab* 2 K 1$_{1}$, אָחָז *of Ahaz* Is 14$_{28}$ (or em. אָחָז הָיָה *Ahaz, there was* to וְאֶחֱזֶה *and I saw*), חֶצְרוֹן *of Hezron* 1 C 2$_{24}$, אלעזר *of Eleazar* CD 5$_{3}$, יְהוֹאָשׁ *of Jehoash* 2 K 14$_{17}$||2 C 25$_{25}$ (יוֹאָשׁ *Joash*), יְהוֹשֻׁעַ *of Joshua* Jg 1$_{1}$, יְהוֹיָדָע *of Jehoiada* 2 C 24$_{17}$, מֹשֶׁה *of Moses* Jos 1$_{1}$, עֻזִּיָּהוּ *of Uzziah* Is 6$_{1}$, שָׁאוּל *of Saul* 2 S 1$_{1}$, שְׁלֹמֹה *of Solomon* 1 K 11$_{40}$.

מוֹת אָדָם *death of a human* Nm 16$_{29}$ (כָּל־אָדָם *of all humans*) Pr 11$_{7}$ Si 10$_{11}$ (מ[ו]ת), אִישֵׁךְ *of your husband* Ru 2$_{11}$, אָבִיו *of his father* 2 C 22$_{4}$, אָבִיהָ וְאִמָּהּ *of her father and mother* Est 2$_{7}$, מוֹת ... בֶּן־ *death of ... the son of* 2 K 14$_{17}$||2 C 25$_{25}$, שְׁנֵי בְּנֵי *of the two sons of* Lv 16$_{1}$, הַיֶּלֶד *of the child* Gn 21$_{16}$, הַמֶּלֶךְ *of the king* Is 6$_{1}$, הַכֹּהֵן *of the priest* Nm 35$_{25.28.32}$ Jos 20$_{6}$, נָבָל *of an outcast* 2 S 3$_{33}$, רָשָׁע *of a wicked one* Ezk 18$_{23}$ 33$_{11}$, יְשָׁרִים *of the upright* Nm 23$_{10}$, הָעֲרֵלִים *of the uncircumcised* Ezk 28$_{10}$ (מוֹתֵי), הַמֵּת *of the dead* Ezk 18$_{32}$, זֶה *of this one* Ec 3$_{19.19}$.

אִישׁ מָוֶת *man of,* i.e. deserving, *death* 1 K 2$_{26}$, אַנְשֵׁי־ *men of,* i.e. deserving 2 S 19$_{29}$, בֶּן־ *son of,* i.e. deserving 1 S 20$_{31}$ (or *son of death = arch villain,* i.e. with מָוֶת as a superlative)* 2 S 12$_{5}$, בְּנֵי־ *sons of,* i.e. deserving 1 S 26$_{16.16}$ (or *son of death = arch villain,* i.e. with מָוֶת as a superlative),* בְּכוֹר מָוֶת *firstborn of death* Jb 18$_{13}$, מַלְאֲכֵי־ *messengers of* Pr 16$_{14}$, הֲרֻגֵי מָוֶת *slain of,* i.e. by, *death* Jr 18$_{21}$, זְבוּבֵי *flies of,* i.e. dead flies Ec 10$_{1}$ (or em. זְבוּב מֵת *a dead fly*), מִשְׁבְּרֵי־ *breakers of* 2 S 22$_{5}$ 1QH 3$_{8.9}$ 9$_{4}$, חֶבְלֵי־ *cords of* Ps 18$_{5}$ 116$_{3}$ 1QH 3$_{28}$, מֹקְשֵׁי *snares of* 2 S 22$_{6}$||Ps 18$_{6}$ (מוֹקְשֵׁי) Pr 13$_{14}$ 14$_{27}$ 21$_{6(mss)}$ (מוֹקְשֵׁי; L מְבַקְשֵׁי *ones who seek*), כְּלֵי־ *weapons of* Ps 7$_{14}$, רשפ[י] מות *flames of death* 4Q525 15$_{5}$, שַׁעֲרֵי מָוֶת *gates of death* Ps 9$_{14}$ (Gnz שַׁעַר *gate of*) 107$_{18}$ Jb 38$_{17}$ 1QH 6$_{24}$ 4QWiles 1$_{10}$, חַדְרֵי־ *chambers of* Pr 7$_{27}$, אהלי מות *tents of death* 4QapPs^{b} 31$_{2}$, גֵי *valley of* 4QapMes 5.2$_{11}$, עֲפַר־מָוֶת *dust of death* Ps 22$_{16}$.

מַר־הַמָּוֶת *bitterness of death* 1 S 15$_{32}$, מְהוּמַת־מָוֶת *tumult of death,* i.e. deadly tumult 1 S 5$_{11}$, פחדי מות *fear of death* Si 9$_{13}$, אימת *dread of* Si 40$_{5}$, אֵימוֹת מָוֶת *dread(s) of death* Ps 55$_{5}$, דֶּרֶךְ *way of* Jr 21$_{8}$, דַּרְכֵי *ways of* Pr 14$_{12}$=16$_{25}$ (or em. יַרְכְּתֵי *innermost parts of*) 4QWiles 1$_{9}$, יוֹם הַמָּוֶת *day of death* Ec 7$_{1}$ 8$_{8}$ Si 30$_{32}$, מחיר מות *price of death* CD 16$_{8.9}$, דבר *matter of* 4QD^{a} 5.2$_{3}$ 10.2$_{1}$ CD 9$_{6.17}$, מִשְׁפַּט־מָוֶת *judgment of,* i.e. liability to, *death* Dt 19$_{6}$ 21$_{22}$=11QT 64$_{9}$ Jr 26$_{11}$ 4QJub^{f} 33$_{13}$ 6.2$_{10}$ ([מ]שפט), חֵטְא *sin of,* i.e. deserving Dt 22$_{26}$=11QT 66$_{6}$, אשמת מות *guilt of,* i.e. deserving, *death* 4QJub^{d} 21$_{22}$, יום מות *day of the death of* CD 5$_{3}$, יוֹם מוֹתִי *day of my death* Gn 27$_{2}$, מוֹתוֹ *of his death* Jg 13$_{7}$ 1 S 15$_{35}$ 2 K 15$_{5}$||2 C 26$_{21}$ (2 K מֹתוֹ) Jr 52$_{11.34}$ (lacking in mss), מוֹתָהּ *of her death* 2 S 6$_{23}$, שְׁנַת־מוֹת *year of the death of* Is 14$_{28}$, עת מות *time of death* Si 9$_{12}$.

<APP> מַחֲנָק *strangling* Jb 7$_{15}$, שֵׁבֶט *shoot* Si 37$_{18(B)}$, שַׁרְבִיט *shoot* Si 37$_{18(D)}$ ([שרביט]ם), חֹק *decree* Si 41$_{3}$.

<ADJ> זֶה *this* Ex 10$_{17}$.

<PREP> לְ of direction, *to, (destined) for* Jr 15$_{2.2}$ 18$_{23}$ 43$_{11.11}$ Pr 11$_{19}$ Si 41$_{1(mg)}$ (הוי למות *alas to death;* B חיים למות perh. *life [says] to death*) 41$_{2}$ (B האח למות *aha to death;* M ה[ר]ע למות *hail to death* [Yadin]), + היה *be* 2 S 15$_{21}$ 4QapMes 5.2$_{5}$ (יהי[ו]), נתן *give* Ps 118$_{18}$, ni. *be given* Ezk 31$_{14}$, לקח pass. *be taken* Pr 24$_{11}$, שׁפת *place* Ps 22$_{16}$, נגע hi. *reach* Si 37$_{2(B)}$ 51$_{6}$, ערה hi. *pour out* Is 53$_{12}$; חכה לְ pi. *wait for* Jb 3$_{21}$.

לְ *until,* + פקד hi. *deposit* 4Q416 2.3$_{6}$, דאב *languish* 4Q418 127$_{1}$; *from* Ps 68$_{21}$ (לַמָּוֶת תּוֹצָאוֹת *escapes from death*); of possession, *of, (belonging) to* Ps 73$_{4}$ (אֵין חַרְצֻבּוֹת לְמוֹתָם *there are no torments to their death;* or em. לָמוֹ תָּם *to them; sound* are their bodies), + היה *be*

11QPsa 19$_9$.

בְּ of time, place, *in, at* Dt 34$_7$ Is 53$_9$ (בְּמֹתָיו *in his deaths* to בְּמָתוֹ or בֹּמָתוֹ *his burial mound** [from בָּמָה III] or בֵּית מֹתוֹ *house of his death,** i.e. his tomb) Ps 6$_6$ 88$_6$ (if em. בַּמֵּתִים *among the dead* to בְּמֹתִים *in Death*) 2 C 24$_{15}$ perh. 4QRitPur 77$_3$, + מות hi. *kill* Jg 16$_{30}$, פרד ni. *be separated* 2 S 1$_{23}$, נפל *fall* Lv 11$_{32}$, לקח *take* Ps 49$_{18}$ Est 2$_7$, נחל *inherit* Si 10$_{11}$ (במ[ו]ת), hi. *give an inheritance* Si 30$_{32}$ (הנח[ל]), קבר ni. *be buried* Jb 27$_{15}$, אבד *perish* Pr 11$_7$, חסה *seek refuge* Pr 14$_{32}$ (or em. בְּתֻמּוֹ *in his integrity*), עשׂה *do* 2 C 32$_{33}$ Si 48$_{14}$, נגע *touch* Lv 11$_{31}$.

בְּ introducing object, + ראה *see* Gn 21$_{16}$; משׁל בְּ *rule over* Si 37$_{18(B)}$ (D שׁלח pi. perh. *send by means of*); חפץ בְּ *delight in* Ezk 18$_{23(mss).32}$ 33$_{11}$.

כְּ *as* Hb 2$_5$ Ca 8$_6$ Ec 3$_{19}$ Lm 1$_{20}$ (or em. כִּי מָוֶת *Death himself* [emphatic כִּי]* or הַמָּוֶת [it is] *death* or כְּמוּת *captivity* is in the house); *according to*, + מות *die* Nm 16$_{29}$ 2 S 3$_{33}$.

מִן of direction, *from* perh. 4QBéat 32$_3$, + נצל hi. *deliver* Jos 2$_{13}$ Ps 33$_{19}$ 56$_{14}$ Pr 10$_2$ 11$_4$, חלץ pi. *deliver* Ps 116$_8$, גאל *redeem* Ho 13$_{14}$, פדה *redeem* Jb 5$_{20}$ Si 51$_2$, קום hi. *raise* Si 48$_5$, חשׂך *withhold* Ps 78$_{50}$; of comparison, *(more) than* Ec 7$_{26}$.

אֶל *to* Pr 12$_{28(mss)}$, + שׁוח *sink down* Pr 2$_{18}$, ירד *go down* Pr 5$_5$ (if em.; see below).

עַל *to*, + נגע hi. *reach* Si 37$_{2(Bmg)}$; *concerning* 1QJubb 35$_8$, + דבר pi. *speak* 4QJubh 35$_8$ ([תדברי על]).

אֵת *with* Is 28$_{18}$, + כרת *cut*, i.e. make, covenant Is 28$_{15}$.

עַד *until*, + היה *be* 2 S 6$_{23}$ 1 K 11$_{40}$, ישׁב *dwell* Nm 35$_{25.28}$ Jos 20$_6$, שׁוב *go back* Nm 35$_{32}$, ראה *see* 1 S 15$_{32}$; *unto*, + נגע hi. *reach* Si 37$_{2(D)}$, חרה *be angry* Jon 4$_9$, עצה ni. *fight* Si 4$_{28}$.

לִפְנֵי *before*, + ברך pi. *bless* Gn 27$_{7.10}$ Dt 33$_1$, אשׁר pi. *pronounce happy* Si 11$_{28}$, צוה pi. *command* Gn 50$_{16}$, כון hi. *prepare* 1 C 22$_5$.

אַחַר *after*, + בוא *come* 1 C 2$_{25}$ (if ins. בָּא *he came*).

אַחֲרֵי *after* Dt 31$_{27}$ Jos 1$_1$ Jg 1$_1$ 2 S 1$_1$, + היה *be* Gn 25$_{11}$ 2 C 22$_4$, חיה *live* 2 K 14$_{17}$||2 C 25$_{25}$, בוא *come* 2 C 24$_{17}$, דבר pi. *speak* Lv 16$_1$, שׁוב *go back* Nm 35$_{28}$, דרשׁ ni. *be sought* Si 46$_{20}$, שׁחת hi. *act corruptly* Dt 31$_{29}$, פשׁע *rebel* 2 K 1$_1$, עשׂה *do* Ru 2$_{11}$, סתם pi. *stop up* Gn 26$_{18}$.

בֵּין *between* 1 S 20$_3$ (+ David).

הַמָּוְתָה *(to) the death* Ps 116$_{15}$ (or em. תְּמוּתָה *death*).

מָוֶת without preposition, *to death*, + שׁוב hi. *bring* Jb 30$_{23}$, ירד *go down* Pr 5$_5$ (or em. אֶל־מָוֶת *to death*).

<COLL> מָוֶת as vocative, Ho 13$_{14}$ Si 41$_{1.2}$; אַל־מָוֶת *not death*, i.e. perh. *immortality** Pr 12$_{28}$ (mss אֶל־ *to* death), הַמָּוְתָה לַחֲסִידָיו appar. *(to) the death of his loyal ones* Ps 116$_{15}$ (or em.; see Prep.).

Also 4QRPc 3.2$_3$.

<SYN> §5 מְשַׁכֶּלֶת *miscarriage*, דִּמְעָה *tears*, דְּחִי *stumbling*, זִק *firebrand*, חֵץ *arrow*, חֶרֶב *sword*, רָעָב *famine*, שְׁבִי *captivity*, רָעָה *evil*; §7 רַע *evil*; §9 בְּלִיַּעַל *Belial*, שְׁאוֹל *Sheol*, אֲבַדּוֹן *Abaddon*; §10 שְׁאוֹל *Sheol*, צַלְמָוֶת *darkness of death*, רְפָאִים *shades*, שַׁחַת *pit*.

<ANT> §1, 2, 7, 9 חַיִּים *life*, §1 ילד ni. inf. *being born*.

⇨ מות *die*.

מוֹתָר 3.0.1 n.m. **abundance**—cstr. מוֹתַר; pl. sf. Q מחסוריכה—**abundance, profit, advantage,** <SUBJ> היה *be* Pr 14$_{23}$. <NOM CL> מוֹתַר הָאָדָם מִן־הַבְּהֵמָה אָיִן *there is no advantage of humans*, i.e. they have no advantage, *over the beasts* Ec 3$_{19}$. <CSTR> מוֹתַר הָאָדָם *advantage of humans* Ec 3$_{19}$. <PREP> לְ of direction, *to* Pr 21$_5$. <COLL> מוֹתָר :: מַחְסוֹר *lack* Pr 14$_{23}$ 21$_5$ 4Q417 1.1$_{17}$.

<ANT> מַחְסוֹר *lack*.

⇨ יתר *exceed*.

[מַז], see מַזְדַּי *Mazdai*.

*__[מַז]__ 0.0.0.2 n.[m.] **extract**—cstr. I מז—<CSTR> מז צמקים *extract of*, i.e. wine or syrup made from, *raisins* Lachish inscr. 30.

Also Hazor bowl inscr. 4-6.

⇨ (?) cf. מִיץ *pressing*.

מִזְבֵּחַ 400.3.46 n.m. **altar**—+ ה- of direction מִזְבֵּחָה; cstr. מִזְבַּח (מִזְבַּחַת); sf. מִזְבְּחִי, מִזְבַּחֲךָ (מִזְבְּחֶךָ), מִזְבְּחוֹ; pl. מִזְבְּחוֹת (מִזְבְּחֹת); sf. מִזְבְּחֹתֶיךָ (מִזְבְּחוֹתֶיךָ), מִזְבְּחֹתָיו, מִזְבְּחוֹתֵיכֶם, מִזְבְּחֹתָם (מִזְבְּחֹתֵיהֶם) מִזְבְּחוֹתֵיהֶם, מִזְבְּחוֹתָם, Kt מזבחותים [2 C 34$_5$])—usu. for sacrifice to Y. (e.g. Gn 8$_{20}$ Ex 20$_{26}$ Lv 1$_5$ Nm 3$_{26}$ Dt 12$_{27}$ Jos 8$_{30}$ Jg 13$_{20}$ 1 S 2$_{28}$ 2 S 24$_{25}$||1 C 21$_{26}$ 1 K

8$_{22}$||2 C 6$_{12}$ Is 19$_{19}$ Ezk 40$_{46}$ Am 9$_1$ Ml 1$_{10}$ Lm 2$_7$ Ne 10$_{35}$ 2 C 1$_6$ 11QT 21$_{10}$), also to gods of Canaanites (e.g. Ex 34$_{13}$ Dt 7$_5$ Jg 2$_2$), Baal (e.g. Jg 6$_{25.28.30}$ 1 K 16$_{32}$ 2 K 21$_3$ Jr 11$_{13}$), host of heaven (2 K 21$_5$||2 C 33$_5$); made of wood (Ex 27$_1$||38$_1$ 30$_1$||37$_{25}$ Ezk 41$_{22}$), earth (Ex 20$_{24}$), stones (Ex 20$_{25}$ Dt 27$_6$ Jos 8$_{31}$), gold (Ex 38$_{38}$ 40$_{5.26}$ Nm 4$_{11}$ 1 K 7$_{48}$||2 C 4$_{19}$), bronze (Ex 38$_{30.39}$ 1 K 8$_{64}$||2 C 7$_7$ 2 K 16$_{14.15}$ Ezk 19$_2$ 2 C 1$_{5.6}$ 4$_1$); usu. as place of sacrifice (e.g. Gn 8$_{20}$ Ex 20$_{24}$ 29$_{38}$ 40$_{29}$ Lv 1$_9$ 2$_2$ 3$_5$ 4$_{19}$ Nm 23$_2$ Dt 12$_{27}$ Jos 22$_{23}$ Jg 6$_{28}$ 1 K 3$_4$ 9$_{25}$ Ezk 43$_{27}$ Ml 1$_7$ 2 C 33$_{16}$ 11QT 20$_{11}$ 22$_6$ 26$_8$ 32$_7$ 34$_{14}$), also as place to seek sanctuary (Ex 21$_{14}$ 1 K 1$_{50.51.53}$ 2$_{28.29}$ 2 K 23$_9$).

<SUBJ> היה *be* Ex 27$_1$ (+ רָבוּעַ *square*) 29$_{37}$ 40$_{10}$ (both + קֹדֶשׁ קָדָשִׁים *a most holy thing*) 2 K 16$_{15}$ (+ לִי לְבַקֵּר *to me for seeking*) Is 19$_{19}$ (+ לַי׳ *to Y.*) Ho 8$_{11}$ (or del.; + לַחֲטֹא *for sinning*), בנה pass. *be built* Jg 6$_{28}$, קרע ni. *be torn* 1 K 13$_{3.5}$, נתץ pu. *be broken down* Jg 6$_{28}$, הרס pass. *be torn down* 1 K 18$_{30}$, חרב *be desolate* Ezk 6$_6$, שׁמם ni. *be desolate* Ezk 6$_4$, אשׁם *be guilty* Ezk 6$_6$, כול hi. *contain* 1 K 8$_{64}$||2 C 7$_7$, יכל *be able* 2 C 7$_7$.

<NOM CL> הַמִּזְבֵּחַ עֵץ *the altar was (of) wood* Ezk 41$_{22}$ (or em. כְּמַרְאֵה : הַמִּזְבֵּחַ *as the appearance. The altar* to כְּמַרְאֵה הַמִּזְבֵּחַ *as the appearance of the altar*), זֶה־מִזְבֵּחַ *this is the altar* 1 C 22$_1$ (or em. הַמִּזְבֵּחַ), הַמִּזְבֵּחַ אֲשֶׁר לִפְנֵי י׳ *the altar that is before Y.* Lv 16$_{18}$, var. 1 K 8$_{64}$ 2 K 16$_{14}$, הַמִּזְבֵּחַ לִפְנֵי הַבָּיִת *the altar was before the house* Ezk 40$_{47}$, מִזְבַּח י׳ אֱלֹהֵינוּ אֲשֶׁר לִפְנֵי מִשְׁכָּנוֹ *the altar of Y. our God which is before his tabernacle* Jos 22$_{29}$, מִזְבַּח הַנְּחֹשֶׁת ... שָׁם לִפְנֵי מִשְׁכַּן י׳ *the bronze altar was ... there before the tabernacle of Y.* 2 C 1$_{5(mss)}$ (L שָׂם *he placed*), מִזְבַּח י׳ אֲשֶׁר לִפְנֵי אוּלָם י׳ *the altar of Y. that was before the porch of Y.* 2 C 15$_8$, הַמִּזְבֵּחַ אֲשֶׁר־לַדְּבִיר *the altar that was*, i.e. belonged, *to the inner sanctuary* 1 K 6$_{22}$, מִזְבַּח הַנְּחֹשֶׁת ... אֲשֶׁר לְאֹהֶל מוֹעֵד *the bronze altar ... which was at the tent of meeting* 2 C 1$_6$.

מִזְבַּח הַבַּעַל אֲשֶׁר לְאָבִיךָ *the altar of Baal which is your father's* Jg 6$_{25}$, הַמִּזְבֵּחַ אֲשֶׁר בְּבֵית־אֵל *the altar that is in Bethel* 1 K 13$_{32}$ 2 K 23$_{15}$, sim. 2 K 16$_{10}$ (in Damascus) 2 C 30$_{14}$ (in Jerusalem), מִזְבַּח הָעוֹלָה ... בַּבָּמָה בְּגִבְעוֹן *the altar of burnt offering was ... at the high place in Gibeon* 1 C 21$_{29}$, הַמִּזְבְּחוֹת אֲשֶׁר עַל־הַגָּג *the altars that were on the roof* 2 K 23$_{12}$, מִזְבְּחוֹתָם כְּגַלִּים *their altars are as (stone) heaps* Ho 12$_{12}$, מִשְׁמַרְתָּם ... הַמִּזְבְּחֹת *their charge was ... the altars* Nm 3$_{31}$, הַמִּזְבֵּחַ ... קָטֹן *the altar was ... too small* 1 K 8$_{64}$.

<OBJ> בנה *build* Gn 8$_{20}$ 12$_{7.8}$ 13$_{18}$ 22$_9$ 26$_{25}$ 35$_7$ Ex 17$_{15}$ 24$_4$ 32$_5$ Nm 23$_{1.14.29}$ Dt 27$_{5.6}$ Jos 8$_{30}$ 22$_{10+7t}$ Jg 6$_{24.26}$ 21$_4$ 1 S 7$_{17}$ 14$_{35.35}$ 2 S 24$_{21.25}$||1 C 21$_{22.26}$ 1 K 9$_{25}$ 18$_{32}$ 2 K 16$_{11}$ 21$_{4.5}$||2 C 33$_{4.5}$ Ezr 3$_2$ 2 C 33$_{15}$, נצב hi. *erect* Gn 33$_{20}$ (or em. מַצֵּבָה *pillar*), קום hi. *erect* 2 S 24$_{18}$||1 C 21$_{18}$ 1 K 16$_{32}$ 2 K 21$_3$||2 C 33$_3$, כון hi. *establish* Ezr 3$_3$ 2 C 33$_{16}$, עשׂה *make* Gn 13$_4$ 35$_{1.3}$ Ex 20$_{24.25}$ 27$_1$||38$_1$ 30$_1$||37$_{25}$ 31$_{8.9}$||35$_{15.16}$ 38$_{1.30}$ Nm 23$_{1(Sam)}$ Dt 16$_{21}$ 1 K 6$_{20}$ (if em.; see below) 7$_{48}$||2 C 4$_{19}$ 1 K 12$_{33}$ 2 K 23$_{12.12.15}$ 2 C 1$_5$ 4$_1$ 7$_7$ 28$_{24}$ 11QT 3$_{14}$ ([יעשו]), רבה hi. *increase* Ho 8$_{11}$ 10$_1$ (if em.; see Prep.), שׂים *place* Ex 40$_{26.29}$ Jr 11$_{13.13}$ 2 C 1$_5$ (mss שָׁם *[was] there*), נתן *give*, i.e. place Ex 40$_{5.6}$, כסה pi. *cover* Ml 2$_{13}$, צפה pi. *cover* 1 K 6$_{20}$ (or em. וַיְצַף *and he covered* to וַיַּעַשׂ *and he made*), 6$_{22}$, חדשׁ pi. *repair* 2 C 15$_8$, רפא pi. *repair* 1 K 18$_{30}$.

בוא hi. *bring* Ex 39$_{38.39}$, סבב po. *go around* Ps 26$_6$, קדשׁ pi. *consecrate* Ex 29$_{44}$ 40$_{10}$ Lv 8$_{15}$ Nm 7$_1$, משׁח *anoint* Ez 30$_{27.28}$ 40$_{10}$ Lv 8$_{11}$ Nm 7$_1$, חטא pi. *cleanse from sin* Lv 8$_{15}$ Ezk 43$_{22}$, כפר pi. *atone for* Lv 16$_{20.33}$ Ezk 43$_{26}$, טהר pi. *purify* Ezk 43$_{26}$ 2 C 29$_{18}$, דשׁן pi. *make fat* 11QPs^a 18$_9$, *clear of ashes* Nm 4$_{13}$, ערך *arrange* Nm 23$_4$, אור hi. *kindle fire upon* Ml 1$_{10}$=CD 6$_{13}$ CD 6$_{12}$, שׁרת pi. *serve* Si 50$_{14.19}$, שׁבר pi. *break* 2 K 11$_{18}$||2 C 23$_{17}$, ערף *break* Ho 10$_2$, נתץ *pull down* Ex 34$_{13}$ Dt 7$_5$ Jg 2$_2$ 6$_{30.31.32}$ 2 K 23$_{12.12.15.15}$ 11QT 2$_6$ ([מזבחו]תיהמה), pi. Dt 12$_3$ 2 C 31$_1$ 34$_{4.7}$, הרס *tear down* Jg 6$_{25}$ 1 K 19$_{10.14}$, סור hi. *remove* 2 K 18$_{22}$||Is 36$_7$||2 C 32$_{12}$ 2 C 14$_2$ 30$_{14}$ 33$_{15}$, קרב hi. *bring near*, i.e. remove 2 K 16$_{14}$, זנח *reject* Lm 2$_7$, ראה *see* 2 K 16$_{10.12}$, זכר *remember* Jr 17$_2$, טמא pi. *defile* 2 K 23$_{16}$ CD 11$_{20}$.

<CSTR> מִזְבַּח י׳ *altar of Y.* Lv 17$_6$ Dt 12$_{27.27}$ 16$_{21}$ 26$_4$ 27$_6$ Jos 9$_{27}$ 22$_{19.28.29}$ 1 K 8$_{22}$||2 C 6$_{12}$ 1 K 8$_{54}$ 18$_{30}$ 2 K 23$_9$ Ml 2$_{13}$ Ne 10$_{35}$ 2 C 8$_{12}$ 15$_8$ 29$_{19.21}$ 33$_{16}$ 35$_{16}$ 11QT 21$_{10}$, אֱלֹהִים *of God* Ps 43$_4$ (mss מִזְבַּחֲךָ *your altar*, O God), אֱלֹהֵי *of the God of* Israel Ezr 3$_2$, הַבַּעַל *of Baal* Jg 6$_{25.28}$, מִזְבְּחוֹת הַבְּעָלִים *altars of the baalim* 2 C 34$_4$, מִזְבַּח סֶמֶל *altar of the image of* jealousy Ezk 8$_5$ (if em.; see below), הָעֹלָה *of burnt offering* Ex 30$_{28}$ 31$_9$||35$_{16}$ 38$_1$ 40$_{6.10.29}$ Lv 4$_{7+6t}$ 1 C 6$_{34}$ 16$_{40}$ 21$_{26.29}$ 2 C 29$_{18}$ (both הָעוֹלָה) 4QRP^c

23$_{6}$ (העולה) 11QT 3$_{14}$ ([העול]ה) 10$_{16}$ (העולה) 22$_{6}$ ([ה]עולה) 23$_{12}$ 26$_{8}$ 27$_{4}$ 52$_{21}$ (all four העולה), הַקְּטֹרֶת *of incense* Ex 30$_{27}$ 31$_{8}$||35$_{15}$ 37$_{25}$ 1 C 6$_{34}$ 28$_{18}$ 2 C 26$_{16.19}$ 11QT 8$_{11}$ (הקטורת), קְטֹרֶת הַסַּמִּים *of fragrant incense* Lv 4$_{7.18(Sam)}$ 11QT 3$_{10}$ ([מזבח] קטורת הסמים), הַזָּהָב *of gold* Ex 38$_{38}$ 40$_{5}$ (+ לִקְטֹרֶת *for incense*) 40$_{26}$ Nm 4$_{11}$ 1 K 7$_{48}$||2 C 4$_{19}$, הַנְּחֹשֶׁת *of bronze* Ex 38$_{30.39}$ 1 K 8$_{64}$||2 C 7$_{7}$ 2 K 16$_{14(mss)}$ (L הַמִּזְבֵּחַ) 16$_{15}$ Ezk 19$_{2}$ 2 C 1$_{5.6}$ 4$_{1}$ (נְחֹשֶׁת), אֲבָנִים *of stones* Ex 20$_{25}$ Dt 27$_{5}$ Jos 8$_{31}$, אֲדָמָה *of earth* Ex 20$_{24}$, מִזְבְּחוֹת הַנֵּכָר *altars of foreignness*, i.e. foreign altars 2 C 14$_{2}$, בֵּית־אֵל *of Bethel* Am 3$_{14}$ (or em. מִזְבַּח *altar of*, or מַצֵּבַת *the pillar of*), מזבחי מצ[רים] perh. *altars of Egypt* 4Qps Ezek^{e} 48$_{2}$, מזבח הוד *altar of glory*, i.e. glorious altar Si 50$_{11}$.

מְשָׁרְתֵי מִזְבֵּחַ *ministers of the altar* Jl 1$_{13}$, מְקוֹם הַמִּזְבֵּחַ *place of the altar* Gn 13$_{4}$, יְסוֹד *base of* Ex 29$_{12}$ (יְסֹד) Lv 4$_{30.34}$ 5$_{9}$ 8$_{15}$ 9$_{9}$ 11QT 34$_{8}$ (יסוד), יְסוֹד מִזְבַּח *base of the altar of* Lv 4$_{7.18.25.30(Sam)}$ 11QT 52$_{21}$, קַרְנוֹת הַמִּזְבֵּחַ *horns of the altar* Ex 29$_{12}$ (קַרְנֹת) Lv 8$_{15}$ 9$_{9}$ 16$_{18}$ 1 K 1$_{50.51}$ 2$_{28}$ Am 3$_{14}$ Ps 118$_{27}$ 11QT 16$_{16}$ ([ה]מזבח), קַרְנֹת מִזְבַּח *horns of the altar of* Lv 4$_{7}$ (קַרְנוֹת) 4$_{18(Sam).25.30.34}$ 11QT 23$_{12}$ (קרנות), קַרְנוֹת מִזְבְּחוֹתֵיכֶם *horns of your altars* Jr 17$_{1}$ (mss מִזְבְּחוֹתָם ,מִזְבְּחוֹתֵיהֶם *of their altars*), זָוִיּוֹת מִזְבֵּחַ *corners of the altar* Zc 9$_{15}$, עזרת המזבח *ledge of the altar* 11QT 16$_{17}$ 23$_{13.14}$ 37$_{4}$ (ה[מז]בח) 11QT^{b} 1$_{16}$ ([ה]מזבח), כַּרְכֹּב הַמִּזְבֵּחַ *edge of the altar* Ex 27$_{5}$, יֶרֶךְ *side of* Lv 1$_{11}$ 2 K 16$_{14}$, קִיר *side of* Lv 1$_{15}$ 5$_{9}$, צַלְעֹת *sides of* Ex 27$_{7}$ 38$_{7}$, גַּב *mound of* Ezk 43$_{13}$ (or em. גַּב to גֹּבַהּ *height of*).

כְּלֵי *vessels of* Ex 38$_{3.30}$ Nm 4$_{14}$ 11QT 33$_{13}$, אֵשׁ *fire of* Lv 6$_{2}$, לַהַב *flame of* Jg 13$_{20}$, דשא [ה]מזבח *ashes of the altar* 4QMMT B$_{32}$, אַבְנֵי מִזְבֵּחַ *stones of the altar* Is 27$_{9}$, דְּמוּת הַמִּזְבֵּחַ *likeness of the altar* 2 K 16$_{10}$, מַרְאֵה *appearance of* Ezk 41$_{22}$ (if em.; see Nom. Cl.), תַּבְנִית *pattern of the altar of* Jos 22$_{28}$, מִדּוֹת *measurements of* Ezk 43$_{13}$, חֻקּוֹת *ordinances of* Ezk 43$_{18}$, שַׁעַר *gate of* Ezk 8$_{5}$ (or em. הַמִּזְבֵּחַ to הַמִּזְרָח *of the east*, or מִזְבַּח to the north of the gate was *the altar of* the image of jealousy), חֲנֻכַּת *dedication offering of*, i.e. for Nm 7$_{10.11.84}$ 2 C 7$_{9}$, מִשְׁמֶרֶת *charge of*, i.e. duties connected with Nm 18$_{5}$ Ezk 40$_{46}$, דְּבַר *matter of* Nm 18$_{7}$, חֲצִי *half of* Ex 27$_{5}$, כָּל־מִזְבֵּחַ *every altar* Am 2$_{8}$, כול מזבח *all the altar of* 11QT 3$_{14}$, כָּל־הַמִּזְבֵּחַ *all the altar* 1 K 6$_{22}$.

<APP> מַעֲשֶׂה *work* Is 17$_{8}$ (or del. הַמִּזְבְּחוֹת), עֵץ *wood* Ezk 41$_{22}$ (if em.; see Nom. Cl.), בָּמָה *high place* 2 K 23$_{15}$, מִקְטָר *place of burning* of incense Ex 30$_{1}$.

<ADJ> גָּדוֹל *great* Jos 22$_{10}$ 2 K 16$_{15}$, אֶחָד *one* 2 C 32$_{12}$, הוּא *that* 1 K 3$_{4}$ 2 K 23$_{15}$, זֶה *this* 2 K 18$_{22}$||Is 36$_{7}$.

<PREP> לְ of benefit, *to, for* Nm 17$_{3.4}$ Jos 9$_{27}$ 1 C 28$_{18}$, + עשׂה *make* Ex 27$_{6}$ 38$_{4}$, נדר *vow* CD 16$_{13}$; of place, *on, at*, + עמד *stand* 2 K 11$_{11}$, hi. *cause to stand* 2 C 23$_{10}$, עלה hi. *cause to go up*, i.e. offer 2 C 29$_{27}$ CD 11$_{17}$; of direction, *to* Ezk 47$_{1}$ 2 C 5$_{12}$, + שׁלח *send* CD 11$_{19}$, עלה hi. *raise* 11QT 23$_{12}$; of possession, *of, (belonging) to* Ezk 45$_{19}$ (הָעֲזָרָה לַמִּזְבֵּחַ *the ledge of the altar*) 11QT 35$_{8}$ (סביב למזבח *the environs of the altar*); introducing object, + קרא *call*, i.e. name Jos 22$_{34}$ Jg 6$_{24}$, רבה hi. *increase* Ho 10$_{1}$ (or em. מִזְבְּחוֹת to לַמִּזְבְּחוֹת).

בְּ of place, *on*, + עלה hi. *cause to go up*, i.e. offer Gn 8$_{20}$ Nm 23$_{2.4.14.30}$, נגשׁ ho. *be brought near* 4QTohB^{b} 1$_{4}$ (הוג[שׁ]); introducing object, + נגע *touch* Ex 29$_{27}$.

מִן of direction, *from* 11QT 31$_{11}$, + שׁפך ni. *be poured* 1 K 13$_{5}$.

אֶל *to*, + בוא *go* Ps 43$_{4}$, יצא *go out* Lv 16$_{18}$, נגשׁ *draw near* Ex 28$_{43}$ 30$_{20}$ Lv 21$_{23}$, hi. *bring near* Lv 2$_{8}$, קרב *draw near* Ex 40$_{32}$ Lv 9$_{7.8}$ Nm 18$_{3}$, hi. *bring near* Lv 1$_{15}$ 5$_{25}$; *upon* + עלה *go up*, i.e. be offered Lv 2$_{12}$, שׁית *place* Ps 84$_{4(ms)}$; שׁעה אֶל *gaze at*, i.e. have regard for Is 17$_{8}$ (or del. הַמִּזְבְּחוֹת).

עַל *upon, over* Ex 29$_{21}$ Lv 1$_{8.12}$ 6$_{2.5}$ 8$_{30}$ Nm 4$_{26}$ 1 C 21$_{26}$ 4QJub^{e} 21$_{8}$ 4QLiturgy 1.2$_{8}$ (המזב[ח]) 11QT 8$_{11}$ ([ע]ל) 34$_{12}$ 35$_{15}$, + היה *be* Is 56$_{7}$ (if ins. יִהְיוּ *they will be*), זרק *toss* Ex 24$_{6}$ 29$_{16.20}$ Lv 1$_{5.11}$ 3$_{2.8.13}$ 7$_{2}$ 8$_{19.24}$ 9$_{12.18}$ 17$_{6}$ Nm 18$_{17}$ 2 K 16$_{13}$ 4QJub^{e} 21$_{7}$ (המזב[ח]) 11QT 22$_{5}$ ([וזר]קו ... [על המזבח]), נזה hi. *sprinkle* Lv 8$_{11}$, שׁפך ni. *be poured out* Dt 12$_{27}$, נסך *pour out* drink offering 11QT 21$_{10}$, עשׂה *do*, i.e. offer Ex 29$_{38}$ Dt 12$_{27}$ Jos 22$_{23}$ Ezk 43$_{27}$ 11QT 23$_{8}$ ([ויעשום]) 27$_{4}$, עלה *go up*, i.e. be offered Is 56$_{7(1QIsa^{a})}$ Ps 51$_{21}$, i.e. grow Ho 10$_{8}$, hi. *cause to go up*, i.e. offer Ex 40$_{29}$ Jos 22$_{23}$ 1 K 3$_{4}$ 9$_{25}$ 12$_{32.33}$ (or del. both) Ezr 3$_{2}$ 1 C 16$_{40}$ 2 C 8$_{12}$ 29$_{21}$ 35$_{16}$, ho. *be caused to go up*, i.e. offered Jg 6$_{28}$, נגשׁ hi. *bring near*, i.e. offer Ml 1$_{7}$, קרב hi. *bring near*, i.e. offer 11QT 21$_{16}$ ([ויקריבו]) 43$_{10}$, בער pi. *burn* Ne 10$_{35}$, קטר pi. *burn* 11QT 23$_{17}$, hi. Lv 4$_{10}$ 9$_{13.17}$ 2 K 16$_{15}$ 1 C 6$_{34.34}$ 2 C 26$_{16}$ 32$_{12}$ 4QJub^{e} 21$_{7}$ (תקט[י]ר)

11QT 20_4 ([המ]זבח]) 20_8 ([ת]קטיר) 21_7 ([על המז]בח]) 20_{11} ([ויק]טירו ... על המזבח]) 22_6 26_8 32_7 34_{14}, שׂרף *burn* 2 K 23_{16} 2 C 34_5, יקד ho. *be kept burning* Lv 6_6, אכל *consume* Lv 6_3 9_{24}, זבח *kill* 2 K 23_{20}, *sacrifice* Ex 20_{24} 2 C 33_{16}, שׂים *place* Gn 22_9 Dt 33_{10}, נתן *give* Lv 17_{11}, i.e. place Lv 1_7 22_{22} Nm 4_{13} 4QJub[d] 21_{13} ([ת]תן ... על ה]מזבח]), פרשׂ *spread* Nm $4_{11.13.14}$, ערך *arrange* 4QRP[c] 23_6, שׁרת pi. *serve* Nm 4_{13}.

עַל *(on)to*, + עלה *go up* Ex 20_{26} 1 S 2_{28} 2 K 16_{12} 23_9 2 C 1_6 Si 50_{11}, hi. *raise* 11QT 33_{15}, קרב *draw near* 2 K 16_{12} 11QT 16_6 ([ויקרב על המז]בח]).

עַל *beside* Jg 6_{28}, + עמד *stand* 1 K 13_1, נצב ni. *stand* Am 9_1; *around* Nm 3_{26}, + פסח pi. *limp* 1 K 18_{26}.

עַל *for*, + כפר pi. *make atonement* Ex 29_{37} Lv 8_{15} 16_{18}, חטא pi. *offer a sin offering* Ex 29_{36} (unless עַל *upon*); *against*, + קרא *cry* 1 K $13_{2.4.32}$, עשׂה *do* 2 K 23_{17}; introducing object, + פקד *visit*, i.e. punish Am 3_{14}.

לִפְנֵי *before* Zc 14_{20} 2 C 29_{19}, + בוא *come* 1 K 8_{31}||2 C 6_{22}, קרב hi. *bring near*, i.e. offer Nm 7_{10}, נוח hi. *place* Dt 26_4, עמד *stand* 1 K 8_{22}||2 C 6_{12}, שׁחה htpal. *worship* 2 K 18_{22}||Is 36_7||2 C 32_{12}, שׁיר pol. *sing* 11QPs[a] 27_5, הרג *kill* 2 K 11_{18}||2 C 23_{17}.

אֶל־פְּנֵי *before*, + קרב hi. *bring near*, i.e. offer Lv 6_7.

מִלִּפְנֵי *from before*, + קום *rise* 1 K 8_{54}.

מֵעִם *from*, + לקח *take* Ex 21_{14}, כרת hi. *cut off* 1 S 2_{33}.

מֵעַל *from (upon)* Nm 17_{11}, + עלה *go up* Jg 13_{20}, ירד hi. *bring down* 1 K 1_{53}, לקח *take* Lv 16_{12} Is 6_6, שׁלח *send*, i.e. stretch, hand 1 K 13_4.

מֵעַל לְ *beside*, + זרח (of leprosy) *arise*, i.e. break out 2 C 26_{19}.

אֵת *with, at*, + שׁית *place* Ps 84_4.

בֵּין *between* Ezk 8_{16} (+ אוּלָם *porch*), + שׂים *place* Ex 40_{30} (+ אֹהֶל *tent*), נתן *give*, i.e. place Ex 30_{18} 40_7 (both + אֹהֶל).

בֵּין ... לְ *between ... and*, + בכה *weep* Jl 2_{17} (+ אוּלָם *porch*).

מִבֵּין *from between*, + קרב hi. *bring near*, i.e. remove 2 K 16_{14} (+ בַּיִת *house* of Y.).

אֵצֶל *beside* 1 K 2_{29}, + עמד *stand* Ezk 9_2, נטה hi. *recline* Am 2_8, שׂים *place* Lv 6_3, נתן *give*, i.e. place 2 K 12_{10} (or em. הַמַּצֵּבָה *the pillar*), נטע *plant* Dt 16_{21} 11QT 52_2 ([אצל מזבח]), שׁלך hi. *throw* Lv 1_{16}, קטר hi. *burn* Lv $1_{16(Gnz)}$, אכל *eat* Lv 10_{12}.

סָבִיב לְ *around*, + הלך *go* 1 K 18_{35}, קום hi. *erect* court Ex 40_{33}, עשׂה *make* trench 1 K 18_{32}.

סְבִיבוֹת *around*, + היה *be* Ezk 6_{13}, זרה pi. *scatter* Ezk 6_5.

מִבַּלְעֲדֵי *apart from*, + בנה *build* Jos 22_{19}.

מִלְּבַד *apart from*, + בנה *build* Jos 22_{29}.

with ה- of direction, הַמִּזְבֵּחָה *upon the altar*, + קטר hi. *burn* Ex $29_{13.18.25}$ Lv $1_{9.13.15.17}$ $2_{2.9}$ $3_{5.11.16}$ $4_{19.26.31.35}$ 5_{12} $6_{8(Sam)}$ $7_{5.31}$ $8_{16.21.28}$ $9_{10.14.20}$ 16_{25} Nm 5_{26} 11QT 15_{13} ([והקטירו המזבחה]) 16_9 ([ויקטי]רו ... המזבחה]), עלה hi. *cause to go up*, i.e. offer Lv 14_{20}, חטא pi. *offer a sin offering* 2 C 29_{24}, זרק *toss* 2 C $29_{22.22.22}$.

without ה- of direction, הַמִּזְבֵּחַ *(upon) the altar*, + קטר hi. *burn* Lv 6_8 11QT 16_{18} 23_{14}; יַעֲלוּ עַל־רָצוֹן מִזְבְּחִי *they will go up with acceptance on my altar* Is 60_7 (or del. עַל־רָצוֹן).

<COLL> מִזְבֵּחַ || חַמָּן *incense altar* Ezk $6_{4.6}$ 2 C $34_{4.7}$ (both +), שֻׁלְחָן *table* Ex 30_{27} 31_8 Nm 3_{31} 1 K 7_{48}||2 C 4_{19} (+) 2 C 29_{18}, מְנוֹרָה *lampstand* Ex 30_{27} 31_8 Nm 3_{31}, אֲרוֹן *ark* Nm 3_{31}, פָּרֹכֶת *veil* Lv 21_{23}, מִשְׁכָּן *tabernacle* Nm 4_{26} 7_1 1 C 21_{29}, אֹהֶל *tent* of meeting Ex 29_{44} Lv $16_{20.33}$, קֹדֶשׁ *sanctuary* Lv 16_{20} Nm 18_5, מִקְדָּשׁ *sanctuary* Lv 16_{33} Lm 2_7 Si 50_{11} (+), בָּמָה *high place* 2 K 18_{22}||Is 36_7||2 C 32_{12} 2 K 23_{15} 2 C 14_2 31_1, בַּיִת *house* 1 C 22_1 (+) 2 K 11_{11}||2 C 23_{10} 2 C 29_{18} (+), גִּלּוּל *idol* Ezk 6_6, פֶּסֶל *image* Dt 7_5 12_3 2 C $34_{4.7}$ (both +), צֶלֶם *image* 2 K 11_{18}||2 C 23_{17}, מַעֲשֶׂה *work* Ezk 6_6, מַצֵּבָה *pillar* Ex 24_4 (+) 34_{13} Dt 7_5 12_3 Is 19_{19} (+) Ho 10_1 (+) 10_2 2 C 14_2 31_1, אֲשֵׁרָה *Asherah* Ex 34_{13} Dt 7_5 12_3 Jg $6_{25.30}$ 2 K 21_3||2 C 33_3 (all three +) Jr 17_2 2 C 14_2 31_1 $34_{4.7}$ (both +).

+ סֶמֶל *image* 2 C 33_{15}, מַסֵּכָה *molten image* 2 C 34_4, אֱלֹהִים *god* 2 C 33_{11}, כְּלִי *vessel* Ex 30_{28} 31_9 36_{16}||39_{39} 40_{10} Lv 8_{11} Nm 3_{31} 7_1 1 K 7_{48}||2 C 4_{19} 2 C 29_{18}, בַּד *pole* Ex 36_{16}||39_{39}, מִכְבָּר *grating* Ex 35_{16}||39_{39}.

מִזְבֵּחַ as vocative 1 K $13_{2.2}$.

שִׁבְעָה מִזְבְּחֹת *seven altars* Nm $23_{1.14.29}$, var. Nm 23_4.

מִזְבֵּחַ לי׳ *an altar to Y.* Gn 8_{20} $12_{7.8}$ 13_{18} Dt 27_5 Jos 8_{30} Jg $6_{24.26}$ 1 S 7_{17} $14_{35.35}$ 2 S $24_{21.25}$||1 C $21_{22.26}$ Is 19_{19} 1 C 21_{18} (||2 S 24_{18} מִזְבֵּחַ לי׳), הַמִּזְבֵּחַ לי׳ *the altar of Y.* Lv 22_{22}, מִזְבֵּחַ לַבַּעַל *an altar to Baal* 1 K 16_{32}, var. 2 K 21_3||2 C 33_3, מִזְבְּחוֹת לַבֹּשֶׁת *altars to shame* Jr 11_{13} (or del.),

מִזְבְּחוֹת לְכָל־צְבָא הַשָּׁמַיִם *altars to all the host of heaven* 2 K 21$_{5}$||2 C 33$_{5}$, מִזְבַּח י׳ בִּירוּשָׁלָ͏ִם *the altar of Y. in Jerusalem* 2 K 23$_{9}$, מִזְבֵּחַ לָאֵל הַנִּרְאֶה אֵלֶיךָ *an altar to the God who appeared to you* Gn 35$_{1}$, sim. Gn 35$_{3}$, מִזְבֵּחַ לְעֹלָה לְמִנְחָה וּלְזָבַח *an altar for burnt offering and cereal offering and sacrifice* Jos 22$_{29}$, הַמִּזְבֵּחַ לֹא לְעוֹלָה וְלֹא לְזָבַח *an altar not for burnt offering or sacrifice* Jos 22$_{26}$, הַמִּזְבֵּחַ לְעֹלָה לְיִשְׂרָאֵל *the altar of burnt offering for Israel* 1 C 22$_{1}$ (if em. מִזְבַּח to הַמִּזְבֵּחַ), מִזְבְּחוֹת לְקַטֵּר לַבָּעַל *altars for burning incense to Baal* Jr 11$_{13}$, הַמִּזְבֵּחַ בְּבֵית־אֵל *the altar in Bethel* 2 K 13$_{4}$ 23$_{17 (mss)}$ (L הַמִּזְבֵּחַ בֵּית־אֵל).

וַיַּעַשׂ מִזְבֵּחַ אֶרֶז *and he made an altar with cedar* 1 K 6$_{20}$ (if em.; see Obj.), כול מזבח העול[ה יעשו נחו]שת טהור *they shall make the whole of the altar of burnt offering (of) pure bronze* 11QT 3$_{14}$.

Also 4QJub^{d} 21$_{7}$ ([המזב]ח) 4QTohB^{c} 2$_{2}$ 4QpsEzek^{a} 4$_{34}$.

<SYN> חַמָּן *incense altar*, שֻׁלְחָן *table*, מְנוֹרָה *lampstand*, אָרוֹן *ark*, פָּרֹכֶת *veil*, מִשְׁכָּן *tabernacle*, אֹהֶל *tent*, קֹדֶשׁ *sanctuary*, מִקְדָּשׁ *sanctuary*, בָּמָה *high place*, בַּיִת *house*, גִּלּוּל *idol*, פֶּסֶל *image*, צֶלֶם *image*, מַעֲשֶׂה *work*, מַצֵּבָה *pillar*, אֲשֵׁרָה *Asherah*.*

⇒ זבח *sacrifice*.

*[מִזְבָּל] n.[m.] **dwelling**, <NOM CL> שְׁאוֹל מִזְבָּל לוֹ *Sheol is his dwelling place* Ps 49$_{15}$ (if em. מִזְּבֻל *without a dwelling place*).

⇒ זְבֻל *dwelling place*.

[מֶזֶג] $_{1}$ n.m. **mixed wine**—מָזֶג—perh. mixed with spices, <OBJ> חסר *lack* Ca 7$_{3}$.

*[מַזְדַּי] 0.0.0.4 pr.n.m. **Mazdaeus**, Persian satrap, alw. abbreviated מז, Samaria coins 14 16 21 48.

[מָזֶה] I $_{1}$ adj. **emaciated**—pl. cstr. מְזֵי—**sucked dry, emaciated, weakened,** מְזֵי רָעָב וּלְחֻמֵי רֶשֶׁף *(they will be) emaciated by famine, devoured* [or *battered*] *by plague* Dt 32$_{24}$ (Sam מזה רעב לחמו *on account of this, famine is his bread*), כְּבוֹדוֹ מְזֵי רָעָב *his honoured one(s) are emaciated by hunger* Is 5$_{13}$ (if em. מְתֵי *men of* hunger; mss מֵתֵי *dying of*).

*[מָזֶה] II $_{1}$ adj. **thin**—pl. cstr. מְזֵי—**thin, weak, emaciated,** מְזֵי רָעָב וּלְחֻמֵי רֶשֶׁף *(they will be) weakened by famine, devoured* [or *battered*] *by plague* Dt 32$_{24}$ (Sam מזה רעב לחמו *on account of this, famine is his bread*), כְּבוֹדוֹ מְזֵי רָעָב *his honoured one(s) are weakened by hunger* Is 5$_{13}$ (if em. מְתֵי *men of* hunger; mss מֵתֵי *dying of*).

*[מָזֶה] III n.m. **storeplace, repository,** <OBJ> אמץ pi. *strengthen* 1QH 5$_{9}$ (if em.; see Cstr.). <CSTR> מזה ברית *repository of the covenant* 1QH 5$_{9}$ (if em. מיה perh. *water*).

⇒ cf. מָזוּ *storehouse*.

מַזֶּה, see מָה *what*, זֶה *this*.

מִזָּה $_{3}$ pr.n.m. **Mizzah,** son of Reuel, and grandson of Esau, <NOM CL> בְּנֵי רְעוּאֵל ... שַׁמָּה וּמִזָּה *the sons of Reuel were ... Shammah and Mizzah* 1 C 1$_{37}$. <APP> אַלּוּף *chief* Gn 36$_{17}$. <COLL> אֵלֶּה בְּנֵי רְעוּאֵל ... שַׁמָּה וּמִזָּה *these are the sons of Reuel: ... Shammah and Mizzah* Gn 36$_{13}$, sim. 36$_{17}$.

*מִזֶּה $_{1}$ n.m. **spurt,** of wine from cup of Y., <OBJ> נגר hi. *pour*, i.e. cause to gush out Ps 75$_{9}$ (unless מִזֶּה *from this*).

⇒ נזה *spurt*.

[מָזוּ] $_{1}$ n.m. **storehouse**—pl. sf. מְזָוֵינוּ—**storehouse, granary,** <SUBJ> פוק hi. *provide* all kinds of food Ps 144$_{13}$. <NOM CL> מְזָוֵינוּ מְלֵאִים *our storehouses are full* Ps 144$_{13}$.

⇒ cf. מָזֶה III *storeplace*.

מְזוּזָה 19.0.1 n.f. **doorpost**—cstr. מְזוּזַת; sf. מְזוּזָתִי, מְזוּזָתָם; pl. מְזוּזֹת (מְזֻזוֹת, מְזוּזוֹת); sf. Q מזוזותיו—**doorpost, gatepost** of house, dwelling place (Ex 12$_{7.22.23}$ 21$_{6}$ Dt 6$_{9}$ 11$_{20}$ Is 57$_{8}$ Ezk 43$_{8}$ Pr 8$_{34}$ 11QT 49$_{13}$), Solomon's palace (1 K 7$_{5}$; or em.; see Nom. cl.), temple (1 S 1$_{9}$ 1 K 6$_{31.33}$ Ezk 41$_{21}$ 43$_{8}$ 45$_{19}$), gate of temple court (Ezk 45$_{19}$ 46$_{2}$), city gate (Jg 16$_{3}$), <SUBJ> רבע pass. *be square* 1 K 6$_{33}$

(if em. מֵאַת רְבִעִית *from a fourth* to מְזוּזוֹת רְבֻעוֹת *square doorposts*) 75 (or em. וְהַמְּחֱזוֹת *and the windows*).

<NOM CL> אַיִל מְזוּזוֹת חֲמִשִׁית *the pillar (and) doorposts were*, i.e. occupied, *a fifth* 1 K 631, הַהֵיכָל מְזוּזַת רְבָעָה *the outer sanctuary was a doorpost of a square*, i.e. it had square doorposts Ezk 4121 (or em. מְזוּזֹת *doorposts of*).

<OBJ> נסע *pull up* Jg 163), נתן *give*, i.e. place Ezk 438, עשׂה *make* 1 K 633, שׁמר *watch* Pr 834, כבס pi. *wash* 11QT 4913.

<CSTR> מְזוּזַת הֵיכַל י׳ *doorpost of the temple of Y.* 1 S 19, הַבַּיִת *of the house* Ezk 4519, מְזוּזוֹת בֵּיתֶךָ *doorposts of your house* Dt 69 1120 (מְזוּזוֹת), מְזוּזַת הַשַּׁעַר *doorpost of the gate* Ezk 462, שַׁעַר *of the gate of* the inner court Ezk 4519, רְבָעָה *of a square*, i.e. square doorpost Ezk 4121 (or em. מְזוּזֹת *doorposts of*), מְזוּזוֹת פְּתָחָי *doorposts of my entrance* Pr 834, מְזוּזוֹת עֲצֵי־שָׁמֶן *doorposts of olive wood* 1 K 633.

<APP> אַיִל *pillar* 1 K 631.

<PREP> בְּ introducing object, + אחז *grasp* Jg 163; אֶל *to*, + נגשׁ hi. *bring near* Ex 216 (+ דֶּלֶת *door*), נגע hi. *apply* Ex 1222; *upon*, + נתן *give*, i.e. place Ezk 4519; עַל *upon* Ex 1223, + נתן *give*, i.e. place Ex 127 Ezk 4519, כתב *write* Dt 69 1120; *beside*, + ישׁב *sit* 1 S 19, עמד *stand* Ezk 462; אֵצֶל *beside*, + נתן *give*, i.e. place Ezk 438; אַחַר *behind*, + שׂים *place* Is 578.

<COLL> מְזוּזָה || מַשְׁקוֹף *lintel* Ex 127.22.23 11QT 4913, סַף *threshold* Ezk 438.8, אָסֹף *threshold* 11QT 4913, דֶּלֶת *door* Jg 163 (+) Is 578 Pr 834 (+), פֶּתַח *entrance* 1 K 75, מַנְעוּל *lock* 11QT 4913; + שַׁעַר *gate* Dt 69 1120, בְּרִיחַ *bar* Jg 163.

שְׁתֵּי הַמְּזוּזוֹת *the two doorposts* Ex 127.22 Jg 163.

<SYN> מַשְׁקוֹף *lintel*, סַף *threshold*, אָסֹף *threshold*, דֶּלֶת *door*, פֶּתַח *entrance*, מַנְעוּל *lock*.*

מָזוֹן 2.0.1 n.[m.] **food**—cstr. Q מזון—**food, provisions**, <OBJ> נשׂא *carry* Gn 4523 (|| לֶחֶם *bread*, בַּר *grain*), נתן *give* 2 C 1123, פוק hi. *provide* Ps 14413 (if em. מִזַּן אֶל־זַן *from kind to kind* to מָזוֹן עַל־מָזוֹן *provisions upon provisions*). <CSTR> מזון אמונ[י]ם *food of the faithful* 4QapMes 5.17. <COLL> מָזוֹן לָרֹב *abundant provisions* 2 C 1123.

<SYN> לֶחֶם *bread*, בַּר *grain*.

⇒ זון *feed*.

מָזוֹר I 3.0.1 n.[m.] **wound** (unless מָזוֹר II *sore* or III *running sore*)—sf. מְזֹרוֹ—**wound(s)**, <SUBJ> גהה *be healed* Ho 513 (or em. יִגְהֶה to יַגְהֶה, i.e. hi.). <OBJ> ראה *see* Ho 513 (|| חֳלִי *sickness*), גהה hi. *heal* Ho 513 (if em.; see Subj.). <CSTR> קלעי מזור *slings of*, i.e. causing, *wounds* 4QapJoseph^c 17=2QapDavid 12 (ק[לעי המזור]). <PREP> לְ of benefit, *to, for*, + דין *plead* Jr 3013 (or em. אֵין־דָּן דִּינֵךְ *there is not one who pleads your cause* to אֵין־רְכֻכִים *there is no softening*).

<SYN> חֳלִי *sickness*.

⇒ זור *press down*.

***מָזוֹר II** 3.0.1 n.[m.] **sore** (unless מָזוֹר I *wound* or III *running sore*)—sf. מְזֹרוֹ—**sore, ulcer, boil**, <SUBJ> גהה *be healed* Ho 513 (or em. יִגְהֶה to יַגְהֶה, i.e. hi.). <OBJ> ראה *see* Ho 513 (|| חֳלִי *sickness*), גהה hi. *heal* Ho 513 (if em.; see Subj.). <CSTR> קלעי מזור *slings of*, i.e. causing, *sores* 4QapJoseph^c 17=2QapDavid 12 (ק[לעי המזור]). <PREP> לְ of benefit, *to, for*, + דין *plead* Jr 3013.

<SYN> חֳלִי *sickness*.

***מָזוֹר III** 3.0.1 n.[m.] **running sore** (unless מָזוֹר I *wound* or II *sore*)—sf. מְזֹרוֹ—<SUBJ> גהה *be healed* Ho 513 (or em. יִגְהֶה to יַגְהֶה, i.e. hi.). <OBJ> ראה *see* Ho 513 (|| חֳלִי *sickness*), גהה hi. *heal* Ho 513 (if em.; see Subj.). <CSTR> קלעי מזור *slings of*, i.e. causing, *running sores* 4QapJoseph^c 17=2QapDavid 12 (ק[לעי המזור]). <PREP> לְ of benefit, *to, for*, + דין *plead* Jr 3013.

<SYN> חֳלִי *sickness*.

⇒ זור *flow*.

***מָזוֹר IV** 1 n.[m.] **trap, net, noose**, <OBJ> שׂים *place* Ob 7 (or em. מָצוֹד *net*).

⇒ זור *draw tight*.

***[מַזּוּרוֹת] I** 0.0.1 n.[f.]pl. **rotten eggs** (unless מַזּוּרוֹת I *catapults* or III *constellations*), <PREP> לְ introducing object, + בקע pi. *hatch* 1QH 227 (למזורות יבקעו אפעה ושוא *they hatch stinking eggs as a viper and false-*

hood).

*[מַזּוֹרוֹת] II 0.0.1 n.[f.]pl. **catapults** (unless מַזּוֹרוֹת I *rotten eggs* or III *constellations*), <PREP> לְ *as*, + בקע ni. *break out* 1QH 2₂₇ (למזורות יבקעו אפעה ושוא *as catapults, wickedness and fraud burst out*).

*[מַזּוֹרוֹת] III 0.0.1 n.[f.]pl. **constellations** (unless מַזּוֹרוֹת I *rotten eggs* or II *catapults*), <PREP> לְ of direction, *to*, + בקע ni. *break out* 1QH 2₂₇.
⇒ מַזָּרוֹת *constellations*.

*מזז 0.0.2 vb. **join** (or **melt, refine** if byform of מסס)*—**Pu.** 0.0.2 ptc. Q ממוזזים—**be joined together, blended,** <SUBJ> זָהָב *gold* 1QM 5₅.₈, כֶּסֶף *silver* 1QM 5₅.₈, נְחֹשֶׁת *bronze* 1QM 5₅.₈. <PREP> כְּ *as*, + מַעֲשֶׂה *work* 1QM 5₈.
⇒ (?) מסס *melt*.

*מֵזַח I 1 n.[m.] **shipyard,** <NOM CL> אֵין מֵזַח עוֹד *there is no longer a shipyard* Is 23₁₀ (or em. מָחוֹז *harbour*).

מֵזַח II 1 n.m.**girdle,** appar. worn next to the skin,* <OBJ> חגר *gird with* Ps 109₁₉ (+ בֶּגֶד *garment*). <PREP> לְ *as*, + היה *be* Ps 109₁₉.
⇒ מְזִיחַ *girdle*.

*מֵזַח III n.[m.] **impudence** (lit. **brow**), <OBJ> רפה pi. *weaken* Jb 12₂₁ (if em.; see Cstr.). <CSTR> מֵזַח אֲפִיקִים *impudence of the mighty* Jb 12₂₁ (if em. מְזִיחַ *girdle of*).
⇒ cf. מֵצַח *brow*.

[מְזִיחַ] 1 n.[m.] **girdle**—cstr. מְזִיחַ—appar. worn next to the skin,* <OBJ> רפה pi. *loosen* Jb 12₂₁ (or em.; see Cstr.). <CSTR> מְזִיחַ אֲפִיקִים *girdle of the mighty* Jb 12₂₁ (or em. מֵזַח *impudence of*).
⇒ מֵזַח II *girdle*.

מֵזִין, see אזן I *hear*.

מַזְכִּיר *recorder*, see זכר I *remember*, Hi. §2.*

*[מַזָּל] 0.0.7 n.[m.] **flow**—cstr. Q מזל—**flow** of lips, **utterance,** <OBJ> כול hi. *endure* 4QMª 11.2₁₇, נתן *give*, i.e. make 1QH 11₅ (others מול ptc. pass. *circumcision*). <CSTR> מזל שפתי *utterance of lips of* 1QH 11₅ (others מול *circumcision of*) 4QShirᵇ 63.2₄, שפתי *of my lips* 4Q 418 222₂ 4QMª 11.2₁₇, שפתיו *of his lips* 4Q416 7₃, שפתיכה *of your lips* 1QSb 3₂₇ (+ מַעֲשֶׂה *deed*), רוח שפת[יה] *of the breath of her lips* 4QBéat 8₂; תרומת מזל *offering of the utterance of* 4QShirᵇ 63.2₄. <PREP> מִן of instrument, *by (means of)* 4QBéat 8₂, + שׁפט *judge* 1QSb 3₂₇ ([ישׁ]פוט). <COLL> מ[ז]ל על כבוד *utterance concerning the glory of* 4QpsHodᶜ 2₂.
Also 4QShirᵇ 22₃.
⇒ נזל *flow*.

מַזְלֵג 2 n.m. **fork,** for extracting meat from pot, <SUBJ> עלה hi. *bring up* 1 S 2₁₄. <NOM CL> הַמַּזְלֵג שְׁלֹשׁ־הַשִּׁנַּיִם בְּיָדוֹ *a three-pronged fork was in his hand* 1 S 2₁₃. <APP> שֵׁן *tooth*, i.e. prong 1 S 2₁₃.
⇒ cf. מִזְלָגָה *fork*.

[מִזְלָגָה] 5.0.1 n.f. **fork**—pl. מִזְלָגוֹת (מִזְלָגֹת); sf. מִזְלְגֹתָיו—as sacrificial implement belonging to altar, <OBJ> עשׂה *make* Ex 27₃‖38₃ (‖ סִיר *pot*, יָע *shovel*, מִזְרָק *basin*, מַחְתָּה *firepan*) 2 C 4₁₆ (or em. הַמִּזְרָקוֹת *the basins*; ‖ סִיר, יָע, + כְּלִי *vessel*), נתן *give*, i.e. place Nm 4₁₄ (‖ יָע, מִזְרָק, מַחְתָּה, (מַחְתָּה), גנב *steal* 4Q523 1₄ (גנ[בו]). <APP> כְּלִי *vessel* Ex 38₃ Nm 4₁₄. <PREP> לְ of benefit, *to, for* 1 C 28₁₇ (if em. לַמִּזְלָגוֹת to הַמִּזְלָגוֹת; ‖ מִזְרָק *basin*, קַשְׂוָה *jar*, + כְּפוֹר *bowl*); בְּ of instrument, *by (means of), with*, + שׁרת pi. *serve* Nm 4₁₄.
<SYN> סִיר *pot*, יָע *shovel*, מִזְרָק *basin*, מַחְתָּה *firepan*, קַשְׂוָה *jar*.
⇒ cf. מַזְלֵג *fork*.

*[מַזָּלָה] n.f. **pit,** <OBJ> כרה *dig* Ps 12₉ (if em. כְּרֻם זֻלּוּת *when worthlessness is exalted* to כְּרֹ מַזָּלוֹת *digging* [= כְּרֹה inf. abs.] *pits*).

מַזָּלוֹת 1.0.2 n.[f.]pl. **planets**—pl. sf. Q מזלותמה—the five planets,* or perh. constellations of the zodiac,* <CSTR> מ[ז]לות השמ[ים] *constellations of the heavens* 8QHymn

14. <PREP> לְ of direction, *to* 8QHymn 1_4 (מ[ז]לות), + קטר pi. *burn incense* 2 K 23_5 (|| יָרֵחַ *moon*, שֶׁמֶשׁ *sun*, + צָבָא *host* of heaven); בְּ of place, *in* 4QBer[b] 1_2.

<SYN> יָרֵחַ *moon*, שֶׁמֶשׁ *sun*.

⇒ cf. מַזָּרוֹת *Mazzaroth*.

מְזִמָּה 19.2.16 n.f. **plan**—מְזִמָּתָה (Jr 11_{15}); cstr. Q מזמת; sf. Q מזמתי, מְזִמָּתוֹ, Q מזמתכה, Si מזמתם (Q מזמתמה); pl. מְזִמּוֹת; cstr. מְזִמּוֹת; sf. מְזִמּוֹתָיו, Q מזמותם—**1. plan, purpose, intention, thinking,*** esp. **private thoughts,*** **a.** of Y., <SUBJ> בצר ni. *be withheld* Jb 42_2. <NOM CL> עַל־בָּבֶל מְזִמָּתוֹ *his plan is against Babylon* Jr 51_{11}. <OBJ> קום hi. *raise up*, i.e. accomplish Jr 23_{20}=30_{24}. <CSTR> מְזִמּוֹת לִבּוֹ *plans of his heart* Jr 23_{20}=30_{24}, מזמת לבכה *plan of your heart* 1QH 4_{21} (+ מַעֲשֶׂה *deed*), חסדו *of his loyalty*, i.e. his loyal plan MasShirShabb 1_1, כבוד[ו] *of his glory*, i.e. his glorious plan 4QShirShabb[c] 3.2_{13}, אפו *of his anger* 4QMyst[c] 3_5. <PREP> בְּ *in, according to* 1QH 4_{21} ([ב]מזמת) perh. 1QH fr. 46_3 4QMyst[c] 3_5, + עשׂה *do* MasShirShabb 1_1.

b. of humans, <SUBJ> היה *be* Is 5_{12} (if em. מִשְׁתֵּיהֶם *their feasts* to מְזִמָּתָם *their purpose*). <OBJ> ידע *know* 1QH 9_{12} (+ רוּחַ *spirit*).

2. wicked plan, scheme, plot, <NOM CL> אֵין אֱלֹהִים כָּל־מְזִמּוֹתָיו *all his wicked schemes are*, i.e. amount to, *'There is no God'* Pr 10_4, [כול מזמות בליעל מחש[בותם *all their thoughts are wicked schemes of Belial* 1QH 2_{16}. <OBJ> עשׂה *do* Jr 11_{15} Ps 37_7, חשׁב *devise* Ps 10_2 21_{12} Ne 4_6 (if em. הַמְּקֹמוֹת אֲשֶׁר תָּשׁוּבוּ *the places where you shall return* to הַמְּזִמּוֹת אֲשֶׁר חָשְׁבוּ *the wicked schemes which they devise*), חמם *devise* Jb 21_{27} (+ מַחֲשָׁבָה *thought*), קום hi. *raise up* 4QBer[a] 7.2_{11} 4QBer[f] 1_6 ([מ]קימי). <CSTR> מזמות בליעל *wicked schemes of Belial* 1QH 2_{16}, כול מעשה *of every creature* 4QMyst[a] $3a.2_{10}$; אִישׁ מְזִמּוֹת *man of wicked schemes* Pr 12_2, בַּעַל־ *possessor of* Pr 24_8, מקימי מזמתמה *ones who raise up their wicked schemes* 4QBer[a] 7.2_{11}, [מ]קימי מזמתכה *ones who raise up your wicked schemes* 4QBer[f] 1_6, כָּל־הַמְּזִמּוֹת *all the wicked schemes* Ne 4_6 (if em.; see Obj.), כָּל־מְזִמּוֹתָיו *all his wicked schemes* Ps 10_4, כול מזמותם *all their wicked schemes* 1QH 5_{10}.

<PREP> לְ *as*, or *for (the purpose of)*, + אמר *mention* Ps 139_{20} (or em. יֹאמְרֻךָ *they mention you* to יַמְרֻךָ *they rebel against you*, i.e. מרה hi.); בְּ of place, accompaniment, *in, with* perh. 4QM[a] 14_4 (ב[מז]מת[ם]) 11QMelch 3_8 (במזמ[ו]ת), + תפשׂ ni. *be caught* Ps 10_2, קום hi. *raise up* CD 5_{19}; כְּ *according to*, + שׁוב hi. *repay* Si 32_{24} (+ פֹּעַל *deed*); מִן of cause, *on account of* Ne 4_6 (if em.; see Subj.). <COLL> מְזִמָּה followed by infinitive of purpose, שׁחת hi. *destroy* Jr 51_{11}, חתף *snatch away* 1QH 5_{10}.

3. discretion, caginess,* <SUBJ> שׁמר *keep* Pr 2_{11} (|| תְּבוּנָה *understanding*) 5_2 (if em. לִשְׁמֹר *to keep* discretion to לִשְׁמָרְךָ that discretion *may keep you*), סתר ni. *be hidden* 1QS 11_6 (+ דֵּעָה *knowledge*). <OBJ> שׁמר *keep* Pr 5_2 (or em. see subj.; + דַּעַת *knowledge*), נצר *keep* Pr 3_{21} (|| תֻּשִׁיָּה *sound wisdom*), מצא *find* Pr 8_{12} (|| דַּעַת *knowledge*, + עָרְמָה *prudence*; or em. דַּעַת מְזִמּוֹת אֶמְצָא *I find knowledge [and] discretion* to מוֹדַעַת מְזִמּוֹת אִמָּצֵא *I am found as the acquaintance of discretion*), נתן *give* Pr 1_4 (|| דַּעַת *knowledge*, + עָרְמָה *prudence*), ידע hi. *make known* perh. 1QH 18_5 (הו[דעתה]). <CSTR> מזמת ערמה *discretion of prudence* 1QS 11_6, ד[עת] *of knowledge* 4QdivProv 1_1 (+ חָכְמָה *wisdom*); אִישׁ מְזִמּוֹת *man of discretion* Pr 14_{17}, מוֹדַעַת *acquaintance of* Pr 8_{12} (if em.; see Obj.). <PREP> בְּ of accompaniment, *with* Si 44_4 (|| מֶחְקָר *searching*).

<SYN> §3 תְּבוּנָה *understanding*, תֻּשִׁיָּה *sound wisdom*, דַּעַת *knowledge*, מֶחְקָר *searching*.

⇒ זמם *plan*.

מִזְמוֹר 57.5.1 n.[m.] **psalm**—Si מזמר—**1. psalm,** as designation in psalm titles, <APP> שִׁיר *song* Ps 30_1 48_1 65_1 66_1 67_1 68_1 75_1 76_1 83_1 87_1 88_1 92_1 98_1 101_1 108_1 4QJonathan 1_1 (מזמו[ר]), הַלְלוּיָהּ *hallelujah* 4QJonathan 1_1 (מזמו[ר]), עֵדוּת *testimony* Ps 80_1.

<COLL> מִזְמוֹר alone as a psalm title, Ps 98_1.

מִזְמוֹר לְדָוִד *a psalm of/to/for David* Ps 3_1 4_1 5_1 6_1 8_1 9_1 12_1 13_1 15_1 19_1 20_1 21_1 22_1 23_1 29_1 30_1 31_1 38_1 39_1 41_1 51_1 62_1 63_1 64_1 65_1 108_1 140_1 141_1 143_1, לְדָוִד מִזְמוֹר *of/to/for David, a psalm* 24_1 40_1 68_1 101_1 109_1 110_1 139_1.

מִזְמוֹר לִבְנֵי־קֹרַח *a psalm of/to/for for the sons of Korah* Ps 48_1 88_1, לִבְנֵי־קֹרַח מִזְמוֹר *of/to/for for the sons of Korah, a psalm* Ps 47_1 49_1 84_1 85_1 87_1.

מִזְמוֹר לְאָסָף *a psalm of/to/for Asaph* Ps 50_1 73_1 75_1

76$_1$ 79$_1$ 82$_1$ 83$_1$, לְאָסָף מִזְמוֹר *of/to/for Asaph, a psalm* Ps 77$_1$ 80$_1$.

לַמְנַצֵּחַ (...) מִזְמוֹר *for the choirmaster (...) a psalm* Ps 4$_1$ 5$_1$ 6$_1$ 8$_1$ 9$_1$ 12$_1$ 13$_1$ 19$_1$ 20$_1$ 21$_1$ 22$_1$ 31$_1$ 39$_1$ 40$_1$ 41$_1$ 49$_1$ 51$_1$ 62$_1$ 64$_1$ 65$_1$ 66$_1$ 67$_1$ 68$_1$ 75$_1$ 76$_1$ 77$_1$ 80$_1$ 84$_1$ 85$_1$ 109$_1$ 139$_1$ 140$_1$, מִזְמוֹר (...) לַמְנַצֵּחַ *a psalm ... for the choirmaster* Ps 88$_1$.

לִידוּתוּן + מִזְמוֹר *for Jeduthun* Ps 39$_{1(Qr)}$, עַל־יְדוּתוּן *according to Jeduthun* Ps 62$_1$ 77$_{1(Qr)}$.

לְהַזְכִּיר + מִזְמוֹר *for offering the token offering* Ps 38$_1$, לְתוֹדָה *for the thank offering* Ps 100$_1$.

מִזְמוֹר + musical directions or names of melodies: בִּנְגִינוֹת *with stringed instruments* Ps 4$_1$ 6$_1$ 67$_1$ 76$_1$, אֶל־הַנְּחִילוֹת perh. *with the flutes* Ps 5$_1$, עַל־הַגִּתִּית *according to the gittith* Ps 8$_1$ 84$_1$, עַל־הַשְּׁמִינִית *according to the sheminith* Ps 6$_1$ 12$_1$, עַל־אַיֶּלֶת הַשַּׁחַר *according to the hind of the dawn* Ps 22$_1$, עַל־מוּת לַבֵּן perh. *according to muth-labben* Ps 9$_{1(mss)}$ (L עַלְמוּת לַבֵּן *'almuth-labben*), אֶל־שֹׁשַׁנִּים *according to lilies* Ps 80$_1$, אַל־תַּשְׁחֵת *do not destroy* Ps75$_1$.

2. psalm, song, music, devotional (Si 44$_5$ 47$_{9[Bmg]}$ 4QShirShabb[d] 1.1$_{40}$ [ר[מזמו]]), at banquets (Si 35$_{4.6}$ 49$_1$); used collectively (Si 44$_5$), <CSTR> חוקרי מזמור *composers of psalms* Si 44$_5$ (+ מָשָׁל *proverb*), קול מזמור *sound of song* Si 35$_6$ 47$_{9(Bmg)}$ (B נגינות שיר *melodies of song*). <PREP> לְ *as*, + זמר pi. *sing* 4QShirShabb[d] 1.1$_{40}$ (ל[מזמו]ר); בְּלֹא *without*, + שׁפך *pour out* conversation Si 35$_4$; כְּ *as* Si 49$_1$ (+ דְּבַשׁ *honey*). <COLL> מזמור על משתה היין *music at a banquet of wine* Si 49$_1$, ר[מזמו] בשמחת אלוהים *a song (sung) with the joy of God* 4Q ShirShabb[d] 1.1$_{40}$.

⇒ זמר I *sing (praise).*

[מַזְמֵרָה] $_4$ n.f. **pruning knife**—pl. מַזְמֵרוֹת; sf. מַזְמְרֹתֵיכֶם—<OBJ> כתת *beat* into spears Jl 4$_{10}$ (|| אֵת *blade*). <PREP> לְ *into* perh. 4QDibHam[a] 19$_2$ ([ ]למזמר), + כתת pi. *beat* swords Is 2$_4$||Mc 4$_3$ (||אֵת *blade*); בְּ of instrument, *by (means of), with,* + כרת *cut* Is 18$_5$.

<SYN> אֵת *blade.*

⇒ זמר II *prune.*

[מְזַמֶּרֶת] I $_5$ n.f. **snuffer**—pl. מְזַמְּרוֹת—**snuffer,** or perh. **knife** to trim wick, as utensil in temple, <SUBJ> עשׂה ni. *be made* 2 K 12$_{14}$. <OBJ> עשׂה *make* 1 K 7$_{50}$|| 2 C 4$_{22}$, לקח *take* 2 K 25$_{14}$||Jr 52$_{18}$. <APP> כְּלִי *vessel* 1 K 7$_{50}$ 2 K 12$_{14}$. <COLL> מְזַמֶּרֶת || סַף *dish* 1 K 7$_{50}$ 2 K 12$_{14}$ (+), מִזְרָק *basin* 1 K 7$_{50}$||2 C 4$_{22}$ 2 K 12$_{14}$ Jr 52$_{18}$, סִיר *pot* 2 K 25$_{14}$||Jr 52$_{18}$, כַּף *ladle* 1 K 7$_{50}$||2 C 4$_{22}$ 2 K 25$_{14}$|| Jr 52$_{18}$, יָעַ *fire-shovel* 2 K 25$_{14}$||Jr 52$_{18}$, מַחְתָּה *firepan* 1 K 7$_{50}$||2 C 4$_{22}$, חֲצוֹצְרָה *trumpet* 2 K 12$_{14}$, + כְּלִי *vessel* 2 K 25$_{14}$||Jr 52$_{18}$; וַיַּעַשׂ ... הַמְזַמְּרוֹת ... זָהָב סָגוּר *and he made ... the snuffers ... of pure gold* 1 K 7$_{50}$||2 C 4$_{22}$.

<SYN> סַף *dish,* מִזְרָק *basin,* סִיר *pot,* כַּף *ladle,* יָעַ *fire-shovel,* מַחְתָּה *firepan,* חֲצוֹצְרָה *trumpet.*

⇒ (?) זמר II *prune.*

*[מְזַמֶּרֶת] II $_5$ n.f. **musical instrument**—pl. מְזַמְּרוֹת—played during the divine meal, <SUBJ> עשׂה ni. *be made* 2 K 12$_{14}$. <OBJ> עשׂה *make* 1 K 7$_{50}$||2 C 4$_{22}$, לקח *take* 2 K25$_{14}$||Jr 52$_{18}$. <APP> כְּלִי *vessel* 1 K 7$_{50}$ 2 K 12$_{14}$. <COLL> מְזַמֶּרֶת || סַף *dish* 1 K7$_{50}$ 2 K12$_{14}$ (+), מִזְרָק *basin* 1 K 7$_{50}$||2 C 4$_{22}$ 2 K 12$_{14}$ Jr 52$_{18}$, סִיר *pot* 2 K 25$_{14}$||Jr 52$_{18}$, כַּף *ladle* 1 K 7$_{50}$||2 C 4$_{22}$ 2 K 25$_{14}$||Jr 52$_{18}$, יָעַ *fire-shovel* 2 K 25$_{14}$||Jr 52$_{18}$, מַחְתָּה *firepan* 1 K 7$_{50}$||2 C 4$_{22}$, חֲצוֹצְרָה *trumpet* 2 K 12$_{14}$, + כְּלִי *vessel* 2 K 25$_{14}$||Jr 52$_{18}$; וַיַּעַשׂ ... הַמְזַמְּרוֹת ... זָהָב סָגוּר *and he made ... the musical instruments ... of pure gold* 1 K 7$_{50}$||2 C 4$_{22}$.

<SYN> סַף *dish,* מִזְרָק *basin,* סִיר *pot,* כַּף *ladle,* יָעַ *fire-shovel,* מַחְתָּה *firepan,* חֲצוֹצְרָה *trumpet.*

⇒ זמר I *sing (praise).*

*[מְזָנִים] n.[m.]pl. **clouds,** <CSTR> שַׁחַק מְזָנִים *rags of clouds,* i.e. ragged clouds Is 40$_{15}$ (if em. מֹאזְנַיִם dust of *the scales;* 1QIsa[a] מזונים).

*[מְזַעֲזֵעַ] I $_1$ n.m. **one who reminds**—pl. sf. מְזַעְזְעֶיךָ—<SUBJ> יקץ *awake* Hb 2$_7$.

מְזַעֲזֵעַ II *shaking,* see זוע *shake.**

מְזַעֲזֵעַ III *barking,* see זעה *bark.**

מִזְעָר I $_{4.3}$ n.[m.] **a little, a few,** of quantity (Is 16$_{14}$ 24$_6$ Si 34$_{19.19[B]}$ 48$_{15}$), of time (Is 10$_{25}$ 29$_{17}$), <SUBJ> שׁאר ni.

remain Is 24₆ Si 48₁₅. <NOM CL> שְׁאָר מְעַט מִזְעָר *the remnant will be a little, a few,* i.e. very few Is 16₁₄ (+ לֹא כַבִּיר *not powerful*), הלא די אנוש נבון מזער *is not a little sufficient for an understanding person?* Si 34₁₉. 19(B). <APP> אֱנוֹשׁ מִזְעָר *people, a few,* i.e. a few people Is 24₆, מְעַט מִזְעָר (of people) *a little, a few,* i.e. very few Is 16₁₄, (of time) *a trifle, a little,* i.e. a very little while Is 10₂₅ 29₁₇.

⇒ cf. זְעֵיר *a little.*

מִזְעָר II, see מִצְעָר II *Mizar.*

מִזְקָא, see מִזְקָה *canal.*

***[מִזְקָה]** 0.0.2 n.f. **canal, conduit**—Q מזקא; pl.Q מזקות —<SUBJ> רוה pi. *draw water* 3QTr 10₃ (מזקות שרוו מהנחל הגדול *the canals that draw water from the great wadi*). <CSTR> כירגר מזקות perh. *cistern of the canals* 3QTr 10₃. <PREP> בְּ of place, *in* 3QTr 2₉ (ובמזקא שבו ככרין עסר *and in the conduit that is,* i.e. ends, *in it are ten talents*).

***[מזר]** vb. **stretch out**—**Qal** pass. **be spread out** (unless from זור *strew, spread out*), <SUBJ> רֶשֶׁת *net* Pr 1₁₇ (if em. מְזֹרָה *scattered* [זרה pu.] to מְזֹרָה or מְזוֹרָה *spread out*). <PREP> בְּעֵינֵי *in the presence of,* + בַּעַל *lord* of wing, i.e. bird Pr 1₁₇ (if em.; see Subj.). <COLL> with adverb, חִנָּם *in vain* Pr 1₁₇ (if em.; see Subj.).

⇒ cf. זור *strew.*

מִזְרֶה 2 n.[m.] **pitchfork,** for winnowing, <PREP> בְּ of instrument, *by (means of), with,* + זרה *winnow* Is 30₂₄ (|| רַחַת *winnowing shovel*) Jr 15₇, pu. *be winnowed* Is 30₂₄ (if em. זֹרֶה *one winnows* to זֹרָה *it is winnowed*).

<SYN> רַחַת *winnowing shovel.*

⇒ זרה I *scatter.*

מַזָּרוֹת 1 pr.n.m. **Mazzaroth,** a star or constellation, prob. the Zodiac,* perh. of the southern hemisphere,* or perh. Venus,* the Hyades,* the boat of Arcturus,* or n.f.pl. **constellations** (=מַזָּלוֹת),* <OBJ> יצא hi. *bring out* Jb 38₃₂ (+ עַיִשׁ *Great Bear*).*

⇒ מַזּוֹרוֹת *constellations.*

מִזְרָח 74.0.29 n.[m.] **sunrise, east**—+ ה- of direction מִזְרָ֫חָה; cstr. מִזְרַח (+ ה- of direction מִזְרְחָה); sf. Q מזרחו —**1.** as cstr. with שֶׁמֶשׁ **(place of) rising** of the sun, **east,** Nm 21₁₁ Dt 4₄₁.₄₇ Jos 1₁₅ 12₁ 13₅ 19₁₂.₂₇.₃₄ Jg 11₁₈ 20₄₃ 21₁₉ 2 K 10₃₃ 41₂₅ 45₆ 45₁₉ Ml 1₁₁ Ps 50₁ 113₃.

2. מִזְרָח alone, **sunrise, east, eastern side,** Ex 27₁₃|| 38₁₃ Nm 2₃ 3₃₈ 32₁₉ 34₁₅ Dt 3₁₇.₂₇ 4₄₉ Jos 4₁₉ 11₃.₈ 12₁.₃.₃ 13₈.₂₇.₃₂ 16₁.₅.₆.₆ 17₁₀ 18₇ 19₁₃ 20₈ (or del.) 1 K 7₂₅||2 C 4₄ Is 41₂ 43₅ 46₁₁ Jr 31₄₀ Am 8₁₂ Zc 8₇ 14₄ Ps 103₁₂ 107₃ Dn 8₉ 11₄₄ Ne 3₂₆.₂₉ 12₃₇ 1 C 12₁₆ 26₁₄.₁₇ 2 C 5₁₂ 29₄ 31₁₄ 2Q apProph 1₉ 3QTr 1₂ 2₁₀.₁₃ 3₁₁ 5₅ 6₂.₉ 8₁.₂ ([מזר[ח]) 9₅.₁₂ 4QMishA 1.1₁ 4Q365a 2.2₄ 4QNarrA 9₂ 11QT 31₁₂ 33₈ 39₁₂.₁₄ 40₉.₁₁ 41₁₁ 46₁₇ Mur 22 1₁₁ Mur 30 1₃ 2₁₆ XḤev/Se 8₉ fr. b₁ ([מז]רח) e-k₃.

<SUBJ> רחק *be distant* Ps 103₁₂.

<CSTR> מִזְרַח הַשֶּׁמֶשׁ *rising of the sun* Nm 21₁₁ (הַשָּׁמֶשׁ) Dt 4₄₁ (שָׁמֶשׁ); ms, Sam^mss מִזְרַח הַשֶּׁמֶשׁ; ms, Sam מִזְרְחָה שֶׁמֶשׁ) 4₄₇ (שָׁמֶשׁ; mss, Sam מִזְרַח שֶׁמֶשׁ; Sam^mss מִזְרְחָה הַשֶּׁמֶשׁ) Jos 1₁₅ (הַשָּׁמֶשׁ) 12₁ (מִזְרְחָה הַשֶּׁמֶשׁ) 13₅ 19₁₂. 27.34 (הַשָּׁמֶשׁ) Jg 11₁₈ (־שֶׁמֶשׁ) 20₄₃ (־שֶׁמֶשׁ) 21₁₉ (מִזְרְחָה הַשֶּׁמֶשׁ) 2 K 10₃₃ Is 41₂₅ 45₆ 59₁₉ Ml 1₁₁ Ps 50₁ 113₃ (all six ־שֶׁמֶשׁ).

מִזְרַח הַגַּיְא *east of the valley* 1 C 4₃₉, יְרִיחוֹ *of Jericho* Jos 4₁₉, יָנוֹחָה *of Janoah* Jos 16₆, הַיַּרְדֵּן *of the Jordan* 1 C 6₆₃, מזרח אחצר *east of Hazor* 3QTr 8₂, בית אחצר *of Beth-hazor* 3QTr 8₁, כחלת *of Cohlith* 3QTr 2₁₃, העיר *of the city* 11QT 46₁₇, בית *of the house of* 11QT 33₈, [החצר] *of the courtyard* XḤev/Se 8 e-k₃, אשיח *of the reservoir of* Solomon 3QTr 5₅ ([מזר[ח]), כלפיהם *of their outlets* 3Q Tr 9₁₂.

אֶרֶץ מִזְרָח *land of the east* Zc 8₇, שַׁעַר הַמִּזְרָח *gate of the east* Ne 3₂₉, רְחוֹב *square of* 2 C 29₄, פְּנֵי *face,* i.e. side, *of* 1 C 5₁₀, קְצֵה מִזְרָח *side of the east of* Jos 4₁₉, פְּאַת ... מִזְרָחָה *side of ... the east* Ex 27₁₃||38₁₃, פנת המזרח *corner of the east* 11QT 41₁₁ 4Q365a 2.2₄ (מזרח).

<APP> רוּחַ *wind,* i.e. side 1 C 9₂₄, קֵדְמָה *east* Ex 27₁₃|| 38₁₃ Nm 2₃ 34₁₅ Jos 19₁₂.₁₃ 11QT 39₁₂.

<PREP> לְ of direction, *to(wards), in* Ne 3₂₆ 1 C 6₆₃ 7₂₈ 26₁₇ 11QT 39₁₄ 40₉, + היה *be* 1 C 9₂₄, ישׁב *dwell* 1 C 5₉, בוא *come* 3QTr 1₂, ברח hi. *put to flight* 1 C 12₁₆,

צפה *watch*, i.e. face 3QTr 6$_9$, עשׂה *make* 11QT 33$_8$ 46$_{17}$, פתח pass. *be opened* XḤev/Se 8$_9$ ([פ]תוח).

לַמִּזְרָחָה *towards the east* 2 C 31$_{14}$.

עַד לְ *as far as*, + הלך *go* 1 C 4$_{39}$.

בְּ of place, *in* 3QTr 2$_{13}$ 9$_{12}$ 11QT 39$_{12}$ 40$_{11}$ XḤev/Se 8 e-k$_3$ ([ב]מזרח).

מִן *from, in, on* Nm 21$_{11}$ Jos 11$_3$ 17$_{10}$ Jg 20$_{43}$ Ml 1$_{11}$ Ps 50$_1$ 2QapProph 1$_9$ 3QTr 2$_{10}$ 3$_{11}$ 4QNarrA 9$_2$, + בוא *come* Jg 11$_{18}$, hi. *bring* Is 43$_5$, קבץ pi. *gather* Ps 107$_3$, עבר *pass* Jos 16$_6$, ראה ni. *appear* 4QMishA 1.1$_1$, עור hi. *stir up* Is 41$_{2.25}$, ידע *know* Is 45$_6$, קרא *call* Is 46$_{11}$, ירא *fear* Is 59$_{19}$, בהל pi. *terrify* Dn 11$_{44}$, הלל pu. *be praised* Ps 113$_3$, עשׂה *make* 11QT 31$_{12}$.

אֶל *to*, + גדל *be great* Dn 8$_9$.

עַד *to*, + שׁוט pol. *go to and fro* Am 8$_{12}$.

ה- of direction, *to(wards), in* Ex 27$_{13}$||38$_{13}$ 32$_{19}$ Nm 34$_{15}$ Dt 3$_{17}$ 4$_{41.49}$ Jos 1$_{18}$ 12$_{1.1.3,3}$ 13$_{8.27}$ 16$_5$ 18$_7$ 20$_8$ (or del.) Jg 21$_{19}$ Jr 31$_{40}$ 1 C 9$_{18}$ 2 C 31$_{14}$ (לַמִּזְרָחָה), + חנה *encamp* Nm 2$_3$ 33$_8$, יצא *go out* Jos 16$_1$, נפל *fall* 1 C 26$_{14}$, עבר *pass* Jos 19$_{13}$, פנה *turn* 1 K 7$_{25}$||2 C 4$_4$, סבב ni. *turn* Jos 16$_6$, נשׂא *lift* eyes Dt 3$_{27}$, בקע ni. *be split* Zc 14$_4$.

מִזְרַח הַשֶּׁמֶשׁ, מִזְרָח, etc., without ה- of direction, *in the east, to(wards) the east, to(wards) the sunrise* Dt 4$_{47}$ Jos 1$_{15}$ 13$_5$ 19$_{34}$ 2 K 10$_{33}$ Ne 12$_{37}$ 3QTr 5$_5$ (מזר[ח]) 8$_{1.2}$ Mur 22 1$_{11}$ Mur 30 1$_3$ 2$_{16}$, + עמד *stand* 2 C 5$_{12}$, שׁוב *turn* Jos 19$_{12.27}$, צפה *watch*, i.e. face 3QTr 6$_2$ 9$_5$.

<COLL> קֶדֶם || מִזְרָח *east* Nm 33$_8$.

|| יָם *west* Dt 3$_{27}$ Jos 11$_3$ 1 K 7$_{25}$||2 C 4$_4$ Zc 14$_4$ Ps 107$_3$ 1 C 9$_{24}$ 11QT 39$_{12}$ 40$_{9.11}$, || מַעֲרָב *west* Is 43$_5$ 45$_6$ 45$_{19}$ Ps 107$_3$ 1 C 7$_{28}$ 12$_{16}$ 11QT 31$_{12}$ Mur 22 1$_{11}$ Mur 30 1$_3$ 2$_{16}$; + מְבוֹא הַשֶּׁמֶשׁ *setting of the sun*, i.e. west Zc 8$_7$; :: מַעֲרָב *west* Ps 103$_{12}$.

|| צָפוֹן *north* Dt 3$_{27}$ Jos 17$_{10}$ (+) 1 K 7$_{25}$||2 C 4$_4$ Is 41$_{25}$ 43$_5$ (+) Am 8$_{12}$ (+) Ps 107$_3$ Dn 11$_{44}$ 1 C 9$_{24}$ 26$_{17}$ 2QapProph 1$_9$ 11QT 31$_{12}$ 39$_{12}$ 40$_{9.11}$ Mur 22 1$_{11}$ Mur 30 1$_3$ 2$_{16}$.

|| תֵּימָן *south* Dt 3$_{27}$ Is 43$_5$ (+), נֶגֶב *south* 1 K 7$_{25}$||2 C 4$_4$ Dn 8$_9$ 1 C 9$_{24}$ 26$_{17}$ 11QT 39$_{13}$, דָּרוֹם *south* 11QT 39$_{12}$ (+) 40$_{9.11}$ Mur 22 1$_{11}$ ([דרו]ם) Mur 30 1$_3$ 2$_{16}$.

+ עֵבֶר הַיַּרְדֵּן *beyond the Jordan* Dt 4$_{49}$ Jos 13$_{27}$, בְּעֵבֶר הַיַּרְדֵּן *beyond the Jordan* Dt 4$_{41.47}$ Jos 1$_{15}$ 12$_1$ 13$_8$, מֵעֵבֶר הַיַּרְדֵּן *beyond the Jordan* Nm 32$_{19}$, מֵעֵבֶר לַיַּרְדֵּן *beyond the Jordan* Nm 34$_{15}$ Jos 18$_7$, מֵעֵבֶר לְיַרְדֵּן יְרִיחוֹ *beyond the Jordan of*, i.e. at, *Jericho* Jos 13$_{32}$ 20$_8$.

מִזְרַח לְ *east of* 1 C 5$_{10}$ 2 C 5$_{12}$, מִזְרְחָה הַשֶּׁמֶשׁ לְ *to the east of* Jg 21$_{19}$, [מזו]רח מן ביתי *east of my house* XḤev/Se 8 fr. b$_1$, מִמִּזְרַח־שֶׁמֶשׁ (וְ)עַד־מְבוֹאוֹ *from the rising of the sun to its setting* Ml 1$_{11}$ Ps 50$_1$ 113$_3$, מִזְרָחָה וָיָמָּה *to the east and to the west*, i.e. from east to west Zc 14$_4$, מזרח צפון *north-east* 11QT 39$_{14}$, נגב מזרח *south-east* 11QT 31$_{10}$.

<SYN> יָם *west*, מַעֲרָב *west*, צָפוֹן *north*, תֵּימָן *south*, נֶגֶב *south*, דָּרוֹם *south*.

<ANT> מַעֲרָב *west*.

Also 4QpsEzek^a 10.2$_1$ ([מזר]ח).

⇨ זרח *arise*, מִזְרָחִי *eastern*.

*[מִזְרָחִי] 0.0.5 adj. **eastern**—fem. sing. Q מזרחית—used attributively of שַׁעַר *gate* 3QTr 2$_7$, פִּנָּה *corner* 3QTr 3$_5$ 7$_{12}$, מִקְצֹעַ *corner* 11QT^b 28$_{01}$ ([במקצ]וע המזרחי צפונה *in the north-east corner*), שִׁית *tunnel* 3QTr 4$_{11}$.

⇨ זרח *arise*, מִזְרָח *east*.

*מְזָרִים I 1 n.[m.]pl. **press**, in which the waters are bound up (unless מְזָרִים I *scatterers*), <PREP> מִן of direction, *from*, + בוא *come* Jb 37$_9$.

מְזָרִים II 1 *scatterers*, i.e. *north wind*, see זרה I *scatter*, Pi. §2.

[מִזְרָע] 1 n.m. **place of sowing**—cstr. מִזְרַע—<SUBJ> יבשׁ *be dry* Is 19$_7$, נדף ni. *be driven away* Is 19$_7$. <CSTR> כֹּל מִזְרַע יְאוֹר *every place of sowing of*, i.e. by, *the Nile* Is 19$_7$.*

⇨ זרע *sow*.

מִזְרָק 32.0.5 n.m. **basin**—cstr. Q מזרק; pl. מִזְרָקִים, מִזְרָקוֹת (מִזְרָקֹת); cstr. מִזְרְקֵי; sf. מִזְרְקֹתָיו—**basin, bowl,** usu. for use with blood (11QT 23$_{12}$ 26$_6$ 34$_7$) at altar; also as table utensil* (for wine, Am 6$_6$), <SUBJ> עשׂה ni. *be made* 2 K 12$_{14}$, מלא *be full* Nm 7$_{13+11t}$.

<NOM CL> קָרְבָּנוֹ ... מִזְרָק אֶחָד *his offering was ... one basin* Nm 7$_{13+10t}$, זֹאת חֲנֻכַּת הַמִּזְבֵּחַ ... מִזְרְקֵי־כֶסֶף *this was the dedication offering of*, i.e. for, *the altar ... basins of silver* Nm 7$_{84}$, שִׁבְעִים הַמִּזְרָק הָאֶחָד *a single*

basin was, i.e. weighed, *seventy (shekels)* Nm 7$_{85}$, תחת הפנא הדרומית אמות תשע ... מזרקות *underneath the south corner at nine cubits are ... basins* 3QTr 3$_{3}$, מזרק הזהב [אשר בי]דו *the basin of gold that is in his hand* 11QT 26$_{6}$.

<OBJ> קרב hi. *bring near*, i.e. offer Nm 7$_{19}$, נתן *give* Ne 7$_{69}$, i.e. place Nm 4$_{14}$, לקח *take* 2 K 25$_{15}$||Jr 52$_{19}$ Jr 52$_{18}$, עשׂה *make* Ex 27$_{3}$||38$_{3}$ 1 K 7$_{40.50}$||2 C 4$_{11.22}$ 1 K 7$_{45}$ 2 C 4$_{8}$.

<CSTR> מזרק הזהב *the basin of gold* 11QT 26$_{6}$, מִזְרְקֵי זָהָב *basins of gold* 2 C 4$_{8}$, ־כֶּסֶף *of silver* Nm 7$_{84}$, ־יַיִן *of wine* Am 6$_{6}$.

<APP> כֶּסֶף *silver* Nm 7$_{13+11t}$, שֶׁקֶל *shekel* Nm 7$_{13+11t}$, קָרְבָּן *offering* Nm 7$_{19}$, זָוִית *corner* of altar Zc 9$_{15}$ (or del. זָוִית or מִזְרָק), כְּלִי *vessel* Ex 38$_{3}$ Nm 4$_{14}$ 1 K 7$_{50}$ 2 K 12$_{14}$ 11QT 33$_{13}$.

<ADJ> אֶחָד *one* Nm 7$_{13+12t}$.

<PREP> לְ of benefit, *to, for* 1 C 28$_{17}$ 11QT 33$_{13}$; בְּ of place, *in* or *from*, + שׁתה *drink* Am 6$_{6}$, עלה hi. *lift up* blood 11QT 23$_{12}$, קבל pi. *receive* blood 11QT 26$_{6}$ ([וקבל]), כנס *collect* blood 11QT 34$_{7}$; of instrument, *by (means of), with*, + שׁרת pi. *serve* Nm 4$_{14}$; כְּ *as*, + היה *be* Zc 14$_{20}$, מלא *be full* Zc 9$_{15}$ (or del.).

<COLL> מִזְרָק || סַף *dish* 1 K 7$_{50}$ 2 K 12$_{14}$ (+) Jr 52$_{19}$, קְעָרָה *dish* Nm 7$_{13+13t}$, כּוֹס *cup* 3QTr 3$_{3}$, קַשְׂוָה *jar* 1 C 28$_{17}$ 3QTr 3$_{3}$ 11QT 33$_{13}$, כִּיּוֹר *bowl* 1 K 7$_{40}$, מְנַקִּית *bowl* Jr 52$_{19}$ 3QTr 3$_{3}$, סִיר *pot* Ex 27$_{3}$||38$_{3}$ 1 K 7$_{45}$ Jr 52$_{18.19}$ 2 C 4$_{11}$, מִזְלָגָה *fork* Ex 27$_{3}$||38$_{3}$ Nm 4$_{14}$ 1 C 28$_{17}$, יָע *shovel* Ex 27$_{3}$||38$_{3}$ Nm 4$_{14}$ 1 K 7$_{40}$||2 C 4$_{11}$ 1 K 7$_{45}$ Jr 52$_{18}$, מְזַמֶּרֶת *snuffer* 1 K 7$_{50}$||2 C 4$_{22}$ 2 K 12$_{14}$ Jr 52$_{18}$, מַחְתָּה *firepan* Ex 27$_{3}$||38$_{3}$ Nm 4$_{14}$ 1 K 7$_{50}$||2 C 4$_{22}$ 2 K 25$_{15}$||Jr 52$_{19}$ 11QT 33$_{13}$, כַּף *ladle* Nm 7$_{13+13t}$ 1 K 7$_{50}$||2 C 4$_{22}$ Jr 52$_{18.19}$, מְנוֹרָה *lampstand* Jr 52$_{19}$, חֲצֹצְרָה *trumpet* 2 K 12$_{14}$.

\+ כּוֹנָנָה *bowl* 11QT 33$_{13}$, כְּפוֹר *bowl* 1 C 28$_{17}$, כְּתֹנֶת *tunic* Ne 7$_{69}$, זָהָב *gold* Ne 7$_{69}$, כְּלִי *vessel* Jr 52$_{18}$ 3QTr 3$_{3}$.

מִזְרְקֵי־כֶסֶף שְׁנֵים עָשָׂר *twelve basins of silver* Nm 7$_{84}$, מִזְרָקוֹת חֲמִשִּׁים *fifty basins* Ne 7$_{69}$, מִזְרְקֵי זָהָב מֵאָה *a hundred basins of gold* 2 C 4$_{8}$, מִזְרָקִים לִפְנֵי הַמִּזְבֵּחַ *basins before the altar* Zc 14$_{20}$, וַיַּעַשׂ ... הַמִּזְרָקוֹת ... זָהָב סָגוּר *and he made ... the basins ... of pure gold* 1 K 7$_{50}$||2 C 4$_{22}$.

<SYN> סַף *dish*, קְעָרָה *dish*, כּוֹס *cup*, קַשְׂוָה *jar*, כִּיּוֹר *bowl*, מְנַקִּית *bowl*, סִיר *pot*, מִזְלָגָה *fork*, יָע *shovel*, מְזַמֶּרֶת *snuffer*, מַחְתָּה *firepan*, כַּף *ladle*, מְנוֹרָה *lampstand*, חֲצֹצְרָה *trumpet*.*

⇒ זרק I *toss*.

[מֵחַ] 2 n.[m.] **fatling**—pl. מֵחִים—of sheep, <SUBJ> אכל *eat* Is 5$_{17}$ (if em. חָרְבוֹת מֵחִים גָּרִים יֹאכֵלוּ *[in] waste places of fatlings sojourners shall eat* to חָרְבוֹת מֵחִים גְּדָיִים יֹאכֵלוּ *[in] waste places fatlings [and] kids shall eat*). <CSTR> חָרְבוֹת מֵחִים appar. *waste places of fatlings* Is 5$_{17}$ (+ כֶּבֶשׂ *ram*; or em. מֵחִים to מְחִיִּם waste places *of the annihilated ones*, i.e. מחה pass; or em. חָרְבוֹת; see Subj.), עֹלוֹת *burnt offerings of* Is 66$_{15}$ (|| אַיִל *ram*, + בָּקָר *cattle*, עַתּוּד *goat*).

<SYN> אַיִל *ram*.

⇒ מחה III *be full of marrow*.

[מֹחַ] 1 n.m. **marrow**—cstr. מֹחַ—<SUBJ> שׁקה pu. *be moistened* Jb 21$_{24}$ (+ עֲטִין perh. *pail*). <CSTR> מֹחַ עַצְמוֹתָיו *marrow of his bones* Jb 21$_{24}$.

⇒ מחה III *be full of marrow*.

מחא I 3 vb. **clap**—**Qal** 3 Impf. יִמְחֲאוּ; inf. מַחְאֲךָ—**clap,** in expression of triumph or approval,* <SUBJ> בֵּן *son* of Ammon Ezk 25$_{6}$ (+ רקע *stamp* with feet, שׂמח *rejoice*), עֵץ *tree* Is 55$_{12}$ (+ פצח *break out* into song), נָהָר *river* Ps 98$_{8}$ (+ רנן pi. *shout joyfully*). <OBJ> כַּף *hand* Is 55$_{12}$ Ps 98$_{8}$, יָד *hand* Ezk 25$_{6}$.

⇒ cf. מחה II *strike*.

***מחא II** 0.0.1 vb. perh. **refuse,** מחא להרים [את הקודשים] perh. *one who refuses to offer the holy things* 4QD^{e} 2.2$_{5}$.

***מחא III** 1 vb. **destroy** (unless from מחה I *wipe* or מָחָה *female prophet*)—**Hi.** 1 Inf. cstr. לַמְחוֹת—**destroy,** <SUBJ> בַּר *son* Pr 31$_{3}$. <OBJ> מֶלֶךְ *king* Pr 31$_{3}$ (וּדְרָכֶיךָ לַמְחוֹת מְלָכִין *and your ways to destroy kings*; or perh. מְלָכִין is from מֶלֶךְ *counsel*).

מחא IV, see מחה III, *be full of marrow*.

[מַחֲבֵא] 1 n.[m.] **hiding place**—cstr. מַחֲבֵא—**hiding**

place, shelter, <CSTR> מַחֲבֵא־רוּחַ *hiding place of,* i.e. from, *the wind* Is 32_2 (|| סֵתֶר *shelter*). <PREP> כְּ *as*, + היה *be* Is 32_2.

<SYN> סֵתֶר *shelter.*

⇨ חבא *hide.*

[מַחֲבֹא] 1 n.[m.] **hiding place**—pl. מַחֲבֹאִים—<CSTR> מִן כֹּל הַמַּחֲבֹאִים *all the hiding places* 1 S 23_{23}. <PREP> מִן partitive, *from among, some of,* + ידע *know* 1 S 23_{23}. <COLL> הַמַּחֲבֹאִים אֲשֶׁר יִתְחַבֵּא שָׁם *the hiding places where he hides himself* 1 S 23_{23}.

⇨ חבא *hide.*

*[מַחֲבָן] n.m. **fertile place**—<NOM CL> מָה הֶעָרִים אֲשֶׁר־הוּא יוֹשֵׁב בָּהֵנָּה הַבְּמַחֲנִים *whether the cities they are dwelling in are fertile places* Nm 13_{19} (if em. הַמַּחֲבָנִים; Sam[ms] מחבנים; + מִבְצָר *fortified place*).

*[מִחְבָן] 1 n.[m.] **fertile land,** perh. **rotten land**—pl. Sam מִחְבָנִים—<PREP> בְּ of place, *in, within,* + ישׁב *dwell* Nm 13_{19}(Sam[ms]) (MT מַחֲנִים *camps*).

[מְחַבְּרָה] 2 n.f. **beam**—pl. מְחַבְּרוֹת—**beam, brace, truss,*** or perh. **clamp, coupling,** made of iron (1 C 22_3), wood (2 C 34_{11}), <PREP> לְ of benefit, *to, for,* + כון hi. *prepare* 1 C 22_3 (|| מַסְמֵר *nail*), קנה *purchase* 2 C 34_{11}.

<SYN> מַסְמֵר *nail.*

⇨ חבר I *join.*

מַחְבֶּרֶת 10.0.2 n.f. **join**—מַחְבֶּרֶת; cstr. Q מחברת; sf. מֶחְבַּרְתּוֹ—**1. join, series** of curtains joined together (unless **place of joining,** i.e. §3), <ADJ> שֵׁנִי *second* Ex $26_{4.5}$||$36_{11.12}$. <PREP> בְּ of place, *in* Ex $26_{4(Sam).4.5.10(Sam)}$||$36_{11.11.12.17}$ ($26_{4.10}$ MT חֹבֶרֶת *series*).

2. join, i.e. **looped pattern,** around edge of shield, <NOM CL> מחברת הצ[ו]רה ... אבני חפץ *the looped pattern of the design shall be ... precious stones* 1QM 5_8. <CSTR> מחברת הצ[ו]רה *looped pattern of the design* 1QM 5_8; צורת מחברת *design of a looped pattern* 1QM 5_5.

3. place of joining of ephod, <PREP> לְעֻמַּת *close by,* + נתן *give,* i.e. place Ex 28_{27}||39_{20}.

⇨ חבר I *join.*

מַחֲבַת 5 n.f. **griddle**—cstr. מַחֲבַת—**1a. griddle, baking tray** of clay or iron, for grain offering, <PREP> עַל *upon* Lv 2_5, + עשׂה ni. *be made* Lv 6_{14} 7_9 (+ מַרְחֶשֶׁת *pan*).

b. plate, <OBJ> לקח *take* Ezk 4_3, נתן *give,* i.e. place Ezk 4_3. <CSTR> מַחֲבַת בַּרְזֶל *plate of iron* Ezk 4_3.

2. cake baked on griddle, <PREP> לְ *in respect of, in connection with* 1 C 23_{29} (+ רָקִיק *wafer,* סֹלֶת *fine flour,* לֶחֶם *bread*).*

⇨ חֲבִתִּים *flat cakes.*

[מַחֲגֹרֶת] 1 n.f. **robe**—cstr. מַחֲגֹרֶת—<SUBJ> היה *be* Is 3_{24} (or del.). <CSTR> מַחֲגֹרֶת שָׂק *robe of sackcloth* Is 3_{24} (or del.; :: פְּתִיגִיל *rich robe*).

<ANT> פְּתִיגִיל *rich robe.*

⇨ חגר *gird.*

מחה I 34.4.5.2 vb. **wipe**—**Qal** 22.2.3.2 Pf. מָחִיתִי ,מָחִיתָ ,מָחָה; impf. יִמְחֶה (Q ימח), 2ms תִּמְחֶה ,אֶמְחֶה (אֶמְחֶנּוּ); + waw וַיִּמַח ,I ומחו; וּמָחִיתִי ,וּמָחָתָה ,וּמָחָה; impv. מְחֵה (מְחֵנִי); ptc. מֹחֶה; inf. abs. מָחֹה; cstr. מְחוֹת—**1. wipe clean,** <SUBJ> Y. 2 K 21_{13} Is 25_8 (|| סור hi. *remove*), אִשָּׁה adulterous *woman* Pr 30_{20}, כֹּהֵן *priest* Nm 5_{23}, impersonal 2 K $21_{13.13}$. <OBJ> Jerusalem 2 K 21_{13}, פֶּה *mouth* Pr 30_{20}, דִּמְעָה *tears* Is 25_8, צַלַּחַת *dish* 2 K 21_{13} (+ הפך *turn over*), אָלָה *curse* Nm 5_{23}. <PREP> אֶל *into,* + מַיִם *water* of bitterness Nm 5_{23}; מֵעַל *from (upon),* + פָּנִים *face* Is 25_8.

2. wipe out, obliterate, annihilate; waste away the flesh (Si 34_1), <SUBJ> Y. Gn 6_7 $7_{4.23}$ Ex $17_{14.14}$ $32_{32.33}$ Dt 9_{14} (+ שׁמד hi. *destroy*) 29_{19} 2 K 14_{27} Is 43_{25} 44_{25} Jr 18_{23} (if em.; see Hi. Subj.) Zc 3_9 (if em. וּמַשְׁתִּי *and I will remove* to וּמָחִיתִי *and I will wipe out*) Ps 9_6 (+ גער *rebuke,* אבד pi. *destroy*) $51_{3.11}$ Si 5_6 1QS 11_3 4QConfess 1.2_5, Israel(ites) Dt 25_{19}=4QCommGenA 4_2, אִישׁ *man* Nimrud ivory inscr. 1_3, מֶלֶךְ *king* Nimrud ivory inscr. 1_3, שֶׁקֶר *falsehood* Si $34_{1(B)}$ (Bmg שֶׁקֶד *watchfulness*), אֲשֶׁר *one who* Kh. Beit Lei graf. 1_2 (מחה [י]שר[א]; others ישר מחר) En-Gedi cave inscr.$_1$; subj. not specified, Pr 31_3 (if em.; see Hi. Subj.).

<OBJ> Moses Ex 32_{32}, אָדָם *human being* Gn 6_7, מֶלֶךְ *king* Pr 31_3 (if em.; see Hi. Subj.), יְקוּם *living form* Gn

$7_{4.23}$, שְׁאֵר *flesh* Si 34_{1} (|| פרע hi. *disturb* sleep), זֵכֶר *memory* Ex 17_{14} Dt 25_{19}=4QCommGenA 4_{2}, שֵׁם *name* Dt 9_{14} 29_{19} 2 K 14_{27} Ps 9_{6}, חַטָּאת *sin* Is 44_{25} Jr 18_{23} (if em.; see Hi. Subj.), פֶּשַׁע *transgression* Is 43_{25} 44_{25} Ps 51_{3} (+ חנן *be gracious*) 1QS 11_{3}, עָוֹן *iniquity* Zc 3_{9} (if em.; see Subj.) Ps 51_{11} (+ סתר hi. *hide* face from sins) Si 5_{6}(+ סלח *pardon*) 4QConfess 1.2_{5}, סֵפֶר *writing* Nimrud ivory inscr. 1_{3} ([הספר]), מִי *whoever* Ex 32_{33}.

<PREP> לְ of direction, *to*, לְעוֹלָם וָעֶד *for ever and ever* Ps 9_{6}; בְּ of time, *in*, + יוֹם *day* Zc 3_{9} (if em.; see Subj.), אַחֲרִית *end* of days 4QCommGenA 4_{2}; of instrument, *by (means of), with*, + צְדָקָה *righteousness* 1QS 11_{3}; כְּ *as* Is 44_{22}; *according to*, + רֹב *abundance* of compassion Ps 51_{3}; מִן of direction, *from*, + סֵפֶר *book* Ex $32_{32.33}$; מִן ... עַד *from ... to*, i.e. both ... and Gn 6_{7} 7_{23} (both מֵאָדָם עַד־בְּהֵמָה עַד־רֶמֶשׂ וְעַד־עוֹף *both humans and beasts and creeping things and birds*); מֵעַל *from upon*, + פָּנִים *face* of earth Gn 6_{7} 7_{4}; מִתַּחַת *from under*, + שָׁמַיִם *heaven* Ex 17_{14} Dt 9_{14} 25_{19} 29_{19} 2 K 14_{27}; לְמַעַן *for the sake of*, + Y. Is 43_{25}. <COLL> inf. abs. + finite form of מחה Ex 17_{14}.

3. pass. ptc. as noun, **annihilated one**, <CSTR> חָרְבוֹת מְחִים *waste places of the annihilated* Is 5_{17} (if em. מֵחִים *of fatlings* to מְחִים).*

Also perh. 4QD^{a} 1c$_{4}$ (מחה[ ]).

<SYN> §1 סור hi. *remove*; §2 פרע hi. *disturb*.

Ni. 9.2.1 Impf. יִמָּחֶה (יִמַּח), 3fs תִּמָּחֶה (תִּמַּח), יִמָּחוּ; + waw וַיִּמָּחוּ; וְנִמְחוּ—**be wiped out, obliterated, annihilated,** <SUBJ> אָדָם *human being* Gn 7_{23}, צֹרֵר *enemy* Ps 69_{29}, שֵׁבֶט *tribe* Dt 25_{6}, יְקוּם *living form* Gn 7_{23}, בְּהֵמָה *beast* Gn 7_{23}, רֶמֶשׂ *creeping thing* Gn 7_{23}, עוֹף *birds* Gn 7_{23}, שֵׁם *name* Dt 25_{6} Ps 109_{13} (+ כרת hi. *cut off*) 4QMyst^{a} 3.2_{8}, צְדָקָה *righteousness* Si $3_{14(A)}$ (C שׁכח ni. *be forgotten*), כָּבוֹד *glory* Si $44_{13(M)}$ ([ימח]ה]; :: עמד *stand*, i.e. remain), חַטָּאת *sin* Ps 109_{14} (:: זכר ni. *be remembered*) Ne 3_{37} (+ כסה pi. *cover*), חֶרְפָּה *reproach* Pr 6_{33}, מַעֲשֶׂה *work* Ezk 6_{6}, כֹּל *everything* 4QAdmon 1_{6} ([נ]מחו]).

<PREP> מִן of direction, *from*, + יִשְׂרָאֵל *Israel* Dt 25_{6} Jg 21_{17}, פֶּה *mouth* 4QMyst^{a} 3.2_{8}, אֶרֶץ *earth* Gn 7_{23}, סֵפֶר *book* Ps 69_{29} (:: כתב ni. *be written*); מִלִּפְנֵי *from before*, + Y. Ne 3_{37}.

<ANT> זכר ni. *be remembered*, עמד *stand*, כתב ni. *be written*.

Hi. 3.0.1 Pf. Q המחיתה; impf. 2ms תֶּמַח (תֶּמְחִי); inf. לְמַחוֹת—**wipe out, cause to be wiped out, blotted out,** <SUBJ> Y. Jr 18_{23} (or em. תֶּמְחִי to תִּמַּח, i.e. qal) Ne 13_{14}(:: זכר *remember*) perh. 4QBark^{e} 5_{3}, בַּר *son* Ps 31_{3} (unless from מחא III *destroy* or מָחָה *female prophet* or מְחוֹת *full measure*; or em. לְמַחוֹת to לִמְחוֹת *to those who wipe out*, i.e. qal, or לְלַחֲנוֹת *to the secondary wives of*). <OBJ> חַטָּאת *sin* Jr 18_{23} (or em.; see Subj.; + כפר pi. *atone*), מֶלֶךְ *king* Pr 31_{3} (or em.; see Subj.), חֶסֶד *kindness* Ne 13_{14}.

<ANT> זכר *remember*.*

מחה II 1 vb. **strike—Qal** 1 + waw וּמָחָה—**strike (against)**, i.e. **reach, meet,** <SUBJ> גְּבוּל *border* Nm 34_{11} (+ ירד *go down*). <PREP> עַל *against*, + כָּתֵף *slope* Nm 34_{11}.

⇒ מְחִי *thrust*, (?) מְחוּיָאֵל *Mehujael*; see also מחא I *clap*.

מחה III 1 vb. **be full of marrow—Pu.** 1 Ptc. מְמֻחָיִם (Qr^{mss} מְמֻחָאִים)—**be full of marrow, flavoured with marrow,** <SUBJ> שֶׁמֶן *fat(ty food)* Is 25_{6} (|| זקק pu. *be purified*).

<SYN> זקק pu. *be purified*.

⇒ מֹחַ *marrow*.

*[**מָחָה**] 1 n.f. **female prophet** (unless from מחא III *destroy* or מחה *wipe*)—pl. cstr. מְחוֹת—<CSTR> מְחוֹת מְלָכִין *female prophets of kings* Pr 31_{3} (+ אִשָּׁה *woman*). <PREP> לְ of direction, *to*, + נתן *give* Pr 31_{3}.

מְחוּגָה 1 n.f. **compass**, or perh. **lathe** for polishing,* used by artisan in making idol, <PREP> בְּ of instrument, *by (means of), with*, + תאר pi. *draw* Is 44_{13} (+ שֶׂרֶד *stylus*, מַקְצֻעָה *knife*).

⇒ חוג *draw a circle*.

[**מָחוֹז**] 1.0.1 n.[m.] **harbour**—cstr. מְחוֹז—**harbour, town,** <NOM CL> אֵין מָחוֹז עוֹד *there is no longer a harbour* Is 23_{10} (if em. מֵזַח *shipyard*). <CSTR> מְחוֹז חֶפְצָם *harbour of their desire* Ps 107_{30}. <APP> עֶגְלָתַיִן *Eglathain*

5/6ḤevBA 44_5. <PREP> בְּ of place, *in* 5/6ḤevBA 44_5; אֶל *to*, + נחה hi. *lead* Ps 107_{30}.*

מְחוּיָאֵל 2 pr.n.m. **Mehujael**—מְחִיָּיאֵל—son of Irad, and great-grandson of Cain, <SUBJ> ילד *beget* Gn 4_{18}. <OBJ> ילד *beget* Gn 4_{18}.
⇒ (?)מחה II *strike* or חיה pi. or hi. *give life* + אֵל *God*.

מַחֲוִים 1 gent. **Mahavite,** <NOM CL> גִּבּוֹרֵי הַחֲיָלִים ... אֱלִיאֵל הַמַּחֲוִים *the mighty ones of valour were ... Eliel the Mahavite* 1 C 11_{46} (or em. הַמַּחֲנִי *the Mahanite*, or הַמַּחֲנַיְמִי *the Mahanaimite*, or הַמְּעוֹנִי *the Meonite*). <APP> אֱלִיאֵל *Eliel* 1 C 11_{46} (or em.; see Nom. Cl.).

מָחוֹל I 6 n.m. **dance**—cstr. מְחוֹל; sf. מְחֹלֵנוּ—**dance, dancing,** <SUBJ> הפך ni. *be turned* into mourning Lm 5_{15}. <CSTR> מְחוֹל מְשַׂחֲקִים *dance of the merrymakers* Jr 31_4; perh. בְּנֵי מָחוֹל *sons of the dance*, i.e. members of the musicians' guild 1 K 5_{11} (but prob. מָחוֹל II *Mahol*). <PREP> לְ *into*, + הפך *turn* mourning Ps 30_{12}; בְּ of accompaniment, *with, in*, + יצא *go out* Jr 31_4, שמח *rejoice* Jr 31_{13}; of instrument, *by (means of), with*, + הלל pi. *praise* Ps 149_3 150_4. <COLL> מָחוֹל || תֹּף *timbrel* Jr 31_4 (+) Ps 149_3 150_4, כִּנּוֹר *lyre* Ps 149_3, שִׂמְחָה *joy* Ps 30_{12} (+); :: מִסְפֵּד *mourning* Ps 30_{12}, אֵבֶל *mourning* Lm 5_{15}.
<SYN> תֹּף *timbrel*, כִּנּוֹר *lyre*.
<ANT> אֵבֶל *mourning*, מִסְפֵּד *mourning*.*
⇒ חול I *whirl*, מְחֹלָה *dance*, מְחוֹלְלָה *dance*.

מָחוֹל II 1 pr.n.m. **Mahol,** father of Heman, Calcol and Darda, <CSTR> בְּנֵי מָחוֹל *sons of Mahol* 1 K 5_{11} (unless מָחוֹל I *dance*).

*[**מְחוֹלְלָה**] 0.0.1 n.f. **dance**—pl. Q מחוללות—<PREP> בְּ perh. of accompaniment, *with, in* 4QMg 5_5 (unless חול pol. ptc. *dancers*).
⇒ חול I *whirl*, מָחוֹל *dance*, מְחֹלָה *dance*.

מְחוֹקֵק *commander*, see חקק *engrave*, Po.

*[**מְחוֹת**] 1 n.f.pl. **full measure**—cstr. מְחוֹת—(unless מְחוֹת = inf. cstr. of מחה *wipe out*), <CSTR> מְחוֹת מְלָכִין *full measure of kings* Pr 31_3. <PREP> לְ *(according) to*, + נתן *give* Pr 31_1.

מַחֲזֶה 4 n.[m.] **vision**—cstr. מַחֲזֵה—of a prophet (Nm $24_{4.16}$ Ezk 13_7), assoc. with revelation, <OBJ> חזה *see* Nm 24_4 (+ אֹמֶר *word*) 24_{16} (+ אֹמֶר, דַּעַת *knowledge*) Ezk 13_7 (|| מִקְסָם *divination*). <CSTR> מַחֲזֵה שַׁדַּי *vision of the Almighty* Nm $24_{4.16}$ (both Sam^{mss} שדה), שָׁוְא־ *of emptiness*, i.e. empty vision Ezk 13_7, [מ]חזה ימינו *vision of our days* 4QMyst^{b} 8_1. <PREP> בְּ of instrument, *by (means of), with*, + היה *be* Gn 15_1.
<SYN> מִקְסָם *divination*.
⇒ חזה *see*.

מֶחֱזָה 4 n.f. **window**, in Solomon's palace complex, <SUBJ> רבע pass. *be square* 1 K 7_5 (if em. הַמְּזוּזוֹת *the doorposts* to הַמֶּחֱזוֹת). <NOM CL> מֶחֱזָה אֶל־מֶחֱזָה *window was towards window* 1 K 7_4. <CSTR> מוּל מֶחֱזָה *front of window* 1 K 7_5 (or del.). <APP> פַּעַם *time* 1 K $7_{4.5}$ (both שָׁלֹשׁ פְּעָמִים *three times*, i.e. in three tiers). <PREP> אֶל *towards, facing* 1 K $7_{4.5}$ (or del.).*
⇒ חזה *see*.

מַחֲזִיאוֹת 2 pr.n.m. **Mahazioth,** son of Heman, musician, <NOM CL> בְּנֵי הֵימָן ... מַחֲזִיאוֹת *the sons of Heman were ... Mahazioth* 1 C 25_4. <PREP> לְ of direction, *to*, + יצא (of lot) *go out* 1 C 25_{30}.
⇒ חזה *see*.

[**מְחִי**] 1 n.[m.] **thrust**—cstr. מְחִי—**thrust, blow,** <OBJ> נתן *give*, i.e. place, against walls Ezk 26_9. <CSTR> מְחִי קָבָלוֹ *stroke of his battering ram* Ezk 26_9.
⇒ מחה II *strike*.

*[**מְחִיגָה**] n.f. **cause of reeling,** <OBJ> נתן *give*, i.e. make 4QDiscourse 2.2_6 (ויתננו לאלוהים על אדירים ומחיג[ה] לפרעה *and he made him as God over the mighty ones, and a cause of reeling to Pharaoh*).
⇒ חוג *make a circle*.

מְחִידָא 2 pr.n.m. **Mehida,** name of family of Nethinim, temple servants in postexilic Judaea, <CSTR> בְּנֵי־

מְחִידָא *sons of Mehida* Ezr 2$_{52}$||Ne 7$_{54}$ (mss both מְחִירָא *Mehira*).

מִחְיָה 8.3.2 n.f. **life**—cstr. מִחְיַת; sf. מִחְיָתֶךָ—**1. (preservation of) life,** in famine (Gn 45$_5$), through work of physician (Si 38$_{14}$), <PREP> לְ of benefit, *for*, + שׁלח *send* Gn 45$_5$; לְמַעַן *for the sake of*, + צלח *succeed* Si 38$_{14}$.

2. sustenance, livelihood, <OBJ> נתן *give* Jg 17$_{10}$ (+ כֶּסֶף *silver*, עֵרֶךְ בְּגָדִים *value of garments*), שׁאר hi. *leave* Jg 6$_4$ (+ שֶׂה *sheep*, שׁוֹר *ox*, חֲמוֹר *ass*). <CSTR> דאגת מחיה *anxiety of*, i.e. for, *livelihood* Si 34$_{1.2}$. <PREP> בְּ of instrument, *by (means of), with*, + ישׁב *dwell* Ps 68$_{11}$ (if em. חַיָּתְךָ *your dwelling place* to מִחְיָתְךָ *your sustenance*).

3. reviving, recovery, among postexilic community (Ezr 9$_{8.9}$), for defeated Ethiopians (2 C 14$_{12}$), <NOM CL> אֵין לָהֶם מִחְיָה *there was no recovery for them* 2 C 14$_{12}$ (unless §5). <OBJ> נתן *give* Ezr 9$_8$ (+ פְּלֵיטָה *remnant*, יָתֵד *tent peg*) 9$_9$ (unless §6; or em. מְנֻחָה *rest*). <APP> מְעַט *a little* Ezr 9$_8$.

4. place of life, i.e. **patch** of flesh,* or **formation of new flesh,*** or perh. **rawness** of flesh, <SUBJ> היה *be* Lv 13$_{24}$ (+ בַּהֶרֶת *spot*). <NOM CL> מִחְיַת בָּשָׂר חַי בַּשְׂאֵת *rawness of living flesh is in the swelling* Lv 13$_{10}$. <CSTR> מִחְיַת בָּשָׂר *rawness of flesh* Lv 13$_{10}$, הַמִּכְוָה *of the burn* Lv 13$_{24}$.

5. as collective, **living beings, survivors,** <OBJ> רום hi. *raise up* 1QH 6$_8$ (|| שְׁאֵרִית *remnant*). <CSTR> עזר שארית ומחיה *assistance of the remnant and the survivors* 1QM 13$_8$. <COLL> מחיה בעמכה *survivors among your people* 1QH 6$_8$, שארית ומחיה לבריתכה *the remnant and survivors of your covenant* 1QM 13$_8$.

6. materials for repair* (unless §3), <OBJ> נתן *give* Ezr 9$_9$. <COLL> מִחְיָה לְרוֹמֵם אֶת־בֵּית אֱלֹהֵינוּ *materials for repair* (or *means of rebuilding*) *to erect the temple of our God* Ezr 9$_9$.

<SYN> §5 שְׁאֵרִית *remnant*.*

⇒ חיה I *live*.

מְחִיָּיאֵל, see מְחוּיאֵל *Mehujael*.

[מְחָיִים] *annihilated ones*, see מחה I *wipe out*.

מְחִיר **מְחִיר** I 15.4.11 n.m. **price**—cstr. מְחִיר; sf. Si מחירך, מְחִירָהּ; pl. sf. מְחִירֵיהֶם—**1. price, cost, value,** <SUBJ> שׁוה *be equal* 1QMyst 1.2$_8$ (מח[יר]) 4Q416 2.2$_7$. <NOM CL> מְחִיר שָׂדֶה עַתּוּדִים *he-goats are the price of a field* Pr 27$_{26}$ (+ לְבוּשׁ *clothing*), אין מחיר *there is no price* Si 6$_{15}$ (+ מִשְׁקָל *weight*) 1QH 10$_{10}$ 4Q416 2.2$_7$ 4QHod[a] 7.2$_8$. <OBJ> שׁקל *weigh*, i.e. pay Si 8$_2$. <CSTR> מְחִיר זֶה perh. *price of this (vineyard)* 1 K 21$_2$ (unless app.), מְחִיר שָׂדֶה *price of a field* Pr 27$_{26}$, מחיר מות *price of death* CD 16$_{8.9}$; כֶּסֶף מְחִיר *money of*, i.e. for, *the price* 1 K 21$_2$, כו]ל מח]יר *any price* 1QMyst 1.2$_8$. <APP> perh. זֶה *this* 1 K 21$_2$ (unless מְחִיר is cstr.).

<PREP> לְ as perh. 4QMyst[a] 6$_{53}$; בְּ of price, *(in exchange) for* 1QS 5$_{17}$, + בוא *come* Lm 5$_4$ (|| כֶּסֶף *money*), קנה *purchase* 2 S 24$_{24}$, שׁבר *buy (food)* Is 55$_1$ (בְּלוֹא מְחִיר *for no price*; || כֶּסֶף), מכר ni. *be sold* 1QMyst 1.2$_6$ (בלוא מחיר; + הוֹן *wealth*), hi. *sell* 4Q416 2.2$_{17}$, לקח *take* 1 K 10$_{28}$||2 C 1$_{16}$, נתן *give* Jr 15$_{13}$, חלק pi. *divide* land Dn 11$_{39}$, רדה *rule* 4QMyst[c] 2b$_3$ (בלוא מחיר); introducing object, + רבה pi. *increase* Ps 44$_{13}$ (+ הוֹן *wealth*); עַד *unto*, + פדה *redeem* CD 16$_8$, קום hi. *fulfil* CD 16$_9$. <COLL> לֹא יִשָּׁקֵל כֶּסֶף מְחִירָהּ *silver cannot be weighed as its price* Jb 28$_{15}$.

2. hire, wages, <OBJ> בוא hi. *bring* Dt 23$_{19}$ (|| אֶתְנַן *fee*). <CSTR> מְחִיר כֶּלֶב *hire of a (temple) servant* Dt 23$_{19}$. <PREP> בְּ of price, *(in exchange) for*, + שׁלח pi. *let go* Is 45$_{13}$ (|| שֹׁחַד *reward*), ירה hi. *teach* Mc 3$_{11}$ (|| שֹׁחַד, כֶּסֶף *money*).

3. money (distinction from §§ 1-2 not alw. clear), <NOM CL> לָמָּה־זֶּה מְחִיר בְּיַד־כְּסִיל *what use is money in the hand of a fool?* Pr 17$_{16}$. <OBJ> אהב *love* Si 34$_{5(B)}$ (+ חָרוּץ *gold*). <PREP> בְּ of price, *(in exchange) for*, + מור hi. *exchange* Si 7$_{18}$ (+ זָהָב *gold*), אהב *love* Si 34$_{5(Bmg)}$ (unless בְּ introducing object); of instrument, *by (means of), with*, + שׁגה *go astray* Si 34$_5$. <COLL> [לוא] יחלתי פניה ... מחיר *I did not seek her favour ... with money* 4QVisSam 7$_3$ (|| הוֹן *wealth*, רְכוּשׁ *possessions*).

<SYN> §1, 2 כֶּסֶף *money*; §2 אֶתְנַן *fee*, שֹׁחַד *reward*; §3 הוֹן *wealth*, רְכוּשׁ *possessions*.*

מְחִיר **מְחִיר** II 1 pr.n.m. **Mehir,** Judahite, son of Chelub, <OBJ> ילד hi. *beget* 1 C 4$_{11}$.

מְחִירָא, see מְחִידָא *Mehida*.

***מחל** 0.0.1 vb. **forgive—Qal** 0.0.1 Pf. Qמחלת—**forgive,** <SUBJ> Y. GnzPs 1_{13} (|| סלח *pardon*, + כפר pi. *make atonement*). <OBJ> חַטָּאת *sin* GnzPs 1_{13}.

Also perh. 4QD^b 4_4.

<SYN> סלח *pardon*.

מַחֲלֵב, see מְחַלֵּב *Mehalleb*.

[מְחַלֵּב] pl.n. **Mehalleb,** or [מַחֲלֵב] **Mahaleb,** town in Asher, perh. ident. with Ahlab at Jg 1_{31}, <SUBJ> היה *be* Jos 19_{29} (if em. מֵחֶבֶל *from the territory of* Achzib).*

מַחְלָה 5 pr.n.f. **Mahlah, 1.** daughter of Zelophehad, <SUBJ> היה *be* Nm 36_{11}. <NOM CL> שֵׁם בְּנוֹת צְלָפְחָד ... מַחְלָה *the names of the daughters of Zelophehad were Mahlah ...* Nm 26_{33}, sim. 27_1 Jos 17_3. <APP> בַּת *daughter* Nm 36_{11}.

2. Manassite, daughter (or perh. son) of Hammolecheth, <OBJ> ילד *bear* 1 C 7_{18}.

מַחֲלָה 4.3 n.f. **sickness, disease,** <SUBJ> היה *be* 1 K 8_{37}||2 C 6_{28} (|| נֶגַע *plague*), פרג hi. *cause* sleep *to be stunted* Si $34_{2(Bmg)}$. <OBJ> שׂים *place* Ex 15_{26}, סור hi. *remove* Ex 23_{25}. <CSTR> שמץ מחלה *whisper of a sickness,* i.e. a slight sickness Si 10_{10}, כָּל־מַחֲלָה *any sickness* Ex 15_{26} (הַמַּחֲלָה) 1 K 8_{37}||2 C 6_{28}. <ADJ> חָזָק *strong,* i.e. serious Si $34_{2(Bmg)}$. <PREP> בְּ of time, *in, during,* + עבר htp. *delay* Si $38_{9(Bmg)}$. <COLL> מְמִתִים מַחֲלָה *caused to die [by] a disease* Ps 17_{14} (if em. מֵחֶלֶד חֶלְקָם *their portion is from the world*).

<SYN> נֶגַע *plague.*

⇨ חלה I *be weak,* מַחֲלֶה *sickness.*

[מַחֲלֶה] 2.0.4 n.m. **sickness**—cstr. מַחֲלֵה; sf. מַחֲלֵהוּ; pl. Q מחלים—**sickness, disease,** <NOM CL> אין מחלה *there is no sickness* 4QHod^e 1_5 (+ נֶגַע *plague*). <OBJ> כול pilp. *endure* Pr 18_{14} (or em. מַחֲלֵהוּ to מְחַלֵּהוּ *makes him sick,* i.e. חלה pi.). <CSTR> מַחֲלֵה מֵעֶיךָ *disease of your bowels* 2 C 21_{15} (+ חֳלִי *sickness*); שערוריות מחלים *horrors of* evil *diseases* 1QpHab 9_1. <ADJ> רַע *evil* 1QpHab 9_1 4QAges^b 1.2_1 (|| מִשְׁפָּט *judgment*) 4Qap Pent 10.1_7 (|| מַכָּה *stroke,* נֶגַע *plague*). <PREP> לְ *for, as* 4QAges^b 1.2_1; בְּ of accompaniment, *with, in* 2 C 21_{15}.

<SYN> נֶגַע *plague,* מַכָּה *stroke,* מִשְׁפָּט *judgment.*

⇨ חלה I *be weak,* מַחֲלָה *sickness.*

[מְחִלָּה] 1.0.1 n.f. **hole**—cstr. מְחִלּוֹת—**hole** in ground, as hiding place (Is 2_{19}), to drain water from laver (11QT 32_{13}), <SUBJ> ירד *go down* 11QT 32_{13}. <CSTR> מְחִלּוֹת עָפָר *holes of the ground* Is 2_{19} (|| מְעָרָה *cave*). <PREP> בְּ of place, *in(to),* + בוא *come* Is 2_{19}.

<SYN> מְעָרָה *cave.*

⇨ חלל III *be pierced.*

[מְחֹלָה] 8 n.f. **dance**—cstr. מְחֹלַת; pl. מְחֹלוֹת (מְחֹלֹת)—**dance, dancing,** not necessarily in a ring,* with music (Jg 11_{34} 1 S 18_6 21_{12} 29_5), in worship (Ex 15_{20} 32_{19}), <OBJ> ראה *see* Ex 32_{19}. <CSTR> מְחֹלַת הַמַּחֲנָיִם perh. *dance of,* i.e. in, *two lines* Ca 7_1 (unless 'of Mahanaim'; or em. מַחֲנַיִם *of,* i.e. *in, the camp;* ms מְחֹלוֹת *dances of*). <PREP> בְּ of accompaniment, *with, in* Is 30_{32} (if em. וּבְמִלְחֲמוֹת *and with battles* to וּבִמְחֹלוֹת *and with dances*) Ca $7_{1(mss)}$, + יצא *go out* Ex 15_{20} 1 S $18_{6(cit)}$ (MT וְהַמְּחֹלוֹת *and the dances;* or em. וְהַמְחֹלְלוֹת *and the dancers*), חול *dance* Jg 21_{21}, ענה *sing* Jg 11_{34} 1 S 21_{12} 29_5; כְּ *as* Ca 7_1. <COLL> מְחֹלָה || תֹּף *timbrel* Ex 15_{20} Jg 11_{34}.

<SYN> תֹּף *timbrel.**

⇨ חול I *whirl,* מָחוֹל *dance,* מְחוֹלָלָה *dance.*

מַחְלוֹן 4 pr.n.m. **Mahlon,** son of Elimelech and Naomi, first husband of Ruth, <SUBJ> מות *die* Ru 1_5. <NOM CL> שֵׁם שְׁנֵי־בָנָיו מַחְלוֹן וְכִלְיוֹן *the names of his two sons were Mahlon and Chilion* Ru 1_2. <CSTR> אֵשֶׁת מַחְלוֹן *wife of Mahlon* Ru 4_{10}. <APP> אֶפְרָתִי *Ephrathite* Ru 1_2. <PREP> לְ of possession, *(belonging) to, of* Ru 4_9.

⇨ (?) חלה *be sick.*

מַחְלִי I 12 pr.n.m. **Mahli, 1.** Levite, son of Merari, <NOM CL> בְּנֵי מְרָרִי מַחְלִי וּמוּשִׁי *the sons of Merari were Mahli and Mushi* Ex 6_{19} Nm 3_{20} 1 C 6_4 23_{21} 24_{26}, var. 1 C 6_{14}. <CSTR> בְּנֵי מַחְלִי *sons of Mahli* Ezr 8_{18} 1 C 23_{21}. <APP> בֵּן *son* Ezr 8_{18}. <PREP> לְ of possession, *(belong-*

ing) to, of 1 C 24_{28}.

2. Levite, son of Mushi and nephew of §1, <NOM CL> בְּנֵי מוּשִׁי מַחְלִי *the sons of Mushi were Mahli* 1 C 23_{23} 24_{30}. <CSTR> בֶּן־מַחְלִי *son of Mahli* 1 C 6_{32}. <APP> בֵּן *son* 1 C 6_{32}.

⇒ מַחְלִי II *Mahli*te.

מַחְלִי II $_{2}$ gent. **Mahlite,** as collective noun, descendants of Mahli, son of Merari, <CSTR> מִשְׁפַּחַת הַמַּחְלִי *clan of the Mahlites* Nm 3_{33} 26_{58}.

⇒ מַחְלִי I *Mahli*.

מַחֲלֻיִים $_{1}$ n.[m.]pl. **sickness, suffering,** <PREP> בְּ of accompaniment, *with, in,* + עזב *leave* 2 C 24_{25}. <ADJ> רַב pl. *many* 2 C 24_{25}.*

⇒ חלה I *be weak*.

[מַחֲלָף] I $_{1}$ n.m. **knife**—pl. מַחֲלָפִים—among temple utensils, <COLL> מַחֲלָפִים תִּשְׁעָה וְעֶשְׂרִים *twenty-nine knives* Ezr 1_{9} (or em. מָחֳלָפִים *replaced*, i.e. חלף ho.; + אֲגַרְטָל *basket,* כְּפוֹר *bowl*).*

⇒ חלף I *pass*.

*__[מַחֲלָף]__ II $_{1}$ n.m. **censer**—pl. מַחֲלָפִים—among temple utensils, <COLL> מַחֲלָפִים תִּשְׁעָה וְעֶשְׂרִים *twenty-nine censers* Ezr 1_{9} (+ אֲגַרְטָל *basket,* כְּפוֹר *bowl*).

*__מַחֲלָף__ III *repaired* (if em. מָחֳלָפִים), see חלף ho. *replace, renew*.

*__מַחֲלָף__ IV *to be changed* (if em. מָחֳלָפִים), a scribal note indicating a manuscript error; see חלף ho. *replace, renew*.

[מַחֲלָפָה] I $_{2}$ n.f. **plait**—pl. cstr. מַחְלְפוֹת—**plait, lock** of hair, perh. of locks as passing through (חלף) each other,* <OBJ> ארג *weave* Jg 16_{13}, גלח pi. *shave* Jg 16_{19}. <CSTR> מַחְלְפוֹת רֹאשִׁי *plaits of my head* Jg 16_{13}, רֹאשׁוֹ *of his head* Jg 16_{19}. <COLL> שֶׁבַע מַחְלְפוֹת *seven plaits of* Jg $16_{13.19}$.*

⇒ חלף I *pass*.

*__[מַחֲלָפָה]__ II $_{2}$ n.f. **copious hair, flowing lock**—pl. cstr. מַחְלְפוֹת—<OBJ> ארג *weave* Jg 16_{13}, גלח pi. *shave* Jg 16_{19}. <CSTR> מַחְלְפוֹת רֹאשִׁי *locks of my head* Jg 16_{13}, רֹאשׁוֹ *of his head* Jg 16_{19}. <COLL> שֶׁבַע מַחְלְפוֹת *seven locks of* Jg $16_{13.19}$.

⇒ חלף II (?) *be sharp*.

[מַחֲלָצָה] I $_{2}$ n.f. **festive robe** (unless מַחֲלָצָה II *white garments*)—pl. מַחֲלָצוֹת—supposedly as taken off (חלץ *draw off*) in ordinary life, in list of fine clothes of women (Is 3_{22}), as clean clothing for high priest (Zc 3_{4}), <OBJ> סור hi. *remove* Is 3_{22} (+ מַעֲטָפָה *tunic,* מִטְפַּחַת *cloak*), לבשׁ hi. *dress with* Zc 3_{4}.

⇒ חלץ I *loosen*.

*__[מַחֲלָצָה]__ II $_{2}$ n.f. **white garments** (unless מַחֲלָצָה I *festive robe*)—pl. מַחֲלָצוֹת—in list of fine clothes of women (Is 3_{22}), as clean clothing for high priest (Zc 3_{4}), <OBJ> סור hi. *remove* Is 3_{22} (+ מַעֲטָפָה *tunic,* מִטְפַּחַת *cloak*), לבשׁ hi. *dress with* Zc 3_{4}.

*__[מַחֲלֻקוֹת]__ $_{0.1}$ n.f. **distribution,** <CSTR> מחשבות מחלקות *plans of,* i.e. for, *the distribution of* Si $41_{21(Bmg)}$ (unless מַחְלְקוֹת pl. of מַחֲלֹקֶת *division*).

⇒ חלק I *divide*.

מַחֲלֹקֶת I $_{43.2.9}$ n.f. **division**—cstr. מַחֲלֹקֶת; sf. מַחֲלֻקְתּוֹ; pl. מַחְלְקוֹת; cstr. מַחְלְקוֹת; sf. מַחְלְקוֹתֵיכֶם, מַחְלְקֹתָם, מַחְלְקוֹתֵיהֶם, (מַחְלְקֹתָם)—**1. (tribal) division** of Israel (unless **allotment** of land to tribes of Israel, i.e. §5), <PREP> לְ *according to,* + נתן *give* as inheritance Jos $12_{7(mss)}$; בְּ *in, according to,* + נתן *give* as inheritance Jos $11_{23(mss)}$ $12_{7(mss)}$, חלק pi. *divide* land Jos $18_{10(mss)}$; כְּ *according to,* + נתן *give* as inheritance Jos 11_{23} (+ לְשִׁבְטֵיהֶם *by their tribes*) 12_{7}, חלק pi. *divide* land Jos 18_{10}.

2. division, course of priests and Levites, <SUBJ> בוא *come* 1 C 27_{1}, יצא *go out* 1 C 27_{1}. <NOM CL> הַמַּחֲלֹקֶת הָאַחַת עֶשְׂרִים וְאַרְבָּעָה אָלֶף *one division was,* i.e. consisted of, *twenty-four thousand* 1 C 27_{1}, הִנֵּה מַחְלְקוֹת הַכֹּהֲנִים וְהַלְוִיִּם *behold the divisions of the priests and Levites* 1 C 28_{21}, מִן־הַלְוִיִּם מַחְלְקוֹת יְהוּדָה

לְבִנְיָמִין *of the Levites some divisions of Judah were (joined) to Benjamin* Ne 11$_{36}$ (mss יְהוּדָה וּבִנְיָמִין there were some divisions of, i.e. joined to, *Judah and Benjamin*), לִבְנֵי אַהֲרֹן מַחְלְקוֹתָם *(belonging) to the sons of Aaron were their divisions* 1 C 24$_{1}$, אֵלֶּה מַחְלְקוֹת הַשֹּׁעֲרִים *these are the divisions of the gatekeepers* 1 C 26$_{19}$, var. 26$_{12}$. <OBJ> עמד hi. *appoint* 2 C 8$_{14}$ 31$_{2}$, פטר *dismiss* 2 C 23$_{8}$.

<CSTR> מַחְלְקוֹת יְהוּדָה *divisions of Judah* Ne 11$_{36}$ (mss יְהוּדָה וּבִנְיָמִין *of Judah and Benjamin*), הַשֹּׁעֲרִים *of the gatekeepers* 1 C 26$_{12.19}$, מַחֲלֹקֶת הַחֹדֶשׁ הַשֵּׁנִי *division of the second month* 1 C 27$_{4}$, [מחל]קת עבודתו *division of his service* 1QSa 2$_{1}$; שָׂרֵי הַמַּחְלְקוֹת *officers of the divisions* 1 C 28$_{1}$, הַכֹּהֲנִים *of the priests* 1 C 28$_{13.21}$ (both + וְהַלְוִיִּם *and the Levites*) 2 C 8$_{14}$ 31$_{2}$ (+ וְהַלְוִיִּם), דְּבַר *matter of*, i.e. concerning 1 C 27$_{1}$. <ADJ> אֶחָד *one* 1 C 27$_{1}$, רִאשׁוֹן *first* 1 C 27$_{2}$.

<PREP> לְ of benefit, *to, for* 1 C 28$_{13}$; *as regards* 1 C 26$_{1}$; שׁמר לְ *keep*, i.e. pay regard, *to* 2 C 5$_{11}$; בְּ *in*, + עמד hi. *appoint* gatekeepers 2 C 8$_{14}$; *according to* 2 C 31$_{16}$ (mss).17, + נתן *give* 2 C 31$_{15}$; כְּ *according to* 2 C 31$_{16}$, + כון ni. *prepare oneself* 2 C 35$_{4(Kt)}$ (Qr hi. *prepare*), קרב hi. *bring near*, i.e. offer 11QT 15$_{5}$ ([כמחלקו]תיהמה); עַל *upon, in, (belonging) to* 1 C 27$_{2+11t}$, + עמד *stand* 2 C 35$_{10}$ (|| עֹמֶד *position*); *according to*, + עמד hi. *appoint* 2 C 31$_{2}$; *in charge of* 1 C 27$_{2.4}$; בְּתוֹךְ *among* 1QSa 2$_{1}$ (בתוך מחל[קת]).

<COLL> מַחְלְקוֹת לְשֹׁעֲרִים *divisions of gatekeepers* 1 C 26$_{1}$ (or em. לַשֹּׁעֲרִים *of the gatekeepers*), … מַחְלְקוֹת … לְכָל־מְלֶאכֶת עֲבוֹדַת בֵּית הָאֱלֹהִים *the divisions … for all the service of the house of God* 1 C 28$_{21}$, וַיֶּחָלְקֵם דָּוִיד מַחְלְקוֹת *and David assigned them to divisions* 1 C 23$_{6}$ (if em. וַיְחַלְּקֵם, i.e. ni.), וּמַחֲלֻקְתּוֹ וּמִקְלוֹת הַנָּגִיד perh. *and as far as his division was concerned, Mikloth was the chief officer* 1 C 27$_{4}$, וּמַחֲלֻקְתּוֹ עַמִּיזָבָד *and (in charge of) his division was Ammizabad* 1 C 27$_{6}$.

3. (military) division, <CSTR> מלחמת המחלקות *war of the divisions* 1QM 2$_{10}$.

4. division of time, **season,** <SUBJ> אבד *perish* 4QapJoseph^{b} 3$_{6}$ (+ מוֹעֵד *season*). <OBJ> נגד hi. *tell* 4QJub^{a} 1$_{4}$ ([מ]חלקות), ספר *recount* 4QCitJub 1.1$_{4}$ ([אספ]ר). <CSTR> מחלקת עתו *division of his time* 4QCit Jub 1.1$_{4}$, עתה *of her time* 4QCitJub 1.1$_{7}$, מחלקות העתים *divisions of the times* 4QJub^{a} 1$_{4}$ ([מ]חלקות [הע]תים) 4QJub^{b} 2$_{1}$ 4QCitJub 1.1$_{2}$ ([מחל]ק[ו]ת) 4QapJerB 9$_{2}$ ([מ]חלקות העתים) 11QMelch 3$_{18}$ ([מח]לקות [העתים]) CD 16$_{3}$; ספר מחלקות *book of the divisions of* the times 4QapJerB 9$_{2}$ ([ספר מ]חלקות) CD 16$_{3}$.

<PREP> בְּ of time, *in* 4QCitJub 1.1$_{2}$ ([במחל]ק[ו]ת) 1.1$_{7}$ 4QBer^{a} 1a.2$_{11}$ ([שבתות ארץ במחל]קותמה *the sabbatical years of the earth in their divisions*), + כתב pass. *be written* 4QCitJub 1.1$_{9}$.

5. division, allotment of inheritance and property (see also §1), <CSTR> מחלקת נחלה ויש *allotment of inheritance and property* Si 42$_{3(M)}$ (B מחלקות; Bmg מחל[ק]ת נחלה וישר *of inheritance and uprightness*), מחל[ק]ת מנה *allotment of a portion* Si 41$_{21(M)}$ (Bmg מחלקות); מחשבות מחלקות *plans of*, i.e. for, *the allotment of* Si 41$_{21(Bmg)}$ (unless מַחֲלֻקוֹת *distribution*). <PREP> עַל *on account of*, + בוש *be ashamed* Si 42$_{3}$.

<COLL> בוש ... מ[ח]שא[ו]ת מחל[ק]ת מנה *be ashamed … of keeping silence with respect to the allotment of a portion*, i.e. of withholding someone's portion Si 41$_{21(M)}$.

6. part, portion, share of land allotted to tribes of Israel (Ezk 48$_{29}$), of land rented (5/6ḤevBA 44$_{25}$), of moon as visible (4QAstrCrypt 1.2$_{11}$), <SUBJ> גלה ni. *be revealed* 4QAstrCrypt 1.2$_{11}$ ([תגלה]). <NOM CL> אֵלֶּה מַחְלְקוֹתָם *these are their portions* Ezk 48$_{29}$. <CSTR> חשבון המחלקת *reckoning of the portion* 5/6ḤevBA 44$_{25}$. <ADJ> אֶחָד *one* 4QAstrCrypt 1.2$_{11}$, הַלֵּזוּ *that* 5/6ḤevBA 44$_{25}$.

7. in pl.n. סֶלַע הַמַּחְלְקוֹת **Rock of Divisions** (unless 'of Smoothness', from מַחֲלֹקֶת II), 1 S 23$_{28}$.*

Also 4QM^{h} 4$_{8}$ ([מחלקו]תם).

<SYN> §2 עֹמֶד *position.*

⇒ חלק I *divide.*

[מַחֲלֹקֶת] II $_{1}$ n.f. **smoothness**—pl. מַחְלְקוֹת—in pl.n. סֶלַע הַמַּחְלְקוֹת **Rock of Smoothness** (unless 'of Divisions', from מַחֲלֹקֶת I), 1 S 23$_{28}$.*

⇒ חלק II *be smooth.*

מָחֲלַת I $_{2}$ n.[f.] **Mahalath,** musical term in two psalm titles, poss. name of melody or instrument or choreography, perh. related to מְחֹלָה *dance* or to the melody's melancholy spirit (cf. חלה *be sick*), <PREP> עַל מָחֲלַת *upon Mahalath* Ps 53$_{1}$, עַל מָחֲלַת לְעַנּוֹת *upon Mahalath Leanoth*, perh. with ref. to responsive singing (cf. ענה *answer*) Ps 88$_{1}$.*

מָחֲלַת II 7 pr.n.f. **Mahalath**—mss מַחֲלַת, mss מַחְלַת—**1.** daughter of Ishmael and wife of Esau, appar. ident. with Basemath at Gn 36$_{3.4.10.13.17}$ (Sam. Mahalath throughout), <SUBJ> ילד *give birth* Gn 36$_{4(Sam)}$. <OBJ> לקח *take (in marriage)* Gn 28$_{9}$ 36$_{3(Sam)}$. <CSTR> בֶּן־ מָחֲלַת *son of Mahalath* Gn 36$_{10(Sam)}$, בְּנֵי *sons of* Gn 36$_{13(Sam).17(Sam)}$. <APP> בַּת *daughter* Gn 28$_{9}$ 36$_{3(Sam)}$, אָחוֹת *sister* Gn 28$_{9}$ 36$_{3(Sam)}$, אִשָּׁה *wife* Gn 36$_{10(Sam).13(Sam).17(Sam)}$.

2. daughter of Jerimoth and granddaughter of David, wife of Rehoboam, <OBJ> לקח *take (in marriage)* 2 C 11$_{18}$. <APP> בַּת *daughter* 2 C 11$_{18(Qr)}$ (Kt בן *son*), אִשָּׁה *wife* 2 C 11$_{18}$.

מַחֲלַת, see מָחֲלַת II, *Mahalath*.

מְחֹלָתִי 2 gent. **Meholathite,** belonging to Abel-meholah, as sing. noun, <APP> Adriel 1 S 18$_{19}$ 2 S 21$_{8}$, בֵּן *son* 2 S 21$_{8}$. <PREP> לְ of direction, *to*, + נתן ni. *be given (in marriage)* 1 S 18$_{19}$; of benefit, *to, for*, + ילד *give birth* 2 S 21$_{8}$.

⇒ cf. אָבֵל II *Abel*.

מַחְמָאֹת 1 n.f.pl. **curd-like things,** in ref. to smooth speech, <SUBJ> חלק *be smooth* Ps 55$_{22}$ (or em.; see Cstr.). <CSTR> מַחְמָאֹת פִּיו *the curd-like things of his mouth* Ps 55$_{22}$ (mss מֵחֶמְאוֹת *than curds*; or em. מֵחֶמְאָה *than butter*).

⇒ חֶמְאָה *curd*.

[מַחְמָד] 13.4.2 n.m. **desirable thing**—cstr. מַחְמַד; sf. Q מחמדו, mss מַחֲמַדֵּנוּ; pl. מַחֲמַדִּים; cstr. מַחֲמַדֵּי; sf. מַחֲמַדֵּי, Si מחמדיך, מַחֲמַדֶּיהָ, מַחֲמַדֵּינוּ, Qr מַחֲמַדֵּיהֶם—**(object of) desire, delight, pleasure; precious thing;** in ref. to children (Ho 9$_{16}$), wife (Ezk 24$_{16}$), male lover (Ca 5$_{16}$), temple (Ezk 24$_{21}$), idols (GnzPs 2$_{21}$); used collectively (Ho 9$_{6}$; unless from מַחְמַד *Machomades*).

<SUBJ> היה *be* Is 64$_{10}$ (+ לְחָרְבָּה *a ruin*), אבד *perish* GnzPs 2$_{21}$. <NOM CL> כֻּלּוֹ מַחֲמַדִּים *all of him is desirable things*, i.e. he is altogether desirable Ca 5$_{16}$. <OBJ> בוא hi. *bring* Jl 4$_{5}$, נתן *give* for food Lm 1$_{11(Qr)}$, לקח *take* 1 K 20$_{6}$ Ezk 24$_{16.25}$, שׂים *place* 1 K 20$_{6}$, ירשׁ *possess* Ho 9$_{6}$ (unless from מַחְמַד *Machomades*), חלל pi. *profane* Ezk 24$_{21.21}$ (if em.; see Cstr.), הרג *kill* Lm 2$_{4}$, מות hi. *kill* Ho 9$_{16}$.

<CSTR> מחמד עין *desirable thing of*, i.e. to, *the eye* Si 36$_{27}$ 45$_{12(Segal)}$ ([עין]), מַחְמַד עֵינֶיךָ *desirable thing of your eyes* 1 K 20$_{6}$ (or em. עֵינֶיךָ to עֵינֵיהֶם *of their eyes*) Ezk 24$_{16}$, עֵינֵיכֶם *of your* (pl.) *eyes* Ezk 24$_{21}$, עֵינֵיהֶם *of their eyes* 1 K 20$_{6}$ (if em.; see above) Ezk 24$_{25}$, מַחֲמַדֵּי עָיִן *desirable things of the eye* Lm 2$_{4}$, מַחְמַד נַפְשְׁכֶם *desirable thing of your* (pl.) *soul* Ezk 24$_{21}$ (if em. מַחְמַל *compassion of*), מַחֲמַדֵּי בִטְנָם *desirable things of their womb* Ho 9$_{16}$, מַחְמַד לְכַסְפָּם *precious things (consisting) of their silver* Ho 9$_{6}$ (unless from מַחְמַד *Machomades*; or em. מַחְמַד כַּסְפָּם); כְּלֵי מַחֲמַדֶּיהָ *her precious vessels* 2 C 36$_{19}$, אֶרֶץ מַחֲמַדִּים *land of desirable things* Is 33$_{17}$ (if em. מֶרְחַקִּים *of distances*), כָּל־מַחְמַד *every desirable thing of* 1 K 20$_{6}$ Si 36$_{27}$, כָּל־מַחֲמַדֶּיהָ *all her desirable things* Lm 1$_{10}$, כָּל־מַחֲמַדֵּינוּ *all our desirable things* Is 64$_{10}$ (mss מַחֲמַדֵּנוּ *our desirable thing*).

<APP> מִקְדָּשׁ *sanctuary* Ezk 24$_{21}$, גָּאוֹן *pride* Ezk 24$_{21}$, מָעוֹז *stronghold* Ezk 24$_{25}$, מָשׂוֹשׂ *joy*.

<ADJ> טוֹב *good* Jl 4$_{5}$.

<PREP> בְּ of place, *among*, + נכר pi. *treat as a stranger* Si 11$_{34}$ (וינכרו[ך]); *against*, + נתן *give* Si 11$_{31}$; עַל *over*, + פרשׂ *spread* hands Lm 1$_{10}$; *(more) than*, + גבר *be mighty* Si 36$_{27}$.

<COLL> מַחְמָד ‖ מַחְמָל *compassion* Ezk 24$_{21}$; + זָהָב *gold* Jl 4$_{5}$, כֶּסֶף *silver* Jl 4$_{5}$, מַמְתַקִּים *sweetness* Ca 5$_{16}$, בַּיִת *house*, i.e. temple Is 64$_{10}$ 2 C 36$_{19}$, אַרְמוֹן *palace* 2 C 36$_{19}$, אֱלִיל *idol* GnzPs 2$_{21}$, בֵּן *son* Ezk 24$_{21.25}$, בַּת *daughter* Ezk 24$_{21.25}$, מַשָּׂא *uplifting*, i.e. desire Ezk 24$_{25}$.

Also 11QPsAp^{a} 6$_{9}$.

<SYN> מַחְמָל *(object of) longing*.

⇒ חמד *desire*, מַחְמֹד *precious thing*.

מַחְמַד* 1 pl.n. **Machomades,** town on Greater Syrtis in Egypt, famous for quicksands, <SUBJ> קבר pi. *bury* Ho 9$_{6}$ (unless cstr. of מַחְמָד *desirable thing*).

[מַחְמֹד] 2 n.[m.] **precious thing**—pl. sf. מַחֲמַדֶּיהָ, Kt מחמודיהם—<SUBJ> היה *be* Lm 1$_{7}$. <OBJ> זכר *remember* Lm 1$_{7}$, נתן *give* for food Lm 1$_{11(Kt)}$. <CSTR> כֹּל מַחֲמַדֶּיהָ *all her precious things* Lm 1$_{7}$.

⇨ חמד *desire,* מַחְמַד *desirable thing.*

מחמודיהם, see מַחְמֹד *precious thing.*

[מַחְמָל] 1 n.[m.] **compassion**—cstr. מַחְמַל—**(object of) compassion** or **longing,** <OBJ> חלל pi. *profane* Ezk 24$_{21}$ (or em.; see Cstr.; || מַחְמַד *desirable thing,* + בֵּן *son,* בַּת *daughter*). <CSTR> מַחְמַל נַפְשְׁכֶם *compassion of your soul* Ezk 24$_{21}$ (or em. מַחְמַד *desirable thing of*).

<SYN> מַחְמַד *desirable thing.**

⇨ חמל *spare.*

[מַחְמָם]* 0.0.0.1 pr.n.[m.] **Mahmam,** <PREP> לְ of possession, *(belonging) to, of* City of David Jar inscr.

מַחְמֶצֶת 2 n.f. **leavened thing,** sour-tasting, <OBJ> אכל *eat* Ex 12$_{19}$ (+ שְׂאֹר *leaven*) 12$_{20}$ (:: מַצָּה *unleavened bread*).

<ANT> מַצָּה *unleavened bread.**

⇨ חמץ I *be sour.*

[מַחֲנָה]* 1 n.f. **mantlet**—pl. מַחֲנוֹת—**mantlet,** shelter for besieging troops, <OBJ> נתן *give,* i.e. place Ezk 4$_{2}$ (unless from מַחֲנֶה *camp;* || דָּיֵק *siege wall,* מָצוֹר *siege enclosure,* כַּר *battering ram*).

<SYN> דָּיֵק *siege wall,* מָצוֹר *siege enclosure,* כַּר *battering ram.*

מַחֲנֶה 215.1.58 n.m.&f. **camp**—cstr. מַחֲנֵה (Q מחני); sf. מַחֲנֶיךָ* (מַחֲנֶךָ), מַחֲנֵהוּ, מַחֲנֵיכֶם, מַחֲנֵיהֶם; du. מַחֲנָיִם (Ca 7$_{1}$); pl. מַחֲנִים, מַחֲנוֹת (מַחֲנֹת); cstr. מַחֲנֹת, Q מחני; sf. Q מחנינו, Q מחניכם, מַחֲנֵיהֶם (Q מחניהמה), Q מחנותם—(fem. when in ref. to persons in a camp*).

1. camp, encampment, a. of Jacob (Gn 32$_{22}$).

b. of Israelites at exodus and on entry to land (Ex 16$_{13.13}$ 19$_{16.17}$ 29$_{14}$ 32$_{17.19.26.27}$ 33$_{7.7.7.11}$ 36$_{6}$ Lv 4$_{12.21}$ 6$_{4}$ 8$_{17}$ 9$_{11}$ 10$_{4.5}$ 13$_{46}$ 14$_{3.8}$ 16$_{26.27.28}$ 17$_{3.3}$ 24$_{10.14.23}$ Nm 4$_{5.15}$ 5$_{2.3.3.4}$ 10$_{2.34}$ 11$_{1+8t}$ 12$_{14.15}$ 13$_{19}$ (Sam מבחנים perh. from בחן *test;* Sam^{ms} מחבנים perh. from מַחֲבָן *fertile place*) 14$_{44}$ 15$_{35.36}$ 19$_{3.7.9}$ 31$_{12.13.19.24}$ Dt 2$_{14.15}$ 29$_{10}$ Jos 1$_{11}$ 3$_{2}$ 5$_{8}$ 6$_{11.11.14.18.23}$ 9$_{6}$ 10$_{6.15.43}$ 18$_{9}$ Ps 78$_{28}$ 106$_{16}$ 2QapMoses 1$_{4}$), of individual Israelite tribes (Nm 1$_{52}$ 2$_{3+10t}$ 10$_{5+6t}$ 4Q Shir^{b} 2.1$_{7}$.

c. in ref. to shrine at Shilo (Jg 21$_{8.12}$); tabernacle and temple as camp of Levites (1 C 9$_{18}$), as camp of Y. (1 C 9$_{19}$ 2 C 31$_{2}$; or em.; see Cstr.).

2. camp, in ref. to towns and settled communities, **a.** Jerusalem as 'the camp' (4QMMT B$_{28.28.30.30.31}$ [[מ]חנה]) B$_{58.60}$).

b. town(s) outside Jerusalem (4QMMT B$_{30.62}$ [[מ]חנות]).

c. community, settlement, as distinct from towns (CD 12$_{23}$; cf. 12$_{18}$), with specific set of rules (4QD^{a} 7.3$_{6}$ 11$_{17}$ 4QD^{b} 8$_{4}$ [[המ]חנה] 4QD^{e} 7.2$_{14}$ [[מ]חניהם] CD 7$_{6}$=19$_{2}$ 9$_{11}$ 10$_{23}$ 12$_{23}$ [המחנ[ו]ת] 13$_{4.5.7.13.13.16.20}$ 14$_{3.9}$ 15$_{14}$ 20$_{26}$; perh. also 1QSa 2$_{15}$ 4QTohA 1.1$_{6}$ 4QTohA 1.2$_{6}$ 4Q Rebukes 1.2$_{3}$ [[מחני]]).

d. of inhabitants of world (GnzPs 2$_{18}$).

3a. (military) camp, (place of) encampment (Ezk 4$_{2}$ [unless from מַחֲנָה *mantlet*] Zc 14$_{15}$ 1QM 6$_{10}$ 7$_{3}$ 7$_{7.7}$ 14$_{2}$ perh. 1Q31 2$_{3}$ 4QapMos^{b} 1.3$_{1}$ 4QM^{a} 1$_{9}$ 8.1$_{17}$ [[מחנות] 4QM^{b} 1$_{8.8}$), of Israelites (Dt 23$_{10+5t}$ Jos 10$_{21}$ 8$_{13}$ Jg 7$_{15}$ 1 S 4$_{3.5.6.6.7}$ 17$_{17}$ 26$_{6}$ 2 S 1$_{2.3}$ 1 K 16$_{16}$ 22$_{34}$||2 C 18$_{33}$ 2 K 3$_{24}$ Am 4$_{10}$ 2 C 22$_{1}$ [or em.; see Prep.]), Ammonites (1 S 11$_{11}$), Assyrians (2 K 19$_{35}$||Is 37$_{36}$||2 C 32$_{21}$ Si 48$_{21}$ [[מ]חנה]), Midianites (Jg 7$_{1+12t}$), Philistines (1 S 13$_{17}$ 14$_{15.19.21}$ 17$_{53}$ 2 S 23$_{16}$||1 C 11$_{18}$), Syrians (2 K 7$_{4+8t}$); in Herodium, during Bar-Kochba revolt (Mur 24 B$_{4}$ [[מחנ]ה] E$_{3}$ MurEpBeth-Mashiko$_{2}$).

3b. army, host, force(s), armed troop (distinction from §3a not alw. clear), Ezk 1$_{24}$ Ps 27$_{3}$ 1 C 12$_{23}$ 1QM 3$_{4.5.14}$ 7$_{1}$ 4QM^{a} 1$_{9.19}$, of Israelites (Ex 14$_{19.20}$ 1 S 28$_{19}$ 1 K 22$_{36}$ 2 K 3$_{9}$), Amorites (Jos 10$_{5}$), Canaanites (Jos 11$_{4}$ Jg 4$_{15.16.16}$), Egyptians (Ex 14$_{20.24.24}$), Kittim (1QM 16$_{3}$), Midianites (Jg 7$_{21.22.22}$ 8$_{10.10.11.11.12}$), Philistines (1 S 17$_{1.4.46}$ 28$_{1.1.5}$ 29$_{1.6}$ 2 S 5$_{24}$||1 C 14$_{15}$ 1 C 11$_{15}$ 14$_{16}$), Syrians

(2 K 6$_{24}$ 7$_{14}$).

4. camp, army, host of Y. (Gn 32$_3$ Jl 2$_{11}$ 1 C 12$_{23}$ 2 C 14$_{12}$ 1QM 4$_9$), gods (4QShirShabb^a 2$_2$ 4QShirShabb^f 20.2$_{13}$).

5. company, group of people (Gn 32$_{8.9.9.11}$ 33$_8$ 50$_9$ 2 K 5$_{15}$); perh. **line** of dancers (Ca 7$_1$).

<SUBJ> היה *be* Gn 32$_9$ 50$_9$ Dt 23$_{15}$ Jg 7$_{1.8}$ 8$_{11}$, שׁאר ni. *remain* Gn 32$_9$, חנה *encamp* Nm 10$_{5.6}$ Jos 10$_5$ Ps 27$_3$ 1 C 11$_{15}$, נסע *set out* Nm 4$_{5.15}$ 10$_{5.6}$, בוא *come* 1QM 7$_3$, יצא *go out* Jos 11$_4$ 1QM 7$_3$, עלה *go up* Jos 10$_5$, רוץ *run* Jg 7$_{21}$ (or em. וַיָּרֻץ *and they ran* to וַיִּקַץ *and they awoke*, i.e. קיץ hi.), נוס *flee* Jg 7$_{22}$, שׁוב *go back* 2 K 5$_{15}$ 1QM 7$_3$, אסף *gather* intrans. Jos 10$_5$, חרד hi. *disperse* intrans. Jg 8$_{12}$ (unless חרד I hi. *startle*), נפל *fall* Jg 4$_{14}$, לחם ni. *fight* 1 S 28$_1$, בטח *have confidence* Jg 8$_{11(mss)}$.

<NOM CL> מַחֲנֵה אֱלֹהִים זֶה *this is the camp of God* Gn 32$_3$, [י]רושלי[ם] מחנה היא *Jerusalem is the camp* 4QMMT B$_{30}$, ירושלים היאה מחנה הקדש *Jerusalem is the camp of holiness* 4QMMT B$_{60}$, הוא מחנה ערי[ה]ם *it is the encampment of their cities* 4QMMT B$_{30}$, רַב מְאֹד מַחֲנֵהוּ *his army is very great* Jl 2$_{11}$, מִי לְךָ כָּל־הַמַּחֲנֶה הַזֶּה *who is all this company to you?*, i.e. what do you mean by it? Gn 33$_8$, מַחֲנֵה הַלְוִיִּם בְּתוֹךְ הַמַּחֲנֹת *the camp of the Levites shall be in the middle of the camps* Nm 2$_{17}$, מַחֲנֵיהֶם עִמָּם *their army was with them* Jg 8$_{10}$, הַמַּחֲנֶה אֲשֶׁר מִצְּפוֹן לָעִיר *the camp that was to the north of the city* Jos 8$_{13}$.

<OBJ> ראה *see* 1 S 28$_5$, שׁמע hi. *cause to hear* 2 K 7$_6$, כתב *write* 1QM 4$_9$, אסף *gather* 1 S 17$_1$, קבץ *gather* 1 S 28$_1$ 29$_1$ 2 K 6$_{24}$, נכה hi. *strike* Gn 32$_9$ Jg 8$_{11}$ 1 C 14$_{15.16}$, פגשׁ *meet* Gn 33$_8$, המם *discomfit* Ex 14$_{24}$ Jg 4$_{15}$ perh. Si 48$_{21}$ ([מ]חנה), חרד hi. *startle* Jg 8$_{12}$ (unless חרד III *disperse*; or em. הֶחֱרִיד *he startled* to הִכְחִיד *he destroyed*, i.e. כחד hi.), כסה pi. *cover* Ex 16$_{13}$, נסע *break up* Nm 10$_2$ (לְמַסַּע אֶת־הַמַּחֲנוֹת *for breaking up the camps*), נתן *give* Jg 7$_{9.14.15}$ 1 S 28$_{19}$, i.e. place Ezk 4$_2$ (unless from מַחֲנֶה *mantlet*), שׂים *place* Jos 8$_{13}$, i.e. make, devoted object Jos 6$_{18}$, בזז *plunder* 2 K 7$_{16}$, שׁסס *plunder* 1 S 17$_{53}$, גאל pi. *defile* 4QTohA 1.1$_6$, טמא pi. *defile* Nm 5$_3$.

<CSTR> מַחֲנֵה י׳ *camp of Y.* 1 C 9$_{19}$, מַחֲנוֹת י׳ *camp(s) of Y.* 2 C 31$_2$ (or em. חַצְרוֹת *courts of*), מַחֲנֵה אֱלֹהִים *camp of God* Gn 32$_3$ 1 C 12$_{23}$, מחני אלוהים *camps of gods* 4QShirShabb^a 2$_2$ 4QShirShabb^f 20.2$_{13}$, אל *of God* 1QM 4$_9$, מַחֲנֵה יִשְׂרָאֵל *camp of Israel* Ex 14$_{19.20}$ Jos 6$_{18.23}$ 7$_{15}$ 1 S 28$_{19}$ 2 S 1$_3$ 2 K 3$_{24}$, [מ]חנות ישראל *camps of Israel* 4QMMT B$_{62}$, מַחֲנֵה הָעִבְרִים *camp of the Hebrews* 1 S 4$_6$, יְהוּדָה *of Judah* Nm 2$_{3.9}$, אֶפְרַיִם *of Ephraim* Nm 2$_{18.24}$ 10$_{22(mss)}$, דָּן *of Dan* Nm 2$_{25.31}$, רְאוּבֵן *of Reuben* Nm 2$_{10.16}$ 10$_{18}$, הַלְוִיִּם *of the Levites* Nm 2$_{17}$, אֲרָם *of the Aramaeans* 2 K 7$_{4+6t}$, אַשּׁוּר *of the Assyrians* 2 K 19$_{35}$||Is 37$_{36}$ Si 48$_{21}$ ([מ]חנה), מִדְיָן *of Midian* Jg 7$_{1.8.13.15}$, מִצְרַיִם *of Egypt* Ex 14$_{20.24.24}$, פְּלִשְׁתִּים *of the Philistines* 1 S 14$_{19}$ 17$_4$ (מַחֲנוֹת *armies of*) 17$_{46}$ 28$_5$ 2 S 5$_{24}$||1 C 14$_{15}$ 2 S 23$_{16}$|| 1 C 11$_{18}$ 1 C 11$_{15}$ 14$_{16}$, סִיסְרָא *of Sisera* Jg 4$_{14}$, מחני כתיים *camps of the Kittim* 1QM 16$_3$, בְּנֵי *of the sons of* Nm 10$_{14.18(mss).22.25}$ Jg 8$_{10}$, מַחֲנוֹת בְּנֵי *camps of the sons of* Levi 1 C 9$_{18}$, מַחֲנֵה מֶלֶךְ *camp of the king of* 2 C 32$_{21}$, מחני קדושיו *camps of his holy ones* 1QM 3$_5$, קדו[שי] *of the holy ones of* Israel 4QTohA 1.1$_6$, הרבים *of the many* 4QRebukes 1.2$_3$ ([מחני]), מחנה הקדש *camp of holiness*, i.e. holy camp 4QMMT B$_{58}$ (מחני הק[ו]דש) B$_{60}$, מחנה ערי[ה]ם *camp of their cities* 4QMMT B$_{30}$.

בני המחנה *sons*, i.e. members, *of the camp* CD 13$_{13}$, באי *ones who come into*, i.e. members of CD 13$_4$, רוב *multitude of* CD 15$_{14}$, יושב [מ]חניהם *inhabitant of their camps* 4QD^e 7.2$_{14}$, [יושבי] המחנות *inhabitants of the camps* 4QD^a 11$_{17}$, פֶּגֶר מַחֲנֶה *corpse of the army of* 1 S 17$_{46}$, פְּקוּדֵי הַמַּחֲנֹת *numbered ones of the camps* Nm 2$_{32}$, סורכי המחנות *commissioners of the camps* 1QM 7$_1$, רוש המחנה *head of the camp* MurEpBeth-Mashiko$_2$, ראשי המחנות *heads of the camps* 1QM 3$_{14}$, ראש [מ]חנות *head of the camps of* 4QMMT B$_{62}$, שרי *commanders of* 4QM^a 1$_{9.19}$, מאד המחנה *property of the camp* CD 9$_{11}$, מושב המחנות *assembly of the camps* CD 12$_{23}$ (המח[נו]ת) 13$_{20}$ 14$_3$ (כל המחנות), מְחֹלַת הַמַּחֲנָיִם perh. *dance of*, i.e. in, *two lines* Ca 7$_1$ (unless 'of Mahanaim'; or em. מַחֲנִים *of*, i.e. in, *the camp*), חצוצרות המחנות *trumpets of the camps* 1QM 3$_4$, קוֹל מַחֲנֶה *sound of an army* Ezk 1$_{24}$, בְּאֹשׁ מַחֲנֵיכֶם *stink of your camp* Am 4$_{10}$, שַׁעַר הַמַּחֲנֶה *gate of the camp* Ex 32$_{26}$, שַׁעֲרֵי מַחֲנוֹת *gates of the camp of* 2 C 31$_2$ (or em.; see above), קְצֵה הַמַּחֲנֶה *edge of the camp* Nm 11$_1$ Jg 7$_{17.19}$ 2 K 7$_8$, קְצֵה מַחֲנֵה *edge of the camp of* 2 K 7$_5$, ע[ב]ר המחנה *side of the camp* 1QM 6$_{10}$, [צ]פון *north(ern part) of* 4QMMT B$_{28}$, דֶּגֶל מַחֲנֵה

standard of the camp of Nm 2$_{3.10.18.25}$ 10$_{14.18.22.25}$.

כָּל־הַמַּחֲנֶה *all the camp* Gn 33$_{8}$ Jos 8$_{13}$ Jg 4$_{15}$ 7$_{14.18.21.22.22(mss)}$ 4QD^{a} 7.2$_{6}$ (כול), כָּל־מַחֲנֶה *all the camp of* Jg 4$_{14}$ 8$_{10}$(כֹּל) perh. 6QapSamKgs 23$_{2}$ ([מח]נה), כָּל־הַמַּחֲנֹת *all the camps* Nm 10$_{25}$ CD 14$_{3}$ (כל המחנות=4QD^{b} 9.5$_{13}$ [כו]ל מחנות) 14$_{9}$ (כל המחנות), כול מחני *all the camps of* 4QShirShabb^{a} 2$_{2}$ 4QShirShabb^{f} 20.2$_{13}$, כָּל־מַחֲנֵהוּ *all his camp* 2 K 5$_{15}$ 6$_{24}$, כָּל־מַחֲנֵיהֶם *all their camps* Jos 10$_{5}$ 1QM 7$_{7}$ (כול מחנהמה) 7$_{7}$ (כול מחניהם).

<APP> עַם *people* Jos 11$_{4}$, רֶכֶב *chariotry* Jos 11$_{4}$, סוּס *horse* Jos 11$_{4}$.

<ADJ> גָּדוֹל *great* 1 C 12$_{23}$, אֶחָד *one* Gn 32$_{9}$, זֶה *this* Gn 33$_{8}$, הֵמָּה *those* Zc 14$_{15}$.

<PREP> לְ of direction, *(in)to* 4QM^{b} 1$_{8}$, + בוא *come* 2 C 22$_{1}$ (or em. לַמִּלְחָמָה *to the battle*) 1QM 7$_{3}$, hi. *bring* 4QMMT B$_{58}$; חצה לְ *divide into* Gn 32$_{8}$.

לְ of benefit, *to, for,* + היה *be* 2 K 3$_{9}$; of possession, *(belonging) to, of* Nm 2$_{9.16.24.31}$ 1 C 9$_{18}$ CD 13$_{7.9}$ 14$_{9}$; introducing predicate, + היה *be* Gn 32$_{11}$; introducing object, + אסף pi. *act as rearguard of* Nm 10$_{25}$.

בְּ of place, *in(to), through, among* Ex 19$_{16}$ 32$_{17}$ Jg 7$_{11}$ 1 S 4$_{6}$ 14$_{19}$ 1QSa 2$_{15}$ 1Q31 2$_{3}$ perh. 4QD^{h} 4.1$_{8}$ ([במ]חניהם) 4QShirShabb^{f} 20.2$_{13}$ perh. 6QapSamKgs 23$_{2}$ (בכל [מח]נה) Mur 24 B$_{4}$ (במ[חנ]ה) E$_{3}$ CD 13$_{16}$, + היה *be* 1 S 14$_{15}$ Zc 14$_{15}$ 4QapMos^{b} 1.3$_{1}$ 4QTohA 1.2$_{6}$ CD 10$_{23}$, ישב *dwell* Nm 13$_{19}$, *remain* Jos 5$_{8}$, שׁאר ni. *remain* Nm 11$_{26}$, עמד *stand* CD 13$_{5}$, בוא *come* Jg 7$_{17.19}$ 1 S 29$_{6}$, יצא *go out* 1 S 28$_{1}$ 29$_{6}$, עלה *go up* 1 S 14$_{21}$, עבר *pass* Ex 32$_{27}$ 1 K 22$_{36}$, hi. *cause to pass* Ex 36$_{6}$, שׁוב *go back* Ex 32$_{27}$, שׂים *place* 4QShir^{b} 2.1$_{7}$ ([בש]נים עשר מחנות *in twelve camps*), הפך htp. *tumble* Jg 7$_{13}$, בקע *break through* 2 S 23$_{16}$||1 C 11$_{18}$, נכה hi. *strike* 2 K 19$_{35}$||Is 37$_{36}$, כחד hi. *destroy* 2 C 32$_{21}$, לין *spend the night* Gn 32$_{22}$ Jos 6$_{11}$, נבא htp. *prophesy* Nm 11$_{26.27}$, קנא pi. *be jealous* Ps 106$_{16}$, נצה ni. *strive* Lv 24$_{10}$, שׁחט *slaughter* Lv 17$_{3}$, מלך hi. *make king* 1 K 16$_{16}$, כבד ni. *be honoured* 4QShir Shabb^{a} 2$_{2}$.

בְּ *against,* + ירד *go down* Jg 7$_{9.11}$, שׂים *place* sword Jg 7$_{22}$; introducing object, + נכה hi. *strike* 2 S 5$_{24}$ Si 48$_{21}$ (Segal) ([ויך במ]חנה).

כְּ *as* 1 C 12$_{23}$.

מִן of direction, *from,* + בוא *come* 2 S 1$_{2}$, יצא *go out* 1 S 13$_{17}$ 17$_{4}$ 2 K 7$_{12}$, hi. *bring out* Ex 19$_{17}$ 1 K 22$_{34}$||2 C 18$_{33}$, נסע *set out* Nm 10$_{34}$, רחק hi. *make distant* Ex 33$_{7}$, שׁלח pi. *send* Nm 5$_{2}$, מלט ni. *escape* 2 S 1$_{3}$; partitive, *from (among),* + יתר ni. *remain* Jg 8$_{10}$.

אֶל *(in)to,* + הלך *go* Jos 9$_{6}$, בוא *come* Gn 32$_{9}$ Lv 14$_{8}$ 16$_{26.28}$ Nm 19$_{7}$ 31$_{24}$ Dt 23$_{12(ms, Sam)}$ Jos 18$_{9}$ Jg 21$_{8}$ 1 S 4$_{3.5.6.7}$ 2 K 3$_{24}$ 7$_{5.10}$, hi. *bring* Nm 31$_{12}$ Jg 21$_{12}$, ירד *go down* Jg 7$_{10}$ 1 S 26$_{6}$, קרב *draw near* Ex 32$_{19}$, שׁוב *go back* Ex 33$_{11}$ Jos 10$_{15.21}$ (or del.) 10$_{43}$ Jg 7$_{15}$ 4QM^{a} 8.1$_{17}$ ([מחנות]), אסף ni. *gather* intrans. Nm 11$_{30}$, שׁלח *send* Jos 10$_{6}$, שׁקף hi. *look down* Ex 14$_{24}$, נפל *fall* 2 K 7$_{4}$.

עַל *upon, over,* + ירד *go down* Nm 11$_{9}$, שׁקף hi. *look down* Ex 14$_{24(Sam)}$, נטשׁ *leave* Nm 11$_{30}$; *according to, by,* + חנה *encamp* Nm 1$_{52}$; *in charge of* 1 C 9$_{19}$ 4QD^{a} 7.3$_{6}$ 4QD^{b} 8$_{4}$ ([המ]חנה).

חוּצָה לְ *outside* 4QMMT B$_{30}$.

חוּץ מִן *outside* 4QMMT B$_{31}$ (חוץ ממ[חנה]).

אֶל־מִחוּץ *(to) outside,* + יצא *go out* Lv 14$_{3}$, hi. *bring out* Lv 4$_{12.21}$ 6$_{4}$, נשׂא *carry* Lv 10$_{4.5}$.

מִחוּץ לְ *outside* Ex 33$_{7}$ 13$_{46}$, + היה *be* Dt 23$_{13}$, חנה *encamp* Nm 31$_{19}$, יצא *go out* 4QM^{a} 1$_{9}$ ([י]צאו), שׂרף *burn* Ex 29$_{14}$ Lv 8$_{17}$ 9$_{11}$, נוח hi. *place* Nm 19$_{9}$ Jos 6$_{23}$, נטה *pitch* tent Ex 33$_{7}$, שׁחט *slaughter* Lv 17$_{3}$ 4QMMT B$_{28}$ ([ישחט]), רגם *stone* Nm 15$_{35}$, סגר ni. *be shut up* Nm 12$_{14.15}$.

אֶל־מִחוּץ לְ *(to) outside,* + יצא *go out* Nm 31$_{13}$ Dt 23$_{11}$ 2QapMoses 1$_{4}$ (ויצא ... מחו[ץ]), hi. *bring* Lv 16$_{27}$ 24$_{14.23}$ Nm 15$_{36}$ 19$_{3}$, שׁלח pi. *send* Nm 5$_{3.4}$, רגם *stone* Nm 15$_{35(mss)}$.

בְּתוֹךְ *among, in the middle of* Nm 2$_{17}$, + בוא *come* 1 S 11$_{11}$, גדל pi. *magnify* glory GnzPs 2$_{18}$.

אֶל־תּוֹךְ *within,* + בוא *come* Dt 23$_{11.12}$.

בְּקֶרֶב *within* Dt 29$_{10}$, + הלך htp. *go* Dt 23$_{15}$, עבר *pass* Jos 1$_{11}$ 3$_{2}$, נפל hi. *cause to fall* Ps 78$_{28}$.

מִקֶּרֶב *from (within),* + מושׁ *depart* Nm 14$_{44}$, המם *discomfit* Dt 2$_{15}$, תמם *come to an end* Dt 2$_{14}$, כרת ni. *be cut off* CD 20$_{26}$.

בֵּין *between,* + היה *be* 1QM 7$_{7}$, בוא *come* Ex 14$_{20.20}$.

לִפְנֵי *before,* + הלך *go* Ex 14$_{19}$, שׁבר ni. *be broken* 2 C 14$_{12}$.

נֶגֶד *before,* + עמד *stand* 1QM 16$_{3}$.

אַחֲרֵי *after,* + רדף *pursue* Jg 4$_{16}$, שׁלח *send* 2 K 7$_{14}$.

עַד לְ *unto (the point of being),* + בוא *come* 1 C 12$_{23}$.

סְבִיבוֹת *round about* Nm 11_{31}, + ראה ni. *be seen* 1QM 7_{7}, שׁטח *spread out* Nm 11_{32}, תקע *sound* trumpet Jg 7_{18}.

סָבִיב לְ *round about*, + היה *be* Ex 16_{13}, עמד *stand* Jg 7_{21}.

הַמַּחֲנֶה without preposition, *in, to the camp*, + בוא *come* Jos 6_{11} 1QM 14_{2}, שׁוב *return* Jos 6_{14}, רוץ hi. *bring quickly* 1 S 17_{17}, עזב *leave* 2 K 7_{7} (lacking in mss), ישׁב *dwell* CD7_{6}=19_{2} (מחנות), אסף ni. *gather* intrans. 4QM^{b} 1_{8}.

<COLL> מַחֲנֶה ‖ דֶּגֶל *standard* Nm 1_{52} 1QM 4_{9}, צָבָא *host* 1QM 4_{9}, עֵדָה *congregation* 1QM 4_{9}, קָהָל *assembly* 1QM 4_{9}, קָרִיא *one called* 1QM 4_{9}, שֵׁבֶט *tribe* 1QM 4_{9}, מִשְׁפָּחָה *clan* 1QM 4_{9}, רֶכֶב *chariotry* Jg $4_{15.16}$, דָּיֵק *siege wall* Ezk 4_{2}, מָצוֹר *siege enclosure* Ezk 4_{2}, כַּר *battering ram* Ezk 4_{2}, מַסָּע *journey* 1QSa 2_{15}.

+ דֶּגֶל *standard* Nm 2_{31}, צָבָא *host* Nm 1_{52} 2_{3+7t} $10_{14.18.22.25}$, חַיִל *army* Jl 2_{11}, בְּהֵמָה *beast* 2 K 3_{9}.

:: מִבְצָר *fortification* Nm 13_{19}.

שְׁנֵי מַחֲנוֹת *two companies* Gn $32_{8.11}$, [שׁ]נים עשר מחנות *twelve camps* 4QShir^{b} 2.1_{7}; כִּי־תֵצֵא מַחֲנֶה *when you go out as an army* Dt 23_{10}, במחנה שיושב *in the camp in which he resided* Mur 24 B_{4} (במחנ[ה]) E_{3}.

Also 1QM 10_{1} 19_{9} (המח[נה]) 4QpsEzek^{e} 16_{1} 4QNarrG 1_{2} 4QShir^{b} 25_{1}.

<SYN> דֶּגֶל *standard*, צָבָא *host*, עֵדָה *congregation*, קָהָל *assembly*, קָרִיא *one called*, שֵׁבֶט *tribe*, מִשְׁפָּחָה *clan*, רֶכֶב *chariotry*, דָּיֵק *siege wall*, מָצוֹר *siege enclosure*, כַּר *battering ram*, מַסָּע *journey*.

<ANT> מִבְצָר *fortification* Nm 13_{19}.

⇨ חנה *encamp*, מַחֲנַיִם *Mahanaim*, מַחֲנֵי־דָן *Mahaneh-dan*.

מַחֲנֵה־דָן 2 pl.n. **Mahaneh-dan, 1.** near Kiriath-jearim, <PREP> לְ introducing object, + קרא *call*, i.e. name Jg 18_{12}.

2. between Zorah and Eshtaol, <PREP> בְּ of place, *in*, + פעם pi. *stir* Jg 13_{25}. <COLL> מַחֲנֵה־דָן בֵּין צָרְעָה וּבֵין אֶשְׁתָּאֹל *Mahaneh-dan, between Zorah and Eshtaol* Jg 13_{25}.

⇨ מַחֲנֶה *camp* + דָּן II *Dan*.

מַחֲנַיִם I 13 pl.n. **Mahanaim**—מַחֲנָיִם; + ה- of direction מַחֲנַיְמָה—city in Gilead, on the R. Jabbok, prob. T. ed-Dhahab el-Garbi, c. 45 km NNE of Dead Sea, <SUBJ> היה *be* Jos 13_{30} (if em.; see Prep.; + גְּבוּל *terrritory*). <OBJ> קרא *call*, i.e. name Gn 32_{3}, נתן *give* Jos 21_{38} 1 C 6_{65} (both + מִגְרָשׁ *land outside city walls*). <CSTR> מְחֹלַת הַמַּחֲנָיִם perh. *dance of Mahanaim* Ca 7_{1} (but prob. *of*, i.e. in, *two lines*, from מַחֲנֶה *camp*). <APP> עִיר *city* Jos 21_{38}. <PREP> בְּ of place, *in* 2 S 19_{33}; מִן of direction, *from* Jos 13_{26}, + היה *be* Jos 13_{30} (or del. prep.), יצא *go out* 2 S 2_{12}; מַחֲנַיִם + ה- of direction, *in, to Mahanaim* 1 K 4_{14}, + בוא *come* 2 S $17_{24.27}$; without prep. or ה- of direction, *to Mahanaim*, + הלך *go* 1 K 2_{8}, בוא *come* 2 S 2_{29}, עבר hi. *bring across* 2 S 2_{8}.*

⇨ חנה *encamp*, מַחֲנֶה *camp*.

*[**מַחֲנַיִם**] **II** 0.0.2 pr.n.m. **Mahanaim,** father of Jonathan, <CSTR> בן מחנים *son of Mahanaim* 5/6ḤevBA $44_{6.18}$.

⇨ חנה *encamp*, מַחֲנֶה *camp*.

[**מַחֲנִי**] gent. **Mahanite,** belonging to Mahanaim, <NOM CL> גִּבּוֹרֵי הַחֲיָלִים ... אֱלִיאֵל הַמַּחֲנִי *the mighty ones of valour were ... Eliel the Mahanite* 1 C 11_{46} (if em. הַמַּחֲוִים *the Mahavite*). <APP> אֱלִיאֵל *Eliel* 1 C 11_{46} (if em.; see Nom. Cl.).

⇨ מַחֲנַיִם *Mahanaim*.

[**מַחֲנַיְמִי**] gent. **Mahanaimite,** belonging to Mahanaim, <NOM CL> גִּבּוֹרֵי הַחֲיָלִים ... אֱלִיאֵל הַמַּחֲנַיְמִי *the mighty ones of valour were ... Eliel the Mahanaimite* 1 C 11_{46} (if em. הַמַּחֲוִים *the Mahavite*). <APP> אֱלִיאֵל *Eliel* 1 C 11_{46} (if em.; see Nom. Cl.).

⇨ מַחֲנַיִם *Mahanaim*.

מַחֲנָק 1 n.[m.] **strangling—1. strangling** (unless §2), <OBJ> בחר *choose* Jb 7_{15}. <APP> מָוֶת *death* Jb 7_{15}.

2. strangler,* an epithet of the death-god (unless §1), <SUBJ> בחר tqtl *choose* neck Jb 7_{15} (וַתִּבְחַר מַחֲנָק נַפְשִׁי מָוֶת מֵעַצְמוֹתָי *and the Strangler has chosen my neck, Death my bones*). <APP> מָוֶת *death* Jb 7_{15}.

⇨ חנק *strangle*.

מַחְסֶה 20.0.3 n.m. **shelter**—מַחֲסֶה; cstr. מַחְסֵה (Q מחסי); sf. מַחְסִי (מַחְסִי), מַחְסֵנוּ, מַחְסֵהוּ, Q מחסיהם—**(place of) shelter,** prob. not **refuge** (מָנוֹס or מָעוֹז),* **a.** for humans, from rain and storm (Is 4_{6} 25_{4} Jb 24_{8}).

b. rocks as shelter for animals (Ps 104_{18}).

c. Y. as shelter (Is 25_{4} Jr 17_{17} Jl 4_{16} Ps 14_{6} 46_{2} 61_{4} $62_{8.9}$ 71_{7} 73_{28} $91_{2.9}$ 94_{22} 142_{6} Pr 14_{26} 11QPsAp[a] 6_{9} [[מח]סך] Mur 6 1_{3}).

d. lies (Is $28_{15.17}$), the flesh (1QH 7_{17}) as shelter.

<SUBJ> היה *be* Is 25_{4} Ps 61_{4} Pr 14_{26}. <NOM CL> סְלָעִים מַחְסֶה לַשְׁפַנִּים *the rocks are a shelter for the rock badgers* Ps 104_{18}, אַתָּה מַחְסִי *you are my shelter* Ps 71_{7} 142_{6}, vars. Jr 17_{17} Ps 91_{9} (or em. מַחְסֶךָ Y. *is your shelter*), י׳ מַחְסֶה לְעַמּוֹ *Y. is a shelter for his people* Jl 4_{16}, ׳׳ מַחְסֵהוּ *Y. is his shelter* Ps 14_{6}, אֱלֹהִים מַחֲסֶה־לָּנוּ *God is a shelter for us* Ps 62_{9}, var. Ps 46_{2}, מַחְסִי בֵּאלֹהִים *my shelter is in God* Ps 62_{8} (or em. חֲסוּ *take shelter*), מחסי בשר אין לי *I do not have shelter of, i.e. in, the flesh* 1QH 7_{17}.

<OBJ> שׂים *place*, i.e. make (into) Is 28_{15}, שׁית *place* Ps 73_{28}, יעה *sweep together* Is 28_{17}, קרא *call* 11QPsAp[a] 6_{9} ([קר]את מח[סך]), הלל pi. *praise* Mur 6 1_{3} ([ה]לל). <CSTR> מחסי עליון *shelter of, i.e. in, the Most High* Mur 6 1_{3}, בשר *of the flesh* 1QH 7_{17}, מַחְסֵה כָזָב *shelter of lies* Is 28_{17}; צוּר מַחְסִי *rock of my shelter* Ps 94_{22}. <APP> עֹז *strength* Ps 71_{7} (מַחֲסִי־עֹז *my shelter, strength,* i.e. my strong shelter), מָעוֹז *stronghold* Is 25_{4}, מִגְדָּל *tower* Ps 61_{4}, חֵלֶק *portion* Ps 142_{6}, אֱלֹהִים *God* Ps 91_{2}. <PREP> לְ *as*, or introducing predicate, + היה *be* Is 4_{6}.

<COLL> || מִסְתּוֹר *shelter* Is 4_{6}, עֹז *strength* Ps 46_{2} (מַחֲסֶה וָעֹז), צֵל *shade* Is 4_{6} (+) 25_{4}, מְצוּדָה *fortress* Ps 91_{2}, מָעוֹז *stronghold* Jl 4_{16}; + סֵתֶר *shelter* Is 28_{17}, סֻכָּה *pavilion* Is 4_{6}, מִשְׂגָּב *stronghold* Ps 94_{22}, עֶזְרָה *help* Ps 46_{2}, מִבְטָח *confidence* Pr 14_{26}, צוּר *rock* Ps 62_{8}; מַחְסֶה as vocative, Ps 91_{2}; מִבְּלִי מַחְסֶה חִבְּקוּ־צוּר *for lack of shelter they embrace the rock* Jb 24_{8}.

<SYN> מִסְתּוֹר *shelter*, צֵל *shade*, עֹז *strength*, מְצוּדָה *fortress*, מָעוֹז *stronghold.*

Also 1QM 15_{10}.*

⇒ חסה *seek shelter*, מַחְסֵיָה *Mahseiah.*

מַחְסוֹם 1 n.[m.] **muzzle,** for mouth of psalmist, <OBJ> שׁמר *keep* Ps 39_{2} (or em. אֶשְׁמְרָה *I will keep* to אָשִׂימָה *I will place*).

⇒ חסם *stop up.*

מַחְסוֹר 13.1.22 n.[m.] **lack**—cstr. מַחְסוֹר; sf. מַחְסוֹרְךָ (מַחְסֹרְךָ, Q מחסורכה), מַחְסֹרוֹ, Q מחסורמה; pl. cstr. Q מחסורי; sf. מַחְסֹרֶיךָ—**lack, want, need, thing needed** (e.g. Jg 19_{20} 4Q416 2.3_{2} 4Q418 127_{1}), <SUBJ> בוא *come* Pr 6_{11}=24_{34}. <NOM CL> אֵין מַחְסוֹר *there is no lack* Ps 34_{10} Pr 28_{27} 1QH 15_{16}, var. Jg 18_{7} (if em.; see Cstr.) 18_{10} 19_{19} Si 40_{26}, כָּל־מַחְסוֹרְךָ עָלָי *all your need is upon me,* i.e. it is for me to provide Jg 19_{20}. <OBJ> חסר *need* Dt 15_{8}, מצא *find* 4Q416 2.3_{2} 4Q418 127_{1}, לקח *take* 4Q418 97_{2} ([מ]חסורכה), יצא hi. *bring out* 4Q418 81_{18}. <CSTR> מַחְסוֹר כָּל־דָּבָר *lack of anything* Jg 18_{7} (if em. אֵין־מַכְלִים דָּבָר *there was no one causing humiliation*) 18_{18} 19_{19}, מחסור צבאם *lack of their host* 4Q416 1_{6} 4Q418 132_{2} ([מחסו]ר), מחסור אוטו *need of his storehouse* 4Q418 126.2_{13}, מחסורי *needs of* 4Q417 1.2_{3}; אִישׁ מַחְסוֹר *man of need* Pr 21_{17} (+ לֹא יַעֲשִׁיר *he will not be rich*), הון מחסורכה perh. *wealth of your need* 4Q417 1.1_{19}, דֵּי מַחְסֹרוֹ *sufficiency of,* i.e. for, *his need* Dt 15_{8}, כָּל־מַחְסוֹרְךָ *all your need* Jg 19_{20}, כול מחסורי *all the needs of* 4Q417 1.2_{3}.

<PREP> לְ of direction. *to* Pr 11_{24} 14_{23} 21_{5} 22_{16} (all four אַךְ לְמַחְסוֹר *[it tends] only to want*), נשׂג hi. *reach*, i.e. be sufficient for 4Q418 126.2_{13}; of benefit, *to, for* perh. 4Q416 1_{4} ([למח]סור) perh. 4Q418 107_{3} perh. 159.2_{5} ([למח]סור), + לוה ni. *borrow* 4Q417 1.1_{21}, לקח *take* 4Q $424\,1_{8}$; בְּ *in, with,* + כבד htp. *glorify oneself* 4Q416 2.2_{20}, קפץ *close* hand 4Q417 1.1_{24} (=4Q418 7_{9} קבץ pi. *gather*) 4Q418 88_{5}; introducing object, + בין hi. *understand* perh. 4Q418 122.1_{5}; לְפִי *according to* 4Q416 1_{6}. <COLL> רֵישׁ || מַחְסוֹר *poverty* Pr 6_{11}=24_{34}; :: מוֹתָר *abundance* Pr 14_{23} 21_{5} 4Q417 1.1_{17}; שלום עד ואין מחסור *peace until [and] there is no lack,* i.e. unfailing peace 1QH 15_{16}.

Also 4QMyst[a] 65_{3} ([מ]חסור) 4Q415 9_{10} 4Q418 16_{3} ([מ]חסורכה) 87_{6} 122.1_{7} 279_{3} 4Q423 12_{1}.

<SYN> רֵישׁ *poverty.*

<ANT> מוֹתָר *abundance.*

⇒ חסר *lack.*

מַחְסֵיָה 2.0.0.10 pr.n.m. **Mahseiah**—I מחסיהו—**1.** father of Neriah, grandfather of Baruch and Seraiah, <CSTR> בֶּן־מַחְסֵיָה *son of Mahseiah* Jr 32_{12} 51_{59}.

2. Arad ost. 23_5, <APP> בֵּן *son* Arad ost. 23_5 ([מחסן]יהו).

3. father of Ishmael, <CSTR> [ב]ן מחסי[הו] *son of Mahseiah* Seal 580 (T. Beit Mirsim?, 7th/6th cent.).

4. appar. son of Elijah, <PREP> לְ of possession, *of, (belonging) to* Seal 585 (T. Beit Mirsim?, 7th/6th cent.).

5. son of Pelatiah, <APP> בֵּן *son* Seal 586 (מח[סי]הו; T. Beit Mirsim?, 7th/6th cent.). <PREP> לְ of possession, *of, (belonging) to* Seal 586 (למח[סי]הו; T. Beit Mirsim?, 7th/6th cent.).

6. appar. father of Shemaiah, Seal 814 (מחסי[הו]; City of David, 7th/6th cent.).

7. appar. son of Nabi, לְ of possession, *of, (belonging) to* Seal 886 (7th cent.).

8. Samaria-Sebaste ost. 1012_1 (מח[סיו]; others [ ]שחן).

9. appar. father of Shebaniah, Bulla D85.

10. father of Jekamiah, <CSTR> בן מחסן[יהו] *son of Mahseiah* Ost. DH79_4.

11. son of Joshua, <APP> בֵּן *son* Bulla DH59.

⇒ מַחְסֶה *refuge* + יְ *Y*.

מחסיהו, see מַחְסֵיָה *Mahseiah*.

*[מְחַפֵּשׂ] n.m. **investigator,** as divine appellative, <SUBJ> חפשׂ *search* Ps 64_7 (if em. חָפֵשׂ מְחַפֵּשׂ וְקֶרֶב אִישׁ appar. *a plot is devised and the mind of a man* to חָפֵשׂ מְחַפֵּשׂ קֶרֶב אִישׁ *the Investigator will search the mind of a man*).

⇒ חפשׂ *search*.

מחץ I 15.1.2.1 vb. **strike through**—**Qal** 14 Pf. מָחַץ, מָחַצְתִּי, מָחֲצָה; impf. יִמְחַץ (יִמְחָץ), 2ms תִּמְחַץ, אֶמְחָצֵם; + waw וָאֶמְחָצֵם, וּמָחֲצָה, וּמָחַץ; impv. מְחַץ; ptc. 1QIsa^a מחצת—**strike through, wound, crush, shatter,** perh. **plunge into** (Ps 68_{24}),* <SUBJ> Y. Dt 32_{39} (|| מות hi. *kill*, :: רפא *heal*) 33_{11} Hb 3_{13} Ps 68_{22} $110_{5.6}$ Jb 5_{18} (|| כאב hi. *hurt*; :: רפא) 26_{12} Si 32_{22} 1QM 12_{11}, Israel(ites) Nm 24_8, Jael Jg 5_{26} (+ הלם *hammer*, מחק *crush*), אִשָּׁה *wife* Jg 5_{26}, worshipper 2 S 22_{39}||Ps 18_{39} (2 S|| כלה pi. *destroy*), perh. אֹיֵב *enemy* Ps 68_{24} (unless מחץ II *dip* or III *run*; or em.; see Prep.), עֹשֶׂה ptc. *one who does* valiantly 1QM 12_{11}, זְרוֹעַ *arm* of Y. Is $51_{9(1QIsa^a)}$ (MT חצב hi. *hew in pieces*; || חלל po. *pierce*), רֶגֶל *foot* Ps 68_{24} (if em.; see Prep.), כּוֹכָב *star* Nm 24_{17}=1QM 11_6, שֵׁבֶט *sceptre* Nm 24_{17}=1QM 11_6 (|| קרר pilp. *tear down*).

<OBJ> רַהַב *Rahab* Is $51_{9(1QIsa^a)}$ (MT חצב hi. *hew in pieces*) Jb 26_{12}, מֶלֶךְ *king* Ps 110_5, גּוֹי *nation* 1QM 12_{11}, אֹיֵב *enemy* 2 S 22_{39}||Ps 18_{39}, צַר *enemy* 1QM 12_{11}, לֹחֵץ *oppressor* Nm 24_8 (if em.; see Coll.), רֹאשׁ *head* Hb 3_{13} Ps 68_{22} 110_6, קָדְקֹד *crown* Ps 68_{22}, פֵּאָה *corner*, i.e. temple of head Nm 24_{17}=1QM 11_6, זְרוֹעַ *arm* Ḥorvat ʿUzza bowl inscr.$_{11}$, חֲלָצַיִם *loins* Nm 24_8 (if em.; see Coll.), מָתְנַיִם *loins* Dt 33_{11} Si 32_{22}, בַּד *limb* Ps 68_{24} (if em.; see Prep.), רֶגֶל *foot* Ps 68_{24} (or em.; see Prep.).

<PREP> בְּ of place, *in*, + דָּם *blood* Ps 68_{24} (unless מחץ II *dip* or III *run*; or em. תִּמְחַץ to תִּרְחַץ *you will wash*, or תִּמְצַח *it will tread*; or em. בְּדָם to בַּדָּם *their limbs*, as obj. of מחץ);* of time, *in*, + יוֹם *day* Ps 110_5; of instrument, *by (means of), with*, + תְּבוּנָה *understanding* Jb 26_{12}; עַל *upon*, + אֶרֶץ *earth* Ps 110_6; מִפְּנֵי *from before* appar. Si $32_{22(Bmg)}$.

<COLL> חִצָּיו יִמְחָץ *he will strike them through with his arrows* Nm 24_8 (or em. חִצָּיו to חֲלָצָיו *his loins*, or לֹחֲצָיו *his oppressors*).

<SYN> מות hi. *kill*, כאב hi. *hurt*, חלל po. *pierce*, כלה pi. *destroy*, קרר pilp. *tear down*.

<ANT> רפא *heal*.*

⇒ מַחַץ *wound*.

*מחץ II 1 vb. **dip** (unless מחץ I *strike through* or III *run*)—**Qal** 1 Impf. 2ms תִּמְחַץ—**dip,** <SUBJ> perh. אֹיֵב *enemy* Ps 68_{24}. <OBJ> רֶגֶל *foot* Ps 68_{24}. <PREP> בְּ of place, *in*, + דָּם *blood* Ps 68_{24} (לְמַעַן תִּמְחַץ רַגְלְךָ בְּדָם *in order that you may dip your foot in blood*).

*מחץ III 1 vb. **run** (unless מחץ I *strike through* or II *dip*)—**Qal** 1 Impf. 3fs תִּמְחַץ—<SUBJ> רֶגֶל *foot* Ps 68_{24}. <PREP> בְּ *to*, + דָּם *blood* Ps 68_{24}.

[מַחַץ] 1.0.1 n.[m.] **wound**—cstr. מַחַץ—<SUBJ> אנשׁ pass. *be incurable* Jb 34_6 (if em. חִצִּי *my arrow[-wound]* to מַחֲצִי *my wound*). <OBJ> רפא *heal* Is 30_{26} (+ שֶׁבֶר *breach*).

<CSTR> מַחַץ מַכָּתוֹ *wound of,* i.e. from, *his blow* Is 30_{26}, מחץ מכתי *wound of,* i.e. from, *my blow* 1QH 9_{27} (מ[חץ]) 4QHod^f 3_3. <PREP> לְ of direction, *to,* + נתן *give* 1QH 9_{27} (ותתן ... מ[חץ]).
⇒ מחץ I *strike through.*

*מחצב vb. **smite—Qal** הֲלוֹא אַתְּ־הִיא הַמַּחְצֶבֶת רַהַב *was it not you who smote Rahab?* Is 51_9 (if em. הַמַּחְצֶבֶת *who hewed*).

מַחְצֵב 3 n.[m.] **hewing,** <CSTR> אַבְנֵי מַחְצֵב *stones of hewing,* i.e. hewn stone 2 K 12_{13} 22_6||2 C 34_{11}.*
⇒ חצב I *hew.*

מֶחֱצָה 2 n.f. **half**—cstr. מֶחֱצַת—<SUBJ> היה *be* Nm $31_{36.43}$. <CSTR> מֶחֱצַת הָעֵדָה *half of,* i.e. belonging to, *the congregation* Nm 31_{43}. <APP> חֵלֶק *portion* Nm 31_{36}.
⇒ חצה I *divide.*

[מַחֲצִית] 16.0.14 n.f. **half**—cstr. מַחֲצִית (מַחֲצַת); sf. מַחֲצִיתוֹ, מַחֲצִיתָהּ, מַחֲצִיתָם—**1. half,** <SUBJ> היה *be* Nm 31_{43} (Sam), כרת ni. *be cut off* 11QT 58_{11}. <NOM CL> כֶּסֶף פְּקוּדֵי הָעֵדָה ... מַחֲצִית הַשֶּׁקֶל *the silver of the mustered ones of the congregation was ... half a shekel* Nm 38_{26}, [מ]חצית [השקל מעה שתים] עשרה *half a shekel is (equivalent to) one hundred and twelve obolos coins* 4QOrd^b 2.1_2, [מ]חצית ההין לפר האחד *half a hin is for one bull* 11QT 14_{14}. <OBJ> נתן *give* Ex $30_{13.13}$ (lacking in Sam) 11QT 39_8 ([ו]נתן), לקח *take* Ex 30_{23}, נשׂא *take* 11QT 39_{10}, חצה *divide* 11QT 58_{14}, קרב hi. *bring near,* i.e. offer Lv $6_{13.13}$ 11QT 21_{15}, שׁלח *send* 11QT 58_{10}, ענשׁ ni. *be punished with* 4QSD $1.1_{5.8.10}$ (ונענש במה את מחצית לחמו *and he shall be punished in them with half of his bread,* i.e. half rations).

<CSTR> מחצית העם *half of the people* 11QT $58_{10.11}$, מַחֲצִית בְּנֵי *half of,* i.e. belonging to, *the sons of* Israel Nm 31_{30} (מֶחֱצַת) $31_{42.47}$ (מֶחֱצַת), הָעֵדָה *of,* i.e. belonging to, *the congregation* Nm 31_{43}(Sam) (MT מֶחֱצַת *half of*), מַטֵּה *of the tribe of* Manasseh Jos 21_{25} 1 C $6_{46.55}$, הָרֶכֶב *of the chariots* 1 K 16_9, מחצית לחמו *half of his bread,* i.e. half rations 4QSD $1.1_{5.8.10}$, מַחֲצִית הַשֶּׁקֶל *half a shekel* Ex $30_{13.13.15}$ 38_{26} 4QOrd^b 2.1_2 ([מ]חצית [השקל]) 11QT $39_{8.10}$ ([השׁ]ק[ל]), מחצית ההין *half a hin* 11QT $14_{14.14}$ ([מ]חצית ההי[ן]) 21_{15} 11QT^b 5_{20}, השׁאר *of the remainder* 11QT 58_{14}; שַׂר מַחֲצִית *commander of half of* the chariots 1 K 16_9.

<APP> אִישׁ *man* 11QT 58_{10}, תְּרוּמָה *offering* Ex 30_{13}, קָרְבָּן *offering* Lv $6_{13.13}$, מִנְחָה *grain offering* Lv $6_{13.13}$, קִנְּמָן־בֶּשֶׂם *cinnamon of spice* Ex 30_{23}, בֶּקַע *half a shekel* Ex 38_{26}, יַיִן *wine* 11QT 14_{14} ([מ]חצית), שֶׁמֶן *oil* 11QT 21_{15}. <PREP> בְּ of accompaniment, *in(to), with,* + בלל pass. *be mixed* 11QT 14_{14} ([ב]לולה); מִן of direction, *from,* + מעט hi. *diminish,* i.e. give less than Ex 30_{15}, לקח *take* Nm $31_{29.30.42.47}$; partitive, *from among, (some) of* 1 C 6_{46}, + נתן *give* Jos 21_{25} 1 C 6_{55}.

2. middle, <CSTR> מַחֲצִית הַיּוֹם *middle of the day* Ne 8_3, מחצית השמים *middle of the heavens* 4QMishA 1.1_2. <PREP> בְּ of place, *in,* + אור hi. *shine* 4QMishA 1.1_2 ([ב]מחצית); עַד *until,* + קרא *read* Ne 8_3 (+ מִן־הָאוֹר *from dawn*).

Also 4QSela 4_2 11QT 4_{15}.
⇒ חצה I *divide.*

מחק 1 vb. **crush—Qal** 1 Pf. מָחֲקָה—**crush,** <SUBJ> Jael Jg 5_{26} (+ הלם *hammer,* מחץ *shatter*), אִשָּׁה *wife* Jg 5_{26}. <OBJ> ראשׁ *head* Jg 5_{26}.
⇒ cf. מחץ *strike through, shatter.*

מְחֹקֵק *commander, sceptre,* see חקק *engrave,* Po.*

*[מְחֹקְקָה] n.f. **decree** of ruler, <PREP> בְּ of accompaniment, *in, with* Si 44_4(M) (במחקק[תם]; B במחקרותם *with their searching out*).

[מֶחְקָר] 1.0.1 n.[m.] **searching**—cstr. Q מחקר; pl. cstr. מֶחְקְרֵי—**1. depth,** or **recess,*** as place to be searched out, <NOM CL> בְּיָדוֹ מֶחְקְרֵי־אָרֶץ *in his hand are the depths of the earth* Ps 95_4 (ms מֶרְחַקֵּי *far places of;** + תּוֹעֲפֹה *peak of mountains*). <CSTR> מֶחְקְרֵי־אָרֶץ *depths of the earth* Ps 95_4 (ms מֶרְחַקֵּי *far places of*).

2. searching out, study, <CSTR> מחקר צדק *study of righteousness* 4QWays^a $1a.2_3$. <PREP> בְּ of instrument, *by (means of), with,* + מצא *find* 4QWays^a $1a.2_3$.*
⇒ חקר I *search.*

*[מַחְקֶרֶת] 0.1 n.f. **searching out**—pl. sf. Si מחקרותם—**searching out, study,** <PREP> of accompaniment, *in, with* Si 44$_{4(B)}$ (M במחקק[תם] *with their decrees*).

*[מחר] vb. **appraise**—**Qal appraise, value,** ptc. as noun, **appraiser, valuer,** <COLL> וְדָרְשׁוּ מֹחֵר בָּתֵּיהֶם *and let their houses be investigated by the appraiser* Ps 109$_{10}$ (דרשׁ qal. pass., מֹחֵר accus. of agency;* if em. וְדָרְשׁוּ מֵחָרְבוֹתֵיהֶם *and let them seek from their ruins*).

מָחָר 52.2.1.2 n.[m.] **morrow, 1. morrow, future,** <CSTR> יוֹם מָחָר *day of the morrow,* i.e. tomorrow, in the future Gn 30$_{33}$ Is 56$_{12}$ Pr 27$_{1}$. <PREP> לְ *at, on,* i.e. tomorrow, in the future Ex 8$_{6}$, + היה *be* Ex 8$_{19}$, אכל *eat* Si 6$_{19}$; *for* tomorrow, + קדשׁ htp. *consecrate oneself* Nm 11$_{18}$ Jos 7$_{13}$, קרא pass. *be invited* Est 5$_{12}$.

2. as adv. **a. tomorrow, in the future** (Ex 13$_{14}$ Dt 6$_{20}$ Jos 4$_{6.21}$ 22$_{24.27.28}$ 4QParGenEx 2$_{10}$ [מח[ר]]), (1) with verb היה *be* Nm 16$_{16}$ 1 S 11$_{9}$, בוא hi. *bring* Ex 10$_{4}$, יצא *go out* 1 S 11$_{10}$ 2 C 20$_{17}$, ירד *go down* 2 C 20$_{16}$, פנה *turn* intrans. Nm 14$_{25}$, סור *turn aside* intrans. Ex 8$_{25}$, שׁלח pi. *send* 2 S 11$_{12}$, סבב hi. *cause to go round,* i.e. send Arad ost. 2$_{6}$, שׁכם hi. *rise early* Jg 19$_{9}$, נצב ni. *stand* Ex 17$_{9}$, נפל *fall* Si 10$_{10}$, עשׂה *do* Ex 9$_{5}$ Jos 3$_{5}$ Est 5$_{8}$ Lachish ost. 9$_{8}$, שׂים *place* Nm 16$_{7}$, נתן *give* Jg 20$_{28}$ Pr 3$_{28}$, ni. *be given,* i.e. allowed Est 9$_{13}$, אמר *say* Jos 22$_{24.27.28}$, שׁאל *ask* Ex 13$_{14}$ Dt 6$_{20}$ Jos 4$_{6.21}$, קדשׁ pi. *consecrate* Ex 19$_{19}$, קצף *be angry* Jos 22$_{18}$, אכל *eat* 2 K 6$_{28}$, מות *die* Is 22$_{13}$, ho. *be killed* 1 S 19$_{11}$.

(2) in nom. cl., שַׁבָּתוֹן שַׁבַּת־קֹדֶשׁ לַי׳ מָחָר *tomorrow is a day of rest, a holy sabbath to Y.* Ex 16$_{23}$, חַג לַי׳ מָחָר *tomorrow there is a feast to Y.* Ex 32$_{5}$, מָחָר חֹדֶשׁ *tomorrow is the new moon* 1 S 20$_{5}$, var. 20$_{18}$, מָחָר אַתָּה וּבָנֶיךָ עִמִּי *tomorrow you and your sons shall be with me* 1 S 28$_{19}$, מח[ר] אות לדור[ות] *in the future it shall be a sign to the generations* 4QParGenEx 2$_{10}$.

<COLL> הַיּוֹם וּמָחָר *today and tomorrow* Ex 19$_{10}$; מָחָר + הַיּוֹם *today* Jos 22$_{18}$ 2 S 11$_{12}$ 2 K 6$_{28}$ Si 10$_{10}$, הַלַּיְלָה *tonight* 1 S 19$_{11}$.

b. כָּעֵת מָחָר **(about) this time tomorrow,** (1) with verb היה *be* 2 K 7$_{18}$, בוא *come* 2 K 10$_{6}$, שׁלח *send* 1 S 9$_{16}$ 1 K 20$_{6}$, שׂים *place,* i.e. make 1 K 19$_{2}$, חקר *search,* i.e. sound out 1 S 20$_{12}$, מטר hi. *rain* Ex 9$_{18}$.

(2) in nom. cl., כָּעֵת מָחָר סְאָה סֹלֶת בְּשֶׁקֶל *about this time tomorrow a seah of fine flour shall be (sold) for a shekel* 2 K 7$_{1}$.

<COLL> מָחָר + הַשְּׁלִשִׁי *the third (day)* 1 S 2$_{12}$.

c. מָחָר כָּעֵת הַזֹּאת **tomorrow at this time,** with verb נתן *give* Jos 11$_{6}$.

Also 4Q417 23$_{3}$ Lachish ost. 21$_{8}$ ([מ]חר) Kh. Beit Lei graf. 1$_{2}$ (ישר מחר; others [א]שר [י]מחה *who obliterates*).*

⇨ מָחֳרָת *morrow.*

[מֹחֵר] *appraiser,* see מחר *appraise.*

[מַחֲרָאָה] 1 n.f. **latrine** or **rubbish dump**—pl. Kt מחראות—<PREP> לְ *into,* + שׂים *place,* i.e. make, house of Baal 2 K 10$_{27(Kt)}$ (למחראות; Qr לְמוֹצָאוֹת *latrines*); הַמַּחֲרָאָה without prep. *on(to) the latrine,* + שׁלך ho. *be cast* Am 4$_{3}$ (if em. וְהִשְׁלַכְתֶּנָה הַהַרְמוֹנָה *and you will cast towards the high place* to וְהָשְׁלַכְתֶּנָה הַמַּחֲרָאָה).

⇨ חֶרֶא *dung.*

*[מַחֲרָב] n.[m.] **laying waste,** <PREP> עַל *for (the purpose of),* + בוא hi. *bring* Jr 15$_{8}$ (if em. עַל־אֵם בָּחוּר *against the mother of a young man* to עַל־מַחֲרָב).

⇨ חרב I *lay waste.*

*[מַחֲרָשׁ] 0.0.1 n.[m.] **scheming**—sf. Q מחרשו—**scheming, devising,** perh. lit. 'ploughing', <NOM CL> מחרשו בסאון רשע *his scheming is in the filth of wickedness* 1QS 3$_{2}$.

⇨ חרשׁ *plough.*

[מַחֲרָשָׁה] 2 n.f. **ploughshare**—sf. מַחֲרַשְׁתּוֹ; pl. מַחֲרֵשֹׁת—<OBJ> לטשׁ *sharpen* 1 S 13$_{20}$ (unless מַחֲרֵשָׁה *goad*). <PREP> לְ charge *for (sharpening)* 1 S 13$_{21}$ (|| אֵת *blade,* שְׁלֹשׁ קִלְּשׁוֹן *three-pronged fork,* קַרְדֹּם *axe,* + דָּרְבָן *goad*).

<SYN> אֵת *blade,* שְׁלֹשׁ קִלְּשׁוֹן *three-pronged fork,* קַרְדֹּם *axe.*

⇨ חרשׁ *plough.*

*[מַחֲרֵשָׁה] 1 n.f. **goad**—sf. מַחֲרֵשָׁתוֹ—<OBJ> לטשׁ *sharpen* 1 S 13$_{20}$ (unless מַחֲרָשָׁה *ploughshare;* || דָּרְבָן

goad; + אֵת blade, קַרְדֹּם axe, מַחֲרֵשָׁה ploughshare).
<SYN> דָּרְבָן goad.*
⇒ חרשׁ engrave.

מָחֳרָת 32.0.4 n.f. **morrow**—Q מוחרת; cstr. מָחֳרַת; sf. מָחֳרָתָם—**1. morrow, next day,** <CSTR> מָחֳרַת הַשַּׁבָּת *morrow of,* i.e. day after, *the sabbath* Lv 23$_{11.15.16}$ 11QT 18$_{12}$ 19$_{13}$ 21$_{13}$ (all three מוחרת), הַפֶּסַח *the passover* Nm 33$_3$ Jos 5$_{11}$, הַחֹדֶשׁ *the new moon* 1 S 20$_{27}$ (+ הַשֵּׁנִי *[on] the second [day]*), הַיּוֹם הַהוּא *that day* 1 C 29$_{21}$; יוֹם הַמָּחֳרָת *day of the morrow,* i.e. the next day Nm 11$_{32}$. <APP> יוֹם *day* Nm 11$_{32(Sam)}$.
<PREP> לְ of time, *on,* + עלה (of dawn) *go up* Jon 4$_7$, hi. *cause to go up,* i.e. offer 1 C 29$_{21}$; of possession, *(belonging) to, of* 1 S 30$_{17}$ (הָעֶרֶב לְמָחֳרָתָם *the evening of their* [? the Amalekites'*] *next day;* or em. לְהַחֲרִימָם *utterly destroying them*); מִן *from,* + ספר *count* Lv 23$_{15}$; *on,* + היה *be* Gn 19$_{34}$ Ex 18$_{13}$ 32$_{30}$ Nm 17$_{23}$ Jg 9$_{42}$ 21$_4$ 1 S 11$_{11}$ 18$_{10}$ 20$_{27}$ 31$_8$ 2 K 8$_{15}$ Jr 20$_3$ 1 C 10$_8$, יצא *go out* Nm 33$_3$, ישׁב *remain* 2 S 11$_{12}$, עשׂה *do* Ex 9$_6$, שׁכם hi. *rise early* Ex 32$_6$ Jg 6$_{38}$ 1 S 5$_{3.4}$ (+ בַּבֹּקֶר *in the morning*) 2 K 6$_{15}$ (if em. מְשָׁרֵת *the servant of* to מִמָּחֳרָת), לון ni. *murmur* Nm 17$_6$, אכל *eat* Jos 5$_{11}$ 4QJub^{d} 21$_{10}$ (... [אכול] [ממח]רת; = 4QJub^{e} מחרת, §2), ni. *be eaten* Lv 7$_{16}$ 19$_6$, נוף hi. *wave* Lv 23$_{11}$, שׁבת *cease* Jos 5$_{12}$; עַד מִן *until after,* + היה *be* 11QT 19$_{13}$ ([תהיינה]) 21$_{13}$, ספר *count* Lv 23$_{16}$ 11QT 18$_{12}$.
<COLL> מָחֳרָת + יוֹם *day* Lv 7$_{16}$ 19$_6$ 2 S 11$_{12}$ 4QJub^{d} 21$_{10}$ ([ביום] ... [וממח]רת).
2. appar. **on the next day,** as adv. of אכל *eat* 4QJub^{e} 21$_{10}$ ([אכול]; but =4QJub^{d} ממחרת, §1, Prep.).
<COLL> מָחֳרָת + יוֹם *day* 4QJub^{e} 21$_{10}$ ([ביום]).*
⇒ מָחָר *morrow.*

[מַחְשֹׂף] 1.0.1 n.[m.] **stripping**—cstr. מַחְשֹׂף—of bark to expose wood (Gn 30$_{37}$), <OBJ> פצל pi. *peel* Gn 30$_{37}$. <CSTR> מַחְשֹׂף הַלָּבָן *stripping of,* i.e. down to, *the white* Gn 30$_{37}$. <APP> פְּצָלָה *stripe* Gn 30$_{37}$. <PREP> לְ perh. *as,* + היה *be* 4QpsJub^{b} 11$_1$ ([יה]יה).
⇒ חשׂף I *make bare.*

*[מַחֲשָׁב] I 0.0.9 n.m. **design**—pl. cstr. Q מחשבי; sf. Q מחשביהם (Q מחשביהמה)—**1. (skilful) design, crafting,** of spirits' garments (4QShirShabb^{f} 23.2$_{10}$), of heavens (4QHod^{a} 7.2$_{21}$).
2. (skilfully crafted) furnishing, decoration, of inner sanctuary (4QShirShabb^{d} 1.2$_{13.14}$).
3. network of fissures (1QH 3$_{33}$), perh. **depth,** of earth (1QH 3$_{32.33}$ 4QBer^{a} 5$_1$ 4QDibHam^{a} 1.7$_7$ 4QShir^{b} 37$_4$; but prob. חשׁב pi. ptc. *ones who scheme*).*
<SUBJ> חושׁ *hasten* 4QShirShabb^{d} 1.2$_{13}$, מלח pu. *be blended* 4QShirShabb^{f} 23.2$_{10}$, המה *moan* 1QH 3$_{32}$ (unless חשׁב pi. ptc. *ones who scheme*), רוע *cry out* 1QH 3$_{33}$ 4QShir^{b} 37$_4$ ([י]רועו); unless in both מחשביה is חשׁב pi. ptc. *ones who scheme*). <NOM CL> כול מחשביהם ... חשׁב *all their designs are ... an artistry* 4QShirShabb^{f} 23.2$_{10}$. <CSTR> מחשבי הדביר *furnishings of the inner sanctuary* 4QShirShabb^{d} 1.2$_{13}$, מחשבי תהום *depths of the abyss* 1QH 3$_{32}$ (unless חשׁב pi. ptc. *ones who scheme*), כול מחשבי *all the furnishings of* 4QShirShabb^{d} 1.2$_{13}$, כול מחשביה *all its designs/depths* 1QH 3$_{33}$ 4QBer^{a} 5$_1$ 4QDibHam^{a} 1.7$_7$ 4QShir^{b} 37$_4$ (unless all four חשׁב pi. ptc. *ones who scheme*), כול מחשביהם *all their designs/furnishings* 4QShirShabb^{d} 1.2$_{14}$ 4QShirShabb^{f} 23.2$_{10}$, כול מחשביהמה *all their designs* 4QHod^{a} 7.2$_{21}$.
⇒ חשׁב *think.*

*[מַחְשָׁב] II 0.0.1 n.m. **fissure, network**—pl. sf. Q מחשביה, <SUBJ> רוע *cry out* 1QH 3$_{33}$ (unless מחשביה is חשׁב pi. ptc. *ones who scheme*). <CSTR> כול מחשביה *all its fissures* 1QH 3$_{33}$ (unless חשׁב pi. ptc. *ones who scheme*).
⇒ חשׁב *weave.*

מַחֲשָׁבָה 56.4.73 n.f. **thought**—מַחֲשֶׁבֶת (מַחֲשָׁבֶת); cstr. מַחֲשֶׁבֶת; sf. Q מחשבתכה, מַחֲשַׁבְתּוֹ; pl. מַחֲשָׁבוֹת (מַחֲשָׁבֹת), L מַחְשָׁבֹת; cstr. מַחְשְׁבוֹת (מַחְשְׁבֹת); sf. מַחְשְׁבוֹתַי (מַחְשְׁבֹתַי), מַחְשְׁבֹתֶיךָ (Q מחשבותיכה, מחשבותך), מַחְשְׁבֹתָיו (מַחְשְׁבוֹתָיו), מַחְשְׁבֹתָם (מַחְשְׁבוֹתָם), מַחְשְׁבֹתֵיכֶם (מַחְשְׁבוֹתֵיכֶם), מַחְשְׁבוֹתֵינוּ, מַחְשְׁבֹתֵיהֶם.
1. thought, purpose, plan, scheme, of Y. (Is 55$_{8.9}$ Jr 18$_{11}$ 29$_{11.11}$ 49$_{29}$ 50$_{45}$ 51$_{29}$ Mc 4$_{12}$ Ps 33$_{11}$ 40$_6$ 92$_6$ Si 43$_{23}$ 1QH 4$_{13}$ 11$_7$ 18$_{22}$ 1QM 13$_2$ 14$_{14}$ [[מ]חשבת] 1QS 3$_{16}$

11$_{11.19}$ 4QD^{a} 1$_{5}$ [[מח]שבות] 4QMyst^{a} 3a.2$_{11.13}$ [[מ]חשבת] 4QapPs^{b} 31$_{5}$ [[מח]שבתיך] 4QShirShabb^{c} 4$_{6}$ [מחשב[תו]] 4Q417 2.1$_{12}$ 4QPrQuot 51$_{13}$ 4QShir^{b} 42$_{7}$), of Belial (1QH 4$_{12}$ 6$_{22}$ 1QM 13$_{4}$ 4QMidrEschat^{a} 3$_{8}$ 4QMidrEschat^{b} 11$_{11}$ [מחשבל] 4QBer^{a} 7.2$_{2}$ [[מ]חשבת] 4QMyst^{a} 3a.2$_{5}$ [[מ]חשבת]), of Melchiresha (4QBer^{f} 1$_{2}$ [[מח]שבות]), of spirits (1QM 13$_{4}$ 4QBer^{a} 7.2$_{3.4.7}$).

Of humans (Gn 6$_{5}$ 2 S 14$_{14}$ Is 55$_{7.8.9}$ 59$_{7.7}$ 65$_{2}$ Jr 4$_{14}$ 11$_{19}$ 6$_{19}$ 18$_{12.18}$ 49$_{30}$ Ezk 38$_{10}$ Ps 33$_{10}$ 56$_{5}$ 94$_{11}$ Jb 5$_{12}$ 21$_{27}$ Pr 6$_{18}$ 12$_{5}$ 15$_{22.26}$ 16$_{3}$ 19$_{21}$ 20$_{18}$ Lm 3$_{60.61}$ [or em.; see Obj.] Est 8$_{3.5}$ 9$_{25}$ Dn 11$_{24.25}$ 1 C 28$_{9}$ 29$_{18}$ Si 13$_{26}$ 36$_{5}$ 37$_{16}$ 41$_{21}$ 1QH 2$_{17}$ [[מחש]בותם] 4$_{14.19}$ 7$_{3}$ perh. 17$_{10}$ [[מח]שבות] 1Qp Hab 3$_{5}$ 1QS 2$_{24}$ 3$_{15}$ 4$_{4.4}$ 5$_{5}$ 4QMidrEschat^{a} 3$_{9}$ 4QAges^{a} 2.2$_{10}$ [מחשב[ותיהם]] 4QD^{a} 6.1$_{15}$ 4QMyst^{a} 1$_{5}$ 4QMyst^{c} 1$_{3}$ 4QAdmonPar 3.2$_{7}$ [[מ]חשבתיכם] 4QAdmon 1.1$_{3}$ 4Q MMT C$_{29}$ 4QapPs^{b} 76$_{2}$ [מחשב[ות]] 4Q416 2.3$_{14}$ 4Q417 2.2$_{12}$ 4Q424 3$_{6}$ CD 2$_{16}$).

<SUBJ> כון ni. *be established* Pr 16$_{3}$ 20$_{18}$ 1QH 4$_{13}$, קום *arise* Jr 51$_{29}$ Pr 15$_{22}$, גבה *be high* Is 55$_{9}$, עמק *be deep* Ps 92$_{6}$, לין *lodge* Jr 4$_{14}$, עלה *go up* 4QD^{a} 6.1$_{15}$, שׁוב *go back* Est 9$_{25}$, פתה pi. *deceive* 4Q417 2.2$_{12}$.

<NOM CL> לֹא מַחְשְׁבוֹתַי מַחְשְׁבוֹתֵיכֶם *my thoughts are not your thoughts* Is 55$_{8}$, מַחְשְׁבוֹתֵיהֶם מַחְשְׁבוֹת אָוֶן *their thoughts are thoughts of iniquity* Is 59$_{7}$, מַחְשְׁבוֹת צַדִּיקִים מִשְׁפָּט *the thoughts of the righteous are justice* Pr 12$_{5}$, תּוֹעֲבַת י׳ מַחְשְׁבוֹת רָע *thoughts of evil are an abomination to Y.* Pr 15$_{26}$, מזמות בליעל [כול מחש]בותם *all their thoughts are plots of Belial* 1QH 2$_{17}$, אופן חוזר מחשבותיו *his thoughts are a revolving wheel* Si 36$_{5}$, שיג ישיח מחשבת עמל perh. *turning aside and musing are*, i.e. produce, *thought of toil*, i.e. toilsome thought Si 13$_{26}$, רַבּוֹת מַחֲשָׁבוֹת בְּלֶב־אִישׁ *many are the plans in the heart of a man* Pr 19$_{21}$, גדולה מ[חשבת כבו]דכה *great is the plan of your glory*, i.e. your glorious plan 1QM 14$_{14}$, ברוב בינה מחשבותיכה *your thoughts will be with much understanding* 4Q416 2.3$_{14}$, מַחְשְׁבוֹת לִבּוֹ לְדֹר וָדֹר *the thoughts of his heart are throughout all generations* Ps 33$_{11}$, עָלַי כָּל־מַחְשְׁבֹתָם לָרָע *all their thoughts are against me for evil* Ps 56$_{6}$, מַחְשְׁבוֹת חָרוּץ אַךְ־לְמוֹתָר *the plans of a diligent one are*, i.e. lead, *surely to abundance* Pr 21$_{5}$, לפני כל פעל היא מחשבת *thought is*, i.e. goes, *before any deed* Si 37$_{16(Bmg, D)}$ (B ראש כל פועל thought is *the beginning of any deed*).

<OBJ> שׁמע *hear* Jr 49$_{20}$ 50$_{45}$, ראה *see* Lm 3$_{60.61}$ (or em. מַלְשְׁנָתָם *their slander*), ידע *know* Is 66$_{18}$ (if ins. יָדַע and transfer מַעֲשֵׂיהֶם וּמַחְשְׁבֹתֵיהֶם *their deeds and their thoughts* to verse 16) Jr 29$_{11.11}$ Mc 4$_{12}$ Ps 84$_{11}$ Jb 21$_{27}$ 4QAges^{a} 2.2$_{10}$ (מחשב[ותיהם]) 4QapPent 10.1$_{5}$ (מחשב[ות]) 4QShir^{b} 42$_{7}$, חשׁב *think* 2 S 14$_{14}$ Jr 11$_{19}$ 18$_{11.18}$ 29$_{11.11}$ 49$_{20.30}$ 50$_{45}$ Ezk 38$_{10}$ Est 8$_{3}$ 9$_{25}$ Dn 11$_{25}$ 4QMidrEschat^{a} 3$_{9}$, pi. Dn 11$_{24}$, חרשׁ *devise* Pr 6$_{18}$, זמם *plot* 1QH 6$_{22}$ (ל[זו]ם), עשׂה *make* Ps 40$_{6}$, כון hi. *establish* 1QS 3$_{15}$ 4Q Myst^{a} 3a.2$_{11}$, כול pilp. *sustain* 4QShirShabb^{c} 4$_{6}$ ([מכ]לכלי מחשב[תו]), כרה I *make deep* 4Q424 3$_{6}$ (unless כרה II *acquire*), נוא hi. *frustrate* Ps 33$_{10}$, פרר hi. *frustrate* Ps 15$_{22}$ Jb 5$_{12}$, שׁוב hi. *revoke* Est 8$_{5}$, עבר hi. *remove* Est 8$_{3}$, עזב *forsake* Is 55$_{7}$, נאץ *spurn* 1QH 4$_{12}$, שׁעע hi *besmear with* Si 41$_{21(Bmg)}$.

<CSTR> מַחְשְׁבוֹת י׳ *thoughts of Y.* Jr 51$_{29}$ Mc 4$_{12}$, מח]שבות אל] *thoughts of God* 4QD^{a} 1$_{5}$, מחשבת בליעל *thought of Belial* 1QH 4$_{12}$ 4QMidrEschat^{a} 3$_{8}$ ([ב]ל[י]על) 4QMidrEschat^{b} 11$_{11}$ (מחשבל prob. error for מחשבת [מ]חשבת בליעל]) 4QMyst^{a} 3a.2$_{5}$ ([מ]חשבת בליעל]), מַחְשְׁבוֹת אָדָם *thoughts of a human being* Ps 94$_{11}$, מַחֲשֶׁבֶת הָמָן *thought of Haman* Est 8$_{5}$, בֶּן־ *of the son of* Est 8$_{5}$, מַחְשְׁבוֹת עַמִּים *thoughts of the peoples* Ps 33$_{10}$, חָרוּץ *of a diligent one* Pr 21$_{5}$, צַדִּיקִים *of the righteous* Pr 12$_{5}$, עֲרוּמִים *of the crafty* Jb 5$_{12}$, מחשבת לבב *thought of the heart* 4QShir^{b} 63.2$_{3}$, כול לבב *of every heart* 4QShir^{b} 22$_{4}$ ([מח]שבת), מַחְשְׁבוֹת לְבַב *thoughts of the heart of* 1 C 29$_{18}$, לִבּוֹ *of his heart* Gn 6$_{5}$ (מַחְשְׁבֹת) Ps 33$_{11}$, מחשבת לבכה *thought of your heart* 1QH 4$_{13}$, מחשב]ות לבם] *thoughts of their heart* 4QapPs^{b} 76$_{2}$.

מַחְשְׁבוֹת שָׁלוֹם *thoughts of peace* Jr 29$_{11}$ (+ וְלֹא לְרָעָה *and not of evil*), מחשבת צדק *thought of righteousness* 1QS 2$_{24}$, מחשבת קודש *thought of holiness* 1QS 4$_{4}$, קודשו *of his holiness* 4QSapDidB 4.2$_{5}$ (קוד[שו]) 4QTime 1.2$_{10}$ (מחש]בת] ק[ו]דש[ו]), קודשכה *of your holiness* 1QS 11$_{19}$, קודשו *of his holiness* 1QM 13$_{2}$, בי[נה] *of understanding* 4QMyst^{b} 300 5$_{1}$, בינתו *of his understanding* 4QPrQuot 51$_{13}$, כבודכה *of your glory* 1QM 14$_{14}$ (מ]חשבת כבו]דכה) 4QpsHod^{b} 3.1$_{24}$ ([מח]שבת), כבודו *of his glory* 1QS 3$_{16}$.

מחשבת רעה *thought of evil* 4QMMT C$_{29}$, מַחְשְׁבוֹת רָע *thoughts of evil* Pr 15$_{26}$, מהשבת רוע *thought of evil* 1QH

7_{3}, רשעה *of wickedness* 1QH 6_{22}, [מח]שבות רשעה *thoughts of wickedness* 1QH 17_{10}, מחשבת רשעם *thought of their wickedness* 1QM 13_{5} 4QBer^{a} 7.2$_{3}$ (רשעמה), ז[מ]ה *of wickedness* 4QD^{a} 6.1$_{15}$, מַחְשְׁבוֹת אָוֶן *thoughts of iniquity* Is 59_{7} Pr 6_{18} 4QMidrEschat^{a} 3_{9}, אוֹנֵךְ *of your iniquity* Jr 4_{14}, מחשבת משטמה *thought of animosity* 1QM 13_{4}, משטמתו *of his animosity* 4QBer^{a} 7.2$_{2}$ ([מ]חשבת), מחשבות נדת *thoughts of impurity of* 4QBer^{a} 7.2$_{4}$, מחשבת זידה *thought of presumptuousness* 1Q29 13_{4}, עמל *of toil* Si 13_{26}, מעשה *of work* 1QS 4_{4}, מחשבות יצר *thoughts of an inclination of* 4QBer^{f} 1_{2} ([מח]שבות יצר) 4QBer^{a} 7.2$_{7}$ 4QAdmon 1.1$_{3}$ 4Q417 2.2$_{12}$ CD 2_{16}, מחשבת יצרו *thought of his inclination* 1QS 5_{5}, מחשבות מחלקות *plans of*, i.e. for, *the allotment of* a portion Si $41_{21(Bmg)}$, [מ]חשבת בית מולדים *plan of the house*, i.e. time, *of birth* 4QMyst^{a} 3a.2$_{13}$.

אנשי מחשבת *men of plan(s)* 4QMyst^{a} 1_{5} 4QMyst^{c} 1_{3}, [מכ]לכלי מחשב[תו] *ones who sustain his plan* 4QShirShabb^{c} 4_{6}, יֵצֶר מַחֲשָׁבוֹת *devising of thoughts* 1 C 28_{9} 4QBéat 7_{4} ([מחשב]ות), יֵצֶר מַחְשְׁבֹת *devising/inclination of the thoughts of* Gn 6_{5} 1 C 29_{18} (מַחְשְׁבוֹת) 4QapPs^{b} 76_{2} ([מחשב]ות), פרי מחשבת *fruit of the thought of* 4QDibHam^{a} 6_{2}, [פרי מ]חשבתיכם *fruit of your thoughts* 4QAdmonPar 3.2$_{7}$, פְּרִי מַחְשְׁבוֹתָם *fruit of their thoughts* Jr 6_{19}, רישית כול מחשבת *beginning of every thought of* 4QShir^{b} 63.2$_{3}$, יחד ... מחשבת *community of ... thought of* 1QS 2_{24}, רזי מחשבת *mysteries of thought* 1QH fr. 17_{3}, [נס]תרי מחשבתו *secrets of his purpose* 4Q417 2.1$_{12}$, [הוות מח]שבות *destruction of plans of* 1QH 17_{10}.

כול מחשבת *every thought* 4QMyst^{a} 3a.2$_{11}$, כול מחשבת *every thought of* 1QH 4_{12} (כל) 1QM 13_{2} 1QS 4_{4} 11_{19} 4QSapDidB 4.2$_{5}$ 4QDibHam^{a} 4_{4} ([מחשב]ת) perh. 4QShir^{b} 23_{4} ([כו]ל מחשב[ ]) 63.2$_{3}$, כול מחשבות *all the thoughts of* 4QBer^{f} 1_{2} ([כל מח]שבות) 4QBer^{a} 7.2$_{7}$ ([כו]ל) 6QapSamKgs 23_{2} ([כל מח]שבות) 4QHod^{b} 13_{4} ([מח]שבות), כול מחשבותך *all your thoughts* 1QH fr. 20_{4}, כול מחש[בותיו] *all his thoughts* 4QShir^{b} 26_{2}, כָּל־ מַחְשְׁבֹתָם *all their thoughts* Ps 56_{6} Lm $3_{60.61}$ 1QH 2_{17} ([כול מחש]בותם) 1QpHab 3_{5} 1QS 3_{15} (both כול).

<APP> סֵפֶר *letter* Est 8_{5}.

<ADJ> רַע *evil* Ezk 38_{10} Est 9_{25}, ירא ni. ptc. *fear-inspiring* 4QD^{a} 1_{5} ([מח]שבות ... הנורא[ות]).

<PREP> לְ introducing object perh. 4Q418 227_{1}, + בין *understand* 4QapPs^{b} 31_{5} ([מח]שבתיך).

בְּ of place, accompaniment, *in, with* 1QH 4_{14} 11_{7} 18_{22} 1QS 4_{4} perh. 4Q178 2_{5} ([במחשבו]ת) perh. 4Q185 1.3$_{15}$ ([במחש]בות) perh. 4QSapDidB 4.2$_{5}$ ([ב]כול מחשבת), + תפשׂ ni. *be caught* 1QH 4_{19}, בוא *come* 4QMidrEschat^{a} 3_{8}, תור *go about* CD 2_{16}; of instrument, *by (means of), with* 4QMidrEschat^{b} 11_{11} (במחשבל prob. error for במחשבת), + כון hi. *establish* 1QS 11_{11} perh. 4Q418 46_{1} ([מחשב]ות), בחן ni. *be proved* 4QTime 1.2$_{10}$ ([במחש]בת); *on account of*, + ברך pass. *be blessed* 1QM 13_{2}, ארר pass. *be cursed* 1QM $13_{4.4}$ 4QBer^{f} 1_{2} ([אר]ור ... [בכל מח]שבות) 4QBer^{a} 7.2$_{2}$ (ב[מ]חשבת) 7.2$_{3}$, זעם pass. *be accursed* 4QBer^{a} 7.2$_{4}$; introducing object, + שׂכל hi. *understand* 1QS 11_{19}, ידע hi. *make known* 4QPrQuot 51_{13} ([ה]ודיענו).

כְּ *according to*, + מלא pi. *fulfil* 1QS 3_{16}, שׁפט *judge* 4QAdmon 1.1$_{3}$; מִן of comparison, *(more) than*, + גבה *be high* Is 55_{9}.

מִן of cause, *on account of*, + שׁמם hi. *be appalled* 1QH 7_{3}.

אַחַר *after*, + הלך *go* Is 65_{2}, תעה *go astray* 1QS 5_{5}.

אַחֲרֵי *after*, + הלך *go* Jr 18_{12}.

<COLL> מַחֲשָׁבָה || עֵצָה *counsel* Jr $49_{20.30}$ 50_{45} Mc 4_{12} Ps $33_{10.11}$ (+) Pr 19_{21} (+) 20_{18} (+) 1QpHab 3_{5} (+) 1QH 4_{13} 4QMMT C$_{29}$, תַּחְבֻּלָה *counsel* Pr 12_{5} 20_{18} (+), דֶּרֶךְ *way* Is $55_{7.8.9}$ 65_{2} (+) 4QAdmon 1.1$_{3}$, מַעֲשֶׂה *deed* Is 66_{18} Ps 92_{6} Pr 16_{3} (+) 1QM 13_{2}, רָעָה *evil* Jr 18_{11} Pr 6_{18} (+) Est 8_{3} (+), כֹּחַ *strength* 1QH 11_{7}.

+ לֵב *heart* Jr 18_{12} 4Q416 2.3$_{14}$, לֵבָב *heart* 1 C 29_{18} 1QS 5_{5}, עַיִן *eye* 1QS 5_{5} CD 2_{16}, אֹמֶר *word* Pr 15_{26}, דָּבָר *word* Ezk 38_{10}, פלא ni. ptc. *wonderful deed* Ps 40_{6}, מְזִמָּה *plan* Jb 21_{28}, נְקָמָה *vengeance* Lm 3_{60}, חֶרְפָּה *reproach* Lm 3_{61}.

אָנֹכִי מַעֲשֵׂיהֶם מַחְשְׁבֹתֵיהֶם perh. *I (am aware of) their deeds and their thoughts* Is 66_{18} (or em.; see Obj.), מחשבתו משיק רבה *by his plan he set alight the great deep* Si $43_{23(Segal)}$, מַחְשְׁבוֹת י׳ לָשׂוּם אֶת־אֶרֶץ בָּבֶל לְשַׁמָּה *the plans of Y. to make the land of Bablyon a desolation* Jr 51_{29}, כול מחשבתם להרע *all their* (Kittim's) *plans are to do evil* 1QpHab 3_{5}, מַחְשְׁבֹתֶיךָ אֵלֵינוּ *your thoughts towards us* Ps 40_{6}, מַחְשְׁבֹתָם לִי *their schemes against me* Lm 3$_{60}$, מַחְשְׁבֹתָם עָלַי *their schemes against me* Lm 3$_{61}$ (or em.; see Obj.).

2. device, (skilful) design, crafting of tabernacle furnishings (Ex 31$_{4}$ 35$_{32.33.35}$), temple furnishings (2 C 2$_{13}$), war engines (2 C 26$_{15}$), treasury (1QH 1$_{13}$); **skill** in design and making of weapons (1QM 5$_{6.8.9.10.11}$).

<SUBJ> נתן ni. *be given*, i.e. assigned 2 C 2$_{13}$. <OBJ> חשב *devise* Ex 31$_{4}$ 35$_{32.35}$ 2 C 2$_{13}$, עשה *make* 2 C 26$_{15}$. <CSTR> מַחֲשֶׁבֶת חוֹשֵׁב *device of a (skilful) designer* 2 C 26$_{15}$; חרש מחשבת *artisan of skill*, i.e. skilful artisan 1QM 5$_{6.9.10.11}$ (מ[ח]שבת), צורת *design of*, i.e. skilful design 1QM 5$_{8}$, חֹשְׁבֵי מַחֲשָׁבֹת *ones who devise designs* Ex 35$_{35}$, מְלֶאכֶת מַחֲשָׁבֶת *craft of design* Ex 35$_{33}$, אוצרות מחשבת *treasuries of (skilful) design* 1QH 1$_{13}$, כָּל־מַחֲשָׁבֶת *any design* 2 C 2$_{13}$. <APP> חִשְּׁבוֹן *war engine* 2 C 26$_{15}$. <COLL> מְלָאכָה + מַחֲשָׁבָה *work* Ex 35$_{35}$, פִּתּוּחַ *engraving* 2 C 2$_{13}$.

Also 4QMyst^{a} 3a.2$_{10}$ ([מח]שבות) 10$_{11}$ ([מחשו]בותם) 4QMyst^{c} 10$_{3}$ ([מחשב]ת) 4QapPent 10.1$_{8}$ ([מח]שבות) 4QBark^{b} 3$_{1}$ 4QHymnSap 3.1$_{3}$ perh. 4QRitMar 6$_{2}$ ([מח]שבות) 4QPrQuot 215$_{3}$ ([מחשב]ת) 4QDinHam^{a} 24$_{3}$ (למחשב[ ]) 4QPrFêtes^{c} 23.1$_{2}$ (למחשבתו) perh. 4QShir^{b} 100$_{2}$ ([מח]שבות).

<SYN> עֵצָה *counsel*, תַּחְבֻּלָה *counsel*, דֶּרֶךְ *way*, מַעֲשֶׂה *deed*, רָעָה *evil*, כֹּחַ *strength*.*

⇨ חשב *think*.

מחשבל, see מַחֲשָׁבָה *thought*.

מַחְשָׁךְ 7.0.4 n.m. **dark place**—pl. מַחֲשַׁכִּים; cstr. מַחֲשַׁכֵּי; sf. Q מחשכיהמה—**dark place, darkness,** as hiding place (Is 29$_{15}$ Ps 74$_{20}$ [or em.; see Obj.]), place of dead (Ps 88$_{7}$ 143$_{3}$ Lm 3$_{6}$), the underworld (1QS 4$_{13}$ 4QM^{a} 8$_{15}$); perh. **dark,** i.e. angry, **thoughts*** (Ps 74$_{20}$; if em.; see Obj.), <SUBJ> מלא *be full* Ps 74$_{20}$ (or em.; see Obj.). <OBJ> שׂים *place*, i.e. make Is 42$_{16}$ (1QIsa^{a} מהשוכים; || מַעֲקָשׁ *crooked place*; :: אוֹר *light*), נתן *give*, i.e. make 4QBark^{a} 1.2$_{9}$ (|| מַעֲקָשׁ; :: אור), מלא *be full of* Ps 74$_{20}$ (if em. מָלְאוּ חֲשַׁכֵּי־אֶרֶץ *the dark places of the earth are full* to מָלְאוּ מַחְשָׁךְ *they are full of dark thoughts*).

<CSTR> מַחֲשַׁכֵּי־אֶרֶץ *dark places of the earth* Ps 74$_{20}$ (or em.; see Obj.) 4QShir^{b} 30$_{2}$ ([מח]שכי ארץ; + תְּהוֹם *deep*), מחשכי אבדונים *dark places of Abaddon(s)* 4QM^{a} 8$_{15(mg)}$ (main text אבנים *of stones*); אש מחשכים *fire of dark places* 1QS 4$_{13}$. <PREP> בְּ of place, *in*, + היה *be* Is 29$_{15}$, ישׁב hi. *cause to sit* Ps 143$_{3}$ Lm 3$_{6}$, שׁית *place* Ps 88$_{7}$ (|| מְצוֹלָה *deep*, + בּוֹר *pit*), בער *burn* 4QM^{a} 8$_{15}$ ([בו]ערת); מַחְשָׁךְ without preposition, *in darkness* Ps 88$_{19}$ (or em. שְׁכֵחֻנִי *they have forgotten me*).

Also 4QBer^{b} 7$_{1}$ 4QBéat 21$_{1}$ ([מ]חשכים).

<SYN> מַעֲקָשׁ *crooked place*, מְצוֹלָה *deep*.

<ANT> אוֹר *light*.*

⇨ חשך *be dark*.

מַ֫חַת 3 pr.n.m. **Mahath, 1.** Gershonite Levite, son of Amasai (1 C 6$_{20}$), or son of Elkanah (1 C 6$_{10}$ if em.; see Nom Cl.), <NOM CL> בְּנֵי אֶלְקָנָה עֲמָשַׂי וְאָחִיו מַחַת *the sons of Elkanah were Amasai and his brother Mahath* 1 C 6$_{10}$ (if em. וַאֲחִימוֹת *and Ahimoth* to וְאָחִיו מַחַת).

<CSTR> בֶּן־מַחַת *son of Mathath* 1 C 6$_{20}$. <APP> בֵּן *son* 1 C 6$_{20}$, אָח *brother* 1 C 6$_{10}$ (if em.; see Nom. Cl.).

2. Kohathite Levite at time of Hezekiah, son of Amasai, <SUBJ> קום *rise* 2 C 29$_{12}$. <APP> בֵּן *son* 2 C 29$_{12}$, לֵוִי *Levite* 2 C 29$_{12}$.

3. Levite at time of Hezekiah, perh. ident with §2, <NOM CL> מַחַת וּבְנָיָהוּ פְּקִידִים *Mahath and Benaiah were overseers* 2 C 31$_{13}$.

מַחְתָּה 22.0.2 n.f. **firepan**—sf. מַחְתָּתוֹ; pl. מַחְתּוֹת (מַחְתֹּת); cstr. מַחְתּוֹת; sf. מַחְתֹּתֶיהָ, מַחְתֹּתָיו—**1. firepan,** utensil of altar, for carrying burning coals or ashes; made of gold (1 K 7$_{50}$||2 C 4$_{22}$), bronze (Ex 27$_{3}$||38$_{3}$), <SUBJ> היה *be* 11QT 3$_{12}$ ([מחתות]תיו יהיו). <OBJ> עשׂה *make* Ex 27$_{3}$||38$_{3}$ 1 K 7$_{50}$||2 C 4$_{22}$, לקח *take* 2 K 25$_{15}$||Jr 52$_{19}$, נתן *give*, i.e. place Nm 4$_{14}$. <APP> כְּלִי *vessel* Ex 38$_{3}$ Nm 4$_{14}$ 11QT 33$_{13}$. <PREP> לְ of benefit, *to, for* 11QT 33$_{13}$; בְּ of instrument, *by (means of), with*, + שׁרת pi. *serve* Nm 4$_{14}$ 1 K 7$_{50}$. <COLL> מְזַמֶּרֶת || מַחְתָּה *snuffer* 1 K 7$_{50}$||2 C 4$_{22}$, כַּף *ladle* 1 K 7$_{50}$||2 C 4$_{22}$ Jr 52$_{19}$, סִיר *pot* Ex 27$_{3}$||38$_{3}$ Jr 52$_{19}$, מִזְרָק *basin* Ex 27$_{3}$||38$_{3}$ Nm 4$_{14}$ 1 K 7$_{50}$||2 C 4$_{22}$ 2 K 25$_{15}$||Jr 52$_{19}$ 11QT 33$_{13}$, סַף *dish* 1 K 7$_{50}$ Jr 52$_{19}$, מְנַקִּית *bowl* Jr 52$_{19}$, קַשְׂוָה *jar* 11QT 33$_{13}$, מִזְלָגָה *fork* Ex 27$_{3}$||38$_{3}$ Nm 4$_{14}$, יָע *shovel* Ex 27$_{3}$||38$_{3}$ Nm 4$_{14}$, מְנוֹרָה *lampstand* Jr 52$_{19}$; וַיַּעַשׂ ... הַמַּחְתּוֹת ... זָהָב סָגוּר *and he made ... the* *firepans ... of pure gold* 1 K 7_{50}||2 C 4_{22}.

2. censer, of bronze (Nm 17_4), <SUBJ> היה *be* Nm 17_3, קדשׁ *be holy* Nm $17_{2.3}$. <OBJ> לקח *take* Lv 10_1 Nm $16_{6.17.18}$ $17_{4.11}$, קרב hi. *bring near,* i.e. offer Nm $16_{17.17.17}$ $17_{3.4}$, רום hi. *raise* Nm 17_2, עשׂה *make* into hammered sheets Nm 17_3, רקע pi. *hammer* into plating Nm 17_4. <CSTR> מַחְתּוֹת הַחַטָּאִים *censers of the sinners* Nm 17_3, הַנְּחֹשֶׁת *of bronze* Nm 17_4; מְלֹא הַמַּחְתָּה *fullness of the censer,* i.e. censer full, of coals Lv 16_{12}. <PREP> בְּ of place, *in,* + נתן *give,* i.e. place Lv 10_1; עַל *upon,* + נתן *give,* i.e. place Nm 16_{17} 17_{11}. <COLL> חֲמִשִּׁים מָאתַיִם מַחְתֹּת *two hundred and fifty censers* Nm 16_{17}.

3. snuffdish, utensil of lampstand, of gold (Ex 25_{38}), <NOM CL> מַחְתֹּתֶיהָ זָהָב טָהוֹר *its snuffdishes shall be (of) pure gold* Ex 25_{38}. <OBJ> עשׂה *make* Ex 37_{23}, כסה pi. *cover* Nm 4_9. <COLL> מַחְתָּה || מֶלְקָחַיִם *tongs* Ex 25_{38}|| 37_{23} Nm 4_9, נֵר *lamp* Ex 37_{23} Nm 4_9; + מְנוֹרָה *lampstand* Nm 4_9, כְּלִי *vessel* Nm 4_9.

<SYN> §1 מְזַמֶּרֶת *snuffer,* כַּף *ladle,* סִיר *pot,* מִזְרָק *basin,* סַף *dish,* מְנַקִּית *bowl,* קַשְׂוָה *jar,* מִזְלָגָה *fork,* יָע *shovel,* מְנוֹרָה *lampstand;* §3 מֶלְקָחַיִם *tongs,* נֵר *lamp.**

⇒ חתה I *take, snatch.*

מְחִתָּה 11.0.1 n.f. **terror**—cstr. מְחִתַּת—**1. terror** (Is 54_{14} Jr 17_{17}); **(cause of) horror** (Jr 48_{39}), **(cause of) dismay** (Pr 21_{15}), <SUBJ> קרב *draw near* Is 54_{14} (+ עֹשֶׁק *oppression*). <NOM CL> מְחִתָּה לְפֹעֲלֵי אָוֶן doing justice *is a (cause of) dismay to evildoers* Pr 12_{15} (:: שִׂמְחָה *joy*). <PREP> לְ *as* or introducing predicate, + היה *be* Jr 17_{17} 48_{39} (|| שְׂחֹק *[object of] laughter*); מִן *from,* + רחק *be far* Is 54_{14}. <COLL> מְחִתָּה לְכָל־סְבִיבָיו *a (cause of) horror to all those around him* Jr 48_{39}.

2. ruin, cause of ruin, <SUBJ> היה *be* 4QTestim$_{24}$=4QapJosh[b] 22.2$_{10}$ (+ פַּח *trap*). <OBJ> שׂים *place,* i.e. make strongholds into Ps 89_{41}. <NOM CL> פִּי־אֱוִיל מְחִתָּה קְרֹבָה *the mouth of a fool is an imminent ruin* Pr 10_{14}, מְחִתַּת דַּלִּים רֵישָׁם *their poverty is the ruin of the poor* Pr 10_{15}, בְּאֶפֶס לְאֹם מְחִתַּת רָזוֹן *without people is the ruin of a ruler,* i.e. without them he is ruined Pr 14_{28} (or em.; see Cstr.), מְחִתָּה לְפֹעֲלֵי אָוֶן the way of Y. *is ruin to evildoers* Pr 10_{29} (:: מָעוֹז *stronghold*), פִּי־כְסִיל מְחִתָּה־לוֹ *the mouth of a fool is ruin to him* Pr 18_7 (+ מוֹקֵשׁ *snare*), מְחִתָּה־לוֹ *there is ruin to him* who opens mouth wide Pr 13_3. <CSTR> מְחִתַּת דַּלִּים *ruin of the poor* Pr 10_{15}, רָזוֹן *of a ruler* Pr 14_{28} (or em. רוֹזֵן *of a ruler*). <ADJ> קָרֹב *near,* i.e. imminent Pr 10_{14}. <COLL> מחתה לכול שכניו *a cause of ruin to all his neighbours* 4QTestim$_{24}$=4QapJosh[b] 22.2$_{10}$.

<SYN> שְׂחֹק *(object of) laughter.*

<ANT> §1 שִׂמְחָה *joy;* §2 מָעוֹז *stronghold.*

⇒ חתת I *be shattered.*

מַחְתֶּ֫רֶת 2 n.f. **breaking in, burglary,** <PREP> בְּ *in (the act of),* + מצא *find* Jr 2_{34}, ni. *be found* Ex 22_1.

⇒ חתר *dig.*

*[**מַחְתּוֹשׁ**] 0.0.1 pr.n.[m.] **Mahtosh,** name in writing exercise, 4QNames$_5$.

[**מַטְאֲטֵא**] I 1 n.[m.] **broom**—cstr. מַטְאֲטֵא—unless מַטְאֲטֵא II *means of destruction,* <CSTR> מַטְאֲטֵא הַשְׁמֵד *broom of destruction* Is 14_{23}. <PREP> בְּ of instrument, *by (means of), with,* + טאטא pilp. *sweep* Is 14_{23}.

⇒ טאטא *sweep.*

*[**מַטְאֲטֵא**] II 1 n.[m.] **means of destruction**—cstr. מַטְאֲטֵא—perh. **implement for pounding, crushing,** unless מַטְאֲטֵא I *broom,* <CSTR> מַטְאֲטֵא הַשְׁמֵד *means of destruction* Is 14_{23}. <PREP> בְּ of instrument, *by (means of), with,* + טאטא pilp. *sweep* Is 14_{23}.

מַטְבֵּחַ 1 n.[m.] **slaughter, place for slaughter,** or **means of slaughter,** <OBJ> כון hi. *prepare* Is 14_{21}.*

⇒ טבח *slaughter.*

מַ֫טָּה 19.0.4 adv. **downwards**—מָ֫טָּה—**1.** מַטָּה, **a. downwards, lower,** אַתָּה תֵרֵד מַטָּה מָּטָּה *you will go down lower (and) lower* Dt 28_{43} (:: מַעְלָה *upwards*).

b. beneath, below, לְמַעַן סוּר מִשְּׁאוֹל מָטָּה *in order to turn from Sheol beneath* Pr 15_{24} (or em. לְמֶ֫טָּה; :: לְמַעְלָה *above*).

2. לְמַטָּה **a. downwards,** (1) with verb היה *be* Dt 28_{13} (:: לְמַעְלָה *upwards*) 11QT 47_2 ([ויהיו] ... למט[ה] ;:: לְמַעְלָה), נתן *give,* i.e. place 11QT 59_{20} (:: לְמַעְלָה), יסף *regenerate* roots 2 K 19$_{30}$||Is 37$_{31}$ (:: לְמַעְלָה), ירד *go down* Ec 3$_{21}$ (+ לָאָרֶץ *to the ground*; :: לְמַעְלָה), שׁוב *go back* 4QDg 1.1$_{3}$ ([שׁב]), ישׁר pi. *direct* waters 2 C 32$_{30}$.

(2) in nom. cl., מִמַּרְאֵה מָתְנָיו וּלְמַטָּה *from the appearance of*, i.e. what appeared to be, *his loins and downwards* Ezk 1$_{27}$ 8$_{2}$ (both :: לְמַעְלָה *upwards*), לְמִבֶּן עֶשְׂרִים שָׁנָה וּלְמָטָּה *from twenty years old and downwards* 1 C 27$_{23}$.

b. beneath, below, מוֹסְדֵי־אֶרֶץ לְמָטָּה *foundations of the earth beneath* Jr 31$_{37}$ (:: מִלְמַעְלָה *above*).

c. לְמַטָּה מִן **less than,** חָשַׂכְתָּ לְמַטָּה מֵעֲוֺנֵנוּ *you have withheld (punishment) less than our iniquities (deserved)* Ezr 9$_{13}$ (or em. מַטֶּה you have withheld *the rod* from our iniquities; mss חָשַׁבְתָּ *you have reckoned*).

3. מִלְּמַטָּה **(from) beneath, (from) below, a.** with verb תאם *be double* Ex 26$_{24}$||36$_{29}$, נתן *give*, i.e. place Ex 27$_{5}$ 28$_{27}$||39$_{20}$, עשׂה *make* Ex 38$_{4}$.

b. in nom. cl., [קר]שים מלמטה *boards from beneath* 4Q365a 5.1$_{17}$,

4. לְמַטָּה לְ **below, beneath,** [ה]מים למ[טה לארץ] *the water beneath the earth* 1QDM 2$_{10}$.

<ANT> (לְ)מַעְלָה *upwards*.

⇒ נטה *stretch out*.

*[מָטֶה] $_{1}$ adj. **reaching**—pl. מָטִים—as noun, **one reaching, one approaching,** <OBJ> חשׂך *hold back* Pr 24$_{11}$ (unless מָטִים is ptc. of מוט *totter*).

⇒ cf. מצא *reach*.

מַטֶּה I $_{252.4.19.2}$ n.m. **staff; tribe**—cstr. מַטֵּה (Q perh. מט [1QM 5$_{1}$]); sf. מַטְּךָ (מַטֶּךָ), מַטֵּהוּ; pl. מַטּוֹת (מַטֹּת); cstr. מַטּוֹת; sf. מַטֹּתָם (מַטֹּתָם), מַטָּיו—**1. staff, rod,** usu. for support; also for punishment (e.g. Is 10$_{5.24}$ 30$_{32}$ [or em.; see Cstr.]), beating out cumin (Is 28$_{27}$), holding bread (Lv 26$_{26}$ Ezk 4$_{16}$ 5$_{16}$ 14$_{13}$ Ps 105$_{16}$ Si 48$_{2}$), **sceptre** (Ps 89$_{45}$ [if em.; see Cstr.] 110$_{2}$), **shaft** of arrow (Hb 3$_{9.14}$ [unless from מַטֶּה II *mace* or מָטוּ *war, company*]), **stem** of vine (Ezk 19$_{11.12.14.14}$), perh. **stalk** of grain (Ps 105$_{16}$).*

<SUBJ> היה *be* Ex 7$_{9.10}$ Ezk 19$_{11.14}$, פרח *sprout* Nm 17$_{20.23}$, ציץ *blossom* Ezk 7$_{10}$ (or em. הַמֻּטֶּה *injustice*), יבשׁ *wither* Ezk 19$_{12}$, הפך ni. *be turned* into serpent Ex 7$_{15}$, רום hi. *raise* Is 10$_{15}$, בלע *swallow* Ex 7$_{12}$, שׁבר ni. *be broken* Jr 48$_{17}$, perh. שׁבע pass. *be sworn* Hb 3$_{9}$ (but prob. שְׁבֻעוֹת *oaths of*; unless מַטֶּה II *mace* or מָטוּ *war, company*).

<NOM CL> מַטֶּה *(it is) a rod* Ex 4$_{2}$, מַטֶּה הוּא בְיָדָם *he is a staff in their hand* Is 10$_{5}$, מַטֵּה הָאֱלֹהִים בְּיָדִי *the rod of God will be in my hand* Ex 17$_{9}$, הַמַּטֶּה אֲשֶׁר בְּיָדוֹ *the staff that was in his hand* 1 S 14$_{27}$, vars. Gn 38$_{18}$ Ex 7$_{17}$ 1 S 14$_{43}$, מַטֵּה אַהֲרֹן בְּתוֹךְ מַטּוֹתָם *the rod of Aaron was among their rods* Nm 17$_{21}$, מַטֶּה אֶחָד לְרֹאשׁ בֵּית אֲבוֹתָם *there shall be one staff for the head of each of their fathers' houses* Nm 17$_{18}$, לְמִי ... הַמַּטֶּה *whose is ... the staff?* Gn 38$_{25}$, מַטֵּהוּ עַל־הַיָּם *his rod is over the sea* Is 10$_{26}$ (or em. עֲלֵיהֶם *against them* or עָלָיו *against him*).

<OBJ> יצא hi. *bring out* Nm 17$_{24}$, נתן *give* Nm 17$_{21.21}$, לקח *take* Ex 4$_{17.20}$ 7$_{9.15.19}$ 17$_{5}$ Nm 17$_{17.17.24}$ 20$_{8.9}$, נטה *stretch out* Ex 8$_{12}$ 9$_{23}$ 10$_{13}$, נשׂא *lift* Is 10$_{24.26}$, רום hi. *raise* Ex 14$_{16}$, נוח hi. *place* Nm 17$_{19.22}$, שׁוב hi. *bring back* Nm 17$_{25}$, שׁלח *send* Ps 110$_{2}$, שׁלך hi. *throw* Ex 7$_{9.10.12}$, חשׂך *withhold* Pr 24$_{11}$ (if em. מָטִים *tottering* [מוט ptc.] to מַטִּים), טבל *dip* 1 S 14$_{27}$ (קְצֵה הַמַּטֶּה *tip of the staff*), בלע *swallow* Ex 7$_{12}$, אכל *consume* Ezk 19$_{12}$, שׁבר *break* Lv 26$_{26}$ Is 14$_{5}$ Ezk 4$_{16}$ 5$_{16}$ 14$_{13}$ Ps 105$_{16}$ Si 48$_{2}$, חתת hi. *shatter* Is 9$_{3}$ (or em.; see Cstr.), שׁבב *shatter* Ps 89$_{45}$ (if em.; see Cstr.), גדע *hew down* Si 32$_{23}$.

<CSTR> מַטֵּה הָאֱלֹהִים *rod of God* Ex 4$_{20}$ 17$_{9}$, אַהֲרֹן *of Aaron* Ex 7$_{12}$ Nm 17$_{21.23.24}$, לֵוִי *of Levi* Nm 17$_{18}$, רְשָׁעִים *of the wicked* Is 14$_{5}$, שִׁכְמוֹ *of*, i.e. for, *his shoulder* Is 9$_{3}$ (or em. מֹטַת *bar of* or מֹטוֹת *bars of*), מַטֵּה בַדֶּיהָ *stem of its branches* Ezk 19$_{14}$ (or em. מַטֵּה to מַטֶּיהָ *its stems*), מַטֵּה עֹז *staff/stem of might*, i.e. mighty staff/stem Jr 48$_{17}$ Ezk 19$_{12}$ (if em. מַטּוֹת *stems of*) 19$_{14}$, עֻזָּהּ *of its might* Ezk 19$_{12}$, עֻזְּךָ־ *of your might* Ps 110$_{2}$, מַטֵּה רֶשַׁע *staff of wickedness* Ezk 7$_{11}$ Si 32$_{23}$, זַעְמִי *of my indignation* Is 10$_{5}$ (if em.; see App.), לֶחֶם־ *of*, i.e. for holding, *bread* Lv 26$_{26}$ Ezk 4$_{16}$ 5$_{16}$ (לֶחֶם) 14$_{13}$ (לָחֶם) Ps 105$_{16}$ Si 48$_{2}$, מוּסָדָה *of appointment*, i.e. appointed staff Is 30$_{32}$ (or em. מוּסָרֹה *of his chastisement*; or em. מַטֵּה to מִטָּה *bed*), מַטּוֹת אֹמֶר *arrows (consisting) of speech* Hb 3$_{9}$ (unless מַטֶּה II *mace* or מָטוּ *war, company*; or em. אֹמֶר to תֹּאמַר *you speak* or אֹמֶר *power* [מַר II with preformative aleph]*), מַטֵּה הוֹדוֹ *sceptre of his majesty*, i.e. his majestic sceptre Ps 89$_{45}$ (if em. מִטְּהָרוֹ *some of his purity*).

קְצֵה הַמַּטֶּה *tip of the staff* 1 S 14$_{27.43}$, שְׁבֻעוֹת מַטּוֹת appar. *oaths of arrows of* Hb 3$_{9}$ (or שׁבע pass. ptc.; or em. שִׂבַּעְתָּ *you have sated* with arrows; unless מַטֶּה II *mace* or מָטוֹ *war, company*), מַעֲבַר מַטֶּה *pass of the staff of* Is 30$_{32}$ (or em.; see above), כָּל־מַטֵּה *every staff of* Ps 105$_{16}$, כָּל־הַמַּטֹּת *all the staffs* Nm 17$_{24}$.

<APP> מַקֵּל *staff* Jr 48$_{17}$, שֵׁבֶט *staff* Is 9$_{3}$ 14$_{5}$ Ezk 19$_{14}$, זַעַם *indignation* Is 10$_{5}$ (or em. מַטֶּה הוּא בְיָדָם זַעְמִי *he is a staff in their hand, my anger* to מַטֵּה זַעְמִי הוּא בְיָדָם *he is the staff of my indignation in their hand*).

<ADJ> אֶחָד *one* Nm 17$_{18}$, זֶה *this* Ex 4$_{17}$, אֵלֶּה *these* Gn 38$_{25}$.

<PREP> לְ *as* or introducing predicate, + היה *be* Ex 4$_{4}$; *into*, + קום *rise*, i.e. grow Ezk 7$_{11}$; introducing object, + חשׂך *withhold* Ezr 9$_{13}$ (if em. לְמַטָּה *less*).

בְּ of instrument, *by (means of), with*, + נכה hi. *strike* Ex 7$_{17}$ 17$_{5}$ Nm 20$_{11}$, חבט ni. *be beaten out* Is 28$_{27}$, נקב *pierce* Hb 3$_{14}$ (unless מַטֶּה II *mace* or מָטוֹ *war, company*), עשׂה *do* Ex 4$_{17}$, טעם *taste* 1 S 14$_{43}$; of accompaniment, *with*, + נטה *stretch* hand Ex 8$_{1.12(Sam).13}$; introducing object, + רום hi. *raise* Ex 7$_{20}$.

מִן of direction, *from*, + יצא *go out* Ezk 19$_{14}$.

עַל *upon*, + כתב *write* Nm 17$_{17.18}$.

בְּתוֹךְ *among* Nm 17$_{21}$.

<COLL> מַטֶּה || שֵׁבֶט *staff, sceptre* Is 10$_{5}$ (+) 10$_{15.24}$ (+) 28$_{27}$ Ezk 19$_{11}$ (+) Si 32$_{23}$, זָדוֹן *presumptuousness* Ezk 7$_{10}$; + פָּתִיל *cord* Gn 38$_{18.25}$, חוֹתָם *seal* Gn 38$_{18}$, חֹתֶמֶת *signet ring* Gn 38$_{25}$, שׁוֹט *scourge* Is 10$_{26}$.

מַטֶּה מַטֶּה שְׁנֵים עָשָׂר מַטּוֹת *twelve staffs* Nm 17$_{17.21}$; מַטֶּה לְבֵית אָב *a staff for each father's house* Nm 17$_{17}$, מַטֶּה לְנָשִׂיא אֶחָד *a staff for each chief* Nm 17$_{21.21}$.

2. tribe, usu. one of the twelve tribes of Israel, constituted by a number of מִשְׁפָּחוֹת *clans*, and equivalent to שֵׁבֶט *tribe*, although מַטֶּה may sometimes refer specif. to a tribe in the process of settlement,* <SUBJ> היה *be* Jos 14$_{4}$, לוה ni. *join oneself* Nm 18$_{2}$, דבק *cling* Nm 36$_{9}$, חנה *encamp* Nm 2$_{5.12.20.22}$ (both, if ins. הַחֹנִים *those who encamped* at 2$_{20}$) 2$_{27}$, לקח *take* Nm 34$_{14.14.14}$ (חֲצִי מַטֵּה *half of the tribe of*) 34$_{15.15}$ (חֲצִי הַמַּטֶּה *half of the tribe*), קרב hi. *bring near*, i.e. offer 11QT^{b} 6$_{13}$ ([המקריבים]), שׁרת pi. *serve* Nm 3$_{6}$ 18$_{2}$, שׁמע *hear* Mc 6$_{9}$, דבר *speak* Nm 36$_{5}$.

<NOM CL> עָלָיו ... מַטֵּה בִּנְיָמִן *next to it shall be ... the tribe of Benjamin* Nm 2$_{22}$ (unless em.; see Subj.).

<OBJ> קרב hi. *bring near* Nm 3$_{6}$ 18$_{2}$, פקד *number* Nm 1$_{49}$, עמד hi. *cause to stand* Nm 3$_{6}$.

<CSTR> מַטּוֹת יִשְׂרָאֵל *tribes of Israel* Nm 31$_{4}$ Jos 22$_{14}$ 4QapJoshua^{b} 1$_{5}$ ([ישראל]) 11QT 19$_{14}$, מַטֵּה אֶפְרַיִם *tribe of Ephraim* Nm 1$_{33}$ (אֶפְרָיִם) 13$_{8}$ (אֶפְרָיִם) Jos 21$_{5.20}$ (אֶפְרָיִם) 1 C 6$_{46}$ (if em.; see below) 6$_{51}$ (אֶפְרָיִם), אָשֵׁר *of Asher* Nm 1$_{41}$ 2$_{27}$ 13$_{13}$ Jos 21$_{6.30}$ 1 C 6$_{47.59}$, בִּנְיָמִן *of Benjamin* Nm 1$_{37}$ 2$_{22}$ 13$_{9}$ 34$_{21}$ Jos 21$_{4.17}$ 1 C 6$_{45}$ 4QapMos^{c} 2.14 ([מ]טה), גָּד *of Gad* Nm 1$_{25}$ 2$_{14}$ 13$_{15}$ Jos 13$_{24}$ 20$_{8}$ 21$_{7.38}$ 1 C 6$_{48.65}$ 4QapMos^{c} 2.15, דָּן *of Dan* Ex 31$_{6}$ 35$_{34}$ 38$_{23}$ Lv 24$_{11}$ Nm 1$_{39}$ 13$_{12}$ Jos 21$_{5.23}$ 1 C 6$_{46}$ (if em.; see below), זְבוּלֻן *of Zebulun* Nm 1$_{31}$ 2$_{7}$ 13$_{10}$ Jos 21$_{7.34}$ 1 C 6$_{48.62}$ (זְבֻלוּן), יְהוּדָה *of Judah* Ex 31$_{2}$||35$_{30}$ 38$_{22}$ Nm 1$_{27}$ 7$_{12}$ 13$_{6}$ 34$_{19}$ Jos 7$_{1.18}$ 21$_{4}$ Si 45$_{25}$ 11QT 23$_{10}$ 24$_{10}$, יוֹסֵף *of Joseph* Nm 13$_{11}$ (or em.; see Prep.), יִשָּׂשכָר *of Issachar* Nm 1$_{29}$ 2$_{5}$ 13$_{7}$ Jos 21$_{6.28}$ 1 C 6$_{47.57}$ (L both יִשָּׂשכָר), לֵוִי *of Levi* Nm 1$_{49}$ 3$_{6}$ 18$_{2}$ Si 45$_{6}$ CD 10$_{5}$, מטה לוי ואהרן *tribe of Levi and Aaron* CD 10$_{5}$, מטות [לוין ויהודה *tribes of Levi and Judah* 11QT^{b} 6$_{13}$, מַטֵּה מְנַשֶּׁה *tribe of Manasseh* Nm 1$_{35}$ 2$_{20}$ 13$_{11}$ 34$_{14}$ Jos 17$_{1}$ 20$_{8}$ 21$_{5.6.25.27}$ 22$_{1}$ 1 C 6$_{46}$ (if del. חֲצִי *half of*) 6$_{47}$ (or em.; see below) 6$_{55.56}$ 12$_{32}$, נַפְתָּלִי *of Naphtali* Nm 1$_{43}$ 2$_{29}$ 13$_{14}$ Jos 21$_{6.32}$ 1 K 7$_{14}$ 1 C 6$_{47.61}$, רְאוּבֵן *of Reuben* Nm 1$_{21}$ 13$_{4}$ Jos 20$_{8}$ 21$_{7.36}$ 1 C 6$_{48.63}$, שִׁמְעוֹן *of Simeon* Nm 1$_{23}$ 2$_{12}$ 13$_{5}$ 34$_{20(mss)}$, הַשִּׁמְעֹנִי *of the Simeonites* Jos 21$_{4}$, מטה גדלי perh. *tribe of Gadli* Ḥorvat 'Uza jar inscr. 1$_{3}$ 2$_{2}$.

מַטֵּה אָבִיהָ *tribe of her father* Nm 36$_{8}$, אֲבִיהֶם *of their father* Nm 36$_{6}$ (mss, Sam אֲבִיהֶן), מַטֵּה אֲבֹתָיו *tribe of his fathers* Nm 13$_{2}$ 36$_{7}$, אֲבֹתֵינוּ *of our fathers* Nm 36$_{4}$, אֲבֹתָם *of their fathers* Nm 1$_{47}$, מַטּוֹת אֲבוֹתֵיכֶם *tribes of your fathers* Nm 33$_{54}$, אֲבוֹתָם *of their fathers* Nm 1$_{16}$ 26$_{55}$ (אֲבֹתָם), אֲבֹתֵיהֶן *of their* (fem.) *fathers* Nm 36$_{4(mss, Sam)}$, מַטֵּה בְנֵי *tribe of the sons of* Asher Nm 10$_{26}$ 34$_{27}$ Jos 19$_{24.31}$, Benjamin Nm 10$_{24}$ Jos 18$_{11.21}$ 1 C 6$_{50}$, Dan Nm 34$_{22}$ Jos 19$_{40.48}$, Ephraim Nm 34$_{24}$ Jos 16$_{8}$, Gad Nm 10$_{20}$ 34$_{14}$, Zebulun Nm 10$_{16}$ 34$_{25}$, Judah Jos 15$_{1.20.21}$ 21$_{9}$ 1 C 6$_{50}$, Joseph Nm 36$_{5}$, Issachar Nm 10$_{15}$ 34$_{26}$ Jos 19$_{23}$, Manasseh Nm 10$_{23}$ 34$_{23}$ Jos 13$_{29}$, Naphtali Nm 10$_{27}$ 34$_{28}$ Jos 19$_{39}$, Reuben Nm 34$_{14}$ Jos 13$_{15}$, Simeon Nm 10$_{19}$ 34$_{20}$ Jos 19$_{1.8}$ 21$_{9}$ 1 C 6$_{50}$, מַטּוֹת בְּנֵי יִשְׂרָאֵל *tribes of the sons of Israel* Nm 36$_{8.9}$ Jos 19$_{51}$ 11QT 21$_{15}$ (בנ[י ישר]אל), מַטֵּה מִשְׁפַּחַת *tribe of the clan of* Nm 36$_{12}$, חֲצִי *of half of* Manasseh 1 C 6$_{46}$ (or del. חֲצִי).

אֲבוֹת הַמַּטּוֹת *fathers' houses of the tribes* Nm 32$_{28}$ Jos 14$_{1}$ 21$_{1}$, נְשִׂיאֵי *leaders of* Nm 7$_{2}$ (הַמַּטֹּת), נְשִׂיאֵי מַטּוֹת *leaders of the tribes of* Nm 1$_{16}$, רָאשֵׁי הַמַּטּוֹת *heads of the tribes* Nm 30$_{2}$ 1 K 8$_{1}$||2 C 5$_{2}$ 11QT 18$_{16}$ ([ראשי ה]מטות), מִשְׁפַּחַת הַמַּטֶּה *clan of the tribe* 1 C 6$_{46}$ (or em. לְמִשְׁפְּחוֹתָם מִמַּטֵּה אֶפְרַיִם וּמִמַּטֵּה דָן *for their clans, from the tribe of Ephraim and from the tribe of Dan*), מִשְׁפַּחַת מַטֵּה *clan of the tribe of* Nm 36$_{6.8}$, מִשְׁפַּחַת חֲצִי מַטֵּה *clan of half of the tribe of* Manasseh 1 C 6$_{56}$ (or em. לְמִשְׁפְּחוֹתָם מֵחֲצִי מַטֵּה *for their clans, from half of the tribe of*), מִשְׁפְּחוֹת מַטֵּה *clans of the tribe of* Jos 21$_{5.6}$ (or em. both לְמִשְׁפְּחוֹתָם מִמַּטֵּה *for their clans, from the tribe of*), צְבָא מַטֵּה *host of the tribe of* Nm 10$_{15+7t}$, שְׁמוֹת מַטּוֹת *names of the tribes of* Nm 26$_{55}$, נַחֲלַת הַמַּטֶּה *inheritance of the tribe* Nm 36$_{3.4}$, מַטֵּה *of the tribe of* Nm 36$_{4.7}$ Jos 15$_{20}$ 16$_{8}$ 19$_{8.23.31.39.48}$, שְׁנֵי הַמַּטּוֹת וַחֲצִי הַמַּטֶּה *of the two and a half tribes* Jos 14$_{3}$, גּוֹרַל מַטֵּה *lot of the tribe of* Jos 18$_{11}$, משבות מטות *dwelling places of the tribes of* 11QT 21$_{15}$, עולת מטה *burnt offering of the tribe of* 11QT 23$_{10}$ 24$_{10}$.

חֲצִי הַמַּטֶּה *half of the tribe* Nm 34$_{13.15}$ Jos 14$_{2.3}$, חֲצִי מַטֵּה *half of the tribe of* Manasseh Jos 13$_{29}$ 21$_{5.6.27}$ 22$_{1}$ Nm 34$_{14}$, מַחֲצִית *half of* Manasseh Jos 21$_{25}$ 1 C 6$_{46.47}$ (if em. מִמַּטֵּה *from the tribe of* to מִמַּחֲצִית) 6$_{55}$ 12$_{32}$, כול המטה *every tribe* 11QT 21$_{2}$, כול מטה ומטה *every tribe* 11QT 22$_{12}$ 23$_{7}$ (כול מ[טה ומטה]), כול המט[ות] *all the tribes* 11QT 21$_{2}$, כֹּל מַטּוֹת *all the tribes of* Nm 31$_{4}$ Jos 22$_{14}$ 11QT 19$_{14}$ (כול).

<APP> אֶפְרַיִם *Ephraim* Jos 14$_{4}$, מְנַשֶּׁה *Manasseh* Jos 14$_{4}$, שֵׁבֶט *tribe* Nm 18$_{2}$ 11QT 21$_{2}$, אָח *brother* Nm 18$_{2}$.

<PREP> לְ of possession, *of, (belonging) to* Ex 31$_{2.6}$|| 35$_{30.34}$ 38$_{22.23}$ Lv 24$_{11}$ Nm 1$_{4+12t}$ 7$_{12}$ 13$_{2+12t}$ (or em. לְמַטֵּה at 13$_{11}$ to לִבְנֵי *[belonging] to the sons of*) 31$_{4.4.4.5.6}$ 34$_{19+9t}$ Jos 7$_{1.18}$ 15$_{21}$ 18$_{21}$ 19$_{51}$ 22$_{14}$ Si 45$_{6.25}$ 4QapMos^{c} 2.1$_{4}$ (ל[מ]טה) 2.1$_{5}$ 11QT 23$_{7}$ (כול מ[טה]) CD 10$_{5}$ Ḥorvat ʿUza jar inscr. 1$_{3}$ 2$_{2}$, + היה *be* Nm 36$_{3.4}$ Jos 13$_{29}$ (לַחֲצִי מַטֵּה *to the half of the tribe of*) 15$_{1}$ 17$_{1}$.

לְ of direction, *to*, + נתן *give* Nm 34$_{13}$ Jos 13$_{15.24}$ 11QT 21$_{2}$ ([ונתנו]) 21$_{2}$ ([ונתנו] ... לכול המט[ות]) 22$_{12.13}$, בוא *come* 4QpsEzek^{c} 4.1$_{1}$ ([ב]א למטותיה[ם]), יצא (of lot) *go out* Jos 17$_{1(ms)}$ 19$_{1.24.40}$, סבב *go around* Nm 36$_{9}$, *call*, i.e. summon Jos 22$_{1}$ (לַחֲצִי מַטֵּה *to the half of the tribe of*); *according to*, + פקד hothp. *be numbered* Nm 1$_{47}$, נחל htp. *inherit* Nm 33$_{54}$; *concerning*, + צוה pi. *command* Jos 14$_{2}$.

מִן partitive, *from (among), (out) of* Nm 34$_{18}$ 36$_{8}$ 1 K 7$_{14}$ 1 C 12$_{32}$, + היה *be* Jos 21$_{4+11}$ (if em. at 21$_{5.6}$; see Cstr.) 1 C 6$_{51}$, + נתן *give* Jos 20$_{8.8.8}$ 21$_{9+11t}$ 1 C 6$_{45+20t}$ (if em. at 6$_{46.46.56}$; see Cstr.), ברר *choose* 11QT 57$_{6}$; of direction, *from*, + סבב *go around* Nm 36$_{7.9}$, קרב hi. *bring near*, i.e. offer 11QT 19$_{14}$ ([ה]ק[ר]בתמה) 21$_{15}$.

אֶל *to*, + סבב *go around* Nm 36$_{7.9(Sam)}$.

עַל *upon, in*, + היה *be* Nm 36$_{12}$; *for, on behalf of* 11QT 19$_{15}$.

<COLL> שְׁנֵי הַמַּטּוֹת *the two tribes* Nm 34$_{15}$ Jos 14$_{3.4}$ (שְׁנֵי מַטּוֹת), תִּשְׁעַת הַמַּטּוֹת *the nine tribes* Nm 34$_{13}$ Jos 14$_{2}$, שנים עשר מטות *the twelve tribes of* 4QapJoshua^{b} 1$_{5}$; הַמַּטּוֹת לִבְנֵי יִשְׂרָאֵל *the tribes of the sons of Israel* Nm 30$_{2}$ 32$_{28}$ Jos 14$_{1}$ 21$_{1}$.

Also 4QBark^{d} 5$_{2}$ ([מ]טותיהם).

<SYN> §1 שֵׁבֶט *staff*, זָדוֹן *presumptuousness*.*

⇒ נטה *stretch out*.

*[מַטֶּה] II 2 n.[m.]pl. **mace** (unless מַטֶּה I *shaft* of arrow or מָטוֹ *war, company*)—pl. cstr. מַטּוֹת; sf. מַטָּיו—<SUBJ> perh. שׁבע pass. *be sworn* Hb 3$_{9}$ (but prob. שְׁבֻעוֹת *oaths of*). <CSTR> מַטּוֹת אֹמֶר *a mace (consisting) of speech* Hb 3$_{9}$; שְׁבֻעוֹת מַטּוֹת appar. *oaths of a mace of* Hb 3$_{9}$ (unless שׁבע pass. ptc.). <PREP> בְּ of instrument, *by (means of), with*, + נקב *pierce* Hb 3$_{14}$. <COLL> שְׁבֻעוֹת מַטּוֹת אֹמֶר *your mace is the oaths of (your) word*, or *the seven-headed mace is (your) word* Hb 3$_{9}$.*

מִטָּה 29.1 n.f. **bed**—cstr. מִטַּת; sf. מִטָּתִי, מִטָּתְךָ, מִטָּתוֹ; pl. מִטּוֹת; cstr. מִטּוֹת; sf. Si מטותם—**bed, couch,** for resting at night (e.g. 1 S 19$_{13}$ Ps 6$_{7}$), in the day (e.g. 2 S 4$_{7}$), in sickness (e.g. Gn 47$_{31}$ 2 K 1$_{4}$), for reclining at feasts (e.g. Ezk 23$_{41}$ Am 6$_{4}$ Est 7$_{8}$); as carried bed (1 S 19$_{15}$), prob. **litter, sedan** (Ca 3$_{7}$), **bier** (2 S 3$_{31}$), <SUBJ> רבד pass. *be spread* Ezk 13$_{41}$ (if em.; see App.). <NOM CL> הִנֵּה מִטָּתוֹ שֶׁלִּשְׁלֹמֹה *behold the litter* (perh. *couch*) *of*

Solomon Ca 37, מִטּוֹת זָהָב וָכֶסֶף עַל רִצְפַת בַּהַט־וָשֵׁשׁ וְדַר וְסֹחָרֶת *there were beds of silver and gold on a pavement of porphyry and marble and mother-of-pearl and turquoise* Est 16 (or em.; see Prep.). <OBJ> שִׂים *place* 2 K 410, שׂחה hi. *cause to swim* with tears Ps 67. <CSTR> מִטַּת אִישׁ *bed of the man of* God 2 K 421, מִטּוֹת שֵׁן *beds of ivory* Am 64, זָהָב וָכֶסֶף *of gold and silver* Est 16; רֹאשׁ הַמִּטָּה *head of the bed* Gn 4731, פְּאַת מִטָּה *corner of a bed* Am 312, חֲדַר הַמִּטּוֹת *chamber of the beds* 2 K 112||2 C 2211. <APP> מִטָּה כְבוּדָּה *couch, wealth,* i.e. sumptuous couch Ezk 2341 (or em. רְבוּדָה *spread* couch).

<PREP> בְּ of place, *in,* + עלה hi. *bring up* 1 S 1915; of accompaniment, *with* Est 16 (if em. מִטּוֹת *[there were] beds of* to בְּמִטּוֹת); מִן of direction, *from,* + ירד *go down* 2 K 14.6.16, hi. *bring down* Si 486; אֶל *in, on, (on)to* 1 S 1916, + אסף *gather,* i.e. draw, feet Gn 4933, שִׂים *place* 1 S 1913, ישׁב *sit* 1 S 2823, נפל *fall* Est 78 (if em.; see below); עַל *upon* Est 78, + ישׁב *sit* Gn 482 1 S 2823(mss) Ezk 2341, שׁכב *lie down* 2 S 47 1 K 214, hi. *cause to lie down* 1 K 1719 2 K 421, ho. *be laid* 2 K 432, סבב *turn* Pr 2614, נפל *fall* Est 78 (or em. עַל to אֶל *[on]to*), הרג *kill* 2 C 2425; *to,* + בוא *go in* Ex 728; סְבִיב לְ *around* Ca 37; אַחֲרֵי *after,* + הלך *go* 2 S 331.

<COLL> מִטָּה || עֶרֶשׂ *couch* Am 312 64 (+) Ps 67, צִיר *hinge* Pr 2614; + כִּסֵּא *chair* 2 K 410, שֻׁלְחָן *table* 2 K 410, מְנוֹרָה *lampstand* 2 K 410, בַּיִת *house* Ex 728, תַּנּוּר *oven* Ex 728, מִשְׁאֶרֶת *kneading bowl* Ex 728.

הַמִּטָּה אֲשֶׁר־עָלִיתָ שָּׁם *the bed (onto) which you have gone* 2 K 14.6.16, מִטָּתוֹ שֶׁלִּשְׁלֹמֹה *the couch of Solomon* Ca 37, כֹּל מַעֲבַר מַטֵּה מוּסָדָה *every burning of a raised bed* Is 3032 (if em. מַטֵּה *staff* to מִטָּה).*

<SYN> עֶרֶשׂ *couch,* צִיר *hinge.**

⇒ נטה *stretch out.*

מֻטָּה, see מוֹטָה *bar.*

[מֻטָּה] 1 n.f. **outspreading**—pl. cstr. מֻטּוֹת—of wings of Assyrian king, <SUBJ> היה *be* Is 88 (+ מְלֹא *fullness* of breadth of land). <CSTR> מֻטּוֹת כְּנָפָיו *outspreadings of his wings,* i.e. his outspread wings Is 88.

⇒ נטה *stretch out.*

מֶטֶה 1.0.1 n.[m.] **injustice, perversity,** <SUBJ> צִיץ *blossom* Ezk 710 (if em. הַמַּטֶּה *the rod*). <OBJ> מלא *be full of* Ezk 99 (|| דָּם *bloodshed*), סור hi. *remove* Is 589 (if em. מוֹטָה *yoke*). <CSTR> אנשי מטה *men of injustice* 1QS 112.

<SYN> דָּם *bloodshed.*

⇒ נטה *stretch out.*

***[מִטְהָר]** n.[m.] **splendour, lustre** or perh. **purity,** <OBJ> שׁבת hi. *cause to cease* Ps 8945 (if em. מִטְּהָרוֹ *some of his purity* to מִטְהָרוֹ; + כִּסֵּא *throne*).

⇒ טהר *be pure.*

***[מָטוֹ]** 2 n.[m.] **war, company** (unless from מַטֶּה I *arrow* or II *mace*)—pl. cstr. מַטּוֹת; sf. מַטָּיו—<SUBJ> perh. שׁבע pass. *be sworn* Hb 39 (but prob. שְׁבֻעוֹת *oaths of*). <CSTR> מַטּוֹת אֹמֶר *war (consisting) of speech* Hb 39; שְׁבֻעוֹת מַטּוֹת appar. *oaths of war of* Hb 39 (unless שׁבע pass. ptc.). <PREP> בְּ of instrument, *by (means of), with,* + נקב *pierce* Hb 314.

מַטְוֶה 1 n.[m.] **yarn,** <OBJ> בוא hi. *bring* Ex 3525. <APP> אַרְגָּמָן *purple (material)* Ex 3525, תְּכֵלֶת *blue (material)* Ex 3525, תּוֹלַעַת *scarlet (material)* Ex 3525 (תּוֹלַעַת שָׁנִי), שֵׁשׁ *fine linen* Ex 3525.

⇒ טוה *spin.*

***[מָטוֹן]** 0.0.1 n.[m.] **hiding place**—pl. cstr. Q מטוני—<CSTR> מטוני פחיה *hiding places of her traps* 1QH fr. 34 (+ מפרש [רשתה] *place of spreading of her net*). <PREP> עַל *upon,* + עמד *stand* 1QH fr. 34 (ו[עמד]).

⇒ (?) טמן *conceal.*

[מְטִיל] I 1 n.[m.] **rod**—cstr. מְטִיל—as description of bones of Behemoth (unless מְטִיל II *strong*), <CSTR> מְטִיל בַּרְזֶל *rod of iron* Jb 4018 (or em. מֵטַל *trap[s] of;* + אָפִיק *tube* of bronze). <PREP> כְּ *as* Jb 4018 (or em.; see Cstr.).

***מְטִיל** II 1 adj. **strong** (unless מְטִיל I *rod*), גְּרָמָיו כִּמְטִיל בַּרְזֶל *his limbs like strong iron* Jb 4018 (or em. מֵטַל *trap[s] of;* + אָפִיק *tube* of bronze).

*[מְטִיל] III n.[m.] **destroyer**, <PREP> לְ *to* Is 50$_6$ (גֵּוִי נָתַתִּי לְמַכִּים וּלְחָיַי לְמֹטְלִים *I gave my back to blows and my cheeks to destroyers* [if em. לְמֹרְטִים *to those who made smooth*, with 1QIsa[a] למטלים]).

מַטִּיף *preacher, teacher*, see נטף *drip*.

*[מְטִל] n.[m.] **trap,** as description of bones of Behemoth, <CSTR> מְטִל בַּרְזֶל *trap(s) of iron* Jb 40$_{18}$ (if em. מְטִיל *rod of*; + אָפִיק *tube* of bronze). <PREP> כְּ *as* Jb 40$_{18}$ (if em.; see Cstr.).

*מִטַּל 2 n.[m.] **dew** (unless טַל *dew* + מִן *some of*)—cstr. מִטַּל—<OBJ> נתן *give* Gn 27$_{28}$ (|| מִשְׁמָן *choice produce*), כלא *withhold* Hg 1$_{10}$ (|| יְבוּל *produce*). <CSTR> מִטַּל הַשָּׁמַיִם *dew of heaven* Gn 27$_{28}$.

<SYN> מִשְׁמָן *choice produce*, יְבוּל *produce*.

⇒ cf. טַל *dew*.

מַטְמוֹן I 5.1 n.[m.] **treasure**—cstr. Si מטמון; pl. מַטְמוֹנִים (מַטְמֹנִים); cstr. מַטְמֻנֵי—**1. (hidden) treasure, hidden store** (Jr 41$_8$). **2. provisions** stored in silo, i.e. grain pit,* <NOM CL> יֶשׁ־לָנוּ מַטְמֹנִים בַּשָּׂדֶה *there are to us hidden stores in the countryside* Jr 41$_8$, בת לאב מטמון שקר *a daughter is a false treasure to her father* Si 42$_9$ (Bmg). <OBJ> נתן *give* Gn 43$_{23}$ Is 45$_3$ (|| אוֹצָר *treasure*). <CSTR> מטמון שקר appar. *treasure of falsehood*, i.e. false treasure Si 42$_9$(Bmg) (M [ ]מטמון ש; B מטמנת *treasure of*; perh. שקר is error for שקד *of*, i.e. which causes, *wakefulness*), מַטְמֻנֵי מִסְתָּרִים *treasures of*, i.e. in, *secret places* Is 45$_3$. <APP> מַטְמֹנִים ... חִטִּים וּשְׂעֹרִים וְשֶׁמֶן וּדְבָשׁ *hidden stores ... wheat and barley and oil and honey* Jr 41$_8$. <PREP> כְּ *as (for)*, + חפשׂ *search* Pr 2$_4$ (|| כֶּסֶף *silver*); מִן of comparison, *(more) than (for)*, + חפר *dig* Jb 3$_{21}$ (or em. וַיַּחְפְּרֻהוּ מִמַּטְמוֹנִים appar. *they dig for it more than [for] treasure* to וַיַּחְפְּרֻהוּם מַטְמוֹנִים *and they dig for themselves crypts* [מַטְמוֹן II]).

<SYN> אוֹצָר *treasure*, כֶּסֶף *silver*.*

⇒ טמן *conceal*.

*[מַטְמוֹן] II n.[m.] **crypt,** for burial, <OBJ> חפר *dig* Jb 3$_{21}$ (if em. וַיַּחְפְּרֻהוּ מִמַּטְמוֹנִים appar. *they dig for it more than [for] treasure* [מַטְמוֹן I] to וַיַּחְפְּרֻהוּם מַטְמוֹנִים *and they dig for themselves crypts*).

⇒ טמן *conceal*.

*[מַטְמֹנֶת] 0.1 n.f. **treasure**—cstr. Si מטמנת—<NOM CL> בת לאב מטמנת שקר *a daughter is to her father a false treasure* Si 42$_9$(B). <CSTR> מטמנת שקר appar. *treasure of falsehood*, i.e. false treasure Si 42$_9$(B) (Bmg, M מטמון *treasure of*; perh. שקר is error for שקד *of*, i.e. which causes, *wakefulness*).

⇒ טמן *conceal*.

מַטָּע 6.0.5 n.m. **planting**—cstr. מַטַּע; sf. Q מטעכה, Kt מטעו, מַטָּעָהּ, Q מטעכם; pl. cstr. מַטָּעֵי; sf. Qr מַטָּעַי, Q מטעיו—**(act of) planting** (Is 60$_{21}$), **(place of) planting, plantation** (Ezk 17$_7$ 31$_4$ 34$_{29}$ Mc 1$_6$ 1QH 8$_{5.21}$), **(object of) planting, plant** (Is 61$_3$ 1QH 8$_{13}$ [מט[ע]] perh. 8$_{20}$), <SUBJ> סתר pu. *be hidden* 1QH 8$_{20}$ ([סותר]). <NOM CL> מטע עציהם על משקלת השמש *the planting of their trees shall be according to the plumb line of the sun* 1QH 8$_{21}$. <OBJ> נטע *plant* 1QH 8$_5$ (נטע[ה]), קום hi. *raise up* Ezk 34$_{29}$.

<CSTR> מַטַּע י׳ *planting of Y.* Is 60$_{21}$ (if em. מטעו [Kt] *his planting*; 1QIsa[a] מטעי י׳ *plantings of Y.*) 61$_3$, שָׁלוֹם *of peace* Ezk 34$_{29}$ (if em.; see Coll.), מטע ברוש ותדהר *planting of juniper and pine* 1QH 8$_5$, עציהם *of their trees* 1QH 8$_{21}$, מַטָּעֵי כָרֶם *planting of vineyards* Mc 1$_6$ (+ עִי *ruin*), מטע פרי *plant of the fruit of* 1QH 8$_{20}$, שחקים *of heaven* 1QH 8$_{13}$ (מט[ע]); נֵצֶר מַטָּעַי *shoot of my planting* Is 60$_{21}$(Qr) (Kt מטעו, 1QIsa[b] מטעיו *of his planting*; + מַעֲשֵׂה יָדַי *work of my hands*), נֵצֶר מַטָּע *shoot of the planting of* Is 60$_{21}$ (if em.; see above; or em. נֹצֵר *guardian of* his plantation), נצר מטעי *shoot of the plantings of* Is 60$_{21}$(1QIsa[a]); עֲרֻגוֹת מַטָּעָהּ *beds of its* (vine's) *planting*, i.e. where it was planted Ezk 17$_4$ (mss עֲרֻגַת *bed of*).

<APP> אֵלָה *terebinth* Is 61$_3$. <PREP> לְ introducing object, + שׂים *place*, i.e. make (into) Mc 1$_6$; עִם *with*, + נוב pol. *bear fruit* 1QH 8$_{13}$ (מט[ע]); סְבִיבוֹת *around*, + הלך *go* Ezk 31$_4$. <COLL> מַטָּע לְשֵׁם *a planting for renown* Ezk 34$_{29}$ (or em. מַטַּע שָׁלוֹם *plantation of peace*), וְקֹרָא לָהֶם ... מַטַּע י׳ *and they shall be called ... the planting*

of Y. Is 61$_3$.
Also 4QBen 1$_5$ 4QRitMar 27$_5$.*
⇒ נטע *plant*, מַטַּעַת *planting*.

[מַטְעָם] 8.6 n.[m.] **delicacy**—sf. Si מטעמו; pl. מַטְעַמִּים (Si מטמים); cstr. Si מטעמי; sf. מַטְעַמּוֹתָיו (מַטְעַמֹּתָיו)—**delicacy, tasty dish,** <NOM CL> מעגל נפש מטעמו *his delicacy is a pollution of the soul* Si 40$_{29(B)}$ (Bmg מעגל נפשו מטעמי זבד *delicacies given as a gift are the pollution of his soul*). <OBJ> עשׂה *make* Gn 27$_{4+5t}$, בוא hi. *bring* Gn 27$_{31}$, נתן *give* Gn 27$_{17}$ (|| לֶחֶם *bread*), אהב *love* Gn 27$_{4.9.14}$, טעם *taste* Si 36$_{24(C)}$, בחן *test* Si 36$_{24(B, Bmg).24}$, בין hi. *understand* Si 36$_{24(B)}$. <CSTR> מטעמי זבד *delicacies of*, i.e. given as, *a gift* Si 36$_{24(Bmg, C)}$ 40$_{29(Bmg)}$, דבר *of speech* Si 36$_{24(B)}$ (מט[ע]מ[י]), כזב *of a lie* Si 36$_{24(B)}$; כל מטעמים *any delicacies* Si 37$_{29(B)}$. <PREP> לְ introducing object, + אוה htp. *desire* Pr 23$_{3.6}$ (both + לֶחֶם *bread*); בְּ of instrument, *by (means of) with*, + אנס ni. *be forced* Si 34$_{21}$; אֶל *towards*, + חנג htp. *dance* Si 37$_{29(Bmg, D)}$ (perh. error for ענג htp. *take delight*); עַל *on account of*, + חנג htp. *dance* Si 37$_{29(D)}$ (perh. error for ענג htp. *take delight*), שׁפך pu. *be poured*, i.e. be caused to slip Si 37$_{29(B)}$; תַּחַת *in place of* Si 33$_{13}$ (שנות לב טוב תחת מטעמים *the sleep of the heart is good in place of delicacies*; + מַאֲכָל *food*).
<SYN> לֶחֶם *bread*.
⇒ טעם *taste*.

מַטַּעַת 0.0.10 n.f. **planting**—cstr. Q מטעת—**(place of) planting, plantation** (1QH 8$_9$); **(object of) planting, plant** (1QH 8$_{6.10}$ 4Q418 81$_{13}$), as description of community council (1QH 6$_{15}$ 1QS 8$_5$ 11$_5$), remnant of Israel and Aaron (CD 1$_7$); in ref. to produce (4QD^e 2.2$_6$ 4QMMT B$_{62}$ [[מ]טעת]), <OBJ> נתן *give* 4QD^e 2.2$_6$ ([לתת]). <CSTR> מטעת עולם *planting of everlastingness*, i.e. everlasting plant 1QH 6$_{15}$ 8$_6$ 1QS 8$_5$ (=4QS^e 2$_{14}$ [מ]שפט *judgment of*) 11$_8$ 4Q418 81$_{13}$ (עו[לם]), אמת *of truth* 1QH 8$_{10}$, ע[צי] *of the trees of* 4QMMT B$_{62}$ ([מ]טעת), [הרביעית] *of the fourth (year)* 4QD^e 2.2$_6$; שורש מטעת *root of planting* CD 1$_7$, עיפי מטעת *branches of a plant of* 1QH 6$_{15}$. <APP> בַּיִת *house* 1QS 8$_5$, סוֹד *council* 1QS 8$_5$. <PREP> לְ *into, as* 1QS 11$_8$ 4Q418 81$_{13}$, + פרח hi. *cause to sprout* 1QH 8$_{6.10}$, כון ni. *be established* 1QS 8$_5$; בְּ of place, *in* perh. 4Q423 2$_7$ ([במטע]), + שׂגשׂג pilp. *grow* 1QH 8$_9$; עַל *concerning* 4QMMT B$_{62}$ (ע[ל מ]טעת). <COLL> מַטַּעַת + נֵצֶר *shoot* 1QH 6$_{15}$ 8$_{6.10}$.
⇒ נטע *plant*, מַטָּע *plant*.

מִטְפַּחַת 2 n.f. **cloak**—מִטְפָּחוֹת—of Ruth (Ru 3$_{15}$), in list of fine clothes of women (Is 3$_{22}$), <NOM CL> הַמִּטְפַּחַת אֲשֶׁר עָלַיִךְ *the cloak that is upon you* Ru 3$_{15}$. <OBJ> יהב *give* Ru 3$_{15}$, שׁית *place* Ru 3$_{15}$, סור hi. *remove* Is 3$_{22}$ (+ מַעֲטָפָה *tunic*, מַחֲלָצָה *festive robe*). <PREP> בְּ introducing object, + אחז *hold* Ru 3$_{15}$.
⇒ טפח I *be broad*.

מטר 17.0.1 vb. **rain—Ni.** 1 3fs תִּמָּטֵר—**1. be rained upon,** <SUBJ> חֶלְקָה *field* Am 4$_7$.
2. be rained down, <SUBJ> גַּחֶלֶת *coal* Ps 140$_{11}$ (if em. מוט Qr ni. *be made to drop*). <PREP> עַל *upon*, + סבב hi. ptc. *one who surrounds* Ps 140$_{11}$ (if em.; see Subj.).
Pu. be rained upon, <SUBJ> אֶרֶץ *land* Ezk 22$_{24}$ (if em. מְטֹהָרָה *purified* to מְמֻטָּרָה).
Hi. 16.0.1 Pf. הִמְטִיר; impf. יַמְטֵר, 3fs תַּמְטִיר, אַמְטִיר; + waw וַיַּמְטֵר, וְהִמְטַרְתִּי; ptc. מַמְטִיר; inf. הַמְטִיר (Q המטר)—**rain** (Is 5$_6$ Am 4$_7$), **(cause it to) rain, send rain,** <SUBJ> Y. Gn 2$_5$ 7$_4$ 19$_{24}$ Ex 9$_{18.23}$ 16$_4$ Ezk 38$_{22}$ Am 4$_{7.7.7(mss)}$ Zc 10$_1$ (if em. מְטַר *rain of* to מַמְטִיר) Ps 11$_6$ 78$_{24.27}$ Jb 20$_{23}$ 1QDM 2$_{10}$, אוֹיֵב *enemy* Ps 55$_4$ (if em. מוט hi. *let drop*), רָשָׁע *wicked one* Ps 55$_4$ (if em. מוט hi.), עָב *cloud* Is 5$_6$, מִי *who?* Jb 38$_{26}$, impersonal Am 4$_7$; subj. not specified, Ps 140$_{11}$ (if em. מוט Kt. hi.).
<OBJ> מָטָר *rain* Is 5$_6$ 1QDM 2$_{10}$, גֶּשֶׁם *rain* Ezk 38$_{22}$ Zc 10$_1$ (if em.; see Subj.), בָּרָד *hail* Ex 9$_{18.23}$, אֶבֶן hail *stone* Ezk 38$_{22}$, מַבֻּל *flood* Jb 20$_{23}$ (if em.; see Prep.), אֵשׁ *fire* Gn 19$_{24}$ Ezk 38$_{22}$ Ps 11$_6$ (or em.; see below), מַבֵּל *fire* Jb 20$_{23}$ (if em.; see Prep.), גָּפְרִית *brimstone* Gn 19$_{24}$ Ezk 38$_{22}$ Ps 11$_6$, פֶּחָם *coal* Ps 11$_6$ (if em.; see below), גַּחֶלֶת *coal* Ps 140$_{11}$ (if em.; see Subj.), לֶחֶם *bread* Ex 16$_4$, מָן *manna* Ps 78$_{24}$, שְׁאֵר *flesh* Ps 78$_{27}$, עוֹף *birds* Ps 78$_{27}$, appar. פַּח *snare* Ps 11$_6$ (or em. פַּחִים אֵשׁ *snares, fire* to פַּחֲמֵי אֵשׁ *coals of fire*), חֵבֶל *pain* Jb 20$_{23}$ (if em.; see Prep.), בַּלָּהָה *terror* Jb 20$_{23}$ (if em.; see Prep.), אָוֶן *trou-*

ble Ps 55$_4$ (if em.; see Subj.).

<PREP> לְ of benefit, *for*, + Israel Ex 16$_4$; *within (a period of)*, + יוֹם *day* Gn 7$_4$.

בְּ of place, *on(to)*, + לְחוּם *flesh* Jb 20$_{23}$ (unless לְחוּם II *warfare*; or em. עָלֵימוֹ בִּלְחוּמוֹ *upon him, on his flesh* to עָלָיו מַבֵּל חֲמוֹ *upon him the fire of his wrath* or מַבֵּל חֲמָתוֹ *the flood of his anger*, or em. בִּלְחוּמוֹ to בְּלַחְמוֹ *as his bread* or חֲבָלִים *pains* or בַּלָּהוֹת *terror*).

כְּ *as*, + עָפָר *dust* Ps 78$_{27}$, חוֹל *sand* Ps 78$_{27}$; *about*, + עֵת *time* Ex 9$_{18}$.

מִן of direction, *from*, + שָׁמַיִם *heaven* Gn 19$_{24}$ Ex 16$_4$.

עַל *upon*, + גּוֹג *Gog* Ezk 38$_{22}$, Israelites Ps 78$_{24.27}$ 1QDM 2$_{10}$ (ע[ליכ]ם), עַם *people* Ezk 38$_{22}$, אֲגַף *troop* Ezk 38$_{22}$, רָשָׁע *wicked one* Ps 11$_6$ Jb 20$_{23}$, חָנֵף *profane one* Jb 20$_{23}$, סבב hi. ptc. *one who surrounds* Ps 140$_{11}$ (if em.; see Subj.), worshipper Ps 55$_4$ (if em.; see Subj.), אֶרֶץ *land* Gn 2$_4$ 7$_4$ Ex 9$_{23}$ Jb 38$_{26}$, מִדְבָּר *steppe* Jb 38$_{26}$, חֶלְקָה *field* Am 4$_7$, כֶּרֶם *vineyard* Is 5$_6$, עִיר *city* Am 4$_{7.7}$, סְדֹם *Sodom* Gn 19$_{24}$, עֲמֹרָה *Gomorrah* Gn 19$_{24}$.

מֵאֵת *from*, + Y. Gn 19$_{24}$.

<COLL> מטר hi. + noun used adverbially, יוֹם *day*, i.e. for (a specified number of) days Gn 7$_4$, מָחָר *tomorrow* Ex 9$_{18}$.

Ho. be rained upon, <SUBJ> אֶרֶץ *land* Ezk 22$_{24}$ (if em. מְטֹהָרָה *purified* to מְמֻטָרָה).

⇒ מָטָר *rain*, (?) מַטְרִי *Matrite*.

מָטָר 38.2.4 n.m. **rain**—cstr. מְטַר; sf. Si מטרו; pl. cstr. מִטְרוֹת—**rain; snowfall** (Si 43$_{18}$), <SUBJ> היה *be* Dt 11$_{17}$ 1 K 8$_{35}$||2 C 6$_{26}$ 1 K 17$_1$ 2 C 7$_{13}$, נתך ni. *be poured* Ex 9$_{33}$, סחף *beat* Pr 28$_3$, חדל *cease* Ex 9$_{34}$.

<NOM CL> אַל־מָטָר עֲלֵיכֶם *let there be no rain upon you* 2 S 1$_{21}$, גֶּבֶר רָשׁ וְעֹשֵׁק דַּלִּים מָטָר סֹחֵף *a poor man who oppresses the poor is a beating rain* Pr 28$_3$.

<OBJ> נתן *give* Dt 11$_{14}$ 28$_{12}$ 1 S 12$_{17.18}$ 1 K 8$_{36}$||2 C 6$_{27}$ 1 K 18$_1$ Is 30$_{23}$ Zc 10$_1$ (or em.; see Cstr.) Jb 5$_{10}$, i.e. make, into powder and dust Dt 28$_{24}$, מטר hi. *rain* Is 5$_6$ 1QDM 2$_{10}$, ריק hi. *pour out* 4QAdmon 1.1$_5$ (הר[י]קו), ירד hi. *send down* 11QM 1.2$_9$, כון hi. *prepare* Ps 147$_8$, שׁאל *ask (for)* Zc 10$_1$, זקק *distil* Jb 36$_{27}$.

<CSTR> מְטַר הַשָּׁמַיִם *rain of heaven* Dt 11$_{11}$, אַרְצְךָ *of your land* Dt 28$_{12}$ (ms, Sam^{mss} מָטָר לְאַרְצְךָ *rain to your land*) 28$_{24}$, ־אַרְצְכֶם *of your* (pl.) *land* Dt 11$_{14}$ (ms, Sam מָטָר לְאַרְצְךָ), זַרְעֲךָ *of*, i.e. for, *your seed* Is 30$_{23}$, ־גֶּשֶׁם *of a shower* Zc 10$_1$ (or em. מַמְטִיר *causing it to rain*), מִטְרוֹת עֻזּוֹ *rains of his strength* Jb 37$_6$ (or em. גֶּשֶׁם מָטָר וְגֶשֶׁם מִטְרוֹת עֻזּוֹ *shower of rain and shower of the rains of his strength* to לַגֶּשֶׁם וּמָטָר עזו he says *to the shower and rain, Be strong*); גֶּשֶׁם מָטָר *shower of rain* Jb 37$_6$ (or em.; see above), גֶּשֶׁם מִטְרוֹת *shower of the rains of* Jb 37$_6$ (or em.; see above), ע[נ]ני מטר *clouds of rain* 4QBer^a 3$_4$, כל מטר *any rain* Si 40$_{16(B)}$.

<PREP> לְ of benefit, *for*, + עשׂה *make* Jr 10$_{13}$=51$_{16}$ Ps 135$_7$ Jb 28$_{26}$ 11QPs^a 26$_{15}$ (למט[ר]); of direction, *to*, + אמר *say* Jb 37$_6$ (if em.; see Cstr.); of possession, *(belonging) to, of* Jb 38$_{28}$; *according to*, + שׁתה *drink* water Dt 11$_{11}$.

כְּ *as* Pr 26$_1$, + ירד *go down* Ps 72$_6$, ערף *drip* Dt 32$_2$; *as for*, + יחל pi. *wait* Jb 29$_{23}$.

מִן *(offering protection) from* Is 4$_6$ (מִסְתּוֹר ... מִמָּטָר *a shelter ... from rain*); of cause, *on account of* 2 S 23$_4$, + המה *stir* Si 43$_{18(B)}$, תמה *marvel* Si 43$_{18(M)}$.

לִפְנֵי *before*, + דעך ni. *be dried up* Si 40$_{16(Bmg)}$ (B מִפְּנֵי *from before*).

<COLL> מָטָר || טַל *dew* Dt 28$_{12}$ 2 S 1$_{21}$ 1 K 17$_1$ Jb 38$_{28}$ (+) 11QM 1.2$_9$, זֶרֶם *downpour* Is 4$_6$, בָּרָד *hail* Ex 9$_{33}$ (+) 9$_{34}$, שֶׁלֶג *snow* Jb 37$_6$ (+) Pr 26$_1$, חֲזִיז *thunder storm* Zc 10$_1$ (+) Jb 28$_{26}$, מַיִם *water* Jb 5$_{10}$ Jb 36$_{27}$ (+) 4QBer^a 3$_4$, קוֹל *voice*, i.e. thunder Ex 9$_{33}$ (+) 9$_{34}$ 1 S 12$_{17.18}$ Jb 28$_{26}$ (+).

+ גֶּשֶׁם *rain* 11QM 1.2$_9$, יוֹרֶה *early rain* Dt 11$_{14}$ 11QM 1.2$_9$, מַלְקוֹשׁ *latter rain* Dt 11$_{14}$ Zc 10$_1$ Jb 29$_{23}$ 11QM 1.2$_9$, שְׂעִירִים *rain (drops)* Dt 32$_2$, רְבִיבִים *showers* Dt 32$_2$ Ps 72$_6$, רוּחַ *wind* Jr 10$_{13}$=51$_{16}$, בָּרָק *lightning* Jr 10$_{13}$=51$_{16}$ Ps 135$_7$ 4QBer^a 3$_4$, נֹגַהּ *brightness* 2 S 23$_4$, חֹרֶב *heat* Is 4$_6$, לֹבֶן *whiteness* Si 40$_{18}$.

<SYN> טַל *dew*, זֶרֶם *downpour*, בָּרָד *hail*, שֶׁלֶג *snow*, חֲזִיז *thunder storm*, מַיִם *water*, קוֹל *voice*, i.e. thunder.*

⇒ מטר *rain*.

מַטָּרָא, see מַטָּרָה *target*.

מַטְרֵד 2 pr.n.f. **Matred**, mother of Mehetabel, who was wife of Hadar, king of Edom, <CSTR> בַּת־מַטְרֵד *daughter of Matred* Gn 36$_{39}$||1 C 1$_{50}$. <APP> בַּת *daughter* Gn

36_{39}||1 C 1_{50} (or em. בַּת מֵי זָהָב *daughter of Mezahab* to מִמֵּי זָהָב *from Mezahab*).

מַטָּרָה 16 n.f. **guard; target**—מַטָּרָא—**1. guard, watch,** <CSTR> חֲצַר הַמַּטָּרָה *court of the guard* Jr $32_{2.8.12}$ 33_{1} $37_{21.21}$ $38_{6.13.28}$ $39_{14.15}$ Ne 3_{25}, שַׁעַר *gate of* Ne 12_{39}.

2. target for archery, <PREP> לְ of direction, *to*, + שׁלח pi. *send* 1 S 20_{20}; *as* or introducing predicate, + היה *be* Jb (if em. לְמַשָּׂא *as a burden to* לְמַטָּרָה), קום hi. *set up* Jb 16_{12}; כְּ *as*, + נצב hi. *set* Lm 3_{12} (כְּמַטָּרָא לַחֵץ *as a target for the arrow*).

⇒ נטר *keep*.

מַטְרִי 1 gent. **Matrite,** Benjaminite clan to which Saul belonged, as collective noun, <CSTR> מִשְׁפַּחַת הַמַּטְרִי *clan of the Matrites* 1 S 10_{21}.

⇒ (?) מטר *rain*.

מִי 423.28.81.3 interrogative (and sometimes relative) pronoun **who?**—(Q מיא).

1. who? whom? whose?, p. 242b
2. who? what?, p. 242b
3. which one(s)?, p. 242b
4. what? with inanimate noun, p. 242b
5. who, as relative pronoun, p. 243a
6. whoever, p. 243a
7. colloquial **what!, what?, why!,** p. 243a
Collocations for §§1-7
a. + perfect, p. 243a
b. + imperfect, p. 243b
(1) מִי + נתן with normal sense, p. 244b
(2) מִי + נתן without normal sense, p. 244b
other collocations, p. 245a
c. + participle as predicate of מִי, p. 245b
d. + participle with article as relative pronoun, p. 245b
e. + infinitive, p. 246a
f. + adjective, p. 246a
g. + pronoun, p. 246a
(1) מִי separated from pronoun, p. 246b
(2) מִי + pronoun + verb, p. 246b
h. + noun, p. 247a
מִי + noun + אֲשֶׁר + verb, p. 247a
other collocations, p. 247a
i. + preposition
(1) לְ *to, for*, p. 247b
(2) כְּ *as*, p. 247b
(3) other prepositions, p. 248a
(1) מִי separated from noun, p. 248b
(2) מִי ... כִּי; מִי + waw of consequence, p. 248b
(3) מִי as first part of subordinate clause, p. 248b
(4) מִי as first element in direct speech, p. 248b
(5) repetition of מִי; מִי + another interrog.; מִי paralleled by noun, p. 249a
j. אֶת־מִי **whom,** p. 249a
k. מִי **(of) whom?, whose?,** p. 249a
l. prefixed with other prepositions, p. 249b

8. whoever, p. 250a
9. מִי אֲשֶׁר **who(ever),** p. 250b

1. who? whom? whose? usu. with ref. to identity of an individual person or group of persons, e.g. מִי אַתְּ *who are you?* Ru 3_{9}, אֶת־מִי אֶשְׁלַח *whom shall I send?* Is 6_{8}, בַּת־מִי אַתְּ *whose daughter are you?* Gn 24_{23}, מִי אַתֶּם *who are you* (pl.)? Jos 9_{8}.

2. who? sometimes with ref. to significance of a person, and thus almost **what?,** e.g. מִי אֲנִי אֲשֶׁר אֶבְנֶה־לּוֹ בַיִת *who am I that I should build him a house?* 2 C 2_{5}, מִי י׳ אֲשֶׁר אֶשְׁמַע בְּקֹלוֹ *who is Y. that I should listen to his voice?* Ex 5_{2}, מִי־אַתְּ בִּתִּי *what are you, my daughter?*, i.e. what is your status? Ru 3_{16}.

3. which one(s)?, out of several, e.g. מִי בְכָל־עֲבָדֶיךָ כְּדָוִד נֶאֱמָן *which among all your servants is as faithful as David?* 1 S 22_{14}, אֶל־מִי מִקְּדֹשִׁים תִּפְנֶה *to which of the holy ones will you turn?* Jb 5_{1}, מִי־אֵל גָּדוֹל כֵּאלֹהִים *what god is as great as God?* Ps 77_{14}.

4. occasionally, with an inanimate noun, **what?,** e.g. מִי שְׁמֶךָ *what is your name?* Jg 13_{17}, מִי־פֶשַׁע יַעֲקֹב

what is the transgression of Jacob? Mc 1$_{5}$ (4QpMic מה *what?*), Gn 33$_{8}$ Dt 4$_{7}$ 2 S 7$_{18}$ Ca 3$_{6}$.

5. occasionally, as relative pronoun, **who,** e.g. רְאוּ מִי הָלַךְ מֵעִמָּנוּ *see who has gone from us* 1 S 14$_{17}$, Gn 21$_{26}$ 43$_{22}$ Dt 21$_{1}$ Jos 24$_{15}$ 1 S 17$_{56}$ 1 K 1$_{20.27}$ Ps 39$_{7}$.

6. perh. indefinite relative pronoun, **whoever,** e.g. מִי־פֶתִי יָסֻר הֵנָּה *whoever is naïve, let him turn here* Pr 9$_{4}$, Zc 4$_{10}$ Is 50$_{8}$ Ec 5$_{9}$ 9$_{4}$* (unless two independent clauses, e.g. *Who is naïve? Let him turn here*).

7. perh. **what!, what?, why!,** as colloquial,* e.g. מִנֹּגַהּ מִמָּטָר (= מִי נֹגַהּ) *why! he's (like) morning light after rain!* 2 S 23$_{4}$, מִבְּנוֹת (= מִי בְּנוֹת) יְרוּשָׁלַםִ: צְאֶינָה וּרְאֶינָה *what! daughters of Jerusalem, come out and see!* Ca 3$_{10-11}$, מִקּוֹל מְחַצְצִים *what! hark to the musicians!* Jg 5$_{11}$ (if em. מִי־חֹצְצִים), כִּי מִיִּשְׂרָאֵל *for what sort of god is the bull god?* Ho 8$_{6}$ (if em. מִי שׁוֹר אֵל), שִׁמְרוּ־מִי בַּנַּעַר בְּאַבְשָׁלוֹם *what! do be careful about the lad Absalom!* 2 S 18$_{12}$, מִי יָקוּם יַעֲקֹב *what? shall Jacob stand?* Am 7$_{2.5}$, מִי אֲנַחֲמֵךְ *what? shall I comfort you?* Is 51$_{19}$, מִטֶּרֶם שׂוּם־אֶבֶן אֶל־אֶבֶן בְּהֵיכַל י׳: מִהְיוֹתָם *before laying one stone upon another in the temple of Y, what was your plight?* Hg 2$_{15-16}$.

a. + perfect of הלך *go* 1 S 14$_{17}$, עלה *go up* Pr 30$_{4}$, עמד *stand* Jr 23$_{18}$, שׂים *place* Gn 43$_{22}$ Ex 2$_{14}$ 4$_{11.11}$ Jb 34$_{13}$ 38$_{5}$, קום hi. *establish* Pr 30$_{4}$ (or em. חזק hi. *strengthen*), שׁית *place* Jb 38$_{36}$, נתן *place* Is 42$_{24}$ Jb 38$_{36}$, שׁלח *send,* i.e. extend, hand 1 S 26$_{9}$, pi. *send away* Jb 39$_{5}$, גלה pi. *remove* clothing Jb 41$_{5}$, אסף *gather* wind Pr 30$_{4}$, צרר *bind* waters Pr 30$_{4}$, נטה *extend* line Jb 38$_{5}$, פתח pi. *release* Jb 39$_{5}$ (מוֹסְרוֹת עָרוֹד מִי פִתֵּחַ *the fetters of the wild ass, who has released?*) 41$_{6}$, ירה *throw,* i.e. lay, cornerstone Jb 38$_{6}$, פלג pi. *make channel* Jb 38$_{25}$, נחה *lead* Ps 60$_{11}$||108$_{11}$, קדם hi. *present* Jb 41$_{3}$, ראה *see* 1 S 23$_{22}$ Is 66$_{8}$, בקשׁ pi. *seek* Is 1$_{12}$.

אמר *say* Jb 36$_{23}$, נגד hi. *tell* Gn 3$_{11}$ Is 41$_{26}$ 45$_{21}$ 48$_{14}$, מלל pi. *speak* Gn 21$_{7}$, יעץ *counsel* Is 23$_{8}$, שׁמע *hear* Is 66$_{8}$ Jr 18$_{13}$, hi. *make known* Is 44$_{7}$ (if em. מִשּׂוּמִי עַם־עוֹלָם וְאֹתִיּוֹת *from my placing a people of eternity; and things to come* to מִי הִשְׁמִיעַ מֵעוֹלָם אוֹתִיּוֹת *who has made known from of old things to come?*) 45$_{21}$, קשׁב hi. *attend* Jr 23$_{18}$, מנה *count* Nm 23$_{10}$, תכן pi. *measure* Is 40$_{13}$, ידע *know* Jb 12$_{9}$, אמן hi. *believe* Is 53$_{1}$.

עשׂה *do* Gn 21$_{26}$ Jg 6$_{29}$ 15$_{6}$ Is 41$_{4}$ 1QH fr. 11$_{5}$ 11QPsApᵃ 3$_{2}$, פעל *do* Is 41$_{4}$, ברא *create* Is 40$_{26}$, פקד *appoint* Jb 34$_{13}$ 36$_{23}$, יעד *appoint* Mc 6$_{9}$ (or em. וּמִי יְעָדָהּ: עוֹד *and who has appointed her? Again* to וּמִי יַעֲדֶה עִיר *and who will adorn a city?* or וּמוֹעֵד הָעִיר *and the assembly of the city*), ילד *give birth* Is 49$_{21}$ Jb 38$_{29}$ (וּכְפֹר שָׁמַיִם מִי יְלָדוֹ *and the frost of heaven, who gave it birth?*), hi. *beget* Jb 38$_{28}$, ברך pi. *bless* Si 34$_{10}$, גדל pi. *bring up* children Is 49$_{21}$ (אֵלֶּה מִי גִדֵּל *these ones, who brought them up?*), יצר *fashion* Is 44$_{10}$, נתך *cast* Is 44$_{10}$, עור hi. *arouse* Is 41$_{2}$, נכה hi. *strike* Dt 21$_{1}$ 2 S 11$_{21}$ 2 K 10$_{9}$, גנב *steal* CD 9$_{11}$, קשׁה hi. *harden oneself* Jb 9$_{4}$, אבד *die* Jb 4$_{7}$ (מִי הוּא נָקִי אָבָד *who, being righteous, died?*).

b. + imperfect of חיה *live* Nm 24$_{23}$, יכל *be able* 1 S 6$_{20}$ 1 K 3$_{9}$ Jb 4$_{2}$ Ec 7$_{13}$ Si 5$_{3}$ 34$_{10}$ 1QH 11$_{24}$ 1QS 11$_{20}$, עצר *detain,* i.e. find, strength 2 C 2$_{5}$ 1QH 10$_{10}$, ערך *be parallel* Ps 89$_{7}$, דמה *be like* Ps 89$_{7}$ GnzPs 1$_{12}$, שׁלם *be complete,* i.e. unscathed Jb 9$_{4}$, שׂבע *be satisfied* Si 42$_{25}$(Bmg M), זכה *be pure* 1QH fr. 4$_{10}$.

הלך *go* Is 6$_{8}$, בוא *come* Jr 49$_{4}$ Jb 41$_{5}$ (בְּכֶפֶל רִסְנוֹ מִי יָבוֹא *into his doubled bridle who can come?*; or em. סִרְיֹנוֹ *his* double *coat of mail*), hi. *bring* Ec 3$_{22}$, עבר *pass* Dt 30$_{13}$, סור *depart* Jr 15$_{5}$, ירד *go down* 1 S 26$_{6}$ Pr 30$_{4}$, hi. *take down* Ob 3, ישׁב *sit* 1 K 1$_{20.27}$, עלה *go up* Dt 30$_{12}$ Jg 1$_{1}$ 20$_{18}$ Ps 24$_{3}$, גוד *attack* 4QMᵃ 1.1$_{17}$, יצב htp. *take stand* Dt 9$_{2}$ 94$_{16}$, עמד *stand* Na 1$_{6}$ Ps 76$_{8}$ 130$_{3}$ 147$_{17}$ (or em. מִי יַעֲמֹד before his cold *who can stand?* to מַיִם יַעֲמֹדוּ *waters stand still*) Pr 27$_{4}$ 4QPrayerᵐ 2$_{2}$ (מי [יעמ]וד), קום *arise* Am 7$_{2.5}$ (both מִי יָקוּם יַעֲקֹב כִּי קָטֹן הוּא perh. *how will Jacob stand, or, who will stand, O Jacob, for he is small?*; or em. hi. who will *raise,* i.e. restore, Jacob?) Na 1$_{6}$ Ps 24$_{3}$ 94$_{16}$, hi. *raise* Gn 49$_{9}$ Nm 24$_{9}$.

מצא *find* Pr 20$_{6}$ (אִישׁ אֱמוּנִים מִי יִמְצָא *a reliable man, who can find?*) 31$_{10}$ (אֵשֶׁת־חַיִל מִי יִמְצָא *a competent woman, who can find?*) Ec 7$_{24}$ (עָמֹק עָמֹק מִי יִמְצָאֶנּוּ *[that which is] deep, deep, who can find it?*), נשׂא *carry* Pr 18$_{14}$ (רוּחַ נְכֵאָה מִי יִשָּׂאֶנָּה *a broken spirit, who can bear it?*), שׂים *place* 2 S 15$_{4}$ Jb 24$_{25}$, נתן *place* Is 41$_{2}$, *cause to be* Is 41$_{2}$, כון hi. *establish* Jb 38$_{41}$, שׁוב *turn back* Y. Jb 9$_{12}$ 11$_{10}$ 23$_{13}$, hand Is 14$_{27}$, action Is 43$_{13}$, desire Jr 2$_{24}$ (תַּאֲנָתָהּ מִי יְשִׁיבֶנָּה *her desire who can turn back?*), יבל hi. *lead* Ps 60$_{11}$||108$_{11}$, יעד hi. *summon* Jr 49$_{19}$=50$_{44}$ Jb

9$_{19}$ 4QMa 11.1$_{17}$, שׁען ni. *lean* Is 50$_{10}$, אמן hi. *believe* Si 36$_{31}$ 37$_{13}$, נוד *shake* Is 51$_{19}$ Jr 15$_5$ Na 3$_7$, שׁכב hi. *lay* Jb 38$_{37}$ (נִבְלֵי שָׁמַיִם מִי יַשְׁכִּיב *the waterskins of heaven, who can lay [flat]?*).

שׁמע *hear* 1 S 30$_{24}$ Is 42$_{23}$, hi. *make known* Is 43$_9$ Ps 106$_2$, אזן hi. *listen* Is 42$_{23}$, קשׁב hi. *attend* Is 42$_{23}$, אמר *say* 2 S 16$_{10}$ Jb 9$_{12}$ 20$_9$ Ec 8$_4$ Si 33$_{10}$ 4QMystc 2b$_3$, מלל pi. *speak* Ps 106$_2$ 4QapPsa 1.1$_7$, דבר pi. *speak* 11QPsa 28$_7$, נגד hi. *tell* 1 S 20$_{10}$ Is 43$_9$ Jb 21$_{31}$ Ec 6$_{12}$ 8$_7$ 10$_{14}$ Si 16$_{22}$ 11QPsa 28$_7$, ספר pi. *relate* Jb 38$_{37}$ 11QPsa 28$_7$, נבא ni. *prophesy* Am 3$_8$, ראה *see* Ps 64$_6$, hi. *show* Ps 4$_7$, שׁור *see* Jb 17$_{15}$ (וְתִקְוָתִי מִי יְשׁוּרֶנָּה *and my hope, who sees it?*) 34$_{29}$, ידע *know* Jr 17$_9$, זכר *remember* Si 16$_{17}$, בין *understand* Ps 19$_{13}$ (שְׁגִיאוֹת מִי־יָבִין *errors, who understands?*) 4QapPsb 31$_5$ ([מח]שבתיך מי יבין *your thoughts, who understands?*) 4QShirShabbb 16$_4$ (מי יבין באלה *who understands these things?*), htpol. *examine* Jb 26$_{14}$ (רַעַם גְּבוּרוֹתָיו מִי יִתְבּוֹנָן *the noise of his mighty deeds who can examine?*) Si 16$_{20}$, שׂיח polel *consider* Is 53$_8$ (אֶת־דּוֹרוֹ מִי יְשׂוֹחֵחַ *his life, who will consider [it]?*).

חפץ *desire* 1QMyst 1.1$_{10}$, פלל htp. *intercede* 1 S 2$_{25}$, צדק *be righteous* 4Q417 1.1$_{16}$, hi. *make righteous* Si 10$_{29}$, בטח *trust* Is 50$_{10}$, ידה hi. *praise* Ps 6$_6$, עדה *adorn* Mc 6$_9$ (if em. וּמִי יְעָדָהּ: עוֹד *and who has appointed her? Again* to וּמִי יַעְדֶּה עִיר *and who will adorn a city?*), פתה pi. *deceive* 1 K 22$_{20}$||2 C 18$_{19}$, שׁפט *judge* 2 C 1$_{10}$, רשׁע hi. *condemn* Jb 34$_{29}$, נחם pi. *console* Is 51$_{19}$ (מִי אֲנַחֲמֵךְ appar. *who am I to console you?*, or, *What! Shall I console you?*; 1QIsaa יְנַחֲמֵךְ who *will console you?*), ישׁע hi. *deliver* 4QPrayerc 3$_2$, חנן ho. *be shown favour* Si 12$_{13}$, חמל *pity* Jr 15$_5$, ירא *fear* Jr 10$_7$ Am 3$_8$, כבד pi. *honour* Si 10$_{29}$, חושׁ *feel (joy)* or *be anxious* or *be sated* Ec 2$_{25}$ (or em. חוס *pity*), נצל hi. *save* 1 S 4$_8$, נתן *give* (see Coll.) Jb 14$_4$ (מִי־יִתֵּן טָהוֹר מִטָּמֵא לֹא אֶחָד *who can bring about pure from impure?; not one*) 31$_{31}$ (מִי־יִתֵּן מִבְּשָׂרוֹ לֹא נִשְׂבָּע *[to] whom has he given of his meat that has not been satisfied?*), כזב hi. *prove false* Jb 24$_{25}$, אכל *eat* Ec 2$_{25}$, hi. *feed* Nm 11$_{4.18}$, שׁקה hi. *give to drink* 2 S 23$_{15}$|| 1 C 11$_{17}$, רפא *heal* Lm 2$_{13}$, אסר *bind*, i.e. commence, battle 1 K 20$_{14}$, כול hi. *endure* Jl 2$_{11}$ 4QMh 6$_5$ 4QMa 11.1$_{17}$, htpalp. *withstand* Si 43$_{3(B)}$, htpol. Si 43$_{3(M)}$, פרר hi. *frustrate* Is 14$_{27}$, גור *dwell* Is 33$_{14.14}$ Ps 15$_1$, שׁכן *dwell* Ps 15$_1$, שׁלם pi. *repay* Jb 21$_{31}$.

<COLL> מִי(־)יִתֵּן *who would give?*, (1) with normal sense of נתן maintained, as transitive construction, *if only someone would give*, Jg 9$_{29}$ (מִי יִתֵּן אֶת־הָעָם הַזֶּה בְּיָדִי *if only someone would give this people into my hand*) Is 27$_4$ (מִי־יִתְּנֵנִי שָׁמִיר *if only someone would give me a thorn*) Jr 9$_1$ (מִי־יִתְּנֵנִי בַמִּדְבָּר מְלוֹן אֹרְחִים *if only someone would give me in the steppe a travellers' inn*) Ps 14$_7$=53$_7$ (מִי יִתֵּן מִצִּיּוֹן יְשׁוּעַת יִשְׂרָאֵל *if only someone would bring about from Zion the salvation of Israel*) 55$_7$ (מִי־יִתֶּן־לִּי אֵבֶר כַּיּוֹנָה *if only someone would give me wings like a dove*) Jb 29$_2$ (מִי־יִתְּנֵנִי כְיַרְחֵי־קֶדֶם *if only someone would cause me to be like the months of old*) 31$_{35}$ (מִי־יִתֶּן־לִי שֹׁמֵעַ לִי *if only someone would give me someone to listen to me*) Ca 8$_1$ (מִי יִתֶּנְךָ כְּאָח לִי *if only someone would make you as a brother to me*).

(2) without normal sense of נתן, as interjection or hypothetical particle, *O that!*, *would (that)*, *would that it were*, *if only (it were)*, + pf. of ידע *know* Jb 23$_3$; impf. of בוא *come* Jb 6$_8$, חרשׁ hi. *be silent* Jb 13$_5$ (+ חרשׁ inf. abs.), צפן hi. *conceal* Jb 14$_{13}$, סתר hi. *conceal* Jb 14$_{13}$, שׁית *place* Jb 14$_{13}$; + inf. of דבר pi. *speak* Jb 11$_5$, מות *die* Ex 16$_3$ 2 S 19$_1$; + waw consecutive and pf. of היה *be* Dt 5$_{29}$; + simple waw and impf. of פתח *open* lips Jb 11$_5$, כתב ni. *be written* Jb 19$_{23}$ (+ אֵפוֹא *therefore*); + nom. cl. Nm 11$_{29}$ Jr 8$_{23}$; + כִּי *that* clause Nm 11$_{29}$; + single noun, עֶרֶב *evening* Dt 28$_{67}$, בֹּקֶר *morning* Dt 28$_{67}$.

מִי לֹא יִרָאֲךָ ... כִּי לְךָ יָאָתָה *who would not fear you ..., for it befits you?* Jr 10$_7$, מִי־שָׂם מְמַדֶּיהָ כִּי תֵדָע *who established its measurements that you might know?* Jb 38$_5$, מִי לֹא־יָדַע בְּכָל־אֵלֶּה כִּי יַד־י׳ עָשְׂתָה זֹּאת *who has not known through all these that the hand of Y. did this?* Jb 12$_9$, מִי יַעֲלֶה־לָּנוּ הַשָּׁמַיְמָה ... וְיַשְׁמִעֵנוּ אֹתָהּ *who could go up for us to the heavens ... that he might tell it us?* Dt 30$_{12}$, מִי יַעֲבָר־לָנוּ אֶל־עֵבֶר הַיָּם ... וְיַשְׁמִעֵנוּ אֹתָהּ *who could cross for us to the other side of the sea ... that he might tell it us?* Dt 30$_{13}$, מִי יְפַתֶּה אֶת־אַחְאָב ... וְיַעַל *who will deceive Ahab ... so that he goes up?* 1 K 22$_{20}$||2 C 18$_{19}$, מִי עָמַד בְּסוֹד י׳ וְיֵרֶא וְיִשְׁמַע אֶת־דְּבָרוֹ *who has stood in the council of Y. to see and hear his word?* Jr 23$_{18}$ (or em. וְיִרְאֵהוּ *to see him*), מִי־הִקְשִׁיב דְּבָרוֹ וַיִּשְׁמָע *who has attended to his word in order to hear?* Jr 23$_{18(Qr)}$ (if em. וַיִּשְׁמָע

and heard), מִי הִקְדִּימַנִי וַאֲשַׁלֵּם *who has presented me (with something) that I should repay (them)?* Jb 41$_{3}$, מִי יָכִין לָעֹרֵב צֵידוֹ כִּי־יְלָדָיו אֶל־אֵל יְשַׁוֵּעוּ *who establishes for the raven its prey when its young cry to God?* Jb 38$_{41}$.

מִי יָגוּר לָנוּ *which one of us can dwell?* Is 33$_{14.14}$ (מִי־), מִי יָלַד־לִי אֶת־אֵלֶּה וַאֲנִי שְׁכוּלָה וְגַלְמוּדָה גֹּלָה וְסוּרָה *who gave birth to these for me when I was barren and sterile, exiled and set apart?* Is 49$_{21}$, אִם־עֲוֹנוֹת תִּשְׁמָר־יָהּ אֲדֹנָי מִי יַעֲמֹד *if you were to keep (account of) iniquities, O Y., who could stand?* Ps 130$_{3}$, אִם ... יַקְהִיל וּמִי יְשִׁיבֶנּוּ *if ... he summons, then who can turn him back?* Jb 11$_{10}$, וְהוּא יַשְׁקִט וּמִי יַרְשִׁעַ *if he silences,* or *is silent, then who can condemn?* Jb 34$_{29}$ (ms יִשְׁקוֹט *is silent*), וְיַסְתֵּר פָּנִים וּמִי יְשׁוּרֶנּוּ *if he hides his face, then who can see him?* Jb 34$_{29}$, וְאִם־לֹא אֵפוֹ מִי יַכְזִיבֵנִי *and if not, then who can prove me false?* Jb 24$_{25}$, הֵן יַחְתֹּף מִי יְשִׁיבֶנּוּ *if he snatches, who can turn him back?* Jb 9$_{12}$, וַעְצֹר בְּמִלִּין מִי יוּכָל *and to stop (you) with words, who is able?* Jb 4$_{2}$.

מִי separated from verb listed above (§§a or b), אַרְיֵה שָׁאָג מִי לֹא יִירָא אֲדֹנָי י׳ דִּבֶּר מִי לֹא יִנָּבֵא *(when) a lion has roared who will not fear? (when) Y. God has spoken who will not prophesy?* Am 3$_{8}$, מִי לֹא יִרָאֲךָ *who would not fear you?* Jr 10$_{7}$, מִי לֹא־יָדַע *who has not known?* Jb 12$_{9}$, מִי בָהֶם הִגִּיד אֶת־אֵלֶּה *who among them has told these things?* Is 48$_{14}$, מִי עָלָה־שָׁמַיִם וַיֵּרַד *who has gone up to heaven and come down (again)?* Pr 30$_{9}$, מִי בָכֶם יַאֲזִין זֹאת יַקְשִׁב וְיִשְׁמַע לְאָחוֹר *who among you will listen to this, will attend and will hear about the future?* Is 42$_{23}$, מִי מֵהֶם עָמַד *which one of them has stood?* Jr 23$_{18}$ (if ins. מֵהֶם), מִי הִשְׁמִיעַ זֹאת מִקֶּדֶם מֵאָז הִגִּידָהּ *who made this known from of old, from of old told it?* Is 45$_{21}$, מִי בָהֶם יַגִּיד זֹאת וְרִאשֹׁנוֹת יַשְׁמִיעֻנוּ *who among them could tell this and make known things past?* Is 43$_{9}$.

מִי־פָעַל וְעָשָׂה *who has acted and effected?* Is 41$_{4}$, מִי־יָצַר אֵל וּפֶסֶל נָסָךְ *who has fashioned a god or cast an image?* Is 44$_{10}$, מִי הֵעִיר מִמִּזְרָח ... יִתֵּן לְפָנָיו גּוֹיִם ... יִתֵּן כֶּעָפָר חַרְבּוֹ *who aroused from the east ... places nations before him ... makes his sword like dust?* Is 41$_{2}$, מִי הִקְשָׁה אֵלָיו וַיִּשְׁלָם *who has hardened himself against him and been unscathed?* Jb 9$_{4}$, מִי ... יִבְטַח בְּשֵׁם י׳ וְיִשָּׁעֵן בֵּאלֹהָיו *who ... trusts in the name of Y. and leans upon his God?* Is 50$_{10}$, מִי בַשַּׁחַק יַעֲרֹךְ לַי׳ יִדְמֶה לַי׳ בִּבְנֵי אֵלִים *who in the cloud(s) is equal to Y., is similar to Y. among the sons of gods?* Ps 89$_{7}$, מִי יְמַלֵּל גְּבוּרוֹת י׳ יַשְׁמִיעַ כָּל־תְּהִלָּתוֹ *who can speak the mighty deeds of Y., make known all his praise?* Ps 106$_{32}$, מִי יַכְזִיבֵנִי וְיָשֵׂם לְאַל מִלָּתִי *who can prove me false and make as nothing my word?* Jb 24$_{25}$.

c. + participle (as predicate of מִי) of ידע *know* 2 S 12$_{22}$ (מִי יוֹדֵעַ וְחַנַּנִי י׳ *who knows if Y. will pity me?*) Is 29$_{15}$ (מִי יוֹדְעֵנוּ *who sees us?*) Jl 2$_{14}$ (מִי־יוֹדֵעַ יָשׁוּב וְנִחָם וְהִשְׁאִיר אַחֲרָיו בְּרָכָה *who knows if he will turn and repent and leave behind him a blessing?*) Jon 3$_{9}$ (מִי יוֹדֵעַ יָשׁוּב וְנִחַם הָאֱלֹהִים וְשָׁב מֵחֲרוֹן אַפּוֹ וְלֹא נֹאבֵד *who knows if God will turn and repent [and] turning from the heat of his anger that we might not die?*) Ps 90$_{11}$ (מִי־יוֹדֵעַ עֹז אַפֶּךָ *who knows the strength of your anger?*) Pr 24$_{22}$ (וּפִיד שְׁנֵיהֶם מִי יוֹדֵעַ *and the ruin of both of them, who knows?*; or em. שׁוֹנִים ruin of *different ones*) Ec 2$_{19}$ (וּמִי יוֹדֵעַ הֶחָכָם יִהְיֶה אוֹ סָכָל *and who knows if he will be wise or foolish?*) 3$_{21}$ 6$_{12}$ (מִי־יוֹדֵעַ מַה־טּוֹב לָאָדָם בַּחַיִּים *who knows what is good for humankind in life?*) 8$_{1}$ Est 4$_{14}$ Si 16$_{21}$ 4QShir[b] 2.2$_{6}$ ([רז]י אלוהים מיא ידע *the mysteries of God, who knows?*).

ראה *see* Is 29$_{15}$ (מִי רֹאֵנוּ *who sees us?*), שׁמע *hear* Is 50$_{10}$ (מִי ... שֹׁמֵעַ *who ... hears?*) Ps 59$_{8}$, קרא *call* Is 41$_{4}$ (מִי ... קֹרֵא הַדֹּרוֹת מֵרֹאשׁ *who ... calls the generations from the beginning?*), בין ni. *be intelligent* Ho 14$_{10}$ (מִי ... נָבוֹן וְיֵדָעֵם *who ... is intelligent [enough] to know them?*), יכח hi. *reprove* Ec 8$_{1}$ (if em. מִי כְּהֶחָכָם *who is like the sage?* to מִי מוֹכִיחַ כְּהֶחָכָם *who reproves like the sage?*), כול pilp. *endure* Ml 3$_{2}$ (מִי מְכַלְכֵּל אֶת־יוֹם בּוֹאוֹ *who can endure the day of his coming?*), אסף *gather* Ps 39$_{7}$ (לֹא־יֵדַע מִי אֹסְפָם *they do not know who gathers them*), תכן pi. *measure* 1QH fr. 16$_{4.5}$, חשׁב *consider* 1QH fr. 16$_{6}$, נחל *inherit* 4Q417 1.1$_{11}$ (מי נוחל כבוד וענ[ו]ל *who inherits glory and injustice*).

d. + participle (with article as relative pronoun), of הלך *go* Ex 10$_{8}$ (מִי וָמִי הַהֹלְכִים *who and who [else] are those who are about to go?*), עמד *stand* Ml 3$_{2}$ (מִי הָעֹמֵד בְּהֵרָאוֹתוֹ *who is one that can stand when he appears?*), אמר *say* 1 S 11$_{12}$ (מִי הָאֹמֵר שָׁאוּל יִמְלֹךְ עָלֵינוּ *who is the one that says, Saul will rule over us?*), ירה hi. *instruct* Jb

36_{22} (הֶן־אֵל יַשְׂגִּיב בְּכֹחוֹ מִי כָמֹהוּ מוֹרֶה *when God raises himself up in his strength, who can instruct like him?*), שׁאר ni. *remain* Hg 2_3 (מִי בָכֶם הַנִּשְׁאָר אֲשֶׁר רָאָה אֶת־הַבַּיִת הַזֶּה *who among you is left who saw this house* in its former glory?), דמה *resemble* GnzPs 4_8.

e. + infinitive, שׁעע hi. *seal* Si $41_{21(\text{Bmg})}$.

f. + adjective, יָרֵא *fearful* Jg 7_3 Is 50_{10}, חָרֵד *trembling* Jg 7_3, עִוֵּר *blind* Is $42_{19.19.19}$, חֵרֵשׁ *deaf* Is 42_{19}, חָכָם *wise* Ho 14_{10} Ps 107_{43} 4QsapHymn 1.2_7. <COLL> מִי חָכָם וְיָבֵן אֵלֶּה *who is wise (enough) to understand these things?* Ho 14_{10}, מִי־חָכָם וְיִשְׁמָר־אֵלֶּה וְיִתְבּוֹנְנוּ חַסְדֵי י׳ *who is wise (enough) to keep these and to consider Y.'s deeds of loyalty?* Ps 107_{43} (if em. וְיִתְבּוֹנְנוּ *and let them consider*); מִי separated from adjective, מִי עִוֵּר כִּי אִם־עַבְדִּי וְחֵרֵשׁ כְּמַלְאָכִי *who is blind like my servant or deaf like my messenger?* Is 42_{19}, מִי עִוֵּר כִּמְשֻׁלָּם וְעִוֵּר כְּעֶבֶד י׳ *who is blind like one who has been recompensed or blind like the servant of Y.?* Is 42_{19}, מִי בָכֶם יְרֵא י׳ *who among you is fearful of Y.?* Is 50_{10}.

g. + pronoun, אָנֹכִי *I* Ex 3_{11} 1 S 18_{18} 2 S 7_{18}||1 C 17_{16} (1 C 29_{14} (אֲנִי) 2 C 2_5 (אֲנִי)), אַתָּה *you* sg. masc. Gn $27_{18.32}$ 1 S 26_{14} (מִי אַתָּה קָרָאתָ אֶל־הַמֶּלֶךְ *who are you who calls to the king?*) 2 S 1_8 Zc 4_7 11QPsAp^a 5_6, אַתְּ *you* sg. fem. Is 51_{12} Ru $3_{9.16}$, הוּא *he* Gn 27_{33} Is 50_9 (מִי־הוּא יַרְשִׁיעֵנִי *who is he that would condemn me?*) Jr 30_{21} (מִי הוּא־זֶה עָרַב אֶת־לִבּוֹ *who is he that pledges his heart?*) Ps 24_{10} (מִי הוּא זֶה מֶלֶךְ הַכָּבוֹד *who is he that is the king of glory?*) Jb 9_{24} (אִם־לֹא אֵפוֹא מִי־הוּא *if not, then who is it?*) 13_{19} (מִי הוּא יָרִיב עִמָּדִי *who is he that would contend with me?*) $17_{3(L)}$ (מִי הוּא לְיָדִי יִתָּקֵעַ *who is he that will be struck into my hand*, i.e. pledge himself to me?; mss 41_2 (מִי־הוּא לְפָנַי יִתְיַצָּב *who is he that can stand before me?*; mss לְפָנָיו *before him*) Si $34_{9(\text{Bmg})}$.

אֲנַחְנוּ *we* 2Q27 1_5, אַתֶּם *you* pl. Jos 9_8 2 K 10_{13}, זֶה *this* masc. Is 63_1 (מִי־זֶה בָּא *who is this, coming?*) Jr 46_7 (מִי־זֶה כַּיְאֹר יַעֲלֶה *who is this that rises like the Nile?*) Jr 49_{19}=50_{44} (מִי־זֶה רֹעֶה אֲשֶׁר יַעֲמֹד לְפָנָי *who is this*, i.e. the, *shepherd who will stand before me?*) Ps 24_8 (מִי זֶה מֶלֶךְ הַכָּבוֹד *who is this that is the king of glory?*) 25_{12} (מִי־זֶה הָאִישׁ יְרֵא י׳ *who is this man, a fearer of Y?*) Jb 38_2 (מִי זֶה מַחְשִׁיךְ עֵצָה בְמִלִּין בְּלִי־דָעַת *who is this that obscures advice with senseless words?*) 42_3 (מִי זֶה מַעְלִים עֵצָה בְּלִי דָעַת *who is this that hides advice without sense?*) Lm 3_{37} (מִי זֶה אָמַר וַתֶּהִי *who is this that commands and it comes about?*) Est 7_5 (מִי הוּא זֶה וְאֵי־זֶה הוּא אֲשֶׁר־מְלָאוֹ לִבּוֹ לַעֲשׂוֹת כֵּן *who is this and where is he whose heart has filled him to do thus?*; or em. מִלֵּא who *has filled* his heart) Si 13_{23} $34_{9.10}$ 11QPs^a $22_{9.9}$, זֹאת *this* fem. (or fem. for neuter) Ca 3_6=8_5 (מִי זֹאת עֹלָה מִן־הַמִּדְבָּר *who is this that is going up from the steppe?*) 6_{10} (מִי־זֹאת הַנִּשְׁקָפָה כְּמוֹ־שָׁחַר *who is this that is leaning out like the dawn?*).

אֵלֶּה *these* Gn 33_5 48_8 Is 60_8, אֲשֶׁר *one that* Jg 21_5 (מִי אֲשֶׁר לֹא־עָלָה *which is the one that did not go up?*) Is 50_{10} 2 C 32_{14} (מִי ... אֲשֶׁר יָכוֹל לְהַצִּיל אֶת־עַמּוֹ מִיָּדִי *who was ... one that was able to save his people from my hand?*), *those that* 2 K 18_{35}||Is 36_{20} (מִי ... אֲשֶׁר־הִצִּילוּ אֶת־אַרְצָם מִיָּדִי *who are ... those that have saved their land from my hand?*), -שֶׁ *one that* Si 16_3 (ממי שהיו לו בנים רבים *than one who has many sons*) 30_{19} (כן מי שיש לו עושר *thus is the one who has wealth*) 4QMMT B_9 (מי שזנת אליו *the one who prostituted herself with him*) CD 20_4 (כמי שלא נפל גורלו *like the one whose lot did not fall*) MurEpBarC^b $_8$ (מי שיתן לך *the one who shall give to you*).

<COLL> **(1)** word(s) separate(s) מִי from pronoun cited, מִי אֵפוֹא הוּא הַצָּד צַיִד *who, therefore, was he who was hunting?* Gn 27_{33}, מִי ... אֲשֶׁר הָלַךְ חֲשֵׁכִים *who ... is one who goes in darkness?* Is 50_{10}; **(2)** מִי־אֵלֶּה כָּעָב תְּעוּפֶינָה וְכַיּוֹנִים אֶל־אֲרֻבֹּתֵיהֶם *who are these flying like the cloud (and) like the doves to their pigeonholes?* Is 60_8; מִי אָנֹכִי כִּי אֵלֵךְ ... וְכִי אוֹצִיא *who am I that I should go ... and that I should take out?* Ex 3_{11}, מִי אָנֹכִי ... כִּי־אֶהְיֶה *who am I ... that I should be?* 1 S 18_{18}, מִי אָנֹכִי ... כִּי הֲבִיאֹתַנִי *of what importance am I ... that you have brought me?* 2 S 7_{18}||1 C 17_{16} (אֲנִי), מִי אֲנִי וּמִי עַמִּי כִּי־נַעְצֹר כֹּחַ לְהִתְנַדֵּב כָּזֹאת *of what importance am I and of what importance is my people that we should find strength to be as generous as this?* 1 C 29_{14}, וּמִי אֲנִי אֲשֶׁר אֶבְנֶה־לּוֹ בַיִת *and who am I to build a house for him?* 2 C 2_5, מִי ... אֲשֶׁר־הִצִּילוּ אֶת־אַרְצָם מִיָּדִי כִּי־יַצִּיל י׳ אֶת־יְרוּשָׁלַםִ מִיָּדִי *who* among all the gods of the land *are ... those that have saved their land from my hand, (to support your belief) that Y. could save Jerusalem from*

my hand? 2 K 18$_{35}$||Is 36$_{20}$, מִי אַתְּ וַתִּירְאִי מֵאֱנוֹשׁ יָמוּת *what kind of person are you that you fear a human being who will die?* Is 51$_{12}$.

h. + noun, 'י *Y.* Ex 5$_2$ Pr 30$_9$, אֵל *God* 2 S 22$_{32}$ Mc 7$_{18}$ Ps 77$_{14}$, *god* Dt 3$_{10}$, אֱלוֹהַּ *God* Ps 18$_{32}$, Abimelech Jg 9$_{28.38}$, Shechem Jg 9$_{28}$, David 1 S 25$_{10}$, פְּלִשְׁתִּי *Philistine* 1 S 17$_{26}$, אִישׁ *man* Gn 24$_{65}$ Nm 22$_9$ Dt 20$_{5.6.7}$ 20$_8$ Jg 10$_{18}$ Jr 9$_{11}$ Ps 34$_{13}$, גֶּבֶר *man* Ps 89$_{49}$ Jb 34$_7$, אָב *father* 1 S 10$_{12}$, בֵּן *son* 1 S 25$_{10}$, אָדוֹן *lord* Ps 12$_5$, בַּעַל *lord* Si 32$_{13}$(Bmg), מַלְאָךְ *angel* 1QM 13$_{14}$, שַׂר *prince* 1QM 13$_{14}$, עֶבֶד *servant* Lachish ost. 2$_3$ 5$_3$ 6$_2$, בָּשָׂר *flesh* Dt 5$_{26}$ 1QH 4$_{29}$, בַּיִת *household* 2 S 7$_{18}$||1 C 17$_{16}$, עַם *people* Dt 33$_{29}$ (מִי כָמוֹךָ עַם נוֹשַׁע בַּי׳ *who is, like you, a people saved by Y.?*) 1 C 29$_{14}$, גּוֹי *nation* Dt 4$_{7.8}$ 1QMyst 1.1$_{10.11}$, חַי *kinsfolk* 1 S 18$_{18}$, צוּר *rock* 2 S 22$_{32}$||Ps 18$_{32}$, שֵׁם *name* Jg 13$_{17}$, אֶחָד *one* Jg 21$_8$, פֶּשַׁע *sin* Mc 1$_5$ (מִי־פֶשַׁע יַעֲקֹב הֲלוֹא שֹׁמְרוֹן perh. *who represents the sin of Jacob? is it not Samaria?*; 4QpMic מָה *what?*), בָּמָה *high place* Mc 1$_5$ (וּמִי בָּמוֹת יְהוּדָה הֲלוֹא יְרוּשָׁלִָם perh. *and who represents the high places of Judah? is it not Jerusalem?*; 4QpMic מָה *what?*).

<COLL> מִי ... כָּל־הַמַּחֲנֶה הַזֶּה אֲשֶׁר פָּגָשְׁתִּי *who ... are all this camp that I have met?* Gn 33$_8$, מִי־אֵל ... אֲשֶׁר־יַעֲשֶׂה כְמַעֲשֶׂיךָ *who is a god ... that can do as your deeds?* Dt 3$_{24}$, מִי הָאִישׁ אֲשֶׁר יָחֵל לְהִלָּחֵם *who is the man that can start to fight?* Jg 10$_{18}$, מִי־גוֹי גָּדוֹל אֲשֶׁר־לוֹ אֱלֹהִים קְרֹבִים אֵלָיו *who is a great people, whose gods are near to it?* Dt 4$_7$, וּמִי גּוֹי גָּדוֹל אֲשֶׁר־לוֹ חֻקִּים ... צַדִּיקִם *and who is a great people, that has righteous ... statutes?* 4$_8$, מִי כָל־בָּשָׂר אֲשֶׁר שָׁמַע קוֹל אֱלֹהִים חַיִּים מְדַבֵּר *who is any mortal that*, i.e. whatever mortal, *has heard the voice of a living God speaking?* Dt 5$_{26}$, מִי־הָאִישׁ אֲשֶׁר בָּנָה *who is the man who has built?*, i.e. whoever has built Dt 20$_5$ (sim. 20$_{6.7}$), מִי־הָאִישׁ הַיָּרֵא וְרַךְ הַלֵּבָב *who is the fearful man whose courage is weak?* Dt 20$_8$||11QT 62$_3$, מִי אֶחָד מִשִּׁבְטֵי יִשְׂרָאֵל אֲשֶׁר לֹא־עָלָה *who is one*, i.e. which one, *of the tribes of Israel did not go up?* Jg 21$_8$.

מִי־הָאִישׁ הַלָּזֶה הַהֹלֵךְ בַּשָּׂדֶה *who is that man walking in the countryside?* Gn 24$_{65}$, מִי־הָאִישׁ הֶחָפֵץ חַיִּים אֹהֵב יָמִים *who is the man who desires life, loves days?* Ps 34$_{13}$, מִי־אֵל כָּמוֹךָ נֹשֵׂא עָוֹן וְעֹבֵר עַל־פֶּשַׁע לִשְׁאֵרִית נַחֲלָתוֹ *who is a God like you that takes away iniquity and passes over sin for a remnant of his inheritance?* Mc 7$_{18}$, מִי י׳ כִּי אֶשְׁמַע בְּקֹלוֹ *of what importance is Y. that I should hear his voice?* Ex 5$_2$, מי עבדך כלב כי זכר אדני את [ע]בדה *who is your servant—a dog—that my lord has remembered his servant* Lachish ost. 2$_3$, מי עבדך כלב כי [של]חת אל עבדך *who is your servant—a dog—that you have sent to your servant?* 5$_3$, מי עבדך כלב כי שלח אדני א[ת ספ]ר מלך *who is your servant—a dog—that my lord has sent the king's document?* 6$_2$.

מִי־אֲבִימֶלֶךְ וּמִי־שְׁכֶם כִּי נַעַבְדֶנּוּ *what is the importance of Abimelech and what is the importance of Shechem that we should serve him?* Jg 9$_{28}$ (sim. 9$_{38}$), מִי הַפְּלִשְׁתִּי הֶעָרֵל הַזֶּה כִּי חֵרֵף מַעַרְכוֹת אֱלֹהִים חַיִּים *of what importance is this uncircumcised Philistine that he reproaches the battlelines of the living God?* 1 S 17$_{26}$, מִי שְׁמֶךָ כִּי־יָבֹא דְבָרְךָ וְכִבַּדְנוּךָ *what is your name, that we might honour you when your word comes (true)?* Jg 13$_{17}$(Qr), מִי־הָאִישׁ הֶחָכָם וְיָבֵן אֶת־זֹאת *who is the man wise enough to understand this?* Jr 9$_{11}$, מִי גֶבֶר יִחְיֶה וְלֹא יִרְאֶה־מָּוֶת יְמַלֵּט נַפְשׁוֹ מִיַּד־שְׁאוֹל *who is a man that lives and does not see death, that rescues his soul from the grasp of Sheol?* Ps 89$_{49}$, מִי אֵלֶּה לָּךְ *what relationship do these have to you?* Gn 33$_5$, מִי לְךָ כָּל־הַמַּחֲנֶה הַזֶּה *what is the significance of all this camp to you?* Gn 33$_8$.

i. + preposition, **(1)** לְ *to, for*, עֹד מִי־לְךָ פֹּה bring out *whomever else belongs to you here* or *who else is yours here?* Gn 19$_{12}$, מַה־לְּךָ פֹה וּמִי לְךָ פֹה *what do you have here and whom do you have here?* Is 22$_{16}$, וְעַתָּה מִי לִי־פֹה *and now, who is there for me here?* Is 52$_5$ (Qr מַה־לִּי *what is there for me?*), מִי־לִי בַשָּׁמָיִם *whom do I have in the heavens?* Ps 73$_{25}$; *with*, [מ]יא לבוז נחשב ביא *who is considered with contempt with me?* 4QM^a 11.1$_{15}$.

(2) כְּ *as*, מִי כְּהֶחָכָם *who is like the sage?* Ec 8$_1$ (or ins. מוֹכִיחַ who *reproves* like the sage?), מִי כָמוֹנִי *who is like me?* Is 44$_7$ (מִי־) Jr 49$_{19}$=50$_{44}$, אֱלֹהִים מִי כָמוֹךָ *O God, who is like you?* Ps 71$_{19}$, מִי־כָמֹכָה בָּאֵלִים י׳ מִי כָּמֹכָה נֶאְדָּר בַּקֹּדֶשׁ *who is like you among the gods, O Y., who is like you majestic in holiness?* Ex 15$_{11}$, מי כמוכה באלים אדוני ומי כאמתכה ומי יצדק לפניכה *who is like you among the gods, O Lord, and who is like your truth, and who shall be righteous before you?* 1QH 7$_{28}$, מי כמוני באלים

who is like me among the gods? 4QM^{h} 6$_{4}$, מיא כמוכה אל ישראל *who is like you, O God of Israel?* 1QM 10$_{8}$, מיא כמוכה בכוח אל ישראל *who is like you in strength, O God of Israel?* 1QM 13$_{13}$, מִי כָמוֹךָ מַצִּיל עָנִי מֵחָזָק מִמֶּנּוּ וְעָנִי וְאֶבְיוֹן מִגֹּזְלוֹ *who is like you, rescuing a poor one from one stronger than him and an utterly poor one from his predator?* Ps 35$_{10}$, מִי כָמוֹךָ עַם נוֹשַׁע בַּי׳ *who is, like you, a people saved by Y.?* Dt 33$_{29}$, מִי־כָמוֹךָ חֲסִין יָהּ וֶאֱמוּנָתְךָ סְבִיבוֹתֶיךָ *who is like you, strong, O Y., with your faithfulness around you?* Ps 89$_{9}$ (or em. מִי־כָמוֹךָ חָסְנְךָ וֶאֱמוּנָתְךָ *who is like you?; your stronghold and your faithfulness* is around you, or כָּמוֹךָ יֶחֱסַן אֱמוּנָתְךָ *like you?; strong is your faithfulness* around you).

מִי בְּכָל־עֲבָדֶיךָ כְּדָוִד *which one of all your servants is like David?* 1 S 22$_{14}$, מִי כָמוֹךָ בְּיִשְׂרָאֵל *who in Israel is like you?* 1 S 26$_{15}$, מִי כְעַמְּךָ כְּיִשְׂרָאֵל *who is like your people, like Israel?* 2 S 7$_{23}$||1 C 17$_{21}$ (כְּעַמְּךָ יִשְׂרָאֵל *like your people Israel*), מיא כעמכה ישראל *who is like your people Israel?* 1QM 10$_{9}$, מִי כְצוֹר *who is like Tyre?* Ezk 27$_{32}$, מִי כַּי׳ אֱלֹהֵינוּ הַמַּגְבִּיהִי לָשָׁבֶת *who is like Y. our God, who raises himself up to sit?* Ps 113$_{5}$, וּמִי כָמוֹנִי אֲשֶׁר־יָבוֹא אֶל־הַהֵיכָל וָחָי *and who is like me, that he might come into the temple to live?* Ne 6$_{11}$, מיא הו[א] כבאי ים ישוב *who like a mariner shall return?* 4QM^{a} 11.1$_{15}$, מי כמעשיך ומי כפועליך *who is like your creatures and who is like your works?* GnzPs 1$_{12}$.

(3) other prepositions, בְּ *in, among*, מִי בֶחָצֵר *who is in the court?* Est 6$_{4}$, מִי גַם־בָּכֶם וְיִסְגֹּר דְּלָתַיִם *who also is among you that might close doors?* Ml 1$_{10}$, מי בכם יסגור דלתו *who among you will close his door* CD 6$_{13}$, מיא בכבודי ידמה ליא *who in my glory resembles me?* 4QM^{a} 11.1$_{15}$, מי בבני האילים *who is among the sons of the gods?* 4QapPs^{b} 15$_{6}$, מי בכם ישיב דבר *who among you shall answer?* 4QapPs^{b} 76$_{10}$, מיא בכם דורש פני אור *who among you seeks the face of light?* 4QMyst^{c} 2b$_{4}$.

מִן *of* Si 46$_{19}$, מִי מִנּוֹשַׁי אֲשֶׁר־מָכַרְתִּי אֶתְכֶם לוֹ *who is (the one) of my creditors to whom I have sold you?* Is 50$_{1}$, שמי מהם שהיא ירא [את התו]רה *whoever of them feared the Torah* 4QMMT C$_{23}$; *among*, מי מבש[ר] כמוהו *who is a messenger like him?* 4QapMos^{c} 2.2$_{11}$.

אֶל *for*, מִי מִשֶּׁלָּנוּ אֶל־מֶלֶךְ יִשְׂרָאֵל *which one of us is for the king of Israel?* 2 K 6$_{11}$.

אֵת *with*, מִי אִתִּי מִי *who is with me, who?* 2 K 9$_{32}$, רֹקַע הָאָרֶץ מי אתי *the one who spread out the earth; who was with me?* Is 44$_{24(Kt)}$ (Qr מֵאִתִּי *by myself*).

כְּמוֹת *like*, מי כמותו *who is like him?* GnzPs 4$_{8}$.

לִפְנֵי *before*, מי הוא לפניו *who is before him?* Si 46$_{3}$.

<COLL> **(1)** word(s) separate(s) מִי from noun cited in main section, מִי־הִגִּיד מֵרֹאשׁ וְנֵדָעָה וּמִלְּפָנִים וְנֹאמַר *who told from the beginning that we might know or from the past that we might say?* Is 41$_{26}$, אֶת־מִי חֵרַפְתָּ וְגִדַּפְתָּ *whom have you reproached and reviled?* 2 K 19$_{22}$||Is 37$_{23}$; עַל־מִי תַּרְחִיבוּ פֶה תַּאֲרִיכוּ לָשׁוֹן *against whom have you made wide wide your mouth, made long your tongue?* Is 57$_{4}$, עַל־מִי אֲדַבְּרָה וְאָעִידָה *to whom shall I speak and bear witness?* Jr 6$_{10}$.

(2) מִי ... כִּי *who (is) ... that?* Gn 3$_{11}$ Is 57$_{11}$; מַה־לְּךָ פֹה וּמִי לְךָ פֹה כִּי־חָצַבְתָּ לְּךָ פֹּה קָבֶר *what do you have here and whom do you have here, that you have hewn for yourself a grave?* Is 22$_{16}$, מִי־הִגִּיד מֵרֹאשׁ וְנֵדָעָה וּמִלְּפָנִים וְנֹאמַר *who told from the beginning that we might know or from the past that we might say?* Is 41$_{26}$, אֶת־מִי נוֹעָץ וַיְבִינֵהוּ וַיְלַמְּדֵהוּ ... וַיְלַמְּדֵהוּ ... יוֹדִיעֶנּוּ *with whom did he take counsel that he might give him wisdom, and teach him ... and teach him ... (and) inform him?* Is 40$_{14}$, אֶת־מִי דָּאַגְתְּ וַתִּירְאִי *about whom are you (so) worried that you fear?* Is 57$_{11}$, עַל־מִי אֲדַבְּרָה וְאָעִידָה וְיִשְׁמָעוּ *to whom shall I speak and bear witness that they might hear?* Jr 6$_{10}$.

(3) מִי as first part of subordinate clause, introduced in main clause by perf. of ידע *know* Gn 21$_{26}$ 43$_{22}$, ni. *be known* Dt 21$_{1}$, hi. *make known* 1 K 1$_{27}$, ראה *see* 1 S 14$_{17}$; impf. of נגד hi. *tell* 2 K 6$_{11}$, ידע *know* Ps 39$_{7}$; inf. of נגד hi. *tell* 1 K 1$_{20}$; impv. of זכר *remember* Jb 4$_{7}$.

(4) מִי as first element in direct speech clause (or following introductory vocative or interjection) with אמר *say* Gn 3$_{11}$ 21$_{7}$ 24$_{65}$ 27$_{18.32.33}$ 33$_{5.8}$ 48$_{8}$ Ex 2$_{14}$ 3$_{11}$ 4$_{11}$ 5$_{2}$ 16$_{3}$ 32$_{26.33}$ Nm 11$_{4.18}$ 22$_{9}$ 24$_{23}$ (אוֹ מִי *or who?*) Dt 20$_{5.8}$ 28$_{67}$ 30$_{12.13}$ Jos 9$_{8}$ Jg 1$_{1}$ 6$_{29}$ 7$_{3}$ 9$_{28.38}$ 10$_{18}$ 13$_{17}$ 15$_{6}$ 18$_{3}$ 20$_{18}$ 21$_{5.8}$ 1 S 6$_{20}$ 10$_{12}$ (וּמִי *and who?*) 11$_{12}$ 18$_{18}$ 20$_{10}$ 22$_{14}$ (וּמִי) 25$_{10}$ 26$_{6.15}$ (וּמִי) 2 S 1$_{8}$ 7$_{18}$||1 C 17$_{16}$ 2 S 12$_{22}$ 15$_{4}$ 16$_{10}$ (וּמִי) 19$_{1}$ 20$_{11}$ 23$_{15}$||1 C 11$_{17}$ 1 K 22$_{20}$||2 C 18$_{19}$ 2 K 9$_{32}$ 10$_{13}$ Is 29$_{15}$ Is 44$_{24}$ 49$_{21}$ 50$_{1}$ (אוֹ מִי) Jr 18$_{13}$ 21$_{13}$ Am 7$_{2.5}$ Ob 3 Na 3$_{7}$ Ps 4$_{7}$ 12$_{5}$ 35$_{10}$ 55$_{7}$ 64$_{6}$ Jb 31$_{31}$ Pr 30$_{9}$ Ru 3$_{9.16}$ Est 6$_{4}$ 7$_{5}$

Ne 6_{11} (וּמִי) Si 13_{23}, שׁמע *hear* Dt 9_{2} Is 48_{14}.

(5) לְמִי ... לְמִי ... לְמִי ... לְמִי ... לְמִי ... לְמִי *whose is? ... whose is? ... whose is? ... whose is? ... whose is? ... whose is?* Pr 23_{29}, מִי ... מִי ... מִי ... מִי ... מִי ... מִי *who? ... who? ... who? ... who? ... who?* 1 S 12_{3}, מִי ... מִי ... מִי ... מִי ... מִי *who? ... who? ... who? ... who?* Jr 49_{19}=50_{44} Pr 30_{4}, מִי ... וּמִי ... וּמִי *who? ... and who? ... and who?* Jr 15_{5}; מִי ... מִי *who? ... who?* Gn 32_{18} Ex 4_{11} 10_{8} 15_{11} Dt 28_{67} Jg 9_{28} 1 S 6_{20} 18_{18} 24_{15} 25_{10} 2 S 7_{18} 20_{11} 22_{32} 1 K 20_{14} 2 K 9_{32} 19_{22} Is 6_{8} 14_{27} 28_{9} 29_{15} 33_{14} 37_{23} 42_{19} 49_{21} 50_{8} 51_{19} 53_{1} 57_{4} 66_{8} Jr 21_{13} 23_{18} Am 3_{8} Mc 1_{5} Na 1_{6} Ml 3_{2} Ps 15_{1} 18_{32} 24_{3} 27_{1} 60_{11} 94_{16} 108_{11} Jb 9_{12} 19_{23} 21_{31} 26_{4} $34_{13.29}$ 36_{23} $38_{5.29.36.37}$ 39_{5} 41_{5} Ec 2_{25} 6_{12} 8_{1} 1 C 7_{16} 29_{14} 2 C 2_{5}; מִי וָמִי *who and who (else)?* Ex 10_{8}, מִי + another interrogative, מָה *what?* Jg 18_{3} 1 S 17_{26} 20_{10} 2 S 16_{10} Is 10_{3} 22_{16} 40_{18} Jr 9_{11} 49_{4} Jon 1_{8} Hg 2_{3} Jb 9_{12} 26_{14} 38_{6} Pr 30_{4} Ec 3_{22} 6_{12} 7_{24} $8_{4.7}$ 10_{14} Lm 2_{13} Est 6_{6}, לָמָּה *why?* 1 S 17_{28} 26_{15} 2 S 11_{21}, -הֲ *is it true that?* Gn 3_{11} Ex 2_{14} Is 66_{8} Jb 5_{1} 38_{28} Ne 6_{11}, הֲלֹא *is it not true that?* Ex 4_{11} Jg $9_{28.38}$ 1 S 9_{20} $26_{14.15}$ 2 S 11_{21} 16_{19} 2 K 6_{11} Is 42_{24} 45_{21} $57_{4.11}$ Mc 1_{5} Hg 2_{3}, אִם *is it true that?* Jos 24_{15} Is 66_{8}, מֵאַיִן *whence?* Jos 9_{8} Jon 1_{8} Na 3_{7}, אַיֵּה *where?* Jg 9_{38} Jb 17_{15}, אֵיפֹה *where?* Is 49_{21} Jb 4_{7}, אֵי־זֶה *where?* Is 50_{1} Est 7_{5} Jon 1_{8} (אֵי־מִזֶּה *from which?*), מַדּוּעַ *why?* Jg 9_{28} 2 S 16_{10}, אִישׁ *which man* Is 40_{13} (מִי־תִכֵּן אֶת־רוּחַ י׳ *who measured the spirit of Y.?*).

מִי paralleled by noun with definite reference, עַל־מִי הֲרִימוֹתָ קּוֹל וַתִּשָּׂא מָרוֹם עֵינֶיךָ עַל־קְדוֹשׁ יִשְׂרָאֵל *against whom have you raised your voice and raised on high your eyes against the holy one of Israel?* 2 K 19_{22}||Is 37_{23} (אֶל־קְדוֹשׁ), עֹד מִי־לְךָ פֹה חָתָן וּבָנֶיךָ וּבְנֹתֶיךָ ... הוֹצֵא *whoever else belongs to you here, be they son-in-law, your sons, or your daughters, bring out* Gn 19_{12}.

מִי ... מִבַּלְעֲדֵי *who ... apart from?* 2 S 22_{32}||Ps 18_{32} 2 S 22_{32}, מִי ... זוּלָתִי *who ... apart from?* Ps 18_{32}.

j. אֶת־מִי **whom,** as object of **(a)** perfect of נגד hi. *tell* Jb 26_{4}, עשׁק *oppress* 1 S 12_{3}, רצץ *oppress* 1 S 12_{3}, חרף pi. *reproach* 2 K 19_{22}, גדף pi. *revile* 2 K 19_{22}, דאג *be concerned (about)* Is 57_{11}. **(b)** impf. of עבד *serve* Jos 24_{15}, עלה hi. *bring up* from dead 1 S 28_{11}, שׁלח *send* Is 6_{8}, ירה hi. *teach* Is 28_{9}, בין hi. *teach* Is 28_{9}.

k. מִי **(of) whom?, whose?,** in cstr., נִשְׁמַת־מִי *whose breath?* Jb 26_{4}, דְּבַר־מִי *whose word?* Jr 44_{28}, אֶת־שׁוֹר מִי *whose ox?* 1 S 12_{3}, חֲמוֹר מִי *whose donkey?* 1 S 12_{3}, מִיַּד־מִי *from whose hand?* 1 S 12_{3}, מִבֶּטֶן מִי *from whose womb?* Jb 38_{29}, בַּת־מִי *whose daughter?* Gn $24_{23.47}$, בֶּן־מִי *whose son?* 1 S $17_{55.56.58}$.

l. לְמִי **to whom?, whose?,** + perfect of עלל po. *act* Lm 2_{20}, חשׁב ni. *be considered* 1QH 3_{24} 18_{26}; + imperfect of עבד *serve* 2 S 16_{19} (לְמִי אֲנִי אֶעֱבֹד perh. *to whom should I give service?*), דמה pi. *liken* Is 46_{5}, שׁוה hi. *equate* Is 46_{5}, משׁל hi. *compare* Is 46_{5} (לְמִי תְדַמְּיוּנִי וְתַשְׁווּ וְתַמְשִׁלוּנִי וְנִדְמֶה *to whom will you liken me or equate me or compare me that we might be alike?*), חפץ *desire* to do honour Est 6_{6}, טוב hi. *act benevolently* Si 12_{1} 14_{5}, זעק *cry out* 11QPs^{a} 24_{14} (לְמִי אזעקה *to whom shall I cry out?*); in nom. cl., לְמִי אוֹי לְמִי אֲבוֹי לְמִי מִדְיָנִים לְמִי שִׂיחַ לְמִי פְּצָעִים חִנָּם לְמִי חַכְלִלוּת עֵינָיִם *to whom is there,* i.e. to whom should one say, *Woe!, to whom is there,* i.e. to whom should one say, *Alas!, to whom is there contention, to whom is there complaint, to whom are there needless bruises, to whom is there dullness of eyes?* Pr 23_{29}, לְמִי הַנַּעֲרָה הַזֹּאת *to whom does this girl belong?* Ru 2_{5}, לְמִי־אַתָּה *to whom do you belong?* Gn 32_{18} 1 S 30_{13}, לְמִי אֵלֶּה לְפָנֶיךָ *to whom do these ahead of you belong?* Gn 32_{18}.

לְמִי זָהָב *to whom is there gold?* Ex 32_{24}, לְמִי־אֶרֶץ *whose is (the) land?* 2 S 3_{12}, למי היין *to whom is the wine?* Si 34_{27}, לְמִי הַחֹתֶמֶת וְהַפְּתִילִים וְהַמַּטֶּה הָאֵלֶּה *whose are these—seal and cords and staff?* Gn 38_{25}, לְמִי כָּל־חֶמְדַּת יִשְׂרָאֵל *to whom does all that is desirable in Israel belong?* 1 S 9_{20}, וּלְמִי אֲנִי עָמֵל וּמְחַסֵּר אֶת־נַפְשִׁי מִטּוֹבָה *and for whom am I toiling and depriving my soul of good?* Ec 4_{8} (Gnz נַפְשׁוֹ *his soul*), בְּשֶׁלְּמִי הָרָעָה הַזֹּאת לָנוּ *on account of whom is this great evil of ours?* Jon 1_{7}, sim. 1_{8} (בַּאֲשֶׁר לְמִי־).

<COLL> לְמִי as first part of subordinate clause, introduced in main clause by impv. of נכר hi. *recognize* Gn 38_{25}.

בְּמִי *by whom?* וַיֹּאמֶר אַחְאָב בְּמִי *and Ahab said, By whom (will what you have said be effected)?* 1 K 20_{14}, דְּעוּ רְאוּ בְּמִי הָיְתָה הַחַטָּאת הַזֹּאת הַיּוֹם *know and see through whom this sin has come about today* 1 S 14_{38} (if em. בַּמָּה *by what?*, i.e. how?).

מִמִּי *than whom?*, + perf. of נעם *be (more) pleasant*

Ezk 32_{19}, *of whom*, + impf. of ירא *fear* Ps 27_1, פחד *fear* Ps 27_1.

עַל־מִי *against whom?*, + perf. of רום hi. *raise* voice 2 K 19_{22}; + impf. of קום *arise* Jb 25_3, ענג htp. *mock* Is 57_4, רחב hi. *make* mouth *wide* Is 57_4, ארך hi. *make* tongue *long* Is 57_4; *upon whom?*, + impf. of אור hi. *cause to shine* 4QConfess 2_5; *to whom?*, + perf. of גלה ni. *be revealed* Is 53_1; + impf. of נוס *flee* Is 10_3, דבר pi. *speak* Jr 6_{10}, עוד *bear witness* Jr 6_{10}; *with whom?* or *on account of whom?*, + perf. of נטשׁ *leave* flock 1 S 17_{28}; *over whom?* or *by whom?*, + perf. of עבר Na 3_{19} (עַל־מִי לֹא־עָבְרָה *over whom has* your evil *not passed?*); *in whom?*, + perf. of בטח *trust* 2 K 18_{20}||Is 36_5; אֶל־מִי *to whom?*, + impf. of דמה pi. *liken* Is $40_{18.25}$ (אֶל־מִי תְדַמְּיוּנִי וְאֶשְׁוֶה *to whom will you liken me that I might be similar [to them]?*), עלה *go up* 1 S 6_{20}, פנה *turn* Jb 5_1; in contracted sentence, אֶל־מִי מִכֻּלָּנוּ *for which one of us all (is your word?)*; אֶת־מִי *with whom?*, + perf. of דמה *be like* Ezk $31_{2.18}$; יעץ ni. *take counsel* Is 40_{14}; in nom. cl., אֶת־מִי־אֵין כְּמוֹ־אֵלֶּה *with whom is there not such as these?* Jb 12_3 אַחֲרֵי מִי *after whom?*, + perf. of יצא *go out* 1 S 24_{15}; + participle, אַחֲרֵי מִי אַתָּה רֹדֵף *after whom do you chase?* 1 S 24_{15}.

<COLL> לְמִי + another interrogative, אָנָה *where?* Gn 32_{18}, הֲלוֹא *is it not true that?* 1 S 9_{20} 2 S 16_{19}; עַל־מִי + another interrogative, הֲלוֹא *is it not true that?* Is 57_4, הֲיֵשׁ *is there?* Jb 25_3, מָה *what?* Is 10_3, אָנָה *where?* Is 10_3, אֵי־מִזֶּה *whence?* 1 S 30_{13}, לָמָּה־זֶּה *why?* 1 S 17_{28}.

8. whoever, as combined relative particle and antecedent (unless, in many cases, מִי introduces simple interrogative clause followed by another, independent, clause, as in §1).

a. as subject of perf., מִי בַז לְיוֹם קְטַנּוֹת וְשָׂמְחוּ *whoever despised a day of small things will rejoice* Zc 4_{10}.

b. as subject of impf., מִי־יָרִיב אִתִּי נַעַמְדָה יָּחַד *whoever would contend with me, let us stand together* Is 50_8.

c. as subject of impv., שִׁמְרוּ־מִי בַּנַּעַר בְּאַבְשָׁלוֹם *be careful, whoever you are, about the lad Absalom* 2 S 18_{12} (mss לִי be careful *for me* or lack לִי/מִי).

d. as subject of ptc., מִי־גָר אִתָּךְ עָלַיִךְ יִפּוֹל *whoever fights with you will fall by you* Is 54_{15} (or del. ־מִי, גָר אִתָּךְ), וּמִי בָחוּר אֵלֶיהָ אֶפְקֹד *and whoever is chosen I shall appoint for them* Jr 49_{19}=50_{44} (or em. וּמִבְחַר אֵילֶיהָ *and the choice of her leaders* I shall visit), אֹהֵב כֶּסֶף לֹא־יִשְׂבַּע כֶּסֶף וּמִי־אֹהֵב בֶּהָמוֹן לֹא תְבוּאָה *one who loves money will not be satisfied with money and whoever is in love with wealth [will] not [be satisfied with] increase* Ec 5_9 (or em. הָמוֹן וְלֹא and whoever loves *wealth without increase*), מי משולח *who is sent* 4QsapHymn A 5_5.

e. in nom. cl., מִי־פֶתִי יָסֻר הֵנָּה *whoever is naïve, let him turn here* Pr $9_{4=16}$, מִי־בַעַל דְּבָרִים יִגַּשׁ אֲלֵהֶם *whoever is a possessor of words*, i.e. disputant, *let him approach them* Ex 24_{14}, מִי־בַעַל מִשְׁפָּטִי יִגַּשׁ אֵלָי *whoever is in dispute with me, let them approach me* Is 50_8, מִי לַי׳ אֵלָי *whoever is for Y., (come) to me* Ex 32_{26}.

f. in extraposed clause, מִי־בָכֶם מִכָּל־עַמּוֹ יְהִי אֱלֹהָיו עִמּוֹ וְיַעַל לִירוּשָׁלַם *whoever among you of all his people, may his God be with him and may he go up to Jerusalem* Ezr 1_3 (||2 C 36_{23} י׳ אֱלֹהָיו עִמּוֹ וְיָעַל *may Y. his God be with him and may he go up*).

9. מִי אֲשֶׁר **who(ever)**, מִי אֲשֶׁר חָטָא־לִי אֶמְחֶנּוּ מִסִּפְרִי *whoever has sinned against me, I shall erase him from my book* Ex 32_{33}, מִי אֲשֶׁר חָפֵץ בְּיוֹאָב וּמִי אֲשֶׁר־לְדָוִד אַחֲרֵי יוֹאָב *whoever is desirous of Joab and whoever (is desirous) of David, follow Joab* 2 S 20_{11}, כִּי־מִי אֲשֶׁר יְחֻבַּר אֶל כָּל־הַחַיִּים יֵשׁ בִּטָּחוֹן *truly, [for] whoever is joined to all the living there is security* Ec $9_{4(Qr)}$.

Also 4QapPent 3_2 4QPrEnosh 3_1 4QapJoseph[b] 3_7 4QMMT C $_3$ 4QsapHymn 1.2_9 4Q418 127_3 161_2 4QpsHod[a] 1_2 4QPseud[b] $5.1_{6.7}$ 4QM[h] $6_{5.7}$ 4QM[a] $11.1_{16.16}$ 4QRitPur 48_4.*

⇒ מִיאָמִן *Miamun*, מִיכָאֵל *Michael*, מִיכָיָהוּ *Micaiah*, מִיכָיְהוּ *Micaiah*.

[מֵיאָה], see מֵאָה *hundred*.

*__[מִיאָמִן]__ 0.0.0.9 pr.n.m. **Miamun**—מאמן—**1.** son of Oded, <APP> בֵּן *son* of Oded Seal 437 ([בן] עדד; 7th/6th cent.).

2. son of Ophai, <APP> בֵּן *son* of Ophai Seal 588 ([בן] עפי; T. Beit Mirsim?; 7th/6th cent.).

3. appar. father of Jehoel, Seal 256 (Lachish, 7th

cent.).

4. appar. father of Maaseiah, Seal 587 (T. Beit Mirsim?; 7th/6th cent.).

5. father of Ahijah, <CSTR> בן מאמ[ן] *son of Miamun* Bulla D21.

6. appar. son of Meshullam, <PREP> לְ of possession, *of, (belonging) to* Bulla D57.

7. appar. father of Zephaniah, Bulla D84.

8. appar. son of Benaiah, <PREP> לְ of possession, *of, (belonging) to* Bulla DH60.

9. appar. son of Zedekiah, Ost. DH79$_5$.*

⇒ מִי *who?* + אמן *be trustworthy.*

[מֵיאָשָׁה], see מֵישָׁא *Mesha.*

***מיד** 1 vb. **shake, convulse—Pol.** + waw וַיְמֹדֶד—**shake, convulse,** unless מדד *measure,* <SUBJ> אֱלוֹהַּ *God* Hb 3$_6$ (|| נתר hi. *cause to jump).* <OBJ> אֶרֶץ *earth* Hb 3$_6$.

<SYN> נתר hi. *cause to jump.*

מֵידְבָא 5 pl.n. **Medeba,** Moabite city, occupied by Reubenites, <OBJ> נתן *give* (of Moses) Jos 13$_9$. <APP> מִישֹׁר *plain* Jos 13$_9$. <PREP> עַל *beside* Jos 13$_{16}$ (+ מִישֹׁר *plain); concerning, for,* + ילל hi. *wail* Is 15$_2$ (+ Dibon, Nebo); עַד appar. *beside* Nm 21$_{30}$ (or em. עַד־נֹפַח אֲשֶׁר *unto Nophah, which is* near Medeba to עַד־נֻפַּח אֵשׁ *until fire was blown* unto Medeba); לִפְנֵי *in front of,* + חנה *encamp* 1 C 19$_7$. <COLL> מֵידְבָא עַד־דִּיבוֹן *Medeba unto Dibon* Jos 13$_9$.

מֵידָד 2 pr.n.m. **Medad,** one of the elders of Israel in the wilderness, who, with Eldad, received a prophetic gift, <SUBJ> כתב pass. *be written,* i.e. registered Nm 11$_{26}$, יצא *go out* to tent of meeting Nm 11$_{26}$, נבא htp. *prophesy* Nm 11$_{26.27}$. <NOM CL> וְשֵׁם הַשֵּׁנִי מֵידָד *and the name of the second was Medad* Nm 11$_{26}$. <OBJ> כלא *restrain* Nm 11$_{27}$. <PREP> עַל *upon,* + נוח *rest* (of spirit) Nm 11$_{26}$.

***[מַיָה]** n.[f.] **water,** <OBJ> לקח *take* Lachish ost. 3$_{18}$ (שלח לקחת מיה perh. *he has sent to take water;* others מזה, i.e. מִזֶּה to take *from here,* or perh. מָזוֹה *provisions;* or em. מִיָּדָה *from his hand).*

⇒ cf. מַיִם *water.*

מֵי הַיַּרְקוֹן, see מַיִם *water,* Coll.

מֵי זָהָב I 2 pr.n. **Me-zahab,** grandfather or grandmother of Mehetabel, Edomite queen (unless מֵי זָהָב II), <CSTR> בַּת מֵי זָהָב Matred, *daughter of Me-zahab* Gn 36$_{39}$||1 C 1$_{50}$.

⇒ מַיִם *water* + זָהָב *gold.*

מֵי זָהָב II 2 pl.n. **Me-zahab,** perh. ident. with Di-zahab at Dt 1$_1$ (unless מֵי זָהָב I), <CSTR> בַּת מֵי זָהָב Matred, *daughter,* or *woman, of Me-zahab* Gn 36$_{39}$||1 C 1$_{50}$.

⇒ מַיִם *water* + זָהָב *gold.*

[מֵיזָן], see יזן, Pu. *be on heat.*

[מֵיטָב] 6 n.[m.] **best, best part**—cstr. מֵיטַב—of land (Gn 47$_{6.11}$ Ex 22$_4$), of field and vineyard (Ex 22$_4$), of flocks and herds (1 S 15$_{9.15}$), <CSTR> מֵיטַב הָאָרֶץ *the best of the land* Gn 47$_{6.11}$, שָׂדֵהוּ *of his land* Ex 22$_4$, כַּרְמוֹ *of his vineyard* Ex 22$_4$, הַצֹּאן וְהַבָּקָר וְהַמִּשְׁנִים *of the flock and the herd and the fatlings* 1 S 15$_{9.15}$ (lacks וְהַמִּשְׁנִים). <OBJ> שׁלם pi. *repay* Ex 22$_4$. <PREP> בְּ of place, *in, among* Gn 47$_{11}$ (+ אֲחֻזָּה *portion),* ישׁב hi. *accommodate* Gn 47$_6$; עַל *on, concerning,* + חמל *take pity* 1 S 15$_{9.15}$.*

⇒ יטב *be good.*

מִיכָא 4 pr.n.m. **Mica,** appar. shortened form of מִיכָאֵל *Michael* or מִיכָיְהוּ *Micaiah* or מִיכָיְהוּ *Micaiah,* **1.** son of Meribbaal/Mephibosheth, ident. with Micah (מִיכָה) at 1 C 8$_{34.35}$||9$_{40.41}$, <NOM CL> וּשְׁמוֹ מִיכָא *and his name was Mica* 2 S 9$_{12}$.

2. Levite, grandson of Asaph and father of Mattaniah, appar. ident with Micah (מִיכָה) at Ne 11$_{17}$ and with Micaiah (מִיכָיָה) at Ne 12$_{35}$, <CSTR> בֶּן־מִיכָא Mattaniah *son of Mica* Ne 11$_{22}$ 1 C 9$_{15}$. <APP> בֵּן *son* of Zichri 1 C 9$_{15}$.

3. Levite and co-signatory of Nehemiah's pledge, perh. ident. with preceding, <NOM CL> אֲחֵיהֶם ... מִיכָא

their brothers were ... Mica Ne 10_{12}.
⇒ מִי *who?* + כְּ *like.*

מִיכָאֵל 13.0.4 pr.n.m. **Michael, 1.** angelic prince and guardian of Israel, Dn $10_{13.21}$ 12_{1} 1QM 9_{15} (+ Sariel, Raphael) 9_{16} (+ Gabriel) $17_{6.7}$. <SUBJ> חזק htp. *exert oneself* Dn 10_{21}, בוא *come* Dn 10_{13}, עמד *arise* Dn 12_{1}, עזר *help* Dn 10_{13}. <OBJ> כתב *write* (name of) on shield 1QM 9_{15} (מיכ[א]ל). <CSTR> משרת מיכאל *the service of Michael* 1QM $17_{6.7}$. <APP> מִיכָאֵל שַׂרְכֶם *Michael, your prince* Dn 10_{21}, מִיכָאֵל הַשַּׂר הַגָּדוֹל הָעֹמֵד עַל־בְּנֵי עַמֶּךָ *Michael, the great prince, who stands with the children of your people* Dn 12_{1}, מִיכָאֵל אַחַד הַשָּׂרִים הָרִאשֹׁנִים *Michael, one of the first princes* Dn 10_{13}, בגבורת מלאך האדיר למשרת מיכאל *by the might of the majestic angel, through the service of Michael* 1QM 17_{6}. <COLL> כִּי אִם־מִיכָאֵל *except Michael* Dn 10_{21}.

2. father of Sethur, chief of Asher, Nm 13_{13}. <CSTR> בֶּן־מִיכָאֵל Sethur, *son of Michael* Nm 13_{13}.

3. one of the sons of Jehoshaphat and brothers of Jehoram, 1 C 21_{2}. <APP> אָח *brother* 2 C 21_{2}, בֵּן *son* 1 C 21_{2}. <PREP> לְ of direction, *to*, + נתן *give* presents 2 C 21_{2}.

4. father of Zebadiah, a returning exile, Ezr 8_{8}. <CSTR> בֶּן־מִיכָאֵל Zebadiah, *son of Michael* Ezr 8_{8}.

5. Gadite, 1 C 5_{13}, <NOM CL> וַאֲחֵיהֶם לְבֵית אֲבוֹתֵיהֶם מִיכָאֵל וּמְשֻׁלָּם *and their brothers, according to the house of their ancestors, were Michael and Meshullam* 1 C 5_{13}.

6. Gadite, son of Jeshishai and father of Gilead, 1 C 5_{14}, <CSTR> בֶּן־מִיכָאֵל Gilead, *son of Michael* 1 C 5_{14}. <APP> בֵּן *son* of Jeshishai 1 C 5_{14}.

7. Kohathite, great-grandfather of Asaph the temple singer, 1 C 6_{25}. <CSTR> בֶּן־מִיכָאֵל Shimea, *son of Michael* 1 C 6_{25}. <CSTR> בֶּן־מִיכָאֵל Gilead, *son of Michael* 1 C 6_{25}. <APP> בֵּן *son* of Baaseiah 1 C 6_{25}.

8. Issacharite chief, 1 C 7_{3}. <NOM CL> וּבְנֵי יִזְרַחְיָה מִיכָאֵל וְעֹבַדְיָה *and the sons of Izrahiah were Michael and Obadiah* 1 C 7_{3}.

9. father of Omri, Issacharite chief at time of David, 1 C 27_{18}. <CSTR> בֶּן־מִיכָאֵל Omri, *son of Michael* 1 C 27_{18}.

10. one of the Manassite chiefs who joined David at Ziklag, 1 C 12_{21}. <SUBJ> נפל *fall*, i.e. desert 1 C 12_{21}. <APP> רֹאשׁ *head* of Manasseh 1 C 12_{21}.

11. Benjamite chief, 1 C 8_{16}. <NOM CL> וּמִיכָאֵל וְיִשְׁפָּה וְיוֹחָא בְּנֵי בְרִיעָה *and Michael and Ishpah and Joha were sons of Beriah* 1 C 8_{16}.
⇒ מִי *who?* + כְּ *like* + אֵל *God.*

מִיכָה 33.0.0.2 pr.n.m. **Micah,** appar. shortened form of מִיכָאֵל *Michael* or מִיכָיְהוּ *Micaiah* or מִיכָיְהוּ *Micaiah*, **1.** Ephraimite, appar. ident. with Micaiah (מִיכָיְהוּ) at Jg $17_{1.4}$, <SUBJ> שׁוב *go back* home Jg 18_{26}, פנה *turn* intrans. 18_{26}, נתן *give* salary 17_{10}, אסף *gather*, i.e. lose, life 18_{23}, אמר *say* to Levite $17_{8.9}$, to Danites 18_{23}, to himself 17_{13}, שׁמע hi. *make* voice *heard*, i.e. raise voice 18_{23}, ידע *know* 17_{13}, ראה *see* 18_{26}, זעק ni. *be summoned* 18_{23}, עשׂה *do* for Levite 18_{4}, *make* cult objects 17_{5} $18_{23.27.31}$, מלא pi. *fill* hand of, i.e. ordain (as priest) $17_{5.12}$, שׂכר *employ* 18_{4}. <CSTR> בֵּית מִיכָה *the house of Micah* Jg $17_{8.12}$ 18_{2+6t}, פֶּסֶל *image of*, i.e made by 18_{31}. <APP> אִישׁ *man* Jg 17_{5}.

<PREP> לְ of direction, *to*, + אמר *say* Jg 18_{23}; of benefit, *to, for*, + יטב hi. *do good* Jg 17_{13}; of possession, *of, (belonging) to* Jg 17_{5} (+ בֵּית אֱלֹהִים *house of God*) 18_{23} (מַה־לְּךָ *what is to you?*, i.e. what do you find wrong?) 18_{23} (מַה־לִּי עוֹד *what else do I have?*) 18_{23} (מַה־לְּךָ *what is to you?*, i.e. what do you find wrong?), + היה *be* Jg 17_{5} (+ לְכֹהֵן *as a priest*) 17_{10} (+ לְאָב לְכֹהֵן *as an advisor and as a priest*) $17_{12.13}$ 18_{4} (all three + לְכֹהֵן) 18_{27}; perh. שׁאל לְ *ask (of)* Jg 18_{15}; בְּ *against*, + פגע *strike* Jg 18_{23}, מִן of comparison, *(more) than* Jg 18_{26} (+ חָזָק *strong*); אֶל *to*, + אמר *say* Jg 17_{9} $18_{23.23}$; עִם *with*, + ישׁב *dwell* Jg 17_{10}.

2. prophet from Moresheth at time of Jotham, Ahaz and Hezekiah, ident. with Micaiah (Kt מיכיה), <SUBJ> היה *be* Jr $26_{18(Qr)}$, אמר *say* Jr $26_{18(Qr).18(Qr)}$, נבא ni. *prophesy* Jr $26_{18(Qr)}$, חזה *see* (in vision) Mc 1_{1}. <OBJ> מות hi. *kill* Jr $26_{18(Qr)}$. <APP> מִיכָה הַמּוֹרַשְׁתִּי *Micah the Moreshethite* Jr $26_{18(Qr)}$ Mc 1_{1} (הַמֹּרַשְׁתִּי). <PREP> אֶל *to*, + היה *be* (of word of Y.) Mc 1_{1}.

3. prophet at time of Jehoshaphat and Ahab, ident. with Micaiah (מִיכָיְהוּ) son of Imla(h) at 1 K $22_{8.9.13.14}$|| 2 C $18_{7.8(Qr).12.13}$ 1 K 22_{15} $22_{24.25.26.28}$||2 C $18_{23.24.25.27}$

and Micah (מִיכָהוּ) son of Imlah at 2 C 18$_{8(Kt)}$, <SUBJ> אמר *say* to Ahab 2 C 18$_{14.14.14}$, דבר pi. *speak* to Ahab 18$_{14}$, נבא htp. *prophesy* about Ahab 18$_{14}$, ראה *see* vision 18$_{14.14}$. <OBJ> שׁבע hi. *adjure* 2 C 18$_{14}$. <PREP> אֶל *to*, + אמר *say* 2 C 18$_{14}$. <COLL> מִיכָה *O Micah* 2 C 18$_{14}$.

4. Benjaminite, son of Meribbaal and father of three or four sons, <OBJ> ילד hi. *beget* 1 C 8$_{34}$||9$_{40}$. <CSTR> וּבְנֵי מִיכָה *and the sons of Micah* 1 C 8$_{35}$||9$_{41}$.

5. Kohathite, elder son of Uzziel, brother of Isshiah (יִשִּׁיָּה), and father of Shamir (Kt Shamur), <NOM CL> בְּנֵי עֻזִּיאֵל מִיכָה ... וְיִשִּׁיָּה *the sons of Uzziel were Micah ... and Isshiah* 1 C 23$_{20}$, בְּנֵי עֻזִּיאֵל מִיכָה *the sons of Uzziel were Micah* 24$_{24}$. <CSTR> לִבְנֵי מִיכָה *of the sons of Micah* 1 C 24$_{24}$, אֲחִי מִיכָה *the brother of Micah* 1 C 24$_{25}$. <APP> מִיכָה הָרֹאשׁ *Micah, the head*, i.e. firstborn 1 C 23$_{20}$.

6. Levite, grandson of Asaph and father of Mattaniah, appar. ident with Mica (מִיכָא) at Ne 11$_{22}$ 1 C 9$_{15}$ and with Micaiah (מִיכָיָה) at Ne 12$_{35}$, <CSTR> בֶּן־מִיכָה Mattaniah, *son of Micah* Ne 11$_{17}$. <APP> בֵּן *son* of Zabdi Ne 11$_{17}$.

7. Reubenite, son of Shimei and father of Reaiah, <NOM CL> מִיכָה בְנוֹ *Micah was his son* 1 C 5$_{5}$ (unless app., *Micah, his son*).

8. father of Abdon (עַבְדּוֹן), one of Josiah's servants, appar. ident. with Micaiah (מִיכָיָה) son of Achbor at 2 K 22$_{12}$, <CSTR> בֶּן־מִיכָה Abdon, *son of Micah* 2 C 34$_{20}$.

9. father of Elijah, <CSTR> בנ[ן] מיכה Elijah, *son of Micah* Seal 527 (T. Beit Mirsim?, 7th/6th cent.).

10. <PREP> לְ of possession, *of, (belonging) to* Seal 313 (6th/5th cent.).

⇒ מִי *who?* + כְּ *like*.

[מִיכָהוּ] 1 pr.n.m. **Micah,** ident. with Micaiah/Micah son of Imla(h) at 1 K 22$_{8+8t}$||2 C 18$_{7+8t}$, <OBJ> מהר *bring quickly* 2 C 18$_{8(Kt)}$. <APP> בֵּן *son* of Imla 2 C 18$_{8(Kt)}$.

⇒ מִי *who?* + כְּ *like* + הוּא *he*.

מִיכָיָה 4 pr.n.m. **Micaiah, 1.** prophet from Moresheth at time of Jotham, Ahaz and Hezekiah, ident. with Micah (Qr), <SUBJ> היה *be* Jr 26$_{18(Kt)}$, אמר *say* Jr 26$_{18(Kt).18(Kt)}$, נבא ni. *prophesy* Jr 26$_{18(Kt)}$. <OBJ> מות hi. *kill* Jr 26$_{18(Kt)}$. <APP> מיכיה הַמּוֹרַשְׁתִּי *Micah the Moreshethite* Jr 26$_{18}$.

2. Levite, grandson of Asaph and father of Mattaniah, appar. ident with Mica (מִיכָא) at Ne 11$_{22}$ 1 C 9$_{15}$ and with Micah (מִיכָה) at Ne 11$_{17}$, <CSTR> בֶּן־מִיכָיָה Mattaniah, *son of Micaiah* Ne 12$_{35}$. <APP> בֵּן *son* of Zaccur Ne 12$_{35}$.

3. father of Achbor (עַכְבּוֹר), one of Josiah's servants, appar. ident. with Micah son of Abdon at 2 C 34$_{20}$, <CSTR> בֶּן־מִיכָיָה Achbor, *son of Micah* 2 K 22$_{12}$.

4. priest assisting in rededication of walls of Jerusalem, <NOM CL> מִיכָיָה ... בַּחֲצֹצְרוֹת *Micaiah ... was on the trumpets* Ne 12$_{41}$. <APP> כֹּהֵן *priest* Ne 12$_{41}$.

⇒ מִי *who?* + כְּ *like* + ׳י Y.

מִיכָיָהוּ 2 pr.n.m. & f. **Micaiah, 1.** one of those sent out by Jehoshaphat to teach, <SUBJ> סבב *go around* Judah 2 C 17$_{7}$, למד pi. *teach* 2 C 17$_{7.7.7}$. <OBJ> (with לְ) שׁלח *send* 2 C 17$_{7}$. <APP> שַׂר *prince* 2 C 17$_{7}$. <PREP> עִם *with* 2 C 17$_{7.7}$. **2.** mother of Abijah and daughter of Uriel, <NOM CL> וְשֵׁם אִמּוֹ מִיכָיָהוּ *and his mother's name was Micaiah* 2 C 13$_{2}$. <APP> בַּת *daughter* of Uriel 2 C 13$_{2}$.

⇒ מִי *who?* + כְּ *like* + ׳י Y.

מִיכָיְהוּ 21.0.0.15 pr.n.m. **Micaiah**—מִכָיְהוּ—**1.** Ephraimite, appar. ident. with Micah at Jg 17$_{5+6t}$ 18$_{2+11t}$, <SUBJ> שׁוב hi. *return* money Jg 17$_{1}$. <NOM CL> וּשְׁמוֹ מִיכָיְהוּ *and his name was Micaiah* Jg 17$_{1}$. <CSTR> בֵּית מִיכָיְהוּ *the house of Micaiah* Jg 17$_{4}$.

2. Micaiah son of Imla(h) (יִמְלָה/א), prophet at time of Jehoshaphat and Ahab, ident. with Micah at 2 C 18$_{14}$, <SUBJ> בוא *come* 1 K 22$_{14}$, דרשׁ *seek* from Y. 1 K 22$_{8}$, אמר *say* 1 K 22$_{14}$||2 C 18$_{13}$ 1 K 22$_{15.15.15}$ 1 K 22$_{25.28.28}$||2 C 18$_{24.27.27}$, דבר pi. *speak* 1 K 22$_{13.13.14}$||2 C 18$_{12.12.18}$ 1 K 22$_{15}$, נבא htp. *prophesy* 1 K 22$_{8.15}$, ראה *see* vision 1 K 22$_{15.15}$. <NOM CL> הוּא מִיכָיְהוּ *he is Micaiah* 2 C 18$_{7}$. <OBJ> קרא *call* 1 K 22$_{13}$, שׁבע hi. *adjure* 1 K 22$_{15}$, שׂנא *hate* 1 K 22$_{8}$, נכה hi. *strike* on cheek 1 K 22$_{24}$||2 C 18$_{23}$, לקח *take* 1 K 22$_{26}$||2 C 18$_{25}$, שׁוב *take back* 1 K 22$_{26}$||2 C 18$_{25}$, מהר pi. *bring quickly* 1 K 22$_{9}$||2 C 18$_{8(Qr)}$. <APP> אִישׁ *man* 1 K 22$_{8}$, בֵּן *son* of Imla(h) 1 K 22$_{8.9}$|| 2 C 18$_{7.8(Qr)}$. <PREP> לְ of direction, *to*, + קרא *call* 2 C

18$_{12}$; בְּ of instrument, *by (means of), through,* + דבר pi. *speak* 1 K 22$_{28}$||2 C 18$_{27}$; אֶל *to,* + אמר *say* 1 K 22$_{14.15.15}$, דבר pi. *speak* 1 K 22$_{13}$||2 C 18$_{12}$; אֵת *with,* + דבר pi. *speak* 1 K 22$_{24}$||2 C 18$_{23}$. <COLL> מִיכָיְהוּ *O Micaiah* 1 K 22$_{15}$.

3. son of Gemariah, Jehoiakim's secretary, <SUBJ> ירד *go down* Jr 36$_{11}$, שׁמע *hear* Jr 36$_{11.13}$, נגד hi. *tell* 36$_{13}$. <APP> בֵּן *son* of Gemariah, Jr 36$_{11}$.

4. father of Nehemiah, <CSTR> לנחמיהו בן מיכיהו *to Nehemiah, son of Micaiah* Seal 30 (Es-Soda [Tartus], 8th cent.).

5. son of Shallum (שלם), <APP> בֵּן *son* of Shallum Seal 368 (8th/7th cent.). <PREP> לְ of possession, *of, (belonging) to* Seal 368.

6. son of Meshullam (משלם), <APP> בֵּן *son* of Meshullam Seal 592 (T. Beit Mirsim?, 7th/6th cent.). <PREP> לְ of possession, *of, (belonging) to* Seal 592.

7. son of Eliaz (אלעז), <APP> בֵּן *son* of Eliaz Seal 590 (T. Beit Mirsim?, 7th/6th cent.). <PREP> לְ of possession, *of, (belonging) to* Seal 590.

8. son of Shahar ([שח[ר), <APP> בֵּן *son* of Shahar Seal 595 (T. Beit Mirsim?, 7th/6th cent.). <PREP> לְ of possession, *of, (belonging) to* Seal 595 ([למכי[הו).

9. son of Hezi (חצי), <APP> בֵּן *son* of Hezi Seal 808 (City of David, 7th/6th cent.). <PREP> לְ of possession, *of, (belonging) to* Seal 595 ([למכי[הו).

10. appar. son of Shebaniah (שבניהו), <PREP> לְ of possession, *of, (belonging) to* Seal 596 597 (both T. Beit Mirsim?, 7th/6th cent.).

11. appar. son of Isaiah ([ישע[הו), <PREP> לְ of possession, *of, (belonging) to* Seal 591 ([למכיהו]; T. Beit Mirsim?, 7th/6th cent.).

12. appar. son of Pelatiah (פלטהו), <PREP> לְ of possession, *of, (belonging) to* Seal 594 ([למכי[הו]; T. Beit Mirsim?, 7th/6th cent.).

13. father of Nemesh (נמש), <CSTR> בן מכיהו Seal 852 (7th cent.).

14. appar. father of Machir (מכר), Seal 749 (c. 700).

15. appar. father of Azrikam (עזריקם), Seal 832 (City of David, 7th/6th cent.).

16. Jerusalem ost. 1$_{2}$.

17. Lachish ost. 11$_{4}$.

18. Ost. DH79$_{1}$.

⇒ מִי *who?* + כְּ *like* + י׳ *Y.*

[מִיכָל] I $_{1}$ n.[m.] perh. **pool** or **stream**—cstr. מִיכַל—עָבְרוּ מִיכַל הַמָּיִם *they have crossed the water pool* 2 S 17$_{20}$ (unless מִיכָל II *collection;* or em. מְכֹל water *container* or מִכֹּה אֶל־ *from here to* the water).

⇒ כול *contain.*

***[מִיכָל] II** $_{1}$ n.[m.] **collection, container, hoard**—cstr. מִיכַל—**collection** of waters, i.e. **pool,** עָבְרוּ מִיכַל הַמָּיִם *they have crossed the water pool* 2 S 17$_{20}$ (unless מִיכָל I *pool;* or em. מְכֹל water *container* or מִכֹּה אֶל־ *from here to* the water).

⇒ כול *contain.*

מִיכַל $_{18}$ pr.n.f. **Michal, 1.** Saul's younger daughter and wife at different times of Adriel (or em. Michal to Merab, as wife of Adriel, at 2 S 21$_{8}$), David (twice), and Palti, <SUBJ> יצא *go out* to greet David 2 S 6$_{20}$, שׁקף ni. *lean* out of window 1 C 15$_{29}$, ירד hi. *let down* David through window 1 S 19$_{12}$, שׁלח pi. *send away* David 1 S 19$_{17.17}$, קרא *meet* David 2 S 6$_{20}$, לקח *take* teraphim 1 S 19$_{13}$, שׂים *place* teraphim on bed, כסה pi. *cover* teraphim 1 S 19$_{13}$, ראה *see* David 1 C 15$_{29}$, אמר *say* 1 S 19$_{11.13.17}$ 2 S 6$_{20}$, נגד hi. *tell* David of Saul's intentions 1 S 19$_{11}$, אהב *love* David (or perhaps Saul) 1 S 18$_{28}$, בזה *despise* David 1 C 15$_{29}$, רמה pi. *deceive* Saul 1 S 19$_{17}$, ילד *give birth* 2 S 21$_{8}$ (or em. Merab), מות *die* 2 S 6$_{23}$.

<NOM CL> וְשֵׁם הַקְּטַנָּה מִיכַל *and the name of the younger was Michal* 1 S 14$_{49}$. <OBJ> בוא hi. *bring* back from Palti 2 S 3$_{13}$, נתן *give* in marriage 1 S 18$_{27}$ 25$_{44}$ 2 S 3$_{14}$, ארשׂ pi. *betroth* 2 S 3$_{14}$, אהב *love* 1 S 18$_{20}$, מות hi. *kill* 1 S 19$_{17}$. <CSTR> חֲמֵשֶׁת בְּנֵי מִיכַל *the five children of Michal* 2 S 21$_{8}$ (or em. Merab). <APP> בַּת *daughter* of Saul 1 S 18$_{20.27.28}$ 25$_{44}$ 2 S 3$_{13}$ 6$_{23}$ 21$_{8}$ (or em. Merab) 1 C 15$_{29}$, אִשָּׁה *wife* of David 1 S 19$_{11}$ 2 S 3$_{14}$. <PREP> לְ of possession, *of, (belonging) to,* + היה *be* child 2 S 6$_{23}$; אֶל *to,* + אמר *say* 1 S 19$_{17.17}$ 2 S 6$_{21}$.

2. Lachish ost. 19$_{3}$ (מכל; others מבל *Mabal* or עמדל *Amdal*).

⇒ perh. מִי *who?* + כְּ *like* + אֵל *God.*

*מיל $_{3}$ vb. **ward off—Qal** $_{3}$ Impf. אֲמִילַם—<SUBJ> worshipper Ps 118$_{10.11.12}$ (בְּשֵׁם י׳ כִּי אֲמִילַם *in the name of Y. I will ward them off*; or em. all three אַפִּילֵם *I caused them to fall*, or אִמָּלֵט *I was delivered*). <OBJ> גּוֹי *nation* Ps 118$_{10.11.12}$ (or em. all three; see Subj.). <PREP> בְּ of accompaniment, *in, with*, + שֵׁם *name* Ps 118$_{10.11.12}$ (or em. all three; see Subj.).

מְיַלֶּדֶת *midwife*, see ילד Pi., §2.

מַיִם $_{580.9.168.3}$ n.m. **water(s)**—מָיִם; cstr. מֵי (מֵימֵי); sf. מֵימֶיךָ, מֵימָיו, Q מימיה, מֵימֵינוּ, מֵימֵיהֶם; + ה- of direction מַיְמָה (מָיְמָה).

1. water for drinking (e.g. Gn 21$_{14}$).

2. water for washing hands (e.g. Ex 30$_{19}$), feet (e.g. Gn 24$_{32}$), person (e.g. 2 K 5$_{12}$), clothes (e.g. Nm 19$_{8}$); specif. ritual purification of vessels (e.g. Lv 6$_{21}$), parts of sacrificial animal (e.g. Lv 1$_{9.13}$ 8$_{21}$).

3. water for other uses or with other effects, e.g. boiling (Is 64$_{1}$), boiling meat (Ex 12$_{9}$), cooking (Ezk 24$_{3}$), damaging clothing (Jr 13$_{1}$), permeating (Ps 109$_{18}$), corroding (Jb 14$_{19}$), dousing flame (Ca 8$_{7}$), drowning (2 K 8$_{15}$), reflecting (Pr 27$_{19}$), determining ordeal (e.g. Nm 5$_{17}$), pouring out as libation (e.g. 2 S 23$_{16}$).

4. water as term for other liquids, **tears** (e.g. Lm 1$_{16}$), **urine** (2 K 18$_{27(Qr)}$), **menstrual discharge** (Is 30$_{22}$; if em. תִּזְרֵם כְּמוֹ דָוָה *you will cast them away like a menstrual garment* to תְּזִירֵם כְּמֵי דָוָה *you will loathe them like an impure discharge*),* **bodily fluids, humours** (Ps 102$_{4}$; if em. כִּי־כָלוּ בְעָשָׁן יָמָי *for my days are consumed in smoke* to כִּי־כָלוּ כְעָשָׁן מֵימָי *for my humours are consumed like smoke*),* appar. **semen** (Is 48$_{1}$ [or em. מִמֵּי *from the semen of* to מִמְּעֵי *from the innards of*]).*

5. water as metaphor for abundance (Am 5$_{24}$), refreshment (e.g. Is 32$_{2}$), weakness (Jos 7$_{5}$), instability (e.g. Gn 49$_{4}$), tempestuousness (e.g. Is 28$_{2}$), what can be drunk (Jb 34$_{7}$), what can be poured (e.g. Ho 5$_{10}$ Ps 22$_{15}$), what runs away (Ps 58$_{8}$), what cannot be recovered (2 S 14$_{14}$).

6. water existing in nature as rain (e.g. Jg 5$_{4}$), clouds (e.g. Jr 10$_{13}$), sea-water (Am 5$_{8}$), river-water (e.g. Ex 2$_{10}$), well-water (e.g. Nm 20$_{17}$), spring-water (2 C 32$_{3}$), cistern-water (e.g. 2 K 18$_{31}$), flood-water (e.g. Gn 7$_{7}$), subterranean water (e.g. Ex 20$_{4}$), melted snow (Jb 24$_{19}$).

7. cosmic **waters,** often as waters of destruction (but mythological allusion not alw. certain; e.g. Gn 1$_{2}$).

8. water in place names, מֵי הַיַּרְקוֹן perh. *Me-jarkon* Jos 19$_{46}$, מִשְׂרְפוֹת מַיִם *Misrephoth-maim* Jos 11$_{8}$ 13$_{6}$ (מִשְׂרְפֹת; or em. מִיָּם Misrephoth *to the west*), שַׁעַר הַמַּיִם *the gate of water*, i.e. Water Gate, in Jerusalem Ne 3$_{26}$ 8$_{1}$ (שַׁעַר־הַמָּיִם) 8$_{3}$ (שַׁעַר־) 8$_{16}$ 12$_{37}$, אָבֵל מָיִם they struck *Abel-maim* 2 C 16$_{4}$ (or em. מִיָּם they struck Abel *from the sea*; ||1 K 15$_{20}$ אָבֵל בֵּית־מַעֲכָה *Abel-beth-maacah*).

<SUBJ> היה *be* Gn 7$_{6.10}$ (= 4QCommGenA 1$_{3}$) 8$_{5}$ 9$_{15}$ (+ לְמַבּוּל become *a flood*) Ex 4$_{9}$ (+ לְדָם turn *into blood*) 7$_{19}$ (+ דָּם become *blood*) Nm 5$_{18}$ (בְּיַד *in the hand of* priest) 20$_{2}$ (+ לָעֵדָה *for the congregation*) 33$_{14}$ Jos 19$_{46}$ (+ גְּבוּל נַחֲלָתָם *the border of their inheritance* was ... the waters of the Jarkon; unless וּמֵי הַיַּרְקוֹן = *and Me-jarkon*, as pl.n., or em. וּמִיָּם *and to the west*) 2 K 3$_{9}$ (+ לַמַּחֲנֶה וְלַבְּהֵמָה *for the camp and for the beasts*) Is 15$_{6}$= Jr 48$_{34}$ (+ [לְ]מְשַׁמָּה *[as a] devastation*) Jr 47$_{2}$ (+ לְנַחַל שׁוֹטֵף turn *into an overflowing stream*) 4QAdmon 1$_{8}$ 11QT 32$_{14}$, יכל *be able* Ca 8$_{7}$, אמן ni. *be reliable* Jr 15$_{18}$, הפך ni. *be changed* Ex 7$_{17.20}$ (both + לְדָם turn *into blood*), גבר *be strong* Gn 7$_{18.19.20.24}$ (= 4QCommGenA 1$_{7}$) 4QParGenEx 2$_{8}$, מלא *be full of* Is 15$_{9}$ (+ דָּם *blood*) Ps 65$_{10}$, ni. *be filled with* 2 K 3$_{17}$ (+ נַחַל *stream*), רבה *be many* Gn 7$_{17.18}$, ערם ni. *be amassed* Ex 15$_{8}$, קוה ni. *be amassed* Gn 1$_{9}$, געש htp. *be in turmoil* Jr 46$_{7.8}$ (or del.).

פחד *fear* 4Q416 1$_{12}$ (+ תְּהוֹם *abyss*), שׁכך *subside* Gn 8$_{1}$, אבד *perish* 11QT 32$_{14}$, חסר *be diminished* Gn 8$_{3}$ (= 4QCommGen 1$_{9}$) 8$_{5}$ (= 4QCommGen 1$_{11}$; הָלוֹךְ וְחָסוֹר perh. *diminishing as they went away*), רפה ni. *be relaxed*, i.e. released Ezk 47$_{8(Qr)}$, כלה *be finished* Gn 21$_{15}$ 4QPatr 5.2$_{3}$, קלל *be light* Gn 8$_{8.11}$ (= 4QCommGen 1$_{14}$), כלא ni. *be restrained* Ezk 31$_{15}$, יבשׁ *be dry* Gn 8$_{7}$ (עַד־ יְבֹשֶׁת הַמַּיִם *until the drying up of the waters*) Jr 50$_{38}$ Jb 12$_{15}$, חרב *be dry* Gn 8$_{13}$ = 4QCommGen 1$_{21}$, שׁתה ni. *be drunk* Is 19$_{5}$ Jr 18$_{14}$ (if em. נתשׁ ni. *be uprooted*), מצה ni. *be drained* Ps 73$_{10}$ (or em. וּמֵי מָלֵא יִמָּצוּ *and waters of a full one are drained* to וּמְלֵיהֶם יָמֹצּוּ *and they suck* up their words), מתק *be sweet* Ex 15$_{25}$, hi. *cause sweetness* Si 38$_{5}$, רפא ni. *be healed* Ezk 47$_{8(Kt).9}$, קור *be cold* Jr 18$_{14}$, זור *be foreign* Jr 18$_{14}$ (or em. מַיִם זָרִים קָרִים *cold foreign waters* to מִמִּצְרַיִם מְקֹרִים be uprooted *from Egypt* flowing *springs* or מֵימֵי קֶדֶם קָרִים *cold* flowing *waters of the east* or מַיִם זָבִים מְקֹרִים *flowing waters;* flowing *springs*).

רפה ni. *be cured* 2 K 2$_{22}$, מתק *be sweet* Pr 9$_{17}$, לקח ho. *be taken* Gn 18$_{4}$, גנב pass. *be stolen* Pr 9$_{17}$, נתן ho. *be placed* Lv 11$_{38}$, בקע ni. *be split* Ex 14$_{21}$ Is 35$_{6}$ 4QAdmon 1$_{4}$, חצה ni. *be divided* 2 K 2$_{8}$, כרת ni. *be cut* Jos 3$_{13}$ 4$_{7.7}$, נתשׁ ni. *be uprooted* Jr 18$_{14}$, זרק pu. *be scattered* Nm 19$_{13.20}$, שׁפך ni. *be poured* 11QT 32$_{14}$, נתך ni. *be poured* 2 S 21$_{10}$, נגר ho. *be poured out* Mc 1$_{4}$ 1QH 4$_{34}$, יצק pu. *be poured* 11QT 49$_{7}$, ho. *be poured out* Si 15$_{16}$ (+ אֵשׁ *fire*), שׁטף *overflow* Is 28$_{2.17}$ perh. 43$_{2}$ Jr 47$_{2}$ Ps 124$_{4}$, גרשׁ *churn up* mud and slime Is 57$_{20}$ (1QIsa[a] htp. waters will *be churned up* into mud and slime).

הלך *go (away)* Gn 8$_{3.5}$ (= 4QCommGen 1$_{11}$), *flow* Jos 4$_{18}$ 1 K 18$_{35}$ Is 8$_{6}$ 11QT 32$_{14}$ Siloam tunnel inscr.$_{5}$, htp. *go (away)* Ps 58$_{8}$, אזל *go (away)* Jb 14$_{11}$, בוא *come* Ezk 47$_{8.9}$ Ps 69$_{2}$ (+ עַד־נֶפֶשׁ *up to [my] throat*), יצא *go out* Ex 17$_{6}$ Nm 20$_{11}$ Jg 15$_{19}$ Ezk 47$_{1.12}$ Zc 14$_{8}$, עלה *go up* Jr 47$_{2}$, גאה *be proud,* i.e. swell Ezk 47$_{5}$, ירד *go down* Jos 3$_{13.16}$ Ezk 47$_{1.8}$, נוס *flee,* i.e. flow away Na 2$_{9}$, זוב *flow* Is 48$_{21}$ (if em. זור *be foreign*) Ps 78$_{20}$ 105$_{41}$, צוף *flow* Lm 3$_{54}$, נזל *flow* Nm 24$_{7}$ (or em. יִזַּל־מַיִם מִדָּלְיוֹ *water flows from his buckets* to יִזַּלּוּ לְאֻמִּים מֵחֵילוֹ *peoples are regarded as worthless next to his might*) Jr 18$_{14}$ (or em.) 147$_{18}$, פכה pi. *trickle* Ezk 47$_{2}$, בוא *come* from Edom 2 K 3$_{20}$, into woman Nm 5$_{22.24.27}$, upon/with food Lv 11$_{34}$, שׁוב *go back* Gn 8$_{3.3}$ (הָלוֹךְ וָשׁוֹב perh. *coming back as they went away*) Ex 14$_{26.28}$ Jos 4$_{18}$, עבר *pass* Is 54$_{9}$ Ps 124$_{5}$ Jb 11$_{16}$, *transgress* Pr 8$_{29}$.

קום *stand* Jos 3$_{16}$, עמד *stand (still)* Jos 3$_{13.16}$ Na 2$_{9}$ Ps 104$_{6}$ 147$_{17}$ (if em. מִי יַעֲמֹד before his cold *who can stand?* to מַיִם יַעַמְדוּ *waters stand still*), נגע hi. *reach* Ps 32$_{6}$, נצב ni. *stand (still)* Ex 15$_{8}$, נשׂא *raise* Gn 7$_{17}$, כסה pi. *cover* Ex 14$_{28}$ Is 11$_{9}$ Ezk 26$_{19}$ Hb 2$_{14}$ Ps 106$_{11}$, אפף *surround* Jon 2$_{6}$ (+ עַד־נֶפֶשׁ *up to [my] throat*), הפך *overturn* earth Jb 12$_{15}$, שׁחק *erode* stones Jb 14$_{19}$, גזל *steal* Jb 24$_{19}$, חיל *writhe* Ps 77$_{17}$, טמא pi. *make unclean* CD 10$_{13}$, ארר pi. *bring curse* Nm 5$_{18+5t}$, הלל pi. *praise* Y. Ps 148$_{4}$, כבה pi. *extinguish* Ca 8$_{7}$ Si 3$_{30}$, שׁחת pi. *destroy* Gn 6$_{17}$ 9$_{15}$, כזב pi. *deceive,* i.e. fail Is 58$_{11}$, גדל pi. *magnify* Ezk 31$_{4}$, ראה *see* Ps 77$_{17.17}$, צבה hi. *cause* womb *to swell* Nm 5$_{22}$, נפל hi. *cause* thigh *to fall* Nm 5$_{22}$, שׁרץ *teem with* Gn 1$_{20.21}$, רחץ *wash* feet Gn 24$_{32}$, שׁקה hi. *quench thirst* Is 43$_{20}$.

<NOM CL> הֵמָּה מֵי מְרִיבָה *they were the waters of Meribah* Nm 20$_{13}$, הֵם מֵי־מְרִיבַת קָדֵשׁ *they are the waters of Meribah of Kadesh* Nm 27$_{14}$, מֵי נֹחַ זֹאת *this is the water of Noah* Is 54$_{9}$, הַמַּיִם אֲשֶׁר בַּיְאֹר *the water that is in the Nile* Ex 7$_{17.20.20}$ (אֲשֶׁר־), הַמַּיִם אֲשֶׁר מִתַּחַת לָרָקִיעַ *the waters that were below the firmament* Gn 1$_{7}$, הַמַּיִם אֲשֶׁר מֵעַל לָרָקִיעַ *the waters that were above the firmament* Gn 1$_{7}$, הַמַּיִם אֲשֶׁר מֵעַל הַשָּׁמָיִם *the waters that are above the heavens* Ps 148$_{4}$, הַמַּיִם אֲשֶׁר־בַּתְּעָלָה *the water that was in the trench* 1 K 18$_{38}$, מַיִם רַבִּים אֲשֶׁר בְּגִבְעוֹן *many waters that are in Gibeon* Jr 41$_{12}$ (or em. בְּגֶבַע *in Geba*), מַיִם עַל־פְּנֵי כָל־הָאָרֶץ *water was on the surface of all the earth* Gn 8$_{9}$, לָנוּ הַמָּיִם *the water is ours* Gn 26$_{20}$, מַיִם סָבִיב לָהּ *waters are around her* Na 3$_{8}$, וְהַמַּיִם לָהֶם חֹמָה *and the water was to them a wall* Ex 14$_{22.29}$, וְאֵין מַיִם *and there is no water* Ex 17$_{1}$ Nm 21$_{5}$, וּבַבּוֹר אֵין־מַיִם כִּי אִם־טִיט *and in the cistern there was not water but only mud* Jr 38$_{6}$, צִמָּאוֹן אֲשֶׁר אֵין־מָיִם *a parched land where there is no water* Dt 8$_{15}$, וּמַיִם אַיִן לִשְׁתּוֹת *and there is no water to drink* Nm 20$_{5}$, אֵין בּוֹ מָיִם *there was no water in it* Gn 37$_{24}$, מִבּוֹר אֵין מַיִם בּוֹ *from a cistern in which there is no water* Zc 9$_{11}$, וּכְגַנָּה אֲשֶׁר־מַיִם אֵין לָהּ *and like a garden that has no water* Is 1$_{30}$.

הַמַּיִם רָעִים *the water is foul* 2 K 2$_{19}$, מֵימָיו נֶאֱמָנִים *his (supply of) water is sure* Is 33$_{16}$, מַיִם עֲמֻקִּים דִּבְרֵי פִי־אִישׁ *deep waters are the words of a man's mouth* Pr 18$_{4}$, מַיִם עֲמֻקִּים עֵצָה בְלֶב־אִישׁ *counsel in the heart of a man is deep waters* Pr 20$_{5}$, וְנִינְוֵה כִבְרֵכַת־מַיִם מֵימֶיהָ *as for Nineveh, its water is like a pool of water* Na 2$_{9}$ (if em. מִימֵי הִיא *from days of it,* i.e. perh. from its foundation), אִישׁ שִׁלְחוֹ הַמָּיִם perh. *each one, his weapon was (as ready to release as) water* Ne 4$_{17}$ (or em. הַמַּיִם to בְּיָדוֹ was *in his hand* or del. שִׁלְחוֹ הַמָּיִם or em. to הֵימִינוּ each man *kept to the right*), [לחיי] אדם מים *for the life of a human is water* Si 39$_{26}$ (+ אֵשׁ *fire,* בַּרְזֶל

iron, מֶלַח *salt*).

<OBJ> בוא hi. *bring* Gn 6$_{17}$ 2 S 23$_{16}$||1 C 11$_{18}$ 2 K 20$_{20}$, אתה hi. *bring* Is 21$_{14}$, שׁוב hi. *turn back* Ex 15$_{19}$, נטה hi. *direct* Si 48$_{17}$, צוף hi. *divert* Dt 11$_{4}$, סתם *block* 2 C 32$_{3}$, ישׁר pi. *divert* 2 C 36$_{23}$, יצא hi. *take out* Nm 20$_{8.10}$ Dt 8$_{15}$ Ne 9$_{15}$, משׁך *draw* 4QHalakhah^a 1$_3$, ירד hi. *cause to go down* Ps 78$_{16}$, עלה hi. *raise* Is 8$_7$ 4QParGenEx 2$_7$, עבר *cross* Jos 4$_{23}$ 2 S 17$_{21}$, הפך *turn* into blood Ps 105$_{29}$, שׁלח *send* Jb 5$_{10}$, pi. *send away* Jb 12$_{15}$, פטר *release* Pr 17$_{14}$ (or em. מַיִם to מִלִּים *words*), שׂים *place* 2 K 6$_{22}$ 4QPatr 5.2$_2$, נתן *give* Gn 24$_{32}$ 43$_{24}$ Ex 17$_2$ Nm 20$_8$ 21$_{16}$ Dt 2$_{28}$ 1 S 25$_{11}$ Is 30$_{20}$ Ho 2$_7$ Ne 9$_{20}$, *place* Ex 30$_{18}$||40$_7$||40$_{30}$ Nm 19$_{17}$ Is 43$_{20}$.

כול hi. *contain* Jr 2$_{13}$, pilp. *provide* 1 K 18$_{4.13}$, חסר *lack* Ezk 4$_{17}$, בקשׁ pi. *seek* Is 41$_{17}$, ריח hi. *smell* Jb 14$_9$, מצא *find* Gn 26$_{32}$ Jr 14$_3$ 2 C 32$_4$, לקח *take* Ex 4$_9$ Nm 5$_{17}$ 1 S 25$_{11}$ 1 K 17$_{10}$, נשׂא *carry* 2 S 23$_{16}$||1 C 11$_{18}$, לכד *capture* Jg 7$_{24.24}$ 2 S 12$_{27}$ (if em. עִיר הַמָּיִם *the city of waters* to הַמָּיִם capture *the waters*; or em. עִיר הַמַּיִם to עִיר הַמְּלוּכָה *the city of royalty*), כנס *gather* Ps 33$_7$, חפר *dig (for)* Ex 7$_{24}$, קור *dig (for)* 2 K 19$_{24}$||Is 37$_{25}$, חשׂף *scoop up* Is 30$_{14}$, תכן pi. *measure* Jb 28$_{25}$, נזל *flow with* Si 14$_{10}$, hi. *cause to flow* Is 48$_{21}$, יבשׁ hi. *dry* Jos 2$_{10}$ 4$_{23}$ 5$_1$ Is 51$_{10}$, מלא *fill* Gn 1$_{22}$ 4QNarrC 1$_8$, *fill with* 1 K 18$_{34}$ 4QapJoshua^b 12$_6$, pi. *fill with* Gn 21$_{19}$ 1 K 18$_{35}$, מצא *find* Ex 15$_{22}$, קבץ pi. *gather* Is 22$_9$.

עצר *restrain* 1QDM 2$_{10}$, צרר *bind* Jb 26$_8$ Pr 30$_4$, יצב hi. *position* Ps 78$_{13}$, שׁאב *draw* Gn 24$_{13}$ Dt 29$_{10}$ Jos 9$_{21.23.27}$ 1 S 7$_6$ 9$_{11}$ 2 S 23$_{16}$||1 C 11$_{18}$ Is 12$_3$, נזה hi. *sprinkle* Nm 8$_7$ 19$_{18.21}$ 4QSD 7.2$_3$ 11QT 49$_{18}$, נטף *drip* Jg 5$_4$, hi. CD 1$_{15}$, נזל *drip* Jr 9$_{17}$, גרע pi. *distill (into)* Jb 36$_{27}$ (if em. כִּי יְגָרַע נִטְפֵי־מָיִם *for he distills drops of water* to נְטָפִים מָיִם distills *drops as/into rain*), קרר hi. *keep* water *cool* Jr 6$_7$ (or em. קור hi. *cause* water *to flow*), כרה *buy* Dt 2$_6$.

שׁתה *drink* Ex 7$_{18.21.24}$ 15$_{23}$ 17$_{1.2.6}$ 34$_{28}$ Nm 20$_{5.11.19}$ 21$_{22}$ 33$_{14}$ Dt 2$_{6.28}$ 9$_{9.18}$ 11$_{11}$ Jg 7$_6$ 15$_{19}$ 1 S 30$_{12}$ 2 S 23$_{16}$|| 1 C 11$_{18}$ 1 K 13$_{8+6t}$ 17$_{10}$ 2 K 3$_{17}$ 6$_{22}$ 18$_{27(Qr).31}$||Is 36$_{12(Qr).16}$ 2 K 19$_{24}$||Is 37$_{25}$ Is 44$_{12}$ Jr 2$_{18.18}$ Ezk 4$_{11.16}$ 12$_{18.19}$ 31$_{14.16}$ Am 4$_8$ Jon 3$_7$ Pr 5$_{15}$ Dn 1$_{12}$ Ezr 10$_6$ 1QH 8$_{13}$ 4QBéat 24.2$_3$, לחך pi. *lick up* 1 K 18$_{38}$, שׁקה hi. *cause*, or *give, to drink* Nm 5$_{24.26.27}$ 20$_{8.17}$ Jg 4$_{19}$ 1 S 30$_{11}$ 2 S 23$_{15}$||1 C 11$_{17}$ Jr 8$_{14}$ 9$_{14}$ 23$_{15}$ Jb 22$_7$ Pr 25$_{21}$ Si 15$_3$, אכל hi. *feed with* 1 K 22$_{27}$||2 C 18$_{26}$, גמא hi. *allow to swallow* Gn 24$_{17}$.

זרק *sprinkle* Ezk 36$_{25}$ 4QTohB^c 1$_9$, זרם po. *pour* (of cloud) Mur88Hb 3$_{10}$ (זרמו מים עבות *the clouds poured rain*; MT זֶרֶם מַיִם עָבָר *the downpour of water passed on*) Ps 77$_{18}$, שׁפך *pour* Ex 4$_9$ 1 S 7$_6$ Am 5$_8$=9$_6$, נסך hi. *pour* 2 S 23$_{16}$, pi. *pour* 1 C 11$_{18}$, יצק *pour* 1 K 18$_{34}$ 2 K 3$_{11}$ Is 44$_3$ Ezk 24$_3$, דלח *stir up* Ezk 32$_{2.13}$, שׁקע hi. *cause to subside* Ezk 32$_{14}$, ראה *see* 2 K 3$_{22}$, שׁאל *ask (for)* Jg 5$_{25}$ 4QapLam^a 1.2$_8$, מאס *reject* Is 8$_6$, ברך pi. *bless* Ex 23$_{25}$, נכה hi. *strike* Ex 7$_{20}$ 2 K 2$_{8.14}$, בקע *split* Is 63$_{12}$, בעה *boil* Is 64$_1$, מדד *measure* Is 40$_{12}$ (or em. מַיִם to יַמִּים *seas*).

<CSTR> מי ים *waters of sea* 1QIsa^a 40$_{12}$ (MT מַיִם; or em. יַמִּים *seas*), מֵי הַיָּם *the waters of the sea* Ex 15$_{19}$ Am 5$_8$=9$_6$ (מֵי־הַיָּם) Ps 33$_7$ 1QpHab 11$_1$ (הים), יַם־סוּף *of the sea of reeds* Dt 11$_4$ Jos 2$_{10}$, הַנָּהָר *of the river* Is 8$_7$, הַבְּרֵכָה *of the pool* Is 22$_{9.11}$, מֵי־שָׁלֶג *waters of snow* Jb 9$_{30(Qr)}$ (בְּמֵי *in/with waters of* snow; Kt בְּמוֹ *in/with* snow), מֵימֵי־שֶׁלֶג *waters of snow* Jb 24$_{19}$ (or em. ־מֵימֵי שֶׁלֶג שְׁאוֹל as *waters of snow* steal dryness and heat, so *Sheol* [steals] those who sin, to שֶׁלֶג מֵימֵי־שְׁאוֹל as *snow* steals dryness and heat, so *the waters of Sheol* steal those who sin).

מימי הכלי *water of the vessel* CD 10$_{13}$, מֵי בְאֵר *water of a well* Nm 20$_{17}$ 21$_{22}$, מֵי־בוֹרוֹ *the water of his cistern* 2 K 18$_{31}$||Is 36$_{16}$, מימי מעי[ן] *waters of the spring* 4Q Béat 24.2$_9$, מֵימֵי הָעֲיָנוֹת *the waters of the springs* 2 C 32$_3$, מֵימֵי הַמַּעְיָנוֹת *the waters of the springs* 2 C 32$_4$ (if em. ־כָּל *all* the springs), מֵי הַיַּרְדֵּן *the waters of the Jordan* Jos 3$_{8.13.13}$ 4$_7$ (מֵימֵי) 4$_{7.18.23}$ 5$_1$, הַיַּרְקוֹן *of the Jarkon* Jos 19$_{46}$ (unless וּמֵי הַיַּרְקוֹן = *and Me-jarkon*, as pl.n., or em. וּמִיָּם *and to the west*), הַשִּׁלֹחַ *of Shiloah* Is 8$_6$, הַמַּבּוּל *of the flood* Gn 7$_{7.10}$ (= 4QCommGenA 1$_3$) 9$_{11}$ (מִמֵּי) 4QCommGenA 1$_3$ (מבול) 4QAdmon 1$_8$ 4QParGenEx 2$_4$ 4QPatr 5.2$_3$ (ה[מבול]), תהומיה *of the abyss* 4QRit Mar 9$_7$, תְּהוֹם רַבָּה *of the great abyss* Is 51$_{10}$.

הַמָּרִים *of the bitter ones*, i.e. bitter waters Nm 5$_{18.19.23.24}$, מימי כזב *waters of falsehood* CD 1$_{15}$, ה[ז]יה *of sprinkling* 4QRitPur 12$_{6.7}$ ([מימ]י הזיה), מֵי נִדָּה *water of*, i.e. for removing, *impurity* Nm 19$_{9.13.20.21.21}$ (both הַנִּדָּה) 31$_{23}$ 1QS 3$_{4.9}$ 4$_{21}$ 4QSD 7.2$_3$ ([מ]י נדה) 4QD^a 6.3$_2$ (הנדה) 4QD^f 2$_{12}$ ([מי] הנדה) 4QD^g 1.2$_{15}$ 4QTohB^c 1$_{5.6}$ (both

(הנדה) 1$_{8}$ ([הנ]דה) 1$_{9}$ (הנדה) 4QNidd 1.1$_{6}$ 11QT 49$_{18}$, מי דוכי *water of purity* 1QS 3$_{9}$ 4QRitPur 12$_{4}$ ([דוכ]י), מימי רחץ *waters of ablution* 1QS 3$_{5}$ 4QRitPur 12$_{5}$ 42.5, מימי רוחץ *waters of ablution* 4QBapt 12$_{7}$, מי קודש *waters of holiness* 1QH 8$_{13}$, מי טהר[ה] *waters of purification* 11QT 50$_{2}$.

מֵי מְרִיבָה *the waters of Meribah* Nm 20$_{13.24}$ Dt 33$_{8}$ Ps 81$_{8}$ 106$_{32}$, מֵי מְרִיבַת קָדֵשׁ *the waters of Meribah of Kadesh* Nm 27$_{14}$ Dt 32$_{51}$ (both ־מֵי) Ezk 47$_{19(mss)}$ (L מְרִיבוֹת) 47$_{28}$, מֵי מֵרוֹם *the waters of Merom* Jos 11$_{5.7}$, מְגִדּוֹ *of Megiddo* Jg 5$_{19}$, יְרִיחוֹ *of Jericho* Jos 16$_{1}$, יְהוּדָה *of Judah* Is 48$_{1}$ (or em. מִמֵּי *from the semen of* to מִמְּעֵי *from the inner parts of* Judah), נֶפְתּוֹחַ *of Nephtoah* Jos 15$_{9}$ 18$_{15}$, נִמְרִים *of Nimrim* Is 15$_{6}$=Jr 48$_{34}$, מֵי גִיחוֹן *the waters of Gihon* Jr 2$_{18}$ (if em. שִׁחוֹר *of [the] Nile*) 2 C 32$_{30}$ (מֵימֵי), נָהָר *of (the) river (Euphrates)* Jr 2$_{18}$, מֵי דִימוֹן *the waters of Dimon* Is 15$_{9}$, מֵי־עֵין שֶׁמֶשׁ *the waters of En-shemesh* Jos 15$_{7}$.

מֵי נֹחַ *water(s) of Noah* Is 54$_{9.9}$ (or del. מֵי־נֹחַ), מֵי מְנֻחוֹת *the waters of rest* Ps 23$_{2}$, תבונה *of understanding* Si 15$_{3}$, חַטָּאת *of sin* Nm 8$_{7}$, רֹאשׁ *of poison* Jr 8$_{14}$ 9$_{14}$ 23$_{15}$ (both ־מֵי), מָצוֹר *of*, i.e. for, *a siege* Na 3$_{14}$, מָלֵא *of a full one*, i.e. abundant waters Ps 73$_{10}$ (or em. וּמֵי מָלֵא יִמָּצוּ *and waters of a full one are drained* to וּמִלֵּיהֶם יָמֹצּוּ *and they suck up their words*), מי רבה *water of abundance*, i.e. abundant water 4QShir^{b} 30$_{4}$, מי צו[ר] *water of a rock* 4QBéat 28$_{2}$.

מֵימֵי הַיְאֹר *the waters of the Nile* Ex 4$_{9}$ 7$_{24}$ Dn 12$_{6.7}$, מִצְרַיִם *of Egypt* Ex 7$_{19}$ 8$_{2}$, יִשְׂרָאֵל *of Israel* 2 K 5$_{12}$, רַגְלֵיהֶם *of their feet*, i.e. their urine 2 K 18$_{27(Qr)}$||Is 36$_{12(Qr)}$ (Kt שֵׁינֵיהֶם *their urine*).

מֵי אָפְסָיִם *water of*, i.e. up to the, *ankles* Ezk 47$_{3}$, מָתְנָיִם *of thighs* Ezk 47$_{4}$, שָׂחוּ *of swimming* Ezk 47$_{5}$.

מִקְוֵה מַיִם *collection of waters* Gn 1$_{10}$ (הַמַּיִם) Lv 11$_{36}$ 4QConfess 2$_{9}$ ([מקו]ה) 4QapMes 5.2$_{3}$, מֵימֵיהֶם *of their waters* Ex 7$_{19}$, חַשְׁרַת־מַיִם *a mass of water* 2 S 22$_{12}$, שִׁפְעַת־מַיִם *a surfeit of water* Jb 23$_{13}$ 38$_{34}$, נִכְבַּדֵּי־מָיִם *heavy ones of water* Pr 8$_{24}$, [תהומ]ות המ[ים] *depths of the waters* 4QJub^{a} 6$_{11}$, חֶשְׁכַת־מַיִם *darkness of waters* 2 S 22$_{12}$, מִשְׁבְּרֵי־מָיִם *the breakers of (the) water(s)* 2 S 22$_{5}$||Ps 18$_{5}$ (if em. מָוֶת *death*) 1QH 3$_{16}$.

אמת המים *conduit of water* 3QTr 5$_{1}$, יציאת המים *out-let*, or *canal*, *of the water* 3QTr 7$_{14}$, עֵין הַמַּיִם *the spring of water* Gn 16$_{7}$ 24$_{13.43}$ (both הַמָּיִם), מוֹצָא מַיִם *spring of water* Is 58$_{11}$, מוֹצָא הַמַּיִם *the spring*, or *canal*, *of water* 2 K 2$_{21}$, מוֹצָאֵי מָיִם *springs of water* Is 41$_{18}$ Ps 107$_{33}$ (וּמֹצָאֵי מַיִם) 107$_{35}$ (מָיִם), מוֹצָא מֵימֵי *the spring*, or *canal*, *of the waters of* Gihon 2 C 32$_{30}$, נבוכי מים *springs of water* 1QH 3$_{15}$, מבוע מים *spring of water* 1QH 8$_{4.16}$, מַבּוּעֵי מַיִם *springs of water* Is 35$_{7}$ (מָיִם) 49$_{10}$, עֵינֹת מַיִם twelve *springs of water* Ex 15$_{27}$||Nm 33$_{9}$, מַעְיְנוֹ־מָיִם *spring of water* Ps 114$_{8}$, כָּל־מַעְיַן־מַיִם *every spring of water* 2 K 3$_{25}$, כָּל־מַעְיְנֵי־מַיִם *all springs of water* 2 K 3$_{19}$, כָּל־מַעְיְנֵי הַמַּיִם *all the springs of water* 1 K 18$_{5}$, מַעְיַן מֵי *spring of the waters of* Jos 15$_{9}$ 18$_{15}$, מְקוֹר מַיִם *spring of water* Jr 2$_{13}$ 17$_{13}$ 4Q418 103.2$_{6}$ 4QBark^{f} 1.1$_{3}$, 4QDibHam^{a} 1.5$_{2}$, גֻּלֹּת מָיִם *springs of water* Jos 15$_{19}$||Jg 1$_{15}$ (or em. גֻּלַּת *spring of*).

בְּאֵר מַיִם *well of water* Gn 21$_{19}$ (מָיִם) 26$_{19}$ Ca 4$_{15}$ CD 19$_{34}$, באר מימי *well of the waters of* 4QBéat 24.2$_{9}$, בְּאֵר הַמָּיִם *the well of water* Gn 21$_{25}$ 24$_{11}$ (הַמָּיִם), בְּאֵרֹת הַמַּיִם *the wells of water* Gn 26$_{18}$, בְּרֵכַת־מַיִם *pool of water* Na 2$_{9}$, בְּרֵכוֹת מָיִם *pools of water* Ec 2$_{6}$, מִיכַל הַמָּיִם perh. *the pool of water* 2 S 17$_{20}$ (or em. מִכֹּל *container of* or מִכֹּה אֶל־ *from here to* the water), אֲגַם־מַיִם *pool of water* Is 41$_{18}$ (or em. אֲגַמִּים *pools*) Ps 107$_{35}$ 114$_{8}$ (מָיִם), אַגְמֵי־מָיִם *pools of water* Is 14$_{23}$, מעמד מים *place of water* Si 43$_{20}$, מקום מים *place of water* CD 11$_{16}$, נַחֲלֵי מַיִם *streams of water* Jr 31$_{9}$ 1QH 9$_{5}$ 4QapJoshua^{a} 11$_{4}$, יִבְלֵי־מָיִם *streams of water* Is 30$_{25}$ 44$_{4}$ (מָיִם; both יובלי in 1QIsa^{a}, i.e. יוּבַל *stream* or יוּבַל *channel*) Ps 18$_{5}$ (if em. חֶבְלֵי שְׁאוֹל *cords of Sheol* to יִבְלֵי מַיִם) Si 50$_{8}$.

פַּלְגֵי־מַיִם *channels of water* Is 32$_{2}$ Ps 1$_{3}$ (פַּלְגֵי מָיִם) 119$_{36}$ Pr 5$_{16}$ (מָיִם) 21$_{1}$ Lm 3$_{48}$ 1QH 10$_{25}$, אֲפִיקֵי מַיִם *channels of water* Jl 1$_{20}$ (מָיִם) Ps 18$_{16}$ (||2 S 22$_{16}$ יָם *of [the] sea*) 42$_{2}$ (אֲפִיקֵי־מָיִם) Ca 5$_{12}$ (מָיִם), מַעֲמַקֵּי־מַיִם *valleys*, i.e. *depths*, *of water* Ezk 27$_{34}$ (מָיִם) Ps 69$_{3.15}$ (מָיִם), שִׁבֹּלֶת מַיִם *current of water* Ps 69$_{16}$, ערפלי מים *clouds of water* 4QBer^{a} 3$_{4}$, נִטְפֵי־מָיִם *drops of water* Jb 36$_{27}$ (or em. נְטָפִים מָיִם *drops as/into rain*), לחת מים *liquid of water* 11QT 49$_{12}$, פֶּרֶץ מָיִם *breach of water* 2 S 5$_{20}$||1 C 14$_{11}$, שֶׁטֶף מַיִם *overflowing of water* Ps 32$_{6}$, זֶרֶם מַיִם *storm of rain* Is 28$_{2}$ Hb 3$_{10}$, הֲמוֹן מַיִם *tumult of water* Jr 10$_{13}$=51$_{16}$ 1QH 2$_{16.27}$ 3$_{14}$ 4QAdmon 1$_{8}$ 11QPs^{a} 26$_{10}$, מִשְׁקַע־מַיִם *stillness of water*, i.e. still water Ezk 34_{18}, רֹחַב מַ֫יִם *breadth*, i.e. sheet, *of water* Jb 37_{10}, אֶרֶץ נַחֲלֵי מָ֫יִם *a land of streams of water* Dt 8_{7} (מָ֫יִם) 10_{7}, שִׁקֲתוֹת הַמָּ֫יִם *the troughs of water* Gn 30_{38}, כָּל־עֲצֵי־מַ֫יִם *all trees of*, i.e. growing by, *water* Ezk 31_{14} 1QH 8_{6} (כול) 8_{9} ([כול ע[צי), כָּל־שֹׁתֵי מָ֫יִם *all drinkers of*, i.e. trees that drink, *water* Ezk $31_{14.16}$ (מָ֫יִם), עִיר הַמָּ֫יִם *the city of waters* 2 S 12_{26} (if em. עִיר הַמְּלוּכָה *the city of royalty*) 12_{27} (or del. עִיר, leaving מַ֫יִם as obj. of לכד *capture*; or em. עִיר הַמָּ֫יִם to עִיר הַמְּלוּכָה).

שֹׁאֲבֵי־מַ֫יִם *drawers of water* Jos $9_{21.23.27}$, חֵמַת מַ֫יִם *skin of water* Gn 21_{14}, צַפַּחַת מָ֫יִם *a jug of water* 1 K 19_{6}, צַפַּחַת הַמַּ֫יִם *the jug of water* 1 S $26_{11.12.16}$, [ק]לחת מי *pot of the water of* 4QTohB^{c} 1_{5}, כֹּל שֶׁרֶץ הַמַּ֫יִם *every swarming creature of the water* Lv 11_{10}, כֹּל מִשְׁעַן־מָ֫יִם *every support of water* Is 3_{1}, שְׁאוֹן מַ֫יִם *roar of waters* Is $17_{12.13}$, קוֹל מַ֫יִם *sound of waters*, i.e. waterfall* Ezk 1_{24} 43_{2} 3QTr 9_{11} (המים), קֹלוֹת מַ֫יִם *sounds of waters*, i.e. waterfall* Ps 93_{4}, חֹמֶר מַ֫יִם *foaming of waters* Hb 3_{15}, מגבל המים *kneaded of*, i.e. with, *water* 1QH 1_{21} 12_{25} ([מגב[ל המים) 13_{15} (מים).

פְּנֵי־מַ֫יִם *(sur)face of waters* Is 18_{2} 19_{8} Ho 10_{7} (מָ֫יִם) Jb 24_{18} (or em. מַ֫יִם to יוֹמָם *at the close of the day*) 26_{10} (מָ֫יִם), פְּנֵי הַמַּ֫יִם *the (sur)face of the water(s)* Gn 1_{2} 7_{18} (both הַמָּ֫יִם) Ex 32_{20} Ec 11_{1} (הַמָּ֫יִם), קְצֵה הַמַּ֫יִם *the edge of the water* Jos 3_{15}, קְצֵה מֵי *the edge of the waters of* Jos 3_{8}, קֵץ מֵי *end of the waters of* 4QCommGenA 1_{3}, [גדות] מים *banks of waters* 1QH 8_{17}, מְעַט־מַ֫יִם *a little (of) water* Gn 18_{4} $24_{17.43}$ Jg 4_{19} 1 K 17_{10}, כָּל־מָ֫יִם *all water (sources)* Is 32_{20}, כָּל־הַמַּ֫יִם *all the water(s)* Ex 7_{20}, כול מי *all the waters of* 1QS 3_{5}, כָּל־מֵימֵי *all the waters of* 2 K 5_{12}, [כ]ול מימיה *all its waters* 4Q415 11_{5}||4Q418 167_{6}.

<APP> מַבּוּל *flood* Gn 6_{17} 7_{6}, יָם *sea* Is 51_{10}, מַ֫יִם *water* Ezk $47_{3.4.5}$, יְאֹר *stream*, i.e. Nile Na 3_{8}, חֲצִי *half* Zc $14_{8.8}$.

<ADJ> עָצוּם *mighty* Is 8_{7}, עָמֹק *deep* Pr 18_{4} 20_{5}, אַדִּיר *majestic* Ex 15_{10} Ps 93_{4} 1QH 8_{19} 4QRP^{c} 6.2_{5} 4QAdmon 1_{4}, עַז *strong* Is 43_{16} Ne 9_{11} 4Q392 2_{4}, קָדוֹשׁ *holy* Nm 5_{17}, זָר *foreign* 2 K 19_{24}, צֹאִי *filthy* CD 10_{11}, זֵידוֹן *seething* Ps 124_{5}, רַב *great, many* Nm 24_{7} (or em. וְזַרְעוֹ בְּמַ֫יִם *and his seed is on* many *waters* to וּזְרֹעוֹ בְּעַמִּים *and his arm is against* many *peoples*) Is 8_{7} 2 S 22_{17}||Ps 18_{17} Is 17_{13} 23_{3} Jr 41_{12} $51_{13.55}$ Ezk 1_{24} $17_{5.8}$ 19_{10} $26_{19.26}$ $31_{5.7.15}$ 32_{13} 43_{2} Ps 29_{3} 32_{6} 93_{4} 107_{23} 144_{7} Ca 8_{7} 2 C 32_{4} 1QH $2_{16.27}$ 11QPs^{a} 26_{10} CD 3_{16}, כַּבִּיר *great* Is 17_{12} 28_{2} Hb 3_{15}, חַי *living*, i.e. fresh, or running, sometimes specif. spring water* Gn 26_{19} Lv $14_{5.6.50.51.52}$ 15_{13} Nm 19_{17} Jr 2_{13} 17_{13} Zc 14_{8} Ca 4_{15} 1QH $8_{7.16}$ 4Q418 103.2_{6} 4QDibHam^{a} 1.5_{2} 11QT 45_{16} CD 19_{34}, זָר *running* 2 K 19_{24}=1QIs^{a} 37_{25} (unless זָר *foreign*; see above) Jr 18_{14},* קַר *cold* Pr 25_{25}, אֵלֶּה *these* Nm $5_{19.22}$ 2 K 2_{21} Ezk $47_{8.9}$.

<PREP> לְ of direction, *to(wards)* 11QPsAp^{a} fr. 3_{2}, + הלך *go* Is 55_{1}, יצא *go out* Jos 16_{1}, פתח ni. *be opened* 1QH 8_{7}, קרא *call* Am 5_{8}=9_{6}; of benefit, *for* Nm 19_{9} (+ לְמִשְׁמֶרֶת *for keeping*, i.e. to be kept, for) 4QAdmon 1_{9}, + עשׂה *make* cistern Is 22_{11}; of purpose, *for (the purpose of obtaining)*, + שׁלח *send* Jr 14_{3}, חפר *dig* CD 3_{16}; *for, in respect of* Am 8_{11}||4QpsEzek^{c} 2_{9} (+ צָמָא *thirst*), + צמא *be thirsty* Ex 17_{3}; *at* or *concerning*, + מרה *rebel* Nm 20_{24}; *as*, + היה *be* (of heart) Jos 7_{5}; introducing object, + היה *become* 1QH 8_{18}, רפא pi. *cure* 2 K 2_{21} (unless לְ of direction after אמר *say*).

בְּ of place, *in(to), on, through* Ex 20_{4} (+ תְּמוּנָה *[drawn] image*, פֶּסֶל *[carved] image*) Lv 11_{9} (+ כֹּל *all* creatures) 11_{10} (+ נֶפֶשׁ living *soul*) 11_{12} (+ כֹּל) Nm 24_{7} (or em. וְזַרְעוֹ בְּמַ֫יִם *and his seed is on* many *waters* to וּזְרֹעוֹ בְּעַמִּים *and his arm is against* many *peoples*) Dt 4_{18} (+ דָּגָה *fish*) 5_{8} (+ תְּמוּנָה *image*) 14_{9} Is 23_{3} Ne 9_{11} (+ כְּמוֹ אֶבֶן *like a stone*) 4QTohB^{c} 1_{5} 4Q392 2_{4} 4QBapt 7.2_{1} 4QRit Pur 4_{5} 7_{4} 12_{4} fr. 11_{3} 42_{5} 51.2_{7} 11QT^{b} $14_{3.21}$.

+ בוא *come* Ps 66_{12} 1QS 5_{13} 4QBapt 2.2_{5} CD 12_{14} (+ אֵשׁ *fire*), hi. *bring* Jr 13_{1} Ezk 27_{26} 4QTohB^{c} 1_{8}, ho. *be brought* Lv 11_{32}, רמשׂ *move* Lv 11_{46} CD 12_{13}, שׁרץ *swarm* 4QJub^{a} 6_{12}, עבר hi. *pass* Nm 31_{23} Is 43_{2}, hi. *transfer* Ezk $47_{3.4}$, נוח *rest* Jos 3_{13}, נוד *shake* (of reed) 1 K 14_{15}, נתן *place* path Is 43_{16}, עשׂה *do*, i.e. conduct, business Ps 107_{23}, קרה pi. *lay beams* Ps 104_{3}, טבל *dip* purificatory agents Lv 14_{51} Nm 19_{18}, blanket 2 K 8_{15}, בשׁל pu. *be cooked* Ex 12_{9} (perh. בְּ of instrument, cooked *with* water), רחץ *wash* Ex 29_{4}||40_{12} Lv $1_{9.13}$ $8_{6.21}$ $14_{8.9}$ 15_{5+11t} $16_{4.24.26.28}$ 17_{15} 22_{6} Nm $19_{7.8.19}$ Dt 23_{12} Ezk 16_{9} 2 K 5_{12} 4QTohA 1.1_{3} 4QNidd 2.1_{3} ([ם]רחץ במי) 4QBapt 12_{5} 4QRit Pur 56_{1} 4QOrd^{c} $1.1_{6.9}$ 11QT 45_{16} 49_{17} 51_{5} CD 10_{11} (perh. all בְּ of instrument),* pu. *be washed* Ezk 16_{4} (perh. בְּ of instrument), htp. *wash oneself* Jb $9_{30(Qr)}$ (perh. בְּ of instrument), שׁטף *wash* Lv 15_{11} 4QTohB^{c} 1_{11}, ni. *be* *washed* Lv 15$_{12}$, pu. *be washed* Lv 6$_{21}$ (perh. בְּ of instrument), כבס pi. *wash* Nm 19$_{8}$ 4QTohA 1.2$_{8.9}$ 4QOrd^{c} 1.1$_{6.9}$ 11QT 49$_{13}$ (perh. בְּ of instrument), pu. *be washed* Lv 15$_{17}$ CD 11$_{4}$, צלל *sink* Ex 15$_{10}$ 1QH 8$_{19}$ ([יצללו]), אבד *perish* 4QRP^{c} 6.2$_{5}$.

at, + קדשׁ hi. *sanctify* Y. Nm 27$_{14}$, מעל *transgress* Dt 32$_{51}$; of accompaniment, *with* 1QH 3$_{24}$, + קדם pi. *precede* Dt 23$_{5}$ Ne 13$_{2}$; of instrument, *with, by (means of)* 4QD^{g} 1.2$_{15}$ 4QapJoshua^{b} 12$_{7}$ (ב[מימיו]) CD 10$_{10}$, + טהר *be cleansed* 4QRitPur 42$_{5}$, pi. *purify* 4QBapt 12$_{7}$, htp. *absolve oneself* 1QS 3$_{4.5}$, כפר pi. *purify* 4QBark^{a} 1.3$_{3}$, נזה hi. *sprinkle* 1QS 3$_{9}$, חטא pi. *remove sin* Lv 14$_{52}$, htp. *be purified of sin* Nm 31$_{23}$, קדשׁ htp. *sanctify oneself* 1QS 3$_{9}$, מהל pass. *be weakened* Is 1$_{22}$; *against*, + נגע *strike*, i.e. touch Nm 19$_{21}$; עצר בְּ *detain* Jb 12$_{15}$; indicating object, + טמא pi. *make unclean* CD 10$_{13}$.

כְּ *as* Gn 49$_{4}$ (=4QCommGenA 4$_{4}$; + פַּחַז *unbridled* as water) Hb 2$_{14}$ Pr 27$_{19}$ (כַּמַּיִם הַפָּנִים לַפָּנִים *like water [when] face is to face*, i.e. when the face is reflected; or em. כְּמוֹ *as* one face to another face, or כְּמַרְאֵה *as the appearance of* one face to another, or מֵי הַפָּנִים *waters of the face*, i.e. *feeling of shame* [כַּמַּיִם הַפָּנִים לַפָּנִים *what shame is for the face*], or em. מֵים as a construct)* 4QWiles 4$_{3}$ 4QBéat 28$_{2}$.

+ היה *be* Jr 15$_{18}$, בוא *come* into body (of curse) Ps 109$_{18}$, הלך *go* 1QH 4$_{34}$ 8$_{34}$, חבא htp. *hide oneself* Jb 38$_{30}$ (or em. כָּאֶבֶן *like a stone* to כְּבָאֶבֶן *as in stone* water hides itself), גלה ni. *be revealed* 1QpHab 11$_{1}$, גלל *roll* Am 5$_{24}$, סבב *encircle* Ps 88$_{18}$, נשׂג hi. *overtake* (of terrors) Jb 27$_{20}$ (or em. כַּמַּיִם terrors overtake him *like water* to יוֹמָם *daily* or בַּיּוֹם *during the day*), נתך *pour out* Jb 3$_{24}$ (of groaning), נגר ni. *be poured* 2 S 14$_{14}$ 1QH 8$_{32}$, נזה hi. *sprinkle* 1QS 4$_{21}$; *as though it were*, etc., + שׁפך *pour* blood Dt 12$_{16.24}$ 15$_{23}$ Ps 79$_{3}$ 4QTestim$_{29}$ 11QT 52$_{12}$ 53$_{5}$, anger Ho 5$_{10}$ CD 19$_{16}$, heart Lm 2$_{19}$, ni. *be poured* Ps 22$_{15}$, המה *make a noise* (of waves) Jr 51$_{55}$ Ps 46$_{4}$, חמר *foam* Ps 46$_{4}$, מסס *melt* 1QH 2$_{28}$, ni. Mc 1$_{4}$, מאס ni. *be rejected* or *melt* Ps 58$_{8}$, בקע htp. *be split open* Mc 1$_{4}$, זכר *remember* trouble Jb 11$_{16}$, שׁתה *drink* iniquity Jb 15$_{16}$, mockery Jb 34$_{7}$.

מִן of direction, *from*, + יצא *go out* Is 48$_{1}$ (or em. מִמֵּי *from the semen of* to מִמְּעֵי *from the inner parts of*), שׁוב *return* 4QBapt 12$_{6}$, משׁה *draw* Moses Ex 2$_{10}$, hi. *draw* worshipper 2 S 22$_{17}$||Ps 18$_{17}$, נצל hi. *rescue* Ps 144$_{7}$; of instrument, *by (means of)*, + היה *be(come)* Ezk 19$_{10}$, ארך *be long* Ezk 31$_{5}$, רבה *be great* Ezk 31$_{5}$, כרת ni. *be cut off* Gn 9$_{11}$, פוץ *overflow* 4QAdmon 1$_{4}$, נקה ni. *be found innocent* Nm 5$_{19}$, perh. שׁקה hi. *water* Ec 2$_{6}$; partitive, *(some) of, (any) of*, + לקח *take* Ex 4$_{9}$, שׁתה *drink* Ex 7$_{24}$, לקק *lap* Jg 7$_{5}$.

אֶל *(in)to*, + פתח *be opened* Jb 29$_{19}$, עבר *pass* Jos 15$_{7}$ 2 S 17$_{20}$ (if em. מִיכַל הַמַּיִם perh. cross *the pool of water* to מִכֹּה אֶל־ pass *from here to* the water), נפל *fall* 2 K 6$_{5}$ 4QSD 7.1$_{7.7}$, ירד hi. *take down* Jg 7$_{4.5}$, נתן *place* soil Nm 5$_{17}$, שׁלך hi. *throw* wood Ex 15$_{25}$, מחה *erase*, i.e. wipe off, words of curse Nm 5$_{23}$; *at, by*, + היה *be* Ezk 31$_{7}$, חנה *encamp* Jos 11$_{5}$, מצא *find* Jr 41$_{12}$, שׁתל pass. *be transplanted* Ezk 17$_{8}$; *against*, + Jr 50$_{38}$ (+ חֹרֶב *drought*; or em. חֶרֶב *sword*).

עַל *at, by* Nm 24$_{6}$ (+ כַּאֲרָזִים *like cedars*) Jg 5$_{19}$, + בוא *come* Jos 11$_{7}$, לקח *take* Ezk 17$_{5}$, נהל pi. *lead* Ps 23$_{2}$, ריב *contend* Dt 33$_{8}$, בחן *test* Ps 81$_{8}$, קצף hi. *anger* Ps 106$_{32}$, שׁכן *dwell* Jr 51$_{13}$, חנה *encamp* Ex 15$_{27}$, זרע *sow* Is 32$_{20}$, שׁתל pass. *be transplanted* Jr 17$_{8}$ Ezk 19$_{10}$; *over* Ps 29$_{3}$ (+ קוֹל י׳ *voice of Y.*) 29$_{3}$ (+ י׳), + זרח *rise* (of sun) 2 K 3$_{22}$, נטה *extend* hand Ex 7$_{19}$ 8$_{2}$, רקע *extend* earth Ps 136$_{6}$, שׁחט *slaughter* bird Lv 14$_{5.50}$, שׁבר pi. *shatter* heads of tannins Ps 74$_{13}$, pass. *be slaughtered* Lv 14$_{6}$; *against*, + נכה hi. *strike* Ex 7$_{17}$.

עַל־פְּנֵי *upon (the surface of)* Ho 10$_{7}$ (+ כְּקֶצֶף perh. *like flotsam*) Jb 24$_{18}$ (+ קַל־הוּא *he is swift*, i.e. swiftly carried off), + רחף pi. *hover* (of wind/spirit) Gn 1$_{2}$, הלך *go* (of ark) Gn 7$_{18}$, זרה *scatter* dust of golden calf Ex 32$_{20}$, שׁלח *send* reed vessels Is 18$_{2}$, pi. *send (away)*, i.e. scatter, bread Ec 11$_{1}$ (+ יָם *sea*), פרשׂ *spread* net Is 19$_{8}$ 1QH 5$_{8}$, ni. *be spread out* 1QH 3$_{26}$, חקק *describe* circle Jb 26$_{10}$, ישׁר pi. *direct* 1QH 6$_{24}$, רעע *break* 1QH 3$_{13}$.

אֵת *with*, + מלא ni. *be filled* 2 K 3$_{20}$, נזה ho. *be sprinkled* 4QRitPur 12$_{7}$.

עַד *unto* Ezk 47$_{19}$ (+ גְּבוּל *border*), + היה *be* Ezk 48$_{28}$ (mss) (L lacks preposition; + גְּבוּל).

בַּעַד *behind*, + סגר hi. *shut up* 4QMyst^{a} 8$_{9}$.

מִפְּנֵי *on account of*, + בוא *come* to ark Gn 7$_{7}$; *from the face of*, + נצל hi. *save* 4QParGenEx 2$_{4}$.

בְּתוֹךְ *in the middle of* 4QTohA 2.2$_{6}$, + היה *be* (of firmament) Gn 1$_{6}$, עשׂה *make* 4QJub^{a} 5$_{12}$ ([מי]ם); *in(side),* + שׂים *place* city fabric Ezk 26$_{12}$.

בֵּין *between,* + בדל hi. *separate* Gn 1$_{6}$ (+ לְמָיִם between upper *and* lower *waters*) 1$_{7.7}$.

מֵעַל *(away) from next to,* + אבד hi. *destroy* beasts Ezk 32$_{13}$.

מִמַּעַל לְ *above* Dn 12$_{6.7}$ (both + אִישׁ *man*).

תַּחַת *below,* + בקע ni. *be split* (of cloud) Jb 26$_{8}$.

מִתַּחַת *below,* + חיל polal *be made to writhe* Jb 26$_{14}$.

בְּלִי *without* Ps 63$_{2}$ (+ אֶרֶץ dry and thirsty *land*), + שׂגה *be great* (of reed) Jb 8$_{11}$.

מֵאֵין *through lack of,* + באשׁ *stink* Is 50$_{2}$.

+ ה- of direction, *to(wards),* + יצא *go out* Ex 7$_{15}$ 8$_{16}$.

<COLL> הַמַּיִם בַּיַּמִּים *the waters in,* i.e. of, *the seas* Gn 1$_{22}$, בַּמַּיִם מִתַּחַת לָאָרֶץ *in the waters under the earth* Ex 20$_{4}$ Dt 4$_{18}$ 5$_{8}$, מְעַט־מַיִם מִכַּדֵּךְ *a little water from your pitcher* Gn 24$_{17.43}$, מְעַט־מַיִם בַּכְּלִי *a little water in the vessel* 1 K 17$_{10}$, מַיִם מִן־הַיְאֹר *water of the Nile* Ex 7$_{18.21}$, מַיִם מִמָּרָה *the water of Marah* Ex 15$_{23}$, מַיִם מִצּוּר *water from a rock* Is 48$_{21}$, מַיִם מִן־הַסֶּלַע *water from the rock* Nm 20$_{8}$ Ne 9$_{15}$ (מִסֶּלַע *from a rock*), מַיִם מִצּוּר הַחַלָּמִישׁ *water from the rock of flint* Dt 8$_{15}$, מַיִם מִגֶּבֶא scoop up *water from a pool* Is 30$_{14}$, מַיִם מִבּוֹרֶךָ drink *water from your cistern* Pr 5$_{15}$, מַיִם מִבֹּאר בֵּית־לֶחֶם אֲשֶׁר בַּשַּׁעַר *water from the cistern of Bethlehem that is by the gate* 2 S 23$_{15.16}$||1 C 11$_{17.18}$ (23$_{15}$||11$_{17}$ בַּשָּׁעַר; 11$_{17.18}$ בּוֹר), מַיִם לְרָחְצָה *water for washing (in)* Ex 40$_{30}$, מַיִם ... לִצְמָאָם *water ... for their thirst* Ne 9$_{15.20}$, מַיִם בִּמְשׂוּרָה *water by measure* Ezk 4$_{11.16}$.

בְּבֹאָם אֶל־אֹהֶל מוֹעֵד יִרְחֲצוּ־מַיִם *when they come to the tent of meeting they are to wash with water* Ex 30$_{20}$, וְכָל־אֲפִיקֵי יְהוּדָה יֵלְכוּ מָיִם *and all the channels of Judah will flow with water* Jl 4$_{18}$, כָּל־הַיָּדַיִם תִּרְפֶּינָה וְכָל־בִּרְכַּיִם תֵּלַכְנָה מָּיִם *all hands will relax and all knees will flow with urine* Ezk 7$_{17}$ (or em. יָדַיִם all *hands*), sim. Ezk 21$_{12}$, עֵינִי יֹרְדָה מַּיִם *my eye is flowing with tears* Lm 1$_{16}$.

מְלוֹא הַסֵּפֶל מָיִם *the fullness of the bowl with water,* i.e. enough water to fill a bowl Jg 6$_{38}$, אֶרֶץ לֹא־שָׂבְעָה מַּיִם *a land unsatisfied with water* Pr 30$_{16}$, הַמַּיִם אֲדֻמִּים כַּדָּם they saw *the water red as blood* 2 K 3$_{22}$.

מַיִם קָרִים עַל־נֶפֶשׁ עֲיֵפָה וּשְׁמוּעָה טוֹבָה מֵאֶרֶץ מֶרְחָק *cold waters upon a weary throat and a good report from a land of distance,* i.e. a far land Pr 25$_{25}$ (or em. שְׁמוּעָה *is a report,* as nom. cl.), לֹא־מַיִם עָיֵף תַּשְׁקֶה *non-water you give a weary one to drink* Jb 22$_{7}$, מַיִם וְשֹׁכְנֵיהֶם *(the) waters and their inhabitants* Jb 26$_{5}$, מַיִם בְּמוּצָק *water as one constrained,* i.e. frozen water Jb 37$_{10}$, מִתָּמָר מֵי מְרִיבַת קָדֵשׁ *from Tamar (unto) the waters of Meribah of Kadesh* Ezk 48$_{28}$ (mss ins עַד *unto*), מַיִם לַחַץ *water (of) oppression* 1 K 22$_{27}$||2 C 18$_{26}$ Is 30$_{20}$ (לָחַץ; or em. in all three מִלַּחַץ water *instead of oppression*, or מֵים cstr. *water of*).*

Also 4QTanḥ 36$_{1}$ 4QD^{g} 1.2$_{13}$ 4QM^{g} 2$_{8}$ 4QMyst^{a} 6.1$_{1.5}$ 4QapJoseph^{a} 2$_{1}$ 4QapJoshua^{b} 13$_{3}$ 4QpsEzek^{a} 9.2$_{4}$ 4QBapt 33$_{1}$ 4Q418 49$_{1}$ 86$_{3}$ 4QPrMercy$_{10}$ 4QHymnSap 2$_{2}$ 4QRitMar 8$_{4}$ 4QPrQuot 132.1$_{1}$ 4QDibHam^{a} 1.7$_{8}$ 4QRitPur 15.1$_{2}$ 229$_{3.3}$ 5QTopon 5$_{3}$ Arad ost. 111$_{8}$ Ophel monumental inscr.$_{2}$.

<SYN> אֹכֶל *food,* תְּהוֹם *abyss.*

<ANT> אֵשׁ *fire.**

⇒ cf. מוֹ *water,* מַיָה *water.*

מִיָּמִן 4.0.18 pr.n.m. **Mijamin**—מִיָּמִין—**1.** priest and co-signatory with Nehemiah, <NOM CL> עַל הַחֲתוּמִים נְחֶמְיָה ... מִיָּמִן *among those that were sealed were Nehemiah ... (and) Mijamin* Ne 10$_{8}$ (or em. הַחוֹתְמִים *those that sealed,* i.e. signed, *were* or אֵלֶּה הַחוֹתְמִים *these were the signatories:*).

2. priest returning with Zerubbabel, Ne 12$_{5}$.

3. husband of foreign wife, descendant of Parosh, <NOM CL> מִבְּנֵי פַרְעֹשׁ רַמְיָה ... וּמִיָּמִן *of the descendants of Parosh were Ramiah ... and Mijamin* Ezr 10$_{25}$.

4. head of sixth priestly course at time of David, <PREP> לְ of direction, *to,* + יצא *go out* (of lot) 1 C 24$_{14}$ (or em. Benjamin).

5. as name of priestly course (derived from §2) and the period during which it holds office, <NOM CL> [בשלישית מי]מין *on the third (day) is Mijamin* 4QMishF^{a} 1$_{4}$, מימין באחד *Mijamin is on the first (day)* 4QMishH 1.2$_{1}$. <CSTR> ביאת מי[מ]ין *arrival of (the priestly course of) Mijamin* 4QMishC^{d} 1.2$_{4}$, [שבת מ]ימין *sabbath of Mijamin* 4QMishD 1$_{6}$. <PREP> בְּ of time, *during (the year of)* 4QOtot 1.7$_{19}$ 4QMishA 1.2$_{11}$ 1.3$_{14}$

(מ]ימין]) 4.313 (מ]ין[מ]ן) 4.44 4QMishBa 1.28 2.24.4 (מ]ין[מימ]ן) 2.26.8 (מ]ין[מ]ין) 2.33 (מ]ין[מ]ין).

Also 4QOtot 1.83 9.11 4QMishH 23.

⇒ מִן *from* + יָמִין *right (side).*

[מִין] 31.4.8 n.m. **kind** (unless all exx. in BH are from לְמִינֵהּ *of itself, of themselves,* reduplicated form of מִן *from*)*—cstr. Si מִין; sf. מִינוֹ (מִינֵהוּ), מִינָהּ (מִינָה); pl. מִינֵהֶם (Q מיניהם); cstr. Q מִינֵי—**1.** usu. in classifications of fauna and flora, **kind, species;** perh. with sense of **likeness** through the generations*; also of different kinds of spirits characterizing a son of light (1QS 314), three kinds of righteousness (CD 416). **2. one's own kind** (Si 1315.16.16).

<NOM CL> מין כל בשר אצלו *each creature's own kind is alongside it* Si 1316, שם *there* (in the sea) ... מין כל חי ... *is every kind of living being* Si 4325(B). <OBJ> אהב *love* Si 1315 (+ הדומה לו *that which is like it*). <CSTR> מין כל בשר *each creature's own kind* Si 1316, מין כל חי *every kind of living being* Si 4325(B), שלושת מיני הצדק *(the) three kinds of righteousness* CD 416, כול מיני רוחותם *all the (different) kinds of their spirits* 1QS 314.

<PREP> לְ *according to, by* Gn 111 (+ עֵץ fruit-producing *tree*) 112 (+ עֵשֶׂב *grass*) 112 (+ עֵץ) 121 (appar. + מַיִם *sea*) 121 (+ עוֹף *bird*) 124 (+ נֶפֶשׁ living *being*) 124.25 (both + חַיָּה *animal*) 125 (+ בְּהֵמָה *beast*) 125 (+ רֶמֶשׂ *small animal*) 620 (+ עוֹף) 620 (+ בְּהֵמָה) 620 (+ רֶמֶשׂ) 714 (+ חַיָּה) 714 (+ בְּהֵמָה) 714 (+ רֶמֶשׂ) 714 (+ עוֹף) Lv 1114 (+ אַיָּה *falcon*) 1115||Dt 1414 (+ עֹרֵב *raven* or *crow*) Lv 1116||Dt 1415 (+ נֵץ *hawk*) Lv 1119||Dt 1418||11QT 481 (למי]נה]; + אֲנָפָה *cormorant* or *heron*) Lv 1122||11QT 483 (+ אַרְבֶּה *[great] locust*) Lv 1122||11QT 483 (+ סָלְעָם *[long-headed] locust*) Lv 1122||11QT 484 (+ חַרְגֹּל *[green] locust*) Lv 1122||11QT 484 (+ חָגָב *[desert] locust*) Lv 1129||11QT 5020 (+ צָב *[thorn-tailed] lizard*) Dt 1413 (+ דַּיָּה), + היה *be* Ezk 4710 (לְמִינָה תִּהְיֶה דְגָתָם *according to its kind will be their fish,* i.e. they will have every kind of fish), למד pi. *teach* 1QS 314, בין hi. *cause to understand* 1QS 314; *as,* + נתן *cause to be* CD 416; בְּ *according to, by* CD 1214 (+ חָגָב *[desert] locust*); אֶל *to,* + חבר pu. *be joined* Si 1316.

<COLL> כָּל־ ... לְמִינוֹ *every ... according to its* (etc.) *kind,* i.e. every kind of Gn 121.25 620 714.14.14.14 Lv 1115|| Dt 1414.*

מֵינֶקֶת *(wet-)nurse,* see ינק *suck,* Hi.

[מֵיסָךְ], see מוּסָךְ *covered way.*

[מֵיפַעַת] 3 pl.n. **Mephaath**—מֵיפַעַת, מֵפַעַת, Kt מופעת—Levitical city in Reuben, on the Moabite plateau, <SUBJ> היה *be* (of territory) Jos 1318. <OBJ> נתן *give* Jos 2137 1 C 664. <APP> מִישׁוֹר *plateau* Jos 1318 Jr 4821(Qr), עִיר *city* of refuge 1 C 664. <PREP> אֶל *to,* + בוא *come* (of judgment) Jr 4821(Qr). <COLL> Mephaath + Jahaz, Kedemoth Jos 1318 2137 1 C 664, + Holon, Jahaz Jr 4821(Qr).

*מִיץ I 1 vb. **press, oppress**—**Qal** 1 Ptc. מֵץ—כִּי־אָפֵס הַמֵּץ כָּלָה *when the oppressor has completely ceased* Is 164 (1QIsa המוץ;* or em. הַמֵּץ to חֹמֵץ *oppressor*).

⇒ מֵץ *extortioner,* מִיץ I *pressure.*

*מִיץ II 1 vb. **churn (milk), press, stir up** (unless מִיץ I *pressure* or II *churning*)—**Qal** 3 Inf. מִיץ—<NOM CL> כִּי מִיץ חָלָב יוֹצִיא חֶמְאָה וּמִיץ־אַף יוֹצִיא דָם וּמִיץ אַפַּיִם יוֹצִיא רִיב *as the churning of milk produces ghee, and the pressing of the nose produces blood, so the stirring up of wrath produces strife* Pr 3033.

⇒ מִיץ II *churning.*

[מֵץ] 1 n.m. **extortioner**—מֵץ—<SUBJ> אפס *cease* Is 164 (or em. הַמֵּץ to חָמוֹץ *oppressor;* 1QIsaa המוץ; + שֹׁד *destruction,* רמס ptc. *one who tramples*).

⇒ מִיץ I *press.*

[מִיץ] I 3 n.m. **pressure** (unless מִיץ II *churning* or מִיץ II *churn*)—cstr. מִיץ—**pressure, pressing,** or perh. **squeezing,** כִּי מִיץ חָלָב יוֹצִיא חֶמְאָה וּמִיץ־אַף יוֹצִיא דָם וּמִיץ אַפַּיִם יוֹצִיא רִיב *for pressure on milk produces butter and pressure on a nostril produces blood and pressure on both nostrils produces strife* Pr 3033.*

⇒ מִיץ I *press.*

*[מִיץ] II 3 n.m. **churning** (unless מִיץ I *pressure* or מִיץ II *churn*)—cstr. מִיץ—**churning, pressing, stir-**

ring, כִּי מִיץ חָלָב יוֹצִיא חֶמְאָה וּמִיץ־אַף יוֹצִיא דָם וּמִיץ אַפַּיִם יוֹצִיא רִיב *for the churning of milk produces butter and the pressing of the nose produces blood, so the stirring up of wrath produces strife* Pr 30$_{33}$.

⇒ מִיץ II *churn.*

*מיר $_{1}$ vb. **procure—Qal** $_{1}$ Ptc. מֵרִים—<SUBJ> כְּסִיל *fool* Pr 3$_{35}$ (וּכְסִילִים מֵרִים קָלוֹן *but fools procure shame*; unless רום hi. ptc. *exalt* or מור ptc. *acquire*). <OBJ> קָלוֹן *shame* Pr 3$_{35}$. <COLL> מיר ‖ נחל *inherit* Pr 3$_{35}$.

[מֵירַב], see מֵרַב *Merab.*

*[מֵירָשׁ] n.m. **new wine** (if em. מֵירָשִׁים to מֵישָׁרִים in all), <APP> יַיִן *wine* Ca 1$_{4}$ (מִיַּיִן מֵירָשִׁים אֲהֵבוּךָ *more than wine, new wine, they love you*; or em. מִמֵּירָשׁ אֲהָבֶךָ *more than new wine your caresses*).* <PREP> לְ *as,* + הלך *go* Ca 7$_{10}$; בְּ of essence, *as,* + הלך htp. *go* Pr 23$_{31}$ (or em.; see below); כְּ *like,* + הלך htp. *go* Pr 23$_{31}$ (if em. בְּמֵישָׁרִים to כְּמֵירָשִׁים); מִן of comparison, *(more) than,* + אהב *love* Ca 1$_{4}$ (or em.; see App.).

⇒ cf. מֵישָׁרִים II (type of) *wine.*

מִישׁ, see מושׁ *depart.*

מֵישָׁא $_{1}$ pr.n.m. **Mesha, 1.** Benjamite, third son of Shaharaim and Hodesh (or em. Horesh, Ada, or Baara), <OBJ> ילד hi. *beget* 1 C 8$_{9}$.

2. father of Rabbi Judan, <COLL> יודן בנו שלרבי מיאשה *Judan, son of Rabbi Mesha* Beth-Shearim tomb inscr. 22 (AHL; Avigad [...]שלרבי [...]שה).

מִישָׁאֵל $_{7}$ pr.n.m. **Mishael—1.** one of Daniel's three companions, renamed Meshach, Dn 1$_{6.7.11.19}$, <SUBJ> עמד *stand* before king Dn 1$_{19}$. <APP> בֵּן *son* Dn 1$_{6}$. <PREP> לְ of direction, *to,* + שׂים *place,* i.e. assign, name Dn 1$_{7}$; כְּ *as,* + מצא ni. *be (found)* Dn 1$_{19}$; עַל *over, in charge of* Dn 1$_{11}$.

2. firstborn son of Uzziel and brother of Elzaphan and Sithri, cousins of Aaron, Ex 6$_{22}$ Lv 10$_{4}$, <SUBJ> קרב *approach* Lv 10$_{4}$, נשׂא *raise,* i.e. remove Lv 10$_{4}$. <NOM CL> וּבְנֵי עֻזִּיאֵל מִישָׁאֵל *and the sons of Uzziel were Mishael and Elzaphan and Sithri* Ex 6$_{22}$. <APP> בֵּן *son* Lv 10$_{4}$ (+ Elzaphan). <PREP> אֶל *to,* + אמר *say* Lv 10$_{4}$, קרא *call* Lv 10$_{4}$.

3. one of the dignitaries who stood beside Ezra as he read the law, Ne 8$_{4}$, <SUBJ> עמד *stand* Ne 8$_{4}$.

⇒ מִי *who* + שֶׁ *which,* + אֵל *God.*

מִישׁוֹר, see מִישׁר *plain.*

מֵישַׁךְ $_{1}$ pr.n.m. **Meshach,** Babylonian name given to Mishael, Daniel's companion, שׂים *appoint* Meshach (as name of Mishael) Dn 1$_{7}$.

מֵישַׁע $_{1}$ pr.n.m. **Mesha,** king of Moab at time of Jehoshaphat and Jehoram, <SUBJ> היה *be* 2 K 3$_{4}$ (+ נֹקֵד *sheepbreeder*), שׁוב hi. *return,* i.e. pay tribute of, beasts 2 K 3$_{4}$. <APP> מֶלֶךְ *king* of Moab 2 K 3$_{4}$.*

מֵישָׁע $_{1}$ pr.n.m. **Mesha,** firstborn son of Caleb, perh. ident. with Mareshah (מָרֵשָׁה) at 1 C 2$_{42}$, to which perh. em. Mesha, <NOM CL> וּבְנֵי כָלֵב ... מֵישָׁע בְּכֹרוֹ *and the sons of Caleb ... were Mesha, his firstborn* 1 C 2$_{42}$. <APP> בְּכוֹר *firstborn* 1 C 2$_{42}$.

מִישֹׁר $_{23.1.3}$ n.m. **plain**—מִישׁוֹר—**1. plain,** esp. **plateau, tableland** of Moab, btw. the Arnon and Heshbon (Jos 13$_{9.16.17.21}$ 20$_{8}$ Dt 3$_{10}$ 4$_{43}$ Jr 48$_{21}$ perh. 2 C 26$_{10}$), and of the Golan (1 K 20$_{23.25}$). **2. plain,** as place of safety and confidence (Ps 26$_{12}$=1QH 2$_{29}$ Ps 27$_{11}$ 143$_{10}$ 11QPs^{a} Si 51$_{15}$ 1QH 3$_{20}$). **3. equity** (Is 11$_{4}$ Ml 2$_{6}$ Ps 45$_{7}$ 67$_{5}$ 1QS^{b} 5$_{22}$).

<SUBJ> היה *be* Jos 13$_{16}$ (+ גְּבוּל *border*), שׁמד ni. *be destroyed* Jr 48$_{8}$ (:: עֵמֶק *valley*). <OBJ> נתן *give* Jos 13$_{9}$. <CSTR> אֹרַח מִישׁוֹר *way of evenness,* i.e. level way Ps 27$_{11}$, אֶרֶץ מִישׁוֹר *land of evenness,* i.e. level ground Ps 143$_{10}$, אֶרֶץ הַמִּישֹׁר *the land of evenness,* i.e. tableland Dt 4$_{43}$ Jr 48$_{21}$, צוּר הַמִּישֹׁר *rock of the plain* Jr 21$_{13}$ (:: עֵמֶק *valley*), כָּל עָרֵי הַמִּישֹׁר *all the towns of the plain* Dt 3$_{10}$ Jos 13$_{21}$, כָּל־הַמִּישֹׁר *all the plain* Jos 13$_{9.16}$, שֵׁבֶט מִישֹׁר *rod of equity* Ps 45$_{7}$. <APP> מֵידְבָא עַד־דִּיבוֹן *Medeba unto Dibon* Jos 13$_{9}$.

<PREP> לְ *as, into,* + היה *be(come)* (of uneven ground)

Is 40$_4$, שׂים *cause* uneven places *to be(come)* Is 42$_{16}$; *in respect of* evenness Zc 4$_7$ (+ הַר *mountain*); בְּ of place, *in, on* plain, level ground Jos 13$_{17}$ (+ עִיר *city*) 20$_8$ (+ Bezer), + היה *be* (of cattle) 2 C 26$_{10}$ (:: שְׁפֵלָה *lowland*), עמד *stand* Ps 26$_{12}$=1QH 2$_{29}$ (רַגְלִי עָמְדָה בְמִישׁוֹר *my foot stands on level ground*, i.e. I stand with confidence), דרך *tread* Si 51$_{15}$(11QPs^a) (דרכה רגלי במישור *my foot treads on level ground*; i.e. I walk with confidence; B באמתה דרכה רגלי *by her truth my foot treads*), הלך *go* to war 1QpHab 3$_1$ (במישור ילכו לכות *through the plain they come to strike*), htp. *go about* 1QH 3$_{20}$ (ואתהלכה במישור לאין חקר *and I go about on level ground*, i.e. in confidence, *without end*), לחם ni. *fight* 1 K 20$_{23.25}$; of accompaniment, *in (a state of), with* equity, + הלך *go* Ml 2$_6$ (|| שָׁלוֹם *peace*), יכח hi. *reprove* meek Is 11$_4$ (|| צֶדֶק *righteousness*) 1QSb 5$_{22}$ ([ול]הוכיח במי[שור]); + ולהתהלך לפניו תמים *and to go about before him with integrity*).

<COLL> כִּי־תִשְׁפֹּט עַמִּים מִישׁוֹר *for you judge the peoples with equity* Ps 67$_5$, במישור לאין חקר *on level ground*, i.e. in confidence, *without end* 1QH 3$_{20}$. <SYN> §2 שָׁלוֹם *peace*, צֶדֶק *righteousness*. <ANT> §2 עֵמֶק *valley*, שְׁפֵלָה *lowland*.

מֵישָׁרִים I$_{16.0.1}$ n.m.pl. **righteousness;** appar. **peace, friendship** (Dn 11$_6$). <NOM CL> אֹרַח לַצַּדִּיק מֵישָׁרִים *(the) way of the righteous person is righteousness* Is 26$_7$. <OBJ> דבר *speak* Is 33$_{15}$ (perh. used adverbially, *righteously*; || צְדָקָה *righteousness*) Pr 16$_{13}$ (if em. יְשָׁרִים *upright ones*; and/or em. דֹּבֵר *one who speaks* to דְּבַר *a word of* or דִּבְרֵי *words of* righteousness) 23$_{16}$ (pi.; perh. used adverbially), נגד hi. *tell* Is 45$_{19}$ (perh. used adverbially, *righteously*; || צֶדֶק *righteousness*), חזה *see* Ps 17$_2$ (+ מִשְׁפָּט *judgment*), כון polel *establish* Ps 99$_4$ (+ מִשְׁפָּט *judgment*, צְדָקָה), לקח *take*, perh. understand Pr 1$_3$ (|| צֶדֶק, מִשְׁפָּט), בין *understand* Pr 2$_9$ (|| צֶדֶק, מִשְׁפָּט), אהב *love* 1 C 29$_{17}$, עשה *do*, i.e. establish Dn 11$_{6.17}$ (if em. וִישָׁרִים עִמּוֹ עָשָׂה appar. *and upright ones will be with him and he will act* to וּמֵישָׁרִים עִמּוֹ יַעֲשֶׂה *and peace he will establish with him*).

<APP> מוּסַר הַשְׂכֵּל *discipline of insight* Pr 1$_3$, כָּל־מַעְגַּל־טוֹב *every way of goodness* Pr 8$_6$. <PREP> לְ of purpose, *for (the purpose of)*, + יצא hi. *take out*, i.e. produce, truth 1QH 4$_{25}$ (+ לָנֶצַח *for ever* or *for victory* you produce their judgment); בְּ of accompaniment, *in (a state of), with*, i.e. righteously Si 39$_{24(Bmg)}$ (appar. ארחותיו במיש[רים] *his ways are with righteousness*; B [Segal] [ארחו]ת תמים יישרו *the ways of upright ones are straight*), דין *judge* Ps 9$_9$ (|| צֶדֶק *righteousness*) 96$_{10}$, שׁפט *judge* Ps 98$_9$ (|| צֶדֶק). <COLL> הַאֻמְנָם ... מֵישָׁרִים תִּשְׁפְּטוּ *do you really ... judge* humankind *righteously* Ps 58$_2$ (|| צֶדֶק *righteousness*), אֲנִי מֵישָׁרִים אֶשְׁפֹּט *I shall judge righteously* Ps 75$_3$, מֵישָׁרִים אֲהֵבוּךָ perh. *rightly do they love you* Ca 1$_4$ (unless מֵישָׁרִים II *wine* or III *smoothness*; or em. מֵירָשׁ *new wine*).

⇒ ישׁר *be straight*.

*מֵישָׁרִים II$_3$ n.m.pl. (a kind of) **wine** (unless in all מֵישָׁרִים III *smoothness* or מֵישָׁרִים IV *gullet* or em. מֵישָׁרִים to מֵירָשִׁים *new wine*), <APP> יַיִן *wine* Ca 1$_4$ (מִיַּיִן מֵישָׁרִים אֲהֵבוּךָ *more than wine, new wine, they love you*). <PREP> לְ *as*, + הלך *go* Ca 7$_{10}$; בְּ of essence, *as*, + הלך htp. *go* Pr 23$_{31}$ (or em.; see below); כְּ *like*, + הלך htp. *go* Pr 23$_{31}$ (if em. בְּמֵישָׁרִים to כְּמֵישָׁרִים); מִן of comparison, *(more) than*, + אהב *love* Ca 1$_4$.

⇒ cf. מֵירָשׁ *new wine*.

*מֵישָׁרִים III$_2$ n.m.pl. **smoothness** (unless in all מֵישָׁרִים II *wine* or מֵישָׁרִים IV *gullet* or em. מֵישָׁרִים to מֵירָשִׁים *new wine*), <CSTR> יֵין מֵישָׁרִים *wine of smoothness*, i.e. smooth wine Ca 1$_4$ (if em. יַיִן *wine* to יֵין). <PREP> לְ in the capacity of, + הלך *go* Ca 7$_{10}$ (הוֹלֵךְ לְדוֹדִי לְמֵישָׁרִים *going to my beloved in the capacity of smoothness*, i.e. smoothly); בְּ of accompaniment, *in (a state of), with*, + הלך htp. *go* Pr 23$_{31}$ (יִתְהַלֵּךְ בְּמֵישָׁרִים *it goes in [a state of] smoothness*, i.e. smoothly).

⇒ ישׁר *be straight*.

*מֵישָׁרִים IV$_2$ n.m.pl. **gullet** (Pr 23$_{31}$ Ca 1$_4$ 7$_{10}$ unless מֵישָׁרִים II *wine* or מֵישָׁרִים III *smoothness* or em. מֵישָׁרִים to מֵירָשִׁים *new wine*), <CSTR> יֵין מֵישָׁרִים *wine of*, i.e. in, *the gullet* Ca 1$_4$ (if em. יַיִן *wine* to יֵין). <PREP> לְ of direction, *into*, + הלך *go* Ca 7$_{10}$ (הוֹלֵךְ לְדוֹדִי לְמֵישָׁרִים *going to my beloved into the gullet*, i.e. down the throat of my beloved); בְּ *in*, + הלך htp. *go* Pr 23$_{31}$ (יִתְהַלֵּךְ בְּמֵישָׁרִים *it goes in the gullet*), ירד *descend* Ps 49$_{15}$ (if em. בָם יְשָׁרִים *the upright* shall rule *over them* to בְּמֵישָׁרִים).

⇒ ישׁר *be straight.*

[מֵיתָר] 9 n.[m.] **cord**—pl. sf. מֵיתָרַי, מֵיתָרֶיךָ, מֵיתָרַיִךְ, מֵיתְרֵיהֶם, מֵיתָרָיו—**1.** usu. **cord, rope,** of tent, esp. tent of meeting; **2.** appar. **string** of bow, Ps 21$_{13}$. **3.** appar. **sinew, (blood) vessels** of heart, Jb 17$_{11}$ (if em. מוֹרָשׁ *desire* or *possession,* i.e. thought).

<SUBJ> נתק ni. *be uprooted* Jr 10$_{20}$ (+ אֹהֶל *tent,* יְרִיעָה *curtain,* בֵּן *son*) Jb 17$_{11}$ (if em.). <NOM CL> וּמִשְׁמֶרֶת בְּנֵי־גֵרְשׁוֹן בְּאֹהֶל מוֹעֵד ... אֶת־מָסַךְ פֶּתַח הֶחָצֵר ... וְאֵת מֵיתָרָיו *and the duty of the sons of Gershon in the tent of meeting was ... the cover of the entrance of the court ... and its cords* Nm 3$_{26}$, וּפְקֻדַּת מִשְׁמֶרֶת בְּנֵי מְרָרִי ... עַמֻּדֵי הֶחָצֵר ... וִיתֵדֹתָם וּמֵיתְרֵיהֶם *and the appointed duty of the sons of Merari ... was the columns of the court ... and their pegs and cords* Nm 3$_{37}$. <OBJ> בוא hi. *bring* Ex 39$_{40}$ (|| יָתֵד *peg*), נשׂא *carry* Nm 4$_{26}$ (|| יָתֵד), ארך hi. *extend* Is 54$_{2}$ (|| יָתֵד, + אֹהֶל *tent,* יְרִיעָה *curtain*), עשׂה *make* Ex 35$_{18}$ (+ יָתֵד). <CSTR> מֵיתְרֵי לְבָבִי *the cords of my heart* Jb 17$_{11}$ (if em. מוֹרָשֵׁי *the desires,* or *thoughts, of;* + זִמָּה *thought*). <APP> כֹּל *all* that Y. commanded Ex 35$_{18}$. <PREP> בְּ of instrument, *with, by (means of),* + כון pol. *direct (bow)* at faces of enemy Ps 21$_{13}$. <COLL> זֹאת מִשְׁמֶרֶת מַשָּׂאָם ... עַמּוּדֵי הֶחָצֵר ... וִיתֵדֹתָם וּמֵיתְרֵיהֶם *this was their duty to carry: ... the columns of the court ... and their pegs and their cords* Nm 4$_{32}$.*

⇒ cf. יֶתֶר *cord.*

מָךְ *poor one,* see מוך *be low.*

***[מַכָּא]** 0.0.0.2 pr.n.m. **Makka, 1.** father of Zadok, <CSTR> בן מכא *son of Makka* Seal 322 (8th cent.). **2.** Seal 464 (T. el-Judeideh).

מַכְאוֹב 16.3.5 n.m. **pain**—cstr. מַכְאוֹב; sf. מַכְאֹבִי (מַכְאוֹבִי), מַכְאֹבֵךְ, מַכְאֹבוֹ, מַכְאוֹבָהּ, Q מכאובנו; pl. מַכְאוֹבִים (מַכְאֹבִים), מַכְאֹבוֹת; sf. מַכְאֹבָיו, מַכְאֹבֵינוּ—**pain, suffering, torture** (Ec 1$_{18}$ 2$_{23}$),* <SUBJ> עלל po. *be dealt out* Lm 1$_{12}$, אנשׁ pass. *be incurable* Jr 30$_{15}$, רבה *increase* Si 3$_{27}$, ירשׁ *possess* 11QPs^{a} 19$_{15}$. <NOM CL> כָּל־יָמָיו מַכְאֹבִים *all his days are pain(s)* Ec 2$_{23}$, יֵשׁ מַכְאוֹב כְּמַכְאֹבִי see if *there is a pain like my pain* Lm 1$_{12}$, רַבִּים מַכְאוֹבִים לָרָשָׁע *many are the pains of the wicked* Ps 32$_{10}$, מַכְאוֹבִי נֶגְדִּי תָמִיד *my pain is continually before me* Ps 38$_{18}$, מכאוב ... עם איש כסיל *pain is ... with the foolish man* Si 34$_{20}$.

<OBJ> ראה *see* Lm 1$_{18}$, ידע *know* Ex 3$_{7}$ 2 C 6$_{29}$, סבל *bear* Is 53$_{4}$, יסף hi. *add* Ec 1$_{18}$, נוח hi. *relieve* Si 38$_{7}$, הפך *transform* Ps 41$_{4}$ (if em.; see Cstr.).

<CSTR> מַכְאוֹב חֲלָלֶיךָ *pain of your slain* Ps 69$_{27}$ (ms חֲלָלְךָ); אִישׁ מַכְאֹבוֹת *man of pains* Is 53$_{3}$, נגע מכאובי *the affliction of my pain* 4QHod^{a} 8$_{2}$, כָּל־מַכְאֹבוֹ *all his pain* Ps 41$_{4}$ (if em. מִשְׁכָּבוֹ *his bed*).

<PREP> לְ of benefit, *to, for* 4QapLam^{a} 1.1$_{14}$ (למכאובנו *for our pain* corrected to למכתינו *for our wounds*), + לקח *take* Jr 51$_{8}$; בְּ of instrument, *by (means of), with,* + יכח ho. *be reproved* Jb 33$_{19}$; כְּ *as* Lm 1$_{12}$; מִן *from* 1QH 9$_{6}$ fr. 4$_{4}$ (ממכ[אוב]); אֶל *of, concerning,* + ספר pi. *tell* Ps 69$_{27}$ (or em. יְסַפֵּרוּ to יֹסִפוּ *they add to*); עַל *(in addition) to,* + יסף *add* Jr 45$_{3}$ perh. 1QpHab 11$_{15}$.

<COLL> מַכְאוֹב || חֳלִי *sickness* Is 53$_{3.4}$, נֶגַע *affliction* 2 C 6$_{29}$ 1QH 9$_{6}$; + יָגוֹן *grief* Jr 45$_{3}$, כַּעַס *vexation* Ec 1$_{18}$ 2$_{23}$, יֵצֶר evil *inclination* 11QPs^{a} 19$_{15}$, שֶׁבֶר *breach* Jr 30$_{15}$, תַּשְׁנִיק *anguish* Si 34$_{20}$, צַעַר *pain* Si 34$_{20}$, נדד ישׁנה *fleeing of sleep* Si 34$_{20}$, פני הפוכות *change of countenance* Si 34$_{20}$.

<SYN> חֳלִי *sickness,* נֶגַע *affliction.**

⇒ כאב *hurt.*

[מַכְבָּדָם], see מַכְבָּרָם *Machbaram.*

מַכְבִּיר *abundance,* see כבר Hi. *multiply.*

מַכְבֵּנָה I 1 pr.n.[m.] **Machbenah** (unless מַכְבֵּנָה II), <CSTR> אֲבִי מַכְבֵּנָה *father of Machbenah* 1 C 2$_{49}$.

מַכְבֵּנָה II 1 pl.n. **Machbenah,** town in the Judaean hills south of Beth-zur and Hebron (possibly ident. with כַּבּוֹן *Cabbon* or מְכֹנָה *Meconah;* unless מַכְבֵּנָה I), <CSTR> אֲבִי מַכְבֵּנָה *father of Machbenah* 1 C 2$_{49}$.*

מַכְבַּנַּי 1 pr.n.m. **Machbannai**, one of David's Gadite warriors, <NOM CL> מַכְבַּנַּי עַשְׁתֵּי עָשָׂר *Machbannai was the eleventh* 1 C 12_{14}.

מַכְבֵּר 1 n.[m.] **cover**, perh. of netted cloth, with which Hazael suffocated Ben-hadad, <OBJ> לקח *take* 2 K 8_{15}, טבל *dip* 2 K 8_{15}, פרשׂ *spread* 2 K 8_{15}.*

⇒ כָּבִיר *braided article*, כְּבָרָה *sieve*, מִכְבָּר *grating, lattice-work*.

מִכְבָּר 6.0.1 n.m. **grating**—cstr. מִכְבַּר—**grating, lattice-work**, around altar, <NOM CL> מִכְבַּר הַנְּחֹשֶׁת אֲשֶׁר־לוֹ *the grating of bronze that was to it* (altar) Ex 35_{16} 38_{30} 39_{39}, המכבר [אשר] מלמעלה לו ... נחושת מ[רוק] *the grating that is above it shall be ... polished bronze* 11QT 3_{15}. <OBJ> עשׂה *make* Ex 27_4||38_4 35_{16} 38_{30}, בוא hi. *bring* Ex 39_{39}. <CSTR> מִכְבַּר הַנְּחֹשֶׁת *the grating of bronze* Ex 35_{16} $38_{5.30}$ 39_{39}. <APP> מַעֲשֵׂה רֶשֶׁת נְחֹשֶׁת *network of bronze* Ex 27_4||38_4. <PREP> לְ of possession, *of (belonging) to* Ex 38_5.

⇒ כָּבִיר *braided article*, כְּבָרָה *sieve*, מַכְבֵּר *cover*.

*[**מַכְבָּרָם**] pr.n.[m.] **Machbaram**, <PREP> לְ of possession, *of (belonging) to* Hazor inscr. 5 (others למכבדם *of Machbadam*).

מַכָּה 48.4.15 n.f. **stroke**—cstr. מַכַּת; sf. מַכָּתִי, מַכָּתְךָ, מַכָּתֵךְ, מַכָּתוֹ; pl. מַכִּים, מַכּוֹת; cstr. מַכּוֹת; sf. Q מכתינו, מַכֹּתְךָ, mss מַכּוֹתֶיךָ (mss מַכֹּתֶיךָ), מַכּוֹתַיִךְ, מַכּוֹתֶיהָ (מַכֹּתֶהָ), מַכֹּתָם (Q מכותם)—**1. stroke, blow, stripe,** <SUBJ> מרק hi. *cleanse* Pr $20_{20(Kt)}$ (or em. מַכּוֹת to מְזַכּוֹת *they purify* or מִכְוֹת *burns*), נעם *be pleasant* Si 36_{23}. <NOM CL> מַכּוֹת חַדְרֵי־בָטֶן *blows are (a scouring for) the chambers of the belly* Pr $20_{30(Qr)}$ (or em.; see Subj.), יש מכה *there is a blow* Si 36_{23}, הספחת מכת עץ *the scab is (from) a blow of wood* 4QD^d 7_1, מכה על מכה *a blow upon a blow* 3QJub 1_2 4QPrMercy$_7$. <OBJ> נכה hi. *strike with* Dt 25_3 Is 14_6 Jr 30_{14} Est 9_5 11QPsAp^a 4_4 ([מ]כה), נתן *give* appar. 2 C 2_9 (or em. מַכֹּלֶת *food*, as || 2 K 5_{25}).

<CSTR> מַכַּת מַכֵּהוּ *blow of the one who struck him* Is 27_7, אוֹיֵב *of an enemy* Jr 30_{14}, מִדְיָן *of Midian* Is 10_{26}, חֶרֶב־ *of the sword* Est 9_5, מכת עץ *blow of wood* 4QD^d 7_1, מַכַּת בִּלְתִּי סָרָה *tireless striking* Is 14_6; מַחַץ מַכָּתוֹ *wound of*, i.e. from, *his blow* Is 30_{26}, מחץ מכתי *wound of*, i.e. from, *my blow* 1QH 9_{27} ([מח]ץ) 4QHod^d 3_3, כול מכה *any blow* 4QD^g 1.1_2. <APP> מוּסָר *discipline* Jr 30_{14}, חִטָּה *wheat* appar. 2 C 2_9 (or em.; see Obj.), כֹּר *cor* appar. 2 C 2_9 (or em.; see Obj.). <ADJ> רַב *great* Dt 25_3, גָּדוֹל *great* 11QPsAp^a 4_4 ([מ]כה גדול[ה]).

<PREP> לְ perh. of benefit, *to, for* 4QShir^b 44.1_4; כְּ *as, according to* Is 10_{26}, + נכה hi. *strike* Is 27_7 (or em. נכה hi. to ho. *be struck*); מִן of comparison, *(more) than*, + נעם *be pleasant* Si 36_{23}; עַל *upon* 3QJub 1_2 perh. 4QTanḥ 14_5 4QPrMercy$_7$.

<COLL> חַבּוּרָה || מַכָּה *blow* Pr 20_{30}, מֻרְדָּף *persecution* Is 14_6; + פֶּצַע *wound* Pr 10_{30}, הֶרֶג *slaughter* Is 27_7 Est 9_5, שׁוֹט *scourge* Is 10_{26}, אַבְדָן *destruction* Est 9_5.

2. wound, <SUBJ> היה *be* Ps 64_8, זרר *be squeezed* Is 1_6, חבשׁ pu. *be bound* Is 1_6, רכך pu. *be made soft* Is 1_6, רפא ni. *be healed* Jr 15_{18}, חלה ni. ptc. *be made sick*, i.e. be severe Jr 10_{19} 30_{12} Na 3_{19}, אנשׁ pass. *be incurable* Jr 15_{18} Mc 1_9, מאן pi. *refuse* Jr 15_{18}, בוא *come* Mc 1_9, נגע *reach* Mc 1_9. <NOM CL> מִכַּף־רֶגֶל וְעַד־רֹאשׁ ... מַכָּה *from the sole of the foot to the head ... is a wound* Is 1_6, מָה הַמַּכּוֹת הָאֵלֶּה בֵּין יָדֶיךָ *what are these wounds between your hands?*, i.e. perh. on your back Zc 13_6. <OBJ> נכה hi. *strike with* 2 K 9_{29}||2 C 22_6 2 K 9_{15}, רפה pi. *heal* Si 3_{28}.

<CSTR> מַכַּת י׳ *the wound of*, i.e. inflicted by, *Y.* Mc 1_9 (if em. מַכּוֹתֶיהָ *her wounds*), מכת לץ *wound of a scorner* Si 3_{28}; דַּם־הַמַּכָּה *blood of the wound* 1 K 22_{35}, כל מכה *all wounds* Si 25_{13}, כָּל־מַכֹּתֶיהָ *all her wounds* Jr 9_8 (מַכֹּתֶהָ) 49_{17} 50_{13}. <APP> שֶׁבֶר *injury* Jr 14_{17}. <ADJ> טְרִי *fresh* Is 1_6, חלה ni. ptc. *severe* Jr 14_{17}, אֵלֶּה *these* Zc 13_6.

<PREP> לְ perh. of benefit, *to, for* 4QapLam^a 1.1_{14} (למכאובנו *for our pain* corrected to למכתינו *for our wounds*); מִן *from, of*, + רפא *heal* Jr 30_{17}, htp. *be healed* 2 K 8_{29}||2 C 22_6 2 K 9_{15}; עַל *on account of*, + שׁרק *hiss* Jr 19_8 49_{17} 50_{13}.

<COLL> חַבּוּרָה || מַכָּה *blow* Is 1_6, פֶּצַע *wound* Is 1_6; + שֶׁבֶר *injury* Jr 10_{19} 30_{12} Na 3_{19}, כְּאֵב *pain* Jr 15_{18}; נִשְׁבְּרָה ... מַכָּה נַחְלָה *she has been injured with ... a*

severe wound Jr 14_{17}.

3. plague, <SUBJ> כתב pass. *be written* Dt 28_{61}. <NOM CL> עַל־פָּנַי תָּמִיד חֳלִי וּמַכָּה *sickness and plague are before me continually* Jr 6_7. <OBJ> עלה hi. *bring up* Dt 28_{61}, יסף *add* Lv 26_{21}, פלא hi. *make wonderful* Dt $28_{59.59.59}$, נכה hi. *strike with* Nm 11_{33}, ראה *see* Dt 29_{21}. <CSTR> מַכּוֹת זַרְעֶךָ *plagues of your seed* Dt 28_{59}, הָאָרֶץ *of the land* Dt 29_{21}; כָּל־מַכָּה *every plague* Dt 28_{61} 1 S 4_8. <ADJ> גָּדוֹל *great* Dt 28_{59} 4QapPent 10.1_8 (גד[ו]לה), רַב *great* Nm 11_{33}, אמן ni. ptc. *enduring* Dt 28_{59}. <PREP> בְּ of instrument, *by (means of), with,* + נכה hi. *strike* 1 S 4_8. <COLL> מַכָּה שֶׁבַע כְּחַטֹּאתֵיכֶם *plagues seven (times as many) as your sins* Lv 26_{21}. <COLL> מַכָּה || חֳלִי *sickness* Dt $28_{59.61}$ Jr 6_7, מַחֲלָה *sickness* 4QapPent 10.1_8, נֶגַע *plague* 4QapPent 10.1_8; + תַּחֲלֻאִים *disceases* Dt 29_{21}.

4. defeat, slaughter, <SUBJ> היה *be* 1 S 4_{10} 14_{14}, רבה *be great* 1 S 14_{30}. <OBJ> נכה hi. *strike with* Jos $10_{10.20}$ Jg 11_{33} 15_8 1 S 6_{19} 14_{14} 19_8 23_5 1 K 20_{21} 2 C 13_{17} 28_5. <ADJ> רִאשׁוֹן *first* 1 S 14_{14}, גָּדוֹל *great* Jos $10_{10.20}$ Jg 11_{33} 15_8 1 S 4_{10} 6_{19} 19_8 23_5 1 K 20_{21} 2 C 28_5, רַב *great* 2 C 13_{17}. <COLL> מַכָּה בַּפְּלִשְׁתִּים *the slaughter among the Philistines* 1 S 14_{30}.

Also perh. 3Q8 1_1 4QAdmonPar 1.1_2 4Q418 87_8.

<SYN> §1, 2 חַבּוּרָה *blow,* מֻרְדָּף *persecution;* §2 פֶּצַע *wound* Is 1_6; §3 חֳלִי *sickness,* מַחֲלָה *sickness,* נֶגַע *plague.*

⇒ נכה hi. *strike.*

מִכְוָה 7 n.f. **(scar of a) burn**—cstr. מִכְוַת—in the skin, <SUBJ> היה *be* Lv 13_{24}, מרק hi. *cleanse away* Pr 20_{30} (if em. וּמַכּוֹת חַדְרֵי־בָטֶן *and wounds* cleanse *the innermost parts* to וּמִכְוֹת חַדְרֵי־בָטֶן; or em. וּמִכְוֹת חַדְרֵי־בָטֶן *and scars of the inner person*).* <NOM CL> מִכְוָה תַּחַת מִכְוָה *a burn for a burn* Ex $21_{25(Sam)}$ (MT כְּוִיָּה *burn*). <CSTR> מִכְוַת־אֵשׁ *burn of,* i.e. made by, *fire* Lv 13_{24}; מִחְיַת הַמִּכְוָה *rawness of the burn* Lv 13_{23}, שְׂאֵת *swelling of* Lv 13_{28}, צָרֶבֶת *scar of* Lv 13_{28}. <PREP> בְּ of place, *in,* + פרח (of leprosy) *break out* Lv 13_{25}; תַּחַת *(in exchange) for* Ex $21_{25(Sam)}$ (MT כְּוִיָּה *burn*).*

⇒ כוה *burn.*

מָכוֹן 17.2.11 n.m. **place; foundation**—cstr. מְכוֹן; sf. מְכוֹנִי, מְכוֹנוֹ; pl. Q מכונים; cstr. Q מכוני; sf. מְכוֹנֶיהָ, Q מכוניהמה—**1. place** of Y.'s dwelling (Ex 15_{17} 1 K $8_{39.43.49}$||2 C $6_{30.33.39}$ Is 18_4 Ps 33_{14} Dn 8_{11} Si 36_{18}), **site** of Y.'s house (Ezr 2_{68}), Mount Zion (Is 4_5), **(dwelling) place,** of worshipper (4QM[a] 11.1_{14}), distress (1QS 10_{15}), uprightness (4QBer[a] 1.2_7), rejoicing (1QH 11_5), eternity (1QH 18_{29}), perh. **dwelling** (4Q418 178_3).

<SUBJ> שׁלך ho. *be thrown down* Dn 8_{11} (ms מְקוֹם *place of*). <NOM CL> מכוני בעדת קודש *my place is in the holy congregation* 4QM[a] 11.1_{14}. <OBJ> פעל *make* Ex 15_{17} (+ לְשִׁבְתְּךָ *for your dwelling*), בנה *build* 1 K 8_{13}||2 C 6_2 (+ לְשִׁבְתְּךָ), מצא *find* 4Q415 11_{12}, בין hi. *understand* perh. 4Q418 227_1.

<CSTR> מְכוֹן שִׁבְתְּךָ, and vars. *place of your dwelling* 1 K $8_{39.43.49}$||2 C $6_{30.33.39}$ Si 36_{18} (שבתיך), ־שִׁבְתּוֹ *of his dwelling* Ps 33_{14}, מִקְדָּשׁוֹ *of his sanctuary* Dn 8_{11} (if not *foundation,* §2; or em. מִקְדָּשׁוֹ to הַמִּקְדָּשׁ *of the sanctuary;* ms מְקוֹם *place of*), מְכוֹן הַר *site of the mountain of* Is 4_5 (+ מִקְרָא *assembly*), מכון צרה *place of distress* with desolation 1QS 10_{15}, רנה *of rejoicing* 1QH 11_5, עולם *of eternity* 1QH 18_{29}, מכוני יוש[ר] *places of uprightness* 4QBer[a] 1.2_7, מכון כול perh. *place of all* 4Q418 227_1=4QHod[a] 7.2_9; בית מכונים perh. *house of dwelling* 4Q415 6_5 ([מכונ]) 4Q418 178_3, מכו[ניכה] *of your dwelling* 4Q 415 2.2_7, כָּל־מְכוֹן *all the site of* Is 4_5.

<APP> שָׁמַיִם *heaven* 1 K $8_{39.43.49}$||2 C $6_{30.33.39}$, מִקְדָּשׁ *sanctuary* Ex 15_{17}, בַּיִת *house* 1 K 8_{13}||2 C 6_2, הַר *mountain* Ex 15_{17}, עִיר *city* Si 36_{18}, יְרוּשָׁלַםִ *Jerusalem* Si 36_{18}.

<PREP> לְ perh. of direction, *to* 4QsapDidB 2_3; בְּ of place, *in* 1QH fr. 7_5, + יצב htp. *stand* 1QH 18_{29} ([להתיצב]), נטע *plant* Ex 15_{17}, נבט hi. *look* Is 18_4, ברך pi. *bless* 1QS 10_{15}, מול *circumcise* 1QH 11_5; מִן of direction, *from,* + שׁמע *hear* 1 K $8_{39.43.49}$||2 C $6_{30.33.39}$ (1 K lacks מִן), שׁגח *gaze* Ps 33_{14}; עַל *upon, over,* + ברא *create* Is 4_5 (or em. וּבָרָא to וּבָא *and he will come*), עמד hi. *set up* Ezr 2_{68}, רחם *have compassion* Si 36_{18}.

2. base, foundation of Y.'s throne (Ps 89_{15} 97_2), of the earth (Ps 104_5); net of wisdom as a strong foundation (Si 6_{29}), <SUBJ> היה *be* Si 6_{29}. <NOM CL> צֶדֶק וּמִשְׁפָּט מְכוֹן כִּסְאֶךָ *righteousness and justice are the foundation of your throne* Ps 89_{15}, var. Ps 97_2. <CSTR> מְכוֹן כִּסְאֶךָ *foundation of your throne* Ps 89_{15}, כִּסְאוֹ *of* *his throne* Ps 97₂, מכון עז *foundation of strength,* i.e. strong foundation Si 6₂₉. <PREP> עַל *upon,* + יסד *establish* Ps 104₅.*

⇒ כון *be upright.*

מְכוֹנָה 25.2.2 n.f. **base**—מְכֹנָה; מְכֻנָתָהּ, מְכוֹנָתוֹ, Si מכונתם; pl. מְכֹנוֹת (Q מכונות); sf. מְכוֹנֹתָיו—**1. base, stand** of laver in temple (1 K 7₂₇₊₁₄ₜ 2 K 25₁₃.₁₆||Jr 52₁₇.₂₀ Jr 27₁₉ 2 C 4₁₄.₁₄), ephah (Zc 5₁₁), altar (Ezr 3₃), <OBJ> עשה *make* 1 K 7₂₇.₃₇.₄₃||2 C 4₁₄ 2 K 16₁₇ 25₁₆||Jr 52₂₀, נתן *give,* i.e. place 1 K 7₃₉, כון hi. *prepare* Zc 5₁₁ (if em. וְהוּכַן *and it shall be prepared* to וְהֵכִנוּ מְכֻנָה *and they shall prepare a stand*), שׁבר pi. *break* 2 K 25₁₃||Jr 52₁₇.

<CSTR> אֹרֶךְ הַמְּכוֹנָה *length of the stand* 1 K 7₂₇, רֹאשׁ *top of* 1 K 7₃₅.₃₅ (הַמְּכֹנָה; or del.), פִּנּוֹת *corners of* 1 K 7₃₄ (הַמְּכֹנָה), מַעֲשֵׂה *construction of* 1 K 7₂₈, מִסְגְּרוֹת הַמְּכֹנוֹת *borders of the stands* 2 K 16₁₇ (if em. הַמִּסְגְּרוֹת *the borders*). <APP> נְחֹשֶׁת *bronze* 1 K 7₂₇, מִסְגֶּרֶת *border* 2 K 16₁₇ (or em.; see Cstr.). <ADJ> אֶחָד *one* 1 K 7₂₇.₃₀.₃₄.₃₈.

<PREP> לְ of possession, *of, (belonging) to* 1 K 7₃₀; of benefit, *to, for* 1 K 7₃₈ perh. 11QT^b fr. 36₂; בְּ of place, *in* 1 K 7₃₂; מִן *from,* i.e. of one piece with 1 K 7₃₄; עַל *upon* 1 K 7₃₈.₄₃||2 C 4₁₄, + כון hi. *establish* Ezr 3₃, נוח ho. *be placed* Zc 5₁₁ (or em. hi. *place*); *concerning,* + אמר *say* Jr 27₁₉; תַּחַת *under* Jr 52₂₀ (unless ins. הַיָּם *the sea* after תַּחַת).

<COLL> מְכוֹנָה + עַמּוּד *pillar* 2 K 25₁₃.₁₆||Jr 52₁₇.₂₀ Jr 27₁₉, יָם *sea* 2 K 25₁₃.₁₆||Jr 52₁₇.₂₀ Jr 27₁₉, בָּקָר *oxen* Jr 52₂₀, כְּלִי *vessel* Jr 27₁₉; הַמְּכֹנוֹת עֶשֶׂר *the ten stands* 1 K 7₂₇, vars. 1 K 7₃₇.₃₈.₄₃||2 C 4₁₄ (if em. עָשָׂה *he made* to עֶשֶׂר).

2. dwelling place, property, estate, <PREP> עַל *in, at,* + שׁקט *be at peace* Si 41₁ 44₆.

3. foundation of hell, <NOM CL> מכונתו א[ש] *its foundation is fire* 4QBéat 15₆.

⇒ כון *be upright.*

[מְכוּרָה] 3 n.f. **origin**—sf. מְכֻרֹתָם; pl. sf. מְכֻרוֹתַיִךְ (מְכֹרֹתַיִךְ)—of Jerusalem (Ezk 16₃), Ammonites (Ezk 21₃₅), Egyptians (Ezk 29₁₄), <NOM CL> מְכֹרֹתַיִךְ ... מֵאֶרֶץ הַכְּנַעֲנִי *your origin was ... from the land of the Canaanites* Ezk 16₃ (|| מוֹלֶדֶת *birth*). <CSTR> אֶרֶץ מְכֻרוֹתַיִךְ *land of your origin* Ezk 21₃₅ (+ בִּמְקוֹם אֲשֶׁר נִבְרֵאת *in the place where you were created*), מְכוּרֹתָם *of their origin* Ezk 29₁₄.

<SYN> מוֹלֶדֶת *birth.*

⇒ (?) כור *dig.*

מָכִי 1.0.0.5 pr.n.m. **Machi, 1.** Gadite, father of Geuel, <CSTR> בֶּן־מָכִי *son of Machi* Nm 13₁₅ (Sam מיכי *Michi*).

2. servant of Gedaliah, <APP> נַעַר *lad,* i.e. servant Arad ost. 110₂.

3. son of Hizziliah, <APP> בֵּן *son* Ḥorvat 'Uza ost. 1₄.

4. appar. son of Shekaniah (שקניה; others יקמיה *Jekamiah*), Seal 153 (Judaea?, 6th cent.).

5. father of Shaul, <CSTR> בן מכי *son of Machi* Seal 936 (8th cent.).

6. father of Azrikam, <CSTR> בן מכי *son of Machi* Bulla D75.

[מִכָּיְהוּ], see מִיכָיְהוּ *Micaiah.*

מָכִיר 22.0.0.1 pr.n.m. **Machir**—I מכר—**1.** eldest son of Manasseh, father of Gilead, <SUBJ> ילד hi. *beget* Nm 26₂₉, לקח *take* 1 C 7₁₅. <OBJ> ילד *bear* 1 C 7₁₄. <CSTR> אֵשֶׁת־מָכִיר *wife of Machir* 1 C 7₁₆, בֶּן־ *son of* Nm 27₁ 32₃₉₍ₘₛ₎ 36₁ Jos 13₃₁ 17₃ 1 C 7₁₇, בְּנֵי *sons of* Gn 50₂₃ Nm 32₃₉ Jos 13₃₁.₃₁ 1 C 2₂₃, בַּת *daughter of* 1 C 2₂₁. <APP> אָב *father* 1 C 2₂₁.₂₃ 7₁₄, בֵּן *son* Gn 50₂₃ Nm 27₁ 32₃₉ 36₁ Jos 13₃₁ 17₃ 1 C 17₁₇. <PREP> לְ of possession, *of, (belonging) to* Nm 26₂₉ Jos 13₃₁.

2. clan descended from preceding, and its territory in Gilead, <SUBJ> ישׁב *dwell* Nm 32₄₀. <APP> אָב *father* Jos 17₁, בֵּן *son* Nm 32₄₀, בְּכוֹר *firstborn* Jos 17₁. <PREP> לְ of direction, *to,* + נתן *give* Nm 32₄₀ Dt 3₁₅; of possession, *of, (belonging) to,* + היה *be* Jos 17₁; מִן of direction, *from,* + ירד *go down* Jg 5₁₄.

3. son of Ammiel, resident of Lo-debar, <SUBJ> נגשׁ hi. *bring near* 2 S 17₂₇. <CSTR> בֵּית מָכִיר *house of Machir* 2 S 9₄.₅. <APP> בֵּן *son* 2 S 9₄.₅ 17₂₇.

4. appar. son of Micaiah, <PREP> לְ of possession, *of, (belonging) to* Seal 749 (c. 700).

⇒ מָכִירִי *Machirite.*

מָכִירִי 1 gent. **Machirite,** as collective sing. noun of descendants of Machir, son of Manasseh, <CSTR> מִשְׁפַּחַת הַמָּכִירִי *clan of the Machirites* Nm 26_{29}.
⇒ מָכִיר *Machir.*

מכך 3 vb. **be brought low—Qal** 1 + waw וַיָּמֹכּוּ—**be brought low, be humiliated, collapse,** <SUBJ> Israelites Ps 106_{43} (or del.; ms וַיִּמַקּוּ *and they pined away*). <PREP> בְּ of cause, *on account of* or of instrument, *by (means of),* + עָוֹן *iniquity* Ps 106_{43}.

Ni. 1 Impf. יִמַּךְ—**sag, sink,** <SUBJ> מְקָרֶה *roof-beam* Ec 10_{18} (|| דלף *drip*). <PREP> בְּ of cause, *on account of,* + עֲצַלְתַּיִם *laziness* Ec 10_{18}.
<SYN> דלף *drip.*

Ho. 1 Pf. הֻמְּכוּ—**be brought low,** <SUBJ> wicked Jb 24_{24} (:: רמם *be exalted*).
<ANT> רמם *be exalted.*
⇒ cf. מוך *be low.*

[מִכַל], see מִיכַל *Michal.*

[מִכְלָא] 3 n.[m.] **fold**—מִכְלָה; pl. cstr. מִכְלְאֹת; sf. מִכְלְאֹתֶיךָ—**fold, enclosure,** for sheep (Hb 3_{17} Ps 78_{70}), goats (Ps 50_{9}), <CSTR> מִכְלְאֹת צֹאן *folds of the sheep* Ps 78_{70}. <PREP> מִן of direction, *from,* + גזר *cut off* Hb 3_{17} (+ רֶפֶת *stall;* or em. גזר to ni. *be cut off*), לקח *take* Ps 50_{9} (|| בַּיִת *house*) 78_{70}.
<SYN> בַּיִת *house.*
⇒ כלא *restrain.*

*****[מִכְלְבֹת]** n.f.pl. **tongs**—<NOM CL> הוּא מִכְלוֹת זָהָב *it was a pair of golden tongs* 2 C 4_{21} (if em. מִכְלוֹת *perfection* to מִכְלְבֹת; or del.). <CSTR> מִכְלוֹת זָהָב *pair of golden tongs* 2 C 4_{21} (if em.; see Nom. Cl.; or del.).

מִכְלָה I, see מִכְלָא *fold.*

מִכְלָה II, see מִכְלוֹת *perfection.*

מִכְלוֹל 2.0.1 n.[m.] **perfection**—cstr. Q מכלול—<OBJ> שׂים *place,* i.e. make 1QSb 3_{25}. <CSTR> מכלול הדר *perfection of adornment* 1QSb 3_{25}; לְבֻשֵׁי מִכְלוֹל *those clothed of,* i.e. in, *perfection* Ezk 23_{12} 38_{4}.
⇒ כלל *be perfect.*

[מִכְלוֹת] 1 n.f.pl. **perfection**—pl. cstr. מִכְלוֹת—<NOM CL> הוּא מִכְלוֹת זָהָב *it was perfection of gold* 2 C 4_{21} (or em. מִכְלְבֹת *tongs of;* or del.). <CSTR> מִכְלוֹת זָהָב *perfection of gold,* i.e. purest gold 2 C 4_{21} (or em.; see Nom. Cl.; or del.).
⇒ כלה *be complete.*

[מַכְלֻל] 1 n.[m.] **ornate robe***—pl. מַכְלֻלִים—<APP> גְּלוֹם *cloak* Ezk 27_{24}, גְּנָז *carpet* Ezk 27_{24}. <PREP> בְּ of instrument, *by (means of), in,* + רכל *trade* Ezk 27_{24}.
⇒ כלל *be perfect.*

[מִכְלָל] 1 n.[m.] **perfection**—cstr. מִכְלַל—<OBJ> חזה *see* Is 33_{17} (if em.; see Cstr.). <CSTR> מִכְלַל־יֹפִי *perfection of beauty* Is 33_{17} (if em. מֶלֶךְ בְּיָפְיוֹ *the king in his beauty*) Ps 50_{2}. <APP> צִיּוֹן *Zion* Ps 50_{2}. <PREP> מִן of direction, *from,* + יפע hi. *shine forth* Ps 50_{2}.
⇒ כלל *be perfect.*

מַכֹּלֶת 1 n.f. **food,** <OBJ> נתן *give* 1 K 5_{25}. <APP> חִטָּה *wheat* 1 K 5_{25} (אֶלֶף כֹּר חִטִּים *a thousand cors of wheat*). <COLL> מַכֹּלֶת לְבֵיתוֹ *food for his household* 1 K 5_{25}.
⇒ אכל *eat.*

[מִכְמָן] 1 n.[m.] **treasure**—pl. cstr. מִכְמַנֵּי—<CSTR> מִכְמַנֵּי הַזָּהָב וְהַכֶּסֶף *the treasures of gold and silver* Dn 11_{43}. <PREP> בְּ *over,* + משׁל *rule* Dn 11_{43} (+ חֲמֻדוֹת *preciousness*).

מִכְמָס 11 pl.n. **Michmas**—מִכְמָשׂ (mss מִכְמָשׁ)—מִכְמָס Ezr 2_{27}||Ne 7_{31} (Ezr mss מִכְמָשׂ); elsewhere מִכְמָשׂ, alw. (except 1 S 13_{5} Is 10_{28} Ne 11_{31}) with mss מִכְמָשׁ **Michmash;** town of Benjamin, Muḫmas, 11 km NNE of Jerusalem, or perh. Kh. el-Hara el-Fawqa, 1 km further N,* <CSTR> אַנְשֵׁי מִכְמָס *men of Michmas* Ezr 2_{27}||Ne 7_{31} (Ezr mss מִכְמָשׂ), מַעֲבַר מִכְמָשׂ *pass of Michmas,* perh. Wadi es-Swenit (מִגְרוֹן *Migron*) 1 S 13_{23} (mss מִכְמָשׁ *Michmash*). <PREP> לְ of place, *at,* + פקד hi. *deposit* Is 10_{28}; בְּ of place, *in, at,* + היה *be* 1 S 13_{2}, חנה *en-*

camp 1 S $13_{5.16}$, אסף ni. *be gathered* 1 S $13_{11(mss)}$; מִן of direction, *from*, + נכה hi. *strike* 1 S 14_{31}; מוּל *in front of* 1 S 14_{5}; מִכְמָשׂ without preposition, *at Michmas* Ne 11_{31}, + אסף ni. *be gathered* 1 S 13_{11}.*

מִכְמָר 2 n.[m.] **net**, prob. not specif. **fishing-net***—pl. sf. מִכְמֹרָיו—<SUBJ> מלא htp. *be filled* 2QapProph 6_{1} ([מכ]מרם יתמל[א]). <CSTR> תּוֹא מִכְמָר *antelope of*, i.e. in, *a net* Is 51_{20}. <PREP> בְּ of place, *in(to)*, + נפל *fall* Ps 141_{10}.*

⇒ כמר *be agitated*, מִכְמֹרֶת *net*.

מִכְמֹ֫רֶת 3.0.2 n.f. **net**—sf. מִכְמַרְתּוֹ—**net**, perh. specif. **fishing net** (Hb $1_{15.16}$);* **snare** (Gn 49_{4} [if em.; see Nom. Cl.]), <SUBJ> פרשׂ ni. *be spread* 1QH 3_{26}. <NOM CL> כְּלֵי חָמָס מִכְמֹרֹתֵיהֶם *weapons of violence are their snares* Gn 49_{5} (if em. מְכֵרֹתֵיהֶם *their plans*). <CSTR> מכמרת חלכאים *net of the wicked* 1QH 3_{26} (+ מְצוֹדָה *net*, פַּח *snare*); פֹּרְשֵׂי מִכְמֹרֶת *those who spread a net* Is 19_{8} (+ חַכָּה *fish-hook*) 1QH 5_{8} (פורשי). <PREP> לְ of direction, *to*, + קטר pi. *burn incense* Hb 1_{16} (|| חֵרֶם *net*), אסף *gather* Hb 1_{15} (|| חֵרֶם *net*, + חַכָּה *fish-hook*). <SYN> חֵרֶם *net*.*

⇒ כמר *be agitated*, מִכְמָר *net*.

מִכְמָשׂ, see מִכְמָס *Michmas*.

מִכְמָשׁ, see מִכְמָס *Michmas*.

מִכְמְתָת 2 pl.n. **Michmethath**, town on border of Ephraim and Manasseh, perh. Kh. Kafr Bēta, Kh. Makhneh el-Foqa, Kh. Juleijil or Kh. Ibn Naser, SE of Shechem, or else a natural feature like the Wadi Bedan, <NOM CL> הַמִּכְמְתָת מִצָּפוֹן *Michmethath is on the north* Jos 16_{6}, הַמִּכְמְתָת אֲשֶׁר עַל־פְּנֵי שְׁכֶם *Michmethath which is before Shechem* Jos 17_{7}. <COLL> וַיְהִי גְבוּל־מְנַשֶּׁה מֵאָשֵׁר הַמִּכְמְתָת *and the border of Manasseh was from Asher to Michmethath* Jos 17_{7}.

מַכְנַדְבַי 1 pr.n.m. **Machnadebai**, husband of non-Jewish wife, <NOM CL> בְּנֵי בִנּוּי ... מַכְנַדְבַי *the sons of Binnui were ... Machnadebai* Ezr 10_{40} (if em. בָּנִי וּבִנּוּי *Bani and Binnui* to בְּנֵי בִנּוּי; or em. מַכְנַדְבַי to וּמִבְּנֵי עַזּוּר/זַכַּי *and of the sons of Azzur/Zaccai*).

מְכֹנָה 1 pl.n. **Meconah**, town in S Judah, perh. ident. with Madmannah at Jos 15_{31}, <PREP> בְּ of place, *in*, + ישׁב *dwell* Ne 11_{28}.

[מִכְנָסַ֫יִם] 5.1.1 n.m.du. **breeches**—du. Si מכנסים; cstr. מִכְנְסֵי—linen undergarments of priests, <SUBJ> היה *be* Ex 28_{42} Lv $6_{3(mss)}$ 16_{4} Ezk 44_{18}, כסה pi. *cover* flesh Ex 28_{42}. <OBJ> לבשׁ *wear* Lv 6_{3} 1QM 7_{10}, עשׂה *make* Ex 28_{42} 39_{28}. <CSTR> מִכְנְסֵי־בַד *breeches of linen* Ex 28_{42} (בָּד) 39_{28} (הַבָּד) Lv 6_{3} 16_{4}, פִּשְׁתִּים *of linen* Ezk 44_{18}. <APP> כָּבוֹד *glory* Si 45_{8} (בכ[ב]וד), עֹז *strength* Si 45_{8}. <PREP> בְּ of instrument, *by (means of)*, *with*, + פאר pi. *adorn* Si 45_{8}. <COLL> מִכְנָסַיִם || פְּאֵר *headdress* Ex 39_{28} (+) Ezk 44_{18} 1QM 7_{10} (+), כֻּתֹּנֶת *tunic* Ex 39_{28} (+) Lv 16_{4} (+) Si 45_{8} 1QM 7_{10}, מְעִיל *robe* Si 45_{8}; + אַבְנֵט *girdle* Ex 39_{28} Lv 16_{4} 1QM 7_{10}, מִצְנֶפֶת *turban* Ex 39_{28} Lv 16_{4}, מִגְבָּעָה *turban* Ex 39_{28} 1QM 7_{10}.

<SYN> כֻּתֹּנֶת *tunic*, מְעִיל *robe*, פְּאֵר *headdress*.

⇒ כנס *gather*.

מֶ֫כֶס 6.0.3.1 n.m. **tribute**—cstr. מֶכֶס; sf. מִכְסָם—tax on spoil for cultic purposes, <SUBJ> היה *be* Nm 31_{37}. <OBJ> רום *raise*, i.e. levy Nm 31_{28}, נתן *give* Nm 31_{41}. <NOM CL> מִכְסָם לַי׳ שְׁנַיִם וּשְׁלֹשִׁים נָפֶשׁ *their tribute for Y. was thirty-two persons* Nm 31_{40}, vars. Nm $31_{38.39}$, המכס ... אחד מן מאה *the tribute shall be ... one per cent* 11QT 60_{7}. <CSTR> מֶכֶס תְּרוּמַת י׳ *tribute of the contribution of*, i.e. for, *Y.* Nm 31_{41}, מכס תרומתמה *tribute of their contribution* 11QT 60_{4}, השלל והבז *of the spoil and the plunder* 11QT 60_{5}. <APP> נֶפֶשׁ *soul*, i.e. individual Nm 31_{28}. <PREP> לְ of benefit, *to*, *for* Bulla D99 (בשלשת למכס *in the third [year] for the tribute*). <COLL> המכס מן השלל ומן הבז ומן הציד *the tribute from the spoil and the plunder and the game* 11QT 60_{7}.*

⇒ כסס *reckon*.

[מִכְסָה] 2.0.1 n.f. **number**—cstr. מִכְסַת; pl. cstr. Sam מִכְסוֹת—**number, amount, reckoning,** <OBJ> חשׁב

pi. *calculate* Lv 27$_{23}$. <CSTR> מִכְסַת נְפָשֹׁת *number of persons* Ex 12$_{4}$ (Sam מִכְסוֹת *numbers of*), מִכְסַת הָעֶרְכְּךָ *amount of your valuation* Lv 27$_{23}$ (Sam מִכְסוֹת), שני מכסה *years of reckoning*, i.e. years reckoned Mur 24 E$_{10}$ ([מ]כסה) F$_{12}$ ([שני]). <PREP> בְּ *according to*, + לקח *take* Ex 12$_{4}$.

⇒ כסס *reckon*.

מִכְסֶה 16.0.1 n.m. **covering**—cstr. מִכְסֵה; sf. מִכְסֵהוּ—of skin for tent of meeting (Ex 26$_{14.14}$||36$_{19.19}$ 35$_{11}$ 39$_{34.34}$ 40$_{19}$ Nm 3$_{25}$ 4$_{25.25}$), of skin for wrapping sacred objects (Nm 4$_{8.10.11.12}$); covering of ark (Gn 8$_{13}$=4QComm GenA 1$_{21}$), of ship (Ezk 27$_{7}$ [if em.; see Subj.]), <SUBJ> היה *be* Ezk 27$_{7}$ (if em. מְכַסֵּךְ *your covering* to מִכְסֵךְ *your covering*). <OBJ> עשׂה *make* Ex 26$_{14}$||36$_{19}$ 35$_{11}$ (+ אֹהֶל *tent*), בוא hi. *bring* Ex 39$_{34.34}$, שׂים *place* Ex 40$_{19}$, נשׂא *carry* Nm 4$_{25.25}$, סור hi. *remove* Gn 8$_{13}$=4QComm GenA 1$_{21}$ ([ו]יסר). <NOM CL> מִשְׁמֶרֶת בְּנֵי־גֵרְשׁוֹן ... הַמִּשְׁכָּן הָאֹהֶל וּמִכְסֵהוּ *the charge of the sons of Gershon was ... the tabernacle, the tent and its covering* Nm 3$_{25(mss, Sam)}$ (L מִכְסֵהוּ), מִכְסֵה הַתַּחַשׁ אֲשֶׁר עָלָיו *the covering of the porpoise skin that is above it* Nm 4$_{25}$. <CSTR> מִכְסֵה הַתֵּבָה *covering of the ark* Gn 8$_{13}$=4QCommGenA 1$_{21}$, הָאֹהֶל *of the tent* Ex 40$_{19}$, עוֹר *of skin of* Nm 4$_{8.10.11.12}$, עֹרֹת *of skins of* Ex 26$_{14}$||36$_{19}$ 39$_{34}$ (עורת) 39$_{34}$, הַתַּחַשׁ *of the porpoise skin* Nm 4$_{25}$. <APP> עוֹר *skin* Ex 26$_{14}$||36$_{19}$. <PREP> בְּ of instrument, *by (means of), with*, + כסה pi. *cover* Nm 4$_{8.11.12}$; אֶל *into*, + נתן *give*, i.e. place Nm 4$_{10}$.

⇒ כסה *cover*.

מְכַסֶּה 4 n.m. **covering**—sf. מְכַסֵּךְ; pl. sf. מְכַסֶּיךָ—of fatty tissue around internal organs (Lv 9$_{19}$), worms covering the dead (Is 14$_{11}$), awning of ship (Ezk 27$_{7}$ [or em.; see Subj.]), clothing (Is 23$_{18}$), <SUBJ> היה *be* Ezk 27$_{7}$ (or em. מְכַסֵּךְ *your covering* to מִכְסֵךְ *your covering*). <NOM CL> מְכַסֶּיךָ תּוֹלֵעָה *your covering is (of) worms* Is 14$_{11}$. <OBJ> מצא hi. *bring* Lv 9$_{19}$ (+ חֵלֶב *fat*, יֹתֶרֶת *appendage* of liver, כִּלְיָה *kidney*). <ADJ> עָתִיק *splendid* Is 23$_{18}$. <PREP> לְ *as* or introducing predicate, + היה *be* Is 23$_{18}$.

⇒ כסה *cover*.

מַכְפֵּלָה 6 pl.n. **Machpelah,** field with cave near Hebron, burial site of the patriarchs and their wives, <NOM CL> בַּמַּכְפֵּלָה אֲשֶׁר לִפְנֵי מַמְרֵא *in Machpelah which is before Mamre* Gn 23$_{17}$. <CSTR> שְׂדֵה הַמַּכְפֵּלָה *field of Machpelah* Gn 23$_{19}$ 49$_{30}$ 50$_{13}$, מְעָרַת *cave of* Gn 23$_{9}$ 25$_{9}$ 2QJub^{a} 23$_{7}$ (מערת המ[כפלה]) 3QJub 3$_{4}$ (מכ[פלה]). <PREP> בְּ of place, *in* Gn 23$_{17}$.

⇒ (?) כפל *double*.

מכר I 80.1.22 vb. **deliver (over)—Qal** 57.0.18 Pf. מָכַר (מְכָרוֹ, מְכָרָנוּ, מְכָרָם), מָכְרָה, מָכַרְתִּי, מָכְרוּ (Q מכרוני, Q מכרוהו), מְכַרְתֶּם; impf. יִמְכֹּר (־יִמְכָּר, Q ימכור), 2ms תִּמְכֹּר (תִּמְכְּרֶנָּה), יִמְכְּרוּ, תִּמְכְּרוּ, נִמְכְּרֶנּוּ; + waw וּמָכַר (וּמְכָרוֹ), וּמָכַרְתִּי, וּמָכְרוּ (Q ומכרוהו, ומכרום), וּמְכָרוּם; וַיִּמְכֹּר (Q וימכור, וַיִּמְכְּרֵם), 3fs וַתִּמְכֹּר, וַיִּמְכְּרוּ; impv. מִכְרָה, מִכְרִי; ptc. מוֹכֵר (מֹכֵר, Q מכיר), מֹכֶרֶת, מוֹכְרִים (sf. מֹכְרֵיהֶן), מֹכְרֵי; inf. abs. מָכֹר (Q מכור); cstr. לִמְכּוֹר (לְמָכְרָהּ, מִכְרָם).

1. deliver over* goods, persons, for the use or possession of others, sometimes for a limited period (e.g. Dt 15$_{12}$ Jg 3$_{8}$ Lv 25$_{15}$), not necessarily by way of sale: (use of) land (e.g. Gn 47$_{20}$ Lv 27$_{20}$ Ezk 48$_{14}$ Mur 30 1$_{1}$), (use of) land with right of redemption (e.g. Lv 25$_{27}$ Ru 4$_{3}$), right to cultivate land until next jubilee (e.g. Lv 25$_{16}$); oft. of transfer of possession of person, as slave (e.g. Gn 37$_{27}$ 45$_{4}$ Ex 21$_{7}$ Am 2$_{6}$ Ne 5$_{8}$), of delivery of daughter in marriage (Gn 31$_{15}$), wife taken in war (Dt 21$_{14}$), kidnapped person (Ex 21$_{16}$ Dt 24$_{7}$); of Y. delivering Israel to their enemies (e.g. Jg 2$_{14}$ 3$_{8}$ 4$_{2}$ Is 50$_{1}$ Ps 44$_{13}$), sometimes specif. as a usufruct for a defined period (e.g. Jg 10$_{7}$), his people's land (Ezk 30$_{12}$); of iniquities delivering a person to Sheol (11Q Ps^{a} 19$_{10}$).

2. specif. **sell** movable or immovable goods in return for valuables, pass ownership, e.g. foodstuffs (Ne 10$_{32}$ 13$_{15.16}$), clothing (Pr 31$_{24}$), animal (Ex 21$_{35}$).

<SUBJ> Y. Jg 2$_{14}$ 3$_{8}$ 4$_{2.9}$ 10$_{7}$ 1 S 12$_{9}$ 23$_{7}$ (if em. נִכַּר *he has alienated* [i.e. נכר pi.] to מָכַר *he has delivered*) Is 50$_{1}$ Ezk 30$_{12}$ Jl 4$_{8}$ Ps 44$_{13}$ 4QpsJub^{a} 1$_{5}$, Egyptians Gn 47$_{20}$, Israel(ites) Lv 25$_{14}$ Dt 14$_{21}$ 21$_{14.14}$ Am 2$_{6}$ 11QT 48$_{6}$, Midianites Gn 37$_{36}$, Philistia Jl 4$_{6.7}$, Sidon Jl 4$_{6.7}$, Tyre Jl 4$_{6.7}$, Tyrians Ne 13$_{16}$, עַם *people* Ne 10$_{32}$, גּוֹי *na-*

tion Jl 4$_3$, Esau Gn 25$_{31}$, Dositheus Mur 30 1$_{1.4}$ 2$_{10.20}$, Judah Gn 37$_{27}$, Kleopos Mur 29 1$_1$ 2$_{10}$, Naomi Ru 4$_3$, אִישׁ *man* Gn 47$_{20}$ Ex 21$_{7.35.37}$ Lv 25$_{27.29}$ 27$_{20}$ Dt 24$_7$ CD 12$_{8.10.10}$ 4QD^f 2$_5$, אִשָּׁה *woman, wife* 2 K 4$_7$ Pr 31$_{24}$, אָב *father* Gn 31$_{15}$, בֵּן *son* Jl 4$_8$, בַּר *son* Mur 29 1$_1$ 2$_{10}$ Mur 30 1$_1$ 2$_{10}$, אָח *brother* Gn 37$_{27}$ 45$_{4.5}$ Lv 25$_{25}$, חֹר *noble* Ne 5$_8$, סָגָן *official* Ne 5$_8$, כֹּהֵן *priest* Gn 47$_{22}$, לֵוִי *Levite* Ezk 48$_{14}$, אָדוֹן *master* Ex 21$_8$, רֵעַ *neighbour* Ex 21$_{35}$, עָמִית *neighbour* Lv 25$_{15.16}$, ישׁב ptc. *one who dwells* 11QT 43$_{14}$, זֹנָה *harlot* Na 3$_4$ (or em. הַמֹּכֶרֶת *who sells* to הַמֻּכֶּרֶת *the one known* [ho. ptc. of נכר I *recognize*]* or הַכֹּמֶרֶת *who ensnares*), גנב ptc. *one who steals* Ex 21$_{16}$, צוּר *rock*, i.e. Y. Dt 32$_{30}$, עָוֹן *iniquity* 11QPs^a 19$_{10}$; subj. not specified, Pr 23$_{23}$ Ne 13$_{15}$.

<OBJ> Israel(ites) Dt 32$_{30}$ Jg 3$_8$ 10$_7$ Is 50$_1$, עַם *people* Ps 44$_{13}$, גּוֹי *nation* Na 3$_4$ (or em.; see Subj.), מִשְׁפָּחָה *clan* Na 3$_4$ (or em.; see Subj.), David 1 S 23$_7$ (if em.; see Subj.), Joseph Gn 37$_{27.36}$ 45$_{4.5}$, Leah Gn 31$_{15}$, Rachel Gn 31$_{15}$, Sisera Jg 4$_9$, אִישׁ *man* Ex 21$_{16}$, אִשָּׁה *woman* Dt 21$_{14}$, אָב *father* 1 S 12$_9$, בֵּן *son* Jl 4$_{6.7}$, of Israel Jg 2$_{14}$ 4$_{2.8}$, בַּת *daughter* Ex 21$_{7.8}$ Jl 4$_8$, אָח *brother* Ne 5$_8$, יַלְדָּה *girl* Jl 4$_3$, צַדִּיק *righteous one* Am 2$_6$, אֶבְיוֹן *poor one* Am 2$_6$, עֶבֶד *slave* CD 12$_{10}$, אָמָה *female slave* CD 12$_{10}$, worshipper 11QPs^a 19$_{10}$, נֶפֶשׁ *soul*, i.e. person Dt 24$_7$, שׁוֹר *ox* Ex 21$_{35.37}$, שֶׂה *sheep* Ex 21$_{37}$, בְּהֵמָה *beast* CD 12$_8$, עוֹף *bird* CD 12$_8$, דָּג *fish* Ne 13$_{16}$, שֶׁבֶר *grain* Ne 10$_{32}$, צַיִד *food* Ne 13$_{15}$, דלה ho. ptc. *vine creeper* Mur 29 2$_{10}$, אֶרֶץ *land* Ezk 30$_{12}$, אֲדָמָה *land* Gn 47$_{22}$, חֶלְקָה *plot of land* Ru 4$_3$, שָׂדֶה *field* Gn 47$_{20}$ Lv 27$_{20}$, בַּיִת *house* Lv 25$_{29}$ Mur 30 1$_4$, נְבֵלָה *carcase* of animal Dt 14$_{21}$ 11QT 48$_6$, שֶׁמֶן *oil* 2 K 4$_7$, עָפָר *dust* 4QActs 1$_6$, אֶבֶן *stone* 4QActs 1$_6$ ([אבניה]), בְּכֹרָה *birthright* Gn 25$_{31}$, סָדִין *garment* Pr 31$_{24}$, מַקָּחָה *ware* Ne 10$_{32}$, מֶכֶר *item of sale* Ne 13$_{15}$ Mur 30 1$_4$, מִמְכָּר *item of sale* Lv 25$_{14}$, מִסְפָּר *number of crops* Lv 25$_{16}$, אֱמֶת *truth* Pr 23$_{23}$, כֹּל *everything* 11QT 43$_{14}$ Mur 30 1$_4$.

<PREP> לְ of direction, *to* Mur 30 1$_4$ 2$_{20}$, + Ishmaelites Gn 37$_{27}$, Israel(ites) Lv 25$_{15.16}$, Sabaeans Jl 4$_8$, עַם *people* Ex 21$_8$, גּוֹי *nation* CD 12$_{8.10.10}$, Jacob Gn 25$_{31}$, Potiphar Gn 37$_{36}$, Pharaoh Gn 47$_{20}$, אִישׁ *man* Lv 25$_{27}$ 27$_{20}$, בֵּן *son* Jl 4$_6$ Ne 13$_{16}$, שַׂר *commander* Gn 37$_{36}$, סָרִיס *eunuch* Gn 37$_{36}$, עָמִית *neighbour* Lv 24$_{14}$, נָכְרִי *foreigner* Dt 14$_{21}$ 11QT 48$_6$, נֹשֶׁה *creditor* Is 50$_1$, שְׁאוֹל *Sheol* 11QPs^a 19$_{10}$.

לְ *as*, + אָמָה *female slave* Ex 21$_7$.

בְּ of place, *in*, + Jerusalem Ne 13$_{16}$; *into*, + יָד *hand*, i.e. power Jg 2$_{14}$ 3$_8$ 4$_2$ 10$_7$ 1 S 12$_9$ 23$_7$ (if em.; see Subj.) Ezk 30$_{12}$ Jl 4$_8$; of time, *in, on*, + date Mur 30 1$_1$, שַׁבָּת *sabbath* Ne 13$_{16}$; of instrument, *by (means of), through*, + זְנוּנִים *prostitution* Na 3$_4$ (or em.; see Subj.), כֶּשֶׁף *sorcery* Na 3$_4$ (or em.; see Subj.); *according to*, + מִסְפָּר *number* of years Lv 25$_{15}$.

בְּ of price, *(in exchange) for* Mur 30 1$_4$, + כֶּסֶף *money* Dt 21$_{14}$ Am 2$_6$ 11QT 43$_{14}$ Mur 30 2$_{20}$, זוז *zuz* Mur 30 2$_{20}$, סֶלַע *tetradrachma* Mur 30 2$_{20}$, הוֹן *wealth* Ps 44$_{13}$ (בְּלֹא־הוֹן *for no wealth*), יַיִן *wine* Jl 4$_3$.

כְּ in phrase כַּיּוֹם *first of all* Gn 25$_{31}$.

מִן of direction, *from*, + גֹּרֶן *threshing floor* CD 12$_{10}$, גַּת *winepress* CD 12$_{10}$; partitive, *(some) of* 4QD^a 6.4$_3$ ([ימכו]רו), + אֲחֻזָּה *property* Lv 25$_{25}$, appar. תְּרוּמָה *tract of land* Ezk 48$_{14}$.

אֶל *to*, + גּוֹי *nation* Jl 4$_8$.

בַּעֲבוּר *for the price of*, + נַעַל *sandal* Am 2$_6$.

ה- of direction, *(in)to*, + Egypt Gn 45$_4$.

<COLL> מכר ‖ נתן *give* Jl 4$_3$, + נתן Dt 14$_{21}$ Jg 2$_{14}$ Pr 31$_{24}$; + מור hi. *exchange* Ezk 48$_{14}$; :: קנה *buy* Pr 23$_{23}$, + קנה Gn 47$_{20.22}$ Lv 25$_{14.15}$ Ne 5$_8$.

מכר + adverb, הֵנָּה *here* Gn 45$_5$, שָׁמָּה *there* Jl 4$_7$, אַחַר *afterwards* 4QD^a 6.4$_3$ ([ימכו]רו); inf. abs. + finite form of מכר, Dt 21$_{14}$.

3. ptc. as noun, **trader,** <SUBJ> לין *lodge* Ne 13$_{20}$, שׁוב *go back* Ezk 7$_{13}$, אמר *say* Zc 11$_5$, אבל htp. *mourn* Ezk 7$_{12}$. <NOM CL> מזרח המכיר *in the east is the trader* Mur 30 1$_3$ 2$_{16}$. <CSTR> מֹכְרֵי כָל־מִמְכָּר *traders of all (kinds of) merchandise* Ne 13$_{20}$. <PREP> כְּ *as*, + היה *be* Is 24$_2$. <COLL> מֹכֵר ‖ רֹכֵל *merchant* Ne 13$_{20}$; :: קֹנֶה *buyer* Is 24$_2$ Ezk 7$_{12}$, + קֹנֶה Zc 11$_5$; + רֹעֶה *shepherd* Zc 11$_5$.

Also 4QPatr 10$_2$.

<SYN> §1 נתן *give*; §3 רֹכֵל *merchant* Ne 13$_{20}$.

<ANT> §1 קנה *buy* Pr 23$_{23}$; §3 קֹנֶה *buyer*.

Ni. 19.0.3 Pf. נִמְכַּר, נִמְכַּרְתֶּם, נִמְכַּרְנוּ; impf. יִמָּכֵר, 3fs תִּמָּכֵר, יִמָּכְרוּ; + waw וְנִמְכַּר, וְנִמְכְּרוּ; ptc. נִמְכָּרִים; inf. הִמָּכְרוֹ—**be delivered over,** of land (Lv 25$_{23.34}$), animal (Lv 27$_{27}$), any devoted object (Lv 27$_{28}$); of person, for theft (Ex 22$_{2}$), as slave (Lv 25$_{42}$ Dt 15$_{12}$ Jr 34$_{14}$ Ps 105$_{17}$ Est 7$_{4}$ Ne 5$_{8}$), to be destroyed (Est 7$_{4}$); of Israelites by Y. (Is 50$_{1}$ 52$_{3}$), **deliver up oneself,** as slave (Lv 25$_{39.47.48.50}$ Ne 5$_{8}$).

<SUBJ> Israelites Lv 25$_{42}$ Is 50$_{1}$, Jerusalem/Zion Is 52$_{3}$, יְהוּדִי *Jew* Ne 5$_{8}$, עַם *people* Est 7$_{4.4}$, Esther Est 7$_{4.4}$, Joseph Ps 105$_{17}$, אָח *brother* Lv 25$_{39.47.48}$ Dt 15$_{12}$ Jr 34$_{14}$ Ne 5$_{8.8}$ (or em. וְנִכְרוּ *that they may be purchased*, i.e. כרה ni.), גַּנָּב *thief* Ex 22$_{2}$, בְּכוֹר *firstborn* Lv 27$_{27}$, חֵרֶם *devoted object* Lv 27$_{28}$, אֶרֶץ *land* Lv 25$_{23}$, שָׂדֶה *field* Lv 25$_{34}$.

<PREP> לְ of direction, *to*, + Israelite Lv 25$_{39}$ Dt 15$_{12}$ Jr 34$_{14}$ Ne 5$_{8}$ (or em.; see Subj.), גּוֹי *nation* Ne 5$_{8}$, אִישׁ *man* Jr 34$_{14}$, גֵּר *sojourner* Lv 25$_{47.50}$, תּוֹשָׁב *inhabitant* Lv 25$_{47.50}$, עֵקֶר *member* of family Lv 25$_{47.50}$, צְמִיתֻת *finality*, i.e. in perpetuity Lv 25$_{23}$.

לְ *as*, + עֶבֶד *slave* Ps 105$_{17}$ Est 7$_{4}$, שִׁפְחָה *female slave* Est 7$_{4}$.

בְּ of price, *for (the value of)*, *(in exchange) for*, + גְּנֵבָה *stolen object* Ex 22$_{2}$, מְחִיר *price* 1QMyst 1.2$_{6}$ (בלוא מחיר *for no price*); *according to, at*, + עֵרֶךְ *valuation* Lv 27$_{27}$; of cause, *on account of*, + עָוֹן *iniquity* Is 50$_{1}$ 4QDibHam^{a} 1.2$_{15}$ (בע]וונותינו]).

<COLL> מכר ni. ‖ שׁלח pu. *be sent away* Is 50$_{1}$; :: גאל ni. *be redeemed* Lv 27$_{27.28}$ Is 52$_{3}$; + adverb, חִנָּם *for nothing* Is 52$_{3}$.

לֹא יִמָּכְרוּ מִמְכֶּרֶת עָבֶד *they shall not be delivered over (with) the delivery of a slave*, i.e. as slaves Lv 25$_{42}$, var. 4QOrd^{a} 2$_{3}$, נִמְכַּרְנוּ ... לְהַשְׁמִיד לַהֲרוֹג וּלְאַבֵּד *we have been delivered up ... in order to destroy, kill and exterminate (us)* Est 7$_{4}$, שְׁנַת הִמָּכְרוֹ *the year when he delivered himself up* Lv 25$_{50}$.

<SYN> שׁלח pu. *be sent away*.

<ANT> גאל ni. *be redeemed*.

Hi. 0.0.1 Impf. 2ms Q תמכיר—**deliver over,** <SUBJ> subj. not specified, 4Q416 2.2$_{18}$. <OBJ> כָּבוֹד *glory* 4Q 416 2.2$_{18}$. <PREP> בְּ of price, *(in exchange) for*, + מְחִיר *price* 4Q416 2.2$_{18}$. <COLL> מכר hi. + ערב *exchange* 4Q416 2.2$_{18}$.

Also perh. 4QapPent 5$_{4}$ (מכיר[ ]).

Htp. 4.1 Pf. הִתְמַכֵּר; + waw וַיִּתְמַכְּרוּ; וְהִתְמַכַּרְתֶּם; inf. הִתְמַכֶּרְךָ—**deliver oneself,** to do evil (1 K 21$_{20.25}$ 2 K 17$_{17}$ Si 47$_{25}$), **offer oneself for sale,** as a slave (Dt 28$_{68}$), all unless מכר II *practise deceit*, <SUBJ> Israelites Dt 28$_{68}$ 2 K 17$_{17}$, Ahab 1 K 21$_{20.25}$, Jeroboam Si 47$_{25}$, בֵּן *son* Si 47$_{25}$. <PREP> לְ of direction, *to*, + רָעָה *evil* Si 47$_{25}$; *as*, + עֶבֶד *slave* Dt 28$_{68}$, שִׁפְחָה *female slave* Dt 28$_{68}$. <COLL> מכר htp. :: קנה *buy* Dt 28$_{68}$; + adverb, שָׁם *there* Dt 28$_{68}$; + לַעֲשׂוֹת הָרַע בְּעֵינֵי י׳ *to do what is evil in the sight of Y.* 1 K 21$_{20.25}$ 2 K 17$_{17}$.

<ANT> קנה *buy*.*

⇒ מֶכֶר *value*, מִמְכָּר *mortgaged property*, מִמְכֶּרֶת *sale*, מַכָּר *trader*, מִכְרִי *Michri*.

***מכר** II 3.1 vb. **practise deceit, guile—Htp.** 3.1 Pf. הִתְמַכֵּר, Si התמכרו; + waw וַיִּתְמַכְּרוּ; inf. הִתְמַכֶּרְךָ—all unless מכר I htp. *deliver oneself*, <SUBJ> Israelites 2 K 17$_{17}$, Ahab 1 K 21$_{20.25}$, Jeroboam Si 47$_{25}$, בֵּן *son* Si 47$_{25}$. <PREP> לְ of direction, *to*, + רָעָה *evil* Si 47$_{25}$. <COLL> מכר + לַעֲשׂוֹת הָרַע בְּעֵינֵי י׳ *to do what is evil in the sight of Y.* 1 K 21$_{20.25}$ 2 K 17$_{17}$.

***[מַכָּר]** I 2 n.[m.] **business assessor**—sf. מַכָּרוֹ; pl. sf. מַכָּרֵיכֶם—**business assessor,** temple official valuing sacrificial animals and offerings (unless מַכָּר II *acquaintance* or מַכָּר III *sale*), <PREP> מֵאֵת *from*, + לקח *take* 1 K 12$_{6.8}$.

⇒ מכר I *deliver (over)*.

[מַכָּר] II 2 n.[m.] **acquaintance**—sf. מַכָּרוֹ; pl. sf. מַכָּרֵיכֶם—**acquaintance** of priest, from whom money is received for repair of temple (unless מַכָּר I *business assessor* or מַכָּר III *sale*), <PREP> מֵאֵת *from*, + לקח *take* 1 K 12$_{6.8}$.

⇒ נכר I *recognize*.

***[מַכָּר]** III 2 n.[m.] **sale**—sf. מַכָּרוֹ; pl. sf. מַכָּרֵיכֶם—**sale** of offerings by priests to raise finance for repair of temple (unless מַכָּר I *business assessor* or מַכָּר II *acquaintance*), <PREP> מֵאֵת *from*, + לקח *take* 1 K 12$_{6.8}$.

⇒ מכר I *sell*.

מֶ֫כֶר 3.0.9 n.m. **value; mortgaged land**—sf. מִכְרָהּ, מִכְרָם—**1. value, price** of water (Nm 20_{19}), mortgaged estate (Dt 18_{8} if em.; see Prep.; unless §4), capable wife (Pr 31_{10}), <NOM CL> רָחֹק מִפְּנִינִים מִכְרָהּ *her value is far beyond that of corals* Pr 31_{10}. <OBJ> נתן *give* Nm 20_{19}. <PREP> לְבַד מִן *apart from*, + אכל *eat* Dt 18_{8} (if em. לְבַד מִמְּכָרָיו *apart from the proceeds of the sale of it* [from מִמְכָּר] to לְבַד מִמְּכָרָיו in same sense) =11QT 60_{15} (לבד ממכר).

2. mortgaged land, land sold (Mur 22 1_{12} Mur 30 $1_{4.7}$ $2_{16.17.22.28}$), **merchandise** (Ne 13_{16}), <OBJ> בוא hi. *bring* Ne 13_{16}, מכר *sell* Ne 13_{16} Mur 30 1_{4}. <CSTR> תחומ[י]ן המכר *boundaries of the item of sale* Mur 30 2_{16}, כָּל־מֶכֶר *all (kinds of) merchandise* Ne 13_{16} (+ דָּג *fish*). <ADJ> זֶה *this* Mur 22 1_{12} Mur 30 $1_{4.7}$ $2_{16.17.22}$. <PREP> לְ *with respect to* Mur 30 $1_{7.28}$; of possession, *of, (belonging) to* Mur 30 2_{22}; בְּ of place, *in* Mur 30 1_{4} 2_{17}; עַל *upon* Mur 30 1_{4} 2_{17}.

3. sale, <OBJ> מרק pi. *complete* Mur 30 2_{24}. <ADJ> זֶה *this* Mur 30 2_{24}.

4. perh. מֶכֶר עַל־הָאָבוֹת is **patrimony, inheritance from father,** without ref. to selling, Dt 18_{8} (unless §1).*

⇒ מכר I *deliver (over).*

מֹכֵר *trader*, see מכר *deliver (over).*

[מִכְרֶה] I 1 n.m. **pit**—cstr. מִכְרֵה—**pit** or **mine*** for salt, <SUBJ> היה *be* Zp 2_{9}. <CSTR> מִכְרֵה־מֶלַח *pit of salt* Zp 2_{9} (+ מִמְשַׁק חָרוּל *ground of nettles*, שְׁמָמָה *desolation*).*

⇒ כרה I *dig.*

***[מִכְרֶה]** II 1 n.m. **heap**—cstr. מִכְרֵה—<SUBJ> היה *be* Zp 2_{9}. <CSTR> מִכְרֵה־מֶלַח *heap of salt* Zp 2_{9} (+ מִמְשַׁק חָרוּל *ground of nettles*, שְׁמָמָה *desolation*; or em. מִכְרֵה־מַלּוּחַ *heap of saltwort*).

***[מְכֵרָה]** I 1 n.f. **counsel**—pl. sf. מְכֵרֹתֵיהֶם—**counsel, plan,** <NOM CL> כְּלֵי חָמָס מְכֵרֹתֵיהֶם *weapons of violence are their plans* Gn 49_{5} (unless מְכֵרָה II *weapon* or III *staff* or IV *beguilement*; or מַכֶּרֶת *circumcision blade*; or em. מִכְמֹרֹתֵיהֶם *their snares*; or em. מִכֹּרֹתֵיהֶם *from their birth*, or em. מְשָׁרֵת *covenanter*, i.e. one cutting [a covenant]).*

***[מְכֵרָה]** II 1 n.f. **weapon**—pl. sf. מְכֵרֹתֵיהֶם—<NOM CL> כְּלֵי חָמָס מְכֵרֹתֵיהֶם *weapons of violence are their weapons* Gn 49_{5} (unless מְכֵרָה I *counsel* or III *staff* or IV *beguilement*, or מַכֶּרֶת *circumcision blade*; or em. מִכְמֹרֹתֵיהֶם *their snares*; or em. מִכֹּרֹתֵיהֶם *from their birth*, or em. מְשָׁרֵת *covenanter*, i.e. one cutting [a covenant]).*

⇒ כור (?) *bore, dig.*

***[מְכֵרָה]** III 1 n.f. **staff**—pl. sf. מְכֵרֹתֵיהֶם—<NOM CL> כְּלֵי חָמָס מְכֵרֹתֵיהֶם *weapons of violence are their staves* Gn 49_{5} (unless מְכֵרָה I *counsel* or II *weapon* or IV *beguilement*, or מַכֶּרֶת *circumcision blade*; or em. מִכְמֹרֹתֵיהֶם *their snares*; or em. מִכֹּרֹתֵיהֶם *from their birth*, or em. מְשָׁרֵת *covenanter*, i.e. one cutting [a covenant]).*

***[מְכֵרָה]** IV 1 n.f. **beguilement**—pl. sf. מְכֵרֹתֵיהֶם—<NOM CL> כְּלֵי חָמָס מְכֵרֹתֵיהֶם *weapons of violence are their beguilements* Gn 49_{5} (unless מְכֵרָה I *counsel* or II *weapon* or III *staff*, or מַכֶּרֶת *circumcision blade*; or em. מִכְמֹרֹתֵיהֶם *their snares*; or em. מִכֹּרֹתֵיהֶם *from their birth*, or em. מְשָׁרֵת *covenanter*, i.e. one cutting [a covenant]).*

⇒ מכר II *practise deceit.*

מִכְרִי 1 pr.n.m. **Michri,** father of Uzzi, Benjaminite, <CSTR> בֶּן־מִכְרִי *son of Michri* 1 C 9_{8}.

⇒ מכר *deliver (over).*

***[מַכֶּרֶת]** 1 n.f. **circumcision blade**—pl. sf. מְכֵרֹתֵיהֶם—<NOM CL> כְּלֵי חָמָס מְכֵרֹתֵיהֶם *weapons of violence are their circumcision blades* Gn 49_{5} (unless מְכֵרָה I *counsel* or II *weapon* or III *staff* or IV *beguilement*; or em. מִכְמֹרֹתֵיהֶם *their snares*; or em. מִכֹּרֹתֵיהֶם *from their birth*, or em. מְשָׁרֵת *covenanter*, i.e. one cutting [a covenant]).*

⇒ כרת *cut.*

מְכֵרָתִי 1 gent. **Mecherathite,** as noun, perh. a variant of בֶּן־הַמַּעֲכָתִי *the Maacathite* in 2 S 23_{24}, <NOM CL> גִּבּוֹרֵי הַחֲיָלִים ... הַמְּכֵרָתִי *the warriors of the armies were ... the Macherathite* 1 C 11_{36}. <APP> חֵפֶר הַמְּכֵרָתִי *Hepher the Macherathite* 1 C 11_{36}.

מִכְשׁוֹל 14.2.12 n.m. **stumbling block**—מִכְשֹׁל; cstr. מִכְשׁוֹל, sf. Q מכשולי; pl. מִכְשֹׁלִים; sf. Si מכשוליך—**(cause of) stumbling** and so falling (e.g. Ezk 3_{20}), sin as a **stumbling block** leading to downfall (e.g. Ezk 18_{30} Ps 119_{165}), **obstacle** to travel (Is 57_{14}), in path of the blind (Lv 19_{14}), Y. as a rock of **stumbling** (צוּר מִכְשׁוֹל) leading to ruin (Is 8_{14}), stumbling alw. implying falling, <SUBJ> היה *be* Ezk 7_{19}. <NOM CL> אין מכשול *there is no stumbling* 1QH 10_{18}, [אין] כול [נגע ומ]כשול בעדתכם *there is not any stroke or stumbling in your congregation* 11QM 1.2_{13}, אֵין לָמוֹ מִכְשׁוֹל *there is not to them any,* i.e. they have no, *cause of stumbling* Ps 119_{165}.

<OBJ> נתן *give, place* Lv 19_{14} Jr 6_{21} Ezk 3_{20} 14_{3} Si 47_{23}, שׂים *place* Ezk $14_{4.7}$ 1QH 4_{15} 1QS 2_{12}, רום hi. *lift up,* i.e. remove, from way Is 57_{14}, רבה hi. *increase* Ezk 21_{20} (or em. הַמְּכְשָׁלִים *those made to stumble,* i.e. כשל ho. ptc.).

<CSTR> מִכְשׁוֹל לֵב *stumbling of heart* 1 S 25_{31}, מִכְשׁוֹל עָוֹן *stumbling block of iniquity* Ezk 18_{30} 44_{12} 4QapJoseph[b] 8_{7} ([מכש]ול עון) 4QHod[b] 7_{9} (עוון), עֲוֹנָם *of their iniquity* Ezk 7_{19} $14_{3.4.7}$ 1QH 4_{15} (עוונם), מכשול עוונו *stumbling block of his iniquity* 1QS $2_{12.17}$; צוּר מִכְשׁוֹל *rock of,* i.e. that causes, *stumbling* Is 8_{14} 4Q Béat 22_{9} ([מכ]שול), נגף מכשול perh. *obstacle of,* i.e. that causes, *stumbling* 4Q418 168_{2}, נגע *affliction of* 1QH 16_{15}, זקי *fetters of* 1QH 8_{35}.

<PREP> לְ as or introducing predicate, + היה *be* 1 S 25_{31} Ezk 18_{30} 44_{12} 1QH 9_{21} ([הייתי]) perh. 4QapJoseph[b] 8_{7} ([למכש]ול) 4QHod[b] 7_{9}; of direction, *(in)to,* + נתן *give* 1QH 9_{27} ([ותתן]), בוש *be put to shame* Si $4_{22(C)}$ (למכשול לך *to your stumbling*); of instrument, *by (means of),* + כשל ni. *stumble* Si $4_{22(A)}$; בְּ of cause, *on account of,* + סוג ni. *turn aside* 1QS 2_{17}; *against,* + כשל *stumble* Jr 6_{21}; כְּ *as,* + היה *be* 4Q415 11_{6} 4Q418 167_{7} ([יהיה]).

<COLL> נֶגֶף ‖ מִכְשׁוֹל *striking* Is 8_{14}; + פּוּקָה *staggering,* i.e. qualm of conscience 1 S 25_{31}, גִּלּוּל *idol* Ezk $14_{3.4.7}$ 44_{12} 1QH 4_{15} 1QS 2_{17}; מכשול מחוקי בריתיך *stumbling from the statutes of your covenant* 1QH 16_{15}, מכשול לפניו *a stumbling block before him* 4Q415 11_{6} 4Q418 167_{7} ([לפנ]יו).

<SYN> נֶגֶף *striking.**

⇒ כשל *stumble.*

***מכשל** vb. **Hi. bring down to destruction,** <SUBJ> Y. Zp 1_{3} (if em. וְהַמַּכְשֵׁלוֹת אֶת־הָרְשָׁעִים *and the stumbling blocks with the wicked* to וְהִמְכְּשַׁלְתִּי אֶת־הָרְשָׁעִים *and I will bring the wicked down to destruction*). <OBJ> רָשָׁע *wicked* Zp 1_{3} (if em.; see Subj.).

⇒ cf. מכך *sink* and כשל *stumble.*

מַכְשֵׁלָה 2 n.f. **ruin**—pl. מַכְשֵׁלוֹת—**1. ruin,** <NOM CL> הַמַּכְשֵׁלָה הַזֹּאת תַּחַת יָדֶךָ *this ruin shall be under your hand,* i.e. rule Is 3_{6}. <ADJ> זֹאת *this* Is 3_{6}.

2. stumbling block, <OBJ> סוף *make an end of* Zp 1_{3} (or em. וְהִכְשַׁלְתִּי *and I will cause to stumble* or וְהִמְכַּשַׁלְתִּי *and I will bring down to destruction,* from מכשל).

⇒ כשל *stumble.*

מִכְתָּב 9.0.0.1 n.m. **writing**—cstr. מִכְתַּב—**1. writing, script,** <NOM CL> הַמִּכְתָּב מִכְתַּב אֱלֹהִים הוּא *the writing was the writing of God* Ex 32_{16}. <CSTR> מִכְתַּב אֱלֹהִים *writing of God* Ex 32_{16}. <PREP> בְּ *in, by (means of),* + עבר hi. *cause to pass,* i.e. make proclamation Ezr 1_{1} 2 C 36_{22}. <COLL> מַעֲשֶׂה ‖ מִכְתָּב *work* Ex 32_{16}; + קוֹל *voice,* i.e. proclamation Ezr 1_{1} 2 C 36_{22}.

2. (piece of) writing, document, perh. **inscription** (Ex 32_{16} 39_{30} Dt 10_{4} Ezr 1_{1}),* i.e. composition (Is 38_{9}), letter (2 C 21_{12} Arad ost. 40_{12}), instructions (2 C 35_{4}), perh. sometimes specifically of writing on papyrus,* <SUBJ> בוא *come* 2 C 21_{12}. <OBJ> כתב *write* Ex 39_{30} Is 10_{1} (if em. וּמְכַתְּבִים עָמָל כִּתֵּבוּ *and writers [who] have kept writing distress* to וּמִכְתְּבֵי[־ם] עָמָל כִּתֵּבוּ *and they [who] keep writing documents of distress*),* בקשׁ pi. *seek* Arad ost. 40_{12}, נתן *give* Arad ost. 40_{9} ([המכתבם]) 40_{12} ([נתתי]), ידע *know (of)* Arad ost. 40_{9} ([המכתבם]). <CSTR> מִכְתַּב שְׁלֹמֹה *writing of Solomon* 2 C 35_{4}, מִכְתַּב פִּתּוּחֵי *writing of the engravings of* a signet Ex 39_{30},

[וּמִכְתְּבֵין־ם] עָמָל *documents of distress* Is 10$_{1}$ (if em.; see Obj.). <ADJ> רִאשׁוֹן *first* Dt 10$_{4}$. <PREP> בְּ *in, according to*, + כון ni. *prepare oneself* 2 C 35$_{4(Kt)}$ (Qr כון hi. *prepare*; mss כְּ *according to*); כְּ *as, according to*, + כתב *write* Dt 10$_{4}$. <COLL> מִכְתָּב לְחִזְקִיָּהוּ *a writing of Hezekiah* Is 38$_{9}$ (or em. מִכְתָּם *Miktam*), [המכתבם] מאדם *the letters from Edom* Arad ost. 40$_{9}$.

<SYN> §1 מַעֲשֶׂה *work*.*

⇒ כתב *write*.

[מִכְתָּה] 1 n.f. **fragment**—sf. מִכְתָּתוֹ—of smashed pot, used collectively, <PREP> בְּ of place, *in*, + מצא ni. *be found* Is 30$_{14}$.

⇒ כתת *crush*.

מִכְתָּם I 6 n.[m.] **Miktam,** in psalm titles, perh. designation of a particular kind of psalm, perh. in ref. to writing on a tablet,* <COLL> מִכְתָּם לְדָוִד *a Miktam of/to/for David* Ps 16$_{1}$ 60$_{1}$, לְדָוִד מִכְתָּם *of/to/ for David, a Miktam* Ps 56$_{1}$ 57$_{1}$ 58$_{1}$ 59$_{1}$, מִכְתָּם לְחִזְקִיָּהוּ *a Miktam of Hezekiah* Is 38$_{9}$ (if em. מִכְתָּב *writing*).*

*מִכְתָּם II 6 n.[m.] **secret prayer,** in psalm titles, <COLL> מִכְתָּם לְדָוִד *a secret prayer of/to/for David* Ps 16$_{1}$ 60$_{1}$, לְדָוִד מִכְתָּם *of/to/ for David, a secret prayer* Ps 56$_{1}$ 57$_{1}$ 58$_{1}$ 59$_{1}$, מִכְתָּם לְחִזְקִיָּהוּ *a secret prayer of Hezekiah* Is 38$_{9}$ (if em. מִכְתָּב *writing*).

*מִכְתָּם III 6 n.[m.] **inscription** on stone slab, in psalm titles, <COLL> מִכְתָּם לְדָוִד *an inscribed psalm of/to/for David* Ps 16$_{1}$ 60$_{1}$, לְדָוִד מִכְתָּם *of/to/for David, an inscribed psalm* Ps 56$_{1}$ 57$_{1}$ 58$_{1}$ 59$_{1}$, מִכְתָּם לְחִזְקִיָּהוּ *an inscribed psalm of Hezekiah* Is 38$_{9}$ (if em. מִכְתָּב *writing*).

*מִכְתָּם IV 6 n.[m.] **gold-lettered inscription,** in psalm titles, <COLL> מִכְתָּם לְדָוִד *a gold-lettered inscription of/to/for David* Ps 16$_{1}$ 60$_{1}$, לְדָוִד מִכְתָּם *of/to/ for David, a gold-lettered inscription* Ps 56$_{1}$ 57$_{1}$ 58$_{1}$ 59$_{1}$, מִכְתָּם לְחִזְקִיָּהוּ *a gold-lettered inscription of Hezekiah* Is 38$_{9}$ (if em. מִכְתָּב *writing*).

⇒ כֶּתֶם *gold*.

*מִכְתָּם V 6 n.[m.] **song sung to the capped reed pipe,** in psalm titles, <COLL> מִכְתָּם לְדָוִד *a song for the flute of/to/for David* Ps 16$_{1}$ 60$_{1}$, לְדָוִד מִכְתָּם *of/to/ for David, a song for the flute* Ps 56$_{1}$ 57$_{1}$ 58$_{1}$ 59$_{1}$, מִכְתָּם לְחִזְקִיָּהוּ *a song for the flute of Hezekiah* Is 38$_{9}$ (if em. מִכְתָּב *writing*).

מַכְתֵּשׁ I 2 n.m. **mortar, hollow, 1. mortar,** <PREP> בְּ of place, *in*, + כתשׁ *pound* Pr 27$_{22}$.

2. hollow, geographical feature, perh. lit. 'molar tooth', <OBJ> בקע *split open* Jg 15$_{19}$. <PREP> מִן of direction, *from*, + יצא (of water) *go out* Jg 15$_{19}$. <COLL> הַמַּכְתֵּשׁ אֲשֶׁר־בַּלֶּחִי *the hollow that is at Lehi* Jg 15$_{19}$.*

⇒ כתשׁ *pound*.

מַכְתֵּשׁ II 1 pl.n. **Machtesh,** a district of Jerusalem, appar. a centre for silverworkers and traders, lit. 'the mortar' or 'the hollow' (as מַכְתֵּשׁ I), perh. at the northern end of the Tyropoean Valley, <CSTR> יֹשְׁבֵי הַמַּכְתֵּשׁ *inhabitants of the Machtesh* Zp 1$_{11}$.

⇒ (?) כתשׁ *pound*.

*[מֵל], [מַל] n.[m.] **hair,** <PREP> לְ of benefit, *to, for*, + שׁרר *abound* with oil Is 57$_{9}$ (if em. וַתָּשֻׁרִי *and you journeyed* to וַתָּשֹׁרִי [qal] or וַתְּשִׁרִי [hi.] *and you abounded*, and em. לַמֶּלֶךְ *to the king* to לְמַלֵּךְ or לְמִלֵּךְ *for your hair*).

⇒ (?) מלל I *wither, hang down*.

מלא 250.8.46.2 vb. **be full—Qal** 101.1.22 Pf. מָלֵא (מְלָאוֹ), מָלְאָה, מָלֵאתָ, מָלֵאתִי (מָלֵתִי), מָלְאוּ (מָלוּ, מָלֵאוּ); impf. 3fs תִּמְלָאֵמוֹ, יִמָּלְאוּ; + waw וּמָלְאָה, וּמָלְאוּ; וַיִּמָּלְאוּ; impv. מִלְאוּ; ptc. מָלֵא, מְלֵאִים; inf. מְלֹאת (מְלֹאות, Q מלואת, Q מליאות, Q מולאת, Q מולואת, Q מולות)—**1a. be full,** <SUBJ> Israelites Zc 9$_{15}$, כְּלִי *vessel* 2 K 4$_{6}$, גַּת *winepress* Jl 4$_{13}$, שֵׂפֶק *sufficiency* Jb 20$_{22}$. <PREP> כְּ *as*, + מִזְרָק *bowl* Zc 9$_{15}$ (or del. כַּמִּזְרָק), זָוִית *corner* Zc 9$_{15}$ (or del. כְּזָוִית). <COLL> מלא ‖ שׁוק hi. *overflow with* Jl 4$_{13}$.

b. be fully set, determined, <SUBJ> לֵב *heart* Ec 8$_{11}$. <PREP> בְּ of place, *within*, + בֵּן *son* of human Ec 8$_{11}$. <COLL> מָלֵא ... לַעֲשׂוֹת רָע *it is fully set ... to do evil* Ec 8$_{11}$.

c. **be full of water, overflow,** <SUBJ> יַרְדֵּן *Jordan* Jos 3_{15} 4QapJoshua^{b} 12_6. <OBJ> מַיִם *water* 4QapJoshua^{b} 12_6 (מי[ם]). <PREP> עַל *upon, over,* + גָּדָה *bank* Jos 3_{15} 4QapJoshua^{b} 12_6. <COLL> מלא + שֶׁטֶף *flood* 4QapJoshua^{b} 12_6; + noun used adverbially, יוֹם *day* Jos 3_{15}.

d. **be satisfied,** <SUBJ> עֶבֶד *servant* Meṣad Ḥashavyahu ost. 1_{12} (השב נא את בגדי ואמלא *return my garment, and I shall be satisfied;* others אם לא *if [it is] not [an obligation]*).

2. with object of material, **a. be full of, be filled with,** <SUBJ> Y. Ezk 16_{30} (if em. אֻמְלָלָה *it is enfeebled* to אֶמְלָא *I am full of*), עַם *people* Is 2_6, Elihu Jb 32_{18}, Jeremiah Jr 6_{11}, Job Jb 36_{17}, Joshua Dt 34_9, Micah Mc 3_8, בֵּן *son* Dt 34_9, עָשִׁיר *rich one* Mc 6_{12}, רָשָׁע *wicked one* Pr 12_{21}, יָד *hand* Is 1_{15}, יָמִין *right hand* Ps 26_{10} 48_{11}, כֶּסֶל *thigh* Ps 38_8, מָתְנַיִם *loins* Is 21_3, פֶּה *mouth* Ps 10_7, שָׂפָה *lip* Is 30_{17}, פָּנִים *face* of world Is 14_{21} 27_6 (unless both §5), עֶצֶם *bone* Jb 20_{11}, אֶרֶץ *earth, land* Gn 6_{13} Lv 19_{29} Is 11_9 Jr 23_{10} 46_{12} 51_5 Ezk 7_{23} Ps 33_5 104_{24} 119_{64} 4QTime 1.2_4, עִיר *city* Ezk 7_{23} 9_9, הַר *mountain* 2 K 6_{17}, גֹּרֶן *threshing floor* Jl 2_{24}, בַּיִת *house* Ex 8_{17} Jg 16_{27} 2 K 5_{13} Is 13_{21}, חָצֵר *court* Ezk 10_4, שֻׁלְחָן *table* Is 28_8 perh. Jb 36_{16} (unless subj. נַחַת *spread* of table), עֲטִין *pail* Jb 21_{24}, מַיִם *water* Is 15_9, מַחְשָׁךְ *dark place* Ps 74_{20}, מִבְחַר *choicest* of valleys Is 22_7.

<OBJ> אִישׁ *man* Jg 16_{27}, אִשָּׁה *woman* Jg 16_{27}, עֹנֵן *soothsayer* Is 2_6, קֹסֵם *diviner* Is 2_6 (if em. מִקֶּדֶם *from the east* to קֹסְמִים), מְעַקֵּד *magician* Is 2_6 (if em. מִקֶּדֶם to מְעַקְּדִים), מְנָאֵף *adulterer* Jr 23_{10}, מֵרַע *evildoer* Jr 23_{10} (if ins. מְרֵעִים), רוּחַ *spirit* Dt 34_9 Mc 3_8 (or del. אֶת־רוּחַ י׳ *the spirit of Y.*), דָּם *blood(shed)* Is 1_{15} 15_9, חָמָס *violence* Gn 6_{13} Ezk 7_{23} Mc 6_{12} Ps 74_{20} (if em.; see below), רַע *evil* Pr 12_{21}, זִמָּה *wickedness* Lv 19_{29}, אָשָׁם *guilt* Jr 51_5, מֻטֶּה *injustice* Ezk 9_9, אָלָה *curse* Ps 10_7, כָּזָב *lie* 4QBéat 17_3 (כזב[ים]), מִרְמָה *deceit* Ps 10_7, תֹּךְ *oppression* Ps 10_7, שֹׁחַד *bribe* Ps 26_{10}, צְוָחָה *outcry* Jr 46_{12}, חֶסֶד *loyalty* Ps 33_5 119_{64}.

תְּנוּבָה *fruit* Is 27_6 (unless §5), בַּר *grain* Jl 2_{24}, חָלָב *milk* Jb 21_{24}, דֶּשֶׁן *fatness* Jb 36_{16}, קִנְיָן *creatures* Ps 104_{24}, עָרֹב *swarm* Ex 8_{17}, אֹחַ *owl* Is 13_{21}, סוּס *horse* 2 K 6_{17}, רֶכֶב *chariot* 2 K 6_{17} Is 22_7, עִיר *city* Is 14_{21} (unless §5), עָנָן *cloud* 2 C 5_{13}, נָוֶה *habitation* Ps 74_{20} (or em. נְאוֹת חָמָס *the habitations of violence* to אֲנָחָה וְחָמָס *sighing and violence*), קִיא *vomit* Is 28_8, דֵּעָה *knowledge* Is 11_9 4QTime 1.2_4, חַלְחָלָה *anguish* Is 21_3, זַעַם *indignation* Is 30_{17}, חֵמָה *anger* Jr 6_{11}, לִבָּה *anger* Ezk 16_{30} (if em.; see Subj.), אֲנָחָה *sighing* Ps 74_{20} (if em.; see above), דִּין *judgment* Jb 36_{17}, מִשְׁפָּט *judgment* Ezk 7_{23} Mc 3_8, צֶדֶק *righteousness* Ps 48_{11}, כֹּחַ *strength* Mc 3_8, גְּבוּרָה *might* Mc 3_8, עֲלוּמִים *vigour* Jb 20_{11}, נֹגַהּ *brightness* Ezk 10_4, נִקְלֶה *burning* Ps 38_8, מִלָּה *word* Jb 32_{18}, מִקְסָם *divination* Is 2_6 (if em. מִקֶּדֶם), תְּהִלָּה *praise* 4QTime 1.2_4.

<PREP> מִפְּנֵי *on account of,* + בָּשָׂר *flesh* Gn 6_{13}.

<COLL> מלא || שׁוק hi. *overflow with* Jl 2_{24}.

b. **have one's fill of, be sated with,** <SUBJ> נֶפֶשׁ *soul,* i.e. desire Ex 15_9, חֶרֶב *sword* of Y. Is 34_6. <OBJ> Israelites Ex 15_9, דָּם *blood* Is 34_6. <COLL> מלא + דשן hothpaal *make oneself fat* Is 34_6.

3a. **be fulfilled, accomplished, completed,** <SUBJ> יוֹם *day* Gn 25_{24} 29_{21} $50_{3.3}$ Lv 8_{33} $12_{4.6}$ Nm $6_{5.13}$ 1 S 18_{26} 2 S 7_{12}||1 C 17_{11} Jr 25_{34} Ezk 5_2 Lm 4_{18} Est 1_5 2_{12} Dn10_3 1QS 7_{20} 8_{26} 4QD^{f} 2_{13} 4QNidd 2.1_3 ([ימים]) 4QRitMar 102_1 4QRitPur 21.7_2 (במילא[ת]) 27.7_1 11.10_2 (במילא[ת]) CD 10_1, שָׁבוּעַ *week* Dn 10_3, חֹדֶשׁ *month* Est 2_{12}, שָׁנָה *year* Lv 25_{30} Jr 25_{12} 29_{10} 1QS $6_{17.18.21.21}$ $7_{20.22}$ 8_{26} 1QSa 1_{10} 4QS^{d} 7_2 4QSD 1.2_7 (במלא[ת]), צָבָא *military service* Is 40_2.

<PREP> לְ of benefit, *to, for* 4QNidd 2.1_3 4QRitPur 21.7_2 (במילא[ת לו]) 27.7_1 ([לו]) 11.10_2 (במילא[ת לו]), + אִישׁ *man* 1QS 7_{20} 8_{26} 4QSD 1.2_7 (במלא[ת] ... [אי]ש), אָב *father* Gn 50_3, אֶזְרָח *native* 1QSa 1_{10}, נדב htp. ptc. *one who volunteers* 1QS $6_{17.18.21.21}$, בָּבֶל *Babylon* Jr 29_{10}, בַּיִת *house* Lv 25_{30}.

<COLL> מלא + בוא *come* Lm 4_{18}, קרב *draw near* Lm 4_{18}; יוֹם מְלֹאת יְמֵי מִלֻּאֵיכֶם *the day when the days of your ordination are accomplished* Lv 8_{33}, sim. Nm 6_{13}.

b. inf. as noun, **fulfilment,** <OBJ> שִׂים *place* 4QShir^{b} 63.3_2. <CSTR> מולות פועלות *the fulfilment of the deeds of* the blameless 4QShir^{b} 63.3_2.

4. **fill,** <SUBJ> Y. Jr 23_{24}, אָדָם *human being* Gn 1_{28}, Noah Gn 9_1, בֵּן *son* Gn 9_1, לֵב *heart* Est 7_5, נֶפֶשׁ *soul,* i.e. creature Gn 1_{22}, תַּנִּין *sea monster* Gn 1_{22}, עוֹף *bird* Gn

1$_{22}$, אַרְבֶּה *locust* Ex 10$_{6}$, שׁוּל *skirt of robe* Is 6$_{1}$, עָנָן *cloud* 1 K 8$_{10}$ Ezk 10$_{3}$, כָּבוֹד *glory* Ex 40$_{34.35}$ Nm 14$_{21}$ (if em. יִמָּלֵא *it will be filled* [i.e. ni.] to יְמַלֵּא) 1 K 8$_{11}$||2 C 5$_{14}$ Ezk 43$_{5}$ 44$_{4}$ Ps 72$_{19}$ (if em. יִמָּלֵא to יְמַלֵּא) 2 C 7$_{1.2}$ Si 42$_{16(M)}$ (כ[בוד]) 4QBark^{a} 1.1$_{3}$, תְּהִלָּה *praise* Hb 3$_{3}$, אֲשֶׁר *(one) who* Est 7$_{5}$; subj. not specified, Jr 51$_{11}$.

<OBJ> אֶרֶץ *earth* Gn 1$_{28}$ 9$_{1}$ Nm 14$_{21}$ (if em.; see Subj.) Jr 23$_{24}$ Hb 3$_{3}$ Ps 72$_{19}$ (if em.; see Subj.) 4QBark^{a} 1.1$_{3}$ ([כל הארץ]), שָׁמַיִם *heaven* Jr 23$_{24}$, מַיִם *water* Gn 1$_{22}$, בַּיִת *house* Ex 10$_{6}$ 1 K 8$_{10.11}$||2 C 5$_{14}$ Ezk 43$_{5}$ 44$_{4}$ 2 C 7$_{1.2}$, מִשְׁכָּן *tabernacle* Ex 40$_{34.35}$, הֵיכָל *temple* Is 6$_{1}$, חָצֵר *court* Ezk 10$_{3}$, שֶׁלֶט *quiver* Jr 51$_{11}$ (or em. מִלְאוּ *fill* to מַלְאוּ *make full ready* [pi. §13]), מַעֲשֶׂה *work* Si 42$_{16(M)}$.

<COLL> מלא || כסה pi. *cover* Hb 3$_{3}$, ברר hi. I *cleanse* or II *sharpen* Jr 51$_{11}$; + רבה *multiply* Gn 1$_{22.28}$ 9$_{1}$, פרה *be fruitful* Gn 1$_{22.28}$ 9$_{1}$; מְלָאוֹ לִבּוֹ לַעֲשׂוֹת כֵּן *his heart has filled him*, i.e. he dares, *to do such a thing* Est 7$_{5}$.

5. fill with, a. with objects, both of thing filled and that with which it is filled, <SUBJ> Y. Ps 110$_{6}$ (or em.; see Obj.), Israel(ites) Is 27$_{6}$ (unless §2) Jr 19$_{4}$, עַם *people* 1 K 18$_{34}$ Ezk 30$_{11}$, Nebuchadnezzar Ezk 30$_{11}$, בֵּן *son* Is 14$_{21}$ (unless §2), of Israel Jr 16$_{18}$, בַּיִת *house* of Judah Ezk 8$_{17}$, עָרִיץ *terrible one* Ezk 30$_{11}$; subj. not specified, Ezk 28$_{16}$ (or em. מִלֵּאתָ *you filled*, i.e. pi.).

<OBJ> 1. thing filled, כַּד *jar* 1 K 18$_{34}$, פָּנִים *face* of world Is 14$_{21}$ 27$_{6}$ (unless both §2), אֶרֶץ *land* Ezk 8$_{17}$ 30$_{11}$, נַחֲלָה *inheritance* Jr 16$_{18}$, גּוֹי *nation* Ps 110$_{6}$ (or em.; see below), מָקוֹם *place* Jr 19$_{4}$, תָּוֶךְ *middle* Ezk 28$_{16}$ (or em.; see Subj.). 2. filled with, חָלָל *slain one* Ezk 30$_{11}$, גְּוִיָּה *corpse* Ps 110$_{6}$ (or em. מָלֵא גְוִיּוֹת *he fills [them] with corpses* to בִּגְוִיּוֹת מִלֵּא גֵאָיוֹת *with corpses he fills the valleys* [pi. §1b] or מִלֵּא גְּוִיּוֹת *he heaps up corpses* [pi. §12] or מְלֵא גֵוות *full of majesty*),* דָּם *blood* Jr 19$_{4}$, מַיִם *water* 1 K 18$_{34}$, תְּנוּבָה *fruit* Is 27$_{6}$ (unless §2), עִיר *city* Is 14$_{21}$ (unless del. עָרִים), תּוֹעֵבָה *abomination* Jr 16$_{18}$, חָמָס *violence* Ezk 8$_{17}$ 28$_{16}$ (or em.; see Subj.).

<PREP> בְּ of accompaniment, *in, with*, + רֹב *abundance* of trade Ezk 28$_{16}$ (or em.; see Subj.). <COLL> מלא || חלל pi. *profane* Jr 16$_{18}$.

b. with obj. and prep., <SUBJ> בַּיִת *house* of Israel Ex 16$_{32(Sam)}$ (מִלְאוּ *fill*; MT מְלֹא *fullness of*). <OBJ> עֹמֶר *omer* Ex 16$_{32(Sam)}$. <PREP> מִן *of, with*, + מָן *manna* Ex 16$_{32(Sam)}$.

6. with obj. יָד, lit. 'fill the hand', **consecrate, ordain** oneself, <SUBJ> בֵּן *son* of Levi Ex 32$_{29}$. <OBJ> יָד *hand* Ex 32$_{29}$. <PREP> לְ of benefit, *to, for*, + Y. Ex 32$_{29}$. <COLL> מלא יָד + adverb, הַיּוֹם *today* Ex 32$_{29}$.

Also 1QSa 1$_{12}$ 5Q16 2$_{3}$ ([ ]מלא) 6$_{1}$.

<SYN> §1a, 2a שׁוק hi. *overflow with*; §4 כסה pi. *cover* Hb 3$_{3}$, ברר hi. I *cleanse* or II *sharpen*; §5 חלל pi. *profane*.

Ni. 36.1.4 Pf. נִמְלָא; impf. יִמָּלֵא, 3fs תִּמָּלֵא, תִּמָּלְאִי, יִמָּלְאוּ (יִמָּלְאוּן), אִמָּלְאָה; + waw וַיִּמָּלֵא, 3fs וַתִּמָּלֵא, וַתִּמָּלְאִי; inf. Q המלא—**1. be filled,** <SUBJ> Tyre Ezk 26$_{2}$ (or em. אִמָּלְאָה הָחֳרָבָה *I am filled, she has been laid waste* to הַמְּלֵאָה הָחֳרָבָה *the full one has been laid waste*, or מְלֵאַת הַחֲרֵבָה *the full one of ruin*, i.e. the one full of ruins) 27$_{25}$, אֶרֶץ *land* Ps 80$_{10(mss)}$ (L pi.), בַּיִת *house* 2 K 10$_{21}$, נַחֲלָה *inheritance* 4Q418 88$_{8}$ (נ[ח]לתכה), חֶסְרוֹן *deficiency* Ec 1$_{15}$ (if em. לְהִמָּנוֹת *to be counted* to לְהִמָּלוֹת *to be filled*). <PREP> בְּ of accompaniment, *in, with*, + אֱמֶת *truth* 4Q418 88$_{8}$. <COLL> מלא ni. + כבד *be heavy* Ezk 27$_{25}$; וַיִּמָּלֵא ... פֶּה לָפֶה *and it was filled ... from one end to the other* 2 K 10$_{21}$.

2. be full of, filled with, a. with object of material, <SUBJ> Y. Ezk 16$_{30}$ (if em. אֻמְלָלָה *it is enfeebled* to אִמָּלֵא *I am filled*), Haman Est 3$_{5}$ 5$_{9}$, Hiram 1 K 7$_{14}$, Oholibah Ezk 23$_{33}$, פֶּה *mouth* Ps 71$_{8}$ 126$_{2}$ Pr 20$_{17}$, לָשׁוֹן *tongue* Ps 126$_{2}$, רֹאשׁ *head* Ca 5$_{2}$, קְוֻצּוֹת *locks of hair* Ca 5$_{2}$, בֶּטֶן *stomach* Ps 17$_{14}$ (if em. תְּמַלֵּא *may you fill*, i.e. pi., to תִּמָּלֵא), גִּיד *sinew* 4QD^{g} 1.2$_{1}$, אֶרֶץ *earth, land* Gn 6$_{11}$ Ex 1$_{7}$ appar. Nm 14$_{21}$ (or em. יְמַלֵּא *it will fill*, i.e. qal) 2 K 3$_{20}$ Is 2$_{7.7.7}$ Ezk 9$_{9}$ Hb 2$_{14}$ appar. Ps 72$_{19}$ (or em. יְמַלֵּא), בַּיִת *house* Is 6$_{4}$ Ezk 10$_{4}$, אָסָם *storehouse* Pr 3$_{10}$, חֶדֶר *room* Pr 24$_{4}$, רְחוֹב *broad place* Zc 8$_{5}$, נַחַל *wadi* 2 K 3$_{17}$, נֵבֶל *jar* Jr 13$_{12.12}$, עָב *cloud* Ec 11$_{3}$.

<OBJ> אֱלִיל *idol* Is 2$_{7}$, בֵּן *son* of Israel Ex 1$_{7}$, יֶלֶד *male child* Zc 8$_{5}$, יַלְדָּה *girl* Zc 8$_{5}$, סוּס *horse* Is 2$_{7}$, זָהָב *gold*, Is 2$_{7}$, כֶּסֶף *silver* Is 2$_{7}$, הוֹן *wealth* Pr 24$_{4}$, מַיִם *water* 2 K 3$_{17.20}$, גֶּשֶׁם *rain* Ec 11$_{3}$, טַל *dew* Ca 5$_{2}$, רְסִיס *drop* Ca 5$_{2}$, יַיִן *wine* Jr 13$_{12.12}$, עָשָׁן *smoke* Is 6$_{4}$, עָנָן *cloud* Ezk 10$_{4}$, חָצָץ *gravel* Pr 20$_{17}$, דָּם *blood* Ezk 9$_{9}$ 4QD^{g} 1.2$_{1}$, חָמָס *violence* Gn 6$_{11}$, שִׁכָּרוֹן *drunkenness* Ezk 23$_{33}$, חָכְמָה *wisdom* 1 K 7$_{14}$, תְּבוּנָה *understanding* 1 K 7$_{14}$, דַּעַת

knowledge 1 K 7_{14}, כָּבוֹד *glory* Nm 14_{21} (or em.; see Subj.) Ps 72_{19} (or em.; see Subj.), תִּפְאֶרֶת *glory* Ps 71_{8}, תְּהִלָּה *praise* Ps 71_{8}, שְׂחוֹק *laughter* Ps 126_{2}, רִנָּה *joyful shout* Ps 126_{2}, יָגוֹן *sorrow* Ezk 23_{33}, חֵמָה *anger* Est 3_{5} 5_{9}, לִבָּה *anger* Ezk 16_{30} (if em.; see Subj.), צפן pass. ptc. *stored thing* Ps 17_{14} (if em.; see Subj.), שָׂבָע *plenty* Pr 3_{10}.

<PREP> בְּ of instrument, *by (means of), with*, + דַּעַת *knowledge* Pr 24_{4}.

<COLL> מלא ni. + פרץ *break through*, i.e. burst Pr 3_{10}; + adverb or noun used adverbially, אָז *then* Ps 126_{2}, אַחַר *afterwards* Pr 20_{17}, יוֹם *day* Ps 71_{8}; תִּמָּלֵא הָאָרֶץ לָדַעַת אֶת־כְּבוֹד י׳ *the earth will be filled with knowing the glory of Y.* Hb 2_{14}.

b. with preposition, <SUBJ> אָפִיק *channel* Ezk 32_{6}. <PREP> מִן *of, with*, + פַּרְעֹה *Pharaoh* Ezk 32_{6}, מֶלֶךְ *king* Ezk 32_{6}, דָּם *blood* Ezk 32_{6} (if em. מִמֶּךָּ *of you* to מִדָּמֵךְ *of your blood*).

3a. have one's fill, be satisfied, <SUBJ> נֶפֶשׁ *soul*, i.e. appetite Ec 6_{7}; subj. not specified, 4Q418 81_{19}. <COLL> מלא ni. + שׂבע *be satisfied* 4Q418 81_{19}.

b. with preposition, **have one's fill of, be sated with,** <SUBJ> אֹזֶן *ear* Ec 1_{8}. <PREP> מִן *of, with*, + שׁמע inf. *hearing* Ec 1_{8}. <COLL> מלא ni. || שׂבע *be satisfied* Ec 1_{8}.

4. be full in number, be complete, <SUBJ> יוֹם *day* Ex 7_{25}, צָבָא *army* 1QM 5_{3}. <COLL> בהמלא צבאם להשלים מערכת *when their army is full (enough) to complete a formation* 1QM 5_{3}.

5. be fully with, fully trust, unless pi., <SUBJ> לֵב *heart* Si 4_{17}. <PREP> בְּ introducing object, + חָכְמוֹת *wisdom* Si 4_{17}. <COLL> עת ימלא לבו *the time when his heart fully trusts* Si 4_{17}.

6. be paid in full, <SUBJ> תְּמוּרָה *recompense* Jb 15_{32} (or em. תִּמָּל ... זְמוֹרָתוֹ *his branch ... will wither*, from מלל). <PREP> בְּ of time, *in, on*, + יוֹם *day* Jb 15_{32} (בְּלֹא יוֹמוֹ *when it is not his day*; or em.; see Subj.).

7. arm oneself with, <SUBJ> אִישׁ *man* 2 S 23_{7} (or em. אִם לֹא *except [with]*; or em. יִמָּלֵא *let him arm himself with* to יְמַלֵּא *let him make full ready* [pi. §13]). <OBJ> בַּרְזֶל *iron* 2 S 23_{7} (or em.; see Subj.), עֵץ *wood*, i.e. shaft, of spear 2 S 23_{7} (or em.; see Subj.).

8. be fulfilled, <COLL> אַל־תֹּאמַר לִפְנֵי הַמָּלְאָךְ *do not say before it has been fulfilled by you* Ec 5_{5} (if em. הַמַּלְאָךְ *the messenger*).

Also 4QMyst[c] 7_{2} (מאל[ת]).

<SYN> §3b שׂבע *be satisfied*.

Pi. 111.7.20.2 Pf. מִלֵּא (מִלָּא), מִלֵּאתָ (מִלֵּאתֶנִי) מִלֵּאתִי, מִלֵּאתֶם, (מִלְאוּהָ, מִלְאוּךָ, Q מלו) מִלְאוּ, (מִלֵּאתִיו, מִלֵּאתִיךָ) מִלֵּאנוּ; impf. יְמַלֵּא (יְמַלֵּה), 2ms תְּמַלֵּא, אֲמַלֵּא (אֲמַלְאֵהוּ); נְמַלֵּא, תְּמַלֶּאנָה 3fpl, יְמַלְאוּ; + waw וּמִלֵּא, וּמִלֵּאתָ, וּמִלֵּאתִי, וַיְמַלֵּא, וָאֲמַלֵּא, וַתְּמַלֵּא 3fs, וַיְמַלְאוּ; (וּמִלְאוּהָ) וּמִלְאוּ (וַיְמַלְאוּם), 3fpl וַתְּמַלֶּאנָה; impv. מַלֵּא, מַלְאוּ; ptc. מְמַלֵּא, מְמַלְאִים; inf. מַלֵּא (מַלְאָם), מַלְאוֹת (מַלֹּאת).

1a. fill, with object only of thing filled; but usu. thing with which it is filled is clear from context, <SUBJ> Y. Ps 81_{11} perh. Jb 20_{23} 1QM 17_{9} (unless §2a), Aramaeans 1 K 20_{27}, Israel(ites) Dt 6_{11} 2 K 3_{25} Ezk 7_{19}, Ben Sira Si 30_{25}, Manasseh 2 K 21_{16}, בַּת *daughter* Ex 2_{16}, נַעֲרָה *young woman* Gn 24_{16}, יֹשֵׁב *inhabitant* Jos 9_{13}, קֹצֵר *reaper* Ps 129_{7}, מְעַמֵּר *binder of sheaves* Ps 29_{7}, עבר ptc. *one who crosses* Is 23_{2} (מִלְאוּךְ *they filled you*; 1QIsa[a] מלאכיך *your messengers*), עזב ptc. *one who forsakes Y.* Is 65_{11}, גֶּפֶן *vine* Ps 89_{10} (mss ni.), חָכְמָה *wisdom* Pr 8_{21}, דֵּעָה *knowledge* 1QMyst 1.1_{7}, כָּבוֹד *glory* 4QNarrC 1_{8}, הָדָר *majesty* 4QMyst[a] 9_{3}.

<OBJ> פֶּה *mouth* Ps 81_{11}, מֵעָה *stomach* Ezk 7_{19}, בֶּטֶן *stomach* Jb 20_{23}, כַּף *hand* Ps 129_{7}, כַּד *jar* Gn 24_{16}, נֹאד *skin bottle* Jos 9_{13}, רַהַט *trough* Ex 2_{16}, מַצְרֵף *crucible* 1QM 17_{9} (unless §2a, and מצרפיו = *his fiery trials*), Tyre Is 23_{2}, תֵּבֵל *world* 1QMyst 1.1_{7}, אֶרֶץ *land* 1 K 20_{27} Ps 80_{10} (mss ni.) 4QNarrC 1_{8}, חֶלְקָה *plot of land* 2 K 3_{25}, מַיִם *water* 4QNarrC 1_{8}, בַּיִת *house* Dt 6_{11}, אוֹצָר *treasury* Pr 8_{21}, מִמְסָךְ *bowl of mixed wine* Is 65_{11}, יֶקֶב *wine-vat* Si 30_{25}(Segal) ([י]קב), חֹצֶן *fold of garment* Ps 129_{7}.

<PREP> לְ of benefit, *to, for*, + מְנִי *Fate* Is 65_{11}; כְּ *as*, + בֹּצֵר *harvester of grapes* Si 30_{25}; מִן *from*, + אֶחָד *one* (drop of water) perh. 4QNarrC 1_{8} (unless מאחד is adv. *secretly*).

<COLL> מלא pi. || שׂבע pi. *satisfy* Ezk 7_{19}; + סתם *stop up* 2 K 3_{25}, נחל hi. *cause to possess* Pr 8_{21}; + adverbial use of חֹדֶשׁ *(when) new* Jos 9_{13}, פֶּה *mouth*, i.e. end 2 K 21_{16} (פֶּה לָפֶה *from end to end*), מאחד perh. *secretly*

4QNarrC 1_{8} (unless *from one*).

b. fill with, (1) with objects both of thing filled and that with which it is filled, <SUBJ> Y. Ex 28_{3} 31_{3}||35_{31} 35_{35} Is 33_{5} Jr 13_{13} 15_{17} 51_{14} Ezk 32_{5} (unless §12a) 35_{8} Hg 2_{7} Jb 8_{21} Ps 17_{14} (or em. תִּמָּלֵא *may it be filled*, i.e. ni.) 83_{17} 107_{9} Jb 22_{18} Si 36_{19} 1QM 12_{12} 19_{4}, Philistines Gn 26_{15}, Elijah 1 K 18_{35}, Hagar Gn 21_{9}, Ishmael Jr 41_{9}, Job Jb 23_{4}, Manasseh 2 K 24_{4}, Nebuchadrezzar Jr 51_{34}, Samuel 1 S 16_{1}, אִישׁ *man* Ezk 9_{7} 10_{2}, בֵּן *son* of man Ezk 3_{3} 24_{4}, מֶלֶךְ *king* 2 K 23_{14} Jr 51_{34}, שַׂר *prince* Jb 3_{15}, נָגִיד *prince* of Tyre Ezk 28_{16} (if em. מָלוּ *they filled* to מִלֵּאתָ *you filled*, i.e. pi.), בַּיִת *house* of Israel Ezk 11_{6}, חָכָם *wise one* Jb 15_{2} (unless §11), חַטָּא *sinner* Pr 1_{13}, אַרְיֵה *lion* Na 2_{13}, רַע *evil* Si 37_{3}, אֲשֶׁר *one who* Gn 44_{1}; subj. not specified, Gn 42_{25} Jr 33_{5} Zp 1_{9} 2 C 16_{14}.

<OBJ> 1. thing or person filled, Babylon Jr 51_{14}, appar. Chaldaeans Jr 33_{5}, Jerusalem 2 K 24_{4}, Zion Is 33_{5} Si 36_{19}, Bezalel 31_{3}||35_{31} 35_{35}, Jeremiah Jr 15_{17}, Oholiab Ex 35_{35}, בֵּן *son* 31_{3}||35_{31} 35_{35}, מֶלֶךְ *king* Jr 13_{13}, כֹּהֵן *priest* Jr 13_{13}, נָבִיא *prophet* Jr 13_{13}, חָכָם *wise one* Ex 28_{3}, יֹשֵׁב *inhabitant* Jr 13_{13}, פֶּה *mouth* Jb 8_{21} 23_{4}, שָׂפָה *lip* Jb 8_{21}, פָּנִים *face* Ps 83_{17} Si 37_{3}, בֶּטֶן *stomach* Ps 17_{14} (or em.; see Subj.) Jb 15_{2} (unless §11), כָּרֵשׂ *stomach* Jr 51_{34}, מֵעֶה *stomach* Ezk 3_{3}, קֶרֶן *horn* 1 S 16_{1}, חֹפֶן *hollow of hand* Ezk 10_{2}, נֶפֶשׁ *soul*, i.e. person Ps 107_{9}, חֵמֶת *skin (bottle)* Gn 21_{9}, אַמְתַּחַת *sack* Gn 44_{1}, כְּלִי *baggage* Gn 42_{25}, סִיר *pot* Ezk 24_{4}, מִשְׁכָּב *bier* 2 C 16_{14}, בְּאֵר *well* Gn 26_{15}, בּוֹר *cistern* Jr 41_{9}, תְּעָלָה *trench* 1 K 18_{35}, חֹר *hole*, i.e. den Na 2_{13}, מְעֹנָה *den* Na 2_{13}, בַּיִת *house* Zp 1_{9} Hg 2_{7} Jb 3_{15} 22_{18} Pr 1_{13}, חָצֵר *court* Ezk 9_{7}, חוּץ *street* Ezk 11_{6}, אֶרֶץ *land* 1QM 12_{12} 19_{4}, הַר *mountain* Ezk 35_{8} (or del. אֶת־הָרָיו), גִּבְעָה *hill* Ezk 35_{8} (if del. אֶת־הָרָיו), גַּיְא *valley* Ezk 32_{5} (or §12a, if em. הַגְּאָיוֹת *the corpses*), מָקוֹם *place* 2 K 23_{14}, תָּוֶךְ *middle* Ezk 28_{16} (if em.; see Subj.), נַחֲלָה *inheritance* 1QM 12_{12} 19_{4}.

2. filled with, אָדָם *humans* Jr 51_{14} (or em. אָדָם to אֹיְבִים *enemies*), פֶּגֶר *corpse* Jr 33_{5}, חָלָל *slain one* Jr 41_{9} Ezk 9_{7} 11_{6} 35_{8}, דָּם *blood* 2 K 24_{4}, עֶצֶם *bone* 2 K 23_{14}, רוּחַ *spirit* Ex 28_{3} 31_{3}||35_{31}, בַּר *grain* Gn 42_{25}, אֹכֶל *food* Gn 44_{1}, מַעֲדָן *delicacy* Jr 51_{34}, בֹּשֶׂם *spice* 2 C 16_{14}, מְגִלָּה *scroll* Ezk 3_{3}, טְרֵפָה *prey* Na 2_{13}, שָׁלָל *spoil* Pr 1_{13}, שֶׁמֶן *oil* 1 S 16_{1}, מַיִם *water* Gn 21_{9} 1 K 18_{35}, עָפָר *dust* Gn 26_{15}, גַּחֶלֶת *coal* Ezk 10_{2}, כֶּסֶף *silver* Jb 3_{15}, חָכְמָה *wisdom* Ex 35_{35}, מִשְׁפָּט *justice* Is 33_{5}, צְדָקָה *righteousness* Is 33_{5}, כָּבוֹד *glory* Hg 2_{7} 1QM 12_{12} 19_{4}, הוֹד *splendour* Si $36_{19(B)}$, שְׂחוֹק *laughter* Jb 8_{21}, תְּרוּעָה *shouting* Jb 8_{21}, שִׁכָּרוֹן *drunkenness* Jr 13_{13}, תּוֹכַחַת *argument* Jb 23_{4}, זַעַם *indignation* Jr 15_{17}, מִרְמָה *deceit* Zp 1_{9}, תַּרְמִית *deceit* Si 37_{3}, חָמָס *violence* 28_{16} (if em.; see Subj.) Zp 1_{9}, קָלוֹן *shame* Ps 83_{17}, רָמוֹת *height* Ezk 32_{5}, קָדִים *east wind* Jb 15_{2} (unless §11), צפן pass. ptc. *stored thing* Ps 17_{14} (or em.; see Subj.), מִבְחַר *choicest* of bones Ezk 24_{4}, טוֹב *good thing* Ps 107_{9} Jb 22_{18}, בְּרָכָה *blessing* 1QM 12_{12} 19_{4}, זַן *kind* 2 C 16_{14}.

<PREP> בְּ of accompaniment, *in, with*, + רֹב *abundance* of trade Ezk 28_{16} (if em.; see Subj.).

<COLL> מלא pi. + סתם pi. *stop up* Gn 26_{15}, שׂבע hi. *satisfy* Ps 107_{9}.

(2) with obj. and prep., <SUBJ> Y. Ps 110_{6} (if em.; see Prep.) Si 36_{19} 4QBéat 14.2_{13}, עַם *people* Ezr 9_{11}, Aaron Lv 9_{17}, Job Jb 40_{31}, גֶּבֶר *man* Ps 127_{5}, קָרִיא *one called* CD 2_{11}. <OBJ> Zion Si 36_{19}, כַּף *hand* Lv 9_{17}, ראשׁ *head* Jb 40_{31}, פָּנִים *face* of world CD 2_{11}, עוֹר *skin* Jb 40_{31}, אַשְׁפָּה *quiver* Ps 127_{5}, אֶרֶץ *land* Ezr 9_{11}, גַּיְא *valley* Ps 110_{6} (if em.; see Prep.), הֵיכָל *temple* Si 36_{19}, יוֹם *day* 4QBéat 14.2_{13}. <PREP> בְּ of instrument, *by (means of), with*, + שֻׂכָּה *barb* Jb 40_{31}, צִלְצַל *spear* Jb 40_{31}, טֻמְאָה *uncleanness* Ezr 9_{11}, גְּוִיָּה *corpse* Ps 110_{6} (if em. מָלֵא בִּגְוִיּוֹת *he fills [them] with corpses*, i.e. qal to מָלֵא גְוִיּוֹת גֵּאָיוֹת *with corpses he fills the valleys*), טוּב *good* 4QBéat 14.2_{13}; מִן of direction, *from*, + פֶּה *mouth*, i.e. end Ezr 9_{11} (מִפֶּה אֶל־פֶּה *from end to end*); *of, with*, + בֵּן *son* Ps 127_{5}, זֶרַע *seed* CD 2_{11}, מִנְחָה *grain offering* Lv 9_{17}, כָּבוֹד *glory* Si 36_{19}, הָדָר *majesty* Si $36_{19(Bmg)}$.

2a. fulfil, accomplish, complete, <SUBJ> Y. Ex 23_{26} 1 K $8_{15.24}$||2 C $6_{4.15}$ Ps $20_{5.6}$ perh. 1QM 17_{9} (unless §1a), Judah Jr 44_{25}, עַם *people* Jr 44_{25}, Jacob Gn $29_{27.28}$, Solomon 1 K 2_{27}, אִשָּׁה *woman* Jr 44_{25}, זָקֵן *old one* Is 65_{20}, קרב hi. ptc. *one who brings near*, i.e. offers perh. 11QT 15_{14}, אַיָּלָה *hind* Jb 39_{2}, רוּחַ *spirit* 1QS 3_{16}, מַעֲרָכָה *battle formation* 4QM[a] $1_{15.16}$ (המ[ע]רכה), מִסְפָּר *number* of years Dn 9_{2}, אֲשֶׁר *one who* GnzPs 3_{7}; subj. not specified, 2 C $36_{21.21}$.

<OBJ> דָּבָר *word* 1 K 2_{27} 2 C 36_{21}, עֵצָה *plan* Ps 20_{5},

פְּעֻלָּה *work* 1QS 3_{16}, מַצְרֵף perh. *fiery trial* 1QM 17_{9} (but prob. §1a, and מצרפיו = *his crucibles*), מִשְׁאָלָה *petition* Ps 20_{6} GnzPs 3_{7}, יוֹם *day* Is 65_{20} 11QT 15_{14}, שָׁבוּעַ *week* Gn $29_{27.28}$, יֶרַח *month* Jb 39_{2}, שָׁנָה *year* 2 C 36_{21}, עֹנָה *period* 4QM^{a} $1_{15.16}$ 4QM^{c} 1_{8} perh. 1_{11} ([במל]אם), מִסְפָּר *number* of days Ex 23_{26}.

<PREP> לְ introducing object, + חָרְבָּה *desolation* Dn 9_{2}; בְּ of instrument, *by (means of), with*, + יָד *hand* 1 K $8_{15.24}$||2 C $6_{4.15}$ Jr 44_{25}; כְּ *as* 1 K 2_{24}||2 C 6_{15} (כַּיּוֹם הַזֶּה *as at this day*); *according to*, + מַחֲשָׁבָה *skilful design* 1QS 3_{16}; אֵת *with*, i.e. for, + psalmist GnzPs 3_{7} (אותי).

<COLL> מלא pi. || דבר pi. *speak* 1 K $8_{15.24}$||2 C $6_{4.15}$ Jr 44_{25}; + נתן *give* Ps 20_{5}.

b. confirm, <SUBJ> Nathan 1 K 1_{14}. <OBJ> דָּבָר *word* 1 K 1_{14}.

3. fill in, set precious stones, <SUBJ> Bezalel and Oholiab Ex 39_{10}, Moses Ex 28_{17}; subj. not specified, Ex 31_{5}||35_{33}. <OBJ> מִלֻּאָה *setting* Ex 28_{17}, טוּר *row* Ex 28_{17}||39_{10}, אֶבֶן *stone* Ex 31_{5}||35_{33}. <PREP> בְּ of place, *in*, + חֹשֶׁן *breastpiece* Ex 28_{17}||39_{10}.

4a. fill bow, **set (arrow)** to bowstring, <SUBJ> Y. Zc 9_{13}. <OBJ> 1. thing filled, קֶשֶׁת *bow* Zc 9_{13}. 2. filled with, Ephraim Zc 9_{13}. <COLL> מלא pi. + דרך *tread*, i.e. bend, bow Zc 9_{13}.

b. with object יָד, **draw bow,** lit. 'fill the hand with', <SUBJ> Jehu 2 K 9_{24}. <OBJ> יָד *hand* 2 K 9_{24}. <PREP> בְּ of instrument, *by (means of), with*, + קֶשֶׁת *bow* 2 K 9_{24}.

5. with obj. יָד, lit. 'fill the hand', **ordain, consecrate as priest,* consecrate** altar (Ezk 43_{26}), oneself (1 C 29_{5} 2 C 29_{31}), <SUBJ> Jeroboam 1 K 13_{33}, Micah Jg $17_{5.12}$, Moses Ex 28_{41} $29_{9.35}$ Si 45_{15} ([וי]מלא), כֹּהֵן *priest* Ezk 43_{26}, קָהָל *assembly* 2 C 29_{31}, בוא ptc. *one who comes* 2 C 13_{9}, מִי *who?* 1 C 29_{5}; subj. not specified, Ex $29_{29.33}$ Lv 8_{33} 16_{32} 21_{10} Nm 3_{3} 11QT 15_{15} 35_{6}.

<OBJ> יָד *hand* 4QShirShabb^{b} 22_{2}, of Aaron Si 45_{15} ([וי]מלא), of Aaron and sons Ex 28_{41} $29_{9.33.35}$ Lv 8_{33}, of sons of Aaron Ex 29_{29} Nm 3_{3}, of son of Micah Jg 17_{5}, of priest Lv 16_{32} 21_{10} Nm 3_{3} 11QT 15_{15} 35_{6}, of Levite Jg 17_{12}, of people 1 K 13_{33}, of altar Ezk 43_{26}, of one devoting oneself 1 C 29_{5} 2 C 13_{9} 29_{31}.

<PREP> לְ of benefit, *to, for*, + Y. 2 C 29_{31}; בְּ of place, *in*, + בֶּגֶד *garment* Ex 29_{29}; of instrument, *by (means of), with*, + פַּר *bull* 2C 13_{9}, אַיִל *ram* 2 C 13_{9}.

<COLL> קדשׁ || מִלֵּא יָד pi. *consecrate* Ex 28_{41} 29_{33}, משׁח *anoint* Lv 16_{32}, טהר pi. *purify* Ezk 43_{26}, כפר pi. *make atonement for* Ezk 43_{26}; + כהן pi. *be priest* Ex 28_{41} Lv 16_{32} Nm 3_{3} Jg 17_{5}, לבשׁ *wear* Lv 21_{10}, יצק ho. (of oil) *be poured* on head Lv 21_{10}; + noun used adverbially, יוֹם *day* Ex 29_{35} Lv 8_{33} 1 C 29_{5} (הַיּוֹם *today*).

6. wholly follow, a. with אַחֲרֵי, <SUBJ> Caleb Nm 14_{24} 32_{12} Dt 1_{36} Jos $14_{8.9.14}$, Joshua Nm 32_{12} Si 46_{6}, Solomon 1 K 11_{6}, אִישׁ *man* Nm 32_{11}, בֵּן *son* Nm 32_{12} Dt 1_{36} Jos 14_{14}, עֶבֶד *servant* Nm 14_{24}; subj. not specified, Si 46_{10}. <PREP> כְּ *as*, + David 1 K 11_{6}, אָב *father* 1 K 11_{6}; אַחֲרֵי *after*, + Y. Nm 14_{24} $32_{11.12}$ Dt 1_{36} Jos $14_{8.9.14}$ 1 K 11_{6} Si $46_{6.10}$.

b. with בְּ, but prob. ni., <SUBJ> לֵב *heart* Si 4_{17}. <PREP> בְּ introducing object, + חָכְמוֹת *wisdom* Si 4_{17}. <COLL> עת ימלא לבו *the time when his heart fully trusts* Si 4_{17}.

7. do fully, as auxiliary verb of קרא *call*, i.e. call loudly (unless §12b). <SUBJ> אִישׁ *man* Jr 4_{5}.

8. give in full, <SUBJ> David 1 S 18_{27}. <OBJ> עָרְלָה *foreskin* 1 S 18_{27}. <PREP> לְ of direction, *to*, + מֶלֶךְ *king* 1 S 18_{27}.

9. replenish, satisfy, <SUBJ> Y. Jr 31_{25}, Job Jb 38_{39}, גַּנָּב *thief* Pr 6_{30}. <OBJ> נֶפֶשׁ *soul* Jr 31_{25}, i.e. appetite Pr 6_{30}, חַיָּה *appetite* Jb 38_{39}. <COLL> מלא pi. || רוה hi. *give to drink* Jr 31_{25}.

10. overflow, <SUBJ> יַרְדֵּן *Jordan* 1 C 12_{16}. <PREP> עַל *over, upon*, + גָּדָה *bank* 1 C 12_{16}.

11. perh. privatively **empty,*** unless §1b, <SUBJ> חָכָם *wise one* Jb 15_{2}. <OBJ> 1. thing emptied, קָדִים *east wind* Jb 15_{2}. 2. emptied from, בֶּטֶן *stomach* Jb 15_{2}.

12a. mass, heap up,* <SUBJ> Y. Ezk 32_{5} (unless §1b) Ps 110_{6} (if em. מָלֵא *he fills* [qal] to מִלֵּא *he heaps up corpses*; or em. מְלֵא גֵוות *full of majesty*).* <OBJ> גְּוִיָּה *corpse* Ezk 32_{5} (if em. הַגֵּאָיוֹת *the valleys* to הַגְּאִיּוֹת) Ps 110_{6} (if em.; see Subj.). <COLL> וּמִלֵּאתִי ... רָמוּתֶךָ *and I will heap ... upon your heights* Ezk 32_{5}.

12b. assemble en masse, <SUBJ> אִישׁ *man* Jr 4_{5} (unless §7). <COLL> קִרְאוּ מַלְאוּ *cry, Assemble en masse* Jr 4_{5} (unless §7).

13. make full ready,* הָבֵרוּ הַחִצִּים מִלְאוּ הַשְּׁלָטִים

sharpen the arrows, make the shields fully ready Jr 51$_{11}$ (if em. מִלְאוּ *fill* to מַלְאוּ), יְמַלֵּא בַרְזֶל וְעֵץ חֲנִית *let him make fully ready the (weapon of) iron and the shaft of the spear* 2 S 23$_{7}$ (if em. יִמָּלֵא *let him arm himself with* [ni. §7] to יְמַלֵּא).

Also perh. 4QWiles 4$_{3}$ perh. 4QM[a] 1$_{20}$ perh. 4QRit Pur 15.1$_{7}$ Kadesh Barnea ost. 2$_{1.1}$ (מל[א]).

<SYN> §1a שׂבע pi. *satisfy;* §2a דבר pi. *speak;* §5 קדשׁ pi. *consecrate,* משׁח *anoint,* טהר pi. *purify,* כפר pi. *make atonement for;* §9 רוה hi. *give to drink* .

Pu. 1 Ptc. מְמֻלָּאִים—**be set with** precious stones (Ca 5$_{14}$), **be set in** gold (Lm 4$_{2}$ [if em.; see Subj.]), <SUBJ> בֵּן *son* of Zion Lm 4$_{2}$ (if em. הַמְסֻלָּאִים *who are weighed* to הַמְמֻלָּאִים *who are set*), גָּלִיל *rod* of gold Ca 5$_{14}$. <PREP> בְּ of place, *in,* + פַּז *pure gold* Lm 4$_{2}$ (if em.; see Subj.); of instrument, *by (means of), with,* + תַּרְשִׁישׁ perh. *chrysolite* Ca 5$_{14}$. <COLL> מלא pu. || עלף pu. *be covered* Ca 5$_{14}$.

<SYN> עלף pu. *be covered.*

Htp. 1 Impf. יִתְמַלְּאוּן—**1. be filled,** <SUBJ> מִכְמָר *net* 2QapProph 6$_{1}$ ([מכ[מרם יתמלו[א).

2. mass oneself, <SUBJ> subj. not specified, Jb 16$_{10}$. <PREP> עַל *against* + Job Jb 16$_{10}$. <COLL> מלא htp. + adverb, יַחַד *together* Jb 16$_{10}$.*

⇒ מָלֵא *full,* מְלֹא *fullness,* מְלֵאָה *full produce,* מִלֻּאָה *setting,* מִלֻּא *consecration, setting,* מִלֻּאת *setting,* מִלּוֹא *citadel,* (?) מַלְיָהוּ *Maliah;* cf. מלה *be full.*

מָלֵא 64.6.10 adj. **full**—Q מלה; cstr. מְלֵא; fem. מְלֵאָה; cstr. מְלֵאַתִי; pl. מְלֵאִים (Q מלאין); fem. מְלֵאוֹת—**1. full, a.** used attributively of סוּס *horse* 1QM 6$_{12}$, רוּחַ *wind* Jr 4$_{12}$, שִׁבֹּלֶת *ear of grain* Gn 41$_{7}$ (|| בָּרִיא *fat*) 41$_{22}$ (|| טוֹב *good*), כֶּסֶף *money,* i.e. price Gn 23$_{9}$ 1 C 21$_{22.24}$, יָרֵחַ *moon* Si 50$_{6}$, בּוֹר *cistern* 3QTr 2$_{1}$.

<COLL> רוּחַ מָלֵא מֵאֵלֶּה *a wind too full for these* Jr 4$_{12}$ (unless *a full wind from these;* or del. מָלֵא), סוסים ... מלאים בתכון ימיהם *horses ... full in their measure of days,* i.e. of full age 1QM 6$_{12}$.

b. used predicatively of יָם *sea* Ec 1$_{7}$, מזו *storehouse* Ps 144$_{13}$, בַּיִת treasure *house* Ezk 28$_{12}$ (if em.; see §2 Coll.).

c. as noun, **full one,** in ref. to vessel, <OBJ> נסע hi. *remove* 2 K 4$_{4}$.

2. full of, a. absolute, (1) used attributively of Naphtali Dt 33$_{23}$ (+ שְׂבַע *satisfied*), בֵּן *son* Is 51$_{20}$, שׁוֹק *thigh* 4QCrypt 1.3$_{4}$, נֶשֶׁר *eagle* Ezk 17$_{3}$ (or em. מְלֵא *full of,* §2b), זַיִת *olive tree* Si 50$_{10}$, גָּבִיעַ *cup* Jr 35$_{5}$, כּוֹס *cup* Ps 75$_{9}$, דוד *pot* 3QTr 4$_{8}$, כַּף *spoon* Nm 7$_{14+12t}$, פֶּלֶג *channel* Ps 65$_{10}$, חֶלְקָה *plot of land* 2 S 23$_{11}$|| 1 C 11$_{13}$, עִיר *city* Is 22$_{2}$ Na 3$_{1}$, בַּיִת *house* Dt 6$_{11}$ Pr 17$_{1}$ Ne 9$_{25}$ 1QDM 2$_{3}$ (בתו[ים) 4QConfess 2$_{8}$, כְּלוּב *cage* Jr 5$_{27}$=Si 11$_{30}$, עֲגָלָה *cart* Am 2$_{13}$, שְׁנַיִם *two* Nm 7$_{14+ 11t}$.

(2) used predicatively of לֵב *heart* Ec 9$_{3}$ Si 10$_{13}$ (לב[ו]), דֶּרֶךְ *way* 2 K 7$_{15}$, עִיר *city* Ezk 36$_{38}$, בַּיִת *house* Jr 5$_{27}$=Si 11$_{30}$, גַּב *rim* of wheel Ezk 1$_{18}$, אוֹפַן *wheel* Ezk 10$_{12}$ (or del. וְהָאוֹפַנִּים and em. מְלֵאִים to מְלֵאוֹת), כָּנָף *wing* Ezk 10$_{12}$ (if em.; see above), אַתָּה *you* (king of Tyre) Ezk 28$_{12}$ (or em.; see Coll.; + כְּלִיל *perfect one*), הִיא *it* (valley) Ezk 37$_{1}$.

<COLL> §§2a (1), (2), מָלֵא *full of,* followed by complement עוֹף *birds* Jr 5$_{27}$=Si 11$_{30}$, צֹאן *flock* of humans Ezk 36$_{38}$, שָׂעִיר *demon* perh. 2QapProph 1$_{7}$, עַיִן *eye* Ezk 1$_{18}$ 10$_{12}$, עֶצֶם *bone* Ezk 37$_{1}$, גַּרְגַּר *olive* Si 50$_{10}$, סֹלֶת *fine flour* Nm 7$_{14+ 11t}$, עֲדָשָׁה *lentil* 2 S 23$_{11}$, שְׂעֹרָה *barley* 1 C 11$_{13}$, עָמִיר *sheaf* Am 2$_{13}$, מַיִם *water* Ps 65$_{10}$, יַיִן *wine* Jr 35$_{5}$, מֶסֶךְ *mixture* Ps 75$_{9}$, קְטֹרֶת *incense* Nm 7$_{14+12t}$, זֶבַח *sacrifice* Pr 17$_{1}$, בֶּגֶד *garment* 2 K 7$_{15}$, נוֹצָה *plumage* Ezk 17$_{3}$ (or em. מְלֵא *full of,* §2b), שֵׂעָר *hair* 4QCrypt 1.3$_{4}$ ([ש[ער), כֶּסֶף *silver* 3QTr 4$_{8}$, כְּלִי *equipment* 2 K 7$_{15}$, טוּב *good thing* Dt 6$_{11}$ Ne 9$_{25}$ 1QDM 2$_{3}$ 4QConfess 2$_{8}$ (both [טוב]), בְּרָכָה *blessing* Dt 33$_{23}$, חָכְמָה *wisdom* Ezk 28$_{12}$ (or em. חָכְמָה to בֵּית־נְכֹתֶיךָ *your treasure house* is full), רַע *evil* Ec 9$_{3}$ Si 10$_{13}$ (לבו רע[ו]), חֵמָה *anger* Is 51$_{20}$, מִרְמָה *deceit* Jr 5$_{27}$=Si 11$_{30(Segal)}$ ([מרמה]).

Preceded by complement תְּשֻׁאָה *noise* Is 22$_{2}$, פֶּרֶק *plunder* Na 3$_{1}$.

b. construct, (1) used attributively of נֶשֶׁר *eagle* Ezk 17$_{3}$ (if em. מָלֵא), קִרְיָה *city* Is 1$_{21}$. <CSTR> מְלֵא נוֹצָה *full of plumage* Ezk 17$_{3}$ (if em. מָלֵא), מְלֵאֲתִי מִשְׁפָּט *full* (fem. sing.) *of justice* Is 1$_{21}$, מְלֵא גֵּוּוֹת *full of majesty* Ps 110$_{6}$ (if em. מָלֵא גְוִיּוֹת).*

(2) as noun, **one full of,** <OBJ> משׁח *anoint* Si 48$_{8}$. <CSTR> מְלֵא יָמִים *one full of days* Jr 6$_{11}$ (+ זָקֵן *aged*

one), מלא תשלומות *one full of retribution* Si 48_8. <PREP> עִם *with* Jr 6_{11}.

3. pregnant, a. used predicatively of אִשָּׁה *woman* 11QT 50_{10}, הֵמָּה *they* (cow, sheep, goat) 11QT 52_6.

b. מְלֵאָה as noun, **pregnant woman,** <CSTR> בֶּטֶן הַמְּלֵאָה *womb of the pregnant woman* Ec 11_5.

4. as noun, **fullness,** unless **full one,** as term for the sea,* <CSTR> מֵי מָלֵא *waters of fullness,* i.e. abundant waters Ps 73_{10} (or em. מִלֵּיהֶם *their words* or מַיִם לֹא מָצְאוּ *they did not find water* or וּמַיִם לֹא יִמְצְאוּ לָמוֹ *and the waters cannot reach them*).*

5. as adverb, **a. full,** i.e. in a full condition, of הלך *go* Ru 1_{21} (:: רֵיקָם *empty*). **b. fully,** of יבשׁ *be dry* Na 1_{10} (or em. הֲלֹא *did not?* and join with following verse). **c. loudly,** of קרא *cry* Jr 12_6 (or em. קָרְאוּ אַחֲרֶיךָ מָלֵא *they cry loudly after you* to קָשְׁרוּ אַחֲרֶיךָ כֻּלָּם *all of them join together against you;* or קָרְאוּ אַחֲרֶיךָ מָלֵא *they cry after you, Fill,* i.e. *fill the ranks, all together!* or *Help! help*).*

Also 4QBéat 31_2.

<SYN> §1 בָּרִיא *fat,* טוֹב *good.**

⇒ מלא *be full.*

מִלֹּא, see מִלּוֹא *citadel.*

[מִלֻּא] 15.0.1 n.m. **consecration, setting**—cstr. Si מלא; pl. מִלֻּאִים (מִלּוּאִים); sf. מִלֻּאֵיכֶם—**1a. consecration (to the priesthood),** <CSTR> אֵיל הַמִּלֻּאִים *ram of the consecration* Ex 29_{22} (מִלֻּאִים) $29_{26.27.31}$ Lv $8_{22.29}$, אילי[ן המלואים] *rams of the consecration* 11QT $15_{3(mg)}$, יְמֵי מִלֻּאֵיכֶם *days of your consecration* Lv 8_{33}. <PREP> לְ of benefit, *to, for* 11QT[b] 1_{12}; *as,* + קטר hi. *burn* 11QT[b] 1_{20} ((והקטירו])). <COLL> מלוא על נפשותמה *a consecration for themselves* 11QT[b] 1_{20}.

b. consecration offering, <NOM CL> מִלֻּאִים הֵם לְרֵיחַ נִיחֹחַ *they are a consecration offering as a pleasing odour* Lv 8_{28}. <CSTR> בְּשַׂר הַמִּלֻּאִים *flesh of the consecration offering* Ex 29_{34}, סַל *basket of* Lv 8_{31}. <PREP> לְ *concerning, in respect of* Lv 7_{37} (הַתּוֹרָה ... לַמִּלּוּאִים *the law ... concerning the consecration offering;* || זֶבַח *sacrifice,* עֹלָה *burnt offering,* מִנְחָה *cereal offering,* חַטָּאת *sin offering,* אָשָׁם *guilt offering*).

2. setting of precious stones, <NOM CL> מלא פז ... קול מזמור *a setting in pure gold ... is the sound of song* with pleasant wine Si $35_{6(Bmg)}$ (B מלואת). <CSTR> מלא פז *settings of,* i.e. in, *pure gold* Si $35_{6(Bmg)}$ (B מלואות); אַבְנֵי מִלֻּאִים *stones of,* i.e. for, *setting* Ex 25_7|| 35_9 35_{27} 1 C 29_2 (אַבְנֵי ... מִלֻּאִים). <PREP> בְּ of place, *in* Si 45_{11} ((במל[ואים]).

<SYN> §1b זֶבַח *sacrifice,* עֹלָה *burnt offering,* מִנְחָה *cereal offering,* חַטָּאת *sin offering,* אָשָׁם *guilt offering.**

⇒ מלא *be full.*

[מְלֹא] 38.0.6.1 n.m. **fullness**—cstr. מְלֹא (מְלוֹא, מְלוֹ); sf. מְלֹאוֹ (מְלוֹאוֹ), מְלֹאָהּ (מְלוֹאָהּ)—**1. fullness,** i.e. **amount that fills,** <SUBJ> היה *be* Is 8_8 4QNarrD 1_3. <NOM CL> יֶשׁ לִי ... מְלֹא כַף־קֶמַח בַּכַּד *there is to me ... a handful of meal in a jar* 1 K 17_{12}, מוּסְדוֹת הַצְּלָעוֹת מְלוֹ הַקָּנֶה *the foundations of the side chambers were the fullness of a reed,* i.e. measured a full reed Ezk 41_8, מְלֹא הָעֹמֶר מִמֶּנּוּ לְמִשְׁמֶרֶת לְדֹרֹתֵיכֶם *an omer full of it shall be for keeping throughout your generations* Ex 16_{32} (Sam מְלָאוֹ *fill* an omer of it), טוֹב מְלֹא כַף ... מִמְּלֹא חָפְנַיִם *one handful is better ... than two handfuls* Ec 4_6.

<OBJ> לקח *take* Ex. 9_8 Lv $16_{12.12}$, לקט pi. *gather* 2 K 4_{39}, נתן *give* Nm 22_{18} 24_{13}, i.e. place Ex 16_{33}, סבב hi. *bring* Arad ost. 2_5, מדד pi. *measure* 2 S 8_2, קמץ *grasp* Lv 2_2 5_{12}, מצה *wring* Jg 6_{38}.

<CSTR> מְלֹא כַף *fullness of the hand,* i.e. handful Ec 4_6, כַּף־קֶמַח *of a hand,* i.e. a handful, *of meal* 1 K 17_{12}, חָפְנַיִם *of both hands,* i.e. two handfuls Ec 4_6, חָפְנָיו *of his hands* Lv 16_{12}, חָפְנֵיכֶם *of your hands* Ex 9_8, קֻמְצוֹ *of his hand* Lv 2_2 5_{12} (מְלוֹא), הָעֹמֶר *of an omer,* i.e. an omer full Ex $16_{32.33}$, החמר *of a homer* Arad ost. 2_5, הַקָּנֶה *of a reed,* i.e. a full reed Ezk 41_8 (מְלוֹ), הַחֶבֶל *of a line,* i.e. a full line 2 S 8_2, הַמַּחְתָּה *of a censer,* i.e. censer full Lv 16_{12}, הַסֵּפֶל *of a bowl,* i.e. a bowlful Jg 6_{38} (מְלוֹא), בִּגְדוֹ *of his garment,* i.e. his garment full 2 K 4_{39}, בֵּיתוֹ *of his house,* i.e. his house full Nm 22_{18} 24_{13}, ־קוֹמָתוֹ *of his height,* i.e. his full height 1 S 28_{20}, רֹחַב־אַרְצְךָ *of the breadth,* i.e. full breadth, *of your land* Is 8_8, יָמֶיךָ *of your days,* i.e. all your days Na 1_{10} (if em. מָלֵא : מִמֵּךְ *fully. From you*), מלא [חכמה] *fullness of wisdom* 4Q NarrD 1_3.

<APP> מָן *manna* Ex 16$_{33}$, פַּקֻּעֹת *gourds* 2 K 4$_{39}$, יַיִן *wine* Arad ost. 2$_{5}$, פִּיחַ *soot* Ex 9$_{8}$, גַּחֶלֶת *coal* Lv 16$_{12}$, קְטֹרֶת *incense* Lv 16$_{12}$, אַזְכָּרָה *token offering* Lv 5$_{12}$, זָהָב *gold* Nm 22$_{18}$ 24$_{13}$, כֶּסֶף *silver* Nm 22$_{18}$ 24$_{13}$, עָמָל *toil* Ec 4$_{6}$ (unless em. וְעָמָל *and*, i.e. with, *toil*), נַחַת *rest* Ec 4$_{6}$ (unless em. וָנַחַת *and*, i.e. with, *rest*).

<PREP> מִן of comparison, *(more) than* Ec 4$_{6}$.

<COLL> מְלֹא קֻמְצוֹ מִסָּלְתָּהּ וּמִשַּׁמְנָהּ *his handful of fine flour and oil* Lv 2$_{2}$, וַיִּפֹּל מְלֹא־קוֹמָתוֹ אַרְצָה *and he fell with his full height to the ground* 1 S 28$_{20}$, השמש רחוק מן השער מלואו *the sun is distant from the gate by its own fullness* CD 10$_{16}$.

2. fullness, i.e. **that which fills, contents,** <SUBJ> אדר hi. *glorify* Is 42$_{10}$ (if em. יוֹרְדֵי הַיָּם *those who go down to the sea* to יַאְדִּירֵהוּ יָם *let the sea glorify him*), שׁיר *sing* Is 42$_{10}$ (unless em.; see above), שׁמע *hear* Is 34$_{1}$, קשׁב hi. *pay attention* Mc 1$_{2}$, רעם *roar* Ps 96$_{11}$||1 C 16$_{32}$ Ps 98$_{7}$, ישׁם *be desolate* Ezk 19$_{7}$.

<NOM CL> מְלֹא כָל־הָאָרֶץ כְּבוֹדוֹ *the fullness of all the earth is his glory* Is 6$_{3}$ (or em. מָלְאָה all the earth *is full of*), מלוא [ש]מים והארץ [כוח גבורותיכה] *the fullness of the heavens and the earth is the strength of your might* 1QH 16$_{3}$, [הדר כ]בודך מלוא כ[ול תבל] *the majesty of your glory is the fullness of all the world* 1QH 16$_{3}$, לַי׳ הָאָרֶץ וּמְלוֹאָהּ *the earth and its fullness is Y.'s* Ps 24$_{1}$, לו ארץ ומלאה *his is the world and its fullness* GnzPs 4$_{3}$, לִי תֵבֵל וּמְלֹאָהּ *mine is the world and its fullness* Ps 50$_{12}$, var. Ps 89$_{12}$.

<OBJ> יסד *found* Ps 89$_{12}$ 4QapPs[b] 15$_{5}$ ([י]סדתם), שׁמם hi. *make desolate* Ezk 30$_{12}$, אכל *devour* Jr 8$_{16}$, שׁטף *overflow* Jr 47$_{2}$, סגר hi. *deliver up* Am 6$_{8}$.

<CSTR> מְלֹא כָל־הָאָרֶץ *fullness of all the earth* Is 6$_{3}$ (or em.; see Nom Cl.), מלוא ה[ש]מים והארץ *fullness of the heavens and the earth* 1QH 16$_{3}$, כ[ול תבל] *of all the world* 1QH 16$_{3}$; מֶגֶד אֶרֶץ וּמְלֹאָהּ *excellence of the earth and its fullness* Dt 33$_{16}$.

<PREP> מִן privative, *of, (so as to be) without*, + ישׁם (of land) *be desolate* Ezk 12$_{10}$ (ms וּמְלוֹאָהּ *and its fullness*), שׁמם (of land) ni. *be made desolate* Ezk 32$_{15}$.

<COLL> מְלֹא || צֶאֱצָא *produce* Is 34$_{1}$; + ישׁב ptc. *one who dwells* Jr 8$_{16}$ Ps 24$_{1}$ 98$_{7}$ GnzPs 4$_{3}$, כָּל־אֲשֶׁר בּוֹ *everything that is in it* Ps 96$_{11}$||1 C 16$_{32}$; אֶרֶץ וּמְלֹאָהּ, and vars. *the earth and its fullness* Dt 33$_{16}$ Is 34$_{1}$ Mc 1$_{2}$ Jr 8$_{16}$ 47$_{2}$ Ezk 19$_{7.12(ms)}$ 30$_{12}$ Ps 24$_{1}$ 4QParGenEx 2$_{13}$ ([הארץ ומ]ל[ו]אה) GnzPs 4$_{3}$, תֵּבֵל וּמְלֹאָהּ *the world and its fullness* Ps 50$_{12}$ 89$_{12}$ 4QapPs[b] 15$_{5}$ ([תבל ו]מלואה), הַיָּם וּמְלֹאוֹ *the sea and its fullness* Is 42$_{10}$ Ps 96$_{11}$||1 C 16$_{32}$ Ps 98$_{7}$, עִיר וּמְלֹאָהּ *the city and its fullness* Am 6$_{8}$.

3. multitude, <SUBJ> היה *be* Gn 48$_{19}$, קרא ni. *be called* Is 31$_{4}$. <CSTR> מְלֹא־הַגּוֹיִם *multitude of the nations* Gn 48$_{19}$, רֹעִים *of shepherds* Is 31$_{4}$.

<SYN> §2 צֶאֱצָא *produce*.*

⇒ מלא *fill*.

מְלֵאָה 3.0.3 n.f. **full produce**—sf. מְלֵאָתְךָ—<SUBJ> קדשׁ *be holy*, i.e. forfeited Dt 22$_{9}$ 4Q418 103.2$_{8}$ (יקד[ש]). <OBJ> אחר pi. *delay* Ex 22$_{28}$ 4QHalakhah[a] 5$_{2}$. <CSTR> ראשית המלאה *choicest of the full produce* 4QHalakhah[a] 5$_{3}$. <APP> זֶרַע *seed* Dt 22$_{9}$, תְּבוּאָה *yield* Dt 22$_{9}$. <PREP> כְּ *as*, + חשׁב ni. *be reckoned* Nm 18$_{27}$. <COLL> מְלֵאָה || דֶּמַע *juice* Ex 22$_{28}$, דָּגָן *grain* Nm 18$_{27}$; + בְּכוֹר *firstborn* Ex 22$_{28}$, בִּכּוּרִים *firstfruits* 4QHalakhah[a] 5$_{2}$, זֶרַע *seed* 4Q418 103.2$_{8}$, תְּבוּאָה *yield* 4Q418 103.2$_{8}$ ([תבוא]ת); מְלֵאָה מִן־הַיָּקֶב *full produce of the wine press* Nm 18$_{27}$.

<SYN> דֶּמַע *juice*, דָּגָן *grain*.

⇒ מלא *be full*.

[מִלֻּאָה] 3.1 n.f. **setting**—cstr. מִלֻּאַת; pl. cstr. Si מלואות; sf. מִלּוּאֹתָם—**setting** of precious stone, <NOM CL> מלואות פז ... קול מזמור *settings in pure gold ... is the sound of song* with pleasant wine Si 35$_{6(B)}$ (Bmg מלא). <OBJ> מלא pi. *set* Ex 28$_{17}$. <CSTR> מִלֻּאַת אֶבֶן *setting of a stone* Ex 28$_{17}$, מלואות פז *settings of*, i.e. in, *pure gold* Si 35$_{6(B)}$ (Bmg מלא). <APP> טוּר *row* Ex 28$_{17}$. <PREP> בְּ of place, *in*, + היה *be* Ex 28$_{20}$, סבב ho. *be enclosed* Ex 39$_{13}$.*

⇒ מלא *be full*.

מַלְאָךְ 213.1.81 n.m. **messenger**—cstr. מַלְאַךְ; sf. מַלְאָכִי, מַלְאָכוֹ; pl. מַלְאָכִים (2 S 11$_{1}$ מלאכים); cstr. מַלְאֲכֵי; sf. מַלְאָכַיִךְ (Q מלאכיכה), 2fs מַלְאָכֵכֶה, מַלְאָכָיו—**1. messenger,** sometimes with task other than conveying of message (e.g. Jos 7$_{22}$ 1 S 19$_{11.14.20}$ 2 K 7$_{15}$ 6$_{32}$ Pr 17$_{11}$);

as description of political envoy (e.g. Is 14$_{32}$ 30$_{4}$ Jr 27$_{3}$ Ezk 17$_{15}$ 2 C 35$_{21}$), spy (Jos 6$_{17.25}$), prophet (Hg 1$_{13}$ 2 C 36$_{15}$), priest (Ml 2$_{7}$), perh. delegate from high priest to enquire after vows (Ec 5$_{5}$);* wind as messenger of Y. (Ps 104$_{4}$).

<SUBJ> אמר *say* Gn 32$_{4}$ Nm 21$_{21}$ 22$_{5}$ Dt 2$_{26}$ Jg 7$_{24}$ 9$_{31}$ 11$_{12.14(mss).17}$ 1 S 6$_{21}$ 11$_{9}$ 2 S 11$_{19.23.25}$ 1 K 19$_{2}$ 20$_{5.9}$ 22$_{13}$||2 C 18$_{12}$ 2 K 5$_{10}$ 6$_{33}$ (if em.; see below) 10$_{8}$ 14$_{8}$ 16$_{7}$ 19$_{9}$||Is 37$_{9}$ Hg 1$_{13}$ Jb 1$_{14}$ Ne 6$_{3}$ 2 C 35$_{21}$, דבר pi. *speak* 1 S 11$_{4}$ 2 S 11$_{19}$ 1 K 22$_{13}$||2 C 18$_{12}$, נגד hi. *tell* 1 S 11$_{9}$ 2 S 11$_{22}$ 2 K 7$_{15}$ 10$_{8}$ Jb 1$_{14}$, נבא htp. *prophesy* 1 S 19$_{20.21.21}$, ברך pi. *bless* 1 S 25$_{14}$, דרשׁ *inquire of* 2 K 1$_{2.16}$, קרא *summon* Nm 22$_{5}$, נחם pi. *comfort* 1 C 19$_{2}$, ראה *see* 1 S 19$_{15}$, ni. *appear* Ml 3$_{1}$.

הלך *go* 2 S 11$_{22}$ 1 K 20$_{9}$ 22$_{13}$||2 C 18$_{12}$ 2 K 1$_{2}$ Is 18$_{2}$, בוא *come* Gn 32$_{7}$ 1 S 11$_{4.9.9}$ 19$_{16}$ 23$_{27}$ 2 S 11$_{22}$ (בוא lacking in mss) 2 K 6$_{32.32}$ 9$_{18}$ 10$_{8}$ Jr 27$_{3}$ Ml 3$_{1}$ Jb 1$_{14}$, hi. *bring* Jos 7$_{22}$, יצא *go out* appar. 2 S 11$_{1}$ (mss הַמְּלָאכִים *the kings*) Ezk 30$_{9}$, hi. *bring out* 1 C 19$_{16}$, עלה hi. *bring up* 1 S 19$_{15}$, ירד *go down* 2 K 6$_{33}$ (or em. הַמֶּלֶךְ *the king*), עבר *pass* Is 23$_{2}$ (if em. מִלְאוּךְ *they filled you*, i.e. מלא pi., to מַלְאָכַיִךְ *your messengers*, as 1QIsa^{a}*), רוץ *run* Jos 7$_{22}$, נדד *flee* Ps 68$_{13(mss)}$, שׁוב *go back* Gn 32$_{7}$ 1 K 20$_{5}$ 2 K 1$_{5}$ 7$_{15}$, hi. *bring back* 2 S 3$_{26}$ 1 K 20$_{9}$, קרא *meet* 1 K 22$_{13}$||2 C 18$_{12}$, נגע hi. *reach* Is 30$_{4}$ (or em. מְלָכָיו *his kings*), שׁלח pass. *be sent* Ezk 23$_{40}$ Pr 17$_{11}$.

רגל pi. *spy on* Jos 6$_{25}$, צלח *succeed* Si 43$_{26}$, נפל *fall* Pr 13$_{17}$ (or em. נפל hi. *cause to fall*), ישׁב *sit* Ml 3$_{1}$, יחל hi. *wait* 2 K 6$_{33}$ (if em.; see above), יצק hi. *set down* Jos 7$_{22}$, כלה pi. *finish* 2 S 11$_{19}$, פנה pi. *prepare* Ml 3$_{1}$, טהר pi. *purify* Ml 3$_{1}$, זקק pi. *refine* Ml 3$_{1}$, לקח *take* Jos 7$_{22}$ 1 S 19$_{14.20}$, שׁמר *watch* 1 S 19$_{11}$, בכה *weep* Is 33$_{7}$, מלט ni. *escape* Jb 1$_{14}$, חרד hi. *startle* Ezk 30$_{9}$, מות hi. *kill* 1 S 19$_{11}$.

<NOM CL> מַלְאַךְ י׳ צְבָאוֹת הוּא *he* (priest) *is the messenger of Y. of hosts* Ml 2$_{7}$, חֲמַת־מֶלֶךְ מַלְאֲכֵי־מָוֶת *the anger of the king is messengers of death* Pr 16$_{14}$.

<OBJ> צוה pi. *command* Gn 32$_{4}$ 2 S 11$_{19}$, ענה *answer* Is 14$_{32}$, שׁלח *send* Gn 32$_{4}$ Nm 20$_{14}$ 21$_{21}$ 22$_{5}$ 24$_{12}$ Dt 2$_{26}$ Jos 6$_{17.25}$ 7$_{22}$ Jg 6$_{35.35}$ 7$_{24}$ 9$_{31}$ 11$_{12.14.17.19}$ 1 S 6$_{21}$ 11$_{3}$ 16$_{19}$ 19$_{11+5t}$ 25$_{14}$ 2 S 2$_{5}$ 3$_{12.14.26}$ 5$_{11}$||1 C 14$_{1}$ 2 S 11$_{4.22}$ 12$_{27}$ 1 K 19$_{2}$ 20$_{2}$ 2 K 1$_{2.16}$ 5$_{10}$ 14$_{8}$ 16$_{7}$ 17$_{4}$ 19$_{9}$||Is 37$_{9}$ Is 42$_{19}$ Ezk 17$_{15}$ 23$_{16}$ Ml 3$_{1}$ Ne 6$_{3}$ 1 C 19$_{2.16}$ 2 C 35$_{21}$ 4QTobit^{e} 4$_{7}$, קרא *meet* 2 K 1$_{3}$, חבא hi. *hide* Jos 6$_{17.25}$, לחץ *press* 2 K 6$_{32}$, עשׂה *make (into)* Ps 104$_{4}$, חפץ *delight in* Ml 3$_{1}$.

<CSTR> מַלְאַךְ י׳ *messenger of Y.* Ml 2$_{7}$, מַלְאֲכֵי הָאֱלֹהִים *messengers of God* 2 C 36$_{16}$, ־גּוֹי *of a nation* Is 14$_{32}$ (or em. גּוֹיִם *of the nations*), בֶּן־הֲדַד *of Ben-hadad* 1 K 20$_{9}$, דָוִד *of David* 1 S 25$_{42}$, יִפְתָּח *of Jephthah* Jg 11$_{13}$, שָׁאוּל *of Saul* 1 S 19$_{20}$, מֶלֶךְ *of the king of* 2 K 1$_{3}$, מַלְאֲכֵי צְבָאוֹת *messengers of armies* Ps 68$_{13(mss)}$ (L מַלְכֵי *kings of*), מַלְאַךְ הַבְּרִית *messenger of the covenant* Ml 3$_{1}$, מלאך שלו[ם] perh. *messenger of peace* 3Q8 1$_{2}$ (but prob. §2), מַלְאֲכֵי שָׁלוֹם *messengers of peace* Is 33$_{7}$ 4QHod^{b} 17$_{3}$ 4Q474 1$_{8}$ (מ[ל]אכי; unless both §2), ־מָוֶת *of death* Pr 16$_{14}$.

יַד הַמַּלְאָכִים *hand of the messengers* 1 S 11$_{7}$ 2 K 19$_{14}$||Is 37$_{14}$ Jr 27$_{3}$ (or em. מַלְאֲכֵיהֶם *of their envoys*), יד מלאכ[י] *hand of the messengers of* 4QMyst^{a} 35$_{2}$ (unless §2), יַד מַלְאָכֶיךָ *hand of your messengers* 2 K 19$_{23}$, מַלְאָכָיו *of his messengers* 2 C 36$_{15}$, קוֹל מַלְאָכֵכֵה *voice of your messengers* Na 2$_{14}$ (or em. מַלְאָכַיִךְ in same sense, or מַאֲכָלֵךְ *your feeding*), עֲצַת מַלְאָכָיו *counsel of his messengers* Is 44$_{26}$.

<APP> חַגַּי *Haggai* Hg 1$_{13}$.

<ADJ> קַל *swift* Is 18$_{2}$, רַע *bad* Pr 13$_{17}$, אַכְזָרִי *cruel* Pr 17$_{11}$, אַחֵר *other* 1 S 19$_{21}$, שְׁלִישִׁ *third* 1 S 19$_{21}$.

<PREP> לְ of direction, *to*, + אמר *say* 1 S 11$_{9}$ 2 S 11$_{19}$.

בְּ introducing object, + לעב hi. *deride* 2 C 36$_{16}$.

בְּיַד *by the hand of*, i.e. by means of, + שׁלח pi. *send* 1 S 11$_{7}$ Jr 27$_{3}$ 2 C 36$_{15}$, חרף pi. *revile* 2 K 19$_{23}$.

כְּ *as* Is 42$_{19}$.

אֶל *to*, + אמר *say* Jg 11$_{13}$ 2 S 11$_{25}$ 2 K 1$_{2.5}$, דבר pi. *speak* Nm 24$_{12}$ 2 K 1$_{3}$.

עַל *upon*, + היה *be* 1 S 19$_{20}$.

לִפְנֵי *before*, + אמר *say* Ec 5$_{5}$ (unless §2; or em. הִמָּלֵאךְ *it has been fulfilled by you*, i.e. מלא ni.).

אַחֲרֵי *after*, + הלך *go* 1 S 25$_{42}$.

<COLL> עֶבֶד || מַלְאָךְ *servant* Is 42$_{19}$ 44$_{26}$, מְשָׁרֵת *minister* Ps 104$_{4}$, נָבִיא *prophet* 2 C 36$_{16}$, שַׂר *officer* Is 30$_{4}$; + צִיר *envoy* Pr 13$_{17}$.

2. heavenly messenger, angel, as good (1 S 29$_{9}$), wise, discerning (2 S 14$_{17.20}$), powerful (2 S 19$_{28}$), malevolent (e.g. 1QM 13$_{11}$ 1QS 3$_{20}$), destructive (e.g. 2 S

מַלְאָךְ

24$_{16.16}$ 2 K 19$_{35}$||Is 37$_{36}$ 1QM 13$_{12}$ 1QS 4$_{12}$), <SUBJ> היה *be* 2 S 24$_{16}$ 4QShir^{b} 35$_{4}$, אמר *say* Gn 16$_{9.10.11}$ 21$_{17}$ 22$_{11.15}$ 31$_{11}$ Nm 22$_{32.35}$ Jg 2$_{1}$ 5$_{23}$ 6$_{12.20}$ 13$_{3.13.16.18}$ 1 K 19$_{5.7}$ Zc 1$_{9.14}$ 2$_{2.7}$ 3$_{6}$ 4$_{1.5}$ 5$_{5.10}$ 6$_{5}$ 1 C 21$_{18}$, דבר *speak* Zc 1$_{9.13.14}$ 2$_{2.7}$ 4$_{1.4.5}$ 5$_{5.10}$ 6$_{4}$, pi. Nm 22$_{35}$ Jg 2$_{4}$ 1 K 13$_{18}$ 2 K 1$_{3.15}$ Zc 2$_{7}$, ענה *answer* Zc 1$_{12}$ 4$_{5}$ 6$_{5}$, קרא *call* Gn 21$_{17}$ 22$_{11.15}$, ברך pass. *be blessed* 11QM 1.2$_{6}$, pi. *bless* Gn 48$_{16}$ Ps 103$_{20}$, הלל pi. *praise* Ps 148$_{2}$, רנן *shout joyfully* 11QPs^{a} 26$_{12}$, עוד hi. *admonish* Zc 3$_{6}$, אוץ hi. *urge* Gn 19$_{15}$ (or em. הָאֲנָשִׁים *the men*), ארר pass. *be cursed* 4QBer^{a} 7.2$_{7}$ ([ארור ... מלא]ך), ראה *see* 1 C 21$_{20}$ (ms הַמֶּלֶךְ *the king*) 11QPs^{a} 26$_{12}$, ni. *appear* Jg 6$_{12}$ 13$_{3.9(ms).21}$ Ex 3$_{2}$, שׁמע *listen* Ps 103$_{20}$, ידע *know* 11QPs^{a} 26$_{12}$, בכה *weep* 4QpsJub^{a} 2.2$_{5}$.

הלך *go* Ex 14$_{19}$ 23$_{23}$ 32$_{34}$ Jg 6$_{21}$, htp. *go about* 1QM 13$_{12}$, נסע *depart* Ex 14$_{19}$, בוא *come* Gn 19$_{1}$ (or em.; see Coll.) Jg 6$_{11}$, hi. *bring* Ex 23$_{20.23}$, יצא *go out* Nm 22$_{32}$ 2 K 19$_{35}$||Is 37$_{36}$ Zc 2$_{7}$ (or em. יֹצֵא to עֹמֵד *standing*) 2$_{7}$ 5$_{5}$ 4QShirShabb^{f} 20$_{9}$ (if em. יצא *he goes out* to יצאו *they go out*), עלה *go up* Gn 28$_{12}$ Jg 2$_{1}$ 13$_{20}$, ירד *go down* Gn 28$_{12}$, עבר *pass* Nm 22$_{26}$, שׁוב *go back* 1 K 19$_{7}$ Zc 4$_{1}$ 4QShirShabb^{f} 20$_{9}$, סור *turn aside* CD 16$_{5}$, רוץ *run* Zc 2$_{7}$, רדף *pursue* Ps 35$_{6}$, עמד *stand* Nm 22$_{24.26}$ 2 S 24$_{16(4QSam^{a})}$||1 C 21$_{15}$ Zc 1$_{11}$ (or em.; see Obj.) 2$_{7}$ (if em.; see above) 3$_{5}$ 1 C 21$_{16}$ 4QpsJub^{a} 2.2$_{5}$, יצב htp. *stand* Nm 22$_{22}$ 11QM 1.2$_{14}$ ([מתיצבי]ם), נצב ni. *stand* Nm 22$_{23.31.34}$, ישׁב *sit* Jg 6$_{11}$, חנה *encamp* Ps 34$_{8}$ 4QBark^{a} 1.2$_{12}$, קרא *meet* Nm 22$_{34}$ Zc 2$_{7}$, פגע *meet* Gn 32$_{2}$, מצא *find* Gn 16$_{7}$, נשׂא *lift* Ps 91$_{11}$, יסף hi. *add* Nm 22$_{26}$ Jg 13$_{21}$, שׁלח *send* Jg 6$_{21}$, i.e. stretch, hand 2 S 24$_{16}$, נגע *touch* Jg 6$_{21}$ 1 K 19$_{5.7}$, רפה hi. *drop* hand 2 S 24$_{16}$||1 C 21$_{15}$, דחה *push* Ps 35$_{5}$, שׁלך *throw* perh. 4QNarrA 1$_{8}$.

אכל *eat* Jg 13$_{16}$, עור hi. *waken* Zc 4$_{1}$, גאל *redeem* Gn 48$_{16}$, ישׁע hi. *save* Is 63$_{9}$, חלץ pi. *deliver* Ps 34$_{8}$, שׁמר *keep* Ex 23$_{20}$ Ps 91$_{11}$, משׁל *rule* 4QpsMos^{e} 1$_{10}$ 2.1$_{6}$ ([מל]אכי), שׁחת pi. *destroy* 2 S 24$_{16}$, hi. 2 S 24$_{16(mss).16}$||1 C 21$_{15.15}$ 1 C 21$_{12}$, כחד hi. *destroy* 2 C 32$_{21}$, נכה hi. *strike* 2 S 24$_{17}$ 2 K 19$_{35}$||Is 37$_{36}$, עשׂה *do* Ps 103$_{20}$, עזר *help* 1QS 3$_{24}$.

<NOM CL> צורות בדניהם מלאכי קודש *the images of their figures are holy angels* 4QShirShabb^{f} 19$_{7}$, מַלְאַךְ י׳ הוּא *it was the angel of Y.* Jg 6$_{22}$ 13$_{16.21}$, יֵשׁ עָלָיו מַלְאָךְ *there is an angel for him* Jb 33$_{23}$, הנה מל[אך] *behold (there was) an angel* 4QJub^{h} 32$_{21}$, מלאכי קודש [בעצ]תם *holy angels are in their assembly* 1QSa 2$_{8}$, מלאכי הקוד[ש בתוכם] *the holy angels are among them* 4QD^{a} 8.1$_{9}$, מלאכי קודש עם צבאותם יחד *the holy angels are together with their hosts* 1QM 7$_{6}$ (=4QM^{a} 1$_{10}$ במערכותמה are *in their battle lines*), מיא מלאך *who is the angel?* 1QM 13$_{14}$.

<OBJ> ראה *see* Nm 22$_{23.25.27.31}$ Jg 6$_{22}$ 2 S 24$_{17}$ 1 C 21$_{16.20}$ (ms הַמֶּלֶךְ *the king*) 1QM 10$_{11}$, hi. *show* 11QPs^{a} 26$_{12}$, ענה *answer* Zc 1$_{11}$ (or em. אֶת־מַלְאַךְ י׳ הָעֹמֵד בֵּין הַהֲדַסִּים *the angel of Y. who was standing among the myrtles* to הָאִישׁ *the man*) 1$_{13}$, צוה pi. *command* Ps 91$_{11}$, שׁלח *send* Gn 24$_{7.40}$ Ex 23$_{20}$ 33$_{2}$ Nm 20$_{16}$ 1 C 21$_{15}$ 2 C 32$_{21}$ 4QapPs^{b} 29$_{2}$ 11QPsAp^{a} 4$_{5}$ ([ישלח]), קרא *meet* Zc 2$_{7}$ Gn 19$_{1}$, עצר *detain* Jg 13$_{15.16}$, עשׂה *make* 1QM 13$_{11}$, ברא *create* 4QJub^{a} 2$_{2}$ ([ברא]).

<CSTR> מַלְאַךְ י׳ *angel of Y.* Gn 16$_{7.9.10.11}$ 22$_{11.15}$ Ex 3$_{2}$ Nm 22$_{22+9t}$ Jg 2$_{1.4}$ 5$_{23}$ 6$_{11.12.21.21.22.22}$ 13$_{3+9t}$ 2 S 24$_{16}$|| 1 C 21$_{15}$ 1 K 19$_{7}$ 2 K 1$_{3}$ 2 K 19$_{35}$||Is 37$_{36}$ Zc 1$_{11}$ (or em.; see Obj.) 1$_{12}$ 3$_{1.5.6}$ 12$_{8}$ Ps 34$_{8}$ 35$_{5.6}$ 1 C 21$_{12.16.18.30}$ 4QpsEzek^{e} 5$_{25}$, הָאֱלֹהִים *of God* Gn 21$_{17}$ (אֱלֹהִים) 31$_{11}$ Jg 6$_{20}$ 13$_{6.9}$ 1 S 29$_{9}$ (אֱלֹהִים) 2 S 14$_{17.20}$ 19$_{28}$ 1 C 21$_{15}$ (if em. הָאֱלֹהִים מַלְאָךְ *God* sent *an angel*), מַלְאֲכֵי אֱלֹהִים *angels of God* Gn 28$_{12}$ 32$_{2}$, מלאכי מלך *angels of the king* 4QShirShabb^{d} 1.2$_{23}$.

מלאך פנים *angel of the presence* 1QSb 4$_{25}$ 3QTJud 5$_{3}$, מלאכי *angels of* 1QH 6$_{13}$ 1QSb 4$_{26}$ 4QJub^{a} 2$_{2}$ ([מלאכי] הפנים), מַלְאַךְ פָּנָיו *angel of his presence* Is 63$_{9}$, מלאך אבות *angel of intercessions* 4QPrEnosh 2$_{1}$.

מלאך כבודו *angel of his glory* 4QShir^{b} 20.1$_{2}$, מלאכי כבוד *angels of glory* 4QShirShabb^{f} 17$_{4}$, כבודו *of his glory* 4QShir^{b} 35$_{4}$, תפארת *of beauty* 4QShirShabb^{f} 17$_{5}$, קודשׁ *of holiness*, i.e. holy angels 1QH 1$_{11}$ (ק[ודש]) 1QM 7$_{6}$ 10$_{11}$ 1QSa 2$_{8}$ 1QSb 3$_{6}$ ([מלאכי] ק[ודש]) 4QJub^{a} 2$_{2}$ (הקו[דש]) 4QpsJub^{a} 2.2$_{5}$ 7$_{6}$ (הקדש) 4QD^{a} 8.1$_{9}$ (הקד[וש]) 15$_{1}$ (הק[דוש]) 4QShirShabb^{f} 19$_{7}$ 20$_{9}$ 23.1$_{8}$ 4QShirShabb^{h} 1$_{3}$ ([מ]לאכי) 11QShirShabb 37$_{1}$ (מלאכ[י] [קודש]) 4Q418 55$_{8}$, קודשו *of his holiness*, i.e. his holy angels 11QM 1.2$_{6.14}$ ([קודשו]), צדק *of righteousness* 6QHymn 5$_{2}$ ([מל]אכי), צדקכה *of your righteousness* 4QBer^{b} 2$_{13}$ ([מ]לאכי), הדעת *of knowledge* 11QShirShabb 10$_{6}$.

מלאך שלו[ם] *angel of peace* 3Q8 1_{2} (unless §1), מלאכי שלום *angels of peace* 4QHod^b 17_{3} 4Q474 1_{8} (מ[ל]אכי; unless both §1), מלאך שלומו *angel of his peace* 4QCitJub 1.1_{8}, שלומכה *of your peace* 4QPrEnosh 1.2_{9}, אמתו *of his truth* 1QS 3_{24}.

מלאכי ממשלתו *angels of his dominion* 1QM 1_{15}, מש[רת] *of authority* 4QBer^a 3_{2}, רום *of loftiness*, i.e. lofty angels 4QShirShabb^d 1.1_{1} ([מ]לאכי), רקיע *of the firmament of* 4QDibHam^a 1.7_{6}, מאורות *of the lights of* 4QShir^b 2.1_{8} (מלא[כי]), ע[ננ]י *of clouds of* rain 4QBer^a 3_{4}, אש *of fire* 4QBer^b 4_{4}, הקולו[ת] *of the sounds* 4QJub^a 2_{2}, הרוחות *of the winds/spirits* 4QJub^a $2_{2.2}$ ([מלאכי הרוחות]), רוחות *of the spirits of* 4QJub^a 2_{2} ([מ]לאכי רוחות]) 2_{2}.

מלאך חושך *angel of darkness* 1QS $3_{20.21}$, משטמה *of animosity* (or *of Mastema*) 1QM 13_{11} CD 16_{5} (המשטמה), מלאכי *angels of* 4QpsJub^a 2.2_{6} (המ[שטמה]) 4QpsEzek^c 3.3_{4} (המשטמות) 4QpsMos^e 1_{10} (המש[ט]מות) 2_{6} (מל[אכי המשטמות]), מַלְאֲכֵי רָעִים *angels of evil* Ps 78_{49} (or em. מַלְאָכִים evil *angels*), מלאכי חבל *angels of destruction* 1QM 13_{12} 1QS 4_{12} 4QTwoWays 2_{7} (מלאכ[י חבל]) 4QShir^a 1_{5} CD 2_{6}, [מלא]ך השחת *angel of the pit* 4QBer^a 7.2_{7}, מלאכי זב[ול] *angels of the dwelling place* 4QShirShabb^f 81_{2}.

אלוהי [מ]לאכי *God of the angels of* 4QShirShabb^d 1.1_{1}, שר מלאכיו *commander of his angels* 4QM^a 1_{3}, רואי מלאכי *ones who see the angels of* 1QM 10_{11}, יד מלאך *hand of the angel of* 1QS 3_{20}, מלאכי *of the angels of* 4QpsEzek^c 3.3_{4} 4QpsMos^e 2.1_{6} (יד מל[אכי]), כול מלאכי *of all the angels of* 1QS 4_{12} perh. CD 2_{6} (בי כל *in the hand of all*), רוחי מלאכי *spirits of the angels of* 4QShir^a 1_{5}.

צבא מלאכים *host of angels* 1QM 12_{8} 4QM^a 5_{1} ([מ]ל[אכי]ם), צבאות *hosts of* 1QM 12_{1}, מִשְׁלַחַת מַלְאֲכֵי *troop of angels of* Pr 78_{49} (or em. מַלְאָכִים *of angels*), רוב כל מלאכים *multitude of all the angels* GnzPs 1_{23}, מוצאי מלאכי *goings out of the angels of* 4QShirShabb^f 23.1_{8}, גבורת מלאך *might of the angel* 1QM 17_{6}, מַרְאֵה מַלְאַךְ *appearance of the angel of* Jg 13_{6}, חָכְמַת *wisdom of* 2 S 14_{20}, חֶרֶב *sword of* 1 C 21_{30}.

כל מלאכים *all the angels* 4QapMes 5.2_{15} (כ[ו]ל) 4QHymnB 1_{2} GnzPs 1_{23}, כול מלאכי *all the angels of* 1QS 4_{12} 4QDibHam^a 1.7_{6} (corrected from מלאכים) 4QTwoWays 2_{7} ([מלאכ]י) 11QM 1.2_{6} CD 2_{6} (כל), כול מלאכיו *all his angels* 11QPs^a 26_{12} 11QPsAp^a 3_{4} ([מ]לאכיו).

<APP> אֱלֹהִים *God* Zc 12_{8}, גִּבּוֹר *mighty one* Ps 103_{20}, לִיץ hi. ptc. *mediator* Jb 33_{23}, בְּלִיַּעַל *Belial* 1QM 13_{11}, רוּחַ *spirit* 1QM 13_{12}.

<ADJ> אַחֵר *another* Zc 2_{7}, רִאשׁוֹן 4QNarrA 1_{8} (הרישו[ן]), רַע *evil* Ps 78_{49}, perh. אַדִּיר *majestic* 1QM 17_{6} (but prob. האדיר is אדר hi. *make glorious*), תַּקִּיף *mighty* 4_{5}.

<PREP> לְ of direction, *to* perh. 11QShirShabb 10_{6}, + אמר *say* 2 S 24_{16}||1 C 21_{15} 1 C 21_{27}, נתן *give* perh. 4QPseud^a 1_{3} (unless §1); introducing predicate, + היה *be* 1QH 1_{11}; introducing object, + ברא *create* 4QJub^a 2_{2} ([ברא]), שׁבע hi. *adjure* 11QPsAp^a 3_{4} (לכול מ[לאכיו]).

בְּ of place, *in* perh. 4QMyst^c $2b_{6}$, + שׂים *place*, i.e. charge with, folly Jb 4_{18}; of cause, *on account of*, or of agent, *by (means of)* 1QS 3_{21} 4_{12}.

כְּ *as* 1 S 29_{9} 2 S 14_{17} 19_{28} 1QSb 4_{25}, + היה *be* Zc 12_{8}, דבר pi. *speak* 4QapMos^c 2.2_{11}.

אֶל *to*, + אמר *say* Nm 22_{34} Jg 6_{12} $13_{15.17}$ Zc 2_{2} 4_{4} 5_{10} 6_{4}; *with*, + שׂור *strive* Ho 12_{5} (or em. אֵל *God**).

עם *with* 1QH 6_{13} 1QM 12_{4} 1QSb 3_{6} 4QShir^b 2.1_{8} (מלא[כי]), + נפל hi. *make fall*, i.e. cast, lot 1QSb 4_{26}.

לִפְנֵי *before*, + עשׂה *do*, i.e. prepare Jg 13_{15}, עמד *stand* Zc $3_{1.3}$ (or del.).

<COLL> מַלְאָךְ || רוּחַ *spirit* 4QBer^b 4_{4} 4QShirShabb^f 17_{5} (+), שַׂר *prince* 1QM 13_{14} 1QS 3_{20}, קָדוֹשׁ *holy one* 1QM $12_{1.4}$, צָבָא *host* Ps 148_{2} 4QShir^b 35_{4} (+); + אֵל *God* 1QS 3_{24} 4QShirShabb^f 23.1_{8}, עֶבֶד *servant* Jb 4_{18}, מְשָׁרֵת *minister* 4QShir^b 35_{4}, כֹּהֵן *priest* 4QShir^b 35_{4}, עַם *people* 4QShir^b 35_{4}.

מַלְאָךְ as vocative 4QBer^a 7.2_{7} (מלא[ך]).

שְׁנֵי הַמַּלְאָכִים *the two angels* Gn 19_{1} (or em. הָאֲנָשִׁים *the men*), מלאך האדיר למשרת מיכאל perh. *the majestic angel of the authority of Michael* 1QM 17_{6} (but prob. *he has made glorious* the might of *the angel for the authority of Michael*).

Also 4QBer^b 2_{12} 4QBer^d 3_{2} ([מ]לאכי) 4QMyst^a 5_{11} (מלכ[י]) 4QapPs^b 1_{10} (מלא[כיו]) 4QShirShabb^f 49_{3} 4Q418 164_{3} (מל[אכיו]) 4QPrFêtes^c 10.2_{5} 4QOrd^b 2.2_{4} ([מ]לאכי) 11QShirShabb 9_{9}.

3. salesman,* <SUBJ> עבר *pass* Is 23$_{2(1QIsa^{a})}$ (unless §1; MT מִלְאוּךְ *they filled you*, i.e. מלא pi.).

<SYN> §1 עֶבֶד *servant*, מְשָׁרֵת *minister*, נָבִיא *prophet*, שַׂר *officer*; §2 רוּחַ *spirit*, שַׂר *prince*, קָדוֹשׁ *holy one*, צָבָא *host*.*

⇨ מַלְאָכִי *Malachi*; cf. מַלְאָכוּת *message*.

מְלָאכָה 166.7.19.1 n.f. **work**—cstr. מְלֶאכֶת; sf. מְלַאכְתְּךָ (מְלַאכְתֶּךָ), מְלַאכְתּוֹ, Q מלאכתמה; pl. cstr. מַלְאֲכוֹת; sf. מַלְאֲכוֹתֶיךָ (Si מלאכתיך)—**1a. work, task, deed, business, trade,** of Y. (Ps 73$_{28}$), in creation (Gn 2$_{2.2.3}$), in judgment (Jr 48$_{10}$ 50$_{25}$); of humans (Gn 39$_{11}$ Jon 1$_{8}$ Ps 107$_{23}$ Pr 18$_{9}$ 22$_{29}$ 24$_{27}$ Si 3$_{17[C]}$ 4$_{29.30(A)}$ 7$_{15}$ 11$_{20}$ 1QS 6$_{2}$ 4QWays^{b} 1$_{14}$ 11QT 47$_{9}$ CD 10$_{19}$ Lachish ost. 13$_{1}$), specif. of potter (Jr 18$_{3}$), perh. playing of timbrels (Ezk 28$_{13}$), particular assignment (4Q424 1$_{6}$); work as prohibited on sabbath and holy days (Ex 12$_{16}$ 20$_{9.10}$||Dt 5$_{13.14}$ Ex 31$_{14.15.15}$ 35$_{2.2}$ Lv 16$_{29}$ 23$_{3+10t}$ Nm 28$_{18.25.26}$ 29$_{1.7.12.35}$ Dt 16$_{8}$ Jr 17$_{22.24}$ 4QJub^{c} 2$_{27}$ 11QT 14$_{10}$ 17$_{11.16}$ 19$_{8}$ 25$_{9}$ 27$_{6.7.10}$ CD 10$_{15}$); work in service of the king (1 S 8$_{16}$ 1 K 5$_{30.30}$ 9$_{23.23}$ 11$_{28}$ Est 3$_{9}$ 9$_{3}$ Dn 8$_{27}$ 1 C 4$_{23}$ 27$_{26}$ 29$_{6}$ 2 C 8$_{9}$), of the sanctuary (Nm 4$_{3}$ Ne 10$_{34}$ 11$_{12.16.22}$ 13$_{10.30}$ 1 C 6$_{34}$ 9$_{13.19.33}$ 23$_{4.24}$ 25$_{1}$ 26$_{30}$ 28$_{13.21}$ 4QRP^{c} 23$_{5.8}$); work of priests dealing with sacrifices (2 C 29$_{34}$), of the Levites as officers and judges (1 C 26$_{29}$), of Israelites, in putting away foreign wives (Ezr 10$_{13}$); work of constructing tabernacle and furnishings (Ex 35$_{21.24.29}$ 36$_{1+8t}$ 38$_{24}$ 40$_{33}$), temple and furnishings (1 K 7$_{14.40}$||2 C 4$_{11}$ 1 K 7$_{51}$||2 C 5$_{1}$ 1 C 22$_{15}$ 28$_{19.20}$ 29$_{1}$ 2 C 8$_{16}$), repairing temple (2 K 12$_{12}$||2 C 24$_{12}$ 2 K 12$_{15.16}$ 22$_{5.5.9}$||2 C 34$_{10.10.17}$ 2 C 24$_{13.13}$ 34$_{12.13}$), rebuilding temple (Hg 1$_{14}$ Ezr 3$_{8.9}$ 6$_{22}$ Ezr 2$_{69}$||Ne 7$_{70}$ Ne 7$_{69}$), rebuilding walls of Jerusalem (Ne 2$_{16}$ 4$_{5+5t}$ 5$_{16.16}$ 6$_{3.3.9.16}$), building Ramah (2 C 16$_{5}$).

b. handiwork, craft, in making tabernacle and temple and their furnishings (distinction from §1a not alw. clear) (Ex 31$_{3.5}$||35$_{31.33}$ 35$_{35.35}$ 36$_{8}$ 38$_{24}$ 39$_{43}$ 1 K 7$_{14.22}$ 1 C 29$_{5}$).

2. (product of) work (Lv 13$_{48}$).

3. use, purpose (Lv 7$_{24}$ 11$_{32}$ 13$_{51}$ Jg 16$_{11}$ Ezk 15$_{3.4.5.5}$ 4QD^{f} 2$_{11}$ [מ]לאכה]]).

4. property, object, livestock (Ex 22$_{7.10}$ Gn 33$_{14}$ 1 S 15$_{9}$ 2 C 17$_{13}$ 1QS 6$_{19.20}$).

5. trading mission (Ps 107$_{23}$ Pr 22$_{29}$; both unless §1).

<SUBJ> היה *be* Ex 36$_{7}$ appar. Ne 4$_{16}$ (mss לִמְלָאכָה *for work*) 2 C 17$_{13}$, עשׂה ni. *be done* Ex 12$_{16}$ 31$_{15}$ 35$_{2}$ Lv 11$_{32}$ 23$_{3}$ Jg 16$_{11}$ Ne 6$_{16}$ 4QD^{f} 2$_{11}$ ([יעשה מ]לאכה]), כלה *be complete* 1 C 28$_{20}$ 2 C 29$_{34}$, תמם *be complete* 1 K 7$_{22}$, שׁלם *be complete* 1 K 7$_{51}$||2 C 5$_{1}$, כון ni. *be established* 2 C 8$_{16}$, שׁבת *cease* Ne 6$_{3}$, בזה ni. *be despised* 1 S 15$_{9}$, מסס ni. *be melted*, i.e. worthless 1 S 15$_{9}$.

<NOM CL> הַמְּלָאכָה הַרְבֵּה וּרְחָבָה *the work is great and widely spaced* Ne 4$_{13}$, הַמְּלָאכָה גְּדוֹלָה *the work is great* 1 C 29$_{1}$, מלאכת צ[דק] היאה *it is a work of righteousness* 4QWays 1$_{14}$, מָה מְלַאכְתְּךָ *what is your business?* Jon 1$_{8}$, הַמְּלָאכָה אֲשֶׁר לְפָנַי *the livestock that is before me* Gn 33$_{14}$, מְלָאכָה הִיא לַאדֹנָי *that is the work of the Lord* Jr 50$_{25}$, מְלֶאכֶת תֻּפֶּיךָ וּנְקָבֶיךָ בָּךְ *the work of your settings and your engravings was within you* Ezk 28$_{13}$, הַמְּלָאכָה אֲשֶׁר לַמֶּלֶךְ *the work which is for the king* Est 9$_{3}$, הַמְּלָאכָה לֹא־לְיוֹם אֶחָד וְלֹא לִשְׁנַיִם *the work is not for one day or two* Ezr 10$_{13}$, עֲלֵיהֶם הַמְּלָאכָה *the work was upon them*, i.e. it was their responsibility 1 C 9$_{33}$ (if em. בַּמְּלָאכָה *in the work*).

<OBJ> כלה pi. *complete* Gn 2$_{2}$ Ex 40$_{33}$, עשׂה *do* Gn 2$_{2.2.3}$ 39$_{11}$ Ex 20$_{9.10}$||Dt 5$_{13.14}$ Ex 31$_{14.15}$ 35$_{2.29.35.35}$ 36$_{1+8t}$ 49$_{43}$ Lv 16$_{29}$ 23$_{3+9t}$ Nm 4$_{3}$ 28$_{18.25.26}$ 29$_{1.7.12.35}$ Dt 16$_{8}$ 1 K 7$_{14.14.40}$||2 C 4$_{11}$ 1 K 7$_{51}$||2 C 5$_{1}$ 1 K 11$_{28}$ 2 K 12$_{12}$||2 C 24$_{12}$ 2 K 12$_{15.16}$ 22$_{5.5.9}$||2 C 34$_{10.10.17}$ Jr 17$_{22.24}$ 18$_{3}$ 48$_{10}$ Hg 1$_{14}$ Ps 107$_{23}$ Est 3$_{9}$ 9$_{3}$ Dn 8$_{27}$ Ezr 3$_{9}$ Ne 2$_{16}$ 6$_{3}$ 11$_{12}$ 13$_{10}$ 1 C 22$_{15}$ 23$_{24}$ 27$_{26}$ 2 C 24$_{13}$ 34$_{13}$ 4QJub^{c} 2$_{27}$ 11QT 14$_{10}$ ([תעשו]) 17$_{11.16}$ 19$_{8}$ ([יעשו]) 25$_{9}$ 27$_{6.7.10}$ 47$_{9}$ CD 10$_{15.19}$ Lachish ost. 13$_{1}$, ברא *create* Gn 2$_{3}$, כון hi. *prepare* Pr 24$_{27}$, קרב hi. *bring near* 1QS 6$_{19}$, צנע hi. *guard* 4Q424 1$_{6}$, שׁבת hi. *cause to cease* Ne 4$_{5}$ 2 C 16$_{5}$, ראה *see* Ex 39$_{43}$, ספר pi. *tell of* Ps 73$_{28}$, שׂכל hi. *cause to understand* 1 C 28$_{19}$, חרם hi. *devote to destruction* 1 S 15$_{9}$.

<CSTR> מְלֶאכֶת י׳ *work of*, i.e. for, *Y.* Jr 48$_{10}$ 1 C 26$_{30}$, הַמֶּלֶךְ *of*, i.e. for, *the king* Dn 8$_{27}$ 1 C 29$_{6}$, שְׁלֹמֹה *of Solomon* 2 C 8$_{16}$, מְלֶאכֶת חָרָשׁ *craft of an artisan* Ex 35$_{35}$.

מְלֶאכֶת עֲבֹדָה *work of labour* Ex 35$_{24}$ (הָעֲבֹדָה) Lv 23$_{7.8.21.25.35.36}$ Nm 28$_{18.25.26}$ 29$_{1.7(mss).12.35}$ Dt 15$_{8(Sam)}$

1 C 9$_{19}$ (הָעֲבֹדָה) Si 7$_{15}$ 11QT 14$_{10}$ ([עבו]דה) 17$_{11.16}$ (both עבודה) 19$_{8}$ ([עבו]דה) 25$_{9}$ ([עבו]דה), עֲבֹדַת *of the labour of* Ex 36$_{1.3}$ 1 C 9$_{13}$ 28$_{13.20}$ (all three עֲבוֹדַת), אֹהֶל *of the tent of* meeting Ex 35$_{21}$, הַקֹּדֶשׁ *of the sanctuary* Ex 38$_{24}$, קֹדֶשׁ הַקֳּדָשִׁים *of the most holy place* 1 C 6$_{34}$, בֵּית *of the house of* Y. Ezr 3$_{8}$ 6$_{22}$ Ne 10$_{34}$ 11$_{22}$ 1 C 23$_{4}$, מלאכ[ת הב]ית *work of the house* 4QRPc 23$_{5}$, מְלֶאכֶת הַשָּׂדֶה *work of*, i.e. in, *the field* 1 C 27$_{26}$.

מְלֶאכֶת עוֹר *work of*, i.e. in, *skin* Lv 13$_{48}$, הָעַמּוּדִים *of*, i.e. on, *the pillars* 1 K 7$_{22}$, הַחוֹמָה *of*, i.e. on, *the wall* Ne 5$_{16}$, תֻּפֶּיךָ וּנְקָבֶיךָ perh. *of your settings and your engravings* Ezk 28$_{13}$ (unless *of your timbrels and your pipes*), מלאכת צ[דק] *work of righteousness* 4QWays 11$_{4}$, מְלֶאכֶת מַחֲשָׁבֶת *craft of design* Ex 35$_{33}$, מַלְאֲכוֹת הַתַּבְנִית *works of*, i.e. according to, *the pattern* 1 C 28$_{19}$.

מְלֶאכֶת רֵעֵהוּ *property of his neighbour* Ex 22$_{7.10}$, מלאכת הרבים *property of the many* 1QS 6$_{20}$.

אַנְשֵׁי מְלָאכָה *men of work* 1 C 25$_{1}$, גִּבּוֹרֵי חֵיל מְלֶאכֶת *mighty ones of ability of*, i.e. for, *the work of* 1 C 9$_{13}$ (or em. חֵיל לִמְלֶאכֶת *of ability for the work of*), שָׂרֵי מְלֶאכֶת *officers of*, i.e. over, *the work of* 1 C 29$_{6}$, עֹשֵׂה מְלָאכָה *one who does work* Ps 107$_{23(mss)}$ Ezr 3$_{9}$ Ne 2$_{16}$ 11$_{12}$ 1 C 23$_{24}$ (all four הַמְּלָאכָה) 2 C 34$_{10}$ (הַמְּלָאכָה) 34$_{13}$ (both mss עֹשֵׂי), עוֹשֵׂה מְלֶאכֶת *one who does the work of* 2 C 24$_{12}$, עֹשֵׂי הַמְּלָאכָה *ones who do the work* Ex 36$_{8}$ 2 K 12$_{12.15.16}$ 2 K 22$_{5.5.9}$||2 C 34$_{10(mss).10.17}$ (2 C all three עוֹשֵׂי) 2 K 22$_{9}$ Ps 107$_{23}$ Est 3$_{9}$ 9$_{3}$ Ezr 3$_{9(mss)}$ Ne 2$_{16(mss)}$ Ne 11$_{12}$ 13$_{10}$ 1 C 22$_{15}$ (מְלָאכָה) 23$_{24(mss)}$ 2 C 24$_{13}$ 34$_{13 (mss)}$, עֹשֵׂי כָל־מְלָאכָה *ones who do any kind of work* Ex 35$_{35}$, עֹשֵׂי מְלֶאכֶת *ones who do the work of* 1 C 27$_{26}$ 2 C 24$_{13(mss)}$ (עוֹשֵׂי).

מרדות מלאכה *chastisement of work* Si 30$_{33}$, צבא מלאכת *service (consisting) of the work of* Si 7$_{15}$, דברי המלאכה *matters of the work* CD 10$_{19}$, אוֹצַר הַמְּלָאכָה *treasury of the work* Ezr 2$_{69}$||Ne 7$_{70}$, רֶגֶל הַמְּלָאכָה *pace of the livestock* Gn 33$_{13}$.

כָּל־מְלָאכָה *all work* Ex 12$_{16}$ Ex20$_{10}$||Dt 5$_{14}$ Ex 31$_{3}$||35$_{31}$ 31$_{5}$ 35$_{35}$ Lv 7$_{24}$ 16$_{29}$ 23$_{3.28.30.31}$ Nm 29$_{7}$ Dt 16$_{8(mss)}$ 1 K 7$_{14}$ Jr 17$_{22.24}$ 1 C 28$_{21}$ 29$_{5}$ 4Q5284 (כול מ[ל]אכ[ה]) 11QT 27$_{6.10}$ (both כול), כָּל־הַמְּלָאכָה *all the work* Ex 35$_{29}$ 36$_{7}$ 39$_{43}$ 1 K 7$_{40}$||2 C 4$_{11(mss)}$ 1 K 7$_{51}$||2 C 5$_{1}$, כָּל־מְלֶאכֶת *all work of* Ex 35$_{24}$ 35$_{33.35}$ 36$_{1.4}$ 38$_{24}$ (כֹּל) Lv 13$_{48}$ 23$_{7+5t}$ Nm 28$_{18.25.26}$ 29$_{1.7(mss).12.35}$ Dt 16$_{8(Sam)}$ Ne 10$_{34}$ 1 C 6$_{34}$ 26$_{30}$ (all three כֹּל) 28$_{13.20}$ 2 C 8$_{16}$ 4QRPc 23$_{5}$ (מלאכ[ות]) 23$_{8}$ 11QT 14$_{10}$ 17$_{11.16}$ 19$_{8}$ 25$_{9}$ (all seven כול), כָּל־מְלַאכְתּוֹ *all his work* Gn 2$_{2.3}$ 1 K 7$_{14}$, כָּל־מְלַאכְתֶּךָ *all your work* Ex 20$_{9}$||Dt 5$_{13}$, כֹּל מַלְאֲכוֹת *all the works of* 1 C 28$_{19}$, כָּל־מַלְאֲכוֹתֶיךָ *all your works* Ps 73$_{28}$.

<ADJ> גָּדוֹל *great* Ne 6$_{3}$, רַב *great* 2 C 17$_{13}$, חִיצוֹן *outer* Ne 11$_{16}$ 1 C 26$_{29}$, זאת *this* Ne 6$_{16}$, כֹּל *everything* 1 C 28$_{19}$.

<PREP> לְ of benefit, *to, for* 1 C 9$_{13}$ (if em.; see Cstr.) 1 C 26$_{29.30}$ 28$_{13}$, + היה *be* Ex 36$_{7}$ Ne 4$_{16(mss)}$, בוא hi. *bring* Ex 35$_{21.29}$ 36$_{3}$, קרב hi. *bring near* 4QRPc 23$_{5.8}$ (יקרי[בו]), נתן *give* Ne 7$_{69}$ perh. 10$_{34}$ 1 C 29$_{5}$ 2 C 8$_{9}$, מצא ni. *be found* Ex 35$_{24}$, עשׂה *do*, i.e. use 1 S 8$_{16}$ Ezk 15$_{3}$, pass. *be made*, i.e. used Ex 38$_{24}$ Lv 7$_{24}$ 13$_{51}$ Ezk 15$_{5.5}$, צלח *succeed*, i.e. be useful Ezk 15$_{4}$, עלה *go up* 2 C 24$_{13}$, קטר hi. *burn*, i.e. offer 1 C 6$_{34}$.

לְ *with respect to*, + שׁמע *obey* 1QS 6$_{2}$; of possession, *of, (belonging) to* Ex 36$_{5}$.

בְּ of accompaniment, *in, with* Pr 22$_{29}$ (אִישׁ מָהִיר בִּמְלַאכְתּוֹ *a man skilled in his work*, or *in his business*) Ne 13$_{30}$ 1 C 9$_{33}$ (or em.; see Nom. Cl.) 28$_{21}$, + היה *be* Si 4$_{29}$, ישׁב *dwell* 1 C 4$_{23}$, ירא htp. *be fearsome* Si 4$_{30(A)}$, רפה htp. *be slack* Pr 18$_{9}$, חזק pi. *strengthen* hands Ezr 6$_{22}$; of instrument, *by (means of), with*, + ישׁן htp. *make oneself old* Si 11$_{20}$ (התי[שן]); of place, *in*, + היה *be* Lv 13$_{48}$.

בְּ introducing object, + עשׂה *do* Ex 31$_{5}$ 1 K 5$_{30}$ 9$_{23}$ Ne 4$_{10.11.15}$ 2 C 34$_{12}$, חזק hi. *hold on to* Ne 5$_{16}$, יאל hi. perh. *require* 4Q5284 (מ[ל]אכ[ה]); *(consisting) of* Ex 31$_{3}$||35$_{31}$; שׁלח בְּ *send*, i.e. put, hand, *to* Ex 22$_{7.10}$.

מִן *from*, + בוא *come* Ex 36$_{4}$, שׁבת *rest* Gn 2$_{2.3}$, רפה *drop* Ne 6$_{9}$.

אֶל *to*, + קרב *draw near* Ex 36$_{2}$, שׁוב *go back* Ne 4$_{9}$.

עַל *over, in charge of* 1 K 5$_{30}$ 9$_{23}$ Ne 11$_{16}$ 1 C 9$_{19}$ 1QS 6$_{20}$; introducing object, + נצח pi. *oversee* Ezr 3$_{8}$ 1 C 23$_{4}$.

עַל *for, at*, + קבץ pass. *be gathered* Ne 5$_{16}$; *concerning*, + יעץ ni. *take counsel* Si 37$_{11}$.

אֵת *with*, + הלך *go* Si 3$_{17(C)}$.

לְנֶגֶד *over* Ne 11$_{22}$.

<COLL> עֲבֹדָה || מְלָאכָה *service* Ex 35$_{21}$ (+) 1 C 25$_{1}$ (+) 26$_{30}$ 27$_{26}$ (+) 2 C 34$_{13}$ (+) CD 10$_{19}$, לָשׁוֹן *tongue*, i.e.

speech Si 4$_{29}$, מָמוֹן *wealth* 1QS 6$_{2}$, הוֹן *wealth* 1QS 6$_{19}$; + מַחֲשָׁבָה *design* Ex 35$_{33}$, יֶלֶד *child* Gn 33$_{13}$.

מְלָאכָה לִתְרוּמַת הַקֹּדֶשׁ *work for the contribution of,* i.e. towards, *the sanctuary* Ex 36$_{6}$, מְלָאכָה בַּנְּחֹשֶׁת *work in bronze* 1 K 7$_{14}$, מְלָאכָה בְּיַד חָרָשִׁים *work by the hand of artisans* 1 C 29$_{5}$, הַמְּלָאכָה לִשְׁלֹמֹה *the work of Solomon* 1 K 9$_{23}$, הַמְּלָאכָה לַבַּיִת *the work of the house* (of Y.) Ne 11$_{12}$, sim. Ne 11$_{16}$ 1 C 23$_{24}$.

Also 11QT 20$_{010}$ (מל[א]כ[ות]).

<SYN> §1 עֲבֹדָה *service,* לָשׁוֹן *tongue,* i.e. *speech;* §4 מָמוֹן *wealth,* הוֹן *wealth.**

[מַלְאָכוּת] 1 n.f. **message**—cstr. מַלְאֲכוּת—**1. message** (if not §2), <CSTR> מַלְאֲכוּת י׳ *message of Y.* Hg 1$_{13}$. <PREP> בְּ of accompaniment, *with,* + אמר *speak* Hg 1$_{13}$.

2. messenger (if not §1), <CSTR> מַלְאֲכוּת י׳ *messenger of Y.* Hg 1$_{13}$. <PREP> בְּ of quality, *as,* + אמר *speak* Hg 1$_{13}$.*

⇒ cf. מַלְאָךְ *messenger.*

מַלְאָכִי 1.0.0.1 pr.n.m. **Malachi,** lit. 'my messenger', **1.** perh. pseudonym for anonymous prophet, <PREP> בְּיַד *by (means of), through,* lit. 'by the hand of' Ml 1$_{1}$.

2. Arad ost. 97.

⇒ מַלְאָךְ *messenger.*

מלאכיה, see מַלְכִּיָּה *Malchi(j)ah.*

מְלֶאכֶת I, see מְלָאכָה *work.*

מְלֶאכֶת II, see מַלְכָּה *queen.*

מִלֵּאת I 1 n.f. **setting** of eyes, or of teeth (if ins. שִׁנָּיו *his teeth*), unless מִלֵּאת II *waterhole,* III *stream,* IV *pool* or V *fullness,* <PREP> עַל *upon, beside,* + ישׁב *sit* Ca 5$_{12}$ (Gnz עַד *unto*).

⇒ מלא *be full.**

מִלֵּאת II 1 n.f. **waterhole, pond,** unless מִלֵּאת I *setting,* III *stream,* IV *pool* or V *fullness,* <PREP> עַל *upon, beside,* + ישׁב *sit* Ca 5$_{12}$ (יֹשְׁבוֹת עַל־מִלֵּאת *set beside waterhole(s);* Gnz עַד *unto*).*

⇒ מלא *be full.*

***מִלֵּאת** III 1 n.f. **stream** (unless מִלֵּאת I *setting,* II *waterhole,* IV *pool* or V *fullness*), <PREP> עַל *upon, beside,* + ישׁב *sit* Ca 5$_{12}$ (Gnz עַד *unto*).

***מִלֵּאת** IV 1 n.f. **pool** (unless מִלֵּאת I *setting,* II *waterhole,* III *stream* or V *fullness*), <PREP> עַל *upon, beside,* + ישׁב *sit* Ca 5$_{12}$ (Gnz עַד *unto*).

***מִלֵּאת** V 1 n.f. **fullness** (unless מִלֵּאת I *setting,* II *waterhole,* III *stream* or IV *pool*), <PREP> עַל *upon, beside,* + ישׁב *sit* Ca 5$_{12}$ (Gnz עַד *unto*).

⇒ מלא *be full.*

מִלְּבַד, see לְבַד *alone.*

מַלְבּוּשׁ 8 n.m. **garment**—sf. מַלְבּוּשֵׁךְ, מַלְבּוּשִׁי, מַלְבּוּשֵׁיהֶם (מַלְבֻּשֵׁיהֶם)—**garment, clothing,** <NOM CL> מַלְבּוּשֵׁךְ שֵׁשׁ וָמֶשִׁי וְרִקְמָה *your clothing was of fine linen and rich fabric and embroidery* Ezk 16$_{13}$(Qr). <OBJ> ראה *see* 1 K 10$_{5}$||2 C 9$_{4}$ (or em. מַלְבִּישָׁיו *his wardrobe attendants,* i.e. לבשׁ hi. ptc.) 2 C 9$_{4}$, יצא hi. *bring out* 2 K 10$_{22}$, לבשׁ *wear* Zp 1$_{8}$, כון hi. *prepare* Jb 27$_{16}$, גאל hi. *defile* Is 63$_{3}$. <CSTR> כָּל־מַלְבּוּשַׁי *all my garments* Is 63$_{3}$. <ADJ> נָכְרִי *foreign* Zp 1$_{8}$. <COLL> מַלְבּוּשׁ || כֶּסֶף *silver* Jb 27$_{16}$; + בֶּגֶד *garment* Is 63$_{3}$.

⇒ לבשׁ *dress.*

מַלְבֵּן 3 n.[m.] **brickmould, brick pavement, 1. brickmould,** <OBJ> חזק hi. *grasp* Na 3$_{14}$. <PREP> בְּ of place, accompaniment, *at, with,* + עבר hi. *cause to pass* 2 S 12$_{31}$(Qr) (Kt מלכן; + מְגֵזָרָה *axe,* חָרִיץ *pickaxe,* מְגֵרָה *saw*); of instrument, *by (means of), with,* + עבד hi. *make work* 2 S 12$_{31}$(Qr) (if em. הֶעֱבִיר *he caused to pass* to הֶעֱבִיד *he made* them *work*).

2. brick pavement, terrace or quadrangle, <NOM CL> בַּמַּלְבֵּן אֲשֶׁר בְּפֶתַח בֵּית־פַּרְעֹה *in the brick pavement that is in the entrance of the house of Pharaoh* Jr 43$_{9}$. <APP> מֶלֶט *mortar* Jr 43$_{9}$. <PREP> בְּ of place, *in,* + טמן *hide* Jr 43$_{9}$.*

⇒ לבן II *make bricks.*

*[מלה] $_{0.0.3}$ vb. **be full—Qal** $_{0.0.3}$ Ptc. Q מלה—**1. be full of,** <SUBJ> Y. Ezk 16$_{30}$ (if em. אֻמְלָה *it is enfeebled* to אֶמְלָה *I am full of*). <OBJ> לִבָּה *anger* Ezk 16$_{30}$ (if em.; see Subj.).

2. ptc. used as noun, **filled place,** i.e. terrace (3QTr 3$_{8.11}$), cistern 3QTr 2$_{1}$),* <CSTR> בור המלה *cistern of the filled place* 3QTr 2$_{1}$. <PREP> בְּ of place, *in* 3QTr 3$_{8.11}$.

Ni. be full of, be filled with, <SUBJ> Y. Ezk 16$_{30}$ (if em. אֻמְלָה *it is enfeebled* to אִמָּלֵה *I am filled*). <OBJ> לִבָּה *anger* Ezk 16$_{30}$ (if em.; see Subj.).

⇒ cf. מלא *be full.*

מִלָּה $_{38.0.7}$ n.f. **word**—cstr. Q מילת; sf. מִלָּתִי, מִלָּתוֹ; pl. מִלִּים (מִלִּין); sf. מִלַּי, מִלֶּיךָ, מִלֵּיהֶם—**word, speech;** derisive **byword** (Jb 30$_{9}$), <SUBJ> כתב ni. *be written* Jb 19$_{23}$, יצא *go out* Ps 19$_{5}$, נטף *drip* Jb 29$_{22}$, עתק hi. *move* Jb 32$_{15}$, קום hi. *raise* Jb 4$_{4}$.

<NOM CL> לֹא־שֶׁקֶר מִלָּי *my words are not falsehood* Jb 36$_{4}$, יֵשׁ מִלִּין *there are words* Jb 33$_{32}$, אֵין מִלָּה בִּלְשׁוֹנִי *there is no word on my tongue* Ps 139$_{3}$, מִלָּתוֹ עַל־לְשׁוֹנִי *his* (Y.'s) *word is upon my tongue* 2 S 23$_{2}$, עוֹד לֶאֱלוֹהַּ מִלִּים *there are yet words for God* Jb 36$_{2}$.

<OBJ> שׁמע *hear* Jb 13$_{17}$ 21$_{2}$ 33$_{1}$ 34$_{2}$ 4QBéat 14.2$_{23}$ 31$_{1}$ ([ש]מעו), ידע *know* Jb 23$_{5}$, נגד hi. *utter* Jb 26$_{4}$, ערך *arrange* Jb 32$_{14}$, יכח hi. *reprove* Jb 6$_{26}$, בחן *test* Jb 12$_{11}$ 34$_{3}$, חקר *search out* Jb 32$_{11}$, יצא hi. *bring out* Jb 8$_{10}$ 15$_{13}$ 4QsapDidA 1$_{4}$, שׁוב hi. *answer (with)* Jb 35$_{4}$, כבר hi. *multiply* Jb 35$_{16}$, שׂים *place*, i.e. make, nothing Jb 24$_{25}$, נתן *give* 4QTanḥ 16$_{3}$, מלא *be full of* Jb 32$_{18}$, מצץ *drain out* Ps 73$_{10}$ (מֵי מָלֵא יִמָּצוּ *waters of fullness will be drained* to מִלֵּיהֶם יָמֹצּוּ *they will drain their words*), תכן pi. *regulate* 4QBark^{a} 1.2$_{10}$.

<CSTR> מילת איש *speech of a man* 4QTanḥ 16$_{3}$; קוֹל מִלִּין *sound of words* Jb 33$_{8}$, מִלַּי *of my words* Jb 34$_{16}$, שֵׂכֶל מִלֶּיךָ *wisdom of your words* Pr 23$_{9}$.

<PREP> לְ introducing predicate, + היה *be* Jb 30$_{9}$; introducing object, + שׁמע *hear* 4QCryptA 1.1$_{2}$ ([ש]מע(ו)).

בְּ of instrument, *by (means of), with,* + יעל hi. *profit* Jb 15$_{3}$, דכא pi. *crush* Jb 19$_{2}$, חשׁך hi. *darken* counsel Jb 38$_{2}$, עלם hi. *conceal* counsel Jb 42$_{3(ms)}$; of benefit, *to, for,* + שׂים *place* Jb 18$_{2}$; introducing object, + עצר *restrain* Jb 4$_{2}$ 29$_{9}$, חבר hi. *join together* Jb 16$_{4}$, בין hi. *understand* 4QCryptA 1.1$_{2}$ (הבי[נ]ו).

עַל perh. *according to* 4QsapDidA 3$_{2}$.

<COLL> מִלָּה ‖ דָּבָר *word* Jb 4$_{2}$ (+) 15$_{3}$ 29$_{22}$ (+) 32$_{11}$ (+) 33$_{1}$, נְגִינָה *song* Jb 30$_{9}$, קַו *line* Ps 19$_{5}$, אֹכֶל *food* Jb 12$_{11}$; + אֹמֶר *word* Jb 6$_{26}$ 4QsapDidA 1$_{4}$, תְּבוּנָה *understanding* Jb 32$_{11}$.

מִלִּים יַעֲנֵנִי *the words with which he would answer me* Jb 23$_{5}$, מִלִּין בְּלִי־דָעַת *words without knowledge* Jb 38$_{2}$ 42$_{3(ms)}$.

Also 4QCryptA 3.1$_{10}$ ([מ]לתי) 4QsapDidA 4$_{4}$ ([מ]לי).

<SYN> דָּבָר *word,* נְגִינָה *song,* קַו *line,* אֹכֶל *food.**

⇒ מלל II *speak.*

מִלֹּו, see מְלֹא *fullness.*

מִלּוֹא I $_{7.0.2}$ n.[m.] **citadel**—מִלֹּא (Q מלה)—**1.** particular structure in Jerusalem, **citadel,** or as pl.n. **Millo,** <OBJ> בנה *build* 1 K 9$_{15.24}$ 11$_{27}$, חזק pi. *strengthen* 2 C 32$_{5}$. <CSTR> בֵּית מִלֹּא *house of the citadel* 2 K 12$_{21}$. <PREP> מִן of direction, *from,* + בנה *build* 2 S 5$_{9}$‖1 C 11$_{8}$. <COLL> הַמִּלּוֹא עִיר דָּוִד *the citadel in the city of David* 2 C 32$_{5}$.

2. mound of earth leading up from the city to the wall,* perh. **esplanade** or **terrace,** <PREP> לְ of direction, *to* perh. 4QM^{c} 1$_{4}$ (למלת; unless *to fill,* from מלא); בְּ of place, *in* 3QTr 3$_{8.11}$.*

⇒ מלא *fill.*

*מִלּוֹא II $_{7}$ pl.n. **Millo**—מִלֹּא—location of palace of Pharaoh's daughter, <OBJ> בנה *build* 1 K 9$_{15.24}$ 11$_{27}$, חזק pi. *strengthen* 2 C 32$_{5}$. <CSTR> בֵּית מִלֹּא *house of the citadel* 2 K 12$_{21}$. <PREP> מִן of direction, *from,* + בנה *build* 2 S 5$_{9}$‖1 C 11$_{8}$. <COLL> הַמִּלּוֹא עִיר דָּוִד *the citadel in the city of David* 2 C 32$_{5}$.

מִלּוֹא III, see בֵּית מִלּוֹא *Beth-millo.*

מַלּוּחַ $_{1}$ n.[m.] **saltwort, mallow,** desert plant growing in salt marshes, *Mesembrianthum forskalii,* or

orache, *Atriplex halimus*; gathered by the poor (Jb 30_4), <OBJ> קטף *pluck* Jb 30_4 (or em. ... הָעֹרְקִים צִיָּה מַלּוּחַ *they flee [to] the desert ... the saltwort* to הָעֹרְקִים צִיָּה וּמְלֵחָה *who flee [into] the desert and the salt-land;** + רֹתֶם *broom*). <CSTR> מִכְרֵה־מַלּוּחַ *heap of saltwort* Zp 2_9 (if em. מֶלַח *salt*). <PREP> כְּ *as*, + קפץ ni. *be contracted* Jb 24_{24} (if em. כַּכֹּל *as the mallow* to כַּמַּלּוּחַ *as saltwort*).*

⇨ מלח *salt.*

מַלּוּךְ 6 pr.n.m. **Malluch, 1.** Levite, Merarite, son of Hashabiah, <CSTR> בֶּן־מַלּוּךְ *son of Malluch* 1 C 6_{29}. <APP> בֵּן *son* 1 C 6_{29}.

2. priest (or priestly family) who returned from exile with Zerubbabel, <SUBJ> עלה *go up* Ne 12_2. <NOM CL> אֵלֶּה הַכֹּהֲנִים וְהַלְוִיִּם ... מַלּוּךְ *these are the priests and the Levites ... Malluch* Ne 12_2. <PREP> לְ of possession, *of, (belonging) to* Ne 12_{14} (if em. מלוכי [Kt] *Malluchi*).

3. member of Bani family, husband of non-Jewish wife, <NOM CL> מִבְּנֵי בָנִי ... מַלּוּךְ *of the sons of Bani were ... Malluch* Ezr 10_{29}.

4. member of Harim family, husband of non-Jewish wife, <NOM CL> וּבְנֵי חָרִם ... מַלּוּךְ *and the sons of Harim were ... Malluch* Ezr 10_{32}.

5. priest, signatory of covenant at time of Nehemiah, <NOM CL> עַל הַחֲתוּמִים ... מַלּוּךְ *upon (the documents) that were sealed are ... Malluch* Ne 10_5 (or em. הַחוֹתְמִים *those who sealed*, i.e. signed, or אֵלֶּה הַחוֹתְמִים *these are the signatories*).

6. lay chief of people, signatory of covenant at time of Nehemiah, <NOM CL> רָאשֵׁי הָעָם ... מַלּוּךְ *the chiefs of the people were ... Malluch* Ne 10_{28}.

⇨ מלך *be king.*

מְלוּכָה I 24.0.4 n.f. **kingship**—מְלֻכָה—**kingship, kingdom, royalty,** <SUBJ> היה *be* 1 K $2_{15.15}$ Ob21 1QM 6_6 4QMa 11.2_{17} (ה[המלוכ]ה), סבב *turn* 1 K 2_{15}. <NOM CL> אֵין־שָׁם מְלוּכָה *there is no kingdom there* Is 34_{12} (unless מְלוּכָה II *king*), וְעוֹד לוֹ אַךְ הַמְּלוּכָה *and what else is there for him except the kingship?* 1 S 18_8, לַי׳ הַמְּלוּכָה *to Y. is the kingship* Ps 22_{29} (unless מְלוּכָה II *king*). <OBJ> נתן *give* 2 S 16_8 1 K 11_{35} (or del. נתן), שׁאל *ask for* 1 K 2_{22}, לקח *take* 1 K 11_{35}, לכד *take* 1 S 14_{47}, חדשׁ *renew* 1 S 11_{14}, שׁוב hi. *restore* 1 K 12_{21}, סבב hi. *turn* 1 C 10_{14}, עשׂה *do*, i.e. exercise 1 K 21_7.

<CSTR> דְּבַר הַמְּלוּכָה *matter of the kingship* 1 S 10_{16}, מִשְׁפַּט *rule of* 1 S 10_{25} (הַמְּלֻכָה), זֶרַע *offspring of*, i.e. of royal descent 2 K 25_{25} Jr 41_1 Ezk 17_{13} Dn 1_3, עִיר *city of*, i.e. royal city 2 S 12_{26} (unless מְלוּכָה II *king*; or em. הַמַּיִם *of water*) $12_{27(mss)}$ (L הַמָּיִם), כִּסֵּא *throne of* 1 K 14_6, צָנִיף *turban of* Is 62_3 (מְלוּכָה). <APP> שֵׁבֶט *tribe* 1 K 11_{35} (or del. אֶת עֲשֶׂרֶת הַשְּׁבָטִים *the ten tribes*). <PREP> לְ of direction, *to*, + צלח *advance* Ezk 16_{13} (unless מְלוּכָה II *king*). <COLL> הַמְּלוּכָה עַל־יִשְׂרָאֵל *the kingship over Israel* 1 S 14_{47}, var. 1 K 21_7, אֵין־שָׁם מְלוּכָה יִקְרָאוּ *they shall name it No Kingdom There* Is 34_{12} (unless מְלוּכָה II *king*).

Also 1Q25 5_6 4Q428 54_1 4QMa 15_7 perh. 4QDibHama 3.2_6 ([מ]לוכה).*

⇨ מלך *be king.*

***מְלוּכָה** II 4 n.f. **king** (unless מְלוּכָה I *kingdom*), <NOM CL> אֵין־שָׁם מְלוּכָה they shall name it *No King There* Is 34_{12}, לַי׳ הַמְּלוּכָה *truly* (לְ emphatic) *Y. is king* Ps 22_{29}. <CSTR> עִיר הַמְּלוּכָה *city of the king* 2 S 12_{26}, כָּל־מְלוּכוֹתָם *all their kings* Jr 10_7 (if em. מַלְכוּתָם *their kingdoms*). <PREP> לְ *to (become)*, + צלח *succeed* Ezk 16_{13}.

⇨ מלך *be king.*

[מַלּוּכִי] 1 pr.n.m. **Malluchi,** priest (or priestly family) who returned from exile with Zerubbabel, <PREP> לְ of possession, *of, (belonging) to* Ne $12_{14(Kt)}$ (Qr מְלִיכוּ *Melichu*; or em. מַלּוּךְ *Malluch*).

⇨ מלך *be king.*

מָלוֹן 8.0.1 n.m. **lodging place**—cstr. מְלוֹן; sf. Q מלונו—<NOM CL> גֶּבַע מָלוֹן לָנוּ *at Geba there is to us a lodging place* Is 10_{29} (or em. גֶּבַע מְלֹנוֹ *Geba is his lodging place*). <OBJ> נתן *give* Jr 9_1. <CSTR> מְלוֹן אֹרְחִים *lodging place of travellers* Jr 9_1, קִצֹּה *of its end*, i.e. its most remote lodging place 2 K 19_{23}||Is 37_{24} (Is 37_{24} if em. מְרוֹם קִצּוֹ *height of its end*). <PREP> בְּ of place, *in, at*, + היה *be* Ex 4_{24}, לין *lodge* Jos 4_3, נתן *give* Gn 42_{27}, נוח hi.

place Jos 4_{3}; אֶל *to*, + בוא *come* Gn 43_{21}, עבר hi. *bring across* Jos 4_{8}; מָלוֹן without prep., *to the lodging place*, + בוא *come* 2 K 19_{23}||Is 37_{24} (Is 37_{24} if em.; see Cstr.).

Also 4QShir^{b} 3_{6}.

⇒ לין *lodge*.

מְלוּנָה $_{2}$ n.f. **hut,** for watching field at night, <PREP> כְּ *as*, + יתר ni. *be left* Is 1_{8} (|| סֻכָּה *booth*), נוד htpol. *sway* Is 24_{20}. <COLL> מְלוּנָה בְמִקְשָׁה *a hut in a cucumber field* Is 1_{8}.

Also perh. 4QBark^{a} 3.2_{2} (מלונתם; others מלכותם).

<SYN> סֻכָּה *booth*.

⇒ לין *lodge*.

מַלּוֹתִי $_{2}$ pr.n.m. **Mallothi,** son of Heman, musician, <NOM CL> לְהֵימָן ... מַלּוֹתִי *(belonging) to Heman were ... Mallothi* 1 C 25_{4}. <PREP> לְ of possession, *(belonging) to, of* 1 C 25_{26}.

⇒ מלל II *speak*.

***[מָלוֹשׁ]** $_{0.0.1}$ n.[m.] perh. **kneading trough,** <CSTR> כול מלוש perh. *every kneading trough* 4QBark^{f} 1.1_{2}.

⇒ לוש *knead*.

מלח I vb. $_{5.1.6}$ **salt—Qal** $_{1.0.2}$ Impf. 2ms תִּמְלָח; ptc. Q מולחים—**salt, season,** <SUBJ> Israelites Lv 2_{13}; subj. not specified, 11QT $34_{10.11}$ (+ רחץ pi. *wash*). <OBJ> קָרְבָּן *offering* Lv 2_{13}, נֵתַח *piece (of meat)* 11QT 34_{10}, קֶרֶב *inner parts* 11QT 34_{11}, כֶּרַע *leg* 11QT 34_{11}. <PREP> בְּ of instrument, *by (means of), with*, + מֶלַח *salt* Lv 2_{13} 11QT $34_{10.11}$.

Ni. $_{1}$ Pf. נִמְלָחוּ—**be grey, be dark*** (unless מלח II ni. *be dissipated* or III ni. *be dark*), <SUBJ> שָׁמַיִם *heaven* Is 51_{6} (|| בלה *be worn out*). <PREP> כְּ *as*, + עָשָׁן *smoke* Is 51_{6}.

Pu. $_{1.1.4}$ Ptc. מְמֻלָּח (ממולח)—ptc. as adj. (מְמֻלָּח is not inflected to agree with the word qualified), **salted, mixed with salt, 1.** used attributively of קְטֹרֶת *incense* Ex 30_{35} (מְמֻלָּח masc., though קְטֹרֶת fem.; or else מְמֻלָּח agrees with רֹקַח *spice mixture*; || טָהוֹר *pure*) Si 49_{1}, מַעֲשֶׂה *work* 4QShirShabb^{f} 20.2_{11} 11QShirShabb 9_{7} ([מ]עשי).

2. used predicatively of מַעֲשֶׂה *work* 4QShirShabb^{f} 19_{4}, מַחֲשָׁב *(skilful) design* 4QShirShabb^{f} 23.2_{10}.

<COLL> ממולח טוהר perh. *blended (in) purity*, i.e. purely blended 4QShirShabb^{f} 19_{4} 20.2_{11} (טוה) 23.2_{10} 11QShirShabb 9_{7}.

<SYN> טָהוֹר *pure*.

Ho. $_{2}$ Pf. הָמְלַחַתְּ; inf. abs. הָמְלֵחַ—**be rubbed with salt water,** <SUBJ> Jerusalem Ezk $16_{4.4}$ (|| חתל ho., pu. *be swaddled*, + רחץ pu. *be washed*, + כרת pu. [of navel] *be cut*).

<SYN> חתל ho., pu. *be swaddled*.

⇒ מַלּוּחַ *saltwort*, מְלֵחָה *saltness*.

מלח II $_{1.0.1}$ vb. **dissipate** (unless מלח I ni. *be grey* or III *be dark*)—**Ni.** $_{1.0.1}$ Pf. נִמְלָחוּ; ptc. Q נמלח—**be dissipated, vanish,** <SUBJ> שָׁמַיִם *heaven* Is 51_{6} (|| בלה *be worn out*), עָשָׁן *smoke* 1QM 15_{10}. <PREP> כְּ *as*, + עָשָׁן *smoke* Is 51_{6}.

<SYN> בלה *be worn out*.

⇒ מֶלַח II *frayed clothing*.

מלח** III vb. **be dark** (unless מלח I ni. *be grey* or II *tear to shreds*)—**Ni.** $_{1}$ Pf. נִמְלָחוּ—**be dark, <SUBJ> שָׁמַיִם *heaven* Is 51_{6} (|| בלה *be worn out*). <PREP> כְּ *as*, + עָשָׁן *smoke* Is 51_{6}.

<SYN> בלה *be worn out*.

[מַלָּח] $_{4.0.2}$ n.m. **mariner**—pl. מַלָּחִים; sf. מַלָּחַיִךְ, מַלְּחֵיהֶם—**mariner, sailor,** <SUBJ> היה *be* Ezk 27_{9}, ירא *fear* Jon 1_{5}, זעק *cry out* Jon 1_{5}, נפל *fall*, i.e. sink Ezk 27_{27} (|| חֹבֵל *sailor*, + חזק hi. ptc. *caulker*), עמד *stand* Ezk 27_{29}. <APP> חֹבֵל *sailor* Ezk 27_{29}. <PREP> כְּ *as* 1QH 3_{14}, + היה *be* 1QH 6_{22} ([הי]יתי). <COLL> כָּל־אֳנִיּוֹת הַיָּם וּמַלָּחֵיהֶם *all the ships of the sea and their mariners* Ezk 27_{9}, מלח באוניה *a mariner in a ship* 1QH 6_{22}, מלחים במצולות *mariners on the deeps* 1QH 3_{14}.

<SYN> חֹבֵל *sailor*.*

מֶלַח I $_{28.3.4}$ n.m. **salt**—cstr. מֶלַח—**1. salt** in domestic use, to season food (Jb 6_{6}), to purify water (2 K $2_{20.21}$), mentioned with iron, fire, water as essentials for life (Si 39_{26}). **2. salt** in ritual use, added to offering (Lv 2_{13}

Ezk 43$_{24}$ 11QT 20$_{13}$ 34$_{10.11}$), scattered in destroyed city (Jg 9$_{45}$), a token of a covenant bond ('covenant of salt', Nm 18$_{19}$ 2 C 13$_{5}$). **3. salt** as occurring naturally (Ezk 47$_{11}$ Zp 2$_{9}$). **4. salt land** (Si 39$_{23}$).

<NOM CL> מֶלַח ... כָל־אַרְצָהּ *all its land is ... salt* Dt 29$_{22}$. <OBJ> קרב hi. *bring near*, i.e. offer Lv 2$_{13}$, שׁבת hi. *let fail* Lv 2$_{13}$, זרע *sow with* Jg 9$_{45}$, שׂים *place* 2 K 2$_{20}$, נתן *give*, i.e. *place* 11QT 20$_{13}$, שׁלך hi. *throw* 2 K 2$_{21}$ Ezk 43$_{24}$. <CSTR> מֶלַח בְּרִית *salt of the covenant of* Lv 2$_{13}$; יָם הַמֶּלַח *Sea of Salt*, i.e. Dead Sea Gn 14$_{3}$ Nm 34$_{3}$ (יָם־הַמֶּלַח) 34$_{12}$ Dt 3$_{17}$ Jos 3$_{16}$ (both יָם־הַמֶּלַח) 12$_{3}$ 15$_{2.5}$ 18$_{19}$ (יָם־הַמֶּלַח), גֵּיא־מֶלַח *Valley of Salt* or *Ge-melah* 2 S 8$_{13}$||1 C 18$_{12}$ (1 C הַמֶּלַח; 2 S mss מֶלֶךְ *of [the] king*) 2 K 14$_{7(Qr)}$ (Kt המלח) Ps 60$_{2}$ 2 C 25$_{11}$ (הַמֶּלַח), נְצִיב מֶלַח *pillar of salt* Gn 19$_{26}$, בְּרִית *covenant of* Nm 18$_{19}$ 2 C 13$_{5}$ 11QT 20$_{14}$ ([בר]ית), מִכְרֵה־ *pit/heap of* Zp 2$_{9}$ (or em. מַלּוּחַ *of saltwort*).

<APP> שְׂרֵפָה *burning* Dt 29$_{22}$.

<PREP> לְ of direction, *to*, + נתן ni. *be given* Ezk 47$_{11}$; *into*, + הפך *turn*, i.e. change Si 39$_{23}$; בְּ of instrument, *by (means of), with*, + מלח *season* Lv 2$_{13}$ 11QT 34$_{10.11}$; כְּ *as*, + שׁכן *rest* Si 43$_{19(B)}$, שׁפך *pour* frost Si 43$_{19(Bmg, M)}$; מִבְּלִי *without*, + אכל ni. *be eaten* Jb 6$_{6}$.

<COLL> מֶלַח || גָּפְרִית *brimstone* Dt 29$_{22}$ (גָּפְרִית וָמֶלַח); + חָרוּל *nettles* Zp 2$_{9}$, בַּרְזֶל *iron* Si 39$_{26}$, אֵשׁ *fire* Si 39$_{26}$, מַיִם *water* Si 39$_{26}$; :: מַשְׁקֶה *irrigated land*.

<SYN> גָּפְרִית *brimstone*.

<ANT> מַשְׁקֶה *irrigated land*.*

⇒ מלח I *salt*.

[מֶ֫לַח] II $_{2}$ n.[m.] **frayed clothing**—pl. מְלָחִים—**frayed clothing, old clothing, rags,** <CSTR> בְּלוֹיֵ מְלָחִים *rags of old clothes* Jr 38$_{11.12}$ (בְּלוֹאֵי ... הַמְּלָחִים; both || סְחָבָה *rag*).

<SYN> סְחָבָה *rag*.*

⇒ מלח II *dissipate*.

מְלֵחָה $_{3.0.1}$ n.f. **salt land,** esp. as unproductive, <OBJ> שׂים *place*, i.e. make Jb 39$_{6}$ (|| עֲרָבָה *steppe*). <CSTR> אֶרֶץ מְלֵחָה *land of saltness* Jr 17$_{6}$ (+ חָרֵר *parched place*). <PREP> לְ *into*, + שׂים *place*, i.e. make Ps 107$_{34}$ (:: אֶרֶץ פְּרִי *land of fruit*, i.e. fruitful land); בְּ of place, *in* 1QH 8$_{24}$. <COLL> הָעֹרְקִים צִיָּה וּמְלֵחָה *who flee [into] the desert and the salt-land* Jb 30$_{4}$ (if em. הָעֹרְקִים צִיָּה ... מַלּוּחַ *they flee [to] the desert ... the saltwort*).*

<SYN> עֲרָבָה *steppe*.

<ANT> אֶרֶץ פְּרִי *land of fruit*.*

⇒ מלח I *salt*.

*[מִלְחִים] n.m. **cleverness**—<CSTR> בְּ *in*, + מִלְחִים *cleverness* Ec 8$_{8}$ (וְאֵין מִשְׁלַחַת בְּמִלְחִים *and there is no deliverance in cleverness*, if em. בַּמִּלְחָמָה *in war*).

מִלְחָמָה I $_{318.4.147}$ n.f. **war**—cstr. מִלְחֶמֶת; sf. מִלְחַמְתִּי, מִלְחַמְתְּךָ (מִלְחַמְתֶּךָ), מִלְחַמְתֵּךְ, מִלְחַמְתּוֹ, מִלְחַמְתָּהּ, מִלְחַמְתָּם; pl. מִלְחָמוֹת; cstr. מִלְחֲמוֹת (מִלְחֲמֹת); sf. Q מלחמותכה, מִלְחֲמֹתֵינוּ (Q מלחמותם), מִלְחֲמֹתָיו.

1. usu. **war, battle, conflict.**

2. perh. by synecdoche, **weapons of war** (Nm 31$_{27}$ Is 3$_{25}$ 21$_{15}$ 22$_{2}$ 30$_{32}$ Ho 1$_{7}$ 2$_{20}$ Ps 76$_{4}$),* and perh. particular weapon, **lance, mace** (Is 30$_{32}$ Ho 1$_{7}$ 2$_{20}$ Ps 76$_{4}$).

3. troops* (Ex 13$_{17}$ Jg 20$_{42}$ 1 S 8$_{12}$ 1 K 5$_{17}$ 20$_{14}$ Jl 4$_{9}$ Ps 27$_{3}$ 89$_{4}$ 2 C 13$_{3}$).

<SUBJ> היה *be* 1 S 14$_{52}$ (+ חָזָק *strong*) 19$_{8}$ 2 S 2$_{17}$ (+ קָשֶׁה *hard*) 3$_{1}$ (+ אָרֹךְ *long*) 3$_{6}$ 10$_{9(mss)}$ 18$_{6.8}$ 21$_{15.18.19.20}$||1 C 20$_{5.6}$ 1 K 14$_{30}$ 15$_{6}$||2 C 13$_{2}$ 1 K 15$_{7.16.32}$ 2 C 15$_{19}$, קרא *befall* Ex 1$_{10}$, קום *arise* Ps 27$_{3}$, עמד *stand*, i.e. arise 1 C 20$_{4}$, בוא *come* 1QM 10$_{6}$, יסף hi. *do again* 1 S 19$_{8}$, שׁוט *go about* 1QH 3$_{35}$, עשׂה ni. *be made* Pr 20$_{18}$ 24$_{6}$ (both if em.; see Obj.), ערך ni. *be prepared* 1QM 2$_{9}$, נצח htp. *be directed* 1QM 16$_{9}$ 17$_{15}$ (המל[חמ]ה מ[תנצח]ת), קרב *be joined* 1 K 20$_{29}$, עלה *go up* 1 K 22$_{35}$||2 C 18$_{34}$, דבק hi. *overtake* Jg 20$_{42}$, נשׂג hi. *overtake* Ho 10$_{9}$, עבר *pass* 1 S 14$_{23}$, שׁוב *go back* 1QM 3$_{2}$, נטשׁ *be left*, i.e. spread out 1 S 4$_{2}$, פוץ ni. *be scattered* 2 S 18$_{8}$, חלק ni. *be divided* 1QM 2$_{13.14}$, כבד *be heavy* Jg 20$_{34}$ 1 S 31$_{3}$||1 C 10$_{3}$, חזק *be strong* 2 K 3$_{26}$ 11QT 58$_{10}$, כתב pass. *be written* 2 C 27$_{7}$.

<NOM CL> לַי׳ הַמִּלְחָמָה *the battle is Y.'s* 1 S 17$_{47}$, מִלְחָמָה לַי׳ בַּעֲמָלֵק *Y. has a war against Amalek* Ex 17$_{16}$, לֹא לַגִּבּוֹרִים הַמִּלְחָמָה *the battle is not to the mighty* Ec 8$_{11}$, sim. 2 C 20$_{15}$, לכה המלחמה *the battle is yours* 1QM 11$_{1.2.4}$, בידכה המלחמה *in your hand is the battle* 1QM 18$_{13}$, [ב]גויתי מלחמות perh. *in my body are*

conflicts 4QShir^{b} 48.2$_{4}$, מלחמת המחלקות בעתש ועשרים הנותרות *the war of the divisions shall be (waged) during the remaining twenty-nine years* 1QM 2$_{10}$ (בעתש error for בתשע), הִנֵּה לָהֶם הַמִּלְחָמָה פָּנִים וְאָחוֹר *behold, the battle was before them and behind* 2 C 13$_{14}$, מֵאֱלֹהִים הַמִּלְחָמָה *the war was of God* 1 C 5$_{22}$, עַד קֵץ מִלְחָמָה *to the end there shall be war* Dn 9$_{26}$, מִלְחֲמוֹת רְחַבְעָם וְיָרָבְעָם כָּל־הַיָּמִים *there were wars of,* i.e. between, *Rehoboam and Jeroboam all the days* 2 C 12$_{15}$, אֶל־בֵּית מֶלֶךְ בָּבֶל מִלְחַמְתִּי *against the house of the king of Babylon is my war* 2 C 35$_{21}$ (if em. בֵּית מִלְחַמְתִּי *house of my war*), יֵשׁ עִמְּךָ מִלְחָמוֹת *there will be with you,* i.e. you will have, *wars* 2 C 16$_{9}$, אֵין מִלְחָמָה *there was no war* 1 K 22$_{1}$, var. 2 C 14$_{5}$.

<OBJ> עשה *make* Gn 14$_{2}$ Dt 20$_{12}$=11QT 62$_{8}$ Dt 20$_{20}$ Jos 11$_{18}$ 1 K 12$_{21}$ 2 K 24$_{16}$ Ezk 17$_{17(ms)}$ Pr 20$_{18}$ 24$_{6}$ (or in both em. עשה to ni. *be made*) 1 C 5$_{10.19}$ 22$_{8}$, ערך *set in array* Gn 14$_{8}$ Jg 20$_{20.22}$ 1 S 17$_{2.8}$ 2 S 10$_{8}$||1 C 19$_{9}$ 1 C 12$_{34.36.37}$ 19$_{17}$ 2 C 13$_{3}$ 14$_{9}$ 1QM 2$_{9}$ 4QM^{a} 1$_{8.16}$ (בע[ר]וך), סדר pi. *set in order* 4QM^{a} 11.2$_{19}$, נצח pi. *direct* 1QM 8$_{9.16}$ (מל[חמה]) 9$_{2.2}$ 16$_{7}$, ראה *see* Ex 13$_{17}$ 1 S 17$_{20}$ Jr 42$_{14}$, צפה *watch* Si 46$_{6}$, ריח hi. *smell* Jb 39$_{25}$, ידע *know* Jg 3$_{1.2}$ Si 47$_{5}$, למד *learn* Is 2$_{4}$||Mc 4$_{3}$, pi. *teach* Jg 3$_{2}$ 1QM 14$_{6}$, זכר *remember* Jb 40$_{32}$, כתב *write* 1QM 4$_{12}$, קרא *encounter* Jos 11$_{20}$, לחם ni. *fight* 1 S 8$_{20}$ 18$_{17}$ 25$_{28}$ 2 C 32$_{8}$ Si 46$_{3}$ ([נל]חם) 4QM^{h} 1$_{3}$, גור *attack with* Ps 140$_{3}$ (or em. גור to גרה pi. *provoke*), גרה pi. *provoke* Ps 140$_{3}$ (if em.; see above), htp. *fight* Dt 2$_{5}$ (if ins. מִלְחָמָה) 2$_{9.19}$ (if ins. מִלְחָמָה) 2$_{24}$, אסר *join* 1 K 20$_{14}$ 2 C 13$_{3}$, חזק hi. *strengthen* 2 S 11$_{25}$, קדשׁ pi. *sanctify,* i.e. prepare Jr 6$_{4}$ Jl 4$_{9}$ Mc 3$_{5}$, סבב *surround with* 1 K 5$_{17}$, שׁוב hi. *repel* Is 28$_{6}$, שׁבר *break* Ho 2$_{20}$, pi. Ps 76$_{4}$, שׁבת hi. *cause to cease* Ps 46$_{10}$.

<CSTR> מִלְחֲמוֹת י׳ *wars of Y.* Nm 21$_{14}$ (מִלְחֲמֹת) 1 S 18$_{17}$ 25$_{28}$ Si 46$_{3}$, מלחמת אלוהים *war of God* 4QShirShabb^{c} 4$_{7}$, אל *of God* 1QM 4$_{12}$ 9$_{5}$ 15$_{12}$, שחקים *of heaven* 4QShirShabb^{c} 4$_{10}$, מִלְחֲמוֹת תֹּעִי *wars of Toi* 2 S 8$_{10}$||1 C 18$_{10}$, רְחַבְעָם וְיָרָבְעָם *of,* i.e. between, *Rehoboam and Jeroboam* 2 C 12$_{15}$, כְּנָעַן *of Canaan* Jg 3$_{1}$, מלחמת גבורי *war of the mighty ones of* heaven 1QH 3$_{35}$, מלמחמת האויב *war of,* i.e. against, *the enemy* 1QM 3$_{11}$ 4QM^{a} 1$_{14}$ (הא[ו]יב), מלחמות זדים *wars of,* i.e. against, *the presumptuous ones* 1QH 6$_{35}$, מלחמות ידיכה *wars of your hands* 1QM 11$_{8}$, מלחמת המחלקות *war of the divisions* 1QM 2$_{10}$, מִלְחֲמוֹת תְּנוּפָה perh. *wars of brandishing (weapons)* Is 30$_{32}$ (unless מִלְחָמָה II *sistrum*; or em.; see Prep.), מלחמות רשעה *wars of wickedness,* i.e. wicked wars 1QH 6$_{29}$ 7$_{7}$, כלה *of destruction,* i.e. destructive wars 4QM^{a} 1$_{14}$, מלחמת היום *battle of the day* 4QM^{a} 1$_{11}$.

אִישׁ מִלְחָמָה *man of war* Ex 15$_{3}$ Jos 17$_{1}$ Jg 20$_{17}$ 1 S 16$_{18}$ 17$_{33}$ 2 S 17$_{8}$ Is 3$_{2}$ Jr 6$_{23(mss)}$ Ezk 39$_{20}$ 11QT 57$_{6}$, מִלְחָמוֹת *of wars* Is 42$_{13}$ 1 C 28$_{3}$, מִלְחֲמוֹת *of the wars of,* i.e. at war with 2 S 8$_{10}$||1 C 18$_{10}$, אַנְשֵׁי הַמִּלְחָמָה *men of war* Nm 31$_{28.49}$ Dt 2$_{14.16}$ Jos 5$_{4.6}$ 6$_{3}$ 10$_{24}$ 1 S 18$_{5}$ 1 K 9$_{22}$|| 2 C 8$_{9}$ (מִלְחָמָה) 2 K 25$_{4.19}$||Jr 52$_{7.25}$ Jr 38$_{4}$ 39$_{4}$ 41$_{3.16}$ 49$_{26}$ 51$_{32}$ Jl 2$_{7}$ (מִלְחָמָה) 4$_{9}$ 1 C 12$_{39}$ 2 C 17$_{13}$ (both מִלְחָמָה) 1QM 2$_{7}$ 9$_{5}$ (both מלחמה) 4QM^{c} 1$_{7}$ ([אנ]שׁי) 11QT 58$_{7.8.16}$ CD 20$_{14}$, מִלְחַמְתָּהּ *of her war,* i.e. her men of war Jr 50$_{30}$, מִלְחַמְתֵּךְ *of your* (fem.) *war,* i.e. your men of war Ezk 27$_{10}$ (or del.) 27$_{27}$, מִלְחַמְתֶּךָ *of your war,* i.e. at war with you Is 41$_{12}$, אנשי מלחמתי *men of my war,* i.e. at war with me 1QH 7$_{22}$ 9$_{22}$ (מלחמ[תי]), עַם הַמִּלְחָמָה *people of war* Jos 8$_{1.3.11(ms)}$ (L הָעָם הַמִּלְחָמָה) 10$_{7}$ 11$_{7}$, גִּבּוֹר מִלְחָמָה *mighty one of war* Ps 24$_{8}$ 1QM 12$_{9}$ (המלח[מה]), גִּבּוֹרֵי *mighty ones of* 2 C 13$_{3}$ 1QH 6$_{33}$ (מלחמות) 1QM 12$_{17}$ (המלחמה), שָׂרֵי מִלְחָמוֹת *commanders of wars,* i.e. military commanders 2 C 32$_{6}$.

עֹשֵׂה מִלְחָמָה *one who makes war* 1 K 12$_{21}$||2 C 11$_{1}$ 2 C 26$_{11}$, עֹשֵׂי *ones who make* 2 K 24$_{16}$ 2 C 26$_{11(mss).13}$ (עוֹשֵׂי), תֹּפְשֵׂי הַמִּלְחָמָה *ones who lay hold of,* i.e. engage in, *war* Nm 31$_{27}$ 11QT 58$_{14}$ (תופשי), מְלֻמְּדֵי מִלְחָמָה *ones trained of,* i.e. in, *war* Ca 3$_{8}$ 1QM 6$_{12}$ (מלומדי), לְמוּדֵי *ones trained of,* i.e. in 1 C 5$_{18}$, עֹזְרֵי הַמִּלְחָמָה *helpers of the war* 1 C 12$_{1}$, עתודי המלחמה *those ready for the battle* 1QM 10$_{5}$, חרוצי *those appointed for* 1QM 16$_{11}$, עֹרְכֵי מִלְחָמָה *ones who set the battle in array* 1 C 12$_{34.36}$, עֱרוּךְ מִלְחָמָה *one arrayed of,* i.e. for battle Jl 2$_{5}$, סדר מלחמה *formation of battle* 1QM 8$_{5}$, סדרי המלחמה *formations of the battle* 1QM 3$_{1.6}$, מערכות *lines of* 1QM 7$_{9}$ 18$_{4}$, דגלי *battalions of* 1QM 5$_{3}$ 9$_{10}$, צְבָא מִלְחָמָה *army of war* Nm 31$_{14}$ (הַמִּלְחָמָה) Is 13$_{4}$ 1 C 7$_{4}$ 12$_{38}$, אנשי נדבת *men of voluntariness of,* i.e. volunteers for 1QM 7$_{5}$, שׁוֹבֵי *ones turned away of,* i.e. averse to Mc 2$_{8}$ (or em. שׁוֹבֵי to שֶׁבֶר *destruction of,* or שְׁבִי *captivity of*),

מְשִׁיבֵי *ones who repel* Is 28$_{6}$, מֵתֵי *dead (ones) of* Is 22$_{2}$.

יד מלחמה *hand*, i.e. power, *of war* 1QM 4$_{3}$, ידי *hands*, i.e. flanks *of* battle 1QM 8$_{12}$ 9$_{7}$, קוֹל מִלְחָמָה *sound of war* Ex 32$_{17}$ Jr 50$_{22}$, דְּמֵי *blood of* 1 K 2$_{5.5}$ (lacking in mss), פְּנֵי הַמִּלְחָמָה *face of the battle* 2 S 10$_{9}$||1 C 19$_{10}$ (2 S mss lack פְּנֵי) 2 S 11$_{15}$, בגדי *garments of* 1QM 7$_{11}$, שערי המלחמה *gates of the war* 1QM 3$_{1.7}$ 16$_{4}$ ([המ[לחמה]).

כְּלֵי מִלְחָמָה *weapons of war* Jg 18$_{11.17}$ (הַמִּלְחָמָה) 2 S 1$_{27}$ Jr 21$_{4}$ (הַמִּלְחָמָה) 51$_{20}$ (or em. כְּלִי *weapon of*) Ezk 7$_{14}$ (if em.; see Prep.) 1 C 12$_{34.38}$ (if em. כְּלֵי צְבָא מִלְחָמָה *weapons of the army of war*) 1QM 8$_{8}$ (המלמחה) 4QpIsa[c] 25$_{3}$, כְּלֵי מִלְחַמְתּוֹ *his weapons of war* Dt 1$_{41}$ 1 S 8$_{12}$ 1QH 6$_{28}$ 1QM 16$_{7}$ perh. 17$_{1}$ (מלחמתה) 17$_{12}$, כְּלֵי מִלְחַמְתָּם *their weapons of war* Jg 18$_{16}$ Ezk 32$_{27}$ 4QPseud[b] 8$_{4}$, כלי מלחמות *weapons of war* 1QH 6$_{31}$ 4QShirShabb[c] 4$_{8}$ ([כ]לי מ[ל]חמו[ת]), כלי מלחמותם *their weapons of war* 1QH 2$_{26}$ 1QpHab 6$_{4}$, קֶשֶׁת מִלְחָמָה *bow of war* Zc 9$_{10}$ 10$_{4}$, ח[צי] מלחמות *arrows of the wars of* 1QH 6$_{29}$, זרקות מלחמה *javelins of war* 1QM 6$_{2.16}$ 8$_{11}$.

כֹּבֶד מִלְחָמָה *heaviness of war* Is 21$_{15}$, עֱזוּז *strength of* Is 42$_{25}$, תְּרוּעַת *alarm of* Jr 4$_{19}$ 49$_{2}$ 1QM 8$_{10}$ 17$_{13}$, חצוצרות *trumpets of* 4QM[c] 1$_{3}$ (המלחמה), יוֹם *day of* Ho 10$_{14}$ Am 1$_{14}$ Jb 38$_{23}$ (יוֹם ...) Pr 21$_{31}$ 1QM 7$_{6}$ (המלחמה) 15$_{12}$ (יום corrected to מועד *appointed time of*) 4QJonathan 3$_{7}$ Kuntillet ʿAjrud add. inscr. 3$_{2.3}$ (both [ים מלח[מה]), יום מלחמתם *day of their war* 1QM 1$_{12}$, שני המלחמה *years of the war* 1QM 2$_{6}$, עֵת מִלְחָמָה *time of war* Ec 3$_{8}$, ק[צי] מלחמות *times of the wars of* 1QM 1$_{8}$, מועד המלחמה *appointed time of the war* 1QM 15$_{5}$ ([המלח[מה]) 15$_{12}$ (יום *day of* corrected to מועד; מלחמה), תעודות *fixed times of* 1QM 2$_{8}$, תעודת מלחמה *convocation of war* 1QSa 1$_{26}$, בֵּית מִלְחַמְתִּי *house of my war*, i.e. with which I am at war 2 C 35$_{21}$ (or em.; see Nom Cl.), שְׁלוֹם הַמִּלְחָמָה *prosperity of the war* 2 S 11$_{7}$, דִּבְרֵי *words of*, i.e. about 2 S 11$_{18.19}$, [הו]דות המלחמה *thanksgivings of war* 4QM[a] 8.1$_{17}$, סֵפֶר מִלְחֲמֹת *book of the wars of* Y. Nm 21$_{14}$, כָּל־מִלְחֲמוֹת *all the wars of* Jg 3$_{1}$, כָּל־מִלְחֲמֹתָיו *all his wars* 2 C 27$_{7}$.

<APP> עַם *people* appar. Jos 8$_{11}$, רַעַם *thunder* of captains Jb 39$_{25}$, תְּרוּעָה *shouting* Jb 39$_{25}$.

<ADJ> רִאשׁוֹן *first* Jg 20$_{39}$, גָּדוֹל *great* 1 C 22$_{8}$, חָזָק *strong* 2 S 11$_{15}$.

<PREP> לְ of direction, *to* (perh. sometimes of benefit, *for*) 1Q31 2$_{4}$ ([למלח[מה]), + הלך *go* 1 S 17$_{13.13(mss)}$ 1 K 22$_{4.6.15}$||2 C 18$_{5.14}$ 2 K 3$_{7}$ 8$_{28}$||2 C 22$_{5}$ Ezk 7$_{14}$ (or em. הַכֹּל וְאֵין הֹלֵךְ לַמִּלְחָמָה *all, but there is none that goes to war* to כְּלֵי מִלְחָמָה *weapons of war*) 2 C 25$_{13}$ 1QM 4$_{6}$ 7$_{4.5}$, בוא *come* Nm 10$_{9}$ (if em.; see below) 31$_{21}$ (or em. מִמִּלְחָמָה *from war*) 32$_{6}$ 1 C 12$_{20}$ 19$_{7}$ 2 C 20$_{1}$ 4QM[a] 1$_{10}$ ([יב]וא ... לנמ[לחמה]), יצא *go out* Nm 21$_{33}$ Dt 23$_{2}$ 3$_{1}$ 20$_{1}$=11QT 61$_{13}$ Dt 21$_{10}$=11QT 63$_{10}$ Dt 29$_{6}$ Jos 8$_{14}$ Jg 3$_{10}$ 20$_{14.20.28}$ 1 S 4$_{1}$ 2 S 21$_{17}$ 1 K 8$_{44}$||2 C 6$_{34}$ 1 K 20$_{18}$ 1 C 7$_{11}$ 1QM 4$_{9}$ 6$_{12}$ 16$_{12}$ 4QM[a] 1$_{12}$ ([ויצאו]) 1$_{15}$ ([ת]צא למלחמה]) 11QT 58$_{5.15}$, עלה *go up* Jg 20$_{18}$ 1 K 20$_{26}$ 2 K 16$_{5}$=Is 7$_{1}$ 4QM[a] 1$_{11}$ ([בע[לות]), עבר *pass* Nm 32$_{27}$ Jos 4$_{13}$, נגשׁ *draw near* Jg 20$_{23}$ 2 S 10$_{13}$||1 C 19$_{14}$ Jr 46$_{3}$ 1QM 4$_{7.11}$, ni. 1 S 7$_{10}$, קרב *draw near* Dt 20$_{3}$ 1QM 10$_{2.3}$ 11QT 61$_{14}$.

לְ of benefit, *for* Nm 32$_{29}$ (חָלוּץ לַמִּלְחָמָה *one equipped for war*) Jos 14$_{11}$ 2 K 18$_{20}$||Is 36$_{5}$ (עֵצָה וּגְבוּרָה לַמִּלְחָמָה *counsel and might for war*) Jr 48$_{14}$ (אַנְשֵׁי־חַיִל לַמִּלְחָמָה *men of ability for war*) Ps 120$_{7}$ 1 C 12$_{9}$ (אַנְשֵׁי צָבָא לַמִּלְחָמָה *men of the army [fit] for war*) 2 C 32$_{2}$ 1QM 6$_{13}$ 11QT 57$_{9}$ (both אנשי חיל למלחמה), + חלץ ni. *equip oneself* Nm 32$_{20}$, למד pi. *train* 2 S 22$_{35}$||Ps 18$_{35}$ Ps 144$_{1}$ 4QapJoseph[b] 2$_{4}$ ([ל[מד]), אזר pi. *gird* with strength 2 S 22$_{40}$||Ps 18$_{40}$, htp. *gird oneself* 1QM 15$_{14}$, חזק *be strong* 2 C 25$_{8}$, htp. *strengthen oneself* 1QM 15$_{12}$, גבר htp. *display arrogance* 4QM[h] 1$_{5}$, אסף *gather* 1 S 17$_{1}$ Zc 14$_{2}$, ni. *be gathered* 2 S 23$_{9}$||1 C 11$_{13}$, ערך pass. *be arrayed* Jr 6$_{23}$=50$_{42}$, קום *rise up* Jr 49$_{14}$ Ob$_{1}$, שׁוב hi. *bring back* 11QT 56$_{16}$, שׁמע pi. *summon* 1 S 23$_{8}$, יעד pass. *be appointed* 1QM 1$_{10}$, חרשׁ pass. *be designated* 4QM[a] 10.2$_{13}$.

לְ *concerning*, + נבא ni. *prophesy* Jr 28$_{8}$; of possession, *of, (belonging) to* 4QJub[f] 37$_{14}$ (גבור למלחמה *mighty one[s] of war*); introducing object, + גרה htp. *fight* Dn 11$_{25}$.

בְּ of place, time, accompaniment, *in(to), among, during, with* Ex 15$_{3(Sam)}$ Zc 10$_{3}$ (or del.) Ec 8$_{8}$ (or em. מִלְחָמָה to מִלְחָם *cleverness*) 1 C 7$_{40}$ 2 C 18$_{3}$ 1QM 3$_{8}$ 16$_{14}$ 18$_{12}$ ([במל[חמה]) 1QpHab 2$_{13}$ 4QShirShabb[c] 4$_{10}$ 4QM[a] 1$_{14}$, + היה *be* 1 S 29$_{4}$, הלך *go* 1 S 17$_{13}$, בוא *come* 1 K 22$_{30.30}$||2 C 18$_{29.29}$, יצא *go out* 2 S 21$_{17(mss)}$ 1 C 14$_{15}$, עלה *go up* 1 S 29$_{9}$, ירד *go down* 1 S 26$_{10}$ 29$_{4}$ 30$_{24}$, הפך *turn* Jg

2039, דבק hi. *pursue closely* 1 S 1422, נוס *flee* 2 S 194, שׁטף *flow*, i.e. dash Jr 86, שׁלח *send*, i.e. stretch out, hand 4QMc 18, נפל *fall* Is 325, עמד *stand* Ezk 135, יצב htp. *stand* 1QSa 121, קום hi. *make stand* Ps 8944, קרב htp. *bring oneself near*, i.e. be engaged in 1QM 1613 (מתקרבי[ם במ]לחמה), לחם ni. *fight* Is 3032 (unless מִלְחָמָה II *sistrum*; or em. וּבְמִלְחֲמוֹת *and with battles* to וּבִמְחֹלוֹת *and with dances*), עשׂה *do*, i.e. help Ezk 1717 (or em. עשׂה to ישׁע hi. *save* by means of), פדה *redeem* Jb 520, רוע hi. *shout* 1 S 1720, זעק *cry* 1 C 520, נתן *give* Is 274 (or del.), חזק *be strong* 1QM 113, pi. *strengthen* hand 1QM 712, רשׁה *be powerful* 1QM 125 4QMa 13 ([ב]מלחמ[ה]), כרת ni. *be cut off* 1QH 635 ([ונ]כרתו), בוס *trample* Zc 105 (or del.), מות *die* Dt 205.6.7 2 S 1911, hi. *kill* 2 S 330, נכה ho. *be struck* Jr 1821.

בְּ of instrument, *by (means of), with*, + לקח *take* Dt 434 Jos 1119 Jg 2122 2 K 1325, תפשׂ *seize* 2 K 147, ישׁע hi. *save* Ezk 1717 (if em.; see above) Ho 17, שׁבר ni. *be broken* Dn 1120.

כְּ *as in*, + נגף ni. *be struck down* Jg 2039.

מִן of direction, *from*, + בוא *come* Nm 3121 (if em.; see above), שׁוב *go back* Jg 813 1QM 310.10 48.13, נוס *flee* 2 S 14 194(ms), שׁקט *be quiet* Jos 1123 1415; partitive, *(some) of, from (out of)*, + קדשׁ hi. *dedicate* 1 C 2627 (מִן־הַמִּלְחָמוֹת וּמִן־הַשָּׁלָל *from the wars and from the booty*, i.e. from the booty taken in wars).

אֶל *to*, + קרב *draw near* Dt 202.3; *concerning*, + יעץ hi. *take counsel* Si 3711(B).

עַל *concerning*, + יעץ hi. *take counsel* Si 3711(Bmg, D).

עַד *unto*, + בוא *come* 1 S 1420.

בְּתוֹךְ *within*, + נפל *fall* 2 S 125.

בְּקֶרֶב *within*, + יצא *go out* 1 K 2039.

לִפְנֵי *before, in the face of*, + חזק pi. *strengthen* 1QH 77.

מִפְּנֵי *on account of*, + יכל *be able* 1 K 517.

אַחַר *after*, + עלה *go up* 1QM 13.

מִלְחָמָה without preposition, *to war*, + בוא *come* Nm 109 (or em. לַמִּלְחָמָה *to war*).

<COLL> מִלְחָמָה || קְרָב *war* Ps 1441 Jb 3823, צָבָא *war* Nm 3127 (+), מַצּוּת *strife* Is 4112, חֶרֶב *sword* Is 325 222 Ho 17 220 Ps 764 Ca 38 1 C 518 (+), קֶשֶׁת *bow* Ho 17 220 Ps 4610 (+) 1 C 518 (+), רֶשֶׁף *flame* of the bow, i.e. arrow Ps 764, חֲנִית *javelin* Ps 4610 (+), מָגֵן *shield* Ps 764 1 C 518 (+), סוּס *horse* Ho 17, פָּרָשׁ *rider* Ho 17, מֵרוֹץ *race* Ec 911, דֶּבֶר *pestilence* Jr 288, רָעָב *famine* Jr 288(mss) Jb 520, צַר *distress* Jb 3823, רָעָה *evil* Jr 288, אַף *anger* Dn 1120, מַסָּה *testing* Dt 434, אוֹת *sign* Dt 434, מוֹפֵת *wonder* Dt 434, יָד mighty *hand* Dt 434, זְרוֹעַ outstretched *arm* Dt 434.

:: שָׁלוֹם *peace* Ps 1207 Ec 38.

[מלח]מה כזו[את] *a war such as this* 4QMa 178.

Also 1QM 11 715 ([מ]לחמה) 718 ([המלחמ]ה) 1115 151.2 1912 1Q36 82 2QapDavid 13 ([מ]לחמה) 4QMa 111 ([ה]מל[חמה]) 113 10.210.12 11.22 ([המל]חמה) 11.216 ([מלח]מה) 1512 192 211.2 ([המלמח]מה) 4QMc 11 4QMf 14 ([מלח]מתם) 323.6 ([מ]לחמה) perh. Mur 484 ([מלח]מה).

<SYN> קְרָב *war*, מַצּוּת *strife*, חֶרֶב *sword*, קֶשֶׁת *bow*, רֶשֶׁף *flame*, סוּס *horse*, פָּרָשׁ *rider*, מֵרוֹץ *race*, דֶּבֶר *pestilence*, רָעָב *famine*, צַר *distress*, רָעָה *evil*, אַף *anger*, מַסָּה *testing*, אוֹת *sign*, מוֹפֵת *wonder*, יָד *hand*, זְרוֹעַ *arm*.

<ANT> שָׁלוֹם *peace*.*

⇒ לחם I *fight*.

*[מִלְחָמָה] II 1 n.f. **adaptation, harmony, sistrum,** like Egyptian ivory or wood clappers or sistrum for beating time in music (unless מִלְחָמָה I *war*), <CSTR> מִלְחֲמוֹת תְּנוּפָה *sistrum of waving* Is 3032. <PREP> בְּ of instrument, *by (means of), with*, + לחם ni. *fight* Is 3032.

מלט I 95.4.10 vb. **escape—Qal** 0.0.2 Pf. Q מלט, Q מלטו—**escape, survive,** <SUBJ> מִי־זֶה *who?* 11QPsa 229, אֵלֶּה *these* CD 721(A) (מלטו; =1910[B] ימלטו prob. ni.). <PREP> בְּ of time, *in*, + קֵץ *time* CD 721(A) (מלטו; =1910[B] ימלטו prob. ni.); of accompaniment, *with, in*, + עָוֶל *injustice* 11QPsa 229. <COLL> מלט :: אבד *perish* 11QPsa 229.

<ANT> אבד *perish*.

Ni. 63.2.3 Pf. נִמְלַט (נִמְלָט), נִמְלְטָה, נִמְלַטְתִּי, נִמְלְטוּ (נמלטו), נִמְלָטְנוּ; impf. יִמָּלֵט, 3fs תִּמָּלֵט, 2ms תִּמָּלֵט, אִמָּלֵט (אִמָּלְטָה), יִמָּלְטוּ, נִמָּלֵט; + waw וְנִמְלַט (וְנִמְלָט), וְנִמְלְטָה, וַיִּמָּלֵט, וָאִמָּלְטָה, וַיִּמָּלְטוּ, וְנִמְלַטְתִּי; impv. הִמָּלֵט, הִמָּלְטִי; ptc. נִמְלָט; inf. הִמָּלֵט—**escape, flee, be delivered** (e.g. Jl 35 Ps 226 Jb 2230 Pr 1121 2826 Dn 121 Si 361[E]), **slip away** (1 S 2029), **slip in** (2 S 46).

<SUBJ> Edom Dn 11$_{41}$, Moab Dn 11$_{41}$, עַם *people* Dn 12$_{1}$, חַיִל *army* 2 C 16$_{7}$, Adrammelech 2 K 19$_{37}$||Is 37$_{38}$, Baanah 2 S 4$_{6}$, Ben-hadad 1 K 20$_{20}$, David 1 S 19$_{10.12.18}$ 20$_{29}$ 22$_{1}$ 23$_{13}$ 27$_{1.1.1}$, Ehud Jg 3$_{26.26}$, Esther Est 4$_{13}$, Ishmael Jr 41$_{15}$, Lot Gn 19$_{17.17.19.20.22}$, Rechab 2 S 4$_{6}$, Sharezer 2 K 19$_{37}$||Is 37$_{38}$, Zedekiah Jr 32$_{4}$ 34$_{3}$ 38$_{18.23}$, אִישׁ *man* Jg 3$_{29}$ 1 S 30$_{17}$ 2 S 1$_{3}$ 1 K 18$_{40}$ 2 K 10$_{24}$ (or em. pi.), אָב *father* Ps 22$_{6}$, בֵּן *son* 1 S 22$_{20}$ 2 K 19$_{37(mss)}$||Is 37$_{38}$ Jr 41$_{15}$, אָח *brother* 2 S 4$_{6}$, מֶלֶךְ *king* 1 K 20$_{20}$ Jr 32$_{4}$ 34$_{3}$ Ezk 17$_{18}$, גִּבּוֹר *mighty one* Jr 46$_{6}$ 4QAdmon 1$_{6}$ (הג[בור]ים), אֹיֵב *enemy* 1 S 19$_{17}$, יֹשֵׁב *inhabitant* Is 20$_{6}$ Zc 2$_{11}$ (if em. הִמָּלְטִי *escape* [subj. Zion] to הִמָּלְטוּ יוֹשְׁבֵי אֶת־ *escape, O you who dwell with*), שְׁבִי *captives* Is 49$_{24}$, פָּרָשׁ *cavalry* 1 K 20$_{20}$.

עשׂה ptc. *one who does* Ezk 17$_{15.15}$ Ml 3$_{15}$, הלך ptc. *one who walks* in wisdom Pr 28$_{26}$, ירא ptc. *one who fears* Si 36$_{1(E)}$, פָּלִיט *escaped one* Am 9$_{1}$, קַל *swift one* Am 2$_{15}$ (if em. יְמַלֵּט *he will not deliver [himself]* to יִמָּלֵט *he will not escape*), חזק hi. ptc. *steadfast one* CD 7$_{14}$, מַלְאָךְ *messenger* Jb 1$_{15}$, worshipper Ps 124$_{7}$, יָפֵחַ *witness* Pr 19$_{5}$, אִי־נָקִי *one not innocent* Jb 22$_{30}$ (or subj. נָקִי *innocent one*, if em. אִי *not* to אֱלֹהִים *God*), טוֹב *good one* Ec 7$_{26}$, רָשָׁע *wicked one* Jb 20$_{20}$ (if em. יְמַלֵּט to יִמָּלֵט), חָנֵף *profane one* Jb 20$_{20}$ (if em.; see above), עַוָּל *wrongdoer* Si 16$_{13}$ (unless pi.), נֶפֶשׁ *soul* Ps 124$_{7}$, זֶרַע *seed* Pr 11$_{21}$, עִיר *city* Jr 48$_{8}$, Zion Zc 2$_{11}$ (or em.; see above), מַלְקוֹחַ *prey* Is 49$_{25}$, סוּס *horse* Ps 33$_{17}$ (if em. יְמַלֵּט to יִמָּלֵט), רֵאשִׁית *chief (ones)* Dn 11$_{41}$ (or em. רֵאשִׁית to שְׁאֵרִית *remnant*), אֶחָד *one* 4QJub^{h} 38$_{5}$ ([אחד]), זֶה *this (one)* Jb 1$_{16.17.19}$, אֵלֶּה *these* Dn 11$_{31}$ CD 19$_{10(B)}$ (=7$_{21[A]}$ מלטו appar. qal), כֹּל *everyone* Jl 3$_{5}$; subj. not specified, 1 K 19$_{17.17}$ Jr 48$_{19}$.

<PREP> לְ of direction, *to*, + אֶרֶץ *land* CD 7$_{14}$.

בְּ of time, *in, at*, + לַיְלָה *night* 1 S 19$_{10}$, עֵת *time* Dn 12$_{1}$, קֵץ *time* CD 19$_{10(B)}$ (=7$_{21[A]}$ מלטו appar. qal); of accompaniment, *with*, + אִישׁ *man* Jr 41$_{15}$, חמד pass. ptc. *desirable thing* Jb 20$_{20}$ (if em.; see Subj.), גָּזֵל *plunder* Si 16$_{13}$ (unless pi.).

כְּ *as*, + צִפּוֹר *bird* Ps 124$_{7}$.

מִן of direction, *from*, + Keilah 1 S 23$_{13}$, מַחֲנֶה *camp* 2 S 1$_{3}$, אִשָּׁה *woman* Ec 7$_{26}$, יָד *hand* 1 S 27$_{1}$ Jr 32$_{4}$ 34$_{3}$ 38$_{18.23}$ Dn 11$_{41}$ 2 C 16$_{7}$, חֶרֶב *sword* 1 K 19$_{17.17}$, פַּח *trap* Ps 124$_{7}$; partitive, *from (among)*, + כֹּל *all* 4QJub^{h} 38$_{5}$ ([כול]).

מִפְּנֵי *from (before)*, + Johanan Jr 41$_{15}$.

אֶל *to*, + אֶרֶץ *land* 1 S 27$_{1}$, מְעָרָה *cave* 1 S 22$_{1}$.

עַל *upon*, + סוּס *horse* 1 K 20$_{20}$; *for*, + נֶפֶשׁ *soul*, i.e. life Gn 19$_{17}$.

ה- of direction, *to*, + Seirah Jg 3$_{26}$, הַר *mountain* Gn 19$_{17.19}$, שָׁם *there* Gn 10$_{20.22}$.

מלט ni. + noun without prep. or ה- of direction, אֶרֶץ *to the land of* 2 K 19$_{37}$||Is 37$_{38}$, צִיּוֹן *to Zion* Zc 2$_{11}$ (if em.; see Subj.).

<COLL> מלט ni. || ברח *flee* 1 S 19$_{12.18}$ 22$_{20}$ (+), נוס *flee* Gn 19$_{20}$ (+) 1 S 19$_{10}$ Jr 46$_{6}$ 48$_{19}$ Am 9$_{1}$, לקח ho. *be taken* Is 49$_{24.25}$, נקה ni. *be unpunished* Pr 19$_{5}$; + פלט pi. *deliver* Ps 22$_{6}$, נצל ni. *be delivered* Is 20$_{6}$.

:: נתן ni. *be given* Jr 32$_{4}$ 34$_{3}$, תפשׂ ni. *be seized* Jr 34$_{3}$, לכד ni. *be captured* Ec 7$_{26}$.

+ adverb, לְבַד *alone* Jb 1$_{15.16.17.19}$, רַק *only* Jb 1$_{15.16.17.19}$.

Inf. abs. + finite verb 1 S 27$_{1}$.

<SYN> ברח *flee*, נוס *flee*, לקח ho. *be taken*, נקה ni. *be unpunished*.

<ANT> נתן ni. *be given*, תפשׂ ni. *be seized*, לכד ni. *be captured*.

Pi. 28.3.5 Pf. מִלֵּט (מִלַּט־, מִלְּטָנוּ, Q מלטם), Q מלטו; impf. יְמַלֵּט (יְמַלְּטֵהוּ), אֲמַלֵּט (אֲמַלֶּטְךָ); + waw וַתְּמַלֵּט (Si וימלטני), וַיְמַלְּטוּ; impv. מַלְּטָה, מַלְּטִי, מַלְּטוּ (מַלְּטוּנִי); ptc. מְמַלֵּט, מְמַלְּטִים; inf. מַלֵּט—**1. deliver, save,** <SUBJ> Y. Is 46$_{4}$ Jr 39$_{18.18}$ Ps 41$_{2}$ 107$_{20}$ 116$_{4}$ Jb 22$_{30}$ perh. Si 16$_{13}$ (unless ni.) 51$_{12}$ 4QpPs^{a} 3.4$_{20}$ 4Q183 1.2$_{3}$ 4QDéluge 4$_{2}$ (אדו[ני]), Bel Is 46$_{2}$, Nebo Is 46$_{2}$, Israelites Jr 51$_{6.45}$, Moabites Jr 48$_{6}$, Bathsheba 1 K 1$_{12}$, David 1 S 19$_{11}$, Job Jb 29$_{12}$, אִישׁ *man* Jr 51$_{6.45}$ Ec 9$_{15}$ (or em. מַלֵּט inf. abs.*), גֶּבֶר *man* Ps 89$_{49}$, אֵם *mother* 1 K 1$_{12}$, מֶלֶךְ *king* 2 S 19$_{10}$, עֶבֶד *servant* 2 S 19$_{6}$, קַל *swift one* Am 2$_{15}$ (or em. יְמַלֵּט *he will not deliver [himself]* to ni. יִמָּלֵט *he will not escape*), גִּבּוֹר *mighty one* Am 2$_{14}$, רָשָׁע *wicked one* Jb 20$_{20}$ (or em. יִמָּלֵט), חָנֵף *profane one* Jb 20$_{20}$ (or em. יִמָּלֵט), שׁמע ptc. *one who hears* Ezk 33$_{5}$, רֹכֵב *rider* Am 2$_{15}$, friends of Job Jb 6$_{23}$, סוּס *horse* Ps 33$_{17}$ (or em. יִמָּלֵט), רֶשַׁע *wickedness* Ec 8$_{8}$ (or em. רֶשַׁע to עֹשֶׁר *riches*).

<OBJ> עַם *people* 2 S 19$_{10}$, כּוּשִׁי *Cushite* Jr 39$_{18}$, Ben

Sira Si 51$_{12}$, Ebed-melech Jr 39$_{18}$, Job Jb 6$_{23}$, שׂכל hi. ptc. *one who considers* Ps 41$_{2}$, צַדִּיק *righteous one* 4QpPs^{a} 3.4$_{20}$ ([צדיקים]), אִי־נָקִי *one not innocent* Jb 22$_{30}$ (or obj. נָקִי *innocent one*, if em. אִי *not* to אֱלֹהִים *God*), עָנִי *poor one* Jb 29$_{12}$, יָתוֹם *orphan* Jb 29$_{12}$, בַּעַל *owner* Ec 8$_{8}$, נֶפֶשׁ *soul*, i.e. life 1 S 19$_{11}$ 2 S 19$_{6}$ 1 K 1$_{12}$ Jr 48$_{6}$ 51$_{6.45}$ Ezk 33$_{5}$ Am 2$_{14.15}$ Ps 89$_{49}$ 116$_{4}$ 1QMyst 1.1$_{4}$, חַיָּה *life* Ps 107$_{20}$ (if em.; see Prep.), עִיר *city* Ec 9$_{15}$, מַשָּׂא *burden* Is 46$_{2}$.

<PREP> בְּ of time, *in, on*, + יוֹם *day* Ps 41$_{2}$ Si 51$_{12}$; of instrument, *by (means of), with*, + חָכְמָה *wisdom* Ec 9$_{15}$; partitive, *(some) of*, + חמד pass. ptc. *desirable thing* Jb 20$_{20}$ (or em.; see Subj.); introducing object, + גֹּזֵל *robber* Si 16$_{13}$ (unless ni.), עַוָּל *unjust one* Si 16$_{13}$ (unless ni.).

מִן of direction, *from*, + רָשָׁע *wicked one* 4QpPs^{a} 3.4$_{20}$, יָד *hand*, i.e. power Ps 89$_{49}$ Jb 6$_{23}$, שְׁחִית *pit* Ps 107$_{20}$ (or em. מִשְּׁחִיתוֹתָם *from their pits* to מִשַּׁחַת חַיָּתָם *their life from the pit*), חָרוֹן *anger* Jr 51$_{45}$, רָז *mystery* 1QMyst 1.1$_{4}$; partitive, *(some) of*, + אִישׁ *man* 2 K 10$_{24}$ (if em.; see Subj.).

<COLL> מלט pi. || נצל hi. *deliver* 2 S 19$_{10}$, פלט pi. *deliver* 4QpPs^{a} 3.4$_{20}$, ישׁע hi. *save* 4Q183 1.2$_{3}$, פדה *ransom* Jb 6$_{23}$ Si 51$_{12}$; + נוס *flee* Jr 48$_{6}$ 51$_{6}$.

+ noun used adverbially, הַיּוֹם *today* 2 S 19$_{6}$, הַלַּיְלָה *tonight* 1 S 19$_{11}$.

Inf. abs + finite form of verb Jr 39$_{18}$.

2. escape from, deliver oneself from, <SUBJ> בֵּן *son* Si 11$_{10(B)}$ (ת[מלטנו]), <OBJ> obj. not specified, Si 11$_{10(B)}$ (ת[מלטנו]).

3. let escape, <SUBJ> אִישׁ *man* 2 K 10$_{24}$ (if em. יִמָּלֵט *he escapes* [ni.] to יְמַלֵּט *he lets escape*).

4. leave undisturbed, <SUBJ> subj. not specified, 2 K 23$_{18}$. <OBJ> עֶצֶם *bone* 2 K 23$_{18}$.

5. lay eggs, <SUBJ> קִפּוֹז *arrow snake* Is 34$_{15}$ (+ קנן pi. *nest*, בקע *hatch*, דגר *incubate*).

<SYN> §1 נצל hi. *deliver*, פלט pi. *deliver*, ישׁע hi. *save*, פדה *ransom*.

Hi. 2.0.1 Pf. הִמְלִיטָה, הִמְלִיט; impf. Q 3fs תמליט—**1. deliver, save,** <SUBJ> Y. Is 31$_{5}$ (+ גנן *protect*, נצל hi. *deliver*, פסח *pass over*).

2. give birth to, be delivered of, <SUBJ> Jerusalem Is 66$_{7}$ (|| ילד *give birth*), הָרָה *pregnant one* 1QH 3$_{9}$. <OBJ> זָכָר *male* Is 66$_{7}$ 1QH 3$_{9}$.

<SYN> ילד *give birth*.

Htp. 2 Impf. יִתְמַלָּטוּ; + waw וָאֶתְמַלְּטָה—**1. escape,** <SUBJ> Job Jb 19$_{20}$ (unless מלט II *be bald* or III *bite* or IV *cleave*). <PREP> בְּ of accompaniment, *with*, + עוֹר *skin* of teeth Jb 19$_{20}$.

2. fly out, <SUBJ> כִּידוֹד *spark* Jb 41$_{11}$ (|| הלך *go*).

<SYN> §2 הלך *go*.

⇒ מְלַטְיָה *Melatiah*.

מלט II 1 vb. **be bald** (unless מלט I *escape* or III *bite* or IV *cleave*)—**Htp.** 1 + waw וָאֶתְמַלְּטָה—**be bald,** <SUBJ> Job Jb 19$_{20}$. <PREP> בְּ of place, *in, on*, + עוֹר *skin* of teeth Jb 19$_{20}$.

***מלט III** 1 vb. **rub, bite** (unless מלט I *escape* or II *be bald* or IV *cleave*)—**Htp.** 1 + waw וָאֶתְמַלְּטָה—**bite oneself, gnaw oneself,** <SUBJ> Job Jb 19$_{20}$. <PREP> בְּ of place, *in, on*, + עוֹר *skin* Jb 19$_{20}$ (וָאֶתְמַלְּטָה בְּעוֹר שִׁנָּי *and I gnawed myself on the skin (with) my teeth*).

***מלט IV** 1 vb. **cleave, stick** (unless מלט I *escape* or II *be bald* or III *bite*)—**Htp.** 1 + waw וָאֶתְמַלְּטָה—**cleave, stick,** <SUBJ> Job Jb 19$_{20}$. <PREP> בְּ *to*, + עוֹר *skin* of teeth Jb 19$_{20}$.

⇒ מֶלֶט *mortar*.

מֶ֫לֶט 1 n.[m.] **mortar,** or **clay floor,** <APP> מַלְבֵּן *brick pavement* Jr 43$_{9}$. <PREP> בְּ of place, *in*, + טמן *hide* Jr 43$_{9}$.

⇒ מלט IV *cleave*.

מְלַטְיָה 1 pr.n.m. **Melatiah,** Gibeonite and repairer of walls of Jerusalem, <SUBJ> חזק hi. *strengthen*, i.e. repair Ne 3$_{7}$. <APP> גִּבְעֹנִי *Gibeonite* Ne 3$_{7}$, אִישׁ *man* Ne 3$_{7}$.

⇒ מלט I *escape* + יְ *Y*.

***[מַלְיָ֫הוּ]** 0.0.0.2 pr.n.[m.] **Maliah, 1.** appar. son of Jehoshua, <PREP> לְ of possession, *of, (belonging) to* Seal 875 (8th/7th cent.).

2. appar. son of Nehemiah, <PREP> לְ of possession, *of, (belonging) to* Bulla D58.
⇒ (?) מלא *be full* + ״י *Y*.

[מְלִיכוּ], see מַלּוּכִי *Malluchi*.

[מְלִילָה] 1.0.1 n.f. **ear of corn**—pl. מְלִילֹת (Q מלילות) —milky ear of corn ready for rubbing out the kernel,* <OBJ> קטף *pluck* Dt 23$_{26}$, אכל *eat* 11QT 19$_{7}$ ([יואכלו]). <APP> לחם חדש אביבות ומלילות *new bread (made of) ears of various cereals* (lit. *ears and ears*) 11QT 19$_{7}$.*
⇒ מלל *rub*.

*מֵלִיץ I 5.1.14 n.m. **interpreter** (if not מֵלִיץ II *one who speaks freely*)—מֵלִיץ, מְלִיצֵי, מְלִיצַי, מְלִיצֶיךָ, Si מְלִיצָיו —**interpreter** (Gn 42$_{23}$ 1QH 18$_{12}$), **spokesperson, mediator** (Is 43$_{27}$ Jb 16$_{20}$ 33$_{23}$ 1QH 2$_{13.14.31}$ 4$_{7.9}$ 6$_{13}$ fr. 2$_{6}$ 4QpPs^{a} 1.1$_{19}$ 4QDiscourse 7$_{2}$ 4QHod^{a} 7.2$_{16}$), **envoy** (2 C 32$_{31}$), **official** (Si 10$_{2}$), <SUBJ> פשע *transgress* Is 43$_{27}$ (+ אָב *father*), תעה hi. *lead astray* 1QH 4$_{7}$ ([התעום]), אמר *say* Jb 33$_{23}$, נגד hi. *tell* Jb 33$_{23}$, חנן *be gracious* Jb 33$_{23}$, מצא *find* Jb 33$_{23}$.

<NOM CL> המה מליצי כזב *they are mediators of lies* 1QH 4$_{9}$ (|| חֹזֶה *seer*), הַמֵּלִיץ בֵּינֹתָם *an interpreter was between them* Gn 42$_{23}$, מְלִיצַי רֵעָי *my cry is my spokesperson* Jb 16$_{20}$ (if em. מְלִיצַי *my spokespersons*; + עֵד *witness*, שָׂהֵד *witness*), מליצי דעת עם כול צעודו *the mediators of knowledge are with all his steps* 1QH fr. 2$_{6}$, אִם־יֵשׁ עָלָיו ... מֵלִיץ *if he has ... a mediator* Jb 33$_{23}$, אין מליץ *there is no mediator* 1QH 6$_{13}$ 4QHod^{a} 7.2$_{16}$, כְּשׁוֹפֵט עָם כֵּן מְלִיצָיו *as the judge of the people, so are its officials* Si 10$_{2}$.

<OBJ> שִׂים *place*, i.e. appoint 1QH 2$_{13}$.

<CSTR> מְלִיצֵי שָׂרֵי *envoys of the princes of* Babylon 2 C 32$_{31}$, מליץ דעת *mediator of knowledge* 1QH 2$_{13}$ 4QpPs^{a} 1.1$_{19}$, מליצי דעת *mediators of knowledge* 1QH fr. 2$_{6}$, מליצי תעות *mediators of error* 1QH 2$_{14}$, כזב *of lies* 1QH 2$_{31}$ 4$_{9}$, רמיה *of deceit* 1QH 4$_{7}$; קנאת מליצי *jealousy of the mediators of* 1QH 2$_{31}$.

<APP> רֵעַ *cry* Jb 16$_{20}$, מַלְאָךְ *messenger* Jb 33$_{23}$.

<ADJ> אֶחָד *one* Jb 33$_{23}$.

<PREP> לְ of benefit, *to, for*, + היה *be* 1QH 2$_{14}$; שמע לְ *listen to* 4QpPs^{a} 1.1$_{19}$ ([שמ]עו); *as*, + חקק *engrave* on tongue 1QH 18$_{12}$; בְּ *in (the matter of)*, + עזב *forsake* 2 C 32$_{31}$.

<COLL> לעמך מליץ *a mediator for your people* 4QDiscourse 7$_{2}$, באלה מליץ *an interpreter in*, i.e. of, *these (things)* 1QH 18$_{12}$.

Also 4QLeqeṭ 1$_{6}$ (ילאצו) 4QapPent 1$_{7}$ (מליץ).

<SYN> חֹזֶה *seer*.

*מֵלִיץ II 5.1.14 n.m. **one who speaks freely** (if not מֵלִיץ I *interpreter*)—מֵלִיץ, מְלִיצֵי, מְלִיצַי, מְלִיצֶיךָ, Si מְלִיצָיו—**one who speaks freely** (Gn 42$_{23}$ 1QH 18$_{12}$), **spokesperson** (Is 43$_{27}$ Jb 33$_{23}$ 1QH 2$_{13.14.31}$ 4$_{7.9}$ 6$_{13}$ fr. 2$_{6}$ 4QpPs^{a} 1.1$_{19}$ 4QDiscourse 7$_{2}$ 4QHod^{a} 7.2$_{16}$), **envoy** (2 C 32$_{31}$), **official** (Si 10$_{2}$), <SUBJ> פשע *transgress* Is 43$_{27}$ (+ אָב *father*), תעה hi. *lead astray* 1QH 4$_{7}$ ([התעום]), אמר *say* Jb 33$_{23}$, נגד hi. *tell* Jb 33$_{23}$, חנן *be gracious* Jb 33$_{23}$, מצא *find* Jb 33$_{23}$.

<NOM CL> המה מליצי כזב *they are speakers of lies* 1QH 4$_{9}$ (|| חֹזֶה *seer*), הַמֵּלִיץ בֵּינֹתָם *an official*, lit. one who spoke freely, *was between them* Gn 42$_{23}$, מְלִיצַי רֵעָי *my cry is my spokesperson* Jb 16$_{20}$ (if em. מְלִיצַי *my spokespersons*; + עֵד *witness*, שָׂהֵד *witness*), מליצי דעת עם כול צעודו *the speakers of knowledge are with all his steps* 1QH fr. 2$_{6}$, אִם־יֵשׁ עָלָיו ... מֵלִיץ *if he has ... a spokesperson* Jb 33$_{23}$, אין מליץ *there is no spokesperson* 1QH 6$_{13}$ 4QHod^{a} 7.2$_{16}$, כְּשׁוֹפֵט עָם כֵּן מְלִיצָיו *as the judge of the people, so are its officials* Si 10$_{2}$.

<OBJ> שִׂים *place*, i.e. appoint 1QH 2$_{13}$.

<CSTR> מְלִיצֵי שָׂרֵי *envoys of the princes of* Babylon 2 C 32$_{31}$, מליץ דעת *speaker of knowledge* 1QH 2$_{13}$ 4QpPs^{a} 1.1$_{19}$, מליצי דעת *speakers of knowledge* 1QH fr. 2$_{6}$, מליצי תעות *speakers of error* 1QH 2$_{14}$, כזב *of lies* 1QH 2$_{31}$ 4$_{9}$, רמיה *of deceit* 1QH 4$_{7}$; קנאת מליצי *jealousy of the speakers of* 1QH 2$_{31}$.

<APP> רֵעַ *cry* Jb 16$_{20}$, מַלְאָךְ *messenger* Jb 33$_{23}$.

<ADJ> אֶחָד *one* Jb 33$_{23}$.

<PREP> לְ of benefit, *to, for*, + היה *be* 1QH 2$_{14}$; שמע לְ *listen to* 4QpPs^{a} 1.1$_{19}$ ([שמ]עו); *as*, + חקק *engrave* on tongue 1QH 18$_{12}$; בְּ *in (the matter of)*, + עזב *forsake* 2 C 32$_{31}$.

<COLL> לעמך מליץ *a spokesperson for your people*

4QDiscourse 7$_{2}$, באלה מליץ *a spokesperson in*, i.e. of, *these (things)* 1QH 18$_{12}$.

Also 4QLeqeṭ 1$_{6}$ (ילאצו) 4QapPent 1$_{7}$ (מליץ).

<SYN> חֹזֶה *seer*.

⇨ ליץ *talk freely*.

מְלִיצָה I $_{2.1}$ n.f. **mocking poem, figure,** <OBJ> נשׂא *take up* Hb 2$_{6}$ (=1QpHab 8$_{6}$ מליצי חידות *interpreters of riddles*), חוד *recite* Hb 2$_{6}$ (if em. חִידוֹת *riddles* to יָחוּדוּ *they will recite*), בין hi. *understand* Pr 1$_{6}$. <PREP> בְּ of accompaniment, *with, in*, + סער hi. *astound* Si 47$_{17}$.<COLL> מְלִיצָה || חִידָה *riddle* Hb 2$_{6}$ (+) Pr 1$_{6}$ Si 47$_{17}$, מָשָׁל *proverb* Hb 2$_{6}$ (+) Pr 1$_{6}$ Si 47$_{17}$, דָּבָר *word* Pr 1$_{6}$, שִׁיר *song* Si 47$_{17}$.

<SYN> מָשָׁל *parable*, חִידָה *riddle*, דָּבָר *word*, שִׁיר *song*.*

⇨ ליץ *scorn*.

***מְלִיצָה** II $_{2.1}$ n.f. **allusive saying, slippery saying, enigma,** <OBJ> נשׂא *take up* Hb 2$_{6}$ (=1QpHab 8$_{6}$ מליצי חידות *interpreters of riddles*), חוד *recite* Hb 2$_{6}$ (if em. חִידוֹת *riddles* to יָחוּדוּ *they will recite*), בין hi. *understand* Pr 1$_{6}$. <PREP> בְּ of accompaniment, *with, in*, + סער hi. *astound* Si 47$_{17}$.<COLL> מְלִיצָה || חִידָה *riddle* Hb 2$_{6}$ (+) Pr 1$_{6}$ Si 47$_{17}$, מָשָׁל *proverb* Hb 2$_{6}$ (+) Pr 1$_{6}$ Si 47$_{17}$, דָּבָר *word* Pr 1$_{6}$, שִׁיר *song* Si 47$_{17}$.

<SYN> מָשָׁל *parable*, חִידָה *riddle*, דָּבָר *word*, שִׁיר *song*.

⇨ מלץ *be smooth*.

***מְלִיצָה** III $_{2.1}$ n.f. **sharp saying, obscure saying,** <OBJ> נשׂא *take up* Hb 2$_{6}$ (=1QpHab 8$_{6}$ מליצי חידות *interpreters of obscure sayings*), חוד *recite* Hb 2$_{6}$ (if em. חִידוֹת *obscure sayings* to יָחוּדוּ *they will recite*), בין hi. *understand* Pr 1$_{6}$. <PREP> בְּ of accompaniment, *with, in*, + סער hi. *astound* Si 47$_{17}$. <COLL> מְלִיצָה || חִידָה *obscure saying* Hb 2$_{6}$ (+) Pr 1$_{6}$ Si 47$_{17}$, מָשָׁל *proverb* Hb 2$_{6}$ (+) Pr 1$_{6}$ Si 47$_{17}$, דָּבָר *word* Pr 1$_{6}$, שִׁיר *song* Si 47$_{17}$.

<SYN> מָשָׁל *parable*, חִידָה *obscure saying*, דָּבָר *word*, שִׁיר *song*.

⇨ לוץ *turn astray*.

***מְלִיצָה** IV $_{2.1}$ n.f. **sweet saying,** <OBJ> נשׂא *take up* Hb 2$_{6}$ (=1QpHab 8$_{6}$ מליצי חידות *interpreters of sweet sayings*), חוד *recite* Hb 2$_{6}$ (if em. חִידוֹת *riddles* to יָחוּדוּ *they will recite*), בין hi. *understand* Pr 1$_{6}$. <PREP> בְּ of accompaniment, *with, in*, + סער hi. *astound* Si 47$_{17}$. <COLL> מְלִיצָה || חִידָה *riddle* Hb 2$_{6}$ (+) Pr 1$_{6}$ Si 47$_{17}$, מָשָׁל *proverb* Hb 2$_{6}$ (+) Pr 1$_{6}$ Si 47$_{17}$, דָּבָר *word* Pr 1$_{6}$, שִׁיר *song* Si 47$_{17}$.

<SYN> מָשָׁל *parable*, חִידָה *riddle*, דָּבָר *word*, שִׁיר *song*.

⇨ מלץ *be pleasant*.

***מְלִיצָה** V $_{2.1}$ n.f. **trope, saying that puts things in different words,** <OBJ> נשׂא *take up* Hb 2$_{6}$ (=1QpHab 8$_{6}$ מליצי חידות *interpreters of tropes*), חוד *recite* Hb 2$_{6}$ (if em. חִידוֹת *riddles* to יָחוּדוּ *they will recite*), בין hi. *understand* Pr 1$_{6}$. <PREP> בְּ of accompaniment, *with, in*, + סער hi. *astound* Si 47$_{17}$.<COLL> מְלִיצָה || חִידָה *riddle* Hb 2$_{6}$ (+) Pr 1$_{6}$ Si 47$_{17}$, מָשָׁל *proverb* Hb 2$_{6}$ (+) Pr 1$_{6}$ Si 47$_{17}$, דָּבָר *word* Pr 1$_{6}$, שִׁיר *song* Si 47$_{17}$.

<SYN> מָשָׁל *parable*, חִידָה *riddle*, דָּבָר *word*, שִׁיר *song*.

⇨ מֵלִיץ *interpreter*.

מלך I $_{347.1.8.1}$ vb. **be king—Qal** $_{297.1.7}$ Pf. מָלַךְ (מָלָךְ), מָלְכוּ, מָלַכְתָּ; impf. יִמְלֹךְ (יִמְלוֹךְ), יִמְלָךְ־, יִמְלוֹךְ), 3fs תִּמְלֹךְ, 2ms תִּמְלֹךְ (תִּמְלוֹךְ), אֶמְלֹךְ (אֶמְלוֹךְ), יִמְלְכוּ; + waw וּמָלַךְ, וּמָלַכְתָּ; וַיִּמְלֹךְ (וַיִּמְלָךְ־), וַיִּמְלְכוּ; impv. מְלָךְ־ (Qr מָלְכָה, Kt מלוכה), מָלְכִי (Kt מלוכי); ptc. מֹלֵךְ, מֹלֶכֶת; inf. abs. מָלֹךְ; cstr. מְלֹךְ (מָלְכוֹ).

Be king, become king, be queen (2 K 11$_{3}$||2 C 22$_{12}$ Est 2$_{4}$), **reign (over),** <SUBJ> Y. Ex 15$_{8}$ 1 S 8$_{7}$ Is 24$_{23}$ 52$_{7}$=11QMelch2$_{23}$ Ezk 20$_{33}$ Mc 4$_{7}$ Zp 3$_{15}$ (if em. מֶלֶךְ יִשְׂרָאֵל *the king of Israel* to יִמְלֹךְ *he will reign*) Ps 47$_{9}$ 93$_{1}$ 96$_{10}$||1 C 16$_{31}$ Ps 97$_{1}$ 99$_{1}$ 146$_{10}$ perh. 1QM 12$_{3}$ 4QMidrEschat[a] 3$_{3}$.

Abijah 1 K 14$_{31(mss)}$||2 C 12$_{16}$ 1 K 15$_{1(mss).2(mss)}$||2 C 13$_{1.2}$, Abijam 1 K 14$_{31}$ 15$_{1.2}$, Absalom 2 S 15$_{10}$, Adonijah 1 K 1$_{5.11.13.18.24}$ 2$_{15}$, Ahab 1 K 16$_{28.29.29}$, Ahasuerus Est 1$_{1.3}$, Ahaz 2 K 15$_{38}$||2 C 27$_{9}$ 2 K 16$_{1.2.2}$||2 C 28$_{1.1}$, Ahaziah (son of Ahab) 1 K 22$_{40.52.52}$, Ahaziah (son of Jehoram) 2 K 8$_{24.25.26.26}$||2 C 22$_{2.2}$ 2 K 9$_{29}$ 2 C 21$_{2}$,

Amaziah 2 K 12$_{22}$||2 C 24$_{27}$ 2 K 14$_{1.2.2}$||2 C 25$_{1.1}$, Amon 2 K 21$_{18.19.19}$||2 C 33$_{20.21.21}$, Asa 1 K 15$_{8}$||2 C 13$_{23}$ 1 K 15$_{9.10}$ 2 C 16$_{13}$, Athaliah 2 K 11$_{3}$||2 C 22$_{12}$, Azariah 2 K 15$_{1.2.2}$, Baal-hanan Gn 36$_{38}$||1 C 1$_{49}$, Baasha 1 K 15$_{28.29.33}$, Bela Gn 36$_{32}$||1 C 1$_{43}$, Ben-hadad 2 K 13$_{24}$, Darius Dn 9$_{2}$, David 1 S 23$_{17}$ 24$_{21.21}$ 2 S 3$_{21}$ 5$_{4.5.5}$ 8$_{15}$||1 C 18$_{14}$ 2 S 16$_{8}$ 1 K 2$_{11.11.11}$||1 C 29$_{27.27.27}$ 1 C 3$_{4.4}$ 4$_{31}$ (mss מֶלֶךְ *king*) 29$_{26}$, Elah 1 K 16$_{6.8}$, Esar-haddon 2 K 19$_{37}$||Is 37$_{38}$, Eshbaal 2 S 2$_{10(\text{mss})}$, Evil-merodach 2 K 25$_{27}$.

Hadad (son of Bedad) Gn 36$_{35}$||1 C 1$_{46}$, Hadad (husband of Mehetabel) Gn 36$_{39(\text{mss})}$||1 C 1$_{50}$, Hadar Gn 36$_{39}$||1 C 1$_{50(\text{mss})}$, Hanun 2 S 10$_{1}$, Hazael 2 K 8$_{15}$, Hezekiah 2 K 16$_{20}$||2 C 28$_{27}$ 2 K 18$_{1.2.2}$||2 C 29$_{1.1}$ 2 C 29$_{3}$, Hoshea 2 K 15$_{30}$ 17$_{1}$, Husham Gn 36$_{34}$||1 C 1$_{45}$, Ish-bosheth 2 S 2$_{10}$.

Jabin Jg 4$_{2}$, J(eh)oahaz (son of Jehu) 2 K 10$_{35}$ 13$_{1}$, J(eh)oahaz (son of) Josiah 2 K 23$_{31.31}$||2 C 36$_{2.2}$ 2 K 23$_{33}$, J(eh)oash (son of Ahaziah) 2 K 12$_{1}$||2 C 24$_{1}$ 2 K 12$_{2.2}$||2 C 24$_{1}$, J(eh)oash (son of Jehoahaz) 2 K 13$_{9.10}$, Jehoiachin 2 K 24$_{6.8.8}$||2 C 36$_{8.9.9}$ 2 K 24$_{12}$, Jehoiakim 2 K 23$_{36.36}$||2 C 36$_{5.5}$ Jr 22$_{15}$, J(eh)oram (son of Jehoshaphat) 1 K 22$_{51}$||2 C 21$_{1}$ 2 K 8$_{16.17.17}$||2 C 21$_{5.5}$ 2 K 8$_{24}$ 2 C 21$_{20.20}$, J(eh)oram (son of Ahab) 2 K 1$_{17}$ 3$_{1.1}$, Jehoshaphat 1 K 15$_{24}$||2 C 17$_{1}$ 1 K 22$_{41.42.42}$||2 C 20$_{31.31.31}$ 2 C 17$_{7}$, Jehu 2 K 9$_{13}$ 10$_{36}$, Jeroboam (son of Nebat) 1 K 11$_{37}$ 14$_{2}$ (if em. לְמֶלֶךְ *as king* to לִמְלֹךְ *to be king*) 14$_{19.20}$, Jeroboam (son of Jehoash) 2 K 14$_{16.23}$, Jobab Gn 36$_{33}$||1 C 1$_{44}$, Joseph Gn 37$_{8.8}$, Josiah 2 K 21$_{26}$ 22$_{1.1}$|| 2 C 34$_{1.1}$ Jr 1$_{2}$ 2 C 34$_{3.8}$, Jotham 2 K 15$_{7}$||2 C 26$_{23}$ 2 K 15$_{32.33.33}$||2 C 27$_{1.1}$ 2 C 27$_{8}$.

Manasseh 2 K 20$_{21}$||2 C 32$_{33}$ 2 K 21$_{1.1}$||2 C 33$_{1.1}$, Menahem 2 K 15$_{14.17}$, Nadab 1 K 14$_{20}$ 15$_{25.25}$, Og Jos 13$_{12}$, Omri 1 K 16$_{22.23.23}$, Pekah 2 K 15$_{25.27}$, Pekahiah 2 K 15$_{22.23}$, Rehoboam 1 K 11$_{43}$||2 C 9$_{31}$ 1 K 12$_{17}$||2 C 10$_{17}$ 1 K 14$_{21.21.21}$||2 C 12$_{13.13.13}$, Rezon 1 K 11$_{24.25}$, Samlah Gn 36$_{36}$||1 C 1$_{47}$, Saul 1 S 11$_{12}$ 13$_{1.1}$ 16$_{1}$, Shallum (son of Jabesh) 2 K 15$_{10.13.13}$, Shallum (son of Josiah) Jr 22$_{11}$, Shaul Gn 36$_{37}$||1 C 1$_{48}$, Sihon Jos 13$_{10.21}$, Solomon 1 K 1$_{13.17.30.35}$ 6$_{1}$ 11$_{42}$||2 C 9$_{30}$ 1 C 29$_{28}$ 2 C 1$_{13}$ Si 47$_{13}$, Uzziah 2 C 26$_{3.3}$, Zechariah 2 K 14$_{29}$ 15$_{8}$, Zedekiah 2 K 24$_{18.18}$||2 C 36$_{11.11}$||Jr 52$_{1.1}$ 2 K 25$_{1}$||Jr 52$_{4}$ Jr 37$_{1}$ 51$_{59}$, Zimri 1 K 16$_{10.11.15}$.

אָדָם *human being* Jb 34$_{30}$, בֵּן *son* Gn 36$_{32.33.35.38}$||1 C 1$_{43.44.46.49}$ 2 S 2$_{10}$ 10$_{1}$||1 C 19$_{1}$ 1 K 1$_{5.11}$ (בֵּן lacking in ms) 1$_{13.17.30}$ 2$_{15}$ 11$_{43}$||2 C 9$_{31}$ 1 K 14$_{20.21.31}$||2 C 12$_{16}$ 1 K 15$_{8}$||2 C 13$_{23}$ 1 K 15$_{24}$||2 C 17$_{1}$ 1 K 15$_{25.25.33}$ 16$_{6.8.28.29.29}$ 22$_{40.41.51}$||2 C 21$_{1}$ 1 K 22$_{52.52}$ 2 K 3$_{1.1.27}$ 8$_{16.24.25}$ 10$_{35}$ 12$_{22}$||2 C 24$_{27}$ 2 K 13$_{1.9.10.24}$ 14$_{1.16.23.29}$ 15$_{1+13t}$ 16$_{1.20}$||2 C 28$_{27}$ 2 K 17$_{1}$ 18$_{1.2.2}$||2 C 29$_{1.1}$ 2 K 19$_{37}$||Is 37$_{38}$ 2 K 20$_{21}$|| 2 C 32$_{33}$ 2 K 21$_{18}$||2 C 33$_{20}$ 2 K 21$_{26}$ 24$_{6}$||2 C 36$_{8}$ Jr 1$_{2}$ 22$_{11}$ 33$_{21}$ 37$_{1}$ Dn 9$_{2}$ 1 C 29$_{26.27.27.27.28}$ 2 C 21$_{2}$ 23$_{3}$, יֶלֶד *child* Ec 4$_{14}$, נַעֲרָה *young woman* Est 2$_{4}$, מֶלֶךְ *king* Gn 36$_{31.31}$||1 C 1$_{43.43}$ Jos 13$_{10.21}$ Jg 4$_{2}$ 1 S 8$_{9.11}$ 12$_{12.14}$ 1 K 15$_{9}$ (mss read עַל *over* for מֶלֶךְ *king of* Judah) 2 K 8$_{16.25}$ 14$_{1.23}$ (mss read עַל *over* for מֶלֶךְ *king of* Israel) 15$_{1.2.2.13.32}$ 16$_{1}$ 18$_{1.2}$ 25$_{27}$ Is 32$_{1}$ Jr 1$_{2}$ 22$_{11}$ 23$_{5}$ 37$_{1}$ (or del. מֶלֶךְ) 51$_{59}$ Pr 8$_{15}$ 2 C 21$_{2}$, מַלְכוּת *kingdom* 2 C 36$_{20}$, עֶבֶד *servant* Pr 30$_{22}$, אָטָד *bramble* Jg 9$_{14}$, גֶּפֶן *vine* Jg 9$_{12}$, זַיִת *olive tree* Jg 9$_{8}$, תְּאֵנָה *fig tree* Jg 9$_{10}$.

<OBJ> מְדִינָה *province* Est 1$_{1}$.

<PREP> לְ of direction, *to, throughout*, + עוֹלָם *eternity* Ex 15$_{18}$ Ps 146$_{10}$, עַד *perpetuity* Ex 15$_{18}$, דּוֹר *generation* Ps 146$_{10}$.

לְ *according to*, + צֶדֶק *righteousness* Is 32$_{1}$.

בְּ of place, *in, at* Arad ost. 88$_{1}$, + Edom Gn 36$_{32}$, Judah 1 K 14$_{21}$, Ashtaroth Jos 13$_{12}$, Damascus 1 K 11$_{24}$, Edrei Jos 13$_{12}$, Hazor Jg 4$_{2}$, Hebron 2 S 5$_{5}$ 15$_{10}$, 1 K 2$_{11}$||1 C 29$_{27}$, Heshbon Jos 13$_{10.21}$, Jerusalem 2 S 5$_{5}$ 1 K 2$_{11}$||1 C 29$_{27}$ 1 K 11$_{42}$||2 C 9$_{30}$ 1 K 14$_{21}$||2 C 12$_{13}$ 1 K 15$_{2}$||2 C 13$_{2}$ 1 K 15$_{10}$ 22$_{42}$||2 C 20$_{31}$ 2 K 8$_{17}$||2 C 21$_{5}$ 2 K 8$_{26}$||2 C 22$_{2}$ 2 K 12$_{2}$||2 C 24$_{1}$ 2 K 14$_{2}$||2 C 25$_{1}$ 2 K 15$_{2}$||2 C 26$_{3}$ 2 K 15$_{33}$||2 C 27$_{1}$ 2 K 16$_{2}$||2 C 28$_{1}$ 2 K 17$_{1}$ 18$_{2}$||2 C 29$_{1}$ 2 K 21$_{1.19}$||2 C 33$_{1.21}$ 2 K 22$_{1}$||2 C 34$_{1}$ 2 K 23$_{31}$||2 C 36$_{2}$ 2 K 23$_{33.36}$||2 C 36$_{5}$ 2 K 24$_{8}$||2 C 36$_{9}$ 2 K 24$_{18}$||2 C 36$_{11}$||Jr 52$_{1}$ Is 24$_{23}$ 2 C 21$_{20}$ 27$_{8}$, Samaria 1 K 16$_{29}$ 22$_{52}$ 2 K 3$_{1}$ 13$_{1.10}$ 14$_{23}$ 15$_{8.13.17.23.27}$, Tirzah 1 K 15$_{33}$ 16$_{8.15.23}$, אֶרֶץ *land* Gn 36$_{31}$, עִיר *city* 1 K 14$_{21}$||2 C 12$_{13}$, הַר *mountain* Is 24$_{23}$ Mc 4$_{7}$.

בְּ of time, + שָׁנָה *year* 1 K 15$_{1.9.25}$ 16$_{8.15.23.29}$ 22$_{41.52}$ 2 K 1$_{17}$ 3$_{1}$ 8$_{16.25}$ 12$_{2}$ 15$_{13.17.23.27.30.32}$, יוֹם *day* Si 47$_{13}$, מוֹעֵד *appointed time* perh. 1QM 12$_{3}$.

בְּ *over*, + כֹּל *all* 2 S 3$_{21}$ 1 K 11$_{37}$.

בְּ of instrument, *by (means of), with*, + יָד mighty *hand* Ezk 20$_{33}$, זְרוֹעַ outstretched *arm* Ezk 20$_{33}$, חֵמָה

anger Ezk 20$_{33}$, חָכְמָה *wisdom* Pr 8$_{15}$, תְּבוּנָה *understanding* Pr 8$_{15}$.

מִן of direction, *from*, + הֹדּוּ *India* Est 1$_{1}$.

עַל *over*, + Aram 1 K 11$_{25}$, Israel 1 S 13$_{1}$ 16$_{1}$ 23$_{17}$ 2 S 2$_{10}$ 5$_{5}$ 8$_{15}$||1 C 18$_{14}$ 1 K 2$_{11}$||1 C 29$_{27}$ 1 K 6$_{1}$ 11$_{42}$||2 C 9$_{30}$ 1 K 15$_{25.25.33}$ 16$_{8.23.29.29}$ 22$_{52.52}$ 2 K 3$_{1}$ 10$_{36}$ 13$_{1.10}$ 14$_{23(mss)}$ 15$_{8.17.23.27}$ 17$_{1}$ 1 C 29$_{26}$ 2 C 1$_{13}$, Israelites Ezk 20$_{33}$, Judah 2 S 5$_{5}$ 1 K 15$_{1}$||2 C 13$_{1}$ 1 K 15$_{9(mss)}$ 22$_{41}$||2 C 20$_{31}$ 2 K 9$_{29}$, עַם *people* 1 S 8$_{7.9.11}$ 12$_{12.14}$ 1 K 14$_{2}$ (if em.; see Subj.), בֵּן *son* of Israel 1 K 12$_{17}$||2 C 10$_{17}$, אָח *brother* Gn 37$_{8}$, אמר ptc. *one who says* 1 S 11$_{12}$, שְׁאֵרִית *remnant* Mc 4$_{7}$, גּוֹי *nation* Mc 4$_{7}$ Ps 47$_{9}$, אֶרֶץ *land* 2 K 11$_{3}$||2 C 22$_{12}$, עֵץ *tree* Jg 9$_{8.10.12.14}$.

עַל *upon*, + כִּסֵּא *throne* Jr 33$_{21}$.

עַד *unto, as far as*, + כּוּשׁ *Ethiopia* Est 1$_{1}$; *until*, + עוֹלָם *eternity* Mc 4$_{7}$ (מֵעַתָּה וְעַד־עוֹלָם *from now and for evermore*).

בְּקֶרֶב *among*, + Israel Zp 3$_{15}$ (if em.; see Subj.).

תַּחַת *instead of, in place of*, + Abijah 1 K 2 C 13$_{23}$, Abijam 1 K 15$_{8}$, Ahab 1 K 22$_{40}$ 2 K 1$_{17}$, Ahaz 2 K 16$_{20}$||2 C 28$_{27}$, Amon 2 K 21$_{26}$, Asa 1 K 15$_{24}$||2 C 17$_{1}$, Azariah 2 K 15$_{7}$, Baal-hanan Gn 36$_{39}$, Baasha 1 K 16$_{6}$, Bela Gn 36$_{33}$||1 C 1$_{44}$, Ben-hadad 2 K 8$_{15}$, Coniah Jr 37$_{1}$, David 1 K 1$_{35}$ 1 C 29$_{28}$, Elah 1 K 16$_{10}$, Hadad Gn 36$_{36}$||1 C 1$_{47}$, Hazael 2 K 13$_{24}$, Hezekiah 2 K 20$_{21}$||2 C 32$_{33}$, Husham Gn 36$_{35}$||1 C 1$_{46}$, J(eh)oahaz 2 K 13$_{9}$, J(eh)oash (son of Ahaziah) 2 K 12$_{22}$||2 C 24$_{27}$, J(eh)oash (son of Jehoahaz) 2 K 14$_{16}$, Jehoiakim 2 K 24$_{6}$||2 C 36$_{8}$, J(eh)oram 2 K 8$_{24}$, Jehoshaphat 1 K 22$_{51}$||2 C 21$_{1}$, Jehu 2 K 10$_{35}$, Jeroboam 1 K 14$_{20.29}$, Jobab Gn 36$_{34}$||1 C 1$_{45}$, Josiah Jr 22$_{11}$, Jotham 2 K 15$_{38}$||2 C 27$_{9}$, Manasseh 2 K 21$_{18}$||2 C 33$_{20}$, Menahem 2 K 15$_{22}$, Nadab 1 K 15$_{28}$, Nahash 1 C 19$_{1}$, Omri 1 K 16$_{28}$, Pekah 2 K 15$_{30}$, Pekahiah 2 K 15$_{25}$, Rehoboam 1 K 14$_{31}$||2 C 12$_{16}$, Samlah Gn 36$_{37}$||1 C 1$_{48}$, Saul 2 S 16$_{8}$, Sennacherib 2 K 19$_{37}$||Is 37$_{38}$, Shallum 2 K 15$_{14}$, Shaul Gn 36$_{38}$||1 C 1$_{49}$, Solomon 1 K 11$_{43}$||2 C 9$_{31}$, Uzziah 2 C 26$_{23}$, Vashti Est 2$_{4}$, Zechariah 2 K 15$_{10}$, אָב *father* Jr 22$_{11}$, בֵּן *son* Gn 36$_{39}$ Jr 37$_{1}$ 2 K 15$_{14.30}$ 1 C 29$_{28}$, מֶלֶךְ *king* 2 S 10$_{1}$||1 C 19$_{1}$ 2 K 3$_{27}$ 8$_{15}$ 13$_{24}$.

אַחֲרֵי *after*, + David 1 K 1$_{13.17.18.30}$, Tibni 1 K 16$_{22}$ (if ins. אַחֲרֵי תִבְנִי).

<COLL> מלך || משׁל *rule* Gn 37$_{8.8}$, שׂרר *rule* Is 32$_{1}$; + היה מֶלֶךְ *be king* 1 K 11$_{37}$, ישׁב עַל־כִּסֵּא *sit on throne* 1 K 1$_{13.17.24.30.35}$ 16$_{11}$ Ps 47$_{9}$, חקק צֶדֶק po. *decree righteousness* Pr 8$_{15}$.

Inf. abs + finite form of verb Gn 37$_{8}$ 1 S 24$_{21}$.

מלך + adverb, שָׁם *there* 1 C 3$_{4}$; + noun used adverbially, שָׁנָה *(for a specified number of) years* 1 S 13$_{1}$ 2 S 2$_{10}$ 5$_{4.5.5}$ 1 K 2$_{11.11}$||1 C 29$_{27.27}$ 1 K 14$_{21}$||2 C 12$_{13}$ 1 K 15$_{2}$||2 C 13$_{2}$ 1 K 15$_{10.25.33}$ 16$_{8.23.23.29}$ 22$_{42}$||2 C 20$_{31}$ 1 K 22$_{52}$ 2 K 3$_{1}$ 8$_{17}$||2 C 21$_{5}$ 2 K 8$_{26}$||2 C 22$_{2}$ 2 K 12$_{2}$||2 C 24$_{1}$ 2 K 13$_{1.10}$ 14$_{2}$||2 C 25$_{1}$ 2 K 14$_{23}$ 15$_{2}$||2 C 26$_{3}$ 2 K 15$_{17.23.27.33}$||2 C 27$_{1}$ 2 K 16$_{2}$||2 C 28$_{1}$ 2 K 17$_{1}$ 18$_{2}$||2 C 29$_{1}$ 2 K 21$_{1.19}$||2 C 33$_{1.21}$ 2 K 22$_{1}$||2 C 34$_{1}$ 2 K 23$_{36}$||2 C 36$_{5}$ 2 K 24$_{18}$||2 C 36$_{11}$||Jr 52$_{1}$ 1 C 3$_{4.4}$ 2 C 9$_{30}$ 21$_{20}$ 27$_{8}$, חֹדֶשׁ *(for a specified number of) months* 2 S 5$_{5}$ 2 K 15$_{8}$ 23$_{31}$||2 C 36$_{2}$ 2 K 24$_{8}$||2 C 36$_{9}$ 1 C 3$_{4}$, יֶרַח *(for a) month* 2 K 15$_{13}$, יוֹם *day*, i.e. period of time 1 K 2$_{11}$||1 C 29$_{27}$ 1 K 11$_{42}$ 14$_{20}$ 2 K 10$_{36}$, *(for a specified number of) days* 1 K 16$_{15}$, עוֹלָם *(to) eternity* 4QMidrEschat^{a} 3$_{3}$, עַד *(to) perpetuity* 4QMidrEschat^{a} 3$_{3}$.

בַּשָּׁנָה הָרְבִיעִית ... לִמְלֹךְ שְׁלֹמֹה *in the fourth year ... of Solomon's reign* 1 K 6$_{1}$, בִּשְׁנַת שְׁמֹנֶה לְמָלְכוֹ *in the eighth year of his reign* 2 K 24$_{12}$, vars. 2 K 25$_{1}$||Jr 52$_{4}$ Jr 1$_{2}$ 51$_{59}$ Est 1$_{3}$ Dn 9$_{2}$ 2 C 17$_{7}$ 29$_{3}$ 34$_{3.8}$, בִּשְׁנַת מָלְכוֹ *in the year when he became king* 2 K 25$_{27}$ (||Jr 52$_{31}$ מַלְכֻתוֹ *of his reign*).

אֹתִי מָאֲסוּ מִמְּלֹךְ *they have rejected me from being king* 1 S 8$_{7}$, vars. 1 S 15$_{23(Gnz)}$ (L מִמֶּלֶךְ *from [being] king*) 16$_{1}$.

Also 4QpIsa^{e} 9$_{2}$ 4QpsEzek^{d} 1.2$_{8}$ 4Q418 206$_{4}$ 4QUnid D 1$_{3}$.

<SYN> משׁל *rule*, שׂרר *rule*.

Hi. 49.0.1 Pf. הִמְלִיךְ, הִמְלַכְתָּ (הִמְלַכְתַּנִי), הִמְלַכְתִּי (הִמְלִיכוּ), (הִמְלַכְתִּיךָ); impf. נַמְלִיךְ (נַמְלֵךְ), Q יַמְלִיכוּ; + waw וְהִמְלַכְתָּ; וַיַּמְלֵךְ (וַיַּמְלִכֵהוּ, וַיַּמְלִיכֶהָ), וָאַמְלִיךְ, וַיַּמְלִיכוּ (וַיַּמְלִכֻהוּ, וַיַּמְלִיכֻהוּ), וַתַּמְלִיכוּ; ptc. מַמְלִיךְ; inf. הַמְלִיךְ (הַמְלִיכוֹ).

Make king, make queen (Est 2$_{17}$), **proclaim king, cause to reign; reign** (intrans.; Dn 9$_{1}$ [if em.; see Subj.]), <SUBJ> Y. 1 S 15$_{11.35}$ 1 K 3$_{7}$||2 C 1$_{8}$ 1 C 28$_{4}$ 2 C 1$_{9.11}$, Aram Is 7$_{6}$, Edom 2 K 8$_{20}$||2 C 21$_{8}$, Ephraim Is 7$_{6}$, Israel(ites) 1 K 12$_{1}$||2 C 10$_{1}$ 1 K 12$_{20}$ 16$_{16}$ 2 K 17$_{21}$ Ho 8$_{4}$ (unless מלך II hi. *seek counsel*) 11QT 57$_{2}$, Manassites

1 C 12$_{32}$, עַם *people* 1 S 11$_{15}$ 1 K 16$_{21}$ (חֲצִי הָעָם *half the people*) 2 K 11$_{12}$||2 C 23$_{11}$ 2 K 14$_{21}$||2 C 26$_{1}$ 2 K 21$_{24}$|| 2 C 35$_{21}$ 2 K 23$_{30}$||2 C 36$_{1}$, קָהָל *assembly* 1 C 29$_{22}$, Abner 2 S 2$_{9}$, Darius Dn 9$_{1}$ (if em. הָמְלַךְ *he was made king* to הִמְלִיךְ *he reigned*), David 1 K 1$_{43}$ 1 C 23$_{1}$, Nebuchadn/rezzar Jr 37$_{1}$ 2 C 36$_{10}$, Neco 2 K 23$_{34}$, Rehoboam 2 C 11$_{22}$, Samuel 1 S 8$_{22}$ 12$_{1}$.

אִישׁ *man* 1 C 12$_{39}$, בֵּן *son* Is 7$_{6}$, מֶלֶךְ *king* 1 K 1$_{43}$ 2 C 36$_{4}$ 2 K 24$_{17}$||2 C 36$_{10}$ Jr 37$_{1}$ Ezk 17$_{16}$ Est 2$_{17}$ Dn 9$_{1}$ (if em.; see above), פַּרְעֹה *Pharaoh* 2 K 23$_{34}$, בַּעַל *lord* Jg 9$_{6.16.18}$, זָקֵן *elder* 2 S 5$_{3}$||1 C 11$_{3}$ (if em. אֶל־הַמֶּלֶךְ *to the king* to לְהַמְלִיכוֹ *to make him king*) 2 K 10$_{5}$, רֹאשׁ *chief* 1 C 11$_{10}$, רָץ *guard* 2 K 11$_{12}$, אֹמֵן *guardian* 2 K 10$_{5}$, עדר ptc. *one who helps* 1 C 12$_{39}$ (mss ערך ptc. *one who arranges*), יֹשֵׁב *inhabitant* 2 C 22$_{1}$, שְׁאֵרִית *remainder* of Israel 1 C 12$_{39}$, אֲשֶׁר *one who* 2 K 10$_{5}$, אֵלֶּה *these* 1 C 12$_{39}$.

<OBJ> Abijah 2 C 11$_{22}$, Abimelech Jg 9$_{6.16.18}$, Ahaziah 2 C 22$_{1}$, Azariah 2 K 14$_{2}$, David 2 S 5$_{3}$||1 C 11$_{3}$ (if em.; see Subj.) 1 C 11$_{10}$ 12$_{32.39.39}$ 28$_{4}$, Eliakim 2 K 23$_{34}$||2 C 36$_{4}$, Esther Est 2$_{17}$, Ish-bosheth 2 S 2$_{9}$, Jehoahaz 2 K 23$_{30}$||2 C 36$_{1}$, J(eh)oash 2 K 11$_{12}$||2 C 23$_{11}$, Jeroboam 1 K 12$_{20}$ 2 K 17$_{21}$, Josiah 2 K 21$_{24}$||2 C 35$_{21}$, Mattaniah 2 K 24$_{17}$, Omri 1 K 16$_{16}$, Rehoboam 1 K 12$_{1}$||2 C 10$_{1}$, Saul 1 S 11$_{15}$ 15$_{11.35}$, Solomon 1 K 1$_{43}$ 1 C 23$_{1}$ 2 C 1$_{8.9.11}$, Tibni 1 K 16$_{21}$, Uzziah 2 C 26$_{1}$, Zedekiah Jr 37$_{1}$ appar. Ezk 37$_{16}$ 2 C 36$_{10}$, אִישׁ *man* 2 K 10$_{5}$, בֵּן *son* Jg 9$_{16}$ 2 S 2$_{9}$ 1 K 16$_{21}$ 2 K 17$_{21}$ 21$_{24}$||2 C 35$_{21}$ 2 K 23$_{30}$||2 C 36$_{1}$ 2 K 23$_{34}$ Jr 37$_{1}$ 1 C 23$_{1}$ 2 C 11$_{22}$ 22$_{1}$ 36$_{10(ms)}$, אָח *brother* 2 C 36$_{4.10}$, דּוֹד *uncle* 2 K 24$_{17}$, מֶלֶךְ *king* 1 S 8$_{22}$ 12$_{1}$ 2 K 8$_{20}$||2 C 21$_{8}$ Is 7$_{6}$ 11QT 57$_{2}$, שַׂר *commander* 1 K 16$_{16}$, עֶבֶד 1 K 3$_{7}$.

<PREP> לְ of benefit, *to, for*, + עַם *people* 1 S 8$_{22}$; as, + מֶלֶךְ *king* Jg 9$_{6}$ 1 S 15$_{11}$; introducing object, + Solomon 1 C 29$_{22}$, בֵּן *son* 1 C 29$_{22}$.

בְּ of place, *in*, + Gilgal 1 S 11$_{15}$, Jerusalem 2 C 36$_{1}$, אֶרֶץ *land* Jr 37$_{1}$, מַחֲנֶה *camp* 1 K 16$_{16}$; of time, *in*, + יוֹם *day* 1 K 16$_{16}$.

כְּ *according to*, + דָּבָר *word* 1 C 11$_{10}$.

מִן of agent, *by (means of), through*, + Y. Ho 8$_{4}$ (unless מלך II hi. *seek counsel*).

אֶל *over*, + Ashurites 2 S 2$_{9}$, Gilead 2 S 2$_{9}$, Jezreel 2 S 2$_{9}$.

עַל *over*, + Benjamin 2 S 2$_{9}$, Edom 2 K 8$_{20}$||2 C 21$_{8}$, Ephraim 2 S 2$_{9}$, Israel 1 S 12$_{1}$ 15$_{35}$ 2 S 2$_{9}$ 1 K 12$_{20}$ 16$_{16}$ 1 C 12$_{39}$ 23$_{1}$ 28$_{4}$, Jerusalem 2 C 36$_{4.10}$, Judah 2 C 36$_{4.10}$, עַם *people* 2 C 1$_{9.11}$, בַּעַל *lord* of Shechem Jg 9$_{18}$, מַלְכוּת *kingdom* of the Chaldaeans Dn 9$_{1}$ (if em.; see Subj.).

בְּתוֹךְ *within*, + Judah Is 7$_{6}$.

עִם *by*, + אֵלוֹן *terebinth* Jg 9$_{6}$.

לִפְנֵי *before*, + Y. 1 S 11$_{15}$.

תַּחַת *instead of, in place of*, + Amaziah 2 K 14$_{21}$||2 C 26$_{1}$, Amon 2 K 21$_{24}$||2 C 35$_{21}$, דָּוִד *David* 1 K 3$_{7}$||2 C 1$_{8}$, Jehoiachin 2 K 24$_{17}$, Jehoram 2 C 22$_{1}$, Josiah 2 K 23$_{34}$, Vashti Est 2$_{17}$, אָב *father* 1 K 3$_{7}$||2 C 1$_{8}$ 2 K 14$_{21}$||2 C 26$_{1}$ 2 K 23$_{30}$||2 C 36$_{1}$ 2 K 23$_{34}$, מֶלֶךְ *king* 2 K 21$_{24}$||2 C 35$_{21}$.

<COLL> מלך hi. || שׂרר hi. *make prince* Ho 8$_{4}$; + משׁח *anoint* 2 K 11$_{12}$||2 C 23$_{11}$ 2 K 23$_{30}$ 1 C 29$_{22}$; + adverb, אֲבָל *however* 1 K 1$_{43}$, שָׁם *there* 1 S 11$_{15}$, שֵׁנִית *a second time* 1 C 29$_{22}$.

<SYN> שׂרר hi. *make prince*.

Ho. $_{1}$ Pf. הָמְלַךְ—**be made king**, Dn 9$_{1}$ (or em. hi. *reign*), <SUBJ> Darius Dn 9$_{1}$, בֵּן *son* Dn 9$_{1}$. <PREP> עַל *over*, + מַלְכוּת *kingdom* of the Chaldaeans Dn 9$_{1}$.*

⇒ מֶלֶךְ I *king*, מֶלֶךְ II *Melech*, מַלְכָּה *queen*, מְלֶכֶת *queen*, מְלוּכָה *kingship*, מַמְלָכָה *kingdom*, מַמְלָכוּת *kingdom*, מַלְכָה *kingdom*, מֹלֶךְ *Molech*, מֹלֶכֶת *sororarch*, מִלְכָּה *Milcah*, מַלְכִּיאֵל *Malchiel*, מַלְכִּיאֵלִי *Malchielite*, מַלְכִּיָּה *Malchijah*, מַלְכִּי־צֶדֶק *Melchizedek*, מַלְכִּי־רֶשַׁע *Melchiresha*, מַלְכִּירָם *Malchiram*, מַלְכִּישׁוּעַ *Malchishua*, מַלְכָּם *Malcam*, מִלְכֹּם *Milcom*, מַלְכִּנֵר *Malchiner*, יַמְלֵךְ *Jamlech*, מַלּוּךְ *Malluch*, מַלּוּכִי *Malluchi*, מִקְנֵמֶלֶךְ *Miknemelech*.

מלך II $_{2}$ vb. **counsel—Ni.** $_{1}$ + waw וַיִּמָּלֵךְ—**take counsel** (unless מלך III ni. *be torn away*), <SUBJ> לֵב *heart* Ne 5$_{7}$. <PREP> עַל *with*, + Nehemiah Ne 5$_{7}$ (וַיִּמָּלֵךְ לִבִּי עָלַי *and my heart took counsel with me*, i.e. I considered [it]).

Hi. $_{1}$ Pf. הִמְלִיכוּ—**seek counsel*** (unless מלך I hi. *make king*), <SUBJ> Israelites Ho 8$_{4}$. <PREP> מִן of agent, *by (means of), through*, + Y. Ho 8$_{4}$.*

⇒ מַלָּךְ *counsellor*, מֹלֶךְ III *counsellor*.

***מלך** III $_{1}$ vb. **tear away, take possession—Ni.** $_{1}$ + waw וַיִּמָּלֵךְ—**be torn away, be snatched** (unless מלך II ni. *take counsel*), <SUBJ> לֵב *heart* Ne 5_{7}. <PREP> עַל *from*, + Nehemiah Ne 5_{7} (וַיִּמָּלֵךְ לִבִּי עָלַי *and my heart was snatched from me*, i.e. I was beside myself).

***מלך** IV vb. **own,** ptc. as noun, **owner,** if em. מֶלֶךְ *king* to מֹלֵךְ, <SUBJ> היה *be* Ec 1_{12} (הָיִיתִי מֹלֵךְ ... בִּירוּשָׁלָם *I was a property-holder ... in Jerusalem*). <PREP> אַחֲרֵי *after*, + בוא *come* Ec 2_{12}.

מַלָּךְ *counsellor*, see מֹלֵךְ III *counsellor*.*

מֶלֶךְ I $_{2518.16.130.70}$ n.m. **king**—cstr. מֶלֶךְ; sf. מַלְכִּי, מַלְכְּךָ, מַלְכְּכֶם, מַלְכָּם; pl. מְלָכִים, מַלְכֵּךְ, מַלְכּוֹ, מַלְכָּהּ, מַלְכֵּנוּ (מְלָכִין; 2 S $11_{1[mss]}$ מְלָאכִים); cstr. מַלְכֵי; sf. מְלָכֶיהָ, מְלָכֵינוּ, מַלְכֵיכֶם, מַלְכֵיהֶם—**king, ruler,** usu. of humans; also of Y. (Nm 23_{21} Dt 33_{5} Is 6_{5} 33_{22} 41_{21} 43_{15} 44_{6} Jr 8_{19} $10_{7.10}$ 46_{18} 48_{15} 51_{57} perh. Ho 10_{3} Zp 3_{15} [or em.; see Cstr.] Zc $14_{9.16.17}$ Ml 1_{14}=5QapMal 1_{3} Ps 5_{3} 10_{16} $24_{7.8.9.10.10}$ 29_{10} $47_{3.7.8}$ 48_{3} 68_{25} 74_{12} 84_{4} 95_{3} 98_{6} 99_{4} 145_{1} 149_{2} perh. Jb 34_{18} perh. Pr 22_{11} perh. Si 38_{2}* 50_{7} 51_{12} 1QH 10_{8} 1QM 12_{8} 4QJub^{a} 1_{28} 4QShirShabb^{a} $1.1_{8.13}$ $1.2_{7.8.14}$ 2_{5} 4QShirShabb^{b} 1_{5} 14.2_{8} 4QShirShabb^{c} 2_{4} 3.2_{12} 4QShirShabb^{d} 1.1_{3} [[מ]ל[ך]] $1.1_{13.17}$ [[המ]לך] 1.1_{28} [[מלך]] $1.1_{31.34.34}$ [[מלכים]] 1.1_{38} [מ]ל[ך] $1.2_{23.24.25.26}$ 3_{1} [[מ]לך] 4QShirShabb^{e} 5_{6} 4QM^{a} 8.1_{13} 4QShirShabb^{f} $14.1_{3.5.7}$ $15.2_{3.7}$ 19_{3} $23.1_{9.11.13}$ $23.2_{2.11}$ 24_{3} 4QHod^{a} $7.1_{11.13}$ 4QShir^{b} 52.3_{4} 11QShirShabb 8_{7} 10_{5} MasShirShabb 2_{2} [[מלך]] $2_{15.18}$ 4_{12}), perh. Molech (Is 57_{9} [or em.; see Prep.]), perh. Milcom (Jr $49_{1.3}$ [or em. both; see Subj.] Zp 1_{5} [or em.; see Prep.]), Leviathan (Jb 41_{26}), trees (Jg $9_{8.15}$).

<SUBJ> היה *be* Gn 17_{16} Dt 33_{5} (or em. לְמֶלֶךְ) Jg $17_{}$ 1 S 8_{19} 12_{14} 15_{26} 2 S 2_{11} 5_{2}||1 C 11_{2} 2 S 15_{21} 1 K 11_{37} 16_{33} 22_{35}||2C 18_{34} 2 K 3_{4} $6_{8.26}$ 15_{5}||2 C 26_{21} 2 K 17_{2} 18_{1} 23_{25} Is 49_{23} Jr 22_{24} Ezk 28_{12} 37_{22} Ho 13_{10} (or em. אֱהִי *shall I be?* to אַיֵּה *where is?*) Ec 1_{12} Ne 13_{26} 1 C 28_{2} 2 C 18_{32}, חיה *live* 1 S 10_{24} 2 S $16_{16.16}$ (lacking in mss) 1 K $1_{25.31.34.39}$ 4_{1} (lacking in ms) 4_{1} 2 K $8_{8.9}$ 11_{12}||2 C 23_{11} 2 K 14_{17}||2 C 25_{25} Is 38_{9} Ps 72_{1} Ne 2_{3}, pi. *let live* 1 K 20_{31}, hi. *cause to live* 2 K 5_{7}, רפא *heal* Ho 5_{13}, htp. *be healed* 2 K 8_{29}=9_{15}, ילד ni. *be born* Ec 4_{13}, זקן *be old* 1 K $1_{1.15}$, דמה *be like* Ezk 31_{2}, יחד htp. perh. *be declared as one* GnzPs 4_{12}, שׁאר ni. *remain* Dt 3_{11}, hi. *leave* 2 K 25_{22}.

אמר *say* Gn $14_{18.21.22}$ Ex $1_{15.18}$ 5_{4} Jg 11_{13} 1 S 17_{56} 21_{3} $22_{16.17.18}$ 28_{13} 2 S $3_{33.38}$ $7_{2.18}$||1 C 17_{16} 2 S $9_{2.3.4}$ 10_{5}||1 C 19_{5} 2 S 11_{20} $13_{25.26}$ $14_{5.8.9.10.12.18.19.20.24}$ $15_{9.19.25.27}$ $16_{2.3.4.10}$ $18_{2.4.25.26.27.29.30.32}$ $19_{1.12.24.26.30.34.39}$ 20_{4} $21_{2.6}$ $24_{2.24}$||1 C 21_{24} 1 K $1_{16.23.28.29.32.33.48}$ $2_{20.22.23.26.30.31.36.42.44}$ $3_{23.24.25.27}$ 11_{18} $12_{6.12}$||2 C $10_{6.12}$ 1 K 12_{28} 13_{6} 15_{18} $20_{1.7.40}$ $22_{3.6.8.8.9.15.16.18.26.27.30.31.34}$||2 C $18_{5.7.7.8.14.15.17.25.26.29.30.33}$ 2 K 1_{11} $3_{6.10.13}$ $5_{5.7}$ $6_{8.11.21.28.30.33}$ (if em.; see below) $7_{12.14}$ $8_{4.6.8.9}$ $9_{18.19}$ 12_{8}||2 C 24_{6} 2 K 13_{14} 14_{9}||2 C 25_{18} 2 K 16_{15} 17_{27} $18_{14.19.29.31}$||Is $36_{4.14.16}$ 2 K $22_{3.12}$||2 C 34_{20} 2 K 23_{21} Is 14_{9} 41_{21} 44_{6} Jr 21_{1} 29_{3} 32_{3} 36_{29} $37_{3.17}$ $38_{5.10.14.16.19}$ 39_{11} Jon 3_{6} Est $1_{10.13.17}$ 3_{11} $5_{3.5.6}$ $6_{3.4.5.6.10}$ $7_{2.5.8.9}$ 8_{7} $9_{12.14.25}$ Dn $1_{3.18}$ $2_{2.3}$ Ezr $1_{1.2}$||2 C $36_{22.23}$ Ne $2_{2.4.6.18}$ 1 C 28_{2} 29_{1} 2 C 2_{10} 12_{6} $18_{3.3}$ 24_{8} $29_{20.24.30}$ $32_{1.9.10}$ 35_{23} Kuntillet 'Ajrud inscr. E1 ([ה]מ[ל]ך), דבר pi. *speak* Ex 1_{17} 2 S $14_{18.19}$ 1 K 2_{38} 12_{12}||2 C 10_{12} 1 K 13_{7} 2 K 1_{9} 8_{4} $25_{6(mss)}$||Jr 52_{9} Jr 32_{4} 38_{25} 39_{5} Dn 1_{19} $11_{27.36}$, htp. 2 S 14_{13} (or em.; pi.), נגד hi. *tell* 1 K 10_{3} 2 K 7_{12}.

קרא *call* Ex 1_{18} Jos 24_{9} 1 S 22_{11} 2 S 9_{9} 21_{2} 1 K 1_{13} $2_{36.42}$ 20_{7} 22_{9}||2 C 18_{8} 2 K 6_{11} 12_{8}||2 C 24_{6} Jr 34_{8}, *read* 2 K 5_{7} 22_{16} 23_{2}||2 C 34_{30}, זעק *cry out* 2 S 19_{5} 2 C 32_{20}, hi. *proclaim* Jon 3_{6}, ענה *answer* 2 S 14_{18} 1 K $1_{28.36}$ 2_{22} 3_{27} 12_{13}||2 C 10_{13} 1 K 13_{6} $20_{4.11}$ Is 14_{9}, צוה pi. *command* 1 S 21_{3} 2 S 9_{11} 14_{8} $18_{5.5.12}$ 21_{14} 1 K 2_{46} 5_{31} 22_{31}||2 C 18_{30} 2 K $16_{15.16}$ 17_{27} 22_{12}||2 C 34_{20} 2 K $23_{4.21}$ Jr 36_{26} 37_{21} $38_{10.27}$ 39_{11} Est 3_{2} Ezr $4_{3.3}$, יסד pi. *decree* Est 1_{8}, שׁבע ni. *swear* 2 S 19_{24} 1 K $1_{13.29.51}$ 2_{23} Jr 38_{16}, hi. *cause to swear* 1 K 2_{42} 22_{16}||2 C 18_{15} 2 C 36_{13}, עוד hi. *admonish* 1 K 2_{42}, זהר ni. *be warned* Ec 4_{13}, הלל pi. *praise* Ps 148_{11}, ידה hi. *praise* Ps 138_{4} (or em.; see Cstr.), שׁיר *sing* Ps 138_{4}, פלל htp. *pray* 2 C 32_{20}, שׁמע *hear* Nm 21_{1} 33_{40} Jos $5_{1.1}$ 9_{1} 11_{1} Jg 5_{3} $11_{17.28}$ 1 S 26_{19} 2 S 8_{9}||1 C 18_{9} 2 S 13_{21} $14_{16.17}$ 1 K 5_{14} $12_{15.16}$||2 C $10_{15.16}$ 1 K 13_{4} 20_{7} 2 K 6_{30} 16_{9} 19_{1}||Is 37_{1} 2 K 20_{12}||Is 39_{1} 2 K 22_{11}||2 C 34_{19} Is 52_{15} Jr 17_{20} 19_{3} 22_{2} 26_{21} 34_{4} $36_{25.30}$ $37_{1.20}$ 38_{19} 50_{43} Ps 138_{4} 2 C 9_{23} 24_{17} 1QMyst 9_{3} 11QT $58_{3(mg)}$, hi. *make proclamation* 1 K 15_{22}, קשׁב hi. *pay attention* Ps 5_{3} Ne 9_{34} 2 C 20_{15}, אמן

hi. *believe* Lm 4$_{12}$.

ראה *see* Gn 26$_8$ Jos 8$_{14}$ 2 S 10$_{19}$ 13$_6$ 20$_{13.22}$ 2 K 3$_{26}$ 6$_{21}$ 8$_{29}$||2 C 22$_6$ 2 K 9$_{16.27}$ 16$_{10.12}$ Is 49$_7$ 52$_{15}$ 62$_2$ Jr 39$_4$ Ezk 21$_{26}$ Ps 48$_5$ Est 5$_2$ Dn 1$_{10}$, htp. *look at one another* 2 K 14$_{8.11}$||2 C 25$_{17.21}$, שׁקף hi. *look out* Gn 26$_8$, בין hi. *understand* Dn 8$_{23}$, *have regard* Dn 11$_{36}$, htpol. *consider* Is 52$_{15}$, ידע *know* Ex 1$_8$ Nm 20$_{14}$ 1 K 1$_{4.18}$ 20$_{13.22}$ Jr 19$_4$ Ec 4$_{13}$ Dn 2$_3$ Arad ost. 40$_{13}$, זכר *remember* 2 S 14$_{11}$ Est 2$_1$ 2 C 24$_{22}$, נכר hi. *recognize* 1 K 20$_{41}$, בשׂר htp. *receive news* 2 S 18$_{32}$, דאג *fear* Jr 38$_{19}$, ירא *fear* Jr 26$_{19}$ Ps 102$_{16}$ 2 C 20$_{15}$, פחד *be afraid* Jr 36$_{24}$, בהל ni. *be terrified* Ps 48$_5$, חתת ni. *be terrified* 2 C 20$_{15}$, שׂער *be horrified* Ezk 27$_{35}$ 32$_{10}$, תמה *be astounded* Ps 48$_5$, שׁמר *keep* 2 K 18$_1$, ni. *beware* 2 K 6$_{9.10}$, נצר *keep* Pr 20$_{28}$ (if em. יִצְּרוּ *they keep* the king to יִצֹּר the king *keeps*), סעד *uphold* Pr 20$_{28}$, בטח *trust* 2 K 18$_1$ 19$_{10}$||Is 37$_{10}$ Ps 21$_8$, אבה *be willing* Dt 2$_{30}$ Jg 11$_{17}$ 2 S 13$_{25}$ 1 K 20$_7$, חפץ *delight in* 1 S 18$_{22}$ 2 S 24$_3$ Est 2$_{14}$ 6$_{6.6.7.9.9.11}$, רצה *be pleased with* 1 C 29$_1$, אוה htp. *desire* Ps 45$_{12}$ (or del.), בחר *choose* 2 S 15$_{15}$, דבק hi. *cling* 2 K 18$_1$, אהב *love* 1 K 11$_1$ Est 2$_{17}$ 2 C 19$_2$, pass. *be loved* Ne 13$_{26}$, רחם pi. *have compassion* Jr 21$_7$, חוס *pity* Jr 21$_7$ Ps 72$_1$, חמל *spare* Jr 21$_7$ 2 C 36$_{17}$.

עבד *serve* 2 S 10$_{19}$ 2 K 18$_1$ Ezk 29$_{19}$, *enslave* Jr 25$_{14}$ 27$_7$, ni. *be served* perh. Ec 5$_8$, hi. *cause to labour* Ezk 29$_{18}$, שׁרת pi. *serve* Is 60$_{10}$ 1QM 12$_{14}$=19$_6$, ברך pass. *be blessed* 1 K 2$_{45}$ 4QShirShabb[d] 1.1$_{28}$ ([מל]ך), pi. *bless* Gn 14$_{18}$ 2 S 13$_{25}$ 19$_{40}$ 1 K 8$_{14}$||2 C 6$_3$, כבד ni. *be honoured* 2 S 6$_{20}$ 4QMyst[a] 9$_3$ ([מ]לך), pi. *honour* Dn 11$_{36}$ 4Q418 158$_5$, דרשׁ *inquire* 1 K 22$_5$||2 C 18$_4$ 2 K 1$_6$ 2 C 19$_2$, בקר pi. *inquire* 2 K 16$_{15}$, בקשׁ pi. *seek* 1 S 26$_{20}$ Jr 26$_{21}$ Dn 1$_{20}$ 2 C 9$_{23}$ 4QpNah 3.1$_2$, שׁאל *ask* 2 S 14$_{18}$ 2 K 8$_6$ Jr 37$_{17}$ 38$_{14}$ Ezk 21$_{26}$ Ps 21$_2$, חלה pi. *entreat* Jr 26$_{19}$, קסם *divine* Ezk 21$_{26}$, חלם *dream* Dn 2$_3$, יעץ *counsel* Jr 49$_{30}$ Mc 6$_5$, ni. *take counsel* 1 K 12$_6$||2 C 10$_6$ 1 K 12$_{28}$ 2 K 6$_8$ 2 C 25$_{17}$ 30$_2$, חשׁב *plan* Jr 49$_{30}$, חדל *leave off* 1 K 22$_{6.15}$ ||2 C 18$_{5.14}$, מאן pi. *refuse* Jr 38$_{19}$.

בכה *weep* 2 S 3$_{32}$ 13$_{36}$ 19$_{1.2}$ 2 K 13$_{14}$, אבל htp. *mourn* 2 S 19$_2$ Ezk 7$_{27}$, קין pol. *lament* 2 S 3$_{33}$, עצב ni. *grieve* 2 S 19$_3$, נחם ni. *be comforted* 2 S 13$_{39}$, גיל *rejoice* Ps 21$_2$, שׂמח *be glad* Ps 21$_2$ 63$_{12}$ 1 C 29$_9$, נשׁק *kiss* 2 S 19$_{40}$, חמל *spare* 2 S 21$_7$, בושׁ hi. *be ashamed* Jr 2$_{26}$, *shame* 2 S 19$_6$, כנע ni. *humble oneself* 2 C 12$_6$, טמא pi. *defile* 2 K 23$_{13}$ Ezk 43$_7$, חלל pi. *profane* Ezk 28$_{12}$, רגז *be disturbed* 2 S 19$_1$, קצף *be angry* Est 1$_{12}$, מרר htpalp. *embitter oneself* Dn 11$_{11}$, שׂער htp. *storm* Dn 11$_{40}$, שׂנא *hate* 1 K 22$_8$||2 C 18$_7$, אכל *eat* 1 S 20$_{24}$ Jr 50$_{17}$ 51$_{34}$, שׁתה *drink* 1 K 20$_{12.16}$ Jr 25$_{26}$ Est 3$_{15}$ 7$_1$, בלע *swallow* Jr 51$_{34}$, כרה *give feast* 2 K 6$_{21}$, קדשׁ pi. *consecrate* 1 K 8$_{64}$ Jr 51$_{28}$, hi. 2 S 8$_{11}$||1 C 18$_{11}$ 2 K 12$_{19}$ 1 C 26$_{26}$ 4QShirShabb[d] 1.1$_{31}$, חנך *dedicate* 1 K 8$_{63}$||2 C 7$_5$.

הלך *go* 2 S 3$_{31}$ 5$_6$ 7$_3$ 8$_3$||1 C 18$_3$ 2 S 13$_{24.25}$ 19$_{1.25}$ 1 K 3$_4$ 20$_{43}$ 22$_6$||2 C 18$_5$ 2 K 3$_{6.7.9.9.9}$ 14$_8$||2 C 25$_{17}$ 2 K 16$_{1.10}$ 19$_{36}$||Is 37$_{37}$ 2 K 23$_{29}$ Is 60$_3$ Jr 49$_3$ (or em. מִלְכֹּם *Milcom*) Am 1$_{15}$ Ec 9$_{14}$ 2 C 18$_3$, hi. *bring* 2 C 36$_6$, htp. *go* 1 S 12$_2$ Ezk 28$_{12}$, בוא *come* Gn 14$_5$ Jos 11$_5$ Jg 5$_{19}$ 1 S 12$_{12}$ 2 S 7$_{18}$||1 C 17$_{16}$ 2 S 13$_6$ 16$_{5.14}$ 19$_{16.25.31}$ 20$_3$ 24$_{21}$ 1 K 1$_1$ 14$_{28}$||2 C 12$_{11}$ 1 K 20$_{43}$ 22$_{30}$||2 C 18$_{29}$ 1 K 22$_{37}$ 2 K 7$_{6.6}$ 11$_8$||2 C 23$_7$ 2 K 14$_{13}$ 15$_{19.29}$ 16$_{11}$ (lacking in mss) 16$_{12}$ 18$_{31}$||Is 36$_{16}$ 2 K 19$_{32}$||Is 37$_{33}$ 2 K 24$_{11}$ 25$_1$||Jr 52$_4$ Jr 17$_{19.25}$ 22$_4$ 36$_{29}$ 37$_{19}$ 39$_1$ 43$_{10}$ 46$_{13}$ Ezk 17$_{12}$ 26$_7$ Zc 9$_9$ Ps 24$_{7.9}$ Est 5$_{4.5.8}$ 7$_1$ Dn 1$_1$ 11$_{13.14.40}$ 2 C 28$_{20}$ 32$_{1.4.21}$ 4QpNah 3.1$_2$, hi. *bring* 1 K 3$_1$ 2 K 17$_{24}$ 24$_{16}$ 25$_6$ Jr 28$_3$ 39$_6$ 52$_{10.11}$ Ezk 17$_{12}$ Ca 1$_4$ 1 C 5$_{26}$ 19$_9$ 2 C 25$_{23}$ 36$_{10}$, ho. *be brought* Ezk 30$_{10}$.

יצא *go out* Gn 14$_{8+5t}$ 17$_6$ 35$_{11}$ Nm 21$_{33}$ Dt 3$_1$ 29$_{6.6}$ 1 S 8$_{20}$ 24$_{15}$ 26$_{20}$ 2 S 11$_{1(mss)}$|| 1 C 20$_1$ (2 S הַמַּלְאכִים appar. *the messengers;* mss הַמְּלָאכִים) 2 S 13$_{39}$ 15$_{16.17}$ 18$_2$ 19$_{20}$ 1 K 20$_{21}$ 2 K 3$_6$ 9$_{21.21}$ 11$_8$||2 C 23$_7$ 2 K 18$_1$ 19$_9$||Is 37$_9$ 2 K 24$_{7.12}$ Jr 17$_{19}$ 29$_2$ 39$_4$ 43$_{10}$ Ec 4$_{13}$ Dn 11$_{11.40}$, hi. *bring out* Gn 14$_{18}$ Ex 6$_{13.27}$ 2 K 24$_{12}$ Ezr 1$_{7.8}$, עלה *go up* Jos 10$_{5+6t}$ 2 S 19$_1$ 1 K 9$_{16}$ 12$_{18}$||2 C 10$_{18}$ 1 K 14$_{25}$||2 C 12$_2$ 1 K 15$_{17}$|| 2 C 16$_1$ 1 K 20$_{1.22}$ 22$_{6.15.29.29}$||2 C 18$_{5.14.28.28}$ 2 K 1$_6$ 3$_{7.21}$ 6$_{24}$ 12$_{18.19}$ 14$_{11}$||2 C 25$_{21}$ 2 K 16$_{5.5}$=Is 7$_{1.1}$ 2 K 16$_{7.9.12}$ 17$_{3.5}$ 18$_{9.13}$||Is 36$_1$ 2 K 23$_2$||2 C 34$_{30}$ 2 K 23$_{29}$||2 C 35$_2$ 2 K 24$_1$|| 2 C 36$_6$ Jr 35$_{11}$ 2 C 18$_{19}$ 29$_{20}$, hi. *cause to go up* 1 K 5$_{27}$ 9$_{15}$ Ezr 4$_2$, i.e. offer 2 S 24$_{22.24}$||1 C 21$_{24}$ 2 K 3$_{26}$, ירד *go down* 1 S 23$_{20}$ 1 K 21$_{18}$ 22$_2$ 2 K 1$_6$ 3$_{12.12(ms).12}$ 6$_{33}$ (if em. הַמַּלְאָךְ *the messenger*) 7$_{17}$ 8$_{29}$||2 C 22$_6$ 2 K 9$_{16}$ 13$_{14}$ Ps 72$_1$ 2 C 20$_{15}$, hi. *bring down* 2 K 11$_{19}$||2 C 23$_{20}$ 2 K 16$_{17}$.

שׁוב *go back* Gn 14$_{5.17}$ 2 S 19$_{15.16}$ 2 K 8$_{29}$=9$_{15}$ 14$_{13}$|| 2 C 25$_{23}$ 2 K 15$_{20}$ 18$_{14}$ 19$_{32.36}$||Is 37$_{33.37}$ 2 K 23$_{25}$ Est 7$_8$ Dn 11$_{13}$ 2 C 19$_1$ 32$_{21}$, hi. *bring back* 2 S 8$_3$ 14$_{13}$ 1 K 2$_{17.19.20}$ 2 K 3$_4$ 16$_6$ Jr 37$_{20}$ 38$_{26}$ Ps 72$_{10}$ Pr 20$_{26}$, יבל hi.

bring Ps 68$_{30}$, קרב *draw near* 2 K 16$_{12}$, hi. *bring near* 2 K 16$_{12}$ Ps 72$_{10}$, סור *turn aside* 2 K 18$_{1}$, hi. *remove* 2 K 16$_{17}$ 18$_{1}$ Est 3$_{10}$ 8$_{2}$ 2 C 15$_{16}$ 36$_{3}$, נגע hi. *reach* Is 30$_{4}$ (if em. מַלְאָכָיו *his messengers* to מְלָכָיו *his kings*), נסע *depart* 2 K 19$_{36}$||Is 37$_{37}$, עבר *pass over* 2 S 15$_{23}$ (lacking in mss) 19$_{19.40.41}$ 24$_{20}$ 1 K 20$_{39}$ 2 K 6$_{9.26.30}$ Mc 2$_{13}$ Ps 48$_{5}$ Dn 11$_{40}$, hi. *allow to pass* Dt 2$_{30}$, *cause to pass* 2 K 16$_{1}$ Ezr 1$_{1}$||2 C 36$_{22}$, *remove* Jon 3$_{6}$ Est 8$_{2.3}$, ברח *flee* 2 S 19$_{10}$ Jr 39$_{4}$, נדד *flee* Ps 68$_{13}$, נוס *flee* Gn 14$_{10.10(ms, Sam)}$ Jos 10$_{16}$ 1 K 12$_{18}$||2 C 10$_{18}$ 2 K 9$_{27}$, חפז ni. *hurry away* Ps 48$_{5}$.

גיח hi. *burst out* Ezk 32$_{2}$, שׁטף *overflow* Dn 11$_{40}$, נהג *lead* Is 20$_{4}$, pass. *be led* Is 60$_{11}$ (or em. נְהוּגִים *led* to נֹהֲגִים *leading*), נחה hi. *lead* Nm 23$_{7}$ 2 K 18$_{11}$, קרא *meet* 1 K 2$_{19}$ 2 K 9$_{21.21}$ 16$_{10}$ 23$_{29}$, קדם pi. *come against* 2 K 19$_{32}$||Is 37$_{33}$, רמס *trample* Ezk 26$_{7}$ 32$_{2}$, רכב *ride* Jr 17$_{25}$ 22$_{4}$ Zc 9$_{9}$ Est 6$_{8}$, hi. *cause to ride* 2 K 13$_{16}$, סבב *go round* 2 K 3$_{9.9.9}$ Ec 9$_{14}$, hi. *turn, change* 1 K 8$_{14}$||2 C 6$_{3}$ 2 K 16$_{17}$ 24$_{17}$ 2C 36$_{4}$, עזב *leave* 2 S 15$_{16}$ 1 K 12$_{13}$||2 C 10$_{13}$ Si 49$_{4}$.

שׁלח *send* Gn 20$_{2}$ Nm 22$_{10}$ Jos 2$_{3}$ 10$_{3}$ 11$_{1}$ 24$_{9}$ 1 S 21$_{3}$ 22$_{11}$ 2 S 5$_{11}$||1 C 14$_{1}$ 2 S 9$_{5}$ 13$_{27}$ 19$_{12}$ 1 K 1$_{44.53}$ 2$_{25.36.42}$ 5$_{15}$ 1 K 7$_{13}$ 12$_{18}$||2 C 10$_{18}$ 1 K 15$_{18}$ 20$_{1.9}$ 2 K 1$_{6}$ 3$_{6}$ 5$_{5}$ 6$_{10}$ 7$_{14}$ 8$_{8}$ 12$_{19}$ 14$_{9}$||2 C 25$_{18}$ 2 K 16$_{10.11}$ 18$_{14.17}$||Is 36$_{2}$ 2 K 19$_{1.4}$||Is 37$_{1.4}$ 2 K 20$_{12}$||Is 39$_{1}$ 2 K 22$_{3.18}$||2 C 34$_{26}$ 2 K 23$_{1}$||2 C 34$_{29}$ Is 20$_{1}$ Jr 21$_{1}$ 26$_{22}$ 29$_{3}$ 36$_{21}$ 37$_{3.7.17}$ 38$_{14}$ 40$_{14}$ Ps 105$_{20}$ Est 1$_{21}$ Dn 11$_{40}$ Ne 2$_{5.6.9}$ 2 C 2$_{2.10}$ 25$_{17}$ 28$_{16}$ 32$_{9}$ 36$_{10}$ 11QT 58$_{3(mg)}$, pi. Ex 6$_{11}$ 2 S 3$_{24}$ 1 K 20$_{41}$, נשׁל pi. *clear out* 2 K 16$_{6}$, אסף *gather* 2 K 5$_{5.7}$ 23$_{1}$||2 C 34$_{29}$ (2 K if em. וַיַּאַסְפוּ *and they gathered* to וַיֶּאֱסֹף *and he gathered*) 2 C 29$_{20}$, ni. *gather oneself* Jos 10$_{5+5t}$, pu. *be gathered* Is 24$_{21}$, יעד ni. *gather oneself* Jos 11$_{5}$ Ps 48$_{5}$, קבץ *gather* 1 K 20$_{1}$ 22$_{6}$||2 C 18$_{5}$ 2 K 6$_{24}$, ni. *gather oneself* Jos 10$_{6}$ GnzPs 2$_{12}$, לקט pi. *gather* Jg 1$_{7}$, פקד *muster* 2 K 3$_{6}$, ni. *be visited*, i.e. punished Is 24$_{21}$, hi. *appoint* 1 K 14$_{27}$||2 C 12$_{10}$ 2 K 7$_{17}$ 25$_{22.23}$||Jr 40$_{7}$ Jr 40$_{5.11}$ 41$_{2.18}$ Est 2$_{3}$ 1 C 26$_{32}$, חבר pi. *bring into alliance* 2 C 20$_{35}$, htp. *make an alliance* 2 C 20$_{35}$, זרה pi. *winnow* Pr 20$_{8.26}$, עור ni. *be roused* Jr 50$_{41}$.

קפץ *shut* mouth Is 52$_{15}$, סגר pu. *be shut up* Is 24$_{21}$, עצר *shut up* 2 K 17$_{4}$, אסר *bind* 2 K 17$_{4}$ 25$_{6}$ Jr 52$_{10}$ 39$_{6}$ 2 C 36$_{6}$, pass. *be bound* Ca 7$_{6}$, כלא *imprison* Jr 32$_{3}$ 4QapPs[b] 33$_{8}$, קום *arise* Ex 1$_{8}$ Jos 24$_{9}$ 2 S 13$_{31}$ 19$_{9}$ 1 K 2$_{19}$ 2 K 7$_{12}$ 16$_{7}$ Is 49$_{7}$ Jon 3$_{6}$ Pr 30$_{31}$ (if em.; see Prep.) Est 7$_{7}$ 1 C 28$_{2}$ 4QpsEzek[d] 1.2$_{3}$, hi. *raise up* Ezk 26$_{7}$, רום *be high* Nm 24$_{7}$ (or em. מַלְכוֹ *his kingdom*, from מֹלֶךְ II), hi. *contribute* Ezr 8$_{25}$ 2 C 30$_{24}$, htpol. *exalt oneself* Dn 11$_{36}$, שׁכם hi. *rise early* 2 C 29$_{20}$, נשׂא *lift* 2 S 3$_{32}$ 1 C 18$_{11}$ 2 K 18$_{14}$ 25$_{27}$||Jr 52$_{31}$ Ezk 29$_{19}$ Am 5$_{26}$ (or em.; see App.) 1 C 21$_{24}$, ni. *lift oneself* 4QM[a] 8.1$_{13}$, pi. *lift*, i.e. promote Est 3$_{1}$ 5$_{11}$.

עמד *stand* 2 S 15$_{17}$ 18$_{4}$ 2 K 10$_{4}$ 11$_{14}$||2 C 23$_{13}$ 2 K 13$_{18}$ 15$_{20}$ 23$_{3}$||2 C 34$_{31}$ Ezk 21$_{26}$ Dn 8$_{23}$ 11$_{2.3.25}$, hi. *cause to stand* Pr 29$_{14}$ 2 C 29$_{24}$, *appoint* Est 4$_{5}$ Dn 11$_{11.13}$, ho. *be propped up* 1 K 22$_{35}$||2 C 18$_{34}$, יצב htp. *stand* Ps 2$_{2}$, שׁען ni. *lean* 2 K 7$_{2(mss).17}$, *rely* 2 C 16$_{7}$, ישׁב *dwell* Nm 21$_{1.34}$ 33$_{40}$ Dt 1$_{4.4}$ 3$_{2}$ 4$_{46}$ Jos 10$_{6}$ 12$_{2}$ 2 S 7$_{1.2}$ 1 K 15$_{18}$||2 C 16$_{2}$ 2 K 15$_{5}$||2 C 26$_{21}$ 2 K 19$_{36}$||Is 37$_{37}$, *sit* 1 S 20$_{24.25}$ 2 S 7$_{18}$||1 C 17$_{16}$ 2 S 19$_{9.9}$ 2 K 22$_{10}$||2 C 18$_{9}$ 2 K 11$_{19}$ Jr 13$_{13.18}$ 17$_{25}$ 22$_{2.4}$ 29$_{16}$ 36$_{22}$ 38$_{7}$ Jon 3$_{6}$ Pr 20$_{8}$ Est 1$_{2}$ 3$_{15}$ 5$_{1}$ 4QM[a] 11.1$_{12}$, hi. *cause to dwell* 2 K 17$_{6.24.26}$, חנה *encamp* Jos 10$_{5+5t}$ 11$_{5}$ 2 K 25$_{1}$ 2 C 32$_{1}$, יחל hi. *wait* 2 K 6$_{33}$ (if em.; see above).

שׁכב *lie down* 2 S 13$_{31}$ 1 K 1$_{21}$ 2 K 14$_{22}$||2 C 26$_{2}$ Is 14$_{18}$, כרע *bow down* 2 C 29$_{29}$, שׁחה htpal. *bow down* 1 K 1$_{47}$ 2$_{19}$ 2 K 19$_{36}$||Is 37$_{37}$ Is 49$_{7}$ Ps 72$_{11}$ 2 C 29$_{29}$, נפל *fall* Ho 7$_{7}$ 2 C 18$_{19}$, hi. *cause to fall* Dn 11$_{11}$, שׁפל hi. *make low* Jr 13$_{18}$, חבא ni. *hide oneself* Jos 10$_{16.17}$, גלה *be exiled* 4QMMT C$_{19}$ (גל[ו]ת), ni. *uncover oneself* 2 S 6$_{20}$, hi. *exile* 2 K 15$_{29}$ 16$_{9}$ 17$_{6.26}$ 18$_{11}$ 24$_{12}$ Jr 20$_{4}$ 24$_{1}$ 27$_{20}$ Est 2$_{6}$ Ezr 2$_{1}$||Ne 7$_{6}$ 1 C 5$_{6.26}$ CD 7$_{14}$, פתח *open* 2 K 13$_{16}$, pi. *set free* Ps 105$_{20}$, מצא *find* 2 S 15$_{25}$ 2 K 9$_{21.21}$ 17$_{4}$ Dn 1$_{20}$ 2 C 20$_{15}$ 32$_{4}$, ni. *be found* Jos 10$_{17}$, כרר pilp. *dance* 2 S 6$_{16}$, רקד pi. *dance* 1 C 15$_{29}$, פזז pi. *leap* 2 S 6$_{16}$, שׂחק pi. *make merry* 1 C 15$_{29}$, לבשׁ *wear* Est 6$_{8}$, pu. *be dressed in* 1 K 22$_{10}$||2 C 18$_{9}$, חפשׂ htp. *disguise oneself* 1 K 22$_{30}$||2 C 18$_{29}$.

לקח *take* Gn 20$_{2}$ Nm 21$_{26}$ 1 S 8$_{11}$ 2 S 8$_{8}$ 9$_{5}$ 20$_{3}$ 21$_{8}$ 24$_{22}$ 1 K 3$_{1}$ 7$_{13}$ 2 K 3$_{26}$ 12$_{19}$ 13$_{16}$ 14$_{13}$ 15$_{29}$ 18$_{31}$||Is 36$_{16}$ 2 K 24$_{7.12}$ Jr 27$_{20}$ 28$_{3}$ 37$_{17}$ 38$_{14}$ Ezk 17$_{12}$ 2 C 16$_{6}$, עשׂר *take a tenth of* 1 S 8$_{11}$, קנה *purchase* 2 S 24$_{24}$||1 C 21$_{24}$, שׂכר *hire* 2 K 7$_{6}$, ירשׁ *possess* 1 K 21$_{18}$ Jr 49$_{1}$ (or em. מִלְכֹּם *Milcom*), לכד *capture* 1 K 9$_{16}$ 2 K 12$_{18}$ 17$_{6}$ 18$_{9}$ Jr 32$_{3.28}$ 34$_{2}$ (if ins. וּלְכָדָהּ *and he will capture it*) 38$_{3}$ Dn 11$_{15}$, שׁבה *capture* 2 K 6$_{21}$, תפשׂ *seize* 2 K 14$_{13}$||2 C 25$_{23}$

2 K 16$_{9}$ 2 K 18$_{13}$||Is 36$_{1}$, ni. *be seized* Jr 38$_{22}$, בזז *plunder* Ezk 29$_{19}$, שׁלל *despoil* Ezk 29$_{19}$.

נתן *give, place* Ex 3$_{19}$ 1 S 8$_{11}$ 17$_{25}$ 2 S 20$_{3}$ 21$_{6.8}$ 1 K 2$_{17.35.35}$ 10$_{13.17}$||2 C 9$_{12.16}$ 1 K 10$_{27}$||2 C 1$_{15}$ 1 K 11$_{18}$ 13$_{7.8}$ 15$_{17}$||2 C 16$_{1}$ 2 K 8$_{6}$ 16$_{12.17}$ 2 K 19$_{17}$||Is 37$_{18}$ 2 K 23$_{5.11}$ Jr 37$_{18}$ 38$_{16}$ 40$_{11}$ 52$_{11}$ Ezk 26$_{7}$ Est 1$_{19}$ 2$_{18}$ 3$_{10}$ 5$_{8}$ 8$_{1.2.7}$ 8$_{11}$ Ezr 7$_{6.11}$ 9$_{9}$ Ne 2$_{8}$ 1 C 29$_{1}$ 2 C 9$_{27}$ 17$_{19}$ (lacking in mss) 24$_{12}$, ni. *be given* Jr 32$_{4}$ 37$_{17}$ Ezr 9$_{7}$, *be placed* Ezk 32$_{29}$, שׂים *place* 1 S 8$_{11}$ 22$_{15}$ 2 S 13$_{33}$ 19$_{20}$ 2 K 6$_{21}$ 13$_{7}$ 18$_{14}$ Jr 43$_{10}$ (if em. וְשַׂמְתִּי *and I will place* to וְשָׂם *and he will place*) Ps 105$_{20}$ Est 2$_{17}$ 3$_{1}$ 10$_{1}$, שׁית *place* 2 S 19$_{29}$, יצג hi. *place* Jr 51$_{34}$, נוח hi. *give rest* Est 3$_{8}$, *leave* 2 S 20$_{3}$, מנה pi. *appoint* Dn 1$_{5.10}$, מוט ni. *be moved* Ps 21$_{8}$, נטה *stretch out* Jr 43$_{10}$ Ezk 30$_{25}$ Dn 11$_{40}$ (if em. יִטַּע *he shall plant* to יַטֶּה), ישׁט hi. *stretch out* Est 4$_{11}$ 5$_{2}$ 8$_{4}$, עטה *wrap* Jr 43$_{10}$, חלק pi. *divide* Dn 11$_{36}$, נצב hi. *set up* 1 C 18$_{3}$, יצק *cast* 1 K 7$_{46}$||2 C 4$_{17}$ (or del.).

נסך hi. *pour out* drink offering 2 K 16$_{12}$, שׁפך *shed* 1 C 28$_{2}$, i.e. cast, siege mound 2 K 19$_{32}$||Is 37$_{33}$ Ezk 26$_{7}$ Dn 11$_{15}$, זרק *toss* 2 K 16$_{12}$, שׁלך hi. *throw* 2 K 23$_{12}$ Jr 26$_{23}$ 36$_{22}$, קלל pilp. *shake* arrows Ezk 21$_{26}$, כסה pi. *cover* Ezk 26$_{7}$ Jon 3$_{6}$, htp. *cover oneself* 2 K 19$_{1}$||Is 37$_{1}$, לוט *cover* 2 S 19$_{5}$, צפה pi. *overlay* 2 K 18$_{16}$, דלח *make turbid* Ezk 32$_{2}$, כול pilp. *provide for* 2 S 19$_{34}$ 20$_{3}$, נשׂא pi. *supply* 1 K 9$_{11}$, גמל *repay* 2 S 19$_{37}$, עשׁר hi. *make rich* Gn 14$_{22}$ 1 S 17$_{25}$.

לחם ni. *fight* Nm 21$_{26}$ Jos 10$_{5+5t}$ 11$_{5}$ 24$_{9}$ Jg 5$_{19}$ 11$_{25}$ 1 S 8$_{20}$ 12$_{9}$ 2 S 8$_{10}$||1 C 18$_{10}$ 1 K 20$_{1}$ 2 K 3$_{21}$ 6$_{8}$ 8$_{29}$=9$_{15}$ 12$_{18}$ 16$_{5.5}$=Is 7$_{1.1}$ 2 K 19$_{8.9}$||Is 37$_{8.9}$ Jr 1$_{18}$ 21$_{2}$ 34$_{1}$ Dn 11$_{11}$ 2 C 35$_{20}$, גרה htp. *fight* Dn 11$_{25}$, נגח htp. *wage war* Dn 11$_{40}$, ערך *set* battle *in array* Gn 14$_{8.8.8.8.8.8}$, צור *besiege* 1 K 20$_{1}$ 2 K 6$_{24}$ 16$_{5}$ 17$_{5}$ 18$_{9}$ Dn 1$_{1}$ 2 C 28$_{20}$, סמך *lean*, i.e. besiege Ezk 24$_{2}$, ריב *strive* Jg 11$_{25}$, מרד *rebel* 2 K 18$_{1}$, פשׁע *rebel* 2 K 3$_{5.7}$, לחץ *oppress* 2 K 13$_{4.22}$, ריב *contend* Ho 5$_{13}$ 10$_{6}$ (unless יָרֵב adj. *great*), נכה hi. *strike, defeat* Gn 14$_{5.17}$ 2 S 8$_{10}$||1 C 18$_{10}$ 1 K 20$_{21}$ 2 K 6$_{21}$ 13$_{16.18}$ 18$_{1}$ 25$_{21}$||Jr 52$_{27}$ Jr 20$_{4}$ 21$_{7}$ 43$_{10}$ 46$_{2.13}$ 49$_{28}$ 2 C 28$_{5}$, נגף ni. *be defeated* 2 S 10$_{19}$, כבשׁ pi. *subdue* 2 S 8$_{11}$, המם *discomfit* Jr 51$_{34}$ (or em. הֲמָמַנִי to חֲמָסַנִי *he has treated me violently*, or הֱתִמַּנִי *he has destroyed me*, or הֱדִמַּנִי *he has destroyed me*), חמס *treat violently* Jr 51$_{34}$ (if em.; see above).

חלה *be sick* 2 K 8$_{7}$ Is 38$_{9}$, ho. *be wounded* 1 K 22$_{34}$||2 C 18$_{33}$ 2 C 35$_{23}$, ספה ni. *be swept away* 1 S 12$_{25}$, מות *die* Ex 2$_{23}$ 2 S 10$_{1}$||1 C 19$_{1}$ 1 K 22$_{35}$||2 C 18$_{34}$ 1 K 22$_{37}$ 2 K 1$_{6}$ 8$_{9}$ 9$_{27}$ 13$_{24}$ Jr 27$_{12}$ 34$_{4}$ 2 C 35$_{23}$, hi. *kill* 2 S 14$_{32}$ 1 K 1$_{51}$ 2$_{26}$ 2 K 5$_{7}$ 16$_{9}$ 23$_{29}$ 25$_{21}$||Jr 52$_{27}$ Jr 26$_{19.21.23}$ 38$_{16}$, הרג *kill* Ezk 26$_{7}$ 2 C 24$_{22}$ 36$_{17}$, ni. *be killed* 4QapJoseph[b] 3$_{12}$, שׁחט *slay* Jr 39$_{6.6}$ 52$_{10}$, תלה *hang* Est 6$_{4}$, קבר ni. *be buried* Jr 22$_{18}$ 2 C 35$_{23}$.

זבח *sacrifice* 1 K 3$_{4}$ 8$_{62}$||2 C 7$_{4}$ 2 C 7$_{5}$ 28$_{22}$, pi. 1 K 8$_{5}$||2 C 5$_{6}$ 2 K 16$_{1}$ 2 C 28$_{22}$, קטר pi. *burn incense* 2 K 16$_{1}$, hi. 2 K 16$_{12}$ Jr 44$_{21}$, שׂרף *burn* 1 K 9$_{16}$ 2 K 23$_{13}$ Jr 21$_{10}$ 34$_{2}$ 36$_{25.27.28.29.32}$ 43$_{10}$, יצת hi. *kindle* Jr 43$_{10}$ (if em. וְהִצַּתִּי *and I will kindle* to וְהִצִּית *and he shall kindle*), קלה *roast* Jr 29$_{22}$.

כרת *cut* 2 K 18$_{1}$ 23$_{13}$, i.e. make, covenant 2 S 5$_{3}$ 2 K 23$_{3}$||2 C 34$_{31}$ Jr 34$_{8}$ Ezk 17$_{12}$, ni. *be cut off* CD 3$_{9}$, hi. *cut off* 1 K 14$_{14}$, קצץ pi. *cut off* 2 K 16$_{17}$ 2 K 24$_{12}$, דמה ni. *be cut off* Ho 10$_{7}$ (or em. שֹׁמְרוֹן מַלְכָּהּ as for *Samaria*, *her king* is cut off, to שֹׁמְרוֹן מַלְכָּהּ *Samaria* is cut off, *her king* is like a splinter) 10$_{15}$, כתת pi. *beat* 2 K 18$_{1}$, קרע *tear* 2 S 13$_{31}$ 2 K 5$_{7.8.8}$ 6$_{30}$ 19$_{1}$||Is 37$_{1}$ 2 K 22$_{11}$||2 C 34$_{19}$ Jr 36$_{22.24}$, בקע *split open* 2 C 32$_{1}$, שׁבר ni. *be broken* Dn 8$_{23}$, pi. *break* 2 K 23$_{13}$ Jr 43$_{10}$, עצם pi. *break bones* Jr 50$_{17}$, פרץ *break down* 2 K 14$_{13}$||2 C 25$_{23}$, דכא pi. *crush* Ps 72$_{1}$, אבד *perish* Zc 9$_{5}$, pi. *destroy* 2 K 13$_{7}$, דמם hi. *destroy* Jr 51$_{34}$ (if em.; see above), שׁמד hi. *destroy* Dn 11$_{40}$, תמם *come to an end* Si 49$_{4}$, hi. *destroy* Jr 51$_{34}$ (if em.; see above).

חרב ni. *be laid waste* 2 K 3$_{23}$, hi. *lay waste* 2 K 19$_{17}$||Is 37$_{18}$, ho. *be laid waste* 2 K 3$_{23}$ (or em. ni.), חרם hi. *devote to destruction* 2 K 19$_{11}$||Is 37$_{11}$ Dn 11$_{40}$, שׁחת pi. *ruin* Ezk 28$_{12}$ 30$_{10}$, hi. 2 C 34$_{11}$ Jr 36$_{29}$ Dn 8$_{23}$ Si 10$_{3}$, נתץ *pull down* 2 K 23$_{12.13}$ Ezk 26$_{7}$, רצץ pi. *crush* 2 K 23$_{12}$ (if em. וַיָּרָץ מִשָּׁם *and he ran from there* to וַיְרַצֵּם שָׁם *and he crushed them there*), דקק hi. *pulverize* 2 K 23$_{13}$, חדל *cease* 2 C 35$_{21}$, שׁבת hi. *cause to cease* Jr 36$_{29}$, בער pi. *remove* 2 C 19$_{2}$, זנח hi. *reject* 2 C 29$_{19}$, ירה *shoot* 2 K 13$_{16}$, hi. 2 K 13$_{16}$ 19$_{32}$||Is 37$_{33}$, ריק hi. *empty*, i.e. draw, sword Ezk 30$_{10}$, עות *blind* 2 K 25$_{6}$ Jr 52$_{10}$ 39$_{6}$, ענשׁ *fine* 2 C 36$_{3}$.

עשׂה *do, make* Gn 14$_{1.1.1.1}$ 1 S 8$_{11}$ 17$_{25}$ 2 S 3$_{24.36}$ 7$_{3}$ 14$_{15.21.22}$ 18$_{4}$ 19$_{38.39}$ 1 K 3$_{28}$ 7$_{40(mss).51}$ 9$_{26}$ 10$_{9.12.16.18}$||2 C

$9_{8.11.15.17}$ 1 K 12_{28} 14_{27}||2 C 12_{10} 1 K $20_{9.22}$ 2 K 16_1 17_8 (or del.) 18_1 19_{11}||Is 37_{11} 2 K $21_{3.11}$ $23_{12.19}$ 24_{13} Jr 15_4 23_5 32_{32} 41_9 44_{17} 52_{20} Ho 10_3 Ca 3_9 Ec $2_{12(mss)}$ 8_4 Est $1_{5.20.21}$ $2_{4.18}$ 5_8 6_6 Dn 8_{23} $11_{3.36}$ Ne 9_{34} 1 C 21_{23} 2 C 2_2 7_6 12_{13} 20_{35} 24_{14} 25_7 30_2 35_{18} 4QpsEzek[a] 16.1_{10} 4QpsEzek[d] 1.2_3, i.e. offer 1 K 8_{64}, פעל *do* Ps 74_{12}, ברא ni. *be created* Ezk 28_{12}, בנה *build* 1 K 3_1 6_2 (ms lacks הַמֶּלֶךְ) 9_{15} 15_{17}||2 C 16_1 1 K 15_{22}||2 C 16_6 2 K 23_{13} Jb 3_{14} Ec 9_{14} Ezr 1_2||2 C 36_{23} 1 C 28_2 2 C 35_3, כלה pi. *finish* 2 S 13_{39} (if em. וַתְּכַל appar. *and it finished* to וַיְכַל) 1 K 3_1, מלא *fill* Ezk 30_{10}, pi. 2 K 23_{13} Jr 51_{34}, יסף hi. *do again* 2 K 24_7 2 C 28_{22}, כון hi. *prepare* 1 C 28_2 29_1 2 C 12_{13} 19_2, עזר *help* Jos 10_{33} 1 K 20_{16} 2 C 19_2 28_{16}, גאל *redeem* Ps 72_1, ישׁע ni. *be saved* Zc 9_9 Ps 33_{16}, hi. *save* 2 S 14_4 2 K 6_{26} 16_7 Ho 13_{10} Ps 72_1, נצל hi. *deliver* 2 S 14_{16} 19_{10} Ps 72_1, מלט ni. *escape* 1 K 20_{20} Jr 32_4 38_{22}, pi. *deliver* 2 S 19_{10}, נתר hi. *release* Ps 105_{20}.

יכל *be able, prevail* 1 K 20_7 2 K 3_{26} $16_{5.5}$=Is $7_{1.1}$ Jr 1_{18} 38_5 Ho 5_{13} 2 C 30_2, צלח hi. *prosper* 1 K 22_{15}||2 C 18_{14} Dn 8_{23} 11_{36}, שׂכל hi. *prosper* 2 K 18_1, *deal wisely* Jr 23_5 Ps 2_{10}, חזק *be strong, prevail* Dn 11_5 2 C 25_7 28_{20} (or em. חֲזָקוֹ *he prevailed against him* to חִזְּקוֹ *he strengthened him*, i.e. pi.), pi. *strengthen* Ezr 6_{22} 2 C 28_{19} (if em.; see above), htp. *strengthen oneself* 1 K 20_{22} 2 C 12_{13}, עזז *be strong*, i.e. prevail Dn 11_{11}, אמץ htp. *exert oneself* 1 K 12_{18}||2 C 10_{18}, גדל *be great* 1 K 10_{23}||2 C 9_{22}, pi. *make great* Est 3_1 5_{11} 10_2, hi. *magnify oneself* Dn 8_{23}, htp. *magnify oneself* Dn 11_{36}, רבה hi. *multiply* Dn 11_{36}, פאר pi. *beautify* Ezr 7_{27}.

חטא *sin* 1 S 19_4 2 K 18_{14} Ezk 28_{12} Ne 13_{26}, hi. *cause to sin* 2 K 21_{11}, רעע hi. *be evil* 2 K 21_{11}, רשׁע hi. *act wickedly* 2 C 20_{35}, פרע pass. *be undisciplined* Si 10_3, hi. *cast off restraint* 2 C 28_{19}, מעל *act unfaithfully* 2 C $28_{19.22}$ 29_{19}, כעס hi. *provoke to anger* 2 K 23_{19} Jr 32_{32}.

מלך *be king* Gn $36_{31.31}$||1 C $1_{43.43}$ Jos $13_{10.21}$ Jg 4_2 1 S $8_{9.11.19(mss)}$ $12_{12.14}$ 1 K 15_9 (mss read עַל *over* for מֶלֶךְ *king of*) 2 K $8_{16.25}$ $14_{1.23}$ (mss read עַל for מֶלֶךְ) $15_{1.32}$ 16_1 18_1 24_{12} Jr 1_2 22_{11} 23_5 37_1 (or del.) 51_{59} Pr 8_{15} Ec 4_{13} 2 C 12_{13} 22_1, hi. *make king* 1 K 1_{43} 2 K 24_{17} Jr 37_1 Ezk 17_{16} 2 C $36_{4.10}$ 4QpsMos[d] 4_2 ([ימלוך]), *make queen* Est 2_{17}, משׁל *rule* Jos $12_{2.4}$ Is 19_4 Dn $11_{3.40}$ Ne 9_{37}, hi. *cause to rule* Dn 11_{36}, דין *judge* Ps 72_1, שׁפט *judge* 1 S $8_{5.6.20}$ 1 K 3_{28} Ps 72_1 Pr 29_{14}, שׁלם hi. *make peace* 2 S 10_{19}.

<NOM CL> י׳ מֶלֶךְ *Y. is king* Ps 10_{16}, vars. Is 33_{22} Ps 24_{10} $47_{3.8}$ 95_3, בָּלָק ... מֶלֶךְ לְמוֹאָב *Balak was ... king of Moab* Nm 22_4, יְהוֹשָׁפָט מֶלֶךְ יְהוּדָה *Jehoshaphat was king of Judah* 2 K 8_{16} (lacking in mss), נִצָּב מֶלֶךְ *a deputy was king* 1 K 22_{48} (mss נְצִיב *deputy*), עַבְדִּי דָוִד מֶלֶךְ עֲלֵיהֶם *my servant David shall be king over them* Ezk 37_{24}, הֲלֹא שָׂרַי יַחְדָּו מְלָכִים *are not my commanders all kings?* Is 10_8, מַלְכֵּךְ נָעַר *your king is a youth* Ec 10_{16}, מַלְכֵּךְ בֶּן־חוֹרִים *your king is a son of nobles* Ec 10_{17}, המלך הוא הקהל *the king is the assembly* CD 7_{16}, הָאַיִל ... מַלְכֵי מָדַי וּפָרָס *the ram is ... the kings of Media and Persia* Dn 8_{20}, הַצָּפִיר הַשָּׂעִיר מֶלֶךְ יָוָן *the he-goat, the buck, is the king of Greece* Dn 8_{21}, הַקֶּרֶן ... הוּא הַמֶּלֶךְ הָרִאשׁוֹן *the horn is ... the first king* Dn 8_{21}, אַשּׁוּר הוּא מַלְכּוֹ *Assyria shall be their king* Ho 11_5.

מֶלֶךְ יִשְׂרָאֵל הוּא *he is the king of Israel* 1 K 22_{32}||2 C 18_{31}, var. 1 K 22_{33}, הוּא מֶלֶךְ *he is king* Jb 41_{26}, vars. Jr 10_{10} 4QShirShabb[d] 1.1_{34} (הו[א] ... מלך), אַתָּה הוּא מַלְכִּי *you are my king* Ps 44_5, אתה ... מלך נכבדים *you are king of the glorious ones* 1QH 10_8, אֲנִי־מֶלֶךְ *I am king* 2 S 19_{23}, vars. Is 43_{15} Ml 1_{14}=5QapMal 1_3 ([א]ני), var. 4QJub[a] 1_{28} ([אנכי] ... מלך), מַלְכֵי חֶסֶד הֵם *they are kings of loyalty* 1 K 20_{31}, התנינים הם מלכי העמים *the serpents are the kings of the peoples* CD $8_{10(A)}$=$19_{23(B)}$ (lacking הם), רֵעֵהוּ מֶלֶךְ *his friend is the king* Pr 22_{11} (or em. רְצוֹן *favour of* the king), מִגְדּוֹל יְשׁוּעוֹת מַלְכּוֹ *his king is a tower of salvation* 1 S $22_{51(Qr)}$||Ps $18_{51(Kt)}$ (מגדל), אֵלֶּה הַמְּלָכִים *these are the kings* Gn 36_{31}||1 C 1_{43}, var. Jos $12_{1.7}$, כָּל־הַמְּלָכִים שְׁלֹשִׁים וְאֶחָד *all the kings were thirty-one (in number)* Jos 12_{24}, הִנֵּה הַמֶּלֶךְ *behold the king* 1 S 12_{13}.

אֵין מֶלֶךְ בְּיִשְׂרָאֵל *there was no king in Israel* Jg 17_6 18_1 21_{25}, sim. Jg 19_1 1 K 22_{48} Jr 8_{19} Ho 3_4=CD 20_{16} Ho 10_3 Mc 4_9, מֶלֶךְ אֵין לָאַרְבֶּה *there is no king to the locusts* Pr 30_{27}, הֲלוֹא־זֶה ... מֶלֶךְ הָאָרֶץ *is this not ... the king of the land?* 1 S 21_{12}, מִי זֶה מֶלֶךְ הַכָּבוֹד *who is the king of glory?* Ps 24_8, sim. Ps 24_{10}, אַיֵּה מֶלֶךְ־חֲמָת *where is the king of Hamath?* 2 K $19_{13(mss)}$||Is 37_{13} (2 K $19_{13[L]}$ אַיּוֹ), אַיֵּה מַלְכְּךָ *where is your king?* Ho 13_{10} (if em; see Subj.), שָׁמָּה ... מְלָכֶיהָ *there are ... her kings* Ezk 32_{29}, קָרוֹב הַמֶּלֶךְ *the king is near (of kin)* 2 S 19_{42}, הַמֶּלֶךְ ...

נָקִי *the king is ... innocent* 2 S 14_{9}, חַי ... הַמֶּלֶךְ *(as) the king is ... alive* 2 S 15_{21}, כֵּן ... הַמֶּלֶךְ *thus is ... the king* 2 S 14_{17}, var. 2 K 18_{21}||Is 36_{6}.

לִקְדוֹשׁ יִשְׂרָאֵל מַלְכֵּנוּ *our king is*, i.e. belongs to, *the holy one of Israel* Ps 89_{19}, מֶלֶךְ לְשָׂדֶה נֶעֱבָד perh. *there is a king to a cultivated field*, i.e. it has a king Ec 5_{8} (or perh. *a king is served by the field*), הַמֶּלֶךְ בִּמְסִבּוֹ *the king was on his couch* Ca 1_{12}, מַלְכָּהּ ... בַגּוֹיִם *her king is ... among the nations* Lm 2_{9}, מֶלֶךְ בִּיהוּדָה *there is a king in Judah* Ne 6_{7}, הַמֶּלֶךְ כְּמַלְאַךְ הָאֱלֹהִים *the king is as the angel of God* 2 S 19_{28}, מַלְכָּהּ כְּקֶצֶף *her king is like a splinter* Ho 10_{7} (if em.; see Subj.).

מלך הכבוד אתנו *the king of glory is with us* 1QM 12_{8}=19_{1}, שְׁלֹשִׁים וּשְׁנַיִם מֶלֶךְ אִתּוֹ *thirty-two kings were with him* 1 K 20_{1}, הַמְּלָכִים אֲשֶׁר אִתּוֹ *the kings who were with him* Gn $14_{5.17}$ 2 K 25_{28}||Jr 52_{32}, הַמֶּלֶךְ ... לִפְנֵי הָאָרוֹן *the king was ... before the ark* 1 K 8_{5}||2 C 5_{6}, מֶלֶךְ יִשְׂרָאֵל ... בְּקִרְבֵּךְ *the king of Israel is ... among you* Zp 3_{15} (or em.; see Cstr.), מַלְכִּי מִקֶּדֶם *my king is from of old* Ps 74_{12}, הַמְּלָכִים ... לְבַדָּם *the kings were ... alone* 1 C 19_{9}, מלך היום *(he is) a king today* Si 10_{10}.

<OBJ> ענה *answer* 1 S 22_{14} 2 S 15_{21} Mc 6_{5}, קרא *call* Jr 46_{17} (or em.; see Cstr.), בשׂר pi. *give news to* 2 S 18_{19}, הלל pi. *praise* 2 C 23_{12}, רום pol. *extol* Ps 145_{1} 4QShir Shabb[d] 1.1_{13} ([מרוממי]), ברך pi. *bless* 2 S 8_{10}||1 C 18_{10} 2 S 14_{22} 1 K 1_{47} 8_{66} Ps 72_{1} 145_{1}, *curse* 1 K $21_{10.13}$, קלל pi. *curse* 2 S 16_{9} Ec 10_{20}, זהר hi. *warn* 2 K 6_{10}, יכח hi. *reprove* Ps 105_{14}||1 C 16_{21}, יסר pi. *discipline* Pr 31_{1}, יעץ *counsel* 1 K 12_{13}, ראה *see* 1 S 16_{1} 2 S 6_{16}||1 C 15_{29} 2 S 24_{20} 2 K 23_{29} Is 6_{5} Ezk 28_{12} 1 C $21_{20(ms)}$, hi. *show* 2 K 8_{13}, חזה *see* Is 33_{22}, שׁמר *watch* 1 S $26_{15(mss)}$, נצר *keep* Pr 20_{28} (or em.; see Subj.), בקשׁ pi. *seek* Ho 3_{5}, שׁמע *hear* 1 C 28_{2}, ידע *know* Ezk 28_{12}, זכר *remember* 4QMMT C$_{23}$, ירא *fear* Dt 3_{1} 1 K 1_{51} Jr 10_{7} Pr 24_{21} Dn 1_{10}, בהל pi. *terrify* Dn 11_{40}.

עבד *serve* Jg 3_{14} 2 K 18_{7} 25_{24}||Jr 40_{9} Jr 25_{11} 27_{6+7t} 28_{14} 30_{9} Ps 72_{1}, שׁרת pi. *serve* 1 K $1_{4.15}$ Est 2_{2} 6_{3} 1 C 27_{1} 28_{1} 2 C 17_{19} GnzPs 4_{12}, שׁקה hi. *give to drink* Jr 25_{18+11t}, שׂמח pi. *gladden* Ho 7_{3} (or em. יְשַׂמְּחוּ *they gladden* to יִמְשְׁחוּ *they anoint*), אשׁר pi. *pronounce happy* Ps 72_{1} חדה pi. *make joyful* Ps 21_{2}.

הלך hi. *lead* Dt 28_{36} 2 C 35_{23}, בוא *come upon* Ezk 32_{2}, hi. *bring* 1 S 15_{20} 2 S 7_{18}||1 C 17_{16} 2 K 23_{29} Is 7_{17} 60_{11} Jr 24_{1} 25_{9} Ezk 17_{12} 26_{7} 2 C 25_{23}, יצא hi. *bring out* Jos 10_{22+8t} 1 K 22_{34}||2 C 18_{33}, עלה hi. *bring up* 2 K 25_{6}||Jr 52_{9} Is 8_{7} (or del.) Ezk 32_{2} 2 C 36_{17}, ירד hi. *bring down* Is 41_{2} (if em.; see above) Si 48_{6}, נגשׁ hi. *bring near* 1 S 15_{32}, קרב *approach* 4QShirShabb[f] 23.2_{2}, hi. *bring near* Jos 8_{23}, קדם pi. *come before* Ps 21_{2}, עבר hi. *bring across* 2 S $19_{16.41(Qr).42}$ 2 C 35_{23}, htp. *provoke to anger* Pr 20_{2}, רכב hi. *cause to ride* 2 K 23_{29} 2 C 35_{23}, קרא *meet* 1 S 18_{6} 2 S $19_{16.17.21.25.26}$ 1 K 21_{18} 2 K 16_{10} 23_{29}||2 C 35_{20}, נשׂג hi. *overtake* 2 K 25_{5}||Jr 52_{8}, שׁלח pi. *send* 2 S 19_{32}, hi. 2 K 15_{37}, נקף hi. *surround* 2 C 23_{7}, שׁוב hi. *bring back* 2 S 15_{25} $19_{11.12.13.44}$ Jr 28_{4}, *bring back (to)* 1 K 2_{30} 12_{16}||2 C 10_{16} 2 K $22_{9.20}$||2 C $34_{16.28}$, מצא *find* 2 K 19_{8}||Is 37_{8}.

קום hi. *raise up* Dt 28_{36} 1 K 14_{14} Is 14_{9} Jr 30_{9}, מלך hi. *cause to reign* 1 S 8_{22} 12_{1} 2 K 8_{20}||2 C 21_{8} Is 7_{6}, רדה hi. *cause to dominate* Is 41_{2} (or em. יַרְדְּ to יוֹרִד *he brings down*, i.e. ירד hi., or יָרֹד *he beats down*, from רדד), משׁח *anoint* Jg 9_{8} Ho 7_{3} (if em.; see above) 8_{10} (if em.; see Cstr.), שׁאל *ask for* 1 S 8_{10} $12_{13.17.19}$, בחר *choose* 1 S 8_{18} 12_{13}, שׂכר *hire* 2 S 10_{6}||1 C 19_{7} 2 K $7_{6.6}$, ישׁע hi. *save* Ps 20_{10}, שׁפט *judge*, i.e. deliver 2 S $18_{19.31}$, עזר *help* 2 C 28_{22}, חזק pi. *strengthen* Jg 3_{12} 2 C 28_{20} (if em.; see Subj.), hi. *seize* Jr 50_{43}, גדל hi. *make great* 2 S $22_{51(Kt)}$|| Ps $18_{51(Qr)}$, עשׁר hi. *enrich* Ezk 27_{33}, כול pilp. *provide for* 2 S 19_{33} 1 K 4_{7} 5_{7}.

נתן *give, place* Dt $2_{24.30}$ $3_{1.3}$ 7_{24} Jos 6_{2} 8_{1} 10_{30} Jg 3_{10} 1 S 8_{6} 12_{13} 2 K $3_{10.13}$ Jr 21_{7} 24_{8} 25_{18} 34_{21} 38_{19} $44_{30.30}$ Ezk 28_{12} Ho $13_{10.11}$ Dn 1_{2} Ne $9_{24.37}$ 13_{26} 2 C 2_{10} 4QpsMos[d] 4_{2} GnzPs 1_{23} ([נת]תו), שׂים *place* Dt $17_{14.15.15}$=11QT $56_{13.14.14}$ 1 S 8_{5} 10_{19}, שׁית *place* Ps 21_{2}, נסך *install* Ps 2_{6}, ישׁב hi. *cause to sit* 2 C 23_{20}, כסה pi. *cover* 1 K 1_{1}, מלא pi. *fill* Jr 13_{13}.

לקח *take* 2 K 24_{12} Jr 43_{10} Ezk 17_{12} Ho 13_{11}, אחז *seize* Ps 48_{5}, תפשׂ *seize* Jos 8_{23} 1 S 15_{8} 2 K 14_{13}||2 C 25_{23} 2 K 25_{6}||Jr 52_{9}, לכד *capture* Jos $10_{39.42}$ $11_{12.17}$ Jg 8_{12}, גרשׁ pi. *drive out* Jos 24_{12}, גלה hi. *exile* Jr 24_{1} 27_{20} Est 2_{6}, גנב *steal* 2 S 19_{42}, אסר *bind* Ps 149_{8}, כלא *imprison* 4QapPs[b] 33_{8}, סור hi. *remove* 1 K 20_{24}, פרשׂ pi. *scatter* Ps 68_{15}, שׁלך hi. *cast* Ezk 28_{12}, טול hi. *throw* Ezk 32_{2}, כשׁל hi. *cause to stumble* 2 C 25_{7} 28_{22}, נפל hi. *cause to fall* 2 C

32_{21}, שׁפל hi. *make low* perh. 4QpsHod^{a} 1_{5} ([מל]כי]), תעה hi. *lead astray* 4QpNah 3.2_{9}, נטשׁ *leave* Ezk 32_{2}, פתה pi. *entice* 2 C 18_{19}, נשׁא hi. *deceive* 2 K 19_{10}||Is 37_{10}, חטא hi. *cause to sin* Ne 13_{26}, חלל pi. *profane* Ezk 28_{12}, נאץ *spurn* Lm 2_{6}.

כנע hi. *subdue* Jg 4_{23}, נכה hi. *strike, defeat* Gn 14_{17} Dt $1_{4.4}$ 3_{1} 4_{46} 29_{6} Jos $10_{28.33.37.39.40}$ $11_{10.12.17}$ $12_{1.7}$ 13_{21} 2 S 8_{3}||1 C 18_{3} 2 S 17_{2} 1 K 16_{16} 22_{34}||2 C 18_{33} 2 K 8_{29}=9_{15} 9_{27} 14_{5}||2 C 25_{3} 2 K 19_{36}||Is 37_{37} Jr 21_{7} Ps 136_{17} (unless from מֶלֶךְ II *kingdom*), נגע pi. *strike* 2 K 15_{5}, hi. *bring* Lm 2_{2} (if em. חִלֵּל מַמְלָכָה *he has profaned the kingdom* to חֲלָלִים מַלְכָּהּ to the land *of the pierced, its king*), מחץ *strike through* Ps 110_{5}, תלה *hang* Jos 8_{29}, רדד *beat down* Is 41_{2} (if em.; see above), חרם hi. *devote to destruction* Jos 2_{10} 10_{24} 11_{12}, אבד pi. *destroy* Ezk 28_{12}, hi. Jr 49_{38}, שׁחת hi. *destroy* 1 S 26_{15} 2 C 35_{21}, אכל *consume* Ezk 28_{12}, מחה hi. *wipe out* Pr 31_{3} (or em. לַמְחוֹת to לְמֹחוֹת *to those who wipe out*, i.e. qal, or מְלָכִין לְלַחֲנוֹת *to the secondary wives of*; or perh. מְלָכִין is from מֶלֶךְ *counsel*), שׁבר *break* GnzPs 1_{24}, הרג *kill* Nm $31_{8.8}$ Ps 135_{10} 136_{18}, מות hi. *kill* Jos 11_{17} 2 K 21_{23} 23_{29}, כרת hi. *cut off* Jg 4_{24}, קבר *bury* 1 K 22_{37} 2 K 23_{29}.

<CSTR> מֶלֶךְ *king of* + pl.n., pr.n. or gent., Achshaph Jos 11_{1} 12_{20}, Admah Gn $14_{2.8}$, Adullam Jos 12_{15}, Ai Jos $8_{1.14.23.29}$ 12_{9}, Amalek 1 S $15_{8.20.32}$, Ammonites (בְּנֵי עַמּוֹן lit. *of the sons of Ammon*) Jg $11_{12.14.28}$ (or em. all three to Moab) 1 S 12_{12} 2 S 10_{1}||1 C 19_{1} Jr 27_{3} 40_{14} 2 C 27_{5} (lacking in mss), Amorites Nm $21_{21.26.29.34}$ 32_{33} Dt 1_{4} 3_{2} 4_{46} Jos 12_{2} $13_{10.21}$ Jg 11_{19} 1 K 4_{19} Ps 135_{11} 136_{19}, Aphek Jos 12_{18}, Arabia 2 K 10_{15}||2 C 9_{14} (2 K if em.; see below), Arad Nm 21_{1} 33_{40} Jos 12_{14}, Aram Jg 3_{10} 1 K 15_{18}||2 C 16_{2} 1 K $20_{1.20.22.23}$ $22_{3.31}$||2 C 18_{30} 2 K $5_{1.5}$ $6_{8.11.24}$ $8_{7.9.28.29}$||2 C $22_{5.6}$ 2 K $9_{14.15}$ $12_{18.19}$ $13_{3.4.7.22.24}$ 15_{37} 16_{5}=Is 7_{1} 2 K 16_{6} (or em. Edom) 16_{7} 2 C $17_{7.7}$ (or em. Israel) $28_{5.23(ms)}$, Aram-naharaim Jg 3_{8}, Arpad 2 K 19_{13}||Is 37_{13}, Assyria 2 K $15_{19.20.20.29}$ 16_{7+5t} 17_{3+8t} $18_{7.9.11.13}$||Is 36_{1} 2 K $18_{14.14.16.17.19}$||Is $36_{2.4}$ 2 K 18_{23} (mss הַמֶּלֶךְ; ||Is 36_{8} הַמֶּלֶךְ אַשּׁוּר) $18_{28.30.31.33}$||Is $36_{13.15.16.18}$ 2 K $19_{4.6.8.10.20.32.36}$||Is 37_{4+6t} 2 K 20_{6}||Is 38_{6} 2 K 23_{29} Is $7_{17.20}$ $8_{4.7}$ 10_{12} $20_{1.4.6}$ Jr $50_{17.18}$ Na 3_{18} Ezr 4_{2} 6_{22} 1 C $5_{6.26.26}$ 2 C $28_{16(ms).21}$ 32_{1+6t} 33_{11} 4QapPs^{b} 33_{8}.

Babylon 2 K $20_{12.18}$||Is $39_{1.7}$ 2 K 24_{1}||2 C 36_{6} 2 K 24_{7+7t} $25_{1.6.8.8.11.20.21}$||Jr $52_{4.9.12.12.15.26.27}$ (2 K 25_{11} if em. הַמֶּלֶךְ) 2 K $25_{22.23.24}$||Jr $40_{7.9}$ 2 K 25_{27}||Jr 52_{31} Is 14_{4} Jr 20_{4} $21_{2.4.7.10}$ 22_{25} 24_{1} $25_{1.9.11.12}$ 27_{6+9t} $28_{2.3.4.11.14}$ $29_{3.21.22}$ $32_{2.3.4.28.36}$ $34_{1.2.3.7.21}$ 35_{11} 36_{29} $37_{1.17.19}$ $38_{3.17.18.22.23}$ 39_{1+7t} $40_{5.11}$ $41_{2.18}$ 42_{11} 43_{10} 44_{30} $46_{2.13.26}$ $49_{28.30}$ $50_{17.18.43}$ $51_{31.34}$ $52_{3.10.11.34}$ Ezk 17_{12} 19_{9} (or del.) $21_{24.26}$ 24_{2} 26_{7} $29_{18.19}$ $30_{10.24.25.25}$ 32_{11} Est 2_{6} Dn 1_{1} Ezr 2_{1}||Ne 7_{6} Ne 13_{6} 4QpIsa^{c} 25_{1} 4QpsEzek^{a} 38_{2} CD 1_{6}, Bashan Nm 21_{33} 32_{33} Dt 1_{4} $3_{1.3.11}$ 4_{47} 29_{6} Jos 9_{10} 12_{4} 13_{30} 1 K 4_{19} Ps 135_{11} 136_{20} Ne 9_{22}, Bela Gn $14_{2.8}$, Bethel Jos 12_{16}.

Canaan Jg $4_{2.23.24.24}$, Chaldaeans 2 C 36_{17}, Cush 2 K 19_{9}||Is 37_{9}, Damascus 2 C 24_{23} (ms לַמֶּלֶךְ דַּרְמֶשֶׂק *to the king at Damascus*), Debir Jos 12_{13}, Dor Jos 12_{23}, Edom Nm 20_{14} Jg $11_{17.17}$ 2 K $3_{9.13.26}$ 16_{6} (if em.) Jr 27_{3} Am 2_{1}, Eglon Jos $10_{3.5.23}$ 12_{12}, Egypt Gn $40_{1.1.5}$ 41_{46} Ex $1_{15.17.18}$ (Sam Pharaoh) 2_{23} $3_{18.19}$ 5_{4} $6_{11.13.27.29}$ $14_{5.8}$ Dt 7_{8} 11_{3} (lacking in Sam) 1 K 3_{1} 9_{16} $11_{18.40}$ 14_{25}||2 C 12_{2} 2 K $17_{4.7}$ 18_{21}||Is 36_{6} 2 K 23_{29}||2 C 35_{20} 2 K $24_{7.7}$ Jr 25_{19} 44_{30} $46_{2.17}$ Ezk $29_{2.3}$ $30_{21.22}$ 31_{2} 32_{2} 2 C 12_{9} $36_{3.4}$ 4QpsEzek^{e} 1_{2} ([מ]לך) Arad ost. 88_{3}, Elam Gn $14_{1.9}$, Ellasar Gn $14_{1.9}$, Gath 1 S $21_{11.13}$ 27_{2} 1 K 2_{39}, Geder Jos 12_{13}, Gerar Gn 20_{2}, Geshur 2 S 3_{3}||1 C 3_{2} 2 S 13_{37}, Gezer Jos 10_{33} 12_{12}, Goiim Gn $14_{1.9}$ Jos 12_{23}, Gomorrah Gn $14_{2.8.10.17}$, Greece Dn 8_{21} 4QpNah 3.1_{2}, Hamath 2 S 8_{9}||1 C 18_{9} 2 K 19_{13}||Is 37_{13}, Hazor Jos 11_{1} 12_{19} Jg 4_{17}, Hebron Jos $10_{3.5.23}$ 12_{10} Royal stamp 1 2 3 4, Hena 2 K 19_{13}||Is 37_{13}, Hepher Jos 12_{17}, Heshbon Dt $2_{24.26.30}$ 3_{6} 29_{6} Jos 9_{10} 12_{5} 13_{27} Jg 11_{19} Ne 9_{22}, Hormah Jos 12_{14}.

Israel 1 S 24_{15} 26_{20} 29_{3} 2 S 6_{20} 1 K $15_{9.16.17.19}$||2 C $16_{1.3}$ 1 K 15_{32} $20_{2.4.7.11.13.21.22.28.31.32.40.41}$ 21_{18} $22_{2.3.4.5.6.8.9.10.18.26.29.30.30.31.32.33.34}$||2 C $18_{4.5.7.8.9.17.25.28.29.29.30.31.32.33}$ 1 K $22_{41.45}$ 2 K $3_{4.5.9.10.11.12.13.13}$ $5_{5.6.7.8}$ $6_{9.10.11.12.21.26}$ 7_{6} $8_{16.25.26}$ $9_{21.27}$ $13_{14.16.18}$ (or del.) $14_{1.8.9.11.13.17}$ ||2 C $25_{17.18.21.23.25}$ 2 K 14_{23} (mss read עַל *over* for מֶלֶךְ *king of*) $15_{1.11.26.29.32}$ 16_{5}=Is 7_{1} 2 K 16_{7} $18_{1.9.10}$ 21_{3} 23_{13} 24_{13} Is 44_{6} Jr 41_{9} Ho 1_{1} 10_{15} Am 1_{1} 7_{10} Mc 1_{14} (if em. מַלְכֵי *kings of*) Zp 3_{15} (or em. יִמְלֹךְ *he will reign*) Pr 1_{1} Ezr 3_{10} Ne 13_{26} 1 C 5_{17} 2 C 8_{11} 16_{7} (if em.; see above) $18_{19.34}$ $20_{34.35}$ 21_{2} (mss, Seb Judah) 22_{5} $28_{5.19}$ (mss, Seb Judah) 29_{27} 30_{26} $35_{3.4}$ 4QparaKings 3_{2} ([מ]לך), Ivvah 2 K 19_{13}||Is 37_{13}.

Jacob Is 41_{21}, Jarmuth Jos $10_{3.5.23}$ 12_{11}, Jericho Jos

$2_{2.3}$ $10_{28.30}$ 12_{9}, Jerusalem Jos $10_{1.3.5.23}$ 12_{10}, Jokneam Jos 12_{22}, Judah 1 K 12_{23}||2 C 11_{3} 1 K $12_{27.27}$ 15_{9} (mss read עַל *over* for מֶלֶךְ *king of*) 15_{17}||2 C 16_{1} 1 K $15_{25.28.33}$ $16_{8.10.15.23.29}$ $22_{2.10.29}$||2 C $18_{9.28}$ 1 K 22_{52} 2 K 1_{17} $3_{1.7.9.12(mss).14}$ 8_{16} (lacking in mss) $8_{16.25.29}$||2 C 22_{6} (2 K lacking in ms) 2 K $9_{16.21}$ 10_{13} 12_{19} $13_{1.10.12}$ $14_{1.9.11.13.17}$ ||2 C $25_{18.21.23.25}$ 2 K $14_{15.23}$ $15_{1.8.13.17.23.27.32}$ 16_{1} 17_{1} $18_{1.14.14.16}$ 19_{10}||Is 37_{10} 2 K 21_{11} $22_{16.18}$||2 C $34_{24.26}$ 2 K 24_{12} $25_{27.27}$||Jr $52_{31.31}$ Is 7_{1} 38_{9} Jr $1_{2.3.3}$ 15_{4} $21_{7.11}$ $22_{1.2.6.11.18.24}$ $24_{1.8}$ $25_{1.3}$ $26_{1.18.19}$ $27_{1.3.12.18.20.21}$ $28_{1.4}$ 29_{3} $32_{1.2.3.4}$ $34_{2.4.6.21}$ 35_{1} $36_{1.9.28.29.30.32}$ 37_{7} 38_{22} $39_{1.4}$ 44_{30} 45_{1} 46_{2} 49_{34} 51_{59} Am 1_{1} Zp 1_{1} Zc 14_{5} Pr 25_{1} Est 2_{6} Dn $1_{1.2}$ 1 C 4_{41} 5_{17} 2 C 16_{7} 18_{3} 19_{1} 20_{25} $21_{2(mss, Seb)}$ (L Israel) 21_{12} 22_{1} 25_{17} $28_{19(mss, Seb)}$ (L Israel) 30_{24} $32_{8.9.23}$ 35_{21} 3QpIsa 1_{4} ([יהו]דה) 4QApocWeeks$_{4}$ 4QapPs[b] 31_{4} ([מ]לך) 33_{8} 4QMMT C_{19} ([יהוד]ה) Arad ost. 40_{13} ([יהוד]ה) Bulla D1.

Kedesh Jos 12_{22}, Kittim 1QM 15_{2} 1QpPs 9_{1} (מל]כי [כתיאים) 4QApocWeeks$_{6}$ ([מל]ך), Lachish Jos $10_{3.5.23}$ 12_{11}, Lair 2 K 19_{13}||Is 37_{13}, Lasharon Jos 12_{18}, Libnah Jos 12_{15}, Maacah 2 S 10_{6}||1 C 19_{7}, Madon Jos 11_{1} 12_{19}, Makkedah Jos 10_{28} 12_{16}, Massa Pr 31_{1} (if transfer athnach), Megiddo Jos 12_{21}, Memshath Royal stamp 16 17 18 19, Moab Nm 21_{26} 22_{10} 23_{7} Jos 24_{9} Jg $3_{12.14.15.17}$ $11_{12.14}$ (both if em.; see above) $11_{17.25.28}$ (if em.; see above) 1 S 12_{9} $22_{3.4}$ 2 K $3_{4.5.7.26}$ Jr 27_{3} Mc 6_{5} 6QapSam Kgs 33_{3} Lachish ost. 8_{3} ([מ]לך), Nineveh Jon 3_{6}.

Persia Dn 10_{1} Ezr $1_{1.1.2}$||2 C $36_{22.22.23}$ Ezr 1_{8} 3_{7} $4_{3.5.5.7}$ 7_{1}, Philistines Gn $26_{1.8}$, Salem Gn 14_{18}, Samaria 1 K 21_{1} 2 K 1_{3}, Sheshach, i.e. Babylon Jr 25_{26}, Shimron Jos 11_{1} $12_{20(mss)}$, Shimron-meron Jos 12_{20} (meron lacking in mss), Shinar Gn $14_{1.9}$, Sidon Jr 27_{3}, Sidonians 1 K 16_{31}, Socoh Royal stamp 11 12 13 14, Sodom Gn $14_{2.8.10.21.22}$, Taanach Jos 12_{21}, Tappuah Jos 12_{17}, Tirzah Jos 12_{24}, Tyre 2 S 5_{11}2 S 5_{11}||1 C 14_{1} 1 K 5_{15} 9_{11} Jr 27_{3} Ezk 28_{12} 2 C $2_{2.10}$, Zeboiim Gn $14_{2.8}$, Ziph Royal stamp 6 7 8 9, Zobah 1 S $14_{47(4QSam^{a})}$ 2 S $8_{3.5}$||1 C $18_{3.5}$ 2 S 8_{12} 1 K 11_{23} 1 C 18_{9}.

מַלְכֵי *kings of*, + pl.n., pr.n. or gent., Amorites Dt 3_{8} 4_{47} 31_{4} Jos 2_{10} 5_{1} 9_{10} $10_{5.6}$ Jos 24_{12}, Arabia Jr 25_{24}, Aram 1 K 10_{29}||2 C 1_{17} 2 C 28_{23}, Assyria 2 K $19_{11.17}$||Is $37_{11.18}$ 2 C 28_{16} 30_{6} 32_{4}, Canaan Jg 5_{19}, Canaanites Jos 5_{1}, Hittites 1 K 10_{29}||2 C 1_{17} 2 K 7_{6}, Egypt 2 K 7_{6}, Elam Jr 25_{25}, Greece 4QpNah 3.1_{3} CD $8_{11(A)}$=$10_{24(B)}$.

Israel 1 K 14_{19} 15_{31} $16_{5.14.20.27.33}$ 22_{37} 2 K 1_{18} 8_{18}||2 C 21_{6} 2 K 10_{34} $13_{8.12.13}$ $14_{15.16.28.29}$ $15_{15.21.31}$ 16_{3}||2 C 28_{2} 2 K $17_{2.8}$ (or del.) $23_{19.22}$ Mc 1_{14} (or em. מֶלֶךְ *king of*) 1 C 9_{1} 2 C 21_{13} 25_{26} 27_{7} $28_{26.27}$ 32_{32} 33_{18} $35_{18.27}$ 36_{8} 4QMMT C_{23} ([ישרא]ל).

Judah 1 S 27_{6} 1 K 14_{29} $15_{7.23}$ 22_{46} 2 K $12_{19.20}$ 14_{18}||2 C 25_{26} 2 K $15_{6.36}$||2 C 27_{7} 2 K 16_{19}||2 C 28_{26} 2 K 18_{5} 20_{20}|| 2 C 32_{32} 2 K $21_{17.25}$ $23_{5.11.12.22.28}$ 24_{5}||2 C 36_{8} Is 1_{1} Jr 1_{18} 8_{1} $17_{19.20}$ $19_{3.4.13}$ 20_{5} 33_{4} 44_{9} Ho 1_{1} Mc 1_{1} 1 C 9_{1} (if ins. וִיהוּדָה *and Judah*) 2 C 34_{11} 35_{27} Si 49_{4}, Media Jr 25_{25} $51_{11.28}$ Est 10_{2} Dn 8_{20}, Midian Nm $31_{8.8}$ Jg $8_{5.12.26}$ 4QapJoseph[b] 3_{12} GnzPs 1_{24}, Persia Est 10_{2} Dn 8_{20} 10_{13} Ezr 9_{9}, Seba Ps 72_{10}, Sheba Ps 72_{10}, Sidon Jr 25_{22}, Tarshish Ps 72_{10}, Tyre Jr 25_{22}, Zimri Jr 25_{25} (or em. Zichri), Zobah 1 S 14_{47}.

מַלְכֵי בֵּית יִשְׂרָאֵל *kings of the house of Israel* 1 K 20_{31}, מלך כל האומים *king of all the peoples* GnzPs 1_{23}, מַלְכֵי עַמִּים *kings of peoples* Gn 17_{16} 1QMyst 9_{3} ([עמ]ים) 4QMyst[a] 60_{4} ([עמי]ם) CD $8_{10(A)}$=$19_{23(B)}$ (העמים), גּוֹיִם *of nations* Is $14_{9.18}$ Jr 10_{7} (הַגּוֹיִם), הָעֶרֶב *of the mixed peoples* 1 K 10_{15} (or em. עֲרַב *of Arabia*, with ||2 C 9_{14}) Jr 25_{24} (or del.).

מֶלֶךְ הָאָרֶץ *king of the land* 1 S 21_{12}, כָּל־הָאָרֶץ *of all the earth* Ps 47_{8}, מַלְכֵי־אֶרֶץ *kings of the earth* Ezk 27_{33} (אֶרֶץ) Ps 2_{2} 76_{13} 89_{28} (both אֶרֶץ) 138_{4} (אָרֶץ; or em. כָּל־מָלְכֵי־אָרֶץ *all the kingdoms of the earth*) Lm 4_{12} 4QsapHymnA 1.1_{13} GnzPs 2_{12}, מַלְכֵי הָאָרֶץ *kings of the earth/land* Jos $12_{1.7}$ 1 K 5_{14} 10_{23}||2 C 9_{22} Ps 102_{16} (הָאָרֶץ) 2 C 9_{23}, אֶרֶץ *of the land of* Jr $25_{20.20}$, הָאֲרָצוֹת *of the lands* Ezr 9_{7}, הָאֲדָמָה *of the earth* Is 24_{21}, מל]כי כול ה]תבל *kings of all the world* 4QpsHod[a] 1_{5}, מַלְכֵי הָאִי *kings of the island* Jr 25_{22}, אִיִּים *of the islands* Ps 72_{10} (מַלְכֵי ...), עֵבֶר הַנָּהָר *of the region beyond the river* 1 K 5_{4}, מֶלֶךְ הַצָּפוֹן *king of the north* Dn 11_{6+6t}, מַלְכֵי הַצָּפוֹן *kings of the north* Jr 25_{26} 1QM 1_{4} 4QpsEzek[c] 4.1_{2} ([מ]לכי), מֶלֶךְ־הַנֶּגֶב *king of the south* Dn 11_{5+7t}.

מלך אלוהים *king of the gods* 4QShirShabb[a] 1.2_{7} 2_{5} 4QShirShabb[b] 1_{5} ([אלו]הים) 4QShirShabb[c] 3.2_{12} ([אלוהי]ן) 4QShirShabb[f] 23.1_{13}, מֶלֶךְ מְלָכִים *king of kings* Ezk 26_{7} 4QapPs[b] 76_{7} 4QShirShabb[d] 1.1_{34} ([מל]כים)

4QM^{a} 8.1_{13} ([המ]לכים), מלך מלכי מלכים *king of the kings of kings* Si 51_{12}, מֶלֶךְ שָׂרִים *king of princes*, or, *of kings** Ho 8_{10} (or em. וְשָׂרִים *and princes*), מלך נשיאי *king of the princes of* 4QShirShabb^{a} 1.2_{14}, נכבדים *of the glorious ones* 1QH 10_{8}, מרוממים *of those who exalt* 4QShirShabb^{d} 3_{1} ([מ]לך) 4QShirShabb^{f} 14.1_{3}, מַלְכֵי צְבָאוֹת *kings of armies* Ps 68_{13} (mss מַלְאֲכֵי *messengers of*).

מלך הטהור *king of the pure one* 4QShirShabb^{d} 1.2_{26} (unless טהור is from טֹהַר *purity, splendour*), הקודש *of holiness* 4QShirShabb^{f} 23.2_{11} MasShirShabb 2_{18}, קודש *of the holiness of* 4QShirShabb^{a} 1.1_{8}, הטוב *of goodness* MasShirShabb 2_{15}, אמת [ו]צדק *of truth and righteousness* 4QShirShabb^{e} 5_{6}, מַלְכֵי חֶסֶד *kings of loyalty* 1 K 20_{31}, מֶלֶךְ הַכָּבוֹד *king of glory* Ps $24_{7.8.9.10.10}$ 1QM 12_{8}=19_{1} 4QShirShabb^{d} 1.1_{3} ([מ]ל[ך]) 1.1_{31} 1.2_{25} 4QShirShabb^{f} 15.2_{7} ([הכבו]ד) 4QShir^{a} 1_{1} ([מ]לך) 4QShir^{b} 52.3_{4} (הכב[ו]ד) 11QShirShabb 8_{7} 10_{5}, מ[ל]ך ההוד *king of splendour* 4QShirShabb^{d} 1.1_{38}, מלך כול קדושי *king of all the holy ones of* 11QShirShabb 30_{4} MasShirShabb 2_{2} (מל[ך כול קדושי]), מֶלֶךְ בַּלָּהוֹת *king of terrors* Jb 18_{14}.

מֶלֶךְ קֶדֶם *king of ancient time* Is 19_{11}, מלכי קדם *kings of the east* 4QM^{a} 11.1_{12}, מֶלֶךְ עוֹלָם *king of eternity*, i.e. everlasting king Jr 10_{10}, מלך כול *king of all* 4QShirShabb^{b} 13_{1} (כו[ל]) 4QShirShabb^{d} 1.1_{28} (מל[ך ה]כול) 4QShirShabb^{e} 6_{2} 4QShirShabb^{f} 24_{3} 11QShirShabb $26b_{1}$ (כו[ל]) 30_{4} MasShirShabb 2_{2} (מל[ך כול]) GnzPs 1_{23} (כל), מל[כי כול] *kings of all* 4QpsHod^{a} 1_{5}.

אֱלֹהֵי ... הַמֶּלֶךְ *God of ... the king* 1 K 13_{6}, אֱלֹהֵי מַלְכֵי *gods of the kings of* 2 C 28_{23}, מַסֵּכוֹת מַלְכְּכֶם *molten images of your king* Am 5_{6} (if em.; see App.), מלאכי מלך *angels of the king* 4QShirShabb^{d} 1.2_{23}, אַנְשֵׁי הַמֶּלֶךְ *men of the king* 2 C 34_{22} (if em. אֲשֶׁר *[those] whom*), אַנְשֵׁי ... מֶלֶךְ *men of ... the king of* Pr 25_{1}, נְשֵׁי הַמֶּלֶךְ *wives of the king* 2 K 24_{15}, לְחֵנוֹת מְלָכִין *secondary wives of kings* Pr 31_{3} (if em.; see Obj.), אֵם הַמֶּלֶךְ *mother of the king* 1 K 2_{19} 2 K 24_{15} 2 C 15_{16} (אֵם ...; unless em. אִמּוֹ *his mother*), בֶּן־ *son of* 2 S 13_{4} $18_{12.20}$ 22_{26}||2 C 18_{25} 2 K $11_{4.12}$||2 C $23_{3.11}$ 2 K 15_{5} Jr 36_{26} 38_{6} Ps 72_{1} (מֶלֶךְ) 2 C 28_{7} Seals 72 (Palestine, 7th cent.) 110 (Beth-Zur, 7th/6th cent.) 209 (c. 700) 252 (7th/6th cent.) 506 507 ([ב]ן) 508 (all three T. Beit Mirsim?, 7th/6th cent.) 719 (Judaea, 7th cent.) 760 (8th cent.) 784 (6th cent.) Bulla 904 (Jerusalem, 7th/6th cent.) Seals 939 940 941 942, בֶּן־מַלְכֵי *son of the kings of* Is 19_{11}, בְּנֵי הַמֶּלֶךְ *sons of the king* Jg 8_{18} 2 S 9_{11} $13_{27.29.30.32.33.35.36}$ 1 K 1_{9} (or del.) $1_{19.25}$ 2 K $10_{6.7.8.13}$ 11_{2}||2 C 22_{11} Zp 1_{8} 1 C 27_{32} 29_{24} 4QM^{a} 11.1_{18}, בְּנֵי ... מֶלֶךְ *sons of ... the king of* 2 C 21_{2}, חֲתַן הַמֶּלֶךְ *son-in-law of the king* 1 S 22_{14}, בַּת־ *daughter of* 2 K 9_{34} (מֶלֶךְ) 11_{2}||2 C 22_{11} Ps 45_{10} (if em.; see below) 45_{14} (מֶלֶךְ; or del.) 2 C 22_{11} Seal 781 (7th cent.), בַּת מֶלֶךְ *daughter of the king of* 2 S 3_{3}||1 C 3_{2} 1 K 16_{31} 2 K 8_{26} (all three בַּת ...) Dn 11_{6} Bulla D14 (המלך), בְּנוֹת־הַמֶּלֶךְ *daughters of the king* 2 S 13_{18} Jr 41_{10} 43_{6}, בְּנוֹת מְלָכִים *daughters of kings* Ps 45_{10} (or em בַּת הַמֶּלֶךְ *daughter of the king*) GnzPs 3_{16}, אֲחֵי ... מֶלֶךְ *brothers of ... the king of* 2 K 10_{13}.

מֶלֶךְ מְלָכִים *king of kings* Ezk 26_{7} 4QapPs^{b} 76_{7} 4QShirShabb^{d} 1.1_{34} (מל[כים]) 4QM^{a} 8.1_{13} ([המ]לכים), מלכי מלכים *kings of kings* Si 51_{12}, שָׂרֵי הַמֶּלֶךְ *princes of the king* Est 1_{18} 6_{9} Ezr 7_{28} 2 C 26_{11}, שָׂרֵי מֶלֶךְ *princes of the king of* Jr $38_{17.18.22}$ $39_{3.3}$, שַׂר מַלְכֵי *prince of the kings of* Dn 10_{13} (if ins. שַׂר), רַבֵּי הַמֶּלֶךְ *chief officers of the king of* Jr 41_{1}, רַבֵּי מֶלֶךְ *chief officers of the king of* Jr 39_{13}, אֲחַשְׁדַּרְפְּנֵי הַמֶּלֶךְ *satraps of the king* Est 3_{12} Ezr 8_{36}, מִשְׁנֶה *second (in command) of* 2 C 28_{7}, אֲסִירֵי *prisoners of* Gn $39_{30(Qr)}$ (אסורי *prisoners of*), אֹיְבֵי *enemies of* 1 S 18_{25} 29_{8} 2 S 18_{32} (both אֹיְבֵי ...) Ps 45_{6} (אוֹיְבֵי).

עֶבֶד הַמֶּלֶךְ *servant of the king* 2 S 18_{29} 2 K 22_{12}||2 C 34_{20} Lachish ost. 3_{19} Seals 69 (T. en-Naṣbeh, 8th/7th cent.) 70 71 (Jerusalem) 125 (T. Qasile, 5th/4th cent.) 504 (ע[בד]) 505 (both T. Beit Mirsim?, 7th/6th cent.) 759 (Umm el-Qanafid, 7th cent.) 917 (8th cent.) Bullae 923 (7th/6th cent.) 924 Seal 932 (7th cent.) Bullae D7 (מלך) D8 D10, עֶבֶד מֶלֶךְ *servant of the king of* 1 S 29_{3} (עֶבֶד ...) 2 K 25_{8} (or em. עֶבֶד to עֹמֵד לִפְנֵי *[who] stood before*), עַבְדֵי הַמֶּלֶךְ *servants of the king* 1 S 22_{17} 2 S 11_{24} 15_{15} 16_{6} 1 K $1_{9.47}$ 2 K 19_{5}||Is 37_{5} Est $3_{2.3}$ 4_{11} 5_{11}, עַבְדֵי מֶלֶךְ *servants of the king of* 1 K 20_{23} (עַבְדֵי ...) 2 K 3_{11} 24_{10} (עַבְדֵי ...; עבדי lacking in mss), נַעֲרֵי־הַמֶּלֶךְ *servants of the king* Est 2_{2} $6_{3.5}$, נַעֲרֵי מֶלֶךְ *servants of the king of* 2 K 19_{6}||Is 37_{6}, סְרִיס הַמֶּלֶךְ *eunuch of the king* Est $2_{3.14.15.21}$, סָרִיסֵי *eunuchs of* Est 4_{5} $6_{2.14}$ (or em. רָצֵי *guards of*), מַשְׁקֵה מֶלֶךְ *butler of the king of* Gn 40_{1},

סֹפֵר הַמֶּלֶךְ *secretary of the king* 2 K 12_{11}||2 C 24_{11}, סֹפְרֵי *secretaries of* Est 3_{12} 8_{9}, רֵעֶה הַמֶּלֶךְ *friend of the king* 1 K 4_{7}, רֵעַ *friend of* 1 C 27_{33}, חֹזֶה *seer of* 1 C 25_{5} 2 C 29_{25} 35_{15} (חוֹזֶה; mss חוֹזֵי *seers of*), מַלְאֲכֵי מֶלֶךְ *messengers of the king of* 2 K 1_{3}, ידיד המלך *beloved one of the king* 4QM[h] 6_{6}, [מרוממי ה]מלך *ones who extol the king* 4QShirShabb[d] 1.1_{13}.

חֵיל מֶלֶךְ *army of the king of* Jr 32_{1} $34_{6.21}$ 38_{3} 46_{2} (חֵיל ...) 1 C 18_{9} (חֵיל ...) 2 C 16_{7}, צְבָא *army of* 2 K 5_{1}, סֹחֲרֵי הַמֶּלֶךְ *traders of the king* 1 K 10_{29}||2 C 1_{16}, פְּקֻדַּת *office*, i.e. officers, *of* 2 C 24_{11}, עֲבֹדַת *service of* 1 C 26_{30}, הֲלִיכוֹת ... מַלְכִּי *processions of ... my king* Ps 68_{25}, עדת המלך *congregation of the king* 4QShirShabb[d] 1.2_{24}, מרוחקי מלך perh. *ones made far of*, i.e. from, *the king* 4Q476 1_{4}.

יַד הַמֶּלֶךְ *hand of the king* 1 S 23_{20} 1 K 10_{13} 13_{6} $22_{6.12}$||2 C $18_{5.11}$ 1 K 22_{15} Est 1_{7} 2_{18} Ne 11_{24} 1 C 18_{17} 2 C 30_{6}, יַד מֶלֶךְ *hand of the king of* Dt 7_{8} Jg 3_{8} 4_{2} (all three יַד ...) 1 S 12_{9} 1 K 22_{3} 2 K 13_{3} 17_{7} (both יַד ...) $18_{30.33}$||Is $36_{15.18}$ 2 K 19_{10}||Is 37_{10} Jr 20_{4} 21_{7} (יַד ...) 21_{10} 22_{25} 27_{6} 29_{21} (all three יַד ...) $32_{3.4.28}$ (יַד ...) 32_{36} 34_{2} 37_{17} 38_{23} 44_{30} 46_{25} Ezk 30_{10} (all three יַד ...) 30_{25} 2 C $28_{5.5}$ 32_{22} (יַד ...) CD 1_{6} (יַד ...), יַד מַלְכֵי *hand of the kings of* Dt 3_{8} (יַד ...) Ezr 9_{7}, יַד מַלְכּוֹ *hand of his king* Zc 11_{6}, יד מלכינו *hand of our kings* 1QM 11_{3}, יד מלכיה[ם] *hand of their kings* 4QparaKings 10_{4}, יְדֵי הַמֶּלֶךְ *hands of the king* 2 K 13_{16} 1 C $25_{2.6}$, יְדֵי ... מֶלֶךְ *hands*, i.e. direction, *of ... the king of* Ezr 3_{10}, כַּף מֶלֶךְ *hand of the king of* 2 K 16_{7} 20_{6}||Is 38_{6} 2 C 32_{11}, כַּף מַלְכֵי *hand of the kings of* 2 C 30_{6}, זְרוֹעַ ... מֶלֶךְ *arm of ... the king of* Ezk 30_{21}, זְרֹעוֹת מֶלֶךְ *arms of the king of* Ezk $30_{24.25}$, עֵינֵי הַמֶּלֶךְ *eyes of the king* 2 S 24_{3} (עֵינֵי ...) Est 1_{21} $2_{4.4}$ 5_{8} 2 C 30_{4}, עֵינֵי מֶלֶךְ *eyes of the king of* Jr 34_{3}, אָזְנֵי הַמֶּלֶךְ *ears of the king* Jr $36_{20.21}$, שִׂפְתֵי־מֶלֶךְ *lips of the king* Pr 16_{10} 4QShirShabb[b] 14.2_{8}, פִּי־ *mouth*, i.e. word of Ec 8_{2}, פִּי הַמֶּלֶךְ *mouth of the king* Est 7_{8}, צַוְּארֵי הַמְּלָכִים *necks of the kings* Jos 10_{24}, רֹאשׁ ... מֶלֶךְ *head of ... the king of* 2 K 25_{27}||Jr 52_{31}, ראש מלכי *head of the kings of* CD $8_{11(A)}$=$19_{24(B)}$.

לֵב הַמֶּלֶךְ *heart of the king* 2 S 14_{1} Jr 4_{9} Pr 21_{1} (מֶלֶךְ) Est 1_{10} Ezr 7_{27}, לֵב מֶלֶךְ *heart of the king of* Ex 14_{8} (לֵב ...) 2 K 6_{11} Ezr 6_{22}, לֵב מְלָכִים *heart of kings* Pr 25_{3}, לְבַב מֶלֶךְ *heart of the king of* Is 10_{12}, מָתְנֵי מְלָכִים *loins of kings* Is 45_{1}, שֹׁד *breast of* Is 60_{16}, עַצְמוֹת מֶלֶךְ *bones of the king of* Am 2_{1}, עַצְמוֹת מַלְכֵי *bones of the kings of* Jr 8_{1}, פְּנֵי הַמֶּלֶךְ *face*, i.e. presence, *of the king* 2 S $14_{24.28.32}$ 2 K 25_{19}||Jr 52_{25} Pr 16_{25} (מֶלֶךְ) Est $1_{10.14}$ Si 7_{5} (מלך), פְּנֵי מֶלֶךְ *face*, i.e. presence, *of the king of* 1 S 22_{4} 2 K 3_{14} (פְּנֵי ...) 4QShirShabb[a] 1.1_{8}, פִּגְרֵי מַלְכֵיהֶם *corpses of their kings* Ezk $43_{7.9}$, רוּחַ הַמֶּלֶךְ *spirit of the king* 2 S 13_{39} (if em. דָּוִד *David* to רוּחַ), רוּחַ ... מֶלֶךְ *spirit of ... the king of* Ezr 1_{1}||2 C 36_{22} 1 C $5_{26.26}$, רוּחַ מַלְכֵי *spirit of the kings of* Jr 51_{11}, זֶרַע הַמֶּלֶךְ *seed*, i.e. offspring, *of the king* 1 K 11_{14} (or em. הַמְּלוּכָה *of the kingship*), שֵׁם הַמֶּלֶךְ *name of the king* Est 3_{12} $8_{8.8.10}$ 2 C 30_{6} (if ins.), שֵׁם ... מֶלֶךְ *name of ... the king of* Jr 46_{17} (if em. שָׁם *there* to שֵׁם), תְּרוּעַת מֶלֶךְ *shout of a king* Nm 23_{21} (or em. תְּרוּעַת to תּוֹרַעַת *majesty of*).

פִּרְדַּת הַמֶּלֶךְ *mule of the king* 1 K $1_{38.44}$.

כְּלֵי מַשְׁקֵה הַמֶּלֶךְ *drinking vessels of the king* 1 K 10_{21}||2 C 9_{20}, מִשְׁתֵּה הַמֶּלֶךְ *feast of the king* 1 S 25_{36}, מַעֲדַנֵּי־מֶלֶךְ *delicacies of a king* Gn 49_{20}, פַּת־בַּג הַמֶּלֶךְ *delicacies of the king* Dn $1_{5.8.13.15}$ (all three פַּתְבַּג), עֹלַת־הַמֶּלֶךְ *burnt offering of the king* 2 K 16_{15}, שְׁלַל ... מֶלֶךְ *spoil of ... the king of* 2 S 8_{12}, גִּנְזֵי הַמֶּלֶךְ *treasuries of the king* Est 3_{9} 4_{7}, אֹצְרוֹת *treasuries of* 1 C 27_{25} 2 C 38_{18}, אוצרות מלכים *treasures of kings* GnzPs 3_{15}, אוֹצְרוֹת מַלְכֵי *treasures of the kings of* Jr 20_{5}, סְגֻלַּת מְלָכִים *treasure of kings* Ec 2_{8}, מִדַּת הַמֶּלֶךְ *tribute of the king* Ne 5_{4}, רְכוּשׁ *property of* 2 C 35_{7}, חמדת מלכים *preciousness*, i.e. treasure, *of kings* GnzPs 3_{15}, חפצי *delights of* GnzPs 2_{27}, שֻׁלְחַן הַמֶּלֶךְ *table of the king* 1 S 20_{29} 2 S 9_{13} 1 K 5_{7}, כִּסֵּא ... הַמֶּלֶךְ *throne of ... the king* 1 K $1_{20.27.37}$, כִּסֵּא הַמְּלָכִים *throne of the kings* 2 K 11_{19} 25_{28}||Jr $52_{32(Qr)}$ (Kt מלכים).

חֲנִית הַמֶּלֶךְ *spear of the king* 1 S $26_{16.22(Qr, mss)}$ (Kt החנית), חֶרֶב מֶלֶךְ *sword of the king of* Ezk 21_{24} 32_{11}, עֲטֶרֶת־מַלְכָּם *crown of their king* 2 S 12_{30}||1 C 20_{2} (2 S ms מַלְכָּהּ *of its king*; or em. מִלְכֹּם *of Milcom*), טַבַּעַת הַמֶּלֶךְ *(signet) ring of the king* Est 3_{12} $8_{8.8.10}$, כְּלֵי ... מֶלֶךְ *instruments of ... the king of* 2 C 29_{27}, אֶבֶן הַמֶּלֶךְ *weight of the king*, i.e. the royal standard weight 2 S 14_{26}, גִּזֵּי *reapings of* Am 7_{1}.

עֵמֶק הַמֶּלֶךְ *valley of the king* Gn 14_{17} 2 S 18_{18}, אֶרֶץ ... מֶלֶךְ *land of ... the king of* Dt $4_{46.47}$ 1 K 4_{19} Ne $9_{22.22}$,

גְּבוּל ... border of ... Jos 12$_{4}$ (or del. גְּבוּל) 12$_{5}$, עִיר ... city of ... Nm 21$_{26}$, עָרֵי הַמְּלָכִים cities of the kings Jos 11$_{12}$, עָרֵי ... מֶלֶךְ cities of the king of Jos 13$_{10}$, קִרְיַת מֶלֶךְ city of the king Ps 48$_{3}$, מְדִינוֹת הַמֶּלֶךְ provinces of the king Est 1$_{16.22}$ 3$_{13}$ 4$_{11}$ 8$_{5.12}$ 9$_{2.12.16.20}$, מַמְלֶכֶת ... מֶלֶךְ kingdom/reign of ... the king of Nm 32$_{33.33}$ Jr 27$_{1}$ 28$_{1}$, מַמְלְכוּת ... kingdom/reign of ... Jos 13$_{21.27.30}$ Jr 26$_{1}$, מַלְכוּת ... הַמֶּלֶךְ reign of ... the king Dn 8$_{1}$ Ezr 8$_{1}$, מַלְכוּת מֶלֶךְ kingdom/reign of the king of Jr 49$_{34}$ Dn 1$_{1}$ (both מַלְכוּת ...) Dn 11$_{9}$ Ezr 4$_{5}$ 7$_{1}$ (both מַלְכוּת ...), עֹל מֶלֶךְ yoke of the king of Jr 27$_{8.11.12}$ 28$_{2.4.11}$ (עֹל ...).

בֵּית הַמֶּלֶךְ house(hold) of the king 2 S 11$_{2.8.9}$ 15$_{35}$ 16$_{2}$ 19$_{19}$ 1 K 9$_{1}$||2 C 7$_{11}$ 1 K 9$_{10}$ 10$_{12}$||2 C 9$_{11}$ 1 K 14$_{26.27}$||2 C 12$_{9.10}$ 1 K 15$_{18(mss, Qr)}$||2 C 16$_{2}$ (1 K Kt מֶלֶךְ) 1 K 16$_{18.18}$ (מֶלֶךְ) 2 K 7$_{9.11}$ 11$_{5.16.19}$||2 C 23$_{5.15.20}$ 2 K 11$_{20(Qr)}$ (Kt מלך) 14$_{14}$||2 C 25$_{24}$ 2 K 15$_{25(Qr)}$ (Kt מלך) 16$_{8}$ 18$_{15}$ 24$_{13}$ 25$_{9}$||Jr 52$_{13}$ Jr 26$_{10}$ 36$_{12}$ 38$_{7.8.11}$ 39$_{8}$ Ho 5$_{1}$ Est 2$_{8.9.13}$ 4$_{13}$ 5$_{1.1}$ 6$_{4}$ 9$_{4}$ Ne 3$_{25}$ 2 C 21$_{17}$ 26$_{21}$ 28$_{21}$, בֵּית מֶלֶךְ house of the king of Jr 21$_{11}$ 22$_{1.6}$ 27$_{18.21}$ 32$_{2}$ 38$_{22}$ 2 C 8$_{11}$ (בֵּית ...), בָּתֵּי מַלְכֵי houses of the kings of Jr 19$_{13}$ 33$_{4}$.

הֵיכַל הַמֶּלֶךְ palace of the king Ps 45$_{16}$ (מֶלֶךְ; or del.) Dn 1$_{4}$ Si 50$_{2}$ (מלך) 50$_{7}$, הֵיכַל מֶלֶךְ palace of the king of 1 K 21$_{1}$ (הֵיכַל ... מֶלֶךְ) 2 K 20$_{18}$||Is 39$_{7}$, הֵיכְלֵי מֶלֶךְ palaces/temples of the king Pr 30$_{28}$ 4QShirShabb^{a} 1.1$_{13}$, היכלי מלכים palaces of kings GnzPs 2$_{26}$, בִּיתַן הַמֶּלֶךְ palace of the king Est 1$_{5}$, מִקְדַּשׁ מֶלֶךְ sanctuary of the king Am 7$_{13}$, דביר מלך inner sanctuary of the king 4QShirShabb^{c} 2$_{4}$ 4QShirShabb^{f} 15.2$_{3}$ (המלך) 19$_{3}$ (דב[יר]), דבירי מלך inner sanctuaries of the king 4QShirShabb^{f} 14.1$_{7}$, [מעון מ]ל[ך] habitation of the king of 4QShirShabb^{d} 1.1$_{46}$, סוכת המלך booth of the king CD 7$_{16}$, סֻכַּת מַלְכְּכֶם booth of your king Am 5$_{6}$ (if em.; see App.), מַחֲנֵה מֶלֶךְ camp of the king of 2 C 32$_{21}$.

מְבוֹא הַמֶּלֶךְ entrance of the king 2 K 16$_{18}$, מבואי מלך entry of the king 4QShirShabb^{f} 14.1$_{5}$, שַׁעַר הַמֶּלֶךְ gate of the king Est 2$_{19.21}$ 3$_{2.3}$ 4$_{2.2.6}$ 5$_{9.13}$ 6$_{10.12}$ 1 C 9$_{18}$, גַּן garden of 2 K 25$_{4}$||Jr 52$_{7}$ Jr 39$_{4}$ Ne 3$_{15}$, חַדְרֵי מַלְכֵיהֶם chambers of their kings Ps 105$_{30}$ (or em. מֶלֶךְ יֶהֱמוּ of the king they croaked), מָעוֹז מֶלֶךְ stronghold of the king of Dn 11$_{17}$, מְקוֹם הַמֶּלֶךְ place of the king Ezk 17$_{16}$, יִקְבֵי wine-vats of Zc 14$_{10}$, בְּרֵכַת pool of Ne 2$_{14}$, קִבְרוֹת הַמְּלָכִים tombs of the kings 2 C 21$_{20}$ 24$_{25}$, קִבְרֵי מַלְכֵי tombs of the kings of 2 C 28$_{27}$.

דֶּרֶךְ הַמֶּלֶךְ way of the king Nm 20$_{17}$ 21$_{22}$, דֶּרֶךְ מַלְכֵי way of the kings of 2 K 8$_{18}$||2 C 21$_{6}$ 2 K 16$_{3}$ 2 C 21$_{13}$, דַּרְכֵי ... מֶלֶךְ ways of ... the king of 2 C 21$_{12}$, דַּרְכֵי מַלְכֵי ways of the kings of 2 K 8$_{18(ms)}$ 2 C 28$_{2}$, מִשְׁפַּט הַמֶּלֶךְ manner of the king 1 S 8$_{9.11}$, מוּסַר מְלָכִים discipline of kings Jb 12$_{18}$ (or em. מוֹסֵר bond of), רָעוֹת מַלְכֵי wickedness of the kings of Jr 44$_{9}$, עֹז מֶלֶךְ strength of a king Ps 99$_{4}$.

דְּבַר־הַמֶּלֶךְ word of the king 1 S 21$_{9}$ 2 S 14$_{17}$ (דְּבַר־ ...) 24$_{4}$||1 C 21$_{4}$ 2 K 18$_{28}$ Ec 8$_{4}$ (מֶלֶךְ) Est 1$_{12.13}$ 2$_{16}$ 3$_{15}$ 4$_{3}$ 5$_{8}$ 8$_{14.17}$ 9$_{1}$ 1 C 21$_{6}$ 26$_{32}$ 2 C 19$_{11}$ Arad ost. 24$_{17}$, דִּבְרֵי words of Is 36$_{13}$ Ne 2$_{18}$ 1 C 29$_{29}$ (דִּבְרֵי ...), דִּבְרֵי ... מֶלֶךְ words of ... the king Pr 31$_{1}$ (unless transfer athnach) Ec 1$_{1}$, דִּבְרֵי מֶלֶךְ words of the king of 2 C 33$_{18}$ Pr 31$_{1}$ (if transfer athnach) 2 C 32$_{8}$ (both דִּבְרֵי ...), אִמְרַת מֶלֶךְ word of the king Pr 20$_{2}$ (if em.; see below), אמרי מלך words of the king 4QShirShabb^{f} 23.1$_{11}$, מִצְוַת הַמֶּלֶךְ command of the king 2 K 18$_{36}$||Is 36$_{21}$ Est 3$_{3}$ Ne 11$_{23}$ 2 C 8$_{15}$ 2 C 24$_{21}$ 29$_{15}$ 30$_{6.12}$ 35$_{10.16}$, מַאֲמַר command of Est 1$_{15}$, טַעַם decree of Jon 3$_{7}$, פִּתְגָם decree of Est 1$_{20}$, דָּתֵי law of Est 3$_{8}$ Ezr 8$_{36}$, נְאֻם־ oracle of Jr 46$_{18}$ 48$_{15}$ 51$_{57}$, מִשְׁלֵי ... מֶלֶךְ proverbs of ... the king of Pr 1$_{1}$, כְּתָב ... writing of ... 2 C 35$_{4}$, אִגְּרוֹת הַמֶּלֶךְ letters of the king Ne 2$_{9}$, ס[פר] המלך letter of the king Lachish ost. 6$_{4}$, סֵפֶר הַמְּלָכִים book of the kings 2 C 16$_{11}$ 24$_{27}$, סֵפֶר מַלְכֵי book of the kings of 1 C 9$_{1}$ 2 C 20$_{34}$ 25$_{26}$ 27$_{7}$ 28$_{26}$ 32$_{32}$ 35$_{27}$ 36$_{8}$.

מִפְקַד ... הַמֶּלֶךְ appointment of ... the king 2 C 31$_{13}$, רִשְׁיוֹן ... מֶלֶךְ permission of ... the king of Ezr 3$_{7}$, מַשְׂאַת הַמֶּלֶךְ present of, i.e. from, the king 2 S 11$_{8}$, מְנָת portion of 2 C 31$_{3}$ (or em. מַתְּנַת present of), גורל מלך lot of the king of 4QapPs^{b} 76$_{7}$, מַשָּׂא מֶלֶךְ burden of a king of Ho 8$_{10}$ (or em. מַשָּׂא to מִמְּשֹׁחַ from anointing), מְלֶאכֶת הַמֶּלֶךְ work of the king Dn 8$_{27}$ 1 C 29$_{6}$, רְצוֹן־מֶלֶךְ favour of a king Pr 14$_{35}$ 16$_{13(mss)}$ (L מְלָכִים of kings) 22$_{11}$ (if em.; see Nom. Cl.).

הַדְרַת־מֶלֶךְ adornment of a king Pr 14$_{28}$ (or em. הֲדַר honour of or עֶזְרַת help of), כבוד המלך glory of the king 4QShirShabb^{a} 1.2$_{8}$ 4QShirShabb^{f} 23.1$_{9}$, מלך of the king of 4QShirShabb^{a} 2$_{5}$ 4QShirShabb^{f} 24$_{3}$, כְּבֹד מְלָכִים glory of kings Pr 25$_{2}$, הו[ד המ]לך splendour of the king 4QShirShabb^{d} 1.1$_{17}$, קודש מלך holiness of the king of

11QShirShabb 10$_{5}$, מִשְׂרְפוֹת ... הַמְּלָכִים *burnings of*, i.e. for, ... *the kings* Jr 34$_{5}$, חֲמַת הַמֶּלֶךְ *anger of the king* 2 S 11$_{20}$ Pr 16$_{14}$ (מֶלֶךְ־) Est 2$_{1}$ 7$_{10}$, זַעַף מֶלֶךְ *anger of the king* Pr 19$_{12}$, אֵימַת *terror of* Pr 20$_{2}$ (or em. חֲמַת *anger of* or אִמְרַת *word of*), מורא מלך *fear of the king of* 23.1$_{13}$, תּוֹעֲבַת מְלָכִים *abomination of kings* Pr 16$_{12}$, שְׁנַת הַמֶּלֶךְ *sleep of the king* Est 6$_{1}$, נֵזֶק *injury of*, i.e. to Est 7$_{4}$, גָּלוּת *exile of* Ezk 1$_{2}$, גָּלוּת ... מֶלֶךְ *exile of ... the king of* 2 K 25$_{27}$||Jr 52$_{31}$.

יוֹם מַלְכֵּנוּ *day of our king* Ho 7$_{5}$ (or em. מַלְכָּם *of their king*), יְמֵי מֶלֶךְ *days of the king* Is 23$_{15}$ Jr 3$_{6}$ (יְמֵי ... הַמֶּלֶךְ) Ps 61$_{7}$, יְמֵי ... מֶלֶךְ *days of ... the king of* Gn 14$_{1.1.1.1}$ Is 7$_{1}$ Jr 1$_{2.3}$ 26$_{18}$ 35$_{1}$ Ho 1$_{1}$ Am 1$_{1.1}$ Zc 14$_{5}$ Ezr 4$_{2.5}$ 1 C 4$_{41}$ 5$_{17.17}$ 2 C 30$_{26}$, יְמֵי מַלְכֵי *days of the kings of* 2 K 23$_{22}$ Is 1$_{1}$ Ho 1$_{1}$ Mc 1$_{1}$ Zp 1$_{1}$ (all four ... יְמֵי), מוֹת הַמֶּלֶךְ *death of the king* Is 6$_{1}$ 14$_{28}$, מוֹת ... מֶלֶךְ *death of ... the king of* 2 K 14$_{17}$||2 C 25$_{25}$.

כָּל־מֶלֶךְ *any king* 1 C 29$_{25}$, כָּל־הַמְּלָכִים *all the kings* Jos 9$_{1}$ 10$_{42}$ 11$_{5}$ (כֹּל) 11$_{18}$ 12$_{24}$ 2 S 10$_{19}$ 1 K 20$_{12(ms)}$ Is 62$_{2}$ Ps 72$_{11}$ (both מְלָכִים) 2 C 9$_{26}$ 4QsapHymnA 10$_{4}$ (כו[ל] מלכים), כָּל־מַלְכֵי *all the kings of* Jos 5$_{1}$ 10$_{6}$ 1 K 5$_{14}$ 10$_{15.23}$||2 C 9$_{14.22}$ (כֹּל) 1 K 10$_{29}$||2 C 1$_{17}$ 1 K 16$_{33}$ (כֹּל) 2 K 18$_{5}$ (כֹּל) Is 14$_{9}$ (כֹּל) 14$_{18}$ Jr 25$_{20.20.22.22.24.24.25.25.25.26}$ Ps 102$_{16}$ 138$_{4}$ (or em.; see above) 2 C 9$_{23}$ (כֹּל) 35$_{18}$ 1QpPs 9$_{1}$ (כול מל[כי]) 4QMyst[a] 60$_{4}$ 4QM[a] 11.1$_{12}$ GnzPs 1$_{24}$ 2$_{12}$, כָּל־מַלְכֵיהֶם *all their kings* Jos 10$_{40}$ 11$_{12.17}$ Ho 7$_{7}$.

<APP> Y. Is 6$_{5}$ Is 43$_{15}$ 44$_{6}$ Zp 3$_{15}$ (or em.; see Cstr.) Zc 14$_{16,17}$ Ps 84$_{4}$ 98$_{6}$, אֵל *God* Ps 68$_{25}$ 4QShirShabb[d] 1.2$_{26}$ 4QShir[b] 52.3$_{4}$, אֱלֹהִים *God* Ps 74$_{12}$ 145$_{1}$.

Abimelech Gn 20$_{2}$ 26$_{1.8}$, Achish 1 S 21$_{11.13}$ 27$_{2}$ 1 K 2$_{39}$, Adonijah 1 K 1$_{25}$, Adoni-zedek Jos 10$_{1.3}$, Agag 1 S 15$_{8.20.32}$, Ahab 1 K 20$_{2.13}$ 21$_{1.18}$ 22$_{41}$ 2 K 21$_{3}$ 2 C 18$_{3.19}$ 4QParaKings 2$_{2}$ ([ה]מלך), Ahasuerus Est 1$_{2.9.10.15.16.17.19}$ 2$_{1.12.16.21}$ 3$_{1.7.8.12}$ 6$_{2}$ 7$_{5}$ 8$_{1.7.10.12}$ 9$_{2.20}$ 10$_{1.3}$, Ahaz 2 K 16$_{1.10.10.11.11}$ (lacking in mss) 16$_{15.16.17}$ 17$_{1}$ Is 1$_{1}$ 7$_{1}$ 14$_{28}$ (or em. אָחָז הָיָה *Ahaz there was* to וָאֶחֱזֶה *and I saw*) Ho 1$_{1}$ Mc 1$_{1}$ 2 C 28$_{16.19.22}$ 29$_{19}$, Ahaziah 2 K 8$_{25.29}$||2 C 22$_{6(mss)}$ 2 K 9$_{16.21.27}$ 10$_{13}$ 12$_{19}$ 2 C 20$_{35}$ 22$_{1}$, Amaziah 2 K 13$_{12}$ 14$_{1.9.11.13.17}$||2 C 25$_{18.21.23.25}$ 2 K 14$_{15.23}$ 15$_{13(mss).17}$ 2 C 25$_{17}$, Amon 2 K 21$_{24}$||2 C 33$_{25}$, Amraphel Gn 14$_{1.9}$, Arioch Gn 14$_{1.9}$, Artaxerxes Ezr 4$_{7}$ 7$_{1.7.11}$ 8$_{1}$ Ne 2$_{1}$ 5$_{14}$ 13$_{6}$, Asa 1 K 15$_{9}$ (mss read עַל *over* for מֶלֶךְ *king of*) 15$_{17}$||2 C 16$_{1}$ 1 K 15$_{18.20.22}$||2 C 16$_{4.6}$ 1 K 15$_{22.25.28.33}$ 16$_{8.10.15.23.29}$ Jr 41$_{9}$ 2 C 15$_{16}$ 16$_{7}$ 21$_{12}$, Azariah 2 K 15$_{1.8.23.27}$ 2 C 22$_{6}$.

Baalis Jr 40$_{14}$, Baasha 1 K 15$_{16.17.19}$||2 C 16$_{1.3}$ 1 K 15$_{32}$ Jr 41$_{9}$, Balak Nm 22$_{10}$ 23$_{7}$ Jos 24$_{9}$ Jg 11$_{25}$ Mc 6$_{5}$, Belshazzar Dn 8$_{1}$, Ben-hadad 1 K 15$_{18}$||2 C 16$_{2}$ 1 K 20$_{1}$ (both mss Ben-hadar) 20$_{20}$ 2 K 6$_{24}$ 8$_{7.9}$, Bera Gn 14$_{2}$, Birsha Gn 14$_{2}$, Chedorlaomer Gn 14$_{1.9}$, Coniah Jr 22$_{24}$, Cushan-rishathaim Jg 3$_{8.10}$, Cyrus Dn 1$_{21}$ 10$_{1}$ Ezr 1$_{1.1.2.7}$||2 C 36$_{22.22.23}$ Ezr 1$_{8}$ 3$_{7}$ 4$_{3.5}$, Darius Hg 1$_{1.15}$ Zc 7$_{1}$ Ezr 4$_{5}$, David 1 S 21$_{12}$ 2 S 3$_{31}$ 5$_{3}$ 6$_{12.16}$||1 C 15$_{29}$ 2 S 7$_{18}$||1 C 17$_{16}$ 2 S 8$_{8.10.11}$||1 C 18$_{10.11}$ 2 S 9$_{5}$ 13$_{21.39}$ (or em.; see Cstr.) 16$_{5.6}$ 17$_{17.21}$ 19$_{12.17}$ 20$_{21}$ 1 K 1$_{1.13.13.28.31.32.37.38.43.47}$ 2 K 11$_{10}$||2 C 23$_{9}$ Jr 30$_{9}$ Ho 3$_{5}$ Ezr 3$_{10}$ 1 C 24$_{31}$ 26$_{26.32}$ 27$_{24.31}$ 28$_{2}$ 29$_{1.9.24.29}$ 2 C 2$_{11}$ 7$_{6}$ 8$_{11}$ 29$_{27}$ 35$_{4}$, Debir Jos 10$_{3}$, Demetrius 4QpNah 3.1$_{2}$ (דמי[טרוס]).

Eglon Jg 3$_{12.14.15.17}$, Esar-haddon Ezr 4$_{2}$, Ethbaal 1 K 16$_{31}$, Evi Nm 31$_{8}$, Evil-merodach 2 K 25$_{27}$||Jr 52$_{31}$, Hadadezer 2 S 8$_{3.5}$||1 C 18$_{3.5}$ 2 S 8$_{12}$ 1 K 11$_{23}$ (mss Hadarezer) 1 C 18$_{9}$, Hazael 2 K 8$_{28.29}$||2 C 22$_{5.6}$ 2 K 9$_{14.15}$ 12$_{18.19}$ 13$_{3.22.24}$, Hezekiah 2 K 18$_{1.9.13}$||Is 36$_{1}$ 2 K 18$_{14.14.16.17}$||Is 36$_{2}$ 2 K 19$_{1.5.10}$||Is 37$_{1.5.10}$ 2 K 20$_{14}$||Is 39$_{3}$ Is 1$_{1}$ 38$_{9}$ Jr 26$_{18.19}$ Ho 1$_{1}$ Mc 1$_{1}$ Pr 25$_{1}$ 1 C 4$_{41}$ 2 C 29$_{18.20.30}$ 30$_{34}$ 31$_{13}$ 32$_{8.9.20.23}$, Hiram 2 S 5$_{11}$||1 C 14$_{1}$ 1 K 5$_{15}$ 9$_{11}$ 2 C 2$_{2.10}$, Hoham Jos 10$_{3}$, Hophra Jr 44$_{30}$, Horam Jos 10$_{33}$, Hoshea 2 K 18$_{1.9.10}$, Hur Nm 31$_{8}$.

Jabin Jos 11$_{1}$ 4$_{2.17.23.24.24}$, Japhia Jos 10$_{3}$, Jeconiah Jr 24$_{1}$ 27$_{20}$ 28$_{4}$ 29$_{2}$ Est 2$_{6}$, Jehoahaz 2 K 14$_{8}$||2 C 25$_{17}$, J(eh)oash 2 K 12$_{7.8.19}$ 13$_{1.10.14}$ 14$_{1.9.11.13.17}$||2 C 25$_{18.21.23.25}$ 2 C 24$_{22}$ perh. Kuntillet 'Ajrud inscr. E1 (א[שיו] ה[מלך]), J(eh)oiachin 2 K 24$_{12}$ 25$_{27.27}$||Jr 52$_{31.31}$ Ezk 1$_{2}$, Jehoiakim Jr 1$_{3}$ 22$_{18}$ 25$_{1}$ 26$_{1.21.22.23}$ 27$_{1}$ (mss Zedekiah) 35$_{1}$ 36$_{1.9.28.29.30.32}$ 45$_{1}$ 46$_{2}$ Dn 1$_{1.2}$, J(eh)onathan Alexander Jannaeus Coin 5, J(eh)oram 2 K 1$_{17}$ 3$_{6}$ 8$_{16.16.25.29}$= 9$_{15.21}$ 11$_{2}$ 12$_{19}$ 2 C 22$_{5.11}$, Jehoshaphat 1 K 22$_{2.10}$||2 C 18$_{9}$ 1 K 22$_{52}$ 2 K 3$_{1.7.12(ms).14}$ 12$_{19}$ 2 C 18$_{3}$ 19$_{1.2}$ 20$_{15.35}$ 21$_{2}$, Jehotham Bulla D1, Jeroboam 1 K 15$_{1}$||2 C 13$_{1}$ 15$_{9}$ 2 K 14$_{23}$ 15$_{1}$ Ho 1$_{1}$ Am 1$_{1}$ 7$_{10}$ 1 C 5$_{17}$, Jobab Jos 11$_{1}$, Jonathan 4QJonathan 2$_{2}$ 3$_{8}$ (ה[מלך]), Josiah 2 K 22$_{3}$ 23$_{23.29}$ Jr 1$_{2}$ 3$_{6}$ 25$_{3}$ Zp 1$_{1}$ 2 C 35$_{16.23}$, Jotham 2 K 15$_{32}$ Is 1$_{1}$ Ho 1$_{1}$ Mc 1$_{1}$ 1 C 5$_{17}$.

Koheleth Ec 1$_{1}$, Lemuel Pr 31$_{1}$, Manasseh 2 K 21$_{11}$

Jr 15$_{4}$ 4QapPs^{b} 33$_{8}$, Melchizedek Gn 14$_{18}$, Merodach-baladan 2 K 20$_{12(mss)}$||Is 39$_{1}$ (2 K 20$_{12[L]}$ Berodach-baladan), Mesha 2 K 3$_{4}$, Nahash 1 S 12$_{12}$ 1 C 19$_{1}$, Nebuchadn/rezzar 2 K 24$_{1}$||2 C 36$_{6}$ 2 K 24$_{10.11}$ 25$_{1.8}$||Jr 52$_{4.12}$ 2 K 25$_{22}$ Jr 21$_{2.7}$ 22$_{25}$ 24$_{1}$ 25$_{1.9}$ 27$_{6.8.20}$ 28$_{3.11.14}$ 29$_{3.21}$ 32$_{28}$ 34$_{1}$ 35$_{11}$ 37$_{1}$ 39$_{1.5.11}$ 43$_{10}$ 44$_{30}$ 46$_{2.13.25}$ 49$_{28.30}$ 50$_{17}$ 51$_{34}$ Ezk 26$_{7}$ 29$_{18.19}$ 30$_{10}$ Est 2$_{6}$ Dn 1$_{1}$ Ezr 2$_{1}$||Ne 7$_{6}$ 2 C 36$_{10.13}$ CD 1$_{6}$, Neco 23$_{29}$||2 C 35$_{2}$ Jr 46$_{2}$, Og Nm 21$_{33}$ 32$_{33}$ Dt 1$_{4}$ 3$_{1.3.11.47}$ 29$_{6}$ 31$_{4}$ Jos 2$_{10}$ 9$_{10}$ 12$_{4}$ 13$_{30}$ 1 K 4$_{19}$ Ps 135$_{11}$ 136$_{20}$ Ne 9$_{22}$, Omri 2 K 8$_{26}$, Pekah 2 K 15$_{29.32}$ 16$_{5}$=Is 7$_{1}$, Piram Jos 10$_{3}$, Pul 2 K 15$_{19}$ 1 C 5$_{26}$, Reba Nm 31$_{8}$, Rekem Nm 31$_{8}$, Rehoboam 1 K 12$_{6.18.18}$ ||2 C 10$_{6.18.18}$ 1 K 12$_{23}$||2 C 11$_{3}$ 1 K 12$_{27.12}$ 14$_{25.27}$||2 C 12$_{2.10}$ 2 C 10$_{13}$ 12$_{13}$, Rezin 2 K 15$_{37}$ 16$_{5}$=Is 7$_{1}$ 2 K 16$_{6}$.

Sargon Is 20$_{1}$, Saul 1 S 18$_{6}$ 29$_{3}$, Sennacherib 2 K 18$_{13}$||Is 36$_{1}$ 2 K 19$_{20.36}$||Is 37$_{21.37}$ 2 C 32$_{1.9.10.22}$, Shallum Jr 22$_{11}$, Shalmaneser 2 K 17$_{3}$ 18$_{9}$, Shemeber Gn 14$_{2}$ (Sam^{mss} Shemebed), Shinab Gn 14$_{2}$, Shishak 1 K 11$_{40}$ 14$_{25}$||2 C 12$_{2}$, Sihon Nm 21$_{21.26.29.34}$ 32$_{33}$ Dt 1$_{4}$ 2$_{24.26.30}$ 3$_{2.6}$ 4$_{46}$ 29$_{6}$ 31$_{4}$ Jos 2$_{10}$ 9$_{10}$ 12$_{2.5}$ 13$_{10.21.27}$ Jg 11$_{19}$ 1 K 4$_{19}$ Ps 135$_{11}$ 136$_{19}$ Ne 9$_{22}$ (if del. וְאֶת־אֶרֶץ *and the land of*), So 2 K 17$_{4}$, Sikkuth Am 5$_{26}$=CD 7$_{14}$ (or em. סִכּוּת to סַכּוּת *Sakkuth* or סֻכַּת *booth of* or מַסֵּכוֹת *molten images of*), Solomon 1 K 1$_{34.39.51}$ 2$_{17.19.22.23.25.29.45}$ 4$_{1}$ 5$_{7.7.27}$ (in all three mss lack Solomon) 6$_{2}$ (ms lacks הַמֶּלֶךְ) 7$_{13.14.40.45}$||2 C 4$_{11.16}$ 1 K 7$_{51}$ 8$_{1.2.5}$||2 C 5$_{6}$ 1 K 9$_{15.26.28}$|| 2 C 8$_{18}$ 1 K 10$_{10.13}$||2 C 9$_{9.12}$ 1 K 10$_{13.16.21.23}$||2 C 9$_{15.20.22}$ 1 K 11$_{1}$ 12$_{2}$||2 C 10$_{2}$ 2 K 23$_{13}$ 24$_{13}$ Jr 52$_{20}$ Pr 1$_{1}$ Ca 3$_{9.11}$ Ne 13$_{26}$ 2 C 7$_{5}$ 8$_{10}$ 30$_{26}$ 35$_{3}$.

Talmai 2 S 3$_{3}$||1 C 3$_{2}$ 2 S 13$_{37}$, Tidal Gn 14$_{1.9}$, Tiglath-pileser 2 K 15$_{29}$ 16$_{7.10}$ 1 C 5$_{6(mss).26(mss)}$ 2 C 28$_{20(mss)}$ (L all three Tillegath-pilneser), Tirhakah 2 K 19$_{9}$||Is 37$_{9}$, Toi 2 S 8$_{9}$||1 C 18$_{9}$, Uzziah 2 K 15$_{13}$ Is 6$_{1}$ Ho 1$_{1}$ Am 1$_{1}$ Zc 14$_{5}$ 2 C 26$_{18.21}$ 3QpIsa 1$_{4}$ ([ל]עזיה), Zalmunna Jg 8$_{5.12}$, Zebah Jg 8$_{5.12}$, Zedekiah 2 K 25$_{2}$||Jr 52$_{5}$ Jr 1$_{3}$ 21$_{1.7}$ 24$_{8}$ 27$_{1(mss).3.12}$ 28$_{1}$ 29$_{3}$ 32$_{1.3.4}$ 34$_{2.4.6.8.21}$ 37$_{1}$ (or del.) 37$_{3.17.18.21}$ 38$_{5.14.16.19}$ 39$_{1.4}$ 44$_{30}$ 49$_{34}$ 51$_{59}$ 4QApocWeeks$_{4}$ ([צד]קיה) 4QMMT C$_{19}$, Zur Nm 31$_{8}$.

Amorite Dt 2$_{24}$, Canaanite Nm 21$_{1}$ 33$_{40}$, גּוֹי *nation* Jr 51$_{28}$.

אִישׁ *man*, i.e. each 2 K 9$_{21}$ Is 14$_{18}$ Jr 25$_{26}$, אָב *father* 2 K 12$_{19}$ 14$_{5}$||2 C 25$_{3}$ 2 K 14$_{29}$ Jr 34$_{5}$, בֵּן *son* Nm 22$_{10}$ Jos 24$_{9}$ Jg 11$_{25}$ 1 S 27$_{2}$ 2 S 8$_{3}$||1 C 18$_{3}$ 2 S 8$_{12}$ 13$_{37}$ 1 K 12$_{23}$||2 C 11$_{3}$ 1 K 15$_{1}$||2 C 13$_{1}$ 1 K 15$_{18}$ 2 K 1$_{17}$ 8$_{9.16.16.25.25.29}$||2 C 22$_{6}$ 2 K 13$_{1}$ 14$_{1.1.8.13.17.17}$||2 C 25$_{17.23.25.25}$ 2 K 14$_{23.23}$ 15$_{1.32.32}$ 16$_{1.5}$=Is 7$_{1}$ 2 K 18$_{1.1.9}$ 20$_{12}$||Is 39$_{1}$ Is 7$_{1.6}$ Jr 1$_{2.3.3}$ 15$_{4}$ 22$_{11.18.24}$ 24$_{1}$ 25$_{1.3}$ 26$_{1}$ 27$_{1.20}$ 28$_{4}$ 35$_{1}$ 36$_{1.9}$ 37$_{1}$ (or del.) 45$_{1}$ 46$_{2}$ Ho 1$_{1}$ Am 1$_{1}$ Zp 1$_{1}$ Pr 1$_{1}$ Ec 1$_{1}$ 2 C 22$_{1.5}$ 30$_{26}$ 35$_{3}$, שַׂר *prince* Is 49$_{7}$, מֹשֵׁל *ruler* Ps 105$_{20}$, אָדוֹן *lord* Gn 40$_{1}$ 1 S 24$_{9}$ 26$_{15.15.17.19}$ 29$_{8}$ 2 S 3$_{21}$ 4$_{8}$ 9$_{11}$ 13$_{33}$ 14$_{9.11(mss).12.15.17.17.18.19.19.22}$ 15$_{15.21.21}$ 16$_{4.9}$ 18$_{28.31.32}$ 19$_{20.21.27.28.28.29.31.36.38}$ 24$_{3.3.21.22}$ 1 K 1$_{2.2.18.20.21.24.27.27.31.36.37.37.43.47}$ 2$_{38}$ 12$_{27}$ 20$_{4.9}$ 2 K 6$_{12.26}$ 8$_{5}$ 18$_{23}$||Is 36$_{8}$ 2 K 19$_{4}$||Is 37$_{4}$ Jr 37$_{20}$ 38$_{9}$ Dn 1$_{10}$ 1 C 21$_{3.23}$ 4QShirShabb^{d} 1.1$_{28}$ ([ה]אדו[ן] מלו[ך]), פַּרְעֹה *Pharaoh* Gn 41$_{46}$ Ex 6$_{11.13.27.29}$ 14$_{8}$ Dt 7$_{8}$ 11$_{3}$ (lacking in Sam) 1 K 3$_{1}$ 9$_{16}$ 11$_{18}$ 2 K 17$_{7}$ 18$_{21}$||Is 36$_{6}$ 2 K 23$_{29}$ Jr 25$_{19}$ 44$_{30}$ 46$_{2.17}$ Ezk 29$_{2.3}$ 30$_{21.22}$ 31$_{2}$ 32$_{2}$.

עֶבֶד *servant* 2 S 10$_{19}$ Jr 25$_{9}$ 27$_{6}$ 43$_{10}$, גֹּאֵל *redeemer* Is 44$_{6}$, קָדוֹשׁ *holy one* Is 43$_{15}$, עַז *strong one* Dn 8$_{23}$ (עַז־פָּנִים *strong one of face*, i.e. impudent), גִּבּוֹר *mighty one* perh. 4QapJoseph^{b} 5$_{3}$, גְּדַפָּן *blasphemer* 4Qps Ezek^{d} 1.2$_{3}$, רִאשׁוֹן *first one* Jr 50$_{17}$, אַחֲרוֹן *last one* Jr 50$_{17}$, רַב pl. *many* 4QpNah 3.2$_{9}$, תַּנִּין *sea monster* Ezk 29$_{3}$, מַיִם *water* Is 8$_{7}$ (or del.), יוֹם *day* Is 7$_{17}$.

<ADJ> גָּדוֹל *great* 2 K 18$_{19.28}$||Is 36$_{4.13}$ Jr 25$_{14}$ 27$_{7}$ Ml 1$_{14}$=5QapMal 1$_{3}$ Ps 47$_{3}$ 95$_{3}$ 136$_{17}$ Ec 9$_{14}$ Nimrud ivory inscr. 1$_{2}$, יָרֵב *great* Ho 5$_{13}$ 10$_{6}$ (unless מֶלֶךְ יָרֵב = *a king, may he contend*, i.e. from ריב *contend*; or em. מֶלֶךְ/מַלְכֵּי רָב *great king*), רַב *great* Ps 48$_{3}$, pl. *many* Jr 50$_{41}$, עַז *strong* Is 19$_{4}$, גִּבּוֹר *mighty* Dn 11$_{3}$, עָצוּם *mighty* Ps 135$_{10}$, אַדִּיר *majestic* Ps 136$_{18}$, חָכָם *wise* Pr 20$_{26}$, חָדָשׁ *new* Ex 1$_{8}$, זָקֵן *old* Ec 4$_{13}$, רִאשׁוֹן *former* Nm 21$_{26}$ Jr 34$_{5}$ Dn 8$_{21}$, רָחוֹק *distant* Jr 25$_{26}$, קָרוֹב *near* Jr 25$_{26}$, עָתִיד *ready* Jb 15$_{24}$, אֶחָד *one* Jos 12$_{9+30t}$ Is 23$_{15}$ Ezk 37$_{22}$, אֵלֶּה *these* Dt 3$_{21}$ Jos 10$_{16.22.24.42}$ 11$_{5.12.18}$ 2 K 3$_{10.13}$.

<PREP> לְ of direction, *to* 1 K 10$_{29}$||2 C 1$_{17}$ 2 K 3$_{13}$ perh. 4QShirShabb^{f} 15.2$_{7}$, + אמר *say* 1 K 1$_{1}$ 2$_{17.38}$ 20$_{2.9.22}$ 2 K 6$_{10}$ 13$_{16.18}$ (or del.) 17$_{26}$ Jr 13$_{18}$ Ezk 28$_{12}$ Ps 45$_{2}$ (unless vocative lamed, *O king!*)* Jb 34$_{18}$ Ec 8$_{4}$ Est 2$_{22}$ 3$_{8}$ 5$_{14}$ 6$_{4}$ Ezr 8$_{22}$ Ne 2$_{3.5.7}$ 1 C 28$_{2}$ 2 C 26$_{18}$ 4QpsEzek^{e} 25$_{5}$ (למל[ך]), ni. *be said* Jos 2$_{2}$, דבר pi. *speak* 1 K 2$_{19}$ Dn 2$_{4}$, נגד hi. *tell* 2 S 14$_{33}$ 17$_{17.21}$ 2 S 18$_{21.25}$ 1 K 1$_{23}$ 2 K 6$_{10.12}$ 7$_{15}$ 22$_{10}$||2 C 34$_{18}$ Jr 36$_{16}$ 51$_{31}$ Dn 2$_{2}$ Si 46$_{20}$, ho. *be*

told Ex 14_{5} 2 S 6_{12} 1 K 2_{29} 2 K 8_{7}, ספר pi. *tell* 2 K $8_{4.5.6}$, pu. *be told* Is 52_{15}, קרא *call* 1 K $1_{28.32}$ 2 K $3_{10.13}$, זעק hi. *call together* 2 S 20_{4}, שׁיר *sing* 4QHod[a] 7.1_{11}, זמר pi. *sing praise* Ps 47_{7} MasShirShabb 2_{18}, רנן *sing joyfully* MasShirShabb 2_{15} ([ורנן]), ידה hi. *give praise* 4QShirShabb[d] 1.1_{38} (למ[ל]ך), חנן htp. *make supplication* Est 4_{8} 8_{3}, שׁמע ni. *be reported* Ne 6_{7}.

אתה *come* Jr 10_{7}, בוא hi. *bring* 1 K 1_{3} 2 C 32_{23} perh. Lachish ost. 5_{10} (א[ב]י), יבל ho. *be brought* Ho 10_{6} (or em. יוּבָל *it shall be brought* to יוֹבִלוּ *they shall bring*, i.e. hi.) Ps 45_{15}, עלה hi. *bring up* 2 K 17_{4}, קרב hi. *bring near* Jg 3_{17}, שׁוב hi. *bring back* 2 K 3_{4} 17_{3}, צעד hi. *make march* Jb 18_{14}, שׁור *journey* Is 57_{9} (or em. וַתָּשֻׁרִי to וַתְּשֻׁרִי or וַתֶּעְשְׁרִי *and you abounded*, from שׁרר, and em. לַמֶּלֶךְ to לְמַלְכֵּךְ or לְמַלֵּךְ *for your hair*), שׁלח *send* Jg 3_{15} 1 K 9_{14} 2 K 12_{19} 16_{8} 2 C 24_{23}.

לקח *take* 1 K 3_{24}, יהב *give* 4QHod[a] 7.1_{13}, נתן *give* Gn $14_{18.21}$ Nm 21_{29} 1 S 2_{10} 2 S 4_{8} 24_{23} 1 K $10_{10.10}$||2 C $9_{9.9}$ 1 K 15_{17}||2 C 16_{1} 2 K 15_{20} 18_{16} Jr 27_{6} 28_{14} Ezk 29_{19} Ps 21_{2} 72_{1} 89_{28} 144_{10} Ezr 1_{2}||2 C 36_{23} Ne $2_{1.6}$ 1 C 28_{2} 2 C 2_{11} 25_{16} 28_{21} 11QT 58_{13}, מלא pi. *give in full* 1 S 18_{27}, שׁאר hi. *leave* Dt 3_{3} Jos 10_{33}, נוח hi. *give rest* 2 S 7_{1}, עשׂה *do* Nm 21_{34} Dt $3_{2.6.21}$ 11_{3} (lacking in Sam) 31_{4} Jos 2_{10} $8_{2.2}$ $9_{10.10.10}$ $10_{1.1.28.28.30.30.39.39}$ 1 K 2_{23} 2 K 6_{30} Lachish ost. 6_{11} (ו[ת]עשו), רבה hi. *make great*, i.e. yield Ne 9_{37}, צרר hi. *cause distress* 2 C 28_{22}, שׁחה htpal. *bow down* 2 S 14_{33} 18_{28} 2 S 24_{20} 1 K $1_{16.23.31.53}$ Zc $14_{16.17}$ Ps 45_{12} (or del.) 1 C 29_{20} 2 C 24_{17}.

לְ of benefit, *to, for* 1 S 19_{4} 2 S 18_{5} Mc 1_{14} Pr $31_{4.4}$ 2 C 35_{21} 1QM 12_{7} perh. 4QShirShabb[c] 3.2_{12} 4QShirShabb[d] 1.1_{3} ([ל[מ]ל[ך]) $1.2_{25.26}$ 4QShirShabb[f] 14.1_{3} perh. 4QsapHymnA 1.1_{13} 4QJonathan 3_{8} ([המלך]) 4QShir[a] 1_{1} (ל[מ]לך) Beersheba jug inscr. T. Qasile ost. 1_{1} Bullae 97 100 ([למלך]) Fiscal Bullae 1* 2*, + היה *be* 2 S $19_{36(ms)}$ 2 K 16_{15} Dn 9_{8} 2 C 28_{22}, יטב *be good* Jr 38_{19}, שׁוה *be suitable* Est 3_{8}, עשׂה *do* 1 K $7_{40.45}$||2 C $4_{11.16}$ Est $5_{4.8}$, ארר *curse* Nm 23_{7}, ירא ni. *be terrible* Ps 76_{13}, שׂים *place* 1 S 8_{11}, בקשׁ pi. *seek* 1 K 1_{2} Est 2_{2}, שׁמר *protect* 2 S $18_{12(mss)}$, חמם *be warm* 1 K $1_{1.2}$, שׂרף *burn* Jr 34_{4}, קרע *tear* 4QpsEzek[c] 3.2_{9}, כון ho. *be prepared* Is 30_{33} (or em. לַמֹּלֶךְ *for Molech*), חדל *cease* 2 C 35_{21}.

לְ of possession, *of, (belonging) to* Gn 14_{22} 40_{5} 1 S 18_{25} 1 K 1_{33} 10_{22}||2 C 9_{21} 1 K $14_{19.25}$||2 C 12_{2} 1 K 14_{29} 15_{1}||2 C 13_{1} 1 K $15_{7.9.23.25.28.31.33}$ $16_{5.8.10.14.15.20.23.27.29}$ 20_{4} 22_{31}||2 C 18_{29} 1 K $22_{39.41.46.52}$ 2 K $1_{17.18}$ 3_{1} 7_{2} (mss הַמֶּלֶךְ) $8_{16.23.25}$ 10_{34} 11_{10}||2 C 23_{9} 2 K $12_{7.20}$ $13_{1.8.10.12}$ $14_{1.15.23.28}$ $15_{1.6.8.11.13.15.17.21.23.26.27.31.32.36}$ 16_{19} 17_{1} $18_{1.9.9.13}$||Is 36_{1} 2 K 20_{20} $21_{17.25}$ 22_{3} $23_{23.28}$ 24_{5} $25_{2.8}$||Jr $52_{5.12}$ Is 38_{9} Jr 1_{3} $25_{1.1.3}$ 32_{1} $36_{1.9}$ 39_{1} 45_{1} 46_{2} Hg $1_{1.15}$ Zc 7_{1} Est 1_{9} 3_{7} 9_{3} $10_{2.3}$ Dn 1_{21} 10_{1} Ezr 1_{1}||2 C 36_{22} Ezr $7_{7.8}$ Ne 1_{1} $2_{1.8}$ 5_{14} 13_{6} 1 C $27_{24.31.33.34}$ 28_{1} 29_{1} 2 C 8_{10} 20_{15} 26_{23} 33_{11} 35_{23} 4QapPs[b] 31_{4} ([ל ... מ[לך]) 33_{8} 4QShirShabb[f] 23.2_{11} Lachish royal bath inscr. T. Beit Mirsim inscr. 1 ([ל[מלך]) Bulla 901 (7th cent.) Weight 43 50 (8th/7th cent.), היה *be* 1 S 8_{11} 18_{18} 27_{6} 1 K $1_{2.4}$ 2 K 17_{3} $24_{1.7}$ Jr 36_{30} Ezk 29_{18} 2 C 1_{12}, מצא ni. *be found* 11QT 59_{13}.

לְ *as* 1 K 14_{4} (or em. לְמַלֵּךְ *to be king*), + ישׁב *sit* 1 C 29_{23}, מלך hi. *cause to reign* Jg 9_{6} 1 S $15_{11.17}$, משׁח *anoint* Jg 9_{8} 1 S 15_{1} 2 S $2_{4.7}$ 5_{3}||1 C 11_{3} 2 S 5_{17} 12_{7} 1 K $1_{34.45}$ 5_{15} $19_{15.16}$ 2 K $9_{3.6.12}$, ni. *be anointed* 1 C 14_{8}, שׂים *place* 1 K 10_{9}, נתן *give* 2 C $9_{8.8}$, כון hi. *establish* 2 S 5_{12}||1 C 14_{2}, בקשׁ pi. *seek* 2 S 3_{17}.

לְ introducing object, + מצא *find*, i.e. befall Ne 9_{32}, בזה *despise* 2 S 6_{11}||1 C 15_{29}, עזר *help* 2 S 8_{5}||1 C 18_{5} Dn 11_{40} 2 C 26_{13} 28_{16}, שׁאל *ask* 2 S 8_{10}||1 C 18_{10}, נשׁק *kiss* 2 S 14_{33}, עטר pi. *crown* Ca 3_{11}, ברך pi. *bless* MasShirShabb 2_{2} ([ו]ברך למל[ך]), גדל hi. *magnify* 4QShirShabb[d] 1.1_{31} (appar. יקדילו is error for יגדילו), צור *besiege* 2 C 28_{19}, ירה hi. *shoot* 2 C 35_{23}, הרג *kill* Ps $135_{11.11}$ $136_{19.20}$.

לְ introducing predicate, + היה *be* Dt 33_{5} (if em.; see subj.) Ezk 37_{22} Zc 14_{9} 1 C 28_{4}, הוה *be* Ne 6_{6}.

לְ *against*, + חטא *sin* Gn 40_{1} 1 S 19_{4} Jr 37_{18}, אנה htp. *seek occasion* 2 K 5_{7}, נתן *give*, i.e. make Jr 1_{18}; *on the part of, in respect of*, + חרה *be angry* 2 S 13_{21}, בלע pu. *be swallowed up* 2 S 17_{16}; *according to*, + מלך *reign* Is 32_{1}; *before* 2 S 19_{29}, + חוב pi. *make guilty* Dn 1_{10}; עמד לְ *stand*, i.e. wait, *for* 1 K 20_{38}, ספד לְ *mourn for* Jr 22_{18} 34_{4}.

בְּ of place, *(with)in, among* 2 S 19_{44} (עֶשֶׂר יָדוֹת ... בַּמֶּלֶךְ *ten portions ... in the king*) Ezk 28_{12} Ho 7_{7}, + היה *be* Jos 5_{1} 1 K 3_{13} 2 K 18_{5}, מצא ni. *be found* Ezk 28_{12}, בער *burn* Est 1_{12}.

בְּ *against*, + עוד hi. *testify* Ne 9_{34}, לחם ni. *fight* Nm

21_{26} 1 S 14_{47} 1QM 14, נשׂא *lift* hand 2 S 18_{28} 20_{21}, רום hi. *lift* hand 1 K $11_{26.27}$, שׁלח *send*, i.e. lift, hand Est 2_{21} 6_{2}, מרד *rebel* 2 K 18_{7} $24_{1.20}$||Jr 52_{3} 2 C 36_{13}, פשׁע *rebel* 2 K $3_{5.6}$, עשׂה *do* Ps 149_{11}.

בְּ of agent, instrument, *by (means of), with*, + שׁבע ni. *swear* Zp 1_{5} (or em. בְּמַלְכָּם *by Milcom*) Ps 63_{12}, ברך htp. *bless oneself* Ps 72_{1}, גלח pi. *shave* Is 7_{20}.

בְּ introducing object, + ראה *see* Ca 3_{11}, בחר *choose* Dt 7_{15} 1 C 28_{2}, רצה *accept* 1 C 28_{2}, פרץ *urge* 2 S $13_{25.27}$ (both 4QSam^{a} פצר *urge*), פגע hi. *entreat* Jr 36_{25}, קלל pi. *curse* Is 8_{21}, עלל htp. *abuse* Jr 38_{19}, קלס htp. *mock* Hb 1_{10}, תעע htp. *mock* 1QpHab 4_{2}, עבד *enslave* Jr 27_{7}, נכה hi. *strike* 2 C 28_{22}.

בְּ *over*, + רדה *rule* 1 K 5_{4}, משׁל *rule* 2 C 9_{26}; *to*, + חתן htp. *become son-in-law* 1 S $18_{22.23.26.27}$, דבק *cling* 2 S 20_{2}; *on account of, concerning*, + גיל *rejoice* Ps 149_{2}.

כְּ *as* 1 K 22_{4} Jr 10_{7}, + היה *be* 2 K 18_{1} Ne 13_{26}, שׁכן *dwell* Jb 29_{25}, עשׂה *do* 2 K 17_{2}, תקף *prevail against* Jb 15_{24}.

מִן of direction, *(away) from*, + היה *be* 2 S 3_{37}, בקשׁ pi. *seek* Si 7_{4}, שׁאל *ask* Ezr 8_{22}, ni. Ne 13_{6}, עמד *stand* Dn 11_{8}, כחד pi. *hide* 2 S 14_{18} Jr 38_{14}, ni. *be hidden* 2 S 18_{13}, עלם ni. *be hidden* 1 K 10_{3}.

מִן *from*, i.e. at the expense of, + אכל *eat* 2 S 19_{43}; *from*, i.e. both (... and) Nimrud ivory inscr. 1_{2} (ממלך גדל [ו]עד [אש] *from great king and unto [private] person*); *from (being)*, + מאס *reject* 1 S 15_{23} (Gnz מִמֶּלֶךְ *from being king*).

מִן of comparison, *(more) than* Jg 11_{25} Ec 4_{13}, + גדל *be great* 1 K 10_{23}||2 C 9_{22}, חזק *be strong* 2 K 3_{26}, יסף hi. *add* 1 K 16_{33}.

מִן introducing object or *on account of*, + ירא *fear* Jr 42_{11}.

מִן *of, with*, + שׂבע hi. *satisfy* Ezk 32_{2}, מלא ni. *be full* Ezk 32_{2}.

לְבַד מִן *apart from* 1 K 10_{15}||2 C 9_{14}.

אֶל *to* Jg 3_{19} 1 K 22_{13}||2 C 18_{12} 2 K 6_{11}, + היה *be* 2 S 19_{36}, אמר *say* Gn 14_{22} Ex 3_{18} 1 S 22_{3} 2 S 4_{8} 7_{3} $9_{3.4.11}$ $13_{6.35}$ 14_{4} $15_{7.15}$ $16_{3.9}$ 18_{28} $19_{20.31.35.42}$ 21_{5} $24_{3.23}$ 1 K 1_{13} 2_{42} 3_{26} 10_{6}||2 C 9_{5} 1 K 12_{23}||2 C 11_{3} 1 K 13_{8} $20_{7.23.28}$ $22_{4.5}$||2 C 18_{4} 1 K 22_{15} 2 K 3_{12} 8_{9} 19_{10}||Is 37_{10} 2 K 20_{14}||Is 39_{3} 2 K 22_{18}||2 C 34_{26} Jr 17_{19} 34_{2} $37_{7.18}$ 38_{4} Ezk 31_{2} 32_{2} Est 6_{6} 2 C 16_{7} 19_{2}, דבר *speak* Jr 38_{19}, pi. Ex $6_{11.27.29}$ 2 S 11_{19} 13_{13} $14_{3.12.15.15}$ 1 K 2_{18} 13_{11} 22_{16}||2 C 18_{15} 2 K $1_{6.15}$ 4_{13} 7_{18} Jr 27_{12} 34_{6} 36_{30} $38_{8.25}$ Dn 9_{6}, קרא *call* 1 S 26_{14} 2 S 14_{33} 2 K 18_{18}, זעק *cry out* 2 S 19_{29}, צעק *cry out* 1 K 20_{39} 2 K 6_{26} $8_{3.5}$, פלל htp. *pray* Ps 5_{3}, רגל pi. *slander* 2 S 19_{28}, שׁמע *listen* 1 K 15_{20}||2 C 16_{4}.

הלך *go* Gn 26_{1} 2 S $19_{27(mss)}$, hi. *bring* 2 K $25_{20(mss)}$||Jr 52_{26}, בוא *come* Ex 3_{18} 1 S 21_{11} 22_{11} 2 S $3_{23.24}$ 5_{3}||1 C 11_{3} (or em. לְהַמְלִיכוֹ *to make him king*) 2 S 13_{24} $14_{3.4(mss).33.33}$ $15_{2.6}$ $19_{6.12.42}$ 1 K $1_{13.15}$ 2_{19} 3_{16} 7_{14} 11_{18} 20_{32} 22_{15}||2 C 18_{14} 2 K 5_{6} 20_{14}||Is 39_{3} 2 K 22_{9}||2 C 34_{16} Jr 27_{3} 36_{20} Est $2_{12.13.14.15}$ $4_{8.11.11.16}$ Dn $11_{6.15}$ Ne 13_{6} 2 C 16_{7} 29_{18}, hi. *bring* 1 K 9_{28}||2 C 8_{18} 2 K 5_{6} Jr 26_{23} Ezk 19_{9} (or del.) 2 C 9_{12}, יצא *go out* 1 K 20_{31} 2 K 18_{31}||Is 36_{16} 2 K $24_{12(mss)}$, עלה hi. *bring up* 2 K 25_{6}||Jr 52_{9}, ירד *go down* 1 K 22_{2}, נגשׁ *draw near* 1 K 20_{22}, ni. 1 K 20_{13}, שׁוב *go back* 2 S 20_{22} 1 K 12_{12}||2 C 10_{12} 1 K $12_{27.27}$ $13_{6.6}$ 2 K 1_{6}, עבר *pass over* 1 S 27_{2} 2 S 19_{37}, ברח *flee* 1 K 2_{39} 11_{40}, נוס *flee* 6QapSamKgs 33_{3}, נפל *fall*, i.e. desert 2 K 25_{11}||Jr 52_{15} (2 K if em. עַל *to*).

שׁלח *send* Nm 20_{14} 21_{21} Dt 2_{26} Jos $10_{3.3.3.3}$ $11_{1.1.1.2}$ Jg $11_{12.14.17.17.19}$ 2 S 8_{10}||1 C 18_{10} 2 S $14_{29.32}$ 19_{15} $20_{2.7.9}$ 2 K 3_{7} $5_{5.7.8}$ 6_{9} $14_{8.9}$||2 C $25_{17.18}$ 2 K 16_{7} $18_{14.17}$||Is 36_{2} Jr 25_{9} $27_{3.3.3.3.3}$ 29_{3} Ho 5_{13} Am 7_{10} 2 C 2_{2}, קבץ *gather* 2 S 3_{21}, קהל ni. *assemble* 1 K 8_{2}||2 C 5_{3}, hi. *assemble* 1 K 8_{1}, בקע hi. *break through* 2 K 3_{26}, נתן *give* 2 S 24_{9}, לקח *take* Jr 38_{14}, ni. *be taken* Est 2_{16}.

אֶל *for*, + בקע *split open* 2 C 32_{1}; *in support of, on behalf of*, + דבר pi. *speak* Est $7_{9(Gnz)}$, שׁמר *guard* 2 K 11_{1} (or del.); *concerning*, + אמר *say* 2 K 19_{32}||Is 37_{33} Jr $22_{11.18}$ 29_{16}, צוה pi. *charge* Ex 6_{13}, פלל htp. *pray* 2 K 19_{20}||Is 37_{21}, שׁמע *hear* 2 K 19_{9}; *against* Ezk 30_{22}; *over*, + שׁמר *watch* 1 S 26_{15}; *beside* 2 K 11_{14}; introducing object, + נגע *reach* Jon 3_{6}.

עַל *upon, over* Jg 8_{26} 1 K 1_{20}, + היה *be* 1 C 29_{25}, עבר *pass*, i.e. befall 1 C 29_{29}, נתן *give*, i.e. impose 2 K 18_{14}, שׂים *place*, i.e. impose 2 K 18_{14}, שׁוה pi. *place* Ps 21_{2}, פרשׂ *spread* Ezk 32_{2}, שׁכן hi. *cause to settle* Ezk 32_{2}, קדר hi. *make dark* Ezk 32_{2}, תקע *clap* hands Na 3_{18}, שׁען ni. *rely* 2 C 16_{7}, עור *rouse oneself*, i.e. guard 4QJonathan 2_{2}.

עַל *beside, with* 2 K 11_{11}||2 C 23_{10} 2 C 23_{13}, + נצב ni.

stand 1 S 22$_{17}$, יעד ni. *gather oneself* 1 K 8$_{5}$||2 C 5$_{6}$.

עַל *against* Ezk 29$_{3}$ 2 C 19$_{2}$ 35$_{21}$, + נבא ni. *prophesy* Ezk 29$_{2}$, הלך *go* Jg 4$_{24}$ 2 C 22$_{5}$, בוא *come* 2 C 28$_{19}$, hi. *bring* Jr 36$_{30}$, עלה *go up* 1 K 20$_{22}$ 2 K 23$_{29}$, קום *rise up* 2 S 18$_{32}$, עמד *stand* Dn 11$_{14}$ 2 C 26$_{18}$, נשׂא *raise* Is 14$_{4}$ Ezk 28$_{12}$ 32$_{2}$, קשׁר *conspire* 2 K 21$_{24}$||2 C 33$_{25}$ Am 7$_{10}$, חשׁב *plot* Dn 11$_{25}$, מרד *rebel* Ne 2$_{19}$, עור hi. *stir* Dn 11$_{25}$, קצף *be angry* 2 K 13$_{18}$, שׂער htp. *storm* Dn 11$_{40}$, חזק *be strong* Dn 11$_{5}$, עוה *do wrong* Est 1$_{16}$.

עַל *concerning* 1QpPs 9$_{1}$ (מל[כי]) 4QpNah 3.1$_{2}$ ([על]), + אמר *say* Jr 36$_{29.30}$, שׁמע *hear* Is 37$_{9}$, כרת *cut*, i.e. make, covenant 2 C 23$_{3}$ (if em. עִם *with*).

עַל *to* Est 1$_{19}$ 3$_{9}$ 5$_{4.8}$ 7$_{3}$ 8$_{5}$ 9$_{13}$ Ne 2$_{5.7}$, + כתב *write* Ezr 4$_{7}$, הלך hi. *bring* 2 K 25$_{20}$, יצא *go out* 2 K 24$_{12}$, שׁלח *send* 2 C 28$_{16}$ 32$_{9}$, נפל *fall*, i.e. desert 2 K 25$_{11}$ (or em. אֶל *to*).

עַל *for, on behalf of*, + דבר pi. *speak* Est 7$_{9}$; *on account of*, + שׁמם *be appalled* Ezk 28$_{12}$, hi. *make appalled* Ezk 32$_{2}$, שׂער *be horrified* Ezk 32$_{2}$.

עַל introducing object, + נקף hi. *surround* 2 K 11$_{8}$, פקד *visit*, i.e. punish Is 24$_{21}$ Jr 25$_{12}$ 36$_{30}$ 46$_{25}$ 50$_{18.18}$, i.e. charge Ezr 1$_{2}$||2 C 36$_{23}$; בטח עַל *trust in* 2 K 18$_{21}$||Is 36$_{6}$.

עִם *with, against* 1 K 8$_{62}$ 10$_{26}$||2 C 1$_{14}$ Pr 30$_{31}$ (וּמֶלֶךְ אֲלְקוּם עִמּוֹ *and a king—God is with him* Pr 30$_{31}$; mss אַל־קוּם appar. against whom *no one stands*; or em. לָקוּם עַל עַמּוֹ *as he stands over his people*) 2 C 32$_{7.9}$ 4QMyst[a] 53$_{12}$ 5QBéat 2.2$_{9}$, + היה *be* 2 S 14$_{17}$ 1 K 1$_{37}$ 2 K 18$_{1}$, דבר pi. *speak* 1 K 1$_{14.22}$, קרא pass. *be invited* Est 5$_{12}$, ישׁב *dwell* 1 C 4$_{23}$, *sit* 1 S 20$_{5}$ 2 S 15$_{19}$, שׁכב *lie down* 2 K 14$_{29}$, נוח *rest* Jb 3$_{14}$, hi. *place* 2 C 9$_{25}$, הלך *go* 2 S 19$_{26}$ 2 K 8$_{28}$, בוא *come* 1 K 13$_{8}$ Est 5$_{14}$ 2 C 25$_{7}$, hi. *bring* Est 5$_{12}$, עבר *pass over* 2 S 19$_{38.41}$, גלה ho. *be exiled* Est 2$_{6}$, שׁלח *send* 11QT 58$_{3(mg)}$, מצא ni. *be found* 2 C 19$_{2}$, חבר pi. *bring into alliance* 2 C 20$_{35}$, htp. *make an alliance* 2 C 20$_{35}$, שׁלם hi. *make peace* 1 K 22$_{45}$, כרת *cut*, i.e. make, covenant 2 C 23$_{3}$ (or em.; see above), לחם ni. *fight* 2 K 13$_{12}$ 14$_{15}$ Dn 11$_{11}$ 2 C 27$_{5}$ (lacking in mss), נגח htp. *wage war* Dn 11$_{40}$, כבשׁ *rape* Est 7$_{8}$, עשׂה *do* 2 C 24$_{22}$, קבר *bury* 2 C 24$_{16}$, ni. *be buried* 2 K 13$_{13}$ 14$_{16}$.

אֵת *with, against* 2 S 16$_{14}$ 17$_{16}$ 1 K 8$_{5}$ 15$_{19}$||2 C 16$_{3}$ 2 K 23$_{2}$ Est 3$_{1}$, + היה *be* 2 K 11$_{8}$||2 C 23$_{7}$, דבר pi. *speak* 2 K 25$_{6}$||Jr 52$_{9}$, הלך *go* 2 S 19$_{27}$ 2 K 3$_{7}$ Jr 51$_{59}$ 2 C 22$_{5}$, בוא *come* 1 K 13$_{7}$, יצא *go out* 1 S 22$_{3}$, עלה *go up* 2 S 19$_{35}$, עבר *pass over* 2 S 19$_{32.34.37.39.41(Kt)}$, ישׁב hi. *cause to sit* Jb 36$_{7}$, מצא ni. *be found* 2 C 29$_{29}$, עשׂה *make* Gn 14$_{2.2.2.2.2}$ Jos 11$_{18}$ 2 K 18$_{31}$||Is 36$_{16}$, ערך *set* battle *in array* Gn 14$_{9.9.9.9}$, לחם ni. *fight* 1 K 22$_{31}$||2 C 18$_{30}$ 2 K 8$_{29}$||2 C 22$_{6}$ 2 K 9$_{15}$ 19$_{9}$||Is 37$_{9}$ Jr 21$_{4}$, חתן htp. *become son-in-law* 1 K 3$_{1}$, ערב htp. *strike a bargin* 2 K 18$_{23}$||Is 36$_{8}$.

מֵאֵת *from* 2 S 15$_{3}$ 4QShir[b] 52.3$_{4}$, + היה ni. *happen* 1 K 1$_{27}$, בוא *come* 1 K 5$_{14}$, שׁאל *ask* 1 K 2$_{19}$, ברח *flee* 1 K 11$_{23}$, נתן ni. *be given* 2 K 25$_{28}$||Jr 52$_{32}$, נשׂא *receive* Si 38$_{2}$, כלה *be determined* Est 7$_{7}$.

מֵעַל *from*, + שׁוב *go back* 2 K 18$_{14}$, עבר hi. *remove* Jon 3$_{6}$, פוץ ni. *be scattered* 2 K 25$_{5}$||Jr 52$_{8}$; *beside*, + עמד *stand* Jr 36$_{21}$.

בַּעַד *on behalf of, for*, + פלל htp. *pray* 1 K 13$_{6}$ (or del. הִתְפַּלֵּל בַּעֲדִי) Ps 72$_{1}$.

בִּגְלַל *on account of*, + נתן *give*, i.e. make Jr 15$_{4}$.

בַּעֲבוּר *on account of*, + כנע hi. *subdue* 2 C 28$_{19}$.

בֵּין *between* Jg 4$_{17}$, + היה *be* 1 K 15$_{16}$ 15$_{32}$, כרת *cut*, i.e. make, covenant 2 K 11$_{17}$||2 C 23$_{16}$ 2 K 11$_{17}$ (or del.).

בְּקֶרֶב *within* 1 K 3$_{28}$.

לִפְנֵי *before, in the presence of* 2 K 21$_{11}$ Est 7$_{9}$ Ne 2$_{1}$ 4Q476 1$_{6}$, + היה *be* 2 K 18$_{1}$ Jr 34$_{4}$ Ne 2$_{1}$, אמר *say* Est 1$_{16}$, דבר pi. *speak* 1 K 3$_{22}$ Est 8$_{3}$, נבא htp. *prophesy* 1 K 22$_{10}$||2 C 18$_{9}$, רוע hi. *shout joyfully* Ps 98$_{6}$, קרא *read* 2 K 22$_{10}$||2 C 34$_{18}$ 2 C 34$_{24}$, ni. *be read* Est 6$_{1}$, כתב *write* 1 C 24$_{6}$, ni. *be written* Est 2$_{23}$, בוא *come* 2 S 19$_{9}$ 1 K 1$_{23.28.32}$ Est 1$_{19}$ 8$_{1}$ 9$_{11.25}$, hi. *bring* 1 K 3$_{24}$ Est 1$_{11}$ 2 C 24$_{14}$, יצא *go out* 2 S 24$_{4}$, צלח *rush* 2 S 19$_{18}$, נשׂא *carry* Is 8$_{4}$ Est 2$_{17}$, נגשׁ hi. *bring near* 2 C 29$_{23}$, מצא *find* favour Est 8$_{5}$, יטב *be good* Ne 2$_{5.6}$, צדק htp. *justify oneself* Si 7$_{5}$, נתן *give*, i.e. place Ezk 28$_{17}$, נטה hi. *extend* Ezr 7$_{28}$ 9$_{9}$, הגה *remove* Pr 25$_{5}$, עמד *stand* Gn 41$_{46}$ 1 K 1$_{2.28}$ 3$_{16}$ 2 K 25$_{8}$||Jr 52$_{12}$ (2 K if em.; see Cstr.) Est 8$_{4}$ Dn 1$_{5.19}$ 2$_{2}$, יצב htp. *stand* Pr 22$_{29}$ Si 38$_{3(Bmg)}$ (B נדיבים *nobles*), כרע *bow down* Ps 72$_{1}$, שׁחה htpal. *bow down* 2 S 14$_{33}$ Ps 72$_{1}$, נפל *fall* 2 S 19$_{19}$ Jr 37$_{20}$, hi. *cause to fall* Jr 38$_{26}$ 1 C 24$_{31}$, בער pu. *burn* Jr 36$_{22}$, הדר htp. *claim honour* Pr 25$_{6}$, חזק pi. *strengthen* Si 45$_{3}$.

מִלִּפְנֵי *from before*, + יצא *go out* Est 8$_{15}$, בקשׁ pi. *seek* Est 4$_{8}$, בעת ni. *be terrified* Est 7$_{6}$; *on account of*, + זעק

cry out 1 S 8_{18}.

מִפְּנֵי *from (before),* + ברח *flee* 1 K 12_2||2 C 10_2, נצל ni. *be delivered* Is 20_6; *on account of* (sometimes perh. introducing object), + ירא *fear* 1 S 21_{13} 1 K 3_{28} Jr 42_{11}, חתת ni. *be terrified* 2 C 32_7, קוץ *dread* Is 7_{16}, שׁמר *keep watch* 2 K 9_{14}, סבב hi. *turn,* i.e. remove 2 K 16_{18}, עשׂה *make* Jr 41_9.

עַל־פְּנֵי *before,* + עבר *pass* 2 S 15_{18}.

נֶגֶד *before,* + דבר pi. *speak* Ps 119_{46}; *against,* + חנה *encamp* 1QM 15_2.

אַחֲרֵי *after,* + היה *be* 2 K 18_1, בוא *come* Ec 2_{12}, רדף *pursue* Jg 8_5 2 K 9_{27} 25_5||Jr 52_8 Jr 39_4, ישׁב *sit* 1 K $1_{20.27}$, מלך *be king* 1 K $1_{13.24}$.

אֵצֶל *beside,* + יתר *remain* Dn 10_{13} (unless em.; see Cstr.), ישׁב *sit* Ne 2_6.

תַּחַת *instead of, in place of,* + מלך *be king* 2 S 10_1||1 C 19_1 2 K 3_{26} 8_{15} 13_{24} 19_{36}||Is 37_{37}, hi. *make king* 2 K 21_{24}||2 C 33_{25}, שׂים *place* 1 K 20_{24}.

<COLL> מֶלֶךְ || רֹזֵן *ruler* Jg 5_3 Hb 1_{10} (+) Ps 2_2 Pr 8_{15} GnzPs 2_{12}, מֹשֵׁל *ruler* GnzPs 2_{12}, נָשִׂיא *prince* Jos 13_{21} (+) Ezk 7_{27} 32_{29}, שַׂר *prince, commander* Is 32_1 Jr 1_{18} 2_{26} 4_9 8_1 17_{25} 24_8 25_{18} 26_{21} 29_2 (+) 32_{32} 34_{21} 36_{21} $44_{17.21}$ $49_{3.38}$ Ezk 17_{12} Ho 3_4=CD 20_{16} Ho $7_{3.5}$ (+) 13_{10} Am 1_{15} Zp 1_8 (both +) Ps 148_{11} Jb 3_{14} Ec $10_{16.17}$ (both +) Lm 2_9 Est $1_{16.16.21}$ Dn $9_{6.8}$ Ezr 7_{28} (+) 8_{25} Ne $9_{32.34}$ 1 C 24_6 2 C 12_6 29_{30} $30_{2.6.12}$ 36_{18} 1QH 10_8 1QpHab 4_2 4QpNah 3.2_9 4QPseud[b] 8_3 Lachish ost. 6_4 (both +), שָׂרָה *queen* Is 49_{23}, גְּבִירָה *queen mother* 2 K 10_{13} Jr 13_{18} 29_2, אָדוֹן *lord* Is 19_4, נָדִיב *noble* Jb 34_{18}, מָשִׁיחַ *anointed one* 1 S 2_{10}, פֶּחָה *governor* Jr 51_{28}, סָגָן *prefect* Jr 51_{28} GnzPs 2_{12} (סגונים), גִּבּוֹר *mighty one* Jr 26_{21} 1QM 12_7 CD 3_9, גָּדוֹל *great one,* i.e. noble Jon 3_7 Pr 25_6 (+), רַב *great one* 1QpHab 4_2 (+), כבד ni. ptc. *honourable one* Ps 149_8 Si 48_6 1QpHab 4_2 (+), עָשִׁיר *rich one* Ec 10_{20}, מְחֹקֵק *commander* Is 33_{22}, שֹׁפֵט *judge* Is 33_{22} Ho 7_7 13_{10} (both +) Ps 2_{10} 148_{11} (+).

|| כֹּהֵן *priest* Jr 1_{18} 2_{26} 4_9 8_1 13_{13} (all three +) 32_{32} 49_3 Lm 2_6 Ezr 9_7 Ne $9_{32.34}$ 4QpNah 3.2_9 4QpsEzek[a] 16.1_{10}, נָבִיא *prophet* Jr 2_{26} 4_9 8_1 13_{13} (all three +) 32_{32} Ne 9_{32}, יוֹעֵץ *counsellor* Mc 4_9 (+) Ezr 7_{28} 8_{25}, חָכָם *wise one* Is 19_{11}, אָב *father* Jr 19_4 (+) Dn $9_{6.8}$ Ne $9_{32.34}$, גּוֹי *nation* Is 41_2 45_1 52_{15} (all three +) $60_{3.11}$ (+) 60_{16} 62_2 Jr 25_{14} 27_7 50_{41} Ps 72_{11} 102_{16} (+) 135_{10} GnzPs 3_{15}, לְאֹם *nation* Ps 148_{11} (+), עַם *people* Jr 1_{18} 29_{16} 50_{41} Est 1_{16} Ne 9_{32} (+) 4QpNah 3.2_9, בַּיִת *house* of Israel Jr 2_{26}, יֹשֵׁב *inhabitant* Jr 8_1 13_{13} $17_{20.25}$ (both +) 19_3 32_{32} Lm 4_{12} 2 C 20_{15} (+), סָרִיס *eunuch* Jr 29_2 (+), חָרָשׁ *artisan* Jr 29_2 (+), מַסְגֵּר *smith* Jr 29_2 (+), אֵל *God* Ps 95_3 Si 7_4 4QShirShabb[f] 14.1_3 4QHod[a] 7.1_{13} 4QM[a] 8.1_{13}, אֱלֹהִים *God* 1 K $21_{10.13}$ (both אֱלֹהִים וָמֶלֶךְ) Is 8_{21} Jr 10_{10} 30_9 46_{25} Ho 3_5 Ps Ps 84_4, צָבָא *host* of heaven Is 24_{21}.

:: חָשֹׁךְ *obscure one* Pr 22_{29}.

מֶלֶךְ as vocative, Jg 3_{19} 5_3 1 S 17_{55} 23_{20} 24_9 26_{17} 2 S $14_{9.19.22}$ 15_{34} 16_4 19_{27} 24_{23} (lacking in mss) 1 K $1_{18.20.24}$ 20_4 2 K $6_{12.26}$ 8_5 Jr 10_7 17_{20} 19_3 22_2 34_4 37_{20} 38_9 Ezk 29_3 Na 3_{18} Ps 2_{10} 5_3 84_4 145_1 Est 7_3 1 C 21_3 2 C 20_{15} 25_7 35_{21} 4QM[a] 8.1_{13} 4QShir[b] 52.3_4 GnzPs 4_{12}.

מֶלֶךְ אֶחָד *one ... king* Jos 12_{9+30t} (all אֶחָד ... מֶלֶךְ) Is 23_{15} Ezk 37_{22}, שְׁנֵי הַמְּלָכִים *the two kings* Dt 3_{21} 2 K 10_4, שְׁנֵיהֶם הַמְּלָכִים *the two kings* Dn 11_{27}, שְׁנֵי מַלְכֵי *two kings of* Dt 3_8 4_{47} Jos 9_{10} 24_{12} Jg 8_{12}, שְׁנֵי מְלָכֶיהָ *its two kings* Is 7_{16}, שְׁלֹשָׁה מְלָכִים *three kings* Dn 11_2, שְׁלֹשֶׁת הַמְּלָכִים *the three kings* 2 K $3_{10.13}$, אַרְבָּעָה מְלָכִים *four kings* Gn 14_9, חֲמֵשֶׁת הַמְּלָכִים *the five kings* Jos $10_{16.17.22.23}$, חֲמֵשֶׁת מַלְכֵי *the five kings of* Nm 31_8 Jos 10_6 4QapJoseph[b] 3_{12}, שְׁלֹשִׁים וּשְׁנַיִם מֶלֶךְ *thirty-two kings* 1 K 20_1, var. 1 K 20_{16}, שִׁבְעִים מְלָכִים *seventy kings* Jg 1_7.

מֶלֶךְ לַי׳ *a king for Y.* 2 C 9_8, מֶלֶךְ לִבְנֵי יִשְׂרָאֵל *a king (belonging) to the sons of Israel* Gn 36_{31}||1 C 1_{43}, הַמְּלָכִים לִיהוּדָה וְיִשְׂרָאֵל *the kings of Judah and Israel* 2 C 16_{11}, מֶלֶךְ לְמוֹאָב *king of Moab* Nm 22_4, מלך מלכ[ים] לכול סודי עולמים *king of kings of all the eternal councils* 4QShirShabb[d] 1.1_{34}, מלך לכולם *a king for all of them* 4QCreatA 1_7.

מֶלֶךְ עַל־אֲרָם *king over Aram* 1 K 19_{15} 2 K 8_{13}, מֶלֶךְ עַל־יִשְׂרָאֵל *king over Israel* 1 S $15_{17.26}$ 2 S 5_3||1 C 11_3 2 S $5_{12.17}$||1 C $14_{2.8}$ (1 C 14_8 עַל־כָּל־יִשְׂרָאֵל *over all Israel*) 2 S 12_7 19_{23} 1 K 1_{34} 4_1 (עַל־כָּל־יִשְׂרָאֵל; ms lacks כָּל־) 11_{37} 14_{14} 19_{16} 2 K $9_{3(mss).12(mss)}$ (both L אֶל *over*) Pr $1_{1(mss)}$ (L מֶלֶךְ יִשְׂרָאֵל *king of Israel*) Ec 1_{12} 1 C 28_4 1 C 29_{25} (מֶלֶךְ ... עַל), מֶלֶךְ עַל־בֵּית יְהוּדָה *king over the house of Judah* 2 S 2_4, מֶלֶךְ עַל־עַמּוֹ *king over his people* 1 S 15_1, vars. 1 K 14_2 (or em.; see Prep.) 2 K $9_{6(mss)}$ (L אֶל), מֶלֶךְ עַל־כָּל־הָאָרֶץ *king over all the earth* Zc 14_9 Ps

47$_{8(mss)}$, sim. Ps 47$_{3}$, מֶלֶךְ עַל־כָּל־בְּנֵי־שָׁחַץ *king over all the sons of pride* Jb 41$_{26}$, מֶלֶךְ עֲלֵיכֶם *king over you* Jg 9$_{15}$ 2 S 3$_{17}$, vars. 2 S 2$_{7}$ 5$_{2}$ Ezk 37$_{24}$ 2 C 2$_{10}$.

מֶלֶךְ בִּירוּשָׁלָם *king in Jerusalem* Ec 1$_{1}$, var. Ec 1$_{12}$, מלך [בהר ציון] *king on Mount Zion* 4QJub^{a} 1$_{28}$.

מְלָכִים לַכִּסֵּא *kings on the throne* Jb 36$_{7}$.

וְמֶלֶךְ ... ׳י *Y. ... and the king* Pr 24$_{21}$, מלך ורכב וסוס ועם רב *a king and chariotry and horses and many people* 11QT 58$_{7}$, מלכים בחיל עוזם *kings with their strong army* 4QPseud^{b} 8$_{3}$.

מָשׁוּחַ מֶלֶךְ *anointed as king* 2 S 3$_{39}$, וַיֵּשֶׁב י׳ מֶלֶךְ *and Y. has sat as king* Ps 29$_{10}$.

יְחִי הַמֶּלֶךְ *may the king live!* 1 S 10$_{24}$ 2 S 16$_{16.16}$ (lacking in mss) 1 K 1$_{25.31.34.39}$ 2 K 11$_{12}$||2 C 23$_{11}$.

Also 1QH fr. 7$_{10}$ 4QD^{a} 12$_{4}$ 4QMyst^{a} 10$_{1}$ 4QpsEzek^{e} 10$_{2}$ ([מ]לכים) 4QShirShabb^{b} 5$_{7}$ (מלן[ך]) 4QShirShabb^{f} 14.1$_{5}$ ([מ]לך) 19$_{8}$ 23.2$_{3.9}$ ([מ]לך) 56$_{1}$ 4QPrayer^{m} 1.2$_{4}$ 4Q476 1$_{2}$ 4QDibHam^{a} 1.3$_{15}$ perh. 27$_{1}$ (מלכ[ ]) 4QPr Fêtes^{c} 196$_{2}$ 4QShir^{b} 99$_{2}$ 11QShirShabb 29$_{1}$ ([מ]לך) 32$_{3}$ Arad ost. 24$_{3}$ En-Gedi cave inscr.$_{6}$ Seal 257 (Lachish, 7th cent.).

<SYN> רֹזֵן *ruler*, מֹשֵׁל *ruler*, נָשִׂיא *prince*, שַׂר *prince, commander*, שָׂרָה *queen*, גְּבִירָה *queen mother*, אָדוֹן *lord*, נָדִיב *noble*, מָשִׁיחַ *anointed one*, פֶּחָה *governor*, סָגָן *prefect*, גִּבּוֹר *mighty one*, גָּדוֹל *great one*, כבד ni. ptc. *honourable one*, מְחֹקֵק *commander*, שֹׁפֵט *judge*, כֹּהֵן *priest*, נָבִיא *prophet*, יוֹעֵץ *counsellor*, חָכָם *wise one*, עָשִׁיר *rich one*, אָב *father*, גּוֹי *nation*, עַם *people*, בַּיִת *house* of Israel, יֹשֵׁב *inhabitant*, אֵל *God*, אֱלֹהִים *God*, צָבָא *host* of heaven Is 24$_{21}$.

<ANT> חָשָׁךְ *obscure one*.*

⇒ מלך *be king*, מַלְכִּיאֵל *Malchiel*, מַלְכִּי *Malchi*, מַלְכִּיאֵלִי *Malchielite*, מַלְכִּיָּה *Malchijah*, מַלְכִּי־צֶדֶק *Melchizedek*, מַלְכִּי־רֶשַׁע *Melchiresha*, מַלְכִּירָם *Malchiram*, מַלְכִּישׁוּעַ *Malchishua*, מַלְכָּם *Malcam*, מַלְכִּנֵר *Malchiner*, עֶבֶד־מֶלֶךְ *Ebed-melech*, רֶגֶם מֶלֶךְ *Regem-melech*.

מֶלֶךְ II $_{2}$ pr.n.m. **Melech,** Benjaminite, son of Micah, <NOM CL> בְּנֵי מִיכָה ... מֶלֶךְ *the sons of Micah were ... Melech* 1 C 8$_{35}$ 9$_{41}$.

⇒ מלך *be king*.

[מֶלֶךְ] III $_{1}$ n.[m.] **counsel**—pl. מְלָכִין—**counsel, advice,** <OBJ> מחה hi. *wipe out* perh. Pr 31$_{3}$ (or em. לַמְחוֹת to לְמֹחוֹת *to those who wipe out*, i.e. qal; but prob. מְלָכִין is from מֶלֶךְ *king*), שׂכל pi. *make foolish* Jb 12$_{17}$ (if em. מוֹלִיךְ יוֹעֲצִים שׁוֹלָל *he leads counsellors away barefoot* to מֶלֶךְ יוֹעֲצִים שִׂכֵּל *he makes foolish the advice of counsellors*; or em. מַלְכֵי יוֹעֲצִים יְשׁוֹלֵל *he plunders the advice of counsellors*), שׁלל po. *plunder* Jb 12$_{17}$ (if em.; see above).

⇒ מלך II *counsel*.

מֹלֶךְ I $_{8}$ pr.n.[m.] **Molech,** a Semitic deity, to whom perh. children were sometimes sacrificed or dedicated in a fire ceremony, or a type of sacrifice (*molk*) of a child or a substitutionary lamb;* alw. with definite article (Lv 20$_{5}$) or pointing of article (except 1 K 11$_{7}$; or em.; see Prep.), <APP> שִׁקֻּץ *abomination* 1 K 11$_{7}$ (or em; see Prep.). <PREP> לְ of direction, *to*, + נתן *give* Lv 20$_{2.3.4}$, עבר hi. *cause to pass*, i.e. burn Lv 18$_{21}$ 2 K 23$_{10}$ Jr 32$_{35}$; of benefit, *to, for*, + בנה *build* high place 1 K 11$_{7}$ (or em. לְמִלְכֹּם *for Milcom*), כון ho. *be prepared* Is 30$_{33}$ (if em. לַמֶּלֶךְ *for the king*); אַחֲרֵי *after*, + זנה *prostitute oneself* Lv 20$_{5}$. <COLL> מֹלֶךְ + כְּמוֹשׁ *Chemosh* 1 K 11$_{7}$.*

⇒ מלך *be king*.

***מֹלֶךְ** II $_{1}$ n.m. **kingdom**—pl. מְלָכִים—<SUBJ> רום *be high* Nm 24$_{7}$ (if em. מַלְכּוֹ *his king* to מָלְכּוֹ *his kingdom*). <OBJ> נכה hi. *strike* Ps 136$_{17}$ (unless from מֶלֶךְ I *king*). <ADJ> גָּדוֹל *great* Ps 136$_{17}$ (unless from מֶלֶךְ I *king*).

⇒ מלך *be king*.

***[מֹלֶךְ]** III n.m. **counsellor,** <SUBJ> היה *be* Ec 1$_{12}$ (אֲנִי קֹהֶלֶת הָיִיתִי מֹלֶךְ עַל־יִשְׂרָאֵל *I Qohelet was counsellor in Jerusalem*; if em. מֶלֶךְ *king*; or vocalize מַלָּךְ*).

⇒ מלך II *counsel*.

***[מְלָךְ]** $_{1}$ n.m. **counsel**—<OBJ> מחא IV *destroy* Pr 31$_{3}$ (לְמֹחוֹת מְלָכִין *to those who destroy* [לְמַמְחוֹת] *counsels* [מְלָכִין], i.e. women).

⇒ מלך II *counsel*.

מַלְכָּא, see מַלְכָּה *queen*.

[מַלְכֹּדֶת] 1 n.f. **snare**—sf. מַלְכֻּדְתּוֹ—<SUBJ> טמן pass. *be hidden* in path Jb 18$_{10}$ (+ חֶבֶל *rope*).
⇒ לכד *capture*.

מַלְכָּה 35.0.1 n.f. **queen**—Q מלכא; cstr. מַלְכַּת; pl. מְלָכוֹת—usu. of wife of non-Israelite king; also of sovereign (1 K 10$_{1.4.10.13}$||2 C 9$_{1.3.9.12}$); as epithet of deity (Jr 7$_{18}$ 44$_{17.18.19.25}$; all five, if em.; see Cstr.).

<SUBJ> אמר *say* 1 K 10$_{4}$||2 C 9$_{3}$ Est 7$_{3}$, דבר pi. *speak* 1 K 10$_{1}$||2 C 9$_{1}$, ענה *answer* Est 7$_{3}$, הלל pi. *praise* Ca 6$_{9}$ (|| פִּלֶגֶשׁ *secondary wife*, + בַּת *daughter*), שׁמע *hear* 1 K 10$_{1.4}$||2 C 9$_{1.3}$, ראה *see* 1 K 10$_{4}$||2 C 9$_{3}$ Ca 6$_{9}$, כתב *write* Est 9$_{29}$, קום pi. *confirm* Est 9$_{29.31}$ (or del.), אמן hi. *believe* 1 K 10$_{4}$||2 C 9$_{3}$, נסה pi. *test* 1 K 10$_{1}$||2 C 9$_{1}$, מאן pi. *refuse* Est 1$_{12}$, חיל htpalp. *writhe in fear* Est 4$_{4}$, הלך *go* 1 K 10$_{10}$||2 C 9$_{9}$, בוא *come* 1 K 10$_{1.4}$||2 C 9$_{1.3}$ Est 1$_{12.17}$, hi. *bring* Est 5$_{12}$, שׁלח *send* Est 4$_{4}$, הפך *turn* 2 C 9$_{12}$, פנה *turn* 1 K 10$_{13}$, מצא *find* Est 7$_{3}$, עמד *stand* Est 5$_{2}$, נתן *give* 1 K 10$_{10}$||2 C 9$_{9}$, נשׂא *lift*, i.e. find, favour Est 5$_{2}$, מכר ni. *be sold* Est 7$_{3}$, עשׂה *do* Est 1$_{9.15}$ 5$_{12}$, עוה *do wrong* Est 1$_{16}$.

<NOM CL> שִׁשִּׁים הֵמָּה מְלָכוֹת *they are sixty queens* Ca 6$_{8(mss)}$ (L מְלָכוֹת; || פִּלֶגֶשׁ *secondary wife*, עַלְמָה *young woman*).

<OBJ> ראה *see* Est 5$_{2}$, בוא hi. *bring* Est 1$_{11.17}$, כבשׁ *rape* Est 7$_{8}$.

<CSTR> מַלְכַּת־שְׁבָא *queen of Sheba* 1 K 10$_{1.4.10.13}$|| 2 C 9$_{1.3.9.12}$, מַלְכַּת הַשָּׁמַיִם *queen of heaven* Jr 7$_{18}$ 44$_{17.18.19.25}$ (all five; if em. מְלֶכֶת *queen of*); דְּבַר־הַמַּלְכָּה *deed of the queen* Est 1$_{17.18}$, משכן המלכא *dwelling place of the queen* 3QTr 6$_{11}$.

<APP> אֶסְתֵּר הַמַּלְכָּה *Esther, the queen* Est 2$_{22}$ 5$_{2.3.12}$ 7$_{1.2.3.5.7}$ 8$_{1.7}$ 9$_{12.29.31}$ (or del.), וַשְׁתִּי הַמַּלְכָּה *Vashti, the queen* Est 1$_{9.11.16.17}$, הַמַּלְכָּה וַשְׁתִּי *the queen, Vashti* Est 1$_{12}$, var. 1$_{15}$, הַמַּלְכָּה בַת־אֲבִיחַיִל *the queen, the daughter of Abihail* Est 9$_{29}$.

<PREP> לְ of direction, *to* Est 5$_{3}$, + אמר *say* Est 7$_{5}$ 8$_{7}$ 9$_{12}$, נגד hi. *tell* 1 K 10$_{1}$||2 C 9$_{1}$ Est 2$_{22}$, ho. *be told* 1 K 10$_{4}$||2 C 9$_{3}$, קרא pass. *be invited* Est 5$_{12}$, נתן *give* 1 K 10$_{13}$||2 C 9$_{12}$ Est 8$_{1}$, ni. *be given* Est 5$_{3}$ 7$_{2.3}$ 9$_{12}$, קטר pi. *burn incense* Jr 44$_{17.18.19.25}$ (all four, if em.; see Cstr.), נסך hi. *pour out* libations Jr 44$_{17.18.19.25}$ (all four, if em.; see Cstr.); of benefit, *to, for*, + עשׂה *make* cakes Jr 7$_{18}$ (if em.; see Cstr.); בְּ *to, with*, + עשׂה *do* Est 1$_{15}$; מִן of direction, *from*, + בקשׁ pi. *seek* Est 7$_{7}$; עִם *with*, + שׁתה *drink* Est 7$_{1}$; מִלִּפְנֵי *before*, + בעת ni. *be terrified* Est 7$_{6}$ (|| מֶלֶךְ *king*).

<COLL> מַלְכָּה as vocative, Est 5$_{3}$ 7$_{1}$.

<SYN> פִּלֶגֶשׁ *secondary wife*, עַלְמָה *young woman*, מֶלֶךְ *king*.*
⇒ מלך I *be king*.

מִלְכָּה 11 pr.n.f. **Milcah, 1.** wife of Abraham's brother, Nahor, <SUBJ> ילד *give birth* Gn 22$_{20.23}$ 24$_{24.47}$. <NOM CL> שֵׁם אֵשֶׁת־נָחוֹר מִלְכָּה *the name of the wife of Nahor was Milcah* Gn 11$_{29}$. <CSTR> אֲבִי־מִלְכָּה *father of Milcah* Gn 11$_{29}$, בֶּן־ *son of* Gn 24$_{15.24}$. <APP> אִשָּׁה *wife* Gn 24$_{15}$, בַּת *daughter* Gn 11$_{29}$.

2. daughter of Zelophehad, <SUBJ> היה *be* Nm 36$_{11}$. <NOM CL> שֵׁם בְּנוֹת צְלָפְחָד ... מִלְכָּה *the name of the daughters of Zelophehad was ... Milcah* Nm 26$_{33}$, vars. Nm 27$_{1}$ Jos 17$_{3}$.
⇒ מלך I *be king*.

מְלֻכָה, see מְלוּכָה *kingship*.

מַלְכוּת 91.2.47 n.f. **kingdom**—cstr. מַלְכוּת; sf. מַלְכוּתִי, (מַלְכֻתוֹ) מַלְכוּתוֹ, (מלכותכה Q ,מַלְכוּתֶךָ) מַלְכוּתְךָ, מַלְכוּתָם, מַלְכוּתָהּ; pl. mss מַלְכֻיוֹת (L מַלְכֻיּוֹת)—**1. kingdom, realm, kingship, rule,** usu. of humans; of Y. (Ps 103$_{19}$ 145$_{11.12.13.13}$ 1QM 12$_{7}$ 4QTobit[e] 6$_{5}$ 4QBer[a] 7a.1$_{5}$ 4QBer[b] 2$_{11}$ [[מ]לכוכה] 4QShirShabb[a] 1.2$_{1}$ [[מלכות]כה] 1.2$_{3}$ 2$_{1.3.4}$ 4QShirShabb[b] 14.1$_{6}$ 4QShirShabb[d] 1.1$_{14.25.32.33}$ [[מלכ]ותו] 1.2$_{10}$ 4QShirShabb[f] 23.1$_{3}$ 23.2$_{11}$ 24$_{3}$ 4QShir[b] 1$_{4}$ MasShirShabb 2$_{20}$ GnzPs 2$_{4}$ 3$_{8}$ 4$_{14}$); of Y., in ref. to Israel (1 C 17$_{14}$ 28$_{5}$).

<SUBJ> כון ni. *be established* 1 S 20$_{31}$ 1 K 2$_{12}$ 2 C 12$_{1}$ (if em.; see Obj.), נשׂא ni. *be exalted* Nm 24$_{7}$ (if em. htp.) 1 C 14$_{2}$, htp. Nm 24$_{7}$ (or em. ni.) 4QBer[a] 7a.1$_{5}$, עמד *stand* Dn 8$_{22}$, סבב *go round* Si 10$_{8}$, מלך *rule* 2 C 36$_{20}$, משׁל *rule* Ps 103$_{19}$, שׁקט *be quiet* 2 C 20$_{30}$, שׁפל *be laid low* 4QpNah 3.4$_{3}$, שׁבר ni. *be broken* Dn 11$_{4}$, חצה

ni. *be divided* Dn 11$_4$, נתשׁ ni. *be plucked up* Dn 11$_4$.

<NOM CL> מַלְכוּתְךָ מַלְכוּת כָּל־עֹלָמִים *your kingdom is a kingdom of all eternity* Ps 145$_{13}$, לכול העולמים היאה מלכותו *his kingdom is to all eternity* 4QTobite 6$_5$.

<OBJ> חזק pi. *strengthen* 2 C 11$_{17}$, hi. *take hold of* Dn 11$_{21}$, כון hi. *establish* 1 C 17$_{11}$ 28$_7$ 2 C 12$_1$ (or em. ni. *be established*), קום hi. *raise up* 1QSb 5$_{21}$, סבב hi. *turn* 1 C 12$_{24}$, הלל pi. *praise* 4QShirShabbd 1.1$_{25}$ ([מה]ללי), שׁבר *break* 4QpsEzekd 1.2$_4$.

<CSTR> מַלְכוּת י׳ *kingdom of Y.* 1 C 28$_5$, מַלְכוּת אֲחַשְׁוֵרוֹשׁ *kingdom of Ahasuerus* Est 3$_6$ 9$_{30}$, יְהוֹשָׁפָט *of Jehoshaphat* 2 C 20$_{30}$, רְחַבְעָם *of Rehoboam* 2 C 12$_1$, שָׁאוּל *of Saul* 1 C 12$_{24}$, מלכות מצרים *kingdom of Egypt* 4QpsEzekd 1.2$_4$, ישראל *of Israel* 11QT 59$_{17}$, מַלְכוּת יְהוּדָה *kingdom of Judah* 2 C 11$_{17}$, כַּשְׂדִּים *of the Chaldaeans* Dn 9$_1$, יָוָן *of Greece* Dn 11$_2$, פָּרַס *of Persia* Dn 10$_{13}$ 2 C 36$_{20}$ (פָּרֶס), מַלְכוּת מֶלֶךְ *kingdom of the king of* Dn 11$_9$, מלכות עמו *kingdom of his people* 1QSb 5$_{21}$ 4QCommGenA 5$_4$, מלכות עד *kingdom of eternity* 4QapMes 2.2$_7$, עולמים *of eternity* 1QM 19$_8$, מַלְכוּת כָּל־עֹלָמִים *kingdom of all eternity* Ps 145$_{13}$, מלכות כבוד *kingdom of the glory*, i.e. glorious kingdom, *of* 4QShirShabbf 24$_3$, מלכות כבודו *kingdom of his glory*, i.e. his glorious kingdom 4QShirShabbd 1.1$_{25}$ 4QShirShabbf 23.2$_{11}$, כ[בוד]כה *of your glory*, i.e. your glorious kingdom 4QShirShabbb 14.1$_6$.

שַׂר מַלְכוּת *prince of the kingdom of* Dn 10$_{13}$, [מה]ללי מלכות *ones who praise the kingdom of* 4QShirShabbd 1.1$_{25}$, ברית המלכות *covenant of the kingship* 4QCommGenA 5$_2$, מלכות *of the kingship of* 4QCommGenA 5$_4$, שמן מלכות *oil of kingship* 4QNarrA 2.2$_6$, כִּסֵּא מַלְכוּת *throne of the kingdom of* 1 C 28$_5$ 4QapMes 2.2$_7$ 11QT 59$_{17}$, היכל מלכות *temple of the kingdom* 1QSb 4$_{26}$, היכל מלכותו *temple of his kingdom* 4QMystc 5$_2$, היכלי מ[לכוכה] *temples of your kingdom* 4QBerb 2$_{11}$, מקדשי מלכות *sanctuaries of the kingdom of* 4QShirShabbf 23.2$_{11}$, שמי מלכותו *heavens of his kingdom* 4QShirShabba 2$_4$, שמי מלכות *heavens of the kingdom of* 4QShirShabbb 14.1$_6$, מְדִינוֹת מַלְכוּתוֹ *provinces of his kingdom* Est 2$_3$, מַלְכוּתֶךָ *of your kingdom* Est 3$_8$.

כְּבוֹד מַלְכוּתוֹ *glory of his kingdom* Ps 145$_{12(Gnz)}$ Est 1$_4$ 4QShirShabbd 1.1$_{32}$ 1.2$_{10}$ 4QShirShabbf 23.1$_3$ 4QShirb 1$_4$ GnzPs 2$_4$ 3$_8$ 4$_{4.14}$, מַלְכוּתְךָ *of your kingdom* Ps 145$_{11}$ 1QM 12$_7$ (מלכותכה), הֲדַר מַלְכוּת *splendour of the kingdom* Dn 11$_{20}$ 4QShirShabbb 32$_2$ ([ה]דר מל[כות]), הֲדַר מַלְכוּתוֹ *splendour of his kingdom* Ps 145$_{12}$ 4QMysta 9$_3$, הדר כול מלכ[ותו] *splendour of all his kingdom* 4QShirShabbd 1.1$_{33}$, הוד מלכותו *splendour of his kingdom* 4QShirShabba 2$_3$, תפארת מלכותו *beauty of his kingdom* GnzPs 3$_{16}$, מלכותכה *of your kingdom* 4QShirShabba 1.2$_3$, תשבחות מלכותכה *praiseworthiness of your kingdom* 4QShirShabba 2$_1$, רום מלכותו *exaltation of his kingdom* 4QShirShabbd 1.1$_{14}$ MasShirShabb 2$_{20}$, מלכות[כה] *of your kingdom* 4QShirShabba 1.2$_1$.

תֹּקֶף כָּל־מַלְכוּתוֹ *strength of all his kingdom* Dn 11$_{17}$, תרבות מלכותו *increase of his kingdom* 4QpUnid 3$_2$, אַחֲרִית מַלְכוּתָם *end of their rule* Dn 8$_{23}$, חֲצִי הַמַּלְכוּת *half of the kingdom* Est 5$_{3.6}$ 7$_2$, כָּל־מַלְכוּת *all the kingdom of* Est 3$_6$, כָּל־מַלְכוּתוֹ *all his kingdom* Est 1$_{20}$ Dn 1$_{20}$ 11$_{17}$ 1 C 29$_{30}$ 2 C 36$_{22}$ 4QShirShabbd 1.1$_{33}$ (כול מלכ[ותו]), כָּל־מַלְכוּתָם *all their royal power* Jr 10$_7$.

<PREP> לְ of direction, *to*, + שׁוב hi. *bring back* 2 C 33$_{13}$, נגע hi. *come* Est 4$_{14}$; *(destined) to*, + ילד ni. *be born* Ec 4$_{14}$ (if em.; see below); of benefit, *to, for*, + בנה *build* 2 C 1$_{18}$ 2 C 2$_{11}$.

בְּ of place, *in(to), throughout* Jr 10$_7$ Est 3$_6$ 9$_{30}$ (if em.; see Coll.) Dn 1$_{20}$, + בוא *come* Dn 11$_9$, עבר hi. *cause* voice *to pass*, i.e. make proclamation 2 C 36$_{22}$, ישׁב *sit* Est 1$_{14}$, עמד hi. *cause to stand* 1 C 17$_{14}$, ילד ni. *be born* Ec 4$_{14}$ (or em. בְּמַלְכוּתוֹ *in his kingdom* to לְמַלְכוּתוֹ *[destined] to his kingship*), חזק htp. *strengthen oneself* 1 C 11$_{10}$, עבד *serve* Ne 9$_{35}$, עשׂה *do* Est 1$_{20}$; of accompaniment, *in, with* Si 44$_3$; *over*, + רדה *rule* 1QM 15$_{15}$ (ב[מ]ל[כות]) 19$_7$ (ר[ד]ינה).

עַל *over*, + מלך ho. *be made king* Dn 9$_1$ (or em. ho. to hi. *reign*), חזק htp. *strengthen oneself* 2 C 1$_1$, ארך hi. *prolong* days 11QT 59$_{21}$.

עִם *with* 1 C 29$_{30}$.

אֵת *against*, + עור hi. *stir up* Dn 11$_2$.

<COLL> מַלְכוּת || מֶמְשָׁלָה *dominion* Ps 145$_{13}$, גְּבוּרָה *might* Ps 145$_{11.12}$ (both +) 1 C 29$_{30}$ Si 44$_3$; + כִּסֵּא *throne* Ps 103$_{19}$.

שֶׁבַע וְעֶשְׂרִים וּמֵאָה מְדִינָה מַלְכוּת אֲחַשְׁוֵרוֹשׁ *the hundred and twenty-seven provinces (of) the kingdom of Ahasuerus* Est 9_{30} (or em. בְּמַלְכוּת *in the kingdom of*), אַרְבַּע מַלְכֻיוֹת *four kingdoms* Dn $8_{22(mss)}$ (L מַלְכֻיּוֹת).

2. royalty, royal status (Est 1_{19}); appar. **royal robes** (Est 5_1), <OBJ> לבשׁ *dress oneself in* Est 5_1 (unless ins. לְבוּשׁ *garment*), נתן Est 1_{19}. <CSTR> בֵּית הַמַּלְכוּת *house of the royalty*, i.e. the royal palace Est 1_9 5_1, מַלְכוּתוֹ *of his royalty*, i.e. his royal palace Est 2_{16} (or del.), כִּסֵּא מַלְכוּתוֹ *throne of his royalty*, i.e. his royal throne Est 1_2 5_1 1 C 22_{10} 4QShirShabb[f] 20.2_2, מַלְכוּתֶךָ *of your royalty*, i.e. your royal throne 2 C 7_{18}, כֶּתֶר מַלְכוּת *crown of royalty*, i.e. royal crown Est 1_{11} 2_{17} 6_8, שֵׁבֶט מַלְכוּתֶךָ *sceptre of your royalty*, i.e. your royal sceptre Ps 45_7, יֵין מַלְכוּת *wine of royalty*, i.e. royal wine Est 1_7, לְבוּשׁ *garment of*, i.e. royal garment Est 5_1 (if ins. לְבוּשׁ) 6_8 8_{15}, דְּבַר־ *word of*, i.e. royal edict Est 1_{19}, הוֹד *majesty of*, i.e. royal majesty Dn 11_{21} 1 C 29_{25}.

3. (period of) reign, <CSTR> מַלְכוּת אֲחַשְׁוֵרוֹשׁ *reign of Ahasuerus* Ezr 4_6, אָסָא *of Asa* 2 C $15_{10.19}$ 16_1, אַרְתַּחְשַׁסְתָּא *of Artaxerxes* Ezr 7_1 8_1, בֵּלְאשַׁצַּר *of Belshazzar* Dn 8_1, דָּוִיד *of David* 1 C 26_{31}, דָּרְיָוֶשׁ *of Darius* Ezr 4_5 Ne 12_{22}, יֹאשִׁיָּהוּ *of Josiah* 2 C 35_{19}, נְבֻכַדְנֶצַּר *Nebuchadnezzar* Dn 2_1, צִדְקִיָּה *of Zedekiah* Jr 49_{34}, מַלְכוּת ... הַמֶּלֶךְ *reign of ... the king* Ezr 8_1 Dn 8_1, מַלְכוּת ... מֶלֶךְ *reign ... of the king of* Jr 49_{34} Ezr 4_5 7_1, מַלְכוּת ... הַפָּרְסִי *reign of ... the Persian* Ne 12_{22}; רֵאשִׁית מַלְכוּת *beginning of the reign of* Jr 49_{34}, תְּחִלַּת מַלְכוּתוֹ *beginning of his reign* Ezr 4_6, שְׁנַת מַלְכֻתוֹ *year of his reign*, i.e. perh. his accession year Jr 52_{31} (or em. מָלְכוֹ *when he became king*). <PREP> לְ of possession, *of, (belonging) to* Dn 2_1 8_1 Est 2_{16} 1 C 26_{31} 2 C 3_2 $15_{10.19}$ $16_{1.12}$ 35_{19}; בְּ of time, *in, during*, + כתב *write* Ezr 4_6, עלה *go up* Ezr 7_1 8_1, זנח hi. *reject* 2 C 29_{19}; עַל *to*, i.e. until Ne 12_{22} (or ins. סֵפֶר דִּבְרֵי הַיָּמִים וְעַד written in *the book of the chronicles until*); עַד *until* Ezr 4_5 Ne 12_{22} (if em.; see above).

Also 1QH 11_5 1QSb 3_5 4QapPs[b] 19.1_5 4QShirShabb[b] 14 (מלכו[ת]) 4QShirShabb[f] 7_3 24_1 35_4 (מ]לכות]) 4Q418 164_4 (מלכו[ת]) 4QBark[a] 3.2_2 4QPrFêtes[c] 51_1 4QapMes 12_2 (מ]לכות]).

<SYN> §1, מֶמְשָׁלָה *dominion*, גְּבוּרָה *might*.*

⇨ מלך I *be king*.

[מַלְכִּי]* 0.0.0.1 pr.n.m. **Malchi,** father of Berechiah, <CSTR> בן מלכי *son of Malchi* Seal 833 (City of David, 7th/6th cent.).

⇨ מֶלֶךְ I *king*.

מַלְכִּיאֵל 3 pr.n.m. **Malchiel,** descendant of Asher and son of Beriah, <NOM CL> בְּנֵי בְרִיעָה חֶבֶר וּמַלְכִּיאֵל *the sons of Beriah were Heber and Malchiel* Gn 46_{17} 1 C 7_{31}. <PREP> לְ of possession, *of, (belonging) to* Nm 26_{45}.

⇨ מֶלֶךְ I *king* + אֵל *God*; מַלְכִּיאֵלִי *Malchielite*.

מַלְכִּיאֵלִי 1 gent. **Malchielite,** as collective noun, of descendants of Malchiel, <CSTR> מִשְׁפַּחַת הַמַּלְכִּיאֵלִי *clan of the Malchielites* Nm 26_{45}.

⇨ מַלְכִּיאֵל *Malchiel*.

מַלְכִּיָּה 16.0.13.17 pr.n.m. **Malchi(j)ah**—מַלְכִּיָּהוּ (Q מלאכיה)—**1.** father of Pashhur, <CSTR> בֶּן־מַלְכִּיָּה *son of Malchiah* Jr 21_1 38_1.

2. priest, son of Passhur, <CSTR> בֶּן־מַלְכִּיָּה *son of Malchiah* Ne 11_{12} 1 C 9_{12}.

3. son of the king, <CSTR> בּוֹר מַלְכִּיָּהוּ *the dungeon of Malchiah* Jr 38_6 (if em.; הַבּוֹר מַלְכִּיָּהוּ *the dungeon [of] Malchiah*). <APP> בֶּן *son* Jr 38_6, appar. בּוֹר *dungeon* Jr 38_6 (or em.; see Cstr.).

4. member of Harim family, husband of non-Jewish wife, <NOM CL> בְּנֵי חָרִם ... מַלְכִּיָּה *the sons of Harim were ... Malchijah* Ezr 10_{31}.

5. son of Harim, repairer of the walls of Jerusalem, perh. ident. with §4, <SUBJ> חזק hi. *strengthen*, i.e. repair Ne 3_{11}. <APP> בֶּן *son* Ne 3_{11}.

6. son of Rechab, ruler of Beth-haccherem and repairer of Dung Gate in Jerusalem, <SUBJ> חזק hi. *strengthen*, i.e. repair Ne 3_{14}, בנה *build* Ne 3_{14}, עמד hi. *set up* Ne 3_{14}. <APP> בֶּן *son* Ne 3_{14}, שַׂר *ruler* Ne 3_{14}.

7. goldsmith and repairer of walls of Jerusalem, <APP> בֶּן *son* Ne 3_{31}.

8. member of Parosh family, husband of non-Jewish wife, <NOM CL> מִבְּנֵי פַרְעֹשׁ ... מַלְכִּיָּה *of the sons of Parosh were ... Malchijah* Ezr 10_{25}.

9. member of Parosh family, husband of non-Jewish wife, <NOM CL> מִבְּנֵי פַּרְעֹשׁ ... מַלְכִּיָּה *of the sons of Parosh were ... Malchijah* Ezr 10$_{25}$ (or em. חֲשַׁבְיָה *Hashabiah*).

10. priest, signatory of covenant at time of Nehemiah, <NOM CL> עַל הַחֲתוּמִים ... מַלְכִּיָּה *upon (the documents) that were sealed are ... Malluch* Ne 10$_{4}$ (mss חִלְקִיָּה *Hilkiah;* or em. עַל הַחֲתוּמִים to הַחוֹתְמִים *those who sealed,* i.e. signed, or אֵלֶּה הַחוֹתְמִים *these are the signatories*).

11. leader of Judah present at Ezra's reading of the Torah, <SUBJ> עמד *stand* Ne 10$_{4}$.

12. Levite musician at dedication of Nehemiah's wall, <SUBJ> עמד *stand* Ne 12$_{42}$.

13. Gershonite Levite, father of Baaseiah (mss Maaseiah) and ancestor of Asaph, <CSTR> בֶּן־מַלְכִּיָּה *son of Malchiah* 1 C 6$_{25}$. <APP> בֵּן *son* 1 C 6$_{25}$.

14. head of priestly family at time of David, <PREP> לְ of direction, *to,* + יצא *go out* 1 C 24$_{9}$.

15. name of priestly course (derived from §14) and its period of office, <NOM CL> [העשירי 30] מלכיה *the tenth (month), 30 (days) is,* i.e. begins with, *Malchijah* 4QMishA 4.1$_{12}$, [בחמישית] ... מלכיה *in the fifth is ... Malchijah* 4QMishF^{a} 1$_{4}$. <CSTR> שבת מלכיה *sabbath of Malchijah* 4QMishD 1$_{5}$, ביאת *arrival of* 4QMishC^{d} 1.2$_{2}$ ([מלכ]יה). <PREP> בְּ of time, *in, at during* 4QMishA 1.2$_{5}$ 4.4$_{3}$ ([מלכי]ה) 4.6$_{8}$ 4QMishB^{a} 1.1$_{6}$ 1.3$_{3}$ ([במלא]כיה) 2.1$_{4}$ 2.2$_{6}$ 2.3$_{6}$ ([במ]לאכיה) 4QMishB^{b} 2$_{4}$ 3$_{4}$ 4QMishC^{d} 1.2$_{3}$ ([ב]מלכיה).

16. name in writing exercise, 4QNames$_{4}$.

17. son of Kareb-or, <APP> בֵּן *son* Arad ost. 24$_{14}$.

18. father of Shemaiah, <CSTR> בן מלכיהו *son of Malchijah* Arad ost. 39$_{2}$.

19. Arad ost. 40$_{3}$, <CSTR> [שלם] מלכיהו *peace of Malchijah* Arad ost. 40$_{3}$.

20. Beersheba graf. 4, <PREP> לְ of possession, *of, (belonging) to* Beersheba graf. 4 ([למלכ]יהו).

21. appar. son of Heleziah, <PREP> לְ of possession, *of, (belonging) to* Seal 176 (Judaea, 7th cent.).

22. son of Hela, <APP> בֵּן *son* Seal 326 (8th/7th cent.). <PREP> לְ of possession, *of, (belonging) to* Seal 326 (8th/7th cent.).

23. servant of Shaphat, <APP> נַעַר *servant* Seal 406 (7th cent.). <PREP> לְ of possession, *of, (belonging) to* Seal 406 (7th cent.).

24. appar. son of Helek, <PREP> לְ of possession, *of, (belonging) to* Seal 598 ([ל]מלכיהו; T. Beit Mirsim?, 7th/6th cent.).

25. son of Pedaiah, <APP> בֵּן *son* Seal 599 (T. Beit Mirsim?, 7th/6th cent.). <PREP> לְ of possession, *of, (belonging) to* Seal 599 (T. Beit Mirsim?, 7th/6th cent.).

26. father of Negbi, <CSTR> בן מלכיהו *son of Malchijah* Seal 620 (T. Beit Mirsim?, 7th/6th cent.).

27. father of Shual, <CSTR> ב[ן] מל[כ]יה[ו] *son of Malchijah* Seal 674 (T. Beit Mirsim?, 7th/6th cent.).

28. Seal 675 ([מלכ]יהו; T. Beit Mirsim?, 7th/6th cent.).

29. appar. father of Manasseh Seal 748 (c. 700).

30. appar. father of Seagiah, Seal 751 (8th/7th cent.).

31. son of Mattan, <APP> בֵּן *son* Seal 761 (8th/7th cent.). <PREP> לְ of possession, *of, (belonging) to* Seal 761 (8th/7th cent.).

32. son of Joiliah, <APP> בֵּן *son* Bullae 931 (7th cent.) D59. <PREP> לְ of possession, *of, (belonging) to* Bullae 931 (7th cent.) D59.

33. son of the king, <APP> בֵּן *son* Seal 942. <PREP> לְ of possession, *of, (belonging) to* Seal 942.

34. father of Elishama, <CSTR> בן מלכיה[ו] *son of Malchijah* Bulla D33.

35. appar. father of Neriah, Bulla D 66.

⇒ מֶלֶךְ I *king* + ״י *Y.*

מַלְכִּיָּהוּ, see מַלְכִּיָּה *Malchi(j)ah.*

מַלְכִּי־צֶדֶק 2.0.3 pr.n.m. **Melchizedek, 1.** king of Salem, priest of God Most High, <SUBJ> יצא hi. *bring out* Gn 14$_{18}$, אמר *say* Gn 14$_{18}$, ברך pi. *bless* Gn 14$_{18}$. <CSTR> דִּבְרָתִי מַלְכִּי־צֶדֶק *manner of Melchizedek* Ps 110$_{4}$. <APP> מֶלֶךְ *king* Gn 14$_{18}$. <PREP> לְ of direction, *to,* + נתן *give* Gn 14$_{18}$.

2. divine being and saviour figure, <SUBJ> שׁוב hi. *bring back* 11QMelch 2$_{5}$ ([מלכי צ]דק), נצל hi. *deliver* 11QMelch 2$_{13}$ ([יצי]ל[מה]), נקם *avenge* 11QMelch 2$_{13}$. <CSTR> נחלת מלכי צדק *inheritance of Melchizedek*

11QMelch $2_{5.5}$ (נחל[ת מלכי צ]דק), גורל *lot of* 11QMelch 2_{8} (מל[כי] צדק). <APP> כֹּהֵן *priest* 4QShirShabb[b] 11_{3} ([מלכי] צדק כוהן בעד[ת אל]) *Melchizedek, priest in the assembly of God*). <PREP> לְ of possession, *of, (belonging) to* 11QMelch 2_{9} (שנת הרצון למלכי צדק *year of favour of Melchizedek*) 11QShirShabb 2_{7} ([כוהנות פ]לא [למלכ]י צדק *the wonderful priesthoods of Melchizedek*).

Also 11QMelch 8_{1} ([מלכי] צדק).*

⇒ מֶלֶךְ I *king* + צֶדֶק *righteousness.*

מַלְכִּירָם 1.0.0.2 pr.n.m. **Malchiram, 1.** son of Jeconiah, <NOM CL> בְּנֵי יְכָנְיָה אַסִּר ... מַלְכִּירָם *the sons of Jeconiah the prisoner, were ... Malchiram* 1 C 3_{18}.

2. Samaria inscr. 108, <PREP> לְ of possession, *of, (belonging) to* Samaria inscr. 108.

3. Seal 250 (7th cent.), <PREP> לְ of possession, *of, (belonging) to* Seal 250 (7th cent.).

⇒ מֶלֶךְ I *king* + רום *be high.*

*[**מַלְכִּי־רֶשַׁע**] 0.0.1 pr.n.m. **Melchiresha,** appar. as name for Satan, <SUBJ> ארר pass. *be cursed* 4QBer[f] 1_{2} ([אר]ור אתה מלכי רשע *cursed are you, O Melchiresha*).

⇒ מֶלֶךְ I *king* + רֶשַׁע *wickedness.*

מַלְכִּי־שׁוּעַ 5 pr.n.m. **Malchishua,** son of Saul, <SUBJ> היה *be* 1 S 14_{49}. <OBJ> ילד hi. *beget* 1 C 8_{33} 9_{39}, נכה hi. *strike* 1 S 31_{2}||1 C 10_{2}. <APP> בֵּן *son* 1 S 31_{2}||1 C 10_{2}.

⇒ מֶלֶךְ I *king* + שׁוּעַ *help.*

מַלְכָּם 1 pr.n.m. **Malcam,** Benjaminite, son of Shaharaim and Hodesh, <OBJ> ילד hi. *beget* 1 C 8_{9}.

⇒ מֶלֶךְ I *king.*

מִלְכֹּם 3 pr.n.[m.] **Milcom,** god of the Ammonites, prob. ident with מֹלֶךְ *Molech,* <SUBJ> הלך *go* Jr 49_{3} (if em. מַלְכָּם *their king*), ירשׁ *possess* Jr 49_{1} (if em. מַלְכָּם). <CSTR> עֲטֶרֶת־מַלְכָּם *crown of Milcom* 2 S 12_{30}||1 C 20_{2} (if em. מַלְכָּם *of their king*). <APP> אֱלֹהִים *god* 1 K 11_{33}, שִׁקֻּץ *detested thing* 1 K $11_{5.7}$ (if em.; see Prep.), תּוֹעֵבָה *abomination* 2 K 23_{13}. <PREP> לְ of benefit, *to, for,* + בנה *build* 1 K 11_{7} (if em. לְמֹלֶךְ *for Molech*) 2 K 23_{13}; introducing object, + שׁחה htpal. *worship* 1 K 11_{33}; בְּ of agent, instrument, *by (means of), with,* + שׁבע ni. *swear* Zp 1_{5} (if em. בְּמַלְכָּם *by their king*); אַחֲרֵי *after,* + הלך *go* 1 K 11_{5}. <COLL> מִלְכֹּם + כְּמוֹשׁ *Chemosh* 1 K 11_{33} 2 K 23_{13}, עַשְׁתֹּרֶת *Ashtoreth* 1 K $11_{5.33}$ 2 K 23_{13}.

⇒ מלך I *be king.*

מלכן, see מַלְבֵּן *brickmould.*

*[**מַלְכִּנֵר**] 0.0.0.1 pr.n.[m.] **Malchiner,** <PREP> לְ of possession, *of, (belonging) to* Seal 911 (8th cent.).

⇒ מֶלֶךְ I *king* + נֵר *lamp.*

[**מַלְכֶת**] 5 n.f. **queen**—cstr. מְלֶכֶת (mss מְלֶאכֶת)—alw. in phrase מְלֶכֶת הַשָּׁמַיִם *the queen of heaven* as epithet of deity (or em. all to מַלְכַּת *queen of*), <CSTR> מְלֶכֶת הַשָּׁמַיִם *queen of heaven* Jr 7_{18} $44_{17.18.19.25}$ (all five mss מְלֶאכֶת). <PREP> לְ of direction, *to,* + קטר pi. *burn incense* Jr $44_{17.18.19.25}$, נסך hi. *pour out* libations Jr $44_{17.18.19.25}$; of benefit, *to, for,* + עשׂה *make* cakes Jr 7_{18}.

⇒ מלך I *be king.*

מֹלֶכֶת 1 n.f. **sororach,** i.e. sister who rules, unless הַמֹּלֶכֶת is pr.n.f. *Hammolecheth,* <SUBJ> ילד *bear* 1 C 7_{18}. <APP> אָחוֹת *sister* 1 C 7_{18}.*

⇒ מלך I *be king.*

מלל I 6.0.1 vb. **wither—Qal** (unless **Ni.**) 4.0.1 Impf. יְמַל, יְמָלוּ; + waw וַיְמַל—**wither, wilt, fade,** <SUBJ> אָדָם *human being* Jb 14_{2} (unless מלל IV ni. *be cut off*), ילד pass. *one born* Jb 14_{2}, wicked Ps 37_{2} Jb 24_{24}, עשׂה ptc. *one who does* injustice Ps 37_{2}, יְקוּם *living form* 1QM 15_{11}, חָצִיר *grass* Ps 90_{6} (if em. יְמוֹלֵל [po.] to יְמַל), זְמוֹרָה *branch* Jb 15_{32} (if em. תְּמוּרָתוֹ ... תִּמָּלֵא *his recompense ... will be paid in full* to זְמוֹרָתוֹ ... תִּמַּל *his branch ... will wither*), קָצִיר *branch* Jb 18_{16}. <PREP> כְּ *as,* + חָצִיר *grass* Ps 37_{2}, ראשׁ *head* of grain Jb 24_{24}. <COLL> מלל || נבל *fade* Ps 37_{2}, יבשׁ *be dry;* + קפץ ni. *be contracted,* i.e. wilt Jb 24_{24}; + adverb, מַהֵר *quickly* 1QM 15_{11}, מְהֵרָה

quickly Ps 37$_{2}$, מִמַּעַל *above* Jb 18$_{16}$.

<SYN> נבל *fade,* יבשׁ *be dry.*

Po. 1 Impf. יְמוֹלֵל—**wither,** <SUBJ> חָצִיר *grass* Ps 90$_{6}$ (or em. יָמַל, i.e. qal; || יבשׁ *be dry;* :: ציץ hi. *flourish*). <PREP> לְ *in, at,* + עֶרֶב *evening* Ps 90$_{6}$.

<SYN> יבשׁ *be dry.*

<ANT> ציץ hi. *flourish.*

Htpo. 1 Impf. יִתְמֹלָלוּ—**wither** (unless מלל IV htpo. *be cut off*), <SUBJ> רָשָׁע *wicked one* Ps 58$_{8}$.

⇨ cf. אמל I *be feeble.*

מלל II 4.1.1 vb. **speak—Pi.** 4.1.1 Pf. מִלֵּל, מִלְּלוּ; impf. יְמַלֵּל, 2ms תְּמַלֶּל־; impv. Si מלל—**speak, utter, declare,** <SUBJ> Job Jb 8$_{2}$, שִׂיב ptc. *elderly one* Si 35$_{3}$, שָׂפָה *lip* Jb 33$_{3}$, מִי *who?* Gn 21$_{7}$ Ps 106$_{2}$ 4QapPs^{a} 1.1$_{7}$. <OBJ> שֵׁם *name* of Y. 4QapPs^{a} 1.1$_{7}$, גְּבוּרָה *mighty deed* Ps 106$_{2}$, דַּעַת *knowledge* Jb 33$_{3}$, אֵלֶּה *these (things)* Jb 8$_{2}$. <PREP> לְ of direction, *to,* + Abraham Gn 21$_{7}$. <COLL> מלל pi. || שׁמע hi. *proclaim* Ps 106$_{2}$; + adverb, עַד־אָן *how long?* Jb 8$_{2}$, perh. בָּרוּר *plainly* Jb 33$_{3}$.

<SYN> שׁמע hi. *proclaim.**

⇨ מִלָּה *word.*

מלל III 1 vb. **scrape—Qal** 1 Ptc. מֹלֵל—**scrape,** with feet, to make signs, <SUBJ> אָדָם *human being* Pr 6$_{13}$ (|| קרץ *wink,* ירה hi. *teach,* i.e. point), אִישׁ *man* Pr 6$_{13}$, בְּלִיַּעַל *wicked one* Pr 6$_{13}$ (or em. אָדָם בְּלִיַּעַל *a human being, a wicked one* to אֲדַם בְּלִיַּעַל *a human being of wickedness*). <PREP> בְּ of instrument, *by (means of), with,* + רֶגֶל *foot* Pr 6$_{13}$.

<SYN> קרץ *wink,* ירה hi. *teach.*

⇨ מְלִילָה *ear of corn.*

מלל IV 4 vb. **cut off, circumcise—Qal** 1 Impv. מֹל—**circumcise,** <SUBJ> Joshua Jos 5$_{2}$. <OBJ> בֵּן *son* of Israel Jos 5$_{2}$. <COLL> מלל + adverb, שֵׁנִית *second (time)* Jos 5$_{2}$.

Ni. 2 + waw וּנְמַלְתֶּם; + waw וַיִּמַּל—**1. be cut off,** <SUBJ> אָדָם *human being* Jb 14$_{2}$ (unless מלל I *wither*).

2. be circumcised, <SUBJ> Abraham and descendants Gn 17$_{11}$. <COLL> וּנְמַלְתֶּם אֵת בְּשַׂר עָרְלַתְכֶם *and you shall be circumcised in respect of the flesh of your foreskin* Gn 17$_{11}$.

Htpo. 1 Impf. יִתְמֹלָלוּ—**be cut off** (unless מלל I *wither*), <SUBJ> רָשָׁע *wicked one* Ps 58$_{8}$.

⇨ cf. מול I *circumcise.*

מִלֲלַי 1 pr.n.m. **Milalai,** priest's son and musician at dedication of walls of Jerusalem, <NOM CL> מִלֲלַי ... בִּכְלֵי שִׁיר דָּוִיד *Milalai ... was with David's instruments of song* Ne. 12$_{36}$. <APP> אָח *brother* Ne 12$_{36}$.

[מַלְמָד] 1.1 n.[m.] **goad**—cstr. מַלְמַד—goad, pointed stick or tipped with iron or with nail driven in at the end (1 S 13$_{21}$; cf. Ec 12$_{11}$), for driving cattle,* used as a weapon (Jg 3$_{31}$ Si 38$_{25}$), <OBJ> תמך *hold* Si 38$_{25}$. <CSTR> מַלְמַד הַבָּקָר *goad of (the) cattle* Jg 3$_{31}$. <PREP> בְּ of instrument, *by (means of), with,* + נכה hi. *strike,* i.e. kill Jg 3$_{31}$.*

⇨ למד *learn.*

מלץ 2 vb. **be smooth—Ni.** 2 Pf. נִמְלְצוּ—**be smooth, pleasant,** <SUBJ> אִמְרָה *word* Ps 119$_{103}$, אֹמֶר *word* Jb 6$_{25(ms)}$ (L מרץ ni. *be grievous*). <PREP> לְ of benefit, *to, for,* + חֵךְ *palate* Ps 119$_{103}$; מִן of comparison, *(more) than,* + דְּבַשׁ *honey* Ps 119$_{103}$. <PREP> מלץ ni. + adverb, מָה *how!* Jb 6$_{25(ms)}$.

⇨ מְלִיצָה II *allusive saying.*

מֶלְצַר 2 n.m. **guardian,** official given charge of Daniel, Hananiah, Mishael and Azariah, <SUBJ> היה *be* Dn 1$_{16}$, ראה *see* Dn 1$_{11}$, שׁמע *hear* Dn 1$_{11}$, נסה pi. *test* Dn 1$_{11}$, נשׂא *take* Dn 1$_{16}$, נתן *give* Dn 1$_{16}$, עשׂה *do* Dn 1$_{11}$. <OBJ> מנה pi. *appoint* Dn 1$_{11}$. <PREP> אֶל *to,* + אמר *say* Dn 1$_{11}$.

מלק 2 vb. **pinch off**—+ waw וּמָלַק—**pinch off, wring** head of bird, <SUBJ> כֹּהֵן *priest* Lv 1$_{15}$ 5$_{8}$. <OBJ> רֹאשׁ *head* Lv 1$_{15}$ 5$_{8}$. <PREP> מוּל *from the front of,* + עֹרֶף *neck* Lv 5$_{8}$ (+ וְלֹא יַבְדִּיל *but he shall not sever [it]*).

מַלְקוֹחַ 7 n.m. **spoil**—cstr. מַלְקוֹחַ—**spoil, booty,** consisting of humans and animals (Nm 31$_{11.26}$), <SUBJ> היה *be* Nm 31$_{32}$, לקח ho. *be taken* Is 49$_{24}$, מלט ni. *be* *delivered* Is 49$_{25}$. <OBJ> לקח *take* Nm 31$_{11}$, בוא hi. *bring* Nm 31$_{12}$, חצה *divide* Nm 31$_{27}$. <CSTR> מַלְקוֹחַ עָרִיץ *spoil of a tyrant* Is 49$_{25}$, הַשְּׁבִי *of the captives* Nm 31$_{25}$; רֹאשׁ מַלְקוֹחַ *head*, i.e. sum, *of the spoil of* Nm 31$_{26}$, כָּל־הַמַּלְקוֹחַ *all the spoil* Nm 31$_{11}$. <APP> שְׁבִי *captives* Nm 31$_{26(Sam)}$, יֶתֶר *remainder* Nm 31$_{32}$. <COLL> מַלְקוֹחַ || שָׁלָל *spoil* Nm 31$_{11}$, שְׁבִי *captives* Nm 31$_{12}$ Is 49$_{24.25}$; + בַּז *prey* Nm 31$_{32}$.

<SYN> שָׁלָל *spoil*, שְׁבִי *captives*.

⇒ לקח *take*.

[מַלְקוֹחַיִם] 1 n.[m.]du. **jaws**—du. sf. מַלְקוֹחָי—<COLL> לְשׁוֹנִי מֻדְבָּק מַלְקוֹחָי *my tongue is made to adhere to my jaws*, i.e. gums Ps 22$_{16}$.

מַלְקוֹשׁ 8.0.4 n.m. **latter rain,** from December to March, constituting some four-fifths of annual rainfall, <SUBJ> היה *be* Jr 3$_{3}$ (or em. וּמַלְקוֹשׁ לוֹא הָיָה *and the latter rain was not* to לָךְ הָיוּ וּלְמוֹקֵשׁ *to you they were and as a snare*), ירה hi. *water* Ho 6$_{3}$ (or em. ירה to רוה hi. *soak*). <OBJ> נתן *give* Dt 11$_{14}$ Jr 5$_{24}$, ירד hi. *send down* Jl 2$_{23}$ 11QM 1.2$_{9}$. <CSTR> עֵת מַלְקוֹשׁ *time of the latter rain* Zc 10$_{1}$, עָב *cloud of* Pr 16$_{15}$. <APP> גֶּשֶׁם *rain* Jr 5$_{24(Qr)}$ 11QM 1.2$_{9}$, מָטָר *rain* Dt 11$_{14}$. <PREP> לְ *for*, i.e. in order to receive, + פער *open* mouth Jb 29$_{23}$; כְּ *as*, + בוא *come* Ho 6$_{3}$. <COLL> מַלְקוֹשׁ || יוֹרֶה *early rain* Dt 11$_{14}$ Jr 5$_{24}$ Jl 2$_{23(mss)}$ 4QAdmonPar 2.2$_{5}$ 11QM 1.2$_{9}$, מוֹרֶה *early rain* Jl 2$_{23}$, גֶּשֶׁם *rain* Jr 5$_{24(Kt)}$ Ho 6$_{3}$ Jl 2$_{23}$; + מָטָר *rain* Zc 10$_{1}$ Jb 29$_{23}$ 11QM 1.2$_{9}$, רְבִיבִים *showers* Jr 3$_{3}$, טַל *dew* 11QM 1.2$_{9}$.

Also 4QSh[b] B$_{6}$ 4QMyst[a] 14$_{2}$.

<SYN> יוֹרֶה *early rain* , מוֹרֶה *early rain*, גֶּשֶׁם *rain*.*

מֶלְקָחַיִם 6.0.1 n.[m.]du. **tongs**—L מֶלְקָחַיִם; sf. מַלְקָחֶיהָ—for removing coal from altar (Is 6$_{6}$); as utensil of lampstand, for use as snuffers (Ex 25$_{38}$||37$_{23}$ Nm 4$_{9}$ 1 K 7$_{49}$||2 C 4$_{21}$ 11QT 9$_{11}$), <NOM CL> מַלְקָחֶיהָ זָהָב טָהוֹר *its tongs shall be (of) pure gold* Ex 25$_{38}$, sim. 1 K 7$_{49}$||2 C 4$_{21}$. <OBJ> עשׂה *make* Ex 37$_{23}$, כסה pi. *cover* Nm 4$_{9}$. <PREP> בְּ of instrument, *by (means of), with*, + לקח *take* Is 6$_{6}$. <COLL> מֶלְקָחַיִם || מַחְתָּה *snuffdish* Ex 25$_{38}$||37$_{23}$, נֵר *lamp* Ex 37$_{23}$ Nm 4$_{9}$ 1 K 7$_{49}$||2 C 4$_{21}$, פֶּרַח *flower* 1 K 7$_{49}$||2 C 4$_{21}$; + מְנֹרָה *lampstand* Nm 4$_{9}$, כְּלִי *vessel* Nm 4$_{9}$.

Also 11QT 9$_{11}$.

<SYN> מַחְתָּה *snuffdish*, נֵר *lamp*, פֶּרַח *flower*.

⇒ לקח *take*.

*__[מַלְקֹט]__ n.[m.] **gleaning,** <CSTR> מַלְקֹט שִׁבֳּלִים *gleaning of sheaves* Is 17$_{5}$ (if em. מְלַקֵּט *one gleaning*).

<PREP> כְּ *as*, + היה *be* Is 17$_{5}$ (if em.; see Cstr.).

⇒ לקט *gather*.

*__[מָלָשׁ]__ 0.0.0.2 pr.n.[m.] **Malash, 1.** Ḥorvat 'Uza jar inscr. 1$_{5}$ ([מל[ש). **2.** Ḥorvat 'Uza jar inscr. 2$_{3}$. **3.** Ḥorvat 'Uza jar inscr. 2$_{5}$. **4.** son of Abariah (or of Reebiah), Seal 910 (others נלש *Nalash*; 7th cent.).

<NOM CL> שני ... מלש *the second is Malash* Ḥorvat 'Uza jar inscr. 1$_{5}$ ([מל[ש) 2$_{3}$. <APP> בֵּן *son* Seal 910 (others נלש *Nalash*; 7th cent.). <PREP> לְ of possession, *of, (belonging) to* Ḥorvat 'Uza jar inscr. 2$_{5}$ Seal 910 (others נלש *Nalash*; 7th cent.).

*__[מַלְשֶׁנֶת]__ n.f. **slander,** <OBJ> שׁמע *hear* Lm 3$_{61}$ (if em. מַחְשְׁבֹתָם *their schemes* to מַלְשְׁנֹתָם). <CSTR> כָּל־מַלְשְׁנֹתָם *all their slander* Lm 3$_{61}$ (if em.; see Obj.).

מֶלְתָּחָה 1 n.f. **clothes store,** or **wardrobe,*** or perh. **cloakroom,*** <CSTR> מֶלְתַּחַת הָאוֹצָר *wardrobe of the treasury* Jr 38$_{11}$ (if em.; see Prep.). <PREP> אֶל *to*, + בוא *come* Jr 38$_{11}$ (if em. תַּחַת *below* to מֶלְתַּחַת *wardrobe of*); עַל *over, in charge of* 2 K 10$_{22}$ (אֲשֶׁר עַל־הַמֶּלְתָּחָה *the one who was in charge of the wardrobe*).

[מַלְתָּעוֹת] 1 n.f.pl. **jawbone**—pl. cstr. מַלְתְּעוֹת—**jawbone,** perh. **fangs,** <OBJ> נתץ *break* Ps 58$_{7}$ (+ שֵׁן *tooth*). <CSTR> מַלְתְּעוֹת כְּפִירִים *jawbone of the young lions* Ps 58$_{7}$ (mss מְתַלְּעוֹת *jawbone of*).*

⇒ (?) נתע *break**; see also מְתַלְּעוֹת *jawbone*.

[מַמְּגוּרָה] 1 n.f. **granary**—pl. מַמְּגֻרוֹת—**granary, silo,** usu. dug in the ground, <SUBJ> הרס ni. *be torn down* Jl 1$_{17}$ (or em. מְגֻרוֹת *granaries* or מִמְּגֻרוֹת *from the granaries*, from מְגוּרָה; || אוֹצָר *treasury*).*

<SYN> אוֹצָר *treasury*.
⇒ אגר *gather*; cf. מְגוּרָה *granary*.

[מְמַד] 1 n.[m.] **measurement**—pl. sf. מְמַדֶּיהָ—of the earth, <OBJ> שׂים *set* Jb 38$_5$.*
⇒ מדד *measure*.

מְמוּכָן 3 pr.n.m. **Memucan**—Kt מומכן—prince at court of King Ahasuerus, <SUBJ> אמר *say* Est 1$_{16}$, ראה *see* Est 1$_{14}$, ישׁב *dwell* Est 1$_{14}$. <NOM CL> הַקָּרֹב אֵלָיו ... מְמוּכָן *the one(s) who were near to him were... Memucan* Est 1$_{14}$ (or em. הִקְרִיב *he brought near*). <OBJ> קרב hi. *bring near* Est 1$_{14}$ (if em.). <CSTR> דְּבַר מְמוּכָן *word of Memucan* Est 1$_{21}$. <APP> שַׂר *prince* Est 1$_{14}$.

[מָמוֹן] 0.1.4 n.[m.] **wealth**—sf. Q ממונו—**wealth, property,** <OBJ> שׁאל *ask (for)* Ps 2$_8$ (if em. מִמֶּנִּי *of me* to מָמוֹנִי *my wealth*). <PREP> לְ *with respect to*, + שׁמע *obey* 1QS 6$_2$ (=4QS^d 2$_7$=4QS^i 3; both ל[הו]ן, from הוֹן *wealth*); בְּ *concerning*, + שׁקר pi. *deal falsely* 4QS^g 3$_3$ ([ב]ממון= 1QS 6$_{25}$ בהון, from הוֹן *wealth*) CD 14$_{20}$ (קר for שׁקר); אַחַר *after*, + לוז ni. *stray* Si 34$_8$. <COLL> מְלָאכָה || מָמוֹן *work* 1QS 6$_2$; + הוֹן *wealth* 1Q27 2$_5$.
<SYN> מְלָאכָה *work*.*

[מָמוֹת] 2 n.[m.] **death**—pl. cstr. מְמוֹתֵי—**(manner of) death,** <OBJ> מות *die* Jr 16$_4$ Ezk 28$_8$. <CSTR> מְמוֹתֵי חָלָל *death of the slain* Ezk 28$_8$, מְמוֹתֵי תַחֲלֻאִים *death of*, i.e. caused by, *diseases* Jr 16$_4$.*
⇒ מות *die*.

מַמְזֵר 2.0.9 n.m. **bastard**—pl. Q ממזרים—in biblical texts, perh. as a quasi-gentilic for a non-Judaean, or specif. an Ashdodite;* as excluded from assembly of Y. (Dt 23$_3$), dwelling in Ashdod (Zc 9$_6$); later, appar. one born as a result of incest or prohibited mixed marriage, excluded from the community (4QMidrEschat^a 3$_4$ 4QMMT B$_{39}$); their spirits mentioned together with other evil spirits (4QShir^a 1$_5$).
<SUBJ> בוא *come* Dt 23$_3$ 4QMidrEschat^a 3$_4$ 4QMMT B$_{39}$, ישׁב *dwell* Zc 9$_6$. <CSTR> רוחות ממזרים *spirits of bastards* 4QShir^a 1$_5$ 4QShir^b 35$_7$ (רוחי) 48.2$_3$ ([רוחות]) 182$_1$ ([רוחי ממזרי[ם]), עדת *assembly of* 4QShir^b 2.2$_3$. <PREP> לְ of possession, *of, (belonging) to* Dt 23$_3$; עַל *concerning* 4QMMT B$_{39}$ ([על]).
Also 1QH fr. 63 fr. 9$_{11}$ 4QPrayer^d 1.1$_9$ ([מ]מזרים).*
⇒ (?) cf. מָזוֹר *sore*.

*[מְמְחִיר] n.[m.] **bargaining,** <CSTR> [מ]מחיר ממכר תגר *bargaining of*, i.e. for, *the wares of a merchant* Si 42$_{5(M)}$. <PREP> עַל *on account of*, + בושׁ *be ashamed* Si 42$_{5(M)}$ ([על]).
⇒ cf. מְחִיר *price*.

*[מָמָךְ] n.[m.] **sinkhole,** a name for Sheol, <OBJ> ירד hi. *bring down* Am 3$_{11}$ (וְהוֹרִד מִמֵּךְ עֻזֵּךְ *and he will bring your strength down to the Sinkhole*; if em. מִמֵּךְ *from you*).

מִמְכָּר 10.2.1 n.m. **mortgaged property**—cstr. מִמְכַּר; sf. מִמְכָּרוֹ; pl. sf. מִמְכָּרָיו—**1. mortgaged property,** land delivered over (מכר *I deliver [over]*) for the use of another, <SUBJ> היה *be* Lv 25$_{28}$, יצא *go out* Lv 25$_{28.33}$. <OBJ> מכר *deliver over* Lv 25$_{14}$, גאל *redeem* Lv 25$_{25}$, קנה *acquire* Lv 25$_{28}$. <CSTR> מִמְכַּר אָחִיו *mortgaged property of his brother* Lv 25$_{25}$, מִמְכַּר־בַּיִת *mortgaged property of*, i.e. consisting of, *a house* Lv 25$_{33}$ (or em. בַּיִת וְעִיר *of a house and city of* to בֵּית עִיר *of a house of the city of* his possession), <PREP> אֶל *to*, + שׁוב *go back* Ezk 7$_{13}$.
2. act of mortgaging, <CSTR> שְׁנַת מִמְכָּרוֹ *year of*, i.e. since, *its mortgaging* Lv 25$_{29}$, שְׁנֵי *years of*, i.e. since Lv 25$_{27}$, כֶּסֶף מִמְכָּרוֹ *value of his mortgaging* Lv 25$_{50}$.
3. value of mortgage of inheritance, <PREP> לְבַד *apart from*, + אכל *eat* Dt 18$_8$ (or em. לְבַד מִמְכָּרָיו *apart from the proceeds of its mortgaging* to לְבַד מִמְכָּרָיו [from מֶכֶר] in same sense, or לְבַד מִכְּמָרִים *apart from the priests*)=11QT 60$_{15}$ (לבד ממכר).
4. item for sale, wares, merchandise, <OBJ> מהר hi. *hasten (after)* Si 42$_{5(B)}$ ([מ]מכר). <CSTR> ממכר תגרו *wares of a merchant* Si 42$_5$; מֹכְרֵי כָל־מִמְכָּר *sellers of all (kinds of) merchandise* Ne 13$_{20}$. <PREP> לְ *with respect to*, + עשׂה *do* CD 13$_{15}$ (:: מִקָּח *buying*); עַל *concerning*, + יעץ ni. *consult* with buyer Si 37$_{11}$.*

⇒ מכר *deliver (over).*

[מִמְכֶּ֫רֶת] 1.0.2 n.f. **sale**—cstr. מִמְכֶּ֫רֶת—**sale** or **transfer of possession,** <CSTR> מִמְכֶּ֫רֶת עֶבֶד *transfer of ownership of a slave* Lv 25_{42}. <COLL> לֹא יִמָּכְרוּ מִמְכֶּ֫רֶת עָבֶד *they shall not be delivered over (as) the transfer of ownership of a slave,* i.e. assigned as slaves Lv 25_{42}, var. 4QOrd[a] 2_3.*

⇒ מכר *deliver (over).*

מַמְלָכָה 117.3.26 n.f. **kingdom**—Si ממלכת; cstr. מַמְלֶ֫כֶת (L מַמְלֶ֫כֶת); sf. מַמְלַכְתּוֹ, מַמְלַכְתְּךָ, מַמְלַכְתִּי; pl. מַמְלָכוֹת; cstr. מַמְלְכוֹת (מַמְלְכֹת)—**1. kingdom, realm,** sometimes perh. **king*** (e.g. 1 S 10_{18} 1 K 10_{20}||2 C 9_{19} 1 K 18_{10} Is 47_5 Jr 1_{15} 25_{26} Ps 68_{33} 79_6 102_{23} 135_{11} Lm 2_2 [or em.; see Obj.] 2 C 12_8), <SUBJ> היה *be* Ex 19_6 Ezk 17_{14} 29_{14}, קרא *call* Ps 79_6, שׁיר *sing* Ps 68_{33}, שׁמע *hear* 2 C 20_{29}, ידע *know* 2 K 19_{19}||Is 37_{20}, עבד *serve* Is 60_{12} Jr 27_8, *worship* Ps 102_{23}, שׁמר *keep* Ezk 17_{14}, שׁוב *go back* 1 K 12_{26} 4QpsMos[d] 1.2_2, קבץ ni. *gather together* Ps 102_{23}, מוט *totter* Ps 46_7, רעשׁ *shake* perh. 4Q418 212_1 (ממל[כה]), עמד *stand* Ezk 17_{14}, נשׂא htp. *exalt oneself* Ezk 17_{14} 29_{14}, שׁקט *be quiet* 2 C 14_4, מצא *find* 1 K 18_{10}, לחם ni. *fight* Is 19_2 Jr 34_1 2 C 17_{10}, לחץ *oppress* 1 S 10_{18}, אבד *perish* Is 60_{12} 4QpsEzek[c] 3.2_7.

<NOM CL> כָּל־הַמַּמְלָכוֹת אֲשֶׁר עַל־פְּנֵי הָאֲדָמָה *all the kingdoms that are upon the face of the earth* Jr 25_{26} (if em.; see Cstr.), נָקִי אָנֹכִי וּמַמְלַכְתִּי מֵעִם י׳ *I and my kingdom are guiltless before Y.* 2 S 3_{28}, מאפרים ממלכת חמס *from Ephraim there was a kingdom of violence* Si 47_{21}.

<OBJ> שׁבע hi. *cause to swear* 1 K 18_{10}, ראה hi. *cause to see* Na 3_5, שׁמע hi. *summon* Jr 51_{27}, יצא hi. *take out* 4QpsEzek[c] 3.2_5 ([א]וציא), שׁלח *send* 1 K 18_{10}, קבץ *gather* Zp 3_8, שׁוב hi. *give back* 2 C 11_1, נתן *give* Nm 32_{33} Dt 3_{13} 1 K 11_{11} 14_8 Ezr 1_2||2 C 36_{23} Ne 9_{22} 2 C 21_3, לקח *take* Dt 3_4 1 K 11_{34}, חזק hi. *grasp,* i.e. possess 4QpsEzek[c] 3.2_5, שׁקה hi. *cause to drink* Jr 25_{26}, נכה hi. *strike* Jr 49_{28}, הרג *kill* Ps 135_{11}, קרע *tear* 1 K $11_{11.13.31}$ 14_8 4QpsEzek[c] 3.2_9 (ממלכ[ה]), שׁבר *break* 4QpsEzek[c] 3.3_1, הרס *tear down* Jr 1_{10}, נתץ *break down* Jr 1_{10} 18_7, נתשׁ *pluck up* Jr 1_{10} 18_7, אבד hi. *destroy* Jr 1_{10} 18_7, שׁחת hi. *destroy* Jr 51_{20}, שׁמד hi. *destroy* Am 9_8, רגז hi. *shake* Is 23_{11}, רעשׁ hi. *shake* Is 14_{16}, חלל pi. *profane* Lm 2_2 (or em. לָאָ֫רֶץ חִלֵּל מַמְלָכָה *to the ground, he has profaned the kingdom* to לְאֶ֫רֶץ חֲלָלִים מַלְכָּהּ *to the land of the pierced its king*), בנה *build* Jr 1_{10} 18_9, נטע *plant* Jr 1_{10} 18_9, כון hi. *establish* Is 9_6 2 C 17_5 Si 46_{13}, סעד *support* Is 9_6.

<CSTR> מַמְלֶ֫כֶת י׳ *kingdom of Y.* 2 C 13_8, מַמְלְכֹת הָאֱלִיל *kingdoms of the idol(s)* Is 10_{10}, מַמְלֶ֫כֶת סִיחֹן *kingdom of Sihon* Nm 32_{33}, עוֹג *of Og* Nm 32_{33} Dt $3_{4.10.13}$, אָבִיו *of his father* 2 C 21_4 (L מַמְלֶ֫כֶת), מַמְלֶ֫כֶת ... מֶ֫לֶךְ *kingdom of ... the king of* Nm $32_{33.33}$, מַמְלֶ֫כֶת כֹּהֲנִים *kingdom of priests* Ex 19_6, ממלכות רוח[י] *kingdoms of the spirits of* 4QShirShabb[d] 1.2_3, קדושים *of the holy ones of* 4QShirShabb[f] 23.2_{11}.

מַמְלְכוֹת הָאָ֫רֶץ *kingdoms of the earth* Dt 28_{25} 2 K $19_{15.19}$||Is $37_{16.20}$ Is 23_{17} Jr 15_4 24_9 25_6 (הַמַּמְלָכוֹת; or em. הַמַּמְלָכוֹת and del. הָאָ֫רֶץ) 29_{18} 34_{14} Ps 68_{33} Ezr 1_2||2 C 36_{23} 2 C $20_{6(ms)}$, אֶ֫רֶץ *of the land of* Jr 34_1, הָאֲרָצוֹת *of the lands* 1 C 29_{30} 2 C 12_8 17_{10} 20_{29}, גּוֹיִם *of nations* Is 13_4 (or em. מַמְלָכוֹת *kingdoms,* nations) Hg 2_{22} (הַגּוֹיִם; or del. מַמְלְכוֹת) 2 C 20_6, צָפוֹנָה *of the north* Jr 1_{15}, אֲרָרַט מִנִּי וְאַשְׁכְּנַז *of Ararat, Minni and Ashkenaz* Jr 51_{27} (or em. מַמְלָכוֹת *kingdoms,* Ararat ...), כְּנָ֫עַן *of Canaan* Ps 135_{11}, חָצוֹר *of Hazor* Jr 49_{28}, ממלכת ישראל *kingdom of Israel* 4QpsEzek[c] 3.2_7, [מצרים] *of Egypt* 4QpsEzek[c] 3.3_1, ממלכת חמס *kingdom of violence* Si 47_{21}.

אֱלוֹהַּ כָּל־גּוֹי וּמַמְלָכָה *god of any nation or kingdom* 2 C 32_{15}, גְּבֶ֫רֶת מַמְלָכוֹת *mistress of the kingdoms* Is 47_5, רֹאשׁ כָּל־הַמַּמְלָכוֹת *head of all the kingdoms* Jos 11_{10} (mss לְכָל־ *of all*), יַד *hand of* 1 S 10_{18}, ראשי ממלכות *heads of the kingdoms of* 4QShirShabb[d] 1.2_3 4QShirShabb[f] 23.2_{11}, מִשְׁפְּחוֹת מַמְלָכוֹת *clans of the kingdoms of* Jr 1_{15} (or del. מִשְׁפְּחוֹת), עָרֵי מַמְלֶ֫כֶת *cities of the kingdom of* Dt 3_{10}, כִּסֵּא מַמְלָכוֹת *throne of kingdoms* Hg 2_{22}, רֵאשִׁית מַמְלַכְתּוֹ *beginning of his kingdom* Gn 10_{10}, צְבִי מַמְלָכוֹת *glory of the kingdoms* Is 13_{19}, שְׁאוֹן *uproar of* Is 13_4 (if em. מַמְלָכוֹת *of kingdoms of*) 1QH 6_7 (מ[מל]כות), חֹזֶק מַמְלְכוֹת *strength of the kingdoms of* Hg 2_{22} (or del. מַמְלְכוֹת), עֲבוֹדַת *service of* 2 C 12_8, ימי ממלכתו *days of his kingdom* 4QpsMos[e] 1_4.

כָּל־ כָּל־מַמְלָכָה *any kingdom* 2 S 9_{19} 2 C 32_{15} (כָּל־ ...), כָּל־הַמַּמְלָכָה *all the kingdom* 1 K $11_{13.34}$, כָּל־הַמַּמְלָכוֹת *all the kingdoms* Dt 3$_{21}$ Jos 11$_{10}$ 1 S 10$_{18}$ 1 K 5$_{1}$ 10$_{20(mss)}$ (L כָּל־מַמְלְכוֹת) Jr 25$_{26}$ (if em.; see above), כֹּל מַמְלְכוֹת *all the kingdoms of* Dt 28$_{25}$ 2 K 19$_{15.19}$||Is 37$_{16.20}$ Is 23$_{17}$ Jr 1$_{15}$ (if del. מִשְׁפְּחוֹת *clans of;* all three כָּל־) 15$_{4}$ 24$_{9}$ 25$_{6}$ (כָּל־הַמַּמְלָכוֹת; or em.; see above) 29$_{18}$ 34$_{1}$ (כָּל־) 34$_{17}$ Ps 135$_{11}$ Ezr 1$_{2}$||2 C 36$_{23}$ 1 C 29$_{30}$ 2 C 17$_{10}$ (both כָּל־) 20$_{6.29}$ (כָּל־) 4QShirShabb[b] 5$_{5}$ (כולממלכו[ת]).

<APP> אֶרֶץ *land* Nm 32$_{33}$, חֶבֶל *territory* Dt 3$_{4.13}$, עִיר *city* Dt 3$_{4}$, בָּשָׁן *Bashan* Dt 3$_{13}$, אֲרָרַט מִנִּי וְאַשְׁכְּנָז *Ararat, Minni and Ashkenaz* Jr 51$_{27}$ (if em.; see Cstr.).

<ADJ> גָּדוֹל *great* Jr 28$_{8}$, שָׁפָל *lowly* Ezk 17$_{14}$ 29$_{14}$, חַטָּא *sinful* Am 9$_{8}$, רָשָׁע *wicked* 4QpsEzek[c] 3.2$_{9}$ (ממלכ[ה] [הרשעה]), הִיא *that* 4QpsEzek[c] 3.2$_{9}$ (ממלכ[ה ... ה]היא), אֵלֶּה *these* Jos 11$_{10}$ Am 6$_{2}$.

<PREP> לְ of direction, *(in)to* perh. 4QPrQuot 10$_{8}$, + קרא *call* Jr 1$_{15}$ (if del. מִשְׁפְּחוֹת *clans of*), עשׂה *do* Dt 3$_{21}$, מצא *find*, i.e. reach Is 10$_{10}$, חצה ni. *be divided* Ezk 37$_{22}$; of benefit, *to, for,* + היה *be* Dt 28$_{25}$, עשׂה ni. *be made* 1 K 10$_{20}$||2 C 9$_{19}$; of possession, *of, (belonging) to* Jos 11$_{10(mss)}$ 2 K 19$_{15}$||Is 37$_{16}$ Jr 15$_{4}$ 24$_{9}$ 29$_{18}$ 34$_{17}$; *concerning,* + אמר *say* Jr 49$_{28}$.

בְּ *upon* Am 9$_{8}$; *over,* + משׁל *rule* 1 K 5$_{1}$ 2 C 20$_{6}$; *against,* + לחם ni. *fight* Is 19$_{2}$.

מִן of direction, *from,* + הלך htp. *go about* Ps 105$_{13}$|| 1 C 16$_{20}$; of comparison, *(more) than,* + היה *be* Ezk 29$_{15}$, יטב *be good,* i.e. better Am 6$_{2}$ (if em. הֲטוֹבִים *are [you] better?* to הֲיִטַבְתֶּם *are you better?*).

עַל *upon, over* Is 9$_{6}$, + היה *be* 2 C 17$_{10}$, קום *arise* 2 C 21$_{4}$, עבר *pass,* i.e. befall 1 C 29$_{30}$, ארך hi. *prolong* days Dt 17$_{20}$ (=11QT 59$_{21}$ מלכותו; Sam על כסא ממלכתו *on his royal throne*), ברך htp. *be blessed* 4QJonathan 2$_{8}$, פקד hi. *appoint* Jr 1$_{10}$, שׁפך *pour* indignation Zp 3$_{8}$; *against,* + בוא hi. *bring* Gn 20$_{9}$, נבא ni. *prophesy* Jr 28$_{8}$; *concerning,* + דבר pi. *speak* Jr 18$_{7}$; *for* 2 C 29$_{21}$.

עִם *with,* + ריב *contend with* 4QTanḥ 1.1$_{2}$.

אֵת *with,* + זנה *prostitute oneself* Is 23$_{17}$.

לִפְנֵי *in the face of, against,* + חזק htp. *show oneself strong* 2 C 13$_{8}$.

<COLL> מַמְלָכָה || גּוֹי *nation* Ex 19$_{6}$ (+) 1 K 18$_{10.10}$ Is 60$_{12}$ Jr 1$_{10}$ 18$_{7.9}$ 27$_{8}$ 29$_{18}$ (+) 51$_{27}$ Ezk 37$_{22}$ Na 3$_{5}$ Zp 3$_{8}$ Ps 46$_{7}$ 79$_{6}$ Ps 105$_{13}$||1 C 16$_{20}$ 2 C 32$_{15}$ perh. 4QConfess 1.2$_{9}$, עַם *people* Jr 34$_{1}$ (+) Ps 102$_{23}$ 105$_{13}$||1 C 16$_{20}$ (+) Ne 9$_{22}$, אֶרֶץ *land* Is 14$_{16}$ Jr 28$_{8}$ Ps 46$_{7}$ (+), עִיר *city* Is 19$_{2}$; + כִּסֵּא *throne* Is 9$_{6}$.

הַמַּמְלָכוֹת אֲשֶׁר שְׁתֵּי מַמְלָכוֹת *two kingdoms* Ezk 37$_{22}$, אַתָּה עֹבֵר שָׁמָּה *the kingdoms to which you are passing over* Dt 3$_{21}$, מַמְלֶכֶת י׳ בְּיַד בְּנֵי דָוִיד *the kingdom of Y. in the hand of the sons of David* 2 C 13$_{8}$, ממלכות ממלכות קדושים perh. *each of the kingdoms of holy ones* 4Q ShirShabb[f] 23.2$_{11}$ (but prob. repetition of ממלכות is error).

2. kingship, sovereignty (distinction from §1 not alw. clear), <SUBJ> אתה *come* Mc 4$_{8}$ (or em.; see Cstr.), בוא *come* Mc 4$_{8}$ (or em.; see Cstr.), קום *stand,* i.e. continue 1 S 13$_{14}$ 24$_{21}$, אמן ni. *be established* 2 S 7$_{16}$, כון ni. *be established* 1 K 2$_{46}$, חזק *be strong* 2 K 14$_{5}$||2 C 25$_{3}$, שׁבת ni. *cease* Is 17$_{3}$.

<NOM CL> לְךָ י׳ הַמַּמְלָכָה *to you, O Y., is the kingship* 1 C 29$_{11}$.

<OBJ> כון hi. *establish* 1 S 13$_{13}$ 2 S 7$_{12}$, קרע *tear* 1 S 28$_{17}$, נתן *give* 1 S 28$_{17}$ 2 C 13$_{5}$, עבר hi. *cause to pass* 2 S 3$_{10}$, נשׂא pi. *exalt* 2 S 5$_{12}$, חזק hi. *grasp* 2 K 15$_{19}$.

<CSTR> מַמְלֶכֶת יִשְׂרָאֵל *kingship of,* i.e. over, *Israel* 1 S 24$_{21}$, מַמְלֶכֶת לְבַת־יְרוּשָׁלִָם *kingship of,* i.e. over, *the daughter of Jerusalem* Mc 4$_{8}$ (or em. מַמְלָכָה *kingship* to the daughter of Jerusalem); חק ממלכת *statute of kingship* Si 47$_{11}$.

<APP> מֶמְשָׁלָה *dominion* Mc 4$_{8}$ (or em.; see Cstr.).

<PREP> לְ of benefit, *for,* + עצר *retain* strength 2 C 22$_{9}$.

<COLL> בַּיִת|| מַמְלָכָה *house* 2 S 7$_{16}$, מִבְצָר *fortification* Is 17$_{3}$; + כִּסֵּא *throne* 2 S 3$_{10}$ 7$_{16}$.

מַמְלַכְתְּךָ אֶל־יִשְׂרָאֵל *your kingship over Israel* 1 S 13$_{13}$ (mss עַל *over*), מַמְלָכָה ... עַל־יִשְׂרָאֵל *kingship ... over Israel* 2 C 13$_{5}$.

3. royalty, <CSTR> זֶרַע הַמַּמְלָכָה *the offspring of royalty,* i.e. royal family 2 K 11$_{1}$||2 C 22$_{10}$, עִיר הַמַּמְלָכָה *city of,* i.e. royal city 1 S 27$_{5}$ 1 C 27$_{25}$ (if ins. בְּעִיר־ הַמַּמְלָכָה), עָרֵי *cities of* Jos 10$_{2}$ 1 S 27$_{5(mss)}$, בֵּית מַמְלָכָה *house of royalty,* i.e. royal palace Am 7$_{13}$, כִּסֵּא הַמַּמְלָכָה *the throne of royalty,* i.e. royal throne 2 C 23$_{20}$, כִּסֵּא מַמְלַכְתּוֹ *throne of his royalty,* i.e. his royal throne Dt 17$_{18}$=11QT 56$_{20}$ Dt 17$_{20(Sam)}$ 2 S 7$_{13}$, מַמְלַכְתֶּךָ *of your royalty,* i.e. your royal throne 1 K 9$_{5}$, קץ ממלכה *period* *of royalty*, i.e. royal period 4QNarrC 1_{13}.

4. (period of) reign, <CSTR> בְּרֵאשִׁית מַמְלֶכֶת יְהוֹיָקִם *in the beginning of the reign of Jehoiakim* Jr 27_1 (or em. בַּשָּׁנָה הָרְבִיעִית לְצִדְקִיָּהוּ *in the fourth year of Zedekiah*), צִדְקִיָּה *of Zedekiah* Jr 28_1 (or em. בַּשָּׁנָה הָרְבִיעִית לְצִדְקִיָּה).

Also 4QVisSam 3.2_5 4QapJoshua[a] 13.1_3 4QParaKings 96_1 (ממלכו[ת]) 4Q392 1_1 2_3 4QShirShabb[b] 21_2 (ממלכו[ת]) 4QShirShabb[f] 20.2_4 4Q416 1_5 4QJonathan 3_6 6QapSamKings 57_1.

<SYN> §1 גּוֹי *nation*, עַם *people*, אֶרֶץ *land*, עִיר *city*; §2 בַּיִת *house*, מִבְצָר *fortification*.*

⇒ מלך I *be king*.

[מַמְלָכוּת] 9.0.1 n.f. **kingdom**—cstr. מַמְלְכוּת—**1. kingdom, realm,** <SUBJ> היה *be* Jos $13_{21.30}$. <OBJ> נתן *give* Jos 13_{12}, שׁוב hi. *give back* 2 S 16_3. <CSTR> מַמְלְכוּת סִיחוֹן *kingdom of Sihon* Jos $13_{21.27}$, עוֹג *of Og* Jos $13_{12.30.31}$, אָבִי *of my father* 2 S 16_3, מַמְלְכוּת ... מֶלֶךְ *kingdom of ... the king of* Jos $13_{21.27.30}$, ממלכות כו[הנים] *kingdom of priests* 4QM[a] 16_3; עָרֵי מַמְלְכוּת *cities of the kingdom of* Jos 13_{31}, יֶתֶר *rest of* Jos 13_{27}, כָּל־מַמְלְכוּת *all the kingdom of* Jos $13_{12.21.30}$.

2. kingship, sovereignty, <OBJ> נתן *give* 1 S 15_{28}, קרע *tear* 1 S 15_{28}, שׁבת hi. *cause to cease* Ho 1_4. <CSTR> מַמְלְכוּת יִשְׂרָאֵל *kingship of*, i.e. over, *Israel* 1 S 15_{28}, בֵּית יִשְׂרָאֵל *of*, i.e. over, *the house of Israel* Ho 1_4.

3. (period of) reign of, <CSTR> רֵאשִׁית מַמְלְכוּת יְהוֹיָקִים *beginning of the reign of Jehoiakim* Jr 26_1.*

⇒ מלך I *be king*.

מִמְסָךְ I 2 n.[m.] **(bowl of) mixed wine** (mixed with water, or perh. spices or honey),* <OBJ> מלא pi. *fill* Is 65_{11} (1QIsa[a] מסכה *molten image*; ‖ שֻׁלְחָן *table*), חקר *search out* Pr 23_{30} (unless מִמְסָךְ II *bowl, amphora*; + יַיִן *wine*).

<SYN> שֻׁלְחָן *table*.*

⇒ מסך *mix*.

***מִמְסָךְ** II 1 n.[m.] **bowl, amphora,** <OBJ> חקר *search out* Pr 23_{30} (unless מִמְסָךְ I *[bowl of] mixed wine*; + יַיִן *wine*).

⇒ מסך *mix*.

מֶמֶר 1 n.[m.] **bitterness,** <NOM CL> בֵּן כְּסִיל ... מֶמֶר לְיוֹלַדְתּוֹ *a foolish son is ... bitterness to the one who bore him* Pr 17_{25} (‖ כַּעַס *vexation*).

<SYN> כַּעַס *vexation*.*

⇒ מרר I *be bitter*.

מַמְרֵא I 9.0.1 pl.n. **Mamre**—Q ממרה—perh. Ḥarām Rāmet, 4 km N of Hebron, <CSTR> אֵלֹנֵי מַמְרֵא *terebinths of Mamre* Gn 13_{18} (+ אֲשֶׁר בְּחֶבְרוֹן *which are at Hebron*) 18_1 (or em. both אֵלוֹן *terebinth of*) 4QAges[a] 2.2_4 (אלוני ממרה). <PREP> לִפְנֵי *before* Gn 23_{17}; עַל־פְּנֵי *before* Gn 23_{19} 25_9 49_{30} 50_{13}; מַמְרֵא without prep. *at Mamre* Gn 35_{27}. <COLL> מַמְרֵא קִרְיַת אַרְבַּע הִיא חֶבְרוֹן *Mamre, Kiriath-arba, that is Hebron* Gn 35_{27}, sim. Gn 23_{19}.

Also 4Q482 1_3 ([מ]מרא).*

⇒ מַמְרֵא II pr.n.m. *Mamre*.

מַמְרֵא II 2 pr.n.m. **Mamre,** Amorite ally of Abram, brother of Aner and Eshcol, <SUBJ> לקח *take* Gn 14_{24}. <CSTR> אֵלֹנֵי מַמְרֵא *terebinths of Mamre* Gn 14_{13} (or em. אֵלוֹן *terebinth of*). <APP> אֱמֹרִי *Amorite* Gn 14_{13}, אָח *brother* Gn 14_{13}.

⇒ מַמְרֵא I pl.n. *Mamre*.

*[**מַמְרֶה**] n.m. **rebellion,** <CSTR> נַחֲלַת מַמְרֶה *inheritance of rebellion* Jb 20_{29} (if em. אִמְרוֹ *his word*).

⇒ מרה *rebel*.

מַמְּרֹרִים 1 n.[m.]pl. **bitterness,** <OBJ> שׂבע hi. *sate with* Jb 9_{18} (or em. מְמֹרְרִים or בִּמְרֹרִים *with bitter things*, from מָרֹר).*

⇒ מרר I *be bitter*.

מִמְשַׁח I 1 n.[m.] **anointing** (unless מִמְשַׁח II *extension* or III *sparkling*), <CSTR> כְּרוּב מִמְשַׁח *cherub of anointing*, i.e. anointed cherub Ezk 28_{14}.*

⇒ משׁח *anoint*.

***מִמְשַׁח** II 1 n.[m.] perh. **extension** (unless מִמְשַׁח I

anointing or III *sparkling*), <CSTR> כְּרוּב מִמְשַׁח *cherub of extension*, i.e. with outstretched wings Ezk 28_{14}.
⇒ מֹשַׁח III *measure*.

***מִמְשַׁח** III 1 n.[m.] **sparkling** (unless I *anointing* or מִמְשַׁח II *extension*), <CSTR> כְּרוּב מִמְשַׁח *cherub of sparkling*, i.e. sparkling cherub Ezk 28_{14}.

מִמְשָׁל 3.0.12 n.[m.] **dominion**—cstr. Q ממשל; sf. Q ממשלו; pl. מִמְשָׁלִים—**1. dominion, rule,** <SUBJ> היה *be* 4QCommGenA 5_1, בוא *come* 4QTime 1.2_9. <NOM CL> מִמְשָׁל רַב מֶמְשַׁלְתּוֹ *his dominion shall be a great dominion* Dn 11_5 (or em.; see Obj.). <OBJ> משׁל *rule with* Dn $11_{3.5}$ (if em. וּמָשַׁל מִמְשָׁל רַב מֶמְשַׁלְתּוֹ *and he shall rule; his dominion shall be great* to ... וּמָשַׁל מִמֶּמְשַׁלְתּוֹ *and he shall rule with* greater dominion *than his dominion*), נתן *give* 4QMyst[a] 6.1_{15}.

<CSTR> ממשל זכר *dominion of male* 4Q415 9_8, [מ]עשיה *of her deeds* 4Q418 43_7 (=4Q417 2.1_9 ממשלת), אור *of light of* day 4QPrQuot 15.6_6, ח[ושך] *of darkness* 4QPrQuot 33.10_{19}, הצדק *of righteousness* 4QTime 1.2_9 (הצדק erased), הטוב *of good* 4QTime 1.2_{9}(with erasure); רוש ממשל *beginning of the dominion of* 4QPrQuot 33.10_{19}, קץ ממשל *period of dominion* 1QM 1_5 (+ יְשׁוּעָה *salvation*), אור ממשל perh. *light of dominion* 4QHod[a] 3.1_{11}, כול ממשלו *all his dominion* 1QS 9_{24}. <ADJ> רַב *great* Dn $11_{3.5}$. <PREP> בְּ of place, time, *in, during* 4QPrQuot 15.6_6 40.2_2 (ב[ממש]ל), + עשׂה *do* 1QS 9_{24}. <COLL> קץ ממשל לכול אנשי גורלו *a period of dominion for all the men of his lot* 1QM 1_5.

2. pl. **rulers,** <SUBJ> ילד ni. *be born* 1 C 26_6 (or em.; see Coll.). <APP> בֵּן *son* 1 C 26_6 (or em.; see Coll.). <COLL> הַמִּמְשָׁלִים לְבֵית אֲבִיהֶם *the rulers of their father's house* 1 C 26_6 (or em. הֵם מֹשְׁלִים *they were rulers*, i.e. משׁל ptc.).

Also 4Q418 206_4 4QPrQuot 1.3_3.*
⇒ משׁל *rule*.

מְמַשֵּׁל *(persistent) teller of proverbs*, see משׁל II *be like*, Pi.

מֶמְשָׁלָה 17.6.64 n.f. **dominion**—Si ממשלת; cstr. מֶמְשֶׁלֶת; sf. Q ממשלתי, מֶמְשַׁלְתְּךָ (mss מֶמְשַׁלְתֶּךָ), מֶמְשַׁלְתּוֹ, Q ממשלתה, Q ממשלתמה; pl. cstr. מֶמְשְׁלוֹת; sf. Q ממשלותך, מַמְשְׁלוֹתָיו (מֶמְשְׁלוֹתָיו), Q ממשלותם.

1. dominion, rule, authority, of Y. (Ps 103_{22} [unless §4] 145_{13} Si $10_{4.5}$ 4QAdmonPar 3.2_9 [[ממ]שלתו]] 4QShir[a] 1_2 [[ממשלתו]] GnzPs 4_9), Belial (1QM $14_{9.10}$ 18_1 1QS $1_{18.23}$ 2_{19} 4QMidrEschat[b] 10_8 4QpsMos[e] 2.1_3 4QBer[a] 7.2_5), angels, supernatural powers (1QM 10_{12} 13_{10} 1QS $3_{20.21.22.23}$), spirits (4QPrayer[e] 1.1_3), humans (1 K 9_{19}‖2 C 8_6 Is 22_{21} Jr 34_1 51_{28} Mc 4_8 Dn 11_5 Si 7_4 10_1 41_6 1QH 7_{23} 1QpHab 2_{13} 1QM 1_6 17_7 1QS 3_{17} 4QpNah 1_{5a} 3.2_4), heavenly bodies over day and night (Gn $1_{16.16}$ Ps $136_{8.9}$ Si 43_6), light (1QS 10_1 4Q408 1_8 4QHod[a] 3.2_6 [[ממשל]תו]]), darkness (1QH 12_6 4Q408 1_{10}), seasons (1QH 12_9), justice (11QMelch 2_9), injustice, evil (Si $41_{6[B]}$ 1QM 17_5 1QS 4_{19} 4QShir[a] 1_6 [[ממשל]ת]]).

<SUBJ> תמם *come to an end* 4QpNah 1_{5a} 4QPrayer[d] 1.1_7, אתה *come* Mc 4_8, בוא *come* Mc 4_8, יפע hi. *shine forth* 4Q408 $1_{8.10}$ (unless both obj.), סור *turn aside*, i.e. end 1QM 1_6, אבד perish Si $41_{6(M)}$ (ממש[ל]ה).

<NOM CL> מִמְשָׁל רַב מֶמְשַׁלְתּוֹ *his dominion shall be a great dominion* Dn 11_5 (or em.; see Prep.), ממשלת מבין סרידה perh. *the rule of an understanding person is a net* Si 10_1 (unless §4; prob. סרידה is error for סדירה *orderliness* or סדורה *[well] ordered*), ביד אלהים ממשלת תבל *dominion over the world is in the hand of God* Si 10_4, sim. Si 10_5, ביד שר אורים ממשלת כול בני צדק *in the hand of the prince of light is dominion over all the sons of righteousness* 1QS 3_{20}, sim. 1QS 3_{21}, באישני לילה ממ]שלותיה *in the middle of the night is her dominion* 4QWiles 1_6, מֶמְשַׁלְתְּךָ בְּכָל־דּוֹר וָדוֹר *your dominion is throughout all generations* Ps 145_{13}, ממ]שלתו בארצות בימים *his dominion is over lands (and) seas* 4QAdmonPar 3.2_9, ממשלתם בכל תבל *their dominion is over all the world* 1QLitPr 3.2_3, ממש]לתו על כול גבורי כוח *his dominion is over all the mighty ones of strength* 4QShir[a] 1_2, ממשלתי על בני [עול] *my dominion is over the sons of injustice* 1QH 7_{23}, מבן עול ממשלת רע *from a son of unrighteousness is the dominion of evil* Si $41_{6(B)}$.

<OBJ> נתן *give* Is 22_{21}, בקשׁ pi. *seek* Si 7_4, יפע hi. *cause to shine* 4Q408 $1_{8.10}$ (unless both subj.), רום hi.

exalt 1QM 17$_7$, סור hi. *remove* 1QM 18$_{11}$ (ממ[ש]לת).

<CSTR> ממשלת כול האל[י]ם *dominion of all the gods* 4QM^a 24$_3$, בליעל *of Belial* 1QM 14$_9$ 1QS 1$_{18.23}$ 4QMidrEschat^b 10$_8$ ([בל]יעל) 4QpsMos^e 2.1$_3$, ישראל *of Israel* 1QM 17$_{17}$, כתיים *of the Kittim* 1QM 1$_6$ 1QpHab 2$_{13}$ (הכתיאים), קדושים *of the holy ones* 1QM 10$_{12}$, מבין *of an understanding person* Si 10$_1$ (unless §4), דורשי *of those who seek* 4QpNah 3.2$_4$, אויב *of the enemy* 1QM 18$_{11}$ (ממ[ש]לת), מֶמְשֶׁלֶת יָדוֹ *dominion of his hand* Jr 34$_1$, רוחי *of the spirits of* his lot 4QPrayer^e 1.1$_3$.

ממשלת אור *dominion of light* 1QS 10$_1$ 4Q408 1$_8$, חושך *of darkness* 1QH 12$_6$ (=4QHod^a 3.2$_7$ ממשלות) 4Q408 1$_{10}$ ([חושך]), יחד *of unity* 4QShir^b 2.1$_9$ ([מ]משלת), משפט *of justice* 11QMelch 2$_9$, רע *of evil* Si 41$_{6(B)}$, רשעה *of wickedness* 1QM 17$_5$ 4QShir^a 1$_6$ (ממשל[ת]), עולה *of injustice* 1QS 4$_{19}$, [עולתכה] *of your injustice* 4QBer^a 7.2$_8$ ([מ]מש[ל]ת]), משטמתו *of his animosity* 1QS 3$_{23}$, עברת *of the fury of* 4QShirShabb^f 23.1$_{12}$, מעשיה *of her deeds* 4Q417 2.1$_9$ (=4Q418 43$_7$ ממשל).

ממשלת כל גבר *dominion of*, i.e. over, *every man* Si 10$_5$, כול בני *of*, i.e. over, *all the sons of* 1QS 3$_{20.21}$ (בני), תבל *of*, i.e. over, *the world* Si 10$_4$ 1QS 3$_{17}$, קץ *of*, i.e. over, *a period* Si 43$_6$, מֶמְשֶׁלֶת הַיּוֹם *dominion of*, i.e. over, *the day* Gn 1$_{16}$, מֶמְשֶׁלֶת בַּיּוֹם *dominion over the day* Ps 136$_8$, מֶמְשֶׁלֶת הַלַּיְלָה *dominion of*, i.e. over, *the night* Gn 1$_{16}$, מֶמְשְׁלוֹת בַּלָּיְלָה *dominion over the night* Ps 136$_9$ (mss מֶמְשֶׁלֶת).

מלאכי ממשלתו *angels of his dominion* 1QM 1$_{15}$, [אנ]שי *men of* 1QM 14$_{10}$, שר ממשלת *prince of the dominion of* 1QM 17$_5$, רוחות ממשלתה *spirits of its dominion* 4QShir^b 1$_3$, אֶרֶץ מֶמְשֶׁלֶת *land of the dominion of* Jr 34$_1$, אֶרֶץ מֶמְשַׁלְתּוֹ *land of his dominion* 1 K 9$_{19}$||2 C 8$_6$ Jr 51$_{28}$ (or em. מֶמְשַׁלְתָּם *of their dominion*), מְקֹמוֹת *places of* Ps 103$_{22}$ (unless §4), גּוֹרל ממשלתו *lot of his dominion* 4QPrQuot 37.12$_{16}$, גב[ור]ות ועוז *might and strength of* GnzPs 4$_9$.

רשית ממשלת *beginning of the dominion of* 1QH 12$_6$ (=4QHod^a 3.2$_7$ ממשלות) 1QS 10$_1$, יומי *days of* 1QS 2$_{19}$, ימי ממשלתו *days of its dominion* 4QpsHod^b 1$_4$, [ק]צי [ממ]שלה *periods of dominion* 4QPrEnosh 4$_1$, קץ [ממשל]ת *period of the dominion of* 4QShir^a 1$_6$, [קצי] ממשלותיו *periods of his dominion* 4QBer^a 7.2$_5$, קץ ממשלתם *period of their dominion* 4QShir^b 35$_8$, קצי *periods of* 4QAges^a 1$_4$ (ממשלותם), כול ממשלת *all the dominion of* 4QPrEnosh 3$_3$, כול ממשלתם *all their dominion* 1QH 12$_9$ 4QMyst^a 10$_9$ (ממ[ש]לותם).

<APP> מַמְלָכָה *kingship* Mc 4$_8$.

<ADJ> רִאשׁוֹן *former* Mc 4$_8$.

<PREP> לְ of benefit, *for* 1QH 12$_9$, + עשׂה *make* Gn 1$_{16.16}$ Ps 136$_{8.9}$, ברא *create* 1QS 3$_{17}$, תכן *regulate* 1QH 1$_{17}$ ([לממשל]תם תכנתה]); of direction, *to* 4QHod^a 3.2$_6$ ([לממשל]תו]); of possession, *of, (belonging) to* 11QMelch 2$_9$.

בְּ of place, time, *in, during* 1QS 1$_{18.23}$ 4$_{19}$ 4Q418 47$_1$ 4QpsHod^b 1$_1$ ([בממש]לת]), + פלא hi. *make wonderful* 1QM 14$_9$, רחם pi. *have compassion* 4QShirShabb^f 23.1$_{12}$, זעם pass. *be accursed* 4QBer^a 7.2$_8$ ([ז]עום ... [במ]מש[ל]ת]), אבד pi. *destroy* 1QpHab 2$_{13}$, אבל htp. *mourn* 4QMidrEschat^b 10$_8$; *under, subject to* 1QM 13$_{10}$ 1QS 3$_{22.23}$.

מִן of comparison, *(more) than*, + משל *rule with* Dn 11$_5$ (if em. וּמָשַׁל מִמְשָׁל רַב מֶמְשַׁלְתּוֹ *and he shall rule; his dominion shall be great* to וּמָשַׁל ... מִמֶּמְשַׁלְתּוֹ *and he shall rule with* greater dominion *than his dominion*); עַל *concerning* 4QpNah 3.2$_4$; לְפִי *according to*, + שׁרת pi. *serve* 1QH 12$_{23}$.

<COLL> מִשְׂרָה || מֶמְשָׁלָה *authority* 1QM 17$_7$.

2. (sphere of) dominion, realm (distinction from §1 not alw. clear), of Y. (Ps 114$_2$ 1QH 13$_{11}$), of angels, spirits (1QH 1$_{11}$ 4QShirShabb^f 23.1$_8$), of humans (2 K 20$_{13}$||Is 39$_2$), <SUBJ> היה *be* Ps 114$_2$ (הָיְתָה ... יִשְׂרָאֵל מַמְשְׁלוֹתָיו *Israel was ... his dominion*; + קֹדֶשׁ *sanctuary*). <OBJ> לכד *capture* 4QNarrC 1$_9$, <CSTR> רוש ממשלות *head of the dominions* 4QShir^b 2.1$_3$, ראשי ממשלות *heads of the dominions of* 4QShirShabb^b 14.1$_6$, רוחי ממשלות *spirits of the dominions of* 4QBer^a 3$_5$, כָּל־ מֶמְשַׁלְתּוֹ *all his dominion* 2 K 20$_{13}$||Is 39$_2$ (+ בַּיִת *house*), כול ממשלתך *all your dominion* 1QH 13$_{11}$, כול ממשלותך *all your dominions* 4QPrEnosh 3$_4$.

<PREP> לְ of direction, *to* 4QShirShabb^f 23.1$_8$; introducing predicate, + היה *be* Ps 114$_{2(ms)}$; בְּ of place, *in* 4QBer^a 2$_2$ ([בם]משלותמה]), + היה *be* 2 K 20$_{13}$||Is 39$_2$ 1QH 1$_{11}$ ([והיו]), ספר pi. *recount* 1QH 13$_{11}$. <COLL> כול ממשלותך בקציהם *all your dominions in their periods*

4QPrEnosh 3_4

3. military might, of Sennacherib, <NOM CL> כָּל־מֶמְשַׁלְתּוֹ עִמּוֹ *all his military might was with him* 2 C 32_9. <CSTR> כָּל־מֶמְשַׁלְתּוֹ *all his military might* 2 C 32_9.

4. perh. **subject** of ruler,* used collectively, <SUBJ> ברך pi. *bless* Ps 103_{22} (unless §1; + מַעֲשֶׂה *work*). <OBJ> בין hi. *cause to understand* Si 10_1 (unless §1).

<SYN> §1 מִשְׂרָה *authority*.

Also 1QM 18_1 4QparaKings 106_1 ([ממשל[ה/ת) 4QM[a] 24_5 4QM[f] 1_7 ([מ]משלתו) 4QPrFêtes 8.3_8 ([מ]משלת) 4Q Shir[b] 1_1 ([מ]משלותם) 4QUnidA 1_1 ([ממש]לת) 6QBen 2_3.*

⇒ משל *rule*.

[מִמְשָׁק] I $_1$ n.[m.] **ground** (unless מִמְשָׁק II *place of possession*)—cstr. מִמְשַׁק—<CSTR> מִמְשַׁק חָרוּל *ground of the nettle,* i.e. ground overrun with nettles Zp 2_9 (or em. מִקְמַשׁ *a heap of*; + מִכְרֵה־מֶלַח *pit of salt*, שְׁמָמָה *desolation*).

*[מִמְשָׁק] II $_1$ n.[m.] **place of possession** (unless מִמְשָׁק I *ground*)—cstr. מִמְשַׁק—<CSTR> מִמְשַׁק חָרוּל *place of possession of,* i.e. possessed by, *the nettle* Zp 2_9 (+ מִכְרֵה־מֶלַח *pit of salt*, שְׁמָמָה *desolation*).

[מֶמְשָׁת] 0.0.0.5 pl.n. **Memshath,** perh. Jebel Zulēqa, 36 km SE of Beersheba, <CSTR> מלך ממשת *king of Memshath* Royal stamp 16 17 18 19.

Also Royal stamp 20.

מַמְתַקִּים $_2$ n.[m.]pl. **sweetness, sweet things,** perh. specif. **sweet drink,** <OBJ> שׁתה *drink* Ne 8_{10} (|| מַשְׁמַנִּים *delicacies*, + מָנָה *portion*). <NOM CL> חִכּוֹ מַמְתַקִּים *his mouth* (or *disposition*) *is sweetness* Ca 5_{16} (+ מַחְמָד *desirable thing*).

<SYN> מַשְׁמַנִּים *delicacies*.

⇒ מתק *be sweet*.

מָן I $_{14.0.1}$ n.m. **manna**—sf. מַנְךָ, Q מנו—daily food of Israelites in desert, explained in Ex 16_{15} as מָן הוּא *what is it?*, though מָן does not usu. mean *what?*; perhaps מַן *how many?*; described as a fine frost (Ex 16_{14}), white like a coriander seed (Ex 16_{31}) and tasting like a wafer made with honey (Ex 16_{31}) or oil (Nm 11_8); appearing on tamarisk bushes in the Sinai region for some weeks around June, it was formerly regarded as a secretion of the tamarisk tree, but now understood as a honeydew excretion of certain insects.*

<SUBJ> היה *be* Jos 5_{12}, ירד *go down* Nm 11_9, שׁבת *cease* Jos 5_{12}. <NOM CL> מָן הוּא *it is manna* Ex 16_{15} (unless *what is it?*, i.e. מָן II), הַמָּן כִּזְרַע־גַּד הוּא *the manna was like seed of coriander* Nm 11_7, אֶל־הַמָּן עֵינֵינוּ *our eyes are (looking) at the manna* Nm 11_6. <OBJ> קרא *call* name Ex 16_{31}, ידע *know* Dt $8_{3.3}$, אכל *eat* Ex $16_{35.35}$ Ps 78_{24} (unless del. לֶאֱכֹל), hi. *feed* Dt $8_{3.3}$, נתן *give,* i.e. place Ex 16_{33}, נוח hi. *place* Ex 16_{33}, מטר hi. *rain* Ps 78_{24}, מנע *withhold* Ne 9_{20}. <APP> מְלֹא *fullness* of omer Ex 16_{33}. <PREP> לְ introducing object, + דרשׁ *seek* 4QShir[b] 10_9. <COLL> מָן + דְּגַן *grain* Ps 78_{24}, לֶחֶם *bread* of angels Ps 78_{24}, מַיִם *water* Ne 9_{20}.*

מָן II $_1$ perh. interrog. pron. **what?,** in ref. to manna, מָן הוּא *what is it?* Ex 16_{15} (unless *it is manna*, i.e. מָן I).

[מַן] I interrog. pron. **who?, how many?—1. who?,** מַן־הוּא רָאָה הֲלִכוֹתֶיךָ אֱלֹהִים *who is it that has seen your processions, O God?* Ps 68_{24} (if em. מִנֵּהוּ : רָאוּ *his portion. They have seen*).

2. how many?,* מַן־הֵיכְלֵי שֵׁן *how many are (your) ivory palaces!* Pr 45_9 (if em. מִן *from*).*

*[מַן] II n.m. **whoever,** מְחַץ מָתְנַיִם קָמָיו וּמְשַׂנְאָיו מַן־יְקוּמוּן *crush the loins of his opponents and of his enemies whoever rises up* Dt 33_{11} (if em. מְשַׂנְאָיו מִן־יְקוּמוּן *of those that hate him, that they rise not again*), מַנֵּה[וּ] רָאָ[ה] הֲלִיכוֹתֶיךָ *whoever has seen your ways* Ps 68_{25} (if em. מִנֵּהוּ : רָאוּ *from him. They have seen*).

[מֵן] I $_{2.1}$ n.[m.] **string**—pl. מִנִּים (מִנִּי, Si מינים)—**string, stringed instrument,** <SUBJ> שׂמח pi. *make glad* Ps 45_9 (מִנִּי appar. pl. or abbrev. for pl.*; or מִן + sf. *from me,* i.e. by my mouth;* or em. מִנִּים). <CSTR> כלי מינים *instruments of strings* Si 39_{15} (+ נֵבֶל *harp*). <PREP> בְּ of instrument, *by (means of), with,* + הלל pi. *praise* Ps

150$_{4}$ (|| עוּגָב *pipe*).*
<SYN> עוּגָב *pipe*.

[מֵן] II 1 n.[m.] **portion**—sf. מְנֵהוּ—<NOM CL> מֵאֹיְבִים מְנֵהוּ *from the enemies shall its portion be* Ps 68$_{24}$ (or em. מְנֵהוּ: רָאוּ *its portion. They have seen* to מַן־הוּא רָאָה *who is it that has seen?*; or del.).

מִן +7717.+55.+c.1300.+106 prep. **from—1a.** before noun with article, מִן־ (מִן Ex 2$_{7}$), -מֵ; **b.** before non-guttural, usu. -מִ, with doubling of following consonant; rarely מִן־; **c.** before gutturals and ר, usu. -מֵ (exceptions מִחוּט, מִהְיוֹת, מִרְדֹּף, מִחוּצָה, מִחוּץ); **d.** before יְ, -מִי assimilating יְ; **e.** before ״י, -מֵ.

2. rarer forms, מִנִּי, מִנֵּי (Is 30$_{11}$).

3. with suffix, מִנִּי (מִמֶּנִּי, מֶנִּי) מִמְּךָ (מִמֶּךָּ, Q ממכה, Q המך), מִמֶּנּוּ, מִמֵּךְ (מִנֵּהוּ, מֶנְהוּ) מִמֶּנּוּ, מִמֶּנָּה, 1cpl מִמֶּנּוּ (mss מִמֵּנוּ), מִכֶּם, מֵהֶם (מֵהֵמָּה, מִנְהֶם), מֵהֵן (mss מֵהֵנָּה, מֵהֶן).

1. of direction,
   a. **(away) from,** p. 337a
   b. **(positioned away) from, to, on, at; from (the side of), in (the direction of), to(wards),** p. 338b
   c. **from (out of), (from) out of,** p. 338b
   d. **in from the outside,** from the perspective of one who is inside, p. 339a
   e. **(originating) from, of,** p. 339a
   f. **from, (at the instigation) of, with (the sanction of),** p. 339a
   g. **starting from,** p. 339a
2. of time,
   a. **from, since,** p. 339b
   b. **after, at (the end of), beyond,** p. 339b
   c. **immediately after,** p. 339b
3. of material, **(out) of, (made) from, (consisting) of,** p. 339b
4. partitive,
   a. **(some) of, (one) of, (any) of, (none) of,**
      (1) as subject of verb, p. 339b
      (2) in nominal clause, p. 340a
      (3) as object of verb, p. 340a
   b. **(out) of, from (among),** p. 340a
5. of comparison,
   a. **(more) than, (better) than, (less) than,** p. 340b
   b. **(more) than (all others),** i.e. most of all, p. 341a
   c. **too much for,** p. 341a
6. privative,
   a. **without, for lack of, away from,** p. 341b
   b. **from (being), from (doing), so as not to be, so as not to do, so that not,** p. 342a
7. locative,* **in, on,** p. 342b
8. of cause, **on account of, because of, for (reason of), through, at,** p. 342b
9. of agent, **by,** p. 343a
10. of instrument, **by (means of), with,** p. 343a
11. **in the estimation of, before,** p. 343b
12. perh. **against, (for protection) from,** p. 343b
13. מִמְּךָ and vars. as noun, **your offspring,** p. 343b
14. מִן ... וָמָעְלָה
    a. positional, p. 343b
    b. temporal, p. 343b
15. מִן in association with other prepositions,
    a. (לְ)מִן ... (וְ)עַד,
       (1) of place, p343b
       (2) class of objects, 344a
       (3) time, p. 344a
    b. מִן ... אֶל *from ... to*, p. 344b
    c. מִן ... לְ, p. 345a
       (1) of place, p. 345a
       (2) of direction, p. 345a
       (3) of time, p. 345a
    d. ה- of direction, p. 345a
16. מִן in compound, followed by other preposition, particle or adverb, p. 345a

1. of direction, **a. (away) from,** e.g. הַחִצִּים מִמְּךָ וָהָלְאָה *the arrows are from you and beyond*, i.e. beyond you 1 S 20$_{22}$, וַיַּרְא אֶת־הַמָּקוֹם מֵרָחֹק *and he saw the place from afar* Gn 22$_{4}$, דַּלּוּ מֵאֱנוֹשׁ *they hang down away from humans* Jb 28$_{4}$, אִם מֵעֵינֵי הָעֵדָה נֶעֶשְׂתָה *if it was done away from the sight of the congregation* Nm 15$_{24}$, כָּבוֹד לָאִישׁ שֶׁבֶת מֵרִיב *it is an honour for a man to* *sit away from strife* Pr 20$_{3}$, וַיָּבֹא אֵלָיו מִכְתָּב מֵאֵלִיָּהוּ *and a letter came to him from Elijah* 2 C 21$_{12}$, וַיָּבֹאוּ ... אִישׁ אִישׁ מִמְּלַאכְתּוֹ *they came ... each one from his work* Ex 36$_{4}$, וַיֵּרֶד מֹשֶׁה מִן־הָהָר *and Moses went down from the mountain* Ex 32$_{15}$, וַנִּסַּע מֵחֹרֵב *and we set out from Horeb* Dt 1$_{19}$, בשובם מן המלחמה *when they retreat from the battle* 1QM 3$_{10}$, לָמָּה תַתְעֵנוּ י׳ מִדְּרָכֶיךָ *why do you make us go astray, O Y., from your paths?* Is 63$_{17}$, הַנִּמְלָט מֵחֶרֶב חֲזָאֵל *the one who escapes from the sword of Hazael* 1 K 19$_{17}$.

כול רעי ומיודעי נדחו ממני *all my friends and acquaintances have been driven away from me* 1QH 4$_{9}$, וַיַּשְׁלִיכוּם מֵרֹאשׁ־הַסֶּלַע *and he threw them from the top of the rock* 2 C 25$_{12}$, הֹקַר רַגְלְךָ מִבֵּית רֵעֶךָ *make your foot stay away from the house of your neighbour* Pr 25$_{17}$, סוּר מֵרָע בִּינָה *to turn aside from evil is understanding* Jb 28$_{28}$, לֹא־רָשַׁעְתִּי מֵאֱלֹהָי *I have not acted wickedly (turning aside) from my God* Ps 18$_{22}$||2 S 22$_{22}$, כָּל־זוֹנֶה מִמֶּךָּ *everyone who plays the prostitute away from you* Ps 73$_{27}$, בָּגְדָה אִשָּׁה מֵרֵעָהּ *a woman is disloyal from,* i.e. in respect to, *her companion* Jr 3$_{20}$, לֹא־אַלְמָן יִשְׂרָאֵל וִיהוּדָה מֵאֱלֹהָיו *Israel and Judah are not widowed from,* i.e. bereft of, *their God* Jr 51$_{5}$, והובדל האיש מן הטהרה *and a man shall be separated,* i.e. excluded, *from the pure food* CD 9$_{21}$.

שְׁאַל מִמֶּנִּי וְאֶתְּנָה גוֹיִם נַחֲלָתֶךָ *ask of me, and I will make the nations your inheritance* Ps 2$_{8}$, מָה־י׳ דּוֹרֵשׁ מִמְּךָ *what does Y. require of you?* Mc 6$_{8}$, וְנִקַּמְתִּי מֵאֹיְבַי *and I will avenge myself of,* i.e. on, *my enemies* 1 S 14$_{24}$, מִכָּל־צָרוֹתָיו הוֹשִׁיעוֹ *he saved him from all his troubles* Ps 34$_{7}$, צְדָקָה תַּצִּיל מִמָּוֶת *righteousness will deliver from death* Pr 10$_{2}$, שָׁמְרֵנִי י׳ מִידֵי רָשָׁע *keep me, O Y., from the hands of the wicked* Ps 140$_{5}$, מֵאִישׁ חֲמָסִים תִּנְצְרֵנִי *may your preserve me from the man of violence* Ps 140$_{5}$, לֹא־הָיָה דָבָר נֶעְלָם מִן־הַמֶּלֶךְ *there was nothing hidden from the king* 1 K 10$_{3}$, רוּחַ קָדְשְׁךָ אַל־תִּקַּח מִמֶּנִּי *do not take your holy spirit from me* Ps 51$_{13}$.

חכרת המך היום [מן] מקצת עפר *I have rented from you today some of the ground* Mur 24 C$_{6}$, חָשַׂךְ אֶת־עַבְדּוֹ מֵרָעָה *he has held his servant back from evil* 1 S 25$_{39}$, אָנֹכִי מָנַעְתִּי מִכֶּם אֶת־הַגֶּשֶׁם *I withheld the rain from you* Am 4$_{7}$, חֲדַל מִמֶּנִּי *desist from me* Jb 7$_{16}$, הֶרֶף מִמֶּנִּי *leave me alone* Dt 9$_{14}$, הַחֲרִישׁוּ מִמֶּנִּי *be silent from me,* i.e. let me have silence Jb 13$_{13}$, וַיִּשְׁבֹּת ... מִכָּל־מְלַאכְתּוֹ *and he rested ... from all his work* Gn 2$_{2}$, וַהֲנִיחֹתִי לְךָ מִכָּל־אֹיְבֶיךָ *and I will give you rest from all your enemies* 2 S 7$_{11}$, הָאָרֶץ שָׁקְטָה מִמִּלְחָמָה *the land had rest from war* Jos 11$_{23}$, אִשָּׁה גְּרוּשָׁה מֵאִישָׁהּ *a woman divorced from her husband* Lv 21$_{7}$ (unless of agent, *by* [§9]), עֶבֶד חָפְשִׁי מֵאֲדֹנָיו *a slave is free from his master* Jb 3$_{19}$, גְּמוּלֵי מֵחָלָב עַתִּיקֵי מִשָּׁדָיִם *ones weaned from milk, ones removed from the breast* Is 28$_{9}$, מָעוֹז מֵאוֹיֵב *a refuge from the enemy* Na 3$_{11}$, צֵל מֵחֹרֶב *a shade from the heat* Is 25$_{4}$, גָּלְתָה יְהוּדָה מֵעֹנִי וּמֵרֹב *Judah has gone into exile from affliction and hard service* Lm 1$_{3}$.*

1b. (positioned away) from, to, on, at; from (the side of), in (the direction of), to(wards), e.g. בֵּית־אֵל מִיָּם וְהָעַי מִקֶּדֶם *Bethel on the west and Ai on the east* Gn 12$_{8}$, הַכְּנַעֲנִי מִמִּזְרָח וּמִיָּם *the Canaanites were to the east and the west* Jos 11$_{3}$, מִימִינוֹ וּמִשְּׂמֹאלוֹ *on his right hand and on his left* 1 K 22$_{19}$, מִקֶּדֶם *in the east* Gn 2$_{8}$, מִכָּל־עֲבָרָיו *on all its sides* Jr 49$_{32}$, לֻחֹת כְּתֻבִים מִשְּׁנֵי עֶבְרֵיהֶם *tablets written on both their sides* Ex 32$_{15}$, יִפֹּל מִצִּדְּךָ אֶלֶף *a thousand may fall at your side* Ps 91$_{7}$; with verb of motion, e.g. וַיִּסַּע לוֹט מִקֶּדֶם *and Lot journeyed eastwards* Gn 13$_{11}$, מֵרָחוֹק בָּרָחוּ *they have fled far away* (lit. from afar) Is 22$_{4}$, וַתְּשַׁלְּחִי צִרַיִךְ עַד־מֵרָחֹק *and you sent your envoys far away* Is 57$_{9}$.

1c. from (out of), (from) out of, e.g. וַיֵּצְאוּ מֵהָעִיר *and they went out from the city* Jr 52$_{7}$, לְהוֹצִיאָם מֵאֶרֶץ מִצְרָיִם *to bring them out of the land of Egypt* Ex 12$_{42}$, מִצָּפוֹן עָשָׁן בָּא *smoke is coming out of the north* Is 14$_{31}$, וַיַּעֲלוּ אֶת־יוֹסֵף מִן־הַבּוֹר *and they brought Joseph up out of the pit* Gn 37$_{28}$, וִישַׁלְּחוּ מִן־הַמַּחֲנֶה כָּל־צָרוּעַ *and let them send every leper out of the camp* Nm 5$_{2}$, קַח־נָא מִפִּיו תּוֹרָה *accept instruction from his mouth* Jb 22$_{22}$, אֵיךְ נִגְנֹב מִבֵּית אֲדֹנֶיךָ כֶּסֶף אוֹ זָהָב *how could we steal silver or gold from the house of your lord?* Gn 44$_{8}$, בְּיָד חֲזָקָה יְגָרְשֵׁם מֵאַרְצוֹ *with a strong hand he will drive them out of his land* Ex 6$_{1}$.

וַיַּצֵּל אֶתְכֶם מִיַּד אֹיְבֵיכֶם *and he delivered you out of the hand of your enemies* 1 S 12$_{11}$, מה אשר יפצה מידו

what is there that can snatch from his hand? 4QTobit^e 6$_7$, י׳ מִשָּׁמַיִם הִשְׁקִיף *Y. looked down from heaven* Ps 14$_2$, י׳ מִצִּיּוֹן יִשְׁאָג *Y. roars from Zion* Am 1$_2$, מִכּוֹסוֹ תִשְׁתֶּה *it drank from his cup* 2 S 12$_3$, וְהִשְׁבַּתִּי חַיָּה רָעָה מִן־הָאָרֶץ *and I will cause the harmful beasts to cease from the land* Lv 26$_6$, וַיִּיקַץ יַעֲקֹב מִשְּׁנָתוֹ *and Jacob awoke from his sleep* Gn 28$_{16}$.

1d. in from the outside, from the perspective of one who is inside,* מַשְׁגִּיחַ מִן־הַחַלֹּנוֹת *gazing in from the windows* Ca 2$_9$, דּוֹדִי שָׁלַח יָדוֹ מִן־הַחֹר *my beloved stretched his hand in from the latch opening* Ca 5$_4$.

1e. (originating) from, of, e.g. אִבְצָן מִבֵּית לָחֶם *Ibzan of Bethlehem* Jg 12$_8$, לשמריו מבארים *belonging to Shemariah of Beeraim* Samaria ost. 1$_2$, אֱנוֹשׁ מִן־הָאָרֶץ *a mortal from the earth* Ps 10$_{18}$, עָפָר מִן־הָאֲדָמָה *dust from the ground* Gn 2$_7$, חֲזִיר מִיָּעַר *a wild boar from the forest* Ps 80$_{14}$, שְׂעִפִּים מֵחֶזְיֹנוֹת לָיְלָה *thoughts from visions of the night* Jb 4$_{13}$, מֵעֵת דְּגָנָם וְתִירוֹשָׁם רָבּוּ *originating from the time when grain and new wine abound** Ps 4$_8$.

1f. from, (at the instigation) of, with (the sanction of), e.g. מֵי׳ הִיא *it was from Y.* Jg 14$_4$, מֵי׳ מַעֲנֵה לָשׁוֹן *from Y. is the answer of the tongue* Pr 16$_1$, לֹא הָיְתָה מֵהַמֶּלֶךְ לְהָמִית אֶת־אַבְנֵר *it was not (at the instigation) of the king to kill Abner* 2 S 3$_{37}$, הֵם הִמְלִיכוּ וְלֹא מִמֶּנִּי *they make kings, but not with my sanction* Ho 8$_4$, וְהִזְהַרְתָּ אוֹתָם מִמֶּנִּי *and you shall warn them from me* Ezk 3$_{17}$, מֵהָאֱלֹהִים הַמִּלְחָמָה *the battle was from God* 1 C 5$_{22}$, מַה־יּוֹכִיחַ הוֹכֵחַ מִכֶּם *what does reproof from you reprove?* Jb 6$_{25}$, זֶה חֵלֶק־אָדָם רָשָׁע מֵאֱלֹהִים *this is the portion of the wicked person from God* Jb 20$_{29}$, תְּשׁוּעַת צַדִּיקִים מֵי׳ *the salvation of the righteous is from Y.* Ps 37$_{39}$, מֵי׳ אִשָּׁה מַשְׂכָּלֶת *from Y. is a prudent wife* Ps 19$_{14}$.

1g. starting from,* e.g. וּבָנוּ מִמְּךָ חָרְבוֹת עוֹלָם *and starting from you they shall rebuild the ancient ruins* Is 58$_{12}$, הֲלֹא מִמִּצְרַיִם וּמִן־הָאֱמֹרִי וּמִן־בְּנֵי עַמּוֹן וּמִן־פְּלִשְׁתִּים וְצִידוֹנִים וַעֲמָלֵק וּמָעוֹן לָחֲצוּ אֶתְכֶם *did they not oppress you, (starting from) Egyptians and Amorites and Ammonites and Philistines, then* (resumptive waw) *Sidonians and Amalekites and Maonites* Jg 10$_{11-12}$, perh. כִּי־יִהְיֶה בְךָ אֶבְיוֹן מֵאַחַד אַחֶיךָ *if there is a poor man among you, (starting) from one of your brothers* Dt 15$_7$.

2. of time, **a. from, since,** e.g. אִם־מִשְּׁנַת הַיֹּבֵל יַקְדִּישׁ שָׂדֵהוּ *if he dedicates his field from the year of the jubilee* Lv 27$_{17}$, הִתְהַלַּכְתִּי לִפְנֵיכֶם מִנְּעֻרַי *I have walked before you since my youth* 1 S 12$_2$, מִבֶּטֶן אִמִּי אֵלִי אָתָּה *from the womb of my mother,* i.e. since I was born, *you have been my God* Ps 22$_{11}$, הֲמִיָּמֶיךָ צִוִּיתָ בֹּקֶר *since (the beginning of) your days, have you commanded the morning?* Jb 38$_{12}$(L); מִקֶּדֶם *from of old* Ps 74$_{12}$, מֵעוֹלָם *from of old* Is 42$_{14}$, מִימֵי קֶדֶם *since the days of old* Is 37$_{26}$, מֵעַתָּה *from now* Jr 3$_4$, מֵעַתָּה וְעַד־עוֹלָם *from this time onward for evermore* Is 9$_6$, מִיּוֹם *from today* Is 43$_{13}$, מִן־הַיּוֹם הַזֶּה וָמָעְלָה *from this day onward* Hg 2$_{18}$, מֵהַיּוֹם הַהוּא וָהָלְאָה *from that day and onwards* 1 S 18$_9$, מִקָּרֹב *from near,* i.e. recently Dt 32$_{17}$, short-lived Jb 20$_5$, soon Ezk 7$_8$.

b. after, at (the end of), beyond, e.g. מִיָּמִים *after some days* Jg 14$_8$, מִיָּמִים רַבִּים *after many days* Jos 23$_1$, מֵרֹב יָמִים *after many days* Is 24$_{22}$, מִיֹּמָיִם *after two days* Ho 6$_2$, כְּמִשְׁלֹשׁ חֳדָשִׁים *after about three months* Gn 38$_{24}$, מִקְצֵה שְׁלֹשֶׁת יָמִים *at the end of three days* Jos 3$_2$, מִקֵּץ שֶׁבַע־שָׁנִים *at the end of seven years* Dt 15$_1$, מֵהַבֹּקֶר *after the morning* 2 S 2$_{27}$, מִן־הַמּוֹעֵד *beyond the appointed time* 2 S 20$_5$; with inf. cstr., כַּחֲלוֹם מֵהָקִיץ *as a dream after waking* Ps 73$_{20}$.

c. immediately after, לָמָּה לֹּא מֵרֶחֶם אָמוּת *why did I not die immediately after (being in) the womb?* Jb 3$_{11}$.

3. of source or origin, **(out) of, (made) from, (consisting) of,** e.g. וַיִּצֶר י׳ אֱלֹהִים מִן־הָאֲדָמָה כָּל־חַיַּת הַשָּׂדֶה *and Y. God formed out of the ground every beast of the field* Gn 2$_{19}$, וַיַּעֲשׂוּ לָהֶם מַסֵּכָה מִכַּסְפָּם ... עֲצַבִּים *and they made for themselves molten images, idols ... from their silver* Hos 13$_2$, נִסְכֵּיהֶם מִדָּם *their libations of blood* Ps 16$_4$, מֵחָמֵץ תּוֹדָה *a thank offering of that which is leavened* Am 4$_5$, אַפִּרְיוֹן ... מֵעֲצֵי הַלְּבָנוֹן *a palanquin ... from the wood of Lebanon* Ca 3$_9$, כְּלֵי תִפְאַרְתֵּךְ מִזְּהָבִי וּמִכַּסְפִּי *your beautiful jewellery of my gold and silver* Ezk 16$_{17}$.

4. partitive (unless §3. of source or origin), **a. (some) of, (one) of, (any) of, (none) of,** (1) as subject of verb, e.g. יָצְאוּ מִן־הָעָם לִלְקֹט *some of the people went* *out to gather* Ex 16_{27}, מִבְּנֵי יְהוּדָה יָשְׁבוּ בְּקִרְיַת הָאַרְבַּע *some of the sons of Judah dwelt in Kiriath-arba* Ne 11_{25}, וַיָּמוּתוּ מֵעַבְדֵי הַמֶּלֶךְ *and some of the servants of the king died* 2 S 11_{24}, לֹא יָלִין מִן־הַבָּשָׂר *none of the flesh shall remain* Dt 16_{4}, לֹא־יִפֹּל מִשַּׂעֲרָתוֹ אַרְצָה *none of the hairs of his head will fall to the ground* 1 K 1_{52}.

(2) in nominal clause, e.g. מִיַּלְדֵי הָעִבְרִים זֶה *this is one of the children of the Hebrews* Ex 2_{6}, מִגֹּאֲלֵנוּ הוּא *he is one of our redeemers*, i.e. a close relative Ru 2_{20}, מֵהֶם עַל־כְּלֵי הָעֲבוֹדָה *some of them were over*, i.e. in charge of, *the vessels of service* 1 C 9_{28}, רְאוּ פֶּן־יֶשׁ־פֹּה עִמָּכֶם מֵעַבְדֵי י׳ *see that there is none of the servants of Y. with you here* 2 K 10_{23}, חָלִלָה לָאֵל מֵרֶשַׁע *let there not be any evil (belonging) to God* Jb 34_{10}.

(3) as object of verb, e.g. אַצִּיגָה־נָּא עִמְּךָ מִן־הָעָם *let me leave with you some of the people* Gn 33_{15}, וָאָקִים מִבְּנֵיכֶם לִנְבִיאִים *and I raised up some of your sons as prophets* Am 2_{11}, קַח אִתְּךָ מִזִּקְנֵי יִשְׂרָאֵל *take with you some of the elders of Israel* Ex 17_{5}, לָקַח לוֹ־מִבְּנוֹת פּוּטִיאֵל *he took (in marriage) one of the daughters of Putiel* Ex 6_{25}, וַיִּקַּח מֵאַבְנֵי הַמָּקוֹם *and he took one of the stones of the place* Gn 28_{11}, וְאָצַלְתִּי מִן־הָרוּחַ אֲשֶׁר עָלֶיךָ *and I will set aside some of the spirit that is upon you* Nm 11_{17}, מִלֶּחֶם אָבִיהָ תֹּאכֵל *she may eat of her father's bread* Lv 22_{13}, הַלְעִיטֵנִי נָא מִן־הָאָדֹם *please let me eat some of the brown stuff* Gn 25_{30}, מִן־הַשֶּׁמֶן יִצֹק הַכֹּהֵן *and the priest shall pour some of the oil* Lv 14_{26}, יִשָּׁקֵנִי מִנְּשִׁיקוֹת פִּיהוּ *let him kiss me with some of the kisses of his mouth* Ca 1_{2}, לֹא־יַשְׁאִירוּ מִמֶּנּוּ עַד־בֹּקֶר *they shall leave none of it until the morning* Nm 9_{12}, ... [חכרתי] מן קצת עפר *I have rented from you ... some of the ground* Mur 24 B_{7}, לוא אתאחר מכול מועדיהם *they are not to delay any of their appointed feasts* 1QS 1_{15}, מיין האגנת תתן *you shall give them some of the wine of*, i.e. from, *the bowls* Arad ost. 1_{9}.

4b. (out) of, from (among), e.g. שְׁנַיִם מִכֹּל *two of each* Gn 6_{19}, אֶחָד מֵהֶם *one of them* Dt 25_{5}, מִכֶּם אֶחָד *one of you* Gn 42_{16}, אֶחָד מֵהַנְּעָרִים *one of the lads* 1 S 16_{18}, [אחת מאמהותי[ו *one of his female servants* 4QT Naph 1_{2}, אַחַת מִשְּׁתֵּי עֵינַי *one of my two eyes* Jg 16_{28}, אלף מן המטה *a thousand from each tribe* 11QT 57_{6}, מְעַט מֵהַרְבֵּה *a few out of many* Jr 42_{2}, אַנְשֵׁי־חַיִל מִכָּל־ יִשְׂרָאֵל *men of ability out of all Israel* Ex 18_{25}, הַטּוֹב וְהַיָּשָׁר מִבְּנֵי אֲדֹנֵיכֶם *the best and most upright of the sons of your lord* 2 K 10_{3}, עשרה אנשים ברורים מן העדה *ten men shall be chosen from among the congregation* CD 10_{5}, ישראל אשר בחרתה לכה מכול עמי הארצות *Israel whom you have chosen for yourself from among all the peoples of the lands* 1QM 10_{9}, מְנָת הַמֶּלֶךְ מִן־רְכוּשׁוֹ *the portion of the king from his own possessions* 2 C 31_{3}, כֹּל הַנּוֹתָרִים מִכֹּל מַחֲנֵה בְנֵי־קֶדֶם *all who remained out of all the army of the sons of the east* Jg 8_{10}.

5. of comparison, **a. (more) than, (better) than, (less) than,** e.g. מָתוֹק מִדְּבַשׁ *sweeter than honey* Jg 14_{18}, עַז מֵאֲרִי *stronger than a lion* Jg 14_{18}, לְאֹם מִלְאֹם יֶאֱמָץ *one nation shall be stronger than the other* Gn 25_{23}, גּוֹיִם גְּדֹלִים וַעֲצֻמִים מִמֶּךָּ *nations greater and mightier than you* Dt 9_{1}, רוח מרוח תגבר *one spirit is more mighty than another* 1QH 9_{16}, וִיגַדֵּל אֶת־כִּסְאוֹ מִכִּסְאֶךָ *and may he make his throne greater than yours* 1 K 1_{47}, גָּבְהוּ דְרָכַי מִדַּרְכֵיכֶם *my ways are higher than your ways* Is 55_{9}, קַלּוּ מִנְּמֵרִים סוּסָיו *his horses are swifter than leopards* Hb 1_{8}.

טוֹב מוֹתִי מֵחַיָּי *my death is better than my life*, i.e. it is better that I should die than live Jon 4_{3}, טוֹב שֵׁם מִשֶּׁמֶן טוֹב *a (good) name is better than precious oil* Ec 7_{1}, טוֹב יֶלֶד מִסְכֵּן וְחָכָם מִמֶּלֶךְ זָקֵן וּכְסִיל *a poor and wise child is better than an old and foolish king* Ec 4_{13}, שְׁמֹעַ מִזֶּבַח טוֹב *to obey is better than sacrifice* 1 S 15_{22}, טוֹבָה חָכְמָה מִפְּנִינִים *wisdom is better than corals*, or *pearls* Pr 8_{11}, טוֹבָה חָכְמָה מִגְּבוּרָה *wisdom is better than might* Ec 9_{16}, טוב לי תורת [פ]יך מאלף אלפים ככרי זהב *the law of your mouth is better to me than a million talents of gold* GnzPs 2_{27}.

צָדְקָה מִמֶּנִּי *she is more righteous than I* Gn 38_{26}, הַאֱנוֹשׁ מֵאֱלוֹהַּ יִצְדָּק *is a human being more righteous than God?* Jb $4_{17(L)}$ (unless מִן *before* [§11]), וַיֶּחְכַּם מִכָּל־הָאָדָם *and he became wiser any (other) human* 1 K 5_{11}, מִכָּל־מְלַמְּדַי הִשְׂכַּלְתִּי *I have insight more than all my teachers* Ps 119_{99}, אַתֶּם הֲרֵעֹתֶם לַעֲשׂוֹת מֵאֲבוֹתֵיכֶם *you have done more evil than your fathers* Jr 16_{12}, הִשְׁחִיתוּ מֵאֲבוֹתָם *they have acted more corruptly than their fathers* Jg 2_{19}.

אֲרֻכָּה מֵאֶרֶץ מִדָּהּ *its measure is longer than the earth* Jb 11$_{9}$, מֵחוֹל יַמִּים יִכְבָּד *it would be heavier than the sand of the seas* Jb 6$_{3}$, הִרְבֵּית רֹכְלַיִךְ מִכּוֹכְבֵי הַשָּׁמָיִם *you increased your merchants more than the stars of the heavens* Na 3$_{16}$, אוֹקִיר אֱנוֹשׁ מִפָּז *I will make humans more rare than fine gold* Is 13$_{12}$, תִּיטַב לַי׳ מִשּׁוֹר *it would be more pleasing to Y. than an ox* Ps 69$_{32}$, הֵיטַבְתְּ חַסְדֵּךְ הָאַחֲרוֹן מִן־הָרִאשׁוֹן *you have made your last kindness better than the first* Ru 3$_{10}$, נִבְחַר מָוֶת מֵחַיִּים *death is chosen rather than life* Jr 8$_{3}$, יש מכה ממכה תנעם *there is a blow that is more pleasant than any other* Si 36$_{23}$, מִשֶּׁלֶג אַלְבִּין *I shall be whiter than snow* Ps 51$_{9}$.

חִזְּקוּ פְנֵיהֶם מִסֶּלַע *they have made their faces harder than rock* Jr 5$_{3}$, תַּקְשִׁיחַ לִבֵּנוּ מִיִּרְאָתֶךָ *you have made our heart harder than your fear*, i.e. so hard that we cannot fear you Is 63$_{1}$, וַיַּחְפְּרֻהוּ מִמַּטְמוֹנִים *and they dig for it more than for hidden treasures* Jb 3$_{21}$, קטן הייתי מאחי *I was smaller than my brothers* 11QPs[a] 28$_{3}$, וַתְּחַסְּרֵהוּ מְעַט מֵאֱלֹהִים *and you have made him a little less than God* Ps 8$_{6}$, לֹא־נֹפֵל אָנֹכִי מִכֶּם *I am not inferior to you* Jb 12$_{3}$; with inf., cstr., טוֹב לַחֲסוֹת בַּי׳ מִבְּטֹחַ בִּנְדִיבִים *it is better to seek refuge in Y. than to trust in princes* Ps 118$_{9}$.

5b. (more) than (all others), i.e. most of all, e.g. וַיִּגְדַּל הַמֶּלֶךְ שְׁלֹמֹה מִכֹּל מַלְכֵי הָאָרֶץ *and king Solomon became greater than any of the (other) kings of the earth* 1 K 10$_{23}$||2 C 9$_{22}$, יָפְיָפִיתָ מִבְּנֵי אָדָם *you are fairer than (any other) people*, i.e. the fairest of people Ps 45$_{3}$, גָּבֹהַּ מִכָּל־הָעָם *taller than any of*, i.e. the tallest of, *the people* 1 S 9$_{2}$, תְּבֹרַךְ מִנָּשִׁים יָעֵל *Jael is blessed more than (other) women*, i.e. the most blessed of women Jg 5$_{24}$.

5c. too much for, e.g. כָבֵד מִמְּךָ הַדָּבָר *the thing is too heavy for you* Ex 18$_{18}$, אין נפלא וחזק ממנו *there is nothing too difficult or too hard for him* Si 39$_{20}$, רַב מִמְּךָ הַדָּרֶךְ *the journey will be too great for you* 1 K 19$_{7}$, מָךְ הוּא מֵעֶרְכֶּךָ *he is too poor for your valuation* Lv 27$_{8}$, קָטֹנְתִּי מִכֹּל הַחֲסָדִים וּמִכָּל־הָאֱמֶת *I am too small for*, i.e. unworthy of, *all the loyalty and faithfulness* Gn 32$_{11}$, הַמְעַט מִכֶּם *is it too little for you?* Nm 16$_{9}$.

With inf. cstr., נָקֵל מִהְיוֹתְךָ לִי עֶבֶד *is it too light a thing that you should be a servant to me?* Is 49$_{6}$, גָּדוֹל רַב־ עֲוֹנִי מִנְּשֹׂא *my iniquity is too great to bear* Gn 4$_{13}$, רַב־ לָכֶם מֵעֲלוֹת יְרוּשָׁלִַם *it is too much for you to go up to Jerusalem* 1 K 12$_{28}$, טְהוֹר עֵינַיִם מֵרְאוֹת רָע *pure one of eyes*, i.e. one too pure, *to see evil* Hb 1$_{13}$, עָצְמוּ מִסַּפֵּר *they are too many to recount* Ps 40$_{6}$.

6. privative, **a. without, for lack of, away from,** e.g. עָמְדוּ מִכֹּחַ נָסִים *fugitives stand without strength* Jr 48$_{45}$, נִבְעַר כָּל־אָדָם מִדַּעַת *all humans are foolish (and) without knowledge* Jr 10$_{14}$, וְשַׁאֲנַן מִפַּחַד רָעָה *and he will be at ease, without dread of evil* Pr 1$_{33}$, בָּתֵּיהֶם שָׁלוֹם מִפָּחַד *their houses are at peace without fear* Jb 21$_{9}$, וָרֵעַ מְיֻדָּעַי מַחְשָׁךְ *and you shattered my acquaintances without pity* Ps 88$_{19}$ (if em. וָרֵעַ מְיֻדָּעַי מַחְשָׁךְ appar. *and friend, my acquaintances are [in] darkness*),* כָּבוֹד לָאִישׁ שֶׁבֶת מֵרִיב *it is an honour for a man to dwell without strife* Pr 20$_{3}$.

תִּשָּׂא פָנֶיךָ מִמּוּם *you will lift up your face without blemish* Jb 11$_{15}$, יזכו מעשיו מכול עול *his works shall be purified (so as to be) without any unrighteousness* 1QS 8$_{18}$, בְּיִרְאַת אֱלֹהֵינוּ תֵּלֵכוּ מֵחֶרְפַּת הַגּוֹיִם *you shall walk in the fear of our God without the reproach of the nations* Ne 5$_{9}$, הֶחֱשֵׁיתִי מִטּוֹב *I have kept silence without good*, i.e. to no avail Ps 39$_{3}$, הֲקָצוֹר קָצְרָה יָדִי מִפְּדוּת *is my hand indeed short without redemption?*, i.e. so that it cannot redeem Is 50$_{2}$, מֵעֹצֶר וּמִמִּשְׁפָּט לֻקָּח *through oppression and without judgment he was taken away* Is 53$_{8}$.

וְנָשַׁמָּה אֶרֶץ מִמְּלֹאָהּ *and the land shall be made desolate (so as to be) without that which fills it* Ezk 32$_{15}$, מִנְעִי קוֹלֵךְ מִבֶּכִי *hold back your voice (so as to be) without weeping* Jr 31$_{16}$, לַיְלָה לָכֶם מֵחָזוֹן *it shall be night to you without vision* Mc 3$_{6}$, מִקֶּשֶׁת אֻסָּרוּ *without a bow they are captured* Is 22$_{3}$, וִיהִי מְתָיו מִסְפָּר *may his men be without number* Dt 33$_{6}$ (from סֵפֶר II; if em. מִסְפָּר *[few in] number*), מִשְׁמַנֵּי הָאָרֶץ יִהְיֶה מוֹשָׁבֶךָ וּמִטַּל הַשָּׁמַיִם מֵעָל *without the oil of earth*, i.e. rain, *will be your dwelling, yes, without the dew of the heavens above** Gn 27$_{39}$.

כול איש אשר מטהר מזובו *every man who purifies himself (so as to be) without his discharge* 11QT 45$_{15}$, וַיְגֹאֲלוּ מִן הַכְּהֻנָּה *and they were defiled away from*, i.e. disqualified from, *the priesthood* Ezr 2$_{62}$||Ne 7$_{64}$, לרצון

לארץ מבשר עולות ומחלבי זבח *so that there may be favour for the land without the flesh of burnt offerings and the fat of sacrifices* 1QS 9_{4}, דאבה נפשכה מכול טוב *your soul languishes for lack of any good thing* 4Q418 127_{1}, בְּשָׂרִי כָּחַשׁ מִשָּׁמֶן *my body has become lean without oil* Ps 109_{24}; with inf. cstr, וְחָשְׁכָה לָכֶם מִקְּסֹם *and it will be dark for you without divination* Mc 3_{6}.

b. from (being), from (doing), so as not to be, so as not to do, so that not, e.g. וְהִשְׁבַּתִּיךְ מִזּוֹנָה *and I will cause you to cease from being a prostitute* Ezk 16_{41}, יֵחַת אֶפְרַיִם מֵעָם *Ephraim will be shattered so as not to be a people* Is 7_{8}, נַכְחִידֵם מִגּוֹי *let us destroy them from being a nation* Ps 83_{5}, וַיְסִרֶהָ מִגְּבִירָה *and he removed her from being queen mother* 1 K 15_{13}||2 C 15_{16}, וְשָׁמַר רַגְלְךָ מִלָּכֶד *and he will keep your feet from being caught* Pr 3_{26}, אֹטֵם אָזְנוֹ מִזַּעֲקַת־דָּל *he shuts his ear from (hearing the) cry of the poor* Pr 21_{13}.

With inf. cstr., חָלִילָה לִּי מֵעֲשׂוֹת זֹאת *far be it from me to do that* Gn 44_{17}, שִׁלַּחְנוּ אֶת־יִשְׂרָאֵל מֵעָבְדֵנוּ *we have let Israel go so as not to serve us* Ex 14_{5}, וַיָּשֻׁבוּ מִלֶּכֶת אֶל־יָרָבְעָם *and they returned so as not to go to Jeroboam* 2 C 11_{4}, צָדוּ צְעָדֵינוּ מִלֶּכֶת בִּרְחֹבֹתֵינוּ *our feet have ranged far without coming into our streets* Lm 4_{18}, גֵּרְשׁוּנִי הַיּוֹם מֵהִסְתַּפֵּחַ בְּנַחֲלַת י׳ *they have driven me out this day from participating in the heritage of Y.* 1 S 26_{19}, עַל הֶעָבִים אֲצַוֶּה מֵהַמְטִיר עָלָיו מָטָר *I will command the clouds not to rain upon it* Is 5_{6}, יִסְּרֵנִי מִלֶּכֶת בְּדֶרֶךְ הָעָם־הַזֶּה *he instructed me not to walk in the way of this people* Is 8_{11}.

זֶרַע יִשְׂרָאֵל יִשְׁבְּתוּ מִהְיוֹת גּוֹי *the offspring of Israel shall cease from being a nation* Jr 31_{36}, וַיֶּחְדַּל מִבְּנוֹת אֶת־הָרָמָה *and he ceased building Ramah* 1 K 15_{21}||2 C 16_{5}, אֲנַחְנוּ מַחְשִׁים מִקַּחַת אֹתָהּ *we keep silence*, i.e. refrain, *from taking it* 1 K 22_{3}.

וַתִּכְהֶיןָ עֵינָיו מֵרְאֹת *and his eyes were dim so that he could not see* Gn 27_{1}, טַח מֵרְאוֹת עֵינֵיהֶם *their eyes are covered so that they cannot see* Is 44_{18}, sim. Ps 69_{24}, לֹא־כָבְדָה אָזְנוֹ מִשְּׁמוֹעַ *his ear is not so heavy that it cannot hear* Is 59_{1}, אֹטֵם אָזְנוֹ מִשְּׁמֹעַ דָּמִים *he shuts his ear from hearing (about) bloodshed* Is 33_{15}, הוּא בֶּן־בְּלִיַּעַל מִדַּבֵּר אֵלָיו *he is such a son of worthlessness*, i.e. a worthless person, *that one cannot speak to him* 1 S 25_{17}, לֹא־קָצְרָה יַד־י׳ מֵהוֹשִׁיעַ *the hand of Y. is not short that it cannot save* Is 59_{1}.

הִזְנִיחָם ... מִכַּהֵן לי׳ *he rejected them ... from serving as priests to Y.* 2 C 11_{14}, אֹתִי מָאֲסוּ מִמְּלֹךְ עֲלֵיהֶם *they have rejected me from being king over them* 1S 8_{7}, אַל־תִּירָא מֵרְדָה מִצְרַיְמָה *do not be afraid of going down to Egypt* Gn 46_{3}, יָרֵא מֵהַבִּיט אֶל־הָאֱלֹהִים *he was afraid of looking at God* Ex 3_{6}.

7. locative,* **in, on,** e.g. וַיִּטַּע י׳ אֱלֹהִים גַּן־בְּעֵדֶן מִקֶּדֶם *and Y. God planted a garden in Eden in the east* Gn 2_{8}, מִמָּחֳרָת *on the next day* Gn 19_{34}, וַיִּשְׁמַע מֵהֵיכָלוֹ קוֹלִי *and in his temple he heard my voice* 2 S 22_{7}||Ps 18_{7}, יֹצֶרְךָ מִבֶּטֶן *the one who formed you in the womb* Is 44_{2}, אִם־תָּשִׁיב מִשַּׁבָּת רַגְלֶךָ *if you turn back your foot on the sabbath* Is 58_{13}, קוֹל נְהִי נִשְׁמַע מִצִּיּוֹן *a sound of wailing is heard in Zion* Jr 9_{18}, תִּשָּׁמַע זְעָקָה מִבָּתֵּיהֶם *may a cry be heard in their houses* Jr 18_{22}, בָּרוּךְ כְּבוֹד־י׳ מִמְּקוֹמוֹ *blessed be the glory of Y. in his place* Ezk 3_{12}, עַם־רַב הֹלְכִים מִדֶּרֶךְ אַחֲרָיו *many people were coming in the road behind him* 2 S 13_{34}, מֵחֵקִי צָפַנְתִּי אִמְרֵי־פִיו *in my bosom I have treasured the words of his mouth* Jb 23_{12}, מֵחֹרֶף עָצֵל לֹא־יַחֲרֹשׁ *in winter the sluggard does not plough* Pr 20_{4}, 2 S 5_{13} Ezk 27_{34} Pr 17_{23} 2 C 15_{8}.

8. of cause, **on account of, because of, for (reason of), through, at,** e.g. לֹא יִסָּפֵר מֵרֹב *it cannot be counted because of multitude* Gn 16_{10}, עֲבָדַי יָרֹנּוּ מִטּוּב לֵב *my servants shall exult on account of gladness of heart* Is 65_{14}, שְׂמַח מֵאֵשֶׁת נְעוּרֶךָ *rejoice on account of the wife of your youth* Pr 5_{18}, פֹּרִיָּה וַעֲנֵפָה הָיְתָה מִמַּיִם רַבִּים *she was fruitful and full of branches on account of the abundant waters* Ezk 19_{10}, מֵרֵיחַ מַיִם יַפְרִחַ *at the scent of water it will bud* Jb 14_{9}, בִּרְכַּי כָּשְׁלוּ מִצּוֹם *my knees are weak through fasting* Ps 109_{24}, מֵעֹצֶר וּמִמִּשְׁפָּט לֻקָּח *through oppression and without judgment he was taken away* Is 53_{8}, לֹא יָכְלוּ לִשְׁתֹּת מַיִם מִמָּרָה *they were not able to drink the water on account of the bitterness* Ex 15_{23}.

הָרִים רָעֲשׁוּ מִמֶּנּוּ *the mountains shake because of him* Na 1_{5}, וַיָּנֻעוּ אַמּוֹת הַסִּפִּים מִקּוֹל הַקּוֹרֵא *and the doorposts of the thresholds shook at the voice of the one who called* Is 6_{4}, סַלְעוֹ מִמָּגוֹר יַעֲבוֹר *his rock shall pass away on account of terror* Is 31_{9}, יִתְמְהוּ מִגַּעֲרָתוֹ *they are astounded at his rebuke* Jb 26_{11}, מִקֶּצֶף י׳ לֹא תֵשֵׁב *on account of the anger of Y. she shall not be inhabited* Jr 50_{12}, זַלְעָפָה אֲחָזַתְנִי מֵרְשָׁעִים *raging has seized me on account of the wicked* Ps 119_{53}, וַיֵּאָנְחוּ בְנֵי־יִשְׂרָאֵל מִן־הָעֲבֹדָה *and the sons of Israel groaned on account of the servitude* Ex 2_{23}, הֲמִיִּרְאָתְךָ יֹכִיחֶךָ *is it on account of your fear (of him) that he reproves you?* Jb 22_{4}, יִנָּחֵם י׳ מִנַּאֲקָתָם *Y. was moved to pity on account of their groaning* Jg 2_{18}.

קָמוּ עֵינָיו מִשֵּׂיבוֹ *his eyes had become dim on account of his old age* 1 K 14_{4}, הוּא מְחֹלָל מִפְּשָׁעֵנוּ *he was wounded on account of our transgressions* Is 53_{4} (unless §10), וַיָּחֶל מְאֹד מֵהַמּוֹרִים *and he was in much pain on account of the archers* 1 S 31_{3}, וַיָּשֹׁחוּ מֵעֹצֶר רָעָה וְיָגוֹן *and they are bowed down on account of oppression, evil and sorrow* Ps 107_{39}, אֶדְאַג מֵחַטָּאתִי *I am anxious because of my sin* Ps 38_{19}, וּבֹשׁ מוֹאָב מִכְּמוֹשׁ *and Moab shall be ashamed (on account) of Chemosh* Jr 48_{13}; with verbs of fearing מִן perh. introducing object, but prob. *on account of*, e.g. לֹא־אִירָא מֵרִבְבוֹת עָם *I will not be afraid (on account) of tens of thousands of people* Ps 3_{7}, לֹא תָגוּר מִמֶּנּוּ *you shall not fear (on account) of him* Dt 18_{22}, מִמִּי אֶפְחָד *(on account) of whom shall I be afraid?* Ps 27_{1}.

With inf. cstr., מֵאַהֲבַת י׳ אֶתְכֶם ... הוֹצִיא י׳ אֶתְכֶם *it is because Y. loves you ... that Y. brought you out* Dt 7_{8}, לֹא־יָכֹל עוֹד לְהָשִׁיב אֶת־אַבְנֵר דָּבָר מִיִּרְאָתוֹ אֹתוֹ *he was not able to answer Abner another word, because he feared him* 2 S 3_{11}, נִבְהֲלוּ הָאִיִּים ... מִצֵּאתֵךְ *the isles are dismayed ... at your going out* Ezk 26_{18}.

9. of agent, **by**, e.g. הָאָרֶץ תֵּעָזֵב מֵהֶם *the land shall be abandoned by them* Lv 26_{43}, דִּבְרֵי חֲכָמִים ... נִתְּנוּ מֵרֹעֶה אֶחָד *the words of the wise are ... given by one shepherd* Ec 12_{11}, הַנִּשְׁכָּחִים מִנִּי־רָגֶל *those who are forgotten by the foot*, i.e. by wayfarers Jb 28_{4}, מַדּוּעַ מִשַּׁדַּי לֹא־נִצְפְּנוּ עִתִּים *why are the times not laid up by the Almighty?* Jb 24_{1}, עָנְיִי מִשֹּׂנְאָי *my affliction by those who hate me* Ps 9_{14}, חֶרְפָּתְךָ מִנִּי־נָבָל *your reproach by the fool* Ps 74_{22}, נולד ממנו מפח נפש *the expiring of the soul is born*, i.e. caused, *by him* Si 30_{12}(B).

10. of instrument, **by (means of), with** (distinction from מִן of cause [§8] not alw. clear), לֹא־יִכָּרֵת כָּל־בָּשָׂר עוֹד מִמֵּי מַבּוּל *never again shall all flesh be cut off by the waters of a flood* Gn 9_{11}, נִבְלְעוּ מִן־הַיַּיִן *they are confused by wine* Is 28_{7}, מִנִּשְׁמַת אֱלוֹהַּ יֹאבֵדוּ *by a breath of God they perish* Jb 4_{9}(L), מֵחֶזְיֹנוֹת תְּבַעֲתַנִּי *you terrify me with visions* Jb 7_{14}, הֲמִבִּינָתְךָ יַאֲבֶר־נֵץ *is it by your wisdom that the hawk flies?* Jb 39_{26}, מִבִּרְכָתְךָ יְבֹרַךְ בֵּית־עַבְדְּךָ *by your blessing they house of your servant shall be blessed* 2 S 7_{29}, וְנָמַסּוּ הָרִים מִדָּמָם *and the mountains shall flow with their blood* Is 34_{3}.

11. in the estimation of, before, וִהְיִיתֶם נְקִיִּם מֵי׳ וּמִיִּשְׂרָאֵל *and your shall be innocent in the estimation of Y. and of Israel* Nm 32_{22}, perh. הֲיִפָּלֵא מֵי׳ דָּבָר *is anything too wonderful*, i.e. difficult, *in the estimation of Y.* Gn 18_{14} (but prob. מִן *too much for* [§5c]).

12. perh. **against, (for protection) from** (but prob. מִן of cause [§8]), הדואג לעמו מחתף ומחזק עירו מצר *he who was anxious for his people against robbery, and strengthened his city against the enemy* Si 50_{4}.

13. מִמְּךָ and vars. as noun, **your offspring,*** קְהַל גּוֹיִם יִהְיֶה מִמֶּךָּ *your offspring shall be a company of nations* Gn 35_{11}, וּמַחֲרִבַיִךְ מִמֵּךְ יֵצֵאוּ *and your offspring shall go forth (more numerous) than your destroyers* Is 49_{17}, וּבָנוּ מִמְּךָ חָרְבוֹת עוֹלָם *and your offspring shall rebuild the ancient ruins* Is 58_{12}, גָּלוּ מִמֵּךְ *your offspring shall go into exile* Mc 1_{16}.

14. מִן ... וָמַעְלָה, **a.** positional, e.g. מֵהַסֶּלַע וָמָעְלָה *from Sela and upward* Jg 1_{36}.

b. temporal, e.g. מֵהַיּוֹם הַהוּא וָמָעְלָה *from that day forward** 1 S 30_{25}.

15. מִן in association with other prepositions, **a.** (לְ)מִן ... (וְ)עַד (1) of place, *from ... as far as, from ... to*, e.g. מִצִּידֹן ... עַד־עַזָּה *from Sidon ... as far as Gaza* Gn 10_{19}, מִנַּחַל מִצְרַיִם עַד־נְהַר־פְּרָת *from the brook of Egypt to the river Euphrates* 2 K 24_{7}, מֵחֲוִילָה עַד־שׁוּר *from Havilah to Shur* Gn 25_{18}, מִיַּם־סוּף וְעַד־יָם פְּלִשְׁתִּים *from the Red Sea to the sea of the Philistines* Ex 23_{31}, מֵאַרְנֹן עַד־יַבֹּק עַד־בְּנֵי עַמּוֹן *from the Arnon to the Jabbok, as far as the sons of Ammon* Nm 21_{24}, מֵחֹרֵב ... עַד־קָדֵשׁ בַּרְנֵעַ *from Horeb ... to Kadesh-barnea* Dt 1_{2}, לְמִדָּן וְעַד־בְּאֵר שֶׁבַע *from Dan to Beer-sheba* Jg 20_{1}, מִגֶּבַע עַד־בְּאֵר שָׁבַע *from Geba to Beer-sheba* 2 K 23_{8}, מִן־הַיַּרְדֵּן וְעַד־יְרוּשָׁלַםִ *from the Jordan as far as Jeru-*

salem 2 S 20$_{2}$, מֵהֹדּוּ וְעַד־כּוּשׁ *from India to Ethiopia* Est 1$_{1}$, מִקְצֵה הָאָרֶץ וְעַד־קְצֵה הָאָרֶץ *from one end of the earth to the other* Dt 13$_{8}$, sim. Gn 47$_{21}$ Dt 4$_{32}$, מִפְּאַת קָדִים עַד־פְּאַת־יָמָּה *from the east side to the west* Ezk 48$_{2}$, מִמִּזְרַח־שֶׁמֶשׁ וְעַד־מְבוֹאוֹ *from the rising of the sun to its setting* Ml 1$_{11}$, מִמָּתְנַיִם וְעַד־יְרֵכַיִם *from the loins to the thighs* Ex 28$_{42}$, מֵרֹאשׁוֹ וְעַד־רַגְלָיו *from his head to his feet* Lv 13$_{12}$, sim. Dt 28$_{35}$ Is 1$_{6}$, מִשְּׂפָתוֹ עַד־שְׂפָתוֹ *from its brim to its brim* 1 K 7$_{23}$, מימן ו[עד שמא]ל *from right to left* Siloam Tunnel inscr.$_{3}$.

(2) class of objects, *from … to, both … and, either … or, neither … nor*, e.g. מִנַּעַר וְעַד־זָקֵן *both youth and old man* Gn 19$_{4}$, מֵאָדָם וְעַד־בְּהֵמָה *both humans and beasts* Ex 9$_{25}$, sim. Ex 11$_{7}$, מֵאִישׁ וְעַד־אִשָּׁה *both man and woman* Jos 6$_{21}$, מִזָּכָר עַד־נְקֵבָה *both male and female* Nm 5$_{3}$, מֵעֹלֵל וְעַד־יוֹנֵק *both infant and suckling* 1 S 15$_{3}$, מִקָּטֹן וְעַד־גָּדוֹל *both small and great* Gn 19$_{11}$, ממלך גדל ו[עד אש] *from great king to common man* Nimrud ivory inscr. 1$_{2}$, מִבְּכוֹר פַּרְעֹה … עַד־בְּכוֹר הַשִּׁפְחָה *from the firstborn of Pharaoh … to the firstborn of the female slave* Ex 11$_{5}$, sim. Ex 12$_{29}$ 13$_{15}$, מֵחֹטֵב עֵצֶיךָ עַד שֹׁאֵב מֵימֶיךָ *both the hewer of your wood and the drawer of your water* Dt 29$_{10}$, מִבֶּן־עֶשְׂרִים שָׁנָה וְעַד־בֶּן־שִׁשִּׁים שָׁנָה *from a son of twenty years to a son of sixty years*, i.e. between twenty and sixty years old Lv 27$_{3}$.

מִנָּבִיא וְעַד־כֹּהֵן *both prophet and priest* Jr 6$_{13}$, מִנֶּפֶשׁ וְעַד־בָּשָׂר *both soul and body* Is 10$_{18}$, מֵעוֹף הַשָּׁמַיִם וְעַד־בְּהֵמָה *both the birds of the air and the beasts* Jr 9$_{9}$, מִגָּדִישׁ וְעַד־קָמָה וְעַד־כֶּרֶם זָיִת *from shocks and standing grain to vineyard of olives* Jg 15$_{5}$, מִן־הָאֶרֶז … וְעַד הָאֵזוֹב *from the cedar … to the hyssop* 1 K 5$_{13}$, מֵעִיר מִבְצָר וְעַד כֹּפֶר הַפְּרָזִי *both fortified city and unwalled village* 1 S 6$_{18}$, מִמִּגְדַּל נוֹצְרִים עַד־עִיר מִבְצָר *both watchtower and fortified city* 2 K 17$_{9}$, מִטּוֹב עַד־רָע *either good or evil* Gn 31$_{24}$, var. 2 S 13$_{22}$, מִשּׁוֹר עַד־חֲמוֹר עַד־שֶׂה *either an ox or an ass or a sheep* Ex 22$_{3}$, מִחוּט וְעַד שְׂרוֹךְ־נַעַל *neither a thread nor the thong of a sandal* Gn 14$_{23}$.

(3) time, *from … until*, e.g. מִנְּעוּרֵינוּ וְעַד־עַתָּה *from our youth until now* Gn 46$_{34}$, מִן־הַבֶּטֶן עַד־יוֹם מוֹתוֹ *from the womb*, i.e. birth, *until the day of his death* Jg 13$_{7}$, לְמִן־הַיּוֹם הִוָּסְדָה וְעַד־עָתָּה *from the day when it was founded until now* Ex 9$_{18}$, לְמִן־הַיּוֹם אֲשֶׁר בָּנוּ אוֹתָהּ וְעַד־הַיּוֹם הַזֶּה *from the day when they built it until this day* Jr 32$_{31}$, מֵעוֹדִי עַד־הַיּוֹם הַזֶּה *from my (coming into) existence until this day* Gn 48$_{15}$, sim. Ex 10$_{6}$, מִיּוֹם הַעֲלֹתִי אֹתָם מִמִּצְרַיִם וְעַד־הַיּוֹם הַזֶּה *from the day when I brought them up out of Egypt until this day* 1 S 8$_{8}$, מִיּוֹם בֹּאֲךָ אֵלַי עַד־הַיּוֹם הַזֶּה *from the day when you came to me until this day* 1 S 29$_{6}$, מִתְּחִלַּת קָצִיר עַד נִתַּךְ־מַיִם עֲלֵיהֶם מִן־הַשָּׁמָיִם *from the beginning of the harvest until water was poured upon them from heaven* 2 S 21$_{10}$, מן היום עד סוף ערב השמטה *from today until the end of the eve of the remittance* Mur 24 E$_{8}$.

מִיּוֹם הָרִאשֹׁן עַד־יוֹם הַשְּׁבִעִי *from the first day until the seventh day* Ex 12$_{15}$, מִן־הַיּוֹם הָרִאשׁוֹן עַד הַיּוֹם הָאַחֲרוֹן *from the first day to the last day* Ne 8$_{18}$, מן השלשה עשר לחדש עד השמנה עשר לחדש *from the thirteenth of the month until the eighteenth of the month* Arad ost. 8$_{2}$, מִשְּׁנַת עֶשְׂרִים וְעַד שְׁנַת שְׁלֹשִׁים וּשְׁתַּיִם *from the twentieth year to the thirty-second year* Ne 5$_{14}$, מִן־הַבֹּקֶר עַד־הָעָרֶב *from the morning until the evening* Ex 18$_{13}$, מֵעֶרֶב עַד־בֹּקֶר *from evening to morning* Ex 27$_{21}$, מֵהַבֹּקֶר וְעַד־עֵת מוֹעֵד *from the morning until the appointed time* 2 S 24$_{15}$, מִיּוֹם עַד־לַיְלָה *from day to night* Is 38$_{12}$, מִן־הָאוֹר עַד־מַחֲצִית הַיּוֹם *from dawn until midday* Ne 8$_{3}$, מֵרֹאשׁ וְעַד־סוֹף *from beginning to end* Ec 3$_{11}$; with inf. cstr., מִהְיוֹת גּוֹי עַד הָעֵת הַהִיא *since the nation came into being until that time* Dn 12$_{1}$, מֵעֲלוֹת הַשַּׁחַר עַד צֵאת הַכּוֹכָבִים *from the going up of the dawn to the coming out of the stars* Ne 4$_{15}$.

b. מִן … אֶל *from … to*, e.g. וַיֵּלֶךְ מִשָּׁם אֶל־הַר הַכַּרְמֶל *and he went from there to Mount Carmel* 2 K 2$_{25}$, ילכו המים מן המוצא אל הברכה *and the water flowed from the spring to the pool* Siloam Tunnel inscr.$_{5}$, מֵאֶרֶץ רְחוֹקָה בָּאוּ אֵלַי מִבָּבֶל *they came to me from a distant land, from Babylon* Is 39$_{3}$, וְיָצָא הַכֹּהֵן מִן־הַבַּיִת אֶל־פֶּתַח הַבָּיִת *and the priest shall go out from the house to the entrance of the house* Lv 14$_{38}$, וַיֵּרֶד מֹשֶׁה מִן־הָהָר אֶל־הָעָם *and Moses went down from the mountain to the people* Ex 19$_{14}$, וַיַּעַל מֹשֶׁה מֵעַרְבֹת מוֹאָב אֶל־הַר נְבוֹ *and Moses went up from the plains of Moab to Mount Nebo* Dt 34$_{1}$, לְהָבִיא עֲצֵי אֲרָזִים מִן־הַלְּבָנוֹן אֶל־יָם יָפוֹא *to bring cedar trees from the Lebanon to the sea at Joppa* Ezr 3$_{7}$, לְהוֹצִיאָם מֵאֶרֶץ מִצְרַיִם אֶל־אֶרֶץ אֲשֶׁר־

תַּרְתִּי לָהֶם *to bring them out from the land of Egypt to a land that I have searched out for them* Ezk 20₆.

וְשָׁלַחְתִּי מֵהֶם פְּלֵטִים אֶל־הַגּוֹיִם *and I will send survivors from them to the nations* Is 66₁₉, נְתַקְּנֻהוּ מִן־הָעִיר אֶל־הַמְסִלּוֹת *let us draw him from the city to the highways* Jg 20₃₂, וַיָּמָד מִשַּׁעַר אֶל־שַׁעַר *and he measured from gate to gate* Ezk 40₂₃; מִזַּן אֶל־זַן *from kind to kind*, i.e. all kinds (of food) Ps 144₁₃, מִן־הַקָּצָה אֶל־הַקָּצָה *from end to end* Ex 26₂₈||36₃₃, מִפֶּה אֶל־פֶּה *from end to end* Ezr 9₁₁, מֵחַיִל אֶל־חָיִל *from strength to strength* Ps 84₈, מִגּוֹי אֶל־גּוֹי מִמַּטֶּה אֶל־מַטֶּה *from tribe to tribe* Nm 36₇, *from nation to nation* Jr 25₃₂, מֵרָעָה אֶל־מֵרָעָה *from evil to evil* Jr 9₂, מִיּוֹם אֶל־יוֹם *from day to day* Nm 30₁₅, מֵעֵת אֶל־עֵת *from time to time* 1 C 9₂₅.

c. מִן ... לְ, (1) of place, *to ... of*, e.g. מִצְּפוֹן לָעִיר *to the north of the city* Jos 8₁₃, מִקֶּדֶם לְבֵית־אֵל *to the east of Bethel* Gn 12₈.

(2) of direction, *from ... to*, e.g. מִשַּׁעַר לָשַׁעַר *from gate to gate* Ex 32₂₇, מִגֶּבַע לְרִמּוֹן *from Geba to Rimmon* Zc 14₁₀.

(3) of time, *from ... to*, e.g. מִיּוֹם־לְיוֹם *from day to day* Ps 96₂, מִבֹּקֶר לָעֶרֶב *from morning to evening* Jb 4₂₀.

d. ה- of direction ... מִן *from ... to*, e.g. מֵחֲצַר עֵינָן שְׁפָמָה *from Hazar-enan to Shepham* Nm 34₁₀, מִבֵּית־אֵל לוּזָה *from Bethel to Luz* Jos 16₂, מִיָּמִים יָמִימָה *from year to year*, lit. from days to days Jg 21₁₉.

16. מִן in compound, followed by other preposition, particle or adverb, e.g. מֵאַחֲרֵי, מֵאַחַר, etc.; see under אָז *then*, אַחַר *after*, אַחֲרֵי *after*, אַיִן *not*, אַיִן *where?*, אֵצֶל *beside*, אֲשֶׁר *which*, אֵת *with*, בֵּין *between*, בְּלִי *nothingness*, בִּלְעֲדֵי *apart from*, בַּעַד *behind*, הָלְאָה *onwards*, זֶה *this*, לְעֻמַּת *close by*, לִפְנֵי *before*, מַטָּה *downwards*, לְבַד *besides*, מַעַל *upwards*, נֶגֶד *before*, עוֹד *still*, עַל *upon*, עִם *with*, פֹּה *here*, פָּנִים *face*, קֶרֶב *middle*, שָׁם *there*, תָּוֶךְ *middle*, תַּחַת *under*.*

מְנָאוֹת, see מְנָת *portion*.

מְנָאֵף *adulterer*, see נאף *commit adultery*, Pi.

[מַנְגִּינָה] 1 n.f. **mocking song**—sf. מַנְגִּינָתָם—<NOM CL> אֲנִי מַנְגִּינָתָם *I am (the subject of) their mocking song* Lm 3₆₃ (or em. אֲנִי־ם נְגִינָתָם in same sense).*

⇒ נגן *play a stringed instrument.*

מְנַגֵּן *musician*, see נגן *play (as stringed instrument)*, Pi.

מְנֻדָּח I *banished one*, see נדח I *thrust*, Pu.

מְנֻדָּח II *widespread*, see נדח III *widen*, Pu.*

מנה 28.3.4.2 vb. **count, appoint**—**Qal** 12.1.1.2 Pf. מָנָה; impf. 2ms תִּמְנֶה; + waw וַיִּמְנוּ; וּמָנִיתִי; impv. מְנֵה; ptc. מוֹנֶה; inf. מְנוֹת—**1. count, number,** <SUBJ> Y. Ps 147₄, perh. Baruch Samaria-Sebaste ost. 1101₃, David 2 S 24₁||1 C 21₁ 1 C 21₁₇, Joab 1 C 27₂₄, אִישׁ *man* Gn 13₁₆, בֵּן *son* 1 C 27₂₄, סֹפֵר *secretary* 2 K 12₁₁, כֹּהֵן *priest* 2 K 12₁₁, worshipper Ps 90₁₂, מִי *who?* Nm 23₁₀; subj. not specified, Jr 33₁₃ Kenyon ost. 4₂. <OBJ> Israel 2 S 24₁|| 1 C 21₁, Judah 2 S 24₁, עָפָר *dust* Gn 13₁₆ Nm 23₁₀ (Sam^mss מֵעֲפַר *any of the dust of*; or em. מִסְפַּר *number of*), כֶּסֶף *money* 2 K 12₁₁, יוֹם *day* Ps 90₁₂, מִסְפָּר *number* Nm 23₁₀ (if em.; see above) Ps 147₄, שַׁעַר *measure* Samaria-Sebaste ost. 1101₃ (others סְאָה *seah*), כֹּל *everything* 5QapMal 1₅. <PREP> בְּ introducing object, + עַם *people* 1 C 21₁₇; מִן partitive, *(some) of*, + עָפָר *dust* Nm 23₁₀(Sam^mss) (or em.; see Obj.). <COLL> מנו 18 לעשר *they counted 18 to give as tithe* Kenyon ost. 4₂.

2. muster, <SUBJ> מֶלֶךְ *king* 1 K 20₂₅. <OBJ> חַיִל *army* 1 K 20₂₅.

3. appoint, assign, <SUBJ> Y. Is 65₁₂. <OBJ> עזב ptc. *one who forsakes* Is 65₁₂, שׁכח ptc. *one who forgets* Is 65₁₂, ערך ptc. *one who arranges* Is 65₁₂, מלא pi. ptc. *one who fills* Is 65₁₂. <PREP> לְ of direction, *to*, + חֶרֶב *sword* Is 65₁₂.

4. reckon as, <SUBJ> אִישׁ *man* Si 40₂₉(B). <OBJ> חַיִּים *life* Si 40₂₈(B) (אין חייו למנות חיים *he should not reckon his life as life*).

5. ptc. as noun, **merchant,*** <SUBJ> אתה hi. *bring* Ps 68₃₂ (if em. מִנֵּי ... יֶאֱתָיו *let them come ... from* to מֹנֵי ... יַאֲתִיו *let the merchants of ... bring*). <CSTR> מֹנֵי מִצְרַיִם *merchants of Egypt* Ps 68₃₂.

Pass. Qal, be appointed, <SUBJ> אֱמֶת *truth* Ps

61$_8$ (if em. מַן *appoint* [pi. impv.] to מֻן *let them be appointed*), חֶסֶד *loyalty* Ps 61$_8$ (if em.).

Ni. 6.1.2 Pf. נִמְנָה; impf. יִמָּנֶה, יִמָּנוּ, Si נמנה; inf. הִמָּנוֹת—**1. be counted, numbered,** <SUBJ> עַם *people* 1 K 3$_8$, עֶבֶד *servant* Is 53$_{12}$, זֶרַע *seed,* i.e. descendants Gn 13$_{16}$, בָּקָר *cattle* 1 K 8$_5$‖2 C 5$_6$, צֹאן *sheep* 1 K 8$_5$‖2 C 5$_6$, אֵלֶּה *these* (sand and dust) 4QpsJub^a 2.1$_7$ (נמ]נים]), חֶסְרוֹן *deficiency* Ec 1$_{15}$ (or em. לְהִמָּלוֹת *to be filled,* i.e. מלא ni.). <PREP> מִן of cause, *on account of,* + רֹב *multitude* 2 K 8$_5$‖2 C 5$_6$; אֵת *with* 1QSb 4$_2$ ([אתו]), + פֹּשֵׁעַ *transgressor* Is 53$_{12}$. <COLL> מנה ni. ‖ ספר ni. *be counted* 1 K 3$_8$ 8$_5$‖2 C 5$_6$.

2. be counted as, reckoned as, <SUBJ> subj. not specified, Si 8$_6$. <PREP> מִן partitive, *(some) of, from among,* + זָקֵן *elderly one* Si 8$_6$.

3. be appointed, apportioned, <SUBJ> perh. wisdom 4Q185 1.2$_9$. <PREP> לְ of direction, *to,* + רָשָׁע *wicked one* 4Q185 1.2$_9$.

<SYN> §1 ספר ni. *be counted.*

Pi. 9.1.1 Pf. מִנָּה, Q מניתי, מִנּוּ; impf. Si ימנה; + waw וַיְמַן; impv. מַן—**1. appoint, send, assign,** <SUBJ> Y. Jon 2$_1$ 4$_{6.7.8}$ Ps 61$_8$ (or em. מַן *appoint* to מֻן *let them be appointed* [pass. qal] or מְנִי *Destiny* or del.; or מן = abbrev. for מלא נון, scribal mark 'plene nun' in ref. to ינצרהו)* Si 38$_{14(Bmg)}$ (B יצלח *it will succeed*), מֶלֶךְ *king* Dn 1$_5$, שַׂר *chief* Dn 1$_{11}$. <OBJ> מֶלְצַר *guardian* Dn 1$_{11}$, דָּג *fish* Jon 2$_1$, תּוֹלַעַת *worm* Jon 4$_7$, קִיקָיוֹן *castor oil plant* Jon 4$_6$, רוּחַ *wind* Jon 4$_8$, קָדִים *east wind* Jon 4$_8$, אֱמֶת *truth* Ps 61$_8$ (or em.; see Subj.), חֶסֶד *loyalty* Ps 61$_8$ (or em.; see Subj.), פְּשָׁרָה *diagnosis* Si 38$_{14(Bmg)}$, רִפְאוּת *healing* Si 38$_{14(Bmg)}$, דָּבָר *thing* Dn 1$_5$. <PREP> לְ of benefit, *to, for,* + רֹפֵא *physician* Si 38$_{14(Bmg)}$; מִן partitive, *(some) of,* + פַּתְבַּג *delicacies* Dn 1$_5$, יַיִן *wine* Dn 1$_5$; עַל *over, in charge of,* + Daniel, Hananiah, Mishael and Azariah Dn 1$_{11}$.

2. apportion, <SUBJ> Y. Ps 16$_5$ (if em. מְנָת *portion of* to מִנִּתָ *you have appointed*), Asher Gn 49$_{20}$ (if em. שְׁמֵנָה *fat* to שֶׁמִּנָּה *who apportions*), מֶלֶךְ *king* Dn 1$_{10}$, אָדוֹן *lord* Dn 1$_{10}$; subj. not specified, Jb 7$_3$ (or em. pu.). <OBJ> מַאֲכָל *food* Dn 1$_{10}$, לֶחֶם *bread* Gn 49$_{20}$ (if em.; see Subj.), מִשְׁתֶּה *drink* Dn 1$_{10}$, לַיְלָה *night* Jb 7$_3$ (or em. pu.), כּוֹס *cup* Ps 16$_5$ (if em.; see Subj.), חֵלֶק *share* Ps 16$_5$ (if em.; see Subj.). <COLL> מנה pi. + נחל ho. *be allotted* Jb 7$_3$.

3. arrange payment (to oneself), <SUBJ> Salome Mur 30 2$_{26}$, אִשָּׁה *wife* Mur 30 2$_{26}$, בַּת *daughter* Mur 30 2$_{26}$. <COLL> מניתי 30 שנה ושנה *I have arranged payment (to myself) of 30 (denarii) each year* Mur 30 2$_{26}$.

Pu. 1 Ptc. מְמֻנִּים—**be appointed,** <SUBJ> שֹׁעֵר *gatekeeper* 1 C 9$_{29}$, לַיְלָה *night* Jb 7$_3$ (if em. מִנּוּ pi. *they have appointed* to מֻנּוּ *they have been appointed*). <PREP> לְ of benefit, *to, for,* + Job Jb 7$_3$ (if em.; see Subj.); עַל *over, in charge of,* + כְּלִי *vessel* 1 C 9$_{29}$, סֹלֶת *fine flour* 1 C 9$_{29}$, יַיִן *wine* 1 C 9$_{29}$, שֶׁמֶן *oil* 1 C 9$_{29}$, לְבוֹנָה *frankincense* 1 C 9$_{29}$, בֹּשֶׂם *spice* 1 C 9$_{29}$.*

⇒ מָנָה *portion,* מָנָה II *portion,* מִנְיָן *number,* מֹנֶה *time,* מְנָת *portion,* (?) מְנִי *Meni.*

מָנָה I 12.2.4 n.f. **portion**—pl. מָנוֹת; cstr. Q מנות; sf. מְנוֹתֶהָ—**portion, share** of food (Est 2$_9$), sent as gifts on feast days (Est 9$_{19.22}$ Ne 8$_{10.12}$ perh. Si 41$_{21}$), of sacrificial animal (Ex 29$_{26}$ Lv 7$_{33}$ 8$_{29}$ 1 S 1$_{4.5}$ 9$_{23}$ 2 C 31$_{19}$ 11QT 22$_{10}$ 11QT^b 5$_2$), **gift** (Si 26$_3$), <NOM CL> אין מנה *there is no portion* 4QPrFêtes^c 280, אשה [ט]ובה מנה *a good wife is a gift* Si 26$_3$ (unless מָנָה II *fate*), בלשוני מנות הוד *on my lips are portions of splendour* 4QPoet^b 1$_4$. <OBJ> שׁלח *send* Ne 8$_{10.12}$, נתן *give* 1 S 1$_{4.5}$ 9$_{23}$ Est 2$_9$ 2 C 31$_{19}$, שׂים *place* 1 S 9$_{23}$.

<CSTR> מנות הוד *portions of splendour* 4QPoet^b 1$_4$, מחל[ק]ת מנה, מִשְׁלוֹחַ מָנוֹת *sending of portions* Est 9$_{19.22}$, *allotment of a portion* Si 41$_{21(M)}$ (Bmg מחלקות). <PREP> לְ *as* or introducing predicate, + היה *be* Ex 29$_{26}$ Lv 7$_{33}$ 8$_{29}$ 11QT 22$_{10}$; of possession, *of, (belonging) to* 11QT^b 5$_2$ (הקבאות למנות *the stomachs of the portions*). <COLL> מָנָה ‖ מַתָּנָה *gift* Est 9$_{22}$, תַּמְרוּק *ointment* Est 2$_9$; + חֵלֶק *portion* Si 26$_3$, מַשְׁמַנִּים *delicacies* Ne 8$_{10}$, מַמְתַקִּים *sweet things* Ne 8$_{10}$; מָנָה אַחַת אַפָּיִם *a portion (consisting of) one of two sides,* i.e. only half a portion 1 S 1$_5$.

<SYN> מַתָּנָה *gift,* תַּמְרוּק *ointment.*

⇒ מנה *count, appoint.*

***מָנָה II** 0.0.1 n.f. **fate**—<NOM CL> אשה [ט]ובה מנה *a good wife is a fate* Si 26$_3$.

מָנֶה I 5.0.5 n.m. **mina**—pl. מָנִים (Q מנין)—unit of weight for precious metals, <SUBJ> היה *be* Ezk 45$_{12}$. <OBJ> עלה hi. *bring up* 1 K 10$_{17}$, נתן *give* Ezr 2$_{69}$||Ne 7$_{70}$ Ne 7$_{71}$. <CSTR> מחצית המנ[ה] *half a mina* 4QOrdª 1.2$_{9}$, משקל ... מנין *weight of ...* twenty *minas* 3QTr 12$_{9}$. <APP> זָהָב *gold* 1 K 10$_{17}$, כֶּסֶף *silver* Ezr 2$_{69}$||Ne 7$_{70}$ Ne 7$_{71}$. <PREP> לְ perh. of benefit, *for* 4QOrdª 1.2$_{10}$.

<COLL> שני מנים *two minas* 4QOrdª 2$_{9}$, שְׁלֹשֶׁת מָנִים *three minas* 1 K 10$_{17}$ (||2 C 9$_{16}$ שְׁלֹשׁ מֵאוֹת *three hundred [shekels]*), עשרת המנים *ten minas* 4QOrdª 1.2$_{10}$, מנין עסרין *twenty minas* 3QTr 12$_{9}$, מָנִים אֲלָפִּים *two thousand minas* Ne 7$_{71}$, מָנִים אַלְפַּיִם וּמָאתָיִם *two thousand two hundred minas* Ne 7$_{70}$, מָנִים חֲמֵשֶׁת אֲלָפִים *five thousand minas* Ezr 2$_{69}$; ונענש שני מנים *and he shall be fined two minas* 4QOrdª 2$_{9}$.

Also 4QOrdª 1.2$_{10}$ 4QBerª 17a$_{1}$.*

*[**מָנֶה**] II 0.0.1 n.[m.] **portion**—cstr. Q מנה—<CSTR> מנה פלאיו *portion of his wonders*, i.e. his wondrous portion 4QShirShabbᵈ 1.2$_{20}$. <PREP> בְּ of accompaniment, *with, in,* + רום pol. *exalt* 4QShirShabbᵈ 1.2$_{20}$.

⇨ מנה *count, appoint.*

[**מֹנֶה**] 2 n.[m.] **time**—pl. מֹנִים—**time, occasion,** <COLL> וְהֶחֱלִף אֶת־מַשְׂכֻּרְתִּי עֲשֶׂרֶת מֹנִים *and he has changed my wages ten times* Gn 31$_{7}$, var. Gn 31$_{41}$.

⇨ מנה *count, appoint.*

מִנְהָג 2.0.1 n.[m.] **driving, custom**—cstr. מִנְהַג—**1. driving** of chariot, <NOM CL> הַמִּנְהָג כְּמִנְהַג יֵהוּא *the driving is like the driving of Jehu* 2 K 9$_{20}$. <CSTR> מִנְהַג יֵהוּא בֶן־נִמְשִׁי *driving of Jehu the son of Nimshi* 2 K 9$_{20}$. <PREP> כְּ *like, as* 2 K 9$_{20}$.

2. custom, <CSTR> מנהג התורה *custom of the law* CD 19$_{3}$. <PREP> כְּ *according to,* + לקח *take (in marriage)* CD 19$_{3}$.

⇨ נהג I *drive.*

[**מִנְהָרָה**] I 1 n.f. **hollow place**—pl. מִנְהָרוֹת—as refuge, <NOM CL> הַמִּנְהָרוֹת אֲשֶׁר בֶּהָרִים *the hollow places that are in the mountains* Jg 6$_{2}$ (|| מְעָרָה *cave,* מְצָד *stronghold*). <OBJ> עשׂה *make* Jg 6$_{2}$.

<SYN> מְעָר *cave,* מְצָד *stronghold.*

*[**מִנְהָרָה**] II 1 n.f. **signal station**—pl. מִנְהָרוֹת—as refuge, <NOM CL> הַמִּנְהָרוֹת אֲשֶׁר בֶּהָרִים *the signal stations that are in the mountains* Jg 6$_{2}$ (|| מְעָרָה *cave,* מְצָד *stronghold*). <OBJ> עשׂה *make* Jg 6$_{2}$.

<SYN> מְעָר *cave,* מְצָד *stronghold.*

⇨ נהר II *shine.*

*[**מָנוֹ**] 0.0.1 pl.n. **Mano,** in list of place names, 4Q522 9.1$_{6}$.

[**מָנוֹד**] 1 n.[m.] **shaking**—cstr. מְנוֹד—**1. (object of) shaking** of head, in derision, <SUBJ> היה *be* Ps 31$_{12}$ (if em. מְאֹד *much*). <OBJ> שׂים *place,* i.e. make Ps 44$_{15}$ (|| מָשָׁל *byword*) 80$_{7}$ (if em. מָדוֹן *strife*). <CSTR> מְנוֹד־רֹאשׁ *shaking of the head* Ps 44$_{15}$.

2. (cause of) grief, <SUBJ> היה *be* Pr 29$_{21}$ (if em. מָנוֹן perh. *insolent one*).

<SYN> מָשָׁל *byword.*

⇨ נוד *move to and fro.*

מָנוֹחַ I 7.2.9 n.m. **resting place**—cstr. מְנוֹחַ; sf. מְנוּחָיְכִי—**1. resting place,** for exiles (Dt 28$_{65}$ Lm 1$_{3}$), Issachar (Gn 49$_{15}$; if מְנֻחָה is מָנוֹחַ with adverbial acc. ־ָה),* bird (Gn 8$_{9}$ perh. Is 34$_{14}$ 4QCommGenA 1$_{15}$); in ref. to home (Ru 3$_{1}$ perh. Si 36$_{4}$).

2. rest (4Q476 2$_{5}$ 4QPrQuot 24.7$_{5}$ 37.12$_{15}$ 41.2$_{3}$), for soul, i.e. self (Ps 116$_{7}$ 1QH 8$_{30}$), wicked (Si 12$_{3}$; or em.; see Nom. Cl.), Israel (1QM 2$_{9}$), eye (1QH 9$_{5}$); after battle (1QM 19$_{9}$).

3. coming to rest, of ark (1 C 6$_{16}$).

<SUBJ> היה *be* Dt 28$_{65}$. <NOM CL> אין מנוח *there is no rest* 1QH 8$_{30}$. <OBJ> ראה *see* Gn 49$_{15}$ (if מְנֻחָה is מָנוֹחַ with adverbial acc. ־ָה),* בקשׁ pi. *seek* Ru 3$_{1}$, מצא *find* Gn 8$_{9}$ Is 34$_{14}$ Lm 1$_{3}$ 4QCommGenA 1$_{15}$, בנה *build* Si 36$_{4}$ (if em.; see Cstr.).

<CSTR> מנוח רשע *rest of a wicked one* Si 12$_{3}$ (or em.; see Nom. Cl.), קודש *of holiness*, i.e. holy rest 4QPrQuot 41.2$_{3}$, שבת *of the sabbath* 4Q476 2$_{5}$, מְנוֹחַ הָאָרוֹן *coming to rest of the ark* 1 C 6$_{16}$; שבת מנוח *sabbath of rest* 1QM 2$_{8}$, מועד *appointed time of* 4QPrQuot

24.7$_5$ ([מו]עד]), בית *house of* Si 36$_4$ (or em. בית to ובנית *and you shall build* a resting place).

<PREP> לְ of direction, *to*, + שׁוב *go back* Ps 116$_7$; of benefit, *for* 1QM 19$_9$; *for (need of)*, + כלה *be dim* 1QH 9$_5$; *pertaining to* Si 12$_3$ (or em. למניח *to one who relieves*, i.e. נוח hi. ptc.); מִן *from (the time of), after*, + עמד hi. *appoint* 1 C 6$_{16}$.

<COLL> מָנוֹחַ לְכַף־רַגְלֶךָ *a resting place for the soul of your foot* Dt 28$_{65}$, var. Gn 8$_9$, מנוח לנ[ו] *rest for us* 4QPrQuot 37.12$_{15}$, מנוח עד הבוקר *rest until the morning* 1QM 19$_9$.

⇒ נוח I *rest*.

מָנוֹחַ II 18.0.0.2 pr.n.m. **Manoah**—I מנח—**1.** father of Samson, <SUBJ> אמר *say* Jg 13$_{8+5t}$, עתר *entreat* Jg 13$_8$, שׁאל *ask* Jg 13$_{17}$, ראה *see* Jg 13$_{19.20.22}$, ידע *know* Jg 13$_{16.21}$, כבד pi. *honour* Jg 13$_{17}$, הלך *go* Jg 13$_{11}$, בוא *come* Jg 13$_{11}$, עלה hi. *cause to go up*, i.e. offer Jg 13$_{16.19}$, קום *rise* Jg 13$_{11}$, נפל *fall* Jg 13$_{20}$, עצר *detain* Jg 13$_{15.16}$, לקח *take* Jg 13$_{19}$, עשׂה *do*, i.e. prepare Jg 13$_{15.16}$, מות *die* Jg 13$_{22}$. <NOM CL> שְׁמוֹ מָנוֹחַ *his name was Manoah* Jg 13$_2$, מָנוֹחַ ... אֵין עִמָּה *Manoah ... was not with her* Jg 13$_9$. <OBJ> ראה hi. *show* Jg 13$_{22}$, שׁמע hi. *cause to hear* Jg 13$_{22}$, מות hi. *kill* Jg 13$_{22}$. <CSTR> קוֹל מָנוֹחַ *voice of Manoah* Jg 13$_9$, קֶבֶר *tomb of* Jg 16$_{31}$. <APP> אִישׁ *husband* Jg 13$_9$, אָב *father* Jg 16$_{31}$. <PREP> לְ of direction, *to*, + אמר *say* Jg 13$_{17.22}$; אֶל *to*, + אמר *say* Jg 13$_{13.16}$, ראה ni. *appear* Jg 13$_{21}$.

2. Seal 11, <PREP> לְ of possession, *of, (belonging) to* Seal 11.

3. father of Maash, <CSTR> בן מנח *son of Manoah* Seal 345 (7th cent.).*

⇒ נוח I *rest*.

מְנוּחָה 21.1.7 n.f. **resting place**—מְנֻחָה; cstr. Q מנוחת; sf. מְנוּחָתִי, מְנוּחָתֶךָ, מְנֻחָתוֹ, Si מנוחתה, Q מנוחתם; pl. מְנוּחֹת (מְנֻחוֹת); cstr. Q מנוחות—**1. resting place,** of Israelites during exodus (Nm 10$_{33}$), Israel in Canaan (Dt 12$_9$ 1 K 8$_{56}$ Is 11$_{10}$), word of Y. (Zc 9$_1$), Issachar (Gn 49$_{15}$; unless מְנֻחָה is מָנוֹחַ with adverbial acc. ־ָה),* Benjaminites (Jg 20$_{43}$; unless pl.n. *Menuhah*; or em.; see Prep.); in ref. to home (Is 32$_{18}$ Mc 2$_{10}$ Ru 1$_9$), dwelling place of Y. as **royal seat*** (Is 66$_1$ Ps 95$_{11}$ 132$_{8.14}$ 4QDibHam^a 1.4$_2$), for ark of covenant (1 C 28$_2$); in title of official (Jr 51$_{59}$).

2. rest, refreshment, peace (Jg 20$_{43}$ [if em.; see Prep.] 2 S 14$_{17}$ Jr 45$_3$ Ps 23$_2$ [unless §1] 1 C 22$_9$), for weary (Is 28$_{12}$), found in wisdom (Si 6$_{28}$); of day of atonement (1QpHab 11$_{6.8}$), eternal rest (4QBéat 14.2$_{14}$).

<SUBJ> היה *be* Is 11$_{10}$. <NOM CL> דַּמֶּשֶׂק מְנֻחָתוֹ *Damascus is its resting place* Zc 9$_1$, זֹאת הַמְּנוּחָה *this is rest* Is 28$_{12}$, זֹאת מְנוּחָתִי *this is my resting place* Ps 132$_{14}$, לֹא זֹאת הַמְּנוּחָה *this is not a resting place* Mc 2$_{10}$, אֵי־ זֶה ... מְנוּחָתִי *where is ... my resting place?* Is 66$_1$. <OBJ> ראה *see* Gn 49$_{15}$ (unless מְנֻחָה is מָנוֹחַ with adverbial acc. ־ָה),* תור *seek* Nm 10$_{33}$, מצא *find* Jr 45$_3$ Ru 1$_9$ Si 6$_{28}$, נתן *give* 1 K 8$_{56}$.

<CSTR> מנוחת יום הכפורים *rest of the day of atonement* 1QpHab 11$_6$, מנוחות עד *rest of eternity*, i.e. eternal rest 4QBéat 14.2$_{14}$; אִישׁ מְנוּחָה *man of rest* 1 C 22$_9$, שַׂר מְנוּחָה *chief of the resting place*, i.e. quartermaster Jr 51$_{59}$, בֵּית מְנוּחָה *house of rest* 1 C 28$_2$, מֵי מְנֻחָה *waters of rest*, i.e. still waters, or waters at a resting place Ps 23$_2$, שבת מנוחתם *sabbath of their rest*, i.e. their restful sabbath 1QpHab 11$_8$.

<APP> מָקוֹם *place* Is 66$_1$.

<ADJ> שַׁאֲנָן *at ease* Is 32$_{18}$.

<PREP> לְ as or introducing predicate, + היה *be* 2 S 14$_{17}$; of direction, *to*, + קום *arise* Ps 132$_8$, ספה ni. *be swept away* 4QBéat 14.2$_{14}$; בְּ of place, *in*, + ישׁב *dwell* Is 32$_{18}$; כְּ perh. *as* 4Q415 13$_5$; מִן privative, *without*, + דרך hi. *tread down* Jg 20$_{43}$ (if em.; see below); אֶל *to*, + בוא *come* Dt 12$_9$ Ps 95$_{11}$; מְנוּחָה without prep. *at the resting place, during (the time of) rest*, + דרך hi. *tread down* Jg 20$_{43}$ (or em. מִמְּנוּחָה *without rest*, or מִנּוֹחָה *from Nohah*), יפע hi. *appear* 1QpHab 11$_6$.

<COLL> מְנוּחָה ‖ אֶרֶץ *land* Gn 49$_{15}$, נַחֲלָה *inheritance* Dt 12$_9$, מַרְגֵּעָה *rest* Is 28$_{12}$; + בַּיִת *house* Is 66$_1$, מִשְׁכָּן *dwelling place* Is 32$_{18}$, נָוֶה *habitation* Is 32$_{18}$; בֵּית מְנוּחָה לַאֲרוֹן בְּרִית י׳ *a house of rest for the ark of the covenant of Y.* 1 C 28$_2$, מנוחה בירוש[לים] *a place of rest in Jerusalem* 4QDibHam^a 1.4$_2$.

Also 1Q56$_2$ 4QparaKings 45$_2$ ([מ]נוחת) 4Q418 237$_1$.

<SYN> §1 אֶרֶץ *land,* נַחֲלָה *inheritance;* §2 מַרְגֵּעָה *rest.**

⇒ נוח I *rest.*

[מָנוֹל] n.m. **possessions,** <SUBJ> נטה *spread* Jb 15$_{29}$ (if em. מִנְלָם perh. *their acquisitions* to מְנֹלָם *their possessions*).*

⇒ (?) נלה II *obtain.*

מָנוֹן I $_{1.1}$ adj. **insolent,** as noun, **insolent** or **disdainful one,*** of slave (Pr 29$_{21}$; unless מָנוֹן II *weak* or III *pained;* or em.; see Subj.), Rehoboam (Si 47$_{23}$), <SUBJ> היה *be* Pr 29$_{21}$ (or em. מָנוֹד *[cause of] grief* or מָנוּן *weak*). <OBJ> עזב *leave* Si 47$_{23}$.*

***מָנוֹן** II $_{1}$ adj. **weak,** as noun, **weak one, weakling,** of slave, <SUBJ> היה *be* Pr 29$_{21}$ (אַחֲרִיתוֹ יִהְיֶה מָנוֹן *in the end he will become a weakling;* unless מָנוֹן I *insolent* or III *pained;* or em. מָנוֹד *[cause of] grief* or מָנוּן *weak*).

***מָנוֹן** III $_{1}$ adj. **pained,** used predicatively with היה *be* Pr 29$_{21}$ (אַחֲרִיתוֹ יִהְיֶה מָנוֹן *in the end he will be pained,* i.e. come to grief; unless מָנוֹן I *insolent* or II *weak;* or em. מָנוֹד *[cause of] grief* or מָנוּן *weak*).

⇒ אנן *complain.*

***מָנוּן** adj. **weak,** as noun, **weak one, weakling,** of slave, <SUBJ> היה *be* Pr 29$_{21}$ (אַחֲרִיתוֹ יִהְיֶה מָנוּן *in the end he will become a weakling,* if em. מָנוֹן *insolent one* or *weak* or *pained*).

מָנוֹס $_{8.0.4}$ n.m. **flight, refuge**—sf. מְנוּסִי—**flight** (e.g. Jr 46$_{5}$), **(place of) refuge, escape,** <SUBJ> היה *be* Ps 59$_{17}$, אבד *perish* Jr 25$_{35}$ Am 2$_{14}$ Ps 142$_{5}$ Jb 11$_{20}$. <NOM CL> מְנוּסִי ... ״י *Y. is ... my refuge* 2 S 22$_{3}$, מנוסי ... [אתה] *you are ... my refuge* 1QH 9$_{28}$, אין מנוס *there is no refuge* 1QH 5$_{29}$ 6$_{33}$ 1QM 14$_{11}$. <OBJ> נוס *flee* Jr 46$_{5}$ (מָנוֹס נָסוּ *they have fled with flight,* i.e. hurriedly), נתן *give* Ps 60$_{6}$ (if em.; see Coll.). <APP> ״י *Y.* Jr 16$_{19}$. <PREP> אֶל *to,* + בוא *come* Jr 16$_{19}$. <COLL> מָנוֹס ‖ פְּלֵיטָה *escape* Jr 25$_{35}$, מִשְׂגָּב *refuge* 2 S 22$_{3}$ Ps 59$_{17}$ 1QH 9$_{28}$, מְצוּדָה *stronghold* 1QH 9$_{28}$, מָעוֹז *stronghold* Jr 16$_{19}$, עֹז *strength* Jr 16$_{19}$, סֶלַע *rock* 1QH 9$_{28}$; + מָגֵן *shield* 2 S 22$_{3}$, קֶרֶן *horn* of salvation 2 S 22$_{3}$; מְנוּסִי בְּיוֹם צָרָה *my refuge in the day of trouble* Jr 16$_{19}$, sim. Ps 59$_{17}$, מָנוֹס לְהִתְנוֹסֵס *a refuge to which to flee* Ps 60$_{6}$ (if em. נֵס *banner* to מָנוֹס).

<SYN> פְּלֵיטָה *escape,* מִשְׂגָּב *refuge,* מְצוּדָה *fortress,* מָעוֹז *stronghold,* עֹז *strength,* סֶלַע *rock.**

⇒ נוס I *flee.*

מְנוּסָה $_{2}$ n.f. **flight**—cstr. מְנֻסַת—<OBJ> נוס *flee* Lv 26$_{36}$. <CSTR> מְנֻסַת־חֶרֶב *flight of,* i.e. from, *the sword* Lv 26$_{36}$. <PREP> בְּ of accompaniment, *with, in,* + הלך *go* Is 52$_{12}$ (‖ חִפָּזוֹן *haste*).

<SYN> חִפָּזוֹן *haste.**

⇒ נוס I *flee.*

[מָנוֹר] $_{4}$ n.[m.] **weaver's beam**—cstr. מְנוֹר—**leash** or **heddle-rod,** cross beam of loom, with ref. to its shape rather than its size,* Goliath's spear being compared with it, <CSTR> מְנוֹר אֹרְגִים *beam of weavers* 1 S 17$_{7}$ 2 S 21$_{19}$‖1 C 20$_{5}$ 1 C 11$_{23}$. <PREP> כְּ *as* 1 S 17$_{7}$ 2 S 21$_{19}$‖ 1 C 20$_{5}$ 1 C 11$_{23}$.*

מְנוֹרָה $_{42.1.1}$ n.f. **lampstand**—מְנֹרָה; cstr. מְנוֹרַת (מְנֹרַת); pl. מְנֹרוֹת; cstr. מְנֹרוֹת—in private house (2 K 4$_{10}$); elsewhere alw. in tabernacle or temple, <SUBJ> היה *be* 11QT 3$_{13}$ ([יהיו]), עשה ni. *be made* Ex 25$_{31}$. <NOM CL> מִשְׁמַרְתָּם ... הַמְּנֹרָה *their charge was ... the lampstand* Nm 3$_{31}$, הִנֵּה מְנוֹרַת זָהָב *behold, there is a lampstand of gold* Zc 4$_{2}$. <OBJ> עשה *make* Ex 25$_{31.31(mss)}$‖37$_{17.17}$ 31$_{8}$‖35$_{14}$ Nm 8$_{4}$ 1 K 7$_{49}$‖2 C 4$_{20}$ 2 C 4$_{7}$, בוא hi. *bring* Ex 39$_{37}$ 40$_{4}$, שׂים *place* Ex 26$_{35}$ 40$_{24}$ 2 K 4$_{10}$, משׁח *anoint* Ex 30$_{27}$, כסה pi. *cover* Nm 4$_{9}$, בער pi. *burn* 2 C 4$_{20}$ 13$_{11}$.

<CSTR> מְנֹרַת הַמָּאוֹר *lampstand of,* i.e. for, *the light* Ex 35$_{14}$ Nm 4$_{9}$, מְנוֹרַת הַזָּהָב *the lampstand of gold* Zc 4$_{2}$ (זָהָב) 2 C 13$_{11}$, מְנֹרוֹת *lampstands of* 1 C 28$_{15}$ 2 C 4$_{7}$, מְנֹרוֹת הַכֶּסֶף *the lampstands of silver* 1 C 28$_{15}$, מנורת קודש *lampstand of holiness,* i.e. holy lampstand Si 26$_{17}$; קְנֵי מְנֹרָה *branches of the lampstand* Ex 25$_{32.32}$‖ 37$_{18.18}$, מַעֲשֵׂה הַמְּנֹרָה *work of the lampstand,* i.e. how it was made Nm 8$_{4}$, יְמִין הַמְּנוֹרָה *right hand side of the lampstand* Zc 4$_{11}$, מִשְׁקַל־מְנוֹרָה וּמְנוֹרָה *weight of each*

lampstand 1 C 28$_{15}$, עֲבוֹדַת *service of* 1 C 28$_{15}$.

<PREP> לְ of possession, *of, (belonging) to* 1 C 28$_{15.15.15}$; בְּ of place, *in, on* Ex 25$_{34}$||37$_{20}$; מִן of direction, *from*, + יצא *go out* Ex 25$_{33}$||37$_{19}$ 25$_{35}$; עַל *upon, above* Si 26$_{17}$, + ערך *arrange* Lv 24$_{4}$; אֶל מוּל פְּנֵי *in front of*, + אור hi. *give light* Nm 8$_{2}$, עלה hi. *set up* Nm 8$_{3}$.

<ADJ> טָהוֹר *pure* Ex 31$_{8}$||35$_{14}$ 39$_{37}$ Lv 24$_{4}$.

<COLL> מְנוֹרָה || כַּף *ladle* Jr 52$_{19}$, סִיר *pot* Jr 52$_{19}$, מִזְרָק *basin* Jr 52$_{19}$, סַף *dish* Jr 52$_{19}$, מְנַקִּית *bowl* Jr 52$_{19}$, מַחְתָּה *firepan* Jr 52$_{19}$; + נֵר *lamp* Ex 35$_{14}$ Nm 4$_{9}$ 1 C 28$_{15.15.15}$ 2 C 4$_{20}$ 13$_{11}$, מֶלְקָחַיִם *tongs* Nm 4$_{9}$, מַחְתָּה *snuffdish* Nm 4$_{9}$, כְּלִי *utensil* Ex 30$_{27}$ 31$_{8}$||35$_{14}$ Nm 4$_{9}$; מְנֹרוֹת הַזָּהָב עֶשֶׂר *ten lampstands of gold* 2 C 4$_{7}$.

<SYN> כַּף *ladle*, סִיר *pot*, מִזְרָק *basin*, סַף *dish*, מְנַקִּית *bowl*, מַחְתָּה *firepan*.*

⇒ cf. נֵר *lamp*.

[מִנְזָר] I $_{1}$ n.[m.] **consecrated one** (unless מִנְזָר II *guard* or III *courtier* or IV *exorcist*)—pl. sf. מִנְּזָרַ֫יִךְ—**consecrated one, prince,** <NOM CL> מִנְּזָרַיִךְ כָּאַרְבֶּה *your consecrated ones are as locusts* Na 3$_{17}$ (|| טִפְסָר *scribe*).

<SYN> טִפְסָר *scribe*.

⇒ נזר *dedicate*.

*__[מִנְזָר]__ II $_{1}$ n.[m.] **guard** (unless מִנְזָר I *consecrated one* or III *courtier* or IV *exorcist*)—pl. sf. מִנְּזָרַ֫יִךְ—<NOM CL> מִנְּזָרַיִךְ כָּאַרְבֶּה *your guards are as locusts* Na 3$_{17}$ (|| טִפְסָר *scribe*).

<SYN> טִפְסָר *scribe*.

*__[מִנְזָר]__ III $_{1}$ n.[m.] **courtier, official** (unless מִנְזָר I *consecrated one* or II *guard* or IV *exorcist*)—pl. sf. מִנְּזָרַ֫יִךְ—<NOM CL> מִנְּזָרַיִךְ כָּאַרְבֶּה *your courtiers are as locusts* Na 3$_{17}$ (|| טִפְסָר *scribe*).

<SYN> טִפְסָר *scribe*.

*__[מִנְזָר]__ IV $_{1}$ n.[m.] **exorcist, conjuror** (unless מִנְזָר I *consecrated one* or II *guard* or III *courtier*)—pl. sf. מִנְּזָרַ֫יִךְ—<NOM CL> מִנְּזָרַיִךְ כָּאַרְבֶּה *your astrologers are as locusts* Na 3$_{17}$ (|| טִפְסָר *scribe*).

<SYN> טִפְסָר *scribe*.

מָנֹחַ *free space*, see נוח I *rest*, Ho. B.

מִנְחָה 211.1.38 n.f. **offering**—cstr. מִנְחַת; sf. מִנְחָתִי, מִנְחָתְךָ, מִנְחָתֵךְ (מִנְחָתוֹ, מִנְחָתָהּ, מִנְחָתָם, מִנְחָתָה (Q מנחתמה); pl. sf. מִנְחֹתֶיךָ (mss מִנְחֹתֶיךָ), מִנְחֹתֵיכֶם, Q מנחותם—**1. gift, present,** <SUBJ> הלך *go* Gn 32$_{21}$, עבר *pass* Gn 32$_{22}$, שׁלח pass. *be sent* Gn 32$_{19}$. <NOM CL> מִנְחָה הִיא *it is a present* Gn 32$_{19}$(Qr), הַמִּנְחָה אֲשֶׁר־בְּיָדָם *the present that was in their hand* Gn 43$_{26}$. <OBJ> בוא hi. *bring* Gn 43$_{26}$ 1 S 10$_{27}$ 1 K 10$_{25}$||2 C 9$_{24}$ 2 C 32$_{23}$ 4QDibHam[a] 1.4$_{10}$, יצא hi. *bring out* Jg 6$_{18}$, ירד hi. *bring down* Gn 43$_{11}$, שׁלח *send* 2 K 20$_{12}$||Is 39$_{1}$, לקח *take* Gn 32$_{14}$ 33$_{10}$ 43$_{15}$ 2 K 8$_{8.9}$, כון hi. *prepare* Gn 43$_{25}$, נוח hi. *place* Jg 6$_{18}$. <APP> זָהָב *gold* 4QDibHam[a] 1.4$_{10}$, כֶּסֶף *silver* 4QDibHam[a] 1.4$_{10}$, אֶבֶן precious *stone* 4QDibHam[a] 1.4$_{10}$, סוּס *horse* 1 K 10$_{25}$||2 C 9$_{24}$, פֶּרֶד *mule* 1 K 10$_{25}$||2 C 9$_{24}$, לֹט *myrrh* Gn 43$_{11}$, בֹּשֶׂם *spice* 1 K 10$_{25}$||2 C 9$_{24}$, נְכֹאת *ladanum* Gn 43$_{11}$, בָּטְנָה *pistachio* Gn 43$_{11}$, שָׁקֵד *almond* Gn 43$_{11}$, כְּלִי *vessel* 1 K 10$_{25}$||2 C 9$_{24}$, שַׂלְמָה *garment* 1 K 10$_{25}$||2 C 9$_{24}$, נֶשֶׁק *weapon* 1 K 10$_{25}$||2 C 9$_{24}$, מְעַט *a little* Gn 43$_{11}$. <ADJ> זֹאת *this* Gn 43$_{15}$. <PREP> בְּ of instrument, *by (means of), with*, + כפר pi. *cover* face, i.e. secure favour Gn 32$_{21}$, חלה pi. *entreat* face, i.e. secure favour Ps 45$_{13}$. <COLL> מִנְחָה || מִגְדָּנוֹת *precious things* 2 C 32$_{23}$; מִנְחָה לְעֵשָׂו אָחִיו *a present for Esau, his brother* Gn 32$_{14}$.

2. tribute, <SUBJ> יבל ho. *be brought* Ho 10$_{6}$ (or em. יוּבַל *it will be bought* to יוֹבִלוּ *they will bring*). <OBJ> בוא hi. *bring* 2 C 17$_{11}$, יבל hi. *bring* Ho 10$_{6}$ (if em.; see Subj.), עלה hi. *bring up* 2 K 17$_{4}$, שׁלח *send* Jg 3$_{15}$, שׁוב hi. *render* 2 K 17$_{3}$ Ps 72$_{10}$, נגשׁ hi. *bring near* 1 K 5$_{1}$, קרב hi. *bring near* Jg 3$_{17.18}$, נשׂא *carry* Jg 3$_{18}$ 2 S 8$_{2.6}$||1 C 18$_{2.6}$, נתן *give* 2 C 17$_{5}$ 26$_{8}$. <CSTR> נֹשְׂאֵי מִנְחָה *ones who carry tribute* Jg 3$_{18}$ (הַמִּנְחָה) 2 S 8$_{2.6}$||1 C 18$_{2.6}$. <COLL> מִנְחָה || אֶשְׁכָּר *payment* Ps 72$_{10}$.

3. offering to Y., of either meat or grain, <SUBJ> עלה *go up*, i.e. be offered 1 K 18$_{29.36}$ 2 K 3$_{20}$, נגשׁ ho. *be brought near*, i.e. offered Ml 1$_{11}$, ערב *be sweet*, i.e. pleasing Ml 3$_{4}$, קטר ho. *be burned* Si 45$_{14}$ (מנ]התו]), שׁבת *cease* Dn 9$_{27}$ (if em.; see Obj.).

<OBJ> בוא hi. *bring* Gn 4$_{3}$ Is 1$_{13}$ 66$_{20.20}$ Ml 1$_{13}$, יבל hi. *bring* Zp 3$_{10}$, עלה hi. *cause to go up*, i.e. offer Is 66$_{3}$,

נגשׁ hi. *bring near*, i.e. offer Am 5$_{25}$ Ml 2$_{12}$ 3$_3$ 11QPs^a 18$_8$, נשׂא *carry* Ps 96$_8$||1 C 16$_{29}$, עבד *serve (with)*, i.e. offer Is 19$_{21}$, ריח hi. *smell*, i.e. accept 1 S 26$_{19}$, רצה *accept* Ml 1$_{10.13}$, נאץ pi. *despise* 1 S 2$_{17}$, שׁבת hi. *cause to cease* Dn 9$_{27}$ (or em. יַשְׁבִּית to יִשְׁבֹּת *it will cease*).

<CSTR> מִנְחַת י׳ *offering of Y.* 1 S 2$_{17}$, יִשְׂרָאֵל *of Israel* 1 S 2$_{29}$, יְהוּדָה וִירוּשָׁלָ͏ִם *of Judah and Jerusalem* Ml 3$_4$, שָׁוְא *of vanity*, i.e. vain offering Is 1$_{13}$, מנחת רצון *offering of acceptance*, i.e. acceptable offering 1QS 9$_5$ CD 11$_{21}$; מַעֲלֵה מִנְחָה *one who makes an offering* Is 66$_3$, ריח מנחותם *aroma of their offerings* 11QShirShabb 9$_4$, רֵאשִׁית כָּל־מִנְחַת *first part of every offering of* 1 S 2$_{29}$, נדבת מנחת *freewill offering of* 1QS 9$_5$, כָּל־מִנְחַת *every offering of* 1 S 2$_{29}$.

<APP> דַּם *blood* of swine Is 66$_3$.

<ADJ> טָהוֹר *pure* Ml 1$_{11}$.

<PREP> בְּ of instrument, *by (means of), with*, + כפר htp. *be atoned for* 1 S 3$_{14}$; introducing object, + בעט *despise* 1 S 2$_{29}$; כְּ *as* 4QapPs^b 46$_5$ CD 11$_{21}$; אֶל *to*, + פנה *turn*, i.e. have regard for Nm 16$_{15}$ (or em. תֹּכַחְתָּם *their argument* or אַנְחָתָם *their sighing* or מִנְחָתָם *their complaint*) Ml 2$_{13}$, שׁעה אֶל *gaze at*, i.e. have regard for Gn 4$_{4.5}$; עַל *upon* Si 50$_9$.

<COLL> זֶבַח || מִנְחָה *sacrifice* 1 S 2$_{29}$ 3$_{14}$ Is 19$_{21}$ Am 5$_{25}$ Dn 9$_{27}$, לְבוֹנָה *frankincense* Is 66$_3$; + קְטֹרֶת *incense* Is 1$_{13}$.

4. specif. **grain offering,** as crushed or parched grain (e.g. Lv 2$_{14}$ perh. 1 C 21$_{23}$), flour (e.g. Lv 6$_{8.13}$ 14$_{10.21}$ 23$_{13}$ Nm 5$_{15}$ 8$_8$ 15$_4$ 28$_5$ 29$_3$ Ezk 46$_{14}$ 1 C 23$_{29}$), baked as bread or cake (e.g. Lv 2$_{4.5.7}$ 6$_{14}$ 7$_9$ Ezk 46$_{20}$), <SUBJ> היה *be* Lv 6$_{16}$ 7$_{9.10}$ Ezk 45$_{17}$ 46$_{11}$, יתר ni. *remain* Lv 10$_{12}$, בוא *come* perh. 4Q365a 2.14, בלל pass. *be mixed* with oil Lv 7$_{10}$ 9$_4$ 14$_{10}$ Nm 8$_8$ 15$_6$ 28$_{9+5t}$ 29$_{3.9.14}$ 11QT 14$_2$ ([ומנ]חה ... בלול[ה]) 14$_5$ ([בלולה]) 14$_{15.17}$ (ב[לולה]), קרב ni. *be brought near*, i.e. offered 11QT 20$_9$, עשׂה ni. *be made* Lv 2$_{8.11}$, אפה ni. *be baked* Lv 7$_9$, אכל ni. *be eaten* Lv 6$_{16}$ 4QMMT B$_{11}$ (המנ[חה נאכלת]), זכר hi. *cause to be remembered* Nm 5$_{15}$, מנע ni. *be withheld* Jl 1$_{13}$, כרת ho. *be cut off* Jl 1$_9$.

<NOM CL> מִנְחָה הִיא *it is a grain offering* Lv 2$_{6(Qr).15(Qr)}$, var. Nm 5$_{15.18}$, זֹאת חֲנֻכַּת הַמִּזְבֵּחַ ... שְׁנֵים־עָשָׂר כְּבָשִׂים ... וּמִנְחָתָם *... this was the dedication offering of the altar ... twelve rams ... and their grain offering* Nm 7$_{87}$, מִנְחָתוֹ שְׁנֵי עֶשְׂרֹנִים סֹלֶת אִשֶּׁה *its grain offering shall be two tenths of an ephah of fine flour, a fire offering* Lv 23$_{13}$, זֶה קָרְבַּן אַהֲרֹן וּבָנָיו ... מִנְחָה *this is the offering of Aaron and his sons ... a grain offering* Lv 6$_{13}$, מִנְחָה עַל־מַחֲבַת קָרְבָּנֶךָ *your offering is a grain offering (baked) on a griddle* Lv 2$_5$, מִנְחַת מַרְחֶשֶׁת קָרְבָּנֶךָ *your offering is a grain offering of*, i.e. cooked in, *a pan* Lv 2$_7$, פְּקֻדַּת אֶלְעָזָר ... מִנְחַת הַתָּמִיד *the charge of Eleazar is ... the continual grain offering* Lv 4$_{16}$, מִנְחָה ... בְּיָדָם *a grain offering was ... in their hand* Jr 41$_5$, בְּיוֹם הַשַּׁבָּת ... מִנְחָה *on the sabbath day shall be (offered) ... a grain offering* Nm 28$_9$, ביום השלישי [פ]רים ... אלים ... ושעיר עזים ... ומנחתם *on the third day there shall be (offered) bulls ... rams ... a he-goat ... and their grain offering* 11QT 28$_8$, vars. 28$_4$ ([ו]מנ[חתמה]) 28$_{11}$, מנחתה ... עליה *its grain offering shall be ... upon it* 11QT 24$_8$, sim. 11QT 34$_{12}$.

<OBJ> בוא hi. *bring* Lv 2$_8$ Jr 17$_{26}$ 41$_5$ 11QT 18$_{13}$ 19$_{11}$, עלה hi. *cause to go up*, i.e. offer Ex 30$_9$ 40$_{29}$ Lv 14$_{20}$ Jos 22$_{23}$ Jg 13$_{19}$ Is 57$_6$ Jr 14$_{12}$ Am 5$_{22}$, נגשׁ hi. *bring near*, i.e. offer Lv 2$_8$, קרב hi. *bring near*, i.e. offer Lv 2$_{8.11.14.14}$ 6$_{7.13}$ 7$_9$ 9$_{17}$ 23$_{16.18.37}$ Nm 5$_{25}$ 6$_{15}$ 15$_{4.9}$ 28$_{12+5t}$ 29$_{9+9t}$ Ezk 46$_{5.5}$ 11QT 15$_9$ 17$_{14}$ 19$_4$ ([ויקריבו]) 23$_5$ ([ויקריבו] ... [ומנחת]מה) 25$_6$ (והק[רבתמה]) 25$_{14}$ 11QT^b 4$_5$ ([ויקריבו]), שׁלח *send* CD 11$_{19}$, עשׂה *make*, i.e. offer Nm 6$_{17}$ 15$_{6.24}$ 29$_3$ 1 K 8$_{64}$ Ezk 45$_{17.24}$ 46$_{7.14.14.15}$, קטר hi. *burn* 2 K 16$_{13.15.15.15}$ Jr 33$_{18}$ 11QT 16$_{9.18}$ ([מנ]חתו) 26$_7$, אפה *bake* Ezk 46$_{20}$, נוף hi. *wave* Nm 5$_{25}$, שׁוב hi. *bring back* Ne 13$_9$, לקח *take* Lv 9$_4$ 10$_{12}$ 14$_{10}$ Nm 5$_{25}$ 8$_8$ Jg 13$_{19.23}$, רצה *accept* Jr 14$_{12}$ Am 5$_{22}$, זכר *remember* Ps 20$_4$, חפץ *desire* Ps 40$_7$, נתן *give*, i.e. place Nm 5$_{18.18}$ Ne 13$_5$, נוח hi. *place* Ezk 42$_{13}$, שׁאר hi. *leave* Jl 2$_{14}$, אכל *eat* Lv 10$_{12}$ Ezk 44$_{29}$, כול hi. *contain* 1 K 8$_{64}$||2 C 7$_7$.

<CSTR> מִנְחַת כֹּהֵן *grain offering of a priest* Lv 6$_{16}$, בִּכּוּרִים *of first fruits* Lv 2$_{14}$, בִּכּוּרֶיךָ *of your first fruits* Lv 2$_{14}$, פִּתִּים *of cake fragments* Lv 6$_{14}$, מנחת החטים *grain offering of the wheat* 11QT 11$_{11}$, שמנו *of its oil* 11QT 24$_5$, נסכו *of its libation* 11QT 26$_7$, סולתו *of its fine flour* 11QT 34$_{12}$, הקורבנים *of the sacrifices* 4Q365a 2.14, מִנְחַת הַבֹּקֶר *grain offering of the morning* Ex 29$_{41}$ Nm 28$_8$ 11QT 13$_{15}$ (מנח[ת ה]בוקר), ־עֶרֶב *of the evening*

1 K 16$_{15}$ Ps 141$_{2}$ Dn 9$_{21}$ Ezr 9$_{4}$ (הָעֶרֶב) 9$_{5}$ (הָעֶרֶב) 11QT 17$_{7}$ (הערב), הַתָּמִיד *of the continuity*, i.e. the continual grain offering Nm 4$_{16}$ Ne 10$_{34}$, מַרְחֶשֶׁת *of*, i.e. cooked in, *a pan* Lv 2$_{7}$, קְנָאֹת *of jealousy* Nm 5$_{15.18.25}$ 4Q365a 2.1$_{5}$ ([מנח]ת הקנאות), זִכָּרוֹן *of remembrance* Nm 5$_{15.18}$.

קָרְבַּן מִנְחָה *offering (consisting) of a grain offering* Lv 2$_{1.4}$, מִנְחָתְךָ *of your grain offering* Lv 2$_{13}$, סֹלֶת הַמִּנְחָה *fine flour of the grain offering* Lv 6$_{8}$, סלת מנחתו *fine flour of its grain offering* 4QJub^{e} 21$_{7}$, תֻּפִינֵי מִנְחַת perh. *baked pieces of a grain offering of* Lv 6$_{14}$ (or em. תֻּפִינֵי to תְּפַתֶּנָּה *you shall crumble it*), תּוֹרַת הַמִּנְחָה *law of the grain offering* Lv 6$_{7}$, עֵת מִנְחַת *time of the grain offering of* Dn 9$_{21}$, כָּל־מִנְחָה *every grain offering* Lv 2$_{11}$ 7$_{9.10}$ 11QT 20$_{9}$ (כול) 20$_{10}$ (כ[ו]ל) (הַמִּנְחָה), כָּל־מִנְחַת *every grain offering of* Lv 6$_{16}$, כָּל־מִנְחָתָם *every grain offering of theirs* Nm 18$_{9}$, כָּל־מִנְחֹתֶךָ *all your grain offerings* Ps 20$_{4}$.

<APP> קָרְבָּן *offering* Nm 6$_{15}$, אִשֶּׁה *fire offering* Lv 23$_{37}$ 11QT 23$_{17}$, מַתַּת *gift* Ezk 46$_{5}$, מַאֲפֶה *something baked* Lv 2$_{4}$, מַרְחֶשֶׁת appar. *(that which is cooked in a) pan* Lv 2$_{7 (Sam)}$, סֹלֶת *fine flour* Lv 6$_{13}$ 14$_{10}$ Nm 8$_{8}$ 15$_{4.6.9}$ 28$_{9+5t}$ 29$_{3.9.14}$ 11QT 14$_{2}$ (ומנ[חה]) 14$_{15.17}$ (ס[ו]לת), אֵיפָה *ephah* Ezk 45$_{24}$ 46$_{5}$, עִשָּׂרוֹן *tenth (of ephah)* Lv 14$_{10}$ Nm 15$_{4.6.9}$ 28$_{9+5t}$ 29$_{3.9.14}$ 11QT 14$_{5.15.17}$, עֲשִׂירִי *tenth* of ephah Lv 6$_{13}$ Nm 28$_{5}$ Ezk 46$_{14}$, בְּרָכָה *blessing* Jl 2$_{14}$.

<ADJ> חָרֵב *dry* Lv 7$_{10}$, חָדָשׁ *new* Lv 23$_{16}$ Nm 28$_{26}$ 4QLiturgy 1.1$_{2}$ ([מ]נחה) 11QT 18$_{13}$ 19$_{11}$.

<PREP> לְ of benefit, *for*, + בנה *build* altar Jos 22$_{29}$; *as, for (the purpose of)* Lv 6$_{13 (Sam)}$ Nm 7$_{13+11t}$ Ezk 45$_{15}$ 1 C 23$_{29}$ 11QT 11$_{11}$, + לקח *take* Lv 14$_{21}$, עשׂה *make*, i.e. offer Nm 28$_{5}$, נתן *give* wheat 1 C 21$_{23}$; *for (the purpose of obtaining)*, + נתן *give* money Ne 10$_{34}$; *in respect of, concerning* Lv 7$_{37}$; *namely, consisting of* Nm 18$_{9}$ 29$_{39}$.

בְּ of time, *at, during*, + קום *rise* Ezr 9$_{5}$; of instrument, *by (means of), with*, + עבד hi. *cause to serve* Is 43$_{23}$.

כְּ *as* 11QT 13$_{15}$ ([כמנח]ת), + היה *be* Lv 5$_{13}$, עשׂה *make*, i.e. offer Ex 29$_{41}$ Nm 28$_{8}$ Ezk 45$_{25}$.

מִן partitive, *(some) of* perh. 4QD^{a} 6.4$_{6}$, + רום hi. *raise*, i.e. offer Lv 2$_{9}$ 6$_{7}$, קמץ *take a handful* Nm 5$_{26}$, יתר ni. *remain* Lv 2$_{3.10}$; *of, with*, + מלא pi. *fill* hand Lv 9$_{17}$; of comparison, *(more) than*, + כפר pi. *atone for* 4QD^{a} 10.1$_{13}$ (ממנ[חה ... ויכפר]).

מֵעַל *from (upon)*, + שׁבת hi. *cause to cease* Lv 2$_{13}$.

עַל *upon* Lv 6$_{8}$, + שׂים *place* Lv 2$_{14}$, נתן *give*, i.e. place Lv 2$_{14}$; *to*, + קרב *be near*, i.e. joined 11QT 20$_{10}$; *besides, along with*, + עשׂה *make*, i.e. offer Lv 14$_{31}$.

עִם *with*, + קטר hi. *burn* 4QJub^{e} 21$_{9}$ ([והקטרת]; = 4QJub^{d} 21$_{9}$ עם מנ[ח]תוה ... והקטרת[ה]) 11QT 20$_{8}$ (ויק[טירו]) 23$_{17}$ 24$_{5}$ (עם] מנחת] ... ויק[טירו]); קרב עם *be near*, i.e. joined, *to* 11QT 20$_{9}$.

מִלְּבַד *besides, apart from*, + קרב hi. *bring near*, i.e. offer Nm 29$_{11+8t}$, עשׂה *make*, i.e. offer Nm 28$_{31}$ 29$_{6.6}$.

לִפְנֵי *before*, + זבח *sacrifice* 11QT 17$_{7}$.

עַד לְ *until*, + ישׁב *sit* Ezr 9$_{4}$.

<COLL> מִנְחָה || זֶבַח *sacrifice* Lv 7$_{37}$ 23$_{37}$ Jos 22$_{29}$ Is 43$_{23}$ (+) Jr 17$_{26}$ 33$_{18}$ Ps 40$_{7}$.

|| שֶׁלֶם *peace offering* Lv 7$_{37}$ (+) Nm 29$_{39}$ 1 K 8$_{64.64}$ 2 K 16$_{13}$ (all three +) Ezk 45$_{15.17}$ Am 5$_{22}$ (+).

|| עֹלָה *burnt offering* Ex 30$_{9}$ 40$_{29}$ Lv 7$_{37}$ 14$_{20.31}$ 23$_{18}$ (both +) 23$_{37}$ Nm 15$_{24}$ 28$_{31}$ 29$_{6+8t}$ (all ten +) 29$_{39}$ Jos 22$_{23.29}$ Jg 13$_{23}$ 1 K 8$_{64.64}$||2 C 7$_{7}$ 2 K 16$_{13.15.15.15}$ Is 43$_{23}$ (+) Jr 14$_{12}$ 17$_{26}$ 33$_{18}$ Ezk 45$_{15.17.17.25}$ Ps 20$_{4}$ 40$_{7}$ (+) Ne 10$_{34}$ CD 11$_{19}$.

|| חַטָּאת *sin offering* Lv 7$_{37}$ 14$_{31}$ (+) Nm 15$_{24}$ (+) 18$_{9}$ Ezk 42$_{13}$ 44$_{29}$ 45$_{17.25}$ 46$_{20}$ (+) 11QT 17$_{14}$ 25$_{14}$ 28$_{8.11}$ (all four +), חֲטָאָה *sin offering* Ps 40$_{7}$ (+).

|| אָשָׁם *guilt offering* Lv 7$_{37}$ 14$_{21}$ (+) Nm 18$_{9}$ Ezk 42$_{13}$ 44$_{29}$ 46$_{20}$ (+).

|| נֶסֶךְ *libation* Ex 29$_{41}$ 30$_{9}$ (both +) Lv 23$_{18.37}$ Nm 6$_{15.17}$ 15$_{24}$ 28$_{8.9.31}$ (all three +) 29$_{6+17t}$ 2 K 16$_{13}$ (+) 16$_{15}$ Is 57$_{6}$ Ezk 45$_{17}$ Jl 1$_{9.13}$ 2$_{14}$ (all three מִנְחָה וָנֶסֶךְ) 4QJub^{e} 21$_{9}$ 11QT 15$_{9}$ 17$_{14}$ 20$_{8}$ 22$_{3}$ 23$_{16}$ 24$_{5.8}$ 25$_{6.14}$ 28$_{8.11}$ 34$_{13}$ (+).

|| מִלֻּא *installation (offering)* Lv 7$_{37}$.

|| לְבוֹנָה *frankincense* Is 43$_{23}$ Jr 17$_{26}$ 41$_{5}$ Ezk 45$_{17}$ Jl 1$_{9.13}$ Ne 13$_{5.9}$ CD 11$_{19}$, קְטֹרֶת *incense* Ex 30$_{9}$ Ps 141$_{2}$, שֶׁמֶן *oil* Ezk 45$_{25}$, עֵץ *wood* CD 11$_{19}$.

מִנְחָה + קָרְבָּן *offering* Nm 18$_{9}$, תּוֹדָה *thank offering* Jr 17$_{26}$, קֹדֶשׁ *holiness*, i.e. holy thing Ezk 42$_{13}$.

תִּכּוֹן ... מַשְׂאַת כַּפַּי מִנְחַת־עָרֶב *let the lifting up of my hands ... be established as the grain offering of the evening* Ps 141$_{2}$.

<SYN> §1 מִגְדָּנוֹת *precious things*; §2 אֶשְׁכָּר *payment*; §3 זֶבַח *sacrifice*, לְבוֹנָה *frankincense*; §4 זֶבַח *sacrifice*,

שְׁלָמִים *peace offering,* עֹלָה *burnt offering,* חַטָּאת *sin offering,* אָשָׁם *guilt offering,* מִלֻּא *installation (offering),* נֶסֶךְ *drink offering,* לְבוֹנָה *frankincense,* קְטֹרֶת *incense*

Also 4QPrFêtes[b] 9_{1} perh. 4QOrd[b] 12_{2} ([מנ]חה).*

*[מְנֻחָה] n.[m.] **complaint,** <PREP> אֶל *to,* + פנה *turn,* i.e. pay attention Nm 16_{15} (if em. מִנְחָתָם *their offering* to מְנֻחָתָם *their complaint*).

⇒ נוח II *sigh.*

מְנֻחוֹת, see מָנַחְתִּי *Manahathite.*

מְנַחֵם I $_{8.0.1.23}$ pr.n.m. **Menahem**—I מנחמו—**1.** king of Israel, son of Gadi, <SUBJ> בוא *come* 2 K 15_{14}, יצא hi. *bring out,* i.e. exact 2 K 15_{20}, עלה *go up* 2 K 15_{14}, סור *turn aside* 2 K 15_{17}, שׁכב *lie down* 2 K 15_{22}, בקע pi. *split* 2 K 15_{16}, נכה hi. *strike* 2 K $15_{14.16}$, מות hi. *kill* 2 K 15_{14}, מלך *be king* 2 K $15_{14.17}$, עשׂה *do* 2 K $15_{17.21}$, נתן *give* 2 K 15_{19}. <CSTR> בֶּן־מְנַחֵם *son of Menahem* 2 K 15_{23}, דִּבְרֵי *deeds of* 2 K 15_{21}. <APP> בֵּן *son* 2 K $15_{14.17}$. <PREP> אֵת *with,* + היה *be* 2 K 15_{19}; תַּחַת *instead of,* + מלך *be king* 2 K 15_{22}.

2. witness to signature of promissory note, <APP> בֵּן *son* XḤev/Se 49_{15}, עֵד *witness* XḤev/Se 49_{15}.

3. 4Q348_{1} ([מנח]ם).

4. Arad ost. 72_{1}. **5.** Samaria-Sebaste ost. 10_{12} ([מנ]חם). **6.** T. Beit Mirsim inscr. 5 ([מנ]חם). **7.** father of Ahikam, Ḥorvat 'Uza ost. 1_{1} (מ[נ]חם). **8.** Seal 182 (Aleppo, 8th/7th cent.). **9.** appar. son of Jobanah, perh. ident. with §10, Seals 197 (Ramat Raḥel) 457 (T. el-Judeideh) 788 (Jerusalem) Jar Stamps 921 ([מנח]ם) 954 ([מנ]ח[ם] יו[בנה]) 956 (מ[נ]חם יו[ב]נה; both T. Beit Mirsim?; all six 8th cent.). **10.** perh. son of Jehobanah, and perh. ident. with §9, Seals 488 (Ramat Raḥel) 771 (Beth-Shemesh; both 8th cent.). **11.** father of Jeremiah, Seal 364 (8th/7th cent.). **12.** father of Hamiohel, Seal 412 (Jerusalem, 7th cent.). **13.** Seal 414 (למנח[ם]; 8th cent.). **14.** son of Hoshea, Seal 428 (7th/6th cent.). **15.** appar. son of Hananiah, Seal 600 (T. Beit Mirsim?, 7th/6th cent.). **16.** son of Ishmael, Seals 601 602 (למנ[חם]; both T. Beit Mirsim?, 7th/6th cent.). **17.** son of Manasseh, Seal 603 (T. Beit Mirsim?, 7th/6th cent.). **18.** appar. son of Pagy, Seal 604 (T. Beit Mirsim?, 7th/6th cent.). **19.** father of Pashhur, Seal 652 (T. Beit Mirsim?, 7th/6th cent.). **20.** appar. father of Calcol, Seal 868 (8th cent.). **21.** appar. father of Obadiah, Bulla D71 (מנחמו). **22.** son of Nimshar, Ost. DH79_{6}.

<CSTR> בן מנחם *son of Menahem* Ḥorvat 'Uza ost. 1_{1} (מ[נ]חם) Seals 364 (8th/7th cent.) 652 (T. Beit Mirsim?, 7th/6th cent.), בת *daughter of* Seal 412 (Jerusalem, 7th cent.).

<APP> בֵּן *son* Seals 428 (7th/6th cent.) 601 602 (למנ[חם בן]) 603 (all three T. Beit Mirsim?, 7th/6th cent.) Ost. DH79_{6}.

<PREP> לְ of possession, *of, (belonging) to* Seals 182 (Aleppo, 8th/7th cent.) 197 (Ramat Raḥel) 414 (למנח[ם]; both 8th cent.) 428 (7th/6th cent.) 600 ([ל]מנחם) 601 602 (למנ[חם]) 603 604 (all four T. Beit Mirsim?, 7th/6th cent.) 788 (Jerusalem, 8th cent.) Ost. DH79_{6}.

⇒ נחם *comfort.*

מְנַחֵם II *comforter,* see נחם *regret,* Pi.

מְנַחֵשׁ *diviner,* see נחשׁ I *practise divination,* Pi.

מָנַחַת I $_{2}$ pr.n.m. **Manahath,** son of Shobal and grandson of Seir the Horite, perh. ancestor of Edomite tribe, <NOM CL> אֵלֶּה בְּנֵי שׁוֹבָל ... מָנַחַת *these are the sons of Shobal ... Manahath* Gn 36_{23}, var. 1 C 1_{40}.

⇒ נוח *rest.*

[מָנַחַת] II $_{1}$ pl.n. **Manahath**—מָנָחַת—place of exile of Benjaminite family of Ehud from Geba, <PREP> אֶל *to,* + גלה hi. *exile* 1 C 8_{6}.

⇒ נוח *rest;* מָנַחְתִּי *Manahathite.*

מָנַחְתִּי $_{1}$ gent. **Manahathite,** belonging to Manahath, as collective sing. noun, **Manahathites,** <CSTR> חֲצִי הַמָּנַחְתִּי *half of the Manahathites* 1 C 2_{52} (if em. הַמְּנֻחוֹת *of the Menuhoth*) 2_{54}.

⇒ מָנַחַת II *Manahath.*

מְנִי $_{1}$ n.[m.] **destiny, 1. destiny,** <OBJ> נחה *guide* Ps

23$_4$ (if em. יְנַחֲמֻנִי *they comfort me* to יַנְחוּ מְנִי *they guide my destiny**).

2. as pr.n. **Meni,** or **Destiny,** name of a god (of fate), <SUBJ> נחה hi. *guide* Ps 61$_8$ (if em. מִמֶּנִּי *than me* to מְנִי *O Destiny*). <CSTR> חֶסֶד וֶאֱמֶת מְנִי *loyalty and faithfulness of Destiny* Ps 61$_8$ (if em. מַן *appoint*, from מנה pi.). <PREP> לְ of benefit, *to, for,* + מלא pi. *fill* bowl of mixed wine Is 65$_{11}$ (+ גַּד *good fortune* or *Gad*).*

⇒ (?) מנה *count.*

מִנִּי I $_1$ pl.n. **Minni,** people and territory in Armenia, <OBJ> שׁמע hi. *summon* Jr 51$_{27}$ (if em.; see Cstr.). <CSTR> מַמְלְכוֹת אֲרָרַט מִנִּי וְאַשְׁכְּנָז *kingdoms of Ararat, Minni and Ashkenaz* Jr 51$_{27}$ (or em. מַמְלְכוֹת *kingdoms,* Ararat ...). <APP> מַמְלָכָה *kingdom* Jr 51$_{27}$ (if em.; see Cstr.).

מִנִּי II, see מִן *from.*

מִנִּי III, see מֵן I *string.*

מְנָיוֹת, see מְנָת *portion.*

מִנְיָמִין $_3$ pr.n.m. **Miniamin**—מִנְיָמִן—**1.** Levite in the time of Hezekiah, <NOM CL> וְעַל־יָדוֹ עֵדֶן וּמִנְיָמִן *and at his hand were Eden and Miniamin,* i.e. assisting him 2 C 31$_{15}$ (mss בִּנְיָמִן *Benjamin*).

2. ancestor of priestly family, <PREP> לְ of possession, *of, (belonging) to,* + היה *be* Ne 12$_{17}$.

4. Asaphite, temple musician, <SUBJ> עמד *stand* Ne 12$_{41}$. <APP> כֹּהֵן *priest* Ne 12$_{41}$.

* **[מִנְיָן]** $_{0.0.1}$ n.[m.] **number**—cstr. Q מנין—<CSTR> מנין כהנים *number of priests* 4QpsEzek^a 4$_3$2. <PREP> לְ perh. of possession, *of, belonging to* 4QpsEzek^a 4$_3$2 (ל[מנין]).

Also perh. 4QDibHam^a 9$_7$.

⇒ מנה *count.*

* **[מָנֵיס]** $_{0.0.1}$ pr.n.[m.] **Manes,** name in writing exercise, 4QNames$_4$.

מִנִּית I $_2$ pl.n. **Minnith,** in Ammon, <CSTR> חִטֵּי מִנִּית *wheat of Minnith* Ezk 27$_{17}$ (or em. חִטִּים וּנְכֹאת *wheat and ladanum;* unless מִנִּית II *rice*). <COLL> וַיַּכֵּם ... עַד בּוֹאֲךָ מִנִּית *and he defeated them ... until you come to,* i.e. as far as, *Minnith* Jg 11$_{33}$.

* **מִנִּית** II $_1$ n.[m.] **rice,** <CSTR> חִטֵּי מִנִּית *wheat of rice,* i.e. rice Ezk 27$_{17}$ (unless מִנִּית I *Minnith*).

[מִנְלֶה] $_1$ n.[m.] perh. **acquisition(s)**—sf. מִנְלָם—<SUBJ> נטה *spread* Jb 15$_{29}$ (or em. מִנְלָם to מִנְלָם *their possessions,* from מָנוֹל, or מְנָלִים *[his] possessions*).

⇒ נלה II *obtain.*

* **[מְנָלִים]** n.[m.]pl. **possessions,** <SUBJ> נטה hi. *cause to decline,* i.e. bring down Jb 15$_{29}$ (if em. יִטֶּה ... מִנְלָם *their acquisitions ... will* not *spread* to יַטֶּה ... מְנָלִים *he shall* not *bring down ... [his] possessions*).

* **מנן** vb. **be disdainful, ungrateful—Hi.** <SUBJ> Israel Ezk 5$_7$ (if em. הֲמָנְכֶם *you are turbulent,* from המן, to הֲמִנְּכֶם *you are disdainful,* inf. with sf.).

* **[מָנֹס]** $_{0.0.1}$ pl.n. **Manos,** site of hidden treasure, <PREP> לְ of possession, *of, (belonging) to* 3QTr 1$_{13}$ (מעבא של מנס *foundry,* or *plastered cistern, of Manos*).

מנע $_{29.8.2}$ vb. **withhold—Qal** $_{25.8.2}$ Pf. מָנַע (מְנָעֲנִי ,מְנָעֲךָ), מָנְעוּ ,מָנַעְתִּי ,מָנָעְתָּ; impf. יִמְנַע (יִמְנָעֲנִי ,יִמְנָעֶנָּה), 2ms תִּמְנַע, אֶמְנַע; + waw וָאֶמְנַע; impv. מְנַע ,מִנְעִי; ptc. מֹנֵעַ (Si מונע)—**withhold, hold back, restrain, refuse** (Si 41$_{19}$), <SUBJ> Y. Gn 30$_2$ Nm 24$_{11}$ 1 S 25$_{26.34}$ Ezk 31$_{15}$ Am 4$_7$ Ps 21$_3$ 84$_{12}$ Pr 30$_7$ Ne 9$_{20}$ 11QPs^a 24$_5$ GnzPs 3$_4$, Jerusalem Jr 2$_{25}$, Jeremiah Jr 42$_4$, Job Jb 22$_7$ 31$_{16}$, Koheleth Ec 2$_{10}$, Rachel zJr 31$_{16}$, בֵּן *son* Pr 1$_{15}$ 3$_{27}$ Si 4$_{3.23}$ 7$_{21.33}$ 12$_4$ 14$_{14}$ 35$_3$ 41$_{19}$ ([ממנ]ע), מֶלֶךְ *king* 2 S 13$_{13}$ 1 K 20$_7$, נָבִיא *prophet* Jr 42$_4$, friend Jb 6$_{14}$ (if em. לַמָּס *to the despairing* to לְמֹנֵעַ *to one who withholds*), רָשָׁע *wicked one* Jb 20$_{13}$, חָנֵף *impious one* Jb 20$_{13}$, חַטָּאת *sin* Jr 5$_{25}$; subj. not specified, Jr 48$_{10}$ Pr 11$_{26}$ 23$_{13}$ Si 14$_4$.

<OBJ> Balaam Nm 24$_{11}$, David 1 S 25$_{34}$, Tamar 2 S 13$_{13}$, אָדוֹן *lord* 1 S 25$_{26}$, דַּל *poor one* Jb 31$_{16}$, עַיִן *eye* Jr

31_{16}, רֶגֶל *foot* Pr 1_{15}, לֵב *heart* Ec 2_{10}, נֶפֶשׁ *soul*, i.e. self Si 14_4, קוֹל *voice* Jr 31_{16}, פְּרִי *fruit* of womb Gn 30_2, בַּר *grain* Pr 11_{26}, לֶחֶם *bread* Jb 22_7, מָן *manna* Ne 9_{20}, גֶּשֶׁם *rain* Am 4_7, נָהָר *river* Ezk 31_{15}, חֶרֶב *sword* Jr 48_{10}, דָּבָר *word* Jr 42_4 Si 4_{23}, שִׁיר *song* Si 35_3, שְׁאֵלָה *request* Si 41_{19} ((ממנ[ע]) GnzPs 3_4, בַּקָּשָׁה *request* 11QPs^a 24_5, מַתָּן *gift* Si 4_3, טוֹב *good* Jr 5_{25} Ps 84_{12} Pr 3_{27}, רָעָה *evil* Jb 20_{13}, מוּסָר *discipline* Pr 23_{13}, חֹפֶשׁ *freedom* Si 7_{21}, חֶסֶד *kindness* Jb 6_{14} (if em. לָמָס *to the despairing* to לְמֹנֵעַ *to one who withholds*) Si 7_{33}, אֲרֶשֶׁת *desire* Ps 21_3.

<PREP> לְ of direction, *from*, + הלך ptc. *one who walks* blamelessly Ps 84_{12}.

בְּ of place, time, *in*, + עוֹלָם *world* Si $4_{23(A)}$, עֵת *time* Si $4_{23(C)}$.

מִן of direction, *from*, + עַם *people* Jr 5_{25} 42_4, Jezaniah Jr 42_4 (or em. Jezaniah to Azariah), Johanan Jr 42_4, Rachel Gn 30_2, גֶּבֶר *man* Pr 30_7, בֵּן *son* Jr 42_4, of Israel Am 4_7, אָח *brother* 2 S 13_{13}, נַעַר *lad* Pr 23_{13}, עֶבֶד *servant* Si 7_{21}, שַׂר *commander* Jr 42_4, בַּעַל *owner*, i.e. one to whom due Pr 3_{27}, רַע *evil one* Si 12_4, רָעֵב *hungry one* Jb 22_7, מִסְכֵּן *poor one* Si 4_3, מֵת *dead one* Si 7_{33}, worshipper 11QPs^a 24_5 GnzPs 3_4, פֶּה *mouth* Ne 9_{20}, דָּם *blood(shed)* Jr 48_{10}, נְתִיבָה *path* Pr 1_{15}, כָּבוֹד *honour* Nm 24_{11}, חֵפֶץ *desire* Jb 31_{16}, שִׂמְחָה *joy* Ec 2_{10}, זֶה *this (one)* 1 K 20_7.

מִן partitive, *(some of), any (of)*, + טוֹבָה *good thing* Si 14_{14}.

מִן privative, *without, so as not to be (in)*, + בְּכִי *weeping* Jr 31_{16}, דִּמְעָה *tears* Jr 31_{16}.

בְּתוֹךְ *within*, + חֵךְ *mouth* Jb 20_{13}.

<COLL> מנע + אצל *withhold* Ec 2_{10}, כלא ni. *be restrained* Ezk 31_{15}, חמל *spare* Jb 20_{13}, צפן hi. *hide* Si $4_{23(A)}$, קפץ *shut up* Si $4_{23(C)}$; :: נתן *give* Ps 21_3 84_{12} Ne 9_{20} Si 7_{33} 12_4 11QPs^a 24_5, שׁקה hi. *give to drink* Jb 22_7, שׁבר hi. *sell grain* Pr 11_{27}, עשׂה *do* GnzPs 3_4.

מְנָעֲךָ י׳ מִבּוֹא בְדָמִים *Y. has held you back from entering into bloodguilt* 1 S 25_{26}, מְנָעַנִי מֵהָרַע אֹתָךְ *he has held me back from harming you* 1 S 25_{34}, בוש ... ממנ[ע] מתת שאלה *be ashamed of ... refusing to grant a request* Si 41_{19}, מִנְעִי רַגְלֵךְ מִיָּחֵף *withhold your foot from (being) bare* Jr 2_{25}.

<ANT> נתן *give*, שׁקה hi. *give to drink*, שׁבר hi. *sell grain*, עשׂה *do*.

Ni. 4 Pf. נִמְנַע; impf. יִמָּנַע, 2ms תִּמָּנַע; + waw וַיִּמָּנְעוּ—**1. be withheld,** <SUBJ> רְבִיבִים *showers* Jr 3_3, מִנְחָה *grain offering* Jl 1_{13}, נֶסֶךְ *drink offering* Jl 1_{13}, אוֹר *light* Jb 38_{15}. <PREP> מִן of direction, *from*, + רָשָׁע *wicked one* Jb 38_{15}, בַּיִת *house* of Y. Jl 1_{13}.

2. hold oneself back, refrain, <SUBJ> Balaam Nm 22_{16}. <COLL> אַל־נָא תִמָּנַע מֵהֲלֹךְ אֵלָי *do not hold yourself back from coming to me* Nm 22_{16}.*

⇒ יִמְנָע *Imna.*

מַנְעוּל 6.0.2 n.[m.] **bolt**—sf. מַנְעֻלָיו (מַנְעוּלָיו)—of door of house (Ca 5_5 11QT 49_{13}), city gate (Ne $3_{3.6.13.14.15}$), hell (4QBéat 15_7), <NOM CL> מנעוליו צומי שחת *its bolts are the fasts of the pit* 4QBéat 15_7. <OBJ> עמד hi. *set up* Ne $3_{3.6.13.14.15}$ (all five ‖ בְּרִיחַ *bar*, דֶּלֶת *door*), כבס pi. *wash* 11QT 49_{13} (‖ מְזוּזָה *doorpost*, מַשְׁקוֹף *lintel*, אַסְּף *threshold*, + דֶּלֶת *door*). <CSTR> כַּפּוֹת הַמַּנְעוּל *handles of the bolt* Ca 5_5.

Also 4Q365a 4_2 ([מ]נעולים).

<SYN> בְּרִיחַ *bar*, דֶּלֶת *door*, מְזוּזָה *doorpost*, מַשְׁקוֹף *lintel*, אַסְּף *threshold*.

⇒ נעל I *lock*.

[מִנְעָל] 1 n.[m.] **bolt**—mss מִנְעָלֶךָ; pl. sf. מִנְעָלֶיךָ—of Asher, <NOM CL> בַּרְזֶל וּנְחֹשֶׁת מִנְעָלֶיךָ *your bolts are iron and bronze* Dt 33_{25} (mss מִנְעָלֶךָ *your bolt* is).

⇒ נעל I *lock*.

[מַנְעַמִּים] 1 n.[m.]pl. **delicacies**—pl. sf. מַנְעַמֵּיהֶם—<PREP> בְּ partitive, *(some) of*, + לחם *eat* Ps 141_4.*

⇒ נעם *be pleasant*.

[מְנַעַנְעִים] 1 n.[m.]pl. **sistrum,** or **sounding rattle,*** <PREP> בְּ of instrument, accompaniment, *by (means of), with*, + שׂחק pi. *make merry* 2 S 6_5 (‖ תֹּף *tambourine*, נֵבֶל *harp*, כִּנּוֹר *lyre*, צֶלְצְלִים *cymbals*).

<SYN> תֹּף *tambourine*, נֵבֶל *harp*, כִּנּוֹר *lyre*, צֶלְצְלִים *cymbals*.*

⇒ נוע *tremble*.

מְנַצֵּחַ *overseer, supervisor, director of music, famous* *one*, see נצח *oversee*, Pi.*

[מְנַקִּית] 4.0.2 n.f. **bowl**—pl. מְנַקִּיּוֹת (מְנַקִּית, Q מנקיאות); sf. מְנַקִּיֹּתָיו (Q מנקיותיו)—for sacrificial use, made of gold (Ex 25_{29}||37_{16} 11QT 3_{12}), <SUBJ> היה *be* 11QT 3_{12}. <NOM CL> תחת הפנא הדרומית אמות תשע ... מנקיאות *underneath the south corner at nine cubits are ... bowls* 3QTr 3_{3}. <OBJ> עשׂה *make* Ex 25_{29}||37_{16}. <APP> כְּלִי *vessel* Ex 37_{16}, נתן *give*, i.e. place Nm 4_{7}, לקח *take* Jr 52_{19}. <PREP> בְּ of place, *in*, + נסך *pour out* Ex $25_{29(Sam)}$, ho. *be poured out* Ex 25_{29}. <COLL> מִזְרָק || מְנַקִּית *basin* Jr 52_{19} 3QTr 3_{3}, סַף *dish* Jr 52_{19}, קְעָרָה *dish* Ex 25_{29}||37_{16} Nm 4_{7}, קַשְׂוָה *jar* Ex 25_{29}||37_{16} Nm 4_{7} 3QTr 3_{3}, כּוֹס *cup* 3QTr 3_{3}, סִיר *pot* Jr 52_{19}, כַּף *ladle* Ex 25_{29}||37_{16} Nm 4_{7} Jr 52_{19}, מַחְתָּה *firepan* Jr 52_{19}, מְנוֹרָה *lampstand* Jr 52_{19}.

<SYN> מִזְרָק *basin*, סַף *dish*, קְעָרָה *dish*, קַשְׂוָה *jar*, כּוֹס *cup*, סִיר *pot*, כַּף *ladle*, מַחְתָּה *firepan*, מְנוֹרָה *lampstand*.*

⇒ (?) נקה *be clean*.

*[מָנֹר] 0.0.0.1 pr.n.[m.] **Manor**, <PREP> לְ of possession, *of, (belonging) to* Seal 758 (c. 700).

מְנֹרָה, see מְנוֹרָה *lampstand*.

מְנַשֶּׁה 146.0.9.4 pr.n.m. **Manasseh**—I מנשׁ—**1.** eldest son of Joseph and Asenath, <SUBJ> היה *be* Gn 48_{5}. <NOM CL> מְנַשֶּׁה הַבְּכוֹר *Manasseh was the firstborn* Gn 48_{14}. <OBJ> ילד *bear* Gn 46_{20}, קרא *call* name Gn 41_{51}, נגשׁ hi. *bring near* Gn 48_{13}, לקח *take* Gn $48_{1.13}$. <CSTR> בֶּן־מְנַשֶּׁה *son of Manasseh* Gn 50_{23} Nm 27_{1} $32_{39.40.41}$ 36_{1} Dt 3_{14} Jos 13_{31} 17_{3} Jg 18_{30} (or em. מֹשֶׁה *of Moses*) 1 K 4_{13} 1 C 7_{17}, רֹאשׁ *head of* Gn $48_{14.17}$. <APP> בֵּן *son* Gn 48_{1}, שְׁנַיִם *two* Gn 48_{13}. <PREP> כְּ *as*, + שׂים *place*, i.e. make Gn 48_{20}; לִפְנֵי *before*, + שׂים *place* Gn 48_{20}. <COLL> מְנַשֶּׁה + אֶפְרַיִם *Ephraim* Gn 46_{20} 48_{1+5t} 51_{23}.

2a. usu. tribe with §1 as eponymous ancestor, with its assoc. territory, <SUBJ> היה *be* Jos 14_{4}, בוא *come* 2 C 30_{1}, שׁלח *send*, i.e. lay, hands 4QpPs^{a} 1.2_{17}, בקשׁ pi. *seek* 4QpPs^{a} 1.2_{17}, ירשׁ hi. *dispossess* Jg 1_{27}, נחל *take possession* Jos 16_{4}, נתן ni. *be given* 4QpPs^{a} 1.2_{17}, עשׂה *do* 2 C 30_{1}.

<NOM CL> בְּנֵי יוֹסֵף ... מְנַשֶּׁה וְאֶפְרָיִם *the sons of Joseph were ... Manasseh and Ephraim* Nm 26_{28}, עַל גְּבוּל נַפְתָּלִי ... מְנַשֶּׁה *on the border of Naphtali was ... Manasseh* Ezk 48_{4}, לִי מְנַשֶּׁה *to me is Manasseh* Ps 60_{9}||108_{9}, הם מנשה *they are Manasseh* 4QpNah 3.3_{9}.

<CSTR> בְּנֵי מְנַשֶּׁה *sons of Manasseh* Nm 1_{34} 2_{20} 7_{54} 10_{23} 26_{29} 34_{23} 36_{12} Jos 13_{29} $16_{4.9}$ $17_{2.2.6.12}$ $22_{30.31}$ Ps 80_{3} (mss) (L לִפְנֵי *before*) 1 C $7_{14.29}$ 9_{3} (בְּנֵי ...), בְּנוֹת *daughters of* Jos 17_{6}, בְּכוֹר *firstborn of* Jos 17_{1}, גדו[ו]לי מנשה *great ones of Manasseh* 4QpNah 3.3_{9}, ... רשׁעי *wicked ones of ...* 4QpPs^{a} 1.2_{17}, מַטֵּה מְנַשֶּׁה *tribe of Manasseh* Nm 1_{35} 2_{20} 13_{11} 34_{14} Jos 17_{1} 20_{8} $21_{5.6.25.27}$ 22_{1} 1 C 6_{46} (if del. חֲצִי *half of*) $6_{47.55.56}$ 12_{32}, שֵׁבֶט *tribe of* Nm 32_{33} (Sam הַמְנַשֶּׁה *of the Manassites*) Jos 13_{29} $22_{1(mss).13.15}$ 1 C $5_{18.23.26}$ 12_{38} 27_{20}, אַלְפֵי *thousands of* Dt 33_{17}, מִשְׁפְּחֹת *clans of* Nm 26_{34} 27_{1}, יַד *hand of* 2 C 34_{9}, גְּבוּל *border of* Jos $17_{7.8.9}$ Ezk 48_{5}, חַבְלֵי־ *portions of* Jos 17_{5}, ... אֶרֶץ *land of ...* Dt 34_{2} 2 C 30_{10}, עָרֵי *cities of* Jos 17_{9} 2 C 34_{6}, חֲצִי *half of* 1 C 6_{46} (or em.; see above), עולת ... מנשה *burnt offering of ... Manasseh* 11QT 24_{13}, כָּל־מְנַשֶּׁה *all Manasseh* Jg 6_{35} 7_{23} 2 C 31_{1} (... כָּל־).

<APP> בֵּן *son* Nm 27_{1} 32_{33} 36_{12} Jos 16_{4} 17_{2} 11QT 24_{13} 44_{13}, מַטֶּה *tribe* Jos 14_{4}, אֶחָד *one (tribe)* Ezk 48_{4}.

<PREP> לְ of direction, *to*, + אמר *say* Jos 17_{17}; of possession, *of, (belonging) to* Nm 1_{10} Jos 17_{10} 1 C 12_{21} 11QT 44_{13}, + היה *be* Jos $17_{8.11}$.

בְּ of place, *in, among, throughout* Jg 6_{15}, + שׁלח *send* Jg 6_{35}.

מִן of direction, *from, out of*, + צעק ni. *be called together* Jg 7_{23}, נתץ pi. *pull down* altars 2 C 31_{1}; partitive, *(some of), from among* 1 C $12_{20.21}$ 2 C 15_{9} $30_{11.18}$.

עַל *to*, + לוה ni. *join oneself* 4QpNah 3.4_{1}, כתב *write* 2 C 30_{1}; *concerning* 4QpNah 3.4_{3}.

בְּתוֹךְ *among* Jg 12_{4}.

אֵת *with* Is 9_{20}.

לִפְנֵי *before*, + עור pol. *arouse* strength Ps 80_{3} (מְנַשֶּׁה lacking in mss).

אַחַר *after*, + בוא *come* 4QpNah 3.4_{6}.

מְנַשֶּׁה without prep. *through Manasseh*, + עבר *pass* Jg 11_{29}.

<COLL> אֶפְרַיִם וּמְנַשֶּׁה *Ephraim and Manasseh* Dt

34_{2} 1 C 9_{3} 2 C 15_{9} $30_{1.10.18}$ 31_{1} 4QpPs^{a} 1.2_{17} 11QT 24_{13}, sim. Jos 17_{17} Is 9_{20} 11QT 44_{13}, מְנַשֶּׁה וְאֶפְרַיִם *Manasseh and Ephraim* Jos 14_{4} 16_{4} 2 C $34_{6.9}$, sim. Is 9_{20}.

2b. as collective gent. noun, **Manassites,** <CSTR> שֵׁבֶט הַמְנַשֶּׁה *tribe of the Manassites* Nm $32_{33(Sam)}$ (MT מְנַשֶּׁה *of Manasseh*) Dt 3_{13} 4_{12} Jos 1_{12} 12_{6} 18_{7} $22_{7.9.10.11.21}$ 1 C $27_{21(mss)}$, חֲצִי *half of* 1 C 27_{21} (mss חֲצִי שֵׁבֶט *half of the tribe of*). <APP> שֵׁבֶט *tribe* Jos 13_{7}. <COLL> חֲצִי שֵׁבֶט הַמְנַשֶּׁה *half the tribe of the Manassites* + בְּנֵי־גָד ... בְּנֵי רְאוּבֵן *sons of Gad ... sons of Reuben* Nm $32_{33(Sam)}$, בְּנֵי־גָד וּרְאוּבֵן *Gad and Reuben* Jos 18_{7}, בְּנֵי־רְאוּבֵן וּבְנֵי־גָד *sons of Reuben and sons of Gad* Jos 4_{12} $22_{9.10.11.21}$, רְאוּבֵנִי ... גָּדִי *Reubenites ... Gadites* Jos 1_{12} 12_{6}.

3. king of Judah, son of Hezekiah, <SUBJ> אמר *say* 2 C 33_{13}, חלה pi. *entreat* 2 C 33_{11}, פלל htp. *pray* 2 C 33_{11}, קשב hi. *pay attention* 2 C 33_{10}, ידע *know* 2 C 33_{13}, זכר *remember* 4QapPs^{b} 33_{8}, קוה pi. *wait* 4QapPs^{b} 33_{8}, שׁוב *go back* 2 K 21_{1}‖2 C 33_{1}, עבר hi. *cause to pass* through fire 2 K 21_{1}‖2 C 33_{1}, קום hi. *raise up* 2 K 21_{1}‖2 C 33_{1}, גבה hi. *make high* 2 C 33_{13}, תעה hi. *lead astray* 2 K 21_{9}‖2 C 33_{9}, שׁחה *bow down* 2 K 21_{1}‖2 C 33_{1}, עבד *serve* 2 K 21_{1}‖2 C 33_{1} 4QapPs^{b} 33_{8} ([עבדתו]ך), כנע ni. *humble oneself* 2 C 33_{11}, כחשׁ pi. *cringe* 4QapPs^{b} 33_{8}.

זבח *sacrifice* 2 C 33_{13}, ענן po. *practice soothsaying* 2 K 21_{1}‖2 C 33_{1}, נחשׁ pi. *divine* 2 K 21_{1}‖2 C 33_{1}, כשׁף pi. *practice sorcery* 2 C 33_{1}, כעס hi. *provoke* 2 K 21_{1}‖2 C 33_{1} 2 K 23_{26}, רעע hi. *do evil* 2 K 21_{11}, חטא *sin* 2 K 21_{17}, hi. *cause to sin* 2 K $21_{11.16}$, שׁפך *shed* blood 2 K 21_{16}, שׁלך hi. *cast* 2 C 33_{13}, שׂים *place* 2 K 21_{1}‖2 C 33_{1} 2 C 33_{13}, סור hi. *remove* 2 C 33_{13}, מלא pi. *fill* 2 K 21_{16}, מלך *be king* 2 K 20_{21}‖2 C 32_{33} 2 K 21_{1}‖2 C 33_{1}, עשׂה *do* 2 K 21_{1}‖2 C 33_{1} 2 K $21_{11.17.20}$‖2 C 33_{22} 2 K 23_{12} 2 C 33_{22} Jr 15_{4}, רבה hi. *increase* guilt 4QapPs^{b} 33_{8}, בנה *build* 2 K 21_{1}‖2 C 33_{1} 2 C 33_{13}, כון hi. *establish* 2 C $33_{13(Kt)}$, שׁכב *lie down* 2 K 21_{18}‖2 C 33_{20}, קבר ni. *be buried* 2 K 21_{18}, כרת ni. *be cut off* 4QapPs^{b} 33_{8} ([א]כרת).

<NOM CL> בֶּן־שְׁתֵּים עֶשְׂרֵה שָׁנָה מְנַשֶּׁה *Manasseh was a son of twelve years,* i.e. twelve years old 2 K 21_{1}‖2 C 33_{1}.

<OBJ> רום hi. *exalt* 4QapPs^{b} 33_{8}, הלך hi. *lead* 2 C 33_{11}, לכד *capture* 2 C 33_{11}, אסר *bind* 2 C 33_{11}, כלא *imprison* 4QapPs^{b} 33_{8}, קבר *bury* 2 C 33_{20}.

<CSTR> דִּבְרֵי מְנַשֶּׁה *deeds of Manasseh* 2 K 21_{17}‖2 C 33_{18}, חַטַּאת *sins of* 2 K 24_{3}.

<APP> אָב *father* 2 K 21_{20}‖2 C 33_{22} 2 C 33_{22}, בֵּן *son* 2 K 20_{21}‖2 C 32_{33} Jr 15_{4}, מֶלֶךְ *king* 2 K 21_{11} Jr 15_{4} 4QapPs^{b} 33_{8}.

<PREP> לְ of direction, *to,* + צרר hi. *cause distress* 2 C 33_{11}; of possession, *of, (belonging) to* 4QapPs^{b} 33_{8}; אֶל *to,* + דבר pi. *speak* 2 C 33_{10}; עַל *against,* + בוא hi. *bring* 2 C 33_{10}; לִפְנֵי *before* 2 K 21_{11}; בִּגְלַל *on account of,* + נתן *give,* i.e. make, a cause of trembling Jr 15_{4}; תַּחַת *instead of,* + מלך *be king* 2 K 21_{18}‖2 C 33_{20}.

4. member of Pahath-moab family, husband of non-Jewish wife, <NOM CL> מִבְּנֵי פַּחַת מוֹאָב ... מְנַשֶּׁה *of the sons of Pahath-moab were ... Manasseh* Ezr 10_{30}.

5. member of Hashum family, husband of non-Jewish wife, <NOM CL> מִבְּנֵי חָשֻׁם ... מְנַשֶּׁה *of the sons of Hashum were ... Manasseh* Ezr 10_{33}.

Also 4Q348_{17} (מנש[ה]).

6. son of the king, <APP> בֵּן *son* Seal 209 (c. 700). <PREP> לְ of possession, *of, (belonging) to* Seal 209 (c. 700).

7. father of Menahem, <CSTR> בן מנש *son of Manasseh* Seal 603 (T. Beit Mirsim?, 7th/6th cent.).

8. appar. son of Malchi(j)ah, <PREP> לְ of possession, *of, (belonging) to* Seal 748 (c. 700).

9. son of Jannaeus, <CSTR> קבר מנשה *tomb of Manasseh* Kfar 'Illar inscr. <APP> בֵּן *son* Kfar 'Illar inscr.

⇒ מְנַשִּׁי *Manassite.*

מְנַשִּׁי 4 gent. **Manassite,** descendant of Manasseh or inhabitant of territory of Manasseh, as collective sing. noun, **Manassites,** <OBJ> נכה hi. *strike* 2 K 10_{33}.

<PREP> לְ of possession, *of, (belonging) to* Dt 4_{43}. <CSTR> חֲצִי שֵׁבֶט הַמְנַשִּׁי *half the tribe of the Manassites* Dt 29_{7} 1 C 26_{32}. <APP> אֶרֶץ *land* 2 K 10_{33}. <COLL> מְנַשִּׁי + גָּדִי ... רְאוּבֵנִי *Reubenites ... Gadites* Dt 4_{43} 29_{7} 1 C 26_{32}, גָּדִי ... רְאוּבֵנִי *Gadites ... Reubenites* 2 K 10_{33}.

⇒ מְנַשֶּׁה *Manasseh.*

[מְנָת] 9.0.2 n.f. **portion**—cstr. מְנָת; pl. cstr. מְנָיוֹת (מְנָאוֹת) —**portion, share** (appar. functions as the cstr. of מָנָה

portion), <SUBJ> היה *be* Ps 63$_{11}$, נתן ni. *be given* Ne 13$_{10}$. <NOM CL> זֶה ... מְנָת־מִדַּיִךְ *this is ... the portion of your measure* Jr 13$_{25}$, י׳ מְנָת־חֶלְקִי *Y. is the portion of my share* Ps 16$_{5}$ (or em.; see Cstr.), רוּחַ זִלְעָפוֹת מְנָת כּוֹסָם *a wind of ragings shall be the portion of their cup* Ps 11$_{6}$, מְנָת הַמֶּלֶךְ ... לָעֹלוֹת *the portion of the king was ... for the burnt offerings* 2 C 31$_{3}$ (or em.; see Cstr.). <OBJ> כנס *gather* Ne 12$_{44}$, נתן *give* Ne 12$_{47}$ 13$_{5}$ (if em.; see Cstr.) 2 C 31$_{4}$, אכל *eat* 2 K 23$_{9}$ (if em. מַצּוֹת *unleavened bread*).

<CSTR> מְנָיוֹת הַמְשֹׁרְרִים וְהַשֹּׁעֲרִים *portions of,* i.e. for, *the singers and the gatekeepers* Ne 12$_{47}$, הַלְוִיִּם וְהַמְשֹׁרְרִים וְהַשֹּׁעֲרִים *of,* i.e. for, *the Levites and the singers and the gatekeepers* Ne 13$_{5}$ (if em. מִצְוַת *commandment of*), הַלְוִיִּם *of,* i.e. for, *the Levites* Ne 13$_{10}$, מְנָת הַכֹּהֲנִים וְהַלְוִיִּם *portion of,* i.e. for, *the priests and Levites* 2 C 31$_{4}$, הַמֶּלֶךְ *of,* i.e. given by, *the king* 2 C 31$_{3}$ (or em. מַתְּנַת *gift of*), ־מִדַּיִךְ *of your measure,* i.e. measured out to you Jr 13$_{25}$ (or em. מֶרְיֵךְ *of your rebellion*), ־חֶלְקִי *of my share,* i.e. my chosen portion Ps 16$_{5}$ (or em. מִנִּתָ *you have appointed,* from מנה), כּוֹסָם *of their cup* Ps 11$_{6}$, שֻׁעָלִים *of jackals* Ps 63$_{11}$, מנת שפתי *portion of my lips* 1QS 10$_{8}$, רוח *of the spirit,* i.e. spiritual portion 4QShirShabb^{d} 1.1$_{40}$, מְנָאוֹת הַתּוֹרָה *portions of,* i.e. prescribed by, *the law* Ne 12$_{44}$.

<APP> גּוֹרָל *lot* Jr 13$_{25}$, מַעֲשֵׂר *tithe* Ne 13$_{5}$ (if em.; see Cstr.), ראשׁ *head,* i.e. choicest portion 4QShirShabb^{d} 1.1$_{40}$.

<PREP> לְ *as* 1QS 10$_{8}$; בְּ of accompaniment, *with,* + זמר pi. *sing praises* 4QShirShabb^{d} 1.1$_{40}$.

<COLL> מְנָת + כּוֹס *cup* Ps 16$_{5}$, פְּרִי *fruit* of praise 1QS 10$_{8}$; מְנָת הַמֶּלֶךְ מִן־רְכוּשׁוֹ *the portion of the king from his own possessions* 2 C 31$_{3}$ (or em.; see Cstr.), מְנָאוֹת הַתּוֹרָה לַכֹּהֲנִים וְלַלְוִיִּם *portions of,* i.e. prescribed by, *the law for the priests and Levites* Ne 12$_{44}$.*

⇒ מנה *count, appoint.*

מָס 1.0.1 adj. **melting,** used as noun, **one who melts, fails, despairs,** לַמָּס מֵרֵעֵהוּ חָסֶד *for one who fails, from their friend is (due) loyalty* Jb 6$_{14}$ (or em. לֹא מָאַס מֵרֵעַ חֶסֶד *a friend does not withhold loyalty* or לַמֹּנֵעַ *to one who withholds;* mss לִמְאֹס *to withhold* from his companion loyalty), לשוב כול מסי לבב *to restore all who are melting of heart,* i.e. whose courage is failing 1QM 10$_{6}$.

⇒ מסס *melt.*

מַס I 23.0.3.1 n.m. **levy**—sf. Q מסם; pl. מִסִּים—**1. levy, (forced) labour,** מַס עֹבֵד being perh. **state slavery** (at Gn 49$_{15}$ of labour willingly undertaken, at 1QSa 1$_{22}$ appar. of menial work, undertaken by mentally impaired),* <SUBJ> היה *be* 1 K 5$_{27}$ (+ שְׁלֹשִׁים אֶלֶף אִישׁ *thirty thousand men*), עבד *serve* Gn 49$_{15}$ Jos 16$_{10}$ 1 K 9$_{21}$ || 2 C 8$_{8(ms)}$ (L lacks עבד). <OBJ> עלה hi. *raise,* i.e. establish 1 K 5$_{27}$ 9$_{15}$, שׁלח *send* to Lebanon 1 K 5$_{27}$. <CSTR> דְּבַר־הַמַּס *an account of the levy* 1 K 9$_{15}$, שָׂרֵי מִסִּים *officers of levies* Ex 1$_{11}$, עבודת המס *the work of the levy* 1QSa 1$_{22}$.

<PREP> לְ *as,* + היה *be(come)* Gn 49$_{15}$ Dt 20$_{11}$=11QT 62$_{8}$ Jos 16$_{10}$ Jg 1$_{30.33}$ Is 31$_{8}$ (unless מָס II *melting*) Pr 12$_{24}$ Lm 1$_{1}$, נתן *cause to be* Jos 17$_{13}$, שׂים *cause to be* Jg 1$_{28}$, עלה hi. *raise,* i.e. establish 1 K 9$_{21}$ || 2 C 8$_{8}$; בְּ perh. *over, in charge of* Jerusalem ost. 2$_{5}$ (but word-division uncertain); עַל *over, in charge of* 2 S 20$_{24}$ (וַאֲדֹרָם עַל־הַמַּס *and Adoram was in charge of the levy* [ms וַאֲדֹנִרָם *and Adoniram*]) 1 K 4$_{6}$ (וַאֲדֹנִירָם ... עַל־הַמַּס *and Adoniram ... was in charge of the levy*) 5$_{28}$ (וַאֲדֹנִירָם עַל־הַמַּס) 12$_{18}$ || 2 C 10$_{18}$ (אֲדֹרָם אֲשֶׁר עַל־הַמַּס *Adoram, who was in charge of the levy* [or em. אֲדֹנִירָם; 2 C הֲדֹרָם]) Seal 782$_{5}$ (7th cent.; לפלאיהו אשר על המס *of Pelaiah, who is in charge of the levy*).

<COLL> מַס־עֹבֵד *serving levy,* i.e. forced labour gang, perh. of state slavery,* Gn 49$_{15}$ Jos 16$_{10}$ 1 K 9$_{21}$ || 2 C 8$_{8}$; מַס + סבל *burden* Gn 49$_{15}$ Ex 1$_{11}$, עבד *serve* Gn 49$_{15}$ Dt 20$_{11}$=11QT 62$_{8}$ Jos 16$_{10}$ 1 K 9$_{21}$ || 2 C 8$_{8(ms)}$ (L lacks עֹבֵד), ירשׁ hi. *dispossess* Jos 16$_{10}$ 17$_{13}$=Jg 1$_{28}$ Jg 1$_{30.33}$, + כבד *be heavy,* i.e. oppressive Jg 1$_{35}$.

Levy constituted by Issachar (Gn 49$_{15}$), Israelites in Egypt (Ex 1$_{11}$), defeated indigenous population (Dt 20$_{11}$=11QT 62$_{8}$ Jos 16$_{10}$ 17$_{13}$=Jg 1$_{28}$ Jg 1$_{30.33.35}$), defeated Assyrian soldiers (Is 31$_{8}$, unless מָס II *melting*), perh. David's Israelite subjects (2 S 20$_{24}$), Solomon's Israelite subjects (1 K 4$_{6}$ 5$_{27.27.28}$ 9$_{15}$), Solomon's non-Israelite subjects (1 K 9$_{21}$||2 C 8$_{8}$), Jerusalem (Lm 1$_{1}$), Rehoboam's Israelite subjects (1 K 12$_{18}$||2 C 10$_{18}$); levy imposed by Egyptians (Ex 1$_{11}$), Babylonians (Lm 1$_{1}$), victorious Israelites (Dt 20$_{11}$=11QT 62$_{8}$ Jos 16$_{10}$ 17$_{13}$=Jg 1$_{28}$ Jg 1$_{30.33.35}$), David (2 S 20$_{24}$), Solomon (1 K 4$_{6}$ 5$_{27.27.28}$ 9$_{15.21}$), Rehoboam (1 K 12$_{18}$||2 C 10$_{18}$); levy imposed in order to build cities (Ex 1$_{11}$), to build temple, palace, and fortifications of Jerusalem (1 K 9$_{21}$), to work in the Lebanon (1 K 5$_{27}$).

2. tax, taxation (but perh. as §1, **levy,** in each case), <OBJ> שׂים *place,* i.e. impose (of Ahasuerus) Est 10$_{1}$ (וַיָּשֶׂם ... מַס עַל־הָאָרֶץ *and he imposed a tax on the land,* unless, as §1, *and he established a levy against,* or, *throughout, the land*), חלק pi. *apportion* 1QpHab 6$_{7}$. <APP> מסם מאכלם *their tax, (which corresponds to) their food (in the biblical text)* 1QpHab 6$_{7}$. <COLL> את עולם ואת מסם *their yoke and their tax,* i.e. the burden of their taxation, or, of their forced labour 1Qp Hab 6$_{7}$.

Also perh. 6Q22 1$_{4}$.*

מַס II 1 n.[m.] **melting,** וְנָס לוֹ מִפְּנֵי־חֶרֶב וּבַחוּרָיו לָמַס יִהְיוּ *and he will flee before the sword and his youths will become as melting,* i.e. their limbs will weaken Is 31$_{8}$ (unless מַס I *levy*).

⇒ מסס *melt.*

מֵסַב 4.0.1 n.[m.] **couch; surroundings; everywhere;** perh. **against**—sf. מְסִבּוֹ; pl. cstr. מְסִבֵּי, מְסִבּוֹת—**1. couch** (perh. **table**), <PREP> בְּ of place, *in, on, at* Ca 1$_{12}$ (עַד־שֶׁהַמֶּלֶךְ בִּמְסִבּוֹ *while the king was on his couch* or *at his table;* or em. בִּמְסִבִּי *around,* i.e. near, *me*).

2. in pl., **surroundings, environs,** <CSTR> מְסִבֵּי יְרוּשָׁלַםִ *the environs of Jerusalem* 2 K 23$_{5}$. <PREP> בְּ of place, *in, throughout,* + קטר hi. *burn (incense)* 2 K 23$_{5}$ (בַּבָּמוֹת בְּעָרֵי יְהוּדָה וּמְסִבֵּי יְרוּשָׁלָםִ *on the high places, throughout the towns of Judah and the environs of Jerusalem;* mss וּבִמְסִבֵּי *and throughout the environs*).

3. as adverb, **all over, everywhere, throughout,** with verb קלע *engrave* 1 K 6$_{29}$ (וְאֵת כָּל־קִירוֹת הַבַּיִת מֵסַב קָלַע ... מִלִּפְנִים וְלַחִיצוֹן *and all the walls of the temple he engraved throughout ... from the inside and on the outside;* or em. מִסָּבִיב *all around* and/or לִפְנִימָה *inwards*). <COLL> במסב perh. *[in] everywhere* 4QPr Quot 10$_{9}$.

4. perh. as prep., **against** (unless מְסִבַּי is סבב hi. ptc. with sf., *those surrounding me*), רֹאשׁ מְסִבָּי עֲמַל שְׂפָתֵימוֹ יְכַסֵּימוֹ perh. *if a head is against me, may the work of their lips cover them* Ps 140$_{10}$ (or em. רֹאשָׁם *their head*).*

⇒ סבב *turn.*

[מְסִבָּה] 1.0.3 n.f. **circle**—Q מסבה; pl. מְסִבּוֹת—**1.** in ref. to motion described, **circle,** וְהוּא מְסִבּוֹת מִתְהַפֵּךְ בְּתַחְבּוּלֹתָיו לְפָעֳלָם *and it* (cloud) *keeps turning [in] circles on his directions to their work* Jb 37$_{12}$ (or ins. יִתְהַלֵּךְ and *it goes about* in circles).

2. geographical, **surroundings, environs,** <CSTR> כָּל־עָרֵי מְסִבּוֹת נַפְתָּלִי *all the cities of the environs of Naphtali* 2 C 16$_{4}$ (if em. כָּל־מִסְכְּנוֹת עָרֵי נַפְתָּלִי *all the supplies of the cities of Naphtali*).

3. architectural, **a. (winding) staircase** within square tower in temple complex,* <CSTR> ב[י]ת מסבה *staircase building* 11QT 30$_{5}$ (others [א]ת מסבה and you are to make *the staircase*), רוחב המסבה *the width of the staircase* 11QT 30$_{10}$. Also 11QT 30$_{3}$.

b. (winding) passage of temple sidechambers, <SUBJ> רחב *be wide* Ezk 41$_{7}$ (if em. וְרָחֲבָה וְנָסְבָה לְמַעְלָה לְמַעְלָה *and it widened and turned upward and upward* to הַמְּסִבָּה and *the winding passage* widened as it went upward).*

⇒ סבב *turn.*

*[מַסְבָּלָא] 0.0.1 pr.n.m. **Masbala,** recipient of letter, <PREP> לְ of benefit, *to, for* 5/6ḤevEp 12$_{2}$.

מַסְגֵּר I 4 n.[m.] **smith, metalworker** (alw. used collectively), <SUBJ> יצא *go out* from Jerusalem Jr 29$_{2}$ (|| חָרָשׁ *artisan*). <OBJ> גלה hi. *exile* 2 K 24$_{14}$ Jr 24$_{1}$ (unless מַסְגֵּר III *women of the harem;* both || חָרָשׁ *artisan*), בוא hi. *bring* to Babylon 2 K 24$_{16}$ Jr 24$_{1}$ (both || חָרָשׁ), הלך hi. *lead away* 2 K 24$_{16}$ (|| חָרָשׁ). <CSTR> וְכָל־הֶחָרָשׁ וְהַמַּסְגֵּר *and all the artisans and the smiths* 2 K 24$_{14}$. <APP>

וְהֶחָרָשׁ וְהַמַּסְגֵּר אֶלֶף *and the artisans and the smiths, a thousand (of them)* 2 K 24$_{16}$. <SYN> חָרָשׁ *artisan*.*
⇒ סגר II *smelt*.

*מַסְגֵּר II 3.0.0.1 n.[m.] **prison,** perh. as a name for Sheol (Ps 142$_{8}$), <CSTR> שער המסגר perh. Azariah, *gatekeeper of the prison* Seal 857. <PREP> מִן of direction, *from, out of*, + יצא hi. *take out* captive Is 42$_{7}$ (|| בֵּית כֶּלֶא *prison*), soul Ps 142$_{8}$; עַל *in(to)*, + סגר pu. *be enclosed* Is 24$_{22}$ (|| בּוֹר *pit*).
<SYN> בֵּית כֶּלֶא *prison*, בּוֹר *pit*.
⇒ סגר *close*.

*מַסְגֵּר III 1 n.[m.] **women of the harem,** unless מַסְגֵּר I *smith*, וְאֶת־שָׂרֵי יְהוּדָה וְאֶת־הֶחָרָשׁ וְאֶת־הַמַּסְגֵּר מִירוּשָׁלַםִ Nebuchadrezzar deported *from Jerusalem the princes of Judah and the artisans and the women of the harem* Jr 24$_{1}$.

מִסְגֶּרֶת I 14 n.f. **panel, rim, stronghold**—cstr. מִסְגֶּרֶת; sf. מִסְגַּרְתּוֹ; pl. מִסְגְּרוֹת (מִסְגְּרֹת) sf. מִסְגְּרֹתֶיהָ.

1. panel, inset of temple stands (1 K 7$_{28+6t}$ 2 K 16$_{17}$), <SUBJ> רבע pu. *be square* 1 K 7$_{31}$ (or del.). <NOM CL> מִסְגְּרֹת לָהֶם *they had panels* 1 K 7$_{28}$, וּמִסְגְּרֹת בֵּין הַשְׁלַבִּים *and (the) panels were among the frames* 1 K 7$_{28}$ (or del.), הַמִּסְגְּרֹת אֲשֶׁר בֵּין הַשְׁלַבִּים *the panels that were among the frames* 1 K 7$_{29}$, וּמִסְגְּרֹתֵיהֶם ... לֹא עֲגֻלּוֹת *and their panels ... were not round* 1 K 7$_{31}$ (or del.; mss וּמִסְגְּרֹתֶיהָ *and its panels*), וּמִסְגְּרֹתֶיהָ מִמֶּנָּה *and its panels were part of it* 1 K 7$_{35}$ (or del. מִמֶּנָּה, leaving וְעַל־רֹאשׁ הַמְּכֹנָה יְדֹתֶיהָ וּמִסְגְּרֹתֶיהָ *and on top of the stand were its handles and its panels*). <OBJ> קצץ pi. *chop up* 2 K 16$_{17}$ (or em.; see Cstr.), סור hi. *remove* 2 K 16$_{17}$ (if em.).
<CSTR> perh. אֶת־הַמִּסְגְּרוֹת הַמְּכֹנוֹת he chopped up *the panels of the stands* 2 K 16$_{17}$ (or em. אֶת־מִסְגְּרוֹת *the panels of* the stands, or move אֶת־הַמִּסְגְּרוֹת to after וַיָּסַר מֵעֲלֵיהֶם and he chopped up the stands *and he removed* the panels *from* them). <APP> לוּחַ bronze *plate* 1 K 7$_{36}$ (if del. עַל *upon* before מִסְגֶּרֶת). <PREP> עַל *upon* 1 K 7$_{29}$ (+ אֲרִי *lion*, בָּקָר *cattle*, כְּרוּב *cherub*); לְמִתַּחַת לְ *below* 1 K 7$_{32}$ (+ אוֹפָן *wheel*; or del.), + פתח pi. *engrave* cherubs, lions, and palms 1 K 7$_{36}$ (or del. מִסְגֶּרֶת).

2. rim, framework of table for bread of presence (Ex 25$_{25.25.27}$||37$_{12.12.14}$), <OBJ> עשׂה *make* Ex 25$_{25}$||37$_{12}$). <APP> טֹפַח *handbreadth*, as width of rim Ex 25$_{25}$||37$_{12}$. <PREP> לְ of benefit, *for*, + עשׂה *make* gold moulding, Ex 25$_{25}$||37$_{12}$; לְעֻמַּת *next to*, + היה *be* (of gold rings) Ex 25$_{27}$||37$_{14}$. <COLL> מִסְגֶּרֶת ... סָבִיב *a rim ... around* Ex 25$_{25}$||37$_{12}$, sim. 25$_{25}$||37$_{12}$.*
⇒ סגר *close*.

*[מִסְגֶּרֶת] II 3 n.f. **stronghold, prison**—pl. sf. מִסְגְּרֹתָם (מִסְגְּרוֹתֵיהֶם, מִסְגְּרֹתֵיהֶם)—<PREP> מִן of direction, *from*, + חרג *shake*, i.e. come trembling Ps 18$_{46}$, רגז *shake*, i.e. come trembling Mc 7$_{17}$; appar. *in, among*, + חגר *gird oneself* 2 S 22$_{46}$||Ps 18$_{46(mss)}$ (ms ויגחרו perh. *and they retreat*; or em. וְיִפְּלוּ מִמְּסִלֹּתָם/מִמַּעְגְּלֹתָם *and they fall away from their roads/their tracks*; 4QSam^{a} יחגרו ממסרותם perh. *they gird themselves with their chains*).*
⇒ סגר *close*.

מַסָּד 1 n.[m.] **foundation**—mss מַסָּד—מִבַּיִת וּמִחוּץ וּמִמַּסָּד עַד־הַטְּפָחוֹת וּמִחוּץ עַד־הֶחָצֵר הַגְּדוֹלָה *outside and inside, and from (the) foundation to the coping and from outside unto the great court* 1 K 7$_{9}$ (or del. second וּמִחוּץ), מַסְּדוֹת הַצְּלָעוֹת מְלוֹ הַקָּנֶה שֵׁשׁ אַמּוֹת אַצִּילָה *the foundations of the side chambers were the fullness of a rod, six cubits per joint* (if em. מוּסְדוֹת [Qr] *foundations*; or em. אֶצְלָהּ *next to it*) Ezk 41$_{8}$.
⇒ יסד *establish*.

[מִסְדְּרוֹן] 1 n.[m.] **porch**—+ ה- of direction הַמִּסְדְּרוֹנָה—**porch, lavatory** or **armoury,** perh. **air-shaft***, וַיֵּצֵא אֵהוּד הַמִּסְדְּרוֹנָה וַיִּסְגֹּר דַּלְתוֹת הָעֲלִיָּה בַּעֲדוֹ וְנָעָל *Ehud went out to the porch and shut the doors of the roof chamber behind him and locked up* Jg 3$_{23(L)}$.*

מסה 4 vb. **melt—Hi.** 4 Pf. הִמְסִיו (ms הִמְסִיו); impf. וַיִּמְסֵם, אַמְסֶה; + waw וַתֶּמֶס—trans., **melt, cause to melt, dissolve, wash away, cause to disintegrate,** <SUBJ> Y. Ps 39$_{12}$ 147$_{18}$ (+ נזל *flow*), אָח *brother*, i.e. fellow-explorer, of Caleb Jos 14$_{8}$, worshipper Ps 6$_{7}$ (|| שׂחה hi.

drown bed with groans [or em. אַמְסֶה *I drown* to אָשִׂיחָה *let me complain*, i.e. שׂיח *complain*], + יגע *be weary*). <OBJ> לֵב melt *heart*, i.e. discourage Jos 14_{8}, עֶרֶשׂ *couch* Ps 6_{7}, חָמוּד *property* Ps 39_{12} (or em. חֶמֶד *property*), שֶׁלֶג *snow* Ps 147_{18}, כְּפוֹר *frost* Ps 147_{18}, קֶרַח *ice* Ps 147_{18}, קָרָה *cold* Ps 147_{18}. <PREP> בְּ of instrument, *by (means of), with*, + דִּמְעָה *tear* Ps 6_{7}; כְּ *as*, + עָשׁ *moth* Ps 39_{12}. <SYN> שׁחה hi. *drown*.*
⇒ מסס cf. *melt*.

מַסָּה I $_{4}$ n.f. **trial, testing**—cstr. מַסַּת; pl. מַסּוֹת (מַסֹּת)—<OBJ> ראה *see* Dt 7_{19} (+ אוֹת *sign*, מוֹפֵת *wonder*, יָד strong *hand*, זְרוֹעַ extended *arm*) 29_{2} (+ אוֹת, מוֹפֵת). <CSTR> מַסַּת נְקִיִּם *testing of innocent ones* Jb 9_{23} (unless מַסָּה III *despair*). <ADJ> גָּדוֹל *great* Dt 7_{19} 29_{2}. <PREP> לְ לעג *mock at* Jb 9_{23} (unless מַסָּה III *despair*); בְּ of accompaniment, *with*, + לקח *take* one nation from among another Dt 4_{34} (|| אוֹת *sign*, מוֹפֵת *wonder*, + מִלְחָמָה *war*, יָד strong *hand*, זְרוֹעַ extended *arm*, מוֹרָא *fearful act*).*
⇒ נסה *try*.

מַסָּה II $_{5}$ pl.n. **Massah,** <OBJ> קרא *call* name Ex 17_{7} (+ עַל־נַסֹּתָם אֶת־י׳ *because of their testing Y.*, + מְרִיבָה *Meribah*). <CSTR> יוֹם מַסָּה *the day of Massah* Ps 95_{8} (+ בַּמִּדְבָּר: אֲשֶׁר נִסּוּנִי אֲבוֹתֵיכֶם *in the wilderness, where your ancestors tested me*, + מְרִיבָה *Meribah*). <PREP> בְּ of place, *in, at*, + נסה pi. *test* Y. Dt 6_{16}, Levi Dt 33_{8} (+ מְרִיבָה *Meribah*), קצף hi. *enrage* Y. Dt 9_{22} (+ תַּבְעֵרָה *Taberah*, קִבְרֹת הַתַּאֲוָה *Kibroth-hattaavah*). <COLL> מַסָּה וּמְרִיבָה *Massah and Meribah* (as composite place name) Ex 17_{7}.*
⇒ נסה *try*.

[מַסָּה] III $_{1}$ n.f. **despair** or **calamity**—cstr. מַסַּת—<CSTR> מַסַּת נְקִיִּם *despair of innocent ones* Jb 9_{23} (unless מַסָּה I *testing*). <PREP> לְ לעג *mock at* Jb 9_{23}.
⇒ מסס *melt*.

[מִסָּה] $_{1}$ n.f. perh. **sufficiency**—cstr. מִסַּת—**sufficiency** or **proportion** or **measure,** וְעָשִׂיתָ חַג שָׁבֻעוֹת ... מִסַּת נִדְבַת יָדְךָ אֲשֶׁר תִּתֵּן *and you are to keep the festival of weeks ... (according to) the sufficiency of generosity*, or, *in proportion to the generosity*, or, *(according to) the measure of the generosity of your hand that you (are able to) give* Dt 16_{10} (or em. כְּמִסַּת *according to the sufficiency of* or כְּמַתְּנַת *according to the gift of* generosity, and/or יִתֶּן לָךְ which *he gives to you*).*

מַסְוֶה $_{3}$ n.[m.] **veil** that Moses wore to protect Israelites from the light of Y. reflected in his face, <OBJ> נתן *place* over face Ex 34_{33}, סור hi. *remove* Ex 34_{34}, שׁוב *return*, i.e. place again, over face Ex 34_{35}.*
⇒ cf. סוּת *vesture*.

מְסוּכָה I $_{1}$ n.f. **hedge,** i.e. obstacle, טוֹבָם כְּחֵדֶק יָשָׁר מִמְּסוּכָה *the best of them is like a thistle, more upright than a hedge* Mc 7_{4} (or em. יְשָׁרָם כִּמְסוּכָה *the most upright of them is like a hedge*).
⇒ סוך *close*.

[מְסוּכָה] II $_{1}$ n.f. **covering, decoration**—sf. מְסֻכָתֶךָ—<NOM CL> כָּל־אֶבֶן יְקָרָה מְסֻכָתֶךָ *every precious stone was your covering* Ezk 28_{13}.
⇒ סכך *screen*.

[מְסוֹלָל] $_{0.0.1}$ n.[m.] **road**—Q מסולל—והיה שמה מסולל ודרך הקודש יקראו לה *and there will be there and there*, perh. everywhere, *a road, which people will call the way of holiness* 1QIsa[a] 38_{5} (MT וְהָיָה־שָׁם מַסְלוּל וָדֶרֶךְ ... יִקָּרֵא לָהּ *and there will be there a road and a way*, which *will be called* the way of holiness).
⇒ סלל *raise*.

[מָסוֹרָה], see [מָסֹרֶת] II *tradition*.

[מַסּוֹרָה], see [מָסֹרֶת] II *tradition*.

[מְסוֹרָה], see [מָסֹרֶת] II *tradition*.

[מְסוּרָה], see [מָסֹרֶת] IV *division*.

מַסָּח I $_{1}$ appar. adv. **by turns** or **all around,** וּשְׁמַרְתֶּם אֶת־מִשְׁמֶרֶת הַבַּיִת מַסָּח *and you are to keep watch over* *the temple by turns* or *all around* 2 K 11$_{6}$ (unless מַסָּח II; or del. מַסָּח).*

*מַסָּח II 1 n.[m.] **detachment, relief body of troops**, וּשְׁמַרְתֶּם אֶת־מִשְׁמֶרֶת הַבַּיִת מַסָּח *and you shall keep the watch of the temple (by) detachment(s)* 2 K 11$_{6}$ (unless מַסָּח I; or del. מַסָּח).*

[מִסְחוֹר], see מִסְחָר *merchandise*.

[מִסְחָר] 1.0.1 n.[m.] **goods**—cstr. מִסְחַר; sf. Q מסחורכה—לְבַד מֵאַנְשֵׁי הַתָּרִים וּמִסְחַר הָרֹכְלִים *apart from (gold deducted from) people of itinerants*, i.e. traders, *and merchants' goods* 1 K 10$_{15}$ (or em. הַתָּרִים to הֶעָרִים people of *the cities*; or מֵאַנְשֵׁי to מֵעָנְשֵׁי apart from *the taxes of* the traders, or מֵאַנְשֵׁי הַתָּרִים to מֵעָנֵי תַרְשִׁישׁ [gold bought by] *the fleet of Tarshish*, and/or וּמִסְחַר to וּמִסַּחַר and [apart] *from [gold deducted from] the trade of merchants*; ||2 C 9$_{14}$ וְהַסֹּחֲרִים מְבִיאִים *when the traders were bringing*), אוטים מסחורכה ופעולתכה perh. *storing your goods and your deed(s)* 4Q418 107$_{4}$.
⇒ סחר *travel*.

מסך I 5.0.1 vb. **mix (wine)**—**Qal** 5 Pf. מָסַכְתִּי, מָסְכָה, מָסַךְ; inf. מְסֹךְ—**mix** wine, usu. with water, but perh. also with other liquids, herbs, honey, etc. (Is 5$_{22}$ Pr 9$_{2.5}$; cf. מֶסֶךְ *mixed wine* Ps 75$_{9}$, מִמְסָךְ *mixture* Is 65$_{11}$ Pr 23$_{30}$, מֶזֶג *mixture* Ca 7$_{3}$),* <SUBJ> י״ *Y.* Is 19$_{14}$, חָכְמוֹת *Wisdom* Pr 9$_{2}$ (unless מסך II; || טבח *slaughter*) 9$_{5}$ (+ שׁתה *drink*, לחם *eat*), אִישׁ mighty *man* Is 5$_{22}$ (|| שׁתה), מֶלֶךְ *king* Ho 7$_{5}$ (if em. מָשַׁךְ יָדוֹ *he extended his hand* to מָסַךְ יֵינוֹ *he mixed his wine*), worshipper Ps 102$_{10}$ (unless מסך II; :: אכל *eat*). <OBJ> שֵׁכָר *strong drink* Is 5$_{22}$, יַיִן *wine* Pr 9$_{2.5}$, יָד *hand* Ho 7$_{5}$ (if em.; see Subj.), רוּחַ *spirit* of distortion Is 19$_{14}$, שִׁקּוּי *drink* Ps 102$_{10}$. <PREP> בְּ of instrument, *with*, or place, *into*, בְּכִי *weeping* Ps 102$_{10}$; בְּקֶרֶב *(in) among* Is 19$_{14}$. <COLL> הוֹי ... אַנְשֵׁי־חַיִל לִמְסֹךְ שֵׁכָר *woe ..., O mighty men, for mixing strong drink* Is 5$_{22}$, וּשְׁתוּ בְּיַיִן מָסָכְתִּי *and drink of the wine I have mixed* Pr 9$_{5}$.

Also 4QBéat 34$_{2}$.

<SYN> שׁתה *drink*. <ANT> אכל *eat*, טבח *slaughter*.*

⇒ מֶסֶךְ *mixed wine*, מִמְסָךְ *mixed wine*, מֶסֶךְ II *bowl*.

*מסך II 2 vb. **draw, pour**—**Qal** 2 Pf. מָסַכְתִּי, מָסְכָה—<SUBJ> י״ *Y.* Ps 75$_{9}$ (if em. מֶסֶךְ *mixed wine* to מָסַךְ), חָכְמוֹת *Wisdom* Pr 9$_{2}$ (unless מסך I), worshipper Ps 102$_{10}$ (unless מסך I; :: אכל *eat*). <OBJ> יַיִן *wine* Pr 9$_{2}$, שִׁקּוּי *drink* Ps 102$_{10}$. <PREP> בְּ of instrument, *with*, or place, *into*, + בְּכִי *weeping* Ps 102$_{10}$; מִן *from*, + זֶה *this* (cup) Ps 75$_{9}$ (if em.; see Subj.). <ANT> אכל *eat*.*

מָסָךְ 25.0.1 n.[m.] **screen**—cstr. מָסַךְ—**1.** vertical **screen, curtain**, at entrance of tent of meeting or tabernacle (Ex 26$_{36}$=36$_{37}$ 26$_{37}$ 35$_{15}$ 39$_{38}$ 40$_{5}$=40$_{28}$ Nm 3$_{25}$ 4$_{25}$ perh. Nm 3$_{31}$), at gate of court of tabernacle (Ex 27$_{16}$=38$_{18}$ 35$_{17}$ 39$_{40}$ 40$_{8}$=40$_{33}$ Nm 3$_{26}$=4QRP^{c} 27$_{1}$ Nm 4$_{26}$), in front of ark (Ex 35$_{12}$ 39$_{34}$ 40$_{21}$ Nm 4$_{5}$ 4QapMoses^{a} 1.2$_{7}$ [[ה]מסך]]).

<NOM CL> וְלְשַׁעַר הֶחָצֵר מָסָךְ *and for the gate of the court there is to be a screen* Ex 27$_{16}$, וּמָסַךְ שַׁעַר הֶחָצֵר מַעֲשֵׂה רֹקֵם *and the screen of the gate of the court is to be the work of an embroiderer* Ex 38$_{18}$, ... וּמִשְׁמַרְתָּם הַמָּסָךְ *and their duty comprised ... the screen* Nm 3$_{31}$, וּמִשְׁמֶרֶת בְּנֵי־גֵרְשׁוֹן ... מָסַךְ פֶּתַח אֹהֶל מוֹעֵד *and the duty of the Gershonites comprised ... the screen of the entrance of the tent of meeting* Nm 3$_{25}$, sim. 3$_{26}$ (מָסַךְ פֶּתַח הֶחָצֵר *the screen of the entrance of the court*). <OBJ> עשׂה *make* Ex 26$_{36}$||36$_{37}$ 35$_{15.17}$, בוא hi. *bring* Ex 39$_{38.40}$, שׂים *place* Ex 40$_{5}$=40$_{28}$, נתן *set in place* Ex 40$_{8}$=40$_{33}$, נשׂא *carry* Nm 4$_{25.26}$.

<CSTR> מָסַךְ הַפֶּתַח *the screen of the entrance* Ex 35$_{15}$ 40$_{5}$=40$_{28}$, מָסַךְ פֶּתַח הָאֹהֶל *the screen of the entrance of the tent* Ex 39$_{38}$, מָסַךְ פֶּתַח הֶחָצֵר *the screen of the entrance of the court* Nm 3$_{26}$=4QRP^{c} 27$_{1}$, מָסַךְ פֶּתַח אֹהֶל מוֹעֵד *the screen of the entrance of the tent of meeting* Nm 3$_{25}$ 4$_{25}$, מָסַךְ שַׁעַר הֶחָצֵר *the screen of the gate of the court* Ex 35$_{17}$ 38$_{18}$ 40$_{8}$=40$_{33}$, מָסַךְ פֶּתַח שַׁעַר הֶחָצֵר *the screen of the entrance of the gate of the court* Nm 4$_{26}$; פָּרֹכֶת הַמָּסָךְ *the veil of*, i.e. constituting, *the screen* Ex 35$_{12}$ 39$_{34}$ 40$_{21}$ Nm 4$_{5}$ 4QapMoses^{a} 1.2$_{7}$ ([המסך]; others [הקודש] the veil of *the sanctuary*). <PREP> לְ of benefit, *for*, + עשׂה *make* Ex 26$_{37}$. <APP> מָסָךְ ... תְּכֵלֶת וְאַרְגָּמָן וְתוֹלַעַת שָׁנִי וְשֵׁשׁ מָשְׁזָר מַעֲשֵׂה רֹקֵם *a screen ... (of)*

blue and purple and crimson and twisted linen, embroiderer's work Ex 26$_{36}$||36$_{37}$ 27$_{16}$, ... אֵת כָּל־אֲשֶׁר צִוָּה י׳ אֶת־מָסַךְ הַפֶּתַח *all that Y. had commanded ... the screen of the entrance* Ex 35$_{15}$, sim. 35$_{17}$ (אֵת מָסַךְ שַׁעַר הֶחָצֵר *the screen of the gate of the court*).

<COLL> מָסָךְ לְפֶתַח הָאֹהֶל *a screen for the entrance of the tent* Ex 26$_{36}$||36$_{37}$, הַמָּסָךְ לְשַׁעַר הֶחָצֵר *the screen for the gate of the court* Ex 39$_{40}$, מָסַךְ הַפֶּתַח לְפֶתַח הַמִּשְׁכָּן *the screen of the entrance, namely the entrance of the tabernacle* Ex 35$_{15}$, הַמָּסָךְ וְכֹל עֲבֹדָתוֹ *the screen and all the work connected with it* Nm 3$_{31}$ (Sam עֲבֹדָתָם *their work* or *work connected with them*).

2. vertical screen as **border defence, bulwark** (Is 22$_{8}$). <OBJ> גלה pi. *remove* Is 22$_{8}$ (+ שַׁעַר *gate*). <CSTR> מָסַךְ יְהוּדָה *the border defence of Judah* Is 22$_{8}$.

3. horizontal screen, **covering,** perh. of cloth (2 S 17$_{19}$), of cloud (Ps 105$_{39}$). <OBJ> לקח *take* 2 S 17$_{19}$, פרשׂ *spread* over top of well 2 S 17$_{19}$. <PREP> לְ *as,* + פרשׂ *spread* cloud Ps 105$_{39}$; עַל *over,* + שׁטח *spread* grain 2 S 17$_{19}$.

⇒ סכך *screen.*

מֶ֫סֶךְ I $_{1}$ n.[m.] **mixed wine, wine** mixed prob. with other liquids, herbs, honey, etc. (but not appar. with water), unless מֶסֶךְ II *bowl,* <SUBJ> מלא *be full* Ps 75$_{9}$ (וְיַיִן חָמַר מָלֵא מֶסֶךְ *and the wine foams, the mixed wine is full,* unless מָלֵא מֶסֶךְ =*full with mixed wine,* as predicate of כּוֹס *cup* in Y.'s hand; || יַיִן *wine*; or em. מֶסֶךְ to מָסַךְ *he draws*). <SYN> יַיִן *wine.**

⇒ מסך I *mix (wine).*

***מֶ֫סֶךְ** II $_{1}$ n.[m.] **bowl,** unless מֶסֶךְ I *mixed wine,* <SUBJ> מלא *be full* Ps 75$_{9}$ (וְיַיִן חָמַר מָלֵא מֶסֶךְ *and the wine foams, the bowl is full*; || יַיִן *wine*; or em. מֶסֶךְ to מָסַךְ *he draws*). <SYN> יַיִן *wine.*

⇒ מסך I *mix (wine).*

מַסֵּכָה I $_{25}$ n.f. **image** (whether forged or cast)—cstr. מַסֵּכַת; pl. מַסֵּכוֹת; sf. מַסֵּכֹתָם—**image** of a deity, **idol** (sometimes perh. collective), <SUBJ> היה *be* Jg 17$_{4}$ (+ בְּ *in* Micah's house), יעל hi. *be of use* Hb 2$_{18}$, כעס hi. *enrage* 1 K 14$_{9}$. <NOM CL> יֵשׁ בַּבָּתִּים הָאֵלֶּה ... מַסֵּכָה *there is, among these houses, an idol* Jg 18$_{14}$. <OBJ> עשׂה *make* Ex 32$_{8}$ Dt 9$_{12.16}$ 27$_{15}$ Jg 17$_{3.4}$ 1 K 14$_{9}$ 2 K 17$_{16}$ Ho 13$_{2}$ Ne 9$_{18}$ 2 C 28$_{2}$ (or em. מִזְבֵּחַ *altar*), specif. make rings into Ex 32$_{4}$, נסך *forge, cast* Is 30$_{1}$ (unless מַסֵּכָה III or IV),* שׂים *place,* i.e. erect, in secret Dt 27$_{15}$, לקח *take* Jg 18$_{17}$ (|| פֶּסֶל *image,* אֵפוֹד *ephod,* תְּרָפִים *teraphim*) 18$_{18}$ (+ פֶּסֶל, אֵפוֹד, תְּרָפִים; or del.), כרת hi. *cut off* Na 1$_{14}$, שׁבר pi. *shatter* 2 C 34$_{4}$ (|| פֶּסֶל, אֲשֵׁרָה *Asherah,* + מִזְבֵּחַ *altar,* חַמָּן *incense altar,* קֶבֶר *grave*), דקק hi. *pulverize* 2 C 34$_{4}$, זרק *scatter* 2 C 34$_{4}$.

<CSTR> אֱלֹהֵי מַסֵּכָה *gods of,* i.e. represented by, or, in the form of, *an image* Ex 34$_{17}$ Lv 19$_{4}$, כָּל־צַלְמֵי מַסֵּכֹתָם *all the images of their idols* Nm 33$_{52}$, אֲפֻדַּת מַסֵּכַת זְהָבֶךָ *the ephod of your idol of gold* Is 30$_{22}$ (+ פֶּסֶל *image*). <APP> עֵגֶל מַסֵּכָה *a calf, an image,* i.e. an image of a calf Ex 32$_{4.8}$ Dt 9$_{12(Sam).16}$ (or del. עֵגֶל) Ne 9$_{18}$, מַסֵּכָה שְׁנֵי עֲגָלִים *an image, two calves* 2 K 17$_{16(Qr)}$ (or del. שְׁנֵי or שְׁנֵי עֲגָלִים; + אֲשֵׁרָה *Asherah*), ומַסֵּכָה תּוֹעֲבַת י׳ מַעֲשֵׂה יְדֵי חָרָשׁ *or an idol, an abomination of Y., a work of an artisan's hands* Dt 27$_{15}$, מַסֵּכָה ... עֲצַבִּים מַעֲשֵׂה חָרָשִׁים *image(s) ..., idols, the work of artisans* Ho 13$_{2}$ (+ עֵגֶל *calf*), פֶּסֶל ... מַסֵּכָה *an image ... an idol* Na 2$_{18}$. <PREP> לְ of direction, *to,* + אמר *say* Is 42$_{17}$ (ms lacks לְמַסֵּכָה *to an idol*; + פֶּסֶל *image*) Ho 13$_{2}$ (or em. לָהֶם *to them* to אֱלֹהִים saying, They are *gods*), שׁחה htpal. *bow down* Ps 106$_{19}$ (+ עֵגֶל *calf*); טהר מִן pi. *purify* Judah *of* 2 C 34$_{3}$ (|| פֶּסֶל, אֲשֵׁרָה *Asherah,* בָּמָה *high place*).

<COLL> פֶּסֶל וּמַסֵּכָה *an image or an idol, an image that is an idol,* or *images and idols* Dt 27$_{15}$ Jg 17$_{3.4}$ 18$_{14}$ (+ אֵפוֹד וּתְרָפִים *ephod and teraphim*) Na 1$_{14}$ (+ קֶבֶר *grave*), אֱלֹהִים אֲחֵרִים וּמַסֵּכוֹת *other gods, and images* 1 K 14$_{9}$, מַסֵּכָה וּמוֹרֵה שָּׁקֶר *an idol and a teacher, a deceit* Hb 2$_{18}$ (1QpHab ומרי perh. *and lords of* or *and teacher[s] of*), וְגַם מַסֵּכוֹת עָשָׂה לַבְּעָלִים *and he also made images of,* or *for, the Baalim* 2 C 28$_{2}$ (or em. מִזְבְּחוֹת *altars* for).

<SYN> פֶּסֶל *image,* אֵפוֹד *ephod,* תְּרָפִים *teraphim,* אֲשֵׁרָה *Asherah,* בָּמָה *high place.*

⇒ נסך *pour.*

מַסֵּכָה II $_{2}$ n.f. **covering,** perh. specif. **veil, pall** (Is 25$_{7}$), **sheet, blanket, counterpane** (Is 28$_{20}$), <SUBJ>

צרר *be cramped* Is 28_{20} (1QIsa[a] מְסַכְסֶכָה *covering;* || מַצָּע *couch*), כנס htp. *be entered* Is 28_{20}, נסך pass., *be woven* over all the nations Is 25_7 (|| לוֹט *covering*).

<SYN> לוֹט *covering,* מַצָּע *couch.*

⇒ נסך *weave.*

*מַסֵּכָה III 1 n.f. **libation** (unless I *image* or IV *scheme*), to seal an alliance, <OBJ> נסך *pour,* i.e. offer Is 30_1 (:: רוח *spirit*). <ANT> רוח *spirit.*

Also 4QD[b] 6.4_6(WA) (מסכתה *its libation;* Baumgarten ממנחה *of a meal offering*).

⇒ נסך *pour.*

*מַסֵּכָה IV 1 n.f. **scheme** (unless I *image* or III *libation*), <OBJ> נסך *weave,* i.e. scheme Is 30_1 (|| עֵצָה *counsel*). <SYN> עֵצָה *counsel.*

⇒ נסך *weave.*

[מַסֵּכָה] V, see מַסֶּכֶת *web.*

*[מְסָכָה] 0.0.1 n.f. **screen**—Q מסכה—<OBJ> עשה *make* 4QRp[c] 8_3 ([ועשיתה]; ||Ex 26_{36} מָסָךְ *screen*). <COLL> מסכה לפתח האוהל *a screen for the entrance of the tent* 4Q RP[c] 8_3.

⇒ סכך *screen.*

[מְסֻכָה], see מְסוּכָה II *covering.*

מִסְכֵּן 4.2 adj. **poor**—sf. Si מסכינך—**1.** used attributively of יֶלֶד *child* Ec 4_{13} (|| חָכָם *wise,* :: זָקֵן *old,* כְּסִיל *fool[ish]*), אִישׁ *man* Ec 9_{15} (|| חָכָם) 9_{15}. **2.** as noun, **poor one, pauper.**

<NOM CL> טוב מסכן וחי בעצמו מעשיר ונגע בבשרו *better is a poor person who is alive in their bone[s] than a rich person whose flesh bears wounds* Si 30_{14} (:: עָשִׁיר *wealthy*). <CSTR> חָכְמַת הַמִּסְכֵּן *the wisdom of a pauper* Ec 9_{16} (+ בְּזוּיָה וּדְבָרָיו אֵינָם נִשְׁמָעִים *is despised and his words are not heard*). <PREP> מִן of direction, *from,* + מנע *withhold* gift Si 4_3 (+ דַּל *poor,* דַּךְ *oppressed,* עָנִי *afflicted*). <COLL> מסכינך appar. *the poor one you know* or *the poor one around you* Si 4_3 (or em. מסכ[י]ן do not withhold a gift from *a poor one*).

<SYN> חָכָם *wise.* <ANT> זָקֵן *old,* כְּסִיל *fool(ish),* עָשִׁיר *wealthy.**

⇒ סכן *be poor;* cf. מִסְכֵּנֻת *poverty.*

מְסַכֵּן I *steward,* see סכן Pi. *be of service.**

מְסַכֵּן II *one who sets up,* see סכן Pi. *set up.**

מְסֻכָּן I 1 n.[m.] **poor** (pu. ptc. of סכן *be poor*), הַמְסֻכָּן תְּרוּמָה עֵץ לֹא־יִרְקַב יִבְחָר *the poor man chooses as an offering a wood that does not rot* Is 40_{20} (unless מְסֻכָּן II or III; or del. הַמְסֻכָּן or תְּרוּמָה or both; or em. הַמְסֻכָּן to הַמְּסַכֵּן *one who is familiar with* [סכן pi. *be familiar with*]* or *one who keeps* [סכן pi. *guard*];* or em. הַמְסֻכָּן תְּרוּמָה to הַמְסַכֵּן תְּמוּנָה *whoever erects* [סכן II *set up*] *an image* chooses a wood that does not rot; or em. מְסֻכָּתוֹ רוֹמֵם *he erects its covering*).*

⇒ סכן *be poor.*

*מְסֻכָּן II 1 n.[m.] **mulberry tree** or **wood,** הַמְסֻכָּן תְּרוּמָה עֵץ לֹא־יִרְקַב יִבְחָר *he chooses as an offering a mulberry tree, a wood that does not rot* Is 40_{20} (unless מְסֻכָּן I or III; or del. הַמְסֻכָּן or תְּרוּמָה or both; or em. הַמְסַכֵּן תְּמוּנָה *whoever erects* [סכן II *set up*] *an image* chooses a wood that does not rot; or em. מְסֻכָּתוֹ רוֹמֵם *he erects its covering*).

*מְסֻכָּן III 1 n.[m.] **sisu tree** or **wood,** הַמְסֻכָּן תְּרוּמָה עֵץ לֹא־יִרְקַב יִבְחָר *he chooses as an offering* (or *tribute*) *a sisu tree, a wood that does not rot* Is 40_{20} (unless מְסֻכָּן I or II; or del. הַמְסֻכָּן or תְּרוּמָה or both; or em. הַמְסַכֵּן תְּמוּנָה *whoever erects* [סכן II *set up*] *an image* chooses a wood that does not rot; or em. מְסֻכָּתוֹ רוֹמֵם *he erects its covering*).

מְסֻכָּן IV *thing formed,* see סכן *form.**

מִסְכְּנוֹת I 7 n.f. **supplies, 1.** appar. **supplies** of food or soldiers, <OBJ> נכה hi. *strike* 2 C 16_4 (or em.; see Cstr.). <CSTR> עָרֵי מִסְכְּנוֹת *cities of supplies,* i.e. store, or garrison, cities (unless מִסְכְּנוֹת II *forced labour*) Ex 1_{11} (of Pharaoh) 2 C 17_{12} (of Jehoshaphat; + בִּירָה *for-*

tress), כָּל־עָרֵי מִסְכְּנוֹת *all the store,* or *garrison, cities* of Solomon (unless מִסְכְּנוֹת II *forced labour*) 1 K 9_{19}|| 2 C 8_6 (+ רֶכֶב cities of *chariotry,* פָּרָשִׁים cities of *cavalry*) 2 C 8_4; כָּל־מִסְכְּנוֹת עָרֵי נַפְתָּלִי *all the supplies of the cities of Naphtali* 2 C 16_4 (unless מִסְכְּנוֹת III *threshing place;* or em. כָּל־עָרֵי מִסְכְּנוֹת נַפְתָּלִי *all the store,* or *garrison, cities of Naphtali* or כָּל־עָרֵי מְסִבּוֹת נַפְתָּלִי *all the cities of the environs of Naphtali;* || 1 K 15_{20} כָּל־כִּנְרוֹת עַל כָּל־אֶרֶץ נַפְתָּלִי *all Chinneroth over all the land of Naphtali* [or em. עַד *unto*]).

2. storehouses, <OBJ> עשׂה *make* 2 C 32_{28} (וּמִסְכְּנוֹת לִתְבוּאַת דָּגָן וְתִירוֹשׁ וְיִצְהָר *and storerooms for the produce of grain, wine, and oil* 2 C 32_{28}; || אֻרְוָה *stall,* אוֹצָר *treasury*).

<SYN> §2 אֻרְוָה *stall,* אוֹצָר *treasury*).

*מִסְכְּנוֹת II 5 n.f. **forced labour,** all unless מִסְכְּנוֹת I *supplies,* <CSTR> עָרֵי מִסְכְּנוֹת *cities of,* i.e. built with, *forced labour* Ex 1_{11} (of Pharaoh) 2 C 17_{12} (of Jehoshaphat; + בִּירָה *fortress*), כָּל־עָרֵי מִסְכְּנוֹת *all the cities of,* i.e. built with, *forced labour* of Solomon 1 K 9_{19}||2 C 8_6 (+ רֶכֶב cities of *chariotry,* פָּרָשִׁים cities of *cavalry*) 2 C 8_4.

*מִסְכְּנוֹת III 1 n.f. **threshing place,** unless מִסְכְּנוֹת I *supplies,* <OBJ> נכה hi. *strike* 2 C 16_4 (or em.; see Cstr.). <CSTR> כָּל־מִסְכְּנוֹת עָרֵי נַפְתָּלִי *all the threshing places of the cities of Naphtali* 2 C 16_4 (or em. כָּל־עָרֵי מִסְכְּנוֹת נַפְתָּלִי *all the store,* or *garrison, cities of Naphtali* or כָּל־עָרֵי מְסִבּוֹת נַפְתָּלִי *all the cities of the environs of Naphtali;* || 1 K 15_{20} כָּל־כִּנְרוֹת עַל כָּל־אֶרֶץ נַפְתָּלִי *all Chinneroth over all the land of Naphtali* [or em. עַד *unto*]).

מִסְכֵּנֻת 1 n.f. **poverty,** <PREP> בְּ of accompaniment, *with, in (a state of)* Dt 8_9 (אֶרֶץ אֲשֶׁר לֹא בְמִסְכֵּנֻת you may eat of *land that is not in a state of poverty*).

⇒ cf. מִסְכֵּן *poor.*

*[מְסַכְסְכָה] 0.0.1 n.f. **covering** (of bed)—Q מסכסכה —<SUBJ> קצר *be short* 1QIsa^a 28_{20} (MT מַסֵּכָה *covering;* || מַצָּע *couch*), כנס htp. *be entered* 1QIsa^a 28_{20}. <SYN> מַצָּע *couch.*

⇒ סכך *weave.*

[מַסֶּכֶת] 2 n.f. **web** or **warp**—מַסֶּכֶת—cloth lying horizontally on the loom, <OBJ> נסע *pull out* Jg 16_{14}. <PREP> עִם *with, into,* + ארג *weave* locks of hair Jg $16_{13.14}$ (if ins. וַתַּאֲרֹג ... עִם־הַמַּסֶּכֶת and he fell asleep *and she wove* the seven locks of his head *into the web*).*

⇒ נסך *weave.*

מְסִלָּה I 27.0.5 n.f. **road**—cstr. מְסִלַּת; sf. מְסִלָּתוֹ; pl. מְסִלּוֹת; sf. מְסִלּוֹתָם, מְסִלֹּתַי; Q [מסלותי]הם—**1.** usu. **(main) road, highway,** connecting cities or countries. **2. paved way,** within temple-palace complex in Jerusalem (1 C $26_{16.18}$ 2 C 9_{11}; at 2 C 9_{11} מְסִלָּה perh. wooden **ramp**). **3.** perh. **byway, beaten track** (Nm 20_{19} 2 S 22_{46}||Ps 18_{46} [if em.]), as distinct from דֶּרֶךְ הַמֶּלֶךְ *the king's highway*). **4. file** of individual soldiers (Jl 2_8); **course** of stars (Jg 5_{20}). **5.** perh. **gate** (2 C $9_{11.18}$).* **6. way, behaviour, conduct** (Is 59_7 Ps 84_6 [unless מְסִלָּה II] Pr 16_{17} 4QJub^{d,f} 21_{22} 4QShir^b 2.1_6).

<SUBJ> היה *be* Is 11_{16} (+ לִשְׁאָר עַמּוֹ *for the remnant of his people*) 11_{16} (+ לְיִשְׂרָאֵל *for Israel*) 19_{23} (מִמִּצְרַיִם אַשּׁוּרָה *from Egypt to Assyria*), שׁמם *be desolated,* i.e. deserted Is 33_8 (+ אֹרַח *way,* עִיר *city*), רום *be high,* i.e. be prepared, built Is 49_{11} (+ דֶּרֶךְ *way*), עלה *go up* Jg 20_{31} 21_{19} 1 C 26_{16}.

<NOM CL> מְסִלּוֹת בִּלְבָבָם appar. *(your) ways are in their heart* Ps 84_6 (unless מְסִלָּה II *praise;* or em. מְסִלֹּתֶיךָ *your ways* or מְסִלָּתְךָ *your way* or מַעֲלוֹת *ascents [to Zion]* or כִּסְלָתְךָ *your confidence*), מְסִלַּת יְשָׁרִים סוּר מֵרָע *the way of upright ones is to turn from evil* Pr 16_{17} (+ דֶּרֶךְ *way*).

<OBJ> עשׂה *make* algum wood (into) 2 C 9_{11} (unless מְסִלָּה III *gatehouse;* or em. מַעֲלוֹת *steps;* || 1 K 10_{12} מִסְעָד perh. *table* or *bench* or *support*), ישׁר pi. *make straight,* i.e. build, prepare, in the steppe Is 40_3=1QS 8_{14}=4QS^e 1.3_5 (|| דֶּרֶךְ *way;* S^e [דרך ... ישׁ]רו), סלל *raise,* i.e. build, prepare Is 62_{10}, סקל pi. *clear* road *of* rocks Is 62_{10}, שׁמר *guard* 4QShir^b 2.1_6 ([ומסל]ת; || דֶּרֶךְ *way* of God).

<CSTR> מְסִלַּת שְׂדֵה כוֹבֵס *fuller's field road* 2 K 18_{17}|| Is 36_2 Is 7_3, מְסִלַּת יְשָׁרִים *the way of upright ones* Pr

16_{17}, ומסל[ת ק]ודשו *and the way of his holiness* 4QShir[b] 2.16; כל מסלות *all roads* 2QapProph 6_2. <APP> דֶּרֶךְ *way* Jr 31_{21}. <ADJ> אֶחָד *one* 1 S 6_{12} (+ דֶּרֶךְ *way*).

<PREP> לְ of place, *at, of* Jg 21_{19} (see Coll.) 1 C 26_{18} (אַרְבָּעָה לַמְסִלָּה *four were on the road*; || פַּרְבָּר *colonnade*); שִׁית לֵב לְ *pay attention to* Jr 31_{21}.

בְּ of place, *on, along* 1 C 26_{16} (עִם שַׁעַר שַׁלֶּכֶת בַּמְסִלָּה הָעוֹלָה *with Shallecheth gate on the road that goes up*; or em. לְשִׁכַּת הַמְסִלָּה the gate of *the chamber of*, i.e. by, *the road* that goes up), + הלך *go* 1 S 6_{12} Jl 2_8 (+ אִישׁ אָחִיו לֹא יִדְחָקוּן *no one presses against their fellow*; + אֹרַח *way*), צעד *step* 4QJub[d] 21_{22} ([ת]צעד; || דרך [[בדרכיהימה]]); 4QJub[f] 21_{22} ([בדרכיהם ותצעד במסלותי]הם)), עמד *stand*, i.e. take up position 2 K 18_{17}||Is 36_2 (if del. in 2 K אֲשֶׁר stood by the channel ..., *which was* by the road), נכה hi. *strike* Benjaminites Jg 20_{31}, עלל po. *glean*, i.e. pick off, stragglers Jg 20_{45}; of instrument, *by (means of)*, or place, *on, along*, + עלה *go up* Nm 20_{19} (Sam mss בְּמִסְלַע *by/along a rocky place*; + דֶּרֶךְ הַמֶּלֶךְ *the king's way*); of accompaniment, *with, in* Is 59_7 (שֹׁד וָשֶׁבֶר בִּמְסִלּוֹתָם *destruction and wreckage are in their ways*, + דֶּרֶךְ *way*, נְתִיבָה *way*, מַעְגָּל *way*).

מִן of direction, *from*, + סבב hi. *remove* body of Amasa 2 S 20_{12} (+ הַשָּׂדֶה *into the countryside*), יגה hi. *remove* body of Amasa 2 S 20_{13} (or em. הגה ho. or סור ho. or נטה ho. *be removed*), נפל *fall (away)* 2 S 22_{46}||Ps $18_{46(mss)}$ (if em. וְיַחְגְּרוּ מִמִּסְגְּרוֹתָם/מִמִּסְגְּרוֹתֵיהֶם *and they gird themselves from their strongholds* to וְיִפְּלוּ מִמְּסִלֹּתָם *and they fall away from their roads*), לחם ni. *fight* Jg 5_{20} (מִמְּסִלּוֹתָם נִלְחֲמוּ עִם־סִיסְרָא *from their courses they* [the stars] *fought with Sisera*).

אֶל *to*, + נתק *draw off* from town Jg 20_{32}; *by, next to* Is 7_3 (+ תְּעָלָה *channel*; unless אֶל = go out [יצא] *to*), בְּתוֹךְ *in the middle of*, + גלל htpo. *roll about* in blood 2 S 20_{12}.

<COLL> אַשְׁרֵי אָדָם ... מְסִלּוֹת בִּלְבָבָם *happy are the people (for whom) ... (your) ways are in their heart* Ps 84_6 (unless מְסִלָּה II; or em.; see Nom. Cl.; mss הָעָם happy are *the people*), בַּמְסִלּוֹת אֲשֶׁר אַחַת עֹלָה בֵית־אֵל וְאַחַת גִּבְעָתָה *along the roads, one of which goes up to Bethel and one to Gibeah* Jg 20_{31}, מִזְרְחָה הַשֶּׁמֶשׁ לִמְסִלָּה הָעֹלָה מִבֵּית־אֵל שְׁכֶמָה *east of a road that goes up from Bethel to Shechem* Jg 21_{19}, מְסִלָּה לֵאלֹהֵינוּ *a road for our God* Is 40_3=1QS 8_{14}=4QS[e] 1.3_5 (Q לאלוהינו), מְסִלּוֹת לְבֵית־י׳ וּלְבֵית הַמֶּלֶךְ perh. *ramps for the temple of Y. and for the palace of the king* 2 C 9_{11} (or em. מַעֲלוֹת *steps*; || 1 K 10_{12} מִסְעָד [sg.] perh. *table* or *bench* or *bannister*).

<SYN> דֶּרֶךְ *way*, פַּרְבָּר *colonnade*.

⇒ סלל *raise*.

*[מְסִלָּה] II 1 n.f. **high praise**—pl. מְסִלּוֹת—<NOM CL> מְסִלּוֹת בִּלְבָבָם *high praises are in their heart* Ps 84_6 (unless מְסִלָּה I; or em. מְסִלֹּתֶךָ *your high praises* or מַעֲלוֹת *ascents [to Zion]* or כִּסְלָתֶךָ *your confidence*).

⇒ סלל *raise*.

*[מְסִלָּה] III 3 n.f. **gatehouse, gateway**—pl. מְסִלּוֹת—all unless מְסִלָּה I *paved way*, <OBJ> עשׂה *make* algum wood (into) 2 C 9_{11} (or em. מַעֲלוֹת *steps*; || 1 K 10_{12} מִסְעָד perh. *table* or *bench* or *support*). <PREP> לְ of place, *at, of* 1 C 26_{18} (אַרְבָּעָה לַמְסִלָּה *four were on the gateway*; || פַּרְבָּר *colonnade*); בְּ of place, *on, along* 1 C 26_{16} (עִם שַׁעַר שַׁלֶּכֶת בַּמְסִלָּה הָעוֹלָה *with Shallecheth gate on the gateway that goes up*; or em. לְשִׁכַּת הַמְסִלָּה the gate of *the chamber of*, i.e. by, *the gateway* that goes up).

מַסְלוּל 1 n.m. **road** between cities, <SUBJ> היה *be* Is 35_8 (1QIsa[a] מְסוֹלָל *road*; + שָׁם *there*). <OBJ> עבר *pass*, i.e. travel by Is 35_8. <PREP> לְ of direction, *to*, + קרא ni. *be called* Is 35_8 (וְדֶרֶךְ הַקֹּדֶשׁ יִקָּרֵא לָהּ *and it* [fem.] *will be called the way of holiness*; or em. לוֹ *it* [masc.]). <COLL> מַסְלוּל וָדֶרֶךְ perh. *a road (for vehicles) and a way (for pedestrians)* Is 35_8 (mss lack וָדֶרֶךְ; or em. וְדֶרֶךְ to טָהוֹר *pure* road or בָּרוּר *purified* road).

⇒ סלל *raise*.

*[מִסְלָע] 1 n.[m.] **rocky place**—Sam מססע—<PREP> בְּ of instrument, *by (means of)*, or place, *on, along*, + עלה *go up* Nm $20_{19(Sam\ mss)}$ (L מְסִלָּה *[main] road*).

⇒ cf. סֶלַע *cliff*.

*[מַסְמָא] 0.0.1 n.f. **sealing stone**—Q מסמא—<NOM CL> תחת המסמא הגדולא שבשילוחו *under the great seal-*

ing stone that is by its water outlet 3QTr 11₆ (others שבשוליחי *that is at its skirts*, i.e. bottom). <ADJ> גָּדוֹל *great* 3QTr 11₆. <PREP> תַּחַת *under* 3QTr 11₆.

[מַסְמֵר] 5.0.1 n.m. **nail**—Q מסמר; pl. מַסְמְרִים, מַסְמְרִים, מַסְמְרוֹת, (מַשְׂמְרוֹת) מַסְמְרוֹת—**1. nail,** of iron (1 C 22₃), of gold (2 C 3₉), used with both wood and metal, in making idols (Is 41₇ Jr 10₄), in construction of temple (1 C 22₃ 2 C 3₉) or of domestic dwelling (CD 12₁₇), in goads for animals (Ec 12₁₁ unless §2). **2.** perh. **sceptre,*** (Ec 12₁₁ unless §1).

<SUBJ> היה *be* CD 12₁₇ (+ עם המת בבתת which is *with the dead person in the house*, || כְּלִי *tool*, יָתֵד *peg*), טמא *be impure* CD 12₁₇, נטע pass. *be embedded* Ec 12₁₁.

<CSTR> כל כלי מסמר או יתד *any tool, nail, or peg* CD 12₁₇.

<PREP> לְ of possession, *of, (belonging) to* 2 C 3₉ (וּמִשְׁקָל לְמִסְמְרוֹת *and the weight of nails* was 50 gold shekels; or del.; or em. לַמִּסְמְרוֹת *of the nails*); of purpose, *(to be used) for* 1 C 22₃ (בַּרְזֶל לָרֹב לַמִּסְמְרִים *iron in abundance for nails*; || מְחַבְּרֹת *join*); בְּ of instrument, *by (means of), with*, + חזק pi. *strengthen*, i.e. fasten, joint Is 41₇, silver and gold Jr 10₄ (|| מַקֶּבֶת *hammer*); כְּ *as* Ec 12₁₁ (דִּבְרֵי חֲכָמִים ... כְּמַשְׂמְרוֹת *words of sages are ... like nails; or sceptres*, || דָּרְבָן *goad*).

<COLL> מסמר ... בכותל *nail ... in the wall* CD 12₁₇, מִסְמְרִים לְדַלְתוֹת הַשְּׁעָרִים *nails for the doors of the gateways* 1 C 22₃, וּכְמַסְמְרוֹת נְטוּעִים בַּעֲלֵי אֲסֻפּוֹת *and like nails embedded* or *sceptres set up (by) leaders of assemblies* or *experts in collected sayings* Ec 12₁₁ (or em. מִבַּעֲלֵי *by leaders of*).*

<SYN> מַקֶּבֶת *hammer*, מְחַבֶּרֶת *join*, יָתֵד *peg*, כְּלִי *tool*.

⇨ (?) סמר *bristle*.

מסס 23.1.15.1 vb. **melt**—**Qal** 3.0.1 Inf. מְסֹס (מְשׂוֹשׂ), Q מוס —**fade away, pine,** perh. **collapse** (Is 10₁₈),* <SUBJ> לֵב *heart* 1QH 2₂₈ (במוס לבי *in the melting of my heart*, i.e. in my terror; + ותחזק נפשי בריתך *then my soul took strength*, or *you strengthened my soul, in your covenant*), לֵבָב *heart* 4QHod[f] 3₅ (למ[ו]ס לבבי; *for the melting of my heart*; ||1QH 2₆ למים *to melt* [hi.] or *to be melted* [ni.]), דֶּרֶךְ *way* Jb 8₁₉ (הֶן־הוּא מְשׂוֹשׂ דַּרְכּוֹ *behold, this is the fading away of his life*, unless מְשׂוֹשׂ דַּרְכּוֹ = *the joy of his life*, i.e. מָשׂוֹשׂ *joy*). <PREP> כְּ *as*, + מַיִם *water* 1QH 2₂₈. <COLL> וּכְבוֹד יַעְרוֹ וְכַרְמִלּוֹ ... יְכַלֶּה וְהָיָה כִּמְסֹס נֹסֵס *and the glory of its forest and its vineyard he will destroy, so that it will be like the fading away of one who is ill* Is 10₁₈ (or em. יְכֻלֶּה *will be destroyed*), מֵי הַשִּׁלֹחַ הַהֹלְכִים לְאַט וּמְשׂוֹשׂ *the waters of Siloam that flow slowly and fading away*, i.e. gently Is 8₆ (unless מְשׂוֹשׂ cstr. of מָשׂוֹשׂ *joy*).

Ni. 20.1.14.1 Pf. נָמַס, נָמַסּוּ; impf. יִמַּס (יִמֶּס) + waw וַיִּמַּס, וַיִּמַּסּוּ, וַיִּמַּס; (וימסן I) וַיִּמַּסּוּ; ptc. נָמֵס; inf. הִמֵּס—**1.** intrans., **melt, evaporate, dissolve, ooze** (Jb 7₅ [if em.]), **disappear**; in conjunction with heart sometimes as idiom, **be discouraged, be frightened, lose heart.**

<SUBJ> לֵב *heart* 2 S 17₁₀ (וְהוּא גַם־בֶּן־חַיִל אֲשֶׁר לִבּוֹ כְּלֵב הָאַרְיֵה הִמֵּס יִמָּס *and even if he be a valiant person, whose heart is like the heart of a lion, it will indeed be melted*, i.e. he will be discouraged) Ezk 21₁₂ (|| רפה *be weak*, of hands, כהה pi. *be weak*, of spirit [or em. Qal, *be weak*], הלך *run* with water, of knees) Na 2₁₁ (+ וּפִק בִּרְכַּיִם וְחַלְחָלָה בְּכָל־מָתְנַיִם *and shaking of knees and trembling in all loins*) Ps 22₁₅ (+ כַּדּוֹנָג my heart was *like wax*; + שפך ni. *be poured*, פרר htp. *be loosened*, of bones) 1QM 8₁₀ (unless להמס hi. *to melt* enemy's heart) 11₉ 14₆=4QM[a] 8.1₃ ([לב [נמ]ס]) 4QM[a] 11.2₁₅ 4QpIsa[a] 8₄ (לב[ם]) and *their heart* will melt; + חתת ni. *be terrified*, of warriors).

לֵבָב *heart* Dt 20₈=11QT 62₄ (וְלֹא יִמַּס אֶת־לְבַב אֶחָיו *that his brothers be not discouraged*; Sam יַמֵּס [hi.] that *he might* not *discourage* his brothers) Jos 2₁₁ (+ וְלֹא־קָמָה עוֹד רוּחַ בְּאִישׁ מִפְּנֵיכֶם *and no one had any spirit left to face you*) 5₁ (+ וְלֹא־הָיָה בָם עוֹד רוּחַ מִפְּנֵי בְּנֵי־יִשְׂרָאֵל *and they had no spirit left to face the Israelites*) 7₅ (+ וַיְהִי לְמָיִם *and it* [heart] *turned to water*) Is 13₇ (|| רפה *be weak*, of hands) 19₁ (+ וְנָעוּ אֱלִילֵי מִצְרַיִם מִפָּנָיו *and the idols of Egypt will shake before him*) 1QH 2₂₆ (unless למיס hi. *to melt* my heart; + אמץ pi. *strengthen*) 4₃₃ (+ רעע *be broken*, of bones, הלך *run* with water, of knees) fr. 4₁₄ 1QM 1₁₄ (unless להמס hi. *to melt* a heart; + אמץ pi.).

קֶרֶב *inward parts* 4QDiscourse 2.2₇ (קרבי[ה]ם *their innards*; || נוע htpol. *palpitate*, of heart), בָּשָׂר *flesh*

1QH 8_{32} (|| נגר ni. *be poured [out]*, of heart, + שׁבר ni. *be broken*, of arm, + הלך *run* like water, of knees), עוֹר *skin* Jb 7_5 (if em. מאס ni. I *be rejected* or II *melt*), מָן *manna* Ex 16_{21} (+ חמם *be hot* [of sun]), אֵסוּר *fetter* Jg 15_{14} (+ כַּפִּשְׁתִּים אֲשֶׁר בָּעֲרוּ בָאֵשׁ the ropes on his arms were *like flax that burns in fire* and his fetters melted from his hands), הַר *mountain* Is 34_3 Mc 1_4 (+ בקע htp. *be split open*) Ps 97_5 (+ אֵשׁ לְפָנָיו תֵּלֵךְ וּתְלַהֵט סָבִיב צָרָיו *fire goes before him and burns around his enemies*) Quntillet ʿAjrud add. inscr. 3_1 (ובזרח אל וימסן הרם *and when God shines the mountains dissolve*).

דּוֹנַג *wax* Ps 22_{15} (|| נדף ni. *be dispersed*, of smoke) 4QHod^{a} 6_3 (ד[ונג]), קֶרַח *ice* Si $3_{15(C)}$ (וכחורב על קרח נמס חטאתיך appar. *and your sins will be like heat over melted ice*; A כחם על כפור להשבית עוניך righteousness towards a father will be *like heat over frost, destroying your iniquities*), רָשָׁע *wicked one* Ps 58_8 (if em. מאס ni. I *be rejected* or II *melt*) 112_{10} (+ כעס *be angry*, חרק *grind* teeth, אבד *disappear*, of desire), אֹיֵב *enemy* 1QM 9_{11} (unless ל[ה]מיס hi. *to melt*, i.e. discourage, enemy).

<PREP> כְּ *as*, + דּוֹנַג *wax* Mc 1_4 Ps 97_5 1QH 4_{33} 8_{32} fr. 4_{14}, מַיִם *water* Mc 1_4 Ps 58_8 (if em. מאס ni. I *be rejected* or II *melt*); מִן of instrument, *by (means of), with, in*, + דָּם *blood* of corpses Is 34_3; מֵעַל *(away) from*, + יָד *hand* Jg 15_{14}; עַל *on account of*, + פֶּשַׁע *sin* 1QH fr. 4_{14}, חֲטָאָה *sin* 1QH fr. 4_{14}, בְּקֶרֶב *within* Egypt Is 19_1 (unless יִמַּס תַּחַת בְּקִרְבּוֹ = the heart of Egypt *will melt in his body*); תַּחַת *below* Y. Mc 1_4; לִפְנֵי *in the presence of*, + אֵשׁ *fire* 4QHod^{a} 6_3; מִפְּנֵי *in the presence of*, + אֵשׁ *fire* Ps 68_3 (+ יֹאבְדוּ רְשָׁעִים מִפְּנֵי אֱלֹהִים *[so] the wicked vanish in the presence of God*); מִלִּפְנֵי *so as not be in the presence of* Y. Ps 97_5 (or del. מִלִּפְנֵי י׳), אָדוֹן *lord* of all the earth Ps 97_5.

<COLL> הִמֵּס יִמָּס *it will indeed be melted* 2 S 17_{10}.

2. appar. **be worthless**, <SUBJ> מְלָאכָה *goods* captured in battle 1 S 15_9 (וְכָל־הַמְּלָאכָה ... נָמֵס *and all the useless ... goods* ; or del. נָמֵס or em. נִמְאָס or נִמְאֶסֶת *rejected*).

Also 3Q8 2_2.

<SYN> §1 רפה *be weak*, כהה pi. *be weak*, הלך *run* with water, נדף ni. *be dispersed*, נוע htpol. *palpitate*, נגר ni. *be poured*.

Hi. 2.0.4 Pf. הֵמַסּוּ—**melt** heart, i.e. **discourage, frighten**, <SUBJ> אִישׁ *man* fearful of battle Dt $20_{8(Sam)}$, אָח *brother* Israelites, who had spied out land Dt 1_{28}. <OBJ> לֵבָב *heart* Dt 1_{28} $20_{8(Sam)}$ 1QH 2_{26} (unless למיס ni. for my heart *to be melted*; + אמץ pi. *strengthen*) 1QM 1_{14} (unless להמס ni. for a heart *to be melted*; + אמץ pi.) 1QM 8_{10} (unless להמס ni. for enemy's heart *to be melted*), אֹיֵב *enemy* 1QM 9_{11} (unless ל[ה]מיס ni. for enemy *to be melted*, i.e. frightened; AHL לר[מוס] *to trample* enemy).

Also 4QDibHam^{c} 14_3 ([]מס) 4QShir^{b} 161_1 ([]ימס).*

⇒ מַס *melting*, מֶס *melting*, מַסָּה III *despair*, תֶּמֶס *melting*; cf. מסה *melt*.

מַסָּע I 1 n.[m.] **quarry**, <APP> אֶבֶן־שְׁלֵמָה מַסָּע *whole stone(s), (of) a quarry*, i.e. perh. undressed 1 K 6_7.*

⇒ נסע I *pull out*.

מַסָּע II 1 n.[m.] **missile, dart** or **arrow**, or other **weapon**, <SUBJ> נשׂג hi. *overtake*, i.e. pierce, Behemoth Jb 40_{18} (unless נסע inf. *journeying**; || חֶרֶב *sword*, חֲנִית *spear*, שִׁרְיָה *javelin*), קום *stand*, i.e. have effect Jb 40_{18}. <SYN> חֶרֶב *sword*, חֲנִית *spear*, שִׁרְיָה *javelin*.*

מַסַּע I 12.0.4 n.[m.] **journey**—pl. cstr. מַסְעֵי; sf. מַסָּעָיו, מַסְעֵיהֶם—**journey, travel, stage of journey, start of journey**, <NOM CL> אֵלֶּה מַסְעֵיהֶם לְמוֹצָאֵיהֶם *these are their travels, (listed) by their points of departure* Nm 33_2, אֵלֶּה מַסְעֵי בְנֵי־יִשְׂרָאֵל *these are the travels of the Israelites* Nm 10_{28} (or em. צִבְאוֹת *armies of*) 33_1. <OBJ> perh. יצא *go out (on)* Nm 33_1 (מַסְעֵי בְנֵי־יִשְׂרָאֵל אֲשֶׁר יָצְאוּ *the journeys of the Israelites that they went on*; unless אֲשֶׁר = *when* they went out from Egypt). <CSTR> מַסְעֵי בְנֵי־יִשְׂרָאֵל *the journeys of the Israelites* Nm 10_{28} (or em.) 33_1; חצוצרות מסעיהם *the trumpets of*, i.e. sounded for, *their journeys* 1QM 3_5 (unless מַסָּע II; + חצוצרות המחנות *the trumpets of the camps*), כֹּל מַסְעֵיהֶם *all their travels* Ex $40_{36.38}$ (כָּל־).

<PREP> לְ of benefit, *for* Nm 10_2 (וְהָיוּ לְךָ לְמִקְרָא הָעֵדָה וּלְמַסַּע אֶת־הַמַּחֲנוֹת *and they will be for you for convocation of the assembly and for the journey of the camp*; unless מַסָּע II; + וְנָסְעוּ הַמַּחֲנוֹת *and they are to*

break camp); *on* travels, *at* start of journey, or *by* stages, + הלך *go* Gen 13_{3} (of Abram; + from Negeb to Bethel) Dt 10_{11}=4QapJoshuaᵃ 3.2_{12}(WA) (of Moses; + לִפְנֵי הָעָם *at the head of the people*; WA [לך] למסע [לפני העם]), נסע *set out* Ex 17_{1} Nm 10_{12} (both of Israelites, from steppe of Sin), תקע *sound* alarm Nm 10_{2}; of possession, *of, (belonging) to* Nm 33_{2} (מוֹצָאֵיהֶם לְמַסְעֵיהֶם *the[ir] points of departure of their journeys*); בְּ *on* travels, journeys Ex 40_{38}, + נסע *set out* Ex 40_{36} (of Israelites), פקד hi. appar. *suffer* 4Dᵃ 11_{19}=4QDᵉ 7.2_{14} (Dᵃ יפ[ק]ידו ... ומסעיהם; Dᵉ [יפ]קידו ... ומס[עיהם]; WA קצי החרון + [יע]מודו/[יעמ]ודו *will stand*, i.e. stay in force; + קצי החרון *the times of anger*); כְּ *in accordance with* 1QSa 2_{15} (לפי כבודו כמ[עמדו] במחניהם וכמסעיהם *according to the honour due him, in accordance with his position in their camps and in accordance with their journeys*; unless מַסַּע II).*

⇒ נסע II *travel*.

*מַסַּע II 1.0.2 n.[m.] **breaking** of camp—sf. Q מסעיהם—**breaking,** or **setting out from,** camp (all unless מַסַּע I), <CSTR> חצוצרות מסעיהם *the trumpets of*, i.e. sounded for, *setting out from them* 1QM 3_{5} (+ חצוצרות המחנות *the trumpets of the camps*). <PREP> לְ of benefit, *for* Nm 10_{2} (וְהָיוּ לְךָ לְמִקְרָא הָעֵדָה וּלְמַסַּע אֶת־הַמַּחֲנוֹת *and they will be for you for convocation of the assembly and for breaking [the] camp[s]*; + וְנָסְעוּ הַמַּחֲנוֹת *and they are to break camp*); כְּ *in accordance with* 1QSa 2_{15} (לפי כבודו כמ[עמדו] במחניהם וכמסעיהם *according to the honour due him, in accordance with his position in their camps and in accordance with their breaking camp*).

⇒ נסע I *pull up, out*.

מִסְעָד I 1 n.[m.] **table, bench, bannister,** or **support** (perh. collective; unless מִסְעָד II), <OBJ> עשׂה *make* almug wood (into) 1 K 10_{12} (|| 2 C 9_{11} מְסִלּוֹת perh. *ramps*; + לְבֵית־י׳ וּלְבֵית הַמֶּלֶךְ *for the temple of Y. and for the palace of the king*).

⇒ סעד *support*.

*מִסְעָד II 1 n.[m.] **step, ramp** (unless מִסְעָד I), <OBJ> עשׂה *make* almug wood (into) 1 K 10_{12} (|| 2 C 9_{11} מְסִלּוֹת perh. *ramps*; + לְבֵית־י׳ וּלְבֵית הַמֶּלֶךְ *for the temple of Y. and for the palace of the king*).

⇒ סעד *support*.

*[מִסְעָר] 0.1 n.f. **storm**—Si מסער—<PREP> בְּ of place, *in*, + מוט htpol. *be tossed about* Si 36_{2}(Bmg) (E ומתמוטט כמסערה אזנו *or one whose ear is tossed about as though from a storm*, i.e. סְעָרָה *storm*).

⇒ סער *storm*.

מִסְפֵּד 16.1.3 n.m. **mourning**—cstr. מִסְפַּד; sf. מִסְפְּדִי—**mourning, wailing, 1. mourning, funeral rites,** for dead (Gn 50_{10} Jr 6_{26} Zc $12_{10.11}$). **2. wailing,** after calamity (Jr 48_{38} Ezk 27_{31} Am $5_{16.16.17}$ Mc $1_{8.11}$ [or em.] Ps 30_{12}), before calamity (Est 4_{2}). **3. wailing,** in contrition (Is 22_{12} Jl 2_{12}). **4. place of mourning** (Mc 1_{11} [if em.]). <SUBJ> גדל *be great* Zc 12_{11} (+ ספד *mourn*), אתה *come* Jb 16_{22} (if em.; see Cstr.), לקח *take* Mc 1_{11} (or em.; see Nom. Cl.; or del. מִסְפַּד בֵּית הָאֵצֶל יִקַּח מִכֶּם עֶמְדָּתוֹ *the mourning of Beth-ezel will take from you its standing place* ; or em. מִסְפֵּד Beth-ezel *is [in] mourning*, or עֲשֶׂה מִסְפֵּד *perform mourning*, O Beth-ezel, or מוּסַד *the establishing of*, or מִיסוֹדוֹ *from its foundation*,* and/or יֻקַּח מִמְּכוֹן עֶמְדָּתוֹ *[it] will be taken from the place of its standing* or יִקְחוּ מִמֵּךְ עֶמְדָּתֵךְ *they will take from you your standing place*).

<NOM CL> כֻּלֹּה מִסְפֵּד *all of it*, or *everywhere*, *is (in) mourning* Jr 48_{38} (or del.), בְּכָל־רְחֹבוֹת מִסְפֵּד *in all streets let there be mourning* Am 5_{16} (+ אמר הוֹ־הוֹ *say, Woe, woe*), וּבְכָל־כְּרָמִים מִסְפֵּד *and in all vineyards let there be mourning* Am 5_{17}, בְּכָל־מְדִינָה ... מִסְפֵּד *in every province ... there was mourning* Est 4_{3} (|| אֵבֶל *mourning*, בְּכִי *weeping*, צוֹם *fasting*, + שַׂק *sackcloth*, אֵפֶר *ash*), מִסְפֵּד בֵּית הָאֵצֶל *Beth-ezel is a place of mourning* (if em. cstr. מִסְפַּד).*

<OBJ> ספד *mourn* Gn 50_{10} (+ אֵבֶל *mourning*), עשׂה *do* Jr 6_{26} (אֵבֶל, + חגר *gird* with sackcloth, פלשׁ htp. *roll* around in ashes) Mc 1_{8} (|| אֵבֶל, + ספד *mourn*, ילל hi. *wail*, הלך *go* barefoot and naked) 1_{11} (if em. מִסְפַּד *mourning of* to עשׂה מִסְפֵּד *perform mourning*), הפך *turn* into dancing Ps 30_{12} (+ שַׂק undo *sackcloth*), תמם

hi. *perfect* Si 38_{17}(B), הום *do noisily* Si 38_{17}(Bmg) (|| אֵבֶל, בְּכִי *weeping*).

<CSTR> מִסְפַּד הֲדַד־רִמּוֹן *the mourning of Hadadrimmon* Zc 12_{11}, מִסְפַּד תַּמְרוּרִים *mourning of bitterness(es)*, i.e. bitter mourning Jr 6_{26}, כול יגו[ן] ומספד מרורים *every (kind of) lamentation of sorrow and mourning of bitterness(es)* 1QH 11_{22}(mg); שְׁנוֹת מִסְפֵּד *years of mourning* Jb 16_{22} (if em. שְׁנוֹת מִסְפָּר *years of a number*, i.e. a few, or a certain number of, years).

<APP> בְּמַר־נֶפֶשׁ מִסְפֵּד מָר *with bitterness of soul, a bitter mourning* Ezk 27_{31} (or del. מִסְפֵּד מָר). <ADJ> גָּדוֹל *great* Gn 50_{10}, כָּבֵד *profound* Gn 50_{10}, מַר *bitter* Ezk 27_{31} (or del.).

<PREP> לְ of possession, *of, (belonging) to* 1QH 11_{22}(mg) (+ קִינָה *lament* of every kind of mourning); of purpose, *for (the purpose of)* perh. 4QpsEzek[c] 5_3 (|| בְּכִי *weeping*), + קרא *call* day Is 22_{12} (|| בְּכִי, + קָרְחָה *baldness*, חֲגֹר *girding* with sackcloth); בְּ of accompaniment, *with, in (a state of)*, + בכה *weep* Ezk 27_{31} (or del. מִסְפֵּד מָר *bitter mourning*; + קרח hi. *make bald*, חגר *gird* with sackcloth), שׁוב *go back* to Y. (|| בְּכִי *weeping*, צוֹם *fasting*, + קרע *tear* clothes); כְּ *as*, + ספד *mourn* Zc 12_{10} (+ מרר hi. *display bitterness*), גדל *be great* Zc 12_{11}; אֶל *to*, + קרא *call* Am 5_{16} (וְקָרְאוּ אִכָּר אֶל־אֵבֶל וּמִסְפֵּד אֶל־יוֹדְעֵי נֶהִי appar. *and they will call a farmworker to lamentation and mourning alongside the experts in dirge*, or em. וְאֶל־מִסְפֵּד יוֹדְעֵי נֶהִי *and to mourning the experts in dirge*).

<COLL> אֶעֱשֶׂה מִסְפֵּד כַּתַּנִּים *I shall make mourning like the jackals* (appar. in ref. to wailing noise) Mc 1_8, כְּמִסְפֵּד עַל־הַיָּחִיד *like mourning over an only child* Zc 12_{10}.

Also 4QBéat 8_1.

<SYN> אֵבֶל *mourning*, בְּכִי *weeping*, צוֹם *fasting*.*

⇒ ספד *mourn*.

מִסְפּוֹא 5.1 n.m. **fodder**, for camels (Gn $24_{25.32}$), for donkeys (Gn 42_{27} 43_{24} Jg 19_{19} Si 33_{25}), <NOM CL> מִסְפּוֹא רַב עִמָּנוּ *there is fodder with us* Gn 24_{25} (|| תֶּבֶן *straw*, + מָקוֹם *place* for humans to spend night), מִסְפּוֹא יֵשׁ *there is fodder* for donkeys (|| תֶּבֶן *straw*, + לֶחֶם *bread*, יַיִן *wine* for humans), לחמור ... מספוא *fodder ... is for a donkey* Si 30_{33} (|| שׁוֹט *whip*, מַשָּׂא *burden*, + מַרְדּוּת מְלָאכָה appar. *rebelliousness of work*, i.e. work grudgingly done, by slave). <OBJ> נתן *give* to camels Gn 24_{32} (|| תֶּבֶן *straw*, + מַיִם washing *water* for humans), to donkey Gn 42_{27} (+ וַיִּפְתַּח ... אֶת־שַׂקּוֹ *and he opened ... his sack* to give) 43_{24} (+ מַיִם washing *water* for humans). <ADJ> רַב *much* Gn 24_{25}. <SYN> תֶּבֶן *straw*, שׁוֹט *whip*, מַשָּׂא *burden*.

[מִסְפָּחָה] 2 n.f. **veil** or **headcovering, shawl**—pl. מִסְפָּחוֹת; sf. מִסְפְּחֹתֵיכֶם—<OBJ> עשׂה *make* Ezk 13_{18} (+ עַל־רֹאשׁ כָּל־קוֹמָה *over the head of every height*, i.e. person of any age; + כֶּסֶת perh. *band*), קרע *tear (off)* Ezk 13_{21} (+ כֶּסֶת).*

מִסְפַּחַת 3 n.f. **scab**, perh. **rash**, <SUBJ> פשׂה *spread* on skin Lv $13_{7.8}$. <NOM CL> מִסְפַּחַת הִיא *it is (only) a scab* Lv 13_6.*

⇒ סַפַּחַת *rash*, שׂפח *cause a rash*.

מִסְפָּר I 133.11.20 n.m. **number**—cstr. מִסְפַּר; sf. מִסְפַּרְכֶם, מִסְפָּרָם; pl. cstr. מִסְפְּרֵי—**1.** usu. **number, total (number)**, or, with non-countable noun, **quantity, amount**; specif. **a certain** (agreed, conventional, etc.) **number** (Dt 25_2 2 S 2_{15}); **report of number** (Est 9_{11}), **final number, limit** (Si 39_{20}); perh. also **statement** or (alphabetic) **order** of names, etc. (e.g. Nm 3_{43} 26_{53} Is 40_{26} Ps 147_4 [both + קרא שֵׁם *call out name*] 1 C $9_{28.28}$ 23_{24}).

<SUBJ> היה *be* Nm 9_{20} (+ עָנָן *cloud*; or em. יָמִים מִסְפָּר *days, a number*, i.e. a few days to יְמֵי מִסְפָּר *days of a number* or יָמִים בְּמִסְפָּר *days in number*) Dt 33_6 (or em. וִיהִי מְתָיו מִסְפָּר appar. *but let his people be a number*, i.e. few, to וְיִהְיוּ *even though* his people be few, or וִיהִי תָמִים מִסְפָּרוֹ *and may his number be perfect*, or em. מִסְפָּר to מִסְפֵּר or מִסְפֵּר *without number* [סֵפֶר II *number*]) Jg 7_6 (+ יֶתֶר *remainder*) 1 S 27_7 2 S 2_{11} Is 10_{19} (+ וּשְׁאָר עֵץ יַעְרוֹ *and the remainder of the trees of its forest* will be a number, i.e. little) Jr 2_{28} 11_{13} (both + אֱלֹהֶיךָ *your gods* will be, i.e. total, the number of your towns) Ho 2_1 (+ כְּחוֹל הַיָּם *like the sand of the sea*; + מדד ni. *be measured*, ספר ni. *be counted*) 1 C 23_3 (+

שִׁשָּׁה + שְׁלֹשִׁים וּשְׁמוֹנָה אֶלֶף *thirty-eight thousand*) 25_1 (+ *six* 25_3) 25_7 (+ מָאתַיִם שְׁמוֹנִים וּשְׁמוֹנָה *two hundred and eighty-eight*) 2 C 29_{32} (+ בָּקָר שִׁבְעִים אֵילִים מֵאָה כְּבָשִׂים מָאתָיִם *seventy cattle, a hundred rams, two hundred lambs*) perh. 4QapJoseph[b] 9_2 (ו[י]בלים מספרם היה perh. *jubilees; their number was*).

שׁאר *remain* Is 21_{17} (if em. וּשְׁאָר מִסְפַּר־ *and the remainder of the number of* the bows to וְשָׁאַר *and* a number of bows *will remain*), צפן ni. *be stored* Jb 15_{20} (or em.; see Coll.), חצץ pu. *be cut off* Jb 21_{21}, כלה *be complete* Si 30_{32} (if em. בעת מספר מצער ימיך *at time of number [when] your days are few* to בעת כלות מספר ימיך *at the time of the completion of the number of your days*).

בוא *come* Est 9_{11} (unless מִסְפָּר II), אתה *come* Jb 16_{22} (or em.; see Cstr.), עלה *go up*, i.e. be registered 1 C 27_{24}, נפל *fall* Nm 14_{29} (if em. לְ your mustered ones will fall *in accordance with* all your number, to וְ your mustered ones *and* all your number will fall).

<NOM CL> (with אַיִן *no, without*, distinction from adverbial usage [see Coll.] sometimes unclear) כִּי־אֵין מִסְפָּר he ceased counting, *for there was no number*, i.e. it was too numerous to be counted Gn 41_{49} (+ הַרְבֵּה *very much*, ספר מְאֹד *count*), שָׁם רֶמֶשׂ וְאֵין מִסְפָּר *moving things are there and there is no number (to them)*, i.e. they cannot be counted Ps 104_{25} (11QPs[a] שם רמש הרבה ואין למספר *moving things are there in plenty and it is not for numbering*, i.e. they cannot be counted), יֶלֶק וְאֵין מִסְפָּר *locusts and there was no number*, i.e. that were too numerous to be counted) Ps 105_{34} (mss יֶלֶק אֵין מִסְפָּר *locusts without number*), וּלְפָנָיו אֵין מִסְפָּר *and before him there is no number*, i.e. his predecessors are too many to be counted Jb 21_{33}, וַעֲלָמוֹת אֵין מִסְפָּר *and girls were no number*, i.e. were too numerous to be counted Ca 6_8.

וְאֵין לָהֶם מִסְפָּר *and there is no number to them*, i.e. they are too numerous to be counted Jr 46_{23}, וְלָהֶם וְלִגְמַלֵּיהֶם אֵין מִסְפָּר *and to them and to their camels there was no number*, i.e. they were too numerous to be counted Jg 6_5 (+ רֹב *abundance*), sim. 7_{12} (+ רֹב), לִתְבוּנָתוֹ אֵין מִסְפָּר *to his understanding there is no number*, i.e. it is too vast to be measured Ps 147_5 (or em. אֵין מְסַפֵּר to אֵין מִסְפָּר *there is no one to recount*),* ולרחמיכה] אין מספר *and to your mercies there is no number*, i.e. limit 1QH 1_5 (+ רַב *great*, גָּדוֹל *great*), וְאֵין מִסְפָּר לָעָם *and there was no number*, i.e. end, *to the people* 2 C 12_3, ואין מספר לעדיכם *and there is no end to your witnesses*, perh. those who testify against you 4QapPs[b] 76_{11}, לַזָּהָב לַכֶּסֶף וְלַנְּחֹשֶׁת וְלַבַּרְזֶל אֵין מִסְפָּר *of gold, of silver, and of bronze and of iron there was no number*, i.e. it was too plentiful to be measured 1 C 22_{16} (or move to 22_{15}, with לְ of possession, and אֵין מִסְפָּר adverbial, *without number*; cf. Coll.).

[על כן לאן] מספר לתשועתו *therefore, there is no limit to his salvation* Si 39_{20} (Segal [ה]יש *is there* a limit?), הֲיֵשׁ מִסְפָּר לִגְדוּדָיו *is there a number to his troops*, i.e. are they few enough to be counted? Jb 25_3, גויתהן מספר יש [לי]מים *(as for) their body, there is a number to the days*, i.e. it has a finite life Si $37_{25 (Dmg)}$, [מס]פר שמות כול צבאם אתכה ... ומ[ספר הקדוש]ים *the number of the names of all their host is with you and the number of the holy ones* 1QM 12_2,

וּמִסְפַּר יָמֶיךָ רַבִּים *and the number of your years is many* Jb 38_{21} (or em. מִסְפָּר to מְסַפֵּר or מִסֵּפֶר *without number* [סֵפֶר II *number*]), ומספר ימיו כפלים *and the number of his days is double* Si 26_1, מִסְפַּר הַצֹּאן שְׁלֹשׁ־מֵאוֹת אֶלֶף *the number of the sheep was three hundred thousand* Nm 31_{36} (Sam צֹאן *sheep*), מִסְפָּרָם ... עֶשְׂרִים־וּשְׁנַיִם אֶלֶף *their number ... was twenty-two thousand* 1 C 7_2, מִסְפָּרָם אֲנָשִׁים עֶשְׂרִים וְשִׁשָּׁה אָלֶף *their number was twenty-six thousand men* 1 C 7_{40}, כֹּל מִסְפַּר רָאשֵׁי הָאָבוֹת ... אַלְפַּיִם וְשֵׁשׁ מֵאוֹת *the total number of the ancestral heads ... was two thousand six hundred* 2 C 26_{12}.

עֶשְׂרִים וְאַרְבַּע מִסְפָּר *twenty-four was (the total) number* 2 S 21_{20} (unless app., *twenty-four [in] number*), מִסְפַּר־חֳדָשָׁיו אִתָּךְ *the number of his months is with you* Jb 14_5.

וְאֵלֶּה מִסְפָּרָם *and these are their number(s)* Ezr 1_9, וְאֵלֶּה מִסְפַּר הַגִּבֹּרִים *and these are the number(s) of the warriors* 1 C 11_{11} (‖2 S 23_8 אֵלֶּה שְׁמוֹת *these are the names of* the warriors; or em. מִסֵּפֶר these are *from the book of* the warriors), וְאֵלֶּה מִסְפְּרֵי רָאשֵׁי הֶחָלוּץ *and these are the numbers of the heads of the armed* 1 C

12_{24} (or em. שֵׁמוֹת these are *the names of*).

חיי אנוש ימים מספר *the life of a person is (but) days, a number,* i.e. a few days Si $37_{25(D)}$ (B חיי איש מספר ימים *the life of a person is [but] a number of days*), טוב חי מספר ימים *the good of a person is,* i.e. lasts, *(but) a number of days* Si $41_{13(Bmg)}$ (M [ט]ובת *the good of;* B טובט חי ימי מספר *the good of a person is days of a number,* i.e. lasts but a few days).

מָה הָאָשָׁם ... מִסְפַּר סַרְנֵי פְלִשְׁתִּים *what is the guilt offering ...? The number of the governors of (the) Philistines* 1 S 6_4, וְעַכְבְּרֵי הַזָּהָב מִסְפַּר כָּל־עָרֵי פְלִשְׁתִּים perh. *and the mice of gold were,* i.e. totalled, *the number of all the cities of (the) Philistines* 1 S 6_{18}, ועו[ד] המספ[ר] appar. *and the number will still be* 4QPrQuot 3_{13} (others ועו[נו ואמרו] המספ[ר] *and they will answer and say ... the number*).

<OBJ> נתן *give* 2 S 24_9||1 C 21_5 Ec 5_{17}, מכר *deliver (over)* Lv 25_{16}, מלא pi. *fulfil,* i.e. allow to live Ex 23_{26}, ידע *know* 2 S 24_2||1 C 21_2 (S + פקד *muster,* C + ספר *count*) CD 2_9=4QD[a] 2.2_9 (unless מִסְפָּר II *account*), בין *understand* Dn 9_2 (+ בַּסְּפָרִים *in/from the documents*), נגד hi. *tell* Jb 31_{37}.

נשׂא *raise,* i.e. count Nm 3_{40} 1 C 27_{23}, מנה *count* Nm 23_{10} (if em. עֲפַר יַעֲקֹב who can count *the dust of Jacob* to מִסְפַּר *the number of*) 23_{10} (וּמִסְפָּר אֶת־רֹבַע יִשְׂרָאֵל) appar. *and [count] the number, the quarter,* or *the dust, of Israel;* Sam וּמִסְפַּר מְרֻבַּעַת *and the number of the quarter of* Israel; Sam mss וּמִי סָפַר *and who can count* a quarter of Israel?; and/or em. אֶת־רֹבַע to תַּרְבֻּעֹת who can count *the dustclouds of* Israel? or אֶת־רִבְבֹת who can count *the myriads of* Israel?) Ps 105_{12} 1 C 27_{23} (obj. elided).

<CSTR> מִסְפַּר כֻּלָּם *the number of all of them* Jb 1_5, מספר כול צבאותם *the number of all their hosts* 1QSa 1_{24}, מספר המש[פחות] *the number of the clans* 1Q29 7_3, מִסְפַּר הָעָם *the number of the people* 2 S 24_2, מִסְפַּר מִפְקַד־הָעָם *the number of the mustering of the people* 2 S 24_9||1 C 21_5.

מִסְפַּר יַעֲקֹב *the number of Jacob* Nm 23_{10} (if em. עֲפַר *the dust of*), מִסְפַּר בְּנֵי יִשְׂרָאֵל *the number of the children of Israel* Dt 32_8 (unless מִסְפָּר III *border;* or ins. שִׁבְעִים the number of the *seventy* children of Israel; or em. אֵל the number of the children of *God* or אֵלִים the number of the children of *gods*) Ho 2_1, מ[ספר הקדוש]ים *the number of the holy ones* 1QM 12_2.

מִסְפַּר שִׁבְטֵי בְנֵי־יַעֲקֹב *the number of the tribes of the sons of Jacob* 1 K 18_{31}, מִסְפַּר שִׁבְטֵי בְנֵי־יִשְׂרָאֵל *the number of the tribes of the sons of Israel* Jos $4_{5.8}$ 1 K 18_{31} (mss), מִסְפַּר שִׁבְטֵי יִשְׂרָאֵל *the number of the tribes of Israel* 1 K $18_{31(mss)}$ Si 45_{11} (שב[טי יש]ראל), מִסְפַּר מְרֻבַּעַת יִשְׂרָאֵל *the number of the quarter of Israel* Nm 23_{10} (Sam).

מִסְפַּר רָאשֵׁי הָאָבוֹת *the number of the ancestral heads* 2 C 26_{12}, מספר אב[ותם] *the number of their ancestors* 4QShir[b] 2.2_4 (or em. ממזר *bastard*), מִסְפַּר סַרְנֵי פְלִשְׁתִּים *the number of the governors of (the) Philistines* 1 S 6_4, מספר החי[י]ם *the number of the living* 4QapPs[b] 31_8 (unless מספר = *from the book of* the living), מִסְפְּרֵי רָאשֵׁי הֶחָלוּץ *the numbers of the heads of the armed* 1 C 12_{24} (or em. שְׁמוֹת *the names of* the heads).

מִסְפַּר כָּל־עָרֵי פְלִשְׁתִּים *the number of all the cities of (the) Philistines* 1 S 6_{18}, מִסְפַּר־קֶשֶׁת גִּבּוֹרֵי בְנֵי־קֵדָר *the number of bows of the warriors of the children of Kedar* Is 21_{17}, מִסְפַּר חֻצוֹת יְרוּשָׁלַםִ *the number of the streets of Jerusalem* Jr 2_{28} (if ins.) 11_{13}, מִסְפַּר הַגִּבֹּרִים *the number(s) of the warriors* 1 C 11_{11} (||2 S 23_8 שְׁמוֹת *the names of;* or em. מִסֵּפֶר *from the book of*).

מִסְפַּר דִּבְרֵי־הַיָּמִים as *a number of,* i.e. in, *the chronicles* of King David 1 C 27_{24} (unless מִסְפָּר II *account;* or em. סֵפֶר in *the book of* the chronicles), [למס]פר סרך עתו *according to the number,* i.e. order, *of the rule of his time* 1QM 15_5 (others [בס]פר *in the book of*), מספר צרותים ושני התגוררם *the number of their troubles and (of) the years of their exile* CD 4_5 (unless מִסְפָּר II *account;* || פֵּרוּשׁ *statement* [or, if II, *explanation*]), מספר דורות עולם *the number of the generations of eternity* 1QH 1_{18} (+ כול שני נצח *all the years of everlastingness,* כול דוריהם *all their generations* [1_{16}]), מספר שני עולם *of the number of the years of eternity* 1QH 1_{24}.

מִסְפַּר פְּקֻדָּתָם *the number of their mustering* 2 C 26_{11} (+ בְּיַד יְעִיאֵל הַסּוֹפֵר *by Jeiel the scribe* or *by Jeiel, who did the counting* [Qr]; or del.), מִסְפַּר שְׁלֹשִׁים אֶלֶף *a total of thirty thousand* 2 C 35$_{7}$, וּבְמִסְפַּר אַרְבָּעִים *and with the number of forty (blows)* Dt 25$_{2}$ (if em. בְּמִסְפָּר: אַרְבָּעִים *with a number; forty*), מספר ופרוש קציהם *the number and statement of their times* CD 2$_{9}$=4QD^{a} 2.2$_{9}$ ([ופרוש קציהם]; unless מִסְפָּר II the *account* and explanation of their times).

מִסְפַּר נַפְשֹׁתֵיכֶם *the number of your souls,* i.e. persons Ex 16$_{16}$, כָּל־זָכָר *of every male* Nm 3$_{22.28.34}$, הַמְלַקְקִים *of those who lapped* Jg 7$_{6}$, הַהֲרוּגִים *of those who had been killed* Est 9$_{11}$ (unless מִסְפָּר II), שֵׁמוֹת *of names* Nm 1$_{2.18.20.22.24.26.28.30.32}$ (all four שֵׁמֹת) 1$_{34.36.38.40.42}$ (all four שֵׁמֹת) 3$_{43}$ 26$_{53}$ 1 C 23$_{24}$, שְׁמֹתָם *of their names* Nm 3$_{40}$, [מס]פר שמות כול צבאם *the number of the names of all their host* 1QM 12$_{2}$.

מִסְפַּר הַיָּמִים *the number of the days* Nm 14$_{34}$ 1 S 27$_{7}$ 2 S 2$_{11}$ Ezk 4$_{4.5}$ (מִסְפַּר יָמִים) 4$_{9}$ Si 37$_{25(B)}$ 41$_{13(Bmg,M)}$ (all three מספר ימים *a number of days*), יָמֶיךָ *of your days* Ex 23$_{26}$ Jb 38$_{21}$ (or em.; see Coll.), מספר ימיו *the number of his days* Si 26$_{1}$, מִסְפַּר יְמֵי־חַיָּיו *the number of the days of his life* Ec 5$_{17(Qr)}$, יְמֵי חַיֵּיהֶם *of the days of their life* Ec 2$_{3}$, יְמֵי־חַיֵּי הֶבְלוֹ *of the days of his life of vanity* Ec 6$_{12}$, שָׁנִים *of years* Lv 25$_{15.50}$ Jb 15$_{20}$ (or em.; see Coll.) Dn 9$_{2}$ (הַשָּׁנִים) CD 4$_{10}$ (מספר השנים), שָׁנָיו *of his years* Jb 36$_{26}$ (or em.; see Coll.), יְרָחִים *of months* Jb 3$_{6}$, חֳדָשָׁיו *of his months* Jb 14$_{5}$ (מִסְפַּר־) 21$_{21}$.

מִסְפַּר הָעֹלָה *the number of burnt offering(s)* 2 C 29$_{32}$, הַצֹּאן *of the sheep* Nm 31$_{36}$ (Sam צאן *of sheep*), תְּבוּאֹת *of harvests* Lv 25$_{16}$, עָרֶיךָ *of your towns* Jr 2$_{28}$ 11$_{13}$, צְעָדַי *of my steps* Jb 31$_{37}$, ומספר גבלותיה *and the number of its borders* 4QCryptA 3.2$_{2}$.

יְמֵי מִסְפָּר *days of a number,* i.e. a few days (see also §2) Nm 9$_{20}$ (if em. יָמִים מִסְפָּר *days, a number,* i.e. a few days) Si 41$_{13(B)}$, שְׁנוֹת מִסְפָּר *years of a number,* i.e. a few, or a certain number of, years Jb 16$_{22}$ (or em. שְׁנוֹת מִסְפֵּד *years of mourning,* or em. מִסְפָּר to מִסַּפֵּר or מִסֵּפֶר *without number* [סֵפֶר II *number*]), עת מספר at *a time of number,* i.e. when little time is left Si 30$_{32}$ (or em. בעת מספר מצער ימיך *at a time of number [when] your days are few* to בעת כלות מספר ימיך *at the time of the completion of the number of your days*).

מְתֵי מִסְפָּר *people of number,* i.e. few in number (used adverbially or adjectivally) Gn 34$_{30}$ Dt 4$_{27}$ Jr 44$_{28}$ (+ שְׁאֵרִית *remainder*) Am 6$_{10}$ (if em. וּנְשָׂאוֹ דוֹדוֹ וּמְסָפְרוֹ perh. *and his paternal uncle and his maternal uncle will pick him up* to וְנִשְׁאֲרוּ מְתֵי מִסְפָּר *and only a few will remain*) Ps 105$_{4}$||1 C 16$_{19}$ (+ מְעַט *few*), אַנְשֵׁי מִסְפָּר *people of number,* i.e. a few people Ezk 12$_{16}$, וּשְׁאָר מִסְפַּר־ *and the remainder of the number of* the bows Is 21$_{17}$ (or em. וְשָׁאַר *and* a number of bows *will remain*), עֹלוֹת מִסְפַּר *burnt offerings of,* i.e. corresponding to, *the number of* all of them Jb 1$_{5}$, תקופות מספר שני עולם *the cycles of the number of the years of eternity* 1QH 1$_{24}$ (+ בכול מועדיהם *with all their appointed days*).

על מ[קום] תפקיד מספר be ashamed *about the place of counting a number,* i.e. of keeping financial records Si 42$_{7(M\ Di\ Lella)}$ (unless מספר obj. of פקד hi. *count*; B על מקום תפקד יד תספור appar. about *the place [where] you count a deposit* or *wherever you make a deposit, count [it]* or *that your hand counts a deposit*; Bmg מפקד יד תחשוב the place [where] *you reckon a deposit*).

כָּל־מִסְפַּרְכֶם *all your number* Nm 14$_{29}$, כול מספרם 4QMyst^{a} 10$_{6}$, כֹּל מִסְפַּר *all the number,* i.e. the total number, *of* 2 C 26$_{12}$ perh. 4Q4QHymnPr 10$_{6}$ (מספר כול; unless מספר = *telling* all).

<APP> לַגֻּלְגֹּלֶת מִסְפַּר נַפְשֹׁתֵיכֶם an omer *per person, (according to) the number of your souls,* i.e. persons Ex 16$_{16}$, מִסְפַּר סַרְנֵי פְלִשְׁתִּים חֲמִשָּׁה טְחֹרֵי זָהָב *the number of the governors of (the) Philistines, five haemorrhoids of gold* 1 S 6$_{4(Qr)}$, בְמִסְפָּר שְׁנֵים עָשָׂר לְבִנְיָמִן ... וּשְׁנֵים עָשָׂר מֵעַבְדֵי דָוִד *according to (an agreed) number, twelve of Benjamin ... and twelve from the servants of David* 2 S 2$_{15}$, בַּחַיִּים מִסְפַּר יְמֵי־חַיֵּי הֶבְלוֹ *in life, the number of the days of his life of vanity* Ec 6$_{12}$, מִסְפָּרָם אַנְשֵׁי מְלָאכָה *their number, (namely, the number of) people of,* i.e. assigned to, *(this) work* 1 C 25$_{1}$.

יָמִים מִסְפָּר *days, a number,* i.e. a few days Nm 9$_{20}$ (or em. יְמֵי מִסְפָּר *days of a number,* i.e. a few days, or יָמִים בְּמִסְפָּר *days in number,* i.e. a few days) Si 37$_{25(D)}$ (B מספר ימים *a number of days*), וּמִסְפָּר אֶת־רֹבַע *and the number, the quarter,* or *the dust,* of Israel Nm 23$_{10}$ (or em. וּמִי סָפַר *and who can count?* and/or תַּרְבֻּעֹת *the dust clouds of* Israel, or אֶת־רִבְבֹת *the myriads of* Israel).

<PREP> לְ *in accordance with* 1 C 27_{1} (+ בֵּן *son* of Israel) Si 45_{11} (+ אֶבֶן *stone* of breastplate) perh. 4QShir[b] 2.24 (בושת פנים למספר *shame [of face] according to the number of*; or em. לממזר shame [of face] *of a bastard*) 11QShirShabb 8_{3} ([נסכיהם למס[פר *their libations in accordance with the number of*) 11QUnid[b] 30_{1}.

לְ *in accordance with*, + שׁלם *be complete* (of years) CD 4_{10}, בוא hi. *bring (in)* 1QSa 1_{24} (+ בסרכו *in accordance with his registration*), יצא hi. *take out* 1QSa 1_{24} (+ בסרכו), לקט *gather* Ex 16_{16}, נפל *fall* Nm 14_{29} (or em. לְ to וְ *and* all your number will fall), נצב hi. *establish* borders Dt 32_{8} (unless מִסְפָּר III *boundary*), פלג pi. *assign* service 1QH 1_{18}, רום hi. *raise* stone Jos 4_{5}, *offer* sacrifice 2 C 35_{7} (לְמִסְפַּר שְׁלֹשִׁים אֶלֶף *in accordance with a number of thirty thousand*, i.e. 30,000 in total), נשׂא *raise* stone Jos 4_{8}, *take* wife Jg 21_{23}, נתן *place* iniquity Ezk 4_{5}, קרא *call*, i.e. recite, prayer 1QM 15_{5} (למס[פר]; others בס[פר] *in the book of*).

בְּ *in accordance with, by* Nm 1_{22} (+ פָּקוּד *mustered one*) 1_{24+9t} (all ten + תּוֹלֵדָה *generation*) $3_{22.28(ms).34}$ (all three + פָּקוּד) $29_{18.21.24(mss).27.30.33.37(mss)}$ (all seven + וּמִנְחָתָם וְנִסְכֵּיהֶם *and their grain offering and their libations* will be in accordance with their number; + כַּמִּשְׁפָּט *[and] according to the law*) Ezr 8_{34} (בְּמִסְפָּר בְּמִשְׁקָל לַכֹּל perh. *everything was by number [and] by weight*; or em. וּבְמִשְׁקָל *and by weight*) 1 C 23_{24} (+ בֵּן *son* of Levi, + לְגֻלְגְּלֹתָם *by their skulls*, i.e. for each person) perh. 4QBéat $15_{1(mg)}$ ([ובמס[פר).

בְּ *in accordance with, by*, + היה *be* Lv 25_{50} (of value of sale) Nm 1_{20} 34_{3}, ילד htp. *be genealogically assigned* Nm 1_{18} (or em. פקד *muster*), חלק ni. *be divided* Nm 26_{53} (or em. pi. *divide*), בוא hi. *bring* 1 C 9_{28} Ezk 20_{37} (if em. בְּמָסֹרֶת הַבְּרִית *into the number*, or *bond*, or *tradition, of the covenant* to בְּמִסְפָּר *according to number*, i.e. in order, or *without counting* [i.e. §2]) appar. 1QH fr. 13_{2}, עבר *pass* 2 S 2_{15}, יצא *go out* 2 C 26_{11} (or del.), hi. *take out* Is 40_{26} (בְּמִסְפָּר ... בְּשֵׁם perh. *in order ... by name*; + רֹב *abundance*) 1 C 9_{28}, לקח *take* Lv 25_{15}, נשׂא *raise*, i.e. count Nm 1_{2}, נשׂא *bear* iniquity Nm 14_{34}, עשׂה *do*, i.e. prepare, sacrifice Nm $15_{12(mss, Sam)}$ (L כְּ *in accordance with*) Ezr 3_{4} (+ כְּמִשְׁפַּט דְּבַר־יוֹם בְּיוֹמוֹ, *according to the rule of*, i.e. that states, *A thing of a [given] day on its day*), עלה hi. *raise*, i.e. offer, burnt offering 1 C 23_{31} (+ כְּמִשְׁפָּט עֲלֵיהֶם *according to a law [imposed] on them*).

בְּ of place, time, *in(to), during* Ec 6_{12}, + בוא *come* Jb 3_{6}.

בְּ *in (respect of)*, מְעַט בְּמִסְפָּר take *a few (in number)* Ezk 5_{3}.

בְּ of instrument, *by (means of), with*, + נכה hi. *strike* Dt 25_{2} (וְהִכָּהוּ לְפָנָיו כְּדֵי רִשְׁעָתוֹ בְּמִסְפָּר׃ אַרְבָּעִים יַכֶּנּוּ *then he* [the judge] *will strike him* [the guilty party] *in his* [the vindicated party] *presence in accordance with the measure of his crime with a number*, i.e. with an agreed, or standard, number [of blows]; *forty blows he will strike him*; or del. וְהִכָּהוּ לְפָנָיו כְּדֵי רִשְׁעָתוֹ and em. וּבְמִסְפַּר אַרְבָּעִים יַכֶּנּוּ *and with the number of forty he will strike him*).

בְּ *as*, + עלה *go up*, i.e. be registered (of census number), as a figure 1 C 27_{24} (unless מִסְפָּר II be registered in the *account*; or em. סֵפֶר in *the book of* the chronicles).

כְּ *in accordance with*, + עשׂה *do*, i.e. prepare, sacrifice Nm $15_{12.12}$ (mss, Sam בְּ *in accordance with*), לקח *take* stones 1 K 18_{31}.

עַל perh. *in accordance with* 4QMyst[a] 10_{6}.

<COLL> **(1)** used adverbially/adjectivally with אַיִן *no, without*, and בְּלִי *without*, יָמִים אֵין מִסְפָּר *days without number* Jr 2_{32}, ימי אין מספר *days of no number* Si $37_{25(D)}$ $41_{13(B)}$, יֶלֶק אֵין מִסְפָּר *locusts without number* Ps $105_{34(mss)}$, גּוֹי ... עָצוּם וְאֵין מִסְפָּר *a nation ... (that) is powerful and without number* Jl 1_{6}.

רָעוֹת עַד־אֵין מִסְפָּר *misfortunes unto no*, i.e. without, *number* Ps 40_{13}, נִפְלָאוֹת עַד־אֵין מִסְפָּר *wonders unto no*, i.e. without, *number* Jb 5_{9} 9_{10} (|| חֵקֶר *investigation*), הגברתה עד אין מס[פר] *you acted mightily (unto) without number*, i.e. on countless occasions 1QH 9_{37}, ותגבר עד לאין מספר *and you acted mightily (unto) without number*, i.e. on countless occasions 1QH 4_{27}, ומתים לאין מספר *and dead*, or *people, without number* 4Q392 1_{8} (or em. מפתים *miracles*), וַעֲצֵי אֲרָזִים לְאֵין מִסְפָּר *and cedar trees without number* 1 C 22_{4}.

ושלום וברכות [עד ב]לי מספר *and peace and blessings unto absence of*, i.e. without, *number* GnzPs 1_{20},

חכמה ובינה ורב קדושתו עד בלי מספר *wisdom and understanding and abundance of his holiness unto absence of number*, i.e. without end GnzPs 4_{7}.

(2) other adverbial usages, וּמִסְפַּר חֻצוֹת יְרוּשָׁלַםִ שַׂמְתֶּם ... מִזְבְּחוֹת *and you have placed ... (as many) altars (as) the number of streets of Jerusalem* Jr 11_{10}, וּמִסְפַּר חֻצוֹת יְרוּשָׁלַםִ קִטְּרוּ לַבַּעַל *and you have offered incense to Baal (as many times as) the number of streets of Jerusalem* Jr 2_{28} (if ins.), מִסְפַּר הַיָּמִים אֲשֶׁר תִּשְׁכַּב עָלָיו תִּשָּׂא אֶת־עֲוֹנָם *(for) the days that you lie upon it you will bear their iniquity* Ezk 4_{4} (or ins. מֵאָה וַחֲמִשִּׁים *one hundred and fifty* days), מִסְפַּר הַיָּמִים אֲשֶׁר־אַתָּה שׁוֹכֵב עַל־צִדְּךָ ... תֹּאכְלֶנּוּ *(for) the number of days that you are lying on your side ... you will eat it* Ezk 4_{9} (or del.), אֲשֶׁר יַעֲשׂוּ ... מִסְפַּר יְמֵי חַיֵּיהֶם *that they should do ... (for) the number of the days of their life* Ec 2_{3}, שֶׁיַּעֲמֹל ... מִסְפַּר יְמֵי־חַיָּיו *that he suffers ... during the number of the days of his life* Ec $5_{17(Qr)}$.

(3) other collocations, מִסְפָּר לַכּוֹכָבִים *(the) number, or order, of the stars* Ps 147_{4} (+ לְכֻלָּם שֵׁמוֹת יִקְרָא *all of them he calls by name*), מִסְפָּרָם לְגֻלְגְּלֹתָם לִגְבָרִים *their number, according to their skulls of men*, i.e. the number of their adult males 1 C 23_{3} 25_{1} (if ins. לְגֻלְגְּלֹתָם לִגְבָרִים), מִסְפַּר שָׁנָיו וְלֹא־חֵקֶר *the number of his years—indeed there is no investigation* Jb 36_{26} (or em. מִסְפָּר to מִסֵּפֶר or מִסֵּפֶר *without number* [סֵפֶר II *number*]), מִסְפַּר הַשָּׁנִים אֲשֶׁר הָיָה דְבַר־י׳ אֶל־יִרְמְיָה *the number of the years (concerning) which the word of Y. came to Jeremiah* Dn $9_{2(L)}$, וּבְנֵי יִשְׂרָאֵל לְמִסְפָּרָם *and the Israelites according to their number*, i.e. and the number of Israelites 1 C 27_{1}, מְתֵי מִסְפָּר בַּגּוֹיִם perh. *few in number compared with the nations* Dt 4_{27}.

(4) מִסְפָּר sg. as predicate of pl. noun or, as nomen regens, as subj. of pl. verb or pl. predicate (which agrees with a pl. nomen rectum), וּמִסְפַּר שָׁנִים נִצְפְּנוּ לֶעָרִיץ *and a (certain) number of years is stored up for the tyrant* Jb 15_{20} (or em. מִסְפָּר to מִסֵּפֶר or מִסֵּפֶר *without number* [סֵפֶר II *number*]), וּמִסְפַּר חֳדָשָׁיו חֻצָּצוּ *and the number of his months is determined* Jb 21_{21}, וּמִסְפַּר יָמֶיךָ רַבִּים *and the number of your years is many* Jb 38_{21} (or em. מִסְפָּר to מִסֵּפֶר or מִסֵּפֶר *without number* [סֵפֶר II *number*]), ומספר ימיו כפלים *and the number of his days is double* Si 26_{1}, וְאֵלֶּה מִסְפָּרָם *and these are their number(s)* Ezr 1_{9}, וְאֵלֶּה מִסְפַּר הַגִּבֹּרִים *and these are the number(s) of the warriors* 1 C 11_{11} (‖2 S 23_{8} שְׁמוֹת *the names of*), also 1 C 23_{27} (see §2); cf. וּשְׁאָר עֵץ יַעְרוֹ מִסְפָּר יִהְיוּ וְנַעַר יִכְתְּבֵם *and the remainder of the tree(s) of its forest will be a number, and a lad will count them* Is 10_{19} (where יִהְיוּ and the suffix of יִכְתְּבֵם do not agree formally with any noun, but semantically agree with עֵץ used collectively, *trees*; cf. Is 21_{17}).

2. perh. as gerund of ספר *count*, i.e. **counting, numbering,** כִּי בְדִבְרֵי דָוִיד הָאַחֲרֹנִים הֵמָּה מִסְפַּר בְּנֵי־לֵוִי perh. *indeed, among the last deeds of David was the numbering of the Levites* 1 C 23_{27}, שם רמש הרבה ואין למספר *many moving things are there and it is not for numbering*, i.e. they cannot be counted 11QPs[a] 104_{25}, [מהם ב]רך הקדישו ומהם שם לימי מספר *one of them he blessed and consecrated it and some of them he appointed as days of counting*, i.e. between one holy day and another Si $36_{9(Segal)}$.

Also 4QapPs[b] 61_{1} (unless מספר = *from the book of* or *telling*) 11QT 3_{17} ([ומס]פר).

<SYN> §1 חֵקֶר *investigation*, מִשְׁקָל *weight*.*

⇒ ספר *count*.

[מִסְפָּר] II 3.0.2 n.[m.] **account, narrative**—cstr. מִסְפַּר—<SUBJ> בוא *come* Est 9_{11} (unless מִסְפָּר I).<OBJ> שׁמע *hear* Jg 7_{15}, ידע *know* CD 2_{9}=4QD[a] 2.2$_{9}$ (unless מִסְפָּר I *number*). <CSTR> מִסְפַּר הַחֲלוֹם *the account of the dream* Jg 7_{15} (+ וְאֶת־שִׁבְרוֹ *and its interpretation*; אִישׁ מְסַפֵּר לְרֵעֵהוּ חֲלוֹם *a man was telling his companion a dream* 7_{13}), מִסְפַּר דִּבְרֵי־הַיָּמִים *the account of the chronicles* of King David 1 C 27_{24} (unless מִסְפָּר I as a *number of*, i.e. in, the chronicles), מִסְפַּר הַהֲרוּגִים *the narrative of those who had been killed* Est 9_{11} (unless מִסְפָּר I), מספר ופרוש קציהם *the account and explanation of their times* CD 2_{9}=4QD[a] 2.2$_{9}$ ([ופרוש קציהם]; unless מִסְפָּר I the *number* and statement of their times), מספר צרותים ושני התגוררם *the number of their troubles and (of) the years of their exile* CD 4_{5} (unless מִסְפָּר I *number*; ‖ פֵּרוּשׁ *explanation* [or, if II, *statement*]). <PREP> בְּ of place, *in(to)*, + עלה *go up*, i.e. be registered (of census number) 1 C 27$_{24}$.

<COLL> פורש שמותיהם לתולדותם וקץ מעמדם ומספר צרותיהם ושני התגוררם *the explanation of their names, according to their generations, and (of) the time of their standing as well as the number of their troubles and (of) the years of their exile* CD 4$_{5}$ (unless מִסְפָּר I *number*).*

⇒ ספר *count.*

*[מִסְפָּר] III $_{1}$ n.[m.] **border**—cstr. מִסְפַּר—יַצֵּב גְּבֻלֹת עַמִּים לְמִסְפַּר בְּנֵי יִשְׂרָאֵל *he establishes the borders of the peoples in accordance with the border of the children of Israel* Dt 32$_{8}$ (unless מִסְפָּר I *number*; + גְּבוּלָה *border*).

מִסְפָּר IV $_{1.0.0.1}$ pr.n.m. **Mispar, 1.** exile returning with Zerubbabel, appar. ident. with Mispereth at Ne 7$_{7}$, <SUBJ> בוא *come* Ezr 2$_{2}$ (or em. מִסְפֶּרֶת *Mispereth* or מְסַפֶּרֶת *Mesappereth*). **2.** <APP> בֵּן *son* Seal 606 (T. Beit Mirsim?; 7th/6th cent.). <PREP> לְ of possession, *of, (belonging) to* Seal 606.

⇒ ספר *count.*

[מְסַפֶּרֶת], see מִסְפֶּרֶת *Mispereth.*

מִסְפֶּרֶת I $_{1}$ pr.n. **Mispereth,** exile returning with Zerubbabel, appar. ident. with Mispar at Ezr 2$_{2}$, <SUBJ> בוא *come* Ne 7$_{7}$ (or em. מְסַפֶּרֶת *Mesappereth*).

⇒ ספר *count.*

*[מִסְפֶּרֶת] II $_{0.1}$ n.f. **scholarship**—sf. Si מספרתם—<PREP> בְּ of accompaniment, *with* Si 44$_{4(Bmg)}$ (חכמי שיח במספרתם *ones who are wise of expression, with their scholarship;* B, M בספרתם in same sense).

⇒ ספר *count.*

*מסר I $_{1}$ vb. **count—Ni.** $_{1}$ + waw וַיִּמָּסְרוּ—**be counted, be provided, be conscripted** (unless מסר III or IV), <SUBJ> חָלוּץ *armed warrior* Nm 31$_{5}$ (or em. Qal *hand over* warriors, or ספר ni. *be counted,* or בחר ni. *be chosen*), אֶלֶף *a thousand* warriors Nm 31$_{5}$ (or em.). <PREP> מִן of direction, *from,* + אֶלֶף *clan* or *thousand* Nm 31$_{5}$ (or em.).*

⇒ מָסֹרֶת III *number.*

*מסר II $_{0.0.2}$ vb. **hand over, hand down—Qal** $_{0.0.1}$ + waw Q וימסור—**hand down, transmit,** <SUBJ> Abraham CD 3$_{3}$. <OBJ> perh. מִצְוָה *commandment* CD 3$_{3}$.

Ni. $_{0.0.1}$ Impf. ימסרו—**be handed over,** <SUBJ> שׁאר ni. ptc. *one who remains* CD 19$_{10(B)}$ (+ מלט ni. *escape;* ||8$_{1[A]}$ סגר hi. *hand over* to sword). <PREP> לְ of direction, *to,* + חֶרֶב *sword* CD 19$_{10(B)}$; בְּ of place/time, *in, at,* + בוא inf. *coming* of messiah CD 19$_{10(B)}$.

⇒ מָסֹרֶת II *tradition.*

מסר III $_{2}$ vb. **deliver up, offer—Qal** $_{1}$ Inf. לִמְסָר־—הָיוּ לִבְנֵי יִשְׂרָאֵל בִּדְבַר בִּלְעָם לִמְסָר־מַעַל בַּי׳ עַל־דְּבַר־פְּעוֹר *they were for the children of Israel's offering* (i.e. *committing*) *trespass against Y. at the behest of Balaam in the matter of Peor* Nm 31$_{16}$ (or em. לָסוּר מֵעַל *to turn away from,* or לִמְעֹל מַעַל *to commit sin* against, Y.).

Ni. $_{1}$ + waw וַיִּמָּסְרוּ—**be delivered up, offered** (unless מסר I or IV), <SUBJ> חָלוּץ *armed warrior* Nm 31$_{5}$ (or em. ספר ni. *be counted,* or בחר ni. *be chosen*), אֶלֶף *a thousand* warriors Nm 31$_{5}$ (or em.). <PREP> מִן of direction, *from,* + אֶלֶף *clan* or *thousand* Nm 31$_{5}$ (or em.).*

*מסר IV $_{1}$ vb. **select—Ni.** $_{1}$ + waw וַיִּמָּסְרוּ—**be selected** (unless מסר I or III), <SUBJ> חָלוּץ *armed warrior* Nm 31$_{5}$ (or em. ספר ni. *be counted,* or בחר ni. *be chosen*), אֶלֶף *a thousand* warriors Nm 31$_{5}$ (or em.). <PREP> מִן of direction, *from,* + אֶלֶף *clan* or *thousand* Nm 31$_{5}$ (or em.).*

*[מֹסָר] $_{1}$ n.[m.] **discipline**—sf. מֹסָרָם—<PREP> בְּ of instrument, *by (means of), with,* + חתם *seal* Jb 33$_{16}$ (or em. מֹסָרָם by *their discipline* to מֻסָרָם by *their discipline,* i.e. מוּסָר, or בְּמַרְאִים *with apparitions,* and/or יַחְתֹּם *he sets a seal* to יְחִתֵּם *he terrifies them,* i.e. חתת hi.).

⇒ יסר *discipline.*

*[מִסְרָב] n.[m.] **obstinacy,** <PREP> בְּ of cause, *because of, through,* + שׁמע not *hear* Jr 13$_{17}$ (if em. בְּמִסְתָּרִים my soul will weep *in hidden places,* i.e. in secret, to בְּמִסְרָבִים if you do not listen *through [acts of] obstinacy*).

⇒ סרב *rebel.*

*[מְסָרֵף] I $_1$ n.m. **maternal uncle***—sf. מְסָרְפוֹ—appar. a surviving relative (unless מְסָרֵף II or III), <SUBJ> נשׂא *take* Am 6$_{10}$, יצא hi. *bring out* Am 6$_{10}$, אמר *say* Am 6$_{10}$ (all + דּוֹד *uncle*; or em. וְנִשְׁאֲרוּ מְתֵי מִסְפָּר *and only a few will remain* to remove, or וַיִּשָּׁאֲרוּ נוֹדְדֵי מִסְפָּר *and there remained a few fugitives* to remove, or וְנָשְׂאוּ דּוֹדוֹ וּפָצְרוּ *and they took his relative and compelled [him]* to remove).

[מְסָרֵף] II $_1$ n.m. **one who burns incense***—sf. מְסָרְפוֹ—specif. **one charged with burning incense** for the dead (in which case שׂרף pi. ptc.; unless מְסָרֵף I or III), <SUBJ> נשׂא *take* Am 6$_{10}$, יצא hi. *bring out* Am 6$_{10}$, אמר *say* Am 6$_{10}$ (all + דּוֹד *uncle*; perh. the conjunction in דּוֹדוֹ וּמְסָרְפוֹ is explicative, *his relative who is charged with burning incense for him*; or em. וְנִשְׁאֲרוּ מְתֵי מִסְפָּר *and only a few will remain* to remove, or וַיִּשָּׁאֲרוּ נוֹדְדֵי מִסְפָּר *and there remained a few fugitives* to remove, or וְנָשְׂאוּ דּוֹדוֹ וּפָצְרוּ *and they took his relative and compelled [him]* to remove).

⇒ סרף *burn,* Pi.

[מְסָרֵף] III, see סרף *anoint with spices,* Pi.

*[מִסְרָר] n.[m.] **stubbornness,** <PREP> בְּ of cause, *because of, through,* + שׁמע not *hear* Jr 13$_{17}$ (if em. בְּמִסְתָּרִים my soul will weep *in hidden places,* i.e. in secret, to בְּמִסְרָרִים if you do not listen *through stubbornness[es]*).

⇒ סרר *be stubborn.*

[מָסֹרֶת] I $_{1.0.1}$ n.f. **bond**—cstr. מָסֹרֶת—**1. bond,** <CSTR> מָסֹרֶת הַבְּרִית *bond of the covenant* Ezk 20$_{37}$ (unless מָסֹרֶת II *tradition* or III *number*; or em.; see Prep.). <PREP> בְּ of place, *in(to),* + בוא hi. *bring* Ezk 20$_{37}$ (or em. בְּמָסֹרֶת הַבְּרִית *into the bond of the covenant* to בְּמוּסַר *into the discipline of* the covenant, or בְּמִסְפָּר *according to number,* i.e. in order, or *without counting* [del. הַבְּרִית]).

2. conjunction of sun and moon at the nodes of the moon (unless מָסֹרֶת II),* במבוא מועדים לימי חודש יחד תקופתם עם מסרותם זה לזה בהתחדשם perh. *at the start of festivals for the days of each month together (with) their circulating, accompanied by their conjunction, one to the other, during their renewal* 1QS 10$_4$=4QS[b] 19$_2$ (תקופותיהמה עם מסרו[ת]ם).

⇒ אסר *bind.*

*[מָסֹרֶת] II $_{1.0.1}$ n.f. **tradition**—cstr. מָסֹרֶת; sf. Q מסרותם—**1. tradition,** <CSTR> מָסֹרֶת הַבְּרִית *tradition of the covenant* Ezk 20$_{37}$ (unless מָסֹרֶת I *bond* or III *number*; or em.; see Prep.). <PREP> בְּ of place, *in(to),* + בוא hi. *bring* Ezk 20$_{37}$ (or em. בְּמָסֹרֶת הַבְּרִית *into the tradition of the covenant* to בְּמוּסַר *into the discipline of* the covenant, or בְּמִסְפָּר *according to number,* i.e. in order, or *without counting* [del. הַבְּרִית]).

2. handing over, transmission (unless מָסֹרֶת I), מבוא מועדים לימי חודש יחד תקופתם עם מסרותם זה לזה בהתחדשם perh. *at the start of festivals for the days of each month together (with) their circulating, accompanied by their handing over, one to the other, during their renewal* 1QS 10$_4$=4QS[b] 19$_2$ (תקופותיהמה עם מסרו[ת]ם).

⇒ מסר II *hand over.*

*[מָסֹרֶת] III $_1$ n.f. **number**—cstr. מָסֹרֶת; pl. Q מסורות; sf. מסורותם—**number, muster-roll,** <CSTR> מָסֹרֶת הַבְּרִית *number of the covenant* Ezk 20$_{37}$ (or em.; see Prep.). <PREP> בְּ of place, *in(to),* + בוא hi. *bring* Ezk 20$_{37}$ (or em. בְּמָסֹרֶת הַבְּרִית *into the number of the covenant* to בְּמוּסַר *into the discipline of* the covenant, or בְּמִסְפָּר *according to number,* i.e. in order, or *without counting* [del. הַבְּרִית]).

⇒ מסר I *count.*

*[מָסֹרֶת] IV $_{0.0.3}$ n.f. **division**—pl. cstr. Q מסורות; sf. מסורותם (מסרותם)—**division, unit** of army, etc.,

<CSTR> [חוּ]קות מסרותם *statutes of*, i.e. rules concerning, *their divisions* 4QShirShabb[f] 23.2$_{13}$, חצוצרות מסורות *the trumpets of the divisions* 1QM 3$_{3}$ (unless מָסֹרֶת V *command post* or מַסֹּרֶת I *collecting point*). <PREP> לְ *in accordance with, by* 1QM 3$_{13}$ (סרך אותות כול העדה למסורותם *the rule of the standards of all the congregation by their divisions*).*

⇒ מסר I *count*.

*[מָסֹרֶת] V 0.0.1 n.f. **command post**—pl. cstr. Q מסורות—<CSTR> חצוצרות מסורות *the trumpets of the command posts* 1QM 3$_{3}$ (unless מָסֹרֶת IV *division* or מַסֹּרֶת I *collecting point*).

*[מַסֹּרֶת] I 0.0.1 n.f. **collecting point**—מסורות—<CSTR> חצוצרות מסורות *the trumpets of the collecting points* 1QM 3$_{3}$ (unless מָסֹרֶת IV *division* or V *command post*).

[מַסֹּרֶת] II, see [מָסֹרֶת] II *tradition*.

[מְסֹרֶת], see [מָסֹרֶת] II *tradition*.

מֹסֵרֹת pl.n. 2 **Moseroth,** station of exodus, appar. ident. with מוֹסֵרָה *Moserah* at Dt 10$_{6}$, <PREP> בְּ of place, *in, at,* + חנה *encamp* Nm 33$_{30}$; מִן of direction, *from,* + נסע *set off* Nm 33$_{31}$.*

⇒ perh. cf. מָסֹרֶת I *bond*.*

*מֹסֶרֶת n.f. **chastisement,** <CSTR> מֹסֶרֶת הַבְּרִית *chastisement of the covenant* Ezk 20$_{37}$ (if em. מָסֹרֶת הַבְּרִית *bond*, or *tradition*, or *number*, *of the covenant*).

<PREP> בְּ of place, *in(to),* + בוא hi. *bring* Ezk 20$_{37}$ (if em.; see Cstr.).

⇒ יסר *discipline*.

מִסַּת, see מִסָּה *sufficiency*.

מִסְתּוֹר 1 n.[m.] **shelter,** <PREP> לְ *as,* + היה *be* Is 4$_{6}$ (appar. of סֻכָּה *booth,* + צֵל *shade,* מַחְסֶה *refuge*).

<COLL> לְצֵל־יוֹמָם מֵחֹרֶב וּלְמַחְסֶה וּלְמִסְתּוֹר מִזֶּרֶם וּמִמָּטָר *as shade during the day from heat and as a refuge and as a shelter from downpour and from rain* Is 4$_{6}$ (1QIsa[a] ענן יומם *a cloud by day* from heat).

⇒ סתר *hide*.

[מַסְתֵּר] 1 n.[m.] **hiding**—cstr. מַסְתֵּר (Q מסתיר [perh. מַסְתִּיר, i.e. סתר hi. ptc.]).

אִישׁ מַכְאֹבוֹת וִידוּעַ חֹלִי וּכְמַסְתֵּר פָּנִים מִמֶּנּוּ *a man of*, i.e. suffering, *pains and known of*, i.e. by, or *debilitated of*, i.e. by (if ידע II), *illness and like a hiding of face from us*, or, *from him*, appar. and he was like one who must hide his face from us, or, like one from whom we must hide our faces (1QIsa[a] יודע חולי וכמסתיר appar. *knowing illness and like one hiding* their face from us).

⇒ סתר *hide*.

מִסְתָּר 10.1 n.[m.] **hiding place**—pl. מִסְתָּרִים; sf. Si מִסְתָּרָיו, מסתרי—**hidden place, hiding place, secret (place),** Wisdom's **secrets** (Si 4$_{18}$), <OBJ> גלה pi. *reveal* Jr 49$_{10}$ (+ וְנֶחְבָּה לֹא יוּכָל *and [when] he tries to hide himself he cannot*; or em. נַחְבֹּה and he is unable *to hide*) Si 4$_{18}$. <CSTR> מַטְמֻנֵי מִסְתָּרִים *hoards of hidden places*, i.e. buried treasure Is 45$_{3}$ (+ אוֹצְרוֹת חֹשֶׁךְ *treasures of darkness*, i.e. hidden treasure).

<PREP> בְּ of place, *in* Lm 3$_{10}$ (+ אֲרִי *lion* [Qr]) + סתר ni. *hide oneself* Jr 23$_{24}$ (+ וַאֲנִי לֹא־אֶרְאֶנּוּ *do I not see him?*), אכל *eat*, i.e. destroy, afflicted one Hb 3$_{14}$, הרג *kill* innocent one Ps 10$_{8}$ (or em. יַהֲרֹג in secret *he kills* to לַהֲרֹג he sits ...in secret *to kill*), ישׁב *sit* Ps 10$_{8}$ (if em.; + בְּמַאְרַב חֲצֵרִים he sits in *ambush of*, i.e. in, *villages* [or em. עֲשִׁרִים in ambush of, i.e. with, *[the] wealthy* or חֲצָרִים of, i.e. among, *[the] reeds*]) 17$_{12}$ (+ וְכִכְפִיר *and like a [young] lion* sitting), ארב *wait in ambush* Ps 10$_{9}$ (+ כְּאַרְיֵה בְסֻכֹּה *like a lion in its lair*), ירה *shoot* person of integrity Ps 64$_{5}$ (+ פִּתְאֹם יֹרֻהוּ וְלֹא יִירָאוּ *suddenly they shoot him and do not fear*; or em. יֵרָאוּ and *are* not *seen*), בכה *weep* Jr 13$_{17}$ (or em. בְּמִסְתָּרִים *in hidden places*, i.e. in secret, to בְּמְסָרְרִים *through stubbornness* or בְּמְסָרְבִים *through obstinacy*).

[מַעְבָּד] I 1.1 n.[m.] **deed**—pl. sf. מַעְבָּדֵיהֶם—<OBJ> נכר hi. *look (at)* Jb 34$_{25}$. <PREP> מִן appar. of cause, *on ac-*

count of, + דחף *push (away)* Si 36_{12} (or em. ממעבד[יה]ם *on account of their deeds* to ממעמד[יה]ם *from their positions* and/or ודחפם *and he pushes them away* to והדפם *and he pushes them way* or ועקרם *and he uproots them*).

⇒ עבד *do.*

*[מַעְבָּד] II 1 n.[m.] **path**—pl. sf. מַעְבָּדֵיהֶם—<OBJ> נכר hi. *look (at)* Jb 34_{25}.

[מַעֲבָד], see מַעְבָּד *deed.*

*[מַעֲבָדְיָה] 0.0.0.1 pr.n.[m.] **Maabadiah**, appar. father of Jaazaniah (יאזניה), Seal 722 (7th cent.).

⇒ עבד *do.*

[מַעֲבֶה] 1.0.1 n.[m.] **thickness**—cstr. מַעֲבֵה—**thickness**, i.e. depth, of the (clay) soil, or perh. **thickness, compactness**, or else **foundry**,* <CSTR> בשואה המעבה של מנס *in the excavation of the foundry of Manos* 3QTr 1_{13},* בְּכִכַּר הַיַּרְדֵּן יְצָקָם הַמֶּלֶךְ בְּמַעֲבֵה הָאֲדָמָה perh. *in the plain of the Jordan the king cast them on account of the thickness of the soil* 1 K 7_{46} (unless בְּמַעֲבֵה הָאֲדָמָה = *in*, or *by means of*, *the thickness of the earth*, i.e. in a clay pit, clay mould, or earthen foundry; ||2 C עֳבִי *thickness* [mss עֲבֵי *thicknesses, deep places*]; or em. בְּמַעְבֶּרֶת אֲדָמָה *at the ford of Adamah*; and/or del. הַמֶּלֶךְ, leaving Hiram as subj.).*

⇒ עבה *be thick.*

[מַעֲבָר] I 3 n.[m.] **pass**—cstr. מַעֲבַר—**1.** mountain **pass** of Michmas (1 S 13_{23}), **ford** of Jabbok (Gn 32_{23}), <OBJ> עבר *cross* Gn 32_{23}. <CSTR> מַעֲבַר יַבֹּק *the ford of Jabbok* Gn 32_{23} (Sam הַיַּבֹּק *the Jabbok*), מַעֲבַר מִכְמָשׂ *the pass of Michmas*, i.e. prob. Wadi es-Swenit (מִגְרוֹן *Migron*) 1 S 13_{23} (mss מִכְמָשׁ *Michmash*; or em. מֵעֵבֶר *across from* Michmas). <PREP> אֶל *to*, + יצא *go out* 1 S 13_{23} (or em. מֵעֵבֶר *across from*).

2. passing, stroke, הָיָה כֹּל מַעֲבַר מַטֵּה מוּסָדָה אֲשֶׁר יָנִיחַ י׳ עָלָיו בְּתֻפִּים וּבְכִנֹּרוֹת *and every passing of the rod of establishment*, i.e. the appointed rod, *that Y. causes to rest upon him will be accompanied by tambourines and harps* Is 30_{32} (unless מַעֲבָר II *burning*; 1QIsa[a] מוסדו *of his establishment*; mss מוּסָרָה *of his punishment*; or em. יַנִּיחַ *places*; or del. אֲשֶׁר יָנִיחַ י׳ עָלָיו).

⇒ עבר *pass.*

*[מַעֲבָר] II 1 n.[m.] **burning**—cstr. מַעֲבַר—unless מַעֲבָר I *passing*, כֹּל מַעֲבַר מַטֵּה מוּסָדָה *every burning of a raised bed* Is 30_{32} (if em. מַטֵּה *rod* to מִטָּה *bed*).*

מַעְבָּרָה 8 n.f. **pass**—pl. מַעְבָּרוֹת (מַעְבָּרוֹת, מַעְבָּרֹת); cstr. מַעְבְּרוֹת—mountain **pass** of Michmas (perh. Is 10_{29}), **passageway**, i.e. **ravine**, near Michmas (1 S 14_{4}), **fords** of Jordan (Jos 2_{7} Jg 3_{28} $12_{5.6}$), of Arnon (Is 16_{2}), perh. of Euphrates (Jr 51_{32}), of Adamah (1 K 7_{46} [if em.]).

<SUBJ> תפשׂ ni. *be seized* Jr 51_{32} (+ אֲגַם *swamp* or *bulwark*). <OBJ> לכד *capture* Jg 3_{28} 12_{5}, עבר *pass (through)* 1 S 14_{4} (אֲשֶׁר בִּקֵּשׁ ... לַעֲבֹר the passageways *that he wanted ... to pass through*). <CSTR> מַעְבְּרוֹת הַיַּרְדֵּן *the fords of the Jordan* Jg 3_{28} $12_{5.6}$, מַעְבֶּרֶת אֲדָמָה *the ford of Adamah* 1 K 7_{46} (if em. מַעֲבֵה הָאֲדָמָה *the thickness of the soil*).

<PREP> בְּ of place, *in, at*, + יצק *cast* metal 1 K 7_{46} (if em. בְּמַעֲבֵה הָאֲדָמָה perh. *on account of the thickness of the soil* to בְּמַעְבֶּרֶת אֲדָמָה *at the ford of Adamah*); of instrument, *by (means of)*, or introducing obj., + עבר *pass* Is 10_{29}; אֶל *by*, + שׁחט *slaughter* Jg 12_{6}; עַל *by* or *to*, + רדף *pursue* Jos 2_{7} (mss עַד *unto*); עַד *unto*, + רדף *pursue* Jos $2_{7(mss)}$; בֵּין *among* 1 S 14_{4}.

<COLL> תִּהְיֶינָה בְּנוֹת מוֹאָב מַעְבָּרֹת לְאַרְנוֹן *the daughters of Moab will be (like this at the) fords of Arnon* Is 16_{2} (or ins. בְּ of place, *at* the fords of Arnon; or em. מֶעֶבְרַת אַרְנוֹן *on account of the fury of*, i.e. directed at, *Arnon*).

⇒ עבר *pass.*

[מַעְגָּל] I 11 n.m. **track**—cstr. מַעְגַּל; pl. cstr. מַעְגְּלֵי; sf. מַעְגְּלוֹתֶיךָ, מַעְגְּלֹתָיו, מַעְגְּלֹתֶיהָ, מַעְגְּלוֹתָם—**track, course** (of life, behaviour).

<SUBJ> כון ni. *be firm* Pr 5_{6} (if em. לֹא תֵדַע *she* [other woman] *does not know* to לֹא יִכֹּנוּ *they* [ways] *are not*

firm), נוע *wander* Pr 5$_6$ (+ אֹרַח *way*), perh. שׁוח *sink down* Pr 2$_{18}$ (unless וְאֶל־רְפָאִים מַעְגְּלֹתֶיהָ = *and to shadows [lead] her ways*, i.e. nom. cl.; + נְתִיבָה *way* [if em. בֵּיתָהּ *her house* sinks down]), לוז ni. *be devious* Pr 2$_{15}$ (if em. וּנְלוֹזִים בְּמַעְגְּלוֹתָם appar. *and [who] are devious in their ways* to וּנְלוֹזִים מַעְגְּלוֹתָם *and their ways are devious*; + אֹרַח *way*).

<OBJ> פלס pi. *make level* or *observe* Is 26$_7$ (+ אֹרַח *way*) Pr 4$_{26}$ 5$_{21}$ (both + דֶּרֶךְ *way*), בין (hi.) *understand* Pr 2$_9$ (or em. וּמֵישָׁרִים understand righteousness and justice *and uprightness*, every way of goodness, to וְתִשְׁמֹר *and you keep [to]* every, or וּתְיַשֵּׁר בְּ *and you keep straight along* every), perh. ידע *know* Pr 5$_6$ (or em. לֹא תֵדָע *she* [other woman] *does not know [them]* to לֹא יִכֹּנוּ *they* [ways] *are not firm*).

<CSTR> מַעְגַּל צַדִּיק *the way of a righteous one* Is 26$_7$, רַגְלֶךָ *of your foot* Pr 4$_{26}$, מַעְגַּל־טוֹב *way of goodness* Pr 5$_{21}$, יֹשֶׁר *of uprightness* Pr 4$_{11}$ (‖ דֶּרֶךְ *way*); כָּל־מַעְגַּל־ *every way of* goodness Pr 2$_9$, כָּל־מַעְגְּלֹתָיו *all his ways* Pr 5$_{21}$.

<APP> וּמֵישָׁרִים כָּל־מַעְגַּל־טוֹב *and uprightness, every way of goodness* Pr 2$_9$ (or em. to וְתִשְׁמֹר *and you keep [to]* every, or וּתְיַשֵּׁר בְּכָל־ *and you keep straight along* every, or וְכָל־ *uprightness and every*)

<PREP> בְּ of place, *in, along* (sometimes perh. of accompaniment, *with*) Is 59$_8$ (וְאֵין מִשְׁפָּט בְּמַעְגְּלוֹתָם *and there is no justice in their ways*; + דֶּרֶךְ *way*, נְתִיבָה *way*), + תמך *hold (fast)* Ps 17$_5$ (or em. verse-division, so that governing verb is מוט ni. *be shaken*), דרך hi. *lead* Pr 4$_{11}$, ישׁר pi. *keep straight* along Pr 2$_9$ (if em. וּמֵישָׁרִים כָּל־ *and uprightness, every* way of goodness, to וּתְיַשֵּׁר בְּכָל־ *and you keep straight along* every), לוז ni. *be devious* Pr 2$_{15}$ (or del. בְּ, leaving מַעְגָּל as subj. of לוז ni.); לְיַד *along*, + פרשׂ *spread* net Ps 140$_6$ (or em. verse-division, so that governing verb is שׁית *place* trap).

<SYN> דֶּרֶךְ *way*.*

⇒ (?) עֲגָלָה *cart*.

*[מַעְגָּל] II 3 n.m. **encampment**—+ ה- of direction מַעְגָּלָה—**encampment**, perh. as a **ring of waggons**, <PREP> בְּ of place, *in(side)*, + שׁכב *lie (asleep)* 1 S 26$_{5.7}$. <COLL> with ה- of direction, *to(wards)*, + בוא *come* 1 S 17$_{20}$.

⇒ עָגֹל *round*.

*[מַעְגָּל] III 2 n.m. **pasture**—pl. cstr. מַעְגְּלֵי; sf. מַעְגָּלֶיךָ —<SUBJ> רעף *drip* Ps 65$_{12}$ (unless מַעְגָּל IV or V). <CSTR> מַעְגְּלֵי־צֶדֶק *pastures of righteousness* Ps 23$_3$. <PREP> בְּ of place, *in, along*, + נחה hi. *lead* Ps 23$_3$.

*[מַעְגָּל] IV 1 n.m. **cart, chariot**—pl. sf. מַעְגָּלֶיךָ— <SUBJ> רעף *drip* Ps 65$_{12}$ (unless מַעְגָּל III or V).

⇒ cf. עֲגָלָה *cart*.

*[מַעֲגַם] n.[m.] **sadness**, מעגמי תעודה אשר פתר perh. *the sadness(es) of testimony that he has interpreted* 4QCryptA 1.2$_8$(WA) (EW מעלמי *the hidden things of* testimony; Pfann [ד]עת[י]מי תעודה אשר פתר[ו]הם *knowledge of the days of appointment*, i.e. appointed days, *the interpretations of which*).

⇒ עגם *be sad*.

מעד 7 vb. **shake**—**Qal** 5 Pf מָעֲדוּ; impf. 3fs תִּמְעַד, אֶמְעַד —**slip, falter, give way**, <SUBJ> קַרְסֹל *ankle* 2 S 22$_{37}$‖ Ps 18$_{37}$ (+ רחב hi. *broaden* steps), רֶגֶל *foot* or *leg* Pr 25$_{19}$ (if em. po.), אָשֻׁר *step* Ps 37$_{31}$, heaven and earth Si 16$_{18}$ (if em. עמד *stand [still]*), worshipper Ps 26$_1$. <PREP> בְּ of cause, *on account of* fear of Y. Si 16$_{18}$ (if em.); כְּ *in accordance with* Si 16$_{18}$ (if em.; or em. כרגשו *in accordance with his restlessness* or *thundering* to ירגשו or ירגזו *they quake* on account of the fear of Y.). <COLL> נָכוֹן לְמוֹעֲדֵי רָגֶל *a blow to*, or *it is established for, ones slipping of feet*, i.e. those whose legs are about to give way Jb 12$_5$.

Pu. 1 Ptc. מוּעֶדֶת—**be out of joint, be sprained**, <SUBJ> רֶגֶל *foot* or *leg* Pr 25$_{19}$ (רֶגֶל מוּעָדֶת *a foot out of joint*; unless a *directed* foot, i.e. יעד ho. ptc.; or em. מוֹעֶדֶת a *slipping* foot, i.e. Qal; ‖ רעע *be broken*, of tooth). <SYN> רעע *be broken*.

Hi. 1 Impv. הַמְעַד—**shake, put out of joint**, <SUBJ> Y. Ps 69$_{24}$ (+ חשׁך *be dark*, of eyes) Hb 3$_6$ (if em. מדד po. *measure* [or em. עמד hi. *stop* or מוט po. *shake* or מוג po. *melt*]), יֹשֵׁב *inhabitant* of Egypt Ezk 29$_7$ (if em.

עמד hi. *support*). <OBJ> מֹתֶן *hip* Ezk 29$_{7}$ (if em.) Ps 69$_{24}$, אֶרֶץ *earth* Hb 3$_{6}$ (if em.). <PREP> לְ of benefit, *for*, + בַּיִת *house* of Irael Ezk 29$_{7}$ (if em.).*

⇨ מַעֲדָן III *faltering*, מְעֹדַנִּית *hesitantly*, מַעֲדַנִּית *hesitantly*.

מַעֲדַי 1 pr.n.m. **Maadai,** Israelite (son of Bani [or em. Bigvai , Bunni, or Bezai]) with foreign wife, <NOM CL> מִבְּנֵי בָנִי מַעֲדַי *of the sons of Bani was Maadai* Ezr 10$_{34}$.

מַעַדְיָה 2 pr.n.m. **Maadiah, 1.** priest who returned with Zerubbabel, <SUBJ> עלה *go up* Ne 12$_{5}$ (or em. מַעַזְיָה *Maaziah*).

2. priest at time of Joiakim, <PREP> לְ of possession, *of, (belonging) to* Ne 12$_{17(mss)}$ לְמַעַדְיָה פִּלְטָי *to Maadiah was Pilti;* L לְמוֹעַדְיָה פִּלְטָי *to Moadiah was Piltai;* or em. לְמַעַזְיָה *to Maaziah* or לְמוֹעֲדֶיהָ *at its appointed times*).

[מַעֲדָן] I 4.0.1 n.[m.] **delicacy**—pl. מַעֲדַנִּים (מַעֲדַנֹּת); cstr. מַעֲדַנֵּי—**delicious food, delicacy** (Gn 49$_{20}$); perh. also **delicateness** (1 S 15$_{32}$ Lm 4$_{5}$), **delight** (1 S 15$_{32}$ Pr 29$_{17}$).

<OBJ> נתן *give* Pr 29$_{17}$ (+ לְנַפְשֶׁךָ give delight[s] to *your soul* or give delicacies *for your appetite;* + נוח hi. *give peace*), *produce* Gn 49$_{20}$=4QCommGenA 6$_{1}$. <CSTR> מַעֲדַנֵּי־מֶלֶךְ *a king's delicacies* Gn 49$_{20}$ (+ לֶחֶם *food;* =4QCommGenA 6$_{1}$ מעדני י[הודה] *the delicacies of Judah;* WA מעדני ה[מלך] *the delicacies of the king*). <PREP> לְ אכל appar. *feed on* Lm 4$_{5}$ (unless לְמַעֲדַנִּים = eat *in accordance with delicateness[es]*, i.e. delicately; + תּוֹלָע wear *scarlet*).

<COLL> מִלֵּא כְרֵשׂוֹ מֵעֲדָנָי הֱדִיחָנִי *he has filled his stomach (with) my delicacies, he has vomited me out* Jr 49$_{34(Qr)}$ (if em. מֵעֲדָנַי *from my delicacies*, i.e. עֵדֶן *delicacy;* or em. מֵעֲדָנַי הִדִּיחָנִי *he has pushed me from my delicacies*), וַיֵּלֶךְ אֵלָיו אֲגַג מַעֲדַנֹּת *and Agag came towards him (with) delicateness(es)*, i.e. delicately, or, *(with) delight(s)*, i.e. happily, 1 S 15$_{32}$ (unless מַעֲדָן II *bond* or III *faltering* or IV *reluctant;* or em. מַעֲנַדֹּת *[in] chains* or מְעֹדַנֹּת or מַעֲדַנֹּת *hesitantly* or מְעֻדֶּנֶת *[as] a pampered woman*).

⇨ עדן *be luxurious.*

[מַעֲדָן] II 2 n.[f.] **bond**—pl. מַעֲדַנֹּת; cstr. מַעַדְנּוֹת—**bond, chain,** <OBJ> קשׁר pi. perh. *untie* Jb 38$_{31}$ (unless מַעֲדֶנֶת *company;* or em. מַעֲנָד *chain*). <CSTR> מַעַדַנּוֹת כִּימָה *the bonds of the Pleiades*, i.e. that unite them in a single constellation Jb 38$_{31}$. <COLL> וַיֵּלֶךְ אֵלָיו אֲגַג מַעֲדַנֹּת *and Agag came towards him (in) chains* 1 S 15$_{32}$ (unless מַעֲדָן I *delicacy* or III *faltering* or IV *reluctant;* or em. מַעֲנַדֹּת *[in] chains* or מְעֹדַנֹּת or מַעֲדַנֹּת *hesitantly* or מְעֻדֶּנֶת *[as] a pampered woman*).

⇨ ענד *bind.*

*[**מַעֲדָן**] III 1 n.[f.] **faltering**—pl. מַעֲדַנֹּת—**faltering (step),** <COLL> וַיֵּלֶךְ אֵלָיו אֲגַג מַעֲדַנֹּת *and Agag came towards him with faltering steps* 1 S 15$_{32}$ (unless מַעֲדָן I *delicacy* or II *bond* or IV *reluctant;* or em. מַעֲנַדֹּת *[in] chains* or מְעֹדַנֹּת or מַעֲדַנֹּת *hesitantly* or מְעֻדֶּנֶת *[as] a pampered woman*).

⇨ מעד *shake.*

*[**מַעֲדָן**] IV 1 n.[f.] **reluctant**—pl. מַעֲדַנֹּת—<COLL> וַיֵּלֶךְ אֵלָיו אֲגַג מַעֲדַנֹּת *and Agag came towards him reluctantly* 1 S 15$_{32}$ (unless מַעֲדָן I *delicacy* or II *bond* or III *faltering;* or em. מַעֲנַדֹּת *[in] chains* or מְעֹדַנֹּת or מַעֲדַנֹּת *hesitantly* or מְעֻדֶּנֶת *[as] a pampered woman*).

⇨ מעד *shake.*

*[**מְעֻדָּנָה**] 0.0.0.1 pr.n.f. **Meuddanah,** daughter of a king, <APP> מעדנה בת המלך *Meuddanah, daughter of the king* Seal 781 (7th cent.). <PREP> לְ of possession, *of, (belonging) to* Seal 781.

⇨ עדן *be luxurious.*

[**מַעֲדַנִּית**] adv. **hesitantly,** וַיֵּלֶךְ אֵלָיו אֲגַג מַעֲדַנֹּת *and Agag came towards him hesitantly* 1 S 15$_{32}$ (if em. מַעֲדַנֹּת *[with] faltering steps* or *[in] chains*).

⇨ מעד *shake.*

*[**מַעֲדֶנֶת**] 1 n.[f.] **company**—cstr. מַעַדְנּוֹת—**company, chorus,** <COLL> הַתְקַשֵּׁר מַעֲדַנּוֹת כִּימָה *can you control the company of the Pleiades*, i.e. prevent their let-

ting loose the spring rains Jb 38$_{31}$ (unless מַעֲדָן II *bond* or מַעֲנָה *bond*).

[מַעֲדֶנֶת] n.f. **pampered woman,** וַיֵּלֶךְ אֵלָיו אֲגַג מַעֲדַנֹּת *and Agag came towards him as a pampered woman* 1 S 15$_{32}$ (if em. מַעֲדַנֹּת *[with] faltering steps* or *[in] chains*).

⇒ עדן *be luxurious.*

מַעְדֵּר 1 n.[m.] **hoe,** <PREP> בְּ of instrument, *by (means of), with,* + עדר ni. *be hoed* (of hill country) Is 7$_{25}$, נפל *fall* (of Lebanon) Is 10$_{34}$ (if em. בְּאַדִּיר Lebanon *as a majestic one* will fall, to בְּמַעְדֵּר *by the hoe;* + בַּרְזֶל by *iron*).*

⇒ עדר *hoe.*

[מָעָה] I 1.0.2 n.f. **particle**—pl. Q מעות, מעת; sf. מְעֹתָיו—
1. particle, grain (of sand), unless מְעֹתָיו *its entrails,* i.e. fem. du./pl. of מֵעֶה *gut,* or from מָעָה II *multitude,* <PREP> כְּ *as* + היה *be* Is 48$_{19}$ (וַיְהִי כַחוֹל זַרְעֶךָ וְצֶאֱצָאֵי מֵעֶיךָ כִּמְעֹתָיו *your seed would have been like the sand and the issue of your belly like its particles,* or *like [the issue of] its entrails;* or em. כַּעֲפָרוֹתָיו *like its dust;* 1QIsa^a וצאצאיכה כמעותיו *and your issue like its particles*).

2. as name of coin of lowest value, **maah,** <NOM CL> בצדו המעת *in its side are the maahs* 3QTr 10$_{8}$ (others בצדו המערבי *on its western side*).* <PREP> כְּ *as* Pr 10$_{20}$ (if em. לֵב רְשָׁעִים כִּמְעָט *the heart of [the] wicked is as little,* i.e. is worth little, to בְּמָעָה *in exchange for a maah,* i.e. is worth but a maah). <COLL> מעות שתין *two maahs* 3QTr 10$_{9}$ (others בעזת שתין *by two supports*).*

*[מָעָה] II 1 n.f. **multitude** (unless מָעָה I *particle*)—pl. sf. מְעֹתָיו—<PREP> כְּ *as* + היה *be* Is 48$_{19}$ (וַיְהִי כַחוֹל זַרְעֶךָ וְצֶאֱצָאֵי מֵעֶיךָ כִּמְעֹתָיו *and your seed would have been as the sand and the issue of your belly like its multitudes*).

[מֵעֶה] 34.3.3.1 n.m. **belly, womb**—du./pl. Si מעים; cstr. מְעֵי; sf. מֵעַי (מֵעָי), מֵעֶיךָ (Q מעיכה), מֵעַיִךְ, מֵעָיו (מְעוֹתָיו), Q מעיה, מֵעֵיהֶם—alw. du./pl., **belly, womb, gut(s), entrails, bowel(s), internal organs,** etc.; exact anatomical reference oft. uncertain, in general, **(the) inside.**

1. oft. as source of procreation in body of a man, perh. **genitals,** Gn 15$_{4}$ 2 S 7$_{12}$ (+ זֶרַע *seed*) 16$_{11}$ (+ בֵּן *son*) 1QIsa^a 39$_{7}$ (+ בֵּן) Is 48$_{1}$ (if em. מַיִם *water,* perh. seminal fluid) 48$_{19}$ (+ צֶאֱצָא, זֶרַע *issue*) 2 C 32$_{21}$ (+ יָצִיא *issue*) appar. 4QRitMar 20$_{3}$ ([מ]עיו לפרי בו[טן] *his genitals, for the fruit of the womb*).

2. womb of a woman, Gn 25$_{23}$ Is 49$_{1}$ Ps 71$_{6}$ (all three + בֶּטֶן *womb*) Ru 1$_{11}$ 4QTob^e 2$_{2}$ 11QT 50$_{10}$; of pregnant beast 4QHalakhah^a 7$_{2}$; perh. of sea, Is 48$_{19}$ (unless מָעָה *particle* of sand).

3. perh. **offspring,** of tomb-builder (Kfar Baram inscr.$_{2}$ [or em. מַעֲשֶׂה *deed*]).

4. belly, as organ of ingestion of liquid by a woman, Nm 5$_{22}$ (+ בֶּטֶן *womb*); of food by a man, Ezk 3$_{3}$ (‖ בֶּטֶן *stomach*) Jb 20$_{14}$ (+ קֶרֶב *inside*); by people in general, Ezk 7$_{19}$ (‖ נֶפֶשׁ *appetite*) Si 40$_{29}$; by fish, Jon 2$_{1.2}$ (+ בֶּטֶן *inside* of Sheol).

5. internal organs, in a man, 2 S 20$_{10}$ (+ חֹמֶשׁ *abdomen*) 2 C 21$_{15.15.18.19}$ Ps 22$_{15}$ (+ לֵב *heart,* עֶצֶם *bone*).

6. inner person, self, as seat of fear or distress, Jr 4$_{19.19}$ (+ לֵב *heart*) Jb 30$_{27}$ Lm 1$_{20}$ (+ לֵב, קֶרֶב *inside*) 2$_{11}$ (+ עַיִן *eye,* כָּבֵד *liver*) Si 4$_{2}$ (‖ קֶרֶב *inside*); of Y.'s sadness or compassion, Is 16$_{11}$ (+ קֶרֶב my *inside*) 63$_{15}$ (+ רַחֲמִים *compassion*) Jr 31$_{20}$ (+ רחם pi. *pity*); of human intention or desire, Ps 40$_{9}$; perh. of sexual arousal or yearning of woman, Ca 5$_{4}$ (+ חֹר *hole,* perh. vagina), of man, Si 51$_{21(B)}$.

7. belly as viewed externally, in description of male lover's body, Ca 5$_{14}$.

<SUBJ> המה *be agitated* Si 51$_{21(B)}$ (+ כתנור *like an oven*), רתח pu. *be boiled,* i.e. agitated Jb 30$_{27}$, המה *make a noise* Is 16$_{11}$ (+ לְמוֹאָב כַּכִּנּוֹר make a noise *for Moab like a harp*) Jr 31$_{20}$ (+ לוֹ *for him* [Ephraim]) Ca 5$_{4}$, חמר pealal *ferment,* i.e. be agitated or twisted in anguish* Lm 1$_{20}$ 2$_{11}$, יצא *go out* 2 C 21$_{15}$ (+ מִן־הַחֹלִי *on account of the illness*) 21$_{19}$ (+ עִם־חָלְיוֹ *with his sickness*).

<NOM CL> מֵעָיו עֶשֶׁת שֵׁן *his belly is a block of ivory*

Ca 5_{14}.

<OBJ> שׁפך *pour (out)* entrails onto ground 2 S 20_{10}, מלא *fill* Ezk 3_3 (+ אֶת הַמְּגִלָּה הַזֹּאת fill gut *with this scroll*) 7_{19}, חמר hi. *cause* insides *to ferment*, i.e. cause distress Si 4_2.

<CSTR> מְעֵי אִמִּי *my mother's womb* Is 49_1 Ps 71_6, מע[י]ן עמו *its mother's womb* 4QHalakhah[a] 7_2, מעי דך *(the) insides of one crushed* Si 4_2, מְעֵי הַדָּג *the fish's inside* Jon $2_{1.2}$ (הַדָּגָה), מִמְּעֵי יְהוּדָה *from the genitals of Judah* Is 48_1 (if em. מִמֵּי *from the [seminal] waters of*); צֶאֱצָאֵי מֵעֶיךָ *the issue(s) of your genitals* Is 48_{19}, הֲמוֹן מֵעֶיךָ *the noise of your bowels* Is 63_{15}, מַחֲלֵה *a sickness*, i.e. disease, *of* 2 C 21_{15}, מִיצִיאֵי מֵעָיו *some of the issue of his (own) genitals* 2 C $32_{21(Qr)}$, סוד מעים perh. *(the) secret (of) the bowels* Si $40_{29(B)}$ (M יסור *punishment*, i.e. agony, of bowels; Bmg יסור מזעים *torture that makes indignant*).

<PREP> בְּ of place, *in(to)* Ru 1_{11} (הַעוֹד־לִי בָנִים בְּמֵעַי *do I still have sons in my womb?*) 4QHalakhah[a] 7_2 (במע[י]ן), + היה *be* Jon 2_1, הפך ni. *be changed* (of food) Jb 20_{14} (+ מְרוֹרַת פְּתָנִים בְּקִרְבּוֹ *asps' venom is in his inside*), מות *die* 11QT 50_{10} (+ בתוכה *inside her*), בוא *come* Nm 5_{22} Kfar Baram inscr.$_2$ (תבא ברכה במעיו perh. *may blessing come to his offspring*; or em. מַעֲשָׂיו upon *his deeds*), סבל *carry* in womb 4QTob[e] 2_2 (במעי[ה]); *against*, + נגף *strike* 2 C 21_{18} (+ לָחֳלִי לְאֵין מַרְפֵּא *for*, i.e. resulting in, *an incurable illness*).

כְּ *as* + היה *be* Is 48_{19} (וַיְהִי כַחוֹל זַרְעֶךָ וְצֶאֱצָאֵי מֵעֶיךָ כִּמְעֹתָיו *your seed would have been like the sand and the issue of your entrails like [the issue of] its entrails*; unless מָעָה *particle*; or em. כַּעֲפְרֹתָיו *like its dust*; 1QIsa[a] וצאצאיכה כמעותיו *and your issue like its particles*).

מִן of direction, *from*, + יצא *go out* Gn 15_4 2 S 7_{12} 16_{11} 1QIsa[a] 39_7 (אשר יצאו ממעיכה *who go out from your [own] genitals*; MT מִמְּךָ *from you*) Is 48_1 (if em. מִמֵּי *from the [seminal] waters of*), פרד ni. *be separated* Gn 25_{23}, גזה *cut* Ps 71_6 (or em. גֹּוזִי you are *the one who severs me* to גֹּחִי *the one who extracts me* or עֻזִּי *my strength*), קרא *call* Is 49_1, פלל htp. *pray* Jon 2_2.

בְּתוֹךְ *inside* Ps 40_9 (+ וְתוֹרָתְךָ *and your law* is inside my entrails), + מסס ni. *melt* (of heart) Ps 22_{15}.

מֵעֶה without preposition, *(from) the belly*, + סתר hi. *hide* Jb 3_{10} (if em. מֵעֵינָי *from my eyes* to מֵעַי *(from) my belly*, i.e. from my mother's womb, || בֶּטֶן *womb*).*

<COLL> מֵעַי מֵעַי אוֹחִילָה קִירוֹת לִבִּי *my bowels, my bowels! I must wait*, or *I am in despair; the walls of my heart!* Jr $4_{19(Qr)}$ (mss, as Kt, אָחוּלָה, or אָחִילָה *I am forced to writhe*).

<SYN> בֶּטֶן *stomach*, קֶרֶב *inside*, נֶפֶשׁ *appetite*.

מָעוֹג I $_1$ **n.[m.] circle. 1. loaf** or perh. **slice (of bread)** or **cake**, <NOM CL> חַי־י׳ אֱלֹהֶיךָ אִם־יֶשׁ־לִי מָעוֹג *(I swear) as Y. your God lives, if I have (even) a loaf* 1 K 17_{12} (unless מָעוֹג II *provisions* or III *round silo* or V *place to which one turns for provisions*; or em. מְאוּמָה *anything*).

2. perh. **circle**, <CSTR> לַעֲגֵי מָעוֹג *mockers of*, i.e. who stand in, *a circle*, or, as §1, *mockers of a cake*, i.e. who mock in pursuit of food Ps 35_{16} (unless מָעוֹג IV *cripple*; or em. לָעֲגוּ לַעַג *they made mockery* or לָעֲגוּ מְעֻוָּג *they mocked one who is encircled* or עָגוּ מְעֻוָּג *they surrounded one who is encircled* or עָגוּ מָעוֹג *they surrounded (in) a circle* or לָעֲגוּ לֹעֲגִים *mochers mocked*).*

⇒ עוג *be round*.

***מָעוֹג** II $_1$ **n.[m.] provisions**, <NOM CL> חַי־י׳ אֱלֹהֶיךָ אִם־יֶשׁ־לִי מָעוֹג *(I swear) as Y. your God lives, if I have (any) provisions* 1 K 17_{12} (unless מָעוֹג I *loaf* or III *round silo* or V *place to which one turns for provisions*; or em. מְאוּמָה *anything*).

⇒ (?) עוג *bake*.

***מָעוֹג** III $_1$ **n.[m.] round silo**, thus provisions kept in a silo, <NOM CL> חַי־י׳ אֱלֹהֶיךָ אִם־יֶשׁ־לִי מָעוֹג *(I swear) as Y. your God lives, if I have (any) provisions* 1 K 17_{12} (unless מָעוֹג I *loaf* or II *provisions* or V *place to which one turns for provisions*; or em. מְאוּמָה *anything*).

***מָעוֹג** IV $_1$ **n.[m.] place to which one turns for provisions**, <NOM CL> חַי־י׳ אֱלֹהֶיךָ אִם־יֶשׁ־לִי מָעוֹג *(I swear) as Y. your God lives, if I have (any) place to turn for provisions* 1 K 17_{12} (unless מָעוֹג I *loaf* or II *provisions* or III *round silo*; or em. מְאוּמָה *anything*).

*מָעוֹג V_1 n.[m.] **lame person,** <CSTR> לַעֲגֵי מָעוֹג *those who mock a lame person* Ps 35_{16} (unless מָעוֹג I *circle;* or em. לָעֲגוּ לַעַג *they made mockery* or לָעֲגוּ מְעֻוָּג *they mocked one who is encircled* or עָגוּ מְעֻוָּג *they surrounded one who is encircled* or עָגוּ מָעוֹג *they surrounded (in) a circle* or לָעֲגוּ לְעֵגִים *mockers mocked).**

מָעוֹז I$_{34.1.9}$ n.m. **refuge** (many refs. may be מָעוֹז II *stronghold*)—mss מָעֹז; cstr. מָעוֹז; sf. מָעוּזִּי (מָעֻזִּי), מָעֻזֵּךְ, מָעוּזּוֹ (מָעֻזּוֹ, Kt מעזה), מָעֻזְּכֶם, מָעֻזְּכֶן, מָעוּזָּם (מָעֻזָּם); pl. מָעֻזִּים; sf. מָעֻזֶּיהָ (Q מעוזיה [i.e. מָעוּזֶּיהָ])—**(place of) refuge** or **of protection;** of Y. (2 S 22_{33} Is $25_{4.4}$ Jr 16_{19} Jl 4_{16} Na 1_7 Ps 27_1 28_8 31_5 37_{39} 43_2 $90_{1[mss]}$ 91_9 [if em.] Si 51_1 1QH 10_{32} perh. Ps 52_9 4QapPs[b] 19.1_3), of heavenly being (Dn 11_1), perh. of people (Ezk 24_{25} Ps 60_9||108_9 1QH $8_{27[Licht]}$ 10_{23}), of rejoicing (Ne 8_{10}), of human body (1QH $8_{32.33}$), of tree (1QH 8_{24}).

<SUBJ> היה *be* Is $25_{4.4}$ (both + Y.; + מַחְסֶה *refuge,* צֵל *shade*) 30_3 (+ לָכֶם ... לְבֹשֶׁת *to you ... as shame;* + צֵל) Ps $90_{1(mss)}$ (+ Y.; L מָעוֹן I *dwelling place* or IV *help*) 1QH 8_{33} (+ לבהלה *turned into terror*), שׁדד pu. *be devastated* Is 23_{14} (or em. מָחוֹז *city*), שׁבת ni. *be made to cease* 1QH 8_{32} (+ נֶפֶשׁ *soul,* לֵב *heart,* בָּשָׂר *flesh*), אמר *say* Is 23_4 (or del. מָעוֹז הַיָּם *the refuge of the sea*).

<NOM CL> אַתָּה מָעוּזִּי *you are my refuge* Ps 31_5, הָאֵל מָעוּזִּי חָיִל *God, my refuge, is (my) valour* 2 S 22_{33} (||Ps 18_{33} הָאֵל הַמְאַזְּרֵנִי *the God who girds me* [with] valour), וַי׳ ... מָעוֹז *and Y. will be ... a refuge* Jl 4_{16} (|| מַחֲסֶה *refuge*), י׳ מָעוֹז־חַיַּי *Y. is the refuge,* or *protection, of my life* Ps 27_1 (+ אוֹרִי וְיִשְׁעִי *my light and my salvation*), מָעוֹז יְשׁוּעוֹת מְשִׁיחוֹ הוּא *he is the protection of the salvation(s) of his anointed* Ps 28_8 (or del. מָעוֹז; + עֹז *strength*), אֶפְרַיִם מָעוֹז רֹאשִׁי *Ephraim is the refuge,* or *protection, of my head,* i.e. my helmet or my chief stronghold Ps 60_9||108_9, מָעוֹז ... דֶּרֶךְ י׳ *a refuge ... is the way of Y.* Pr 10_{29} (mss מָעֹז; :: מְחִתָּה *destruction* for evildoers), כִּי־חֶדְוַת י׳ הִיא מָעֻזְּכֶם *for rejoicing of,* i.e. in, *Y. is your protection* Ne 8_{10} (or em. כִּי־י׳ הוּא מָעֻזֵּנוּ *for Y. is our protection*), היא ... מעוז קודש קו[ד]שים *it is ... the protection of (the) holy of holies* 4QS[e] $1.2_{17(WA)}$ (others מעון *dwelling place;* ||1QS 8_8 היאה ... מעון, ||4QS[d] 2_2 מעון ... [היא]), [וכאבי]ון אין מעוז לו *and like a poor one (who) has no protection* 1QH $8_{27(Licht)}$.

<OBJ> בקשׁ pi. *seek* Na 3_{11} (+ מִבְצָר *fortified town*), שׂים *place* Ps 52_9 (הַגֶּבֶר לֹא יָשִׂים אֱלֹהִים מָעוּזּוֹ *the person who does not make God his refuge* or *the person whose refuge God does not appoint*) 91_9 (if em. עֶלְיוֹן שַׂמְתָּ מְעוֹנֶךָ *you have made Elyon your dwelling place* to מָעוּזֶּךָ *your refuge;* || מַחֲסֶה *refuge*) perh. 1QH 10_{23}, לקח *take* Ezk 24_{25}, עצר *retain* protection 1QH $8_{24(AHL)}$ (Licht מַעְיָן *spring*), חלל pi. *profane* Dn 11_{31}, שׁמד hi. *destroy* Is 23_{11} (unless מָעֻזְנֶיהָ *her refuges* is from מָעוֹזֶן *refuge* or מָעֻזָּן *mart;* 1QIsa[a] מעוזיה; or em. מְעוֹנֶיהָ *her dwelling places*).

<CSTR> מעוז חיל גבורים *the protection of an army of mighty ones* 1QH 10_{23}, מעוז קודש קו[ד]שים *the protection of (the) holy of holies* 4QS[e] $1.2_{17(WA)}$ (others, ||1QS 8_8=4QS[d] 2_2 מעון *dwelling place*), מעוז מרום *the refuge of height,* i.e. heaven 1QH 10_{32}, מָעוֹז הַיָּם *the refuge of,* i.e. from, or, by, *the sea,* i.e. harbour city Is 23_4 (or del.), מִצְרָיִם *of Egypt* Ezk 30_{15}, פַּרְעֹה *of Pharaoh* Is $30_{2.3}$ (both || צֵל *shade*), מֶלֶךְ הַצָּפוֹן *of the king of the north* Dn 11_7, מָעוֹז־חַיַּי *the refuge,* or *protection, of my life* Ps 27_1 Si 51_1, מָעוֹז רֹאשִׁי *the refuge,* or *protection, of my head,* i.e. my helmet or my chief stronghold Ps 60_9||108_9, מעוז מותני *the protection of my hips* 1QH 8_{33}, מָעוֹז יְשׁוּעוֹת מְשִׁיחוֹ *the protection of the salvation(s) of his anointed* Ps 28_8 (or del. מָעוֹז).

רֹאשׁ הַמָּעוֹז *the top of the fortified place* Jg 6_{26} (mss מָעוֹן *dwelling place*), עָרֵי מָעֻזּוֹ *the cities of his refuge* Is 17_9 (or em. מָעֻזֵּךְ *your refuge*), צוּר מָעוֹז *a rock of refuge* Ps 31_3=$71_{3(mss)}$ (L מָעוֹן *of a dwelling place,* in which to live; || מְצוּדָה *refuge*), צוּר מָעֻזֵּךְ *the rock of your refuge* Is 17_{10}, אֱלֹהֵי מָעוּזִּי *the God of my protection* Ps 43_2 (or em. אֱלֹהִים עֻזִּי for you, *O God, are my strength*), פנות מעוז appar. *corners,* i.e. towers, *of protection* Si 50_2 (if em. מעון corners of *[the holy] place*), מִבְצְרֵי מָעֻזִּים *fortified towns of refuge(s)* Dn 11_{39}

<APP> י׳ מָעוּזָּם *Y., their refuge* Ps 37_{39}, הָאֵל מָעוּזִּי *God, my refuge* 2 S 22_{33} (||Ps 18_{33} הָאֵל הַמְאַזְּרֵנִי *the God who girds me*), יָם מָעוֹז הַיָּם *(the) sea, (that is to say) the refuge of the sea* Is 23_4 (or del. יָם or מָעוֹז הַיָּם), סִין מָעוֹז מִצְרָיִם *Sin, the protection of Egypt* Ezk 30_{15}, הַמִּקְדָּשׁ הַמָּעוֹז *the sanctuary, the refuge* Dn 11_{31}, אֶת־מָעוּזָּם מְשׂוֹשׂ

תִּפְאַרְתָּם אֶת־מַחְמַד עֵינֵיהֶם וְאֶת־מַשָּׂא נַפְשָׁם בְּנֵיהֶם וּבְנוֹתֵיהֶם *their refuge*, or *protection, the joy of their glory, the delight of their eyes and the desire of their soul, their sons and their daughters* Ezk 24_{25} (or del. בְּנֵיהֶם וּבְנוֹתֵיהֶם or em. וּבְנֵיהֶם *and their sons* and daughters), חומת הבחן פ[נת יקר] ... מעוז קודש קו[ד]שים *the wall of the fortress*, or *of testing, a cornerstone of preciousness ... the protection of (the) holy of holies* 4QSe 1.$2_{17(WA)}$ (others, ||1QS 8_8=4QSd 2_2 מעון *dwelling place*).

<ADJ> זֶה *this* Jg 6_{26} (mss מָעוֹן *dwelling place*).

<PREP> לְ *as* Na 1_7 (or comparative לְ, טוֹב י׳ לְמָעוֹז *Y. is better than a refuge;** or em. טוֹב י׳ לְמָעוֹז *Y. is good as a refuge* to לְמְחַכֵּי־לוֹ מָעוֹז Y. is good, *to those who wait for him [he is] a refuge*) Dn 11_1 (|| מַחֲזִיק as *one who strengthens*) perh. 1QHb 1_1; בְּ of place, *in(to)*, + בוא *come* Dn 11_7, עוז *take refuge* Is 30_2; of essence, *consisting of*, 1QH 10_{32} (ומשענתי במעוז מרום *and my support is the refuge of height*, i.e. heaven); חזק בְּ hi. *hold on to* Is 27_5; עַל *upon*, + שׁפך *pour* anger Ezk 30_{15}; *against*, + גרה htp. *fight* Dn $11_{10(Gnz)}$; עַד *unto*, i.e. until he has reached, + גרה htp. *fight* Dn 11_{10} (Gnz עַל fight *against*).

<COLL> מָעוֹז לַדָּל *a refuge for the poor* Is 25_4, מָעוֹז לָאֶבְיוֹן *a refuge for the poor* Is 25_4, וּמָעוֹז לִבְנֵי יִשְׂרָאֵל *and a refuge for the children of Israel* Jl 4_{16}, וּלְמָעוֹז לוֹ *and as a protection for him* Dn 11_1 (ms לִי as *my own* protection), מָעוֹז ... לָנוּ בְּדֹר וָדֹר you have been *a refuge ... for us through generation and generation* Ps $90_{1(mss)}$ (L מָעוֹן I *dwelling place* or IV *help*; mss לְדֹר *to generation* and generation), מָעוֹז לַתֹּם *a refuge of integrity* Pr 10_{29} (mss מָעֹז; or em. לַתָּם *for the upright*), מָעוֹז מֵאוֹיֵב *a refuge from an enemy* Na 3_{11}, ונשבת מעוזי מגויתי *and my protection has been made to cease from my body* 1QH 8_{32}.

אספרה שמך מעוז חיי *I will recount your name, O refuge of my life* Si 51_1, י׳ עֻזִּי וּמָעֻזִּי וּמְנוּסִי בְּיוֹם צָרָה *O Y., my strength and my protection and my refuge on a day of trouble* Jr 16_{19}, מָעוֹז בְּיוֹם צָרָה *a refuge on a day of trouble* Na 1_7, מָעוּזָּם בְּעֵת צָרָה *their refuge in a time of trouble* Ps 37_{39}.

Also perh. 4Q418 115_1 ([מעוזכן]).

<SYN> מָנוֹס *refuge*, מַחֲסֶה *refuge*, מְצוּדָה *refuge*, צֵל *shade*, עֹז *strength*, מַחֲזִיק *one who strengthens*.

<ANT> מְחִתָּה *destruction*.*

⇒ עוז *take refuge*.

***מָעוֹז** II 24.1.9 n.m. **strength**—cstr. מָעוֹז; sf. מָעֻזִּי (מָעוּזִּי), מָעֻזָּם (מָעוּזָּם), מָעֻזְּכֶן, מָעֻזְּכֶם, (מעזה Kt) מָעֻזּוֹ, מָעֻזֵּךְ; pl. מָעֻזִּים; cstr. מָעוּזֵּי; sf. מָעֻזְנֶיהָ (Q מעוזיה [i.e. מָעוּזֶּיהָ])—**1. stronghold** (Jg 6_{26} Is $23_{4.11.14}$ Ezk 24_{25} 30_{15} Na 3_{11} Ps 69_9 108_9 Dn $11_{7.10.19.31.38.39}$ 1QH 10_3 4QSe 1.$2_{17(WA)}$); of Y. (2 S 22_{33} Is $25_{4.4}$ [unless both מָעוֹז I *refuge*] Jr 16_{19} perh. Jl 4_{16} perh. Na 1_7 Ps 27_1 28_8 [unless both מָעוֹז I] 37_{39} $90_{1[mss]}$ [unless both מָעוֹז I] Si 51_1 [unless מָעוֹז I] 1QH 10_{32}), of way of Y. Pr 10_{29}; of rejoicing (Ne 8_{10}).

2. **strength**, of army (1QH 10_{23}), Y. (Is 17_9 27_5), king (Dn 11_1), worshipper (Ps 43_2), poor person 1QH 8_{27} children (Ezk 24_{25}), city (Is 17_{10}), towers (Si 50_2), tree (1QH 8_{24}), body (1QH 8_{32}), loins (1QH 8_{33}), salvation (Ps 28_8).

<SUBJ> היה *be* Is $25_{4.4}$ (both + Y.; + מַחְסֶה *refuge*, צֵל *shade*) Ps $90_{1(mss)}$ (+ Y.; L מָעוֹן I *dwelling place* or IV *help*) 1QH 8_{33} (+לבהלה turned *into terror*), שׁדד pu. *be devastated* Is 23_{14} (or em. מָחוֹז *city*), שׁבת ni. *be made to cease* 1QH 8_{32} (+ נֶפֶשׁ *soul*, לֵב *heart*, בָּשָׂר *flesh*), אמר *say* Is 23_4 (or del. מָעוֹז הַיָּם *the stronghold of the sea*).

<NOM CL> הָאֵל מָעוּזִּי חָיִל *God, my stronghold, is (my) valour* 2 S 22_{33} (||Ps 18_{33} הָאֵל הַמְאַזְּרֵנִי *the God who girds me* [with] valour), וַי׳... מָעוֹז *and Y. will be ... a refuge* Jl 4_{16} (unless מָעוֹז I *refuge*; || מַחֲסֶה *refuge*), י׳ מָעוֹז־חַיַּי *Y. is the refuge*, or *strength, of my life* Ps 27_1 (+ אוֹרִי וְיִשְׁעִי *my light and my salvation*), מָעוֹז יְשׁוּעוֹת מְשִׁיחוֹ הוּא *he is the strength of the salvation(s) of his anointed* Ps 28_8 (or del. מָעוֹז; + עֹז *strength*), אֶפְרַיִם מָעוֹז רֹאשִׁי *Ephraim is the stronghold of my head*, i.e. my chief stronghold Ps 60_9||108_9, ... מָעוֹז דֶּרֶךְ י׳ *a stronghold ... is the way of Y.* Pr 10_{29} (mss מָעֹז; :: מְחִתָּה *destruction* for evildoers), כִּי־חֶדְוַת י׳ הִיא מָעֻזְּכֶם *for rejoicing of*, i.e. in, *Y. is your strength* Ne 8_{10} (or em. כִּי־י׳ הוּא מָעֻזֵּנוּ *for Y. is our strength*), היא ... מעוז קודש קו[ד]שים *it is ... the stronghold of (the) holy of holies* 4QSe 1.$2_{17(WA)}$ (others מעון *dwelling place*; ||1QS 8_8 [היא] ... מעון ([וכאב]ון אין), ||4QSd 2_2 היאה ... מעון)

מעוז לו *and like a poor one (who) has no strength* 1QH 8_{27}(Licht).

<OBJ> בקשׁ pi. *seek* Na 3_{11} (+ מִבְצָר *fortified town*), לקח *take* Ezk 24_{25}, עצר *retain* strength 1QH 8_{24}(AHL) (Licht מַעְיָן *spring*), חלל pi. *profane* Dn 11_{31}, שׁמד hi. *destroy* Is 23_{11} (unless מָעֻזֶּנֶיהָ *its refuges* is from מָעוֹזֶן *refuge* or מַעֲזָן *mart;* 1QIsa[a] מעוזיה; or em. מְעֹנֶיהָ *its dwelling places*).

<CSTR> מעוז חיל גבורים *the strength of an army of mighty ones* 1QH 10_{23}, מעוז קודש קו[ד]שים *the stronghold of (the) holy of holies* 4QS[e] 1.2_{17}(WA) (others, ||1QS 8_8=4QS[d] 2_2 מעון *dwelling place*), מעוז מרום *the stronghold of height,* i.e. heaven 1QH 10_{32} (unless מָעוֹז I *refuge*), מָעוּזֵי אַרְצוֹ *the fortresses of his own land* Dn 11_{19}, מָעוֹז הַיָּם *the stronghold of,* i.e. by, *the sea,* i.e. harbour city Is 23_4 (or del.), מִצְרָיִם *of Egypt* Ezk 30_{15}, מָעוֹז־חַיַּי *the strength of my life* Ps 27_1 Si 51_1, מָעוֹז רֹאשִׁי *the stronghold, of my head,* i.e. my chief stronghold Ps 60_9||108_9, מעוז מותני *the strength of my hips* 1QH 8_{33}, מָעוֹז יְשׁוּעוֹת מְשִׁיחוֹ *the strength of the salvation(s) of his anointed* Ps 28_8 (or del. מָעוֹז), מֶלֶךְ הַצָּפוֹן *of the king of the north* Dn 11_7.

רֹאשׁ הַמָּעוֹז *the top of the fortified place* Jg 6_{26} (mss מָעוֹן *dwelling place*), עָרֵי מָעֻזּוֹ *the cities of his strength* Is 17_9 (or em. מָעֻזֵּךְ *your strength*), צוּר מָעֻזֵּךְ *the rock of your strength* Is 17_{10} (unless מָעוֹז I *refuge*), אֱלֹהֵי מָעוּזִּי *the God of my strength* Ps 43_2 (or em. אֱלֹהִים עֻזִּי for you, *O God, are my strength*), פנות מעוז appar. *corners,* i.e. towers, *of strength* Si 50_2 (if em. מעון corners of *[the holy] place*), מִבְצְרֵי מָעֻזִּים *fortified towns of strength(s)* Dn 11_{39}.

<APP> הָאֵל מָעוּזִּי *God, my stronghold* 2 S 22_{33} (||Ps 18_{33} הָאֵל הַמְאַזְּרֵנִי *the God who girds me*), יָם מָעוֹז הַיָּם *(the) sea, (that is to say) the stronghold of the sea* Is 23_4 (or del. מָעוֹז הַיָּם or יָם), סִין מָעוֹז מִצְרָיִם *Sin, the stronghold of Egypt* Ezk 30_{15}, הַמִּקְדָּשׁ הַמָּעוֹז *the sanctuary, the stronghold* Dn 11_{31}, אֶת־מָעוּזָּם מְשׂוֹשׂ תִּפְאַרְתָּם אֶת־מַחְמַד עֵינֵיהֶם וְאֶת־מַשָּׂא נַפְשָׁם בְּנֵיהֶם וּבְנוֹתֵיהֶם *their strength, the joy of their glory, the delight of their eyes and the desire of their soul, their sons and their daughters* Ezk 24_{25} (or del. בְּנֵיהֶם וּבְנוֹתֵיהֶם or em. וּבְנֵיהֶם *and their sons* and daughters), חומת הבחן פנות יקר[... מעוז קודש קו[ד]שים *the wall of the fortress,* or *of testing, a cornerstone of preciousness ... the stronghold of (the) holy of holies* 4QS[e] 1.2_{17}(WA) (others, ||1QS 8_8=4QS[d] 2_2 מעון *dwelling place*).

<ADJ> זֶה *this* Jg 6_{26} (mss מָעוֹן *dwelling place*).

<PREP> לְ *to,* + שׁוּב פָּנִים *turn face* Dn 11_{19}; *as* Na 1_7 (or comparative טוֹב י׳ לְמָעוֹז, לְ *Y. is better than a fortress;** or em. טוֹב י׳ לְמָעוֹז *Y. is good as a stronghold* to לִמְחַכֵּי־לוֹ מָעוֹז Y. is good, *to those who wait for him [he is] a stronghold*) Dn 11_1 (|| מַחֲזִיק as *one who strengthens*) perh. 1QH[b] 1_1; בְּ of place, *in(to),* + בוא *come* Dn 11_7; of essence, *consisting of,* 1QH 10_{32} (ומשענתי במעוז מרום *and my support is the stronghold of the height,* i.e. heaven); בְּ חזק hi. *hold on to* Is 27_5; עַל *upon,* + שׁפך *pour* anger Ezk 30_{15}; *against,* + גרה htp. *fight* Dn 11_{10}(Gnz); עַד *unto,* i.e. until he has reached, + גרה htp. *fight* Dn 11_{10} (Gnz עַל fight *against*).

<COLL> מָעוֹז לַדָּל *a stronghold for the poor* Is 25_4, וּמָעוֹז לִבְנֵי *a stronghold for the poor* Is 25_4, מָעוֹז לָאֶבְיוֹן יִשְׂרָאֵל *and a stronghold for the children of Israel* Jl 4_{16}, וּלְמָעוֹז לוֹ *and as a stronghold for him* Dn 11_1 (ms לִי as *my own* stronghold), מָעוֹז ... לָנוּ בְּדֹר וָדֹר you have been *a stronghold ... for us through generation and generation* Ps 90_1(mss) (unless מָעוֹז I *refuge;* L מָעוֹן I *dwelling place* or IV *help;* mss לְדֹר *to generation* and generation), מָעוֹז לַתֹּם *a stronghold of integrity* Pr 10_{29} (mss מָעֹז; or em. לַתָּם *for the upright*), ונשבת מעוזי מגויתי *and my strength has been made to cease from my body* 1QH 8_{32}.

אספרה שמך מעוז חיי *I will recount your name, O strength of my life* Si 51_1 (unless מָעוֹז I *refuge*), י׳ עֻזִּי וּמָעֻזִּי וּמְנוּסִי בְּיוֹם צָרָה *O Y., my strength and my stronghold and my refuge on a day of trouble* Jr 16_{19}.

Also perh. 4Q418 115_1 (]מעוזכ[).

<SYN> מָנוֹס *refuge,* מַחֲסֶה *refuge,* מְצוּדָה *refuge,* צֵל *shade,* עֹז *strength,* מַחֲזִיק *one who strengthens.*

<ANT> מְחִתָּה *destruction.*

⇨ עזז *be strong.*

*[מָעוֹז] 0.1 n.m. **arrogance**—<NOM CL> תחתת גאון אדם מעוז *the beginning of the pride of a human is arrogance* Si 10_{12}.

⇒ יעז *be insolent.*

*[מָעֹוזֶן] $_{1}$ n.[m.] **refuge**—pl. sf. מָעֻזֶּנֶיהָ (unless from מָעוֹז *refuge* or מַעֲזָן *mart*)—<OBJ> שׁמד hi. *destroy* Is 23$_{11}$ (or em. to מְעוֹנֶיהָ *its dwelling places;* 1QIsa^{a} מעוזיה *its refuges*).

⇒ עוז *take refuge.*

*[מָעוּזְיָה] $_{0.0.8}$ pr.n.m. **Mauzzijah**—Q מעזיה, מעוזיה, מועזיה, מיעוזיה (WA), מגוזיה (WA)—priestly family and weekly cycle associated with it.

<NOM CL> [בשנה] הראישונה ... מועזי[ה] *in the first year is ... Mauzzijah* 4QMishF^{a} 1$_{2}$, מעוזיה ... בשנה] הראישונה] *Mauzzijah ... is in the first year* 4QMishF^{b} 1$_{01}$, [ה]שנה הרישונ[ה] בחו[דש ... מו]עזיה *for the first year in the (first) month ... is Mauzzijah* 4QMishF^{b} 1$_{4}$.

<CSTR> שבת מעוזיה *the sabbath of Mauzzijah* 4QMishA 4.3$_{2}$.

<PREP> בְּ of place/time, *in, during (the priestly course of)* 4QOtot 8$_{3}$ ([ב]מעוזיה הפסח *in Mauzzijah is the Passover*) 4QMishA 4.3$_{6}$ (4ב [ב]מעוזיה יום הזכרון *on the fourth of Mauzzijah is the day of remembrance*) 4.6$_{7}$ ([3ב] במעזיה הפסח ה[שני] *on the third of Mauzzijah is the second Passover*) 4QMishB^{a} ([ודוקה בארבעה] במעזיה בארבעה בוא appar. *and the new moon,* or *full moon,* or *lunar observation, is in the fourth [week] of Mauzzijah, on the fourth [day] of it;* WA מגוזיה [i.e. ג for ע]) 2.1$_{8}$ (ב[דל]יה במג[וזיה] בוא [הפסח] *in Delaiah; in Mauzzijah [in it] is the Passover;* others ב[גמול בשל]שה במ[עזיה] *in Gamul; on the third of Mauzzijah* [in it] is the Passover) 2.2$_{1.2}$ (השבי[עי במעוזיה] במיעזיה הואה יום הזכרון *the seventh is in Mauzzijah; in Mauzzijah is the day of remembrance;* others השבי[עי] במועזיה הואה יום הזכ[ר]ון *the seventh is in Mauzzijah, which is the day of remembrance*).

⇒ עוז *take refuge.*

*[מְעוּט] $_{0.1.1}$ n.[m.] **small thing, diminution**—Q מעוט; pl. Si מעוטים—<OBJ> בזה *despise* Si 19$_{1}$ (ובוזה מעוטים [ית]ערער *and one who despises small things will be stripped [even of these];* unless מְעוּטִים *reduced things,* i.e. מעט pass. ptc.). <CSTR> מעוט האדם *diminution of humankind* 4QpIsa^{c} 4.2$_{8}$ (unless מעט *be few* inf., or מְעַט *the few [remaining] of* humankind). <PREP> לְ *concerning, about* 4QpIsa^{c} 4.2$_{8}$ (פשרו למעוט האדם *its interpretation is about the diminution of humankind*).

⇒ מעט *be few.*

מָעוֹךְ $_{1}$ pr.n.m. **Maoch,** Gittite, father of Achish, appar. ident. with Maacah (מַעֲכָה) at 2 K 2$_{39}$, <CSTR> בֶּן־מָעוֹךְ *son of Maoch* 1 S 27$_{2}$.

מָעוּךְ *animal that is pressed,* see מעך *press.*

מָעוֹן I $_{19.1.29}$ n.[m.] **dwelling place**—cstr. מְעוֹן; sf. מְעוֹנְךָ, מְעוֹנוֹ, מְעוֹנָהּ; pl. cstr. Q מעוני; sf. Q מעוניהם—**dwelling place, abode, dwelling, place, home, a.** of Y. (Dt 26$_{15}$ 1 S 2$_{29.32}$ [or em. both] Jr 25$_{30}$ Zc 2$_{17}$ Ps 26$_{8}$ [or em.] 68$_{6}$ 2 C 30$_{27}$ 36$_{15}$ Si 50$_{2}$ [or em. מָעוֹז *refuge*] 1QH 12$_{2}$ fr. 9$_{7}$ 1QS 8$_{8}$=4QS^{d} 2$_{2}$ 1QS 10$_{3}$=4QS^{b} 8.2$_{1}$=4QS^{f} 1.2$_{2}$ 1QSb 4$_{25}$ 1QM 12$_{2}$ 4QShirShabb^{d} 1.2$_{19}$=4QShirShabb^{f} 8$_{3}$= 11QShirShabb 2$_{2}$ 4QShirShabb^{d} 1.2$_{23}$ 4QHod^{a} 7.1$_{12}$ 4QM^{a} 11.1$_{15}$ 4QShir^{a} 1$_{3}$ 4QShir^{b} 41$_{1}$ 11QShirShabb 3$_{10}$ 11QPsa^{a} 24$_{4}$ GnzPs 2$_{26}$ perh. 1QH^{b} 2$_{1}$ [others מַעְיָן *spring*] 4QShirShabb^{g} 1$_{2}$ 4QPrQuot 20$_{3}$).

b. of angels (4QBer^{b} 2$_{13}$ 4QShirShabb^{a} 2$_{5.6}$ perh. 4QShirShabb^{c} 11$_{4}$ [[ומעונ[י]] 4QShirShabb^{d} 1.2$_{45}$ [[מעונ[י]]])] 4QapJoshua^{c} 9.2$_{8}$.

c. of worshipper (4QHod^{a} 2$_{1}$), in ref. to God as refuge (Dt 33$_{27}$ [if em.] Ps 71$_{3}$ Ps 90$_{1}$ [in both, mss מָעוֹז *refuge*] 91$_{9}$ [or em. מָעוֹז]), of desert dwellers (1 C 4$_{41}$ [if em.]), on hill (Jg 6$_{26[mss]}$ [L מָעוֹז *refuge*]).

d. of wild animals (Jr 9$_{10}$ 49$_{33}$ 51$_{37}$ Na 2$_{12}$ 1QH 5$_{13}$).

e. of light (1QS 10$_{1}$=4QS^{d} 3.2$_{11}$), of holiness (1QS 10$_{12}$ [others מַעְיָן *spring*]), of knowledge (1Q36 12$_{2}$).

<SUBJ> היה *be* Ps 90$_{1}$ (י׳ מָעוֹן אַתָּה הָיִיתָ לָּנוּ בְּדֹר וָדֹר *O Y., you have been a dwelling place for us through generation and generation;* unless מָעוֹן II *help* or III *reminder of sin;* mss מָעוֹז *refuge,* לְדֹר *to generation* and generation), כרת ni. *be cut off* Zp 3$_{7}$ (or em. מְעוֹנָהּ *her dwelling place* to מֵעֵינֶיהָ cut off *from her eyes*).

<NOM CL> היאה ... מעון קודש קודשים *it is ... the dwelling place of (the) holy of holies* 1QS 8$_{8}$=4QS^{d} 2$_{2}$

([... והיא]; ||4QS^{e} $1.2_{17[WA]}$ היא ... מעוז קודש קו[ד]שים *it is ... the refuge* [מָעוֹז I], or *stronghold* [מָעוֹז II], *of (the) holy of holies* [others [מעון]), מְעֹנָה אֱלֹהֵי קֶדֶם *the God of antiquity is his dwelling place* Dt 33_{27} (if em. מְעֹנָה *a dwelling place*, i.e. מְעוֹנָה), אַיֵּה מְעוֹן אֲרָיוֹת *where is the dwelling place of lions?* Na 2_{12} (+ מִרְעֶה *pasture* [or em. מְעָרָה *cave*), במרומי רום מעון שו[די] *in the heights of height is the dwelling place of Shaddai* 4QShir^{b} 41_{1}.

<OBJ> שִׂים *place*, i.e. cause to be Jr 10_{22} 91_{9} (unless מָעוֹן II *help*; or em. עֶלְיוֹן שַׂמְתָּ מְעוֹנֶךָ *you have made Elyon your dwelling place* to מָעוּזֶּךָ *your refuge*; ||מַחֲסֶה *refuge*), שׂגב pi. *set on high* Ps 107_{41} (if em. מֵעֹנִי *from affliction*),* שׁית *cause* valley *to be* Ps 84_{7} (if em. מַעְיָן *spring* to מָעוֹן), אהב *love* Ps 26_{8} (or em. עֲבֹדַת *the service of* your house) GnzPs 2_{26}, נכה hi. *strike* 1 C 4_{41} (if em. הַמְּעוּנִים *the Maonites* to הַמְּעוֹנִים *the dwelling places* or מְעוֹנֵיהֶם *their dwelling places*; + אָהֳלֵיהֶם *their tents* [or em. אָהֳלֵי חָם *the tents of Ham*]), שׁמד hi. *destroy* Is 23_{11} (if em. מָעֻזְנֶיהָ *her strongholds* to מְעוֹנֶיהָ *her dwelling places*).

<CSTR> מעון קודש *a dwelling place of holiness* 1QS 10_{12} (others מַעְיָן *spring*) 1QH $12_{2(AHL)}$=4QHod^{b} 8.2_{8} (1Q קו[ד]ש; 4Q מ[עון קודש]; ||4QHod^{a} 2_{1} מעון שלו[ם] *a dwelling place of peace*) 1QSb 4_{25}, מעון הקודש *the dwelling place of holiness* 4QM^{a} 11.1_{15} (מ[עו]ן glory *of the dwelling place of*) 11.1_{20}, מעון קודש קודשים *the dwelling place of (the) holy of holies* 1QS 8_{8}=4QS^{d} 2_{2} (||4QS^{e} $1.2_{17[WA]}$ מעוז קודש קו[ד]שים *the refuge* [מָעוֹז I], or *stronghold* [מָעוֹז II], *of [the] holy of holies* [others [מעון]), מְעוֹן קָדְשׁוֹ *the dwelling place of his holiness* Jr 25_{30} (or del. מְעוֹן) Zc 2_{17} Ps 68_{6} 2 C 30_{27}, מְעוֹן קָדְשְׁךָ *the dwelling place of your holiness* Dt 26_{15} 1QM 12_{2} 11Q Psa^{a} 24_{4} (both קודשכה).

מעון שו[די] *the dwelling place of Shaddai* 4QShir^{b} 41_{1}, מעון פלא *the dwelling place of wonder* 4QShirShabb^{d} 1.2_{19}=4QShirShabb^{f} 8_{3}=11QShirShabb 2_{2} (פל[א]) 11Q ShirShabb 3_{10} (מע[ון פלא]), מעוני פלא *the dwelling places of wonder* 4QShirShabb^{d} 1.2_{23}, מע[ני פלאיהמה] *the dwelling places of their wonders* 4QBer^{b} 2_{13}, מעון כבוד *(the) dwelling place of glory* 1QS 10_{3}=4QS^{b} 8.2_{1}=4QS^{f} 1.2_{2}, מעון כבודכה *the dwelling place of your glory* 1QH fr. 9_{7}, מע[ון] כבוד מלכותו majesty *of the dwelling place of the glory of his kingship* 4QShir^{a} 1_{3}, מעון שלו[ם] *a dwelling place of peace* 4QHod^{a} 2_{1} (||1QH $12_{2[AHL]}$ [קו]דש *of holiness*, ||4QHod^{b} 8.2_{8} (מ[עון קודש]), מעון דעת *a dwelling place of knowledge* 1Q36 12_{2} (others מַעְיַן *spring of*), מעון חיים *a dwelling place of life* 1QH^{b} 2_{1} (others מעין *spring of*).

מְעוֹן בֵּיתֶךָ *the dwelling place of your house* Ps 26_{8} (or em. עֲבֹדַת *the service of* your house; + וּמְקוֹם מִשְׁכַּן כְּבוֹדֶךָ *and the site of the dwelling of your glory*) Gnz Ps 2_{26}, מְעוֹן תַּנִּים *a dwelling place of jackals* Jr 9_{10} 10_{22} 49_{33} 51_{37}, מְעוֹן אֲרָיוֹת *the dwelling place of lions* Na 2_{12} 1QH 5_{13}, מְעוֹן אֹיְבַי *dwelling place of my enemies* Ps 69_{19} (if em. לְמַעַן *on account of* to לִמְעוֹן), מעון חוקו *the dwelling place of its statute*, i.e. appointed for it 1QS 10_{12}=4QS^{d} 3.2_{11} (חוק[ו]), מעוני עומדם *the dwelling places of their standing* 4QShirShabb^{a} 2_{5}.

צוּר מָעוֹן *a rock of a dwelling place*, i.e. in which to live Ps 71_{3} (mss, ||Ps 31_{3} מָעוֹז *of refuge*; unless מָעוֹן II *help*), רֹאשׁ הַמָּעוֹן *the top of the dwelling place* Jg 6_{26} (mss) (L מָעוֹז *fortified place*), פנות מעון appar. *the corners*, i.e. towers, *of the (holy) dwelling place* Si 50_{2} (or em. מָעוֹז corners of *strength* [מָעוֹז II]; + בהיכל מלך *in the palace of [the divine] king*), כבוד [מע]ון *the glory of the dwelling place of* holiness 4QM^{a} 11.1_{15}, הדר מע[ון] *the majesty of the dwelling place of* the glory of his kingship 4QShir^{a} 1_{3}, [בכו]ל [מ]עון *in every dwelling place* 4QapJoshua^{c} 9.2_{8}.

<APP> מְעוֹן קָדְשְׁךָ ... הַשָּׁמַיִם *the dwelling place of your holiness ... the heavens* Dt 26_{15}, לִמְעוֹן קָדְשׁוֹ לַשָּׁמָיִם *to the dwelling place of his holiness, to the heavens* 2 C 30_{27}, גַּלִּים מְעוֹן תַּנִּים *ruins, a dwelling place of jackals* Jr 9_{10} 51_{37}, שְׁמָמָה מְעוֹן תַּנִּים *a devastation, a dwelling place of jackals* Jr 10_{22}, מְעוֹן תַּנִּים שְׁמָמָה *a dwelling place of jackals, a devastation* Jr 49_{33}, מְעוֹנָהּ כֹּל אֲשֶׁר־פָּקַדְתִּי עָלֶיהָ so that *her dwelling place, everything with which I visited her* would not be cut off Zp 3_{7} (or em. מֵעֵינֶיהָ so that everything ... would not be cut off *from her eyes*).

חומת הבחן פנת יקר ... מעון קודש קודשים *the wall of the fortress*, or *of testing, a cornerstone of preciousness ... the dwelling place of (the) holy of holies* 1QS 8_{8}=4QS^{d} 2_{2} ([חומת הבחן פנת יקר]; ||4QS^{e} $1.2_{17[WA]}$ ... פ[נת יקר]

מעוז קודש קו[ד]שים *a cornerstone of preciousness ... the refuge* [מָעוֹז I], or *stronghold* [מָעוֹז II], *of [the] holy of holies* [others מעון]).

<ADJ> זֶה *this* Jg $6_{26(mss)}$ (L מָעוֹז *refuge*).

<PREP> לְ of direction, *to*, + אסף ni. *be gathered* 1QS 10_{3}=4QS^{b} 8.2_{1}=4QS^{f} 1.2_{2} ([האספם]), בוא *come* (of prayer) 2 C 30_{27}, פרשׂ (pi.) *extend* hands in prayer 11QPsa^{a} 24_{4}; *as*, + היה *be(come)* Jr 49_{33} (of Hazor [or em. הֶחָצֵר *the court*]) 51_{37} (of Babylon), נתן *give*, i.e. cause (Jerusalem) to be Jr 9_{10}; *for*, + יסד pi. *establish* Ps 8_{3} (if em. לְמַעַן *on account of*);* *from*, + גאל *redeem* Ps 69_{19} (if em. לְמַעַן *on account of*).

בְּ of place, *in* Ps 68_{6} (אֱלֹהִים בִּמְעוֹן קָדְשׁוֹ a father of orphans ... is *God in the dwelling place of his holiness*) 1QH 5_{13} (עני במעון אריות *a poor one [who is] in the dwelling place of lions*) fr. 9_{7} 1QSb 4_{25} (כמלאך פנים במעון קודש *like an angel of presence in the dwelling place of holiness*) 1QM 12_{2} ([מס]פר שמות כול צבאם אתכה במעון קודשכה *the number of the names of all their host is with you in the dwelling place of your holiness*) perh. 1QH^{b} 2_{1} (others מַעְיָן *spring*) 4QBer^{b} 2_{13} (רוחי קודשכה במע[וני פלאיהמה] *the spirits of your holiness in the dwelling places of their wonders*) 4QShirShabb^{d} 1.2_{19} (סוד שני במעון פלא *a second council in the dwelling place of wonder*; =11QShirShabb 2_{2} ([סוד שני] [ב]מעון פל[א]; =4QShirShabb^{f} 8_{3} [סו]ד) 1.2_{23} (מלאכי מלך במעוני פלא *the angels of [the] king in the dwelling places of wonder*) 11QShirShabb 3_{10} ([כוהני] קרוב במע[ון פלא] *priests of proximity in the dwelling place of wonder*), + perh. ברך pu. *be blessed* 4QapJoshua^{c} 9.2_{8} ([ויברך בכו]ל [מ]עון] *and he will be blessed in every dwelling place*), שכן *dwell* 1QH 12_{2}=4QHod^{a} 2_{1} (both [אשכנ]ה; ||4QHod^{b} 8.2_{8} [אשכנה ... במ[עון]), ספר pi. *relate* Y.'s glory 4QShirShabb^{a} 2_{5}, הלל pi. *praise* Y. 4QHod^{a} 7.1_{12} (+ אהל ישועה in *the tent of salvation*, perh. זמר pi. *praise* Y. 4QM^{a} 11.1_{20}; perh. *in comparison with* 4QShirShabb^{a} 2_{6} (וכוהנתנו מה במעוניהם *and what is our priesthood compared to their dwelling places?*, i.e. to the positions they hold).

מִן of direction, *from* Ps $68_{6(mss)}$ (אֱלֹהִים מִמְּעוֹן קָדְשׁוֹ a father of orphans ... is *God from the dwelling place of his holiness*) perh. 1Q36 12_{2} (others מַעְיָן *spring*) 4QShirShabb^{g} 1_{2}, + שׁקף hi. *look down* Dt 26_{15}, נתן *give* voice Jr 25_{30} (+ מִמָּרוֹם *from on high*; or del. מָעוֹן), נער *roar* or עור ni. *be roused* Zc 2_{17}.

אֶל *(in)to*, + אסף ni. *be gathered* 4QS^{d} 3.2_{11} ([ובה]אספו; ||1QS 10_{1} עַל *[in]to*).

עַל *(in)to*, + אסף ni. *be gathered* 1QS 10_{1} (|| 4QS^{d} 3.2_{11} אֶל *[in]to*); *on*, + חמל *have mercy* 2 C 36_{15} (|| עַם Y.'s *people*).

<COLL> ולאל אומר ... מעון קודש *and to God I say, (You are) ... a dwelling place of holiness* 1QS 10_{12} (others מַעְיָן *spring*; + מכין טובי מקור דעת *preparer of my goodness, source of knowledge*; others מָכוֹן *place* of my goodness).

[בכו]ל [מ]עון מן השמי[ם] perh. *in every dwelling place of heaven* 4QapJoshua^{c} 9.2_{8}.

לָמָּה תִבְעֲטוּ בְּזִבְחִי וּבְמִנְחָתִי אֲשֶׁר צִוִּיתִי מָעוֹן appar. *why do you kick at my sacrifice(s) and my cereal offering(s), which I commanded in (my) dwelling place?* 1 S 2_{29} (or em. לָמָּה תַבִּיט זִבְחִי וּמִנְחָתִי תְּעוֹיֵן *why do you look at my sacrifice[s] and eye my cereal offering[s]?*), וְהִבַּטְתָּ צַר מָעוֹן בְּכֹל אֲשֶׁר־יֵיטִיב אֶת־יִשְׂרָאֵל appar. *and you will see an enemy in*, or *of*, *(my) dwelling place, with all the good things that he (Y.) gives Israel* 1 S 2_{32} (or del.; or em. צַר מְעַיֵּן *an enemy eyeing* or *distressed, eyeing* all the good things, and or אֵיטִיב *the good things that I give*).

<SYN> מַחֲסֶה *refuge*, עַם *people*.*

⇒ עון *dwell*.

***מָעוֹן II** 3 n.[m.] **help**, <SUBJ> היה *be* Ps 90_{1} (יי מָעוֹן אַתָּה הָיִיתָ לָּנוּ בְּדֹר וָדֹר *O Y., you have been a help for us through generation and generation*; unless מָעוֹן I *dwelling place* or III *reminder of sin*; mss מָעוֹז *refuge*, לְדֹר *to generation* and generation). <OBJ> שׂים *set* Ps 91_{9} (unless מָעוֹן I *dwelling place*). <CSTR> צוּר מָעוֹן *a rock of help* Ps 71_{3} (||Ps 31_{3} מָעוֹז *of refuge*; unless מָעוֹן I *dwelling place*).

***מָעוֹן III** 1 n.[m.] **reminder of sin** (unless מָעוֹן I *refuge* or II *help*), <SUBJ> היה *be* Ps 90_{1} (אֲדֹנָי מָעוֹן אַתָּה הָיִיתָ לָּנוּ *Lord, you have been our reminder of sin*).

⇒ עָוֹן *sin*.

מָעוֹן IV $_5$ pl.n. **Maon,** town in hill country of Judah, home of Nabal and Abigail, near to where David hid from Saul, perh. T. Ma'īn 13 km S of Hebron, <NOM CL> בָּהָר ... מָעוֹן *in the mountain(s) were ... Maon* Jos 15$_{55}$. <CSTR> מִדְבַּר מָעוֹן *the steppe of Maon* 1 S 23$_{24}$. $_{25.25}$. <PREP> בְּ of place, *in* 1 S 25$_2$ (וְאִישׁ בְּמָעוֹן *and there was a man in Maon*). <COLL> וַיִּרְדֹּף אַחֲרֵי־דָוִד מָעוֹן *and he pursued David (to) Maon* 1 S 23$_{25(mss)}$.

מָעוֹן V $_3$ pr.n.m. **Maon, 1.** descendant of Caleb, son of Shammai and father of Beth-zur, <NOM CL> וּבֶן־שַׁמַּי מָעוֹן וּמָעוֹן אֲבִי בֵית־צוּר *and the son of Shammai was Maon and Maon was the father of Beth-zur* 1 C 2$_{45}$.

2. a people that oppressed Israel, perh. ident. with Maonites and assoc. with Mā'an, near Petra, <SUBJ> לחץ *(op)press* Israel Jg 10$_{12}$ (or em. מִדְיָן *Midian*).

<PREP> מִיַּד *from (the power of)* Jg 10$_{12}$ (or em.).

מְעוֹן, see בֵּית מְעוֹן *Beth-meon*, בֵּית בַּעַל מְעוֹן *Beth-baal-meon*, and בַּעַל מְעוֹן *Baal-Meon*.

[מְעוֹנָה] $_{9.4}$ n.f. **dwelling place**—מְעֹנָה; sf. מְעוֹנָתוֹ (מְעֹנָתוֹ); pl. מְעוֹנוֹת; cstr. מְעֹנוֹת; sf. מְעוֹנֹתֶינוּ, מְעֹנֹתָיו (Q מעונותיהם) מְעוֹנֹתָם, (מעונותיה Si) מְעוֹנֹתֶיהָ, ([מ]עונותיו) —**dwelling place, abode,** of Y. (Ps 76$_3$ 4Q392 1$_5$ perh. 3$_4$), of king (Jr 21$_{13}$), **lair** of wild animals (Am 3$_4$ Na 2$_{13}$ Ps 104$_{22}$ Jb 37$_8$ 38$_{40}$), of Wisdom (Si 14$_{27}$), of light (1QH 12$_5$), of darkness (1QH 12$_7$=4QHod[a] 3.2$_7$).

<SUBJ> היה *be* Ps 76$_3$ (+ בְּצִיּוֹן his dwelling place *was in Zion*; || סֹךְ *booth*)

<NOM CL> מְעֹנָה אֱלֹהֵי קֶדֶם *the God of antiquity is a dwelling place* Dt 33$_{27}$ (or em. מְעֹנָה *his refuge*, i.e. מָעוֹן, or מִמַּעַל *above* is the God of antiquity [+ וּמִתַּחַת *and below*] or מְעַנֶּה *one who humbles*, i.e. ענה pi. ptc. [and em. וּמִתַּחַת to וּמְחַתֵּת *and one who shatters*]).

<OBJ> מלא pi. *fill* with prey Na 2$_{13}$ (|| חֹר *hole*).

<CSTR> מְעֹנוֹת אֲרָיוֹת *dwelling places of lions* Ca 4$_8$ (+ הַרְרֵי נְמֵרִים *mountains of leopards* [or em. חֹרֵי *holes of*]).

<PREP> בְּ of place, *in(to)* 4Q392 1$_5$ 3$_4$ (ובמ[עונותיו *and in his dwelling places*), + בוא *come* Jr 21$_{13}$, שׁכן *dwell* Jb 37$_8$ Si 14$_{27}$ (+ צֵל *shade*), שׁחח *lie low* Jb 38$_{40}$ (|| סֻכָּה *booth*); מִן of direction, *from* 1QH 12$_5$ (מבוא אור ממ[עונתו *with the entrance of daylight from its dwelling place*; ||4QHod[a] 3.2$_6$ [עם] מבא אור לממשל[תו] *with the entrance of the sun to its government*), + נתן *give* voice Am 3$_4$ (or del. מִמְּעֹנָתוֹ *from his dwelling place*), שׁור *look* Ca 4$_8$; אֶל *(in)to*, + אסף ni. *be gathered* (of darkness) 1QH 12$_7$=4QHod[a] 3.2$_7$ ([האספו]); *in*, + רבץ *lie down* Ps 104$_{22}$.

<SYN> חֹר *hole*, סֹךְ *booth*, סֻכָּה *booth*, הַר *mountain*.*
⇒ עון *dwell*.

[מְעוּנִי] $_4$ gent. **Maonite**—pl. מְעוּנִים—perh. in ref. to (originally north-Arabian) people of Maon (see מָעוֹן V, §2), who became temple servants, <OBJ> נכה hi. *strike* 1 C 4$_{41(Qr)}$ (Kt מעינים perh. *Meinim*; or em. הַמַּעְיָנִים *the springs* or הַמְּעוֹנִים *the dwelling places* or מְעוֹנֵיהֶם *their dwelling places*; + אָהֳלֵיהֶם *their tents* [or em. אָהֳלֵי חָם *the tents of Ham*]). <CSTR> בְּנֵי־מְעוּנִים *the sons of (the) Maonites* Ezr 2$_{50(Qr)}$||Ne 7$_{52}$ (Kt מעינים perh. *Meinim*). <PREP> מִן partitive, *some of* 2 C 20$_1$ (if em. וְעִמָּהֶם מֵהָעַמּוֹנִים *and with them* [the Ammonites] *were some of the Ammonites* to מֵהַמְּעוּנִים and with them were *some of the Maonites*); עַל *against*, + עזר *help* 2 C 26$_7$ (+ עַרְבִי *Arabian*; mss עַמּוֹנִי *Ammonite[s]*).

מְעוֹנֵן *diviner by brontomancy*, see ענן *divine*, Po.*

מְעוֹנְנִים, see ענן *divine*, Pi.

מְעוֹנֹתַי $_1$ pr.n.m. **Meonothai,** descendant of Judah, father of Ophrah, and appar. son of Othniel (if em.), וּבְנֵי עָתְנִיאֵל חֲתַת: וּמְעוֹנֹתַי הוֹלִיד אֶת־עָפְרָה *and the sons of Othniel were Hathath. And Meonothai was the father of Ophrah* 1 C 4$_{14}$ (or em. וּמְעוֹנֹתָי: וּמְעוֹנֹתַי Hathath *and Meonothai. And Meonothai* was the father of, or וּמְעוֹנֹתָי: וְהוֹלִיד Hathath *and Meonothai. And he was the father of*).

[מָעוּף] $_1$ n.[m.] **darkness**—cstr. מְעוּף—הִנֵּה צָרָה וַחֲשֵׁכָה מְעוּף צוּקָה וַאֲפֵלָה מְנֻדָּח *behold, distress and darkness, gloom of constraint, and obscurity, one driven out* Is 8$_{22}$ (or em. מְעוּף to מוּעַף, *gloom of*, as 8$_{23}$, or to מֵעִיף

one hastening distress, i.e. עוף hi. *cause to fly*, or to מֵעוּף *from flying*, i.e. inescapable [distress and darkness], or to מוּעָף *one plunged into darkness*, i.e. עוף ho. *be made dark*, as || to מְנֻדָּח; and/or מְנֻדָּח to מִנֹּגַהּ darkness *without brightness* or אֲפֵלַת *the darkness of* one who is driven out).

⇒ עוף *be dark*.

[מָעוֹר] 1 n.[m.] **nakedness**—pl. sf. מְעוֹרֵיהֶם—in pl., **genitalia**, <PREP> עַל נבט hi. *look at* Hb 2_{15} (or del.; ||1QpHab 11_3 אל מועדיהם *at their appointed times*).

⇒ עור *be naked*.

מָעֹז, see מָעוֹז I *refuge* and II *stronghold*.

מַעַזְיָה 1 pr.n.m. **Maaziah**—**1.** priest and co-signatory with Nehemiah, <NOM CL> עַל הַחֲתוּמִים נְחֶמְיָה ... מַעַזְיָה *upon those that were sealed are Nehemiah ... (and) Maaziah* Ne 10_7 (or em. הַחוֹתְמִים *those that sealed*, i.e. signed, *were* or אֵלֶּה הַחוֹתְמִים *these are the signatories*).

2. priest who returned with Zerubbabel, <SUBJ> עלה *go up* Ne 12_5 (or em. מַעַזְיָה *Maaziah*).

3. priest at time of Joiakim, <PREP> לְ of possession, *of, (belonging) to* Ne 12_{17} (if em. לְמוֹעַדְיָה פִּלְטָי *to Moadiah was Piltai* to לְמַעַזְיָה *to Maaziah* was Piltai).

מַעַזְיָהוּ 1 pr.n.m. **Maaziah**, head of twenty-fourth priestly course at time of David, <PREP> לְ of direction, *to*, + יצא *go out* (of lot) 1 C 24_{18}.

*__[מַעֻזֵּן]__ 1 n.[m.] **mart**—pl. sf. מָעֻזְנֶיהָ—<OBJ> שׁמד hi. *destroy* Is 23_{11} (unless from מָעוֹז *refuge* or מָעוֹזֶן *refuge*).

מעט I $_{23.4.10}$ vb. **be few**—**Qal** $_{8.1.4}$ Pf. Q מעטו; impf. יִמְעַט (יִמְעָט), תִּמְעָטוּ; + waw וַיִּמְעֲטוּ; ptc. Q [מ]עוט, perh. מְעָטָה; Si, Q מעוטים; inf. מְעֹט (Q perh. מעוט)—**be reduced, be diminished, be (too) few, be (too) small.**

<SUBJ> רָעֵב *hungry one* Ps 107_{39} (|| שׁחח *be laid low*), אָדָם *humankind* 4QpIsa[c] 4.2_8 (פשרו למעוט האדם *its interpretation is about the diminution of humankind*; unless מְעוּט *small thing, diminution*, or מְעַט *the few [remaining] of* humankind), בַּיִת *household* Ex 12_4, גּוֹלָה *diaspora* Jr 29_6 (:: רבה *be large*), אֹהֶל *tent* of Jacob, i.e. returning exiles Jr 30_{19} (|| צער *be small* [or del.], + רבה hi. *increase* [or del.]), כבד hi. *make numerous*), שְׁאָר *remnant* of archers Is 21_{17} (or em. וּשְׁאָר *and the remnant* of the number, to וְשָׁאַר *and* a number of archers of warriors of the sons of Kedar *will be left [but] will be reduced*), קֶשֶׁת *bow*, i.e. archer Is 21_{17} (if em.), הוֹן *wealth* Pr 13_{11} (+ רבה hi. *increase* wealth), שׁנה *year* Lv 25_{16} (:: רבב *be large*) 4QD[e] $6.2_{10(mg)}$ ([מ]עטו), יוֹם *day* CD 10_9=4QD[a] 8.3_7=4QD[e] 6.4_{18} (D[a] [מעט]ו ימו; D[e] [מע]טו), תְּלָאָה *hardship* Ne 9_{32}.

<PREP> בְּ of cause, *on account of*, + מַעַל *transgression* CD 10_9=4QD[a] 8.3_7=4QD[e] 6.4_{18} ([מעט]ו; D[e] [מע]טו); מִן of direction, *from* 5QRègle 24_3 ([מ]עטו [מ]יום [ב]רואם *from the day of his creating them they have diminished*); of comparison, *than*, i.e. too small (etc.) *for*, + היה inf. *being* Ex 12_4 (אִם־יִמְעַט הַבַּיִת מִהְיֹת מִשֶּׂה *if the household is too small for there being a lamb*, i.e. to have a lamb); of instrument, *by (means of), through*, + עֹצֶר *oppression* Ps 107_{39}, רָעָה *misfortune* Ps 107_{39}, יָגוֹן *weariness* Ps 107_{39}, perh. הֶבֶל *vanity* Pr 13_{11} (הוֹן מֵהֶבֶל יִמְעָט *wealth is diminished by vanity*, but perh. *wealth [gained] by vanity is diminished*; or em. מְבֹהָל *hastily gained* wealth is diminished); לִפְנֵי *in the presence of*, i.e. appear small to, Y. Ne 9_{32}; מִדֵּי *for the sufficiency of*, + מַרְעִיל *covering* CD 10_{11} (see Coll.).

<COLL> וּלְפִי מֹעֹט הַשָּׁנִים תַּמְעִיט *and in accordance with the diminution of the years, you are to reduce* Lv 25_{16}, ובוזה מעוטים [ית]ערער *and one who despises reduced things will be stripped (even of these)* Si 19_1 (unless מְעוּטִים *small things*, i.e. noun מעוט), במים צואים ומעוטים מדי מרעיל איש *in water (that is) dirty or reduced for the sufficiency of covering*, i.e. insufficient to cover, *a man* CD 10_{11}=4QD[a] $8.3_{9(WA)}$ ([במים] [צואים ומעו]טים [מדי מרעיל איש]; others [ומו]עטים, either וּמֹעֲטִים *and reducing*, i.e. qal ptc., or וּמוּעָטִים *and reduced*, i.e. pu. ptc.), [מ]עוט אל ימעו]יט] *one must not reduce that which is (already) reduced* 4QHalakhah[a] 6_2 (unless מעוט = מְעַט one must not [further] reduce *a little*), perh. אָח עֲשׂוּיָה לְבָרָק מְעֻטָּה לְטָבַח *alas (it is)*

made like lightning, reduced (enough) for slaughter Ezk 21_{20} (unless adj. מָעֹט *small* or עטה pu. ptc. *sharpened;* or em. מְרֻטָה, מֹרְטָה, or מֹרָטָה *polished*).

<SYN> שׁחח *be laid low,* צער *be small.*

<ANT> רבב *be large,* רבה *be large*).

Pi. 1.2 Pf. מִעֲטוּ; impv. Si מעט—**become few** or perh. **reduce output** (Ec 12_3); **withdraw** (Si 3_{18}); **make few** (Si 35_8), <SUBJ> בֵּן *son* Si 3_{18}, טֹחֲנָה *woman working at mill* or *molar* Ec 12_3 (+ בטל *be idle*). <OBJ> נֶפֶשׁ *soul* Si 3_{18} (+ שׁפל hi. *abase* soul). <PREP> מִן of direction, *from,* + גְּדוּלָּה world's *greatness* Si 3_{18}. <COLL> כל לאמר ומעט הרבה *finish speaking and make few (words count for) many* Si 35_8 (or em. כַּלֵּל אֹמֶר בִּמְעַט הַרְבֵּה *perfect [your] speech; with a few [words] let there be many [thoughts expressed],* i.e. מְעַט *few*).

Pu. 0.0.2 Q Ptc. מועט—as ptc., **something reduced,** i.e. **a few, a little,** <SUBJ> מִקְדָּשׁ *sanctuary* Ezk 11_{16} (if em. וָאֱהִי לָהֶם לְמִקְדָּשׁ מְעַט *and I was to them as a sanctuary a little while* to מְעָט as a *diminished* sanctuary). <PREP> לְ *as* few, i.e. as a minimum CD 13_1 (עשרה אנשים למועט *ten men as a minimum*) 4QD[a] 10.1_6 ([שכר] שני [ימים לממוע[ט] *two days' wages at least;* WA, ||CD 14_{13} לממעיט wages *of the one who pays least,* i.e. hi. ptc. [others לממעט]); בֵּין ... לְ *between ... and* 1QS 4_{16} (לפי נחלת איש בין רוב למועט *in accordance with a person's inheritance, abundance,* i.e. much, *or little*).

<COLL> [במים צואים ומו]עטים [מדי מרעיל איש] *in water (that is) dirty or reduced for the sufficiency of covering,* i.e. insufficient to cover, *a man* 4QD[a] 8.3_9 (unless וּמוֹעֲטִים *and reducing,* i.e. qal ptc.; ||CD 10_{11}, WA ומעוטים *and reduced,* i.e. qal pass. ptc.), 4QpIsa[c] 4.2_{17}(Horgan) ([פשרו למועט[ה האדם]) *its interpretation is about the reduced one,* i.e. few, *of humankind;* others מיעט[]; unless מועט = מְעַט *few of* humankind).

Hi. 13.1.2 Pf. Si המעיטם; impf. תַּמְעִיטִי, יַמְעִיט, 2ms תַּמְעִיט (Q תמעט ,תַּמְעִיטֶנִי), תַּמְעִיטוּ; + waw וְהִמְעַטְתָּה, וְהִמְעַטְתִּים; ptc. מַמְעִיט—**reduce** in number, as punishment (Lv 26_{22} Jr 10_{24} Si 48_2 perh. Ps 107_{38}), perh. **diminish** power (Ezk 29_{15}), perh. **waste** breath (4Q416 2.2_6); **reduce in size** (Nm 26_{54} 33_{54}); **collect less, few(er)** (Ex $16_{17.18}$ Nm 11_{32} 35_8 2 K 4_3); **pay less, least** (Ex 30_{15} Lv 25_{16} CD 14_{13}).

<SUBJ> Y. Jr 10_{24} (+ יסר pi. *discipline*) Ezk 29_{15} Ps 107_{38} (+ רבה *increase* intrans.), Moses Nm 26_{54} (:: רבה hi. *increase,* + נתן ho. *be given*), Elijah Si 48_2, Israelites Nm 33_{54} (:: רבה hi.) 35_8 (:: רבה hi., + נתן *give*), אִשָּׁה impoverished *woman* 2 K 4_3, דַּל *poor one* Ex 30_{15} (:: רבה hi. [of rich one]), land purchaser Lv 25_{16} (:: רבה hi.), חַיָּה (wild) *animal* Lv 26_{22} (|| כרת hi. *cut off,* שׁכל pi. *bereave* [lacking in Gnz]); subj. not specified Ex $16_{17.18}$ (both :: רבה hi.) Nm 11_{32} CD 14_{13} 4QHalakhah[a] 6_2 4Q416 2.2_6+4Q417 1.2_8 (for all six, see Coll.).

<OBJ> Israelites Lv 26_{22} Jr 10_{24}, Ephraim Si 48_2, Egypt Ezk 29_{15}, בְּהֵמָה *beast* Ps 107_{38}, מִקְנָה *price* Lv 25_{16}, נַחֲלָה *inheritance* Nm 26_{54} 33_{54}, עִיר *city* Nm 35_8, כְּלִי *vessel* 2 K 4_3, מְעַט *a little* or מָעוּט *that which is reduced* 4QHalakhah[a] 6_2, רוּחַ perh. *breath* 4Q416 2.2_6+4Q417 1.2_8.

<PREP> לְ of benefit, *for,* + מְעַט *few* Nm 26_{54} 33_{54}; בְּ of instrument, *by (means of), with,* + דבר *word* 4Q416 2.2_6+4Q417 1.2_8; cause, *on account of,* + קִנְאָה *zeal* Si 48_2; מִן of comparison, give less *than,* + מַחֲצִית *half* shekel Ex 30_{15}; מֵאֵת *from (with),* + מְעַט *few* Nm 35_8.

<COLL> וַיִּלְקְטוּ הַמַּרְבֶּה וְהַמַּמְעִיט *and the one who collected more* (manna) *and the one who collected less (both) gathered* Ex 16_{17}, וְלֹא הֶעְדִּיף הַמַּרְבֶּה וְהַמַּמְעִיט לֹא הֶחְסִיר *and the one who collected more* (manna) *had not exceeded and the one who collected less had not fallen short* Ex 16_{18}, הַמַּמְעִיט אָסַף עֲשָׂרָה חֳמָרִים *the one who collected few(est) gathered ten homers* (of quails) Nm 11_{32}, שכר שני ימים לכל חדש לממעיט *(for) every month two days' wages of the one who pays least* CD 14_{13} (others לממעט; ||4QD[a] 10.1_6 [שכר] שני [ימים לממוע[ט] *two days' wages at least,* i.e. pu. ptc.; WA לממעי[ט]).

אַל־תַּמְעִיטִי *collect not a few,* i.e. collect many 2 K 4_3, וַיְבָרְכֵם וַיִּרְבּוּ מְאֹד וּבְהֶמְתָּם לֹא יַמְעִיט *and he blessed them, so they increased greatly, and their beasts he did not reduce in number,* i.e. he increased Ps 107_{38}.

וּלְפִי מְעֹט הַשָּׁנִים תַּמְעִיט *and in accordance with the diminution of the years, you are to reduce* Lv 25_{16}, [מ]עוט אל ימע[יט] *one must not reduce that which is (already) reduced* or *one must not (further) reduce a little* 4QHalakhah[a] 6_2, ובדבריכה אל תמעט רוחכה perh.

and with your words do not waste your breath 4Q416 2.2_{6}+4Q417 1.2_{8}, מִן־הַמַּמְלָכוֹת תִּהְיֶה שְׁפָלָה ... וְהִמְעַטְתִּים לְבִלְתִּי רְדוֹת בַּגּוֹיִם *it will be the lowest of the kingdoms ... and I shall diminish them so as not to rule over the nations* Ezk 29_{15} (or del. מִן־הַמַּמְלָכוֹת תִּהְיֶה שְׁפָלָה).

<SYN> כרת hi. *cut off*, שׁכל pi. *bereave*.

<ANT> רבה hi. *increase*.*

⇒ מְעַט *few*, מִעוּט *reduction*, מָעֹט *small*.

***מעט** II $_{1}$ vb. **draw—Pu.** ptc. מְמֹעָטָה—**be drawn (out), stretched,** <SUBJ> בָּרָק *lightning* Ezk 21_{20} (בָּרָק מְמֹעָטָה לְטָבַח *lightning drawn out for slaughter*).

[מָעֹט] $_{1}$ adj. **small**—fem. מְעֻטָּה—**small,** אָח עֲשׂוּיָה לְבָרָק מְעֻטָּה לְטָבַח *alas (it is) made like lightning, small (enough) for slaughter* Ezk 21_{20} (unless מְעֻטָּה = מעט pass. ptc., *removed*, or עטה pu. ptc. *sharpened*; or em. מְרֻטָּה, מֹרָטָה, or מֹרָטָה *polished*).

⇒ מעט *be few*.

מְעַט $_{101.11.12}$ n.[m.] **few**—Q perh. מיעט, מעוט; מְעָט; cstr. מְעַט; pl. מְעַטִּים—**1a.** as noun, **(a) few, (a) little,** <SUBJ> היה *be* Gn 30_{30} (כִּי מְעַט אֲשֶׁר־הָיָה לְךָ *for the little you had*) 47_{9} (מְעַט וְרָעִים הָיוּ יְמֵי שְׁנֵי חַיַּי *few and wretched have been the days of the years of my life*) 4QTobit[e] 2_{8} (אם יהיה לך מעט *if you have little*), יצר ni. *be formed* Si 49_{14}, שׁאר *remain* Is 16_{14} (if em. וּשְׁאָר מְעַט *and a remnant of a few of* to וְשָׁאַר *and a few will remain*), ni. *remain* Lv 25_{52} Is 16_{14} (if em. וּשְׁאָר מְעַט *and a remnant of a few of* to וְנִשְׁאַר *and a few will remain*) Jr 42_{2}, לקח ho. *be taken* Gn 18_{4}, פרץ *break through*, i.e. increase in size Gn 30_{30}.

<NOM CL> כִּי מְעַט הֵמָּה *for they were few* Jos 7_{3}, עִיר קְטַנָּה וַאֲנָשִׁים בָּהּ מְעָט *there was a small town and the people in it were few* Ec 9_{14}, וְהָעִיר רַחֲבַת יָדַיִם ... וְהָעָם מְעַט בְּתוֹכָהּ *and the city was wide of hands ... but the people were few inside it* Ne 7_{4}, כִּי־אַתֶּם הַמְעַט מִכָּל־הָעַמִּים *for you were the smallest of all the peoples* Dt 7_{7}, בעין כושל מעט הוא חלקו *in the eye of one who stumbles*, perh. old person, *their share is small* Si 14_{9} (erased מעטהו; or em. כושל to כִּילַי *villain* or בּוֹצֵעַ *slanderer* or *extortioner* or כְּסִיל *fool* and/or בעין to בְּעֵינֵי *in the eyes of*), מעט לו ואין דיו perh. if *he has little and there is not enough for him* 5Q14 1_{5}.

טוֹב־מְעַט לַצַּדִּיק *better is (the) little of the righteous one* than the abundance of evildoers Ps 37_{16}, טוֹב־מְעַט בְּיִרְאַת י׳ *better is a little with the fear of Y.* than a great treasure with turmoil in it Pr 15_{16}, טוֹב־מְעַט בִּצְדָקָה *better is a little with righteousness* than an abundance of produce(s) without justice Pr 16_{8}.

יֶשׁ־לִי ... כִּי אִם ... מְעַט־שֶׁמֶן *I have ... only ... a little oil* 1 K 17_{12}, וּשְׁאָרוֹ מְעַט *and his remnant will be a few of* Is 16_{14} (if em. וּשְׁאָר מְעַט *and a remnant of a few of*), זֶה שִׁבְתָּהּ הַבַּיִת מְעָט appar. *this staying of hers at home has been little* Ru 2_{7} (or em. וְלֹא שָׁבְתָה [בַּשָּׂדֶה] מְעָט *and she has not rested [even] a little while [in the field]* or וְלֹא שָׁבָה הַבַּיְתָה מְעָט *and she has not returned home [even] a little while*, both as §1c).

הַמְעַט הוּא אִם־רָב *is it few or many?* Nm 13_{18}, הַמְעַט מִתַּזְנוּתָיִךְ *are there (too) few of your prostitutions?* Ezk $16_{20(Qr)}$, הַמְעַט מִכֶּם כִּי־הִבְדִּיל אֱלֹהֵי יִשְׂרָאֵל אֶתְכֶם *is it (too) little for you that the God of Israel has set you apart?* Nm 16_{9}, הֲלֹא־מְעַט יָמַי וַחֲדָל *are my days not few (enough)?; then, cease* Jb $10_{20(Qr)}$ (Kt יֶחְדָּל *let him cease*; or em. וְחָדֵל *and fleeting* or יְמֵי חֶלְדִּי *the days of my duration*), הַמְעַט מִמְּךָ תַּנְחֻמוֹת אֵל *are God's consolations (too) few for you?* Jb 15_{11}.

הַמְעַט מִכֶּם הַלְאוֹת אֲנָשִׁים כִּי תַלְאוּ *is it (too) little for you wearing people*, or *treating people as helpless, that you weary*, or *treat as helpless*, my God as well? Is 7_{13}, הַמְעַט קַחְתֵּךְ אֶת־אִישִׁי וְלָקַחַת גַּם אֶת־דּוּדָאֵי בְּנִי *is your taking of my husband (so) little that (you) take my son's mandrakes as well?* Gn 30_{15} (or em. וְלָקַחַתְּ *that you would take*), הַמְעַט כִּי הֶעֱלִיתָנוּ מֵאֶרֶץ ... כִּי־תִשְׂתָּרֵר עָלֵינוּ *is it (too) little that you brought us up from a land* flowing with milk and honey ... *that you* also *need to lord it over us?* Nm 16_{13}, הַמְעַט לָנוּ אֶת־עֲוֹן פְּעוֹר אֲשֶׁר לֹא־הִטַּהַרְנוּ מִמֶּנּוּ *is it (so) little for us with the sin of Peor*, or *is the sin of Peor (so) little for us, that we have not cleansed ourselves of it?* Jos 22_{17}, הַמְעַט מִכֶּם הַמִּרְעֶה הַטּוֹב תִּרְעוּ וְיֶתֶר מִרְעֵיכֶם תִּרְמְסוּ *is the good pasture (too) little for you to graze that you must trample the rest of your pastures?* Ezk 34_{18} (or ins. כִּי is it too little for you *that* you graze?).

<OBJ> בוא hi. *bring* Hg 1$_{6}$ (:: הַרְבֵּה *much*), עבר *pass* 2 S 16$_{1}$ 19$_{37}$ (if em. כִּמְעַט your servant will *hardly* pass to כִּי מְעַט *for* your servant will pass *a little*), ירד hi. *take down* Gn 43$_{11.11}$, לקח *take* 1 K 17$_{10}$ Ezk 5$_{3}$, נטשׁ *leave* 1 S 17$_{28}$, אכל *eat* Ec 5$_{11}$ (:: הַרְבֵּה *much*), שׁקה hi. *give to drink* Gn 24$_{43}$ Jg 4$_{19}$, גמא hi. *allow to swallow* Gn 24$_{17}$, טעם *taste* 1 S 14$_{29.43}$, שׁבר *buy (food)* Gn 43$_{2}$ 44$_{25}$, אסף *gather* Dt 28$_{38}$, מעט hi. *reduce* 4QHalakhah^{a} 6$_{2}$ ([מ]עוט אל ימע[יט]) *one must not [further] reduce a little*; unless מעוט = מְעוּט *that which is reduced*, i.e. מעט pass. ptc.), ראה *see* Si 43$_{32}$.

<CSTR> מְעַט־מַיִם *a little (of) water* Gn 18$_{4}$ 24$_{17.43}$ Jg 4$_{19}$ 1 K 17$_{10}$, אֹכֶל *food* Gn 43$_{2}$ 44$_{25}$, שֶׁמֶן *oil* 1 K 17$_{12}$, רֶגַע *moment* Is 26$_{20}$ Ezr 9$_{8}$ (unless in both כִּמְעַט־ = *just* a moment, as §2b), מְעַט־גּוֹי *a few (of) nation(s)* Dn 11$_{23}$, perh. מעט דבר *a little (of) word*, i.e. with few words Si 20$_{13}$ (unless חכם במעט דבר נפשו = *as for a wise person, the object of his desire is [acquired] by few [words]*, i.e. מְעַט abs. and דְּבַר cstr.; or em. מְעַט דְּבָרִים *a few words*).

מְעַט צֳרִי *a little (of) balm* Gn 43$_{11}$, דְּבַשׁ *honey* Gn 43$_{11}$ 1 S 14$_{29.43}$, מְעַט הַצֹּאן *a few of the sheep*, i.e. the few sheep 1 S 17$_{28}$, מְעַט מִזְעָר perh. *a little of a few*, i.e. very few, very little (unless app., *a few, a few*, in same sense) Is 10$_{25}$ (§3) 16$_{14}$ (perh. here מְעַט adj., as §1f) 29$_{17}$ (§3), מְעַט שֵׁנוֹת *a few (more of) sleeps* Pr 6$_{10}$=24$_{33}$, מְעַט תְּנוּמוֹת *a few (more of) slumberings* Pr 6$_{10}$=24$_{33}$, מְעַט חִבֻּק יָדַיִם *a little (more of) clasping of hands* Pr 6$_{10}$=24$_{33}$, מעוט האדם appar. *the few (left) of humankind* 4QpIsa^{c} 4.2$_{8}$ (unless מְעוֹט *diminution of*, i.e. מעט inf.) 4.2$_{17(Horgan)}$ ([מועט] האדם); others [מיעט]; unless מוּעַט *something reduced*, or *a few, of*, i.e. מעט pu. ptc.).

וּשְׁאָר מְעַט *and a remnant of a few of* Is 16$_{14}$ (or em. וְנִשְׁאַר or וְשָׁאַר *and* a few *will remain* or וּשְׁאָרוֹ *and his remnant* will be a few of), מְתֵי מְעָט *people of a few*, i.e. a few people Dt 26$_{5}$ 28$_{62}$ (מְעָט).

<APP> מִנְחָה *gift* Gn 43$_{11}$.

<PREP> לְ of direction, *to*, + פנה *turn* Hg 1$_{9}$ (or em. פָּנֹה אֶל־הַרְבֵּה וְהִנֵּה לִמְעָט *turning to much and behold (it was turning) to little* to וְהָיָה or וְהָיָה *and it became* as little); of benefit, *to, for*, + מעט hi. *reduce in size* Nm 26$_{54}$ 33$_{54}$ (both :: רַב *many*); *as*, + היה *be* 2 C 29$_{34}$ (רַק הַכֹּהֲנִים הָיוּ לִמְעָט *but the priests were as a few*, i.e. too few); *concerning, about* 4QpIsa^{c} 4.2$_{8}$ (פשרו למעוט האדם appar. *its interpretation is about the few [left] of humankind*; unless מְעוֹט *diminution of*, i.e. מעט inf.) 4.2$_{17(Horgan)}$ (פשרו למועט] האדם]); others [מיעט]; unless מוּעַט *something reduced*, or *a few, of*, i.e. מעט pu. ptc.).

בְּ of instrument, *by (means of), with* perh. Si 20$_{13}$ (חכם במעט דבר נפשו *as for a wise person, the object of his desire is [acquired] by few [words]*, unless מעט דבר = by *a little word* is his desire [expressed]), + עצם *be powerful* Dn 11$_{23}$, ישׁע hi. *save* 1 S 14$_{6}$ (:: רַב *many*).

כְּ *as* (cf. §2) Pr 10$_{20}$ (or em. לֵב רְשָׁעִים כִּמְעָט *the heart of [the] wicked is as little*, i.e. is worth little, to בְּמָעָה *in exchange for a maah*, i.e. is worth but a maah; or em. כִּי מְעַט *little indeed*, i.e. emphatic כִּי),* + היה *be* Ps 105$_{12}$||1 C 16$_{19}$ (בִּהְיוֹתָם מְתֵי מִסְפָּר כִּמְעַט וְגָרִים בָּהּ *when they were people of number, as a few, and sojourning there*; 1 C בִּהְיוֹתְכֶם *when you were*), יתר hi. *leave* Is 1$_{9}$ (or em. לוּלֵי י׳ צְבָאוֹת הוֹתִיר שָׂרִיד כִּמְעָט כִּסְדֹם הָיִינוּ *had Y. of hosts not left us a remnant as a few*, i.e. a small remnant, *we should have been like Sodom* to שָׂרִיד כִּמְעַט had Y. of hosts not left us *a remnant*, we should *nearly* have been like Sodom, as §2a; or em. כִּי מְעַט *little indeed*, i.e. emphatic כִּי).*

כְּ *as though it were (for)*, + היה *be* Ezr 9$_{8}$ (unless כִּמְעַט = *hardly*, as §2b), חבה *hide* Is 26$_{20}$ (unless כִּמְעַט = *hardly*), חבא ni. *hide* 4QpsEzek^{a} 4$_{3}$ (יחבא כמעט perh. *let him hide as though it were for a little [while]*), בער *burn* (of anger) Ps 2$_{12}$ (unless כִּמְעַט = *hardly*), נתן *give* 2 C 12$_{7}$ (unless כִּמְעַט = cause to be *hardly*).

כְּ *in accordance with* 4QTobit^{e} 2$_{8}$.

בֵּין ... לְ *between* many *and* few Si 42$_{4(B,M)}$ (על מקנה בין רב למעט be ashamed *about a purchase, be it of much or of little*; Bmg חשׁבון of *an account*) 1QSa 1$_{18}$ ([בי]ן רוב למועט ... יכבדו איש מרעהו *between abundance and little*, i.e. be it great or small, ... *each person is to honour their companion*) 4Q417 2.1$_{20}$=4Q418 43$_{15}$ (417 :: רוֹב *abundance*; 418 ל[מעט]; :: רַב *many*), + חלק ni. *be divided* Nm 26$_{56}$ (:: רַב).

מֵאֵת *from (with)*, + מעט hi. *collect fewer* Nm 35$_{8}$ (:: רַב *many*).

<COLL> טָעַמְתִּי מְעַט *I tasted a little* 1 S 14$_{29}$, sim. 14$_{43}$, יְמֵי שְׁנֵי מְגוּרַי שְׁלֹשִׁים וּמְאַת שָׁנָה מְעַט וְרָעִים הָיוּ יְמֵי שְׁנֵי

חַיַּי *the days of the years of my sojourning were one hundred and thirty years; few and wretched have been the days of the years of my life* Gn 47$_{9}$.

וְאִם־מְעָט וְאֹסִפָה *and if that were (too) little I would have added* 2 S 12$_{8}$, כַּלֵּל אֹמֶר בִּמְעַט הַרְבֵּה *perfect (your) speech; with a few (words) let there be many (thoughts expressed)* Si 35$_{8}$ (if em. כל לאמר ומעט הרבה *finish speaking and make few [words count for] many*, i.e. מעט pi.).

כִּי־אַתֶּם הַמְעַט מִכָּל־הָעַמִּים *for you were the smallest of all the peoples* Dt 7$_{7}$, הַמְעַט מִתַּזְנוּתָיִךְ *are there (too) few of your prostitutions?* Ezk 16$_{20(Qr)}$, הַמְעַט מִכֶּם *is it (too) little for you?* Nm 16$_{9}$ Is 7$_{13}$ Ezk 34$_{18}$, הַמְעַט מִמְּךָ *are they (too) few for you?* Jb 15$_{11}$, מְעַט מֵהַרְבֵּה *a few from many* Jr 42$_{2}$, מעט ראיתי ממעשיו *few have I seen of his deeds* Si 43$_{32}$, מְעַט בְּמִסְפָּר *few in number* Ezk 5$_{3}$, כִּמְעַט לִפְלֵיטָה *as though it were a few for a remnant* 2 C 12$_{7}$ (unless כִּמְעַט = *hardly*, as §2b), טוֹב־מְעַט לַצַּדִּיק *better is (the) little of the righteous one* Ps 37$_{16}$, טוֹב־מְעַט בְּיִרְאַת י׳ *better is a little with the fear of Y.* Pr 15$_{16}$, טוֹב־מְעַט בִּצְדָקָה *better is a little with righteousness* Pr 16$_{8}$.

הַמְעַט *is it/are they little/few?* Gn 30$_{15}$ Nm 13$_{18}$ 16$_{9.13}$ Jos 22$_{17}$ Is 7$_{13}$ Ezk 16$_{20}$ 34$_{18}$ Jb 15$_{11}$, הֲלֹא־מְעַט *are they not few?* Jb 10$_{20}$.

מְעַט *few, little* + רַב *many* Nm 13$_{18}$ 26$_{54.56}$ 33$_{54}$ 35$_{8}$ Dt 26$_{5}$ 28$_{38}$ 1 S 14$_{6}$ Si 42$_{4}$ 4Q418 43$_{15}$ ([ל]מעט), גָּדוֹל *great* Dt 26$_{5}$ Ne 7$_{4}$, חָזָק *strong* Nm 13$_{18}$, עָצוּם *mighty* Dt 26$_{5}$, רָפֶה *weak* Nm 13$_{18}$ (Sam רָפֵא), רַע *bad* Gn 47$_{9}$, הַרְבֵּה *much* Hg 1$_{6.9}$ Ec 5$_{11}$, הָמוֹן *abundance* Ps 37$_{16}$, רֹב *abundance* Pr 16$_{8}$ 1QSa 1$_{18}$ 4Q417 2.1$_{20}$, אוֹצָר *treasure* Pr 15$_{16}$.

1b. a little, as adv. of עבד *serve* 2 K 10$_{18}$ (:: הַרְבֵּה *much*) Si 6$_{19}$, חסר pi. *make less* Ps 8$_{6}$ (וַתְּחַסְּרֵהוּ מְּעַט מֵאֱלֹהִים *and you have made him a little less than heavenly beings*), דרך *tread*, i.e. advance 1QM 9$_{11}$, שׁחת hi. *destroy* Si 5$_{15}$ (מעט והרבה אל תשחת *in little or in much do not be destructive*).

1c. a little while (but distinction from §1b not alw. clear), as adv. of היה *be* Ezk 11$_{16}$ (or em. וָאֱהִי לָהֶם לְמִקְדָּשׁ מְעַט *and I was to them as a sanctuary a little while* to מְעֻט as a *diminished* sanctuary, i.e. מעט pu.), רמם *be raised* Jb 24$_{24}$ (רוֹמּוּ מְּעַט וְאֵינֶנּוּ *they were raised up for a little while, then ceased to be*; or em. רֻמּוֹ *his being high* was for a little while), קצף *be angry* Zc 1$_{15}$ (קָצַפְתִּי מְּעָט *I was angry for a little while*), חלל hi. *begin* Ho 8$_{10}$ (וַיָּחֵלּוּ מְּעָט *and they began a little while*; or em. חדל *cease* or חלה *desist*), שׁוב *go back* Ru 2$_{7}$ (if em. זֶה שִׁבְתָּהּ הַבַּיִת מְעָט appar. *this staying of hers at home has been little* to וְלֹא שָׁבָה הַבַּיְתָה מְעָט *and she has not returned home [even] a little while*), שׁבת *rest* Ru 2$_{7}$ (if em. וְלֹא שָׁבְתָה [בַּשָּׂדֶה] מְעָט to זֶה שִׁבְתָּהּ הַבַּיִת מְעָט *and she has not rested [even] a little while [in the field]*).

1d. מְעַט מְעַט **little by little,** + impf. of גרשׁ pi. *expel* nations from before Israel Ex 23$_{30}$, נשׁל *clear* nations from before Israel Dt 7$_{22}$.

1e. as predicative adj., **few, little,** יִהְיוּ יָמָיו מְעַטִּים *may his days be few* Ps 109$_{8}$, יִהְיוּ דְבָרֶיךָ מְעַטִּים *let your words be few* Ec 5$_{1}$, מעט רעה כרעת אשה *(any) evil is little compared with the evil of a woman* Si 25$_{19}$.

1f. appar. as indeclinable attributive adj., **little, few** (unless מְעַט is app., or cstr., under §1a), סִכְלוּת מְעָט *a little folly* Ec 10$_{1}$, עֵזֶר מְעָט *a little help* Dn 11$_{34}$, אֲנָשִׁים מְעָט *a few people* Ne 2$_{12}$, וּשְׁאָר מְעַט מִזְעָר *and a little, small, remnant* Is 16$_{14}$ (or em. וְנִשְׁאַר or וְשָׁאַר *and* a small few *will remain* or וּשְׁאָרוֹ *and its remnant* will be a small few), גּוֹיִם לֹא מְעָט *nations not few*, i.e. many nations Is 10$_{7}$, דברים מעט *few words* CD 20$_{24}$ (others מעט[ים], i.e. declinable attributive adj.).

1g. adj. as noun, **little thing,** אין קטן ומעט עמו ואין נפלא וחזק ממנו perh. *there is no small thing or little thing compared with him and nothing more wonderful or strong than he* Si 39$_{20}$.

2. כִּמְעַט, **a. almost, nearly,** + pf. of היה *be* Is 1$_{9}$ (or em. לוּלֵי י׳ צְבָאוֹת הוֹתִיר שָׂרִיד כִּמְעָט כִּסְדֹם הָיִינוּ *had Y. of hosts not left us a remnant as a few*, i.e. a small remnant, *we should have been like Sodom*, as §1a, to שָׂרִיד כִּמְעַט had Y. of hosts not left us *a remnant*, we should *nearly* have been like Sodom) Pr 5$_{14}$, דמה *be like* Is 1$_{9}$ (if em.), נטה *be extended* Ps 73$_{2(Qr)}$ (וַאֲנִי כִּמְעַט נָטָיוּ רַגְלָי *as for me, my legs were almost extended*, i.e. I nearly fell right down; + כְּאַיִן appar. *almost*), שׁכב *lie down* Gn 26$_{10}$, שׁכן *dwell* Ps 94$_{17}$, כלה pi. *destroy* Ps 119$_{87}$; + ptc. of נטה *be extended* Ps 73$_{2(Kt)}$ (appar. וַאֲנִי כִּמְעַט

נָטוּי רַגְלָי *and I am almost extended [on] my legs*, i.e. I nearly fell right down; + כְּאַיִן appar. *almost*).

<COLL> כִּמְעַט קָט וַתַּשְׁחִיתִי מֵהֵן בְּכָל־דְּרָכָיִךְ perh. *almost, only (and) you were more corrupt than them in all your ways* Ezk 16$_{47}$ (or em. קָטֹן hardly *less*, as §2b, or כִּי־אִם עָטַפְתְּ *rather, you were feeble* and became more corrupt).

b. just, hardly, + impf. of עבר *pass* 2 S 19$_{37}$ (or em. כִּי מְעַט *for* your servant will pass *a little*), בער *burn* Ps 2$_{12}$ (וְתֹאבְדוּ דֶרֶךְ כִּי־יִבְעַר כִּמְעַט אַפּוֹ *and you die along the way when his anger hardly blazes*, i.e. at the very onset of his anger; unless כְּ + מְעַט as §1a, when his anger burns *as though it were for a little*); + pf. of נטה hi. *incline* ear 11QSi 51$_{16}$ (+ הַרְבֵּה *much*); waw consec. and pf. of נתן *cause to be* 2 C 12$_{7}$ (וְנָתַתִּי לָהֶם כִּמְעַט לִפְלֵיטָה *and I shall cause them to be hardly [as] a remnant*; unless כְּ + מְעַט as §1a, I shall give to them *as though it were a few*, for a remnant).

<COLL> חֲבִי כִמְעַט־רֶגַע appar. *hide just (for) a moment*, or, as §1a, *hide as though it were (for) a little (of a) moment* Is 26$_{20}$ (or em. חֲבֶה *hide*), וְעַתָּה כִּמְעַט־רֶגַע הָיְתָה תְחִנָּה *and now, just (for) a moment*, or, as §1a, *as though it were (for) a little (of a) moment, there has been compassion* Ezr 9$_{8}$, כִּמְעַט שֶׁעָבַרְתִּי מֵהֶם עַד שֶׁמָּצָאתִי *(it was) hardly that I had passed*, i.e. I had hardly passed, *from them before I found* Ca 3$_{4}$.

c. very soon or **immediately** or **suddenly,** introducing apodosis, + impf. of כנע hi. *humble* Ps 81$_{15}$ (לוּ עַמִּי שֹׁמֵעַ ... כִּמְעַט אוֹיְבֵיהֶם אַכְנִיעַ *if my people would listen ... very soon I would humble their enemies*; or em. שָׁמַע *had listened*), שׁוב hi. *take back* hand Ps 81$_{15}$, נשׂא *raise* Jb 32$_{22}$ (כִּי לֹא יָדַעְתִּי אֲכַנֶּה כִּמְעַט יִשָּׂאֵנִי עֹשֵׂנִי *for I do not know how to give flattering titles, or else very soon my maker would take me away*).

Also perh. 4QMᵃ 11.2$_{18}$ (כ]מעט]).

3. עוֹד מְעַט *(in) a little yet*, i.e. **soon,** + waw consec. and pf. of כלה *be complete* Is 10$_{25}$, בוא *come* Jr 51$_{33}$, שׁוב *go back* Is 29$_{17}$, סקל *stone* Ex 17$_{4}$, פקד *punish* Ho 1$_{4}$, שׁבת hi. *end* Ho 1$_{4}$, בין htpol. *examine* Ps 37$_{10}$=4Qp Psᵃ 1.2$_{5}$; + simple waw and impf. of חשׁב ni. *be reckoned* Is 29$_{17}$; + simple waw and nom. cl., וְעוֹד מְעַט וְאֵין רָשָׁע *and soon there will be no evildoer* Ps 37$_{10}$=4Qp Psᵃ 1.2$_{5}$; in nom. cl., followed by simple waw and ptc., עוֹד אַחַת מְעַט הִיא וַאֲנִי מַרְעִישׁ אֶת־הַשָּׁמַיִם *it is one more little time when I shake the heavens* Hg 2$_{6}$.

<ANT> §1a רַב *many*, הַרְבֵּה *much*, הָמוֹן *abundance*; §1b הַרְבֵּה *much*.*

⇨ מעט *be few*.

[מַעֲטֶה] 1 n.[m.] **garment**—cstr. מַעֲטֵה—<OBJ> נתן *give* Is 61$_{3}$ (or del. נתן; + תַּחַת רוּחַ כֵּהָה *instead of a dimmed spirit*; + פְּאֵר *turban*), שׂים *place* Is 61$_{3}$ (if del. נתן *give*), התל pi. *mock* Si 11$_{4(A)}$ (if em. בעטה א[פ]ר do not mock *one who is enveloped in ashes* to מעטה אבד do not mock *the garment of one who is lost*; B בעוטה אזור do not mock *one who wears a loincloth*). <CSTR> מַעֲטֵה תְהִלָּה *a garment of praise* Is 61$_{3}$, מעטה אבד *the garment of one who is lost* Si 11$_{4(A)}$ (if em.).

⇨ עטה *wrap*.

[מַעֲטָפָה], see מַעֲטֶפֶת *covering*.

[מַעֲטֶפֶת] 1 n.f. **garment**—pl. מַעֲטָפוֹת—appar. **shawl** or **coat,** in list of women's jewellery and fine clothing, <OBJ> סור hi. *remove* Is 3$_{22}$.*

⇨ עטף *wrap*.

מָעַי 1 pr.n.m. **Maai**—מָעַי—priest, appar. brother of Zechariah, <NOM CL> מָעַי ... בִּכְלֵי־שִׁיר דָּוִיד *Maai ... was with David's instruments of song* Ne 12$_{36}$ (ms מְעַי *Mei*). <APP> אָח *brother* Ne 12$_{36}$.

מְעִי I 1 n.[m.] **ruin,** <SUBJ> היה *be* Is 17$_{1}$ (וְהָיְתָה מְעִי מַפָּלָה *and it* [Damascus] *will be a ruin, a falling down* or *a ruin of a falling down* [if מְעִי cstr.]; or em. לְעִי be *as a ruin [of]*; or em. וְהָיְתָה הִמָּ עִי *and behold it will become a heap of rubble*; or del. מְעִי or מַפָּלָה).*

⇨ (?) עוה *bend*; עִי *ruin*.

מְעִי II, see מָעַי *Maai*.

[מְעִי] III, see מֵעֶה *belly*.

מְעִיל 28.2.1 n.m. **robe**—cstr. מְעִיל; sf. מְעִילְךָ, מְעִילוֹ (מְעִלוֹ);

pl. מְעִילֵיהֶם—a loosely fitting outer garment, **a.** in sacral use, as part of Aaron's priestly attire (Ex $28_{4.31}$||39_{22} 28_{34}||39_{26} 29_{5} $39_{23.24.25}$ Lv 8_{7} Si $45_{8.12}$ [or em. מֵעַל *upon*]), of David perh. as priest (1 C 15_{27}).

b. in non-sacral use, of Samuel, as child (1 Sam 2_{19}), as adult (1 S 15_{27}), as ghost (1 S 28_{14}), of Jonathan (1 S 18_{4}), Saul (1 S $24_{5.12.12}$), Job (Jb 1_{20}), Job's comforters (Jb 2_{12}), princesses (2 S 13_{18}), princes (Ezk 26_{16}).

<SUBJ> קרע ni. *be torn* 1 S 15_{27}.

<NOM CL> הַמְּעִיל אֲשֶׁר עָלָיו *the robe that was upon him* 1 S 18_{4}, הַמְּעִיל אֲשֶׁר־לְשָׁאוּל *the robe that belonged to Saul* 1 S 24_{5}.

<OBJ> נתן *give* 1 S 18_{4}, עשׂה *make* Ex 28_{4} (+ חֹשֶׁן *breastplate*, אֵפוֹד *ephod*, כְּתֹנֶת *tunic*) 28_{31}||39_{22}, לבשׁ *wear* 2 S 13_{18} (or em. מְעִילִים wear *robes* to מֵעוֹלָם wear *from of old*, i.e. always wear; + כְּתֹנֶת *tunic*), hi. *dress* Aaron *in* Ex 29_{5} (+ כְּתֹנֶת, אֵפוֹד, חֹשֶׁן) Lv 8_{7} (+ אֵפוֹד) 1 S 2_{19}, יעט *cover with* Is 61_{10} (or em. עטה hi. *wrap in*), סור hi. *remove* Ezk 26_{16} (+ בִּגְדֵי רִקְמָתָם perh. *the garments of their status*), פשׁט htp. *strip oneself of* 1 S 18_{4}, קרע *tear* in mourning Jb 1_{20} 2_{12} Ezr 9_{3} (all three + ראשׁ *head*) 9_{5} (+ בֶּגֶד perh. specif. inner *garment*).

<CSTR> מְעִיל צְדָקָה *a robe of righteousness* Is 61_{10}, מְעִיל בּוּץ *a robe of linen* 1 C 15_{27} (+ אֵפוֹד *ephod*), מְעִיל הָאֵפוֹד *the robe of the ephod* Ex 28_{31}||39_{22} 29_{5}; שׁוּלֵי הַמְּעִיל *the skirts of the robe* Ex 28_{34}||39_{26} $39_{24.25}$, כְּנַף־הַמְּעִיל *the edge of the robe* 1 S 24_{5}, כְּנַף מְעִילוֹ *the edge of his robe* 1 S 15_{27}, כְּנַף מְעִילְךָ *the edge of your robe* 1 S $24_{12.12}$, פִּי־הַמְּעִיל *the mouth*, i.e. opening, *of the robe* Ex 39_{23}.

<APP> כ[ב]וד ועוז ... מעיל adorned him with *glory and strength ... a robe* Si $45_{8.12}$ (or em. עטרת פז מעיל ומצנפת *a diadem of fine gold, a robe and a turban* to מֵעַל מִצְנַפְתּוֹ a diadem of fine gold [was] *upon his turban*).

<ADJ> קָטֹן *small* 1 S 2_{19}.

<PREP> בְּ of instrument, be dressed *in, with*, + פאר pi. *adorn* Si 45_{8} (|| כְּתֹנֶת *tunic*, מִכְנָסַיִם *breeches*) 45_{12} (or em. מְעִיל *robe* to מֵעַל *upon*), כרבל pulp. *be wrapped* 1 C 15_{27}; כְּ *as* Jb 29_{14} (כִּמְעִיל ... מִשְׁפָּטִי *my vindication was ... like a robe*; || צָנִיף *turban*); *as (though it were)*, + לבשׁ *wear* 4QapPs[b] 15_{10}, עטה *be wrapped in* Is 59_{17} (+ קִנְאָה be wrapped in *zeal*) Ps 109_{29} (+ בֹּשֶׁת be wrapped in *shame*).

<COLL> וְהוּא עֹטֶה מְעִיל *and he was wrapped in a robe* 1 S 28_{14}.

<SYN> צָנִיף *turban*, כְּתֹנֶת *tunic*, מִכְנָסַיִם *breeches*.*

[מְעִים], see מֵעֶה *belly*.

[מְעַיִם], see מֵעֶה *belly*.

מַעְיָן 23.1.15 n.[m.] **spring**—Gnz מְעַיָן; cstr. מַעְיַן (Q, מעיין, מַעְיְנוֹ); sf. מַעְיָנוֹ; pl. מַעְיָנִים, מַעְיָנוֹת; cstr. מַעְיְנֵי, מַעְיְנֹת (מַעְיָנַי); sf. מַעְיָנַי, מַעְיְנֹתֶיךָ—**spring, (water) source,** sometimes specif. of primordial waters (Gn 7_{11} 8_{2} Pr 8_{24} 4QCommGenA 1_{5} 4QBer[a] 5_{9}).

<SUBJ> היה *be* pure Lv 11_{36} (|| בּוֹר *cistern*), חרב *be dry* Ho 13_{15} (|| מָקוֹר *source*), יבשׁ *be dry* Si 14_{10} (or em. יָבֵשׁ [that is] *dry*) 1QH 6_{17} (+ מקור עולם *a source of eternity*), רפשׂ ni. *be muddied* Pr 25_{26} (|| מָקוֹר), פתח ni. *be opened* 1QH 12_{13} (מעין גבור[תכה נפתח לי] *a spring of your strength is opened for me*), בקע ni. *be split open* Gn 7_{11} Pr 8_{24} (if em. מַעְיָנוֹת נִכְבַּדֵּי־מָיִם *springs, ones drenched of*, i.e. with, *water* to מַעְיָנוֹת נִבְקָעִים before *wells were split open*) 4QCommGenA 1_{5}, סכר ni. *be closed* Gn 8_{2}, חתם pass. *be sealed* Ca 4_{12} (|| גַּן *garden*, גַּל *spring*), הלך *go*, i.e. flow Ps 104_{10} (+ נַחַל *stream*, הַר *mountain*), יצא *go out* Jl 4_{18} (+ אָפִיק *channel*), נזל *flow* Si 14_{10}, שׁקה hi. *water* Jl 4_{18}, פוץ *spread* Pr 5_{16} (+ פֶּלֶג *channel*).

<NOM CL> כָּל־מַעְיָנַי בָּךְ *all my springs are in you*, appar. you are the source of all I have Ps 87_{7} (or em. כֻּלָּם עֹנֵי בָךְ *all of them sing of you* or כָּל־מַעְיָנַי בָךְ *all your springs* or כָּל־מְעֻנֵּי בָךְ *all who are humbled by you* or כָּל־מְעוֹנָם בָּךְ *all whose dwelling is in you*), בְּאֵין מַעְיָנוֹת *when there were no springs* Pr 8_{24} (|| תְּהוֹם *abyss*; or em. מַעְיְנוֹת *springs of*), מַעְיָן ... צַדִּיק *a well ... is a righteous one* Pr 25_{26}, מַעְיָן ... אֲחֹתִי *my sister ... is a spring* Ca 4_{12} (Gnz מְעַיָן).

<OBJ> סתם *block* 2 K $3_{19.25}$ (both + עִיר *city*, חֶלְקָה *field*, עֵץ *tree*) 2 C 32_{4} (+ נַחַל *stream*), נכה hi. *strike* 1 C 4_{41} (if em. מְעוּנִים *Maonites* [Qr]; + אֹהֶל *tent*), פתח *open* Is 41_{18} (|| נָהָר *river*, + אֲגַם *pool*, מוֹצָא *spring*), בקע *split open* Ps 74_{15} (|| נַחַל *stream*, + נָהָר *river*), שׁית *cause* val-

ley *to be* Ps 84$_7$ (or em. שִׁית to שׁתה *drink* [from] a spring and/or מַעְיָן to מֵעַיִן drink *from a spring;* or מַעְיָן to מָעוֹן cause valley to be a *dwelling place;* + בְּרָכָה *pool*), שׁלח pi. *send out* Ps 104$_{10}$, עצר *retain* 1QH 8$_{24}$ (AHL מָעוֹז *strength*), סתר (pi.) *conceal* 1QH 5$_{26}$ (|| סוֹד *secret* of truth).

<CSTR> מַעְיַן גַּנִּים *a spring of gardens* Ca 4$_{15}$ (|| בְּאֵר *well*), מַעְיַן מֵי נֶפְתּוֹחַ *the source of the waters of Nephtoah* Jos 15$_9$ 18$_{15}$, מַעְיְנֵי־מַיִם *sources of water* 1 K 18$_5$ (מַעְיְנֵי הַמַּיִם) 2 K 3$_{19}$, מַעְיְנוֹ־מָיִם *a source of water* Ps 114$_8$, מַעְיְנוֹת־מָיִם *springs of water* Pr 8$_{24}$ (if em. מַעְיָנוֹת נִכְבַּדֵּי־מָיִם *springs, ones drenched of,* i.e. with, *water*), מַעְיְנֹת תְּהוֹם *(the) springs of (the) abyss* Gn 7$_{11}$ 8$_2$ 4Q CommGenA 1$_5$ 4QBer^a 5$_9$ (מעיני תהום).

מעין קודש *a spring of holiness* 1QS 10$_{12}$ (others מָעוֹן *dwelling place*), מעין דעת *a spring of knowledge* 1Q36 12$_2$ (others מָעוֹן), מעין חיים *a spring of life* 1QH 8$_{12}$ 1QH^b 2$_1$ (others מָעוֹן), מעיין משפט *a spring of judgment* 4Q424 2$_2$, מַעַיְנֵי הַיְשׁוּעָה *the springs of salvation* Is 12$_3$, מעין אור *a spring of light* 1QS 3$_{19}$ (others מָעוֹן; || מָקוֹר *source*), מעין כבוד *a spring of glory* 1QS 11$_7$ (|| מָקוֹר, מִקְוֶה *collection* of water), מעין הגב[ורה] *the spring of strength* 1QH 1$_5$, מעין גבור[תכה] *a spring of your strength* 1QH 12$_{13}$, מעין בינה *a spring of understanding* 1QH 5$_{26}$ (|| סוֹד *secret* of truth), מעין אור *a spring of light* 1QH 6$_{17}$, מעין רז *a spring of secret(s)* 1QH 8$_6$.

כָּל־הַמַּעְיָנוֹת *all the springs* 2 C 32$_4$, כָּל־מַעְיָנַי *all my springs* Ps 87$_7$ (or em. כָּל־מַעְיָנַיִךְ *all the springs of* you, or כֻּלָּם עֹנֵי *all of them sing of* you, or כָּל־מְעֻנַּי *all who are humbled of,* i.e. by, you, or כָּל־מְעוֹנָם *all whose dwelling* is in you), כָּל־מַעְיְנֹת *all (the) springs of* Gn 7$_{11}$ 4QCommGenA 1$_5$ (כול מעינות), כָּל־מַעְיְנֵי *all (the) sources of* 1 K 18$_5$ 2 K 3$_{19}$ (כָּל־מַעְיְנֵי־).

<APP> מִקְוֶה *collection* of water Lv 11$_{36}$, נִכְבָּד *heavy one,* i.e. one drenched with water Pr 8$_{24}$ (or em. מַעְיָנוֹת נִכְבַּדֵּי־מָיִם *springs, ones drenched of,* i.e. with, *water* to מַעְיְנוֹת־מָיִם *springs of water* or מַעְיָנוֹת נִבְקָעִים before *wells were split open* or מַעְיָנוֹת נִבְכֵי־מָיִם *wells, sources of water*).

<PREP> לְ *as, into,* + הפך *turn* flint Ps 114$_8$ (|| אֲגַם *pool*); בְּ of place, *in* 1QS 3$_{19}$ perh. 1QH^b 2$_1$ (in both, others מָעוֹן *dwelling place*), + בוא *come* 1QH 8$_{12}$ (בלי]בוא זר ב[מעין *a stranger will not come into the spring of* life); perh. of accompaniment, *with,* 1QH 8$_6$ (+ עצי חיים *trees of life* with a spring of secret[s]); מִן of direction, *from* perh. 1Q36 12$_2$ (others מָעוֹן *dwelling place*), + שׁאב *draw* water Is 12$_3$; אֶל *to,* + הלך *go* 1 K 18$_5$ (|| נַחַל *stream*), יצא *go out* (of border) Jos 18$_{15}$, תאר *depart* (of border) Jos 15$_9$; עִם *with* 1QS 11$_7$.

<SYN> בּוֹר *cistern,* בְּאֵר *well,* מִקְוֶה *collection* of water, נַחַל *stream,* אֲגַם *pool,* נָהָר *river,* מָקוֹר *source,* גַּל *spring,* תְּהוֹם *abyss,* גַּן *garden,* סוֹד *secret.**

⇒ cf. עַיִן *spring.*

[מְעַיָן], see מַעְיָן *spring.*

[מְעִינִי] 2 gent. perh. **Minaean**—pl. Kt מעינים—appar. in ref. to non-Semitic people, <OBJ> נכה hi. *strike* 1 C 4$_{41}$(Kt) (Qr מְעוּנִים *Maonites;* or em. הַמַּעְיָנִים *the springs* or הַמְּעוֹנִים *the dwelling places* or מְעוֹנֵיהֶם *their dwelling places;* + אָהֳלֵיהֶם *their tents* [or em. אָהֳלֵי חָם *the tents of Ham*]). <CSTR> בְּנֵי־מְעוּנִים *the sons of (the) Minaeans* Ezr 2$_{50}$(Kt) (Qr, ||Ne 7$_{52}$ מְעוּנִים *Maonites*).*

מעך 3.0.2 vb. **press—Qal** 2.0.1 Impf. Q ימעכו; ptc. מָעוּךְ, מְעוּכָה—**1.** appar. **press, squeeze** foodstuffs, <COLL> [כאש]ר ימעכו ויצא משקיהם *when they press so their liquid goes out* 4QṬohA 2.1$_7$, [מש]קיהם יוצא כאש[ר י]מעך *their liquid goes out when he presses* 4Q Leqeṭ 1$_5$.

2. pass., **be pressed,** <SUBJ> חֲנִית *spear* 1 S 26$_7$. <PREP> בְּ of place, *in,* + אֶרֶץ *ground* 1 S 26$_7$.

3. pass. ptc. as noun, perh. **animal that is pressed,** perh. in ref. to squeezing of testicles for castration, <OBJ> קרב hi. *offer (in sacrifice)* Lv 22$_{24}$ (|| כתת pass. *be crushed,* נתק pass. *be torn,* כרת pass. *be cut*), perh. עשׂה *do,* i.e. prepare (for sacrifice) Lv 22$_{24}$. <SYN> כתת pass. *be crushed,* נתק pass. *be torn,* כרת pass. *be cut.*

Pi. press, <SUBJ> מִצְרַיִם *Egypt* Ezk 23$_{21}$ (if em. בַּעֲשׂוֹת מִמִּצְרַיִם דַּדַּיִךְ לְמַעַן שְׁדֵי נְעוּרָיִךְ *when ones of Egypt handled your nipples for the sake of the breasts of your youth* to בַּעֲשׂוֹת מִצְרַיִם דַּדַּיִךְ לְמַעֵךְ *when Egypt squeezed your nipples to press* the breasts). <OBJ> דַּד *nipple* Ezk 23$_{21}$ (if em.).

Pu. 1 Pf. מֹעֲכוּ—**be pressed,** <SUBJ> שַׁד *breast* Ezk 23_{3} (+ עשׂה pi. *squeeze*) 23_{21} (if em. בַּעֲשׂוֹת מִמִּצְרַיִם דַּדַּיִךְ לְמַעַן שְׁדֵי נְעוּרָיִךְ *when ones of Egypt handled your nipples for the sake of the breasts of your youth* to בַּעֲשׂוֹת מִמִּצְרַיִם דַּדַּיִךְ לְמֹעַךְ *when your nipples were squeezed by Egypt, so that* the breasts of your youth *could be pressed*).

Hi. crush, כפיר החרון [להמ]עיכו כשח[ל] *the lion of anger to crush him like a young lion* 4QpHos[b] 2_{2} (others כפיר החרון כי אנוכי כשח[ל] *the lion of anger; for I am like a lion*).

מַעֲכָה I 18 pr.n.m.&f. **Maacah, 1.** appar. son of Nahor and Reumah, <OBJ> ילד *give birth (to)* Gn 22_{24}.

2. secondary wife of Caleb and mother of Sheber, Tirhanah, Shaaph, and Sheva (or em. ילד hi. *beget*, of Caleb, for last two). <SUBJ> ילד *give birth* 1 C 2_{48}. <APP> פִּילֶגֶשׁ *secondary wife* 1 C 2_{48}.

3. sister of Machir, <NOM CL> וְשֵׁם אֲחֹתוֹ מַעֲכָה *and his sister's name was Maacah* 1 C 7_{15} (or em. אֲחֹתָם *their sister*, i.e. sister of Huppim and Shuppim [and daughter of Machir]; ms אִשְׁתּוֹ *his wife*, i.e. Machir's wife, as §4).

4. wife of Machir and mother of Peresh and Sheresh, <SUBJ> ילד *give birth* 1 C 7_{16}, קרא *call* child's name 1 C 7_{16}. <NOM CL> וְשֵׁם אִשְׁתּוֹ מַעֲכָה *and his wife's name was Maacah* 1 C $7_{15(ms)}$. <APP> אִשָּׁה *wife* 1 C 7_{16}.

5. wife of eponymous ancestor of Gibeon (or ins. Jeiel as son of Gibeon and husband of Maacah, as §6), <NOM CL> וְשֵׁם אִשְׁתּוֹ מַעֲכָה *and his wife's name was Maacah* 1 C 8_{29}.

6. wife (or sister, if em.) of Jeiel, <NOM CL> וְשֵׁם אִשְׁתּוֹ מַעֲכָה *and his wife's name was Maacah* 1 C 8_{29} (if ins. Jeiel) 9_{35} (mss אֲחֹתוֹ *his sister*).

7. father of Achish, king of Gath, appar. ident. with Maoch (מָעוֹךְ) at 1 S 27_{2}, <CSTR> בֶּן־מַעֲכָה *son of Maacah* 1 K 3_{39}.

8. daughter of Talmi, wife of David, and mother of Absalom, <CSTR> בֶּן־מַעֲכָה *son of Maacah* 2 S 3_{3}||1 C 3_{2}. <APP> בַּת *daughter* 2 S 3_{3}||1 C 3_{2}.

9. father of one of David's warriors, Hanan, <CSTR> בֶּן־מַעֲכָה *son of Maacah* 1 C 11_{43}.

10. father of David's chief of Simeonites, Shephatiah, <CSTR> בֶּן־מַעֲכָה *son of Maacah* 1 C 27_{16}.

11. daughter of Absalom, favourite wife of Rehoboam, and mother of Abijah, Attai, Ziza, and Shelomith (or em. Shelomoth), <OBJ> לקח *take* in marriage 2 C 11_{20}, אהב *love* 2 C 11_{20}. <CSTR> בֶּן־מַעֲכָה *son of Maacah* 2 C 11_{22}. <APP> בַּת *daughter* 2 C $11_{20.21}$.

12. daughter of Abishalom and mother of Abijam/Abijah (if em.), <NOM CL> וְשֵׁם אִמּוֹ מַעֲכָה *and his mother's name was Maacah* 1 K 15_{2}||2 C 13_{2} (if em. מִיכָיָהוּ *Micaiah*). <APP> בַּת *daughter* 1 K 15_{2}||2 C 13_{2} (if em. מִיכָיָהוּ *Micaiah* to מַעֲכָה *Maacah* and אוּרִיאֵל מִן־גִּבְעָה daughter of *Uriel from Gibeah* to אֲבִישָׁלוֹם *Abishalom*).

13. daughter of Abishalom and mother of Asa, <SUBJ> עשׂה *make* an abomination for Asherah 1 K 15_{13}||2 C 15_{16}. <NOM CL> וְשֵׁם אִמּוֹ מַעֲכָה *and his mother's name was Maacah* 1 K 15_{10}. <OBJ> סור hi. *remove* from status of queen-mother 1 K 15_{13}||2 C 15_{16}. <APP> בַּת *daughter* 1 K 15_{10}, אֵם *mother* 1 K 15_{13}||2 C 15_{16}.

מַעֲכָה II 3 pl.n. **Maacah,** appar. land of the Maacathites; also perh. the people themselves, <NOM CL> וְאִישׁ־טוֹב וּמַעֲכָה לְבַדָּם בַּשָּׂדֶה *and Ish-tob and Maacah alone were in the field (of battle)* 2 S 10_{8} (unless אִישׁ־טוֹב וּמַעֲכָה = *the men of Tob and [of] Maacah*). <CSTR> מֶלֶךְ מַעֲכָה *the king of Maacah* 2 S 10_{6}||1 C 19_{7}, אֲרַם מַעֲכָה *Aram of Maacah* 1 C 19_{6}.

⇒ מַעֲכַת *Maacath*, מַעֲכָתִי *Maacathite.*

מַעֲכָה III, see אָבֵל בֵּית־מַעֲכָה *Abel-beth-maacah.*

מַעֲכַת 1 pr.n.m. **Maacath,** (ancestor of) unvanquished people on N border of Israel, <SUBJ> ישׁב continue to *dwell* among Israelites Jos 13_{13} (|| גְּשׁוּר *Geshur*). <SYN> גְּשׁוּר *Geshur.*

⇒ מַעֲכָה *Maacah.*

מַעֲכָתִי 8 gent. **Maacathite,** descendant of Maacath/inhabitant of Maacah, **1.** sing., individual **Maacathite,** <APP> בֶּן־אֲחַסְבַּי הַמַּעֲכָתִי *the son of Ahasbai, the Maacathite* 2 S 23_{34} (if del. בֶּן־ Ahasbai, *son of* the

Maacathites, as §2), אֶשְׁתְּמֹעַ הַמַּעֲכָתִי *Eshtemoa, the Maacathite* 1 C 4_{19} (or em. אֶשְׁתְּמֹעַ to יִשְׁעִי *Ishi*).

2. sing. used collectively, **Maacathites,** <OBJ> ירשׁ hi. *(dis)possess* Jos 13_{13} (|| גְּשׁוּרִי *Geshurite*). <CSTR> גְּבוּל ... הַמַּעֲכָתִי *the border of ... the Maacathites* Dt 3_{14} (Sam מַכְעָתִי *Machathites*) Jos 12_{5} 13_{11} (all three || גְּשׁוּרִי *Geshurite*), בֶּן־הַמַּעֲכָתִי *a son of the Maacathites,* i.e. a Maacathite 2 S 23_{34} (or del. בֶּן־, leaving הַמַּעֲכָתִי in app. to Ahasbai, as §1) 2 K 25_{23}||Jr 40_{8}.

⇒ מַעֲכָה *Maacah.*

מעל $_{35.0.10}$ vb. **sin—Qal** $_{35.0.10}$ Pf. מָעַל, מָעַלְתָּ, מָעַלְנוּ, מָעֲלוּ, מְעַלְתֶּם; impf. יִמְעַל, 3fs תִּמְעֹל, תִּמְעֲלוּ; + waw וַיִּמְעַל; 3fs וּמָעֲלָה; 3fs וַתִּמְעֹל, וַיִּמְעֲלוּ; ptc. Q מועל, מועלה; inf. מְעֹל (Q מעול, מָעוֹל, מְעָל־, מַעֲלוֹ, מַעֲלָם)—**sin, commit (sin), be sinful, transgress,** esp. **commit sacrilege,** as redressed by the אָשָׁם *reparation offering.**

<SUBJ> Moses Dt 32_{51} Ne 1_{8}, Aaron Dt 32_{51}, Achan Jos 22_{20} 1 C 2_{7}, Saul 1 C 10_{13}, Uzziah 2 C 26_{16} (+ שׁחת hi. *corrupt*) 26_{18}, Ahaz 2 C 28_{19} (+ פרע hi. *set free*) 28_{22} 29_{19}, Shecaniah Ezr 10_{2}, Reubenites, Gadites, and Manassites Jos $22_{16.31}$ 1 C 5_{25} (+ זנה *prostitute oneself*), Israel Dn 9_{7}.

אִישׁ *man* Nm 5_{6} Dn 9_{7} Ezr $10_{2.6}$ 4QHalakhah^{a} 1_{13} ([איש]) CD 7_{1} 9_{16}, אִשָּׁה *woman* Nm $5_{6.12}$ (+ שׂטה *stray*) Ezr 10_{2}, יֶלֶד *child* Ezr 10_{2}, אָב *father* Ezk 20_{27} 2 C 29_{6} (+ עשׂה רַע *do evil,* עזב *leave* Y., סבב פָּנִים hi. *turn face* from tabernacle, נתן עֹרֶף *give,* i.e. display, *neck,* i.e. be stubborn) 30_{7}, אָח *brother* 2 C 30_{7}, בֵּן *son* of Israel Nm 31_{16} (if em. לִמְסָר־ *to commit* sin to לִמְעֹל *to commit* sin) Jos 7_{1}, יֹשֵׁב *inhabitant* of Jerusalem Ezk 15_{8} Dn 9_{7}, יְהוּדִי *Judaean* Ne 13_{27}, מֶלֶךְ *king* of Israel Ezk 17_{20}, שַׂר *prince,* i.e. leader, of priests 2 C 36_{14} (+ טמא pi. *defile*), צַדִּיק *righteous one* Ezk 18_{24} (|| חטא *sin*), שָׁב *repentant one* CD 15_{13}=4QD^{a} 8.1_{4}=4QD^{e} 6.2_{6} (both [השב]), נֶפֶשׁ *soul* Lv $5_{15.21}$ (both || חטא) 5_{27} (+ טמא ni. *defile oneself*), פֶּה *mouth* of king Pr 16_{10}.

עַם *people* Ezr 10_{10}, בַּיִת *house* of Israel Ezk $39_{23.26}$, קָהָל *congregation* Ezr 10_{2}, אֶרֶץ *land* Ezk 14_{13} (+ חטא), appar. עִיר *city* 4Q418 159.2_{2}, Jerusalem 2 C 12_{2} (or del. מעל), Israelites Ne 1_{8}.

<OBJ> מַעַל *sin* Lv $5_{15.21}$ Nm $5_{6.12.27}$ 31_{16} (if em. לִמְסָר־ *to commit* sin to לִמְעֹל *to commit* sin) Jos 7_{1} $22_{16.20.31}$ Ezk 14_{13} 15_{8} 17_{20} 18_{24} 20_{27} 39_{26} Dn 9_{7} 1 C 10_{13} 2 C 28_{19} 26_{14} 4QHalakhah^{a} 1_{13} 4QpsEzek^{c} 3.2_{3} 5_{1} ([מעלו]) 4Q Myst^{b} 4_{4}.

<PREP> בְּ of place/time, *in, at, during,* + מַיִם *waters* of Meribah Dt 32_{51} (perh. בְּ *in respect of*), שֶׁבֶת *dwelling* Ezk 39_{26}.

בְּ of accompaniment, *with, in (a state of),* + שְׁגָגָה *inadvertence* Lv 5_{15}.

בְּ *against* 4QD^{f} 3_{6}, + Y. Lv 5_{21} 26_{40} Nm 5_{6} Nm 31_{16} (if em. לִמְסָר־ *to commit* sin to לִמְעֹל *to commit* sin) Dt 32_{51} (or em. בִּי׳ *against Y.* to בִּדְבָרִי *against my word*) Jos 22_{31} Ezk 17_{20} 20_{27} $39_{23.26}$ Dn 9_{7} 1 C 10_{13} 2 C 12_{2} (or del. מעל בְּ) 26_{16} $28_{19.22}$ 30_{7} 4QpsEzek^{c} 5_{1}(אשר [מעלו בי] their sin *that they sinned against me*), אֱלֹהִים *God* Jos 22_{16} Ezr 10_{2} Ne 13_{27} 1 C 5_{25} 2 C 26_{16} 30_{7}, אִישׁ *man,* i.e. husband Nm $5_{12.27}$, שְׁאֵר *flesh,* i.e. kin 4Q418 101.2_{5} CD 7_{1} (in both perh. בְּ *in respect of*), צאן my *flock* 4Q Bapt 14_{3}, חֵרֶם *ban* Jos 7_{1} 22_{20} 1 C 2_{7}, מִשְׁפָּט *judgment,* i.e. justice Pr 16_{10} (perh. בְּ *in respect of* judgment), תּוֹרָה *law* CD 9_{16} (perh. בְּ *in respect of*).

בְּ *in respect of,* + אָדָם *human being* 4QD^{f} 3_{6}, בְּהֵמָה *beast* 4QD^{f} 3_{6}.

כְּ *in accordance with,* + תּוֹעֵבָה *abomination* 2 C 36_{14}.

עַל *concerning* 1 C 10_{13}; בְּתוֹךְ *among,* + בֵּן *son* of Israel Dt 32_{51}.

<COLL> מַעַלְנוּ וַנֹּשֶׁב *we have sinned by marrying* foreign women Ezr 10_{2}, מְעַלְתֶּם וַתֹּשִׁיבוּ *you have sinned by marrying* Ezr 10_{6}, לִמְעֹל ... לְהֹשִׁיב *by sinning ... in marrying* foreign women Ne 13_{27}, וַיּוֹסֶף לִמְעוֹל *and he continued to sin* 2 C 28_{22}, הִרְבּוּ לִמְעָל־ *they increased (their) sinning* 2 C $36_{14(Qr)}$, כל דבר אשר ימעל איש בתורה *everything concerning which one sins against the law* CD 9_{16}, ועד לכלה ועד למעול *either to the point of destroying or to the point of sinning* 4QapJoshua^{a} 3.1_{7}.

Also 4QMyst^{a} 7_{6} (אשר מ[על] *who sinned*) 4QPrFêtes $54_{2(mg)}$ (מעלת *you have sinned*).

<SYN> חטא *sin.**

⇒ מַעַל *sin.*

מַעַל I $_{29.3.32}$ n.[m.] **sin**—מַעַל; cstr. מַעַל (Q מועל); sf. מַעֲלוֹ (Q מעלו), מַעַלְכֶה (מועלכה), מעלנו, מעלכם, מַעֲלָם (Q

מועלם)—**sin, sinning, sinfulness, transgression,** esp. **sacrilege,** as redressed by the אָשָׁם *reparation offering;** perh. **deceit** (Jb 21_{34} Si 41_{18}).

<SUBJ> שׁאר ni. *remain* Jb 21_{34} (+ הֶבֶל *vanity*), כתב pass. *be written (down)* 2 C 33_{19} (|| חַטָּאת *sin*), מצא ni. *be found* in our hand 4QMMT C_9 (|| שֶׁקֶר *deceit*, רָעָה *evil*)

<NOM CL> מָה־הַמַּעַל *what is the sin?* Jos 22_{16}, מעל עשק *oppression is a sin* Si 10_7.

<OBJ> נשׂא *bear* Ezk 39_{26} (or em. נשׁה *forget*), מעל *commit (sin)* Lv $5_{15.21}$ 26_{40} (+ עָוֺן *sin*) Nm 5_6 (+ חַטָּאת *sin*) $5_{12.27}$ Jos 7_1 $22_{16.20.31}$ Ezk 14_{13} 17_{20} 18_{24} (|| חַטָּאת *sin*) 20_{27} 39_{26} (|| כְּלִמָּה *insult*) Dn 9_7 1 C 10_{13} 2 C 28_{19} 36_{14} 4QHalakhah^{a} 11_3 4QMyst^{b} 4_4 4QpsEzek^{c} 3.2_3 5_1 ([מעלו]), מסר appar. *commit (sin)* Nm 31_{16} (or em. לִמְסָר־מַעַל *to commit sin* to לָסוּר מֵעַל *to turn away from*, or לִמְעֹל מַעַל *to commit sin*), רבה hi. *increase* 1QH fr. 45_5 (+ זָדוֹן *presumptuousness*), פלא hi. *do wonderfully*, i.e. commit sin exceedingly Si 48_{16} (:: יֹשֶׁר *uprightness*), כפר hi. *atone (for)* 4QPrFêtes 54_2, שׁבת hi. *cause to cease* 4QCreatA 1_2, ספר pi. *recount* 1QS 10_{23}= 4QS^{f} 3_6 ([מעל] ... [תס]פר; :: צְדָקָה *righteousness*).

<CSTR> מַעַל הַגּוֹלָה *the sin of the diaspora* Ezr 9_4 10_6, מעל האדם *the sin of the (first) human being* CD 10_8= 4QD^{a} 8.3_7=4QD^{e} 6.4_{18} (D^{e} מועל [ה]אדם), מעל אנשים *the sin(s) of people* 1QS 10_{23}=4QS^{f} 3_6 ([מעל]), מעל אבותי *the sin(s) of my ancestors* 1QH 4_{34}, מעל ישראל *Israel's sinning* CD 20_{23}, מעל חטאת *transgression of sin* 1QS 9_4 (|| אַשְׁמָה *guilt* of sin).

אשמת מעל *the guilt of sin* 1QH 4_{30} 11_{11} (+ תועבות נדה *abominations of [menstrual] impurity*) 4QWiles 4_5 (אשמות מע[ל] *guilty deeds of sin*) 4QHod^{b} 7_3, קץ מעל *the time of* Israel's *sinning* CD 20_{23}, קץ מועלם *the time of their sinning* 4QpHos^{a} 1_9, כול חללי מעל *all the battle-victims (because) of sin* 1QM 3_8, מרבי מעל *increasers of sin* 1QH fr. 45_5, כל המעל *all the transgression* 4QHalakhah^{a} 11_3, כָּל־מַעֲלָם *all their sin(s)* Ezk 39_{26} (or del. כָּל־).

<ADJ> זֶה *this* Jos $22_{16.31}$ Ezr 9_2.

<PREP> בְּ of accompaniment, *(along) with, in (a state of)* perh. 4Q416 2.3_3 4QBéat 16_6 (|| עֹשֶׁק *oppression*), + ידה htp. *confess* Lv 26_{40}, רצה *atone (for)* 4QDibHam^{a} 1.6_6 (+ עָוֺן *sin*); *in (a state of), involved with*, + היה *be* Ezr 9_2.

בְּ of instrument, *by (means of), with*, + מרד *rebel* against God 1QpHab 1_6 ([מרדו]; || עֹשֶׁק *oppression*).

בְּ of cause, *on account of* perh. 4QpsEzek^{c} 5_1 4Q423 2_4, + מות *die* Ezk 18_{24} 1 C 10_{13}, גלה ho. *be exiled* 1 C 9_1, מעט *be reduced* (of days) CD 10_8=4QD^{a} 8.3_7=4QD^{e} 6.4_{18} (D^{a} [מעטו ימו]; D^{e} [מע]טו), נדח hi. *expel* Dn 9_7, סתר hi. *hide* face CD 1_3=4QD^{c} 1_{10} (ב[מע]לם ... הסת[יר]), קצף *be angry* 4QpsMos^{e} 2.1_6, נקם *take vengeance* 4QAdmonPar 3.2_6, קום hi. *establish* 4QAdmonPar 3.2_6 (WA).

בְּ appar. *about, concerning*, + ידע *know* Jos 22_{22} (|| מֶרֶד *rebellion*).

עַל *concerning*, + בושׁ *be ashamed* Si 41_{18}, חרד *be fearful* Ezr 9_4, אבל htp. *be in mourning* Ezr 10_6, כפר pi. *atone* for 1QS 9_4, perh. נתן *give* heart, i.e. pay attention to 4QMMT C_9.

עִם *with*, + זכר *remember* guilt with, i.e. and, sin 1QH 4_{34}.

כְּפִי *in accordance with*, + יכח hi. *reprove* CD 20_4.

בַּעַד *for*, + כפר pi. *atone* 1QH 17_{12} (בע[ד]; + חַטָּאָה *sin*, עָוֺן *sin*).

בַּעֲבוּר *on account of*, + דרשׁ *seek* revenge 4QpsEzek^{c} 3.2_3.

<COLL> מַעַל בַּי׳ *a sin against Y.* Lv 5_{21} Nm 5_6 31_{16} (or em. לִמְסָר־מַעַל בַּי׳ *to commit a sin against Y.* to לָסוּר מֵעַל י׳ *to turn away from Y.*) Jos 22_{22} 2 C 28_{19}, מַעַל בְּאִישָׁהּ *a sin against her husband* Nm 5_{27}, מעל בַּחֵרֶם *a sin against the ban* Jos 7_1 22_{20}, כי במועלם אשר עזבהו *for in their sin when*, or *in that, they left him* CD 1_3=4QD^{c} 1_{10} (כי ב[מע]לם [אשר עזבוה]ו; but perh. here and at 4QpHos^{b} 1_9 4QpsMos^{e} 2.1_6 4Q423 2_4 מ[ו]עלם, מועלכה, etc. is מעל inf. cstr., in same sense as מַעַל), צדקות אל ... ומעל אנשים עד תום פשעם *the righteous deeds of God ... and the sin(s) of people right up to the fullness of their sinfulness* 1QS 10_{23}=4QS^{f} 3_6 [צ]דקות אל ... [ומעל אנשים [עד ת]ום פשעם]).

Also 1QH fr. 1_8 ([מ]על; others [ג]על *abhorrence*) 4QD^{a} $7.1_{3(WA)}$ (מועלו *his sin*; DJD וע לו) 4QpsMos^{e} 2.2_3 (but prob. מעליהם = *from over them*) 4QMMT C_4 ([החמ]ס והמעל *the violence and the sin*).

<SYN> חַטָּאת *sin*, אַשְׁמָה *guilt*, כְּלִמָּה *insult*, מֶרֶד *rebellion*, עֹשֶׁק *oppression*, שֶׁקֶר *deceit*, רָעָה *evil*.

<ANT> יֹשֶׁר *uprightness*, צְדָקָה *righteousness*.*

⇒ מעל *sin*.

מַ֫עַל II $141.2.32$ n.[m.] **height**—מֶ֫עַל; + ה- of direction מַ֫עְלָה (מֶ֫עְלָה, Q מעלא)—**1.** as noun, **height**, <CSTR> מרומי מעל *the heights of high*, i.e. the highest heavens Si 26_{16} (Segal אֵל the heights of *God*).

2-14, as adverb or in adverbial constructions.

2. לְמַעְלָה **above, on top, on high, upwards; upside down** (Jg 7_{13}); **in the future** (1 C 17_{17} [if em.]); **exceedingly** (1 C 22_5 23_{17} $29_{3.25}$ 2 C 1_1 20_{19}).

With verb היה *be* Dt 28_{13} (|| לְרֹאשׁ *as [the] head*, :: לְמַטָּה *below*, לְזָנָב *as [the] tail*) 11QT 47_2 ([ל]מעלה); :: לְמַטָּה *below*) 59_{20} (|| לְרֹאשׁ, :: לְמַטָּה, לְזָנָב), נשׂא ni. *be raised* 1 C 14_2, רבה *be many* Ezr 9_6 1 C 23_{17}, רום *be high* 1QH 7_{24} (unless תָּרֵם *you raise* my horn upwards, i.e. רום hi.), hi. *raise* 4QapPs^b 33_{10}, perh. 1QH 7_4, גדל hi. *magnify* 1 C 22_5 29_{25} 2 C 1_1, הלל pi. *praise* 2 C 20_{19} (unless לְמַעְלָה *exceedingly* modifies preceding גָּדוֹל in an exceedingly *loud* voice), פרשׂ *extend* wings Ex 25_{20}||37_9, שׁוב *go back* 4QD^g 1.1_3 (ושב הדם למ]עלה] *and the blood runs upwards*; || לְמַטָּה *downwards*), בוא *come* 11QT 32_{11}, hi. *bring* Ps 74_5 (or em. כְּמֵבִיא לְמַ֫עְלָה *as one bringing*, i.e. wielding, *upwards* axes to לוֹ עָלֶה bringing *for himself foliage*), עלה *go up* Ec 3_{21} (:: לְמַטָּה *below*).

הפך *turn* tent Jg 7_{13}, פנה *turn* (intrans.) Is 8_{21}, סבב ni. *turn* (intrans.) Ezk 41_7, רחב *be wide* Ezk 41_7 (or em. וְרָחֲבָה וְנָסְבָה לְמַעְלָה לְמַעְלָה *and it widened and turned ever upwards* to וְרָחֲבָה הַמְּסִבָּה *and the staircase widened* the higher it went, or וְרֹחַב הַמְּסִבָּה *and the width of the staircase* went higher and higher, i.e. grew greater as it grew higher), עשׂה *do*, i.e. produce, fruit 2 K 19_{30}||Is 37_{31} (:: לְמַטָּה *below*).

רום hi. *raise* 4QapJoseph^b 16_3 ([למעל[ה), גבה hi. *make high* Is 7_{11} (:: שְׁאֹלָה *to Sheol*, i.e. underneath, downwards [if em. שְׁאָלָה *question*]), perh. נתן *give* 1 C 29_3 (נָתַתִּי לְבֵית־אֱלֹהַי לְמַעְלָה *I gave exceedingly to the house of my God*, unless לְמַעְלָה = I gave to the house of my God *on high*).

ראה *see* 1 C 17_{17} (if em. וּרְאִיתַנִי כְּתוֹר הָאָדָם הַמַּעֲלָה appar. *and you saw me as a line of humanity, the progeny*, i.e. you saw in me all my descendants, or *and you saw me after the manner of humans, O Height* to לְמַעְלָה *above*, i.e. in the future).

In nom. cl., אֹרַח חַיִּים לְמַעְלָה לְמַשְׂכִּיל *(the) way of life is upwards for an intelligent one* Pr 15_{24}, וְהַחַמָּנִים אֲשֶׁר־לְמַעְלָה *and the incense altars that were above* 2 C 34_4, עַל־כֵּן רֹחַב־לַבַּיִת לְמַעְלָה *therefore, the width of the temple was upwards*, i.e. increased with height Ezk 41_7, כִּי מוּסַב־הַבַּיִת לְמַעְלָה לְמַעְלָה *for the enclosure of the temple was ever upwards* Ezk 41_7 (or em. מוּסָב the temple *being oriented* and/or לְמַעְלָה לְמַעְלָה to מִמַּעֲלֶה לְמַעֲלֶה *from ascent to ascent*, i.e. in stages).

<COLL> לְמַעְלָה לְמַעְלָה *upwards (and) upwards* Ezk $41_{7.7}$ (or em. מִמַּעֲלֶה לְמַעֲלֶה *from ascent to ascent*; + סָבִיב סָבִיב *all around*), עֲוֹנֹתֵינוּ רָבוּ לְמַעְלָה רֹאשׁ *our sins have increased upwards (towards the) head* Ezr 9_6 (or em. לְמַעֲלָה מֵעַל הָרֹאשׁ *upwards, over the head*; + וְאַשְׁמָתֵנוּ גָדְלָה עַד לַשָּׁמָיִם *and our guilt has increased unto the heavens*), למעלה מעל בית הכיור *above, over the house of the laver* 11QT 32_{11} (Yadin מעל לבית in same sense; 11Q19 מע]ל [לבית), sim. 11QT 7_6 ([למ]עלה] מעל כול ה *above, over all the*), למעלה על גוי *above, over a nation* 4QapPs^b 33_{10}, וְהַחַמָּנִים אֲשֶׁר־לְמַעְלָה מֵעֲלֵיהֶם *and the incense altars that were above, on top of them* 2 C 34_4.

Also 4Q418 107_2 8QHymn 2_4 11QT 10_{13} (ל]מ]עלה).

3. לְמַעְלָה לְ as prep, **above,** [חצים עלו למע]לה לרקיע *arrows went up above the firmament* 4QJub^a 2_4 (:: לְמַטָּה לְ *below*), ויתרוממו למעלה לכול *and exalted themselves above everything* 4QConfess 2_6.

Also perh. 11QT 6_2.

4. מִלְמַעְלָה **above, on top**; sometimes perh. **from above** (Jos $3_{13.16}$), with verb גבר *be mighty*, i.e. arise, מדד ni. *be measured* Jr 31_{37} (:: לְמַטָּה *below*), נטה pass. *be turned* Ezk 1_{22}, פרד pass. *be divided* Ezk 1_{11}, כתב pass. *be written* 5/6ḤevBA 44_{26}, ירד *go down* Jos $3_{13.16}$, סכך *surround* 1 K 8_7, כסה pi. *cover* 2 C 5_8, שׂים *place* Ex 40_{19}, נתן *place* Ex 25_{21} 39_{31} 40_{20}, פרשׂ *spread* garment Nm 4_6, כלה pi. *complete* Gn 6_{16}, קרם *cover* with skin Ezk 37_8 (or em. ni., *be covered*).

Without verb, מִכְסֵה עֹרֹת תְּחָשִׁים מִלְמַעְלָה *a covering of badgers' skins above* Ex 26_{14}||36_{19}, מִכְסֵה הַתַּחַשׁ אֲשֶׁר־עָלָיו מִלְמָעְלָה *the covering of badger (skin) that is over it, above* Nm 4_{25}, וְהַיָּם עֲלֵיהֶם מִלְמָעְלָה *and the sea was over them, above* 1 K 7_{25}||2 C 4_4, וּכְבוֹד אֱלֹהֵי־יִשְׂרָאֵל עֲלֵיהֶם מִלְמָעְלָה *and the glory of the God of Israel was over them, above* Ezk 10_{19} 11_{22}, דְּמוּת ... עָלָיו מִלְמָעְלָה *a likeness was over him, above* Ezk 1_{26} (or del. עָלָיו, leaving מִלְמָעְלָה as predicate of nom. cl.).

In nom. cl., וּמִלְמַעְלָה אֲבָנִים יְקָרוֹת *and above were precious stones* 1 K 7_{11}, ירידתו מלמעלא *its descent is from above* 3QTr 10_2.

<COLL> מִלְמַעְלָה + unit of measurement, אַמָּה *(one) cubit* Gn 6_{16}, חֲמֵשׁ עֶשְׂרֵה אַמָּה *fifteen cubits* Gn 7_{20}.

עַל ... מִלְמַעְלָה *over ... above*, עַל־הָאָרֹן מִלְמָעְלָה *over the ark, above*, i.e. above the ark Ex 25_{21} 40_{20}, עַל־הָאָרוֹן וְעַל־בַּדָּיו מִלְמָעְלָה *over the ark and over its poles, above*, i.e. above ark and poles 1 K 8_7||2 C 5_8, עַל־הַמִּצְנֶפֶת מִלְמָעְלָה *over the turban, above*, i.e. above the turban Ex 39_{31}, עַל־רָאשֵׁיהֶם מִלְמָעְלָה *over their heads, above*, i.e. above their heads Ezk 1_{22}, עָלָיו מִלְמָעְלָה *over it, above*, i.e. above it Ex 40_{19} Nm 4_{25} (in ref. to tabernacle) Ezk 1_{26} (in ref. to throne; or del. עָלָיו), עֲלֵיהֶם מִלְמָעְלָה *over them, above*, i.e. above them 1 K 7_{25}||2 C 4_4 (in ref. to oxen) Ezk 10_{19} 11_{22} (both מִלְמָעְלָה; in ref. to wheels) 37_8 (עֲלֵיהֶם ... מִלְמָעְלָה; in ref. to bones).

הַשָּׁמַיִם מִלְמַעְלָה *the heavens above* Jr 31_{37}, כול שמלמ[מע]לה כתוב *everything that is written above* 5/6 ḤevBA 44_{26}.

5. מִלְמַעְלָה מִן as prep., **above,** ומלמעלה מזה עמודים *and above this are columns* 11QT 10_{11}, מלמעלה מן הארון *above the ark* 11QT 7_9(Yadin) (הכפורת אשר מלמ[עלה מן הארון] *the mercy seat, which is above the ark*; others מלמע]לה שתים] the mercy seat, which is *above, two* cubits) 10_{12}.

6. perh. מִלְמַעְלָה לְ as prep, **above,** in nom. cl., והמכבר [אש]ר מלמעלה לו *and the grating that is above it* 11QT 3_{15}.

Also 11QT 10_{16}.

7. מִמַּעַל **above,** with verb קדר *be dark* Jr 4_{28}, ספן pass. *be covered* with cedar 1 K 7_3, מלל ni. *wither* Job 18_{16} (:: מִתַּחַת *below*), עלה *go up* Is 14_{13}, רעף hi. *drip* Is 45_8, דרשׁ *seek* Jb 3_4, אמץ pi. *strengthen* clouds Pr 8_{28}, שׁמד hi. *destroy* fruit Am 2_9 (:: מִתַּחַת), משׁל *rule* 4QAstrCrypt 1.2_8 ([תו]משל ... ממעו[ל]); without verb, בַּשָּׁמַיִם מִמַּעַל *in the heavens above* Ex 20_4||Dt 5_8 Dt 4_{39} Jos 2_{11} 1 K 8_{23} (all five :: מִתַּחַת *below*), צוה pi. *command* clouds Ps 78_{23}.

In nom. cl., וְכֹתָרֹת ... גַּם־מִמַּעַל *and there were also capitals ... above* 1 K 7_{20}.

<COLL> הַשָּׁמַיִם ... מִמַּעַל *the heavens ... above* Is 14_{13}, שָׁמַיִם מִמַּעַל *(the) heavens above* Is 45_8 4Q392 1_4, הַשָּׁמַיִם מִמָּעַל *the heavens above* Jr 4_{28}, הרקיע ממעו[ל] *the firmament above* 4QAstrCrypt 1.2_8, שְׁחָקִים מִמָּעַל *(the) clouds above* Pr 8_{28}, אֱלוֹהַּ מִמָּעַל *God above* Jb 3_4 31_2 (|| מִמְּרוֹם *above*), אֵל מִמָּעַל *God above* Jb 31_{28}, וְעַל־הַשְּׁלַבִּים כֵּן מִמָּעַל *and over the frames it was thus, above* 1 K 7_{29}.

8. מִמַּעְלָה **above,** with verb עצר *detain* heavens 1QDM 2_{10} (ממ]עלה]; + למ[טה לארץ] *below the earth*), ראה hi. *show (oneself)* 4QapMos[c] 2.2_7. <COLL> השמים [ממ]עלה *the heavens above* 1QDM 2_{10}, באש בעורה ממעלה [ב]שמים *in a blazing fire above, in the heavens* 4QapMos[c] 2.2_7.

Also 4QShirShabb[f] 31_3.

9. מַעְלָה **upwards, high(er),** with verb לקח ni. *be taken* in whirlwind Si 48_9, עלה *go up* Dt 28_{43} (:: מַטָּה *downwards*). <COLL> מַעְלָה מָּעְלָה *higher (and) higher* Dt 28_{43}.

Also 4QDiscourse 7_3 4QapPs[b] 69_9 4QShirShabb[f] 2_2 ([מ]עלה)) 4QNarrB 107_2.

10. מַעְלָה לְ as prep., **above,** מעלה לראשי[נו] *above our heads* 4QapJoshua[a] 6.2_5, ברוך [ה]אדו[ן] מלך ה[כול מעלה לכול ברכה *blessed be the lord, the king of everything, above every blessing* 4QShirShabb[d] 1.1_{28}.

11. מִמַּעַל לְ as prep., **above,** with verb שׂים *place* Gn 22_9 Jr 43_{10}, נתן *place* Ex 28_{27}||39_{20} Jr 52_{32}, עמד *stand* Is 6_2.

With noun, appar. אֲדֹנָי *Adonai* Is 6_2, אֶבֶן *stone* Jr 43_{10}, עֵץ *wood* Gn 22_9, מַיִם *waters* Dn $12_{6.7}$ (both ... אִישׁ אֲשֶׁר the *man ... who was* above the waters of the river), שָׁמַיִם *heavens* 4QMyst[a] 8_{10} (שמים ממעל לשמים *heaven above heaven*), רָקִיעַ *firmament* Ezk 1_{26}, חֵשֶׁב *band* of ephod Ex 28_{27}||39_{20}, כִּסֵּא *throne* Jr 52_{32}, רֶגֶל *feet* Lv 11_{21} (+ אֲשֶׁר־לוֹ כְרָעַיִם *that has legs* above its feet), לִשְׁכָּה

chamber Jr 35$_{4}$ (+ לִשְׁכַּת הַשָּׂרִים אֲשֶׁר *the chamber of the princes, which* was above the chamber of Maaseiah).

12. מִן ... וָמַעְלָה **from ... and above/and over,** once appar. in implicit ref. to age, **and older** (2 K 3$_{21}$); with noun שָׁנָה *year* Ex 30$_{14}$ 38$_{26}$ (both + עֶשְׂרִים *twenty*) Lv 27$_{7}$ (+ שִׁשִּׁים *sixty*) Nm 1$_{3+14t}$ (all fifteen + עֶשְׂרִים) 4$_{3+6t}$ (all seven + שְׁלֹשִׁים *thirty*) 8$_{24}$ 14$_{29}$ 26$_{2.4}$ 32$_{11}$ Ezr 3$_{8}$ (all five + עֶשְׂרִים) 1 C 23$_{3}$ (+ שְׁלֹשִׁים) 23$_{24.27}$ (if em. וּלְמַעְלָה, as §13) 2 C 25$_{5}$ (all three + עֶשְׂרִים) 1QM 2$_{4}$ (+ חֲמִשִּׁים *fifty*) 4QM^{a} 4$_{2}$ (מבן] עשרים [ש]נה [ו]מעלה] *from anyone of twenty years and upwards*) 11QT 17$_{8}$ (+ עֶשְׂרִים) CD 10$_{8}$=4QD^{a} 8.3$_{7}$ (מבן] ששים שנה ומע]לה] *from anyone of sixty years and over*), חֹדֶשׁ *(one) month* Nm 3$_{15+6t}$ 26$_{62}$, יוֹם *(to)day* 1 S 16$_{13}$ 30$_{25}$ Hg 2$_{15.18}$, סֶלַע *rock* Jg 1$_{36}$, שְׁכֶם *shoulder* 1 S 9$_{2}$ 10$_{23}$, חֹגֵר *one girding,* i.e. warrior 2 K 3$_{21}$.

<COLL> מִבֵּית לַכֹּתֶרֶת וָמַעְלָה *from inside the crown and upwards* 1 K 7$_{31}$ (or em. לַכְּתֵפֹת inside *the walls;* or del. לַכֹּתֶרֶת וָמַעְלָה).

13. מִן ... וּלְמַעְלָה **from ... and above/and over,** with noun, מֹתֶן *thigh* Ezk 1$_{27}$ (מַרְאֵה מָתְנָיו *from the appearance of his thighs*) 8$_{2}$ (both :: וּלְמַטָּה *and below*), אֲרִיאֵל *altar* Ezk 43$_{15}$, שָׁנָה *year* 1 C 23$_{27}$ (or em. וּמַעְלָה, as §12; + עֶשְׂרִים *twenty* years) 2 C 31$_{16}$ (+ שָׁלֹשׁ *three*) 31$_{17}$ (+ עֶשְׂרִים).

14. עַד־לְמַעְלָה **exceedingly** (or perh. **from then on**), with verb גדל *be great* 2 C 17$_{12}$ (הֹלֵךְ וְגָדֵל עַד־לְמַעְלָה *increasing at every stage exceedingly* or *increasing at every stage from then on*), חזק hi. *grow strong* 2 C 26$_{8}$; in nom. cl., עַד־לְמַעְלָה חָלְיוֹ *from then on,* or *exceedingly (grave), was his illness* 2 C 16$_{12}$.

<SYN> §2 לְרֹאשׁ *as [the] head;* §7 מִמָּרוֹם *above.*

<ANT> §2 לְמַטָּה *below,* לְזָנָב *as [the] tail,* שְׁאֹלָה *to Sheol;* §3 לְמַטָּה לְ *below;* §7 לְמַטָּה *below;* מִתַּחַת *below;* §9 מַטָּה *downwards;* §13 וּלְמַטָּה *and below.*

⇒ עלה *go up.*

[מַעַל] III, see מַעֲלֶה *height.*

[מֹעַל] I 1 n.[m.] **raising**—cstr. מֹעַל—<CSTR> מֹעַל יְדֵיהֶם *raising of their hands* Ne 8$_{6}$. <PREP> בְּ of accompaniment, *accompanied by, with* or of instrument, *by (means of), with,* + ענה *reply* amen Ne 8$_{6}$.

⇒ עלה *go up.*

[מֹעַל] II, see מַעַל *sin.*

מַעֲלָה I 47.0.8 n.f. **step; ascent**—Q מעלהא; pl. מַעֲלוֹת (מַעֲלֹת); cstr. מַעֲלוֹת; sf. Qr מַעֲלוֹתָיו (Kt מעלותו), מַעֲלֹתֵהוּ—**1. step** of altar (Ex 20$_{26}$), of throne (1 K 10$_{19.20}$||2 C 9$_{18.19}$ 2 K 9$_{13}$), of gateway (Ezk 40$_{6+5t}$ 11QT 30$_{4}$), of vestibule (Ezk 40$_{49}$), of court (Ezk 43$_{17}$), of terrace (11QT 46$_{7}$), of city (Ne 3$_{15}$ 12$_{37}$); of (winding) staircase (11QT 30$_{10}$ 31$_{9}$ 42$_{7}$); **2.** perh. **flight of steps, staircase** (Ne 12$_{37}$ [if em. מַעֲלֶה *ascent*]). **3. stage, degree** of sundial (2 K 20$_{9+6t}$ Is 38$_{8.8.8.8.8}$); **4. upper room** or **roof** (Am 9$_{6}$ [or em. עֲלִיָּה *upper room*]); **5.** (act of) **ascent,** i.e. **return** from exile (Ezr 7$_{9}$ perh. 1 C 17$_{17}$), **pilgrimage** to Jerusalem (Ps 84$_{6}$ [if em. מְסִלָּה *road*]); **6.** perh. title of Y., **Height** (1 C 17$_{17}$).

<SUBJ> ירד *go down* Ne 3$_{15}$, עלה *go up* Ezk 40$_{49}$ (or em. וּבַמַּעֲלוֹת אֲשֶׁר יַעֲלוּ *and at the steps that go up* to וּבְמַעֲלוֹת עֶשֶׂר *and by ten steps* they go up), פנה *turn* (intrans.) Ezk 43$_{17}$.

<NOM CL> מַעֲלוֹת בִּלְבָבָם *ascents (to Zion),* i.e. pilgrimages, *are in their heart* Ps 84$_{6}$ (if em. מְסִלּוֹת appar. *[your] ways*), וּמַעֲלוֹת ... עֹלוֹתָיו *and* seven *steps are its ascents* Ezk 40$_{26(Qr)}$ (or em. עֹלוֹתָיו to מַעֲלוֹ *its height* or וּמַעֲלוֹת to וּבְמַעֲלוֹת *and by* seven *steps* and עֹלוֹתָיו to יַעֲלוּ־בוֹ *they will go up by it*), וּמַעֲלוֹת ... מַעֲלוֹ *and* seven *steps are its ascent* Ezk 40$_{26}$ (if em.) 40$_{31(Kt).34(Kt).37(Kt)}$ (in all three Qr מַעֲלָיו eight steps were *its ascents*).

<OBJ> ידע *know* Ezk 11$_{5}$, בנה *build* Am 9$_{6}$ (or em. עֲלִיָּה *upper room*), יסד (pi.) *establish* Ezr 7$_{9}$ (if em. יְסֻד *establishing of* to יִסַּד / יָסַד *he established*), עשׂה *make* 11QT 46$_{7}$, שׂפה *cover* with gold 11QT 30$_{9}$.

<CSTR> מַעֲלוֹת עִיר דָּוִיד *the steps of the city of David* Ne 12$_{37}$, מַעֲלוֹת אָחָז *the stages,* i.e. sundial, *of Ahaz* 2 K 20$_{11}$ Is 38$_{8}$ (or ins. עֲלִיַּת sundial of *the upper chamber of* Ahaz; 1QIsa^{a} מעלות עלות אחז), מַעֲלוֹת רוּחֲכֶם *the ascent of your spirit,* i.e. what comes to mind Ezk 11$_{5}$ (or em. מַעֲלַת *the ascent of*).

שִׁיר הַמַּעֲלוֹת *song of (the) ascents* Ps 120$_{1}$ 121$_{1(mss)}$

(L לַמַּעֲלוֹת *of the ascents*) 122_{1} 123_{1} 124_{1} 125_{1} 126_{1} 127_{1} 128_{1} 129_{1} 130_{1} 131_{1} 132_{1} 133_{1} 134_{1}.

יְסֻד הַמַּעֲלָה *the establishing of the ascent* from Babylon Ezr 7_{9} (or em. יִסַּד/יָסַד *he established* the ascent), בית מעלות *building of steps*, perh. staircase or stairwell 11QT 42_{7}, גֶּרֶם הַמַּעֲלוֹת *the bone*, i.e. surface, *of the steps* 2 K 9_{13}, צֵל הַמַּעֲלוֹת *the shadow of*, i.e. on, *the stages*, i.e. sundial Is 38_{8}, שֵׁשׁ מַעֲלוֹת *six steps* 1 K 10_{19}||2 C 9_{18} 1 K 10_{20}||2 C 9_{19} (הַמַּעֲלוֹת), שְׁמֹנֶה מַעֲלוֹת *eight steps* Ezk $40_{34.37}$, עֶשֶׂר מַעֲלוֹת *ten stages* 2 K $20_{9.9.10.10.11}$ Is $38_{8.8}$.

<APP> כול בית המסבה הזואת ... מעלותיו *all this staircase building ... its steps* 11QT 31_{9}, וּרְאִיתַנִי כְּתוֹר הָאָדָם הַמַּעֲלָה appar. *and you saw me as a line of humanity, the progeny*, i.e. you saw in me all my descendants, or *and you saw me after the manner of humans, O Height* 1 C 17_{17} (or em. וּרְאִיתַנִי to וְרְאִיתִנִי *and I saw myself* or וַתַּרְאֵנִי/וְהִרְאִיתַנִי *and you showed me*, as it were a line; and/or כְּתוֹר to בְּתוֹךְ *in the middle of* humanity or מִתּוֹר and you have shown me *more than* a human being *can fathom*; and/or הַמַּעֲלָה to לְמַעְלָה *above*, i.e. in the future, or to הָעֹלָם shown me *eternity*; or הַמַּעֲלָה = you showed me *the return* from exile; ||2 S 7_{19} וְזֹאת תּוֹרַת הָאָדָם *and this is the law*, or *form*, *of humanity*).

<PREP> לְ of possession, *of*, *(belonging) to* Ps 121_{1} (11QPs^{a}, mss שִׁיר הַמַּעֲלוֹת *song of ascents*), perh. 8Q Hymn 1_{4} (ל[מע]ל[ו]ת); of benefit, *for*, + עשׂה *make* 11QT 30_{4} (ועשי[תה]).

בְּ of place, *in, on, at* Ezk 40_{49} (or em. וּבַמַּעֲלוֹת אֲשֶׁר יַעֲלוּ אֵלָיו ... אֶחָד מִפֹּה וְאֶחָד מִפֹּה *and at the steps that go up to it ... one was here and one was here* to וּבְמַעֲלוֹת עֶשֶׂר *and by ten steps* they go up to it, i.e. בְּ of instrument), + ירד *go down* Is 38_{8}, שׁוב *go back*, of shadow 2 K $20_{11(\text{mss})}$, of sun Is 38_{8}, hi. *turn* shadow *back* 2 K 20_{11}.

בְּ of instrument, *by (means of), with*, + עלה *go up* Ex 20_{26} Ezk $40_{6.22.26}$ (if ins. בְּ and em. עֹלוֹתָיו *its ascents* to יַעֲלוּ־בוֹ *they go up by it*) 40_{49} (if em. וּבַמַּעֲלוֹת *and at the steps* to וּבְמַעֲלוֹת *and by* ten *steps*).

עַל *upon*, + עלה *go up* Ne 12_{37}, ירד *go down* Ne 12_{37} (if em. בַּמַּעֲלֶה *on the ascent* to וַיֵּרְדוּ בַּמַּעֲלָה *and they went down by the staircase*).

תַּחַת *below* 3QTr 1_{2} 2_{1} 12_{4}.

עַד *unto* Ne 3_{15}.

<COLL> מַעֲלוֹת שֶׁבַע *seven steps* Ezk $40_{22.26}$ (if em. שִׁבְעָה *seven*), מַעֲלוֹת שְׁמֹנֶה *eight steps* Ezk 40_{31}, מַעֲלוֹת עֶשֶׂר *ten steps* Ezk 40_{49} (if em. וּבַמַּעֲלוֹת *and at the steps* to וּבְמַעֲלוֹת *and by* ten *steps*), שתים עשרה מעלה *twelve steps* 11QT 46_{7}.

הַמַּעֲלָה מִבָּבֶל *the ascent from Babylon* Ezr 7_{9}, בַּמַּעֲלָה לַחוֹמָה perh. *on*, or *by*, *the staircase to the wall* Ne 12_{37} (if em. בַּמַּעֲלֶה *on the ascent*), תחת המעלהא של השית העליונא *below the steps of the upper pit* 3QTr 12_{4}, תחת המעלות הבואת למזרח *below the steps that come to the east* 3QTr 1_{2}.

וַתָּשָׁב הַשֶּׁמֶשׁ עֶשֶׂר מַעֲלוֹת בַּמַּעֲלוֹת אֲשֶׁר יָרֵדָה *and the sun went back ten degrees, by the (same) degrees that it had gone down* Is 38_{8} (or em. אֲשֶׁר יָרַד הַצֵּל *that the shadow had gone down*).

ורוחב המסבה עולה מעלות *and the width of the staircase going up (by) steps* 11QT 30_{10}, למעלות משני צדי השערים *for the steps at both sides of the gates* 11QT 30_{4}.*

⇒ עלה *go up*.

***מַעֲלָה II** 15.0.1 n.f. **extolment**—pl. מַעֲלוֹת—<NOM CL> ערבה באף ... מעלה *sweet to the nose*, i.e. *pleasing, is ... extolment* 11QPs^{a} Zion 14. <CSTR> שִׁיר הַמַּעֲלוֹת *song of extolments* Ps 120_{1} $121_{1(\text{mss})}$ (L לַמַּעֲלוֹת *of the extolments*) 122_{1} 123_{1} 124_{1} 125_{1} 126_{1} 127_{1} 128_{1} 129_{1} 130_{1} 131_{1} 132_{1} 133_{1} 134_{1}.

⇒ עלה II pi. *extol*.

מֹעֲלָה, see מַעַל *height*.

מַעֲלֶה 19.1.1 n.m. **ascent**—cstr. מַעֲלֵה; sf. Kt מעלו; pl. sf. Qr מַעֲלָיו—**1. ascent, elevation, hill.**

<NOM CL> וּמַעֲלוֹת ... מַעֲלָיו *and* seven *steps are its ascents*, i.e. its elevation Ezk 40_{26} (if em. עֹלוֹתָיו *its ascents* Ezk $40_{26(\text{Qr})}$ $40_{31(\text{Qr}).34(\text{Qr}).37(\text{Qr})}$ (in all three Kt מַעֲלוֹ eight steps were *its elevation*).

<OBJ> ידע hi. *make known* 1QPrLit 3.2_{7} (מעלי; others מעשי *deeds*).

<CSTR> [חול] מעלה *a hill of sand* Si $25_{20(\text{Segal})}$, מַעֲלֵה

הָעִיר *the ascent of*, i.e. to, *the city* 1 S 9_{11}, מַעֲלֵה הַזֵּיתִים *the ascent*, i.e. hill, *of the olive trees* 2 S 15_{30}, מַעֲלֵה קִבְרֵי בְנֵי־דָוִיד *the ascent of*, i.e. to, *the graves of the sons of David* 2 C 32_{33} (or em. קִרְיַת־דָּוִיד *the city of David*), מעלי עולם *ascents of eternity* 1QPrLit 3.2_{7} (others מעשי *deeds of*; or em. פֹּעֲלֵי *deeds of*; + יסורי כבוד *the instructions of glory*).

<PREP> לְ of direction, + סבב ho. *be encircled*, i.e. oriented Ezk 41_{7} (if em. כִּי מוּסַב־הַבַּיִת לְמַעְלָה לְמַעְלָה *for the enclosure of the temple was ever upwards* to מוּסָב the temple *being oriented* and/or כִּי מוּסָב הַבַּיִת מִמַּעְלָה לְמַעְלָה *for the house was oriented from height to height*, i.e. in stages).

בְּ of place, *in, on, at*, + קבר *bury* 2 C 32_{33} (or em. מַעֲלֵה קִבְרֵי בְנֵי־דָוִיד on *the ascent of*, i.e. to, *the graves of the sons of David* to קִרְיַת־דָּוִיד in *the city of David*); of instrument, *by (means of), with*, + עלה *go up* 1 S 9_{11} 2 S 15_{30}, ירד *go down* Ne 12_{37} (if ins. וַיֵּרְדוּ; perh. בְּ of place).

כְּ *as* Si $25_{20(Segal)}$ (כמעלה [חול ... אשת לשון] *like a hill of sand ... is a vituperative wife*).

מִן of direction, *from*, + סבב ho. *be encircled* Ezk 41_{7} (if em.).

<COLL> בְּמַעֲלֵה לַחוֹמָה *on*, or *by, the ascent to the wall* Ne 12_{37} (or em. בְּמַעֲלָה *on the step*, or perh., *staircase* of the wall).

2. in geographical descriptions, though distinction between מַעֲלֵה as common noun, **ascent,** or as part of pl.n., **Ascent** or **Maaleh-**, is sometimes uncertain.

<NOM CL> מַעֲלֵה אֲדֻמִּים אֲשֶׁר נֹכַח לַנָּחַל *the ascent of Adummim, which is opposite the stream* Jos 15_{7}, מַעֲלֵה־גוּר אֲשֶׁר אֶת־יִבְלְעָם *the ascent of Gur, which is by Ibleam* 2 K 9_{27}.

<CSTR> מַעֲלֵה אֲדֻמִּים *ascent of Adummim* Jos 15_{7} 18_{17}, מַעֲלֵה־גוּר *ascent of Gur* 2 K 9_{27}, מַעֲלֵה הֶחָרֶס *ascent of Heres* Jg 8_{13}, מַעֲלֵה הַלּוּחִית *the ascent of Luhith* Is 15_{5} Jr $48_{5(Qr)}$, מַעֲלֵה עַקְרַבִּים *ascent of Akrabbim* Nm 34_{4} Jos 15_{3} Jg 1_{36}, מַעֲלֵה בֵית־חוֹרֹן *ascent of Beth-horon* Jos 10_{10}, מַעֲלֵה הַצִּיץ *the ascent of Ziz* 2 C 20_{16} (or em. חֲצִיץ of *Haziz*); דֶּרֶךְ מַעֲלֵה *the way of the ascent of* Jos 10_{10}.

<PREP> מִלְ *from (by)*, + שׁוּב *go back* Jg 8_{13} (or em. מִן *from*); מִנֶּגֶב לְ *south of*, + סבב ni. *go around* Nm 34_{4}, יצא *go out* Jos 15_{3}; נֹכַח לְ *opposite* Jos 15_{7} $18_{17(mss)}$; בְּ of place, *in, on, at*, + עלה *go up* Is 15_{5} Jr 48_{5} (if em. בֶּכִי go up *weeping* to בּוֹ *on it*) 2 C 20_{16} (perh. בְּ of instrument, *by [means of]* in all three), נכה hi. *strike* 2 K 9_{27}; מִן of direction, *from* Jg 1_{36}, + שׁוּב *go back* Jg 8_{13} (if em. מִלְ *from [by]*); נֹכַח *opposite* Jos 18_{17} (mss נֹכַח לְ *opposite*).

3. platform, <CSTR> מַעֲלֵה הַלְוִיִּם *the platform of the Levites* Ne 9_{4}. <PREP> עַל *upon*, + קום *stand* Ne 9_{4}.

⇒ עלה *go up*.

[מַעֲלִיל] 1 n.[m.] **deed**—pl. sf. Kt מעליליכם—<ADJ> רַע *evil* Zc $1_{4(Kt)}$ (Qr מַעֲלָל *deed*). <PREP> בְּ of instrument, *by (means of), with*, + מרה (hi.) *rebel (against)* 4QAdmon 1_{2} (במ]עלי[ליהם; unless וַיֹּאמְרוּ = ויאמרו *and they said*, i.e. used the name of, God, in their deeds); מִן of direction, *from*, + שׁוּב *go back* Zc $1_{4(Qr)}$ (|| דֶּרֶךְ *way*, i.e. behaviour).

Also 4QapPs[b] 46_{6} [מ]עלילם *their deeds*; others [ב]עלילם *in their furnace*; or em. [מ/ב]עלולם *from in their whirlwind*).

<SYN> דֶּרֶךְ *way*, i.e. behaviour.

⇒ עלל *do*.

[מַעֲלָל] 41.0.4 n.m. **deed**—pl. מַעֲלָלִים; cstr. מַעַלְלֵי; sf. מַעֲלָלֶיךָ, מַעֲלָלַיִךְ, מַעֲלָלָיו, Q[מ]עלליהם, מַעֲלָלֵינוּ, מַעַלְלֵיהֶם (Q מעלליהמה), מַעַלְלֵיכֶם—**deed,** usu. in ref. to evil deeds; Y.'s deeds (Ps 77_{12} 78_{7} perh. Mc 2_{7} [unless Jacob's deeds]); youth's actions (Jr 20_{11}), good person's deeds (Pr 14_{14} [if em.]), person's deeds GnzPs 4_{21}.

<SUBJ> היה *be* Ho 7_{2} (+ נֶגֶד *before* Y.'s presence), עשׂה *do* Jr 4_{18} (|| דֶּרֶךְ *way*, i.e. behaviour), מרה *rebel* Is 3_{8} (|| לָשׁוֹן *tongue*, i.e. speech), נתן *give*, allow, to repent Ho 5_{4}, סבב *encircle* Ho 7_{2}.

<NOM CL> כִּי־לְשׁוֹנָם וּמַעַלְלֵיהֶם אֶל־י׳ *for their speech and their deeds are (directed) against Y.* Is 3_{8}, וּמַעַלְלֵיכֶם אֲשֶׁר לֹא־טוֹבִים *and your deeds that are not good* Ezk 36_{31}, אִם־אֵלֶּה מַעֲלָלָיו *if these are his* (Jacob's) *deeds* or *are these his* (Y.'s) *deeds?* Mc 2_{7}.

<OBJ> יטב hi. *improve* Jr $7_{3.5}$ 18_{11} 26_{13} (all four || דֶּרֶךְ *way*, i.e. behaviour) 35_{15} (+ דֶּרֶךְ), רעע hi. *make evil* Mc 3_{4}, ראה *see* Jr 11_{18} (if em. hi. *show*), זכר *remember* Ezk

36_{31} (+ דֶּרֶךְ, עָוֹן *sin*, תּוֹעֵבָה *abomination*) Ps $77_{12(Qr)}$ (Kt hi. *invoke*), שׁכח *forget* Ps 78_7 (+ מִצְוָה *commandment*), שׁוב hi. *return*, i.e. repay Ho 4_9 (|| דֶּרֶךְ).

<CSTR> מַעַלְלֵי־יָהּ *the deeds of Yah* Ps 77_{12}, אֵל *of God* Ps 78_7; רֹעַ מַעֲלָלֶיךָ *the evil of your* (sg.) *deeds* Dt 28_{20} (or del.), מַעַלְלֵיכֶם *of your* (pl.) *deeds* Is 1_{16} Jr 4_4 $21_{12(Qr)}$ 23_2 25_5 44_{22} (+ תּוֹעֵבָה *abomination*), מַעַלְלֵיהֶם *of their deeds* Jr $21_{12(Kt)}$ 23_{22} 26_3 Ho 9_{15} Ps 28_4 (+ פֹּעַל *deed*, מַעֲשֶׂה *deed*) 11QT 59_7 (רוע מעלליהמה), פְּרִי מַעֲלָלָיו *the fruit of his deeds* Jr 17_{10} (|| דֶּרֶךְ *way*, i.e. behaviour) 32_{19} GnzPs 4_{21} (both + דֶּרֶךְ), מַעַלְלֵיכֶם *of your deeds* Jr 21_{14}, מַעַלְלֵיהֶם *of their deeds* Is 3_{10} Mc 7_{13}.

<ADJ> רַע *evil* Zc $1_{4(Qr)}$ (Kt מַעֲלִיל *deed*) Ne 9_{35}.

<PREP> בְּ of instrument, *by (means of), with* perh. 4QDiscourse 2.2_3 (+ נִדַּת מַעֲשֵׂי *impurity of deeds of*), + כעס hi. *anger* Ps 106_{29}, זנה *prostitute oneself* Ps 106_{39} (|| מַעֲשֶׂה *deed*), נכר htp. *disguise oneself* Pr 20_{11} (+ פֹּעַל *deed*); כְּ *in accordance with*, + עשׂה *do* Zc 1_6 (|| דֶּרֶךְ *way*, i.e. behaviour), שׁוב hi. *return*, i.e. repay Ho 12_3 (|| דֶּרֶךְ); מִן of direction, *from*, + שׁוּב *go back* Zc $1_{4(Qr)}$ (Kt מַעֲלִיל *deed*; || דֶּרֶךְ *way*, i.e. behaviour) Ne 9_{35}; of instrument, *by (means of), with*, + שׂבע *be satisfied* Pr 14_{14} (if em. מֵעָלָיו a good person gains satisfaction *more than he* [one whose mind turns aside] *does* or *by himself* to מִמַּעֲלָלָיו *by his deeds*); partitive, *(any) of, (some) of*, + נפל hi. *cause to fall*, i.e. relinquish Jg 2_{19} (+ דֶּרֶךְ *way*, i.e. behaviour).

<COLL> רֹעַ מַעֲלָלֶיךָ אֲשֶׁר עֲזַבְתָּנִי *the evil of your deeds by which you deserted me* Dt 28_{20} (or del.), רַע מַעֲלָלִים *(one who is) evil of deeds*, i.e. whose deeds are evil 1 S 25_3 (+ קָשֶׁה *hard*, i.e. obdurate).

Also 4QapPs^b 4_1 4QpsEzek^a (both [מ]עלליה).

<SYN> מַעֲשֶׂה *deed*, לָשׁוֹן *tongue*, i.e. speech, דֶּרֶךְ *way*, i.e. behaviour.

⇒ עלל *do*.

מַעֲמָד 5.1.46 n.[m.] **place**—cstr. מַעֲמַד; sf. Q מעמדי, מַעֲמָדְךָ, Q מעמדו, מעמדה, מַעֲמָדָם (Q מעמדמה)—**place, position, standing (up)** (i.e., as gerund, 1QS 6_{12} 1QM 4_4 14_6 18_{13}), **station, (holding) office.**

<NOM CL> מאתכה מעמדי *from*, or *because of, you is my standing*, perh. my ability to stand 1QH 2_{22}, כִּי מַעֲמָדָם לְיַד־בְּנֵי אַהֲרֹן *for their place was next to the sons of Aaron* 1 C 23_{28} (or em. הֶעֱמִידָם *he positioned them*), ולכול גבוריהם אין מעמד *and for all their warriors there will be no place* or *no standing*, i.e. they will be felled 1QM 14_8=4QM^a 8.1_6 (ולגבו[ריהמה] אין מע[מד] *and for their warriors there will be no place*), אני עם אלים מעמד[י] *as for me, my place is with the angels* 4QHod^a 7.1_9.

<OBJ> ראה *see* 1 K 10_5||2 C 9_4, חזק hi. *hold*, i.e. maintain 1QH 5_{29}=4QHod^c 1.4_1 ([מ]עמד) 1QSa 2_5 4QMyst^a 10_2 ([מ]עמד) 4QShirShabb^f 23.2_8 (in both perh. חזק pi. *hold*), ערך *array*, i.e. set up 1QM 9_{10}, perh. פקד hi. *appoint* 1QH 16_5.

<CSTR> מַעֲמַד מְשָׁרְתָיו *the (order of) standing of those who ministered to him* 1 K $10_{5(Qr)}$||2 C 9_4 (|| מוֹשָׁב *[order of] seating*; + מַלְבּוּשׁ *clothing*), מעמד איש *the position of (one) person* after another 1QM 5_4, מעמד האיש *the standing (up) of the person* questioning the community 1QS 6_{12}, מעמד רשעים *standing (up) of (the) wicked* 1QM 4_4.

מעמד צדק perh. *a place of righteousness* 1QH 16_5, מעמד רצ[ונך] perh. *place of your will* 1QH 16_{13}, מעמד פלאיהם *the station(s) of their wonders* 4QShirShabb^f 23.2_7, מעמד קודשים *office of holiness(es)*, i.e. most holy office 4QShirShabb^f 23.2_8, מעמד עולמים *a place of eternities* 1QM 13_{16}, מעמד מים יקרים every *place*, or perh. *stagnant pool,* of cold waters* Si $43_{20(B)}$.

בית מעמדו *the place of his standing* 1QS $2_{22.23}$, חדל מעמד *cessation of standing (up) of* (the) wicked 1QM 4_4, חזוק מעמד *strength of standing*, i.e. strength to stand up 1QM 14_6=4QM^a 8.1_4 (חזוק; + אמוץ מתנים/ [אומץ מ]תנים *strength of hips*), סרך מעמד *the rule of the position of* (one) person after another, i.e. the rule that states that one person should stand behind another 1QM 5_4.

כול עונות מעמדמה *all the periods of their (holding) office* 4QBer^a 7.2_6, כל מעמד *every place of* cold waters Si $43_{20(B)}$, [כול] מעמד perh. *every place of* your will 1QH 16_{13}, כול מע[מדיהם] *all their stations* 4QShirShabb^d 1.1_{12}.

<PREP> לְ of direction, *to*, + שׁוּב *go back* 1QM $6_{1.4}$,

פשט *spread out* (intrans.) 1QM 8_{6}; of possession, *of, (belonging) to* 1QM 17_{9} (רזיו למעמדכם perh. *his secrets of your station [in life]*); of purpose, *for (the purpose of)* perh. 1QM 13_{16}, + חזק pi. *strengthen* hips 1QSa 1_{17}; introducing obj., + ברך pi. *bless* 4QShirShabb^{d} 1.1_{12} ([יברך] ... מע]מדיהם]).

בְּ of place/time, *in, during* 1QS 6_{12} (אשר לוא במעמד האיש *which is not during the standing [up] of the person*, i.e. which is not while the person is standing) 4QShirShabb^{f} 23.2_{7} (במעמד פלאיהם רוחות רוקמה *in the station[s] of their wonders are colourful spirits*) perh. 4QpsMos^{d} 3_{7} 4QShirShabb^{f} 7_{4} 11QShirShabb 3_{10}(Newsom) (במע]מדי]; others במעו]ן פלא] *in a dwelling place of wonder*) 4QOrd^{c} 1.1_{11} (ב]מע]מד), + עמד *stand* 1QSa 1_{22}, יצב htp. *position oneself* 1QH 3_{21} 11_{13} fr. 7_{11}=4QHod^{a} 7.2_{15} (במעמ]ד]), קום htpol. *raise oneself* 1QH fr. 1_{11} (ואתקו]ממה]), רנן pi. *exult* 4QShirShabb^{f} 20.2_{14} (ו]רננו אחד אחד במעמד]ו] *and they exult, each one in their place*), שׁרת pi. *minister* 1QM 2_{3}, עוד *witness* 4QPrQuot 11_{4}; חזק בְּ hi. *hold (on to)* 1QH 4_{36}.

כְּ *in accordance with*, + ישׁב *sit* 1QSa 2_{15} (כמ]עמדו]), perh. עשׂה *make* standing 1QH 16_{13} (וככול]] *and in accordance with every* place).

מִן of place, *from*, + הרס *throw* Is 22_{19} (|| מַצָּב *position*), פרד hi. *separate* (trans.) 1QH fr. 5_{2}, דחף *push (away)* Si 36_{12} (if em. ממעבד]יה]ם *on account of their deeds*, i.e. מַעְבָּד, to ממעמד]יה]ם *from their positions*; or em. ודחפם *and he pushes them away* to והדפם *and he pushes them away* or ועקרם *and he uproots them*).

אֶל *to* perh. 4QJub 2.5_{15}(WA) (אל מע]מדו] *to his place*; others אל מש]קהו] *to his drink*)

עַל *at, in* 2 C 35_{15} (וְהַמְשֹׁרְרִים בְּנֵי־אָסָף עַל־מַעֲמָדָם *and the singers, the sons of Asaph, were at their station*) 4QM^{a} 1_{15}, + יצב htp. *position oneself* 1QM $8_{3.17}$ (יתיצבו]]) 16_{5} 17_{11} (התיצ]בם ... מעמד]ו]); *upon*, + קפא hi. *cause to freeze* Si 43_{20}.

<COLL> לאין מעמד *to non-standing*, i.e. so that none can stand 1QM 18_{13} (perh. + מגנתה *you have handed over*) 4QM^{a} 11.2_{17}, במעמד העמדתני *in the place you have positioned me* 1QH fr. 1_{11}, למעמ]ד לצב]ואת עבודתו מעשו *for the office of*, i.e. among, *the hosts, (that is to say) his service, his work* 1QSa 1_{17}.

במעמד עם *in place with*, i.e. alongside 1QH 3_{21}, כמ]עמדו] במחניהם *in accordance with his position in their camps* 1QSa 2_{15}, בית מעמדו ביחד אל *the place of his standing in the community of God* 1QS 2_{22}, במעמד יומם *in the (liturgical) office, daily* 4QPrQuot 11_{4}.

איש במעמדו *each one in their place* 1QM 2_{3}, איש למעמדו *each one in their place* 1QM 8_{6}, איש על מעמדו *each one in their place* 1QM 16_{5} 17_{11} (אי]ש על מעמד]ו]), אחד אחד במעמד]ו] *each one in their place* 4QShirShabb^{f} 20.2_{14}.

Also 4QShirShabb^{f} 37_{2} (מע]מדיה]ם]) 4QparaKings 46_{3} 11QShirShabb 8_{10}.*

⇒ עמד *stand.*

מַעֲמָד 1 n.[m.] **standing ground, firm place,** <NOM CL> וְאֵין מָעֳמָד *where there was no standing ground* Ps 69_{3} (+ טָבַעְתִּי בִּיוֵן מְצוּלָה *I sank in (the) mud of (the) depth*).

⇒ עמד *stand.*

מַעֲמָסָה 1 n.f. **burden,** אֶבֶן מַעֲמָסָה *a stone of burden*, i.e. heavy weight, such as used in sport of weightlifting or as barricade Zc 12_{3}.*

⇒ עמס *raise.*

[מַעֲמָק] 5.0.3 n.[m.] **depth**—pl. מַעֲמַקִּים; cstr. מַעֲמַקֵּי; sf. Q מעמקיה—<OBJ> שׂים *place*, i.e. cause depths to be, a passage Is 51_{10} (+ תְּהוֹם *abyss*; 1QIsa^{a} adds בְּ places a passage *in* the depths of the sea). <CSTR> מַעֲמַקֵּי־יָם *depths of (the) sea* Is 51_{10} 4Q418 119_{4} (מעמקי הים), מַיִם *of (the) waters* Ezk 27_{34} (מַיִם) Ps $69_{3.15}$ (מַיִם), מעמקי תהום *the depths of (the) abyss* 4QapJoseph^{b} 1_{30}. <PREP> בְּ of place, *in(to)* perh. 4QapJoseph^{b} 1_{30} 4QBéat 5_{11}, + שׁבר ni. *be broken* Ezk 27_{34}, בוא *come* Ps 69_{3}, שׂים *place* 1QIsa^{a} 51_{10}; מִן of direction, *from*, + נצל ni. *be rescued* Ps 69_{15} (+ מְשׁוֹעָה *from destruction* [if em. מְשֹׂנְאַי *from those who hate me*]), קרא *call* to Y. Ps. 130_{1}.

⇒ עמק *be deep.*

[מַעַן], see לְמַעַן *for the sake of.*

[מַעֲנָד] n.[f.] **bond, chain,** <OBJ> קשׁר pi. perh. *untie*

Jb 38$_{31}$ (if em. מַעֲדָן *bond;* unless מַעֲדֶנֶת *company*). <CSTR> מַעַדַנּוֹת כִּימָה *the bonds of the Pleiades,* i.e. that unite them in a single constellation Jb 38$_{31}$ (if em. מַעַדְנוֹת *bonds of*). <COLL> וַיֵּלֶךְ אֵלָיו אֲגַג מַעֲדַנֹּת *and Agag came towards him (in) chains* 1 S 15$_{32}$ (if em. מַעֲדַנֹּת *[in] chains* or *[with] faltering steps*).
⇒ ענד *bind.*

מַעֲנָה 2 n.f. **furrow**—pl. sf. Kt מענותם—**furrow** or specif. **plough furrow,** area at end of field where plough is turned,* <OBJ> חצב *cut* 1 S 14$_{14}$ (if em.; see Cstr.). <CSTR> חֲצִי מַעֲנָה *half a furrow* 1 S 14$_{14}$ (or em. חֲצִי to חֹצְבֵי *ones cutting*). <PREP> לְ appar. introducing obj., + ארך hi. *lengthen* Ps 129$_{3(Kt)}$ (מענותם; Qr מַעֲנִיתָם *their furrow;* or em. עֲוֹנוֹתָם *their sins* or עַנְוָתָם *their humility*). <COLL> כְּבַחֲצִי מַעֲנָה צֶמֶד שָׂדֶה perh. *as* (if the dead lay) *in half a furrow, (indeed, that which could be covered by) a yoke (of oxen), (even) a field* 1 S 14$_{14}$ (or em. וּבְחִצִּים וּבְאַבְנֵי הַשָּׂדֶה *with both arrows and the stones of the field*).*
⇒ (?) ענה *be occupied;* cf. מַעֲנִית *furrow.*

מַעֲנֶה I 7.3.7 n.m. **answer**—cstr. מַעֲנֵה—<NOM CL> וְאֵין מַעֲנֶה *and there is no answer* Pr 29$_{19}$ (unless ענה hi. ptc. *answering,* i.e. he does not answer; + כִּי יָבִין *although he understands*), כִּי אֵין מַעֲנֵה אֱלֹהִים *for there is no answer of,* i.e. from, *God* Mc 3$_{7}$, כִּי אֵין מַעֲנֶה בְּפִי שְׁלֹשֶׁת הָאֲנָשִׁים *for there was no answer in the mouth(s) of the three men* Jb 32$_{5}$, ואין פה ... ולא מענה לשון *and there is no mouth* for the spirit of destruction *and no answer of the tongue* for all the children of guilt 1QH 7$_{11}$, יש מחריש מאין מענה *there is one who is silent because of there being no answer* Si 20$_{6}$, מֵי׳ מַעֲנֵה לָשׁוֹן *from Y. comes,* or *to Y. belongs, the answer of a tongue* Pr 16$_{1}$ (+ מַעַרְכֵי *disposition* of heart).
<OBJ> מצא *find* Jb 32$_{3}$ 1QH 17$_{17}$ (א]מצ[אה; + לספר צדקותיך *to recount your deeds of righteousness*), נשׂג hi. *reach,* i.e. find Si 35$_{14}$ (|| מוּסָר *discipline*), נתן *give* 1QH 2$_{7}$ (+ לע[רול] שפתי *to the uncircumcision of my lips*), כון hi. *establish* 1QH 11$_{34}$ (+ תְּחִנָּה *supplication*), נכר hi. *recognize* 1QH 7$_{13}$.
<CSTR> מַעֲנֵה אֱלֹהִים *an answer of,* i.e. from, *God* Mc 3$_{7}$, מַעֲנֵה־פִיו *the answer of his mouth* Pr 15$_{23}$ (+ דָּבָר *word*), מַעֲנֵה לָשׁוֹן *the answer of a tongue* Pr 16$_{1}$ Si 4$_{24}$ 1QH 2$_{7}$ 7$_{11.13}$ (+ יֵצֶר מַעֲשֶׂה *thought of action,* i.e. intended deed) 11$_{34}$ 16$_{6}$ 17$_{17}$; כול מענה *every answer of* the tongue 1QH 7$_{13}$.
<PREP> בְּ of instrument, *by (means of), with* Pr 15$_{23}$ (שִׂמְחָה לָאִישׁ בְּמַעֲנֵה־פִיו *a person's joy is [provided] by the answer of his mouth*) 1QH 16$_{6}$ (+ דַּעַת *knowledge*), + ידע ni. *be known* (of understanding) Si 4$_{24}$ (|| אֹמֶר *word*).
Also 1QH fr. 8$_{2}$ ([מענ[ה) 40$_{2}$ 4QShir^{b} 70$_{2}$ (אוזן ומענ[ה] *ear and answer*) perh. 4QPrayer^{i} 1$_{3}$ (unless המענות אשר = *the dwelling places that*).
<SYN> אֹמֶר *word,* מוּסָר *discipline.*
⇒ ענה *answer.*

*[**מַעֲנֶה**] II 1.2 n.[m.] **purpose**—sf. מַעֲנֵהוּ (Si מענו)—<PREP> לְ of benefit, *for,* + פעל *make* Pr 16$_{4}$ (or em. לַמַּעֲנֵהוּ appar. God has made everything *for its purpose* to לְמַעֲנוֹ=לַמַּעֲנֵהוּ *for his own sake,* i.e. prep. לְמַעַן), פרע *loosen,* i.e. unleash, storehouse of weather Si 43$_{14}$ (M) (unless למענו = *for his own sake*), ברא *create* storehouse Si 43$_{14(Bmg)}$ (unless למענו = *for his own sake;* B למען appar. *so that* he created), צלח *be successful* Si 43$_{26(B, Bmg)}$ (unless למענו = *for his own sake;* Bmg [second reading] למען appar. *so that* a messenger was successful).
⇒ ענה *be troubled.*

מְעֹנָה, see מְעוֹנָה *dwelling place.*

[**מַעֲנִית**] 1 n.f. **furrow**—pl. sf. Qr מַעֲנִיתָם—<PREP> לְ appar. introducing obj., + ארך hi. *lengthen* Ps 129$_{3(Qr)}$ (מַעֲנִיתָם; Kt מענותם *their furrow;* or em. עֲוֹנוֹתָם *their sins* or עַנְוָתָם *their humility*).
⇒ (?) ענה *be occupied;* cf. מַעֲנָה *furrow.*

מעסר, see מַעֲשֵׂר *tenth, tithe.*

מַעַץ 1 pr.n.m. **Maaz,** great-great-grandson of Judah, <SUBJ> היה *be* son of Ram 1 C 2$_{27}$.

[מַעֲצֵבָה] 1 n.f. **(place of) pain,** <PREP> לְ perh. of cause, *on account of,* + שׁכב *lie down* Is 50_{11}.
⇒ עצב *hurt.*

מַעֲצָד 2 n.[m.] **axe, billhook,** a cutting tool, <PREP> בְּ of instrument, *by (means of), with,* + כרת *cut* tree Jr 10_{3}, סעף pi. *lop* boughs Is 10_{33} (if em. בְּמַעֲרָצָה *with terror,* i.e. frighteningly, to בְּמַעֲצָדה *with his axe*). <APP> מַעֲשֵׂה יְדֵי־חָרָשׁ בַּמַּעֲצָד *the work of the hands of an artisan, by an axe* Jr 10_{3}. <COLL> חָרַשׁ בַּרְזֶל מַעֲצָד appar. *he has fashioned the iron of an axe* or *iron into an axe* Is 44_{12} (or ins. יָחֵד *sharpens* an axe, or בְּ *with* an axe, and understand חָרַשׁ בַּרְזֶל as *an artisan of iron* sharpens, or, is with, an axe; or del. מַעֲצָד; or em. מַעֲצָד to גֹּלֶם עָצַד the artisan of iron *cuts a model*).*
⇒ עצד *cut.*

*[מַעֲצָדָה] n.f. **axe,** <PREP> בְּ of instrument, *by (means of), with,* + סעף pi. *lop* boughs Is 10_{33} (if em. בְּמַעֲרָצָה *with terror,* i.e. frighteningly, to בְּמַעֲצָדָה *with an axe*).
⇒ עצד *cut.*

*[מַעֲצָה] n.f. **disobedience,** <PREP> בְּ *in,* + הלך *walk* Jr 7_{24} (if em. בְּמֹעֵצוֹת *in counsels* to בְּמַעֲצוֹת) Ps 81_{13} (if em. בְּמוֹעֲצוֹתֵיהֶם *in their counsels* to בְּמַעֲצוֹתֵיהֶם); מִן *(because) of,* + נפל *fall* Ps 5_{11} (if em. מִמֹּעֲצוֹתֵיהֶם *(because) of their counsels* to מִמַּעֲצוֹתֵיהֶם), אכל *consume* Ho 11_{6} (if em. מִמֹּעֲצוֹתֵיהֶם *(because) of their counsels* to מִמַּעֲצוֹתֵיהֶם).
⇒ cf. מוֹעֵצָה II *disobedience.*

מַעֲצוֹר 1.1 n.[m.] **stopping, restraint, impediment,** <NOM CL> כִּי אֵין לַי׳ מַעֲצוֹר לְהוֹשִׁיעַ בְּרַב אוֹ בִמְעָט *for Y. has no stopping to save,* i.e. there is no stopping Y.'s saving, *whether it be by many or by few* 1 S 14_{6}, ואין מעצור לתשועתו *and there is no stopping (of) his salvation* Si 39_{18}.
⇒ עצר *stop.*

מַעְצָר 1 n.[m.] **stopping, restraint, impediment,** <NOM CL> אִישׁ אֲשֶׁר אֵין מַעְצָר לְרוּחוֹ *a person for whose spirit there is no stopping,* i.e. who cannot control themselves Pr 25_{28}.
⇒ עצר *stop.*

מַעֲקֶה 1.0.1 n.[m.] **parapet,** <OBJ> עשׂה *make* Dt 22_{8}= 11QT 65_{6} (+ לְגַגֶּךָ *for your roof*/לגגו *for its roof*).*

[מַעֲקָשׁ] n.[m.] 1.0.1 **rough place**—pl. מַעֲקַשִּׁים—<OBJ> שׂים *place,* i.e. cause to be Is 42_{16} (+ לְמִישׁוֹר *as even ground;* + מַחְשָׁךְ *darkness*), נתן *give,* i.e. cause to be 4QBark[a] 1.2_{9} (+ לְמִישׁוֹר; + מַחְשָׁךְ *darkness*).
⇒ עקשׁ *twist.*

[מַ֫עַר] 2 n.[m.] **nakedness**—cstr. מַ֫עַר; sf. מַעְרֵךְ—**1. nakedness** of woman, or perh. specif. **pudenda,** <OBJ> ראה hi. *show* nations Na 3_{5} (|| קָלוֹן *shame*).

2. empty space, bare place, <CSTR> מַעַר־אִישׁ *nakedness of,* i.e. empty space on, *each one* 1 K 7_{36} (or em. מַעַר־ to תֹּאַר־ *form of* each; or כְּמַעַר *in accordance with the empty space of* to מֵעֵבֶר *on the other side of* each). <PREP> כְּ *in accordance with,* + פתח pi. *engrave* 1 K 7_{36} (or em.).
<SYN> §1 קָלוֹן *shame.*
⇒ ערה *be naked.*

מַעֲרָב I 14.0.15 n.[m.] **west**—cstr. Q מערב; + ה- of direction מַעֲרָבָה (מַעְרָבָה)—**1. (the) west.**

<NOM CL> מערב יורשי בר אבשי *west are the heirs of Bar-abishai,* i.e. they own the land to the west Mur 22. 1_{9} (:: מִזְרָח *east*), sim. 22.1_{3}, תחומ[י] המכר הזה ... מערב הדרך *the boundaries of this sale,* i.e. the land being sold, *is ... west of the road* Mur 30 2_{16}.

<CSTR> מערב הדרך *west of the road* Mur 30 1_{3} 2_{16} (both :: מִזְרָח *east,* צָפוֹן *north,* דָּרוֹם *south*), מַעֲרַב־גָּבַע *west of Geba* Jg 20_{33} (if em. מַעֲרֵה־גָבַע *empty space of Geba*), מערב ההיכל *west of the temple* 11QT 35_{10}, מערב צפונו *the west of its north,* i.e. (on) its northwest (side) 11QT 30_{7}; שער המערב *the gate of the west* 11QT 38_{6}, פנת המערב *the corner of the west* 11QT 41_{1} [פנת] [המ]ער[ב] 44_{15}, צפון המערב *the north of the west,* i.e. the northwest 11QT 46_{14}.

<APP> אֶרֶץ *land* Ps 107_{3}, מָקוֹם *place* Jg 20_{33} (if em. מַעֲרֵה *cave*).

<PREP> לְ of direction, *to(wards), in, on* 1 C 7_{28} (וְלַמַּעֲרָב גֶּזֶר וּבְנֹתֶיהָ *and to the west were Gezer and its villages*; :: מִזְרָח *east*) 26_{16} (לְשֻׁפִּים וּלְחֹסָה לַמַּעֲרָב appar. *for Shuppim and for Hosah it was to the west* [or em. לִשְׁנַיִם לְחֹסָה *for two*, i.e. for the second, *it was for Hosah* in the west, or לַסִּפִּים לְחֹסָה *for the thresholds it was for Hosah* in the west) 26_{18} (לַפַּרְבָּר לַמַּעֲרָב *at the colonnade towards the west*), + עשׂה *make* a place 11QT 35_{10}, ברח hi. *cause to flee* 1 C 12_{16} (or em. וַיַּבְרִיחוּ *and he caused* all [the inhabitants of] the valleys *to flee* to the west, to וַיִּבְרַח *and he blocked* all the valleys to the west; :: מִזְרָח *east*).

בְּ of place, *in, on* 11QT 30_{7} (רחוק מקיר ההיכל שבע אמות במערב צפונו *far from the wall of the temple seven cubits on the west of its north*, i.e. with seven cubits of distance on its northwest side 11QT 30_{7}.

מִן of direction, *from* Ps 75_{7} (mss לֹא ... מִמַּעֲרָב וְלֹא מִמִּדְבַּר הָרִים *elevation is not ... from the west and not from the steppe*; L מִדְבָּר *steppe of* mountains; or em. twice לֹא *if only*; :: מוֹצָא *east*) 3QTr 12_{1} (ביאתו מן המ[ע]רב *the entrance to it is from the west*), + רחק *be distant* Ps 103_{12} (:: מִזְרָח *east*), בוא *come* Dn 8_{5}, קבץ pi. *gather* Is 43_{5} (:: מִזְרָח) Ps 107_{3} (:: מִזְרָח, צָפוֹן *north*, יָם *south* [or em. יָמִין *south*]), גיח hi. *burst out* Jg 20_{33} (if em. מִמַּעֲרֵה־גֶבַע *from the empty space of Geba* to מִמַּעֲרַב־גֶּבַע *from west of Geba* or מִמַּעֲרָב לַגִּבְעָה *from west of Gibeah*).

מִן *in, on* Mur 30 2_{15} (וא]בנים והכל[את שעליו מהמערב *and rocks and pens that are upon it in the west*; :: דָּרוֹם *south*), + ירא *fear* Y. Is 59_{19} (mss ראה *see*; :: מִזְרַח־שֶׁמֶשׁ *rising of sun*, i.e. east), ידע *know* Y. Is 45_{6} (if em. מַעֲרָבָה *west*; :: מִזְרַח שֶׁמֶשׁ; or em. מַעֲרָבָהּ *its* [sun's] *setting*, i.e. §2), עשׂה *make* gates 11QT 31_{13} (מהערב *on the west*; :: מִזְרָח *east*, צָפוֹן *north*).

<COLL> מֵעֵבֶר לַיַּרְדֵּן מַעֲרָבָה *on the other side of the Jordan (and) westward* 1 C 26_{30}, וַיַּשְּׁרֵם לְמַטָּה־מַּעֲרָבָה לְעִיר דָּוִיד *and he directed them downwards, towards the west of the city of David* 2 C 32_{30} (or em. מִזְרָחָה *towards the east*), בָּנָה חוֹמָה ... מַעְרָבָה לְגִיחוֹן *he built a wall ... towards the west of Gihon* 2 C 33_{14} (or em. נֶגְבָּה *towards the south*), מִמַּעֲרָב לַגִּבְעָה *from west of Gibeah* Jg 20_{33} (if em. מִמַּעֲרֵה־גֶבַע *from the empty space of Geba*).

ומערב צפון לכול בית מושב ישב *and west (and) north*, i.e. northwest, *of any place of residence he will dwell* 4QṬohA 1_{2}, לצפון המערב לעיר *to the north of the west*, i.e. the northwest, *of the city* 11QT 46_{14}.

בשלף של השוא הצופא מערב בדרום *in the fallow land of Ha-shaweh, looking west, in the south*, i.e. oriented southwest 3QTr 8_{11}, בהבסה ראש הסלע הצופא מערב perh. *in the treading at the top of the rock looking west* 3QTr 11_{5}.

2. setting (of sun), <PREP> מִן *in*, + ידע *know* Y. Is 45_{6} (if em. מִמַּעֲרָבָה *in [the] west* to מִמַּעֲרָבָהּ *in its* [sun's] *setting*; :: מִזְרָח *rising* of sun). <ANT> מִזְרָח *rising* of sun.

<ANT> §1 מִזְרָח *east*, מוֹצָא *east*, צָפוֹן *north*, יָם *south*, דָּרוֹם *south*, מִזְרַח־שֶׁמֶשׁ *rising of sun*, i.e. east; §2 מִזְרָח *rising* of sun.

⇨ ערב *become evening.*

[מַעֲרָב] II 9 n.m. **merchandise**—sf. מַעֲרָבֵךְ; pl. sf. מַעֲרָבַיִךְ—<SUBJ> נפל *fall* into sea Ezk 27_{27} (|| הוֹן *wealth*, עִזָּבוֹן *merchandise*) 27_{34} (or del.). <OBJ> ערב *trade (in)* Ezk 27_{9} (or del.) 27_{27}, נתן *give*, i.e. pay for goods with, Ezk $27_{13.17}$ (or in both ins. בְּ give *in exchange for* merchandise). <CSTR> עֹרְבֵי מַעֲרָבֵךְ *traders of*, i.e. in, *your merchandise* Ezk 27_{27}, רֹב הוֹנַיִךְ וּמַעֲרָבַיִךְ *the abundance of your wealth(s) and your merchandise(s)* Ezk 27_{33} (+ עִזָּבוֹן *merchandise*). <PREP> בְּ of instrument, *by (means of), with, in* Ezk 27_{25} (if em. אֳנִיּוֹת תַּרְשִׁישׁ שָׁרוֹתַיִךְ מַעֲרָבֵךְ appar. *ships of Tarshish were your travellers*, i.e. traders, *in respect of your merchandise* to בְּמַעֲרָבֵךְ *in your merchandise*); *in exchange for*, + היה *be* (or iron, cassia, and cane) Ezk 27_{19}, נתן *give* Ezk $27_{13.17}$ (if ins. בְּ in both).

<SYN> הוֹן *wealth*, עִזָּבוֹן *merchandise*.*

⇨ ערב II *exchange*, or ערב IV *offer, deliver.*

***מַעֲרָבָה** 1 n.f. **west,** <PREP> מִן *in*, + ידע *know* Y. Is 45_{6} (:: מִזְרַח שֶׁמֶשׁ *rising of sun*, i.e. east; or em. מִמַּעֲרָבָה *in [the] west* to מִמַּעֲרָב in same sense, i.e. מַעֲרָב, §1, or to מִמַּעֲרָבָהּ *in its* [sun's] *setting*, i.e. מַעֲרָב, §2).

<ANT> מִזְרַח שֶׁמֶשׁ *rising of sun*, i.e. east.

⇨ ערב *become evening.*

[מַעֲרָבִי] 0.0.5 adj. **western**—Q מערבי; fem. מערבית—used attributively of צַד *side* 3QTr 6_{12} 10_{8} (others המאת in its side are *the maahs*, i.e. (מָעָה) 10_{13}, פִּנָּה *corner* 3_{10}, בַּיִת *house* of lying down, i.e. graveyard 11_{16}.

⇒ ערב *become evening*.

[מַעֲרֶה] I $_{1}$ n.[m.] **empty space** (unless מַעֲרֶה II *approaches*)—cstr. מַעֲרֵה—without trees or houses, <CSTR> מַעֲרֵה־גָּבַע *empty space of Geba* Jg 20_{33} (or em. מַעֲרַב־גֶּבַע *west of Geba* or מַעֲרָב לַגִּבְעָה *west of Gibeah*). <APP> מָקוֹם *place* Jg 20_{33} (or em.). <PREP> מִן of direction, *from*, + גיח hi. *burst out* Jg 20_{33} (or em.); בְּעַד *on behalf of*, + היה *be*, i.e. serve as (of ruined city) Is 32_{14} (if em. מְעָרוֹת *caves* to מַעֲרוֹת *empty places*; and/or del. בְּעַד, leaving מַעֲרוֹת as complement of היה).

⇒ ערה *be naked*.

*[מַעֲרֶה] II $_{1}$ n.[m.] **approaches** (unless מַעֲרֶה I *empty space*)—cstr. מַעֲרֵה—**approaches, vicinity,** <CSTR> מַעֲרֵה־גָּבַע *approaches to* or *vicinity of Geba* Jg 20_{33}. <APP> מָקוֹם *place* Jg 20_{33}. <PREP> מִן of direction, *from*, + גיח hi. *burst out* Jg 20_{33}.

מְעָרָה I 40.0.4 n.f. **cave**—Q מערא; cstr. מְעָרַת; pl. מְעָרוֹת; cstr. מְעָרוֹת—**cave** (perh. **cave country** at 1 K $18_{4.13}$), as temporary dwelling place in time of danger (Gn 19_{30} Jg 6_{2} 1 S 13_{6} 2 S 24_{13}||1 C 11_{15} [or em. מְצוּדָה *stronghold* in both] 1 K $18_{4.13}$ $19_{9.13}$ Is 2_{19} Ezk 33_{27} Ps 57_{1} 142_{1} 4QparaKings $2_{1[WA]}$ perh. Is 32_{14} [unless מְעָרָה II *empty space* or em. מַעֲרֶה in same sense]), as lair of wild animals (Na 2_{12} [if em. מִרְעֶה *pasture*]), as acquisition (Gn $23_{9.11.17.20}$ 49_{32} 50_{13}), as place of burial (Gn $23_{19.20}$ 25_{9} 49_{29} 50_{13} Jos 10_{27}), of refuge in battle (Jos $10_{16.17}$ 1 S 22_{1} perh. 1 S $17_{23[Kt]}$), of detention in battle (Jos $10_{18.22.27}$ 1 S 24_{11}), of ambush or of planning criminal or guerrilla action (Jg 20_{33} [if em.] 1 S $24_{4.9}$); as place to relieve oneself (1 S $24_{4.8}$), to conceal treasure (3QTr 2_{3} $6_{1.7}$ 7_{8}), perh. to rinse butchered meat (3QTr 2_{3}).

<SUBJ> היה *be(come)* (of Y.'s house) Jr 7_{11}, קום *arise*, i.e. be transferred Gn $23_{17.20}$.

<NOM CL> וְשָׁם מְעָרָה *and a cave was there* 1 S 24_{4}, וּמְעָרָה הוּא לִכְפִרִים *which was a cave of (young) lions* Na 2_{12} (if em. מִרְעֶה *pasture*; + מְעוֹן אֲרָיוֹת *a dwelling place of lions*), במערא שאצלה *in the cave that is next to it* 3QTr 7_{8} (others שאצל ה *that is next to the fountain*).

הַמְּעָרָה אֲשֶׁר־בּוֹ *the cave that is in it* Gn 23_{11} (+ שָׂדֶה *field*) 23_{17} (+ עֵץ, שָׂדֶה *tree*) 23_{20} 49_{32} (both || שָׂדֶה), הַמְּעָרָה אֲשֶׁר בִּשְׂדֵה עֶפְרוֹן הַחִתִּי *the cave that is in the field of Ephron the Hittite* Gn 49_{29}, מְעָרַת הַמַּכְפֵּלָה אֲשֶׁר־לוֹ אֲשֶׁר בִּקְצֵה שָׂדֵהוּ *the cave of Mach-pelah, which was his, which was at the end of his field* Gn 23_{9}, מְעָרַת שְׂדֵה הַמַּכְפֵּלָה אֲשֶׁר עַל־פְּנֵי מַמְרֵא *the cave of the field of Mach-pelah, which is opposite Mamre* Gn $23_{19(mss)}$ (L lacks אֲשֶׁר), בַּמְּעָרָה אֲשֶׁר בִּשְׂדֵה הַמַּכְפֵּלָה אֲשֶׁר עַל־פְּנֵי־מַמְרֵא *in the cave that is in the field of Mach-pelah, which is opposite Mamre* Gn 49_{30}.

<OBJ> נתן *give* Gn $23_{9.9.11}$, קנה *buy* Gn 49_{30} 50_{13}, עשׂה *make* Jg 6_{2} (|| מִנְהָר *hollow*, מְצָדָה *stronghold*).

<CSTR> מְעָרַת פָּרִצִים *a cave of violent ones* Jr 7_{11}, מְעָרַת הַמַּכְפֵּלָה *the cave of Mach-pelah* Gn 23_{9} 25_{9}, מְעָרַת שְׂדֵה הַמַּכְפֵּלָה *the cave of the field of Mach-pelah* Gn 23_{19} 50_{13}, מְעָרַת עֲדֻלָּם *the cave of Adullam* 1 S 22_{1} 2 S 23_{13}||1 C 11_{15} (or in both em. מְצֻדַת *stronghold of* Adullam), מערת העמוד *the cave of the pillar* 3QTr 6_{1}, מערת בית המרה *the cave of Beth-hammarah* 3QTr 2_{3} (others המדח the cave of *rinsing*), מערות פְּלִשְׁתִּים appar. *the caves of (the) Philistines* 1 S 17_{23} (Qr מַעַרְכוֹת *the battle-lines of*), מְעָרוֹת צֻרִים *caves of rocks* Is 2_{19} (|| מְחִלָּה *hole*).

מִקְנֵה ... הַמְּעָרָה *the purchase of ... the cave* Gn 49_{32}, פִּי הַמְּעָרָה *the mouth of the cave* Jos $10_{18.22.27}$, פֶּתַח הַמְּעָרָה *(at) the entrance of the cave* 1 K 19_{13}, יַרְכְּתֵי הַמְּעָרָה *the recesses of the cave* 1 S 24_{4}, שְׁתֵּי מְעָרוֹת *two caves* 1 K $18_{4.13}$ (if em. מְעָרָה one *cave* in both).

<APP> שָׂדֶה *field* Gn 23_{17}.

<PREP> בְּ of place, *in(to), at* Ezk 33_{27} (|| מְצָדָה *stronghold*, + שָׂדֶה *field*, חָרְבָּה *ruin*) 3QTr 2_{3} (במערת בית המרה ... עשתות זהב *in the cave of Beth-hammarah ... there are 65 ingots of gold*; others המדח the cave of *rinsing*) 4QparaKings $2_{1(WA)}$ ([חמש]ים במ[ערת] *fifty in the cave*), + היה *be* Ps 142_{1}, בוא *come* Is 2_{19}, ברח *flee*

Ps 57$_{1}$, חבא ni. *hide oneself* Jos 10$_{16.17}$, htp. *hide oneself* 1 S 13$_{6}$ (|| חוֹחַ *hole*, סֶלַע *rock*, צְרִיחַ *tunnel*, בּוֹר *cistern*), hi. *hide* prophets 1 K 18$_{4.13}$, נתן *give* Saul into David's hands in the cave 1 S 24$_{11}$, חפר *dig* (perh. pass. *be buried*) 3QTr 6$_{1}$ ([ב]מערת) 6$_{7}$ 7$_{8}$, ישׁב *dwell* Gn 19$_{30}$, קבר *bury* Gn 49$_{30}$ 50$_{13}$.

מִן of direction, *from*, + עלה *go up* 1 S 17$_{23(Kt)}$, קום *arise* 1 S 24$_{8}$, יצא *go out* 1 S 24$_{9}$, hi. *take out* five kings Jos 10$_{22.23}$.

אֶל *(in)to*, + בוא *come* 2 S 23$_{13}$ 1 K 19$_{9}$, ירד *go down* 1 C 11$_{15}$, מלט ni. *escape* 1 S 22$_{1}$; *at, in*, + קבר *bury* Gn 23$_{19}$ 25$_{9}$ (+ שָׂדֶה *field*) 49$_{29}$, שׁלך hi. *throw* bodies Jos 10$_{27}$.

עַל *in charge of, over*, + פקד hi. *appoint* sentries Jos 10$_{18}$.

בְּעַד *on behalf of*, + היה *be*, i.e. serve as (of ruined city) Is 32$_{14}$ (unless מְעָרָה II *empty space* or em. מַעֲרֶה in same sense; and/or del. בְּעַד, leaving מְעָרָה as complement of היה).

<COLL> במערא של הכנא של הרגם *in the cave of the base of the rock* 3QTr 6$_{7}$, במערת בית המרה הישן בדביר השלישי *in the cave of Old Beth-hammarah, in the third chamber* 3QTr 2$_{3}$ (others המדה הישן ברובד השלישי in the cave of *old rinsing, on the third ledge*), בַּמְּעָרָה בְּמַקֵּדָה *in the cave at Makkedah* Jos 10$_{16.17}$.

הַמְּעָרָה אֲשֶׁר נֶחְבְּאוּ־שָׁם *the cave where they had hidden* Jos 10$_{27}$, וַיָּבֹא־שָׁם אֶל־הַמְּעָרָה וַיָּלֶן שָׁם *and he entered there into the cave and passed the night there* 1 K 19$_{9}$, וְשָׁם מְעָרָה וַיָּבֹא שָׁאוּל לְהָסֵךְ אֶת־רַגְלָיו *and a cave was there, and Saul entered to cover his legs*, i.e. to relieve himself 1 S 24$_{4}$.

<SYN> שָׂדֶה *field*, מִנְהָר *hollow*, מְצָדָה *stronghold*, חוֹחַ *hole*, מְחִלָּה *hole*, סֶלַע *rock*, צְרִיחַ *tunnel*, בּוֹר *cistern*.

*[מְעָרָה] II $_{1}$ n.f. **empty space**—pl. מְעָרוֹת—<PREP> בְּעַד *on behalf of*, + היה *be*, i.e. serve as (of ruined city) Is 32$_{14}$ (unless מְעָרָה I *cave* or em. מַעֲרֶה *empty space*; and/or del. בְּעַד, leaving מְעָרָה as complement of היה).

מְעָרָה III $_{1}$ pl.n. **Mearah,** Sidonian town, perh. 'Aṯlīt 23 km NNE of Caesarea, <NOM CL> וּמְעָרָה אֲשֶׁר לַצִּידֹנִים עַד־אֲפֵקָה *and Mearah, which belongs to the Sidonians, up to Aphek* Jos 13$_{4}$ (or em. מֵעַזָּה *from Gaza* or מֵעָרָה *from Arah*).

[מַעֲרָךְ] $_{1}$ n.[m.] **disposition**—pl. cstr. מַעַרְכֵי—**disposition, arrangement,** <NOM CL> לְאָדָם מַעַרְכֵי־לֵב *a human being's are the dispositions of (the) heart* Pr 16$_{1}$ (+ מֵי׳ מַעֲנֵה לָשׁוֹן *from Y. comes*, or *to Y. belongs, the answer of a tongue*). <CSTR> מַעַרְכֵי־לֵב *dispositions of (the) heart* Pr 16$_{1}$.

⇒ ערך *array*.

מַעֲרָכָה $_{20.2.63}$ n.f. **array**—cstr. Q מערכת; pl. Si מערכות; cstr. (מַעַרְכֹת) מַעַרְכוֹת; sf. Q מער[כותיו], מערכותמה—**array, row, 1.** of persons, usu. of troops, **battle-line,** perh. sometimes **battle, army;** perh. **row** of worshippers or **array** of all humankind (1QS 10$_{14}$).

<SUBJ> אסר ni. *be bound*, i.e. be constituted 1QM 5$_{3}$ (על אלף איש תאסר המערכה *the battle-line will be constituted of a thousand men*), נצב ni. *be positioned* 4QM^{a} 1$_{11}$, יצא *go out* 1QM 16$_{12}$=4QM^{a} 11.2$_{10}$ 4QM^{a} 1$_{15}$ ([תו]צא) 4QM^{c} 1$_{9}$, עלה *go up* 4QM^{a} 1$_{11}$ (ובע[לות]), קום *arise* 4QM^{a} 1$_{12}$ (יקו[מו]), עמד *stand (still)* 4QM^{a} 1$_{11.15}$, עבר *pass* 4QM^{a} 1$_{11}$, מלא *fulfil* period 4QM^{a} 1$_{16}$ (המ[ע]רכה), ארב *wait in ambush* 4QM^{a} 1$_{12}$.

<OBJ> שׁלם hi. *complete*, i.e. constitute 1QM 5$_{3(mg)}$, ערך *array* 1 S 17$_{21}$, סדר pi. *order* 1QM 5$_{16.16}$ 14$_{3}$ 15$_{6}$ 4QM^{a} 1$_{13}$ (מער[כותיו]), כנע hi. *humble* 1QM 6$_{5(mg)}$, חרר pi. *reproach* 1 S 17$_{10.26.36}$ perh. 17$_{45}$.

<CSTR> מערכת אנשים *row of people*, i.e. worshippers, or *array of humankind*, i.e. all humanity 1QS 10$_{14}$.

מערכות המלחמה *the lines of battle* 1QM 7$_{9}$ 18$_{4}$, מערכת פנים *a battle-line of faces*, i.e. the front line 1QM 5$_{3(mg)}$, מערכות הפנים *the battle-lines of faces*, i.e. the front lines 1QM 9$_{4}$, מערכת אנשי הבינים *the battle-line of the men of the interval*, i.e. of the skirmishers 1QM 6$_{9}$, מערכות הבנים *the battle-lines of the interval*, i.e. of skirmishing 4QM^{c} 1$_{6}$, מערכת האויב *the battle-line of the enemy* 1QM 3$_{7}$ 6$_{2.5(mg)}$ (מערכת אויב) 8$_{8.12}$ 4QM^{a} 1$_{5}$ (מערכות), מערכת כתיים *the battle-line of (the) Kittim* 1QM 16$_{6}$ 17$_{12}$ ([מע]רכת) 18$_{4}$ ([מ]ערכות כ[תיים]) 4QM^{a} 13$_{5}$ (כתיאים), מערכות גויים *the battle-lines of (the) nations* 4QM^{c} 1$_{3}$, מַעַרְכוֹת פְּלִשְׁתִּים *the battle-lines of (the)*

Philistines 1 S 17$_{23(Qr)}$ (Kt appar. מְעָרוֹת *caves of*; or em. מַחֲנוֹת *camps of*) 23$_3$ 11QPs^a 28$_{14}$ (מן]ערכות [פלשתים]), מַעַרְכוֹת יִשְׂרָאֵל *the battle-lines of Israel* 1 S 17$_8$ (מַעַרְכֹת) 17$_{10.45}$, מַעַרְכוֹת אֱלֹהִים חַיִּים *the battle-lines of the living God* 1 S 17$_{26.36}$ (מַעַרְכֹת).

כול אנשי המערכה *all the men of the battle-line* 1QM 7$_{12}$, אנש]י המע]רכה *the men of the battle-line* 4QM^a 1$_{12}$, אלף מערכת *a thousand (soldiers) of the battle-line of* the skirmishers 1QM 6$_9$, דגלי המערכה *the battalions of the battle-line* 1QM 17$_{10}$, אנשי סרך המערכות *the men of the rule of,* i.e. governing, *the battle-lines* 1QM 6$_{10(mg)}$, כול ראשי המערכות *all the heads of the battle-lines* 1QM 19$_{12}$=4QM^b 1$_{11}$ (וכו]ל]), אֱלֹהֵי מַעַרְכוֹת *the God of the battle-lines of* Israel 1 S 17$_{45}$, עֹדְרֵי מַעֲרָכָה *helpers of,* i.e. those constituting, *a battle-line* 1 C 12$_{39}$ (mss עֹרְכֵי *arrayers of,* i.e. those arrayed as).

מקום המערכה *the place of the battle-line* 1QM 19$_9$= 4QM^b 1$_9$, ימין המערכה *the right of the battle-line* 1QM 6$_8$ (+ ולשמאולה *and to its left*), עברי המערכה *the sides of the battle-line* 1QM 9$_{11}$, סדר מערכות *the order of the lines* of battle 1QM 7$_9$, שתי המערכות *the two battle-lines* 1QM 6$_4$ 7$_{18}$, שלוש מערכות *three battle-lines* 4QM^a 1$_{11.12}$, שבע המערכות *the seven battle-lines* 1QM 5$_{16}$ 9$_4$ (שבע מערכות), כול המערכות *all the battle-lines* 1QM 15$_6$ 4QM^c 1$_{12}$ (לכו]ל המ]ערכות), כול מערכות *all the battle-lines of* 1QM 18$_{4.4}$ ([מ]ערכות) 4QM^c 1$_6$.

<APP> בסדר מערכות המלחמה מערכה לקראת מערכה *in the order of the lines of battle, battle-line opposite battle-line* 1QM 7$_9$, אַנְשֵׁי מִלְחָמָה עֹדְרֵי מַעֲרָכָה *men of war, helpers of,* i.e. those constituting, *a battle-line* 1 C 12$_{39}$ (mss עֹרְכֵי *arrayers of,* i.e. those arrayed as).

<ADJ> למערכה האחת *to one battle-line,* i.e. per battle-line 1QM 5$_4$ 6$_{11}$ (למערכה [א]חת), המערכה הראישונה *the first battle-line* 1QM 8$_2$ 4QM^a 1$_{15}$ (הר]אישונה]) 10.2$_{12}$ (הראיש]ונה]), מערכה אחרת *another battle-line* 1QM 16$_{12}$=4QM^a 11.2$_{10}$, המערכה השנית *the second battle-line* 4QM^a 1$_{15}$ (והשנית *and the second one,* with ellipsis of noun) 1$_{16}$ (המ]ע]רכה) 4QM^c 1$_9$.

<PREP> לְ of direction, *to, into, up to* perh. 4QM^a 10.2$_{12}$ 13$_5$ (ל]מערכת]), + הלך *go* 4QM^a 1$_5$, יצא *go out* 1QM 3$_7$, קרב *approach* 1QM 8$_8$, נגשׁ *approach* 4QM^c 1$_6$, נגע hi. *reach* 4QM^a 11.2$_{20}$ (למ]ערכת]), שׁלך hi. *throw* weapons 1QM 8$_{12}$.

לְ of possession, *of, (belonging) to* 1QM 5$_4$ (ושבעה סדרי פנים למערכה האחת *and seven rows of faces will belong to each battle-line*) 6$_{11}$ (חמשים למערכה [א]חת *fifty will belong to each battle-line*).

לְ of benefit, *for,* + תקע *strike,* i.e., blow, trumpet 4QM^c 1$_9$ (לכו]ל המ]ערכות (יתקעו]), 1$_{12}$, שׂים *place,* i.e. set, ambush 4QM^a 1$_{12}$.

בְּ of place, *in, among* 1QM 8$_{17}$ (מעמדם במערת *their standing in the battle-line of*) 4QM^a 1$_{10}$ (כיא מלאכי קודש במערכותמה יחד] *for angels of holiness are within their battle-lines together*) 4QM^c 1$_3$, + ברך pi. *bless* 1QS 10$_{14}$ (others מִן *from out of,* i.e. מ for ב), נכה hi. *strike* 1 S 4$_2$ (or em. ho. *be struck*).

מִן of direction, *from, from out of, from among,* + בוא *come* 1 S 4$_{16}$ (or em. מַחֲנֶה *camp*), יצא *go out* 1QM 9$_{13}$, עלה *go up* 1 S 17$_{23(Qr)}$, רוץ *run* 1 S 4$_{12}$, נוס *flee* 1 S 4$_{16}$, ברך pi. *bless* 1QS 10$_{14}$ (others בְּ *among,* for מִן), חרף pi. *reproach* 11QPs^a 28$_{14}$ (ממ]ערכות פלשתים]) *reproaching from the battle-lines of the Philistines*).

אֶל *to(wards),* + הלך *go* 1 S 23$_3$, יצא *go out* 1 S 17$_{20}$, שׁלך hi. *throw* weapons 1QM 6$_2$, קרא *call* 1 S 17$_8$.

בֵּין *between,* + קרב htp. *approach* or *enter battle* 4QM^c 1$_7$, עמד *stand* 1QM 6$_{1.4}$ 7$_{18}$ (ועמ]דו]) 8$_4$ 16$_{4.12}$, שׂים *place,* i.e. make, space 4QM^a 1$_{11}$.

אֶל־בֵּין *to between,* + יצא *go out* 1QM 7$_{9.14}$.

מִתּוֹךְ *from inside,* + יצא *go out* 1QM 9$_4$.

עִם *with,* + יצא *go out* 1QM 7$_{17.17}$.

אַחַר *after,* + סדר *order* 1QM 5$_{16}$ (מערכה אחר מערכה *battle-line after battle-line*), עמד *stand* 4QM^a 1$_{11}$ (מערכה אחר מערכה).

לְיַד *alongside,* + בוא *come* 1QM 8$_2$, נגע hi. *arrive* 1QM 17$_{12}$ (ליד מע]רכת]), עמד *stand* 1QM 16$_6$.

לִפְנֵי *in front of,* + עמד *stand* 1QM 16$_{13}$=4QM^a 11.2$_{11}$ (ועו]מד לפני המער]כ]ה]) 4QM^c 1$_1$.

לִקְרַאת *opposite,* + ערך *array* 1 S 17$_{21}$ (מַעֲרָכָה לִקְרַאת מַעֲרָכָה *battle-line opposite battle-line*), סדר pi. *order* 1QM 7$_9$ (מערכה לקראת מערכה).

<COLL> לבוא המערכה *to come (back) to the battle-line* 1QM 3$_{10}$, וַיָּרָץ הַמַּעֲרָכָה *and he ran towards the battle-line* 1 S 17$_{22.48}$, עם כול מערכה ומערכה *with each battle-line* 1QM 7$_{17}$, בַּמַּעֲרָכָה בַּשָּׂדֶה *among the battle-*

line in the field 1 S 4_{2}.

Also 1Q33 2_{4} 4QM^{a} 1_{7} ([המער]כה) 1_{7}.

2. of row of lamps, <CSTR> בוא hi. *bring* נֵרֹת מַעֲרָכָה *the lamps of the row* (i.e. the lamps that Aaron was ordered to array [ערך] at Ex 27_{21}) Ex 39_{37}.

3. of row of array of shewbread (מַעֲרֶכֶת), <OBJ> שִׂים *place,* i.e. cause to be (arrayed as) Lv 24_{6}=11QT 8_{9} ([ושמת ... מערכות]). <CSTR> שְׁתֵּי מַעֲרָכוֹת *two rows* Lv $24_{6(\text{Sam})}$, שתי המערכות *the two rows* 11QT 8_{9}. <PREP> עַל *upon,* + נתן *place* pure frankincense Lv 24_{7}=11QT 8_{9} ([ונתת]ה; if em. in Lv מַעֲרֶכֶת *row [of shewbread]*). <COLL> שְׁתַּיִם מַעֲרָכוֹת שֵׁשׁ הַמַּעֲרֶכֶת *two rows, six in each row (of shewbread)* Lv 24_{6}, [שתים מערכות] *two rows* 11QT 8_{9}.

4. appar. of row of logs on altar, <OBJ> סדר pi. *order* Si 50_{14}. <CSTR> מערכות עליון *the rows (of logs) of the Most High* Si 50_{14}. <PREP> עַל *by* or *(leaning) over,* + נצב ni. *be positioned* Si 50_{12}.

5. ordered array of stones or **level ground** or **correct (building) procedure** for building altar, <PREP> בְּ of place, *in, on* level ground, or instrument, *by (means of), with* ordered array of stones, or, correct procedure, + בנה *build.*

⇨ ערך *array.*

מַעֲרֶכֶת 9 n.f. **array**—מַעֲרֶכֶת; cstr. מַעֲרֶכֶת—**1. row (of shewbread).**

<NOM CL> שֵׁשׁ הַמַּעֲרֶכֶת *six is the row,* i.e. there are six in each row Lv 24_{6}, וּמַעֲרֶכֶת לֶחֶם עַל־הַשֻּׁלְחָן הַטָּהוֹר *and a row of (shew)bread is on the pure table* 2 C 13_{11} (or em. לֶחֶם הַמַּעֲרֶכֶת *the bread of the row [of shewbread]*).

<CSTR> מַעֲרֶכֶת תָּמִיד *a row (of shewbread) of continuity* 2 C 2_{3}, מַעֲרֶכֶת לֶחֶם *the row of (shew)bread* 2 C 13_{11} (or em. לֶחֶם הַמַּעֲרֶכֶת *the bread of the row [of shewbread]*), לֶחֶם הַמַּעֲרֶכֶת *the bread of the row (of shewbread)* Ne 10_{34} 1 C 9_{32} (הַמַּעֲרֶכֶת) 23_{29} 2 C 13_{11} (if em.), שֻׁלְחַן הַמַּעֲרֶכֶת *the table of the row (of shewbread)* 1 C 28_{16} (שֻׁלְחֲנוֹת *the tables of*) 2 C 29_{18}.

<PREP> appar. לְ of purpose, *for (the purpose of),* + קטר hi. *offer incense* 2 C 2_{3} (with ellipsis of prep.); עַל *upon,* + נתן *place* pure frankincense Lv 24_{7} (or em. מַעֲרָכוֹת *rows,* i.e. מַעֲרָכָה).

<COLL> שְׁתַּיִם מַעֲרָכוֹת שֵׁשׁ הַמַּעֲרֶכֶת *two rows, six in each row (of shewbread)* Lv 24_{6} (Sam שְׁתֵּי *two* rows).

2. perh. **meal,** as set out in order (1QSa 2_{22}). <CSTR> כול מע[רכת] perh. *every meal* 1QSa 2_{22}. <PREP> לְ *in respect of, concerning,* + עשׂה *do* 1QSa 2_{22} (יעש[ו] לכול מע[רכת]).

⇨ ערך *array.*

[מַעֲרֹם] 1.2 n.[m.] **nakedness**—pl. sf. Si מערמיה, מַעֲרֻמֵּיהֶם (Si מערומיהם)—**1. nakedness,** of abyss and heart (Si 42_{18}), Wisdom (11QPs^{a} Si 51_{19}); perh. specif. **pudenda** (2 C 28_{15} Si $51_{19[\text{11QPs}^{a}]}$; perh. **secret** (Si 42_{18}). **2. naked person,** of Judaean captives (2 C 28_{15}).

<OBJ> לבשׁ hi. *clothe,* i.e. cover up 2 C 28_{15}, בין htpol. *examine* Si $51_{19(\text{11QPs}^{a})}$ (or ins. בְּ; see Prep.). <CSTR> כָּל־מַעֲרֻמֵּיהֶם *all their nakedness(es)* 2 C 28_{15} Si $42_{18(\text{B})}$ (כל מערומיהם; M lacks כָּל־). <PREP> בְּ בין htpol. *look upon, examine* Si 42_{18} $51_{19(\text{11QPs}^{a})}$ (if ins. בְּ in broken text).

⇨ עור *be naked.*

***[מַעֲרָף]** 0.1 n.[m.] **drop (of rain)**—cstr. Si מערף—<SUBJ> רפא hi. *heal* Si 43_{22}, perh. פרע *release* dew Si 43_{22} (unless טַל *dew* is subj., in app. with מַעֲרָף), דשׁן pi. *fatten,* i.e. refresh Si 43_{22} (unless טַל is subj.). <CSTR> מערף ענן *a drop of cloud* Si 43_{22}. <APP> perh. מערף ענן טל *a drop of cloud, dew* Si 43_{22}.

⇨ ערף *drip.*

***[מַעֲרָץ]** n.[m.] **terror,** <NOM CL> וְהוּא מַעֲרִצְכֶם *and he will be your terror,* i.e. the one who strikes terror into you Is 10_{13} (if em. מַעֲרִצְכֶם [mss מַעֲרִצְכֶם] *the one who terrifies you;* ‖ מוֹרָא your *fear*).

⇨ ערץ *be terrified.*

מַעֲרָצָה 1 n.f. **terror,** <PREP> בְּ of instrument, *by (means of), with,* + סעף pi. *lop* boughs Is 10_{33} (or em. בְּמַעֲרָצָה *with terror,* i.e. frighteningly, to בְּמַעֲצָדָה *with an axe* or בְּמַעֲצָדֹה *with his axe*).

⇨ ערץ *be terrified.*

מַעֲרָת 1 pl.n. **Maarath,** town in hill country of Judah, perh. Kh. Qūfīn, 12 km SW of Bethlehem, <NOM CL> בָּהָר ... מַעֲרָת *in the mountain(s) was ... Maarath* Jos 15_{59}. <APP> עִיר *city* Jos 15_{59}.

מַעֲשֶׂה I $_{234.40.293}$ n.m. **deed**—Si perh. מעשי; cstr. מַעֲשֵׂה (Si, Q perh. מעשי); sf. מַעֲשֶׂךָ, מַעֲשֵׂהוּ, מַעֲשֵׂנוּ; pl. מַעֲשִׂים; sf. מַעֲשַׂי, מַעֲשֶׂיךָ (Q מעשיכה, מעשייכה), מַעֲשַׂיִךְ (מַעֲשָׂיִךְ), מַעֲשָׂיו (Q מעשו), Q מַעֲשֶׂיהָ, מַעֲשֵׂינוּ, מַעֲשֵׂיכֶם, מַעֲשֵׂיהֶם (Q מעשיהמה).

1a. usu. **deed, action** (of God: Ex 32_{16} 34_{10} Dt 32_4 $11_{3.7}$ Jos 24_{31} Jg $2_{7.10}$ Is $5_{12.19}$ 10_{12} 19_{25} $28_{21.21}$ 29_{23} 60_{21} 64_7 66_3 Jr 51_{10} Ps $8_{4.7}$ 19_2 28_5 33_4 60_{21} 64_{10} $92_{5.6}$ 102_{26} 103_{22} 106_{13} $107_{22.24}$ $111_{2.6.7}$ 118_{17} 138_8 143_5 $145_{4.17}$ Jb 14_{15} 34_{19} 37_6 Ec 3_{11} 7_{13} 8_{17} 11_5 Si 2_{18} $16_{15.22}$ $36_{15.20}$ $38_{8[mg]}$ 39_{33} 42_{15} 143_5 1QS 1_{19} 4_4 10_{17} 1QH $1_{26.30}$ $4_{20.31.32}$ 5_{36}=4QHod^c 1.4_{10} 1QH 7_{32} 11_4 12_{28} 13_{19} 16_8 17_{18} 1QM 10_8 $13_{1.2.9}$ 14_{12} 4QJub^a 2_3 4QTime 1.$2_{6.10}$ 4QBer^a 1.2_6 4Q392 1_7 4QShirShabb^e 23.2_{12} 4Q417 1.1_6 2.1_{13} 4Q418 102_2 4Q423 4_2 4QHod^a 7.2_{11} 4QDibHam^a 7_4 4QShir^b 63.2_1 4QPrFêtes^c 97.1_9 4QRitPur 5_{16} 4QapMes 2.2_{10} 11QPs^a 18_4 24_9 28_7 11QHymn^a 1_5 11QHymn^b$_2$ 11QShirShabb $10_{4.6}$ Mas ShirShabb 1_6 CD 1_1=4QD^c 1_9 CD 13_7=4QD^b 9.4_4 GnzPs $1_{10.12.12}$ $4_{10.22.23}$; of angels: 4QBer^b 2_{10}; of a woman: Pr 31_{31}).

b. sometimes sg. used in place of pl. or collectively, **deeds, activity, behaviour** (Ex 34_{10} Lv 18_3 Dt 11_7 15_{10} Jos 24_{31} Jg $2_{7.10}$ 13_{12} 1 K 13_{11} Is 5_{19} 10_{12} 19_{14} $28_{21.21}$ Jr 51_{10} Ezk 16_{30} Ps 33_4 62_{13} 64_{10} $107_{24[mss]}$ $111_{2[mss]}$ $118_{17[mss]}$ Ec 3_{11} 4_3 7_{13} $8_{14.14}$ 9_{10} 11_5 2 C 17_4 Si $39_{19.33}$ 47_8).

c. esp. as nomen regens, oft. **product, produce, production, work, working, making, manufacture,** by a person (Gn 40_{17} Ex 23_{16} $26_{1.31.36}$||$36_{8.35.37}$ 27_{16}||36_{18} $28_{6.15.32.39}$||$39_{3.8.22.29}$ 28_{11} 32_{16} 39_{27} Jr $10_{9.9}$ Hos 13_2 Mc 6_{16} Jb 37_6 Pr 16_{11} Si 34_{26} $45_{10.11}$ 49_1 1QM 5_{5+5t} 7_{11} 4QJub^a 2_3 4QShirShabb^e 23.2_7 11QT 7_{14}); by means of a process (Ex 28_8||39_5 Si $43_{4[M]}$ 4QShirShabb^c 2_3 4QShirShabb^e 14_6) or an instrument or material employed for the resulting product (Nm 31_{20} Is 32_{17} Hb 3_{17} Ec 8_{11} 2 C 16_{14} 1QH $5_{8.16}$ 4QapJoshua^a 15.1_2 11QT 50_{17} 59_3 GnzPs 2_{20}), and esp. the hand (see Cstr.); also **work (giving the appearance) of,** in ref. to the outer form of an end-product (and sometimes almost equivalent to §2, כְּמַעֲשֵׂה *as, like*) (Ex 27_4||38_4 28_{14} 28_{22}||39_{15} 1 K 7_{17+5t} Is 3_{24} 2 C 3_{10} 1QM $5_{5.7.9}$ 4QShirShabb^e 23.2_9); **work achieved, achievement** (2 C 20_{37}); **(process of) production** (1 C 9_{31}); also in ref. more to the **construction, structure, composition, make-up, design** of a finished product (Nm 8_4 1 K $7_{8.28.33.33}$ 2 K 16_{10} Ezk $1_{16.16}$ 1QM 10_{14} 4QCommGenD 1_2 4QShirShabb^d 1.1_{44} 4QShirShabb^e $19_{4.6.6}$ 20.2_4 4QBark^a 1.1_3).

d. labour, work(ing), task, occupation, trade, business (Gn 5_{29} 46_{33} 47_3 Ex $5_{4.13}$ $23_{12.16}$ Nm 31_{51} Jg 19_{16} 25_2 Isa 54_{16}=CD 6_8 Is 59_6 Ezk 46_1 Ps 104_{13} Ec 2_{17} 1 C 23_{28} 1QS 4_4 1QSa 1_{22} 11QT $43_{16.17}$ CD 12_{18} perh. 1 S 20_{19}).

e. creation, creature, created being (Is 29_{16} Ps 103_{22} $104_{24.31}$ 139_{14} $145_{9.10.17(Gnz)}$ Dn 9_{14} Si 15_{19} 16_{26} 38_8 $42_{15[Bmg,M].16.22}$ $43_{2[M].25[B].28.32}$ 1QS 11_{20} 1QH $1_{6.33}$ 3_{23} 9_{36} $10_{11.36}$ $11_{24.30}$ $13_{6.8}$ 14_{16} 15_{20} fr. 2_7 fr. 5_8 4QJub^a 2_1 4QMyst^a 3a.$2_{10.15}$ 4QShirShabb^a 1_5 4QShirShabb^d 1.1_{35} 4QShirShabb^e 19_3 4Q423 5_4 4QShir^b 63.4_1 11QPs^a 18_7 4QPrFêtes^c 131.2_7 4QShir^b 10_{10} GnzPs 2_{22} 4_{11}).

f. object of mockery (Jr 10_{15}=51_{18}), **substance** (4QShirShabb^e 20.2_{10}), perh. cultic **apparatus** (collective) (2 C 4_6).

g. (act of) **sexual intercourse** (4QD^e $5_{18.18}$=4QD^f $3_{11.12}$).

h. perh. **event, episode, story** (4QTob^e 6_1 1 S 20_{19} Ps 45_2 Est 10_2 4QMMT B$_2$ C$_{27}$).

<SUBJ> היה *be* Ex 28_{32} (+ לְפִיו will be *at its mouth*) Jg 13_{12} (מַה־יִּהְיֶה מִשְׁפַּט־הַנַּעַר וּמַעֲשֵׂהוּ *what will be the character of the lad and his behaviour?*) Is 19_{15} (וְלֹא־יִהְיֶה לְמִצְרַיִם מַעֲשֶׂה *and there will be[long] to Egypt no deed*) 29_{15} (וְהָיָה בְמַחְשָׁךְ מַעֲשֵׂיהֶם *so that their deeds are [done] in darkness*) 32_{17} (וְהָיָה מַעֲשֵׂה הַצְּדָקָה שָׁלוֹם *and the produce of righteousness will be peace;* || עֲבֹדָה *service*) 1QS 4_{23} (+ לבושת will be put *to shame*) 4QShirShabb^d 1.1_{35} (+ [בר]צון דעתו *at the desire of his knowing*) 4QapMes 2.2_{10} (ונכ[ב]דות שלוא היו מעשה אדני *and glorious acts that were not a deed of my Lord*).

גדל *be great* Ps 92_6 (:: מַחֲשָׁבָה *thought*), רבב *be many* Ps 104_{24}, יכל ho. *be able* 1QH 11_{24}, יעל hi. *be of use* Is 57_{12} (|| צְדָקָה *righteousness*), עשׂה ni. *be done* Gn 20_9

Ec 1_{14} 2_{17} 4_3 8_9 4QMyst[a] 3a.2_6, יסד ni. *be established* 11QPs[a] 102_{26} (MT qal, *establish* work), שׁמר htp. *be observed* Mc 6_{16} (or em. qal, *observe* deed; + חֻקָּה *statute*), גלה pu. *be revealed* Si 16_{15}, כתב pass. *be written (down)* Est 10_2, זור *be strange* Is 28_{21} (|| עֲבֹדָה *service*), דרשׁ pass. *be sought* Ps 111_2, שׁכח ni. *be forgotten* Si $38_{8(mg)}$, שׁבת *cease* Si 38_8, אבד *disappear* 1QH fr. 3_{10} ([ויאבד]), מחה ni. *be erased* Ezk 6_6 (or del.), רקב *rot* Si 14_{19} (+ פֹּעַל *deed*), perh. מלח pu. *be salted*, i.e. blended 4QShirShabb[e] 19_3 20_{10}.

ברך pass. *be blessed* Is 19_{25}, pi. *bless* Ps 103_{22} (+ צָבָא *host*) 4QShir[b] 63.4_1, זכה htp. *be purified* 1QS 8_{18}, חטא htp. *be purified from sin* Nm 31_{20} (or em. pi., *purify from sin*, with מַעֲשֶׂה as obj.), יצק ho. *be poured (out)*, i.e. by being fashioned from molten metal, Si $43_{4[M]}$, רדד ho. *be hammered work (giving the appearance) of a slope* 1 K 7_{29} (if em. מַעֲשֵׂה מוֹרָד *work [giving the appearance] of a slope* to מַעֲשֵׂה מֻרָד *hammered work*).

חושׁ hi. *hasten* intrans. Is 5_{19} (unless trans., with מַעֲשֵׂה as obj., or em. יָחִישָׁה *may it hasten/may he hasten [it]* to יָחִישׁ י׳ *Y. will hasten* his activity), appar. בוא *come* Is 66_{18} (or em. בָּאָה deeds are *coming* to בָּא I [Y.] *am coming*, and ins. יֹדֵעַ *I, who know* their deeds, am coming; :: מַחֲשָׁבָה *thought*), ho. *be brought* Jr 10_9 (or del. מַעֲשֵׂה חָרָשׁ *the work of an artisan* is brought; and replace with מַעֲשֵׂה חֲכָמִים כֻּלָּם *all of them are the work of experts*, from end of verse), עלה *go up*, i.e. be accepted by God CD 5_5, יצב htp. *take one's stand* 1QH 10_{11}, עצר *gather* strength 1QH 10_{11}, יפע hi. *shine*, i.e. become visible CD $20_{3.6}$, אמר *say* Is 29_{16} (|| יֵצֶר *created being*), ספר pi. *recount* wonders 1QH 11_{24}, נגד hi. *tell*, i.e. proclaim, glory Ps 19_2, כחשׁ pi. *deceive* Hb 3_{17} (or em. מַעֲשֵׂה־זַיִת *the produce of the olive* deceives, to מַעֲשֵׂהוּ/מַעֲשֵׂה זַיִת *the olive* deceives *[its] produce*, i.e. fails to produce what is expected), הלל pi. *praise* Pr 31_{31} (or em. מַעֲשֶׂיהָ *her deeds* to בַּעְלָהּ or אִישָׁהּ *her husband*).

<NOM CL> בגדי קודש ... מעשה חשב *the garments of holiness were ... the work of a skilled person* Si 45_{10}, מַעֲשֵׂה חֲכָמִים כֻּלָּם *all of them are the work of experts* Jr 10_9, חשן משפט ... מעשה אורג *the breastplate of judgment ... was the work of a weaver* Si 45_{11}, ... והלוהב מעשה חרש מחשבת *and the blade is ... the work of a thoughtful artisan* 1QM 5_{10}, sim. 5_{11} (והכידנים *and the javelins* are), ויד הכידן ... מעשה חושב *and the hand(grip) of the javelin is ... the work of a skilled person* 1QM 5_{14}, וּמָסַךְ שַׁעַר הֶחָצֵר מַעֲשֵׂה רֹקֵם *and the screen of the gate of the tent was the work of an embroiderer* Ex 38_{18}.

וְהַלֻּחֹת מַעֲשֵׂה אֱלֹהִים הֵמָּה *and the tablets were the work of God* Ex 32_{16} (+ מִכְתָּב *writing*), פלאות מעשי י׳ *the deeds of Y. are wonders* Si $11_{4(A)}$ (+ פֹּעַל *deed*), מה נורא מעשי י׳ *how awe-inspiring are the deeds of Y.* Si $43_{2(B)}$, שמש ... מעשי [ע]ליון *(the) sun ... is a creation of the Most High* Si $43_{2(M)}$, שמש ... מעשי מוצק *(the sun) ... is a thing that has been poured out*, i.e. fashioned from molten metal Si $43_{4(M)}$, מעשי גדיל שפה *(the) edge is workings (giving the appearance) of a cord* 1QM 5_5, וְכֹתָרֹת ... מַעֲשֵׂה שׁוּשַׁן *and (the) capitals ... were work (giving the appearance) of a lotus* 1 K 7_{19}, ... וּפִיהָ מַעֲשֵׂה־כֵן *and its mouth was ... work (giving the appearance) of a stand* 1 K 7_{31} (or del. מַעֲשֵׂה־כֵן).

וְעַמֵּךְ כֻּלָּם ... מַעֲשֵׂה יָדַי *and your people, all of them, are ... the work of my hands* Is 60_{21} (1QIsa[a,b] ידיו *his hands*), וּמַעֲשֵׂה יָדְךָ כֻּלָּנוּ *and all of us are the work of your hand* Is 64_7, כִּי־מַעֲשֵׂה יָדָיו כֻּלָּם *for all of them are the work of his hands* Jb 34_{19}, מַעֲשֵׂי יָדָיו אֱמֶת וּמִשְׁפָּט *the works of his hands are truth and justice* Ps 111_7 (mss מַעֲשֵׂה *the work of*; or del. אֱמֶת or מִשְׁפָּט), חַמּוּקֵי יְרֵכַיִךְ כְּמוֹ חֲלָאִים מַעֲשֵׂה יְדֵי אָמָּן *the curves of your thighs are ... the work of an artisan's hands* Ca 7_2 (Gnz חַמּוּקֵי), עֲצַבֵּיהֶם ... מַעֲשֵׂה יְדֵי אָדָם *their idols are ... the work of human hands* Ps 115_4 (||135_{15} עֲצַבֵּי הַגּוֹיִם *the idols of the nations*; mss מַעֲשֵׂי *the works of* in both), כִּי־חֻקּוֹת הָעַמִּים הֶבֶל הוּא ... מַעֲשֵׂה יְדֵי־חָרָשׁ *for the statutes of the peoples are vanity ..., the product of the hands of an artisan* Jr 10_3 (or em. חִתַּת *the terror of*, i.e. that which inspires terror in).

מַעֲשֵׂה הָרָעָה מְהֵרָה *the product of evil is speed* Ec 8_{11} (or em. preceding פִּתְגָּם for no *sentence* is carried out, to פִּתְגָּם for *no sentence of*, i.e. on, an evil *deed* is carried out quickly; or em. מַעֲשֶׂה to מֵעֹשֵׂי no sentence is carried out quickly *on account of those who do* evil),

הֶבֶל הֵמָּה מַעֲשֵׂה תַּעְתֻּעִים *they are vanity, an object of mockery* Jr 10$_{15}$=51$_{18}$, כנ[ו]ל [מעשי]הם ק[וד]שי דבקי פלא *all their constructions are of acts of holiness of those that cling to wonder* 4QShirShabb^{e} 19$_{4}$, אלוהים חיים כול מעשיהם *all their constructions are,* i.e. they are completely made up of, *living gods* 4QShirShabb^{e} 19$_{6}$.

מַעֲשֵׂהוּ כָּל־אַבְנֵי־כִיס *all the stones,* i.e. *weights, of a bag are his work* Pr 16$_{11}$, וצדק כול מעשיך *and all your deeds are righteousness* 1QH 13$_{19}$, צדק כול מעשיו *all his deeds are righteousness* 4Q418 102$_{2}$, ואמת כול מעשיו *and all his deeds are truth* 1QS 10$_{17}$=4QS^{f} 1.4$_{3}$ ((ואמת כול מ[עש]יו]), perh. אמת מעשיהם *their deeds are truth* 1QH 13$_{4}$, [וכול מעשיה טומאה ונאצ]ה ותבל *and all their deeds are impurity and offence and depravity* 4QJub^{d} 21$_{21}$, אֶפֶס מַעֲשֵׂיהֶם *their deeds are nothing* Is 41$_{29}$, מַעֲשֵׂיהֶם מַעֲשֵׂי אָוֶן *their deeds are deeds of iniquity* Is 59$_{6}$ (+ פֹּעַל *deed*).

מָה־הַמַּעֲשֶׂה הַזֶּה *what is this thing?* Gn 44$_{15}$, ומה [מע]שה *and what is the deed (of)?* 4QMyst^{b} 6$_{2}$, מַה־מַּעֲשֵׂיכֶם *what are your occupations?* Gn 46$_{33}$ 47$_{3}$, וְכֵן כָּל־מַעֲשֵׂה יְדֵיהֶם *and like this is every work of their hands* Hg 2$_{14}$, אשר מעשיך הכול *whose deeds are,* i.e. constitute, *the totality (of creation)* 1QH 16$_{8}$, מַעֲשֵׂה חָרָשִׁים כֻּלֹּה *all of it is the work of artisans* Ho 13$_{2}$, וְזֶה מַעֲשֵׂה הַמְּנֹרָה *and this is the structure of the lampstand* Nm 8$_{4}$, sim. 1 K 7$_{28}$ (מְכוֹנָה of the *stand* [or em. מְכֹנוֹת *stands*]), כִּי לֹא אֱלֹהִים הֵמָּה כִּי אִם־מַעֲשֵׂה יְדֵי־אָדָם *for they were not gods but the product of human hands* 2 K 19$_{18}$||Is 37$_{19}$, כִּי אֵין מַעֲשֶׂה ... בִּשְׁאוֹל *for there is no activity ... in Sheol* Ec 9$_{10}$ (:: חֶשְׁבּוֹן *thought,* דַּעַת *knowledge,* חָכְמָה *wisdom*).

כִּי רַע עָלַי הַמַּעֲשֶׂה *for evil (it seemed) to me was the labour* Ec 2$_{17}$, הלוא כל מעשיו נחמד[ים] *are not all his created beings desirable?* Si 42$_{22}$, וְכִי מַעֲשָׂיו טוֹב לְךָ מְאֹד *and because his deeds have been very good for you* 1 S 19$_{4}$, מעשה אל כלם טובים *the deed(s) of God, all of them are good* Si 39$_{33}$, גְּדֹלִים מַעֲשֵׂי י׳ *great are the deeds of Y.* Ps 111$_{2}$ (mss מַעֲשֵׂה *deeds of*), [כ]יא כופלים כל מעשי אל *for all the deeds of God are double(d)* 4Q392 1$_{7}$, מַה־נּוֹרָא מַעֲשֶׂיךָ *how awe-inspiring are your deeds* Ps 66$_{3}$, נִפְלָאִים מַעֲשֶׂיךָ *wonderful are your creations* Ps 139$_{14}$ (or del.), נפלאות נפלאים מעשיכה *wonders of wonders are your creations* 11QPs^{a} 139$_{14}$.

וּמַעֲשֵׂהוּ בַכַּרְמֶל *whose business was at Carmel* 1 S 25$_{2}$, וּבַסַּל ... מַעֲשֵׂה אֹפֶה *and in the basket ... was the product of a baker* Gn 40$_{17}$, באומר אלהים מעשיו *by the word of God are,* i.e. came into being, *his creations* Si 42$_{15(Bmg,M)}$ (B רצונו *his will;* perh. + פֹּעַל *deed*), בתמים מעשי[מה] perh. *with perfection are their deeds* 4QBer^{b} 2$_{10}$, וְכָל־מַעֲשֵׂהוּ בֶּאֱמוּנָה perh. *and every deed of his is (done) reliably* Ps 33$_{4}$, כיא כול מעשיהם באמתכה perh. *for all their deeds are (done) for the purpose of your truth* 1QH 6$_{9}$, כיא בהולל מעשיהם *for through madness are their deeds (effected)* 1QH 4$_{8}$, ובחושך כול מעשיהם perh. *and as darkness are all their deeds* 1QM 15$_{9}$.

וּלְשַׁעַר הֶחָצֵר מָסָךְ ... מַעֲשֵׂה רֹקֵם *and for the gate of the court there is to be a screen ... the work of an embroiderer* Ex 27$_{16}$, ומעשיהם לנדה לפניו *and their deeds are as impurity before him* CD 2$_{1}$ (+ הוֹן *wealth*), sim. 1QS 5$_{19}$ (+ וכול *and all* their deeds; + הון), ולרוח עולה ... מעשי תועבה *and to the spirit of iniquity belong ... deeds of abomination* 1QS 4$_{10}$=4QS^{c} 2$_{8}$ ([ולרוח עולה] ... [תו]עבה), לכה ... כול מעשי הצדקה *to you ... belong all the deeds of righteousness* 1QH 1$_{26}$, לאל עליון ... כול מעשי צדקה *to God most high belong all deeds of righteousness* 1QH 4$_{31}$, ולבני האדם ... מעשי הרמיה *and to the children of humankind belong ... deeds of deceit* 1QH 1$_{27}$ (+ עֲבֹדָה *service*).

שְׂבָכִים מַעֲשֵׂה שְׂבָכָה גְּדִלִים מַעֲשֵׂה שַׁרְשְׁרוֹת לַכֹּתָרֹת *trellises, work (giving the appearance) of a trellis, (and) cords, work (giving the appearance) of chains pertained to the capitals* 1 K 7$_{17}$ (or em. וַיַּעַשׂ שְׁתֵּי שְׂבָכִים לְכַסּוֹת אֶת־הַכֹּתֶרֶת *and he made two trellises to cover the capital*).

וכשמו כן מעשיו *and just like his name, so are his deeds* Si 2$_{18}$, מעשה לוטש כן היין *the product of a smith (thus) is wine* Si 34$_{26}$ (mg כי היית *because you were*), וּמַעֲשֵׂה הָאוֹפַנִּים כְּמַעֲשֵׂה אוֹפַן הַמֶּרְכָּבָה *and the structure of the wheels was in accordance with the structure of the wheel of a chariot* 1 K 7$_{33}$ (or em. אוֹפַן to אוֹפַנֵּי *the wheels of*), מַרְאֵה הָאוֹפַנִּים וּמַעֲשֵׂיהֶם כְּעֵין תַּרְשִׁישׁ ... וּמַרְאֵיהֶם וּמַעֲשֵׂיהֶם כַּאֲשֶׁר יִהְיֶה הָאוֹפַן בְּתוֹךְ הָאוֹפָן *the appearance of the wheels and their composition(s) was like the glow of topaz ... and their appearance(s) and their composition(s) was as if a wheel was inside a wheel* Ezk 1$_{16}$ (or del. first וּמַעֲשֵׂיהֶם and/or וּמַרְאֵיהֶם).

מִתַּחַת לָאֲרָיוֹת וְלַבָּקָר לֹיוֹת מַעֲשֵׂה מוֹרָד *below the lions and the oxen were spirals, work (giving the appearance) of a slope* 1 K 7$_{29}$ (unless מוֹרָד = *hammered*, i.e. רדד ho. ptc., and em. מַעֲשֵׂה hammered *work*; and/or em. לֹיוֹת to לְוָיוֹת *wreaths*), וְעַל רֹאשׁ הָעַמּוּדִים מַעֲשֵׂה שׁוֹשָׁן *and on the top(s) of the columns was work (giving the appearance of) a lotus* 1 K 7$_{22}$ (or del.), מעשה כל בשר נגדו *the activity of all flesh is before him* Si 39$_{19}$, [ב]תוך רוחי הדר מעשי רוקמות פלא *among the spirits of splendour are the products of wonderful acts of embroidery* 4QShirShabb^{e} 14$_{6}$.

<OBJ> עשׂה *do* Gn 20$_{9}$ 44$_{15}$ Ex 18$_{20}$ 23$_{12}$ Nm 16$_{28}$ Dt 11$_{3}$ (|| אוֹת *sign*) 11$_{7}$ 14$_{29}$ 28$_{21}$ Jos 24$_{31}$ Jg 2$_{7.10}$ 1 S 8$_{8}$ 1 K 13$_{11}$ 2 K 23$_{19}$ Is 19$_{15}$ 29$_{16.16}$ Jr 7$_{13}$ Ezk 16$_{30}$ Ec 2$_{11}$ (+ עָמָל *toil*) 3$_{11}$ Si 51$_{30}$ 4QD^{e} 5$_{18}$=4QD^{f} 3$_{11}$, *make* Ex 26$_{1.31.36}$|| 36$_{8.35.37}$ 27$_{4}$||38$_{4}$ 28$_{6.15.22.39}$||39$_{3.8.15.29}$ 28$_{14}$ 38$_{18}$ 39$_{22.27}$ Dt 27$_{15}$ Ps 104$_{24}$ Dn 9$_{14}$ 2 C 3$_{10}$ 4QJub^{a} 2$_{3}$ ([ע]שה), *prepare* 11QT 50$_{17}$, פעל *do* Is 26$_{12}$ (or em. גַּם כָּל־ *and all* our works you have done, to כְּגֹמֶל you have acted *in accordance with the recompense of* our deeds) 1QpHab 12$_{8}$.

ברא *create* Si 16$_{26}$ 1QH 13$_{8}$, כון hi. *establish* 1QS 11$_{16}$ =4QS^{j} 1$_{3}$ ([מעש]יו), polel *establish* Ps 90$_{17.17}$ (lacking in mss), יסד *establish* Ps 102$_{26}$ (11QPs^{a} יסד ni. *be established*, with מַעֲשֶׂה as subj.) 1QS 3$_{25}$, שׂים *place* Dt 27$_{15}$ Ec 3$_{17}$ (if em. שָׁם there is a time ... for every deed *there* to שָׂם *he has appointed* for every deed ... a time), perh. בוא *bring* 4QPrayers^{a} 3$_{6}$, גדל hi. *make great* Ec 2$_{4}$, כלה pi. *complete* Ex 5$_{13}$, בצע pi. *complete* Is 10$_{12}$, תמם hi. *perfect* 4QBer^{c} 1$_{3}$ ([לה]תם; WA [ושמר]תם *and you kept*; + [חטא] מכול *from every sin*), שׁמר *observe* Mc 6$_{16}$ (if em. htp., *be observed*, of deed).

בוא hi. *bring* to judgment Ec 12$_{14}$, מלא *fill* Si 42$_{16(M)}$, מצא *find* Ec 3$_{11}$, לקח *take* Nm 31$_{51}$, אסף *gather* Ex 23$_{16}$, סור hi. *remove* Jb 33$_{17}$ (or em. מַעֲשֶׂה to remove a person *a deed*, perh. remove the deed from the person, to מִמַּעֲשֵׂהוּ *from his behaviour* or מֵעַוְלָה *from iniquity* or מֵעֻשֶּׂה *from what is hidden*, i.e. עשׂה II *hide*),* בלה pi. *wear out*, i.e. use up Is 65$_{22}$, שׁנה pi. *change* 1QH 5$_{36}$= 4QHod^{c} 1.4$_{10}$ ([משנים]), חושׁ hi. *hasten* trans. Is 5$_{19}$ (unless intrans., with מַעֲשֵׂהוּ as subj., or em. יָחִישָׁה *may it hasten/may he hasten [it]* to יָחִישׁ י׳ *Y. will hasten* his activity), עבד *serve* Dt 4$_{28}$=11QT 59$_{3}$.

בחן *test* Si 34$_{26}$, ברר pi. *purify* 1QS 4$_{20}$ 1QM 13$_{1}$, חטא pi. *purify from sin* Nm 31$_{20}$ (if em. htp. *be purified of sin*), דוח hi. *rinse* 2 C 4$_{6}$, קטר hi. *offer as incense* 4QMidrEschat^{a} 1$_{7}$, קדשׁ hi. *consecrate* Si 32$_{11(Bmg)}$ (B מַעֲשֵׂר *tithe*), שׁקל *weigh* 4Q418 123.2$_{6}$ (שקול מעשיכה *the weighing of your deeds*), רפה hi. *drop* Ps 138$_{8}$, נכה hi. *strike* Hg 2$_{17}$, חבל pi. *ruin* Ec 5$_{5}$ (or em. qal, *take away*), פרץ *break up* 2 C 20$_{37}$, שׁמד hi. *destroy* 4QD^{a} 1$_{3}$ ([ימשי]ד), אבד pi. *destroy* 2 K 19$_{18}$||Is 37$_{19}$.

רעע hi. *make evil* 4QJub^{h} 35$_{13}$, רשׁע hi. *condemn* 4QShir^{b} 48.2$_{5}$, שׂנא *hate* 4QShir^{b} 18.2$_{7}$, תעב pi. *abominate* 1QH 16$_{11}$, הלל po. *make foolish* 1QH 4$_{17}$=4QHod^{d} 1$_{5}$ ([להולל]), כחשׁ pi. *deceive* Hb 3$_{17}$ (if em. מַעֲשֵׂה־זַיִת *the produce of the olive* deceives, to מַעֲשֵׂהוּ/ מַעֲשֵׂה זַיִת *the olive* deceives *[its] produce*, i.e. fails to produce what is expected).

ראה *see* Ex 34$_{10}$ Dt 11$_{7}$ Jg 2$_{7}$ Is 5$_{12}$ (|| פֹּעַל *deed*) 29$_{23}$ Jon 3$_{10}$ (+ דֶּרֶךְ *way*) Ps 8$_{4}$ 107$_{24}$ (נִפְלָאָה *wonder*) Ec 1$_{14}$ 4$_{3}$ 7$_{13}$ 8$_{17}$ Si 15$_{19(A)}$ (+ מִפְעָל *deed*) 4QJub^{a} 2$_{3}$ 4QJub^{d} 21$_{21}$ ([ראיתי] ... מע[שי]), שׁמע *hear (of)* 11QPs^{a} 24$_{9}$, ידע *know (about)* Jos 24$_{31}$ Jg 2$_{10}$ Is 66$_{18}$ (if ins. ידע :: מַחֲשָׁבָה *thought*) Jb 37$_{7}$ (if em. אַנְשֵׁי מַעֲשֵׂהוּ so that all *the people of his making* [i.e. whom he has made] might know, to אֱנוֹשׁ/אֲנָשִׁים so that every *person*/all *people* might know his deeds) Ec 11$_{5}$ 1QH 1$_{7}$ 4$_{32}$ 7$_{13}$ 13$_{8}$ ([ותדע]) CD 2$_{8}$, i.e. have experience of 4QD^{e} 5$_{18}$=4QD^{f} 3$_{12}$ (D^{e} [ידע]ה; D^{f} [מעשה]), hi. *inform (about)* Ex 18$_{20}$ 1QH 13$_{10}$ ([הודעתה]) 1QLitPr 3.2$_{7}$ (others מַעֲלֶה *ascent*; or em. פֹּעַל *deed*), למד *learn* Ps 106$_{35}$, זכר *remember* Si 42$_{15}$, פקד *notice* 1QS 5$_{24}$=4QS^{d} 1.2$_{3}$=4QS^{g} 1$_{5}$ (S^{g} ... [פוקדי]ם [מעשי]הם; + רוּחַ *spirit*) CD 5$_{16}$=4QD^{a} 3.2$_{3}$ (CD מ[ע]שיהם; 4QD^{a} [פקד אל] את מעשי[הם] *God noticed their deeds*), שׁכח *forget* Am 8$_{7}$ Ps 106$_{13}$ (or em. אֵל *forget* God; + עֵצָה *counsel*).

אמר *say* Ps 45$_{2}$, ספר pi. *recount* 1 K 13$_{11}$ Jr 51$_{10}$ Ps 107$_{22}$ 118$_{17}$ 1QM 13$_{9}$+4QM^{a} 7$_{2}$ (|| מִשְׁפָּט *judgment*) 11QPs^{a} 18$_{4}$ 28$_{7}$, נגד hi. *tell*, i.e. proclaim Is 57$_{12}$ Si 16$_{22}$ (erased מָה *what?*) perh. 11QPs^{a} 28$_{6}$ (unless עִלּוּ = עלו *they have praised* my works, i.e. עלה pi., not עָלוּ proclaim *concerning him* and [proclaim] my works), שׂכל hi. *teach (about)* Ps 64_{10} (|| פֹּעַל *deed*), שׁבח pi. *praise* Ps 145_{4} (|| גְּבוּרָה *strength*), ידה hi. *praise* Ps 145_{10} (+ חָסִיד *devotee*) 4QShirShabb^{d} 1.1_{44} ([להו]דו[ת]), ברך pi. *bless* Dt 28_{12} Jb 1_{10} 1QS 1_{19}, רצה *desire*, i.e. find acceptable Ec 9_{7}, כתב *write (down)* 4QTob^{e} 6_{1} ([כתבו]) 4QMMT C_{27}.

<CSTR> מַעֲשֵׂה י׳ *the activity of Y.* Ex 34_{10} Dt 11_{7} Jos 24_{31} Jg 2_{7} Jr 51_{10} Ps $107_{24(mss)}$ $111_{2(mss)}$ (L מַעֲשֵׂי *the deeds of* in both), מַעֲשֵׂי י׳ *the deeds of Y.* Ps 107_{24} 111_{2} (mss מַעֲשֵׂה in both) Si $11_{4(A)}$ $43_{2(B)}$, מַעֲשֵׂי יָהּ *the deeds of Yah* Ps 118_{17} (mss מַעֲשֵׂה *the activity of*), מעשה אל every *deed of God* Si 36_{15}, *the deeds of God* Si 39_{33}, מַעֲשֵׂה הָאֱלֹהִים *the activity of God* Ec 7_{13} (or em. מַעֲשֵׂי *the deeds of*) 8_{17} 11_{5} (or em. מַעֲשֵׂי), מעשי אל *the deeds of God* Si 42_{15} 1QS 4_{4} 1QH 5_{36}=4QHod^{c} 1.4_{10} ([אל]) CD 1_{1}=4QD^{c} 1_{9} (מעש[י] אל) CD 2_{14} 13_{7}=4QD^{b} 9.4_{4} ([מ]עשי אל) 4Q392 1_{7}, מעשה אדני *a deed of my Lord* 4QapMes 2.2_{10}, [מ]עשי אלוחי פדותי *the deeds of the God of my redemption* 4QShir^{b} 63.2_{1}, מעשי אדון הכול *the deeds of the Lord of all* 11QPs^{a} 28_{7}, מעשי [ע]ליון appar. *a creation of the Most High* Si $43_{2(M)}$, מעשי ימין עוצך *the deeds of the right hand of your strength* 1QH 17_{18}.

מעשי דויד *the deeds of David* CD 5_{5}, מעשי איש *the deeds of a man* 4QShir^{b} 63.3_{2}, מעשי גבר *the deeds of a man* 1QS 4_{20}, מַעֲשֵׂה אִשָּׁה *the deed(s) of a woman* Ezk 16_{30}, מעשה צדיק *the deed of a righteous person* 4QMyst^{a} 3a.2_{3}, מַעֲשֵׂה הַצַּדִּיקִים *the deed(s) of the righteous* Ec 8_{14}, מַעֲשֵׂה הָרְשָׁעִים *the deed(s) of the wicked* Ec 8_{14}, מעשי חסידיך *the deeds of your devoted ones* 11QPs^{a} 22_{6}, מעשי ישבי *the deeds of the dwellers of* 4QapPs^{b} 69_{5a}, מע[שי בני ה]אדם *the deeds of the children of humankind* 4QJub^{d} 21_{21}, מעשי רו[חות] רקיע פלא *deeds of spirits of a firmament of wonder* 4QShirShabb^{e} 19_{3} (=11QShirShabb 6_{4} מעש[י רוחו]ת רקיע פלא).

מעשי הדור *the deeds of* that *generation* 4QJub^{i} 23_{22}, מעשי דור ודור *the deeds of each generation* 4QD^{e} 2.2_{21}, מעשי כול *the deeds of all* 4QShir^{b} 52.3_{3}, מעשה כל בשר *the activity of all flesh* Si 39_{19}, מַעֲשֵׂה יִשְׂרָאֵל *the behaviour of Israel* 2 C 17_{4}, מַעֲשֵׂה אֶרֶץ־מִצְרַיִם *the behaviour of the land of Egypt* Lv 18_{3}, מַעֲשֵׂה אֶרֶץ־כְּנַעַן *the behaviour of the land of Canaan* Lv 18_{3}, מעשי ארץ *the deeds of the land (of)* 4QMyst^{b} 1a.1_{3}, מַעֲשֵׂה בֵּית־אַחְאָב every *deed of the house of Ahab* Mc 6_{16}.

מַעֲשֵׂה אֹפֶה *the product of a baker* Gn 40_{17}, מעשה לוטש *the work of a smith* Si 34_{26}, מַעֲשֵׂה אֹרֵג *the work of a weaver* Ex 28_{32}||39_{22} 39_{27} Si 45_{11} (אורג), מעשי אורג *the products of a weaver* 4QShirShabb^{e} 23.$2_{7.10}$ 11QShirShabb 9_{7} ([מ]עשי אורג]), מַעֲשֵׂה רֹקֵם *the work of an embroiderer* Ex 26_{36}||36_{37} 27_{16}||36_{18} 28_{39}||39_{29}, מַעֲשֵׂה רֹקֵחַ *the work of a perfumer* Ex 30_{25} $30_{9 35}$||37_{29} (30_{35} רוֹקֵחַ) Si 49_{1} (רוקח).

מַעֲשֵׂה חֹשֵׁב *the work of a skilled person* Ex $26_{1.31}$||$36_{8.35}$ $28_{6.15}$||$39_{3.8}$ Si 45_{10} 1QM $5_{5.14}$ 7_{11} (all three חושב) 11QT 7_{14} ([מ]עשי חוש[ב]), מַעֲשֵׂה חֲכָמִים *the work of experts* Jr 10_{9}.

מַעֲשֵׂה חָרָשׁ וִידֵי צוֹרֵף *the work of an artisan and the hands of a (gold)smith* Jr 10_{9} (or del. מַעֲשֵׂה חָרָשׁ and replace with מַעֲשֵׂה חֲכָמִים כֻּלָּם *all of them are the work of experts* from end of verse), מעשה חרש מחשבת *the work of an artisan of a thought*, i.e. a thinking one 1QM $5_{6.9.10.11}$ (מ[ח]שבת), מַעֲשֵׂה חָרַשׁ אֶבֶן פִּתּוּחֵי חֹתָם *the work of an engraver of a stone of inscribings of a signet ring* Ex 28_{11}, מַעֲשֵׂה חָרָשִׁים *the work of artisans* Ho 13_{2}.

מַעֲשֵׂה עִזִּים *the product of goats* Nm 31_{20} 11QT 50_{17}, מַעֲשֵׂה־זַיִת *the produce of the olive* Hb 3_{17} (or em. מַעֲשֵׂהוּ / מַעֲשֶׂה זַיִת *the olive* deceives *[its] produce*, i.e. fails to produce what is expected), מַעֲשֵׂה הַחֲבִתִּים *the making of flat cakes* 1 C 9_{31}, מעשי רוק[מה] *the products of embroidery* 4QShirShabb^{c} 2_{3}, מַעֲשֵׂה שְׂבָכָה *work (giving the appearance) of a trellis* 1 K 7_{17} (or del., see Nom. Cl.), מַעֲשֵׂה שַׁרְשְׁרוֹת *work (giving the appearance) of chains* 1 K 7_{17} (or del., see Nom. Cl.), מעשי גדיל *workings (giving the appearance) of a cord* 1QM $5_{5.7}$, מַעֲשֵׂה עֲבֹת *work (giving the appearance) of cords* Ex 28_{14} 28_{22}||39_{15}, מַעֲשֵׂה שׁוּשַׁן *work (giving the appearance of) a lotus* 1 K $7_{19.22}$ (שׁוֹשָׁן; or del.), מעשי אופירים *products of fine gold* 4QShirShabb^{e} 23.2_{9}.

מַעֲשֵׂה מוֹרָד *work (giving the appearance) of a slope* 1 K 7_{29} (unless מוֹרָד = *hammered*, i.e. רדד ho. ptc., and em. מַעֲשֶׂה hammered *work*), מַעֲשֵׂה־כֵן *work (giving the appearance) of a stand* 1 K 7_{31} (or del.), מַעֲשֵׂה צַעֲצֻעִים *work (giving the appearance) of images* 2 C 3_{10} (or em. מֵעֵצִים *from pieces of wood*), מעשי צורת מחשבת

the workings of the shape of a thought, i.e. the work put into a considered design 1QM 5$_{8}$, מעשי עמוד מחשבת *the workings of a column of thought*, i.e. the work put into a considered column 1QM 5$_{9}$, מַעֲשֵׂה אֵפֹד *the work of*, i.e. that went into producing, *(the) ephod* Ex 28$_{15}$||39$_{8}$ (Sam הָאֵפוֹד), מעשי רוקמות פלא *the products of acts of embroidery of wonder* 4QShir Shabb[e] 14$_{6}$, מעשי אש *the workings*, i.e. effects, *of fire* 1QH 5$_{16}$, מַעֲשֵׂה רֶשֶׁת נְחֹשֶׁת *a product (consisting) of a network of bronze* Ex 27$_{4}$||38$_{4}$.

מעשה ידים *the work of hands* 4QapJoshua[a] 15.1$_{2}$, מַעֲשֵׂה יְדֵי חָרָשׁ *the work of the hands of an artisan* Dt 27$_{15}$ Jr 10$_{3}$ (יְדֵי־), מַעֲשֵׂה יְדֵי אָמָּן *the work of an artisan's hands* Ca 7$_{2}$, מַעֲשֵׂה יְדֵי יוֹצֵר *the work of a potter's hands* Lm 4$_{2}$ (KtOr מַעֲשֵׂי *the products of*), מַעֲשֵׂה יְדֵי אָדָם *the work of human hands* Dt 4$_{28}$=11QT 59$_{3}$ (מעשי) 2 K 19$_{18}$ ||Is 37$_{19}$ (יְדֵי־אָדָם) Ps 115$_{4}$||135$_{15}$ (mss מַעֲשֵׂי *the works of* in both) 2 C 32$_{19}$ (הָאָדָם; ms מַעֲשֵׂי).

מַעֲשֵׂה יָדַי *the work of my hands* Is 19$_{25}$ 29$_{23}$ 60$_{21}$ (1QIsa[a,b] ידיו *his hands*) perh. 4QDibHam[c] 131$_{4}$, מַעֲשֵׂה יָדֵינוּ *the work of our hands* Ho 14$_{4}$ Ps 90$_{17.17}$ (lacking in mss).

מַעֲשֵׂה יָדְךָ *the work of your* [sg.] *hand* Dt 2$_{7}$ (יָדֶךָ; mss יָדֶיךָ *your hands*) 14$_{29}$ (or em. מַעֲשֶׂיךָ *your deeds*) 16$_{15}$ (mss) 24$_{19 (mss)}$ 28$_{12}$ (יָדֶךָ; mss יָדֶיךָ) 30$_{9}$ (יָדֶךָ; mss יָדֶיךָ; or em. יְדֵיכֶם *your* [pl.] *hands*) Is 64$_{7}$, מַעֲשֵׂה יָדֶיךָ *the work of your* [sg.] *hands* Dt 2$_{7 (mss)}$ 16$_{15}$ 24$_{19}$ (mss יָדְךָ *of your hand* in both) 28$_{12 (mss)}$ 30$_{9 (mss)}$ Mc 5$_{12}$ Ps 8$_{7 (mss)}$ (L מַעֲשֵׂי *works of*) 4QPs[b] 92$_{5}$ (L מַעֲשֵׂי) Ps 102$_{26}$ (mss, 4QPs[b] מַעֲשֵׂי) 138$_{8 (mss)}$ (L מַעֲשֵׂי) 143$_{5}$ (mss מַעֲשֵׂי) Jb 14$_{15}$ Ec 5$_{5}$ (mss מַעֲשֵׂי) 1QLitPr 3.2$_{7}$ 4QDibHam[a] 7$_{4}$ (מעשי ידיכה) 4QPr Fêtes[c] 97.1$_{9}$ (מ[ע]שי ידיכה), מַעֲשֵׂה יְדֵיכֶם *the work of your* [pl.] *hands* Dt 30$_{9}$ (if em. יָדְךָ *your* [sg.] *hand*; mss יָדֶיךָ *your* [sg.] *hands*) 31$_{29}$ Jr 25$_{6.7}$ (or del.) 44$_{8 (mss)}$ (L מַעֲשֵׂי *the works of*) Hg 2$_{17}$.

מַעֲשֵׂה יָדָיו *the work of his hands* 1 K 16$_{7}$ Is 2$_{8}$ 5$_{12}$ 17$_{8}$ (+ אֲשֶׁר עָשׂוּ אֶצְבְּעֹתָיו *what his fingers made*) Jb 1$_{10}$ 1QIsa[a,b] 60$_{21}$ (MT יָדַי *my hands*) Ps 19$_{2}$ (Gnz מַעֲשֵׂי *the works of*) 28$_{5}$ (mss מַעֲשֵׂי) 111$_{7 (mss)}$ (L מַעֲשֵׂי) Jb 34$_{19}$ 4Q ParGenEx 9$_{1 (WA)}$ (others יעשו his hands *move*), מַעֲשֵׂה יְדֵיהֶם *the work of their hands* 2 K 22$_{17}$ (||2 C 34$_{25}$ מַעֲשֵׂי) Is 65$_{22}$ Jr 1$_{16 (mss)}$ (L מַעֲשֵׂי *the works of*) 25$_{14}$ 32$_{30}$ (or del.) Hg 2$_{14}$ Ps 28$_{4}$ (mss מַעֲשֵׂי) 64$_{10}$ (if em. מַעֲשֵׂהוּ *his work*) Lm 3$_{64}$ GnzPs 2$_{20}$.

מַעֲשֵׂי אֶצְבְּעֹתֶיךָ *the works of your fingers* Ps 8$_{4}$ (mss מַעֲשֵׂה *work of*).

מעשה [גבורתך] *the deed of your strength* 1QH 13$_{10}$, מעשי גבורתום appar. *the deeds of his strength* 1QS 1$_{21}$, מַעֲשֵׂה תָקְפּוֹ וּגְבוּרָתוֹ perh. every *episode of*, i.e. concerning, *his might and his strength* Est 10$_{2}$, מעשי פלאך *the deeds of your wonder* 1QS 11$_{20}$=4QS[j] 1$_{8}$ (1QS פלאכה) 1QH 7$_{32}$ 11$_{4}$ (פלאכה) GnzPs 1$_{10}$, *the creations of your wonder* 1QH 10$_{11}$ (פלאכה), מעשי פלאים *deeds of wonders* 4QBer[a] 1.2$_{6}$, מעשי חדשות פל[א] *deeds of new things of wonder*, i.e. wonderful new deeds 4QShir Shabb[c] 4$_{11}$.

מעשי טוב *deeds of goodness* 1QS 1$_{5}$, מַעֲשֵׂה הַצְּדָקָה *the produce of righteousness* Is 32$_{17}$, מעשי צדקה *deeds of righteousness* 1QH 1$_{26}$ (הצדקה) 4$_{31}$, מעשה צ[דק] *a deed of righteousness* 4Q418 159.2$_{4}$, מעשה צדקי *a deed of my righteousness* Si 16$_{22}$ (erased מה צדק *what is righteousness?*), מעשי כבודו *the deeds of his glory* 4Q ShirShabb[e] 23.2$_{12}$ 4QPoet[b] 1$_{3}$ MasShirShabb 1$_{6}$, [מעש]י ק[ו]דש[ו] *the deeds of his holiness* 4QTime 1.2$_{10}$ (others [מחש]בת *the calculation of*), מעשי אמתכה *the deeds of your truth* 1QH 1$_{30}$ 1QM 13$_{9}$ 1QM 14$_{12}$=4QM[a] 8.1$_{10}$, מעשי אמתו *the deeds of his truth* 1QS 1$_{19}$ 1QM 13$_{1.2}$ 11QShirShabb 10$_{6}$ ([אמת]ו).

מעשי רמיה *deeds of deceit* 1QH 1$_{27}$ (הרמיה) fr. 3$_{10}$ 1QS 4$_{23}$ 4QBer[c] 1$_{2}$ ([מ]עשי), מ[עושי שקר *deeds of falsehood* 1QpHab 10$_{12}$, [מע]שה אף *deed of anger* 4QMyst[b] 1a.1$_{4}$, [מע]ש[י תעותם] *the deeds of their error* 4QJub[a] 1$_{11}$, [מעשי תעות לבם] *the deeds of the error of their heart* 4QJub[a] 1$_{11}$, מַעֲשֶׂה הָרָעָה *the product of evil* Ec 8$_{11}$, [מעש]י רשעה *deeds of wickedness* 4QParGenEx 1$_{12}$, מַעֲשֵׂי אָוֶן *deeds of iniquity* Is 59$_{6}$, מעשה עולה *deed of iniquity* 1QH 16$_{11}$, מעשי עול[ה] *deeds of iniquity* 1QH 2$_{3}$, מעשי נדה *deeds of impurity* 1QH fr. 3$_{16}$ ([מ]עשי) 4Q Shir[b] 18.2$_{7}$, מעשי אשמה *deeds of wickedness* 4QShir[b] 48.2$_{5}$, מעשי רשע אשמתכה *the deeds of the wickedness of your guilt* 1QS 2$_{5}$, מעשי תועבה *deeds of abomination* 1QS 4$_{10}$=4QS[c] 2$_{8}$ ([תו]עבה) 1QpHab 12$_{8}$ (תועבות), מעשי ההבל *deeds of vanity* 1QS 5$_{18}$=4QS[d] 1.1$_{10}$ ([מע]שי), מעשי אפעה *deeds of nothing* 1QH 3$_{17}$=4QHod[f] 4.1$_{6}$

(מעש]י אפעה]),מעשי פלצות *deeds of,* i.e. inspiring, *shuddering* 1QH 3_{12}, מַעֲשֵׂה תַּעְתֻּעִים *an object of mockery* Jr 10_{15}=51_{18}.

מעשי התורה *events of,* i.e. recorded in, *the law* 4Q MMT C_{27}, מעשי תורה perh. *events of (the) law* 4QMMT C_{24} (others מב[ק]שי *seekers of* or עושי *doers of*), *deeds of,* i.e. in obedience to, *(the) law* 4QMidrEschat^{a} 1_{7}, מַעֲשֵׂה עֲבֹדַת בֵּית הָאֱלֹהִים *the labour of the service of the house of God* 1 C 23_{28}, מַעֲשֵׂה הָעוֹלָה perh. *the apparatus of the burnt offering* 2 C 4_{6}.

מעשי עולם *deeds of eternity* 1QLitPr 3.2_{7} (others מעלי *ascents of;* or em. פֹּעֲלֵי *deeds of;* + יסורי כבוד *the instructions of glory*), מעשי רוח *deeds of spirit,* i.e. spirit-inspired deeds, or *beings of spirit,* or *breath,* i.e. living beings 4QShirShabb^{a} 1_{5}.

מעשי שמים וארץ *the construction(s),* or *creatures, of heaven and earth* 4QBark^{a} 1.1_{3}, מעשי חיה ובני כנף *the construction(s) of beasts and winged animals* 1QM 10_{14}, מַעֲשֵׂה הַמְּנֹרָה *the structure of the lampstand* Nm 8_{4}, מַעֲשֵׂה הַמְּכוֹנָה *the structure of the stand* 1 K 7_{28} (or em. הַמְּכֹנוֹת *the stands*), מַעֲשֵׂה הָאוֹפַנִּים *the structure of the wheels* 1 K 7_{33}, מַעֲשֵׂה אוֹפַן *the structure of the wheel of* 1 K 7_{33} (or em. אוֹפַנֵּי *the wheels of*), מעשי תבנ]יתו] *the construction(s) of its structure* 4QShir Shabb^{d} 1.1_{44}, מעשי פנו]תו] *the construction(s) of its corner(s)* 4QShirShabb^{e} 20.2_{4} (=11QShirShabb 7_{6} מ]עשי] פנותו), מעשי נוגה *substance(s) of shining* 4QShirShabb^{e} 20.2_{10}, מעשי ל[בנ]י הוד *constructions of bricks of majesty* 4QShirShabb^{e} 19_{6} (=11QShirShabb j_{6} מע]שי לבני [הוד]), מעשי לב[נ]י] *constructions of bricks of* 11QShir Shabb 4_{4}, מעשה ה[תבה] *of the construction of the ark* 4QCommGenD 1_{2}.

מעשי ... גדול *great of ... deeds of* wonders 4QBer^{a} 1.2_{6} (+ נוֹרָאָה *fearful deed,* רְפוּאָה *act of healing*), גבורות מעשיו *the mighty acts of his deeds* 4QTime 1.2_{6} 4Q417 2.1_{13}, [כב]וד מעשיו *the glory of his deeds* 11QShirShabb 10_{4}, תמהי מעשה *marvels of a deed,* i.e. marvellous deeds Si 48_{14}, תמהי מעשהו *the marvels of his creation* Si $43_{25(B)}$ (Bmg מעשיו *of his created beings*), פקודת מעשי *the noticing,* or *punishment, of a deed* 4Q416 7_{2}, כָּל־אַנְשֵׁי מַעֲשֵׂהוּ *all the people of his making,* i.e. whom he has made Jb 37_{7} (or em. אֱנוֹשׁ/אֲנָשִׁים so that every *person*/all *people* might know his deeds).

כול מחשבת מעשה *every thought of,* i.e. thinking about, *a deed* 1QS 4_{4}, כול יצר מעשה *every thought of,* i.e. thinking about, *a deed* 1QH 7_{13}, פירוש מעשיהם *the detailing of their deeds* CD 4_{6}, עבודת מעשו *the service of his deeds* 1QSa 1_{18} (erased עבודתו מעשו *his service, his deeds*), כול עבודת מעשיהם *all the service of their deeds* 4QMyst^{c} 1_{3} (WA מעשי[הם]) 4QShir^{b} 63.3_{3}, כול פעולת מעשיהם *all the enacting,* or *reward, of their deeds* 1QS $4_{16.25}$ (מעשיהן), גְּמֻל מַעֲשֵׂינוּ *the recompense of our deeds* Is 26_{12} (if em. גַּם כָּל־ *and all* our works to כִּגְמֻל *in accordance with the recompense of*), ממשלת מעשיה *the governing of its deeds* 4Q417 2.1_{9}= 4Q418 43_{7} (ממשל מ[עשיה]).

רשע מעשיו *the wickedness of his deeds* 4Q417 1.1_{8}, [רוע] מעשי *the wickedness of my deeds* 1QH 17_{19}, פשעי מעשיהם *the sins of their deeds* 1QS 3_{22}, נדת מעשי *the impurity of the deeds of* 4QDiscourse 2.2_{3} (+ מַעֲלָל *deed*), חושך מעשיכה *the darkness of your deeds* 1QS 2_{7}.

חשבון מעשה *the calculation of the construction of* 4QCommGenD 1_{2}, ימי המעשה *the days of labour* 11QT $43_{16.17}$, שֵׁשֶׁת יְמֵי הַמַּעֲשֶׂה *the six days of labour* Ezk 46_{1} (:: שַׁבָּת *sabbath,* חֹדֶשׁ *month*), יוֹם הַמַּעֲשֶׂה perh. *the day of the (previous) event* or *of labour* 1 S 20_{19} (unless מַעֲשֶׂה III *evening feast;* or em. הַמּוֹעֵד *of the festival*), בִּכּוּרֵי מַעֲשֶׂיךָ *the firstfruits of your labours* Ex 23_{16}, [מקצה דברי ה]מעשים *some of the words of,* i.e. concerning, *the events* 4QMMT B_{2}, כֹּל כְּלִי מַעֲשֶׂה *every ornament of labour,* i.e. that required labour for its production Nm 31_{51}, כלי מעשה *a tool of,* i.e. for, *work* CD 12_{18}, כֹּחַ מַעֲשָׂיו *the might of his deeds* Ps 111_{6}, פְּרִי מַעֲשֶׂיךָ *the fruit of your labours* Ps 104_{13} (unless מַעֲשֶׂה II *cloud* or IV *storehouse;* or del. פְּרִי or em. פְּרֹשׂ לְעָבֶיךָ *the spreading of your clouds* or מֵרִי אֲסָמֶיךָ/שָׁמֶיךָ *drenching* [רוה hi.] *your storehouses/heavens*), כָּל־כִּשְׁרוֹן הַמַּעֲשֶׂה *every success(ful outcome) of a deed* Ec 4_{4} (+ עָמָל *labour*), פִּתְגָם מַעֲשֵׂה *a sentence of,* i.e. on, *a deed of* evil Ec 8_{11}, מִרְקַחַת מַעֲשֶׂה *perfume of making,* i.e. a compound of perfumes 2 C 16_{14}.

רשית מעשי[כה] *the beginning of your creation(s)* 4Q PrFêtes^{c} 131.2_{7}, מקצת מעשי *some of the events of* 4Q

MMT C$_{27}$, [רו]ב מעש[י] *abundance of deeds of* 4QHod^f 4.1$_6$ (=1QH 3$_{17}$ [כול] *all* the deeds of), רוב מעשיו *the abundance of his deeds* 11QPs^a 18$_4$, רב כל מעשיך *the abundance of all your* [masc.] *deeds* GnzPs 1$_{12}$, רֹב מַעֲשַׂיִךְ *the abundance of your* [fem.] *products* Ezk 27$_{16}$ (or em. מַעֲשַׂיִךְ to מַעֲרָבֵךְ *your merchandise*) 27$_{18}$ (or del.).

כָּל־מַעֲשֶׂה *every deed* Ec 8$_9$ 12$_{14}$ 2 C 31$_{21}$ 1QS 3$_{25}$ 1QH 10$_8$ 4Q417 1.1$_6$ (all three כול) 2.1$_{10}$ (כול מ[עש]ה), כֹּל מַעֲשֶׂה *every deed of* Mc 6$_{16}$ Ec 8$_{17}$ Si 36$_{15}$ 1QH 16$_{11}$ 4QMyst^a 3a.2$_3$ 37$_2$ (all three כול), כָּל־מַעֲשֶׂה *every product of* Nm 31$_{20}$ 11QT 50$_{17}$ (כול), *all the work of* Dt 2$_7$ 14$_{29}$ (or em. כָּל־מַעֲשֶׂיךָ *all your deeds*) 16$_{15}$ 24$_{19}$ (both כֹּל) 28$_{12}$ 30$_9$ (כֹּל) 2 K 22$_{17}$ (ms lacks כֹּל) Hg 2$_{14.17}$, *all the activity of* Dt 11$_7$ Jos 24$_{31}$ Jg 2$_7$, perh. every *episode of* Est 10$_2$.

ראש כול מעשה *the beginning of every deed* Si 37$_{16}$ (|| פֹּעַל *deed*, :: דָּבָר *word* [B]/מַאֲמָר *word* [Bmg, D], מַחֲשֶׁבֶת *thought*), מזמות כול מעשה *the devisings of every deed* or *creature* 4QMyst^a 3a.2$_{10}$ (+ מַחֲשָׁבָה *thought*), חבלי כול מעשה *the pains of every deed* or *creature* 4QMyst^a 3a.2$_{15}$, יצר כל מעשה *the forming of every creation* 4Q423 5$_4$.

כָּל־הַמַּעֲשֶׂה *all the deed(s)* 1 K 13$_{11}$, *every deed* Ec 3$_{17}$, *all the event* 4QTob^e 6$_1$ ([כול]), *the whole of creation* 1QH fr. 2$_7$ (כו[ל המע]שה), כָּל־הַמַּעֲשִׂים *all the things* Nm 16$_{28}$ 1 S 8$_8$ 2 K 23$_{19}$ Jr 7$_{13}$ Ec 1$_{14}$.

כֹּל מַעֲשֵׂי *all the works of* 2 C 34$_{25}$, כול מעשי *all the deeds of* 1QS 1$_{5.19}$ 2$_5$ 4$_{4.20.23}$ 5$_{18}$=4QS^d 1.1$_{10}$ (כ[ל מע]שי) 1QH 1$_{26.30}$ 2$_3$ 3$_{12.17}$ ([כול]; =4QHod^f 4.1$_6$ ([רו]ב מעש[י] *abundance of deeds of*) 4$_{31}$ 4QJub^a 1$_{11}$ (כ[ל מע]שי) 1$_{11}$ ([כל מעשי]) 4QJub^d 21$_{21}$ (כול מע[שי]) 4Q392 1$_7$ (כל) 4QShirShabb^a 1$_5$ 4QShirShabb^e 23.2$_{12}$ 4QShir^b 18.2$_7$ 11QShirShabb 10$_6$ GnzPs 1$_{10}$ (כל), *all the creations of* 1QH 10$_{11}$, סוד רישית כול מעשי *the secret of the origins of all the deeds of* a person 4QShir^b 63.3$_2$.

כָּל־מַעֲשֵׂינוּ *all our works* Is 26$_{12}$ (or em. גַּם כָּל־ *and all* to כִּגְמֹל *in accordance with the recompense of* our deeds).

כָּל־מַעֲשֵׂךָ *all your activity* Dt 15$_{10}$ (mss מַעֲשֶׂיךָ all *your deeds*), כָּל־מַעֲשֶׂיךָ *all your* (sg.) *deeds* Dt 14$_{29}$ (if em. כָּל־מַעֲשֵׂה יָדְךָ *all the work of your hand*) 15$_{10(mss)}$ Si 7$_{36}$ 30$_{31}$ 32$_{11}$ (מ[ע]שיך) 34$_{22}$ 35$_{23}$ 1QH 4$_{20}$ 13$_{19}$ (both כול) 1Q26 1$_6$ 1QSb 2$_{27}$ 4QJub^d 21$_{15.24}$ (all four כול מעשיכה) 4QPrEnosh 2$_5$ ([כ]ול מעשי[כ]ה) 4Q418 148.1$_3$ ([כ]ול מעשיכה) 4Q423 4$_2$ (מעשיכה) 4QRitPur 5$_{16}$ (כול [מע]ש[י]כ[ה]) GnzPs 4$_{22}$, *all your created beings* Ps 145$_{10}$ 1QH 1$_6$ (מעשיכה) 1$_{33}$ 3$_{23}$ (both כול מעשיכה) 9$_{36}$ (כול מעש[י]כה) 10$_{36}$ ([כ]ול מעשיכה) 11$_{24.30}$ (both כול מעשיכה) 13$_8$ 14$_{16}$ 15$_{20}$ (all three כול מעשיך) fr. 5$_8$ ([כול מעשיכ]ה), פי כל מעשך from *the mouth(s) of all your creatures* GnzPs 2$_{22}$.

כ[ו]ל [מע]שיכם *all your* (pl.) *deeds* 4QJub^h 36$_8$.

כָּל־מַעֲשֵׂהוּ *all its construction* 2 K 16$_{10}$, *all his deeds* Is 10$_{12}$ 19$_{14}$ (or em. מַעֲשֶׂיהָ *all her deeds*) Ps 33$_4$ 2 C 32$_{30}$ Si 47$_8$ 1QH 16$_{14}$ (כול מעש[הו]), כָּל־מַעֲשָׂיו *all his deeds* Ps 145$_{17}$ Si 14$_{19}$ 1QS 10$_{17}$=4QS^f 1.4$_3$ (1QS כול; 4QS [כול מ]עש[יו]) 1QS 11$_{16}$=4QS^j 1$_3$ (1QS כול; 4QS מעש[יו]) 1QH 4$_{32}$ (כול) 4Q417 2.1$_{12}$ ([כול מ]עשיו) 4Q418 102$_2$ (כול) 11QHymn^b 2 ([כ]ול) GnzPs 4$_{10}$, כָּל־מַעֲשָׂיו *all his created beings* Ps 103$_{22}$ 145$_{9.17(Gnz)}$ Dn 9$_{14}$ Si 42$_{16(B).22(M)}$ 43$_{28}$ 4QJub^a 2$_1$ ([כל]מעשו) 2$_3$ (כל [מ]עשו) 4QShirShabb^d 1.1$_{35}$ (כול) 4Q423 7$_4$ (כ[ל מע]שיי) 4QHod^a 7.2$_{11}$ 11QPs^a 18$_7$ (both כול) GnzPs 4$_{11}$.

כָּל־מַעֲשֶׂיהָ *all her deeds* Is 19$_{14}$ (if em. מַעֲשֵׂהוּ *his deeds*) 4QD^a 1$_3$ (כול).

כָּל־מַעֲשֵׂיהֶם *all their deeds* Am 8$_7$ Ps 33$_{15}$ 1QS 5$_{19}$ 1QM 15$_9$ 1QH 1$_9$ 4$_{17}$ (all four כול; =4QHod^d 1$_5$ ([כו]ל)) 1QH 6$_9$ (כול) 4QJub^d 21$_{21}$ ([כול מעשיהם]) 21$_{23}$ ([כול מ]עשיהמה) 4QMyst^c 1$_{6(WA)}$ (כול) 4QPrayer^m 1.2$_8$ (כול מעשיהמה) 4QM^h 2$_4$ (כול מע[שיהם]), *all their constructions* 4QShirShabb^e 19$_4$ (כ[ו]ל [מעשי]הם; =11QShirShabb 6$_6$ [כול מע]שיהם) 19$_6$ perh. 11QShirShabb 9$_3$ (מעשיה[ם]), [קץ]כול מעשיהם *the end of all their deeds* 4QCreatA$_6$.

<APP> עֵץ *wood* Dt 4$_{28}$=11QT 59$_3$ 2 K 19$_{18}$||Is 37$_{19}$, אֶבֶן *stone* Dt 4$_{28}$=11QT 59$_3$ 2 K 19$_{18}$||Is 37$_{19}$ Lm 4$_2$ (if em. נֵבֶל *pitcher*) 1QM 5$_{6.8}$, נְחֹשֶׁת *bronze* 1QM 5$_6$, בַּרְזֶל *iron* 1QM 5$_{10.11}$, כֶּסֶף *silver* Jr 10$_9$ Ps 115$_4$||135$_{15}$ 1QM 5$_6$ 11QT 59$_3$, זָהָב *gold* Ex 28$_6$ 28$_{15.22}$||39$_{8.15}$ Nm 31$_{51}$ Jr 10$_9$ Ps 115$_4$||135$_{15}$ Si 45$_{10}$ 1QM 5$_6$ 11QT 59$_3$, חֲלִי *ornament* Ca 7$_2$.

תְּכֵלֶת *blue (material)* Ex 26$_{36}$||36$_{37}$ 27$_{16}$||38$_{18}$ 28$_6$ 28$_{8.15}$||39$_{5.8}$ 39$_{22}$ (כְּלִיל תְּכֵלֶת *a complete one of blue*) 39$_{29}$

Si 45_{10}, אַרְגָּמָן *purple (material)* Ex 26_{36}||36_{37} 27_{16}||38_{18} 28_{6} $28_{8.15}$||$39_{5.8}$ 39_{29} Si 45_{10}, שֵׁשׁ *fine linen* Ex 26_{36}||36_{37} 27_{16}||38_{18} 28_{6} $28_{8.15}$||$39_{5.8}$ $39_{27.29}$, תּוֹלֵעָה *scarlet (material)* Ex 26_{36}||36_{37} 27_{16}||38_{18} 28_{6} $28_{8.15}$||$39_{5.8}$ 39_{29}, קְטֹרֶת *incense* Ex 30_{35}||37_{29} Si 49_{1}, רֹקַח *perfume* Ex $30_{25.35}$, שֶׁמֶן *oil* Ex 30_{25}||37_{29}, קֶרֶן *horn* 1QM 5_{14}.

מִזְבֵּחַ *altar* Is 17_{8} (or del. מִזְבֵּחַ), מִכְבָּר *grating* Ex 27_{4}||38_{4}, שְׂבָכָה *trellis* 1 K 7_{17} (or em., see Nom. Cl.), מָסָךְ *screen* Ex 26_{36}||36_{37} 27_{16}, כּוּר *furnace* Si 34_{26} $43_{4(M)}$, כְּלִי *instrument* Si $43_{2(M)}$, נֵבֶל *pitcher* Lm 4_{2} (or em. אֶבֶן *stone*).

חֹשֶׁן *breastplate* Ex 28_{15}||39_{8}, אֵפֹד *ephod* Ex 28_{6}, אַבְנֵט *girdle* Ex 28_{39}||39_{29}, מְעִיל *robe* Ex 39_{22}, כְּתֹנֶת *tunic* Ex 39_{27}, לֹיָה *spiral* 1 K 7_{29} (or em. לִוְיָה *garland*), גְּדִיל *cord* 1 K 7_{17} (or em.; see Nom. Cl.), שַׁרְשְׁרָה *chain* Ex 28_{14} 28_{22}||39_{15}, מִגְבָּלָה *cord* Ex 28_{14}, מִקְשֶׁה perh. *plaiting* Is 3_{24} (appar. מַעֲשֶׂה מִקְשֶׁה *work [giving the appearance of] plaiting*, or del. מַעֲשֶׂה).

אֵלֶּה *these (things)* Ezk 16_{30}, כָּלִיל *whole one* Ex 39_{27}, עֲבֹדָה *service* 1QSa $1_{18(erased)}$, שָׂפָה *edge* Ex 28_{32}, צוּרָה *shape* 1QM $5_{5.14}$ 7_{11}, בֶּדֶן *shape* 1QM $5_{6.8}$, קֹדֶשׁ *holiness* Ex 37_{29}, הֶבֶל *vanity* Jr 10_{3}, מַאֲכָל *food* Gn 40_{17}, perh. פְּרִי *fruit* Dt 30_{9}, נֵצֶר *shoot* Is 60_{21}, מַטָּע *planting* 1QIsa[a,b] 60_{21}.

שָׁמַיִם *heavens* Ps 8_{4} 102_{26}, אַשּׁוּר *Assyria* Is 19_{25}, יֶלֶד *child* Is 29_{23} (or del. יֶלֶד), כְּרוּב *cherub* Ex $26_{1.31}$||$36_{8.35}$ 2 C 3_{10}, אֱלֹהִים *gods* Dt 4_{28}=11QT 59_{3} 2 C 32_{19}, פֶּסֶל *statue* Dt 27_{15}, מַסֵּכָה *image* Dt 27_{15}, תּוֹעֵבָה *abomination* Dt 27_{15}.

<ADJ> זֶה *this* Gn 44_{15} 1 K 7_{8} 4QTob[e] 6_{1}, אֵלֶּה *these* Nm 16_{28} Jr 7_{13} Ne 6_{14}, גָּדוֹל *great* Dt 11_{7} Jg 2_{7} 1QH 7_{32} ([הגדולים]) 10_{11} 1QM 10_{8} 4QJub[a] 2_{3} 4QTob[e] 6_{3} (מע[שו]; WA מע]שי] *the works of* the great one), טוֹב *good* perh. Ec 12_{14}, רַע *evil* Ec 4_{3} Ezr 9_{13} perh. Ec 12_{14}, perh. טָמֵא *impure* 4QMyst[a] $3a.2_{3}$ (וכול מעשה הצדיק הטמ[אה] perh. *and every impure deed of a righteous person*), קָדוֹשׁ *holy* 4QShir[b] 15_{6} ([הקדושי]ם]).

<PREP> לְ of direction, *to(wards)* Ps $145_{17(Gnz)}$ (י׳ ... חָסִיד לְכָל־מַעֲשָׂיו *Y. ... is loyal to all his created beings*) perh. 4QParGenEx 1_{12} ([ולמעש]י]) 4Q417 20_{3} 29.1_{6} 4Q 418 275_{1} 4QUnidA 1_{8} (למעש ה), + שׁחה htpal. *bow down* Is 2_{8} Jr 16_{1} Mc 5_{12} 4QJub[a] 1_{11} (מע]ש]י) GnzPs 2_{20}, נתן *give* heart to, i.e. examine Ec 8_{9}, אמר *say* Ho 14_{4} (but perh. לְ *of, [as a statement] concerning*), יפע hi. *cause* mighty deeds *to shine* on 4QHod[a] 7.2_{11}.

לְ of possession, *of, (belonging) to* 2 K 16_{10} (תַּבְנִיתוֹ לְכָל־מַעֲשֵׂהוּ *the design of all its construction*) 1QS 3_{14} (אותותם למעשיהם *the[ir] signs of their deeds*) 1QH 1_{9} (ומשפט לכול מעשיהם perh. *and the judgment of all their deeds*) 3_{12} (ומשברי שחת לכול מעשי פלצות perh. *and the breakers of the pit belong to*, i.e. are possessed by, *deeds of shuddering*) 13_{6} (perh. [ושמ]חת עד למעשה *and joy of eternity belongs to a creature of*) 4QShirShabb[e] 19_{6} (צורות כבוד למעשי *shapes of glory of the constructions of*; =11QShirShabb 6_{7} [צורות [כבוד] [למע]שי]).

לְ of benefit, *to, for* perh. 11QShirShabb 10_{6}, + כול pilp. *provide* 1QH 9_{36} (מעש]י[כה]), חרת *engrave* statutes 4QShirShabb[a] 1_{5}, פתח ni. *be opened* 1QH 3_{17} ([לכול] *for all* the deeds), זבח *sacrifice* children 4QJub[a] 1_{11} ([ויזבחו ... לכל מעשי]), נתן *place* sabbath as sign 4QJub[a] 2_{1} ([ויתן ... לכל [מעשו]), שמר *keep* 4QShir[b] 10_{10} ([שומר] ח[סד באמת לכול מעשיו *the one who truly maintains loyalty for all his creatures*).

לְ of purpose, *for (the purpose of)*, + יצא hi. *take out*, i.e. produce, instrument Isa 54_{16}=CD 6_{8}.

לְ *about, concerning*, + דרשׁ *seek*, i.e. investigate 1QS 6_{14} (+ שֵׂכֶל *intelligence*) 6_{17} (+ רוּחַ *spirit*), פקד *take note* CD 13_{11}=4QD[b] 9.4_{8} ([יפקדהו]), פרשׁ pi. *explain* 4Q417 2.1_{10} ([פ]רש ... מ[עש]ה).

לְ *against* 4QShir[b] 52.3_{3} (משפטים למעשי כול *judgments against the deeds of all*).

לְ *as*, + חשׁב ni. *be considered* Lm 4_{2}.

לְ כסף *yearn for* Jb 14_{15}.

בְּ of place, *in, throughout, among, during (the execution of)* Ps $145_{17(Gnz)}$ (י׳ ... חָסִיד בְּכָל־מַעֲשָׂיו *Y. ... is loyal in all his deeds*; || דֶּרֶךְ *way*) 1QS 11_{20}=4QSj 1_{8} (but perh. בְּ = what is a human being *compared with* all your wonderful creations?) 1QH 4_{20} (אין הולל בכול מעשיך *there is no folly in all your deeds*) 10_{11} (ומי בכול מעשי פלאכה *and who among all the creations of your wonder* could gather strength?) 11_{24} (ומי בכול מעשיכה *and who among all the creations of your wonder* is able to relate?) 17_{18} (וארוך אפים [במשעטיכה] ומעשי ימין

עוזך *and patience in the execution of your judgments and the deeds of the right hand of your strength*) 1QH fr. 2_{7} (but perh. בְּ = what is dust *compared with* the whole of creation?) 4Q417 1.1_{6} (כיא מה הואה יחיד בכול מעשה *for he is unique in every deed*) GnzPs 4_{22} (א]ין כחש ב[כל מעשיך *there is no deceit in any of your deeds;* || דָּבָר *word*) perh. 1Q26 1_{6} 1QLitPr 3.2_{7} 1Q40 9_{1} (במעש[]) 4Q418 $238_{2(mg)}$ 4Q423 4_{2}.

+ היה *be* Si 30_{31} (+ עֶלְיוֹן be *supreme*) 34_{22} (+ צָנוּעַ be *modest*), בוא *come* Kfar Baram inscr. (במע[ש]יו), מצא ni. *be found* GnzPs 4_{23} (|| פֹּעַל *deed*), אמן pu. *be established* 1QS 4_{4} (unless pi. *trust* in), ערב htp. *be mixed* into, i.e. share in 1QH 16_{14} ([מעש]הו; + רוּחַ *spirit*), חנן *be gracious* 1QSb 2_{27}, ארר pass. *be cursed* 1QS 2_{5}, ברך pass. *be blessed* 1QM 13_{2}, pi. *bless* Dt 2_{7} 14_{29} 15_{10} (+ מִשְׁלַח יָד *enterprise*) 16_{15} (+ תְּבוּאָה *produce*) 24_{19} 4QJubd 21_{24}.

יתר hi. *make abundant* Dt 30_{9}, ספר pi. *recount* wonderful deeds 1QH 1_{30}, זכר *remember*, i.e. be mindful of, what is to come Si 7_{36}, אור hi. *illuminate* face, i.e. smile Si 32_{11} (מ[ע]שיך ה[א]ר), צלח hi. *prosper* 2 C 32_{30} 4QJubh 36_{8} (כ[ו]ל [מע]שיכם), הלך htp. *walk* 4Q417 2.1_{12} ([בכול מ]עשיו), ישר *go straight*, i.e. behave well 4QJubd 21_{15} ([תי]שר), שמר *keep* soul, i.e. show restraint Si 35_{23} (|| דֶּרֶךְ *way*), תעה hi. *lead astray* Is 19_{14}.

בְּ of instrument, *by (means of), with, through* 1QH 5_{16} (כ[ז]הב במעשי אש *like silver [refined] through the workings*, i.e. effects, *of fire*) perh. 2QapMoses 1_{6} (עם אחד [במעש]יך *one people through your deeds*), + בחן ni. *be tested* 4QTime 1.2_{10} (במעש[י]; others [במחש]בת *by the calculation of*), חדש pi. *renew* covenant 4QPrFêtesc 97.1_{9} ([ותחדש] ... [ב]מעשי), טמא *be impure* Ps 106_{39} (|| מַעֲלָל *deed*), כבד pi. *honour* father Si 3_{8} (unless בְּ of place, *throughout;* :: מַאֲמָר *word*), נתן *give* praise Si 47_{8} (unless בְּ of place), כעס hi. *anger* Dt 31_{29} 1 K 16_{7} 2 K 22_{17}||2 C 34_{25} Jr $25_{6.7}$ (or del.) 32_{30} (or del.) 44_{8}, כסה htp. *cover oneself* Is 59_{6} (unless מַעֲשֶׂה II *hidden thing*).

בְּ of cause, *on account of* perh. 4QapPsb 93_{1}, + בין ni. *be intelligent* perh. 4QShirShabbb 20_{2} (במ[ש]י), רנן pi. *exult* Ps 92_{5} (|| פֹּעַל *deed*), פאר htp. *glorify oneself* 11QPsa 22_{6}, ברך pi. *bless* 4QShirShabbe 23.2_{12}, הלל pi. *praise* God's name 1QM 14_{12}=4QMa 8.1_{10} (... [ב]מעשי נהלל[ה]), בוא *come* Ezr 9_{13} (+ אַשְׁמָה *sin*).

בְּ of accompaniment, *with, in addition to,* + ספר pi. *recount* 1QS 1_{21}.

בְּ introducing obj., + חלל hi. *begin* 2 C 31_{21}, עשׂה *do* 2 C 31_{21}.

בְּ *concerning* 4QRitPur 5_{16} (הצדיק בכול מע[ש]י[כ]ה] *the one who is righteous concerning all your deeds*), + שׂכל hi. *teach* 1QH 11_{4} CD 13_{7}=4QDb 9.4_{4} (... ישכיל] במ[עשי]), perh. ירה hi. *teach* 1QpHab 10_{12} (unless להרותם במ[ע]שי = *to saturate*, or *impregnate, them with deeds of*).

בְּ *for (the price of)*, + סחר *trade* Ezk 27_{18} (or del. בְּרֹב מַעֲשַׂיִךְ *for the abundance of your products*).

בְּ *in charge of, over,* + משׁל *rule* 1QH 10_{8} GnzPs 4_{11}, hi. *cause to rule* Ps 8_{7}.

בְּ *upon,* + שׁען ni. *lean* 4Q418 159.2_{4}.

בְּ *in accordance with,* + שׁפט *judge* 1QSb 3_{27} (ישׁ[פוט]).

בְּ *towards, (in connection) with* 1QH 11_{30} (והמון] חסדיה בכול מעשיכה *and the abundance of your acts of loyalty towards all your created beings*), + צדק *be righteous* 1QH 1_{6}, פנה *turn* to, i.e. look at Ec 2_{11}.

בְּ *against* 1QH 10_{36} (ומשפט ב[כ]ול מעשיכה) perh. *and judgment against all your created beings*).

בין בְּ hi. *understand (about)* 1QH 12_{28} ([ומה] יבין במע[שיו] *and what does he* [human] *understand about his* [God's] *deeds?*) 5QRègle 1_{9} (במעש[]) CD 1_{1}=4QDc 1_{9} (במעש[י]) CD 2_{14} 4QDe 2.2_{21} 4Q418 158_{4}, htpol. *consider* 1QH 7_{32} 4QMMT C_{23}; שׂוח בְּ polel *consider* Ps 143_{5} (|| פֹּעַל *deed*); דבק בְּ *cling to* 1QS 1_{5}; בטח בְּ *trust (in)* Jr 48_{7} (or em. בְּמַעֲשַׂיִךְ וּבְאוֹצְרוֹתַיִךְ *in your deeds and in your treasures* to בְּמְצָדוֹתַיִךְ בְּמָעֻזַּיִךְ *in your fortresses [and] in your strongholds*); שׂמח בְּ *rejoice in* Ps 104_{31} Ec 3_{22}.

כְּ *as* Ps 86_{8} (וְאֵין כְּמַעֲשֶׂיךָ *and there is nothing like your deeds*) Si 49_{1} (שם יאשיהו כקטרת סמים המללח מעשה רוקח *the name of Josiah is like incense of spices, that has been blended, the work of a perfumer*) 4QShirShabbc 2_{3} ([כ]מעשי) 4QShirShabbe 23.2_{7} (+ רוחות רוקמה *spirits of embroidery*) 23.2_{9} (+ דמות רוח כבוד *the appearance of a spirit of glory*) 23.2_{10} (+ חֵשֶׁב perh. *conception*) 11QShirShabb 9_{7} ([כ]מעשי).

כְּ *in accordance with* Ex 28_{8}||39_{5} (... וְחֵשֶׁב אֲפֻדָּתוֹ

כְּמַעֲשֵׂהוּ *and the belt of its ephod ... is to be [made] in accordance with its production*) 1 K 7$_{33}$ (וּמַעֲשֵׂה הָאוֹפַנִּים כְּמַעֲשֵׂה *and the structure of the wheels was in accordance with the structure of*) 1QM 5$_{7}$ (כמעשי גדיל שפה *[the] edge is in accordance with the workings of a cord*) GnzPs 1$_{12}$ (מי כמעשיך *who is in accordance with your deeds?*; || פֹּעַל *deed*).

כְּ *in accordance with*, + היה *be* 1 K 7$_{8}$ (or del. היה, leaving חָצֵר *court* as subj. of nom. cl.), מזז pu. *be welded* 1QM 5$_{8}$, חרץ pu. *be cut* 1QM 5$_{9}$, יצא *go out* (of recompense) Si 16$_{14}$, הלך *go* 2 C 17$_{4}$, נגע hi. *reach* (of end or recompense) Ec 8$_{14.14}$, יכח hi. *reprove* 1QH 18$_{13}$, ידע *know* how to distinguish good and evil 4Q417 2.1$_{8}$ ([כ]מעש]יהם]), עשׂה *do* Ex 23$_{24}$ Lv 18$_{3.3}$ Dt 3$_{24}$ (|| גְּבוּרָה *strength*) 1 S 8$_{8}$ 2 K 23$_{19}$ 1QM 10$_{8}$, *make* Ex 28$_{15}$||39$_{8}$, ישׁע hi. *deliver* 1QM 11$_{4}$, זכר *remember* Ne 6$_{14}$, שׁלם pi. *recompense* Jr 25$_{14}$ (+ פֹּעַל *deed*) Ps 62$_{13}$, htp. *be recompensed* 11QPs^{a} 22$_{10}$, נתן *give* recompense Ps 19$_{4}$ (or del. תֵּן לָהֶם *give to them*; + פֹּעַל *deed*, מַעֲלָל *deed*), שׁוב hi. *repay* recompense Ps 19$_{4}$ (if del. תֵּן לָהֶם) Lm 3$_{64}$.

מִן of direction, *from*, + בוא *come* Jg 19$_{16}$ (+ שָׂדֶה *field*), שׁוב hi. *turn* (trans.) 4QapPs^{b} 69$_{5a}$, סור *depart* 4QJub^{d} 21$_{23}$ ([סורה מכול מ]עשיהמה] *depart from all their deeds*; || תּוֹעֵבָה *abomination*), hi. *remove* Jb 33$_{17}$ (if ins. מִן), פרע hi. *release* Ex 5$_{4}$, נוא hi. *restrain* 4QM^{h} 2$_{4}$ ([מע]שיהם]); ידע *rest* Jb 37$_{7}$ (if em. אַנְשֵׁי מַעֲשֵׂהוּ so that all *the people of his making* [i.e. whom he has made] might know, i.e. ידע I, to אֱנוֹשׁ מִמַּעֲשֵׂהוּ so that every *person*/*all people* might rest *from his labour*, i.e. ידע II).

מִן of comparison, *(more) than* Si 43$_{28}$ (גדול מכל מעשיו *greater than all his created beings*) 4QMyst^{a} 7$_{3}$ ([רחו]ק ... ממעש[ה] *further ... than a deed*).

מִן of cause, *on account of*, + סחר *trade* Ezk 27$_{16}$ (or em. מַעֲשַׂיִךְ *your products* to מַעֲרָבֵךְ *your merchandise*).

מִן of instrument, *by (means of), through*, + שׂבע *be satisfied* Ps 104$_{13}$ (if em. מִפְּרִי מַעֲשֶׂיךָ *for the sake of the fruit of your labours* to מִמַּעֲשֶׂיךָ *through your* [God's] *actions*).

מִן partitive, *(some) of* MasShirShabb 1$_{6}$, + ראה *see* Si 43$_{32}$.

מִן perh. *after*, + נחם pi. *comfort* Gn 5$_{29}$ (+ עִצָּבוֹן *pain*).

עַל *upon*, + שׁען ni. *lean* 1QS 5$_{18}$=4QS^{d} 1.1$_{10}$ (כו[ל מע]שי).

עַל *over* or *greater than* Si 42$_{16(B)}$ (וכבוד י׳ על כול מעשיו perh. *just as the glory of Y. is over all his created beings*) 11QPs^{a} 18$_{7}$ (ותפארתו על כול מעשיו perh. *and his glory is over all his created beings*).

עַל *towards* Ps 145$_{9}$ (וְרַחֲמָיו עַל־כָּל־מַעֲשָׂיו *and his mercy is towards all his created beings*) Dn 9$_{14}$ (כִּי־צַדִּיק י׳ אֱלֹהֵינוּ עַל־כָּל־מַעֲשָׂיו *for Y. our God is righteous towards all his created beings*); *on account of, for*, + ברך pi. *bless* 4QJub^{a} 2$_{3}$ (ונ[ברכהו] על כל [מ]עשו *and we blessed him for all his deeds*) GnzPs 4$_{10}$, ידה hi. *praise* 4QTob^{e} 6$_{3}$ (ומודים אותו על מע[שו] *and praising him for his deed[s]*).

עַל *for (the purpose of)*, + עֵת *time* Ec 3$_{17}$ (or em. שָׁם there is a time ... for every deed *there* to שָׂם *he has appointed* a time, or שֵׁם *[there is] a name* for every deed, or זְמָן *[there is a] time* for every deed, or שֹׁמֵר *[there is] one who guards against* every deed, or מִשְׁפָּט *[there is] a judgment* against every deed, or מִשֹּׁם *[there is] observation* of every deed; + חֵפֶץ *thing*).

עַל *against*, + היה *be* (of anger) 4QJub^{i} 23$_{22}$.

עַל *over, in charge of* 1 C 9$_{31}$ (וּמַתִּתְיָה ... עַל מַעֲשֵׂה הַחֲבִתִּים *and Mattithiah ... was in charge of the making of flat cakes*) 23$_{28}$ (כִּי מַעֲמָדָם ... עַל ... מַעֲשֵׂה עֲבֹדַת בֵּית הָאֱלֹהִים *for their position was ... over ... the labour of the service of the house of God*).

עַל *concerning*, + דבר pi. *speak* 2 C 32$_{19}$.

אֶל *(on)to*, + גלל *roll* Pr 16$_{3}$ (or em. גלה pi. *reveal*; + מַחֲשָׁבָה *thought*); בין אֶל *understand* Ps 28$_{5}$ (|| פְּעֻלָּה *deed*) 33$_{15}$ CD 1$_{10}$=4QD^{a} 2.1$_{14}$ ([מעש]יהם]); נבט אֶל hi. *look at* Si 36$_{15}$; שׁעה אֶל *look at* Is 17$_{8}$.

לְפִי *in accordance with*, + דרשׁ *seek*, i.e. investigate 1QS 5$_{21}$ (+ שֵׂכֶל *intelligence*), שׁאל *ask* 1QS 6$_{18}$ (+ שֵׂכֶל), כתב *write*, i.e. inscribe, name 1QS 5$_{23}$=4QS^{g} 1$_{3}$ ([לפי] ... [ולכתו]ב); =4QS^{d} 1.2$_{3}$ ni. *be inscribed*; + שֵׂכֶל).

כְּפִי *in accordance with*, + עשׂה *do*, i.e. undertake, service 1QSa 1$_{22}$.

אַחַר *after*, + קצף htp. *become angry* Si 35$_{19(B)}$ (+ דָּבָר *thing*), קפץ htp. *jump about* Si 35$_{19(E)}$ (+ דָּבָר).

תַּחַת *instead of* Is 3$_{24}$ (or del. מַעֲשֶׂה).

נֶגֶד *in front of* 1QH fr. 5$_{8}$ (מעשיכ[ה]).

לְנֶגֶד *in front of*, + ספר pi. *recount* wonderful deeds 1QH 1$_{33}$ 3$_{23}$.

לְעֵינֵי *in the sight of*, + גלה ni. *be revealed* 1QH 14$_{16}$, עשׂה *do*, i.e. perform, acts of judgment 1QH 15$_{20}$.

<COLL> [שבעה] מעשים *seven things* 4QJub^{a} 2$_{3}$, מעשיו בתורה *his deeds in*, i.e. that are consistent with, *the law* 1QS 5$_{21}$ (=4QS^{d} 1.2$_{1}$ את מעשיהם *their deeds*) 6$_{18}$ 4QS^{d} 1.2$_{3}$=4QS^{g} 1$_{3}$ (ומעשו בתור[ה]) 4QS^{d} 1.2$_{3}$=4QS^{g} 1$_{5}$ (S^{d} מעשיהם *their deeds*; S^{g} [ומעשי]הם ב[תורה]), מעשיהם בדורותם *their deeds through their generations* 1QS 3$_{14}$, כול מעשיו בכוח גבורתו *all his deeds in the might of his strength* 1QH 4$_{32}$, אשר לא ידעו שמעשיו תחת השמים *who did not know him whose works* are revealed *under the heavens* Si 16$_{15}$, נבון בוחן מעשה מעשה *an intelligent one, testing every deed* Si 34$_{26}$, תן עדות למראש מעשיך appar. *give evidence of, from of old, your deeds* Si 36$_{20}$, מַעֲשֵׂה חָרָשׁ אֶבֶן פִּתּוּחֵי חֹתָם תְּפַתַּח *you are to inscribe* the two stones *(as though you were doing) the work of an engraver of a stone of inscribings of a signet ring* Ex 28$_{11}$.

Also 1QH 13$_{3}$ 4QD^{a} 7.3$_{6}$ ([מ]עשים) 4QMyst^{a} 3a.2$_{2.16}$ 3c$_{6}$ 44$_{2}$ (מעש[י]) 4Q365a 5.1$_{7}$(WA) ([מ]עשה) 4QapPs^{b} 45$_{6}$ 4QapJerB 8$_{1.3}$ 4QpsEzek^{a} 36.2$_{2}$ 4QShirShabb^{e} 7$_{10}$ (מעש[י]) 4QShirShabb^{e} 17$_{7}$ 33$_{2}$ (מעש[י]) 61$_{1}$ 4Q415 2.1$_{2}$ 4$_{1}$ 4Q416 18$_{4}$ 4Q417 2.1$_{7.9.19}$ (מעש[ן]) 4Q418 55$_{7}$ (מעשנ[ה]) 81$_{7}$ 101.1$_{2}$ ([מ]עשיו) 148.2$_{8}$ 198$_{2}$ 216$_{1}$ (מעש[ן]) 4QPoet^{b} 1$_{1}$ 4QSap^{b} 15$_{2}$ 4QRitMar 12$_{15}$ 16$_{1}$ 4QPrQuot 26$_{2}$ ([מ]עשים) 4QPrFêtes^{c} 3.8$_{1}$ 184.1$_{4}$ 4QShir^{b} 63.2$_{5}$ 4QOrd^{b} 25$_{1}$ ([מ]עשים).

2. כְּמַעֲשֵׂה, as prep., **like (the construction of), as though it were** (difference from uses under כְּ *as*, in §1, Prep., not alw. clear), **a.** followed by noun: מַרְאָה *mirror* 1QM 5$_{4}$, לְבֵנָה *tile* Ex 24$_{10}$, שָׂפָה *edge* 1 K 7$_{26}$|| 2 C 4$_{5}$. **b.** preceded by verb: מרק pass. *be polished* 1QM 5$_{4}$. **c.** preceded by subj. of nom. cl.: שָׂפָה *edge* 1 K 7$_{26}$|| 2 C 4$_{5}$. <COLL> וְתַחַת רַגְלָיו כְּמַעֲשֵׂה לִבְנַת הַסַּפִּיר *and below his feet, it was like tile(s) of sapphire* Ex 24$_{10}$.

<SYN> §1 פֹּעַל *deed*, פְּעֻלָּה *deed*, מַעֲלָל *deed*, נִפְלָאָה *wonder*, דֶּרֶךְ *way*, עֲבֹדָה *service*, גְּבוּרָה *strength*, מַרְאֶה *appearance*, אוֹצָר *treasure*, צְדָקָה *righteousness*, אוֹת *sign*, מִשְׁפָּט *judgment*, תּוֹעֵבָה *abomination*, יֵצֶר *created being*.

<ANT> §1 דָּבָר *word*, מַאֲמָר *word*, מַחֲשָׁבָה *thought*, מַחֲשֶׁבֶת *thought*, חֶשְׁבּוֹן *thought*, דַּעַת *knowledge*, חָכְמָה *wisdom*, שַׁבָּת *sabbath*, חֹדֶשׁ *month*.*

⇒ עשׂה *do*.

*[מַעֲשֶׂה] II $_{2}$ n.m. **covering**—pl. sf. מַעֲשֵׂיהֶם, מַעֲשֶׂיךָ—**1. covering,** <PREP> בְּ of instrument, *by (means of), with*, + כסה htp. *cover oneself* Is 59$_{6}$ (unless מַעֲשֶׂה I *deed*). **2. cloud,** <CSTR> פְּרִי מַעֲשֶׂיךָ *fruit of your clouds* Ps 104$_{13}$ (unless מַעֲשֶׂה I *deed* or IV *storehouse*).

⇒ עשׂה *hide*.

*מַעֲשֶׂה III $_{1}$ n.m. **evening, evening feast,** <CSTR> יוֹם הַמַּעֲשֶׂה *day of the evening feast* 1 S 20$_{19}$ (unless מַעֲשֶׂה I *deed*).

*[מַעֲשֶׂה] IV $_{1}$ n.m. **storehouse**—pl. sf. מַעֲשֶׂיךָ—<CSTR> פְּרִי מַעֲשֶׂיךָ *supplies of your storehouses* Ps 104$_{13}$ (unless מַעֲשֶׂה I *deed* or II *cloud*).

⇒ עשׂה *gather*.

מַעֲשַׂי $_{1}$ pr.n.m. **Maasai,** priest who returned from exile, son of Adiel, perh. ident. with Amashsai (עֲמַשְׁסַי [or em. עֲמָשַׁי/עֲמָסַי *Amasai*]) at Ne 11$_{13}$. <NOM CL> וּמִן־הַכֹּהֲנִים ... מַעְשַׂי *and from among the priests were ... Maasai* 1 C 9$_{12}$. <APP> בֶּן *son* 1 C 9$_{12}$.

⇒ עשׂה *do*.

מַעֲשֵׂיָה $_{17.0.0.2}$ pr.n.m. **Maaseiah, 1.** father of the Zephaniah who was a priest during the reign of Zedekiah, <CSTR> בֶּן־מַעֲשֵׂיָה Zephaniah *son of Maaseiah* Jr 21$_{1}$ 29$_{25}$ 37$_{3}$.

2. father of Jezaniah and/or Azariah, colleague(s) of Johanan son of Kareah, <CSTR> בֶּן־מַעֲשֵׂיָה *son of Maaseiah* Jr 42$_{1}$ 43$_{2}$ (if em. הוֹשַׁעְיָה *Hoshaiah* in both).

3. father of the Zedekiah who prophesied falsely during the reign of Zedekiah, <CSTR> בֶּן־מַעֲשֵׂיָה Zedekiah *son of Maaseiah* Jr 29$_{21}$ (or del.).

4. priest, of family of Jeshua son of Jozadak, married to foreign woman, <NOM CL> מִבְּנֵי יֵשׁוּעַ ... מַעֲשֵׂיָה *from* *among the descendants of Jeshua ... were Maaseiah* Ezr 10_{18}.

5. priest, of family of Harim, married to foreign woman, <NOM CL> וּמִבְּנֵי חָרִם מַעֲשֵׂיָה *and from among the descendants of Harim were Maaseiah* Ezr 10_{21}.

6. priest, of family of Pashhur, married to foreign woman, <NOM CL> וּמִבְּנֵי פַּשְׁחוּר ... מַעֲשֵׂיָה *and from among the descendants of Pashhur were ... Maaseiah* Ezr 10_{22}.

7. Israelite, of family of Pahath-moab, married to foreign woman, <NOM CL> וּמִבְּנֵי פַּחַת מוֹאָב ... מַעֲשֵׂיָה *and from among the descendants of Pahath-moab were ... Maaseiah* Ezr 10_{30}.

8. son of Ananiah and father of the Azariah who helped to repair the walls of Jerusalem, <CSTR> בֶּן־מַעֲשֵׂיָה *son of Maaseiah* Ne 3_{23}. <APP> בֵּן *son* Ne 3_{23}.

9. Judaean leader present at Ezra's reading of the law, <SUBJ> עמד *stand* Ne 8_4.

10. one of the interpreters at Ezra's reading of the law, Levite (if del. וְ *and* the Levites; or del. וְהַלְוִיִּם *and the Levites* and/or Maaseiah), <SUBJ> בין hi. *explain* Ne $8_{7.7}$, קרא *read*, שׂים *place*, i.e. apply, intelligence Ne 8_7. <APP> לֵוִי *Levite* Ne 8_7 (if em.).

11. family head, co-signatory with Nehemiah, <NOM CL> רָאשֵׁי הָעָם ... מַעֲשֵׂיָה *the heads of the people were ... Maaseiah* Ne 10_{26}.

12. Judahite leader of postexilic community, son of Baruch, <NOM CL> מִבְּנֵי יְהוּדָה ... מַעֲשֵׂיָה *from among the descendants of Judah were ... Maaseiah* Ne 11_5. <APP> בֵּן *son* Ne 11_5.

13. Benjaminite ancestor of leader of postexilic community, son of Ithiel and father of Kolaiah, <CSTR> בֶּן־מַעֲשֵׂיָה *son of Maaseiah* Ne 11_7. <APP> בֵּן *son* Ne 11_7.

14. trumpet-blowing priest at rededication of walls of Jerusalem, <NOM CL> וְהַכֹּהֲנִים ... מַעֲשֵׂיָה *and the priests were ... Maaseiah* Ne 12_{41}.

15. another priest at rededication of walls of Jerusalem, <NOM CL> וְהַכֹּהֲנִים ... מַעֲשֵׂיָה *and the priests were ... Maaseiah* Ne 12_{41}.

16. son of Malchijah and father of Michael, ancestor of Asaph the musician (L בַּעֲשֵׂיָה *Baaseiah*), <CSTR> בֶּן־מַעֲשֵׂיָה *son of Maaseiah* 1 C $6_{25(mss)}$. <APP> בֵּן *son* 1 C $6_{25(mss)}$.

17. father of Eliakim, <CSTR> בן מעשיה *son of Maaseiah* Seal 242 (6th cent.; others מעשיו *Maaseio*).

18. appar. father of Ishmael, <PREP> לְ of possession, *of, (belonging) to* Seal 427 (7th cent.).

19. father of Elishama, <CSTR> בן מעשיהו *son of Maaseiah* Bulla 930 (7th/6th cent.).

⇒ עשׂה *do* + יה *Y*.

מַעֲשֵׂיָהוּ 7.0.0.7 pr.n.m. **Maaseiah, 1.** keeper of the threshold during the reign of Zedekiah and son of Shallum, <SUBJ> שׁמר *keep*, i.e. protect, *threshold* Jr 35_4. <CSTR> לִשְׁכַּת מַעֲשֵׂיָהוּ *chamber of Maaseiah* Jr 35_4. <APP> בֵּן *son* Jr 35_4.

2. Levitical musician at time of David, <NOM CL> וְעִמָּהֶם ... מַעֲשֵׂיָהוּ *and with them were ... Maaseiah* 1 C 15_{18}, וּמַעֲשֵׂיָהוּ ... בִּנְבָלִים *and Maaseiah ... was on harps* 1 C 15_{20}. <APP> אָח *brother* 1 C 15_{18}, perh. שֹׁעֵר *gatekeeper* 1 C 15_{18} (or del. שֹׁעֵר).

3. one of the officers who entered a covenant with Jehoiada; son of Adaiah (or em. עִדּוֹ *Iddo* and/or em. Maaseiah to שְׁמַעְיָה *Shemaiah*). <SUBJ> בוא *come* to Jerusalem 2 C 23_1, סבב go *around* Judah 2 C 23_1, קבץ *gather* Levites and community heads 2 C 23_1. <OBJ> לקח *take* 2 C 23_1. <APP> שַׂר *prince* 2 C 23_1, בֵּן *son* 2 C 23_1.

4. administrative officer of Uzziah, <APP> שֹׁטֵר *officer* 2 C 26_{11}. <PREP> בְּיַד *by (the hand of)* 2 C 26_{11} (+ בְּמִסְפַּר פְּקֻדָּתָם *in accordance with the number of their mustering* by Maaseiah).

5. appar. son of Ahaz killed by Zichri, <OBJ> הרג *kill* 2 C 28_7. <APP> בֵּן the king's *son* 2 C 28_7.

6. governor of Jerusalem sent by Josiah to deliver money for repair of the temple, <SUBJ> בוא *come* to Hilkiah 2 C 34_8, נתן *give* money 2 C 34_8 (or em. נתך hi. *pour*), חזק pi. *strengthen* temple 2 C 34_8. <OBJ> שׁלח *send* 2 C 34_8. <APP> שַׂר *prince* 2 C 34_8.

7. appar. son of Jahmaliah, Seal 51 (Palestine, 7th cent.).

8. appar. father of Meshullam, <PREP> לְ of possession, *of, (belonging) to* Seal 55 (T. el-Judeideh).

9. appar. father of Isaiah (ישעיה[ו]), <PREP> לְ of possession, *of, (belonging) to* Seal 294 (Hebron, 8th cent.).

10. appar. son of Miamun, <PREP> לְ of possession, *of, (belonging) to* Seal 587 (למע[שיהו]; T. Beit Mirsim?; 7th/6th cent.).

11. appar. son of Ashiah, <PREP> לְ of possession, *of, (belonging) to* Seal 605 (למעשי[הו]; T. Beit Mirsim?; 7th/6th cent.).

12. appar. son of Hilkiah, <PREP> לְ of possession, *of, (belonging) to* Seal 607 (למעשי[הו]; T. Beit Mirsim?; 7th/6th cent.).

13. father of Jaazaniah (יאזנה[ו]), <CSTR> [ב]ן מעשיהו *son of Maaseiah* Seal 848 (City of David; 7th/6th cent.).

14. son of (perh.) Huzphith (חצפ[ית]), <APP> בֵּן *son* Bulla D60. <PREP> לְ of possession, *of, (belonging) to* Bulla D60.

⇒ עשׂה *do* + ׳י *Y.*

[מַעֲשֵׂיו] pr.n.m. **Maaseio,** father of Eliakim, <CSTR> בן מעשיו *son of Maaseio* Seal 242 (6th cent.; others מעשיה *Maaseiah*).

⇒ עשׂה *do* + ׳י *Y.*

מַעֲשֵׂר 32.1.10 n.m. **tenth, tithe**—Q מעסר; cstr. מַעְשַׂר; sf. Si מעשרך, מַעְשְׂרוֹ; pl. מַעַשְׂרוֹת; sf. מַעְשְׂרֹתֵיכֶם—**1. tenth,** as a fraction in measurements (e.g. Ezk $45_{11.14}$); not always clearly differentiated from (2).

2. tithe, a tax for religious purposes, not necessarily of an exact tenth.*

<SUBJ> היה *be* Lv 27_{31} (+ קֹדֶשׁ לְ׳ *holiness of,* i.e. consecrated to, *Y.*; || עֲשִׂירִי *a tenth,* + כֹּל אֲשֶׁר־יַעֲבֹר תַּחַת הַשָּׁבֶט *everything that passes under the staff*) perh. Ml 3_{10} (וִיהִי טֶרֶף *and let it* [tithe] *be food* in my house, unless וִיהִי = *and let there be*), פגל pu. *be defiled* 3QTr 1_{10} (מפוגל; others מפי גל *at the mouth of the rock*), יצא *go out* to battle 11QT 58_{5} (+ חֲמִישִׁית *a fifth*).

<NOM CL> ומעשר האיפה [העשרון] *and the tithe of the ephah is the tenth* 4QOrd^{b} 2.1_{5}, מַעְשַׂר הָאָרֶץ ... לַי׳ every *tenth of the (produce of) the land ... belongs to Y.* Lv 27_{30} (+ קֹדֶשׁ *holiness*), וללויים מעשר הדגן ... ומעשר מן הדבש *and to the Levites belongs a tithe of the grain ... and a tithe of the honey* 11QT 60_{6}, מעשר הבקר והצון לכוהנים הוא *the tithe of the cattle and the sheep belongs to the priests* 4QMMT B_{63}, בתל ... מעסר *on the hill is ... a tithe* 3QTr 1_{10}, מעשרה בה *its tithe is with it,* i.e. it is subject to the tithe 4QD^{e} 3.2_{17} (if em. מעסדה), וְחֹק הַשֶּׁמֶן ... מַעְשַׂר הַבַּת מִן־הַכֹּר *and the rule for oil ... is (that there should be) a tenth of a bath from (each) cor* Ezk 45_{14} (or del. מִן־הַכֹּר).

<OBJ> בוא hi. *bring* Dt 12_{6} (|| עֹלָה *burnt offering,* זֶבַח *sacrifice,* תְּרוּמָה *contribution,* נֶדֶר *vowed offering,* נְדָבָה *voluntary offering,* בְּכוֹר *firstborn;* or del. מַעְשֵׂר and/or תְּרוּמָה, זֶבַח and נֶדֶר) 12_{11} (|| מִבְחַר *choice,* עֹלָה, זֶבַח, תְּרוּמָה, + נֶדֶר) Am 4_{4} (|| זֶבַח) Ml 3_{10} Ne 10_{38} (|| פְּרִי *fruit,* רֵאשִׁית *first[fruits],* תְּרוּמָה) 13_{12} 1 C 31_{5} (+ רֵאשִׁית, תְּבוּאָה *produce*) $31_{6.6.12}$ (|| קֹדֶשׁ *holiness* [or del.], תְּרוּמָה), יצא hi. *take out* Dt 14_{28}, עלה hi. *take up* to temple Ne 10_{39}.

נתן *give* to king Gn 14_{20} 11QT 58_{13}, to Levites Nm $18_{21.24}$ (both + לְנַחֲלָה *as an inheritance*) 18_{26} (+ בְּנַחֲלַתְכֶם *as your inheritance* [Sam בְּנַחֲלֹתֵיכֶם *as your inheritances*), to Levite, orphan, sojourner, and widow Dt 26_{12}, *place* Ne 13_{5} (|| תְּרוּמָה *contribution,* + כְּלִי *sacred vessel,* מִנְחָה *cereal offering,* לְבוֹנָה *frankincense*) 2 C 31_{6} (+ עֲרֵמוֹת עֲרֵמוֹת place *in separate heaps*), נוח hi. *place* Dt 14_{28}, לקח *take* Nm $18_{26.28}$, שׁלח *send* 11QT 58_{5} Arad ost. 5_{10} (י[שלח] לך את המע[שר] *who sends you the tithe;* others המע[רב] *the merchandise*), רום hi. *raise,* i.e. contribute Nm $18_{24.26}$, נשׂא *raise,* i.e. have same weight as Ezk 45_{11} (לָשֵׂאת מַעְשַׂר הַחֹמֶר הַבָּת *so that a tenth of a homer has the same weight as a bath;* || עֲשִׂירִי *a tenth*), קדשׁ hi. *consecrate* Si 32_{11} (mg מַעֲשֶׂה *deed*), גאל *redeem,* i.e. give payment instead of tithed produce Lv 27_{31} (if del. partitive מִן redeem *some of* tithe; + חֲמִישִׁית *a fifth*), אכל *eat* Dt 12_{17} (|| תְּרוּמָה *contribution,* נֶדֶר *vowed offering,* בְּכוֹר *firstborn*) 12_{17} 14_{23} (|| בְּכוֹר, + עַשֵּׂר תְּעַשֵּׂר *you must tithe*) 26_{12}, עשׂר pi. *tithe* Dt 26_{12} (or em. hi. *tithe*).

<CSTR> מַעְשַׂר בְּנֵי־יִשְׂרָאֵל *the tithe(s) of the children of Israel* Nm 18_{24}, מעשר העם *a tenth of the people* 11QT 58_{5}, מַעְשַׂר בָּקָר וָצֹאן every *tithe of cattle and sheep* Lv 27_{32} 2 C 31_{6}, מעשר הבקר והצון *the tithe of the cattle and the sheep* 4QMMT B_{63}, מעשר בה[מתם]

the tithe of their beasts 4QD^{e} 2.2$_{7}$ (WA [בןקר] *of cattle*; || פְּדוּי *redemption*).

מַעְשַׂר הָאָרֶץ every *tenth of the (produce of) the land* Lv 27$_{30}$, מַעְשַׂר דְּגָנְךָ וְתִירֹשְׁךָ וְיִצְהָרֶךָ *the tithe of your grain, your new wine, and your new oil* Dt 12$_{17(mss)}$ (L וְתִירֹשְׁךָ *and your new wine*) 14$_{23}$ (Sam mss דְּגָנֶיךָ *your grains*), מַעְשַׂר הַדָּגָן הַתִּירוֹשׁ וְהַיִּצְהָר *the tithe of the grain, the new wine, and the new oil* Ne 13$_{5.12}$ 11QT 60$_{6}$ (both וְהַתִּירוֹשׁ *and of the new wine*), מַעְשַׂר תְּבוּאָתְךָ every *tithe of your produce* Dt 14$_{28}$ 26$_{12}$, מַעְשַׂר קָדָשִׁים *a tithe of holinesses*, i.e. of things consecrated to Y. 2 C 31$_{6}$ (or ins. כָּל־תְּבוּאַת שָׂדֶה a tithe of *all the produce of the field*).

מַעְשַׂר הַחֹמֶר *a tenth of a homer* Ezk 45$_{11}$, מַעְשַׂר הַבַּת *a tenth of a bath* Ezk 45$_{14}$, מעשר האיפה *a tenth of an ephah* 4QOrd^{b} 2.1$_{5}$, מַעֲשֵׂר מִן הַמַּעֲשֵׂר *a tenth of the tithe* Ne 10$_{39}$.

שְׁנַת הַמַּעֲשֵׂר *the year of the tithe* Dt 26$_{12}$ (or em. שֵׁנִית הַמַּעֲשֵׂר *the second [of the] tithe*), כָּל־מַעְשַׂר *every tithe* Nm 18$_{21}$, כָּל־הַמַּעֲשֵׂר *all the tithe(s)* Ml 3$_{10}$, כָּל־מַעְשַׂר *every tenth of* Lv 27$_{30.32}$, *tithe of* Dt 14$_{28}$ 26$_{12}$, כֹּל מַעְשְׂרֹתֵיכֶם *all your tithes* Nm 18$_{28}$.

<APP> תְּרוּמָה *contribution* Nm 18$_{26}$, מִצְוָה *commandment* of, i.e. that commanded for, the Levites Ne 13$_{5}$ (or em. מְנָת *portion*), כֹּל *everything* commanded Dt 12$_{11}$.

<ADJ> שֵׁנִי *second* 3QTr 1$_{10}$.

<PREP> לְ of purpose, *for (the purpose of)* Ne 12$_{44}$ (+ נִשְׁכָּה *chamber* for; || רֵאשִׁית *first(fruits)*, תְּרוּמָה *contribution*) 11QT 37$_{10}$ (|| זֶבַח *sacrifice*, בִּכּוּר *firstfruits*).

בְּ partitive, *(some) of, (any) of*, or *in connection with*, + קבע *rob* Ml 3$_{8}$ (|| תְּרוּמָה *contribution*).

מִן partitive, *(some) of, (any) of* Nm 18$_{26}$ (מַעֲשֵׂר מִן־הַמַּעֲשֵׂר *a tenth of the tithe*; cf. Cstr.), + גאל *redeem*, i.e. give payment instead of tithed produce Lv 27$_{31}$ (or del. מִן, leaving מַעֲשֵׂר as obj. of גאל), רום hi. *raise*, i.e. contribute Nm 18$_{26.28}$.

עַל *over, in charge of* 2 C 31$_{12}$.

<COLL> מַעֲשֵׂר מִכֹּל *a tenth of everything*, appar. in ref. to booty Gn 14$_{20}$, מַעְשַׂר הַכֹּל לָרֹב *the tithe of everything, in abundance* 2 C 31$_{5}$, מעשר מן הדבש *a tenth of the honey* 11QT 60$_{9}$, מַעֲשֵׂר מִן־הַמַּעֲשֵׂר *a tenth of the tithe* Nm 18$_{26}$, מַעְשַׂר הַבַּת מִן־הַכֹּר *a tenth of a bath from (each) cor* Ezk 45$_{14}$ (or del. מִן־הַכֹּר).

כָּל־מַעֲשַׂר בְּיִשְׂרָאֵל *all the tithes in Israel* Nm 18$_{21}$, וְכָל־מַעְשַׂר בָּקָר וָצֹאן ... הָעֲשִׂירִי יִהְיֶה־קֹּדֶשׁ לַי׳ *and as for every tithe of cattle and sheep ..., the tenth (part) will be holiness of*, i.e. consecrated to, *Y.* Lv 27$_{32}$.

Also 4QBer^{a} 17$_{1}$.

<SYN> עֲשִׂירִי *tenth*, רֵאשִׁית *first(fruits)*, מִבְחָר *choice*, תְּרוּמָה *contribution*, קֹדֶשׁ *holiness*, עֹלָה *burnt offering*, זֶבַח *sacrifice*, נֶדֶר *vowed offering*, נְדָבָה *voluntary offering*, בְּכוֹר *firstborn*, בִּכּוּר *firstfruit*, פְּדוּי *redemption*, פְּרִי *fruit*.*

⇒ עֶשֶׂר *ten*.

[מַעֲשַׁקָּה] 2 n.f. **extortion**—pl. מַעֲשַׁקּוֹת—<CSTR> בֶּצַע מַעֲשַׁקּוֹת *gain of*, i.e. from, *extortion(s)* Is 33$_{15}$ (+ שֹׁחַד *bribe*), רַב מַעֲשַׁקּוֹת *(one who is) great of extortion(s)*, i.e. who extorts greatly Pr 28$_{16}$ (or em. רַב to יֶרֶב *multiplies* extortion; + בֶּצַע *extortion*).

⇒ עשק *oppress*.

מֹף 1.0.2 pl.n. **Memphis,** Egyptian capital city, 20 km S of Cairo, ident. with נֹף at Is 19$_{13}$ Jr 2$_{16}$ 44$_{1}$ 46$_{14.19}$ Ezk 30$_{13.16}$, <SUBJ> קבר pi. *bury* Ho 9$_{6}$. <PREP> בְּ of place, *in*, + הרג *kill* 4QpsEzek^{b} 1.2$_{6}$; מִן of direction, *from*, + יצא hi. *bring out* 4QpsEzek^{b} 1.2$_{6}$.

***[מִפְאָר]** 0.0.1 n.m. **beauty, glory**—<NOM CL> ואדם מפאר עליון *but humankind is the glory of the Most High* 11QPs^{a} 154,(10)17-18.

⇒ cf. תִּפְאֶרֶת *beauty*.

מְפִבֹשֶׁת, see מְפִיבֹשֶׁת *Mephibosheth*.

מִפְגָּע 1 n.[m.] **target** for archery, <PREP> לְ introducing object, + שׂים *place*, i.e. make into Jb 7$_{20}$; בְּ of place, *at* Jb 36$_{32}$ (if em. בְּמַפְגִּיעַ perh. *the assailant* [פגע hi. ptc.] to בַּמִּפְגָּע *[to strike] at the target*).*

⇒ מגע *meet*.

[מַפָּח] 1.1 n.m. **expiring**—cstr. מַפַּח—**1. breathing out** of life, i.e. expiring in death (Jb 11$_{20}$, unless §2). **2.**

breathing out of the life, i.e. **heartache, disappointment** (Si 30$_{12}$). <SUBJ> ילד pass. *be born* Si 30$_{12}$ (Bmg), ni. *be born,* i.e. caused Si 30$_{12}$(B). <NOM CL> תִּקְוָתָם מַפַּח־נָפֶשׁ *their hope is (for) the expiring of the soul,* or, *their hope is (nothing but) disappointment* Jb 11$_{20}$. <CSTR> מַפַּח־נָפֶשׁ *expiring of the soul* Jb 11$_{20}$ Si 30$_{20}$.*

⇒ נפח *breathe.*

מַפֻּחַ 1 n.m. **bellows,** <SUBJ> חרר ni. *be set aglow* Jr 6$_{29}$ (or em. מַפֻּחִים אֵשׁ תַּם *the bellows* snort and blow, *the fire is made ready*).* <NOM CL> מַפֻּחַ לְגֶחָלִים *bellows are for (live) coals* Pr 26$_{21}$ (if em. פֶּחָם *charcoal*).*

⇒ נפח *breathe.*

מְפִיבֹשֶׁת 15.0.2 pr.n.m. **Mephibosheth**—מְפִי־בֹשֶׁת, מְפִבֹשֶׁת—**1.** son of Saul and Rizpah, <OBJ> ילד *bear* 2 S 21$_{8}$, לקח *take* 2 S 21$_{8}$, נתן *give* 2 S 21$_{8}$, יקע hi. *expose* 2 S 21$_{8}$. <APP> בֵּן *son* 2 S 21$_{8}$.

2. son of Jonathan, ident. with מְרִיב בַּעַל *Merib-baal* at 1 C 8$_{34.34}$ 9$_{40}$. <SUBJ> אמר *say* 2 S 9$_{6}$ 19$_{26.31}$, ירא *fear* 2 S 9$_{6}$, אכל *eat* 2 S 9$_{6.10.11.13}$, הלך *go* 2 S 19$_{26}$, בוא *come* 2 S 9$_{6}$, ירד *go down* 2 S 19$_{25}$, קרא *meet* 2 S 19$_{25}$, נפל *fall* 2 S 9$_{6}$, שׁחה htpol. *bow down* 2 S 9$_{6}$, ישׁב *dwell* 2 S 9$_{13}$, עשׂה *do,* i.e. prepare 2 S 19$_{25}$, כבס pi. *wash* 2 S 19$_{25}$. <NOM CL> שְׁמוֹ מְפִיבֹשֶׁת *his name was Mephibosheth* 2 S 4$_{4}$. <OBJ> רמה pi. *deceive* 2 S 19$_{26}$. <CSTR> נַעַר מְפִי־בֹשֶׁת *servant of Mephibosheth* 2 S 16$_{1}$. <APP> בֵּן *son* 2 S 9$_{6.10}$ 19$_{25}$ 21$_{7}$. <PREP> לְ of direction, *to,* + אמר *say* 2 S 9$_{6}$ 19$_{25}$, שׁוב hi. *restore* 2 S 9$_{6}$; of possession, *of, (belonging) to* 2 S 9$_{12.12}$ 16$_{4}$; עַל introducing object, + חמל *spare* 2 S 21$_{7}$; עִם *with,* + הלך *go* 2 S 19$_{26}$, עשׂה *do* 2 S 9$_{6}$. <COLL> מְפִיבֹשֶׁת as vocative, 2 S 9$_{6}$ 19$_{26}$.

3. appar. error for אישׁ בשׁת *Ish-bosheth,* <CSTR> ראשׁ מפיבשׁת *head of Mephibosheth* 2 S 4$_{14}$(4QSam[a]) (MT אִישׁ־בֹּשֶׁת *Ish-bosheth*).

4. name in writing exercise, 4QNames$_{5}$.

מֻפִּים I 1 pr.n.m. **Muppim,** son of Benjamin, perh. ident. with שְׁפוּפָם *Shephupham* at Nm 26$_{39}$ (mss, Sam שׁוּפָם *Shupham*), and שֻׁפִּים *Shuppim* at 1 C 7$_{12}$, <NOM CL> בְּנֵי בִנְיָמִן ... מֻפִּים *the sons of Benjamin were ... Muppim* Gn 46$_{21}$ (unless מֻפִּים II *defects*).

***מֻפִּים** II 1 n.[m.]pl. **defects** in the scribe's archetype, a gloss by the scribe of a manuscript, Gn 46$_{21}$ (unless מֻפִּים I *Muppim*).

מֵפִיץ I 1 n.[m.] **scatterer, disperser** (unless מֵפִיץ II *club*), <NOM CL> אִישׁ ... מֵפִיץ *a man* who bears false witness ... *is a scatterer* Pr 25$_{18}$ (or em. מַפֵּץ *hammer;* ‖ חֶרֶב *sword,* חֵץ *arrow*).

<SYN> חֶרֶב *sword,* חֵץ *arrow.*

⇒ פוץ *be scattered.*

***מֵפִיץ** II 1 n.[m.] **club,** or perh. **hammer,** as weapon (unless מֵפִיץ I *scatterer*), <NOM CL> אִישׁ ... מֵפִיץ *a man* who bears false witness ... *is a club* Pr 25$_{18}$ (or em. מַפֵּץ *hammer;* ‖ חֶרֶב *sword,* חֵץ *arrow*).

<SYN> חֶרֶב *sword,* חֵץ *arrow.*

⇒ פוץ *be scattered;* cf. מַפֵּץ *hammer.*

[מַפָּל] 2 n.m. **refuse; fold (of flesh)**—cstr. מַפַּל; pl. cstr. מַפְּלֵי—**1. refuse,** what is discarded, <OBJ> שׁבר hi. *sell* Am 8$_{6}$ (or del.). <CSTR> מַפַּל בַּר *refuse of the wheat* Am 8$_{6}$ (or del.).

2. fold of Leviathan's flesh, <SUBJ> דבק *cling together* Jb 41$_{15}$. <CSTR> מַפְּלֵי בְשָׂרוֹ *the folds of his flesh* Jb 41$_{15}$.

⇒ נפל *fall.*

[מִפְלָאָה] 1 n.f. **wondrous work**—pl. cstr. מִפְלְאוֹת—<CSTR> מִפְלְאוֹת תְּמִים דֵּעִים *the wondrous works of the one perfect of knowledge* Jb 37$_{16}$ (or em. נִפְלְאוֹת *wondrous works of*). <APP> מִפְלָשׂ *poising* of clouds Jb 37$_{17}$. <PREP> עַל *about, concerning,* + ידע *know* Jb 37$_{16}$.

⇒ פלא *be wonderful.*

***[מִפְלָג]** 0.0.9 n.[m.] **division, channel**—cstr. Q מפלג; sf. Q מפלגו; pl. sf. Q מפלגיו, Q מפלגיה, Q מפלגיהם, Q מפלגיהן—**1. division, class** of followers of good and evil spirits (1QH 12$_{23}$ [[למפלגן יהם]] 1QS 4$_{15.16}$), perh. of angels (4QShirShabb[f] 23.17), of features of the earth (1QM 10$_{12}$), <CSTR> מפלג כבודו *division of his glory*

4QPrQuot 1.3$_7$; חוקי מפלגיה *boundaries of its divisions* 1QM 10$_{12}$ (unless §3), כול מפלג *every division of* 4QPrQuot 1.3$_7$, כול מפלגו *every division of his* 4QPrQuot 15.6$_{11}$, כול מפלגיו *all his divisions* 4QShirShabb^f 23.1$_7$. <PREP> לְ *according to, in,* + שׁרת pi. *serve* 1QH 12$_{23}$ (למפלג[יהם]); בְּ of place, *(with)in* 1QS 4$_{16}$ 4QPrQuot 1.3$_7$; partitive, *(some) of,* + נחל *inherit* 1QS 4$_{15}$; מִן of direction, *from* 4QShirShabb^f 23.1$_7$.

2. channel (of water), <PREP> עִם *with* 1QH 8$_{21}$ (פפחתה מקורם עם מפלגי[הם] *you have opened their spring with their channels*).

3. separation,* <CSTR> חוקי מפלגיה *boundaries of its separations* 1QM 10$_{12}$ (unless §1).

4. course of wood between stone in a wall, <OBJ> תמם hi. *destroy* 1QH 3$_{30}$ (להתם כול עץ לח ויבש מפלגיהם *to destroy all timber, (both) fresh and dry, their courses,* i.e. the courses of wood between those of stone).

Also 5QRègle 27$_5$ ([מ]פלגיכה).

⇨ פלג *divide.*

[מִפְלַגָּה] 1.0.1 n.f. **division**—pl. מִפְלַגּוֹת; sf. Q מפלגותם—of lay family groups (2 C 35$_{12}$), followers of good and evil spirits (1QS 4$_{17}$), <PREP> לְ *according to,* + נתן *give* 2 C 35$_{12}$; בֵּין *between,* + נתן *give,* i.e. place, enmity 1QS 4$_{17}$. <COLL> מִפְלַגּוֹת לְבֵית־אָבוֹת לִבְנֵי הָעָם *divisions of the fathers' houses of the sons of the people* 2 C 35$_{12}$.*

⇨ פלג *divide.*

מַפָּלָה 3 n.f. **ruin**—מַפָּלָה—**ruin(s),** <SUBJ> היה *be* Is 17$_1$ (if em.; see Cstr.). <CSTR> מְעִי מַפָּלָה *heap of ruins* Is 17$_1$ (or del. מְעִי). <PREP> לְ *as,* + שׂים *place,* i.e. make into Is 23$_{13}$ 25$_2$ (|| גַּל *heap*).

<SYN> גַּל *heap.*

⇨ נפל *fall.*

מַפֵּלָה, see מַפָּלָה *ruin.*

מִפְלָט 1 n.[m.] **refuge,** from wind and tempest, <SUBJ> ברך pass. *be blessed* Ps 144$_2$ (if em. מְפַלְטִי *my deliverer* to מִפְלָטִי *my refuge*). <NOM CL> מִפְלָטִי ... י׳ *Y. is ... my refuge* 2 S 22$_2$||Ps 18$_3$ (if em. מְפַלְטִי *my deliverer*). <OBJ> חושׁ hi. *seek with haste* or perh. *hasten to** Ps 55$_9$. <APP> י׳ *Y.* Ps 144$_2$ (if em.; see Subj.).*

⇨ פלט *escape.*

מִפְלֶצֶת 4 n.f. **horrible image**—מִפְלֶצֶת; sf. מִפְלַצְתָּהּ—made for Asherah, <OBJ> עשׂה *make* 1 K 15$_{13}$||2 C 15$_{16}$, כרת *cut down* 1 K 15$_{13}$||2 C 15$_{16}$, שׂרף *burn* 1 K 15$_{13}$|| 2 C 15$_{16}$.*

⇨ פלץ *shudder.*

[מִפְלָשׂ] 1 n.[m.] **poising**—pl. cstr. מִפְלְשֵׂי—**poising, balancing,** <OBJ> בין *understand* Jb 36$_{29}$ (if em.; see Cstr.). <CSTR> מִפְלְשֵׂי עָב *poising of the clouds* Jb 36$_{29}$ (if em. מִפְרְשֵׂי *spreading out of*) 37$_{16}$. <APP> מִפְלָאָה *wondrous work* Jb 37$_{16}$, תְּשֻׁאָה *crash (of thunder)* Jb 36$_{29}$ (if em.; see Cstr.). <PREP> עַל *about, concerning,* + ידע *know* Jb 37$_{16}$.*

⇨ פלס *weigh.*

[מַפֶּלֶת] 8.1 n.f. **downfall**—cstr. מַפֶּלֶת; sf. מַפַּלְתֵּךְ, מַפַּלְתָּם, מַפַּלְתּוֹ, מַפַּלְתֵּךְ—**1. downfall** of person (Si 5$_{13[A]}$), wicked (Pr 29$_{16}$), Pharaoh (Ezk 32$_{10}$), Tyre (Ezk 26$_{15.18}$ 27$_{27}$), **fall** of tree, in ref. to Pharaoh (Ezk 31$_{16}$), <NOM CL> לשון אדם מפלתו *the tongue of a person is his downfall* Si 5$_{13(A)}$ (C מפליטו *his deliverer*). <CSTR> קוֹל מַפַּלְתֵּךְ *sound of your downfall* Ezk 26$_{15}$, מַפַּלְתּוֹ *of its fall* Ezk 31$_{16}$, יוֹם מַפַּלְתֵּךְ *day of your downfall* Ezk 32$_{10}$, מַפַּלְתֵּךְ *of your* (fem.) *downfall* Ezk 26$_{18}$ 27$_{27}$. <PREP> בְּ introducing object, + ראה *see* Pr 29$_{16}$.

2. felled tree trunk, <PREP> עַל *upon,* + שׁכן *dwell* Ezk 31$_{13}$ (|| פֹּארָה *bough*).

3. carcass, <OBJ> ראה *see* Jg 14$_8$. <CSTR> מַפֶּלֶת הָאַרְיֵה *carcass of the lion* Jg 14$_8$ (+ גְּוִיָּה *body*).

<SYN> §2, פֹּארָה *bough.*

⇨ נפל *fall.*

מִפְּנֵי, see פָּנִים *face.*

[מִפְעָל] 3.2 n.[m.] **deed**—cstr. Si מפעל; pl. cstr. מִפְעֲלוֹת; sf. מִפְעָלָיו—**deed, work** of Y. (Ps 46$_9$ 66$_5$ Pr 8$_{22}$), humans (Si 15$_{15}$ 16$_{12}$), <OBJ> חזה *see* Ps 46$_9$, ראה *see* Ps 66$_5$, נכר hi. *recognize* Si 15$_{19}$. <CSTR> מִפְעֲלוֹת י׳ *deeds*

of Y. Ps 46$_9$, אֱלֹהִים of God Ps 66$_5$, מפעל איש *deed of a person* Si 15$_{19(A)}$ (B אנוש *of a person*); קֶדֶם מִפְעָלָיו *the beginning of his works* Pr 8$_{22}$, כל מפעל *every deed of* Si 15$_{19}$. <PREP> בְּ *according to*, + שׁפט *judge* Si 16$_{12}$.
⇒ פעל *do.*

מֵפָעַת, see מֵיפַעַת *Mephaath.*

[מַפָּץ] 1.0.2 n.[m.] **shattering**—cstr. Q מפץ; sf. מַפָּצוֹ—**shattering** (Ezk 9$_2$ 4QpsHod^c 3$_4$), **shattering blow** (4QS^h A$_3$), <OBJ> נתן *give* 4QpsHod^c 3$_4$ (ל[תת]; unless מַפֵּץ *club*). <CSTR> מפץ אב[ן] *shattering blow of a stone* 4QS^h A$_3$; כְּלִי מַפָּצוֹ *weapon of his shattering*, i.e. his shattering weapon Ezk 9$_2$. <PREP> בְּ of instrument, *by (means of), with* 4QS^h A$_3$.
⇒ נפץ I *shatter.*

מַפֵּץ 1.0.1 n.[m.] **club,** or perh. **hammer,** as weapon, <SUBJ> עלה *go up* Na 2$_2$ (if em. מֵפִיץ *scatterer* to מַפֵּץ). <NOM CL> מַפֵּץ־אַתָּה לִי *you are a club to me* Jr 51$_{20}$, מַפֵּץ ... אִישׁ *a man* who bears false witness ... *is a club* Pr 25$_{18}$ (if em. מֵפִיץ *club*), מפץ לכול עמי הארצות *(they shall be) a club to all the peoples of the lands* 1QH 4$_{26}$. <APP> כְּלִי *weapon* Jr 51$_{20}$.
⇒ נפץ I *shatter*; cf. מֵפִיץ II *club.*

מִפְקָד 5.2.0.1 n.[m.] **muster**—cstr. מִפְקַד—**1a. muster, counting, census,** <OBJ> חשב *consider* Si 42$_7$. <CSTR> מִפְקַד־הָעָם *muster of the people* 2 S 24$_9$||1 C 21$_5$, מפקד יד *counting of hand* Si 42$_{7(Bmg)}$; מִסְפַּר מִפְקַד *number of the muster of* 2 S 24$_9$||1 C 21$_5$.

b. שַׁעַר הַמִּפְקָד as pl.n. **Muster Gate,** Ne 3$_{31}$.

2. appointed place, or perh. **mustering place,** <CSTR> מִפְקַד הַבַּיִת *appointed place of the house* Ezk 43$_{21}$ (+ מִחוּץ לַמִּקְדָּשׁ *outside the sanctuary*). <PREP> בְּ of place, *in*, + שׂרף *burn* Ezk 43$_{21}$.

3. appointment, <CSTR> מִפְקַד יְחִזְקִיָּהוּ הַמֶּלֶךְ *appointment of*, i.e. by, *Hezekiah the king* and Azariah the chief officer of the house of God 2 C 31$_{13}$; עת מפקד *time of appointment*, i.e. appointed time Si 35$_{11}$ (unless §4 or error for מפטר *departure*).

<PREP> בְּ of time, *in, at*, + אחר htp. *delay* Si 35$_{11}$; of instrument, *by (means of), through* 2 C 31$_{13}$.

4. farewell,* <CSTR> עת מפקד *time of farewell* Si 35$_{11}$ (unless §3).

5. guard,* <COLL> מִפְקָד followed by list of names T. ʿIra ost. 1$_1$.*
⇒ פקד *visit.*

[מִפְרָץ] I 1 n.[m.] **landing place**—pl. sf. מִפְרָצָיו—for ships, <PREP> עַל *at, beside*, + שׁכן *dwell* Jg 5$_{17}$.
⇒ פרץ *break through.*

***[מִפְרָץ]** II 1 n.[m.] **wadi**—pl. sf. מִפְרָצָיו—<PREP> עַל *at, beside*, + שׁכן *dwell* Jg 5$_{17}$.
⇒ (?) פרץ *break through.*

[מַפְרֶקֶת] 1 n.f. **neck**—sf. מַפְרַקְתּוֹ—<SUBJ> שׁבר ni. *be broken* 1 S 4$_{18}$.
⇒ פרק *tear apart.*

[מִפְרָשׂ] 2.0.2 n.[m.] **spreading**—cstr. Q מפרש; sf. מִפְרָשֵׂךְ; pl. cstr. מִפְרְשֵׂי—**1. spreading out, expanse,** <OBJ> בין *understand* Jb 36$_{29}$ (or em.; see Cstr.). <CSTR> מִפְרְשֵׂי עָב *spreading out of the clouds* Jb 36$_{29}$ (or em. מִפְלְשֵׂי *poising of*), מפרש שחקים *expanse of the skies* 1QM 10$_{11}$. <APP> תְּשֻׁאָה *crash (of thunder)* Jb 36$_{29}$ (or em.; see Cstr.).

2. place of spreading, <CSTR> מפרש [רשתה] *place of spreading of her net* 1QH fr. 3$_4$ (=4QHod^b מפרשי *places of spreading of*; + מטוני פחיה *hiding places of her traps*). <PREP> עַל *upon*, + עמד *stand* 1QH fr. 3$_4$ (עמד[ו]).

3. sail, <SUBJ> היה *be* Ezk 27$_7$ (+ שֵׁשׁ־בְּרִקְמָה מִמִּצְרַיִם *linen with embroidery from Egypt*).
⇒ פרשׂ *spread.*

***[מִפְשָׂע]** 0.0.1 n.[m.] **marching,** <CSTR> ידי מפשע *signal(s) of marching* 1QM 8$_7$.
⇒ פשׂע *march.*

מִפְשָׂעָה n.f. **buttocks,** <PREP> עַד *unto*, + כרת *cut garment* 1 C 19$_4$ (||2 S 10$_4$ שְׁתוֹתֵיהֶם *their buttocks*).*
⇒ פשׂע *march* or פשׂע *cover.*

מַפְתֵּחַ 3.1 n.m. **key**—cstr. מַפְתֵּחַ—<NOM CL> מקום ידים רבות מפתח *a place of many hands (where) there is a key* Si 42$_{6(M)}$. <OBJ> לקח *take* Jg 3$_{25}$, נתן *give*, i.e. place, on shoulder Is 22$_{22}$. <CSTR> מַפְתֵּחַ בֵּית־דָּוִד *key of the house of David* Is 22$_{22}$. <PREP> עַל *over*, i.e. in charge of 1 C 9$_{27}$ (or em. הֵם עַל־הַמַּפְתֵּחַ *they were over the key* to עֲלֵיהֶם מִפְתָּחוֹ *upon them was*, i.e. they were in charge of, *its opening*).

Also XḤev/Se 8 c2 (המפ[תח]).*

⇒ פתח *open*.

[מִפְתָּח] 1.0.1 n.[m.] **opening**—cstr. מִפְתַּח—**opening (up)**, <NOM CL> מִפְתַּח שְׂפָתַי מֵישָׁרִים *the opening of my lips is uprightness*, i.e. my utterance is upright Pr 8$_{6}$, עֲלֵיהֶם מִפְתָּחוֹ *upon them was*, i.e. they were in charge of, *its opening* 1 C 9$_{27}$ (if em. הֵם עַל־הַמַּפְתֵּחַ *they were over*, i.e. in charge of, *the key*). <CSTR> מִפְתַּח שְׂפָתַי *opening of my lips* Pr 8$_{6}$, מפתח חסדיו *opening up of his mercies* 1QS 10$_{4}$ (=4QS^{d} 9$_{1}$ חסדי *of the mercies of* eternity). <PREP> לְ *concerning* 1QS 10$_{4}$.

⇒ פתח *open*.

מִפְתָּן 8 n.[m.] **threshold**—cstr. מִפְתַּן—**threshold,** as viewed from inside a building,* <CSTR> מִפְתַּן דָּגוֹן *threshold of Dagon* 1 S 5$_{5}$, הַשַּׁעַר *of the gate* Ezk 46$_{2}$, הַבַּיִת *of the house* Ezk 9$_{3}$ 10$_{4.18}$ (all three הַבָּיִת) 47$_{1}$. <PREP> אֶל *to*, + עלה ni. *be taken up* Ezk 9$_{3}$; *at, by*, + כרת pass. *be cut off* 1 S 5$_{4}$; עַל *upon, at, over*, + כרת pass. *be cut off* 1 S 5$_{4(mss)}$, דרך *tread* 1 S 5$_{5}$, שׁחה htpal. *worship* Ezk 46$_{1}$, דלג *leap* Zp 1$_{9}$; *to*, + רום *rise* Ezk 10$_{4}$; מֵעַל *from (upon)*, + יצא *go out* Ezk 10$_{18}$; מִתַּחַת *from below*, + יצא *go out* Ezk 47$_{1}$.*

מֵץ, see מֵיץ *extortioner*.

מֹץ 8.0.1 n.m. **chaff**—Q מוץ; cstr. מֹץ—<SUBJ> עבר *pass* Is 29$_{5}$ Zp 2$_{2}$ (if em.; see Prep.), סער po. *be storm-driven* Ho 13$_{3}$. <CSTR> מֹץ הָרִים *chaff of*, i.e. on, *the mountains* Is 17$_{13}$. <OBJ> נדף *drive* Ps 1$_{4}$, גנב *steal*, i.e. sweep away Jb 21$_{18}$. <PREP> כְּ *as* Ps 1$_{4}$ 1QH 7$_{23}$, + היה *be* Is 5$_{24}$ (if em. כְּמַק *as rottenness*) 29$_{5}$ Ho 13$_{3}$ Ps 35$_{5}$ Jb 21$_{18}$, רדף pu. *be chased* Is 17$_{13}$, סער po. *be storm-driven* Hb 3$_{14}$ (if em. כְּמוֹ *as [though]* to כְּמֹץ, and transfer to follow יִסְעֲרוּ [emended to יְסֹעֲרוּ]), עבר *pass* Zp 2$_{2}$ (or em. עָבַר יוֹם as chaff *a day has passed* to עֹבֵר as *passing* chaff), שׂים *place*, i.e. make, hills Is 41$_{15}$. <COLL> מֹץ || גַּלְגַּל *tumbleweed* Is 17$_{13}$; + תֶּבֶן *straw* Jb 21$_{18}$, אָבָק *dust* Is 29$_{5}$, עָשָׁן *smoke* Ho 13$_{3}$; מֹץ לִפְנֵי רוּחַ *chaff before the wind* Ps 35$_{5}$ 1QH 7$_{23}$.*

<SYN> גַּלְגַּל *tumbleweed*.

מצא I 457.32.66 vb. **find—Qal** 308.26.34 Pf. מָצָא (מְצָאוֹ, מְצָאַתְנִי) מָצָאתָ (מְצָאתַם, מְצָאֻתְנוּ, מְצָאַתְנוּ) מָצְאָה (מְצָאָהּ, מְצָאתִיהָ, מְצָאתִיהוּ, מְצָאתִיו, מְצָתִי) מָצָאתִי, מָצָאת (מְצָאתָהּ, מְצָאתִים), מְצָאתֶם (מְצָאֻהוּ, Q מצאוכה, מְצָאוּנִי, מְצָאוּ) מָצְאוּ (מְצָאוּנָה, מְצָאֻנְהוּ) מָצָאנוּ; impf. יִמְצָא (יִמְצָאֲךָ, יִמְצָאֶכָּה, יִמְצָאֶהוּ, יִמְצָאֶנּוּ, Q ימצאנה), 3fs תִּמְצָא (תִּמְצָאֲךָ), 2ms תִּמְצָא (תִּמְצָאֵם, תִּמְצָאֶנּוּ), אֶמְצָא (אֶמְצָאֲךָ, אֶמְצָאֵהוּ, Si אמצאנו), יִמְצְאוּ (יִמְצָאוּ, יִמְצָאֻנְנִי, יִמְצָאֻהוּ, יִמְצָאוּנְהָ), 3fpl תִּמְצֶאןָ, תִּמְצְאוּ (תִּמְצָאוּ, תִּמְצְאוּן, תִּמְצָאֻהוּ), נִמְצָא; + waw וּמָצָא (וּמְצָאוּךָ) וּמָצְאוּ, (וּמְצָאתָהּ) וּמָצָאת, וּמָצָאָה, (וּמְצָאָנוּ, וּמְצָאָהּ, וּמְצָאֻהוּ), וּמְצָאתֶם; וַיִּמְצָא (וַיִּמְצָאֵהוּ, וַיִּמְצָאָהּ, וַיִּמְצָאֵם), 3fs וַתִּמְצָא, וָאֶמְצָא (וָאֶמְצָאֲךָ), וַיִּמְצְאוּ (Q וימצאוכה; וַיִּמְצָאֻהוּ); impv. מְצָא, מִצְאוּ, מְצֶאןָ; ptc. מוֹצֵא (מוֹצְאוֹ, sf. מֹצְאִי, Si מוצאו), מֹצֵאת (מוֹצֵאת, מוֹצְאֵת), מֹצְאִים (Q מוצאיה, מֹצְאֵיהֶם), מֹצְאֵי, מֹצְאוֹת; inf. מְצֹא (מְצוֹא, Q מצאת, Q מצאך, מֹצַאֲכֶם).

1. find what is sought, missed, **a.** thing (Gn 2$_{20}$ 8$_{9}$ 26$_{19.32}$ 27$_{20}$ 31$_{32.33.34.35.37}$ Ex 5$_{11}$ 15$_{22}$ 16$_{25.27}$ Dt 22$_{14.17}$= 11QT 65$_{9.12}$ 1 S 9$_{4.4}$ 20$_{21.36}$ 1 K 18$_{5}$ Is 58$_{3.13}$ Jr 2$_{24}$ 6$_{16}$ 14$_{3}$ 45$_{3}$ Ho 2$_{8}$ Am 8$_{12}$ Jon 1$_{3}$ Ps 69$_{1}$ 84$_{4}$ 107$_{4}$ 132$_{5.6}$ Jb 20$_{8}$ 32$_{3.13}$ 33$_{10}$ Pr 2$_{5}$ 4$_{22}$ Ru 1$_{9}$ Ec 7$_{28}$ 11$_{1}$ 12$_{10}$ Lm 1$_{3.6}$ 2$_{16}$ Ne 5$_{8}$ 1 C 4$_{40}$ Si 11$_{10}$ 51$_{18[B]}$ 4Q185 1.1$_{12}$ 4QCommGenA 1$_{15}$ 4Q416 2.2$_{8}$ 2.3$_{3}$ 4Q418 127$_{1}$ GnzPs 3$_{1}$).

b. person (Gn 18$_{26.28.30}$ 19$_{11}$ 38$_{20.22.23}$ 41$_{38}$ Jos 2$_{22}$ 2 S 17$_{20}$ 1 K 1$_{3}$ 13$_{28}$ 18$_{12}$ 21$_{20.20}$ 2 K 2$_{17}$ 9$_{21.35}$ Is 41$_{12}$ Jr 5$_{1}$ 41$_{12}$ Ezk 22$_{30}$ Ho 2$_{9}$ Jb 17$_{10}$ Pr 7$_{15}$ 18$_{22}$ 20$_{6}$ 31$_{10}$ Ca 3$_{1.2.4}$ 5$_{6}$ Ec 7$_{28.28}$ Ezr 8$_{15}$ 2 C 20$_{16}$ Si 6$_{14}$ Si 51$_{16}$), wisdom personified (Pr 1$_{28}$ 8$_{17.35}$ Si 6$_{27}$ 51$_{20.26.27}$ 4Q185 1.2$_{12}$).

c. Y. (Dt 4$_{29}$ Jr 29$_{13}$ Ho 5$_{6}$ perh. Ps 32$_{6}$ [unless §4; or em.; see Coll.]) Jb 23$_{3}$ 4QapMes 2.2$_{4}$.

2. find, meet, encounter (Gn 4$_{14.15}$ 16$_{7}$ 32$_{20}$ 37$_{15.17}$ Nm 15$_{32.33}$ 35$_{27}$ Dt 22$_{23.25.27}$=11QT 66$_{7}$ Dt 22$_{28}$ 32$_{10}$ Jg 1$_{5}$ 21$_{12}$ 1 S 9$_{11.13.13}$ 10$_{2.3}$ 23$_{17}$ 24$_{20}$ 30$_{11}$ 1 K 11$_{29}$ 13$_{14.24}$

18$_{10}$ 19$_{19}$ 20$_{36.37}$ 2 K 4$_{29}$ 10$_{13}$||2 C 22$_{8}$ 2 K 10$_{15}$ 19$_{8}$||Is 37$_{8}$ Jr 2$_{34}$ 50$_{7}$ Ho 12$_{5}$ Ps 89$_{21}$ Ca 3$_{3}$ 5$_{7.8}$ 8$_{1}$ Ec 9$_{15}$ [or em.; see Subj.] 2 C 34$_{15}$ 11QT 66$_{4}$), **befall, overtake** (Gn 44$_{34}$ Ex 18$_{8}$ Nm 20$_{14}$ Dt 4$_{30}$ 31$_{17.17.21}$ Jos 2$_{23}$ Jg 6$_{15}$ perh. Jb 31$_{29}$* [unless §4] Est 8$_{6}$ Ne 9$_{32}$ 4QapJoshua^{a} 3.1$_{3}$), of (punishment for) sin (Nm 32$_{23}$ 2 K 7$_{9}$).

3. find, discover, come across, oft. unexpectedly (Gn 11$_{2}$ 30$_{14}$ 36$_{24}$ 37$_{32}$ 44$_{8}$ Lv 5$_{22.23}$ Dt 22$_{3}$ 24$_{1}$ Jg 15$_{15}$ 17$_{8.9}$ 1 S 31$_{8}$||1 C 10$_{8}$ 2 K 4$_{39}$ 22$_{8}$||2 C 34$_{14}$ 2 K 23$_{24}$ Is 34$_{14}$ Ho 9$_{10}$ Pr 25$_{16}$ Ne 7$_{5}$ 2 C 29$_{16}$ 32$_{4}$ CD 9$_{15}$), **find (written)** Ne 7$_{5}$ 8$_{14}$.

4. find (one's way to), i.e. **reach** (Is 10$_{10.14}$ perh. Ho 12$_{9}$ Ps 21$_{9}$ [or em.; see Subj.] 21$_{9}$ 32$_{6}$ [unless §1c] 116$_{3}$ 119$_{143}$ Jb 3$_{22}$ 11$_{7a}$ [or em.; see Prep.] perh. 31$_{29}$* [unless §2] 37$_{23}$ [unless §5] perh. Ec 7$_{27}$),* **hit,** of axe head (Dt 19$_{5}$), archers (1 S 31$_{3}$||1 C 10$_{3}$), **catch (hold of),** of fire (Ex 22$_{7}$).

5. find (out), discover, learn answer to riddle (Jg 14$_{12.18}$), mysteries of Y. (Jb 11$_{7}$), deeds of Y. (Ec 3$_{11}$ 8$_{17.17.17}$), perh. Y. himself (Jb 37$_{23}$ [unless §4]), future events (Ec 7$_{14}$ [unless §10]), appointed times (CD 6$_{19}$), sum (Ec 7$_{27}$ [unless §4]), consequences of righteousness (4QWays^{b} 1a.2$_{14}$).

6. find out, detect wrongdoing (Gn 44$_{16}$ 1 S 12$_{5}$ 29$_{3.6.8}$ 2 K 17$_{4}$ Jr 2$_{5}$ 23$_{11}$ Ps 10$_{15}$ [or em.; see Subj.] 17$_{3}$ 36$_{3}$).

7. find (to be so), through examination, experience (Ec 7$_{26.27.29}$ Dn 1$_{20}$ Ne 9$_{8}$ 1 C 20$_{2}$ 2 C 25$_{5}$ Si 34$_{8[Bmg]}$ 4QMMT C$_{30}$), **find to be sound** (Si 34$_{22}$).

8. find, i.e. **obtain, gain, achieve** harvest (Gn 26$_{12}$), booty (Nm 31$_{50}$ Jg 5$_{30}$ 1 S 14$_{30}$ Ps 119$_{162}$ [or em.; see Obj.] 2 C 20$_{25}$), fortified cities (2 S 20$_{6}$), wealth, prosperity, good (Ho 12$_{9}$ Jb 31$_{25}$ Pr 1$_{13}$ 16$_{20}$ 17$_{20}$ 18$_{22}$ 19$_{8}$ Si 6$_{14}$ 40$_{18}$), joy (Si 15$_{6[A, Bmg]}$), ransom (Jb 33$_{24}$), reward (perh. 2 S 18$_{22}$ [or em.; see Subj.] Si 12$_{2}$), scroll (Ezk 3$_{1}$), wisdom, knowledge (Pr 3$_{13}$ 8$_{9.12}$ 24$_{14}$ Si 40$_{19}$), vision (Lm 2$_{9}$), life (Pr 8$_{35}$ 21$_{21}$), peace, rest (Ca 8$_{10}$ [or em.; see Subj.] Si 6$_{28}$ 11$_{19}$ 34$_{21}$), support (Si 3$_{31}$ 4QBéat 14.2$_{7}$), glory (Si 4$_{13}$), time (Si 12$_{16}$), favour (usu. מצא חֵן בְּעֵינֵי *find favour in the sight of,* Gn 6$_{8}$ 18$_{3}$ 19$_{19}$ 30$_{27}$ 32$_{6}$ 33$_{8.10.15}$ 34$_{11}$ 39$_{4}$ 47$_{45.49}$ 50$_{4}$ Ex 33$_{12.13.13.16.17}$ 34$_{9}$ Nm 11$_{11.15}$ 32$_{5}$ Dt 24$_{1}$ Jg 6$_{17}$ 1 S 1$_{18}$ 16$_{22}$ 20$_{3.29}$ 25$_{8}$ 27$_{5}$ 2 S 14$_{22}$ 15$_{25}$ 16$_{4}$ 1 K 11$_{19}$ Jr 31$_{2}$ Pr 3$_{4}$ 28$_{23}$ Ru 2$_{2.10.13}$ Est 5$_{8}$ 7$_{3}$ 8$_{5}$ Si 3$_{18}$ 42$_{1}$ 44$_{23}$ 4QDibHam^{a} 3.2$_{18}$ 4QPrFêtes^{c} 99.1$_{1}$); **experience** distress (Jr 10$_{18}$ [or em.; see Subj.] Ps 116$_{3}$), dishonour (Pr 6$_{33}$).

9. find (from one's resources), i.e. **afford** (Lv 12$_{8}$ 25$_{26.28}$ 1 S 25$_{8}$), **find sufficient** (Nm 11$_{22.22}$ Jg 21$_{14}$ [unless all three מצא II *suffice*]), **find (possible to do)** (Jg 9$_{33}$ 1 S 10$_{7}$ Ec 9$_{10}$ Si 12$_{11}$ 34$_{6}$), **find (courage, strength, skill)** (2 S 7$_{27}$||1 C 17$_{25}$ Is 57$_{10}$ Ps 76$_{6}$ 4Q424 3$_{7}$), **provide** (Pr 9$_{12}$ [or em.; see Subj.] Si 15$_{6[B]}$).

10. מצא אַחֲרֵי **find fault with*** (Ec 7$_{14}$ [unless §5]).

<SUBJ> Y. Gn 18$_{26.28.30}$ 44$_{16}$ Dt 32$_{10}$ Jr 23$_{11}$ Ezk 22$_{30}$ Ho 9$_{10}$ Ps 10$_{15}$ (or em. בַּל־תּוֹצִא *you will not allow to escape* [i.e. יצא hi.]) 17$_{3}$ 89$_{21}$ Jb 33$_{10}$ Ne 9$_{8}$, מַלְאָךְ *angel* Gn 16$_{7}$ Jb 33$_{24}$.

Adullamite Gn 38$_{20.22.23}$, Ephraim Ho 12$_{9}$, Israel(ites) Ex 15$_{22}$ Dt 4$_{29}$ 22$_{3}$ 1 S 12$_{5}$ Is 41$_{12}$ 57$_{10}$ 58$_{3.13}$ Jr 2$_{34}$ 5$_{1}$ 6$_{16}$ 29$_{13}$ Ho 5$_{6}$ 12$_{5}$ Am 8$_{12}$, Judah(ites) Jg 1$_{5}$ Lm 1$_{3}$ 2 C 20$_{16}$, Philistines 1 S 31$_{8}$||1 C 10$_{8}$, Shilonite 1 K 11$_{29}$, Simeon(ites) Jg 1$_{5}$, עַם *people* Gn 47$_{25}$ Ex 5$_{11}$ 16$_{27}$ 1 S 14$_{30}$ Jr 31$_{2}$ Ps 73$_{10}$ (if em. מֵי מָלֵא *waters of fullness* to מַיִם לֹא מָצְאוּ *they did not find water*) 2 C 20$_{25}$, גּוֹי *nation* 1 K 18$_{10}$, מַמְלָכָה *kingdom* 1 K 18$_{10}$, Abraham Gn 18$_{3}$, Achish 1 S 29$_{3.6.8}$, Ahab 1 K 18$_{5.12}$, Ahaziah 2 K 9$_{21}$, Ahijah 1 K 11$_{29}$, Amaziah 2 C 25$_{5}$, Anah Gn 36$_{24}$, Baruch Jr 45$_{3}$, Ben Sira Si 51$_{16.18(B).20.27}$, David 1 S 16$_{22}$ 20$_{3.29}$ 27$_{5}$ Ps 132$_{5}$ 1 C 20$_{2}$, Elijah 1 K 19$_{19}$ 21$_{20}$, Esther Est 5$_{8}$ 7$_{3}$ 8$_{5}$, Ezra Ezr 8$_{15}$, Gehazi 2 K 4$_{29}$, Gideon Jg 6$_{17}$, Hadad 1 K 11$_{19}$, Hilkiah 2 K 22$_{8}$||2 C 34$_{14}$ 2 K 23$_{24}$ 2 C 34$_{15}$, Isaac Gn 26$_{12}$, Jacob/Israel Gn 32$_{6}$ 33$_{8.10.15}$ 47$_{29}$, Jehoram 2 K 9$_{21}$, Jehoshaphat 2 C 20$_{25}$, Jehu 2 K 10$_{13}$||2 C 22$_{8}$ 2 K 10$_{15}$, Joab 2 S 14$_{22}$, Job Jb 11$_{7.7}$ (or em.; see Prep.) 17$_{10}$ 23$_{3}$, Johanan Jr 41$_{12}$, Jonah 1$_{3}$, Joseph Gn 37$_{17}$ 39$_{4}$ 50$_{4}$, Koheleth Ec 7$_{26+6t}$ 12$_{10}$, Laban Gn 30$_{27}$ 31$_{32.33.34.35.37}$, Moses Ex 33$_{12.13.13.16.17}$ 34$_{9}$ Nm 11$_{11.15}$, Nehemiah Ne 7$_{5.5}$, Noah Gn 6$_{8}$, Obadiah 1 K 18$_{5}$, Reuben Gn 30$_{14}$, Ruth Ru 2$_{2.10.13}$, Samson Jg 15$_{15}$, Saul 1 S 9$_{4.4.11.13.13}$ 10$_{2}$, Sheba 2 S 20$_{6}$, Shechem Gn 34$_{11}$, Ziba 2 S 16$_{4}$.

אָדָם *human being* Pr 3$_{13}$ Ec 3$_{11}$ 7$_{14}$ 8$_{17.17}$, אִישׁ *man* Gn 19$_{11}$ 37$_{15}$ Lv 25$_{26}$ Nm 31$_{50}$ Dt 22$_{14.17}$=11QT 65$_{9.12}$ Dt 22$_{23.25.27}$=11QT 66$_{7}$ Dt 22$_{28}$ 24$_{1}$ Jg 14$_{18}$ 17$_{8.9}$ 21$_{12}$ 1 S 10$_{3}$ 24$_{20}$ 31$_{3}$ 1 K 20$_{37}$ 2 K 2$_{17}$ Ps 76$_{6}$ Si 44$_{23}$ perh. 4Q418 103.2$_{5}$ 4Q424 3$_{7}$ 11QT 66$_{4}$, אִשָּׁה *woman* Dt 24$_{1}$ Pr 7$_{15}$,

אָב *father* Jr 2$_{5}$, אֵם *mother* Ho 2$_{8.9}$, בֵּן *son* Gn 27$_{20}$ Nm 32$_{5}$ 1 S 9$_{4.4}$ 2 S 20$_{6}$ Jr 41$_{12}$ Ezk 3$_{1}$ Pr 2$_{5}$ 3$_{4}$ 24$_{14}$ Si 3$_{18}$ 6$_{27.28}$ 11$_{10}$ 12$_{2}$ 34$_{21.22}$ 42$_{1}$, of Israel Ex 16$_{25}$ Nm 15$_{32}$, בַּת *daughter* of Jerusalem Ca 5$_{8}$, כַּלָּה *daughter-in-law* Ru 1$_{9}$, מֶלֶךְ *king* 2 S 15$_{25}$ 2 K 9$_{21}$ 17$_{4}$ Dn 1$_{20}$ 2 C 32$_{4}$, מַלְכָּה *queen* Est 7$_{3}$, פַּרְעֹה *Pharaoh* Gn 41$_{38}$, שַׂר *commander* Jr 41$_{12}$, חֹר *noble* Ne 5$_{8}$, סָגָן *official* Ne 5$_{8}$, רַב־שָׁקֵה *Rabshakeh* 2 K 19$_{8}$||Is 37$_{8}$, עֶבֶד *servant* Gn 19$_{19}$ 26$_{19.32}$ 41$_{38}$ 44$_{8}$ 2 S 7$_{27}$||1 C 17$_{25}$ 2 S 17$_{20}$ 1 K 1$_{3}$ Is 41$_{12}$, שִׁפְחָה *female servant* 1 S 1$_{18}$, צָעִיר *insignificant one*, i.e. servant Jr 14$_{3}$, נַעַר *lad* 1 S 9$_{4.4.11.13.13}$ 20$_{21.36}$ 25$_{8}$, רֵעַ *friend* Gn 38$_{20.22.23}$ Jb 32$_{3.13}$, מֵרֵעַ *friend* Jg 14$_{12}$, female lover Ca 3$_{1.2.4}$ 5$_{6}$, כֹּהֵן *priest* 2 K 22$_{8}$||2 C 34$_{14}$ 2 K 23$_{24}$ Ne 8$_{14}$ 2 C 29$_{16}$, לֵוִי *Levite* Ne 8$_{14}$, נָבִיא *prophet* 1 K 11$_{29}$ 13$_{14.28}$ Lm 2$_{9}$, מֵלִיץ *mediator* Jb 33$_{24}$, worshipper Ps 69$_{21}$ Ps 116$_{3}$ 132$_{6}$, יֹשֵׁב *inhabitant* Jr 10$_{18}$ (or em. יִמָּצֵאוּ *they shall be found out* [מצא I ni.] or *they shall be drained* [מצא III ni.] or יֶאְשָׁמוּ *they shall be guilty*) 2 C 20$_{16}$.

חָכָם *wise one* Ec 8$_{17}$, שׂכל hi. ptc. *one who considers* Pr 16$_{20}$, רדף ptc. *one who pursues* Jos 2$_{22}$ Pr 21$_{21}$, בקשׁ pi. ptc. *one who seeks* Jr 2$_{24}$, שׁחר pi. ptc. *one who seeks* Pr 8$_{17}$, יחל pi. ptc. *one who hopes* 4QapMes 2.2$_{4}$, מצא ptc. *one who finds* Pr 8$_{35}$, שׁמר ptc. *one who keeps* Pr 19$_{8}$, *sentry* Ca 3$_{3}$ 5$_{7}$, perh. פעל ptc. *one who does* good Si 3$_{31}$, תמך ptc. *one who holds* Si 4$_{13}$, ירא ptc. *one who fears* Y. Si 15$_{6(A, Bmg)}$, נתן ptc. *one who gives* Si 51$_{26}$, הרה ptc. *one who conceives* Ho 2$_{8.9}$, הלך ptc. *one who goes* Gn 32$_{20}$, בוא ptc. *one who enters* covenant CD 6$_{19}$.

גֹּאֵל *avenger* of blood Nm 35$_{27}$, מוֹרֶה *archer* 1 S 31$_{3}$|| 1 C 10$_{3}$, warrior Jg 1$_{5}$, אֹיֵב *enemy* 1 K 21$_{20}$ Lm 2$_{16}$ Si 12$_{16}$, שׂנא ptc. *one who hates* Si 12$_{11}$, pi. ptc. Jb 31$_{29}$, מַר *bitter one* Jb 3$_{22}$, עָמֵל *troubled one* Jb 3$_{22}$, יכח hi. ptc. *one who rebukes* Pr 28$_{23}$, חַטָּא *sinner* Pr 1$_{13}$, נֹאֵף *adulterer* Pr 6$_{33}$, עִקֵּשׁ *crooked one* Pr 17$_{20}$, פְּתִי *simple one* Pr 1$_{28}$, לֵץ *scorner* Pr 1$_{28}$, נֶפֶשׁ *soul*, i.e. person Lv 5$_{22.23}$, ראשׁ *head*, i.e. chief Ne 8$_{14}$, יָד *hand* Lv 12$_{8}$ 25$_{28}$ Jg 9$_{33}$ 1 S 10$_{7}$ 23$_{17}$ 25$_{8}$ Is 10$_{10.14}$ Ps 21$_{9}$ (or em. תָּבוֹא *it will come*) Jb 31$_{25}$ Ec 9$_{10}$, יָמִין *right hand* Ps 21$_{9}$.

אַרְיֵה *lion* 1 K 13$_{24}$ 20$_{36}$, אַיָּל *deer* Lm 1$_{6}$, צִפּוֹר *bird* Ps 84$_{4}$, לִילִית *nightjar* Is 34$_{14}$, יוֹנָה *dove* Gn 8$_{9}$ 4QComm GenA 1$_{15}$, בַּרְזֶל *iron (axe head)* Dt 19$_{5}$, אֵשׁ *fire* Ex 22$_{5}$, יְגִיעַ *product of labour* Ho 12$_{9}$.

תְּלָאָה *hardship* Ex 18$_{8}$ Nm 20$_{14}$ Ne 9$_{32}$, צַר *distress* Ps 119$_{143}$, צָרָה *distress* Dt 31$_{17.21}$ 4QapJoshua[a] 3.1$_{3}$, מֵצַר *distress* Ps 116$_{3}$ (or em. מְצוּרֵי to מְצָדֵי *nets of*), מָצוֹק *distress* Ps 119$_{143}$, רַע *evil* Gn 44$_{34}$ Jb 31$_{29}$, רָעָה *evil* Dt 31$_{17.17.21}$ Est 8$_{6}$, חַטָּאת *sin* Nm 32$_{23}$, עָוֹן *(punishment for) iniquity* 2 K 7$_{9}$, חָכְמָה *wisdom* Pr 8$_{12}$ (or em. דַּעַת מְזִמּוֹת אֶמְצָא *I find knowledge [and] discretion* to מוֹדַעַת מְזִמּוֹת אִמָּצֵא *I am found as the acquaintance of discretion*) Si 15$_{6(B)}$ perh. 4Q185 1.2$_{12}$ (but prob. obj.), בְּשׂוֹרָה *news* 2 S 18$_{22}$ (אֵין־בְּשׂוֹרָה מֹצֵאת perh. *there is no news that finds a reward*; or em. מוּצֵאת *that is paid for* [i.e. יצא ho.]), דָּבָר *thing* Dt 4$_{30}$.

אֶחָד *one* 2 K 4$_{39}$, שֵׁנִי *second one* Gn 32$_{20}$, שְׁלִישִׁי *third one* Gn 32$_{20}$, רַב pl. *many* Si 34$_{6}$, -שֶׁ *one who* GnzPs 3$_{1}$, מִי *who?* Pr 20$_{6}$ 31$_{10}$, זֹאת *this* Jg 6$_{13}$, אֵלֶּה *these* 1 C 4$_{40}$.

Subj. not specified, Gn 2$_{20}$ (or em. pass. ptc.)* 4$_{14.15}$ 11$_{2}$ Nm 11$_{22.22}$ (unless both מצא II *suffice*) 15$_{33}$ Jos 2$_{23}$ 1 S 30$_{11}$ Jr 50$_{7}$ Ps 32$_{6}$ (or em.; see Coll.) 36$_{3}$ 107$_{4}$ 119$_{162}$ (or em.; see Obj.) Jb 20$_{8}$ 37$_{23}$ Pr 4$_{22}$ 8$_{9.35}$ 18$_{22.22}$ 25$_{16}$ Ca 8$_{10}$ (unless מוֹצֵאת is יצא hi. ptc. *one who brings out*; mss מוֹצֵאת; or em.; see Obj.) Ec 9$_{15}$ (or em. pass. ptc. or ni.) 11$_{1}$ Si 6$_{14}$ 34$_{8(Bmg)}$ 40$_{18.19}$ CD 9$_{15}$ 4Q185 1.1$_{12}$ 4Q MMT C$_{30}$ 4Q416 2.2$_{8}$.

<OBJ> Y. Dt 4$_{29}$ Jr 29$_{13}$ Ho 5$_{6}$ 12$_{5}$ Jb 23$_{3}$ 37$_{23}$ 4QapMes 2.2$_{4}$, אֱלֹהִים *god* Gn 31$_{32}$, תְּרָפִים *images* Gn 31$_{35}$, Egyptian 1 S 30$_{11}$, Israel(ites) Ex 18$_{8}$ Nm 20$_{14}$ Dt 4$_{30}$ Jg 6$_{13}$ Ho 9$_{10}$ Ne 9$_{32}$, Judah(ites) 2 C 25$_{5}$, Shunammite 1 K 1$_{3}$, עַם *people* Dt 31$_{17.17.21}$ 32$_{10}$ Jr 50$_{7}$ Est 8$_{6}$, הָמוֹן *multitude* 2 C 20$_{16}$, שְׁאֵרִית *remnant* perh. 4QapPs[b] 33$_{1}$, Abishag 1 K 1$_{3}$, Adoni-bezek Jg 1$_{5}$, Ahab 1 K 21$_{20}$, Ahimaaz 2 S 17$_{20}$, Azariah Dn 1$_{20}$, Cain Gn 4$_{14.15}$, Daniel Dn 1$_{20}$, David 1 S 23$_{17}$ Ps 89$_{21}$, Elijah 1 K 18$_{10.12}$ 2 K 2$_{17}$, Elisha 1 K 19$_{19}$, Esau Gn 32$_{20}$, Hananiah Dn 1$_{20}$, Ishmael Jr 41$_{12}$, Jehonadab 2 K 10$_{15}$, Jehu 2 K 9$_{21}$, Jeroboam 1 K 11$_{29}$, Jonathan 2 S 17$_{20}$, Joseph Gn 37$_{15}$, Mishael Dn 1$_{20}$, Saul 1 S 10$_{3}$ 31$_{3.8}$||1 C 10$_{3.8}$.

אָדָם *human being* Ec 7$_{28}$, אִישׁ *man* Gn 41$_{38}$ Nm 15$_{32.33}$ Jos 2$_{23}$ 1 S 10$_{2}$ 30$_{11}$ 1 K 13$_{14.24}$ 20$_{36.37}$ 2 K 4$_{29}$ 7$_{9}$ Is 41$_{12}$ Jr 5$_{1}$ Ezk 22$_{30}$ Pr 20$_{6}$ Ec 9$_{15}$ (or em. pass. ptc. or ni.) Si 34$_{8(Bmg)}$, אִשָּׁה *woman, wife* Gn 38$_{20.22.23}$ Jg 21$_{14}$ (unless מצא II *suffice*) Pr 18$_{22}$ 31$_{10}$ Ec 7$_{26.28}$ 11QT 66$_{4}$, אָב *father* Gn 44$_{34}$, בֵּן *son* Nm 32$_{23}$ 1 K 19$_{19}$ 2 K 10$_{15}$ Jr 41$_{12}$ 2 C 22$_{8}$

(or del. בְּנֵי), אָח *brother* Gn 37$_{17}$ Nm 20$_{14}$ 2 K 10$_{13}$||2 C 22$_{8}$ (2 C if del. בְּנֵי *sons of*), מֶלֶךְ *king* 2 K 19$_{8}$||Is 37$_{8}$, שַׂר *prince* 2 C 22$_{8}$, עֶבֶד *servant* Ps 89$_{21}$, שִׁפְחָה *female servant* Gn 16$_{7}$, נַעַר *lad* Pr 7$_{15}$, בְּתוּלָה *young woman* Dt 22$_{23.28}$ Jg 21$_{12}$, נַעֲרָה *girl* Dt 22$_{23(Qr).25(Qr).28(Qr)}$ Jg 21$_{12}$ 1 S 9$_{11}$, רֵעַ *neighbour* Dt 19$_{5}$ 2 K 7$_{9}$, צַדִּיק *righteous one* Gn 18$_{26.28.30}$, אֶבְיוֹן *poor one* Jr 2$_{34}$, חָכָם *wise one* Jb 17$_{10}$, מְנַחֵם *comforter* Ps 69$_{21}$, רֹאֶה *seer* 1 S 9$_{13.13}$, worshipper Ps 116$_{3}$ 119$_{143}$, אֹהֵב *friend* Si 6$_{14}$, מְאַהֵב *lover* Ho 2$_{9}$, female lover Ca 3$_{3}$ 5$_{7}$, דּוֹד *beloved* Ca 5$_{6.8}$ 8$_{1}$, עֵזֶר *help*, i.e. helper Gn 2$_{20}$ (or em. pass. ptc.),* שׂנא ptc. *one who hates* Ps 21$_{9}$, רֹצֵחַ *killer* Nm 35$_{27}$, אֹיֵב *enemy* 1 S 24$_{20}$.

גֻּלְגֹּלֶת *skull* 2 K 9$_{35}$, לְחִי *jawbone* Jg 15$_{15}$, יָד *hand* Ps 76$_{6}$, כַּף *palm (of hand)* 2 K 9$_{35}$, רֶגֶל *foot* 2 K 9$_{35}$, לֵב *heart*, i.e. courage 2 S 7$_{27}$, לֵבָב *heart* Ne 9$_{8}$, נְבֵלָה *corpse* 1 K 13$_{28}$, פֶּגֶר *corpse* 2 C 20$_{25}$, אָתוֹן *she-ass* 1 S 9$_{4.4}$, פֶּרֶא *wild ass* Jr 2$_{24}$, בְּהֵמָה *cattle* 2 C 20$_{25}$ (if em. בָּהֶם *among them* to בְּהֵמָה), חָצִיר *grass* 1 K 18$_{5}$, צִיץ *flower* 4Q185 1.1$_{12}$, גֶּפֶן *vine* 2 K 4$_{39}$, דּוּדָאִים *mandrakes* Gn 30$_{14}$, לֶחֶם *bread* Ex 16$_{25}$ Ec 11$_{1}$, דְּבַשׁ *honey* Pr 25$_{16}$, תֶּבֶן *straw* Ex 5$_{11}$, קוֹץ *thorns* Ex 22$_{5}$.

עִיר *city* 2 S 20$_{6}$, בִּקְעָה *valley* Gn 11$_{2}$, בְּאֵר *well* Gn 26$_{19}$, יֵמִם *hot spring(s)* Gn 36$_{24}$, מַיִם *water* Gn 26$_{32}$ Ex 15$_{22}$ Jr 14$_{3}$ Ps 73$_{10}$ (if em.; see Subj.) 2 C 32$_{4}$, דֶּרֶךְ *way* Ps 107$_{4}$, נְתִיבָה *path* Ho 2$_{8}$, פֶּתַח *entrance* Gn 19$_{11}$, בַּיִת *house* Ps 84$_{4}$, מִשְׁכָּן *dwelling place* Ps 132$_{5.6}$, מָקוֹם *place* Ps 132$_{5.6}$, מָכוֹן *place* 4Q415 11$_{12}$, מִרְעֶה *pasture* Lm 1$_{6}$ 1 C 4$_{40}$, אֳנִיָּה *ship* Jon 1$_{3}$.

אוֹצָר *treasure* Si 40$_{18(B)}$, סִימָה *treasure* Si 40$_{18(Bmg)}$, כֶּסֶף *money* Gn 44$_{8}$, אוֹן *wealth* Ho 12$_{9}$, הוֹן *wealth* Pr 1$_{13}$ Si 6$_{14}$, כֹּפֶר *ransom* Jb 33$_{24}$, תַּשְׁלֻמֶת *reward* Si 12$_{2}$, קָרְבָּן *offering* Nm 31$_{50}$, כְּלִי *jewellery* Nm 31$_{50}$, *object* 2 C 20$_{25}$, כּוּמָז *ornament* Nm 31$_{50}$, אֶצְעָדָה *bracelet* Nm 31$_{50}$, צָמִיד *bracelet* Nm 31$_{50}$, טַבַּעַת *ring* Nm 31$_{50}$, עָגִיל *anklet* Nm 31$_{50}$, עֲטָרָה *crown* 1 C 20$_{2}$, שָׁלָל *spoil* Jg 5$_{30}$ 1 S 14$_{30}$ Ps 119$_{162}$ (or em. כְּמוֹצֵא *as one who finds* to כִּי מוֹצָא *for [your] utterance* is), רְכוּשׁ *possessions* 2 C 20$_{25}$, בֶּגֶד *garment* 2 C 20$_{25(mss)}$, כַּבִּיר *much* Jb 31$_{25}$, חֵץ *arrow* 1 S 20$_{21.36}$, אֲבֵדָה *lost object* Lv 5$_{22.23}$ Dt 22$_{3}$ CD 9$_{15}$.

חֵן *favour* Gn 6$_{8}$ 18$_{3}$ 19$_{19}$ 30$_{27}$ 32$_{6}$ 33$_{8.10.15}$ 34$_{11}$ 39$_{4}$ 47$_{25.29}$ 50$_{4}$ Ex 33$_{12.13.13.16.17}$ 34$_{9}$ Nm 11$_{11.15}$ 32$_{5}$ Dt 24$_{1}$ Jg 6$_{17}$ 1 S 1$_{18}$ 16$_{22}$ 20$_{3.29}$ 25$_{8}$ 27$_{5}$ Jr 31$_{2}$ Pr 3$_{4}$ 28$_{23}$ Ru 2$_{2.10.13}$ Est 5$_{8}$ 7$_{3}$ 8$_{5}$ Si 3$_{18(C)}$ 42$_{1}$ 44$_{23}$ 4QDibHam[a] 3.2$_{18}$ ([חן]) 4QPrFêtes[c] 99.1$_{1}$, רַחֲמִים *compassion* Si 3$_{18(A)}$, מִשְׁעָן *support* Si 33$_{1}$ 4QBéat 14.2$_{7}$ ([מ]שען]), חֵפֶץ *pleasure* Is 58$_{3.13}$ 4Q416 2.2$_{8}$, טוֹב *good* Pr 16$_{20}$ 17$_{20}$ 18$_{22}$ 19$_{8}$ perh. Si 51$_{18(B)}$, צְדָקָה *righteousness* Pr 21$_{21}$ (or del. צְדָקָה), כָּבוֹד *glory* Pr 21$_{21}$ Si 4$_{13}$ GnzPs 3$_{1}$.

נֶגַע *stroke* Pr 6$_{33}$, טֻמְאָה *uncleanness* 2 C 29$_{16}$, קָלוֹן *dishonour* Pr 6$_{33}$, צָרָה *distress* Ps 116$_{3}$, יָגוֹן *grief* Ps 116$_{3}$, רָעָה *evil* 1 S 29$_{6}$ 2 S 14$_{22}$ 15$_{25}$ 16$_{4}$ 1 K 11$_{19}$ Jr 23$_{11}$, רֶשַׁע *wickedness* Ps 10$_{15}$, עָוֹן *iniquity* Gn 44$_{16}$ perh. Ho 12$_{9}$ Ps 36$_{3}$, עָוֶל *wrong* Jr 2$_{5}$, זִמָּה *wickedness* Ps 17$_{3}$ (if em. זַמֹּתִי *I have planned* to זַמֹּתִי or זִמָּתִי *my wickedness*, as part of first half-verse), עֶרְוָה *nakedness*, i.e. indecency Dt 24$_{1}$, קֶשֶׁר *conspiracy* 2 K 17$_{4}$.

שָׁלוֹם *peace* Ca 8$_{10}$ (unless מוֹצְאֵת is hi. ptc. of יצא *one who brings out*; mss מוֹצאת; or em. כְּמוֹצְאֵת שָׁלוֹם *as one who finds peace* to כְּמוֹצֵאת שָׁלוֹם *as one who is handed over as a surety* [מצא ho. ptc.] or מוֹצָא שָׁלוֹם *star of the evening*), מָנוֹחַ *rest* Gn 8$_{9}$ Is 34$_{14}$ Jr 45$_{3}$ Lm 1$_{3}$ 4QCommGenA 1$_{15}$, מְנוּחָה *rest* Ru 1$_{9}$ Si 6$_{28}$, מַרְגּוֹעַ *rest* Jr 6$_{16}$, נַחַת *rest* Si 11$_{19}$ 34$_{21}$, קֶבֶר *grave* Jb 3$_{22}$, חַיָּה *life*, i.e. vigour Is 57$_{10}$ (or em. חַיָּתֵךְ *your life* to דֵּי חַיָּתֵךְ *sufficiency of your life*), חַיִּים *life* Pr 8$_{35}$ 21$_{21}$, בְּתוּל *virginity* Dt 22$_{14.17}$=11QT 65$_{9.12}$.

חָכְמָה *wisdom* Jb 32$_{13}$ Pr 3$_{13}$ 8$_{17.35}$ Si 6$_{27}$ 40$_{19}$ 51$_{20.27}$ 4Q185 1.2$_{12}$ (unless subj.) 4Q424 3$_{7}$, חָכְמוֹת *wisdom* Pr 1$_{28}$ 24$_{14}$, שֶׂכֶל *understanding* Pr 3$_{4}$, דֵּעָה *knowledge* Si 51$_{16(11QPs^a)}$, דַּעַת *knowledge* Pr 2$_{5}$ 8$_{9}$, לֶקַח *instruction* Si 51$_{16(B)}$, אֹמֶר *word* Pr 4$_{22}$, דָּבָר *word* Am 8$_{12}$ Pr 4$_{22}$ Ec 12$_{10}$ Ne 5$_{8}$ Si 34$_{22}$, חִידָה *(answer to) riddle* Jg 14$_{12.18}$, מַעֲנֶה *answer* Jb 32$_{3}$, סֵפֶר *book* 2 K 22$_{8}$||2 C 34$_{14}$ Ne 7$_{6}$ 2 C 34$_{15}$, חָזוֹן *vision* Lm 2$_{9}$, חֲלוֹם *dream* Jb 20$_{8}$, תְּנוּאָה *occasion (for accusation)* Jb 33$_{10}$, מַעֲשֶׂה *deed* Ec 3$_{11}$ 8$_{17.17.17}$, יוֹם *day* Lm 2$_{16}$.

שַׁעַר *measure* Gn 26$_{12}$, חֶשְׁבּוֹן *sum* Ec 7$_{27.28}$, דַּי *sufficiency* Lv 12$_{8}$ 25$_{28}$ Is 57$_{10}$ (if em.; see above), חֵקֶר *depth* of Y. Jb 11$_{7}$, תַּכְלִית *completeness* Jb 11$_{7}$, תּוֹצָאָה *consequence* 4QWays[b] 1a.2$_{14}$, מַחְסוֹר *thing needed* 4Q416 2.3$_{3}$ 4Q418 127$_{1}$, כֹּל *everything* Ec 9$_{10}$, מְאוּמָה *anything* 1 S 12$_{5}$ 29$_{3}$ Ec 7$_{14}$, מָה *what?* Gn 31$_{37}$ 1 S 29$_{8}$, זֶה *this* Ec 7$_{27.29}$, זֹאת *this* Gn 37$_{32}$, אֲשֶׁר *that which* 1 S 10$_{7}$ 25$_{8}$ Ezk 3$_{1}$, -שֶׁ *one who* Ca 3$_{1.2.4}$.

<PREP> לְ of benefit, *to, for* perh. 4QapPs^b 33$_1$, + Y. Ps 132$_5$, Ephraim Ho 12$_{9.9}$, עַם *people* Nm 11$_{22.22}$ (unless both מצא II *suffice*), עֵדָה *assembly* Jg 21$_{14}$ (unless מצא II *suffice*), כַּף *sole* of foot Gn 8$_9$, נֶפֶשׁ *soul*, i.e. self Jr 6$_{16}$, לִילִית *nightjar* Is 34$_{14}$.

לְ introducing object, + עַם *people* Ne 9$_{32}$, אָב *father* Ne 9$_{32}$, מֶלֶךְ *king* Ne 9$_{32}$, שַׂר *prince* Ne 9$_{32}$, כֹּהֵן *priest* Ne 9$_{32}$, נָבִיא *prophet* Ne 9$_{32}$, אֹיֵב *enemy* Ps 21$_9$, שׂנא ptc. *one who hates* Ps 21$_{9(mss)}$, מַמְלָכָה *kingdom* Is 10$_{10}$, חַיִל *wealth* Is 10$_{14}$.

לְ *in respect to*, + אִשָּׁה *woman* Dt 22$_{14}$=11QT 65$_9$, בַּת *daughter* Dt 22$_{17}$=11QT 65$_{12}$.

בְּ of place, *in, among*, + Y. Jr 2$_5$, Bezek Jg 1$_5$, Dothan Gn 37$_{17}$, Sodom Gn 18$_{26}$, עִיר *city* Dt 22$_{23}$ Ec 9$_{15}$ (or em. pass. ptc. or ni.), אֶרֶץ *land* Gn 11$_2$, חֶלְקָה *plot of land* 2 K 9$_{21}$, שָׂדֶה *field* Gn 30$_{14}$ 16$_{25}$ Dt 22$_{25.27}$ 1 S 30$_{11}$ Ps 132$_6$ 11QT 66$_4$, מִדְבָּר *steppe* Gn 36$_{24}$ Jr 31$_2$ (or em. כַּמִּדְבָּר *as in the steppe*), נַחַל *wadi* Gn 26$_{19}$, סוֹף *end* of wadi 2 C 20$_{16}$, דֶּרֶךְ *way* Ex 18$_8$ 1 K 11$_{29}$ (unless em. בַּדֶּרֶךְ to וַיְסִירֵהוּ מִן־הַדֶּרֶךְ *and he turned aside from the way*) 13$_{24}$, בַּיִת *house* 2 K 22$_8$ 23$_{24(mss)}$ (L בֵּית *in the house of*), הֵיכָל *temple* 2 C 29$_{16}$, חוּץ *outside* Ca 8$_1$, מָקוֹם *place* 11QT 66$_4$.

David 1 S 29$_{3.6}$ Jr 23$_{11}$ 2 C 34$_{15}$, Hoshea 2 K 17$_4$, אִשָּׁה *woman* Dt 24$_1$, בֵּן *son* 2 C 20$_{25}$ (or em.; see Obj.), עֶבֶד *servant* 1 S 29$_8$, friends of Job Jb 17$_{10}$, פֶּה *mouth* of sack Gn 44$_8$, יָד *hand* 1 S 12$_5$, עַיִן *eye*, i.e. sight Gn 6$_8$ 18$_3$ 19$_{19}$ 30$_{27}$ 32$_6$ 33$_{8.10.15}$ 34$_{11}$ 39$_4$ 47$_{25.29}$ 50$_4$ Ex 33$_{12.13.13.16.17}$ 34$_9$ Nm 11$_{11.15}$ 32$_5$ Dt 24$_1$ Jg 6$_{17}$ 1 S 1$_{18}$ 16$_{22}$ 20$_{3.29}$ 25$_8$ 27$_5$ 2 S 14$_{22}$ 15$_{25}$ 16$_4$ 1 K 11$_{19}$ Pr 3$_4$ Ru 2$_{2.10.13}$ Est 5$_8$ 7$_3$ Si 3$_{18(C)}$ 42$_1$ 44$_{23}$ 4QDibHam^a 3.2$_{18}$ ([בעיניכה]), חֵפֶץ *desire* GnzPs 3$_1$, זֹאת *this* 4QapMes 2.2$_4$, אֵלֶּה *these* Ec 7$_{28}$ 4Q 415 11$_{12}$.

בְּ of time, *in, during, after*, + יוֹם *day* Is 58$_3$, חֹדֶשׁ *month* Jr 2$_{24}$, שָׁנָה *year* Gn 26$_{12}$, אַחֲרִית *end* Dt 4$_{30}$ Si 34$_{22}$, רֹב *multitude* of days Ec 11$_1$, עֵת *time* Si 33$_1$ 4Q Béat 14.2$_7$, מַחֲלֹקֶת *division* of time 4QCitJub 1.1$_7$, חַיִּים *life* 4Q418 103.2$_9$; *in (the act of)*, + מַחְתֶּרֶת *breaking in* Jr 2$_{34}$.

בְּ of accompaniment, *in, with*, + טָהֳרָה *purity* Si 51$_{20}$; of instrument, *by (means of), with*, + קֶשֶׁת *bow* 1 S 31$_3$|| 1 C 10$_3$; partitive, *some (part) of*, + Jezebel 2 K 9$_{35}$.

כְּ *as* Ho 9$_{10}$; *as in*, + מִדְבָּר *steppe* Jr 31$_2$ (if em.; see above); *as (to)*, + קֵן *nest* Is 10$_{14}$; *(at) about*, + יוֹם *day*, i.e. now 1 S 9$_{13}$.

מִן of direction, *from*, + Y. Lm 2$_9$ Si 4$_{13}$; of time, *from*, + יוֹם *day* 1 S 29$_{3.6.8}$ Ne 9$_{32}$; partitive, *out of, from among*, + יֹשֵׁב *inhabitant* Jg 21$_{12}$, כְּלִי *object* Gn 31$_{37}$, אֶלֶף *thousand* Ec 7$_{28}$; *(some of)*, + כֹּהֵן *priest* Ezr 8$_{15}$, לֵוִי *Levite* Ezr 8$_{15}$.

אֵל *at, beside*, + מַיִם *water* Jr 41$_{12}$.

עַל *at, beside*, + עַיִן *spring* Gn 16$_7$; *against*, + Job Jb 33$_{10}$.

עִם *with*, + אֲשֶׁר *one who* Gn 31$_{32}$; *at* 1 S 10$_2$.

עַד *until*, + יוֹם *day* 1 S 29$_{3.6.8}$ Ne 9$_{32}$, תַּכְלִית *perfection* Jb 11$_7$ (or em. תַּגִּעַ *you will reach*).

מִקְצָת *some of*, + דָּבָר *deed* 4QMMT C$_{30}$.

כְּדֵי *sufficient for*, + גְּאֻלָּה *redemption* Lv 25$_{26}$.

לִפְנֵי *before*, + אֵל *God* Si 3$_{18(A)}$, מֶלֶךְ *king* Est 8$_5$.

אַחֲרֵי *after (the death of)* or (find fault) *with*,* + אָדָם *person* Ec 7$_{14}$.

מצא *find at, in*, + noun without preposition, בַּיִת *house* Ru 1$_9$, בֵּית־אֵל *Bethel* Ho 12$_5$.

<COLL> מצא || אפף *surround* Ps 116$_3$, בין *understand* Pr 2$_5$ 8$_9$, ראה *see* Lm 2$_{16}$, נשׂג hi. *attain to* Si 34$_{22}$, נגע hi. *reach* Si 11$_{10}$; + בקשׁ pi. *seek* Dt 4$_{29}$ Jos 2$_{22}$ 2 S 17$_{20}$ 1 K 1$_3$ 2 K 2$_{17}$ Is 41$_{12}$ Jr 2$_{24}$ 5$_1$ 29$_{13}$ Ezk 22$_{30}$ Ho 2$_9$ 5$_6$ Am 8$_{12}$ Pr 2$_5$ Ca 3$_{1.2}$ 5$_6$ Ec 7$_{28}$ 8$_{17}$ 12$_{10}$ 1 C 4$_{40}$ Si 6$_{27}$ 11$_{10}$ 51$_{26}$ 4Q 185 1.1$_{12}$, דרשׁ *seek* Dt 4$_{29}$ Jr 29$_{13}$ Ps 10$_{15}$, חפשׂ *search for* Pr 2$_5$, pi. Gn 31$_{35}$, שׁחר pi. *seek* Pr 1$_{28}$ 7$_{15}$ 8$_{17}$, קוה pi. *wait for* Ps 69$_{21}$ Lm 2$_{16}$.

+ adverb, אָז *then* 4Q416 2.2$_8$ 4Q418 107$_1$ ([תמצ[א), אַחֲרֵי *afterwards* Pr 28$_{23}$ (ms אַחֲרָיו *with him* or *by it* [reproof]; or em. אַחֲרָיו and move to end of verse), לְאָחוֹר *afterwards* Si 6$_{28}$, כֵּן *as soon as* 1 S 9$_{13}$, perh. *in sufficient quantity* Jg 21$_{14}$, שָׁם *there* Gn 18$_{28.30}$ 1 S 10$_3$ Ezr 8$_{15}$, אֲשֶׁר *(the place) where* Ex 5$_{11}$ Jg 17$_{8.9}$, הַרְבֵּה *much* Si 51$_{16}$.

לִמְצֹא *to find*, preceded by לאה *be weary* Gn 19$_{11}$, מהר pi. *hasten* Gn 27$_{20}$, בקשׁ pi. *seek* Ec 12$_{10}$, יכל *be able* Ec 8$_{17}$.

עֵת מְצֹא *time of finding* Ps 32$_6$ (or em. מָצוֹק *of distress* or מָצוֹר *of distress*), משניהם מוצא אוצר *better than both of them is finding treasure* Si 40$_{18(B)}$, var. 40$_{19}$,

מוֹצֶא אֲנִי מַר מִמָּוֶת אֶת־הָאִשָּׁה *I find the woman to be more bitter than death* Ec 7_{26}, וַיִּמְצָאֵם עֶשֶׂר יָדוֹת עַל כָּל־הַחַרְטֻמִּים *and he found them ten times better than all the magicians* Dn 1_{20}, במצאך מקצת דברינו כן *when you find some of our practices to be correct* 4QMMT C_{30}, לא ימצא להשחיתך *he will not find it possible to destroy you* Si 12_{11}, מָצָאתָ אֶת־לְבָבוֹ נֶאֱמָן לְפָנֶיךָ *you found his heart faithful before you* Ne 9_{8}, וַיִּמְצָאָהּ מִשְׁקַל כִּכַּר־זָהָב *and he found it (to be) a weight of a talent of gold* 1 C 20_{2}, וַיִּמְצָאֵם שְׁלֹשׁ־מֵאוֹת אֶלֶף *and he found them (to be) three hundred thousand* 2 C 25_{5}, לא מצאו להנצל מרעה *they do not find it possible to deliver themselves from evil* Si $34_{6(B)}$, אשרי איש מצא תמים *happy is the man whom one finds,* i.e. is found, *to be without fault* Si $34_{8(Bmg)}$, וָאֶמְצָא כָּתוּב בּוֹ *and I found written in it (the following)* Ne 7_{5}, sim. Ne 8_{14}.

11. pass. **be found, i.e. be present,** <SUBJ> אִישׁ *man* Ec 9_{15} (if em. מָצָא *one found* to מָצוּא *there was present*), עֵזֶר *help* Gn 2_{20} (if em. מָצָא to מָצוּא).* <PREP> לְ of benefit, *for*, + אָדָם *human being* Gn 2_{20} (if em.; see Subj.); בְּ of place, *in*, + עִיר *city* Ec 9_{15} (if em.; see Subj.).

Also 4QapJoshua^{b} 10_{4} 4QpsEzek^{c} 1_{6} 4QpsEzek^{d} 9_{1} 4Q418 97_{3} 148.1_{2} 4QNarrB 1_{5} 4QDibHam^{a} 7_{15} 4QPrFêtes^{c} 59_{2} 4QapMes 2.3_{7} (מצא[ו]).

<SYN> אפף *surround*, בין *understand*, ראה *see*, נשׂג hi. *attain to*, נגע hi. *reach*.

Ni. $142.7.32$ Pf. נִמְצָא, 3fs Q נמצאת, נִמְצֵאת, נִמְצֵאתִי, נִמְצְאוּ (נִמְצָאוּ); impf. יִמָּצֵא, 3fs תִּמָּצֵא, תִּמָּצְאִי, יִמָּצְאוּן, 3fpl תִּמָּצֶאנָה; + waw וַיִּמָּצֵא, 3fs וַתִּמָּצֵא, וַיִּמָּצְאוּ; וְנִמְצָא, וְנִמְצֵאתִי, וְנִמְצָאוּ; ptc. נִמְצָא, נִמְצָאָה, נִמְצָאִים (נִמְצָאִים; sf. נִמְצָאַיִךְ), נִמְצָאוֹת (נִמְצָאֹת); inf. cstr. הִמָּצְאוֹ, abs. הִמָּצֵא.

1. (of what is sought, missed, lost) **be found, a.** thing (Gn $44_{9.10.12.16.17}$ Dt 22_{20} 1 S 9_{20} $10_{2.16}$ 2 K 22_{13}‖2 C 34_{21} 2 K 23_{2}‖2 C 34_{30} Jr 50_{20} [§ 4] Jb 28_{12} [unless §4; or em.; see Subj.] 28_{13} Ezr 2_{62}‖Ne 7_{64} CD 9_{14}). **b.** person (Gn $18_{29.30.31.32}$ Jos 10_{17} 1 S 10_{21} 1 C 26_{31} CD 9_{16}), Tyre (Ezk 26_{21}). **c.** Y. (Is 55_{6} 65_{1} Jr 29_{14} 1 C 28_{9} 2 C $15_{2.4.15}$).

2. be found, encountered, met (Dt 21_{1} Jg $20_{48.48}$ Is 13_{15} 22_{3} [unless all three §5]), of wisdom (Pr 8_{12} [if em.; see Coll.]), of words of Y. (Jr 15_{16} [or em.; see Subj.]).

3. a. be present, of persons (Gn 19_{15} Dt 17_{2}=11QT 55_{15} Dt 18_{10}=11QT 60_{17} Dt 20_{11}=11QT 62_{7} 1 S $13_{15.16}$ Jr 5_{26} 41_{3} Ec 9_{15} [if em.; see Subj.] Est 1_{5} 4_{16} Ezr 8_{15} 1 C 4_{41} 29_{17} 2 C 5_{11} 29_{29} 30_{21} 31_{1} $34_{32.33}$ $35_{7.17.18}$ Si 12_{17}), of Y. (Ps 46_{2}).

b. be (found), exist, remain (Gn 47_{14} Ex 9_{19} 12_{19} 1 S 13_{19} 2 S $17_{12.13}$ 2 K $12_{11.19}$ 14_{14}‖2 C 25_{24} 2 K 16_{8} 18_{15} 19_{4}‖Is 37_{4} 2 K 20_{13}‖Is 39_{2} 2 K 22_{9}‖2 C 34_{17} 2 K $25_{19.19}$‖Jr $52_{25.25}$ Is 30_{14} 35_{9} 51_{3} 65_{8} Jr 41_{8} Zp 3_{13} Ps 37_{36} Jb 42_{15} Pr 10_{13} Dn 11_{19} Si 6_{10} 1QH 4_{20} 1QS $6_{2.24}$ 4QpPs^{a} 1.2_{7} 4Q185 1.1_{12} 4QD^{a} 11_{6} 4Q418 69.2_{8} 4QHod^{b} 8.1_{3} 11QT 59_{14}), **be found in someone's possession** (Ex $35_{23.24}$ Dt 21_{17} 1 S 9_{8} $13_{22.22}$ 21_{4} 1 C 28_{9}), **be found (written)** (Est 6_{2} Dn 12_{1} [unless §10] Ne 13_{1}).

4. be found, i.e. **discovered, detected,** of what is stolen (Ex 21_{16} $22_{3.3}$), evil, falsehood (1 S 25_{28} 1 K 1_{52} 1QS $10_{22.23}$ 4QMMT C_{9} [[י]מצא]), wrongdoing (Jr 50_{20} Ezk 28_{15} Mc 1_{13} Ml 2_{6} Jb 19_{28} 2 C 36_{8} GnzPs 4_{23}), conspiracy (Jr 11_{9} 4QD^{a} 5.1_{10} [[נמ]צא]), good (1 K 14_{13} 2 C 19_{3}), breach in building (2 K 12_{6}), shed blood (Jr 2_{34}), perh. **be found out (as guilty)** (Jr 10_{18} [if em.; see Subj.]).

5. be caught, be captured, be seized,* of thief (Ex $22_{1.6.7}$ Dt 24_{7} Jr 2_{26} Pr 6_{31}), Israel among thieves (Jr 48_{27}), people having unlawful sexual intercourse (Dt $22_{22.28}$=11QT 66_{10}), Babylon (Is 13_{15} [unless §2] Jr 50_{24}), cities (Jg 20_{48} [unless §2]), rulers (Is 22_{3} [unless §2]).

6. be found (to be so), through examination, experience (Dn 1_{19} Ezr 10_{18} 1 C 24_{4} 2 C 2_{16} Si $34_{8[B]}$ $44_{16.17.20}$ 46_{20} 4QpsJub^{a} $2.2_{8.8}$ 4QpsJub^{b} 7_{1} 4QSD 1.2_{5} 4Q424 1_{12}), **be found to be correct** (Est 2_{23}).

7. be found (out), through study, revelation (1QS 8_{11} 9_{13} CD 15_{10}).

8. be (found to be) sufficient (Jos 17_{16} Zc 10_{10} [unless both מצא II ni. *be sufficient*]).

9. be gained (Ho 14_{9} Pr 16_{31}).

10. be left over, survive (Is $37_{31[1QIsa^{a}]}$); perh. ptc. as noun, **survivor(s), refugee(s)*** (Dn 12_{1} [unless §3]).

11. be reached, of wisdom (Jb 28_{12}).

<SUBJ> Y. Is 55_{6} 65_{1} Jr 29_{14} Ps 46_{2} (or em.; see below) 1 C 28_{9} 2 C $15_{2.4.15}$, Babylon Jr 50_{24}, Chaldaeans Jr 41_{3}, Israel(ites) Jr 48_{27} Ezr 8_{15} 2 C 31_{1} 35_{18}, Jews Est 4_{16},

Judah 2 C 35_{18}, Meunites 1 C $4_{41(Qr)}$, Tyre Ezk 26_{21}, עַם *people* Dt 20_{11}=11QT 62_7 1 S $13_{15.16}$ 2 K 25_{19}||Jr 52_{25} Est 1_5 Dn 12_1 1 C 28_9, שְׁאֵרִית *remnant* 2 K 19_4||Is 37_4, Abraham Si 44_{20} 4QpsJub^a 2.2_8 ([א]ברהם) 4QpsJub^b 7_1, Eliezer Ezr 10_{18}, Enoch Si 44_{17}, Gedaliah Ezr 10_{18}, Jarib Ezr 10_{18}, Maaseiah Ezr 10_{18}, Noah Si 44_{17}, Samuel Si 46_{20}, Saul 1 S 10_{21}.

אָדָם *human being* Ex 9_{19}, אִישׁ *man* Ex 21_{16} Dt 17_2=11QT 55_{15} Dt $22_{22.29}$ 24_7 2 K 25_{19}||Jr 52_{25} Jr 41_8 Ec 9_{15} (if em. qal) Si $34_{8(B)}$ 1QH 4_{20} 1QS $6_{2.24}$ 4QpPs^a 1.2_7 11QT 59_{14}, אִשָּׁה *woman* Dt 17_2=11QT 55_{15} Jb 42_{15}, אָב *father* 2 S 17_{12}, בֵּן *son* 1 S 10_{21} 1 C 24_4 4Q418 69.2_8, of Israel 2 C 30_{21} 35_{17}, בַּת *daughter* Gn 19_{15}, יֶלֶד *youth* Dn 1_{19}, נַעֲרָה *girl* Dt $22_{28(Qr)}$=11QT 66_{10}, בְּתוּלָה *young woman* Dt 22_{28}=11QT 66_{10}, מֶלֶךְ *king* Jos 10_{17} Dn 11_{19}, שַׂר *prince* 4QpsJub^a 2.2_8 ([שר]), מְאֹד *Grand One* Ps 46_2 (if em. מְאֹד *very*), שֹׁפֵט *judge* 4QBark^f 1.1_6, כֹּהֵן *priest* 2 C 5_{11}, יֹשֵׁב *inhabitant* Jr 10_{18} (if em. יִמְצָאוּ *they shall find*, i.e. experience [distress] to יִמָּצֵאוּ *they shall be found out*), בַּעַל *owner* CD 9_{16}, אֹהֵב *friend* Si 6_{10}, חָבֵר *companion* Si 6_{10}, רֵעַ *neighbour* 1QS 6_{10}, גַּנָּב *thief* Ex $22_{1.6.7}$ Jr 2_{26} Pr 6_{31}.

עבר hi. ptc. *one who burns* child Dt 18_{10}=11QT 60_{17}, קֹסֵם *diviner* Dt 18_{10}=11QT 60_{17}, מְנַחֵשׁ *diviner* Dt 18_{10}=11QT 60_{17}, מְעֹנֵן *soothsayer* Dt 18_{10}=11QT 60_{17}, מְכַשֵּׁף *sorcerer* Dt 18_{10}=11QT 60_{17}, חבר ptc. *one who casts spell* Dt 18_{10}=11QT 60_{17}, שׁאל ptc. *one who consults* ghosts Dt 18_{10}=11QT 60_{17}, דרשׁ ptc. *one who inquires* of the dead Dt 18_{10}=11QT 60_{17}, חֹזֶה *seer* 1QH 4_{20}, חָרָשׁ *smith* 1 S 13_{19}, חָלָל *slain one* Dt 21_1, פָּרִיץ *ravenous one* Is 35_9, צַדִּיק *righteous one* Si 44_{17}, רָשָׁע *wicked one* Jr 5_{26} Ps 37_{36}, גִּבּוֹר *mighty one* 1 C 26_{31}, אֹיֵב *enemy* Si 12_{17}.

לָשׁוֹן *tongue* of deceit Zp 3_{13}, דָּם *blood* Jr 2_{34}, עוֹר *skin* Ex 35_{23}, אָתוֹן *female ass* 1 S 9_{20} $10_{2.16}$, בְּהֵמָה *beast* Ex 9_{19}, שֹׁרֶשׁ *root* Jb 19_{28}, שְׂאֹר *leaven* Ex 12_{19}, פְּרִי *fruit* Ho 14_9, צִיץ *flower* 4Q185 1.1_{12}, תִּירוֹשׁ *new wine* Is 65_8, אַרְגָּמָן *purple (material)* Ex 35_{23}, תְּכֵלֶת *blue (material)* Ex 35_{23}, תּוֹלֵעָה *scarlet (material)* Ex 35_{23}, שֵׁשׁ *fine linen* Ex 35_{23}, עֵז *(hair of) goat* Ex 35_{23}, עֵץ *wood* Ex 35_{24}, שֹׁרֶשׁ *root* Is $37_{31(1QIsa^a)}$ (הנמצא שרש *the surviving root*; MT הַנִּשְׁאָרָה שֹׁרֶשׁ *the surviving* remnant shall be *a root*), חֶרֶשׂ *sherd* Is 30_{14}, צְרוֹר *pebble* 2 S 17_{13}, אֶבֶן *(precious) stone* 1 C 28_9, זָהָב *gold* 2 K 12_{19} perh. 14_{14}||2 C 25_{24} 2 K 16_8, כֶּסֶף *silver, money* Gn 47_{14} 2 K 12_{11} perh. 14_{14}||2 C 25_{24} 2 K 16_8 18_{15} 22_9||2 C 34_{17}, גָּבִיעַ *cup* Gn $44_{9.10.12.16.17}$, כְּלִי *vessel* 2 K 14_{14}||2 C 25_{24}, עֲטָרָה *crown* Pr 16_{31}, חֶרֶב *sword* 1 S $13_{22.22}$, חֲנִית *spear* 1 S $13_{22.22}$, גְּנֵבָה *stolen object* Ex $22_{3.3}$, אֲבֵדָה *lost object* CD 9_{14}.

הַר *hill country* Jos 17_{16}, עִיר *city* Jg 20_{48}.

רָעָה *evil* 1 S 25_{28} 1 K 1_{52} 4QMMT C$_9$ ([י]מצא), חַטָּאת *sin* Jr 50_{20}, עָוֶל *wrong* GnzPs 4_{23}, עַוְלָה *wrong* Ezk 28_{15} Ml 2_6 4QHod^b 8.1_3 ([עולה]), פֶּשַׁע *transgression* Mc 1_{13}, מִרְמָה *deceit* 1QS 10_{22}, כָּזָב *lie* 1QS 10_{22}, שֶׁקֶר *falsehood* 4QMMT C$_9$ ([י]מצא), מַעַל *unfaithfulness* 4QMMT C$_9$ ([י]מצא), שִׁקּוּץ *detested thing* 1QS 10_{23}, קֶשֶׁר *conspiracy* Jr 11_9 4QD^a 5.1_{10} (נמ]צא קש[ר), בֶּדֶק *breach* 2 K 12_6.

שָׂשׂוֹן *joy* Is 51_3 Si 15_6, שִׂמְחָה *gladness* Is 51_3 Si 15_6, חָכְמָה *wisdom* Jb 28_{12} (or em. תָּבוֹא *it comes* or תֵּצֵא *it comes out*) 28_{13} Pr 8_{12} (if em.; see Coll.) 10_{13}, שֶׂכֶל *understanding* 1QS 9_{13}, בְּתוּל *virginity* Dt 22_{20}.

דָּבָר *word* Jr 15_{16} (or em. מִנֹּאֲצַי *from those who despise*), *thing* 1 K 14_{13} Est 2_{23} 2 C 19_3 1QS 8_{11}, סֵפֶר *book* 2 K 22_{13}||2 C 34_{21} 2 K 23_2||2 C 34_{30}, כְּתָב *enrolment* Ne 7_{64}, חֹק *statute* 4QD^a 11_6, רֶבַע *quarter* of shekel 1 S 9_8, עֲשָׂרָה *ten* Gn 18_{32}, עֶשְׂרִים *twenty* Gn 18_{31}, שְׁלֹשִׁים *thirty* Gn 18_{30}, אַרְבָּעִים *forty* Gn 18_{29}, מֵאָה וַחֲמִשִּׁים אֶלֶף וּשְׁלֹשֶׁת אֲלָפִים וְשֵׁשׁ מֵאוֹת *a hundred and fifty-three thousand six hundred* 2 C 2_{16}, כֹּל *everything* Dt 21_{17} 2 K 20_{13}||Is 39_2 1QS 9_{20}, אֵלֶּה *these* Ezr 2_{62}||Ne $7_{64(mss)}$.

Subject not specified, Jg 20_{48} 1 S 21_4 Is 13_{15} 22_3 (or em. נִמְצָאַיִךְ to אַמִּיצַיִךְ or נֶאֱמָצַיִךְ *your mighty ones*) Zc 10_{10} (unless מצא II *be sufficient*) Est 6_2 Ne 13_1 2 C 29_{29} $34_{32.33}$ 35_7 36_8 CD 15_{10} 4QCommGenA 3_5.

<PREP> לְ of benefit, *to, for*, + Israelites Zc 10_{10} (unless מצא II ni. *be sufficient*), בֵּן *son* Jos 17_{16} (unless מצא II ni.), אֲבֵדָה *lost object* CD 9_{16}.

לְ of possession, *of, (belonging) to*, + Saul 1 S 13_{22}, Jonathan 1 S 13_{22}, אִישׁ *man* Dt 21_{17}, נַעֲרָה *girl* Dt $22_{20(Qr)}$, מֶלֶךְ *king* 11QT 59_{14}.

לְ of agent, *by* Is 65_1 (נִמְצֵאתִי לְלֹא בִקְשֻׁנִי *I was found by those who did not seek me* Is 65_1), + Benjamin 2 C 15_2, Israel 2 C 15_4, Judah 2 C $15_{2.15}$, Asa 2 C 15_2, Solomon 1 C 28_9, אִישׁ *man* 1QS 8_{11}, בֵּן *son* 1 C 28_9, גּוֹלָה *ex-*

iles Jr 29$_{14}$.

בְּ of place, *in, on, within, among* 4QCommGenA 3$_{5}$, + Benjamin 2 C 34$_{32}$, Hebronites 1 C 26$_{31}$, Israel(ites) Dt 18$_{10}$=11QT 60$_{17}$ Jr 41$_{8}$ 2 C 34$_{33}$, Jerusalem 2 C 30$_{21}$ 34$_{32}$, Judah 4QD^{a} 5.1$_{10}$ ([נמ]צא), Susa Est 1$_{5}$ 4$_{16}$, Zion Is 51$_{3}$, עַם *people* Jr 5$_{26}$, Adonijah 1 K 1$_{52}$, David 1 S 25$_{28}$, Job Jb 19$_{28}$, אִישׁ *man* Jr 11$_{9}$ 1QS 6$_{24}$, מֶלֶךְ *king* Ezk 28$_{15}$, יֹשֵׁב *inhabitant* Jr 11$_{9}$ Mc 1$_{13}$, גַּנָּב *thief* Jr 48$_{27}$, פֶּה *mouth* Zp 3$_{13}$, שָׂפָה *lip* Ml 2$_{6}$ Pr 10$_{13}$ 1QS 10$_{22}$, לָשׁוֹן *tongue* 1QS 10$_{23}$, יָד *hand* Gn 44$_{16.17}$ Ex 21$_{16}$ 22$_{3}$ 1 S 9$_{8}$ 13$_{22}$ 4QMMT C$_{9}$ ([י]מצא).

אֶרֶץ *land* Gn 47$_{14}$ 1 S 13$_{19}$ Jb 28$_{13}$ 42$_{15}$ 4QpPs^{a} 1.2$_{7}$, אֲדָמָה *land* Dt 21$_{1}$, שָׂדֶה *field* Ex 9$_{19}$, גְּבוּל *border* 1 S 13$_{19(mss)}$, דֶּרֶךְ *way* Pr 16$_{31}$, בַּיִת *house* Ex 12$_{19}$ 2 K 14$_{14}$‖2 C 25$_{24(mss)}$ 2 K 22$_{9}$‖2 C 34$_{17}$ 2 K 23$_{2}$, אוֹצָר *treasury* 2 K 12$_{19}$ 14$_{14}$ 16$_{8}$ 18$_{15}$ 20$_{13}$‖Is 39$_{2}$, בִּירָה *fortress* Est 1$_{5}$, עִיר *city* Dt 20$_{11}$=11QT 62$_{7}$ 2 K 25$_{19.19}$‖Jr 52$_{25.25}$ Ec 9$_{15}$ (if em. qal), שַׁעַר *gate*, i.e. city Dt 17$_{2}$=11QT 55$_{15}$, אַמְתַּחַת *sack* Gn 44$_{12}$, כָּנָף *wing*, i.e. skirt of garment Jr 2$_{34}$, מְכִתָּה *fragment* Is 30$_{14}$, אֶשְׁכּוֹל *cluster* Is 65$_{8}$, תּוֹרָה *law* 4QD^{a} 11$_{6}$, מַעֲשֶׂה *deed* GnzPs 4$_{23}$; of time, *in, during* צָרָה *distress* Ps 46$_{2}$, יוֹם *day* Si 6$_{10}$, עֵת *time* 4Q424 1$_{12}$; *in (the act of)*, + מַחְתֶּרֶת *breaking in* Ex 22$_{1}$.

כְּ *like*, + Daniel Dn 1$_{19}$, בַּת *daughter* Jb 42$_{15}$.

מִן of time, *from, since*, + יוֹם *day* 1 S 25$_{28}$; of agent, *by*, + Y. Ho 14$_{9}$; partitive, *from among*, + בֵּן *son* Ezr 10$_{18}$, כֹּל *all* Dn 1$_{19}$; of cause, *on account of*, + רוּחַ *wind* 4Q 185 1.1$_{12}$.

עַל *against*, + Jehoiakim 2 C 36$_{8}$.

עִם *with*, + Jehoshaphat 2 C 19$_{3}$, Jonathan 1 S 13$_{16}$, Saul 1 S 13$_{15.16}$, מֶלֶךְ *king* 2 C 19$_{3}$.

אֵת *with* 1 C 28$_{9}$, + אִישׁ *man* Ex 35$_{23}$, מֶלֶךְ *king* 2 C 29$_{29}$, אֲשֶׁר *one who* Gn 44$_{9.10}$, כֹּל *everyone* Ex 35$_{24}$.

עַד *until*, + עֵת *time* Si 46$_{20}$.

לְפִי *according to*, + עֵת *time* 1QS 9$_{13}$ (=4QS^{e} 3$_{9}$ לפני *before*).

בְּקֶרֶב *among*, + Israel(ites) Dt 17$_{2}$=11QT 55$_{15}$.

מצא ni. *be found*, + noun without preposition, בַּיִת *in the house* 2 K 12$_{11}$ 14$_{14}$ 16$_{8}$ 18$_{15}$ 2 C 34$_{30}$.

<COLL> מצא ni. ‖ היה *be* Ml 2$_{6}$, ספה ni. *be captured* Is 13$_{15}$, תפשׂ *be caught* Jr 50$_{24}$; + בקשׁ pi. *seek* Is 65$_{1}$ Ps 37$_{36}$, pu. *be sought* Jr 50$_{20}$ Ezk 26$_{21}$ Est 2$_{23}$, דרשׁ *seek* Is 55$_{6}$ 1 C 28$_{9}$ 2 C 15$_{2}$ 1QS 8$_{11}$, ni. *be sought* 1 C 26$_{31}$.

+ adverb, אֲבָל *however* 2 C 19$_{3}$, אוּלַי *perhaps* Gn 18$_{29.30.31.32}$, פֹּה *here* 1 C 28$_{9}$, שָׁם *there* Gn 18$_{29.30.31.32}$ 2 S 17$_{12.13}$ 2 K 12$_{6}$ Is 35$_{9}$ 41$_{3}$ 1 C 4$_{41}$ (שָׁמָּה) Si 12$_{17}$ 4Q CommGenA 3$_{5}$, מֵאַיִן *where?* Jb 28$_{12}$ (or em.; see Subj.), מְאֹד *much* Ps 46$_{2}$, עוֹד *again* 1QH 4$_{20}$ 4Q418 69.2$_{8}$ 4Q Hod^{b} 8.1$_{3}$ ([עו]ד); inf. abs. + finite form of מצא Ex 22$_{3}$.

מוֹדַעַת מְזִמּוֹת אִמָּצֵא *I am found as the acquaintance of discretion* Pr 8$_{12}$ (if em. דַּעַת מְזִמּוֹת אֶמְצָא *I find knowledge [and] discretion*), אַחַת הַמְּקוֹמֹת אֲשֶׁר נִמְצָא שָׁם *one of the places where he is to be found* 2 S 17$_{12}$, כֹּל אֲשֶׁר־יִמָּצֵא שָׁם בֶּדֶק *any place where a breach is found* 2 K 12$_{6}$, וַיִּמָּצֵא כָתוּב *and it was found written* Est 6$_{2}$, vars. Dn 12$_{1}$ Ne 13$_{1}$, וַיִּמָּצְאוּ בְנֵי־אֶלְעָזָר ... רַבִּים מִן־בְּנֵי אִיתָמָר *and the sons of Eleazar were found ... to be more than the sons of Ithamar* 1 C 24$_{4}$, כול הנמצא לעשות *all that is found out (as necessary) to do* 1QS 9$_{20}$, var. CD 15$_{10}$.

נמצא תמים *he was found to be without fault* Si 34$_{8(B)}$ 44$_{16.17}$, vars. Si 44$_{20}$ (נאמן *steadfast*) 46$_{20}$ (נבון *understanding*) 4QpsJub^{a} 2.2$_{8}$ (כחש *weak*) 4QpsJub^{a} 2.2$_{8}$ (נאמן) 4QpsJub^{b} 7$_{1}$ (נאמן) 4QSD 1.2$_{5}$ ([נאמן]) 4Q424 1$_{12}$ (perh. חָנֵף *profane*).

Also 1QM 15$_{11}$ 4QD^{f} 3$_{6}$.

<SYN> היה *be*, ספה ni. *be captured*, תפשׂ *be caught*.

Hi. 7 Pf. הִמְצִיאוּ ,הִמְצִיתִךָ; impf. יַמְצִאֶנּוּ (יַמְצִאֵהוּ); + waw וַיַּמְצִאוּ; ptc. מַמְצִיא—**1. cause to meet, deliver up,** <SUBJ> Y. Zc 11$_{6}$, Abner 2 S 3$_{8}$. <OBJ> Ishbosheth 2 S 3$_{8}$, אָדָם *human beings* Zc 11$_{6}$, אִישׁ *man*, i.e. each one Zc 11$_{6}$. <PREP> בְּ *into*, + יָד *hand* 2 S 3$_{8}$ Zc 11$_{6}$.

2. cause to befall, cause to overtake, cause to come, <SUBJ> Y. Jb 34$_{11}$ (+ שׁלם pi. *requite*) 37$_{13}$ (or em. יַמְצִאֵהוּ *he causes it to come* to יְאַמְּצֵהוּ *he strengthens it*). <OBJ> impersonal Jb 34$_{11}$ 37$_{13}$ (or em.; see Subj.). <PREP> לְ of benefit, *for*, + חֶסֶד *loyalty* Jb 37$_{13}$ (or em.; see Subj.), שֵׁבֶט *rod*, i.e. correction Jb 37$_{13}$ (or em.; see Subj.), אֶרֶץ *land* Jb 37$_{13}$ (or em. לְאַרְצוֹ to אֻמְלַל אֶרֶץ *the land languishes*); כְּ *according to*, + אֹרַח *way* Jb 34$_{11}$.

3. bring, present, <SUBJ> בֵּן *son* Lv 9$_{12.13.18}$.

<OBJ> דָּם *blood* Lv 9$_{12.18}$, עוֹלָה *burnt offering* Lv 9$_{12}$. <PREP> לְ *according to*, + נֵתַח *piece* Lv 9$_{13}$; אֶל *to*, + Aaron Lv 9$_{12.13.18}$.

Ho. be found (as), handed over (as), <SUBJ> female lover Ca 8_{10} (if em. כְּמוֹצֵאת שָׁלוֹם *as one who finds peace* to כְּמוּצֵאת שָׁלוֹם *as one who is handed over as a surety*).*

*מצא II 5 vb. **suffice—Qal** 3 Pf. מָצְאוּ; + waw וּמָצָא—**suffice, be sufficient** (unless מצא I *find sufficient*), <SUBJ> אִשָּׁה *woman*, Jg 21_{14}; subj. not specified, Nm $11_{22.22}$. <PREP> לְ of benefit, *to, for*, + עַם *people* Nm $11_{22.22}$, עֵדָה *assembly* Jg 21_{14}.

Ni. 2 Impf. יִמָּצֵא—**be sufficient** (unless מצא I ni. *be [found to be] sufficient*), <SUBJ> הַר *hill country* Jos 17_{16}; subj. not specified, Zc 10_{10}. <PREP> לְ of benefit, *to, for*, + Israelites Zc 10_{10}, בֵּן *son* Jos 17_{16}.

*מצא III 2 vb. **drain—Ni.** 2 Impf. Sam יִמָּצֵא; + waw Sam וְנִמְצָא—**be drained out, be drained dry,** <SUBJ> דָּם *blood* Lv $1_{15(Sam)}$ (MT וְנִמְצָה), שְׁאָר ni. ptc. *what remanins* of blood Lv $5_{9(Sam)}$ (MT יִמָּצֵה), יֹשֵׁב *inhabitant* Jr 10_{18} (if em. יִמְצָאוּ *they shall experience* [מצא I] to יִמָּצְאוּ *they shall be drained dry*). <PREP> אֶל *at*, + קִיר *side* of altar Lv $1_{15(Sam)}$, יְסוֹד *base* of altar Lv $5_{9(Sam)}$.*
⇒ cf. מצה *drain.*

מֹצָא, see מוֹצָא I *going out.*

מַצָּב 10.0.1 n.m. **standing place**—cstr. מַצַּב; sf. מַצָּבֶךָ—**1. standing place,** <CSTR> מַצַּב רַגְלֵי *standing place of the feet of* the priests Jos $4_{3.9}$. <PREP> מִן of direction, *from*, + נשׂא *take up* Jos 4_3; עַל *upon, at* 4QMᵃ 11. 2_{20}; תַּחַת *under*, i.e. at, + קום hi. *raise* stones Jos 4_9.

2. military post, garrison, <SUBJ> יצא *go out* 1 S 13_{23}, חרד *tremble* 1 S 14_{15} (+ מַשְׁחִית *destroyer*). <NOM CL> מַצַּב פְּלִשְׁתִּים אָז בֵּית לָחֶם *the garrison of the Philistines was then at Bethlehem* 2 S 23_{14}, מַצַּב פְּלִשְׁתִּים אֲשֶׁר מֵעֵבֶר הַלָּז *the garrison of the Philistines that is on yonder side* 1 S 14_1. <CSTR> מַצַּב פְּלִשְׁתִּים *garrison of the Philistines* 1 S 13_{23} $14_{1.4.11}$ 2 S 23_{14}, הָעֲרֵלִים *of the uncircumcised* 1 S 14_6; אַנְשֵׁי הַמַּצָּב *men of the garrison* 1 S 14_{12} (or em. הַמַּצָּבָה *of the guard*). <PREP> אֶל *to*, + עבר *pass over* 1 S $14_{1.4(mss).6}$, גלה ni. *show oneself* 1 S 14_{11}; עַל *to*, + עבר *pass over* 1 S 14_4.

3. position, office, <PREP> מִן of direction, *from*, + הדף *thrust* Is 22_{19} (‖ מַעֲמָד *post*).
<SYN> §3 מַעֲמָד *post.*
⇒ נצב *stand.*

מֻצָּב I 1 n.[m.] perh. **siege mound,** <COLL> וְצַרְתִּי עָלַיִךְ מֻצָּב *and I will besiege you with a mound* Is 29_3 (‖ מְצוּרָה *siegeworks*).
<SYN> מְצוּרָה *siegeworks.**
⇒ נצב *stand.*

מֻצָּב II, see נצב II *stand*, Ho.

מַצָּבָה 1 n.f. **guard,** <CSTR> אַנְשֵׁי הַמַּצָּבָה *men of the guard* 1 S 14_{12} (or em. הַמַּצָּב *of the garrison*). <COLL> וְחָנִיתִי לְבֵיתִי מַצָּבָה *and I will encamp at my house as a guard* Zc 9_8 (if em. מִצָּבָה perh. *against an army*).
⇒ נצב *stand.*

מַצֵּבָה 38.0.4 n.f. **pillar**—מַצֵּבֶת; cstr. מַצְּבַת (מַצֶּבֶת); sf. מַצַּבְתָּהּ; pl. מַצֵּבוֹת (מַצֵּבֹת); cstr. מַצְּבוֹת; sf. מַצְּבוֹתֶיךָ, מַצְּבֹתָם (מַצְּבוֹתָם, מַצְּבֹתֵיהֶם, Q מצבותיהם)—**1. pillar, memorial stone,** commemorating appearance of Y. (Gn $28_{18.22}$ 31_{13} $35_{14.14}$), making of covenant (Gn $31_{45.51.52.52}$); at Rachel's tomb (Gn $35_{20.20}$); erected by Moses (Ex 24_4), by Absalom as personal memorial (2 S $18_{18.18}$); assoc. with cult of Canaanites (Ex 23_{24} 34_{13} Dt 7_5 12_3 4QapPent 2_5 11QT 2_6 [[מצבות]יהמה]]), Egyptians (Jr 43_{13}), Tyre (Ezk 26_{11}); built by Israelites (1 K 14_{23} 2 K 17_{10} Ho 3_4 $10_{1.2}$), prohibited for Israelites (Lv 26_1 Dt 16_{22} 11QT 51_{20} 52_2), assoc. with Baal (2 K 3_2 $10_{26.27}$), removed, destroyed by Israelites (2 K 18_4 23_{14} 2 C 14_2 31_1), by Y. (Mc 5_{12}); in Egypt for Y. (Is 19_{19}).

<SUBJ> היה *be* Is 19_{19}, ירד *go down* Ezk 26_{11} (or em. תֵּרֵד *it will go down* to יוֹרִד *he will bring down*).

<NOM CL> עֵדָה הַמַּצֵּבָה *the pillar is a witness* Gn 31_{52}, הִנֵּה הַמַּצֵּבָה *behold the pillar* Gn $31_{51(L)}$, הִיא מַצֶּבֶת קְבֻרַת־רָחֵל *it is the pillar of Rachel's tomb* Gn 35_{20}, מַצֶּבֶת אֲשֶׁר בְּעֵמֶק־הַמֶּלֶךְ *the pillar that is in the valley of the king* 2 S 18_{18}, אֵין מַצֵּבָה *there is no pillar* Ho 3_4.

<OBJ> יצא hi. *bring out* 2 K 10_{26}, ירד hi. *bring down*

Ezk 26$_{11}$ (if em.; see Subj.), עבר *pass* Gn 31$_{52}$, שׂים *place as* Gn 28$_{18.22}$, קום hi. *erect* Lv 26$_{1}$ Dt 16$_{22}$ 11QT 51$_{20}$ 52$_{2}$, רום hi. *set up (as)* Gn 31$_{45}$, נצב hi. *erect* Gn 35$_{14.14.20}$ 2 S 18$_{18}$ 2 K 17$_{10}$, ירה *erect* Gn 31$_{51}$, בנה *build* Ex 24$_{4}$ 1 K 14$_{23}$, עשׂה *make* 2 K 3$_{2}$, יטב hi. *make good* Ho 10$_{1}$, משׁח *anoint* Gn 31$_{13}$, שׁבר pi. *break* Ex 23$_{24}$ 34$_{13}$ Dt 7$_{5}$ 12$_{3}$ 2 K 18$_{4}$ 23$_{14}$ Jr 43$_{13}$ 2 C 14$_{2}$ 31$_{1}$ 4QapPent 2$_{5}$ ([תשברון]) 11QT 2$_{6}$ ([מצבות]יהמה תשברון]), כרת hi. *cut off* Mc 5$_{12}$, נתץ *pull down* 2 K 10$_{27}$ (or em.; see Cstr.), שׂרף *burn* 2 K 10$_{26}$ (or em.; see Cstr.), שׁדד po. *destroy* Ho 10$_{2}$, סור hi. *remove* 2 K 3$_{2}$, שׂנא *hate* Dt 16$_{22}$.

<CSTR> מַצֶּבֶת הַבַּעַל *pillar of Baal* 2 K 3$_{2}$ 10$_{27}$ (מַצְּבַת הַבַּעַל; mss מַצְּבוֹת *pillars of*; or em. מִזְבַּח *altar of*), מַצְּבוֹת בֵּית־הַבַּעַל *pillars of the house of Baal* 2 K 10$_{26}$ (mss מַצֶּבֶת *pillar of*; or em. אֲשֵׁרַת *Asherah of*), בֵּית־שֶׁמֶשׁ *of Beth-shemesh*, i.e. Heliopolis Jr 43$_{13}$, עֻזֵּךְ *of your strength*, i.e. your strong pillars Ezk 26$_{11}$, מַצֶּבֶת קְבֻרַת *pillar of the tomb of* Gn 35$_{20}$, אֶבֶן *of stone* Gn 35$_{14}$; אֵלוֹן הַמַּצֵּבָה *terebinth of the pillar* Jg 9$_{6}$ (if em. מֻצָּב *established* terebinth).

<PREP> לְ introducing object, *call*, i.e. name 2 S 18$_{18}$.

<COLL> מַצֵּבָה || גַּל *heap* Gn 31$_{51.52}$, אֲשֵׁרָה *Asherah* Ex 34$_{13}$ Dt 7$_{5}$ 12$_{3}$ 16$_{22}$ (+) 1 K 14$_{23}$ 2 K 17$_{10}$ 18$_{4}$ 23$_{14}$ 2 C 14$_{2}$ 31$_{1}$ 11QT 51$_{20}$, פֶּסֶל *carved image* Lv 26$_{1}$ Dt 7$_{5}$ 12$_{3}$ Mc 5$_{12}$, אֱלִיל *worthless gods* Lv 26$_{1}$, מִזְבֵּחַ *altar* Ex 24$_{4}$ (+) 34$_{13}$ Dt 7$_{5}$ 12$_{3}$ Is 19$_{19}$ (+) Ho 10$_{1.2}$ 2 C 14$_{2}$ 31$_{1}$, בָּמָה *high place* 1 K 14$_{23}$ 2 K 18$_{4}$ 2 C 14$_{2}$ 31$_{1}$, זֶבַח *sacrifice* Ho 3$_{4}$, אֵפֹד *ephod* Ho 3$_{4}$ (+), תְּרָפִים *teraphim* Ho 3$_{4}$ (+); + אֶבֶן מַשְׂכִּית *figured stone*, בָּתֵּי אֱלֹהֵי־מִצְרַיִם *houses of the gods of Egypt* Jr 43$_{13}$.

שְׁתֵּים עֶשְׂרֵה מַצֵּבָה *twelve pillars* Ex 24$_{4}$ (Sam אֲבָנִים *stones*).

2. appar. **stump** of tree, <NOM CL> בְּשַׁלֶּכֶת מַצֶּבֶת בָּם *in felling*, i.e. when it is felled, *the stump is (still) among them* Is 6$_{13}$ (or em. with 1QIsa[a] משלכת מצבת במה *cast away from the site of a high place**), זֶרַע קֹדֶשׁ מַצַּבְתָּהּ *seed of holiness is its stump* Is 6$_{13}$ (or del.).

<SYN> §1, גַּל *heap*, אֲשֵׁרָה *Asherah*, פֶּסֶל *carved image*, אֱלִיל *worthless gods*, מִזְבֵּחַ *altar*, בָּמָה *high place*, זֶבַח *sacrifice*.*

⇒ נצב *stand*.

מִצְּבָיָה 1 gent. **Mezobaite,** as noun, a particular **Mezobaite,** <NOM CL> גִּבּוֹרֵי הַחֲיָלִים ... הַמְּצֹבָיָה *the warriors of the armies were ... the Mezobaite* 1 C 11$_{47}$ (or em. מִצֹּבָה *from Zobah* or הַצֹּבָתִי *the Zobathite*). <APP> יַעֲשִׂיאֵל *Jaasiel* 1 C 11$_{47}$ (or em.; see Nom. Cl.).

מַצֶּבֶת, see מַצֵּבָה *pillar*.

מְצַד 11.0.1 n.f. **stronghold**—מְצַד; pl. מְצָדוֹת; cstr. מְצָדוֹת—**stronghold, mountain fastness,** <SUBJ> תפשׂ ni. *be seized* Jr 48$_{41}$. <NOM CL> מְצָדוֹת סְלָעִים מִשְׂגַּבּוֹ *strongholds of rocks shall be his refuge* Is 33$_{16}$. <OBJ> עשׂה *make* Jg 6$_{2}$. <CSTR> מְצַד מִדְבָּרָה *stronghold of the steppe* 1 C 12$_{9}$, מְצָדוֹת עֵין־גֶּדִי *strongholds of En-gedi* 1 S 24$_{1}$, סְלָעִים *of rocks* Is 33$_{16}$. <PREP> לְ *at*, + בדל ni. *defect* 1 C 12$_{9}$; בְּ of place, *in* Ezk 33$_{27}$ 3QTr 9$_{17}$ (unless pl.n. *Mezad*), + ישׁב *dwell* 1 S 23$_{14}$ 24$_{1}$ Jr 51$_{30}$ 1 C 11$_{7}$, סתר htp. *hide oneself* 1 S 23$_{19}$; עַד לְ *to*, + בוא *come* 1 C 12$_{17}$. <COLL> מְצַד || מְעָרָה *cave* Jg 6$_{2}$ Ezk 33$_{27}$, מִנְהָרָה *hollow place* Jg 6$_{2}$, קִרְיָה *city* Jr 48$_{41}$.

<SYN> מְעָרָה *cave*, מִנְהָרָה *hollow place*, קִרְיָה *city*.*

מְצָדָה, see מְצוּדָה *stronghold*.

מצה 7 vb. **drain—Qal** 4 Pf. מָצִית; impf. יִמְצוּ; + waw וַיִּמֶץ; וּמָצִית—**1. drain,** <SUBJ> Jerusalem Is 51$_{17}$, Oholibah Ezk 23$_{34}$, רָשָׁע *wicked one* Ps 75$_{9}$. <OBJ> כּוֹס *cup* Ezk 23$_{34}$, קֻבַּעַת *cup* Is 51$_{17}$, שֶׁמֶר pl. *dregs* Ps 75$_{9}$. <COLL> מצה || שׁתה *drink* Is 51$_{17}$ Ezk 23$_{34}$.

2. wring out, <SUBJ> Gideon Jg 6$_{38}$. <OBJ> טַל *dew* Jg 6$_{38}$, מְלֹא *fullness* Jg 6$_{38}$, מַיִם *water* Jg 6$_{38}$. <PREP> מִן of direction, *from*, + גִּזָּה *fleece* Jg 6$_{38}$.

Also perh. 4QDibHam[a] 26$_{9}$.

<SYN> §1 שׁתה *drink*.

Ni. 3 Impf. יִמָּצוּ, יִמָּצֶה; + waw וְנִמְצָה—**be drained out,** <SUBJ> דָּם *blood* Lv 1$_{15}$, שׁאר ni. ptc. *what remains* of blood Lv 5$_{9}$, מַיִם *water* Ps 73$_{10}$ (or em. מֵי מָלֵא יִמָּצוּ *waters of fullness will be drained* to מִלֵּיהֶם יָמֹצּוּ *they will drain their words*, from מצץ *drain*). <PREP> לְ of agent, *by*, + רָשָׁע *wicked one* Ps 73$_{10}$ (or em.; see Subj.); אֶל *at*, + יְסוֹד *base* of altar Lv 5$_{9}$; עַל *at*, + קִיר *side* of altar Lv 1$_{15}$.*

⇒ (?) מֹצָה *Mozah,* מְצִירוֹק *emission of spittle;* cf. מצא III *drain,* מצץ *drain.*

מֹצָה 1.0.0.1 pl.n. **Moza,** town in Benjamin, perh. Qalōnyā, 7.5 km WNW of Jerusalem, <SUBJ> היה *be* Jos 18$_{26}$. <APP> עִיר *city* Jos 18$_{26}$.

Also Jerusalem jar handle inscr. (המצה) Stamp/Coins 31 32 (both 6th/5th cent.).

⇒ (?) מצה *drain.*

מַצָּה I 53.0.4 n.f. **unleavened bread**—pl. מַצּוֹת (מַצֹּת)—**1. unleavened bread, cakes,** flat bread made of barley meal and water, at ordinary meals (Gn 19$_{3}$ Jg 6$_{19.20.21.21}$ 1 S 28$_{24}$), the Exodus (Ex 12$_{39}$), Passover (Ex 12$_{8}$ Nm 9$_{11}$), sacrificial meals (Ex 29$_{2.23}$ Lv 2$_{4.4.5}$ 6$_{9}$ 7$_{12.12}$ 8$_{2.26.26}$ 10$_{12}$ Nm 6$_{15.15.17.19.19}$ 1 C 23$_{29}$ 11QT 15$_{9}$ [[מצה]] 20$_{12}$ [מ[צות]]); as food of priests (2 K 23$_{9}$ [or em.; see Obj.]).

2. (festival of) Unleavened Bread, usu. חַג הַמַּצּוֹת *festival of Unleavened Bread,* occupying the seven days after Passover (Ex 12$_{15.17.18.20}$ 13$_{6.7}$ 23$_{15.15}$ 34$_{18.18}$ Lv 23$_{6.6}$ Nm 28$_{17}$ Dt 16$_{3.8.16}$ Jos 5$_{11}$ Ezk 45$_{21}$ Ezr 6$_{22}$ 2 C 8$_{13}$ 30$_{13.21}$ 35$_{17}$ 4QMishE[a] 1$_{3}$ 4Q365a 1$_{2}$ [[המצו]ת] 11QT 11$_{10}$ 17$_{11}$).

<SUBJ> היה *be* Lv 2$_{5}$, אכל ni. *be eaten* Ex 13$_{7}$ Nm 28$_{17}$ Ezk 45$_{21}$.

<OBJ> אפה *bake* Gn 19$_{3}$ 1 S 28$_{24}$, אכל *eat* Ex 12$_{15.18.20}$ 13$_{6}$ 23$_{15}$ 34$_{18}$ Lv 23$_{6}$ Nm 28$_{27 (ms, Sam)}$ Dt 16$_{3.8}$ Jos 5$_{11}$ Jg 6$_{21}$ 2 K 23$_{9}$ (or em. מְנָיוֹת *portions*), שׁמר *keep* Ex 12$_{17}$ (הַמַּצּוֹת appar. *the [feast of] unleavened bread;* Sam הַמִּצְוָה *the commandment*), לקח *take* Jg 6$_{20}$ 11QT 15$_{9}$ ([מצה]).

<CSTR> חַג הַמַּצּוֹת *feast of unleavened bread* Ex 23$_{15}$ 34$_{18}$ Lv 23$_{6}$ Dt 16$_{16}$ Ezr 6$_{22}$ (מַצּוֹת) 2 C 8$_{13}$ 30$_{13.21}$ 35$_{17}$ 4QMishE[a] 1$_{3}$ 4Q365a 1$_{2}$ ([המצו]ת) 11QT 11$_{10}$ 17$_{11}$, לֶחֶם מַצּוֹת *bread (consisting) of unleavened bread* Ex 29$_{2}$ 4QD[e] 3.2a$_{1}$ (ל[ח]ם המצ[ו]ת), עֻגֹת מַצּוֹת *cakes of unleavened bread* Ex 12$_{39}$, חַלַּת מַצָּה *cake of unleavened bread* Lv 8$_{26}$ Nm 6$_{19}$ 11QT 15$_{9}$ ([חלת מצה]), חַלֹּת מַצֹּת *cakes of unleavened bread* Ex 29$_{2}$ Lv 2$_{4}$ 7$_{12}$ (both חַלּוֹת), רְקִיק מַצָּה *wafer of unleavened bread* Nm 6$_{19}$, רְקִיקֵי מַצּוֹת *wafers of unleavened bread* Ex 29$_{2}$ Lv 2$_{4}$ 7$_{12}$ Nm 6$_{15}$ 1 C 23$_{29}$ (הַמַּצּוֹת), אֵיפַת־קֶמַח מַצּוֹת *an ephah of flour of,* i.e. made into, *unleavened cakes* Jg 6$_{19}$, סַל הַמַּצּוֹת *basket of unleavened bread* Ex 29$_{23}$ Lv 8$_{2.26}$ Nm 6$_{15}$ (מַצּוֹת) 6$_{17}$.

<APP> עָבוּר *produce* Jos 5$_{11}$, לֶחֶם *bread* Dt 16$_{3}$.

<PREP> בְּ introducing object, + נגע *touch* Jg 6$_{19}$; עַל *with,* + אכל *eat* Nm 9$_{11}$.

<COLL> מַצָּה + קָלוּי *parched grain* Jos 5$_{11}$, בָּשָׂר *meat* Jg 6$_{20.21}$, מְרֹרִים *bitter herbs* Nm 9$_{11}$; מַצּוֹת תֵּאָכֵל *it shall be eaten unleavened* Lv 6$_{9}$, אִכְלוּהָ מַצּוֹת *eat it unleavened* Lv 10$_{12}$, מ[צות] יוא[כ]לום *they shall eat them unleavened* 11QT 20$_{12}$, מַצּוֹת עַל־מְרֹרִים יֹאכְלֻהוּ *they shall eat it with unleavened bread and bitter herbs* Ex 12$_{8}$.*

מַצָּה II 3 n.f. **strife, contention,** <OBJ> נתן *give* Pr 13$_{10}$, אהב *love* Pr 17$_{19}$. <PREP> לְ of benefit, *for,* + צום *fast* Is 58$_{4}$ (|| רִיב *strife*).

<SYN> רִיב *strife.*

⇒ נצה I *fight.*

מֻצְהָב, see צהב *gleam,* Ho.*

[מִצְהָלָה] 2 n.f. **neighing**—pl. cstr. מִצְהֲלוֹת; sf. מִצְהֲלוֹתַיִךְ—of horses (Jr 8$_{16}$), of Jerusalem (Jr 13$_{27}$), <OBJ> ראה *see* Jr 13$_{27}$ (+ נִאוּפִים *adultery,* זִמָּה *wickedness*). <CSTR> קוֹל מִצְהֲלוֹת אַבִּירָיו *sound of the neighings of his stallions* Jr 8$_{16}$. <APP> שִׁקּוּץ *abomination* Jr 13$_{27}$.

⇒ צהל *neigh.*

[מָצוֹד] I 3 n.[m.] **net**—cstr. מְצוֹד; sf. מְצוּדוֹ; pl. מְצוֹדִים—**net, snare,** <NOM CL> לִבָּהּ ... מְצוֹדִים *her heart is ... snares* Ec 7$_{26}$ (|| חֵרֶם *net*), חָמַד רָשָׁע מְצוֹד רָעִים *the desire of the wicked is (for) the net of evil ones* Pr 12$_{12}$ (if em.; see Obj.). <OBJ> חמד *desire* Pr 12$_{12}$ (unless מָצוֹד II *stronghold;* or em. חָמַד to חֶמֶד *desire of,* or em. מְצוֹד רָעִים to מְצוּד רֵעִים *game of friends,* or em. חָמַד רָשָׁע מְצוֹד רָעִים *the wicked one desires the net of evil ones* to חֹמֶר רֹעֵשׁ מְצוּדַת רָעִים *the stronghold of evil ones is quaking clay,* or יִשָּׁמֵד יְסוֹד רָעִים *the foundation of evil ones will be destroyed*), מצא *find,* i.e. reach Ps 116$_{3}$ (or em.; see Cstr.). <CSTR> מְצוֹד רָעִים *net of evil* *ones* Pr 12_{12} (unless מָצוֹד II *stronghold;* or em.; see Obj.), מְצָדֵי שְׁאוֹל *nets of Sheol* Ps 116_{3} (if em. מְצָרֵי *distress of*). <PREP> מִן of direction, *from*, + נצל ni. *deliver oneself* Pr 6_{5} (if em. מִיַּד *from the hand* to מִמָּצוֹד). <COLL> מְצוּדוֹ עָלַי הִקִּיף *he has surrounded me with his net* Jb 19_{6} (unless מָצוֹד II *siegeworks*).

<SYN> חֵרֶם *net*.*

⇒ צוד *hunt*.

[מָצוֹד] II 3.0.1 n. [m.] **stronghold, siegeworks**—cstr. מְצוֹד; sf. מְצוּדוֹ; pl. מְצוֹדִים—**1. stronghold,** <SUBJ> אבד *perish* Pr 12_{12} (if em.; see Obj.). <OBJ> חמד *desire* Pr 12_{12} (or em. חָמַד רָשָׁע מְצוֹד *the wicked desires the stronghold of* to חֹמֶר רֹעֵשׁ מְצוּדַת *crumbling clay is the stronghold of*,* or em. חָמַד רָשָׁע *the wicked desires* to אָבַד the stronghold of evil ones *perishes*). <CSTR> מְצוֹד רָעִים *stronghold of evil ones* Pr 12_{12} (unless מָצוֹד I *net;* or em. מְצוֹד רֵעִים *game of friends*).

2. watchtower, <PREP> עַל *upon*, + עמד *stand* CD 4_{12}.

3. siegeworks, <OBJ> בנה *build* Ec 9_{14} (mss מְצוֹרִים *siegeworks*). <ADJ> גָּדוֹל *great* Ec 9_{14} (mss מְצוֹרִים *siegeworks*). <COLL> מְצוּדוֹ עָלַי הִקִּיף *he has surrounded me with his siegeworks* Jb 19_{6} (unless מָצוֹד I *net*).*

⇒ (?) צוד *hunt;* cf. מְצוּדָה II *stronghold*, מְצוּדָה II *stronghold*.

*[מָצוֹד] n.[m.] **game,** <OBJ> חמד *desire* Pr 12_{12} (if em.; see Cstr.). <CSTR> מְצוֹד רֵעִים *game of friends* Pr 12_{12} (if em. מְצוֹד רָעִים *net/stronghold of evil ones*).

מְצוּדָה I 2.1.3 n.f. **net**—pl. מְצֹדוֹת; cstr. Q מצודות; sf. Si מְצוּדֹתֶיהָ, Q מצודותם—**net, snare,** <NOM CL> פשרו שלושת מצודות בליעל *its interpretation is,* i.e. concerns, *the three nets of Belial* CD 4_{15}. <CSTR> מצודות בליעל *nets of Belial* CD 4_{15}, רשעה *of wickedness* 1QH 3_{26} (+ מִכְמֹרֶת *net*, פַּח *snare*); כול מצודות *all the nets of* 1QH 3_{26}. <ADJ> רָעָה *evil* Ec 9_{12}. <PREP> בְּ of place, *in(to)*, + אחז ni. *be held* Ec 9_{12}, בוא hi. *bring* Ezk 19_{9} (or em. בַּמְּצֻרֶת *into custody* or בַּמַּצָּרָה *into the guard-house;* + סוּגַר *cage*), תפשׂ ni. *be caught* 1QH 4_{12}, נפל *fall* Si 9_{3}; עַל *concerning*, + אמר *say* CD 4_{15}. <COLL> שלושת מצודות *three nets of* CD 4_{15}.*

⇒ צוד *hunt*.

[מְצוֹדָה] II 1 n.f. **stronghold**—sf. מְצֹדָתָהּ—<SUBJ> היה *be* Is 29_{7} (or em. מְצֹרֹתֶיהָ *her siegeworks*, from מְצוּרָה; 1QIs^{a} מצרתה).

⇒ cf. מָצוֹד II *stronghold*, מְצוּדָה II *stronghold*.

מְצוּדָה I 4 n.f. **net, prey**—sf. מְצוּדָתִי—**1. net,** <OBJ> נתן *give*, i.e. place Ezk 19_{8} (if em. מִמְּדִינוֹת *from the provinces* to מְצוּדוֹת *nets*). <PREP> בְּ of place, *in(to)*, + תפשׂ *be caught* Ezk 12_{13} 17_{20} (both + רֶשֶׁת *net*), בוא hi. *bring* Ps 66_{11} (unless מְצוּדָה III *steppe;* or em. בַּמָּצוֹר or בַּמְּצוּרָה *into distress*).

2. prey, <PREP> לְ *as* or introducing predicate, + היה *be* Ezk 13_{21}.

3. eyrie,* dwelling place and lookout of bird of prey (unless מְצוּדָה II *stronghold*), <PREP> עַל *upon*, + לין htpol. *dwell* Jb 39_{28} (עַל־שֶׁן־סֶלַע וּמְצוּדָה *on the crag of a cliff and,* i.e. as, *a lookout*).

⇒ צוד *hunt*.

מְצוּדָה II 17.0.2 n.f. **stronghold**—מְצֻדָה; cstr. מְצֻדַת; sf. מְצוּדָתִי (מְצֻדָתִי); pl. מְצוּדוֹת—**1. stronghold, mountain fastness,** <SUBJ> ברך pu. *be blessed* Ps 144_{2}. <NOM CL> מְצֻדָתִי ... ׳׳ *Y. is ... my stronghold* 2 S 22_{2}||Ps 18_{3}, מְצוּדָתִי אָתָּה *you are my stronghold* Ps 31_{4} 71_{3}, var. 1QH 9_{28} ((אתה] ... מצודתי), חֹמֶר רֹעֵשׁ מְצוּדַת רָעִים *crumbling clay is the stronghold of evil ones* Pr 12_{12} (if em. חָמַד רָשָׁע מְצוֹד רָעִים *the wicked one desires the net of evil ones*).* <OBJ> לכד *capture* 2 S 5_{7}||1 C 11_{5}.

<CSTR> מְצֻדַת צִיּוֹן *stronghold of Zion* 2 S 5_{7}||1 C 11_{5}, עֲדֻלָּם *of Adullam* 1 S 22_{1} 2 S 23_{13}||1 C 11_{15} (all three, if em. מְעָרַת *cave of*), מְצוּדַת רָעִים *stronghold of evil ones* Pr 12_{12} (if em.; see Subj.); בֵּית מְצוּדוֹת *house of strongholds* Ps 31_{3}. <APP> ׳׳ *Y.* Ps 144_{2}, אֱלֹהִים *God* Ps 91_{2}.

<PREP> בְּ of place, *in* 2 S 23_{14}||1 C 11_{16}, + היה *be* 1 S 22_{4}, ישׁב *dwell* 1 S 22_{5} 2 S 5_{9}; בטח בְּ *trust in* Jr 48_{7} (if em. בְּאוֹצְרוֹתַיִךְ *in your treasures* to בִּמְצֻדוֹתַיִךְ *in your strongholds*); אֶל *to*, + בוא *come* 2 S 23_{13} (if em.; see Cstr.), עלה *go up* 1 S 24_{23}(mss), ירד *go down* 2 S 5_{17} 1 C 11_{15} (if em.; see Cstr.), מלט ni. *escape* 1 S 22_{1} (if em.;

see Cstr.); עַל *upon, in,* + לין htpol. *dwell* Jb 39$_{28}$ (unless מְצוּדָה I, §3 *eyrie*); *to,* + עלה *go up* 1 S 24$_{23}$.

<COLL> מְצוּדָה || מִשְׂגָּב *stronghold* Ps 144$_{2}$ (+) 1QH 9$_{28}$, מַחְסֶה *refuge* Ps 91$_{2}$, מָנוֹס *refuge* 1QH 9$_{28}$, סֶלַע *rock* 2 S 22$_{2}$||Ps 18$_{3}$ Ps 31$_{4}$ 71$_{3}$ 1QH 9$_{28}$ 4QapPs^{b} 24$_{7}$, חֶסֶד *loyalty* Ps 144$_{2}$; + שֶׁן־סֶלַע *crag of rock* Jb 39$_{28}$, צוּר מָעוֹז *rock of refuge* Pr 31$_{3}$, צוּר מָעוֹן *rock of a dwelling* Ps 71$_{3}$, מְפַלֵּט *deliverer* 2 S 22$_{2}$||Ps 18$_{3}$ Ps 144$_{2}$ 4QapPs^{b} 24$_{7}$ (מפלט[י]); מְצוּדָה as vocative, Ps 91$_{2}$.

2. siegeworks, <OBJ> קום hi. *raise up* Is 29$_{3}$(mss, 1QIs^{a}) (L מֻצָּרֹת *siegeworks*).

<SYN> §1 מִשְׂגָּב *stronghold,* מַחְסֶה *refuge,* מָנוֹס *refuge,* סֶלַע *rock,* חֶסֶד *loyalty.*

⇒ cf. מָצוֹד II *stronghold,* מְצוּדָה II *stronghold.*

***מְצוּדָה III** 1 n.f. **steppe, place of wandering,** <PREP> בְּ of place, *in(to),* בוא hi. *bring* Ps 66$_{11}$ (unless מְצוּדָה I *net*).

⇒ צוד *wander.*

מִצְוָה 181.9.45 n.f. **commandment**—cstr. מִצְוַת; sf. מִצְוָתְךָ, מִצְוָתוֹ; pl. מִצְוֹת (מִצְוֹות); cstr. מִצְוֹת (Q מצוות); sf. מִצְוֹתַי (מצוותיQ), מִצְוֹתֶיךָ (מצוותיכהQ), מִצְוֹתָיו (מצוותיוQ), (מצוותו Q)—**command(ment), 1.** of humans (e.g. Is 29$_{13}$ Jr 35$_{14.16.18.18}$ Pr 6$_{20}$ 2 C 29$_{25}$), of king (1 K 2$_{43}$ 2 K 18$_{36}$||Is 36$_{21}$ Est 3$_{3}$ Ne 11$_{23}$ Ne 12$_{24.45}$ 2 C 8$_{14.15}$ 24$_{21}$ 29$_{15}$ 30$_{6.12}$ 35$_{10.15.16}$); **obligation** (Ne 10$_{33}$); perh. **due** of Levites, singers and gate keepers (Ne 13$_{5}$ [or em.; see Cstr.]); perh. **terms** of deed transferring property (Jr 32$_{11}$).

2. of Y., **a.** singular, used collectively (e.g. Ex 24$_{12}$ Nm 15$_{31}$ Dt 5$_{31}$ 6$_{1}$ 7$_{11}$ 8$_{1}$ 11$_{8}$ 15$_{5}$ 19$_{9}$ Jos 22$_{3}$ Ps 19$_{9}$ 119$_{96}$ 2 C 14$_{3}$ 31$_{21}$ Si 6$_{37}$ 10$_{19}$ 15$_{15}$ 35$_{18[Bmg, E].23[B, Bmg]}$ 37$_{12[B, D]}$ 44$_{20}$ 45$_{5}$ 1QpHab 5$_{5}$ 1QS 8$_{17}$ 4QD^{c} 1$_{6}$ GnzPs 1$_{10}$); particular command (1 S 13$_{13}$ 1 K 13$_{21}$ Ml 2$_{1.4}$ Jb 23$_{12}$ 2 C 29$_{25}$).

b. plural (e.g. Gn 26$_{5}$ Ex 15$_{26}$ 16$_{28}$ 20$_{6}$||Dt 5$_{10(Qr)}$ Lv 4$_{2}$ 22$_{31}$ 26$_{3}$ 27$_{34}$ Nm 15$_{22}$ 36$_{13}$ Dt 4$_{2}$ 5$_{29}$ 8$_{6}$ 11$_{1}$ 13$_{5}$ 26$_{17}$ 28$_{1}$ 30$_{8}$ Jg 2$_{17}$ 3$_{4}$ 1 K 2$_{3}$ 3$_{14}$ 6$_{12}$ 9$_{6}$||2 C 7$_{19}$ 1 K 14$_{8}$ 2 K 17$_{13}$ 18$_{6}$ Is 48$_{18}$ Ps 78$_{7}$ 89$_{32}$ 112$_{1}$ 119$_{6+20t}$ Ec 12$_{13}$ Dn 9$_{4}$ Ezr 7$_{11}$ 9$_{10}$ Ne 1$_{5}$ 9$_{13}$ 10$_{30}$ 1 C 28$_{7}$ 29$_{19}$ 34$_{31}$ Si 35$_{23[Bmg]}$ 37$_{12[Bmg]}$ 45$_{17}$ 1QSb 1$_{1}$ 4QpHos^{a} 2$_{4}$ 11QT 59$_{16}$ CD 2$_{18}$).

3. of wisdom (e.g. Pr 2$_{1}$ 3$_{1}$ 4$_{4}$ 7$_{1.2}$).

<SUBJ> היה *be* Is 29$_{13}$, פלא ni. *be wonderful,* i.e. difficult Dt 30$_{11}$, כתב pass. *be written* Dt 30$_{10}$, למד pu. *be learned* Is 29$_{13}$, אור hi. *enlighten* Ps 19$_{9}$, חכם pi. *make wise* Ps 119$_{98}$.

<NOM CL> נֵר מִצְוָה *the commandment is a lamp* Pr 6$_{23}$, אֵלֶּה הַמִּצְוֹת *these are the commandments* Lv 27$_{34}$ Nm 36$_{13}$ 1QDM 2$_{11}$ (אל[ה] מצו[ות]), זֹאת הַמִּצְוָה *this is the commandment* Dt 6$_{1}$, מִצְוַת הַמֶּלֶךְ הִיא *it was the commandment of the king* 2 K 18$_{36}$||Is 36$_{21}$, מה הוא המצו[ה] *what is the commandment?* 4QMyst^{a} 3$_{22}$, כֵּן מִצְוַת דָּוִיד *such was the commandment of David* 2 C 8$_{14}$, אֲלֵיכֶם הַמִּצְוָה הַזֹּאת *this command is for you* Ml 2$_{1}$, מִצְוַת הַמֶּלֶךְ עֲלֵיהֶם *there was a commandment of the king concerning them* Ne 11$_{23}$, בְּיַד־י׳ הַמִּצְוָה בְּיַד־נְבִיאָיו *the commandment was by Y. through his prophets* 2 C 29$_{25}$, רְחָבָה מִצְוָתְךָ מְאֹד *your commandment is very broad* Ps 119$_{96}$, מִצְוַת י׳ בָּרָה *the commandment of Y. is pure* Ps 19$_{9}$, כָּל־מִצְוֹתֶיךָ אֱמוּנָה *all your commandments are reliability,* i.e. reliable Ps 119$_{86}$, sim. Ps 119$_{151}$, כָּל־מִצְוֹתֶיךָ צֶּדֶק *all your commandments are righteousness,* i.e. righteous Ps 119$_{172}$, מִצְוֹתֶיךָ שַׁעֲשֻׁעָי *your commandments are my delight* Ps 119$_{143}$, טוב לי מצוות רצונך מכל [אב]נים טובות *your gracious commandments are better to me than any precious stones* GnzPs 2$_{29}$.

<OBJ> צוה pi. *command* Lv 27$_{34}$ Nm 36$_{13}$ Dt 4$_{2.40}$ 6$_{2.17}$ 7$_{11}$ 8$_{1.11}$ 10$_{13}$ 11$_{8.13.22.27}$ 13$_{19}$=11QT 55$_{13}$ Dt 15$_{5}$ 19$_{9}$ 26$_{13}$ 27$_{1}$ 28$_{1.13.15.45}$ 30$_{8.11}$ 31$_{5}$ Jos 22$_{5}$ Jg 3$_{4}$ 1 S 13$_{13}$ 1 K 2$_{43}$ 8$_{58}$ 13$_{21}$ 2 K 17$_{34}$ 18$_{6}$ Jr 35$_{14.16}$ Ne 1$_{7}$ 9$_{14}$ 1QH fr. 2$_{8}$ (מצו[תכה צויתו]) 1QDM 2$_{1}$ ([מצוו]תי) 2$_{11}$ (מצ[וות]) 4QpsMos^{e} 2.14, דבר pi. *speak* Nm 15$_{22}$ Dt 5$_{31}$, למד *learn* Ps 119$_{73}$, pi. *teach* Dt 5$_{31}$ 6$_{1}$, דרשׁ *seek* 1 C 28$_{8}$ 4QD^{c} 1$_{6}$, שׁמע *hear,* i.e. obey Jg 2$_{17}$ 3$_{4}$, לקח *accept* Pr 10$_{8}$ Si 35$_{18}$ (Bmg, E), כתב *write* Dt 24$_{12}$ 2 K 17$_{37}$, שׁלח *send* Ml 2$_{4}$ 4QpsMos^{e} 1$_{5}$, נתן *give* Ex 24$_{12}$ 1 K 9$_{6}$||2 C 7$_{19}$ Ne 9$_{13}$ 13$_{5}$ (or em.; see Cstr.) Si 45$_{17}$ 4QapPs^{b} 69$_{5}$ ([נתן]), שׂים *place* Si 45$_{5}$, שׁלך hi. *cast* 4QpHos^{a} 2$_{4}$, עלה hi. *cause to go up,* i.e. offer 2 C 35$_{16}$, עמד hi. *cause to stand,* i.e. place, obligations Ne 10$_{33}$, זכר *remember* Nm 15$_{39.40}$ 4QBark^{d} 2.1$_{15}$ ([מצותיכ[ה]), ירא *fear* Pr 13$_{13}$, אהב *love* Ps 119$_{47.48.127}$, חפץ *delight in* Ps 119$_{166(ms)}$, צפן *treasure* Pr 2$_{1}$ 7$_{1}$.

שׁמר *keep* Gn 26$_{5}$ Ex 16$_{28}$ 20$_{6}$||Dt 5$_{10}$ Lv 22$_{31}$ 26$_{3}$ Dt 4$_{2.40}$ 5$_{29}$ 6$_{2.17}$ 7$_{9.11}$ 8$_{1.2.6.11}$ 10$_{13}$ 11$_{1.8.22}$ 13$_{5.19}$=11QT 55$_{13}$ Dt

15_{5} 19_{9} $26_{17.18}$ 27_{1} $28_{1.9.13.45}$ $30_{10.16}$ Jos 22_{5} 1 S 13_{13} 1 K 2_{3} 3_{14} 6_{12} $8_{58.61}$ 1 K 9_{7} $11_{34.38}$ 13_{21} 14_{8} 2 K $17_{13.19.37}$ 18_{6} 23_{3} 35_{18} Ps 89_{32} 119_{60} Pr 4_{4} 7_{2} 19_{16} Ec 8_{5} 12_{13} Dn 9_{4} Ne $1_{5.7.9}$ 10_{30} 1 C 29_{19} 34_{31} Si 15_{15} 35_{23} 37_{12} 44_{20} 1QH 16_{13} ([מצוו]ת[יך]) 16_{17} ([מצוו]ותיך) 1QpHab 5_{5} 1QDM 2_{1} ([ושׁ]מרתה ... [מצוו]תי) 1QSb 1_{1} 4QCommGenC 4_{3} 4QpsEzek^{a} 16.2_{8} ([שׁמ]רו) 4QsapHymnA 1.1_{2} ([שׁו]מרי) 11QT 59_{16} CD $2_{18.21}$ 3_{2} 19_{2}, נצר *keep* Ps 78_{7} 119_{115} Pr 3_{1} 6_{20}, עשׂה *do* Lv 22_{31} $26_{14.15}$ Nm $15_{22.39.40}$ Dt 5_{31} $6_{1.25}$ 7_{11} 8_{1} 11_{22} 15_{5} 19_{9} 27_{10} $28_{1.13.15}$ 30_{8} Jos 22_{5} 2 K 17_{37} Ps 119_{166} Ne 1_{9} 10_{30} 1 C 28_{7} 2 C 14_{3} 30_{12} 35_{16} perh. 4Q417 1.2_{13} (מצו[ ]), קום hi. *fulfil* Jr $35_{14.16}$ CD 9_{7}, כבד hi. *glorify* GnzPs 4_{6}.

שׁכח *forget* Dt 26_{13} Ps 119_{176}, עזב *forsake* 1 K 18_{18} 2 K 17_{16} 2 C 7_{19} Ezr 9_{10}, פרר hi. *break* Nm 15_{31} Ezr 9_{14} 4QpsMos^{e} 2.1_{4}, עבר *transgress* Est 3_{3} 2 C 24_{20} Si 10_{19}, סתר hi. *hide* Ps 119_{19} (or em. אִמְרָתֶךָ *your word*).

<CSTR> מִצְוַת י׳ *commandment of Y.* Jos 22_{3} 1 S 13_{13} 2 C $24_{20(mss)}$, מִצְוֹת *commandments of* Lv $4_{2.13.22.27}$ 5_{17} Nm 15_{39} Dt 4_{2} 6_{17} 8_{6} 10_{13} $11_{27.28}$ $28_{9.13}$ Jg 2_{17} 3_{4} 1 K 18_{18} 2 K $17_{16.19}$ Ezr 7_{11} Ne 10_{30} 1 C 28_{8} 2 C 24_{20} 4QapMos^{c} 2.2_{5} (מצוות [י]הוה), מִצְוֹת ... אֲדֹנֵינוּ *commandments ... of our Lord* Ne 10_{30}, מִצְוַת אֱלֹהֵינוּ *commandment of our God* Ezr 10_{3}, מִצְוַת ... אֱלֹהֵיכֶם *commandment of ... your God* Jos 22_{3}, מִצְוֹת אֱלֹהָי *commandments of my God* Ps 119_{115}, מִצְוֹת ... אֱלֹהָיו *commandments ... of his God* Lv 4_{22}, אֱלֹהֶיךָ *of your God* Dt 8_{6} $10_{13(ms, Sam)}$ $28_{9.13}$, אֱלֹהֵיכֶם *of your* (pl.) *God* Dt 4_{2} 6_{17} $11_{27.28}$ 1 C 28_{8}, אֱלֹהֵיהֶם *of their God* 2 K $17_{16.19}$, מצות אל *commandments of God* 4QCommGenC 4_{3} 4QD^{a} 1_{17} CD 2_{18} $3_{2.6.12}$ 5_{21} 8_{19}=19_{32} 9_{7}, עליון *of the Most High* Si 44_{20}, עשׂיהם *of their maker* CD 2_{21}.

מִצְוַת *commandment of* + pr.n. Asaph 2 C 35_{10} (מִצְוַת ...), Gad 2 C 29_{25}, David Ne $12_{24.45}$ 2 C 8_{14} 29_{25} 35_{15}, Heman 2 C 35_{10} (מִצְוַת ...), Jeduthun 2 C 35_{10} (מִצְוַת ...), Jehonadab Jr 35_{18}, Moses 2 C 8_{13}, Nathan 2 C 29_{25}, Solomon Ne 12_{45}.

מִצְוַת אִישׁ *commandment of the man of* God Ne 12_{24} 2 C 8_{14} (both מִצְוַת ...), אֲנָשִׁים *of men* Is 29_{13}, אָבִיךָ *of your father* Pr 6_{20}, אֲבִיכֶם *of your father* Jr 35_{18} (מִצְוַת ...), אֲבִיהֶם *of their father* Jr $35_{14.16}$, בְּנוֹ *of his son* Ne 12_{45} (מִצְוַת ...), הַמֶּלֶךְ *of the king* 2 K 18_{36}||Is 36_{21} Est 3_{3} Ne 11_{23} 2 C 8_{15} 24_{21} 29_{15} $30_{6.12}$ $35_{10.16}$, הַשָּׂרִים *of the princes* 2 C 30_{12} (מִצְוַת ...), הַנָּבִיא *of the prophet* 2 C 29_{25} (מִצְוַת ...), חֹזֵה *of the seer of* the king 2 C 29_{25} (מִצְוַת ...) 35_{15} 2 C 35_{10} (מִצְוַת ... חוֹזֶה), מצות קדושים *commandment(s) of the holy ones* 4QapMes 2.2_{2}, יוריהם *of their teacher* CD 3_{8}, מִצְוַת שְׂפָתָיו *commandment of his lips* Jb 23_{12}, מצות דברו *commandment of his word* GnzPs 4_{6}, מצוות רצונך *commandments of your pleasure*, i.e. your gracious commandments GnzPs 2_{29}, מִצְוַת הַלְוִיִּם וְהַמְשֹׁרְרִים וְהַשֹּׁעֲרִים *due of the Levites and the singers and the gatekeepers* Ne 13_{5} (or em. מְנָיוֹת *portions of*).

שׁומר מצוה *one who keeps the commandment(s)* Si $37_{12(B, D)}$ (Bmg מצותיו *of his commandments*), שֹׁמְרֵי מִצְוֹתָי *ones who keep my commandments* Ex 20_{5} CD 19_{2}, מִצְוֹתָיו *his commandments* Dt $5_{10(Qr)}$ $7_{9(Qr)}$ (both Kt מצותו *his commandment*; mss מִצְוֹתַי) Dn 9_{4} Ne 1_{5} 1QSb 1_{1} (שׁומרי) 4QConfess 6_{4} ([שׁומ]רי מצות[יו]) 4QsapHymnA 1.1_{2} ([שׁו]מרי כול מצוותיו), שׁומרי מצוותיך *ones who keep your commandments* 1QH 16_{13} ([מצוו]ת[יך]) 16_{17} ([מצוו]ותיך), שׁומרי מצות *ones who keep the commandments of* 4QCommGenC 4_{3}, דורשׁי מצוותו *ones who seek his commandment(s)* 4QD^{c} 1_{6}, יְרֵא מִצְוָה *one who fears the commandment* Pr 13_{13}, מִשְׁמֶרֶת מִצְוַת *charge of the commandment of* Jos 22_{3}, דֶּרֶךְ־מִצְוֹתֶיךָ *way of your commandments* Ps 119_{32}, נְתִיב *path of* Ps 119_{35}, דִּבְרֵי מִצְוֹת *matters of the commandments of* Y. Ezr 7_{11}.

כָּל־הַמִּצְוָה *all the commandment* Dt 5_{31} 6_{25} 8_{1} $11_{8.22}$ 15_{5} 19_{9} 27_{1} Dt 31_{5} 1QS 8_{17}, כָּל־מִצְוָתְךָ *all your commandment* Dt 26_{13}, כָּל־הַמִּצְוֹת *all the commandments* Lv 26_{14} Nm 15_{22} 4Q365a 1_{5} (כול), כָּל־מִצְוֹת *all the commandments of* Lv 4_{2} (כֹּל) $4_{13.22.27(mss, Sam)}$ 5_{17} Nm 15_{39} 2 K 17_{16} Ne 10_{30} 1 C 28_{8} 4QapMos^{c} 2.2_{5} (כול מצו[ות]), כָּל־מִצְוֹתַי *all my commandments* Lv 26_{15} Nm 15_{40} (מִצְוֹתָי) Dt 5_{29} (mss, Sam lack כָּל־) 1 K 6_{12} 4QpsMos^{e} 2.1_{4} 11QT 55_{13} (כול מצוותי), כָּל־מִצְוֹתֶיךָ *all your commandments* Dt $26_{13(ms, Sam)}$ Ps $119_{6.86.151}$, כָּל־מִצְוֹתָיו *all his commandments* Dt 13_{19} 26_{18} $28_{1.15}$ 30_{8} Jr 35_{18} 4QsapHymnA 1.1_{2} (כול).

<APP> קוֹל *voice* CD 3_{8}, מַעֲשֵׂר *tithe* Ne 13_{5} (or em.; see Cstr.), תּוֹרָה *law* Si 45_{5}.

<ADJ> טוֹב *good* Ne 9_{13}, אֵלֶּה *these* Lv 26_{14} Nm 15_{22},

זאת *this* Dt 6$_{25}$ 11$_{22}$ 15$_5$ 19$_9$ 30$_{11}$ Ml 2$_{1.4}$.

<PREP> לְ *to* perh. 4Q365a 1$_5$, + אזן *listen* Ex 15$_{26}$, קשׁב hi. *pay attention* Is 48$_{18}$, שׁמע *listen* Ne 9$_{29}$ CD 3$_8$; יאב לְ *long for* Ps 119$_{131}$; introducing object, + עשׂה *do* 4QapMos^c 2.2$_5$ ([יע]שה לכול מצ[ות]).

בְּ of accompaniment, *in* perh. 4QD^a 1$_{14}$ ([במצו]ת]), + הלך *walk* 1 K 6$_{12}$ 2 C 17$_4$ perh. 4QapLam^b 1$_7$; of cause, *because of, at* Ezr 10$_3$ (הַחֲרֵדִים בְּמִצְוַת אֱלֹהֵינוּ *those who tremble at the commandment of our God*); *according to*, + עמד hi. *place* 2 C 29$_{25}$, הלל pi. *praise* Ne 12$_{24}$, ידה hi. *give thanks* Ne 12$_{24}$, רגם *stone* 2 C 24$_{21}$, חלל hi. *begin* 2 C 31$_{21}$; *against* 4QD^a 1$_{17}$; introducing object, + אמן hi. *trust* Ps 119$_{66}$, בין htpol. *consider* Si 6$_{37}$, חזק hi. *grasp* CD 3$_{12}$, מאס *reject* CD 8$_{19}$=19$_{32}$ 19$_5$; חפץ בְּ *delight in* Ps 112$_1$ 4QUnidC 1$_1$ (במצ[ו]תו), שׁעע בְּ pilp. *delight in* Ps 119$_{47}$.

כְּ *according to* 2 C 35$_{15.16}$, + הלך *go* 2 C 30$_6$, בוא *come* 2 C 29$_{15}$, עמד *stand* 2 C 35$_{10}$, יכח hi. *reprove* CD 7$_2$, נתן *give* Dt 26$_{13}$, עשׂה *do* Dt 31$_5$ 2 K 17$_{34}$, שׁמר *keep* Ne 12$_{45}$, עלה hi. *cause to go up*, i.e. offer 2 C 8$_{13}$, הלל pi. *praise* Ne 12$_{24(mss)}$, ידה hi. *give thanks* Ne 12$_{24(mss)}$.

מִן of direction, *from*, + סור *turn aside* Dt 17$_{20}$ Dn 9$_5$ 2 C 8$_{15(mss)}$ (L lacks מִן) 1QS 8$_{17}$, סוג ni. *turn back* 4QapMes 2.2$_2$, שׁגה *go astray* Ps 119$_{21}$, hi. *cause to stray* Ps 119$_{10}$, זנה *act as prostitute* 11QT 59$_{14}$.

מִן partitive, *some of*, + חטא *sin (in respect of)* Lv 4$_2$, עבר *transgress* Dt 26$_{13}$, עשׂה *do* Lv 4$_{13.22.27}$ 5$_{17}$; *from among, from out of* CD 10$_3$.

אֶל *to*, + שׁמע *listen*, i.e. obey Dt 11$_{13.27.28}$ 28$_{13}$ Ne 9$_{16}$, קשׁב hi. *pay attention* Ne 9$_{34}$, נבט hi. *look* Ps 119$_6$, כון pol. *direct* way GnzPs 1$_{10}$, נשׂא *lift* hands Ps 119$_{48}$.

עַל *to*, + שׁמע *listen*, i.e. obey Jr 35$_{18}$; *against*, + יעץ ni. *take counsel* CD 3$_6$, דבר pi. *speak* rebellion CD 5$_{21}$.

בֵּין *between*, i.e. concerning 2 C 19$_{10}$ (+ לְחֻקִּים וּלְמִשְׁפָּטִים *and statutes and ordinances*).

<COLL> מִצְוָה || תּוֹרָה *law* Gn 26$_5$ Ex 16$_{28}$ 24$_{12}$ Jos 22$_5$ 2 K 17$_{13}$ (+) 17$_{34.37}$ Ps 19$_9$ Pr 3$_1$ 6$_{20.23}$ 7$_2$ Ne 9$_{13.14.29}$ (+) 2 C 14$_3$ 31$_{21}$ 4QapPs^b 69$_5$ GnzPs 4$_6$.

|| חֹק *statute* Dt 4$_{40}$ 5$_{31}$ 6$_{1.2(Sam).17}$ 7$_{11}$ 26$_{17}$ 27$_{10}$ 1 K 3$_{14}$ 8$_{58.61}$ 2 K 17$_{37}$ Jr 32$_{11}$ Ps 119$_{48}$ (+) Ezr 7$_{11}$ (+) Ne 1$_7$ 9$_{13.14}$ 10$_{30}$ 1 C 29$_{19}$ 2 C 19$_{10}$ 34$_{31}$ Si 45$_{17}$ (+) 4QD^a 1$_{17}$ CD 19$_5$.

|| חֻקָּה *statute* Gn 26$_5$ Ex 15$_{26}$ (+) Lv 26$_{3.15}$ (+) Dt 6$_2$ 8$_{11}$ 10$_{13}$ 11$_1$ 28$_{15.45}$ 30$_{10.16}$ 1 K 2$_3$ 6$_{12}$ (+) 9$_6$||2 C 7$_{19}$ 1 K 11$_{34.38}$ 2 K 17$_{13.34}$ 23$_3$ Ps 89$_{32}$ (+) 4QpsEzek^a 16.2$_8$ 4QpsMos^e 2.1$_4$ 11QT 59$_{16}$.

|| מִשְׁפָּט *ordinance* Lv 26$_{15}$ (+) Nm 36$_{13}$ Dt 5$_{31}$ 6$_1$ 7$_{11}$ 8$_{11}$ 11$_1$ 26$_{17}$ 30$_{16}$ 1 K 2$_3$ 6$_{12}$ 8$_{58}$ 2 K 17$_{34.37}$ Ps 19$_9$ (+) Dn 9$_5$ Ne 1$_7$ 9$_{13.29}$ (+) 10$_{30}$ 1 C 28$_7$ 2 C 19$_{10}$ Si 45$_{17}$ (+).

|| פִּקּוּד *precept* Ps 19$_9$, עֵדָה *testimony* Dt 6$_{17}$ 1 K 2$_3$ 2 K 23$_3$ Ne 9$_{34}$ 1 C 29$_{19}$ 2 C 34$_{31}$, עֵדוּת *testimony* Ps 19$_9$, מִשְׁמֶרֶת *charge* Gn 26$_5$ Dt 11$_1$, אֹמֶר *word* Jb 23$_{12}$ (+) Pr 2$_1$ 7$_1$.

+ אִמְרָה *word* Ps 119$_{172}$, דָּבָר *word* Nm 15$_{31}$ Dt 4$_2$ Pr 4$_4$ 13$_{13}$ 2 C 34$_{31}$, שְׁבוּעָה *oath* 1 K 2$_{43}$, יִרְאָה *fear* of Y. Ps 19$_9$ Si 6$_{37}$, תּוֹכְחוֹת מוּסָר *reproofs of discipline* Pr 6$_{23}$.

מִצְוֹת י׳ אֲשֶׁר לֹא תֵעָשֶׂינָה *the commandments of Y. (concerning) that which should not be done* Lv 4$_{2.13.22.27}$ 5$_{17}$, מִצְוַת שְׂפָתָיו וְלֹא אָמִישׁ *as for the commandment of his lips, I have not departed (from it)* Jb 23$_{12}$, מִצְוַת הַמֶּלֶךְ הַשָּׂרִים בִּדְבַר י׳ *the commandment of the king and the princes by the word of Y.* 2 C 30$_{12}$, מצות אל ביד משה *the commandments of God by the hand of Moses* CD 5$_{21}$, כול מצ[ות י]הוה בפי משה משיחו *all the commandments of Y. by the mouth of Moses, his anointed one* 4QapMos^c 2.2$_5$, מִצְוַת מֹשֶׁה לַשַּׁבָּתוֹת וְלֶחֳדָשִׁים וְלַמּוֹעֲדוֹת *the commandment of Moses pertaining to the sabbaths and the new moons and the festivals* 1 C 8$_{13}$, מִצְוַת הַמֶּלֶךְ עַל־הַכֹּהֲנִים וְהַלְוִיִּם *the commandment of the king for the priests and Levites* 2 C 8$_{15}$, סֵפֶר הַמִּקְנָה הֶחָתוּם ... הַמִּצְוָה וְהַחֻקִּים perh. *the deed of purchase, the sealed copy ... (containing) the terms and conditions* Jr 32$_{11}$ (unless *according to commandment and statutes*).

Also 1QH 17$_7$ 4QJub^e 21$_5$ ([מצות]יו) 4QpsJub^a 3.2$_{10}$ 4QPrayers^a 1$_4$ 4QapPs^b 86$_6$ 4Q417 19$_4$ 4Q418 197$_2$ 4QDibHam^b 121$_2$ ([מצו]ותיכה) 6QBen 3$_2$.

<SYN> תּוֹרָה *law*, חֹק *statute*, חֻקָּה *statute*, מִשְׁפָּט *ordinance*, פִּקּוּד *precept*, עֵדָה *testimony*, עֵדוּת *testimony*, מִשְׁמֶרֶת *charge*, אֹמֶר *word*.*

⇒ צוה *command*.

[מְצוֹלָה], see מְצוֹלָה *depth*.

מְצוֹלָה 12.0.8 n.f. **depth**—מְצֻלָה; pl. מְצוֹלֹת (מְצֻלוֹת); cstr.

מְצֻלוֹת (מְצוּלוֹת)—**depth, the deep,** perh. as a term for the underworld;* perh. **hollow** (Zc 1₈), <SUBJ> יבשׁ hi. *dry up* Zc 10₁₁, בלע *swallow* Ps 69₁₆.

<OBJ> רתח hi. *cause to boil* Jb 41₂₃.

<CSTR> מְצוּלוֹת יְאֹר *depths of the Nile* Zc 10₁₁, מְצֻלוֹת יָם *depths of the sea* Mc 7₁₉ Ps 68₂₃ 1QH 3₆ (מ]צולות ים]); יְוֵן מְצוּלָה *mire of the deep* Ps 69₃, יארי מצולות *channels of depths* 4QBerᵃ 5₁₀, כֹּל מְצוּלוֹת *all the depths of* Zc 10₁₁.

<PREP> לְ *as* or introducing predicate, + היה *be* 1QH 8₁₉; בְּ of place, *in(to)* Zc 1₈ Ps 107₂₄ 1QH 3₆ (בנמ]צולות ים]) 3₁₄ 4Q392 2₅, + ירד *go down* Ex 15₅, שׁלך hi. *cast* Mc 7₁₉ Ne 9₁₁, טבע pi. *drown* GnzPs 1₂₄, שׁוב hi. *bring back* Ps 68₂₃(mss), שׁית *place* Ps 88₇; מִן of direction, *from*, + שׁוב hi. *bring back* Ps 68₂₃; מְצוּלָה without preposition, *into the deep*, + שׁלך hi. *cast* Jon 2₄ (or del.).

<COLL> מְצוּלָה ‖ מַעֲמַקִּים *depths* Ps 69₃, מַחְשָׁךְ *darkness* Ps 88₇, + תְּהוֹם *deep* Ex 15₅, לְבַב יַמִּים *heart of the seas* Jon 2₄, יָם *sea* Jb 41₂₃, שִׁבֹּלֶת *stream* Ps 69₁₆, נָהָר *flood* Jon 2₄, בּוֹר *pit* Ps 88₇, בְּאֵר *pit* Ps 69₁₆.

Also 4Q418 119₂.₃ 227₃.*

<SYN> מַעֲמַקִּים *depths*, מַחְשָׁךְ *darkness*.

⇒ cf. צלל *sink*.

מָצוֹק 6.1 n.[m.] **distress, anguish,** <SUBJ> מצא *find* Ps 119₁₄₃ (‖ צַר *distress*). <CSTR> אִישׁ מָצוֹק *man of*, i.e. in, *distress* 1 S 22₂ (+ אֲשֶׁר לוֹ נֹשֶׁא *who had a creditor*, i.e. was in debt, מַר־נֶפֶשׁ *bitter of soul*), עֵת מָצוֹק *time of distress* Ps 31₂₂ (if em. עִיר מָצוֹר *city of fortification*) Ps 32₆ (if em. עֵת מְצֹא *time of finding*), תחנוני מצוק *supplications of (one in) distress* Si 32₁₆(B). <PREP> בְּ of cause, *on account of*, + אכל *eat* Dt 28₅₃.₅₇ Jr 19₉, שׁאר hi. *leave* Dt 28₅₅. <COLL> מָצוֹק אֲשֶׁר־יָצִיק לְךָ אֹיִבֶךָ *the distress with which your enemy shall distress you* Dt 28₅₃.₅₅.₅₇ (all three ‖ מָצוֹר *siege*), var. Jr 19₉ (‖ מָצוֹר).

<SYN> צַר *distress*, מָצוֹר *siege*.

⇒ צוק *press upon*.

מָצוּק 2.1 n.[m.] **pillar**—pl. cstr. מְצֻקֵי—**1. pillar,** <NOM CL> הַשֵּׁן הָאֶחָד מָצוּק מִצָּפוֹן perh. *the one crag was (as) a pillar from the north* 1 S 14₅ (or del.), לַי׳ מְצֻקֵי אֶרֶץ *(belonging) to Y. are pillars of the earth* 1 S 2₈. <CSTR> מְצֻקֵי אֶרֶץ *pillars of the earth* 1 S 2₈. <PREP> עַל *upon*, + שׁית *place* the world 1 S 2₈.

2. solid casting, <OBJ> מהם *melt* Si 43₄ (unless מהם = *from them*). <NOM CL> כור נפוח מהם מצוק *the furnace that is blown*, i.e. glowing, *from them is a solid casting* Si 43₄(B) (unless מהם = vb. *melt*; Bmg, M מוצק).

⇒ צוק *pour out*.

מְצוּקָה 7.2.5 n.f. **distress**—pl. cstr. Si מצוקות; sf. מְצוּקוֹתַי, מְצוּקֹתֵיהֶם, מְצֻקוֹתֵיהֶם (מְצוּקוֹתֵיהֶם, Q מצוקותיכה, Q מצוקותיהמה, Q מצוקותם)—**distress, anguish, affliction,** <SUBJ> בעת pi. *terrify* Jb 15₂₄ (‖ צַר *distress*). <CSTR> מצוקות שלהבת *distress of*, i.e. caused by, *flame* Si 51₄; יוֹם ... מְצוּקָה *day of ... distress* Zp 1₁₅ (‖ צָרָה *trouble*), [ז]מן מצוקה *time of distress* Si 32₂₆, כול מצוקות *all distresses* 4QJubᵃ 1₈ (כל מ]צוקות]) 4QPseudᵇ 1₇ (‖ צָרָה *trouble*). <PREP> בְּ of accompaniment, *with*, + מהר pi. *hasten* 1QH 5₁₇; מִן of direction, *from* 1Q25 4₂ 4QDᵃ 9.3₁₄ 4QPseudᵇ 1₇, + יצא hi. *bring out* Ps 25₁₇ (+ צָרָה *trouble*) 107₂₈, נצל hi. *deliver* Ps 107₆ 4QapPsᵃ 2₄ ([ממצ]וקותיהם יצילם]), ישׁע hi. *save* Ps 107₁₃.₁₉ Si 51₄ 4QJubᵃ 1₈ (יושיעום כל מ]צוקות]) 4QapMosᵃ 1.14 (להושיעכ]ה]).

<SYN> צַר *distress*, צָרָה *trouble*.

⇒ צוק *press upon*.

מָצוֹר I 20.0.1 n.[m.] **siege**—cstr. מְצוֹר; sf. מְצוּרֵךְ; pl. mss מְצוּרִים—**1. siege,** perh. **distress** (Dt 28₅₃.₅₅.₅₇ Jr 19₉ Ps 32₆ [if em.; see Cstr.] 66₁₁ [if em.; see Prep.]), <OBJ> נתן *give*, i.e. place Ezk 4₂ (unless §2; ‖ דָּיֵק *siege-wall*, סֹלְלָה *mound*, כַּר *battering ram*, מַחֲנֶה *camp*), שׂים *place* Mc 4₁₄ (unless §2).

<CSTR> מְצוֹר יְרוּשָׁלַםִ *siege of Jerusalem* Ezk 4₇; מֵי מָצוֹר *water of*, i.e. for, *a siege* Na 3₁₄, עֵת *time of* Ps 31₂₂ (if em. עִיר *city of* fortification) 32₆ (if em. עֵת מְצֹא *time of finding*), יְמֵי הַמָּצוֹר *days of the siege* Ezk 5₂, מְצוּרֵךְ *of your siege* Ezk 4₈, עִיר מָצוֹר perh. *city of siege* Ps 31₂₂ (but prob. *city of fortification*, i.e. fortified city, from מָצוֹר II).

<PREP> בְּ *in, into (a state of)*, + היה *be* Ezk 4₃ Zc 12₂, בוא *come* Dt 20₁₉ 2 K 24₁₀ 25₂‖Jr 52₅, hi. *bring* Ps 66₁₁ (if em. בַּמְּצוּדָה *into the net*), ישׁב *dwell* Jr 10₁₇ 2 C 32₁₀,

נתן *give*, i.e. place 4QActs 1$_{4}$ ([ויתן]); בְּ of cause, *on account of*, + אכל *eat* Dt 28$_{53.57}$ Jr 19$_{9}$ (all three || מָצוֹק *distress*), שׁאר hi. *leave* Dt 28$_{55}$ (|| מָצוֹק); אֶל *to*, + כון hi. *direct* face Ezk 4$_{7}$.

2. siegeworks, <OBJ> בנה *build* Dt 20$_{20}$ Ec 9$_{14(mss)}$ (מְצוּרִים; L מְצוֹדִים *siegeworks*).

<SYN> §1 דָּיֵק *siege-wall*, סֹלְלָה *mound*, כַּר *battering ram*, מַחֲנֶה *camp*, מָצוֹק *distress*.

⇒ צור *besiege*.

מָצוֹר II 6.0.2 n.[m.] **fortification, 1. fortification, fortress,** <OBJ> בנה *build* Zc 9$_{3}$, פתח *open* 1QH 6$_{30}$. <CSTR> [עולם] מצור *stronghold of everlastingness*, i.e. everlasting stronghold 1QH 6$_{30}$, עִיר מָצוֹר *city of fortification*, i.e. fortified city Ps 31$_{22}$ (unless *city of siege*, i.e. besieged city, from מָצוֹר I; or em. עֵת מָצוֹר *time of siege* or עֵת מָצוֹק *time of distress*) 60$_{11}$ 1QH 6$_{25}$, עָרֵי *cities of*, i.e. fortified cities 2 C 8$_{5}$. <PREP> לְ of benefit, *for*, + בנה *build* cities 2 C 11$_{5}$.

2. watchtower, <PREP> עַל *upon*, + יצב htp. *stand* Hb 2$_{1}$ (or em. מַצּוֹרִי *my watch*).*

⇒ צור *besiege*.

*[מָצוֹר] III 0.0.2 n.[m.] **creature**—cstr. Q מצור—**creature(s), formation,** <NOM CL> הוא מצוררק *he is a formation of spittle*, i.e. formed from semen 4QSj 1$_{9}$. <CSTR> מצור ימים *creatures of the seas* 4QBer^{a} 5$_{9}$, מצוררק *formation of spittle*, i.e. one formed from semen 4QSj 1$_{9}$ (=1QS 11$_{21}$ מצירוק *emission of spittle*). <APP> חֹמֶר *clay* 4QSj 1$_{9}$.

⇒ צור *form*.

מָצוֹר IV 5 pl.n. **Egypt,** <SUBJ> היה *be* Ezk 27$_{8}$ (if em.; see Cstr.). <CSTR> יְאֹרֵי מָצוֹר *streams of Egypt* 2 K 19$_{24}$||Is 37$_{25}$ Is 19$_{6}$ (both unless מָצוֹר V *whey*; both or em. יְאֹרֵי־ם צוּר *streams of the mountain*),* עָרֵי *cities of* Mc 7$_{12}$ (unless מָצוֹר V *whey*; or em. עָרֵי to עַד *to*; or em. וְעָרֵ־ם צוּר *and the cities of the rock*),* חַכְמֵי *skilled ones of* Ezk 27$_{8}$ (if em. חֲכָמַיִךְ צוֹר *your skilled ones, O Tyre*). <PREP> לְמִנֵּי *from*, + בוא *come* Mc 7$_{12}$ (unless מָצוֹר V *whey*; or em. וּלְמִנֵּי־ם צוֹר *and from Tyre*; or em. צֹר *Tyre*); עַד *to, as far as*, + בוא *come* Mc 7$_{12}$ (if em.; see Cstr.).*

⇒ cf. מִצְרַיִם *Egypt*.

*מָצוֹר V 4 n.m. **whey,** i.e. glacier rivulets, <CSTR> יְאֹרֵי מָצוֹר *streams of whey* Is 19$_{6}$ 37$_{25}$ (both unless מָצוֹר IV *Egypt*; both or em. יְאֹרֵי־ם צוּר *streams of the mountain*), עָרֵי *cities of* Mc 7$_{12}$ (unless מָצוֹר IV *Egypt*; or em. עָרֵי to עַד *to*; or em. וְעָרֵ־ם צוּר *and the cities of the rock*). <PREP> לְמִנֵּי *from*, + בוא *come* Mc 7$_{12}$ (unless מָצוֹר IV *Egypt*; or em. וּלְמִנֵּי־ם צוֹר *and from Tyre*; or em. צֹר *Tyre*); עַד *to, as far as*, + בוא *come* Mc 7$_{12}$ (if em.; see Cstr.).

מְצוּרָה I 8 n.f. **fortification**—pl. מְצֻרוֹת (מְצֻרֹת, מְצוּרוֹת)—**1. fortification, fortress,** <OBJ> חזק pi. *strengthen* 2 C 11$_{11}$, נצר *guard* Na 2$_{2}$ (or em. מַצָּרָה *watch*). <CSTR> עָרֵי מְצוּרָה *cities of fortification*, i.e. fortified cities 2 C 14$_{5}$, מְצֻרוֹת *of fortifications*, i.e. fortified cities 2 C 11$_{10.23}$ 12$_{4}$ (both הַמְּצֻרוֹת) 21$_{3}$. <PREP> בְּ of place, *in*, + נתן *give*, i.e. place 2 C 11$_{11}$.

2. siegeworks, <OBJ> קום hi. *raise* Is 29$_{3}$ (|| מֻצָּב *siege mound*).

<SYN> §2 מֻצָּב *siege mound*.

*[מְצוּרָה] II n.f. **distress,** <PREP> בְּ of place, *in(to)*, + בוא hi. *bring* Ps 66$_{11}$ (if em. בַּמְּצוּדָה *into the net*).

מצוררק, see מָצוֹר III *creature*.

[מַצּוּת] 1.1 n.f. **strife**—cstr. Si מצות; sf. מַצֻּתֶךָ—<SUBJ> היה *be* Si 34$_{26(Bmg)}$. <CSTR> מצות לצים *strife of scorners* Si 34$_{26}$; אַנְשֵׁי מַצֻּתֶךָ *men of your strife*, i.e. who strive with you Is 41$_{12}$ (|| מִלְחָמָה *war*). <PREP> לְ of benefit, *for* Si 34$_{26(B)}$.

<SYN> מִלְחָמָה *war*.

⇒ נצה I *fight*.

*[מצח] vb. **tread, Qal,** <SUBJ> רֶגֶל *foot* Ps 68$_{24}$ (if em. תִּמְחַץ perh. *you will wound* to תִּמְצַח *it will tread*). <PREP> בְּ of place, *in*, + דָּם *blood* Ps 68$_{24}$.

מֵצַח 13.1.1 n.m. **forehead**—cstr. מֵצַח; sf. מִצְחוֹ (Gnz מָצְחוֹ),

מִצְחֵךְ (מִצְחֵךְ), מִצְחָם; pl. cstr. מִצְחוֹת—**forehead, brow,** sometimes as indicative of a person's attitude (Is 48₄ Jr 3₃ Ezk 3₇), <SUBJ> היה *be* Jr 3₃. <NOM CL> מִצְחֵךְ נְחוּשָׁה *your forehead is bronze* Is 48₄. <OBJ> נתן *give,* i.e. make, hard Ezk 3₈.₉, עזז hi. *make strong* Si 8₁₆. <CSTR> מֵצַח אַהֲרֹן *forehead of Aaron* Ex 28₃₈, אִשָּׁה זוֹנָה *of a woman, a prostitute* Jr 3₃ (or em. אִשָּׁה זוֹנָה to נְחֻשָׁה *of bronze*), מִצְחוֹת הָאֲנָשִׁים *foreheads of the men* Ezk 9₄, מצחות נאנחים ונאנקים *foreheads of those who sigh and groan* CD 19₁₂; חִזְקֵי־מֵצַח *ones hard of forehead,* i.e. with a hard forehead Ezk 3₇. <PREP> בְּ of place, *in(to),* + טבע *sink* 1 S 17₄₉, זרח (of leprosy) *emerge* 2 C 26₁₉, צרע pu. *be struck with leprosy* 2 C 26₂₀; אֶל *upon,* + נכה hi. *strike* 1 S 17₄₉; עַל *upon,* + היה *be* Ex 28₃₈.₃₈, תוה hi. *place a mark* Ezk 9₄=CD 19₁₂; לְעֻמַּת *alongside,* + נתן *give,* i.e. make Ezk 3₈. <COLL> מֵצַח || עֹרֶף *neck* Is 48₄, פָּנִים *face* Ezk 3₈, לֵב *heart* Ezk 3₇.

<SYN> עֹרֶף *neck,* פָּנִים *face,* לֵב *heart.*

[מִצְחָה] 1 n.f. **greaves**—cstr. מִצְחַת—**greaves,** armour protecting the shins, <NOM CL> מִצְחַת נְחֹשֶׁת עַל־רַגְלָיו *greaves of bronze were upon his legs* 1 S 17₆. <CSTR> מִצְחַת נְחֹשֶׁת *greaves of bronze* 1 S 17₆.*

***[מְצִירוֹק]** 0.0.2 n.[m.] **emission of spittle,** i.e. of semen (unless from צִירוּק *lump of clay,* cf. with metathesis, קרץ *nip, pinch*), <NOM CL> הואה מצירוק *he is an emission of spittle* 1QS 11₂₁ (=4QSj 1₉ מצורר֯ק *formation of spittle*), אני מצירוק *I am an emission of spittle* 4QShirᵇ 28₃. <APP> חֹמֶר *clay* 1QS 11₂₁, יֵצֶר *creature* of clay 4QShirᵇ 28₃.

⇨ מצה *drain* + רֹק *spittle.*

[מְצִלָּה] 1 n.f. **bell**—pl. cstr. מְצִלּוֹת—<SUBJ> היה *be* Zc 14₂₀(MSS). <CSTR> מְצִלּוֹת הַסּוּס *bells of the horse(s)* Zc 14₂₀; כָּל־מְצִלּוֹת *all the bells of* Zc 14₂₀(mss). <PREP> עַל *upon,* + היה *be* Zc 14₂₀.

⇨ צלל *tingle.*

***[מַצְלַ֫חַת]** 0.1 n.f. **success,** <NOM CL> יש עת אשר בידו מצלחת *there is a time when success is in his* (physician's) *hand* Si 38₁₃ (unless צלח hi. ptc. *he shows success with his hand*).

⇨ צלח *prosper.*

מְצִלְתַּ֫יִם 13 n.f.du. **cymbals**—מְצִלְתָּיִם—<NOM CL> עִמָּהֶם ... מְצִלְתַּיִם *with them were ... cymbals* 1 C 16₄₂. <APP> כְּלֵי־שִׁיר ... מְצִלְתַּיִם *instruments of song ... cymbals* 1 C 15₁₆, מְצִלְתַּיִם נְחֹשֶׁת *cymbals, bronze,* i.e. bronze cymbals 1 C 15₁₉. <PREP> בְּ of accompaniment, *with, to (the accompaniment of)* Ne 12₂₇ 1 C 25₆ 2 C 5₁₂, + עמד *stand* Ezr 3₁₀(mss), hi. *position* Ezr 3₁₀ 1 C 15₁₆ 2 C 29₂₅, עלה hi. *bring up* ark 1 C 15₂₈, שׂחק pi. *make merry* 1 C 13₈, נבא ni. *prophesy* 1 C 25₁(Qr); of instrument, *by (means of), with,* + רום hi. *raise* sound 2 C 5₁₃; introducing object, + שׁמע hi. *sound* 1 C 15₁₉. <COLL> מְצִלְתַּיִם || חֲצוֹצְרָה *trumpet* Ezr 3₁₀ 1 C 13₈ 15₂₈ 16₄₂ 2 C 5₁₃, כִּנּוֹר *lyre* Ne 12₂₇ 1 C 13₈ 15₁₆.₂₈ 16₅ (both +) 25₁.₆ 2 C 5₁₂ 29₂₅, נֵבֶל *harp* Ne 12₂₇ 1 C 13₈ 15₁₆.₂₈ 16₅ (both +) 25₁.₆ 2 C 5₁₂ 29₂₅, שִׁיר *song* Ne 12₂₇ 1 C 13₈; + שׁוֹפָר *ram's horn* 1 C 15₂₈, כְּלֵי־הַשִּׁיר *instruments of song* 2 C 5₁₃, var. 1 C 16₄₂.

<SYN> חֲצוֹצְרָה *trumpet,* כִּנּוֹר *lyre,* נֵבֶל *harp,* שִׁיר *song.*

⇨ צלל *tingle.*

***[מָצָן]** n.[m.] **thicket, place of thorns,** vocalization uncertain, as name for the underworld, the Thicket, <PREP> אֶל *to,* + לקח *take* Jb 5₅ (if em. אֶל־מִצִּנִּים *from thorns* to perh. אֶל־מָצָנִים *to the Thicket*).

מִצְנֶ֫פֶת 12.1.1 n.f. **turban**—מִצְנָפֶת; cstr. מִצְנֶפֶת—usu. of high priest; of king (Ezk 21₃₁), <OBJ> עשׂה *make* Ex 28₄.₃₉||39₂₈, לבשׁ *dress with* Si 45₁₂, שׂים *place* Ex 29₆||Lv 8₉, סור hi. *remove* Ezk 21₃₁. <CSTR> מִצְנֶפֶת בַּד *turban of linen* Lv 16₄, שֵׁשׁ *of fine linen* Ex 28₃₉||39₂₈. <APP> בֶּגֶד *garment* Ex 28₄. <PREP> בְּ of instrument, *by (means of), with,* + צנף *wind (the head)* Lv 16₄; עַל *upon,* + היה *be* Ex 28₃₇, נתן *give,* i.e. place Ex 29₆||Lv 8₉(Sam) Ex 39₃₁, שׂים *place* Lv 8₉; אֶל מוּל פְּנֵי *at the front of,* + היה *be* Ex 28₃₇.

<COLL> מִצְנֶפֶת || עֲטָרָה *crown* Ezk 21₃₁ Si 45₁₂, מִגְבָּעָה *headdress* Ex 39₂₈ (+), אַבְנֵט *girdle* Ex 28₄ 28₃₉||39₂₈ (+) Lv 16₄, אֵפֹד *ephod* Ex 28₄, חֹשֶׁן *breastpiece* Ex 28₄, מְעִיל

robe Ex 28$_4$ Si 45$_{12}$, כְּתֹנֶת *tunic* Ex 28$_4$ 28$_{39}$||39$_{28}$ Lv 16$_4$ (+), מִכְנָסַיִם *breeches* Ex 39$_{28}$ Lv 16$_4$ (both +).

Also 4QapJoseph[b] 12$_2$.

<SYN> עֲטָרָה *crown*, אַבְנֵט *girdle*, אֵפֹד *ephod*, חֹשֶׁן *breastpiece*, מְעִיל *robe*, כְּתֹנֶת *tunic*.

⇒ צנף *wind*.

מַצָּע 1 n.m. **couch,** <SUBJ> קצר *be short* Is 28$_{20}$ (קָצַר הַמַּצָּע מֵהִשְׂתָּרֵעַ *the bed is too short to stretch oneself [on it]*). <PREP> בְּ of place, *in, on*, + קלל pi. *curse* Ec 10$_{20}$ (if em. בְּמַדָּעֲךָ *in your thought*).

⇒ יצע *extend*.

[מִצְעָד] 3.0.9 n.[m.] **step**—Q מצעדם; pl. cstr. מִצְעֲדֵי; sf. מִצְעָדָיו, Q מצעדיכה, Q מצעדי—usu. **step;** also **footstep, heel** (Dn 11$_{43}$), **flight,** i.e. descent, of arrow into the deep (1QH 3$_{17}$), <NOM CL> מֵיְ׳ מִצְעֲדֵי־גֶבֶר *the steps of a man are from Y.* Ps 37$_{23}$ Pr 20$_{24}$ (גָּבֶר; both + דֶּרֶךְ *way*), מאתכה מצעדי *my steps are from you* 1QH 2$_{23.33}$, לא מצעד לקול רגלי *there is no step to the sound of my feet*, i.e. I cannot take a step 1QH 8$_{34}$ (+ פַּעַם *footstep*). <CSTR> מִצְעֲדֵי־גֶבֶר *steps of a man* Ps 37$_{23}$ Pr 20$_{24}$ (גָּבֶר), מצעדי דעת *steps of knowledge* 4QUnidA 2$_4$. <PREP> בְּ of place, *in, at* Dn 11$_{43}$; of accompaniment, *in, with* 4QUnidA 2$_4$, + כבד pi. *honour* 4Q416 2.3$_{16}$ (|| רוֹשׁ *poverty*); עִם *with* 1QH 3$_{25}$ 9$_{33}$, + שמע hi. *make* voice *heard* 1QH 3$_{17}$.

Also 4QHod[a] 7.2$_9$.

⇒ צעד *step*.

מִצְעָר I 5.2.2 n.m. **small thing**—cstr. מִצְעַר—**1. small thing, small one,** of city (Gn 19$_{20}$), beginning (Jb 8$_7$), <SUBJ> היה *be* Jb 8$_7$ (+ אַחֲרִיתְךָ יִשְׂגֶּה מְאֹד *your future will be very great*). <NOM CL> הִיא מִצְעָר *it is a small one*, var. Gn 19$_{20}$.

2. a few, <NOM CL> מצער ימיך *your days are few* Si 30$_{32}$. <CSTR> מִצְעַר אֲנָשִׁים *a few men* 2 C 24$_{24}$. <PREP> בְּ of accompaniment, *with*, + בוא *come* 2 C 24$_{24}$.

3. a little while (Is 63$_{18}$ [or em.; see Prep.] Si 33$_{10}$ [Bmg] 1QH 6$_8$), <OBJ> פקד *appoint* Si 33$_{10(Bmg)}$ (B מוֹעֵד *appointed time*). <PREP> לְ of time, *for, in*, + ירשׁ *possess* Is 63$_{18}$ (or em. לַמִּצְעָר יָרְשׁוּ עַם *the people possessed for a little while* to לָמָּה צָעֲרוּ *why do they have little regard for?*), קוּם hi. *raise up* survivors 1QH 6$_8$.

Also 4QpsEzek[a] 3$_6$.

⇒ צער *be insignificant*.

מִצְעָר II 1 pl.n. **Mizar,** mountain mentioned in assoc. with Mount Hermon, <CSTR> הַר מִצְעָר *Mount Mizar* Ps 42$_7$ (mss מִזְעָר *Mizar*).

מִצְפָּה 40 pl.n. **Mizpah**—+ ה- of direction הַמִּצְפָּתָה—alw. with article or pointing of article (except Ho 5$_1$), **1.** in Gilead, <OBJ> קרא *call*, i.e. name Gn 31$_{49}$ (Sam המצבה). <PREP> לְ *at*, + היה *be* Ho 5$_1$; בְּ of place, *in, at*, + דבר pi. *speak* Jg 11$_{11}$, חנה *encamp* Jg 10$_{17}$; הַמִּצְפָּה without preposition, *to Mizpah*, + בוא *come* Jg 11$_{34}$.

2. in Benjamin, perh. T. en-Naṣbeh, 12 km N of Jerusalem, <OBJ> בנה *build* 1 K 15$_{22}$||2 C 16$_6$. <CSTR> אַנְשֵׁי ... הַמִּצְפָּה *men of ... Mizpah* Ne 3$_7$ (or em. הַמִּצְפֶּה *of Mizpeh*), שַׂר הַמִּצְפָּה *ruler of Mizpah* Ne 3$_{19}$ (or em.; see below), פֶּלֶךְ *district of* Ne 3$_{15.19}$ (if ins. חֲצִי פֶּלֶךְ *half the district of*), <PREP> בְּ of place, *in, at* Jr 41$_{10}$, + היה *be* 2 K 25$_{25}$ Jr 41$_3$ (or em. בַּמִּשְׁתֶּה *at the feast*), שׁאר ni. *remain* Jr 41$_{10}$ (or del.), ישׁב *dwell* Jr 40$_{10}$, אמר *say* Jr 40$_{15}$, שׁבע ni. *swear* Jg 21$_1$, שׁפט *judge* 1 S 7$_6$, אכל *eat* Jr 41$_1$; מִן of direction, from, + יצא *go out* 1 S 7$_{11}$ Jr 41$_6$, שׁבה *take captive* Jr 41$_{14.16}$ (if em. הֵשִׁיב *he had brought back* to שָׁבָה *he had taken captive*); בֵּין *between*, שׂים *place* 1 S 7$_{12}$; with ה- of direction, *to, at*, + בוא *come* Jr 40$_{6.8.12.13}$ 41$_1$, סבב *go round* 1 S 7$_{16}$, קבץ *gather* 1 S 7$_5$, ni. *gather* intrans. 1 S 7$_6$, htp. 1 S 7$_{6(mss).7}$; הַמִּצְפָּה without preposition, *to, at Mizpah*, + בוא *come* 2 K 25$_{23}$, עלה *go up* Jg 20$_3$ 21$_{5.8}$, צעק hi. *call together* 1 S 10$_{17}$, קהל ni. *be assembled* Jg 20$_1$.

3. appar. ident. with מִצְפֶּה *Mizpeh* at Jos 11$_8$, <CSTR> אֶרֶץ הַמִּצְפָּה *land of Mizpah* Jos 11$_3$.*

מִצְפֶּה I 2.1 n.m. **watchtower,** <PREP> עַל *upon* Si 37$_{14(B)}$ (Bmg, D שֵׁן *crag*), + עמד *stand* Is 21$_8$; *to*, + בוא *come* 2 C 20$_{24}$. <COLL> הַמִּצְפֶּה לַמִּדְבָּר *the watchtower of the steppe* 2 C 20$_{24}$.

⇒ צפה *look out*.

מִצְפֶּה II 6.0.1 pl.n. **Mizpeh**—Q מצפא; cstr. מִצְפֵּה—**1.** in Judah, <NOM CL> בַּשְּׁפֵלָה ... הַמִּצְפֶּה *in the lowland was ... Mizpeh* Jos 15$_{38}$. <APP> עִיר *city* Jos 15$_{38}$.

2. in Benjamin, perh. en-Nebī Samwīl, 8 km NW of Jerusalem, unless ident. with מִצְפָּה *Mizpah*, <SUBJ> היה *be* Jos 18$_{26}$ (הַמִּצְפֶּה). <CSTR> אַנְשֵׁי ... הַמִּצְפֶּה *men of ... Mizpah* Ne 3$_{7}$ (if em. הַמִּצְפָּה *of Mizpah*).

3. appar. ident. with הַמִּצְפָּה at Jos 11$_{3}$, near Hermon, <CSTR> בִּקְעַת מִצְפֶּה *valley of Mizpeh* Jos 11$_{8}$ 4QSela 9.14 (מצפא).

4. in Moab, <CSTR> מִצְפֵּה מוֹאָב *Mizpeh of Moab* 1 S 22$_{3}$. <COLL> וַיֵּלֶךְ דָּוִד ... מִצְפֵּה מוֹאָב *and David went ... to Mizpeh of Moab* 1 S 22$_{3}$.

5. in Gilead, perh. ident. with רָמַת הַמִּצְפֶּה *Ramath-mizpeh* at Jos 13$_{26}$, <OBJ> עבר *pass* Jg 11$_{29}$ (or del.). <CSTR> מִצְפֵּה גִּלְעָד *Mizpeh of Gilead* Jg 11$_{29}$ (or del.) 11$_{29}$. <PREP> מִן of direction, *from*, + עבר *pass* Jg 11$_{29}$.

⇒ צפה *look out.*

[מַצְפּוֹן] 1 n.[m.] **hidden treasure**—pl. sf. מַצְפֻּנָיו—**hidden treasure**, perh. **hiding place,*** <SUBJ> בעה ni. *be sought* Ob$_{6}$. <PREP> אֶל *to*, + לקח *take* Jb 5$_{5}$ (if em. אֶל־מִצִּנִּים *from thorns* to אֶל־מַצְפֻּנִים).*

⇒ צפן *hide.*

מצץ 1 vb. **suck**—**Qal** 1 Impf. תָּמֹצּוּ—**suck, draw milk,** <SUBJ> אהב ptc. *one who loves* Is 66$_{11}$ (|| ינק *suck*), עַם *people* Ps 73$_{10}$ (if em. מֵי מָלֵא יִמָּצוּ *waters of fullness will be sucked* [i.e. מצה ni.] to מִלֵּיהֶם יָמֹצּוּ *they will suck their words*). <OBJ> מִלָּה *word* Ps 73$_{10}$ (if em.; see Subj.).

<SYN> ינק *suck.**

⇒ cf. מצה *drain.*

מֻצָּק *cast object, casting*, see יצק Ho.

מֵצַר 3.0.2 n.[m.] **distress**—pl. מְצָרִים; cstr. מְצָרֵי—**1. distress, torment,** <SUBJ> מצא *find* Ps 116$_{3}$ (or em.; see Cstr.; || חֶבֶל *cord*, + צָרָה *distress*, יָגוֹן *grief*). <CSTR> מְצָרֵי שְׁאוֹל *torments of Sheol* Ps 116$_{3}$ (or em. מְצָרֵי to מְצֹדֵי *nets of*); עוני מצר[יו] *affliction of his torments* 4QBéat 2.2$_{5}$ (unless מצר[פו] *of his hardship*; + צוּקָה *distress*). <PREP> מִן of direction, *from (out of)*, + קרא *call* Ps 118$_{5}$ (unless §3); בֵּין *among, within*, + נשׂג hi. *overtake* Lm 1$_{3}$.

2. narrow place, <PREP> בְּ of place, *in*, + נשׂג hi. *overtake* 1QH 5$_{29}$.

3. Confinement, as name for the underworld,* <PREP> מִן of direction, *from (out of)*, + קרא *call* Ps 118$_{5}$ (unless §1).

<SYN> §1 חֶבֶל *cord.**

⇒ צרר *bind, be narrow.*

*[**מֶצֶר**] 0.0.0.1 pr.n.m. **Mezer**, son of Shallum, <APP> בֵּן *son* Seal 608 ([ב]ן; T. Beit Mirsim?, 7th/6th cent.) Bulla WSS 556 ([ב]ן; others מצרי *Mizri* or משלם *Meshullam*). <PREP> לְ of possession, *of, (belonging) to* Bulla WSS 556 ([ל]מצר).*

[מַצָּרָה] I n.f. **watch,** <OBJ> נצר *guard* Na 2$_{2}$ (if em. מְצֻרָה *fortress*).

*[**מַצָּרָה**] II n.f. **guard-house,** <PREP> בְּ of place, *in(to)*, + בוא hi. *bring* Ezk 19$_{9}$ (if em. בַּמְּצֹדוֹת *into the nets* to בַּמַּצָּרָה *into the guard-house*).

מִצְרִי I 30 gent. **Egyptian**—fem. מִצְרִית; pl. מִצְרִים; fem. מִצְרִיֹּת—**1.** as attributive adj. of אִישׁ *man* Gn 39$_{1}$ Ex 2$_{11.19}$ Lv 24$_{10}$ 1 S 30$_{11}$ 2 S 23$_{21}$||1 C 11$_{23}$, אִשָּׁה *woman, wife* Ex 1$_{19}$ 1 C 4$_{18}$ (if ins. אִשָּׁה מִצְרִיָּה *an Egyptian wife*), נַעַר *lad* 1 S 30$_{13}$, עֶבֶד *slave* 1 C 2$_{34}$, שִׁפְחָה *female slave* Gn 16$_{1}$.

2. as sing. noun, a particular **Egyptian, a.** masc., <OBJ> תעב pi. *abhor* Dt 23$_{8}$, נכה hi. *strike* Ex 2$_{12}$, הרג *kill* Ex 2$_{14}$ 2 S 23$_{21}$||1 C 11$_{23}$, טמן *hide* Ex 2$_{12}$. <CSTR> יַד הַמִּצְרִי *hand of the Egyptian* 2 S 23$_{21.21}$||1 C 11$_{23.23}$, בֵּית *house of* Gn 39$_{2}$ (... בֵּית) 39$_{5}$. <APP> אָדוֹן *lord* Gn 39$_{2}$. <PREP> אֶל *to*, + ירד *go down* 2 S 23$_{21}$||1 C 11$_{23}$.

b. fem., <SUBJ> ילד *bear* Gn 21$_{9}$ 25$_{12}$. <OBJ> לקח *take* Gn 16$_{3}$, נתן *give* Gn 16$_{3}$. <CSTR> בֶּן־ ... הַמִּצְרִית *son of ... the Egyptian* Gn 21$_{9}$. <APP> Hagar Gn 16$_{3}$ 21$_{9}$ 25$_{12}$, שִׁפְחָה *female slave* Gn 16$_{3}$ 25$_{12}$.

3. as collective singular noun, **Egyptians,** <PREP> לְ of possession, *of, (belonging) to* Ezr 9$_{1}$.

4. as pl. noun, **Egyptians,** <SUBJ> אמר *say* Gn 12$_{12}$, ראה *see* Gn 12$_{12.14}$, אכל *eat* Gn 43$_{32.32}$, יכל *be able* Gn

43$_{32}$, נתן *give*, i.e. place Dt 26$_6$, רעע hi. *harm* Dt 26$_6$, ענה pi. *afflict* Dt 26$_6$, הרג *kill* Gn 12$_{12}$. <OBJ> כסה pi. *cover* Jos 24$_7$. <PREP> לְ *to* Gn 43$_{32}$ (if em. לְמִצְרַיִם *to the Egyptians* to לְמִצְרִים); עַל *upon*, + בוא hi. *bring* Jos 24$_7$; בֵּין *between*, + שִׂים *place* Jos 24$_7$.*

⇒ מִצְרַיִם *Egypt*.

*מִצְרִי II 0.0.0.2 pr.n.m. **Mizri, 1.** appar. son of Shebaniah, <PREP> לְ of possession, *of, (belonging) to* Bulla D61.

2. son of Shecaniah, <APP> בֵּן *son* Judaean ost. DH 79$_{10}$.*

3. son of Shallum, <APP> בֵּן *son* Bulla WSS 556 ([ב]ן; others מצר *Mezer* or משלם *Meshullam*). <PREP> לְ of possession, *of, (belonging) to* Bulla WSS 556 (ל[מצר]).

[מֻצְרִי] *Musri*, see מִצְרַיִם II *Mizraim*.

מִצְרַיִם I 674.0.34.2 pr.n.m. **Egypt**—מִצְרָיִם; + ה- of direction מִצְרַיְמָה (מִצְרָיְמָה)—**1.** son of Ham, <SUBJ> ילד *beget* Gn 10$_{13}$||1 C 1$_{11}$. <NOM CL> בְּנֵי חָם ... מִצְרַיִם *the sons of Ham were ... Egypt* Gn 10$_6$||1 C 1$_8$ (+ Cush, Put, Canaan).

2a. territory and state in NE Africa. **b. Egyptians** (distinction from §2a not alw. clear), e.g. Gn 41$_{56}$ 43$_{32}$ 45$_2$ 46$_{34}$ 47$_{15}$ 50$_3$ Ex 1$_{13}$ 3$_9$ 6$_5$ 7$_5$ 8$_{17}$ 9$_{11}$ 10$_6$ 12$_{30}$ 14$_4$ 32$_{12}$ Nm 14$_{13}$ 20$_{15}$ 33$_3$ Jos 24$_6$ Jg 6$_9$ 1 S 4$_8$ 6$_6$ Is 19$_{16}$ 23$_5$ Ezk 29$_{12}$ 30$_{23}$.

<SUBJ> היה *be* Gn 47$_{15}$ Is 19$_{16}$ Ezk 29$_{14}$ Jl 4$_{19}$, אמר *say* Gn 47$_{15}$ Ex 12$_{33}$ 14$_{25}$ 32$_{12}$ Nm 14$_{13}$ (or em. וְאָמְרוּ אֶל־ *and they will say to* to וְגַם כָּל־ *and also all*), נדר *vow* Is 19$_{21}$, שׁמע *hear* Gn 45$_2$ Nm 14$_{13}$, ידע *know* Ex 7$_5$ 14$_{4.18}$ Is 19$_{21}$ Ezk 30$_{26}$, דרשׁ *inquire of* Is 19$_3$, חרד *tremble* Is 19$_{16}$, פחד *fear* Is 19$_{16}$, בכה *weep* Gn 50$_3$, שׂמח *rejoice* Ps 105$_{38}$, ברך pass. *be blessed* Is 19$_{25}$, שׁתה *drink* Ex 7$_{18.21.24}$, נסע *march* Ex 14$_{10}$, בוא *come* Gn 47$_{15}$ Ex 14$_{17}$ Is 19$_{23}$, hi. *bring* Gn 47$_{15}$, עלה *go up* Jr 46$_8$, קום *rise* Ex 12$_{30}$, שׁוב *go back* Is 19$_{22}$, שׁלח pi. *send* Ex 12$_{33}$ 1 S 6$_6$, רדף *pursue* Ex 14$_{9.23}$ Jos 24$_6$, מהר pi. *hasten* Ex 12$_{33}$, נוס *flee* Ex 14$_{25.27}$, נשׂג hi. *overtake* Ex 14$_9$, פוץ ni. *be scattered* Ezk 29$_{13}$, קבץ pi. *gather* Ho 9$_6$.

עבד *serve* Is 19$_{21.23}$, hi. *make serve* Ex 1$_{13}$ 6$_5$, רעע hi. *deal harshly* Nm 20$_{15}$, כבד pi. *harden* heart 1 S 6$_6$, עשׂה *squeeze* Ezk 23$_{21}$ (if em.; see Prep.), לחץ *oppress* Ex 3$_9$, סקל *stone* Ex 8$_{22}$, יהב *give* Gn 47$_{15}$, נתן *give* Ezk 17$_{15}$, שׁלם pi. *pay* vows Is 19$_{21}$, מכר *sell* Gn 47$_{20}$, יסד ni. *be founded* Ex 9$_{18}$, לחם ni. *fight* Is 19$_2$, חיל *be in pain* Is 23$_5$, חפר *dig* Ex 7$_{24}$, כחד pi. *conceal* Gn 47$_{15}$, יכל *be able* Ex 7$_{21.24}$, עזר *help* Is 30$_7$, חזק *be firm* Ex 12$_{33}$, כסה pi. *cover* Jr 46$_8$, לאה ni. *weary oneself* Ex 7$_{18}$, חיה *live* Gn 47$_{15}$, מות *die* Gn 47$_{15}$, אבד *perish* Ex 10$_7$, hi. *destroy* Jr 46$_8$, קבר pi. *bury* Nm 33$_4$.

<NOM CL> מִצְרַיִם אָדָם וְלֹא־אֵל *Egypt is human and not God* Is 31$_3$, עֶגְלָה יְפֵה־פִיָּה מִצְרָיִם *a beautiful heifer is Egypt* Jr 46$_{20}$, כּוּשׁ עָצְמָה וּמִצְרַיִם *Cush was her might, Egypt too* Na 3$_9$.

<OBJ> ראה *see* Ex 14$_{13.30}$, זכר *remember* Ezk 23$_{27}$, קרא *call to* Ho 7$_{11}$, עבד *serve* Ex 14$_{12.12}$, שׁוב hi. *bring back* Ezk 29$_{14}$, תעה hi. *lead astray* Is 19$_{13.14}$, נער pi. *shake off* Ex 14$_{27}$, פוץ hi. *scatter* Ezk 29$_{12}$ 30$_{23.26}$, זרה pi. *disperse* Ezk 29$_{12}$ 30$_{23.26}$, קבץ pi. *gather* Ezk 29$_{13}$, נהל pi. *supply* Gn 47$_{15}$, נתן *give* Is 43$_3$, סוך pilp. *provoke* Is 19$_2$, נגף *strike* Ex 12$_{23.27}$ Jos 24$_5$ Is 19$_{22}$, נכה hi. *strike* Ex 3$_{20}$ 1 S 4$_8$ Ps 136$_{10}$, שׁבר *break* 4QpsEzek^{d} 1.2$_5$, נצל pi. *despoil* Ex 3$_{22}$ 12$_{36}$, סכר pi. *deliver up* Is 19$_4$, רפא *heal* Is 19$_{22}$, סמך *support* Ezk 30$_6$.

<CSTR> אֱלֹהֵי מִצְרַיִם *gods of Egypt* Ex 12$_{12}$ Jr 43$_{12.13}$, אֱלִילֵי *idols of* Is 19$_1$ 1QM 14$_1$, גִּלּוּלֵי *idols of* Ezk 20$_{7.8}$, בְּנֵי *sons of* Ezk 16$_{26}$, בַּת־ *daughter of* Jr 46$_{11.19.24}$ (all three מִצְרָיִם), בְּכוֹרֵי *firstborn of* Ps 135$_8$ (מִצְרָיִם), חַרְטֻמֵּי *magicians of* Gn 41$_8$ Ex 7$_{11.22}$, יֹשְׁבֵי *inhabitants of* Ezk 29$_6$ 4QNarrC 1$_{14}$ ([יו]שבי ... מצרים), שְׁבִי *captives of* Is 20$_4$, הֲמוֹן *multitude of* Ezk 30$_{10}$ 32$_{18}$, מִשְׁפַּחַת *clan of* Zc 14$_{18}$, סֹמְכֵי מִצְרַיִם *ones who support Egypt* Ezk 30$_6$, מַכֵּה *one who struck* Ps 136$_{10}$.

מֶלֶךְ מִצְרַיִם *king of Egypt* Gn 40$_{1.1}$ (מִצְרָיִם) 40$_5$ 41$_{46}$ (מִצְרָיִם) Ex 1$_{15.17}$ (מִצְרָיִם) 1$_{18}$ (Sam פַּרְעֹה *Pharaoh*) 2$_{23}$ 3$_{18.19}$ 5$_4$ 6$_{11.13}$ (both מִצְרָיִם) 6$_{27.29}$ 14$_{5.8}$ Dt 7$_8$ (מִצְרָיִם) 11$_3$ (lacking in Sam) 1 K 3$_1$ (מִצְרָיִם) 9$_{16}$ 11$_{18.40}$ 14$_{25}$||2 C 12$_2$ 2 K 17$_{4.7}$ (מִצְרָיִם) 18$_{21}$||Is 36$_6$ 2 K 23$_{29}$||2 C 35$_{20}$ 2 K 24$_{7.7}$ (מִצְרָיִם) Jr 25$_{19}$ 44$_{30}$ 46$_{2.17}$ Ezk 29$_2$ (מִצְרָיִם) 29$_3$ 30$_{21.22}$ 31$_2$ 32$_2$ 2 C 12$_9$ 36$_{3.4}$ 4QpsEzek^{e} 1$_2$ ([מ]לך) Arad ost. 88$_3$.

יַד מִצְרַיִם *hand of the Egyptians* Ex 3$_8$ 14$_{30}$ (מִצְרָיִם)

18$_{9}$ (מִצְרָיִם) 18$_{10.10}$ (מִצְרָיִם) Jg 6$_{9}$ 1 S 10$_{18}$ 4QBibPar 14.1$_{5}$, עֵינֵי *eyes of* Ex 3$_{21}$ 11$_{3}$ (both מִצְרָיִם) 12$_{36}$ Nm 33$_{3}$ (כָּל־מִצְרַיִם *of all the Egyptians*), לֵב *heart of* Ex 14$_{17}$, לְבַב *heart of* Is 19$_{1}$, ־רוּחַ *spirit of* Is 19$_{3}$, מִקְנֵה *cattle of* Ex 9$_{4,6}$ (both מִצְרָיִם), צֵל *shadow of* Is 30$_{2}$ (מִצְרָיִם) 30$_{3}$, עֶרְוַת *nakedness*, i.e. shame, *of* Is 20$_{4}$ (מִצְרָיִם), סִבְלֹת *burdens of* Ex 6$_{6.7}$ (מִצְרָיִם), בָּתֵּי *houses of* Ex 8$_{17}$ 10$_{6}$ (כָּל־מִצְרַיִם), מָעוֹז *stronghold of* Ezk 30$_{15}$ (מִצְרָיִם), רֶכֶב *chariot(s) of* Ex 14$_{7}$, מַחֲנֵה *camp*, i.e. army Ex 14$_{20.24.24}$ (מִצְרָיִם), חֵיל *army of* Dt 11$_{4}$, מֹטֹת *bars*, i.e. power, *of* Ezk 30$_{18}$ (or em. מֹטוֹת to מַטּוֹת *staffs of*), שֵׁבֶט *sceptre of* Zc 10$_{11}$, חרב מצר[ים] *sword of Egypt* 4QpsEzek[a] 1$_{6}$, מזבחי מצ[רים] *altars of Egypt* 4QpsEzek[e] 48$_{2}$.

אֶרֶץ מִצְרַיִם *land of Egypt* Gn 13$_{10}$ 21$_{21}$ (מִצְרָיִם) 41$_{19.29}$ (מִצְרָיִם) 41$_{30}$ (מִצְרָיִם) 41$_{33}$ (מִצְרָיִם) 41$_{34.36}$ (מִצְרָיִם) 41$_{41.43.44.45.46}$ (all five מִצְרָיִם) 41$_{48.53}$ (מִצְרָיִם) 41$_{54.55.56}$ 45$_{8}$ (both מִצְרָיִם) 45$_{18.19.20.26}$ (מִצְרָיִם) 46$_{20}$ 47$_{6+6t}$ 48$_{5}$ 50$_{7}$ (מִצְרָיִם) Ex 4$_{20}$ (אַרְצָה מִצְרָיִם) 5$_{12}$ (מִצְרָיִם) 6$_{13}$ (מִצְרָיִם) 6$_{26.28}$ 7$_{3}$ (both מִצְרָיִם) 7$_{4.19.21}$ 8$_{1.2.3.12.13}$ (all six מִצְרָיִם) 8$_{20}$ 9$_{9}$ (מִצְרָיִם) 9$_{9}$ (מִצְרָיִם) 9$_{22}$ (מִצְרָיִם) 9$_{22.23}$ (both מִצְרָיִם) 9$_{24.25}$ 10$_{12.12}$ (מִצְרָיִם) 10$_{13.14.15}$ (מִצְרָיִם) 10$_{21}$ (מִצְרָיִם) 10$_{22}$ 11$_{3.5.6}$ (מִצְרָיִם) 11$_{9}$ (מִצְרָיִם) 12$_{1.12.12.13}$ (מִצְרָיִם) 12$_{17}$ (מִצְרָיִם) 12$_{29.41}$ (מִצְרָיִם) 12$_{42}$ (מִצְרָיִם) 12$_{51}$ 13$_{15.18}$ 16$_{1}$ (both מִצְרָיִם) 16$_{3.6.32}$ (both מִצְרָיִם) 19$_{1}$ (מִצְרָיִם) 20$_{2}$ 22$_{20}$ 23$_{9}$ (both מִצְרָיִם) 29$_{46}$ 32$_{1.4.7.8}$ (all three מִצְרָיִם) 32$_{11.23}$ 33$_{1}$ (מִצְרָיִם) Lv 11$_{45}$ 18$_{3}$ 19$_{34}$ (מִצְרָיִם) 19$_{36}$ (מִצְרָיִם) 22$_{33}$ 23$_{43}$ 25$_{38.42.55}$ (all four מִצְרָיִם) 26$_{13.45}$ Nm 1$_{1}$ 3$_{13}$ 8$_{17}$ 9$_{1}$ 14$_{2}$ 15$_{41}$ 26$_{4}$ (מִצְרָיִם) 33$_{1.38}$ Dt 1$_{27}$ (מִצְרָיִם) 5$_{6.15}$ 6$_{12}$ 8$_{14}$ 9$_{7}$ 10$_{19}$ (מִצְרָיִם) 11$_{10}$ 13$_{6}$=11QT 54$_{16}$ Dt 13$_{11}$ 15$_{15}$ 16$_{3.3}$ 20$_{1}$ (מִצְרָיִם)=11QT 61$_{14}$ Dt 24$_{22}$ (מִצְרָיִם) 29$_{1.15}$ (מִצְרָיִם) 29$_{24}$ (מִצְרָיִם) 34$_{11}$ (מִצְרָיִם) Jos 24$_{17}$ Jg 2$_{12}$ 19$_{30}$ 1 S 12$_{6}$ 27$_{8}$ (both מִצְרָיִם) 1 K 6$_{1}$ 8$_{9.21}$ (both מִצְרָיִם) 9$_{9}$||2 C 7$_{22}$ 1 K 12$_{28}$ (מִצְרָיִם) 2 K 17$_{7.36}$ Is 11$_{16}$ (מִצְרָיִם) 19$_{18.19.20}$ 27$_{13}$ Jr 2$_{6}$ 7$_{22}$ (all five מִצְרָיִם) 7$_{25}$ 11$_{4.7}$ 16$_{14}$ 23$_{7}$ 24$_{8}$ (all three מִצְרָיִם) 31$_{32}$ (מִצְרָיִם) 32$_{20.21}$ (מִצְרָיִם) 34$_{13}$ 42$_{14.16}$ (מִצְרָיִם) 43$_{7.11}$ (מִצְרָיִם) 43$_{12.13}$ (מִצְרָיִם) 44$_{1}$ (מִצְרָיִם) 44$_{8.12.12.13.14}$ (מִצְרָיִם) 44$_{15.24}$ (מִצְרָיִם) 44$_{26}$ (מִצְרָיִם) 44$_{26}$ (מִצְרָיִם) 44$_{27.28.28}$ 46$_{13}$ Ezk 19$_{4}$ (both מִצְרָיִם) 20$_{5.6}$ (both מִצְרָיִם) 20$_{8.9}$ (both מִצְרָיִם) 20$_{10.36}$ (both מִצְרָיִם) 23$_{19}$ (מִצְרָיִם) 23$_{27}$ (מִצְרָיִם) 29$_{9.10.12.19.20}$ (both מִצְרָיִם) 30$_{13.13.25}$ (both מִצְרָיִם) 32$_{15}$ Ho 2$_{17}$ 7$_{16}$ (both מִצְרָיִם) 11$_{5}$ 12$_{10}$ 13$_{4}$ Am 2$_{10}$ (all three מִצְרָיִם) 3$_{1.9}$ (מִצְרָיִם) 9$_{7}$ Mc 6$_{4}$ 7$_{15}$ (מִצְרָיִם) Zc 10$_{10}$ Ps 78$_{12}$ 81$_{6.11}$ (both מִצְרָיִם) Dn 9$_{15}$ 11$_{42}$ 2 C 6$_{5}$ 20$_{10}$ (מִצְרָיִם) 1QDM 1$_{1}$ ([ארץ מ]צרים) 2$_{6}$ ([מצרים]) 4QBibPar 14.1$_{4}$ 4QJub[h] 40$_{6}$ 4QapJoshua[b] 12$_{5}$ (אר[ץ]) 4QpsEzek[a] 16.2$_{6}$ (מצ[רים]) 4QpsMos[d] 3$_{4}$ (מ[צרים]) 3$_{5}$ (מצר[ים]).

אַדְמַת מִצְרַיִם *farmland of Egypt* Gn 47$_{20.26}$, גְּבוּל *border of* Gn 47$_{21}$ Ex 10$_{14}$ (מִצְרָיִם) 10$_{19}$ (מִצְרָיִם) 1 K 5$_{1}$ (מִצְרָיִם) 2 C 9$_{26}$ (מִצְרָיִם), מלכות מצרים *kingdom of Egypt* 4QpsEzek[d] 1.2$_{4}$, שערי *gates*, i.e. cities, *of* 4QpsEzek[a] 1$_{5}$ (שער[י]) 8$_{1}$ (מצ[רי]ם), דֶּרֶךְ מִצְרַיִם *way of Egypt* Is 10$_{24.26}$ (both מִצְרָיִם) Jr 2$_{18}$ Am 4$_{10}$ (or em. דֶּרֶךְ to דֶּבֶר *pestilence of*), נְהַר *river of* Gn 15$_{18}$, נַחַל *wadi of* Nm 34$_{5}$ (נַחְלָה מִצְרָיִם) Jos 15$_{4.47}$ (מִצְרָיִם) 1 K 8$_{65}$||2 C 7$_{8}$ (מִצְרָיִם) 2 K 24$_{7}$ Is 27$_{12}$ (מִצְרָיִם), יְאוֹר *Nile of* Am 8$_{8}$ (מִצְרָיִם) 9$_{5}$ (יְאֹר מִצְרָיִם), יְאֹרֵי *streams of* Is 7$_{18}$ (מִצְרָיִם), שִׁיחוֹר *Shihor of* 1 C 13$_{5}$, ־יַם *sea of* Is 11$_{15}$, מֵימֵי *waters of* Ex 7$_{19}$ 8$_{2}$ (מִצְרָיִם), צֹעַן מִצְרָיִם *Zoan of Egypt* Nm 13$_{22}$.

שְׁבוּת מִצְרַיִם *fortunes of Egypt/the Egyptians* Ezk 29$_{14}$, טוּב *good things of* Gn 45$_{23}$ (מִצְרָיִם), חֲמֻדוֹת *precious things of* Dn 11$_{43}$ (מִצְרָיִם), יְגִיעַ *(product of) labour of* Is 45$_{14}$, אֵטוּן *linen of* Pr 7$_{16}$ (מִצְרָיִם), חָכְמַת *wisdom of* 1 K 5$_{10}$ (מִצְרָיִם), מַשָּׂא *oracle of*, i.e. concerning Is 19$_{1}$, עֳנִי *affliction of* Ex 3$_{17}$, דֶּבֶר *pestilence of* Am 4$_{10}$ (if em.; see above), מִדְוֵה *disease of* Dt 7$_{15(mss)}$ 28$_{60}$, מַדְוֵי *diseases of* Dt 7$_{15}$ 28$_{60(mss)}$, שְׁחִין *boil(s) of* Dt 28$_{27}$, חַטַּאת *(punishment for) sin of* Zc 14$_{19}$ (מִצְרָיִם), חֶרְפַּת *reproach of* Jos 5$_{9}$, גְּאוֹן *pride of* Ezk 32$_{12}$, תּוֹעֲבַת *abomination of* Gn 46$_{34}$ Ex 8$_{22.22}$, יוֹם *day of* Ezk 30$_{9}$ (מִצְרָיִם).

כָּל־מִצְרַיִם *all Egypt/the Egyptians* Gn 41$_{55}$ 45$_{9}$ (מִצְרָיִם) 47$_{15}$ Ex 7$_{24}$ 9$_{11}$ (מִצְרָיִם) 10$_{6}$ 12$_{30}$ Nm 33$_{3}$ Dt 7$_{18}$ (both מִצְרָיִם).

<APP> עַם *people* Is 19$_{25}$, אֶרֶץ *land* Jr 37$_{7}$, מִשְׁעֶנֶת *staff* 2 K 18$_{21}$||Is 36$_{6}$.

<PREP> לְ of direction, benefit, *to, for* Gn 43$_{32}$ (or em. לְמִצְרִים *to the Egyptians*) Gn 50$_{11}$ Is 23$_{5}$ 4QParGenEx 3$_{6}$, + היה *be* Is 19$_{15.17}$, אמר *say* Gn 41$_{55}$, עתר ni. *be entreated* Is 19$_{22}$, בוא *come* 4QActs 1$_{6}$, יבל ho. *be brought* Ho 12$_{2}$ (or em. יבל hi. *bring*), שׁוב *go back* Jr 37$_{7}$ 4QActs 1$_{8}$ (למצרי[ם]), ידע ni. *make oneself known* Is 19$_{21}$, יהב *give* Gn 47$_{15}$, נתן *give* Gn 47$_{15}$, שׁבר *sell grain* Gn 41$_{56}$, עשׂה *do* Ex 18$_{8}$ 19$_{4}$ Dt 7$_{18}$; *(in relation) to*, + היה *be* Is 19$_{24}$; *concerning* Jr 46$_{2}$; of possession, *of, (belonging) to* Gn 45$_{9}$.

בְּ of place, *in(to)*, Gn 42$_{1.2}$ 45$_{13}$ 50$_{26}$ Ex 3$_{7}$ 4$_{18}$ 12$_{27}$ 14$_{11}$ Nm 11$_{18}$ 1 K 12$_{2}$||2 C 10$_{2}$ Ps 106$_{7}$ Ne 9$_{9}$ 1QM 1$_{4}$ 4QBib Par 14.1$_{6}$ 4QpsJub[b] 2$_{2}$ ([במצר]ים) CD 3$_{5}$, + היה *be* Ex 1$_{5}$ 9$_{18}$ 11$_{6(mss, Sam)}$ 12$_{30}$ Dt 6$_{21}$ 16$_{12}$ 24$_{18}$ 1 S 2$_{27}$ 1 K 11$_{40}$ 4QpsEzek[a] 1$_{3}$ ([במ]צרים), דבר pi. *speak* Ex 14$_{12}$, נגד hi. *tell* Jr 46$_{14}$, שׁמע *hear* 1 K 11$_{21}$, אכל *eat* Nm 11$_{5}$, בוא *come* Is 19$_{23}$, ישׁב *dwell* Gn 50$_{22}$ Ex 12$_{40}$ Nm 20$_{15}$ 1 K 12$_{2}$ (or em. וַיֵּשֶׁב ... בְּמִצְרָיִם *and he dwelt ... in Egypt* to ... וַיָּשָׁב מִמִּצְרָיִם *and he returned ... from Egypt*), נפל *fall* Ezk 30$_{4.6}$, ילד *bear* Nm 26$_{59}$, pu. *be born* Gn 46$_{27}$, קבר *bury* Gn 47$_{29}$, עשׂה *do* Nm 14$_{22}$ Dt 1$_{30}$ 4$_{34}$ 6$_{22}$ Jos 9$_{9}$ Ps 106$_{21}$ 4Q185 1.1$_{15}$, pass. *be done* Ex 3$_{16}$, נתן ni. *be given* 4QNarrC 1$_{13}$, שׂים *place* Ps 78$_{43}$, עבד *serve* Jos 24$_{14}$, זנה *prostitute oneself* Ezk 23$_{3}$, נכה hi. *strike* Nm 33$_{4}$ Ps 78$_{51}$, עשׂה *squeeze* Ezk 23$_{21(mss)}$, שׁבת ni. *cease* Ezk 30$_{18}$.

בְּ *upon, against*, + בוא *come* Ezk 30$_{4}$ Jr 46$_{20(mss)}$, נתן *give*, i.e. place Ex 7$_{4}$ Ezk 30$_{8.16}$, שׂים *place* Ex 15$_{26}$, לחם ni. *fight* Ex 14$_{25}$, סוך pilp. *provoke* Is 19$_{2}$, עשׂה *do* Ex 14$_{31}$ Jos 24$_{7}$ Ezk 30$_{19}$; of accompaniment, *with*, + היה *be* Ex 9$_{11}$; introducing object, + עלל htp. *make sport of* Ex 10$_{2}$ 1 S 6$_{6}$, משׁל *rule over* Is 19$_{4}$.

מִן of direction, *from* Ezk 27$_{7}$ Ho 11$_{11}$ 4QDibHam[a] 1.1$_{9}$, + היה *be* Is 19$_{23}$, קרא *call* Ho 11$_{1}$, אתה *come* Ps 68$_{32}$ (or em. אתה hi. *bring*), בוא *come* 2 C 12$_{3}$, hi. *bring* Gn 43$_{2}$, יצא *go out* Ex 13$_{3.8}$ 23$_{15}$ 34$_{18}$ Nm 11$_{20}$ 22$_{5.11}$ Dt 4$_{45.46}$ 16$_{6}$ 23$_{5}$ 24$_{9}$ 25$_{17}$ Jos 2$_{10}$ 5$_{4.4.5.6}$ 2 K 21$_{15}$ Jr 37$_{5}$ Mc 7$_{15(ms)}$ Hg 2$_{5}$ Ps 114$_{1}$ 2 C 5$_{10}$ 4QapPent 2$_{10}$, hi. *bring out* Ex 3$_{10.11.12}$ 6$_{27}$ 12$_{39}$ 13$_{9.14.16}$ 14$_{11}$ 18$_{1}$ Nm 20$_{16}$ 23$_{22}$ 24$_{8}$ Dt 4$_{20.37}$ 6$_{21}$ 9$_{12.26}$ 16$_{1}$ 26$_{8}$ Jos 24$_{6}$ 1 S 12$_{8}$ 1 K 8$_{16.51.53}$ Jr 26$_{23}$, נסע hi. *cause to set out* Ps 80$_{9}$, עלה *go up* Gn 13$_{1}$ 45$_{25}$ Nm 32$_{11}$ Jg 11$_{13.16}$ 1 S 15$_{2.6}$, hi. *bring up* Ex 17$_{3}$ Nm 20$_{5}$ 21$_{5}$ Jos 24$_{32}$ Jg 2$_{1}$ 6$_{8.13}$ 1 S 8$_{8}$ 10$_{18}$ 2 S 7$_{6}$ Ho 12$_{14}$ Ne 9$_{18}$, שׁוב *go back* 1 K 12$_{2}$||2 C 10$_{2}$ (1 K if em.; see above), נשׂא *carry* Gn 47$_{30}$, גרשׁ pu. *be expelled* Ex 12$_{39}$, שׁבר *buy grain* Gn 42$_{3}$, שׁאל *ask* Ex 12$_{35}$, פדה *redeem* 2 S 7$_{23}$||1 C 17$_{21}$, ישׁע hi. *save* Jg 10$_{11}$ (if ins. הוֹשַׁעְתִּי), שׁאר ni. *remain* Is 11$_{11}$, עשׂה *squeeze* Ezk 23$_{21}$ (or em. בַּעֲשׂוֹת מִמִּצְרַיִם appar. *when they squeezed from Egypt* to בַּעֲשׂוֹת מִצְרַיִם *when the Egyptians squeezed* or בְּעָשׂוֹת מִמִּצְרַיִם *when they were squeezed by the Egyptians*).

מִן of time, *since (being in)*, נשׂא *forgive* Nm 14$_{19}$, עזב *forsake* Ezk 23$_{8}$; of cause, *on account of*, or of agent, *by (means of), through*, + בושׁ *be ashamed* Is 20$_{5}$ Jr 2$_{36}$, עשׂה pu. *be squeezed* Ezk 23$_{21}$ (if em.; see above).

אֶל *to*, + שׁלח *send* Jr 26$_{22}$, מכר *deliver (over)* Gn 37$_{36}$.

עַל *over*, + שׁוב *go back* Ex 14$_{26}$, נטה *stretch hand* Ex 7$_{5}$, נוף *wave* hand Is 19$_{16}$, קִין pol. *chant a lamentation* Ezk 32$_{16}$; *over*, i.e. in charge of, + קום *arise* Ex 1$_{8}$.

עַל *upon, against* Is 20$_{3}$, + בוא hi. *bring* Ex 11$_{1}$, נפל *fall* Ps 105$_{38}$, נבא ni. *prophesy* Ezk 29$_{2}$, יעץ *counsel* Is 19$_{12}$, ריק hi. *empty*, i.e. draw, sword Ezk 30$_{11}$, חזק (of famine) *be severe* Gn 47$_{20}$; *concerning* 4QHos[b] 17$_{1}$; introducing object, + פקד *visit*, i.e. punish Jr 9$_{25}$ 46$_{25}$; בטח על *trust in* 2 K 18$_{21.24}$||Is 36$_{6.9}$.

עַל־פְּנֵי *opposite* Gn 25$_{18}$ Jos 13$_{3}$ 1 S 15$_{7}$.

בְּתוֹךְ *among, within*, + יצא *go out* Ex 11$_{4}$, עשׂה *do* Dt 11$_{3}$, שׁלח *send* Ps 135$_{9}$ (or del.).

מִתּוֹךְ *from among*, + יצא hi. *bring out* Ex 7$_{5}$.

בְּקֶרֶב *among, within*, + עשׂה *do* Jos 24$_{5}$, מסס ni. *melt* Is 19$_{1}$, בקק ni. *be devastated* Is 19$_{3}$.

בֵּין *between*, + פלה hi. *separate* Ex 11$_{7}$ (+ Israel).

מִצְרַיִם with ה- of direction, *to Egypt*, + בוא *come* Gn 12$_{11.14}$ 41$_{57}$ 46$_{6.8.26.27}$ 48$_{5}$ Ex 1$_{1}$, hi. *bring* Gn 37$_{28}$ 46$_{7}$ 2 C 36$_{4}$, ירד *go down* Gn 12$_{10}$ 26$_{2}$ 46$_{3.4}$ Nm 20$_{15}$ Dt 10$_{22}$ 26$_{5}$, hi. *bring down* Gn 37$_{25}$, ho. *be brought down* Gn 39$_{1}$, שׁוב *go back* Gn 50$_{14}$ Ex 4$_{21}$ 13$_{17}$ Nm 14$_{3.4}$, מכר *deliver (over)* Gn 45$_{4}$.

מִצְרַיִם without prep. or ה- of direction, *to Egypt*, + בוא *come* 1 S 12$_{8}$ 1 K 11$_{17.18}$ 2 K 23$_{34}$ 25$_{26}$ Is 19$_{1}$ Jr 26$_{21}$ 41$_{17}$ 42$_{15.17.18.19}$ 43$_{2}$ Ps 105$_{23}$ 2 C 26$_{8}$ Lachish ost. 3$_{16}$, hi. *bring* Dn 11$_{8}$, ירד *go down* Gn 43$_{15}$ Jos 24$_{4}$ Is 30$_{2}$ 31$_{1}$ 52$_{4}$ 4QpsJub[b] 1$_{3}$, שׁוב *go back* Ex 4$_{19}$ Ho 8$_{13}$ 9$_{3}$, hi. *bring back* Dt 28$_{68}$ 11QT 56$_{16}$, ברח *flee* 1 K 11$_{40}$, שׁלח *send* Jr 26$_{22}$ Ezk 17$_{15}$, דבק *keep close* Jr 42$_{16}$, נתן *give* hand Lm 5$_{6}$.

<COLL> אָהֳלֵי־חָם + מִצְרַיִם *tents of Ham* Ps 78$_{51}$, אֶרֶץ־חָם *land of Ham* Ps 105$_{23}$, כּוּשׁ *Cush* Is 11$_{11}$ 20$_{3.4.5}$ 43$_{3}$ 45$_{14}$ Ezk 29$_{10}$ 30$_{4.9}$ Na 3$_{9}$ Ps 68$_{32}$, כּוּר הַבַּרְזֶל *the oven of iron* Dt 4$_{20}$ 1 K 8$_{51}$ Jr 11$_{4}$, עַם לֹעֵז *a people who speak a foreign language* Ps 114$_{1}$, בֵּית עֲבָדִים *house of slaves* Ex 13$_{3.14}$ 20$_{2}$ Dt 5$_{6}$ 6$_{12}$ 8$_{14}$ 13$_{6}$=11QT 54$_{16}$ Dt 13$_{11}$ Jos 24$_{17}$ Jg 6$_{8}$ Jr 34$_{13}$ Mc 6$_{4}$.

מִצְרַיִם as vocative, Ps 135$_{9}$ (or del.).

מִצְרַיִם אֲשֶׁר בָּרַח *Egypt where he had fled* 1 K 12$_{2}$||

2 C 10$_{2}$.

Also 4QOrd^{a} 2$_{3}$ 4QIsa^{c} 28$_{1}$ 4QpsJub^{a} 1$_{5}$ 4QActs 1$_{2}$ 4QpsEzek^{a} 21$_{3}$ (מ]צרים]) 31$_{2}$ 4QpsEzek^{e} 5$_{4}$ 70$_{2}$ 4Qps Mos^{d} 1.17 (מ]צרים]) 3QNarrA 1$_{10}$.*

⇒ מִצְרִי *Egyptian.*

מִצְרַיִם II $_{7}$ pl.n. **Mizraim, Musri,** perh. Muṣri, a region of N. Syria near Que (Cilicia),* <CSTR> מַלְכֵי מִצְרַיִם *kings of* 2 K 7$_{6}$. <PREP> מִן of direction, *from* 1 K 10$_{28}$‖2 C 1$_{16}$ (or em. מִמֻּצְרִי *from Musri*), + יצא *go out* 1 K 10$_{29}$ (or em. מִמֻּצְרִי), hi. *bring out* 2 C 1$_{17}$ 9$_{28}$; מִצְרַיִם with ה- of direction, *to Mizraim,* + hi. *bring back* Dt 17$_{16}$.*

אָבֵל מִצְרַיִם, *Abel-mizraim,* see אָבֵל II *Abel,* §8.

מְצֹרָע, see צרע *be leprous.*

מַצְרֵף 2.0.14 n.[m.] **crucible; affliction**—cstr. Q מצרף; pl. sf. Q מצרפיו (Q מצרפותיו)—**1. crucible,** <OBJ> מלא pi. *fill* perh. 1QM 17$_{9}$ (but prob. §2). <CSTR> מצרף אל *crucible of God* 1QM 17$_{9}$; בחוני מצרף *ones tested of,* i.e. in, *a crucible* 1QM 17$_{1}$, ברורי *ones purified of,* i.e. in 1QH fr. 18$_{4}$, חללי *slain ones of* 4QM^{a} 10.2$_{11}$. <NOM CL> מַצְרֵף לַכֶּסֶף *the crucible is for silver* Pr 17$_{3}$ 27$_{21}$ (both ‖ כּוּר *smelting-pot*). <PREP> בְּ of place, *in(to),* + בוא hi. *bring* 1QH 5$_{16}$ (במצרן[ף]), בחן *test* 1QM 16$_{15}$, חזק htp. *strengthen oneself* 1QM 17$_{9}$.

2. affliction, hardship, trial, <SUBJ> ירד *go down* 4QMidrEschat^{a} 4$_{4}$ (יור[ד]). <OBJ> מלא pi. *complete* 1QM 17$_{9}$ (unless §1). <CSTR> צרת מצרף *distress of affliction* 1QS 8$_{4}$, עוני מצרןפו] *affliction of his hardship* 4QBéat 2.2$_{5}$ (unless מצרן[יו] *of his afflictions;* צוּקָה *distress*), עת המצרף *time of the trial* 4QpPs^{a} 1.2$_{18}$ 4QMidr Eschat^{a} 4$_{1}$ 4QMidrEschat^{b} 8$_{3}$ (מצ[רף]), ימי מצרפותיו *days of his trials* CD 20$_{27}$. <APP> נִסּוּי *trial* 1QS 1$_{17}$. <PREP> מִן of cause, *on account of,* + שׁוב *go back* 1QS 1$_{17}$ (‖ אֵימָה *dread,* פַּחַד *fear*); אַחֲרֵי *after,* + בין hi. *instruct* 4QMidrEschat^{a} 4$_{4}$ (יבינו[ן]).

<SYN> §1 כּוּר *smelting-pot;* §2 אֵימָה *dread,* פַּחַד *fear.*

⇒ צרף *refine.*

מַק 2 n.m. **rottenness**—מָק—**rottenness,** or **stench,** <SUBJ> היה *be* Is 3$_{24}$ (:: בֹּשֶׂם *perfume*). <PREP> כְּ *as,* + היה *be* Is 5$_{24}$ (or em. כַּמּוֹץ *as chaff;* + אָבָק *dust*).

<ANT> בֹּשֶׂם *perfume.*

⇒ מקק *rot.*

מַקֶּבֶת I $_{4}$ n.f. **hammer**—pl. מַקָּבוֹת—<SUBJ> ni. שׁמע *be heard* 1 K 6$_{7}$ (‖ גַּרְזֶן *axe*). <OBJ> שׂים *place* Jg 4$_{21}$. <APP> כְּלִי *instrument* of iron 1 K 6$_{7}$. <PREP> בְּ of instrument, *by (means of), with,* + יצר *shape* Is 44$_{12}$ (or em. יצר to יצר pi. *fasten;* + מַעֲצָד *axe*), חזק pi. *fasten* Jr 10$_{4}$ (‖ מַסְמֵר *nail*).

<SYN> גַּרְזֶן *axe,* מַסְמֵר *nail.*

⇒ (?) נקב *pierce.*

[מַקֶּבֶת] II $_{1}$ n.f. **excavation**—cstr. מַקֶּבֶת—**excavation,** or perh. **fissure,*** <CSTR> מַקֶּבֶת בּוֹר *excavation of a pit,* i.e. quarry Is 51$_{1}$ (or del. בּוֹר; ‖ צוּר *rock*). <PREP> אֶל *to,* + נבט hi. *look* Is 51$_{1}$. <COLL> מַקֶּבֶת בּוֹר נֻקַּרְתֶּם *the quarry from which you were dug* Is 51$_{1}$.

<SYN> צוּר *rock.*

⇒ נקב *pierce.*

מַקֵּדָה 9.0.0.1 pl.n. **Makkedah,** town in lowland of Judah, <NOM CL> מַקֵּדָה ... בַּשְּׁפֵלָה *in the lowland were ... Makkedah* Jos 15$_{41}$. <OBJ> לכד *capture* Jos 10$_{28}$. <CSTR> מֶלֶךְ מַקֵּדָה *king of Makkedah* Jos 10$_{28}$ 12$_{16}$. <APP> עִיר *city* Jos 15$_{41}$. <PREP> בְּ of place, *in* Jos 10$_{16.17}$; מִן of direction, *from* Ḥorvat 'Uzza ost. 1$_{4}$; עַד *as far as,* + נכה hi. *strike* Jos 10$_{10}$; מַקֵּדָה without prep., *at Makkedah* Jos 10$_{21}$.

מְקַדֵּה, *immigrant trader,* see קדה *trade.**

מִקְדָּשׁ 74.5.81 n.m. **sanctuary**—cstr. מִקְדַּשׁ; sf. מִקְדָּשִׁי, מִקְדָּשֵׁנוּ, מִקְדָּשָׁהּ (מִקְדָּשׁוֹ), מִקְדָּשׁוֹ (מִקְדָּשֶׁךָ), מִקְדָּשְׁךָ מִקְדָּשָׁם; pl. מִקְדָּשִׁים; cstr. מִקְדְּשֵׁי; sf. מִקְדָּשַׁי, מִקְדָּשֶׁיךָ, מִקְדְּשֵׁיכֶם—**1. sanctuary, sacred place** (but not Temple building, which is בֵּית הַמִּקְדָּשׁ *house of the sanctuary*),* usu. of Y.; in ref. to the precincts of the tabernacle (e.g. Ex 25$_{8}$ Lv 12$_{4}$ 16$_{33}$ [unless from מִקְדָּשׁ *holiest part*] 21$_{23}$), of the temple (e.g. Is 63$_{18}$ Jr 51$_{51}$ Ezk 5$_{11}$ 43$_{21}$

45_{4} Ps 74_{7} Dn 9_{17} 1 C 22_{19} Si 51_{12} 11QT 43_{12} CD 12_{1}), perh. of heavenly sanctuary (Ps 68_{36});* of Moab (Is 16_{12}), of Tyre (Ezk 28_{18}); Y. as a sanctuary (Is 8_{14} Ezk 11_{16} [or em. both; see Prep.]), the holy ones as a sanctuary for Y. (4QShir^{b} 35_{2}).

2. holy things (Nm 10_{21}).

3. consecrated part of offering (Nm 18_{29} [unless from מִקְדָּשׁ *holiest part*]).

<SUBJ> היה *be* Ezk 37_{28} $45_{3.4}$ (or em. מִגְרָשׁ *land outside city wall*) $48_{8.10.21}$, בנה ni. *be built* 4QJub^{a} 1_{27}, חלל ni. *be profaned* Ezk 7_{24} (if em. מְקַדְּשֵׁיהֶם *those sanctifying them* [i.e. קדשׁ pi. ptc.] to מִקְדְּשֵׁיהֶם *their sanctuaries*) 25_{3}, חרב *be desolate* Am 7_{9}, רנן *shout for joy* Si $47_{10(Bmg)}$ (B משפט *justice*).

<NOM CL> מִקְדַּשׁ־מֶלֶךְ הוּא *it is the sanctuary of the king* Am 7_{13}, המקדש [משכן אוהל מועד] *the sanctuary is the tabernacle of the tent of meeting* 4QMMT B_{29}.

<OBJ> ירא *revere* Lv 19_{30} 26_{2}, שׁכן pi. *cause to dwell* 11QT 47_{4} ([מקד]שי) 47_{11}, נשׂא *carry* Nm 10_{21}, ברא *create* 11QT 29_{9}, עשׂה *make* Ex 25_{8}, כון hi. *establish* 11QT 29_{9}, pol. Ex 15_{17}, בנה *build* Ps 78_{69} 1 C 22_{19} 2 C 20_{8} Si 51_{12} 4QpsMos^{e} 1_{5}, נצב hi. *erect* Si 47_{13}, נתן *give*, i.e. place Ezk 37_{26}, כול pilp. *provide for* Si 45_{24}, רום hi. *raise*, i.e. offer Nm 18_{29} (unless from מִקְדָּשׁ *holiest part*), כפר pi. *make atonement for* Lv 16_{33} (unless from מִקְדָּשׁ), חטא pi. *cleanse* Ezk 45_{18}, קדשׁ pi. *sanctify* 11QT 29_{8} ([מ]קדשי) 46_{11}, גאל pi. *defile* 11QT 47_{13}, טמא pi. *defile* Lv 20_{3} Nm 19_{20} Ezk 5_{11} 23_{38} 1QpHab 12_{9} 4QpsMos^{e} 2.1_{8} 11QT 45_{10} 47_{18} CD 5_{6} 20_{23}, חלל pi. *profane* Lv $21_{12.33}$ Ezk 23_{39} 24_{21} 28_{18} 44_{7} Dn 11_{31} 11QT 35_{7} ([מק]דש) 46_{11}, נאר pi. *spurn* Lm 2_{7}, עזב *abandon* 4QJub^{a} 1_{10} ([עזבו] ... מקדש[י]), שׁמם hi. *make desolate* Lv 26_{31} 4QMidrEschat^{a} 3_{6} ([מקדו]ש), בוס pol. *trample* Is 63_{18}, שׁלח pi. *send*, i.e. set, on fire Ps 74_{7}.

<CSTR> מִקְדַּשׁ י׳ *sanctuary of Y.* Nm 19_{20} Jos 24_{26} Ezk 48_{10} 1 C 22_{19}, אֲדֹנָי *of my Lord* Lm 2_{20}, מקדש אל *sanctuary of God* 1QpHab 12_{9} 4QWays^{b} 12_{2} ([מ]קדש אל), מִקְדַּשׁ אֱלֹהָיו *sanctuary of his God* Lv 21_{12}, [מק]דש אלוהיהמה *sanctuary of their God* 11QT 35_{5}, מִקְדַּשׁ מֶלֶךְ *sanctuary of the king* Am 7_{13}, הַקֹּדֶשׁ *of holiness*, i.e. holy sanctuary Lv 16_{33} (unless from מִקְדָּשׁ *holiest part*) 11QT 46_{10} (הקודש), הַבַּיִת *of the house* Ezk 48_{21}, מִקְדְּשֵׁי בֵּית *sacred places of the house of* Y. Jr 51_{51}, מקד[ש] [י]שראל *sanctuary of Israel* 4QMidrEschat^{a} 3_{6}, מִקְדְּשֵׁי יִשְׂרָאֵל *sanctuaries of Israel* Am 7_{9}, מקדש אדם *Sanctuary of Humans* 4QMidrEschat^{a} 3_{6},* עולמים *of everlastingness*, i.e. everlasting sanctuary 4QShir^{b} 35_{2}, מקדש הקו[דש] *sanctuary of holiness*, i.e. holy sanctuary 4QpsMos^{e} 2.1_{1}, קודשו *of his holiness*, i.e. his holy sanctuary 4QShirShabb^{d} 1.1_{11} ([קודשו]) 1.1_{42} ([קודש]ו), מקדשי קודש [קודשים] *sanctuaries of the holiest holiness* 4QShirShabb^{a} 1.1_{7}, מקדש פלא *sanctuary of wonder*, i.e. wonderful sanctuary 4QShirShabb^{d} 1.2_{22}, מקדשי *sanctuaries of*, i.e. wonderful sanctuaries 4QShirShabb^{e} 5_{5}, מקדשי מלכות *sanctuaries of the kingdom of* his glory 4QShirShabb^{f} 23.2_{11}, מקדש כול *sanctuary of all* 4QShirShabb^{f} 23.2_{4}.

נֹשְׂאֵי הַמִּקְדָּשׁ *ones who carry the sanctuary* Nm 10_{21}, מְשָׁרְתֵי הַמִּקְדָּשׁ *ministers of the sanctuary* Ezk 45_{4}, מִשְׁמֶרֶת *charge of* Nm 3_{38}, מִשְׁמֶרֶת מִקְדָּשִׁי *charge of my sanctuary* Ezk 44_{15}=CD 4_{1}, עֲוֹן הַמִּקְדָּשׁ *guilt of*, i.e. connected with, *the sanctuary* Nm 18_{1}, שַׁעַר *gate of* Ezk 44_{1}, שערי המקדש *gates of the sanctuary* 1QM 2_{3}, מוֹצָאֵי הַמִּקְדָּשׁ *exits of the sanctuary* Ezk 44_{5}, עזרת מקדש *court of the sanctuary* Si 50_{11}, מְקוֹם מִקְדָּשִׁי *place of my sanctuary* Is 60_{13}, מִקְדָּשׁוֹ *of his sanctuary* Dn $8_{11(ms)}$, מִקְדָּשֵׁנוּ *of our sanctuary* Jr 17_{12}, מְכוֹן מִקְדָּשׁוֹ *place of his sanctuary* Dn 8_{11} (or em. מִקְדָּשׁוֹ to הַמִּקְדָּשׁ *of the sanctuary*), עיר המקדש *city of the sanctuary* 4QActs 1_{7} 4QSD 7.2_{6} ([עיר המ]קדש) 11QT $45_{12.17}$ CD $12_{1.2}$, עיר מקדשי *city of my sanctuary* 11QT $47_{9.13}$, בֵּית מִקְדָּשָׁם *house of their sanctuary* 2 C 36_{17}, כְּלֵי הַמִּקְדָּשׁ *vessels of the sanctuary* Ne 10_{40}, הון המקדש *wealth of the sanctuary* CD 6_{16}, טהרת *pure thing(s) of* 4QMMT B_{54} (טה[ר]ת) 11QT 47_{17}, עצמות *bones of* 4QMMT B_{59} ([ע]צמות המק[דש]), עורות *skins of* 11QT 47_{17}, טמא *defilement of* CD 4_{18}, משאי מקד[ש] *utterances of the sanctuary* 4QBer-a 2_{1}, חוקות מקדשיו *statutes of his sanctuaries* 4QShirShabb^{d} 1.2_{21}, כול המקדש *all the sanctuary* 11QT 45_{8} 11QT^{c} 3_{4}.

<APP> מָכוֹן *place* Ex 15_{17}, קֹדֶשׁ *holiness*, i.e. holy place Ezk 45_{3}, מָעוֹז *fortress* Dn 11_{31}, הַר *mountain* Ex 15_{17}.

<ADJ> שָׁמֵם *desolate* Dn 9_{17}.

<PREP> לְ as or introducing predicate, + היה be Is 814 (or em. לְמַקְשִׁיר as one who conspires or לְמוֹקֵשׁ as a snare) Ezk 1116 (or em. לְמוֹקֵשׁ), קדשׁ hi. sanctify 4QShirb 352 ([יקדי]שׁ); of direction, to perh 4QOrdb 154 ([למקד]שׁ) 5214.18, + בוא come 2 C 308 4QMMT B5 hi. bring 4QMMT B20 ([להביא]ם למקד[שׁ]); of benefit, to, for, + היה be Ezk 454, בנה build 1 C 2810; of possession, of, (belonging) to 4QShirShabba 1.17 4QShirShabbd 1.142; in respect of, i.e. for use in, + טהר be pure 11QT 4716.

בְּ of place, in Jos 2426 Ps 966 4QShirShabbd 1.222 11QTc 34, + היה be Ezk 447.11, ברך pi. bless 4QShirShabbd 1.111 ([לברך]), שׁמר keep Ezk 448, זבח sacrifice 11QT 4712.16, שׁחט slaughter 4QMMT B35, הרג ni. be killed Lm 220, אכל eat 4QWaysb 122 ([במו]קדשׁ).

מִן of direction, from Ps 6836 11QT 4312 5217, + יצא go out Lv 2112 Ezk 4712 2 C 2618, מושׁ depart 11QT 311, חלל hi. begin Ezk 96, סתר hi. hide face CD 13; introducing object, + ירא fear 4QMMT B49 11QT 4611.

אֶל to 4QRitPur 563 (ל[א]), + בוא come Lv 124 Is 1612 Ezk 2339 449.16 Ps 7317 4QDa 6.24 ([תבו]) 11QT 458.10.10 468 11QTb 1211 CD 612, hi. bring 1QM 711; over, + אמר say Ezk 253; against, + נטף hi. drip, i.e. speak Ezk 217.

עַל upon, + שׁכן dwell 11QT 462 ([ישכ]ון ... על מקד[שׁי]), מֵעַל אור hi. cause face to shine Dn 917; for 2 C 2921; מֵעַל from, + רחק be far Ezk 86; לְתוֹךְ inside, + בוא come 11QT 5220; בְּתוֹךְ inside, + היה be 11QT 463, זבח sacrifice 11QT 5215; אֶל־תּוֹךְ inside, + בוא come 11QT 4611; מִחוּץ לְ outside, + שׂרף burn Ezk 4321; סָבִיב לְ around, + עשׂה make 11QT 469; בֵּין between, + בדל hi. separate 11QT 4610.

מִקְדָּשׁ without prep., into the sanctuary, + בוא come Lm 110.

<COLL> מִקְדָּשׁ || בָּמָה high place Am 79, רֶגֶל foot Is 6013, שֵׁם name 11QT 4711, עִיר city Si 5112; + אֹהֶל מוֹעֵד tent of meeting Lv 1633, בַּיִת house Ezk 447.11 Am 713 1 C 2810 Si 4713.

Also 1QDM 413 ([מקד]שׁ) 1Q39 103 4QHalakhaha 66 4QAdmonPar 1.26 4QpsEzeka 457 4QShirShabbf 86 115 411 4QBapt 133 ([ה]מקד[שׁ]) 4QOrdb 10.27 203 11QTb 1212 11QTc 35 ([המקד]שׁ).

<SYN> בָּמָה high place, רֶגֶל foot, שֵׁם name, עִיר city.*

⇒ קדשׁ be holy.

***מִקְדָּשׁ** 2 n.[m.] **holiest part**—cstr. מִקְדַּשׁ; sf. מִקְדְּשׁוֹ—(unless from מִקְדָּשׁ sanctuary), <OBJ> רום hi. raise, i.e. offer Nm 1829, כפר pi. make atonement for Lv 1633. <CSTR> מִקְדַּשׁ הַקֹּדֶשׁ holiest part of the sanctuary Lv 1633.

⇒ קדשׁ be holy.

[מַקְהֵל] 2 n.[m.] **assembly**—pl. מַקְהֵלִים, מַקְהֵלוֹת—<PREP> בְּ of place, in, + ברך pi. bless Ps 2612 6827 (or em. בְּמוֹ קְהִלּוֹת in the assemblies).*

⇒ קהל assemble.

מַקְהֵלֹת 2 pl.n. **Makheloth,** station of exodus, <PREP> בְּ of place, + חנה encamp Nm 3325; מִן of direction, from, + נסע set out Nm 3326.*

⇒ קהל assemble.

מִקְוֵא, see מִקְוֶה II collection.

מִקְוָה 1 n.f. **reservoir,** <OBJ> עשׂה make Is 2211.

⇒ קוה collect.

מִקְוֶה I 5.0.6 n.m. **hope**—cstr. מִקְוֵה—in ref. to Y. (Jr 148 1713 5017), <SUBJ> היה be Jr 148. <NOM CL> יֵשׁ־מִקְוֶה there is hope Ezr 102 1QH 320 66 914 fr. 17, אֵין מִקְוֶה there is no hope 1 C 2915 (unless מִקְוֶה III abode) 4QparaKings 1422. <OBJ> עזב forsake Jr 1713 (unless מִקְוֵה II Pool). <CSTR> מִקְוֵה יִשְׂרָאֵל hope of Israel Jr 148 1713 (unless both מִקְוֵה II Pool), אֲבוֹתֵיהֶם of their fathers Jr 507 (unless מִקְוֵה II Pool or III abode; + נָוֶה habitation). <APP> ״ Y. Jr 1713 507 (unless both מִקְוֵה II Pool), ישׁע hi. ptc. saviour Jr 148 (unless מִקְוֵה II Pool). <PREP> לְ against, + חטא sin Jr 507 (unless מִקְוֵה II Pool). <COLL> מִקְוֵה as vocative, Jr 148 1713; מקוה לאיביך hope for your enemies 4QapPsb 283.*

⇒ קוה wait.

[מִקְוֶה] II 7.5.9 n.m. **collection**—cstr. מִקְוֵה (מִקְוֵא; Q מקוי); pl. sf. Q מקויהם—**1. collection of waters, reservoir, pool; Pool, Fountain, Source,** as appellative for Y. (Is 33$_{21}$ [if em.; see Nom. Cl.] Jr 14$_8$ 17$_{13}$ 50$_7$ 1QS 11$_6$),* <SUBJ> היה *be* Lv 11$_{36}$, לבשׁ *dress oneself* Si 43$_{20}$, כרה ni. *be dug* Si 50$_3$, סתר ni. *be hidden* 1QS 11$_6$. <NOM CL> יי׳ לָנוּ מִקְוֵה־נְהָרִים *Y. will be for us a Source of rivers* Is 33$_{21}$ (if em. מְקוֹם *place of*; or em. to מְקֹר־ם *Source of*),* מקוה זדון חטא *a reservoir of presumptuousness is sin* Si 10$_{13}$. <OBJ> קפא hi. *congeal*, i.e. freeze Si 43$_{20(Bmg)}$ (B מקורו *its spring*), נתן *give* 4QConfess 2$_9$ (ה[מקו]), עזב *forsake* Jr 17$_{13}$ (unless מִקְוֶה I *hope*).

<CSTR> מִקְוֵה יִשְׂרָאֵל *Pool of Israel* Jr 14$_8$ 17$_{13}$ (unless both מִקְוֶה I *hope*), אֲבוֹתֵיהֶם *of their fathers* Jr 50$_7$ (unless מִקְוֶה I), מִקְוֵה מַיִם *collection of waters* Gn 1$_{10}$ (הַמַּיִם) Lv 11$_{36}$ 4QConfess 2$_9$ (ה[מקו]) 4QapMes 5.2$_3$, מֵימֵיהֶם *of their waters* Ex 7$_{19}$, נְהָרִים *of rivers* Is 33$_{21}$ (if em.; see Nom. Cl.) 1QM 10$_{13}$ (מקוי נהרות), מקוה זדון *reservoir of presumptuousness* Si 10$_{13}$, גבורה *of might* 1QS 11$_6$ 4QBer^{a} 1.2$_5$ (גבורות), כָּבוֹד *of glory* 1QH 12$_{29}$ (מקוי) 4QShir^{b} 52.3$_2$ (מקוי הכבוד); כָּל־מִקְוֵה *every collection of* Ex 7$_{19}$ 4QapMes 5.2$_3$, כול מקויהם perh. *all their reservoirs* 4QMyst^{a} 6.1$_{14}$ (unless *all their hopes*, i.e. מִקְוֶה I).

<APP> יי׳ *Y.* Jr 17$_{13}$ 50$_7$ (unless both מִקְוֶה I *hope*), ישׁע hi. ptc. *saviour* Jr 14$_8$ (unless מִקְוֶה I), מַעְיָן *spring* Lv 11$_{36}$, בּוֹר *cistern* Lv 11$_{36}$, עָרְמָה *prudence* 1QS 11$_6$.

<ADJ> אֶחָד *one* Gn 1$_9$ (if em.; see Prep.).

<PREP> לְ *as*, + לקח pu. *be taken* 1QH 12$_{25}$ ([לק]חתי); לְ *against*, + חטא *sin* Jr 50$_7$ (מִקְוֶה I *hope*), introducing object, + קרא *call*, i.e. name Gn 1$_{10}$; אֶל *(in)to*, + נפל *fall* CD 11$_{16}$ (if em. מקום *place*), קוה ni. *be gathered* Gn 1$_9$ (if em. מָקוֹם *place* to מִקְוֵ־ם* or מִקְוָם* [contraction of מִקְוֵיהֶם *their collection*]); עַל *over*, + נטה *stretch* hand Ex 7$_{19}$.

<COLL> מִקְוֶה || מָקוֹר *source* 1QH 12$_{25.29}$ 1QS 11$_6$; + מַעְיָן *spring* 1QS 11$_6$, נַחַל *wadi* 4QapMes 5.2$_3$, אֲגַם *pool* Ex 7$_{19}$, נָהָר *river* Ex 7$_{19}$, יְאֹר *Nile* Ex 7$_{19}$; ויחסום הרים מקוה *and he dammed the mountains for a reservoir* Si 48$_{17}$.

2. heap, <CSTR> מקוי אפר *heap of ashes* 1QH fr. 3$_6$, עפר *of dust* 1QH 12$_{25}$. <COLL> מִקְוֶה || מָקוֹר *source* 1QH 12$_{25}$.

3. company, <SUBJ> לקח *take* 1 K 10$_{28}$||2 C 1$_{16}$ (or em.; see Cstr.). <CSTR> מִקְוֵה סֹחֲרֵי הַמֶּלֶךְ *the company of the king's merchants* 1 K 10$_{28}$||2 C 1$_{16}$ (מִקְוֵא; or em. מִקְּוֹא *from Ko* or מִקְּוֵה *from Kue*).

4. droves (of horses), <OBJ> לקח *take* 1 K 10$_{28}$||2 C 1$_{16}$ (or em. מִקְּוֹא *from Ko* or מִקְּוֵה *from Kue*).

<SYN> §§1, 2 מָקוֹר *source*.*

⇒ קוה *collect*.

*מִקְוֶה III 2 n.m. **abode**—cstr. מִקְוֵה—**abode** (Jr 50$_7$ [unless מִקְוֶה I *hope* or II *Pool*]), **abiding** (1 C 29$_{15}$ [unless מִקְוֶה I]), <NOM CL> אֵין מִקְוֶה *there is no abiding* 1 C 29$_{15}$. <CSTR> מִקְוֵה אֲבוֹתֵיהֶם *abode of their fathers* Jr 50$_7$. <APP> יי׳ *Y.* Jr 50$_7$. <PREP> לְ *against*, + חטא *sin* Jr 50$_7$.

מָקוֹם 401.10.65.4 n.m.&f. **place**—מָקֹם; cstr. מְקוֹם; sf. מְקוֹמִי, מְקֹמָה (מְקוֹמָה), מְקוֹמוֹ (מְקֹמוֹ), (מקומכה Q, מְקוֹמֶךָ) מְקוֹמֵךְ, מְקוֹמֵנוּ, מְקוֹמְכֶם, מְקוֹמָם; pl. מְקֹמוֹת (מְקוֹמוֹת, מְקוֹמֹת); cstr. מְקֹמוֹת; sf. מְקוֹמֹתֵיכֶם, מְקֹמֹתָם (מְקֹמֹתָם, Q מקומותמה).

1. place, location, site, in ref. to city (e.g. Gn 12$_6$ 18$_{24}$ 19$_{12}$ 28$_{19}$ Dt 21$_{19}$), land (e.g. Gn 29$_{26}$ Ex 3$_8$ 23$_{20}$ Nm 10$_{29}$ 14$_{40}$ 32$_1$ Jg 11$_{19}$ 1 S 12$_8$).

2. dwelling place, abode, home (e.g. Gn 18$_{33}$ 32$_1$ Ex 16$_{29}$ Nm 24$_{11}$ Jg 7$_7$ 9$_{55}$ 19$_{28}$ 1 S 2$_{20}$ 26$_{25}$ 2 S 19$_{40}$ Ps 26$_{10}$ 103$_{16}$ Am 4$_6$ Jb 2$_{11}$ 7$_{10}$ 18$_{21}$ 20$_9$ 2 C 25$_{10}$), of Y. (Ps 26$_8$ 132$_5$ Is 26$_{21}$ Ho 5$_{15}$ Mc 1$_3$), of lion (Jr 4$_7$).

3. sanctuary, sacred site, of Y. (e.g. Gn 12$_{6.8}$ 13$_{14}$ 22$_4$ 28$_{11.16}$ Ex 20$_{24}$ Dt 12$_5$ Jos 9$_{27}$ perh. 2 K 5$_{11}$ Jr 7$_{12}$ Is 60$_{13}$ Ezr 8$_{17}$ Ne 1$_9$), of other gods (e.g. Dt 12$_2$ Ezk 6$_{13}$ 2 C 33$_{19}$).*

4. space, room (e.g. Gn 24$_{23}$ 1 S 26$_{13}$ Jr 7$_{32}$).

5. (plot of) land, property, estate, fief (Jg 9$_{55}$ 19$_{28}$ 1 S 2$_{20}$ 27$_5$ 2 S 19$_{40}$ Is 5$_8$* 7$_{23}$ Mur 22 1$_2$ 5/6ḤevBA 44$_6$).*

6. tomb (e.g. Is 45$_{19}$ Jr 7$_{32}$ 19$_{11\text{-}12}$ Ezk 39$_{11}$ Jb 16$_{18}$ Si 8$_{10}$),* מָקוֹם אֶחָד *one place*, i.e. **Sheol** (Ec 6$_6$).*

7. place for refuge (e.g. Ex 21$_{13}$).

8. place at meal (1 S 9$_{22}$ 20$_{25}$).

9. site of leprosy (2 K 5.11).

10. position (e.g. Jos 8$_{19}$ Is 46$_7$), rightful place, normal position (e.g. Gn 29$_3$ Jos 4$_{18}$ 1 S 3$_2$ 5$_3$ 6$_2$ 2 S 6$_{17}$ 1 K 8$_6$||2 C 5$_7$).

11. office, post (1 K 20$_{24}$).

12. reason (Si 4$_5$).

13. opportunity (to speak) (Si 13$_{22}$).

14. direction (Ezk 10$_{11}$).

15. (the) place, perh. as reverential periphrasis for Y. (Est 4$_{14}$).*

16. מְקוֹם cstr. **(in) place of, instead of** (e.g. 1 K 21$_{19}$ Is 33$_{21}$ Ezk 39$_{11}$ Ho 2$_{1}$ Ps 44$_{20}$).*

<SUBJ> היה *be* Dt 11$_{24}$ 2 K 22$_{19}$ Is 7$_{23}$ Ezk 45$_{4}$ Jb 16$_{18}$ 11QT 35$_{13}$, שׁאר ni. *remain* Jr 8$_{3}$, נפל *fall* 5/6ḤevBA 44$_{10.13}$, ידע ni. *be known* Na 3$_{17}$, נכר hi. *recognize* Ps 103$_{16}$ Jb 7$_{10}$, קרא ni. *be called,* i.e. named 5/6ḤevBA 44$_{7.8.9}$ ([מקום שנקרה]) 5/6ḤevBA 44$_{11.11.14}$, שׁור *behold* Jb 20$_{9}$, כחשׁ pi. *deny* Jb 8$_{18}$, רחק *be distant* Dt 12$_{21}$ 11QT 53$_{1}$ ([ירח]ק ... [המקום]), פנה pass. *be empty* MurEpBar$^{b}_{5}$ (appar. פניו is error for פנוי), פקד ni. *be missing,* i.e. empty 1 S 20$_{25.27}$, בדל ho. *be separated* 11QT 16$_{12}$ 35$_{13}$, עשׂה pass. *be made* 11QT 37$_{10}$, אבד *be destroyed* 4Q MMT C$_{5}$.

<NOM CL> הַמָּקוֹם ... אַדְמַת־קֹדֶשׁ הוּא *the place ... is holy ground* Ex 3$_{5}$, var. Jos 5$_{15}$, הַמָּקוֹם קֹדֶשׁ *the place is holy* Ezk 42$_{13}$, י׳ לָנוּ מְקוֹם־נְהָרִים יְאֹרִים *Y. is to us a place of rivers (and) streams* Is 33$_{21}$ (or em.; see Cstr.), מְקוֹם סַפִּיר אֲבָנֶיהָ *its stones are a place of sapphires* Jb 28$_{6}$, הַמָּקוֹם מְקוֹם מִקְנֶה *the place was a place of cattle* Nm 32$_{1}$, כִּסֵּא כָבוֹד ... מְקוֹם מִקְדָּשֵׁנוּ *a throne of glory ... is the place of our sanctuary* Jr 17$_{12}$, מְקוֹמִי אֲשֶׁר בְּשִׁילוֹ *my place which was in Shiloh* Jr 7$_{12}$.

זֶה הַמָּקוֹם *this is the place* Ezk 46$_{20}$ 5/6ḤevBA 44$_{13}$, vars. Ezk 43$_{7.7}$ (if em. אֶת־ ... וְאֵת to זֶה ... וְזֶה) Jb 18$_{21}$, [ירושלים] היא המקום *Jerusalem is the place* 4QMMT B$_{32}$, var. B$_{60}$, אלה המקומות *these are the places* 5/6 ḤevBA 44$_{10}$, הִנֵּה־נָא הַמָּקוֹם *behold the place* 2 K 6$_{1}$, הִנֵּה מָקוֹם אִתִּי *behold, there is a place by me* Ex 33$_{21}$, הִנֵּה־שָׁם מָקוֹם *behold, there was a place there* Ezk 46$_{19}$, יֵשׁ ... מָקוֹם *there is ... a place* Jb 28$_{1}$, הֲיֵשׁ בֵּית־אָבִיךָ מָקוֹם לָנוּ לָלִין *is there room for us to lodge in the house of your father?* Gn 24$_{23}$, גַּם־מָקוֹם לָלוּן *there is also room to lodge* Gn 24$_{25}$, אֵין־מָקוֹם לַבְּהֵמָה *there was no place for the beast* Ne 2$_{14}$, sim. Si 13$_{22}$, אֶפֶס מָקוֹם *there is no place* Is 5$_{8}$, מֵאֵין מָקוֹם *because there is no place* Jr 7$_{32}$ 19$_{11}$, כָּל־שֻׁלְחָנוֹת ... בְּלִי מָקוֹם *all tables ... are without a place* Is 28$_{8}$, לֹא מְקוֹם זֶרַע *it is not a place of grain* Nm 20$_{5}$.

רַב הַמָּקוֹם בֵּינֵיהֶם *the space between them was great* 1 S 26$_{13}$, מַה־נּוֹרָא הַמָּקוֹם הַזֶּה *how awesome is this place!* Gn 28$_{17}$, אֵי־זֶה מָקוֹם *where is the place?* Is 66$_{1}$, vars. Jb 28$_{12.20}$ 38$_{19}$, צַר־לִי הַמָּקוֹם *the place is too narrow for me* Is 49$_{20}$, מקום שלחזקיא *the place which belongs to Hezekiah* Mur 22 1$_{2}$.

<OBJ> ראה *see* Gn 24$_{4}$ Dt 12$_{13}$ 1 S 23$_{22}$ 26$_{5}$ Jr 42$_{18}$ Ezk 43$_{7}$ (if ins. הֲרָאִיתָ *have you seen?*), hi. *show* 2 K 6$_{6}$, ידע *know* Jb 28$_{23}$ Ru 3$_{4}$, pi. *cause to know* Jb 38$_{12}$, עבר *pass* 2 K 6$_{9}$, נוח hi. *leave* Ec 10$_{4}$, נתן *give* Nm 10$_{29}$ Jos 1$_{3}$ 20$_{4}$ Jg 18$_{10}$ 20$_{36}$ 1 S 9$_{22}$ 27$_{5}$ Jr 7$_{14}$ Ezk 39$_{11}$ Si 4$_{5}$ 38$_{12 (Segal)}$ ([תן]) 11QT 48$_{14}$, שׂים *place* Ex 21$_{13}$ 2 S 7$_{10}$||1 C 17$_{8}$ 1 K 8$_{21}$, עשׂה *make* 2 K 6$_{2}$ Na 1$_{8}$ (יַעֲשֶׂה כָלָה מְקוֹמָהּ *he will make an end of her place;* or em. מְקוֹמָה *of opposition* or בְּקָמָיו *of those who rise up against him*) 11QT 35$_{10}$ 37$_{13}$ 42$_{12}$ 46$_{13.17}$ 48$_{14}$, כון hi. *prepare* Ex 23$_{20}$ 1 C 15$_{1.3}$, פנה pi. *prepare* Gn 24$_{31}$, תקן pi. *prepare* MurEpBar$^{b}_{5}$, יסד *establish* Ps 104$_{8}$, חזק pi. *strengthen* MurEpBar$^{b}_{7}$, מלא *fill* Jr 19$_{4}$, pi. 2 K 23$_{14}$, בדל hi. *separate* 11QT 48$_{12}$, חלק pi. *apportion* 5/6ḤevBA 44$_{6.7.8.9}$ ([מקום]), חכר *rent* 5/6ḤevBA 44$_{6.17}$.

מצא *find* Ps 132$_{5}$, תור *seek out* Dt 1$_{33}$, בחר *choose* Dt 12$_{5.14.21.26}$ 14$_{23.24}$ 15$_{20}$ 16$_{2.6.11.15.16}$ 17$_{10}$=11QT 56$_{5}$ Dt 18$_{6}$ 23$_{17}$ 26$_{2}$ 31$_{11}$ Jos 9$_{27}$ Ne 1$_{9}$ 4QapMos^{a} 1.1$_{8}$ 11QT 52$_{9.16}$ 53$_{1}$ ([המקום אשר בחרתי]) 56$_{5}$ 60$_{13}$, אהב *love* Ps 26$_{8}$, רחב hi. *widen* Is 54$_{2}$ 4QSD 2$_{5}$ ([הרחי]בי), פאר pi. *beautify* Is 60$_{13}$, כבד pi. *glorify* Is 60$_{13}$, שׁפט *judge* 1 S 7$_{16}$ (unless אֶת = *with*), נכר pi. *treat as foreign,* i.e. profane Jr 19$_{4}$, אבד pi. *destroy* Dt 12$_{2}$, שׁחת hi. *destroy* Gn 19$_{13}$ 2 K 18$_{25}$, שׁמם hi. *make desolate* perh. 1QH fr. 5$_{5}$.

<CSTR> מְקוֹם הַכְּנַעֲנִי וְהַחִתִּי וְהָאֱמֹרִי וְהַפְּרִזִּי וְהַחִוִּי וְהַיְבוּסִי *place of the Canaanites and the Hittites and the Amorites and the Perizzites and the Hivvites and the Jebusites* Ex 3$_{8}$, שְׁכֶם *of Shechem* Gn 12$_{6}$, הַתֹּפֶת *of Topheth* Jr 19$_{13}$, דָּוִד *of David* 1 S 20$_{25.27}$ 2 C 3$_{1}$, הַמֶּלֶךְ *of the king* Ezk 17$_{16}$, גְּדֹלִים *of the great ones* Pr 25$_{6}$, רֹאִים *of those who see* Jb 34$_{26}$, מְקוֹם לֹא־יָדַע־אֵל *the place of one who did not know God* Jb 18$_{21}$, פְּלֹנִי אַלְמוֹנִי *of such and such a place* 1 S 21$_{3}$ 2 K 6$_{8}$ (פְּלֹנִי אַלְמֹנִי), מְקוֹם מֵתִים *place of the dead* Jb 33$_{22}$ (if em.; see Prep.), מקומות ישראל *places of Israel* Kfar Alma inscr.

מְקוֹם תַּנִּים *place of jackals* Ps 44$_{20}$ (or em. מֹק מָתְנַיִם

festering of loins [i.e. מקק inf. cstr.]; mss תַּנִּין *of dragons*), מְקוֹם הַשְּׁחִין *place of the boil* Lv 1319.

מְקוֹם כִּסְאִי *place of my throne* Ezk 437, מִקְדָּשִׁי *of my sanctuary* Is 6013, מִקְדָּשֵׁנוּ *of our sanctuary* Jr 1712, הַקֹּדֶשׁ *of the holiness*, i.e. the holy place/sanctuary Lv 1017 1413, קָדְשׁוֹ *of his holiness*, i.e. his holy place Ps 243 Ezr 98, [מקו]ם קו[דשך] *place of your holiness*, i.e. your holy place 4QapPsb 3311, מְקוֹם קָדוֹשׁ appar. *place of the holy one*, i.e. holy place Ec 810 (mss מָקוֹם holy *place*), הַמִּזְבֵּחַ *of the altar* Gn 134, הָאָרוֹן *of the ark* 1 K 87||2 C 58, שֵׁם *of the name* of Y. Is 187, מקום היד *place of the hand*, i.e. latrine* 1QM 77 11QT 4613 (יד), ידים *of hands*, i.e. where people have access Si 426, מְקוֹם רַגְלַי *place of my feet* Is 6013, כַּפּוֹת *of the soles of* my feet Ezk 437, דַּם *of the blood of* the guilt offering Lv 1428, הַדֶּשֶׁן *of the ashes* Lv 116, הָעֹלָה *of the burnt offering* Lv 429, מִקְנֶה *of cattle* Nm 321, זֶרַע וּתְאֵנָה וְגֶפֶן וְרִמּוֹן *of grain and figs and vines and pomegranates* Nm 205, אֶרֶץ *of a land of* darkness Is 4519, ־נְהָרִים יְאֹרִים *of rivers (and) streams* Is 3321 (or em. מְקוֹר *source of* or מִקְוֵה *collection of*), סַפִּיר *of sapphires* Jb 286.

מְקוֹם אָהֳלֵךְ *place of your tent* Is 542 4QSD 25 ([אוה]לך), מִשְׁכַּן *of the dwelling place of* your glory Ps 268, שַׁעַר *of the gate* Zc 1410, הַגֹּרֶן *of the threshing floor* 1 C 2122, הַמֻּנָּח *of free space* Ezk 4111, מקום המערכה *place of the battle line* 1QM 199, מְקוֹם הַחֵצִי *place of the arrow* 1 S 2037, הַשֶּׁבֶת *of the seat* 1 K 1019||2 C 918, בִּינָה *of understanding* Jb 2812.20, הַמִּשְׁפָּט *of justice* Ec 316, הַצֶּדֶק *of righteousness* Ec 316, מְקֹמוֹת מֶמְשַׁלְתּוֹ *places of his dominion* Ps 10322.

מקום היין *place of wine* Si 324, מים *of water* CD 1116 (or em.; see Prep.), גורלו *of his lot* 1QS 223, תהו ובו[הו] *of emptiness and void* 4QCreatA 15, ר[שעה] *of wickedness* 1QH fr. 55, עשרה *of ten (men)* CD 132.

מְקוֹם שָׁם קֶבֶר *a place where there is a grave* Ezk 3911, מְקוֹם זֶה *the place which* Ps 1048, מְקוֹם אֲשֶׁר *the place where* Gn 3920 403 Lv 433 72 1413 1 S 294 2 S 1521 Ezk 613 Est 43 817 Ne 414, מְקוֹם שֶׁ- *the place where* Ec 17 113.

מקום יביט *the place where he looks* Si 3414, תגור *where you sojourn* Si 4119, תגור *where she sojourns* Si 4211, תפקד *where you deposit* Si 427, עומדם *where they had stood* 1QM 143.

אַנְשֵׁי הַמָּקוֹם *men of the place* Gn 267.7 2922 3822 Jg 1916, מְקֹמוֹ *of his place* Ezr 14, מְקֹמָהּ *of her place* Gn 3821, שֵׁם הַמָּקוֹם *name of the place* Gn 2214 2819 322.31 3317 3515 Ex 177 Nm 113.34 213 Jos 59 726 Jg 25 2 S 520|| 1 C 1411 2 C 2026, אַבְנֵי *stones of* Gn 2811 1QJuba 2720, שַׁעַר מְקֹמוֹ *gate of his place* Dt 2119=11QT 644 Ru 410 (מְקוֹמוֹ), רֹחַב מָקוֹם *width of the place of* Ezk 4111, ת[חומי המ]קום *borders of the place* Mur 22 111, תְּפִלַּת הַמָּקוֹם *prayer of the place* 2 C 640 715.

אַחַד הַמְּקֹמוֹת *one of the places* Jg 1913 2 S 179.12 (both הַמְּקוֹמֹת), [מקצת] מקומות *some of the places* 4QMMT C5.

כָּל־מָקוֹם *any/every place* Nm 1831 Dt 1213 Jos 13 Is 723 Am 83 Ml 111 Pr 153 1QS 63 (כול) 4QapMes 2.34 ([מקו]ם) 11QT 4811 5119 (both כול).

כָּל־הַמָּקוֹם *every place* Gn 1826 2013 Ex 2024 Dt 1124.

כָּל־הַמְּקֹמוֹת *all the places* Dt 122 1 S 716 (הַמְּקוֹמוֹת) 1 S 3031 Jr 83 249 2914 (הַמְּקוֹמוֹת) 4012 455 Ezk 3412 (הַמְּקוֹמֹת) Ezr 14 Ne 46 (or em. הַמְּזִמּוֹת *the wicked schemes*).

כָּל־מְקֹמוֹת *all the places of* Ps 10322 Kfar Alma inscr. Kfar Baram inscr. (both מקומות).

כֹּל מְקוֹמֹתֵיכֶם *all your places* Am 46, כָּל־מְקוֹמֹתָם *all their places* Ne 1227.

<APP> יִשְׂרָאֵל *Israel* 1 S 716 (unless אֵת = *with*), כָּסִפְיָא *Casiphia* Ezr 817.17, אֶרֶץ *land* Jg 1810 Ezk 2135, מְדִינָה *province* Est 43, עִיר *city* Est 817, גַּיְא *valley* Ezk 3911, מָרוֹם *height* Jr 1712, בַּיִת prison *house* Gn 3920 403, מִשְׁכָּן *dwelling place* Ps 1325, דְּבִיר *inner sanctuary* 1 K 86|| 2 C 57, קֹדֶשׁ הַקֳּדָשִׁים *the holy of holies*, i.e. most holy place 1 K 616 86||2 C 57, מְנוּחָה *resting place* Is 661, עַמּוּד *column* 11QT 4212.

<ADJ> קָדוֹשׁ *holy* Ex 2931 Lv 69.19.20 76 1013 1624 249 Ec 810(mss) 4QapPsb 313, טָהוֹר *pure* Lv 412 64 1014 (or em. טָהוֹר to קָדוֹשׁ *holy*) Nm 199, טָמֵא *impure* Lv 1440.41.45, רַע *evil* Nm 205, קָרוֹב *near* CD 1114 (קרוב לגוים *near gentiles*), רָחוֹק *distant* 11QT 664, צַר *narrow* Nm 2226, אמן ni. ptc. *firm* Is 2223.25, חָרֵב *devastated* Jr 3312 (+ מֵאֵין אָדָם וְעַד־בְּהֵמָה *without human beings or beasts*), אַחֵר *another* Nm 2313.27 Ezk 123 Est 414 4QDa 114.5a, אֶחָד *one* Gn 19 (or em.; see Prep.) Ec 320 66, הוּא *that* Gn 2131 2214 2811.19 323 Nm 113.34 1324 Dt 123 1710 Jos 59 726 Jg 25 1517 1812 1 S 2328 2 S 216 520||1 C 1411 2 S 68||

1 C 13_{11} 2 C 20_{26} MurEpBar$^{b}_{7}$, זֶה *this* Gn $19_{13.14}$ 20_{11} $28_{16.17}$ Nm 20_{5} Dt 1_{31} 9_{7} 11_{5} 26_{9} 29_{6} 1 S 12_{8} 1 K $8_{29.30.35}$|| 2 C $6_{20.21.26}$ 1 K $13_{8.16}$ 2 K 6_{9} 18_{25} $22_{16.17.19.20}$||2 C $34_{24.25.27.28}$ Jr $7_{3.6.7.20}$ 14_{13} $16_{2.3.9}$ $19_{3.4.6.7.12}$ $22_{3.11}$ 24_{5} 27_{22} $28_{3.3.4.6}$ 29_{10} 32_{37} $33_{10.12}$ 40_{2} 42_{18} 44_{29} 51_{62} Zp 1_{4} Hg 2_{9} 2 C 6_{40} $7_{12.15}$ 1QJub^{a} 27_{20} ([הזה]) Mur 22 1_{11} ([המ]קום ה[זה]) Kfar Alma inscr. Kfar Baram inscr., אֵלֶּה *these* 1 S 7_{16}

<PREP> לְ of direction, *to* Ne 4_{7} perh. 4QTohB^{a} 2_{6}, + הלך *go* Jg 7_{7} 9_{55} 19_{28} 1 S 2_{20} 14_{46} 2 C 25_{10}, שׁוב *go back* Gn 18_{33} 32_{1} Nm 24_{25} Jos 4_{18} 1 S 5_{11} 26_{25} 2 S 19_{40} 2 C 25_{10}, hi. *bring back* Gn 29_{3} 1 S 5_{3}, קרב *draw near* Jb 33_{22} (if em. לַמְּמִתִים *to those who cause death* to לִמְקוֹם מֵתִים *to the place of the dead*, abbreviated as לִמ׳ מתים),* שׁלח pi. *send* 1 S 6_{2}; בֵּין ... לְ *between ... and*, + היה *be* 1QM 7_{7} (+ מַחֲנֶה *camp*).

לְ of benefit, *to, for* 1 S 30_{31}, + עשׂה *do* Jr 7_{14} 19_{12}; *according to* Gn 36_{40}; appar. *from* or perh. *in respect of*, + גלה *be exiled* 2 S 15_{19} (ms מִן *from*); introducing object, + קרא *call*, i.e. name Gn 21_{31} 35_{7} Nm 13_{24} Jg 15_{17} 18_{12} 1 S 23_{28} 2 S 2_{16} 6_{8}||1 C 13_{11} Jr 19_{6}, נשׂא *forgive* Gn $18_{24.26}$.

בְּ of place, *in, at, to* Gn 20_{11} 28_{16} Jr 16_{3} Pr 15_{3} Est 4_{3} 8_{17} Ezr $8_{17.17}$ 1 C 16_{27} 4QTohC 1_{8} 4QCreatA 1_{5} 4QapPs^{b} 31_{3} 4QShir^{b} 37_{2} 4QapMes 2.3_{4} ([בכל מקו[ם]), + היה *be* Lv 13_{19} 2 S 15_{21} Jr 16_{2} 33_{12} Kfar Alma inscr. Kfar Baram inscr. (twice), שׁאר ni. *remain* Jr 8_{3}, אמר ni. *be said* Ho 2_{1}, דבר pi. *speak* Is 45_{19}, ברך pi. *praise* Ps 103_{22}, ראה ni. *appear* Dt 16_{16} 31_{11}, שׁמע ni. *be heard* Jr 33_{10}, זכר *remember* 4QapPs^{b} 33_{11} (במקו[ם]), כתב *write* CD 13_{12}, pass. *be written* 4QD^{a} $11_{4.5a}$, בוא *come* Ex 20_{24} 2 S 17_{12}, עלה *go up* Gn 35_{13}, hi. *cause to go up*, i.e. offer Dt $12_{13.14}$, נגשׁ ho. *be brought near*, i.e. offered Ml 1_{11}, קרב *draw near* Jg 19_{13}, קבץ ni. *gather oneself* Ne 4_{14}, דרך *tread* Dt 11_{24} Jos 11_{3}, חנה *encamp* Nm 9_{17}, ישׁב *dwell* Dt 23_{17}, hi. *cause to dwell* 1 S 12_{8}, שׁכן pi. *allow to dwell* Jr $7_{3.6}$, שׁכב *lie down* Gn 28_{11} 1 S $3_{2.9}$, נוח hi. *place* Nm 19_{9}, יצג hi. *place* 2 S 6_{17}, נצב hi. *erect* Gn 35_{14}, עמד *stand* Nm 22_{26} Pr 25_{6}, קום *stand* Ps 24_{3}, שׁבת hi. *rest* CD 11_{14} (or em. qal), חבא ni. *hide oneself* 2 S 17_{9}, מצא *find* 11QT 66_{4}, מושׁ *be lacking* 1QS $6_{3.6}$ 13_{2}.

נתן *give* Jr 14_{13} Am 4_{6} Hg 2_{9} Ezr 9_{8} 1 C 21_{25}, i.e. *make* Jr 24_{9}, ערך *arrange* battle Jg 20_{22}, שׁלך hi. *cast* Am 8_{3}, בנה *build* 2 C 3_{1} 33_{19}, עשׂה ni. *be done* Gn 29_{26}, שׂמח *rejoice* Dt 16_{11} 11QT 52_{16}, חגג *celebrate festival* Dt 16_{15}, שׂרף *burn* 11QT 16_{12}, קטר pi. *burn incense* Jr 19_{4}, זבח *sacrifice* Dt 16_{2} 11QT 51_{19}, שׁחט *slaughter* Lv $4_{24.29.33}$ 7_{2} 14_{13}, ni. *be slaughtered* Lv 6_{18}, בשׁל pi. *boil* Ex 29_{31}, אכל *eat* Lv $10_{13.14.17}$ 24_{9} Nm 18_{31} Dt 12_{18} 14_{23} 15_{20} 16_{7} 1 K $13_{8.16.22}$ 11QT 52_{9}, ni. *be eaten* Lv $6_{9.19}$ 7_{6}, שׁתה *drink* 1 K $13_{8.16,22}$, לקק *lick* 1 K 21_{19}, שׁפך *shed* blood Jr 7_{6} 22_{3}, *pour* speech Si 35_{4}, כבס pi. *wash* Lv 6_{20}, רחץ *wash* Lv 16_{24}, תקע *fasten* as peg Is 22_{23}, pass. *be fastened* Is 22_{25}, ספק *strike* Jb 34_{26}, דכה pi. *crush* Ps 44_{20} (or em.; see Cstr.), בקק *make useless* Jr 19_{7}, פקד *punish* Jr 44_{29}, שׁפט *judge* Ezk 21_{35}, מות *die* Jr 22_{12} 42_{22} Ezk 17_{16}, קבר *bury* 11QT $48_{11.12}$.

בְּ *against, upon*, + יצת ni. *be kindled* 2 K 22_{17}, נתך ni. *be poured out* 2 C 34_{25}.

בְּ introducing object, + בחר *choose* Dt 12_{18} 14_{25} 16_{7} 17_{8} 2 C 7_{12} 4QMMT B_{32} ([בחר בו]) B_{60}, פגע *reach* Gn 28_{11}.

כְּ *as*, + היה *be* Jr 19_{13}.

מִן of direction, *from* Ne 4_{6} (or em.; see Cstr.) Si 41_{18} (Bmg) 4QapJoseph^{a} 8_{2}, + שׁאר ni. *remain* Ezr 1_{4}, נגד hi. *tell* Dt 17_{10}=11QT 56_{5}, שׁרק *hiss* Jb 27_{23}, ברך pass. *be blessed* Ezk 3_{12} (or em.; see below), בקשׁ pi. *seek* Ne 12_{27}, ראה *see* Gn 13_{14}, שׁמע *hear* 2 C 6_{21}, הלך pi. *go* Ec 8_{10}, בוא *come* Ezk 38_{15} Jb 2_{11}, hi. *bring* 4QWay^{b} 12_{4} (א[יבי]), יצא *go out* Gn 19_{14} 16_{29} Is 26_{21} Jr 4_{11} Mc 1_{3} Ru 1_{7} 4QHalakhah^{a} 1_{4} 1_{4}, hi. *bring out* Gn 19_{12}, נסע *set out* Jos 3_{3}, מושׁ *depart* Is 46_{7}, נדד *wander* Pr 27_{8}, עתק *move* Jb 14_{18} 18_{4}, גיח hi. *burst out* Jg 20_{33}, נתר *spring* Jb 37_{1}, חושׁ hi. *be dislodged* 1QS 8_{8}, שׁוב *go back* Jr 40_{12}, קום *arise* Jos 8_{19} Jg 20_{33} 4QM^{a} 1_{13}, רום *arise* Ezk 3_{12} (if em. בָּרוּךְ *blessed* to בְּרוּם *when* the glory of Y. *arose*) 1QS 2_{23}, עמד *stand*, i.e. arise Est 4_{14}, גלה *be exiled* 2 S 15_{19} (ms) Ezk 12_{3}, שׁלח pi. *send* Jr 24_{5}, סור hi. *remove* 1 K 20_{24}, לקח *take* Jr 13_{7} 28_{3}, שׂער pi. *sweep away* Jb 27_{21}, קבץ pi. *gather* Jr 29_{14}, נצל hi. *deliver* Ezk 34_{12}, שׁחה htpal. *bow down* Zp 2_{11}, אבד pi. *destroy* Dt 12_{3}, בלע pi. *destroy* Jb 8_{18}, כרת hi. *cut off* Zp 1_{4}, שׁבת hi. *cause to cease* Jr 16_{9}, דעך ni. *disappear* Jb 6_{17}, עור hi. *stir up* Jl 4_{7}, רגז *shake* Jb 9_{6}, רעשׁ *shake* Is 13_{13}.

בושׁ מִן *be ashamed of* Si 41_{19}.

אֶל *to(wards), into, at* 1 K 10$_{19}$ 2 K 6$_8$, + הלך *go* Gn 13$_4$ 22$_3$ 30$_{25}$ Nm 23$_{13}$ Dt 14$_{25}$ 26$_2$ Jr 7$_{12}$ Ec 1$_7$ 3$_{20}$ 6$_6$, בוא *come* Gn 22$_9$ Dt 12$_{26}$ 18$_6$=11QT 60$_{13}$ Dt 29$_6$ 1 S 20$_{19}$ 26$_5$ 2 S 2$_{23}$ 4QapMos^a 1.1$_8$ (ל[א]) 11QT 45$_5$ (וב[א]) 53$_9$, hi. *bring* Ex 23$_{20}$ Nm 20$_5$ 32$_{17}$ Dt 26$_9$ 1 K 5$_8$ 8$_6$||2 C 5$_7$ 2 K 22$_{16}$ Is 14$_2$, יבל ho. *be brought* Is 18$_7$, יצא hi. *bring out* Lv 4$_{12}$ 6$_4$ 14$_{45}$, עלה *go up* Nm 14$_{40}$ Dt 17$_8$, hi. *bring up* Ex 3$_8$ 1 C 15$_3$, ירד *go down* Ps 104$_8$, נסע *set out* Nm 10$_{29}$, שׁכם hi. *rise early (to go)* Gn 19$_{27}$, דרשׁ *resort* Dt 12$_5$, שׁאף *pant*, i.e. hasten Ec 1$_5$, קוה ni. *be gathered* Gn 1$_9$ (or em. מִקְוֶ־ם *pool* [i.e. מִקְוֶה II with enclitic mem]* or מִקְוֵם [contraction of מִקְוֵיהֶם *their collection*]*), שׁוב *go back* 1 S 29$_4$ Ho 5$_{15}$ 1QM 14$_3$, hi. *bring back* Jr 27$_{22}$ 28$_{3.4.6}$ 29$_{10.14}$ 32$_{37}$ Ne 1$_9$ 2 C 24$_{11}$, לקח *take* Nm 23$_{27}$, גלה *be exiled* Ezk 12$_3$, ברח *flee* Nm 24$_{11}$, נפל *fall* CD 11$_{16.16}$ (or em. מקור *spring* or מקוה *pool*), שׁלך hi. *cast* Lv 1$_{16}$ 14$_{40}$, שׁפך *pour* Lv 14$_{41}$, פרשׂ *spread* wings 1 K 8$_7$, נוף hi. *wave* hand 2 K 5$_{11}$, שׁלח *send* 2 K 6$_{10}$, פתח *open* 1 K 8$_{29}$||2 C 6$_{20}$, אמר *say* Gn 20$_{13}$, פלל htp. *pray* 1 K 8$_{29.30.35}$||2 C 6$_{20.21.26}$, שׁמע *hear* 1 K 8$_{30}$, זבח *sacrifice* Dt 16$_6$, ידע po. *cause to know*, i.e. direct 1 S 21$_3$ (or em. ידע to יעד ni. *make appointment*), נתן *give*, i.e. place Gn 39$_{20}$ 40$_3$ Jos 9$_{27}$ 2 S 11$_{16}$.

אֶל *upon, against*, + דבר pi. *speak* Jr 40$_2$, נתך ni. (of wrath) *be poured out* Jr 7$_{20}$.

אֶל *concerning*, + דבר pi. *speak* Jr 51$_{62}$.

עַל *upon, at* 2 C 9$_{18}$, + היה *be* Kfar Alma inscr., עמד *stand* Ex 3$_5$ Jos 5$_{15}$, נתן *give* Jr 45$_5$, i.e. place Lv 14$_{28}$, שׁכן hi. *cause to dwell* 11QT 53$_9$ 56$_5$, ספר *count* Si 42$_7$.

עַל *to*, + בוא *come* Ex 18$_{23}$, פרשׂ *spread* wings 2 C 5$_8$.

עַל *against* 2 C 34$_{27}$, + דבר pi. *speak* 2 K 22$_{19}$, בוא hi. *bring* 2 K 22$_{20}$||2 C 34$_{28}$ Jr 19$_3$ 2 C 34$_{24}$, עלה *go up* 2 K 18$_{25}$.

עַל introducing object, + בין htpol. *look at* Ps 37$_{10}$.

עַד *unto* 1 K 5$_{23}$, + הלך *go* Gn 13$_3$, בוא *come* Dt 1$_{31}$ 9$_7$ 11$_5$ 1 S 20$_{37}$ 1QM 19$_9$, עבר *pass* Gn 12$_6$ Jg 11$_{19}$, ישׁב *remain* Zc 14$_{10}$.

אֵת *with*, i.e. near to, + שׁפט *judge* perh. 1 S 7$_{16}$ (unless אֵת = object marker).

בְּקֶרֶב *within* Gn 18$_{24}$.

אַחֲרֵי *after*, + הלך *go* Ezk 10$_{11}$.

מָקוֹם without prep., *to the place, in the place* Ec 3$_{16}$, + הוה *be* Ec 11$_3$ (יְהוּא; mss הוּא *it is*) Si 42$_{11}$, ישׁט hi. *stretch out* hand Si 34$_{14}$, בושׁ *be ashamed* Si 42$_6$.

<COLL> הַמָּקוֹם (...) אֲשֶׁר ... שָׁם and vars. *the place (...) where*, + verb היה *be* Gn 13$_3$ 2 S 15$_{21}$ 1 K 5$_8$ Is 7$_{23}$ 1QS 6$_{3.6}$, הלך *go* Jr 45$_5$, pi. 1 S 30$_{31}$, נדח hi. *drive* Jr 8$_3$ 24$_9$ 29$_{14}$, ni. *be driven* Jr 40$_{12}$, גלה hi. *exile* Jr 22$_{12}$, פוץ ni. *be scattered* Ezk 34$_{12}$, עמד *stand* Gn 19$_{27}$, ישׁב *dwell* 2 K 6$_1$, חנה *encamp* 1 S 26$_5$, שׁכן *settle* Nm 9$_{17}$, גור *sojourn* Ezr 1$_4$, שׁכב *lie down* 1 S 26$_5$ Ru 3$_4$, נפל *fall* 2 S 2$_{23}$, מצא ni. *be found* 2 S 17$_{12}$, אמר *promise* to place name 2 C 6$_{20}$, דבר pi. *speak* Gn 35$_{15}$, חפץ *desire* to go and live Jr 42$_{22}$, בחר *choose* to set name (unless מָקוֹם is obj. of בחר, i.e. the place that he will choose to set his name there) Dt 12$_{5.21}$ 14$_{23.24}$ 16$_{2.6.11}$ 26$_2$ Ne 1$_9$, פקד hi. *appoint* 1 S 29$_4$, עבד *serve* Dt 12$_2$, נתן *give* Ezk 6$_{13}$, אסר pass. *be bound* Gn 40$_3$, סתר ni. *hide oneself* 1 S 20$_{19}$, ערך *arrange* battle Jg 20$_{22}$, בשׁל pi. *boil* Ezk 46$_{20}$.

+ nom. cl., e.g. הַמָּקוֹם אֲשֶׁר אַתָּה שָׁם *the place where you are* Gn 13$_{14}$, Jg 18$_{10}$ 2 S 11$_{16}$.

הַמָּקוֹם (...) אֲשֶׁר ... שָׁמָּה *the place (...) to which, at which*, + verb היה *be* Ru 1$_7$, בוא *come* Gn 20$_{13}$, hi. *bring* Dt 12$_{11}$, נוס *flee* Ex 21$_{13}$, טמן *hide* Jr 13$_7$, מכר *deliver (over)* Jl 4$_7$.

מָקוֹם ... אֲשֶׁר ... מִשָּׁם *a place ... from which*, + verb ראה *see* Nm 23$_{13}$, גלה hi. *exile* Jr 29$_{14}$.

הַמָּקוֹם אֲשֶׁר and vars., *the place where*, + verb היה *be* 1 S 23$_{22}$, ברא ni. *be created* Ezk 21$_{35}$, אמר ni. *be said* Ho 2$_1$, דבר pi. *speak* Gn 35$_{13.14.15}$, שׁמע *hear* Ne 4$_{14}$, זכר hi. *cause to be remembered* Ex 20$_{24}$, לקק *lick* 1 K 21$_{19}$, שׁוב *go back* Ne 4$_6$ (or em.; see Cstr.), נגע hi. *reach* Est 4$_3$ 8$_{17}$, שׁלח *send*, i.e. direct 1 K 5$_{23}$, פנה *turn* Ezk 10$_{11}$, שׁכן pi. *cause to dwell* 11QT 60$_{13}$, אסר pass. *be bound* Gn 39$_{20}$ Dn 39$_{20}$, שׁחט *slaughter* Lv 4$_{24.33}$ 7$_2$ 14$_{13}$, ni. *be slaughtered* Lv 6$_{18}$; + nom. cl. Nm 22$_{26}$.

הַמָּקוֹם אֲשֶׁר־אָמַר־לוֹ הָאֱלֹהִים *the place of which God had told him* Gn 22$_{3.9}$, sim. Nm 10$_{29}$ 14$_{40}$ 1 K 8$_{29}$ 13$_{22}$ 2 K 6$_{10}$ Jr 33$_{10}$.

מְקוֹם שֶׁ- *the place where*, + נפל *fall* Ec 11$_3$, הלך *go*, i.e. flow Ec 1$_7$.

מָקוֹם || עִיר *place* Am 4$_6$, מִשְׁכָּן *dwelling place* Jb 18$_{21}$, מוֹצָא *mine* Jb 28$_1$, דֶּרֶךְ *way* Jb 28$_{23}$ 38$_{19}$ (+); + מַעֲמָד *standing place* 1QS 2$_{23}$, אֶרֶץ *land* Gn 30$_{25}$ Jr 7$_7$, הַר

mountain Ps 24$_{3}$, יַרְכָּה *flank* Ezk 38$_{15}$, מָעוֹן *habitation* Ps 26$_{8}$, בַּיִת *house* Jb 7$_{10}$, קֵן *nest* Pr 27$_{8}$, מַחֲנֶה *camp* 4Q MMT B$_{60}$.

מָקוֹם לַחֲנֹתְכֶם *a place for you to encamp* Dt 1$_{33}$, מָקוֹם לָשֶׁבֶת שָׁם *a place in which to dwell* 2 K 6$_{2}$, מקום לקללך *a reason to curse you* Si 4$_{5}$, מקום לקבור *a place to bury* 11QT 48$_{14}$.

שלושה מקומות *three places* 11QT 46$_{17}$.

Also 1QSb 3$_{26}$ 4QPrQuot 122$_{2}$.

<SYN> עִיר *place*, מִשְׁכָּן *dwelling place*, מוֹצָא *mine*, דֶּרֶךְ *way*.*

⇒ קום *arise*.

*[מְקוֹמָה] n.f. **opposition**, <OBJ> עשׂה *make* Na 1$_{8}$ (כָּלָה יַעֲשֶׂה מְקוֹמָה *he will make a full end of opposition*; if em. מְקוֹמָהּ *her place*).

⇒ קום *arise*.

מָקוֹר I 18.2.39 n.m. **source**—cstr. מְקוֹר (מְקֹר); sf. מְקוֹרְךָ (Q מקורכה), מְקוֹרוֹ (Si מקורה), מְקוֹרָהּ (מְקֹרָהּ), Q מקורם —**source, spring, fountain,** in ref. to Y. (Jr 2$_{13}$ 17$_{13}$), wife (Pr 5$_{18}$); source of menstrual blood (Lv 20$_{18.18}$), blood in childbirth (Lv 12$_{7}$), bodily discharge of man (1QM 7$_{6}$ 4QOrd^{c} 1.1$_{4}$ [ממקו[ר]ו] 1.1$_{7}$), presumptuousness (Si 10$_{13}$), knowledge, in ref. to Y. (1QS 10$_{12}$); **Fountain,** as appellative for Y. (Jr 17$_{13}$ 1QS 11$_{6}$).

<SUBJ> היה *be* Zc 13$_{1}$ Pr 5$_{18}$, פתח ni. *be opened* Zc 13$_{1}$ 1QH 11$_{19}$ 4QHod^{e} 1$_{4}$, ברך pass. *be blessed* Pr 5$_{18}$, נבע hi. *pour out* wickedness Si 10$_{13}$, כול hi. *contain* 4Q 418 103.2$_{6}$, סתר ni. *be hidden* 1QS 11$_{6}$, בושׁ *be ashamed* Ho 13$_{15}$ (or em. יֵבוֹשׁ *it will be ashamed* to יֵבַשׁ *it will be dry* or יוֹבִישׁ *it will make dry*), כזב pi. *lie* 1QSb 1$_{3}$ (יכז[ב]), נזל *flow* Jr 18$_{14}$ (if em. קָרִים *cold* to מְקֹרִים *springs*).*

<NOM CL> מְקוֹר חַיִּים פִּי צַדִּיק *the mouth of the righteous is a fountain of life* Pr 10$_{11}$, תּוֹרַת חָכָם מְקוֹר חַיִּים *the teaching of the wise is a fountain of life* Pr 13$_{14}$, יִרְאַת י׳ מְקוֹר חַיִּים *the fear of Y. is a fountain of life* Pr 14$_{27}$, מְקוֹר חַיִּים שֵׂכֶל בְּעָלָיו *understanding is a fountain of life for those who possess it* Pr 16$_{22}$, נַחַל נֹבֵעַ מְקוֹר חָכְמָה *the fountain of wisdom is a gushing stream* Pr 18$_{4}$ (unless מָקוֹר II *convocation*), אני ... מקור הנדה *I am ... a source of impurity* 1QH 12$_{2}$, עיני מקור מים *my eye is a spring of water* 4QBark^{f} 1.1$_{3}$, מְקוֹר מָשְׁחָת צַדִּיק מָט לִפְנֵי־רָשָׁע *the righteous who totters before the wicked is a polluted fountain* Pr 25$_{26}$, עִמְּךָ מְקוֹר חַיִּים *with you is the fountain of life* Ps 36$_{10}$.

<OBJ> גלה pi. *uncover* Lv 20$_{18}$, ערה pi. *make naked* Lv 20$_{18}$, פתח *open* 1QH 2$_{18}$ 8$_{21}$ 18$_{10}$ ([מקו]ר) 18$_{12}$ ([מקו]רי) 18$_{13}$ ([מ]קור) 4Q418 81$_{1}$, יבשׁ hi. *make dry* Jr 51$_{36}$ Ho 13$_{15}$ (if em.; see Subj.), קפא hi. *congeal*, i.e. freeze Si 43$_{20}$(B, M) (Bmg מקוה *the pool*), עזב *forsake* Jr 2$_{13}$ 17$_{13}$ 4QDibHam^{a} 1.5$_{2}$ ([עזבו]), שׂים *place* 4QShir^{b} 63.3$_{1}$.

<CSTR> מְקוֹר מַיִם *source of water* Jr 2$_{13}$ 17$_{13}$ 4Q Bark^{f} 1.1$_{3}$ 4Q418 103.2$_{6}$ 4QDibHam^{a} 1.5$_{2}$ CD 11$_{16}$ (if em. מקום *place of*), מקור נוזלים *source of streams* 1QH 8$_{4}$, מְקוֹר דִּמְעָה *source of tears* Jr 8$_{23}$, דָּמֶיהָ *of her blood* Lv 12$_{7}$ (מְקֹר) 20$_{18}$, חַיִּים *of life* Ps 36$_{10}$ Pr 10$_{11}$ 13$_{14}$ 14$_{27}$ 16$_{22}$ 1QH 8$_{14}$, יִשְׂרָאֵל *of Israel* Ps 68$_{27}$ (unless מָקוֹר II *convocation*; or em.; see Prep.), מק[ור ז]והר *source of brightness* 4QBer^{a} 1.2$_{4}$, מקור חושך *source of darkness* 1QS 3$_{19}$, הטוהר *of purity* 4QShir^{b} 52.3$_{2}$ ([מ]קור), נדה *of impurity* 1QH 1$_{22}$ (הנדה) 12$_{25}$, הקודש *of holiness* 4Q ShirShabb^{a} 1.1$_{7}$ 15$_{2}$ ([ה]קודש), דעת *of knowledge* 1QH 2$_{18}$ 12$_{29}$ 1QS 10$_{12}$, דעתו *of his knowledge* 1QS 11$_{3}$, מבינה *of understanding* 4QBer^{a} 1.2$_{6}$, חָכְמָה *of wisdom* Pr 18$_{4}$ (unless מָקוֹר II *convocation*), ערמה *of prudence* 4Q Ber^{a} 1.2$_{6}$, צדקה *of righteousness* 1QS 11$_{6}$, צדקתו *of his righteousness* 1QS 11$_{5}$, אמתכה *of your truth* 1QH 18$_{13}$ ([מ]קור), תהלה *of praise* 4QShir^{b} 63.3$_{1}$, עולם *of everlastingness*, i.e. everlasting source 1QH 6$_{17}$ 8$_{8.20}$ ([מק]ור) 10$_{31}$ 18$_{15}$ ([עולם]) 1QSb 1$_{3}$ (ע[ו]לם) 4Q418 81$_{1}$; [בר]כת המקו[ר] *blessing of the source* 1QpPs 8$_{2}$.

<APP> י׳ *Y.* Jr 2$_{13}$ 17$_{13}$, שָׂפָה *lip* 4Q418 81$_{1}$.

<PREP> לְ of direction, *to*, + פתח ni. *be opened* 1QH 10$_{31}$; *as* or introducing predicate, + היה *be* 1QH 6$_{17}$ 8$_{8}$, קרץ pu. *be nipped off* 1QH 12$_{25}$ ([קו]רצתי); introducing object, + אמן hi. *believe* 1QH 8$_{14}$.

בְּ of place, *in* 4QShir^{b} 44.1$_{1}$, + נתן *give*, i.e. place 1QH 8$_{4}$ ([נ]תתני), סתר pu. *be hidden* 1QH 8$_{20}$ (סותר[במקו]ר), הלל pi. *praise* 4Q418 81$_{1}$.

כְּ *as* 4Q418 103.2$_{6}$.

מִן of direction, *from* 1QS 3$_{19}$ 11$_{5}$ 4QShirShabb^{a} 1.1$_{7}$ 15$_{2}$ ([מ]מקור), + פתח *open* 1QS 11$_{3}$, נכר hi. *regard* 1QSb

3$_{19}$ (להכנ[י]רכה), שׁמע hi. *proclaim* 1QH 18$_{15}$ (להשמ[יע]); *free of (impurity emanating from)*, + היה *be* pure 1QM 7$_6$, טהר *be pure* Lv 12$_7$ 4QOrd^c 1.1$_4$ (ממקו[ר]ו) 1.1$_7$; partitive, *(ones) from among* Ps 68$_{27}$ (unless מָקוֹר II *convocation*; or em. בְּמִקְרָאֵי *among the assemblies of*).

אֶל *(in)to* 4QD^e 2.2$_3$, נפל *fall* CD 11$_{16}$ (if em.; see Cstr.).

<COLL> מָקוֹר || מַעְיָן *spring* Ho 13$_{15}$ Pr 25$_{26}$ 1QH 6$_{17}$ (+) 1QS 3$_{19}$ 10$_{12}$ (both מעון), מַבּוּעַ *spring* 1QH 8$_4$, מִקְוֶה *reservoir* 1QH 12$_{25.29}$ 1QS 11$_6$, יָם *sea* Jr 51$_{36}$, עֶרְוָה *nakedness* Lv 20$_{18}$.

מקור לאבל *a fountain for mourning* 1QH 11$_{19}$, מקור לברכת עד *a fountain for everlasting blessing* 4QHod^e 1$_4$.

Also 4Q418 127$_1$ 4QHod^a 7.1$_{21}$ 4QBéat 21$_{7.7}$.

<SYN> מַעְיָן *spring*, מַבּוּעַ *spring*, יָם *sea*, עֶרְוָה *nakedness*.*

⇒ קור *dig*.

*[מָקוֹר] II 2 n.[m.] **convocation** (unless מָקוֹר *source*)—cstr. מְקוֹר—<NOM CL> נַחַל נֹבֵעַ מְקוֹר חָכְמָה *the convocation of Wisdom is a gurgling stream* Pr 18$_4$.

<CSTR> מְקוֹר יִשְׂרָאֵל *convocation of Israel* Ps 68$_{27}$, חָכְמָה *of Wisdom* Pr 18$_4$. <PREP> מִן *in*, + ברך pi. *bless* Ps 68$_{27}$.

⇒ קור *call, invoke*.

[מִקָּח] 1.0.1 n.[m.] **taking, buying**—cstr. מִקַּח—**1. taking,** <NOM CL> אֵין ... מִקַּח־שֹׁחַד *there is no ... taking of bribes* 2 C 19$_7$ (|| מַשֹּׂא *lifting* of face, i.e. partiality, עַוְלָה *injustice*). <CSTR> מִקַּח־שֹׁחַד *taking of bribes* 2 C 19$_7$.

2. buying, <PREP> לְ *with respect to*, + עשׂה *do* CD 13$_{15}$ (:: מִמְכָּר *selling*).

<SYN> §1 מַשֹּׂא *lifting* of face, i.e. partiality, עַוְלָה *injustice*.

<ANT> מִמְכָּר *selling*.

⇒ לקח *take*.

[מַקָּחָה] 1 n.f. **ware**—pl. מַקָּחוֹת—<OBJ> בוא hi. *bring* Ne 10$_{32}$ (+ שֶׁבֶר *grain*), מכר *sell* Ne 10$_{32}$.

⇒ לקח *take*.

[מִקְטָר] 1 n.[m.] **place of burning**—cstr. מִקְטַר—**place of burning, incense altar,** <OBJ> עשׂה *make* Ex 30$_1$ (unless em. מִזְבַּח קְטֹרֶת *an altar of incense*),* סור hi. *remove* 2 C 30$_{14}$ (if em. הַמְקַטְּרוֹת *the incense altars*, i.e. מִקְטֶרֶת pl.), שׁלך hi. *cast* 2 C 30$_{14}$ (if em.; see above). <CSTR> מִקְטַר קְטֹרֶת *place of burning incense* Ex 30$_1$, כָּל־הַמְקָטָרוֹת *all the incense altars* 2 C 30$_{14}$ (if em.; see Obj.). <APP> מִזְבֵּחַ *altar* Ex 30$_1$.*

⇒ קטר *smoke*.

מֻקְטָר 1 n.m. **incense,** perh. **frankincense,*** <SUBJ> נגשׁ ho. *be brought near*, i.e. offered Ml 1$_{11}$ (unless קטר ho. ptc.;* + מִנְחָה *offering*).*

⇒ קטר *smoke*.

מִקְטֶ֫רֶת 2.0.2 n.f. **censer; incense**—cstr. Q מקטרת; sf. מִקְטַרְתּוֹ—**1. censer,** i.e. cup or casket for incense,* <NOM CL> בְּיָדוֹ מִקְטֶרֶת *in his hand was a censer* 2 C 26$_{19}$, מִקְטַרְתּוֹ בְּיָדוֹ *his censer was in his hand* Ezk 8$_{11}$.

2. incense in such a utensil, or **offering of incense,*** <OBJ> ערך *arrange* 1QM 2$_5$. <CSTR> מקטרת ניחוח *incense of soothing*, i.e. soothing incense 1QM 2$_5$ (+ לרצון אל *for the acceptance of God*), מקטרת קודשכ[ה וני]חו[ח] רצונכה *incense of your holiness and the soothing of your acceptance*, i.e. holy and soothing incense acceptable to you 4QRitPur 29.7$_{11}$.*

⇒ קטר *smoke*.

[מְקַטֶּ֫רֶת] 1 n.f. **incense altar**—pl. מְקַטְּרוֹת—**incense altar** or perh. utensils for smoke cult,* <OBJ> סור hi. *remove* 2 C 30$_{14}$ (or em. הַמְקְטָרוֹת *the incense altars*, i.e. מִקְטָר pl.; + מִזְבֵּחַ *altar*), שׁלך hi. *cast* 2 C 30$_{14}$ (or em.; see above). <CSTR> כָּל־הַמְקַטְּרוֹת *all the incense altars* 2 C 30$_{14}$ (or em.; see Obj.).*

⇒ קטר *smoke*.

מַקֵּל 18 n.m.&f. **rod**—cstr. מַקַּל (מַקֵּל); sf. מַקְלִי, מַקְלוֹ, מַקֶּלְכֶם; pl. מַקְלוֹת—**1. rod,** used by Jacob in breeding sheep (Gn 30$_{37+5t}$), ruler (Jr 48$_{17}$); of almond (Jr 1$_{11}$); **staff** of traveller (Gn 32$_{11}$ Ex 12$_{11}$), carried when riding ass (Nm 22$_{27}$); of shepherd (1 S 17$_{40.43}$), given symbolic names (Zc 11$_{7.10.14}$); as weapon (Ezk 39$_9$).

2. perh. **penis,*** in supposed divination* (Ho 4$_{12}$).
<SUBJ> נגד hi. *tell*, i.e. give oracles Ho 4$_{12}$, שׁבר ni. *be broken* Jr 48$_{17}$. <NOM CL> מַקֶּלְכֶם בְּיֶדְכֶם *your staff shall be in your hand* Ex 12$_{11}$. <OBJ> ראה *see* Jr 1$_{11}$, לקח *take* Gn 30$_{37}$ 1 S 17$_{40}$ Zc 11$_{7.10}$, שׂים *place* Gn 30$_{41}$, יצג hi. *place* Gn 30$_{38}$, פצל pi. *peel* Gn 30$_{38}$, גדע *hew down* Zc 11$_{10.14}$.
<CSTR> מַקֵּל שָׁקֵד *rod of almond* Jr 1$_{11}$, לִבְנֶה *of storax* Gn 30$_{37}$ (מַקֵּל; + לוּז *almond*, עַרְמוֹן *plane*), תִּפְאָרָה *of glory*, i.e. glorious rod Jr 48$_{17}$, מַקֵּל יָד *staff of hand* Ezk 39$_{9}$.
<APP> מַטֶּה *rod* Jr 48$_{17}$, נֹעַם *pleasantness*, as name of staff Zc 11$_{10}$.
<ADJ> לַח *fresh* Gn 30$_{37}$, שֵׁנִי *second* Zc 11$_{14}$.
<PREP> לְ introducing object, + קרא *call*, i.e. name Zc 11$_{7}$.
בְּ of place, *in, among*, + פצל pi. *peel* Gn 30$_{37}$, יחם pi. *conceive* Gn 30$_{41}$; of instrument, *by (means of), with*, + בער pi. *kindle* fire Ezk 39$_{9}$, נכה hi. *strike* Nm 22$_{27}$; of accompaniment, *with*, + בוא *come* 1 S 17$_{43}$, עבר *cross* Gn 32$_{11}$; introducing object, + שׂלק hi. *set fire to* Ezk 39$_{9}$ (|| חֵץ *arrow*, קֶשֶׁת *bow*, רֹמַח *spear*, נֶשֶׁק *weapons*, מָגֵן *shield*, צִנָּה *[large] shield*).
אֶל *at, by*, + יחם *conceive* Gn 30$_{39}$.
עַל *upon* Gn 30$_{37}$.
<COLL> שְׁנֵי מַקְלוֹת *two staffs* Zc 11$_{7}$.
<SYN> חֵץ *arrow*, קֶשֶׁת *bow*, רֹמַח *spear*, נֶשֶׁק *weapons*, מָגֵן *shield*, צִנָּה *(large) shield*.*

מִקְלוֹת 4 pr.n.m. **Mikloth, 1.** Benjaminite, son of Jeiel and Maacah, <SUBJ> ילד hi. *beget* 1 C 8$_{32}$ 9$_{38}$, ישׁב *dwell* 1 C 8$_{32}$. <NOM CL> בְּנוֹ הַבְּכוֹר עַבְדּוֹן ... וּמִקְלוֹת *his firstborn son was Abdon ... then Mikloth* 1 C 8$_{31}$ (if ins. וּמִקְלוֹת) 9$_{37}$.
2. officer of David, <NOM CL> וּמַחֲלֻקְתּוֹ וּמִקְלוֹת הַנָּגִיד perh. *and as for his division, Mikloth was chief officer* 1 C 27$_{4}$ (or del.).

מִקְלָט 20.0.1 n.[m.] **refuge**—cstr. מִקְלַט; sf. מִקְלָטוֹ—**refuge, asylum,** for one who kills a person without intent, <CSTR> מִקְלַט הָרֹצֵחַ *refuge of*, i.e. for, *the killer* Jos 21$_{13.21.27.32.38}$; עָרֵי מִקְלָט *cities of refuge* Nm 35$_{6}$ (הַמִּקְלָט) 35$_{11.13.14}$ Jos 20$_{2}$ 1 C 6$_{42.52}$ (all three הַמִּקְלָט) 4QHalakhah^{a} 2$_{1}$ (ע[וי]ר המקלט), עִיר מִקְלָטוֹ *city of his refuge*, i.e. his city of refuge Nm 35$_{25.26.27.28.32}$, עִיר מִקְלָט *city of the refuge of* Jos 21$_{13.13.27.32.38}$.
<PREP> לְ of benefit, *for*, + היה *be* Nm 35$_{12.15}$ Jos 20$_{3}$.
<COLL> מִקְלָט מִגֹּאֵל *refuge from the avenger* Nm 35$_{12}$, var. Jos 20$_{3}$.*

*[מִקְלִיחַ] 0.0.1 pr.n.[m.] **Makliah,** name in writing exercise, 4QNames$_{5}$.

[מִקְלַעַת] 4 n.f. **carving**—cstr. מִקְלַעַת; pl. מִקְלָעוֹת; cstr. מִקְלְעוֹת—<NOM CL> אֶרֶז ... מִקְלַעַת פְּקָעִים וּפְטוּרֵי צִצִּים *the cedar was (in the form of) ... carving of gourds and open flowers* 1 K 6$_{18}$, עַל־פִּיהָ מִקְלָעוֹת *at its mouth there were carvings* 1 K 7$_{31}$. <OBJ> קלע *carve* 1 K 6$_{32}$.
<CSTR> מִקְלַעַת פְּקָעִים וּפְטוּרֵי צִצִּים *carving of gourds and open flowers* 1 K 6$_{18}$, מִקְלְעוֹת כְּרוּבִים וְתִמֹרֹת וּפְטוּרֵי צִצִּים *carvings of cherubim and palms and open flowers* 1 K 6$_{29.32}$; פִּתּוּחֵי מִקְלָעוֹת *engraved decorations (consisting) of carvings of* 1 K 6$_{29}$.
⇒ קלע *carve*.

*[מִקְמְיָהוּ] 0.0.0.1 pr.n.m. **Mekimiah,** father of Nahum, <CSTR> בן מקמיהו *son of Mekimiah* Bulla D64.
⇒ קום *rise* + י׳ *Y*.

*[מִקְמָשׁ] n.[m.] **pile,** <CSTR> מִקְמַשׁ חָרוּל *a heap of wild vetch* Zp 2$_{9}$ (if em. מִמְשַׁק *ground of*).

*[מֶקֶן] 0.0.0.1 pr.n.[m.] **Meken,** <PREP> לְ of possession, *of, (belonging) to* Seal 735 (9th/8th cent.).

מִקְנָה 15.1 n.f. **purchase**—cstr. מִקְנַת; sf. מִקְנָתוֹ—**1. purchase, person or thing purchased,** <SUBJ> מול ni. *be circumcised* Gn 17$_{12.13.27}$, אכל *eat* Ex 12$_{44}$. <OBJ> מול *circumcise* Ex 12$_{44}$. <CSTR> מִקְנַת־כֶּסֶף *purchase of*, i.e. one purchased for, *money* Gn 17$_{12.27}$ Ex 12$_{44}$ (כָּסֶף), מִקְנַת כַּסְפֶּךָ *purchase of your money* Gn 17$_{13}$, כַּסְפּוֹ *of his money* Gn 17$_{23}$; סֵפֶר הַמִּקְנָה *deed of purchase* Jr 32$_{11.12(Qr^{Or})}$ (L הַסֵּפֶר) 32$_{12.14.16}$, שְׂדֵה מִקְנָתוֹ *field of his purchase*, i.e. purchased by him Lv 27$_{22}$, כָּל־מִקְנַת

every purchase of Gn 17$_{23}$. <APP> אִישׁ *man* Gn 17$_{27}$, בֵּן *son* Gn 17$_{12}$, זָכָר *male* Gn 17$_{12.23}$, עֶבֶד *servant* Ex 12$_{44}$, סֵפֶר *deed* appar. Jr 32$_{12}$. <PREP> עַל *on account of*, + בושׁ *be ashamed* Si 42$_{4}$ (+ בין רב למעט *whether much or little*). <COLL> מִקְנָה :: יְלִיד *one who is born* Gn 17$_{12.13.23.27}$.

2. possession (though purchase), <PREP> לְ *as*, + קום *arise*, i.e. pass over to Gn 23$_{18}$.

3. purchase price, <OBJ> רבה hi. *increase* Lv 25$_{16}$, מעט hi. *reduce* Lv 25$_{16}$. <CSTR> כֶּסֶף מִקְנָתוֹ *money of his purchase price* Lv 25$_{51}$.

<ANT> §1 יְלִיד *one who is born.*

⇒ קנה *acquire.*

מִקְנֶה I 76.0.6 n.m. **cattle**—cstr. מִקְנֵה; sf. מִקְנֶךָ, מִקְנֵהוּ, מִקְנֵנוּ, תִּקְנְךָ; pl. cstr. מִקְנֵי; pl. sf. מִקְנֶיךָ, Q מקנינו, מִקְנֵיכֶם, מִקְנֵיהֶם, (מִקְנֵהֶם, Q מקניהמה)—**(possessions consisting of) cattle, livestock,** usu. of cows and sheep in herds and flocks, but also camels (Ex 9$_{3}$ Jb 1$_{3}$ 1 C 5$_{21}$), horses (Ex 9$_{3}$), asses (Ex 9$_{3}$ Jb 1$_{3}$ 1 C 5$_{21}$); **(purchased) property** (Gn 49$_{32}$; or em.; see Cstr.) or goods,* including servants (Jb 1$_{3}$).

<SUBJ> היה *be* Gn 26$_{14.14}$ 30$_{29}$ Nm 32$_{1.26}$ Jb 1$_{3}$ Ec 2$_{7}$ 2 C 26$_{10}$, רבה *be many* 1 C 5$_{9}$, נגד hi. *tell* perh. Jb 36$_{33}$ (or em. מְקַנֵּא *the one who arouses jealousy*), זכר ni. *be remembered* appar. Ex 34$_{19}$ (or em. תִּזָּכֵר to הַזָּכָר *male*; Sam^{mss} זכר hi. *mention*), רעה *graze* Is 30$_{23}$, שׁתה *drink* Nm 20$_{19}$ 2 K 3$_{17}$, ישׁב *dwell* Dt 3$_{19}$ Jos 1$_{14}$, הלך *go* Ex 10$_{26}$, עלה *go up* Ex 12$_{38}$ Jg 6$_{5}$, אסף ni. *be gathered* Gn 29$_{7}$, פרץ *break out*, i.e. increase Jb 1$_{10}$ 4Q418 126.2$_{15}$, מות *die* Ex 9$_{6}$.

<NOM CL> וּמִקְנֵיהֶם ... הֲלוֹא לָנוּ הֵם *as for their cattle ... will they not be ours?* Gn 34$_{23}$, לִי ... מִקְנְךָ *to me are ... your cattle* Ex 34$_{19}$ (if em.; see Subj.), לַעֲבָדֶיךָ מִקְנֶה *to your servants are cattle* Nm 32$_{4}$, מִקְנֶה רַב לָכֶם *there is to you much cattle* Dt 3$_{19}$, מִקְנֵה הַבְּהֵמָה אֶל־אֲדֹנִי *the livestock is to my lord*, i.e. at his disposal Gn 47$_{18}$, מִקְנְךָ אֲשֶׁר בַּשָּׂדֶה *your cattle that are in the field* Ex 9$_{3}$.

<OBJ> בוא hi. *bring* Gn 47$_{17}$, עוז hi. *bring into safety* Ex 9$_{19}$, נוס hi. *cause to flee* Ex 9$_{20}$, יהב *give* Gn 47$_{16}$, סגר hi. *hand over* Ps 78$_{48}$ 4QParGenEx 3$_{9}$, שׂים *place* Jg 18$_{21}$, לקח *take* Gn 36$_{6}$ 46$_{6}$ Ezk 38$_{13}$ 1 C 7$_{21}$, נצל hi. *snatch* Gn 31$_{9}$, בזז *plunder* Nm 31$_{9}$, שׁבה *capture* 1 C 5$_{21}$, רכשׁ *collect* Gn 31$_{18}$, עשׂה *make*, i.e. acquire Ezk 38$_{12}$ 2 C 32$_{29}$, נהג *drive* Gn 31$_{18.18}$ 1 S 23$_{5}$, עזב *leave* Ex 9$_{21}$, זכר hi. *mention* Ex 34$_{19}$(Sam^{mss}), מות hi. *kill* Ex 17$_{3}$.

<CSTR> מִקְנֵה יִשְׂרָאֵל *cattle of Israel* Ex 9$_{4.7}$, מִצְרַיִם *of Egypt* Ex 9$_{4.6}$, ־אַבְרָם *of Abram* Gn 13$_{7}$, ־לוֹט *of Lot* Gn 13$_{7}$, אֲבִיכֶם *of your father* Gn 31$_{9}$, בְּנֵי *of the sons of* Israel Ex 9$_{6}$.

מִקְנֵה בָקָר *cattle (consisting) of herds* Gn 26$_{14}$ 47$_{17}$ (הַבָּקָר) 2 C 32$_{29}$ (מִקְנֵה־ ...), צֹאן *of flocks* Gn 26$_{14}$ 47$_{17}$ (הַצֹּאן) 2 C 32$_{29}$, הַבְּהֵמָה *of the beasts* Gn 47$_{18}$, קִנְיָנוֹ *of his acquisition*, i.e. acquired by him Gn 31$_{18}$, מִקְנֵה הַשָּׂדֶה וְהַמְּעָרָה *the property purchased (consisting) of the field and the cave* Gn 49$_{32}$ (or em. מִקְנַת *purchase of*).

אַנְשֵׁי מִקְנֶה *men of cattle* Gn 46$_{32.34}$, שָׂרֵי *overseers of* Gn 47$_{6}$ 1 C 28$_{1}$ (שָׂרֵי ...), רֹעֵי מִקְנֵה *herders of the cattle of* Gn 13$_{7}$, קוֹל מִקְנֶה *sound of cattle* Jr 9$_{9}$, המון מקנה *multitude of cattle* 1QM 12$_{12}$, הֲמוֹן מִקְנֵיהֶם *multitude of their cattle* Jr 49$_{32}$, אָהֳלֵי מִקְנֶה *tents of cattle* Gn 4$_{20}$ (if em. אֹהֶל וּמִקְנֶה *tent and cattle*) 2 C 14$_{14}$, אֶרֶץ *land of* Nm 32$_{4}$, מְקוֹם *place of* Nm 32$_{1}$.

כֹּל מִקְנֵה *all the cattle of* Ex 9$_{6}$, כָּל־מִקְנֵהוּ *all his cattle* Gn 31$_{18}$, כָּל־מִקְנֵהֶם *all their cattle* Gn 47$_{17}$ Nm 31$_{9}$.

<APP> סוּס *horse* Ex 9$_{3}$, חֲמוֹר *ass* Ex 9$_{3}$ 1 C 5$_{21}$, גָּמָל *camel* Ex 9$_{3}$ 1 C 5$_{21}$, בָּקָר *herd* Ex 9$_{3}$ 12$_{38}$ Ec 2$_{7}$, צֹאן *flock* Ex 9$_{3}$ 12$_{38}$ Ec 2$_{7}$ 1 C 5$_{21}$, פֶּטֶר *firstborn* Ex 34$_{19}$, נֶפֶשׁ *soul*, i.e. person 1 C 5$_{21}$.

<ADJ> רַב *many* Nm 32$_{1}$ Jos 22$_{8}$ 2 C 26$_{10}$, עָצוּם *numerous* Nm 32$_{1}$, כָּבֵד *heavy*, i.e. numerous Ex 12$_{38}$, זָכָר *male* Ex 34$_{19}$ (if em.; see Subj.), הוּא *that* 1 S 30$_{20}$.

<PREP> לְ of benefit, *for* Jos 14$_{4}$ 4QapJoshua^{a} 19.2$_{6}$, + היה *for* Ezk 45$_{4}$ (if em. מִקְדָּשׁ לַמִּקְדָּשׁ *a sacred place for the sanctuary* to מִגְרָשׁ לְמִקְנֶה *land outside city wall for cattle*), עשׂה *make* booths Gn 33$_{17}$, בנה *build* fence Nm 32$_{16}$.

בְּ of place, *among* 4QRitMar 9$_{5}$; of accompaniment, *with*, + שׁוב *go back* Jos 22$_{8}$, רום htpol. *exalt oneself* 1QH 10$_{25}$ (appar. אמקנה is error for במקנה); *in respect of* Gn 13$_{2}$ (+ כָּבֵד *heavy*, i.e. rich); of price, *(in exchange) for*, + נתן *give* Gn 47$_{16.17}$, נהל pi. *refresh* with food Gn 47$_{17}$; *against*, + היה *be* Ex 9$_{3}$.

מִן partitive, *from (among), (some) of*, + מות *die* Ex $9_{6.7}$.

אֵת *with*, + היה *be* Gn 34_5.

לִפְנֵי *before*, + נהג *drive* 1 S 30_{20}.

מִפְּנֵי *on account of*, + נשׂא *bear* Gn 36_7.

בֵּין *between*, + פלה hi. *separate* Ex 9_4.

<COLL> מִקְנֶה || בְּהֵמָה *beast* Gn 34_{23} 36_6 Nm 31_9 32_{26} 2 K 3_{17} 4QParGenEx 3_9, בְּעִיר *beast* Ps 78_{48}.

+ בָּקָר *herd* 1 S 30_{20} Jb 1_3, צֹאן *flock* 1 S 30_{20} Jb 1_3, גָּמָל *camel* Jr 49_{32} Jb 1_3, אָתוֹן *she-ass* Jb 1_3, מִרְמָשׂ *reptile* 4QRitMar 9_5, כָּל־אֲשֶׁר לְךָ בַּשָּׂדֶה *all that you have in the field* Ex 9_{19}.

|| אִשָּׁה *wife* Nm 32_{26} Dt 3_{19} Jos 1_{14}, בֵּן *son* Ex 17_3, טַף *infants* Nm 31_9 $32_{16.26}$ Dt 3_{19} Jos 1_{14} Jg 18_{21}, עֶבֶד *slave* Ex $9_{20.21}$, עֲבֻדָּה *service*, i.e. household servants Gn 26_{14} Jb 1_3.

|| קִנְיָן *acquisition* Gn 34_{23} 36_6 Jos 14_4 Ezk $38_{12.13}$ 1QH 10_{25}, רְכֻשׁ *property* Gn 31_{18} 46_6 1 C 28_1 2 C 32_{29} (+), חַיִל *wealth* Nm 31_9, נְכָסִים *riches* Jos 22_8, כְּבוּדָּה *property* Jg 18_{21}, שָׁלָל *plunder* Ezk 38_{13} (+).

|| זָהָב *gold* Gn 13_2 Jos 22_8 Ezk 38_{13} 1QM 12_{12} (both +), כֶּסֶף *silver* Gn 13_2 47_{18} (+) Jos 22_8 Ezk 38_{13} 1QM 12_{12} (both +), נְחֹשֶׁת *bronze* Jos 22_8, בַּרְזֶל *iron* Jos 22_8, אֶבֶן precious *stone* 1QM 12_{12} (+), שַׂלְמָה *garment* Jos 22_8, עִיר *city* 2 C 32_{29} (+).

אֲבִי יֹשֵׁב אֹהֶל וּמִקְנֶה *ancestor of whoever dwells in a tent and (among) cattle* Gn 4_{20} (or em.; see Cstr.), מִקְנֵה הַשָּׂדֶה וְהַמְּעָרָה מֵאֵת בְּנֵי־חֵת *the property purchased from the sons of Heth (consisting) of the field and the cave* Gn 49_{32} (or em.; see Cstr.), כָּל־רְכוּשׁ וּמִקְנֶה לַמֶּלֶךְ וּלְבָנָיו *all the property and cattle of the king and his sons* 1 C 28_1.

<SYN> בְּהֵמָה *beast*, בְּעִיר *beast*, אִשָּׁה *wife*, בֵּן *son*, טַף *infants*, עֶבֶד *slave*, עֲבֻדָּה *service*, קִנְיָן *acquisition*, רְכֻשׁ *property*, כְּבוּדָּה *property*, חַיִל *wealth*, נְכָסִים *riches*, זָהָב *gold*, כֶּסֶף *silver*, נְחֹשֶׁת *bronze*, בַּרְזֶל *iron*, שַׂלְמָה *garment*.*

⇒ קנה *acquire*.

מִקְנֵיָהוּ 2.0.0.6 pr.n.m. **Mikneiah**—I מקניו—**1.** Levite, musician at time of David, <SUBJ> נצח pi. *supervise* 1 C 15_{21}. <NOM CL> מִקְנֵיָהוּ ... עִמָּהֶם *with them were ... Mikneiah* 1 C 15_{18}. <APP> אָח *brother* 1 C 15_{18}.

2. Arad ost. 60_4.

3. son of Jehomalach (or of Jehucal), <APP> בֵּן *son* Seal 162 (Palestine, 7th cent.). <PREP> לְ of possession, *of, (belonging) to* Seal 162 (Palestine, 7th cent.).

4. appar. father of Zaphan, Seal 654 (T. Beit Mirsim?, 7th/6th cent.).

5. Seal $272_{1.3}$ (8th cent.) (both מקניו), <APP> עֶבֶד *servant* of Y. Seal $272_{1.3}$ (both 8th cent.). <PREP> לְ of possession, *of, (belonging) to* Seal 272_3 (8th cent.).

6. appar. father of Ahimelech, Bulla D26.

⇒ קנה *acquire* + ׳י Y.

מִקְנִיו, see מִקְנֵיָהוּ *Mikneiah*.

*[**מִקְנְמֶלֶךְ**] 0.0.0.2 pr.n.m. **Miknemelech, 1.** father of Temachel, <CSTR> בן מקנמלך *son of Miknemelech* Seal 318 (7th cent.).

2. Seal 609 (T. Beit Mirsim?, 7th/6th cent.), <PREP> לְ of possession, *of, (belonging) to* Seal 609 (T. Beit Mirsim?, 7th/6th cent.).

⇒ קנה *acquire* + מלך *be king*.

מִקְסָם 2 n.[m.] **divination**—cstr. מִקְסַם—<SUBJ> היה *be* Ezk 12_{24} (|| חָזוֹן *vision*). <OBJ> אמר *speak* Ezk 13_7 (|| מַחֲזֶה *vision*), מלא *be full of* Is 2_6 (if em. מִקֶּדֶם *from the east*). <CSTR> מִקְסַם חָלָק *divination of flattery* Ezk 12_{24}, כָּזָב *of a lie* Ezk 13_7. <ADJ> חָלָק *smooth* Ezk $12_{24 (mss)}$ (מִקְסָם חָלָק).

<SYN> חָזוֹן *vision*, מַחֲזֶה *vision*.

⇒ קסם *practise divination*.

מָקַץ 1 pl.n. **Makaz,** one of Solomon's administrative centres, perh. in the Shephelah, <PREP> בְּ of place, *in* 1 K 4_9.

מִקְצוֹעַ, see מִקְצֹעַ *corner*.

מִקְצֹעַ 12.0.11 n.m. **corner**—מִקְצוֹעַ; cstr. מִקְצֹעַ; pl. מִקְצֹעֹת (Q מקצועות); cstr. מִקְצְעֹת (מקצועות), מִקְצוֹעֵי; sf. מִקְצְעוֹתָיו—**1. corner (piece)** of altar (Ex 26_{24}||36_{29} Ezk 41_{22}), tabernacle (Ex 26_{23}||36_{28}, if em.; see Cstr.).

2. **corner** of pool (3QTr 2_{13} perh. 11_{1}), of staircase tower in temple complex (11QT $30_{8.8}$), gatehouse of temple court (11QT 36_{3}), side chambers of temple court (11QT $36_{7.7}$ 44_{11}), **(inner) corner, angle** of court (Ezk $46_{21.21.21.22}$ 11QT 36_{12} 37_{13}).

3. perh. pl.n. **the Angle**, a corner in the wall of Jerusalem (Ne $3_{19.20.24.25}$ 2 C 26_{9}).

<NOM CL> מִקְצֹעֹתָיו לוֹ *its corner pieces were to it* Ezk 41_{22}, המקצוע אשר אצל בני יהודה *the corner that is next to the sons of Judah* 11QT 44_{11}.

<CSTR> מִקְצֹעַ הֶחָצֵר *corner of the court* Ezk $46_{21.21}$, מִקְצוֹעֵי *corners of* Ezk 46_{21}, מִקְצֹעוֹת *corners of* Ezk 46_{22} 11QT 37_{13} (מקצועות), מְקֻצְעֹת הַמִּשְׁכָּן *corners of the tabernacle* Ex 26_{23}||36_{28} (if em. מְקֻצְעֹת *corners of*, i.e. קצע pu. ptc.).

<ADJ> שֵׁנִי *second* 11QT 36_{12}, צְפוֹנִי *northern* 3QTr 2_{13}, המזרחי צפונה *north-eastern* 11QT^b 10_{6} (ב]מקצ[וע]).

<PREP> לְ *as* or introducing predicate, + היה *be* Ex 26_{24}; of benefit, *for*, + עשׂה *make* Ex 26_{23}||36_{28} (if em.; see Cstr.) 36_{29}.

בְּ of place, *in* Ezk $46_{21.21.22}$ 3QTr 11_{1} 11QT^b 10_{6} (ב]מקצ[וע]), + חפר *dig* 3QTr 2_{13}.

מִן of direction, *from* 11QT 30_{8} $36_{3.7}$ 44_{11}, + חזק hi. *repair* Ne 3_{20}.

אֶל *to* 11QT 30_{8} 36_{7}, + עבר hi. *cause to pass* Ezk 46_{21}.

עַל *at*, + בנה *build* towers 2 C 26_{9}.

עַד *to*, + חזק hi. *repair* Ne 3_{24}.

מִנֶּגֶד *from opposite*, + חזק hi. *repair* Ne 3_{25}.

<COLL> פִּנָּה + מִקְצֹעַ *corner* Ne 3_{24} 11QT 36_{12}; הַנֶּשֶׁק הַמִּקְצֹעַ *the armoury at the angle* Ne 3_{19}, המקצוע השני לחצר *the second (inner) corner of the court* 11QT 36_{12}; שְׁנֵי הַמִּקְצֹעֹת *the two corners* Ex 26_{24}||36_{29}, ארבעת מקצועות *(the) four corners* 3QTr 11_{1}, אַרְבַּעַת מִקְצוֹעֵי *the four corners of* Ezk $46_{21.22}$ (מִקְצֹעֹת) 11QT 37_{13} (מקצועות).

Also 11QT^b 32_{1}.

⇒ קצע *have corners.*

[מַקְצֻעָה] I $_{1}$ n.f. **knife** (unless מַקְצֻעָה II *square*)—pl. מַקְצֻעוֹת—**knife, scraping tool,** for shaping wood, <PREP> בְּ of instrument, *by (means of), with*, + עשׂה *make* Is 44_{13} (+ שֶׂרֶד *stylus*, מְחוּגָה *compass*).*

⇒ קצע I *scrape.*

*[מַקְצֻעָה] II $_{1}$ n.f. **square** (unless מַקְצֻעָה I *knife*)—pl. מַקְצֻעוֹת—**square,** for working with wood, <PREP> בְּ of instrument, *by (means of), with*, + עשׂה *make* Is 44_{13} (+ שֶׂרֶד *stylus*, מְחוּגָה *compass*).

⇒ קצע II *make a corner.*

מִקְצָת, see קְצָת *end.*

מקק $_{10}$ vb. **rot—Ni.** $_{9}$ Pf. נָמַקּוּ; impf. 3fs תִּמַּק, יִמַּקּוּ, 3fpl תִּמַּקְנָה; + waw וְנָמַקּוּ, וְנְמַקֹּתֶם; ptc. נְמַקִּים—**1. rot, decay,** <SUBJ> צבא *host* of heaven Is 34_{4}, עַיִן *eye* Zc 14_{12}, לָשׁוֹן *tongue* Zc 14_{12}, בָּשָׂר *flesh* Zc 14_{12} (if em. הָמֵק *causing* his flesh *to rot* to הָמֵק יִמַּק *it will utterly rot*). <PREP> בְּ of place, *in*, + חֹר *hole*, i.e. socket, of eye Zc 14_{12}, פֶּה *mouth* Zc 14_{12}.

2. fester, <SUBJ> מָתְנַיִם *loins* Ps 44_{20} (if em. בִּמְקוֹם תַּנִּים *in the place of jackals* to בְּמֹק מָתְנַיִם *with festering of loins*), לְחִי *jaw* Ps 102_{6} (if em. לַחְמִי: מִקּוֹל אַנְחָתִי *my bread. Because of the sound of my groaning* to לְחָיַי יִמַּקּוּ לְאַנְחָתִי *my jaws fester from my groaning*),* חַבּוּרָה *wound* Ps 38_{6} (|| באשׁ hi. *stink*). <PREP> מִפְּנֵי *on account of*, + אִוֶּלֶת *folly* Ps 38_{6}.

3. pine away, <SUBJ> אִישׁ *man* Ezk 4_{17} (+ שׁמם ni. *be appalled*), אָח *brother* Ezk 4_{17}, שׁאר ni. ptc. *one who remains* Lv $26_{39.39}$, בַּיִת *house* of Israel Ezk 24_{23} 33_{10}. <PREP> בְּ of place, *in*, + אֶרֶץ *land* Lv 26_{39}; of cause, *on account of*, + עָוֹן *iniquity* Lv $26_{39.39}$ Ezk 4_{17} 24_{23}, חַטָּאת *sin* Ezk 33_{10}, פֶּשַׁע *transgression* Ezk 33_{10}.

<SYN> §2 באשׁ hi. *stink.*

Hi. $_{1}$ Inf. abs. הָמֵק—**cause to rot,** <SUBJ> Y. Zc 14_{12} (or em. הָמֵק יִמַּק *it* [flesh] *will utterly rot*, i.e. ni.). <OBJ> בָּשָׂר *flesh* Zc 14_{12} (or em.; see Subj.).

Perh. **Haphtil** $_{1}$ Impf. 3fs תַּמְתִּיק—**putrefy** (unless מתק hi. *cause sweetness*), <SUBJ> רָעָה *evil* Jb 20_{12}. <PREP> בְּ of place, *in*, + פֶּה *mouth* Jb 20_{12}.*

⇒ מַק *rottenness.*

מִקְרָא $_{23.0.14}$ n.m. **convocation**—cstr. מִקְרָא; sf. Q מקראם; pl. cstr. מִקְרָאֵי; sf. מִקְרָאֶיהָ—**1. convocation, assembly,** on the sabbath and other sacred days;

perh. **place of assembly** (Is 4$_{5}$ Ps 68$_{27}$ [if em.; see Cstr.]), **day of assembly** (Is 1$_{13}$)*, <SUBJ> היה *be* Ex 12$_{16.16}$ Lv 23$_{7.21.24.27.36}$ Nm 28$_{25.26}$ 29$_{1.7.12}$ 11QT 19$_{8}$ ([מקרא]) 25$_{3}$ ([מן]קרא ... יהיה[]) 27$_{8}$. <NOM CL> אֵלֶּה ... מִקְרָאֵי קֹדֶשׁ *these are ... the holy convocations* Lv 23$_{4}$, בַּיּוֹם הַשְּׁבִיעִי ... מִקְרָא־קֹדֶשׁ *on the seventh day shall be ... a holy convocation* Lv 23$_{3.8}$, vars. Lv 23$_{35}$ Nm 28$_{18}$ 11QT 17$_{10}$. <OBJ> קרא *proclaim* Lv 23$_{2.4.37}$.

<CSTR> מִקְרָא־קֹדֶשׁ *convocation of holiness*, i.e. holy convocation Ex 12$_{16.16}$ Lv 23$_{3+7t}$ Nm 28$_{18.25.26}$ 29$_{1.7.12}$ 4QOrd[b] 3$_{1}$ ([קודש]) 11QT 17$_{10}$ ([קו]דש]) 19$_{8}$ ([מקרא קודש]) 25$_{3}$ ([מן]קרא קודש]) 27$_{8}$ 11QT[b] 7$_{24}$ (both קודש), מִקְרָאֵי קֹדֶשׁ *convocations of holiness*, i.e. holy convocations Lv 23$_{2.4.37}$, מִקְרָאֵי יִשְׂרָאֵל *assemblies of Israel* Ps 68$_{27}$ (if em. מְקוֹר *source of*); קְרֹא מִקְרָא *proclaiming of convocation(s)* or *festival(s)** Is 1$_{13}$. <APP> מוֹעֵד *appointed feast* Lv 23$_{4}$, שַׁבָּת *sabbath* Lv 23$_{3}$, שַׁבָּתוֹן *solemn rest* Lv 23$_{24}$, זִכְרוֹן *memorial* Lv 23$_{24}$. <PREP> מִן *from*, + ברך pi. *bless* Ps 68$_{27}$ (if em.; see Cstr.); עַל *over*, + ברא *create* Is 4$_{5}$ (+ מָכוֹן *site* of Mount Zion).

2. as verbal noun, **assembling, summoning,** <CSTR> מקרא העדה *summoning of the congregation* 1QM 3$_{2}$, השרים *of the commanders* 1QM 3$_{3}$, אנשי הבנים *of the men of the interval*, i.e. skirmishers 1QM 3$_{7}$; חצוצרות המקרא *trumpets of summoning* 1QM 7$_{13.15}$ 8$_{3}$ 9$_{3}$ 16$_{12}$ (חצ[ו]צרות) (המקר[א]) 4QM[a] 10.2$_{11}$ ([חצוצרות]) 4QM[c] 1$_{0}$, מקראם *of their summoning* 1QM 3$_{1}$, מקרא *of summoning of* 1QM 3$_{2.3.7}$. <PREP> לְ of benefit, *for*, + היה *make* Nm 10$_{2}$. <COLL> מִקְרָא הָעֵדָה *summoning the congregation* Nm 10$_{2}$ (+ מַסַּע אֶת־ הַמַּחֲנוֹת *breaking the camps*).

3. reading, what is read, <PREP> בְּ introducing object, + בין *understand* Ne 8$_{8}$.

Also 4QRP[b] 15$_{4}$.*

⇒ קרא *call*.

*[מִקְרָה] 0.0.5 n.f. **beam-work**—sf. Q מקראה; cstr. Q מקרת; pl. sf. Q מקרותיו—**beam-work, rafter** (cf. מְקָרֶה *beam-work*), <NOM CL> מקרותיו כבית הכיות *its rafters shall be like (those of) the house of the laver* 11QT 33$_{9}$. <CSTR> מקרת שני עשר העמודים *beam-work of the twelve columns* 11QT 34$_{15}$, הגג *of the roof* 11QT 39$_{2}$, גגו *of its roof* 11QT 36$_{6}$ ([מ]קרת גגו[ן]); גובה המקרה *height of the beam-work* 11QT 36$_{10}$. <PREP> מִן of direction, *from*, + ירד *go down* 11QT 34$_{15}$; עַד *to* 11QT 36$_{6}$ ([עד] [מ]קרת) 39$_{2}$.

Also 11QT 5$_{6}$.

⇒ קרה *lay beams*.

מִקְרֶה 10.0.2 n.m. **accident**—cstr. מִקְרֵה (מִקְרֶה); sf. מִקְרֶהָ—**1. accident, chance,** <SUBJ> היה *be* 11QT 45$_{7}$ 46$_{18}$, קרה *chance upon* Ru 2$_{3}$ (וַיִּקֶר מִקְרֶהָ חֶלְקַת הַשָּׂדֶה *her chance came upon*, i.e. by chance she came upon, *the plot of land*). <NOM CL> מִקְרֶה הוּא *it is an accident* 1 S 20$_{26}$. <CSTR> מקרה לילה *accident of the night*, i.e. emission of semen 11QT 45$_{7}$. <COLL> מִקְרֶה הוּא הָיָה לָנוּ *it has happened to us by chance* 1 S 6$_{9}$.

2. fate, fortune, <SUBJ> קרה *befall* Ec 2$_{14}$. <NOM CL> מִקְרֶה אֶחָד לָהֶם *there is one fate to them*, i.e. they have the same fate Ec 3$_{19}$, vars. Ec 9$_{2.3}$. <CSTR> מִקְרֵה הַכְּסִיל *fate of the fool* Ec 2$_{15}$, מִקְרֶה בְנֵי־הָאָדָם *fate of the sons of human beings* Ec 3$_{19}$, הַבְּהֵמָה *of the beasts* Ec 3$_{19}$. <ADJ> אֶחָד *one* Ec 2$_{14}$ 3$_{19}$ 9$_{2.3}$. <PREP> כְּ *as, according to*, + קרה *befall* Ec 2$_{15}$.

Also perh. 4QT 25$_{8}$.

⇒ קרה *befall*.

*[מְקָרָה] n.f. **living room,** <CSTR> עֲלִיַּת הַמְּקָרָה *upper chamber of the living room* Jg 3$_{20}$ (if em. הַמְּקֵרָה *of coolness*).

מְקָרֶה 1 n.m. **beam-work, rafter** (cf. מִקְרָה *beam-work*), of roof, ceiling, <SUBJ> מכך ni. *sink in* Ec 10$_{18}$.

⇒ קרה *lay beams*.

מְקֵרָה 2 n.f. **coolness** or **cool place, summer palace,*** <CSTR> חֲדַר הַמְּקֵרָה *chamber of the coolness*, i.e. the cool chamber Jg 3$_{24}$, עֲלִיַּת *upper chamber of* Jg 3$_{20}$ (or em. הַמְּקָרָה *of the living room*).*

קרר *be cold*.

*[מְקַרְקַר] 1 n.[m.] **echoing shout**—cstr. מְקַרְקַר—**echoing shout, echo sound** (unless קרר ptc. pilp. *tear down*), <NOM CL> לַאדֹנָי י׳ צְבָאוֹת ... מְקַרְקַר קִר *to*

my Lord, Y. of hosts is the echoing sound of a clamour Is 22$_5$. <CSTR> מְקַרְקַר קִר *the echoing sound of a clamour* Is 22$_5$.

*[מִקְרָשׁ] n.[m.] **frame,** <CSTR> מִקְרַשׁ עֶרֶשׂ *frame of a bed* Am 3$_{12}$ (if em. דְּמֶשֶׁק appar. *damask of*). <PREP> בְּ of place, *on*, + ישׁב *sit* Am 3$_{12}$ (if em.; see Cstr.).
⇒ cf. קֶרֶשׁ *board.*

מִקְשָׁה I$_{9.1}$ n.f. **hammered work,** of cherubim (Ex 25$_{18}$ 37$_7$), lampstand (Ex 25$_{31.36}$||37$_{17.22}$ Nm 8$_{4.4}$), trumpets (Nm 10$_2$ Si 50$_{16}$), setting for apples of gold (Pr 25$_{11}$; if em.; see Cstr.), <NOM CL> כֻּלָּהּ מִקְשָׁה אַחַת *the whole of it shall be one piece of hammered work* Ex 25$_{36}$|| 37$_{22}$, זֶה מַעֲשֵׂה הַמְּנֹרָה מִקְשָׁה *this is the work of the lampstand,* i.e. how it was made, *hammered work* Nm 8$_4$, מִקְשָׁה הִיא *it was hammered work* Nm 8$_{4(Qr)}$. <CSTR> מִקְשָׁיוֹת כֶּסֶף *hammered work of silver* Pr 25$_{11}$ (if em. מַשְׂכִּיּוֹת *images of silver*); חצוצרות מקשה *trumpets of hammered work* Si 50$_{16}$. <APP> זָהָב *gold* Ex 25$_{36}$||37$_{22}$ Nm 8$_4$, כֶּסֶף *silver* Nm 10$_2$. <ADJ> אֶחָד *one* Ex 25$_{36}$|| 37$_{22}$. <PREP> בְּ of place, *in* Pr 25$_{11}$ (if em.; see Cstr.). <COLL> מִקְשָׁה תַּעֲשֶׂה אֹתָם *you shall make them of hammered work* Ex 25$_{18}$ Nm 10$_2$, vars. Ex 37$_{7.17}$, מִקְשָׁה תֵּעָשֶׂה הַמְּנוֹרָה *the lampstand shall be made of hammered work* Ex 25$_{31}$.

מִקְשָׁה II$_2$ n.f. **cucumber field,** <CSTR> תֹּמֶר מִקְשָׁה *post of,* i.e. scarecrow in, *a cucumber field* Jr 10$_5$. <PREP> בְּ of place, *in* Is 1$_8$ (|| כֶּרֶם *vineyard*).
<SYN> כֶּרֶם *vineyard.*

מִקְשֶׁה $_1$ n.[m.] **locks of hair,** <APP> מַעֲשֶׂה מִקְשֶׁה *work, locks of hair,* i.e. well-dressed hair Is 3$_{24}$ (or del. מַעֲשֶׂה; :: קָרְחָה *baldness*). <PREP> תַּחַת *instead of,* + היה *be* Is 3$_{24}$ (if del. em.; see App.).
<ANT> קָרְחָה *baldness.**

מַר I$_{38.3.1}$ adj. **bitter**—מָר; cstr. מַר; f.sg. מָרָה; cstr. מָרַת; m.pl. מָרִים; cstr. מָרֵי—**bitter, poisonous*** (Ps 64$_4$), **1a.** attributively of גּוֹי *nation* Hb 1$_6$ (unless מַר II *strong*), נֶפֶשׁ *soul* Jb 21$_{25}$, זְעָקָה *cry* Est 4$_1$, צְעָקָה *cry* Gn 27$_{34}$, מִסְפֵּד *mourning* Ezk 27$_{31}$, עֳנִי *affliction* 2 K 14$_{26}$ (if em. מֹרֶה to הַמַּר), דָּבָר *word* Ps 64$_4$, יוֹם *day* Am 8$_{10}$ Zp 1$_{14}$ (if em.; see §2a).

1b. (1) מַר־נֶפֶשׁ *bitter of soul,* i.e. embittered, attributively of אִישׁ *man* 1 S 22$_2$.

(2) מָרֵי נֶפֶשׁ *bitter of soul,* i.e. angry (unless מַר II *strong*), attributively of אִישׁ *man* Jg 18$_{25}$, הֵמָּה *they* 2 S 17$_8$.

2a. predicatively of קוֹל *sound* of day of Y. Zp 1$_{14}$ (or em. הַמַּר *of the bitter* day), זֵכֶר *remembrance* Si 41$_{1(M, Yadin)}$ (מה מר [ז]כרך *how bitter is the remembrance of you*), אַחֲרִית *end* Pr 5$_4$ (|| חַד *sharp*), רָעָה *evil* Jr 4$_{18}$ (זֹאת רָעָתֵךְ כִּי מָר *this is [the result of] your evil; surely it is bitter;* or em. מַר כִּי *bitter; surely* to מֶרְיֵךְ *your rebelliousness* has reached), הֵם *they* Ex 15$_{23}$ (מַיִם *waters*), מָה *what?* 4Q416 2.3$_{15}$ (:: מָתוֹק *sweet*), עזב inf. *forsaking* Jr 2$_{19}$ (רַע וָמַר עָזְבֵךְ אֶת־י׳ *your forsaking of Y. is evil and bitter*).

2b. מָרַת נֶפֶשׁ *bitter of soul,* i.e. embittered, predicatively of הִיא *she* 1 S 1$_{10}$ (Hannah).

3. as adverb, **a. bitterly, in bitterness,** (1) מַר + בכה *weep* Is 33$_7$, הלך *go* Ezk 3$_{14}$ (unless מַר II *strong;* + בַּחֲמַת רוּחִי *in the wrath of my spirit*), appar. ברך pi. *bless* Si 41$_{1(B)}$ (מה [מ]ר יברך *how bitterly does one bless;* M [ז]כרך how bitter is *your remembrance*).

(2) מָרָה + זעק *cry* Ezk 27$_{30}$.

b. as complement to object, מוֹצֶא אֲנִי מַר מִמָּוֶת אֶת־הָאִשָּׁה *I find the woman more bitter than death* Ec 7$_{26}$ (unless מַר II *strong*).

4. as noun, **a. bitter one,** <SUBJ> צעק *cry* Si 4$_6$. <OBJ> דאב hi. *cause to languish* Si 4$_1$ (+ עָנִי *afflicted one*). <CSTR> מר נפש *one bitter of soul* Si 4$_1$, מָרֵי נֶפֶשׁ *ones bitter of soul* Jb 3$_{20}$ (+ עָמֵל *sufferer*) Pr 31$_6$ (unless מַר II *strong;* or em. מָרִי *bitter one,* i.e. with archaic gen. ending;* + אבד ptc. *one perishing*), מר רוח *one bitter of spirit* Si 4$_6$. <PREP> לְ of direction, *to,* + נתן *give* Jb 3$_{20}$ Pr 31$_6$.

b. bitterness, bitter thing, (1) מַר, <SUBJ> סור *turn aside,* i.e. depart 1 S 15$_{32}$. <NOM CL> לְשָׁלוֹם מַר לִי מָר *for the sake of (my) welfare there was to me bitterness (upon) bitterness* Is 38$_{17}$ (for מָר 1QIsa[a] reads מאודה *much*), כָּל־מַר מָתוֹק *every bitter thing is sweet*

Pr 27₇. <OBJ> שׂים *place* Is 5₂₀ (:: מָתוֹק *sweet[ness]*). <CSTR> מַר־נֶפֶשׁ *bitterness of soul* Ezk 27₃₁, נַפְשִׁי *of my soul* Is 38₁₅ Jb 7₁₁ (|| צַר *distress*) 10₁, מר רוח *bitterness of spirit* Si 7₁₁, מַר־הַמָּוֶת *bitterness of death* 1 S 15₃₂; כָּל־מַר *every bitter thing* Pr 27₇. <PREP> לְ *as* + שׂים *place* Is 5₂₀ (:: מָתוֹק *sweet[ness]*); בְּ of accompaniment, *with, in* Si 7₁₁, + בכה *weep* Ezk 27₃₁, דבר *speak* Jb 10₁, שׂיח *complain* Jb 7₁₁; עַל *in*, + דדה htp. *go* Is 38₁₅ (or em. דדה to נדד *toss about*, or ידה hi. *give thanks* despite).

(2) מָרָה, <SUBJ> היה *be* 2 S 2₂₆.

(3) מָרִים, <CSTR> מֵי הַמָּרִים *waters of bitterness*, used in an ordeal* Nm 5₁₈.₁₉ (both + ארר pi. *effect curse*) 5₂₃.₂₄ (unless §4c or from מָרָה II *instruction* or מָרָה *disputed matter*; + ארר pi.) 5₂₇ (if em. הַמַּיִם *the waters* to מֵי הַמָּרִים). <PREP> לְ *for, as a cause of*, + בוא *enter* Nm 5₂₄.₂₇.

c. perh. specif. **illness,*** <PREP> לְ *for, as (a cause of)*, + בוא *enter* Nm 5₂₄ (unless §4b).

<SYN> §2a חַד *sharp*; §4b צַר *distress*.

<ANT> §2a מָתוֹק *sweet*; §4b מָתוֹק *sweet(ness)*.*

⇒ מרר I *be bitter*.

*מַר II ₉ adj. **strong** (unless מַר I *bitter*), **1a.** attributively of גּוֹי *nation* Hb 1₆, מַר I *bitterness* Is 38₁₇ (הִנֵּה לְשָׁלוֹם מַר־לִי מָר *it was for (my) good that I had strong bitterness*).

b. מָרֵי נֶפֶשׁ *strong of soul*, i.e. tough, attributively of אִישׁ *man* Jg 18₂₅, הֵמָּה *they* 2 S 17₈.

c. מָרֵי נָפֶשׁ *strong of soul, i.e. warriors* Pr 31₆ (וְיַיִן לְמָרֵי נָפֶשׁ *and give wine to the warriors*).

2. used predicatively, as complement to object, מוֹצֶא אֲנִי מַר מִמָּוֶת אֶת־הָאִשָּׁה *I find the woman stronger than death* Ec 7₂₆.

3. as noun, **strength, power, vigour,** <CSTR> מַטּוֹת אֶמַּר *arrows of power* Hb 3₉ (מַר with preformative aleph; if em. אֹמֶר *of speech*), יָמַי *days of* Ps 102₂₃ (if em. יָמַי: אֹמַר *my days. I say*).

4. as adverb, **strengthened,** + הלך *go* Ezk 3₁₄ (+ בַּחֲמַת רוּחִי *in the wrath of my spirit*).

מַר III ₁ n.[m.] **drop** (unless מַר IV *dust*), <PREP> כְּ *as* Is 40₁₅ (+ שַׁחַק *dust*, דַּק *fine one*, i.e. dust). <COLL> מַר מִדְּלִי *a drop from a bucket* Is 40₁₅ (or em. מִדְּלִי to מִדֶּל *of a cloud/thunderbolt*).

*מַר IV ₁ n.[m.] **dust** (unless מַר III *drop*), <PREP> כְּ *as* Is 40₁₅ (+ שַׁחַק *dust*, דַּק *fine one*, i.e. dust). <COLL> מַר מִדְּלִי *dust*, i.e. droplets, *of the balances* Is 40₁₅ (if em. מִדְּלִי appar. *from a bucket*).

*מַר V ₂ n.[m.] **abortion,** <CSTR> מֵי הַמָּרִים *waters of*, i.e. that cause an, *abortion* Nm 5₁₈.₂₄ (unless מרר IV ptc. *flowing*).

מֹר I ₁₂ n.m. **myrrh**—מוֹר; cstr. מָר־; sf. מוֹרִי—a fragrant resin, in non-religious use burned as incense (Ca 3₆) or powdered and kept in a perfume bag around the neck (Ca 1₁₃), or mixed with oil as a perfume for clothes (Ps 45₉) or bed (Pr 7₁₇), or as massage (Est 2₁₂); in a religious context, as an ingredient of oil for anointing tabernacle furniture (Ex 30₂₃), <SUBJ> עבר *pass*, i.e. flow Ca 5₅.₁₃ (both מוֹר עֹבֵר *flowing myrrh*). <NOM CL> מֹר ... כָּל־בִּגְדֹתֶיךָ *all your garments are ... myrrh* Ps 45₉. <OBJ> נוף *sprinkle* Pr 7₁₇ (as second obj.; + מִשְׁכָּב *bed*), ארה *pluck* Ca 5₁, נטף *drip* Ca 5₅.₅.₁₃. <CSTR> מָר־דְּרוֹר *myrrh of flowing* or perh. *of pearls*,* i.e. as solidified drops or lumps Ex 30₂₃; צְרוֹר הַמֹּר *bag of myrrh* Ca 1₁₃, שֶׁמֶן *oil of* Est 2₁₂, קְטֹרֶת *smoke of* Ca 3₆ (מוֹר; if em.; see Coll.), הַר *mountain of* Ca 4₆ (הַמּוֹר). <APP> בֹּשֶׂם *spice* Ex 30₂₃, פְּרִי *fruit* Ca 4₁₄. <PREP> עִם *with* Ca 4₁₄.

<COLL> בֹּשֶׂם || קְצִיעָה *cassia* Ps 45₉, אָהָל *aloe* Ps 45₉ Pr 7₁₇ Ca 4₁₄, לְבוֹנָה *frankincense* Ca 3₆ 4₆.₁₄ (+); + בֹּשֶׂם *spice* Ca 5₁ Est 2₁₂, קִנָּמוֹן *cinnamon* Ex 30₂₃ Pr 7₁₇ Ca 4₁₄, קִדָּה *cassia* Ex 30₂₃, נֵרְדְּ *nard* Ca 4₁₄, כֹּפֶר *henna* Ca 4₁₄, כַּרְכֹּם *saffron* Ca 4₁₄, קָנֶה aromatic *cane* Ex 30₂₃ Ca 4₁₄, תַּמְרוּק *ointment* Est 2₁₂, שֶׁמֶן *oil* Ex 30₂₃.

מְקֻטֶּרֶת מוֹר לְבוֹנָה *burned in myrrh (and) frankincense* Ca 3₆ (or em. מִקְּטֹרֶת rising up *from the smoke of* myrrh).

<SYN> קְצִיעָה *cassia*, אָהָל *aloe*, לְבוֹנָה *frankincense*.*

*מֹר II n.[m.] **foam,** <CSTR> מֹר יָם *foam of the sea* Ho

11$_4$ (if em. מְרִימֵי *ones who raise,* i.e. רום hi.). <PREP> כְּ *as,* + היה *be* Ho 11$_4$ (if em.; see Cstr.).

מרא I 1.0.1 vb. **be rebellious—Qal** 1 Ptc. מֹרְאָה—**be rebellious,** <SUBJ> עִיר *city* Zp 3$_1$ (unless from מֻרְאָה *crissum, excrement;* or em. מֹרָה *rebellious;* || גאל ni. *be defiled*).

<SYN> גאל ni. *be defiled.*

Hi. 0.0.1 Impf. Q ימרא—**provoke,** <SUBJ> אִישׁ *man* CD 11$_{12}$ (=4QD^f 5.1$_7$ ימר, i.e. מרה hi.). <OBJ> עֶבֶד *servant* CD 11$_{12}$, אָמָה *female servant* CD 11$_{12}$, שׂכר ptc. *hired labourer* CD 11$_{12}$. <PREP> בְּ of time, *on,* + שַׁבָּת *sabbath* CD 11$_{12}$.

⇒ cf. מרה *be rebellious.*

מרא II 1 vb. **beat, strike** (unless מרא IV *act the man*) —**Hi.** 1 Impf. 3fs תַּמְרִיא—**beat** the air with wings, i.e. **flap** wings, or **strike** the ground with foot, <SUBJ> רְנָנָה *female ostrich* Jb 39$_{18}$ (or em. רְנָנִים to יְעֵנִים *ostriches*). <PREP> בְּ of place, *in, on,* + מָרוֹם *height* Jb 39$_{18}$.*

***[מרא] III** vb. **graze, feed on the fat of the land,** <SUBJ> עֵגֶל *calf* Is 11$_6$ (if em. וּמְרִיא *and the fatling* to יִמְרְאוּ *they will graze;* cf. 1QIsa^a ימרו), כְּפִיר *young lion* Is 11$_6$ (if em.; see above). <COLL> מרא + adverb, יַחְדָּו *together* Is 11$_6$ (if em.; see Subj.).

⇒ מְרִיא *fatling.*

***מרא IV** 1 vb. **act the man** (unless מרא II *beat strike*) —**Hi.** 1 Impf. 3fs תַּמְרִיא—**act the man,** of ostrich speeding across the desert instead of caring for her chicks, <SUBJ> רְנָנָה *female ostrich* Jb 39$_{18}$ (or em. רְנָנִים to יְעֵנִים *ostriches*). <PREP> בְּ of accompaniment, *with,* + מָרוֹם *height,* i.e. proudly Jb 39$_{18}$.

מָרָא 1 pr.n.f. **Mara**—mss מָרָה—**1.** as name for Naomi, lit. 'bitterness' or 'bitter one', <OBJ> קרא *call,* i.e. name Ru 1$_{20}$.

2. Seal 208 (En-Gedi, 6th cent.; others נרא *Neriah;* others נרת *Narath*), <PREP> לְ of possession, *of, (belonging) to* Seal 208 (En-Gedi, 6th cent.).

⇒ מרר I *be bitter.*

מְרֹאדַךְ בַּלְאֲדָן, see מְרֹדַךְ בַּלְאֲדָן *Merodach-baladan.*

מַרְאָה 12.0.6 n.f. **vision; mirror**—cstr. מַרְאוֹת (מַרְאֹת)—**1. vision,** as means of revelation, <NOM CL> מַרְאוֹת כַּמַּרְאֶה appar. *(there were) visions like the vision* that I had seen Ezk 43$_3$ (or del. מַרְאוֹת). <OBJ> ראה *see* Ezk 1$_1$ Dn 10$_{7.7.8}$, נגד hi. *tell* 1 S 3$_{15}$. <CSTR> מַרְאוֹת אֱלֹהִים *visions of God* Ezk 1$_1$ 8$_3$ 40$_2$, מראת כב[ו]ד *visions of glory,* i.e. glorious visions 1QLitPr 3.2$_6$, מַרְאֹת הַלַּיְלָה *visions of the night* Gn 46$_2$, מראת [הסנה] *vision of the bush* 4QParGenEx 3$_4$. <ADJ> גָּדוֹל *great* Dn 10$_8$, זֹאת *this* Dn 10$_8$. <PREP> בְּ *in* or of instrument, *by (means of), with,* + אמר *say* Gn 46$_2$, ראה ni. *appear* 4QParGen Ex 3$_4$ ([ויראה]), ידע htp. *make oneself known* Nm 12$_6$, בוא hi. *bring* Ezk 8$_3$ 40$_2$, חדש pi. *renew* 1QLitPr 3.2$_6$; of cause, *on account of,* + הפך ni. *come upon* Dn 10$_{16}$. <COLL> מַרְאָה || חֲלוֹם *dream* Nm 12$_6$; + דָּבָר *word* 1QLit Pr 3.2$_6$.

2. mirror, <CSTR> מַרְאֹת הַצֹּבְאֹת *mirrors of the serving women* Ex 38$_8$, מראת פנים *mirror of a face,* i.e. face mirror 1QM 5$_{5.11}$; מעשה מראת *work of a mirror of* 1QM 5$_5$. <PREP> בְּ *from, out of,* + עשׂה *make* Ex 38$_8$; כְּ *as,* + לבן pu. *be made white* 1QM 5$_{11}$.

<SYN> §1 חֲלוֹם *dream.*

Also 4QparaKings 105$_3$.*

⇒ ראה *see.*

מַרְאֶה 103.6.22 n.m. **sight**—cstr. מַרְאֵה (Q מראי); sf. Qr מַרְאֵךְ, מַרְאֵהוּ, מַרְאֶהָ; pl. cstr. Q מראי; appar. pl. (but prob. sg.) sf. מַרְאַיִךְ, מַרְאָיו, מַרְאֵינוּ, מַרְאֵיהֶם, מַרְאֵיהֶן—**1. appearance, visible form, figure, countenance,** <SUBJ> ראה ni. *be seen* Dn 1$_{13.13.15}$, בחר pass. *be chosen,* i.e. choice Ca 5$_{15}$, כסה pi. *cover* Nm 9$_{16}$, שׁחת ho. *be spoilt* Is 52$_{14}$ (if em. מִשְׁחַת *disfigurement* to מָשְׁחַת).

<NOM CL> מִשְׁחַת מֵאִישׁ מַרְאֵהוּ *his appearance was a disfigurement,* i.e. disfigured, *beyond (that of) a human* Is 52$_{14}$ (or em.; see Subj.), מַרְאֵה שָׁלִשִׁים כֻּלָּם *all of them were,* i.e. had, *the appearance of officers* Ezk 23$_{15}$, לֹא מַרְאֶה *there was (to him) no (such) form* that we should desire him Is 53$_2$, זֶה מַרְאֵיהֶן *this was their appearance* Ezk 1$_5$, הִיא מַרְאֵה דְּמוּת כְּבוֹד־י׳ *it was the*

appearance of the likeness of the glory of Y. Ezk 1$_{28}$, מַרְאַיִךְ נָאוֶה *your countenance is comely* Ca 2$_{14}$, מַרְאֵיהֶן רַע *their appearance was bad* Gn 41$_{21}$, מַרְאֵה הַנֶּגַע עָמֹק מֵעוֹר בְּשָׂרוֹ *the appearance of the plague spot is deeper than the skin of his body* Lv 13$_3$, sim. Lv 13$_{20.25.30}$ 14$_{37}$, אֵין־מַרְאֵהוּ עָמֹק מִן־הָעוֹר *its appearance is not deeper than the skin* Lv 13$_{31}$, sim. Lv 13$_{4.32.34}$.

מַרְאֵה כְּבוֹד י׳ כְּאֵשׁ אֹכֶלֶת *the appearance of the glory of Y. was like a devouring fire* Ex 24$_{17}$, מַרְאֵיהֶם כְּגַחֲלֵי־אֵשׁ בֹּעֲרוֹת *their appearance was like (that of) burning coals of fire* Ezk 1$_{13}$, מַרְאֵיהֶן כַּלַּפִּידִם *their appearance as like (that of) torches* Na 2$_5$, מַרְאֵהוּ כַּלְּבָנוֹן *his appearance is like (that of) the Lebanon* Ca 5$_{15}$, מַרְאֵהוּ כְּמַרְאֵה מַלְאַךְ הָאֱלֹהִים *his appearance was like that of the angel of God* Jg 13$_6$, מַרְאֵהוּ כְּמַרְאֵה סוּסִים *his appearance was like that of horses* Jl 2$_4$, מַרְאֵהוּ כְּמַרְאֵה נְחֹשֶׁת *his appearance was like that of bronze* Ezk 40$_3$, מַרְאֵה הָאוֹפַנִּים ... כְּעֵין תַּרְשִׁישׁ *the appearance of the wheels was ... like the gleam of beryl* Ezk 1$_{16}$, var. 10$_9$, מַרְאֵיהֶם ... כַּאֲשֶׁר יִהְיֶה הָאוֹפַן בְּתוֹךְ הָאוֹפָן *their appearance was as though a wheel was within a wheel* Ezk 1$_{16}$, כְּמַרְאֵה הַקֶּשֶׁת ... כֵּן מַרְאֵה הַנֹּגַהּ *as the appearance of the bow ... so was the appearance of the brightness* Ezk 1$_{28}$, הַמַּרְאֶה כַּמַּרְאֶה appar. *the appearance was like the appearance* Ezk 41$_{21}$ (or em.; see Cstr.), מַרְאֵיהֶם דְּמוּת אֶחָד לְאַרְבַּעְתָּם *as for their appearance(s), the form of one was to all four of them*, i.e. they all had the same form Ezk 10$_{10}$.

<OBJ> ראה *see* Ezk 10$_{22}$, hi. *show* Nm 8$_4$ Ca 2$_{14}$, נכר hi. *recognize* Jb 4$_{16}$, שׁחר hi. *blacken* Si 25$_{17}$, הפך *change* 4QD^a 6.1$_7$.

<CSTR> מַרְאֵה מַלְאַךְ *appearance of the angel of* Y. Jg 13$_6$, כְּבוֹד *of the glory of* Y. Ex 24$_{17}$, [מר]אי פלא *appearance of wonder*, i.e. wonderful appearance 11QShirShabb 4$_6$, מַרְאֵה אָדָם *appearance of a human being* Ezk 1$_{26}$ Dn 10$_{18}$, מראה איש *appearance of a man* Si 25$_{17}$, מַרְאֵה־גָבֶר *appearance of a man* Dn 8$_{15}$, הַיְלָדִים *of the youths* Dn 1$_{13}$, שָׁלִשִׁים *of officers* Ezk 23$_{15}$, מָתְנָיו *of his loins* Ezk 1$_{27.27}$ 8$_2$, סוּסִים *of horses* Jl 2$_4$.

מַרְאֵה הַנֶּגַע *appearance of the disease* Lv 13$_3$, צָרַעַת *of leprosy* Lv 13$_{43}$, מראי הבשר *appearance of the flesh* 4QD^a 6.1$_2$, מראי שבולת *figures of grain* of gold 1QM 5$_{11}$.

מַרְאֵה דְּמוּת *appearance of the likeness of* Ezk 1$_{28}$, מראי תבנית *appearance of the form of* 4QShirShabb^d 1.2$_3$, שני *of scarlet* 4QShirShabb^f 23.2$_8$, חור *of white* 4QShirShabb^f 23.2$_9$, מַרְאֵה־זֹהַר *appearance of brightness* Ezk 8$_2$ 10$_1$, הַנֹּגַהּ *of the brightness* Ezk 1$_{28}$, ־אֵשׁ *of fire* Nm 9$_{15.16}$ Ezk 1$_{27.27}$ 8$_2$ (or em. אִישׁ *of a man*) 4QShirShabb^f 20.2$_{10}$ (מראי אש), מראי להבי *appearance of flames of* fire 4QShirShabb^f 15.2$_3$, גחלי *of coals of* fire 4QShirShabb^d 1.2$_6$, שבולי *of streams of* fire 4QShirShabb^f 20.2$_{10}$, מַרְאֵה הַלַּפִּידִים *appearance of torches* Ezk 1$_{13}$, הַבָּזָק *of lightning* Ezk 1$_{14}$ (or em. הַבָּרָק *of lightning*), בָּרָק *of lightning* Ezk 1$_{14}$ (הַבָּרָק; if em.; see above) Dn 10$_6$, הַקֶּשֶׁת *of the bow* Ezk 1$_{28}$, הָאוֹפַנִּים *of the wheels* Ezk 1$_{16}$ 10$_9$, אֶבֶן *of a stone of* sapphire Ezk 1$_{26}$, נְחֹשֶׁת *of bronze* Ezk 40$_3$, הַמִּזְבֵּחַ *of the altar* Ezk 41$_{21}$ (if em. כַּמַּרְאֶה: הַמִּזְבֵּחַ *like the appearance. An altar*), הַלְּשָׁכוֹת *of the chambers* Ezk 42$_{11}$.

אִישׁ מַרְאֶה *man of appearance*, i.e. handsome man 2 S 23$_{21(Qr)}$ (or em. אִישׁ מִדָּה *a man of [great] stature*; Kt אשר *whose* appearance), יְפֵה מַרְאֶה *beautiful of*, i.e. in, *appearance* (masc. sing.) 1 S 17$_{42}$ (mss עֵינַיִם *of eyes*) 11QPs^a 28$_9$ (יפי המראה), יְפַת־ *beautiful of* (fem. sing.) Gn 12$_{11}$ 29$_{17}$ 39$_6$ 2 S 14$_{27}$, יְפוֹת *beautiful of* (fem. pl.) Gn 41$_{2.4}$ (יְפֹת הַמַּרְאֶה), טֹבַת *good of* (fem. sing.) Gn 24$_{16}$ 26$_7$ 2 S 11$_2$ Est 1$_{11}$ 2$_{3.7}$, טוֹבֵי *good of* (masc. pl.) Dn 1$_4$, טוֹבוֹת *good of* (fem. pl.) Est 2$_2$, רָעוֹת מַרְאֶה *bad of*, i.e. in, *appearance* Gn 41$_{3.4}$ (הַמַּרְאֶה), כבוד מראי *glory of the appearance*, i.e. glorious appearance, *of* scarlet 4QShirShabb^f 23.8$_8$, יפי מראיה *beauty of her appearance* 4Q418 167$_5$.

<PREP> לְ *in, with respect to* Jos 22$_{10}$ (מִזְבֵּחַ גָּדוֹל לְמַרְאֶה *an altar great in appearance*, i.e. large, conspicuous).

בְּ of cause, *on account of*, + תעב pi. *abhor* Si 11$_2$.

כְּ *as* Lv 13$_{43}$ Jg 13$_6$ Ezk 1$_{13.26.26.27.27}$ 8$_{2.2}$ 10$_1$ 40$_3$ 41$_{21}$ 42$_{11}$ Jl 2$_4$ Dn 8$_{15}$ 10$_{6.18}$ 4QShirShabb^f 20.2$_{10}$, + היה *be* Nm 9$_{15}$, ראה *see* 4QD^a 6.1$_{10}$, רוץ *run* 4QShirShabb^d 1.2$_6$, רצא *run* Ezk 1$_{14}$ (or em. יצא *go out*), שׁוּב *go back* Ezk 1$_{14}$; *according to*, + עשׂה *make* Nm 8$_4$.

אֶל *at*, + נבט hi. *look* 1 S 16$_7$, טול ho. *be thrown down* Jb 41$_1$.

מִן of direction, *from* Ezk 1$_{27.27}$ 8$_{2}$.

בְּתוֹךְ *within* 4QShirShabb[f] 23.2$_{9}$.

<COLL> מַרְאֶה ‖ תֹּאַר *form* Gn 29$_{17}$ 39$_{6}$ Is 52$_{14}$ 53$_{2}$ Est 2$_{7}$ Si 11$_{2}$ 11QPs[a] 28$_{9}$, בָּשָׂר *flesh* Gn 41$_{3.4}$, הָדָר *splendour* Is 53$_{2}$, עַיִן *eye*, i.e. gleam Ezk 1$_{16}$ (+) 1$_{27}$ 8$_{2}$ 10$_{9}$ (+), קוֹל *voice* Ca 2$_{14.14}$, מַעֲשֶׂה *work*, i.e. structure Ezk 1$_{16.16}$.

+ תְּמוּנָה *form* Nm 12$_{8}$ Jb 4$_{16}$, דְּמוּת *likeness* Ezk 1$_{5.13.16.26.28}$ 10$_{10.22}$ 4QShirShabb[f] 20.2$_{10}$, פָּנִים *face* Si 25$_{17}$, גֹּבַהּ קוֹמָתוֹ *the exaltation of his stature* 1 S 16$_{7}$.

מַרְאֶה used adverbially, *clearly*, + דבר pi. *speak* Nm 12$_{8}$ (+ פֶּה אֶל־פֶּה *mouth to mouth*, לֹא בְחִידֹת *not in riddles*).

נִרְאָה מַרְאֵיהֶם טוֹב *their appearance was seen (to be) good* Dn 1$_{15}$.

2. (eye) sight, seeing, <SUBJ> אפס *cease* Si 41$_{2}$ (Bmg) (unless המראה = *rebelliousness*). <NOM CL> טוֹב מַרְאֵה עֵינַיִם מֵהֲלָךְ־נָפֶשׁ *better is sight of the eyes than the wandering of desire* Ec 6$_{9}$. <CSTR> מַרְאֵה עֵינַיִם *sight of the eyes* Ec 6$_{9}$, עֵינֵי *of the eyes of* Lv 13$_{12}$, עֵינֶיהָ *of her eyes* Ezk 23$_{16}$, מַרְאֵי עֵינֶיךָ *sights of your eyes* Ec 11$_{9}$; כָּל־מַרְאֵה *all the sight of* Lv 13$_{12}$. <PREP> לְ *to, in* Gn 2$_{9}$ (נֶחְמָד לְמַרְאֶה *desirable to the sight*) Lv 13$_{12}$; *at*, + עגב *lust* Ezk 23$_{16}$; בְּ *in, according to*, + הלך pi. *walk* Ec 11$_{9}$. <COLL> מַרְאֶה ‖ דֶּרֶךְ *way* Ec 11$_{9}$, תִּקְוָה *hope* Si 41$_{2(Bmg)}$.

3a. sight, thing seen, spectacle, <OBJ> ראה *see* Ex 3$_{3}$ Dt 28$_{34.67}$. <CSTR> מַרְאֵה עֵינֶיךָ *sight of your eyes*, i.e. that which your eyes see Dt 28$_{34.67}$ Si 9$_{7}$, עֵינָיו *of his eyes* Is 11$_{3}$ 4QDivProv 1$_{3}$ (עינו), מראי דמיונים *sight of spectacles* 1QM 6$_{13}$, מראי עו[למים] *sight of everlastingness*, i.e. everlasting sight 4QShirShabb[d] 1.2$_{8}$; חזות מראה *a glimpse of a sight* Si 42$_{22}$, כול מראי *every sight of* 1QM 6$_{13}$. <ADJ> גָּדוֹל *great* Ex 3$_{3}$, זֶה *this* Ex 3$_{3}$. <PREP> לְ *to*, + בעל pass. *be accustomed* 1QM 6$_{13}$; *according to*, + שׁפט *judge* Is 11$_{3}$; בְּ of cause, *on account of*, + נבל htp. *act foolishly* Si 9$_{7}$; מִן of cause, *on account of*, + אמר *say* Dt 28$_{67}$, שׁגע pu. *be made mad* Dt 28$_{34}$; אַחֲרֵי *after*, + הלך *go* 4QDivProv 1$_{3}$ ([ההולך אחר]). <COLL> מַרְאֶה ‖ מִשְׁמָע *hearing* Is 11$_{3}$.

3b. specif. **vision,** <SUBJ> אמר ni. *be told* Dn 8$_{26}$, עלה *go up* Ezk 11$_{24}$. <OBJ> ראה *see* Ezk 8$_{4}$ 11$_{24}$ 43$_{3.3.3}$ Si 49$_{8}$ 4QpsEzek[a] 4$_{5}$, ידע hi. *cause to know* 4QVisSam 1$_{5}$ (הו[דיעני]), בין hi. *cause to understand* Dn 8$_{16}$. <CSTR> מראה האלוהים *vision of God* 4QVisSam 1$_{5}$, כבודך *of your glory* GnzPs 2$_{24}$, הקודש *of holiness*, i.e. holy vision GnzPs 4$_{17}$, מַרְאֵה הַמַּרְאֶה appar. *the vision of the vision* Ezk 43$_{3}$ (or del. כַּמַּרְאֶה), הָעֶרֶב וְהַבֹּקֶר *of the evening and the morning* Dn 8$_{26}$; כבוד מראה *glory of the vision* GnzPs 3$_{26}$. <PREP> בְּ *in* or of instrument, *by (means of), with*, + בוא hi. *bring* Ezk 11$_{24}$ (+ בְּרוּחַ אֱלֹהִים *in the spirit of God*), ראה *see* GnzPs 2$_{7}$ 3$_{11}$ 4$_{17}$; *concerning* Dn 10$_{1}$; introducing object, + בין hi. *understand* Dn 9$_{23}$; כְּ *as* Ezk 8$_{4}$ 43$_{3}$ (or del.) 43$_{3.3}$; עַל *on account of*, + שׁמם htpo. *be appalled* Dn 8$_{27}$. <COLL> מַרְאֶה ‖ דָּבָר *word* Dn 9$_{23}$ 10$_{1}$ (+) GnzPs 2$_{24}$ 3$_{26}$ (+); + מַרְאָה *vision* Ezk 43$_{3}$, נבא pass. ptc. *prophecy* GnzPs 2$_{7}$ 3$_{10}$ 4$_{17}$, רוּחַ *spirit* GnzPs 4$_{17}$.

Also 4QVisSam 3.1$_{6}$ ([מ]ראה) 4QTobit[e] 7.2$_{6}$ ([מ]ראה) 11QShirShabb 5$_{7}$ ([מ]רא[י]).

<SYN> §1 תֹּאַר *form*, בָּשָׂר *flesh*, הָדָר *splendour*, עַיִן *eye*, i.e. gleam, קוֹל *voice*, מַעֲשֶׂה *work*, i.e. structure; §2 דֶּרֶךְ *way*, תִּקְוָה *hope*; §3a מִשְׁמָע *hearing*; §3b דָּבָר *word*.
⇒ ראה *see*.

*[מַרְאָה] n.f. **edict,** <NOM CL> מַרְאַת י׳ טְהוֹרָה *the edict of Y. is pure* Ps 19$_{10}$ (if em.; see Cstr.). <CSTR> מַרְאַת י׳ *edict of Y.* Ps 19$_{10}$ (if em. יִרְאַת: עֵינָיִם *eyes. The fear of* to מַרְאַת: עֵינָי *my eyes. The edict of*).

[מַרְאָה], see מֻרְאָה *crissum, excrement*.

[מֻרְאָה], or [מֹרְאָה] 2 n.f. **crissum, excrement**—sf. מֻרְאָתוֹ—**1. crissum,** area or feathers around the cloaca of a bird* or perh. crop, pouchlike element of the gullet, <OBJ> סור hi. *remove* Lv 1$_{16}$ (+ נוֹצָה *feathers*).

2. excrement, הוֹי מֹרְאָה וְנִגְאָלָה *woe to the excrement and defiled* oppressing city Zp 3$_{1}$ (unless from מרא I *be rebellious*).

מֵרוֹן, see שִׁמְרוֹן מְראוֹן *Shimron-meron*.

מָרֵאשָׁה, see מָרֵשָׁה *Mareshah*.

[מְרַאֲשׁוֹת] 10 n.[f.]pl. **place of head**—pl. cstr. מְרַאֲשֹׁתֵי; sf. מְרַאֲשֹׁתָיו (Kt מראשתו), מְרַאֲשֹׁתֵיכֶם—usu. **place of**

head of one lying down, perh. **head support** (Gn 28$_{11.18}$); **position on head** (Jr 13$_{18}$), <COLL> צַפַּחַת הַמַּיִם מְרַאֲשֹׁתֵי שָׁאוּל *the jar of water at the head of Saul* 1 S 26$_{12}$, צַפַּחַת הַמַּיִם אֲשֶׁר מְרַאֲשֹׁתָיו *the jar of water that was at his head* 1 S 26$_{16(Qr)}$, sim. 1 S 26$_{11}$, הִנֵּה מְרַאֲשֹׁתָיו עֻגַת רְצָפִים *behold, there was at his head a cake baked on hot stones* and a jar of water 1 K 19$_{6}$; וַיָּשֶׂם מְרַאֲשֹׁתָיו *and he put (it) at the place of his head* Gn 28$_{11}$, vars. Gn 28$_{18}$ 1 S 19$_{13.16}$, חֲנִיתוֹ מְעוּכָה־בָאָרֶץ מְרַאֲשֹׁתָיו *his spear was stuck in the ground at his head* 1 S 26$_{7}$; יָרַד מְרַאֲשׁוֹתֵיכֶם עֲטֶרֶת תִּפְאַרְתְּכֶם *your glorious crown has come down from your head* Jr 13$_{18}$ (or em. מֵרָאשֵׁיכֶם or מֵרָאשׁוֹתֵיכֶם *from your heads*).*

מֵרַב 4.0.0.1 pr.n.f. **Merab**—I מירב—**1.** elder daughter of Saul, <SUBJ> נתן ni. *be given* 1 S 18$_{19}$, ילד *bear* 2 S 21$_{8}$ (mss). <NOM CL> שֵׁם הַבְּכִירָה מֵרַב *the name of the first-born was Merab* 1 S 14$_{49}$, הִנֵּה ... מֵרַב *here is ... Merab* 1 S 18$_{17}$. <OBJ> נתן *give* 1 S 18$_{17.19}$. <CSTR> בְּנֵי מֵרַב *sons of Merab* 2 S 21$_{8(mss)}$. <APP> בַּת *daughter* 1 S 18$_{17}$ 2 S 21$_{8(mss)}$.

2. appar. daughter of Ishmael, <PREP> לְ of possession, *of, (belonging) to* Seal 589 (מ[י]רב; T.Beit-Mirsim?, 7th/6th cent.).

3. mother of Oniah, <CSTR> בן מירב *son of Merab* Seal 730 (8th/7th cent.).*

[מַרְבָד] 2 n.[m.] **cover**—pl. מַרְבַדִּים—for couch (Pr 7$_{16}$), <OBJ> רבד *deck with* Pr 7$_{16}$, עשׂה *make* Pr 31$_{22}$. <APP> חֲטֻבוֹת *multicoloured cloth* of Egyptian linen Pr 7$_{16}$.

⇨ רבד *deck.*

מִרְבָּה 1 n.f. **much,** <OBJ> כול hi. *contain* Ezk 23$_{32}$ (or em. מַרְבָּה *it makes much,* i.e. רבה hi.).

⇨ רבה *be much.*

מַרְבֶּה 2 n.[m.] **abundance**—cstr. מַרְבֵּה—**1. abundance,** used adverbially, **in abundance,** with חלק pu. *be divided* (of spoil) Is 33$_{23}$ (or em. to pi. *divide;* 1QIsa^{a} מרובה *much,* i.e. רבה pu. ptc.).

2. increase, <CSTR> מַרְבֵּה הַמִּשְׂרָה *increase of dominion* Is 9$_{6}$ (or em.; see Prep.). <PREP> לְ of possession, *of, (belonging) to* Is 9$_{6}$ (or em. לָמוֹ רַבָּה *to him dominion is great,* i.e. he bears great dominion, or לוֹ מַרְבָּה *to him* dominion *is increased;* 1QIsa^{a} למ רבה).*

⇨ רבה *be much.*

מַרְבִּית 5 n.f. **increase**—cstr. מַרְבִּית; sf. מַרְבִּיתָם—**1. increase,** in ref. to descendants, <SUBJ> מות *die* 1 S 2$_{33}$. <CSTR> כָּל־מַרְבִּית בֵּיתְךָ *all the increase of your house* 1 S 2$_{33}$.

2. interest, perh. specifically on a loan of food,* **profit,** <PREP> בְּ of price, *(in exchange) for,* + נתן *give* food Lv 25$_{37}$ (|| נֶשֶׁךְ *interest*).

3. majority (1 C 12$_{29}$), **multitude** (2 C 30$_{18}$), <SUBJ> שׁמר *keep* 1 C 12$_{29}$, טהר htp. *purify oneself* 2 C 30$_{18}$, אכל *eat* 2 C 30$_{18}$. <CSTR> מַרְבִּית הָעָם *multitude of the people* 2 C 30$_{18}$ (+ רַבַּת *many*). <PREP> עַל *for,* + פלל htp. *pray* 2 C 30$_{18}$.

4. greatness, <CSTR> חֲצִי מַרְבִּית חָכְמָתְךָ *half of the greatness of your wisdom* 2 C 9$_{6}$.

<SYN> §2 נֶשֶׁךְ *interest.*

Also perh. 4Q523 1$_{6}$ (מ[ר]בית).*

⇨ רבה *be much.*

מרבעל, see מְרִיב בַּעַל *Merib-baal.*

מַרְבֵּץ 2.0.1 n.[m.] **resting place**—cstr. מַרְבַּץ—of beasts, <CSTR> מַרְבַּץ־צֹאן *resting place of sheep* Ezk 25$_{5}$ (|| נָוֶה *pasture*), מרבץ בקר *resting place of cattle* Is 65$_{10}$ (1QIsa^{a}) (MT רֵבֶץ *resting place of;* || נָוֶה). <PREP> לְ as or introducing predicate, + היה *be* Zp 2$_{15}$, נתן *give,* i.e. make into Ezk 25$_{5}$. <APP> שַׁמָּה *desolation* Zp 2$_{15}$. <COLL> מַרְבֵּץ לַחַיָּה *a resting place for (wild) beasts* Zp 2$_{15}$.

<SYN> נָוֶה *pasture.*

⇨ רבץ *lie down.*

מַרְבֵּק 4.1 n.[m.] **stall, 1. stall,** for fattening calves, <CSTR> עֵגֶל־מַרְבֵּק *calf of the stall,* i.e. fatted calf 1 S 28$_{24}$, עֶגְלֵי *calves of* Jr 46$_{21}$ Ml 3$_{20}$. <PREP> מִתּוֹךְ *from (out of)* Am 6$_{4}$ (|| צֹאן *flock*).

2. fattening, <OBJ> כלה pi. *finish* Si 38$_{26}$.

<SYN> §1 צֹאן *flock.*

מַרְגּוֹעַ $_{1}$ n.[m.] **(place of) rest,** <OBJ> מצא *find* Jr 6$_{16}$ (+ לְנַפְשְׁכֶם *for your soul*). <PREP> לְ of direction, *to*, + הלך *go* Jr 31$_{2}$ (if em. לְהַרְגִּיעוֹ *to give him rest* to לְמַרְגִּיעוֹ *to his rest*).

⇒ רגע *be at rest.*

[מַרְגְּלוֹת] $_{5}$ n.[f.]pl. **place of feet**—pl. sf. מַרְגְּלֹתָיו (Kt מרגלתו)—**place of feet** of one lying down, **feet,** <NOM CL> מַרְגְּלֹתָיו כְּעֵין נְחֹשֶׁת קָלָל *his feet were as the gleam of burnished bronze* Dn 10$_{6}$ (‖ זְרוֹעַ *arm*, + עַיִן *eye*, פָּנִים *face*, גְּוִיָּה *body*). <OBJ> גלה pi. *uncover* Ru 3$_{4.7}$. <COLL> אִשָּׁה שֹׁכֶבֶת מַרְגְּלֹתָיו *a woman was lying at his feet* Ru 3$_{8}$, var. Ru 3$_{14}$.

<SYN> זְרוֹעַ *arm.*

⇒ רגל *go about.*

*[**מַרְגָּלִית**] $_{0.0.1}$ n.f. **jewel**—pl. Q מרגליות—<APP> חֵפֶץ *delight* GnzPs 2$_{29}$. <PREP> בְּ of place, *in*, + צרר *bind* stone Pr 26$_{8}$ (if em. בְּמַרְגֵּמָה *in a sling*); מִן of comparison, *than* GnzPs 2$_{29}$.

מַרְגֵּמָה I $_{1}$ n.f. **sling** (unless מַרְגֵּמָה II *heap of stones*), <PREP> בְּ of place, *in*, + צרר *bind* stone Pr 26$_{8}$ (or em. בְּמַרְגָּלִית *in a jewel*).

⇒ רגם *stone.*

***מַרְגֵּמָה** II $_{1}$ n.f. **heap of stones** (unless מַרְגֵּמָה I *sling*), <PREP> בְּ of place, *in* Pr 26$_{8}$ (כִּצְרוֹר אֶבֶן בְּמַרְגֵּמָה *like a pebble* [צְרוֹר] *in a heap of stones*; or em. בְּמַרְגָּלִית *in a jewel*).

⇒ רגם *stone.*

מַרְגֵּעָה n.f. **(place of) rest,** <NOM CL> זֹאת הַמַּרְגֵּעָה *this is the rest* Is 28$_{12}$ (‖ מְנוּחָה *rest*).

<SYN> מְנוּחָה *rest.*

⇒ רגע *be at rest.*

מרד $_{25.2.4}$ vb. **rebel—Qal** $_{25.2.4}$ Pf. מָרַד, מָרַדְתָּ, מָרְדוּ (מָרָדְנוּ, מָרַדְנוּ (מָרֶדוּ)); impf. Si יִמְרוֹד, תִּמְרְדוּ (תִּמְרֹדוּ); + waw וַיִּמְרֹד (וַיִּמְרָד־), וַיִּמְרְדוּ; ptc. מֹרְדִים (מוֹרְדִים), מֹרְדֵי; inf. מְרֹד (מְרוֹד, מָרְדְכֶם)—**rebel (against), revolt,** <SUBJ> Israelites Dn 9$_{5.9}$ Ne 2$_{19}$, Jews Ne 6$_{6}$, Gadites Jos 22$_{16.18.19.19.29}$, Reubenites Jos 22$_{16.18.19.19.29}$, חֲצִי *half* of tribe of Manasseh Jos 22$_{16.18.19.19.29}$, עַם *people* Jr 2$_{31}$ (if em. רַדְנוּ *we have roamed* to מָרַדְנוּ *we have rebelled*), גּוֹי *nation* Ezk 2$_{3.3}$, עֵדָה *congregation* Nm 14$_{9}$, Hezekiah 2 K 18$_{7.20}$‖Is 36$_{5}$, Jehoiakim 2 K 24$_{1}$, Jeroboam 2 C 13$_{6}$, Nehemiah Ne 6$_{6}$, Zedekiah 2 K 24$_{20}$‖Jr 52$_{3}$‖2 C 36$_{13}$, אִישׁ *man* 1QpHab 8$_{11}$, אָב *father* Ne 9$_{26}$, בֵּן *son* 2 K 18$_{7}$ 2 C 13$_{6}$, of Israel Ezk 2$_{3.3}$, עֶבֶד *servant* 2 C 13$_{6}$ Si 20$_{36}$, נָסִיךְ *prince* Si 16$_{7(B)}$ (A מרה *be rebellious*), כֹּהֵן *priest* 1QpHab 8$_{16}$, זֶרַע *seed* of royalty Ezk 17$_{15}$, אֵלֶּה *these* Gn 14$_{4}$, כֹּל *all* CD 8$_{4}$ (=4QD^{a} 3.4$_{2}$ מוררים, i.e. ptc. of מרר II *rebel* or pl. of מָרֹר *bitter plague*); subj. not specified, Ezk 20$_{38}$ Jb 24$_{13}$.

<OBJ> בֵּן *son* of Israel Jos 22$_{19}$, אוֹר *light* Jb 24$_{13}$ (מֹרְדֵי־אוֹר *ones who rebel of*, i.e. against, *the light*; or em. אוֹר to אֵל *God*).

<PREP> בְּ *against* 4QPrFêtes^{c} 233$_{2}$ (מ]רדנו]), + Y. Nm 14$_{9}$ Jos 22$_{16.18.19.29}$ Ezk 2$_{3}$ Dn 9$_{9}$ Ne 9$_{26}$ 1QpHab 8$_{11}$, Nebuchadnezzar 2 K 24$_{1}$ 2 C 36$_{13}$, מֶלֶךְ *king* 2 K 18$_{7.20}$‖Is 36$_{5}$ 2 K 24$_{1.20}$‖Jr 52$_{3}$‖2 C 36$_{13}$ Ezk 17$_{15}$.

בְּ of accompaniment, *with*, *in*, + גְּבוּרָה *might* Si 16$_{7(B)}$.

עַל *against*, + מֶלֶךְ *king* Ne 2$_{19}$, אָדוֹן *lord* 2 C 13$_{6}$.

<COLL> מרד ‖ פשׁע *transgress* Ezk 2$_{3}$(+) 20$_{38}$, חטא *sin* Dn 9$_{5}$, עוה *commit iniquity* Dn 9$_{5}$, רשׁע hi. *do wickedly* Dn 9$_{5}$; + מרה hi. *be rebellious* Ne 9$_{26}$, מעל *act treacherously* Jos 22$_{16}$, שׁוב מֵאַחֲרֵי *go back from (following) after* Jos 22$_{29}$, סור *turn aside* Dn 9$_{5}$.

:: עבד *serve* Gn 14$_{4}$ 2 K 18$_{7}$.

+ noun used adverbially, הַיּוֹם *today* Jos 22$_{16.18}$, שָׁנָה *year* Gn 14$_{4}$ (שְׁלֹשׁ־עֶשְׂרֵה שָׁנָה מָרָדוּ *[in] the thirteenth year they rebelled*).

אַל־תִּמְרֹדוּ בִּבְנֹתְכֶם לָכֶם מִזְבֵּחַ *do not rebel by building an altar for yourselves* Jos 22$_{19(mss)}$, var. Jos 22$_{16}$, וַיִּמְרָד־בּוֹ לִשְׁלֹחַ מַלְאָכָיו *and he rebelled against him by sending his messengers* Ezk 17$_{15}$.

<SYN> פשׁע *transgress*, חטא *sin*, עוה *commit iniquity*, רשׁע hi. *do wickedly*.

<ANT> עבד *serve.**

⇒ מֶרֶד I *rebellion*, II *Mered*, מַרְדּוּת I *rebelliousness.*

מֶרֶד I $_{1.0.1}$ n.[m.] **rebellion,** against Y., <PREP> בְּ of

accompaniment, *with, in* Jos 22_{22} (|| מַעַל *unfaithful act*); of cause, *on account of*, + שׁלח htp. *be sent away* 4QDa 11_{7} (unless בְּ of accompaniment, *[being] in rebellion, let him be sent*).
<SYN> מַעַל *unfaithful act.**
⇨ מרד *rebel.*

מֶ֫רֶד II 2 pr.n.m. **Mered**—מֶ֫רֶד—Judahite, son of Ezrah and husband of Pharaoh's daughter, Bithiah, <SUBJ> לקח *take (in marriage)* 1 C 4_{18}. <NOM CL> בְּנֵי עֶזְרָה ... מֶרֶד *the sons of Ezrah were ... Mered* 1 C $4_{17(\text{Seb, mss})}$ (L בֶּן־ *son of*). <PREP> לְ of possession, *of, (belonging) to* 1 C 4_{18} (if ins. וּלְמֶרֶד *and to Mered* were two wives, an Egyptian wife and a Jewish wife).
⇨ מרד *rebel.*

מרדוף, see מִרְדָּף *pursuit.*

מַרְדּוּת I 1 n.f. **rebelliousness,** <CSTR> נַעֲוַת הַמַּרְדּוּת *perverse one* (fem.) *of rebelliousness*, i.e. perverse, rebellious woman 1 S 20_{30}.*
⇨ מרד *rebel.*

*[**מַרְדּוּת**] II 0.2 n.f. **chastisement**—cstr. Si מרדות—**chastisement, discipline,** <NOM CL> מרדות מלאכה [לע]בד *the chastisement of work is for a slave* Si 30_{33} (Segal). <CSTR> מרדות פותה וכסיל *chastisement of the simple one and the fool* Si $42_{8(\text{Bmg})}$ (B מוסר *chastisement of*), מלאכה *of work* Si 30_{33}. <PREP> עַל *on account of*, + בושׁ *be ashamed* Si $42_{8(\text{Bmg})}$.
⇨ רדה *rule.*

[**מְרֹדַךְ**] pr.n.m. **Merodach**—מְרֹדַךְ—Marduk, god of Babylon, <SUBJ> חתת *be dismayed* Jr 50_{2} (+ בֵּל *Bel*).
⇨ מְרֹדַךְ בַּלְאֲדָן *Merodach-baladan*, אֱוִיל מְרֹדַךְ *Evil-merodach*, מָרְדֳּכַי *Mordecai.*

מְרֹדַךְ בַּלְאֲדָן 2 pr.n.m. **Merodach-baladan**—mss מְרֹאדַךְ בַּלְאֲדָן (1QIsaa מרודך בלאדן)—son of Baladan and king of Babylon at time of Hezekiah, 2 K $20_{12(\text{mss})}$|| Is 39_{1} (2 K L בְּרֹאדַךְ בַּלְאֲדָן *Berodach-baladan*), <SUBJ> שׁלח *send* 2 K $20_{12(\text{mss})}$||Is 39_{1}, שׁמע *send* 2 K $20_{12(\text{mss})}$|| Is 39_{1}. <APP> בֵּן *son* 2 K $20_{12(\text{mss})}$||Is 39_{1}, מֶלֶךְ *king* 2 K $20_{12(\text{mss})}$||Is 39_{1}.
⇨ מְרֹדַךְ *Merodach.*

מָרְדֳּכַי 60 pr.n.m. **Mordecai**—מָרְדֳּכַי—**1.** uncle (or cousin) and adoptive father of Esther, <SUBJ> אמר *say* Est 4_{13}, דבר *speak* Est 10_{3}, pi. Est 7_{9}, נגד hi. *tell* Est 2_{22} 3_{4} 4_{7} 6_{2}, צוה pi. *command* Est $2_{10.20}$ 8_{9}, זעק *cry* Est 4_{1}, שׁמע *hear* Est 3_{4}, ידע *know* Est 2_{11} 4_{1}, כתב *write* Est $9_{20.23.29}$, רצה pass. *be favoured* Est 10_{3}, דרשׁ *seek* Est 10_{3}, זוע *tremble* Est 5_{9}, הלך *go* Est 9_{4}, htp. Est 2_{11}, בוא *come* Est 4_{1} 8_{1}, יצא *go out* Est 4_{1} 8_{15}, עבר *pass* Est 4_{17}, *transgress* Est 3_{3}, שׁוב *go back* Est 6_{12}, שׁלח *send* Est 9_{20}, קום *rise* Est 5_{9}, pi. *confirm* Est 9_{29}, *impose obligation* Est $9_{20.31}$, ישׁב *sit* Est $2_{19.21}$ 5_{13} 6_{10}, כרע *bow down* Est $3_{2.5}$, שׁחה htpal. *prostrate oneself* Est $3_{2.5}$, לקח *take*, i.e. adopt Est $2_{5.16}$, קבל pi. *accept* Est 4_{4}, קרע *tear* Est 4_{1}, לבשׁ *put on* Est 4_{1}, עשׂה *do* Est 4_{17}.

<NOM CL> שְׁמוֹ מָרְדֳּכַי *his name was Mordecai* Est 2_{5}, אִם מִזֶּרַע הַיְּהוּדִים מָרְדֳּכַי *if Mordecai is of the offspring of the Jews* Est 6_{13}, גָּדוֹל מָרְדֳּכַי בְּבֵית הַמֶּלֶךְ *Mordecai was great in the house of the king* Est 9_{4}, מָרְדֳּכַי ... מִשְׁנֶה לַמֶּלֶךְ ... וְגָדוֹל לַיְּהוּדִים *Mordecai was ... second in rank to the king ... and great to*, i.e. popular among, *the Jews* Est 10_{3}.

<OBJ> ראה *see* Est $5_{9.13}$, קרה *befall* Est 4_{7}, לבשׁ hi. *dress* Est 4_{4} 6_{11}, תלה *hang* Est 5_{14} 6_{4}, שׂים *place* Est 8_{2}, גדל pi. *promote* Est 10_{2}.

<CSTR> דֹּד מָרְדֳּכַי *uncle of Mordecai* Est 2_{15}, עַם *people of* Est 3_{6} (מָרְדֳּכַי), מַאֲמַר *command of* Est 2_{20}, דִּבְרֵי *words of* Est 3_{4} 4_{9} (מָרְדֳּכַי), שֵׁם *name of* Est 2_{22} (מָרְדֳּכַי), פַּחַד־ *fear of* Est 9_{3}, גְּדֻלַּת *greatness of* Est 10_{2}.

<APP> אִישׁ *man* Est 9_{4}, בֵּן *son* Est 2_{5}, יְהוּדִי *Jew* Est 5_{13} 6_{10} 8_{7} $9_{29.31}$ 10_{3}.

<PREP> לְ *to, for (oneself)*, + לקח *take*, i.e. adopt Est $2_{5.15}$; of direction, *to*, + אמר *say* Est 3_{3} 8_{7}, נגד hi. *tell* Est 4_{12}, ידע ni. *be made known* Est 2_{22}, נתן *give* Est 8_{2}; of benefit, *to, for*, + עשׂה *do, make* Est $6_{3.10}$ 7_{9}, כון hi. *prepare* Est 6_{4} 7_{10}.

בְּ *against*, + שׁלח *send*, i.e. lay, hands on Est 3_{6}

אֶל *to*, + אמר *say* Est 3_{4}, צוה pi. *charge (with message)* Est 4_{10}, שׁוב hi. *reply* Est 4_{15}, יצא *go out* Est 4_{6}.

עַל *concerning*, + צוה pi. *charge* Est 4$_{5}$; introducing object, + צוה pi. *command* Est 4$_{17}$; *against* Est 5$_{9}$.

מֵעַל *from (upon)*, + סור hi. *remove* sackcloth Est 4$_{4}$.

עִם *with*, i.e. for, + עשׂה *do* Est 6$_{3}$.

לִפְנֵי *before*, + נפל *fall* Est 6$_{13}$.

<COLL> מָרְדֳּכַי הוֹלֵךְ וְגָדוֹל *Mordecai became greater and greater* Est 9$_{4}$.

2. exile returning with Zerubbabel, <SUBJ> בוא *come* Ezr 2$_{2}$||Ne 7$_{7}$.

⇒ מְרֹדַךְ *Merodach.*

*[מִרְדּוֹף] 0.0.4 n.[m.] **pursuit**—cstr. Q מרדף (מרדוף)—<SUBJ> חשׂך *hold back*, i.e. relent Is 14$_{6}$ (if em.; see Coll.). <NOM CL> מִרְדֹּף רָעָה לְמוֹתוֹ *the (reward of) the pursuit of evil is truly death itself* Pr 11$_{19}$ (if em. מְרַדֵּף *one who pursues*). <CSTR> חצוצרות המרדף *trumpets of the pursuit* 1QM 3$_{2.9.}$ 7$_{13}$ 9$_{6}$ (מרדוף). <COLL> רֹדֶה בָאַף גּוֹיִם מִרְדֹּף בְּלִי חָשָׂךְ *angrily ruling nations with unrelenting pursuit* Is 14$_{6}$ (if em. מֻרְדָּף *persecution*).

Also perh. 4QapJosephᵇ 7$_{3}$ (מרדפיהם; unless *from their pursuers*, i.e. רדף ptc.).

⇒ רדף *pursue.*

מֻרְדָּף 1 n.[m.] **persecution,** <SUBJ> חשׂך *hold back*, i.e. relent Is 14$_{6}$ (or em.; see Coll.; || מַכָּה *blow*). <COLL> רֹדֶה בָאַף גּוֹיִם מֻרְדָּף בְּלִי חָשָׂךְ *angrily ruling nations with unrelenting persecution* Is 14$_{6}$ (or em. מִרְדּוֹף *pursuit* or מְרַדֵּף the staff *that persecuted*).

<SYN> מַכָּה *blow.*

⇒ רדף *pursue.*

מרה I 45.5.13 vb. **be rebellious—Qal** 23.2 Pf. מָרָה, מָרְתָה, (מָרֶתָה), מָרִיתָ, מָרִיתִי, מָרוּ, מְרִיתֶם, מָרִינוּ; + waw Si ומרה, וּמְרִיתֶם; ptc. מֹרֶה (מוֹרֶה), מֹרִים; inf. abs. מָרוֹ—**be rebellious (against),** <SUBJ> Israel(ites) appar. 2 K 14$_{26}$ (or em. הַמַּר *the bitter* affliction) Is 1$_{20}$ Ps 105$_{28}$ (or em. שָׁמְרוּ *they kept* not), עַם *people* 1 S 12$_{15}$ Is 65$_{2}$ (if em. סוֹרֵר *stubborn* to מוֹרֶה *rebellious*), בַּיִת *house* of Israel Is 63$_{10}$, Jerusalem Jr 4$_{17}$, Samaria Ho 14$_{1}$, עִיר *city* Zp 3$_{1}$, קָהָל *congregation* Nm 20$_{10}$, Aaron Nm 20$_{24}$ 27$_{14}$, Moses Nm 20$_{24}$ 27$_{14}$, אִישׁ *man* 1 K 13$_{21.26}$, בֵּן *son* Dt 21$_{18.20}$ Ezk 2$_{8}$ (if em. מֶרִי *rebellion* to מֹרֶה *rebellious*) perh. Si 30$_{12}$(B), נָסִיךְ *prince* Si 16$_{7}$(A) (B מרד *rebel*), שׁוֹרֵר *watcher* Ps 5$_{11}$, דּוֹר *generation* Ps 78$_{8}$, worshipper Lm 1$_{18.20.20}$ 3$_{42}$, לֵב *heart* Jr 5$_{23}$; subj. not specified, Is 50$_{5}$ Jb 20$_{29}$ (if em. אִמְרוֹ *his word* to מֹרֵא *rebellious one*).

<OBJ> Y. Jr 4$_{17}$, פֶּה *mouth*, i.e. command Nm 20$_{24}$ 27$_{14}$ 1 S 12$_{15}$ 1 K 13$_{21.26}$ Lm 1$_{18}$, דָּבָר *word* Ps 105$_{28}$ (or em.; see Subj.).

<PREP> לְ *at*, + מַיִם *waters* of Meribah Nm 20$_{24}$.

בְּ of place, *in*, + מִדְבָּר *steppe* of Zin Nm 27$_{14}$; of time, *during*, + מְרִיבָה *strife* Nm 27$_{14}$; of accompaniment, *with, in*, + גְּבוּרָה *might* Si 16$_{7}$(A); *against* Si 30$_{12}$(B), + אֱלֹהִים *God* Ho 14$_{1}$ Ps 5$_{11}$.

<COLL> מרה || סרר *be stubborn* Dt 21$_{18.20}$ Jr 5$_{23}$ Ps 78$_{8}$, פשׁע *transgress* Lm 3$_{42}$.

+ מאן pi. *refuse* Is 1$_{20}$, סוג ni. *turn back* Is 50$_{5}$, סור *turn aside* Jr 5$_{23}$.

:: שׁמע *listen*, i.e. obey Dt 21$_{18.20}$, שׁמר *keep* commandment 1 K 13$_{21}$.

+ adverb, מְאֹד *very* 2 K 14$_{26}$ (or em.; see Subj.), עוֹלָם *(in) ancient times* Si 16$_{7}$(A).

מָרוֹ מָרִיתִי *I have been very rebellious* Lm 1$_{20}$.

Also perh. 4QpIsaᶜ 46$_{2}$.

<SYN> סרר *be stubborn*, פשׁע *transgress.*

<ANT> שׁמע *listen.*

Hi. 22.3.13 Pf. Q המרה, הִמְרוּ; impf. יַמְרֶה, 2ms Si תמר, יַמְרוּ (יַמְרוּהוּ), תַּמְרוּ; + waw וַתֶּמֶר, וַיַּמְרוּ (Q ויאמרו), וַתַּמְרוּ; ptc. מַמְרִים; inf. לַמְרוֹת, הַמְרוֹתָם, Q אמרות, Si המראה—**1. be rebellious (against), defy, provoke,** <SUBJ> Israel(ites) Ex 23$_{21}$ (if em. תַּמֵּר *you shall* not *show bitterness* [i.e. מרר hi.] to תֶּמֶר *you shall* not *be rebellious*) Dt 1$_{26.43}$ 9$_{7.23.24}$ 31$_{27}$ Ezk 20$_{8}$ Ps 78$_{17.40.56}$ 107$_{11}$, Judah Is 3$_{8}$, Jerusalem Is 3$_{8}$ Ezk 5$_{6.7}$ (if em. הֲמָנְכֶם *your being turbulent* to הַמְרוֹתְכֶם *your being rebellious*), עַם *people* 1 S 12$_{14}$, בַּיִת *house* of Israel Ezk 20$_{13}$, אִישׁ *man* Josh 1$_{18}$ Ps 139$_{20}$ (if em. יֹאמְרֻךָ *they mention you* to יַמְרֻךָ *they rebel against you*, i.e. מרה I hi.) 4QDᶠ 5.1$_{7}$ (=CD 11$_{12}$ ימרא, i.e. מרא I hi.), גֶּבֶר *man* perh. 4QMystᵃ 3a.2$_{8}$ (ג[בר]), אָב *father* Ps 106$_{7.33}$ (or em. הֵמֵרוּ *they made bitter*, i.e. מרר I hi.) 106$_{43}$ (unless מרר III *be strong*) Ne 9$_{26}$ 4QDibHamᵃ 1.2$_{8}$, בֵּן *son* Ezk 20$_{21}$ Si 3$_{23}$, שָׂרָה *noble lady* Est 1$_{18}$ (if em. תֹּאמַרְנָה *they will say* to

תַּמְרֶינָה *they will be rebellious*), הֵתֵל *mocker* Jb 17$_{2}$ (if em. הֲתֻלִים *mockery* to הֹתְלִים *mockers*), קָרוֹב *near one* 1QH 14$_{14}$, אֲשֶׁר *one who* 1QS 6$_{26}$ 4QOrd[a] 2$_{5}$ perh. 4QDibHam[a] 7$_{14}$, אֵלֶּה *these* Si 39$_{31}$; subj. not specified, Jb 17$_{2}$ (or em.; see above) 4QpPs[a] 1.2$_{3}$.

<OBJ> Y. Ps 78$_{40.56}$ Ps 139$_{20}$ (if em.; see Subj.) 4QAdmon 1.1$_{2}$, עֶלְיוֹן *the Most High* Ps 78$_{17.56}$ 106$_{7}$ (if em.; see Prep.), עֶבֶד *servant* 4QD[f] 5.1$_{7}$, אָמָה *female servant* 4QD[f] 5.1$_{7}$ ([אמתו]), שָׂכִיר *hired labourer* 4QD[f] 5.1$_{7}$ ([שכירו]), פֶּה *mouth*, i.e. command Dt 1$_{26.43}$ 9$_{23}$ Jos 1$_{18}$ 1 S 12$_{14}$ Si 39$_{31}$ 1QH 14$_{14}$ 1QS 6$_{26}$ 4QDibHam[a] 1.2$_{8}$, דָּבָר *word* 4Q185 1.2$_{3}$ 4QAdmon 1.2$_{9}$ 4QMyst[a] 3a. 2$_{8}$, עַיִן *eye*, i.e. presence Is 3$_{8}$, רוּחַ *spirit* Ps 106$_{33}$ (or em.; see Subj.), מִשְׁפָּט *ordinance* Ezk 5$_{6}$, אֹמֶר *word* Ps 107$_{11}$.

<PREP> לְ *as*, or *for (the purpose of)*, + מְזִמָּה *wicked scheme* Ps 139$_{20}$ (if em.; see Subj.).

בְּ of place, *in, at*, + מִדְבָּר *steppe* Ezk 20$_{13}$ Ps 78$_{40}$, צִיָּה *desert* Ps 78$_{17}$, יָם *sea* Ps 106$_{7}$; of time, *on*, + שַׁבָּת *sabbath* 4QD[f] 5.1$_{7}$ ([ב]שב[ת]); of accompaniment, *in, with*, + עֵצָה *counsel* Ps 106$_{43}$ 3 (unless מרר III *be strong*), חֹק *statute* Si 39$_{31}$, מַעֲלָל *deed* 4QAdmon 1.1$_{2}$ (במ]עלי[ליהם); *against*, + Y. Ezk 20$_{8.13.21}$ 23$_{21}$ (if em.; see Subj.), יוֹתֵר *excess* Si 3$_{23}$ (ביותר ממך אל תמר perh. *do not rebel against what is beyond you*).

מִן *from*, + יוֹם *day* Dt 9$_{24}$; of comparison, *than*, + גּוֹי *nation* Ezk 5$_{7}$ (if em.; see Subj.).

לְמִן *from*, + יוֹם *day* Dt 9$_{7}$.

עַל *beside, at*, + יָם *sea* Ps 106$_{7}$ (or em. עַל־יָם to עֶלְיוֹן *[against] the Most High*).

עִם *with, against* + Y. Dt 9$_{7.24}$ 31$_{27}$.

<COLL> מרה hi. || עצב *grieve* Ps 78$_{40}$, נאץ *spurn* Ps 107$_{11}$, שׁנה pi. *change*, i.e. pervert 1QH 14$_{14}$.

+ מרד *rebel* Ne 9$_{26}$, חטא *sin* Ps 78$_{17}$, זיד hi. *be presumptuous* Dt 14$_{3}$, מאס *reject* ordinances Ezk 20$_{13}$.

:: שׁמע *listen*, i.e. obey Dt 14$_{3}$ 9$_{23}$ Jos 1$_{18}$ 1 S 12$_{14}$ Ezk 20$_{8}$, עבד *serve* 1 S 12$_{14}$, אמן hi. *believe* Dt 9$_{23}$, ירא *fear* 1 S 12$_{14}$, הלך *walk* in statutes Ezk 20$_{13.21}$, שׁמר *keep* ordinances Ezk 20$_{21}$, testimonies Ps 78$_{56}$.

+ adverb, כַּמָּה *how often!* Ps 78$_{40}$.

כול הממרים לשוב מעונם *all who rebel (by refusing) to turn back from their iniquity* 4QpPs[a] 1.2$_{3}$.

2. perh. inf. as noun, **rebelliousness,** <SUBJ> אפס *cease* Si 41$_{2(Bmg)}$ (unless המראה = *the sight*; || תִּקְוָה *hope*).

<SYN> §1 עצב *grieve*, נאץ *spurn*, שׁנה pi. *change*; §2 תִּקְוָה *hope*.

<ANT> שׁמע *listen*, עבד *serve*, אמן hi. *believe*, ירא *fear*, הלך *walk*, שׁמר *keep*.

Also 1Q41 1$_{1}$ 4QPrFêtes[c] 131.1$_{15}$ ([המ]רותם) 11QMelch 5$_{3}$.*

⇒ מְרִי *rebelliousness*, מְרָתַיִם *Merathaim*, יִמְרָה *Imrah*.

***מרה II** $_{0.0.1}$ vb. **change—Hi.** $_{0.0.1}$ Impf. Q תמר (Q תאמר)—**exchange,** <SUBJ> subj. not specified, 4Q416 2.2$_{6}$ (תמר=4Q418 8$_{6}$ תאמר). <OBJ> רוּחַ *spirit* 4Q416 2.2$_{6}$. <PREP> בְּ of price, *(in exchange) for*, + הוֹן *wealth* 4Q 416 2.2$_{6}$.

⇒ cf. מור I *change*.

מרה III graze—Htp. graze, feed, <SUBJ> Israelites Is 61$_{6}$ (if em. תִּתְיַמָּרוּ *you will boast* [אמר htp.] to תִּתְמָרוּ *you will graze*).*

⇒ מְרִיא *fatling*.

***מרה IV** $_{1}$ vb. **be strong,** מִי כָמֹהוּ מוֹרֶה *who is as powerful as he?* Jb 36$_{22}$ (unless ירה ptc. *teacher*).

***[מָרָה] I** $_{1}$ n.[f.] **instruction, revelation** (unless from מַר I *bitter* or מָרֶה *disputed matter*)—pl. מָרִים—<CSTR> מֵי הַמָּרִים *waters of instruction* Nm 5$_{24}$.

⇒ ירה *teach*.

מָרָה II $_{5}$ pl.n. **Marah**—+ ה- of direction מָרָתָה—bitter spring in route of Exodus, perh. En Hawāra, 75 km SE of Suez, <OBJ> קרא *call* name Ex 15$_{23}$. <PREP> בְּ of place, *in, at*, + חנה *encamp* Nm 33$_{8}$; מִן *from, of* Ex 15$_{23}$ (מַיִם מִמָּרָה *the water of Marah*), + נסע *set out* Nm 33$_{9}$; with ה- of direction, *to Marah*, + בוא *come* Ex 15$_{23}$.

⇒ מרר I *be bitter*.

***[מָרֶה]** $_{1}$ n.m. **disputed matter** (unless from מַר I *bitter* or מָרָה II *instruction, revelation*)—pl. מָרִים—

disputed matter, contention, <CSTR> מֵי הַמָּרִים *waters of contention* Nm 5$_{24}$.
⇒ מרר *rebel.*

[מֹרָה] 2 n.f. **bitterness**—cstr. מֹרַת (מָרַּת)—<SUBJ> היה *be* Gn 26$_{35}$. <NOM CL> מֹרָה בְּלֶב־חֹרְשֵׁי רָע *bitterness is in the heart of those who devise evil* Pr 12$_{20}$ (if em. מִרְמָה *deceit*). <OBJ> ידע *know* Pr 14$_{10}$. <CSTR> מֹרַת רוּחַ *bitterness of spirit* Gn 26$_{35}$, מָרַּת נַפְשׁוֹ *bitterness of its soul* Pr 14$_{10}$ (or em. נַפְשׁוֹ to נֶפֶשׁ *of the soul*).*
⇒ מרר I *be bitter.*

מֹרֶה, see מוֹרֶה *Moreh.*

*[מַרְהֵבָה] 0.0.1 n.f. **raging** or **onslaught,** <SUBJ> היה *be* 1QH 3$_{25}$ 4Q418 176$_{3}$ (both if מדהבה is error for מרהבה), שׁבת *cease* Is 14$_{4(1QIsa^a)}$ (MT מַדְהֵבָה *distress;* + נֹגֵשׂ *oppressor*). <NOM CL> [א]ין עוד מדהבה *there shall no longer be raging* 1QH 12$_{18}$ (if מדהבה is error for מרהבה).
⇒ רהב *storm.*

*[מְרוֹ] 1 n.[m.] **violent man**—with prosthetic aleph אִמְרוֹ—**violent man, oppressor,** <CSTR> נַחֲלַת אִמְרוֹ *portion of a violent man* Jb 20$_{29}$ (unless אִמְרוֹ *his word,* from אֹמֶר).
⇒ מרה *be rebellious.*

*[מְרוֹגֶלֶת] 0.0.1 n.f. **clothing for legs,** <NOM CL> והבטן מרוגלת הנה והנה *and as for the belly, clothing for legs is on either side* 1QM 5$_{13}$ (unless רגל ptc. pu. *bound* or *towards the legs,* i.e. downward).
⇒ רֶגֶל *foot.*

[מָרוּד] 3.1 n.[m.] **wandering**—pl. מְרוּדִים; sf. מְרוּדַי, מְרוּדֶיהָ—**1. wandering, homelessness,** <OBJ> זכר *remember* Lm 3$_{19}$ (|| עֳנִי *affliction,* + לַעֲנָה *wormwood,* רֹאשׁ *poison*). <CSTR> יְמֵי ... מְרוּדֶיהָ *days of her ... wandering* Lm 1$_{7}$ (or em. מְרוּרֶיהָ *her bitterness;* || עֳנִי *affliction*).

2. homeless one, <OBJ> בוא hi. *bring* Is 58$_{7}$ (+ רָעֵב *hungry one*). <APP> עָנִי *poor one* Is 58$_{7}$. <PREP> עַל *for* Si 32$_{19}$ (אנחה על מרודיה *there is sighing for her homeless ones* Si 32$_{19}$; or em. מורידה *the one who causes it* [a tear] *to fall*).
<SYN> §1 עֳנִי *affliction.*
⇒ רוד *wander.*

מֵרוֹז 1 pl.n. **Meroz,** in northern Israel, perh. Kh. Mārūs, 4 km NW of Hazor, <OBJ> ארר *curse* Jg 5$_{23}$.

[מְרוֹחַ] 1 n.[m.] **crushing**—cstr. מְרוֹחַ—<SUBJ> היה *be* Lv 21$_{20}$ (+ יַלֶּפֶת *scab,* גָּרָב *eczema,* תְּבַלֻּל *confusion* of sight, דַּק *thin one,* גִּבֵּן *hunchbacked,* שֶׁבֶר *fracture* of hand or foot). <CSTR> מְרוֹחַ אָשֶׁךְ *crushing of testicle,* i.e. one that has crushed testicles (and may therefore not serve at altar) Lv 21$_{20}$.
⇒ מרח *rub.*

מָרוֹם 54.10.30 n.m. **height**—cstr. מְרוֹם; pl. מְרוֹמִים (מְרֹמִים); cstr. מְרוֹמֵי (מְרֹמֵי); sf. מְרוֹמָיו—**1. height, elevated place, on high,** <NOM CL> מָרוֹם מֵרִאשׁוֹן מְקוֹם מִקְדָּשֵׁנוּ *an elevated place from the beginning is the place of our sanctuary* Jr 17$_{12}$.

<OBJ> תפשׂ *hold* Jr 49$_{16}$, בצר pi. *fortify* Jr 51$_{53}$ (or §2, if em.; see Cstr.).

<CSTR> מְרוֹם הָרִים *height of the mountains* 2 K 19$_{23}$||Is 37$_{24}$, גִּבְעָה *of the hill* Jr 49$_{16}$, מְרוֹמֵי שָׂדֶה *heights of the field,* i.e. upland fields Jg 5$_{18}$, מְרוֹם יִשְׂרָאֵל *height of Israel* Ezk 17$_{23}$ 20$_{40}$ 34$_{14}$ 4QpPs^{a} 1.3$_{11}$ (ישר[אל]), ־צִיּוֹן *of Zion* Jr 31$_{12}$ (unless §4), עֻזָּהּ *of her strength,* i.e. her strong height Jr 51$_{53}$ (or em. מְרוֹם to מָרוֹם *to heaven,* i.e. §2),* קִצּוֹ *of its end,* i.e. farthest height Is 37$_{24}$ (or em. מְלוֹן *lodging place of,* with ||2 K 19$_{23}$), שִׁבְתּוֹ *of his dwelling* Ob$_{3}$ (or em. מֵרִים *making high,* i.e. רום hi.), מְרֹמֵי קָרֶת *heights of the city* Pr 9$_{3.14}$.

יֹשְׁבֵי מָרוֹם *inhabitants of the height* Is 26$_{5}$, תֹּפְשֵׂי מְרוֹם *ones who hold the height of* Jr 49$_{16}$, הַר מְרוֹם *mountain of the height of* Israel Ezk 17$_{23}$ 20$_{40}$ 4QpPs^{a} 1.3$_{11}$, הָרֵי *mountains of* Ezk 34$_{14}$, [ה]רי מרום *mountains of the height* 4QSh B$_{3}$, רֹאשׁ־מְרוֹמִים *top of the heights* Pr 8$_{2}$, גַּפֵּי מְרֹמֵי *summits of the heights of* Pr 9$_{3}$.

<APP> יַרְכָּה *distant part* of Lebanon 2 K 19$_{23}$||Is 37$_{24}$, קִרְיָה lofty *city* Is 26$_{4}$, חָגוּ *cleft* of rock Ob$_{3}$, כִּסֵּא *throne*

Jr 17$_{12}$.

<PREP> לְ of direction, *to(wards)*, + רום hi. *lift* horn Ps 75$_6$ (unless §4); בְּ of place, *on*, + רנן pi. *shout for joy* Jr 31$_{12}$ (unless §4), שׁכן *dwell* Ob$_3$, שׂום *place* Hb 2$_9$, מרא hi. *flap wings* Jb 39$_{18}$; עַל *upon* Jg 5$_{18}$.

מָרוֹם without prep., *on the height, to the height*, + עלה *go up* 2 K 19$_{23}$||Is 37$_{24}$, ישׁב *sit* Pr 9$_{14}$, שׁכן *dwell* Is 33$_{16}$, חצב *hew* tomb Is 22$_{16}$.

2. height (of heaven), heaven, sky, on high, <SUBJ> אמל pulal *languish* Is 24$_4$ (if em.; see §3 Cstr.).

<CSTR> מרומי אל *heights of God* Si 43$_{9(B)}$, מרום עליון *height of the Most High* 4QPseud^{b} 5.1$_3$, הקודש *of the holiness*, i.e. holy height 4QBen 1$_4$, מְרוֹם קָדְשׁוֹ *height of his holiness*, i.e. his holy height Ps 102$_{20}$, מרומי רום *heights of the height*, i.e. highest heights 4QShirShabb^{a} 1.1$_{20}$ 1.2$_4$ 2$_4$ 4QShirShabb^{d} 1.1$_{34}$ 4QShir^{b} 41$_1$, רומים *of the heights* MasShirShabb 1$_9$, מעל *of the height* Si 26$_{16}$, מקדשי *of the sanctuaries of* 4QShirShabb^{f} 23.2$_{11}$, עומדכה *of your standing place* 4QBer^{a} 1.2$_1$ ([מ]רומי)), כ[בודו] *of his glory*, i.e. his glorious heights 11QShirShabb 10$_2$, מרום כסא *height of the throne of* 11QShirShabb 7$_2$.

אֱלֹהֵי מָרוֹם *God of the height* Mc 6$_6$ (unless §4), אלוהי מרומים *God of the heights* 4QShirShabb^{d} 1.1$_{30}$, כוהני מרומי *priests of the heights of* 4QShirShabb^{a} 1.1$_{20}$, ראשי מרומים *chiefs of the heights* 4QShirShabb^{d} 1.1$_{34}$, יושבי מרומי *inhabitants of the heights of* MasShirShabb 1$_9$, רוש מרו[מ]ים *top of heaven*, i.e. uppermost heaven 4QShirShabb^{d} 1.1$_{43}$, צְבָא הַמָּרוֹם *the host of heaven* Is 24$_{21}$, שער מרום *gate of the height of* 4QBen 1$_4$, שערי המרום *gates of the height* 4QCommGenB 2$_5$, שערי מרומי *gates of the heights of* 4QShirShabb^{a} 1.2$_4$, נבלי מרום *jars*, i.e. clouds, *of heaven* Si 43$_8$, מעוז מרום *strength of*, i.e. from, *on high* 1QH 10$_{32}$, תואר מרום *form of the height* Si 43$_1$, כול מרומי *all the heights of* 4QShirShabb^{a} 2$_4$ 4QShirShabb^{d} 1.1$_{34}$ 4QShirShabb^{f} 23.2$_{11}$.

<PREP> לְ of direction, place, *to(wards), on* 4QPseud^{b} 5.1$_3$, + עלה *go up* Ps 68$_{19}$, שׁוב *go back* Ps 7$_8$ (unless §4; or em. שׁוּבָה *go back* to שֵׁבָה *sit*)=11QMelch 1$_{11}$, דלל *be brought low (through looking)* Is 38$_{14}$ (unless §4), ישׁב *sit* Ps 7$_8$ (if em.; see above), רום pol. *exalt* 4QShirShabb^{d} 1.1$_{33}$.

בְּ of place, *on, in* Ps 93$_4$ Jb 16$_{19}$ 1QM 14$_{14}$ (במרומי[כה]) 4QBer^{a} 1.2$_1$ (ב[מ]רומי) 4QShirShabb^{a} 2$_4$ 4QShirShabb^{f} 23.2$_{11}$ 4QPrQuot 15.6$_2$ (במרומ[ים]) 4QShir^{b} 41$_1$, + שׁמע hi. *cause to be heard* Is 58$_4$, זכר *remember* Si 16$_{17}$, הלל pi. *praise* Ps 148$_1$, קלס pi. *praise* Si 47$_{15}$, שׂמח *rejoice* 1QM 17$_8$, שׁקף hi. *look down* Ps 102$_{20}$, זרח *arise* Si 26$_{16}$ (זור[חת]), זהר hi. *shine* Si 43$_{9(B)}$ (M שׂרק hi. *shine*), פקד *visit*, i.e. punish Is 24$_{21}$, שׁפט *judge* perh. 1QH fr. 46$_4$ 4QHod^{b} 12$_3$, עשׂה *do* Jb 25$_2$, אמץ pi. *strengthen* Si 45$_{2(B)}$ (Bmg במוראים *with fear*).

מִן *from, of* Is 24$_{18}$ (אֲרֻבּוֹת מִמָּרוֹם *windows of heaven*) Jb 31$_2$ Si 40$_{11}$, + שׁאג *roar* Jr 25$_{30}$, שׁלח *send* 2 S 22$_{17}$||Ps 18$_{17}$ Ps 144$_7$ Lm 1$_{13}$, ערה ni. (of spirit) *be poured* Is 32$_{15}$.

אֶל *to*, + שׁוב *go back* Si 40$_{11}$.

עַד *unto* Ps 71$_{19}$.

מֵעַל לְ *above* 4QShirShabb^{d} 1.1$_{34}$.

מָרוֹם without prep., *on high, in heaven, to heaven*, + שׁכן *dwell* Is 33$_5$ 57$_{15}$ (unless §4), בצר pi. *fortify* fortress Jr 51$_{53}$ (if em. מְרוֹם *height of* [§1] to מָרוֹם);* in nom. cl., מָרוֹם מִשְׁפָּטֶיךָ *your judgments are on high* Ps 10$_5$ (unless §4; or em. סָרוּ *they have turned away*; + מִנֶּגְדּוֹ *beyond him*), אַתָּה מָרוֹם לְעֹלָם *you are on high for ever* Ps 92$_9$ (unless §4).

<COLL> מָרוֹם || שָׁמַיִם *heaven* Ps 102$_{20}$ 148$_1$ Jb 16$_{19}$, מָעוֹן *habitation* Jr 25$_{30}$.

+ מַעַל *above* Jb 31$_2$, קָדוֹשׁ *holy (place)* Is 57$_{15}$.

:: אֲדָמָה *earth* Is 24$_{21}$, אֶרֶץ *earth* Si 40$_{11}$ 47$_{15}$.

3a. (of social status) **height, exaltation, on high,** <ADJ> רַב pl. *many* Ec 10$_6$. <PREP> לְ of direction, place, *to, on*, + שׂים *place* Jb 5$_{11}$; בְּ of place, *in, on*, + נתן ni. *be given*, i.e. placed Ec 10$_6$; מִן of direction, *from*, + דבר pi. *speak* Ps 73$_8$. <COLL> מְרוֹמִים :: שֵׁפֶל *low estate* Ec 10$_6$.

3b. height, i.e. **most exalted one(s),** <SUBJ> אמל pulal *languish* Is 24$_4$.

<CSTR> מְרוֹם עַם־הָאָרֶץ *height*, i.e. most exalted, *of the people of the earth* Is 24$_4$ (or em. הַמָּרוֹם עִם *exalted [place]*, i.e. heaven, *with* the earth).

4. height, as divine title, **Exalted One*** (unless §§1, 2, 5), <SUBJ> אמר *say* Is 57$_{15}$. <NOM CL> אַתָּה מָרוֹם לְעֹלָם *you are the Exalted One for ever* Ps 92$_9$. <CSTR>

מְרוֹם־צִיּוֹן *Exalted One of Zion* Jr 31_{12}; אֱלֹהֵי מָרוֹם *God of the height*, i.e. the Exalted One Mc 6_{6}. <PREP> לְ of direction, *to*, + שׁוּב *turn* Ps 7_{8}, רום hi. *lift* horn Ps 75_{6}; *for*, + דלל *be brought low (through looking)* Is 38_{14}; בְּ of cause, *on account of*, + רנן pi. *shout for joy* Jr 31_{12}. <COLL> מָרוֹם + רָם *high one* Is 57_{15}, נִשָּׂא *lofty one* Is 57_{15}; מָרוֹם as vocative, *O Exalted One*, Ps 10_{5} 56_{3}.

5. as adverb, **on high, upwards, haughtily,** with נשׂא *lift* eyes 2 K 19_{22}||Is 37_{23} Is 40_{26}, לחם *fight* Ps 56_{3} (unless §4; or em. רוֹמְמֵנִי *lift me up*, i.e. רום pol., and join with 56_{4}), חלף hi. *renew* strength appar. Si $43_{30(B)}$ (מרומים; Bmg מרומםיו *O you who extol him*).

Also 4QShirShabb[a] 1.2_{2} 4QShirShabb[b] 23_{2} 4QShir Shabb[c] 3.2_{9} 11QShirShabb 8_{7}.

<SYN> §2 שָׁמַיִם *heaven*, מָעוֹן *habitation*.

<ANT> §2 אֲדָמָה *earth*, אֶרֶץ *earth*; §3a שֵׁפֶל *low estate*.*

⇒ רום *be high*.

מֵרוֹם 2 pl.n. **Merom,** perh. Mērūn, 12 km SW of Hazor, <CSTR> מֵי מֵרוֹם *waters of Merom* Jos $11_{5.7}$.

⇒ רום *be high*.

מֵרוֹץ 1 n.[m.] **race,** <NOM CL> לֹא לַקַּלִּים הַמֵּרוֹץ *the race is not to the swift* Ec 9_{11} (|| מִלְחָמָה *battle*).

<SYN> מִלְחָמָה *battle*.

⇒ רוץ *run*.

[מְרוּצָה] I 4 n.f. **running**—cstr. מְרוּצַת (מְרֻצַת); sf. מְרוּצָתָם (Qr מְרֻצָתָם)—**1. (mode of) running,** <OBJ> ראה *see* 2 S 18_{27}. <CSTR> מְרֻצַת אֲחִימַעַץ בֶּן־צָדוֹק *running of Ahimaaz the son of Zadok* 2 S 18_{27}, מְרוּצַת הָרִאשׁוֹן *running of the first one* 2 S 18_{27}. <PREP> כְּ *as* 2 S 18_{27}.

2. course, way of life, <NOM CL> מְרוּצָתָם רָעָה *their course is evil* Jr 23_{10} (+ גְּבוּרָה *might*). <PREP> בְּ of place, *in(to)*, + שׁוּב *go back* Jr 8_{6} (+ מִלְחָמָה *battle*).

⇒ רוץ *run*.

מְרוּצָה II 1 n.f. **extortion,** <OBJ> עשׂה *do* Jr 22_{17} (||עֹשֶׁק *oppression*, + בֶּצַע *gain*, דָּם *blood[shed]*). <PREP> עַל *(looking) towards* Jr 22_{17}.

<SYN> עֹשֶׁק *oppression*.

⇒ רצץ *crush*.

[מְרוּקִים] 1.0.1 n.[m.]pl. **cosmetic treatment**—pl. sf. מְרוּקֵיהֶם—for women, with oil, spices and ointments, <CSTR> יְמֵי מְרוּקֵיהֶם *days of their cosmetic treatment* Est 2_{12}.

Also 1Q38 1_{1}.

⇒ מרק I *rub*.

מָרוֹר, see מָרֹר *bitter thing*.

מְרוֹרָה, see מְרֵרָה *bitter thing, poison*.

מָרוֹת 1 pl.n. **Maroth,** appar. in Judah, <CSTR> יוֹשֶׁבֶת מָרוֹת *inhabitant of Maroth* Mc 1_{12}.

מַרְזֵחַ 2 n.m. **feasting**—cstr. מִרְזַח—**1. feasting,** or perh. **place of feasting** or **group of those feasting,*** <SUBJ> סור *pass away* Am 6_{7}. <CSTR> מִרְזַח סְרוּחִים *the feasting of those who sprawl about* Am 6_{7}.

2. funeral meal, <CSTR> בֵּית מַרְזֵחַ *house of a funeral meal*, i.e. where one is being held Jr 16_{5}.*

מרח 1 vb. **rub—Qal** 1 Impf. יִמְרְחוּ—**rub, spread by rubbing,** <OBJ> דְּבֵלָה *fig-cake* Is 38_{21} (||Is 38_{27} שׂים *place*). <PREP> עַל *upon*, + שְׁחִין *boil* Is 38_{21}.*

⇒ מָרוֹחַ *crushing*.

מֶרְחָב 6.0.3 n.[m.] **broad place**—cstr. mss מֶרְחַב; pl. cstr. מֶרְחֲבֵי—**1. broad place,** assoc. with deliverance (2 S 22_{20}||Ps 18_{20} Ps 31_{9} 118_{5}), in heart of worshipper (1QH 5_{33}), as pasture for sheep (Ho 4_{16}), for walking (4QBéat 14.2_{11}).

2. broad place, perh. as term for Y.'s heavenly dwelling* (Ps 118_{5}).

3. broad place, perh. as term for Sheol (Ho 4_{16} Ps 18_{20} 31_{9}).*

4. expanse of land (Hb 1_{6} 1QH 6_{31}).

<OBJ> פתח *open* 1QH 5_{33}. <CSTR> מֶרְחַבְיָהּ *broad place of Y.* Ps $118_{5(mss)}$ (L מֶרְחָב יָהּ in *a broad place Y.* answered me), מרחב רגלכה *broad place of*, i.e. for, *your foot* 4QBéat 14.2_{11}, מֶרְחֲבֵי־אֶרֶץ *expanses of the*

earth Hb 1$_{6}$. <PREP> לְ of direction, *to*, + הלך *go* Hb 1$_{6}$, יצא hi. *bring out* 2 S 22$_{20}$||Ps 18$_{20}$ 4QBéat 14.2$_{11}$ ([ויוציאכה]); *as*, + פתח *open* 1QH 6$_{31}$; בְּ of place, *in*, + עמד hi. *cause to stand* Ho 4$_{16}$, ענה *answer* Ps 118$_{5}$. <COLL> מרחב אין קץ *an expanse without end* 1QH 6$_{31}$.*

⇒ רחב *be broad.*

מֶרְחָק 19.0.2 n.m. **distance**—pl. מֶרְחַקִּים (מַרְחַקִּים); cstr. מֶרְחַקֵּי—**distance, distant place, afar,** <SUBJ> אזן hi. *hear* Is 8$_{9}$, אזר htp. *gird oneself* Is 8$_{9}$, חתת *be shattered* Is 8$_{9}$. <CSTR> מֶרְחַקֵּי־אָרֶץ *distant places of the earth* Is 8$_{9}$ Ps 95$_{4(ms)}$ (L מֶחְקְרֵי *depths of*); אֶרֶץ מֶרְחָק *land of distance*, i.e. distant land Is 13$_{5}$ 46$_{11}$ Jr 4$_{16}$ (הַמֶּרְחָק) 6$_{20}$ Pr 25$_{25}$, מַרְחַקִּים *of distances*, i.e. that stretches far Is 33$_{17}$ (or em. מַחֲמַדִּים *of desirable things*) Jr 8$_{19}$, בֵּית הַמֶּרְחָק *house of distance*, i.e. last house 2 S 15$_{17}$, כֹּל מֶרְחַקֵּי *all the distant places of* Is 8$_{9}$. <APP> אִי *island* 1QpHab 3$_{10}$, קָצֶה *end* of heaven Is 13$_{5}$, דֶּרֶךְ *way*, i.e. journey 11QT 43$_{12}$ (במרחק מן המקדש דרך שלושת ימים *at a distance from the sanctuary, a journey of three days*). <PREP> בְּ of place, *in, at*, + זכר *remember* Zc 10$_{9}$, ישב *dwell* 11QT 43$_{12}$; מִן of direction, *from*, + בוא *come* Is 10$_{3}$ 30$_{27}$ Ezk 23$_{40}$ 1QpHab 3$_{10}$, hi. *bring* Jr 5$_{15}$ Pr 31$_{14}$, נגד hi. *tell* Jr 31$_{10}$, ידע *know* Ps 138$_{6}$, *in (the direction of), to(wards)*, + נוס *flee* Is 17$_{13}$. <COLL> מֶרְחָק + עַם *people* Is 8$_{9}$ Zc 10$_{9}$.

⇒ רחק *be distant.*

*[מַרְחֶשְׁוָן] 0.0.2 pr.n.[m.] **Marcheshvan,** eighth month of postexilic Jewish calendar, October/November, <PREP> לְ of possession, *of, belonging to* 4QMish C^{b} 5$_{7}$ (למ[רח]שון) Mur 22 1$_{1}$ 5/6ḤevBA 44$_{1}$.

מַרְחֶשֶׁת 2 n.f. **pan,** perh. specif. with lid,* <CSTR> מִנְחַת מַרְחֶשֶׁת *grain offering of*, i.e. cooked in, *a pan* Lv 2$_{7}$. <PREP> בְּ of place, *in*, + עשׂה ni. *be made* Lv 7$_{9}$ (+ מַחֲבַת *griddle*).*

מרט 14 vb. **make smooth**—**Qal** 7 + waw וָאֶמְרְטָה (וָאֶמְרְטֵם); ptc. מֹרְטִים; pass. מְרוּטָה; inf. מָרְטָה—**1. polish,** <SUBJ> Y. Ezk 21$_{16}$ (if em. הִיא מֹרָטָה *it has been polished* to הוּא מְרָטָהּ *he has polished it*); subj. not specified, Ezk 21$_{16}$ (or em. לְמָרְטָה to לִמְרַצֵּחַ *to the slayer*). <OBJ> חֶרֶב *sword* Ezk 21$_{16}$ (or em.; see Subj.) 21$_{16}$ (if em.; see Subj.).

2. pull out hair (of), <SUBJ> Ezra Ezr 9$_{3}$ (+ קרע *tear* garments), Nehemiah Ne 13$_{25}$ (+ נכה hi. *strike*); subj. not specified, Is 50$_{6}$ (1QIsa^{a} טלל hi. *cause to fall*; || נכה hi.). <OBJ> אִישׁ *man* Ne 13$_{25}$. <PREP> מִן partitive, *(some) of*, + שֵׂעָר *hair* Ezr 9$_{3}$.

3. pass. **a. be rubbed raw,** <SUBJ> כָּתֵף *shoulder* Ezk 29$_{18}$ (|| קרח ho. *be made bald*).

b. be polished, <SUBJ> חֶרֶב *sword* Ezk 21$_{14}$ (or em. מֹרָטָה, i.e. pu.; + חדד ho. *be sharpened*) 21$_{16}$ (if em. מְעֻטָּה appar. *small* to מְרוּטָה) 21$_{33}$ (+ פתח pass. *be opened*, i.e. unsheathed). <PREP> לְ *for (the purpose of)*, + כָּלָה *destruction* Ezk 21$_{33}$ (if em. לְהָכִיל perh. *to endure*).

<SYN> §2 נכה hi. *strike*; §3 קרח ho. *be made bald.*

Ni. 2 Impf. יִמָּרֵט—**lose hair,** through leprosy, <SUBJ> רֹאשׁ *head* Lv 13$_{40}$ (+ קֵרֵחַ הוּא *he is bald*) 13$_{41}$ (+ גִּבֵּחַ הוּא *he is bald [of the forehead]*). <PREP> מִן of direction, *from*, + פֵּאָה *corner* Lv 13$_{41}$.

Pu. 5 Pf. מֹרָטָה; ptc. מְמֹרָט (מורט)—**1. be polished,** <SUBJ> נְחֹשֶׁת *bronze* 1 K 7$_{45}$, חֶרֶב *sword* Ezk 21$_{14}$ (if em. מְרוּטָה, i.e. qal ptc. pass. to מֹרָטָה) 21$_{15}$ (+ חדד ho. *be sharpened*) 21$_{16}$ (|| חדד ho.).

2. be smooth-skinned, <SUBJ> גּוֹי *nation* Is 18$_{2}$ (|| משׁך pu. *be tall*), עַם *people* Is 18$_{7}$ (|| משׁך pu.).

<SYN> §1 חדד ho. *be sharpened*; §2 משׁך pu. *be tall.*

מְרִי 23 n.[m.] **rebellion**—מֶרִי; sf. מֶרְיְךָ, מִרְיָם—**1. rebellion, rebelliousness, defiance.**

2. rebellious one(s) (Ezk 2$_{7.8}$ 44$_{6}$ [or em.; see Prep.] Pr 17$_{11}$ [if מְרִי is subj.]).

<SUBJ> היה *be* Ezk 2$_{8}$. <NOM CL> חַטַּאת־קֶסֶם מֶרִי *rebellion is (as) the sin of divination* 1 S 15$_{23}$ (+ פצר hi. inf. *stubbornness*), מְרִי הֵמָּה *they are rebellion*, i.e. rebellious Ezk 2$_{7}$ (mss בֵּית מְרִי *house of rebellion*), מְרִי שִׂחִי perh. *my complaint is*, i.e. calls for, *defiance* Jb 23$_{2}$. <OBJ> ידע *know* Dt 31$_{27}$ (+ עֹרֶף stiff *neck*), בקשׁ pi. *seek* Pr 17$_{11}$. <APP> בַּיִת *house* of Israel Ezk 44$_{6}$ (or em.; see Prep.). <CSTR> עַם מְרִי *people of rebellion*,

i.e. rebellious people Is 30$_{9}$, בְּנֵי־מֶ֫רִי *sons of rebellion,* i.e. rebels Nm 17$_{10}$, בֵּית מְרִי *house of rebellion,* i.e. rebellious house Ezk 2$_{5.6.7(mss).8}$ (הַמֶּ֫רִי) 3$_{9.26.27}$ 12$_{2}$ (הַמֶּרִי) 12$_{2.3.9}$ (הַמֶּ֫רִי) 12$_{25}$ (הַמֶּרִי) 17$_{12}$ (הַמֶּרִי) 24$_{3}$ (הַמֶּרִי) 44$_{6}$ (הַמֶּרִי; if em.; see Prep.). <PREP> בְּ of accompaniment, *in,* or of cause, *on account of,* + נתן *give,* i.e. appoint Ne 9$_{17}$; אֶל *to,* + אמר *say* Ezk 44$_{6}$ (or em. בֵּית הַמֶּרִי *the house of rebellion*).

⇨ מרה *be rebellious.*

מְרִיא 8.0.1 n.[m.] **fatling**—pl. מְרִיאִים; cstr. מְרִיאֵי; sf. מְרִיאֵיכֶם—an animal, usu. ox, raised specif. for slaughtering, often in sacrifice, <SUBJ> רבץ *lie down* Is 11$_{6}$ (or em. וּמְרִיא *and the fatling* to יִמְרְאוּ *they will graze*). <NOM CL> מְרִיאֵי בָשָׁן כֻּלָּם *all of them are fatlings of Bashan* Ezk 39$_{18}$. <OBJ> זבח *sacrifice* 2 S 6$_{13}$ 1 K 1$_{9.19.25}$. <CSTR> מְרִיאֵי בָשָׁן *fatlings of Bashan* Ezk 39$_{18}$; חֵלֶב מְרִיאִים *fat of fatlings* Is 1$_{11}$ 4QDiscourse 10$_{4}$ ([מריא]ים), שֶׁלֶם מְרִיאֵיכֶם *peace offerings of your fatlings* Am 5$_{22}$. <PREP> בְּ introducing object, + נהג *lead* Is 11$_{6}$; עִם *with,* + ירד *go down* Is 34$_{7}$ (if em. אַבִּירִים *bulls* to מְרִיאִים). <COLL> מְרִיא ‖ שׁוֹר *ox* 2 S 6$_{13}$ 1 K 1$_{19.25}$, בָּקָר *cattle* 1 K 1$_{9}$, עֵגֶל *calf* Is 11$_{6}$, צֹאן *sheep* 1 K 1$_{9.19.25}$, כְּפִיר *young lion* Is 11$_{6}$; + פַּר *bull* Is 1$_{11}$ Ezk 39$_{18}$, אַיִל *ram* Is 1$_{11}$ Ezk 39$_{18}$, כַּר *ram* Ezk 39$_{18}$, כֶּבֶשׂ *sheep* Is 1$_{11}$, עַתּוּד *(male) goat* Is 1$_{11}$ Ezk 39$_{18}$.

<SYN> שׁוֹר *ox,* בָּקָר *cattle,* עֵגֶל *calf,* צֹאן *sheep,* כְּפִיר *young lion.*

⇨ מרא III *graze.*

*[**מָרִיב**] n.[m]. **contention,** <NOM CL> עַמְּךָ מְרִיבֵי הַכֹּהֵן *with you is my contention, O priest* Ho 4$_{4}$ (if em. עַמְּךָ כִּמְרִיבֵי כֹהֵן appar. *your people are as those who contend with a priest*).

⇨ ריב *strive.*

מְרִיבָה I 2 n.f. **strife**—cstr. מְרִיבַת—<SUBJ> היה *be* Gn 13$_{8}$. <CSTR> מְרִיבַת הָעֵדָה *strife of the congregation* Nm 27$_{14}$. <PREP> בְּ of time, *during,* + מרה *be rebellious* Nm 27$_{14}$.

Also 1QpHab 1$_{9}$ ([מ]ריבה).

⇨ ריב *strive.*

מְרִיבָה II 11 pl.n. **Meribah**—cstr. מְרִיבַת; pl. cstr. מְרִיבוֹת—source of water, place of Israelite rebellion during Exodus, **1.** located at Rephidim, <OBJ> קרא *call* name Ex 17$_{7}$ (+ מַסָּה *Massah*).

2. located at Kadesh, <CSTR> מֵי מְרִיבָה *waters of Meribah* Nm 20$_{13.24}$ Dt 33$_{2}$ (if em.; see Prep.) 33$_{8}$ (+ מַסָּה *Massah*) Ps 81$_{7}$ 106$_{32}$, מֵי מְרִיבַת קָדֵשׁ *waters of Meribah of Kadesh* or *of Meribath-Kadesh* Nm 27$_{14}$ Dt 32$_{51}$ Ezk 47$_{19}$ (מְרִיבוֹת) 48$_{28}$. <PREP> כְּ *as at,* + קשׁה hi. *harden* heart Ps 95$_{8}$ (+ מַסָּה *Massah*); מִן of direction, *from,* + בוא *come* Dt 33$_{2}$ (if em. מֵרִבְבֹת קֹדֶשׁ *from ten thousands of holy ones* to מִמְּרִבַת קָדֵשׁ *from Meribah of Kadesh*).

⇨ ריב *strive.*

מְרִיב בַּ֫עַל 4.0.0.1 pr.n.[m.] **Merib-baal**—מְרִיב בָּֽעַל (מְרִי־בַ֫עַל, I מרבבעל)—**1.** son of Jonathan, ident. with מְפִיבֹשֶׁת *Mephibosheth* at 2 S 4$_{4}$ 2 S 9$_{6.10.11.12.13}$ 16$_{1.4}$ 19$_{25.26.31}$ 21$_{7}$, <SUBJ> ילד hi. *beget* 1 C 8$_{34}$ 1 C 9$_{40}$. <NOM CL> בֶּן־יְהוֹנָתָן מְרִיב בָּֽעַל *the son of Jonathan was Merib-baal* 1 C 8$_{34}$ 9$_{40}$.

2. Samaria ost. 2$_{7}$.

⇨ ריב *strive* + בַּעַל *Baal.*

מְרִיבוֹת קָדֵשׁ, see מְרִיבָה II *Meribah.*

מְרִיבַת קָדֵשׁ, see מְרִיבָה II *Meribah.*

מְרָיָה 1 pr.n.m. **Meraiah,** head of priestly family at time of Joiakim, <NOM CL> לִשְׂרָיָה מְרָיָה *(belonging) to Seraiah was Meraiah* Ne 12$_{12}$.

מֹרִיָּה, see מוֹרִיָּה *Moriah.*

מְרָיוֹת 7 pr.n.m. **Meraioth, 1.** priest, son of Zerahiah, ancestor of Ezra and Zadok, <SUBJ> ילד hi. *beget* 1 C 5$_{33}$. <NOM CL> מְרָיוֹת בְּנוֹ *Meraioth was his son* 1 C 6$_{37}$. <OBJ> ילד hi. *beget* 1 C 5$_{32}$. <CSTR> בֶּן־מְרָיוֹת *son of Meraioth* Ezr 7$_{3}$. <APP> בֵּן *son* Ezr 7$_{3}$.

2. son of Ahitub and father of Zadok, <CSTR> בֶּן־מְרָיוֹת *son of Meraioth* Ne 11$_{11}$ 1 C 9$_{11}$. <APP> בֵּן *son* Ne 11$_{11}$ 1 C 9$_{11}$.

3. head of priestly family, <PREP> לְ of possession, *of, (belonging) to* Ne 12$_{15}$ (or em. לִמְרֵמוֹת *of Meremoth*).

*מָרִים I $_{5}$ n.m. **blessing**—pl. מָרִים—<CSTR> מֵי מָרִים *waters of blessing* Nm 5$_{18.19}$ (מֵי הַמָּרִים הַמְאָרְרִים *the waters of blessing that [also] curse*, i.e. that bless or curse; :: ארר pi. *curse*) 5$_{23}$. <PREP> לְ *for*, + בוא *enter* Nm 5$_{24.27}$.

מָרִים II *flowing*, see מרר IV *flow*.

מָרִים III *rebellion*, see מרר VI *be rebellious*.

*מְרָים I n.m. **desire**—<NOM CL> מְרַיִם כְּסִילִים קָלוֹן *the desire of fools is shame(ful)* Pr 3$_{35}$ (if em. כְּסִילִים מְרִים קָלוֹן *fools exalt shame*). <CSTR> מְרַיִם כְּסִילִים *the desire of fools* Pr 3$_{35}$.
⇒ רום *desire*.

מִרְיָם II $_{15.0.1}$ pr.n.f. **Miriam, 1.** sister of Aaron and Moses, daughter of Amram, <SUBJ> היה *be* Nm 12$_{10}$, אמר *say* Nm 12$_{1}$, דבר pi. *speak* Nm 12$_{1.8}$, ענה *answer* Ex 15$_{21}$, שׁמע *hear* Nm 12$_{5}$, ירא *fear* Nm 12$_{5}$, יצא *go out* Nm 12$_{4.5}$, אסף ni. *be gathered*, i.e. brought in Nm 12$_{10.15}$, סגר ni. *be shut up* Nm 12$_{15}$ 4QapMos^{c} 2.1$_{9}$ (ותסג[ר]), לקח *take* Ex 15$_{20}$, יאל ni. *be foolish* Nm 12$_{10}$, חטא *sin* Nm 12$_{10}$, כלם ni. *be put to shame* Nm 12$_{10}$, צרע pu. *be struck with leprosy* Nm 12$_{10.10}$, מות *die* Nm 20$_{1}$, קבר ni. *be buried* Nm 20$_{1}$.

<NOM CL> בְּנֵי עַמְרָם ... מִרְיָם *the children of Amram were ... Miriam* 1 C 5$_{29}$.

<OBJ> קרא *call* Nm 12$_{5}$, שׁלח *send* Mc 6$_{4}$, ילד *bear* Nm 26$_{59}$.

<APP> אָחוֹת *sister* Ex 15$_{20}$ Nm 26$_{59}$, נְבִיאָה *female prophet* Ex 15$_{20}$.

<PREP> לְ of direction, *to*, + עשׂה *do* Dt 24$_{9}$; introducing object, + רפא *heal* Nm 12$_{10}$; בְּ of agent, *by means of, through*, + דבר pi. *speak* Nm 12$_{1}$; *against*, + חרה (of anger) *be kindled* Nm 12$_{5}$; אֶל *to*, + אמר *say* Nm 12$_{4}$, פנה *turn* Nm 12$_{10}$; עַל *against*, + שׁית *place* Nm 12$_{10}$; אַחֲרֵי *after*, + יצא *go out* Ex 15$_{20}$.

2. Judahite, <OBJ> הרה *conceive* 1 C 4$_{17}$ (or em. יוֹלֶד יֶתֶר וְיָלוֹן וַתַּהַר *and Jalon, and she conceived* to *and Jether begat*), ילד hi. *beget* 1 C 4$_{17}$ (if em.).*

*[מְרִירָה] n.f. *act of violence*—<OBJ> כתב *write* Jb 13$_{26}$ (if em. מְרֹרוֹת *bitter things* to מְרִרוֹת *acts of violence*).
⇒ מרר *be strong*.

מְרִירוּת $_{1}$ n.f. **bitterness,** <PREP> בְּ of accompaniment, *with* perh. 4Q418 200$_{1}$ ([במרירן]), + אנח ni. *sigh* Ezk 21$_{11}$ (+ שִׁבָּרוֹן *breaking* of loins).*
⇒ מרר I *be bitter*.

מְרִירִי I $_{2.1}$ adj. **bitter**—pl. cstr. מְרִירֵי—**1.** used attributively of קֶטֶב *destruction*, i.e. pestilence Dt 32$_{24}$ (unless מְרִירִי III *mighty*).

2. as noun, **a. bitter one,** <CSTR> מרירי יום *bitter ones of day*, i.e. those whose day is bitter Si 11$_{4}$. <PREP> בְּ introducing object, + קלס pi. *mock* Si 11$_{4}$.

b. poisonous one, <CSTR> מְרִירֵי יָם *Poisonous Ones of Yam* Jb 3$_{5}$ (if em. יוֹם *of the day*).* <PREP> כְּ *as*, + בעת pi. *terrify* Jb 3$_{5}$ (unless מְרִירִי II *demon*; or em. כַּמְרִירֵי *darkness of*).
⇒ מרר I *be bitter*.

*[מְרִירִי] II $_{2}$ n.m. **demon,** name of a demon, **Meriri**—pl. cstr. מְרִירֵי—<CSTR> מְרִירֵי יוֹם *demons of the day* Jb 3$_{5}$ (unless מְרִירִי I *bitter*); קֶטֶב מְרִירִי *devastation of Meriri* Dt 32$_{24}$ (unless מְרִירִי I *bitter* or III *mighty*; || רֶשֶׁף *Resheph*, בְּהֵמוֹת *Behemoth*). <PREP> כְּ asseverative, + בעת pi. *terrify* Jb 3$_{5}$ (unless מְרִירִי I *bitter*).

*מְרִירִי III $_{1}$ adj. **mighty**, used attributively of קֶטֶב *destruction* Dt 32$_{24}$ (unless מְרִירִי I *bitter* or II *Meriri*).
⇒ מרר IV *be strong*.

מֹרֶךְ $_{1}$ n.[m.] **faintness, despair,** <OBJ> בוא hi. *bring* into heart Lv 26$_{36}$.
⇒ רכך *be tender*.

מֶרְכָּב $_{3}$ n.m. **saddle, chariotry**—sf. מֶרְכָּבוֹ—**1.**

means for riding (Lv 15_{9}),* such as **saddle, seat** of litter (Ca 3_{10}), <SUBJ> טמא *be unclean* Lv 15_{9}. <OBJ> עשׂה *make* of purple Ca 3_{10} (unless מֶרְכָּבוֹ אַרְגָּמָן is nom. cl., *its seat was of purple*; or em. אַלְגֻּמִּן *of algum*; || עַמּוּד *post*, רְפִידָה *support*). <CSTR> כָּל־הַמֶּרְכָּב *any saddle* Lv 15_{9}. <PREP> עַל *upon*, + רכב *ride* Lv 15_{9}.

2. chariotry, or perh. **chariot depot,*** <PREP> לְ of benefit, *for*, + היה *be* 1 K 5_{6}.

<SYN> §1 עַמּוּד *post*, רְפִידָה *support*.*

⇒ רכב *ride*.

מֶרְכָּבָה 44.1.11 n.f. **chariot**—cstr. מִרְכֶּבֶת; sf. מֶרְכַּבְתּוֹ; pl. מַרְכָּבוֹת; cstr. מַרְכְּבוֹת (מַרְכְּבֹת); sf. מַרְכְּבֹתֶיךָ, מַרְכְּבוֹתָיו (מַרְכְּבֹתָיו), מַרְכְּבֹתֵיהֶם—**1. chariot, chariotry,** for war (e.g. Ex 14_{25} 15_{4} Jos $11_{6.9}$ Jg 4_{15} 5_{28} 1 K 20_{33} 22_{35}||2 C 18_{34} Jr 4_{13} Mc 5_{9} Na 3_{2} Hg 2_{22} 2 C 14_{8} 35_{24} 1QM 11_{10}).

2. chariot for transport (e.g. Gn 46_{29} 2 K $5_{21.26}$).

3. chariot in ceremonial use (Gn 41_{43} 1 S $8_{11.11}$ 2 S 15_{1} Is 22_{18} 4QJub^{h} 40_{6}).

4. chariot in prophetic vision (Zc $6_{1.2.2.3.3}$ Si 49_{8} 4QpsEzek^{a} 4_{6}).

5. chariot in the cult of the sun (2 K 23_{11}).

6. chariot as bearing the cherubim in the temple (1 C 28_{18}).

7. heavenly **chariot** for Y.'s battles (Is 66_{15} Hb 3_{8} 4QBer^{a} 1.2_{2}); in the heavenly sanctuary (4QShirShabb^{d} 1.2_{15} 4QShirShabb^{f} $20.2_{3.4}$ [[למרכבו]ת] $20_{5.8.11}$).

<SUBJ> הלל pi. *praise* 4QShirShabb^{d} 1.2_{15}, יצא *go out* Zc 6_{1}, i.e. be imported 1 K 10_{29}, רקד *skip*, i.e. jolt Na 3_{2}.

<NOM CL> שָׁמָּה מַרְכְּבוֹת כְּבוֹדֶךָ *there shall be your glorious chariots* Is 22_{18}, כַּסּוּפָה מַרְכְּבֹתָיו *his chariots are as the stormwind* Is 66_{15} Jr 4_{13}.

<OBJ> יצא hi. *bring out*, i.e. import 2 C 1_{17}, עלה hi. *bring up* 2 C 1_{17}, נהג pi. *drive* Ex 14_{25}, אסר *bind*, i.e. prepare Gn 46_{29}, ירה *throw* Ex 15_{4}, עשׂה *make*, i.e. acquire 2 S 15_{1}, רתם *attach* Mc 1_{13}, הפך *overthrow* Hg 2_{22}, שׂרף *burn* Jos $11_{6.9}$ 2 K 23_{11}, אבד hi. *destroy* Mc 5_{9}.

<CSTR> מַרְכְּבֹת פַּרְעֹה *chariots of Pharaoh* Ex 15_{4}, מַרְכְּבוֹת עַמִּי־נָדִיב appar. *chariots of my people, the noble*, i.e. my noble people Ca 6_{12} (unless *of Amminadib*; mss עַמִּינָדָב *of Amminadab*; or em. מֶרְכַּבַת עִם נָדִיב *a chariot* [archaic form, or cstr. with following preposition] *with a prince*),* מִרְכֶּבֶת הַמִּשְׁנֶה *chariot of the second one* Gn 41_{43}, מַרְכְּבוֹת הַשֶּׁמֶשׁ *chariots of the sun* 2 K 23_{11}, מרכבות דבירו *chariots of his inner shrine* 4QShirShabb^{d} 1.2_{15}, מַרְכְּבוֹת כְּבוֹדֶךָ *chariots of your glory*, i.e. your glorious chariots Is 22_{18} 4QBer^{a} 1.2_{2} (כבודכה), מרכבות כבודו *chariots of his glory*, i.e. his glorious chariots 4QShirShabb^{f} $20.2_{3.5}$, הדרו *of his splendour*, i.e. his splendid chariots 11QShirShabb 10_{7} ([מר]כבות), [ה]פלא *of wonder*, i.e. wonderful chariots 4QShirShabb^{f} 20.2_{11}.

שלישי מרכבותיו *officers of his chariots* 1QM 11_{10}, כסא מרכבה *throne of the chariot* 4QShirShabb^{f} 20.2_{8}, אוֹפַן הַמֶּרְכָּבָה *the wheel of the chariot* 1 K 7_{33}, מַרְכְּבֹתָיו *of his chariots* Ex 14_{25} (אֹפַן), קוֹל מַרְכָּבוֹת *sound of chariots* Jl 2_{5}, פַּעֲמֵי מַרְכְּבוֹתָיו *hoofbeats of his chariots* Jg 5_{28}, אֻרְיוֹת ... מֶרְכָּבוֹת *stalls of*, i.e. for, ... *chariots* 2 C 9_{25}, תַּבְנִית הַמֶּרְכָּבָה *plan of the chariot* 1 C 28_{18}, כבוד מרכבות *glory of the chariots of* 4QShirShabb^{f} 20.2_{11}. נגה מרכבה *brightness of the chariot* 4QpsEzek^{a} 4_{6}, זני מרכבה *kinds of chariot* Si 49_{8}.

<APP> סוּסֶיךָ מַרְכְּבֹתֶיךָ יְשׁוּעָה *your horses, your victorious chariot(s)* Hb 3_{8}, הַמֶּרְכָּבָה הַכְּרֻבִים זָהָב *the golden chariot (for) the cherubim* 1 C 28_{18}.

<ADJ> רִאשׁוֹן *first* Zc 6_{2}, שֵׁנִי *second* Zc 6_{2} 4QJub^{h} 40_{6} ([ה]שנית), שְׁלִשִׁי *third* Zc 6_{3}, רְבִיעִי *fourth* Zc 6_{3}.

<PREP> לְ of possession, *of, (belonging) to* Is 2_{7} 4QShirShabb^{f} 20.2_{4} (למרכבו[ת]).

בְּ of place, *in(to)* Zc $6_{2.2.3.3}$, + עלה *go up* 1 K 12_{18}||2 C 10_{18}, hi. *take up* 1 K 20_{33}, רכב hi. *cause to ride* Gn 41_{43}, עמד hi. appar. *prop oneself up* 2 C 18_{34}, ho. *be propped up* 1 K 22_{35}, שׂים *place* 1 S 8_{11}; of accompaniment, *with*, + יצא *go out* 2 C 14_{8}.

מִן of direction, *from*, + עבר hi. *remove* 2 C 35_{24}.

אֶל *in*, + נכה hi. *strike* 2 K 9_{27}, עלה hi. *take up* 2 K 10_{15}.

עַל *upon, in*, + רכב *ride* Hb 3_{8}, hi. *cause to ride* 4QJub^{h} 40_{6}.

מֵעַל *from (upon)*, + ירד *go down* Jg 4_{15}, נפל *fall*, i.e. get down 2 K 5_{21}, הפך *turn* 2 K 5_{26}.

לִפְנֵי *before*, + רוץ *run* 1 S 8_{11}.

מַרְכְּבוֹת without prep., *in, among the chariots of*, +

שִׂים *place* Ca 6_{12} (or em. שִׂים to שׂמח pi. *make glad*).

<COLL> סוּס || מֶרְכָּבָה *horse* Jos $11_{6.9}$ 2 S 15_1 Jr 4_{13} (+) Mc 5_9 Na 3_2 Hg 2_{22} 2 C 9_{25}, חַיִל *army* Ex 15_4 2 C 14_8.

אַרְבַּע מַרְכָּבוֹת *four chariots* Zc 6_1, שְׁלֹשׁ מֵאוֹת מַרְכָּבוֹת *three hundred chariots* 2 C 14_8.

Also 4QShirShabb^f 37_1 ([מר]כבות) 47_1 ([מ]רבו[ת]) 11QShirShabb 6_3 ([מרכב).

<SYN> סוּס *horse*, חַיִל *army*.*

⇒ רכב *ride*.

[מַרְכֹּלֶת] 1 n.f. **market place**—sf. מַרְכֻלְתֵּךְ—**market place** or **trading**, <PREP> בְּ of place, *in* Ezk 27_{24} (or em. בָּם רְכֻלָּתֵךְ *in them was your trade*).*

⇒ רכל *trade*.

מִרְמָה I 39.1.8 n.f. **deceit**—pl. מִרְמוֹת—**deceit, treachery,** perh. **self-deceit** (Pr 14_8) or **disillusionment** (Pr $14_{8.25}$)* or **slander** (Ps 5_7), <SUBJ> מושׁ *depart* Ps 55_{12}, מצא ni. *be found* 1QS 10_{22}.

<NOM CL> תַּחְבֻּלוֹת רְשָׁעִים מִרְמָה *the counsels of the wicked are deceit* Pr 12_5, דִּבְרֵי־פִיו ... מִרְמָה *the words of his mouth are ... deceit* Ps 36_4, var. Jr 9_7 (if em.; see Obj.), אִוֶּלֶת כְּסִילִים מִרְמָה *the folly of fools is self-deceit* Pr 14_8, יָפִחַ כְּזָבִים מִרְמָה *a witness of lies is deceit,* i.e. a false witness is a deceiver Pr 14_{25}, לֹא מִרְמָה בְּפִיו *there was no deceit in his mouth* Is 53_9, מִרְמָה בְּמִרְמָה *there is deceit with,* i.e. upon, *deceit* Jr 9_5 (if em.; see Prep.), מִרְמָה בְּלֶב־חֹרְשֵׁי רָע *deceit is in the heart of those who devise evil* Pr 12_{20} (or em. מָרָה *bitterness*), מרמה בלבבם perh. *deceit is in their heart* 4QapPs^b 85_3.

<OBJ> דבר pi. *speak* Jr 9_7 (or em. דִּבֵּר בְּפִיו to דִּבְרֵי פִּיו *the words of his mouth* are deceit) Ps 34_{14}, נגד hi. *tell* Pr 12_{17}, הגה *imagine* Ps 38_{13}, צמד hi. *join together,* i.e. frame Ps 50_9, כון hi. *prepare* Jb 15_{35}, קרב hi. *bring near* 4QJub^f 39_9 ([ותקרב]), מלא pi. *fill with* Zp 1_9, שׁית *place* Pr 26_{24}, עשׂה *do* Dn 11_{23}, צלח hi. *cause to prosper* Dn 8_{25}.

<CSTR> אִישׁ־מִרְמָה *man of deceit* Ps 5_6 (... אִישׁ) 43_1, ... אַנְשֵׁי *men of ...* Ps 55_{24} 1QH 4_{20} (אנשי מרמה), לב מרמה *heart of deceit,* i.e. deceitful heart 4QBéat 2.2_3 5_7, שִׂפְתֵי מִרְמָה *lips of deceit,* i.e. deceitful lips Ps 17_1, לְשׁוֹן *tongue of* Ps 52_6 Si 51_6, פִּי־ *mouth of* Ps 109_2, דִּבְרֵי *words of* Ps 35_{20}, מֹאזְנֵי *balances of,* i.e. deceptive balances Ho 12_8 Am 8_5 Pr 11_1 20_{23}, אַבְנֵי *stones of,* i.e. deceptive weights Mc 6_{11}.

<PREP> לְ *according to,* i.e. deceitfully, + שׁבע ni. *swear* Ps 24_1.

בְּ of accompaniment, *with, in* Jr 9_5, + ענה *answer* Gn 34_{13} (or em. בְּמִרְמָה וַיְדַבֵּרוּ *with deceit, and they spoke* to וַיְדַבְּרוּ בְמִרְמָה *and they spoke with deceit*), דבר pi. *speak* Gn 34_{13} (if em.; see above), הלך *walk* 1QpHab 3_5, בוא *come* Gn 27_{35}, סבב *surround* Ho 12_1.

עַל *upon,* i.e. towards, + חושׁ hi. *hasten* Jb 31_5.

בְּתוֹךְ *among,* + ישׁב *dwell* appar. Jr 9_5 (or שִׁבְתְּךָ בְּתוֹךְ *your dwelling is among* to שֵׁב: תּוֹךְ בְּתוֹךְ *to repent. There is oppression with oppression,* deceit with deceit).

<COLL> מִרְמָה || כַּחַשׁ *lie* Ho 12_1, כָּזָב *lie* 1QS 10_{22}, נֵכֶל *craft* 1QpHab 3_5, תֹּךְ *oppression* Ps 10_7 (מִרְמוֹת וָתֹךְ) 55_{12}, עַוְלָה *injustice* Ps 43_1, חָמָס *violence* Zp 1_9, דָּם *blood(shed)* Ps 5_7 55_{24}, הַוָּה *destruction* Ps 38_{13} 55_{12} (+), בֶּלַע *destruction* Ps 52_6, אָוֶן *iniquity* Ps 36_4 Jb 15_{35} (+).

+ שֶׁקֶר *falsehood* Ps 109_2, שָׁוְא *vanity* Jb 31_5, אָלָה *curse* Ps 10_7, רַע *evil* Ps 34_{14}, רָעָה *evil* Ps 50_9, רֶשַׁע *wickedness* Mc 6_{11}.

:: מִשְׁפָּט *justice* Pr 12_5, צֶדֶק *righteousness* Pr 12_{17}.

בָּתֵּיהֶם מְלֵאִים מִרְמָה *their houses are full of deceit* Jr 5_{27}, פִּיהוּ מָלֵא מִרְמוֹת *his mouth is full of deceit* Ps 10_7 (mss) (L וּמִרְמוֹת *and deceit*), מִרְמָה אֲחַזְיָה *treachery, O Ahaziah!* 2 K 9_{23}.

Also 4Q418 87_2.

<SYN> כַּחַשׁ *lie*, כָּזָב *lie*, נֵכֶל *craft*, תֹּךְ *oppression*, עַוְלָה *injustice*, חָמָס *violence*, דָּם *blood(shed)*, הַוָּה *destruction*, בֶּלַע *destruction*, אָוֶן *iniquity*.

<ANT> מִשְׁפָּט *justice*, צֶדֶק *righteousness*.*

⇒ רמה *deceive*.

מִרְמָה II 1 pr.n.m. **Mirmah**, Benjaminite, son of Shaharaim, <OBJ> ילד hi. *beget* 1 C 8_{10}.

מְרֵמוֹת 6.0.0.2 pr.n.m. **Meremoth**—I מרימות—**1.** priest, repairer of the walls of Jerusalem, son of Uriah, and co-signatory with Nehemiah, <SUBJ> חזק hi. *strength-*

en, i.e. repair Ne 3$_{4.21}$. <NOM CL> עַל הַחֲתוּמִים ... מְרֵמוֹת *upon (the documents) that were sealed are ... Meremoth* Ne 10$_{4}$ (or em. עַל הַחֲתוּמִים to הַחוֹתְמִים *those who sealed*, i.e. signed, or אֵלֶּה הַחוֹתְמִים *these are the signatories*). <CSTR> יַד־מְרֵמוֹת *hand of Meremoth* Ezr 8$_{33}$. <APP> בֵּן *son* Ezr 8$_{33}$ Ne 3$_{4.21}$, כֹּהֵן *priest* Ezr 8$_{33}$.

2. priest (or priestly family) who returned from exile with Zerubbabel, <SUBJ> עלה *go up* Ne 12$_{3}$. <NOM CL> אֵלֶּה הַכֹּהֲנִים וְהַלְוִיִּם ... מְרֵמוֹת *these are the priests and the Levites ... Meremoth* Ne 12$_{2}$. <PREP> לְ of possession, *of, (belonging) to* Ne 12$_{15}$ (if em. לִמְרָיוֹת *of Meremoth*).

3. husband of non-Jewish wife, <NOM CL> מִבְּנֵי בָנִי ... מְרֵמוֹת *of the sons of Bani were ... Meremoth* Ezr 10$_{36}$.

4. Arad ost. 50$_{1}$.

5. appar. recipient of goods at Samaria, Samaria ost. 33$_{3}$ (מר]מות]; others מנת[ ]).

6. Seal 754 (מרימות; c. 700), <PREP> לְ of possession, *of, (belonging) to* Seal 754 (c. 700).

מִרְמָס 7.0.1 n.[m.] **trampling place**—cstr. מִרְמַס—**trampling place, trampled ground,** <NOM CL> מרמס גיזעו לכול עוברי דרך *its stump shall be a trampling place to all who pass by in the way* 1QH 8$_{8}$. <OBJ> שׂים *place*, i.e. make (into) Is 10$_{6}$ (+ חֹמֶר *mud*), נתן *give*, i.e. make (into) Dn 8$_{13}$, רעה *graze on* Ezk 34$_{19}$. <CSTR> מִרְמַס שֶׂה *trampling place of sheep* Is 7$_{25}$ (|| מִשְׁלַח *place of letting loose*), רַגְלֵיכֶם *of your feet* Ezk 34$_{19}$ (|| מִרְפָּשׂ *muddied waterhole*). <PREP> לְ *as* or introducing predicate, + היה *be* Is 5$_{5}$ Is 7$_{25}$ 28$_{18}$ Mc 7$_{10}$ (+ טִיט *mud*).

<SYN> מִרְפָּשׂ *muddied waterhole*, מִשְׁלָח *place of letting loose*.

⇒ רמס *trample*.

*[**מִרְמָשׂ**] 0.0.1 n.[m.] **reptile,** 4QRitMar 9$_{5}$ (+ מִקְנֶה *cattle*).

⇒ רמשׂ *creep*.

*[**מְרָנְיוֹ**] pr.n.[m.] **Meraniah,** appar. recipient of goods at Samaria, Samaria ost. 42$_{3}$ (others אדניו *Adonijah*).

מֵרֹנֹתִי 2 gent. **Meronothite,** as noun, an individual **Meronothite,** <SUBJ> חזק hi. *strengthen*, i.e. repair Ne 3$_{7}$. <NOM CL> עַל־הָאֲתֹנוֹת ... הַמֵּרֹנֹתִי *over the she-asses was ... the Meronothite* 1 C 27$_{30}$. <APP> יָדוֹן *Jadon* Ne 3$_{7}$, יֶחְדְּיָהוּ *Jehdeiah* 1 C 27$_{30}$, אִישׁ *man* Ne 3$_{7}$.

מֶרֶס 1 pr.n.m. **Meres,** prince at court of King Ahasuerus, <SUBJ> ראה *see* Est 1$_{14}$, ישׁב *dwell* Est 1$_{14}$. <NOM CL> הַקָּרֹב אֵלָיו ... מֶרֶס *the one(s) who were near to him were ... Meres* Est 1$_{14}$. (or em. הִקְרִיב *he brought near*). <OBJ> קרב hi. *bring near* Est 1$_{14}$ (if em.; see Nom. Cl.). <APP> שַׂר *prince* Est 1$_{14}$.

מַרְסְנָא 1 pr.n.m. **Marsena,** prince at court of King Ahasuerus, <SUBJ> ראה *see* Est 1$_{14}$, ישׁב *dwell* Est 1$_{14}$. <NOM CL> הַקָּרֹב אֵלָיו ... מַרְסְנָא *the one(s) who were near to him were ... Marsena* Est 1$_{14}$. (or em. הִקְרִיב *he brought near*). <OBJ> קרב hi. *bring near* Est 1$_{14}$ (if em.; see Nom. Cl.). <APP> שַׂר *prince* Est 1$_{14}$.

*[**מַרְסַרְזְרֻכִן**] pr.n.[m.] **Marsarzeruchin,** <CSTR> [ב]ן מרסרזר[כן] *son of Marsarzeruchin* T. en-Naṣbeh inscr. 4.

מֵרַע, see רעע *be evil*, Hi.

[**מֵרֵעַ**] 9 n.m. **friend**—sf. מֵרֵעֲךָ, מֵרֵעֵהוּ (מֵרֵעֵהוּ); pl. מֵרֵעִים—of bridegroom (Jg 14$_{11}$ 15$_{2.6}$), of king's adviser (Gn 26$_{26}$; unless מַרְעֶה *pasturage supervisor*), <SUBJ> היה *be* Jg 14$_{11}$, הלך *go* Gn 26$_{26}$ (unless from מַרְעֶה *pasturage supervisor*), רחק *be distant* Pr 19$_{7}$ (+ אָח *brother*), מאס *refuse* Jb 6$_{14}$ (if em. לַמָּס מֵרֵעֵהוּ *to the despairing one from his friend* [i.e. מִן *from* + רֵעַ *friend*] to לֹא מָאַס מֵרֵעַ *a friend does not refuse*), פרד ni. *separate oneself*, i.e. withdraw Pr 19$_{4(mss)}$ (L מֵרֵעֵהוּ *from his friend*, i.e. מִן + רֵעַ). <OBJ> לקח *take* Jg 14$_{11}$, תור hi. *search out* appar. Pr 12$_{26}$ (or em. יָתֵר מִרְעֵהוּ *he seeks out his pasture* or יָסַר מֵרָעָה *he turns aside from evil*). <APP> אֲחֻזַּת *Ahuzath* Gn 26$_{26}$ (unless מַרְעֶה *pasturage supervisor*). <PREP> לְ of possession, *of, (belonging) to*, + היה *be* Jg 14$_{20}$; of direction, *to*, + נתן

give Jg 15$_{2.6}$; אֶל *to*, + עשׂה *do*, i.e. show, loyalty 2 S 3$_{8}$ (|| אָח *brother*). <COLL> שְׁלֹשִׁים מֵרֵעִים *thirty friends* Jg 14$_{11}$.

<SYN> אָח *brother*.

⇒ רעה *associate with*.

*[מַרְעֶה] $_{1}$ n.m. **pasturage supervisor** (unless from מֵרֵעַ *friend*)—sf. מֵרֵעֵהוּ—<SUBJ> הלך *go* Gn 26$_{26}$. <APP> אֲחֻזַּת *Ahuzath* Gn 26$_{26}$.

מִרְעֶה $_{13}$ n.m. **pasture**—cstr. מִרְעֵה; sf. מִרְעֵהוּ, מִרְעֵיכֶם—**pasture, grazing land,** usu. for sheep; for cattle (Jl 1$_{18}$), wild ass (Jb 39$_{8}$), stag (Lm 1$_{6}$), young lion (Na 2$_{11}$; or em; see Nom. Cl.), <SUBJ> היה *be* Is 32$_{14}$ (|| מָשׂוֹשׂ *joy*). <NOM CL> מִרְעֶה לְצֹאנָם שָׁם *there was pasture for their flocks there* 1 C 4$_{41}$, אֵין מִרְעֶה *there is no pasture* Gn 47$_{24}$ Jl 1$_{18}$, מִרְעֶה הוּא לַכְּפִרִים *it is the pasture of the young lions* Na 2$_{11}$ (or em. מְעָרָה *cave*). <OBJ> רעה *feed on* Ezk 34$_{14}$ (|| נָוֶה *pasture*) 34$_{18}$, בקשׁ pi. *seek* 1 C 4$_{39}$, תור *seek out* Jb 39$_{8}$ Pr 12$_{26}$ (if em. יָתֵר מֵרֵעֵהוּ *he searches out his friend* to יָתֻר מִרְעֵהוּ *he seeks out his pasture*), מצא *find* Lm 1$_{6}$ 1 C 4$_{40}$. <CSTR> מִרְעֵה עֲדָרִים *pasture of flocks* Is 32$_{14}$; יֶתֶר מִרְעֵיכֶם *rest of your pasture* Ezk 34$_{18}$. <APP> הַר *mountain* Jb 39$_{8}$. <ADJ> טוֹב *good* Ezk 34$_{14.18}$ 1 C 4$_{40}$, שָׁמֵן *fat* Ezk 34$_{14}$ 1 C 4$_{40}$. <PREP> בְּ of instrument, *by (means of), with*, + רעה *feed* Ezk 34$_{14}$.

<SYN> נָוֶה *pasture*, מָשׂוֹשׂ *joy*.

⇒ רעה *pasture*.

[מַרְעִית] $_{10.1.4}$ n.f. **pasturing**—cstr. Si מרעית; sf. מַרְעִיתִי, מַרְעִיתֶךָ, מַרְעִיתָם, מַרְעִיתוֹ, (Q מרעיתכה) מַרְעִיתָם (Q מרעיתמה)—**1. pasturing, shepherding,** <CSTR> צֹאן מַרְעִיתִי *sheep of my pasturing* Jr 23$_{1}$ Ezk 34$_{31}$, מַרְעִיתֶךָ *of your pasturing* Ps 74$_{1}$ 79$_{13}$ (מַרְעִיתֶךָ) 4QD^{a} 11$_{13}$ (צון; + עם פדותכה *people of your redemption*), מַרְעִיתוֹ *of his pasturing* Ps 100$_{3}$, עַם מַרְעִיתוֹ *people of his pasturing* Ps 95$_{7}$ (+ צֹאן יָדוֹ *sheep of his hand*), עם מרעיתכה *people of your pasturing* 4Q418 172$_{10}$. <PREP> בְּ perh. of instrument, *by (means of), with* 4Q418 173$_{5}$.

2. pasture, pasturage, <NOM CL> מרעית עשיר דלים *the poor are the pasture of the rich* Si 13$_{19}$, בְּכָל־שְׁפָיִים מַרְעִיתָם *on all the bare heights shall be their pasture* Is 49$_{9}$. <OBJ> שׁדד *despoil* Jr 25$_{36}$. <CSTR> מרעית עשיר *pasture of the rich* Si 13$_{19}$. <PREP> כְּ *according to*, + שׂבע *be satisfied* Ho 13$_{6}$ (or em. כְּמוֹ רְעִיתִים *when I fed them* or כִּרְעוֹתָם *when they fed*).

3. flock, <SUBJ> פוץ ni. *be scattered* Jr 10$_{21}$. <CSTR> כָּל־מַרְעִיתָם *all their flock* Jr 10$_{21}$.

Also 4Q418 172$_{11}$ 173$_{2}$ ([מר]עיתמה).

⇒ רעה *pasture*.

מַרְעֲלָה $_{1}$ pl.n. **Maralah,** on border of Zebulun, <COLL> וְעָלָה גְבוּלָם לַיָּמָּה מַרְעֲלָה *and their border goes up westward (to) Maralah* Jos 19$_{11}$.

מַרְפֵּא I $_{15.2.9}$ n.m. **healing**—מַרְפֵּה; cstr. מַרְפֵּא—**healing, remedy, health,** <SUBJ> היה *be* 1QH 2$_{8}$, פתח ni. *be opened up* 4QHod^{a} 7.2$_{4}$. <NOM CL> לְשׁוֹן חֲכָמִים מַרְפֵּא *the speech of the wise is healing* Pr 12$_{18}$, צִיר אֱמוּנִים מַרְפֵּא *a faithful messenger is healing* Pr 13$_{17}$, חַיֵּי בְשָׂרִים לֵב מַרְפֵּא *a mind of health is the life of the flesh* Pr 14$_{30}$ (unless מַרְפֵּא II), מַרְפֵּא לָשׁוֹן עֵץ חַיִּים *the healing of the tongue is a tree of life* Pr 15$_{4}$ (unless מַרְפֵּא II), אִמְרֵי־נֹעַם ... מַרְפֵּא לָעָצֶם *pleasant words are ... health to the body* Pr 16$_{24}$, מרפא כל מערף ענן טל *the dripping of the cloud of dew is the healing of all* Si 43$_{22}$, לְכָל־בְּשָׂרוֹ מַרְפֵּא *to all his flesh (they are) healing* Pr 4$_{22}$, יש מרפא לשון *there is healing of tongue*, i.e. soothing speech Si 36$_{28}$, אֵין מַרְפֵּא *there is no healing* Pr 6$_{15}$ 29$_{1}$, vars. Jr 14$_{19}$ 2 C 21$_{18}$ 36$_{16}$ 1QH 2$_{26}$ (unless from מַרְפֵּה *remission*), מַרְפֵּא בִּכְנָפֶיהָ *healing is in its (sun's) wings* Ml 3$_{20}$.

<OBJ> עלה hi. *bring up* Jr 33$_{6}$.

<CSTR> מַרְפֵּא לָשׁוֹן *healing of tongue*, i.e. soothing speech Pr 15$_{4}$ Si 36$_{28}$ (unless both מַרְפֵּא II), מרפא [ע]ולם *healing of everlastingness*, i.e. everlasting healing 1QH 9$_{25}$; עֵת מַרְפֵּא *time of healing* Jr 8$_{15}$ (מַרְפֵּה; unless from מַרְפֶּה *relaxation*) 14$_{19}$.

<PREP> לְ as or introducing predicate 1QS 4$_{6}$, + היה *be* 1QH 9$_{25}$; לְ of benefit, *for*, + אור hi. *cause to shine* 4QDiscourse 2.2$_{8}$, זרח *shine* 4QJub^{a} 2$_{12}$ ([ל]מרפה); יחל לְ pi. *hope for* CD 8$_{4}$.

<COLL> אֲרוּכָה || מַרְפֵּא *healing* Jr 33$_{6}$, מָתוֹק *sweet-*

ness Pr 16$_{24}$; + שָׁלוֹם *peace* Jr 8$_{15}$ 14$_{19}$, חַיִּים *life* Pr 4$_{22}$; :: בְּעָתָה *terror* Jr 8$_{15}$ 14$_{19}$, קִנְאָה *jealousy* Pr 14$_{30}$, פַּח *trap* 1QH 2$_{8}$.

Also 4QParaKings 39$_{5}$.
<SYN> אֲרוּכָה *healing*, מָתוֹק *sweetness*.
<ANT> בְּעָתָה *terror*, קִנְאָה *jealousy*, פַּח *trap*.
⇒ רפא *heal*.

מַרְפֵּא II 3.1 n.m. **calmness**—cstr. מַרְפֵּא—**1. calmness,** <SUBJ> נוח hi. *appease* Ec 10$_{4}$ (unless from מַרְפֶּה *relaxation*; or em. יַנִּיחַ to יָנִיא *it frustrates*, i.e. נוא hi.). <NOM CL> חַיֵּי בְשָׂרִים לֵב מַרְפֵּא *a mind of calmness*, i.e. a calm mind, *is the life of the flesh* Pr 14$_{30}$ (unless מַרְפֵּא I; :: קִנְאָה *jealousy*).

2. gentleness, <NOM CL> יש מרפא לשון *there is gentleness of tongue* Si 36$_{28}$ (unless מַרְפֵּא I), מַרְפֵּא לָשׁוֹן עֵץ חַיִּים *gentleness of the tongue is a tree of life* Pr 15$_{4}$ (unless מַרְפֵּא I). <CSTR> מַרְפֵּא לָשׁוֹן *gentleness of the tongue*, i.e. of speech Pr 15$_{4}$ Si 36$_{28}$ (unless both מַרְפֵּא I).
⇒ רפה *relax*.

מַרְפֵּה, see מַרְפֵּא I *healing*, מַרְפֶּה *relaxation*.

*[**מַרְפֶּה**] 3.0.1 n.m. **relaxation**—מַרְפֶּה, Q מרפא—**relaxation, remission,** <SUBJ> נוח hi. *appease* Ec 10$_{4}$ (unless from מַרְפֵּא II *calmness*). <NOM CL> אין מרפא *there is no remission* 1QH 2$_{26}$ (unless from מַרְפֵּא I *healing*). <CSTR> עֵת מַרְפֵּה *time of healing* Jr 8$_{15}$ (unless from מַרְפֵּא I *healing*).

[**מִרְפָּשׂ**] 1 n.[m.] **muddied waterhole**—cstr. מִרְפַּשׂ—as a result of trampling, <OBJ> שׁתה *drink* Ezk 34$_{19}$ (|| מִרְמָס *trampling place*). <CSTR> מִרְפַּשׂ רַגְלֵיכֶם *muddied waterhole of your feet*, i.e. that your feet have muddied Ezk 34$_{19}$.
<SYN> מִרְמָס *trampling place*.
⇒ רפשׂ *trample*.

מרץ I 4.0.2 vb. **be sick—Ni.** 3.0.2 Pf. נִמְרְצוּ; ptc. נִמְרָץ, נִמְרֶצֶת—**be sickening, painful, grievous,** <SUBJ> אֹמֶר *word* Jb 6$_{25}$ (unless מרץ II ni. *be forceful* or III *be victorious*; or em. מלץ ni. *be pleasant*), קְלָלָה *curse* 1 K 2$_{8}$ (unless מרץ II or III), חֶבֶל *destruction* Mc 2$_{10}$, חֵבֶל *labour pains* 1QH 3$_{8.12}$. <COLL> מרץ ni. + adverb מָה *how!* Jb 6$_{25}$ (unless מרץ II ni. *be bitter* or III *be victorious*).

Hi. 1 Impf. יַמְרִיצְךָ—**sicken,** <SUBJ> מָה *what?* Jb 16$_{3}$. <OBJ> friends of Job Jb 16$_{3}$.
⇒ מֶרֶץ *agony*.

*מרץ II 4 vb. **be forceful, be difficult—Ni.** 3 Pf. נִמְרְצוּ; ptc. נִמְרֶצֶת, נִמְרָץ—<SUBJ> אֹמֶר *word* Jb 6$_{25}$ (unless מרץ I *be sick* or III *be victorious*), קְלָלָה *curse* 1 K 2$_{8}$ (unless מרץ I or III), חֶבֶל *destruction* Mc 2$_{10}$ (unless מרץ I *be sick*). <COLL> מרץ ni. + adverb מָה *how!* Jb 6$_{25}$ (unless מרץ I *be sick* or III *be victorious*).

Hi. 1 Impf. יַמְרִיצְךָ—**provoke** (unless מרץ I *sicken*), <SUBJ> מָה *what?* Jb 16$_{3}$. <OBJ> friends of Job Jb 16$_{3}$.

*מרץ III 2 vb. **be victorious** (unless מרץ I *be sick* or II *be forceful*)—**Ni.** 2 Pf. נִמְרְצוּ; ptc. נִמְרֶצֶת—**be victorious,** <SUBJ> אֹמֶר *word* Jb 6$_{25}$, קְלָלָה *curse* 1 K 2$_{8}$. <COLL> מרץ ni. + adverb מָה *how!* Jb 6$_{25}$.

*[**מֶרֶץ**] 0.0.1 n.[m.] **agony,** <CSTR> חבלי מרץ *labour pains of agony* 1QH 3$_{11}$ 6$_{21}$ ([חבלי מרץ]).
⇒ מרץ *be sick*.

מְרֻצָתָם, see מְרוּצָה I *running*.

מַרְצֵעַ 2 n.[m.] **awl,** pointed hand tool, used to pierce ear of slave, <OBJ> לקח *take* Dt 15$_{17}$, נתן *give*, i.e. place Dt 15$_{17}$. <PREP> בְּ of instrument, *by (means of), with*, + רצע *pierce* Ex 21$_{6}$.*
⇒ רצע *pierce*.

[**מַרְצֶפֶת**] 1 n.f. **pavement**—cstr. מַרְצֶפֶת—**pavement** or **plastered floor,** in temple, <CSTR> מַרְצֶפֶת אֲבָנִים *pavement of stones* 2 K 16$_{17}$. <PREP> עַל *upon*, + נתן *give*, i.e. place 2 K 16$_{17}$.*
⇒ רצף *inlay*.

מרק I 4.0.1 vb. **rub—Qal** 2.0.1 Impv. מִרְקוּ; ptc. pass.

מָרוּק, Q מרוקה—**1. polish,** <SUBJ> פָּרָשׁ *cavalry* Jr 46_{4}. <OBJ> רֹמַח *spear* Jr 46_{4}.

2. pass. **be polished,** <SUBJ> נְחֹשֶׁת *bronze* 2 C 4_{16} 1QM 5_{4}.

Pu. $_{1}$ + waw וּמֹרַק—**be scoured,** <SUBJ> כְּלִי bronze *vessel* Lv 6_{21} (+ שׁטף pu. *be rinsed*).

Hi. $_{1}$ Impf. 3fs Kt תמריק—**cleanse away,** <SUBJ> חַבּוּרָה *blow* Pr $20_{30(Kt)}$ (Qr תַּמְרוּק *massage*), מַכָּה *burn* Pr 20_{30} (if em. מַכּוֹת *blows* to מִכְוֹת *burns*). <PREP> בְּ introducing object, + רַע *evil* Pr $20_{30(Kt)}$ (or em. רֵעַ to רַע *will* or מֵעִים *inward parts*).*

⇒ מְרוּקִים *cosmetic treatment*, תַּמְרוּקִים *cosmetic treatment*.

*מרק II $_{0.0.2}$ vb. **complete—Pi.** $_{0.0.2}$ Inf. מרק—**complete (a transaction),** <SUBJ> Salome Mur 30 1_{5} 2_{24}, אִשָּׁה *wife* Mur 30 1_{5} 2_{24}, בַּת *daughter* Mur 30 1_{5} 2_{24}. <OBJ> מֶכֶר *sale* Mur 30 2_{24}. <PREP> לִפְנֵי *before*, + לֹקֵחַ *purchaser* Mur 30 1_{5} 2_{24}. <COLL> אחראים וערבים למרק *guarantors and sureties to complete*, i.e. that I will complete, the sale Mur 30 2_{24}.

מָרָק $_{3.0.1}$ n.[m.] **broth**—cstr. Qr מְרַק—<OBJ> אכל *eat* Is $65_{4(Qr,\ 1QIsa^a)}$ (|| בָּשָׂר *flesh*), שׂים *place* Jg 6_{19} (|| בָּשָׂר), שׁפך *pour* Jg 6_{20} (+ בָּשָׂר, מַצָּה *unleavened bread*), ריק hi. *empty* Ezk 24_{10} (if em. הַרְקַח הַמֶּרְקָחָה *add the spice* to הָרֵק הַמָּרָק *empty the broth*), רחק hi. *remove* Ezk 24_{10} (if em. הַרְקַח הַמֶּרְקָחָה *add the spice* to הַרְחֵק הַמָּרָק *remove the broth*). <CSTR> מְרַק פִּגֻּלִים *broth of foul things* Is $65_{4(Qr,\ 1QIsa^a)}$ (Kt פרק *fragment[s] of*), מרק זבחם *broth of their sacrifices* 4QMMT B_{8}. <PREP> בְּ of accompaniment, *with* 4QMMT B_{8}.

<SYN> בָּשָׂר *flesh*.

[מֶרְקָח] $_{1}$ n.[m.] **perfume**—pl. מֶרְקָחִים—**perfume, spices,** <CSTR> מִגְדְּלוֹת מֶרְקָחִים *raised beds of perfume* Ca 5_{13} (or em. מִגְדָּנוֹת *precious things of*, or מְגַדְּלוֹת *yielding* perfume, i.e. גדל pi.; + בֹּשֶׂם *spice*).

⇒ רקח *mix ointment*.

מֶרְקָחָה $_{2}$ n.f. **pot of ointment** (Jb 41_{23}), **spice** (Ezk 24_{10}; or em.; see Obj.), <OBJ> רקח hi. appar. *add spice* Ezk 24_{10} (or em. הַרְקַח הַמֶּרְקָחָה *add the spice* to הַרְחֵק הַמָּרָק *remove the broth* or הָרֵק הַמָּרָק *empty the broth*). <PREP> כְּ *as*, + שׂים *place*, i.e. make Jb 41_{23} (|| סִיר *pot*).

<SYN> סִיר *pot*.

⇒ רקח *mix ointment*.

מִרְקַחַת $_{3.1}$ n.f. **ointment mixture**—מִרְקַחַת—<OBJ> עשׂה *make* Si 38_{8}. <CSTR> מִרְקַחַת מַעֲשֶׂה *ointment mixture of work*, i.e. by the art of perfumery 2 C 16_{14}; רֹקְחֵי הַמִּרְקַחַת *ones who mixed the ointment* 1 C 9_{30}, רֹקַח מִרְקַחַת *blend of an ointment mixture* Ex 30_{25}. <APP> מַעֲשֶׂה *work* of perfumer Ex 30_{25}. <PREP> בְּ *according to* or of instrument, *by means of*, + רקח pu. *be mixed* 2 C 16_{14}. <COLL> הַמִּרְקַחַת לַבְּשָׂמִים *the ointment mixture of the spices* 1C 9_{30}.*

⇒ רקח *mix ointment*.

מרר I $_{16.2}$ vb. **be bitter—Qal** $_{6}$ Pf. מַר (מָר), מָרָה—**be bitter,** <SUBJ> נֶפֶשׁ *soul* 1 S 30_{6} 2 K 4_{27}, שֵׁכָר *strong drink* Is 24_{9}; impersonal, Is $38_{17.17}$ Ru 1_{13} Lm 1_{4}. <PREP> לְ of benefit, *to, for*, + Zion Lm 1_{4}, Hezekiah Is $38_{17.17}$, Naomi Ru 1_{13}, אֵם *mother* 2 K 4_{27}, מֶלֶךְ *king* Is $38_{17.17}$, שֹׁתֶה *drinker* Is 24_{9}; מִן of cause, *on account of*, + בַּת *daughter* Ru 1_{13}. <COLL> מרר + adverb, מְאֹד *exceedingly* Ru 1_{13}.

Pi. $_{3}$ Pf. אֲמָרֵר; + waw וַיְמָרְרוּ (וַיְמָרֲרֻהוּ)—**1. show bitterness (to),** <SUBJ> Isaiah Is 22_{4}, בַּעַל *lord* of arrows, i.e. archer Gn 49_{23}. <OBJ> Joseph Gn 49_{23}. <COLL> בְּ of accompaniment, *with, in*, בְּכִי *weeping* Is 22_{4} (אֲמָרֵר בַּבֶּכִי *let me show bitterness in weeping*, i.e. weep bitterly). <COLL> וַיְמָרֲרֻהוּ וָרֹבּוּ וַיִּשְׂטְמֻהוּ *and they showed him bitterness and shot at and harassed him* Gn 49_{23}.

2. make bitter (unless מרר III pi. *strengthen*), <SUBJ> Egyptians Ex 1_{14}. <OBJ> חַיִּים *life* Ex 1_{14}. <PREP> בְּ of instrument, *by (means of), with*, + עֲבֹדָה *labour* Ex 1_{14}.

Hi. $_{5.1}$ Pf. הֵמַר; impf. 2ms תַּמֵּר; impv. Si המר; inf. abs. הָמֵר—**1. show bitterness** (Ex 23_{21}; or em.; see Subj.), **show bitter grief** (Zc $12_{10.10}$), <SUBJ> Israel(ites) Ex 23_{21} (or em. תַּמֵּר *you shall* not *be rebellious*, i.e. מרה hi.), בֵּן *son* Si 38_{17} (unless מרר III ni. *strengthen oneself*); subj. not specified, Zc $12_{10.10}$. <PREP> בְּ *against*, + Y. Ex 23_{21} (or em.; see Subj.); עַל *on account of*, + בְּכוֹר *firstborn* Zc 12_{10}, אֲשֶׁר *one who* Zc 12_{10}.

2. make bitter, cause bitterness, <SUBJ> שַׁדַּי *the Almighty* Jb 27_2 Ru 1_{20}, אָב *father* Ps 106_{33} (if em. הִמְרוּ *they provoked* [i.e. מרה hi.] to הֶמָרוּ), בֵּן *son* perh. Si 3_{23} (but prob. תמר is מרה hi.). <OBJ> נֶפֶשׁ *soul* Jb 27_2, רוּחַ *spirit* Ps 106_{33} (if em.; see Subj.). <PREP> לְ *to* or introducing object, + Naomi Ru 1_{20}; בְּ of accompaniment, *with, in*, + יוֹתֵר *excess* perh. Si 3_{23} (but prob. תמר is מרה hi.). <COLL> מרר hi. + adverb, מְאֹד *much* Ru 1_{20}.

Htp. $_{0.1}$ Impv. Si התמרר—**show bitter grief,** <SUBJ> בֵּן *son* Si $38_{16(B)}$ (Bmg htpalp.; + נהה *lament*, זוב hi. *cause* tears *to flow*).

Htpalp. $_{2.1}$ Impf. יִתְמַרְמַר; + waw וַיִּתְמַרְמַר; impv. Si התמרמר—**1. be enraged** (unless מרר III *strengthen oneself*), <SUBJ> מֶלֶךְ *king* Dn 11_{11}, צָפִיר *male goat* Dn 8_7. <PREP> אֶל *against*, + אַיִל *ram* Dn 8_7.

2. show bitter grief, <SUBJ> בֵּן *son* Si $38_{16(Bmg)}$ (B htp.; + זוב hi. *cause* tears *to flow*, נְהִי *lamentation*).*

⇒ מַר I *bitter*, מֹר *myrrh*, מֹרָה *bitterness*, מְרִירוּת *bitterness*, מֶמֶר *bitterness*, מַמְרֹרִים *bitterness*, תַּמְרוּרִים *bitterness*, מְרִירִי *bitter*, מָרָא *Mara*, מָרָה *Marah*.

*מרר II $_1$ vb. **flow—Hi.** $_1$ Inf. הָמִיר—**flow,** <SUBJ> אֶרֶץ *earth* Ps 46_3 (unless from מור hi. *change*).

*מרר III $_{5.1}$ vb. **be strong—Qal, be strong, harden,** <SUBJ> אָב *father* Ps 106_{43} (if em. יַמְרוּ from מרה I hi. *be rebellious* to יָמֹרוּ). <PREP> בְּ of accompaniment, *in, with*, + עֵצָה *counsel* Ps 106_{43}.

Ni. $_{0.1}$ Impv. Si המר—**strengthen oneself** (unless מרר I hi. *show bitterness*), <SUBJ> בֵּן *son* Si 38_{17}.

Pi. 2 + waw וַיְמָרְרוּ (וַיְמָרֲרֻהוּ)—**strengthen** (unless מרר I pi. *make bitter*), <SUBJ> Egyptians Ex 1_{14}, בַּעֲלֵי חִצִּים *masters of arrows*, i.e. *archers* Gn 49_{23}. <OBJ> Joseph Gn 49_{23}, חַיִּים *life* Ex 1_{14}. <PREP> בְּ of instrument, *by (means of), with*, + עֲבֹדָה *labour* Ex 1_{14}.

Htpalp. 2 Impf. יִתְמַרְמַר; + waw וַיִּתְמַרְמַר—**strengthen oneself** (unless מרר I htpalp. *be enraged*), <SUBJ> מֶלֶךְ *king* Dn 11_{11}, צָפִיר *male goat* Dn 8_7. <PREP> אֶל *against*, + אַיִל *ram* Dn 8_7.

[מָרֹר] $_{3.0.11}$ n.m. **bitter thing**—pl. מְרֹרִים (מְרוֹרִים, Q perh. מוררים); cstr. Q מרורי—**bitter thing, bitterness,** perh. **bitter plague** (4QDª 3.4_2), **bitter herb** for passover meal (Ex 12_8 Nm 9_{11}), <SUBJ> דקר *pierce* perh. 4QDª 3.4_2 ([וידקרום]; unless מוררים is ptc. of מרר II *rebel*; =CD 8_4 מורדים, i.e. ptc. of מרד *rebel*). <OBJ> שׂבע hi. *sate with* Lm 3_{15} (|| לַעֲנָה *wormwood*).

<CSTR> מרורי נפש *bitterness of soul* 1QH 5_{12} 1Qp Hab 9_{11}, יום *of the day* 1QH 5_{34}; אשת מרורים *woman of bitterness*, i.e. bitter woman 4QapLamª 2_7, רעת *evil of*, i.e. bitter evil 1QS 4_{13} (+ יָגוֹן *sorrow*), אבל *mourning of*, i.e. bitter mourning 1QH 11_{19}, מספד *lamentation of*, i.e. bitter lamentation 1QH 11_{22}, כול מוררים perh. *all bitter plagues* 4QDª 3.4_2 (unless מוררים is ptc. of מרר II *rebel*). <PREP> לְ of direction, *into*, + פרח *break out* 1QH 8_{28} (+ כְּאֵב *pain*); *as*, + יפע hi. *appear* 1QH 5_{32}; בְּ of accompaniment, *with, in*, + שׁמע *hear* 1QH 5_{12}, נתן *give*, i.e. deliver up 1QpHab 9_{11} (+ נֶגַע *plague*), דכא htp. *be crushed* 1QH 8_{37} ([וידכ]או במרורי[ם]); of instrument, *by (means of)* or of cause, *on account of*, + עשׁשׁ *waste away* 1QH 5_{34} (+ כַּעַס *anger*); עַל *upon*, i.e. with, + אכל *eat* Ex 12_8 Nm 9_{11}.*

<SYN> לַעֲנָה *wormwood*.

[מְרֵרָה] $_1$ n.f. **gall**—sf. מְרֵרָתִי—<OBJ> שׁפך *pour* onto ground Jb 16_{13} (+ כִּלְיָה *kidney*).*

⇒ מרר I *be bitter*.

[מְרֹרָה] I $_4$ n.f. **bitter thing**—cstr. מְרוֹרַת; sf. מְרֹרָתִי; pl. מְרֹרוֹת (מְרֹרֹת)—**1. bitter thing,** <OBJ> כתב *write* Jb 13_{26} (unless מְרֹרָה II *strong thing*). <CSTR> אַשְׁכְּלֹת מְרֹרֹת *clusters of bitter things* Dt 32_{32} (|| רֹאשׁ *poison*).

2. gall, bile, <CSTR> [מר]ורת הדג *gall of the fish* 4QTobitᵉ 5_2. <PREP> מִן of direction, *from*, + הלך *go* Jb 20_{25} (|| גֵּוָה *body*).

3. poison, venom, <NOM CL> מְרוֹרַת פְּתָנִים בְּקִרְבּוֹ *it (his bread) is the poison of asps within him* Jb 20_{14}. <CSTR> מְרוֹרַת פְּתָנִים *poison of asps* Jb 20_{14}.

<SYN> §1 רֹאשׁ *poison*; §2 גֵּוָה *body*.*

⇨ מרר I *be bitter*.

*[מְרֹרָה] II $_1$ n.f. **strong thing** (unless מְרֹרָה I *bitter thing*)—pl. מְרֹרוֹת—<OBJ> כתב *write* Jb 13$_{26}$.
⇨ מרר III *be strong*.

מְרָרִי I $_{39.0.2}$ pr.n.m. **Merari**, third son of Levi and clan claiming descent from him, <SUBJ> היה *be* Nm 3$_{17}$. <NOM CL> בְּנֵי לֵוִי ... מְרָרִי *the sons of Levi were ... Merari* Gn 46$_{11}$ 1 C 5$_{27}$ 6$_{1}$, אֵלֶּה שְׁמוֹת בְּנֵי־לֵוִי ... מְרָרִי *these are the names of the sons of Levi ... Merari* Ex 6$_{16}$. <CSTR> בֶּן־מְרָרִי *son of Merari* 1 C 6$_{32}$, בְּנֵי *sons of* Ex 6$_{19}$ Nm 3$_{20.36}$ 4$_{29.33.42.45}$ 7$_{8}$ 10$_{17}$ Jos 21$_{7.34.40}$ Ezr 8$_{19}$ 1 C 6$_{4.14.29.48.62}$ 9$_{14}$ 15$_{6.17}$ 23$_{21}$ 24$_{26.27}$ 26$_{10.19}$ 2 C 29$_{12}$ 34$_{12}$, מִשְׁפְּחֹת *clans of* Nm 3$_{33.35}$, נשי מררי *prince of Merari* 1QM 4$_{1}$, אות *ensign of* 1QM 4$_{1}$. <APP> בֵּן *son* 1 C 6$_{32}$, אֵלֶּה *these* Nm 3$_{17}$. <PREP> לְ of possession, *of, (belonging) to* Nm 3$_{33}$ 26$_{57}$ 1 C 23$_{6}$.
⇨ מְרָרִי II *Merarite*.

מְרָרִי II $_1$ gent. **Merarite**, descendant of Merari, as sing. noun used collectively, **Merarites**, <CSTR> מִשְׁפַּחַת הַמְּרָרִי *clan of the Merarites* Nm 26$_{57}$.
⇨ מְרָרִי I *Merari*.

מָרֵשָׁה I $_6$ pl.n. **Mareshah**—מָרֵאשָׁה—in lowland of Judah, perh. T. Sandaḥanne, 25 km WNW of Hebron, <OBJ> בנה *build* 2 C 11$_{8}$. <NOM CL> בַּשְּׁפֵלָה ... מָרֵאשָׁה *in the lowland was ... Mareshah* Jos 15$_{44}$ (mss מָרֵשָׁה). <CSTR> יוֹשֶׁבֶת מָרֵשָׁה *inhabitants of Mareshah* Mc 1$_{15}$. <APP> עִיר *city* Jos 15$_{44}$. <PREP> לְ *at* 2 C 14$_{9}$; מִן *(originating) from, of* 2 C 20$_{37}$; עַד *as far as*, + בוא *come* 2 C 14$_{8}$.

מָרֵשָׁה II $_2$ pr.n.m. **Mareshah, 1.** son of Caleb and father of Hebron, <NOM CL> בְּנוֹ מִשְׁנֵה מָרֵשָׁה *his second son was Mareshah* 1 C 2$_{42}$ (if ins.). <CSTR> בְּנֵי מָרֵשָׁה *sons of Mareshah* 1 C 2$_{42}$. <APP> אָב *father* 1 C 2$_{42}$.

2. son of Laadah and great-grandson of Judah (unless name of town founded by Laadah), <CSTR> אֲבִי מָרֵשָׁה *father of Mareshah* 1 C 4$_{21}$.

מִרְשַׁעַת $_1$ n.f. **wickedness**, i.e. wicked one, as descr. of Athaliah, <APP> עֲתַלְיָהוּ *Athaliah* 2 C 24$_{7}$ (or em. מַרְשַׁעַת *seductress*, i.e. רשע hi. ptc.).
⇨ רשע *be wicked*.

מֹרַשְׁתִּי, see מוֹרַשְׁתִּי *Morashtite*.

מְרָתַיִם $_1$ pl.n. **Merathaim**, name for Babylon, perh. 'double rebelliousness', unless name of bay in Southern Babylonia, <CSTR> אֶרֶץ מְרָתַיִם *land of Merathaim* Jr 50$_{21}$ (if em.; see Prep.). <APP> הָאָרֶץ מְרָתַיִם *the land Merathaim* Jr 50$_{21}$ (or em.; see Prep.; + פְּקוֹד *Pekod*). <PREP> עַל *concerning* Jr 50$_{21}$ (or em. עַל־הָאָרֶץ *concerning the land* to עֲלֵה אֶרֶץ *go up to the land of* Merathaim).
⇨ מרה I *be rebellious*.

מַשָּׂא I $_{37.4.14.1}$ n.m. **burden**—cstr. מַשָּׂא (cstr. מַשׂא, Si משוא); sf. מַשָּׂאוֹ, Si משאה, מַשַּׂאֲכֶם, Q משואם; pl. cstr. Q, Sam משאי; sf. Q משאיה[ם]—**1. load, burden,** carried by animal, donkey, mule (Ex 23$_{5}$ 2 K 5$_{17}$ Si 30$_{33}$ Arad ost. 3$_{4}$), camel (2 K 8$_{9}$), etc. (Is 46$_{1.2}$).

2. load, burden, carried by humans, Levites (Nm 4$_{15+8t}$ [but see also §6 *assigned duty*]), carried on sabbath (Jr 17$_{21.22.27}$ Ne 13$_{15.19}$).

3. consignment, goods, as the contents of such a load (2 K 5$_{17}$ 8$_{9}$ Is 46$_{2}$ Ne 13$_{15.19}$ Arad ost. 3$_{4}$).

4. weight carried by pillars (4QShirShabb[d] 1.1$_{41}$), peg (Is 22$_{25}$); **weight** of a heavy object (Si 6$_{21}$ perh. 1QH 1$_{12}$).

5. mental **load** (Si 51$_{26}$), **burden** of sin (Ps 38$_{5}$), of suffering (Jb 7$_{20}$), of punishment to be executed (Is 30$_{27}$ [if em.]), of responsibility for people (Nm 11$_{11.17}$ Dt 1$_{12}$=1QDM 2$_{7}$ [or מַשָּׂא II *utterance*] 2 S 15$_{33}$ Jr 23$_{33}$ [if em.] Ezk 24$_{25}$ Jb 7$_{20(TiqSof)}$ perh. 4QPrayers[a] 1$_{2}$), children as a burden for their parents (Ezk 24$_{25}$).

6. assigned duty, responsibility, task, business (Nm 4$_{15}$ Si 38$_{2}$ [unless מַשָּׂא II *utterance*] 1QSa 1$_{19.20}$ perh. 1QM 10$_{12}$ 4QBer[a] 2$_{1}$ 4QShirShabb[f] 23.1$_{5}$).

7. (as verbal noun of נשׂא *raise*), i.e. **raising, lifting up, holding up, transport(ing)** (Nm 4$_{24}$ perh. 1 C 15$_{22.22.28}$ 19$_{7}$ Si 32$_{15}$ 1QM 10$_{12}$ 4QBer[a] 2$_{1}$ 4QShirShabb[d]

1.1$_{42}$), esp. in adverbial construction following אַיִן *there is no* **carrying,** i.e. he (etc.) no longer carries, is unable to carry, etc. (2 C 20$_{25}$ 35$_{3}$ 4QShir[b] 17$_{3}$).

8. perh. **exaltation** (11QShirShabb 8$_{6}$).

9. perh. **music** (1 C 15$_{22.22.28}$).

10. perh. **tribute** (2 C 17$_{11}$), but see מַשָּׂא III *tribute*.

<SUBJ> היה *be* Is 46$_{1}$ (הָיוּ עֲצַבֵּיהֶם מַשָּׂא *their idols have become a burden*, if מַשָּׂא moved from near end of verse), נתן pass. qal *be given* 2 K 5$_{17}$, כרת ni. *be cut*, i.e. removed Is 22$_{25}$.

<NOM CL> נְשֻׂאֹתֵיכֶם עֲמוּסוֹת מַשָּׂא לַעֲיֵפָה *your carried things are borne, a burden for a weary (beast)* Is 46$_{1}$ (or move מַשָּׂא to earlier clause and em. to כְּמַעֲמָסוֹת נְשֻׂאוֹת לִבְהֵמָה עֲיֵפָה *as burdens carried by a weary beast*), מספוא ושוט ומשא לחמור *fodder and a whip and a burden is the donkey's lot* Si 30$_{33}$, לְאֵין מַשָּׂא *such that there was no carrying*, i.e. so that they were unable to carry 2 C 20$_{25}$, אֵין־לָכֶם מַשָּׂא בַּכָּתֵף *there is not to you carrying*, i.e. you no longer carry/you are no longer to carry (the ark), *on the shoulder* 2 C 35$_{3}$, גבורה אין משא perh. *strength (for which) there is not carrying*, i.e. which a mortal cannot possess 4QShir[b] 17$_{3}$.

כִּי־אֵין עִם־י׳ אֱלֹהֵינוּ עַוְלָה וּמַשֹּׂא פָנִים וּמִקַּח־שֹׁחַד *for with Y. our God there is no iniquity or raising of the face*, i.e. favouritism, *or taking of a bribe* 1 C 19$_{7}$, כי אלהי משפט הוא ואין עמו משוא פנים *for he is a God of judgment and with him there is no raising of the face*, i.e. favouritism Si 32$_{15}$, אֵלֶּה מַשָּׂא בְנֵי־קְהָת *these things are the burden of*, i.e. must be carried by, *the sons of Kohath* Nm 4$_{15}$ (Sam מַשָּׂאֵי *the burdens of*), וְכָבֵד מַשָּׂאָה *and heavy is his burden* Is 30$_{27}$ (if em. וְכֹבֶד מַשָּׂאָה *and [with] heaviness of burden*), אַתֶּמָה מַשָּׂא or אַתֶּם הַמַּשָּׂא *you are the*, or *a*, *burden* Jr 23$_{33}$ (if em. אֶת־מַה־מַשָּׂא and you will tell them *the*, *What-is-(the)-pronouncement*).

<OBJ> נשׂא *raise*, i.e. carry Dt 1$_{12}$=1QDM 2$_{7}$ (... [אשא] [מש]אכם how *can I carry ... your load?*; || טֹרַח *burden*, רִיב *dispute*) 2 K 7$_{8}$ (6QKgs משואם; MT מִשָּׁם *from there*) Jr 17$_{21.27}$ Si 38$_{2}$ (unless מַשָּׂא II *utterance*) 51$_{26}$, carry out 1QSa 1$_{20}$, impose Ne 5$_{7(mss)}$ (L נשׁא ... מַשָּׁא *cause to be indebted with ... a debt*), בוא *come* through city gates Ne 13$_{19}$, hi. *bring* through city gates Jr 17$_{21.24}$ (+ מְלָאכָה *work*) Ne 13$_{15}$, to Jehoshaphat 2 C 17$_{11(ms)}$ (+ מִנְחָה *gift*), יצא hi. *take out* of house Jr 17$_{22}$ (+ מְלָאכָה *work*), perh. שׁלם pi. *repay* Hazor ost. 11 ([מ]שא ז שלם *this burden he repaid*; others]שא ז של[[Phoenician] or]שא זי ל[[Aramaic]), נתן *give*, i.e. assign (duty) 1QSa 1$_{19}$, שׂים *place* Nm 11$_{11}$, לקח *take* 2 K 8$_{9}$ Ezk 24$_{25}$ (|| מָשׂוֹשׂ *joy*, מַחְמַד *desire*), כול pilp. *provide (with)* 4QShirShabb[f] 23.1$_{5}$ ([לכ]לכלם *to provide them*, unless לְכֻלָּם *for all of them* tasks for everyone), מלט pi. *rescue* Is 46$_{2}$, חלל pi. *defile* Ezk 24$_{21}$ (if em. מַחְמָל *burden*).

<CSTR> מַשָּׂא צֶמֶד־פְּרָדִים *a load of*, i.e. carried by, *a yoke of mules* 2 K 5$_{17}$, משא צמד חמרם *a load of*, i.e. carried by, *a yoke of donkeys* Arad ost. 3$_{4}$, מַשָּׂא אַרְבָּעִים גָּמָל *a load of*, i.e. carried by, *forty camels* 2 K 8$_{9}$.

משא רוחות perh. *the raising of winds* or *the task of spirits* (unless, as §2, *the pronouncement of spirits*) 1QM 10$_{12}$, משא עדה *the business of (the) congregation* 1QSa 1$_{20}$, משאי מקד[ש] perh. spirits of *the raising(s) up*, or *tasks*, *of the sanctuary* (unless, as §2, *of the pronouncements of*) 4QBer[a] 2$_{1}$, משאי כול perh. *tasks of all*, i.e. every kind of task or tasks for everyone 4QShirShabb[f] 23.1$_{5}$, משא אלוהים perh. *the exaltation of God* or *the exaltation of*, i.e. by, *heavenly beings* 11QShirShabb 8$_{6}$.

מַשָּׂא הָעָם *the burden of the people* Nm 11$_{11}$ (כָּל־ burden of *all* the people) 11$_{17}$, משא הריב perh. *the burden of*, i.e. responsibility for, *the dispute* 4QPrayers[a] 1$_{2}$, מַשָּׂא בְנֵי־קְהָת *the burden of the sons of Kohath* Nm 4$_{15}$ (Sam מַשָּׂאֵי *the burdens of*), מַשָּׂא מֶלֶךְ שָׂרִים *the burden of a king of princes* Ho 8$_{10}$ (unless מַשָּׂא III *tribute** or מַשָּׂא is inf. qal of נשׂא *lift up*, i.e. appoint;* or em. מְשֹׁחַ *anointing* a king, and/or ins. וְ *and* princes), מַשָּׂא נַפְשָׁם *the burden of their soul* Ezk 24$_{25}$, מַשָּׂא נַפְשְׁכֶם *the burden of your soul* Ezk 24$_{21}$ (if em. מַחְמַל *burden of* [mss מַחְמַד *desire of*]; || מַחְמַד), מַשָּׂא עָוֹן *burden of guilt* Ho 14$_{3}$ (if em. תִּשָּׂא *you will forgive*),* מַשֹּׂא פָנִים *raising of the face*, i.e. favouritism 1 C 19$_{7}$ Si 32$_{15}$ (משוא).

עמודי משא *the columns of*, i.e. that must bear, *the burden of* 4QShirShabb[d] 1.1$_{41}$ (=4QShirShabb[f] 6$_{2}$

[עמודי]), אבן משא *a stone of weight*, i.e. heavy stone Si 6_{21} (or em. מַסָּה *of testing*), כֶּסֶף מַשָּׂא *silver of*, i.e. as, *tribute* 2 C 17_{11} (ms וּמַשָּׂא silver *and tribute*).

קול משא *the sound of the exaltation of* 11QShir Shabb 8_6, כול רוחי משאי *all the spirits of the raising(s) up*, or *tasks, of* the sanctuary (unless, as §2, *of the pronouncements of*) 4QBer[a] 2_1, מִשְׁמֶרֶת מַשָּׂאָם *the observance of their burden*, i.e. the burden assigned them Nm $4_{31.32}$ (+ כְּלֵי *the vessels of* the observance; ms כָּל־כְּלֵי *all the vessels of*), עֲבֹדַת מַשָּׂא *service of carrying* Nm 4_{47} (+ עֲבֹדַת עֲבֹדָה *service of working*), כָּל־מַשָּׂא *every (kind of) consignment* Ne 13_{15}, כָּל־מַשָּׂא *every burden of* Ho 14_3 (if em.; see above), כָּל־מַשָּׂאָם *all their burden* Nm $4_{24.24}$.

<APP> אֲדָמָה *soil* 2 K 5_{17} (or del. אֲדָמָה), מִנְחָה *gift* 2 K 8_9, גָּאוֹן *pride* Ezk 24_{21} (if em. מַחְמָל *burden*), מָעוֹז *refuge* Ezk 24_{25}, בֵּן *son* Ezk 24_{25} (or del. בְּנֵיהֶם וּבְנוֹתֵיהֶם *their sons and their daughters*, or em. וּבְנֵיהֶם *and their sons* and their daughters), שַׂר *prince* 1 C 15_{28} (or em. הַשַּׂר הַמַּשָּׂא appar. *the officer [of] the transport/the music* to בְּמַשָּׂא the officer *in charge of transport/music*).

<ADJ> זֶה *this* perh. Hazor ost. 11 ([מ]שא ז שלם *this burden he repaid*; others]שא ז של[[Phoenician] or]שא זי ל[[Aramaic]), כָּבֵד *heavy* Ps 38_5.

<PREP> לְ of benefit, *for* 1QH 1_{12} (|| עֲבֹדָה *service*) perh. 4QShirShabb[f] 81_3 11QShirShabb 8_8; of possession 4QShirShabb[d] 1.1_{42}+4QShirShabb[f] 6_3 ([כול רוחי] דעת ואור למשא *all the spirits of knowledge and of light, for lifting up*); *in connection with* Nm 4_{24} (זֹאת עֲבֹדַת מִשְׁפְּחֹת הַגֵּרְשֻׁנִּי לַעֲבֹד וּלְמַשָּׂא *this is the service of the clans of the Gershonite[s] with regard to working and carrying*), + היה *be* Nm 4_{27} (of עֲבֹדָה *service*; || עֲבֹדָה); *as* or introducing predicate, + היה *be* upon David 2 S 15_{33} 19_{36} Jb 7_{20} (or em. לְמַטָּרָה *as a target*).

בְּ of place/time, *at, during* perh. 11QShirShabb 8_9 ([במש[א); of accompaniment, *with*, + בוא *come* through city gates Jr 17_{27} (if ins. בוֹ *with it*); introducing obj., + נשׂא *raise*, i.e. carry Nm 11_{17}; בְּ *in, concerning*, + יסר *instruct* 1 C 15_{22} (יָסֹר בַּמַּשָּׂא *he gave instruction in music* or *transport*, i.e. יסר inf. abs., unless יָסֹר is noun, an *instructor* in music/transport; or em. יָשַׂר *he ruled* over, i.e. was in charge of, from שׂרר); בְּ *over, in charge of* 1 C 15_{22} (וּכְנַנְיָהוּ ... בְּמַשָּׂא *and Chenaniah ... was in charge of transport* or *music*; or del. בְּמַשָּׂא and/or em. וּכְנַנְיָהוּ *and Conaniah*; mss וּבְנָיָהוּ *and Benaiah*) 15_{28} (if em. הַשַּׂר הַמַּשָּׂא appar. *the officer [of] the transport/music* to בְּמַשָּׂא the officer *in charge of transport/music*), שׂרר *rule* 1 C 15_{22} (if em. יסר *give instruction* in).

כְּ *as*, + כבד *be heavy* Ps 38_5.

מִן privative, *without, so as not to have* Ho 8_{10} (וַיָּחֵלּוּ מְּעַט מִמַּשָּׂא appar. *and they began a little, without the burden of* a king; unless מַשָּׂא III *tribute** or מַשָּׂא is inf. qal of נשׂא;* or em. מְעַט and they began *to diminish* on account of the burden of a king, or וְיֶחֱלוּ/וְיֶחְדְּלוּ *and they will cease/desist* a little from the burden of a king, and/or מִמְּשֹׁחַ cease/desist *from anointing* a king); partitive, *(some) of, (any) of* perh. 4QparaKings 106_1(WA) ([ממשא]; others ממשל[ת] *government*).

אֶל *to*, + שׂים *place*, i.e. assign Nm 4_{19} (Seb, mss עַל *to*; || עֲבֹדָה *service*).

עַל *to*, + שׂים *place*, i.e. assign Nm 4_{19}(Seb, mss); *concerning*, + פקד *visit*, i.e. give instructions Nm 4_{49} (|| עֲבֹדָה *service*).

עִם *with*, + צוה pi. *command (to go)* Arad ost. 3_4.

אֵת *with* Nm 4_{27} (if em. וּפְקַדְתֶּם עֲלֵיהֶם מִשְׁמֶרֶת אֵת כָּל־מַשָּׂאָם *and you are to visit upon them observance of all their burden* to וּפְקֻדָּתָם עֲלֵיהֶם בְּשֵׁמוֹת *and their visitation will be upon them by names* with all their burden [or del. אֵת כָּל־מַשָּׂאָם]).

תַּחַת *under*, i.e. because of, + רבץ *lie down*, i.e. buckle Ex 23_5.

<COLL> למשאם ... לעבודתם *for their burden ... for their service*, i.e. for carrying them ... for serving them 1QH 1_{12}, משאו בע[בוד]ת העדה *his duty within the service of the congregation* 1QSa 1_{19}, עמודי משא לזבול רום רומים *the columns of*, i.e. that must bear, *the burden the dwelling place of the height of heights* 4QShir Shabb[d] 1.1_{41} (=4QShirShabb[f] 6_2 [עמודי] משא [ל]זבול), למשא יחד רקיע זו[ ]רו[ם רומ[ים *of lifting up together the firmament of splendour* 4QShirShabb[d] 1.1_{42}+4QShir Shabb[f] 6_3.

וּפְקַדְתֶּם עֲלֵיהֶם מִשְׁמֶרֶת אֵת כָּל־מַשָּׂאָם *and you are to visit upon them observance of all their burden* Nm

4_{27} (or em. וּפְקֻדָּתָם עֲלֵיהֶם בְּשֵׁמוֹת *and their visitation will be upon them by names* with all their burden [or del. [אֵת כָּל־מַשָּׂאָם]).

מַשָּׂא עַל *a burden upon* 2 S 15_{33} 19_{36} (if em. אֶל appar. *for*), מַשָּׂא לַעֲיֵפָה *a burden for a weary (beast)* Is 46_1 (or move מַשָּׂא to earlier clause) Jb 7_{20} (or em.; see Prep.).*

⇒ נשׂא *lift*.

מַשָּׂא II 29.1.4 n.m. **utterance**—cstr. מַשָּׂא; pl. cstr. Q משאי—**pronouncement, utterance, speech** (2 K 9_{25} Is 13_1 14_{28} 15_1 17_1 19_1 $21_{1.11.13}$ 22_1 23_1 30_6 Jr 23_{33+7t} Ezk 12_{10} Na 1_1 Hb 1_1 Zc 9_1 12_1 Ml 1_1 Pr 30_1 31_1 2 C 24_{27} Si 9_{18} 38_2 [unless מַשָּׂא I *burden*]* perh. 1QM 10_{12} 4QBer^a 2_1), specifically of **utterance of praise** (1Q Myst 1.1_8 11QShirShabb 10_6).*

<SUBJ> היה *be* Jr 23_{36} (כִּי הַמַּשָּׂא יִהְיֶה לְאִישׁ דְּבָרוֹ *for then the pronouncement [of Y.] would be for a person their own word* [or em. הֲמַשָּׂא for *should a pronouncement* be?; + דִּבְרֵי אֱלֹהִים *the words of God*), i.e. come to prophet Is 14_{28} (or em. אָחָז הָיָה in the year of the death of the king *Ahaz, there came* to me וָאֶחֱזֶה *and I saw* this pronouncement), רבה *be many* 2 C $24_{27(Qr)}$ (יִרֶב הַמַּשָּׂא עָלָיו appar. *may the pronouncement concerning him multiply*; Kt רֹב הַמַּשָּׂא *the abundance of the pronouncement*), שׂנא pu. *be made odious* or שׁנה pu. *be changed*, i.e. perverted Si 9_{18} (ומשא על פיהו משונא *and words by his mouth are made odious* or *are perverted*; or em. מַשִּׁיא and *one who deceives* with his mouth is hated).

<NOM CL> נכון הדבר לבוא ואמת המשא *established is the word to come and dependability*, i.e. dependable, *the pronouncement* 1QMyst 1.1_8, מַה־מַּשָּׂא י׳ *what is the pronouncement of Y.?* Jr 23_{33}, אֶת־מַה־מַּשָּׂא and you will say to them *the, What is (the) pronouncement?* Jr 23_{33} (or em. אַתֶּמָה מַשָּׂא/אַתֶּם הַמַּשָּׂא *you are a/the burden*, as §1), הַנָּשִׂיא הַמַּשָּׂא הַזֶּה *this oracle is*, i.e. concerns, *the prince* Ezk 12_{10} (or del. הַמַּשָּׂא or ins. עַל־ this oracle is *about* the prince).

<OBJ> נשׂא *raise*, i.e. utter 2 K 9_{25} Pr 30_1 (if ins. נשׂא), receive Si 38_2 (unless מַשָּׂא I *burden*), חזה *see*, appar. learn in a vision Is 13_1 (or em. אָחָז הָיָה in the year of the death of the king *Ahaz, there came* to me וָאֶחֱזֶה *and I learned* this pronouncement *in a vision*) Hb 1_1 Lm 2_{14} (if em. מַשְׂאֵת *burden*), אמר *(attempt to) say* Jr $23_{34.38}$ (or del.) 23_{38}, *designate* word *as* Jr 23_{38}, זכר *remember* Jr 23_{36} (or em. hi. *mention*), יסר pi. *teach* Pr 31_1 (or em. מֶלֶךְ מַשָּׂא the words of Lemuel, *a king; a pronouncement* that his mother taught him, to מֶלֶךְ מַשָּׂא the words of Lemuel, *king of Massa*, whose mother taught him).

<CSTR> מַשָּׂא י׳ *the pronouncement of Y.* Jr $23_{33.34.36.38}$ (or del.) 23_{38}, מַשָּׂא דְבַר־י׳ *the pronouncement of the word of Y.* Zc 9_1 12_1 Ml 1_1 (unless in all three מַשָּׂא and דְּבַר are in app.), מַשָּׂא מֹשֶׁה *the pronouncement of Moses* 2 C 24_9 (if em. מַשְׂאַת *the tax of*, i.e. imposed by, Moses, to כְּמַשָּׂא *in accordance with the pronouncement of* Moses).

מַשָּׂא בָּבֶל *the pronouncement of*, i.e. on, *Babylon* Is 13_1, מוֹאָב *of*, i.e. on, *Moab* Is 15_1, דַּמֶּשֶׂק *of*, i.e. on, *Damascus* Is 17_1, נִינְוֵה *of*, i.e. on, Nineveh Na 1_1, מִצְרָיִם *of*, i.e. on, *Egypt* Is 19_1, דּוּמָה *of*, i.e. on, *Dumah* Is 21_{11} (mss אֱדוֹם *Edom*), צֹר *of*, i.e. on, *Tyre* Is 23_1, מִדְבַּר־יָם *of*, i.e. on, *the steppe of the west* Is 21_1 (or em. מִדְבָּר יֶהֱמֶה of, i.e. on, *[the] steppe; he makes a noise*), גֵּיא חִזָּיוֹן *of*, i.e. on, *the valley of vision* Is 22_1, בַּהֲמוֹת נֶגֶב *of*, i.e. on, *the beasts of the south* Is 30_6.

משא רוחות perh. *the pronouncement of spirits* (unless, as §1, *the raising of winds* or *the task of spirits*) 1QM 10_{12}, משאי מקד[ש] perh. spirits of *the pronouncements of the sanctuary* (unless, as §1, *of the raising(s) up*, or *tasks*, *of*) 4QBer^a 2_1, משאי קודש perh. *pronouncements of holiness* 11QShirShabb 10_6, מַשְׂאוֹת שָׁוְא וּמַדּוּחִים perh. *pronouncements of vanity and enticement* Lm 2_{14} (if em. מַשְׂאוֹת *pronouncements of*, i.e. מַשְׂאֵת *burden*).

רֹב הַמַּשָּׂא *the abundance of the pronouncement* 2 C $24_{27(Kt)}$ (Qr יִרֶב appar. *may* the pronouncement *multiply*), כול רוחי משאי *all the spirits of the pronouncements of* the sanctuary (unless, as §1, *of the raising(s) up*, or *tasks*, *of*) 4QBer^a 2_1.

<APP> דָּבָר *word* of Y. Zc 9_1 12_1 Ml 1_1 (unless all three מַשָּׂא דְבַר־י׳ = *the pronouncement of the word of Y.*), of Agur Pr 30_1 (or em. הַמַּשָּׂא to מִמַּשָּׂא words of Agur *from Massa* or הַמַּשָּׂאִי words of Agur *the Massaite* or הַנֹּשֵׂא

מְשָׁלוֹ words of Agur, *who utters his proverb;* or ins. אֲשֶׁר נָשָׂא *who uttered;* or em. דִּבְרֵי אָגוּר בִּן־יָקֶה *the words of Agur son of Jakeh* to דְּבָרַי גּוּר בְּנִי וְקָחֵם *fear my words, O son, and accept them* and הַמַּשָּׂא to וְשׁוּב *and repent)* 31$_1$ (or em. מֶלֶךְ מַשָּׂא the words of Lemuel, *a king; a pronouncement* to מֶלֶךְ מַשָּׂא the words of Lemuel, *king of Massa),* נְאוּם *oracle* Zc 12$_1$ Pr 30$_1$ (or em.).

<ADJ> מַשָּׂא זֶה *this* 2 K 9$_{25}$ Is 14$_{28}$ Ezk 12$_{10}$ (or del. מַשָּׂא).

<PREP> כְּ *in accordance with,* + בוא hi. *bring* 2 C 24$_9$ (if em. מַשְׂאַת bring *the tax of,* i.e. imposed by, Moses, to כְּמַשָּׂא *in accordance with the pronouncement of* Moses).

<COLL> מַשָּׂא *oracle of,* i.e. on, + pl.n., etc. as title of following oracle Is 13$_1$ 15$_1$ 17$_1$ 19$_1$ 21$_{1.11}$ 22$_1$ 23$_1$ 30$_6$ Na 1$_1$, מַשָּׂא בַּעְרָב perh. *pronouncement on the Arabians* or *on the steppe* Is 21$_{13}$ (or del.); perh. מַשָּׂא as a heading on its own, without a following description Zc 9$_1$; הַמַּשָּׂא ... עַל־יִשְׂרָאֵל *a pronouncement ... on* Zc 12$_1$, עָלָיו *the pronouncement concerning him* (Joash) 2 C 24$_{27}$, מַשָּׂא ... אֶל־יִשְׂרָאֵל בְּיַד מַלְאָכִי *a pronouncement ... to Israel through Malachi/my messenger* Ml 1$_1$.

Also 4QShirShabb[f] 23.1$_1$ ([משאיה]ם) 4Q410 1$_9$ 4Q418 15$_1$.

<SYN> §1 עֲבֹדָה *service;* §2 דָּבָר *word.**

⇒ נשׂא I *lift;* cf. מַשְׂאֵת II *utterance.*

*[מַשָּׂא] III $_1$ n.[m.] **tribute** (unless מַשָּׂא I *burden* or מַשָּׂא is inf. qal of נשׂא *lift*)*—cstr. מַשָּׂא—<CSTR> מַשָּׂא מֶלֶךְ שָׂרִים *tribute of the king of princes* Ho 8$_{10}$. <PREP> מִן of cause, *on account of,* + חלל hi. *begin* to be few Ho 8$_{10}$.

⇒ נשׂא *lift.*

מַשָּׂא IV $_2$ pr.n.m. **Massa, 1.** a son of Ishmael, Gn 25$_{14}$|| 1 C 1$_{30}$. **2.** territory and people named after the preceding, <CSTR> מֶלֶךְ מַשָּׂא *king of Massa* Pr 31$_1$ (if em. מֶלֶךְ מַשָּׂא the words of Lemuel, *a king; a pronouncement,* i.e. מַשָּׂא I, which his mother taught him). <PREP> מִן of direction, *from,* or partitive, *one of* Pr 30$_1$ (if em. דִּבְרֵי אָגוּר בִּן־יָקֶה הַמַּשָּׂא *the words of Agur son of Jakeh, the pronouncement,* i.e. מַשָּׂא I, to מִמַּשָּׂא *from/of Massa).**

מַשֹּׂא, see מַשָּׂא I *burden.*

מַשָּׂאָה $_1$ n.f. **burden,** בָּא מִמֶּרְחָק בֹּעֵר אַפּוֹ וְכֹבֶד מַשָּׂאָה *coming from afar (with) his anger burning and (with) heaviness of burden* Is 30$_{27}$ (or em. וְכָבֵד מַשָּׂאהּ *and heavy is his burden* [i.e. מַשָּׂא] or כָּבֵד מַשִּׂיאָהּ *his liver is fuming* [i.e. נשׂא III hi.]).*

⇒ נשׂא I *lift.*

*[מַשְׂאָה] n.f. **smoke signal**—<CSTR> כֹּבֶד מַשְׂאָה *heavy of a column of smoke,* i.e. a dense smoke signal Is 30$_{27}$ (if em. כֹּבֶד מַשָּׂאָה *(?) heavy is the burden).*

⇒ cf. מַשְׂאֵת III *smoke signal.*

[מַשָּׂאִי] gent. **Massaite,** i.e. descendant of Massa, דִּבְרֵי אָגוּר בִּן־יָקֶה הַמַּשָּׂאִי *the words of Agur son of Yakeh, the Massaite* Pr 30$_1$ (if em. הַמַּשָּׂא *the pronouncement).*

מַשְׂאֵת I $_{12.2.1.}$ n.f. **gift; offering**—cstr. מַשְׂאַת; pl. מַשְׂאֹת (Si משאות); cstr. מַשְׂאוֹת (מַשְׂאֹת); sf. מַשְׂאוֹתֵיכֶם—**1. gift** from king (2 S 11$_8$ Est 2$_{18}$ [used collectively] Si 38$_2$), specif. **portion** of food as gift from a ruler (Gn 43$_{34.34.34}$ perh. Jr 40$_5$), from military officer (perh. Jr 40$_5$).

2. offering to Y. (Ezk 20$_{40}$ Ps 141$_2$).

3. tribute, tax as given to ruler (Am 5$_{11}$ 2 C 24$_{6.9}$).

4. perh. **elevation, position** of honour (Ps 62$_5$ [if em.]).

5. perh. **raising** as verbal noun of נשׂא *raise* (1QM 18$_3$).

6. perh. mental **burden** of reproach (Zp 3$_{18}$).

<SUBJ> רבה *be great* Gn 43$_{34}$, כון ni. *be established* Ps 141$_2$ (+ מִנְחָה as an *offering),* יצא *go out,* i.e. be sent, to Uriah 2 S 11$_8$.

<NOM CL> יש בשת משאת עון *there is a shame (that is) a burden of iniquity* Si 4$_{21}$(C) (A בֹּשֶׁאת), מַשְׂאֵת עָלֶיהָ חֶרְפָּה *a burden upon her was reproach* Zp 3$_{18}$ (or em. מַשְׂאֵת to מִי נָשָׂא *who has raised,* i.e. uttered, a reproach against her? or מַשְׂאֵת עָלַיִךְ to נֹשְׂאִם עָלַיִךְ they were *uttering against you* a reproach or שְׂאֵת עָלָיו *the uttering*

against him of a reproach).

<OBJ> נשׂא *raise*, i.e. receive (gifts) Si 38_2, give (portion of food) Gn 43_{34}, נתן *give* Jr 40_5 (|| אֲרֻחָה *ration of food* [or del.]) Est 2_{18} (+ כְּיַד הַמֶּלֶךְ appar. *in accordance with the authority of the king*; or del.), לקח *take* Am 5_{11}, בוא hi. *bring* 2 C $24_{6.9}$, דרשׁ *seek* Ezk 20_{40} (רֵאשִׁית מַשְׂאוֹתֵיכֶם *the best of your offerings*; + תְּרוּמָה *contribution*), נדח hi. *push aside* Ps 62_5 (if em. מִשְּׂאֵתוֹ *from his eminence* they take counsel to push [him] to מַשְׂאֵתוֹ / מַשְׂאֵתִי they take counsel to push aside *his/my position*).

<CSTR> מַשְׂאַת הַמֶּלֶךְ *a present of*, i.e. from, *the king* 2 S 11_8, מַשְׂאַת בִּנְיָמִן *the portion of Benjamin* Gn 43_{34}, מַשְׂאַת מֹשֶׁה *the tax of*, i.e. imposed by, *Moses* 2 C 24_6 (+ וְהַקָּהָל *and of the congregation*; or em. וְהִקְהִל *and he assembled*) 24_9 (or em. כְּמַשָּׂא *in accordance with the pronouncement of* Moses), מַשְׂאַת־בַּר *a tribute of grain* Am 5_{11} (or em. מַשְׂאֹת *tributes of*), מַשְׂאַת כַּפַּי *the offering of my hands* Ps 141_2, מַשְׂאֹת כֻּלָּם *the portions of all of them* Gn 43_{34}, משאת עון *a burden of iniquity* Si 42_1, משאת יד אל ישראל *the raising of the hand of the God of Israel* against the whole multitude of Belial 1QM 18_3, רֵאשִׁית מַשְׂאוֹתֵיכֶם *the best of your offerings* Ezk 20_{40}.

<APP> בֹּשֶׁת *shame* Si 42_1.

<PREP> מִן of comparison, *(more) than*, + רבה *be great* Gn 43_{34}; אֶל *for*, + שׁמר *keep (watch)* Lachish ost. 4_{10} (+ אוֹת *sign*).

<SYN> שׁוֹפָר *horn*, אֲרֻחָה *ration of food*.*

⇒ נשׂא I *lift*.

*[מַשְׂאֵת] II $_1$ n.f. **utterance**—pl. cstr. מַשְׂאוֹת—<OBJ> חזה *see*, appar. learn in a vision Lm 2_{14} (or em. מַשָּׂא *pronouncement*). <CSTR> מַשְׂאוֹת שָׁוְא וּמַדּוּחִים perh. *pronouncements of vanity and enticement* Lm 2_{14} (or em. מַשְּׂאוֹת *pronouncements of*, i.e. מַשָּׂא II).

⇒ cf. מַשָּׂא II *utterance*.

*מַשְׂאֵת III $_{3.0.0.1}$ n.f. **beacon, fire-signal**—cstr. מַשְׂאַת; pl. cstr. I משאת—**beacon, fire-signal**, appar. in form of column of flame or smoke, <SUBJ> עלה *go up* Jg 20_{40}, חלל hi. *begin* to go up Jg 20_{40}. <OBJ> נשׂא *raise*, i.e. light (beacon) Jr 6_1 (|| שׁוֹפָר *horn*), עלה hi. *cause to rise up* Jg 20_{38}. <CSTR> מַשְׂאַת הֶעָשָׁן *signal of smoke* Jg 20_{38}, משאת לכש *beacons of Lachish* Lachish ost. 4_{10}. <APP> עַמּוּד *column* Jg 20_{40}. <PREP> שׁמר אֶל *watch for* Lachish ost. 4_{10}.

<SYN> שׁוֹפָר *horn*.

⇒ נשׂא *lift*.

[מַשְׁבָּלָה], see מַסְבָּלָא *Masbala*.

מִשְׂגָּב I $_{17.0.2}$ n.f. **stronghold**—mss מִשְׁגָּב; cstr. מִסְגַּב; sf. מִשְׂגַּבּוֹ, מִשְׂגַּבִּי—<SUBJ> היה *be* Ps $9_{10.10}$ (וִיהִי י׳ מִשְׂגָּב לַדָּךְ מִשְׂגָּב לְעִתּוֹת בַּצָּרָה *and may Y. be a stronghold of the oppressed one, a stronghold of times in distress*; or em. וַיְהִי *and Y. was* and/or הַצָּרָה times of *distress*; mss מִשְׁגָּב for second מִשְׂגָּב) 59_{17} (+ לִי *you have been a stronghold to me/my stronghold*; || מָנוֹס *refuge*), ברך pass. *be blessed* Ps 144_2 (|| צוּר *rock*, חֶסֶד *loyalty* [or em. חֹסֶן *stronghold*], מְצוּדָה *fortress*, מָגֵן *shield*), יבשׁ hi. *be put to shame* Jr 48_1 (unless מִשְׂגָּב = *Misgab*), חתת *be dismayed* Jr 48_1 (unless pl.n.).

<NOM CL> מְצָדוֹת סְלָעִים מִשְׂגַּבּוֹ *fortresses of rocks are his stronghold* Is 33_{16}, [אתה אלי] ... משגבי *you, O my God, are ... my stronghold* 1QH 9_{28} (|| מָנוֹס *refuge*, סֶלַע *rock*, מְצוּדָה *fortress*), כִּי־אֱלֹהִים מִשְׂגַּבִּי *for God is my stronghold* Ps $59_{10=18}$ (or ins. אַתָּה for *you*, O God, are), אַךְ־הוּא ... מִשְׂגַּבִּי *indeed he is ... my stronghold* Ps $62_{3=7}$ (|| צוּר *rock*, יְשׁוּעָה *salvation*), ואין לו משגב *and he has no stronghold* 4QapJoshua[b] 22.1_3, מִשְׂגָּב־לָנוּ אֱלֹהֵי יַעֲקֹב *our stronghold is the God of Jacob* Ps $46_{8=12}$.

<OBJ> שׁחח hi. *prostrate* Is 25_{12} (if del. מִבְצַר *the fortification of* the stronghold of your walls), שׁפל hi. *make low* Is 25_{12} (if em.), נגע hi. *cause to reach* ground Is 25_{12} (if em.).

<CSTR> מִשְׂגַּב חוֹמֹתֶיךָ *the stronghold of your walls*, i.e. your walled stronghold Is 25_{12}; מִבְצַר מִשְׂגַּב *the fortification of the stronghold of* your walls Is 25_{12} (or del. מִבְצַר).

<APP> י׳ *Y.* Ps 144_2, אֱלֹהִים *God* 2 S 22_3 (|| מָגֵן *shield*, קֶרֶן *horn*, יֶשַׁע *salvation*, מָנוֹס *refuge*), אֵל *God* Ps 18_3 (|| מָגֵן, קֶרֶן), מִשְׂגָּב *stronghold* Ps 9_{10}.

<PREP> לְ *as*, + היה *be* (of Y.) Ps 94_{22} (|| צוּר *rock*), ידע

ni. *be known* (of Y.) Ps 48$_4$; חסה בְּ *trust in* 2 S 22$_3$||Ps 18$_3$ Ps 144$_2$.

<SYN> מָגֵן *shield,* קֶרֶן *horn,* יֶשַׁע *salvation,* חֶסֶד *loyalty,* יְשׁוּעָה *salvation,* מָנוֹס *refuge,* סֶלַע *rock,* צוּר *rock,* מְצוּדָה *fortress.*

⇒ שׂגב *be high.*

מִשְׂגָּב II 1 pl.n. **Misgab,** perh. ident. with Kir-moab, הֹבִישָׁה הַמִּשְׂגָּב וָחָתָּה *Misgab has been put to shame* (fem.) *and dismayed* (fem.) Jr 48$_1$ (or em. הֹבִישׁ ... וָחַת, i.e. masc. with מִשְׂגָּב *stronghold* as subj.).

⇒ שׂגב *be high.*

מַשֶּׂגֶת, see נשׂג Hi. ptc., *overtaking.*

***מִשֶּׂה** 1 n.m. **place where sheep can be eaten,** <SUBJ> היה *be* Ex 12$_4$ (אִם־יִמְעַט הַבַּיִת מִהְיֹת מִשֶּׂה *if the house is too small to be a place where sheep can be eaten;* unless *too small for a lamb,* i.e. שֶׂה + מִן of comparison).

[מַשּׁוֹא], see מַשָּׂא *burden.*

[מְשׂוּכָה] 1 n.f. **hedge**—cstr. מְשֻׂכַת—<CSTR> מְשֻׂכַת כִּמְשֻׂכַת חָדֶק *a hedge of briar* Pr 15$_{19}$ (or em. כִּמְשֻׂכַת *like a hedge of* to מְשֻׂכֶּכֶת *hedged about with* briar, i.e. שׂוך polal). <CSTR> כְּ *as* Pr 15$_{19}$ (or em.; + דֶּרֶךְ עָצֵל *the way of an idler*).*

⇒ שׂוך *close.*

[מְשׂוּכָה] 1 n.f. **hedge**—sf. מְשׂוּכָתוֹ (or em. מְשׂוּכָתוֹ, i.e. מְס/שׂוּכָה, in same sense, from שׂוך/ס *close*)—**hedge** of vineyard (Is 5$_5$) as protective barrier; the area protected by such a barrier, **enclosure** (Pr 18$_{11}$ [if em.]), <OBJ> סור hi. *remove* Is 5$_5$ (|| גָּדֵר *wall*). <PREP> בְּ of place, *in* Pr 18$_{11}$ (if em. הוֹן עָשִׁיר ... כְּחוֹמָה נִשְׂגָּבָה בִּמְשֻׂכִּיתוֹ *the wealth of a rich person is ... like a fortified wall, in,* or perh. *according to, his imagination* to נִשְׂגָּב בִּמְשֻׂכָּתוֹ and like a wall *he is fortified within his enclosure*). <SYN> גָּדֵר *wall.**

⇒ שׂכך *cover.*

***[מָשׂוֹר]** 0.0.1 n.[m.] **measure,** [מ]שור במשורה perh. *measure by measure* 4Q418 1$_1$.

⇒ מְשׂוּרָה *measure.*

מַשּׂוֹר 1 n.m. **saw,** <SUBJ> גדל htp. *magnify oneself* Is 10$_{15}$ (|| גַּרְזֶן *axe*). <OBJ> נוף hi. *wave,* i.e. wield Is 10$_{15}$. <SYN> גַּרְזֶן *axe.*

***מִשׂוֹרָה** 0.0.2 n.f. **government, dominion,** <SUBJ> היה *be* 1QIsa^a 9$_5$ (+ על שכמו *upon his shoulder;* MT מִשְׂרָה *government*). <CSTR> מרבה משורה *the increase of dominion* 1QIsa^a 9$_{6(mg)}$ (MT מִשְׂרָה).

⇒ שׂרר *rule.*

מְשׂוּרָה 4.0.2 n.f. **measure** or specif. **capacity** (Lv 19$_{35}$ 1 C 23$_{29}$), <SUBJ> היה *be* 1QIsa^a 9$_5$ (unless from מִשׂוֹרָה *government;* + על שכמו *upon his shoulder;* MT מִשְׂרָה *government*). <CSTR> מרבה משורה *the increase of measure* 1QIsa^a 9$_{6(mg)}$ (unless from מִשׂוֹרָה *government;* MT מִשְׂרָה *government*), כָּל־מְשׂוּרָה *every (assessment of) capacity* 1 C 23$_{29}$ (|| מִדָּה *size*). <APP> מִשְׁפָּט *judgment,* i.e. measuring Lv 19$_{35}$ (|| מִדָּה *size,* מִשְׁקָל *weight*), שִׁשִּׁית הַהִין *a sixth of a hin* Ezk 4$_{11}$. <PREP> לְ *for (looking after)* 1 C 23$_{29}$; בְּ *in connection with,* + עשׂה *do,* i.e. practise, iniquity Lv 19$_{35}$; *in accordance with* (a restricted) measure perh. 4Q418 1$_1$ ([מ]שור במשורה perh. *measure by measure*), + שׁתה *drink* water Ezk 4$_{11.16}$ (+ בְּשִׁמָּמוֹן *in horror;* || מִשְׁקָל *weight*), שׁקה hi. *give* water *to drink* 4QMyst^a 6.1$_5$. <SYN> מִדָּה *size,* מִשְׁקָל *weight.**

⇒ מָשׂוֹר *measure.*

מָשׂוֹשׂ I 17 n.m. **joy**—cstr. מְשׂוֹשׂ; sf. מְשׂוֹשִׂי, מְשׂוֹשָׂהּ—**joy,** appar. **joyful sound** (Is 24$_{8.8}$), **joyful place** (Is 32$_{14}$), perh. **object of joy** (Is 60$_{15}$ 65$_{18}$ Ezk 24$_{25}$ Ho 2$_{13}$ Ps 48$_3$ Lm 2$_{15}$).

<SUBJ> היה *be,* i.e. serve as (of ruined city) Is 32$_{14}$ (if del. בְּעַד *on behalf of,* i.e. as, leaving מָשׂוֹשׂ as complement of היה), שׁבת *cease* Is 24$_{8.8}$ (|| שְׁאוֹן *tumult*), גלה *be exiled* Is 24$_{11}$ (|| שִׂמְחָה *joy*), שׁבת *cease* Lm 5$_{15}$ (+ מָחוֹל *dancing,* אֵבֶל *mourning*).

<NOM CL> הֶן־הוּא מְשׂוֹשׂ דַּרְכּוֹ *behold, this is the joy*

of his way, appar. this is the best he may expect Jb 8_{19} (unless מָשׂוֹשׂ II *rottenness*; or inf. cstr. of מוס *be rotten* or of מסס *melt*).

<OBJ> שׂושׂ *rejoice*, i.e. experience Is 62_5 (וּמְשׂוֹשׂ חָתָן עַל־כַּלָּה יָשִׂישׂ עָלַיִךְ אֱלֹהָיִךְ *and the joy of the groom over the bride your God will feel concerning you*) 66_{10}, מאס *reject* Is 8_6 (see Coll.), ברא *create*, i.e. turn into Is 65_{18} (הִנְנִי בוֹרֵא אֶת־יְרוּשָׁלַם גִּילָה וְעַמָּהּ מָשׂוֹשׂ *behold, I am turning Jerusalem into an object of rejoicing and her people into an object of joy*), שׂים *set*, i.e. make Is 60_{15}, לקח *take* Ezk 24_{25} (|| מַשָּׂא *burden*, מַחְמָד *desire*), שׁבת hi. *end* Ho 2_{13} (|| מוֹעֵד *appointed time*).

<CSTR> מְשׂוֹשׂ לִבֵּנוּ *the joy of our heart* Lm 5_{15}, מְשׂוֹשׂ חָתָן *the joy of the bridegroom* Is 62_5, מְשׂוֹשׂ הָאָרֶץ *the joy of the land* Is 25_{11}, מְשׂוֹשׂ תִּפְאַרְתָּם *the joy of their glory*, perh. the part of their glory that gave them most joy Ezk 24_{25}, מְשׂוֹשׂ פְּרָאִים *the joy of wild donkeys*, i.e. a reason for them to rejoice, or *a joyful place of*, i.e. for, *wild donkeys* Is 32_{14}, מְשׂוֹשׂ דּוֹר וָדוֹר *(object of) joy of generation and generation* Is 60_{15}, מְשׂוֹשׂ כָּל־הָאָרֶץ *(the object of joy) of the whole land* or *world* Ps 48_3, מְשׂוֹשׂ דַּרְכּוֹ *the joy of his way* Jb 8_{19} (unless מָשׂוֹשׂ II *rottenness*; see Nom. Cl.), מְשׂוֹשׂ תֻּפִּים *the joy of*, i.e. associated with, or *the joyful sound of, tambourines* Is 24_8, כִּנּוֹר *of (the) harp* Is 24_8.

כָּל־בָּתֵּי מָשׂוֹשׂ *all the households of joy*, i.e. every happy home Is 32_{13} (+ קִרְיָה עַלִּיזָה *joyful town*), קִרְיַת מְשׂוֹשִׂי *the city of my joy* Jr 49_{25} (or em. מָשׂוֹשׂ of *joy*; || תְּהִלָּה *praise*), כָּל־מְשׂוֹשָׂהּ *all her (objects of) joy* Ho 2_{13}.

<APP> מְעָרָה *cave* or *empty space* Is 32_{14} (|| מִרְעֶה *pasture*), גָּאוֹן *pride* Is 60_{15}, מָעוֹז *stronghold* Ezk 24_{25}, בֵּן *son* Ezk 24_{25} (or del. בְּנֵיהֶם וּבְנוֹתֵיהֶם *their sons and their daughters*, or em. וּבְנֵיהֶם *and their sons* and their daughters), חַג *festival* Ho 2_{13}, חֹדֶשׁ *month*, i.e. new moon festival Ho 2_{13}, שַׁבָּת *sabbath (celebration)* Ho 2_{13}, עִיר *city* Ps 48_3, הַר *mountain* Ps 48_3, קִרְיָה *city* Ps 48_3, יַרְכָה *distant part* Ps 48_3, יָפֶה *fair one* Ps 48_3.

<PREP> בְּ of place, *in*, + הלל pu. *be praiseworthy* Ps 48_3, בְּעַד *on behalf of*, + היה *be*, i.e. serve as (of ruined city) Is 32_{14} (or del. בְּעַד, leaving מָשׂוֹשׂ as complement of היה).

<COLL> מְשׂוֹשׂ חָתָן עַל־כַּלָּה *the joy of the groom over the bride* Is 62_5, הָעִיר שֶׁיֹּאמְרוּ ... מָשׂוֹשׂ לְכָל־הָאָרֶץ *the city of which they would say ... The whole land's*, or *world's, object of joy* Lm 2_{15} (or del. שֶׁיֹּאמְרוּ or מָשׂוֹשׂ לְכָל־הָאָרֶץ; + כְּלִילָה *perfect one* or *crown* of beauty), יַעַן כִּי מָאַס הָעָם הַזֶּה מֵי הַשִּׁלֹחַ הַהֹלְכִים לְאַט וּמְשׂוֹשׂ אֶת־רְצִין perh. *because this people has rejected the waters of Siloam that flow slowly and joy (of) in favour of Rezin* Is 8_6 (unless וּמְשׂוֹשׂ is inf. of מסס *melt* or משׂשׂ *melt*, and/or del. אֶת־רְצִין).

<SYN> שִׂמְחָה *joy*, גִּילָה *rejoicing*, מַחְמָד *desire*, תְּהִלָּה *praise*, מַשָּׂא *burden*, מוֹעֵד *appointed time*, שָׁאוֹן *tumult*, מִרְעֶה *pasture*.

⇨ שׂושׂ *rejoice*.

*[מָשׂוֹשׂ] II 1 vb. **rottenness** (unless מָשׂוֹשׂ I *joy*)—cstr. מְשׂוֹשׂ—<NOM CL> הֶן־הוּא מְשׂוֹשׂ דַּרְכּוֹ *behold, this is the rottenness of his way* Jb 8_{19}. <CSTR> מְשׂוֹשׂ דַּרְכּוֹ *the rottenness of his way* Jb 8_{19}.

מִשְׂחָק 1 n.[m.] **(object of) laughter,** <NOM CL> וְרֹזְנִים מִשְׂחָק לוֹ *and governors are his object of laughter*, i.e. are ridiculed by him Hb 1_{10}.

⇨ שׂחק *laugh*.

*[מִשְׂטָם] 0.0.1 n.[m]. **hostility,** <CSTR> וכול משטם *and all hostility* 4QAcademyFr 1_5 (+ תֶּבֶל *confusion*, אַשְׁמָה *guilt*).

⇨ שׂטם *be hostile*.

מַשְׂטֵמָה I 2.0.14 n.f. **hostility**—sf. Q משטמתו; pl. Q משטמות—<NOM CL> עַל רֹב עֲוֹנְךָ וְרַבָּה מַשְׂטֵמָה perh. *because of the abundance of your iniquity, (then) great is (your) hostility (towards me)* Ho 9_7 (unless מַשְׂטֵמָה II *cord*; or em. עֲוֹנָם *their iniquity* and/or replace מַשְׂטֵמָה in 9_8 with וְרַבָּה מַשְׂטֵמָה), מַשְׂטֵמָה בְּבֵית אֱלֹהָיו *there is hostility in the house of his God* Ho 9_8 (unless מַשְׂטֵמָה II *cord*; or em. וְרַבָּה מַשְׂטֵמָה *and great is [the] hostility* in the house).

<CSTR> מלאך משטמה *an angel of hostility*, as definition of Belial 1QM 13_{11}, מלאך המשטמה *the angel of hostility* CD 16_5 (=4QD[e] 6.2_{18} המשט]מה]; 4QD[f] 4.2_6 מלא]ך]), מלאכי המ]שטמה] *the angels of hostility* 4Qps

Jub^{a} 2.2$_{6}$, מלאכי המשטמות *the angels of hostilities* 4QpsEzek^{c} 3.3$_{4}$ 4QpsMos^{e} 1$_{10}$ (המש]ט[מות) 2.1$_{6}$ (מל]אכי]).

שר המ]ש[טמה *the prince of hostility* 4QpsJub^{a} 2.1$_{9}$ (+ שׂטם hi. *accuse*) 2.2$_{6}$ ([שר המשטמה]) 2.2$_{13}$ (+ מלאכי] הקדש[*the angels of holiness*) 2.2$_{14}$ (המ]ש[טמה; + Belial) 2.2$_{14}$ ([שר המשטמה]) 11QapPs^{a} 2$_{4}$ (ש]ר המשט[מה; + שֵׁד *demon*) MasJub 1$_{5}$.

ממשלת משטמתו *the government of his hostility*, i.e. hostile dominion of angel of darkness 1QS 3$_{23}$, מחשבת משטמה *thought of hostility*, i.e. hostile plans of Belial 1QM 13$_{4}$, [מ]חשבת משטמתו *the thought of his hostility*, i.e. hostile plans of Belial 4QBer^{a} 7.2$_{2}$ (|| אַשְׁמָה *guilt*, רֶשַׁע *wickedness*, + נִדָּה *impurity*).

Also 4QShir^{b} 152$_{3}$ ([מ]שטמ[ה]) 4QBéat 19$_{4}$ 6QHymn 9$_{1}$.

<SYN> אַשְׁמָה *guilt*, רֶשַׁע *wickedness*.*

⇒ שׂטם *be hostile*.

*מַשְׂטֵמָה II $_{2}$ **cord, noose, fetter, snare** (unless מַשְׂטֵמָה I *hostility*), <NOM CL> מַשְׂטֵמָה בְּבֵית אֱלֹהָיו *a snare in the house of his God* Ho 9$_{8}$ (|| פַּח *trap*). <OBJ> ררה *cast* Ho 9$_{7}$ (if em. רַבָּה *great is* to רֹרֵה *one casting*).

<SYN> פַּח *trap*.

מֵשִׂים $_{1}$ n.[m.] **attention,** ellipsis for מֵשִׂים לֵב *setting to heart*, מִבְּלִי מֵשִׂים לָנֶצַח יֹאבֵדוּ *they perish forever without any attention (being paid)* Jb 4$_{20}$.

[מְשֻׂכָה], see מְשׂוּכָה *hedge*.

מַשְׂכִּיל I $_{14}$ n.[m.] **maskil,** usu. as (part of) title of thirteen psalms, **psalm of success,*** <OBJ> זמר pi. *sing* Ps 47$_{8}$. <APP> שִׁיר יְדִידֹת *a song of love(s)* Ps 45$_{1}$ (mss יְדִידוּת *a loved one*), תְּפִלָּה *prayer* Ps 142$_{1}$. <COLL> מַשְׂכִּיל לְדָוִד *a maskil of*, or *for*, *David* Ps 32$_{1}$, מַשְׂכִּיל לְדָוִד *a maskil of*, or *for*, *David* Ps 52$_{1}$ (preceded by לַמְנַצֵּחַ perh. *for the director*) 53$_{1}$ (preceded by לַמְנַצֵּחַ עַל־מָחֲלַת perh. *for the director, to the tune of Mahalath*) 54$_{1}$ 55$_{1}$ (both preceded by לַמְנַצֵּחַ בִּנְגִינֹת perh. *for the director, with stringed instruments*) 142$_{1}$ (followed by בִּהְיוֹתוֹ בַמְּעָרָה תְפִלָּה *when he was in the cave, a prayer*).

מַשְׂכִּיל לִבְנֵי־קֹרַח *a maskil of*, or *for*, *the descendants of Korah* Ps 42$_{1}$ (preceded by לַמְנַצֵּחַ), לִבְנֵי־קֹרַח מַשְׂכִּיל *a maskil of*, or *for*, *the descendants of Korah* Ps 44$_{1}$ (preceded by לַמְנַצֵּחַ) 45$_{1}$ (לִבְנֵי־קֹרַח מַשְׂכִּיל; preceded by לַמְנַצֵּחַ עַל־שֹׁשַׁנִּים perh. *for the director, to the tune of Shoshannim* [or em. שֶׁשֹּׁנִים *of those that change*]).

מַשְׂכִּיל לְאָסָף *a maskil of*, or *for*, *Asaph* Ps 74$_{1}$ 78$_{1}$, מַשְׂכִּיל לְאֵיתָן הָאֶזְרָחִי *a maskil of*, or *for*, *Ethan the Ezrahite* 89$_{1}$, מַשְׂכִּיל לְהֵימָן הָאֶזְרָחִי *a maskil of*, or *for*, *Heman the Ezrahite* 88$_{1}$ (preceded by שִׁיר מִזְמוֹר לִבְנֵי קֹרַח לַמְנַצֵּחַ עַל־מָחֲלַת לְעַנּוֹת *a song, a psalm of, or for, the descendants of Korah; for the director, to the tune of Mahalath le-annoth*).

⇒ שׂכל hi. *prosper*.

מַשְׂכִּיל II $_{14}$ n.[m.] **responsive song,** usu. as (part of) title of thirteen psalms, <OBJ> זמר pi. *sing* Ps 47$_{8}$. <APP> שִׁיר יְדִידֹת *a song of love(s)* Ps 45$_{1}$ (mss יְדִידוּת *a loved one*), תְּפִלָּה *prayer* Ps 142$_{1}$. <COLL> לְדָוִד מַשְׂכִּיל *a responsive song of*, or *for*, *David* Ps 32$_{1}$, מַשְׂכִּיל לְדָוִד *a responsive song of*, or *for*, *David* Ps 52$_{1}$ (preceded by לַמְנַצֵּחַ perh. *for the director*) 53$_{1}$ (preceded by לַמְנַצֵּחַ עַל־מָחֲלַת perh. *for the director, to the tune of Mahalath*) 54$_{1}$ 55$_{1}$ (both preceded by לַמְנַצֵּחַ בִּנְגִינֹת perh. *for the director, with stringed instruments*) 142$_{1}$ (followed by בִּהְיוֹתוֹ בַמְּעָרָה תְפִלָּה *when he was in the cave, a prayer*).

מַשְׂכִּיל לִבְנֵי־קֹרַח *a responsive song of*, or *for*, *the descendants of Korah* Ps 42$_{1}$ (preceded by לַמְנַצֵּחַ), לִבְנֵי־קֹרַח מַשְׂכִּיל *a responsive song of*, or *for*, *the descendants of Korah* Ps 44$_{1}$ (preceded by לַמְנַצֵּחַ) 45$_{1}$ (לִבְנֵי־קֹרַח מַשְׂכִּיל; preceded by לַמְנַצֵּחַ עַל־שֹׁשַׁנִּים perh. *for the director, to the tune of Shoshannim* [or em. שֶׁשֹּׁנִים *of those that change*]).

מַשְׂכִּיל לְאָסָף *a responsive song of*, or *for*, *Asaph* Ps 74$_{1}$ 78$_{1}$, מַשְׂכִּיל לְאֵיתָן הָאֶזְרָחִי *a responsive song of*, or *for*, *Ethan the Ezrahite* 89$_{1}$, מַשְׂכִּיל לְהֵימָן הָאֶזְרָחִי *a responsive song of*, or *for*, *Heman the Ezrahite* 88$_{1}$ (preceded by שִׁיר מִזְמוֹר לִבְנֵי קֹרַח לַמְנַצֵּחַ עַל־מָחֲלַת לְעַנּוֹת *a song, a psalm of, or for, the descendants of Korah; for the director, to the tune of Mahalath le-annoth*).

⇨ שׂכל II *lay crosswise.*

*מַשְׂכִּיל III $_{14}$ n.[m.] **instructive** or **skilful song,** usu. as (part of) title of thirteen psalms, <OBJ> זמר pi. *sing* Ps 47$_{8}$. <APP> שִׁיר יְדִידֹת *a song of love(s)* Ps 45$_{1}$ (mss יְדִידוּת *a loved one*), תְּפִלָּה *prayer* Ps 142$_{1}$. <COLL> לְדָוִד מַשְׂכִּיל *an instructive song of,* or *for, David* Ps 32$_{1}$, מַשְׂכִּיל לְדָוִד *an instructive song of,* or *for, David* Ps 52$_{1}$ (preceded by לַמְנַצֵּחַ perh. *for the director*) 53$_{1}$ (preceded by לַמְנַצֵּחַ עַל־מָחֲלַת perh. *for the director, to the tune of Mahalath*) 54$_{1}$ 55$_{1}$ (both preceded by לַמְנַצֵּחַ בִּנְגִינֹת perh. *for the director, with stringed instruments*) 142$_{1}$ (followed by בִּהְיוֹתוֹ בַמְּעָרָה תְפִלָּה *when he was in the cave, a prayer*).

מַשְׂכִּיל לִבְנֵי־קֹרַח *an instructive song of,* or *for, the descendants of Korah* Ps 42$_{1}$ (preceded by לַמְנַצֵּחַ), לִבְנֵי־קֹרַח מַשְׂכִּיל *an instructive song of,* or *for, the descendants of Korah* Ps 44$_{1}$ (preceded by לַמְנַצֵּחַ) 45$_{1}$ (לִבְנֵי־קֹרַח מַשְׂכִּיל; preceded by לַמְנַצֵּחַ עַל־שֹׁשַׁנִּים perh. *for the director, to the tune of Shoshannim* [or em. שֶׁשֹּׁנִים *of those that change*]).

מַשְׂכִּיל לְאָסָף *an instructive song of,* or *for, Asaph* Ps 74$_{1}$ 78$_{1}$, מַשְׂכִּיל לְאֵיתָן הָאֶזְרָחִי *an instructive song of,* or *for, Ethan the Ezrahite* 89$_{1}$, מַשְׂכִּיל לְהֵימָן הָאֶזְרָחִי *an instructive song of,* or *for, Heman the Ezrahite* 88$_{1}$ (preceded by שִׁיר מִזְמוֹר לִבְנֵי קֹרַח לַמְנַצֵּחַ עַל־מָחֲלַת לְעַנּוֹת *a song, a psalm of, or for, the descendants of Korah; for the director, to the tune of Mahalath le-annoth*).

⇨ שׂכל I *be wise.*

מַשְׂכִּיל IV *instructor,* see שׂכל hi. *be intelligent.**

מַשְׂכִּית I $_{6.0.2}$ n.f. **image**—sf. מַשְׂכִּיתוֹ; pl. Q משכיות; cstr. מַשְׂכִּיּוֹת; sf. מַשְׂכִּיֹּתָם—**1. image,** perh. a **relief,** of stone (Lv 26$_{1}$) or silver (Pr 25$_{11}$) for cultic use (Lv 26$_{1}$ Nm 33$_{52}$ Ezk 8$_{12}$ 11QT 51$_{21}$).

2. perh. **ornament** or (if em.) **carving** (Pr 25$_{11}$).

3. imagination, thought (Ps 73$_{7}$ Pr 18$_{11}$).

<SUBJ> appar. עבר *pass,* i.e. overreach oneself Ps 73$_{7}$ (unless מַשְׂכִּית II *desire*; or em. עָבְרוּ *they have passed* to עָבְדוּ *they have served* the imaginations of the[ir] heart, or עֲבָדָיו *their deeds* are, i.e. they fulfil, the images of their heart, and/or מַשְׂכִּיּוֹת *images of* to בְּשֻׂכִּיַּת they pass *with,* i.e. fulfil, *the expectation of* their heart).

<NOM CL> עֲבָדָיו מַשְׂכִּיּוֹת לֵבָב *their deeds are,* i.e. they fulfil, *the imaginations of the(ir) heart* Ps 73$_{7}$ (if em. עָבְרוּ the imaginations of their heart *have passed*), כְּחוֹמָה נִשְׂגָּבָה מַשְׂכִּיתוֹ *like a fortified wall is his imagination* Pr 18$_{11}$ (if del. בְּ *in* or *according to, his imagination*; or em. מַשְׂכִּיתוֹ to נְכָסָיו *his possessions* are like a fortified wall), פִּתּוּחֵי זָהָב וּמַשְׂכִּיּוֹת כֶּסֶף דָּבָר דָּבֻר עַל־אָפְנָיו, perh. *inscriptions of gold and carvings of silver is a word spoken at its (appropriate) occasion* Pr 25$_{11}$ (if em. תַּפּוּחֵי *apples of* gold and בְּ *in* ornaments of silver to וּ).

<OBJ> אבד pi. *destroy* Nm 33$_{52}$ (+ צֶלֶם *image*), עבד *serve* Ps 73$_{7}$ (if em. עבר *pass,* with מַשְׂכִּית as subj.).

<CSTR> מַשְׂכִּיּוֹת לֵבָב *the imaginations of the(ir) heart* Ps 73$_{7}$ (unless מַשְׂכִּית II *desire*; or em. שֻׂכִּיַּת *the expectation of*), מַשְׂכִּיּוֹת כֶּסֶף perh. *ornaments of silver* Pr 25$_{11}$; אֶבֶן מַשְׂכִּית *a stone of,* i.e. with an, *image* Lv 26$_{1}$ (unless מַשְׂכִּית II *desire*) 11QT 52$_{2}$ ([א]בן [מ]שכית), אבני משכיות *stones of,* i.e. with, *images* 11QT 51$_{21}$, חַדְרֵי מַשְׂכִּיתוֹ *the chambers of his idol* Ezk 8$_{12}$ (or em. חֲדַר *the chamber of* and/or מִסְתָּרָם of *their secret*; + אֵין י׳ רֹאֶה אֹתָנוּ *Y. cannot see us*).

<PREP> בְּ of place, *in* Pr 18$_{11}$ (הוֹן עָשִׁיר ... כְּחוֹמָה נִשְׂגָּבָה בְּמַשְׂכִּיתוֹ *the wealth of a rich person is ... like a fortified wall, in,* or perh. *according to, his imagination*; or del. בְּ, leaving nom. cl.; or em. נִשְׂגָּב בִּמְשֻׂכָּתוֹ and like a wall *he is fortified in his enclosure*) 25$_{11}$ (תַּפּוּחֵי זָהָב בְּמַשְׂכִּיּוֹת כֶּסֶף perh. *apples of gold in ornaments of silver,* or em. תַּפּוּחֵי to פִּתּוּחֵי *inscriptions of* gold and/or בְּ to וּ *and* carvings of silver, as part of nom. cl.).*

⇨ שׂכה *look.*

*מַשְׂכִּית II $_{2}$ n.f. **desire** (unless מַשְׂכִּית I *image*)—pl. cstr. מַשְׂכִּיּוֹת—<SUBJ> עבר *pass,* i.e. overreach oneself Ps 73$_{7}$. <CSTR> מַשְׂכִּיּוֹת לֵבָב *desires of the(ir) heart* Ps 73$_{7}$; אֶבֶן מַשְׂכִּית *stone of desire,* i.e. wishing stone Ps 73$_{7}$.

[מַשְׂכֹּרֶת] $_{4.0.2}$ n.f. **recompense**—sf. מַשְׂכֻּרְתִּי, מַשְׂכֻּרְתֶּךָ

(Q משכרתכה, [משכור]), מַשְׂכֻּרְתֵּךְ—specif. **wages** (Gn 29$_{15}$ 31$_{7.14}$ perh. 4Q418 261$_{2}$); more generally, **reward, recompense** (Ru 2$_{12}$ perh. 4Q418 137$_{3}$), <SUBJ> היה *be* Ru 2$_{12}$ (וּתְהִי מַשְׂכֻּרְתֵּךְ שְׁלֵמָה מֵעִם־י׳ *and may your reward from Y. be complete;* + פֹּעַל *deed*). <NOM CL> מַה־מַּשְׂכֻּרְתֶּךָ *what are your wages,* i.e. what should I pay you? Gn 29$_{15}$. <OBJ> חלף hi. *change,* appar. reduce Gn 31$_{7.41}$ (both + עֲשֶׂרֶת מֹנִים change wages *ten times*) 4Q418 261$_{2}$ ([משכור]). <PREP> בְּ perh. *in connection with* 4Q418 137$_{3}$ (+ עֲבֹדָה *service*).

⇒ שׂכר *hire.*

*[מִשְׂמָחָה] 0.1 n.f. **celebration**—sf. Si משמחותם—<PREP> בְּ of place/time, *at, during* perh. Si 44$_{4}$(B) (ומושלים במשמחותם *tellers of proverbs at their celebrations;* others בְּמִשְׁמְרוֹתָם and [priestly] rulers *with their watches* or מַשְׂמְרוֹתָם tellers of proverbs with *their nails,* i.e. pointed sayings.).

[מַשְׂמֵר], see מַסְמֵר *nail.*

[מַשְׂמְרָה], see מַסְמֵר *nail.*

[מְשַׂנֵּא], see שׂנא, Pi. ptc., *adversary.*

מִשְׂפָּח I 1 n.[m.] perh. **bloodshed,** <SUBJ> פרח *sprout* like poison Ho 10$_{4}$ (if em. מִשְׁפָּט *judgment*). <OBJ> זכר *remember* 1QM 17$_{2}$ (others read משפט *judgment*). <CSTR> perh. משפח [נדב ו]אבי[ה]וא בני אהרון *bloodshed of Nadab and Abihu, the sons of Aaron* 1QM 17$_{2}$ (others read משפט *judgment of*). <COLL> וַיְקַו לְמִשְׁפָּט וְהִנֵּה מִשְׂפָּח *and he looked for judgment and behold, bloodshed* Is 5$_{7}$ (unless מִשְׂפָּח II *legal infringement;* || צְעָקָה *outcry,* :: מִשְׁפָּט *judgment,* צְדָקָה *righteousness*).

<SYN> צְעָקָה *outcry.*

<ANT> מִשְׁפָּט *judgment,* צְדָקָה *righteousness.**

*מִשְׂפָּח II 1 n.[m.] **legal infringement, breaking of law** (unless מִשְׂפָּח I *bloodshed*), <COLL> וַיְקַו לְמִשְׁפָּט וְהִנֵּה מִשְׂפָּח *and he looked for justice, and behold, a breaking of law* Is 5$_{7}$ (|| צְעָקָה *outcry,* :: מִשְׁפָּט *judgment,* צְדָקָה *righteousness*).

<SYN> צְעָקָה *outcry.*

<ANT> מִשְׁפָּט *judgment,* צְדָקָה *righteousness.*

מִשְׂרָה 2.0.5 n.f. **government, dominion**—cstr. Q משרת—<SUBJ> היה *be* Is 9$_{5}$ (or del.; + עַל־שִׁכְמוֹ *upon his shoulder;* 1QIsa^{a} מְשׂוּרָה *measure*). <OBJ> רום hi. *raise,* perh. establish or exalt 1QM 17$_{7}$ (|| מֶמְשָׁלָה *government*).

<CSTR> משרת מיכאל *the government of Michael* 1QM 17$_{6.7}$, משרת אשמתו *the government of his wickedness,* perh. his wicked régime 1QM 13$_{4}$=4QBer^{a} 7.2$_{3}$ (unless from מַשְׂרֵת *pan*), משרת [רשעתכה ואשמתכה] *the government of your evil and wickedness,* i.e. your evil and wicked régime 4QBer^{b} 6$_{8}$.

מלאכי מש[רת] *angels of the government of* 4QBer^{a} 3$_{2}$ (others מש[לחות] *of missions*), מַרְבֵּה הַמִּשְׂרָה *the increase of dominion* Is 9$_{6}$(Qr) (or em. לְמַרְבֵּה הַמִּשְׂרָה *of the increase of dominion* to לָמוֹ רַבָּה *for him great is* the dominion or לוֹ מְרֻבָּה *for him* the dominion *will be increased;* Kt לם רבה appar. *for them great is* the dominion; 1QIsa^{a} מְשׂוּרָה *government*).

<APP> גְּבוּרָה *strength* 1QM 17$_{6}$.

<PREP> לְ appar. *namely, that is to say* 1QM 17$_{6}$; בְּ of place/time, *during, throughout,* or of cause, *on account of,* + זעם pass. *be cursed* 1QM 13$_{4}$=4QBer^{a} 7.2$_{3}$ (unless from מַשְׂרֵת *pan*) 4QBer^{a} 7.2$_{9}$+4QBer^{b} 6$_{8}$ ([ז]עום); || מֶמְשָׁלָה *government* ([במ]מש[לת]); of instrument, *by (means of), through* 1QM 17$_{6}$ (with ellipsis of בְּ).

<SYN> מֶמְשָׁלָה *government.*

⇒ cf. שׂרר *rule.*

[מִשְׂרָפָה] n.f. 4 **burning**—pl. cstr. מִשְׂרְפוֹת—in ref. to fires of destruction (Is 33$_{12}$), appar. ceremonial fires of funeral (Jr 34$_{5}$).

<SUBJ> היה *be* Is 33$_{12}$ (וְהָיוּ עַמִּים מִשְׂרְפוֹת־שִׂיד *and peoples will become burnings of,* i.e. will be burnt to, *lime*). <CSTR> מִשְׂרְפוֹת־שִׂיד *burnings of,* i.e. into, *lime* Is 33$_{12}$, מִשְׂרְפוֹת אֲבוֹתֶיךָ *the burnings (in honour) of your ancestors* Jr 34$_{5}$. <PREP> כְּ *in accordance with* Jr 34$_{5}$ (וּכְמִשְׂרְפוֹת אֲבוֹתֶיךָ ... כֵּן יִשְׂרְפוּ־לָךְ *and in accordance with the burnings [in honour] of your ancestors ... so they will burn,* i.e. make fires, *for you;* mss בְּ and *with*

the fires of; or del. יִשְׂרְפוּ־לָךְ; or em. וּכְמִשְׂרְפוֹת to וְכִבְכוֹת *and as the weeping of*, i.e. as they wept for your ancestors, and יִשְׂרְפוּ to יִבְכּוּ so *they will weep* for you). <COLL> perh. as part of pl.n., מִשְׂרְפוֹת מַיִם *Misrephoth-maim* Jos 11_8 13_6 (מִשְׂרְפֹת).
⇒ שׂרף *burn.*

מִשְׂרְפוֹת מַ֫יִם 2 pl.n. **Misrephoth-maim**—מִשְׂרְפֹת מָ֫יִם—perh. Kh. el-Mušērefe, on border of Lebanon and Israel (or em. מִיָּם Misrephoth *in the west*), <PREP> עַד *unto* Jos 13_6 (+ כָּל־יֹשְׁבֵי הָהָר מִן־הַלְּבָנוֹן *all the dwellers of the hill country from Lebanon* up to Misrephoth-maim), + רדף *pursue* Jos 11_8 (+Sidon, Mizpeh).

מַשְׂרֵקָה 2 pl.n. **Masrekah,** native town or territory of fifth king of Edom, <PREP> מִן of direction, *from* Gn 36_{36}||1 C 1_{47}.

מַשְׂרֵת 1.0.1 n.f. **pan** or **tray** or some other utensil for baking or serving cakes, <OBJ> לקח *take* 2 S 13_9 (or em. וַתִּקַּח אֶת־הַמַּשְׂרֵת *and she took the pan* or *tray* to וַיִּקְרָא אֶת־הַמְשָׁרֶת *and he called the [female] attendant;* + יצק *pour*, i.e. serve food), משרת אשמתו *the pan*, i.e. underworld fires, *of his punishment** 1QM 13_4= 4QBer^a 7.2$_3$ (unless *the government of his wickedness*, i.e. from מִשְׂרָה *government*). <PREP> זעם pass. *be cursed* 1QM 13_4=4QBer^a 7.2$_3$ (unless from מִשְׂרָה *government*).*

***משׂשׂ** 1 vb. **melt—Qal** 1 Inf. מְשׂוֹשׂ—**melt, trickle,** מֵי הַשִּׁלֹחַ הַהֹלְכִים לְאַט וּמְשׂוֹשׂ *the waters of Shiloh that go softly and trickle* Is 8_6 (unless from מָשׂוֹשׂ *joy*; or em. וּמָשׂוֹשׂ, i.e. inf. abs.).
⇒ cf. מסס *melt.*

מַשׁ I 2 pr.n.m. **Mash,** one of four sons of Aram, in ref. to Mesopotamian people, appar. ident. with Meshech at 1 C 1_{17} and Mesha (מֵשָׁא II), <NOM CL> וּבְנֵי אֲרָם ... מַשׁ *and the sons of Aram were ... Mash* Gn 10_{23} (Sam מֵשָׁא),* בְּנֵי שֵׁם ... מַשׁ *the sons of Shem were ... Mash* 1 C $1_{17(mss)}$ (L מֶשֶׁךְ *Meshech*).*

***מַשׁ** II n.[m.] **swamp,** <OBJ> ערק *gnaw* Jb 30_3 (הָעֹרְקִים צִיָּה אוֹ מַשׁ *they gnaw the desert or swamp;* if em. אֶמֶשׁ *twilight*).

***[מַשׂ]** III 1 n.m. **statue**—sf. מַשָּׂם—<SUBJ> עלה *go up* Jb 20_6 (if em. שִׂיאוֹ *his height* to מַשּׂוֹ *his statue*). <OBJ> רצץ *crush* 2 K 23_{12} (unless מִשָּׁם *from there*).

***[משׂא]** vb. **sweep away—Qal, sweep away, destroy,** <SUBJ> subj. not specified, Ezk 17_9. <OBJ> גֶּפֶן *vine* Ezk 17_9. <PREP> מִן *from*, + שֹׁרֶשׁ *root* Ezk 17_9 (לְמַשְׂאוֹת אוֹתָהּ מִשָּׁרָשֶׁיהָ *to destroy it* [vine] *from its roots;* if em. לְמַשְּׂאוֹת *to lift*, i.e. נשׂא qal inf.).

מַשָּׁא 3 n.m. **debt**—cstr. מַשָּׁא—<OBJ> נשׁא *lend*, i.e. cause to be indebted with Ne 5_7 (mss מַשָּׂא ... נשׂא *impose ... a burden*), עזב *abandon*, i.e. cancel Ne 5_{10}, נטשׁ *abandon*, i.e. cancel Ne 10_{32} (or ins. נשׂא *raise*, i.e. *remove*). <CSTR> מַשָּׁא כָל־יָד *debt of every hand*, perh. from whomsoever Ne 10_{32}. <ADJ> זֶה *this* Ne 5_{10}.*
⇒ נשׁא *lend.*

מֵשָׁא I 1 pl.n. **Mesha, 1.** area in Arabia, perh. ident. with Massa (מַשָּׂא II), <PREP> מִן *of direction*, from, + היה *be* Gn 10_{30} (וַיְהִי מוֹשָׁבָם מִמֵּשָׁא בֹּאֲכָה סְפָרָה *and their dwelling was from Mesha until you come to Sephar*).

מֵשָׁא II 1.0.1 pr.n.m. **Mesha,** one of four sons of Aram, appar. ident. with Mash at Gn 10_{23} and Meshech at 1 C 1_{17}, Mash, and Meshech at 1 C 1_{17}, <NOM CL> וּבְנֵי אֲרָם ... מֵשָׁא *and the sons of Aram were ... Mash* Gn $10_{23(Sam)}$ (MT מַשׁ *Mash*),* בני ארם ... משא אשר בעבר פורת *the sons of Aram, ... Mesha, who are across the Euphrates* 1QM 2_{11}. <APP> בֵּן *son* of Aram 1QM 2_{11}. <PREP> בְּ *against*, + לחם ni. *fight* 1QM 2_{11}.

[מַשְׁאָב] 1 n.[m.] perh. **watering hole**—מַשְׁאַבִּים—<PREP> בֵּין *among*, + תנה pi. *recite* righteous deeds of Y., or חצץ pi. *divide* flocks Jg 5_{11} (מִקּוֹל מְחַצְצִים בֵּין מַשְׁאַבִּים שָׁם יְתַנּוּ perh. *louder than the sound of those who divide [their flocks], among the watering holes, there let them recite;* or em. קוֹל מְחַצְּצִים *the sound*

*of trumpeters).**
⇒ שׁאב *draw (water).*

[מַשָּׁאָה] 2 n.f. **debt**—cstr. מַשַּׁאת; pl. מַשָּׁאוֹת—<OBJ> נשׁה hi. *lend,* i.e. cause to be indebted with Dt 24_{10} (ms, Sam נשׁא *lend*) Ne 5_{11} (if em. מְאַת *the hundred [shekels] of* silver), ערב *guarantee* Pr 22_{26}, שׁוב hi. *return* Ne 5_{11} (if em. מְאַת *the hundred [shekels] of* silver; + בַּיִת *house,* שָׂדֶה *field,* כֶּרֶם *vineyard,* זַיִת *olive,* דָּגָן *grain,* יִצְהָר *new oil*). <CSTR> מַשַּׁאת מְאוּמָה *a loan of anything* Dt 24_{10}, מַשַּׁאת הַכֶּסֶף *the loan(s) of money* Ne 5_{11} (if em. מְאַת *the hundred [shekels] of* silver).
⇒ נשׁא *lend.*

מְשׁוֹאָה 3.1.2 n.f. **devastation**—מְשׁוֹאָה—<SUBJ> ערק *gnaw* wilderness Jb 30_3 (|| שֹׁאָה *destruction,* אֶמֶשׁ *evening* [ms אֱנוֹשׁ *human being;* or em. אֵם *the mother of* destruction and devastation]).

<OBJ> שׂבע hi. *sate* Jb 38_{27} (|| שֹׁאָה *destruction,* + אֶרֶץ לֹא־אִישׁ מִדְבָּר לֹא־אָדָם בּוֹ *land without people, steppe in which there is no human*), משׁשׁ pi. *grope* Jb 30_3 (if em. אֶמֶשׁ *evening* to יְמַשְׁשׁוּ *they grope*).

<CSTR> מְשֻׁאוֹת נֶצַח *devastations of eternity,* i.e. everlasting ruins Ps 74_3 (if em. מַשֻּׁאוֹת *deceptions of*); ... יוֹם מְשׁוֹאָה *a day of ... devastation* Zp 1_{15} (|| שֹׁאָה *destruction,* מְצוּקָה *distress,* צָרָה *distress,* חֹשֶׁךְ *darkness,* אֲפֵלָה *darkness,* עָנָן *cloud,* עֲרָפֶל *cloud*) Si 51_{10} (|| צָרָה), ... אֵם מְשׁוֹאָה *the mother of ... devastation* Jb 30_3 (if em. אֶמֶשׁ *evening*).

<PREP> לְ of direction, *to* 1QH 9_6 (ואני משאה למשואה *as for me, I go from destruction to devastation;* erased משאה אל משואה in same sense; || נֶגַע *wound,* מִשְׁבָּר *point of delivery*), + רום hi. *raise* feet, i.e. step Ps 74_3 (if em. מַשֻּׁאָה *deception*); אֶל *to* 1QH $9_{6(\text{erased})}$; עִם *with* 1QH 5_{30} (יחד תולנתם עם שאה משואה *their complaint went together with destruction and devastation*).

<COLL> שֹׁאָה וּמְשֹׁאָה *destruction and devastation* Jb 30_3 (שׁוֹאָה) 38_{27} Zp 1_{15} Si 51_{10} (שואה ומשואה) (וּמְשׁוֹאָה) 1QH 5_{30} (משואה).

<SYN> שֹׁאָה *destruction,* אֶמֶשׁ *evening,* חֹשֶׁךְ *darkness,* אֲפֵלָה *darkness,* עָנָן *cloud,* עֲרָפֶל *cloud,* מְצוּקָה *distress,* צָרָה *distress,* נֶגַע *wound,* מִשְׁבָּר *point of delivery.**

[מַשֻּׁאָה] 2 n.f. **deception**—pl. מַשּׁוּאוֹת; cstr. מַשֻּׁאוֹת—perh. as name for the underworld (Ps 73_{18}),* <SUBJ> נדח hi. *push aside* Ps 62_5 (if em. מִשְּׂאֵתוֹ *from his eminence* they take counsel to push [him] to מַשֻּׁאוֹת they counsel *deceptions* to push [him] aside). <OBJ> יעץ *counsel* Ps 62_5 (if em.), חזה *see* Lm 2_{14} (if em. מַשְׂאֹת *pronouncement*). <CSTR> מַשְׂאוֹת שָׁוְא וּמַדּוּחִים perh. *deceptions of vanity and enticement* Lm 2_{14} (if em. מַשְׂאוֹת *pronouncements of,* i.e. מַשָּׂא *burden*), מַשֻּׁאוֹת נֶצַח *deceptions of eternity* Ps 74_3 (if em. מְשֻׁאוֹת *devastations of*). <PREP> לְ appar. of instrument, *by (means of), through,* + נפל hi. *cause* evildoers *to fall* Ps 73_{18}; appar. *against,* + רום hi. *raise* feet, Ps 74_3 (or em. מַשֻּׁאָה to מְשֹׁאָה step to *destruction* or פַּעַם *foot* to כַּף raise *hand* against).*
⇒ נשׁא *deceive.*

מַשָּׁאוֹן 1 n.[m.] **deception,** <PREP> בְּ of instrument, *by (means of),* + כסה ni. *be covered,* i.e. concealed (of hatred) Pr 26_{26}.
⇒ נשׁא *deceive.*

מִשְׁאָל 2 pl.n. **Mishal,** Levitical city in Asher, ident. with Mashal (מָשָׁל) at 1 C 6_{59}, perh. T. Kishon, 8.5 km SE of Acco, <SUBJ> היה *be* Jos 19_{26} (+ גְּבוּל their *border,* i.e. territory was ... Mishal). <OBJ> נתן *give* to Gershonites Jos 21_{30}||1 C 6_{59} (if em. מָשָׁל *Mashal;* + מִגְרָשׁ *land outside city walls*).*

[מִשְׁאָלָה] 2.0.1 n.f. **request**—pl. cstr. מִשְׁאֲלֹת (Q משאלות); sf. מִשְׁאֲלֹתֶיךָ—<OBJ> נתן *give* Ps 37_4, מלא pi. *fulfil* Ps 20_6 GnzPs 3_7. <CSTR> מִשְׁאֲלֹת לִבֶּךָ *the requests of your heart* Ps 37_4, משאלות לבי *the requests of my heart* GnzPs 3_7; כול משאלות *all the requests of* GnzPs 3_7, כָּל־מִשְׁאֲלוֹתֶיךָ *all your requests* Ps 20_6.
⇒ שׁאל *ask.*

[מִשְׁאֶרֶת] 4 n.f. **kneading trough** or **tray**—sf. מִשְׁאַרְתֶּךָ; pl. sf. מִשְׁאֲרוֹתֶיךָ, מִשְׁאֲרֹתָם—<SUBJ> ברך pass. *be blessed* Dt 28_5 (|| טֶנֶא *basket,* + פְּרִי *fruit*), ארר pass.

be cursed Dt 28_{17} (|| טֶנֶא, + פְּרִי), צרר pass. *be wrapped* Ex 12_{34} (וַיִּשָּׂא הָעָם אֶת־בְּצֵקוֹ טֶרֶם יֶחְמָץ מִשְׁאֲרֹתָם צְרֻרֹת בְּשִׂמְלֹתָם עַל־שִׁכְמָם *and the people took away their dough before it was leavened, their kneading trays wrapped in their cloaks, upon their shoulder*). <PREP> בְּ of place, *in(to)*, + בוא *come* Ex 7_{28} (|| תַּנּוּר *oven*, + בַּיִת, חֶדֶר *chamber*, מִטָּה *couch*). <SYN> טֶנֶא *basket*, תַּנּוּר *oven*.*

מְשֻׁבָה, see מְשׁוּבָה I *going back*.

[מִשְׁבְּצָה] 9.0.1 n.f. **(ornamental) setting**—cstr. Q משבצתו; pl. מִשְׁבְּצוֹת (מִשְׁבְּצֹת); pl. cstr. מִשְׁבְּצוֹת (מִשְׁבְּצֹת) —**setting** of stones and chains on ephod and breastplate, or perh. **chequerwork** or **plaiting**, <OBJ> עשׂה *make* Ex 28_{13} 39_{16} (|| טַבַּעַת *ring*), נתן *give*, i.e. place perh. Ex 28_{25}||39_{18}. <CSTR> מִשְׁבְּצוֹת זָהָב *settings of gold* Ex 28_{11}||39_{6} (מִשְׁבְּצֹת) 28_{13} (מִשְׁבְּצֹת) $39_{13.16}$ (מִשְׁבְּצֹת) Ps 45_{14}; מֻסַבֹּת מִשְׁבְּצוֹת *ones encircled of*, i.e. by, *settings of* Ex 28_{11}||39_{6} (מִשְׁבְּצֹת) 39_{13}, שְׁתֵּי הַמִּשְׁבְּצוֹת *the two settings* Ex 28_{25}||39_{18} (הַמִּשְׁבְּצֹת), שְׁתֵּי מִשְׁבְּצֹת *two settings of* Ex 39_{16}. <PREP> מִן perh. partitive, *(some) of*, or of comparison, *(more) than* Ps 45_{14} (מִמִּשְׁבְּצוֹת זָהָב לְבוּשָׁהּ *of*, or *brighter than*, *settings of gold is her clothing*; or em. בְּמִשְׁבְּצוֹת her clothing is *with settings of* gold, or מִשְׁבֶּצֶת all wealth, *set* in gold, with לְבוּשָׁהּ as part of following clause); עַל *on*, + נתן *give*, i.e. place Ex 28_{14} 28_{25}||39_{18}.

Also 4QUnidD$_{2}$.

<SYN> טַבַּעַת *ring*.

⇒ שׁבץ *decorate*.

[מַשְׁבֵּר] 1.0.6 n.[m.] **mouth of cervix**—cstr. מִשְׁבַּר; sf. Q perh. משברי; pl. Q משברים; cstr. Q משברי; sf. משבריה —at 1QH $3_{8.9.10}$ (and perh. $3_{11.12}$) with wordplay with מִשְׁבָּר *breaker*.

<SUBJ> חושׁ *hasten* (intrans.) 1QH 3_{11} (|| חֵבֶל *labour pain*).

<OBJ> פתח *open* or pi. *release* 1QH $11_{32(mg)}$ (פתחתה משברי *you have opened/released my cervix*, i.e. eased my [birth] pains; unless מִשְׁבְּרִי you have released [me] *from my breaking*; + ומיגוני נחמתני *and from my distress you have consoled me*).

<CSTR> מַשְׁבֵּר בָּנִים *the point of delivery (of sons)* Ho 13_{13}, משברי מות *the point(s) of delivery of*, i.e. from, *death* 1QH $3_{8.9}$; כול משברים *all the points of delivery* 1QH 3_{11}.

<PREP> לְ of direction, *to* 1QH 9_{7} (ואני ... מחבלים למשברים *as for me, I go from birthpangs to point[s] of delivery*; || מְשׁוֹאָה *devastation*, נֶגַע *wound*); בְּ of place/time, *at*, + עמד *stand*, i.e. be ready Ho 13_{13}, perh. *through*, + מלט hi. *give birth* 1QH 3_{9}; מִן of direction, *from*, + מלט ni. *escape*, i.e. *be born* 1QH 3_{10}; עַל *at*, + מרץ *be sickening* 1QH 3_{8} (וחבל נמרץ על משבריה להחיל בכור הריה perh. *and pain was sickening at her cervix so as to cause writhing in the furnace of conception*); עַד *unto*, + בוא *come* (of children) 2 K 19_{3}||Is 37_{3} (+ וְכֹחַ אַיִן לְלֵדָה *but there is no strength to give birth* [or em. לַיֹּלֵדָה *the woman giving birth has* no strength]) 1QH 3_{8}.

<SYN> חֵבֶל *labour pain*, מְשׁוֹאָה *devastation*, נֶגַע *wound*.

⇒ (?) שׁבר *break*.

[מִשְׁבָּר] I 5.0.8 n.[m.] **surf, breaker** (wave of sea)—pl. Q משברים; cstr. מִשְׁבְּרֵי; sf. מִשְׁבָּרֶיךָ, Q משבריהם—at 1QH $3_{8.9.10}$ (and perh. $3_{11.12}$) with wordplay with מַשְׁבֵּר *mouth of cervix*; perh. **rage*** (Ps 88_{8}).

<SUBJ> אפף *surround* 2 S 22_{5} (mss, ||Ps 18_{5} חֶבֶל *cord*; || נַחַל *stream* of Belial, חֶבֶל *cord* of Sheol, מוֹקֵשׁ *snare* of death) 1QH $9_{4(\text{Licht})}$ ([אפפוני] the breakers of death *surround me*), עבר *pass* over drowning person Jon 2_{4}=Ps 42_{8}, perh. פתח *open* Sheol 1QH 3_{16} (ומשברי מים בהמון קולם ובהתרגשם יפתחו ש]או[ל perh. *and the breakers of the waters by the din of their noise and by their storming about will open Sheol*), עוף htpol. *fly about* 1QH 8_{31} (ויתעופפו עלי משברים *and breakers fly about over me*; Licht [פחי] *the traps of* [the] breakers fly about), רגשׁ htp. *be stormy* 1QH 3_{16}, הום *make a noise* 1QH 6_{23} (=4QHod^{c} 2.2$_{2}$ [מ]שבריהם ... המו; || גַּל *wave*).

<NOM CL> ומשברי שחת לכול מעשי פלצות perh. *and the breakers of (the) pit will be (destined) to all the deeds of shuddering*, i.e. that make one shudder 1QH

3_{12} (=4QHod^b 2_2 [ומש]ברי שחת לכול [מעשי פלצות]; + הרית אפאה perh. *she who is pregnant with nothingness*).

<OBJ> ענה pi. *oppress*, i.e. send in oppression Ps 88_8 (or em. עִנִּיתָ *you have oppressed* to אֵנִיתָ לִי *you have brought upon me*; + חֵמָה *anger*).

<CSTR> מִשְׁבְּרֵי־יָם *the breakers of (the) sea* Ps 93_4, מִשְׁבְּרֵי־מָוֶת *the breakers of death* 2 S 22_5 (mss, ||Ps 18_5 חֶבְלֵי *the cords of* death; or em. מַיִם breakers of *water*) 1QH $3_{8.9}$ 9_4, מִשְׁבְּרֵי־מַיִם *the breakers of (the) water(s)* 2 S 22_5||Ps 18_5 (if em.) 1QH 3_{16}, משברי שחת *the breakers of (the) pit* 1QH 3_{12} (=4QHod^b 2_2 [מש]ברי [פחי]); משברים *the traps of (the) breakers* 1QH 8_{31}(Licht) (others עלי breakers fly about *over me*), כָּל־מִשְׁבָּרֶיךָ *all your breakers* Jon 2_4=Ps 42_8 (|| גַּל *wave*) Ps 88_8 (perh. *all your outburst*),* כול משבריהם *all their breakers* 1QH 6_{23} (=4QHod^c 2.2_2 [כל מ]שבריהם).

<APP> מַיִם *water(s)* Ps 93_4.

<PREP> בְּ of place, *in, among*, + מלט hi. *give birth* 1QH 3_9; מִן of direction, *from*, + מלט ni. *escape* 1QH 3_{10}; of comparison, *(more) than* Ps 93_4 (if em. אַדִּירִים מִשְׁבְּרֵי more than the sound of many *majestic* waters, *the breakers of* the sea, to אַדִּיר מִמִּשְׁבְּרֵי *more majestic than the breakers of* the sea); עַד *unto*, + בוא *come* (of sons) 1QH 3_8.

<SYN> גַּל *wave*, נַחַל *stream*, חֶבֶל *cord*, מוֹקֵשׁ *snare*.*

⇒ שׁבר *break*.

[מִשְׁבָּר] II, see מַשְׁבֵּר *mouth of cervix*.

[מִשְׁבָּת] I $_1$ n.[m.] **cessation**—pl. sf. מִשְׁבַּתֶּהָ—**cessation, inactivity,** <CSTR> עַל *at, concerning*, + שׂחק *laugh* Lm 1_7 (unless מִשְׁבָּת II *shattering*; or em. מִשְׁבַּתֶּהָ *her inactivity* to שִׁבְתָּהּ *her sitting down* or שְׁבִיתָהּ *her captivity*).

⇒ שׁבת *cease*.

*__[מִשְׁבָּת]__ II $_1$ n.[m.] **shattering** (unless מִשְׁבָּת I *inactivity*)—pl. sf. מִשְׁבַּתֶּהָ—<CSTR> עַל *at, concerning*, + שׂחק *laugh* Lm 1_7.

*__[מִשְׁגָּה]__ $_{0.0.3}$ n.f. **error**—sf. Q משגתם; pl. sf. Q משגותם —<CSTR> משגת א[ש]מה *the error of their wickedness*, i.e. their wicked error 4QMidrEschat^a 1_9 (others א[ונ]מה *of their iniquity*). <PREP> בְּ of instrument, *by means of*, or of cause, *on account of*, + לבט ni. *be ruined* 1QH 2_{19}, תפשׂ ni. *be seized* by Belial 4QMidrEschat^a 1_9 ([ית]פשו); לִפְנֵי *on account of* or *in accordance with*, + ענשׁ ni. *be punished* CD 3_5.

⇒ שׁגה *err*.

מִשְׁגֶּה $_{1.0.2}$ n.m. **mistake,** about money (Gn 43_{12}), <NOM CL> אוּלַי מִשְׁגֶּה הוּא *perhaps it was a mistake* Gn 43_{12}. <PREP> בְּ of accompaniment, *with, in (a state of)*, + טעה *err* GnzPs 3_{18} (if em. משם appar. מֵשַׁם *desolation* to משגה; || הֶבֶל *vanity*).

Also 4QD^b 14_1 4QRitPur 7_3.

⇒ שׁגה *err*.

[מִשְׁגֶּה] n.f. **mistake,** <SUBJ> לין *pass the night*, i.e. remain with Job Jb 19_4 (if em. מְשׁוּגָתִי *my mistake*, from שׁוג *err*, to מִשְׁגָּתִי *my mistake*; + שׁגה *err*).

⇒ שׁגג *err*.

משׁה $_3$ vb. **pull—Qal** $_1$ Pf. מְשִׁיתִהוּ—**pull out,** <SUBJ> בַּת *daughter* of Pharaoh Ex 2_{10}. <OBJ> מֹשֶׁה *Moses* Ex 2_{10}, יֶלֶד *child* Ex 2_{10}. <PREP> מִן of direction, *from*, + מַיִם *water(s)* Ex 2_{10}.

Hi. $_2$ Impf. יַמְשֵׁנִי—as Qal, **pull out,** <SUBJ> Y. 2 S 22_{17}||Ps 18_{17} (|| לקח *take*, + נצל hi. *rescue*). <OBJ> David 2 S 22_{17}||Ps 18_{17}. <PREP> מִן of direction, *from*, + מַיִם *water(s)* 2 S 22_{17}||Ps 18_{17}. <SYN> לקח *take*.

[מַשֶּׁה] $_{1.0.1}$ n.m. **debt**—cstr. מַשֵּׁה—**loan, debt,** or perh. **part of patrimony,*** <OBJ> נשׁה hi. *lend*, i.e. cause to be indebted with Dt 15_2=11QMelch 2_3, שׁמט *annul* Dt 15_2 (if em. שָׁמוֹט כָּל־בַּעַל מַשֵּׁה יָדוֹ *every possessor of a debt of his hand*, with which he caused his neighbour to be indebted, *is to annul* to שָׁמוֹט כָּל־בַּעַל מַשֶּׁה אֶת־ מַשֵּׁה יָדוֹ *every possessor of a debt*, i.e. creditor, *is to annul the debt of his hand*). <CSTR> מַשֵּׁה יָדוֹ *a debt of his hand*, i.e. that he owns Dt 15_2 (=11QMelch 2_3 יד *a* debt of *a hand*); כָּל־בַּעַל מַשֶּׁה *every possessor of a debt*, i.e. creditor, *of* Dt 15_2=11QMelch 2_3 (or em.).*

⇒ נשׁה I *lend*.

מֹשֶׁה 762.4.75 pr.n.m. **Moses**—Q מושה—son of Amram and Jochebed, brother of Aaron and Miriam, husband of Zipporah, father of Gershom and Eliezer, leader of Israelite exodus from Egypt and law-giver.

<SUBJ> היה *be* Ex 3_{1} 4_{14} $18_{2.17}$ $24_{12.18}$ $34_{1.27}$ Dt 33_{4}, יאל hi. *be pleased, undertake* Ex 2_{21} Dt 1_{5}, אמן ni. *be trustworthy* Nm 12_{7}, hi. *believe* Nm 20_{12}, יכל *be able* Ex $18_{17.17}$ 33_{17} 40_{35} Nm 11_{11} Dt 1_{5} 31_{1}, כון ni. *be ready* Ex 34_{1}, בושׁ pol. *be delayed* Ex 32_{1}, קצף *be angry* Ex 16_{20} Lv 10_{16} Nm 31_{14}, רמם ni. *be full of worms* Nm 17_{9}, מרה *be rebellious* Nm 20_{23} 27_{12}.

ראה *see* Ex $2_{11.11.11}$ $3_{1.3.4}$ $4_{18.21}$ 6_{1} 7_{1} $10_{25.25.29}$ 24_{9} 31_{1} $32_{19.25}$ $33_{17.17}$ 39_{43} Nm $11_{11.23}$ $27_{12.12}$ Dt $1_{5.5.5}$ 5_{1} $32_{48.48}$, ho. *be caused to see* Ex 25_{1}, חזה *see*, i.e. select Ex 18_{17}, נבט hi. *look* Ex 3_{6} Nm 12_{8}, שׁמע *hear* Ex $18_{17.24}$ 32_{17} Lv 10_{20} Nm 7_{89} 9_{8} 11_{10} 16_{4} Dt 1_{5} 5_{1}, ידע *know* Ex 10_{1} 32_{21} 33_{1} 34_{29} Nm 11_{16} Dt 5_{1} $31_{25.25}$, hi. *cause to know* Ex $18_{15.17}$.

בוא *come* Ex $3_{1.13.15}$ $5_{1.22}$ 6_{10} $7_{10.26}$ 9_{1} $10_{1.3}$ 18_{7} 19_{7} $24_{3.18}$ $33_{8.9}$ $34_{34.35}$ $40_{32.35}$ Lv 9_{23} Nm 7_{89} $17_{8.23}$ 20_{6} Dt $1_{5.5}$ 31_{1} 32_{48}, hi. *bring* Ex $4_{4.4}$ 18_{17} $40_{1.1.21}$ Nm 16_{12} $20_{3.3.12}$ 31_{54}, הלך *go* Ex $3_{6.11.15}$ 4_{10+5t} $5_{1.4}$ 7_{14} 8_{21} $10_{8.9.9.25}$ 12_{31} 17_{5} $19_{10.23}$ $32_{7.33}$ 33_{1} Nm 16_{25} Dt $5_{1.1}$ $31_{1.14}$ 32_{44}, יצא *go out* Ex $2_{11.11}$ $8_{8.25.26}$ $9_{29.33}$ 10_{16} 11_{4} 12_{31} 18_{7} 33_{8} $34_{34.34}$ Lv 9_{23} Nm 11_{24} $12_{4.4}$ 31_{13} Dt 31_{1}, hi. *bring out* Ex $3_{6.11.11}$ $4_{4.4}$ 6_{26} 14_{11} 16_{2} 19_{17} Lv 24_{13} Nm 17_{24} $20_{7.10}$ Dt 5_{1} 1 S 12_{8}, עלה *ascend* Ex 17_{10} $19_{3.20.23}$ 24_{1+5t} 32_{30} 33_{1} $34_{1.4}$ Nm 20_{27} 27_{12} Dt 1_{5} $5_{1.1.1}$ $32_{48.48}$ 34_{1}, hi. *bring up* Ex 17_{3} $32_{1.7.23}$ $33_{1.12}$ $40_{1.25.29}$ Nm 16_{12} $20_{3.23}$ 21_{5}, ירד *descend* Ex $19_{14.21.23.25}$ $32_{1.7.15}$ $34_{29.29}$ Nm 20_{28} Dt $5_{1.1.1}$, מושׁ *depart* Nm 14_{44}, שׁוב *return* Ex $4_{18.18.19.20.21}$ 5_{22} 24_{13} 32_{31} 33_{11}, hi. *bring back, turn away* Ex $4_{4.4}$ 19_{8} 34_{35} Nm 17_{25} Ps 106_{23}, ho. *be brought back* Ex 10_{8}.

קום *arise* Ex 2_{17} 12_{31} 24_{13} Nm 16_{25} Dt $5_{1.1}$, hi. *raise* Ex $40_{1.18.18.33}$ Nm 7_{1}, שׁכם hi. *rise early* Ex 8_{16} 9_{13} 24_{4} 34_{4}, רום hi. *raise* Ex 14_{15} 17_{11} Nm 20_{11} 31_{25}, עמד *stand* Ex 3_{4} 9_{8} 18_{17} 32_{26} Nm 16_{18} Dt $5_{1.1.1}$ Jr 15_{1} Ps 106_{23} CD 5_{18}, hi. *cause to stand* Nm 3_{5} 8_{5} 11_{24} $27_{18.22}$, נצב ni. *stand* Ex 7_{14} 17_{9} 33_{17} 34_{1}, יצב htp. *stand* Ex 8_{16} 9_{13} Dt $31_{14.14}$, ישׁב *sit, dwell* Ex $2_{15.15.21}$ 17_{12} $18_{13.14}$ Dt 5_{1}, hi. *cause to dwell* 1 S 12_{8}, חנה *encamp* Ex 18_{5} Nm 33_{8}, שׁחה htpal *bow down* Ex 18_{7} 24_{1} 34_{8}, קדד *bow down* Ex 34_{8}, נפל *fall* Nm 14_{5} $16_{4.20}$ 17_{9} 20_{6}, htp. *prostrate oneself* Dt $5_{1.1.1}$, שׁכב *lie down* Dt 31_{16}.

אמר *say* Ex $2_{11.14.14}$ 3_{3+9t} 4_{1+6t} $5_{1.1.22}$ $6_{12.30}$ $7_{8.14.19.26}$ 8_{1+6t} $9_{13.29}$ $10_{3.9.25.29}$ 11_{4} $12_{1.21}$ 13_{3} 14_{13} 15_{1} 16_{6+9t} $17_{2.4.9.10.15}$ $18_{2.15}$ $19_{3.10.14.23.25}$ $20_{20.22}$ $24_{8.13}$ 31_{12} 32_{11+7t} $33_{5.12.12.17}$ 34_{8} $35_{1.4.4.30}$ Lv 1_{1} 4_{1} $6_{1.17}$ $7_{22.28}$ $8_{5.31.31}$ $9_{1.6.7}$ $10_{3.4.6.16}$ 11_{1} 12_{1} 15_{1} $17_{1.1}$ 18_{1} 19_{1} 20_{1} $21_{1.1.16}$ $22_{1.17}$ $23_{1.9.23.33}$ 24_{13} 25_{1} 27_{1} Nm 5_{11} $6_{1.22}$ 8_{1} $9_{8.9}$ $10_{29.35.35}$ $11_{11.16.21.29}$ 12_{13} 13_{17} $14_{13.41}$ $15_{1.17}$ 16_{4+7t} $17_{1.11}$ 18_{25} 20_{10} $25_{5.10}$ 26_{3} $27_{6.15}$ $28_{1.1}$ 30_{1} $31_{3.15}$ $32_{6.20.29}$ 33_{50} $34_{1.13}$ 36_{5} Dt 1_{5+11t} $5_{1.1.1}$ $27_{9.11}$ 29_{1} $31_{1.7.10.22.25}$ 32_{45} 33_{1+9t} Jos 1_{13} 14_{9} 1QDM 2_{5} ([יאמר]) 4QD[a] 3.2_{10} CD 5_{8} 8_{14} 19_{26}.

דבר *speak* Dt 5_{1}, pi. *speak* Ex $4_{10.14}$ 5_{22} $6_{9.10.12.27.29}$ $7_{1.7}$ 9_{1} 11_{1} 12_{1} $14_{1.15}$ 16_{11} $19_{3.19}$ 20_{19} $25_{1.1}$ 31_{12} 33_{17} 34_{29+5t} Lv 1_{1} 4_{1} 6_{17} $7_{22.28}$ $10_{5.12}$ 11_{1} 12_{1} 15_{1} 16_{2} 17_{1} 18_{1} 19_{1} $21_{16.24}$ $22_{1.17}$ $23_{1.9.23.33.44}$ $24_{13.23}$ 25_{1} 27_{1} Nm $5_{5.11}$ $6_{1.22}$ 7_{89} 8_{1} $9_{4.9}$ 11_{24} 14_{39} $15_{1.17}$ $16_{4.23.25.28}$ $17_{12.16.21}$ 18_{25} 19_{1} 20_{7} 26_{3} $27_{6.15}$ 30_{2} 31_{3} 33_{50} Dt $1_{1.3.5.5.5}$ 4_{45} 5_{1} 27_{9} $31_{1.25.30.30}$ $32_{44.45}$ Jos 4_{12} 13_{33} Jg 1_{20} 1QDM 2_{11} 4_{3} ([ידבר]) 4QOrd[a] 5_{7} 4Q Zedek 3_{6}.

ספר pi. *recount* Ex 10_{1} 18_{8} 24_{3}, נגד hi. *tell* Ex 4_{28} $19_{3.9}$ Dt 5_{1} 29_{1}, ענה *answer* Ex 4_{1}, צוה pi. *command* Ex 16_{24} 25_{1} 34_{31} 36_{6} Lv 6_{1} 8_{31} $9_{5.21}$ 10_{16} 24_{1} Nm 5_{1} $27_{18.23}$ 28_{1} 32_{28} $34_{1.13}$ 35_{1} 36_{5} Dt 1_{5+8t} 5_{1+23t} 27_{1+8t} $29_{1.1.1}$ $31_{1.10.22.25.25}$ 33_{4} Jos $1_{7.13}$ 4_{10} $8_{31.33.35}$ $11_{12.15}$ $22_{2.5}$ 2 K 18_{12} 21_{8} 1 C 6_{34} 15_{15} 1QS 8_{15}, pu. *be commanded* Ex 34_{34} Lv 8_{31} 10_{12} Nm 3_{16}, שׁבע ni. *swear* Jos 14_{9}, זהר hi. *instruct* Ex 18_{17}, למד pi. *teach* Dt $1_{5.5.5}$ 5_{1} $31_{16.22}$, באר pi. *explain* Dt 1_{5}, עוד hi. *warn* Ex 19_{21} Dt 1_{5} 5_{1} 29_{1} 31_{25} 32_{45}, בטא pi. *speak impetuously* Ps 106_{32}.

קרא *call, read* Ex 12_{21} $17_{6.15}$ 19_{7} 24_{6} 33_{7} 34_{31} 36_{2} Lv 9_{1} 10_{4} Nm 11_{2} 13_{16} 16_{12} Dt 5_{1} 29_{1} $31_{7.14.30}$ Ps 99_{6} 1QDM 1_{11} 2_{5} ([יקרא]), שׁיר *sing* Ex $15_{1.1}$, רום pol. *exalt* Ex 15_{1}, נוה hi. *glorify* Ex 15_{1}, ברך pi. *bless* Ex 39_{43} Lv 9_{23} Dt 33_{1}, עתר *pray* Ex 8_{26} 10_{16}, hi. *make supplication* Ex $8_{4.5.25}$ 9_{27} 10_{16}, חנן htp. *make supplication* Dt 1_{5}, פלל htp. *intercede* Nm 11_{2} $21_{7.7}$ Dt $5_{1.1}$, חלה pi. *entreat* Ex 32_{11}, שׁאל *ask* Ex 18_{7}, צעק *cry out* Ex 8_{8} 14_{15} 15_{24} 17_{4} Nm 12_{13}.

עשׂה *do, make* Ex $4_{14.14.21.30}$ $7_{6.6.10.20}$ 8_{12} 11_{10} 14_{11} $17_{4.}$

6 18_{14+5t} $40_{16.16}$ Lv 8_4 Nm 4_{17} $8_{5.5.20.23}$ $10_{1.1}$ 16_{28} $17_{26.26}$ 20_{27} $21_{8.9.34.34}$ 27_{22} 31_{31} Dt $5_{1.1.1}$ $34_{10.12}$ 2 K 18_4 1 C 21_{29} 2 C 1_3, עבד *serve* Ex 3_{11} 10_8 12_{31}, ישׁע hi. *help* Ex 2_{17}, מלא pi. *fill* hand, i.e. ordain Si 45_{15}, משׁח *anoint* Ex 40_{1+5t} Lv $8_{10.10.10}$ Nm $7_{1.1}$ Si 45_{15}, כפר pi. *atone* Ex 32_{30} Lv 8_{15} 4QDibHam^a 1.2_9, טהר pi. *purify* Nm $8_{5.5.5}$, חטא pi. *purify* Lv 8_{15}, קדשׁ pi. *consecrate* Ex 13_1 $19_{10.14.23}$ $40_{1.1.1}$ Lv $8_{10.10.10.15.30}$ Nm $7_{1.1}$ Dt 32_{48}, hi. *consecrate* Nm 20_{12} 27_{12}, רחץ *wash* Ex $40_{1.31.32}$ Lv $8_{6.21}$.

שׂרף *burn* Ex 32_{19} Lv 8_{17} Dt 5_1 4QOrd^a 1.2_{17}, קטר hi. *cause to smoke* Ex 40_{27} Lv $8_{16.20.21.28}$, זבח *sacrifice* Ex 5_1 8_{21}, כרת *make covenant* Dt $28_{69.69}$ CD 15_9, hi. *cut* Nm 4_{17}, נתח pi. *cut into pieces* Lv 8_{20}, פסל *cut into shape* Ex 34_4 Dt $5_{1.1}$, חצה *divide* Nm $31_{25.42}$, בקע *split* Ex 14_{15}, בדל ni. *be separated* Nm 16_{20}, hi. *separate* Nm 8_5 Dt 4_{41}, נחל pi. *distribute* Jos 13_{32}, רבה hi. *make much* Nm 26_{52}, מעט hi. *reduce* Nm 26_{52}.

נתן *give, place* Ex 7_8 17_2 18_{25} 30_{11} 34_{33} 40_{1+11t} Lv 8_{6+6t} Nm $3_{5.44.51}$ $7_{4.6.6.6.6}$ $11_{11.11}$ 16_{12} $27_{6.18}$ $31_{25.25.41.47}$ $32_{33.40}$ Dt 1_{5+5t} 5_1 $29_{1.1.1}$ 31_9 Jos $1_{14.15}$ 9_{24} 12_6 13_{8+5t} $14_{3.3}$ 17_4 18_7 $22_{4.7}$ 2 C 5_{10}, שׂים *place* Ex 4_{14} 8_8 17_{14} 18_{17} 19_7 24_6 40_{1+11t} Lv $8_{6.9.9.24}$ Nm $21_{8.9}$ Dt 1_5 4_{44} $5_{1.1}$ 31_{16} Ps 105_{26}, סמך *lay* hand Nm $27_{18.23}$ Dt 34_9.

לקח *take* Ex $4_{4.4.14.20.20}$ 7_{14} $9_{8.10}$ 13_{19} 14_{11} $17_{5.5}$ $24_{6.6.8}$ 30_{11} 32_{19} 33_7 34_4 $40_{1.19}$ Lv 8_{1+9t} Nm 1_{17} 3_{40+5t} $7_{4.6}$ $8_{5.5}$ 11_{16} $12_{1.1}$ 17_{16} $20_{7.9.23}$ 25_4 $27_{18.22}$ $31_{25.25.47.51.54}$ Dt $1_{5.5}$ $5_{1.1}$ 4QOrd^a 5_4, נשׁל *take off* Ex 3_4, תפשׂ *lay hold of* Dt 5_1, אחז *hold* Ex 4_4, צרר *bind* Nm 25_{16}, חבשׁ *bind* Lv 8_{13}, כלא *restrain* Nm 11_{28}.

אסף *gather* Ex 3_{15} 4_{29} Nm $11_{16.24}$ 21_{16}, ni. *return to a place* Nm 11_{30}, *be gathered* Nm 27_{12} 31_1 Dt 32_{48}, קהל hi. *cause to assemble* Ex 35_1 Lv 8_1 Nm 1_{17} 8_5 $20_{7.10}$ Dt 1_5, קרא *meet* Ex 5_{20} 7_{14} 18_7 Nm 31_{13}, קרב *approach* Ex 3_4 32_{19} 40_{32} Dt 5_1, hi. *bring near* Ex $40_{1.1}$ Lv $8_{6.13.17.21.24}$ Nm 3_5 $8_{5.5}$ 27_5, נגשׁ ni. *draw near* Ex 20_{21} 24_2, hi. *bring near* Lv 8_{13}.

שׁלח *send* Ex $4_{4.4}$ 24_4 Nm $13_{3.16.17.26}$ 14_{36} 16_{12} 20_{14} 21_{32} 31_6 32_6 Dt 1_5 Jos $14_{7.11}$, pi. *send away* Ex 18_{27}, פרע hi. *cause to leave* Ex 5_4, נהג *drive* Ex 3_1, ירשׁ hi. *drive out* Jos 13_{12}, נחה *lead* Ex 32_{33}, נסע hi. *lead out* Ex 15_{22}, ברח *flee* Ex 2_{15}, נוס *flee* Ex 4_3, פנה *turn* Ex 2_{11} 32_{15} Dt $5_{1.1}$, סור *turn aside* Ex $3_{3.4}$ 34_{34}, עבר *pass over* Ex 17_5 Dt $1_{5.5.5.5}$ 31_1 34_1, hi. *cause to pass over* Nm 27_6 32_2, רכב hi. *cause to ride* Ex 4_{20}.

הרה *conceive* Nm 11_{11}, ילד *bear* Nm 11_{11}, גדל *grow up* Ex 2_{11}, אמץ pi. *strengthen* Dt 1_5, חזק pi. *make strong* Dt 1_5, hi. *take hold of* Ex 4_4, אכל *eat* Ex 34_{27} Dt $5_{1.1}$, שׁתה *drink* Ex 34_{27} Dt $5_{1.1}$, שׁקה hi. *cause to drink* Ex 2_{17} 32_{19} Nm 20_7, רעה *pasture* Ex 3_1, נוח hi. *cause to rest, place* Ex 17_{11} 32_9 Nm $17_{16.22}$ 1 K 8_9, נבל *wither* Ex $18_{17.17}$, מות *die* Ex 10_{25} Dt 1_5 31_{14} 32_{48} 34_5 Jos 1_2.

נכה hi. *strike* Ex 2_{11} 7_{14} $17_{5.6}$ Nm 20_{11} 25_{16} Dt 4_{46} Jos 12_6 $13_{12.21}$, שׁבר pi. *shatter* Ex 32_{19} 34_1 Dt $5_{1.1}$, טחן *grind* Ex 32_{19} Dt 5_1, כתת *crush* Dt 5_1, הרג *kill* Ex $2_{14.14}$, מות hi. *kill* Ex 16_2 17_3 Nm 16_{12} 17_6, שׁחט *slaughter* Lv $8_{15.19.23}$, רעע hi. *harm* Nm 16_{15}, נקר pi. *gouge out* Nm 16_{12}, יקע hi. *expose* Nm 25_4, פשׁט hi. *strip* Nm $20_{23.28}$, זרה *scatter* Ex 32_{19}, זרק *scatter* Ex $9_{8.10}$ $24_{6.8}$ Lv $8_{19.24}$, נזה hi. *sprinkle* Lv $8_{10.30}$ Nm 8_5, שׁפך *pour out* Ex 4_4, יצק *pour out* Lv $8_{10.15}$.

נוף hi. *wave* Lv 8_{29} Nm $8_{5.5}$, שׁלך hi. *throw* Ex $4_{3.3}$ 15_{24} 32_{19} Dt $5_{1.1}$, נטה *stretch out* Ex $9_{22.23}$ $10_{12.13.21.22}$ $14_{15.21.26.27}$ 33_7, פרשׂ *spread out* Ex $9_{29.33}$ 40_{19}, גבל hi. *circumscribe* Ex $19_{10.23}$, בנה *build* Ex 17_{15} 24_4, ערך *arrange* Ex $40_{1.23}$, יסף hi. *do again* Ex $10_{25.29}$ Dt 1_5, מהר pi. *hasten* Ex 34_8, חדל *cease* Ex 14_{11}, כלה pi. *finish* Ex 34_{33} 40_{33} Nm 7_1 16_{28} Dt 31_{24} 32_{45}, רפה hi. *leave off* Dt 5_1, שׁבת hi. *cause to cease* Ex 5_4.

מעל *sin* Dt 32_{48}, באשׁ hi. *cause to be despised* Ex 5_{20}, שׁית *lay* sin, i.e. penalize Nm 12_{11}, נקם *avenge* Nm 31_1, ירא *fear* Ex 2_{14} 3_6 Nm 21_{34}, יגר *fear* Dt 5_1, סתר hi. *hide* Ex 3_6, טמן *conceal* Ex 2_{11}, סכך *cover* Ex 40_1, hi. *cover* Ex 40_{21}, לבשׁ hi. *dress* Ex $40_{1.1}$ Lv $8_{6.13}$ Nm $20_{23.28}$, אפד *dress in ephod* Lv 8_6, חגר *gird* Lv $8_{6.6.13}$.

כתב *write* Ex 17_{14} 24_4 34_{27} Nm $17_{16.16}$ 33_2 Dt $31_{9.16.22.24}$ 4QZedek 3_6 4QDibHam^a 1.3_{12}, דרשׁ *seek* Lv $10_{16.16}$, בחר *choose* Ex 18_{25}, שׁמר *guard* Nm 3_{38} Ps 99_6, ni. *take heed* Ex 10_{25}, שׁפט *judge* Ex $18_{13.15}$, שׂרר htp. *cause oneself to rule* Nm $16_{12.12}$, פקד *number* Ex $30_{11.11}$ Nm $1_{1.19.44.48}$ 3_{5+6t} 4_{21+7t} $26_{63.64}$, hi. *appoint* Nm 1_{48}, נשׂא *lift* head, i.e. number Ex 30_{11} Nm $1_{1.48}$ $4_{1.21}$ 26_1 31_{25}, *lift* eyes Dt 1_5, *lift*, i.e. forgive Ex 10_{16}, *bear* burden Nm $11_{11.11.16}$ Dt $1_{5.5}$, *take* Nm 3_{40} 16_{15}, htp. *exalt oneself* Nm 16_3, מצא *find* favour Ex $33_{12.12.12.17}$ 34_8 Nm $11_{11.11}$,

נשׁק *kiss* Ex 18$_{7}$.

<NOM CL> הוּא אַהֲרֹן וּמֹשֶׁה *it was Aaron and Moses* Ex 6$_{26}$, הוּא מֹשֶׁה וְאַהֲרֹן *it was Moses and Aaron* Ex 6$_{27}$, מֹשֶׁה וְאַהֲרֹן בְּכֹהֲנָיו *Moses and Aaron were among his priests* Ps 99$_{6}$, בְּנֵי עַמְרָם ... מֹשֶׁה *the children of Amram were ... Moses* 1 C 5$_{29}$ 23$_{13}$, מֹשֶׁה בֶּן־שְׁמֹנִים שָׁנָה *Moses was the son of eighty years,* i.e. eighty years old Ex 7$_{7}$, מֹשֶׁה בֶּן־מֵאָה וְעֶשְׂרִים שָׁנָה *Moses was the son of one hundred and twenty years,* i.e. one hundred and twenty years old Dt 34$_{7}$, הָאִישׁ מֹשֶׁה גָּדוֹל מְאֹד *the man Moses was very great* Ex 11$_{3}$, הָאִישׁ מֹשֶׁה עָנָו מְאֹד *the man Moses was very humble* Nm 12$_{3}$, מושה ... עם אלוהים בענן *Moses was ... with God in the cloud* 4QapMos^{c} 2.2$_{10}$, לֹא־כֵן עַבְדִּי מֹשֶׁה *my servant Moses is not so* Nm 12$_{7}$.

<OBJ> קרא *call* Ex 2$_{10}$, צוה pi. *command* Ex 4$_{28}$ 6$_{13}$ 7$_{1.6}$ 12$_{28.50}$ 18$_{17}$ 19$_{7}$ 25$_{1}$ 31$_{1.1}$ 34$_{4.8}$ 38$_{22}$ 39$_{1+8t}$ 40$_{16+7t}$ Lv 7$_{38}$ 8$_{4+5t}$ 9$_{10}$ 16$_{34}$ 24$_{23}$ 27$_{34}$ Nm 1$_{19.54}$ 2$_{33.34}$ 3$_{42.51}$ 4$_{49}$ 8$_{3.20.22}$ 9$_{5}$ 15$_{36}$ 17$_{26}$ 20$_{9}$ 26$_{4}$ 27$_{11.22}$ 30$_{1.17}$ 31$_{17.21.31.41.47}$ 36$_{10}$ Dt 1$_{3.5.5}$ 5$_{1}$ 28$_{69}$ 34$_{9}$ Jos 9$_{24}$ 11$_{15.15.20}$ 14$_{5}$ 17$_{4}$ 2 K 18$_{6}$ Ml 3$_{22}$ Ne 1$_{7.8}$ 1 C 22$_{13}$ Si 45$_{1}$, ירה hi. *teach* Ex 4$_{10.14}$, זכר *remember* Is 63$_{11}$ (or del. מֹשֶׁה), ידע *know* Ex 33$_{12.17}$ Dt 34$_{10}$, hi. *cause to know* Ex 33$_{12.12}$, יעץ *advise* Ex 18$_{17}$, ענה *answer* Ex 19$_{19}$ Dt 1$_{5}$ Ps 99$_{6.6}$, שׁוב hi. *bring back* word to Jos 14$_{7}$, בכה *bewail* Dt 34$_{8}$.

ראה *see* Ex 4$_{14}$ 34$_{30}$, hi. *cause to see* Ex 25$_{1}$ 33$_{17}$ Nm 8$_{4}$ Dt 34$_{1.1}$, שׁמע *hear* Ex 6$_{12}$, hi. *cause to hear* Si 45$_{1}$, פגשׁ *meet* Ex 4$_{21.27}$, פגע *meet* Ex 5$_{20}$, קרא *meet* Ex 4$_{14.27}$, קרה *befall* Nm 11$_{23}$, נגשׁ hi. *bring near* Si 45$_{1}$, שׂים *place* Ex 2$_{14}$ 33$_{17}$, נתן *set* Ex 7$_{1}$, עשׂה *do, make* Ex 32$_{9}$ Nm 14$_{11}$ Dt 5$_{1}$ 1 S 12$_{6}$, ילד *bear* Ex 6$_{20}$ Nm 26$_{59}$, שׁלח *send* Ex 3$_{6.11.13.14.15}$ 4$_{28}$ 5$_{22}$ 7$_{14}$ Nm 16$_{28.28}$ Dt 34$_{10}$ Jos 24$_{5}$ 1 S 12$_{8}$ Mc 6$_{4}$ Ps 105$_{26}$ 4QParGenEx 3$_{4}$, גרשׁ pi. *expel* Ex 10$_{9}$, אמץ pi. *strengthen* Si 45$_{1}$, חזק pi. *make strong* Si 45$_{1}$, נצל hi. *deliver* Ex 18$_{2}$, ירא *fear* Jos 4$_{14}$, קצף hi. *enrage* Ps 106$_{32}$, הרג *kill* Ex 2$_{15}$ Nm 11$_{11.11}$, מות hi. *kill* Ex 4$_{21}$, קבר *bury* Dt 34$_{5}$, מחה *wipe out* Ex 32$_{31}$, סקל *stone* Ex 17$_{4}$.

<CSTR> אל משה *God of Moses* 4QConfess 2$_{3}$, חֹתֵן *father-in-law of* Ex 18$_{1+6t}$ Nm 10$_{29}$ Jg 1$_{16}$ 4$_{11}$, אֵשֶׁת *wife of* Ex 18$_{2}$, בֶּן־ *son of* 1 C 26$_{24}$, בְּנֵי *sons of* 1 C 23$_{15}$, מְשָׁרֵת *servant of* Nm 11$_{28}$ Jos 1$_{1}$ Si 46$_{1}$, פְּקוּדֵי *numbered ones of,* i.e. those numbered by Nm 26$_{63.64}$.

יַד *hand of* Ex 9$_{35}$ 34$_{29}$ 35$_{29}$ Lv 8$_{36}$ 10$_{11}$ 26$_{46}$ Nm 4$_{37.45.49}$ 9$_{23}$ 10$_{13}$ 15$_{23}$ 17$_{5}$ 27$_{23}$ 33$_{1}$ 36$_{13}$ Jos 14$_{2}$ 20$_{2}$ 21$_{2.8}$ 22$_{9}$ Jg 3$_{4}$ 1 K 8$_{53.56}$ Ps 77$_{21}$ Ne 8$_{14}$ 9$_{14}$ 10$_{30}$ 2 C 33$_{8}$ 34$_{14}$ 35$_{6}$ 1QH 17$_{12}$ 1QM 10$_{6}$ 1QS 1$_{3}$ 4QS^{e} 3$_{6}$ 4QD^{a} 1.3$_{2}$ 11$_{2}$ 4QapJoshua^{a} 22.1$_{3}$ 4QparaKings 104$_{7}$ 4Q418 184$_{1}$ 4Q419 1$_{2}$ 4Q423 11$_{1}$ 4QDibHam^{a} 1.5$_{14}$ 3.2$_{16}$ ([יד]) 4$_{8}$ (מוש[ה]) CD 5$_{21}$, יְדֵי *hands of* Ex 17$_{12}$, יְמִין *right hand of* Is 63$_{12}$, פְּנֵי *face of* Ex 34$_{35.35}$ 4QDibHam^{a} 6$_{12}$, עֵינֵי *eyes of* Nm 11$_{10}$ 25$_{6}$, פִּי *mouth,* i.e. command, *of* Ex 38$_{21}$ 4QapMos^{c} 2.2$_{5}$, קול *voice of* 4QD^{a} 1$_{16}$ 4QapJoshua^{a} 26$_{3}$ ([מ]ושה), דְּבַר *word of* Ex 8$_{9.27}$ 12$_{35}$ 32$_{28}$ Lv 10$_{7}$, מַשָּׂא *pronouncement of* 2 C 24$_{9}$ (if em.; see below).

יְמֵי *days of* Si 46$_{7}$, תּוֹלְדֹת *generations of* Nm 3$_{1}$, סֵפֶר *book of* Ne 13$_{1}$ 2 C 25$_{4}$ 35$_{12}$ 2QJuridical 1$_{3}$ 4QMMT C$_{10.21}$ (ס[פר מו]שה), תּוֹרַת *law of* Jos 8$_{31.32}$ 23$_{6}$ 1 K 2$_{3}$ 2 K 14$_{6}$ 23$_{25}$ Ml 3$_{22}$ Dn 9$_{11.13}$ Ezr 3$_{2}$ 7$_{6}$ Ne 8$_{1}$ 2 C 23$_{18}$ 30$_{16}$ 1QS 5$_{8}$ 8$_{22}$ 4QS^{b} 9$_{7}$ 4QD^{a} 11$_{6}$ 4QOrd^{b} 3$_{5}$ CD 15$_{2.9.12}$ 16$_{2.5}$, מִצְוַת *commandment of* 2 C 8$_{13}$, חוקות *statutes of* 4QapMos^{c} 2.2$_{2}$, מַשְׂאַת *tax of,* i.e. imposed by 2 C 24$_{6.9}$ (or em. מַשְׂאַת to כְּמַשָּׂא *according to the pronouncement of*), אַף *anger of* Ex 32$_{19}$, מוֹת *death of* Jos 1$_{1}$, אֵבֶל *mourning of,* i.e. for Dt 34$_{8}$ 4QapJoshua^{a} 14$_{3}$.

<APP> אִישׁ *man* Ex 11$_{3}$ 32$_{1.23}$ Nm 12$_{3}$ Dt 33$_{1}$ Jos 14$_{6}$ Ps 90$_{1}$ Ezr 3$_{2}$ 1 C 23$_{14}$ 2 C 30$_{16}$ 4QapMos^{c} 2.2$_{10}$, עַם *people* Is 63$_{11}$ (or em. עַמּוֹ *his people* to עַבְדּוֹ *his servant*), עֶבֶד *servant* Ex 14$_{31}$ Nm 12$_{7.8}$ Dt 34$_{5}$ Jos 1$_{1.2.7.13.15}$ 8$_{31.33}$ 9$_{24}$ 11$_{12.15}$ 12$_{6.6}$ 13$_{8}$ 14$_{7}$ 18$_{7}$ 22$_{2.4.5}$ 1 K 8$_{53.56}$ 2 K 18$_{12}$ 21$_{8}$ Is 63$_{11}$ (if em.; see above) Ml 3$_{22}$ Ps 105$_{26}$ Dn 9$_{11}$ Ne 1$_{7.8}$ 9$_{14}$ 10$_{30}$ 1 C 6$_{34}$ 2 C 1$_{3}$ 24$_{6}$ 4QapPent 2$_{2}$ 4QapJoshua^{a} 22.1$_{2}$ 4QDibHam^{a} 1.5$_{14}$ 6$_{12}$ (עב[ד]) 4QDibHam^{b} 122$_{1}$ (עב[ד]), מָשִׁיחַ *anointed one* 4QapMos^{c} 2.2$_{5}$, בָּחִיר *chosen one* Ps 106$_{23}$, אָדוֹן *lord* Nm 11$_{28}$.

<ADJ> זֶה *this* Ex 32$_{1.23}$ (unless both זֶה מֹשֶׁה as divine title* *the One of Moses*).

<PREP> לְ of direction, *to, towards,* + דבר pi. *speak* Ex 32$_{33}$ 4QCommGenA 4$_{2}$, אמר *say* Ex 3$_{13}$ 4$_{4.18}$ 6$_{26}$ 10$_{25}$ Nm 21$_{16}$, נגד hi. *tell* Ex 16$_{22}$ Nm 11$_{24}$, ספר pi. *recount* Nm 13$_{26}$, שׁחה htpal. *bow down* Ex 11$_{4}$; introducing object, + שׁמע *hear* 4QapJoshua^{a} 3.2$_{5}$, אמן hi. *believe* Ex 4$_{1.4}$, נשׁק *kiss* Ex 4$_{27}$, קרא *call* Ex 8$_{4}$ 9$_{27}$ 10$_{16}$ 12$_{31}$ 19$_{20}$, נוח hi. *cause to rest* Ex 33$_{12}$, קנא pi. *envy* Ps 106$_{16}$; of benefit, *to, for* Dt 1$_{5}$, + היה *be* Lv 8$_{29}$ Nm 10$_{1}$ Ps 99$_{6}$, רעע *be evil* Ps 106$_{32}$, ידע hi. *make known* Ps 103$_{7}$, נתן *give* Ex

2_{21} 24_{12} Ps 99_{6}, עשׂה *do, make* Ex 18_{1} Nm 11_{11} 21_{8} Dt 5_{1}, לקח *take* Nm 27_{18}, שׁמר ni. *take heed* Ex 10_{25}, קנא pi. *be jealous* Nm 11_{29}, פסל *cut into shape* Ex 34_{1} Dt 5_{1}, כתב *write* Ex 34_{27}, שׁלח *send* Nm 13_{1}; ישׁב לְ *wait for* Ex 24_{13}; *against*, + חטא *sin* Ex 10_{16}; *concerning*, + היה *be* Ex $32_{1.23}$; *on the part of*, + חרה *burn (with anger)* Nm 16_{15}; of possession, *of, (belonging) to* Ps 90_{1}.

בְּ introducing object, + בחר *choose* Si 45_{1}, אמן hi. *believe* Ex 14_{31} 19_{9}; *against*, + דבר pi. *speak* Nm $12_{1.8}$ $21_{5.7}$, חרה *be kindled* Ex 4_{14}; of agent, *by, through*, + דבר pi. *speak* Nm 12_{2}; *with*, + דבר pi. *speak* Nm 12_{8}, אנף htp. *be angry* Dt $1_{5.5}$, עבר htp. *become furious* Dt 1_{5}.

כְּ *as, like*, + קום *arise* Dt 34_{10}.

מִן *from* Ex 18_{17} Nm 11_{11}, + רפה *relax*, i.e. withdraw Ex 4_{21} (or em. וַיֶּרֶף hi. *and he refrained* from).

אֶל *to* Ex 32_{26} 6Q22 1_{3}, + אמר *say* Ex $3_{14.15}$ $4_{1.4.10.19.21}$ $5_{4.20}$ $6_{1.2}$ $7_{1.8.14.19.26}$ $8_{1.12.16}$ $9_{1.8.13.22.27}$ $10_{1.8.9.12.21}$ $11_{1.9}$ $12_{1.43}$ $14_{11.15.26}$ $16_{2.4.28}$ $17_{5.14}$ $18_{6.17}$ $19_{9.10.21.23}$ $20_{19.22}$ $24_{1.12}$ 30_{34} 31_{12} $32_{9.17.33}$ $33_{5.12.17}$ $34_{1.27}$ 36_{5} Lv 1_{1} 16_{2} 21_{1} Nm 3_{40} $7_{4.11}$ 9_{6} $11_{11.16.23}$ $12_{4.11.14}$ $14_{2.11}$ $15_{35.37}$ 16_{3} $17_{25.27}$ $20_{12.23}$ $21_{8.34}$ 25_{4} 26_{1} $27_{6.12.18}$ $31_{25.49}$ 32_{25} Dt 1_{5+7t} 5_{1+5t} $31_{14.16}$ 34_{1} 4QBibPar 7_{3} 4QTestim$_{1}$ 4QapPent4_{4}, דבר *speak* Ex 6_{29}, pi. Ex 4_{30} $6_{2.10.13.28.29}$ 7_{8} 9_{12} 13_{1} $14_{1.11}$ 16_{11} 25_{1} $30_{11.17.22}$ 31_{1} 32_{7} $33_{1.11}$ 40_{1} Lv 1_{1} 4_{1} $5_{14.20}$ $6_{1.12.17}$ $7_{22.28}$ 8_{1} 10_{19} 11_{1} 12_{1} 13_{1} $14_{1.33}$ 15_{1} 16_{1} 17_{1} 18_{1} 19_{1} 20_{1} 21_{16} $22_{1.17.26}$ $23_{1.9.23.26.33}$ $24_{1.13}$ 25_{1} 27_{1} Nm $1_{1.48}$ 2_{1} $3_{5.11.14.44}$ $4_{1.17.21}$ $5_{1.4.5.11}$ $6_{1.22}$ $7_{89.89}$ (if em.; see below) $8_{1.5.23}$ $9_{1.9}$ 10_{1} 11_{24} 13_{1} 14_{26} $15_{1.17.22}$ $16_{20.23}$ $17_{1.9.16}$ 18_{25} 19_{1} 20_{7} $25_{10.16}$ 26_{52} 28_{1} 31_{1} 33_{50} $34_{1.16}$ $35_{1.9}$ Dt $1_{5.5}$ $5_{1.1.1.1}$ 32_{48} Jos 1_{3} 11_{23} $14_{6.10}$ Ps 99_{6}, htp. Nm 7_{89} (or em. מִדַּבֵּר to pi. מְדַבֵּר), קרא *call* Ex 3_{4} 8_{21} 10_{24} 19_{3} 24_{16} Lv 1_{1}, צעק *cry out* Nm 11_{2}, צוה pi. *give charge* Ex 16_{34}.

בוא *come* Ex $18_{5.6.15.15}$ 19_{9} Nm 13_{26} 21_{7}, hi. *bring* Ex $18_{17.26}$ 36_{3} 39_{33} Lv 24_{11} Nm 31_{12} 32_{2}, שׁוב *return* Nm 17_{15}, ירד *descend*, i.e. bow down Ex 11_{4}, קרב *approach* Nm 31_{48} Dt 1_{5} 5_{1}, hi. *bring near* Nm 15_{33} Dt 1_{5}, נגשׁ *draw near* Ex 34_{30} Nm 32_{6}, יעד ni. *gather oneself* Nm $10_{1.1}$, אסף ni. *be gathered* Ex 32_{26}, קהל hi. *cause to assemble* Dt 31_{25}, לקח *take* Lv 24_{1}, נתן *give* Ex 31_{18} Nm 17_{21} Dt $5_{1.1.1.1}$, ראה ni. *appear* Ex $3_{1.15}$ $4_{1.4}$ Nm 20_{6}, שׁמע *listen* Ex $6_{9.12.30}$ $7_{1.20}$ 9_{12} 11_{9} 16_{20} Dt 1_{5} $5_{1.1}$ Jos 1_{17}; *in the presence of*, + הסה hi. *silence* Nm 13_{30}.

עַל *unto*, + קרא *call* Ex 5_{1} 1QDM 1_{1} ([ו]יקרא), בכה *weep* Nm 11_{11}; *upon* Nm $11_{16.24}$, + ראה *look* Ex 5_{20}, שׂים *set* Nm 11_{11}; *over*, + פאר htp. *show one's glory*, i.e. command Ex 8_{5}, שׂכך *cover* Ex 33_{17}; *against*, + לון ni. *murmur* Ex 15_{24} 16_{6} Nm $14_{2.36}$ 17_{6}, hi. *murmur* Ex 16_{2} 17_{3} Nm 17_{16}, קהל ni. *assemble* Nm 16_{3} 17_{7} 20_{2}, hi. *cause to assemble* Nm 16_{18}, נצה hi. *strive* Nm 26_{9}; *before*, + עמד *stand* Ex 18_{13}, נצב ni. *stand* Ex 18_{14}.

מֵעַל *from upon*, + קלל hi. *make light* Ex 18_{17}.

עִם *with* Ex $18_{17.17}$ 19_{23}, + היה *be* Jos $1_{5.17}$ 3_{7}, דבר pi. *speak* Ex 19_{9} 31_{18} 33_{9} Nm 11_{16} 4QpsJub^{a} 1_{6} 4QapPent 1_{2}, ריב *strive* Ex $17_{2.2}$ Nm 20_{3}, יצב htp. *stand* Ex 34_{4} Nm 11_{16}, עלה *ascend* Ex 24_{2} 34_{1}, שׁלח *send* Ex 33_{12}.

אֵת *with*, + היה *be* Nm 1_{1}, נשׂא *bear* burden Ex 18_{17} Nm 11_{16}, כרת *make covenant* Ex 34_{27}, דבר pi. *speak* Ex 34_{31} Nm 3_{1}.

לִפְנֵי *before* 4QpsJub^{c} 1_{2}, + עמד *stand* Ex 9_{11} 17_{6} Nm 27_{2}, הלך *go* Ex 32_{33}, קרב *approach* Nm 9_{6}, קרא *proclaim* Ex 33_{17}, דבר pi. *speak* Nm 36_{1}; *against*, + קום *arise* Nm 16_{2}.

מִלִּפְנֵי *from before*, + יצא *go out* Ex 35_{20}, לקח *take* Ex 36_{3}.

עַל־פְּנֵי *in front of*, + עבר *pass over* Ex 34_{4}, hi. *cause to pass over* Ex 33_{17}.

אַחֲרֵי *after*, + נבט hi. *look* Ex 33_{8}, הלך *go* Nm 16_{25}.

תַּחַת *beneath*, + שׂים *place* Ex 17_{12}.

כְּמוֹ *as, like*, + קום hi. *raise* Dt 5_{1}.

<COLL> מֹשֶׁה וְאַהֲרֹן *Moses and Aaron* (and vars.) Ex 4_{29} $5_{1.4.20}$ $6_{13.27}$ $7_{6.8.10.20}$ $8_{4.8.21}$ $9_{8.27}$ $10_{3.8.16}$ 11_{10} $12_{1.28.31.43.50}$ $16_{2.6}$ 17_{10} 24_{9} 40_{31} Lv 9_{23} 11_{1} 14_{33} 15_{1} Nm $1_{17.44}$ 2_{1} $3_{38.39}$ 4_{1+6t} 8_{20} 9_{6} 12_{4} 13_{26} $14_{2.5.26}$ 15_{33} $16_{3.18.20}$ $17_{6.7.8}$ 20_{2+5t} $26_{9.64}$ 33_{1} Jos 24_{5} 1 S $12_{6.8}$ Ps 77_{21} 99_{6} 105_{26} 106_{16} CD 5_{18}, אַהֲרֹן וּמֹשֶׁה *Aaron and Moses* (and vars.) Ex $6_{20.26}$ Nm 3_{1} 26_{59} 1 C 5_{29} 23_{13}, מֹשֶׁה וְאֶלְעָזָר *Moses and Eleazar* (and vars.) Nm 20_{28} $26_{1.3.63}$ 27_{2} 31_{12+5t} 32_{2}, מֹשֶׁה וּמִרְיָם *Moses and Miriam* (and vars.) Nm 12_{4} 26_{59} Mc 6_{4} 1 C 5_{29}, מֹשֶׁה ... וְחוּר *Moses ... and Hur* Ex 17_{10}, מֹשֶׁה וִיהוֹשֻׁעַ *Moses and Joshua* (and vars.) Ex 24_{13} Dt 31_{14} 32_{44}, מֹשֶׁה ... נָדָב *Moses ... Nadab* Ex $24_{1.9}$, מֹשֶׁה ... וַאֲבִיהוּא *Moses ... and Abihu* Ex $24_{1.9}$, מֹשֶׁה וּשְׁמוּאֵל *Moses and Samuel* Jr 15_{1}; מֹשֶׁה as vocative, Ex 3_{14}.

Also 1Q62 2_1 4QMidrEschat[a] 1.2_3 4QMyst[a] 74_2 4QapPent 9_5 4QapJoshua[a] 22.1_1 4QapJoshua[b] 17_4 4QPrFêtes[c] 2_4 11QMelch 1_{12}.*

⇒ משה *pull out.*

[מַשּׁוּאָה], see מַשָּׁאָה *deception.*

מְשׁוֹאָה, see מְשֹׁאָה *devastation.*

*__[מָשׁוֹב]__ 0.0.11 n.[m.] **going back**—cstr. Q משוב—**1. return, coming back, withdrawal** of troops, <CSTR> משוב גורל *the return of the lot of* 1QM 1_{13}, משוב שלום *the withdrawal of,* i.e. in, *peace* 1QM 3_{11} (unless בְּמְשׁוּב = *at the returning of* peace, i.e. inf. of שׁוב; =4QM[f] 11_4 [בבמ]שוב [שלום]); חצוצרות המשוב *the trumpets of,* i.e. for signalling, *withdrawal* 1QM 3_{10} 8_2 (+ מִקְרָא trumpets of *summoning*) 8_{13} 4QM[c] 1_8 (חצו[צ]רות המשו[ו]ב), חצוצרות דרך המשוב *the trumpets of,* i.e. for signalling, *the way,* perh. route, *of withdrawal* 1QM 3_{10}, תהלת המשוב *the hymn of the return (from battle)* 1QM 14_2. <PREP> לְ of benefit, *for,* + אזר htp. *gird oneself* 1QM 1_{13}; בְּ of cause, *on account of, at* 1QM 3_{11} גילות אל במשוב *rejoicings of God at the withdrawal of,* i.e. in, peace; unless בְּמְשׁוּב = *at the returning of* peace, i.e. inf. of שׁוב; =4QM[f] 11_4 [בבמ]שוב]). <COLL> המשוב ממלחמת האויב *withdrawal from the battle against the enemy* 1QM 3_{10}.

2. appar. **restoration,** <CSTR> משוב חיו *the restoration of his life* 1QS 3_1 (unless לְמְשׁוּב = he was not strong enough for his life *to return,* i.e. inf. of שׁוב; others and ||4QS[c] לְמֵשִׁיב *as one who restores* or *for the restorer of* his life), [מ]שוב ר[חמי] חסדיו *the restoration of the compassion(s) of his acts of loyalty* 4QShirShabb[d] 1.1_{23}, משוב חסדים *the restoration of acts of loyalty* 1QM 3_6. <PREP> לְ of benefit, *for,* + חזק *be strong,* i.e. steadfast (enough) 1QS 3_1 (unless לְ of inf.; see Cstr.); appar. חכה לְ *wait for* 4QShirShabb[d] 1.1_{23} (unless ל[מ]שׁוב = wait for the compassion of his acts of loyalty *to return,* i.e. inf. of שׁוב; others ל[ה]שׁוב *for being returned*).

3. appar. **turning,** <CSTR> משוב יד גבורתו *the turning of the hand of his strength* 4QShirShabb[d] 1.1_{39} (+ למשפטי שלומים *to judgments of recompense*). <PREP> בְּ of time, *at, during,* + רצה pi. *make* thanksgiving *acceptable* 4QShirShabb[d] 1.1_{39} (unless בְּ introduces מְשׁוּב as inf. of שׁוב, *when* the hand *turns*).

⇒ שׁוב *go back.*

מְשׁוֹבָב 1 pr.n.m. **Meshobab,** prince (נָשִׂיא) of Simeon who heads genealogical listing, <NOM CL> וְהוּא מְשׁוֹבָב *and it* (genealogical listing) *was Meshobab* 1 C 4_{34} (if ins. הוּא; or del.).

⇒ שׁוב *go back.*

[מְשׁוּבָה] I 12.2 n.f. **going back**—מְשֻׁבָה; cstr. מְשׁוּבַת; sf. מְשׁוּבָתִי, Si משובתו, משובתינו, מְשׁוּבָתָם; pl. sf. מְשֻׁבוֹתַיִךְ, מְשֻׁבוֹתֵיהֶם, מְשׁוּבֹתֵיכֶם, מְשׁוּבֹתֵינוּ—**1.** as description of condition, **going back, apostasy, rebellion,** in pl. perh. **act of apostasy, rebellion** (Jr 2_{19} 3_{22} 5_6 14_7 Ezk 37_{23} [if em.]); perh. **indecisiveness** or **aversion** to instruction (Pr 1_{32}); perh. **illness** (Jr 2_{19} 3_{22} Ho 14_5).

<SUBJ> רבב *be many* Jr 14_7, עצם *be mighty* Jr 5_6 (|| פֶּשַׁע *sin*), נצח ni. *endure* Jr 8_5, יכח hi. *reprove* Jr 2_{19} (|| רָעָה *evil*), הרג *kill* Pr 1_{32} (unless מְשׁוּבָה II *idleness;* || שַׁלְוָה *tranquillity*). <OBJ> רפא *heal* Jr $3_{22(mss)}$ (L רפה *heal*) Ho 14_5.

<CSTR> מְשׁוּבַת פְּתָיִם *the indecisiveness of the naïve* Pr 1_{32} (unless מְשׁוּבָה II *idleness*); כֹּל מְשׁוּבֹתֵיהֶם *all their acts of apostasy* Ezk 37_{13} (if em. מוֹשְׁבֹתֵיהֶם all *their dwelling places*). <APP> מַדּוּעַ שׁוֹבְבָה הָעָם הַזֶּה יְרוּשָׁלַםִ מְשֻׁבָה נִצַּחַת *why does this people, Jerusalem, rebel* (fem. sg.) *(with) a persistent rebellion?* Jr 8_5 (Q Or שׁוֹבְבוּ *rebel* [pl.]; ms lacks יְרוּשָׁלַםִ).

<PREP> לְ of direction, *to,* + תלא pass. *be hung,* i.e. attached Ho 11_7 (or em. תְּלוּאִים לִמְשׁוּבָתִי my people *are attached to apostasy from me* to נִלְאָה מִמְּשׁוּבָתוֹ *is wearied by its apostasy* or חוֹלִאִים לִמְשׁוּבָתָם *are diseased by their apostasy* or תְּלוּאִים לַעֲצַבִּים *are attached to idols*).

בְּ of accompaniment, *with, in (a state of),* + חטא *sin* Ezk 37_{23} (if em. מוֹשָׁב *dwelling place*).

מִן of direction, *from,* + ישׁע hi. *save* Ezk 37_{23} (if em. מוֹשָׁב *dwelling place*); of instrument, *by (means of), through,* + לאה ni. *be wearied* Ho 11_7 (if em. תְּלוּאִים

נִלְאָה לִמְשׁוּבָתִי *attached to apostasy from me* to מִמְּשׁוּבָתוֹ *wearied by its apostasy*).

עַל *on account of* or *by*, + חלל ni. *be profaned*, i.e. feel defiled (of Josiah) Si 49$_{2}$ (or em. נִחַל *was profaned* to נֶחְלָה *was made weak*, i.e. was sickened, i.e. חלה I ni., or *was distressed*, i.e. חלה IV ni.).

<COLL> מְשׁוּבָתִי *apostasy from me* Ho 11$_{7}$ (or em.).

2. as description of (female) person, **one who goes back, rebel, apostate,** <SUBJ> הלך *go* to non-Israelite places of worship Jr 3$_{6.7}$, שׁוב *go back* to Y. Jr 3$_{6.6.12}$, עשׂה *do* Jr 3$_{6}$, פשׁע *sin* Jr 3$_{12}$, פזר pi. *scatter* ways, i.e. stray Jr 3$_{12}$, זנה *prostitute oneself* Jr 3$_{6}$, נאף pi. *commit adultery* Jr 3$_{8}$, צדק pi. *justify* self Jr 3$_{11}$, ידע *know*, i.e. recognize, *sin* Jr 3$_{12}$, שׁמע not *hear* Y.'s voice Jr 3$_{12}$. <OBJ> שׁלח pi. *send away* Jr 3$_{8}$. <APP> מְשֻׁבָה יִשְׂרָאֵל *apostate Israel* Jr 3$_{6.8.11}$ (all three + בָּגֵדָה יְהוּדָה *treacherous Judah*) 3$_{12}$. <PREP> בְּ of place, *(up)on*, + נפל hi. *cause* face *to fall* upon, i.e. be displeased with Jr 3$_{12}$; אֶל *to*, + נתן *give* document of separation Jr 3$_{8}$.

3. appar. as description of action, **turning back, ability to turn back** (trans.) (Si 43$_{23[Bmg]}$), <SUBJ> perh. נשׁק hi. *set alight* great ocean Si 43$_{23(Bmg)}$ (תַּ[שִּׁ]יק]; alternatively תַּ[שִּׁ]יק, i.e. נשׁק hi. appar. *seal*; תַּעֲ[שִׁ]יק, i.e. עשׁק hi. *overpower*; B מחשבתו *his thinking*). <COLL> משובתו *his* (Y.'s) *turning back* or *his ability to turn back* forces of chaos Si 43$_{23(Bmg)}$.

<SYN> §1 שַׁלְוָה *tranquillity*, רָעָה *evil*, פֶּשַׁע *sin*.

⇨ שׁוב *go back*.

*[מְשׁוּבָה] II $_{1}$ n.f. **idleness** (unless מְשׁוּבָה I *going back*)—cstr. מְשׁוּבַת—<SUBJ> הרג *kill* Pr 1$_{32}$ (|| שַׁלְוָה *tranquillity*). <CSTR> מְשׁוּבַת פְּתָיִם *the idleness of the naïve* Pr 1$_{32}$.

<SYN> שַׁלְוָה *tranquillity*.

⇨ שׁוב *sit* (byform of ישׁב *sit*).

[מְשׁוּגָה] $_{1}$ n.f. **mistake**—sf. מְשׁוּגָתִי—**error, inadvertent sin,** <SUBJ> לין *pass the night*, i.e. remain with Job Jb 19$_{4}$ (or em. מְשֻׁגָּתִי *my mistake*, from שׁגג *err*; + שׁגה *err*).

⇨ cf. שׁגג *err*, שׁגה *err*.

מָשׁוֹט $_{1}$ n.[m.] **oar,** <OBJ> תפשׂ *seize* Ezk 27$_{29}$ (וְיָרְדוּ מֵאָנִיּוֹתֵיהֶם כֹּל תֹּפְשֵׂי מָשׁוֹט מַלָּחִים כֹּל חֹבְלֵי הַיָּם *and all who seize an oar, mariners, all the sailors of the sea, will go down*; mss מֵאֳנִיּוֹתֵיהֶם; or del. מַלָּחִים and/or em. וְכֹל חֹבְלֵי *and all the sailors of* or וְחֹבְלֵי *and the sailors of*, without כֹּל). <CSTR> כֹּל תֹּפְשֵׂי מָשׁוֹט *all who seize an oar* Ezk 27$_{29}$.

⇨ שׁוט *row*.

מִשּׁוֹט $_{1}$ n.[m.] **oar**—pl. sf. מִשּׁוֹטָיִךְ—<OBJ> עשׂה *make* Ezk 27$_{6}$ (+ אַלּוֹנִים מִבָּשָׁן *of oaks from Bashan*, + קֶרֶשׁ *plank*, נֵס perh. *mast*, מִפְרָשׂ perh. *sail*, מְכַסֶּה perh. *awning*).

⇨ שׁוט *row*.

*[מְשׁוּכִים] $_{0.0.2}$ pl.n. **Meshuchim**—Q המשוכים—area of land undergoing sale in vicinity of En-gedi, <SUBJ> קרא ni. *be called* 5/6ḤevBA 44$_{8.15}$ (both + מקום the *place* called Meshuchim; + חוֹרַת *Horath*).

*[מְשׁוּלֶּמֶת] $_{0.0.0.1}$ pr.n.f. **Meshullemeth,** <PREP> לְ of possession, *of, (belonging) to* Seal 856.

⇨ שׁלם *be complete*.

[מְשׁוּסָה] $_{1.0.1}$ n.f. **plunder**—Kt משוסה—<PREP> לְ *as*, + היה *be(come)* (of exiled Israelites) 11QT 59$_{8}$ (|| בַּז *spoil*, אָכְלָה *food*), נתן *give* Jacob Is 42$_{24(Kt)}$ (or em. מְשׁוֹסֶה give to a *plunderer*, i.e. po. ptc. of שׁסה *plunder*; Qr מְשִׁסָּה [1QIsa[a] משיסה] *plunder*; + לְבֹזְזִים and Israel *to plunderers*). <SYN> בַּז *spoil*, אָכְלָה *food*.

⇨ שׁסס *plunder*.

משׁח I $_{71.3.6}$ vb. **anoint**—**Qal** $_{65.3.6}$ Pf. מָשַׁח (מָשַׁחְתָּ, מְשָׁחוֹ), מָשַׁחְתָּ, Q משחתי (מְשַׁחְתִּיךָ, מְשַׁחְתִּיו), מָשְׁחוּ, מְשַׁחְנוּ; impf. יִמְשַׁח, 2ms תִּמְשַׁח (תִּמְשַׁח), יִמְשָׁחוּ; + waw וַיִּמְשַׁח, וּמְשַׁחְתּוֹ (וַיִּמְשָׁחֻהוּ), וַיִּמְשָׁחוּ, וַיִּמְשָׁחֵם, וַיִּמְשָׁחֶךָ, וימשחני Q); impv. מְשַׁחוּ, מִשְׁחוּ, מָשְׁחֻהוּ; ptc. Si מושח (מֹשְׁחִים), מָשׁוּחַ, cstr. Q משוח, מְשֻׁחִים; inf. abs. מָשׁוֹחַ; cstr. מְשֹׁחַ (Q מושחני, מְשָׁחֳךָ, מָשְׁחוֹ), מָשְׁחָה.

1. anoint, smear with oil, rather than pour (יצק) oil, usu. on the head (Ex 29$_{7}$||Lv 8$_{12}$ 1 S 10$_{1}$ 2 K 9$_{3.6}$), **a. anoint** as priest, Aaron and his own sons (Ex 28$_{41}$

29$_7$||Lv 8$_{12}$ Ex 29$_{36}$ 30$_{30}$ 40$_{13.15.15}$ Lv 6$_{13}$ [pass.] 8$_{10.11}$ Nm 3$_3$ [pass.] Si 45$_{15}$ CD 12$_{23}$ [pass.]); later priests (Lv 16$_{32}$ Nm 35$_{25}$ 1 C 29$_{22}$ 4QapMos^a 1.1$_{9[WA]}$ 4QapMos^b 1.1$_1$).

b. anoint as king (esp. with לְמֶלֶךְ *as king*) (Jg 9$_{8.15}$ 1 S 15$_{1.17}$ 24$_7$ 33$_9$ [pass.] 2 S 5$_3$||1 C 11$_3$ 2 S 5$_{17}$||1 C 14$_8$ [1 C pass.] 2 S 12$_7$ 1 K 5$_{15}$ 2 K 23$_{30}$); future or would-be king (1 S 16$_{3.12.13}$ 2 S 19$_{11}$ 1 K 1$_{34.39.45}$ 19$_{15.16}$ 2 K 9$_{3.6.12}$ 11$_{12}$||2 C 23$_{11}$ Ps 45$_8$ 89$_{21}$ 11QPs^a 28$_{8.11.13}$ perh. Si 48$_8$); other leader (e.g. with לְנָגִיד *as ruler;* 1 S 9$_{16}$ 10$_1$ 1 C 29$_{22}$ Si 46$_{13}$ 48$_8$ 1QIsa^a 52$_{14}$ [unless משח II *mar*]).

c. anoint prophet (1 K 19$_{16}$ [לְנָבִיא *as prophet*] Is 61$_1$ Si 48$_8$).

d. anoint cultic objects (Ex 30$_{26}$ 40$_{9.10.11}$ Lv 8$_{10.11}$ Nm 7$_1$), pillar (Gn 31$_{13}$), holy place (Dn 9$_{24}$), sacrificial animal (Ex 29$_{36}$).

e. anoint person for secular festivity (Am 6$_6$ Ps 45$_8$).

<SUBJ> Y. 1 S 10$_1$ (+ יצק *pour* oil) 15$_{17}$ 2 S 12$_7$ (+ נצל hi. *deliver*) 2 K 9$_3$ 9$_6$ (both + יצק) 9$_{12}$ 1QIsa^a 52$_{14}$ (משחתי *I have anointed;* unless משח II *mar*) Is 61$_1$ (+ בשׂר pi. *proclaim good news,* חבשׁ *bind* brokenhearted, קרא *call,* i.e. announce, freedom) Ps 89$_{21}$ 2 C 22$_7$, appar. Lv 7$_{36}$ 16$_{32}$ (or em. יִמְשַׁח whom *he anoints* to יִמְשְׁחוּ whom *they anoint,* i.e. who has been anointed, or מָשׁוּחַ who *is anointed;* + מלא יָד pi. *fill the hand,* i.e. ordain, כהן pi. *serve as priest*) Nm 35$_{25}$ Dn 9$_{24}$ (+ כלא pi. *restrain* sin, תמם hi. *bring* sin *to an end,* כפר pi. *expiate* sin, בוא hi. *bring* righteousness, חתם *seal,* i.e. bring an end to, vision and prophet), אֱלֹהִים *God* Ps 45$_8$.

Moses Ex 28$_{41}$ (+ מלא יָד pi. *fill the hand,* i.e. ordain, קדשׁ pi. *consecrate,* כהן pi. *serve as priest*) 29$_7$||Lv 8$_{12}$ (+ יצק *pour* oil) Ex 29$_{36}$ 30$_{26.30}$ 40$_{9.10.11}$ (all five + קדשׁ pi.) 40$_{13}$ (+ קדשׁ pi., כהן pi.) 40$_{15.15}$ (+ כהן pi.) Lv 8$_{10}$ 8$_{11}$ Nm 7$_{1.1}$ (all four + קדשׁ pi.) Si 45$_{15}$ (+ מלא יָד pi.).

Samuel 1 S 9$_{16}$ (+ ישׁע hi. *save*) 15$_1$ 16$_{3.12.13}$ (+ צלח *rush,* of spirit) Si 46$_{13}$ (+ כון מַמְלֶכֶת hi. *establish kingship*) 11QPs^a 28$_{11}$ (+ שׂים *place,* i.e. appoint, as leader and ruler), Nathan 1 K 1$_{34}$ (or del. וְנָתָן הַנָּבִיא *and Nathan the prophet*) 1$_{39}$ (if ins. וְנָתָן הַנָּבִיא) 1$_{45}$ (וְנָתָן הַנָּבִיא lacking in ms), Elijah 1 K 19$_{15.16}$ Si 48$_8$, נָבִיא *prophet,* in ref. to Samuel 11QPs^a 28$_8$ (|| גדל pi. *magnify*) 28$_{13}$, to Nathan 1 K 1$_{34}$ (or del. וְנָתָן הַנָּבִיא *and Nathan the prophet*) 1$_{39}$ (if ins. וְנָתָן הַנָּבִיא) 1$_{45}$ (וְנָתָן הַנָּבִיא lacking in ms).

Zadok 1 K 1$_{34.39}$ (both + תקע *strike,* i.e. sound, trumpet) 1$_{45}$, Jehoiada 2 K 11$_{12}$||2 C 23$_{11}$ (+ נתן *place* crown and testimony, מלך hi. *appoint as king,* נכה hi. *strike,* i.e. clap, hands), כֹּהֵן *priest* 1 K 1$_{34.39.45}$.

Jacob Gn 31$_{13}$ (+ נדר *vow*), אִישׁ *man* of Jabesh-gilead 2 S 2$_4$, בֵּן *son* of Jehoiada 2 C 23$_{11}$, זָקֵן *elder* of Israel 2 S 5$_3$||1 C 11$_3$ (+ כרת בְּרִית *make a covenant*), בַּיִת *house* of Judah 2 S 2$_7$, שֵׁבֶט *tribe* of Israel 2 S 19$_{11}$, עַם *people* of the land (of Judah) 2 K 23$_{30}$ (+ מלך hi. *appoint* as king), קָהָל *assembly* of Israel 1 C 29$_{22}$ (+ מלך hi. *appoint as king*), שַׂר *prince,* i.e. military officer perh. 2 K 11$_{12}$, leaders of Judah and Israel Am 6$_6$, רֵאשִׁית *first,* i.e. best, *(one)* Am 6$_6$ (וְרֵאשִׁית שְׁמָנִים יִמְשָׁחוּ *and spread on themselves the best of oils*).

עֵץ *tree* Jg 9$_{8.15}$; subj. not specified, Lv 16$_{32}$ (if em. יִמְשַׁח whom *he anoints* to יִמְשְׁחוּ whom *they anoint,* i.e. who has been anointed) 2 S 5$_{17}$ (||1 C 14$_8$ pass.) 1 K 5$_{15}$.

<OBJ> Aaron (alone) Ex 29$_7$||Lv 8$_{12}$ Ex 40$_{13}$ Si 45$_{15}$, Aaron and his sons Ex 28$_{41}$ 30$_{30}$ Lv 7$_{36}$, sons alone Ex 40$_{15}$, Zadok 1 C 29$_{22}$ (with לְ introducing obj.), כֹּהֵן *priest* Lv 16$_{32}$ (or em. pass., the priest who *is anointed*) Nm 35$_{25}$, אָב *father* Ex 40$_{15}$, בֵּן *son* Ex 40$_{15}$ 1 K 1$_{34}$ 19$_{16}$ 2 C 22$_7$, אִישׁ *man* 1 S 9$_{16}$, קָטֹן *little,* i.e. youngest, *one* 1 S 16$_{12.13}$, אֲשֶׁר *the one whom* I say 1 S 16$_3$.

Absalom 2 S 19$_{11}$, David 1 S 16$_{12.13}$ 2 S 2$_{4.7}$ 5$_3$||1 C 11$_3$ 2 S 5$_{17}$ 12$_7$ Ps 89$_{21}$ 11QPs^a 28$_{8.11.13}$ (ד[ו]יד), Elisha Si 48$_8$, Hazael 1 K 19$_{15}$, Jehoahaz 2 K 23$_{30}$, Jehu 1 K 19$_{16}$ 2 K 9$_{3.6.12}$ 2 C 22$_7$, Joash 2 K 11$_{12}$||2 C 23$_{11}$, Saul 1 S 9$_{16}$ 10$_1$ 15$_{1.17}$, Solomon 1 K 1$_{34.39.45}$ 5$_{15}$ 1 C 29$_{22}$, מֶלֶךְ *king* Jg 9$_8$ Ps 45$_8$ Si 48$_8$ (if em. מְלֵא = *one full of* to מַלְכֵי *kings of* recompense), עֶבֶד Y.'s *servant,* i.e. David Ps 89$_{21}$, נָגִיד *leader* Si 46$_{13}$, מָלֵא *one full* of recompense, in ref. to Elisha or perh. Jehu Si 48$_8$ (unless מלא = מְ[מַ]לֵּא *one who would fulfil* recompense, i.e. Elisha; or em. מַלְכֵי *kings of* recompense, i.e. Jehu and Hazael), נָבִיא *prophet* Si 48$_8$, appar. the prophet Is 61$_1$.

מַצֵּבָה *standing stone* Gn 31$_{13}$, מִזְבֵּחַ *altar* Ex 29$_{36}$ 30$_{26.26}$ 40$_{10}$ Lv 8$_{11}$ Nm 7$_1$, קֹדֶשׁ *holiness,* i.e. holy of holies Dn 9$_{24}$, אֹהֶל *tent* of meeting Ex 30$_{26}$, אֲרוֹן *ark* Ex 30$_{26}$, מִשְׁכָּן *tabernacle* Ex 40$_9$ Lv 8$_{10}$ Nm 7$_1$, שֻׁלְחָן *table*

Ex 30_{26}, כְּלִי *vessel* Ex $30_{26.26.26}$ 40_{10} Lv 8_{11} Nm $7_{1.1}$, מְנוֹרָה *lampstand* Ex 30_{26}, כִּיּוֹר *bowl* Ex 30_{26} 40_{11} Lv 8_{11}, כֵּן *stand* Ex 30_{26} 40_{11} Lv 8_{11}, כֹּל *everything* in tabernacle Ex 40_{9} Lv 8_{10}.

אָטָד *bramble* Jg 9_{15}, מַרְאֶה *appearance* of Y.'s servant 1QIsa^{a} 52_{14} (unless משׁח II *mar*), תֹּאַר *form* of Y.'s servant 1QIsa^{a} 52_{14} (unless משׁח II), שֶׁמֶן anoint king with *oil* of rejoicing Ps 45_{8}.

<PREP> לְ of benefit, *for*, or *on behalf of*, + י׳ *Y.* 1 S 16_{3} 1 C 29_{22}; *as*, i.e. so as to be, + מֶלֶךְ *king* Jg 9_{15} 1 S $15_{1.17}$ 2 S $2_{4.7}$ 5_{3}||1 C 11_{3} 2 S 5_{17} 12_{7} 1 K $1_{34.45}$ 5_{15} $19_{15.16}$ 2 $19_{15.16}$ 2 K $9_{3.6.12}$, נָגִיד *leader* 1 S 9_{16} 10_{1} 1 C 29_{22}, כֹּהֵן *priest* 1 C 29_{22}; introducing obj., + Zadok 1 C 29_{22}; בְּ of place, *at, in*, + Gihon 1 K 1_{45}; of instrument, *by (means of), with*, + שֶׁמֶן *oil* Ex 30_{26} Nm 35_{25} Ps 89_{21} Si 45_{15} 11QPs^{a} 28_{11}; מִן of comparison, *(more) than*, + אִישׁ *man* 1QIsa^{a} 52_{14} (unless משׁח II *mar*), בֵּן *son* of humankind 1QIsa^{a} 52_{14} (unless משׁח II), חָבֵר *companion* Ps 45_{8}; עַל anoint someone so as to be *over, in charge of*, + עֵץ *tree* Jg 9_{8} (cf. 9_{15} אַתֶּם מֹשְׁחִים אֹתִי לְמֶלֶךְ עֲלֵיכֶם if *you are going to anoint me as king over you*), שֵׁבֶט *tribe* of Israel 2 S 19_{11}, נַחֲלָה Y.'s *inheritance* 1 S 10_{1} (cf. 15_{1} לִמְשָׁחֲךָ לְמֶלֶךְ עַל־עַמּוֹ *to anoint you as king over his people*); בְּקֶרֶב *in the middle of*, + אָח *brother* 1 S 16_{13}.

<COLL> משׁח + adverb, שָׁם *there* Gn 31_{13} 2 S 2_{4} 1 K 1_{34}.

וַיִּמְשַׁח אֹתוֹ לְקַדְּשׁוֹ *and he anointed him to consecrate him* Lv 8_{12}, sim. Ex 29_{36}, אֲשֶׁר מְשָׁחוֹ י׳ לְהַכְרִית Jehu, *whom Y. anointed in order to destroy* the household of Ahab 2 C 22_{7}, בְּיוֹם מָשְׁחוֹ אֹתָם *on the day of his anointing them* Lv 7_{36}, רוּחַ אֲדֹנָי י׳ עָלָי יַעַן מָשַׁח י׳ אֹתִי *the spirit of my Lord Y. is upon me, because Y. has anointed me* Is 61_{1}, משמשחו *after he had anointed him* 11QPs^{a} 28_{13}.

2. smear with oil, shield, in preparation for battle (Is 21_{5}), wafers (Ex 29_{2} Lv 2_{4} 7_{12} Nm 6_{15}); with dye, walls of room (Jr 22_{14}), <SUBJ> Shallum (Jehoahaz) Jr 22_{14} (וּמָשׁוֹחַ appar. *and I shall smear* to וּמָשׁוּחַ *and smeared*, of house), שַׂר *prince*, i.e. military officer Is 21_{5} (or em. משׁך *pull*, i.e. wield, shield). <OBJ> בַּיִת *house*, i.e. palace Jr 22_{14} (or em.), מָגֵן *shield* Is 21_{5} (or em.). <PREP> בְּ of instrument, *by (means of), with*, + שָׁשַׁר *vermilion* Jr 22_{14} (or em.; + סָפוּן בָּאָרֶז *panelled with cedar* [or em. סָפוֹן *I shall panel*]).

3. pass., **a. be anointed,** <SUBJ> David 2 S 3_{39}, כֹּהֵן *priest* Lv 16_{32} (if em. יִמְשַׁח whom *he anoints* to מָשׁוּחַ who *is anointed*) Nm 3_{3} (+ מלא יָד pi. *fill the hand*, i.e. ordain to priesthood, כהן pi. *serve as priest*). <COLL> וְאָנֹכִי הַיּוֹם רַךְ וּמָשׁוּחַ מֶלֶךְ *and I am today soft*, i.e. inexperienced, *even though anointed as king* 2 S 3_{39} (or em. רַךְ וְשַׁח מִמְּלֹךְ *too inexperienced and lowly to rule*).

b. be smeared with oil, of wafers (Ex 29_{2} Lv 2_{4} 7_{12} Nm 6_{15}), of shield in preparation for battle (2 S 1_{21} [if em.]); with dye, of walls of room (Jr 22_{14} [if em.]), <SUBJ> מַצָּה *unleavened bread* Ex 29_{2}, רָקִיק *wafer* of unleavened bread Lv 2_{4} 7_{12} Nm 6_{15}, בַּיִת *house*, i.e. palace Jr 22_{14} (if em. וּמָשׁוֹחַ appar. *and I shall smear* to וּמָשׁוּחַ *and smeared*; + סָפוּן *panelled* [or em. סָפוֹן *I shall panel*]), מָגֵן *shield* 2 S $1_{21(\text{mss})}$ (if em. בְּלִי מָשׁוּחַ Saul's shield *without the one anointed one* with oil, to בַּל־מָשׁוּחַ *not smeared* with oil). <PREP> בְּ of instrument, *by (means of), with*, + שֶׁמֶן *oil* Ex 29_{2} Lv 2_{4} 7_{12} Nm 6_{15} (all four || בלל pass. *be mixed*) 2 S $1_{21(\text{mss})}$ (if em.), שָׁשַׁר *vermilion* Jr 22_{14} (if em.).

c. as noun, **anointed one, 'messiah'**, equivalent to מָשִׁיחַ *anointed one*), <SUBJ> עמד *stand*, i.e. appear CD 12_{23} (or em. מָשִׁיחַ). <CSTR> משוח אהרן ישראל *the anointed one of Aaron and Israel* CD 12_{23} (or em.). <PREP> בְּלִי *without* 2 S $1_{21(\text{mss})}$ (מָגֵן שָׁאוּל בְּלִי מָשׁוּחַ *the shield of Saul without the one anointed* with oil; or em. בַּל Saul's shield *not smeared* with oil; or כְּלִי *the weapon of* the one anointed; L מָשִׁיחַ *anointed one*).

d. as adj., **anointed,** used attributively of כֹּהֵן *priest* 4QapMos^{a} $1.1_{9(\text{WA})}$ 4QapMos^{b} $1.1_{1(\text{WA})}$ (others מָשִׁיחַ in same sense).

4. inf. as gerund(ive), **anointing, being anointed,** לְמָשְׁחָה בָהֶם *for their being ordained in them* (clothes) Ex 29_{29} (+ מלא יָד pi. *fill the hand*, i.e. ordain).

<SYN> §1 גדל pi. *magnify*; §3b בלל pass. *be mixed*.

Ni. $_{5}$ Pf. נִמְשַׁח; inf. הִמָּשַׁח—**be anointed,** <SUBJ> Aaron Lv 6_{13}, David 1 C 14_{8}, מִזְבֵּחַ *altar* Nm $7_{10.84.88}$. <PREP> לְ *as*, i.e. so as to be, + מֶלֶךְ *king* 1 C 14_{8}. <COLL> בְּיוֹם הִמָּשַׁח אֹתוֹ *on the day of his/its being anointed* Lv 6_{13} Nm $7_{10.84}$, אַחֲרֵי הִמָּשַׁח אֹתוֹ *after its being anointed* Nm 7_{88}.

Pu. be anointed, <SUBJ> כְּרוּב *cherub* Ezk 28$_{14}$ (if em. מִמְשַׁח appar. the cherub of *the extension of* the one who protects, to מִמְשָׁח an *anointed* cherub, who protects).*

⇒ מָשִׁיחַ *anointed one,* מִשְׁחָה I *anointing,* מָשְׁחָה I *anointing,* מְשִׁיחָה *anointing.*

*משׁח II 0.0.1 vb. **mar—Qal** 0.0.1 Pf משחתי—<SUBJ> appar. Y. 1QIsa^{a} 52$_{14}$ (unless משׁח I *anoint*). <OBJ> מַרְאֶה *appearance* of Y.'s servant 1QIsa^{a} 52$_{14}$, תֹּאַר *form* of Y.'s servant 1QIsa^{a} 52$_{14}$. <PREP> מִן privative, *so as not to be,* + אִישׁ *man* 1QIsa^{a} 52$_{14}$, בֵּן *son* of humankind 1QIsa^{a} 52$_{14}$.*

*משׁח III 0.0.2 vb. **measure—Qal** 0.0.2 Impv. Q משח—**measure** (unless both times noun מֶשַׁח *distance*), <OBJ> אַמָּה *cubit* 3QTr 7$_{6}$ 9$_{1}$. <PREP> בְּ of place, *at, in,* + שׁוֹבֶךְ *dovecote* or *hollow* or *gutter* 3QTr 9$_{1}$, perh. רוּחַ *side* 3QTr 7$_{6}$; מִן of direction, *from,* + שׁוּל *edge* 3QTr 9$_{1}$.

⇒ מִשְׁחָה II *measurement,* מָשְׁחָה II *prescribed portion,* מִמְשָׁח *extension.*

*[מֶשַׁח] 0.0.2 n.[m.] **distance**—Q משח; cstr. Q משח—used adverbially (unless both times verb משׁח *measure*), <CSTR> משח אמות עסרין *(at) a distance of twenty cubits* 3QTr 7$_{6}$. <COLL> משח משולו אמות שלוש *(at) a distance from its edge of three cubits* 3QTr 9$_{1}$; בְּ ... משח *at ... (at) a distance (of)* 3QTr 7$_{6}$ 9$_{1}$.

⇒ משׁח III *measure.*

מִשְׁחָה I 23.0.1 n.f. **anointing**—cstr. מִשְׁחַת; pl. sf. Q משחותיהם—**1. anointing,** <CSTR> מִשְׁחַת־קֹדֶשׁ the oil of *anointing of holiness* Ex 30$_{25.25.31}$, מִשְׁחַת י׳ the oil of *anointing of,* perh. by, *Y.* Lv 10$_{7}$, מִשְׁחַת אֱלֹהָיו the oil of *anointing of,* perh. by, *his God* Lv 21$_{12}$; שֶׁמֶן הַמִּשְׁחָה *the oil of anointing* Ex 25$_{6}$||35$_{8}$ 29$_{7}$||Lv 8$_{10}$ Ex 29$_{21}$||Lv 8$_{30}$ Ex 31$_{11}$ 35$_{15}$||39$_{38}$ 35$_{28}$ 37$_{29}$ (שֶׁמֶן הַמִּשְׁחָה קֹדֶשׁ *the oil of anointing, a holy thing;* ||Ex 30$_{25}$ שֶׁמֶן מִשְׁחַת־קֹדֶשׁ *oil of anointing of holiness*) 40$_{9}$ Lv 8$_{2.12}$ 21$_{10}$ Nm 4$_{16}$, שֶׁמֶן מִשְׁחַת־קֹדֶשׁ *oil of anointing of holiness* Ex 30$_{25.25.31}$, שֶׁמֶן מִשְׁחַת י׳ *the oil of anointing of,* perh. by, *Y.* Lv 10$_{7}$, נֵזֶר שֶׁמֶן מִשְׁחַת אֱלֹהָיו *the consecration,* or *distinction, of the oil of anointing of,* perh. by, *his God* Lv 21$_{12}$.

2. oil, 3QTr 12$_{12}$ (ומשחותיהם *and their oils,* unless מִשְׁחָה II, §1 *measurement*).*

⇒ משׁח I *anoint.*

[מִשְׁחָה] II 2.0.1 n.f. **measurement**—cstr. מִשְׁחַת; pl. sf. Q משחותיהם—**1. measurement,** ופרושה ומשחותיהם ופרוט כל/ופרוטכל אחד ואח[ד] *and the explanation and their measurements and the protocol of/the detailing of each and every thing* 3QTr 12$_{12}$ (unless מִשְׁחָה I, §3 *oil*).

2. prescribed portion of priests from sacrifices, <NOM CL> זֹאת מִשְׁחַת אַהֲרֹן וּמִשְׁחַת בָּנָיו *this is the prescribed portion of Aaron and the prescribed portion of his sons* Lv 7$_{35}$ (+ מֵאִשֵּׁי י׳ *from the fire offerings of Y.*). <CSTR> מִשְׁחַת אַהֲרֹן *the prescribed portion of Aaron* Lv 7$_{35}$, מִשְׁחַת בָּנָיו *the prescribed portion of his sons* Lv 7$_{35}$.

⇒ משׁח III *measure.*

*[מִשְׁחָה] III 2.0.1 n.f. **consecrated portion**—cstr. מִשְׁחַת—**consecrated portion** of priests from sacrifices (unless מִשְׁחָה II *prescribed portion*), <NOM CL> זֹאת מִשְׁחַת אַהֲרֹן וּמִשְׁחַת בָּנָיו *this is the consecrated portion of Aaron and the consecrated portion of his sons* Lv 7$_{35}$ (+ מֵאִשֵּׁי י׳ *from the fire offerings of Y.*). <CSTR> מִשְׁחַת אַהֲרֹן *the consecrated portion of Aaron* Lv 7$_{35}$, מִשְׁחַת בָּנָיו *the consecrated portion of his sons* Lv 7$_{35}$.

⇒ משׁח I *anoint.*

מָשְׁחָה I 2 n.f. **anointing**—sf. מָשְׁחָתָם—state or fact of being anointed, <SUBJ> היה *be* Ex 40$_{15}$ (לִהְיֹת לָהֶם מָשְׁחָתָם לִכְהֻנַּת עוֹלָם לְדֹרֹתָם *so that for them their anointing will be for [the purpose of being] a priesthood of eternity throughout their generations*). <PREP> לְ *for (the purpose of),* + היה *be* Ex 29$_{29}$. <COLL> לְמָשְׁחָה בָהֶם *for anointing in them,* i.e. to be anointed in them Ex 29$_{29}$.*

⇒ משׁח I *anoint.*

מָשְׁחָה II 1 n.f. **prescribed portion** of priests from

sacrifices, <PREP> לְ *as*, + נתן *give* holy things Nm 18$_8$ (+ חֹק as an eternal *statute*).*
⇒ משח III *measure*.

*[**מִשְׁחוֹר**] n.[m.] **darkness,** <PREP> לְ *as, (turned) into*, + הפך ni. *be changed* (of splendour) 1QH 5$_{32}$ ([למשחו]ר; others [למשחי]ת *into destruction*; || אֲפֵלָה *darkness*, + הוֹד *splendour*, מָאוֹר *light* of face). <SYN> אֲפֵלָה *darkness*.
⇒ שׁחר *be black*.

מַשְׁחִית I $_{10.0.2}$ n.[m.] **destruction, ruin,** <CSTR> בַּעַל מַשְׁחִית *lord of destruction*, i.e. one who destroys Pr 18$_9$, חָרָשֵׁי מַשְׁחִית *artisans of*, i.e. those skilful in bringing about, *destruction* Ezk 21$_{36}$, הַר־הַמַּשְׁחִית *mountain of destruction* 2 K 23$_{13}$ (unless *of the destroyer*, i.e. מַשְׁחִית II), משפט משחית perh. *judgment of destruction* 4Q Béat 8$_3$ (unless מַשְׁחִית II). <PREP> לְ *as, as (a cause of), for (the purpose of)*, + היה *be* Ex 12$_{13}$ Ezk 5$_{16}$ 2 C 22$_4$, עזר *help* 2 C 20$_{33}$, נקם ni. *take revenge* Ezk 25$_{15}$ (לְמַשְׁחִית אֵיבַת עוֹלָם *for destruction [with] eternal enmity*); *into*, + הפך ni. *be changed* Dn 10$_8$ 1QH 5$_{32}$; *to (the point of)*, i.e. utterly, + הרג *kill* Ezk 9$_6$.*
⇒ שׁחת *be ruined*.

מַשְׁחִית II *destroyer*, see שׁחת *be ruined*, hi.

מִשְׁחָר I $_1$ n.[m.] **dawn** (unless מִשְׁחָר II *radiance*), <CSTR> רֶחֶם מִשְׁחָר from *the womb of dawn* Ps 110$_3$ (or em. מֵרֶחֶם מִשַּׁחַר go from *the womb towards the dawn** or רֶחֶם שַׁחַר from *the womb of dawn*).*
⇒ שַׁחַר *dawn*.

***מִשְׁחָר** II $_1$ n.[m.] **radiance** (unless מִשְׁחָר I *dawn*), <NOM CL> מִשְׁחָר לְךָ טַל יַלְדֻתֶיךָ *the dew of your boyhood is your radiance* Ps 110$_3$.

[**מַשְׁחֵת**] $_1$ n.[m.] **destruction**—sf. מַשְׁחֵתוֹ—<CSTR> כְּלִי מַשְׁחֵתוֹ *his weapon of destruction* Ezk 9$_1$ (or del.).
⇒ שׁחת *be spoiled*.

[**מִשְׁחַת**] $_1$ n.f. **disfigurement**—cstr. מִשְׁחַת—<NOM CL> כֵּן־מִשְׁחַת מֵאִישׁ מַרְאֵהוּ וְתֹאֲרוֹ מִבְּנֵי אָדָם perh. *(his) appearance was so great a disfigurement from (that of) a man and his form from (that of) human beings* Is 52$_{14}$ (or em. מָשְׁחַת his appearance *was disfigured*, so as not be a man's, i.e. שׁחת ho., or מָשְׁחַת *disfigurement*; 1QIsa^a משחתי *I have anointed** or *marred* his face).
⇒ שׁחת *be spoiled*.

מָשְׁחָת $_2$ n.[m.] **blemish**—sf. מָשְׁחָתָם—**1. blemish,** <NOM CL> כִּי מָשְׁחָתָם בָּהֶם *for (their) disfigurement is with them* (sacrificial beasts from foreigners) Lv 22$_{25}$ (|| מוּם *blemish*), כֵּן־מָשְׁחַת מֵאִישׁ מַרְאֵהוּ וְתֹאֲרוֹ מִבְּנֵי אָדָם perh. *(his) appearance was so great a disfigurement from (that of) a man and his form from (that of) human beings* Is 52$_{14}$ (if em. מִשְׁחַת *disfigurement*, i.e. מִשְׁחָה). **2. blemished (sacrificial) animal,** <OBJ> זבח *sacrifice* Ml 1$_{14}$ (unless מָשְׁחָת is שׁחת ho. ptc.). <SYN> מוּם *blemish*.
⇒ שׁחת *be spoiled*.

מִשְׁטוֹחַ $_1$ n.[m.] **spreading place**—cstr. מִשְׁטַח—**1.** place for spreading nets to catch fish, <COLL> מִשְׁטוֹחַ לַחֲרָמִים *a spreading place of*, i.e. for, *nets* Ezk 47$_{10}$.

2. perh. place for spreading out game, וַיִּשְׁטְחוּ לָהֶם מִשְׁטוֹחַ סְבִיבוֹת הַמַּחֲנֶה *and they spread for themselves a spreading place*, i.e. they heaped up the quail in a pile, *around the camp* Nm 11$_{32}$ (if em. שָׁטוֹחַ and they kept on *spreading*, i.e. inf. of שׁטח; Sam שָׁחוֹט *slaughtering*; Sam mss שְׁחוּטָה *that which was slaughtered*).

3. perh. place for spreading out priestly linen, <CSTR> פנת המשטח *the corner of the spreading place* 3QTr 7$_{11}$ (others הַמִּשְׁמָרָה *of the guardhouse* or *fortress*).
⇒ שׁטח *spread*.

[**מִשְׁטָח**] $_2$ n.[m.] **spreading place**—cstr. מִשְׁטַח—place for spreading nets to catch fish, <SUBJ> היה *be* Ezk 26$_5$ (מִשְׁטַח חֲרָמִים תִּהְיֶה בְּתוֹךְ הַיָּם *a [mere] spreading place for nets it* [Tyre] *will become in the middle of the sea*) 26$_{14}$ (וּנְתַתִּיךְ לִצְחִיחַ סֶלַע מִשְׁטַח חֲרָמִים תִּהְיֶה לֹא תִבָּנֶה עוֹד *and I will make you* [Tyre] *a shining of rock*, i.e. a bare rock; *a [mere] spreading place for nets you will become; you will not be rebuilt*; or em. תִּהְיִי/תִּבָּנִי *you will be/you will* not *be* rebuilt) 47$_{10}$ (מִשְׁטוֹחַ לַחֲרָמִים יִהְיוּ *a spreading place of,* i.e. for, *nets they will become*; or em. יִהְיֶה *it* [river] *will become*). <CSTR> מִשְׁטַח חֲרָמִים *a spreading place of,* i.e. for, *nets* Ezk 26$_{5.14}$.

⇒ שׁטח *spread.*

[מִשְׁטָר] 1 n.[m.] **writing**—sf. מִשְׁטָרוֹ—**writing** in the heavens, i.e. the pattern of the stars, or the **ordinance(s)** by which they rule the earth, or that **rule,*** <OBJ> שׂים *place,* i.e. impose, upon the earth Jb 38$_{33}$.

⇒ cf. שֹׁטֵר *official.*

מֶשִׁי 2 n.[m.] **fine cloth,** prob. not **silk,** <NOM CL> מַלְבּוּשֵׁךְ ... מֶשִׁי *your clothing was ... (of) fine cloth* Ezk 16$_{13}$ (רִקְמָה *embroidery,* שֵׁשׁ *fine linen;* + זָהָב *gold,* כֶּסֶף *silver*). <OBJ> כסה pi. *cover* adolescent Jerusalem, *with* Ezk 16$_{10}$ (|| רִקְמָה, שֵׁשׁ, תַּחַשׁ *fine leather*). <SYN> רִקְמָה *embroidery,* שֵׁשׁ *fine linen,* תַּחַשׁ *fine leather.*

מֻשִׁי, see מוּשִׁי *Mushi.*

מְשֵׁיזַבְאֵל 3 pr.n.m. **Meshezabel, 1.** grandfather of Meshullam, one of those who helped repair the walls of Jerusalem, <CSTR> בֶּן־מְשֵׁיזַבְאֵל *son of Meshezabel* Ne 3$_4$.

2. one of the leaders of returning exiles, <NOM CL> רָאשֵׁי הָעָם ... מְשֵׁיזַבְאֵל *the heads of the people were ... Meshezabel* Ne 10$_{22}$.

3. descendant of Zerah and father of Pethahiah, the latter perh. a Persian governor, <CSTR> בֶּן־מְשֵׁיזַבְאֵל *son of Meshezabel* Ne 11$_{24}$.

⇒ אֵל *God.*

מָשִׁיחַ 39.1.23 n.m. **anointed one**—cstr. מְשִׁיחַ; sf. מְשִׁיחִי, מְשִׁיחוֹ, מְשִׁיחֶךָ; pl. cstr. Q משיחי; sf. מְשִׁיחָי, L מְשִׁיחֶיךָ (Q משיחיכה), Q משיחיה.

1. in ref. to **king** (1 S 2$_{10.35}$ 16$_6$ Ps 2$_2$ 20$_7$ 28$_8$ 89$_{39.52}$ 132$_{10}$ appar. Hb 3$_{13}$ Ps 84$_{10}$ Lm 4$_{10}$ perh. Ps 20$_7$ 28$_8$ 89$_{39.52}$ 4QNarrA 2.2$_6$ perh. 4QTime 1.2$_9$), specif. Saul (1 S 12$_{3.5}$ 24$_{7.7.11}$ 26$_{9.11.16.23}$ 2 S 1$_{14.16.21}$ Si 46$_{19}$), David (2 S 19$_{22}$ 22$_{51}$||Ps 18$_{51}$ 2 S 23$_1$ Ps 132$_{17}$ appar. 2 C 6$_{42}$), Zerubbabel (perh. Dn 9$_{25.26}$), Cyrus (Is 45$_1$ perh. Dn 9$_{25.26}$).

2. in ref. to **priest** (Lv 4$_{3.5.16}$ 6$_{15}$ perh. Hb 3$_{13[mss]}$ 4QapMos^a 1.1$_9$ 4QapMos^b 1.1$_1$ 4QapMes 4.8$_{11}$), specif. Joshua ben Jozadak (perh. Dn 9$_{25.26}$); 2 S 1$_{21}$ הַכֹּהֵן הַמָּשִׁיחַ *the priest, the anointed one* or *the priest who is anointed.*

3. in ref. to **prophets** (1QM 11$_7$ appar. Ps 105$_{15}$||1 C 16$_{22}$), specif. Moses (4QapMos^c 2.2$_5$); people of Israel (perh. Hb 3$_{13[mss]}$).

4. in ref. to eschatological figure, a 'messiah', whether royal or priestly, 1QS 9$_{11}$ 1QSa 2$_{12.14.20}$ 1Q30 1$_2$ 4QCommGenA 5$_4$ 4QD^e 2.2$_{14}$ 4QBer^b 10$_{13}$ 4Qpara Kings 16$_2$ 4QapMes 1.2$_{10}$ 11QMelch 2$_{18}$ CD 2$_{12}$ 6$_1$=4QD^b 2$_6$=6QD 3$_4$ CD 12$_{23}$ 14$_{19}$=4QD^a 10.1$_{11}$ CD 19$_{10}$ 20$_1$.

<SUBJ> קום ho. *be raised* 2 S 23$_1$, לכד ni. *be captured* Lm 4$_{20}$, כרת ni. *be cut off* Dn 9$_{26}$ (+ וְאֵין לוֹ *and there is none of him,* i.e. he will be no more).

אחר htp. not *delay* 4QapMes 1.2$_{10}$ ([משיחו]), בוא *come* 1QS 9$_{11}$ 1QSa 2$_{14}$ (יבוא מש[יח] *the anointed one of* Israel *will come*) 4QCommGenA 5$_4$ CD 19$_{10}$ 4QapMes 1.2$_{10}$ ([משיחו] ... [לבוא] ... י[בוא]), hi. *bring* sacrificial beast Lv 4$_3$, blood of sacrificial beast Lv 4$_{5.16}$, עמד *arise* CD 12$_{23}$ 14$_{19}$=4QD^a 10.1$_{11}$ (if em. at 4QD מְמוֹד *arising of,* i.e. cstr.; CD [עמוד משי]ח) (if em. מָשׁוּחַ *one who is anointed*) 20$_1$.

שׁלח *send,* i.e. extend, hand to bread 1QSa 2$_{20}$ ([ישל]ח), כפר pi. *atone (for)* iniquity CD 14$_{19}$=4QD^a 10.1$_{11}$ (CD [משי]ח; 4QD [ויכפר]; unless וִיכֻפַּר *and* their iniquity *will be atoned for,* i.e. pu.), רפא *heal* battle-victims 4QapMes 1.2$_{10}$ ([משיחו]), חיה pi. *revive* dead 4QapMes 1.2$_{10}$ ([משיחו]), בשׂר pi. *announce (good news) (to)* humble 4QapMes 1.2$_{10}$ ([משיחו]).

עשׂה *prepare* cereal offering Lv 6$_{15}$, חטא *sin* Lv 4$_{3.3}$, קרב hi. *present* offering Lv 4$_3$, שׁחט *slaughter* sacrificial beast Lv 4$_5$, סמך *rest* hands on sacrificial beast Lv 4$_3$.

<NOM CL> המבשר הו[אה] משיח הרו[ח] *the bringer of good news is the anointed one of the spirit* 11QMelch 2$_{18}$, עֵד מְשִׁיחוֹ *his anointed one is a witness* 1 S 12$_5$ (+ י״

Y.), אַךְ נֶגֶד י׳ מְשִׁיחוֹ *surely his anointed one is in the presence of Y.* 1 S 16_{6}, כִּי־מְשִׁיחַ י׳ הוּא *for he is Y.'s anointed one* 1 S $24_{7.11}$.

<OBJ> הלך hi. *lead* 1QSa 2_{12} ([אלה את] יולי[ך] *God leads* the anointed one; others [אל] יוליד *God begets* the anointed one), חזק hi. *hold* by hand Is 45_{1}, עוד hi. *call to witness* Si 46_{19}, ענה *answer* Ps 20_{7}, ילד hi. *beget* 1QSa 2_{12} ([אל] יוליד *God begets* the anointed one; others [אלה את] יולי[ך] *God leads* the anointed one), ישע hi. *save* Ps 20_{7} perh. Hb 3_{13} (if em. לְיֵשַׁע אֶת־ appar. *for the salvation of* your anointed one to לוֹשַׁע אֶת־ *to save*; or em. object-marker אֶת־ to עַם for the salvation of *the people of* your anointed one), קלל pi. *curse* 2 S 19_{22}, שׁחת pi. *destroy* 2 S 1_{14}, מות pol. *kill* 2 S 1_{16}.

<CSTR> מְשִׁיחַ י׳ *Y.'s anointed one* 1 S $24_{7.7.11}$ $26_{9.11.16.23}$ 2 S $1_{14.16}$ 19_{22} Lm 4_{20}, מְשִׁיחַ אֱלֹהֵי יַעֲקֹב *the anointed one of the God of Jacob* 2 S 23_{1}, משיח ישראל *the anointed one of Israel* 1QSa 2_{14} (מש[יח]) 2_{20} 4Qpara Kings 16_{2} ([מ]שיח ישר[א]ל), משיח אהרון וישראל *the anointed one of Aaron and Israel* 1QS 9_{11} (משיחי appar. *anointed ones of*) CD 12_{23} (אהרן; if em. מָשׁוּחַ *one who is anointed*) 14_{19}=4QD^{a} 10.1_{11} (CD [משי]ח אהרן) CD 19_{10} (אהרן).

משיח הצדק *the messiah of righteousness* 4QComm GenA 5_{4}, [מש]יח הקודש *the anointed one of holiness* 1Q30 1_{2}, משיחי הקודש *the anointed ones of holiness* CD 6_{1}=4QD^{b} 2_{6}=6QD 3_{4} (if em. משיחו *his anointed one, holiness* in CD), משיחי רוח הקדש *the anointed ones of the spirit of holiness* 4QD^{e} 2.2_{14}, משיחי רוח קדשו *the anointed ones of his spirit of holiness* 4Q Ber^{b} 10_{13} (קוד[שו]; others משיחו *his anointed one,* the spirit of his holiness) CD 2_{12}, משיח הרו[ח] *the anointed one of the spirit* 11QMelch 2_{18}.

קֶרֶן מְשִׁיחוֹ *the horn of his anointed one* 1 S 2_{10} (+ מֶלֶךְ *king*), מָעוֹז יְשׁוּעוֹת מְשִׁיחוֹ *the strength of the salvation(s) of his anointed* Ps 28_{8} (or del. מָעוֹז), יֵשַׁע עַם מְשִׁיחֶךָ *the salvation of the people of your anointed one* Hb 3_{13} (if em. יֵשַׁע עַם appar. *salvation of;* mss מְשִׁיחֶךָ *your anointed ones*).

פי ... משיחו through *the mouth of... his anointed one* 4QapMos^{c} 2.2_{5}, פְּנֵי מְשִׁיחֶךָ *the face of your anointed one* Ps 84_{10} (+ מָגֵן *shield*) 132_{10} (+ עֶבֶד *servant*) 2 C 6_{42} (mss) (L מְשִׁיחֶיךָ *of your anointed ones*), עִקְּבוֹת מְשִׁיחֶךָ *the footsteps of your anointed one* Ps 89_{52}.

עמוד משיח *the arising of the anointed one of* Aaron and Israel CD 14_{19}=4QD^{a} 10.1_{11} (CD [ממוד משי]ח; or em. עֲמוֹד *arising of*), [כסא ה[משיח *the throne of the anointed one* 4QTime 1.2_{9} (others [ה[מלך *of the king*), כול משיחיה *all its/her anointed ones* 4QapMes 4.8_{11}.

<APP> קֹדֶשׁ *holiness* CD 2_{12} (or em. משיחי *anointed ones of* holiness) CD 6_{1} (or em., as ||6QD 3_{4}, (משיחי), רוּחַ *spirit* of holiness 4QBer^{b} 10_{13} (others משיחי; others נח[ה על משיחו] a spirit of holiness *rests upon his anointed one*), *breath* of our nostrils Lm 4_{20}.

כֹּהֵן *priest* Lv $4_{3.5.16}$ 6_{15} 4QapMos^{a} 1.1_{9} 4QapMos^{b} 1.1_{1} (WA מָשׁוּחַ *anointed* priest, in both), גֶּבֶר *man* 2 S 23_{1}, צֶמַח *shoot* of David 4QCommGenA 5_{4}, זֶרַע *seed,* i.e. offspring, of David 2 S 22_{51}||Ps 18_{51}, אָדוֹן *lord* 1 S 24_{7} 26_{16}, נָגִיד *leader* Dn 9_{25} 11QMelch 2_{18} ([משיח נגיד]), חֹזֶה *seer* 1QM 11_{7}.

מֹשֶׁה *Moses* 4QapMos^{c} 2.2_{5}, דָּוִד *David* 2 S 22_{51}||Ps 18_{51}, שָׁאוּל *Saul* 2 S 1_{21} (if del. בְּלִי the shield of Saul *without* the one anointed with oil, i.e. Saul himself; mss מָשׁוּחַ *anointed [one]*; or em. בַּל־מָשׁוּחַ *not anointed* with oil), כּוֹרֶשׁ *Cyrus* Is 45_{1}.

<ADJ> קֹדֶשׁ *holy* 4QapMes 1.2_{10} (משיחו הקדש] *his holy anointed one*).

<PREP> לְ of direction, *to,* + אמר *say* Is 45_{1}; of benefit, *to, for,* + עשׂה *do* 1 S 24_{7} 2 S 22_{51}||Ps 18_{51}, ערך *array,* i.e. prepare, lamp Ps 132_{17}; שׁמע לְ *listen to,* i.e. obey 4QapMes 1.2_{1}.

בְּ *against,* + דבר pi. *speak* CD 6_{1}=4QD^{b} 2_{6}=6QD 3_{4} (6QD [דברו]), שׁלח *send* hand, i.e. strike 1 S $26_{9.11.23}$, נגע *strike* Ps 105_{15}||1 C 16_{22} (+ נָבִיא *prophet*).

עַל *against,* + דבר pi. *speak* 4QD^{e} 2.2_{14} 4QBer^{b} 10_{13} (both [דברו]; others נח[ה על משיחו] a spirit of holiness *rests upon his anointed one*), יסד ni. *establish oneself* or *plot* Ps 2_{2} (or em. סוד ni. *take counsel* or יעד ni. *be called to meeting;* + י׳ *Y.*; or del. עַל־י׳ וְעַל־מְשִׁיחוֹ *against Y. and against his anointed one*), יצב htp. *take one's stand* Ps 2_{2} (+ י׳ *Y.*; or del. עַל־י׳ וְעַל־מְשִׁיחוֹ); *over,* + שׁמר *keep (guard)* 1 S 26_{16}.

עַד *unto (the appearance of)* Dn 9_{25} 11QMelch 2_{18} ([עד משיח]).

עִם *with, against,* + עבר htp. *become angry* Ps 89$_{39}$ (+ עֶבֶד *servant*).

לִפְנֵי *in the presence of* 4QapMos^{a} 1.1$_{9}$ 4QapMos^{b} 1.1$_{1}$ (WA מָשׁוּחַ *anointed* priest, in both), + הלך htp. *go (about)* 1 S 2$_{35}$.

נֶגֶד *in the presence of,* + ענה *answer* 1 S 12$_{3}$ (+ י׳ Y.).

בְּיַד *through,* + נגד hi. *tell* 1QM 11$_{7}$, ידע hi. *inform* CD 2$_{12}$, עזב *leave* 4QapMes 9$_{3}$ (unless ב[י]ד leave *in the hand of* an anointed one).

בְּלִי *without* 2 S 1$_{21}$ (or del. בְּלִי; mss מָשׁוּחַ the shield of Saul *anointed* with oil / the shield of Saul without the *one anointed* with oil, i.e. Saul himself; or em. בַּל־מָשׁוּחַ *not anointed* with oil).

<COLL> י׳ ומשיחו *Y. and his anointed one* Si 46$_{19}$, הַכֹּהֵן הַמָּשִׁיחַ ... הַכֹּהֵן *the priest, the anointed one ..., the priest* Lv 4$_{5.16}$, הַכֹּהֵן הַמָּשִׁיחַ תַּחְתָּיו מִבָּנָיו *the priest, the one anointed in place of him, from among his sons* Lv 6$_{15}$.

הַכֹּהֵן הַמָּשִׁיחַ אֲשֶׁר מִלֵּא אֶת־יָדוֹ *the priest, the anointed one, whose hand he has filled,* i.e. whom he has consecrated Lv 4$_{5}$(Sam), [ה]כוהן המשיח אשר יוצק על ר[ו]אשו שמן משיחה *the priest, the anointed one, upon whose head is poured the oil of anointing* 4QapMos^{a} 1.1$_{9}$ (WA מָשׁוּחַ *anointed* priest).

מְשִׁיחַ י׳ ... אֲשֶׁר אָמַרְנוּ בְּצִלּוֹ נִחְיֶה בַגּוֹיִם *Y.'s anointed one ..., in whose shade we thought we could live among the nations* Lm 4$_{20}$.

מָשִׁיחַ בַּשָּׁמֶן *an anointed one with oil* 1 S 1$_{21}$ (mss מָשׁוּחַ either in same sense or with verbal force, *anointed* with oil), משיח בשמן מלכות *an anointed one with oil of kingship* 4QNarrA 2.2$_{6}$.

נביא ומשיחי אהרון וישראל *a prophet and the anointed one(s) of Aaron and Israel* 1QS 9$_{11}$, משיח מאהרן ומישראל *an anointed one from Aaron and from Israel* CD 20$_{1}$ (cf. Cstr.).*

⇒ משח *anoint.*

*[מְשִׁיחָה] 0.0.2 n.f. **anointing**—Q משיחה; cstr. Q משיחת—<CSTR> שמן המשיחה *the oil of anointing* of anointed priest 4QapMos^{a} 1.1$_{9}$, שמן משיחת כהונתם *the oil of the anointing of their priesthood* 1QM 9$_{8}$ (4QM^{c}5 שמן כהונתם *the oil of their priesthood,* without משיחת).

⇒ משח I *anoint.*

*[מְשִׁיכָה] 0.0.1 n.f. **drawing (of water)**—Q משיכה—<OBJ> משך *draw* 4QHalakhah^{a} 1$_{5}$ (למשוך מים מן הבור המשיכה *to draw water from the cistern, the drawing*).

⇒ משך *pull.*

[מְשִׁיסָה], see מְשִׁסָּה *plunder.*

*[מְשִׁיר] n.[m.] **song,** <OBJ> שׁיר *sing* Ps 137$_{3}$ (if em.; see Cstr.). <CSTR> מְשִׁיר צִיּוֹן *song of Zion* Ps 137$_{3}$ (if em. מְשִׁיר *one of the sons of*). <COLL> מְשִׁירִי אֲהוֹדֶנּוּ *(with) my song I will praise him* Ps 28$_{7}$ (if em. מִשִּׁירִי *with my song*).

⇒ cf. שִׁיר *song.*

משך I 36.2.6 vb. **pull**—**Qal** 30.1.4 Pf. מָשַׁךְ, מָשְׁכָה, מְשַׁכְתִּיךָ, מָשְׁכוּ; impf. יִמְשׁוֹךְ (Si ימשך), 2ms תִּמְשֹׁךְ (תִּמְשְׁכֵנִי), אֶמְשְׁכֵם; + waw וַיִּמְשֹׁךְ; וּמָשַׁכְתִּי, וּמָשַׁכְתָּ, 2ms וַתִּמְשֹׁךְ, וַיִּמְשְׁכוּ; impv. מְשֹׁךְ (מָשְׁכֵנִי), מִשְׁכוּ; ptc. מֹשֵׁךְ (מֹשְׁכִים, מֹשְׁכֵי); inf. מְשֹׁךְ (מְשׁוֹךְ, מָשְׁכוֹ).

1. of horizontal movement, **drag (along, off, away), haul (along, off, away), pull (along, off, away).**

<SUBJ> Y. Jr 31$_{3}$ (unless משך =*prolong,* as §4) Ho 11$_{4}$ Ps 28$_{3}$ (unless §19 or משך II *seize*) perh. Jb 24$_{22}$ (unless §4 or משך II *seize*; or em. מֶשֶׁךְ *acquisition of*), אַבִּיר *mighty one/bull,* in ref. to Y. Jb 24$_{22}$ (if em. אַבִּירִים although he has dragged off *mighty ones* to אַבִּיר־ם and the *mighty one* will haul away), Job (as representative of humankind) Jb 40$_{25}$ (unless משך II *seize*; + שׁקע hi. *depress* tongue of Leviathan), (male) lover Ca 1$_{4}$ (or em. מָשְׁכֵנִי *pull me* to מְשֻׁכָּךְ appar. *oil has made you attractive,* with שֶׁמֶן *oil* as subj., i.e. as §15; + בוא hi. *bring*), עָנִי *poor one* Ps 10$_{9}$ (יַחְטֹף עָנִי בְּמָשְׁכוֹ בְרִשְׁתּוֹ the wicked one *catches the poor one when* the poor one *pulls against his net,* unless בְּמָשְׁכוֹ בְרִשְׁתּוֹ = *when he pulls him into his net*; or del. יַחְטֹף עָנִי and em. לְמָשְׁכוֹ *to drag him* into his net; or משך II *seize*), wicked rich perh. Jb 24$_{22}$ (or em. מֶשֶׁךְ *acquisition of*); subj. not specified, Ezk 32$_{20}$ (unless §19; or em. מָשְׁכוּ אוֹתָהּ וְכָל־הֲמוֹנֶיהָ *they have dragged her and all her multitudes* to וְהָשְׁכַּב כָּל־הֲמוֹנָם *and all her multitude*

will be laid low).

<OBJ> Israel Jr 31$_{3}$ (unless משך = *prolong*, as §4) Ho 11$_{4}$, (female) lover Ca 1$_{4}$ (or em. מָשְׁכֵנִי *pull me* to מְשָׁכֻךָ appar. *they have made you* [male lover] *attractive*, i.e. see §15), עָנִי *poor one* Ps 10$_{9}$ (יַחְטֹף עָנִי בְּמָשְׁכוֹ בְרִשְׁתּוֹ the wicked one *catches the poor one when he pulls him into his net*, unless בְּמָשְׁכוֹ בְרִשְׁתּוֹ = *he pulls against his net*; or em. לְמָשְׁכוֹ *to drag him* into his net), הָמוֹן *multitude* of Egypt Ezk 32$_{20}$ (unless §19; or em.), Egypt Ezk 32$_{20}$ (or em.), אַבִּיר *mighty one* or *bull* Jb 24$_{22}$ (unless §4 or משך II *seize*; or em. וּמָשַׁךְ *although he has dragged off* to וּמֶשֶׁךְ *although the acquisition of* mighty ones/bulls, or אַבִּירִים *bulls/mighty ones* to אֶבְיוֹנִים *poor ones* or אֹבְדִים *lost ones* or אַבִּיר־ם and *the mighty one* will haul away, or אַבִּיר יָמָו although *the mighty one* has prolonged [i.e. as §4] *his days*), לִוְיָתָן *Leviathan* Jb 40$_{25}$ (unless משך II *seize*), נֶפֶשׁ *soul* of worshipper Ps 28$_{3}$ (if em. אַל־תִּמְשְׁכֵנִי *do not haul me off* to אַל־תִּמְשֹׁךְ נַפְשִׁי *do not haul off my soul*), עָוֹן *iniquity* Is 5$_{18}$ (מֹשְׁכֵי הֶעָוֹן *draggers of sin*), חַטָּאָה *sin* Is 5$_{18}$.

<PREP> בְּ perh. of place, *in(to)*, + רֶשֶׁת *net* Ps 10$_{9}$; of instrument, *by (means) of, with*, + חֶבֶל *cord* Is 5$_{18}$ Ho 11$_{4}$, עֲבֹת *rope* Ho 11$_{4}$, חַכָּה *hook* Jb 40$_{25}$ (unless משך II *seize*), כֹּחַ *strength* Jb 24$_{22}$ (unless משך II *seize* or unless אַבִּיר *mighty one*; or em. וּמָשַׁךְ *although he has dragged off* bulls/mighty ones to וּמֶשֶׁךְ *although the acquisition of* bulls/mighty ones, or אַבִּירִים *bulls/mighty ones* to אַבִּיר יָמָו although *the mighty one* has prolonged [i.e. as §4] *his days* with his [full] strength); perh. *against*, + רֶשֶׁת *net* Ps 10$_{9}$; כְּ *as with*, + עֲבֹת *rope* Is 5$_{18}$; עִם *with*, + רָשָׁע *wicked one* Ps 28$_{3}$ (unless §19 or משך II *seize*), פֹּעֵל evil*doer* Ps 28$_{3}$ (unless משך II; or ins. אַל־תְּאַבְּדֵנִי *do not destroy me* with evildoers); אַחֲרֵי *behind, after*, + (male) lover Ca 1$_{4}$ (if אַחֲרֶיךָ taken with preceding מָשְׁכֵנִי *pull me* rather than with following נָּרוּצָה *let us run*; or em. מָשְׁכֵנִי to מְשָׁכֻךָ appar. *they have made you* [male lover] *attractive*, i.e. see §15).

<COLL> הוֹי מֹשְׁכֵי הֶעָוֹן *woe to those who drag along sin* Is 5$_{18}$, מְשַׁכְתִּיךָ חָסֶד *I have dragged you along (with) loyalty* Jr 31$_{3}$ (unless *I have prolonged to you loyalty*, as §4), הֲתִמְשֹׁךְ *are you able to drag?* Job 40$_{25}$(ms).

2. of vertical movement, **pull, pull up,** <SUBJ> perh. אָח *brother*, i.e. Joseph's brothers Gn 37$_{28}$, אִישׁ *man* Jr 38$_{13}$ perh. Gn 37$_{28}$ (i.e. Midianite traders). <OBJ> Joseph Gn 37$_{28}$ (|| עלה hi. *raise*), Jeremiah Jr 38$_{13}$ (|| עלה hi.). <PREP> בְּ of instrument, *by (means) of, with*, + חֶבֶל *cord* Jr 38$_{13}$.

3. pull out lambs from flock, <SUBJ> זָקֵן *elder* Ex 12$_{21}$ (or em. מהר pi. *hasten*; || לקח *take*).

4. prolong, <SUBJ> Y. Jr 31$_{3}$ (unless משך = *drag along*, as §1) Ps 36$_{11}$ 85$_{6}$ Jb 24$_{22}$ (unless §1) Ne 9$_{30}$ (unless משך = *be patient*, as §16); subj. not specified, Ps 109$_{12}$.

<OBJ> Israel Jr 31$_{3}$ (as indirect obj.; unless משך = *drag along*, as §1), אַבִּיר *(life of) mighty one* Jb 24$_{22}$ (unless §1), חֶסֶד *loyalty* Jr 31$_{3}$ (unless as §1) Ps 36$_{11}$ 109$_{12}$ Ne 9$_{30}$ (if ins. חֶסֶד *loyalty*; unless משך = *be patient*, as §16), צְדָקָה *righteousness* Ps 36$_{11}$, אַף *anger* Ps 85$_{6}$, יֹבֵל *ram's horn* Ex 19$_{13}$ (בִּמְשֹׁךְ הַיֹּבֵל *at the prolonging of [the sound of] the ram's horn*; or em. שׁתק *be silent*), יוֹם *day* Jb 24$_{22}$ (if em. אַבִּירִים although he has dragged off [i.e. as §1] *bulls/mighty ones* to אַבִּיר יָמָו although *the mighty one* has prolonged *his days*), שָׁנָה *year* Ne 9$_{30}$ (unless משך = *be patient*, as §16, or ins. חֶסֶד *loyalty*, with שָׁנִים רַבּוֹת adverbial, *for many years*).

<PREP> לְ perh. of direction, *to(wards)*, + יֹדֵעַ *one who knows* Y. Ps 36$_{11}$, יָשָׁר *upright one* Ps 36$_{11}$; בְּ appar. of instrument, *by (means of), with*, + קֶרֶן *horn* Jos 6$_{5}$ (בִּמְשֹׁךְ בְּקֶרֶן הַיֹּבֵל *at the prolonging [of sound] by means of the ram's horn*); perh. of accompaniment, *with, in (a state of)*, + כֹּחַ *strength* Jb 24$_{22}$ (if em. אַבִּירִים although he has dragged off [i.e. as §1] *bulls/mighty ones* to אַבִּיר יָמָו although *the mighty one* has prolonged *his days*); עַל *for* or *on account of*, + אָב *father*, i.e. ancestor Ne 9$_{30}$ (perh. משך = *be patient*, as §16).

<COLL> מְשַׁכְתִּיךָ חָסֶד *I have prolonged to you loyalty* Jr 31$_{3}$ (unless *I have dragged you along (with) loyalty*, as §1), אַל־יְהִי־לוֹ מֹשֵׁךְ חָסֶד *may he not have one who prolongs loyalty*, i.e. stays loyal Ps 109$_{12}$.

5. sow seeds, <SUBJ> זֹרֵעַ *sower* Ps 126$_{2}$ (if em. מֶשֶׁךְ־ *the bag of* seed to מֹשֵׁךְ *sowing* seed). <OBJ> זֶרַע *seed* Am 9$_{13}$ (or em. בְּמֹשֵׁךְ הַזָּרַע reach *the sower of the seed* to בְּמֹשֵׁךְ *the sower* or בְּזֹרֵעַ *the sower*; || דרך *tread* grapes) Ps 126$_{2}$ (if em. מָשֵׁךְ־).

6. appar. **extend** hand, perh. **make common cause** with,* <SUBJ> appar. מֶלֶךְ *king* Ho 7$_{5}$ (unless משׁך II *seize*; or em. מָשַׁךְ יָדוֹ *he extended his hand* to מָשַׁךְ יֵינוֹ or מָסַךְ *he mixed his wine* or הִשְׁכִּירוּ אֹתוֹ *they made him drunk*). <OBJ> יָד *hand* Ho 7$_{5}$ (unless משׁך II *seize*; or em.; see Subj.).

7. appar. **pull away,** i.e. **pervert** law, <SUBJ> אִישׁ *man* Si 35$_{17}$. <OBJ> תּוֹרָה *law* Si 35$_{17}$. <PREP> אַחַר *in accordance with,* + צֹרֶךְ *need* Si 35$_{17(B)}$ (ואחר צרכו ימשך *and in accordance with what he requires he will pervert* the law; Bmg, E ויאחר צרכו למשוך/למשך *and he will delay what he requires to pervert* the law).

8. draw water, <OBJ> מַיִם *water* 4QHalakhah^{a} (+ מן הבור *from the cistern*).

9. perh. **bring,** <PREP> אֶל *to* 4QMMT B$_{9(WA)}$ (מושכת אליו perh. *bringing to him*; others מי שזנת אליו *whoever prostituted herself with him* or מושבת אליו *an object that was returned to him*).

10. draw bow, and perh. more generally, **wield** weapon, **a.** as verb, <SUBJ> אִישׁ *man* 1 K 22$_{34}$||2 C 18$_{33}$, Tarshish, Pul, and Lud Is 66$_{19}$ (or em. מֹשְׁכֵי קֶשֶׁת *who draw a bow* to מֶשֶׁךְ וְרֹשׁ *Meshech and Rosh* and/or פּוּל *Pul* to פּוּט *Put*; ms lacks קֶשֶׁת *bow*, leaving מֹשְׁכֵי תֻבַל *the archers of Tubal*); subj. not specified, Jg 5$_{14}$ (unless here משׁך = *hold* staff, as §17; or משׁך II *seize*). <PREP> לְ of direction, *to (the point of)*, + תֹּם *completeness* 1 K 22$_{34}$||2 C 18$_{33}$ (מָשַׁךְ ... לְתֻמּוֹ a man *pulled* on his bow *to his completeness*, i.e. as far as he could, unless תֹּם = in his *innocence*, i.e. by happenstance); בְּ *against, on* (or perh. introducing obj.), + קֶשֶׁת *bow* 1 K 22$_{34}$||2 C 18$_{33}$; introducing obj., or (hold) *onto*, + שֵׁבֶט *spear* Jg 5$_{14}$ (unless שֵׁבֶט = hold *staff*, as §17; or משׁך II *seize*).

b. ptc. as noun, **one who draws (bow), archer,** מֹשְׁכֵי תֻבַל *the archers of Tubal* Is 66$_{19(ms)}$.

11. appar. **draw up, march** (intrans. Jg 5$_{14}$ 20$_{37}$), trans. (Jg 4$_{6}$), <SUBJ> Barak Jg 4$_{6}$ (+ לקח *take*), אֹרֵב *ambush party* Jg 20$_{37}$; subj. not specified, Jg 5$_{14}$ (unless משׁך = *wield* spear or *hold* staff, as §10 or §17). <PREP> בְּ perh. *under the authority of*, + שֵׁבֶט *staff* Jg 5$_{14}$ (unless as §10 or §17).

12. appar. **draw, mislead** enemy troops, <SUBJ> Deborah Jg 4$_{7}$. <OBJ> Sisera Jg 4$_{7}$, רֶכֶב *chariot(ry)* Jg 4$_{7}$, הָמוֹן *multitude* Jg 4$_{7}$. <PREP> אֶל *to*, + Barak Jg 4$_{7}$, נַחַל *river* Jg 4$_{7}$.

13. perh. **stimulate** (unless §20), <SUBJ> Koheleth Ec 2$_{3}$ (or em. שׂמך or סמך *support* or שׂמח pi. *gladden*; + נהג *lead*). <OBJ> בָּשָׂר *flesh* Ec 2$_{3}$ (or em.). <PREP> בְּ of instrument, *by (means of), with,* + יַיִן *wine* Ec 2$_{3}$ (or em.).

14. follow, trail behind, <SUBJ> אָדָם *human being* Jb 21$_{33}$ (unless משׁך II *seize*). <PREP> אַחֲרֵי *behind, after,* + רַע (corpse of) *evil one* Jb 21$_{33}$ (unless משׁך II *seize*; + וּלְפָנָיו אֵין מִסְפָּר *and in front of him there is no number [of people]*).

15. appar. **make attractive, cause to follow,** <SUBJ> appar. שֶׁמֶן *oil* Ca 1$_{4}$ (if em. מָשְׁכֵנִי *pull me*, i.e. as §1, to מְשָׁכֻךְ *they have made you* [male lover] *attractive*; + בוא hi. *bring*). <OBJ> (male) lover Ca 1$_{4}$ (if em.).

16. perh. **be patient,** <SUBJ> Y. Ne 9$_{30}$ (unless משׁך = *prolong* days/loyalty, as §4). <PREP> עַל *concerning* or *on account of*, + אָב *father*, i.e. ancestor Ne 9$_{30}$ (unless as §4). <COLL> וַתִּמְשֹׁךְ עֲלֵיהֶם שָׁנִים רַבּוֹת *and you were patient with them/on their account (for) many years* Ne 9$_{30}$ (unless as §4).

17. hold, <SUBJ> subj. not specified, Jg 5$_{14}$ (unless משׁך = *wield* spear, as §10). <PREP> בְּ introducing object, or (hold) *onto*, + שֵׁבֶט *staff* Jg 5$_{14}$ (unless שֵׁבֶט = *spear*, as §10).

18. carry, bear, <SUBJ> עֶגְלָה *calf* Dt 21$_{3}$. <PREP> בְּ introducing obj., עֹל *yoke* Dt 21$_{3}$=11QT 63$_{1}$ (משכה] [בעול).

19. lay out for burial* (unless §1), <SUBJ> Y. Ps 28$_{3}$; subj. not specified, Ezk 32$_{20}$. <OBJ> הָמוֹן *multitude* of Egypt Ezk 32$_{20}$, worshipper Ps 28$_{3}$. <PREP> עִם *with*, + רָשָׁע *wicked one* Ps 28$_{3}$.

20. sustain* (unless §13), <SUBJ> Koheleth Ec 2$_{3}$. <OBJ> בָּשָׂר *flesh* Ec 2$_{3}$. <PREP> בְּ of instrument, *by (means of), with,* + יַיִן *wine* Ec 2$_{3}$.

Also 4QparaKings 6$_{2}$ 4QNarrA 17$_{1}$ 4QRitPur 226$_{3}$.

<SYN> §2 עלה hi. *raise*; §3 לקח *take*; §5 דרך *tread* grapes

Ni. 3.1.1 Impf. Si ימשך, 3fs תִּמָּשֵׁךְ, יִמָּשֵׁכוּ; inf. Q המשך —**1. be delayed** or **be prolonged,** <SUBJ> יוֹם *day*

Is 13$_{22}$, קֵץ end *time* 1QpHab 7$_{12}$, דָּבָר *word* of Y. Ezk 12$_{25.28}$. <PREP> עַל perh. *on account of*, + אִישׁ *man* of truth 1QpHab 7$_{12}$. <COLL> לֹא־תִמָּשֵׁךְ עוֹד *it will not be further delayed* Ezk 12$_{25.28}$ (־לֹא).

2. be pulled away, i.e. **disappear,** <SUBJ> פֹּעַל *work* of human being's hands Si 14$_{19}$. <PREP> אַחֲרֵי *after*, + דּוֹר *generation* of flesh and blood Si 14$_{19}$.

Pu. 3 Ptc. מְמֻשָּׁךְ (מְמֻשָּׁכָה)—**1.** appar. **be tall** (unless משׁך II *be scented*), <SUBJ> עַם *people* Is 18$_{2.7}$ (both || מרט pu. *be smooth-skinned*).

2. be delayed, <SUBJ> תּוֹחֶלֶת *hope* Pr 13$_{12}$ (תּוֹחֶלֶת מְמֻשָּׁכָה ... תַּאֲוָה בָאָה *hope delayed ... a desire come [true]*).

<SYN> §1 מרט pu. *be smooth-skinned*.*

⇒ מֶשֶׁךְ I *trail, acquisition*; מְשִׁיכָה *drawing*.

*משׁך II 7 vb. **seize** (unless משׁך I *pull*)—**Qal** 7 Pf. מָשַׁךְ; impf. יִמְשׁוֹךְ, 2ms תִּמְשֹׁךְ (תִּמְשְׁכֵנִי)—**seize, hold on,** <SUBJ> Y. Ps 28$_3$ Jb 24$_{22}$, אָדָם *human being* Jb 21$_{33}$, Job (as representative of humankind) Jb 40$_{25}$, Koheleth Ec 2$_3$ (if em.; see Prep.), מֶלֶךְ *king* Ho 7$_5$, רָשָׁע *wicked one* Ps 10$_9$; subj. not specified, Jg 5$_{14}$. <OBJ> לִוְיָתָן *Leviathan* Jb 40$_{25}$, עָנִי *poor one* Ps 10$_9$, אַבִּיר *mighty one* Jb 24$_{22}$, worshipper Ps 28$_3$, יָד *hand* Ho 7$_5$. <PREP> לְ introducing object, + שֵׁבֶט *spear* Jg 5$_{14}$; בְּ of instrument, *by (means) of, with*, + כֹּחַ *strength* Jb 24$_{22}$, חַכָּה *hook* Jb 40$_{25}$, רֶשֶׁת *net* Ps 10$_9$; introducing object, + חָכְמָה *wisdom* Ec 2$_3$ (if em. יַיִן *wine* to חָכְמָה; unless משׁך I §13 *stimulate* or §20 *sustain*); עִם *with*, + רָשָׁע *wicked one* Ps 28$_3$, פֹּעֵל evildoer Ps 28$_3$; אַחֲרֵי *behind, after*, + רַע (corpse of) *evil one* Jb 21$_{33}$.

*משׁך III 1 vb. **scent**—**Pu.** 1 Ptc. מְמֻשָּׁךְ—**be scented** (unless משׁך I pu. *be tall*), <SUBJ> עַם *people* Is 18$_{2.7}$ (both || מרט pu. *be smooth-skinned*).

<SYN> §1 מרט pu. *be smooth-skinned*.

[מֶשֶׁךְ] I 2 n.[m.] **trail; acquisition**—(unless מֶשֶׁךְ II *bag[ful]*)—cstr. מֶשֶׁךְ—**1. trail** of seed, as drawn along (משׁך *drag*) in sowing, <OBJ> נשׂא *raise*, i.e. leave Ps 126$_6$ (or del. נשׂא and em. ־מֶשֶׁךְ *trail of* seed to מֹשֵׁךְ *sowing* seed). <CSTR> מֶשֶׁךְ־הַזָּרַע *the trail of seed* Ps 126$_6$ (or em. מֹשֵׁךְ *sowing* seed). **2. acquisition,** as a drawing up (משׁך §2 *pull up*), <NOM CL> מֶשֶׁךְ חָכְמָה מִפְּנִינִים *the acquisition of wisdom is* better *than corals* Jb 28$_{18}$ (unless מֶשֶׁךְ III *price*), וּמֶשֶׁךְ אַבִּירִים בְּכוֹחוֹ *although the acquisition of bulls/mighty ones is within his power* Jb 24$_{22}$ (unless וּמָשַׁךְ *although he has dragged off* bulls/mighty ones by his strength). <CSTR> מֶשֶׁךְ חָכְמָה *acquisition of wisdom* Jb 28$_{18}$ (unless מֶשֶׁךְ III *price*), מֶשֶׁךְ אַבִּירִים *acquisition of bulls/mighty ones* Jb 24$_{22}$ (if em.).*

⇒ משׁך *pull*.

[מֶשֶׁךְ] II 2 n.[m.] **(leather) pouch, bag, bagful** (unless מֶשֶׁךְ I *pulling along*)—cstr. מֶשֶׁךְ—**bag, bagful,** for seeds, wisdom as corals, <NOM CL> וּמֶשֶׁךְ חָכְמָה מִפְּנִינִים appar. *and a bag(ful) of wisdom is* better *than corals* Jb 28$_{18}$. <OBJ> נשׂא *raise*, i.e. carry Ps 126$_6$ (or del. נשׂא and em. ־מֶשֶׁךְ *bag of* seed to מֹשֵׁךְ *sowing* seed). <CSTR> מֶשֶׁךְ־הַזָּרַע *the bag of seed* Ps 126$_6$ (or em. מֹשֵׁךְ *sowing* seed), מֶשֶׁךְ חָכְמָה appar. *a bag(ful) of wisdom* Jb 28$_{18}$. <PREP> בְּ of place, *in*, חטף *seize* Ps 10$_9$ (if em. בְּמָשְׁכוֹ = *when he pulls him* to בְּמַשְׁכּוֹ *in his bag*).*

⇒ משׁך I *pull* or II *seize*.

*[מֶשֶׁךְ] III 1 n.[m.] **price** (unless מֶשֶׁךְ I *acquisition*), <NOM CL> מֶשֶׁךְ חָכְמָה מִפְּנִינִים *the price of wisdom is above corals* Jb 28$_{18}$. <CSTR> מֶשֶׁךְ חָכְמָה *price of wisdom* Jb 28$_{18}$.

מֶשֶׁךְ IV 9 pl.n. **Meshech,** people and territory in Asia Minor, perh. Phrygia, <SUBJ> נתן *give*, i.e. exchange, goods Ezk 27$_{13}$ (+ Javan, Tubal).

<NOM CL> בְּנֵי יֶפֶת ... מֶשֶׁךְ *the sons of Japheth were ... Meshech* Gn 10$_2$||1 C 1$_5$ (+ Gomer, Magog, Madai, Javan, Tubal, Tiras; Sam mss appar. מוֹשֵׁךְ *Moshech* at Gn 10$_2$), בְּנֵי שֵׁם ... מֶשֶׁךְ *the sons of Shem were ... Meshech* 1 C 1$_{17}$ (mss מַשׁ *Mash*; as ||Gn 10$_{23}$, where Sam has מַשָּׁא *Mesha*; + Elam, Asshur, Arpachshad, Lud, Aram, Uz, Hul, Gether), יָוָן תֻּבַל וָמֶשֶׁךְ הֵמָּה רֹכְלָיִךְ *Javan and Tubal and Meshech, they were your traders* Ezk 27$_{13}$, שָׁם מֶשֶׁךְ תֻּבַל וְכָל־הֲמוֹנָהּ *there are Meshech, Tubal, and all its multitude* Ezk 32$_{26}$ (mss וְתֻבַל *and*

Tubal; or em. גְּבוּרָתוֹ and all *its strength*).

<CSTR> נְשִׂיא רֹאשׁ מֶשֶׁךְ וְתֻבָל *the prince of Rosh, Meshech, and Tubal* or *chief prince of Meshech and Tubal* Ezk 38$_{2.3}$ 39$_{1}$ (both וְתֻבָל).

<PREP> אֶל *to*, + שׁלח pi. *send (away)* survivors Is 66$_{19}$ (if em. מֹשְׁכֵי קֶשֶׁת *who draw a bow to* מֶשֶׁךְ וְרֹשׁ *Meshech and Rosh*; + Tarshish, Pul [or em. Put], Lud, Rosh, Tubal, Javan).

<COLL> אוֹיָה־לִי כִּי־גַרְתִּי מֶשֶׁךְ *alas for me, for I sojourn (in) Meshech* Ps 120$_{5}$ (or em. מַשָּׂא in *Massa*; + Kedar).

[מֹשֵׁךְ] *one who draws the bow, archer*, see משׁך I *pull*, §10b.

מִשְׁכָּב 46.3.9 n.m. **bed, lying down**—cstr. מִשְׁכַּב; sf. מִשְׁכָּבִי, מִשְׁכָּבְךָ (מִשְׁכָּבֶךָ), מִשְׁכָּבֵךְ, מִשְׁכָּבוֹ, מִשְׁכָּבָהּ, מִשְׁכָּבָם, מִשְׁכַּבְכֶם; pl. cstr. מִשְׁכְּבֵי; sf. מִשְׁכְּבוֹתָם.

1. bed, whether bedstead or mat and covers (sometimes perh. more generally **place to lie down** [e.g. Lv 15$_{21}$ Ezk 32$_{25}$]), usu. as place of resting or sleeping.

2. bedding,* any element such as mat, quilt or covering (Lv 15$_{4}$).

3. specif. **marital bed** or as place of fornication, usu. in ref. to worship of other deities (Gn 49$_{4}$=4QCommGenA 4$_{5}$ Is 57$_{7.8}$ Pr 7$_{17}$ Is 57$_{7.8}$ Ezk 23$_{17}$ perh. Ho 7$_{14}$ Ca 3$_{1}$ Si 47$_{20}$).

4. sickbed (Ex 21$_{18}$=4QHalakhah[a] 3.1$_{3}$ 2 S 13$_{5}$ Ps 41$_{4}$ Jb 33$_{19}$); **deathbed** (1 K 1$_{47}$ Si 46$_{19}$ 47$_{20}$ perh. 4QṬohC 1$_{7}$).

5. perh. **prayer mat** (Ps 149$_{5}$), or **place of lying down** in ecstasy or prayer (Is 57$_{8}$).*

6. dining couch (3QTr 11$_{16}$).*

7. bier (2 C 16$_{14}$).

8. grave (Is 57$_{2}$ Ezk 32$_{25}$ 2 C 16$_{14}$).*

9. other functions of the bed: as place for planning evil (Mc 2$_{1}$ Ps 36$_{5}$), for private thoughts or words (Ps 4$_{5}$ Ec 10$_{20}$), for respite from daily terrors (Jb 7$_{13}$), as perfumed (Pr 7$_{17}$ 2 C 16$_{14}$); as asset seized by creditor (Pr 22$_{27}$).

<SUBJ> היה *be* Lv 15$_{26}$ (+ כְּמִשְׁכַּב נִדָּתָהּ *like the bed of*, i.e. affected by, *her menstruation*; || כְּלִי *vessel*, i.e. object for sitting in or on), טמא *be impure* Lv 15$_{4}$ (|| כְּלִי) 15$_{24}$, לקח ho. *be taken* by creditor Pr 22$_{27}$ (if em. qal, *take* bed), נשׂא *raise*, i.e. give relief from Jb 7$_{13}$ (|| עֶרֶשׂ *couch*).

<NOM CL> מִשְׁכָּבִי קֶבֶר *my couch is the grave* Ps 88$_{6}$ (if em. שֹׁכְבֵי *ones who lie down [in]*).

<OBJ> לקח *take* Pr 22$_{27}$ (or em. ho., *be taken*), שׂים *place* Is 57$_{7}$, נתן *give*, i.e. place Ezk 32$_{25}$, נגשׁ hi. *present* to David 2 S 17$_{28}$ (or ins. עַרְשׂת *couches of*, i.e. for, lying down, i.e. as §2; + סַף *bowl*, כְּלִי יוֹצֵר *potter's vessel*), בוא hi. *bring* to David 2 S 17$_{28}$ (if ins. בוא hi.; or ins. עַרְשׂת), הפך *turn* Ps 41$_{4}$ (or em. מִשְׁכָּבוֹ *his bed* to מַכְאֹבוֹ *his pain*; + בְּחָלְיוֹ *in his sickness* [or em. בַּחֲלוֹתוֹ *when he was sick* or לְחָיִל *into strength*]).

נגע hi. *touch* 4QṬohC 1$_{7}$ (unless מַגָּע *contact* of, i.e. with, the bed), עלה *go up (onto)* Gn 49$_{4}$=4QCommGenA 4$_{5}$, רחב *make wide* (appar. to accommodate many lovers) Is 57$_{8}$, נוף *sprinkle (with)* myrrh, aloes, and cinnamon Pr 7$_{17}$ (or em. נַפְתִּי *I have sprinkled* to הֲנִפֹתִי/הֲנַפְתִּי *I have waved*, i.e. נוף hi., or נָטַפְתִּי *I have dripped*, or נָפַתִּי *I have caused to flow*), מלא pi. *fill (with)* spices and ointments 2 C 16$_{14}$ (+ קֶבֶר *grave*).

<CSTR> מִשְׁכְּבֵי אָבִיךָ *your father's bed(s)* Gn 49$_{4}$=4QCommGenA 4$_{5}$ (אביכה), מִשְׁכַּב נִדָּתָהּ *the bed of*, i.e. affected by, *her menstruation* Lv 15$_{26}$.

חֲדַר מִשְׁכָּבְךָ *your bedroom* Ex 7$_{28}$ (Sam חדרי מִשְׁכָּבֶיךָ *your bedrooms*; + מִטָּה *couch*) 2 K 6$_{12}$ (מִשְׁכָּבֶךָ) Ec 10$_{20}$ (mss) (L חַדְרֵי מִשְׁכָּבְךָ *your bedrooms*), חֲדַר מִשְׁכָּבוֹ *his bedroom* 2 S 4$_{7}$ (+ מִטָּה), בית המשכב *the building of the dining couch(es)*, i.e. refectory (unless *the place of lying down*, i.e. graveyard, as §2) 3QTr 11$_{16}$, כָּל־מִשְׁכָּבוֹ *all his bed* Ps 41$_{4}$ (or em. מִשְׁכָּבִי all *my bed* or מַכְאֹבוֹ/בִי all *his/my pain*), מגע המשכב *contact of*, i.e. with, *the bed* 4QṬohC 1$_{7}$ (unless מַגֵּעַ a man *touching* the bed), כָּל־הַמִּשְׁכָּב *every bed* Lv 15$_{4.24.26}$.

<PREP> לְ of direction, *(on)to, upon*, + נפל *fall* Ex 21$_{18}$=4QHalakhah[a] 3.1$_{3}$ (וְלֹא יָמוּת וְנָפַל לְמִשְׁכָּב *and does not die but falls upon a bed*; 4Q ולוא י]מו[ת ונפל [למשכ]בו *and does not die but falls upon his bed*.

בְּ of place, *in, on*, + שׁכב *lie down* 2 S 11$_{13}$ (וַיֵּצֵא בָעֶרֶב לִשְׁכַּב בְּמִשְׁכָּבוֹ עִם־עַבְדֵי אֲדֹנָיו וְאֶל־בֵּיתוֹ לֹא יָרָד *and in the evening he left to lie on his bed, in the company of the servants of his master, but he did not go to his house*), hi. *lay* 2 C 16$_{14}$; *against*, + נגע *strike*, i.e. touch Lv 15$_{5.21.23}$ (both ‖ כְּלִי *vessel*, i.e. object for sitting in or on).

כְּ *as*, + היה *be* Lv 15$_{26}$.

מֵעַל *from (upon)*, + קום *arise* 2 S 11$_{2}$ (+ לְעֵת הָעֶרֶב *at evening time*).

עַל *upon* Lv 15$_{23}$ (וְאִם עַל־הַמִּשְׁכָּב הוּא *and if he*, i.e. the one touching, *is on the bed;* Sam הִיא if *she*, i.e. menstruant, is on the bed) Jb 33$_{15}$ (בִּתְנוּמוֹת עֲלֵי מִשְׁכָּב *in slumbers on a bed*) 4QapPent 10.1$_{6}$ Ketef Hinnom inscr. 1$_{8}$ ([אנ]חה על מש[כב] *groaning upon his bed;* others [ח העלם ש[*eternity*), + יכח ho. *be reproved* by pain Jb 33$_{19}$, שׁכב *lie down* Lv 15$_{4.24.26}$ (all three כָּל־הַמִּשְׁכָּב אֲשֶׁר יִשְׁכַּב עָלָיו *every bed that he lies upon* [15$_{26}$ תִּשְׁכַּב *she lies*]) 2 S 13$_{5}$, שׁחה htpal. *prostrate oneself*, i.e. bow down or perh. lie down 1 K 1$_{47}$, נוח *rest* Is 57$_{2}$ Si 40$_{5}$ 46$_{19}$, בוא hi. *bring* groaning Si 47$_{20}$ (but perh. עַל *on account of* marriage bed; ‖ צֶאֱצָא *offspring*), ילל hi. *howl* Ho 7$_{14}$ (or em. מִשְׁכְּבוֹתָם howl upon *their beds* to מִזְבְּחוֹתָם howl over *their sacrifices*), בקשׁ pi. *seek* beloved (in a dream or in the bed) Ca 3$_{1}$ (+ בַּלֵּילוֹת *in the night-times*).

פעל *do*, perh. mentally enact, evil Mc 2$_{1}$ (or del. וּפֹעֲלֵי רָע woe to ... *and the doers of evil* or em. וּפֹעַל/וּפָעֳלֵי who plan iniquity and evil behaviour/deeds), חשׁב *reckon*, i.e. plan, iniquity Mc 2$_{1}$ (if em.) Ps 36$_{5}$, אמר *say* Ps 4$_{5}$ (רִגְזוּ וְאַל־תֶּחֱטָאוּ אִמְרוּ בִלְבַבְכֶם עַל־מִשְׁכַּבְכֶם וְדֹמּוּ *tremble, and do not sin; say in your heart, on your beds, and be silent;* or em. וְעַל־מִשְׁכַּבְכֶם דֹּמּוּ *and on your beds be silent* or אִמְרוּ בִלְבַבְכֶם וְאַל־תֶּחֱטָאוּ רִגְזוּ עַל־מִשְׁכַּבְכֶם וְדֹמּוּ *say in your heart*, i.e. ponder, *and do not sin; tremble upon your beds and be silent*), דמם *be silent* Ps 4$_{5}$ (if em.), רגז *tremble* Ps 45 (if em.), רנן pi. *exult* Ps 149$_{5}$ (or em. עַל מִשְׁכְּבוֹתָם perh. *upon their prayer mats* to עַל מִשְׁפְּחוֹתָם *according to their clans* or בְּשִׂמְחַת עוֹלָם *with a rejoicing of eternity*), הרג *kill* 2 S 4$_{11}$.

<COLL> נָתְנוּ מִשְׁכָּב לָהּ *they have set a place for her to lie down* or *they have made a grave for her* Ezk 32$_{25}$.

10. lying (down), in ref. to sexual relations (Lv 18$_{22}$ 20$_{13}$ Nm 31$_{17.18.35}$ Jg 21$_{11.12}$ Is 57$_{8}$ Ezk 23$_{17}$ 1QSa 1$_{10}$ 4QDe 2.2$_{17}$=6QD 5$_{3}$), death (perh. 3QTr 11$_{16}$), sleep (2 S 4$_{5}$), rest (4QṬohA 1.1$_{1}$).

<OBJ> שׁכב *lie down* (i.e. cognate accusative) Lv 18$_{22}$ 20$_{13}$ 2 S 4$_{5}$ 4QDe 2.2$_{17}$=6QD 5$_{3}$ ([ישכב]) 4QṬohA 1.1$_{1}$ (‖ מוֹשָׁב *dwelling*), ידע *know*, i.e. experience Nm 31$_{18.35}$ Jg 21$_{11}$, אהב *love* Is 57$_{8}$ (or em. אָהַבְתְּ מִשְׁכָּבָם *you have loved their lying down*, i.e. having sex with them, to אַהֲבַת מִשְׁכָּבִים perh. you make a covenant for yourself with them [for] *love of lyings down*, i.e. on account of sexual desire; + יָד חָזִית perh. *you have seen their penises*).

<CSTR> משכב יגון *a lying down of grief* 4QṬohA 1.1$_{1}$, משכב יצועי *the lying down of*, i.e. on, *my bed* 1QS 10$_{14}$, מִשְׁכַּב הַצָּהֳרָיִם *the lying down of noon*, i.e. siesta 2 S 4$_{5}$, משכבי זכר *the lyings down of a male* 1QSa 1$_{10}$, מִשְׁכְּבֵי אִשָּׁה *the lyings down of*, acts of intercourse with, *a woman* Lv 18$_{22}$ 20$_{13}$ 4QDe 2.2$_{17}$ (=6QD 5$_{3}$ [אשה]), מִשְׁכַּב זָכָר *lying down of*, i.e. intercourse with, *a male* Nm 31$_{17.18.35}$ Jg 21$_{11.12}$, מִשְׁכַּב דֹּדִים *lying down of love*, i.e. love-making Ezk 23$_{17}$.

אַהֲבַת מִשְׁכָּבִים *love of lyings down*, i.e. sexual desire Is 57$_{8}$ (if em. אָהַבְתְּ מִשְׁכָּבָם *you have loved their lying down*, i.e. having sex with them), בית המשכב *the place of lying down*, i.e. graveyard (unless *building of the dining couch*, i.e. refectory, as §1) 3QTr 11$_{16}$, עַרְשׁוֹת מִשְׁכָּב *couches of*, i.e. for, *lying down* 2 S 17$_{28}$ (if ins. עַרְשׁוֹת).

<PREP> לְ of purpose, *for (the purpose of)* Ezk 23$_{17}$; *in respect of*, + ידע *know* a man Nm 31$_{17}$ Jg 21$_{12}$, woman 1QSa 1$_{10}$.

עִם *with*, i.e. during, + רנן pi. *exult* 1QS 10$_{14}$ (בראשית צאת ובוא לשבת וקום ועם משכב יצועי *when I start to go out or to come in to sit down or to stand up and while I am lying on my bed*).

Also 4QBarka 5$_{1}$ ([מ]שכבי) 4QṬohBc 1$_{12}$ ([מש[כבו ומוש[בו] *his lying down and his dwelling*).

<SYN> §1 כְּלִי *vessel*, i.e. object for sitting in or on, עֶרֶשׂ *couch*, צֶאֱצָא *offspring;* §2 מוֹשָׁב *dwelling*.*

מִשְׁכָּן 139.0.6 n.m. **tabernacle**—cstr. מִשְׁכַּן; sf. מִשְׁכָּנִי, Q (מִשְׁכָּנִי) מִשְׁכְּנוֹ, מ[ו]שכנכה; pl. מִשְׁכָּנוֹת; cstr. מִשְׁכְּנוֹת; sf. Q משכנותי, מִשְׁכְּנוֹתָיו, מִשְׁכְּנוֹתֶיךָ, (מִשְׁכְּנֹתֶיךָ) מִשְׁכְּנֹתֶיהָ, מִשְׁכְּנוֹתֵינוּ, מִשְׁכְּנֹתָם, (מִשְׁכְּנֵיהֶם) מִשְׁכְּנֹתֶיהָ.

1. oft. (tent) **Tabernacle** as **dwelling-place** of Y. during the wilderness journeys: its construction commanded (Ex 20), its elements fashioned (Ex 36), its structure consecrated (Ex 40); it is dismantled, transported and reassembled during the journeying of the Israelites; all sacrifice is to take place at its entrance (e.g. Lv 1$_{3.5}$); in Canaan, it is erected at Shiloh; it is brought to Jerusalem by David (2 S 6$_{17}$), and lodged in the Temple by Solomon (1 K 8$_{4}$), where, at least acc. to Chronicles, it remains (cf. 2 C 29$_{5}$).

2. rarely, **tabernacle,** a smaller inner sanctuary within the Tabernacle proper, and covered by a tent (אֹהֶל) (Ex 26$_{13}$).

3. the temple as **dwelling place** of Y. (Ps 43$_{3}$ 84$_{2}$ Ezk 37$_{27}$), or Jerusalem (Ps 46$_{5}$).

4. dwelling, dwelling-place, of humans (Nm 16$_{24.27}$ 24$_{5}$ Is 32$_{18}$ 54$_{2}$ Jr 9$_{18}$ 30$_{18}$ 51$_{30}$ Ezk 25$_{4}$ Hb 1$_{6}$ Ps 78$_{28}$ [if em.] 87$_{2}$ Jb 18$_{21}$ 21$_{28}$), sometimes specif. **tent** (Ca 1$_{8}$).

5. grave, viewed as a dwelling-place (Is 22$_{16}$ Ps 49$_{12}$ [if em.] perh. 3QTr 6$_{11}$).

6. dwelling of wild ass (Jb 39$_{6}$).

7. pl. sometimes appar. used of one dwelling place (Ps 43$_{3}$ 49$_{12}$ 84$_{2}$ 132$_{5.7}$ Jb 18$_{21}$ 39$_{6}$).*

<SUBJ> היה *be(come)* Ex 26$_{6}$||36$_{13}$ (+ אֶחָד *one,* i.e. whole) 40$_{9}$ (+ קֹדֶשׁ *holiness,* i.e. made sacred) Ezk 37$_{27}$ (וְהָיָה מִשְׁכָּנִי עֲלֵיהֶם *and my tabernacle,* or perh. *my presence, will be over them*), טוב *be good* Nm 24$_{5}$ (|| אֹהֶל *tent*), שׁכן *dwell* Jos 22$_{19}$, קום ho. *be erected* Ex 40$_{17}$ Nm 9$_{15(Sam)}$ (MT hi. *erect* tabernacle), ירד ho. *be taken down* Nm 10$_{17}$, פקד pu. *be mustered,* i.e. described in detail Ex 38$_{21}$, נסע *set off* Nm 1$_{51}$, חנה *encamp* Nm 1$_{51}$.

<NOM CL> וּמִשְׁמֶרֶת בְּנֵי־גֵרְשׁוֹן ... הַמִּשְׁכָּן *and the responsibility of the Gershonites ... was the tabernacle* Nm 3$_{25}$ (|| אֹהֶל *tent* of meeting), קִרְבָּם בָּתֵּימוֹ עוֹלָם מִשְׁכְּנֹתָם לְדֹר וָדֹר appar. *their inside is their home(s) for ever, their dwelling places for generation upon generation* Ps 49$_{12}$ (or em. קְבָרִים *graves* are, or קִבְרָם *their grave* is; + בַּיִת *house*), אֵלֶּה מִשְׁכְּנוֹת עַוָּל *these are the dwelling places of an unjust one* Jb 18$_{21}$ (|| מָקוֹם *place* [sg.]).

קָדֹשׁ מִשְׁכַּן עֶלְיוֹן *holy is the dwelling place of the Most High* Ps 46$_{5}$ (if em. קְדֹשׁ מִשְׁכְּנֵי עֶלְיוֹן *the holy one,* i.e. holiest, *of the dwelling places of the Most High*), מַה־יְּדִידוֹת מִשְׁכְּנוֹתֶיךָ *how beloved are your dwelling places,* O Y. of hosts, perh. with pl. in ref. to single dwelling place (Jerusalem) Ps 84$_{2}$.

מִשְׁכָּנִי אֲשֶׁר בְּתוֹכָם *my tabernacle, which is among them* Lv 15$_{31}$, וּמִשְׁכַּן י׳ ... בַּבָּמָה בְּגִבְעוֹן *and the tabernacle of Y. ... was in the high place at Gibeon* 1 C 21$_{29}$ (mss ins. אֲשֶׁר the high place *that was* at Gibeon; || מִזְבַּח *altar*), משכנו בציון *his dwelling place is in Zion* 4QapPs 1$_{10}$ (WA משכני בצפיכ[ן] appar. *my dwelling place is with your spies*).

<OBJ> בוא hi. *bring* Ex 39$_{33}$ (or em. הַמִּשְׁכָּן to הַבְּגָדִים *the* priestly *garments*), נשׂא *raise,* i.e. carry Nm 1$_{50}$ 10$_{17}$ 1 C 23$_{26}$, כסה pi. *cover,* of curtains Ex 26$_{13}$, of cloud Nm 9$_{15}$ (Sam ho. *be erected,* of tabernacle), קום hi. *erect* Ex 26$_{30}$ 40$_{2.18}$ Nm 1$_{51}$ 7$_{1}$ 9$_{15}$ 10$_{21}$, מלא *fill* (of glory of Y.) Ex 40$_{34.35}$.

עשׂה *make* Ex 26$_{1}$||36$_{8}$ (+ עֶשֶׂר יְרִיעֹת *[of] ten curtains*) 35$_{11}$ 1 C 21$_{29}$, חקק *hew out* Is 22$_{16}$ (+ קֶבֶר *grave*), ירד hi. *take down* Nm 1$_{51}$, שׂים *place,* i.e. appoint Jb 39$_{6}$ (שַׂמְתִּי ... מִשְׁכְּנוֹתָיו מְלֵחָה *I have appointed saltland [as] his dwelling places;* || בַּיִת *house* [sg.]), נתן *give,* i.e. place Lv 26$_{11}$ (or em. בְּרִית *covenant*) Ezk 25$_{4}$ (|| טִירָה *encampment*), מצא *find* Ps 132$_{5}$, נטשׁ *abandon* Ps 78$_{60}$ (|| אֹהֶל *tent*), ירשׁ *possess* Hb 1$_{6}$.

קדשׁ pi. *sanctify* Ex 40$_{9}$ Lv 8$_{10}$ Nm 7$_{1.1}$ (|| מִזְבֵּחַ *altar*) Ps 46$_{5}$ (if em. קְדֹשׁ *the holy one,* i.e. holiest, *of* the dwelling places of the Most High, to קִדֵּשׁ מִשְׁכָּנוֹ the Most High *has sanctified his dwelling place;* + עִיר־אֱלֹהִים *the city of God*), משׁח *anoint* Ex 40$_{9}$ Lv 8$_{10}$ Nm 7$_{1.1}$, שׁרת pi. *minister (to)* Nm 1$_{50}$, רחם pi. *take pity (on)* Jr 30$_{18}$ (|| אֹהֶל *tent;* or del. אֹהֶל and em. מִשְׁכָּן to שְׁבִית *captivity*).

שׁלך hi. *throw (down)* Jr 9$_{18}$ (or em. הִשְׁלִיכוּ מִשְׁכְּנוֹתֵינוּ *they have thrown down our dwelling places* to הָשְׁלַכְנוּ מִמִּשְׁכְּנוֹתֵינוּ *we have been thrown from our dwelling places* or הִשְׁלַכְנוּ *we have thrown down* our dwelling places), יצת hi. *set ablaze* Jr 51$_{30}$ (|| בְּרִיחַ *bar*), טמא pi. *defile* Lv 15$_{31}$ Nm 19$_{13}$, חלל pi. *profane* Ps 74$_{7}$ (+ לָאָרֶץ so as to fall *to the ground*).

<CSTR> מִשְׁכַּן י׳ *the tabernacle of Y.* Lv 17$_{4}$ Nm 16$_{9}$

(+ עֲבֹדַת *service of* the tabernacle of Y.) 16$_{24.27}$ (if in both em. מִשְׁכַּן־קֹרַח דָּתָן וַאֲבִירָם *the dwelling place of Korah, Dathan and Abiram* Nm 16$_{24.27}$ (to מִשְׁכַּן י׳ *the tabernacle of Y.*) 17$_{28}$ 19$_{13}$ 31$_{30.47}$ (both + שֹׁמְרֵי מִשְׁמֶרֶת *the keepers of the service of* the tabernacle of Y.) Jos 22$_{19}$ 1 C 16$_{39}$ 21$_{29}$ 2 C 1$_{5}$ 29$_{6}$, מִשְׁכְּנֵי עֶלְיוֹן *the dwelling places of the Most High* Ps 46$_{5}$ (or em. מִשְׁכָּנוֹ the Most High has sanctified *his dwelling place* or מִשְׁכַּן holy is *the dwelling place of* the Most High), משכן אלוהי[ ] דעת *the dwelling place of the God of knowledge* 4QShir Shabb^{f} 20.2$_{7}$.

משכן רוש רום כבוד מלכותו *the dwelling place of the head of the height of the glory of his kingship* 4QShir Shabb^{d} 1.2$_{10}$, מִשְׁכַּן כְּבוֹדֶךָ *the dwelling place of your glory* Ps 26$_{8}$ (+ מְקוֹם *the place of* the dwelling place of; + מְעוֹן *dwelling place*) 74$_{7(mss)}$ (מִשְׁכַּן־; L שְׁמֶךָ *of your name*), מִשְׁכַּן־שְׁמֶךָ *the dwelling place of your name* Ps 74$_{7}$ (mss כְּבוֹדֶךָ *of your glory*).

מִשְׁכַּן שִׁלוֹ *the tabernacle of*, i.e. at, *Shiloh* Ps 78$_{60}$ (mss שִׁילֹה/שִׁלֹה), מִשְׁכַּן בֵּית אֱלֹהִים *the tabernacle of the house of God* 1 C 6$_{33}$ (+ כָּל־עֲבֹדַת *all the service of*), מִשְׁכַּן אֹהֶל מוֹעֵד *the tabernacle of the tent of meeting* Ex 39$_{32}$ 40$_{2.6.29}$ (both אֹהֶל־; in Sam, all four הַמִּשְׁכָּן אֹהֶל מוֹעֵד *the tabernacle, the tent of meeting*, i.e. app.) 1 C 6$_{17}$ (אֹהֶל־), מִשְׁכַּן הָעֵדֻת *the tabernacle of the testimony* Ex 38$_{21}$ Nm 1$_{50.53.53}$ (מִשְׁמֶרֶת מִשְׁכַּן הָעֵדוּת *the service of the tabernacle of the testimony*) 10$_{11}$.

משכן המלכא *the dwelling place of the queen* 3QTr 6$_{11}$, מִשְׁכְּנוֹת יַעֲקֹב *the dwelling places of Jacob* Ps 87$_{2}$ (+ כֹּל *all* the dwelling places of), מִשְׁכַּן־קֹרַח דָּתָן וַאֲבִירָם *the dwelling place of Korah, Dathan and Abiram* Nm 16$_{24.27(mss)}$ (L קֹרַח; or in both del. דָּתָן וַאֲבִירָם or em. קֹרַח דָּתָן וַאֲבִירָם to י׳ the tabernacle of *Y.*), מִשְׁכְּנוֹת עַוָּל *the dwelling places of an unjust one* Jb 18$_{21}$, מִשְׁכְּנוֹת רְשָׁעִים *the dwelling places of wicked ones* Jb 21$_{28}$ (+ אֹהֶל *the tent of* the dwelling places [ms lacks אֹהֶל]; or del. אֹהֶל or מִשְׁכְּנוֹת), מִשְׁכְּנוֹת הָרֹעִים *the dwelling places of the shepherds* Ca 1$_{8}$, מִשְׁכְּנוֹת מִבְטַחִים *dwelling places of security* Is 32$_{18}$.

תַּבְנִית הַמִּשְׁכָּן *the model of the tabernacle* Ex 25$_{9}$, פְּקוּדֵי הַמִּשְׁכָּן *the mustered ones*, i.e. inventory, *of the tabernacle* Ex 38$_{21}$, עֲבֹדַת הַמִּשְׁכָּן *the service of the tabernacle* Ex 39$_{32(Sam)}$ (+ כָּל־ *all* the service of) 39$_{40}$ (+ כָּל־כְּלֵי *all the vessels of*, i.e. used in, *the service of*) Nm 3$_{7.8}$ (or del.), עֲבֹדַת מִשְׁכַּן *the service of the tabernacle of* Ex 39$_{32}$ (+ כָּל־ *all* the service of) Nm 16$_{9}$ 1 C 6$_{33}$ (+ כָּל־), מִשְׁמֶרֶת מִשְׁכַּן *the service of the tabernacle of* Nm 1$_{53}$ 31$_{30.47}$ (both + שֹׁמְרֵי *the keepers of* the service of), פְּקֻדַּת כָּל־הַמִּשְׁכָּן *responsibility of*, i.e. for, *all the tabernacle* Nm 4$_{16}$.

אֲחֹרֵי הַמִּשְׁכָּן *the back [parts] of the tabernacle* Ex 26$_{12}$, יַרְכְּתֵי הַמִּשְׁכָּן *the recesses of the tabernacle* Ex 26$_{22}$||36$_{27}$, פֶּתַח הַמִּשְׁכָּן *the entrance of the tabernacle* Ex 35$_{15}$ 40$_{6(Sam).29(Sam)}$, פֶּתַח מִשְׁכַּן *(at) the entrance of the tabernacle of* the tent of meeting Ex 40$_{6.29}$, צִדֵּי הַמִּשְׁכָּן *the sides of the tabernacle* Ex 26$_{13}$, צֶלַע(־)הַמִּשְׁכָּן *the side of the tabernacle* Ex 26$_{20.26.27}$||36$_{25.31.32(Sam, mss)}$ 26$_{35}$, יֶרֶךְ הַמִּשְׁכָּן *the side of the tabernacle* Ex 26$_{35}$ (Gnz, Sam)||40$_{22.24}$ Nm 3$_{29.35}$, חֲצַר הַמִּשְׁכָּן *the courtyard of the tabernacle* Ex 27$_{9}$, קַרְקַע הַמִּשְׁכָּן *the floor of the tabernacle* Nm 5$_{17}$ (or em. הַמִּזְבֵּחַ of *the altar*).

קַרְשֵׁי הַמִּשְׁכָּן *the planks of the tabernacle* Ex 26$_{17}$||36$_{22}$ (+ כֹּל *all* the planks of) 36$_{32}$ Nm 3$_{36}$ 4$_{31}$, קַרְשֵׁי צֶלַע(־)הַמִּשְׁכָּן *the planks of the side of the tabernacle* Ex 26$_{26.27.27}$||36$_{31.32.32(Sam, mss)}$, מְקֻצְעֹת הַמִּשְׁכָּן appar. *the cornered pieces of the tabernacle* Ex 26$_{23}$||36$_{28}$ (or em. מִקְצֹעֹת *corners of*).

כֹּל כְּלֵי הַמִּשְׁכָּן *all the vessels of the tabernacle* Ex 27$_{19}$, כָּל־כְּלֵי עֲבֹדַת הַמִּשְׁכָּן *all the vessels of*, i.e. used in, *the service of the tabernacle* Ex 39$_{40}$, יִתְדֹת הַמִּשְׁכָּן *the tentpegs of the tabernacle* Ex 35$_{18}$ 38$_{31}$ (+ כָּל־ *all* the tentpegs of), יְרִיעֹת הַמִּשְׁכָּן *the curtains of the tabernacle* Nm 4$_{25}$, יְרִיעוֹת מִשְׁכְּנוֹתַיִךְ *the curtains of your dwelling places* Is 54$_{2}$ (+ אֹהֶל *tent*), אֹהֶל מִשְׁכְּנוֹת *the tent of the dwelling places of* wicked ones Jb 21$_{28}$ (ms lacks אֹהֶל; or del. אֹהֶל or מִשְׁכְּנוֹת).

נֹשְׂאֵי הַמִּשְׁכָּן *the bearers of the tabernacle* Nm 10$_{17}$, קְדֹשׁ מִשְׁכְּנֵי *the holy one*, i.e. holiest, *of the dwelling places of* the Most High Ps 46$_{5}$ (or em. קְדֹשׁ מִשְׁכַּן *holy is the dwelling place of* the Most High, or קִדֵּשׁ מִשְׁכָּנוֹ the Most High *has sanctified his dwelling place*), כָּל־הַמִּשְׁכָּן *all the tabernacle* Nm 4$_{16}$, כֹּל מִשְׁכְּנוֹת *all the dwelling places of* Jacob Ps 87$_{2}$.

<APP> דְּבִיר *inner sanctuary* 4QShirShabb^{d} 1.2$_{10}$,

מִשְׁכָּן *tabernacle* Ex 38$_{21}$, אֹהֶל *tent* Ps 78$_{60}$, specif. tent of meeting Ex 39$_{32(Sam)}$ (MT מִשְׁכַּן אֹהֶל מוֹעֵד *the tabernacle of the tent of meeting,* i.e. cstr.) 39$_{33}$ (or em. הַמִּשְׁכָּן to הַבְּגָדִים *the* priestly *garments*) 40$_{2(Sam).6(Sam).29(Sam)}$ (in all three, MT מִשְׁכַּן אֹהֶל מוֹעֵד) Nm 3$_{25}$.

<PREP> לְ of possession, of,*(belonging) to* Ex 26$_{15.18}$|| 36$_{20.23}$ (הַקְּרָשִׁים לַמִּשְׁכָּן *the planks of the tabernacle*) 38$_{20}$ (כָּל־הַיְתֵדֹת לַמִּשְׁכָּן וְלֶחָצֵר *all the tentpegs of the tabernacle and of the court*; or del. לַמִּשְׁכָּן וְ) 40$_{5.28}$ (both מָסַךְ הַפֶּתַח לַמִּשְׁכָּן *the screen of the entrance of the tabernacle*) Nm 1$_{50}$ (עַל־מִשְׁכַּן הָעֵדֻת ... וְעַל כָּל־ אֲשֶׁר־לוֹ *in charge of the tabernacle of the testimony ... and in charge of all that pertains to it*; or em. בּוֹ everything that is *inside it*); of direction, *to,* + בוא *come* Ps 132$_{7}$ (|| הֲדֹם רַגְלָיִם *footstool*).

סָבִיב לְ *around,* + קום hi. *establish* courtyard Ex 40$_{3}$ (|| מִזְבֵּחַ *altar*), חנה *encamp* Nm 1$_{50.53}$, נפל hi. *cause* birds *to drop* Ps 78$_{28}$ (or em. qal *fall*, of birds; סָבִיב לְמִשְׁכְּנֹתָיו *around his dwelling places*; or em. מִשְׁכְּנֹתָם/ מִשְׁכְּנֹתֵיהֶם/מִשְׁכְּנֵיהֶם *around their dwelling places;* + מַחֲנֶה *camp*); מִסָּבִיב לְ *from around,* + עלה *go up,* i.e. depart Nm 16$_{24}$ (|| אֹהֶל *tent*).

בְּ of place, *in* Ex 40$_{9}$ Lv 8$_{10}$ (both הַמִּשְׁכָּן וְאֶת־כָּל־ אֲשֶׁר־בּוֹ *the tabernacle and everything that is inside it*) Nm 1$_{50}$ (עַל־מִשְׁכַּן הָעֵדֻת ... וְעַל כָּל־אֲשֶׁר־בּוֹ *in charge of the tabernacle of the testimony ... and in charge of everything that is inside it*; if em. לוֹ all that *pertains to it*) 4$_{16}$ (כָּל־הַמִּשְׁכָּן וְכָל־אֲשֶׁר־בּוֹ *all the tabernacle and everything that is inside it*) perh. 4QBéat 28$_{3}$, + ישׁב *dwell* Is 32$_{18}$ (|| מְנוּחָה *resting place,* + נָוֶה *dwelling place*), הלך htp. *go about* 2 S 7$_{6}$||1 C 17$_{5}$ (if ins. הלך htp. and em. מִן *from* to בְּ at 1 C), נפל *fall* in praise 4Q ShirShabb[f] 20.2$_{7}$ ([במשכ]ן), חפר *dig* 3QTr 6$_{11}$ (unless pass. *be buried*).

מִן of direction, *from,* + היה *be* 1 C 17$_{5}$ (or ins. הלך htp. *go about,* and/or em. מִן *from* to בְּ *in,* as ||2 S 17$_{6}$), שׁלך ho. *be thrown,* i.e. be forcibly removed Jr 9$_{18}$ (if em. הִשְׁלִיכוּ מִשְׁכְּנוֹתֵינוּ *they have thrown down our dwelling places* to הָשְׁלַכְנוּ מִמִּשְׁכְּנוֹתֵינוּ *we have been thrown from our dwelling places*), סבב hi. *turn face* 2 C 29$_{6}$.

מֵעַל *from (above),* + עלה ni. *arise,* i.e. depart (of cloud) Ex 40$_{36}$ Nm 10$_{11}$, of Israelites Nm 16$_{24}$ (+ מִסָּבִיב *from around* tabernacle).

עַל *over* Ex 26$_{7}$||36$_{14}$ (לְאֹהֶל עַל־הַמִּשְׁכָּן *for a tent over the tabernacle*) 40$_{38}$ (כִּי עֲנַן י׳ עַל־מִשְׁכָּן יוֹמָם *for a cloud of Y. was over the tabernacle through the day*; or em. הֶעָנָן *the cloud* was), + היה *be* (of cloud) Nm 9$_{15.20}$, שׁכן *dwell* (of cloud) Nm 9$_{18.22}$, ארך hi. *prolong stay* (of cloud) Nm 9$_{19.22}$ (or del. עַל־הַמִּשְׁכָּן *over the tabernacle*), פרשׂ *spread* tent Ex 40$_{19}$ (or em. אֹהֶל *tent* to קְלָעִים *hangings* or יְרִיעוֹת *curtains*), perh. שׂים *place* covering of tent Ex 40$_{19}$ (unless עָלָיו *over it* refers to tent, not tabernacle); *in charge of,* + פקד hi. *appoint* Levites Nm 1$_{50}$; *at, by,* + רעה *graze* kids Ca 1$_{8}$; סָבִיב עַל *around* Nm 3$_{23}$ 4$_{26}$ (both הֶחָצֵר אֲשֶׁר עַל־הַמִּשְׁכָּן ... סָבִיב *the court that was around the tabernacle;* || מִזְבֵּחַ *altar*).

אֶל *(in)to,* + היה *be* 1 C 17$_{5}$ (if ins. אֶל־מִשְׁכָּן *to tabernacle;* and/or ins. הלך htp. *go about* from tabernacle to tabernacle), בוא hi. *bring* Ex 40$_{21}$ Ps 43$_{3}$ (+ הַר־קֹדֶשׁ *mountain of* your *holiness*), קרב *approach* Nm 17$_{28}$.

לִפְנֵי *in front of* Jos 22$_{29}$ (מִזְבַּח י׳ ... אֲשֶׁר לִפְנֵי מִשְׁכָּנוֹ *the altar of Y. ... that is in front of his tabernacle*), + שׁרת pi. *minister* 1 C 6$_{17}$, חנה *encamp* Nm 3$_{38}$ (|| אֹהֶל *tent* of meeting), קרב hi. *present* offering Lv 17$_{4}$ Nm 7$_{3}$, עזב *leave* Zadok and other priests 1 C 16$_{39}$, שׂים *place* 2 C 1$_{5}$ (וּמִזְבַּח הַנְּחֹשֶׁת ... שָׂם *and the altar of bronze ... he placed* before the tabernacle of Y.; mss שָׁם the altar of bronze ... *was there* before the tabernacle of Y.).

אַחֲרֵי *behind,* + חנה *encamp* Nm 3$_{23}$.

<COLL> וָאֶהְיֶה מִתְהַלֵּךְ בְּאֹהֶל וּבְמִשְׁכָּן perh. *and I have been going about in a tent, that is to say, a tabernacle* 2 S 7$_{6}$ (or del. וּבְ ;אֹהֶל ||1 C 17$_{5}$ וָאֶהְיֶה מֵאֹהֶל אֶל־אֹהֶל וּמִמִּשְׁכָּן *and I have been from tent to tent, that is to say, from a tabernacle* [or ins. אֶל־מִשְׁכָּן from tabernacle *to tabernacle* or em. as 2 S]).

הַמִּשְׁכָּן ... כֵּלָיו *the tabernacle ... (and) its vessels* Ex 25$_{9}$ 39$_{33}$ (or em. הַמִּשְׁכָּן to הַבְּגָדִים *the* priestly *garments*) 40$_{9}$ Nm 1$_{50}$ 3$_{36}$ 4$_{16}$ 7$_{1}$ 1 C 23$_{26}$, לְכֹל כְּלֵי הַמִּשְׁכָּן בְּכֹל עֲבֹדָתוֹ וְכָל־יְתֵדֹתָיו *indeed, all the vessels of the tabernacle for all its servicing and all its tentpegs* Ex 27$_{19}$ (Sam וְעָשִׂיתָ אֶת־כֹּל *and you are to make all* the vessels), אֶת־הַמִּשְׁכָּן אֶת־אָהֳלוֹ אֶת־מִכְסֵהוּ אֶת־קְרָסָיו וְאֶת־קְרָשָׁיו אֶת־בְּרִיחָו אֶת־ עַמֻּדָיו וְאֶת־אֲדָנָיו *the tabernacle—its tent and its cover;*

its clasps and its planks; its bars, its posts, and its sockets Ex 35$_{11}$ (mss וְאֶת־אָהֳלוֹ *and its tent*), … אֶת־הַמִּשְׁכָּן אֶת־הָאֹהֶל וְאֶת־כָּל־כֵּלָיו קְרָסָיו קְרָשָׁיו בְּרִיחָיו וְעַמֻּדָיו וַאֲדָנָיו *the tabernacle … the tent and all its vessels; its clasps, its planks, its bars and its posts and its sockets* Ex 39$_{33}$ (Qr) (or em. הַמִּשְׁכָּן to הַבְּגָדִים *the* priestly *garments*), הַמִּשְׁכָּן … אֲדָנָיו … קְרָשָׁיו … בְּרִיחָיו … עַמֻּדָיו *the tabernacle … its clasps … its planks … its bars … its posts* Ex 40$_{18}$, קַרְשֵׁי הַמִּשְׁכָּן וּבְרִיחָיו וְעַמֻּדָיו וַאֲדָנָיו *the planks of the tabernacle and its bars and its posts and its sockets* Nm 3$_{36}$ 4$_{31}$ (וְעַמּוּדָיו), הַמִּשְׁכָּן … הֶחָצֵר סָבִיב *the tabernacle … the court around (it)* Ex 38$_{31}$.

הַמִּשְׁכָּן לְאֹהֶל מוֹעֵד *the tabernacle of the tent of meeting* (cf. Cstr.) Ex 39$_{40}$, הַמִּשְׁכָּן לְאֹהֶל הָעֵדֻת *the tabernacle of*, or, *that is to say, the tent of the testimony* Nm 9$_{15}$, חֹצְבִי מָרוֹם קִבְרוֹ חֹקְקִי בַסֶּלַע מִשְׁכָּן לוֹ perh. *hewing on high his grave, carving in the rock his (eternal) dwelling place* Is 22$_{16}$, מִשְׁכָּנוֹת לֹּא־לוֹ *dwelling places (that are) not his* Hb 1$_{6}$, מִשְׁכָּנוֹת לַאֲבִיר יַעֲקֹב *dwelling places for the mighty one*, or *bull*, *of* Jacob, Ps 132$_{5}$ (|| מָקוֹם *place* [sg.])

Also 4QDibHam^{a} 1.4$_{1}$ (מ[ש]כנכה).

<SYN> מִזְבֵּחַ *altar*, אֹהֶל *tent*, מְנוּחָה *resting place*, מָקוֹם *place*, בַּיִת *house*, הֲדֹם רַגְלַיִם *footstool*, טִירָה *encampment*, בְּרִיחַ *bar*.*

[מֹשֶׁכֶת] 1 n.f. **belt**—pl. cstr. מֹשְׁכוֹת—**belt,** of Orion, less prob. **cord** by which he is dragged along (משׁך),* <OBJ> פתח pi. *release*, i.e. prevent Orion from bringing on the autumnal rains Jb 38$_{31}$ (מַעֲדָן *bond*). <CSTR> מֹשְׁכוֹת כְּסִיל *the belt of Orion* Jb 38$_{31}$. <SYN> מַעֲדָן *bond*.*

משׁל I 81.14.71 vb. **rule—Qal** 78.10.49 Pf. מָשַׁל, מָשְׁלָה, מָשַׁלְתָּ; impf. יִמְשֹׁל (יִמְשׁוֹל ,יִמְשָׁל־), 3fs תִּמְשֹׁל, 2ms תִּמְשֹׁל (תִּמְשָׁל־), יִמְשְׁלוּ (יִמְשָׁלוּ, Q ימושולו); + waw וּמָשַׁל, וּמָשַׁלְתָּ, Q ומשלו; וַיִּמְשְׁלוּ; ptc. מֹשֵׁל (מוֹשֵׁל), מוֹשֵׁל, מֹשְׁלָה, Si מושלת, מֹשְׁלִים, מוֹשְׁלִים, מֹשְׁלֵי, מֹשְׁלוֹ, Qr מֹשְׁלָיו, Q מושליו); impv. מְשָׁל־; inf. מְשֹׁל (מָשֹׁל, Q משול, מְשָׁל־)—**1a. rule, dominate, subjugate, (have) control, have charge, master; implement (rule)** (Dn 11$_{3.4.5}$ [if em.]); **assume authority, presume** (Ex 21$_{8}$ CD 13$_{12}$).

<SUBJ> Y. Jg 8$_{23}$ Is 63$_{19}$ Ps 89$_{10}$ (+ שׁבח pi. *calm* waves, דכא pi. *crush* Rahab, פזר pi. *scatter* enemies) 1QpHab 5$_{13}$, אֱלֹהִים *God* Ps 59$_{14}$ 66$_{7}$, Adam appar. 4QapPs^{b} 1$_{7}$, Cain Gn 4$_{7}$, Joseph Gn 37$_{8.8}$, Sihon Jos 12$_{2}$, Og Jos 12$_{5}$, Job Jb 17$_{6}$ (or em. לִמְשֹׁל he has placed me *to rule* peoples, to לְמָשָׁל *as a proverb of* peoples; unless מֹשֶׁל II, §3 *proverb*), Gideon Jg 8$_{22.23}$, Israel Dt 15$_{6}$ (|| עבט hi. *lend*, :: עבט *borrow*) Mc 5$_{1}$ (§1b) appar. 4QapPs^{a} 76$_{15}$ (perh. §1b), Philistines Jg 14$_{4}$ 15$_{11}$.

אִישׁ *man* Gn 3$_{16}$ (unless משׁל II *be like*) Jg 9$_{2.2}$ Jr 22$_{30}$ (+ ישׁב עַל־כִּסֵּא *sit upon throne*) Zc 6$_{13}$ (+ נשׂא הוֹד *raise*, perh. be clothed in, *majesty*, ישׁב *sit*, i.e. be enthroned; or del. משׁל or ישׁב) 2 C 7$_{18}$ (+ קום כִּסֵּא hi. *establish throne*) Si 41$_{2}$(Bmg) (איש נוקש ומושל בכל *a man trapped, although ruling over everything*, unless ומושל = a man trapped *and dominated*, i.e. pu.; B איש כושל ינקש בכל *a stumbling man will trip against everything*; Bmg איש כושל ונוקש בכל *a man stumbling and tripping against everything* [M איש כשל ונוקש ב[כל]]) CD 13$_{12}$ 4Q424 3$_{6}$.

אִשָּׁה *woman* Is 3$_{12}$ (+ נגשׂ *rule*; or em. נָשִׁים *women* to נֹשִׁים *creditors*), i.e. Eve 4QapPs^{b} 1$_{7}$, appar. Jacob 4QNarrC 1$_{10}$, בֵּן *son* Jg 8$_{22.22.23}$ 9$_{2}$, specif. sons of Aaron, i.e. priests 1QS 9$_{7}$=4QS^{d} 3.1$_{7}$ ([בני אה]רן [ימש]ל[ו] *the sons of Aaron will have charge*) 4QpsMos^{e} 1$_{2}$, צֶמַח *shoot* of David Zc 6$_{13}$ (or del. משׁל) 4QpIsa^{a} 8$_{20}$ ([צמח]), זֶרַע *seed*, i.e. offspring 4QJub^{h} 32$_{19}$ (לזורעכה … וי]משלו] *to your offspring … and they will rule*) 11QT 59$_{15}$.

מֶלֶךְ *king* Jos 12$_{2.5}$ Is 19$_{4}$ (+ אָדוֹן *lord*) Dn 11$_{3}$ (+ עשׂה כִּרְצוֹנוֹ *do as he pleases*) 11$_{4.43}$ Ne 9$_{37}$ (+ כִּרְצוֹנָם *as they please*) 4QJub^{h} 32$_{19}$ ([ומלכים … וימש]לו *and kings … and they will rule*) 11QT 59$_{19}$, שַׂר *prince* Dn 11$_{5}$ (מִן־ שָׂרָיו *one of his princes*; + חזק *be strong*), אָדוֹן *lord*, i.e. master of enslaved woman Ex 21$_{8}$, עָשִׁיר *wealthy one* Pr 22$_{7}$ (+ לוה hi. *lend*).

חכם *wise one* Si 9$_{17}$ (if em. מושל עמו חכם *the ruler of his people is a sage*, as §1b, to בעמו a sage rules *over his people* [others עמי *my people*]), עֶבֶד *servant* Gn 24$_{2}$ Pr 17$_{2}$ 19$_{10}$ Lm 5$_{8}$ (+ פֹּרֵק אֵין מִיָּדָם *there is no deliverer from their hand*), כֹּהֵן wicked *priest* 1QpHab 8$_{9}$, מַלְאָךְ *angel* of hostility 4QpsMos^{e} 1$_{10}$ 2.1$_{6}$ ([מל]אכי), אֹיֵב *enemy* 11QT 59$_{20}$, שֹׂנֵא *one who hates* Israel's ancestors Ps 106$_{41}$ (+ נתן בְּיַד *place in the hand of* nations,

לחץ *oppress*, כנע תַּחַת יַד ni. *be humbled under the hand of* enemy), רָשָׁע *wicked one* Pr 29$_2$ (|| רדה *rule* [if em. רבה *be many*]), זֵד *arrogant person* Ps 19$_{14}$ (or em. זָר *stranger*), גּוֹי *nation* Dt 15$_6$ Jl 2$_{17}$, אַחֲרוֹן *last (nation)* 4QpsEzek^a 44$_4$ + 4QpsEzek^c 3.2$_6$ (ה[אח]רון).

בָּשָׂר *flesh* perh. 1QH fr. 19$_2$, *mortal* Si 48$_{12}$, זְרוֹעַ *arm* of Y. Is 40$_{10}$, יָד *hand* of diligent Pr 12$_{24}$ (+ היה לְמַס *become for*, i.e. subject to, *levy*), לָשׁוֹן *tongue* Si 37$_{18(B)}$ (ומושלת בם כליל לשון *and [the] tongue rules over them completely*; B mg, D ומשלח perh. *and* the perfection of the tongue *dispatches* them), perh. לֵבָב *heart* 4QMyst^c 2a$_3$ (מה נכבד לבב והוא ממש[ל] מושל perh. *how honoured is the heart when it implements rule,* unless מָשָׁל *proverb*; others מִמְשָׁל *rule* for מוֹשֵׁל *ruling*), נֶפֶשׁ *soul*, i.e. desire Si 23$_{6(Segal)}$ (+ פחז hi. *make reckless*), רוּחַ *spirit* perh. 4Q415 9$_9$, specif. perverted spirit 1QH 13$_{15}$ fr. 12$_6$ (ר[וח ... משל; others [ר]וח ... מע[ן]), spirit of Belial CD 12$_2$=4QD^f 5.1$_{18}$.

תַּעֲלוּל *capriciousness* or *child* Is 3$_4$ (+ שַׂר *prince*), מַלְכוּת *kingship* of Y. Ps 103$_{19}$ (+ כון כִּסֵּא hi. *establish* throne), שֶׁמֶשׁ *sun* 4QJub^a 2$_8$ (ה[שמ]ש), יָרֵחַ *moon* 4QJub^a 2$_8$, כּוֹכָב *star* 4QJub^a 2$_8$ Gn 1$_{18}$ (+ מֶמְשֶׁלֶת *rule*, בדל hi. *divide*), מָאוֹר *luminary* Gn 1$_{18}$, אוֹרָה *light* 4QAst Crypt 1$_7$ ([ת]משול אורה); subj. not specified, Jb 41$_{25}$ (if em. אֵין־עַל־עָפָר מָשְׁלוֹ *there is not on dust his like*, i.e. מֹשֶׁל II, to מֹשְׁלוֹ *one who can dominate him*) 1QS 9$_{22}$ (כעבד למושל בו *like a servant to the one who rules over him*; || רדה *rule*; =4QS^d 3.2$_7$ (כעבד למוש[ל בו]).

<OBJ> עַם *people* Jb 17$_6$ (or em. לְמֹשֶׁל he has placed me *to rule* peoples, to לְמָשָׁל *as a proverb of* peoples; unless מָשָׁל II, §3 *proverb*), לִוְיָתָן *Leviathan* Jb 41$_{25}$ (if em. אֵין־עַל־עָפָר מָשְׁלוֹ *there is not on dust his like*, i.e. מֹשֶׁל II, to מֹשְׁלוֹ *one who can dominate him*), perh. מִמְשָׁל *rule* Dn 11$_{3.5}$ (if em. וּמָשַׁל מִמְשָׁל רַב מֶמְשַׁלְתּוֹ *and he will rule; a mighty rule will be his government* to וּמָשַׁל מִמְשָׁל רַב מִמֶּמְשַׁלְתּוֹ *and he will rule*, i.e. implement, *a rule greater than that of his* [king of the south's] *government*) 4QMyst^c 2a$_3$ (מה נכבד לבב והוא ממש[ל] מושל perh. *how honoured is the heart when it implements rule,* unless מָשָׁל *proverb*; others מִמְשָׁל *rule* for מוֹשֵׁל *ruling*), מֹשֶׁל *rule* Dn 11$_4$.

<PREP> לְ of direction, *(un)to*, + אֶפֶס *end* of earth Ps 59$_{14}$ (unless לְ relates to ידע *know* to the ends of the earth that God rules in/over Israel), יוֹם *day* 4QAst Crypt 1$_7$ ([ת]משול ... ליום); of benefit, *to, for*, + Y. Is 40$_{10}$.

בְּ of place/time, *at, during*, + Jerusalem Is 28$_{14}$ (§1b; but perh. בְּ *over* Jerusalem), Israel Mc 5$_{14}$ (§1b) Ps 59$_{14}$ 2 C 7$_{18}$ (but perh. in all three בְּ *over* Israel), עַם *people* 2 C 23$_{20}$ (§1b; but perh. בְּ *over* the people), עֵת *time* Jg 14$_4$; of instrument, *by (means of), with*, + פֶּה *mouth*, i.e. command, of fools Pr 26$_{7(Gnz)}$ (§1b; L מָשָׁל *proverb*), גְּבוּרָה *strength* Ps 66$_7$ (but perh. בְּ of cause, *on account of*); of accompaniment, *with, in (a state of)*, + יִרְאָה *fear* 2 S 23$_{3(mss)}$ (§1b).

בְּ *over, in charge of* Si 23$_{6(Segal)}$ perh. 4QWays^b 1.2$_6$ 4QpsMos^e 1$_2$ 4Q415 9$_9$ 4Q416 2.1$_{19}$ 4Q424 3$_6$, + Israel Dt 15$_6$ Jg 14$_4$ Is 63$_{19}$ (+ לֹא־נִקְרָא שִׁמְךָ עֲלֵיהֶם *your name has not been called over them*) Mc 5$_{14}$ (§1b) Ps 59$_{14}$ (but perh. in both בְּ of place, *in*) Lm 5$_8$ 2 C 7$_{18}$ (but perh. בְּ of place, *in*) 1QpHab 8$_9$ (but perh. בְּ of place, *among*) perh. 4QapJoshua^a 3.1$_{11}$ 4QpsMos^e 1$_{10}$ 2.1$_6$, Egypt Is 19$_4$, Judah Is 3$_4$ Jr 22$_{30}$ (but perh. בְּ of place, *in*), Jerusalem Is 3$_4$ 28$_{14}$ (§1b; but perh. בְּ of place, *in*), Salcah Jos 12$_5$ (or em. בְּ to מִן *from*), Bashan Jos 12$_5$ (בְּכָל־הַבָּשָׁן *over all Bashan*), Gilead Jos 12$_5$ (חֲצִי הַגִּלְעָד over *half of Gilead*, with ellipsis of בְּ).

תֵּבֵל *world* 4QPrEnosh 1.2$_7$ (§1b), מִדְרָךְ *step* 4QJub^h 32$_{19}$ (וימש[לו; מדרוך), אֶרֶץ *land* Gn 45$_{8.26}$ (both §1b) appar. 4QpsEzek^c 3.2$_6$ (ובכו[ל הא]רץ perh. rule *even over all the land*; =4QpsEzek^a 44$_4$ [ובכול [הארץ]), הַר *mountain* Jos 12$_5$ (or em. בְּ to מִן *from*), מַמְלָכָה *kingdom* 1 K 5$_1$ (§1b) 2 C 20$_6$ (§1b).

חַטָּאת *sin* Gn 4$_7$, רוּחַ *spirit* Pr 16$_{32}$ (§1b) 4QsapDidB 5$_3$, specif. spirit of Elisha Si 48$_{12}$, appar. תְּהִלָּה *praise* Si 15$_{10}$ (ומשל בה ילמדנה [A] *and the one who masters*, or, as מֹשֵׁל II, *who declaims proverbs about, it will teach it*), מִשְׁפָּט *judgment*, i.e. administration of justice 1QS 9$_7$=4QS^d 3.1$_7$ ([ימש]ל[ו ב]משפט), טוֹב *good* Si 37$_{18(B)}$, רָעָה *evil* Si 37$_{18(B)}$, חַיִּים *life* Si 37$_{18(B)}$, מָוֶת *death* Si 37$_{18(B)}$, הוֹן *(disbursement of) wealth* 1QS 9$_7$=4QS^d 3.1$_7$ ([ימש]ל[ו]), גֵּאוּת *swelling* of sea Ps 89$_{10}$.

אָדָם *humankind* 2 S 23$_3$ (§1b) perh. Hb 1$_{14}$ (§1b) 1QpHab 5$_{13}$, עַם *people* Is 3$_4$ 2 C 23$_{20}$ (§1b; but perh. בְּ of place, *among* the people) Si 9$_{17}$ (if ins. בְּ a sage rules *over* his people), גּוֹי *nation* Dt 15$_{6}$ Ps 22$_{29}$ (§1b; or em. וּמֹשֵׁל appar. *and ruler* to וּמָשְׁלוֹ *and his rule* is over the nations, i.e. מֹשֵׁל I, or וְהוּא מֹשֵׁל *and he rules*, as §1a) 4QpIsa^{a} 8$_{20}$ (הג[ואי]ם) 4QJub^{h} 32$_{19}$ ([וי]משלו בכול [ה]גוים *and they will rule over all the nations*), נַחֲלָה *inheritance* Jl 2$_{17}$.

אִישׁ *man* Jg 8$_{22.23.23.23}$ 15$_{11}$ CD 12$_{2(mg)}$=4QD^{f} 5.1$_{18}$, אִשָּׁה *woman* Gn 3$_{16}$ (unless משל II *be like*), בֵּן *son* Pr 17$_{2}$ 11QPs^{a} 28$_{11(mg)}$ (§1b), יָלוּד *one born* of woman 1QH 13$_{15}$, אָב *father*, i.e. ancestor of Israel Ps 106$_{41}$, אָח *brother* Gn 37$_{8}$, עֶבֶד *servant* 1QS 9$_{22}$=4QS^{d} 3.2$_{7}$ ([כעבד למושל] *like a servant to the one who rules* over him), רָשׁ *pauper* Pr 22$_{7}$, מֶלֶךְ *king* 2 C 9$_{26}$ (§1b) 11QT 59$_{20}$, שַׂר *prince* Pr 19$_{10}$, בַּעַל *lord* of Shechem Jg 9$_{2.2}$, אֹיֵב *enemy* 11QT 59$_{19}$, כְּסִיל *fool* Ec 9$_{17}$ (§1b; or em. מָשָׁל *proverb*), worshipper Ps 19$_{14}$.

גְּדִי *kid* 11QPs^{a} 28$_{4}$ (§1b), מַעֲשֶׂה every *created thing* 1QH 10$_{8}$ (§1b), אֵלֶּה *these (animals)* 4QapPs^{b} 1$_{7}$, דָּגָה *fish* 4QapPs^{b} 1$_{7}$ ([דגת הים] all *the fish of the sea*), perh. רֶמֶשׂ *scurrying creatures* Hb 1$_{14}$ (§1b), יוֹם *day* Gn 1$_{18}$ 4QJub^{a} 2$_{8}$, לַיְלָה *night* Gn 1$_{18}$ 4QJub^{a} 2$_{8}$.

קִנְיָן *property* Ps 105$_{21}$ (§1b), מִכְמָן *treasury* Dn 11$_{43}$ (or em. מַטְמוֹן *treasury*), חֶמְדָּה *preciousness* Dn 11$_{43}$, כֹּל *everything* Gn 24$_{2}$ Ps 103$_{19}$ 1 C 29$_{12}$ Si 41$_{2(Bmg)}$ (unless משל pu., with בְּ of agent, *by* everything) perh. 2Q apProph 6$_{3}$ 4QapPs^{a} 76$_{15}$ (perh. §1b) 4QNarrC 1$_{10(WA)}$ ([ב]כול; §1b).

כְּ *in accordance with*, + רָצוֹן *will* 4QJub^{h} 32$_{19}$ (י]משלו... כרצונם] *they will rule ... according to their wish*) 11QT 59$_{19}$.

מִן of direction, *from*, + Aroer Jos 12$_{2}$, Teman Jos 12$_{2}$, Salcah Jos 12$_{5}$ (if em. בְּ to מִן *from*), הַר *mountain* Jos 12$_{5}$ (if em. בְּ to מִן *from*), נָהָר *river* 1 K 5$_{1}$||2 C 9$_{26}$ (§1b).

עַד *unto*, + Jabbok Jos 12$_{4}$, נַחַל *stream* Jos 12$_{2}$, יָם *sea* Jos 12$_{2.2}$, גְּבוּל *border* Jos 12$_{5.5}$ (if ins. עַד after הַגִּלְעָד *Gilead*) 1 K 5$_{1}$ (§1b).

עַל *upon*, + כִּסֵּא *throne* Zc 6$_{13}$ (or del. משל); *over, in charge of*, + יִשְׂרָאֵל *Israel* 11QT 15$_{19}$, אֶרֶץ *land* 2 C 9$_{26}$ (§1b), עַם *people* Pr 28$_{15}$ (§1b), גְּוִיָּה *body* Ne 9$_{37}$.

תּוֹךְ *within*, + נַחַל *stream* Jos 12$_{2}$ (or em. בְּתוֹךְ in same sense).

בְּתוֹךְ *within*, + רָקִיעַ *firmament* 4QAstCrypt 1$_{7}$ ([ת]משול ... בתוך הרקיע).

<COLL> לֹא־יִמְשֹׁל לְמָכְרָהּ *he must not presume to deliver her over* Ex 21$_{8}$, אל ימשול איש ... להביא איש אל העדה *a person ... must not presume to bring someone into the congregation* CD 13$_{12}$, לעולם אכרית זרעו ממשול עוד *I shall cut off his seed for ever, so as not to rule longer* 11QT 59$_{15}$, ימשלו/ומשלו לעולם *(and) they will rule for ever* 4QNarrC 1$_{10}$, וְאֶל־אִישֵׁךְ תְּשׁוּקָתֵךְ וְהוּא יִמְשָׁל־בָּךְ perh. *your desire will be towards your husband so he will control you* Gn 3$_{16}$ (unless משל II *be like*; or ins. וְאֵלַיִךְ תְּשׁוּקָתוֹ וְאַתְּ תִּמְשְׁלִי בוֹ *and because his desire is towards you, you will [be able to] control him*), וְאֵלֶיךָ תְּשׁוּקָתוֹ וְאַתָּה תִּמְשָׁל־בּוֹ perh. *its desire will be towards you, so you can control it* Gn 4$_{7}$.

הֲמָלֹךְ תִּמְלֹךְ עָלֵינוּ אִם־מָשׁוֹל תִּמְשֹׁל בָּנוּ *will you really reign over us or will you really rule over us?* Gn 37$_{8}$, מַה־טּוֹב לָכֶם הַמְשֹׁל בָּכֶם שִׁבְעִים אִישׁ... אִם־מְשֹׁל בָּכֶם אִישׁ אֶחָד *what is good for you, the ruling of seventy men over you ... or the ruling of one man over you?* Jg 9$_{2}$, וּבִמְשֹׁל רָשָׁע יֵאָנַח עָם *and at the ruling of a wicked one people groan* Pr 29$_{2}$ (mss רְשָׁעִים *wicked ones*).

מֹשֵׁל עוֹד *ruling again* Jr 22$_{30}$, מֹשֵׁל בִּגְבוּרָתוֹ עוֹלָם *ruling by his strength forever* Ps 66$_{7}$, אַל־יִמְשְׁלוּ־בִי *let them not rule over me* Ps 19$_{14}$, מַטֵּה־עֹז שֵׁבֶט לִמְשׁוֹל *a staff of strength, a rod for ruling (with)* Ezk 19$_{14}$, ... לֹא־נָאוֶה לְעֶבֶד מְשֹׁל בְּשָׂרִים *it is not fitting ... for a servant to rule over princes* Pr 19$_{10}$.

1b. ptc. as noun, **ruler, one who controls,** etc. (appar. sg. used collectively at Is 16$_{1}$ [or em.]); at Is 28$_{14}$, perh. play on מֹשֵׁל *teller of proverbs* may be intended (+ אַנְשֵׁי לָצוֹן *men of mockery*); sometimes distinction between these two senses uncertain (e.g. Is 52$_{5}$).

<SUBJ> היה *be(come)* 1 K 5$_{1}$||2 C 9$_{26}$ (1 K וּשְׁלֹמֹה הָיָה מוֹשֵׁל *and Solomon was ruler*; 2 C וַיְהִי מוֹשֵׁל *and he became ruler*) Mc 5$_{1}$ (מִמְּךָ לִי יֵצֵא לִהְיוֹת מוֹשֵׁל בְּיִשְׂרָאֵל *from you for my sake he will come out to become a ruler in/over Israel*; or em. מִמְּךָ יֵצֵא יֶלֶד *from you a child will come out* to become; + אֶלֶף *clan* [or em. אַלֻּף *chief*]) Si 7$_{6(A)}$ (אל תבקש להיות מושל אם אין לך חיל להשבית זדון *do not seek to be a ruler if you have no strength to make impudence cease*), כבד ni. *be honoured* Si 10$_{24}$

(|| שֹׁפֵט *judge*, שַׂר *prince* [B]), הלל poal *be mad* Is 52_5 (if em. ילל hi. *howl*).

בוא *come* 2 C 23_{20} (|| שַׂר *prince*, אַדִּיר *majestic one*) 1QpHab 4_{12} (מושלי[הם] *their rulers*), עבר *pass* or *succeed (one another)* 1QpHab 4_{10}, יצא *go out* Jr 30_{21} (|| אַדִּיר *majestic one* [or em. אַדִּירוֹ מִמֶּנּוּ *his majestic one* will be *one of his own* to אַדִּיר מֵהֶם he will be *more majestic than them*]), נגשׁ ni. *approach* Jr 30_{21}, עמד *arise* 4QpNah 3.1_3 (+ מֶלֶךְ *king*), נפל *fall* 4QpNah 3.2_9 ([מוש]לים]; || נִכְבָּד *honoured one* [נכב]דים]), שׁלח *send* ram Is 16_1 (or em. שִׁלְחוּ־כַר מֹשֵׁל־אֶרֶץ *send a ram, O ruler of the land* to שָׁלְחוּ־כַר/כָּרִם לְמֹשְׁלֵי־ *they sent a ram/rams to the rulers of* the land), ירד hi. *take down* 2 C 23_{20} (if em. וַיּוֹרֶד *and he* [Jehoiada] *brought down* the king, to וַיּוֹרִדוּ *and they brought down*), דלה *hang down* Pr 26_7(Gnz) דַּלְיוּ שֹׁקַיִם מִפִּסֵּחַ וּמֹשֵׁל בְּפִי כְסִילִים appar. *legs hang down [uselessly] from a lame person and*, i.e. as does, *one who rules by the command of fools*; L וּמָשָׁל *and*, i.e. as does, *a proverb* from the mouth of fools; or em. דַּלְיוּ to דָּלוּ, i.e. דלל, in same sense), ישׁב hi. *seat* king on throne 2 C 23_{20}.

בזה *despise* (or perh. בזז *plunder*) 1QpHab 4_5, שׂחק *laugh* 1QpHab 4_5, ילל hi. *howl* Is 52_5 (or em. הלל po. *be mad* or pi. *praise* rulers), נקף hi. *surround* enemies 1QpHab 4_5, תפשׂ *capture* enemies 1QpHab 4_5, הרס *tear down* fortifications 1QpHab 4_5, שׁחת pi. or hi. *destroy* earth 1QpHab 4_{12} (מושלי[הם] *their rulers*), חנן *take pity* Si 13_{12} (if em. אכזרי יתן מושל ולא יחמל *a cruel one implements rule and does not show mercy*, i.e. מֹשֵׁל I, to מושל אכזרי לא יחן ולא יחמל *a cruel ruler has no pity and shows no mercy*), חמל *have mercy* Si 13_{12} (if em.), שׁמע *hear* Is 28_{14}, אזן hi. *listen* Si 30_{27}(E [Segal]) ([האזינו]; || שַׂר *prince*), קשׁב hi. *attend* Pr 29_{12}, פתח pi. *release* Joseph Ps 105_{20} (or em. וַיְפַתְּחֵהוּ *and he released him* to יְרוֹמְמֵהוּ *he elevates him [as]* ruler; || מֶלֶךְ *king*).

<NOM CL> י׳ המושל *Y. is the ruler* 4QNarrC 1_7(mg), אַתָּה מוֹשֵׁל בַּכֹּל *you are ruler over everything* 1 C 29_{12} (+ וְהָעֹשֶׁר וְהַכָּבוֹד מִלְּפָנֶיךָ *and glory and wealth are before you*, וּבְיָדְךָ כֹּחַ וּגְבוּרָה וּבְיָדְךָ לְגַדֵּל וּלְחַזֵּק לַכֹּל *and in your hand is power and strength and in your hand is [the power] to magnify and to strengthen everyone*), וְאַתָּה מוֹשֵׁל בְּכֹל מַמְלְכוֹת הַגּוֹיִם *and you are ruler over all the kingdoms of the nations* 2 C 20_6 (ms הָאָרֶץ kingdoms *of the earth*; + וּבְיָדְךָ כֹּחַ וּגְבוּרָה וְאֵין עִמְּךָ לְהִתְיַצֵּב *and in your hand is power and strength and there is none who can take a stand alongside you*), ... הנה אתה מושל בכל מעשה *behold, you are ... ruler over every created thing* 1QH 10_8 (|| שַׂר *prince*, מֶלֶךְ *king*, אָדוֹן *lord*).

מושל עמו חכם *the ruler of his people is a sage* Si 9_{17} (or ins. בְּ a sage rules *over* his people, as §1a; others עמי *my people*), טוֹב ... מֹשֵׁל בְּרוּחוֹ מִלֹּכֵד עִיר *better is ... one who controls his temper than one who captures a city* Pr 16_{32}, אֲרִי־נֹהֵם וְדֹב שׁוֹקֵק מֹשֵׁל רָשָׁע *a growling lion and a prowling bear is a wicked ruler* Pr 28_{15}.

מֹשְׁלֵי הָעָם הַזֶּה אֲשֶׁר בִּירוּשָׁלָםִ *rulers of this people, who are in/over Jerusalem* Is 28_{14}, כִּי לַי׳ הַמְּלוּכָה וּמֹשֵׁל perh. *for indeed Y. is the king and ruler* or *for to Y. belong kingship and ruler*, i.e. king Ps 22_{29} (or em. וְהוּא מֹשֵׁל for to Y. is the kingship *and he rules*; or em. וּמָשְׁלוֹ *and his rule* is over the, i.e. מֹשֵׁל I).

וְכִי הוּא מֹשֵׁל בְּכָל־אֶרֶץ מִצְרָיִם *and that he was ruler over all the land of Egypt* Gn 45_{26}, וּמֹשֵׁל עַל־מֹשֵׁל *and ruler will be against ruler* or *and there will be ruler upon ruler* Jr 51_{46} (Or lacks וְ *and*), כְּרֶמֶשׂ לֹא־מֹשֵׁל בּוֹ *like scurrying creatures, there is no ruler over them*, i.e. humankind, or *like scurrying creatures, who have no ruler over them* Hb 1_{14} (=1QpHab 5_{13} כרמש למשל בו *like scurrying creatures, to rule over them*, i.e. humankind), אֲשֶׁר אֵין־לָהּ ... מֹשֵׁל *who has no ... ruler* Pr 6_7 (|| קָצִין *judge*, שֹׁטֵר *officer*).

<OBJ> שׂים *place*, i.e. appoint (as) Ps 105_{21} (|| אָדוֹן *lord*) 11QPs^a 28_4 (|| רֹעֶה *shepherd*) 28_{11}(mg) (|| נָגִיד *leader*), רום pol. *elevate (as)* Ps 105_{20} (if em. וַיְפַתְּחֵהוּ *and he released him* to יְרוֹמְמֵהוּ *he elevates him [as]* ruler), קרב hi. *bring near* Jr 30_{21}, לקח *take* Jr 33_{26} 2 C 23_{20}, הלל pi. *praise* Is 52_5 (if em. ילל hi. rulers *howl*).

<CSTR> מֹשֵׁל עַמּוֹ *the ruler of his people* Ps 105_{20} (if em. מֹשֵׁל עַמִּים וַיְפַתְּחֵהוּ *the ruler of peoples and he released him* to מֹשֵׁל עַמּוֹ יְרוֹמְמֵהוּ *he elevates him [as] ruler of his people*) Si 9_{17} (מושל עמו; or ins. בְּ ruling *over* his people, as §1a; others עמי *my people*), משלי קהל *rulers of (the) congregation* Si 30_{27}(E), מושלי

הכתיאים *the rulers of the Kittim* 1QpHab 4$_{5.10}$ 4Qp Nah 3.1$_3$ (מושלי כתיים]) 3.1$_4$ ([מושלי הכתיים]), מֹשֵׁל־אֶרֶץ *(the) ruler(s) of (the) land* Is 16$_1$ (or em. מֹשְׁלֵי־ *rulers of*), מֹשְׁלֵי הָעָם הַזֶּה *rulers of this people* Is 28$_{14}$.

שֵׁבֶט מֹשְׁלִים *the rod of rulers* Is 14$_5$ (|| רָשָׁע *evildoer*) Ezk 19$_{11}$ (if em. שִׁבְטֵי *rods of*), [נ]חלת כול מושלים *the inheritance of all rulers* 4Q423 5$_4$, עֶבֶד מֹשְׁלִים *the servant of rulers* Is 49$_7$, זַעֲקַת מוֹשֵׁל *the outcry of a ruler* among, or over, fools Ec 9$_{17}$ (or em. מִשְׁלֵי the noise of *the proverbs of* fools), פְּנֵי־מוֹשֵׁל *faces of*, i.e. an audience with, *a ruler* Pr 29$_{26}$, רוּחַ הַמּוֹשֵׁל *the spirit*, i.e. anger, *of the ruler* Ec 10$_4$.

<APP> perh. לְבָנוֹן *Lebanon* 4QpNah 1.2$_7$.

<ADJ> אַכְזָרִי *cruel* Si 13$_{12}$ (if em. אכזרי יתן מושל ולא יחמל *a cruel one implements rule and does not show mercy*, i.e. מָשַׁל I, to מושל אכזרי לא יחן ולא יחמל *a cruel ruler has no pity and shows no mercy*), רָשָׁע *wicked* Pr 28$_{15}$, צַדִּיק *righteous* 2 S 23$_3$ 4Q417 1.1$_{13}$.

<PREP> לְ of direction, *to*, + שׁלח *send* ram Is 16$_1$ (if em. מֹשֵׁל־אֶרֶץ appar. send a ram, *O ruler of [the] land* to לְמֹשְׁלֵי־ send a ram *to the rulers of* the land).

לְ of possession, *of, (belonging) to* 1QSb 5$_{28}$ (שבט מושלים *a sceptre of rulers*, but perh. *a rod for*, i.e. to strike, *rulers*, i.e. לְ of benefit) perh. 4QpNah 1.2$_7$.

לְ *as* Gn 45$_8$ (with ellipsis of לְ; || אָדוֹן *lord*, אָב *father [figure]*), 4QPrEnosh 1.2$_7$ (|| שַׂר *prince*) perh. 4QMyst^c 2b$_2$ (והוא למש[ל] perh. *and he will be as a ruler*) 4Q Prayer^c 1$_{11}$ (+ [וישח[ת *and he destroyed*, unless מָשָׁל *proverb*); + וירד *and he will subjugate*, unless מָשָׁל *proverb*), + היה *be* 4QapPs^a 76$_{15}$ (unless לִמְשֹׁל *to rule*, as §1b, not לְמֹשֵׁל *as a ruler*); כְּ *as*, + דבר pi. *speak*, i.e. pronounce, judgments 4Q417 1.1$_{13}$ ([דב]ר).

עַל *concerning* 1QpHab 4$_{5.10}$ (ע[ל]; both + פֵּשֶׁר its *interpretation* concerns); *against* or *upon, in addition to* Jr 51$_{46}$ (מֹשֵׁל עַל־מֹשֵׁל *ruler will be against ruler* or *there will be ruler upon ruler*).

אֵת *with*, + לחם *eat* Pr 23$_1$.

בְּיַד *into the hand of*, + נתן ni. *be given* 1QpHab 4$_5$ 4QpNah 3.1$_4$ ([נתנה ביד מושלי הכתיים] *was given into the hand of the rulers of the Kittim*).

לִפְנֵי *before*, + מאן pi. *refuse (to show obedience)* Si 4$_{27}$.

<COLL> מושל בכול תבל ארצכה *ruler over all the world of your earth* 4QPrEnosh 1.2$_7$(mg), מוֹשֵׁל בַּכֹּל *ruler over everything* 1 C 29$_{12}$ 4QNarrC 1$_{10}$(WA) (מושל [ב]כול), מֹשֵׁל בַּגּוֹיִם *ruler over the nations* Ps 22$_{29}$ (or em. מָשְׁלוֹ *his rule* is over the nations, i.e. מֹשֶׁל I), מֹשֵׁל בְּכָל־אֶרֶץ מִצְרָיִם *ruler over all the land of Egypt* Gn 45$_{8.26}$, מוֹשֵׁל בְּכָל־הַמַּמְלָכוֹת *ruler over all the kingdoms* 1 K 5$_1$, מוֹשֵׁל בְּכֹל מַמְלְכוֹת הַגּוֹיִם *ruler over all the kingdoms of the nations* 2 C 20$_6$ (ms הָאָרֶץ kingdoms of *the earth*), מוֹשֵׁל בְּכָל־הַמְּלָכִים *ruler over all the kings* 2 C 9$_{26}$.

מֹשְׁלֵי הָעָם הַזֶּה אֲשֶׁר בִּירוּשָׁלָם *rulers of this people, who are in/over Jerusalem* Is 28$_{14}$, מוֹשֵׁל בְּיִשְׂרָאֵל *ruler in/over Israel* Mc 5$_1$, מֹשֵׁל רָשָׁע עַל עַם־דָּל *a wicked ruler over a poor people* Pr 28$_{15}$, הַמּוֹשְׁלִים בָּעָם *the rulers among/over the people* 2 C 23$_{20}$, מוֹשֵׁל בָּאָדָם צַדִּיק מוֹשֵׁל יִרְאַת אֱלֹהִים *a righteous ruler over humankind, a ruler of*, i.e. with, *reverence for God* 2 S 23$_3$ (mss בְּיִרְאַת *with reverence for*), מושל בבני בריתו *ruler over the children of his covenant* 11QPs^a 28$_{11}$(mg), מוֹשֵׁל בַּכְּסִילִים *a ruler among*, or *over, fools* Ec 9$_{17}$ (or em. מִשְׁלֵי כְסִילִים *proverbs of fools*).

מושל בגדיותיו *ruler over his kids* 11QPs^a 28$_4$, מֹשֵׁל בְּכָל־קִנְיָנוֹ *ruler over all his property* Ps 105$_{21}$, מֹשֵׁל בְּרוּחוֹ *one who controls his temper* Pr 16$_{32}$.

מֹשֵׁל בְּפִי כְסִילִים appar. *one who rules by the command of fools* Pr 26$_7$(Gnz) (L מָשָׁל *proverb*), מֹשְׁלִים אֶל־זֶרַע אַבְרָהָם יִשְׂחָק וְיַעֲקֹב *rulers for the seed of Abraham, Isaac and Jacob* Jr 33$_{26}$, מֹשֵׁל מַקְשִׁיב עַל־דְּבַר־שָׁקֶר כָּל־מְשָׁרְתָיו רְשָׁעִים *a ruler who listens to a lie, all his ministers will be wicked* Pr 29$_{12}$, ומושלים במשמרותם *and [priestly] rulers with their watches* Si 44$_4$ (unless משלים = *tellers of proverbs* with their nails, i.e. pointed sayings, as משל II).

Also 4QpsEzek^e 64$_1$ (מושלי) 4QMyst^a 26$_1$ (מו[של]) 4QMyst^c 2b$_2$ (unless מָשָׁל *proverb*) 6QHymn 6$_3$ (מ[ושלים]).

<SYN> §1a עבט hi. *lend*, רדה *rule*; §1b שֹׁפֵט *judge*, קָצִין *judge*, מֶלֶךְ *king*, שַׂר *prince*, אָדוֹן *lord*, אַדִּיר *majestic one*, נִכְבָּד *honoured one*, נָגִיד *leader*, שֹׁטֵר *officer*, אָב *father (figure)*, רֹעֶה *shepherd*, רָשָׁע *evildoer*.

<ANT> §1a עבט *borrow*.

Pu. 0.1 Ptc. Si מושל—**be dominated,** <SUBJ> אִישׁ *man* Si 41_{2}(Bmg) (איש נוקש ומושל בכל *a man trapped and dominated by everything,* unless ומושל = a man trapped, *although ruling* over everything, as Qal; B איש כושל ינקש בכל *a stumbling man will trip against everything;* Bmg איש כושל ונוקש בכל *a man stumbling and tripping against everything* [M איש כשל ונוקש [בכל]). <PREP> בְּ of agent, *by,* + כֹּל *everything* Si 41_{2} (Bmg) (unless Qal).

Hi. 3.4.21 Pf. Q המשיל (המשילו, המשילך, המשליכה, המשילמה), המשלת[ה] ([ה]משלתנו); impf. Q ימשיל, 2ms Si תמשיל (Q תמשל, תַּמְשִׁילֵהוּ); + waw וְהִמְשִׁילָם; Si וימשילהו, 2ms Q ותמשל (Si ותמשילם); inf. הַמְשֵׁל (Si המשילם)—**give dominion, control (over), cause to rule (over); let** child **have its own way** (Si 30_{11}); perh. **entrust (to), give responsibility (for)** (Si 45_{17}); perh. **make competent, skilful** (4Q418 81_{15}); perh. as Qal, **rule** (Jb 25_{2}).

<SUBJ> Y. Ps 8_{7} (+ כֹּל שַׁתָּה תַחַת־רַגְלָיו *everything you have placed under his feet*) 4QBer^{b} 4_{2} 4QparaKings 104_{4}(WA) (המשלתה *you have given* your kings *dominion* over your people; others [ו]הכשלתה perh. *and you will cause [them] to stumble* among peoples) 4QPar GenEx 1_{9} 4Q416 $2.3_{12.17}$=4Q418 $9_{12.18}$ 4Q418 $81_{3.9.15}$ 4Q 423 2_{2} 4QDibHam^{a} 8_{6} perh. Si 45_{17} 4QMyst^{a} $13b_{2}$ 4Q Myst^{c} 3_{6} 4QPrFêtes^{c} 191_{4} ([ה]משלתנו), Moses perh. Si 45_{17}, Solomon 47_{19}, מַשְׂכִּיל *instructor* 4QS^{e} 1.3_{19} (למש]כיל]); =1QS 9_{20}=4QS^{b} 8.1_{3}=4QS^{d} 3.2_{4} להשכילם *to instruct them* for להמשילם *to give them dominion*), מֶלֶךְ *king* Dn 11_{39} (+ עָשָׂה כִּרְצוֹנוֹ *do as he pleases,* חלק pi. *distribute* land, רבה hi. *increase* glory).

<OBJ> Aaron Si 45_{17}, אָדָם *Adam* 4QDibHam^{a} 8_{6} ([אדם]), *human being* 4QParGenEx 1_{9} ([אדם]), perh. *humankind* 4QBer^{b} 4_{2} perh. 4QMyst^{c} 3_{6} ([אדם]), אֱנוֹשׁ *humankind* Ps 8_{7}, אִישׁ *man* 4Q424 1_{10} 3.2, אִשָּׁה *woman* Si 47_{19}, perh. specif. *wife* Si 30_{28}, אָב *father* 4Q416 2.3_{17} 4QDibHam^{a} 8_{6} (אדם א[בינו] *Adam, our father*), בֵּן *son* Si 30_{11} (+ ואל תשא לשחיתותיו *and do not overlook his misbehaviour*) 30_{28} (+ אל תתן שלך לאחר *do not give what is yours to another*), specif. son of humankind, i.e. human being Ps 8_{7}, אֵם *mother* 4Q416 2.3_{17}, אֹהֵב *friend* Si 30_{28}, רֵעַ *companion* Si 30_{28}, מֶלֶךְ *king* 4Qpara Kings 104_{4}(WA) (מלכיכ[ה] המשלתה *you have given your kings dominion* over your people; others מלכיה[ם ו]הכשלתה perh. *their kings, and you will cause [them] to stumble* among peoples), אֲשֶׁר *one who* recognizes king Dn 11_{39}.

<PREP> בְּ of place/time, *in, during,* + נְעוּרִים *(time of) youth* Si 30_{11}; perh. *in connection with,* + חָכְמָה *wisdom* of hands, i.e. dexterity, craftsmanship 4Q418 81_{15}.

בְּ *over, in charge of* 4QparaKings 38_{8}(WA) ([ה]משילו בכלם *he caused him to rule over all of them;* others שילו [ ]לם *Shiloh …*) 4Q416 2.3_{17} perh. 4Q418 246_{2} 4Q410 4_{1} ([ה]משיל ב[ן]) ([המ]שילו ב[ן]), + עַם *people* 4Q paraKings 104_{4}(WA) (מלכיכ[ה] המשלתה בעמך *you have given your kings dominion over your people;* others מלכיה[ם ו]הכשלתה בעמ[ן] perh. *their kings, and you will cause [them] to stumble among peoples*), אִשָּׁה *wife* 4Q416 2.4_{2}=4Q418 10_{5} (המש]יל בה]) 4Q416 2.4_{3} 4Q 416 2.4_{6}=4Q418 10_{7} ([ימ]שיל בה]), רדף ptc. *one who pursues* knowledge 4Q424 3_{2}.

גְּוִיָּה *body* Si 47_{19}, מַעֲשֶׂה *creation* Ps 8_{7}, גַּן *garden* 4Q423 2_{2}, אוֹצָר *treasury* 4Q418 81_{9}, הוֹן *wealth* 4Q424 1_{10}, נַחֲלָה *inheritance* 4Q416 2.3_{12}=4Q418 9_{12} 418 81_{3} (ובנ]חלתו]), חֹק *statute* Si 45_{17}, מִשְׁפָּט *judgment* Si 45_{17}.

אֲשֶׁר *that which* is on the earth 4QMyst^{c} 3_{6}, רַבִּים *many* Dn 11_{39}, perh. כֹּל *all* 4QS^{e} 1.3_{19} (להמשילם בכול *to give them dominion over all;* =1QS 9_{20} להשכילם כול הנמצא לעשות *to teach them everything that there is to do;* =4QS^{b} 8.1_{3}=4QS^{d} 3.2_{4} להשכילם בכול *to instruct them in everything* that there is to do [4QS^{d} 3.2_{4} [בכל]).

<COLL> המשילו לאכול פר[י האדמה] appar. *he gave him authority to eat the fruit of the earth* 4QParGenEx 1_{9}, המשילך להתהלך ברצונכה appar. *he has given you authority to go about as you please* 4Q416 2.4_{7}=4Q418 10_{8} ([המש]ילך להתהלך ברצונכה), ובו המשילכה לעבדו ולשמרו *and over it he gave you charge to work it and to protect it* 4Q423 2_{2}.

איש רע עין אל תמשל בהו[ן] *do not let an avaricious person have control of wealth* 4Q424 1_{10}, הַמְשֵׁל וָפַחַד עִמּוֹ *ruling,* or, *allowing to rule, and terror are with him* Jb 15_{2}.

Also 4QRitMar 4_{4} ([ה]משיל]) 4Q418 228_{2} perh. 4Q Myst^{a} 19_{1} (המשל, unless מָשָׁל *proverb*).*

⇨ מֹשֶׁל *rule*, מִמְשָׁל *rule*, מֶמְשָׁלָה *rule*, מֶמְשֶׁלֶת *rule*.

משל II $_{18.2}$ vb. **be like—Qal** $_{10.1}$ Impf. יִמְשֹׁל, יִמְשְׁלוּ (יִמְשָׁלוּ); ptc. מֹשֵׁל (Si מושל, מֹשְׁלִים, Si מושלים); impv. מְשֹׁל; inf. מְשֹׁל.

1a. tell, recite, proverbs, etc. (cf. מָשָׁל *proverb*), <SUBJ> Israelites Ezk 12$_{23}$ 18$_{2}$ (or del. משל), Ezekiel Ezk 17$_{2}$ (|| חוד *propound riddle*) 24$_{3}$ (+ אמר *say*). <OBJ> מָשָׁל *proverb* Ezk 12$_{23}$ 17$_{2}$ 18$_{2}$ (or del. משל) 18$_{3}$ (or em. מְשֹׁל הַמָּשָׁל *the reciting of* this *proverb* to מֹשֵׁל הַמָּשָׁל *a reciter of* this *proverb*, as §1b) 24$_{3}$. <PREP> בְּ of place, *in*, + Israel Ezk 18$_{3}$; *about, concerning*, + appar. תְּהִלָּה *praise* Si 15$_{10}$ (ומשל בה ילמדנה [A] *and the one who declaims proverbs about it*, or, as משל I, *one who has mastery over it, will teach it*); אֶל *to*, + בַּיִת *house* of Israel Ezk 17$_{2}$, of rebellion (i.e. Jerusalem) Ezk 24$_{3}$ (or em. עַל *about, concerning*); עַל *about, concerning*, + Jerusalem Ezk 16$_{44}$ (§1b) 24$_{3}$ (if em. אֶל *to*). <COLL> וְלֹא־יִמְשְׁלוּ אֹתוֹ עוֹד בְּיִשְׂרָאֵל *and they will not recite it again in Israel* Ezk 12$_{23}$, אִם־יִהְיֶה לָכֶם עוֹד מְשֹׁל הַמָּשָׁל הַזֶּה *if there will again be reciting of this proverb* Ezk 18$_{3}$ (or em. מֹשֵׁל *a reciter of*), וְאֶל־אִישֵׁךְ תְּשׁוּקָתֵךְ וְהוּא יִמְשָׁל־בָּךְ perh. *your desire will be towards your husband so he will be like you* Gn 3$_{16}$ (unless משל I *rule*).*

1b. ptc. as noun, **teller of proverbs, sage, bard;** at Is 28$_{14}$, perh. play on מֹשֵׁל *ruler* (+ אַנְשֵׁי לָצוֹן *men of mockery*). <SUBJ> היה *be* Ezk 18$_{3}$ (if em. מְשֹׁל הַמָּשָׁל there will be no more *reciting of* this *proverb* to מֹשֵׁל הַמָּשָׁל there will no longer be *a reciter of* this *proverb*), אמר *say* Nm 21$_{27}$ (or em. הַמֹּשְׁלִים *the bards* would say to בְּמְשָׁלִים they used to say *in proverbial sayings*) Ezk 16$_{44}$, שׁמע *hear* Is 28$_{14}$, משל *tell proverb* Ezk 16$_{44}$. <NOM CL> מֹשְׁלֵי הָעָם הַזֶּה אֲשֶׁר בִּירוּשָׁלָםִ *the tellers of proverbs of*, i.e. to, *this people, who are in Jerusalem* Is 28$_{14}$; כָּל־הַמֹּשֵׁל *everyone who tells proverbs* Ezk 16$_{44}$. <CSTR> מֹשֵׁל הַמָּשָׁל *a reciter of* this *proverb* 18$_{3}$ (if em. מְשֹׁל הַמָּשָׁל *the reciting of* this *proverb*, as §1a). <COLL> ומושלים במשמרותם *and tellers of proverbs with their nails*, i.e. pointed sayings Si 44$_{4}$ (unless משלים = *[priestly] rulers* with their watches; others במשמחותם tellers of proverbs *at their celebrations*).

2. perh. **be like,** אֶל־אִישֵׁךְ תְּשׁוּקָתֵךְ וְהוּא יִמְשָׁל־בָּךְ *your desire will be for your husband, and he will be like you* (in desire).*

<SYN> §1a חוד *propound riddle*.

Ni. $_{4}$ Pf. נִמְשַׁל, נִמְשַׁלְתָּ; + waw וְנִמְשַׁלְתִּי—**be like(ned), be comparable,** <SUBJ> אָדָם *humankind* Ps 49$_{13.21}$ (both + דמה ni. *be destroyed* or *be silent*), מֶלֶךְ *king* of Babylon Is 14$_{10}$, worshipper Ps 28$_{1}$ 143$_{7}$. <PREP> כְּ *as*, i.e. be comparable with, + בְּהֵמָה *beast* Ps 49$_{13.21}$; אֶל be likened *to*, i.e. be like, + מֶלֶךְ *king* of nations Is 14$_{10}$ (+ חֻלֵּיתָ כָמוֹנוּ *you have been made weak*, or *made alone, like us*); עִם be comparable *with*, + יֹרֵד *one who goes down* to the pit Ps 28$_{1}$ 143$_{7}$. <COLL> נִמְשַׁל כַּבְּהֵמוֹת נִדְמוּ appar. *they* (humankind) *are like (the) beasts that are destroyed*, or *silent* Ps 49$_{13.21}$ (mss in both נִדְמָה they are like the beasts, *destroyed* or *silent*).

Pi. $_{1}$ Ptc. מְמַשֵּׁל—ptc. as noun, **teller of proverbs,** <NOM CL> הֲלֹא מְמַשֵּׁל מְשָׁלִים הוּא *is he not (merely) a teller of proverbs?* Ezk 21$_{5}$. <CSTR> מְמַשֵּׁל מְשָׁלִים *a teller of proverbs* Ezk 21$_{5}$.

Hi. $_{1}$ Impf. וְתַמְשִׁלוּנִי—**liken, compare,** <SUBJ> Israel(ites) Is 46$_{5}$ (|| דמה pi. *liken*, + שׁוה hi. *make equal*). <OBJ> Y. Is 46$_{5}$. <PREP> לְ of comparison, *to, with*, + מִי *whom?* Is 46$_{5}$.

<SYN> דמה pi. *liken*.

Htp. $_{1}$ + waw וָאֶתְמַשֵּׁל—**be like(ned), be comparable,** <SUBJ> Job Jb 30$_{19}$. <PREP> כְּ *as*, i.e. be comparable with, + עָפָר *dust* and ashes Jb 30$_{19}$.*

⇨ מָשָׁל *proverb*, מֹשֶׁל *likeness*.

מָשָׁל I $_{39.5.2}$ n.m. **proverb**—cstr. מְשַׁל; sf. מְשָׁלוֹ; pl. מְשָׁלִים; cstr. מִשְׁלֵי—**proverb, (proverbial) saying, maxim, parable, prediction, prophecy, didactic** or **moral verse** or **theme, discourse** (whether or not there is any element of comparison, as relation to משל II *be like* may suggest), specif. sometimes assoc. with Solomon (1 K 5$_{12}$ Pr 1$_{1}$ 10$_{1}$ [or del.] 25$_{1}$ Si 47$_{17}$); assoc. with infamy or derision (Dt 28$_{37}$=11QT 59$_{2}$ 1 K 9$_{7}$||2 C 7$_{20}$ Jr 24$_{9}$ Ezk 14$_{8}$ Mc 2$_{4}$ Ps 44$_{15}$ 69$_{12}$); perh. sg. used collectively (Si 44$_{5}$ 47$_{17}$).

<SUBJ> יצא *go out*, i.e. escape Si 6$_{35}$ (אל יצאך *may* a proverb of understanding *not escape you*; || שִׂיחָה *discourse*), דלה *hang down* Pr 26$_{7}$ (דַּלְיוּ שֹׁקַיִם מִפִּסֵּחַ וּמָשָׁל

בְּפִי כְסִילִים *legs hang down [uselessly] from a lame person and,* i.e. as does, *a proverb from the mouth of fools;* or em. דִּלְיוּ to דַּלּוּ in same sense Gnz וּמֹשֵׁל appar. *and,* i.e. as does, *one who rules* by the command of fools), עלה *go up* Pr 26$_9$ (חוֹחַ עָלָה בְיַד־שִׁכּוֹר וּמָשָׁל בְּפִי כְסִילִים *a thorn goes up into the hand of a drunkard and a proverb into the mouth of fools*), דבר ni./ntp. *be spoken* 4QMyst^b 1a.2b$_1$ (|| חִידָה *riddle*), אמר *say* 1 S 24$_{14}$ perh. Ezk 12$_{22}$ (מָה־הַמָּשָׁל הַזֶּה לָכֶם ... לֵאמֹר *what is this proverb of yours ... that says?*) 18$_2$.

<NOM CL> מָה־הַמָּשָׁל הַזֶּה *what is this proverb?* Ezk 12$_{22}$, sim. Ezk 18$_2$ (if em. מַה־לָּכֶם אַתֶּם מֹשְׁלִים אֶת־הַמָּשָׁל הַזֶּה *what is it to you, you recite,* i.e. why do you recite, *this proverb* to מַה־לָּכֶם הַמָּשָׁל הַזֶּה *what is this proverb,* i.e. what does this proverb mean, *to you?*), זִכְרֹנֵיכֶם מִשְׁלֵי־אֵפֶר *your reminders are proverbs of ashes* Jb 13$_{12}$ (+ גַּב *response*), גַּם־אֵלֶּה מִשְׁלֵי שְׁלֹמֹה *these too are proverbs of Solomon* Pr 25$_1$.

<OBJ> נשׂא *raise,* i.e. declaim Nm 23$_{7.18}$ 24$_{3.15.20.21.23}$ Is 14$_4$ Mc 2$_4$ (|| נְהִי *lament*) Hb 2$_6$ (or del.; + חִידָה *riddle,* מְלִיצָה *satire;* =1QpHab 7$_6$ appar. מְלִיצֵי *interpreters of* riddles) Jb 27$_1$ 29$_1$ (both שְׂאֵת מְשָׁלוֹ *the raising,* i.e. declaiming, *of his discourse*) Si 44$_5$ (but perh. נושאי משל בכתב [B] *bearers of proverbs in writing,* perh. those who transfer spoken proverbs into written form; || מִזְמוֹר *psalm*), אמר *say* 4QMyst^b 1a.2b$_1$, דבר pi. *speak* 1 K 5$_{12}$, משׁל *tell (proverb)* Ezk 12$_{23}$ 17$_2$ (|| חִידָה *riddle*) 18$_2$ (or del. משׁל) 18$_3$ (or em. מְשֹׁל הַמָּשָׁל *the reciting of* this *proverb* to מֹשֵׁל הַמָּשָׁל *a reciter of* this *proverb,* i.e. cstr.) 21$_5$ (מְמַשֵּׁל מְשָׁלִים *a teller of proverbs,* i.e. pi.) 24$_3$, בין *understand* Pr 1$_6$ (|| מְלִיצָה *satire,* + דָּבָר *word* of sages, חִידָה *riddle*) Si 3$_{29}$ (+ חָכְמָה *wisdom*), אזן pi. *evaluate* or *listen intently (to)* Ec 12$_9$, חקר pi. *investigate* Ec 12$_9$, תקן pi. *correct* or *arrange* Ec 12$_9$ (or del. תקן pi.), עתק hi. *transcribe* Pr 25$_1$, שׁבת hi. *end* Ezk 12$_{23}$, שׂים *place,* i.e. cause to be (as) Ps 44$_{15}$ (|| מְנוֹד־רֹאשׁ *shaking of the head*).

<CSTR> מִשְׁלֵי שְׁלֹמֹה *the proverbs of Solomon* Pr 1$_1$ 10$_1$ (or del.) 25$_1$, מְשַׁל הַקַּדְמֹנִי *the proverb of an ancient one* 1 S 24$_{14}$ (mss מָשָׁל הַקַּדְמֹנִי *a proverb, the ancient one;* i.e. app.; or em. מְשַׁל הַקַּדְמֹנִיִּים *the proverb of the ancient ones*), מְשַׁל עַמִּים *a proverb of,* i.e. among, *peoples* Jb 17$_6$ (if em. לִמְשֹׁל *to rule,* to לְמָשָׁל *as a proverb of;* unless מֹשֶׁל II, §3 *proverb;* + תֹּפֶת לְפָנִים perh. *spitting of faces,* i.e. someone to spit at), מִשְׁלֵי כְסִילִים *proverbs of fools* Ec 9$_{17}$ (if em. מוֹשֵׁל בַּכְּסִילִים *a ruler among,* or *over, fools*), משל בינה *a proverb of,* i.e. conducive to, *understanding* Si 6$_{35}$, משלי חכמים *the proverbs of wise ones* Si 3$_{29}$, מִשְׁלֵי־אֵפֶר *proverbs of ashes* Jb 13$_{12}$.

נושאי משל *declaimers,* or *bearers, of proverb(s)* Si 44$_{5(B)}$, מְמַשֵּׁל מְשָׁלִים *a teller of proverbs* Ezk 21$_5$, זַעֲקַת מִשְׁלֵי *the outcry,* i.e. noise, *of the proverbs of* fools Ec 9$_{17}$ (if em. מוֹשֵׁל בַּכְּסִילִים the outcry of *a ruler among,* or *over, fools*), מֹשֵׁל הַמָּשָׁל *a reciter of* this *proverb* Ezk 18$_3$ (if em. מְשֹׁל הַמָּשָׁל *the reciting of* this *proverb,* i.e. obj.), שְׂאֵת מְשָׁלוֹ *the raising,* i.e. declaiming, *of his discourse* Jb 27$_1$ 29$_1$.

<APP> מָשָׁל הַקַּדְמֹנִי *a proverb, the ancient one* 1 S 24$_{14(mss)}$ (L מְשַׁל הַקַּדְמֹנִי *the proverb of an ancient one*).

<ADJ> הַמָּשָׁל הַזֶּה *this proverb* Is 14$_4$ Ezk 12$_{22.23}$ 18$_{2.3}$, מְשָׁלִים הַרְבֵּה *many proverbs* Ec 12$_9$.

<PREP> לְ of direction, *to,* + נטה hi. *extend* ear, i.e. listen Ps 49$_5$ (|| חִידָה *riddle*); *as,* i.e. remembered in, + היה *be* Dt 28$_{37}$=11QT 59$_2$ (|| שְׁנִינָה *taunt* [11QT perh. שְׁנִינָה in same sense], שַׁמָּה *desolation* [Sam appar. שֵׁם *name;* 11QT [שמ[ה], without לְ, i.e. שָׁמָּה *there*]) 1 S 10$_{12}$ (עַל־כֵּן הָיְתָה לְמָשָׁל *therefore it became [as] a proverb*) 1 K 9$_7$ (|| שְׁנִינָה *taunt*) Ps 69$_{12}$ (+ שַׂק make *sackcloth* my clothing, נְגִינָה *[mocking] song,* חֶרְפָּה *reproach*), נתן *give,* i.e. cause to become Jr 24$_9$ (|| שְׁנִינָה *taunt,* חֶרְפָּה *reproach,* קְלָלָה *curse*) 2 C 7$_{20}$ (|| שְׁנִינָה), שׂים hi. *place* Ezk 14$_8$ (or em. qal; mss שמם hi. *appal,* so as to be as a proverb; || אוֹת *sign*), יצג hi. *place* Jb 17$_6$ (if em. לִמְשֹׁל he has placed me *to rule* peoples, to לְמָשָׁל he has set me up *as a proverb of* peoples; unless מֹשֶׁל II *proverb*).

בְּ of instrument, *by (means of), with,* + אמר *say* Nm 21$_{27}$ (if em. הַמֹּשְׁלִים *the bards* would say to בִּמְשָׁלִים they used to say *in proverbs*), פתח *open* mouth Ps 78$_2$ (|| חִידָה *riddle*), סער hi. *amaze* Si 47$_{17}$ (מ[שׁ]ל; || שִׁיר *song,* חִידָה).

<COLL> וַיִּשָּׂא מְשָׁלוֹ וַיֹּאמַר *and he* (Balaam) *uttered his prediction, saying* Nm 23$_{7.18}$ 24$_{3.15.20.21.23}$, עַל־כֵּן הָיְתָה לְמָשָׁל הֲגַם שָׁאוּל בַּנְּבִאִים *therefore, Is Saul too among the prophets?, became [as] a proverb* 1 S 10$_{12}$,

כַּאֲשֶׁר יֹאמַר מְשַׁל הַקַּדְמֹנִי מֵרְשָׁעִים יֵצֵא רֶשַׁע *as the proverb of an ancient one says, From (the) wicked wickedness goes out* 1 S 24$_{14}$ (mss מָשָׁל הַקַּדְמֹנִי *a proverb, the ancient one;* or em. מְשַׁל הַקַּדְמֹנִיִּים *the proverb of the ancient ones*), אֶפְתְּחָה בְמָשָׁל פִּי אַבִּיעָה חִידוֹת מִנִּי־קֶדֶם *let me open my mouth with a proverb, let me produce riddles from antiquity* Ps 78$_{2}$.

מָשָׁל ... בְּכָל־הָעַמִּים *a proverb ... among all the peoples* Dt 28$_{37}$ (בְּכֹל הָעַמִּים) 1 K 9$_{7}$||2 C 7$_{20}$, מָשָׁל בַּגּוֹיִם *a proverb among the nations* Ps 44$_{15}$, מָשָׁל ... בְּכָל־הַמְּקֹמוֹת אֲשֶׁר־אַדִּיחֵם שָׁם *a proverb ... in all the places I push them to* Jr 24$_{9}$ (or del. בְּכָל־הַמְּקֹמוֹת אֲשֶׁר־אַדִּיחֵם שָׁם).

מָה־הַמָּשָׁל הַזֶּה לָכֶם עַל־אַדְמַת יִשְׂרָאֵל *what is this proverb of yours concerning the land of Israel?* Ezk 12$_{22}$, sim. Ezk 18$_{2}$ (מַה־לָּכֶם אַתֶּם מֹשְׁלִים אֶת־הַמָּשָׁל הַזֶּה *what is it to you, you recite,* i.e. why do you recite, *this proverb?;* or em. מַה־לָּכֶם הַמָּשָׁל הַזֶּה *what is this proverb,* i.e. what does this proverb mean, *to you?*), שְׁלֹשֶׁת אֲלָפִים מָשָׁל *three thousand proverbs* 1 K 5$_{12}$ (|| שִׁיר 1005 *songs*).

Also 4QMyst^{c} 1$_{2}$ ([מ]של; || חִידָה *riddle*).

<SYN> שִׁיר *song,* מִזְמוֹר *psalm,* אוֹת *sign,* חִידָה *riddle,* שִׂיחָה *discourse,* שְׁנִינָה *taunt,* חֶרְפָּה *reproach,* מְלִיצָה *satire,* מְנוֹד־רֹאשׁ *shaking of the head,* נְהִי *lament,* קְלָלָה *curse,* שַׁמָּה *desolation.**

⇒ משל II *be like.*

מָשָׁל II 1 pl.n. **Mashal,** Levitical city in Asher, ident. with Mishal (מִשְׁאָל) at Jos 19$_{26}$ 21$_{30}$. <OBJ> נתן *give* to Gershonites 1 C 6$_{59}$ (||Jos 21$_{30}$ מִשְׁאָל *Mashal;* + מִגְרָשׁ *land outside city walls*).

מֹשֵׁל I *ruler, one who controls,* see משל I *rule,* §1b.

מֹשֵׁל II *teller of proverbs, sage, bard,* see משל II *be like,* §1b.

מֹשֶׁל I 2.2 n.[m.] **rule**—Si מושל; cstr. Si מושל; sf. מָשְׁלוֹ—**rule, government, dominion;** perh. **mastery** (Si 50$_{27}$). <NOM CL> וּמָשְׁלוֹ מִיָּם עַד־יָם וּמִנָּהָר עַד־אַפְסֵי־אָרֶץ *and his rule will be from sea to sea and from (the) river unto the ends of (the) earth* Zc 9$_{10}$, מוסר שכל ומושל אופנים לשמעון perh. *Simeon had discipline, intelligence,* or *discipline of,* i.e. leading to, *intelligence, and mastery of (different) situations* Si 50$_{27}$ (unless מֹשֶׁל II *uttering of proverbs, ability to utter proverbs;* or *proverbial wisdom*), מָשְׁלוֹ בַּגּוֹיִם *his rule is over the nations* Ps 22$_{29}$ (if em. מֹשֵׁל *ruler* over the nations). <OBJ> נתן *give,* i.e. implement Si 13$_{12}$ (or em. אכזרי יתן מושל ולא יחמל *a cruel one implements rule and does not show mercy* to מושל אכזרי לא יחן ולא יחמל *a cruel ruler has no pity and shows no mercy,* i.e. משל I, §1b), משל *rule* Dn 11$_{4}$ (מָשְׁלוֹ אֲשֶׁר מָשָׁל *the rule that he ruled,* i.e. implemented). <CSTR> מושל אופנים perh. *mastery of (different) situations* Si 50$_{27}$ (unless מֹשֶׁל II).

<PREP> בְּ of place/time, *during,* or of instrument, *by (means of), with,* + כרה *dig* Nm 21$_{18}$ (if em. בִּמְחֹקֵק בְּמִשְׁעֲנֹתָם *with a staff, with their sticks* [Sam appar. בִּמְחֹקֵק וּבְמִשְׁעֲנֹתָם *with a staff, that is with their stick*] to בִּמְחֹקְקֹתָם וּבְמָשְׁלָם *with their statutes and during/with their rule*); כְּ *in accordance with,* + חצה ni. *be divided* Dn 11$_{4}$.*

⇒ משל I *rule.*

מֹשֶׁל II 2.1 n.[m.] **likeness**—cstr. מְשֹׁל (Si מושל); sf. מָשְׁלוֹ—**1. like(ness),** <NOM CL> אֵין־עַל־עָפָר מָשְׁלוֹ *there is not on dust his like* Jb 41$_{25}$ (or em. מֹשְׁלוֹ *one who can dominate him,* i.e. משל I). **2.** perh. **uttering of proverbs, ability to utter proverbs;** or **proverbial wisdom** (unless מֹשֶׁל I *mastery* of different situations). <NOM CL> מוסר שכל ומושל אופנים לשמעון perh. *Simeon had discipline, intelligence,* or *discipline of,* i.e. leading to, *intelligence, and the uttering of,* or *ability to utter, proverbs,* or *the proverbial wisdom, of,* i.e. for/drawn from, *(different) occasions* Si 50$_{27}$ (or em. מְשָׁלֵי *proverbs of,* i.e. for/drawn from). <CSTR> מושל אופנים perh. *the uttering of,* or *ability to utter, proverbs of,* i.e. for, *(different) occasions* Si 50$_{27}$ (or em.). **3.** perh. as מָשָׁל, **proverb,** <CSTR> מְשֹׁל עַמִּים *a proverb of,* i.e. among, *peoples* Jb 17$_{6}$ (unless לִמְשֹׁל *=to rule,* i.e. משל I; or em. לְמָשָׁל *as a proverb of;* i.e. מָשָׁל + תֹּפֶת לְפָנִים; perh. *spitting of faces,* i.e. someone to spit at). <PREP> לְ *as,* + יצג hi. *place* Jb 17$_{6}$ (unless משל I; or em. מָשָׁל).

⇨ משׁל *be like.*

[מִשְׁלוֹחַ], see מִשְׁלַח *extending.*

[מִשְׁלוֹחַת], see מִשְׁלַחַת *undertaking.*

[מִשְׁלָח] 7.0.3 n.[m.] **extending**—cstr. מִשְׁלַח, sf. Q משלחם—(in unvocalized texts, forms might belong instead to מִשְׁלֹחַ *extending*) **extending, moving** of limbs (1QS 10$_{13}$), specif. **activity, enterprise** (Dt 28$_{20}$ 1QS 9$_{23}$ 4QShirShabb^{d} 1.1$_{36}$).

<OBJ> עשׂה *do* Dt 28$_{20}$ (or del. אֲשֶׁר תַּעֲשֶׂה *that you do*).

<CSTR> מִשְׁלַח יָדְךָ *the extending of your* (sg.) *hand* Dt 12$_{18}$ 15$_{10}$ 23$_{21}$ (or em. מִשְׁלַח יָדְךָ to מַעֲשֶׂיךָ *your activities*) 28$_{8.20}$ (יָדְךָ; mss, Sam יָדֶיךָ *your* [sg.] *hands* in all five), מִשְׁלַח יֶדְכֶם *the extending of your* (pl.) *hand* Dt 12$_{7}$ (Sam יְדֵיכֶם *your* [pl.] *hands*), משלח כפים *extending of hands,* i.e. activity 1QS 9$_{23}$ (=4QS^{d} 3.2$_{8}$ [משלח כפים]; =4QS^{e} 1.4$_{5}$ [משל]ח כפים]; =4QS^{f} 1.1$_{1}$ [כפים] משלוח, i.e. מִשְׁלֹחַ *extending*), משלח ידי ורגלי *the extending,* i.e. moving, *of my hand/hands and foot/feet* 1QS 10$_{13}$; כֹּל מִשְׁלַח *every extending of* hand(s) Dt 12$_{7.18}$ 15$_{10}$ 23$_{21}$ (or em. כֹּל מִשְׁלַח יָדְךָ *all the extending of your hand,* i.e. activity, to כָּל־מַעֲשֶׂיךָ *all your activities*) 28$_{8.20}$ (כָּל־) 1QS 9$_{23}$ (כול משלח; =4QS^{d} 3.2$_{8}$ [כל משלח]; =4QS^{e} 1.4$_{5}$ [כ]ול משל[ח]; =4QS^{f} 1.1$_{1}$ [כו]ל משלוח *every extending of hands,* i.e. מִשְׁלַח *extending*), ר[א]שית משלח at *the beginning of the extending,* i.e. moving, *of* my hand/hands and foot/feet 1QS 10$_{13}$.

<PREP> בְּ of place, *in (the execution of)* 4QShirShabb^{d} 1.1$_{36}$ (כול מעשיו במשלחם *all his created beings in their activity*), + עשׂה *do* God's will 1QS 9$_{23}$ (+ מִמְשָׁל *domain;* =4QS^{d} 3.2$_{8}$ [לע]שות ... בכל משלח כפים]; =4QS^{e} 1.4$_{5}$ [לעשות ... בכ]ול משל[ח כפים]; =4QS^{f} 1.1$_{1}$ מִשְׁלַח *extending*), שׂמח *rejoice* Dt 12$_{7.18}$, ברך pi. *bless* Dt 15$_{10}$ (+ מַעֲשֶׂה *activity*) 23$_{21}$ (or em. מִשְׁלַח יָדְךָ *the extending of your hand,* i.e. activity, to מַעֲשֶׂיךָ *your activities*), שׁלח pi. *send (away)* curse, confusion, and reproach Dt 28$_{20}$; perh. *in connection with,* + צוה pi. *command* a blessing Dt 28$_{8}$ (+ אָסָם *storehouse*).

<COLL> כֹּל מִשְׁלַח יָדְךָ עַל־הָאָרֶץ *all the extending of your hand,* i.e. activity, *upon the land* Dt 23$_{21}$ (or em. כָּל־מַעֲשֶׂיךָ *all your activities* upon the land).

2. appar. place in which (only) beasts are let loose, **grazing ground,** מִשְׁלַח שׁוֹר *a grazing ground of oxen* Is 7$_{25}$. <PREP> לְ *as,* + היה *be(come)* Is 7$_{25}$ (|| מִרְמָס *trampling place*).

<SYN> §2 מִרְמָס *trampling place.*

⇨ שׁלח *send.*

[מִשְׁלֹחַ] 3.0.5 n.[m.] **extending**—cstr. מִשְׁלוֹחַ (L מִשְׁלֹחַ) —**1.** in verbal sense, **extending, giving, sending** of presents (Est 9$_{19.22}$). **2.** specif. **extending** of hand, i.e. **(military) attack** (1QM 1$_{1}$). **3. dominion** or **possession** (Is 11$_{14}$). **4. activity, enterprise** (4QD^{f} 1.1$_{1}$).

<NOM CL> אֱדוֹם וּמוֹאָב מִשְׁלוֹחַ יָדָם *Edom and Moab are the extending of their hand,* i.e. their dominion or possession Is 11$_{14(L)}$ (or ins. בְּ *within* the extending of their hand, i.e. their grasp, or em. בֶּאֱדוֹם ... יִשְׁלְחוּ *against Edom* and Moab *they will send their hand,* i.e. attack; + מִשְׁמַעַת *hearing,* i.e. vassal or servant), perh. ראשית משלוח יד בני אור *first, the extending of the hand,* i.e. attack, *of the children of light* 1QM 1$_{1}$ (unless רֵאשִׁית part of cstr., *the first [part] of* the attack).

<OBJ> עשׂה *make* Est 9$_{19}$ (הַיְּהוּדִים ... עֹשִׂים אֶת יוֹם ... מִשְׁלוֹחַ מָנוֹת *the Jews ... make* the fourteenth *day* of the month of Adar [a day of] ... *sending of presents*).

<CSTR> מִשְׁלוֹחַ מָנוֹת *sending of presents* Est 9$_{19.22}$, משלוח [כפים] *extending of hands,* i.e. activity 4QD^{f} 1.1$_{1}$ (=1QS 9$_{23}$ משלח כפים *extending of hands,* i.e. מִשְׁלַח *extending*), מִשְׁלוֹחַ יָדָם *the extending of their hand,* i.e. their dominion or possession Is 11$_{14(L)}$ (or em. יִשְׁלְחוּ *they will send* their hand, i.e. attack), משלוח ידכה *the extending of your hand* 4Q418 87$_{13}$, משלוח יד בני אור *the extending of the hand,* i.e. attack, *of the children of light* 1QM 1$_{1}$.

יְמֵי ... מִשְׁלוֹחַ *days of,* i.e. for ... *sending of* presents Est 9$_{22}$, perh. ראשית משלוח יד *the first (part) of the extending of the hand,* i.e. attack, *of* the children of light 1QM 1$_{1}$ (unless רֵאשִׁית adverbial, *first,* the attack of the children of light, i.e. nom. cl.), [כו]ל משלוח [כפים] *every extending of hands,* i.e. activity 4QS^{f} 1.1$_{1}$ (=1QS 9$_{23}$ כול משלח כפים *every extending of hands,* i.e. מִשְׁלַח

extending), כול משלוח *every extending (of)* 4Q418 91_2.

<PREP> בְּ of place, *in (the action of)* perh. 4Q418 91_2, + עשׂה *do* God's will 4QS[f] 1.1_1 (לעשות ... בכו[ל משלוח] [כפים] *to do* his will *in every extending of hands*, i.e. activity; =1QS 9_{23} מִשְׁלַח *extending*; + מִמְשָׁל *domain*).

<COLL> מִשְׁלוֹחַ מָנוֹת אִישׁ לְרֵעֵהוּ *the sending of presents, each person to their neighbour* Est $9_{19.22}$ (+ וּמַתָּנוֹת לָאֶבְיוֹנִים *and gifts to the poor*).

Also 4Q418 159.1_5 ([מ]שלוח).

⇒ שׁלח *send.*

מִשְׁלַחַת 2.0.1 n.f. **undertaking**—cstr. מִשְׁלַחַת; pl. sf. Q משלוחתיו (משלחתו, משלוחתו)—**1. undertaking** or perh. **mission,** <CSTR> כול משלוחתיו *all his undertakings* 4QShir[b] 16_2 4QShirShabb[f] 23.1_{13} (משלחותו).

<PREP> לְ of purpose, *for (the purpose) of, on,* + יצא hi. *take out,* i.e. send 4QShirShabb[f] 23.1_{13} ([ויוציאם] *and he sends them out*); מִן of comparison, *(more) than,* + רום *be high,* i.e., be too exalted, for 4QShirShabb[f] 23. 1_{11}, שׁפל *be low(ly)* 4QShirShabb[f] 23.1_{11} ([ישפלו]).

2. perh. **sending (a replacement)** for oneself to battle, i.e. **deputation, substitution,** or **setting aside, laying down** of weapons, or **discharging** of oneself from battle, <NOM CL> וְאֵין שִׁלְטוֹן בְּיוֹם הַמָּוֶת וְאֵין מִשְׁלַחַת בַּמִּלְחָמָה *and there is,* i.e. one has, *no authority over the day of death and there is no sending (a replacement) into the battle* Ec 8_8 (or em. בְּיוֹם הַמִּלְחָמָה *on the day of battle*). <COLL> מִשְׁלַחַת בַּמִּלְחָמָה perh. *sending (a replacement) into the battle* Ec 8_8 (or em.).

3. perh. **sending, dispatching** of troop of angels, or **company** of angels (unless as §1, **undertaking, mission**), <OBJ> שׁלח pi. *send out* (i.e. cognate accusative) Ps 78_{49} (or em. וְצָרָה he sent out against them the heat of his anger, fury, and rage *and distress,* a sending, to וְצִוָּה and rage *and he commanded* the dispatching of, or, a company of, angels). <CSTR> מִשְׁלַחַת מַלְאֲכֵי רָעִים *dispatching of angels of evil ones* Ps 78_{49} (ms מַלְאָכִים of evil *angels*; or em. מְשַׁלֵּחַ אֶת־ *sending out the* angels of). <APP> עֶבְרָה *anger* Ps 78_{49} (or em.), זַעַם *anger* Ps 78_{49} (or em.), חָרוֹן *heat* of anger Ps 78_{49} (or em.), צָרָה *distress* Ps 78_{49} (or em.).

Also perh. 1Q40 8_1 ([מ]שלחות) 11QShirShabb e_2 ([משׁ]לחות).

⇒ שׁלח *send.*

מְשֻׁלָּם I 25.0.0.17 pr.n.m. **Meshullam.**

1. son of Zerubbabel and brother of Hananiah and Shelomith, <NOM CL> וּבְנֵי־זְרֻבָּבֶל מְשֻׁלָּם וַחֲנַנְיָה *and the sons of Zerubbabel were Meshullam and Hananiah* 1 C $3_{19(\text{Seb})}$ (or ins. בְּבָבֶל the sons of Zerubbabel [born] *in Babylon*).

2. grandfather of Shaphan the scribe, <CSTR> בֶּן־מְשֻׁלָּם Azaliah *son of Meshullam* 2 K 22_3.

3. Kohathite overseer of temple repairs at time of Josiah, <SUBJ> פקד ho. *be appointed* 2 C 34_{12}, נצח pi. *oversee* 2 C 34_{12}.

4. son of Elpaal, descendant of Benjamin, וּזְבַדְיָה וּמְשֻׁלָּם ... בְּנֵי אֶלְפָּעַל *and Zebadiah and Meshullam ... were sons of Elpaal* 1 C 8_{17}.

5. Gadite chief, son of Abihail, <NOM CL> וַאֲחֵיהֶם לְבֵית אֲבוֹתֵיהֶם מִיכָאֵל וּמְשֻׁלָּם *and their brothers, by their ancestral houses, were Michael and Meshullam* 1 C 5_{13}.

6. prominent person present (and perh. resident) at Ahava, <SUBJ> אתה *come* Ezr 8_{16} (if em. וָאֲצַוֶּה אוֹתָם *and I commanded them* to [go to] Iddo [Qr] to וְאָמְרָם לָאֲתוֹת *and their command was to come* to Iddo). <OBJ> יצא hi. *take out* Ezr $8_{16(\text{Kt})}$, צוה pi. *command* Ezr $8_{16(\text{Qr})}$. <APP> רֹאשׁ *head* Ezr 8_{16} (or em. רָאשִׁים, in app. with Meshullam, to אֲנָשִׁים I sent *men* to Meshullam). <PREP> לְ of direction, *to,* or perh. *for,* i.e. to fetch, + שׁלח *send* Ezr 8_{16}.

7. one of four men who assisted (or perh. opposed) Ezra in connection with communal repudiation of intermarriage, perh. ident. with preceding, <SUBJ> עזר *help* Jonathan and Jahzeiah Ezr 10_{15}.

8. Judaean leader at time of Ezra, perh. ident. with preceding, <SUBJ> עמד *stand* to left of Ezra Ne 8_4 (or del. Meshullam or em. מִשְּׂמֹאל *on the left*).

9. priest and co-signatory with Nehemiah, <NOM CL> עַל הַחֲתוּמִים נְחֶמְיָה ... מְשֻׁלָּם *upon those that were sealed are Nehemiah ... (and) Meshullam* Ne 10_8 (or em. הַחוֹתְמִים *those that sealed,* i.e. signed, *were* or

הַחוֹתְמִים אֵלֶּה *these are the signatories*).

10. leading figure, appar. priest, who took part in dedication of walls of Jerusalem, perh. ident. with preceding, <SUBJ> הלך *go* Ne 12_{33}.

11. chief of returning exiles and co-signatory with Nehemiah, <NOM CL> רָאשֵׁי הָעָם ... מְשֻׁלָּם *the heads of the people were ... Meshullam* Ne 10_{21}.

12. son of Zadok, father of Hilkiah, and grandfather of Seraiah (Ne 11_{11}) or Azariah (1 C 9_{11}), a priest (or ancestor of priest, if ins. בֶּן־ *son of* before Seraiah/Azariah) who lived in Jerusalem after the exile, <CSTR> בֶּן־מְשֻׁלָּם Hilkiah/Azariah *son of Meshullam* Ne 11_{11} 1 C 9_{11}. <APP> בֶּן *son* of Zadok Ne 11_{11} 1 C 9_{11}.

13. son of Meshillemith (or em. Meshillemoth) and father of Jahzerah (or em. Johanan or Jedaiah), ancestor of Maasai, another priest living in Jerusalem after the exile, <CSTR> בֶּן־מְשֻׁלָּם Jahzerah *son of Meshullam* 1 C 9_{12} (or em.). <APP> בֶּן *son* of Meshillemith 1 C 9_{12} (or em.).

14. head of priestly family of Ezra at time of Joiakim, <NOM CL> לְעֶזְרָא מְשֻׁלָּם *(belonging) to (the family of) Ezra was Meshullam* Ne 12_{13}.

15. head of priestly family of Ginnethon at time of Nehemiah, <NOM CL> לְגִנְּתוֹן מְשֻׁלָּם *(belonging) to (the family of) Ginnethon was Meshullam* Ne 12_{16}.

16. head of family of gatekeepers at time of Nehemiah (or em. שַׁלּוּם *Shallum*), <SUBJ> שׁמר *keep (watch)* Ne 12_{25}, שׁער *act as gatekeeper* Ne 12_{25} (or em. שֹׁמְרִים שֹׁעֲרִים appar. *sentries, namely gatekeepers* to שֹׁעֲרִים שֹׁמְרִים *gatekeepers keeping* watch, or שֹׁמְרִים בַּשְּׁעָרִים watch-*keepers at the gates*).

17. son of Joed (Ne 11_7 יוֹעֵד, or em. יוֹדַע *Joda*) or Hodaviah (1 C 9_7 הוֹדַוְיָה, or em. הוֹדִיָּה *Hodiah*, or וִיהוּדָה *and Judah*) and father of Sallu, a Benjaminite chief who lived in Jerusalem after the exile, <CSTR> בֶּן־מְשֻׁלָּם Sallu *son of Meshullam* Ne 11_7 1 C 9_7. <APP> בֶּן *son* of Joed Ne 11_7 (or em. יוֹדַע of *Joda*), of Hodaviah 1 C 9_7 (or em. בֶּן־הוֹדַוְיָה *son of Hodaviah* to בֶּן־הוֹדִיָּה *son of Hodiah* or וִיהוּדָה *and Judah*, i.e. unconnected to Meshullam).

18. another Benjaminite chief, son of Shephatiah (or Reuel, if del. Shephatiah), living in Jerusalem after the exile, <NOM CL> וּמִבְּנֵי בִנְיָמִן סַלּוּא ... וּמְשֻׁלָּם *and of the descendants of Benjamin were Sallu ... and Meshullam* 1 C 9_8. <APP> בֶּן *son* of Shephatiah 1 C 9_8 (or del. בֶּן־שְׁפַטְיָה *son of Shephatiah*, leaving בֶּן־רְעוּאֵל *son of Reuel* in app. with Meshullam).

19. Israelite married to foreign woman, <NOM CL> וּמִבְּנֵי בָּנִי מְשֻׁלָּם *and from the descendants of Bani was Meshullam* Ezr 10_{29} (ms Bachi; or em. Binnui, Bunni, Bigvai, or Bezai).

20. one who helped repair walls of Jerusalem, son of Berechiah and father-in-law of Tobiah's son, <SUBJ> חזק hi. *strengthen* wall Ne $3_{4.30}$. <CSTR> בַּת־מְשֻׁלָּם *the daughter of Meshullam* Ne 6_{18}. <APP> בֶּן *son* of Berechiah Ne $3_{4.30}$ 6_{18}.

21. one who helped repair Jeshanah Gate, son of Besodeiah, <SUBJ> חזק hi. *strengthen* wall Ne 3_6, קרה pi. *put on roof* Ne 3_6, עמד hi. *erect* doors, locks, and bars Ne 3_6. <APP> בֶּן *son* Ne 3_6.

22. father of the Zechariah who was a gatekeeper in postexilic times, <CSTR> בֶּן־מְשֻׁלָּם *son of Meshullam* 1 C 9_{21} (if em. מְשֶׁלֶמְיָה *Meshelamiah*).

23. son of Nedabiah (נדביהו), <APP> בֶּן *son* Arad ost. 39_3.

24. appar. father of Shemijah and perh. servant of Elnathan, [שמיה משלם נער אלנת[ן *Shemijah (son of) Meshullam, servant of Elnathan* Arad ost. 110_1.

25. appar. father of Maaseiah (מעשיהו), Seal 55 (T. el-Judeideh).

26. appar. father of Neriah (נריהו), Seal 56.

27. appar. son of Elnathan (אלנתן), <PREP> לְ perh. of possession, *of, (belonging) to* Seal 189 190 (למ[שלם]; both Gibeon, 8th cent.).

28. appar. son of Ahimelech (אח[י]מלך), Seal 358 (Lachish, 8th cent.) 792_1 (Lachish, 8th cent.),

29. father of Jekamiah (יקמיהו), <CSTR> בן משלם *son of Meshullam* Seal 575 (T. Beit Mirsim?, 7th/6th cent.).

30. father of Micaiah (מכיהו), <CSTR> בן משלם *son of Meshullam* Seal 592 (T. Beit Mirsim?, 7th/6th cent.).

31. appar. father of Ashiah (אשיהו), <PREP> לְ perh. of possession, *of, (belonging) to* Seal 610 (T. Beit Mirsim?, 7th/6th cent.).

32. son of Rephaiah (רפאיהו), <APP> בֶּן *son* Seal 611

(T. Beit Mirsim?, 7th/6th cent.). <PREP> לְ perh. of possession, *of, (belonging) to* Seal 611.

33. appar. son of Ospi (אספי), <PREP> לְ perh. of possession, *of, (belonging) to* Seal 757 (8th–6th cent.).

34. father of Jedaiah (ידעיהו), <CSTR> בן משלם *son of Meshullam* Seal 812 (City of David, 7th/6th cent.).

35. father of Azaliah (אצליהו), <CSTR> בן משלם *son of Meshullam* Seal 853 (7th cent.).

36. son of Shallum, <APP> בֵּן *son* Bulla WSS 556 (בן[ן]; others מצרי *Mizri* or מצר *Mezer*). <PREP> לְ of possession, *of, (belonging) to* Bulla WSS 556 (ל[מצר]).

37. appar. father of Miamun, Bulla D57.

38. father of Neriah, <CSTR> בן משלם *son of Meshullam* Bulla D67.

⇒ שׁלם *be whole.*

מְשֻׁלָּם II, see שׁלם, Pu. *be made complete.*

מְשִׁלֵּמוֹת $_2$ pr.n.[m.] **Meshillemoth, 1.** appar. ident. with Meshillemith at 1 C 9$_{12}$, son of Immer and father of Ahzai (||1 C 9$_{12}$ Meshullam), ancestor of Amashsai (or em. Amasai; ||1 C 9$_{21}$ Maasai), a priest living in Jerusalem after returning from exile, <CSTR> בֶּן־מְשִׁלֵּמוֹת *son of Meshillemoth* Ne 11$_{13}$. <APP> בֵּן *son* of Immer Ne 11$_{13}$.

2. father of the Berechiah (or em. Zechariah) who was an Ephraimite leader at the time of Ahaz, <CSTR> בֶּן־מְשִׁלֵּמוֹת *son of Meshillemoth* 2 C 28$_{12}$.

⇒ שׁלם *be whole.*

מְשֶׁלֶמְיָה $_1$ pr.n.m. **Meshelemiah,** father of the Zechariah who was a gatekeeper in postexilic times, <CSTR> בֶּן־מְשֶׁלֶמְיָה *son of Meshelemiah* 1 C 9$_{21}$ (or em. Meshullam).

⇒ שׁלם *be whole.*

מְשֶׁלֶמְיָהוּ $_3$ pr.n.m. **Meshelemiah,** Korahite gatekeeper at time of David, <NOM CL> לַקָּרְחִים מְשֶׁלֶמְיָהוּ *to the Korahites belonged Meshelemiah* 1 C 26$_1$ (or em. אֲשֶׁר־הֵקִים הַמֶּלֶךְ דָּוִיד לְמִשְׁמָר to לַקָּרְחִים *whom King David appointed for keeping guard*), וְלִמְשֶׁלֶמְיָהוּ בָּנִים *and Meshelemiah had sons* 1 C 26$_{2.9}$ (+ וְאַחִים *and brothers*).

⇒ שׁלם *be whole* + ׳י Y.

מְשִׁלֵּמִית $_1$ pr.n.m. **Meshillemith,** appar. ident. with Meshillemoth at Ne 11$_{13}$, son of Immer and father of Meshullam (||Ne 11$_{13}$ Ahzai), ancestor of Maasai (||Ne 11$_{13}$ Amashsai), a priest living in Jerusalem after returning from exile, <CSTR> בֶּן־מְשִׁלֵּמִית *son of Meshillemith* 1 C 9$_{12}$ (or em. Meshillemoth). <APP> בֵּן *son* of Immer 1 C 9$_{12}$ (or em.).

⇒ שׁלם *be whole.*

מְשֻׁלֶּמֶת $_{1.0.0.2}$ pr.n.f. **Meshullemeth**—I משולמת—**1.** daughter of Haruz and mother of Amon, <NOM CL> וְשֵׁם אִמּוֹ מְשֻׁלֶּמֶת *and the name of his mother was Meshullemeth* 2 K 21$_{19}$. <APP> בַּת *daughter* of Haruz 2 K 21$_{19}$.

2. <PREP> לְ perh. of possession, *of, (belonging) to* Seal 856.

3. daughter of Elikon, <APP> בַּת *daughter* ost. DH 72$_6$.*

⇒ שׁלם *be whole.*

[מְשֻׁלָּשׁ] $_1$ n.[m.] **triad**—cstr. מִשְׁלֹשׁ—<CSTR> מִשְׁלֹשׁ חֳדָשִׁים *triad of months* Gn 38$_{24}$. <PREP> כְּ *around,* + היה *be* Gn 38$_{24}$ (וַיְהִי כְּמִשְׁלֹשׁ חֳדָשִׁים *and it came to pass around a triad of months [later];* or em. כְּמִשְׁלֹשׁ *around after three* months; Sam appar. כְּמִשְׁלֹשֶׁת in same sense).

⇒ שָׁלֹשׁ *three.*

*** [מְשַׁם]** $_{0.0.1}$ n.[m.] **desolation,** <PREP> בְּ of accompaniment, *with, in (a state of),* + טעה *err* GnzPs 3$_{18}$ (or em. משם to מִשְׁגֶּה *error;* || הֶבֶל *vanity*). <SYN> הֶבֶל *vanity.*

⇒ שׁמם *be desolate.*

מְשַׁמָּה I $_{7.0.1}$ n.f. **devastation**—pl. מְשַׁמּוֹת—**(place of) devastation,** or **horror,** <SUBJ> היה *be(come)* Is 15$_6$ Jr 48$_{34}$ (both + מֵי נִמְרִים *the waters of Nimrim*) Ezk 5$_{15}$ (|| חֶרְפָּה *reproach,* גְּדוּפָה *reproach,* מוּסָר *discipline;* or del. מוּסָר וּמְשַׁמָּה *(a symbol) of discipline and destruc-*

tion). <OBJ> נתן *give*, i.e. turn (land, hill country) into Ezk 6$_{14}$ (|| שְׁמָמָה *desolation*) 33$_{28}$ (or del. מְשַׁמָּה; || שְׁמָמָה) 33$_{29}$ (|| שְׁמָמָה) 35$_{3}$ (or em. וּמְשַׁמָּה to וְשַׁמּוֹתָ *and you will become desolate*; || שְׁמָמָה). <PREP> לְ of direction, *to*, + נתן *give*, i.e. hand (over) Ezk 35$_{7(mss)}$ (לִשְׁמָמָה וּמְשַׁמָּה; L לִשְׁמָמָה וּשְׁמָמָה *to desolation and desolation*) 4QJub^{a} 1$_{13}$ (ונת]תי אותם ... לש]בי ולמ]שמות[ולאכל]) *and I shall give them over to captivity and to destructions and to devouring*). <COLL> מְשַׁמָּה לַגּוֹיִם *(a symbol) of destruction for the nations* (or del. מְשַׁמָּה; mss בַּגּוֹיִם *among the nations*), שְׁמָמָה וּמְשַׁמָּה *desolation and destruction* Ezk 6$_{14}$ 33$_{28}$ (or del. וּמְשַׁמָּה) 33$_{29}$ 35$_{3}$ (or em. וּמְשַׁמָּה to וְשַׁמּוֹתָ *and you will become desolate*) 33$_{7(mss)}$.

Also perh. 4Q418 148.2$_{5}$.

<SYN> שְׁמָמָה *desolation*, חֶרְפָּה *reproach*, גְּדוּפָה *reproach*, מוּסָר *discipline*.*

⇒ שׁמם *be desolate*.

*[מְשַׁמָּה] II pl.n. **Meshammah**, <COLL> וְנָתַתִּי לָהּ אֶת־כְּרָמֶיהָ מְשַׁמָּה *and I will give her vineyards (in) Meshammah* Ho 2$_{17}$ (if em. מִשָּׁם *from there*; || עֵמֶק עָכוֹר *valley of Achor*).

[מַשְׁמָן] 1 n.[m.] **rich food**—pl. מַשְׁמַנִּים—**1. rich food, delicacy**, <OBJ> אכל *eat* Ne 8$_{10}$ (|| מַמְתַּק *sweet food*, + מָנָה *present*). **2. fatling**, <CSTR> מֵיטַב ... הַמַּשְׁמַנִּים *the best of ... the fatlings* 1 S 15$_{9}$ (if em. הַמִּשְׁנִים *those born in second batch*; + צֹאן *sheep*, בָּקָר *cattle*, כַּר *ram*). <SYN> §1 מַמְתַּק *sweet food*.

⇒ שׁמן *be fat*.

[מִשְׁמָן] 6 n.m. **fat**—cstr. מִשְׁמַן; pl. cstr. מִשְׁמַנֵּי; sf. מִשְׁמַנָּיו, מִשְׁמַנֵּיהֶם—**1.** of body, **fat, fattest, healthiest, part** (Is 17$_{4}$). **2.** of person, **fat, healthy, sturdy, strong(est)** (Ps 78$_{31}$ perh. Is 10$_{16}$ Dn 11$_{24}$). **3.** of crops, **choice produce** (Gn 27$_{28}$). **4.** of land, **choice**, i.e. **most fertile, area** (Gn 27$_{39}$ perh. Is 10$_{16}$). **5.** of city, perh. **best**, or **strongest** (Dn 11$_{24}$).

<SUBJ> היה *be* Gn 27$_{39}$ (הִנֵּה מִשְׁמַנֵּי הָאָרֶץ יִהְיֶה מוֹשָׁבֶךָ וּמִטַּל הַשָּׁמַיִם מֵעָל *behold, your dwelling place will be the most fertile areas of the land and of the dew of the skies above*; or em. מִשְׁמַנֵּי/מִשְּׁמַנֵּי *and away from the most fertile areas of* the land ... and away from the dew of the skies, i.e. שָׁמָן *choice part* or שֶׁמֶן *oil*), רזה ni. *become thin* Is 17$_{4}$ (|| כָּבוֹד *glory*).

<OBJ> נתן *give* Gn 27$_{28}$ (מִטַּל הַשָּׁמַיִם וּמִשְׁמַנֵּי הָאָרֶץ וְרֹב דָּגָן וְתִירֹשׁ *of the dew of the skies and the choice produce of the land and abundance of grain and new oil*; or em. מִשְׁמַנֵּי/וּמִשְּׁמַנֵּי *and of the choice produce of*, i.e. שָׁמָן *choice part* or שֶׁמֶן *oil*).

<CSTR> מִשְׁמַן בְּשָׂרוֹ *the fat of his flesh* Is 17$_{4}$, מִשְׁמַנֵּי הָאָרֶץ *the choice produce/areas of the land* Gn 27$_{28.39}$ (or em. מִשְּׁמַנֵּי/מִשְׁמַנֵּי, i.e. מִן *of/away, from* + שָׁמָן *choice part* or שֶׁמֶן *oil*), מִשְׁמַנֵּי מְדִינָה *the strongest cities/people, or most fertile areas, of a province* Dn 11$_{24}$; בְּשָׂרִי כָּחַשׁ מִשְּׁמֶן *my flesh of fatness, i.e. well-fed body, has grown gaunt* Ps 109$_{24}$ (if em. מִשֶּׁמֶן, i.e. with broken cstr. chain). <PREP> בְּ of place, *in(to)*, or *against*, + בוא *come* Dn 11$_{24}$, שׁלח pi. *send (away)* thinness Is 10$_{16}$; partitive, *(some) of, among*, + הרג *kill* Ps 78$_{31}$ (|| בָּחוּר *youth*).

<SYN> כָּבוֹד *glory*, בָּחוּר *youth*.

⇒ שׁמן *be fat*.

מַשְׁמַנָּה, see מִשְׁמַנָּה *Mishmannah*.

מִשְׁמַנָּה 1 pr.n.m. **Mishmannah**—מַשְׁמַנָּה—one of the Gadite warriors supporting David, <NOM CL> מִשְׁמַנָּה הָרְבִיעִי *Mishmannah was the fourth* 1 C 12$_{11}$ (mss מַשְׁמַנָּה *Mashmannah*).

⇒ שׁמן *be fat*.

[מִשְׁמָע] I 1.0.4 n.[m.] **hearing**—cstr. מִשְׁמַע—<CSTR> מִשְׁמַע אָזְנָיו *the hearing of his ears* Is 11$_{4}$ 4QdivProv 1$_{3}$ ([מ]שמע אוזניו) (both :: מַרְאֶה *seeing*), משמע משפטים *the hearing of judgments* 1QSa 1$_{11}$, משמע אלוהים *the hearing of divine beings* 4QShirShabb^{d} 1.2$_{12}$. <PREP> לְ *in accordance with, by*, + יכח hi. *reprove* Is 11$_{4}$ (וְלֹא־לְמִשְׁמַע אָזְנָיו יוֹכִיחַ ... וְהוֹכִיחַ בְּמִישׁוֹר לְעַנְוֵי־אָרֶץ *and not in accordance with the hearing of his ears will he reprove ... but he will reprove with equity for the sake of the humble of the land*; or em. עֲנִיֵּי *the poor of* the land); perh. of agent, *by*, + כבד ni. *be honoured* 4QShir Shabb^{d} 1.2$_{12}$, שמע ni. *be heard* 4QShirShabb^{d} 1.2$_{12}$ (erased); בְּ of place/time, *at*, + יצב htp. *stand* perh. be present 1QSa 1_{11}; אַחַר *after, in accordance with,* + הלך *go* 4QdivProv 1_3 (כל רע[ההולך אחר [מ]שמע *every evil one, who goes,* i.e. behaves, *in accordance with the hearing of* his ears).

Also 4QSap[b] 10_5.

<ANT> מַרְאֶה *seeing.*

⇒ שׁמע *hear.*

מִשְׁמָע II 4 pr.n.m. **Mishma, 1.** fifth son of Ishmael, Gn 25_{14}||1 C 1_{30}. **2.** son of Mibsam and father of Hammuel (and Zaccur and Shimei, unless em.), descendant of Simeon, <NOM CL> מִשְׁמָע בְּנוֹ *Mishma was his* (Mibsam's) *son* 1 C 4_{25}, וּבְנֵי מִשְׁמָע חַמּוּאֵל בְּנוֹ זַכּוּר בְּנוֹ שִׁמְעִי בְנוֹ *and the sons of Mishma were Hamuel, his son, Zaccur, his son, and Shimei, his son* 1 C 4_{26} (or del. וּבְנֵי מִשְׁמָע, with חַמּוּאֵל בְּנוֹ *Hamuel was his son* referring to Mishma in preceding verse). <CSTR> בְּנֵי מִשְׁמָע *the sons of Mishma* 1 C 4_{26} (or del.).

⇒ שׁמע *hear.*

[מִשְׁמַעַת] 4 n.f. **hearing**—sf. מִשְׁמַעְתֶּךָ, מִשְׁמַעְתּוֹ, מִשְׁמַעְתָּם—**1. hearing** (1 S 22_{14}, or em., as §3, Is 11_{14}, if em.). **2.** appar. **servant** or **vassal (nation)** (Is 11_{14}, or em. as §1). **3.** perh. **retinue, court,** or **bodyguard** (2 S 23_{23}||1 C 11_{25}), perh. more generally **subjects** (1 S 22_{14}, if em.).

<NOM CL> וּבְנֵי עַמּוֹן מִשְׁמַעְתָּם *and the children of Ammon are their hearing,* i.e. one hearing them, i.e. a vassal or servant Is 11_{14} (or ins. בְּ *within* their hearing, as §1, i.e. obedient to them; + מִשְׁלַח יָד *extending of hand,* i.e. dominion or possession). <PREP> אֶל *to,* + סור *depart* 1 S 22_{14} (or em. וְסָר אֶל־מִשְׁמַעְתֶּךָ *and one turning to your hearing,* i.e. acting at your bidding, to וְשַׂר *and an officer* over your retinue, or *prince* over your subjects; as §3); *over, in charge of* 1 S 22_{14} (if em.), + שׂים *place* Benaiah 2 S 23_{23} (or em. עַל *over, in charge of,* as ||1 C 11_{25}, and/or em. מִשְׁמַעְתּוֹ *his retinue* to מִשְׁמַרְתּוֹ *his watch* or אֶל־מִשְׁמַעְתּוֹ *over his retinue* to לְמַשְׁמִעֵהוּ appointed him *as his herald*); עַל *over, in charge of,* + שׂים *place* Benaiah 1 C 11_{25} (or em. מִשְׁמַעְתּוֹ *his retinue* to מִשְׁמַרְתּוֹ *his watch* or מִשְׁפַּחְתּוֹ *his clan*).

⇒ שׁמע *hear.*

מִשְׁמָר I 22.1.6.1 n.m. **watch**—cstr. מִשְׁמַר; sf. מִשְׁמָרוֹ (Q משמרוה), מִשְׁמַרְכֶם, pl. sf. מִשְׁמָרָיו—**1.** with verbal sense, **guard(ing), watch(ing)** (Ezk 38_7 Pr 4_{23} [if em.] Ne 7_3 12_{25} [if em.] Si 42_{11} CD 12_5, **custody, imprisonment** (Gn $40_{3.4.7}$ 41_{10} $42_{17.19.30}$ [if em.] Lv 24_{12} Nm 15_{34}).

2. of person, **guard, sentry, lookout** (Jr 51_{12} Jb 7_{12} Ne $4_{3.16.17}$).

3. of object, **barrier** (Jr 51_{12} Jb 7_{12}), **prison,** as punishment, to restrict free movement, or while decision about one's fate is taken (Gn $40_{3.4.7}$ 41_{10} $42_{17.19.30}$ [if em.] Lv 24_{12} Nm 15_{34}).

4. as abstract, **protection** (1QH 9_{33} 4QJub[d] 21_{20} 4QHod[f] 1_1).

5. (cultic) service (Ne 13_{14}).

6. (priestly) course, division (Ne $12_{24.24.25}$ [or em.] 1 C $26_{16.16}$ 11QT 45_5).

<SUBJ> היה *be* Ne 4_{16} (mss ins. לְ the night was for us *for* guarding; see Coll.) 4QJub[d] 21_{20} (והייה משמרוה [עו]ל הטוב perh. *and his protection,* or *watch, will be over the good person*), בוא *come* 11QT 45_5 ([וב]א משמר אל מקומו *and a priestly division will come to its place,* i.e. will commence its duties).

<NOM CL> ומשמר שלומכה לפלט נפשי *and the protection of,* i.e. afforded by, *your peace is to rescue my soul* 1QH 9_{33} (|| תּוֹכֵחָה *reproof*), על בני האדם משמרו *(incumbent) upon human beings is his observation,* i.e. close watch over him CD 12_5 (=4QD[f] 5.1_{20} [על בני]).

<OBJ> שׂים *place* Jb 7_{12} (see Coll.), עמד hi. *position* Ne 4_3, חזק pi. *strengthen,* i.e. carefully keep, watch Jr 51_{12} Si $42_{11(M)}$ (על בת חז[ק] משמר *over a daughter keep close watch;* Bmg hi. *strengthen*), נתן *give* 1QH fr. 2.1_5, שׁמר *keep* Ne 12_{25} (if em. שֹׁמְרִים שְׁעָרִים מִשְׁמָר appar. *sentries, namely gatekeepers, by shift* to שֹׁעֲרִים שֹׁמְרִים *gatekeepers keeping* watch, or שֹׁמְרִים בַּשְּׁעָרִים watch-*keepers at the gates*).

<CSTR> מִשְׁמַר בֵּית שַׂר הַטַּבָּחִים *the custody,* or *prison, of the house(hold) of the captain of the guard* Gn 40_3 (mss) (L הַטַּבָּחִים) 41_{10}, מִשְׁמַר בֵּית אֲדֹנָיו *the custody,* or *prison, of the house(hold) of his master* Gn 40_7, בֵּית מִשְׁמַרְכֶם *the house,* i.e. place, *of your (im)prison-*

(ment) Gn 42_{19}, משמר שלומכה *the protection of*, i.e. afforded by, *your peace* 1QH 9_{33}, משמר צדקכה *the protection of*, i.e. afforded by, *your righteousness* 1QH fr. 2.1_5, משמר גבורים *the protection of*, i.e. afforded by, *mighty ones* 4QHod[f] 1_1.

אַנְשֵׁי הַמִּשְׁמָר *the men of the guard* Ne 4_{17}, כָּל־מִשְׁמָר *all guarding* Pr 4_{23}.

<PREP> לְ of purpose, *for (the purpose of)*, + היה *be* Ne 4_{16}(mss) (see Coll.), קום hi. *establish* 1 C 26_1 (if em. אֲשֶׁר־הֵקִים לַקָּרְחִים *belonging to the Korahites* to אֲשֶׁר־הֵקִים הַמֶּלֶךְ דָּוִד לְמִשְׁמָר *whom King David appointed for watching*); as, + היה *be* Ezk 38_7 (וְהָיִיתָ לָהֶם לְמִשְׁמָר *and you are to be for them as a watch*, i.e. you are to be watching/on guard for them; or em. לָהֶם to לִי *for me*).

בְּ of place/time, *in, at, during* perh. Arad ost. 111_2, + היה *be* Gn $40_{4.7}$, נתן *give*, i.e. place Gn 40_3 41_{10} 42_{30} (if ins. בְּמִשְׁמָר *in prison*), נוח hi. *place* Lv 24_{12} Nm 15_{34}, עמד hi. *position* Ne 7_3 (+ מִשְׁמֶרֶת *watch*); of accompaniment, *with, (in) a state of*, + נצר *keep* Pr 4_{23} (if em. מִכָּל־מִשְׁמָר נְצֹר לִבֶּךָ appar. *more than any guarding, keep your heart,** or *yourself* to בְּכָל־ *in all guarding, guard your heart*, i.e. whatever you guard make sure you guard yourself); *in connection with*, + עשׂה *do* Nm 13_{14} (אֲשֶׁר עָשִׂיתִי בְּבֵית אֱלֹהַי וּבְמִשְׁמָרָיו *that I performed in connection with the house of my God and in connection with his/its rituals*; or del. וּבְמִשְׁמָרָיו).

מִן of comparison, *(more) than*, + נצר *keep* Pr 4_{21} (or em. בְּ of accompaniment).

אֶל *(in)to*, + אסף *gather*, i.e. place Gn 42_{17}.

לְעֻמַּת *opposite* Ne 12_{24} (see Coll.) 1 C 26_{16} (see Coll.).

<COLL> שֹׁמְרִים שֹׁעֲרִים מִשְׁמָר appar. *sentries, namely gatekeepers, by shift* Ne 12_{25} (or em. שֹׁעֲרִים שֹׁמְרִים *gatekeepers keeping* watch, or שֹׁמְרִים בַּשְּׁעָרִים watch-*keepers at the gates*).

וַיִּהְיוּ יָמִים בְּמִשְׁמָר *and they were (some) days in custody* or *prison* Gn 40_4 (or em. בַּמִּשְׁמָר *in the prison*), וַיֶּאֱסֹף אֹתָם אֶל־מִשְׁמָר שְׁלֹשֶׁת יָמִים *and he gathered them into custody*, or *prison, three days* Gn 42_{17}.

וַיַּנִּיחֻהוּ בַּמִּשְׁמָר לִפְרֹשׁ לָהֶם עַל־פִּי י׳ *and they placed him in the prison*, or *in custody, to clarify for themselves concerning the command of Y.* Lv 24_{12}, וַיַּנִּיחוּ אֹתוֹ בַּמִּשְׁמָר כִּי לֹא פֹרַשׁ מַה־יֵּעָשֶׂה לוֹ *and they placed him in the prison*, or *in custody, for what was to be done to him had not been clarified* Nm 15_{34}.

הַחֲזִיקוּ הַמִּשְׁמָר הָקִימוּ שֹׁמְרִים *strengthen the watch*, or *barrier; position guards* Jr 51_{12}, הֲיָם־אָנִי אִם־תַּנִּין כִּי־תָשִׂים עָלַי מִשְׁמָר *am I Yam or Tannin that you set a watch over me?* Jb 7_{12}.

וַנַּעֲמִיד מִשְׁמָר עֲלֵיהֶם יוֹמָם וָלַיְלָה מִפְּנֵיהֶם *and we set a watch*, or *posted a guard, over them* (walls, repair works, or workers), or, *against them* (Sanballat and Tobiah), *day and night on their account* Ne 4_3 (or em. עָלֶיהָ *over it*, i.e. Jerusalem), וְהָיוּ־לָנוּ הַלַּיְלָה מִשְׁמָר וְהַיּוֹם מְלָאכָה appar. *and they were for us (by) night a guard and (by) day a workforce* Ne 4_{16} (mss *and ... was*; mss וְהָיָה ... לְמִשְׁמָר ... לִמְלָאכָה *and* for us the night *was for guarding* and the day *for working*).

אִישׁ בְּמִשְׁמָרוֹ וְאִישׁ נֶגֶד בֵּיתוֹ *each one at his watch and each one in front of his house* Ne 7_3 (or del. וְאִישׁ נֶגֶד בֵּיתוֹ), לְהַלֵּל לְהוֹדוֹת ... מִשְׁמָר לְעֻמַּת מִשְׁמָר *to praise (and) to give thanks ... shift opposite shift*, i.e. in continuous (priestly) shifts Ne 12_{24} (or em. וּלְהוֹדוֹת *and to give thanks*), לְשֻׁפִּים וּלְחֹסָה לַמַּעֲרָב ... מִשְׁמָר לְעֻמַּת מִשְׁמָר *to Shuppim and to Hosah it fell for the west (gate) ..., shift by shift* 1 C 26_{16} (unless מִשְׁמָר לְעֻמַּת מִשְׁמָר is nom. cl., *shift followed shift*, or em. לְשֻׁפִּים to לִשְׁנַיִם *as two*, appar. as a double lot, or לַסִּפִּים *that is, the thresholds*, as gloss on הָאֲסֻפִּים place of *the storehouses* in 26_{15}), שֹׁמְרִים שֹׁעֲרִים מִשְׁמָר appar. *sentries, namely gatekeepers, by shift* Ne 12_{25} (or em. שֹׁעֲרִים שֹׁמְרִים *gatekeepers keeping* watch, or שֹׁמְרִים בַּשְּׁעָרִים watch-*keepers at the gates*).

<SYN> תּוֹכֵחָה *reproof.**

⇨ שׁמר *keep*.

***מִשְׁמָר II** 1 n.m. **muzzle,** <OBJ> שׂים *place* Jb 7_{12} (הֲיָם־אָנִי אִם־תַּנִּין כִּי־תָשִׂים עָלַי מִשְׁמָר *Am I the sea or a sea-monster that you set a muzzle on me?*; unless מִשְׁמָר I *watch* or III *wakefulness*).

⇨ שׁמר *keep*.

***מִשְׁמָר III** 1 n.m. **wakefulness,** <OBJ> שׂים *set* Jb 7_{12} (הֲיָם־אָנִי אִם־תַּנִּין כִּי־תָשִׂים עָלַי מִשְׁמָר *Am I the sea or a sea-monster that you set wakefulness on me?*; unless

מִשְׁמָר I *watch* or II *muzzle*).
⇒ שׁמר *keep*.

*[מִשְׁמָרָה] 0.0.1 n.f. perh. **guardhouse** or **fortress**, <CSTR> פנת המשמרה *the corner of the guardhouse* or *fortress* 3QTr 7$_{11}$ (others הַמִּשְׁטָח *the spreading place*).
⇒ שׁמר *keep*.

מִשְׁמֶרֶת 78.1.9 n.f. **watch**—מִשְׁמֶרֶת; cstr. מִשְׁמֶרֶת; sf. מִשְׁמַרְתִּי, מִשְׁמַרְתְּךָ, מִשְׁמַרְתּוֹ, מִשְׁמַרְתָּם, מִשְׁמַרְתָּם; pl. מִשְׁמָרוֹת; cstr. מִשְׁמְרוֹת; sf. מִשְׁמְרוֹתָם (מִשְׁמְרֹתָם, Q משמרותמה, מִשְׁמְרוֹתֵיהֶם)—**1.** usu. priestly **watch, vigil, guard, (religious) observance** (e.g. Gn 26$_5$ 4QJub^f 21$_{23}$), **duty, guard-duty, shift** (Ne 12$_9$ 1 C 9$_{23}$).

2. division of priests, Levites, or Israelites (e.g. 1QM 2$_{2.3.4}$ 4QM^d 1$_3$).

3. guardianship, custody (Nm 18$_8$ 2 S 20$_3$ 1Q36 16$_2$).

4. something to keep watch over (Ex 12$_6$).

5. something reserved (for later usage) (Ex 16$_{23.32.33.34}$ Nm 17$_{25}$ 19$_9$ 4QṬohB^b 1$_8$).

6. (duty of) protection (1 S 22$_{23}$ 1 C 12$_{30}$).

7. appar. **place of watching, (sentry) post** (Is 21$_8$ Hb 2$_1$ 2 C 7$_6$).

<NOM CL> מִשְׁמֶרֶת בְּנֵי־גֵרְשׁוֹן בְּאֹהֶל מוֹעֵד וְהָאֹהֶל *the duty of the Gershonites was in the tent of meeting and comprised the tent* Nm 3$_{25}$, וּמִשְׁמַרְתָּם בְּיַד אִיתָמָר *and their duty is to be under the control of Ithamar* Nm 4$_{28}$, [ומשמרותן] ראשי אבות העדה שנים וחמשים *and the divisions of the heads of the fathers of the congregation are fifty-two* 4QM^d 1$_3$, perh. וּמִשְׁמֶרֶת בְּנֵי אַהֲרֹן אֲחֵיהֶם לַעֲבֹד בֵּית י׳ *and the duty of the sons of Aaron, their brothers, was to serve the house of Y.* 1 C 23$_{32}$ (unless וּמִשְׁמֶרֶת obj. of שׁמר *keep* watch over, with Levites as subj. of שׁמר and עבד; or em. מִשְׁמֶרֶת, without וְ, as nom. cl.).

וְזֹאת מִשְׁמֶרֶת מַשָּׂאָם *and this is the observance of their burden*, i.e. the burden assigned them Nm 4$_{31}$, כִּי־מִשְׁמֶרֶת אַתָּה עִמָּדִי *for you are a (duty of) protection with me*, i.e. I promise to protect you 1 S 22$_{23}$, כִּי עֲלֵיהֶם מִשְׁמֶרֶת *for (incumbent) upon them was guard-duty* 1 C 9$_{27}$ (or em. מִשְׁמַרְתּוֹ *its guard duty*, i.e. the duty of guarding it), לְאֵלֶּה מַחְלְקוֹת הַשֹּׁעֲרִים ... מִשְׁמָרוֹת לְעֻמַּת אֲחֵיהֶם *pertaining to these were the divisions of the gatekeepers ..., shifts in parallel with their brothers* 1 C 26$_{12}$.

<OBJ> שׁמר *keep* Gn 26$_5$ Lv 8$_{35}$ 18$_{30}$ 22$_9$ Nm 1$_{53}$ 9$_{19.23}$ 31$_{30.47}$ 3$_{7.7.8.28.32}$ (both שֹׁמְרֵי מִשְׁמֶרֶת *keepers of the watch of*) 3$_{38}$ 8$_{26}$ (+ עֲבֹדָה *service*) 18$_{3.3.4}$ (+ עֲבֹדָה) 18$_{5.5}$ 31$_{30.47}$ (both שֹׁמְרֵי מִשְׁמֶרֶת) Dt 11$_1$ Jos 22$_3$ 1 K 2$_3$ (+ חֻקָּה *statute*, מִצְוָה *commandment*, מִשְׁפָּט *judgment*, עֵדוּת *testimony*) 2 K 11$_5$ (שֹׁמְרֵי מִשְׁמֶרֶת) 11$_{6.7}$ Ezk 40$_{45.46}$ (both שֹׁמְרֵי מִשְׁמֶרֶת) 44$_8$ (or del.) 44$_{8.14}$ (both שֹׁמְרֵי מִשְׁמֶרֶת) 44$_{15}$=CD 4$_1$ Ezk 44$_{16}$ 48$_{11}$ Zc 3$_7$ (+ דֶּרֶךְ *way* of Y.) Ml 3$_7$ (if ins. מִשְׁמֶרֶת) 3$_{14}$ Ne 12$_{45.45}$ 1 C 12$_{30}$ 23$_{32.32}$ (or del. מִשְׁמֶרֶת) 23$_{32}$ (unless מִשְׁמֶרֶת introduces nom. cl.) 2 C 13$_{11}$ 23$_6$ 4QJub^f 21$_{23}$ ([משמר]ת; 4QJub^d [ו]שמ[ור משמ]רת), נתן *give* Nm 18$_8$, *cause to be* Ezk 44$_{14}$ (+ עֲבֹדָה *service*), עמד hi. *establish* Ne 7$_3$ (+ מִשְׁמָר *watch*) 13$_{30}$ (+ מְלָאכָה *work*), נפל hi. *let fall*, i.e. cast (lot) 1 C 25$_8$ (or em. גּוֹרָלוֹת מִשְׁמָרוֹת appar. *they cast lots, namely, duties*, i.e. they cast lots for duties, to גּוֹרָלוֹת they cast *lots of*, i.e. for, duties; mss מִשְׁמֶרֶת *duty*).

<CSTR> מִשְׁמֶרֶת י׳ *the watch of Y.* Lv 8$_{35}$ Nm 9$_{19.23}$ 1 K 2$_3$ 2 C 13$_{11}$ 23$_6$, משמר[ת אל]עליון *the observance of El Elyon* 4QJub^f 21$_{23}$ (4QJub^d [משמ]רת אל עליון), מִשְׁמֶרֶת אֱלֹהֵיהֶם *the observance of their God* Ne 12$_{45}$, מִשְׁמֶרֶת כָּל־הָעֵדָה *the watch (on behalf) of all the congregation* Nm 3$_7$, מִשְׁמֶרֶת בְּנֵי יִשְׂרָאֵל *the watch (on behalf) of the children of Israel* Nm 3$_{8.38}$, מִשְׁמֶרֶת בְּנֵי־גֵרְשׁוֹן *the duty of the Gershonites* Nm 3$_{25}$, מִשְׁמֶרֶת בְּנֵי מְרָרִי *the duty of the Merarites* Nm 3$_{36}$, מִשְׁמֶרֶת בְּנֵי אַהֲרֹן *the duty of*, or *watch of*, i.e. over, *the sons of Aaron* 1 C 23$_{32}$, מִשְׁמֶרֶת בֵּית־שָׁאוּל *the protection of the household of Saul* 1 C 12$_{30}$.

מִשְׁמֶרֶת הַבַּיִת *the watch of*, i.e. over, *the house*, i.e. temple 2 K 11$_6$ Ezk 40$_{45}$ (הַבַּיִת) 44$_{14}$ (הַבַּיִת), מִשְׁמֶרֶת בֵּית הַמֶּלֶךְ *the watch of*, i.e. over, *the house of the king* 2 K 11$_5$, מִשְׁמֶרֶת בֵּית־י׳ *the watch of*, i.e. over, *the house of Y.* 2 K 11$_7$, מִשְׁמֶרֶת מִשְׁכַּן י׳ *the watch of*, i.e. over, *the tabernacle of Y.* Nm 31$_{30.47}$, מִשְׁמֶרֶת מִשְׁכַּן הָעֵדוּת *the watch of the tabernacle of the testimony* Nm 1$_{53}$, מִשְׁמֶרֶת אֹהֶל מוֹעֵד *the watch of*, i.e. over, *the tent of testimony* Nm 18$_4$ 1 C 23$_{32}$ (אֹהֶל־), מִשְׁמֶרֶת כָּל־הָאֹהֶל *the watch of*, i.e. over, *all the tent* Nm 18_{3}, מִשְׁמֶרֶת הַמִּזְבֵּחַ *the observance of (duties connected with) the altar* Nm 18_{5} Ezk 40_{46}, מִשְׁמֶרֶת הַקֹּדֶשׁ *the observance of holiness*, or *of (duties connected with) the sanctuary* Nm $3_{28.32}$ 18_{5} 1 C 23_{32} (or del.), מִשְׁמֶרֶת קָדָשָׁי perh. *the observance of my holy rites* Ezk 44_{8} (or del.), מִשְׁמֶרֶת הַמִּקְדָּשׁ *the watch of*, i.e. over, *the sanctuary* Nm 3_{38}, מִשְׁמֶרֶת מִקְדָּשִׁי *the watch of*, i.e. over, *my sanctuary* Ezk 44_{15}=CD 4_{1}, מִשְׁמֶרֶת מַשָּׂאָם *the observance of their burden*, i.e. the burden assigned them Nm $4_{31.32}$.

[משמרותן ראשי אבות העדה] *the divisions of the heads of the fathers of the congregation* 4QM^{d} 1_{3}, מִשְׁמְרוֹת יֹשְׁבֵי יְרוּשָׁלִָם *the watches of*, i.e. by, *the residents of Jerusalem* Ne 7_{3}, מִשְׁמֶרֶת תְּרוּמֹתָי *the custody of my contributions* Nm 18_{8}, מִשְׁמֶרֶת חֻקֹּתָיו וּמִשְׁפָּטָיו וּמִצְוֹתָיו *the observance of his statutes and his judgments and his commandments* Dt 11_{1} (if em. מִשְׁמַרְתּוֹ וְחֻקֹּתָיו *his observance and his statutes* and his judgments and his commandments; Sam, ms מִשְׁמַרְתּוֹ חֻקֹּתָיו *his religious observance, namely his statutes* and his judgments and his commandments), מִשְׁמֶרֶת מִצְוַת י׳ *the observance of the commandment of Y.* Jos 22_{3}, מִשְׁמֶרֶת הַטָּהֳרָה *the observance of purity* Ne 12_{45}.

ראשי המשמרות *the heads of the (priestly) divisions* 1QM 2_{2}, ראשי משמרותם *the chiefs of their divisions* 1QM $2_{3.4}$, [א]נשי משמרת *the men of the guardianship*, i.e. the guardians, of your secrets 1Q36 16_{2}, שֹׁמְרֵי מִשְׁמֶרֶת *keepers of the watch of*, i.e. over Nm $3_{28.32}$ $31_{30.47}$ 2 K $11_{5.7}$ (if em. וְשָׁמְרוּ *and they are to keep* to וְשֹׁמְרֵי *and keepers of*) Ezk $40_{45.46}$ 44_{14}, שֹׁמְרֵי מִשְׁמַרְתִּי *the keepers of my observance* Ezk 44_{8}, פְּקֻדַּת מִשְׁמֶרֶת *the appointment of the duty of* Nm 3_{36}, כְּלֵי מִשְׁמֶרֶת *the vessels of*, i.e. pertaining to, *the observance of* Nm 4_{32}, בֵּית־מִשְׁמֶרֶת *(in) a place of custody* 2 S 20_{3}, גּוֹרָלוֹת מִשְׁמָרוֹת *lots of*, i.e. for, *duties* 1 C 25_{8} (if em. גּוֹרָלוֹת *lots*, i.e. app.; mss מִשְׁמֶרֶת *duty*).

<APP> חֻקָּה *statute* Gn 26_{5} Dt $11_{1(Sam, ms)}$ (L מִשְׁמַרְתּוֹ וְחֻקֹּתָיו *his observance and his statutes* and his judgments and his commandments; or em. מִשְׁמֶרֶת חֻקֹּתָיו *the observance of his statutes*), מִצְוָה *commandment* Gn 26_{5} Dt $11_{1(Sam, ms)}$, מִשְׁפָּט *judgment* Dt $11_{1(Sam, ms)}$, תּוֹרָה *law* Gn 26_{5}, גּוֹרָל *lot* 1 C 25_{8} (or em. גּוֹרָלוֹת מִשְׁמָרוֹת appar. *they cast lots, namely, duties*, i.e. they cast lots for duties, to גּוֹרָלוֹת *lots of*, i.e. for, duties; mss מִשְׁמֶרֶת *duty*), מַחֲלֹקֶת *division* 1 C 26_{12}.

<PREP> לְ perh. of direction, *to* 4QM^{a} 1_{7}.

לְ of purpose, *for (the purpose of)*, or perh. *by, in accordance with* shifts Ne 12_{9} (אֲחֵיהֶם לְנֶגְדָּם לְמִשְׁמָרוֹת *their brothers were opposite them for duties* or *by shifts*) 1 C 9_{23} (וְהֵם ... עַל־הַשְּׁעָרִים ... לְמִשְׁמָרוֹת *and they ... were in charge of the gates ... for guard-duties* or *by shifts*; or em. שֹׁמְרִים *[as] guards*), + יחשׂ htp. *be genealogically enrolled* 2 C 31_{16} (|| עֲבֹדָה *service*, מַחֲלֹקֶת *division*) 31_{17} (|| מַחֲלֹקֶת).

לְ appar. *to, in charge of*, + שׂים *place* Ezk 44_{8}.

לְ *as* Ex 16_{32} (מְלֹא הָעֹמֶר מִמֶּנּוּ לְמִשְׁמֶרֶת *the fullness of an omer of it is to be as something reserved*; Sam מַלְאוּ *fill* an omer of it as something reserved; or em. מִמֶּנּוּ to מִמָּן/מָן an omer *of manna*), + היה *be* Ex 12_{6} Nm 19_{9}, נוח hi. *place*, i.e. set aside Ex $16_{23.33.34}$ 4QṬoh B^{b} 1_{8} (והנ]יחוהו למשמרת]) perh. *and they shall set them aside as something reserved*), שׁוב hi. *take back* Nm 17_{25}, שׁמר *keep (watch)* Nm 3_{38}.

בְּ of accompaniment, *with* perh. Si $44_{4(B)}$ (ומושלים במשמרותם *and [priestly] rulers with their watches*; others במשמחותם tellers of proverbs at *their celebrations*, i.e. מִשְׂמָחָה; or מַשְׂמְרוֹתָם tellers of proverbs with *their nails*, i.e. pointed sayings.

בְּ perh. *over, in charge of*, + שׁרת pi. *minister* 1QM 2_{2}= 4QM^{d} 1_{5} ([י]שׁ[רתו]).

בְּ *as*, + פקד *appoint* Gershonites their tasks as a duty Nm 4_{27} (or em. בְּמִשְׁמֶרֶת *as a duty* to בְּשֵׁמוֹת *by names* [and/or em. וּפְקַדְתֶּם *and you are to appoint* to וּפְקֻדָּתָם *and their appointment* will be]).

בְּ *in connection with*, + עשׂה *do* to Levites Nm 8_{26}.

אֶל *over, in charge of*, + שׂים *place* Benaiah 2 S 23_{23} (if em. מִשְׁמַעְתּוֹ *his retinue* to מִשְׁמַרְתּוֹ *his watch*).

עַל appar. *at, by*, + עמד *stand* Hb 2_{1} (|| מָצוֹר *rampart* [or em. מַצּוֹר *guard post*]) 2 C 7_{6}, נצב ni. *stand* Is 21_{8} (|| מִצְפֶּה *watchtower*).

עַל *over, in charge of*, + שׂים *place* Benaiah 2 S 23_{23} (if em. מִשְׁמַעְתּוֹ *his retinue* to מִשְׁמַרְתּוֹ *his watch*), יצב htp. *take one's stand* 1QH fr. 4_{5} ([ו]יתיצבו]), עמד hi. *establish* (|| עֲבֹדָה *service*, מַחֲלֹקֶת *division*) 2 C 8_{14} 35_{2}.

<COLL> משמרת לרזיכה *the guardianship of your secrets* 1Q36 16$_{2}$, מִשְׁמָרוֹת לַכֹּהֲנִים וְלַלְוִיִּם *watches of the priests and of the Levites* Ne 13$_{30}$, מִשְׁמֶרֶת לְדֹרֹתֵיכֶם *something reserved for your generations* Ex 16$_{32.33}$, מִשְׁמֶרֶת עַד־הַבֹּקֶר *something reserved until the morning* Ex 16$_{23}$, מִשְׁמֶרֶת לְמֵי נִדָּה *something reserved for waters of impurity* Nm 19$_{9}$, לְמִשְׁמֶרֶת לְאוֹת לִבְנֵי־מֶרִי *something reserved as a sign to children of rebelliousness* Nm 17$_{25}$, מִשְׁמָרוֹת לְעֻמַּת אֲחֵיהֶם *shifts in parallel with their brothers* 1 C 26$_{12}$.

Also 4QSela 9.2$_{14}$ ([משׁ]מרות).

<SYN> עֲבֹדָה *service*, מַחֲלֹקֶת *division*, מִצְפֶּה *watchtower*, מָצוֹר *rampart*.*

⇒ שׁמר *keep*.

*[מְשַׁמֵּשׁ] 0.0.0.1 pr.n.m. **Meshammesh,** father of Jehu (יהוא), <CSTR> בן משמשׁ *the son of Meshammesh* Seal 570 (T. Beit Mirsim?, 7th/6th cent.).

*[מְשָׁנָה] n.f. **bladder,** <CSTR> זִרְמַת מְשָׁנָה *effusion of the bladder* Ps 90$_{5}$ (if em. זְרַמְתָּם שֵׁנָה *you overwhelm them, sleep*).

מִשְׁנֶה I 35.0.10 n.[m.] **second**—cstr. מִשְׁנֵה (Q משׁנא); sf. מִשְׁנֵהוּ (Q [מ]שׁניהו); pl. מִשְׁנִים; cstr. Q משׁני; sf. Q משׁניו, משׁניכם—**1. second** in rank or importance, **deputy,** second-in-command (Gn 41$_{43}$ 1 S 23$_{17}$ Est 10$_{3}$ Ne 11$_{17}$ 1 C 5$_{12}$ 15$_{18}$ 16$_{5}$ 2 C 28$_{7}$ 31$_{12}$ 35$_{24}$ 1QM 2$_{1}$=4QM[d] 1$_{4}$ perh. Ne 11$_{9}$ 4QpsEzek[d] 9$_{3}$ 4QShirShabb[e] 13$_{4}$); second, or, deputizing, rank (2 K 23$_{4}$ 25$_{18}$||Jr 52$_{24}$ 11QT 31$_{4}$ 4QShirShabb[a] 3.2$_{5}$ 11QShirShabb 1$_{8}$ 6$_{9}$); next one (4QShirShabb[b] 3$_{4}$ 4QShirShabb[e] 11$_{3}$); perh. successor (4QAdmon 1.2$_{9}$).

2. second child or perh. **younger brother** (1 S 8$_{2}$ 17$_{13}$ 2 S 3$_{3}$).

3. animal of the **second brood** (1 S 15$_{9}$ [or em.]).

4. copy, duplicate, equivalent (Dt 17$_{18}$ 3QTr 12$_{11}$ perh. Dt 15$_{18}$ 17$_{18}$ Jr 16$_{18}$ 17$_{18}$ Jb 42$_{10}$).

5. second quarter of Jerusalem, the **Mishneh** (2 K 22$_{14}$||2 C 34$_{22}$ Zp 1$_{10}$ perh. Ne 11$_{9}$), area to NW of the earlier city.

6. double (share), twice as much* (Gn 43$_{12.15}$ Ex 16$_{5.22}$ Is 61$_{7}$ [or del.] 61$_{7}$ [unless מִשְׁנֶה III *the best*] Zc 9$_{12}$ [unless מִשְׁנֶה II *equivalent*]; perh. Dt 15$_{18}$ Jr 16$_{18}$ [unless both מִשְׁנֶה II] 17$_{18}$ Jb 42$_{10}$).

In some constructions under Cstr. and App., perh. מִשְׁנֶה used as adjective, **second.**

<SUBJ> היה *be* Ex 16$_{5}$ (see Coll.).

<NOM CL> וִיהוּדָה בֶן־הַסְּנוּאָה עַל־הָעִיר מִשְׁנֶה *and Judah son of Hassenuah was over the city (as) second-in-command* Ne 11$_{9}$ (or em. הַסְּנָאָה *Hassenaah;* unless הָעִיר מִשְׁנֶה *the city, [the] second quarter,* i.e. the second quarter of the city, or *Mishneh,* as app.), כִּי מָרְדֳּכַי הַיְּהוּדִי מִשְׁנֶה לַמֶּלֶךְ אֲחַשְׁוֵרוֹשׁ וְגָדוֹל לַיְּהוּדִים *for Mordecai the Jew was a deputy to King Artaxerxes and the greatest of the Jews* Est 10$_{3}$ (or em. בַּיְּהוּדִים *among,* i.e. of, the Jews), וּבַקְבֻּקְיָה מִשְׁנֶה *and Bakbukiah was second-in-command* Ne 11$_{17}$ (:: ראשׁ *head*), יוֹאֵל הָרֹאשׁ וְשָׁפָם הַמִּשְׁנֶה *Joel was the head and Shapham the second most important* 1 C 5$_{12}$ (or em. שְׁבָט *Shebat* or שָׁפָן *Shaphan;* :: ראשׁ *head*), וְעִמָּהֶם אֲחֵיהֶם הַמִּשְׁנִים *and with them were their brothers, those of second rank* 1 C 15$_{18}$, אָסָף הָרֹאשׁ וּמִשְׁנֵהוּ זְכַרְיָה *Asaph was the head and his deputy was Zechariah* 1 C 16$_{5}$ (:: ראשׁ *head*).

וַעֲלֵיהֶם נָגִיד כָּנַנְיָהוּ הַלֵּוִי וְשִׁמְעִי אָחִיהוּ מִשְׁנֶה *and over them was a prince, Conaniah the Levite, and Shimei, his brother, a second-in-command* or *and over them Conaniah, the Levite, was prince and Shimei, his brother, was second-in-command* 2 C 31$_{12(Qr)}$ (:: נָגִיד *prince*), הַמִּשְׁנֶה אֲשֶׁר־לוֹ *the deputy that was his,* i.e. his deputy Gn 41$_{43}$ 2 C 35$_{24}$ (unless in one or both אֲשֶׁר־לוֹ defines רֶכֶב/מִרְכֶּבֶת *the chariot of* the deputy), כִּי מִשְׁנֶה שְׂכַר שָׂכִיר עֲבָדְךָ שֵׁשׁ שָׁנִים appar. *for (a) double (share compared with),* i.e. twice as much as, or, *a duplicate (of),* i.e. the same as, *the wage of an employee is your servant,* i.e. your servant has been (worth to you), *(for) six years* Dt 15$_{18}$ (unless מִשְׁנֶה II *equivalent;* mss מִשְׁנֵה *a double portion,* or *a duplicate, of* the wages), בשׁית שבצח בצפון ... משׁנא הכתב הזא perh. *in the pit that is by the bare rock, to the north ... there is a duplicate of this document* 3QTr 12$_{11}$ (others ... משׁנה הזא and/or שׁכינה in the *neighbouring* pit or שׁכנה in the pit *of [the] presence* or שׁבצהב צפון in the pit *that is in Zehab, north of*).

תַּחַת בָּשְׁתְּכֶם מִשְׁנֶה appar. *despite your shame, (there will be) a double portion* Is 61$_{7}$ (or em. תַּחַת כִּי *because* your shame was double and/or בָּשְׁתָּם *their shame*; or תַּחַת בֹּשֶׁת [without מִשְׁנֶה] *instead of shame* and reproach, exultation will be their portion), perh. וּמִשְׁנֵהוּ אֲבִינָדָב *and his* (Jesse's) *second child*, or *his* (Eliab's) *younger brother, was Abinadab* 1 S 17$_{13}$ (unless מִשְׁנֵהוּ in app. with אֱלִיאָב as predicate of וְשֵׁם שְׁלֹשֶׁת בָּנָיו *and the name(s) of his three sons were* ... Eliab, his second / his younger brother; :: בְּכוֹר *firstborn*, שְׁלִישִׁי *third [child]*), וּמִשְׁנֵהוּ כִלְאָב *and his* (David's) *second child*, or *his* (Amnon's) *younger brother, was Chileab* 2 S 3$_{3}$ (or em. דָּנִיֵּאל *Daniel*, as ||1 C 3$_{1}$, or דְּלוּיָה *Deluijah*; :: בְּכוֹר *firstborn*, שְׁלִישִׁי *third [child]*, רְבִיעִי *fourth [child]*, חֲמִישִׁי *fifth [child]*, שִׁשִּׁי *sixth [child]*).

<OBJ> ירשׁ *possess* Is 61$_{7}$ (unless מִשְׁנֶה III *the best*), לקח *take* Gn 43$_{12}$, לקט *glean* Ex 16$_{22}$, כתב *write (down)* Dt 17$_{18}$ Jos 8$_{32.32}$ (or del. אֲשֶׁר כָּתַב *that he wrote down*), שׁלם pi. *recompense* Jr 16$_{18}$ (unless מִשְׁנֶה II *equivalent*; + רִאשׁוֹנָה *first [of all]*), שׁוב hi. *repay* Zc 9$_{12}$ (unless מִשְׁנֶה II *equivalent*; see Coll.), הרג *kill* 2 C 28$_{7}$.

<CSTR> מִשְׁנֵה הַמֶּלֶךְ *the king's deputy* 2 C 28$_{7}$, [משני פלא[the princes of *those second in rank (in respect) of wonder* 4QShirShabb[e] 13$_{3.7}$ ([משנ[י פלא]), משני [נשי]אי פלא *the deputies of the princes of wonder* 4QShir Shabb[e] 13$_{4}$, משנא הכתב *a duplicate of the document* 3QTr 12$_{11}$ (others משנה), מִשְׁנֵה־כֶסֶף *a double share of silver* Gn 43$_{15(mss)}$ (L מִשְׁנֶה *a double share [of] silver*, i.e. app.), מִשְׁנֵה שְׂכַר שָׂכִיר *a double share of*, i.e. twice as much as, or, *a duplicate of*, i.e. the same as, *the wage of an employee* Dt 15$_{18(mss)}$ (unless מִשְׁנֶה II *equivalent*), מִשְׁנֵה עֲוֹנָם וְחַטָּאתָם *a double share of*, i.e. twice as much as, or, *a duplicate of*, i.e. the same as, *their iniquity and their sin* Jr 16$_{18}$ (unless מִשְׁנֶה II *equivalent*), מִשְׁנֵה הַתּוֹרָה *a copy*, or *the second promulgation*, or, *exposition, of the law* Dt 17$_{18}$, מִשְׁנֵה תּוֹרַת מֹשֶׁה *a copy*, or *the second promulgation*, or, *exposition, of the law of Moses* Jos 8$_{32}$.

כֹּהֵן הַמִּשְׁנֶה *the priest of the second rank*, i.e. deputy high priest 2 K 23$_{4}$ (if em. כֹּהֲנֵי *the priests of*; + הַכֹּהֵן הַגָּדוֹל *the high priest*, שֹׁמְרֵי הַסַּף *the keepers of the threshold*) 25$_{18(mss)}$||Jr 52$_{24}$ (L 2 K כֹּהֵן מִשְׁנֶה perh. *a priest of second rank*; + כֹּהֵן הָרֹאשׁ *the priest of the head*, i.e. high priest, שְׁלֹשֶׁת שֹׁמְרֵי הַסַּף *the three keepers of the threshold*), נשיאי משנה *princes of second rank* 4QShirShabb[a] 3.2$_{5}$, נש]יאי משני[*the princes of those second in rank (in respect) of* wonder 4QShir Shabb[e] 13$_{3.7}$ ([נשיאי משׁ[ני]), [לשון מ]שניהו *the tongue of his deputy* 4QShirShabb[b] 3$_{4}$, [לשון] משניו *the tongue of his deputies* 4QShirShabb[e] 11$_{3}$ (=4QShirShabb[c] 1.2$_{27}$ [לשון משניו]); :: שְׁלִישִׁי *third [in line]*), מִרְכֶּבֶת הַמִּשְׁנֶה *the chariot of the deputy* Gn 41$_{43}$, רֶכֶב הַמִּשְׁנֶה *the chariot of his deputy* 2 C 35$_{24}$, שֵׁם מִשְׁנֵהוּ *the name of his second-born child* 1 S 8$_{2}$ (:: בְּכוֹר *firstborn*), ... מֵיטַב הַמִּשְׁנִים *the best of ... those born in second batch* 1 S 15$_{9}$ (ms הַשְּׁמֵנִים *the fatlings*; or em. הַמַּשְׁמַנִּים/הַשְּׁמַנִּים in same sense, or הַמְּעִילִים *the garments*; + צֹאן *sheep*, בָּקָר *cattle*, כַּר *ram*), כְּפוֹרֵי כֶסֶף מִשְׁנִים perh. *bowls of silver of additional kinds*, i.e. various kinds of silver bowls Ezr 1$_{10}$ (or em. מְשֻׁנִּים *different* bowls, or אֲלָפִים שְׁנַיִם the bowls of silver were *two thousand*).

<APP> אֶלְקָנָה מִשְׁנֵה הַמֶּלֶךְ *Elkanah, the king's deputy* 2 C 28$_{7}$, כֶּסֶף מִשְׁנֶה *silver, a double share*, i.e. double the silver Gn 43$_{12}$ (+ מִשְׁגֶּה *mistake*), מִשְׁנֶה־כֶסֶף *a double share (of) silver* Gn 43$_{15}$ (mss מִשְׁנֵה *a double share of*, i.e. cstr.), מִשְׁנֶה שְׂכַר שָׂכִיר appar. *a double share (compared with)*, i.e. twice as much as, or, *a duplicate (of)*, i.e. the same as, *the wage of an employee* Dt 15$_{18}$ (unless מִשְׁנֶה II *equivalent*; mss מִשְׁנֵה *a double share*, or, *duplicate, of*, i.e. cstr.), מִשְׁנֶה שְׁנֵי הָעֹמֶר לָאֶחָד *a double share, two omers for one*, or *for each person* Ex 16$_{22}$, מִשְׁנֶה שִׁבָּרוֹן break them with *a double share of*, i.e. twice as much, or, *a duplicate (of)*, i.e. the same, *breaking* Jr 17$_{18}$, perh. וּמִשְׁנֵהוּ אֲבִינָדָב *and his* (Jesse's) *second child*, or *his* (Eliab's) *younger brother, Abinadab* 1 S 17$_{13}$ (unless וּמִשְׁנֵהוּ אֲבִינָדָב = *and his second child/younger brother was Abinadab*, i.e. nom. cl.), אֲחֵיהֶם הַמִּשְׁנִים *their brothers, those of second rank* 1 C 15$_{18}$, שִׁמְעִי אָחִיהוּ מִשְׁנֶה *Shimei, his brother, a second-in-command* 2 C 31$_{12}$ (unless *Shimei, his brother, was second-in-command*, i.e. nom. cl.), הכוהן המשנה *the priest, the second one*, i.e. the deputy (high) priest 11QT 31$_{4}$ (+ [הכוהן הג]דול *the high priest*), הָעִיר מִשְׁנֶה *the city, (the) second quarter*, i.e. the second quarter

of the city, or *Mishneh* Ne 11₉ (unless הָעִיר מִשְׁנֶה and Judah son of Hassenuah was over *the city [as] second-in-command*, i.e. nom. cl.).

<PREP> לְ *as*, + היה *be* 1 S 23₁₇; *unto*, + יסף hi. *increase* Jb 42₁₀; בְּ of place, *among, in* 4QShirShabb[e] 13₄ (השׁשׁי במשני [נשׂ]אי פלא *the sixth among the deputies of the princes of wonder*) perh. 11QShirShabb 6₉, + ישׁב *dwell* 2 K 22₁₄||2 C 34₂₂; מִן of direction, *from*, + היה *be* (of wailing) Zp 1₁₀ (+ שַׁעַר הַדָּגִים *the Fish Gate*); עַל *over, in charge of* Ne 11₉ (וִיהוּדָה ... עַל־הָעִיר מִשְׁנֶה *and Judah ... was over the city, [the] second quarter*, i.e. the second quarter of the city, or *Mishneh*, i.e. app.; or *and Judah ... was over the city [as] second-in-command*, i.e. nom. cl.); אַחַר *after, behind*, + סרך *order* heads of priests 1QM 2₁=4QM[d] 1₄ ([יסרוכו אחר] *they will order after*).

<COLL> כוהן הראשׁ ומשנהו *the priest of the head*, i.e. high priest, *and his deputy* 1QM 2₁=4QM[d] 1₄ (הרואשׁ), וְהָיָה מִשְׁנֶה עַל אֲשֶׁר־יִלְקְטוּ יוֹם יוֹם *and it will be a double share compared with what they glean each day* Ex 16₅, מִשְׁנֶה מֵאֶחָיו *second in command of*, i.e. over, *his brothers* Ne 11₁₇, מִשְׁנֶה שִׁבָּרוֹן שָׁבְרֵם *break them with a double share of*, i.e. twice as much, or, *a duplicate (of)*, i.e. the same, *breaking* Jr 17₁₈, גַּם־הַיּוֹם מַגִּיד מִשְׁנֶה אָשִׁיב לָךְ appar. *even the day announces (it): a double share I shall repay to you* Zc 9₁₂ (unless מִשְׁנֶה II *equivalent*; or em. גְּמוּל יוֹם מְגֻרַיִךְ *[as] recompense for the day of your sojournings*, a double share), בִּירוּשָׁלַםִ בַּמִּשְׁנֶה *in Jerusalem in the second quarter* or *Mishneh* 2 K 22₁₄|| 2 C 34₂₂.

Also perh. 11QShirShabb 1₈ (משני perh. מִשְּׁנֵי *from two*).

<ANT> ראשׁ *head*, נָגִיד *prince*, בְּכוֹר *firstborn*, שְׁלִישִׁי *third*, רְבִיעִי *fourth (child)*, חֲמִישִׁי *fifth (child)*, שִׁשִּׁי *sixth (child)*.*

⇒ שׁנה II *repeat*.

*מִשְׁנֶה II ₃ n.[m.] **equivalent** (unless מִשְׁנֶה I *second*) —מִשְׁנֵה—<OBJ> שׁלם pi. *recompense* Jr 16₁₈, שׁוב hi. *repay* Zc 9₁₂. <CSTR> מִשְׁנֵה עֲוֹנָם וְחַטָּאתָם *the equivalent of their iniquity and their sin* Jr 16₁₈, מִשְׁנֵה שְׂכַר שָׂכִיר *equivalent of the wage of an employee* Dt 15₁₈(mss). <APP> מִשְׁנֶה שְׂכַר שָׂכִיר *the equivalent, the cost*, i.e. the equivalent of the cost, *of a hired servant* Dt 15₁₈ (mss מִשְׁנֵה *equivalent of*). <COLL> מִשְׁנֶה שְׂכַר שָׂכִיר עֲבָדְךָ *at the equivalent of the cost of a hired servant he has served you* Dt 15₁₈.

*מִשְׁנֶה III ₁ n.[m.] **the best (portion)** (unless מִשְׁנֶה I *second*), <OBJ> ירשׁ *possess* Is 61₇.

מְשִׁסָּה ₆ n.f. **plunder**—Q משיסה; pl. מְשִׁסּוֹת—<PREP> לְ *as*, + היה *be* 2 K 21₁₄ Is 42₂₂ (with ellipsis of לְ in MT) Jr 30₁₆ (all three || בַּז *spoil*) Hb 2₇ Zp 1₁₃ (שְׁמָמָה *desolation*), נתן *give* Jacob Is 42₂₄(Qr) (Kt appar. מְשׁוּסָּה *plunder*; or em. מְשׁוֹסֶה give to a *plunderer*, i.e. po. ptc. of שׁסה *plunder*; Qr מְשִׁסָּה [1QIsa[a] משיסה] *plunder*; + לְבֹזְזִים and Israel *to plunderers*).

<COLL> הָיוּ ... לִמְשִׁסָּה וְאֵין־אֹמֵר הָשַׁב *they have become ... as plunder, and there is none to say, Hold back* Is 42₂₂(mss), וְהָיוּ שֹׁאסַיִךְ לִמְשִׁסָּה *and your plunderers will become as plunder* Jr 30₁₆ (Qr mss שֹׁסַיִךְ, Kt mss appar. שֹׁאֲסַיִךְ, i.e. ptc. of שׁסס *plunder*), וְהָיִיתָ מְשִׁסּוֹת לָמוֹ *and you will become as plunder for them* Hb 2₇, וְהָיוּ לְבַז וְלִמְשִׁסָּה לְכָל־אֹיְבֵיהֶם *and they will become as spoil and as plunder for all their enemies* 2 K 21₁₄.

<SYN> בַּז *spoil*, שְׁמָמָה *desolation*.

⇒ שׁסס *plunder*.

[מִשְׁעוֹל] ₁ n.[m.] **(narrow) pathway**—cstr. מִשְׁעוֹל (Sam משעל)—<CSTR> מִשְׁעוֹל הַכְּרָמִים *a pathway of*, i.e. through, *the vineyards* Nm 22₂₄. <PREP> בְּ of place, *in, on*, + עמד *stand* (of angel) Nm 22₂₄ (+ בְּמָקוֹם צָר *in a narrow place* 22₂₆). <COLL> מִשְׁעוֹל הַכְּרָמִים גָּדֵר מִזֶּה וְגָדֵר מִזֶּה *a pathway of*, i.e. through, *the vineyards, with a fence on one side and a fence on the other side* Nm 22₂₄.

⇒ cf. שֹׁעַל *hollow hand*.

מִשְׁעִי I ₁ n.[f.] **cleansing** (of new-born child), <PREP> לְ of purpose, *for (the purpose of)*, + רחץ pu. *be washed* Ezk 16₄ (unless לְמִשְׁעִי adverbial, you were not washed *cleanly*; + כרת pu. *be cut*, of umbilical cord, מלח ho.

be rubbed in salt, + חתל pu./ho. *be swaddled;* unless מִשְׁעִי II *rubbing* or III *midwife*).
⇒ שׁעה II *smooth, anoint,* or שׁעע *smooth, anoint.*

*מִשְׁעִי II 1 n.[f.] **rubbing,** <PREP> לְ of purpose, *for (the purpose of),* + רחץ pu. *be washed* Ezk 16$_4$ (לֹא־רֻחַצְתְּ לְמִשְׁעִי *you were not washed (ready) for rubbing (with oil);** unless מִשְׁעִי I *cleansing* or III *midwife*).
⇒ שׁעה *smear.*

*מִשְׁעִי III 1 n.[f.] **midwife,** <PREP> לְ of agent, *by,* + רחץ pu. *be washed* Ezk 16$_4$ (לֹא־רֻחַצְתְּ לְמִשְׁעִי *you were not washed by the midwife;* + כרת pu. *be cut,* of umbilical cord, מלח ho. *be rubbed in salt,* חתל pu./ho. *be swaddled;* unless מִשְׁעִי I *cleansing* or II *rubbing*).

*מִשְׁעִי IV 1 n.[f.] **smoothness,** <PREP> לְ of agent, *by,* + רחץ pu. *be washed* Ezk 16$_4$ (לֹא־רֻחַצְתְּ לְמִשְׁעִי *you were not washed to smoothness,* i.e. smooth; + כרת pu. *be cut,* of umbilical cord, מלח ho. *be rubbed in salt,* חתל pu./ho. *be swaddled;* unless מִשְׁעִי I *cleansing* or II *rubbing*).

[מִשְׁעָל], see מִשְׁעוֹל *pathway.*

מִשְׁעָם 1 pr.n.m. **Misham,** a son of Elpaal, descendant of Benjamin, <NOM CL> וּבְנֵי אֶלְפַּעַל עֵבֶר וּמִשְׁעָם וָשָׁמֶד *and the sons of Elpaal were Eber and Misham and Shamed* 1 C 8$_{12}$ (mss Ebed, Shamer).

מַשְׁעֵן 1 n.[m.] **support, sustenance,** or (if em.) perh. **rod** as symbol of ruler, <OBJ> סור hi. *remove* Is 3$_1$. <APP> מִשְׁעָן *support,* i.e. sustenance Is 3$_{1.1}$ (or del. מִשְׁעָן both times). <COLL> מַשְׁעֵן וּמַשְׁעֵנָה כֹּל מִשְׁעַן־לֶחֶם וְכֹל מִשְׁעַן־מָיִם *support and support,* perh. every kind of sustenance, *all sustenance (consisting) of food and all sustenance (consisting) of water* Is 3$_1$ (or del. כֹּל מִשְׁעַן־לֶחֶם וְכֹל מִשְׁעַן־מָיִם, in which case מַשְׁעֵן וּמַשְׁעֵנָה perh. *rod and staff,* i.e. every kind of ruler). <SYN> מַשְׁעֵנָה *support,* מִשְׁעָן *support.*
⇒ שׁען *lean.*

מִשְׁעָן I 4.3.2 n.[m.] **support**—cstr. מִשְׁעַן; sf. Q משעני—in general, **support, help** (2 S 22$_{19}$||Ps 18$_{19}$ Si 33$_1$ 36$_{29}$ 42$_{26}$ 1QH 10$_{23}$); appar. **sustenance** (Is 3$_{1.1}$ [or del.]); appar. **staff, stick** as support (1QS 11$_4$).

<SUBJ> היה *be* 2 S 22$_{19}$ (וַיְהִי י׳ מִשְׁעָן לִי *and Y. was a support for me* or *my support;* mss, ||Ps 18$_{19}$ לְמִשְׁעָן was *as a support* to me/*as* my *support*), מצא ni. *be found* Si 33$_1$ (ובעת מוטו ימצא משען *and at the time he totters support will be found,* unless יִמְצָא *he will find* support; + פועל טוב יקראנו בדרכיו *a good deed will encounter him along his ways*).

<NOM CL> והויא עולם משען ימיני *and he who is forever the staff of my right hand* 1QS 11$_4$ (unless והויא עולם = *and exists for ever,* with משען ימיני as nom. cl., *support is at my right hand;* + וגבורתו משענת ימיני *and his strength is the staff of my right hand* 11$_5$, i.e. מִשְׁעֶנֶת).

<OBJ> נתן *give,* i.e. cause to be 1QH 10$_{23}$ (ולא נתתה משעני על בצע *and you have not caused my support to be on,* i.e. caused me to rely on, *[unjust] gain*), סור hi. *remove* Is 3$_{1.1}$ (or del. מִשְׁעָן both times), מצא *find* perh. Si 33$_1$ 4QBéat 14.2$_7$ ([מ]שען), עמד hi. *establish* Si 36$_{29(C)}$, בקשׁ pi. *seek* Si 42$_{26}$ (אין ביראת י׳ מחסור ואין לבקש עמה משׁ[ע]ן [B] *in reverence for Y. there is no lack and no need to seek [additional] support beside it*).

<CSTR> מִשְׁעַן־לֶחֶם *sustenance (consisting) of food* Is 3$_1$ (or del.), מִשְׁעַן־מָיִם *sustenance (consisting) of water* Is 3$_1$ (or del.), משען ימיני *the staff of my right hand* 1QS 11$_4$ (unless as nom. cl., *support is at my right hand*); עמוד משען perh. *a pillar of support* Si 36$_{29(B, D)}$ (D עמוד מ[שע]ן; unless מִשְׁעָן in app. with עַמּוּד and preceding nouns), כָּל מִשְׁעַן־ *every sustenance (consisting) of* food/water Is 3$_{1.1}$ (or del. both times).

<APP> (see Cstr. and Coll.) perh. עַמּוּד *column* Si 36$_{29(B, D)}$ (D מ[שע]ן), perh. עֵזֶר *help* Si 36$_{29(B)}$, perh. מִבְצָר *fortification* Si 36$_{29(B)}$, perh. עִיר *city* Si 36$_{29(D)}$ (מ[שע]ן), perh. קִנְיָן *acquisition* Si 36$_{29(B)}$, מַשְׁעֵן *sustenance* Is 3$_1$ (or del. מִשְׁעָן), מַשְׁעֵנָה *sustenance* Is 3$_1$ (or del. מִשְׁעָן).

<PREP> לְ *as,* + היה *be* 2 S 22$_{19(mss)}$||Ps 18$_{19}$ (וַיְהִי[־]י׳ מִשְׁעָן לִי *and Y. was as a support for me* or *my support*).

מַשְׁעֵן וּמַשְׁעֵנָה כֹּל מִשְׁעַן־לֶחֶם וְכֹל מִשְׁעַן־מָיִם <COLL> *support and support*, perh. every kind of sustenance, *all sustenance (consisting) of food and all sustenance (consisting) of water* Is 3_1 (or del. כֹּל מִשְׁעַן־לֶחֶם וְכֹל מִשְׁעַן־מָיִם, in which case מַשְׁעֵן וּמַשְׁעֵנָה perh. *rod and staff*, i.e. every kind of ruler).

Also perh. 4Q418 45.24 ([משענ]ן).

<SYN> מַשְׁעֵן *support*, מַשְׁעֵנָה *support*.

⇒ שׁען *lean*.

*[מִשְׁעָן] II 0.0.0.1 pr.n.m. **Mishan**, son of Shahar (שחר), <APP> בֵּן *son* Seal 612 (T. Beit Mirsim?, 7th/6th cent.). <PREP> לְ perh. of possession, *of, (belonging) to* Seal 612.

⇒ שׁען *lean*.

מַשְׁעֵנָה 1 n.f. **support, sustenance,** or (if em.) perh. **staff** as symbol of ruler, <OBJ> סור hi. *remove* Is 3_1. <APP> מַשְׁעֵן *support*, i.e. sustenance Is $3_{1.1}$ (or del. מַשְׁעֵן both times). <COLL> מַשְׁעֵן וּמַשְׁעֵנָה כֹּל מִשְׁעַן־לֶחֶם וְכֹל מִשְׁעַן־מָיִם *support and support*, perh. every kind of sustenance, *all sustenance (consisting) of food and all sustenance (consisting) of water* Is 3_1 (or del. כֹּל מִשְׁעַן־לֶחֶם וְכֹל מִשְׁעַן־מָיִם, in which case מַשְׁעֵן וּמַשְׁעֵנָה perh. *rod and staff*, i.e. every kind of ruler). <SYN> מַשְׁעֵן *support*, מִשְׁעָן *support*.*

⇒ שׁען *lean*.

מִשְׁעֶנֶת 11.0.7 n.f. **support**—cstr. מִשְׁעֶנֶת; sf. מִשְׁעַנְתִּי, מִשְׁעַנְתּוֹ, מִשְׁעַנְתֶּךָ; pl. sf. מִשְׁעֲנֹתָם (Q משענותם)—**stick, staff** for walking during convalescence (Ex 21_{19}) or as a support for a weak person (2 K 18_{21}||Is 36_6 Ezk 29_6) or for an old person (Zc 8_4), as an aid on journeys or as substitute for absent owner (Jg 6_{21} 2 K 4_{29} perh. Ps 23_4 1QS 11_5), for digging well (Nm 21_{18}),* a channel of owner's miraculous powers (Jg 6_{21} 2 K $4_{29.31}$); in some of the preceding refs., מִשְׁעֶנֶת perh. also, or instead, a sign of owner's high status; appar. **support** in general, as מִשְׁעָן (1QH 7_{16} 10_{32} 1QM 4_{13} 17_4 4QpsHod^c 2_5).

<SUBJ> היה *be* Ezk 29_6 (יַעַן הֱיוֹתָם מִשְׁעֶנֶת קָנֶה לְבֵית יִשְׂרָאֵל *because they were a staff [consisting] of a reed for the house of Israel*, or *the house of Israel's staff [consisting] of a reed*); or em. הֱיוֹתְךָ because *you were*), נחם pi. *comfort* Ps 23_4 (or em. נחה hi. *guide*; || שֵׁבֶט *staff*).

<NOM CL> הַמִּשְׁעֶנֶת אֲשֶׁר בְּיָדוֹ *the staff that was in his hand* Jg 6_{21}, וְאִישׁ מִשְׁעַנְתּוֹ בְּיָדוֹ מֵרֹב יָמִים *and each one, a stick is in their hand on account of the abundance of days (lived)* Zc 8_4 (+ זְקֵנִים זְקֵנוֹת *old men [and] old women*), עִמָּדִי שִׁבְטְךָ וּמִשְׁעַנְתֶּךָ *with me are your rod and your staff* Ps 23_4 (if del. preceding כִּי־אַתָּה *for*, or *indeed, you are with me*; your rod and your staff, they comfort me), וגבורתו משענת ימיני *and his strength is the staff of my right hand* 1QS 11_5 (+ משען ימיני perh. *the staff of my right hand* 11_4), כי לא [על הון בצע משׁ]ענתי *for not upon the wealth of (unjust) gain is my support* 1QH7_{16} (others [נשׁ]ענתי *have I relied*), ומשענתי במעוז מרום *and my support consists in the refuge of the height*, i.e. heaven 1QH 10_{32}, ומשענתם בלוא חו[יל] perh. *and their support is without strength* 1QM 17_4 (+ לתהו ולבהו תשוקתם *their desire is towards formlessness and emptiness*).

<OBJ> לקח *take* 2 K 4_{29} (+ בְּיָדְךָ *in your hand*), שׂים *place* on sick child's face 2 K $4_{29.31}$, כתב *write* on banners 1QM 4_{13}.

<CSTR> משענת אל *God's support* 1QM 4_{13} (|| עֵזֶר *God's help*, + יְשׁוּעָה *salvation*, נֵצַח *victory*, שִׂמְחָה *rejoicing*, הוֹדָה *thanksgiving*, תְּהִלָּה *praise*, שָׁלוֹם *peace*), מִשְׁעֶנֶת קָנֶה *a staff (consisting) of a (mere) reed* 2 K 18_{21}||Is 36_6 (both מִשְׁעֶנֶת הַקָּנֶה *the staff (consisting) of a broken reed*) Ezk 29_6, משענת ימיני *the staff of my right hand* 1QS 11_5, משענת רום השמים *the support of the height of heaven* 4QpsHod^c 2_5; קְצֵה הַמִּשְׁעֶנֶת *the end*, i.e. tip, *of the staff* Jg 6_{21}.

<APP> perh. מִצְרַיִם *Egypt* 2 K 18_{21}||Is 36_6 (unless מִצְרַיִם in app. with קָנֶה staff consisting of a broken *reed*).

<PREP> בְּ of instrument, *with, (by means of)*, + כרה *dig* Nm 21_{18} (בִּמְחֹקֵק בְּמִשְׁעֲנֹתָם *with a staff, with their sticks*; Sam appar. בִּמְחֹקֵק וּבְמִשְׁעֲנֹתָם *with a staff, that is with their stick*; or em. בִּמְחֹקְקֹתָם וּבְמָשְׁלָם *with their statutes and during/with their rule*); עַל *upon*, i.e. with the aid of 4QpsHod^c 2_5 (וכפותיו על משענת רום השמים perh. *and its branches were*, i.e. relied, *upon the support of the height of heaven*), + הלך htp. *go about* Ex

21$_{19}$; בטח עַל *rely on, trust in* 2 K 18$_{21}$||Is 36$_{6}$.

Also 4QBark (משענותם אשר *their staffs, which*) 4Q UnidA 1$_{6}$ (רוח ומשענתו *spirit, and his staff*).

<SYN> שֵׁבֶט *staff*, עֵזֶר *help*.

⇒ שׁען *lean*.

מִשְׁפָּחָה 304.2.22 n.f. **clan**—cstr. מִשְׁפַּחַת; sf. מִשְׁפַּחְתִּי, מִשְׁפַּחְתּוֹ, מִשְׁפַּחְתָּם; pl. מִשְׁפָּחוֹת (מִשְׁפָּחֹת); cstr. מִשְׁפְּחוֹת (מִשְׁפְּחֹת); sf. מִשְׁפְּחֹתָיו, מִשְׁפְּחוֹתֶיהָ, מִשְׁפְּחֹתֵיכֶם, מִשְׁפְּחֹתָם, מִשְׁפְּחֹתֵיהֶם, מִשְׁפְּחוֹתֵיהֶם, מִשְׁפְּחוֹתָם, Q משפחותמה (מִשְׁפְּחוֹתָם)—**clan; species** (Gn 8$_{19}$), **type** (Jr 15$_{3}$).

<SUBJ> היה *be* Nm 26$_{40}$ (or em.; see Nom. Cl.), ברך ni. *be blessed* Gn 12$_{3}$ 28$_{14}$, רבה hi. *increase* 1 C 4$_{27}$, חנה *encamp* Nm 3$_{23.29.35}$, ישׁב *dwell* 1 C 2$_{55}$, פוץ ni. *be spread out* Gn 10$_{18}$, אכל *eat* Jr 10$_{25}$, כלה pi. *destroy* Jr 10$_{25}$, שׁמם hi. *devastate* Jr 10$_{25}$, כרת ni. *be cut off* CD 3$_{1}$, תעה *err* CD 3$_{1}$, ספד *wail* Zc 12$_{12+8t}$, יהב *give* Ps 96$_{7}$ || 1 C 16$_{28}$, נתן *give* Gn 24$_{41}$, בוא *come* Zc 14$_{18}$, עלה *go up* Zc 14$_{17.18}$, קום *arise* 2 S 14$_{7}$, קרב *approach* Jos 7$_{14}$, שׁחה htpal. *bow down* Ps 22$_{28}$, שׁמע *hear* Jr 2$_{4}$, קרא *call* Jr 10$_{25}$, לכד ni. *be taken by lot* Jos 7$_{17}$ (if em. qal) 1 S 10$_{21}$.

<NOM CL> מִשְׁפַּחְתִּי הַצְּעִרָה *my clan is the least* 1 S 9$_{21}$, אֵלֶּה מִשְׁפְּחֹת בְּנֵי־נֹחַ *these are the clans of the sons of Noah* Gn 10$_{32}$, sim. Ex 6$_{14.15.19.24}$ Nm 26$_{7+11t}$ 1 C 4$_{2}$ 6$_{4}$, אֵלֶּה הֵם מִשְׁפְּחֹת הַלֵּוִי *these are the clans of the Levites* Nm 3$_{20}$, sim. Nm 3$_{21.27.33}$, בְּנֵי רְאוּבֵן ... מִשְׁפַּחַת הַחֲנֹכִי *the sons of Reuben were ... the clan of the Hanochites* Nm 26$_{5}$ (or em.; see below), sim. Nm 26$_{23}$ (or em.; see below), מִשְׁפַּחְתָּם אֲשֶׁר עִמָּכֶם *their clans which are with you* Lv 25$_{45}$, לְגֵרְשׁוֹן מִשְׁפַּחַת הַלִּבְנִי *to Gershon was the clan of the Libnites* Nm 3$_{21}$, sim. Nm 3$_{21+6t}$ 26$_{5+59t}$ (if em. חֲנוֹךְ *Hanoch* to לַחֲנוֹךְ *to Hanoch* at 26$_{5}$, תּוֹלָע *Tola* to לְתוֹלָע *to Tola* at 26$_{23}$, אִיעֶזֶר *Iezer* to לְאִיעֶזֶר *to Iezer* at 26$_{30}$, אַשְׂרִיאֵל *Asriel* to לְאַשְׂרִיאֵל *to Asriel* at 26$_{31}$, שֶׁכֶם *Shechem* to לְשֶׁכֶם *to Shechem* at 26$_{31}$, שְׁמִידָע *Shemida* to לִשְׁמִידָע *to Shemida* at 26$_{32}$, חֵפֶר *Hepher* to לְחֵפֶר *to Hepher* at 26$_{32}$, and if ins. לְאַרְדְּ *to Ard* at 26$_{40}$), מִשְׁפְּחֹת הַשּׁוּחָמִי ... אַרְבָּעָה וְשִׁשִּׁים אֶלֶף וְאַרְבַּע מֵאוֹת *the clans of the Shuhamites were ... sixty-four thousand and four hundred* Nm 26$_{43}$.

<OBJ> בחר *choose* Jr 33$_{24}$, יצא hi. *bring out* Jos 6$_{23}$, לקח *take* Jr 25$_{9}$, לכד *take by lot* Jos 7$_{14.17}$ (or em.; see Subj.), פקד *appoint* Jr 15$_{3}$, כתב *write* 1QM 4$_{10}$ 1QSa 1$_{21}$, ילד hi. *beget* 1 C 4$_{8}$, בוא hi. *bring* Jr 25$_{9}$, עלה hi. *bring up* Am 3$_{1}$, קרב hi. *bring near* Jos 7$_{17.17}$, מכר *deliver (over)* Na 3$_{4}$ (or em. הַמֹּכֶרֶת *the one who delivers [over]* to הַכֹּמֶרֶת *the one who ensnares*), שׁלח *send* Jr 25$_{9}$, שׂים *put* Ps 107$_{41}$, נוח hi. *place* Jos 6$_{23}$, סלח *forgive* Dt 29$_{17}$, קרא *call* Jr 1$_{15}$, שׁלח pi. *let go* Jg 1$_{25}$, מאס *reject* Jr 33$_{24}$.

<CSTR> מִשְׁפַּחַת הָאָזְנִי *clan of the Oznites* Nm 26$_{16}$, הָאֲחִירָמִי *of the Ahiramites* Nm 26$_{38}$, הָאִיעֶזְרִי *of the Iezerites* Nm 26$_{30}$, הָאֵלֹנִי *of the Elonites* Nm 26$_{26}$, הָאַרְאֵלִי *of the Arelites* Nm 26$_{17}$, הָאַרְדִּי *of the Ardites* Nm 26$_{40}$, הָאֲרוֹדִי *of the Arodites* Nm 26$_{17}$, הָאַשְׁבֵּלִי *of the Ashbelites* Nm 26$_{38}$, הָאַשְׂרְאֵלִי *of the Asrielites* Nm 26$_{31}$, הַבַּכְרִי *of the Becherites* Nm 26$_{35}$, הַבַּלְעִי *of the Belaites* Nm 26$_{38}$, הַבְּרִיעִי *of the Beriites* Nm 26$_{44}$, הַגּוּנִי *of the Gunites* Nm 26$_{48}$, הַגִּלְעָדִי *of the Gileadites* Nm 26$_{29}$, הַגֵּרְשֻׁנִּי *of the Gershonites* Nm 26$_{57}$, הַדָּנִי *of the Danites* Jg 13$_{2}$ 18$_{11}$, הַזַּרְחִי *of the Zerahites* Nm 26$_{13.20}$ Jos 7$_{17.17}$, הַחֶבְרִי *of the Heberites* Nm 26$_{45}$, הַחֶבְרֹנִי *of the Hebronites* Nm 3$_{27}$ 26$_{58}$, הַחַגִּי *of the Haggites* Nm 26$_{15}$, הַחוּפָמִי *of the Huphamites* Nm 26$_{39}$, הַחֶלְקִי *of the Helekites* Nm 26$_{30}$, הֶחָמוּלִי *of the Hamulites* Nm 26$_{21}$, הַחֲנֹכִי *of the Hanochites* Nm 26$_{5}$, הַחֶפְרִי *of the Hepherites* Nm 26$_{32}$, הַחֶצְרוֹנִי *of the Hezronites* Nm 26$_{6.21}$ (הַחֶצְרֹנִי).

הַיַּחְלְאֵלִי *of the Jahleelites* Nm 26$_{26}$, הַיַּחְצְאֵלִי *of the Jahzeelites* Nm 26$_{48}$, הַיָּכִינִי *of the Jachinites* Nm 26$_{12}$, הַיָּמִינִי *of the Jaminites* Nm 26$_{12}$, הַיִּמְנִי *of the Imnites* Nm 26$_{44}$ (if em. הַיִּמְנָה *of Imnah*), הַיִּצְהָרִי *of the Izharites* Nm 3$_{27}$, הַיִּצְרִי *of the Jezerites* Nm 26$_{49}$, הַיָּשׁוּבִי *of the Jashubites* Nm 26$_{24}$, הַיִּשְׁוִי *of the Ishvites* Nm 26$_{44}$, הַכַּרְמִי *of the Carmites* Nm 26$_{6}$, הַלִּבְנִי *of the Libnites* Nm 3$_{21}$ 26$_{58}$, הַמּוּשִׁי *of the Mushites* Nm 3$_{33}$ 26$_{58}$, הַמַּחְלִי *of the Mahlites* Nm 3$_{33}$ 26$_{58}$, הַמַּטְרִי *of the Matrites* 1 S 10$_{21}$, הַמָּכִירִי *of the Machirites* Nm 26$_{29}$, הַמַּלְכִּיאֵלִי *of the Malchielites* Nm 26$_{45}$, הַמְּרָרִי *of the Merarites* Nm 26$_{57}$, הַנְּמוּאֵלִי *of the Nemuelites* Nm 26$_{12}$, הַנַּעֲמִי *of the Naamites* Nm 26$_{40}$.

הַסַּרְדִּי *of the Seredites* Nm 26$_{26}$, הָעָזִּיאֵלִי *of the Uzzielites* Nm 3$_{27}$, הָעַמְרָמִי *of the Amramites* Nm 3$_{27}$, הָעֵרִי *of the Erites* Nm 26$_{16}$, הָעֵרָנִי *of the Eranites* Nm 26$_{36}$,

הַפּוּנִי *of the Punites* Nm 2623, הַפַּלֻּאִי *of the Palluites* Nm 265, הַפַּרְצִי *of the Perezites* Nm 2620, הַצְּפוֹנִי *of the Zephonites* Nm 2615, הַקְּהָתִי *of the Kohathites* Nm 2657 1 C 639, הַקָּרְחִי *of the Korahites* Nm 2658, הַשָּׁאוּלִי *of the Shaulites* Nm 2613, הַשּׁוּחָמִי *of the Shuhamites* Nm 2642, הַשּׁוּנִי *of the Shunites* Nm 2615, הַשּׁוּפָמִי *of the Shuphamites* Nm 2639, הַשִּׁכְמִי *of the Shechemites* Nm 2631, הַשִּׁלֵּמִי *of the Shillemites* Nm 2649, הַשֵּׁלָנִי *of the Shelanites* Nm 2620, הַשְּׁמִידָעִי *of the Shemidaites* Nm 2632, הַשִּׁמְעִי *of the Shimeites* Nm 321 Zc 1213, הַשִּׁמְרֹנִי *of the Shimronites* Nm 2624, הַשֻּׁתַלְחִי *of the Shuthelahites* Nm 2635, הַתּוֹלָעִי *of the Tolaites* Nm 2623, הַתַּחֲנִי *of the Tahanites* Nm 2635.

מִשְׁפַּחַת אֱלִימֶלֶךְ *clan of Elimelech* Ru 21.3, יְהוּדָה *of Judah* Jos 717 (or em. מִשְׁפְּחֹת) Jg 177, מִצְרַיִם *of Egypt* Zc 1418, רָם *of Ram* Jb 322, הַיִּמְנָה *of Imnah* Nm 2644 (or em.; see above).

מִשְׁפְּחוֹת (or מִשְׁפְּחֹת) הַגֵּרְשֻׁנִּי *clans of the Gershonites* Nm 321.23 424, הַזְּבוּלֹנִי *of the Zebulunites* Nm 2627, הַיִּתְרִי *of the Ithrites* 1 C 253, הַכְּנַעֲנִי *of the Canaanites* Gn 1018, הַלֵּוִי *of the Levites* Ex 619 Nm 320 1 C 64, הַלְוִיִּם *of the Levites* Jos 2127.40, הַמִּשְׁרָעִי *of the Mishraites* 1 C 253, הַפּוּתִי *of the Puthites* 1 C 253, הַצָּרְעָתִי *of the Zorathites* 1 C 42, הַקְּהָתִי *of the Kohathites* Nm 327.30 418.37 Jos 214.10, הַקָּרְחִי *of the Korahites* Ex 624, הָרֻאוּבֵנִי *of the Reubenites* Nm 267, הַשּׁוּחָמִי *of the Shuhamites* Nm 2643, הַשִּׁמְעֹנִי *of the Simeonites* Nm 2614, הַשֻּׁמָתִי *of the Shumathites* 1 C 253.

מִשְׁפְּחוֹת (or מִשְׁפְּחֹת) אֲחַרְחֵל *clans of Aharhel* 1 C 48, דָּן *of Dan* Nm 2642, יְהוּדָה *of Judah* Nm 2622 Jos 717 (if em.; see above), יִשְׂרָאֵל *of Israel* Jr 311, יִשָּׂשכָר *of Issachar* Nm 2625 1 C 75, לֵוִי *of Levi* Nm 2658, מְנַשֶּׁה *of Manasseh* Nm 2634 271, מְרָרִי *of Merari* Nm 333.35, נַפְתָּלִי *of Naphtali* Nm 2650, רְאוּבֵן *of Reuben* Ex 614, שִׁמְעוֹן *of Simeon* Ex 615, קִרְיַת יְעָרִים *of Kiriath-jearim* 1 C 253, סֹפְרִים *of the scribes* 1 C 255.

משפחות אל *clans of God* 1QM 410, מִשְׁפַּחַת אֲבִי *clan of the father of* Nm 3612, sim. 1 S 1818 11QT 5717, מִשְׁפַּחַת בְּנֵי *clan of the sons of* Nm 361, מִשְׁפַּחַת לִבְנֵי *clan of the sons of* 1 C 655 (or em.; see below), מִשְׁפְּחֹת ... בֶּן־ *clans of the son of* Nm 271, מִשְׁפְּחֹת בְּנֵי *clans of the sons of* Gn 1032 Nm 329 428.33.41.42.45 2618.37.47 361.12 Jos 2120.26.34 1 C 651.55 (if em. מִשְׁפַּחַת לִבְנֵי *clan of the sons of*), מִשְׁפַּחַת בֵּית *clan of the house of* Jg 91 2 S 165 Zc 1212.12.13, מִשְׁפְּחוֹת בֵּית *clans of the house of* Jr 24 1 C 421, מִשְׁפַּחַת הַמַּטֶּה *clan of the tribe* 1 C 647, מַטֵּה *of the tribe of* Nm 366.8, מִשְׁפְּחֹת מַטֵּה *clans of the tribe of* Jos 215.6, מִשְׁפְּחוֹת שִׁבְטֵי *clans of the tribes of* 1 S 921, מַמְלְכוֹת *of the kingdoms of* Jr 115, [משפחת הגוי[ם *clan of the nations* 4QCitJub 1.22, מִשְׁפְּחוֹת גּוֹיִם *clans of the nations* Ps 2228 || 1 C 1628, עַמִּים *of the peoples* Ps 967 , מִשְׁפַּחַת גֵּר *clan of a sojourner* Lv 2547, משפחות בוגדים *clans of traitors* Si 164(B) (A משפחת בגדים) 164(B) (משפחת), מִשְׁפְּחֹת הָאֲדָמָה *clans of the earth* Gn 123 2814 Am 32, משפחות האדמה *clans of the earth* 4QBer[b] 513, מִשְׁפְּחוֹת הָאָרֶץ *clans of the earth* Zc 1417, הָאֲרָצוֹת *of the lands* Ezk 2032, צָפוֹן *of the north* Jr 259, מִשְׁפַּחַת חֲצִי *clan of the half of* 1 C 656.

מַטֵּה, עֵקֶר מִשְׁפַּחַת *offshoot of the clan of* Lv 2547, מִשְׁפַּחַת *tribe of the clan of* Nm 3612, שֵׁבֶט מִשְׁפְּחֹת *tribe of the clans of* Nm 418, [מספר המש[פחות *number of the clans of* 1Q29 73, מושב משפחות *dwelling places of clans* 1QM 1014, פְּקוּדֵי מִשְׁפְּחֹת *numbered ones of clans of* Nm 437.41.42.45, עֲבֹדַת *service of* Nm 424.28.33, זֶבַח מִשְׁפָּחָה *sacrifice of*, i.e. attended by, *clan* 1 S 2029, בּוּז־מִשְׁפָּחוֹת *contempt of clans* Jb 3134, שְׁתֵּי הַמִּשְׁפָּחוֹת *two of the clans* Jr 3324, כָּל־הַמִּשְׁפָּחָה *all the clan* 1 S 206 2 S 147 Am 31, כָּל־מִשְׁפַּחַת *all the clan of* Jg 125 91, sim. 1 C 427, כֹּל הַמִּשְׁפָּחוֹת *all the clans* Zc 1214, כָּל־מִשְׁפְּחֹת *all the clans of* Gn 123 (כֹּל) 2814 Nm 2643 Jos 623 1 S 921 Jr 115 24 259 311 Am 32 (both כֹּל) Ps 2228 1 C 75 (כֹּל) 1QSa 115 4QMyst[a] 672 4QRitPur 546 (all three כול משפחות).

<APP> אַרְבַּע *four* Jr 153, אֶרֶץ *land* Zc 1212, דּוֹר *generation* Est 928, מְדִינָה *province* Est 928, עִיר *city* Est 928, אִיעֶזֶר *Iezer* Nm 2630 (or em.; see Nom. Cl.), אַרְדְּ *Ard* Nm 2640 (or ins.; see Nom. Cl.), אַשְׂרִיאֵל *Asriel* Nm 2631 (or em.; see Nom. Cl.), חֲנוֹךְ *Hanoch* Nm 265 (or em.; see Nom. Cl.), חֵפֶר *Hepher* Nm 2632 (or em.; see Nom. Cl.), נַעֲמָן *Naaman* Nm 2640 (or ins.; see Nom. Cl.), שֶׁכֶם *Shechem* Nm 2631 (or em.; see Nom. Cl.), שְׁמִידָע *Shemida* Nm 2632 (or em.; see Nom. Cl.), תּוֹלָע *Tola* Nm 2623 (or em.; see Nom. Cl.).

<PREP> לְ *according to* Gn 105 (if ins. אֵלֶּה בְּנֵי יֶפֶת *these are the sons of Japheth*) 1020.31 3640 Ex 617.25 1221 Nm 122+10t 318.19.20 438.42 2612+14t Jos 1323.28.31 1520 168

17$_{2}$ 18$_{28}$ 19$_{8.16.23.31.39.48}$ 21$_{7.33.40}$ 1 C 5$_{7}$ 64$_{7.48}$ 4QapJerB 8$_{4}$, + היה *be* Nm 1$_{20}$ 4$_{36.40.44}$ 26$_{20}$ Jos 13$_{29}$ 15$_{1}$ 16$_{5}$ 17$_{2}$ 18$_{21}$, יצא *go out* Gn 8$_{19}$ Jos 19$_{1.17.24.32.40}$, נסע *journey* Nm 2$_{34}$, עלה *go up* Jos 18$_{11}$ 19$_{10}$, יסד *establish* 4QD^{a} 11$_{10}$, עמד hi. *station* Ne 4$_{7}$, קרב *draw near* Nm 27$_{1}$ Jos 7$_{14}$, hi. *bring near* 1 S 10$_{21}$, נחל htp. *inherit* Nm 33$_{54}$, נתן *give* Jos 13$_{15.24}$, חלק ni. *be divided* 1QM 2$_{14}$ ([מ]שפחותם]), פרד ni. *be separated* Gn 10$_{5}$ (or em.), פקד *visit*, i.e. number Nm 3$_{15.39}$ 4$_{29.34.46}$, נשׂא *lift* head, i.e. count Nm 1$_{2}$ 4$_{2.22}$, בכה *weep* Nm 11$_{10}$.

לְ of possession, *of, (belonging) to* Nm 3$_{30.35}$ 36$_{1.6}$ 1 C 6$_{39}$; of direction, *to, towards*, + הלך *go* Jg 21$_{24}$, יצא *go out* Jos 21$_{4}$; of benefit, *to, for* Jos 21$_{26.34}$ 1 C 6$_{55}$, + היה *be* Jg 18$_{19}$ CD 20$_{13}$; *as for* Jos 21$_{20}$.

בְּ of place/time 1 C 6$_{45}$ 4QBer^{a} 18$_{1}$; *against*, + שׂים *set* face Lv 20$_{5}$; *over, in charge of* 1 C 4$_{38}$.

כְּ *as*, + היה *be* Ezk 20$_{32}$.

מִן of direction, *from*, + נסע *set out* Jg 18$_{11}$, קנה *buy* Lv 25$_{45}$, לקח *take* Jr 3$_{14}$; of cause, *on account of*, + חרב *be desolate* Si 16$_{4.4(B)}$; partitive, *(some) of, from among* Lv 25$_{49}$ Nm 27$_{11}$ 36$_{1.8.12}$ Jos 21$_{5.6.27.40}$ Jr 8$_{3}$ Jb 32$_{2}$ Ru 2$_{1.3}$ 1 C 6$_{46.51.56}$, + היה *be* Jos 21$_{10}$ Jg 13$_{2}$ 17$_{7}$, לקח *take (for marriage)* Gn 24$_{40}$ 11QT 57$_{17}$, נשׂא *take (for marriage)* 11QT 57$_{19}$, יצא *go out* 2 S 16$_{5}$, שׁלח *send* Jg 18$_{2}$.

אֶל *to*, + הלך *go* Gn 24$_{38}$, בוא *come* Gn 24$_{41}$, שׁוב *go back* Lv 25$_{10.41}$, דבר pi. *speak* Jg 9$_{1}$.

עַל *against*, + חשׁב *plan* Mc 2$_{3}$; *upon*, + שׁפך *pour out* Jr 10$_{25}$; *according to*, + ילד htp. *register oneself by genealogy* Nm 1$_{18}$.

בְּתוֹךְ *within, among*, + בוא *come* 1QSa 1$_{9}$.

מִתּוֹךְ *from (among)*, + גרע ni. *be diminished* Nm 27$_{4}$.

סָבִיב לְ *round about* Jos 15$_{12}$ 18$_{20}$.

<COLL> מִשְׁפָּחָה || אֲחֻזָּה *possession* Lv 25$_{10.41}$; + אִישׁ *man* Jg 1$_{25}$, אֶבְיוֹן *poor* Ps 107$_{41}$, אֶפֶס *end* Ps 22$_{28}$, בֵּית אָב *house of father* Gn 24$_{38.40}$ Nm 1$_{2+13t}$ 2$_{34}$ 3$_{15.20}$ 4$_{2+7t}$, שֵׁבֶט *tribe* Dt 29$_{17}$ Jg 18$_{19}$ 21$_{24}$, אֻמָּה *people* 4QD^{a} 11$_{10}$, גּוֹי *nation* Jr 10$_{25}$ Ezk 20$_{32}$ Na 3$_{4}$, לָשׁוֹן *tongue*, i.e. language Gn 10$_{5.20.31}$, מָקוֹם *place* Gn 36$_{40}$.

מִשְׁפָּחָה as vocative, Jr 2$_{4}$ Ps 96$_{7}$ || 1 C 16$_{28}$.

מִשְׁפָּחוֹת מִשְׁפָּחוֹת לְבָד *each clan by itself* Zc 12$_{12.14}$, sim. Est 9$_{28}$.

Also 1QM 3$_{16}$ ([משפח]ותיו]) 4QBer^{b} 5$_{9}$ 4QMyst^{a} 66$_{2}$ 4QsapHymnA 12$_{2}$ 4QPrFêtes^{c} 36$_{1}$.

<SYN> אֲחֻזָּה *possession*.*

מִשְׁפָּט 421.20.420 n.m. **judgment**—cstr. מִשְׁפַּט; sf. מִשְׁפָּטִי, מִשְׁפָּטֶךָ (משפטכה Q), מִשְׁפָּטוֹ, מִשְׁפָּטָהּ, Q משפטכם, מִשְׁפָּטָם, מִשְׁפָּטָן (משפטמה Q); pl. מִשְׁפָּטִים (משפטות Q); cstr. מִשְׁפְּטֵי; sf. מִשְׁפָּטַי, מִשְׁפָּטֶיךָ (משפטיכה Q), מִשְׁפָּטַיִךְ, מִשְׁפָּטָיו, מִשְׁפְּטֵיהֶם (משפטיהמה Q)—**1. judgment, a. act of judgment**, <SUBJ> היה *be* Lv 24$_{22}$, דרשׁ *seek* 1QH 17$_{6}$, פרח *sprout* Ho 10$_{4}$, תמך *take hold* Jb 36$_{17}$.

<NOM CL> כִּי הַמִּשְׁפָּט לֵאלֹהִים הוּא *for the judgment is to God* Dt 1$_{17}$, כיא לאל המשפט *for to God is the judgment* 1QS 11$_{10}$, כִּי לְכָל־חֵפֶץ יֵשׁ עֵת וּמִשְׁפָּט *for to every matter there is a time and a judgment* Ec 8$_{6}$ (unless §6), כיא [אמת כול מ]שפטיו *for true are all his judgments* 1QSb 4$_{27}$.

<OBJ> שׁפט *judge* Dt 16$_{18}$=11QT 51$_{12}$ Zc 7$_{9}$, ידע *know* Ec 8$_{5}$ (unless §6), נתן *give* 1QpHab 5$_{4}$, נטה hi. *pervert* 11QT 51$_{17}$ 57$_{20}$.

<CSTR> מִשְׁפַּט י׳ *judgment (pertaining to the affairs) of Y.* 2 C 19$_{8}$, מִשְׁפַּט אֶחָד appar. *judgment (consisting) of one (judgment)* Lv 24$_{22}$ (or em. מִשְׁפָּט one *judgment*), מִשְׁפַּט הָאוּרִים *judgment (by means) of the Urim* Nm 27$_{21}$, האורים והתומים *(by means) of the Urim and the Thummim* 11QT 58$_{18.20}$, מִשְׁפַּט־צֶדֶק *judgment of righteousness* Dt 16$_{18}$=11QT 51$_{12}$ 51$_{17}$ 57$_{20}$, אֱמֶת *of truth* Zc 7$_{9}$, יושר *of uprightness* Si 4$_{9}$, משפט כול הגוים *judgment of all the nations* 1QpHab 5$_{4}$, קצי *of the ends of* 1QH 17$_{10}$.

בַּעַל מִשְׁפָּטִי *lord of my judgment*, i.e. my legal opponent Is 50$_{8}$,* רוּחַ מִשְׁפָּט *spirit of judgment* Is 4$_{4}$ 28$_{6}$.

<ADJ> אֶחָד *one* Lv 24$_{22}$ (if em.; see above).

<PREP> לְ *for (the purpose of)* 1QS 9$_{5}$, + היה *be* 1QSa 1$_{25}$, בוא *come* 2 S 15$_{2.6}$, ירד *go down* Is 34$_{5}$, עלה *go up* Jg 4$_{5}$ hi. *bring up* 1QpHab 10$_{4}$ 1QS 5$_{12}$, ישׁב *sit* Ps 122$_{5}$ 11QT 57$_{13}$, עמד *stand* Nm 35$_{12}$ Jos 20$_{6}$ hi. *appoint* 2 C 19$_{8}$ 4QPrayer^{c} 2$_{6}$, קום *arise* Is 54$_{17}$ Ps 76$_{10}$, קרב *come near* Is 41$_{1}$ Ml 3$_{5}$, כון pol. *establish* Ps 9$_{8}$, עור *rouse oneself* 4Q418 69.2$_{7}$.

בְּ of place, time 1QH 1$_{6}$ 4QMyst^{a} 56$_{2}$, + בוא *enter* Ps 143$_{2}$ (unless §1d), עשׂה *do* Lv 19$_{15.35}$, מעל *sin* Pr 16$_{10}$,

נטה hi. *thrust away* Pr 18$_{5}$ (unless §1d), נכר hi. *recognize* face, i.e. show partiality Pr 24$_{23}$ (unless §1d) 11QT 51$_{12}$; of instrument, *by (means of)* 1QH 17$_{13}$ fr. 6$_{2}$ fr. 57$_{3}$ 4QOrd^{a} 5$_{3}$, + שׁאל *ask* Nm 27$_{21}$||11QT 58$_{18.20}$; of accompaniment, *in (a state of), with,* + בוא *come* Is 3$_{14}$, נכר hi. *recognize* face, i.e. show partiality Dt 1$_{17}$; introducing object, + קוץ *abhor* Si 4$_{9}$; to indicate comparison, + דמה *be like* 4QM^{a} 11.1$_{17}$.

מִן *from* 1QH 17$_{10.11}$ 4Q417 4.2$_{5}$; introducing object or *on account of,* + ירא *be afraid of* Ps 119$_{120}$, פחד *fear* 1QH fr. 4$_{9}$.

<COLL> מִשְׁפָּט || בָּעֵר *burning* Is 4$_{4}$, חֶסֶד *kindness* Zc 7$_{9}$, רַחֲמִים *compassion* Zc 7$_{9}$; + דִּין *judgment* Jb 36$_{17}$, עֵת *time* Ec 8$_{5.6}$, תּוֹרָה *law* 11QT 57$_{13}$.

b. sentence, decision, <SUBJ> היה *be* 1QS 6$_{23}$ 7$_{25}$, כתב pass. *be written* Ps 149$_{9}$, שׁלם *be complete* CD 9$_{20}$, יצא *go out* GnzPs 4$_{20}$.

<NOM CL> לוֹ אֵין מִשְׁפַּט־מָוֶת *to him there is no sentence of death* Dt 19$_{6}$, כן המשפט *thus is the sentence* CD 8$_{16}$ || 19$_{29}$ (משפט) 20$_{1}$, כֵּן מִשְׁפָּטֶךָ *thus is your sentence* 1 K 20$_{40}$, vars. CD 8$_{1}$||19$_{13}$, מִשְׁפַּט־מָוֶת לָאִישׁ הַזֶּה *a sentence of death is to this man* Jr 26$_{11}$, אֵין־לָאִישׁ הַזֶּה מִשְׁפַּט־מָוֶת *there is no sentence of death to this man* Jr 26$_{16}$, [כי מ]שפט מות הו[אה] *for it is a sentence of death* 4QD^{a} 6.2$_{10}$, כי משפט מות *for (it is) a sentence of death* 4QJub^{f} fr. 4$_{3}$, אֵין מִשְׁפָּטָם *there is no sentence upon them* Jr 49$_{12}$, מִשְׁפָּטִי לֶאֱסֹף *my decision is to gather* Zp 3$_{8}$, יָשָׁר מִשְׁפָּטֶיךָ *your decisions are upright* Ps 119$_{137}$, מֵי׳ כָּל־מִשְׁפָּטוֹ *its every decision is from Y.* Pr 16$_{33}$, אמת משפטיך בנו *your sentences against us are correct* CD 20$_{30}$, שלים משפטו *his sentence is fulfilled* 4QD^{a} 11$_{16}$.

<OBJ> אמר *say* Dt 17$_{11}$, דבר pi. *speak,* i.e. pronounce 2 K 25$_{6}$ Jr 1$_{16}$ 4$_{12}$ 12$_{1}$ 39$_{5}$||52$_{9}$ 4Q417 1.1$_{13}$, זכר *remember* Ps 105$_{5}$||1 C 16$_{12}$, חרץ *decide* 1 K 20$_{40}$ 1QS 8$_{10}$, כון hi. *determine* 1QH 1$_{9}$, פלג pi. *divide,* i.e. decide 1QH 1$_{16}$, נתן *give* 1QpHab 10$_{4}$, קבל pi. *accept* 4QD^{a} 11$_{1}$|| 4QD^{e} 7.1$_{16}$, יכח hi. *argue* 1QS 9$_{17}$, מלא *be full* Ezk 7$_{23}$, סור hi. *remove* Zp 3$_{15}$, נשׂא *lift* Ex 28$_{30}$, עשׂה *do,* i.e. decide Ezk 18$_{8}$ Ps 105$_{5}$||1 C 16$_{12}$ 4Q418 121$_{1}$, שׁאל *ask* Is 58$_{2}$ 4QM^{h} 1$_{6}$, דרשׁ *seek* 4QSela 9.2$_{10}$, שׁמע *hear* 1 K 3$_{28}$ 1QH 10$_{34}$ hi. *proclaim* Si 48$_{7}$, צדק hi. *pronounce righteous* 1QH 9$_{9}$ 1QM 11$_{14}$, שׁפט *judge* 1 K 3$_{28}$ Ezk 16$_{38}$ 23$_{45.45}$ Zc 8$_{16}$ 4QBark^{a} 1.2$_{7}$.

<CSTR> מִשְׁפַּט בְּנֵי *decision of the sons of* Ex 28$_{30}$, משפט סוד *decision of the council* 4QAges^{a} 1$_{10}$, מִשְׁפְּטֵי־פִיו *sentences of his mouth* Ps 105$_{5}$||1 C 16$_{12}$ (פִּיהוּ), משפט האורים והתומים *decision of the Urim and the Thummim* 4QpIsa^{d} 1$_{5}$ 4QSela 9.2$_{10}$.

מִשְׁפַּט אֱמֶת *decision of truth* Ezk 18$_{8}$, משפט אמתכה *decision of your truth* 1QH fr. 5$_{10}$ 1QM 11$_{14}$, מִשְׁפַּט שָׁלוֹם *decision of peace* Zc 8$_{16}$, משפט צדק *decision of righteousness* 1QH fr. 5$_{1}$ 1QS 9$_{17}$ 1QSb 2$_{26}$ 4Q418 121$_{1}$ 214$_{2}$ 4QM^{h} 1$_{6}$, הצדק *of righteousness* 1QH 1$_{26}$ 4Q417 3$_{2}$ (הצד[ק]), מִשְׁפְּטֵי־צֶדֶק *decisions of righteousness* Is 58$_{2}$ 4QMyst^{a} 80$_{3}$ ([מ]שפטי) 4QsapDidA 3$_{1}$ ([מ]שפטי צד[ק]) 4QShir^{b} 43$_{4}$ (צד[ק]).

משפט שקר *decision of falsehood* GnzPs 4$_{20}$, מִשְׁפַּט־מָוֶת *sentence of death* Dt 19$_{6}$ 21$_{22}$||11QT 64$_{9}$ Jr 26$_{11.16}$ 4QJub^{f} fr. 4$_{3}$ 4QD^{a} 6.2$_{10}$ ([מ]שפט), משפט נקמות *sentence of vengeance* 4QShir^{b} fr. 35$_{1}$, משפטי נקם *sentences of vengeance* Si 48$_{7}$, משפט רשעה *sentence of evil* 1QS 8$_{10}$, מִשְׁפַּט דָּמִים *sentence of bloodshed* Ezk 7$_{23}$, נֹאֲפוֹת *of adulterers* (fem.) Ezk 23$_{45}$, מִשְׁפְּטֵי נֹאֲפוֹת *sentences of adulterers* (fem.) Ezk 16$_{38}$, מִשְׁפַּט שֹׁפְכוֹת *sentence of those who shed* blood Ezk 23$_{45}$, מִשְׁפְּטֵי שֹׁפְכֹת *sentences of those who shed* blood Ezk 16$_{38}$, עוני *of affliction* 4QBark^{a} 1.2$_{7}$, משפט כל *sentence of all* CD 8$_{1}$.

חֹשֶׁן מִשְׁפָּט *breastpiece of decision* Ex 28$_{15}$ Si 45$_{10}$, הַמִּשְׁפָּט *of the decision* Ex 28$_{29.30}$, חֵטְא מִשְׁפַּט *sin (worthy) of the sentence of* Dt 21$_{22}$||11QT 64$_{9}$, דְּבַר הַמִּשְׁפָּט *word of judgment,* i.e. decision Dt 17$_{9}$, דְּבַר מִשְׁפָּט *word of judgment,* i.e. decision 2 C 19$_{6}$, שכל משפטכה *prudence of your decision* 1QH 9$_{31}$, כול משפט *every decision* 1QH 1$_{26}$.

<ADJ> משפט הזה *this decision* CD 8$_{18}$||19$_{32}$||20$_{8}$, [המשפ]טים הצדיקים *the righteous judgments* 4QMyst^{a} 55$_{2}$.

<PREP> לְ of purpose, *in order to obtain,* + פלא ni. *be difficult* Dt 17$_{8}$; בְּ *according to,* + שׁפט *judge* Ezk 7$_{27}$, בחר *choose* 1QH 9$_{10}$, צדק *be righteous* 1QH 9$_{15}$ 4Q417 1.1$_{16}$, hi. *pronounce righteous* 4Q418 7$_{2}$, זכה *be pure* 1QH fr. 4$_{10}$; of accompaniment, *with, in,* + חנן *be gracious* 1QSb 2$_{26}$, רצה *be pleased* 4Q424 3$_{8}$; כְּ *according to* CD 8$_{18}$||19$_{32}$||20$_{8}$ 4Q417 3$_{2}$, + אור hi. *give light* 4Q

pIsa^{d} 1$_{5}$; עַל *according to*, + עשׂה *do*, i.e. practise Dt 17$_{11}$; *against*, + שׁוב hi. *answer* 1QH 1$_{26}$ (or em. על *against* to עול *injustice*); introducing object, + כזב pi. *declare false* Jb 34$_{6}$ (or em.; see below); עַל פִּי *according to*, + יצא *go out* 11QT 58$_{21}$.

<COLL> מִשְׁפָּט || דִּין *plea* 1QH 9$_{9}$, רִיב *dispute* 1QH 10$_{35}$, דֶּרֶךְ *way* Ezk 7$_{27}$, חָמָס *violence* Ezk 7$_{23}$, דָּם *blood* Ezk 16$_{38}$, נֶגַע *wound* 1QH 9$_{10}$, תּוֹכֵחָה *rebuke* Si 48$_{7}$, תּוֹרָה *law* Dt 17$_{11}$; + אֱמֶת *truth* Zc 8$_{16}$, דַּעַת *knowledge* 1QS 9$_{17}$, מוֹפֵת *wonder* Ps 105$_{5}$||1 C 16$_{12}$, נִפְלָאוֹת *wonders* Ps 105$_{5}$||1 C 16$_{12}$ (נִפְלָאֹת), עֵצָה *counsel* 1QS 6$_{23}$, עֲבֹדָה *service* 1QH 1$_{17}$.

c. case to be judged, cause, <SUBJ> היה *be* 2 S 15$_{4}$ 1QS 6$_{9}$, יצא *go out* Ps 17$_{2}$, עבר *pass over* Is 40$_{27}$.

<NOM CL> מִשְׁפָּטִי אֶת־י׳ *my cause is with Y.* Is 49$_{4}$, לאל משפטי *to God is my cause* 1QS 11$_{2}$, כִּי לָכֶם הַמִּשְׁפָּט *for to you is the case to be judged* Ho 5$_{1}$, אם משפט לתורת *if the case is about the law of* CD 13$_{5}$, אלה המשפטים *these are the cases* 1QS 6$_{24}$, משפטי בצדקת אל *my cause is with the righteousness of God* 1QS 11$_{12}$.

<OBJ> נתן *give* Ezk 23$_{24}$, דרשׁ *investigate* 4Q424 3$_{4}$, בין *understand* 4Q424 3$_{2}$, ערך *set in order* Jb 13$_{18}$ 23$_{4}$, עשׂה *do*, i.e. uphold 1 K 8$_{45}$||2 C 6$_{35}$ 1 K 8$_{49}$||2 C 6$_{39}$ 1 K 8$_{59.59}$ Mc 7$_{9}$ Ps 9$_{5}$ 140$_{13}$, קרב hi. *bring near* Nm 27$_{5}$, יצא hi. *bring out* 1QH 4$_{25}$, סור hi. *remove* Jb 27$_{2}$ 34$_{5}$, פרר hi. *frustrate* Jb 40$_{8}$, מאס *reject* Jb 31$_{13}$, שׁפט *judge* Jr 5$_{28}$ Lm 3$_{59}$ 1QS 6$_{24}$, ריב *conduct (a legal case)* 1QSa 1$_{14.20}$.

<CSTR> מִשְׁפַּט עַבְדּוֹ *cause of his servant* 1 K 8$_{59}$, עַבְדִּי *of my servant* Jb 31$_{13}$, אֲמָתִי *of my female servant* Jb 31$_{13}$, עַמּוֹ *of his people* 1 K 8$_{59}$, אֶבְיוֹנִים *of the poor* Jr 5$_{28}$ Ps 140$_{13}$, משפט האוב *case of the medium* CD 12$_{3}$, רעיהם *of their companions* CD 20$_{10}$, משפט ... הידעוני *case of ... the necromancer* CD 12$_{3}$, משפט כול *case of every* 1QS 10$_{16.18}$; משמע משפטים *hearing of cases* 1QSa 1$_{11}$, כל משפט *every case* CD 14$_{12}$.

<APP> דִּין *plea* Ps 140$_{13}$.

<PREP> לְ *concerning, in relation to*, + דבר pi. *speak* CD 14$_{12}$, שׁאל ni. *be asked* 1QS 6$_{9}$; of cause, *on account of*, + עור hi. *rouse* Ps 35$_{23}$, קיץ hi. *awake* Ps 35$_{23}$; of instrument, *by (means of), with*, + רשׁע hi. *condemn* 1QS 5$_{6}$; כְּ *in accordance with*, + שׁפט ni. *be judged* CD 12$_{3}$ 20$_{10}$; אֶל *concerning*, + שׁאל ni. *be asked* 1QS 7$_{21}$; עַל *concerning* or *despite*, + כזב ni./pu. *be declared a liar* Jb 34$_{6}$ (if em. אֲכַזֵּב *I shall declare false*).

<COLL> מִשְׁפָּט || דִּין *plea* Jr 5$_{28}$, רִיב *dispute* Mc 7$_{9}$ Ps 35$_{23}$, עַוָּתָה *lack of justice* Lm 3$_{59}$, דֶּרֶךְ *way* Is 40$_{27}$ 1QS 11$_{2}$, נֶפֶשׁ *soul* Jb 27$_{2}$, לֵבָב *heart* 1QS 11$_{2}$, פְּעֻלָּה *recompense* Is 49$_{4}$; + דִּין *plea* Ps 9$_{5}$, רִיב *dispute* 2 S 15$_{4}$ 1QS 5$_{6}$ 1QSa 1$_{14}$ CD 14$_{12}$, עֵצָה *counsel* 1QS 6$_{9}$, דָּבָר *matter* 1QS 6$_{9}$.

d. place/seat of judgment, court, <NOM CL> פשרו הוא בית המשפט *its interpretation is the house of judgment* 1QpHab 10$_{3}$. <OBJ> צוה pi. *appoint* Ps 7$_{7}$. <CSTR> אֻלָם הַמִּשְׁפָּט *hall of judgment* 1 K 7$_{7}$, בית המשפט *house of judgment* 1QpHab 8$_{2}$ 10$_{3}$, מְקוֹם הַמִּשְׁפָּט *place of judgment* Ec 3$_{16}$.

<PREP> בְּ of place/time, + בוא *enter* Ps 143$_{2}$ (unless §1a) Jb 9$_{32}$ 22$_{4}$, hi. *bring* Jb 14$_{3}$ Ec 11$_{9}$ 12$_{14}$ 1QH fr. 4$_{11}$, נטה hi. *thrust away* Pr 18$_{5}$ (unless §1a), הלך *go* Jb 34$_{23}$, נתן *set* 4QapPs^{b} fr. 45$_{4}$, קום *stand* Ps 1$_{5}$ (unless §1e), ישׁב *sit* 4QapPs^{b} fr. 76-7$_{12}$, ריב *conduct (a legal case)* 4QMyst^{a} 59$_{2}$, נכר hi. *recognize* face, i.e. show partiality Pr 24$_{23}$ (unless §1a); מִן of direction, place, *from, out of*, + לקח pu. *be taken* Is 53$_{8}$ (unless §2), בדל hi. *separate* 4QS^{d} 7$_{1}$; אֶל *to*, + נגשׁ ni. *draw near* Dt 25$_{1}$; עַל *upon*, + ישׁב *sit* Is 28$_{6}$; מִשְׁפָּט without preposition, *(in) a court*, + דבר pi. *speak* Is 32$_{7}$ (unless §2).

<COLL> מִשְׁפָּט || עֵצָה *counsel* 4QS^{d} 7$_{1}$, טָהֳרָה *purification ritual* 4QS^{d} 7$_{1}$, צֶדֶק *righteousness* Ec 3$_{16}$, עֹצֶר *oppression* Is 53$_{8}$.

e. execution of judgment, <SUBJ> בוא *come* Jr 48$_{21}$ 1QS 11$_{14}$ (or obj. of hi.; see below), יצא *go out* Ho 6$_{5}$ (if em. מִשְׁפָּטֶיךָ אוֹר יֵצֵא *your judgments are light (that) goes out* to מִשְׁפָּטִי כָאוֹר יֵצֵא *my judgment goes out as the light*), נגע *reach* Jr 51$_{9}$, נשׂא ni. *be lifted* Jr 51$_{9}$.

<NOM CL> עַד־הֵנָּה מִשְׁפַּט מוֹאָב *thus far is the judgment of Moab* Jr 48$_{47}$, מִשְׁפָּטֶיךָ אוֹר *your judgments are light* Ho 6$_{5}$ (or em.; see Subj.), צֶדֶק מִשְׁפָּטֶיךָ *your judgments are righteous* Ps 119$_{75}$, אמת וצדיק ... משפטו *true and righteous is ... his judgment* 1QS 1$_{26}$, בְּכָל־הָאָרֶץ מִשְׁפָּטָיו *his judgments are in all the earth* Ps 105$_{7}$||1 C 16$_{14}$, כי להם המשפט *for to them is the judgment* CD 13$_{7}$, בי[ד]כה משפט כולם *by your hand is the judgment*

of all of them 1QH 5_{4} fr. 13_{4}, בידו משפט כלם *by his hand is the judgment of all of them* 4QMyst^{b} 11_{2}, [בידו] משפט כול חי *the judgment of every living thing is in his hand* 4QS^{f} 4_{3}, בידו משפט כול חי *in his hand is the case of every living thing* 1QS 10_{16}, כיא את אל משפט כול חי *for with God is the judgment of every living thing* 1QS 10_{18}, [בי]דכה משפט הצאן *by your hand is the judgment of the flock* 4Q418 172_{13}, באפכה כול משפטי נגע *in your anger are all the judgments of a wound* 1QH 11_{8}, כיא מאתכה משפט *for from you is the judgment* 4QShir^{b} 3_{4}, בכול מוסדי ארץ משפטי יוד *in all the foundations of the earth are the judgments of Yod*, i.e. Y. 4QShir^{b} 10_{12} (or em. ידו of *his hand*).

<OBJ> עשׂה *do*, i.e. carry out Ezk 5_{8} 39_{21} Ps 9_{17} 119_{84} 149_{9} 1QS 5_{12} CD 1_{2} 4QpNah 1-2_{4} 4QpPs^{a} 3.4_{15} 4QapPs^{b} 76-7_{13}, בוא hi. *bring* 1QS 11_{14} (or subj. of qal; see above) 4QD^{e} 5_{15} || 4QD^{f} 3_{8}, כון hi. *accomplish* 1QS 10_{20}, ראה *see* Ezk 39_{21}, זכר *remember* 1QM 17_{2}, ספר pi. *recount* 1QM 13_{9}, שׁקה hi. *cause to drink* 1QM 12_{10} 19_{2}.

<CSTR> משפט אל *judgment of*, i.e. performed by, *God* 1QM $6_{3.5}$, משפטי אל *judgments of*, i.e. performed by, *God* 11QMelch 2_{13} ([א]ל) 2_{23} ([משפט]י), משפט [משחי]ת *judgment of the destroyer* 4QBéat 8_{3}, משפטי אש *judgments (by means) of fire* 1QpHab 10_{13}.

מִשְׁפַּט מוֹאָב *judgment of*, i.e. against, *Moab* Jr 48_{47}, משפט [נדב ואבי]הוא *judgment of Nadab and Abihu* 1QM 17_{2}, קורח *of Korah* 4Q423 5_{2}, רשעה *of wickedness* 4QpPs^{a} 3-10.4_{11}, משפטי רשעה *judgments of wickedness* 1QpHab 9_{1}, משפט רשעים *judgment of the wicked* 1QH 2_{24}, אויב *of the enemy* 4QBéat 10_{5} ([משפ]ט), הצאן *of the flock* 4Q418 172_{13} 239_{2} ([מ]ש[פט הצא]ן), [מ]שפטי ערים perh. *judgments of cities* 4QHod^{a} 10_{4}, משפטי נגע *judgments of a wound* 1QH 11_{8} fr. 3_{16}, משפטי נגיעי *judgments of my wounds* 1QH 13_{3}, משפטי שלומים *judgments of retributions* 4QShirShabb^{d} 1.1_{39}.

משפטי גבורות *judgments of the strength of* 1QM 13_{9}, צדק *of righteousness* 1QH 1_{23} 4QpsHod^{b} 2_{3}, אמת *of truth* 4QapPs^{b} fr. 76_{13}, משפט אף *judgment of anger* 1Q36 16_{3} ([מש]פט), הארורה *of the curse* 4QD^{e} 5_{15}, עתי *of the times of* 4QCitJub 1.1_{5}, קצי *of the ends of* 4QSD 7.2_{10}, כול *of every* 4QS^{f} 4_{3}, כולם *of all of them* 1QH 5_{4} 4QMyst^{b} 11_{2} 4Q418 1_{3}.

רְצוּץ מִשְׁפָּט *broken of*, i.e. by, *judgment* Ho 5_{11}, זיקות *flaming arrows of* Si 43_{13}(M), זקי *fetters of* 1QH 8_{37}, פחי *calamities of* 1QH 18_{25}, נגועי *stricken of*, i.e. by 4QWays^{a} 2_{4} ([משפ]ט), עיין *spring of* 4Q424 2_{2}, יום המשפט *day of the judgment* 1QpHab 12_{14} 13_{3} 3QpIsa 1_{6} 4QTohB^{a} 2_{5} ([יו]ם), מועד משפט *appointed time of judgment* 1QS 4_{20}, קץ *end (of a period) of* 1QH 6_{29} 4QPrEnosh fr. 1.1_{6}, קץ משפטכ[ה] *end (of a period) of your judgment* 1QH fr. 58_{5}, נקם משפטי *vengeance of the judgments of* God 11QMelch 2_{13}, כול משפטי *all the judgments of* 1QH 11_{8}.

<ADJ> משפטים גדולים *great judgments* 1QS 5_{12} 4QAges^{b} 1_{1}.

<PREP> לְ *for (the purpose of)* 4QJub^{i} fr. 19_{2} 4QAges^{b} 1_{1} 4QShirShabb^{d} 1.1_{39}, + בוא *come* 1QpHab 10_{13}, שׂים *place* Hb 1_{12}, יסד pi. *establish* 1QH 5_{8} (or em. יסדתני *you have established me to* יסרתני *you have instructed me*), נתן *give* 2QapDavid 2_{4} 4QpPs^{a} 2_{19}, ברא ni. *be created* Si 39_{29}, רשׁע hi. *condemn* 1QH 7_{12}; *amounting to* 1QH fr. 3_{16}.

בְּ of place/time, *in, during* 4QCitJub 1.1_{5} 4QapJoseph^{b} 2_{8} 11QMelch 2_{23} 11QShirShabb 10_{3}, + קום *stand* Ps 1_{5} (unless §1d), רצה ni. *be accepted* 1QpHab 7_{16}, רום hi. *raise* 1QM 14_{5}, ספה *be snatched away* 4QSD 7.2_{10}; of accompaniment, *with, in*, + כרת hi. *cut off* 1QH $4_{20.26}$; introducing object, + אחז *hold* Dt 32_{41}, ראה *see* 4QpPs^{a} 3.4_{11}; of instrument, *by (means of), with*, + נגע *strike* 1QpHab 9_{1}, אכל *devour* 1QM 6_{3}, בעת ni. *be terrified* 1QH 1_{23}, נפל hi. *cause to fall* 1QM 6_{5}, כבד ni. *be honoured* 1QH 2_{24}, קדשׁ htp. *cause oneself to be hallowed* 1QM 17_{2}, רעע *break* 4Q418 69.2_{9}.

עַל *on account of*, + כלם ni. *be ashamed* Si 41_{16}; עַד *until*, + נקה ni. *be exempt from punishment* 4QRitPur 7_{20}; לְמַעַן *for the sake of*, + גיל *rejoice* Ps 48_{12}||97_{8}; לִפְנֵי *before* 4QHod^{a} 10_{4}.

<COLL> מִשְׁפָּט || אֵל *God* 1QM 15_{13}, הוֹכִיחַ *reproof* Hb 1_{12}, רִיב *dispute* CD 1_{2}; + יָד *hand* Ezk 39_{21}, מַעֲשֶׂה *deed* 1QM 13_{9}, מִרְדָּף *persecution* 8QHymn 2_{5}, תַּחֲלֻאִים *diseases* 1QH fr. 3_{16}.

Also 1QM 15_{13} 1Q36 16_{4} 4QPrEnosh fr. 1.1_{6} 2_{4} 8QHymn 2_{5}.

2. justice, perh. **just one** (e.g. Ps 37_{28}), <SUBJ> גלל

ni. *flow* Am 5_{24}, יצא *go out* Hb $1_{4.4.7}$, סוג ho. *be moved away* Is 59_{14}, רחק *be far* Is 59_{9}, שׁוב *return* Ps 94_{15}, שׁכן *abide* Is 32_{16}, רנן *sing* Si 47_{10} (or em. משפט *justice* to מקדש *sanctuary*).

<NOM CL> אֵין מִשְׁפָּט *there is no justice* Is $59_{8.15}$ Jb 19_{7}, מה משפט *what is justice?* 4Q418 69.2_{5}, מִשְׁפָּטֶךָ תְּהוֹם רַבָּה *your justice is (like) the great deep* Ps 36_{7}, כִּי כָל־דְּרָכָיו מִשְׁפָּט *for all his ways are justice,* i.e. just Dt 32_{4}, צֶדֶק וּמִשְׁפָּט מְכוֹן כִּסְאֶךָ *righteousness and justice are the foundation of your throne* Ps 89_{15}, sim. Ps 97_{2} (כִּסְאוֹ *his throne*), אמת ומשפט וצדק מכון כסאו *truth and justice and righteousness are the foundation of his throne* 11QPs^{a} 26_{11}, מַעֲשֵׂי יָדָיו אֱמֶת וּמִשְׁפָּט *the works of his hands are truth and justice* Ps 111_{7}, כִּמְעִיל וְצָנִיף מִשְׁפָּטִי *my justice was like a cloak and a turban* Jb 29_{14}, מֵי׳ מִשְׁפַּט־אִישׁ *the justice of,* i.e. due to, *a man is from Y.* Pr 29_{26}, מַחְשְׁבוֹת צַדִּיקִים מִשְׁפָּט *the thoughts of the righteous are justice,* i.e. just Pr 12_{5}, ממקור צדקתו משפטי *from the fountain of his righteousness is my justice* 1QS 11_{5} (or em. משפטו *his justice*).

<OBJ> גזל *rob* Is 10_{2}, הפך *turn* Am 5_{7} 6_{12}, סור hi. *remove* Jb 27_{2}, נטה hi. *pervert* Ex 23_{6} Dt 16_{19} 24_{17} 27_{19} 1 S 8_{3} 11QT $51_{13.13}$ 57_{19}, עות pi. *make crooked,* i.e. pervert Jb 8_{3} 34_{12}, ענה pi. *afflict* appar. Jb 37_{23} (or transfer athnach; see Cstr.), ליץ hi. *scorn* Pr 19_{28}, שׂנא *hate* Jb 34_{17}, תעב pi. *abhor* Mc 3_{9}.

אהב *love* Is 61_{8} Ps 33_{5} 37_{28} 99_{4}, בין *understand* Jb 32_{9} Pr 2_{9} 28_{5} (unless §6), hi. Si $35_{16.16}$, דין *judge* Jr 21_{12}, דרשׁ *seek* Is 1_{17} 16_{5} 4QCryptA 3.2_{5} 4QWays^{a} 1a.2b.$_{3}$ (ש[ידרו]), בחר *choose* Jb 34_{4}, ידע *know* Mc 3_{1}, יצא hi. *cause to appear* Is $42_{1.3}$ Ps 37_{6}, כתב *write* 1QM 4_{6}, יצג hi. *set down* Am 5_{15}, נתן *give* Zp 3_{5} Ps 72_{1} Jb 36_{6}, לקח *receive* Pr 1_{3} 4Q418 228_{3}, עשׂה *do,* i.e. practise or execute Gn $18_{19.25}$ Dt 10_{18} 2 S 8_{15} || 1 C 18_{14}, 1 K 3_{28} 10_{9} || 2 C 9_{8} Jr $22_{3.15}$ 23_{5} 33_{15} Ezk $18_{5.19.21.27}$ $33_{14.16.19}$ 45_{9} Mc 6_{8} Ps 99_{4} 103_{6} 119_{121} 146_{7} Pr $21_{3.7.15}$ Si 20_{4} 32_{22} 1QH 10_{36} 1QS 1_{5} 5_{4} (|| 4QS^{d} 1_{3}) 8_{2} 9_{15} 2QapMoses 1_{2} 4QapJoseph^{b} $1_{17.23}$ 4QDéluge 2_{3}, שׂים *place* Is 28_{17} 42_{4} Jr 5_{1} 7_{5} 9_{23}, שׁמר *keep* Is 56_{1} Ho 12_{7} Ps 106_{3} 1QS 10_{25}, מלא *be filled with* Mc 3_{8}, pi. *fill* Is 33_{5}, רבה hi. *increase* GnzPs $1_{7.20}$ 4_{24}, רגע hi. *make twinkle,* i.e. appear suddenly Is 51_{4}, דבר pi. *speak* Is 32_{7} (unless §1d) Ps 37_{30}, שׁיר *sing* Ps 101_{1}, שׁמע *hear,* i.e. understand 1 K 3_{11}.

<CSTR> משפט אל *justice of God* 1QM 4_{6}, מִשְׁפַּט אֶבְיֹנְךָ *justice of,* i.e. due to, *your poor* Ex 23_{6}, עֲנִיִּים *of the poor* Jb 36_{6}, עֲנִיֵּי *of the poor of* Is 10_{2}, אַלְמָנָה *of a widow* Dt 10_{18} 27_{19}, גֵּר *of a sojourner* Dt 24_{17} 27_{19}, יָתוֹם *of an orphan* Dt 10_{18} 24_{17} 27_{19}, מִשְׁפַּט־אִישׁ *justice of,* i.e. due to, *a man* Pr 29_{26}, [מ]שפט עולם *justice of eternity,* i.e. perpetual justice 4QS^{e} 2_{14}, משפט עוז *justice of strength* 1QS 10_{25}.

אֱלֹהֵי מִשְׁפָּט *God of justice* Is 30_{18} Ml 2_{17} (הַמִּשְׁפָּט) Si 32_{15}, מורה משפט *teacher of justice* 4QapPs^{b} 1_{1}, מְלֵאֲתִי מִשְׁפָּט *full of justice* Is 1_{21}, שַׂגִּיא ... מִשְׁפָּט *great of ... justice* Jb 37_{23} (if transfer athnach; see Obj.), אֹרַח *path of* Is 40_{14}, אָרְחוֹת *paths of* Pr 2_{8} 17_{23}, נְתִיבוֹת *paths of* Pr 8_{20}, מֹאזְנֵי *scales of* Pr 16_{11}, קו משפט *line of justice* 1QH 6_{26}, שֹׁמְרֵי מִשְׁפָּט *those who keep justice* Ps 106_{3}, גֵּזֶל מִשְׁפָּט *robbery,* i.e. misappropriation, *of justice* Ec 5_{7}, עושי משפט *deeds of justice* 1QS 8_{3}, ברית *covenant of* 1QS 8_{9}, ממשלת *dominion of* 11QMelch 2_{9}.

<APP> צֶדֶק *righteousness* 4QBark^{e} 5_{2}, אֱמֶת *truth* 4QWays^{a} 1a.2b$_{3}$. <ADJ> מִשְׁפָּט מְעֻקָּל *crooked justice* Hb 1_{4}.

<PREP> לְ *about, in relation to* Jb 9_{19}; introducing object, + קוה pi. *wait for* Is 5_{7} 59_{11}; *in accordance with* 1QS 8_{6}, + יסר pi. *discipline* Is 28_{26}, שׂרר *rule* Is 32_{1}, כון ni. *be established* 4QS^{e} 2_{14}; *as,* + חשׁב *consider* Jb 35_{2}.

בְּ of accompaniment, *in, with* 4QBark^{e} 5_{2}, + גבה *be exalted* Is 5_{16}, שׁבע ni. *swear* Jr 4_{2}, דרך hi. *lead* Ps 25_{9}, נטר *keep* a grudge 1QS 7_{8}, לון ni. *murmur* 1QS 7_{18}; of instrument, *by (means of), with,* + דין *judge* Ps 72_{2}, כול pilp. *manage* Ps 112_{5}, חיה pi. *keep alive* Ps 119_{149} (if em. כְּמִשְׁפָּטֶךָ *according to your justice* to בְּמִשְׁפָּטֶךָ) 119_{156} (if em. כְּמִשְׁפָּטֶיךָ *in accordance with your ordinances* to בְּמִשְׁפָּטֶךָ), סעד *sustain* Is 9_{6}, עמד hi. *cause to stand* Pr 29_{4}, עשׂה *make* Jr 17_{11}, רעה *tend* Ezk 34_{16}, פדה ni. *be ransomed* Is 1_{27}, ארשׂ pi. *betroth oneself* Ho 2_{21}.

כְּ *according to,* + חיה pi. *keep alive* Ps 119_{149} (or em.; see above) 119_{156} (if em. מִשְׁפָּטֶיךָ *your ordinances* to מִשְׁפָּטֶךָ *your justice*); מִן of direction, place, *from, out of,* + לקח pu. *be taken* Is 53_{8} (מֵעֹצֶר וּמִמִּשְׁפָּט לֻקָּח *he was taken from power and justice,* i.e. from his just position of power;* unless §1d); עַל *on account of,* +

בוש *be ashamed* Si 42$_{2(M)}$; *against*, + נפל *fall* 1QH 3$_{27}$; בְּלֹא *without* Pr 16$_8$, + בנה *build* Jr 22$_{13}$, יתר hi. *leave over* Si 30$_{38}$, ספה ni. *be swept away* Pr 13$_{23}$, עשק *oppress* Ezk 22$_{29}$, נקם *take vengeance* 4QMyst^{a} 7$_5$; בְּלִי *without*, + צחה *slander* 1QS 7$_4$.

<COLL> מִשְׁפָּט || י׳ *Y.* Ps 101$_1$, אוֹר *light* 1QS 11$_5$, בֶּגֶד *garment* Dt 24$_{17}$, לֶחֶם *bread* Ps 146$_7$, נֶפֶשׁ *soul* Jb 27$_2$, דֶּרֶךְ *way* Ps 25$_9$, אֱמוּנָה *faithfulness* Jr 5$_1$, אֱמֶת *truth* Is 59$_{14}$ Ps 89$_{15}$, חָכְמָה *wisdom* Ps 37$_{30}$, חֶסֶד *kindness* Mc 6$_8$, חָסִיד *godly one* Pr 2$_8$, טוֹב *good* Jb 34$_4$, יְשָׁרָה *uprightness* Mc 3$_9$, מֵישָׁרִים *uprightness* Ps 99$_4$, נְכֹחָה *uprightness* Is 59$_{14}$, צֶדֶק *righteousness* Is 32$_1$ Jr 22$_{13}$ Jb 8$_3$ 29$_{14}$, צְדָקָה *righteousness* Is 1$_{27}$ 5$_{16}$ 32$_{16}$ 56$_1$ 59$_{9.14}$ Am 5$_7$ Ps 36$_7$ 106$_3$ Pr 8$_{20}$ GnzPs 4$_{24}$, תְּבוּנָה *understanding* Is 40$_{14}$, חֻקָּה *statute* Ezk 18$_{19.21}$, תּוֹרָה *law* Is 42$_4$ 51$_4$, עֲרָפֶל *cloud* Ps 97$_2$, אָוֶן *iniquity* Pr 19$_{28}$ 21$_{15}$, חָמָס *violence* Ezk 45$_9$, מִרְמָה *deceit* Pr 12$_5$, שֹׁחַד *bribe* 1 S 8$_3$ 11QT 57$_{19}$.

+ אהבת חסד *love of loyalty* 1QS 5$_4$ (||4QS^{d} 1$_3$) 8$_2$ 4QBark^{e} 5$_2$, אֱמֻן *faithfulness* 1QS 10$_{25}$, אֱמֶת *truth* Jr 4$_2$ Ps 111$_7$ 1QM 4$_6$ 1QS 1$_5$ 5$_4$ 8$_2$ 4QWays^{a} 1a.2b$_3$ 4QPrayer^{d} 1.1$_6$ 11QPs^{a} 26$_{11}$ GnzPs 1$_7$, גְּבוּרָה *might* Mc 3$_8$, כֹּחַ *strength* Mc 3$_8$ Jb 37$_{23}$ (if transfer athnach; see above), חֶסֶד *kindness* Jr 9$_{23}$ Ho 2$_{21}$ 12$_7$ Ps 101$_1$, עֲנָוָה *humility* 1QS 5$_4$||4QS^{d} 1$_3$, הצנע לכת *modesty of going* 1QS 5$_4$ (||4QS^{d} 1$_3$) 8$_2$ 4QBark^{e} 5$_2$, יְשׁוּעָה *salvation* Is 59$_{11}$, מוּסָר *discipline* Pr 1$_3$, מֵישָׁרִים *uprightness* Pr 1$_3$ 2$_9$, צֶדֶק *righteousness* Is 16$_5$ Ho 2$_{21}$ Ps 37$_6$ 72$_2$ 89$_{15}$ 97$_2$ 119$_{121}$ Pr 1$_3$ 2$_9$ Ec 5$_7$ 1QM 4$_6$ 4QapJoseph^{b} 1$_{23}$ 18$_3$ 11QPs^{a} 26$_{11}$ GnzPs 1$_{20}$, צְדָקָה *righteousness* Gn 18$_{19}$ 2 S 8$_{15}$||1 C 18$_{14}$ 1 K 10$_9$||2 C 9$_8$ Is 5$_7$ 9$_6$ 28$_{17}$ 33$_5$ Jr 4$_2$ 9$_{23}$ 22$_{3.15}$ 23$_5$ 33$_{15}$ Ezk 18$_{5.19.21.27}$ 33$_{14.16.19}$ 45$_9$ Am 5$_{24}$ Ps 33$_5$ 72$_1$ 99$_4$ 103$_6$ Pr 21$_3$ 1QS 1$_5$ 5$_4$ (||4QS^{d} 1$_3$) 8$_2$, רַחֲמִים *compassion* Ho 2$_{21}$, תּוֹרָה *law* Si 42$_{2(M)}$, חֹק *statute* Si 42$_{2(M)}$, פְּרִי *fruit* Am 6$_{12}$, רוּחַ *spirit* Mc 3$_8$, שְׂאֵת *dignity* Hb 1$_7$, כָּבוֹד *glory* 1QM 4$_6$.

3. ordinance, <SUBJ> היה *be* Nm 15$_{16}$, כתב pass. *be written* CD 5$_9$, עזר *help* Ps 119$_{175}$.

<NOM CL> כָּל־מִשְׁפָּטָיו לְנֶגְדִּי *all his ordinances are before me* 2 S 22$_{23}$||Ps 18$_{23}$ (if em. 2 S מִשְׁפָּטוֹ *his ordinance* to מִשְׁפָּטָיו), מִשְׁפָּטֶיךָ לָאָרֶץ *your ordinances are to the earth* Is 26$_9$, מָרוֹם מִשְׁפָּטֶיךָ מִנֶּגְדּוֹ *your ordinances are on high away from him* Ps 10$_5$, מִשְׁפְּטֵי־י׳ אֱמֶת *the ordinances of Y. are truth*, i.e. true Ps 19$_{10}$, מִשְׁפָּט לֵאלֹהֵי יַעֲקֹב *it is an ordinance of the God of Jacob* Ps 81$_5$, מִשְׁפָּטֶיךָ טוֹבִים *your ordinances are good* Ps 119$_{39}$, וּלְעוֹלָם כָּל־מִשְׁפַּט צִדְקֶךָ *and every ordinance of your righteousness is forever* Ps 119$_{160}$ (or em. כָּל־מִשְׁפַּט *every ordinance of* to כָּל־מִשְׁפְּטֵי *all the ordinances of*).

אֵלֶּה הַמִּשְׁפָּטִים *these are the ordinances* Ex 21$_1$ Lv 26$_{46}$ Nm 36$_{13}$ Dt 4$_{45}$ 6$_1$ (זֹאת) 12$_1$ 1QS 8$_{20}$ 4QD^{e} 7.1$_{15}$ ([אלה המ]שפטים), מָה ... הַמִּשְׁפָּטִים *what are ... the ordinances* Dt 6$_{20}$, אֲשֶׁר־לוֹ ... מִשְׁפָּטִים צַדִּיקִם *to whom are ... righteous ordinances* Dt 4$_8$, כן המשפט *thus is the ordinance* CD 15$_7$ 16$_{12}$, זה משפט [תור]ת הצרעת *this is the ordinance of the law of the skin disease* 4QD^{a} 6.1$_{13}$, [מ]שפט הזב את זובו *(this is) the ordinance of the one who discharges his discharge* 4QD^{a} 6.1$_{14}$, המשפטים האלה על פי כול החוקים *these ordinances are according to all the statutes* 4QD^{a} 11$_5$.

<OBJ> שמע *hear* Dt 5$_1$ 7$_{12}$ 4QMMT B$_{52.53.53}$, דבר *speak* Dt 5$_1$, pi. Dt 4$_{45}$ 5$_{31}$, אמר *say* 11QT 56$_6$, נגד hi. *declare* Ps 147$_{19}$ 11QT 56$_2$, כתב *write* 2 K 17$_{37}$, ספר pi. *recount* Ex 24$_3$ Ps 119$_{13}$, עוד hi. *invoke* 1QSa 1$_{11}$, ידע *know* Jr 5$_{4.5}$ 8$_7$ Ps 147$_{20}$ 4Q418 221$_4$ hi. *cause to know* Ezk 20$_{11}$ CD 15$_{11}$, דרשׁ *investigate* 1QS 6$_7$ 8$_{24}$ 4Q418 81$_7$, ראה *see* 4QMMT B$_{53}$, זכר *remember* Ml 3$_{22}$ Ps 119$_{52}$, למד *learn* Dt 5$_1$ Ps 119$_7$, pi. *teach* Dt 4$_{1.5.14}$ 5$_{31}$ 6$_1$ Ps 119$_{108}$ Ezr 7$_{10}$ Si 45$_{5.17}$ 11QPs^{a} 24$_8$, ירה hi. *teach* Dt 33$_{10}$, נתן *give* Lv 26$_{46}$ Dt 11$_{32}$ Ezk 20$_{25}$ Ne 9$_{13}$ 4QD^{a} 11$_{12}$, צוה pi. *charge* Nm 36$_{13}$ Dt 6$_{20}$ 7$_{11}$ 8$_{11}$ 1 K 8$_{58}$ 2 K 17$_{34}$ Ml 3$_{22}$ Ne 1$_7$ 1 C 22$_{13}$ 2 C 33$_8$, שׂים *place* Ex 15$_{25}$ 21$_1$ Jos 24$_{25}$ 4QShir^{b} 63.3$_3$.

עשׂה *do*, i.e. practise Lv 18$_{4.5}$ 19$_{37}$ 20$_{22}$ 25$_{18}$ Dt 4$_{1.5.14}$ 5$_{1.31}$ 6$_1$ 7$_{11.12}$ 11$_{32}$ 12$_1$ 26$_{16.16}$ 33$_{21}$ 1 K 6$_{12}$ 11$_{33}$ 2 K 17$_{37}$ Ezk 5$_7$ 11$_{12.20}$ 18$_{17}$ 20$_{11+5t}$ 36$_{27}$ 37$_{24}$ Ezr 7$_{10}$ Ne 9$_{29}$ 10$_{30}$ 1 C 22$_{13}$ 28$_7$ 2 C 33$_8$ 4QD^{a} 11$_{12.18}$ 4QMMT B$_{53}$, פעל *do* Zp 2$_3$, שׁמר *keep* Lv 18$_{5.26}$ 19$_{37}$ 20$_{22}$ 25$_{18}$ Dt 5$_1$ 7$_{11.12}$ 8$_{11}$ 11$_1$ 26$_{16.17}$ 30$_{16}$ 1 K 2$_3$ 8$_{58}$ 9$_4$||2 C 7$_{17}$ Ezk 11$_{20}$ 18$_9$ 20$_{18.19.21}$ 36$_{27}$ Ps 119$_{106}$ Ne 1$_7$ 10$_{30}$, נגע hi. *apply* Si 50$_{19}$, רום hi. *exalt* 4QShirShabb^{d} 1.1$_{25}$, יכח hi. *acknowledge (as just)* 1QS 10$_{11}$, בחן *test* 1QSb 3$_{23}$ ([לב]חון), שׁוה pi. *to consider* Ps 119$_{30}$ (or em. שִׁוִּיתִי *I have considered* to אִוִּיתִי *I have desired*).

געל *abhor* Lv 26$_{15}$, מאס *reject* Ezk 20$_{13}$ 4QD^{e} 7.1$_{11}$, מור hi. *exchange* 1QH 14$_{20}$ 4QBer^{a} 7.2$_{12}$, מרה hi. *be* rebellious (against) Ezk 5$_{6}$, עזב *forsake* Is 58$_{2}$.

<CSTR> מִשְׁפַּט י׳ *ordinance of Y.* Jr 8$_{7}$, מִשְׁפְּטֵי־י׳ *ordinances of Y.* Ps 19$_{10}$, משפט אל *ordinance of God* 1QS 9$_{25}$, משפטי אל *ordinances of God* 1QS 3$_{5}$ 4$_{2}$, מִשְׁפַּט אֱלֹהָיו *ordinance of his God* Is 58$_{2}$, אֱלֹהֵיהֶם *of their God* Jr 5$_{4.5}$, משפט בני *ordinance of the sons of* 1QSa 1$_{2}$, משפט ... אנושי *ordinance of ... the men of* 1QSa 1$_{2}$, משפט הרבים *ordinance of the many* 4QD^{e} 7.1$_{11}$, משפטי היחד *ordinances of the community* 1QS 6$_{15}$ 4QD^{e} 3.3$_{19}$ (הי[חד]), ישראל *of Israel* 4QMMT B$_{53}$, מִשְׁפְּטֵי הַגּוֹיִם *ordinances of the nations* Ezk 5$_{7}$||11$_{12}$.

משפטי צדק *ordinances of righteousness* 1QS 3$_{1}$ 4$_{4}$, מִשְׁפַּט צִדְקֶךָ *ordinance of your righteousness* Ps 119$_{160}$ (or em.; see below), מִשְׁפְּטֵי צִדְקֶךָ *ordinances of your righteousness* Ps 119$_{7.62.106.160}$ (if em. מִשְׁפַּט *ordinance of*) 119$_{164}$, צדקו *of his righteousness* CD 20$_{30}$, משפטי אמתכה *ordinances of your truth* 4QPrayer^{e} 1$_{4}$, קודשכה *of your holiness* 4QD^{a} 11$_{12}$, משפט התורה *ordinance of the law* 11QT 50$_{7.17}$, משפטי התורה *ordinances of the law* CD 14$_{8}$, משפטות התורא *ordinances of the law* 1QSa 1$_{11}$, משפט תורת *ordinance of the law of* 4QD^{a} 6.1$_{13}$ (תו[רת]), משפט היסורים *ordinance of the instructions* CD 7$_{7}$ (=19$_{4}$ היסודים *the founding principles*; or em. האסרים *the vows*, i.e. אִסָּר), משפט היסודים *ordinance of the founding principles* CD 19$_{4}$ (=7$_{7}$; see above), משפט ה[ט]הרה *ordinance of purity* 4QOrd^{c} 1$_{6}$.

משפט הנדבות *ordinance of the freewill offerings* CD 16$_{13}$, העריות *of,* i.e. concerning, *nakedness* CD 5$_{9}$, עת ועת *of a time and a time,* i.e. each time CD 12$_{21}$, המת *of the dead* 4QMMT B$_{74}$, משפט ... החלל *ordinance ... of the slain* 4QMMT B$_{74}$, משפט נתק הרוש והז[קן] *ordinance of the scab of the head and the beard* 4QD^{a} 6.1$_{5}$||4QD^{h} 4.2$_{10}$, משפט הזב *ordinance of the one who discharges* 4QD^{a} 6.1$_{14}$||4QD^{g} 1.2$_{3}$, מִשְׁפְּטֵי־פִיךָ *ordinances of your mouth* Ps 119$_{13}$, משפטי פיהו *ordinances of his mouth* 4QShirShabb^{d} 1.1$_{39}$, משפטי שקט *ordinances of quietness* 4QShirShabb^{a} 1.2$_{11}$, משפט כול *ordinance of all* 4QparaKings fr. 23$_{2}$.

אֹרַח מִשְׁפָּטֶיךָ *path of your ordinances* Is 26$_{8}$, חוק המשפט *statute of the ordinance* 11QT 50$_{6}$, חֻקַּת מִשְׁפָּט *statute of an ordinance* Nm 27$_{11}$ 35$_{29}$, תורת המשפט *law of the ordinance* 11QT 29$_{4}$, קו משפטו *line of his ordinance* 1QS 10$_{9}$, דעת משפטי *knowledge of the ordinances of* 1QS 3$_{1}$, פרוש המשפטים *explanation of the ordinances* CD 14$_{18}$ 4QD^{a} 11$_{18}$.

קנאת משפט *zeal of,* i.e. for, *the ordinance* 4QBer^{a} 2$_{3}$, משפטי *of,* i.e. for, *the ordinances of* 1QS 4$_{4}$ 4QPrayer^{e} 1$_{4}$, משפ[טיכה] *of,* i.e. for, *your ordinances* 1QH fr. 17$_{2}$, משפטיו *of,* i.e. for, *his ordinances* 1QS 2$_{15}$, ריב משפטיכה *dispute of,* i.e. over, *your ordinances* 1QM 12$_{5}$.

כָּל־מִשְׁפָּט *every ordinance of* Ps 119$_{160}$ (or em.; see below), כול ... משפט *every ... ordinance* 1QS 5$_{16}$||4QS^{b} 9$_{10}$, כול המשפט *all the ordinance* 4QapMos^{b} 1.3$_{1}$, כָּל־הַמִּשְׁפָּטִים *all the ordinances* Ex 24$_{3}$ 4Q419 1$_{1}$ (כול המשפ[טים]) 4QM^{a} 4$_{3}$ (המשפט[י]ם) 4QDibHam^{a} 3.2$_{14}$, כָּל־מִשְׁפָּטֵי *all the ordinances of* Ps 119$_{160}$ (if em. מִשְׁפַּט *ordinance of*) Ps 119$_{13}$ CD 14$_{8}$ (both כֹּל) 1QH 7$_{35}$ 1QS 6$_{15}$ 4QShirShabb^{a} 1.1$_{5}$ (all three כול), כָּל־מִשְׁפָּטַי *all my ordinances* Lv 19$_{37}$ 20$_{22}$, כול משפטיך *all your ordinances* 1QH 14$_{20}$ 4Q408 1$_{6}$ (כול מש[פטיך]), כָּל־מִשְׁפָּטָיו *all his ordinances* Nm 9$_{3}$ 2 S 22$_{23}$ (if em. מִשְׁפָּטוֹ *his ordinance*) 1QDM 2$_{7}$ 1QSb 3$_{23}$ 4QapMos^{c} 2.2$_{4}$ (all three כול), כול משפטיהמה *all their ordinances* 1QSa 1$_{5}$.

<ADJ> אֶחָד *one* Nm 15$_{16}$, זֶה *this* 1QS 8$_{19}$ CD 12$_{21}$ 4QD^{a} 6.1$_{3}$ 4QapMos^{b} 1.3$_{1}$ 11QT 15$_{3}$ 29$_{4}$ 50$_{6}$, אֵלֶּה *these* Nm 35$_{24}$ Dt 7$_{12}$ CD 12$_{19}$ 20$_{27}$ 4QD^{a} 11$_{5}$ 4QM^{a} 4$_{3}$ 4QDibHam^{a} 3.2$_{14}$ (הא[לה]) 5QRègle 9$_{3}$, יָשָׁר *upright* Ne 9$_{13}$, טוֹב *good* 4QPrEnosh fr. 1.2$_{5}$, רִאשׁוֹן *first* 1QS 9$_{10}$ (רשונים) CD 20$_{31}$.

<PREP> לְ *for* 1QH 7$_{35}$ 4QapMos^{c} 2.2$_{4}$ 4QShirShabb^{a} 1.2$_{11}$, + יחל pi. *wait* Ps 119$_{43}$, כתב *enroll* 1QS 6$_{22}$, צפה pi. *watch closely* 1QS 9$_{25}$, חרת *engrave* 4QShirShabb^{a} 1.1$_{5}$; *about, in relation to* 2 C 19$_{10}$, + שׁוב hi. *answer* 1QS 5$_{16}$||4QS^{b} 9$_{10}$; *in accordance with,* + עמד *stand* Ps 119$_{91}$, הלך htp. *walk* CD 12$_{21}$; introducing object, + שׂים *place* 1 S 30$_{25}$.

בְּ introducing object, + מאס *reject* Lv 26$_{43}$ Ezk 5$_{6}$ 20$_{16}$ 1QS 3$_{5}$ 4QD^{a} 11$_{5}$, בין hi. *cause to understand* 1QS 6$_{15}$ 1QSa 1$_{5}$, pol. *understand* CD 14$_{8}$, חזק hi. *preserve* CD 20$_{27}$; *against,* + חטא *sin* Ne 9$_{29}$; *according to* CD 14$_{22}$ 4QD^{a} 7.2$_{9}$ 4Q416 6$_{1}$, + יסר *instruct* 1QSa 1$_{8}$, htp. *be instructed* CD 20$_{31}$, שׁפט *judge* Ezk 23$_{24}$ 44$_{24}$ 4QD^{e} 7.1$_{15}$, ni. *be judged* 1QS 9$_{10}$ CD 20$_{31}$, רצה *make accept-*

able 4QShirShabbd 1.139; of accompaniment, *in (accordance with), with,* + הלך *walk* Ezk 3724 Ps 8931 1QS 820; of instrument, *by (means of), with* 4QBarka 1.34, + חיה *live* Ne 929, pi. *keep alive* Ps 119156 (if em. כְּמִשְׁפָּטֶיךָ *in accordance with your ordinances* to בְּמִשְׁפָּטֶיךָ), משל hi. *cause to rule* Si 4517, פחד pi. *frighten* 1QS 42.

כְּ *according to* Nm 296+7t 1QS 819 4QDa 6.13 (|| 4QDg 1.111) 6.43 4QapMosb 1.31 4QMMT B74 4QMa 43 11QT 153.9 1715 185 194 235 256.15 285.8 11QTb 45.9 521.24 61, + היה *be* 11QT 2210, בדל hi. *separate* CD 73, נזר hi. *keep separate* CD 72, עלה hi. *offer* sacrifice 1 C 2331, טהר *be (regarded as) pure* 11QT 507, עשׂה *do,* i.e. practise Lv 510 916 Nm 93.14 1524 2 K 1734 Ezk 57||1112 Ezr 34 4QDf 315 11QT 273 5017, הלך htp. *walk* CD 77 1221 194, חיה pi. *keep alive* Ps 119156 (or em.; see above), אכל *eat* 4QOrdc 16.10, תקע *give a trumpet blast* 4QMc fr. 112, נזה ho. *be sprinkled* 4QDd 8.24, זנה *fornicate* 4QDe 7.113.

מִן *from* 4QDe 3.319, + סור *turn aside* Ps 119102 Dn 95; אֶל *to,* + שׁמע *listen* Dt 41; *for* Ps 11920 (תַּאֲבָה אֶל־ מִשְׁפָּטֶיךָ *longing for your ordinances*); עַל *according to* 4QDibHama 3.214, + שׁפט *judge* Nm 3524, בדל hi. *separate* CD 1219; *on account of,* + הלל pi. *praise* Ps 119164, ידה hi. *give praise* Ps 11962; *concerning* CD 1613; *against,* + רום hi. *raise* hand CD 2030; עַל פִּי *according to,* + הלך htp. *walk* 1QSa 12, עשׂה *do,* i.e. practise 4Q419 11 11QT 566; עִם *with* 4QShirShabba 1.117; אֵת of instrument, *by (means) of, with,* + כפר *make atonement* 4QTohBc 14; חוּצָה מִן *outside* the ordinance, i.e. illegally 4QDe 7.112; מִשְׁפָּט without preposition *(by) an ordinance,* + ברר *cleanse* 4QPrEnosh fr. 1.25.

<COLL> אֵל || מִשְׁפָּט *God* 1QS 215, אֱמֶת *truth* Ezk 189 1QH 1420, דֶּרֶךְ *way* Ps 11930, חֹק *statute* Ezk 1112 2018.25 3627 Ps 815 Si 455, חֻקָּה *statute* Lv 184 2518 2615.43 1 K 612 Ezk 56.7 1120 189.17 2011+5t 3724 Ps 1823, מִצְוָה *commandment* 1 K 612 Ne 929 CD 72, תּוֹרָה *law* Ps 8931 11QPsa 248, סֵפֶר *book* 1QS 67, שַׁבָּת *sabbath* Ezk 2016.24, גִּלּוּל *idol* Ezk 2016.18.24.

+ דָּבָר *word* Ps 14719 4QapMosc 2.24, דָּם *blood* 2 C 1910, דֶּרֶךְ *way* Jr 54.5, חֹק *statute* Ex 1525 Lv 2646 Dt 41.5.8.14 51.31 61.20 711 1132 2616.17 Jos 2425 1 S 3025 1 K 858 2 K 1737 Ml 322 Ps 14719 Ezr 710 Ne 17 913 1030 1 C 2213 2 C 1910 338 Si 4517.17 CD 2030 4QWiles 54 4QDa 1112 4QMMT B52 4QDibHama 3.214, חֻקָּה *statute* Lv 185.26 1937 2022 Nm 93.14 Dt 811 111 3016 2 S 2223 1 K 23 1133 2 K 1734 Ezk 56, טָהֳרָה *purification regulation* 4QMMT B52, יָשָׁר *upright (one)* 1 K 1133, מִצְוָה *commandment* Nm 3613 Dt 531 61 711 811 111 2617 3016 1 K 23 858 2 K 1734.37 Dn 95 Ne 17 913 1030 1 C 287 2 C 1910, הוֹרָה *teaching* 4QShirShabba 1.117, מִשְׁמֶרֶת *watch* Dt 111, עֵדָה *testimony* Dt 620 1 K 23 Si 455 CD 2030, סוֹד *secret counsel* 4QShirb 63.33, צְדָקָה *righteousness* Dt 3321, תּוֹרָה *law* Lv 2646 Nm 1516 Dt 3310 2 K 1734.37 Ml 322 Ne 913 2 C 1910 338 1QS 516 (||4QSb 910||4QSd 19) 622, מַעֲשֶׂה *matter* 4QShirShabba 1.15.

4. custom, manner, perh. **destiny** (e.g. Jg 1312), **rank** (Si 3816), <SUBJ> היה *be* Jg 1312 1 S 811. <NOM CL> כֹּה מִשְׁפָּטוֹ *thus was his custom* 1 S 2711, מֶה מִשְׁפַּט הָאִישׁ *what is the manner of the man?* 2 K 17, כומז אודם ... משפט שיר *an ornament of ruby is ... the custom of song* Si 355, הוא משפט בריאתם *that is the manner of their creation* CD 1215, בידו משפטי כול *in his hand are the manners of all* 1QS 317. <OBJ> ידע *know* 1 S 213 2 K 1726.26, צוה pi. *charge* 1 C 2419, ירה hi. *teach* 2 K 1727, דבר pi. *speak* 1 S 1025, נגד *declare* 1 S 89, ראה ho. *be shown* Ex 2630.

<CSTR> מִשְׁפַּט אֱלֹהֵי *manner of the God of* 2 K 1726.26.27, דָּוִיד *of David* 2 C 814, צִדֹנִים *of the Sidonians* Jg 187, הַגּוֹיִם *of the nations* 2 K 1733, מִשְׁפַּט הַבָּנוֹת *custom of the daughters* Ex 219, הַכֹּהֲנִים *of the priests* 1 S 213, הַמֶּלֶךְ *of the king* 1 S 89.11, הַמְּלֻכָה *of kingship* 1 S 1025, מִשְׁפַּט־הַנַּעַר *manner,* or *destiny, of the lad* Jg 1312, משפט אנוש *manner of a human being* 4Q418 773, [ר]וחו *of his spirit* 4Q417 2.118, משפט שיר *custom of song* Si 355, משפט בריאתם *manner of their creation* CD 1215, משפטי כסיל *manners of a fool* 4QMystc 2a1, משפטי כול *manners of all* 1QS 317; כול משפטיהן *all their manners* 1QS 418.

<ADJ> זֶה *this* Ex 2131 Jos 615, רִאשׁוֹן *former* Gn 4013 2 K 1734.40.

<PREP> בְּ introducing object, + בין *understand* 4Q418 773; כְּ *as, like,* + נתן *give* Gn 4013; *in accordance with, after,* + גדד htpo. *lacerate oneself* 1 K 1828, בער pi. *burn* 2 C 420, בשׁל pi. *boil* 2 C 3513, דבר pi. *speak*

CD 14_8, דרשׁ *seek* 1 C 15_{13}, ידע *know* 4Q417 2.1_{18}, חנן *be gracious* Ps 119_{132}, ישׁב *dwell* Jg 18_7, עמד *stand* 2 K 11_{14} 1 C 6_{17} 2 C 30_{16}, hi. *appoint* 2 C 8_{14}, אסף *gather* (people) *together* or *bury* Si 38_{16} (perh. כמשפטו אסוף שׁארו *according to his rank bury his body*), עבד *serve* 2 K 17_{33}, עשׂה *do*, i.e. practise Ex 21_9 2 K $17_{34.40}$ Ne 8_{18}, i.e. make 2 C 4_7, ni. *be done* Ex 21_{31}, שׁמר *keep* CD 10_{14}, בוא *enter* 1 C 24_{19}, סבב *go around* Jos 6_{15}, קום hi. *set up* Ex 26_{30}; עַל *according to*, + ישׁב *sit* Jr 30_{18}; *concerning* 1QS 4_{18}.

<COLL> מִשְׁפָּט || כומז *ornament* Si 35_5; + Y. 1 S 2_{13}, תּוֹרָה *law* 2 C 30_{16}.

5. legal right, entitlement, <SUBJ> היה *be* Dt 18_3. <NOM CL> לוֹ מִשְׁפַּט הַבְּכֹרָה *the entitlement of the firstborn's privilege is his* Dt 21_{17}, לְךָ מִשְׁפַּט הַגְּאֻלָּה *yours is the legal right of redemption* Jr 32_7, לְךָ מִשְׁפַּט הַיְרֻשָּׁה *yours is the legal right of possession* Jr 32_8, לוֹ הַמִּשְׁפָּט *the entitlement is his* Ezk 21_{32}. <OBJ> נטה hi. *turn aside*, i.e. obstruct Lm 3_{35}, ידע *know* CD 9_{15} (לא ידע מוצאיה את משפטה *its finder did not know its entitlement*, i.e. its owner CD 9_{15}).

<CSTR> מִשְׁפַּט הַגְּאֻלָּה *legal right of redemption* Jr 32_7, הַיְרֻשָּׁה *of possession* Jr 32_8, גָּבֶר *of a man* Lm 3_{35}, מִשְׁפַּט הַבְּכֹרָה *entitlement of the firstborn's privilege* Dt 21_{17}, מִשְׁפַּט הַכֹּהֲנִים *entitlement of the priests* Dt 18_3.

<PREP> לְ *about, in relation to*, + יצא *go out* 1QS 5_3 (יצא תכון הגורל ... למשפט *the fixed rule of a lot shall go out ... in relation to the entitlement*); בְּ *over* 4QBer[a] fr. $17b_2$, + משׁל *rule* 1QS 9_7.

<COLL> מִשְׁפָּט || גְּאֻלָּה *redemption* Jr 32_8; + דָּבָר *thing* 1QS 5_3, הוֹן *wealth* 1QS 5_3 9_7 4QBer[a] fr. $17b_2$, תּוֹרָה *law* 1QS 5_3.

מִשְׁפַּט הַגְּאֻלָּה לִקְנוֹת *legal right of redemption by purchase* Jr 32_7.

6. just measure, specification, proper measure, moderation, restraint, discretion, <NOM CL> כִּי לְכָל־חֵפֶץ יֵשׁ עֵת וּמִשְׁפָּט *for to every matter there is a time and a proper measure* Ec 8_6 (unless §1),* <OBJ> בין *understand* Pr 28_5 (unless §2),* ידע *know* Ec 8_5 (unless §1).* <CSTR> כָּל־מִשְׁפָּטָיו *all its specifications* 1 K 6_{38} (if em. מִשְׁפָּטוֹ *its specification*). <APP> יום משפטו *(each) day its just measure* 1QS 10_7. <PREP> לְ *according to*, + יסר pi. *discipline* Jr 30_{11} || 46_{28}, כלה *be complete* 1 K 6_{38}; בְּ of accompaniment, *in, with*, + יסר pi. *discipline* Jr 10_{24}; כְּ *according to* Ezk 42_{11}, + בוא hi. *bring* 1 K 5_8. <COLL> מִשְׁפָּט || תְּכוּן *arrangement* 1QS 10_7; + דָּבָר *detail* 1 K 6_{38}, עֵת *time* Ec 8_5.

Also 1QH 14_4 fr. 14_3 fr. 39_1 1QM 15_{13} 1QNoah 2_2 1QDM 2_7 1Q36 16_4 4QAges[a] 1_{10} 4QWiles 5_4 4Q185 1.2_3 4QD[a] 5.1_3 8.2_2 9.3_{10} 4QD[f] 4.2_{16} 4QD[g] 1.2_7 4QTohB[a] 2_1 4QTohD 2_2 4QMyst[a] 6.2_{17} 53_5 4QMyst[b] 5_2 7_3 10_2 4QPrEnosh 1.1_6 2_4 6_1 4QapJoseph[b] 3_5 18_3 4QapPs[b] fr. 19.1_2 4QparaKings fr. 104_8 4QShirShabb[f] fr. 48_1 4Q417 1.1_{14} 4Q418 126.2_6 147_7 212_2 4Q419 4_2 4QWays[a] 3_1 4Q424 1_9 4QPatr 3.2_2 4QM[a] fr. $3_{1.2}$ 4QM[f] fr. 35_2 4QM[g] 6_3 4QM[h] 2_5 4QRitMar fr. 76_1 4QDibHam[a] 9_6 4QShir[b] 18.3_8 59.3_3 67_2 71_2 137_4 4QOrd[b] 14_6 39_1 4QapMes $2.1+3_8$ 6QapSamKgs 21_2 8QHymn 2_5 11QShirShabb 28_3.

<SYN> י״ Y., אֵל *God*, אהבת חסד *love of loyalty*, אֵמֻן *faithfulness*, אֱמוּנָה *faithfulness*, אֱמֶת *truth*, גְּאֻלָּה *redemption*, גְּבוּרָה *might*, הַצְנֵעַ לֶכֶת *modesty of going*, חָכְמָה *wisdom*, חֶסֶד *kindness*, חָסִיד *godly one*, טוֹב *good*, יְשׁוּעָה *salvation*, יָשְׁרָה *uprightness*, כֹּחַ *strength*, מֵישָׁרִים *uprightness*, נְכֹחָה *uprightness*, עֲנָוָה *humility*, צֶדֶק *righteousness*, צְדָקָה *righteousness*, רַחֲמִים *compassion*, תְּבוּנָה *understanding*.

יָד *hand*, לֵבָב *heart*, נֶפֶשׁ *soul*, אוֹר *light*, בֶּגֶד *garment*, דָּבָר *thing, matter*, דֶּרֶךְ *way*, הוֹן *wealth*, כּוּמָז *ornament*, לֶחֶם *bread*, סֵפֶר *book*, עֲרָפֶל *cloud*, טָהֳרָה *purification ritual*, חֹק *statute*, חֻקָּה *statute*, מִצְוָה *commandment*, עֵצָה *counsel*, שַׁבָּת *sabbath*, תּוֹרָה *law*, תְּכוּן *arrangement*.

אָוֶן *iniquity*, בַּעַר *burning*, גִּלּוּל *idol*, דָּם *blood*, חָמָס *violence*, מֻרְדָּף *persecution*, מִרְמָה *deceit*, נֶגַע *wound*, עַוָּתָה *lack of justice*, עֹצֶר *oppression*, שֹׁחַד *bribe*, תַּחֲלֻאִים *diseases*, הוֹכִיחַ *reproof* Hb 1_{12}, תּוֹכֵחָה *rebuke*, דִּין *plea*, פְּעֻלָּה *recompense*, רִיב *dispute*.*

⇒ שׁפט *judge*.

מְשֹׁפֵט *adversary*, see שׁפט Po. *judge*.

מִשְׁפְּתַיִם I$_2$ n.[m.]du. **fire-places, ash-heaps** (unless מִשְׁפְּתַיִם II *saddle-bags* or III *divided sheepfolds* or IV *double wall* or V *grazing places*), <PREP> בֵּין *between, among*, + ישׁב *sit* Jg 5_{16}, רבץ *lie down* Gn 49_{14}, שׁכב *lie down* Ps 68_{14} (if em. שְׁפַתַּיִם perh. *hooks* to מִשְׁפְּתַיִם).*

*מִשְׁפְּתַיִם II $_2$ n.[m.]du. **saddle-bags** of a mule (unless מִשְׁפְּתַיִם I *fire-places* or III *divided sheepfolds* or IV *double wall* or V *grazing places*), <PREP> בֵּין *between, among*, + ישׁב *sit* Jg 5_{16}, רבץ *lie down* Gn 49_{14}.

*מִשְׁפְּתַיִם III $_2$ n.[m.]du. **divided sheepfolds** (unless מִשְׁפְּתַיִם I *fire-places* or II *saddle-bags* or IV *double wall* or V *grazing places*), <PREP> בֵּין *between, among*, + ישׁב *sit* Jg 5_{16}, רבץ *lie down* Gn 49_{14}.

*מִשְׁפְּתַיִם IV $_2$ n.[m.]du. **double wall** (unless מִשְׁפְּתַיִם I *fire-places* or II *saddle-bags* or III *divided sheepfolds* or V *grazing places*), <PREP> בֵּין *between, among*, + ישׁב *sit* Jg 5_{16}, רבץ *lie down* Gn 49_{14}.

*מִשְׁפְּתַיִם V $_2$ n.[m.]du. **grazing places** (unless מִשְׁפְּתַיִם I *fire-places* or II *saddle-bags* or III *divided sheepfolds* or IV *double wall*), <PREP> בֵּין *between, among*, + ישׁב *sit* Jg 5_{16}, רבץ *lie down* Gn 49_{14}.
⇒ שׁפה [?] *graze*.

[מֶשֶׁק] I $_1$ n.[m.] **acquisition, possession** (unless מֶשֶׁק II *libation*)—cstr. מֶשֶׁק—<CSTR> בֶּן־מֶשֶׁק בֵּיתִי *the son of the acquisition of my house*, i.e. my heir Gn 15_2 (or em. בֶּן־מֶשֶׁק בַּת בֵּיתִי *son of Meshek, the daughter of my house*, i.e. מֶשֶׁק III).*
⇒ מִמְשָׁק *ground*.

*[מֶשֶׁק] II $_1$ n.[m.] **libation** (unless מֶשֶׁק I *acquisition*) —cstr. מֶשֶׁק—<CSTR> בֶּן־מֶשֶׁק בֵּיתִי *the son of the libation of my grave* (בַּיִת *grave*), i.e. the one who pours libations for me as my heir Gn 15_2.

*[מֶשֶׁק] III $_1$ pr.n.f. **Meshek**, <CSTR> בֶּן־מֶשֶׁק *son of Meshek* Gn 15_2. <APP> בַּת בֵּיתִי *daughter of*, i.e. one who belongs to, *my house* Gn 15_2 (if ins. בַּת).

[מַשָּׁק] I $_1$ n.[m.] **rushing about** (unless מַשָּׁק II *swarm*) —cstr. מַשַּׁק—**rushing about** or **infestation** or **assault**, <CSTR> מַשַּׁק גֵּבִים *rushing about of locusts* Is 33_4. <PREP> כְּ *as*, + שׁקק *rush about* Is 33_4.*
⇒ שׁקק *rush about*.

*[מַשָּׁק] II $_1$ n.[m.] **swarm**—cstr. מַשַּׁק—(unless מַשָּׁק I *rushing about*), <CSTR> מַשַּׁק גֵּבִים *swarm of locusts* Is 33_4. <PREP> כְּ *as*, + שׁקק *rush about* Is 33_4.
⇒ נשׁק *arrange*.

[מְשֻׁקָּד] *shaped like almond blossom*, see שׁקד II *shape like almond*.

מַשְׁקֶה I $_{13}$ n.m. **cup-bearer**—cstr. מַשְׁקֵה; sf. מַשְׁקֵהוּ; pl. מַשְׁקִים; sf. מַשְׁקָיו—**1. cup-bearer,** <SUBJ> היה *be* Gn 40_{13} Ne 1_{11}, אסר pass. *be bound* Gn 40_5, חטא *sin* Gn 40_1, חלם *dream* Gn 40_5. <OBJ> ראה *see* 1 K 10_5||2 C 9_4. <CSTR> מַשְׁקֵה מֶלֶךְ־מִצְרַיִם *cup-bearer of the king of Egypt* Gn 40_1; שַׂר הַמַּשְׁקִים *chief of the cup-bearers* Gn $40_{2.9.20.21.23}$ 41_9.

<COLL> מַשְׁקֶה || אֹפֶה *baker* Gn $40_{2.20}$; + אֹפֶה *baker* Gn $40_{1.5}$, חָכְמָה *wisdom* 1 K 10_5||2 C 9_4, בַּיִת *house* 1 K 10_5||2 C 9_4, מַאֲכָל *food* 1 K 10_5||2 C 9_4, מוֹשָׁב *seat* 1 K 10_5||2 C 9_4, מַלְבּוּשׁ *robe* 1 K 10_5||2 C 9_4, מַעֲמָד *attendance* 1 K 10_5||2 C 9_4.

2. office of cup-bearer, <PREP> עַל *to*, + שׁוב hi. *restore* Gn 40_{21}.
⇒ שׁקה hi. *cause to drink*.

מַשְׁקֶה II $_{6.1.10}$ n.m. **drink; irrigated land**—cstr. מַשְׁקֵה; pl. cstr. Q משקי; sf. Q משקיהם—**1. drink,** <SUBJ> יצא *go out* 4QTohA 2.1_7 4QLeqet 1_5. טמא *be impure* Lv 11_{34}, שׁתה ni. *be drunk* Lv 11_{34}, <OBJ> חסר hi. *cause to lack* Is 32_6, עצר *restrain* 1QH 4_{11}. <CSTR> מַשְׁקֵה הַמֶּלֶךְ *drink of the king* 1 K 10_{21}||2 C 9_{20}, משקה הרבים *drink of the many* 1QS 6_{20} 7_{20} 4QLeqet 1_3, משקה דעת *drink of knowledge* 1QH 4_{11}, כְּלֵי מַשְׁקֶה *vessels of drink*, i.e. drinking vessels, *of* 1 K 10_{21}||2 C 9_{20}, כָּל־מַשְׁקֶה *every drink* Lv 11_{34}. <PREP> בְּ introducing object, + נגע *touch* 1QS 6_{20} 7_{20} 4QLeqet 1_3.

2. irrigated land, <NOM CL> כִּי כֻלָּהּ מַשְׁקֶה *for all of it was irrigated land* Gn 13_{10}. <OBJ> הפך *turn* Si 39_{23},

נתן *give* 1QH 8₄. <CSTR> מַשְׁקֵה יִשְׂרָאֵל *irrigated land of Israel* Ezk 45₁₅, משקי גן *irrigated lands of the garden* 1QH 8₄. <PREP> לְ *for* 4QOrd[b] 13₆; מִן *(originating) from, of* Ezk 45₁₅. <COLL> מַשְׁקֶה + מַבּוּעַ *spring* 1QH 8₄, מָקוֹר *fountain* 1QH 8₄.

Also 4QTohA 2.1₆ 2.2₁₂.

⇒ שׁקה hi. *cause to drink.*

מִשְׁקוֹל 1 n.[m.] **weight,** <PREP> בְּ *according to,* + אכל *eat* Ezk 4₁₀.

⇒ שׁקל *weigh,* שֶׁקֶל *shekel,* מִשְׁקָל *weight.*

מַשְׁקוֹף 3.0.6 n.m. **lintel**—pl. sf. Q משקופיו—<OBJ> כבס pi. *wash* 11QT 49₁₃. <CSTR> רְבֻעֵי מַשְׁקוֹף *square (ones) of lintel,* i.e. with square lintels 1 K 7₅ (if em. רְבֻעִים שָׁקֶף *square [ones with respect to] frame,* i.e. with square frames). <PREP> מִן *from* 4Q365a 2.2₆(erased) 11QT 36₁₀; אֶל *to,* + נגע hi. *apply* Ex 12₂₂; עַל *upon,* + נתן *place* Ex 12₇, ראה *see* Ex 12₂₃; עד *unto* 4Q365a 2.2₆= 11QT 41₁₅ 11QT 36₉ 41₁₅ 42₂. <COLL> מַשְׁקוֹף + שְׁתֵּי הַמְּזוּזֹת *two doorposts* Ex 12₇.₂₂.₂₃, מַנְעוּל *lock* 11QT 49₁₃, מְזוּזָה *doorpost* 11QT 49₁₃, אָסַף *threshold* 11QT 49₁₃.

⇒ שׁקף *overhang.*

מִשְׁקָל 49.3.17 n.m. **weight**—cstr. מִשְׁקַל; sf. מִשְׁקָלוֹ, מִשְׁקָלָהּ, מִשְׁקָלָם—**weight, full weight, value,** <SUBJ> היה *be* 1 K 10₁₄||2 C 9₁₃ 2 K 25₁₆||Jr 52₂₀ 2 C 9₁₃ 4QWays[a] 3₂, ni. 4Q418 77₄, חקר ni. *be ascertained* 1 K 7₄₇=2 C 4₁₈, כתב ni. *be written* Ezr 8₃₄.

<NOM CL> אֵין מִשְׁקָל *there was no weight* 1 C 22₃.₁₄ Si 6₁₅ 26₁₅, בֶּקַע מִשְׁקָלוֹ *half a shekel was its weight* Gn 24₂₂, עֲשָׂרָה זָהָב מִשְׁקָלָם *ten (units of) gold was their weight* Gn 24₂₂, חֲמִשִּׁים שְׁקָלִים מִשְׁקָלוֹ *fifty shekels was its weight* Jos 7₂₁, מִשְׁקָל לְמִסְמְרוֹת לִשְׁקָלִים חֲמִשִּׁים *the weight of the nails was fifty shekels* 2 C 3₉, שְׁלֹשִׁים וּמֵאָה מִשְׁקָלָהּ *one hundred and thirty (shekels) was its weight* Nm 7₁₃||7₁₉₊₁₀ₜ, מִשְׁקַל קֵינוֹ שְׁלֹשׁ מֵאוֹת מִשְׁקַל נְחֹשֶׁת *the weight of his spear was three hundredweight of bronze* 2 S 21₁₆, מִשְׁקָל שֵׁשׁ מֵאוֹת *(the) weight was six hundred (shekels)* 1 C 21₂₅, מִשְׁקַל נִזְמֵי הַזָּהָב ... אֶלֶף וּשְׁבַע־מֵאוֹת זָהָב *the weight of the rings of gold was ... one thousand and seven hundred (shekels of) gold* Jg 8₂₆, מִשְׁקַל הַשִּׁרְיוֹן חֲמֵשֶׁת־אֲלָפִים שְׁקָלִים *the weight of the armour was five thousand shekels* 1 S 17₅, מִשְׁקָלָהּ כִּכַּר זָהָב *its weight was a talent of gold* 2 S 12₃₀, מִשְׁקַל כִּכַּר־זָהָב *(it was) the weight of a talent of gold* 1 C 20₂, כלוה משקל ככרין שבעשרה *all of it was the weight of seventeen talents* 3QTr 1₄, הכל משקל ככרין *all was the weight of* seventy-two *talents* 3QTr 12₉.

<OBJ> עשׂה *make* Jb 28₂₅, נתן *give* 1C 28₁₅, קבל pi. *receive* Ezr 8₃₀, תכן *measure* 4Q418 126.2₃.

<CSTR> משקל איש ואיש *value of each man* 1QS 9₁₂, מִשְׁקַל נִזְמֵי *the weight of the rings of* Jg 8₂₆, נְחֹשֶׁת *of bronze* 2 S 21₁₆, הַנְּחֹשֶׁת *of the bronze* 1 K 7₄₇=2 C 4₁₈, הַכֶּסֶף *of the silver* Ezr 8₃₀, הַזָּהָב *of the gold* 1 K 10₁₄= 2 C 9₁₃ Ezr 8₃₀, הַכֵּלִים *of the vessels* Ezr 8₃₀, קֵינוֹ *of his spear* 2 S 21₁₆, הַשִּׁרְיוֹן *of the armour* 1 S 17₅, מְנוֹרָה *of the lamp stand* 1 C 28₁₅, כִּכַּר־זָהָב *of a talent of gold* 1 C 20₂, משקל ככרין *weight of talents* 3QTr 1₄ 12₉, קצים *of the ends* 4Q418 77₄ (ו[מ]שקל), צדק *of righteousness* 4Q418 126.2₃, צדקה *of righteousness* 4QBark[b] 4₃.

מֹאזְנֵי מִשְׁקָל *balances of weight,* i.e. for weighing Ezk 5₁, כָּל־הַמִּשְׁקָל *all the weight* Ezr 8₃₄.

<APP> הַזָּהָב מִשְׁקָל *the gold, weight* 1 C 28₁₆ (or em. מִשְׁקָל *weight* to בְּמִשְׁקָל *according to weight*).

<PREP> לְ *in accordance with,* + הלך htp. *walk* 1QS 9₁₂.

בְּ *according to* Gn 43₂₁ Ezr 8₃₄ 4Q415 6₅ 4Q418 87₁₂ 4QBark[b] 4₃, + אכל *eat* Ezk 4₁₆, עשׂה *do* 4Q424 3₁, שׁוב hi. *bring back* Lv 26₂₆, נתן *give* 1 C 28₁₄₊₆ₜ 28₁₆ (if em.; see above), נבע hi. *pour out* Si 16₂₅, תכן *measure* 4QBark[a] 1.2₁₀; *in respect of* 4QsapDidB 1+3₆, + עשׂה *do* Lv 19₃₅.

עִם *by (means of), with,* + כון hi. *determine* 4Q415 11₈.

<COLL> שֶׁקֶל || מִשְׁקָל *shekel* Nm 7₁₃||7₁₉₊₁₀ₜ, מְשׂוּרָה *capacity* Ezk 4₁₆ Lv 19₃₅ (+), מִדָּה *measure* Lv 19₃₅ (+) Jb 28₂₅, תֹּכֶן *arrangement* 1QS 9₁₂, מִסְפָּר *number* Ezr 8₃₄, מְחִיר *price* Si 6₁₅, צָנוּעַ *modesty* Si 16₂₅

Also 4QMyst[a] 20₂ 32₄ 4Q418 77₃ 172₂.

<SYN> שֶׁקֶל *shekel,* מְשׂוּרָה *capacity,* מִדָּה *measure,* תֹּכֶן *arrangement,* מִסְפָּר *number,* מְחִיר *price,* צָנוּעַ *modesty.*

⇒ שׁקל *weigh.*

[מִשְׁקֹלֶת] 2.0.2 n.f. **levelling implement**—מִשְׁקָלֶת; cstr. מִשְׁקֹלֶת—mason's **level** or **plumbline,** <OBJ> נטה *stretch out* 2 K 21$_{13}$, שׂים *place* 1QH 6$_{26}$. <CSTR> מִשְׁקֹלֶת בֵּית *levelling implement of the house of* 2 K 21$_{13}$, משקלת א[מת] *levelling implement of truth* 1QH 6$_{26}$, השמש *of the sun* 1QH 8$_{22}$. <PREP> לְ *as,* + שׂים *place* Is 28$_{17}$; עַל *upon,* + פנה *turn* 1QH 8$_{22}$. <COLL> מִשְׁקֹלֶת || קָו *plumb-line* 2 K 21$_{13}$ Is 28$_{17}$ 1QH 8$_{22}$; + כָּפִּים *beam* 1QH 6$_{26}$, סוֹד *foundation* 1QH 6$_{26}$. <SYN> קָו *plumb-line.**

⇒ שׁקל *weigh.*

מִשְׁקֹלֶת, see מִשְׁקֹלֶת *levelling implement.*

[מִשְׁקָע] 1 n.[m.] **what is settled**—cstr. מִשְׁקַע—<OBJ> שׁתה *drink* Ezk 34$_{18}$. <CSTR> מִשְׁקַע־מַיִם *what is settled of the water,* i.e. clear water Ezk 34$_{18}$. <COLL> מִשְׁקָע || מִרְעֶה *pasture* Ezk 34$_{18}$.

⇒ שׁקע *sink.*

[מִשְׁרָה] 1 n.f. **juice**—cstr. מִשְׁרַת—<OBJ> שׁתה *drink* Nm 6$_{3}$. <CSTR> מִשְׁרַת עֲנָבִים *juice of grapes* Nm 6$_{3}$; כָּל־מִשְׁרַת *all the juice of* Nm 6$_{3}$.

מִשְׁרָעִי 1 gent. **Mishraite,** as collective noun, **Mishraites,** <NOM CL> וּמִשְׁפְּחוֹת קִרְיַת יְעָרִים ... הַמִּשְׁרָעִי *and the clans of Kiriath-jearim (were) ... the Mishraites* 1 C 2$_{53}$ (+ יִתְרִי *Ithrites,* פּוּתִי *Puthites,* שֻׁמָתִי *Shumathites).*

מְשָׁרֵת *minister,* see שׁרת Pi. *serve.*

משׁשׁ I 10 vb. **feel—Qal** 3 Impf. אֲמֻשְּׁךָ, יְמֻשֵּׁנִי; + waw וַיְמֻשֵּׁהוּ—**feel,** <SUBJ> Isaac Gn 27$_{21.22}$, אָב *father* Gn 27$_{12}$. <OBJ> Jacob Gn 27$_{12.21.22}$.

Pi. 6 Pf. מִשַּׁשְׁתָּ; impf. יְמַשְׁשׁוּ, יְמַשֵּׁשׁ; + waw וַיְמַשֵּׁשׁ; ptc. מְמַשֵּׁשׁ—**grope, search with hands,** <SUBJ> Laban Gn 31$_{34.37}$ (both :: מצא *find*), Israelites Dt 28$_{29}$, Job's mockers Jb 30$_{3}$ (if em. אֶמֶשׁ *evening* to יְמַשְׁשׁוּ *they grope*), חָכָם *wise one* Jb 5$_{14}$ (|| פגשׁ pi. *encounter*), עִוֵּר *blind one* Dt 28$_{29}$, ראשׁ *chief* Jb 12$_{25}$ (|| תעה hi. *cause to wander about*). <OBJ> אֹהֶל *tent* Gn 31$_{34}$, חֹשֶׁךְ *darkness* Jb 12$_{25}$, מְשֹׁאָה *devastation* Jb 30$_{3}$ (if em.; see Subj.), שׁוֹאָה *devastation* Jb 30$_{3}$ (if em.; see Subj.), כְּלִי *vessel* Gn 31$_{37}$, כֹּל *all* Gn 31$_{34.37}$. <PREP> בְּ of place, time, *in, during,* + אֲפֵלָה *darkness* Dt 28$_{29}$, צָהֳרַיִם *noon* Dt 28$_{29}$ Jb 5$_{14}$; כְּ *as,* + לַיְלָה *night* Jb 5$_{14}$.

<SYN> פגשׁ pi. *encounter,* תעה hi. *cause to wander about.*

<ANT> מצא *find.*

Hi. 1 Impf. יָמֵשׁ—**feel,** <SUBJ> subj. not specified, Ex 10$_{21}$. <OBJ> חֹשֶׁךְ *darkness* Ex 10$_{21}$.

⇒ ימשׁ *touch,* מושׁ II *feel.*

***משׁשׁ II** 1.1 vb. **arrive—Qal** 0.1 Impf. 3fs Si תמושׁ—**arrive** (unless from מושׁ I *depart),* <SUBJ> רָעָה *evil* Pr 17$_{13}$ appar. Si 40$_{10(Bmg)}$, כָּלָה *destruction* appar. Si 40$_{10(B)}$. <PREP> בַּעֲבוּר *on account of,* + רָשָׁע *wicked one* Si 40$_{10(Bmg)}$.

Hi. 1 Impf. יָמֵשׁ—**arrive** (unless משׁשׁ I *feel),* <SUBJ> חֹשֶׁךְ *darkness* Ex 10$_{21}$.

מִשְׁתֶּה 46.5 n.m. **feast**—cstr. מִשְׁתֵּה; pl. sf. מִשְׁתָּיו, מִשְׁתֵּיכֶם, מִשְׁתֵּיהֶם—**1. feast,** <SUBJ> היה *be* Jg 14$_{17}$.

<NOM CL> הִנֵּה־לוֹ מִשְׁתֶּה *behold (there was) to him a feast* 1 S 25$_{36}$, טוֹב־לֵב מִשְׁתֶּה תָמִיד *a good heart (has) a perpetual feast* Pr 15$_{15}$, מִשְׁתֶּה וְיוֹם טוֹב *(there was) a feast and a holiday* Est 8$_{17}$. <OBJ> אכל *eat* Gn 19$_{3}$ 26$_{30}$, שׁתה *drink* Gn 26$_{30}$, עשׂה *make* Gn 19$_{3}$ 21$_{8}$ 26$_{30}$ 29$_{22}$ 40$_{20}$ Jg 14$_{10}$ 2 S 3$_{20}$ 1 K 3$_{15}$ Is 25$_{6.6}$ Jb 1$_{4}$ Est 1$_{3.5.9}$ 2$_{18.18}$ 5$_{4.5.8.12}$ 6$_{14}$ 9$_{19}$, שׁית *set* Jr 51$_{39}$.

<CSTR> מִשְׁתֵּה אֶסְתֵּר *feast of Esther* Est 2$_{18}$, הַמֶּלֶךְ *of the king,* i.e. a royal feast 1 S 25$_{36}$, נָשִׁים *of,* i.e. for, *women* Est 1$_{9}$, שְׁמָנִים *of fat things* Is 25$_{6}$, שְׁמָרִים *of matured wines* Is 25$_{6}$, הַיַּיִן *of wine* Est 5$_{6}$ 7$_{2.7.8}$ Si 34$_{31}$ 35$_{5.5.5}$ 49$_{1}$; יוֹם מִשְׁתֶּה *day of a feast,* i.e. festival Est 9$_{17.18}$, יְמֵי הַמִּשְׁתֶּה *days of the feast* Jg 14$_{12}$ Jb 1$_{5}$, מִשְׁתֶּה *of a feast,* i.e. festive days Est 9$_{22}$, בֵּית־מִשְׁתֶּה *house of a feast,* i.e. banquet house Jr 16$_{8}$ Ec 7$_{2}$ (:: אֵבֶל *mourning)* Est 7$_{8}$ (מִשְׁתֵּה *of the feast of).*

<ADJ> גָּדוֹל *great* Gn 21$_{8}$ Est 2$_{18}$, תָּמִיד *perpetual* Pr 15$_{15}$, שָׂמֵחַ *joyful* Est 5$_{14}$. <PREP> בְּ of time, *during* Si 34$_{31}$, + אמר *say* Est 5$_{6}$ 7$_{2}$; כְּ *as* 1 S 25$_{36}$; מִן *from,* + קום *arise* Est 7$_{7}$; אֶל *to,* + בוא *come* Est 5$_{4.5.8.14}$, hi. *bring* Est

5_{12} 6_{14}; עַל *upon* Si $35_{5.5}$ 49_1, + יפה *be beautiful* Si 35_5; מִשְׁתֶּה without preposition *(at) a feast*, + היה *be* Is 5_{12}. <COLL> מִשְׁתֶּה || מַצָּה *unleavened bread* Gn 19_3, שִׂמְחָה *joy* Est 8_{17} $9_{17.18.22}$; + שִׂמְחָה *joy* Est 9_{19}, יוֹם טוֹב *holiday* Est 9_{19}; מִשְׁתֵּה שִׁבְעַת יָמִים *seven day feast* Est 1_5.

2. drink, <OBJ> מנה pi. *appoint* Dn 1_{10} (+ מַאֲכָל *food*), נתן *give* Ezr 3_7 (+ מַאֲכָל *food*, שֶׁמֶן *oil*). <CSTR> יֵין מִשְׁתָּיו *wine of his drink*, i.e. his own wine Dn $1_{5.8}$ (both || פַּתְבַּג *portion* of the king), יֵין מִשְׁתֵּיהֶם *wine of their drink*, i.e. their own wine Dn 1_{16} (+ פַּתְבַּג *portion*).

<SYN> מַצָּה *unleavened bread*, שִׂמְחָה *joy*, פַּתְבַּג *portion*.

<ANT> אֵבֶל *mourning*.

⇒ שׁתה *drink*.

מַשְׁתִּין, see שׁין Hi. *urinate*.*

[מַת] I 22.2.2 n.m. **man**—pl. מְתִים (מְתִם); cstr. מְתֵי; sf. מְתֶיךָ, מְתָיו—<SUBJ> היה *be* Dt 33_6 Ps 105_{12}||1 C 16_{19}, אמר *say* Jb 31_{31}, דרך *tread* Jb 22_{15}, hi. *attain to* Si 15_7, ירא *fear* Is 41_{14} (unless מֹת *louse*), נאק *groan* Jb 24_{12} (or em. מְתִים to מֵתִים *the dying*), נפל *fall* Is 3_{25}, שׁאר ni. *remain* Dt 4_{27}, שׁוב *return* Jr 44_{28}, תעב pi. *abhor* Jb 19_{19}.

<NOM CL> אֲנִי מְתֵי מִסְפָּר *I am few men in number* Gn 34_{30}, כְּבוֹדוֹ מְתֵי רָעָב *his glory is hungry men* Is 5_{13} (or *men dying of hunger* [מֵת, ptc. of מות *die*], or em. מְתֵי to מְזֵי *empty of*, i.e. by, hunger). <OBJ> חרם hi. *destroy* Dt 3_6, נכה hi. *smite* Jg 20_{48} (if em. מְתֹם *entire* to מְתִים), חרשׁ hi. *make silent* Jb 11_3, ידע *know* Jb 11_{11}, עזר *help* Is 41_{14} (unless מֹת *louse*), שׁאר hi. *spare* Dt 2_{34}, עמד hi. *station* Ne 4_7 (if em.; see Cstr.).

<CSTR> מְתֵי יִשְׂרָאֵל *men of Israel* Is 41_{14} (unless מֹת *louse*), מִסְפָּר *of number*, i.e. numerable, few in number Gn 34_{30} Dt 4_{27} Jr 44_{28} Ps 105_{12}||1 C 16_{19}, מְעָט *of few*, i.e. few men Dt 26_5 28_{62}, עוֹלָם *of eternity*, i.e. men of the eternal home, the dead Ps 143_3 (if em.; see Prep.), רָעָב *of hunger*, i.e. hungry men Is 5_{13} (or em.; see Nom. Cl.), אָוֶן *of iniquity* Jb 22_{15}, שָׁוְא *of vanity* Ps 26_4 Jb 11_{11} Si 15_7, אָהֳלִי *of my tent* Jb 31_{31}, סוֹדִי *of my company*, i.e. my friends Jb 19_{19}, מתי עם *men of kinsmen*, i.e. clan members Si 7_{16}, מְתֵי חֲנִית/חֲנִיתוֹת *men of*, i.e. armed with, *spears* Ne 4_7 (if em. מִתַּחְתִּיּוֹת *from the lowest parts*); תולעת מתים *worm of men* (unless *of the dead*) 1QH 6_{34} 11_{12}, מֵרוֹם מְתֶךָ *at the sound of your men*, i.e. soldiers Is 33_3 (if em. מֵרוֹמְמֻתֶךָ *your lifting up*), כָּל־מְתֵי *all the men of* Jb 19_{19}.

<APP> אִשָּׁה *woman* Dt 3_6, עִיר *city* Dt 3_6. <PREP> בְּ of accompaniment, *in (a state of), with*, + גור *sojourn* Dt 26_5, שׁאר ni. *remain* Dt 28_{62}; of comparison, *(more) than*, + חשׁב hi. *esteem* Si 7_{16}; כְּ *as, like*, + ישׁב hi. *cause to dwell* Ps 143_3 (if em. מֵתֵי *the dead ones of* to מְתֵי; הוֹשִׁיבַנִי בְמַחֲשַׁכִּים כְּמְתֵי עוֹלָם *he caused me to dwell in the dark places like the men of the eternal home*);* מִן *from*, + פלט pi. *deliver* Ps $17_{14.14}$ (or em. מִמְתִים to מְמִיתָם *slay them*, i.e. ptc. used as impv.*); אֶל *to* perh. Ḥorvat 'Uza bowl inscr. (Beit-Arieh)9; עִם *with*, + ישׁב *sit* Ps 26_4. <COLL> מַת || אִישׁ *man* Si 15_7, גְּבוּרָה *might* Is 3_{25}, נַעֲלָם *dissembler* Ps 26_4, נֶפֶשׁ *soul* Jb 24_{12}, תּוֹלֵעָה *worm* Is 41_{14} (unless מֹת *louse*); + אִשָּׁה *woman* Dt 2_{34} 3_6, טַף *children* Dt 2_{34} 3_6.

<SYN> אִישׁ *man*, גְּבוּרָה *might*, נֶפֶשׁ *soul*.*

*[מַת] II adv. **truly,** מַת אֵב אָנֹכִי אֶת־גְּאוֹן יַעֲקֹב *truly I am the foe of Jacob's pride* Am 6_8 (if em. מְתָאֵב *loathing* to מַת אֵב, i.e. אֵב is stative ptc. of איב).*

מֵת *dead one*, see מות *die*.

*[מֹת] 1 n.m. **louse** (unless מַת I *man*)—pl. cstr. מְתֵי—<SUBJ> ירא *fear* Is 41_{14}. <OBJ> עזר *help* Is 41_{14}. <CSTR> מְתֵי יִשְׂרָאֵל *lice of Israel* Is 41_{14}. <COLL> מֹת || תּוֹלֵעָה *worm* Is 41_{14}, vocative Is 41_{14}.

מַתְבֵּן 1 n.[m.] **heap of straw,** <SUBJ> דושׁ ni. *be trampled down* Is 25_{10}.

⇒ תֶּבֶן *straw*.

מֶתֶג 4 n.m. **bridle**—sf. מִתְגִּי—or perh. **muzzle*** (2 K 19_{28} =Is 37_{29} Ps 32_9 Pr 26_3), <NOM CL> מֶתֶג לַחֲמוֹר *a bridle is for the ass* Pr 26_3 (|| שֵׁבֶט *rod*, שׁוֹט *whip*). <OBJ> שׂים *place* 2 K 19_{28}||Is 37_{29} (|| חָח *hook*), לקח *take* 2 S 8_1 (unless מֶתֶג הָאַמָּה *Metheg-ammah*). <CSTR> מֶתֶג הָאַמָּה *bridle of the cubit* 2 S 8_1 (unless pl.n. *Metheg-ammah*). <PREP> בְּ of instrument, *by (means of), with*, + בלם

restrain Ps 32$_{9}$ (+ רֶסֶן *halter*).

<SYN> חָח *hook*, שֵׁבֶט *rod*, שׁוֹט *whip*.*

⇒ מֶתֶג הָאַמָּה *Metheg-Ammah*.

מֶתֶג הָאַמָּה 1 appar. pl.n. **Metheg-ammah,** unless 'bridle of the cubit', <OBJ> לקח *take* 2 S 8$_{1}$.

⇒ מֶתֶג *bridle*.

מִתּוֹךְ, see תָּוֶךְ *midst*.

מָתוֹק 12.0.3 adj. **sweet**—מְתוּקָה; pl. מְתוּקִים—**1.** in nom. cl., used predicatively of נֹפֶת *flowing honey* Pr 24$_{13}$ (|| טוֹב *good*), פְּרִי *fruit* Ca 2$_{3}$, שְׁנָת *sleep* Ec 5$_{11}$, אוֹר *light* Ec 11$_{7}$, מָה *what?* Jg 14$_{18}$ (|| עַז *strong*) 4Q416 2.3$_{15}$ (:: מַר *bitter*), מַר *bitter thing* Pr 27$_{7}$ (|| נֹפֶת *flowing honey*).

<COLL> מָתוֹק with מִן of comparison, *sweeter than*, + דְּבַשׁ *honey* Jg 14$_{18}$ Ps 19$_{11}$.

2. used as noun, **sweet thing, sweetness,** <SUBJ> יצא *go out* Jg 14$_{14}$ (|| מַאֲכָל *food*). <NOM CL> מָתוֹק לַנֶּפֶשׁ *(they are) sweetness to the soul* Pr 16$_{24}$ (|| מַרְפֵּא *healing*). <OBJ> שׂים *place* Is 5$_{20}$ (:: מַר *bitterness*). <PREP> לְ *for*, + היה *be* Ez 3$_{3}$; *as*, + שׂים *place* Is 5$_{20}$ (:: מַר *bitterness*).

Also 4QMyst^{b} 12$_{1}$ ([מ]תוק) 4QM^{h} 1$_{8}$.

<SYN> טוֹב *good*, מַאֲכָל *food*, נֹפֶת *flowing honey*, מַרְפֵּא *healing*.

<ANT> מַר *bitter, bitterness*.

⇒ מתק *be sweet*.

***מָתוֹר** 0.0.1 n.[m.] **following after,** <CSTR> מתור שרירות *following after the stubbornness of* his heart 1QS 3$_{3}$. <PREP> בְּ of time, *in, during*, + צדק *be righteous* 1QS 3$_{3}$.

⇒ תור *follow*.

מְתוּשָׁאֵל 2 pr.n.m. **Methushael,** antediluvian Cainite, son of Mehujael and father of Lamech, <SUBJ> ילד *beget* Gn 4$_{18}$. <OBJ> ילד *beget* Gn 4$_{18}$.*

⇒ (?) מַת *man*, שְׁאוֹל *Sheol*.

מְתוּשֶׁלַח 6.0.1 pr.n.m. **Methuselah**—מְתוּשָׁלַח—antediluvian Sethite, son of Enoch and father of Lamech, lived 969 years, <SUBJ> חיה *live* Gn 5$_{25.26}$, ילד hi. *beget* Gn 5$_{25.26}$, מות *die* Gn 5$_{27}$. <OBJ> ילד hi. *beget* Gn 5$_{21.22}$. <CSTR> יְמֵי מְתוּשֶׁלַח *days of Methuselah* Gn 5$_{27}$.

<COLL> חֲנוֹךְ מְתוּשֶׁלַח לָמֶךְ *Enoch, Methuselah, Lamech* 1 C 1$_{3}$.

Also 1QNoah 8$_{2}$ (מתושל[ח]).

מתח 1 vb. **spread out**—Qal 1 + waw וַיִּמְתָּחֵם—<SUBJ> Y. Is 40$_{22}$. <OBJ> שָׁמַיִם *heavens* Is 40$_{22}$. <PREP> כְּ *as*, + אֹהֶל *tent* Is 40$_{22}$.

<SYN> נטה *stretch out*.*

⇒ אַמְתַּחַת *sack*, מִתְחָה *spreading out*.

***מִתְחָה** n.f. **spreading out,** <NOM CL> מְעֹנָה אֱלֹהֵי קֶדֶם וּמִתְחַת זְרֹעֹת עוֹלָם *the Everlasting God is (your) dwelling and the spreading of the everlasting arms*, i.e. the heavens Dt 33$_{27}$ (if em. וּמִתַּחַת *and beneath* are the everlasting arms). <CSTR> מִתְחַת זְרֹעֹת עוֹלָם *spreading out of the arms of everlastingness*, i.e. of the everlasting arms Dt 33$_{27}$ (if em.; see Nom Cl.).

⇒ מתח *spread out*.

מָתַי 43.1.3 interrog. adv. **when?, 1. when?,** with verb, היה *be* 4QpsEzek^{a} 2$_{3.9}$, אבד *be destroyed* Ps 41$_{6}$, מות *die* Ps 41$_{6}$, יבשׁ *be dry* Jr 12$_{4}$, עשׂה *do* Gn 30$_{30}$ Ps 119$_{84}$, נחם pi. *comfort* Ps 119$_{82}$, בוא *come* Ps 42$_{3}$ 101$_{2}$, עבר *pass* Am 8$_{5}$, קום *arise* Jb 7$_{4}$, קיץ hi. *awake* Pr 23$_{35}$, קבץ *gather* 4QpsEzek^{b} 1.2$_{3}$, ראה ni. *appear* Ps 42$_{3}$, שׁמע *hear* Jr 42$_{1}$, שׂכל hi. *have understanding* Ps 94$_{8}$.

2. עַד־מָתַי **how long?,** lit. 'until when', **a.** in nom. cl., עַד־מָתַי אֲדֹנָי *how long, O Lord?* Is 6$_{11}$, עַד־מָתַי לָעֵדָה הָרָעָה הַזֹּאת *how long (remains) for this wicked congregation?* Nm 14$_{27}$, עַד־מָתַי הֲיֵשׁ *how long are there* false prophets? Jr 23$_{26}$, עַד־מָתַי הֶחָזוֹן *how long is the vision?* Dn 8$_{13}$, עַד־מָתַי קֵץ *how long (until) the end of* the wonders? Dn 12$_{6}$.

b. as interj. Hb 2$_{6}$ Ps 6$_{4}$ 90$_{13}$.

c. with verb, היה *be* Ex 10$_{7}$ Ne 2$_{6}$, אבל *mourn* Jr 12$_{4}$, htp. *be in mourning* 1 S 16$_{1}$, חסר *lack* Si 51$_{24}$, מאן pi. *refuse* Ex 10$_{3}$, חרף pi. *reproach* Ps 74$_{10}$, שׂנא *hate* Pr 1$_{22}$, עשׁן *be angry* Ps 80$_{5}$, שׁפט *judge* Ps 82$_{2}$, שׁכר htp. *make oneself drunk* 1 S 1$_{14}$, גדד htpo. *lacerate oneself* Jr 47$_{5}$,

אמר *say* 2 S 2$_{26}$, עלז *exult* Ps 94$_{3.3}$, ראה *see* Jr 4$_{21}$, יכל *be able* Ho 8$_{5}$, רחם pi. *have mercy* Zc 1$_{12}$, אהב *love* Pr 1$_{22}$, חמד *desire* Pr 1$_{22}$, שׁכב *lie down* Pr 6$_{9}$, קום *arise* Pr 6$_{9}$, פסח *pass over* 1 K 18$_{21}$, חמק htp. *turn hither and thither* Jr 31$_{22}$, שׁוב *return* Ne 2$_{6}$, לין *lodge* Jr 4$_{14}$, נשׂא *lift* Ps 82$_{2}$.

3. לְמָתַי **for when,** + עתר hi. *make supplication* Ex 8$_{5}$.

4. אַחֲרֵי מָתַי עֹד **how much longer?,** lit. 'after when more', + טהר *be pure* Jr 13$_{27}$.*

מְתִים, see מַת *man*.

*[**מָתָךְ**] n.[m.] **intoxicating drink, wine,** <CSTR> מְסַפֵּחַ הַמָּתָךְ *of the outpouring of wine* Hb 2$_{15}$ (if em. מְסַפֵּחַ חֲמָתְךָ *joining your anger*).
⇨ נתך *pour out.*

*[**מַתָּךְ**] 0.0.1 n.[m.] **outpouring,** <SUBJ> נפל *fall* 1QH 3$_{28}$ (+ גּוֹרָל *lot*). <CSTR> מתך חמה *outpouring of anger* 1QH 3$_{28}$.
⇨ נתך *pour out.*

[**מַתְכֹּנֶת**] 5.1 n.f. **measurement**—cstr. מַתְכֹּנֶת; sf. מַתְכֻּנְתָּהּ, מַתְכֻּנְתּוֹ—**measurement, specification, specified number,** <SUBJ> היה *be* Ezk 45$_{11}$. <OBJ> גרע *diminish* Ex 5$_{8}$, עשׂה *make* Ex 5$_{8}$, שׂים *set* Ex 5$_{8}$. <CSTR> מַתְכֹּנֶת הַלְּבֵנִים *specified number of the bricks* Ex 5$_{8}$. <PREP> בְּ *according to,* + עשׂה *make* Ex 30$_{32.37}$, שׁתה *drink* Si 34$_{27}$; עַל *according to,* + עמד hi. *erect* 2 C 24$_{13}$.

מַתְּלָאָה 1 interj. **what a weariness!,** contraction of מָה *what* and תְּלָאָה *weariness,* <NOM CL> הִנֵּה מַתְּלָאָה *behold, what a weariness (is this)!* Ml 1$_{13}$.
⇨ מָה *what,* תְּלָאָה *weariness.*

*[**מְתַלָּה**] 0.0.1 n.f. **deception**—pl. Q מתלות—<OBJ> חזה *see* Is 30$_{10}$(1QIsa[a]).
⇨ תלל *mock, deceive.*

[**מְתַלְּעָה**] 3.0.1 n.f. **tooth, jaw**—pl. cstr. מְתַלְּעוֹת; sf. מְתַלְּעֹתָיו, Q מתלעותם—**tooth** or **jaws, jawbone,** <NOM CL> מְתַלְּעוֹת לָבִיא לוֹ *the teeth of a lion are his* Jl 1$_{6}$ (|| שֵׁן *tooth*), מַאֲכָלוֹת מְתַלְּעֹתָיו *his teeth are knives* Pr 30$_{14}$ (|| שֵׁן *tooth*), מתלעותם כחנית חדה *their teeth are like a sharp spear* 1QH 5$_{10}$ (|| שֵׁן *tooth*). <OBJ> שׁבר pi. *shatter* Jb 29$_{17}$ (|| שֵׁן *tooth*), פצה *open* Hb 3$_{14}$ (if em. לְהָפִיצֵנִי עֲלִיצֻתָם כְּמוֹ *to scatter me, their rejoicing as to* כְּמוֹ יִפְצִין מְתַלְּעוֹת *when they were opening their jaws*).* <CSTR> מְתַלְּעוֹת לָבִיא *teeth of a lion* Jl 1$_{6}$, עַוָּל *of an unjust one* Jb 29$_{17}$.
<SYN> שֵׁן *tooth.**

מְתֹם 3 n.[m.] **well-being, 1. well-being,** <NOM CL> אֵין־בּוֹ מְתֹם *there is no well-being in him* Is 1$_{6}$, אֵין־מְתֹם בִּבְשָׂרִי *there is no well-being in my flesh* Ps 38$_{4}$ (or em. אֵין־ם תֹּם בִּבְשָׂרִי *there is no,* i.e. encl. mem, *soundness, in my flesh;* || שָׁלוֹם *peace*) 38$_{8}$ (:: נִקְלֶה *burning*).

2. entirety, <CSTR> עִיר מְתֹם *city of entirety,* i.e. entire city Jg 20$_{48}$ (or em. מְתֹם to מְתִים *men*).
<SYN> שָׁלוֹם *peace.*
<ANT> נִקְלֶה *burning.**
⇨ תם *be complete,* מַת *man.*

[**מִתְמוֹטֵט**] *totterer,* see מוט *be shaken,* Htpol.

מַתָּן I 5.7 n.m. **gift**—sf. מַתָּנָם—collective **gifts,** <SUBJ> כפה *subdue* Pr 21$_{14}$ (|| שֹׁחַד *bribe*), נחה hi. *lead* Pr 18$_{16}$, עמד *stand* Si 11$_{17}$ (|| רָצוֹן *favour*), רחב hi. *enlarge* Pr 18$_{16}$. <OBJ> נתן *give* Gn 34$_{12}$ Si 7$_{33}$ (|| חֶסֶד *loyalty*), רבה hi. *increase* Gn 34$_{12}$ (|| מֹהַר *bride-gift*), מנע *withhold* Si 4$_{3}$. <CSTR> מתן '' *gift of Y.* Si 11$_{17}$; אִישׁ מַתָּן *man of gifts,* i.e. generous man Pr 19$_{6}$ Si 3$_{17}$, תְּרוּמַת מַתָּנָם *offering of their gifts* Nm 18$_{11}$, חסר מתן *(one) lacking of a gift,* i.e. in sustenance Si 10$_{27}$ (|| הוֹן *wealth*), חיי מתן *life of gifts,* i.e. a beggar's life Si 40$_{28}$. <PREP> בְּתוֹךְ *in the midst of,* + היה *be* Si 4$_{31}$.
<SYN> הוֹן *wealth,* חֶסֶד *loyalty,* רָצוֹן *favour,* מֹהַר *bride-gift,* שֹׁחַד *bribe.*
⇨ נתן *give.*

מַתָּן II 2.0.0.19 pr.n.m. **Mattan, 1.** priest of Baal, <OBJ> הרג *kill* 2 K 11$_{18}$||2 C 23$_{17}$. <APP> כֹּהֵן *priest* of Baal 2 K

11_{18}||2 C 23_{17}.

2. father of Shephatiah, <CSTR> בֶּן־מַתָּן *son of Mattan* Jr 38_{1}.

3. Kh. el-Meshash ost. 1682.2_{2}, <APP> בֵּן *son* Kh. el-Meshash ost. 1682.2_{2}.

4. Seal 374 (7th cent.), <PREP> לְ of possession, *of, (belonging) to* Seal 374 (7th cent.).

5. appar. father of Tanḥum, Seal 404 (Lachish, 8th cent.; others מגן *Magen*) 493 (Ramat Raḥel, 8th cent.; others מגן *Magen*).

6. father of Hubba, <CSTR> בן מתן *son of Mattan* Seal 552 (T. Beit Mirsim?, 7th/6th cent.).

7. father of Jehoaz, <CSTR> בן מתן *son of Mattan* Seal 574 (T. Beit Mirsim?, 7th/6th cent.).

8. son of Adonihai, <APP> בֵּן *son* Seal 613 (T. Beit Mirsim?, 7th/6th cent.). <PREP> לְ of possession, *of, (belonging) to* Seal 613 (T. Beit Mirsim?, 7th/6th cent.).

9. son of Pelatiah, <APP> בֵּן *son* Seal 614 (T. Beit Mirsim?, 7th/6th cent.), Seal 615 (T. Beit Mirsim?, 7th/6th cent.), Seal 616 (T. Beit Mirsim?, 7th/6th cent.) ([בן]). <PREP> לְ of possession, *of, (belonging) to* Seal 614 (T. Beit Mirsim?, 7th/6th cent.), Seal 615 (T. Beit Mirsim?, 7th/6th cent.), Seal 616 (T. Beit Mirsim?, 7th/6th cent.).

10. son of Hodaviah, <APP> בֵּן *son* Seal 617 (T. Beit Mirsim?, 7th/6th cent.). <PREP> לְ of possession, *of, (belonging) to* Seal 617 (T. Beit Mirsim?, 7th/6th cent.).

11. son of Jehozarah, <APP> בֵּן *son* Seal 618 (T. Beit Mirsim?, 7th/6th cent.) ([ב]ן). <PREP> לְ of possession, *of, (belonging) to* Seal 618 (T. Beit Mirsim?, 7th/6th cent.).

12. father of Obadiah, <CSTR> בן מתן *son of Mattan* Seal 634 (T. Beit Mirsim?, 7th/6th cent.).

13. appar. father of Neriah, Seal 745 (c. 700).

14. father of Malchiah, <CSTR> בן מתן *son of Mattan* Seal 761 (8th/7th cent.).

15. master of Nethibiah, <CSTR> נער מתן *servant of Mattan* Seal 783 (7th cent.).

16. appar. father of Ahikam, Seal 865.

17. appar. son of Ahab, <PREP> לְ of possession, *of, (belonging) to* Seal 876.

18. father of Ahimiah, <CSTR> בת מתן *daughter of Mattan* Bulla D15.

⇒ נתן *give*.

*[מֹתֶן] n.[m.] **strength,** <CSTR> לֵב מָתְנוֹ *heart of his strength* Ec 7_{7} (וִיאַבֵּד אֶת־לֵב מָתְנוֹ *and it [slander] destroys the heart of his strength,* i.e. his stout heart; if em. מַתָּנָה *gift*).

מַתָּנָה I $_{17.3.3}$ n.f. **gift**—cstr. מַתְּנַת; sf. Q מתנתך, Si מתנתו; pl. מַתָּנוֹת (מַתָּנֹת); cstr. מַתְּנוֹת (מַתְּנֹת); sf. מַתְּנֹתֵיכֶם, מַתְּנוֹתָם (Q מתנותמה)—**1. gift, offering, bribe. 2. dedication** (Nm 18_{7}),* <SUBJ> היה *be* Ezk $46_{16.17}$, אבד pi. *destroy* Ec 7_{7} (unless מַתָּנָה II *violence*; or em. מַתָּנָה *gift* to מָתְנוֹ *his strength* or מְתָנָה *strength*).

<NOM CL> לָכֶם מַתָּנָה *to you is a gift* Nm 18_{6}, מתנה לו ולזרעו *(they are) a gift to him and to his seed* Si 45_{21}. <OBJ> נתן *give* Gn 25_{6} Lv 23_{38} Ezk $46_{16.17}$ 2 C 21_{3} Si 3_{17}, נשׂא *lift* Ezk 20_{31}, בוא hi. *bring* 11QT 29_{6}, לקח *take* Ps 68_{19}, שׂנא *hate* Pr 15_{27}.

<CSTR> מַתְּנַת יָדוֹ *gift of his hand* Dt 16_{17}, מַתְּנֹת קָדְשֵׁיהֶם *gifts of their holiness,* i.e. their holy offerings Ex 28_{38}, מת[נות ד]מעיהם *gifts of their tithes* 4QT 6_{7}; עֲבֹדַת מַתָּנָה *service of dedication* Nm 18_{7}, ... מִשְׁלוֹחַ מַתָּנוֹת *sending of ... gifts* Est 9_{22}, כָּל־מַתְּנֹת *all the gifts of* Ex 28_{38}, כֹּל מַתְּנֹתֵיכֶם *all your gifts* Nm 18_{29}, כול מתנותמה *all their gifts* 11QT 29_{6}. <ADJ> רַב *many* 2 C 21_{3}.

<PREP> לְ *namely, even,* + קדשׁ hi. *consecrate* Ex 28_{38}; בְּ of instrument, *by (means of), with,* + טמא pi. *make impure* Ezk 20_{26}, חלל pi. *profane* Ezk 20_{39}; כְּ *according to* Dt 16_{17} Si 32_{12}; מִן *from among,* + רום hi. *offer* Nm 18_{29}; מֵאֵת *from* 4QT 6_{7}; מִלְּבַד *besides* Lv 23_{38}.

<COLL> בְּמִשְׁעֲנֹתָם וּמִמִּדְבָּר מַתָּנָה a pit which they dug *with their staves as a gift from the steppe* Nm 21_{18} (if em. בְּמִשְׁעֲנֹתָמוֹ מִמִּדְבָּר).*

מַתָּנָה || נְדָבָה *freewill offering* Lv 23_{38}, נֶדֶר *votive offering* Lv 23_{38}, שַׁבָּת *sabbath* Lv 23_{38}, בֶּצַע *gain* Pr 15_{27}, עֹשֶׁק *extortion* Ec 7_{7}; + גִּלּוּל *idol* Ezk 20_{39}, מָנָה *portion* Est 9_{22}, נֶדֶר *votive offering* 11QT 29_{6}.

Also 11QPsAp[a] 4_{12}.

<SYN> נְדָבָה *freewill offering,* נֶדֶר *votive offering,* שַׁבָּת *sabbath,* בֶּצַע *gain,* עֹשֶׁק *extortion,* מָנָה *portion.**

⇒ נתן *give.*

*מַתָּנָה II 1 n.f. **violence,** <SUBJ> אבד pi. *destroy* Ec 7_{7} (unless מַתָּנָה I *gift;* or em. מַתָּנָה *violence* to מָתְנוֹ *his strength* or מָתְנָה *strength).*
⇒ ינה *be violent, oppress.*

מַתָּנָה III 2 pl.n. **Mattanah,** station of Israelites in Moab, <PREP> מִן *from* Nm 21_{19}; מַתָּנָה without preposition or ה- of direction *(to) Mattanah* Nm 21_{18} (unless מַתָּנָה I *gift).*
⇒ נתן *give.*

*[מָתְנָה] n.f. **strength,** וִיאַבֵּד אֶת־לֵב מָתְנָה *and it (slander) destroys a heart of strength,* i.e. stout heart Ec 7_{7} (if em. מַתָּנָה *gift).*

מַתְּנַי 3 pr.n.m. **Mattenai, 1.** member of Hashum clan, husband of non-Jewish wife, <NOM CL> מִבְּנֵי חָשֻׁם מַתְּנַי *from the sons of Hashum were Mattenai* Ezr 10_{33}.

2. member of Bani clan, husband of non-Jewish wife, <NOM CL> מִבְּנֵי בָנִי ... מַתְּנַי *from the sons of Bani were ... Mattenai* Ezr 10_{37} (+ יַעֲשָׂו *Jaasu).*

3. head of priestly clan in the days of Joiakim, <NOM CL> וּלְיוֹיָרִיב מַתְּנַי *and for Joiarib was Mattenai* Ne 12_{19}.
⇒ נתן *give.*

מִתְנִי 1 gent. **Mithnite,** as sing. noun, <NOM CL> גִּבּוֹרֵי הַחֲיָלִים ... הַמִּתְנִי *the warriors of the armies were ... the Mithnite* 1 C 11_{43}. <APP> יוֹשָׁפָט *Joshaphat* 1 C 11_{43}.

מַתַּנְיָה 13.0.0.1 pr.n.m. **Mattaniah, 1.** original name of Zedekiah, king of Judah, <OBJ> מלך hi. *make king* 2 K 24_{17}. <APP> דּוֹד *uncle* 2 K 24_{17}.

2. member of Elam clan, husband of non-Jewish wife, <NOM CL> מִבְּנֵי עֵילָם מַתַּנְיָה *from the sons of Elam were Mattaniah* Ezr 10_{26}.

3. member of Zattu clan, husband of non-Jewish wife, <NOM CL> מִבְּנֵי זַתּוּא ... מַתַּנְיָה *from the sons of Zattu were ... Mattaniah* Ezr 10_{27} (+ יְרֵמוֹת *Jeremoth).*

4. member of Pahath-moab clan, husband of non-Jewish wife, <NOM CL> מִבְּנֵי פַּחַת מוֹאָב ... מַתַּנְיָה *from the sons of Pahath-moab were ... Mattaniah* Ezr 10_{30}.

5. member of Bani clan, husband of non-Jewish wife, <NOM CL> מִבְּנֵי בָנִי ... מַתַּנְיָה *from the sons of Bani were ... Mattaniah* Ezr 10_{37}.

6. Levite who lived in postexilic Jerusalem, son of Mica, <SUBJ> שׁמר *keep* Ne 12_{25} (+ בַּקְבֻּקְיָה *Bakbukiah).* <NOM CL> מִן־הַלְוִיִּם ... מַתַּנְיָה *from the Levites were ... Mattaniah* Ne 11_{17} 1 C 9_{15}, הַלְוִיִּם ... מַתַּנְיָה *the Levites were ... Mattaniah* Ne 12_{8}. <CSTR> בֶּן־מַתַּנְיָה *son of Mattaniah* Ne 11_{22} 12_{35} 13_{13} 2 C 20_{14}. <APP> בֵּן *son* Ne $11_{17.22}$ 12_{35} 1 C 9_{15}.

7. appar. father of Zephaniah, Seal 716 (6th cent.).*
⇒ נתן *give,* מַתַּנְיָהוּ *Mattaniah.*

מַתַּנְיָהוּ 3.0.0.15 pr.n.m. **Mattaniah, 1.** Levitical musician and prophet, son of Heman, <NOM CL> בְּנֵי הֵימָן ... מַתַּנְיָהוּ *the sons of Heman were ... Mattaniah* 1 C 25_{4}, הַתְּשִׁיעִי מַתַּנְיָהוּ *the ninth was Mattaniah* 1 C 25_{16}. <APP> בֵּן *son* 1 C 25_{16}.

2. son of Asaph, Levite who cleansed temple during reign of Hezekiah, <NOM CL> מִן־בְּנֵי אָסָף ... מַתַּנְיָהוּ *from the sons of Asaph were ... Mattaniah* 2 C 29_{13}.

3. son of Neriah, <APP> בֵּן *son* Lachish ost. 1_{5}.

4. Beersheba graf. 6, <PREP> לְ of possession, *of, (belonging) to* Beersheba graf. 6 (למתנ[יהו]).

5. appar. son of Azariah, <PREP> לְ of possession, *of, (belonging) to* Seal 268 (Jerusalem, 7th cent.).

6. appar. father of Hodiah, Seal 367 (8th/7th cent.).

7. father of Ezer, <CSTR> בן מתניהו *son of Mattaniah* Seal 369 (8th/7th cent.).

8. father of Jehoshua, <CSTR> בן מתניהו *son of Mattaniah* Seal 521 (T. Beit Mirsim?, 7th/6th cent.).

9. son of Semachiah, <PREP> לְ of possession, *of, (belonging) to* Seal 619 (T. Beit Mirsim?, 7th/6th cent.). <APP> בֵּן *son* Seal 619 (T. Beit Mirsim?, 7th/6th cent.).

10. appar. father of Benaiah, Seal 721 (7th cent.).

11. appar. son of Ishmael, <PREP> לְ of possession, *of, (belonging) to* Seal 778 (T. el-Ḥesi, 7th/6th cent.).

12. appar. father of Athaiah, Seal 889 (7th cent.).

13. Decanter inscr. (7th cent.), <PREP> לְ of possession, *of, (belonging) to* Decanter inscr. (7th cent.).

14. father of Aḥijah, <CSTR> [ב]ן מת[ניהו] *son of Mattaniah* Bulla D20.

15. appar. son of Amariah, <PREP> לְ of possession, *of, (belonging) to* Bulla D62.

16. son of Uriah, <PREP> לְ of possession, *of, (belonging) to* Bulla D63. <APP> בֵּן *son* Bulla D63.

17. appar. father of Athaiah, Bulla DH58.

⇒ נתן *give*, מַתַּנְיָה *Mattaniah*.

מָתְנַיִם 47.3.6 n.m.du. **loins**—מָתְנַיִם (Q מותנים); cstr. מָתְנֵי (Q מתניה); sf. מָתְנַי (Q מותני), מָתְנֶיךָ, מָתְנָיו (Q מתנו), מָתְנֶיהָ, מָתְנֵינוּ, מָתְנֵיכֶם, מָתְנֵיהֶם—**loins,** or perh. rather **musculature** linking upper part of body with lower,* <SUBJ> חגר pass. *be girded* Ex 12_{11} Dn 10_{5}, מלא *be full* Is 21_{3}, קום *arise* Dt 33_{11}, הלל htp. *boast* 1QH 10_{33}, מקק ni. *fester* Ps 44_{20} (if em. בִּמְקוֹם תַּנִּים *in the place of jackals* to בְּמַק מָתְנַיִם *with festering of loins*).

<OBJ> מחץ *strike through* Dt 33_{11} Si 32_{22}, בקע pi. *split* Si 30_{12}, רצץ pi. *crush* Si 30_{12}, עמד hi. *cause to stand* Ezk 29_{7}, חזק pi. *make strong* Na 2_{2} 1QS 1_{17}, פתח pi. *loose* Is 45_{1} (וּמָתְנֵי מְלָכִים אֲפַתֵּחַ perh. *and I will open the loins of kings*, i.e. make kings run [to open doors before him]),* מעד hi. *shake* Ps 69_{24}, אזר *gird* Jr 1_{17}, חגר *gird* 2 K 4_{29} 9_{1} Pr 31_{17}, שנס pi. *gird* 1 K 18_{46}.

<CSTR> מָתְנֵי אָבִי *loins of my father* 1 K 12_{10}||2 C 10_{10}, אִישׁ *of a man* Jr 13_{11}, מְלָכִים *of kings* Is 45_{1}, מתניה המש[ר]תים *loins of the servants* 4QparaKings 9_{3}, מתני אכזרי *loins of a cruel one* Si 32_{22}; אֵזוֹר מָתְנָיו *girdle of his loins* Is 11_{5}, זַרְזִיר מָתְנַיִם *strong of loins* Pr 30_{31} (or em. מָתְנַיִם to מִתְנַשֵּׂא *exalted*, i.e. strutting, with זַרְזִיר as *cockerel*), חזוק מותנים *strength of loins* 1QH 2_{7}, מעוז מותני *strength of my loins* 1QH 8_{33}, אמוץ מתנים *might of loins* 1QM 14_{7}, מַרְאֵה מָתְנָיו *appearance of his loins* Ezk $1_{27.27}$ 8_{2}, שִׁבְּרוֹן מָתְנַיִם *breaking of loins* Ezk 21_{11}, מֵי מָתְנָיִם *waters of*, i.e. up to the, *loins* Ezk 47_{4}, כָּל־מָתְנַיִם *all loins* Ezk 29_{7} (מָתְנָיִם) Am 8_{10} Na 2_{11}.

<PREP> בְּ of place, *on, by* 1 K 2_{5} Ezk $9_{2.3.11}$ 23_{15} Na 2_{11} Jb 40_{16}, + אזר pass. *be girded* 2 K 1_{8}, חגר *gird* 1 K 20_{32}, שׂים *put* Gn 37_{34} 1 K 20_{31} Ps 66_{11}, אסר *bind* Jb 12_{18}; מִן *from*, + היה *be* Ex 28_{42}, ראה *see* Ezk 8_{2}; of comparison, *(more) than*, + עבה *be thick* 1 K 12_{10}||2 C 10_{10}; אֶל *to*, + דבק *cling* Jr 13_{11}; עַל *upon* Jr 13_{4} 48_{37}, + היה *be* Ezk 44_{18}, עלה hi. *bring up* Am 8_{10}, צמד pu. *be bound* 2 S 20_{8}, אסר pass. *be bound* Ne 4_{12}, שׂים *put* Jr $13_{1.2}$; מֵעַל *from upon*, + פתח pi. *loose* Is 20_{2}.

<COLL> מֹתֶן || חֲלָצַיִם *loins* Is 11_{5}, יָד *hand* Jr 48_{37}, כָּתֵף *shoulder* Ezk 29_{7}, זְרוֹעַ *arm* Pr 31_{17}, שָׁרִיר *muscle* Jb 40_{16}, ראשׁ *head* 1 K $20_{31.32}$ Ezk 23_{15} 44_{18} Am 8_{10} Si 30_{12}, לֵב *heart* 1QH 10_{33}, עַיִן *eye* Ps 69_{24}, רֶגֶל *foot* 1 K 2_{5} Is 20_{2}, כֹּחַ *strength* 1QH 2_{7}.

<SYN> חֲלָצַיִם *loins*, יָד *hand*, כָּתֵף *shoulder*, זְרוֹעַ *arm*, שָׁרִיר *muscle*, ראשׁ *head*, לֵב *heart*, עַיִן *eye*, רֶגֶל *foot*, כֹּחַ *strength*.*

מִתְנַקֵּם *avenger*, see נקם *avenge*, Htp.

מתק I 5.5.1 vb. **be sweet**—**Qal** 3.1.1 Pf. מָתְקוּ; impf. יִמְתְּקוּ; + waw וַיִּמְתְּקוּ (Q וימתוקו)—**be sweet, become sweet,** <SUBJ> מַיִם *water* Ex 15_{25} Pr 9_{17} (|| נעם *be pleasant*), רֶגֶב *clod* Jb 21_{33}, חַיִּים *life* Si 40_{18}, דָּבָר *word* 4QapJoseph[b] 3_{5}. <PREP> לְ *in the estimation of* Jb 21_{33}; מִן of comparison, *(more) than*, + נֹפֶת *flowing honey* 4QapJoseph[b] 3_{5}.

<SYN> נעם *be pleasant*.

Hi. 2.4 Pf. Si המתיקו; impf. Si ימתיק, 3fs תַּמְתִּיק, נַמְתִּיק; ptc. Si ממתיק—**cause sweetness, make (oneself) sweet,** <SUBJ> Y. Ps 55_{15}, worshipper Ps 55_{15}, מַיִם *water* Si 38_{5}, רָעָה *evil* Jb 20_{12} (unless מקק haphtil *putrefy**), שְׁאֵלָה *request* Si 40_{30}, זֵכֶר *remembrance* Si 49_{1}, עֹז *strength* Si 40_{30}. <OBJ> סוֹד *counsel* Ps 55_{15}. <PREP> לְ *in the estimation of*, + אִישׁ *man* Si 40_{30}; בְּ *in*, + פֶּה *mouth* Jb 20_{12} (unless מקק haphtil *putrefy**), חֵךְ *palate* Si 49_{1}; of instrument, *by (means of), through*, + עֵץ *wood* Si 38_{5}; כְּ *as, like*, + אֵשׁ *fire* Si 40_{30}. <COLL> מתק + adv. יַחְדָּו *together* Ps 55_{15}.*

⇒ מֶתֶק *sweetness*, מֹתֶק *sweetness*, מָתָק *sweetness*, מָתֵק *sweetness*, מָתוֹק *sweet*, מַמְתַּקִּים *sweetness*, מִתְקָה *Mithkah*.

***מתק** II 1 vb. **suck**—**Qal** 1 Pf. מָתְקוּ—**1. suck,** <SUBJ> appar. רִמָּה *worm* Jb 24_{20}. <OBJ> corpse of evil doer Jb 24_{20} (unless מָתֹק I *sweetheart*).

2. suckle, <SUBJ> רִגְבֵי־נַחַל *the waters of the river*

Jb 21$_{33}$. <OBJ> wicked Jb 21$_{33}$.

*[**מָתָק**] 1 n.m. **sweetness**—sf. מְתָקוֹ—**sweetness, lover** (unless מתק II *suck*), <CSTR> רֶחֶם מְתָקוֹ *womb of his sweetheart* Jb 24$_{20}$.
⇒ מתק *be sweet.*

*[**מָתֶק**], see מֹתֶק *sweetness.*

[**מֹתֶק**] or [מָתֶק]* 2.0.1 n.m. **sweetness**—cstr. מֹתֶק—<SUBJ> יסף hi. *add* Pr 16$_{21}$ (+ חָכָם *wise*). <NOM CL> מֶתֶק רֵעֵהוּ מֵעֲצַת־נָפֶשׁ *the sweetness of his friend is from the counsel of the soul* Pr 27$_{9}$ (or em. מֶתֶק רֵעֵהוּ מֵעֲצַת to מִתְקָרְעָה מֵעַצֶּבֶת the soul *is torn by pain*). <CSTR> מֶתֶק שְׂפָתַיִם *sweetness of lips* Pr 16$_{21}$ (or em. מֶתֶק *sweetness* to מֶתֶג *bridle*, i.e. control, of lips), מֶתֶק רֵעֵהוּ *sweetness of his friend* Pr 27$_{9}$ (or em.; see Nom. Cl.). <PREP> בְּ of accompaniment, *in (a state of), with,* + שׂכל hi. *cause to consider* 4QBéat 5$_{9}$.*
⇒ מתק *be sweet.*

[**מֹתֶק**] 1 n.[m.] **sweetness**—sf. מָתְקִי—<OBJ> חדל ho. *be made to leave off* Jg 9$_{11}$ (|| תְּנוּבָה *fruit*).
<SYN> תְּנוּבָה *fruit.*
⇒ מתק *be sweet.*

מִתְקָה 2 pl.n. **Mithkah,** station of Israelites in wilderness, <PREP> בְּ of place, *in,* + חנה *encamp* Nm 33$_{28}$; מִן of direction, *from,* + נסע *set out* Nm 33$_{29}$.*
⇒ מתק *be sweet.*

*[**מִתְקָל**] 0.0.1 n.m. **offence**—cstr. Q מתקל—<OBJ> שׁמר ni. *keep oneself (from)* 4QBéat 14.2$_{26}$. <CSTR> מתקל לשון *offence of the tongue* 4QBéat 14.2$_{26}$.

מִתְרְדָת 2 pr.n.m. **Mithredath, 1.** treasurer of Cyrus, <SUBJ> ספר *count* Ezr 1$_{8}$. <CSTR> יַד מִתְרְדָת *hand of Mithredath* Ezr 1$_{8}$. <APP> גִּזְבָּר *treasurer* Ezr 1$_{8}$.

2. Persian petitioner against rebuilding of Jerusalem, <SUBJ> כתב *write* Ezr 4$_{7}$.

[**מַתָּת**] 6.3 n.f. **gift**—מַתָּת; cstr. מַתַּת; sf. Si מתתו—<SUBJ> היה *be* Ezk 46$_{11}$. <NOM CL> מַתַּת אֱלֹהִים הִיא *it is the gift of God* Ec 3$_{13}$, זֹה מַתַּת אֱלֹהִים הִיא *this is the gift of God* Ec 5$_{18}$. <OBJ> נתן *give* 1 K 13$_{7}$. <CSTR> מַתַּת אֱלֹהִים *gift of God* Ec 3$_{13}$ 5$_{18}$, יָדוֹ *of his hand* Ezk 46$_{5.11}$, שֶׁקֶר *of falsehood*, i.e. false gift Pr 25$_{14}$. <APP> מִנְחָה *offering* Ezk 46$_{5}$. <PREP> בְּ of cause, *on account of,* + הלל htp. *boast* Pr 25$_{14}$; כְּ *as, like,* + נתן *give* Si 32$_{12}$; עַל *on account of,* + בושׁ *be ashamed* Si 42$_{7}$ (+ לֶקַח *acquisition*); אַחֲרֵי *after,* + נאץ *spurn* Si 41$_{22}$; אַחַר *after,* + חרף pi. *reproach* Si 41$_{22(M)}$.
⇒ נתן *give.*

מַתַּתָּה 1 pr.n.m. **Mattathah,** member of Hashum clan, husband of non-Jewish wife, <NOM CL> מִבְּנֵי חָשֻׁם ... מַתַּתָּה *from the sons of Hashum were ... Mattathah* Ezr 10$_{33}$.
⇒ נתן *give.*

מַתִּתְיָה 4.0.2.3 pr.n.m. **Mattithiah, 1.** member of Nebo clan, husband of non-Jewish wife, <NOM CL> מִבְּנֵי נְבוֹ ... מַתִּתְיָה *from the sons of Nebo were ... Mattithiah* Ezr 10$_{43}$.

2. assistant to Ezra the scribe, <SUBJ> עמד *stand* Ne 8$_{4}$.

3. Levite, son of Shallum, <NOM CL> מַתִּתְיָה ... בֶּאֱמוּנָה *Mattithiah was ... in the office of trust* 1 C 9$_{31}$.

4. Levite who served under David, prob. ident. with מַתִּתְיָהוּ at 1 C 15$_{18.21}$ 25$_{3.21}$, <NOM CL> מִשְׁנֵהוּ ... מַתִּתְיָה *second to him was ... Mattithiah* 1 C 16$_{5}$.

5. son of Simeon, <APP> בַּר *son* 4Q348$_{14}$.

6. father of Johanan, <CSTR> בן מת[תיה] *son of Mattithiah* 4QRebukes 1.2$_{3}$.

7. high priest, <APP> כֹּהֵן *priest* Antigonus Coin 30 31 ([כה]ן) 34 ([כה]ן), חָבֵר *friend* Antigonus Coin 30.
⇒ נתן *give,* מַתִּתְיָהוּ *Mattithiah.*

מַתִּתְיָהוּ 4.0.0.1 pr.n.m. **Mattithiah, 1.** Levite appointed by David as musician, son of Jeduthun, prob. ident. with מַתִּתְיָה at 1 C 16$_{5}$, <SUBJ> נצח pi. *lead* music 1 C 15$_{21}$, הלל pi. *praise* 1 C 25$_{3}$, נבא ni. *prophesy* 1 C 25$_{3}$. <NOM CL> עִמָּהֶם ... מַתִּתְיָהוּ *with them were ... Mattithiah* 1 C 15$_{18}$, מַתִּתְיָהוּ ... בְּכִנֹּרוֹת *Mattithiah ... were with* *lyres* 1 C 15$_{21}$, בְּנֵי יְדוּתוּן ... מַתִּתְיָהוּ *the sons of Jeduthun were ... Mattithiah* 1 C 25$_{3}$, לְאַרְבָּעָה עָשָׂר מַתִּתְיָהוּ *to the fourteenth was Mattithiah* 1 C 25$_{21}$. <OBJ> עמד hi. *appoint* 1 C 15$_{18}$. <APP> אָח *brother* 1 C 15$_{18}$, בֵּן *son* 1 C 25$_{21}$, מִשְׁנֶה *second* 1 C 15$_{18}$.

2. appar. father of Pelaiah, Seal 782 (7th cent.).

⇨ נתן *give*, מַתִּתְיָה *Mattithiah*.

נ

נָא I 405.4.10.3 part. **please**—Q נה—**please**, occurs only in reported speech, usu. attached to imperatives or jussives for politeness' sake; freq. used by inferior persons in address to superior persons*; less prob. as emphasis or as notation of logical consequence*; often linked with preceding word by maqqeph, and often with daghesh forte when vowel precedes.

Preceded by, **1.** imperative of קרה hi. *cause (good fortune) to occur* Gn 24_{12}, אמר *say* Gn 12_{13} Jg 12_{6} 2 S 20_{16} 1 K 2_{17} 2 K 4_{13} 18_{19}||Is 36_{4} Jr 18_{11} Ezk 17_{12} Hg 2_{2}, דבר pi. *speak* Gn 50_{4} Ex 11_{2} Jg 9_{2} 2 S 13_{13} 2 K 18_{26}||Is 36_{11}, נגד hi. *tell* Gn 24_{23} 32_{30} 37_{16} Jos 7_{19} Jg $16_{6.10}$ 1 S 9_{18} 10_{15} 23_{11} 2 S 1_{4} 2 K 9_{12} Jr 36_{17} 38_{25} Jon 1_{8}, ספר pi. *tell* Gn 40_{8} 2 K 8_{4}, קרא *call* Jg 7_{3} 2 S 17_{5} Jb 5_{1}, *read* Is $29_{11.12}$ Lachish ost. 6_{5}, ברך pi. *bless* 1 C 29_{20} Si 45_{25} 50_{22}, ראה *see* 1 S 14_{29} 16_{17} 2 S 7_{2} 13_{28} Jr 5_{1}, hi. *show* Ex 33_{18} Jg 1_{24}, נבט hi. *look* Gn 15_{5} Is 64_{8}.

ידע *know* 1 K 20_{7} 2 K 5_{7}, hi. *make known* Ex 33_{13} 4QD[a] 1_{19}, נכר hi. *recognize* Gn 37_{32} 38_{25}, בין *understand* Ps 50_{22}, hi. 4QAdmonPar 2.2_{2}, שׁמע *hear* Gn 37_{6} Nm 12_{6} 16_{8} 20_{10} 1 S $22_{7.12}$ 28_{22} Is 7_{13} 51_{21} Jr 5_{21} $28_{7.15}$ 37_{20} 38_{20} Ezk 18_{25} Mc $3_{1.9}$ 6_{1} Zc 3_{8} Jb 13_{6} 33_{1} 42_{4} Lm 1_{18} 4Q185 1.1_{13}, שׁאל *ask* Dt 4_{32} Jg 18_{5} Jr 18_{13} 30_{6} Hg 2_{11} Jb 8_{8} 12_{7}, דרשׁ *inquire* 1 K 22_{5}||2 C 18_{4} Jr 21_{2}, חלה pi. *entreat* 1 K 13_{6} Ml 1_{9}, פלל htp. *pray* Jr 37_{3}, שׁבע ni. *swear* Jos 12_{12}, שׁמר ni. *beware* Jg 13_{4} 1 S 19_{2}, זכר *remember* Jg 16_{28} 2 K 20_{3}||Is 38_{3} (+ אָנָּא *please*) Mc 6_{5} Jb 4_{7} 10_{9} Ne 1_{8} 4QDibHam[a] 6_{6} ([ז]כור), יאל hi. *be pleased* Jg 19_{6} 2 K 6_{3}, קסם *divine* 1 S 28_{8}, אבל htp. *behave as a mourner* 2 S 14_{2}, לבשׁ *dress in* 2 S 14_{2}, גמא hi. *allow to swallow* Gn 24_{17}, שׁקה hi. *give to drink* Gn $24_{43.45}$ Jg 4_{19}, לעט hi. *feed* Gn 25_{30}.

הלך *go* Gn 27_{9} 37_{14} Ex 10_{11} Nm $22_{6.17}$ $23_{13.27}$ Jg 19_{11} 1 S 23_{22} 2 S 13_{7} Is 1_{18} Jr 7_{12} Ec 2_{1}, בוא *come* Gn 16_{2} Ezk 33_{30} Jb 17_{10}, hi. *bring* Ex 4_{6}, נגשׁ *draw near* Gn $27_{21.26}$ 45_{4}, hi. *bring near* 1 S 30_{7}, קרב hi. *bring near* Ml 1_{8}, יצא *go out* Jg 9_{38} Is 7_{3}, עלה *go up* 1 K 18_{43}, שׁוט *go about* 2 S 24_{2}, רוץ *run* 2 K 4_{26}, סור *turn aside* Gn 19_{2} Nm 16_{26}, נטה hi. *incline* Gn 24_{14}, עבר hi. *cause to pass* 2 S 24_{10}||1 C 21_{8}, שׁוב *go back* Jr 18_{11} 25_{5} 35_{15} Zc 1_{4} Ps 80_{15} Jb 6_{29}, hi. *bring back* Ne 5_{11} Meṣad Ḥashavyahu ost. 1_{12}, שׁלח *send* Ex 4_{13} 2 S 13_{17} 2 K 4_{22} Jb 1_{11} 2_{5}, pi. 1 S 20_{29}, ישׁב *remain* Nm 22_{19} 2 K $2_{2.4.6}$ Jr 36_{15} 4QParaKings 9_{6}, לין *lodge* Jg 19_{9}, עמד *stand* 2 S 1_{9} Is 47_{12}, קום *arise* Gn 27_{19} 1 K 14_{2}, נשׂא *lift, forgive* Gn 13_{14} 27_{3} 31_{12} Gn 50_{17} (+ אָנָּא *please*) 50_{17} Ex 10_{17} 1 S 15_{25} 25_{28} Ezk 8_{5} Zc 5_{5}, סלח *pardon* Nm 14_{19} Am 7_{2} 4QDibHam[a] 4_{7} ([נא]), פקח *open* 2 K 6_{17}, hi. *explain* Lachish ost. 3_{5}.

מצא *find* 1 S 20_{36}, לקח *take* Gn 22_{2} 33_{11} 48_{9} 1 S 9_{3} 17_{17} 26_{11} 1 K $17_{10.11}$ 2 K 5_{15} Jon 4_{3} Jb 22_{22}, קנה *purchase* Jr 32_{8}, רצה *accept* Ps 119_{108}, נתן *give* Gn 30_{14} 34_{8} Jg 8_{5} 1 S 25_{8} 2 K 5_{22}, יהב *give*, i.e. come Gn 38_{16}, שׂים *place* Gn 24_{2} 47_{29} Jos 7_{19} Jr 38_{12} Hg $2_{15.18}$ 17_{3}, עדה *deck oneself* Jb 40_{10}, ספח *attach* 1 S 2_{36}, סכן hi. *agree with* Jb 22_{21}, פרד ni. *separate oneself* Gn 13_{9}, עשׂה *do* 4QDibHam[a] 1.2_{7} (+ אָנָּא *please*), פקד *attend to* 2 K 9_{34}, *count* 1 S 14_{17}, ערב htp. *make a bargain* 2 K 18_{23}||Is 36_{8}, כבד pi. *honour* 1 S 15_{30}, בחן *test* Ml 3_{10}, נסה pi. *test* Dn 1_{12}, שׁפט *judge* Is 5_{3}, ישׁע hi. *save* 2 K 19_{19} Ps 118_{25} (+ אָנָּא), נצל hi. *deliver* Gn 32_{12} Jg 10_{15}, רפא *heal* Nm 12_{13}, חזק pi. *strengthen* Jg 16_{28}, סעד *sustain* Jg 19_{8}, צלח hi. *prosper* Ps 118_{25} (+ אָנָּא) Ne 1_{11}, אזר *gird* Jb 38_{3} 40_{7}, חתר *dig* Ezk 8_{8}, חדל *cease* Am 7_{5}, סכל pi. *make foolish* 2 S 15_{31}, נכה hi. *strike* 1 K $20_{35.37}$ 2 K 6_{18}, מחה *blot out* Ex 32_{32}, הרג *kill* Nm 11_{15}.

2. imperfect, jussive or cohortative of היה *be* Gn 26_{28} Jg 6_{39} 15_{2} 2 S 14_{17} 24_{17}||1 C 21_{17} 1 K 22_{13}||2 C 18_{12} 2 K 2_{9} Ps 119_{76} Ca 7_{9} Ne $1_{6.11}$ (+ אָנָּא *please*) 2 C 6_{40}, חיה *live* 1 K 20_{32}, גדל *be great* Nm 14_{17}, אמר *say* 1 S 16_{16} Ps $118_{2.3.4}$ 124_{1} 129_{1}, דבר pi. *speak* Gn 44_{18} 1 S 25_{24} 2 S $14_{12.15.18}$ Ps 122_{8}, נגד hi. *tell* 2 K 7_{12} Is 19_{12}, ידע hi. *make known* Is 5_{5}, הלל pi. *praise* Si 44_{1}, חוד *propound a riddle* Jg 14_{12}, שׁיר *sing* Is 5_{1}, יעץ *give counsel* 1 K 1_{12}, פגע *entreat* Jr 27_{18}, שׁמע *hear* 1 S 26_{19}, זכר

remember 2 S 14$_{11}$ Si 42$_{15}$, בחר *choose* 2 S 17$_{1}$, ירא *fear* Jr 5$_{24}$.

הלך *go* Ex 3$_{18}$ 4$_{18}$ 5$_{3}$ 34$_{9}$ 2 S 13$_{24.26}$ 15$_{7}$ 2 K 2$_{16}$ 6$_{2}$ Jr 40$_{15}$ Ru 2$_{2}$, בוא *come* Jg 13$_{8}$ 2 S 13$_{5.6}$ 2 K 5$_{8}$ Jr 17$_{15}$, יצא *go out* 2 S 22$_{3}$, hi. *bring out* Gn 19$_{8}$ Jg 19$_{24}$, עלה *go up* Gn 50$_{5}$, ירד *go down* Gn 18$_{21}$ 4QAges^{a} 2.2$_{6}$, עבר *pass* Gn 33$_{14}$ Nm 20$_{17}$ Dt 3$_{25}$ Jg 11$_{17.19}$ 2 S 16$_{9}$, סור *turn aside* Ex 3$_{3}$, שׁוב *go back* 2 S 19$_{38}$ 1 K 17$_{21}$ Dn 19$_{16}$ 4QDibHam^{a} 1.2$_{11}$ 1.4$_{11}$, רוץ *run* 2 S 18$_{19.22}$, מלט ni. *escape* Gn 19$_{20}$ 1 S 20$_{29}$, עזב *leave* Ne 5$_{10}$, נפל *fall* 2 S 24$_{14}$||1 C 21$_{13}$ Jr 37$_{20}$ 42$_{2}$, ישׁב *dwell* Gn 44$_{33}$ 47$_{4}$, עמד *stand* 1 S 16$_{22}$ Is 47$_{13}$ Ezr 10$_{14}$, קום *arise* 2 S 2$_{14}$ Ca 3$_{2}$, שׂים *place* 1 K 20$_{31}$, יצג hi. *place* Gn 33$_{15}$, נתן ho. *be given* 2 K 5$_{17}$, לקח *take* 2 K 7$_{13}$, ho. *be brought* Gn 18$_{4}$, לקט pi. *glean* Ru 2$_{7}$, עשׂה *make* Jos 22$_{26}$ 2 K 4$_{10}$, כון hi. *prepare* 1 C 22$_{5}$, נסה pi. *test* Jg 6$_{39}$, אמן ni. *be confirmed* 1 K 8$_{26}$, עצר *detain* Jg 13$_{15}$, סלח *pardon* 2 K 5$_{18}$, נשׁק *kiss* 1 K 19$_{20}$, יקר *be precious* 2 K 1$_{13}$, רעע hi. *act wickedly* Jg 19$_{23}$, נכה hi. *strike* 1 S 26$_{8}$, מות ho. *be put to death* Jr 38$_{4}$, גמר *be ended* Ps 7$_{10}$.

3. perfect with waw consecutive of עשׂה *do* Gn 40$_{14}$.

4. noun, אֵל נָא רְפָא נָא לָהּ *O God, pray heal her* Nm 12$_{13}$ (or em. אַל נָא *do not*), אל נא זוכר *pray, let God remember* GnzPs 4$_{13}$.

5. particle, **a.** הִנֵּה־נָא **behold, please,** followed immediately by (1) perfect of שׁמע *hear* 1 K 20$_{31}$, ידע *know* Gn 12$_{11}$ 2 K 4$_{9}$ 5$_{15}$, יאל hi. *be pleased* Gn 18$_{27.31}$, מצא *find* Gn 19$_{19}$, עצר *restrain* Gn 16$_{2}$, זקן *be old* Gn 27$_{2}$, רפה *decline* Jg 19$_{9}$, עשׂה *do* 2 S 14$_{21}$, ערך *arrange* Jb 13$_{18}$, פתח *open* mouth Jb 33$_{2}$.

(2) vocative noun, הִנֶּה נָּא־אֲדֹנַי סוּרוּ נָא *behold, please, my lords, turn aside, I pray* Gn 19$_{2}$.

(3) nominal clause, e.g. הִנֵּה־נָא לִי שְׁתֵּי בָנוֹת *behold, please, I have two daughters* Gn 19$_{8}$, הִנֵּה־נָא הָעִיר הַזֹּאת קְרֹבָה לָנוּס שָׁמָּה *behold, please, this city is near enough to flee there* Gn 19$_{20}$, Jg 13$_{3}$ 1 S 9$_{6}$ 2 S 13$_{24}$ 1 K 22$_{13}$ 2 K 2$_{16.19}$ 6$_{1}$ Jb 40$_{16}$.

(4) noun as subject of verbal clause, הִנֵּה־נָא רוּחַ אֱלֹהִים רָעָה מְבַעִתֶּךָ *behold, please, an evil spirit from God is terrifying you* 1 S 16$_{15}$.

(5) predicate of nominal clause, of which הִנֵּה־נָא is subject, הִנֵּה־נָא בְהֵמוֹת *behold, please Behemoth* Jb 40$_{15}$.

b. אַל־נָא **please let not, do not,** (1) followed (not alw. immediately) by imperfect, jussive or cohortative of היה *be* Gn 13$_{8}$ Nm 12$_{12}$, הלך *go* 2 S 13$_{25}$, עבר *pass* Gn 18$_{3}$, מושׁ *depart* Jg 6$_{18}$, עזב *leave* Nm 10$_{31}$, מנע ni. *refrain* Nm 22$_{16}$, כחד pi. *hide* 1 S 3$_{17}$ 2 S 14$_{18}$, שׂים *place* heart, i.e. have regard 1 S 25$_{25}$, שׁית *place*, i.e. impute, sin Nm 12$_{11}$, נשׂא *lift* face, i.e. show partiality Jb 32$_{21}$, חרה *be kindled*, i.e. angry Gn 18$_{30.32}$, רעע hi. *act wickedly* Gn 19$_{7}$, עשׂה *do* Jr 44$_{4}$, אבד *perish* Jon 1$_{14}$ (+ אָנָּא *please*), קבר *bury* Gn 47$_{29}$.

(2) אַל־נָא as interjection, **please let it not be so!, Oh no!,** Gn 19$_{18}$ 33$_{10}$.

c. אִם־נָא **if now, please,** alw. in phrase אִם־נָא מָצָאתִי חֵן *if now I have found favour,* Gn 18$_{3}$ 30$_{27}$ 33$_{10}$ 47$_{29}$ 50$_{4}$ Ex 33$_{13}$ 34$_{9}$ Jg 6$_{17}$ 1 S 27$_{5}$.

d. אִם יֶשְׁךָ־נָּא **if you now, please,** אִם יֶשְׁךָ־נָּא מַצְלִיחַ דַּרְכִּי *if you will now prosper my way* Gn 24$_{42}$.

e. אוֹי־נָא **woe now!,** אוֹי־נָא לִי *woe now to me!* Jr 4$_{31}$ 45$_{3}$, אוֹי־נָא לָנוּ *woe now to us!* Lm 5$_{16}$.

f. אַיֵּה־נָא **where now, please?,** אַיֵּה־נָא אֱלֹהֵיהֶם *where now is their God?* Ps 115$_{2}$.

g. נֶגְדָה־נָּא לְ **may it please be in the presence of!,** נֶגְדָה־נָּא לְכָל־עַמּוֹ *may it be in the presence of all his people* Ps 116$_{14.18}$ (or em. both לְנֶגֶד עֵינֵי כָל־ *in the sight of all* his people!).*

נָא II 1 adj. **raw,** used adverbially of אכל *eat* meat Ex 12$_{9}$.

נֹא 5 pl.n. **No, Thebes**—cstr. נֹא—**No,** i.e. **Thebes,** after Memphis, the most important Egyptian city, on the Nile, 700 km S of Mediterranean Sea, <SUBJ> היה *be* Ezk 30$_{16}$, בקע ni. *be breached* Ezk 30$_{16}$, ישׁב *sit* Na 3$_{8}$. <CSTR> נֹא אָמוֹן *No-amon,* i.e. Thebes of Amon Na 3$_{8}$; הֲמוֹן נֹא *multitude of Thebes* Ezk 30$_{15}$ (or em. נֹף *of Noph,* i.e. Memphis). <PREP> בְּ *against,* + עשׂה *do* judgment Ezek 30$_{14}$; מִן *of,* Jr 46$_{25}$ (אָמוֹן מִנֹּא *Amon of Thebes*); of comparison, *(more) than,* + יטב hi. *be good* Na 3$_{8}$; סָבִיב לְ *around* Na 3$_{8}$.

נֹאד 6 n.m. **skin bottle**—cstr. נֹאד (נאוד); sf. נֹאדְךָ; pl.

cstr. נֹאדוֹת—**skin bottle, skin,** perh. **parchment** for writing (Ps 56$_9$),* <SUBJ> בקע pu. *be split open* Jos 9$_4$, htp. Jos 9$_{13}$, צרר pu. *be tied up,* i.e. mended Jos 9$_4$. <OBJ> לקח *take* Jos 9$_4$ 1 S 16$_{20}$, מלא pi. *fill* Jos 9$_{13}$ (+ חֲדָשִׁים *[when] new*), פתח *open* Jg 4$_{19}$, שׁלח *send* 1 S 16$_{20}$. <CSTR> נֹאוד הֶחָלָב *the skin of milk* Jg 4$_{19}$, נֹאד יַיִן *skin of wine* 1 S 16$_{20}$, נֹאדוֹת יַיִן *skins of wine* Jos 9$_{4.13}$ (הַיַּיִן). <ADJ> בָּלֶה *worn* Jos 9$_4$. <PREP> בְּ of place, *in,* + שׂים *place* tears Ps 56$_9$; כְּ *as,* + היה *be* Ps 119$_{83}$ (or כְּנֹאד *as a skin bottle* to כְּנָאד *as one grieving,* from נוד II); *as in,* + כנס *gather* Ps 33$_7$ (if em. כַּנֵּד *as in a heap* to כַּנֹּד); כְּמוֹ *as in,* + נצב ni. *stand* Ex 15$_8$ (if em. כְּמוֹ נֵד *as in a heap*). <COLL> נֹאד בְּקִיטוֹר *a skin bottle in the smoke* Ps 119$_{83}$ (or em.; see Subj.).*

⇒ cf. נֹד III *wineskin.*

נאה 3.1.1 vb. **be fitting—Qal** 0.1 Pf. Si נאתה—**be fitting,** <SUBJ> תְּהִלָּה *praise* Si 15$_9$. <PREP> בְּ of place, *in,* + פֶּה *mouth* Si 15$_9$.

Pi. adorn, <SUBJ> שֶׁמֶן *oil* Ps 141$_5$ (if em. יָנִי *let it* not *refuse* to יְנָא *let it* not *adorn*).

Pal. 3.0.1 Pf. נָאווּ, נַאֲוָה—**1. be comely, beautiful,** <SUBJ> לְחִי *cheek* Ca 1$_{10}$, צַוָּאר *neck* Ca 1$_{10}$, רֶגֶל *foot* Is 52$_7$=11QMelch 2$_{15}$. <PREP> בְּ of accompaniment, *with,* + תֹּר *plait* Ca 1$_{10}$, חָרוּז *necklace* Ca 1$_{10}$; עַל *upon,* + הַר *mountain* Is 52$_7$=11QMelch 2$_{15}$. <COLL> נאה pal. + adverb, מָה *how!* Is 52$_7$=11QMelch 2$_{15}$ ([מה]).

2. befit, <SUBJ> קֹדֶשׁ *holiness* Ps 93$_5$. <PREP> לְ introducing object, + בַּיִת *house* Ps 93$_5$.*

⇒ נָאֶה *fitting,* נָאוֶה *comely, fitting,* נַאֲהֲבַת *Nahabath.*

*[נָאָה] 12 n.f. **pleasant place** (unless נָוָה *pasture*)—pl. cstr. נְאוֹת—**pleasant place, oasis,** <SUBJ> דשׁא *sprout* Jl 2$_{22}$, רעף *drip* Ps 65$_{13}$, יבשׁ *be dry* Jr 23$_{10}$, יצת ni. *be burned* Jr 9$_9$ (or em. נִצְּתוּ to נִצּוּ *they are laid waste,* from נצה II ni.), דמם ni. *be destroyed* Jr 25$_{37}$, אבל *mourn* Am 1$_2$.

<OBJ> ירשׁ *possess* Ps 83$_{13}$, מלא *be full of* Ps 74$_{20}$, אכל *devour* Jl 1$_{19.20}$, הרס *tear down* Lm 2$_2$.

<CSTR> נְאוֹת אֱלֹהִים *oases of God* or perh. *finest oases** Ps 83$_{13}$, יַעֲקֹב *of Jacob* Lm 2$_2$, הָרֹעִים *of the shepherds* Am 1$_2$, מִדְבָּר *of the steppe* Jr 9$_9$ 23$_{10}$ Jl 1$_{19.20}$ (הַמִּדְבָּר) 2$_{22}$ Ps 65$_{13}$, דֶּשֶׁא *of grass* Ps 23$_2$, הַשָּׁלוֹם *of peace* Jr 25$_{37}$, חָמָס *of violence* Ps 74$_{20}$ (or em. אֲנָחָה וְחָמָס *sighing and violence*).

<PREP> בְּ of place, *in,* + רבץ hi. *cause to lie down* Ps 23$_2$.

עַל *for (the sake of),* + נשׂא *raise* a dirge Jr 9$_9$.

<COLL> הַר + נָוֶה *mountain* Jr 9$_9$, גִּבְעָה *hill* Ps 65$_{13}$, מִבְצָר *stronghold* Lm 2$_2$, מַמְלָכָה *kingdom* Lm 2$_2$, ראשׁ *top* of Carmel Am 1$_2$, אָפִיק *channel* Jl 1$_{20}$, מַיִם *waters* Ps 23$_2$.

⇒ נאה *be fitting, comely.*

*[נָאֶה] 0.2.1 adj. **fitting**—f.sg. Si נאה, m.pl. Si נאים—**fitting, suitable,** used predicatively, נאים דברים יפים על משתה היין *fine words are fitting at a banquet of wine* Si 35$_5$, לא כל בשת נאה לשמר *not every kind of shame is suitable to keep,* i.e. to be regarded as shameful Si 41$_{16(B, C)}$, לו נאה תפארת ועוז *for him beauty and strength are fitting* GnzPs 3$_{24}$.

⇒ נאה *be fitting.*

*[נַאֲהֲבַת] 0.0.0.1 pr.n.f. **Nahabath,** daughter of Remaliah, <APP> בַּת *daughter* Seal 60 (Palestine, 7th cent.). <PREP> לְ of possession, *of (belonging) to* Seal 60 (Palestine, 7th cent.).

⇒ נאה *be fitting* + בַּת *daughter;* or אהב *love* (i.e. *beloved*).

*נאו 2 vb. **praise** (unless from נָאוֶה *fitting*)—**Pi.** 2 Inf. נַאֲוָה—**praise, laud,** <SUBJ> יָשָׁר *upright one* Ps 33$_1$; subj. not specified, Ps 93$_5$ 147$_1$. <OBJ> תְּהִלָּה *Luminous One* Ps 33$_1$ 147$_1$. <PREP> לְ *in,* + בַּיִת *house* Ps 93$_5$. <COLL> כִּי־נָעִים נָאוָה *how pleasant to praise* Ps 147$_1$, רַנְּנוּ ... לַיְשָׁרִים נָאוָה *rejoice ..., O upright, in praising* Ps 33$_1$, נַאֲוָה־קֹדֶשׁ *lauding by the saints* Ps 93$_5$.

נָאוֶה 11.4 adj. **comely, fitting**—m.s. נָאוֶה, f.s. נָאוָה (נָוָה), cstr. נָוַת—**1. comely, beautiful, a.** used predicatively of אֲנִי *I* (female lover) Ca 1$_5$ (+ שְׁחוֹר *dark*), אַתְּ *you* (female lover) Ca 6$_4$ (|| יָפֶה *fair*), רַעְיָה *beloved* Ca 6$_4$, מִדְבָּר *mouth* Ca 4$_3$, מַרְאֶה *countenance* Ca 2$_{14}$ (|| עָרֵב *sweet*).

<COLL> נָאוָה כִּירוּשָׁלָ‍ִם *comely as Jerusalem* Ca 6_4.

b. as noun, **comely one,** <SUBJ> חלק pi. *divide spoil* Ps 68_{13} (or em. נְוַת בַּיִת תְּחַלֵּק *the comely one of the house divides* to בִּנְאוֹת יְחֻלַּק *in meadows* the spoil *is divided* or בֵּית נְכֹת יְחֻלָּק *the treasure house shall be divided up*; unless נְוַת is ptc. of נוה I *dwell*). <OBJ> דמה *destroy* Jr 6_2 (or em. הַנָּוָה וְהַמְּעֻנָּגָה דָּמִיתִי *the comely and the delicate one I will destroy* to הֲלִנְוֵה מַעֲנָג דָּמְתָה *is she like a pasture of delight?*). <CSTR> נְוַת בַּיִת *the comely one of the house* Ps 68_{13} (or em.; see Subj.). <APP> בַּת *daughter* of Zion Jr 6_2.

2. fitting, suitable (+ לְ *for, to*), used predicatively of תְּהִלָּה *praise* Ps 33_1 (unless נָאוָה is from נאוה pi. *praise*; + לַיְשָׁרִים *for the upright*) 147_1 (unless נָאוָה is from נאוה pi. *praise*), שְׂפָה *lip*, i.e. speech Pr 17_7 (+ לְנָבָל *for a fool*, or *outcast*, לְנָדִיב *for a prince*), עֹשֶׁר *wealth* Si 14_3 (+ ללב קטן *for a small heart*, i.e. mean person), חָרוּץ *gold* Si 14_3 (+ לאיש רע עין *to a man evil of eye*, i.e. a miser), תַּעֲנוּג *luxury* Pr 19_{10} (+ לִכְסִיל *for a fool*), כָּבוֹד *honour* Pr 26_1 (+ לִכְסִיל), משל inf. *ruling* Pr 19_{10} (+ לְעֶבֶד *for a servant*), זָדוֹן *presumptuousness* Si 10_{18} (+ לאנוש *for a human*), עַזּוּת *strong anger* Si 10_{18} (+ לילוד אשה *for one born of woman*), בֹּשֶׁת *shame* Si $41_{16(M)}$ (+ לבוש *to be ashamed*, i.e. regard as shameful), פֶּשַׁע *transgression* Ps 36_2 (if em. נְאֻם *utterance of*; + לָרָשָׁע *for the wicked*).

<SYN> §1a יָפֶה *fair*, עָרֵב *sweet*.*

⇒ נאה *be fitting*.

נְאוּפִים 2 n.[m.]pl. **adultery**—sf. נְאֻפַיִךְ—**adultery** or more prob. **tokens of adultery,*** or **urge to commit adultery,** <NOM CL> כָּל־הַלַּיְלָה יֵשׁ נְאוּפֵיהֶם *their adultery lasts all night* Ho 7_6 (if em. יָשֵׁן אֹפֵהֶם *their baker sleeps*).* <OBJ> ראה *see* Jr 13_{27} (+ מִצְהָלָה *neighing*, זִמָּה *wickedness*). <APP> שִׁקּוּץ *abomination* Jr 13_{27}. <COLL> בָּלָה נְאוּפִים *a woman worn out by adultery* Ezk 23_{43} (or em. הֲלֹא כָאֵלֶּה נָאֲפוּ *have they not, like these, committed adultery?*).*

⇒ נאף *commit adultery*.

נָאוֹר* 1 n.[m.] **Shining One,** in ref. to Y., <NOM CL> נָאוֹר אַתָּה אַדִּיר מֵהַרְרֵי־טָרֶף *splendid are you, more majestic than the eternal mountains* Ps 76_5.

⇒ אור *be light*.

נְאוֹת, see נָוֶה *pasture*.

נאכר, see נֵכָר *foreignness*.

נאם 1 vb. **utter a prophetic oracle—Qal** 1 + waw וַיִּנְאֲמוּ—**utter a prophetic oracle,** <SUBJ> נָבִיא *prophet* Jr 23_{31}. <OBJ> נְאֻם *oracle* Jr 23_{31} (for וַיִּנְאֲמוּ נְאֻם *and they utter an oracle* mss read נְאֻם י׳ *[it is] an oracle of* Y.).

⇒ נְאֻם *utterance*.

[נְאֻם] 376.0.1 n.m. **utterance**—cstr. נְאֻם (L נְאוּם)—**utterance,** usu. of Y., given through prophet, **prophetic oracle,** <OBJ> נאם *utter* Jr 23_{31} (for וַיִּנְאֲמוּ נְאֻם *and they utter an oracle* mss read נְאֻם י׳ *[it is] an oracle of Y.*). <NOM CL> נְאֻם־פֶּשַׁע לָרָשָׁע *the utterance of transgression is to the wicked* Ps 36_2 (or em. נָעִים transgression is *pleasant* or נָאוָה *fitting* or נָאַץ *spurned* by).

<CSTR> נְאֻם י׳ *utterance of Y.* Gn 22_{16} Nm 14_{28} 1 S 2_{30} 2 K $9_{26.26}$ 19_{33}||Is 37_{34} 2 K 22_{19}||2 C 34_{27} Is 14_{22} 30_1 31_9 41_{14} $43_{10.12}$ 49_{18} $52_{5.5}$ 54_{17} 55_8 59_{20} $66_{2.17.22}$ Jr $1_{8.15.19}$ $2_{3.9.12.29}$ 3_{1+7t} $4_{1.9.17}$ 5_{9+5t} 6_{12} $7_{11.13.19.30}$ (L נְאוּם; mss נְאֻם) 7_{32} $8_{1.13.17}$ 9_{2+5t} 12_{17} $13_{11.14.25}$ $15_{3.6.9.20}$ $16_{5.11.14.16}$ 17_{24} 18_6 $19_{6.12}$ $21_{7.10.13.14}$ $22_{5.16.24}$ 23_{1+17} (mss at 23_{31}) $25_{7.9.12.31}$ $27_{8.11.15.22}$ 28_4 29_{9+7t} $30_{3.10.11.17.21}$ 31_{1+13t} $32_{5.30.44}$ 33_{14} $34_{5.17.22}$ 35_{13} $39_{17.18}$ 42_{11} 44_{29} 45_5 $46_{5.23.26.28}$ 48_{12+7t} $49_{2.6.13.16}$||Ob 4 Jr 49_{30+5t} 50_{4+6t} 51_{24+6t} Ezk $13_{6.7}$ 16_{58} 37_{14} Ho $2_{15.18.23}$ 11_{11} Jl 2_{12} Am $2_{11.16}$ $3_{10.15}$ 4_{3+5t} $9_{7.8.12.13}$ Ob 8 Mc 4_8 5_9 Zp $1_{2.3.10}$ 3_8 Hg 1_{13} $2_{4.4.14.17.23}$ Zc 1_4 $2_{9.10.10.14}$ 8_{17} 10_{12} 11_6 $12_{1.4}$ 13_8 Ml 1_2 Ps 110_1.

נְאֻם אֲדֹנָי י׳ *utterance of Adonai, Y.* Is 56_8 Jr 2_{22} Ezk 5_{11} $11_{8.21}$ $12_{25.28}$ $13_{8.16}$ 14_{11+5t} 15_8 16_{8+7t} 17_{16} $18_{3.9.23.30.32}$ 20_{3+5t} $21_{12.18}$ $22_{12.31.34}$ 24_{14} 25_{14} $26_{5.14.21}$ 28_{10} 29_{20} 30_6 31_{18} $32_{8.14.16.31.32}$ 33_{11} $34_{8.15.30.31}$ $35_{6.11}$ $36_{14.15.23.32}$ $38_{18.21}$ 39_{5+5t} $43_{19.27}$ $44_{12.15.27}$ $45_{9.15}$ 47_{23} 48_{29} Am 4_5 $8_{3.9.11}$.

נְאֻם י׳ צְבָאוֹת *utterance of Y. of hosts* Is $14_{22.23}$ 17_3 22_{25} Jr 8_3 25_{29} 30_8 49_{26} Na 2_{14} 3_5 Hg 1_9 $2_{4.8.9.23.23}$ Zc $1_{3.16}$ $3_{9.10}$ 5_4 $8_{6.11}$ $13_{2.7}$.

נְאֻם אֲדֹנָי י׳ צְבָאוֹת *utterance of Adonai, Y. of hosts* Is 3$_{15}$ Jr 2$_{19}$ 49$_5$ 50$_{31}$, הָאָדוֹן י׳ צְבָאוֹת *of the Lord, Y. of hosts* Is 1$_{24}$ 19$_4$, אֲדֹנָי י׳ אֱלֹהֵי הַצְּבָאוֹת *of Adonai Y., the God of hosts* Am 3$_{13}$, נְאֻם י׳ אֱלֹהֵי יִשְׂרָאֵל *utterance of Y., the God of Israel* 1 S 2$_{30}$ Is 17$_6$ Am 6$_{8.14}$ (הַצְּבָאוֹת), י׳ צְבָאוֹת אֱלֹהֵי יִשְׂרָאֵל *of Y. of hosts, the God of Israel* Zp 2$_9$, נאם אל *utterance of God* CD 19$_8$.

נְאֻם ... אֲבִיר יִשְׂרָאֵל *utterance of ... the mighty one of Israel* Is 1$_{24}$, נְאֻם ... גֹּאֲלֵךְ קְדוֹשׁ יִשְׂרָאֵל *utterance of ... your redeemer, the holy one of Israel* Is 41$_{14}$ (unless *your redeemer is the holy one of Israel*).

נְאֻם בִּלְעָם *utterance of Balaam* Nm 24$_{3.15}$, דָּוִד *of David* 2 S 23$_1$, הַגֶּבֶר *of the man* Nm 24$_{3.15}$ 2 S 23$_1$ Pr 30$_1$, נְאֻם ... בֶּן־ *utterance of ... the son of* Nm 24$_{3.15}$ (both בְּנוֹ) 2 S 23$_1$, נְאֻם הַמֶּלֶךְ *utterance of the king* Jr 46$_{18}$ 48$_{15}$ 51$_{57}$ (all three + י׳ צְבָאוֹת שְׁמוֹ *Y. of hosts is his name*), שֹׁמֵעַ *of the one who hears* the words of God Nm 24$_{4.16}$, פֶּשַׁע *of transgression* Ps 36$_2$ (or em.; see Nom. Cl.).

<COLL> נְאֻם י׳ לַאדֹנִי *the utterance of Y. to my lord* Ps 110$_1$, נְאֻם הַגֶּבֶר לְאִיתִיאֵל לְאִיתִיאֵל וְאֻכָל *the utterance of the man to Ithiel, to Ithiel and Ucal* Pr 30$_1$.*

⇒ נאם *utter a prophetic oracle.*

* [נֶאֱמָנוּת] 0.0.3 n.f. **trustworthiness, assurance,** <NOM CL> ברית אל נאמנות להם *the covenant of God is an assurance to them* CD 7$_5$=19$_1$ 14$_2$. <COLL> בקרוה נאמנות *they shall examine her with regard to her trustworthiness* 4QOrd^a 2$_9$.

⇒ אמן *be trustworthy.*

נאף 31 vb. **commit adultery—Qal** 16 Impf. יִנְאַף, 2ms תִּנְאָף; + waw 3fs וַתִּנְאַף, וַיִּנְאֲפוּ; ptc. נֹאֵף, נֹאֶפֶת, נֹאֲפוֹת (נֹאֶפֶת); inf. abs. נָאֹף (נאוֹף)—**1. commit adultery (with),** of man with wife of someone else (Jr 29$_{23}$), of woman with strangers (Ezk 16$_{32}$), with images of other gods (Ezk 23$_{37}$), <SUBJ> Israelite(s) Ex 20$_{14}$||Dt 5$_{18}$ Jr 7$_9$, Judah Jr 3$_9$, אִישׁ *man* Lv 20$_{10.10}$, בֵּן *son* Jr 5$_7$, נָבִיא *prophet* Jr 23$_{14}$; subj. not specified, Pr 6$_{32}$. <OBJ> אִשָּׁה *woman* Lv 20$_{10}$ Pr 6$_{32}$, אֶבֶן *stone* Jr 3$_9$, עֵץ *tree* Jr 3$_9$. <COLL> נאף || גנב *steal* Ex 20$_{14}$||Dt 5$_{18}$ Jr 7$_9$, רצח *murder* Ex 20$_{14}$||Dt 5$_{18}$ Jr 7$_9$; + שׁבע ni. *swear* in vain Jr 7$_9$, קטר pi. *burn incense* to Baal Jr 7$_9$, הלך *go* after foreign gods Jr 7$_9$, in lies Jr 23$_{14}$.

2. ptc. as noun, **adulterer, a.** masc., <SUBJ> מות ho. *be put to death* Lv 20$_{10.10}$. <CSTR> עֵין נֹאֵף *eye of the adulterer* Jb 24$_{15}$.

b. fem., <SUBJ> מות ho. *be put to death* Lv 20$_{10}$. <NOM CL> נֹאֲפֹת הֵנָּה *they are adulterers* Ezk 23$_{45}$. <CSTR> מִשְׁפַּט נֹאֲפוֹת *judgment of adulterers* Ezk 23$_{45}$ (+ שׁפך ptc. *one who sheds* blood), מִשְׁפְּטֵי *judgments of* Ezk 16$_{38}$ (+ שׁפך ptc.).

3. inf. abs. as noun, (act of) **adultery,** <SUBJ> פרץ *break through* Ho 4$_2$ (|| אלה *curse*, כחשׁ pi. *deceive*, רצח *murder*, גנב *steal*).

Also perh. 4QErr 1$_5$ (ה[נ]אף; others האנף).

<SYN> §1 גנב *steal*, רצח *murder*; §3 אלה *curse*, כחשׁ pi. *deceive*, רצח *murder*, גנב *steal*.

Pi. 15 Pf. נִאֲפוּ, נִאֵפָה; impf. 3fpl תְּנָאַפְנָה; + waw וַיְנַאֲפוּ; ptc. מְנָאֵף, מְנָאֶפֶת, מְנָאֲפִים—**1. commit adultery (with),** of man with wife of someone else (Jr 29$_{23}$), of woman with strangers (Ezk 16$_{32}$), in ref. to idolatry (Ezk 23$_{37}$), <SUBJ> Israel Jr 3$_8$, Ahab Jr 29$_{23}$ (+ דבר pi. *speak* lying words), Oholah Ezk 23$_{37.37}$, Oholibah Ezk 23$_{37.37}$, Zedekiah Jr 29$_{23}$, אִשָּׁה *wife* Ezk 16$_{32}$ (+ לקח *receive* strangers), בֵּן *son* Jr 29$_{23}$, כַּלָּה *bride* Ho 4$_{13.14}$ (both || זנה *prostitute oneself*), מְשׁוּבָה *apostate one* Jr 3$_8$. <OBJ> אִשָּׁה *woman, wife* Jr 29$_{23}$ Ho 3$_1$ Ps 20$_{30}$, גִּלּוּל *idol* Ezk 23$_{37}$.

2. ptc. as noun, **adulterer, a.** masc., <NOM CL> כֻּלָּם מְנָאֲפִים *they are all adulterers* Jr 9$_1$ (+ בֹּגֵד *traitor*) Ho 7$_4$. <OBJ> מלא *be full of* Jr 23$_{10}$. <CSTR> זֶרַע מְנָאֵף *offspring of an adulterer* Is 57$_3$ (or em. מְנָאֵף וַתִּזְנֶה *an adulterer, and she prostituted herself* to מְנָאֶפֶת וְזֹנָה *of an adulterer* (fem.) *and a prostitute*). <PREP> בְּ *against*, + היה *be* Ml 3$_5$ (|| מְכַשֵּׁף *sorcerer*, + שׁבע ni. ptc. *one who swears* falsely); עִם *with* Ps 50$_{18}$.

b. fem. <CSTR> זֶרַע מְנָאֶפֶת *offspring of an adulterer* Is 57$_3$ (if em.; see §2a, Cstr.).

<SYN> §1 זנה *prostitute oneself*; §2 מְכַשֵּׁף *sorcerer*.*

⇒ נִאוּפִים *adultery*, נַאֲפוּפִים *adultery*.

נֹאֵף *adulterer*, see נאף *commit adultery.*

[נַאֲפוּפִים] 1 n.[m.]pl. **adultery**—pl. sf. נַאֲפוּפֶיהָ—**adultery** or more prob. **tokens of adultery,*** such as jewellery or tattoos, <OBJ> סור hi. *remove* Ho 2_4 (|| זְנוּנִים *prostitution*).

<SYN> זְנוּנִים *prostitution*.*

⇨ נאף *commit adultery*.

נאץ 24.1.13 vb. **have contempt—Qal** 8.1.9 Pf. נָאַץ, 2ms Q נאצת, נאצו (נָאֲצוּ); impf. יִנְאַץ, 2ms תִּנְאַץ, יְנָאֲצוּן; + waw וַיִּנְאַץ—**have contempt (for), despise, spurn, disdain,** <SUBJ> Y. Dt 32_{19} Jr 14_{21} Lm 2_6 1QH 12_{12} perh. 4QapPs[b] 13_1, Israelites Ps 107_{11}, עַם *people* Jr 33_{24}, בֵּן *son* Si $41_{22(B)}$, פֶּתִי *simple one* Pr 1_{30}, לֵץ *scorner* Pr 1_{30}, אֱוִיל *fool* Pr 15_5, כְּסִיל *fool* Pr 1_{30}, לֵב *heart* Pr 5_{12}; subj. not specified, Jr 15_{16} (if em.; see Obj.). <OBJ> עַם *people* Jr 33_{24}, מֶלֶךְ *king* Lm 2_6, כֹּהֵן *priest* Lm 2_6, עֵצָה *counsel* Ps 107_{11}, מַחֲשָׁבָה *plan* 1QH 12_{12}, תּוֹכַחַת *reproof* Pr 1_{30} 5_{12}, מוּסָר *discipline* Pr 15_5, דָּבָר *word* Jr 15_{16} (if em. נִמְצְאוּ *they were found* [מצא ni.] to מִנֹּאֲצֵי *from those who despise*). <PREP> בְּ of accompaniment, *with in (a state of)*, + זַעַם *indignation* Lm 2_6; מֵאַחֲרֵי *after*, + מַתַּת *gift* Si $41_{22(B)}$ (Bmg שְׁאֵלָה *request*). <COLL> נאץ || מרה hi. *be rebellious (against)* Ps 107_{11}; + שׂנא *hate* Pr 5_{12}; :: אבה *be willing* Pr 1_{30}.

Also 1Q25 4_6 4QMyst[a] 71_3 4QapJoseph[a] 4_1 4QapPs[b] 19.1_6 4QparaKings 12_6 47_4 122_2.

<SYN> מרה hi. *be rebellious (against)*.

<ANT> :: אבה *be willing*.

Pi. 15.0.4 Pf. נִאֵץ, נִאַצְתָּ, נִאֲצוּ (נאצו); impf. יְנָאֵץ, יְנַאֲצֻנִי; + waw וַיְנַאֲצוּנִי; ptc. מְנַאֲצַי, מְנַאֲצֶיךָ; inf. abs. נִאֵץ—**have contempt (for), revile, spurn;** perh. **cause to have contempt** (2 S 12_{14}; or em.; see Obj.), <SUBJ> David 2 S 12_{14}, עַם *people* Nm 14_{11} Dt 31_{16} Is 1_4 Ps 74_{18}, גּוֹי *nation* Is 1_4, אִישׁ *man* Nm 16_{30} 1 S 2_{17}, בֵּן *son* Is 1_4, זֶרַע *offspring* Is 1_4, בצע ptc. *one who extorts* Ps 10_3, רָשָׁע *wicked one* Ps 10_{13}, אֹיֵב *enemy* Ps 74_{10}; subj. not specified, Nm 14_{23} Is 5_{24} 60_{14} Jr 23_{17} 1QH 12_{22} 15_{22} 1QS 5_{19} CD 1_2.

<OBJ> Y. Nm $14_{11.23}$ 16_{30} Dt 31_{16} 2 S 12_{14} (if del. אֹיְבֵי *enemies of*) Jr 23_{17} (or em. מְנַאֲצַי דִּבֶּר *those who spurn me; Y. has spoken* to מְנַאֲצֵי דְבַר *those who spurn the word of* Y.) Ps $10_{3.13}$ CD 1_2, Israel(ites) Is 60_{14}, אֹיֵב *enemy* 2 S 12_{14} (or del. אֹיְבֵי), קָדוֹשׁ *holy one* Is 1_4, worshipper 1QS 12_{22} 15_{22}, שֵׁם *name* Ps $74_{10.18}$, מִנְחָה *offering* 1 S 2_{17}, אִמְרָה *word* Is 5_{24}, דָּבָר *word* Jr 23_{17} (if em.; see above) 1QS 5_{19}.

<PREP> לְ of direction, *to*, + נֵצַח *everlastingness* Ps 74_{10}; בְּ of instrument, *by (means of)* or of cause, *on account of*, + דָּבָר *matter* 2 S 12_{14}.

<COLL> נאץ pi. || מאס *despise* Is 5_{24}, עזב *forsake* Is 1_4; + חרף pi. *reproach* Ps $74_{10.18}$, פרר hi. *break covenant* Dt 31_{16}; :: אמן hi. *believe in* Nm 14_{11}; + adverb, עַד־אָנָה *how long?* Nm 14_{11}, עַל־מֶה *why?* Ps 10_{13}.

<SYN> מאס *despise*, עזב *forsake*.

<ANT> אמן hi. *believe in*.

Htpo. 1 Ptc. מִנֹּאָץ—**be treated with contempt, reviled,** <SUBJ> שֵׁם *name* Is 52_5 (תָּמִיד כָּל־הַיּוֹם שְׁמִי מִנֹּאָץ *continually all the day my name is reviled*; or em. שְׁמִי־ם נֻאָץ pass. qal, or מְנֹאָץ pu. with same meaning).*

⇨ נֶאָצָה *reviling*, נְאָצָה *disgrace*.

[נֶאָצָה] 3.0.2 n.f. **reviling**—Q נצה; pl. נֶאָצוֹתֶיךָ, נֶאָצוֹת—**reviling, blasphemy,** <OBJ> אמר *say* Ezk 35_{12}, שׁמע *hear* Ezk 35_{12}, עשׂה *do* Ne $9_{18.26}$ 4QTestim$_{28}$ (ועשו[ע]); || חֲנֻפָּה *impiousness*). <CSTR> כָּל־נֶאָצוֹתֶיךָ *all your revilings* Ezk 25_{12}. <ADJ> גָּדוֹל *great* Ne $9_{18.26}$ 4QTestim$_{28}$. <PREP> בְּ of accompaniment, *in, with* 1QH 14_2.

<SYN> חֲנֻפָּה *impiousness*.*

⇨ נאץ *have contempt*.

נְאָצָה 2 n.f. **disgrace,** <NOM CL> [נאצ]ה היאה *it is a disgrace* 4QJub[f] 33_{13}. <CSTR> יוֹם־צָרָה וְתוֹכֵחָה וּנְאָצָה *day of distress and rebuke and disgrace* 2 K 19_3||Is 37_3.*

⇨ נאץ *have contempt*.

נאק 2 vb. **groan—Qal** 2 Impf. יִנְאָקוּ; + waw וְנָאַק—**groan,** <SUBJ> פַּרְעֹה *Pharaoh* Ezk 30_{24}, מַת *man* Jb 24_{12} (מְתִים; ms מֵתִים *the dead*; + שׁוע pi. *cry for help*). <OBJ> נְאָקָה *groaning* Ezk 30_{24}. <PREP> מִן of direction, *from* + עִיר *city* Jb 24_{12}.

⇨ נְאָקָה *groaning*.

[נְאָקָה] 4 n.f. **groaning**—cstr. נַאֲקַת; sf. נַאֲקָתָם; pl. cstr. נַאֲקוֹת—**groaning, groan,** <OBJ> שׁמע *hear* Ex 2$_{24}$ 6$_{5}$, נאק *groan* Ezk 30$_{24}$. <CSTR> נַאֲקַת בְּנֵי יִשְׂרָאֵל *groaning of the sons of Israel* Ex 6$_{5}$, נַאֲקוֹת חָלָל *groans of a slain one* Ezk 30$_{24}$. <PREP> מִן of cause, *on account of*, + נחם ni. *be moved to pity* Jg 2$_{18}$. <COLL> נַאֲקָתָם מִפְּנֵי לֹחֲצֵיהֶם וְדֹחֲקֵיהֶם *their groaning because of those who maltreated and oppressed them* Jg 2$_{18}$.

⇒ נאק *groan*.

נאר I 2 vb. **repudiate** (unless נאר II *curse*)—**Pi.** 2 Pf. נֵאֵר, נֵאַרְתָּה—**repudiate, spurn,** <SUBJ> Y. Ps 89$_{40}$ (+ חלל pi. *defile*) Lm 2$_{7}$ (|| זנח *reject*). <OBJ> בְּרִית *covenant* Ps 89$_{40}$, מִקְדָּשׁ *sanctuary* Lm 2$_{7}$.

<SYN> זנח *reject*.

*נאר II 2 vb. **curse** (unless נאר I *repudiate*)—**Pi.** 2 Pf. נֵאֵר, נֵאַרְתָּה—**curse,** <SUBJ> Y. Ps 89$_{40}$ (+ חלל pi. *defile*) Lm 2$_{7}$ (|| זנח *reject*). <OBJ> בְּרִית *covenant* Ps 89$_{40}$, מִקְדָּשׁ *sanctuary* Lm 2$_{7}$.

<SYN> זנח *reject*.

נֹב 7 pl.n. **Nob**—+ ה- of direction נֹבֶה—priestly city, perh. Rās el-Mešārif, 2 km N of Jerusalem, <NOM CL> בְּנֵי בִנְיָמִן ... נֹב *the sons of Benjamin were ... (at) Nob* Ne 11$_{32}$. <OBJ> נכה hi. *strike* 1 S 22$_{19}$. <APP> עִיר *city* 1 S 22$_{19}$. <PREP> בְּ of place, *in* 1 S 22$_{11}$ perh. 2 S 21$_{16}$ (יִשְׁבִּי בְּנֹב *Ishbi was in Nob* 2 S 21$_{16[Qr]}$; unless pr.n. *Ishbi-benob*), + עמד *stand* Is 10$_{32}$; נֹב with ה- of direction, *to Nob*, + בוא *come* 1 S 21$_{2}$ 22$_{9}$.

נבא 115.0.9 vb. **prophesy—Qal** 0.0.3 Ptc. pass. Q נבואיו—pass. ptc. as noun, **thing prophesied, prophecy,** in psalm titles, <CSTR> כל נבואיו *all his* (Y.'s) *prophecies* GnzPs 2$_{7}$ 3$_{11}$ 4$_{17}$ (all three + מַרְאֶה *vision*). <PREP> בְּ *in* or of instrument, *by (means of), with*, + ראה *see* GnzPs 2$_{7}$ 3$_{11}$ 4$_{17}$.

Ni. 87.0.6 Pf. נִבָּא, נִבֵּאתָ, (נִבֵּיתָ), נִבֵּאתִי, נִבְּאוּ (נִבָּאוּ); impf. יִנָּבֵא, 2ms תִּנָּבֵא, תִּנָּבְאוּ; + waw וְנִבֵּאתָ, וְנִבְּאוּ, וַיִּנָּבֵא, וַיִּנָּבְאוּ; impv. הִנָּבֵא (Q אנבא); ptc. נִבָּא, נִבְּאִים (נִבָּאִים), נִבְּאֵי; inf. הִנָּבֵא (הִנָּבְאוֹ, הִנָּבְאֹתוֹ), הִנָּבְאִי—**prophesy,** usu. of prophet giving word of Y.; in ecstatic state (1 S 10$_{11}$ 19$_{20}$), with music (1 C 25$_{1.2.3}$); of 'false' prophets (1 K 22$_{12}$||2 C 18$_{11}$ Jr 5$_{31}$ 14$_{14.15.16}$ 20$_{6}$ 23$_{16.21.25.26.32}$ 27$_{10.14.15.16.16}$ 28$_{6}$ 29$_{9.21.31}$ 37$_{19}$ Ezk 13$_{2.16}$ CD 6$_{1}$), prophesying by Baal (Jr 2$_{8}$); of Y. giving prophetic word through spirit (GnzPs 1$_{14}$).

<SUBJ> Y. GnzPs 1$_{14}$, Ahab Jr 29$_{21}$, Amos Am 7$_{15.16}$, Asaph 1 C 25$_{2}$, Azariah 2 C 15$_{8}$ (if em.; see Obj.), Ezekiel Ezk 11$_{13}$ 12$_{27}$ 37$_{4.7.7}$, Hananiah Jr 28$_{6}$, Isaiah 3QpIsa 1$_{3}$ ([ישע]יה[ו]), Jeduthun 1 C 25$_{3}$, Jeremiah Jr 11$_{21}$ 19$_{14}$ 25$_{15.30}$ 26$_{9.12}$ 32$_{3}$, Micah Jr 26$_{18}$, Pashhur Jr 20$_{6}$, Saul 1 S 10$_{11}$, Shemaiah Jr 29$_{31}$, Uriah Jr 26$_{20}$, Zedekiah Jr 29$_{21}$, מוֹרַשְׁתִּי *Morashtite* Jr 26$_{18}$.

אִישׁ *man* Jr 26$_{11}$ Zc 13$_{3.3}$, בֵּן *son* Jr 26$_{20}$ 29$_{21}$ Jl 3$_{1}$ 1 C 25$_{1(Qr)}$ (Kt הנביאים *the prophets*) 2 C 15$_{8}$ (if em.; see Obj.), of man (in ref. to Ezekiel) Ezk 4$_{7}$ 6$_{2}$ 11$_{4.4}$ 13$_{2.2}$ (if em. הַנִּבְּאִים *who prophesy* to הִנָּבֵא *prophesy*) 13$_{17}$ 21$_{2.7.14.19.33}$ 25$_{2}$ 28$_{21}$ 29$_{2}$ 30$_{2}$ 34$_{2.2}$ 35$_{2}$ 36$_{1.3.6}$ 37$_{9.9.12}$ 38$_{2.14}$ 39$_{1}$ 4QpsEzek^{a} 2$_{5.6.7}$ 4QpsEzek^{b} 1.1$_{7}$ ([הנבא]), בַּת *daughter* Jl 3$_{1}$, נָבִיא *prophet* 1 S 19$_{20}$ 1 K 22$_{12}$||2 C 18$_{11}$ Jr 2$_{8}$ 5$_{31}$ 14$_{14.15.16}$ 23$_{16.21.25.26.26}$ (if em. נְבִיאֵי *prophets of* to נִבְּאֵי *who prophesy*) 27$_{10.14.15.16.16}$ 28$_{6.8.9}$ 29$_{9}$ 32$_{3}$ 37$_{19}$ Ezk 13$_{2}$ (or em.; see above) 13$_{16}$ 38$_{17}$ Am 2$_{12}$ Zc 13$_{4}$, חֹזֶה *seer* (Amos) Am 7$_{12.13}$, קֹסֵם *diviner* Jr 27$_{10}$ 29$_{9}$, עֹנֵן *soothsayer* Jr 27$_{10}$, כַּשָּׁף *sorcerer* Jr 27$_{10}$, חֹלֵם *dreamer* Jr 27$_{10}$, סוג hi. ptc. *one who moves* boundary CD 6$_{1}$, מִי *who?* Am 3$_{8}$; subj. not specified, Jr 23$_{32}$.

<OBJ> דָּבָר *word* Jr 20$_{1}$ 25$_{30}$ 26$_{12}$ 28$_{6}$, נְבוּאָה *prophecy* 2 C 15$_{8}$ (if ins. אֲשֶׁר נִבָּא עֲזַרְיָהוּ בֶּן־ *which Azariah the son of Oded had prophesied*), חֲלוֹם false *dream* Jr 23$_{32}$, שֶׁקֶר *falsehood* Jr 14$_{14}$ 23$_{25.26}$ 27$_{10.14.16}$ 29$_{21}$ CD 6$_{1}$, כתב pass. ptc. *thing written* Jr 25$_{13}$.

<PREP> לְ of direction, *to*, + Israelites Jr 27$_{10}$ 37$_{19}$, עַם *people* Jr 14$_{16}$ 27$_{14.16.16}$, גּוֹלָה *exiles* Jr 29$_{9.21.31}$, Zedekiah Jr 27$_{14}$ 37$_{19}$, כֹּהֵן *priest* Jr 27$_{16.16}$; *concerning*, + מִלְחָמָה *war* Jr 28$_{8}$, דֶּבֶר *pestilence* Jr 28$_{8}$, רָעָב *famine* Jr 28$_{8(mss)}$ (L רָעָה *evil*), שָׁלוֹם *peace* Jr 28$_{9}$, עֵת *time* Ezk 12$_{27}$; introducing object, + שֶׁקֶר *falsehood* Jr 27$_{15}$.

בְּ of time, *in*, + יוֹם *day* Jr 26$_{18}$ Ezk 38$_{17}$; *in, by (the name of)*, + בַּעַל *Baal* Jr 2$_{8}$, שֵׁם *name* Jr 11$_{21}$ 14$_{14.15}$ 23$_{5}$ 26$_{9}$ 27$_{15}$ 29$_{9.21}$; of accompaniment, *with*, + שֶׁקֶר *falsehood* Jr 5$_{31}$ 20$_{6}$ 29$_{9}$, כִּנּוֹר *lyre* 1 C 25$_{1(Qr)}$, נֵבֶל *harp* 1 C 25$_{1(Qr)}$, מְצִלְתַּיִם *cymbals* 1 C 25$_{1(Qr)}$; of instrument, *by* (*means of*), *through*, + רוּחַ *spirit* GnzPs 1_{14}.

כְּ *as, according to*, + דָּבָר *word* Jr 26_{20}.

אֶל *to*, + Israel Am 7_{15}, עַם *people* Am 7_{15}, הַר *mountain* Ezk 36_1; *against*, + נָבִיא *prophet* Ezk 13_2, אֲדָמָה *land* Ezk 21_7, אֶרֶץ *land* Jr 28_8, עִיר *city* Jr 25_{30} $26_{11.12}$, בַּיִת *house* Jr 26_{12}, הַר *mountain* Ezk 6_2, יַעַר *forest* Ezk 21_2; *concerning*, + Jerusalem Ezk 13_{16}.

עַל *to*, + עֶצֶם *bone* Ezk 37_4 4QpsEzek^a 2_5, רוּחַ *breath* Ezk 37_9 4QpsEzek^a 2_7; *against*, + Gog Ezk 39_1, Magog Ezk 38_2, אִישׁ *man* Ezk 11_4, בֵּן *son* Ezk 25_2, בַּת *daughter* Ezk 13_{17}, פַּרְעֹה *Pharaoh* Ezk 29_2, מֶלֶךְ *king* Ezk 29_2, נָשִׂיא *prince* Ezk 38_8, רֹעֶה *shepherd* Ezk 34_2, אֶרֶץ *land* Jr 26_{20}, גּוֹי *nation* Jr 25_{13}, מַמְלָכָה *kingdom* Jr 28_8, עִיר *city* Jr 26_{20}, Egypt Ezk 29_2, Jerusalem Ezk 4_7, Sidon Ezk 28_{21}, הַר *mountain* Ezk 35_2; *concerning*, + Israel Am 7_{16}, Judah and Jerusalem 3QpIsa 1_3 (ע]ל יהודה [וירושלם), אֲדָמָה *land* Ezk 36_6; *according to*, + פֶּה *mouth*, i.e. word GnzPs 1_{14}; *under*, + יָד *hand*, i.e. charge 1 C 25_2.

עִם *with*, + נָבִיא *prophet* 1 S 10_{11}.

<COLL> נבא ni. || נטף hi. *drip*, i.e. preach Ezk $21_{2.7}$ Am 7_{16}; + חזה *see* vision Ezk 13_{16}, ראה *see* vision Jl 3_1, חלם *dream* Jl 3_1, שִׂים פָּנִים אֶל/עַל *set face to/against* Ezk 6_2 13_{17} $21_{2.7}$ 25_2 28_{21} 29_2 35_2 38_2; with following prophetic message introduced by (finite form of) אמר *say* Jr 25_{30} Ezk 13_2 21_{14} 30_2 34_2 $36_{1.6}$ $37_{4.9.12}$ 39_1, inf. cstr. לֵאמֹר *saying* 1 K 22_{12}||2 C 18_{11} Jr 23_{25} $26_{9.18}$ 27_{16} 32_3 37_{19}.

+ adverb or noun used adverbially, כֵּן *thus* 1 K 22_{12}||2 C 18_{11}, לָכֵן *therefore* Ezk 36_3 37_{12} 38_{14}, מַדּוּעַ *why?* Jr 26_9 32_3, עוֹד *again* Zc 13_3, שָׁם *there* Am 7_{12}, שָׁנָה *year* Ezk 38_{17}.

<SYN> נטף hi. *drip*, i.e. preach.

Htp. 28 Pf. הִנַּבֵּאתִי, הִנַּבְּאוּ; impf. יִתְנַבֵּא; + waw וַיִּתְנַבֵּא, וַיִּתְנַבְּאוּ, וְהִתְנַבִּיתָ; ptc. מִתְנַבֵּא, מִתְנַבְּאִים, מִתְנַבְּאוֹת; inf. הִתְנַבּוֹת—**rave** (1 S 18_{10} Jr 29_{26}), **prophesy,** in ecstatic state (Nm $11_{25.26.27}$ 1 S $19_{20.21.21.24}$), with music (1 S $10_{5.6.10}$), of prophets of Baal (1 K 18_{29}); of prophet giving word of Y. (1 K $22_{8.18}$||2 C $18_{7.17}$ Jr 26_{20} 29_{27} Ezk 37_{10} 2 C 20_{37}), 'false' prophets (1 K 22_{10}||2 C 18_9 Jr 14_{14} Ezk 13_{17}), prophesying by Baal (Jr 23_{13}).

<SUBJ> Eldad Nm 11_{27}, Eliezer 2 C 20_{37}, Jeremiah Jr 29_{27}, Medad Nm 11_{27}, Micaiah 1 K $22_{8.18}$||2 C 18_{17}, Saul 1 S $10_{6.10.13}$ $19_{23.24}$, Uriah Jr 26_{20}, עֲנְּתֹתִי *Anathothite* Jr 29_{27}, אִישׁ *man* Nm $11_{25.26}$ 1 K 22_8||2 C 18_7 Jr 26_{20}, בֵּן *son* 1 K 22_8 Jr 26_{20} 2 C 20_{37}, בַּת *daughter* Ezk 13_{17}, זָקֵן *elder* Nm 11_{25}, נָבִיא *prophet* 1 S 10_5 1 K 18_{29} 22_{10}||2 C 18_9 Jr 23_{13}, מַלְאָךְ *messenger* 1 S $19_{20.21.21}$.

<OBJ> חָזוֹן false *vision* Jr 14_{14}, קֶסֶם *divination* Jr 14_{14}, תַּרְמִית *deceit* of heart Jr 14_{14}, טוֹב *good* 1 K $22_{8.18}$||2 C 18_{17}, רַע *evil* 1 K 22_8.

<PREP> לְ of direction, *to*, + Israelites Jr 14_{14}, עַם *people* Jr 29_{27}, Zephaniah Jr 29_{27}, בֵּן *son* Jr 29_{27}, כֹּהֵן *priest* Jr 29_{27}; introducing object, + טוֹבָה *good* 2 C 18_7, רַע *evil* 2 C 18_{17}, רָעָה *evil* 2 C 18_7.

בְּ of place, *in*, + מַחֲנֶה *camp* Nm $11_{26.27}$; *in, by (the name of)*, + בַּעַל *Baal* Jr 23_{13}, שֵׁם *name* Jr 26_{20}.

מִן *from (out of)*, + לֵב *heart* Ezk 13_{17}.

עַל *against*, + Jehoshaphat 2 C 20_{37}; *concerning*, + מֶלֶךְ *king* 1 K $22_{8.18}$||2 C $18_{7.17}$.

עִם *with*, + נָבִיא *prophet* 1 S 10_6.

בְּתוֹךְ *among, within*, + נָבִיא *prophet* 1 S 10_{10}, בַּיִת *house* 1 S 18_{10}.

לִפְנֵי *before*, + Jehoshaphat 1 K 22_{10}||2 C 18_9, Samuel 1 S 19_{24}, מֶלֶךְ *king* 1 K 22_{10}||2 C 18_9.

<COLL> נבא htp. || שׁגע pu. *be mad* Jr 29_{26}; + הפך ni. *be turned* into another man 1 S 10_6.

<SYN> שׁגע pu. *be mad*.*

⇒ נְבוּאָה *prophecy*, נָבִיא *prophet*, נְבִיאָה *prophet* (fem.), נָבִי *Nabi*.

נבב 4 vb. **hollow out**—**Qal** 4 Ptc. pass. נָבוּב; cstr. נְבוּב—pass. ptc. as adj., **hollow,** of pillar (Jr 52_{21}), altar (Ex 27_8||38_7), empty-minded man (Jb 11_{12}), **1.** attributively of אִישׁ *man* Jb 11_{12} (or em. נְבוֹב man is an *offspring*).

2. predicatively in nom cl. with עַמּוּד *pillar* Jr 52_{21}.

3. adverbially of עשׂה *make* altar Ex 27_8||38_7 (נְבוּב לֻחֹת *hollow one of boards*, i.e. hollow with boards).

נְבוֹ I 1 pr.n.m. **Nebo,** Babylonian deity Nabu, <SUBJ> קרס *stoop* Is 46_1 (+ בֵּל *Bel*).

⇒ נְבוּזַרְאֲדָן *Nebuzaradan*, נְבוּכַדְנֶאצַּר *Nebuchadnezzar*, נְבוּכַדְרֶאצַּר *Nebuchadrezzar* נְבוּשַׁזְבָּן *Nebu* shazban.

נְבוֹ II 12.0.1 pl.n. **Nebo, 1.** mountain in Moab, from which Moses viewed promised land, Jebel en-Nebā, 15 km E of northern tip of Dead Sea, and c. 1250 m above it, <CSTR> הַר־נְבוֹ *Mount Nebo* Dt 32$_{49}$ 34$_{1}$ (+ פִּסְגָּה *Pisgah*) 1QDM 1.1$_{2}$ ([הר נבו]). <PREP> אֶל *to*, + עלה *go up* 1QDM 1.1$_{2}$ ([א]ל הר נבו); לִפְנֵי *before*, + חנה *encamp* Nm 33$_{47}$ (+ הָרֵי הָעֲבָרִים *mountains of Abarim*). <COLL> הַר הָעֲבָרִים הַזֶּה הַר־נְבוֹ *this mountain of the Abarim, Mount Nebo* Dt 32$_{49}$.*

2. town in NW Moab, allocated to Reuben, prob. Kh. el-Mukhayyat, 2 km SW of Mount Nebo, <SUBJ> שׁדד pu. *be devastated* Jr 48$_{1}$. <OBJ> נכה hi. *conquer* Nm 32$_{3}$, בנה *build* Nm 32$_{38}$. <APP> אֶרֶץ *land* Nm 32$_{3}$. <PREP> אֶל *to* Jr 48$_{1}$; עַל *over*, + ילל hi. *wail* Is 15$_{2}$; *against*, + בוא *come* Jr 48$_{22}$; עַד *as far as*, + ישׁב *dwell* 1 C 5$_{8}$.

3. town in Judah, perh. Nūbā, 12 km NW of Hebron, <CSTR> אַנְשֵׁי נְבוֹ *men of Nebo* Ne 7$_{33}$, בְּנֵי *sons of* Ezr 2$_{29}$ 10$_{43}$, כפר נבו *village of Nebo* (or *Chepharnebo*) 3QTr 9$_{11}$. <ADJ> אַחֵר *other* Ne 7$_{33}$.

נְבוֹ, see סַמְגַּר נְבוֹ *Samgar-nebo*.

[נָבוּא] *thing prophesied*, see נבא *prophesy*.

נְבוּאָה 3.4.2 n.f. **prophecy**—cstr. נְבוּאַת; sf. Q נבואתה, Si נבואתם—**1. prophecy,** as word of Y. (2 C 15$_{8}$ 11QPs^{a} 27$_{11}$), false (Ne 6$_{12}$), written (2 C 9$_{29}$). **2. giving of prophecy, office of prophet** (Si 46$_{1.13}$).

<SUBJ> נתן ni. *be given* appar. 11QPs^{a} 27$_{11}$. <OBJ> דבר pi. *speak* Ne 6$_{12}$, שׁמע *hear* 2 C 15$_{8}$, נבא ni. *prophesy* 2 C 15$_{8}$ (or em.; see App.). <CSTR> נְבוּאַת אֲחִיָּה הַשִּׁילוֹנִי *prophecy of Ahijah the Shilonite* 2 C 9$_{29}$ (|| דָּבָר *word*, + חָזוֹת *vision*). <APP> הַנְּבוּאָה עֹדֵד הַנָּבִיא *the prophecy, (namely that of) Oded the prophet* 2 C 15$_{8}$ (or ins. אֲשֶׁר נִבָּא עֲזַרְיָהוּ בֶן־ *which Azariah the son of* Oded *had prophesied*). <PREP> לְ perh. *as* MasUnid 14; בְּ *in* or of instrument, *by (means of), through* Si 44$_{3}$, + דבר pi. *speak* 11QPs^{a} 27$_{11}$; *in (the giving of)* Si 46$_{1.13}$, + נשׂא *raise* voice Si 46$_{20}$ (בנבוא[ה]); עַל *in*, + כתב pass. *be written* 2 C 9$_{29}$.

<SYN> דָּבָר *word*.*

⇒ נבא *prophesy*.

*****[נָבוֹב]** n.[m.] **offspring,** אִישׁ נָבוֹב יְלַבְּבוֹ עַיִר *man is an offspring that an ass produces* Jb 11$_{12}$ (if em. אִישׁ נָבוּב יִלָּבֵב וְעַיִר *a hollow man will gain understanding; and an ass*).

⇒ נוב *bear fruit*.

נבוד, see כָּבוֹד *glory*.

נְבוּזַרְאֲדָן 15.0.1 pr.n.m. **Nebuzaradan**—נְבוּזַר־אֲדָן, Q נבוזרדן—chief cook (רַב־טַבָּחִים) of Nebuchadrezzar and head of Babylonian forces who captured Jerusalem, <SUBJ> הלך hi. *bring* 2 K 25$_{20}$||Jr 52$_{26}$, בוא *come* 2 K 25$_{8}$||Jr 52$_{12}$, hi. *bring* 4QpsEzek^{a} 16.14, גלה hi. *exile* 2 K 25$_{11}$||Jr 52$_{15}$ Jr 39$_{9}$ 52$_{30}$, שׁלח *send* Jr 39$_{13}$, pi. Jr 40$_{1}$, נוח hi. *leave* Jr 43$_{6}$, שׁאר hi. *leave* 2 K 25$_{12(mss)}$||Jr 52$_{16}$ Jr 39$_{10}$, לקח *take* 2 K 25$_{20}$||Jr 52$_{26}$ Jr 39$_{11.13}$ 40$_{1}$ 4QpsEzek^{a} 16.14, נתן *give* Jr 39$_{10.13}$, שׂים *place* Jr 39$_{11}$, פקד hi. *place in charge* Jr 41$_{10}$, עשׂה *do* Jr 39$_{11}$, נכה hi. *strike* 4QpsEzek^{a} 16.14, שׂרף *burn* 2 K 25$_{8}$||Jr 52$_{12}$. <CSTR> יַד נְבוּזַרְאֲדָן *hand of Nebuzaradan* Jr 39$_{11}$. <APP> רַב־טַבָּחִים *chief of (the) cooks* 2 K 25$_{8}$||Jr 52$_{12}$ 2 K 25$_{11.12(mss).20}$||Jr 52$_{15.16.26}$ Jr 39$_{9.10.11.13}$ 40$_{1}$ 41$_{10}$ 43$_{6}$ 52$_{30}$ 4QpsEzek^{a} 16.14, עֶבֶד *servant* 2 K 25$_{8}$. <PREP> אֶל *to*, + דבר pi. *speak* Jr 39$_{11}$.*

⇒ נְבוֹ II *Nebo*.

*****[נְבוֹךְ]** 0.0.1 n.[m.] **spring**—pl. cstr. נבוכי—<CSTR> נבוכי מים *springs of water* 1QH 11$_{15}$. <PREP> עַל *over*, + רתח *boil* 1QH 11$_{15}$.

נְבוּכַדְנֶאצַּר, see נְבוּכַדְרֶאצַּר *Nebuchadrezzar*.

נְבוּכַדְרֶאצַּר 61.0.1 pr.n.m. **Nebuchadrezzar**—Kt נבוכדנצור, Kt נבוכדראצור, נְבוּכַדְנֶאצַּר, נְבֻכַדְנֶאצַּר, נְבֻכַדְנֶצַּר—**Nebuchadrezzar** (e.g. Jr 21$_{2}$ + 32t), less accurately **Nebuchadnezzar** (e.g. 2 K 24$_{11}$ + 26t), king of Babylon who conquered Jerusalem and exiled its people, <SUBJ> דבר pi. *speak* Jr 39$_{5}$, צוה pi.

command Jr 39$_{11}$, שׁבע hi. *cause to swear* 2 C 36$_{13}$, יעץ *take counsel* Jr 49$_{30}$, חשׁב *plan* Jr 49$_{30}$, חלם *dream* Dn 2$_{1}$.

הלך hi. *lead* 2 C 36$_{6}$, בוא *come* 2 K 24$_{11}$ 25$_{1}$||Jr 52$_{4}$ Jr 39$_{1}$ 46$_{13}$ Dn 1$_{1}$, hi. *bring* Jr 24$_{1}$ 28$_{3}$ 2 C 36$_{7.10}$, ho. *be brought* Ezk 30$_{10}$, יצא *go out* Jr 43$_{10}$, hi. *bring out* Ezr 1$_{7}$, עלה *go up* 2 K 24$_{1}$||2 C 36$_{6}$ Jr 35$_{11}$, קום hi. *raise* Ezk 26$_{7}$, שׁלח *send* 2 C 36$_{10}$, בקשׁ pi. *seek* Jr 44$_{30}$, שׁבה *capture* Jr 43$_{10}$, גלה *exile* Jr 27$_{20}$, hi. Jr 24$_{1}$ 29$_{1}$ 52$_{28}$ Est 2$_{6}$ Ezr 2$_{1}$||Ne 7$_{6}$, שׁאר hi. *leave* 2 K 25$_{22}$, לקח *take* Jr 27$_{20}$ 28$_{3}$, שׁלל *despoil* Ezk 29$_{19}$, בזז *plunder* Ezk 29$_{19}$, נשׂא *lift* Ezk 29$_{19}$, עטה *grasp* Jr 43$_{10}$, אסר *bind* 2 C 36$_{6}$, נטה *spread* Jr 43$_{10}$, כסה pi. *cover* Ezk 26$_{7}$, יצג hi. *place*, i.e. make into Jr 51$_{34(Qr)}$, נתן *give*, i.e. place Ezk 26$_{7}$ Ezr 1$_{7}$ 2 C 36$_{7}$, שׁפך *pour*, i.e. raise, siege-mound Ezk 26$_{7}$, מלא *fill* Ezk 30$_{10}$.

חנה *encamp* 2 K 25$_{1}$||Jr 52$_{4}$, בנה *build* 2 K 25$_{1}$||Jr 52$_{4}$, צור *besiege* Jr 39$_{1}$ Dn 1$_{1}$, לחם ni. *fight* Jr 21$_{2}$ 34$_{1}$, נכה hi. *strike* Jr 29$_{21}$ 43$_{10}$ 46$_{2.13}$ 49$_{28}$, הרג *kill* Ezk 26$_{7}$, המם *discomfit* Jr 51$_{34(Qr)}$, בלע *swallow* Jr 51$_{34(Qr)}$, רמס *trample* Ezk 26$_{7}$, יצת hi. *kindle* Jr 43$_{10}$ (if em. וְהִצַּתִּי *and I will kindle* to וְהִצִּית *and he shall kindle*), שׂרף *burn* Jr 43$_{10}$, נתץ *break down* Ezk 26$_{7}$, שׁבר pi. *break* Jr 43$_{10}$, עצם pi. *break bones* Jr 50$_{17}$, שׁחת pi. *destroy* Ezk 30$_{10}$, ריק hi. *empty*, i.e. draw, sword Ezk 30$_{10}$, מלך hi. *make king* Jr 37$_{1}$ 2 C 36$_{10}$, עבד *serve* Ezk 29$_{18.19}$, hi. *make serve* Ezk 29$_{18}$.

<OBJ> בוא hi. *bring* Jr 25$_{9}$ Ezk 26$_{7}$, עבד *serve* Jr 27$_{8}$ 28$_{14}$, לקח *take* Jr 43$_{10}$.

<CSTR> עַבְדֵי נְבֻכַדְנֶאצַּר *servants of Nebuchadnezzar* 2 K 24$_{10}$, יַד נְבוּכַדְנֶאצַּר *hand of Nebuchadnezzar* Jr 27$_{6}$ 32$_{28}$ 1 C 5$_{41}$ (נְבֻכַדְנֶאצַּר) CD 1$_{6}$, נְבוּכַדְרֶאצַּר *of Nebuchadrezzar* Jr 21$_{7}$ 22$_{25}$ 29$_{21}$ 44$_{30}$ 46$_{26}$ Ezk 30$_{10}$, עֹל נְבֻכַדְנֶאצַּר *yoke of Nebuchadnezzar* Jr 28$_{11}$, מַלְכוּת נְבֻכַדְנֶצַּר *reign of Nebuchadnezzar* Dn 2$_{1}$.

<APP> מֶלֶךְ *king* 2 K 24$_{1}$||2 C 36$_{6}$ 2 K 24$_{10.11}$ 25$_{1.8}$||Jr 52$_{4.12}$ 2 K 25$_{22}$ Jr 21$_{2.7}$ 22$_{25}$ 24$_{1}$ 25$_{1.9}$ 27$_{6.8.20}$ 28$_{3.11.14}$ 29$_{3.21}$ 32$_{28}$ 34$_{1}$ 35$_{11}$ 37$_{1}$ 39$_{1.5.11}$ 43$_{10}$ 44$_{30}$ 46$_{2.13.25}$ 49$_{28.30}$ 50$_{17}$ 51$_{34}$ Ezk 26$_{7}$ 29$_{18.19}$ 30$_{10}$ Est 2$_{6}$ Dn 1$_{1}$ Ezr 2$_{1}$||Ne 7$_{6}$ 2 C 36$_{10.13}$ CD 1$_{6}$, עֶבֶד *servant* Jr 25$_{9}$ 27$_{6}$ 43$_{10}$, אֹיֵב *enemy* Jr 44$_{30}$.

<PREP> לְ of direction, *to*, + נתן *give* Jr 27$_{6}$ Ezk 29$_{19.20}$; of possession, *of, (belonging) to* 2 K 25$_{8}$||Jr 52$_{12}$ Jr 25$_{1}$ 32$_{1}$ 52$_{29.30}$, + היה *be* 2 K 24$_{1}$ Ezk 29$_{18}$; בְּ *against*, + מרד *rebel* 2 K 24$_{1}$ 2 C 36$_{13}$; אֶל *to*, + עלה hi. *bring up* Jr 39$_{5}$, שׁלח *send* Jr 29$_{3}$; *for*, + שׁלח *send* Jr 25$_{9}$; עַל *upon, for*, + היה ni. *be gone* Dn 2$_{1}$; לִפְנֵי *before*, + בוא hi. *bring* Dn 1$_{18}$.

Also 4QpsMos^{d} 6$_{1}$ (נבוכדרא[צר]) 6$_{2}$ ([נבוכ]דראצר).
⇒ נְבוֹ II *Nebo*.

נָבוֹן *intelligent one*, see בין ni. *understand*.

נְבוּשַׁזְבָּן 1 pr.n.m. **Nebushazban,** official of Nebuchadnezzar, <SUBJ> בוא *come* Jr 39$_{3}$ (if em. שַׂר־סְכִים *Sarsechim*), שׁלח *send* Jr 39$_{13}$, ישׁב *sit* Jr 39$_{3}$ (if em.; see above), לקח *take* Jr 39$_{13}$, נתן *give*, i.e. place Jr 39$_{13}$. <OBJ> ראה *see* Jr 39$_{3}$ (if em.; see Subj.). <APP> רַב־סָרִיס *Rabsaris*, appar. 'chief eunuch' Jr 39$_{3}$ (if em.; see Subj.) 39$_{13}$.
⇒ נְבוֹ II *Nebo*.

נָבוֹת 22 pr.n.m. **Naboth,** Jezreelite, owner of vineyard, <SUBJ> אמר *say* 1 K 21$_{3.4.6}$, דבר pi. *speak* 1 K 21$_{4}$, ברך pi. *curse* 1 K 21$_{9.13}$, נתן *give* 1 K 21$_{2.3.6.15}$, מאן pi. *refuse* 1 K 21$_{15}$, חפץ *desire* 1 K 21$_{6}$, סקל pu. *be stoned* 1 K 21$_{14.15}$, מות *die* 1 K 21$_{9.13.14.15.16}$. <NOM CL> אֵין נָבוֹת חַי כִּי־מֵת *Naboth is not alive, but dead* 1 K 21$_{15}$. <OBJ> יצא hi. *bring out* 1 K 21$_{9.13}$, ישׁב hi. *cause to sit* 1 K 21$_{9.12}$, עוד hi. *testify against* 1 K 21$_{9.13}$, סקל *stone* 1 K 21$_{9.13}$. <CSTR> דַּם נָבוֹת *blood of Naboth* 1 K 21$_{19}$ 2 K 9$_{26}$ (דְּמֵי), כֶּרֶם *vineyard of* 1 K 21$_{7.15.16.18}$, שְׂדֵה *field of* 2 K 9$_{25}$, חֶלְקַת *plot of* 2 K 9$_{21.25(mss)}$. <APP> יִזְרְעֵאלִי *Jezreelite* 1 K 21$_{1.4.6.7.15.16}$ 2 K 9$_{21.25}$. <PREP> לְ of direction, *to* 1 K 21$_{3}$, + אמר *say* 1 K 21$_{6}$, נתן *give* 1 K 21$_{2.6}$; of possession, *of, (belonging) to*, + היה *be* 1 K 21$_{1}$; אֶל *to*, + דבר pi. *speak* 1 K 21$_{2.6}$; אֵת *with*, + ישׁב *dwell* 1 K 21$_{8}$; נֶגֶד *opposite*, + ישׁב *sit* 1 K 21$_{12}$, hi. *cause to sit* 1 K 21$_{9}$.

נבח 1 vb. **bark—Qal** 1 Inf. לִנְבֹּחַ—**bark,** <SUBJ> כֶּלֶב *dog* Is 56$_{10}$ (as description of sentries, כְּלָבִים אִלְּמִים לֹא יוּכְלוּ לִנְבֹּחַ *dumb dogs that cannot bark*).

נֹבַח I 1 pr.n.m. **Nobah,** Manassite, <SUBJ> הלך *go*

Nm 32$_{42}$, לכד *capture* Nm 32$_{42}$, קרא *call*, i.e. name Nm 32$_{42}$.

נֹבַח II 2 pl.n. **Nobah,** a town and perh. a region in Gilead, previously called קְנָת *Kenath*, <OBJ> קרא *call*, i.e. name Nm 32$_{42}$. <PREP> מִקֶּדֶם לְ *east of* Jg 8$_{11}$.

נִבְחַז 1 pr.n.[m.] **Nibhaz,** god of the Avvites, a community in western Elam,* perh. the deity Ibnaḫaza,* <OBJ> עשׂה *make* 2 K 17$_{31}$ (mss נִבְחַן *Nibhan*; + תַּרְתָּק *Tartak*).*

נִבְחַן, see נִבְחַז *Nibhaz*.

נבט 69.17.26 vb. **look—Pi.** 1 + waw וְנִבַּט—**look,** <SUBJ> subj. not specified, Is 5$_{30}$. <PREP> לְ *at, across*, + אֶרֶץ *land* Is 5$_{30}$.

Hi. 68.17.26 Pf. הִבִּיט, Q הבטתה, הִבִּ֫יטוּ, הִבַּטְתֶּם; impf. יַבִּיט, 2ms תַּבִּיט (תַּבֵּט), אַבִּיט (אַבִּ֫יטָה), יַבִּ֫יטוּ; + waw וְהִבִּ֫יטוּ; וַיַּבֵּט, 3fs וַתַּבֵּט, 2ms וַתַּבֵּט; impv. הַבֵּט (הַבֵּיט, הַבִּ֫יטָה, הַבֶּט־), הַבִּ֫יטוּ; ptc. מַבִּיט; inf. הַבִּיט (הַבִּיטִ׳, Si הביטך, Q הביטכה, Si הביטו, הַבִּיטָם).

1. look, behold, regard, consider, regard favourably, accept graciously* (Am 5$_{22}$ Hb 1$_{13}$ Ps 13$_{11}$ 80$_{11}$ 84$_{11}$ Lm 4$_{11}$); of house, **overlook** (Si 42$_{11}$), <SUBJ> Y. perh. Nm 23$_{21}$ (unless subj. impersonal) Is 18$_{4}$ 63$_{5.15}$ 64$_{8}$ 66$_{2}$ Am 5$_{22}$ Hb 1$_{3}$ (or em. תַּבִּיט *you behold* to אַבִּיט *I* [Habakkuk] *behold*) 1$_{13.13}$ Ps 10$_{14}$ 13$_{4}$ 33$_{13}$ 74$_{20}$ 80$_{15}$ 84$_{10}$ 102$_{20}$ 104$_{32}$ 142$_{5}$ Jb 28$_{24}$ Lm 1$_{11}$ 2$_{20}$ 3$_{63}$ 4$_{16}$ 5$_{1}$ Si 15$_{18}$ 16$_{19}$ 39$_{20}$ 42$_{18(M)}$ 1QpHab 1$_{6}$ ([הביט]) 1QS 11$_{19}$ 4QBark[c] 1.2$_{1}$ 4QapLam[b] 1$_{5}$.

Israelites Is 22$_{8.11}$ Hb 1$_{5}$, עַם *people* Ex 33$_{8}$ Is 8$_{22}$ 51$_{6}$, לְאֹם *nation* Is 51$_{6}$, עֵדָה *assembly* Ps 22$_{18}$, בַּיִת *house* Zc 12$_{10}$ Si 42$_{11}$, Philistine 1 S 17$_{42}$, Abram Gn 15$_{5}$, Ben Sira Si 51$_{19(B).21}$, Eli 1 S 23$_{2}$, Elijah 1 K 19$_{6}$, Elisha 2 K 3$_{14}$, Habakkuk Hb 1$_{3}$ (if em.; see above), Hezekiah Is 38$_{11}$, Job Jb 35$_{5}$, Jonah Jon 2$_{5}$, Lot Gn 19$_{17}$, Moses Ex 3$_{6}$ Nm 12$_{8}$ 2QapMoses 1$_{5}$ ([מושה]), Ornan 1 C 21$_{21}$, Samuel 1 S 16$_{7}$, Saul 1 S 24$_{9}$, אֱנוֹשׁ *human being* Jb 36$_{25}$, אִישׁ *man* Nm 21$_{9}$ 1QS 3$_{7}$ 4QCryptA 3.2$_{10}$, אִשָּׁה *wife* Gn 19$_{26}$, אֵם *mother* Jg 5$_{28}$ (if em. וַתְּיַבֵּב *and she cried aloud* to וַתַּבֵּט), בֵּן *son* Si 9$_{8}$ 36$_{15}$ 41$_{21}$ 4Q417 2.1$_{18}$, שַׂר *prince* Si 30$_{30}$, מֹשֵׁל *ruler* Si 30$_{30}$, יֹעֵץ *counsellor* Si 37$_{9}$ (Bmg, D).9, נַעַר *servant* 1 K 18$_{43.43}$, worshipper Ps 91$_{8}$ 119$_{6.15.18}$ 1QH 4$_{27}$ 18$_{20}$ 19$_{17}$ 21$_{4}$, עִוֵּר *blind one* Is 42$_{18}$.

אֹהֵב *friend* Si 37$_{4}$, רֵעַ *neighbour* perh. Si 34$_{14}$, יֹשֵׁב *inhabitant* Zc 12$_{10}$, עבר ptc. *one who passes by* Lm 1$_{12}$, שׁכם hi. ptc. *one who rises early* Is 5$_{12}$, שׁקה hi. ptc. *one who gives to drink* Hb 2$_{15}$, רדף ptc. *one who pursues* righteousness Is 51$_{1.2}$, בקשׁ pi. ptc. *one who seeks* Y. Is 51$_{1.2}$, עָרוּם *shrewd one* perh. 4QBéat 5$_{13}$, מֵלִיץ *mediator* 1QH 12$_{11}$, חֹזֶה *seer* 1QH 12$_{11}$, מאס ptc. *one who refuses* to enter covenant 1QS 3$_{3}$, יצר ptc. *one who forms* Ps 94$_{9}$, עַיִן *eye* Ps 92$_{12}$ Jb 39$_{29}$ Pr 4$_{25}$ 1QS 11$_{3.6}$, אוֹרָה *light* of heart perh. 1QS 11$_{3}$, אֹרַח *path* Jb 6$_{19}$ (or em. אָרְחוֹת *paths of* to אֹרְחוֹת *caravans of*, i.e. אֹרְחָה pl.), מִי *who?* Si 42$_{25}$, כֹּל *anyone* 1QH 18$_{3}$; subj. not specified, Ps 34$_{6}$ 4QMyst[b] 1.2$_{1.2.3}$ 4Q416 2.1$_{5}$ 2.3$_{15}$.

<OBJ> Israelites Lm 4$_{16}$, אָדָם *human being* Is 38$_{11}$, בֹּגֵד *traitor* Hb 1$_{13}$, יָמִין *right hand* (or adverbial *to the right*) Ps 142$_{5}$, פָּנִים *face* Ps 84$_{10}$, תְּמוּנָה *form* of Y. Nm 12$_{8}$, תֹּאַר *form* Si 42$_{25(Bmg)}$, שֹׁרֶשׁ *root* of injustice 4Q416 2.3$_{15}$, שָׁמַיִם *heaven* Jb 35$_{5}$, שֶׁלֶם *peace offering* Am 5$_{22}$, פֹּעַל *deed* Is 5$_{12}$, פלא ni. ptc. *wonderful thing* Ps 119$_{18}$, אתה ptc. *that which is to come* 42$_{18(M)}$, כַּעַס *anger* Ps 10$_{14}$, עָמָל *trouble* Hb 1$_{3}$ Ps 10$_{14}$, אָוֶן *misfortune* Nm 23$_{21}$, צַר *distress* appar. 2 S 23$_{2}$, רֵישׁ *poverty* Si 37$_{9}$, חֹשֶׁךְ *darkness* 1QS 3$_{3}$, שֶׁבֶת *sitting* Lm 3$_{63}$, קִימָה *rising up* Lm 3$_{63}$, הוֹד *splendour* Si 42$_{25(M)}$, מָבוֹא *entrance* Si 42$_{11}$, אֹרַח *path* Ps 119$_{15}$, דֶּרֶךְ *way* Si 37$_{9(Bmg, D)}$, of, i.e. towards, the sea 1 K 18$_{43}$, אֲשֶׁר *one who* Zc 12$_{10}$.

<PREP> לְ *to(wards), at*, + אֶרֶץ *earth* Ps 104$_{32}$, קָצָה *end* of earth Jb 28$_{24}$, בְּרִית *covenant* Ps 74$_{20}$, נֹכַח *front*, i.e. ahead Pr 4$_{25}$; *as* or *rather than*, + דֶּרֶךְ *way* of light 1QS 3$_{3}$; introducing object, + כֹּל *everything* Si 15$_{18}$.

בְּ of place, *in*, + Jacob Nm 23$_{21}$, מָכוֹן *place* Is 18$_{4}$, כֹּל *everything* 1 S 23$_{2}$; of time, *in, on*, + יוֹם *day* Is 22$_{8}$; of instrument, *by (means of), with*, + עַיִן *eye* Ps 84$_{10}$.

בְּ *at* or introducing object, + שׁוּר perh. *watcher* Ps 92$_{12}$, עֹשֶׁק *oppression* 1QpHab 1$_{6}$ ([הביט]), מַעַל *unfaithfulness* 1QpHab 1$_{6}$ ([הביט]), פלא ni. ptc. *wonderful thing* 1QS 11$_{3}$, כָּבוֹד *glory* 1QH 18$_{20}$, אוֹר *light* 1QS 3$_{7}$, עֹמֶק *depth* of mysteries 1QS 11$_{19}$, רָז *mystery* perh. 1QS 11$_{3}$ 4QMyst[b] 1.2$_{2}$ 4Q416 2.1$_{5}$ 4Q417 2.1$_{18}$, הוה ptc.

event 1QS 11$_6$, קַדְמֹנִי *former thing* 4QCryptA 3.2$_{10}$ (בקד[מ]וניות), שֹׁרֶשׁ *root* of wisdom 4QMyst^b 1.2$_3$, חָכְמָה *wisdom* Si 51$_{19(B)}$ (בו[ה]) 51$_{21}$, תּוּשִׁיָּה *wisdom* 1QS 11$_6$, מְזִמָּה *discretion* 1QS 11$_6$, דֵּעָה *knowledge* 1QS 11$_6$, אֵלֶּה *these (things)* 4Q418 123.2$_5$.

מִן of direction, *from*, + שָׁמַיִם *heaven* Is 63$_{15}$ Ps 33$_{13}$ 80$_{15}$ 102$_{20}$, רָחוֹק *distance* Jb 36$_{25}$, עוֹלָם *everlastingness* Si 39$_{20}$.

לְמִן *from*, + רָחוֹק *distance* Jb 39$_{29}$.

אֶל *to, at*, + Y. Ex 3$_6$ Ps 34$_6$ 2QapMoses 1$_5$, Abraham Is 51$_2$, Sarah Is 51$_2$, אִשָּׁה *wife* Si 41$_{21(M [Yadin])}$ (אל [אשת]), אָב *father* Is 51$_2$, מֶלֶךְ *king* 2 K 3$_{14}$, נָחָשׁ *serpent* Nm 21$_9$, עָנִי *humble one* Is 66$_2$, נָכֶה *contrite one* Is 66$_2$, עשׂה ptc. *one who does* Is 22$_{11}$, אֶרֶץ *earth* Is 8$_{22}$ 51$_6$ Ps 102$_{20}$, צוּר *rock* Is 51$_1$, הֵיכָל *temple* Jon 2$_5$, יְסוֹד *foundation* of world Si 16$_{19}$, קֶצֶב *extremity* of mountains Si 16$_{19}$, נֶשֶׁק *weapon* Is 22$_8$, שֻׁלְחָן *table* Si 37$_{4(B)}$, מַרְאֶה *appearance* 1 S 16$_7$, גֹּבַהּ *exaltation* 1 S 16$_7$, יְפִי *beauty* Si 9$_8$, בְּרִית *covenant* 1QH 4$_{27}$, תָּעוּת *error* 1QH 12$_{11}$, מִצְוָה *commandment* Ps 119$_6$, מַעֲשֶׂה *work* Si 36$_{15}$, עָמָל *trouble* Hb 1$_{13}$, אֲשֶׁר *one who* Zc 12$_{10}$ (if em. אֵלַי אֵת to אֶל־ or אֵלָי), זֶה *this (one)* Is 66$_2$.

עַל *on, at*, + יָד *hand* Si 30$_{30}$, מָעוֹר *nakedness* Hb 2$_{15}$, שַׁחַת *destruction* Si 37$_{4(Bmg, D)}$.

עִם *with, among*, + יֹשֵׁב *inhabitant* Is 38$_{11}$.

עַד *unto*, + עוֹלָם *everlastingness* Si 39$_{20}$.

בְּעַד *through*, + אֶשְׁנָב *window* Jg 5$_{28}$ (if em.; see Subj.).

אַחֲרֵי *after, behind*, + Lot Gn 19$_{17}$, Moses Ex 33$_8$, Saul 1 S 24$_9$.

מֵאַחֲרֵי *from behind*, + Lot Gn 19$_{26}$.

ה- of direction, *towards*, + שָׁמַיִם *heaven* Gn 15$_5$.

<COLL> נבט hi. || ראה *see* Nm 23$_{21}$ 2 K 3$_{14}$ Is 5$_{12}$ 22$_{11}$ 38$_{11}$ 63$_{15}$ Hb 1$_5$ Lm 1$_{11.12}$ 2$_{20}$; + ראה 1 S 17$_{42}$ Is 42$_{18}$ Ps 10$_{14}$ 22$_{18}$ 33$_{13}$ 80$_{15}$ 84$_{10}$ 84$_{10}$ 142$_5$ Jb 28$_{24}$ 35$_5$ Lm 5$_1$ 1 C 21$_{21}$ 4QapLam^b 1$_5$, hi. *cause to see* Hb 1$_3$.

|| שׂכל hi. *consider* 4QMyst^b 1.2$_2$, רצה *accept* Is 5$_{22}$, שׁמע *hear* Is 42$_{18}$ 51$_1$ Ps 92$_{12}$ 94$_9$.

+ חזה *see* Jb 36$_{25}$, שׁור *behold* Jb 35$_5$, שׁקף hi. *look down* Ps 102$_{20}$, ישׁר hi. *look straight ahead* Pr 4$_{25}$, בין hi. *understand* 4Q417 2.1$_{18}$, htpol. *consider* 4Q416 2.3$_{15}$, שׂיח *meditate* Ps 119$_{15}$, קוה pi. *hope* Jb 6$_{19}$, נגע *touch* Ps 104$_{32}$.

+ adverb, אֵיכָה *how?* 1QH 21$_4$ (א[יכ]ה), מָה *how?* 2QapMoses 1$_5$.

יָרֵא מֵהַבִּיט *he was afraid to look* Ex 3$_6$, מקום יביט *the place to which he looks* Si 34$_{14}$.

2. cause to be seen, display, <SUBJ> עֶצֶם *self* Si 43$_{1(Bmg)}$ (עצם שמים *heaven itself*). <OBJ> נְהָרָה *light* Si 43$_{1(Bmg)}$ (B מרביט הדרו *shows its splendour*).

Also 1QH fr. 2.2$_{11}$ 4QTanḥ 14$_4$ perh. 4QCryptA 1$_5$ perh. 4Q417 2.1$_3$ 4QPrFêtes^c 16$_6$.

<SYN> §1 ראה *see*, שׂכל hi. *consider*, שׁמע *hear*, רצה *accept*.*

⇒ מַבָּט *expectation*, נְבָט *Nebat*.

נְבָט 25.1.1 pr.n.m. **Nebat,** father of Jeroboam I, <CSTR> בֶּן־נְבָט *son of Nebat* 1 K 11$_{26}$ 12$_{2.15}$||2 C 10$_{2.15}$ 1 K 15$_1$ 16$_{3.26.31}$ 21$_{22}$ 22$_{53}$ 2 K 3$_3$ 9$_9$ 10$_{29}$ 13$_{2.11}$ 14$_{24}$ 15$_{9.18.24.28}$ 17$_{21}$ 23$_{15}$ 2 C 9$_{29}$ 13$_6$ Si 47$_{23}$ 4QMMT C$_{19}$.

⇒ נבט *look*.

*[נָבִי] 0.0.0.3 pr.n.[m.] **Nabi, 1.** father of Zephaniah, <CSTR> בן נבי *son of Nabi* Seal 258 (others נבי[א] *of the prophet*; Lachish, 7th cent.).

2. father of Sheanaph, <CSTR> בן נבי *son of Nabi* Seal 343 (7th cent.).

3. appar. father of Oreb, Seal 785 (8th/7th cent.).

4. appar. father of Mahseiah, Seal 886 (7th cent.).

⇒ נבא *prophesy*.

נָבִיא 325.5.44.2 n.m. **prophet**—Q נבי, I נבא; cstr. Q נביא; sf. נְבִיאֲךָ, נְבִיאֲכֶם; pl. נְבִיאִים (נְבִאִים); cstr. נְבִיאֵי (נְבִאֵי); sf. נְבִיאַי, נְבִיאֶיךָ, נְבִיאַיִךְ, נְבִיאָיו (נְבִאָיו), נְבִיאֶיהָ, נְבִיאֵינוּ, נְבִיאֵיכֶם, נְבִיאֵיהֶם.

Male spokesman, usu. for Y., or for Israel before Y.; pl. נְבִיאִים *prophets* may include female prophets (sg. marked as נְבִיאָה *prophet [f.]*); related terms are רֹאֶה *seer*, חֹזֶה *seer*, אִישׁ אֱלֹהִים *man of God*.

1. of prophets of Y. (e.g. Dt 18$_{15}$ Jg 6$_8$ 1 S 3$_{20}$ 22$_5$ 2 S 7$_2$ 1 K 11$_{29}$ 16$_7$ 18$_4$ 19$_{10}$ 2 K 5$_8$ Jr 1$_5$ 7$_{25}$ 44$_4$ Ezk 2$_5$ Am 2$_{11}$ Hg 1$_1$ Zc 1$_1$ Ml 3$_{23}$ Ps 105$_{15}$ Dn 9$_6$ Ezr 9$_{11}$ Ne 9$_{26}$ 2 C 20$_{20}$ 11QPs^a 28$_8$), ecstatic prophets (e.g. Nm 11$_{29}$ 1 S 10$_5$ 19$_{20}$), 'false' prophets (e.g. Dt 13$_2$ 1 K 22$_{10}$||2 C

18$_9$ Is 9$_{14}$ Jr 5$_{13.31}$ 14$_{14}$ 27$_9$ 29$_8$ Ezk 13$_3$ 22$_{28}$ Mc 3$_5$ Zp 3$_4$ 1QH 12$_{16}$), Abraham (Gn 20$_7$).

2. of prophets of other deities: of Asherah (1 K 18$_{19}$), of Baal (1 K 18$_{19.22.25.40}$ 19$_1$ 2 K 10$_{19}$ Jr 2$_8$ 23$_{13}$).

3. of Aaron as spokesman for Moses acting as a god (Ex 7$_1$).

<SUBJ> היה *be* Ex 7$_1$ Nm 12$_6$ 1 K 1$_8$ Jr 5$_{13}$ 28$_8$ 32$_2$ Ezk 2$_5$ 13$_{4.9}$ 33$_{33}$ Ne 6$_{14}$ 2 C 28$_9$, חיה *live* Zc 1, יצר ni. *be formed as* Si 49$_{75}$, כול pilp. *endure* Si 49$_9$ (נ[ב]יא).

אמר *say* Dt 13$_2$=11QT 54$_8$ Jg 6$_8$ 1 S 22$_5$ 2 S 24$_{11}$ 1 K 13$_{26.29}$ 18$_{36}$ 20$_{13.22.38}$ 22$_{6.12}$||2 C 18$_{5.11}$ 2 K 5$_8$ 9$_{1.4}$ 20$_1$||Is 38$_1$ 2 K 20$_{14}$||Is 39$_3$ Jr 2$_{26}$ 14$_{13.15}$ 23$_{16.25.33.34}$ 25$_2$ 26$_{11}$ 27$_{9.14.16}$ 28$_{1.5.6.15}$ 32$_2$ 37$_{19}$ 42$_4$ 45$_1$ Ezk 13$_{4.9}$ 22$_{28}$ Zc 1$_4$ 13$_4$ Ne 6$_7$ 2 C 12$_5$ 25$_{15.16}$ 28$_9$ 11QMelch 2$_{15}$, דבר *speak* Jr 28$_6$, pi. Dt 13$_{2.6}$=11QT 54$_{8.15}$ Dt 18$_{18.20.22.22}$=11QT 61$_{3.4}$ 1 K 13$_{26}$ 14$_2$ 2 K 5$_8$ Jr 23$_{16.28}$ 25$_2$ 34$_6$ 45$_1$ Ezk 13$_4$ 14$_9$ Dn 9$_6$ 2 C 25$_{15}$ 1QpHab 7$_8$ 1Q29 ([יד]בר ... הנב[יא]) 4QTestim 1$_7$ 4QapMos^a 1.1$_4$ 11QT 61$_{07}$ ([ידבר הנביא]), נגד hi. *tell* 1 K 14$_2$ 2 K 6$_{12}$ Jr 42$_4$, ספר pi. *tell* Jr 23$_{26.28.32(mss)}$, קרא *call* 1 K 18$_{25}$ 2 K 9$_1$ 20$_{11}$ Mc 3$_5$ Zc 1$_4$ Ne 6$_7$, זעק *cry out* Hb 1$_1$ 2 C 32$_{20}$, צעק *cry out* 1 K 20$_{38}$, שׁוע pi. *cry for help* Hb 1$_1$, צוה pi. *command* Jr 36$_8$ 51$_{59}$, עוד hi. *warn* Ne 9$_{26}$ 2 C 24$_{19}$, קדשׁ pi. *consecrate*, i.e. declare, war Mc 3$_5$.

נאם *utter a prophetic oracle* Jr 23$_{31}$, נבא ni. *prophesy* 1 S 10$_5$ 19$_{20}$ 1 K 22$_{10}$||2 C 18$_9$ Jr 2$_8$ 5$_{31}$ 14$_{14.15}$ 23$_{16.25.26}$ 27$_{9.14.15.16}$ 28$_{5.8.9}$ 29$_8$ 32$_2$ 37$_{19}$ Ezk 13$_{2.16}$ 38$_{17}$ Am 2$_{12}$ Zc 13$_4$ 2 C 15$_8$ (if em.; see App.), htp. 1 K 18$_{25}$ 22$_{10}$||2 C 18$_9$ Jr 14$_{14}$ 23$_{13.21}$, פגע *intercede* Jr 27$_{18}$, פלל htp. *pray* Jr 37$_3$ 42$_{2.3}$ 2 C 32$_{20}$, דרשׁ *inquire* Jr 37$_6$ Ezk 14$_7$, שׁאל *ask* Jr 23$_{33}$, ירה hi. *teach* Is 9$_{14}$, למד pi. *teach* 4QapPs^b 69$_4$, שׂכל *enlighten* 4QapPs^b 69$_4$, גלה *reveal* 1QS 1$_3$, pi. *uncover* iniquity Lm 2$_{14}$, גיל *rejoice* Hb 3$_1$, עלז *exult* Hb 3$_1$.

חזה *see* Ezk 13$_{4.9.16}$ 22$_{28}$ Hb 1$_1$, ראה *see* 2 S 7$_2$ Ezk 13$_3$ Hb 3$_1$ Lm 2$_{14}$, צפה *watch* Ho 9$_8$ (if transfer athnach), שׁמע *hear* 1 K 13$_{26}$ Jr 23$_{21}$ 26$_7$ 28$_5$ 42$_4$ Ezk 13$_2$ Hb 3$_1$, ידע *know* Jr 14$_{18}$ 2 C 25$_{16}$, ni. *be known* Jr 28$_9$, חשׁב *think* Jr 23$_{26}$, חלם *dream* Jr 23$_{25}$, קסם *divine* Ezk 13$_9$ 22$_{28}$ Mc 3$_{11}$, ירא *fear* Hb 3$_1$, pi. *cause to fear* Ne 6$_{14}$, אמן ni. *prove trustworthy* Si 36$_{21}$ 4QapMos^a 1.1$_6$ ([נ]אמן), שׁכח hi. *cause to forget* Jr 23$_{26}$, כחשׁ pi. *deceive* Zc 13$_4$, נשׁא hi. *deceive* Jr 29$_8$, פתה pu. *be deceived* Ezk 14$_9$ 1QH 12$_{16}$, כתב *write* 2 C 26$_{22}$ 4QDibHam^a 1.3$_{13}$, ni. *be written* Ezk 13$_9$, אכל *eat* 1 K 18$_{19}$, נשׁך *bite* Mc 3$_5$.

הלך *go* 2 S 24$_{11}$ 1 K 13$_{23.26}$ 20$_{38}$ 2 K 9$_4$ Jr 2$_8$ 23$_{14}$ 28$_{11}$ Ezk 13$_3$ 4QpsEzek^a 16.1$_6$, hi. *bring* 1 K 13$_8$, בוא *come* 1 K 1$_{22.23.32.29}$ 2 K 9$_4$ 20$_1$||Is 38$_1$ 2 K 20$_{14}$||Is 39$_3$ 2 K 23$_{18}$ Ezk 13$_9$ Ps 51$_2$ 2 C 12$_5$ 1QS 9$_{11}$, יצא *go out* 2 C 28$_9$, עלה *go up* 1 K 14$_5$ 2 K 23$_2$ Ezk 13$_4$, ירד *go down* 1 S 10$_5$ 1 K 13$_8$, hi. *bring down* 1 K 1$_{32}$, נגשׁ *draw near* 1 K 18$_{36}$ 20$_{22}$, ni. 1 K 20$_{13}$, רוץ *run* Jr 23$_{21}$, תעה *go astray* Is 28$_7$, hi. *lead astray* Jr 23$_{13.32(mss)}$ Mc 3$_5$, טעה hi. *lead astray* Ezk 13$_9$, שׁגה *swerve* Is 28$_7$, פוק *reel* Is 28$_7$, פנה *turn* Jr 2$_{26}$, שׁוב hi. *bring back* 1 K 13$_{20.26.29}$ Jr 23$_{21}$ Ml 3$_{23}$ Ne 9$_{26}$ 4QapMos^a 1.1$_4$ ([להש]יבכה), סור hi. *remove* 1 K 20$_{38}$, שׁלח *send* Jr 29$_1$, אסף *gather*, i.e. cure 2 K 5$_3$, רכב hi. *cause to ride* 1 K 1$_{32.38.44}$.

ישׁב *dwell* 1 K 13$_{11.25}$, עמד *stand* 1 K 20$_{38}$ Jr 23$_{21}$, קום *arise* Dt 13$_2$=11QT 54$_8$ Dt 34$_{10}$ Si 48$_1$ 4QapMos^a 1.1$_4$, נוח *rest*, i.e. wait Hb 3$_1$ (or em. חכה pi. *wait*), hi. *place* 1 K 13$_{29}$, יחל pi. *wait* Ezk 13$_4$, שׁחה htpal. *bow down* 1 K 1$_{23}$, נדח hi. *thrust aside* Dt 13$_6$ 27$_{14}$, דחה ni. *be thrust down* Jr 23$_{11(mss)}$, דחח ni. *be thrust down* Jr 23$_{11}$, נפל *fall* Jr 23$_{11}$ 37$_{13}$, כשׁל *stumble* Ho 4$_5$, רגז *tremble* Hb 3$_1$ (or em. יִרְגְּזוּ אֲשֻׁרָי *my steps tremble*), מנע *withhold* Jr 42$_4$, נשׂא *lift* 1 K 13$_{29}$ 2 K 19$_2$||Is 37$_2$, מצא *find* 1 K 11$_{29}$ 13$_{26}$ Lm 2$_9$, סחר *trade* Jr 14$_{18}$, טוח *daub* Ezk 13$_{9.16}$ 22$_{28}$, כסה htp. *cover oneself* 1 K 11$_{29}$, חפשׂ htp. *disguise oneself* 1 K 20$_{38}$, בחר *choose* 1 K 18$_{25}$, משׁח *anoint* 1 K 1$_{34.45}$ 11QPs^a 28$_{8.13}$, חרץ *decide* 1 K 20$_{38}$, חזק pi. *strengthen* Jr 23$_{14}$, יעל hi. *benefit* Jr 23$_{32(mss)}$.

חנף *be impious* Jr 23$_{11}$, נאף *commit adultery* Jr 23$_{14}$, זיד hi. *be presumptuous* Dt 18$_{20}$=11QT 61$_{07}$ (הנביא] ... [יזיד), פחז *be wanton* Zp 3$_4$, בושׁ *be ashamed* Jr 2$_{26}$ Zc 13$_4$, תמה *be astonished* Jr 4$_9$, הבל hi. *cause to become vain* 23$_{16}$, לקח *take* 1 K 18$_{25}$ Jr 23$_{31}$ 28$_{10}$, גנב pi. *steal* Jr 23$_{30}$.

נתן *give* Dt 13$_2$=11QT 54$_8$, שׂים *place* 1 K 18$_{25}$, יצק *pour* 2 K 9$_4$, שׁפך *shed* perh. Lm 4$_{13}$, לבשׁ *wear* Zc 13$_4$, כלא pass. *be kept imprisoned* Jr 32$_2$, עצר *shut up* Si 48$_1$ (ע[צ]ר), גדר *build wall* Ezk 13$_4$, עשׂה *do* 1 K 18$_{25}$ Jr 32$_{32}$, מעט hi. *diminish* Si 48$_1$, חדל *cease* 2 C 25$_{16}$, שׁבר

break Jr 28_{12} Si 48_1, נכה ho. *be struck* Zc 13_5, גדד htpo. *lacerate oneself* 1 K 18_{25}, תמם *be consumed* Jr 14_{15}, אבד *perish* Jr 27_{15}, הרג ni. *be killed* Lm 2_{20}, מות *die* Dt 18_{20}=11QT 61_2 1 K 13_{29} Jr 26_8 28_{17} 38_9, ho. *be put to death* Dt 13_6=11QT 54_{15} 4QapMos^a 1.1_4, קבר *bury* 1 K 13_{29}.

<NOM CL> אֲנִי נָבִיא *I am a prophet* 1 K 13_{18}, לֹא־נָבִיא אָנֹכִי *I am not a prophet* Am 7_{14} Zc 13_5, נְבִאִים הֵם *they are prophets* Jr 27_{18}, כָּל־עַם י׳ נְבִיאִים *all the people of Y. are prophets* Nm 11_{29}, נָבִיא הוּא *he is a prophet* Gn 20_7, var. 4QapMos^a 1.1_6, נָבִיא ... הוּא הַזָּנָב *the prophet ... is the tail* Is 9_{14}, אֱוִיל הַנָּבִיא *the prophet is a fool* Ho 9_7, ההרים [המה] הנביא[ים] *the mountains are the prophets* 11QMelch 2_{17}, נְבִיאֵי הַבַּעַל אַרְבַּע מֵאוֹת וַחֲמִשִּׁים אִישׁ *the prophets of Baal are four hundred and fifty men* 1 K 18_{22}, נָבִיא פַּח יָקוֹשׁ עַל־כָּל־דְּרָכָיו *as for the prophet, a fowler's trap is on all his paths* Ho 9_8 (unless transfer athnach).

הִנֵּה נָתָן הַנָּבִיא *here is Nathan the prophet* 1 K 1_{23}, שָׁם אֲחִיָּה הַנָּבִיא *there is Ahijah the prophet* 1 K 14_2, יֵשׁ נָבִיא בְּיִשְׂרָאֵל *there is a prophet in Israel* 2 K 5_8, אֵין־עוֹד נָבִיא *there is no longer a prophet* Ps 74_9, הַאֵין פֹּה נָבִיא לַי׳ *is there not a prophet of Y. here?* 1 K 22_7||2 C 18_6 2 K 3_{11}, אַיֵּה נְבִיאֵיכֶם *where are your prophets?* Jr $37_{19(Qr)}$, הַנָּבִיא אֲשֶׁר בְּשֹׁמְרוֹן *the prophet who is in Samaria* 2 K 5_3, sim. 2 K 6_{12}, הַנָּבִיא אֲשֶׁר מִגַּת הַחֵפֶר *the prophet who was from Gath-hepher* 2 K 14_{25}, sim. Jr 28_1, נְבִיאֵיכֶם אֲשֶׁר־בְּקִרְבְּכֶם *your prophets who are among you* Jr 29_8.

<OBJ> צוה pi. *command* Dt $18_{18.20}$ 14_{14} $23_{32(mss)}$ Zc 1_6, קרא *call* 1 K 1_{10} 2 K 10_{19}, ענה *answer* Jr 23_{37}, נכר hi. *recognize* 1 K 20_{38}, זכר hi. *mention* Si 49_9 (נ[ב]יא) 49_{10}, פתה pi. *deceive* Ezk 14_9, ראה hi. *show* Hb 1_1, שׁמע *hear* 2 C 15_8 (or em.; see App.), עלה hi. *bring up* Jr 38_{10}, ירד hi. *bring down* 1 K 18_{40}, קום hi. *raise up* Dt $18_{15.18}$= 4QTestim 1_5 Jr 29_{15} 11QT 61_{02} ([נביא ... אקים]) 61_{05} ([נביא אקים]), עמד hi. *set up* Ne 6_7, שׁלח *send* Jg 6_8 1 K 14_4 Jr 7_{25} $14_{14.15}$ $23_{21.32(mss)}$ 25_4 26_5 27_{14} 28_9 $29_{8.19}$ 35_{15} 37_6 44_4 Ezk 13_4 Hg 1_{12} Ml 3_{23} 2 C 24_{19} 25_{15} 4QDibHam^a 1.3_{13} ([ש]לחתה) 11QPs^a 28_8, שׁוב hi. *bring back* 1 K 13_{23} 2 C 24_{19}, עבר hi. *cause to pass away* Zc 13_2, סור hi. *remove* Is 3_2, גלה hi. *exile* Jr 29_1, נטשׁ *forsake* Jr 23_{33}, שׁלך hi. *cast* Jr 38_9, ילד *give birth to* Jr 2_{26}.

מצא *find* 1 K 13_{23}, קדשׁ hi. *consecrate as* Jr 1_5, משׁח *anoint* Si 48_8, חתם *seal* Dn 9_{24}, קבץ *gather* 1 K $18_{19.20}$ 22_6||2 C 18_5, חבא hi. *hide* 1 K 18_4, סתר hi. *hide* Jr 36_{26}, תפשׂ *seize* 1 K 18_{40} Jr 26_8 37_{13}, לקח *take* 1 K 18_4 2 K 6_{12} Jr 36_{26} 38_{14} 43_6, נתן *give* 4QapPs^b 69_4, i.e. place Jr 20_2, כול pilp. *provide for* 1 K 18_4, קנה hi. *cause to possess* Zc 13_5 (or em. אָדָם הִקְנַנִי *a human has caused me to possess* to אֲדָמָה קִנְיָנִי *the land is my possession*), ישׁע hi. *save* Jr 2_{26}, כלא *imprison* Jr 32_2, עצם pi. *close eyes* Is 29_{10}, מלא pi. *fill* with drunkenness Jr 13_{13}, שׁתה hi. *give to drink* Jr 23_{15}, אכל *devour* Jr 2_{30}, hi. *feed* Jr 23_{15}, נכה hi. *strike* Jr 20_2 2 C 25_{15}, כרת hi. *cut off* 1 K 18_4, שׁמד hi. *destroy* Ezk 14_9, הרג *kill* 1 K 18_{13} $19_{1.10.14}$ Ne 9_{26}, מות hi. *kill* 1 K 13_{23}, שׁחט *kill* 1 K 18_{40}, קבר *bury* 1 K 13_{29}.

<CSTR> נביא אלוהים *prophet of God* 11QPs^a 28_{13}, נְבִיאֵי י׳ *prophets of Y.* 1 K $18_{4.13.13}$, אָבִיךָ *of your father* 2 K 3_{13}, אִמֶּךָ *of your mother* 2 K 3_{13}, כָּל־חֹזֶה *of every seer* 2 K $17_{13(Qr)}$ (or em. כָּל־נָבִיא וְכָל־חֹזֶה *every prophet and every seer*), הָאֲשֵׁרָה *of Asherah* 1 K 18_{19}, הַבַּעַל *of Baal* 1 K $18_{19.22.25.40}$ 2 K 10_{19}, יִשְׂרָאֵל *of Israel* Ezk $13_{2.16}$ 38_{17}, יְרוּשָׁלִַם *of Jerusalem* Jr $23_{14.15}$, שֹׁמְרוֹן *of Samaria* Jr 23_{13}, תַּרְמִת *of the deceit of* Jr 23_{26} (or em. וְנִבְּאֵי *and who prophesy*, i.e. נבא ni.), חֲלֹמוֹת *of dreams* Jr $23_{32(mss)}$ (L נִבְּאֵי), נְבִיאֵי מִלִּבָּם appar. *those who prophesy by their own heart* Ezk 13_2 (or em. לִנְבִיאֵי מִלִּבָּם to אֲלֵיהֶם *to them*), נביאי כזב *prophets of falsehood* 1QH 12_{16}.

בֶּן־נָבִיא *son of a prophet* Am 7_{14} Seal 258 (נבי[א]; others נבי *of Nabi*; Lachish, 7th cent.), בְּנֵי הַנְּבִאִים *sons of the prophets* 1 K 20_{35} 2 K $2_{3.5.7.15}$ $4_{1.38.38}$ 5_{22} 6_1 9_1, פי הנביא *mouth of the prophet* 4QapMos^a 1.1_1, פִּי הַנְּבִאִים *mouth of the prophets* Zc 8_9, פי נביאי *mouth of the prophets of* 1QH 12_{16}, פִּי כָּל־נְבִיאָיו *mouth of all his prophets* 1 K 22_{22}||2 C 18_{21}, כָּל־נְבִיאֶיךָ *of all your prophets* 1 K 22_{22}||2 C $18_{21(mss)}$ (L lacks כָּל־), צַוַּאר ... הַנָּבִיא *neck of ... the prophet* Jr $28_{10.12}$, אָזְנֵי ... *ears of ...* Jr 29_{29}, לֵב הַנְּבִאִים *heart of the prophets* Jr 23_{26}, עַצְמוֹת הַנָּבִיא *bones of the prophet* 2 K 23_{18}, הַנְּבִיאִים *of the prophets* Jr 8_1, דְּמֵי ... הַנְּבִיאִים *blood of the prophets* 2 K 9_7.

דְּבַר הַנָּבִיא *word of the prophet* Jr 28$_{9}$ 11QT 54$_{11}$, דִּבְרֵי הַנָּבִיא *words of the prophet* Dt 13$_{4}$ Hg 1$_{12}$ 1 C 29$_{29}$ 2 C 9$_{29}$ 12$_{15}$ (all four דִּבְרֵי ...) CD 7$_{10}$ (דברי ...) Lachish ost. 6$_{5}$ (ה[נבא]; others ה[שרם] *of the princes*), הַנְּבִיאִים *of the prophets* 1 K 22$_{13}$||2 C 18$_{12}$ (2 C הַנְּבִאִים) Jr 23$_{16}$ (הַנְּבִאִים) 26$_{5}$ (... הַנְּבִיאִים) 27$_{14}$ (הַנְּבִאִים) 1QpHab 2$_{9}$ 7$_{5}$ (both ... דברי), נְבִיאֵיכֶם *of your prophets* Jr 27$_{16}$, מִצְוַת ... הַנָּבִיא *commandment of ... the prophet* 2 C 29$_{25}$, [משפ]טי ... הנב[יא] *ordinances of ... the prophet* 11QM 2$_{1}$, מִדְרַשׁ הַנָּבִיא *discourse of the prophet* 2 C 13$_{22}$, ספר ... הנביא *book ... of the prophet* 4QMidr Eschat^{a} 3$_{15.16}$ 4$_{3}$ 6$_{1}$ ([ספר] ... הנב[יא]) 4QMidrEschat^{b} 1$_{2}$ (ספר ... הנ[ביא]) 1$_{5}$ ([... הנביא]) 1$_{6}$ ([ספר ... הנביא]) 1$_{9}$ (ספר ה[נביא]) 2$_{2}$ ([ספר ... הנביא]) 2$_{13}$ ([הנ[ביא]) 4QMg 7$_{1}$ ([ספר ...]) 4QSD 2$_{3}$ (ס[פר]), ספרי הנביאים *books of the prophets* 4QMMT C$_{10}$ (ספרי הנ[ביאים]) C$_{17}$ ([ספרי] [הנביאים]) CD 7$_{17}$, חֲזוֹן ... הַנָּבִיא *vision of ... the prophet* 2 C 32$_{32}$, חלמות נביאים *dreams of prophets* 11QPs^{a} 22$_{14}$.

עִיר הַנָּבִיא *city of the prophet* 1 K 13$_{29}$, חֶבֶל נְבִיאִים *band of prophets* 1 S 10$_{5.10}$ (נְבִאִים), לַהֲקַת *company of* 1 S 19$_{20}$ (or em. קְהִלַּת *assembly of*), חסדי נביאיך *loyalties of your prophets* 11QPs^{a} 22$_{5}$, עֲוֹן הַנָּבִיא *punishment of the prophet* Ezk 14$_{10}$, קֶשֶׁר נְבִיאֶיהָ *conspiracy of its prophets* Ezk 22$_{25}$ (or em. אֲשֶׁר נְשִׂיאֶיהָ *whose princes*), חַטֹּאת נְבִיאֶיהָ *sins of her prophets* Lm 4$_{13}$, יְמֵי ... הַנָּבִיא *days of ... the prophet* 2 C 35$_{18}$, קצי ... [הנביאים] *ages of ... the prophets* 1QSb 1$_{27}$.

יֶתֶר הַנְּבִיאִים *rest of the prophets* Ne 6$_{14}$, כָּל־נָבִיא *every prophet* 2 K 17$_{13(mss)}$, כָּל־הַנְּבִיאִים *all the prophets* 1 K 22$_{10.12}$||2 C 18$_{9.11}$ (הַנְּבִאִים), כָּל־נְבִיאֵי *all the prophets of* 2 K 17$_{13(Qr)}$ (Kt נביאו *his prophet*), כָּל־נְבִיאָיו *all his prophets* 1 K 22$_{22}$||2 C 18$_{21}$, כָּל־נְבִיאֶיךָ *all your prophets* 1 K 22$_{22}$||2 C 18$_{21(mss)}$ (L lacks כָּל־).

<APP> Shilonite 1 K 11$_{29}$, Ahijah 1 K 11$_{29}$ 14$_{2.18}$, Azariah 2 C 15$_{8}$ (if em.; see below), Daniel 4QMidr Eschat^{a} 4$_{3}$, Elijah 1 K 18$_{36}$ Ml 3$_{23}$ 2 C 21$_{12}$, Elisha 2 K 6$_{12}$ 9$_{1}$, Ezekiel 4QMidrEschat^{a} 3$_{16}$ 4QMidrEschat^{b} 2$_{13}$ (הנב[יא]) CD 3$_{21}$, Gad 1 S 22$_{5}$ 2 S 24$_{11}$, Habakkuk Hb 1$_{1}$ 3$_{1}$, Haggai Hg 1$_{1.3.12}$ 2$_{1.10}$, Hagui 11QM 2$_{1}$ (הנב[יא]), Hananiah Jr 28$_{1.5.10.12.15.17}$, Isaiah 2 K 19$_{2}$||Is 37$_{2}$ 2 K 20$_{1}$||Is 38$_{1}$ 2 K 20$_{11.14}$||Is 39$_{3}$ 2 C 26$_{22}$ 32$_{20.32}$ 4QMidr Eschat^{a} 3$_{15}$ 6$_{1}$ ([יש]עיה הנב[יא]) 4QMidrEschat^{b} 1$_{2}$ ([ישעיה הנ[ביא]) 1$_{5}$ 1$_{6}$ (both [ישעיה הנביא]) 4QMg 7$_{1}$ 4QSD 2$_{3}$ 11QMelch 2$_{15}$ ([יעש]יה) CD 4$_{13}$ 7$_{10}$, Jehu 1 K 16$_{7.12}$, Jeremiah Jr 20$_{2}$ 25$_{2}$ 28$_{5+5t}$ 29$_{1.29}$ 32$_{2}$ 34$_{6}$ 36$_{8.26}$ 37$_{2.3.6.13}$ 38$_{9.10.14}$ 42$_{2.4}$ 43$_{6}$ 45$_{1}$ 46$_{1.13}$ 47$_{1}$ 49$_{34}$ 50$_{1}$ 51$_{59}$ Dn 9$_{2}$ 2 C 36$_{12}$ 4QpsEzek^{a} 16.1$_{2.6}$ 25$_{1}$ ([יר]מיהו הנב[יא]) 4QpsEzek^{e} 3$_{5}$ ([י]רמיה), Job Si 49$_{9}$ (נ[ב]יא), Jonah 2 K 14$_{25}$, Nathan 2 S 7$_{2}$||1 C 17$_{1}$ 2 S 12$_{25}$ 1 K 1$_{8+8t}$ Ps 51$_{2}$ 1 C 29$_{29}$ 2 C 9$_{29}$ 29$_{25}$, Oded 2 C 15$_{8}$ (or ins. אֲשֶׁר נִבָּא עֲזַרְיָהוּ בֶּן־ *which Azariah the son of* Oded *prophesied*), Samuel 2 C 35$_{18}$, Shemaiah 2 C 12$_{5.15}$, Zechariah Zc 1$_{1.7}$ 4QMidrEschat^{b} 2$_{2}$ ([זכריה הנביא]) CD 19$_{7}$.

אִישׁ *man* Jg 6$_{8}$ Zp 3$_{4}$, i.e. each Jr 23$_{30}$ Zc 13$_{4}$, בֵּן *son* 1 K 16$_{7}$ 2 K 14$_{25}$ 19$_{2}$||Is 37$_{2}$ 2 K 20$_{1}$||Is 38$_{1}$ Jr 28$_{1}$ Zc 1$_{1.7}$ 1 C 25$_{1(Kt)}$ 2 C 15$_{8}$ (if em.; see above) 26$_{22}$ 32$_{20.32}$ CD 4$_{13}$ 7$_{10}$, נַעַר *lad* 2 K 9$_{4}$, עֶבֶד *servant* 1 K 14$_{18}$ 2 K 9$_{7}$ 17$_{23}$ 21$_{10}$ 24$_{2}$ Jr 7$_{25}$ 25$_{4}$ 26$_{5}$ 29$_{19}$ 35$_{15}$ 44$_{4}$ Ezk 38$_{17}$ Am 3$_{7}$ Zc 1$_{6}$ Dn 9$_{6.10}$ Ezr 9$_{11}$ 1QS 1$_{3}$ 1QpHab 2$_{9}$ 7$_{5}$ 1QSb 1$_{27}$ (עבדיו [הנביאים]) 4QpHos^{a} 1.2$_{5}$ 4QPrayers^{b} 2$_{4}$ 4QpsMos^{e} 2.1$_{5}$ 4QDibHam^{a} 1.3$_{13}$, חֹזֶה *seer* 2 S 24$_{11}$, תַּחֲלִיף *successor* Si 48$_{8}$, נְבוּאָה *prophecy* 2 C 15$_{8}$ (הַנְּבוּאָה עֹדֵד הַנָּבִיא *the prophecy, [namely that of] Oded the prophet*; or em.; see above), עַיִן *eye* Is 29$_{10}$.

<ADJ> זָקֵן *old* 1 K 13$_{11.25.29}$, רִאשׁוֹן *former* Zc 1$_{4}$ 7$_{7.12}$, נָבָל *foolish* or *outcast* Ezk 13$_{3}$, אֶחָד *one* 1 K 13$_{11}$ 20$_{13}$, הוּא *that* Dt 13$_{4.6}$=11QT 54$_{11.15}$ Dt 18$_{20}$=11QT 61$_{2}$ Ezk 14$_{9}$.

<PREP> לְ of direction, *to*, + אמר *say* 1 K 18$_{25}$ Ezk 13$_{2}$ (or em.; see Cstr.) 2 C 25$_{15}$, ספר pi. *tell* 1 K 13$_{11}$, קרא ni. *be called*, i.e. be named 1 S 9$_{9}$.

לְ of benefit, *to, for*, + היה *be* Jr 23$_{11}$, חבשׁ *saddle* 1 K 13$_{23.26}$, עשׂה *do* Jr 38$_{9}$, ni. *be done* Jr 5$_{13}$.

לְ *as*, + קום hi. *raise up* sons Am 2$_{11}$, אמן ni. *be attested* 1 S 3$_{20}$, משׁח *anoint* 1 K 19$_{16}$; *concerning* Jr 23$_{9}$; of possession, *of, (belonging) to* Hb 3$_{1}$.

לְ introducing object, + קרא *call* 1 K 13$_{2}$, מצא *find*, i.e. befall Ne 9$_{32}$, בדל hi. *set apart* 1 C 25$_{1(Kt)}$ (Qr הַנִּבְּאִים *who prophesy*), התל pi. *mock* 1 K 18$_{25}$, רעע hi. *harm* Ps 105$_{15}$.

בְּ of place, *within, among* 1 S 10$_{11.12}$ 19$_{24}$ Jr 5$_{13}$, + ראה *see* Jr 23$_{13.14}$; *with*, + דבר pi. *speak* Nm 12$_{6}$; of agent, instrument, *by (means of), through*, ענה *answer*

1 S 28_{6}, עלה hi. *bring up* Ho 12_{14}, שׁמר ni. *be preserved* Ho 12_{14}, חצב *hew* Ho 6_{5}; introducing object, + אמן hi. *believe* 2 C 20_{20}, רעע hi. *harm* 1 C 16_{22}, תעע htp. *mock* 2 C 36_{16}.

בְּיַד *by means of, through* 2 C 29_{25}, + היה *be* 1 K 16_{7} Hg $1_{1.3}$ 2_{1}, אמר *say* 11QMelch 2_{15} ([ביד]), דבר pi. *speak* 1 K 14_{18} 16_{12} 2 K 14_{25} 17_{23} 21_{10} 24_{2} Jr 37_{2} 50_{1} Ezk 38_{17} CD 4_{13} 4QPrayers[b] 2_{4} (דבר[תה]), ספר pi. *tell* 1QpHab 2_{9}, ענה *answer* 1 S 28_{15}, צוה pi. *command* Ezr 9_{11} 1QS 1_{3} 4QpsMos[e] 2.1_{5} (ב[י]ד), קרא *proclaim* Zc 7_{7}, דמה pi. *use parables* Ho 12_{11}, עוד hi. *testify* 2 K 17_{13} Ne 9_{30}, קום hi. *promise* CD 3_{21}, כתב pass. *be written* CD 19_{7}, שׁלח *send* 2 S 12_{25} Zc 7_{12} 4QpHos[a] 1.2_{5} ([ביד]), נתן *give* Dn 9_{10}.

מִן of direction, *from*, + בוא *come* 2 C 21_{12}, בקשׁ pi. *seek* Ezk 7_{26}, אבד *perish* Jr 18_{18}=4QMidrEschat[b] 4_{6} ([תאבד]); *from* (+ עַד *to*, i.e. both … and) Jr 6_{13} 8_{10}; of cause, *on account of*, + גור *fear* Dt 18_{22}=11QT 61_{4}; partitive, *one of, from among* 1 K 18_{13} 20_{41}.

אֶל *to*, + היה *be* 2 S 24_{11} 1 K 13_{20} Jr 37_{6} 46_{1} 47_{1} 49_{34} Hg 2_{10} Zc 1_{7} Dn 9_{2}, אמר *say* 2 S 7_{2}||1 C 17_{1} 1 K 20_{38} 22_{6}||2 C 18_{5} Jr $23_{33.37}$ 26_{16} $28_{5.15}$ 42_{2} Zc 7_{3} 13_{5}, דבר pi. *speak* Jr 14_{14} 23_{21} 46_{13}, גלה *reveal* Am 3_{7}, שׁמע *listen* Dt 18_{15} Jr 27_{9} Dn 9_{6}11QT 61_{02} ([נביא ... אליו תשמעון]), ידע htp. *make oneself known* Nm 12_{6}, הלך *go* 2 K $3_{13.13}$, בוא *come* 1 K 14_{2} Ezk $14_{4.7}$, שׁלח *send* 2 K 19_{2}||Is 37_{2} Jr 29_{1} 37_{3}.

אֶל *against* Ezk 13_{4}, + היה *be* Ezk 13_{9}, נבא ni. *prophesy* Ezk 13_{2}.

עַל *upon, over*, + בוא (of sun) *set* Mc 3_{6}, קדר *be dark* Mc 3_{6}, שׁפך *pour* 1 K 18_{25}, עמד *stand* 1 S 19_{20}; *to* Ezk 13_{3}, + דבר pi. *speak* Ho 12_{11}; *against* Jr $23_{30.31.32(mss)}$, + בוא hi. *bring* Jr 23_{11}, נטה *stretch* hand Ezk 14_{9}; *concerning*, + אמר *say* Jr 14_{15} 23_{15} Mc 3_{5}; introducing object, + צוה pi. *command* Am 2_{12}.

עִם *with*, + נבא ni. *prophesy* 1 S 10_{11}, htp. 1 S 10_{5}.

אֵת *with* Jr 23_{28} 27_{18}.

מֵאֵת *from*, + בוא *come* Lachish ost. 3_{20}, יצא *go out* Jr 23_{15}, דרשׁ *inquire* 1 K 22_{7}||2 C 18_{6} 2 K 3_{11}.

בְּתוֹךְ *among*, + נבא htp. *prophesy* 1 S 10_{10}.

לִפְנֵי *before* 1 S 10_{5} 2 K 5_{3}, + נפל *fall* Jr 42_{2}.

מִלִּפְנֵי *from before*, + כנע ni. *humble oneself* 2 C 36_{12}.

<COLL> נָבִיא || חֹזֶה *seer* Is 29_{10} Mc 3_{6} (+) 1 C 29_{29} 2 C 12_{15}, רֹאֶה *seer* 1 S 9_{9} (+) 1 C 29_{29}, קֹסֵם *diviner* Is 3_{2} Jr 27_{9} 29_{8} Mc 3_{6} (+), עֹנֵן *soothsayer* Jr 27_{9}, כַּשָּׁף *sorcerer* Jr 27_{9}, מַלְאָךְ *messenger* 2 C 36_{16}, כֹּהֵן *priest* 2 K 10_{19} (+) 2 K 23_{2} Is 28_{7} Jr 2_{8} (+) 2_{26} 4_{9} 5_{31} (+) 6_{13} $8_{1.10}$ 13_{13} 14_{18} 18_{18} $23_{11.33.34}$ $26_{7.8.11.16}$ 29_{1} 32_{32} Ezk 7_{26} (+) Mc 3_{11} Zp 3_{4} (+) Zc 7_{3} Lm 2_{20} 4_{13} Ne 9_{32}, חָכָם *wise one* Jr 18_{18}, שֹׁפֵט *judge* Is 3_{2}, זָקֵן *elder* Is 3_{2} Ezk 7_{26} (+), נָזִיר *Nazirite* Am $2_{11.12}$ (+), מָשִׁיחַ *anointed one* Ps 105_{15}||1 C 16_{22} 1QS 9_{11} (+), מֶלֶךְ *king* Jr 2_{26} 4_{9} (+) 8_{1} 13_{13} 32_{32} Lm 2_{9} (+) Ne 9_{32}, שַׂר *prince* Jr 2_{26} 4_{9} (+) 8_{1} 32_{32} Lm 2_{9} (+) Ne 9_{32}, ראשׁ *head*, i.e. chief Mc 3_{11}, חָסִיד *loyal one* 11QPs[a] 22_{5}, עַם *people* 2 K 23_{2} Jr $23_{33.34}$ $26_{7.8}$ 29_{1}, יֹשֵׁב *inhabitant* 2 K 23_{2} (+) Jr 8_{1} 13_{13} 32_{32}, אִישׁ *man* 2 K 23_{2} (+) Jr 32_{32} Ho 9_{7} (אִישׁ הָרוּחַ *man of the spirit*), אָב *father* Zc 1_{5} (+) Ne 9_{32}, חֲלוֹם *dream* 1 S $28_{6.15}$ Jr 27_{9} 29_{8} (+), חָזוֹן *vision* Dn 9_{24}, אוּרִים *Urim* 1 S 28_{6}.

+ נְבִיאָה *prophet* (fem.) Ne 6_{14}, חֹלֵם *dreamer* Dt $13_{2.4.6}$=11QT $54_{8.11.15}$, עֹבֵד *worshipper* 2 K 10_{19}, עֶבֶד *servant* 2 K 9_{7}, תפשׂ ptc. *one who handles* law Jr 2_{8}, רֹעֶה *shepherd*, i.e. ruler Jr 2_{8}.

:: זָקֵן *elder* Is 9_{14}.

נְבִיא לַי׳ *a prophet of Y.* 1 S 3_{20} 1 K 18_{22} 22_{7}||2 C 18_{6} 2 K 3_{11} 2 C 28_{9}, שנים עשר הנביאים *the twelve prophets* Si 49_{10}, מֵאָה נְבִאִים *a hundred prophets* 1 K 18_{4}, נְבִיאֵי הָאֲשֵׁרָה אַרְבַּע מֵאוֹת *the four hundred prophets of Asherah* 1 K 18_{19}, נְבִיאֵי הַבַּעַל אַרְבַּע מֵאוֹת וַחֲמִשִּׁים *the four hundred and fifty prophets of Baal* 1 K 18_{19}.

נוֹתַרְתִּי נָבִיא *I remain as a prophet* 1 K 18_{22}.

Also 4QBibPar 6_{6} 4QSD 7.2_{8} (הנ[ביאים]) 4QapJoshua[b] 36_{2} 4QparaKings 31_{5} (נ[ב]יאים) 4QNarrA 13_{3} (הנבי[ ]) Lachish ost. 16_{5}.

<SYN> חֹזֶה *seer*, רֹאֶה *seer*, קֹסֵם *diviner*, עֹנֵן *soothsayer*, כַּשָּׁף *sorcerer*, מַלְאָךְ *messenger*, כֹּהֵן *priest*, חָכָם *wise one*, שֹׁפֵט *judge*, זָקֵן *elder*, נָזִיר *Nazirite*, מָשִׁיחַ *anointed one*, מֶלֶךְ *king*, שַׂר *prince*, ראשׁ *head*, חָסִיד *loyal one*, עַם *people*, יֹשֵׁב *inhabitant*, אִישׁ *man*, אָב *father*, חֲלוֹם *dream*, חָזוֹן *vision*, אוּרִים *Urim*.

<ANT> זָקֵן *elder*.*

→ נבא *prophesy*.

נְבִיאָה $_{6.0.1}$ n.f. **prophet** (fem.), prophesying with song (Ex 15$_{20}$), as judge (Jg 4$_{4}$), giving word of Y. (2 K 22$_{14}$|| 2 C 34$_{22}$), opponent of Nehemiah (Ne 6$_{14}$), married to Isaiah (Is 8$_{3}$), <SUBJ> אמר *say* Jg 4$_4$ 2 K 22$_{14}$||2 C 34$_{22}$, קרא *call* Jg 4$_4$, הלך *go* Jg 4$_4$, שׁלח *send* Jg 4$_4$, משׁך *draw* Jg 4$_4$, ישׁב *sit* Jg 4$_4$, *dwell* 2 K 22$_{14}$||2 C 34$_{22}$, הרה *conceive* Is 8$_3$, ילד *give birth* Is 8$_3$, לקח *take* Ex 15$_{20}$, שׁפט *judge* Jg 4$_4$. <APP> Deborah Jg 4$_4$, Huldah 2 K 22$_{14}$||2 C 34$_{22}$, Miriam Ex 15$_{20}$, Noadiah Ne 6$_{14}$, אִשָּׁה *wife* Jg 4$_4$, אָחוֹת *sister* Ex 15$_{20}$. <PREP> לְ introducing object, + זכר *remember* Ne 6$_{14}$ (+ נָבִיא *prophet*); אֶל *to*, + אמר *say* Jg 4$_4$, דבר pi. *speak* 2 K 22$_{14}$||2 C 34$_{22}$, הלך *go* 2 K 22$_{14}$||2 C 34$_{22}$, עלה *go up* Jg 4$_4$, קרב *draw near* Is 8$_3$, שׁלח *send* 2 K 22$_{14}$||2 C 34$_{22}$; אַחֲרֵי *after*, + יצא *go out* Ex 15$_{20}$.

Also 4QNarrA 15$_2$.*

⇒ נבא *prophesy*.

נְבָיוֹת $_5$ pr.n.m. **Nebaioth**—נְבָיֹת—**1.** firstborn son of Ishmael, <NOM CL> אֵלֶּה שְׁמוֹת בְּנֵי יִשְׁמָעֵאל ... נְבָיֹת *these are the names of the sons of Ishmael ... Nebaioth* Gn 25$_{13}$, אֵלֶּה תֹּלְדוֹתָם ... נְבָיוֹת *these are their genealogies ... Nebaioth* 1 C 1$_{29}$. <CSTR> אֲחוֹת נְבָיוֹת *sister of Nebaioth* Gn 28$_9$ 36$_3$. <APP> בְּכֹר *firstborn* Gn 25$_{13}$ 1 C 1$_{29}$.

2. Arabian tribe, <CSTR> אֵילֵי נְבָיוֹת *rams of Nebaioth* Is 60$_7$ (+ קֵדָר *Kedar*).

*[נבך] vb. **pour out, Qal,** <SUBJ> worshipper Ps 69$_{11}$ (if em. וָאֶבְכֶּה *and I wept* to וָאֶבֹּכָה *and I poured out*). <PREP> בְּ of accompaniment, *with, in*, + צוֹם *fasting* Ps 69$_{11}$ (if em.; see Subj.).

Hi. cause to flow, <SUBJ> Y. Ps 84$_7$ (if em. עֹבְרֵי בְּעֵמֶק הַבָּכָא *ones who pass through the valley of Baca* to עֹבְרֵי בְּעֵמֶק הִבְכָא *he caused brooks to flow in the valley*).

⇒ נֵבֶךְ I *spring*.

[נֵ֫בֶךְ] I $_1$ n.[m.] **spring**—pl. cstr. נִבְכֵי—<NOM CL> אֵין ... נִבְכֵי־מָיִם *there were no ... springs of water* Pr 8$_{24}$ (if em.; see Cstr.). <CSTR> נֵבֶךְ יַעְזֵר *spring of Jazer* Jr 48$_{32}$ (if em. מִבְּכִי *more than for the weeping of* Jazer), נִבְכֵי־יָם *springs of the sea* Jb 38$_{16}$ (unless נֵבֶךְ II *sandy depths*; + תְּהוֹם *deep*), מָיִם *of water* Pr 8$_{24}$ (if em. נִכְבַּדֵּי *heavy ones of*, i.e. perh. springs filled with). <APP> מַעְיָן *spring* Pr 8$_{24}$ (if em.; see Cstr.). <PREP> לְ *for, on account of*, + בכה *weep* Jr 48$_{32}$ (if em.; see Cstr.); עַד *to*, + בוא *come* Jb 38$_{16}$ (unless נֵבֶךְ II *sandy depths*). <COLL> נֵבֶךְ as vocative, *O Jazer* Jr 48$_{32}$ (if em.; see Cstr.).*

⇒ נבך *pour out*.

*[נֵ֫בֶךְ] II $_1$ **sandy depths** (unless נֵבֶךְ I *spring*)—pl. cstr. נִבְכֵי—<CSTR> נִבְכֵי־יָם *sandy depths of the sea* Jb 38$_{16}$ (+ תְּהוֹם *deep*). <PREP> עַד *to*, + בוא *come* Jb 38$_{16}$.

נבל I $_{20.1.2}$ vb. **wither—Qal** $_{20.1.2}$ Pf. נָבֵל, נָבְלָה; impf. יִבּוֹל, 2ms תִּבֹּל, יִבְּלוּ (יִבּוֹלוּן); + waw וַנָּבֶל; ptc. נֹבֵל (Si נוֹבֵל), נֹבֶלֶת; inf. abs. נָבֹל; cstr. נְבֹל—**1. wither, fade, drop, decay, crumble away,** <SUBJ> Israelites Is 64$_5$, מֵרַע *wicked one* Ps 37$_2$, עשׂה ptc. *one who does* wrong Ps 37$_2$, בטח ptc. *one who trusts* in riches Pr 11$_{28}$ (if em. יִפֹּל *he will fall* to יִבֹּל), צָבָא *host* of heaven Is 34$_4$, עָלֶה *leaf* Is 1$_{30}$ 34$_{4.4}$ (unless נֹבֶלֶת is n.f. I *withered fruit* or II *unripe figs*) Jr 8$_{13}$ Ezk 47$_2$ Ps 1$_3$ 1QH 16$_{26}$, צִיץ *flower* Is 28$_1$ 40$_{7.8}$, צִיצָה *blossom* Is 28$_4$ (צִיצַת נֹבֵל; or em. צִיצַת נֵבֶל *blossom of a young shoot*), עַיִן *eye*, i.e. bloom Is 28$_4$ (if em. יִבְלָעֶנָּה *he swallows it* to יִבֹּל עֵינָהּ *its bloom withers*), אֶרֶץ *earth* Is 24$_4$ (or del.), תֵּבֵל *world* Is 24$_4$, הַר *mountain* Jb 14$_{18}$ (or em. יִפּוֹל *it will fall*), זֶה *this (leaf)* Si 14$_{18}$.

<PREP> כְּ *as*, + עָלֶה *leaf* Is 64$_5$, נֵץ *flower* 1QH 18$_{32}$; מִן of direction, *from*, + גֶּפֶן *vine* Is 34$_4$, תְּאֵנָה *fig tree* Is 34$_4$; לִפְנֵי *before* 1QH 18$_{32}$, + חֹם *heat* 1QH 16$_{26}$.

<COLL> יבשׁ || נבל *be dry* Is 40$_{7.8}$, מלל *wither* Ps 37$_2$, אמל pulal *languish* Is 24$_4$, אבל *mourn* Is 24$_4$, תמם *come to an end* Ezk 47$_{12}$; + מקק ni. *rot* Is 34$_4$, גלל ni. *be rolled up* Is 34$_4$, נפל *fall* Jb 14$_{18}$; :: קום *stand* Is 40$_8$.

2. wear oneself out (Ex 18$_{18.18}$), **lose heart** (2 S 22$_{46}$||Ps 18$_{46}$), <SUBJ> עַם *people* Ex 18$_{18.18}$, Moses Ex 18$_{18.18}$, בֵּן *son* of foreigner 2 S 22$_{46}$||Ps 18$_{46}$. <COLL> נָבֹל תִּבֹּל *you will utterly wear yourself out* Ex 18$_{18}$.

<SYN> §1 יבשׁ *be dry*, מלל *wither*, אמל pulal *languish*, אבל *mourn*, תמם *come to an end*.

<ANT> §1 קום *stand*.*

⇨ נְבֵלָה *corpse,* נֹבֶלֶת *withered fruit.*

נבל II 5.1.1 vb. **be foolish—Qal** 1 Pf נָבַלְתָּ—**be foolish,** <SUBJ> Ithiel and Ucal Pr 30$_{32}$ (+ נשׂא htp. *exalt oneself,* זמם *plot evil*).

Pi. 4 Impf. 2ms תְּנַבֵּל; + waw וַיְנַבֵּל; ptc. מְנַבֵּל—**treat as a fool, spurn, dishonour,** <SUBJ> Y. Jr 14$_{21}$ Na 3$_{6}$, Jeshurun Dt 32$_{15}$ (+ נטשׁ *forsake*), בֵּן *son* Mc 7$_{6}$ (+ קום *rise up* against). <OBJ> אָב *father* Mc 7$_{6}$, עִיר *city* Na 3$_{6}$, צוּר *rock* of salvation Dt 32$_{15}$, כִּסֵּא *throne* of glory Jr 14$_{21}$.

Hi. 0.0.1 Inf. Q הביל—**make foolish,** <PREP> בְּ of instrument, *by (means of), with,* + פַּחַז *wantonness* 4QWiles 1$_{15}$.

Htp. 0.1 Inf. Si התנבל—**act foolishly,** <SUBJ> בֵּן *son* Si 9$_{7}$. <PREP> בְּ of cause, *on account of,* + מַרְאֶה *sight* of eyes Si 9$_{7}$.*

⇨ נָבָל I *foolish,* V *Nabal,* נְבָלָה *folly,* נַבְלוּת *lewdness.*

*__נבל__ III 5.1.1 vb. **be sacrilegious; treat with contempt—Qal** 1 Pf. נָבַלְתָּ—**be sacrilegious,** <SUBJ> Ithiel and Ucal Pr 30$_{32}$ (+ נשׂא htp. *exalt oneself,* זמם *plot evil*).

Pi. 4 Impf. 2ms תְּנַבֵּל; + waw וַיְנַבֵּל; ptc. מְנַבֵּל—**treat with contempt, spurn, dishonour,** <SUBJ> Y. Jr 14$_{21}$ Na 3$_{6}$, Jeshurun Dt 32$_{15}$ (+ נטשׁ *forsake*), בֵּן *son* Mc 7$_{6}$ (+ קום *rise up* against). <OBJ> אָב *father* Mc 7$_{6}$, עִיר *city* Na 3$_{6}$, צוּר *rock* of salvation Dt 32$_{15}$, כִּסֵּא *throne* of glory Jr 14$_{21}$.

Hi. 0.0.1 Inf. Q הביל—**dishonour,** <PREP> בְּ of instrument, *by (means of), with,* + פַּחַז *wantonness* 4QWiles 1$_{15}$.

Htp. 0.1 Inf. Si התנבל—**act sacrilegiously,** <SUBJ> בֵּן *son* Si 9$_{7}$. <PREP> בְּ of cause, *on account of,* + מַרְאֶה *sight* of eyes Si 9$_{7}$.

⇨ נָבָל II *outcast, sacrilegious,* V *Nabal,* נְבָלָה II *sacrilege,* נַבְלוּת *lewdness.*

*__נבל__ IV 5.1.1 vb. **act ignominiously—Qal** 1 Pf. נָבַלְתָּ—**act ignominiously,** <SUBJ> Ithiel and Ucal Pr 30$_{32}$ (+ נשׂא htp. *exalt oneself,* זמם *plot evil*).

Pi. 4 Impf. 2ms תְּנַבֵּל; + waw וַיְנַבֵּל; ptc. מְנַבֵּל—**treat ignominiously,** <SUBJ> Y. Jr 14$_{21}$ Na 3$_{6}$, Jeshurun Dt 32$_{15}$ (+ נטשׁ *forsake*), בֵּן *son* Mc 7$_{6}$ (+ קום *rise up* against). <OBJ> אָב *father* Mc 7$_{6}$, עִיר *city* Na 3$_{6}$, צוּר *rock* of salvation Dt 32$_{15}$, כִּסֵּא *throne* of glory Jr 14$_{21}$.

Hi. 0.0.1 Inf. Q הביל—**dishonour, treat ignominiously,** <PREP> בְּ of instrument, *by (means of), with,* + פַּחַז *wantonness* 4QWiles 1$_{15}$.

Htp. 0.1 Inf. Si התנבל—**act ignominiously,** <SUBJ> בֵּן *son* Si 9$_{7}$. <PREP> בְּ of cause, *on account of,* + מַרְאֶה *sight* of eyes Si 9$_{7}$.

⇨ נָבָל IV *ignominious.*

נָבָל I 18.4.3 adj. **foolish** (unless נָבָל II *outcast, sacrilegious person,* or IV *low-class*)—pl. masc. נְבָלִים, fem. נְבָלוֹת—**1.** attributively of עַם *people* Dt 32$_{6}$ (:: חָכָם *wise*) Ps 74$_{18}$, גּוֹי *nation* Dt 32$_{21}$ Si 49$_{5}$ 50$_{26}$ (unless נָבָל III *noble*) 11QM 2$_{1}$ ([הנבו]ל), נָבִיא *prophet* Ezk 13$_{3}$, דָּבָר *word* 1QS 7$_{9}$ CD 10$_{17}$ (|| רֵק *empty*).

2. as noun, **fool, a.** masc., <SUBJ> היה *be* Jr 17$_{11}$, אמר Ps 14$_{1}$||53$_{2}$, דבר pi. *speak* Is 32$_{6}$, שׂבע *be satisfied* Pr 30$_{22}$. <CSTR> אֲבִי נָבָל *father of a fool* Pr 17$_{21}$ (+ כְּסִיל *fool*), בְּנֵי *sons of* Jb 30$_{8}$ (+ בְּלִי־שֵׁם *without a name,* i.e. disreputable), לב נבל *heart of a fool* Si 36$_{5}$, חֶרְפַּת נָבָל *reproach of a fool* Ps 39$_{9}$, מוֹת *death of* 2 S 3$_{33}$, אַחַד הַנְּבָלִים *one of the fools* 2 S 13$_{13}$. <PREP> לְ of benefit, *to, for* Pr 17$_{7}$ (:: נָדִיב *noble*); of direction, *to,* + קרא ni. *be called,* i.e. be named Is 32$_{5}$ (:: נָדִיב), יצע hi. *extend* Si 42$_{7}$; מִן of direction, *from* Ps 74$_{22}$.

b. fem., <CSTR> אַחַת הַנְּבָלוֹת *one of the foolish women* Jb 2$_{10}$.

Also 4QapJoseph^{a} 1$_{10}$.

<SYN> §1 רֵק *empty.*

<ANT> §1 חָכָם *wise;* §2 נָדִיב *noble.*

⇨ נבל II *be foolish.*

*__נָבָל__ II 18.4.3 adj. **outcast, sacrilegious person** (unless נָבָל I *foolish* or IV *low-class*)—pl. masc. נְבָלִים, fem. נְבָלוֹת—**1.** attributively of עַם *people* Dt 32$_{6}$ (:: חָכָם *wise*) Ps 74$_{18}$, גּוֹי *nation* Dt 32$_{21}$ Si 49$_{5}$ 50$_{26}$ 11QM 2$_{1}$ ([הנבו]ל), נָבִיא *prophet* Ezk 13$_{3}$, דָּבָר *word* 1QS 7$_{9}$ CD 10$_{17}$ (|| רֵק *empty*).

2. as noun, **outcast, sacrilegious person, a.** masc.,

<SUBJ> היה *be* Jr 17_{11}, אמר Ps 14_1||53_2, דבר pi. *speak* Is 32_6, שׂבע *be satisfied* Pr 30_{22}. <CSTR> אֲבִי נָבָל *father of a sacrilegious* son Pr 17_{21} (+ כְּסִיל *fool*), בְּנֵי *sons of* an outcast Jb 30_8 (+ בְּלִי־שֵׁם *without a name*, i.e. disreputable), לב נבל *heart of a sacrilegious person* Si 36_5, חֶרְפַּת נָבָל *reproach of an outcast* Ps 39_9, מוֹת *death of* 2 S 3_{33}, אַחַד הַנְּבָלִים *one of the sacrilegious* 2 S 13_{13}. <PREP> לְ of benefit, *to, for* Pr 17_7 (:: נָדִיב *noble*); of direction, *to*, + קרא ni. *be called*, i.e. be named Is 32_5 (:: נָדִיב), יצע hi. *extend* Si 42_7; מִן of direction, *from* Ps 74_{22}.

b. fem., <CSTR> אַחַת הַנְּבָלוֹת *one of the outcast women* Jb 2_{10}.

Also 4QapJoseph[a] 1_{10}.

<SYN> §1 רֵק *empty*.

<ANT> §1 חָכָם *wise*; §2 נָדִיב *noble*.

⇒ נבל III *treat with contempt*.

*נָבָל III$_{1}$ adj. **noble, 1.** attributively of גּוֹי *nation* Si 50_{26}.

2. in nom. cl., used predicatively, נָבָל שמוֹ *his name is noble* 1 S 25_{25} (unless נָבָל V *Nabal*).

*נָבָל IV$_{18.4.3}$ adj. **low-class, ignominious** (unless נָבָל I *foolish* or II *outcast, sacrilegious person*)—pl. masc. נְבָלִים, fem. נְבָלוֹת—**1.** attributively of עַם *people* Dt 32_6 (:: חָכָם *wise*) Ps 74_{18}, גּוֹי *nation* Dt 32_{21} Si 49_5 50_{26} 11QM 2_1 (הנבו[ל]), נָבִיא *prophet* Ezk 13_3, דָּבָר *word* 1QS 7_9 CD 10_{17} (|| רֵק *empty*).

2. as noun, **low-class, ignominious person, a.** masc., <SUBJ> היה *be* Jr 17_{11}, אמר Ps 14_1||53_2, דבר pi. *speak* Is 32_6, שׂבע *be satisfied* Pr 30_{22}. <CSTR> אֲבִי נָבָל *father of a ignominious* son Pr 17_{21} (+ כְּסִיל *fool*), בְּנֵי *sons of* a low-class person Jb 30_8 (+ בְּלִי־שֵׁם *without a name*, i.e. disreputable), לב נבל *heart of an ignominious person* Si 36_5, חֶרְפַּת נָבָל *reproach of an ignominious person* Ps 39_9, מוֹת *death of* 2 S 3_{33}, אַחַד הַנְּבָלִים *one of the ignominious* 2 S 13_{13}. <PREP> לְ of benefit, *to, for* Pr 17_7 (:: נָדִיב *noble*); of direction, *to*, + קרא ni. *be called*, i.e. be named Is 32_5 (:: נָדִיב), יצע hi. *extend* Si 42_7; מִן of direction, *from* Ps 74_{22}.

b. fem., <CSTR> אַחַת הַנְּבָלוֹת *one of the low-born women* Jb 2_{10}.

Also 4QapJoseph[a] 1_{10}.

<SYN> §1 רֵק *empty*.

<ANT> §1 חָכָם *wise*; §2 נָדִיב *noble*.

⇒ נבל IV *act ignominiously*.

נָבָל V$_{22}$ pr.n.m. **Nabal,** livestock farmer and first husband of Abigail, <SUBJ> היה *be* 1 S 25_{37}, אמר *say* 1 S 25_{10}, ענה *answer* 1 S 25_{10}, שׁאל *ask* 1 S 25_5, ידע *know* 1 S 25_{10}, לקח *take* 1 S 25_{10}, נתן *give* 1 S $25_{5.10}$, גזז *shear* sheep 1 S 25_4, טבח *slaughter* 1 S 25_{10}, מות *die* 1 S $25_{38.39}$. <NOM CL> שֵׁם הָאִישׁ נָבָל *the name of the man was Nabal* 1 S 25_3, var. 1 S 25_{25} (unless נָבָל II *noble*). <OBJ> נגף *strike* 1 S 25_{38}. <CSTR> אֵשֶׁת נָבָל *wife of Nabal* 1 S 25_{14} 27_3 30_5 2 S 2_2 3_3, לֵב *heart of* 1 S 25_{36}, יַד *hand of* 1 S 25_{39}, רָעַת *evil of* 1 S 25_{39}. <APP> אִישׁ *man, husband* 1 S $25_{19.25}$, כַּרְמְלִי *Carmelite* 1 S $27_{3(mss)}$ 30_5 2 S 2_2 3_3. <PREP> לְ of direction, *to*, + נגד hi. *tell* 1 S $25_{5.19.36.37}$; of benefit, *to, for*, + יתר ni. *remain* 1 S 25_{34}; *concerning*, + שׁאל *ask* 1 S 25_5; of possession, *of, (belonging) to* 1 S $25_{5.36}$; כְּ *as*, + היה *be* 1 S 25_{26}; מִן of direction, *from*, + יצא *go out* 1 S 25_{37}; אֶל *to*, + דבר pi. *speak* 1 S 25_9, בוא *come* 1 S $25_{5.36}$, שׂים *place* heart, i.e. pay attention 1 S $25_{25(mss)}$; עַל *upon*, i.e. with 1 S 25_{36}; *to*, + שׂים *place* heart, i.e. pay attention 1 S 25_{25}; עִם *with* 1 S 25_{25}; בְּקֶרֶב *within*, + מות *die* 1 S 25_{37}.

⇒ נָבָל *be foolish*.

נֵ֫בֶל I$_{11.1.0.22}$ n.m. **jar**—cstr. נֵ֫בֶל; pl. cstr. נִבְלֵי; sf. נִבְלֵיהֶם—normally an **amphora,** i.e. with two or four handles and a narrow neck;* prob. not **leather bottle;** usu. for storing wine or oil; the clouds as jars (Jb 38_{37} Si 43_8).

<SUBJ> מלא ni. *be filled* with wine Jr $13_{12.12}$, כתת pass. *be crushed* Is 30_{14}. <NOM CL> עֲלֵיהֶם ... נֵבֶל יַיִן *upon them was ... a jar of wine* 1 S 16_1. <OBJ> עלה hi. *bring up* 1 S 1_{24}, נשׂא *carry* 1 S 10_3, שׁכב hi. *cause to lie down*, i.e. tilt Jb 38_{37}, לקח *take* 1 S 25_{18}, נפץ pi. *shatter* Jr 48_{12} (+ כְּלִי *vessel*).

<CSTR> נֵבֶל יוֹצְרִים *jar of the potters*, i.e. earthenware jar Is 30_{14}, נֵבֶל יַיִן *jar of wine* 1 S 1_{24} 10_3 2 S 16_1 (both יַיִן) Ne 5_{18} (if em. כָּל־ *all* wine) Samaria ost. 1_2

([י]ין) 3_2 ([י]ין) 5_3 6_3 7_3 ([נבל י]ין) 8_2 ([י]ין) 9_3 ([נ]בל י[ין]) 10_3 11_1 ([נ]בל יין) 12_3 13_2 14_3 15_2 ([נ]בל י[ין]) 89_1 ([נ]בל י[ין]), נִבְלֵי־ *jars of* 1 S 25_{18}, נבל שמן *jar of oil* Samaria ost. 16_2 17_2 18_2 19_2 20_2 ([נבל ש]מן) 21_2 53_2 54_2 55_2 59_1 72_2 73_2 ([נבל]), נִבְלֵי־חֶרֶשׂ *jars of earthenware* Lm 4_2, נִבְלֵי שָׁמַיִם *jars of heaven* Jb 38_{37}, נבלי מרום *jars of heaven* Si 43_8; כְּלֵי הַנְּבָלִים *vessels of the jars* Is 22_{24}, שֵׁבֶר נֵבֶל *breaking of a jar of* Is 30_{14}, כלי צבא נבלי מרום perh. *a mechanism of*, i.e. for, *the host of the jars of heaven* Si 43_8, כָּל־נֵבֶל *every jar* Jr $13_{12.12}$.

<APP> מַעֲשֵׂה *work* of potter's hands Lm 4_2. <PREP> לְ *as*, + חשב ni. *be reckoned* Lm 4_2; בְּ of place, *in* Samaria ost. 53_2 72_2 73_2 ([בנבל]). <COLL> שְׁנַיִם נִבְלֵי־יַיִן *two jars of wine* 1 S 25_{18}.

Also Kenyon ost. $2_{7.9}$.*

⇨ cf. נֵבֶל II *harp*.

נֵבֶל II $_{27.3.3}$ n.m. **harp**—נֵבֶל (נָבֶל) נֶבֶל; cstr. נֵבֶל; pl. נְבָלִים; נְבָלֶיךָ—<SUBJ> היה *be* Is 5_{12}, עור *awake* Ps 57_9||108_3, ערב hi. *make sweet* Si 40_{21}. <NOM CL> לִפְנֵיהֶם נֵבֶל *before them shall be a harp* 1 S 10_5, כנור נבלי לתכון קודשו *my lyre (and) my harp are according to the pattern of his holiness* 1QS 10_9. <OBJ> עשׂה *make* 1 K 10_{12}||2 C 9_{11}, נכה hi. *strike* 4QSd 9_8.

<CSTR> נֵבֶל עָשׂוֹר *harp of ten (strings)* Ps 33_2 144_9 1QM 4_5 (unless app. *a harp, one of ten [strings]*), נבל [שמ]חה *harp of joy* 1QH 19_{23}; פִּי הַנֵּבֶל *mouth*, i.e. sound, *of the harp* Am 6_5, הֶמְיַת נְבָלֶיךָ *sound of your harps* Is 14_{11} (1QIsaa המית נבלתך *noisy throng of your dead*, i.e. נְבֵלָה *corpse*), זִמְרַת נְבָלֶיךָ *melody of your harps* Am 5_{23} (or em. נִבְלֵיכֶם *of your* [pl.] *harps*), [שי]רות נבל *songs of the harp* Si 39_{15}, כְּלִי־נֶבֶל *instrument (consisting) of a harp* Ps 71_{22}, כְּלֵי נְבָלִים *instruments (consisting) of harps* 1 C 16_5.

<APP> כְּלִי *instrument* 1 C 15_{16}, perh. עָשׂוֹר *ten (strings)* Ps 33_2 144_9 1QM 4_5 (but prob. cstr. *harp of ten [strings]*).

<PREP> בְּ of instrument, accompaniment, *by (means of), with, on* Ne 12_{27} 1 C $15_{.20}$ 25_6 2 C 5_{12} 1QM 4_5, + הלל pi. *praise* Ps 150_3, זמר pi. *praise* Ps 144_8 1QH 19_{23}, ידה hi. *praise* Ps 33_2, שׂחק pi. *make merry* 2 S 6_5||1 C 13_8, נבא ni. *prophesy* 1 C $25_{1(Qr)}$, בוא *come* 2 C 20_{28}, עלה hi. *bring up* 1 C 15_{28}, עמד hi. *position* 1 C 15_{16} 2 C 29_{25}.

עַל *to (the accompaniment of)*, + נגד hi. *tell (of)* Ps 92_4.

עִם *with*, + נתן *give*, i.e. play Ps 81_3.

<COLL> נֵבֶל || כִּנּוֹר *lyre* 1 S 10_5 2 S 6_5||1 C 13_8 1 K 10_{12}||2 C 9_{11} Is 5_{12} Ps 33_2 57_9||108_3 71_{22} (+) 81_3 (+) 150_3 Ne 12_{27} 1 C $15_{16.28}$ 16_5 (+) $25_{1.6}$ 2 C 5_{12} 20_{28} 29_{25} 1QH 19_{23} 1QS 10_9, עָשׂוֹר *ten-stringed harp* Ps 92_4, חָלִיל *flute* 1 S 10_5 Is 5_{12} Si 40_{21} 1QH 19_{23} 1QS 10_9 (+), חֲצוֹצְרָה *trumpet* 1 C 13_8 15_{28} 2 C 20_{28}, תֹּף *tambourine* 1 S 10_5 2 S 6_5||1 C 13_8 Is 5_{12} Ps 81_3 (+), מְצִלְתַּיִם *cymbals* Ne 12_{27} 1 C 13_8 $15_{16.28}$ 16_5 (+) $25_{1.6}$ 2 C 5_{12} 29_{25}, צֶלְצְלִים *cymbals* 2 S 6_5, מְנַעַנְעִים *sistrum* 2 S 6_5, שִׁיר *song* Am 5_{23} (+) Ne 12_{27} 1 C 13_8, יַיִן *wine* Is 5_{12}.

+ שׁוֹפָר *rams' horn* 1 C 15_{28}, הִגָּיוֹן *music* Ps 92_4, כלי מינים *instruments of strings* Si 39_{15}.

Also Si $47_{9(Bmg)}$.

<SYN> כִּנּוֹר *lyre*, עָשׂוֹר *ten-stringed harp*, חָלִיל *flute*, חֲצוֹצְרָה *trumpet*, תֹּף *tambourine*, מְצִלְתַּיִם *cymbals*, צֶלְצְלִים *cymbals*, מְנַעַנְעִים *sistrum*, שִׁיר *song*, יַיִן *wine*.*

⇨ cf. נֵבֶל I *jar*.

*[**נֹבֶל**] III n.[m.] **young shoot, sprig,** <CSTR> צִיצַת נֵבֶל *blossom of a young shoot* Is 28_4 (if em. צִיצַת נֹבֵל *fading blossom*).

נְבָלָה $_{13}$ n.f. **sacrilege, outrage,** serious **disorderly conduct,** less prob. **folly,** in ref. to sexual offences (Gn 34_7 Dt 22_{21} Jg $19_{23.24}$ $20_{6.10}$ 2 S 13_{12} Jr 29_{23}), retaining devoted object (Jos 7_{15}), impious speech (Is 9_{16} 32_6), impious behaviour (1 S 25_{25}); **disgrace** (Jb 42_8), <NOM CL> נְבָלָה עִמּוֹ *sacrilege is with him* 1 S 25_{25}. <OBJ> דבר *speak* Is 9_{16}, pi. Is 32_6 (+ אָוֶן *iniquity*), עשׂה *do* Gn 34_7 Dt 22_{21} Jos 7_{15} Jg 19_{23} 20_6 (|| זִמָּה *wickedness*) 20_{10} 2 S 13_{12} Jr 29_{23} Jb 42_8. <CSTR> דְּבַר הַנְּבָלָה *thing of sacrilege* Jg 19_{24}, כָּל־הַנְּבָלָה *all the sacrilege* Jg 20_{10}. <ADJ> זֹאת *this* Jg $19_{23.24}$ 2 S 13_{12}. <PREP> כְּ *according to*, + עשׂה *do* Jg 20_{10}. <COLL> נְבָלָה + בְּיִשְׂרָאֵל *in Israel* Gn 34_7 Dt 22_{21} Jos 7_{15} Jg $20_{6.10}$ Jr 29_{23}, לֹא־יֵעָשֶׂה כֵן בְּיִשְׂרָאֵל *such a thing should not be done in Israel* 2 S 13_{12}.

<SYN> זִמָּה *wickedness.**
⇒ נבל III *be sacrilegious, treat with contempt.*

נְבֵלָה 48.0.7 n.f. **corpse**—cstr. נִבְלַת; sf. נִבְלָתִי, נִבְלָתְךָ, נִבְלָתוֹ, נִבְלָתָהּ, נִבְלָתָם, (נבלתמה) נִבְלָתָם—**1. corpse** of humans, oft. collectively, **corpses** (Dt 28$_{26}$ Is 5$_{25}$ 26$_{19}$ Jr 7$_{33}$ 9$_{21}$ 16$_{4}$ 19$_{7}$ 34$_{20}$ Ps 79$_{2}$ 4QTanḥ 1.1$_{3}$), perh. as something outcast or sacrilegious.*

<SUBJ> היה *be* Dt 28$_{26}$ 1 K 13$_{24}$ 2 K 9$_{37(Qr)}$ Is 5$_{25}$ Jr 7$_{33}$ 16$_{4}$ 34$_{20}$ 36$_{30}$, בוא *come* 1 K 13$_{22}$, לין *remain (overnight)* Dt 21$_{23}$=11QT 64$_{11}$, נפל *fall* Jr 9$_{21}$, קום *arise* Is 26$_{19}$, שׁלך ho. *be cast* 1 K 13$_{24.25.28}$ Jr 36$_{30}$. <OBJ> ראה *see* 1 K 13$_{25}$ 4QTanḥ 1.1$_{3}$, מצא *find* 1 K 13$_{28}$, אכל *eat* 1 K 13$_{28}$, ירד hi. *bring down* Jos 8$_{29}$, נשׂא *lift* 1 K 13$_{29}$, שׁלך hi. *cast* Jos 8$_{29}$ Jr 26$_{23}$, נוח hi. *place* 1 K 13$_{30}$, נתן *give* Jr 19$_{7}$ Ps 79$_{2}$. <CSTR> נִבְלַת הָעָם *corpses of the people* Jr 7$_{33}$, הָאָדָם *of human beings* Jr 9$_{21}$, עֲבָדֶיךָ *of your servants* Ps 79$_{2}$, נבלת כוהניכה *corpses of your priests* 4QTanḥ 1.1$_{3}$, נִבְלַת אִיזֶבֶל *corpse of Jezebel* 2 K 9$_{37}$, אִישׁ־ *of the man of* God 1 K 13$_{29}$; המית נבלתך *noisy throng of your corpses* Is 14$_{11(1QIsa^a)}$ (MT הֶמְיַת נְבָלֶיךָ *sound of your harps*). <PREP> אֵצֶל *beside*, + עמד *stand* 1 K 13$_{24.24.25.28}$.

2. carcass of animal, oft. of a clean animal that dies of itself (e.g. Lv 7$_{24}$ 17$_{15}$ 22$_{8}$ Dt 14$_{21}$ Ezk 4$_{14}$ 44$_{31}$), or of an unclean animal regardless of how it died (e.g. Lv 11$_{8.11}$).*

<SUBJ> חיה *live* 4QHalakhah^a 11$_{4}$ (נב[לות]). <OBJ> שׁקץ pi. *abominate* Lv 11$_{11}$, נשׂא *carry* Lv 11$_{28.40}$ 4QMMT B$_{23}$ (הנוש]א]), נתן *give* Dt 14$_{21}$, מכר *deliver (over)* Dt 14$_{21}$ 11QT 48$_{6}$, אכל *eat* Dt 14$_{21}$ Ezk 4$_{14}$ 44$_{31}$ 11QT 48$_{6}$. <CSTR> נִבְלַת בְּהֵמָה *carcass of a beast* Lv 5$_{2}$ 4QMMT B$_{22}$ ([הבהמה]), חַיָּה *of an animal* Lv 5$_{2}$, שֶׁרֶץ *of swarming thing* Lv 5$_{2}$; חֵלֶב נְבֵלָה *fat of a carcass* Lv 7$_{24}$, [ע]ור נבלת *hide of the carcass of* 4QMMT B$_{22}$, כָּל־ נְבֵלָה *any carcass (of what dies of itself)* Dt 14$_{21}$ Ezk 44$_{31}$ 11QT 48$_{6}$ (כול). <PREP> בְּ of instrument, *by means of, with*, + טמא *be impure* Lv 22$_{8}$; introducing object, + נגע *touch* Lv 5$_{2}$ 11$_{8.24.27.36.39}$ Dt 14$_{8}$; מִן partitive, *some of*, + נשׂא *carry* Lv 11$_{25}$ 11QT 51$_{4}$, נפל *fall* Lv 11$_{35.37.38}$, אכל *eat* Lv 11$_{40}$. <COLL> נְבֵלָה || טְרֵפָה *savaged beast* Lv 7$_{24}$ 17$_{15}$ 22$_{8}$ Ezk 4$_{14}$ 44$_{31}$, עֶצֶם *bone* 11QT 51$_{4}$, בָּשָׂר *flesh* Ps 79$_{2}$; + בָּשָׂר Lv 11$_{11}$ Dt 14$_{8}$ Ezk 4$_{14}$; נבלה בעוף ובבהמה *the carcass of a winged thing or a beast* 11QT 48$_{6}$.

3. carcass of idols, used collectively, <CSTR> נִבְלַת שִׁקּוּצֵיהֶם *carcasses of their detestable things* Jr 16$_{18}$. <PREP> בְּ of instrument, *by (means of), with*, + חלל pi. *profane* Jr 16$_{18}$.

<SYN> §2 טְרֵפָה *savaged beast*, בָּשָׂר *flesh.**
⇒ נבל I *wither.*

[נַבְלוּת] I 1.0.1 n.f. **lewdness**—sf. נַבְלֻתָהּ—**lewdness, shamelessness, sexual misconduct,** perh. **foolishness, degeneration,*** <SUBJ> שׁמע ni. *be heard* 1QS 10$_{22}$ (+ כַּחַשׁ *deceit*). <NOM CL> [אם נבלות] בדברי *is there any lewdness in my words?* 4QShir^b 18.2$_{5}$. <OBJ> גלה pi. *uncover* Ho 2$_{12}$ (unless נַבְלוּת II *ruin*).

Also perh. 4QpIsa^c 26$_{6}$.
⇒ נבל II *be foolish.*

*__[נַבְלוּת]__ II 1 n.f. **ruin** (unless נַבְלוּת I *lewdness*)—sf. נַבְלֻתָהּ—**ruin, degeneration, withering away,** <OBJ> גלה pi. *uncover* Ho 2$_{12}$.
⇒ נבל I *wither.*

נְבַלָּט 1 pl.n. **Neballat,** in Benjamin, Bēt Nebālā, 35 km NW of Jerusalem, <NOM CL> בְּנֵי בִנְיָמִן ... נְבַלָּט *the sons of Benjamin were ... (at) Neballat* Ne 11$_{34}$.

*__נֹבֶלֶת__ I 1 n.f. **unripe fig(s)** or **withered fruit** (unless נֹבֶלֶת is ptc. of נבל *wither*), <PREP> כְּ *as*, + נבל *wither* Is 34$_{4}$ (כְּנֹבֶלֶת מִתְּאֵנָה *as unripe figs from a fig tree*).

נֹבֶלֶת II *withered*, see נבל I *wither.*

נבע I 10.6.7 vb. **gush—Qal** 1 Ptc. נֹבֵעַ—**gush,** <SUBJ> נַחַל *stream* Pr 18$_{4}$.

Pi. 0.1 Pf. Si ניבע—**pour out, utter,** <SUBJ> Ben Sira Si 50$_{27}$ (unless hi.). <OBJ> מוּסָר *discipline* Si 50$_{27}$, מָשָׁל *proverb* Si 50$_{27}$ (unless מושל is ptc. of משל *use a proverb*). <PREP> בְּ *according to*, + פִּתּוּר *interpretation* Si 50$_{27}$.

Hi. 9.5.7 Pf. Si הביע, Q הבעתה; impf. יַבִּיעַ, 3fs Si תביע,

יַבִּיעוּ (יַבִּיעוּן), אַבִּיעָה, 3fs תַּבַּעְנָה; impv. Q הביעו, Q הבענה; ptc. Si מביע—**pour out, burst out, spout, utter,** perh. **belch** (Ps 59$_8$),* <SUBJ> Ben Sira Si 16$_{25}$ (|| חוה pi. *declare*) 50$_{27}$ (unless pi.), אִשָּׁה *woman* appar. Si 42$_{14(B)}$, בַּת *daughter* Si 42$_{14(Bmg)}$ 1QM 19$_7$ ([ב]נות), בֹּגֵד *traitor* Ps 59$_8$, פעל ptc. *one who does evil* Ps 94$_4$ (+ דבר pi. *speak*, אמר htp. *boast*), חבא pu. ptc. *one hidden* 1QH 16$_{18}$, יָדִיד *beloved* perh. 4QHod^a 7.1$_{17}$ (+ נגד hi. *tell*), גיל ptc. *one who rejoices* 4QBéat 2.2$_2$, worshipper Ps 71$_{16}$ (if em. אָבוֹא *I will come* to אַבִּיעַ) 78$_2$ (+ פתח *open* mouth), פֶּה *lip* Pr 15$_{2.28}$ (+ הגה *meditate*) 19$_{28}$ (if em. יְבַלַּע *it swallows* to יַבִּיעַ), שָׂפָה *lip* Ps 119$_{171}$ Pr 10$_{32}$ (if em. יֵדְעוּן *they know* to יַבִּיעוּן), מָקוֹר *source* Si 10$_{13}$, חָכְמוֹת *wisdom* Pr 1$_{23}$ (|| ידע hi. *make known*), שִׂמְחָה *joy* 4QHod^a 7.2$_4$ ([ש]מחה תביע), יוֹם *day* Ps 19$_3$ (|| חוה pi.), שֶׁמֶשׁ *sun* Si 43$_{2(B)}$; subj. not specified, Ps 145$_7$ (|| רנן pi. *sing joyfully*) 4QMyst^c 1$_1$ ([א]ביעה; + חלק pi. *apportion* words).

<OBJ> רוּחַ *spirit* Pr 1$_{23}$ Si 16$_{25}$ 4QMyst^c 1$_1$ ([א]ביעה), זֵכֶר *remembrance* Ps 145$_7$, תְּהִלָּה *praise* Ps 119$_{171}$, אֹמֶר *speech* Ps 19$_3$ 4QBéat 24.2$_1$, חִידָה *riddle* Ps 78$_2$, מוּסָר *discipline* Si 50$_{27}$, מָשָׁל *proverb* Si 50$_{27}$ (unless מושל is ptc. of משל *use a proverb*), רָצוֹן *acceptance* Pr 10$_{32}$ (if em.; see Subj.), חֶרְפָּה *reproach* Si 42$_{14(Bmg)}$, אִוֶּלֶת *folly* Pr 15$_2$, רָעָה *evil* Pr 15$_{28}$, זִמָּה *wickedness* Si 10$_{13}$, אָוֶן *iniquity* Pr 19$_{28}$ (if em.; see Subj.), חַמָּה *heat* Si 43$_{2(B)}$.

<PREP> לְ of direction, *to*, + פֶּתִי *simple one* Pr 1$_{23}$, יוֹם *day* Ps 19$_3$; בְּ of place, *in*, + דֶּרֶךְ *way* 4QBéat 2.2$_2$; of instrument, *by (means of), with*, + פֶּה *mouth* Ps 59$_8$; of accompaniment, *with, in*, + קוֹל *voice* 1QM 19$_7$, תְּבוּנָה *understanding* Si 50$_{27}$, שִׂמְחָה *joy* 4QHod^a 7.1$_{17}$, צָרָה *distress* appar. Si 43$_{2(B)}$; *according to*, + מִשְׁקָל *measure* Si 16$_{25}$; introducing object, + גְּבוּרָה *mighty deed* Ps 71$_{16}$ (if em.; see Subj.).

<COLL> נבע hi. + adverb, פִּתְאֹם *suddenly* 1QH 16$_{18}$; יַבִּיעוּן בְּפִיהֶם חֲרָבוֹת בְּשִׂפְתוֹתֵיהֶם *they belch with their mouths, swords with their lips*, i.e. they belch swords from their mouths and lips* Ps 59$_8$.

Also perh. 4QpHos^b 20$_2$ 4Q418 228$_2$.

<SYN> חוה pi. *declare*, ידע hi. *make known*, רנן pi. *sing joyfully*.*

⇒ מַבּוּעַ *spring*.

***נבע** II 1 vb. **ferment—Hi.** 1 Impf. יַבִּיעַ—**cause to ferment,** <SUBJ> זְבוּב dead *fly* Ec 10$_1$ (or del.; + באשׁ hi. *cause to stink*). <OBJ> שֶׁמֶן *ointment* Ec 10$_1$ (or del.).

***נבק** 1 vb. **pour—Qal** 1 + waw וְנָבְקָה—**pour, flow** (unless בקק ni. *be devastated*), <SUBJ> רוּחַ *spirit* of Egypt Is 19$_3$. <PREP> בְּקֶרֶב *within*, + Egypt Is 19$_3$.

2. trans. **pour out,** <SUBJ> worshipper Ps 69$_{11}$ (if em. וָאֶבְכֶּה *and I wept* to וָאֶבְּקָה *and I poured out*). <OBJ> נֶפֶשׁ *soul* Ps 69$_{11}$ (if em.; see Subj.). <PREP> בְּ of accompaniment, *with, in*, + צוֹם *fasting* Ps 69$_{11}$ (if em.; see Subj.).

***[נֶבֶשׁ]** 0.0.0.1 n.[f.] **soul**—sf. I נבשכם—**soul,** i.e. life, <PREP> בְּ of price, *at the cost of* Arad ost. 24$_{18}$ (דבר המלך אתכם בנבשכם *the word of the king is with*, i.e. incumbent upon, *you at the cost of your life*).

⇒ cf. נֶפֶשׁ *soul*.

נִבְשָׁן 1 pl.n. **Nibshan,** town in the Judaean steppe, perh. Kh. el-Maqārī, 17 km SSW of Jericho, <NOM CL> בַּמִּדְבָּר ... הַנִּבְשָׁן *in the steppe was ... Nibshan* Jos 15$_{62}$.

נֶגֶב I 112.0.3 n.m. **south country**—cstr. נֶגֶב; + ה- of direction נֶגְבָּה—**1. south country, a. Negeb,** the region south of the hill country of Judah and north of the Sinai peninsula, <SUBJ> ישׁב *be inhabited* Zc 7$_7$, ירשׁ *possess* Ob$_{19}$. <OBJ> ראה hi. *show* Dt 34$_3$, פשׁט *raid* 1 S 30$_{14}$, נכה hi. *strike*, i.e. defeat Jos 10$_{40}$, לקח *take* Jos 11$_{16}$.

<CSTR> נֶגֶב יְהוּדָה *Negeb of Judah* 1 S 27$_{10}$ 2 S 24$_7$, עֲרָד *of Arad* Jg 1$_{16}$, כָּלֵב *of Caleb* 1 S 30$_{14}$, הַכְּרֵתִי *of the Cherethites* 1 S 30$_{14}$, הַיְּרַחְמְאֵלִי *of the Jerahmeelites* 1 S 27$_{10(L)}$ (mss הַיְּרַחְמְאֵלִי), הַקֵּינִי *of the Kenites* 1 S 27$_{10}$; בַּהֲמוֹת נֶגֶב *beasts of the Negeb* Is 30$_6$ (unless נֶגֶב II *provision*), אֶרֶץ הַנֶּגֶב *land of the Negeb* Gn 20$_1$ (אַרְצָה) 24$_{62}$ Nm 13$_{29}$ Jos 15$_{19}$ Jg 1$_{15}$, עָרֵי *cities of* Jr 13$_{19}$ (unless נֶגֶב II) 32$_{44}$ 33$_{13}$ Ob$_{20}$ 2 C 28$_{18}$ (... עָרֵי), יַעַר *forest of* Ezk 21$_2$ (if em.; see Prep.) 21$_3$, רָאמַת נֶגֶב *Ramah of the Negeb* or *Ramath-negeb* Jos 19$_8$, רָמוֹת־נֶגֶב *Ramoth of the Negeb* or *Ramoth-negeb* 1 S 30$_{27}$, כָּל־

הַנֶּגֶב *all the Negeb* Jos 11_{16}.

<APP> אֶרֶץ *land* Jos 10_{10} 11_{16}.

<PREP> בְּ of place, *in(to)* Dt 1_{7} Jos 12_{8} 15_{21} (בַּנֶּגְבָּה) Jg 1_{16} Is 21_{1} Ps 126_{4}, + עלה *go up* Nm $13_{17.22}$, ישׁב *dwell* Nm 33_{40}.

מִן of direction, *from*, + הלך *go* Gn 13_{3}, בוא *come* Jr 17_{26}.

אֶל *to*, + יצא *go out* 2 S 24_{7}; *against*, + פשׁט *make a raid* 1 S $27_{10(mss).10(mss).10}$ 30_{1}.

עַל *against*, + פשׁט *make a raid* 1 S $27_{10.10.10(mss)}$ 30_{14}.

ה- of direction, *(towards), in*, + נסע *journey* Gn 12_{9}, עלה *go up* Gn 13_{1}.

הַנֶּגֶב/נֶגֶב without preposition or ה- of direction, *in the Negeb* Ezk 21_{2} (or em. יַעַר הַשָּׂדֶה נֶגֶב *the forest land [in] the Negeb* to יַעַר הַנֶּגֶב *the forest of the Negeb*), + ישׁב *dwell* Nm 21_{1} Jg 1_{9}.

<COLL> הַנֶּגֶב || הַר *hill country* Dt 1_{7} Jos 10_{10} 11_{16} 12_{8} Jg 1_{9} Jr 17_{26} 32_{44} 33_{13}, שְׁפֵלָה *lowland* Dt 1_{7} Jos 10_{10} 11_{16} 12_{8} Jg 1_{9} Jr 17_{26} 32_{44} 33_{13} Ob$_{19}$ Zc 7_{7} 2 C 28_{18}, עֲרָבָה *Arabah* Dt 1_{7} Jos 11_{16} 12_{8}, אֶשֶׁד *slope* Jos 10_{10} 12_{8}, מִדְבָּר *steppe* Jos 12_{8}, חוֹף *shore* Dt 1_{7}, יְהוּדָה *Judah* Jr 32_{44}.

הַנֶּגֶב לִיהוּדָה *the Negeb of Judah* 2 C 28_{18}.

b. in ref. to Egypt, <CSTR> מֶלֶךְ־הַנֶּגֶב *king of the south* Dn 11_{5+7t}, זְרֹעוֹת *arms*, i.e. armies, *of* Dn 11_{15}. <PREP> בְּ of place, *in(to)*, + בוא *come* Dn 11_{29}.

2. south, <CSTR> נֶגֶב יְרוּשָׁלָםִ *south of Jerusalem* Zc 14_{10}, כִּנְרוֹת *of Chinneroth* Jos 11_{2} (or em. נֶגְבָּה מִנֶּגֶד *to the south, opposite*, or del.); פְּאַת נֶגֶב *southern side* Ex 26_{18}||36_{23} (נֶגְבָּה) 27_{9}||38_{9} Nm 34_{3} 35_{5} Jos 18_{15} (נֶגְבָּה) Ezk 47_{19} $48_{16.28.33}$ (נֶגְבָּה), גְּבוּל נֶגֶב *boundary of the south* Nm 34_{3} Jos $15_{2.4}$ 18_{19}, שַׁעַר *gate of* Ezk $46_{9.9}$.

<APP> רוּחַ *wind*, i.e. side 1 C 9_{24}.

<PREP> לְ of direction, *to(wards), in* 1 C 26_{17} 11QT 38_{14} 39_{12}, + יצא *go out* 11QT 4_{2} ([יוצאים לנגבה]).

מִן of direction, *from, in, on* (the south of), *to* (the south of) Jos $15_{7.8}$ $18_{5.13}$ 19_{34} Jg 21_{19} 1 S 14_{5} Ezk 21_{3} 40_{2} (or em. נֶגְדִּי *opposite me*, or del.) 47_{1} perh. Si $37_{4(Bmg)}$ (D מנוב appar. *away from fruit*; B מנגד *opposite*, i.e. aloof), + היה *be* Nm 34_{4}, עלה *go up* Jos 15_{3}, סבב ni. *turn* Nm 34_{4}.

אֶל *to*, + גדל *be great* Dn 8_{9}; אֶל מִן *to*, + יצא *go out* Jos 15_{3}.

מֵאֵצֶל *from beside*, קום *arise* 1 S 20_{41} (or em. נֶגֶב to אַרְגָּב *mound*).

מִמּוּל *from opposite* 1 K 7_{39}||2 C 4_{10} (קֵדְמָה מִמּוּל נֶגֶב *eastwards opposite the south*, i.e. in the south-east).

ה- of direction, *to(wards), in* Jos 11_{2} (if em.; see Cstr.) $17_{9.10}$ 18_{16} Ezk 47_{19} $48_{10.17}$, + היה *be* Jos 15_{1} 18_{19} 1 C 9_{24}, מושׁ *depart* Zc 14_{4}, ראה *see* Gn 13_{14}, עבר *pass* Jos 18_{13}, פנה *turn* 1 K 7_{25}||2 C 4_{4}, סבב ni. *turn* Jos $18_{14.14}$, נגח *push* Dn 8_{4}, נפל *fall* 1 C 26_{15}, פרץ *spread* Gn 28_{14}, שׂים *place* Ex 40_{24}.

נֶגֶב without preposition or ה- of direction, *to, in the south* Jos 11_{2} (or em.; see Cstr.), + עשׂה *make* 11QT 31_{10} (נגב מזרח *in the south-east*).

<COLL> נֶגֶב || צָפוֹן *north* Gn 13_{14} 28_{14} Nm 35_{5} 1 K 7_{25}||2 C 4_{4} Ezk $48_{10.16.17}$ Dn 8_{4} 1 C 9_{24} 26_{17} 11QT 38_{14} 39_{12}; :: צָפוֹן Jos 17_{10} 18_{5} 1 S 14_{5} Ezk $21_{3.9}$ $46_{9.9}$ Zc 14_{4}.

|| מִזְרָח *east* 1 K 7_{25}||2 C 4_{4} Dn 8_{9} 1 C 9_{24} 26_{17} 11QT 39_{13}, קֶדֶם *east* Gn 13_{14} 28_{14} Nm 35_{5} Ezk $48_{10.16.17}$ 11QT 39_{12}, יָם *west* Gn 13_{14} 28_{14} Nm 35_{5} Jos 19_{34} 1 K 7_{25}||2 C 4_{4} Ezk $48_{10.16.17}$ Dn 8_{4} 1 C 9_{24} 11QT 38_{14} 39_{12}.

+ תֵּימָן *south* Ex 26_{18}||36_{23} 27_{9}||38_{9} Jos 15_{1} Ezk $47_{19.19}$ 48_{28}.

Also 4QSela 8_{1} ([הנג]ב).

<SYN> §1a הַר *hill country*, שְׁפֵלָה *lowland*, עֲרָבָה *Arabah*, אֶשֶׁד *slope*, מִדְבָּר *steppe*, חוֹף *shore*, יְהוּדָה *Judah*; §2 צָפוֹן *north*, מִזְרָח *east*, קֶדֶם *east*, יָם *west*.*

<ANT> §2 צָפוֹן *north*.

*נֶגֶב II 2 n.[m.] **provision** (unless נֶגֶב I *south country*), <CSTR> בַּהֲמוֹת נֶגֶב *beasts of provision*, i.e. pack animals Is 30_{6}, עָרֵי הַנֶּגֶב *cities of provision*, i.e. store cities Jr 13_{19}.

*[נֶגֶב] III 0.0.0.2 pr.n.[m.] **Negeb,** appar. father of Tanhum, Seals 187 (Gibeon, 8th cent.) 776 (Beth-Shemesh, 8th cent.).

*[נֶגְבִּי] 0.0.0.1 pr.n.m. **Negbi,** son of Malchijah, <APP> בֵּן *son* Seal 620 (T. Beit Mirsim?, 7th/6th cent.). <PREP> לְ of possession, *of, (belonging) to* Seal 620 (T. Beit Mirsim?, 7th/6th cent.).

נגד 371.7.32.1 vb. **tell**—**Hi.** 336.6.32 Pf. הִגִּיד (הִגִּידָה), הִגִּידָה, הִגַּדְתָּ (הִגַּדְתָּה), הִגַּדְתִּי, הִגִּידוּ (Q הגדו); impf. יַגִּיד (יַגֵּד), תַּגִּיד, 2ms תַּגִּיד, 3fs (יַגִּידָה, יַגִּידֶהָ, Si יגידנו, יַגֶּדְךָ, יַגֶּד־ נַגִּידָה (נַגִּידָה), נַגִּיד, תַּגִּידוּ, יַגִּידוּ, (אַגִּידֶנּוּ, אַגִּידָה) אַגִּיד, תַּגִּידִי (נַגִּידֶנּוּ); + waw וְהִגִּיד, וְהִגִּידָה, וְהִגַּדְתָּ, וְהִגַּדְתִּי, וְהִגִּידוּ, וַיַּגִּידוּ, (וָאַגִּד) וָאַגִּיד, (וַתַּגֶּד־) וַתַּגֵּד 3fs ,(וַיַּגֶּד־) וַיַּגֵּד; וְהִגַּדְתֶּם (וַיַּגִּדוּ), וַנַּגֶּד־; impv. הַגֵּד (הַגֶּד־, הַגִּידָה, Q הגידנה), הַגִּידִי, הַגִּידוּ; ptc. מַגִּיד, מַגִּידֵי, מַגֶּדֶת; inf. abs. הַגֵּד (הַגֵּיד); cstr. הַגִּיד (Kt לגיד).

1. tell, declare, announce, report, make known, inform; explain, expound (e.g. Gn 41_{24} Jg 14_{12} Dn 2_{2}), <SUBJ> Y. Dt 4_{13} 1 S 3_{13} 23_{11} 2 S 7_{11}||1 C 17_{10} (or em. וְהִגִּיד לְךָ *and he declares to you* to וְהִגְדִּילְךָ *and he will make you great*) 2 K 4_{27} Is 42_{9} 43_{12} 44_{8} 45_{19} 46_{10} $48_{3.5}$ 57_{12} Jr 33_{3} 42_{3} Mc 6_{8} (or em. הֻגַּד *it has been declared*, i.e. ho.) Zc 9_{12} (or em. גַּם־הַיּוֹם מַגִּיד *also today [I] declare* to גְּמוּל יוֹם מְגֻרֵיךְ *recompense of*, i.e. for, *the day of your sojourning*) Ps 111_{6} 147_{19} Jb 11_{6} 36_{9} 1QM $11_{5.8}$ 1QDM 1.1_{6} 4QJub[a] 1_{5} 4QMidrEschat[b] 3_{10} ([ה]גיד) 11QT 51_{7}, idols Is $41_{22.22.23}$.

Archite 2 S 14_{35}, Chaldaeans Dn 2_{2}, Cushite 2 S 18_{21}, Edomite 1 S $22_{22.22}$ Ps 52_{2}, Israel(ites) Dt 26_{3} 2 S 1_{20} Is 48_{20} Jr 5_{20} Mc 1_{10} (or em. אַל תָּגִילוּ *do not rejoice*), Shuhite Jb 26_{4}, עַם *people* Ex 13_{8}, גּוֹי *nation* Jr 31_{10}, Jerusalem Is 3_{9}, Judah Is 3_{9}.

Abiathar 1 S 22_{21} 2 S 15_{28} 17_{16}, Abigail 1 S $25_{19.36}$, Abra(ha)m Gn 12_{18} 21_{26}, Ahab 1 K 19_{1}, Ahijah 1 K 14_{3}, Ahimaaz 2 S 15_{28} $17_{17.21}$, Balaam Nm 23_{3}, Baruch Jr 36_{17}, Bildad Jb 26_{4}, Boaz Ru 3_{4}, David 1 S 19_{18} 24_{19} (or em. הִגְדַּלְתָּ *you have made great*), Doeg 1 S $22_{22.22}$ Ps 52_{2}, Eliakim 2 K 18_{37}||Is 36_{22}, Elisha 2 K 6_{12}, Esther Est $2_{10.20}$ 8_{1}, Ezekiel Ezk 24_{19} Si 49_{8}, Gabriel Dn 9_{23}, Gad 2 S 24_{13}, Gehazi 2 K 4_{31}, Ham Gn 9_{22}, Hathach Est $4_{7.8.9}$, Hoshaiah Lachish ost. 3_{1} (להגן[ד]), Hushai 2 S 14_{35}, Isaiah Is 21_{10} Si 48_{25}, Jacob Gn $29_{12.15}$ $31_{20.27}$ 32_{6} 49_{1}, Jehu 2 K 9_{12}, Jeremiah Jr 16_{10} $38_{15.25.27}$ $42_{4.20.21}$, Joab 2 S 11_{18} 14_{33}, Joah 2 K 18_{37}||Is 36_{22}, Job Jb 31_{37} $38_{4.18}$ 42_{3}, Jonah Jon $1_{8.10}$, Jonathan, son of Abiathar 2 S 15_{28} $17_{17.21}$, Jonathan, son of Saul 1 S $14_{1.43.43}$ $19_{2.3.7}$ 20_{9}, Joseph Gn 37_{5} 46_{31} 47_{1} 4QapJoseph[b] $1_{25.28}$ perh. 3_{7}, Micah Mc 3_{8}, Micaiah Jr 36_{13}, Michal 1 S 19_{11}, Mordecai Est 2_{22} 3_{4} 4_{7} 6_{2}, Moses Ex 4_{28} $19_{3.9}$ Dt 5_{5} 30_{18}, Naaman 2 K 5_{4}, Nehemiah Ne $2_{12.16.18}$, Obadiah 1 K $18_{12.16}$, Rahab Jos $2_{14.20}$, Rebekah Gn 24_{23} 4QJub[g] 27_{7} (א[ג]יד), Ruth Ru 2_{19} 3_{16}, Samson Jg 14_{2+6t} 16_{6+6t}, Samuel 1 S $3_{15.18}$ 8_{9} $9_{18.19}$ $10_{16.16}$ 15_{16} Si 46_{20}, Saul 1 S 10_{15}, Shaphan 2 K 22_{10}||2 C 34_{18}, Shebna 2 K 18_{37}||Is 36_{22}, Solomon 1 K 10_{3}||2 C 9_{2}, Zadok 2 S 15_{28} 17_{16}.

אָדָם *human being* Ps 64_{10} Dn 10_{21} 11_{2} (both כְּמַרְאֵה אָדָם *one with the appearance of a human being*), אִישׁ *man, husband* Gn 32_{30} 37_{17} Jg 13_{6} 14_{15} 1 S $4_{13.14}$ $9_{6.8}$ 27_{11} 2 S 1_{4} $18_{10.11}$ 2 K $7_{9.10}$ Jr 4_{5} 9_{11} Dn 9_{23} 4QD[f] 3_{15} 4QapJoshua[a] 26_{2} (ה[ג]יד), אִשָּׁה *woman, wife* Jg 13_{10} 14_{17} 1 S 19_{11} 25_{37} 27_{11} 2 S 11_{5} 2 K $4_{2.7}$, אָב *father* Gn 9_{22} Dt 32_{7}, בֵּן *son* Gn 45_{26} Jos 7_{19} 1 S 14_{1} 2 S 13_{4} 15_{28} 2 K 18_{37}||Is 36_{22} Ezr 2_{59}||Ne 7_{61}, of man, in ref. to Ezekiel Ezk 23_{36} 37_{18} 40_{4} 43_{10}, בַּת *daughter* Ca 5_{8}, אָח *brother* Gn 42_{29} $43_{6.7}$ 44_{24} 45_{13}, נַעַר *lad* Nm 11_{27} 1 S $25_{8.12.14}$ 2 S $1_{5.6.13}$ 17_{18}, נַעֲרָה *young woman* Gn $24_{28(Qr)}$ Est 4_{4}, עֶבֶד *servant* Gn 26_{32} 1 S $18_{24.26}$ 2 S 12_{18} 2 K 6_{11} Est $3_{4.6}$ Lachish ost. 3_{1} (להגן[ד]), שִׁפְחָה *female servant* 2 S 17_{17}, סָרִיס *eunuch* Est 4_{4}, גֹּאֵל *redeemer* Ru 4_{4}.

מֶלֶךְ *king* 2 S 19_{7} 1 K 1_{20} 2 K 7_{12}, פַּרְעֹה *Pharaoh* Jub[h] 40_{1}, נָשִׂיא *prince* Ex 16_{22}, שַׂר *prince, chief* 2 K 5_{4} Jr $36_{16.16.20}$ 4QJub[h] 40_{2} ([שר] ... [וי]גיד), אָדוֹן *lord* 1 K 1_{20}, שֹׁפֵט *judge* Dt 17_{9}=11QT 56_{1} ([והג]ידו) Dt 17_{10}=11QT 56_{2} ([והגי]דו) Dt 17_{11}=11QT 56_{3} 11QT $56_{4.7}$, סֹפֵר *scribe* 2 K 18_{37}||Is 36_{22} 2 K 22_{10}||2 C 34_{18}, מַזְכִּיר *recorder* 2 K 18_{37}||Is 36_{22}, כֹּהֵן *priest* Dt $17_{9.10.11}$ 2 S 17_{16}, נָבִיא *prophet* 1 K 14_{3} 2 K 6_{12}, worshipper Ps 38_{19} 40_{5} $71_{17.18}$ 75_{10} (or em. אָגִיל *I will rejoice*) 142_{3} 4QapPs[b] 1_{1} GnzPs 3_{27}, אַשָּׁף *conjuror* Dn 2_{2}, חַרְטֹם *magician* Dn 2_{2}, חָכָם *wise one* Is 19_{12} Jb 15_{18}, צַדִּיק *righteous one* Ps 92_{16}.

מֵרֵעַ *companion* Jg $14_{12.12.13.14}$, יָדִיד *beloved* perh. 4QHod[a] 7.1_{17}, חלק ptc. *one who shares* Pr 29_{24}, שׁמע ptc. *one who hears* CD 9_{12}, יָפֵחַ *witness* Pr 12_{17}, עֵד *witness* Pr 12_{17}, מֵלִיץ *mediator* Jb 33_{23}, מַגִּיד *messenger* Jr 51_{31}, מַלְאָךְ *messenger* 1 S 11_{9} 2 S 11_{22} 2 K 7_{15} 10_{8} Jb 1_{15} 33_{23}, רָץ *runner* Jr 51_{31}, צֹפֶה *sentry* 2 S 18_{25} 2 K $9_{18.20}$, מְצַפֶּה *sentry* Is 21_{6}, פָּלִיט *escaped one* Gn 14_{13} 2 K 9_{15} Is 45_{21} 66_{19} Jr 50_{28}, נוס ptc. *one who flees* Jr 50_{28}, יֹשֵׁב *inhabitant* Is 42_{12} Jr 4_{5}, דּוֹר *generation* Ps 22_{32} 145_{4}, בַּיִת *house(hold)* Gn $24_{49.49}$, of Jacob Is 48_{6} (or em. עוד hi. *testify*).

פֶּה *mouth* Ps 51$_{17}$, קוֹל *voice* Jr 4$_{15}$, לֵב *heart* Si 37$_{14}$, נֶפֶשׁ *soul* 11QPs^a 19$_9$, רֵעַ *roar* Jb 36$_{33}$, עוֹף *birds* Jb 12$_7$, בַּעַל *possessor* of wings, i.e. bird Ec 10$_{20}$, מַקֵּל *staff* Hos 4$_{12}$, גִּבְעָה *hill* 11QPs^a 28$_6$, שָׁמַיִם *heavens* Ps 50$_6$ 97$_6$, רָקִיעַ *firmament* Ps 19$_2$, עָפָר *dust* Ps 30$_{10}$, סוֹף *end* Si 11$_{27}$, אֶחָד *one* Jb 33$_{23}$, זֶה *this* Jb 1$_{16.17.19}$, אֵלֶּה *these* Ezr 2$_{59}$||Ne 7$_{61}$, מִי *who?* Gn 3$_{11}$ 1 S 20$_{10}$ Is 41$_{26}$ 43$_9$ 44$_7$ 45$_{21}$ 48$_{14}$ Ec 6$_{12}$ 8$_7$ 10$_{14}$ Si 16$_{22}$ 11QPs^a 28$_7$, אֲשֶׁר *one who* Lv 14$_{35}$, -שֶׁ *one who* Ca 1$_7$.

Subj. not specified, Gn 41$_{24}$ 48$_2$ (or em. ho.) Lv 5$_1$ Jg 4$_{12}$ 9$_{7.42}$ 14$_{19}$ 1 S 14$_{33}$ 17$_{31}$ 18$_{20}$ 19$_{21}$ 23$_{1.25}$ 24$_2$ 2 S 2$_4$ 3$_{23}$ 4$_{10}$ 10$_5$||1 C 19$_5$ 2 S 11$_{10}$ 15$_{31}$ 19$_9$ 1 K 1$_{23}$ 2$_{39}$ 20$_{17}$ 2 K 7$_{11}$ 9$_{36}$ Is 41$_{26}$ 58$_1$ Jr 46$_{14}$ 48$_{20}$ 50$_2$ Am 4$_{13}$ (or em. מַגִּיד לְאָדָם מַה־שֵּׂחוֹ *declaring to humans what is his thought* to מְמַגֵּד לָאֲדָמָה שִׂיחהּ *making abundant its plants for the earth*) Ps 9$_{12}$ 92$_3$ Est 4$_{12}$ 2 C 20$_2$ 1QM 10$_1$ 11QT 55$_{18}$.

<OBJ> 1. thing made known, עַם *people* Est 2$_{10.20}$ 3$_6$, מוֹלֶדֶת *kindred* Est 2$_{10.20}$, בַּיִת *house* Ezr 2$_{59}$||Ne 7$_{61}$, זֶרַע *seed*, i.e. descent Ezr 2$_{59}$||Ne 7$_{61}$, יָד *hand* Ne 2$_{18}$, זְרוֹעַ *arm*, i.e. strength Ps 71$_{18}$, לֵב *heart* Jg 16$_{17.18.18}$, שֵׁם *name* Gn 32$_{30}$, כָּבוֹד *glory* Gn 45$_{13}$, תְּהִלָּה *praise* Is 42$_{12}$ Ps 51$_{17}$.

דָּבָר *word, matter* Gn 44$_{24}$ Ex 4$_{28}$ 19$_9$ Dt 5$_5$ 17$_9$=11QT 56$_1$ ((והג]ידו]) Dt 17$_{10.11}$ Jos 2$_{14.20}$ 1 S 3$_{18}$ 18$_{26}$ 19$_7$ 25$_{36.37}$ 2 S 11$_{18}$ 1 K 10$_3$ ||2 C 9$_2$ 2 K 6$_{12}$ 18$_{37}$||Is 36$_{22}$ Jr 16$_{10}$ 36$_{13.16.20}$ 42$_4$ Ps 147$_{19}$ Ec 10$_{20}$ Est 4$_{9.12}$ 4QJub^a 1$_5$ ((הדב[רים]) 4QapJoseph^b 1$_{28}$, מִלָּה *word* Jb 26$_4$, פָּרָשָׁה *exact statement* Est 4$_7$, רשׁם pass. ptc. *that which is inscribed* Dn 10$_{21}$, חִידָה *riddle* Jg 14$_{12+6t}$ 4QMyst^b 1b$_1$, חֲלוֹם *dream* Dn 2$_2$ 4QJub^h 40$_1$ ([חלמותיו]), מַרְאָה *vision* 1 S 3$_{15}$, אוֹת *sign* Ex 4$_{28}$, בְּרִית *covenant* Dt 4$_{13}$, תּוֹרָה *law* 11QT 56$_{3.7}$, מִשְׁפָּט *judgment* 11QT 56$_2$ ((והגי[דו]), *manner* 1 S 8$_9$, דֶּרֶךְ *way* Jr 42$_3$, i.e. errand 1 S 9$_{6.8}$, fate Si 46$_{20}$.

קרה ptc. *that which befalls* Gn 42$_{29}$, אתה ptc. *that which is to come* Is 41$_{23}$, היה ni. ptc. *future event* Si 48$_{25}$, רִאשׁוֹן *former thing* Is 41$_{22}$ 48$_3$, אַחֲרִית *end* Is 46$_{10}$, בצר pass. ptc. *fortified*, i.e. closely guarded, *thing* Jr 33$_3$, תַּעֲלֻמָה *secret* Jb 11$_6$, סתר ni. ptc. *hidden thing* Si 48$_{25}$, חָדָשׁ *new thing* Is 42$_9$, גָּדוֹל *great thing* Jr 33$_3$.

צֶדֶק *righteousness* Ps 50$_6$ 97$_6$ Pr 12$_{17}$, צְדָקָה *righteousness* Is 57$_{12}$ Ps 22$_{32}$ 4QapMes 5.2$_7$ (צד[ק]ות), יֹשֶׁר *uprightness* Jb 33$_{23}$, מֵישָׁר *uprightness* Is 45$_{19}$, אֱמֶת *truth* Ps 30$_{10}$ Dn 11$_2$, אֱמוּנָה *faithfulness* Ps 92$_3$ 11QPs^a 19$_9$, חֶסֶד *loyalty* Ps 92$_3$ 4QapJoseph^b 1$_{25}$, חַטָּאת *sin* Is 3$_9$ 58$_1$ Mc 3$_8$, פֶּשַׁע *transgression* Is 58$_1$ Mc 3$_8$ Jb 36$_9$, עָוֹן *iniquity* Ps 38$_{19}$, תּוֹעֵבָה *abomination* Ezk 23$_{36}$, מִרְמָה *deceit* Pr 12$_{17}$.

מַעֲשֶׂה *deed* Is 57$_{12}$ Ps 19$_2$ Si 16$_{22}$, עֲלִילָה *deed* Ps 9$_{12}$, פֹּעַל *deed* Ps 64$_{10}$ Jb 36$_9$, נִפְלָאָה *wonderful deed* Ps 71$_{17}$ Jb 42$_3$, נְקָמָה *vengeance* Jr 50$_{28}$, כֹּחַ *strength* Ps 111$_6$, גְּבוּרָה *might* Ps 71$_{18}$ GnzPs 3$_{27}$, צָרָה *distress* Ps 142$_3$, שִׂיחָה *anxiety* Si 37$_{14}$, בַּיִת *house* Ezk 43$_{10}$, מִסְפָּר *number* Jb 31$_{37}$, זַן *kind* of chariot Si 49$_8$, קֵץ *time* 1QM 1$_{18}$ ((ק[צי]).

אֵלֶּה *these* Is 48$_{14}$, זאת *this* Is 43$_9$ 45$_{21}$ Jr 5$_{20}$ 9$_{11}$, הֵמָּה *those things* 11QT 51$_7$, אֲשֶׁר *that which, one who* Gn 45$_{13}$ 49$_1$ Jg 14$_6$ 1 S 15$_{16}$ 24$_{19}$ 2 S 18$_{21}$ 2 K 7$_{12}$ Is 21$_6$ 41$_{22}$ 46$_{10}$ Ru 2$_{19}$ 3$_4$, כֹּל *everything* 1 S 9$_{19}$ 19$_{18}$ 2 S 11$_{22}$ 1 K 19$_1$ Ezk 40$_4$ Ru 3$_{16}$ Ec 10$_{14}$ Est 4$_7$ 4QAcademyFr 1$_3$ ((כו[ל]); obj. not specified, Is 44$_7$ 4QHod^a 7.1$_{17}$.

2. person(s) to whom made known, Y. Jb 31$_{37}$ Si 16$_{22}$, Israel(ites) Dt 32$_7$, David 2 S 15$_{31}$, בַּיִת *house(hold)* 2 K 7$_{9.11}$, *house* of Israel Ezk 43$_{10}$.

<PREP> לְ of direction, *to* or introducing indirect object 4QapJoshua^a 26$_2$ (ה[ג]יד) 4QparaKings 12$_6$ 4Q sapHymnA 1.2$_3$ 4QapMes 5.2$_7$ 4QAcademyFr 1$_3$, + Y. Dt 26$_3$, Aramaean Gn 31$_{20}$, Hebrew Gn 14$_{13}$, Jews Ne 2$_{18}$, Naamathite Jb 12$_7$, Babylon Is 21$_{10}$, Egypt Is 19$_{12}$, Israel(ites) Dt 4$_{13}$ 5$_5$ 17$_9$=11QT 56$_1$ ([והג]ידו לכה]) Dt 17$_{10}$=11QT 56$_2$ ((והגי[דו]) Dt 17$_{11}$=11QT 56$_3$ Dt 30$_{18}$ 1 K 1$_{20}$ Is 41$_{22}$ Mc 3$_8$ Ps 147$_{19}$ 1QM 10$_1$ 11$_{5.8}$ 11QT 55$_{18}$ 56$_{4.7}$, עַם *people* 1 S 8$_9$ 2 S 19$_9$ Is 58$_1$ Jr 16$_{10}$ 42$_{3.4}$ Ezk 24$_{19}$ Hos 4$_{12}$ Ps 22$_{32}$ 111$_6$.

Aaron Ex 4$_{28}$, Abiathar 2 S 15$_{35}$, Abigail 1 S 25$_{14}$, Abimelech, king of Gerar Gn 21$_{26}$, Abimelech, son of Jerubbaal Jg 9$_{42}$, Abram Gn 14$_{13}$, Absalom 2 S 17$_{18}$, Ahab 1 K 18$_{12.16}$, Ahimaaz 2 S 17$_{17}$, Balak Nm 23$_3$, Ben-hadad 1 K 20$_{17}$, Boaz Ru 4$_4$, Daniel Dn 10$_{21}$ 11$_2$, David 1 S 18$_{26}$ 19$_{2.3.7.11}$ 20$_{9.10}$ 22$_{21}$ 23$_{1.25}$ 25$_{12}$ 2 S 1$_{4.5.6.13}$ 2$_4$ 4$_{10}$ 7$_{11}$||1 C 17$_{10}$ (or em.; see Subj.) 2 S 10$_5$||1 C 19$_5$ 2 S 11$_{5.10.18.22}$ 12$_{18}$ 17$_{16.17.21}$ 24$_{13}$ 4QMidrEschat^b 3$_{10}$ ((ה[גיד]), Delaiah Jr 36$_{13}$, Delilah Jg 16$_{6+6t}$, Eli 1 S 3$_{13.18}$ 4$_{14}$, Elisha 2 K 4$_2$, Elishama Jr 36$_{13}$, Elnathan Jr 36$_{13}$, Esther Est 2$_{22}$ 4$_{4.8.9}$, Gemariah Jr 36$_{13}$, Haman Est 3$_{4.6}$,

Hezekiah 2 K 1837||Is 3622.

Isaac Gn 2632 4QJubg 277 (א[ג]יד), Jacob/Israel Gn 4526 482, Jaush Lachish ost. 31 (להג[ד] ל[אד]ני יאו[ש]), Jehoshaphat 2 C 202, Jehu 2 K 936 108, Jezaniah Jr 423.4, Jezebel 1 K 191, Joab 2 S 323 1810.11, Job Jb 115.16.17.19 116, Johanan Jr 423.4, Jonadab 2 S 134, Jonathan 2 S 1717, Joseph Gn 3716, Joshua Jos 719, Jotham Jg 97, Laban Gn 2915 3120.27, Mordecai Est 412, Moses Ex 1622 Nm 1127 4QJuba 15 11QT 517, Nabal 1 S 258.19.36.37, Oholah Ezk 2336, Oholibah Ezk 2336, Rachel Gn 2912, Ruth Ru 34, Samson Jg 1412.13, Samuel 1 S 1918, Saul 1 S 96.8.18.19 1016 1433.43.43 1516 1820.24 1921 2222 242 Ps 522, Shimei 1 K 239, Sisera Jg 412, Zadok 2 S 1535, Zedekiah Jr 3613 3815, Zophar Jb 127.

אָדָם *human being* Gn 311 Am 413 (or em.; see Subj.) Mc 68 (or em.; see Subj.) Jb 3323 Ec 612 87 1014 Ne 212, אִישׁ *man, husband* Gn 436.7 Jg 1310 1 S 119 2519 2 K 427.31 Jon 110, אִשָּׁה *woman, wife* Jg 136 1416.16.17 1 S 2514 1 K 143 2 K 47, אָב *father* Gn 4424 4513 Jg 142.6.9.16 1 S 141, אֵם *mother* Jg 142.6.9.16, חָמוֹת *mother-in-law* Ru 219 316, בֵּן *son* Ex 138 Jg 1417 Jr 3613 423.4 Ezk 3718, of Israel Ex 193, אָח *brother* Gn 922 375, דּוֹד *uncle* 1 S 1015, נַעַר *lad* 1 S 96.8 1016, עֶבֶד *servant* Gn 4424 1 S 2311 2 S 1711|| 1 C 1710 2 K 712 912 Est 34.

אָדוֹן *lord* Gn 326 2 K 54 Lachish ost. 31 (להג[ד] ל[אד]ני), מֶלֶךְ *king* 2 S 1433 1528 1717.21 1821.25 1 K 123 2 K 611.12 715 2210||2 C 3418 Jr 3616 5131 Ec 1020 Dn 22 Si 4620 4QJubh 402 ([וי]גיד ... [למלך]), מַלְכָּה *queen* 1 K 103||2 C 92 Est 222, פַּרְעֹה *Pharaoh* Gn 1218 4124 4631 471, שַׂר *prince* Jr 3613.17 3825.27 423.4, חֹר *noble* Ne 218, כֹּהֵן *priest* Lv 1435 2 S 1535 Ne 218, שֹׁעֵר *gatekeeper* 2 K 710, סֹפֵר *scribe* Jr 3613, סָגָן *official* Ne 218, חָכָם *wise one* 4QJubh 401 ([החכמים ו]יגיד [להמה]), חַרְטֹם *magician* 4QJubh 401 ([חרטומי ... ו]יגיד [להמה]), מֵרֵעַ *companion* Jg 1415, female lover Ca 17, דּוֹד *beloved* Ca 58, מַלָּח *mariner* Jon 18, רָשָׁע *wicked one* Jb 369, בַּיִת *house(hold)* Gn 2428, of Jacob/Israel Is 485 581 Ezk 404, שְׁאֵרִית *remnant* of Judah Jr 4220.21, דּוֹר *generation* Ps 7118, כֹּל *everyone* Ps 7118, עוֹלָם *eternity*, i.e. for ever Ps 7510 (or em.; see Subj.).

בְּ of place, *in, among*, + Arnon Jr 4820, Egypt Jr 4614, Gath 2 S 120 Mc 110 (or em.; see Subj.), Jezreel 2 K 915, Judah Jr 45, Zion Jr 5028, עַם *people* Ps 912, עִיר *city* 1 S 413, בַּיִת *house* Jr 520, גּוֹי *nation* Jr 502, אִי *coastland* Is 4212 Jr 3110, הַר *mountain* 11QT 517, אֹזֶן *ear* Jr 3620; of time, + יוֹם *day* Ex 138, בֹּקֶר *morning* Ps 923, לַיְלָה *night* Ps 923; of instrument, *by (means of), with*, + קוֹל *voice* Is 4820; of accompaniment, *with, in*, + אֱמֶת *truth* 11QT 564.

כְּ *as*, + Sodom Is 39; *concerning, according to*, + דָּבָר *word, thing* Gn 2428 1 S 2512 Jr 3827, כֹּל *everything* Jr 4220.

מִן of direction, *from*, + Dan Jr 415, מָקוֹם *place* Dt 1710 11QT 564; of time, *from, since*, + ראשׁ *beginning* Is 4126, רֵאשִׁית *beginning* Is 4610, קֶדֶם *ancient time* Is 4610; of comparison, *(more) than*, + צֹפֶה *sentry* Si 3714.

אֶל *to* 4QpPsa 1.45, + Y. Ex 199, Eli 1 S 315.

עַל *concerning* 11QT 5518, + Y. Jb 3633, Bigthana Est 62, David and followers 1 S 2711, Joseph 4QJubh 402 ([וי]גיד על[יו]), Teresh Est 62, אָדָם *human being* Si 1127, אִשָּׁה *woman* 4QDf 315 ([אשה] ... יגיד על[ה]), סָרִיס *eunuch* Est 62.

אֵת *with*, + מִי *whom?* Jb 264.

לִפְנֵי *before*, + Y. Ps 1423, Saul 1 S 1731.

עַל־אֹדוֹת *concerning*, + בְּאֵר *well* Gn 2632.

עַל־פִּי *according to*, + דָּבָר *word* Gn 437.

מִפִּי *according to* 4QapJoshuaa 262 (ה[ג]יד).

<COLL> נגד hi. **a.** with object clause introduced by

(1) כִּי *that* Gn 311 1218 2912 3120 Dt 263 3018 Jg 412 149 1 S 313 1016 2221 2 S 711 1218 197 Jr 4820 5131 Ps 9216 1QM 101 4QMidrEschatb 310 (ה[גיד]).

(2) וְ *that* 1 C 1710.

(3) אֲשֶׁר *that* Est 34 1QDM 1.16.

(4) -שֶׁ *that* Ca 58.

(5) הֲ interrogative Gn 2423 436 Jb 3818.

(6) אִם *if, whether* Gn 2449.49.

(7) אוֹ מָה *if (by chance)* 1 S 2010.

(8) מִי *who?* 1 K 120 2 K 611.

(9) מָה *what?* Gn 2915 Jos 719 1 S 1015 1443 2 S 14 1 K 143 2 K 42 Is 4122 Jr 3825 Ezk 2419 3718 Am 413 (or em.; see Subj.) Mc 68 Ec 612 81 Ne 212.

(10) אֵי־זֶה *where?* 1 S 918.

(11) אֵיפֹה *where?* Gn 3716 Jb 384.

(12) אֵיכָה *where?* Ca 17.

(13) בַּמֶּה *wherein?* Jg 16$_{6.10.13.15}$.

(14) מַדּוּעַ *why?* 2 S 13$_4$.

(15) אֵיךְ *how?* Jr 36$_{17}$.

(16) כַּאֲשֶׁר *how?, when?* Ec 8$_7$.

(17) בַּאֲשֶׁר לְמִי *on account of whom?* Jon 1$_8$.

(18) לֵאמֹר *saying*, followed by direct speech Gn 45$_{26}$ Ex 13$_8$ Lv 14$_{35}$ 1 S 14$_{33}$ 18$_{24}$ 19$_{2.11}$ 23$_1$ 24$_2$ 25$_{14}$ 27$_{11}$ 2 S 2$_4$ 3$_{23}$ 4$_{10}$ 11$_{10}$ 15$_{31}$ 17$_{16}$ 19$_9$ 1 K 1$_{23}$ 2$_{39}$ 20$_{17}$ 2 K 4$_{31}$ 5$_4$ 7$_{10}$ 9$_{18.20}$ 10$_8$ 22$_{10}$||2 C 34$_{18}$ 2 C 20$_2$ 1QM 11$_5$; finite form of אמר Gn 46$_{31}$ 47$_1$ 48$_2$ Nm 11$_{27}$ Jg 13$_{10}$ 14$_2$ 16$_{17}$ 1 S 14$_{43}$ 2 S 11$_5$ 18$_{10}$ Is 46$_{10}$ Jr 31$_{10}$ Ps 52$_2$.

b. assoc. with other verbs, (1) || ספר pi. *tell* Ps 19$_2$ 11QPs^a 28$_7$ (+), אמר *say* Ex 19$_3$ Dt 17$_{11}$ (+) 32$_7$ Jr 4$_5$ (+) 4QMyst^b 1b$_1$ 11QT 56$_3$, דבר *speak* Is 45$_{19}$, pi. Ps 40$_6$ 11QPs^a 28$_7$, בשׂר pi. *announce* 2 S 1$_{20}$, שׁמע hi. *announce* Is 41$_{26}$ 43$_9$ (+) 43$_{12}$ 44$_8$ (+) 45$_{21}$ 48$_{3.5}$ (both +) 48$_{20}$ Jr 4$_{5.15}$ 5$_{20}$ 46$_{14}$ 50$_2$ 4QHod^a 7.1$_{17}$ (+), ירה hi. *teach* Dt 17$_{11}$ (+) Jb 12$_7$.

(2) + נבע hi. *utter* 4QHod^a 7.1$_{17}$, קרא *proclaim* Is 44$_7$, ראה hi. *show* Est 4$_8$, שׁבח pi. *praise* Ps 145$_4$, ידה hi. *praise* Ps 30$_{10}$ 11QPs^a 19$_9$, הלל pi. *praise* 11QPs^a 19$_9$, עוד hi. *bear witness* 11QPs^a 28$_6$, שׁפך *pour* complaint Ps 142$_3$.

(3) :: כחד pi. *hide* Jos 7$_{19}$ 1 S 3$_{18}$ Is 3$_9$ Jr 38$_{25}$ Jb 15$_{18}$, עלם hi. *hide* 2 K 4$_{27}$, מנע *withhold* Jr 42$_4$.

c. + adverb, לָמָּה *why?* Gn 12$_{18}$, הַיּוֹם *today* Dt 26$_3$ 1 S 24$_{19}$ 2 S 19$_7$ Jr 42$_{21}$ Zc 9$_{12}$ (or em.; see Subj.), יוֹם *day*, i.e. within a specified number of days Jg 14$_{12.14}$, מֵאָז *from of old* Is 48$_{3.5}$, עַד־הֵנָּה *thus far* Ps 71$_{17}$, עַד־כֵּן *still* Ne 2$_{16}$.

Inf. abs. + finite form of נגד hi. Jg 14$_{12}$ 1 S 10$_{16}$ 22$_{22}$ Jr 36$_{16}$.

2. denounce, inform against (Dt 13$_{10.10}$ [if em.; see Subj.] Jr 20$_{10.10}$ perh. Jb 17$_5$ 21$_{31}$), <SUBJ> Israelites Dt 13$_{10}$ (if em. הָרֹג תַּהַרְגֶנּוּ *you shall surely kill him* to הַגֵּד תַּגִּידֶנּוּ *you shall surely inform against him*), מִי *who* Jb 21$_{31}$; subj. not specified, Jr 20$_{10.10}$ perh. Jb 17$_5$ (but prob. §3). <OBJ> Jeremiah Jr 20$_{10}$, אִשָּׁה *wife* Dt 13$_{10}$ (if em.; see Subj.), בֵּן *son* Dt 13$_{10}$ (if em.; see Subj.), אָח *brother* Dt 13$_{10}$ (if em.; see Subj.), רֵעַ *friend* Dt 13$_{10}$ (if em.; see Subj.) perh. Jb 17$_5$, דֶּרֶךְ *way* Jb 21$_{31}$. <PREP> לְ *for (the purpose of obtaining)*, + חֵלֶק *portion* perh. Jb 17$_5$; עַל *to*, + פָּנִים *face* Jb 21$_{31}$. <COLL> Inf. abs. + finite form of נגד hi. Dt 13$_{10}$ (if em.; see Subj.).

3. invite,* unless §2, <SUBJ> subj. not specified, Jb 17$_5$. <OBJ> רֵעַ *friend* Jb 17$_5$. <PREP> לְ of direction, *to*, + חֵלֶק *portion*, i.e. feast Jb 17$_5$.

4. ptc. as noun, מַגִּיד **messenger,** <SUBJ> בוא *come* 2 S 15$_{13}$, רוץ *run* Jr 51$_{31}$, אמר *say* 2 S 15$_{13}$, נגד hi. *tell* Jr 51$_{31}$. <OBJ> קרא *meet* Jr 51$_{31}$.

Also 4QapJoseph^a 9$_1$ ([ה]גדתי) 4QapJoseph^b 8$_1$ 4QHymnPr 3$_2$ 4QPrFêtes^c 5.2$_5$ 11QMelch 5$_2$.

<SYN> §1 ספר pi. *tell*, אמר *say*, דבר qal, pi. *speak*, בשׂר pi. *announce*, שׁמע hi. *announce*, ירה hi. *teach*.

<ANT> כחד pi. *hide*, עלם hi. *hide*, מנע *withhold*.

Ho. 35.1.0.1 Pf. הֻגַּד (ms הוגד); + waw וְהֻגַּד; וַיֻּגַּד; inf. abs. הֻגֵּד—**be told, announced, reported,** <SUBJ> חָזוּת *vision* Is 21$_1$, impersonal Gn 22$_{20}$ 27$_{42}$ 31$_{22}$ 38$_{13.24}$ Ex 14$_5$ 17$_4$ Jos 9$_{24.24}$ 10$_{17}$ Jg 9$_{25.47}$ 1 S 15$_{12.31(ms)}$ 19$_{19}$ 23$_{7.13}$ 27$_4$ 2 S 6$_{12}$ 10$_{17}$||1 C 19$_{17}$ 2 S 19$_2$ 21$_{11}$ 1 K 1$_{51}$ 2$_{29.41}$ 18$_{13}$ 2 K 6$_{13}$ 8$_7$ Is 7$_2$ 40$_{21}$ Mc 6$_8$ (if em. הִגִּיד *he has declared* to הֻגַּד) Lachish ost. 3$_{13}$, חֹק *statute*, i.e. appointed time Si 14$_{12}$, חֲצִי *half* 1 K 10$_7$||2 C 9$_6$, כֹּל *everything* Ru 2$_{11.11}$.

<PREP> בְּ of time, *in, on*, + יוֹם *day* Gn 31$_{22}$.

לְ of direction, *to*, + Israel(ites) Dt 17$_4$ Is 40$_{21}$, בַּיִת *house* of David Is 7$_2$, Abimelech Jg 9$_{25.47}$, Abraham Gn 22$_{20}$, Ben-hadad 2 K 8$_7$, Boaz Ru 2$_{11}$, David 2 S 6$_{12}$ 15$_{31(ms)}$ 10$_{17}$||1 C 19$_{17}$ 2 S 21$_{11}$, Isaiah Is 21$_2$, Joab 2 S 19$_2$, Joshua Jos 10$_{17}$, Judah Gn 38$_{24}$, Laban Gn 31$_{22}$, Rebekah Gn 27$_{42}$, Samuel 1 S 15$_{12}$, Saul 1 S 19$_{19}$ 23$_{7.13}$ 27$_4$, Solomon 1 K 1$_{51}$ 2$_{29.41}$, Tamar Gn 38$_{13}$, אָדָם *human being* Mc 6$_8$ (if em.; see Subj.), בֵּן *son* Si 14$_{12}$, מֶלֶךְ *king* Ex 14$_5$ 2 S 6$_{12}$ 1 K 2$_{29}$ 2 K 6$_{13}$ 8$_7$, מַלְכָּה *queen* 1 K 10$_7$||2 C 9$_6$, אָדוֹן *lord* 1 K 18$_{13}$, עֶבֶד *servant* Jos 9$_{24}$ Lachish ost. 3$_{13}$.

מִן of time, *from, since*, + ראשׁ *beginning* Is 40$_{21}$.

<COLL> נגד ho. + **a.** כִּי *that* Gn 31$_{22}$ Ex 14$_5$ Jg 9$_{47}$ 1 S 23$_{7.13}$ 27$_4$ 1 K 2$_{29.41}$.

b. מָה *what?* Mc 6$_8$ (if em.; see Subj.).

c. לֵאמֹר *saying* Gn 22$_{20}$ 38$_{13.24}$ Jos 10$_{17}$ 1 S 15$_{12.31(ms)}$ 19$_{19}$ 2 S 6$_{12}$ 1 K 1$_{51}$ 2 K 6$_{13}$ 8$_7$ Is 7$_2$ Lachish ost. 3$_{13}$.

d. direct speech without particle, 2 S 19$_2$.

inf. abs. + finite form of נגד ho. Jos 9$_{24}$ Ru 2$_{11}$.

וַיֻּגַּד לְרִבְקָה אֶת־דִּבְרֵי עֵשָׂו *and it was told to Rebekah,* i.e. someone told her, *the words of Esau* Gn 27$_{42}$, הֻגֵּד הֻגַּד לַעֲבָדֶיךָ אֵת אֲשֶׁר צִוָּה י׳ *it has indeed been told to your servants how Y. commanded* Moses to give the land Jos 9$_{24}$, וַיֻּגַּד לְדָוִד אֵת אֲשֶׁר־עָשְׂתָה רִצְפָּה *and it was told to David what Rizpah had done* 2 S 21$_{11}$, sim. 1 K 18$_{13}$.

Also perh. 1Q30 7$_{2}$.*

⇨ נֶ֫גֶד *in front of,* perh. נָגִיד *leader.*

נֶ֫גֶד I $_{151.8.44}$ prep. **in front of**—sf. נֶגְדִּי, נֶגְדְּךָ (נֶגְדֶּךָ, Q נגדכה), נֶגְדּוֹ, נֶגְדָּהּ, נֶגְדְּכֶם, נֶגְדָּם (Q נגדמה); ה- of direction נֶגְדָּה—**1.** נֶגֶד alone, **a. in front of, before. b. in the presence of. c. opposite, against** (Jb 10$_{17}$ Ec 4$_{12}$ Si 37$_{5}$ 51$_{2}$ 1QH 10$_{24}$), **over against** (Ps 23$_{5}$ 31$_{20}$ 138$_{1}$).* **d.** perh. **toward** (Ps 52$_{11}$ 88$_{2}$).* **e.** with reflexive suffix, **in front of oneself,** i.e. straight ahead (Jos 6$_{5.20}$ Jr 31$_{39}$ Am 4$_{3}$ Ne 12$_{37}$ Pr 4$_{25}$).

Followed by noun or suffix in ref. to noun, Y. 1 S 12$_{3}$ 16$_{6}$ 2 S 22$_{13}$||Ps 18$_{13}$ Is 40$_{17}$ 49$_{16}$ 59$_{12}$ Ps 38$_{10}$ 39$_{6}$ 69$_{20}$ 88$_{2}$ 89$_{37}$ 109$_{15}$ 119$_{168}$ Jb 26$_{6}$ Pr 15$_{11}$ Si 39$_{19}$ 4QapPs^{b} 31$_{5}$ 4QDibHam^{a} 1.3$_{3}$, אֱלֹהִים *gods* Ps 138$_{1}$, Aramaeans 1 K 20$_{27}$, Israel Dt 31$_{11}$ 1 S 15$_{30}$ 2 S 12$_{12}$, עַם *people* Ex 34$_{10}$ 1 K 21$_{13}$, גּוֹי *nation* Is 61$_{11}$, קָהָל *assembly* of Israel Jos 8$_{35}$ 1 K 8$_{22}$||2 C 6$_{12}$ 2 C 6$_{13}$ Si 50$_{13}$, חַיִל *army* 1QM 15$_{2}$, תּוֹדָה *thanksgiving company* Ne 12$_{37}$, תַּהֲלוּכָה *procession* Ne 12$_{37}$.

Aristobulos 4QMishC^{b} 3$_{6}$ ([אר]יסטבולוס), Jacob Gn 33$_{12}$, Job Jb 10$_{17}$ (unless נֶגֶד II *blow*), Joseph Gn 47$_{15}$, Naboth 1 K 21$_{10.13}$, אִישׁ *man* Ne 8$_{3}$, i.e. each Jos 6$_{5.20}$, אִשָּׁה *woman* Jos 8$_{35}$ Ne 8$_{3}$, i.e. each Am 4$_{3}$, אָב *father* Ps 78$_{12}$, בֵּן *son* Ps 31$_{20}$ Pr 4$_{25}$ (+ לְנֹכַח *in front*) 1QH 10$_{24}$ 13$_{11}$ 4QBark^{a} 1.3$_{2}$, אָח *brother* Gn 31$_{32.37}$ 1 C 8$_{32}$ 9$_{38}$, טַף *infants* Jos 8$_{35}$, מֶלֶךְ *king* Ps 119$_{46}$ 1QM 15$_{2}$, מָשִׁיחַ *anointed one* 1 S 12$_{3}$, זָקֵן *elder* 1 S 15$_{30}$ Is 24$_{23}$ Ru 4$_{4}$, כֹּהֵן *priest* Jos 8$_{33}$ 2 C 8$_{14}$, לֵוִי *Levite* Jos 8$_{33}$ 2 C 7$_{6}$, worshipper Ps 38$_{18}$ 44$_{16}$ 51$_{5}$, ירא ptc. *one who fears* Y. Ps 22$_{26}$ (or em. נְגִידִי *O my Prince*) 4QapPs^{b} 31$_{4}$ 33$_{5}$ ([ירא]יך), חָסִיד *loyal one* Ps 52$_{11}$, גֵּר *sojourner* Jos 8$_{35}$, ישב ptc. *one who sits* Ru 4$_{4}$, בין hi. *one who understands* Ne 8$_{3}$, צֹרֵר *enemy* Ps 23$_{5}$, עָר *enemy* Si 37$_{5.6(Bmg)}$, קום ptc. *one who rises up* Si 51$_{13}$, חַי *living one* Ec 6$_{8}$, פָּנִים *face* Ex 10$_{10}$ Is 5$_{21}$ (+ בְּעֵינֵיהֶן *in their own eyes*) Ho 7$_{2}$ Lm 3$_{35}$, עַיִן *eye* Jl 1$_{16}$ 1QH 10$_{4}$ ([נגד עיני])=4QHod$_{f}$ 3$_{2}$.

Jericho Jos 3$_{16}$, עִיר *city* Jos 8$_{11}$, הַר *mountain* Ex 19$_{2}$, סַף *threshold* Ezk 41$_{16}$, פֶּתַח *entrance* Ezk 40$_{13}$ 3QTr 1$_{8}$, שַׁעַר *gate* Ezk 40$_{23}$ Ne 3$_{31}$ 3QTr 2$_{7}$, בַּיִת *house* Ne 3$_{10.23.29}$ 7$_{3}$, בִּנְיָן *building* Ezk 42$_{1.1}$, נִשְׁכָּה *chamber* Ne 3$_{30}$, רִצְפָּה *pavement* Ezk 42$_{3}$, חוֹמָה *wall* Ne 13$_{21}$, גִּזְרָה *space* Ezk 42$_{1}$, גַּנָּה *garden* 3QTr 11$_{6}$, מַחֲנֶה *camp* 1QM 16$_{3}$, שֶׁמֶשׁ *sun* Nm 25$_{4}$ 2 S 12$_{12}$, אוּר *fire* Is 47$_{14}$, קַו *line* Jr 31$_{39(Qr)}$ (Kt קוה), מַעֲשֶׂה *work* 1QH fr. 5$_{8}$ (מעשיכ[ה]), חַטָּאת *sin* 4QPrFêtes^{b} 41$_{1}$, אֶחָד *one* Ec 4$_{12}$, עֶשְׂרִים *twenty (cubits)* Ezk 42$_{3}$.

With verb, היה *be* Ho 7$_{2}$ Ps 89$_{37}$ 109$_{15}$ Si 51$_{13}$, גדל pi. *magnify* 1QH 26$_{18}$ ([ת]גדלכה), רבב *be many* Is 59$_{12}$ 31$_{5}$, צמח hi. *cause to grow* Is 61$_{11}$, דבר pi. *speak* Ps 119$_{46}$, ספר *tell* 4QapPs^{b} 31$_{4}$, זמר pi. *sing praise* Ps 138$_{1}$, צעק *cry out* Ps 88$_{2}$, גיל *rejoice* 4QapPs^{b} 33$_{5}$, קרא *read* Dt 31$_{11}$ Jos 8$_{35}$ Ne 8$_{3}$, ענה *answer,* i.e. testify 1 S 12$_{3.3}$, עוד hi. *testify* 1 K 21$_{13}$, נכר hi. *recognize* Gn 31$_{32}$, ידע hi. *make known* 4Q418 135$_{2}$, כבד pi. *honour* 1 S 15$_{30.30}$, ישר hi. *look straight ahead* Pr 4$_{25}$.

הלך *go* Gn 33$_{12}$ Ec 6$_{8}$, בוא *come* Dt 31$_{11}$, יצא *go out* Jr 31$_{39}$ Am 4$_{3}$, עלה *go up* Jos 6$_{5.20}$ Ne 12$_{37}$, עבר *pass* Jos 3$_{16}$, חנה *encamp* Ex 19$_{2}$ 1 K 20$_{27}$ 1QM 15$_{2.2}$, ישב *sit* 1 K 21$_{13}$ Is 47$_{14}$, *dwell* 1 C 8$_{32}$ 9$_{38}$, hi. *cause to sit* 1 K 21$_{10}$, ברך *kneel* 2 C 6$_{13}$, עמד *stand* Jos 8$_{33}$ 1 K 8$_{22}$||2 C 6$_{12}$ Ec 4$_{12}$ 2 C 7$_{6}$ 1QM 16$_{3}$, לין *lodge* Ne 13$_{21}$, סתר *hide* 1QH 13$_{11}$, שים *place* Gn 31$_{37}$ 1QH 10$_{4}$ ([ות]שם … [נגד])=4QHod$_{f}$ 3$_{2}$, ערך *arrange,* i.e. spread, table Ps 23$_{5}$, נטה hi. *turn aside* Lm 3$_{35}$, חדש pi. *renew* Jb 10$_{17}$ (unless נֶגֶד II *blow*), גבר hi. *show one's might* 1QH 10$_{24}$, חזק hi. *repair* Ne 3$_{10.23.29.30}$, *hold* shield Si 37$_{5.6(Bmg)}$, קנה *purchase* Ru 4$_{4}$, שלם pi. *pay* vows Ps 22$_{26}$ (or em.; see above), עשה *do* Ex 34$_{10}$ 2 S 12$_{12.12}$ Ps 78$_{12}$ 4QBark^{a} 1.3$_{2}$, שרת pi. *serve* 2 C 8$_{14}$, כרת ni. *be cut off* Jl 1$_{16}$, יקע hi. *expose* Nm 25$_{4}$, מות *die* Gn 47$_{15}$.

2. נֶגְדָּה **before, in the presence of,** followed by noun, עַם *people* Ps 116$_{14.18}$; with verb, שלם pi. *pay* vows Ps 116$_{14.18}$.

3. with preposition, **a.** לְנֶגֶד **in front of, before, in**

the presence of, opposite, against (Pr 21$_{30}$ Dn 10$_{13}$ 1QH 10$_{15}$), **comparable to** (1QH 18$_{10}$ 20$_{31}$), **over,** i.e. in charge of (Ne 11$_{22}$), followed by noun or suffix in ref. to noun, Y. Ps 50$_{8}$ 90$_{8}$ Pr 21$_{30}$ 1QH 20$_{31}$, מַלְאָךְ *angel* Nm 22$_{32}$, Israelites Is 1$_{7}$, Daniel Dn 8$_{15}$ 10$_{13.16}$, Elijah 2 K 1$_{13}$, Habakkuk Hb 1$_{3}$, Hashabiah Ne 12$_{24}$, Jeshua Ne 12$_{24}$, Joshua Jos 5$_{13}$, Mattaniah Ne 12$_{9}$, Sherebiah Ne 12$_{24}$, בֵּן *son* Ne 12$_{24}$ 1 C 5$_{11}$ 1QH 13$_{15}$, אִישׁ *man* perh. 4QMyst[a] 7$_{5}$, גֶּבֶר *man* perh. 4QMyst[b] 6$_{5}$ perh. 7$_{2}$, אָח *brother* Ne 12$_{9}$, worshipper 2 S 22$_{23}$||Ps 18$_{23}$ Ps 16$_{8}$ (or em. לִנְגִידִי *as my leader*) Ps 39$_{2}$, דרשׁ ptc. *one who seeks* 1QH 10$_{15}$, בֹּנֶה *builder* Ne 3$_{37}$, זָר *stranger* Ps 54$_{5}$ (or em. לִנְגִידִים *as my leader*), זֵד *presumptuous one* Ps 54$_{5(mss)}$ (or em.; see above) 86$_{14}$ (or em. לִנְגִידִים), רָם *haughty one* 1QS 11$_{1}$, עָרִיץ *terrible one* Ps 54$_{5}$ (or em.; see above), רַב pl. *many* 1QH 12$_{28}$, פָּנִים *face* 1QH 12$_{15}$, רֹאשׁ *head*, i.e. chief Ne 12$_{24}$, עַיִן *eye* 2 S 22$_{26}$||Ps 18$_{25}$ Ps 5$_{5}$ 26$_{3}$ 36$_{2}$ 101$_{3.7}$ Jb 4$_{16}$ 1QS 10$_{11}$ 4QapPs[b] 31$_{5}$ (ע[ינ]ך) 33$_{8}$ 4QBéat 2.2$_{7}$, בַּיִת *house* Ne 3$_{28}$, מַעֲשֶׂה *work* 1QH 9$_{33}$ 11$_{23}$, מְלָאכָה *work* Ne 11$_{22}$, כָּבוֹד *glory* 1QH 18$_{10}$ GnzPs 1$_{3}$.

With verb, היה *be* 1QH 10$_{15}$, ספר pi. *tell* 1QH 9$_{33}$ 11$_{23}$, שׁוב hi. *reply* 1QS 11$_{1}$, אכל *devour* Is 1$_{7}$, כרע *fall to one's knees* 2 K 1$_{13}$, ישׁב *dwell* 1 C 5$_{11}$, יצב htp. *stand* GnzPs 1$_{3}$, עמד *stand* Jos 5$_{13}$ Dn 8$_{15}$ 10$_{13.16}$ 4QAdmonPar 3.2$_{7}$, כון ni. *be established* Ps 101$_{7}$, ירט *be precipitate* Nm 22$_{32}$, כעס hi. *provoke* Ne 3$_{37}$, שׂים *place* Ps 54$_{5}$ 86$_{14}$ (or em. both; see above) 1QH 12$_{15}$ 4QLam[b] 1$_{9}$, שׁוה pi. *place* Ps 16$_{8}$ (or em.; see above), שׁית *place* Ps 90$_{8}$ 101$_{3}$ 4QBéat 2.2$_{7}$ ([וישיתה]), גבר hi. *show one's might* 1QH 13$_{15}$, חזק hi. *repair* Ne 3$_{28}$, פלא hi. *do wondrously* 1QH 12$_{28}$, כפה *subdue* 4QapPs[b] 31$_{5}$.

b. מִנֶּגֶד (1) **from before, from opposite, away from (the presence of)** (1 S 26$_{20}$ Ps 10$_{5}$), **aloof from** (Ps 38$_{12}$), followed by noun or suffix in ref. to noun, Y. 1 S 26$_{20}$, male lover Ca 6$_{5}$, worshipper Ps 38$_{12}$ (if em. מִנֶּגֶד נִגְעִי *aloof from my plague* to מִנֶּגְדִּי *aloof from me*), רָשָׁע *wicked one* Ps 10$_{5}$, עַיִן *eye* Is 1$_{16}$ Jr 16$_{17}$ (+ מִלִּפְנֵי *from the presence of*) Am 9$_{3}$ Jon 2$_{4}$ Ps 31$_{23}$ Si 39$_{19}$, נֶגַע *plague* Ps 38$_{12}$ (or em.; see above), עֲלֹת *ascent* Ne 3$_{19}$, מִקְצֹעַ *angle* Ne 3$_{25}$, מִגְדָּל *tower* Ne 3$_{25.27}$.

With verb, נפל *fall* 1 S 26$_{20}$, סבב hi. *turn* Ca 6$_{5}$, סור hi. *remove* Is 1$_{16}$, גרשׁ ni. *be expelled* Jon 2$_{4}$, גזר ni. *be cut off* Ps 31$_{23}$, יצב htp. *stand* Ps 5$_{5}$, עמד *stand* Ps 38$_{12}$, צפן ni. *be hidden* Jr 16$_{17}$, סתר ni. *hide oneself* Am 9$_{3}$ Si 39$_{19B)}$ (Bmg pu. *be hidden*), חזק pi. *repair* Ne 3$_{19}$, hi. Ne 3$_{25.27}$.

(2) as adverb, **in front, opposite, at a distance, aloof** (2 S 18$_{13}$ Ob$_{11}$ Si 37$_{4[B]}$ 37$_{9}$), with ראה *see* Dt 32$_{52}$ 2 K 3$_{22}$ 4$_{25}$, שׁלך hi. *cast* soul, i.e. risk life Jg 9$_{17}$, חנה *encamp* Nm 2$_{2}$, ישׁב *sit* Gn 21$_{16.16}$, יצב htp. *stand* 2 S 18$_{13}$, עמד *stand* 2 K 2$_{7}$ (+ מֵרָחֹק *at a distance*) Ob$_{11}$ Si 37$_{4(B)}$, קום *stand* Si 37$_{9}$, תלא pass. *be suspended* Dt 28$_{66}$; in nom. cl. 2 K 2$_{15}$.

c. מִנֶּגֶד לְ (1) **in front of, opposite,** followed by noun, Gibeah Jg 20$_{34}$; with verb, בוא *come* Jg 20$_{34}$.

(2) **from before, from the presence of,** followed by noun, אִישׁ *man* Pr 14$_{7}$, כְּסִיל *fool* Pr 14$_{7}$; with verb, הלך *go* Pr 14$_{7}$.

d. כְּנֶגֶד (1) **corresponding to, fit for,** עֵזֶר כְּנֶגְדּוֹ *help*, i.e. a helper, *corresponding to him* Gn 2$_{18.20}$.

(2) **before,** or perh. **in contrast with, contrary to,** with noun, אֶרֶץ *earth* GnzPs 1$_{9}$; with verb, רבה hi. *increase* righteousness GnzPs 1$_{9}$.

e. עַד־נֶגֶד **as far as opposite,** followed by noun, קֶבֶר *grave* Ne 3$_{16}$, שַׁעַר *gate* Ne 3$_{26}$, מִגְדָּל *tower* Ne 3$_{25}$; with verb, ישׁב *dwell* Ne 3$_{26}$, חזק hi. *repair* Ne 3$_{16}$.

Also 4QpHos[b] 1$_{2}$ 4QJub[f] 11$_{2}$ ([נג]ד) 4QapElisée 3$_{2}$ (לנגדו) 4Q418 127$_{3}$ 128$_{2}$ 4QPrayer[i] 1$_{1}$.*

⇨ נגד *tell*; cf. נֶגֶד III *honest*.

*[נֶגֶד] II $_{1}$ n.[m.] **blow**—sf. נֶגְדִּי—**blow, affliction** (unless נֶגֶד I *before*), <OBJ> חדשׁ pi. *renew* Jb 10$_{17}$.

*[נֶגֶד] III adj. **honest,** used as noun, **honest things, forthright things,** <OBJ> דבר pi. *speak* Pr 8$_{6}$ (if em. נְגִידִים *noble things* to נְגָדִים).

⇨ cf. נֶגֶד I *before*.

*[נִגְדָּל] n.[m.] **fortified city,** <PREP> כְּ *as* Ca 6$_{4.10}$ (both if em. כַּנִּדְגָּלוֹת *bannered troops* [דגל ni. ptc.] to כַּנִּגְדָּלוֹת).

⇨ גדל *be great*.

נגה 6.2 vb. **shine—Qal** 3 Pf. נָגַהּ; impf. יִגַּהּ—**shine,** <SUBJ> אוֹר *light* Is 9$_1$ Jb 22$_{28}$, שָׁבִיב *flame* Jb 18$_5$ (:: דעך *be extinguished*). <PREP> עַל *upon*, + ישׁב ptc. *one who dwells* Is 9$_1$, דֶּרֶךְ *way* Jb 22$_{28}$.

<ANT> דעך *be extinguished.*

Hi. 3.2 Impf. יַגִּיהַּ, 2ms Si תגיה—**1. give light to, brighten,** <SUBJ> Y. 2 S 22$_{29}$||Ps 18$_{29}$ (Ps + אור hi. *light* lamp). <OBJ> חֹשֶׁךְ *darkness* 2 S 22$_{29}$||Ps 18$_{29}$.

2. cause to shine, cause wrath to blaze (Si 16$_{11}$; or em.; see Subj.), <SUBJ> Y. Si 16$_{11}$ (or em. יניח *he will place*, i.e. נוח hi.), בֵּן *son* appar. Si 36$_4$ (or em. תנוח *you will rest*), יָרֵחַ *moon* Is 13$_{10}$ (+ הלל hi. *cause to shine*, חשך *be dark*). <OBJ> אוֹר *light* Is 13$_{10}$, רֹגֶז *wrath* Si 16$_{11}$ (or em.; see Subj.). <PREP> עַל *upon, against*, + רָשָׁע *wicked one* Si 16$_{11}$ (or em.; see Subj.). <COLL> נגה hi. + adverb, אַחַר *afterwards* Si 36$_4$ (or em.; see Subj.).*

⇒ נֹגַהּ I *brightness*, II *Nogah*, נְגֹהָה *brightness*.

נֹ֫גַהּ I 19.0.7 n.f. **brightness**—Q נוגה; cstr. נֹגַהּ; sf. Q נגהו (Q נוגהו), נָגְהָם—**brightness, shining, light,** <SUBJ> היה *be* Hb 3$_4$ (or em. תִּהְיֶה *it will be* to תַּחְתָּיו *beneath him*).

<OBJ> ברא *create* Is 4$_5$, מלא *be full of* Ezk 10$_4$, אסף *gather*, i.e. remove Jl 2$_{10}$ 4$_{15}$, אור hi. *make shine* 4Q Wiles 1$_8$.

<NOM CL> נֹגַהּ לָאֵשׁ *there was brightness to the fire*, i.e. it was bright Ezk 1$_{13}$, נֹגַהּ לוֹ סָבִיב *there was brightness to it round about* Ezk 1$_{4.27}$, אֵין נֹגַהּ לוֹ *there is no brightness to him* Is 50$_{10}$, var. Am 5$_{20}$, נֹגַהּ כָּאוֹר *there was brightness like the light* Hb 3$_4$ (if em.; see Subj.).

<CSTR> נֹגַהּ אֵשׁ *brightness of a fire of* flame Is 4$_5$, בְּרַק *of the flash of* your spear Hb 3$_{11}$, זַרְחֵךְ *of your rising* Is 60$_3$, כְּבוֹד *of the glory of* Y. Ezk 10$_4$, נגה מרכבה *brightness of the chariot* 4QpsEzek[a] 4$_6$;* אוֹר נֹגַהּ *light of the brightness* Pr 4$_{18}$, אור נגהו *light of its brightness* 4QUnidD 1$_3$, מַרְאֵה הַנֹּגַהּ *appearance of the brightness* Ezk 1$_{28}$, שביבי נוגה *flames of brightness* 4QBer[a] 1.2$_3$, נוגהו *of its brightness* 1QH 14$_{18}$, מעשי [נ]וגה *works of brightness* 4QShirShabb[f] 20.2$_{11}$, עדי נגה *ornament of brightness* 11Q22 1$_2$.

<PREP> לְ of place, direction, *to* perh. 4QUnidD 1$_1$, + הלך *go* Is 60$_3$, pi. Hb 3$_{11}$; of benefit, *to, for*, + אור hi. *give light* Is 60$_{19}$.

כְּ *as*, + יצא *go out* Is 62$_1$.

מִן of direction, *from*, + בער *blaze* 2 S 22$_{13}$, עבר *pass* Ps 18$_{13}$ (or em. עבר to בער); of cause, *on account of* 2 S 23$_4$; privative, *without* Is 8$_{22}$ (אֲפֵלָה מִנֹּגַהּ *darkness without light*; if em. מְנֻדָּח *thrust* into darkness).

<COLL> נֹגַהּ || אוֹר *light* Is 60$_{3.19}$ Am 5$_{20}$ (both +) Hb 3$_{11}$; + לַפִּיד *torch* Is 62$_1$, אֹפֶל *darkness* Am 5$_{20}$.

נֹגַהּ נֶגְדּוֹ *the brightness before him* 2 S 22$_{13}$||Ps 18$_{13}$. Also 4QBer[a] 13$_1$ (וגה[נ]).

<SYN> אוֹר *light.*

⇒ נגה *shine.*

נֹ֫גַהּ II 2 pr.n.m. **Nogah,** son of David, <SUBJ> ילד ni. *be born* 1 C 3$_7$. <NOM CL> אֵלֶּה שְׁמוֹת הַיְּלוּדִים אֲשֶׁר הָיוּ־לוֹ בִּירוּשָׁלָם ... נֹגַהּ *these are the names of the children whom he had in Jerusalem ... Nogah* 1 C 14$_6$. <APP> אֵלֶּה *these* 1 C 3$_7$.

⇒ נגה *shine.*

[נְגֹהָה] 1 n.f. **brightness**—pl. נְגֹהוֹת—<PREP> לְ קוה pi. *wait for* Is 59$_9$ (|| אוֹר *light*, :: אֲפֵלָה *darkness*).*

<SYN> אוֹר *light.*

<ANT> אֲפֵלָה *darkness.*

⇒ נגה *shine.*

נגח 11.0.3 vb. **gore—Qal** 4 Impf. יִגַּח (יִגָּח)—**gore,** <SUBJ> שׁוֹר *ox* Ex 21$_{28.31.32}$ 4QHalakhah[a] 8$_3$ ([יגח ... איש]). <OBJ> אִישׁ *man* Ex 21$_{28}$ 4QHalakhah[a] 8$_3$ ([יגח שור]), אִשָּׁה *woman* Ex 21$_{28}$ 4QHalakhah[a] 8$_3$ ([יגח]), בֵּן *son* Ex 21$_{31}$, בַּת *daughter* Ex 21$_{31}$, עֶבֶד *slave* Ex 21$_{32}$, אָמָה *female slave* Ex 21$_{32}$.

Pi. 6.0.3 Impf. יְנַגַּח, 2ms תְּנַגַּח, תְּנַגְּחוּ, נְנַגֵּחַ; + waw Q ונגחו; ptc. מְנַגֵּחַ; inf. Q נגח—**gore, push,** <SUBJ> Israelites Ps 44$_6$ (|| בוס *trample*) 1QSb 5$_{27}$ (תנכח; appar. error for תנגח), מֶלֶךְ *king* 1 K 22$_{11}$||2 C 18$_{10}$, בְּכוֹר *firstborn* Dt 33$_{17}$, אַיִל *ram* Dn 8$_4$, perh. עַתּוּד *he-goat* Ezk 34$_{21}$ (+ הדף *thrust*), subj. not specified, 4QapPs[b] 46$_{7.7}$. <OBJ> Aramaeans 1 K 22$_{11}$||2 C 18$_{10}$, עַם *people* Dt 33$_{17}$ perh. 1QSb 5$_{27}$ ([עמ]ים), חלה ni. ptc. *weak one* Ezk 34$_{21}$, צַר *adversary* Ps 44$_6$, רַב pl. *many* 4QapPs[b] 46$_7$. <PREP> בְּ of agent, instrument, *by (means of), with,* + Y. Ps 44$_6$,

קֶרֶן *horn* Dt 33_{17} Ezk 34_{21} 4QapPs^{b} 46_{7}, אֵלֶּה *these (horns)* 1 K 22_{11}||2 C 18_{10}; כְּ *as*, + פַּר *bull* 1QSb 5_{27} ([כפו]ר); ה- of direction, *to*, + יָם *west* Dn 8_{4}, צָפוֹן *north* Dn 8_{4}, נֶגֶב *south* Dn 8_{4}. <COLL> עַמִּים יְנַגַּח יַחְדָּו אַפְסֵי־אָרֶץ *he will gore the peoples, all of them, (to) the ends of the earth* Dt 33_{17}.

<SYN> בוס *trample*.

Htp. 1 Impf, יִתְנַגַּח—**join in combat,** <SUBJ> מֶלֶךְ *king* Dn 11_{40}. <PREP> בְּ of time, *at*, + עֵת *time* Dn 11_{40}; עִם *with*, + מֶלֶךְ *king* Dn 11_{40}.

⇒ נַגָּח *prone to gore*.

נַגָּח 2.0.1 adj. **prone to gore,** used predicatively, שׁוֹר נַגָּח הוּא מִתְּמוֹל שִׁלְשֹׁם *the ox was prone to gore three days ago*, i.e. in the past Ex $21_{29.31}$ 4QHalakhah^{a} 8_{4} ([שור]).

⇒ נגח *gore*.

נָגִיד 44.2.2 n.m. **leader**—cstr. נְגִיד (נְגִד); pl. נְגִידִים; cstr. נְגִידֵי—**1. leader, prince, ruler, a.** in general (Ps 76_{13} Jb 29_{10} 31_{37} Pr 28_{16} Si $41_{19[Bmg]}$).

b. king of Israel (2 C 6_{5} Si 46_{13}), in ref. to Saul (1 S 9_{16} 10_{1}), David (1 S 13_{14} 25_{30} 2 S 5_{2}||1 C 11_{2} 2 S 6_{21} 7_{8}|| 1 C 17_{7} Is 55_{4} 1 C 5_{2} 4QDibHam^{a} 1.4_{7} 11QPs^{a} 28_{11}), Solomon (1 K 13_{5} 1 C 29_{22}), Jeroboam (1 K 14_{7}), Jehu (1 K 16_{2}), Hezekiah (2 K 20_{5}); Judah as leading tribe (1 C 28_{4}).

c. foreign rulers (Dn $9_{25.26}$ 11_{22}), specif. of Tyre (Ezk 28_{2}).

2. leader, commander, chief officer, of temple (Jr 20_{1} Ne 11_{11}||1 C 9_{11} 2 C 31_{13} 35_{8}), gatekeepers (1 C 9_{20}), treasuries (1 C 26_{24}), offerings (2 C 31_{12}), fortress (2 C 11_{11}), palace (2 C 28_{7}), house of Aaron (1 C 12_{28}), tribe (1 C 27_{16} 2 C 19_{11}), family (2 C 11_{22}); in army (1 C 13_{1} 27_{4} [or del.] 2 C 32_{21}).

3. נְגִידִים **noble things** (Pr 8_{6}; or em.; see Obj.).

4. Leader, Prince, as divine appellative (Ps 16_{8} 22_{26} 54_{5} 86_{14}; all four, if em.).*

<SUBJ> היה *be* 2 S 7_{8}||1 C 17_{7} 1 K 13_{5} 1 C 9_{20} 11_{2} 2 C 6_{5}, אמר *say* Ezk 28_{2}, בוא *come* Dn 9_{26}, עלה *go up* 2 K 20_{5}, נתן *give* 2 C 35_{8}, i.e. make Ezk 28_{2}, עשׂה *make* Ezk 28_{2}, רבה hi. *increase* wealth Ezk 28_{2}, שׁטף ni. *be swept away* Dn 11_{22}, שׁבר ni. *be broken* Dn 11_{22}, מות *die* Ezk 28_{2}.

<NOM CL> נָגִיד אֱלִיעֶזֶר *the chief officer was Eliezer* 1 C 27_{16}, שְׁבֻאֵל ... נָגִיד *Shebuel was ... chief officer* 1 C 26_{24}, sim. 1 C 27_{4} (or del.) 2 C 19_{11} 31_{13}, עֲלֵיהֶם נָגִיד כּוֹנַנְיָהוּ *over them the chief officer was Conaniah* 2 C 31_{12}, הוּא־פָקִיד נָגִיד *he* (Pashhur) *was the overseer, the chief officer* in the house of Y. Jr 20_{1}, נָגִיד חֲסַר תְּבוּנוֹת וְרַב מַעֲשַׁקּוֹת *a ruler lacking in understanding is also great of oppression*, i.e. a great oppressor Pr 28_{16} (or del. נָגִיד), מִן־הַכֹּהֲנִים ... נְגִיד בֵּית הָאֱלֹהִים *of the priests was ... the chief officer of the house of God* Ne 11_{11}|| 1 C 9_{11}.

<OBJ> דבר pi. *speak* noble things (§3) Pr 8_{6} (or em. נְגָדִים *honest things*, from נגד III), ירד hi. *bring down* Ezk 28_{2}, משׁח *anoint* Si 46_{13}, נתן *give*, i.e. place, make 1 K 14_{7} 16_{2} Is 55_{4} 2 C 11_{11}, שׂים *place*, i.e. make 11QPs^{a} 28_{11}, חלל pi. *pierce* Ezk 28_{2}, הרג *kill* Ezk 28_{2} 2 C 28_{7}, כחד hi. *destroy* 2 C 32_{21}.

<CSTR> נְגִיד עַמִּי *leader of my people* 2 K 20_{5}, צֹר *of Tyre* Ezk 28_{2}, בְּרִית *of the covenant* Dn 11_{22}, הַבַּיִת *of the house* 2 C 28_{7}, בֵּית *of the house of* God Ne 11_{11}|| 1 C 9_{11} (Ne נְגִד) 2 C 31_{13}, נְגִידֵי בֵּית *leaders of the house of* God 2 C 35_{8}; עַם נָגִיד *people of the leader* Dn 9_{26}, רוּחַ נְגִידִים *spirit of leaders* Ps 76_{13}, קוֹל *voice of* Jb 29_{10}, כָּל־נָגִיד *every leader* 1 C 13_{1}.

<APP> Azariah 1 C 9_{11}, Azrikam 2 C 28_{7}, Hezekiah 2 K 20_{5}, Hilkiah 2 C 35_{8}, Jehiel 2 C 35_{8}, Jehoiada 1 C 12_{28}, Seraiah Ne 11_{11}, Zechariah 2 C 35_{8}, מָשִׁיחַ *anointed one* Dn 9_{25}, פָּקִיד *overseer* Jr 20_{1}, רֹעֶה *shepherd* 4QDibHam^{a} 1.4_{7}, חֲסַר *one lacking* understanding Pr 28_{16} (or del. נָגִיד).

<PREP> לְ of direction, *to*, + אמר *say* Ezk 28_{2}; *as* 1 C 5_{2}, + היה *be* 2 S 5_{2}, משׁח *anoint* 1 S 9_{16} 10_{1} 1 C 29_{22}, עמד hi. *appoint* 2 C 11_{22}, צוה pi. *appoint* 1 S 13_{14} 25_{30} 2 S 6_{21}, בחר *choose* 1 C 28_{4}; *namely*, 1 C 13_{1}; *as*, + שׁוה pi. *place*, i.e. make Ps 16_{8} (if em. לְנֶגְדִּי *before me* to לִנְגִידִי *as my leader*), שׂים *place*, i.e. regard Ps 54_{5} 86_{14} (both if em. לְנֶגְדָּם *before them* to לִנְגִידִ־ם *as my leader*); introducing object, + רפא *heal* 2 K 20_{5}.

כְּ *as*, + היה *be* 4QDibHam^{a} 1.4_{7}; כְּמוֹ *as* Jb 31_{37}.

בּוֹשׁ מִן *be ashamed of* Si $41_{19(Bmg)}$.

אֶל *to*, + אמר *say* 2 K 20_{5}.

עַל *against*, + בוא *bring* Ezk 28$_{2}$.

עִם *with* 1 C 12$_{28}$.

עַד *until (the time of)* Dn 9$_{25}$.

<COLL> נָגִיד || שַׂר *commander* 1 C 13$_{1}$ (+) 2 C 32$_{21}$, מְצַוֶּה *commander* Is 55$_{4}$, גִּבּוֹר *mighty one* 2 C 32$_{21}$.

+ מֹשֵׁל *ruler* 11QPs^{a} 28$_{11}$, מֶלֶךְ *king* Ps 76$_{13}$, ראשׁ *head* 2 C 11$_{22}$, מֵישָׁר *uprightness* Pr 8$_{6}$.

נָגִיד as vocative, נְדָרַי אֲשַׁלֵּם נְגִידִי *my vows I will pay, O my Prince* Ps 22$_{26}$ (if em. נֶגֶד *before*).

נָגִיד עַל־עַמִּי יִשְׂרָאֵל *ruler over my people Israel* 1 S 9$_{16}$ 1 K 14$_{7}$ 16$_{2}$ 1 C 11$_{2}$ 17$_{7}$ 2 C 6$_{5}$, sim. 1 S 13$_{14}$ 25$_{30}$ 2 S 5$_{2}$ 6$_{21}$ 7$_{8}$ 1 K 1$_{35}$ 4QDibHam^{a} 1.4$_{7}$, נגידים על עם *rulers over the people* Si 46$_{13}$, נגיד לעמו *ruler of his people* 11QPs^{a} 28$_{11}$, נָגִיד בְּאֶחָיו *leader among his brothers* 2 C 11$_{22}$, הַנָּגִיד לְאַהֲרֹן *the chief officer of (the house of) Aaron* 1 C 12$_{28}$, פָּקִיד נָגִיד בְּבֵית י׳ *the overseer, the chief officer in the house of Y.* Jr 20$_{1}$, נָגִיד עַל־הָאֹצָרוֹת *chief officer over the treasuries* 1 C 26$_{24}$, הַנָּגִיד לְבֵית־יְהוּדָה לְכֹל דְּבַר־הַמֶּלֶךְ *the ruler of the house of Judah in every matter of the king* 2 C 19$_{11}$.

<SYN> שַׂר *commander*, מְצַוֶּה *commander*, גִּבּוֹר *mighty one*.*

⇒ perh. נגד hi. *tell* or נֶגֶד *before*.

[נְגִינָה] 14.1.3 n.f. **music (of stringed instruments)**—נְגִינַת; sf. נְגִינָתִי, נְגִינָתָם; pl. נגינות (נְגִינֹת); cstr. נְגִינוֹת; sf. נגינותי (נְגִינוֹתָי)—**1. music (of stringed instruments),** <NOM CL> כול נגינתי לכבוד אל *all my music shall be for the glory of God* 1QS 10$_{9}$. <OBJ> נגן pi. *play* Is 38$_{20}$, כון hi. *prepare* Si 47$_{9}$ ([הכין]). <CSTR> נגינות שיר *music of*, i.e. for, *song* Si 47$_{9}$; כול נגינתי *all my music* 1QS 10$_{9}$. <PREP> בְּ of accompaniment, *with, to (the accompaniment of)* (alw. pl.) Hb 3$_{19}$ Ps 4$_{1}$ 6$_{1}$ 54$_{1}$ 55$_{1}$ 67$_{1}$ 76$_{1}$, + המה *murmur* 1QH 13$_{30}$ (+ כִּנּוֹר *harp*); מִן *from*, + שׁבת *cease* Lm 5$_{14}$ (or תמם *cease*, if em. מִנְּגִינָתָם *from their music* to מִנְּגִינָה תַּמּוּ *they have ceased from music*);* עַל *with, to (the accompaniment of)* Ps 61$_{1}$ (נְגִינַת; mss נְגִינֹת).

2. (mocking) song, <SUBJ> היה *be* Jb 30$_{9}$ (|| מִלָּה *by-word*) Lm 3$_{14}$ 1QH 10$_{11}$. <NOM CL> אֲנִי־ם נְגִינָתָם *I am (the subject of) their mocking song* Lm 3$_{63}$ (if em. אֲנִי מַנְגִּינָתָם *I am [the subject of] their mocking song*). <OBJ> זכר *remember* Ps 77$_{7}$ (or em. וְהָגִיתִי *and I meditate on* or נִגַּנְתִּי *I play*). <CSTR> נְגִינוֹת שׁוֹתֵי שֵׁכָר *the songs of drunkards* Ps 69$_{13}$ (or em. וּנְגִינוֹת to וַיְנַגְּנוּ בִי *and they make songs about me*). <APP> שְׂחֹק *laughter* Lm 3$_{14}$.

<SYN> §2 מִלָּה *by-word*.*

⇒ נגן *play a stringed instrument.*

נגיע, see נֶגַע *stroke.*

נִגְלָה *revealed matter*, see גלה Ni. *reveal.*

נגן 15.1.1 vb. **play (a stringed instrument)—Qal** 1 Ptc. נֹגְנִים—ptc. as noun, **musician,** <NOM CL> אַחַר נֹגְנִים *behind are musicians* Ps 68$_{26}$ (+ שָׁרִים *singers*).

Pi. 14.1.1 + Impf. יְנַגֵּן; + waw וְנִגֵּן; ptc. מְנַגֵּן, Si מְנַגְּנוֹת; inf. נַגֵּן—**1. play (a stringed instrument), accompany with a stringed instrument** (11QPs^{a} 27$_{10}$), <SUBJ> Bethlehemite 1 S 16$_{18}$, David 1 S 16$_{23}$ 18$_{10}$ 19$_{9}$, אִישׁ *man* 1 S 16$_{16.16.17}$, בֵּן *son* 1 S 16$_{18}$, מְנַגֵּן *musician* 2 K 3$_{15}$, worshipper Ps 33$_{3}$ (+ שִׁיר *sing*) 77$_{7}$ (if em. נְגִינָתִי *my song* to נִגַּנְתִּי *I play*);* subj. not specified, Ezk 33$_{32}$ 11Q
Ps^{a} 27$_{10}$. <OBJ> נְגִינָה *music (of stringed instruments)* Is 38$_{20}$, שִׁיר *song* 11QPs^{a} 27$_{10}$. <PREP> בְּ of time, *in*, + לַיְלָה *night* Ps 77$_{7}$ (if em.; see Subj.); of instrument, *by (means of), with*, + יָד *hand* 1 S 16$_{16.23}$ 18$_{10}$ 19$_{9}$; of accompaniment, *with*, + תְּרוּעָה *shout* Ps 33$_{3}$; introducing object, + כִּנּוֹר *lyre* 1 S 16$_{16}$; כְּ *as*, + יוֹם *day* 1 S 18$_{10}$ (כְּיוֹם בְּיוֹם *as [he did] day by day*); עַל *over*, + פגע pass. ptc. *stricken one* 11QPs^{a} 27$_{10}$. <COLL> אִישׁ יֹדֵעַ מְנַגֵּן *a man skilful at playing the lyre* 1 S 16$_{16}$, יֹדֵעַ נַגֵּן *(one) skilful at playing* 1 S 16$_{18}$, אִישׁ מֵיטִיב לְנַגֵּן *a man skilful at playing* 1 S 16$_{17}$, מֵטִב נַגֵּן *one who plays well* Ezk 33$_{32}$, הֵיטִיבוּ נַגֵּן *play well* Ps 33$_{3}$.

2. ptc. as noun, **musician, a.** masc., <SUBJ> נגן pi. *play* 2 K 3$_{15}$. <OBJ> לקח *take* 2 K 3$_{15}$.

b. fem., <PREP> עִם *with*, + דמך *sleep* Si 9$_{4}$.*

⇒ נְגִינָה *music (of stringed instruments).*

נֹגֵן *musician*, see נגן *play (a stringed instrument).*

נגע I $_{150.11.65}$ vb. **touch—Qal** $_{107.3.51}$ Pf. נָגַע, נָגְעָה, נָגְעוּ, נְגַעֲנוּךָ; impf. יִגַּע, 3fs תִּגַּע (תִּגַּע), יִגְּעוּ, תִּגְּעוּ (תִּגְּעוּ); + waw וַיִּגַּע, 3fs וַתִּגַּע; impv. גַּע; ptc. נֹגֵעַ (נוֹגֵעַ), נֹגַעַת, נֹגְעִים (Q נוגעים), Q נוגעי, נֹגַעַת, נוגעת; ptc. pass. נָגוּעַ, Q נגועי; inf. נְגֹעַ (נְגֹעַ), גַּעַת, לִנְגֹּעַ, נָגְעֵךְ, נָגְעוֹ.

1a. touch (Gn 3$_{3}$ Ex 19$_{12.12}$ 29$_{37}$ 30$_{29}$ Lv 5$_{2.3}$ 6$_{11.20}$ 7$_{19.21}$ 11$_{8+6t}$ 12$_{4}$ 15$_{5+9t}$ 22$_{4.5.6}$ Nm 4$_{15}$ 16$_{26}$ 19$_{11+5t}$ 31$_{19}$ Dt 14$_{8}$ Jg 6$_{21}$ 2 S 23$_{7}$ 1 K 6$_{27.27.27}$ 19$_{5.7}$ 2 K 13$_{21}$ Is 6$_{7}$ 52$_{11}$ Ho 4$_{2}$ Hg 2$_{12.13}$ Jb 6$_{7}$ (unless נגע II *rest*) Lm 4$_{14.15}$ Est 5$_{2}$ Dn 8$_{5.18}$ 10$_{10.16}$ Si 13$_{1}$ 1QS 5$_{13}$ 6$_{16.20}$ 7$_{19.20}$ 8$_{17}$ 4QS^{d} 1$_{7}$ 4QD^{g} 1.2$_{7}$ 4QSD 1.2$_{6}$ [[י]גע]] 4QTohA 1.1$_{4.4.5.6.7}$ [[יגע]] 1.1$_{8.8}$ 2.1$_{3.4.7.7.7}$ [[הנוג[ע]] 2.1$_{8}$ 2.2$_{6}$ 3.1$_{8}$ [[י]גע]] 3.2$_{8}$ 4QTohB^{c} 1$_{10.12.13}$ 2$_{4}$ 4QTohC 1$_{5.6}$ 4QNidd 2.1$_{2}$ 4QLeqet 1$_{3}$ 4Q416 2.2$_{16}$ 11QT 32$_{15}$ 49$_{21}$ 50$_{5.8.12.21}$ 51$_{1}$ [[יגע]] 51$_{2}$ [[הנוגע]] 63$_{14}$ CD 10$_{13}$ 12$_{17}$), the heart (1 S 10$_{26}$), sexually (Gn 20$_{6}$ Pr 6$_{29}$ Ru 2$_{9}$), causing harm (Gn 26$_{11.29}$ Ex 19$_{13}$ Jos 9$_{19}$ 2 S 14$_{10}$ Jr 12$_{14}$ Zc 2$_{12.12}$ Ps 105$_{15}$||1 C 16$_{22}$ Jb 1$_{11}$ 2$_{5}$ 5$_{19}$ 19$_{21}$ 4QapJoseph^{b} 3$_{10}$ 11QPsAp^{a} 6$_{8}$), **strike** (Gn 32$_{26.32}$ Ezk 17$_{10}$ Am 9$_{5}$ Ps 104$_{32}$ 144$_{5}$ Jb 1$_{19}$ perh. 1Qp Hab 9$_{1}$), with plague (1 S 6$_{9}$).

b. reach, arrive (at), overtake (Jg 20$_{34.41}$ 2 S 5$_{8}$ Is 16$_{8}$ Jr 4$_{10.18}$ 48$_{32}$ 51$_{9}$ Jon 3$_{6}$ Mc 1$_{9}$ Jb 4$_{5}$ Dn 9$_{21}$ Si 32$_{21}$ [Bmg] 34$_{22}$ [unless §1a] 1QH 19$_{21}$ 11QPsAp^{a} 6$_{10}$).

c. of time, **arrive** (Ezr 3$_{1}$ Ne 7$_{72}$).

<SUBJ> Y. 1 S 10$_{26}$ Am 9$_{5}$ Ps 104$_{32}$ 144$_{5}$ Jb 1$_{11}$ 2$_{5}$, מַלְאָךְ *angel* Jg 6$_{21}$ 1 K 19$_{5.7}$, Israelites Lv 11$_{8}$ Dt 14$_{8}$ Is 52$_{11}$, בַּיִת *house* perh. 4QpsEzek^{a} 36.2$_{1}$, עַם *people* Ex 19$_{12}$, עֵדָה *congregation* Nm 16$_{26}$, Abimelech Gn 20$_{6.29}$, Esther Est 5$_{2}$, Gabriel Dn 8$_{18}$ 9$_{21}$, אָדָם *human being* Gn 3$_{3}$ 11QT 32$_{15}$ 50$_{8}$, אִישׁ *man* Gn 32$_{26.33}$ Lv 15$_{5}$ 22$_{5}$ 2 S 23$_{7}$ 2 K 13$_{21}$ Hg 2$_{12}$ Dn 9$_{21}$ 1QS 5$_{13}$ 6$_{16.20}$ 7$_{19.20}$ 8$_{17}$ 11QT 50$_{5.21}$ 51$_{1}$ ([יגע ... איש]), אִשָּׁה *woman, wife* Gn 3$_{3}$ 12$_{4}$ 11QT 63$_{14}$, בֵּן *son* Nm 4$_{15}$, נַעַר *lad* Ru 2$_{9}$, מֶלֶךְ *king* Ps 105$_{15}$||1 C 16$_{22}$, נָשִׂיא *prince* Jos 9$_{19}$, כֹּהֵן *priest* Lm 4$_{14}$, נָבִיא *prophet* Lm 4$_{14}$, שָׁכֵן *neighbour* Jr 12$_{14}$.

דבר pi. ptc. *one who speaks* 2 S 14$_{10}$, נגע ptc. *one who touches* Zc 2$_{12}$, זוב ptc. *one who has a discharge* (masc.) Lv 15$_{11.12}$ 4QTohA 1.1$_{4}$, (fem.) 4QTohA 1.1$_{4.5.6}$, ספר ptc. *one who counts* 4QTohA 1.1$_{7}$ ([יגע]), טָמֵא *unclean one* Nm 19$_{22}$ Hg 2$_{13}$ 4QTohA 3.1$_{8}$ CD 10$_{13}$, כִּדְמוּת *one with the likeness of* human being Dn 10$_{16.18}$.

יָד *hand* Ex 19$_{13}$ 1 S 6$_{9}$ Jb 19$_{21}$ Dn 10$_{10}$, כָּנָף *wing* 1 K 6$_{27.27.27}$, דָּם *blood(shed)* Ho 4$_{2}$, בָּשָׂר *flesh* Lv 7$_{19}$, נֶפֶשׁ *soul* Lv 5$_{2.3}$ 7$_{21}$ 22$_{6}$ Jb 6$_{7}$ (unless נגע II *rest*), רוּחַ *wind* Ezk 17$_{10}$ Jb 1$_{19}$.

צָפִיר *he-goat* Dn 8$_{5}$, נְטִישָׁה *vine-tendril* Jr 48$_{32}$, שָׂרֹק *vine-tendril* Is 16$_{8}$, חֶרֶב *sword* Jr 4$_{10}$, מִשְׁפָּט *judgment* 51$_{9}$, חַטָּאָה *sin* 1QH 19$_{21}$, רַע *evil* Jb 5$_{19}$, רָעָה *evil* Jg 20$_{34.41}$, אָסוֹן *harm* Si 34$_{22}$, מַכָּה *wound* Mc 1$_{9}$, דֶּבֶר *pestilence* 11QPsAp^{a} 6$_{8}$, נֶגַע *plague* 11QPsAp^{a} 6$_{10}$ ([נגע]), יָגוֹן *grief* 1QH 19$_{21}$, שַׁוְעָה *cry* of poor Si 32$_{21(Bmg)}$, חֹדֶשׁ *month* Ezr 3$_{1}$ Ne 7$_{72}$, דָּבָר *matter* Jon 3$_{6}$, זֶה *this* Is 6$_{7}$, כֹּל *all* Lv 6$_{11.20}$ Nm 19$_{16}$ 31$_{19}$ 2 S 5$_{8}$ 4QTohB^{c} 1$_{10}$ 4Q Nidd 2.1$_{2}$ 11QT 49$_{21}$.

Subj. not specified, Gn 26$_{11}$ Ex 19$_{12}$ 29$_{37}$ 30$_{29}$ Lv 11$_{24+5t}$ 15$_{5+6t}$ 22$_{4}$ Nm 19$_{11.13.18.21}$ Jr 4$_{18}$ Zc 2$_{12}$ Jb 4$_{5}$ Pr 6$_{29}$ Lm 4$_{15}$ Si 13$_{1}$ 4QS^{d} 1$_{7}$ 4QD^{g} 1.2$_{7.10}$ ([הנו[גע]) 4QTohA 1.1$_{8.8}$ 2.1$_{7}$ ([הנג[ע]) 2.2$_{6}$ 4QTohB^{c} 1$_{13}$ ([ה]נוגע) 4QTohC 1$_{6}$ 4QapJoseph^{b} 3$_{10}$ 4Q416 2.2$_{16}$ 11QT 50$_{12}$ 51$_{2}$ ([הנוגע]) CD 12$_{17}$ (הנו[גע]).

<OBJ> Isaac Gn 26$_{29}$, Ruth Ru 2$_{9}$, Jazer Jr 48$_{32}$, טָמֵא *unclean thing* Is 52$_{11}$, לֶחֶם *food* 4QTohA 2.1$_{7}$ ([הנוג[ע]), מַשְׁקֶה *drink* 1QS 7$_{20}$.

<PREP> לְ introducing object perh. 4Q417 26$_{1}$, + טָהֳרָה *pure things* 4QS^{d} 1$_{7}$.

בְּ introducing object 4QD^{g} 1.2$_{7.10}$ ([הנו[גע]) 4QTohA 2.1$_{7.7.8}$ 3.1$_{8}$ ([י]גע]) 3.2$_{8}$ 4QTohB^{c} 1$_{10}$ ([בו]) 2$_{4}$ 4QTohC 1$_{5}$ 4QNidd 2.1$_{2}$ ([ב[ו]) 11QT 51$_{1}$ ([יגע בו]) 51$_{2}$ ([הנוגע בהמה]), + Israelites Zc 2$_{12}$, Philistines 1 S 6$_{9}$, Jerusalem Mc 1$_{9}$, Daniel Dn 8$_{18}$ 10$_{10.18}$, Elijah 1 K 19$_{5.7}$, Job Jb 5$_{19}$ 19$_{21}$, אָדָם *human being* Lv 22$_{5.6}$ 4QTohA 1.1$_{8}$, אִישׁ *man* Gn 26$_{11}$ Lv 22$_{5}$ 11QT 50$_{8}$, אִשָּׁה *woman, wife* Gn 26$_{11}$ Lv 15$_{19}$ 2 S 14$_{10}$ Pr 6$_{29}$ 4QTohA 1.1$_{6}$, בֵּן *son* Si 34$_{22}$, מָשִׁיחַ *anointed one* Ps 105$_{15}$||1 C 16$_{22}$, נגע ptc. *one who touches* Ex 19$_{13}$, זוב ptc. *one who has a discharge* 4QTohA 1.1$_{4}$, בְּלִיַּעַל *worthless one* 2 S 23$_{7}$, ישב *inhabitant* Jos 9$_{19}$.

חֹלֶד *weasel* 11QT 50$_{21}$, עַכְבָּר *mouse* 11QT 50$_{21}$, חֹמֶט *lizard* 11QT 50$_{21}$, כֹּחַ *lizard* 11QT 50$_{21}$, לְטָאָה *lizard* 11QT 50$_{21}$, צָב *lizard* 11QT 50$_{21}$, תִּנְשֶׁמֶת *lizard* 11QT 50$_{21}$, בְּהֵמָה *beast* Lv 7$_{21}$ 11$_{26}$, שֶׁרֶץ *swarming things* Lv 22$_{5.6}$ 11QT 50$_{21}$.

רֹאשׁ *head*, i.e. top, of sceptre Est 5$_{2}$, לֵב *heart* 1 S 10$_{26}$, בָּבָה *apple* of eye Zc 2$_{12}$, כַּף *socket* of hip joint Gn

32$_{26.33}$, עֶצֶם *bone* Nm 19$_{16.18}$ 2 K 13$_{21}$ 1QH 19$_{21}$ 11QT 50$_{5}$, דָּם *blood(shed)* Ho 4$_{2}$ 4QTohA 1.1$_{7}$ ([ינגע בדם]) 1.1$_{8}$ 11QT 50$_{5}$, בָּשָׂר *flesh* Lv 6$_{20}$ 15$_{7}$ Jg 6$_{21}$, נְבֵלָה *carcass* Lv 5$_{2}$ 11$_{8.24.27.36.39}$ Dt 14$_{8}$, מֵת *dead one* Nm 19$_{11.13.16.18}$ 11QT 50$_{5}$, חָלָל *slain one* Nm 19$_{16.18}$ 31$_{19}$ 11QT 50$_{5}$.

פְּרִי *fruit* Gn 3$_3$, גֶּפֶן *vine* Ezk 17$_{10}$, מַצָּה *unleavened bread* Jg 6$_{21}$, הַר *mountain* Ex 19$_{12}$ Ps 104$_{32}$ 144$_5$, קָצֶה *end* Ex 19$_{12}$, לְבוּשׁ *garment* Lm 4$_{14}$, אֹהֶל *tent* Ex 30$_{29}$ ([באה]ליך), אֲרוֹן *ark* Ex 30$_{29}$, שֻׁלְחָן *table* Ex 30$_{29}$, מִזְבֵּחַ *altar* Ex 29$_{37}$ 30$_{29}$, מְנֹרָה *lampstand* Ex 30$_{29}$, כֵּן *stand* Ex 30$_{29}$, כִּיּוֹר *laver* Ex 30$_{29}$, גֶּבֶא *cistern* CD 10$_{13}$, צִנּוֹר *conduit* 2 S 5$_8$, בַּיִת *house* 11QT 50$_{12}$, קִיר *wall* 1 K 6$_{27.27}$, שַׁעַר *gate* Mc 1$_9$, פִּנָּה *corner* Jb 1$_{19}$, מִשְׁכָּב *bed* Lv 15$_{5.21.23.27}$, כְּלִי *vessel* Ex 30$_{29}$ Lv 15$_{12.22.23.27}$ 4QTohA 1.1$_{4.4}$, דָּבָר *thing* Lv 5$_2$, אִשֶּׁה *fire offering* Lv 6$_{11}$.

קֹדֶשׁ *holiness*, i.e. holy thing Lv 12$_4$, טָהֳרָה *pure things* 1QS 5$_{13}$ 6$_{16}$ 7$_{19}$ 8$_{17}$ 4QTohA 2.1$_3$ 4QSD 1.2$_6$ (י[גע] [בטהרה]) 11QT 49$_{21}$ 63$_{14}$, טֻמְאָה *uncleanness* Lv 5$_3$ 7$_{21}$, טָמֵא *unclean thing* Lv 7$_{19.21}$ 22$_4$, שֶׁקֶץ *abomination* Lv 7$_{21}$, זוֹב *discharge* 4QTohB^c 1$_{12}$ ([ב]זובו]), שִׁכְבָה *lying down* of seed, i.e. ejaculate 4QTohA 2.1$_4$, קֶבֶר *grave* Nm 19$_{16.18}$ 11QT 50$_5$, נַחֲלָה *heritage* Jr 12$_{14}$ 4QapJoseph^b 3$_{10}$ ([בנחלת[ה]), אֶרֶץ *earth* Am 9$_5$ Dn 8$_5$, עָפָר *dust* CD 12$_{17}$ (הנ[ו]גע), אֶבֶן *stone* CD 12$_{17}$ (הנ[ו]גע), עֵץ *wood* CD 12$_{17}$ (הנ[ו]גע), מַיִם *water* Nm 19$_{21}$ 11QT 32$_{15}$, מַשְׁקֶה *drink* 1QS 6$_{20}$ 4QLeqet 1$_3$, זֶפֶת *pitch* Si 13$_1$, אֵלֶּה *these* Lv 11$_{31}$ Hg 2$_{13}$, כֹּל *all* Lv 15$_{10.11}$ Nm 16$_{26}$ 19$_{22}$ Jb 1$_{11}$.

בְּ of instrument, *by (means of), with*, + כָּנָף *skirt* Hg 2$_{12}$, מִשְׁפָּט *judgment* perh. 1QpHab 9$_1$ (unless נגועו is from נֶגַע *stroke*).

בְּ of time, *in, during*, + רִאשׁוֹן *first (year)* 1QS 7$_{19}$, שֵׁנִי *second (year)* 1QS 7$_{20}$.

כְּ *(at) about*, + עֵת *time* Dn 9$_{21}$.

אֶל introducing object 11QPsAp^a 6$_8$ ([אל[יך]), + Daniel Dn 9$_{21}$, אִשָּׁה *woman, wife* Gn 20$_6$, מֶלֶךְ *king* Jon 3$_6$, כָּנָף *wing* 1 K 6$_{27}$, עֶצֶם *bone* Jb 2$_5$, בָּשָׂר *flesh* Jb 2$_5$, קֹדֶשׁ *holiness*, i.e. holy thing Nm 4$_{15}$, לֶחֶם *bread* Hg 2$_{12}$, נָזִיד *pottage* Hg 2$_{12}$, יַיִן *wine* Hg 2$_{12}$, שֶׁמֶן *oil* Hg 2$_{12}$, מַאֲכָל *food* Hg 2$_{12}$, שָׁמַיִם *heaven* Jr 51$_9$.

עַל *upon*, + פָּנִים *face* of countryside Nm 19$_{16}$ 11QT 50$_5$.

עַל introducing object, + Benjaminites Jg 20$_{34.41}$, שָׂפָה *lip* Is 6$_7$ Dn 10$_{16}$.

עַד *as far as*, + Job Jb 4$_5$, Jazer Is 16$_8$, לֵב *heart* Jr 4$_{18}$, נֶפֶשׁ *soul* Jr 4$_{10}$.

<COLL> נגע || רעע hi. *harm* Ps 105$_{15}$||1 C 16$_{22}$, בוא *come* Jb 4$_5$ Pr 6$_{29}$ (+); + עשׂה רָעָה *do harm* Gn 26$_{29}$.

2. pass. a. be stricken, plagued, <SUBJ> אִישׁ *man* Is 53$_4$, worshipper Ps 73$_{14}$, עֲדִי *ornament* 4QWiles 1$_5$. <COLL> נגע pass. + noun used adverbially, יוֹם *day* Ps 73$_{14}$; חֲשַׁבְנֻהוּ נָגוּעַ *we considered as plagued* Is 53$_4$ (+ נכה ho. *be struck*, ענה pu. *be afflicted*), נגועי שחת *plagued with corruption* 4QWiles 1$_5$.

b. as noun, **one stricken, plagued,** <CSTR> נגועי [משפ[ט] *ones stricken of*, i.e. by, *judgment* 4QWays^a 2$_4$, עוונות *of*, i.e. by, *iniquity* 4QShir^a 1$_{7(mg)}$ ([נגוע[י]); לבב נג[ועים] *heart of ones stricken* 4QWays^b 9$_2$, קצי נגוע[י] *periods of ones stricken* 4QShir^a 1$_{7(mg)}$. <PREP> עַל *upon* 4QWays^a 2$_4$.

Also 4QMyst^a 15$_2$.

<SYN> §1 רעע hi. *harm*, בוא *come*.

Ni. $_1$ + waw וַיִּנָּגְעוּ—**(pretend to) be defeated,** <SUBJ> Joshua and Israel Jos 8$_{15}$. <PREP> לִפְנֵי *before*, + עַם *people* Jos 8$_{15}$, אִישׁ *man* Jos 8$_{15}$, מֶלֶךְ *king* Jos 8$_{15}$.

Pi. $_3$ Pf. נִגְּעוּ; + waw וַיְנַגַּע—**strike, afflict (with),** <SUBJ> Y. Gn 12$_{17}$ 2 K 15$_5$ 2 C 26$_{20}$. <OBJ> 1. person stricken, Uzziah 2 C 26$_{20}$, מֶלֶךְ *king* 2 K 15$_5$ (+ וַיְהִי מְצֹרָע *and he became a leper*), פַּרְעֹה *Pharaoh* Gn 12$_{17}$, בַּיִת *house(hold)* Gn 12$_{17}$. 2. stricken with, נֶגַע *plague* Gn 12$_{17}$. <PREP> עַל *on account of*, + דָּבָר *matter* Gn 12$_{17}$.

Pu. $_{1.0.8}$ Pf. Q נוגע; impf. Q ינוגע, יְנֻגָּעוּ; ptc. Q מנוגע, Q מנוגעים—**be stricken, afflicted,** <SUBJ> אִישׁ *man* Is 53$_{8(1QIsa^a)}$ 1QM 7$_4$ 1QSa 2$_{3.4.10}$ CD 14$_{15}$ (ינו[ג]ע), רָשָׁע *wicked one* Ps 73$_5$, הלל ptc. *one who acts foolishly* Ps 73$_5$, כֹּל *all* 1QSa 2$_5$; subj. not specified, 1QSa 2$_6$ 11QT 45$_{18}$ (+ צָרוּעַ *leper*) 48$_{14}$.

<PREP> לְ appar. of benefit, *for, on behalf of*, + עַם *people* Is 53$_{8(1QIsa^a)}$ (or em. לָמוֹ *for them* to לַמָּוֶת *to death*).

בְּ of place, *in*, + בָּשָׂר *flesh* 1QSa 2$_{5.6}$; of instrument, *by (means of), with*, + צָרַעַת *leprosy* 11QT 48$_{14}$, נֶגַע *disease* 4QD^e 2.2$_{12}$ 11QT 48$_{14}$, נֶתֶק *scall* 11QT 48$_{14}$, טֻמְאָה

impurity 1QM 7$_{4}$, אֶחָד *one* 1QSa 2$_{3}$, אֵלֶּה *these* 1QSa 2$_{4}$.

מִן of cause, *on account of*, + פֶּשַׁע *transgression* Is 53$_{8(1QIsa^a)}$; עִם *with*, + אָדָם *human being* Ps 73$_{5}$.

Hi. 38.9.6 Pf. הִגִּיעַ ,הִגַּעַתְּ ,הִגִּיעוּ; impf. יַגִּיעַ (יַגִּיעֶנָּה), 3fs תַּגִּיעַ, 2ms Si תגיע ,יַגִּיעוּ; + waw וְהִגַּעְתֶּם ,וְהִגִּיעוּ ,וְהִגַּעְתִּיהוּ; וַיַּגַּע, 3fs וַתַּגַּע ,וַיַּגִּיעוּ; ptc. מַגִּיעַ (Q מגע), מַגַּעַת ,מַגִּיעֵי; inf. Q הגיע (הַגִּיעֵנוּ), הגיעם Q).

1. reach (as far as), extend to (Gn 28$_{12}$ Is 8$_{8}$ Zc 14$_{5}$ Ps 32$_{6}$ Jb 20$_{6}$ 2 C 3$_{11.11.12}$ 28$_{9}$), i.e. afford (Lv 5$_{7}$), **reach, arrive (at), come, attain to, draw near** (1 S 14$_{9}$ Is 30$_{4}$ Ps 88$_{4}$ 107$_{18}$ Est 4$_{3.14}$ 6$_{14}$ 8$_{17}$ Dn 8$_{17}$ 12$_{12}$ Si 12$_{5}$ 37$_{2.12[B].30[B]}$ 51$_{6}$ 1QH 14$_{24}$ [[תגיע]] 16$_{29}$ 1QM 17$_{11}$= 4QM^{a} 11.2$_{20}$), of time (Ezk 7$_{12}$ Ca 2$_{12}$ Ec 12$_{1}$ Est 2$_{12.15}$ 9$_{1}$), **reach one's goal** (Si 11$_{10}$ 32$_{21[B]}$), **reach the age** (CD 15$_{5}$).

<SUBJ> Israelites Ps 107$_{18}$, Philistines 1 S 14$_{9}$, Esther Est 4$_{14}$, אִישׁ *man* 1QM 17$_{11}$, בֵּן *son* Si 11$_{10}$ 12$_{5}$ CD 15$_{5}$, מַלְאָךְ *messenger* Is 30$_{4}$, סָרִיס *eunuch* Est 4$_{14}$, חכה pi. ptc. *one who waits* Dn 12$_{12}$, פחד pi. ptc. *one who fears* Si 37$_{12(B)}$, רבה hi. ptc. *one who increases* Si 37$_{30(B)}$, זוע hi. ptc. *one who is greedy* Si 37$_{30(Bmg)}$, ראשׁ *head* Jb 20$_{6}$, i.e. top Gn 28$_{12}$, יָד *hand* Lv 5$_{7}$, כָּנָף *wing* 2 C 3$_{11.11.12}$, נֶפֶשׁ *soul* Si 51$_{6}$ 1QH 14$_{24}$ ([נפ]שי תגיע), חַיָּה *life* Si 51$_{6}$, חַיִּים *life* Ps 88$_{4}$ 1QH 16$_{29}$ ([חיי]), צָפִיר *he-goat* Dn 8$_{17}$, מַיִם *water* Ps 32$_{6}$, נָהָר *river* Is 8$_{8}$, גַּיְא *valley* Zc 14$_{5}$, זַעַף *anger* 2 C 28$_{9}$, דִּין *judgment* Si 37$_{2}$ (or em. דון to דין *sorrow*), שַׁוְעָה *cry* of poor Si 32$_{21(B)}$, דָּבָר *word* Est 4$_{3}$ 8$_{17}$ 9$_{1}$, דָּת *decree* Est 4$_{3}$ 8$_{17}$ 9$_{1}$, תֹּר *turn* Est 2$_{12.15}$, יוֹם *day* Ezk 7$_{12}$, שָׁנָה *year* Ec 12$_{1}$, עֵת *time* Ca 2$_{12}$.

<OBJ> Hanes Is 30$_{4}$, מָקוֹם *place* Est 4$_{3}$ 8$_{17}$, דַּי *sufficiency*, i.e. sufficient for Lv 5$_{7}$.

<PREP> לְ *to, at* or introducing object, + יָד *hand*, i.e. side, of battle line 1QM 17$_{11}$ ([ליד]), כָּנָף *wing* 2 C 3$_{11}$, מַעֲרָכָה *battle line* 4QM^{a} 11.2$_{20}$ ([למ]ערכת), עָב *cloud* Jb 20$_{6}$, קִיר *wall* 2 C 3$_{11.12}$, מַלְכוּת *kingdom* Est 4$_{14}$, שַׁחַת *pit* 1QH 16$_{29}$, שְׁאוֹל *Sheol* Ps 88$_{4}$ Si 51$_{6}$, מָוֶת *death* Si 51$_{6}$, יוֹם *day* Dn 12$_{12}$; of benefit, *for*, + עֵת *time* Est 4$_{14}$.

בְּ *in accordance with* or *despite*, + טוֹבָה *good* Si 12$_{5}$.

אֶל *to* or introducing object, + Azal (or em. אֵצֶל to אֶצְלוֹ *beside it*), Jonathan 1 S 14$_{9}$, בֵּן *son* Si 37$_{12(B)}$, נַעַר *lad* 1 S 14$_{9}$, חָסִיד *loyal one* Ps 32$_{6}$, זֵד *presumptuous one* Si 12$_{5}$, זָרָא *abhorrence* Si 37$_{30(B)}$, מָוֶת *death* Si 37$_{2(B)}$.

אֶל־אֵצֶל *to beside, to the side of*, + גַּיְא *valley* Zc 14$_{5}$ (if em.; see above).

עַל *to*, + מָוֶת *death* Si 37$_{2(Bmg)}$.

עַד *as far as*, + צַוָּאר *neck* Is 8$_{8}$, שַׁעַר *gate* of death 107$_{18}$ 1QH 14$_{24}$ ([תגיע]), מָוֶת *death* Si 37$_{2(D)}$.

עַד לְ *as far as*, + שָׁמַיִם *heaven* 2 C 28$_{9}$.

אֵצֶל *beside, near*, + אַיִל *ram* Dn 8$_{17}$.

ה- of direction, *to*, + שָׁמַיִם *heaven* Gn 28$_{12}$.

<COLL> נגע hi. || עלה *go up* Jb 20$_{6}$, בוא *come* Ec 12$_{1}$, מצא *find* Si 11$_{10}$; הִגִּיעַ דְּבַר־הַמֶּלֶךְ וְדָתוֹ לְהֵעָשׂוֹת *the word of the king and his decree had arrived*, i.e. the time had come for them, *to be executed* Est 9$_{1}$, יגיעו לעבור על הפקודים *they reach the age to pass over to the registrants* CD 15$_{5}$.

2a. cause to touch, touch with (Ex 4$_{25}$ 12$_{22}$ Is 6$_{7}$ Jr 1$_{9}$ perh. 4QTohC 1$_{7}$ 4QOrd^{b} 2.2$_{1}$), **let touch** (4Q MMT B$_{4}$). **b. cause to reach,** i.e. **extol** (Si 13$_{23}$), **cast down** (Is 25$_{12}$ 26$_{5}$ Ezk 13$_{14}$ Lm 2$_{2}$). **c. join, bring together** (Is 5$_{8}$). **d. bring near,** i.e. **offer** (Si 50$_{19}$).

<SUBJ> Y. Is 25$_{12}$ 26$_{5}$ Jr 1$_{9}$ Ezk 13$_{14}$ Lm 2$_{2}$, Israelites Ex 12$_{22}$, Simeon (Si 50$_{19}$), Zipporah Ex 4$_{25}$, אִישׁ *man* perh. 4QTohC 1$_{7}$ (י[א]ש), בֵּן *son* Si 50$_{19}$, כֹּהֵן *priest* Si 50$_{19}$, אֶחָד *one* of the seraphim Is 6$_{7}$, כֹּל *all* Si 13$_{23}$; subj. not specified, Is 5$_{8}$ 4QMMT B$_{4}$ (מגיע[י]ם).

<OBJ> בַּיִת *house* Is 5$_{8}$, קִיר *wall* Ezk 13$_{14}$, מִבְצָר *fortification* Is 25$_{12}$ Lm 2$_{2}$, קִרְיָה *city* Is 26$_{5}$, מִשְׁכָּב *bed* perh. 4QTohC 1$_{7}$, מִשְׁפָּט *due* Si 50$_{19}$, שֵׂכֶל *wisdom* Si 13$_{23}$.

<PREP> לְ *to* or introducing object, + רֶגֶל *foot* Ex 4$_{25}$, אֶרֶץ *ground* Is 25$_{12}$ Lm 2$_{2}$; בְּ *to, with*, + בַּיִת *house* Is 5$_{8}$; introducing object 4QMMT B$_{4}$ (מגיע[י]ם), + טָהֳרָה *pure things* 4QOrd^{b} 2.2$_{1}$; אֶל *to* or introducing object, + Y. Si 50$_{19}$, מַשְׁקוֹף *lintel* Ex 12$_{22}$, מְזוּזָה *doorpost* Ex 12$_{22}$, אֶרֶץ *ground* Ezk 13$_{14}$; עַל *upon* or introducing object, + פֶּה *mouth* Is 6$_{7}$ Jr 1$_{9}$; מִן of instrument, *with*, + דָּם *blood* Ex 12$_{22}$; עַד *as far as*, + עָפָר *dust* Is 25$_{12}$ 26$_{5}$, עָב *cloud* Si 13$_{23}$.

<COLL> נגע hi. || בוא *come* Ezk 7$_{12}$, קרב hi. *bring near* Is 5$_{8}$, שׁפל hi. *make low* Is 25$_{12}$ 26$_{5}$; + שׁחח hi. *lay low* Is 25$_{12}$ 26$_{5}$, הרס *tear down* Lm 2$_{2}$.

3. befall, happen, <SUBJ> מָה *what* Est 9$_{26}$, impersonal Ec 8$_{14.14}$. <PREP> כְּ *according to*, + מַעֲשֶׂה *deed* Ec 8$_{14.14}$; אֶל *to*, + Jews Est 9$_{26}$, צַדִּיק *righteous one* Ec 8$_{14}$, רָשָׁע *wicked one* Ec 8$_{14}$.

Also 1Q25 2$_1$ ([לה]גיע) 1Q39 10$_1$.

<SYN> §1 עלה *go up*, בוא *come*, מצא *find*; §2 בוא *come*, קרב hi. *bring near* Is 5$_8$, שׁפל hi. *lay low*.*

⇒ נֶגַע *stroke, plague*.

*נגע II $_1$ vb. **rest** (unless נגע I *touch*)—**Qal** $_1$ Inf. לִנְגּוֹעַ—**rest**, <SUBJ> נֶפֶשׁ *soul* Jb 6$_7$ (מֵאֲנָה לִנְגּוֹעַ נַפְשִׁי *my soul refuses to rest*).

*[נגע] III vb. **sit**—**Qal**, <SUBJ> רֵעַ *friend* Ps 38$_{12}$ (if em. מִנֶּגֶד נִגְעִי יַעֲמֹדוּ *they stand aloof from my plague* to מִנֶּגֶד נָגְעוּ *they sit aloof*).

נֶ֫גַע $_{78.2.49}$ n.m. **stroke, plague**—נֶגַע; cstr. נֶ֫גַע; sf. נִגְעִי, נִגְעוֹ (Q נגעכה) נִגְעֵךְ (Si נִגְעֹה); pl. נְגָעִים (Q נגיעים, Q נגועים); cstr. נִגְעֵי (נגיעי); sf. Q נגיעי, Q נגיעיכה, Q נגיעיה, Q נגיעיהם—**1. stroke, blow, assault,** in violent crime (Dt 17$_8$ 21$_5$), punishment (2 S 7$_{14}$ Pr 6$_{33}$), <SUBJ> היה *be* Dt 21$_5$=11QT 63$_4$ 1QH 17$_{25}$. <OBJ> מצא *find* Pr 6$_{33}$. <CSTR> נִגְעֵי בְּנֵי *strokes of the sons of* 2 S 7$_{14}$; כָּל־נֶגַע *every assault* Dt 21$_5$=11QT 63$_4$. <PREP> בְּ of instrument, *by (means of), with*, + יכח hi. *reprove* 2 S 7$_{14}$; בֵּין ... לְ *between ... and*, בֵּין נֶגַע לָנֶגַע *between one kind of assault and another* Dt 17$_8$. <COLL> נֶגַע || שֵׁבֶט *rod* 2 S 7$_{14}$, דָּם *blood(shed)* Dt 17$_8$, דִּין *plea* Dt 17$_8$, רִיב *dispute* Dt 21$_5$=11QT 63$_4$, קָלוֹן *dishonour* Pr 6$_{33}$.

2. plague, disease, affliction, caused by Y. (Gn 12$_{17}$ Ex 11$_1$ perh. Is 53$_8$ Ps 39$_{11}$ 89$_{33}$ Si 10$_{13}$ 1QpHab 9$_{11}$ 4QParGenEx 3$_6$ 4QDibHam 1.6$_7$), angels (1QS 3$_{14.23}$ 4$_{12}$); sometimes specif. **skin disease*** (Lv 13$_{2+29t}$ 14$_{3.32}$ Dt 24$_8$ 4QD^a 6.1$_7$ [[הנגע]] 6.1$_{13}$ 4QD^g 1.1$_8$ [[הנגע]] 4QD^h 4.2$_4$ [[הנגע]]), sometimes in ref. to diseased spot in the skin (e.g. Lv 13$_{6.17.29.42}$) or (by metonymy) to a diseased person (Lv 13$_{4.12.13.17.31}$); in cloth garment or object of leather (Lv 13$_{47+16t}$), sometimes in ref. to diseased spot (e.g. Lv 13$_{49.50.51.56}$), diseased garment (Lv 13$_{50.55}$); in (walls of) house (Lv 14$_{34+10t}$).

<SUBJ> היה *be* Lv 13$_{9.29.42.47.49.52}$, עמד *stand*, i.e. be unchanged Lv 13$_4$, פרח *break out* Lv 14$_{43}$ 1QH 16$_{27}$ 4QD^a 6.1$_7$ ([פר]ח הנגע), פשׂה *spread* Lv 13$_{5.6.51.53.55}$ 14$_{39.44.48}$, סור *depart* Lv 13$_{58}$, שׁוב *go back* Lv 14$_{43}$ 11QPs^a 24$_{12}$, קרב *draw near* Ps 91$_{10}$, נגע *reach* 11QPsAp^a 6$_{10}$ ([נגע]), פגשׁ *meet* 4Q418 7$_8$, הפך *change* Lv 13$_{55}$, ni. *be changed* Lv 13$_{17}$, כהה pi. *be dim* Lv 13$_{6.56}$, מאר ni. *be painful* 1QH 13$_{28}$ 4Q418 243$_5$, חלה *make sick* 1QH 19$_{22}$, כבס hothp. *be washed* Lv 13$_{55.56}$, רפא ni. *be healed* Lv 14$_{3.48}$ 4QD^a 6.1$_{13}$ ([נרפא]) 4QD^g 1.1$_8$ ([נרפא] [הנגע]), שׁבת *cease* 4QHod^a 7.2$_6$.

<NOM CL> צָרַעַת מַמְאֶרֶת הַנֶּגַע *the disease is a malignant leprosy* Lv 13$_{51}$, נֶגַע צָרַעַת הוּא *it is the disease of leprosy* Lv 13$_{3.20(Kt).25(Kt).27(Kt)}$ (all three Qr הִיא) 13$_{49}$, נֶגַע הִיא *it is a plague* Lv 13$_{22(Qr)}$ (Kt הוא), [זה הנ]גע *this is an affliction* 4QTohA 1.1$_4$, אין נגע *there is no affliction* 1QH 18$_{19}$ ([אין]) 19$_{22}$, var. 4QM^g 8$_9$ ([א]ין), בְּרֹאשׁוֹ נִגְעוֹ *his disease is on his head* Lv 13$_{44}$, נגע בבשרו *a disease is in his flesh* Si 30$_{14}$, בּוֹ הַנֶּגַע *the disease is in him* Lv 13$_{45.54.57}$, vars. 13$_{46}$ 14$_{32.40}$ 11QT 46$_0$ ([בו נגע]), הַנֶּגַע בְּקִירֹת הַבַּיִת *the disease is in the walls of the house* Lv 14$_{37}$, נֶגַע בְּאַפּוֹ *affliction is in his anger* Ps 30$_6$ (if em. רֶגַע *[for] a moment*), כול נגיעיהם ... בממשלת משטמתו *all their afflictions are ... on account of the rule of his animosity* 1QS 3$_{23}$, נֶגַע לָמוֹ perh. *the affliction was due to them* Is 53$_8$ (1QIsa^a נוגע *he was afflicted*, i.e. נגע pu.).

<OBJ> ראה *see* Lv 13$_{3+6t}$ 14$_{36.37}$, ידע *know* 1 K 8$_{38}$|| 2 C 6$_{29}$, בוא hi. *bring* Ex 11$_1$ Si 10$_{13}$ ([ויבא]), סור hi. *remove* Ps 39$_{11}$, שׁלח *send* 4QParGenEx 3$_6$, נתן *give*, i.e. place Lv 14$_{34}$, נגע pi. *afflict with* Gn 12$_{17}$, סגר hi. *shut up* Lv 13$_{4.31.50}$, טהר pi. *declare purified* Lv 13$_{13.17}$, שׂרף *burn* Lv 13$_{55}$, קרע *tear* Lv 13$_{56}$.

<CSTR> נֶגַע צָרַעַת *disease of leprosy* Lv 13$_2$ (צָרָ֫עַת) 13$_{3.9.20.25.27.47}$ (צָרָ֫עַת) 13$_{49}$ 14$_3$ (־הַצָּרַעַת) 14$_{32.34.54}$ Dt 24$_8$ (־הַצָּרַעַת) 11QT 49$_4$ (הצרעת), צָרַעַת *of leprosy of* Lv 13$_{59}$ 11QT 46$_0$ ([נגע צרעת]), הַנֶּתֶק *of the scall* Lv 13$_{31}$, נגע נדה *disease of impurity* 4QRitPur 1.12$_{16}$ 34.5$_{17}$ (הנדה), נֶגַע לְבָבוֹ *affliction of his heart* 1 K 8$_{38}$, נגיעי [בנ]י *afflictions of the sons of* 1QH 4$_8$, נגע מכשול *affliction of*, i.e. that causes, *stumbling* 1QH 8$_{24}$ 4QM^g 8$_9$ ([מכשול]), נגע מכאובי *the affliction of my pain* 4QHod^a 2$_2$, רע *of evil* 11QPs^a 24$_{12}$ (unless רע is attributive adj.).

רוב נגיעים *multitude of afflictions* 1QS 4$_{12}$, פקודת

נגיעיהם *visitation of,* i.e. for, *their afflictions* 1QS 3_{14}, משפטי נגע *judgments of affliction* 1QH 19_8 fr. 3_{16}, נגיעי *of my afflictions* 1QH 9_{33}, [טמאות נגע] *impurity of disease* 4QMMT B_{71}, מַרְאֵה הַנֶּגַע *appearance of the disease* Lv 13_3, שְׂאֵת *swelling of* Lv 13_{43}, עוֹר הַנֶּגַע *skin of the diseased person* Lv 13_{12}, תורת נגע *law of,* i.e. concerning, *disease* CD 13_5, תּוֹרַת נֶגַע *law of,* i.e. concerning, *the disease of* Lv 13_{59}, עת הנגע *time of the affliction* 4QNidd 4_6, כָּל־נֶגַע *any disease/affliction* 1 K 8_{37}|| 2 C 6_{28} 4QD^a $6e_2$ (כול; נגע erased) 4Q417 2.2_9 (כול) 4QBark^a 1.1_{11} (ל[מכו]), *any disease/affliction of* Lv 14_{54} 1QH 8_{24} 4QM^g 8_9 (both כול), כול נגיעיהם *all their afflictions* 1QH 9_{18} 1QS 3_{23}.

<ADJ> גָּדוֹל *great* Gn 12_{17}, אֲדַמְדָּם *reddish* Lv 13_{42}, לָבָן *white* Lv 13_{42}, רַע *evil* 11QPs^a 24_{12} (unless רע is noun, *of evil*), אֶחָד *one* Ex 11_1.

<PREP> לְ of benefit, *for* or *concerning* Lv 14_{54}; introducing predicate, + היה *be* Lv 13_2; לְ ... מִן *from ... to,* ממכאוב לנגע *from pain to affliction* 1QH 17_6.

בְּ of place, *in* Lv 13_3; *into (a state of), during,* + בוא *come* 4QDibHam 1.5_{18} (בנג[י]עים), שמר ni. *take heed* Dt 24_8; introducing object, + רצה *accept* 1QH 17_{10} 4QBéat 2.2_4, מאס *reject* 4QDibHam 1.6_7; of instrument, *by (means of), with* 4QRitPur 1.12_{16} 11QT 49_4, + רצה *satisfy,* i.e. expiate, iniquity 4Q183 1.2_7 (בנגיע[יה]ם), פקד *visit,* i.e. punish Ps 89_{33}, נגע pu. *be stricken,* ענה pi. *afflict* 1QpHab 9_{11}, pu. *be afflicted* 4QD^e 2.2_{12}, perh. ידע hi. *humiliate* 1QH 16_{27} (מ[וד]ע; unless ידע hi. *cause to know,* and בְּ introducing object).

כְּ *as* Lv 14_{35}.

מִן *from* perh. 4QRitPur 34.5_{17}, + טהר pi. *purify* 11QPs^a 24_{12}, רפא ni. *be healed* 4QD^g 1.2_2 (נרפא הנ[גע]) 4QD^h 4.2_4 ([הנגע]); of instrument, *by (means of), with,* + נגף ni. *be stricken* 4QBark^a 1.1_{11} ([הנגף] ... [מכו]ל).

עַל *on account of,* + ברך pi. *bless* 4Q417 2.2_9 ([ברן]).

עִם *with* 1QH 9_{18}.

לִפְנֵי *before, in the face of,* + חזק pi. *strengthen* 1QH 9_{32}, hi. *be strong* 1QH 12_{36}, אמץ pi. *strengthen* 1QH 10_7 (נג[ע]) עמד hi. *establish* 1QH 17_{10}, קום htpol. *raise oneself up* 1QH 22_6 (תקומם[ ]).

מִנֶּגֶד *aloof from,* + עמד *stand* Ps 38_{12} (or em. מִנֶּגֶד נִגְעִי *aloof from my plague* to מְנַגְּדַי *aloof from me,* or em. מִנֶּגֶד נִגְעִי יַעֲמֹדוּ *they stand aloof from my plague* to מִנֶּגֶד נָגְעוּ *they sit aloof,* i.e. נגע III).

<COLL> נֶגַע || מַחֲלָה *sickness* 1 K 8_{37}||2 C 6_{28} 4QapPent 10.1_8, מַכָּה *plague* 4QapPent 10.1_8, צָרַעַת *leprosy* 11QT 48_{15}, נֶתֶק *scall* 11QT 48_{15}, מַכְאֹב *pain* 2 C 6_{29}, שֵׁבֶט *rod* Ps 89_{33}, מִשְׁפָּט *judgment* 1QH 17_{10}, נִסּוּי *trial* 4QDibHam^a 1.6_7, יִסּוּר *punishment* 4QBéat 2.2_4; + רָעָה *evil* Ps 91_{10}, תִּגְרָה *hostility* Ps 39_{11}.

נגעים לאין [מרפא] *diseases with no cure* 4QapPent 10.1_8.

Also perh. 1QH 21_4 1QpHab 9_1 (unless נגועו is from נגע *touch*) 4QTohD 3_1 4Q415 19_3 4Q418 87_8.

<SYN> §1 שֵׁבֶט *rod,* דָּם *blood(shed),* דִּין *plea,* רִיב *dispute,* קָלוֹן *dishonour;* §2 מַחֲלָה *sickness,* מַכָּה *plague,* צָרַעַת *leprosy,* נֶתֶק *scall,* מַכְאֹב *pain,* שֵׁבֶט *rod,* מִשְׁפָּט *judgment,* נִסּוּי *trial,* יִסּוּר *punishment.**

⇒ נגע I *touch.*

נגף 49.0.13 vb. **strike—Qal** 25.0.6 Pf. נָגַף (נְגָפָנוּ, נְגָפוֹ); impf. יִגֹּף, 3fs Q תגוף, 2ms תִּגֹּף (תִּגּוֹף), אֶגּוֹף; + waw וַיִּגֹּף, וַנִּגְּפוּ; וַיִּגֹּף (וַיִּגְּפֵנוּ, וַיִּגְּפֵהוּ), וָאֶגֹּף; ptc. נֹגֵף; inf. abs. נָגֹף; cstr. לִנְגֹּף (Q לנגוף, נָגְפוֹ)—**strike,** causing injury or death, **plague** (Ex 7_{27} 32_{35} Jos 24_5 4QParGenEx 3_8), **strike down, defeat, rout** (Jg 20_{35} 1 S 4_3 2 C 13_{15} 14_{11} 1QM 1_{13} 3_9), **stumble** (Pr 3_{23}), <SUBJ> Y. Ex 7_{27} $12_{23.27}$ 32_{35} Jos 24_5 Jg 20_{35} 1 S 4_3 26_{10} 2 S 12_{15} Is 19_{22} Zc $14_{12.18}$ Ps 89_{24} 2 C $13_{15.20}$ 14_{11} $21_{14.18}$ 1QM 3_9 4QParGenEx 3_8 perh. 4Q496 11_1, מַשְׁחִית *destroyer* Ex 12_{23}, אִישׁ *man* Ex 21_{22}, בֵּן *son* 1QM 1_{13}, יֹשֵׁב *inhabitant* Ps 91_{12}, יָד *hand* of Y. 4QM^a 1_4, רֶגֶל *foot* Pr 3_{23}, שׁוֹר *ox* Ex 21_{35}.

<OBJ> 1. person or thing struck, Benjamin(ites) Jg 20_{35}, Cushites 2 C 14_{11}, Egypt(ians) Ex $12_{23.27}$ Jos 24_5 Is 19_{22}, Israel(ites) 1 S 4_3 2 C 13_{15}, עַם *people* Ex 32_{35} Zc 14_{12}, גּוֹי *nation* Zc 14_{18}, Jehoram 2 C 21_{18}, Jeroboam 2 C $13_{15.20}$, Nabal 1 S 25_{38}, Saul 1 S 26_{10}, אִשָּׁה *woman* Ex 21_{22}, בֵּן *son* 1QM 3_9, יֶלֶד *child* 2 S 12_{15}, שׂנא pi. ptc. *one who hates* Ps 89_{24}, רֶגֶל *foot* Ps 91_{12}, שׁוֹר *ox* Ex 21_{35}, מִקְנֶה *cattle* 4QParGenEx 3_8, גְּבוּל *border,* i.e. territory Ex 7_{27}, רִשְׁעָה *wickedness* 1QM 1_{13}.

2. struck with, מַגֵּפָה *plague* Zc $14_{12.18}$ 2 C 21_{14} 4QpsHistB 1_2.

<PREP> לְ of instrument, *by (means of), with,* + חֳלִי

sickness 2 C 21$_{18}$.

בְּ of place, *in*, + מֵעֶה *bowels* 2 C 21$_{18}$; of instrument, *by (means of), with*, + צְפַרְדֵּעַ *frog* Ex 7$_{27}$, דֶּבֶר *pestilence* 4QParGenEx 3$_{8}$ ([בדב]ר); *against, upon*, + עַם *people* 2 C 21$_{14}$, אִשָּׁה *wife* 2 C 21$_{14}$, בֵּן *son* 2 C 21$_{14}$, אֶבֶן *stone* Ps 91$_{12}$, רְכוּשׁ *possessions* 2 C 21$_{14}$.

לִפְנֵי *before*, + Israel Jg 20$_{35}$, Judah 2 C 13$_{15}$ 14$_{11}$, Philistines 1 S 4$_{3}$, Abijah 2 C 13$_{15}$, Asa 2 C 14$_{11}$.

אַחֲרֵי *after*, + זֹאת *this* 2 C 21$_{18}$.

<COLL> נגף || כתת *crush* Ps 89$_{24}$; + מות *die* Ex 21$_{35}$ 1 S 25$_{38}$ 1 C 13$_{20}$, אנשׁ ni. *be incurably sick* 2 S 12$_{15}$; + adverb, לָמָּה *why?* 1 S 4$_{3}$; וְנָגַף י׳ אֶת־מִצְרַיִם נָגֹף וְרָפוֹא *and Y. will strike Egypt, striking and healing* Is 19$_{22}$.

Also 4Q415 11$_{7}$ 6QapSamKings 44.1$_{9}$ ([וי]גף).

<SYN> כתת *crush* Ps 89$_{24}$.

Ni. 23.0.6 Pf. נִגַּף, נִגְּפוּ (נִגְּפוּ); impf. יִנָּגֵף, 3fs Q תנגף, תִּנָּגְפוּ; + waw וַיִּנָּגֵף, וַיִּנָּגְפוּ (וַיִּנָּגְפוּ) וְנִגַּפְתֶּם; ptc. נִגָּף, נִגָּפִים; inf. abs. נִגּוֹף; cstr. הִנָּגֵף (Q הנגפם)—usu. **be defeated, routed; be stricken** by plague (4QBark^{a} 1.1$_{11}$ [[הנגף]]), <SUBJ> Aramaeans 2 S 10$_{15}$||1 C 19$_{16}$, Benjaminites Jg 20$_{36}$, Israel(ites) Lv 26$_{17}$ Dt 1$_{42}$ 28$_{25}$ Jg 20$_{32.39.39}$ 1 S 4$_{2.10}$ 1 K 8$_{33}$||2 C 6$_{24}$, Judah 2 K 14$_{12}$||2 C 25$_{22}$, Philistines 1 S 7$_{10}$, עַם *people* 2 S 18$_{7}$ 1 K 8$_{33}$||2 C 6$_{24}$, Abner 2 S 2$_{17}$, אִישׁ *man* 2 S 2$_{17}$, בֵּן *son* of Israel Nm 14$_{42}$, of Ammon, Moab, Mount Seir 2 C 20$_{22}$, מֶלֶךְ *king* 2 S 10$_{19}$, עֶבֶד *servant* 2 S 10$_{19}$||1 C 19$_{19}$ 2 S 18$_{7}$, אֹיֵב *enemy* Dt 28$_{7}$ 1QM 3$_{2}$ 9$_{2.3}$, עָנָו *humble one* 4QBark^{a} 1.1$_{11}$ ([הנגף]), רִשְׁעָה *evil* 4QM^{g} 4$_{1}$.

<PREP> כְּ *as (in)*, מִלְחָמָה *battle* Jg 20$_{39}$.

מִן of instrument, *by (means of), with*, + נֶגַע *plague* 4QBark^{a} 1.1$_{11}$ ([הנגף] ... מכו]ל נגע]).

לִפְנֵי *before* 1QM 17$_{15}$ 6QapSamKings 32$_{2}$, + Benjaminites Jg 20$_{32.39}$, Israel(ites) Dt 28$_{7}$ 1 S 7$_{10}$ 2 S 10$_{15.19}$|| 1 C 19$_{16.19}$ 2 K 14$_{12}$||2 C 25$_{22}$ 1QM 9$_{3}$, Philistines 1 S 4$_{2}$, אֹיֵב *enemy* Lv 26$_{17}$ Nm 14$_{42}$ Dt 1$_{42}$ 28$_{25}$ 1 K 8$_{33}$||2 C 6$_{24}$, עֶבֶד *servant* 2 S 2$_{17}$.

<COLL> נגף ni. + adverb, שָׁם *there* 2 S 18$_{7}$, כְּבָרִאשֹׁנָה *as formerly* Jg 20$_{32}$; inf. abs. + finite form of נגף ni. Jg 20$_{39}$ (נִגּוֹף נִגָּף הוּא לְפָנֵינוּ *they are surely smitten before us*); יִתֵּן י׳ אֹיְבֶיךָ ... נִגָּפִים *Y. will cause your enemies ... to be defeated* Dt 28$_{7}$, var. Dt 28$_{25}$.

Also 4Q415 11$_{9}$.

Htp. 1.0.1 Impf. יִתְנַגְּפוּ; inf. Q התנגפי—**stumble,** <SUBJ> רֶגֶל *foot* Jr 13$_{16}$. <PREP> עַל *upon*, + הַר *mountain* of twilight Jr 13$_{16}$.

Also 4QShir^{b} 18.3$_{9}$.*

⇒ נֶגֶף *striking*, מַגֵּפָה *plague*.

נֶגֶף 7.1.2 n.m. **striking**—נֶגֶף—**1a. striking,** <CSTR> אֶבֶן נֶגֶף *stone of striking* Is 8$_{14}$ (|| מִכְשׁוֹל *stumbling*) 1Q38 1$_{2}$.

1b. obstacle, against which one strikes the foot, <CSTR> נגף מכשול perh. *obstacle of*, i.e. that causes, *stumbling* 4Q418 168$_{2}$. <PREP> בְּ of instrument, *by (means of), with* or of cause, *on account of*, + תקל ni. *stumble* Si 35$_{20(B)}$ (E בדרך *in the [same] way*).

2. plague, <SUBJ> היה *be* Ex 12$_{13}$ 30$_{12}$ Nm 8$_{19}$ Jos 22$_{17}$, שׁחת hi. *destroy* Ex 12$_{13}$, חלל hi. *begin* Nm 17$_{11.12}$.

Also 4Q418 167$_{7}$.

<SYN> §1a מִכְשׁוֹל *stumbling*.*

⇒ נגף *strike*.

נגר I 10.0.3 vb. **pour** (unless all forms are from גרר *drag*)*—**Ni.** 4.0.1 Pf. נִגְּרָה; + waw Q וינגר; ptc. נִגָּרִים, נִגָּרוֹת—**1. be poured out, be spilt, flow,** <SUBJ> עַיִן *eye* Lm 3$_{49}$, לֵב *heart* 1QH 16$_{32}$ (|| מסס ni. *melt*), מַיִם *water* 2 S 14$_{14}$. <PREP> כְּ *as*, + מַיִם *water* 1QH 16$_{32}$; ה- of direction, *upon*, + אֶרֶץ *ground* 2 S 14$_{14}$.

2. be stretched out (unless נגר II *smite*), <SUBJ> יָד *hand* Ps 77$_{3}$. <COLL> נגר ni. + noun used adverbially, לַיְלָה *in the night* Ps 77$_{3}$.

3. fem. ptc. as noun, **torrent,*** יִגֶל יְבוּל בֵּיתוֹ נִגָּרוֹת בְּיוֹם אַפּוֹ *a flood will sweep away his house, torrents on the day of his wrath* Jb 20$_{28}$ (if em. יִגֶל יְבוּל *the produce of* his house *will depart*).

<SYN> §1 מסס ni. *melt*.

Hi. 5.0.1 Impf. יַגִּירֻהוּ; + waw וַיַּגֵּר, וְהִגַּרְתִּי, 2ms וַתַּגֵּר; impv. הַגִּרֵם; ptc. Q מגיר—**1. pour** (Ps 75$_{9}$), **pour down, hurl down** (Mc 1$_{6}$), <SUBJ> Y. Mc 1$_{6}$ Ps 75$_{9}$; subj. not specified, 4QapLam^{a} 1.2$_{8}$. <OBJ> אֶבֶן *stone* Mc 1$_{6}$. <PREP> לְ of direction, *into*, + גַּיְא *valley* Mc 1$_{6}$; מִן of direction, *from*, + זֶה *this* Ps 75$_{9}$.

2. deliver up, <SUBJ> Y. Jr 18$_{21}$ (unless נגר II *smite*; || נתן *give*), הַר *mountain* of Seir Ezk 35$_{5}$; subj. not specified, Ps 63$_{11}$ (unless נגר II; or em. ho.). <OBJ> בֵּן *son* Jr 18$_{21}$ Ezk 35$_{5}$; obj. not specified, Ps 63$_{11}$ (or em. ho.). <PREP> בְּ of time, *in,* + עֵת *time* Ezk 35$_{5}$; עַל *to,* + יָד *hand,* i.e. power, of sword Jr 18$_{21}$ Ezk 35$_{5}$ Ps 63$_{11}$ (or em. ho.).

Ho. 1.0.1 Ptc. מֻגָּרִים (Q מוגרים)—**1. be poured out,** <SUBJ> מַיִם *water* Mc 1$_{4}$ 1QH 12$_{34}$ (both + מסס ni. *melt*). <PREP> בְּ of place, + מוֹרָד *slope* Mc 1$_{4}$ 1QH 12$_{34}$.

2. be delivered up, <SUBJ> enemies Ps 63$_{11}$ (if em. יַגִּירֻהוּ *they shall deliver him up* to [i.e. hi.] יֻגְּרוּ *they shall be delivered up*). <PREP> עַל *to,* + יָד *hand,* i.e. power, of the sword Ps 53$_{11}$ (if em.; see Subj.).*

***נגר II** 3 vb. **smite—Pi.** 1 Pf. נִגְּרָה—**smite** (unless נגר I ni. *be stretched out*), <SUBJ> יָד *hand* Ps 77$_{3}$. <COLL> יָדִי לַיְלָה נִגְּרָה *at night his hand* (י־ as 3 ms sf.) *strikes (me)* Ps 77$_{3}$.

Hi. 2 Impf. יַגִּירֻהוּ; impv. הַגִּרֵם—**1. smite** (unless נגר I hi. *deliver up*), <SUBJ> Y. Jr 18$_{21}$. <PREP> עַל *by means of, with,* + יָד *hand,* i.e. edge, of sword Jr 18$_{21}$.

2. be smitten (unless נגר I hi. *deliver up*), <SUBJ> subj. not specified, Ps 63$_{11}$. <PREP> עַל *by means of, with,* + יָד *hand,* i.e. edge, of sword Ps 63$_{11}$. <COLL> יַגִּירֻהוּ *may they be smitten by him* (i.e. הוּ־ as dative of agency) Ps 63$_{11}$.

[נֶגֶרֶת] *torrent,* see נגר I *pour,* Ni. §3.*

נגשׂ 23.0.2 vb. **press—Qal** 19.0.2 Pf. נָגַשׂ; impf. יִגֹּשׂ, 2ms תִּגֹּשׂ, תִּנְגְּשׂוּ; ptc. נֹגֵשׂ (נוֹגֵשׂ), נֹגְשִׂים (sf. Q נוגשיכה, נֹגְשַׂיִךְ), נֹגְשֵׂי (נֹגְשֵׂיהֶם, נֹגְשָׂיו)—**1. oppress,** <SUBJ> Israelites Is 58$_{3}$. <OBJ> עָצֵב *labourer* Is 58$_{3}$.

2. exact (payment) of, be a creditor,* in connection with debts (Dt 15$_{2.3}$), tribute (2 K 23$_{35}$), <SUBJ> Israelites Dt 15$_{3}$, Jehoiakim 2 K 23$_{35}$, בַּעַל *owner* of loan, i.e. creditor Dt 15$_{2}$ 1QDM 1.3$_{6}$ ([יגוש]) 11QMelch 2$_{3}$ ([יגוש]). <OBJ> 1. thing exacted, זָהָב *gold* 2 K 23$_{35}$, כֶּסֶף *silver* 2 K 23$_{35}$. 2. person of whom exacted, עַם *people* 2 K 23$_{35}$, אִישׁ *man* 1QDM 1.3$_{6}$ ([יגוש איש]), אָח *brother* Dt 15$_{2}$ 1QDM 1.3$_{6}$ 11QMelch 2$_{3}$ (both ... [יגוש אחיו]), רֵעַ *neighbour* Dt 15$_{2}$ 11QMelch 2$_{3}$ (... [יגוש רעהו]), נָכְרִי *foreigner* Dt 15$_{3}$ 1QDM 1.3$_{6}$ ([הנ]כרי יגוש]).

3. ptc. as noun, **ruler, oppressor, taskmaster, exactor (of tribute)** (Dn 11$_{20}$), **(ass-)driver** (Jb 39$_{7}$), <SUBJ> יצא *go out* Ex 5$_{10}$ Zc 10$_{4}$, עבר *pass* Zc 9$_{8}$, אמר *say* Ex 5$_{10.13}$, אוץ *urge on* Ex 5$_{13}$, נתן *give* Ex 5$_{6}$, שׂים *place* Ex 5$_{6.14}$, יסף hi. *add* Ex 5$_{6}$, גרע *diminish* Ex 5$_{6}$, שׁבת *cease* Is 14$_{4}$ 4QHod^{e} 1$_{2}$. <NOM CL> נֹגְשָׂיו מְעוֹלֵל *his oppressors are children* Is 3$_{12}$ (or em. נֹגְשִׂים עוֹלְלוּ *creditors levy distress,* from עלל II *impose burden,* as of a tax-gatherer).* <OBJ> צוה pi. *command* Ex 5$_{6}$, עבד *serve* 4Q416 2.2$_{17}$, עבר hi. *cause to pass* Dn 11$_{20}$, שׂים *place,* i.e. make Is 60$_{17}$.

<CSTR> נֹגְשֵׂי הָעָם *taskmasters of the people* Ex 5$_{10}$, פַּרְעֹה *of Pharaoh* Ex 5$_{14}$, נֹגֵשׂ חֲבֵרוֹ *ruler of his companion* Jb 40$_{19}$ (if em.; see Coll.); קוֹל נֹגֵשׂ *voice of the taskmaster* Jb 3$_{18}$, תְּשֻׁאוֹת נוֹגֵשׂ *shouts of the driver* Jb 39$_{7}$, שֵׁבֶט הַנֹּגֵשׂ *rod of the taskmaster* Is 9$_{3}$, כָּל־נוֹגֵשׂ *every ruler* Zc 10$_{4}$.

<PREP> בְּ *over,* + רדה *rule* Is 14$_{2}$; מִפְּנֵי *on account of* Ex 3$_{7}$.

<COLL> נֹגֵשׂ + שֹׁבֶה *captor* Is 14$_{2}$, שֹׁטֵר *official* Ex 5$_{6.10}$, פְּקֻדָּה *oversight,* i.e. overseers Is 60$_{17}$, מַדְהֵבָה *distress* Is 14$_{4}$; הֶעָשׂוּי נֹגֵשׂ חֲבֵרוֹ *the one who is made to be the ruler of his companion* Jb 40$_{19}$ (if em. הָעֹשׂוֹ יַגֵּשׁ חַרְבּוֹ *let the one who made him draw his sword*).

Ni. 4 Pf. נִגַּשׂ; + waw וְנִגַּשׂ—**be hard pressed, oppressed, distressed** (1 S 14$_{24}$), <SUBJ> עַם *people* 1 S 13$_{6}$ Is 3$_{5}$, אִישׁ *man* 1 S 14$_{24}$ Is 3$_{5}$, עֶבֶד *servant* Is 53$_{7}$ (+ ענה ni. *be afflicted*). <PREP> בְּ of agent, *by,* + אִישׁ *man* Is 3$_{5}$, רֵעַ *neighbour* Is 3$_{5}$.

Ho. be oppressed, <SUBJ> רֶגֶל *foot* 2 S 3$_{34}$ (if em. הֻגָּשׁוּ *brought near* to הֻגָּשׂוּ). <PREP> לְ of instrument, *by (means of), with,* + נְחֹשֶׁת du. *fetters* 2 S 3$_{34}$ (if em.; see Subj.).*

נֹגֵשׂ *oppressor,* see נגשׂ *press.*

נגשׁ 125.4.31 vb. **draw near—Qal** 68.0.7 Impf. יִגַּשׁ (יִגָּשׁ), 2ms תִּגַּשׁ, יִגְּשׁוּ (יִגַּשׁוּ, יִגָּשׁוּ), תִּגְּשׁוּ (תִּגַּשׁוּ); + waw וַיִּגַּשׁ, 3fs וַתִּגַּשׁ, וַיִּגְּשׁוּ (וַיִּגָּשׁוּ), 3fpl וַתִּגַּשְׁןָ; impv. גַּשׁ (גֶּשׁ־, גְּשָׁה־), גֹּשִׁי, גְּשׁוּ (גֹּשׁוּ); inf. גֶּשֶׁת (גִּשְׁתּוֹ, גִּשְׁתָּם)—**draw near, approach,**

used absolutely (Gn 18$_{23}$ 27$_{21.26.27}$ 29$_{10}$ 33$_{6.7}$ 45$_4$ Ex 24$_2$ Jos 8$_{11}$ 1 S 17$_{16}$ 2 S 1$_{15}$ 1 K 18$_{36}$ 20$_{28}$ 22$_{24}$||2 C 18$_{23}$ 2 K 4$_{27}$ 5$_{13}$ Is 41$_1$ Jr 42$_1$ Jl 4$_9$ 2 C 29$_{31}$), for sexual purposes (Ex 19$_{15}$), for battle (Jg 20$_{23}$ 2 S 10$_{13}$||1 C 19$_{14}$ Jr 46$_3$ Jl 4$_9$ 1QM 4$_{7.11}$); in legal contexts, to receive judgment (Ex 24$_{14}$), to give judgment (1QSa 1$_{13}$), of the approach of one's legal opponent (Is 50$_8$); in cultic contexts, of priest's approach to altar (Ex 28$_{43}$ 30$_{20}$ Lv 21$_{21.21.23}$ Ezk 44$_{13}$), bringing of offerings (2 C 29$_{31}$); perh. **meet** (Ps 91$_7$); **move away**, i.e. make room (Is 49$_{20}$).

<SUBJ> Egyptians Jr 46$_3$, Israelites Is 49$_{20}$, Philistine 1 S 17$_{16}$, עַם *people* Ex 19$_{15}$ Jos 8$_{11}$ 2 S 10$_{13}$||1 C 19$_{14}$ 1 K 18$_{30.30}$ Jr 42$_1$, לְאֹם *nation* Is 41$_1$, שֵׁבֶט *tribe* Nm 4$_{19}$, קָהָל *assembly* 2 C 29$_{31}$.

Abimelech Jg 9$_{52}$, Abraham Gn 18$_{23}$, Aaron Ex 24$_2$ 28$_{43}$ 30$_{20}$ 34$_{30}$, Abihu Ex 24$_2$, David 1 S 17$_{40}$ 30$_{21}$, Elijah 1 K 18$_{21.36}$, Gehazi 2 K 4$_{27}$, Jacob Gn 27$_{21.22.26.27}$ 29$_{10}$ 33$_3$, Jezaniah Jr 42$_1$, Joab 2 S 10$_{13}$||1 C 19$_{14}$, Johanan Jr 42$_1$, Joseph Gn 33$_7$, Judah Gn 44$_{18}$, Leah Gn 33$_7$, Lot Gn 19$_9$, Nadab Ex 24$_2$, Rachel Gn 33$_7$, Ruth Ru 2$_{14}$, Saul 1 S 9$_{18}$, Zedekiah 1 K 22$_{24}$||2 C 18$_{23}$.

אִישׁ *man* Gn 43$_{19}$ Lv 21$_{21.21.23}$ 1 K 20$_{28}$ CD 8$_{7(A)}$=19$_{19(B)}$, בֵּן *son* Ex 28$_{43}$ 30$_{20}$ Nm 32$_{16}$ 1 K 22$_{24}$||2 C 18$_{23}$ 2 K 2$_5$ Jr 42$_1$ 1QM 4$_{7.11}$ 4QD^a 5.2$_6$, of Israel Ex 34$_{30}$ Nm 8$_{19}$ Jos 3$_9$ Jg 20$_{23}$, of Judah Jos 14$_6$, יֶלֶד *child* Gn 33$_{6.7}$, אָח *brother* Gn 45$_{4.4}$, שַׂר *commander* Jr 42$_1$, גִּבּוֹר *warrior* Jl 4$_9$, עֶבֶד *servant* 2 K 5$_{13}$, שִׁפְחָה *servant* (fem.) Gn 33$_6$, כֹּהֵן *priest* 4QM^c 1$_6$, לֵוִי *Levite* Ezk 44$_{13.13}$, נָבִיא *prophet* 1 K 18$_{36}$ 20$_{22}$, זָקֵן *elder* Ex 24$_2$, בַּעַל *possessor* of judgment, i.e. legal opponent Is 50$_8$, צַר *adversary* Ezr 4$_2$, אֶזְרָח *native* 1QSa 1$_{13}$, נשׂא ptc. *one who carries* 4QMMT B$_{23}$ ([י]גשׁ).

ראשׁ *head* Jos 21$_1$, פִּנָּה *corner*, i.e. ruler 1 S 14$_{38}$, דֶּבֶר *pestilence* Ps 91$_7$, קֶטֶב *destruction* Ps 91$_7$, רָעָה *evil* Am 9$_{10}$ (if em. תַּגִּישׁ appar. *it will* not *bring near* [i.e. hi.] to תִּגַּשׁ), מִי *who?* Ex 24$_{14}$ Jr 30$_{21}$, אֶחָד *one* 2 S 1$_{15}$ Jb 41$_{16}$, אֵלֶּה *these* Ezk 9$_6$; subj. not specified, Is 65$_5$.

<OBJ> עַם *people* 1 S 30$_{21}$ (mss אֶל *to*), Samuel 1 S 9$_{18}$ (mss אֶל), קֹדֶשׁ *holiness*, i.e. holy thing Nm 4$_{19}$ (mss, Sam אֶל).

<PREP> לְ of direction, *to*, + מִלְחָמָה *battle* (or perh. of benefit, *for*) Jg 20$_{23}$ 2 S 10$_{13}$||1 C 19$_{14}$ Jr 46$_3$ 1QM 4$_{7.11}$, מַעֲרָכָה *battle-line* 4QM^c 1$_6$, זִמָּה *wickedness* CD 8$_{7(A)}$=19$_{19(B)}$, עֲבֹדָה *service* 4QD^a 5.2$_6$, טָהֳרָה *pure food* 4QMMT B$_{23}$ ([י]גשׁ).

לְ of benefit, *for*, + בֵּן *son* Is 49$_{20}$ (גְּשָׁה־לִּי *move away*, i.e. make room, *for me*).

בְּ of place, *in, at*, + Gilgal Jos 14$_6$; *to* or introducing object, + עַם *people* Is 65$_5$, אֶחָד *one* Jb 41$_{16}$.

אֶל *to* Is 50$_8$, + Y. Jr 30$_{21}$ Ezk 44$_{13}$, Philistine 1 S 17$_{40}$, עַם *people* 1 S 30$_{21(mss)}$ 1 K 18$_{21}$, Aaron Ex 24$_{14}$, Eleazar Jos 21$_1$, Elijah 1 K 18$_{30.30}$, Elisha 2 K 2$_5$, Hur Ex 24$_{14}$, Isaac Gn 27$_{22}$, Joseph Gn 44$_{18}$ 45$_4$, Joshua Jos 14$_6$ 21$_1$, Moses Ex 34$_{30}$ Nm 32$_{16}$, Samuel 1 S 9$_{18(mss)}$, Zerubbabel Ezr 4$_2$, אִישׁ *man* Gn 43$_{19}$, אִשָּׁה *woman* Ex 19$_{15}$, אָב *father* Gn 27$_{22}$, בֵּן *son* Jos 21$_1$, מֶלֶךְ *king* 1 K 20$_{22}$, כֹּהֵן *priest* Jos 21$_1$, ישׁב ptc. *one who dwells* Ps 91$_7$, ראשׁ *head* Jos 21$_1$ Ezr 4$_2$, מִזְבֵּחַ *altar* Ex 28$_{43}$ 30$_{20}$ Lv 21$_{23}$, קֹדֶשׁ *holiness*, i.e. holy thing Nm 4$_{19(mss, Sam)}$, i.e. sanctuary Nm 8$_{19}$ Ezk 44$_{13}$.

עַל *to*, + אִישׁ *man* Ezk 9$_6$, קֹדֶשׁ *holiness*, i.e. holy thing Ezk 44$_{13}$.

עַד *to*, + אָח *brother* Gn 33$_3$, פֶּתַח *entrance* Jg 9$_{52}$.

בְּתוֹךְ *within*, + שַׁעַר *gate* 1 S 9$_{18}$.

לִפְנֵי *before*, + Aramaeans 1 C 19$_{14}$.

<COLL> נגשׁ + בוא *come* Ex 28$_{43}$ 30$_{20}$ Lv 21$_{23}$ Jos 8$_{11}$ Jg 9$_{52}$; + adverb, אַחַר *afterwards* Gn 33$_7$, הֲלֹם *hither* 1 S 14$_{38}$ Ru 2$_{14}$, הֵנָּה *here* Jos 3$_9$, הָלְאָה *there* Gn 19$_9$ (גֶּשׁ־הָלְאָה *approach there*, i.e. stand back).

Followed by infinitive of purpose, of הדף *thrust* 2 K 4$_{27}$, כהן pi. *serve as priest* Ezk 44$_{13}$, שׁרת pi. *serve* Ex 28$_{43}$ 30$_{20}$, קטר hi. *burn* Ex 30$_{20}$, שׂרף *burn* Jg 9$_{52}$, קרב hi. *bring near*, i.e. offer Lv 21$_{21.21}$, רִיב *contend* 1QSa 1$_{13}$.

וַיִּירְאוּ מִגֶּשֶׁת אֵלָיו *and they were afraid to draw near to him* Ex 34$_{30}$.

Also perh. 4QOrd^b 3$_{23}$ MasJub 2$_3$.

Ni. 17.0.8 Pf. נִגַּשׁ, נִגְּשׁוּ, נִגַּשְׁתֶּם; + waw וְנִגַּשׁ, וְנִגְּשָׁה, וְנִגְּשׁוּ; ptc. נִגָּשִׁים, Q נגשות; inf. Q הנגשו—**draw near, approach,** used absolutely (Gn 33$_{7,7}$ Ex 34$_{32}$ Dt 20$_2$=11QT 61$_{15}$ Dt 21$_5$=11QT 63$_3$ 1QM 16$_{13}$), for judgment (Dt 25$_1$), for battle (1 S 7$_{10}$ 11$_{20.21}$ 4QM^a 1$_{14}$); of priests in sanctuary (Ex 19$_{22}$ 4QapMoses^a 1.2$_7$ [ונג[ש]]).

<SUBJ> Israelites 1 S 11$_{20.21}$, Philistines 1 S 7$_{10}$, עַם

people Is 29_{13}, Joseph Gn 33_{7}, Leah Gn 33_{7}, Moses Ex 20_{21} 24_{2}, Rachel Gn 33_{7}, אִישׁ *man* Dt 25_{1} 4QRitPur $41_{2(mg)}$ (ש[אי]), יְבֵמֶת *sister-in-law* Dt 25_{9}, אִשָּׁה *woman* 4QRitPur $41_{2(mg)}$, בֵּן *son* of Israel Ex 34_{32} Dt 21_{5}=11QT 63_{3}, יֶלֶד *child* Gn 33_{7}, מֹשֵׁל *ruler* Jr 30_{21}, שַׂר *commander* Ezr 9_{1}, כֹּהֵן *priest* Ex 19_{22} Dt 20_{2}=11QT 61_{15} Dt 21_{5}=11QT 63_{3} 1QM 16_{13} 19_{11} perh. 1Q29 2_{4} ((הכונ[הן]) 4QapMosesª 1.2$_{7}$ (ש[ונג] ... הכו[הן]) 4QMª 10.2$_{13}$, נָבִיא *prophet* 1 K 20_{13}, חֹרֵשׁ *plougher* Am 9_{13}, דרך ptc. *one who treads* grapes Am 9_{13}, מַעֲרָכָה *battle-line* 4QMª 1_{14} ((מערכו[ת]).

<PREP> לְ of direction, *to*, + אֲרוֹן *ark* 4QapMosesª 1.2$_{7}$ (ש[ונג]), מִלְחָמָה *battle* (or perh. of benefit, *for*) 1 S 7_{10} 4QMª 1_{14}.

בְּ of accompaniment, *with*, + פֶּה *mouth*, i.e. speech Is 29_{13}; *to* or introducing object, + קֹצֵר *reaper* Am 9_{13}, משך ptc. *one who draws out*, i.e. sows, seeds Am 9_{13}, דֶּרֶךְ *path* 4QBéat 14.2$_{6}$.

אֶל *to*, + Y. Ex 19_{22} 24_{2} Jr 30_{21}, Ahab 1 K 20_{13}, Ezra Ezr 9_{1}, אִישׁ *man* Dt 25_{9}, מֶלֶךְ *king* 1 K 20_{13}, עֲרָפֶל *thick cloud* Ex 20_{21}, מִשְׁפָּט *(place of) judgment* Dt 25_{1}, עִיר *city* 1 S 11_{20}, חוֹמָה *wall* 2 S 11_{21}.

<COLL> נגשׁ ni. + adverb, לְבַד *alone* Ex 24_{2}, מַדּוּעַ *why?* 2 S 11_{20}, לָמָּה *why* 2 S 11_{21}, שָׁם *there* 1QM 19_{11}.

Followed by infinitive of purpose, of לחם ni. *fight* 2 S 11_{20}.

Hi. 37.4.15 Pf. Q הגיש, 2ms Q הגשתם (Q הגשתנו), הִגִּישׁוּ (Q הגישני), הִגַּשְׁתֶּם; impf. יַגֵּשׁ (Q יגיש, Si יגישך), 3fs תַּגִּישׁ, Q אגישנו, יַגִּישׁוּ, תַּגִּישׁוּ (תַּגִּשׁוּן); + waw וְהִגִּישׁוֹ (וְהִגִּישָׁהּ); וַיַּגֵּשׁ (וַיַּגֶּשׁ־, וַיַּגִּשׁ, Si ויגישהו), 3fs וַתַּגֵּשׁ, וַיַּגִּשׁוּ (וַיַּגִּישׁוּ), וַתַּגִּשׁוּן; impv. הַגִּישָׁה (הַגִּשָׁה), הַגִּישׁוּ (הַגִּשׁוּ); ptc. מַגִּישׁ, מַגִּישִׁים (מַגִּשִׁים), מַגִּישֵׁי; inf. Si הגיש (Q לגיש, Si הגשת, Q הגישבי, Q הגישו).

1. bring near, present, bring, in cultic contexts, of offerings (Ex 32_{6} Lv 2_{8} 8_{14} Jg 6_{19} Am 5_{25} Ml $1_{7.8.8}$ 2_{12} 3_{3} 2 C 29_{23} Si 40_{16} 11QPsª 18_{8}), in legal contexts, of bringing evidence (Is $41_{21.22}$ 45_{21}); perh. **draw** sword (Jb 40_{19}; or em.; see Obj.).

<SUBJ> Y. Si 45_{5} 1QH 6_{13} 8_{21} 20_{23} 1QS 11_{13} 4QAgesᵇ 1_{3} 4QBarkª 1.1$_{11}$, Gileadite 2 S 17_{29}, Israelites Ex 32_{6} 1 S 15_{32}, עַם *people* 1 S 13_{9} 14_{34}, מַמְלָכָה *kingdom* 1 K 5_{1}, בַּיִת *house* of Israel Am 5_{25}, Aaron Si 40_{16}, Abiathar 1 S 23_{9} (unless §3) $30_{7.7}$, Ahijah 1 S 14_{18} (unless §3), Barzillai 2 S 17_{29}, Gideon Jg 6_{19} (unless §3), Jacob Gn $27_{25.25}$, Joseph Gn $48_{10.13}$, Machir 2 S 17_{29}, Moses Lv 8_{14}, Shobi 2 S 17_{29}, Tamar 2 S 13_{11}.

אִשָּׁה *woman* 1 S 28_{25}, בֵּן *son* 1 S 30_{7} 2 S 17_{29} 2 K $4_{5.6}$ Ml 3_{3} CD 4_{2}, אָדוֹן *master* Ex $21_{6.6}$, נָדִיב *noble* Si 13_{9}, כֹּהֵן *priest* Lv 2_{8} 1 S 23_{9} (unless §3) 30_{7} Ml 1_{7} 2 C 29_{23} CD 4_{2}, לֵוִי *Levite* CD 4_{2}, מַשְׂכִּיל *instructor* 1QS 9_{16}, worshipper 1QH 6_{19}, פָּלִיט *escaped one* Is 45_{21} (unless §3), שַׁאֲנָן *one at ease* Am 6_{3} (unless §3), בטח ptc. *one who trusts* Am 6_{3} (unless §3), נקב ptc. pass. *distinguished one* Am 6_{3}, עשׂה ptc. *one who makes* Jb 40_{19} (or em.; see Obj.).

יָד *hand* Si $32_{12(B)}$ (בהגשת יד var. בהגיש יד *according to the bringing near of [your] hand*, i.e. according to your means; B בהשגת, i.e. נשׂג hi.), idols Is $41_{21.22}$ (unless §3), רָעָה *evil* Am 9_{10} (unless §3; or em. תִּגַּשׁ *it will* not *draw near*, i.e. qal); subj. not specified, Ml 2_{12} 11QPsª 18_{8}.

<OBJ> (object not expressed, Gn 27_{25} 48_{13} Jg 6_{19} 1 S 28_{25} 2 S 13_{11} 2 K 4_{5} Is 41_{22}), Agag 1 S 15_{32}, Ephraim Gn 48_{13}, Manasseh Gn 48_{13}, Moses Si 45_{5}, עֶבֶד *slave* Ex $21_{6.6}$, אִישׁ *man* 1QS 9_{16} perh. 1QH 6_{19}, בֵּן *son* Gn 48_{10} Si 13_{9}, יָתוֹם *orphan* 4QBarkª 1.1$_{11}$, מֶלֶךְ *king* 1 S 15_{32}, מַשְׂכִּיל *instructor* 1QS 11_{13}, worshipper 1QH 6_{13} 8_{21}, אֶבְיוֹן *poor one* 4QBarkª 1.1$_{11}$, דַּל *poor one* 4QBarkª 1.1$_{11}$, עָנִי *afflicted one* 4QBarkª 1.1$_{11}$, עִוֵּר *blind one* Ml 1_{8}, פִּסֵּחַ *lame one* Ml 1_{8}, חֹלֶה *sick one* Ml 1_{8}.

פַּר *bull* Lv 8_{14}, שׁוֹר *ox* 1 S 14_{34}, עֵגֶל *calf* 1 S 28_{25}, שֶׂה *sheep* 1 S 14_{34}, צֹאן *sheep* 2 S 17_{29}, שָׂעִיר *he-goat* 2 C 29_{23}, צַיִד *game* Gn 27_{25}, בָּשָׂר *flesh* Jg 6_{19}, דָּם *blood* 4QCommMal 1.2$_{2}$ CD 4_{2}, חֵלֶב *fat* Si 40_{16} CD 4_{2}, שְׁפוֹת *cream* 2 S 17_{29}, חֶמְאָה *curds* 2 S 17_{29}, חִטָּה *wheat* 2 S 17_{29}, שְׂעֹרָה *barley* 2 S 17_{29}, לֶחֶם *bread* Ml 1_{7}, מַצָּה *unleavened bread* 1 S 28_{25}, לְבִיבָה *cake* 2 S 13_{11}, קֶמַח *flour* 2 S 17_{29}, קָלִי *parched grain* 2 S 17_{29}, פּוֹל *beans* 2 S 17_{29}, עֲדָשָׁה *lentils* 2 S 17_{29}, מָרַק *broth* Jg 6_{19}, דְּבַשׁ *honey* 2 S 17_{29}, עוֹלָה *burnt offering* 1 S 13_{9} Si 40_{16}, שֶׁלֶם *peace offerings* Ex 32_{6}, מִנְחָה *grain offering* Lv 2_{8} Ml 2_{12} 3_{3} (מַגִּישֵׁי מִנְחָה) 11QPsª 18_{8}, *tribute* 1 K 5_{1}, נִיחֹחַ *soothing odour* 4Q419 1_{6}.

אֲרוֹן *ark* 1 S 14_{18} (unless §3), אֵפֹד *ephod* 1 S 23_{9} (un less §3) 30$_{7.7}$, מִשְׁכָּב *bed* 2 S 17$_{29}$, סַף *basin* 2 S 17$_{29}$, כְּלִי *vessel* 2 S 17$_{29}$ 2 K 4$_{5.6}$, שֶׁבֶת *seat* Am 6$_{3}$ (unless §3), עֲצֻמָה *evidence* Is 41$_{21.22}$ (unless §3), חֶרֶב *sword* Jb 40$_{19}$ (or em. הֶעָשׂוֹ יַגֵּשׁ חַרְבּוֹ *let the one who made him draw his sword* to הֶעָשׂוּי נֹגֵשׂ חֲבֵרוֹ *the one who is made to be the ruler of his companion*).

<PREP> לְ of direction, *to, into*, + Y. Ml 2$_{12}$, עַם *people* 2 S 17$_{29}$, David 1 S 30$_{7}$ 2 S 17$_{29}$, Isaac Gn 27$_{25.25}$, עֲרָפֶל *cloud* Si 45$_{5}$, בִּינָה *understanding* 1QH 6$_{13}$.

בְּ of place, *in(to)*, + מִדְבָּר *steppe* Am 5$_{25}$, דֶּרֶךְ *way* 4QBark^{a} 1.1$_{11}$; of instrument, *by (means of), with*, + רַחֲמִים *compassion* 1QS 11$_{13}$, רָצוֹן *favour* 1QH 8$_{21}$; of accompaniment, *with, in*, + צְדָקָה *righteousness* Ml 3$_{3}$.

כְּ *according to*, + גֹּדֶל *greatness* of mercy 1QH 8$_{21}$.

מִן partitive, *some of*, + בֵּן *son* 4QAges^{b} 1$_{3}$.

אֶל *to*, + Y. Ex 21$_{6}$, Amnon 2 S 13$_{11}$, David 1 S 30$_{7}$, Israel (Jacob) Gn 48$_{10.13}$, Samuel 1 S 15$_{32}$, Saul 1 S 13$_{9}$ 14$_{34}$, אִשָּׁה *wife* 2 K 4$_{5.6}$, דֶּלֶת *door* Ex 21$_{6}$, מְזוּזָה *doorpost* Ex 21$_{6}$, מִזְבֵּחַ *altar* Lv 2$_{8}$.

עַל *upon*, + מִזְבֵּחַ *altar* Ml 1$_{7}$.

לִפְנֵי *before* 4QParGenEx 2$_{9}$, + קָהָל *assembly* 2 C 29$_{23}$, Saul 1 S 28$_{25}$, מֶלֶךְ *king* 2 C 29$_{23}$, עֶבֶד *servant* 1 S 28$_{25}$.

לְעֻמַּת *corresponding to*, + רַחֲמִים *compassion* 4QAges^{b} 1$_{3}$.

לְפִי *according to*, + שֶׂכֶל *insight* 1QH 6$_{19}$, טוּב *goodness* 4QAges^{b} 1$_{3}$.

<COLL> נגשׁ hi. || קרב pi. *bring near* Is 41$_{21}$ 11QPs^{a} 18$_{8}$, עלה hi. *cause to go up*, i.e. offer Ex 32$_{6}$ 1 S 13$_{9}$ (+), קטר hi. *burn incense* Si 40$_{16}$; + קרב hi. *bring near* Lv 2$_{8}$ Ml 1$_{8}$, דשׁן pi. *make* altar *fat* 11QPs^{a} 18$_{8}$.

Followed by infinitive of purpose, of אכל *eat* 2 S 13$_{11}$ 17$_{29}$, זבח *sacrifice* Ml 1$_{8}$.

כדי כן יגישך *in like measure he will bring you near* Si 13$_{9}$.

2. appar. **draw near**, <SUBJ> שָׁנָה *year* 4QD^{f} 3$_{2}$ ([והגיש[ה] שנת ה[יובל] *and the year of the Jubilee approaches*).

3. perh. **divine**, through approach to the deity* (unless §1), <SUBJ> Abiathar 1 S 23$_{9}$, Ahijah 1 S 14$_{18}$, Gideon Jg 6$_{19}$, כֹּהֵן *priest* 1 S 23$_{9}$, פָּלִיט *escaped one* Is 45$_{21}$, שַׁאֲנָן *one at ease* Am 6$_{3}$, בטח ptc. *one who trusts* Am 6$_{3}$; subj. not specified, Is 41$_{22}$ Am 9$_{10}$. <OBJ> אֲרוֹן *ark* 1 S 14$_{18}$, אֵפוֹד *ephod* 1 S 23$_{9}$, שֶׁבֶת *seat* Am 6$_{3}$, רָעָה *evil* Am 9$_{10}$.

Also 4QDibHam^{a} 10$_{1}$ 4QOrd^{b} 8$_{2}$.

<SYN> §1 קרב pi. *bring near*, עלה hi. *cause to go up*, i.e. offer, קטר hi. *burn incense*.

Ho. 2.0.1 Pf. Q הוגשתי, הֻגָּשׁוּ; ptc. מֻגָּשׁ—**be brought near** (2 S 3$_{34}$ [or em.; see Subj.] 1QH 6$_{18}$ 4QTohB^{b} 1$_{4}$ [[הוג]שׁ]), **be offered** (Ml 1$_{11}$; or em.; see Subj.), <SUBJ> worshipper 1QH 6$_{18}$, רֶגֶל *foot* 2 S 3$_{34}$ (or em. הֻגָּשׁוּ *oppressed*),* מֻקְטָר *incense* Ml 1$_{11}$ (or em. מֻגָּשׁ *offering* [מֻקְטָר = קטר ho. *be burned*]), מִנְחָה *offering* Ml 1$_{11}$ (or em.; see above), כְּלִי *vessel* 4QTohB^{b} 1$_{4}$ ([הוג]שׁ). <PREP> לְ of direction, *to*, + שֵׁם *name* Ml 1$_{11}$, נְחֹשֶׁת du. *fetters* 2 S 3$_{34}$ (or em.; see Subj.); בְּ of place, *into, onto*, + יַחַד *community* 1QH 6$_{18}$, מִזְבֵּחַ *altar* 4QTohB^{b} 1$_{4}$ ([הוג]שׁ).

Htp. 1 Impv. הִתְנַגְּשׁוּ—**draw near**, <SUBJ> פָּלִיט *escaped one* Is 45$_{20}$. <COLL> נגשׁ htp. + בוא *come* Is 45$_{20}$; + adverb, יַחְדָּו *together* Is 45$_{20}$.*

נָד I *wanderer*, see נוד I *move to and fro*.

נָד II *one grieving, lamenter*, see נוד II *grieve*.

נֵד I 6.0.1 n.m. **heap**—Q ניד; cstr. נֵד—**heap, wall, hill, mountain, dam, dike**, alw. of waters (except Is 17$_{11}$; or em.; see Cstr.), <CSTR> נֵד קָצִיר *heap of the harvest* Is 17$_{11}$ (unless em. נָד *it has fled* [from נדד I] or *it is burned up* [from נדד I] or נָד *it has fled* [from נוד]). <ADJ> אֶחָד *one* Jos 3$_{13.16}$ (unless both נֵד III *mud-bank*). <PREP> כְּ *as in*, + כנס *gather* Ps 33$_{7}$ (or em. כַּנֹּד *as in a skin bottle*); כְּמוֹ *as in*, + נצב ni. *stand* Ex 15$_{8}$ (unless נֵד II *mist*; or em. נִצְּבוּ כְמוֹ־נֵד to נִצְּבוּ כְּמוֹ נֵד *they swelled up* [צבה ni.] *like a wineskin*; or em. כְּמוֹ־נֵד to כְּמוֹ נֹאד *as a skin bottle*), hi. *cause to stand* Ps 78$_{13}$. <COLL> יַעַמְדוּ נֵד *they shall stand in a heap* Jos 3$_{13}$ (unless נֵד III *mud-bank*), var. 4QapJoshua^{b} 12$_{2}$, קָמוּ נֵד *they rose up in a heap* Jos 3$_{16}$ (unless נֵד III).*

***נֵד** II 1 n.[m.] **mist** (unless נֵד I *heap*), <PREP> כְּמוֹ *as*, +

נצב ni. *stand* Ex 15$_{8}$.

* **נֵד** III $_{2}$ n.m. **mud-bank** (unless נֵד I *heap*), <ADJ> אֶחָד *one* Jos 3$_{13.16}$. <COLL> יַעַמְדוּ נֵד *they shall stand up (as) a mud-bank* Jos 3$_{13}$, קָמוּ נֵד *they stood up (as) a mud-bank* Jos 3$_{16}$.

[נֹד] I $_{1}$ n.[m.] **wandering** (unless נֹד II *grief, lament*)—sf. נֹדִי—**wandering** or **variability** of circumstances, thus **misery,*** <OBJ> ספר *count* Ps 56$_{9}$ (or em. נְדֻדַי *my tossings*).

⇒ נוד *wander* or נדד I *flee*.

* **[נֹד]** II $_{1}$ n.[m.] **grief, lament** (unless נֹד I *wandering*)—sf. נֹדִי—**grief, lament,** <OBJ> ספר *write down* Ps 56$_{9}$.

⇒ נוד II *grieve*.

* **[נֹד]** III n.[m.] **wineskin,** <PREP> כְּמוֹ *as*, + צבה ni. *swell up* Ex 15$_{8}$ (if em. נִצְּבוּ כְמוֹ־נֵד *they stood as a heap* to נִצְּבוּ כְּמוֹ נֵד *they swelled up like a wineskin*).

⇒ נאד *skin bottle*.

נדא $_{1}$ vb. **drive away—Hi.** + waw Kt וידא—**drive away,** <SUBJ> Jeroboam 2 K 17$_{21(Kt)}$ (Qr, mss נדח hi. *drive away*). <OBJ> Israel 2 K 17$_{21(Kt)}$. <PREP> מֵאַחֲרֵי *from (following)*, + Y. 2 K 17$_{21(Kt)}$ (mss lack מֵאַחֲרֵי י׳).*

נדב $_{17.1.14}$ vb. **impel—Qal** $_{3.1}$ Pf. נָדַב (Si נדבו), נָדְבָה; impf. יִדְּבֶנּוּ—**impel, stir,** <SUBJ> לֵב *heart* Ex 25$_{2}$ 35$_{29}$ Si 45$_{23}$, רוּחַ *spirit* Ex 35$_{21}$. <OBJ> Phinehas Si 45$_{23}$, אִישׁ *man* Ex 25$_{2}$ 35$_{21.29}$, אִשָּׁה *woman* Ex 35$_{29}$, בֵּן *son* Si 45$_{23}$ (ב[ן]). <COLL> נדב || נשׂא *lift*, i.e. stir Ex 35$_{21}$; + infinitive of purpose of בוא hi. *bring* Ex 35$_{29}$.

<SYN> נשׂא *lift*.

Ni. $_{0.0.3}$ Ptc. Q נדבים, Q נדבי—**offer oneself, volunteer,** <SUBJ> subj. not specified, 1QS 1$_{7.11}$. <PREP> לְ of benefit, *for*, + אֱמֶת *truth* 1QS 1$_{11}$. <COLL> הנדבים לעשות חוקי אל *those who volunteer to perform the statutes of God* 1QS 1$_{7}$.

Also 4QPsAp[a] 5$_{3}$.

Pu. $_{0.0.1}$ Ptc. מנודבים—**be freely devoted,** <SUBJ> subj. not specified, 4QapLam[b] 1$_{3}$.

Htp. $_{14.0.10}$ Pf. הִתְנַדְּבוּ, הִתְנַדַּבְתִּי; impf. Q יתנדב; + waw וַיִּתְנַדְּבוּ; ptc. מִתְנַדֵּב, מִתְנַדְּבִים (Q מתנדים); inf. הִתְנַדֵּב (הִתְנַדֶּב־, הִתְנַדְּבָם)—**1. offer oneself, volunteer,** for war (Jg 5$_{2.9}$), for service of Y. (2 C 17$_{16}$), holiness, truth (1QS 5$_{6.10}$); with infinitive (see Coll.), **offer willingly** to do something (Ne 11$_{2}$ 1QS 5$_{1.10.21.22}$ 6$_{13}$ 1QpMic 8$_{7}$).

<SUBJ> Israelite 1QS 6$_{13}$, עַם *people* Jg 5$_{2}$, רֹב *multitude* 1QS 5$_{22}$, Amasiah 2 C 17$_{16}$, אִישׁ *man* Ne 11$_{2}$ 1QS 5$_{1.10}$ 1Q31 1$_{1}$ (המתנדבי[ם]), בֵּן *son* 2 C 17$_{16}$ 1QS 5$_{21}$, מְחֹקֵק *commander* Jg 5$_{9}$; subj. not specified, 1QS 5$_{6.8}$ 1QpMic 8$_{7}$. <PREP> לְ of benefit, *for*, + Y. 2 C 17$_{16}$, קֹדֶשׁ *holiness* 1QS 5$_{6}$, אֱמֶת *truth* 1QS 5$_{10}$; בְּ of place, *among*, + עַם *people* Jg 5$_{9}$, יַחַד *community* 1QS 5$_{21.22}$. <COLL> נדב htp. + infinitive of ישׁב *dwell* Ne 11$_{2}$, הלך htp. *walk* 1QS 5$_{10}$, שׁוּב *go back* 1QS 5$_{1.22}$, קום hi. *establish* covenant 1QS 5$_{21}$, פקד *visit*, i.e. observe, statutes 1QS 5$_{21}$, חזק hi. *hold fast* 1QS 5$_{1}$, יסף ni. *join (oneself to)* 1QS 6$_{13}$ 1QpMic 8$_{7}$; + adverb, יַחַד *together* 1QS 5$_{10}$.

2. make a freewill offering, <SUBJ> עַם *people* 1 C 29$_{9.14.17}$, David 1 C 29$_{14.17}$, שַׂר *commander* 1 C 29$_{6}$, ראשׁ *head* Ezr 2$_{68}$, מִי *who?* 1 C 29$_{5}$; subj. not specified, Ezr 3$_{5}$. <OBJ> נְדָבָה *freewill offering* Ezr 3$_{5}$, אֵלֶּה *these* 1 C 29$_{17}$, perh. מָה *what?* 4QapPent 10.1$_{6}$. <PREP> לְ of direction, *to*, + Y. Ezr 3$_{5}$ 1 C 29$_{9.17}$, בַּיִת *house* of Y. Ezr 2$_{68}$; בְּ of accompaniment, *with, in*, + לֵב whole *heart* 1 C 29$_{9}$, יֹשֶׁר *uprightness* of heart 1 C 29$_{17}$, שִׂמְחָה *joy* 1 C 29$_{17}$; כְּ *as, according to*, + זֹאת *this* 1 C 29$_{14}$. <COLL> נדב htp. + infinitive of purpose, of עמד hi. *erect* house of Y. Ezr 2$_{68}$, מלא pi. *fill* hand, i.e. consecrate oneself 1 C 29$_{5}$.

3. be given as a freewill offering, <COLL> כָּל־הִתְנַדֵּב *everything that had been given as a freewill offering* Ezr 1$_{6}$.

⇒ נְדָבָה *freewill*, נָדִיב *willing*, נְדִיבָה *nobility*, נָדָב *Nadab*, נְדַבְיָה *Nedabiah*, אֲבִינָדָב *Abinadab*, אֲחִינָדָב *Ahinadab*, יְהוֹנָדָב *Jehonadab*, עַמִּינָדָב *Amminadab*.*

נָדָב $_{20}$ pr.n.m. **Nadab, 1.** son of Aaron and Elisheba, <SUBJ> ילד ni. *be born* Nm 26$_{60}$, ראה *see* Ex 24$_{9}$, עלה *go up* Ex 24$_{1.9}$, קרב hi. *bring near*, i.e. offer Lv 10$_{1}$ Nm

3$_{4}$ 26$_{61}$, שחה htpal. *worship* Ex 24$_{1}$, כהן pi. *serve as priest* Ex 28$_{1}$, לקח *take* Lv 10$_{1}$, נתן *give*, i.e. place Lv 10$_{1}$, שׂים *place* Lv 10$_{1}$, מות *die* Lv 10$_{1}$ Nm 3$_{4}$ 26$_{61}$ 1 C 24$_{2}$. <NOM CL> הַבְּכוֹר נָדָב *the firstborn was Nadab* Nm 3$_{2}$, בְּנֵי אַהֲרֹן נָדָב *the sons of Aaron were Nadab* 1 C 5$_{29}$ 24$_{1}$. <OBJ> קרב hi. *bring near* Ex 28$_{1}$, ילד *bear* Ex 6$_{23}$, אכל *consume* Lv 10$_{1}$. <APP> אִישׁ *man*, i.e. each one Lv 10$_{1}$, בֵּן *son* Ex 28$_{1}$ Lv 10$_{1}$. <PREP> לְ of possession, *(belonging) to*, + היה *be* Nm 3$_{4}$.

2. king of Israel, son of Jeroboam, <SUBJ> מלך *be king* 1 K 14$_{20}$ 15$_{25}$, הלך *go* 1 K 15$_{25}$, עשׂה *do* 1 K 15$_{25.31}$, צור *besiege* 1 K 15$_{27}$. <OBJ> נכה hi. *strike* 1 K 15$_{25}$, מות hi. *kill* 1 K 15$_{27}$. <CSTR> דִּבְרֵי נָדָב *deeds of Nadab* 1 K 15$_{31}$. <APP> בֵּן *son* 1 K 14$_{20}$ 15$_{25}$. <PREP> עַל *against*, + קשׁר *conspire* 1 K 15$_{25}$.

3. Judahite, son of Shammai, <NOM CL> בְּנֵי שַׁמַּי נָדָב *the sons of Shammai were Nadab* 1 C 2$_{28}$. <CSTR> בְּנֵי נָדָב *sons of Nadab* 1 C 2$_{30}$.

4. Benjaminite, son of Jeiel and Maacah, 1 C 8$_{30}$||9$_{36}$.

⇒ נדב *impel*.

נְדָבָה 26.0.13 n.f. **freewill**—cstr. נִדְבַת; pl. נְדָבוֹת (נְדָבֹת); cstr. נִדְבוֹת; sf. נִדְבוֹתָם, נִדְבֹתֵיכֶם, נִדְבֹתֶיךָ (Q נדבותמה)—

1a. freewill, voluntariness, generosity, <NOM CL> עַמְּךָ נְדָבֹת *your people will be voluntariness*, i.e. will offer themselves voluntarily Ps 110$_{3}$ (or em. עִמְּךָ נְדִבֹת *with you is honour*, i.e. נְדִיבָה). <CSTR> נדבת [לב] *generosity of heart* 1QH 6$_{24}$, נדבת מלחמה *voluntariness of battle* 1QM 7$_{5}$; אנשי נדבת *men of the voluntariness of*, i.e. volunteers for, battle 1QM 7$_{5}$, גֶּשֶׁם נְדָבוֹת *rain of generosity*, i.e. abundant rain Ps 68$_{10}$. <PREP> בְּ of accompaniment, *with*, + זבח *sacrifice* Ps 54$_{8}$ (unless §2, or בִּנְדָבָה *for [your] generosity*),* אהב *love* 1QH 6$_{24}$ ([ואהבתה]).

1b. as adverb, **freely, voluntarily, generously,** of אהב *love* Ho 14$_{5}$ 1QH 6$_{26}$ 7$_{10}$, נדר *vow* Dt 23$_{24}$ (unless אֱלֹהֶיךָ נְדָבָה *your generous God* [with suff. in construct chain*]) 11QT 53$_{13}$.

2. freewill offering, usu. of sacrificial offering; of contributions for building and furnishing sanctuary (Ex 35$_{29}$ 36$_{3}$ Ezr 1$_{4}$ 8$_{28}$ 2 C 31$_{14}$), <SUBJ> נתן *give* Lv 23$_{38}$ Dt 16$_{10}$. <NOM CL> הַכֶּסֶף הַזָּהָב נְדָבָה לי׳ *the silver (and) the gold are a freewill offering to Y.* Ezr 8$_{28}$, נְדָבָה זֶבַח קָרְבָּנוֹ *the sacrifice of his offering is a freewill offering* Lv 7$_{16}$. <OBJ> קרא *call* Am 4$_{5}$, שׁמע hi. *proclaim* Am 4$_{5}$, בוא hi. *bring (as)* Ex 35$_{29}$ 36$_{3}$ Dt 12$_{6}$, עשׂה *do*, i.e. offer (as) Lv 22$_{23}$ Ezk 46$_{12.12}$, נדב htp. *offer* Ezr 3$_{5}$, אכל *eat* Dt 12$_{17}$, רצה *accept* Ps 119$_{108}$ (unless §3), יסף hi. *add* 4Q416 4.2$_{7}$ (נדב[ה]).

<CSTR> נִדְבוֹת הָאֱלֹהִים *freewill offerings of God* 2 C 31$_{14}$, נִדְבַת יָדְךָ *freewill offering of your hand* Dt 16$_{10}$, נִדְבוֹת פִּי *freewill offerings of my mouth* Ps 119$_{108}$ (unless §3), נדבת שפתים *freewill offering of the lips* 4QS^{d} 7$_{5}$ (=1QS 9$_{4}$ תרומת *offering of*), נדבות רצונכה *freewill offerings of your acceptance*, i.e. acceptable to you 4QPrFêtes^{c} 131.2$_{6}$, נדבת מנחת *freewill offering (consisting) of an offering of* acceptance, i.e. acceptable freewill offering 1QS 9$_{5}$; מִסַּת נִדְבַת *sufficiency of the freewill offering of* Dt 16$_{10}$, משפט הנדבות *ordinance of the freewill offerings* CD 16$_{13}$, כָּל־נִדְבוֹתֵיכֶם *all your freewill offerings* Lv 23$_{38}$, כָּל־נִדְבוֹתָם *all their freewill offerings* Lv 22$_{18}$.

<APP> עוֹלָה *burnt offering* Ezk 46$_{12}$, שֶׁלֶם *peace offering* Ezk 46$_{12}$.

<PREP> לְ *as* 4QRP^{c} 23$_{7}$, + קרב hi. *bring near*, i.e. offer Lv 22$_{18.21}$; introducing object, + רום hi. *contribute* 2 C 35$_{8}$; בְּ of accompaniment, *with*, + זבח *sacrifice* Ps 54$_{8}$; *as* Nm 15$_{3}$, + רצה *accept* 1QS 9$_{24}$ (=4QS^{d} 8$_{8}$ כנדבה); כְּ *as*, + רצה *accept* 4QS^{d} 8$_{8}$ (=1QS 9$_{24}$ בנדבה); עַל *over*, i.e. in charge of 2 C 31$_{14}$; עִם *with* Ezr 1$_{4}$; לְבַד מִן *besides* 11QT 29$_{5}$, + עשׂה *do*, i.e. offer Nm 29$_{39}$ 11QT 29$_{2}$ ([תעשו ... לבד מנדריכמה ונדבותיכמה] *you shall offer ... besides your votive offerings and your freewill offerings*); מִלְּבַד *besides* Lv 23$_{38}$.

<COLL> נְדָבָה || נֶדֶר *votive offering* Lv 7$_{16}$ 22$_{18}$ 23$_{38}$ Nm 29$_{39}$ Dt 12$_{6}$ 4Q416 4.2$_{7}$ (נדב[ה]); + נֶדֶר Lv 22$_{21.23}$ Nm 15$_{3}$ Dt 12$_{17}$, עוֹלָה *burnt offering* Dt 12$_{6}$, זֶבַח *sacrifice* Dt 12$_{6}$, מַעֲשֵׂר *tithe* Dt 12$_{6.17}$, תְּרוּמָה *offering* Dt 12$_{6.17}$ 2 C 31$_{14}$, בְּכוֹר *firstborn* Dt 12$_{6.17}$, תּוֹדָה *thank-offering* Am 4$_{5}$.

נְדָבָה לְבֵית הָאֱלֹהִים *freewill offering for the house of God* Ezr 1$_{4}$.

3. perh. **noble utterance,*** <OBJ> רצה *favour with*

Ps 119_{108} (unless §2). <CSTR> נִדְבוֹת פִּי *noble utterances of my mouth* Ps 119_{108} (unless §2).

<SYN> נֶדֶר *votive offering.**

⇒ נדב *impel.*

נְדַבְיָה 1.0.0.2 pr.n.m. **Nedabiah**—I נדביהו—**1.** son of Jeconiah, <NOM CL> בְּנֵי יְכָנְיָה אַסִּר ... נְדַבְיָה *the sons of Jeconiah the prisoner were ... Nedabiah* 1 C 3_{18}.

2. Weight 55 (Lachish, 7th/6th cent.), <PREP> לְ of possession, *of, (belonging) to* Weight 55 (Lachish, 7th/6th cent.).

3. father of Meshullam, <CSTR> בן נדביהו *son of Nedabiah* Arad ost. 39_3.

⇒ נדב *impel* + יו *Y.*

נדביהו, see נְדַבְיָה *Nedabiah.*

***נִדְגָּלוֹת** I 1 n.f.pl. **admirable sights, conspicuous sights, heavenly phenomena,** perh. **stars,** יָפָה אַתְּ רַעְיָתִי כְּתִרְצָה נָאוָה כִּירוּשָׁלִָם אֲיֻמָּה כַּנִּדְגָּלוֹת *you are beautiful as Tirzah, my beloved, lovely as Jerusalem, awe-inspiring as (these) admirable* or *conspicuous sights,* or *as the stars* Ca 6_4, sim. 6_{10} (|| לְבָנָה *moon,* חַמָּה *sun*).

⇒ דגל II *look.*

נִדְגָּלוֹת II *bannered troops,* see דגל I *raise the standard.*

נדד I 28.1.5 vb. **flee**—**Qal** 23.1.4 Pf. Si נדד, נָדְדָה, נָדְדוּ (נָדֵדוּ); impf. יִדּוֹד (Q ינדד), יִדֹּדוּן (Q ידודו); + waw 3fs וַתִּדַּד; ptc. נֹדֵד (נודד), נֹדֶדֶת, נֹדְדִים; inf. נְדֹד—**1. flee, escape, depart, wander about,** <SUBJ> Ephraim Ho 7_{13} 9_{17}, Madmenah Is 10_{31}, עַם *people* Is 33_3 Ezk 31_{12} (if em. וַיֵּרְדוּ *and they went down* to וַיִּדְּדוּ *and they fled*), אִישׁ *man* Pr 27_8 4QDa 5.2_8, מֶלֶךְ *king* Ps $68_{13.13}$ (unless נדד III *bow down;* or em. both hi.), קָצִין *ruler* Is 22_3, נֹדֵד *fugitive* Is 21_{15}, worshipper Ps 55_8, ראה ptc. *one who sees* Na 3_7 Ps 31_{12}, פֶּתִי *simple one* 4QpNah 3.3_5, רָשָׁע *wicked one* Jb 15_{23} (or em.), בְּהֵמָה *beast* Jr 9_9, עוֹף *bird* Is 16_2 Jr 4_{25} 9_9, צִפּוֹר *bird* Pr 27_8, קָצִיר *harvest* Is 17_{11} (if em. נֵד *heap of* to נַד *it has fled*), שְׁנָה *sleep* Si 34_{20} (or em. נדד ישינה *sleep has fled* to נדדי ש[י]נה *restlessness of sleep*), שֵׁנָה *sleep* Gn 31_{40} Est 6_1 Dn 2_1 (if em. נִהְיְתָה *it was gone* to נָדְדָה *it fled*), מוֹרֶה *early rain* 4QMidrEschatb 4_{14} (המ[ור]ה).

<PREP> לְ *for (the purpose of obtaining),* + לֶחֶם *bread* Jb 15_{23}.

בְּ of place, *among,* + גּוֹי *nation* Ho 9_{17}; of time, *in, on,* + יוֹם *day* Is 17_{11} (if em.; see Subj.).

מִן of direction, *from,* + Y. Ho 7_{13}, worshipper Ps 31_{12}, עַיִן *eye* Gn 31_{40}, עִיר *city* Na 3_7, קֵן *nest* Pr 27_8, מָקוֹם *place* Pr 27_8, צֵל *shadow* Ezk 31_{12} (if em.; see Subj.); of cause, *on account of,* + קוֹל *sound* Is 33_3.

עַל *upon,* i.e. from, + Nebuchadnezzar Dn 2_1 (if em.; see Subj.).

מִתּוֹךְ *from (among),* + קָהָל *assembly* 4QpNah 3.3_5.

מִפְּנֵי *from (before),* + חֶרֶב *sword* Is 21_{15}, קֶשֶׁת *bow* Is 21_{15}, כֹּבֶד *weight* of battle Is 21_{15}.

<COLL> נדד || עוז hi. *flee for safety* Is 10_{31}, נפץ *be scattered* Is 33_3, הלך *go* Jr 9_9.

+ adverb, יַחַד *together* Is 22_3.

אַרְחִיק נְדֹד *I would make distance to wander,* i.e. wander far away Ps 55_8, ינדד לעב[וד את הגואים] *he departs in order to serve the gentiles* 4QDa 5.2_8.

2. flutter, <SUBJ> subj. not specified, Is 10_{14} (|| פצה *open* mouth, + צפף pilp. *chirp*). <OBJ> כָּנָף *wing* Is 10_{14}.

3. ptc. as noun, **fugitive,** <SUBJ> נדד *flee* Is 21_{14}. <OBJ> גלה pi. *uncover* Is 16_3 (+ נִדָּח *outcast*), קדם pi. *meet* with bread Is 21_{14}. <PREP> לְ introducing object, + קבץ pi. *gather* Jr 49_5.

Also 4QSapDidB 4.2_1.

<SYN> §1 עוז hi. *flee for safety;* §2 פצה *open.*

Poal 1 + waw וְנוֹדַד—**fly away,** <SUBJ> גֹּבַי *locust* Na 3_{17}.

Hi. 1 Impf. יְנִדֻּהוּ—**chase away, expel,** <SUBJ> צָבָא *army* Ps $68_{13.13}$ (if em. יִדֹּדוּן יִדֹּדוּן *they flee, they flee* [i.e. qal] to יְנִדּוּן יְנִדּוּן); subj. not specified, Jb 18_{18} (or em. יְנַדֻּהוּ *they cast him,* from; נדה II; + הדף *thrust*). <OBJ> מֶלֶךְ *king* Ps $68_{13.13}$ (both if em.; see Subj.), רָשָׁע *wicked one* Jb 18_{18} (or em.; see Subj.). <PREP> מִן of direction, *from,* + תֵּבֵל *world* Jb 18_{18} (or em.; see Subj.).

Ho. 2 Impf. יֻדַּד; ptc. מֻנָּד—**be chased away, be discarded,** <SUBJ> חָנֵף *impious one* Jb 20_8 (+ עוף *fly*),

קוֹץ *thorns* 2 S 23$_{6}$ (unless קוֹץ *wick*). <PREP> כְּ *as*, + חִזָּיוֹן *vision* Jb 20$_{8}$.

Htpo. 1.0.1 Impf. Q יִתְנֹדְדוּ, אתנודד—**flee away, recoil in horror,** <SUBJ> ראה ptc. *one who sees* Ps 64$_{9}$ (unless נדד III *bow down* or נוד htpol. *shudder*).

Also 4QBéat 23$_{2}$.*

⇒ נָד *wandering*, נְדֻדִים *restlessness*, perh. נִדָּה *impurity*.

*[נדד] II 1 vb. **be burned up** (unless נדד I *flee*)—**Qal, be burned up,** <SUBJ> קָצִיר *harvest* Is 17$_{11}$ (if em. נֵד *heap of* or *fire of* to נָד *it is burned up*). <PREP> בְּ of time, *in, on*, + יוֹם *day* Is 17$_{11}$ (if em. see Subj.).

*נדד III 3 vb. **bow down—Qal** 3 Impf. אֶדַּדֶּה, יִדּוֹן—**bow down, prostrate oneself,** <SUBJ> Hezekiah Is 38$_{15}$ (unless דדה htp. *go*), מֶלֶךְ *king* Is 38$_{15}$ Ps 68$_{13.13}$ (unless both נדד I *flee*), worshipper Ps 42$_{5}$ (if em. אֲדַדֵּם appar. *I shall lead them* [דדה htp.] to אֶדַּדֶּ־ם *I shall prostrate myself*, + enclitic mem). <PREP> עַל *on account of*, + מַר *bitterness* of soul Is 38$_{15}$ (unless דדה htp. *go*). <COLL> אֶדַּדֶּה כָל־שְׁנוֹתַי *I shall prostrate myself all my years* Is 38$_{15}$ (unless דדה htp. *go*).

Htpo. 1 יִתְנֹדְדוּ—**be brought low** (unless נדד I *flee*), <SUBJ> ראה ptc. *one who sees* Ps 64$_{9}$ (or em. רֹאֵה בָם *one who sees them* to רֹהֲבִים *the arrogant*).

נֹדֵד *fugitive*, see נדד I *flee*.

נְדֻדִים 1 n.[m.]pl. **restlessness, tossings,** through sleeplessness, <OBJ> שׂבע *be sated with* Jb 7$_{4}$, ספר *count* Ps 56$_{9}$ (if em. נֹדִי *my wandering* to נְדֻדַי). <CSTR> נדדי שנ[י]נה *restlessness of sleep* Si 34$_{20}$ (if em. נדד ישינה *sleep has fled*).

⇒ נדד I *flee*.

נדה I 2.1.1 vb. **thrust aside—Pi.** 2 Ptc. מְנַדִּים, sf. מְנַדֵּיכֶם—**thrust aside, postpone** (Am 6$_{3}$), **exclude** (Is 66$_{5}$), <SUBJ> אָח *brother* Is 66$_{5}$; subj. not specified, Am 6$_{3}$ (unless נדה II pi. *escape*). <OBJ> Israelites Is 66$_{5}$. <PREP> לְ introducing object, + יוֹם *day* Am 6$_{3}$ (unless נדה II pi. *escape*); לְמַעַן *for the sake of*, + שֵׁם *name* Is 66$_{5}$.

Pu. 0.0.1 Ptc. Q מנודה—**be excluded,** 4QRitPur 1.12$_{17}$.

Htp. 0.1 Impf. Si יתנדה—**distance oneself,** <SUBJ> אֹהֵב *friend* Si 6$_{11}$. <PREP> מִן of direction, *from*, + בֵּן *son* Si 6$_{11}$.

⇒ perh. נִדָּה II *flow*.

*נדה II 2 vb. **throw—Qal Pass. be thrown, be hurled,** <SUBJ> יֹשֵׁב *inhabitant* Ex 15$_{16}$ (if em. יִדְּמוּ *they are silent* [from דמם] to יֻדּוּ־ם *they are hurled* [qal pass., with enclitic mem]), רָשָׁע *wicked one* Ps 31$_{18}$ (if em. יִדְּמוּ to יֻדּוּ־ם). <PREP> לְ *into*, + שְׁאוֹל *Sheol* Ps 31$_{18}$ (if em.; see Subj.); כְּ *as*, + אֶבֶן *stone* Ex 15$_{16}$ (if em.; see Subj.).

Pi. 1 Ptc. מְנַדִּים—**1. cast, fling,** <SUBJ> יָד *hand* of wicked Ps 36$_{12}$ (if em. תְּנִדֵנִי *let it* not *cause me to wander* [נוד hi.] to תְּנַדֵּנִי *let it* not *fling me*); subj. not specified, Jb 18$_{18}$ (if em. יְנִדֻּהוּ *they expel him* [נדד I hi.] to יְנַדֻּהוּ *they cast him*). <OBJ> רָשָׁע *wicked one* Jb 18$_{18}$ (if em.; see Subj.), worshipper Ps 36$_{12}$ (if em.; see Subj.). <PREP> מִן of direction, *from*, + תֵּבֵל *world* Jb 18$_{18}$ (if em.; see Subj.).

2. escape (unless נדה I *postpone*), <SUBJ> subj. not specified, Am 6$_{3}$. <PREP> לְ *from*, + יוֹם *day* Am 6$_{3}$.

Hi. 1 + waw וַיַּדּוּ—**fling** (unless ידה pi. *throw*), <SUBJ> אוֹיֵב *enemy* Lm 3$_{53}$. <OBJ> אֶבֶן *stone* Lm 3$_{53}$. <PREP> בְּ of place, *at*, + (inhabitant of) Jerusalem Lm 3$_{53}$.

*נדה III 2 vb. **be impure—Pi.** 2 Ptc. מְנַדִּים, sf. מְנַדֵּיכֶם—**make impure, declare impure,** <SUBJ> אָח *brother* Is 66$_{5}$ (unless נדה I pi. *exclude*); subj. not specified, Am 6$_{3}$ (unless נדה I pi. *postpone* or II pi. *escape*). <OBJ> Israelites Is 66$_{5}$. <PREP> לְ introducing object, + יוֹם *day* Am 6$_{3}$ (unless נדה II pi. *escape*); לְמַעַן *for the sake of*, + שֵׁם *name* Is 66$_{5}$.

⇒ נִדָּה I *impurity*.

נֵדֶה 1 n.m. **gift,** given to prostitute, <OBJ> נתן *give* Ezk 16$_{33}$ (+ נָדָן *gift*).

נִדָּה I 29.0.68 n.f. **impurity** (unless נִדָּה II *flow of blood*)—

cstr. נִדַּת; sf. נִדָּתָהּ, Q נדתם; pl. Q נדות; cstr. Q נדות—**1. impurity**, perh. as requiring distance (cf. נדד *drive away*),* in ref. to menstruation (e.g. Lv 12$_{2.5}$ 15$_{19+8t}$ 18$_{19}$ Ezk 18$_{6}$ 22$_{10}$ Ezk 36$_{17}$ 4QSD 7.2$_{15}$ 4QD^{a} 6.2$_{2.6}$ 4QTohA 1.1$_{7.8}$ 11QT 48$_{16.17}$), prohibited marriage (Lv 20$_{21}$ 11QT 66$_{13}$), sexual intercourse (CD 12$_{2}$), immorality, idolatry (e.g. Zc 13$_{1}$ Ezr 9$_{11.11}$ 1QpHab 8$_{13}$ 1QH 19$_{11}$ fr. 3$_{16}$ 1QM 13$_{5}$ 1QS 4$_{5.10}$ 11$_{14}$ 4QpNah 3.3$_{1}$ 4QDiscourse 2.2$_{3}$ 4QShir^{b} 18.2$_{7}$ CD 3$_{17}$). **2. impure thing, abomination** (e.g. Ezk 7$_{19.20}$ Lm 1$_{17}$ CD 2$_{1}$ 1QS 5$_{19}$ 10$_{24}$), in ref. to cultic objects (2 C 29$_{5}$).

<SUBJ> היה *be* Lv 15$_{24}$. <NOM CL> נִדָּה הִיא *it is impurity* Lv 20$_{21(Qr)}$ 11QT 66$_{13}$. <OBJ> יצא hi. *bring out* 2 C 29$_{5}$, שׁבת hi. *cause to cease* 1QS 10$_{24}$, טמא hi. *defile with* 4QHalakhah^{a} 1$_{6}$ ([הט]מיא).

<CSTR> נדת אנוש *impurity of a human being* 1QS 11$_{14}$, נִדַּת עַמֵּי *impurity of the peoples of* the lands Ezr 9$_{11}$, נִדַּת דְּוֺתָהּ *impurity of her menstruation* Lv 12$_{2}$ 4QSD 7.2$_{15}$ 4QD^{a} 6.2$_{6}$ ([דאותה]) 6.2$_{8}$ (נדת ד[אותה]), נדת טמאה *impurity of uncleanness* 1QpHab 8$_{13}$ 4QapPs^{b} 69$_{2.2}$, נִדַּת טֻמְאָתָהּ *impurity of her uncleanness* Lv 18$_{19}$, נדת טמאתם *impurity of their uncleanness* 1QM 13$_{5}$ 4QBer^{a} 3.2$_{4}$ (ט[מאתמה]) 4QNidd 2.2$_{1}$ ([טמאתם]) 11QT 45$_{10}$ 48$_{16}$ (both טמאתמה) 48$_{17}$, נדות טמאה *impurities of uncleanness* 4QRitPur 1.12$_{9}$, נדת תועב[ותיהם] *impurity of their abominations* 4QShir^{b} 43$_{7}$, מעשי *of the deeds of* 4QDiscourse 2.2$_{3}$.

גלולי נדה *idols of impurity* 1QS 4$_{5}$, אנשי *men of* 4QBapt 2.2$_{8}$, רוח *spirit of* 1QS 4$_{22}$, טמאי נ[דה] *ones unclean (because) of impurity* 4QTohB^{c} 1.2$_{6}$, טְמֵאַת הַנִּדָּה *woman unclean (because) of impurity*, i.e. menstruation Ezk 22$_{10}$, סוד נדתם *council of their impurity* 4QAges^{b} 1$_{2}$ (corrected to טמאתם *their uncleanness*), דם הנדה *blood of impurity* 4QTohA 1.1$_{8}$, מחשבות נדת *thoughts of impurity of* 4QBer^{a} 7.2$_{4}$, ערות נדה *nakedness*, i.e. indecency, *of impurity* 4QRitPur 29.7$_{9}$, מִשְׁכַּב נִדָּתָהּ *bed of her impurity* Lv 15$_{26}$.

אֶרֶץ נִדָּה *land of impurity* Ezr 9$_{11}$, דרכי נדה *ways of impurity* 1QS 4$_{10}$ CD 3$_{17}$, מעשי *deeds of* 1QH fr. 3$_{16}$ 4QShir^{b} 18.2$_{7}$, תועבת *abomination of* 4Q419 1$_{11}$, תועבות *abominations of* 1QH 19$_{11}$, [ע]ון *iniquity of* 4QD^{a} 6.2$_{2}$, נגע *disease of* 4QRitPur 1.12$_{16}$ 34.5$_{17}$ (הנדה), עבודת נדת *service of the impurity of* 1QM 13$_{5}$, סרך הנדות *rule of impurities* 4QNidd 1.1$_{5}$, יְמֵי נִדַּת *days of the impurity of* Lv 12$_{2}$ 4QSD 7.2$_{15}$ 4QD^{a} 6.2$_{6}$ ([י]מי), נִדָּתָהּ *of her impurity* Lv 15$_{25}$, טֻמְאַת הַנִּדָּה *uncleanness of impurity*, i.e. of menstruation Ezk 36$_{17}$, טֻמְאַת נִדָּתָהּ *uncleanness of her impurity* Lv 15$_{26}$, עֵת־נִדָּתָהּ *time of her impurity* Lv 15$_{25}$ 4QD^{a} 6.2$_{3}$ ([עת נדתה]).

מֵי נִדָּה *water of*, i.e. for removing, *impurity* Nm 19$_{9.13.20.21.21}$ (both הַנִּדָּה) 31$_{23}$ 1QS 3$_{4.9}$ 4$_{21}$ 4QD^{a} 6.3$_{2}$ (הנדה) 4QD^{f} 2$_{12}$ ([מ]י הנדה) 4QD^{g} 1.2$_{15}$ 4QTohB^{c} 1.2$_{2}$ ([מי נדה]) 1.2$_{5.6}$ (both הנדה) 1.2$_{8}$ (הנ[דה]) 1.2$_{9}$ (הנדה) 4QNidd 1.1$_{6}$ 11QT 49$_{18}$ 51$_{0}$ ([מי נדה]), מקור נדה *source of impurity* 1QH 9$_{22}$ (הנדה) 20$_{25}$, רוב *abundance of* 4QHod^{b} 7$_{4}$, כול נדת *every (kind of) impurity of* 1QpHab 8$_{13}$, כול נדתם *all their impurity* 4QOrd^{b} 30$_{1}$.

<APP> אִשָּׁה *woman* Ezk 18$_{6}$, רִיק *vain thing* 1QS 10$_{24}$.

<PREP> לְ *as* or introducing predicate 1QS 5$_{19}$ CD 2$_{1}$, + היה *be* Ezk 7$_{19}$ Lm 1$_{17}$ 4QapPs^{b} 69$_{2}$ ([היתה]), נתן *give*, i.e. make into Ezk 7$_{20}$; of benefit, *for*, + פתח ni. *be opened* Zc 13$_{1}$.

בְּ *in (a state of), during* Lv 15$_{33}$ 18$_{19}$ 4QRitPur 33.4$_{9}$ 4QOrd^{b} 30$_{1}$ ([ב]כול נדתם) 4QBéat 18$_{4}$, + היה *be* Lv 15$_{19}$ 4QD^{g} 1.2$_{8}$ ([תהיה בנד[תה]) 4QapPs^{b} 69$_{2}$ ([היתה]) 11QT 48$_{16}$, בוא *come* 11QT 45$_{10}$, שׁכב *lie down* Lv 15$_{20}$, גלל htpo. *wallow* 1QH 4$_{19}$, נגע *touch* 4QTohA 1.1$_{7}$ (יג[ע]), עזב *leave* 4QNidd 2.2$_{1}$ ([עזבו[הו]).

בְּ of cause, *on account of* Ezr 9$_{11}$ perh. 4QpNah 3.3$_{1}$; of instrument, *by (means of), with* perh. 4QDiscourse 2.2$_{3}$, + טמא *defile* CD 12$_{2}$ 11QT 48$_{17}$, פעל *do* 1QpHab 8$_{13}$.

כְּ *as in*, + טמא *be impure* Lv 12$_{5}$ 4QD^{a} 6.2$_{8}$ (... [טמאה [כנדת]); *as (though it were)*, + זנח pi. *reject* 4QapPs^{b} 46$_{6}$ (or em. זנח hi. *reject*); *according to* 4QShir^{b} 2.2$_{8}$ 43$_{7}$.

מִן *from, of* 4QRitPur 1.12$_{9}$, + טהר *be clean* 4QTohA 1.1$_{7}$ (מ[נד]תה), ni. *cleanse oneself* 4QRitPur 1.12$_{2}$ ([מ]נדת]) , pi. *cleanse* 1QS 11$_{14}$.

אֶל *to*, + קרב *draw near* Ezk 18$_{6}$.

עַל *over*, i.e. beyond, + זוב *have discharge* Lv 15$_{25}$.

עִם *with* 4QPrFêtes^{a} 1$_{3}$.

<COLL> נִדָּה || חַטָּאת *sin* Zc 13$_{1}$ 1QS 11$_{14}$, עֶרְוָה *nakedness* 1QH 9$_{22}$ 20$_{25}$ (+); + פתל ni. ptc. *tortuous thing*

1QS 10_{24}.

Also 4QD^{g} 1.2$_{9}$ 4QNidd 3$_{3}$ 4QapJoshua^{a} 1$_{1}$ 4Q417 4.2$_{2}$ 4Q418 20$_{2}$ 4QRitMar 295$_{2}$ 4QPrFêtes^{c} 184.1$_{13}$ 4QRitPur 1.12$_{10.11}$.

<SYN> חַטָּאת *sin*, עֶרְוָה *nakedness*.*

⇒ נדד III *be impure*.

*נִדָּה II 29.0.68 n.f. **flow of blood** (unless נִדָּה I *impurity*)—cstr. נִדַּת; sf. נִדָּתָהּ, Q נדתם; pl. Q נדות; cstr. Q נדות—**1. flow of blood,** causing ritual impurity, in ref. to menstruation (e.g. Lv 12$_{2.5}$ 15$_{19+8t}$ 18$_{19}$ Ezk 18$_{6}$ 22$_{10}$ Ezk 36$_{17}$ 4QSD 7.2$_{15}$ 4QD^{a} 6.2$_{2.6}$ 4QTohA 1.1$_{7.8}$ 11QT 48$_{16.17}$), prohibited marriage (Lv 20$_{21}$ 11QT 66$_{13}$), sexual intercourse (CD 12$_{2}$), immorality, idolatry (e.g. Zc 13$_{1}$ Ezr 9$_{11.11}$ 1QpHab 8$_{13}$ 1QH 19$_{11}$ fr. 3$_{16}$ 1QM 13$_{5}$ 1QS 4$_{5.10}$ 11$_{14}$ 4QpNah 3.3$_{1}$ 4QDiscourse 2.2$_{3}$ 4QShir^{b} 18.2$_{7}$ CD 3$_{17}$).

2. impure thing, abomination (e.g. Ezk 7$_{19.20}$ Lm 1$_{17}$ CD 2$_{1}$ 1QS 5$_{19}$ 10$_{24}$), in ref. to cultic objects (2 C 29$_{5}$).

<SUBJ> היה *be* Lv 15$_{24}$. <NOM CL> נִדָּה הִיא *it is impurity* Lv 20$_{21(Qr)}$ 11QT 66$_{13}$. <OBJ> יצא hi. *bring out* 2 C 29$_{5}$, שׁבת hi. *cause to cease* 1QS 10$_{24}$, טמא hi. *defile with* 4QHalakhah^{a} 1$_{6}$ (הט[מיא]).

<CSTR> נדת אנוש *impurity of a human being* 1QS 11$_{14}$, נִדַּת עַמֵּי *impurity of the peoples of* the lands Ezr 9$_{11}$, נִדַּת דְּוֹתָהּ *flow of blood of her menstruation* Lv 12$_{2}$ 4QSD 7.2$_{15}$ 4QD^{a} 6.2$_{6}$ ([דאותה]) 6.2$_{8}$ (נדת ד[אותה]), נדת טמאה *impurity of uncleanness* 1QpHab 8$_{13}$ 4QapPs^{b} 69$_{2.2}$, נִדַּת טֻמְאָתָהּ *impurity of her flow of blood* Lv 18$_{19}$, נדת טמאתם *impurity of their uncleanness* 1QM 13$_{5}$ 4QBer^{a} 3.2$_{4}$ (ט[מאתמה]) 4QNidd 2.2$_{1}$ ([טמאתם]) 11QT 45$_{10}$ 48$_{16}$ (both טמאתמה) 48$_{17}$, נדות טמאה *impurities of uncleanness* 4QRitPur 1.12$_{9}$, נדת תוע[בותיהם] *impurity of their abominations* 4QShir^{b} 43$_{7}$, מעשי *of the deeds of* 4QDiscourse 2.2$_{3}$.

גלולי נדה *idols of impurity* 1QS 4$_{5}$, אנשי *men of* 4QBapt 2.2$_{8}$, רוח *spirit of* 1QS 4$_{22}$, טמאי נ[דה] *ones unclean (because) of impurity* 4QTohB^{c} 1.2$_{6}$, טְמֵאַת הַנִּדָּה *woman unclean (because) of the flow of blood* , i.e. menstruation Ezk 22$_{10}$, סוד נדתם *council of their impurity* 4QAges^{b} 1$_{2}$ (corrected to טמאתם *their uncleanness*), דם הנדה *blood of impurity* 4QTohA 1.1$_{8}$, מחשבות נדת *thoughts of impurity of* 4QBer^{a} 7.2$_{4}$, ערות נדה *nakedness*, i.e. indecency, *of impurity* 4QRitPur 29.7$_{9}$, מִשְׁכַּב נִדָּתָהּ *bed of her impurity* Lv 15$_{26}$.

אֶרֶץ נִדָּה *land of impurity* Ezr 9$_{11}$, דרכי נדה *ways of impurity* 1QS 4$_{10}$ CD 3$_{17}$, מעשי *deeds of* 1QH fr. 3$_{16}$ 4QShir^{b} 18.2$_{7}$, תועבת *abomination of* 4Q419 1$_{11}$, תועבות *abominations of* 1QH 19$_{11}$, [ע]ון *iniquity of* 4QD^{a} 6.2$_{2}$, נגע *disease of* 4QRitPur 1.12$_{16}$ 34.5$_{17}$ (הנדה), עבודת נדת *service of the impurity of* 1QM 13$_{5}$, סרך הנדות *rule of impurities* 4QNidd 1.1$_{5}$, יְמֵי נִדַּת *days of the impurity of* Lv 12$_{2}$ 4QSD 7.2$_{15}$ 4QD^{a} 6.2$_{6}$ ([ימ]י), נִדָּתָהּ *of her impurity* Lv 15$_{25}$, טֻמְאַת הַנִּדָּה *uncleanness of flow of blood*, i.e. of menstruation Ezk 36$_{17}$, טֻמְאַת נִדָּתָהּ *uncleanness of her impurity* Lv 15$_{26}$, עֵת־נִדָּתָהּ *time of her flow of blood* Lv 15$_{25}$ 4QD^{a} 6.2$_{3}$ ([עת נדתה]).

מֵי נִדָּה *water of*, i.e. for removing, *impurity* Nm 19$_{9.13.20.21.21}$ (both הַנִּדָּה) 31$_{23}$ 1QS 3$_{4.9}$ 4$_{21}$ 4QD^{a} 6.3$_{2}$ (הנדה) 4QD^{f} 2$_{12}$ ([מי] הנדה) 4QD^{g} 1.2$_{15}$ 4QTohB^{c} 1.2$_{2}$ ([מי נדה]) 1.2$_{5.6}$ (both הנדה) 1.2$_{8}$ (הנ[דה]) 1.2$_{9}$ (הנדה) 4QNidd 1.1$_{6}$ 11QT 49$_{18}$ 51$_{0}$ ([מי נדה]), מקור נדה *source of impurity* 1QH 9$_{22}$ (הנדה) 20$_{25}$, רוב *abundance of* 4QHod^{b} 7$_{4}$, כול נדת *every (kind of) impurity of* 1QpHab 8$_{13}$, כול נדתם *all their impurity* 4QOrd^{b} 30$_{1}$.

<APP> אִשָּׁה *woman* Ezk 18$_{6}$, רֵק *vain thing* 1QS 10$_{24}$.

<PREP> לְ *as* or introducing predicate 1QS 5$_{19}$ CD 2$_{1}$, + היה *be* Ezk 7$_{19}$ Lm 1$_{17}$ 4QapPs^{b} 69$_{2}$ ([היתה]), נתן *give*, i.e. make into Ezk 7$_{20}$; of benefit, *for*, + פתח ni. *be opened* Zc 13$_{1}$.

בְּ *in (a state of), during* Lv 15$_{33}$ 18$_{19}$ 4QRitPur 33.4$_{9}$ (בנד[ה]) 4QOrd^{b} 30$_{1}$ ([ב]כול נדתם) 4QBéat 18$_{4}$, + היה *be* Lv 15$_{19}$ 4QD^{g} 1.2$_{8}$ (תהיה בנד[תה]) 4QapPs^{b} 69$_{2}$ ([היתה]) 11QT 48$_{16}$, בוא *come* 11QT 45$_{10}$, שׁכב *lie down* Lv 15$_{20}$, גלל htpo. *wallow* 1QH 4$_{19}$, נגע *touch* 4QTohA 1.1$_{7}$ (יג[ע]), עזב *leave* 4QNidd 2.2$_{1}$ (עזבו[הו]).

בְּ of cause, *on account of* Ezr 9$_{11}$ perh. 4QpNah 3.3$_{1}$; of instrument, *by (means of), with* perh. 4QDiscourse 2.2$_{3}$, + טמא *defile* CD 12$_{2}$ 11QT 48$_{17}$, פעל *do* 1QpHab 8$_{13}$.

כְּ *as in*, + טמא *be impure* Lv 12$_{5}$ 4QD^{a} 6.2$_{8}$ ([כנדת] ... [כנדת]); *as (though it were)*, + זנח pi. *reject* 4QapPs^{b} 46$_{6}$ (or em. זנח hi. *reject*); *according to* 4QShir^{b} 2.2$_{8}$ 43$_{7}$.

מִן *from, of* 4QRitPur 1.12$_{9}$, + טהר *be clean* 4QTohA 1.1$_{7}$ (מ]נד[תה), ni. *cleanse oneself* 4QRitPur 1.12$_{2}$ ([מ]נדתה), pi. *cleanse* 1QS 11$_{14}$.

אֶל *to*, + קרב *draw near* Ezk 18$_{6}$.

עַל *over*, i.e. beyond, + זוב *have discharge* Lv 15$_{25}$.

עִם *with* 4QPrFêtes^{a} 1$_{3}$.

<COLL> נִדָּה || חַטָּאת *sin* Zc 13$_{1}$ 1QS 11$_{14}$, עֶרְוָה *nakedness* 1QH 9$_{22}$ 20$_{25}$ (+); + פתל ni. ptc. *tortuous thing* 1QS 10$_{24}$.

Also 4QD^{g} 1.2$_{9}$ 4QNidd 3$_{3}$ 4QapJoshua^{a} 1$_{1}$ 4Q417 4.2$_{2}$ 4Q418 20$_{2}$ 4QRitMar 295$_{2}$ 4QPrFêtes^{c} 184.1$_{13}$ 4Q RitPur 1.12$_{10.11}$.

<SYN> חַטָּאת *sin*, עֶרְוָה *nakedness*.

⇒ perh. נדה *cast, throw* or perh. נדד I *flee*.

נדח I 55.3.15 vb. **thrust—Qal** 2 impf. יִדַּח; inf. לִנְדֹּחַ—**1. thrust** (unless נדח II *wield an axe*), <SUBJ> Israelites Dt 20$_{19}$. <OBJ> גַּרְזֶן *axe* Dt 20$_{19}$. <PREP> עַל *against*, + עֵץ *tree* Dt 20$_{19}$.

2. thrust away, banish (unless דחח ni. *be pushed*), <SUBJ> perh. Y. 2 S 14$_{14}$. <OBJ> נִדָּח *banished one* 2 S 14$_{14}$. <PREP> מִן of direction, *from*, + Y. 2 S 14$_{14}$.

Also perh. 4QMidrEschat^{b} 29$_{3}$.

Ni. 24.1.8 Pf. נִדְּחָה, Q נדחתי, נִדְּחוּ; + waw וְנִדַּחְתָּ, וְנִדַּחְתֶּם; ptc. נִדָּח נִדָּחָה (נִדַּחַת), (נִדַּחֲכֶם, נִדָּחוֹ, נִדָּחֵךְ), נִדָּחִים, נִדְּחֵי, נִדָּחַי (נִדְחֵי, Q נדחיו)—**1. be thrust out, be driven away, be banished,** <SUBJ> Ammonites Jr 49$_{5}$, Jews Jr 40$_{12}$, שְׁאֵרִית *remnant* of Judah Jr 43$_{5}$, אִישׁ *man*, i.e. each one Jr 49$_{5}$, בֵּן *son* of Israel 4QTobit^{e} 6$_{8}$, רֵעַ *friend* 1QH 12$_{9}$, מֹדָע *acquaintance* 1QH 12$_{9}$, perh. worshipper 4QapPs^{b} 79$_{4}$, תֻּשִׁיָּה *effective aid* Jb 6$_{13}$. <PREP> בְּ of place, *among*, + גּוֹי *nation* 4QTobit^{e} 6$_{8}$ (בהמה ... [הגוים]); מִן of direction, + Job Jb 6$_{13}$, worshipper 1QH 12$_{9}$; לִפְנֵי *before*, i.e. straight ahead of, + אִישׁ *man*, i.e. each one Jr 49$_{5}$. <COLL> הַמְּקֹמוֹת אֲשֶׁר נִדְּחוּ שָׁם *the places where they were banished* Jr 40$_{12}$, הַגּוֹיִם אֲשֶׁר נִדְּחוּ שָׁם *the nations where they were banished* Jr 43$_{5}$.

2. go astray, <SUBJ> שׁוֹר *ox* Dt 22$_{1}$=11QT 64$_{14}$, שֶׂה *sheep* Dt 22$_{1}$=11QT 64$_{14}$, חֲמוֹר *ass* 11QT 64$_{14}$.

3. (allow oneself to) be drawn away, led astray, <SUBJ> Israelite Dt 4$_{19}$ 30$_{17}$, חֲסַר *one lacking* in sense 11QPs^{a} 18$_{6}$, פֶּתִי *simple one* 11QPs^{a} 18$_{6}$. <PREP> מִן of direction, *from*, + מָבוֹא *entrance* 11QPs^{a} 18$_{6}$.

4. ptc. as noun, **a.** masc., **banished one(s), outcast(s),** <SUBJ> היה *be* Dt 30$_{4}$ Ne 1$_{9}$, בוא *come* Is 27$_{13}$ Jr 49$_{36}$, גור *sojourn* Is 16$_{4}$, שׁחה htpal. *worship* Is 27$_{13}$. <OBJ> בוא hi. *bring* Ne 1$_{9}$, שׁוב hi. *bring back* 2 S 14$_{13}$ 4QNarrG 1$_{1}$ (ב[י]שׁיב), אסף *gather* Is 11$_{12}$ 1QLitPr 1$_{1}$ ([ואספתה נדחינו]), כנס pi. *gather* Ps 147$_{2}$, קבץ pi. *gather* Is 56$_{8}$ Ne 1$_{9}$ Si 51$_{12}$, נדח *banish* 2 S 14$_{14}$, סתר pi. *hide* Is 16$_{3}$. <CSTR> נִדְחֵי יִשְׂרָאֵל *outcasts of Israel* Is 11$_{12}$ 56$_{8}$ Ps 147$_{2}$ Si 51$_{12}$, מוֹאָב *of Moab* Is 16$_{4(mss)}$, עֵילָם *of Elam* Jr 49$_{36(Qr, mss)}$ (Kt עולם *of everlastingness*). <APP> מוֹאָב *Moab* appar. Is 16$_{4}$. <PREP> לְ of benefit, *to, for*, + היה *be* Is 16$_{4}$. <COLL> נדח ni. ptc. || נפץ pass. ptc. *dispersed one* Is 11$_{12}$, אֹבֵד *lost one* Is 27$_{13}$; + נֹדֵד *fugitive* Is 16$_{3}$.

הַנִּדָּחִים בְּאֶרֶץ מִצְרָיִם *the banished ones in the land of Egypt* Is 27$_{13}$.

b. fem., (1) **banished one(s), outcast(s),** <OBJ> קרא *call*, i.e. name Jr 30$_{17}$, קבץ pi. *gather* Mc 4$_{6}$ Zp 3$_{19}$. <COLL> נִדַּחַת || צֹלֵעָה *lame one* Mc 4$_{6}$ Zp 3$_{19}$.

(2) **strayed one,** of sheep, <OBJ> שׁוב hi. *bring back* Ezk 34$_{4.16}$. <COLL> נִדַּחַת || אֹבֶדֶת *lost one* Ezk 34$_{4.16}$.

Also 4QparaKings 21$_{2}$ 23$_{2}$.

<SYN> §4a נפץ pass. ptc. *dispersed one*, אֹבֵד *lost one*; §4b צֹלֵעָה *lame one*, אֹבֶדֶת *lost one*.

Pu. 1.0.1 Ptc. מְנֻדָּח, Q מנודחים—**1. be thrust** (unless נדח III pu. *be widespread*), <SUBJ> עַם *people* Is 8$_{22}$ (or em.; see Coll.). <COLL> אֲפֵלָה מְנֻדָּח *thrust (into) darkness* Is 8$_{22}$ (or em. מִנֹּגַהּ *without brightness*).

2. ptc. as noun, **banished one, exile,** <SUBJ> תעה *wander* 4QPrFêtes^{c} 12.1$_{1}$. <OBJ> שׁוב hi. *bring back* 4QPrFêtes^{c} 12.1$_{1}$ (משיב]).

Hi. 27.2.6 Pf. הִדִּיחֲךָ (הִדִּיחָם), הִדַּחְתָּם (Q הדחתו), הִדַּחְתִּי (הִדַּחְתִּים, הִדַּחְתִּיךָ), הִדִּיחוּ, הִדַּחְתֶּם; impf. Q ידיחני, 2ms Si תדיח, 3fs אַדִּיחֵם, תַּדִּיחֶנּוּ; + waw וְהִדַּחְתִּי, וְהִדִּיחַ (וְהִדַּחְתִּיו); וַתַּדִּחֵם, וַיַּדִּיחוּ, וַיַּדַּח; impv. הַדִּיחֵמוֹ; inf. הַדִּיחַ (הַדִּיחִי, הַדִּיחֲךָ (Q הדיחכה), Si הדיחם).

1. thrust (unless נדח II *impel*), <SUBJ> Absalom 2 S 15$_{14}$. <OBJ> רעה *evil* 2 S 15$_{14}$. <PREP> עַל *upon*, + David 2 S 15$_{14}$, עֶבֶד *servant* 2 S 15$_{14}$.

2. thrust away, (cause to) turn aside, lead

astray, <SUBJ> Jehoram 2 C 21$_{11}$, Jeroboam 2 K 17$_{21}$ (Qr, mss) (Kt נדא hi. *drive away*) Si 47$_{24}$, אִישׁ *man* Dt 13$_{14}$=11QT 55$_{3}$ (אנש[י]ם), אִשָּׁה *woman, wife* Dt 13$_{11}$=11QT 55$_{06}$ ([להדיחכה]) Pr 7$_{21}$, בֵּן *son* Dt 13$_{11}$=11QT 55$_{06}$ ([להדיחכה]) Dt 13$_{14}$=11QT 55$_{3}$ (ב[ני]) 2 K 17$_{21(Qr)}$, בַּת *daughter* Dt 13$_{11}$=11QT 55$_{06}$ ([להדיחכה]), אָח *brother* Dt 13$_{11}$=11QT 55$_{06}$ ([להדיחכה]), רֵעַ *friend* Dt 13$_{11}$, נָבִיא *prophet* Dt 13$_{6}$=11QT 54$_{17}$, חֹלֵם *dreamer* Dt 13$_{6}$=11QT 54$_{17}$; subj. not specified, Ps 62$_{5}$ 1QM 14$_{9}$ (הדיחונ[ו]).

<OBJ> Israel(ites) Dt 13$_{6}$=11QT 54$_{17}$ Dt 13$_{11}$=11QT 55$_{06}$ ([להדיחכה]) 2 K 17$_{21(Qr)}$ Si 47$_{24}$ 1QM 14$_{9}$ (הדיחונ[ו]), Judah 2 C 21$_{11}$, אִישׁ *man* Ps 62$_{5}$, נַעַר *lad* Pr 7$_{21}$, יֹשֵׁב *inhabitant* Dt 13$_{14}$=11QT 55$_{3}$ (י[ו]שבי).

<PREP> בְּ of instrument, *by (means of), with*, + חֵלֶק *smoothness* of speech Pr 7$_{21}$; מִן of direction, *from*, + אֲדָמָה *land* Si 47$_{24}$ ([מ]אדמתם), דֶּרֶךְ *way* Dt 13$_{6}$=11QT 54$_{17}$, שְׂאֵת *eminence* Ps 62$_{5}$, בְּרִית *covenant* 1QM 14$_{9}$; מֵעַל *from (following)*, + Y. Dt 13$_{11}$=11QT 55$_{06}$ ([להדיחכה]); מֵאַחֲרֵי *from (following)*, + Y. 2 K 17$_{21(Qr)}$.

<COLL> נדח hi. || נטה hi. *lead astray* Pr 7$_{21}$; + חטא hi. *cause to sin* 2 K 17$_{21(Qr)}$.

3. chase away, scatter, <SUBJ> רֹעֶה *shepherd* Jr 23$_{2}$, אֲרִי *lion* Jr 50$_{17}$. <OBJ> Israel (as sheep) Jr 50$_{17}$, צֹאן *flock* Jr 23$_{2}$. <COLL> נדח hi. + פוץ hi. *scatter* Jr 23$_{2}$.

4. thrust out, drive away, banish, <SUBJ> Y. Dt 30$_{1}$ Jr 8$_{3}$ 16$_{15}$ 23$_{3.8}$ 24$_{9}$ 27$_{10.15}$ 29$_{14.18}$ 32$_{37}$ 46$_{28}$ Ezk 4$_{13}$ Jl 2$_{20}$ Ps 5$_{11}$ Dn 9$_{7}$ 4QDibHam^{a} 1.5$_{12}$ 1.6$_{13}$ ([הדחתם]), עַם *people* 1QH 12$_{8}$, Israelites 2 C 13$_{9}$, Nebuchadrezzar Jr 51$_{34}$ (if em. הֱדִיחָנִי *he has vomited me* [i.e. דוח hi.] to הֱדִיחָנִי).

<OBJ> Israelites Dt 30$_{1}$ Jr 27$_{10.15}$ 29$_{14.18}$ 32$_{37}$, Jacob (i.e. Israel) Jr 46$_{28}$ Dn 9$_{7}$ 4QDibHam^{a} 1.5$_{12}$ 1.6$_{13}$ ([ישר]אל ... [הדחתם]), עַם *people* 4QDibHam^{a} 1.5$_{12}$ 1.6$_{13}$ ([הדחתם]), Jerusalem Jr 51$_{34}$ (if em.; see Subj.), אִישׁ *man* Dn 9$_{7}$, בֵּן *son* Si 8$_{19}$, of Aaron 2 C 13$_{9}$, of Israel Jr 16$_{15}$ Ezk 4$_{13}$, זֶרַע *offspring* Jr 23$_{8}$, עֶבֶד *servant* Jr 46$_{28}$, כֹּהֵן *priest* 2 C 13$_{9}$, לֵוִי *Levite* 2 C 13$_{9}$, worshipper 1QH 12$_{8}$, שׁוֹרֵר *watcher*, i.e. enemy Ps 5$_{11}$, יֹשֵׁב *inhabitant* Dn 9$_{7}$, שְׁאֵרִית *remnant* Jr 8$_{3}$ 23$_{3}$ 24$_{9}$, צְפוֹנִי *northerner* Jl 2$_{20}$, פָּנִים *face* Jl 2$_{20}$, סוֹף *end*, i.e. rear Jl 2$_{20}$, טוֹבָה *good*, i.e. prosperity Si 8$_{19}$.

<PREP> כְּ *as* 1QH 12$_{8}$ (כצפור מקנה *as a bird from its nest*); מִן *of direction, from*, + אֶרֶץ *land* 1QH 12$_{8}$; אֶל *to*, + אֶרֶץ *land* Jl 2$_{20}$; מֵעַל *from*, + בֵּן *son* Si 8$_{19}$.

<COLL> נדח hi. + רחק hi. *make distant*, i.e. remove Jl 2$_{20}$.

הַגּוֹיִם אֲשֶׁר הִדִּיחֲךָ י׳ ... שָׁמָּה *the nations where Y. ... has banished you* Dt 30$_{1}$, vars. Jr 29$_{14.18}$ 46$_{28}$ Ezk 4$_{13}$, הַמְּקֹמוֹת ... אֲשֶׁר הִדַּחְתִּים שָׁם *the places ... where I have banished them* Jr 8$_{3}$, vars. Jr 24$_{9}$ 29$_{14}$, הָאֲרָצוֹת אֲשֶׁר הִדִּיחָם שָׁמָּה *the lands where he has banished them* Jr 16$_{15}$, vars. Jr 23$_{3.8}$ 32$_{37}$ Dn 9$_{7}$ 4QDibHam^{a} 1.5$_{12}$ 1.6$_{13}$ ([הדחתם]).

Also 4QPrFêtes^{c} 183$_{6}$.

<SYN> §3 נטה hi. *lead astray*.

Ho. 1 Ptc. מֻדָּח—**be chased away,** <SUBJ> צְבִי *gazelle* Is 13$_{14}$.*

⇒ מַדּוּחִים *enticement*.

*נדח II 3 vb. **impel, wield**—**Qal** 1 Inf. לִנְדֹּחַ—**wield,** <SUBJ> Israelites Dt 20$_{19}$. <OBJ> גַּרְזֶן *axe* Dt 20$_{19}$. <PREP> עַל *against*, + עֵץ *tree* Dt 20$_{19}$.

Ni. 1 + waw Sam ונדח, וְנִדְּחָה—**be at work (with an axe),** <SUBJ> יָד *hand* Dt 19$_{5}$ (+ לִכְרֹת הָעֵץ *to cut down a tree*). <PREP> בְּ of accompaniment, *with*, + גַּרְזֶן *axe* Dt 19$_{5}$.

Hi. 1 + waw וְהִדִּיחַ—**impel** (unless נדח I hi. *thrust*), <SUBJ> Absalom 2 S 15$_{14}$. <OBJ> רָעָה *evil* 2 S 15$_{14}$. <PREP> עַל *upon*, + David 2 S 15$_{14}$, עֶבֶד *servant* 2 S 15$_{14}$.

*נדח III 1 vb. **widen**—**Pu.** 1 Ptc. מְנֻדָּח—**be widespread** (unless נדח I pu. *be thrust*), <SUBJ> אֲפֵלָה *darkness* Is 8$_{22}$ (אֲפֵלָה מְנֻדָּח *widespread darkness*).

נִדָּח *outcast, banished one(s), strayed one(s)*, see נדח I Ni. *be thrust out*.

נִדַּחַת *banished one(s)*, see נדח I *thrust*, Ni.

נָדִיב 27.5.13 adj. **willing; noble**—m.s. cstr. נְדִיב; f.s. נְדִיבָה; m.pl. נְדִיבִים; cstr. נְדִיבֵי; sf. Q נדיבכה, נְדִיבֵמוֹ (Q נדיביהמה)—**1.** used attributively of רוּחַ *spirit* Ps 51$_{14}$

(unless רוּחַ נְדִיבָה is *spirit of willingness*).

2. used predicatively or as noun, **a. willing (one), generous (one),** <SUBJ> בוא hi. *bring* Ex 35$_{5.22}$ 2 C 29$_{31}$. <CSTR> נְדִיב לֵב *willing one of heart,* i.e. whose heart is willing Ex 35$_{22}$ 2 C 29$_{31}$, לִבּוֹ *of his heart* Ex 35$_{5}$, נדיבי לב *willing ones of heart* 1QM 10$_{5}$; כָּל־נָדִיב *every willing one* 1 C 28$_{21}$, כֹּל נְדִיב *every willing one of* Ex 35$_{5.22}$ C 29$_{31}$. <APP> עָתוּד *one prepared* 1QM 10$_{5}$. <PREP> לְ of direction, *to,* + דבר pi. *speak* 1QM 10$_{5}$; perh. *namely, that is to say* 1 C 28$_{21}$ (or del. לְ). <COLL> כָּל־נָדִיב בַּחָכְמָה *every willing one who has a skill* 1 C 28$_{21}$.

b. noble (one), prince, often as military leader (e.g. Ps 47$_{10}$ 83$_{12}$ Is 13$_{2}$ Jb 12$_{21}$),* <SUBJ> בוא *come* CD 6$_{8}$ (נדיבי העם הם הבאים *the nobles of the people are those who come*), שׂרר *rule* Pr 8$_{16}$, יעץ *counsel* Is 32$_{8}$, קרב *draw near* Si 13$_{9}$, נגשׁ hi. *bring near* Si 13$_{9}$, אסף ni. *gather* intrans. Ps 47$_{10}$, קום *stand* Is 32$_{8}$, כרה *dig* Nm 21$_{18}$=CD 6$_{4}$. <OBJ> תעה hi. *cause to wander* Ps 107$_{40}$, שׁית *place,* i.e. make Ps 83$_{12}$, שׁפט *judge* 1QSb 3$_{27}$ ([ישׁ]פוט), נכה hi. *strike* Pr 17$_{26}$.

<CSTR> נְדִיבֵי הָעָם *nobles of the people* Nm 21$_{18}$=CD 6$_{4}$ CD 6$_{8}$, עַמּוֹ *of his people* Ps 113$_{8}$, עַמִּים *of the peoples* Ps 47$_{10}$; בַּת נָדִיב *daughter of a noble* Ca 7$_{2}$, פְּנֵי־ *face of* Pr 19$_{6}$, לב נ[דיבים *heart of nobles* Si 8$_{2}$, בֵּית נָדִיב *house of the noble* Jb 21$_{28}$, פִּתְחֵי נְדִיבִים *entrances of the nobles* Is 13$_{2}$, מַרְכְּבוֹת עַמִּי־נָדִיב appar. *chariots of my people, the noble,* i.e. my noble people Ca 6$_{12}$* (unless *of Ammi-nadib;* mss עַמִּינָדָב *of Amminadab*), [כו]ל נדינים *all nobles* 1QSb 3$_{27}$.

<APP> בֵּן *son* Ps 146$_{3}$, שֹׁפֵט *judge* Pr 8$_{16}$.

<PREP> לְ of benefit, *to, for* Pr 17$_{7}$; introducing object, + בוז *despise* Si 8$_{4}$; בְּ *in,* + בטח *trust* Ps 118$_{9}$ 146$_{3}$; אֶל *to,* + אמר *say* Jb 34$_{18}$; עַל *upon* 1Q25 1$_{7}$, + שׁפך *pour* contempt Ps 107$_{40}$ Jb 12$_{21}$; עִם *with,* + ישׁב hi. *cause to sit* 1 S 2$_{8}$ Ps 113$_{8.8}$ 4Q416 2.3$_{11}$; לִפְנֵי *before, in the presence of,* + יצב htp. *stand* Si 38$_{3}$(B) (Bmg מלכים *kings*), שׁפל hi. *make low* Pr 25$_{7}$; מִפְּנֵי *on account of,* + גור *fear* Si 7$_{6}$; בֵּין *among,* + ישׁב hi. *cause to sit* Si 11$_{1}$.

<COLL> נָדִיב || נָסִיךְ *prince* Ps 83$_{12}$, מֶלֶךְ *king* Jb 34$_{18}$, שַׂר *prince* Nm 21$_{18}$=CD 6$_{4}$ Pr 8$_{16}$; אָפִיק *mighty one* Jb 12$_{21}$, צַדִּיק *righteous one* Pr 17$_{26}$, רָשָׁע *wicked one* Jb 21$_{28}$; :: נָבָל *fool* or *outcast* Is 32$_{5}$ Pr 17$_{7}$.

לֹא־יִקָּרֵא עוֹד לְנָבָל נָדִיב *the fool,* or *outcast, will no longer be called noble* Is 32$_{5}$.

Also 1QH fr. 47$_{2}$ 4Q415 2.1$_{7}$ 4Q418 149$_{2}$ 177$_{5}$ 4QBark^{e} 3$_{2}$ 4QM^{a} 11.1$_{12}$ 4QDibHam^{a} verso 2.7$_{1}$.

<SYN> נָסִיךְ *prince,* מֶלֶךְ *king,* שַׂר *prince.*

<ANT> נָבָל *fool* or *outcast.**

⇒ נדב *impel,* עַמִּי־נָדִיב *Ammi-nadib.*

[נְדִיבָה] 3 n.f. **nobility**—sf. נְדִבָתִי; pl. נְדִיבוֹת—**1. nobility, honour** (Jb 30$_{15}$ [mss נְתִיבָתִי *my path*] Ps 110$_{3}$ [if em; see Nom Cl.]). **2. noble thing** (Is 32$_{8}$), **noble deed** (Ps 110$_{3}$ [if em; see Nom Cl.]).* <SUBJ> רדף ni. *be pursued* Jb 30$_{15}$ (if em.; see Obj.). <NOM CL> עִמְּךָ נְדָבֹת *with you shall be noble deeds** Ps 110$_{3}$ (if em. עַמְּךָ נְדָבֹת *your people will be voluntariness,* i.e. will offer themselves voluntarily). <OBJ> רדף *pursue* Jb 30$_{15}$ (or em. תִּרְדֹּף *it pursues* to תֵּרָדֵף *it is pursued;* + יְשׁוּעָה *prosperity*), יעץ *counsel* Is 32$_{8}$.*

⇒ נדב *impel.*

[נָדָן] I 1 n.[m.] **sheath**—sf. נְדָנָהּ—for sword, <PREP> אֶל *to,* + שׁוב hi. *bring back* 1 C 21$_{27}$.

[נָדָן] II 1 n.[m.] **gift**—pl. sf. נְדָנַיִךְ—given by prostitute to lover, <OBJ> נתן *give* Ezk 16$_{33}$ (+ נֵדֶה *gift*).

נדף I 9.1.3 vb. **drive—Qal** 3.1.1 Impf. יִדְּפֶנּוּ, 3fs תִּדְּפֶנּוּ, 2ms תִּנְדֹּף (Si תנדוף)—**drive about, blow away, defeat** (Jb 32$_{13}$ Si 33$_{9}$[Bmg]), <SUBJ> Y. Ps 68$_{3}$ (or em. תִּנָּדְפוּ *may they be driven away,* i.e. ni.) Jb 32$_{13}$ Si 33$_{9}$(Bmg) (B הדף *push away;* || כנע hi. *humble*), אִישׁ Jb 32$_{13}$, רוּחַ *wind* Ps 1$_{4}$. <OBJ> Job Jb 32$_{13}$, perh. Og 4QapJoseph^{c} 1$_{2}$, אֹיֵב *enemy* Ps 68$_{3}$ (or em.; see Subj.) Si 33$_{9}$(Bmg), שׂנא pi. ptc. *one who hates* Ps 68$_{3}$ (or em.; see Subj.), מֹץ *chaff* Ps 1$_{4}$.

<SYN> כנע hi. *humble.*

Ni. 6.0.2 Pf. נִדַּף; ptc. נִדָּף; inf. הִנָּדֵף—**be driven about, be driven away, be blown away,** <SUBJ> אֹיֵב *enemy* Ps 68$_{3}$ (if em. תִּנְדֹּף *may you drive away* [qal] to תִּנָּדְפוּ *they are blown away,* i.e. 3 mpl with prefixed t-)* Si 33$_{9}$(Bmg), שׂנא pi. ptc. *one who hates* Ps 68$_{3}$

(if em.; see above), פעל ptc. *one who does*, i.e. gets Pr 21$_{6}$ (if em.; see below), עָלֶה *leaf* Lv 26$_{36}$ Jb 13$_{25}$ (unless both נדף II ni. *be dried up*), קַשׁ *stubble* Is 41$_{2}$, מִזְרָע *place of sowing* Is 19$_{7}$ (unless נדף II *dry up*; || יבשׁ *be dry*), עָשָׁן *smoke* Ps 68$_{3}$, הֶבֶל *breath*, i.e. vapour Pr 21$_{6}$ (unless נדף II; or em. נִדָּף to רֹדֵף *pursuing*; or em. פֹּעַל אוֹצָרוֹת ... הֶבֶל נִדָּף מְבַקְשֵׁי־מָוֶת *the getting of treasures ... is a vapour driven [by] them that seek death* to פֹּעַל אוֹצָרוֹת ... הֶבֶל נִדָּף בְּמוֹקְשֵׁי־מָוֶת *one who gets treasures ... is needlessly driven into the snares of death*).*

<PREP> מִלִּפְנֵי *from before* 4QapPs[b] 46$_{8}$ ([ו]ינדפו [מ]לפני).*

Also 4Q178 2$_{4}$.

<SYN> יבשׁ *be dry*.

***נדף II** $_{3}$ vb. **dry up** (unless נדף I *drive*)—**Ni.** $_{3}$ Ptc. נִדָּף—**be dried up,** <SUBJ> עָלֶה *leaf* Lv 26$_{36}$ Jb 13$_{25}$, הֶבֶל *breath*, i.e. vapour Pr 21$_{6}$, מִזְרָע *place of sowing* Is 19$_{7}$.

נדר $_{31.0.10}$ vb. **vow—Qal** $_{31}$ Pf. נָדַר (נָדֶר), נָדֳרָה, נָדַרְנוּ, נָדַרְתָּ (Q נדרתה), נָדַרְתִּי; impf. יִדֹּר (Q ידור), 3fs תִּדֹּר (Q תדור), 2ms תִּדֹּר (תִּדּוֹר), תִּדְּרוּ; + waw וְנָדְרוּ; וַיִּדַּר, 3fs וַתִּדֹּר, וַיִּדְּרוּ; impv. נִדְרוּ; ptc. נֹדֵר; inf. לִנְדֹּר—**make a vow,** <SUBJ> Egyptians Is 19$_{21}$, Israel(ites) Nm 21$_{2}$ Dt 12$_{11.17}$ 23$_{22.23.24}$ Ps 76$_{12}$ 11QT 53$_{10.11.12.13.14}$, Judah Jr 44$_{25}$, Absalom 2 S 15$_{7}$, David Ps 132$_{2}$, Hannah 1 S 1$_{11}$, Jacob Gn 28$_{20}$ 31$_{13}$, Jephthah Jg 11$_{30}$, Jonah Jon 2$_{10}$, אִישׁ *man* Nm 6$_{2}$ 30$_{3}$ Jon 1$_{16}$ 11QT 53$_{14}$ CD 16$_{13}$, אִשָּׁה *woman* Nm 6$_{2}$ 30$_{4.11}$ 11QT 53$_{16}$, אָב *father* Jg 11$_{39}$, עֶבֶד *servant* 2 S 15$_{8}$, נָזִיר *Nazirite* Nm 6$_{21.21}$, נכל ptc. *deceptive one* Ml 1$_{14}$; subj. not specified, Lv 27$_{8}$ Ec 5$_{1.4.4}$ 4Q416 2.4$_{8}$ (נ[ו]דר) CD 16$_{18}$.

<OBJ> נֶדֶר *vow* Gn 28$_{20}$ 31$_{13}$ Nm 6$_{2.21}$ 21$_{2}$ 30$_{3.4}$ Dt 12$_{11.17}$ 23$_{22}$ Jg 11$_{30.39}$ 1 S 1$_{11}$ 2 S 15$_{7.8}$ Is 19$_{21}$ Jr 44$_{25}$ Jon 1$_{16}$ Ec 5$_{3}$ 4Q416 2.4$_{8}$ ([נ[ו]דר נד[ר) 11QT 53$_{11.14.16}$, קָרְבָּן *offering* Nm 6$_{21}$, מְאוּם *anything* CD 16$_{13}$.

<PREP> לְ of direction, *to*, + Y. Gn 31$_{13}$ Nm 21$_{2}$ 30$_{3.4}$ Dt 12$_{11}$ 23$_{22.24}$ Jg 11$_{30.39}$ 2 S 15$_{7}$ Is 19$_{21}$ Ec 5$_{1}$ 11QT 53$_{14.16}$, אָבִיר *mighty one* of Jacob Ps 132$_{2}$, מִזְבֵּחַ *altar* CD 16$_{13}$.

בְּ of place, *in*, + חֶבְרוֹן *Hebron* 2 S 15$_{7}$; of instrument, *by (means of), with*, + פֶּה *mouth* 11QT 53$_{10.13}$.

עַל *according to*, + נֵזֶר *Naziriteship* Nm 6$_{21}$.

מִלְּבַד *besides*, + אֲשֶׁר *that which* Nm 6$_{21}$.

נדר + noun without preposition, בַּיִת *in the house* Nm 30$_{11}$.

<COLL> נדר || שׁבע ni. *swear* Nm 30$_{3}$ Ps 132$_{2}$; + אסר *vow* Nm 30$_{3.4.11}$ 11QT 53$_{14.16}$, דבר pi. *speak* Dt 23$_{24}$, קדשׁ hi. *consecrate* 11QT 53$_{10}$.

+ adverb, שָׁם *there* Gn 31$_{13}$ (בֵּית־אֵל ... אֲשֶׁר נָדַרְתָּ לִּי שָׁם *Bethel ... where you made a vow to me*); noun used adverbially, נְדָבָה *voluntarily* Dt 23$_{24}$ 11QT 53$_{13}$.

נדר + vow specified by (1) direct speech introduced by אמר *say* Gn 28$_{20}$ Nm 21$_{2}$ Jg 11$_{30}$ 1 S 1$_{11}$ 2 S 15$_{8}$.

(2) direct speech without אמר Ps 132$_{2}$.

(3) infinitive of נזר hi. *separate oneself* Nm 6$_{2}$, קטר pi. *burn incense* Jr 44$_{25}$, נסך hi. *pour out* drink offering Jr 44$_{25}$, מות hi. *put to death* 4QTohB[a] 2$_{4}$ ([ונ]דרו לא להמית *and they shall vow not to put to death*), עשׂה *do* 11QT 53$_{13}$.

יַפְלִא לִנְדֹּר *he makes a special vow* Nm 6$_{2}$, תֶּחְדַּל לִנְדֹּר *you leave off making a vow* Dt 23$_{23}$.

<SYN> שׁבע ni. *swear*.*

⇒ נֶדֶר *vow*.

נֶ֫דֶר $_{60.0.12}$ n.m. **vow**—נֶ֫דֶר; cstr. נֶ֫דֶר (נֶ֫דֶר); sf. נִדְרִי, נִדְרוֹ, נְדָרֶיךָ, נְדָרָהּ; pl. נְדָרִים; sf. נְדָרַי (נְדָרֶי), נְדָרֶ֫יךָ (Q נדריכה), נְדָרֶ֫יהָ, נְדָרֵ֫ינוּ, נִדְרֵיכֶם, נִדְרֵיהֶם—**1. vow,** <SUBJ> קום *stand* Nm 30$_{5.6.8.10.12}$ 11QT 53$_{19.20}$ 54$_{4}$, שׁלם pu. *be paid* Ps 65$_{2}$.

<NOM CL> נדרים בפיהם *vows are in their mouths* 4QS[d] 1$_{12}$, נְדָרֶיהָ עָלֶיהָ *her vows are (binding) upon her* Nm 30$_{7}$, sim. 30$_{9}$, עָלַי ... נְדָרֶיךָ *your vows*, i.e. the vows that I made to you, *are ... (binding) upon me* Ps 56$_{13}$.

<OBJ> נדר *vow* Gn 28$_{20}$ 31$_{13}$ Nm 6$_{2.21}$ 21$_{2}$ 30$_{3.4}$ Dt 23$_{22}$ Jg 11$_{30.39}$ 1 S 1$_{11}$ 2 S 15$_{7.8}$ Is 19$_{21}$ Jr 44$_{25}$ Jon 1$_{16}$ Ec 5$_{3}$ 4Q416 2.4$_{8}$ ([נ[ו]דר נד[ר) 11QT 53$_{11.14.16}$, שׁמע *hear* Nm 30$_{5}$ 11QT 53$_{17.20}$, דרשׁ *require* Dt 23$_{22}$ 11QT 53$_{11}$, קום hi. *establish* Nm 30$_{14.15}$ Jr 44$_{25}$ 11QT 54$_{2}$ ([כול [נדר] ... יקי]מנו), פלא hi. *make difficult* Lv 27$_{2}$, פרר hi. *annul* Nm 30$_{9.13.14}$, שׁלם pi. *pay* Dt 23$_{22}$ 2 S 15$_{7}$ Is 19$_{21}$ Na 2$_{1}$ Ps 22$_{26}$ 50$_{14}$ 61$_{9}$ 66$_{13}$ 116$_{14.18}$ Jb 22$_{27}$ Pr 7$_{14}$ Ec 5$_{3}$

11QT 53_{11}, עשׂה *do* Jg 11_{39} Jr $44_{25.25}$.

<CSTR> נֵדֶר אַלְמָנָה וּגְרוּשָׁה *vow of a widow or a divorced woman* Nm 30_{10} 11QT 54_4, נֵדֶר נָזִיר *vow of a Nazirite* Nm 6_2, נִזְרוֹ *of his consecration* Nm 6_5; בַּר־נְדָרָי *son of my vows* Pr 31_2, יְמֵי נֶדֶר *days of the vow of* Nm 6_5, כָּל־נֵדֶר *any vow* Nm 30_{14} Dt 23_{19} (נֵדֶר) 11QT 54_2 ([כול נדר]), כול נדר *any vow of* 11QT 54_4, כָּל־נְדָרֶיהָ *all her vows* Nm $30_{5.6.12.15}$ 11QT $53_{19.20}$ (both כול).

<APP> כֹּל *everything* Nm 30_{10} 11QT 54_4.

<PREP> לְ of benefit, *for*, + בוא hi. *bring* Dt 23_{19}; *concerning* or *consisting of* Nm 30_{13}; introducing object, + שׁמע *hear* Ps 61_6.

בְּ of instrument, *by (means of)* CD 6_{15}.

כְּפִי *according to*, + עשׂה *do* Nm 6_{21}.

לְבַד מִן *besides* 11QT 29_2 ([לבד מנדריכמה]).

אַחַר *after (making)*, + בקר pi. *inquire* Pr 20_{25}.

<COLL> נֵדֶר || שְׁבוּעָה *oath* Nm $30_{3.14}$ (+) 4QS^{d} 1_{12} 11QT 53_{14}, אִסָּר *vow* Nm 30_3 (+) $30_{4.5.5.6.8.12.13.14}$ (+) 30_{15} 11QT 53_{14} (+) $53_{16.17.19.20}$, חֵרֶם *ban* 4QS^{d} 1_{12} CD 6_{15}; + מִבְטָא *impetuous utterance* Nm $30_{7.9}$, זֶבַח *sacrifice* Jon 1_{16} Pr 7_{14}, תּוֹדָה *thank-offering* Ps 50_{14} 56_{13}, עוֹלָה *burnt offering* Ps 66_{13}.

2. votive offering, i.e. offering made in payment of a vow (distinction from §1 not alw. clear), <NOM CL> נֶדֶר ... זֶבַח קָרְבָּנוֹ *the sacrifice of his offering is ... a votive offering* Lv 7_{16}.

<OBJ> נדר *vow* Dt $12_{11.17}$, בוא hi. *bring* Dt 12_6, נשׂא *take* Dt 12_{26} 11QT 53_9, אכל *eat* Dt 12_{17}, זבח *sacrifice* 1 S 1_{21}, פלא pi. *make special* Lv 22_{21} Nm $15_{3.8}$, יסף hi. *add* 4Q416 4.2_7.

<CSTR> מִבְחַר נִדְרֵיכֶם *choicest of your votive offerings* Dt 12_{11}, כָּל־נְדָרֶיךָ *all your votive offerings* Dt 12_{17} 11QT 53_9 (כול נדריכה), כָּל־נִדְרֵיכֶם *all your votive offerings* Lv 23_{38}, כָּל־נִדְרֵיהֶם *all their votive offerings* Lv 22_{18}.

<PREP> לְ *as*, + קרב hi. *bring near*, i.e. offer Lv 22_{18}, רצה ni. *be accepted* Lv 22_{23}; מִלְּבַד *besides* Lv 23_{38}; לְבַד מִן *besides*, + עשׂה *do*, i.e. offer Nm 29_{39}.

<COLL> נֶדֶר || נְדָבָה *freewill offering* Lv 7_{16} 22_{18} 23_{38} Nm 29_{39} Dt 12_6 4Q416 4.2_7 ([נדבו[ה]); + נְדָבָה Lv $22_{21.23}$ Nm 15_3 Dt 12_{17}, עוֹלָה *burnt offering* Dt $12_{6.11}$, זֶבַח *sacrifice* Dt $12_{6.11}$ 1 S 1_{21}, מַעֲשֵׂר *tithe* Dt $12_{6.11.17}$, תְּרוּמָה *offering* Dt $12_{6.11.17}$, בְּכוֹר *firstborn* Dt $12_{6.17}$, קֹדֶשׁ *holy thing* Dt 12_{26}.

Also 4Q418 130_3.

<SYN> §1 שְׁבוּעָה *oath*, אִסָּר *vow*, חֵרֶם *ban*; §2 נְדָבָה *freewill offering*.*

⇒ נדר *vow*.

נֹהַּ 1 n.[m.] **pre-eminence,** <NOM CL> לֹא נֹהַּ בָּהֶם *there shall be no pre-eminence among them* Ezk 7_{11}.*

נהג I $_{30.4.3}$ vb. **drive—Qal** $_{20.4.3}$ Pf. נָהַג, Q נהגה, נָהֲגוּ; impf. יִנְהַג (יִנְהָג), אֶנְהָגְךָ, יִנְהֲגוּ (יִנְהָגוּ); + waw וַיִּנְהַג, וַיִּנְהֲגוּ; impv. נְהַג; ptc. נֹהֵג, נֹהֲגִים; pass. נְהוּגִים—**1. drive, lead (away), urge on** animals (Gn 31_{18} Ex 3_1 1 S 23_5 30_{20} 2 K 4_{24} Is 11_6 Jb 24_3 Si 38_{25} 4QJub^{h} 35_{10}), cart (2 S 6_3|| 1 C 13_7), perh. chariot (2 K 9_{20}), people (1 S 30_{22} Ca 8_2 Lm 3_2 4QTNaph 1_8), as captives (1 S 30_2 Is 20_4), army to battle (1 C 20_1 2 C 25_{11}); of Y. leading Israel as flock (Ps 80_2); **lead one's life, conduct oneself** (Si 3_{26} [unless ni.]); of the mind, **give guidance** (Ec 2_3).

<SUBJ> Y. Lm 3_2, Amalekites 1 S 30_2, Ahio 2 S 6_3|| 1 C 13_7, Amaziah 2 C 25_{11}, Esau 4QJub^{h} 35_{10}, David 1 S 23_5, Jacob Gn 31_{18}, Jehu 2 K 9_{20}, Joab 1 C 20_1, Laban 4QTNaph 1_8, Moses Ex 3_1, Uzziah 2 S 6_3||1 C 13_7, אִישׁ *man* 1 S 30_{22}, אֵם *mother* 2 K 4_{24}, בֵּן *son* 2 S 6_3 2 K 9_{20}, נַעַר *lad* Is 11_6, מֶלֶךְ *king* Is 20_4, רֹעֶה *shepherd* Ps 80_2, אהב ptc. *one who loves* Si 3_{26} (unless ni.), female lover Ca 8_2, תמך ptc. *one who holds* goad Si 38_{25}, פאר htp. *one who glories* Si 38_{25}, לֵב *heart* Ec 2_3, שֵׁבֶט *rod* Ps 23_4 (if em. יְנַחֲמֻנִי *they will comfort me* to יְנַהֲגֻנִי *they will lead me*, i.e. נהג pi.), מִשְׁעֶנֶת *staff* Ps 23_4 (if em.; see above); subj. not specified, 1 S 30_{20} Jb 24_3.

<OBJ> (object not expressed, 1 S $30_{2.20.22}$ 2 K 4_{24} 2 K 9_{20}), Joseph, i.e. Israel Ps 80_2, עָם *people* 2 C 25_{11}, Hannah 4QTNaph 1_8, אִשָּׁה *woman, wife* 1 S $30_{2.22}$, אֵם *mother* 4QTNaph 1_8, בֵּן *son* 1 S 30_{22}, בַּת *daughter* 4QTNaph 1_8, נַעַר *lad* Is 20_4, זָקֵן *elder* Is 20_4, שְׁבִי *captives* Is 20_4, גָּלוּת *exiles* Is 20_4, חַיִל *army* 1 C 20_1, worshipper Ps 23_4 (if em.; see Subj.) Lm 3_2, male lover Ca 8_2, מִקְנֶה *cattle* Gn 31_{18} 1 S 23_5, בָּקָר *herd* 1 S 30_{20}, צֹאן *flock* Ex 3_1 1 S 30_{20} 4QJub^{h} 35_{10}, חֲמוֹר *ass* Jb 24_3, אָתוֹן *she-ass* 2 K 4_{24}, רְכוּשׁ *possessions* Gn 31_{18}, עֲגָלָה *cart*

2 S 6_{3}, chariot 2 K 9_{20}.

<PREP> בְּ of accompaniment, *with*, + שִׁגָּעוֹן *madness* 2 K 9_{20}, טוֹבָה *good* Si 3_{26} (unless ni.); of instrument, *by (means of), with*, + חָכְמָה *wisdom* Ec 2_{3}; introducing object, + אַלּוּף *ox* Si 38_{25}, עֵגֶל *calf* Is 11_{6}, כְּפִיר *young lion* Is 11_{6}, מְרִיא *fatling* Is 11_{6}, עֲגָלָה *cart* 1 C 13_{7}.

כְּ *as*, + צֹאן *flock* Ps 80_{2}.

אֶל *to* 4QapMoses[c] 2.1_{10}.

לִפְנֵי *before*, + מִקְנֶה *cattle* 1 S 30_{20}.

אַחַר *behind*, + מִדְבָּר *steppe* Ex 3_{1}.

<COLL> נהג + הלך *go* 1 S $30_{2.22}$ 2 K 4_{24} 2 C 25_{11}, hi. *lead* Lm 3_{2}, בוא hi. *bring* Ca 8_{2}; + adverb, כֵּן *so* Is 20_{4}.

2. pass. **a. be led in procession,** <SUBJ> מֶלֶךְ *king* Is 60_{1}.

b. be led away, as captives, <SUBJ> בְּתוּלָה *young woman* Lm 1_{4} (if em. נוּגוֹת *are grieved* [i.e. יגה ni.] to נְהוּגוֹת *are led away*).

Also Si $38_{27(Bmg)}$ 40_{23}.

Ni. 0.1 **be led**—Si Impf. ינהג—**be led** (into Sheol), <SUBJ> אהב ptc. one who loves (riches) Si 3_{26} (unless qal).*

Pi. 10 Pf. נִהַג, נִהַגְתָּ; impf. יְנַהֵג (יְנַהֲגֵנוּ, יְנַהֶגְךָ, יְנַהֲגֵם); + waw וַיְנַהֵג (וַיְנַהֲגֵהוּ, וַיְנַהֲגֵם), 2ms וַתְּנַהֵג—**1. lead** people (Is 49_{10} 63_{14} Ps 48_{15} 78_{52}), **lead away,** as captives (Gn 31_{26} Dt 4_{27} 28_{37}). **2. drive on** wind (Ex 10_{13} Ps 78_{26}). **3. drive,** or perh. **cause to drive** chariot (Ex 14_{25}), <SUBJ> Y. Ex 10_{13} 14_{25} (unless subj. Egyptians) Dt 4_{27} 28_{37} Is 63_{14} Ps 48_{15} 78_{26}, Jacob Gn 31_{26}, רחם pi. ptc. *one who has compassion* Is 49_{10}.

<OBJ> Egyptians perh. Ex 14_{25}, Israelites Dt 4_{27} 28_{37} Ps 48_{15}, עַם *people* Is 63_{14} Ps 78_{52}, בַּת *daughter* Gn 31_{26}, אָסוּר *prisoner* Is 49_{10}, רוּחַ *wind* Ex 10_{13}, תֵּימָן *south wind* Ps 78_{26}, מֶרְכָּבָה *chariot* Ex 14_{25}, אֲשֶׁר *one who* Is 49_{10}.

<PREP> בְּ of place, *in(to)*, + אֶרֶץ *land* Ex 10_{13}, מִדְבָּר *steppe* Ps 78_{52}; of instrument, *by (means of), with*, + עֹז *strength* Ps 78_{26}; of accompaniment, *with, in*, + כְּבֵדֻת *heaviness* Ex 14_{25}.

כְּ *as*, + שׁבה pass. ptc. *captive* Gn 31_{26}, עֵדֶר *flock* Ps 78_{52}.

ה- of direction, *to*, + שָׁם *there* Dt 4_{27} 28_{37}.

<COLL> נהג pi. + נהל pi. *lead* Is 49_{10}, נסע hi. *lead out* Ps$78_{26.52}$; + noun used adverbially, יוֹם *day* Ex 10_{13}, לַיְלָה *night* Ex 10_{13}, עַלְמוּת perh. *everlastingness*, i.e. for ever Ps $48_{15(mss)}$ (L עַל־מוּת perh. *against death*; or em. עַל־עֲלָמוֹת *according to Alamoth*).

Pu. be led away, <SUBJ> אָמָה *female slave* Na 2_{8} (if em. מְנַהֲגוֹת *lament*, i.e. נהג II pi.). <PREP> כְּ *as with*, + קוֹל *voice* of doves Na 2_{8} (if em.; see Subj.).*

⇒ מִנְהָג *driving, custom*.

נהג II 1 vb. **lament—Pi.** 1 Ptc. מְנַהֲגוֹת—**lament,** <SUBJ> אָמָה *female slave* Na 2_{8} (or em. מְנֹהָגוֹת *lead away* [i.e. נהג I pu.]; + תפף po. *beat* breast). <PREP> כְּ *as with*, + קוֹל *voice* of doves Na 2_{8}.*

נהה I 3.1 vb. **lament—Qal** 2.1 + waw וְנָהָה; impv. נְהֵה—**lament (with), wail (with),** <SUBJ> בֵּן *son* Si $38_{16(B)}$ (+ מרר htp. *show bitter grief*, זוב hi. *cause* tears *to flow*), of man, in ref. to Ezekiel Ezk 32_{18}, worshipper Ps 102_{8} (if em. וָאֶהְיֶה *and I am* to וָאֶנְהֶה *and I lament*); subj. not specified, Mc 2_{4}. <OBJ> נְהִי *lamentation* Mc 2_{4}, קִינָה *dirge* Si $38_{16B)}$. <PREP> עַל *concerning, over*, + הָמוֹן *multitude* Ezk 32_{18}.

Ni. 1 + waw וַיִּנָּהוּ—**lament,** i.e. follow repentantly (unless נהה II *follow* or III *turn away*), <SUBJ> בַּיִת *house* of Israel 1 S 7_{2}. <PREP> אַחֲרֵי *after*, + Y. 1 S 7_{2}.

⇒ נְהִי *lamentation*, נִי *wailing*.

***נהה II** 1 vb. **follow** (unless נהה I *lament* or III *turn away*)—**Ni.** 1 + waw וַיִּנָּהוּ—**follow, adhere (to),** <SUBJ> בַּיִת *house* of Israel 1 S 7_{2}. <PREP> אַחֲרֵי *after*, + Y. 1 S 7_{2}.

***נהה III** 1 vb. **turn** (unless נהה I *lament* or II *follow*)—**Ni.** 1 + waw וַיִּנָּהוּ—**turn,** <SUBJ> בַּיִת *house* of Israel 1 S 7_{2}. <PREP> אַחֲרֵי *after*, + Y. 1 S 7_{2}.

***[נָהוֹר]** n.[m.] **light,** <CSTR> נה[ור]י אורים *lights of flames* 4QBer[a] 1.2_{3}.

⇒ נהר II *shine*.

נְהִי 7.1 n.[m.] **lamentation**—נְהִי—**lamentation, wailing,** <SUBJ> שׁמע ni. *be heard* Jr 31_{15}. <NOM CL> ונהי קינה perh. *and let there be lamentation (and) a dirge*

Si 38$_{16(Bmg)}$ (B נהה *lament*). <OBJ> נהה *lament with* Mc 2$_{4}$, נשׂא *raise* Jr 9$_{9.17}$, למד pi. *teach* Jr 9$_{19}$. <CSTR> יוֹדְעֵי נֶהִי *ones who know*, i.e. are skilled in, *lamentation* Am 5$_{16}$, קוֹל נְהִי *sound of lamentation* Jr 9$_{18}$. <APP> קוֹל *voice* Jr 31$_{15}$. <COLL> נְהִי || בְּכִי *weeping* Jr 9$_{9}$ (בְּכִי וְנֶהִי) 31$_{15}$, קִינָה *dirge* Jr 9$_{9.19}$; + מִסְפֵּד *wailing* Am 5$_{16}$, מָשָׁל *proverb* Mc 2$_{4}$.

<SYN> בְּכִי *weeping*, קִינָה *dirge*.

⇒ נהה I *lament*.

*נְהִיָה I $_{1.0.1}$ n.f. **lamentation** (unless נְהִיָה II *the future*), <OBJ> נהה *lament with* Mc 2$_{4}$ (+ נְהִי *lamentation*).

נְהִיָה II *the future*, see היה Ni. *be*.

נהל I $_{10.0.2}$ vb. **lead** (many refs may be נהל II *give rest*)—**Pi.** $_{9.0.2}$ Pf. נִהַלְתָּ; impf. יְנַהֵל (יְנַהֲלֵנִי ,יְנַהֲלֵם), 2ms תְּנַהֲלֵנִי; + waw וַיְנַהֲלוּם ,וַיְנַהֲלֵם; ptc. מְנַהֵל; inf. Q נהל.

1. lead, guide, <SUBJ> Y. Ex 15$_{13}$ Is 40$_{11}$ 49$_{10}$ Ps 23$_{2}$ 31$_{4}$ 4QapMes 2.2$_{13}$ 1QH 23$_{7}$, אִישׁ *man* 2 C 28$_{15}$; subj. not specified, Is 51$_{18}$. <OBJ> עַם *people* Ex 15$_{13}$, אָסוּר *prisoner* Is 49$_{10}$, נתשׁ pass. ptc. *uprooted one* 4QapMes 2.2$_{13}$, עול ptc. *one who gives suck* Is 40$_{11}$, worshipper Ps 23$_{2}$ 31$_{4}$, שִׁבְיָה *captives* 2 C 28$_{15}$, אֲשֶׁר *one who* Is 49$_{10}$. <PREP> לְ introducing object, + Jerusalem Is 51$_{18}$; בְּ of instrument, *by (means of), with*, + חֲמוֹר *ass* 2 C 28$_{15}$, יָמִין *right hand* perh. 1QH 23$_{7}$, עֹז *strength* Ex 15$_{13}$; מִן partitive, *(from) among*, + בֵּן *son* Is 51$_{18}$; אֶל *to*, + נָוֶה *habitation* Ex 15$_{13}$; עַל *beside*, + מַבּוּעַ *spring* Is 49$_{10}$, מַיִם *water* Ps 23$_{2}$; לְמַעַן *for the sake of*, + שֵׁם *name* Ps 31$_{4}$. <COLL> נהל pi. || נחה hi. *lead* Ps 31$_{4}$; + נחה *lead* Ex 15$_{13}$, נהג pi. *lead* Is 49$_{10}$, בוא hi. *bring* 2 C 28$_{15}$, רבץ hi. *cause to lie down* Ps 23$_{2}$.

2. supply, provide with, <SUBJ> Joseph Gn 47$_{17}$. <OBJ> Egyptians Gn 47$_{17}$. <PREP> בְּ of time, *in*, + שָׁנָה *year* Gn 47$_{17}$; of price, *(in exchange) for*, + מִקְנֶה *cattle* Gn 47$_{17}$; introducing object, + לֶחֶם *food* Gn 47$_{17}$.

3. give rest, <SUBJ> Y. 2 C 32$_{22}$ (or em. וַיְנַהֲלֵם to וַיָּנַח לָהֶם *and he gave them rest*, i.e. נוח hi.). <OBJ> Hezekiah 2 C 32$_{22}$ (or em.; see Subj.), יֹשֵׁב *inhabitant* 2 C 32$_{22}$ (or em.; see Subj.). <PREP> מִן *from*, + סָבִיב *round about*, i.e. on all sides 2 C 32$_{22}$ (or em.; see Subj.).

<SYN> §1 נחה hi. *lead*.

Htp. $_{1}$ Impf. אֶתְנַהֲלָה—**lead on, travel by stages,** <SUBJ> Jacob Gn 33$_{14}$. <PREP> לְ *according to*, + אַט *gentleness*, i.e. gently Gn 33$_{14}$, רֶגֶל *foot*, i.e. pace Gn 33$_{14}$.*

⇒ נַהַל *Nahal*, נַהֲלָל *Nahalal*, נַהֲלֹל I *watering place*, II *Nahalol*.

*נהל II $_{10.0.2}$ vb. **give rest** (unless נהל I *lead*)—**Pi.** $_{9.0.2}$ Pf. נִהַלְתָּ; impf. יְנַהֵל (יְנַהֲלֵנִי ,יְנַהֲלֵם), 2ms תְּנַהֲלֵנִי; + waw וַיְנַהֲלוּם ,וַיְנַהֲלֵם; ptc. מְנַהֵל; inf. Q נהל—**give rest,** <SUBJ> Y. Ex 15$_{13}$ Is 40$_{11}$ 49$_{10}$ Ps 23$_{2}$ 31$_{4}$ 2 C 32$_{22}$ (or em. וַיְנַהֲלֵם to וַיָּנַח לָהֶם *and he gave them rest*, i.e. נוח hi.) 4QapMes 2.2$_{13}$ 1QH 23$_{7}$, Joseph Gn 47$_{17}$ (וַיְנַהֲלֵם בַּלֶּחֶם *and he gave them rest with bread*), אִישׁ *man* 2 C 28$_{15}$; subj. not specified, Is 51$_{18}$. <OBJ> Egyptians Gn 47$_{17}$, Hezekiah 2 C 32$_{22}$ (or em.; see Subj.), יֹשֵׁב *inhabitant* 2 C 32$_{22}$ (or em.; see Subj.), עַם *people* Ex 15$_{13}$, אָסוּר *prisoner* Is 49$_{10}$, נתשׁ pass. ptc. *uprooted one* 4QapMes 2.2$_{13}$, עול ptc. *one that gives suck* Is 40$_{11}$, worshipper Ps 23$_{2}$ 31$_{4}$, שִׁבְיָה *captives* 2 C 28$_{15}$, אֲשֶׁר *one who* Is 49$_{10}$.

<PREP> לְ introducing object, + Jerusalem Is 51$_{18}$; בְּ of instrument, *by (means of), with*, + חֲמוֹר *ass* 2 C 28$_{15}$, יָמִין *right hand* perh. 1QH 23$_{7}$, עֹז *strength* Ex 15$_{13}$; בְּ of time, *in*, + שָׁנָה *year* Gn 47$_{17}$; of price, *(in exchange) for*, + מִקְנֶה *cattle* Gn 47$_{17}$; introducting object, + לֶחֶם *food* Gn 47$_{17}$; מִן *from*, + סָבִיב *round about*, i.e. on all sides 2 C 32$_{22}$ (or em.; see Subj.); מִן partitive, *(from) among*, + בֵּן *son* Is 51$_{18}$; אֶל *to*, + נָוֶה *habitation* Ex 15$_{13}$; עַל *beside*, + מַבּוּעַ *spring* Is 49$_{10}$, מַיִם *water* Ps 23$_{2}$; לְמַעַן *for the sake of*, + שֵׁם *name* Ps 31$_{4}$.

<COLL> נהל pi. || נחה hi. *lead* Ps 31$_{4}$; + נחה *lead* Ex 15$_{13}$, נהג pi. *lead* Is 49$_{10}$, בוא hi. *bring* 2 C 28$_{15}$, רבץ hi. *cause to lie down* Ps 23$_{2}$.

<SYN> §1 נחה hi. *lead*.

Htp. $_{1}$ Impf. אֶתְנַהֲלָה—**continue on,** <SUBJ> Jacob Gn 33$_{14}$. <PREP> לְ *according to*, + אַט *gentleness*, i.e. gently Gn 33$_{14}$, רֶגֶל *foot*, i.e. pace Gn 33$_{14}$.

⇒ נַהַל *Nahal*, נַהֲלָל *Nahalal*, נַהֲלֹל I *watering place*, II *Nahalol*.

*[נַ֫הַל] 0.0.0.1 pr.n.[m.] **Nahal,** appar. father of Neriah, Seal 934 (7th cent.).
⇒ נהל *lead.*

נַהֲלָל 2 pl.n. **Nahalal,** town in Zebulun, appar. ident. with נַהֲלֹל *Nahalol* at Jg 130, perh. T. en-Naḥl, 8 km ESE of Haifa, <SUBJ> היה *be* Jos 1915. <OBJ> נתן *give* Jos 2135. <APP> עִיר *city* Jos 1915.*
⇒ נהל *lead.*

[נַהֲלֹל] I 1 n.[m.] **watering place** (unless נַהֲלֹל II *thornbush*)—pl. נַהֲלֹלִים—**watering place,** or perh. **pasture,** <CSTR> כֹּל הַנַּהֲלֹלִים *all the watering places* Is 719 (‖ נַעֲצוּץ *thornbush*). <PREP> בְּ of place, *in, on,* + נוח *rest* Is 719.*
⇒ נהל *lead.*

*[נַהֲלֹל] II 1 n.[m.] **thornbush** (unless נַהֲלֹל I *watering place*)—pl. נַהֲלֹלִים—**shrub, thorny bush,** <CSTR> כֹּל הַנַּהֲלֹלִים *all the thornbushes* Is 719 (‖ נַעֲצוּץ *thornbush*). <PREP> בְּ of place, *in, on,* + נוח *rest* Is 719.
<SYN> נַעֲצוּץ *thornbush.*

נַהֲלֹל III 1 pl.n. **Nahalol,** town in Zebulun, appar. ident. with נַהֲלָל *Nahalal* at Jos 1915 2123, perh. T. en-Naḥl, 8 km ESE of Haifa, <CSTR> יֹשְׁבֵי נַהֲלֹל *inhabitants of Nahalol* Jg 130.
⇒ נהל *lead.*

נהם I 5 vb. **growl—Qal** 5 Impf. יִנְהֹם; + waw וְנָהַמְתָּ, וְנִהֲמוּתֶם; ptc. נֹהֵם—**1. growl,** <SUBJ> גּוֹי *nation,* as lion Is 529 (+ שׁאג *roar*) 530, אֲרִי *lion* Pr 2815 (unless §3), לָבִיא *lion* Is 306 (if em. מֵהֶם *from them* to נֹהֵם), לַיִשׁ *lion* Is 306 (if em.; see above). <PREP> בְּ of time, *in,* + יוֹם *day* Is 530; כְּ *as,* + נְהָמָה *roar* of sea Is 530; עַל *over,* + טֶרֶף *prey* Is 530.

2. groan, <SUBJ> עַם *people* Ezk 2423, אִישׁ *man,* i.e. each Ezk 2423, בֵּן *son* Pr 511 (unless §3). <PREP> בְּ of time, *in, at,* + אַחֲרִית *end* Pr 511; אֶל *to,* + אָח *brother* Ezk 2423.

3. perh. **growl with hunger,*** <SUBJ> בֵּן *son* Pr 511, אֲרִי *lion* Pr 2815 (‖ שׁקק II *be thirsty*).
<SYN> שׁקק II *be thirsty.*
⇒ נְהָמָה *yearning.*

*[נהם] II vb. **sleep—Pi. put to sleep,** <SUBJ> subj. not specified, Jb 1120 (if em. מָנוֹס אָבַד מִנְהֶם *escape has perished from them* to מָנוֹס אִבֵּד מְנַהֵם *he who puts to sleep destroys their escape* [unless hi.]).

Hi. put to sleep, <SUBJ> subj. not specified, Jb 1120 (if em. מָנוֹס אָבַד מִנְהֶם *escape will perish from them* to מָנוֹס אֹבֵד מַנְהִם *he who puts to sleep destroys their escape* [unless Pi.]).
⇒ cf. נום I *be drowsy.*

נַ֫הַם 2 n.[m.] **growling,** <NOM CL> נַהַם כַּכְּפִיר זַעַף מֶלֶךְ *the raging of a king is a growling like (that of) the lion* Pr 1912, נַהַם כַּכְּפִיר אֵימַת מֶלֶךְ *the terror of,* i.e. inspired by, *a king is a growling like (that of) a lion* Pr 202 (or em. אֵימַת to חֲמַת *wrath of* or אִמְרַת *word of*).
⇒ נהם *growl.*

[נְהָמָה] I 2.0.1 n.f. **growling**—cstr. נַהֲמַת; sf. Q נהמתי—**1. growling, roaring,** <CSTR> נַהֲמַת לָבִיא *growling of a lion* Ps 389 (if em. לִבִּי groaning *of my heart*), נַהֲמַת יָם *roaring of the sea* Is 530. <PREP> כְּ *as,* + נהם *growl* Is 530; מִן of instrument, *by (means of), with,* + שׁאג *roar* Ps 389 (if em.; see Cstr.).

2. groaning, <SUBJ> בוא *come* 1QH 1833. <CSTR> לִבִּי נַהֲמַת לִבִּי *groaning of my heart* Ps 389 (or em. לִבִּי to לָבִיא growling *of a lion*). <PREP> מִן of cause, *on account of,* + שׁאג *roar* Ps 389 (or em.; see Cstr.).
⇒ נהם *growl.*

*נְהָמָה II 1 n.f. **yearning**—<CSTR> נַהֲמַת לִבִּי *yearning of my heart* Ps 389. <PREP> מִן of cause, *on account of,* + שׁאג *roar* Ps 389 (or em.; see Cstr.).
⇒ נהם I *growl, be hungry.*

נהק 2 vb. **bray—Qal** 2 Impf. יִנְהַק, יִנְהָקוּ—**bray,** <SUBJ> פֶּרֶא *wild ass* Jb 65 (‖ געה *low*), צָעִיר *young one* Jb 307. <PREP> עַל *upon,* + דֶּשֶׁא *grass* Jb 65; בֵּין *among,* + שִׂיחַ *bush* Jb 307.
<SYN> געה *low.*

נהר I $_{3}$ vb. **flow** (unless נהר III *be noisily excited*)—**Qal** $_{3}$ Impf. יִנְהֲרוּ; + waw וְנָהֲרוּ—**flow, stream,** <SUBJ> עַם *people* Mc 4$_{1}$, גּוֹי *nation* Is 2$_{2}$ Jr 51$_{44}$. <PREP> אֶל *to,* + בֵּל *Bel* Jr 51$_{44}$, הַר *mountain* Is 2$_{2}$; עַל *to,* + הַר *mountain* Mc 4$_{1}$. <COLL> נהר + adverb, עוֹד *again* Jr 51$_{44}$.*

⇒ נָהָר *river.*

נהר II $_{3.0.1}$ vb. **shine** (unless נהר III *be noisily excited*)—**Qal** $_{3}$ + waw וְנָהֲרוּ, וְנָהַרְתְּ—**shine, be radiant (with joy),** <SUBJ> Israelites Jr 31$_{12}$, Zion Is 60$_{5}$; subj. not specified, Ps 34$_{6}$. <PREP> אֶל *on account of* or *concerning,* + טוּב *goodness* Jr 31$_{12}$; עַל *on account of* or *concerning,* + בֵּן *son* of flock and herd Jr 31$_{12}$, דָּגָן *grain* Jr 31$_{12}$, תִּירוֹשׁ *new wine* Jr 31$_{12}$, יִצְהָר *fresh oil* Jr 31$_{12}$.

Hi. $_{0.0.1}$ Impf. יהיר (unless יהיר is אור hi. or noun)—**cause to shine,** <SUBJ> Y. 4QapPs[b] 1$_{5}$. <OBJ> כּוֹכָב *star* 4QapPs[b] 1$_{5}$ (כוב[ים]), כְּסִיל *(star of) Orion* 4QapPs[b] 1$_{5}$.*

⇒ נְהוֹר *light,* נְהָרָה *light.*

***נהר** III $_{6}$ **be noisily excited** (unless נהר I *flow* or II *shine*)—**Qal** $_{6}$ Impf. יִנְהֲרוּ; + waw וְנָהֲרוּ, וְנָהַרְתְּ—**be noisily excited, come in noisy excitement,** <SUBJ> Israelites Jr 31$_{12}$, Zion Is 60$_{5}$, עַם *people* Mc 4$_{1}$, גּוֹי *nation* Is 2$_{2}$ Jr 51$_{44}$; subj. not specified, Ps 34$_{6}$. <PREP> אֶל *to,* + בֵּל *Bel* Jr 51$_{44}$, הַר *mountain* Is 2$_{2}$; *on account of* or *concerning,* + טוּב *goodness* Jr 31$_{12}$; עַל *to,* + הַר *mountain* Mc 4$_{1}$; *on account of* or *concerning,* + בֵּן *son* of flock and herd Jr 31$_{12}$, דָּגָן *grain* Jr 31$_{12}$, תִּירוֹשׁ *new wine* Jr 31$_{12}$, יִצְהָר *fresh oil* Jr 31$_{12}$. <COLL> נהר + adverb, עוֹד *again* Jr 51$_{44}$.

נָהָר I $_{119.2.11}$ n.m. **river**—cstr. נְהַר; pl. נְהָרִים, נְהָרוֹת (נְהָרֹת); cstr. נַהֲרֵי, נַהֲרוֹת; sf. נַהֲרֹתַיִךְ, נַהֲרוֹתֶיךָ, נַהֲרֹתֶיהָ, נַהֲרֹתָם (נַהֲרוֹתָם) (נַהֲרֹתֶיהָ)—**1. river, stream, torrent;** oft. specif. of Euphrates as הַנָּהָר *the river* (Gn 31$_{21}$ 36$_{37}$||1 C 1$_{48}$ Ex 23$_{31}$ Nm 22$_{5}$ Jos 24$_{2.3.14.15}$ 2 S 10$_{16}$||1 C 19$_{16}$ 1 K 5$_{1.4.4}$ 14$_{15}$ Is 27$_{12}$ Ezr 8$_{36}$ Ne 2$_{7.9}$ 3$_{7}$ 2 C 9$_{26}$ Si 39$_{22}$ [כנהר]), נָהָר *(the) river* (Is 7$_{20}$ Jr 2$_{18}$ Mc 7$_{12}$ Zc 9$_{10}$ Ps 72$_{8}$ 80$_{12}$ Si 44$_{21}$), נְהָרוֹת Ps 89$_{26}$ (if וֹת־ is fem. sg. ending)*; הַנָּהָר הַגָּדוֹל *the great river,* as designation of Euphrates (Gn 15$_{18}$ Dt 1$_{7}$ Jos 1$_{4}$), Tigris (Dn 10$_{4}$).

2. flood, current of sea (Is 44$_{27}$ Jon 2$_{4}$ Ps 24$_{2}$ 93$_{3.3.3}$; perh. Ps 46$_{5}$; 89$_{26}$).*

<SUBJ> היה *be* Gn 2$_{10}$, הלך *go,* i.e. flow Ezk 31$_{4}$ (or em. הֹלֵךְ *going* to הֹלִיכָה *it caused to flow,* i.e. hi.), בוא *come* Ezr 8$_{15}$, יצא *go out,* i.e. flow Gn 2$_{10}$, שׁטף *overflow* Is 43$_{2}$ Ca 8$_{7}$ 1QH 16$_{14}$ GnzPs 4$_{24}$, פשׁע *transgress,* i.e. overflow Jb 40$_{23}$ (if em. יַעֲשֹׁק *it oppresses* to יִפְשַׁע), שׁקה hi. *water* Gn 2$_{10}$ 1QH 14$_{16}$ ([ישקו]), סבב *surround* Jon 2$_{4}$, בזא *divide* Is 18$_{2.7}$, נשׂא *lift up* Ps 93$_{3.3.3}$, גרשׁ *churn up* 1QH 16$_{14}$, חרב *be dry* Is 19$_{5}$ Jb 14$_{11}$, יבשׁ *be dry* Is 19$_{5}$ Jb 14$_{11}$, זנח hi. *stink* Is 19$_{6}$, מחא *clap* Ps 98$_{8}$, עשׁק *oppress* Jb 40$_{23}$ (or em.; see above).

<NOM CL> הַנָּהָר הָרְבִיעִי הוּא פְרָת *the fourth river is the Euphrates* Gn 2$_{14}$, הֲלֹא טוֹב ... נַהֲרוֹת דַּמֶּשֶׂק *are not the rivers of Damascus ... better* than all the waters of Israel? 2 K 5$_{12}$, נָהָר *there is a river* Ps 46$_{5}$.

<OBJ> הלך hi. *cause to flow* Ezk 31$_{4}$ (if em.; see Subj.) 32$_{14}$, עבר *cross* Gn 31$_{21}$ Is 47$_{2}$, פתח *open* Is 41$_{18}$, חבשׁ pi. *bind* Jb 28$_{11}$, שׂים *place,* i.e. make Is 42$_{15}$ 43$_{19}$ 50$_{2}$ Ps 107$_{33}$, נתן *give* Is 43$_{20}$, חרב hi. *dry up* Na 1$_{4}$, יבשׁ hi. *dry up* Is 44$_{27}$ Ps 74$_{15}$, מנע *restrain* Ezk 31$_{15}$, רפס *foul* by treading Ezk 32$_{2}$, בקע pi. *split* the earth *with* Hb 3$_{9}$ (or em. pi. to ni. [subj. earth] *break out into*).

<CSTR> נְהַר מִצְרַיִם *river of Egypt* Gn 15$_{18}$ (or em. נַחַל *stream of*), נַהֲרוֹת בָּבֶל *rivers of Babylon* Ps 137$_{1}$, דַּמֶּשֶׂק *of Damascus* 2 K 5$_{12}$, נהרות עדן *rivers of Eden* 1QH 14$_{16}$, נַהֲרֵי־כוּשׁ *rivers of Cush* Is 18$_{1}$ Zp 3$_{10}$, נְהַר אַהֲוָא *river (of) Ahava* Ezr 8$_{31}$, גּוֹזָן *of Gozan* 2 K 17$_{6}$ 18$_{11}$ 1 C 5$_{26}$, כְּבָר *(of) Chebar* Ezk 1$_{1.3}$ 3$_{15.23}$ 10$_{15.20.22}$ 43$_{3}$ 4QpsEzek[e] 65$_{4}$ (נה[ר]), נהר סור *river (of) Sur* 4QpsMos[d] 3$_{7}$, נְהַר־פְּרָת *river (of the) Euphrates* Gn 15$_{18}$ Dt 1$_{7}$ 11$_{24}$ Jos 1$_{4}$ 2 S 8$_{3(Qr)}$||1 C 18$_{3}$ (2 S Kt lacks פרת) 2 K 23$_{29}$ 24$_{7}$ Jr 46$_{2.6.10}$, נַהֲרוֹת אֵיתָן *rivers of continuity,* i.e. continuously flowing Ps 74$_{15}$, נַהֲרֵי נַחֲלֵי *rivers of the streams of* honey Jb 20$_{17}$ (or del. or em. יִצְהָר *of oil,* and join with preceding, or em. נָהָר *of oil* or נִהֲרֵי *of my oil,* i.e. נָהָר II), נהרי אור *rivers of fire* 4QShirShabb[f] 15.2$_{2}$.

שֵׁם־הַנָּהָר *name of the river* Gn 2$_{13.14}$, מֵי *waters of* Is 8$_{7}$ Jr 2$_{18}$ (נָהָר), שִׁבֹּלֶת *stream of* Is 27$_{12}$, מקוי נהרות *collection,* i.e. reservoir, *of rivers* 1QM 1$_{13}$, רְחֹבוֹת הַנָּהָר *Rehoboth of,* i.e. on, *the river* Gn 36$_{37}$||1 C 1$_{48}$, עֵבֶר

הַנָּהָר *region beyond the river* 1 K 5$_{4.4}$ Ezr 8$_{36}$ Ne 2$_{7.9}$ 3$_{7}$, שַׁעֲרֵי הַנְּהָרוֹת *gates of the rivers* Na 2$_{7}$, מְקוֹם נְהָרִים *place of rivers* Is 33$_{21}$ (or del. נְהָרִים), מַבְּכֵי נְהָרוֹת *sources of the rivers* Jb 28$_{11}$ (if em. מִבְּכִי *without trickling*), בזאי נהרות *mockeries of rivers* 1QH 16$_{14}$, כָּל־הַנְּהָרוֹת *all the rivers* Na 1$_{4}$, כול נהרות *all the rivers of* 1QH 14$_{16}$.

<APP> אַהֲוָא *Ahava* Ezr 8$_{21}$, אֲמָנָה *Amana* 2 K 5$_{12(Qr)}$ (Kt אבנה *Abana*), פַּרְפַּר *Pharpar* 2 K 5$_{12}$, פְּרָת *Euphrates* 1 C 5$_{9}$, יְאֹר *stream* Is 33$_{21}$ (or del. נְהָרִים), פְּלַגָּה *stream* Jb 20$_{17}$ (or em.; see Cstr.).

<ADJ> גָּדוֹל *great* Gn 15$_{18}$ Dt 1$_{7}$ Jos 1$_{4}$ Dn 10$_{4}$, עָצוּם *mighty* Is 8$_{7}$, רַב pl. *many* Is 8$_{7}$, צַר *narrow* or *gleaming* Is 59$_{19}$, שֵׁנִי *second* Gn 2$_{13}$, שְׁלִישִׁי *third* Gn 2$_{14}$, רְבִיעִי *fourth* Gn 2$_{14}$.

<PREP> לְ of direction, *to*, + בוא hi. *bring* 1 C 5$_{26}$.

בְּ of place, *in, on, at, by*, + ראה *see* Ezk 10$_{15.10}$, ישׁב hi. *cause to dwell* 2 K 17$_{6}$, נוח hi. *place* 2 K 18$_{11}$ (if em. וַיַּנְחֵם *and he led them* [i.e. נחה hi.] to וַיַּנִּחֵם *and he placed them*), שׂים *place* Ps 89$_{26}$, נצב hi. *set up* 1 C 18$_{3}$, שׁוב hi. *restore* 2 S 8$_{3}$; *through* perh. 4QapPs[b] 6$_{2}$, + עבר *pass* Is 43$_{2}$ Ps 66$_{6}$, גיח hi. *burst out* Ezk 32$_{2}$ (or em. בְּנַחֲרָתְךָ *with your snorting* or בְּנְחִירֶיךָ *with your nostrils*); *in* or of instrument, *by (means of)*, + קדשׁ htp. *sanctify oneself* 1QS 3$_{5}$; *against* Hb 3$_{8}$, + חרה *burn* Hb 3$_{8}$; introducing object, + ראה *look at*, i.e. enjoy Jb 20$_{17}$ (or em.; see Cstr.), נוס pol. *drive on* Is 59$_{19}$.

כְּ *as* Is 66$_{12}$ Ps 78$_{16}$ GnzPs 4$_{24}$, + היה *be* Is 48$_{18}$, בוא *come* Is 59$_{19}$, געשׁ htp. *be in turmoil* Jr 46$_{7.8}$, רוה pi. *saturate* Si 39$_{22}$.

מִן of direction, *from* Gn 15$_{18}$ (or em.; see Cstr.) Zc 9$_{10}$, + היה *be* Dt 11$_{24.24}$, נסע *journey* Ezr 8$_{31}$, משׁל *rule* 1 K 5$_{1}$ 2 C 9$_{26}$, רדה *have dominion* Ps 72$_{8}$, נחל hi. *cause to inherit* Si 44$_{21}$.

לְמִן *from* 1 C 5$_{9}$.

אֶל *to*, + שׁלח *send* Ps 80$_{12}$, קבץ *gather* Ezr 8$_{15}$; *beside* Jr 46$_{10}$, + ישׁב *dwell* Ezk 3$_{15}$, ראה *see* Ezk 43$_{3}$.

עַל *over*, + נטה *stretch* hand Ex 7$_{19}$ 8$_{1}$, נוף hi. *wave* hand Is 11$_{15}$; *upon*, + כון pol. *establish* Ps 24$_{2}$; *on, beside* Nm 22$_{5}$ 24$_{6}$ Ezk 1$_{1}$ 4QpsMos[d] 3$_{7}$, + היה *be* Jr 46$_{2}$ Ezk 1$_{3}$, קרא *call* fast Ezr 8$_{21}$, ראה *see* Ezk 3$_{23}$ 10$_{22}$, עלה *go up* 2 K 23$_{29}$, ישׁב *sit* Ps 137$_{1}$, בכה *weep* Ps 137$_{1}$.

עַל־יַד *beside*, + היה *be* Dn 10$_{4}$, כשׁל *stumble* Jr 46$_{6}$.

עַד *unto, as far as* Gn 15$_{18}$ Mc 7$_{12}$, + היה *be* Jos 1$_{4.4}$ 2 K 24$_{7}$, בוא *come* Dt 1$_{7.7}$, שׁית *place* border Ex 23$_{31}$.

בְּעֵבֶר *beyond* Jos 24$_{15(Kt)}$ Is 7$_{20}$ (בְּעֶבְרֵי), + ישׁב *dwell* Jos 24$_{2}$, עבד *serve* Jos 24$_{14}$.

מֵעֵבֶר *(from) beyond* Jos 24$_{15(Qr)}$ 2 S 10$_{16}$||1 C 19$_{16}$, + לקח *take* Jos 24$_{3}$.

מֵעֵבֶר לְ *(from) beyond* Is 18$_{1}$, + זרה pi. *scatter* 1 K 14$_{15}$, יבל hi. *bring* Zp 3$_{10}$.

<COLL> נָהָר || נַחַל *stream* Is 11$_{15}$ (+) 66$_{12}$ Ps 74$_{15}$ (+), יְאֹר *Nile* Ex 7$_{19}$ 8$_{1}$ Is 19$_{6}$ Jr 46$_{7.8}$ (all three +) Si 39$_{22}$, יָם *sea* Is 50$_{2}$ Na 1$_{4}$ (both +) Hb 3$_{8}$ Zc 9$_{10}$ (+) Ps 24$_{2}$ 66$_{6}$ 72$_{8}$ (both +) 80$_{12}$ 89$_{26}$ Jb 14$_{11}$ (+) 1QS 3$_{5}$, אֲגַם *pool* Ex 7$_{19}$ 8$_{1}$ Is 41$_{18}$ 42$_{15}$ (both +), מַעְיָן *spring* Is 41$_{18}$ Ps 74$_{15}$ (+), מַיִם *water* Is 43$_{2.20}$ Ezk 31$_{15}$ (+) 32$_{2.14}$ Ca 8$_{7}$ (both +) 1QS 3$_{5}$ (+), דֶּרֶךְ *way* Is 43$_{19}$.

+ נֹזֵל *stream* Ps 78$_{16}$, מוֹצָא *spring* Is 41$_{18}$ Ps 107$_{33}$, מִקְוֶה *collection* of waters Ex 7$_{19}$, גַּל *wave* Is 48$_{18}$ Jon 2$_{4}$, מִשְׁבָּר *breaker* Jon 2$_{4}$.

הָלְכוּ בַּצִּיּוֹת נָהָר *they* (waters) *flowed through the desert (as) a river* Ps 105$_{41}$, נָהָר יוּצַק יְסוֹדָם *their foundation was washed away by a river* Jb 22$_{16}$.

Also 4QpsEzek[a] 9$_{13}$ 14$_{1}$ 16$_{17}$.

<SYN> נַחַל *stream*, יְאֹר *Nile*, יָם *sea*, אֲגַם *pool*, מַעְיָן *spring*, מַיִם *water*, דֶּרֶךְ *way*.*

⇒ נהר I *flow*.

*[נָהָר] II n.[m.] **oil,** <CSTR> פְּלַגּוֹת נָהָר *streams of oil* Jb 20$_{17}$ (if em. נַהֲרֵי *rivers of*; or em. to נָהֳרִי *of my oil*).

נְהָרָה 1.1 n.f. **light,** <SUBJ> יפע hi. *shine* Jb 3$_{4}$ (+ חֹשֶׁךְ *darkness*). <OBJ> נבט hi. *cause to be seen* Si 43$_{1(Bmg)}$ (B הדרו *its splendour*).

⇒ נהר II *shine*.

נַהֲרַיִם *Naharaim*, see אֲרָם *Aram*, §2a.

נוא 8.0.8 vb. **restrain—Qal** 1 Impf. Kt תנואון—see Hi. §2.

Hi. 8.0.8 Pf. הֵנִיא; impf. יָנִיא (יָנִי, Q יניאה, Q יאנה), Qr תְּנִיאוּן; + waw וַיָּנִיאוּ; inf. abs. Sam הָנֵא; cstr. Q הניא—**1a. restrain, oppose,** woman in making of vow, <SUBJ>

אִישׁ *husband* Nm 30$_{9}$ (+ פרר hi. *annul*) 30$_{12}$, אָב *father* Nm 30$_{6.6}$ 11QT 53$_{20.21}$. <OBJ> אִשָּׁה *woman* Nm 30$_{6.6.9}$ 11QT 53$_{20.21}$, אַלְמָנָה *widow* Nm 30$_{12}$, גְּרוּשָׁה *divorced woman* Nm 30$_{12}$. <PREP> בְּ of time, *on*, + יוֹם *day* Nm 30$_{6.9}$ 11QT 53$_{20}$. <COLL> inf. abs. + finite form of נוא hi. Nm 30$_{6(Sam)}$ 11QT 53$_{20}$.

1b. annul, make ineffectual, oath made by woman, <SUBJ> אִישׁ *man, husband* CD 16$_{10}$ (ה[אישׁ]) 16$_{11.11.12}$ (both :: קום hi. *let stand*). <OBJ> שְׁבוּעָה *oath* CD 16$_{10.11.11.12}$. <PREP> בְּ *according to*, + רָצוֹן *will* perh. 4Q416 2.4$_{9}$ (+ פרר hi. *annul*).

2. discourage, <SUBJ> אָב *father* Nm 32$_{9}$, בֵּן *son* of Gad and Reuben Nm 32$_{7(Qr)}$ (Kt תנואון appar. qal, in same sense). <OBJ> לֵב *heart* Nm 32$_{7(Qr)}$ 4QM^{h} 2$_{4}$. <PREP> מִן *from*, + מַעֲשֶׂה *work* 4QM^{h} 2$_{4}$ (מכול מעו[שיהם]). <COLL> נוא hi. + adverb, לָמָּה *why?* Nm 32$_{7(Qr)}$; + מֵעֲבֹר discourage *from crossing over* Nm 32$_{7(Qr)}$, לְבִלְתִּי־בֹא discourage *from entering* Nm 32$_{9}$.

3. hinder, frustrate, <SUBJ> Y. Ps 33$_{10}$ (|| פרר hi. *frustrate*). <OBJ> מַחֲשָׁבָה *plan* Ps 33$_{10}$.

4. refuse, <SUBJ> רֹאשׁ *head* Ps 141$_{5}$ (or em. יָנִי *let it* not *refuse* to יִנְאָ *let it* not *adorn* [נאה pi.] or יָנִיר *let it* not *shine* [ניר II]). <OBJ> שֶׁמֶן *oil* Ps 141$_{5}$ (or em.; see Subj.).

<SYN> §3 פרר hi. *frustrate*.

<ANT> §1b קום hi. *let stand*.*

⇒ תְּנוּאָה *opposition*.

נוב 4.0.5 vb. **flow**—**Qal** 3 Impf. יָנוּב, יְנוּבוּן—**flow (with), be full of sap, prosper,** <SUBJ> צַדִּיק *righteous one* Ps 92$_{15}$ (+ דְּשֵׁנִים וְרַעֲנַנִּים יִהְיוּ *they will be fat*, i.e. full of sap, *and green*), רָשָׁע *wicked one* Ps 58$_{10}$ (if em. יָבִינוּ *they experience* to יְנוּבוּ), פֶּה *mouth* of righteous Pr 10$_{31}$ (:: כרת ni. *be cut off*), חַיִל *wealth* Ps 62$_{11}$. <OBJ> חָכְמָה *wisdom* Pr 10$_{31}$. <PREP> בְּ of time, *in*, + שֵׂיבָה *old age* Ps 92$_{15}$. <COLL> נוב + adverb, עוֹד *still* Ps 92$_{15}$.

<ANT> כרת ni. *be cut off*.

Pol. 1.0.5 Impf. יְנוֹבֵב, 3fs Q תנובב; ptc. Q מנובב—**make flourish, cause to prosper, produce (fruit),** <SUBJ> דָּגָן *grain* Zc 9$_{17}$, תִּירוֹשׁ *new wine* Zc 9$_{17}$, אֶרֶץ *land* 4QapPs^{b} 1$_{8}$ ([הארץ]) 11QM 1.2$_{10}$; subj. not specified, 1QH 16$_{13}$. <OBJ> בָּחוּר *young man* Zc 9$_{17}$, בְּתוּלָה *young woman* Zc 9$_{17}$, פְּרִי *fruit* 1QH 16$_{13}$ 4QSh B$_{3}$ ([פרי]ן) 4QapPs^{b} 1$_{8}$ 11QM 1.2$_{10}$. <PREP> לְ of benefit, *for*, + Israelites 11QM 1.2$_{10}$; בְּ of place, *in, on*, + הַר *mountain* 4QSh B$_{3}$ (ב[ה]רי); of instrument, *by (means of), with*, + חֶרֶט *stylus* 4QparaKings 25$_{4}$; עִם *with* 1QH 16$_{13}$.*

⇒ נוֹב *what flows, fruit*, נִיב *what flows*, תְּנוּבָה *sap, fruit*.

[נוֹב] 1.2 n.[m.] **what flows**—cstr. Kt נוב—**flow, fruit,** in ref. to praise (Is 57$_{19[Kt]}$), item of jewellery (Si 35$_{5[Bmg]}$), <OBJ> ברא *create* Is 57$_{19(Kt)}$. <CSTR> נוב שְׂפָתַיִם *fruit of the lips* Is 57$_{19(Kt)}$ (Qr נִיב *fruit of*), נוב זיר perh. *fruit (consisting) of a setting* Si 35$_{5(Bmg)}$ (B ניב זהב *fruit of gold*). <PREP> מִן of direction, *(away) from*, + עמד *stand* appar. Si 37$_{4(Bmg, D)}$ (B מנגד *opposite*, i.e. aloof); עַל *upon* Si 35$_{5(Bmg)}$.

⇒ נוב *bear fruit*.

נוֹבִי, see נֵיבַי *Nebai*.

נוּגוֹת, see יגה I *be grieved*.

נוד I 24.2.1 vb. **move to and fro**—**Qal** 18.2.1 Pf. נָדוּ; impf. יָנוּד, 3fs Si תנוד, 2ms תָּנוּד, Q ינודו, תְּנֻדוּ; + waw וַיָּנֻדוּ; impv. נוּדִי, נֻדוּ; ptc. נָד; inf. נוּד—**1. sway,** <SUBJ> קָנֶה *reed* 1 K 14$_{15}$. <PREP> בְּ of place, *in*, + מַיִם *water* 1 K 14$_{15}$.

2a. wander, flee, <SUBJ> Israel Jr 4$_{1}$, Chaldaeans Jr 50$_{8}$, אָדָם *human being* Jr 50$_{3}$, אִישׁ *man* 4QMidr Eschat^{b} 8$_{8}$ ([אנשׁי]), כֹּהֵן *priest* Lm 4$_{15}$ (if em. נָצוּ perh. *they fled* to נָדוּ), נָבִיא *prophet* Lm 4$_{15}$ (if em.; see above), יֹשֵׁב *inhabitant* Jr 49$_{30}$, נֶפֶשׁ *soul* Ps 11$_{1}$ (unless subj. צִפּוֹר *bird*), בְּהֵמָה *beast* Jr 50$_{3}$, צִפּוֹר *bird* perh. Ps 11$_{1}$ Pr 26$_{2}$, קָצִיר *harvest* Is 17$_{11}$ (if em. נֵד *heap of* the harvest to נָד *it has fled*), חֶרְפָּה *reproach* Si 34$_{2(Bmg)}$ (B hi.). <PREP> מִתּוֹךְ *from within*, + Babylon Jr 50$_{8}$. <COLL> נוד || נוס *flee* Jr 49$_{30}$, הלך *go* Jr 50$_{3}$, יצא *go out* Jr 50$_{8}$, עוף *fly* Pr 26$_{2}$; + adverb, מְאֹד *much*, i.e. far away Jr 49$_{30}$; נודו הַרְכֶם צִפּוֹר *flee to your mountain (as) a bird* Ps 11$_{1(Kt)}$ (unless, *flee to your mountain, O bird[s]*; Qr נוּדִי), רע נאמן תנוד חרפה appar. *reproach flees (from)* *a faithful friend* Si 34$_{2(Bmg)}$ (B hi.).

2b. ptc. as noun, **wanderer,** <SUBJ> היה *be* Gn 4$_{12.14}$. <NOM CL> באין אשה נע ונד *without a wife there is*, i.e. one without a wife is, *a vagabond and a wanderer* Si 36$_{30}$. <COLL> || נוע ptc. *fugitive* Gn 4$_{12.14}$ (both נָע וָנָד) Si 36$_{30}$.

3. shake head, i.e. **show grief, sympathize,** <SUBJ> Naamathite Jb 2$_{11}$, Shuhite Jb 2$_{11}$, Temanite Jb 2$_{11}$, Bildad Jb 2$_{11}$, Eliphaz Jb 2$_{11}$, Jeremiah Jr 16$_5$, Zophar Jb 2$_{11}$, אִישׁ *man*, i.e. each one Jb 2$_{11}$, אָח *brother* Jb 42$_{11}$, אָחוֹת *sister* Jb 42$_{11}$, ידע ptc. *one who knows* Jr 48$_{17}$ Jb 42$_{11}$, רֵעַ *friend* Jb 2$_{11}$, סָבִיב *one round about* Jr 48$_{17}$, מִי *who?* Is 51$_{19}$ Jr 15$_5$ Na 3$_7$; subj. not specified, Jr 22$_{10}$ Ps 69$_{21}$ (unless נוד II *grieve, lament*). <PREP> לְ *for, on account of*, + Jerusalem Is 51$_{19}$ Jr 15$_5$, Nineveh Na 3$_7$, Moab Jr 48$_{17}$, Job Jb 2$_{11}$ 42$_{11}$, אָב *father* Jr 16$_5$, אֵם *mother* Jr 16$_5$, בֵּן *son* Jr 16$_5$, בַּת *daughter* Jr 16$_5$, מֵת *dead one* Jr 22$_{10}$. <COLL> נוד || בכה *weep* Jr 22$_{10}$; + נחם pi. *comfort* Is 51$_{19}$ Na 3$_7$ Ps 69$_{21}$ Jb 2$_{11}$ 42$_{11}$, חמל *have compassion* Jr 15$_5$, ספד *lament* Jr 16$_5$.

<SYN> §2a נוס *flee*, הלך *go*, יצא *go out*, עוף *fly*; §2b נוע ptc. *fugitive*; §3 בכה *weep* Jr 22$_{10}$.

Hi. 3.1 Impf. יָנִיד, 3fs Si תניד, 2ms תְּנִדֵנִי; inf. הָנִיד—**1. cause to wander, cause to flee,** i.e. make destitute (Si 34$_{2[B]}$), <SUBJ> Y. 2 K 21$_8$, יָד *hand* of wicked Ps 36$_{12}$ (or em. תְּנַדֵּנִי *let it* not *fling me*, from נדה II *throw*), חֶרְפָּה *reproach* Si 34$_{2(B)}$. <OBJ> רֶגֶל *foot* of Israel 2 K 21$_8$, רֵעַ *friend* Si 34$_{2(B)}$, worshipper Ps 36$_{12}$ (or em.; see Subj.). <PREP> מִן of direction, *from*, + אֲדָמָה *land* 2 K 21$_8$.

2. shake the head, <SUBJ> עבר ptc. *one who passes* Jr 18$_{16}$. <PREP> בְּ introducing object, + ראשׁ *head* Jr 18$_{16}$.

Htpol. 3 Impf. 2ms תִּתְנוֹדֵד; + waw וְהִתְנוֹדְדָה; ptc. מִתְנוֹדֵד—**1. sway, move to and fro,** <SUBJ> אֶרֶץ *earth* Is 24$_{20}$. <PREP> כְּ *as*, + מְלוּנָה *hut* Is 24$_{20}$. <COLL> נוד htpol. + נוע *stagger* Is 24$_{20}$.

2. shake the head, in mockery, <SUBJ> Moab Jr 48$_{27}$.

3. pity oneself, <SUBJ> Ephraim Jr 31$_{18}$.*

⇨ נִיד *shaking*, נִידָה *shaking of head*, מָנוֹד *shaking*, נוֹד *Nod*.

***נוד II** 1 vb. **grieve, lament—Qal** 1 Ptc. נוּד—ptc. as noun, **one grieving, lamenter,** <PREP> לְ קוה pi. *look for* Ps 69$_{21}$ (unless נוד I *shake the head;* נוּד as qal ptc. or em. נָד); כְּ *as*, + היה *be* Ps 119$_{83}$ (if em. כִּנֹאד *as a skin bottle* to כְּנָאד *as one grieving*).

⇨ נֹד II *grief*.

נוֹד 1 pl.n. **Nod,** prob. symbolic name of land to which Cain was exiled, <CSTR> אֶרֶץ־נוֹד *land of Nod* Gn 4$_{16}$ (+ קִדְמַת עֵדֶן *east of Eden*).*

⇨ נוד *move to and fro*.

נוּד *one grieving, lamenter,* see נוד II *grieve*.

נוֹדָב 1 pr.n.m. **Nodab,** Arabian tribe, <PREP> עִם *with*, + עשׂה *make* war 1 C 5$_{19}$.

נוה I 2 vb. **dwell—Qal** 2 Impf. יִנְוֶה; ptc. נְוַת—**1. dwell, remain** (unless נוה III *aim at*), <SUBJ> גֶּבֶר *man* Hb 2$_5$ (or em. יִרְוֶה *he shall* not *be sated* or יִבָּנֶה *he shall* not *be built up*).

2. fem. ptc. as noun, **(female) dweller, inhabitant,** unless from נָאוֶה *comely*, <SUBJ> חלק pi. *divide* spoil Ps 68$_{13}$ (or em. נְוַת בַּיִת תְּחַלֵּק *the inhabitant of the house divides* to בִּנְאוֹת יְתַחֲלֵק *in meadows* spoil *is divided* or בֵּית נְכֹת יְחֻלַּק *the treasure house shall be divided up*). <CSTR> נְוַת בַּיִת *the inhabitant of the house* Ps 68$_{13}$ (or em.; see Subj.).

⇨ נָוֶה *habitation*, נָוָה *pasture*, (?) נָיוֹת *Naioth*.

נוה II 1.1 vb. **glorify—Hi.** 1 Impf. אַנְוֵהוּ—**glorify** or **beautify** (unless נוה III hi. *admire*), <SUBJ> Moses Ex 15$_2$ (|| רום pol. *exalt*), בֵּן *son* of Israel Ex 15$_2$. <OBJ> אֵל *God* Ex 15$_2$.

<SYN> רום pol. *exalt*.*

Htp. 0.1 Impf. Si. יתנוה—**boast,** <SUBJ> עָשִׁיר *rich one* Si 13$_3$.

⇨ cf. נאה *be fitting, comely*.

***נוה III** 2 vb. **aim at—Qal** 1 Impf. יִנְוֶה—**aim at, achieve, settle,** (unless נוה I *dwell*), <SUBJ> גֶּבֶר *man* Hb 2$_5$.

Hi. 1 Impf. אַנְוֵהוּ—**admire** (unless נוה II hi. *glorify*), <SUBJ> Moses Ex 15$_{2}$ (|| רום pol. *exalt*), בֵּן *son* of Israel Ex 15$_{2}$. <OBJ> אֵל *God* Ex 15$_{2}$.

<SYN> רום pol. *exalt*.

[נָוָה] I 14 n.f. **pasture** (unless cstr. נְאוֹת is from נָאָה *pleasant place, oasis*)—cstr. נְוַת; pl. נָוֹת; cstr. נְאוֹת—**1. pasture, meadow,** <SUBJ> היה *be* Zp 2$_{6}$, דשא *sprout* Jl 2$_{22}$, רעף *drip* Ps 65$_{13}$, יבשׁ *be dry* Jr 23$_{10}$, יצת ni. *be burned* Jr 9$_{9}$ (or em. נִצְּתוּ to נִצּוּ *they are laid waste,* from נצה II ni.), דמם ni. *be destroyed* Jr 25$_{37}$ (unless §2), חטא *be missing* Jb 5$_{24}$ (if em. נָוְךָ *your abode* to נָוְתֵךְ *your pasture*),* אבל *mourn* Am 1$_{2}$.

<OBJ> ירשׁ *possess* Ps 83$_{13}$, פקד *visit* Jb 5$_{24}$ (if em.; see Subj.), אכל *devour* Jl 1$_{19.20}$, שׂים *place*, i.e. make Ml 1$_{3}$ (if em.; see Cstr.).

<CSTR> נְאוֹת אֱלֹהִים *pastures of God* or perh. *finest pastures** Ps 83$_{13}$, הָרֹעִים *of the shepherds* Am 1$_{2}$, מִדְבָּר *of the steppe* Jr 9$_{9}$ 23$_{10}$ Jl 1$_{19.20}$ (הַמִּדְבָּר) 2$_{22}$ Ml 1$_{3}$ (if em. לְתַנּוֹת *for the jackals* to נְוֹת) Ps 65$_{13}$, דֶּשֶׁא *of grass* Ps 23$_{2}$, הַשָּׁלוֹם *of peace* Jr 25$_{37}$ (unless §2).

<PREP> בְּ of place, *in*, + רבץ hi. *cause to lie down* Ps 23$_{2}$, חלק htp. *be divided* Ps 68$_{13}$ (if em. נְוַת בַּיִת תְּחַלֵּק *the inhabitant of the house divides* to בִּנְוֹת יִתְחַלֵּק *in meadows* spoil *is divided*).

עַל *for (the sake of)*, + נשׂא *raise* a dirge Jr 9$_{9}$.

<COLL> נָוָה + הַר *mountain* Jr 9$_{9}$, גִּבְעָה *hill* Ps 65$_{13}$, ראשׁ *top* of Carmel Am 1$_{2}$, אָפִיק *channel* Jl 1$_{20}$, מַיִם *waters* Ps 23$_{2}$, גְּדֵרָה *fold* for sheep Zp 2$_{6}$, כָּרָה *cistern* for shepherd Zp 2$_{6}$.

2. habitation, abode, <OBJ> הרס *tear down* Lm 2$_{2}$, שׁלם pi. *restore* Jb 8$_{6}$, מלא *be full of* Ps 74$_{20}$ (or em.; see Cstr.). <CSTR> נְאוֹת יַעֲקֹב *habitations of Jacob* Lm 2$_{2}$, נְוַת צִדְקֶךָ *habitation of your righteousness*, i.e. your righteous habitation Jb 8$_{6}$, נְאוֹת חָמָס *habitations of violence* Ps 74$_{20}$ (or em. אֲנָחָה וְחָמָס *sighing and violence*). <COLL> נָוָה + מִבְצָר *stronghold* Lm 2$_{2}$, מַמְלָכָה *kingdom* Lm 2$_{2}$.

⇒ נוה I *dwell*.

[נָוָה] II *(female) dweller, inhabitant,* see נוה I *dwell*.

נָוֶה I 32.1 n.m. **habitation**—cstr. נְוֵה; sf. נָוְךָ, נָוֵהוּ, נְוֵהֶם, נְוֵהֶן—**1. habitation, abode** of Y. (Ex 15$_{13}$ 2 S 15$_{25}$ Kh. Beit Lei graf. 6$_{2}$), of Israel (Is 32$_{18}$ Jr 10$_{25}$ 25$_{30}$), of jackals (Is 34$_{13}$ 35$_{7}$); in ref. to city (Is 27$_{10}$ 33$_{20}$), land (Jr 31$_{23}$), Y. as habitation of Israel (Jr 50$_{7}$).

<SUBJ> היה *be* Is 34$_{13}$, שׁלח pu. *be deserted* Is 27$_{10}$, עזב ni. *be forsaken* Is 27$_{10}$. <NOM CL> עִיר בְּצוּרָה ... נָוֶה *the fortified city is ... a habitation* deserted and forsaken Is 27$_{10}$. <OBJ> ראה hi. *let see* 2 S 15$_{25}$, פקד *visit* Jb 5$_{24}$ (or em. נָוְתֵךְ *your pasture*), ברך pi. *bless* Jr 31$_{23}$ Pr 3$_{33}$, קבב *curse* Jb 5$_{3}$, שׁמם hi. *make desolate* Jr 10$_{25}$ Ps 79$_{7}$.

<CSTR> נוה יה *habitation of Yah* Kh. Beit Lei graf. 6$_{2}$ (others נקה יה *Yah has acquitted*), נְוֵה חָכָם *habitation of a wise one* Pr 21$_{20}$, צַדִּיק *of a righteous one* Pr 24$_{15}$, צַדִּיקִים *of the righteous* Pr 3$_{33}$, תַּנִּים *of jackals* Is 34$_{13}$, קָדְשֶׁךָ *of your holiness*, i.e. your holy habitation Ex 15$_{13}$, שָׁלוֹם *of peace* Is 32$_{18}$, צֶדֶק־ *of righteousness* Jr 31$_{23}$ 50$_{7}$.

<APP> י׳ Y. Jr 50$_{7}$, יְרוּשָׁלַםִ *Jerusalem* Is 33$_{20}$, אֹהֶל *tent* Is 33$_{20}$, הַר *mountain* Jr 31$_{23}$.

<ADJ> שַׁאֲנָן *at ease* Is 33$_{20}$.

<PREP> לְ *against*, + חטא *sin* Jr 50$_{7}$, ארב *lie in wait* Pr 24$_{15}$; בְּ of place, *in* Is 35$_{7}$ Pr 21$_{20}$, + ישׁב *dwell* Is 32$_{18}$; אֶל *to*, + נהל pi. *lead* Ex 15$_{13}$; עַל *upon*, + זרה pu. *be scattered* Jb 18$_{15}$; *against*, + שׁאג *roar* Jr 25$_{30}$.

<COLL> נָוֶה + בַּיִת *house* Pr 3$_{33}$, מִשְׁכָּן *dwelling place* Is 32$_{18}$, אֹהֶל *tent* Jb 5$_{24}$ 18$_{15}$, חָצִיר *grass*, i.e. habitation Is 34$_{13}$ (1QIsa[a] חצר *court*), מְנוּחָה *resting place* Is 32$_{18}$, רֵבֶץ *resting place* Pr 24$_{15}$, מִקְוֵה *hope* Jr 50$_{7}$.

נָוֶה as vocative, Jr 31$_{23}$.

2. pasture, grazing land, meadow (distinction from §1 not alw. clear), <SUBJ> היה *be* Ezk 34$_{14}$. <NOM CL> בְּכָל־עָרָיו נְוֵה רֹעִים *in all its cities there shall be pasture for shepherds* Jr 33$_{12}$. <OBJ> ראה *see* Jr 4$_{25}$ (if em. וְהִנֵּה *and behold* to הַנָּוֶה), שׁמם hi. *make appalled* Jr 49$_{20}$ 50$_{45}$.

<CSTR> נְוֵה רֹעִים *pasture of*, i.e. for, *shepherds* Jr 33$_{12}$, צֹאן־ *of sheep* Is 65$_{10}$, גְּמַלִּים *of camels* Ezk 25$_{5}$, אֵיתָן *of continuity* Jr 49$_{19}$ 50$_{44}$, מַעֲנָג *of delight* Jr 6$_{2}$ (if em.; see Prep.), נוה צמחים *pasture of shoots* Si 43$_{21(B)}$ (Bmg צור *rock of*).

<ADJ> טוֹב *good* Ezk 34$_{14}$.

<PREP> לְ introducing predicate, + היה *be* Is 65$_{10}$; introducing object, + נתן *give*, i.e. make into Ezk 25$_{5}$; indicating comparison, + דמה *be like* Jr 6$_{2}$ (if em. הַנָּוָה וְהַמְּעֻנָּגָה דָּמִיתִי *the comely and the delicate one I will destroy* to הֲלִנְוֵה מַעֲנָג דָּמְתָה *is she like a pasture of delight?*); בְּ of place, *in, on*, + רבץ *lie down* Ezk 34$_{14}$, שׁתל pass. *be planted* Ho 9$_{13}$; מִן of direction, *from*, + לקח *take* 2 S 7$_{8}$||1 C 17$_{7}$ (+ מֵאַחַר הַצֹּאן *from after the sheep*); אֶל *to*, + עלה *to up* Jr 49$_{19}$ 50$_{44}$, שׁוב pol. *bring back* Jr 50$_{19}$; עַל *(on)to*, + שׁוב hi. *bring back* Jr 23$_{3}$. <COLL> נָוֶה || מִרְעֶה *pasture* Ezk 34$_{14}$, רֵבֶץ *resting place* Is 65$_{10}$, מִרְבָּץ *resting place* Ezk 25$_{5}$.

<SYN> מִרְעֶה *pasture*, רֵבֶץ *resting place*, מִרְבָּץ *resting place*.*

⇒ נוה I *dwell*.

*[נָוֶה] II $_{0.0.0.1}$ pr.n.[m.] **Naveh**, Ḥorvat ʿUza jar inscr. 2$_{8}$.

נוח I $_{142.15.14.1}$ vb. **rest**—**Qal** $_{33.9.2.1}$ Pf. נָחָה, נַחְתִּי, נָחוּ; impf. יָנוּחַ, 3fs תָּנוּחַ, 2ms תָּנוּחַ, אָנוּחַ, יָנוּחוּ; + waw וְנָחָה, וַיָּנוּחוּ, 3fs וַתָּנַח, וַיָּנַח, וַנָּנַח, וְנָחוּ; ptc. Q נחה; inf. abs. נוֹחַ; cstr. נוֹחַ (נוּחַ, נְחֹה).

1. rest, settle down; rest upon, i.e. form alliance with (Is 7$_{2}$), <SUBJ> Aram Is 7$_{2}$ (unless נחה II *turn to*), אָדָם *human being* Pr 21$_{16}$, חַיָּה *beast* 2 S 21$_{10}$, אַרְבֶּה *locust* Ex 10$_{14}$, דְּבוֹרָה *bee* Is 7$_{19}$, עוֹף *birds* 2 S 21$_{10}$, יָד *hand* Is 25$_{10}$ Ps 38$_{3}$ (if em. וַתִּנְחַת *it came down* to וַתָּנַח), כַּף *sole* Jos 3$_{13}$, רוּחַ *spirit* Nm 11$_{25.26}$ 2 K 2$_{15}$ Is 11$_{2}$, אֲרוֹן *ark* Nm 10$_{36}$, תֵּבָה *ark* Gn 8$_{4}$ 4QCommGenA 1$_{10}$, שֵׁבֶט *sceptre* Ps 125$_{3}$, חָכְמָה *wisdom* Pr 14$_{33}$, כַּעַס *anger* Ec 7$_{9}$, רֹגֶז *anger* Si 5$_{6(A)}$, בְּרָכָה *blessing* Si 44$_{23}$.

<PREP> בְּ of place, *in*, + קָהָל *assembly* Pr 21$_{16}$, לֵב *heart* Pr 14$_{33}$, חֵיק *bosom* Ec 7$_{9}$, נַעֲצוּץ *thorn-bush* Is 7$_{19}$, גְּבוּל *border*, i.e. territory Ex 10$_{14}$, נָקִיק *cleft* of rock Is 7$_{19}$, הַר *mountain* Is 25$_{10}$, נַהֲלֹל *watering place* Is 7$_{19}$, נַחַל *wadi* Is 7$_{19}$, מַיִם *water* Jos 3$_{13}$; of time, *in, on*, + חֹדֶשׁ *month* Gn 8$_{4}$, יוֹם *day* Gn 8$_{4}$ 4QCommGenA 1$_{10}$.

עַל *upon*, + Ephraim Is 7$_{2}$ (unless נחה II *turn to*), Eldad Nm 11$_{26}$, Elisha 2 K 2$_{15}$, Medad Nm 11$_{26}$, אִישׁ *man* Nm 11$_{25}$, בֵּן *son* 2 S 21$_{10}$, זָקֵן *elder* Nm 11$_{25}$, worshipper Ps 38$_{3}$ (if em.; see Subj.), רָשָׁע *wicked one* Si 5$_{6(A)}$, רֹאשׁ *head* Si 44$_{23}$, חֹטֶר *shoot* Is 11$_{2}$, נֵצֶר *branch* Is 11$_{2}$, הַר *mountain* Gn 8$_{4}$ 4QCommGenA 1$_{10}$, גּוֹרָל *lot* Ps 125$_{3}$.

<COLL> נוח :: נסע *journey* Nm 10$_{36}$; + adverb, יוֹמָם *by day* 2 S 21$_{10}$, לַיְלָה *by night* 2 S 21$_{10}$.

2. have rest, repose, <SUBJ> Y. Ex 20$_{11}$, Jews Est 9$_{18.22}$, Daniel Dn 12$_{13}$, Job Jb 3$_{26}$, Samuel Si 46$_{19}$, בֵּן *son* appar. Si 36$_{4}$ (if em. תגיה appar. *you will cause to shine* [i.e. נגה hi.] to תנוח *you will rest*) Si 40$_{5}$, עֶבֶד *servant* Dt 5$_{14}$, אָמָה *female servant* Dt 5$_{14}$, יְגִיעַ *weary one* Jb 3$_{17}$, עָנִי *poor one* Si 34$_{4.4}$, עָשִׁיר *rich one* Si 34$_{3}$, הלך ptc. *one who goes* Is 57$_{2}$, שׁוֹר *ox* Ex 23$_{12}$, חֲמוֹר *ass* Ex 23$_{12}$, נֶפֶשׁ *soul* Antinoopolis inscr.2, אֶרֶץ *earth* Is 14$_{7}$, שְׁאָר *remainder* of Jews Est 9$_{16}$ (or em. נָקוֹם or נִקּוֹם *taking vengeance* or נִחוֹם *gaining satisfaction*) 9$_{17}$, שַׁוְעָה *cry for help* Si 32$_{21}$, אֲפֵלָה *darkness* 4Q392 1$_{5}$, impersonal Is 23$_{12}$ Jb 3$_{13}$ Ne 9$_{28}$ Si 34$_{4.21}$ ([ינוח]).

<PREP> לְ of benefit, *to, for*, + Israelites Ne 9$_{28}$, Job Jb 3$_{13}$, בֵּן *son* Si 34$_{21}$ ([ינוח לך]), בְּתוּלָה *young woman* Is 23$_{12}$, עָנִי *poor one* Si 34$_{4}$.

בְּ of place, *in*, + צְרוֹר *bundle* of life Antinoopolis inscr.2; of time, *in, on*, + יוֹם *day* Ex 20$_{11}$ Est 9$_{17.18.22}$.

מִן *from*, + אֹיֵב *enemy* Est 9$_{16}$ (or em.; see Subj.) 9$_{22}$.

עַל *upon*, + מִשְׁכָּב *bed* Is 57$_{2}$ Si 40$_{5}$ 46$_{19}$.

לִפְנֵי *before*, + Y. 4Q392 1$_{5}$.

<COLL> נוח || נפשׁ ni. *be refreshed* Ex 23$_{12}$, שׁקט *be quiet* Is 14$_{7}$ Jb 3$_{13}$ (+) 3$_{26}$, שׁלו *be at ease* Jb 3$_{26}$; + ישׁן *sleep* Jb 3$_{13}$; + adverb, אָז *then* Jb 3$_{13}$, אַחַר *afterwards* Si 36$_{4}$ (if em.; see Subj.), שָׁם *there* Is 23$_{12}$ Jb 3$_{17}$.

3. cease speaking, <SUBJ> נַעַר *lad* 1 S 25$_{9}$.

4. wait quietly for (unless נוח II *sigh*), <SUBJ> Habakkuk Hb 3$_{16}$. <PREP> לְ introducing object, + יוֹם *day* Hb 3$_{16}$.

<SYN> §2 נפשׁ ni. *be refreshed*, שׁקט *be quiet*, שׁלו *be at ease*.

<ANT> §1 נסע *journey*.

Hi. A. $_{33.2.4}$ Pf. הֵנִיחַ, הֵנִיחוּ; impf. יָנִיחַ (וִינִיחֲךָ), 3fs תָּנִיחַ; + waw וְהֵנִיחַ, וְהֵנַחְתִּי (וְהֵנִחוֹתִי), וַיָּנַח (וַיְנִיחֵנִי); impv. הָנִיחוּ; ptc. מֵנִיחַ; inf. הָנִיחַ (הֲנִיחִי, Q הניחנו).

1. cause to rest, give rest to, <SUBJ> Y. Ex 33$_{14}$ Dt 3$_{20}$ 12$_{10}$ 25$_{19}$ Jos 1$_{13.15}$ 21$_{44}$ 22$_{4}$ 23$_{1}$ 2 S 7$_{1.11}$ 1 K 5$_{18}$ Is

14$_{3}$ 57$_{18}$ (if em. וְאַנְחֵהוּ *and I will lead him* [i.e. נחה hi.] to וַאֲנִחֵהוּ *and I will give him rest*) 1 C 22$_{9.18}$ 23$_{25}$ 2 C 14$_{5.6}$ 15$_{15}$ 20$_{30}$ 32$_{22}$ (if em. וַיְנַהֲלֵם *and he led them* to וַיָּנַח לָהֶם *and he gave them rest*) Si 47$_{13}$ 4QMidrEschat^{a} 3$_{7}$ 4QDibHam^{a} 3.2$_{2}$ 4Q417 1.1$_{22}$ 4Q418 8$_{9}$, עַם *people* Is 28$_{12}$, בֵּן *son* Pr 29$_{17}$, רוּחַ *spirit* of Y. Is 63$_{14}$ (unless §5; or em. תַּנְחֵנוּ *it led him* or תַּנְחֵם *it led them*, i.e. נחה hi.), זֶה *this* Gn 5$_{29}$ (if em. יְנַחֲמֵנוּ *he will comfort us* to יְנִיחֵנוּ *he will give us rest*).

<OBJ> Israel(ites) Is 57$_{18}$ (if em.; see Subj.) 63$_{14}$ (unless §5; or em.; see Subj.) Pr 29$_{17}$, Lamech and family Gn 5$_{29}$ (if em.; see Subj.).

<PREP> לְ of direction, *to* or introducing object, + Israel(ites) Dt 12$_{10}$ 25$_{19}$ Jos 1$_{13}$ 21$_{44}$ 22$_{4}$ 23$_{1}$ Is 14$_{3}$ 1 C 22$_{18}$ 4QMidrEschat^{a} 3$_{7}$ 4QDibHam^{a} 3.2$_{2}$, Judah 2 C 14$_{6}$ 15$_{15}$, עַם *people* 1 C 23$_{25}$, Asa 2 C 14$_{5}$, David 2 S 7$_{11}$, Jehoshaphat 2 C 20$_{30}$, Moses Ex 33$_{14}$, Solomon 1 K 5$_{18}$ Si 47$_{13}$, בֵּן *son* 1 C 22$_{9}$, אָח *brother* Dt 3$_{20}$ Jos 1$_{15}$, מֶלֶךְ *king* 2 S 7$_{1}$, עֶבֶד *servant* 2 S 7$_{11}$, עָיֵף *weary one* Is 28$_{12}$, יֹשֵׁב *inhabitant* 2 C 32$_{22}$ (if em.; see Subj.), נֶפֶשׁ *soul* 4Q417 1.1$_{22}$.

כְּ *as (likewise to)*, + Israelites Jos 1$_{15}$, בְּהֵמָה *beast* Is 65$_{15}$; *according to*, + כֹּל *everything* Jos 21$_{44}$.

מִן privative, *from, (so as to be) without*, + בֵּן *son* of Belial 4QMidrEschat^{a} 3$_{7}$, אֹיֵב *enemy* Dt 12$_{10}$ 25$_{19}$ Jos 23$_{1}$ 2 S 7$_{1.11}$ 1 C 22$_{9}$, עֹצֶב *pain* Is 14$_{3}$, רֹגֶז *turmoil* Is 14$_{3}$, עֲבֹדָה *service* Is 14$_{3}$, סָבִיב *round about*, i.e. on every side Jos 21$_{44}$ 2 S 7$_{1}$ 1 K 5$_{18}$ 1 C 22$_{9.18}$ 2 C 14$_{6}$ 15$_{15}$ 20$_{30}$ Si 47$_{13}$.

2. pacify, satisfy, <SUBJ> Y. Ezk 5$_{13}$ 16$_{42}$ 21$_{22}$ 24$_{13}$. <OBJ> חֵמָה *anger* Ezk 5$_{13}$ 16$_{42}$ 21$_{22}$ 24$_{13}$. <PREP> בְּ *upon*, + Israelites Ezk 5$_{13}$, עִיר *city* Ezk 24$_{13}$, זוֹנָה *prostitute* Ezk 16$_{42}$.

3. relieve, <SUBJ> רֹפֵא *physician* Si 38$_{7}$. <OBJ> מַכְאוֹב *pain* Si 38$_{7}$. <PREP> בְּ of instrument, *by (means of), with*, + תְּרוּפָה *medicine* Si 38$_{7}$.

4. quieten, still, cause to cease, <SUBJ> עַם *people* 1QM 17$_{14}$ (ינח[ו]). <OBJ> קוֹל *sound* of alarm 1QM 17$_{14}$.

5. (as **Hi. B**), **cause to rest upon, set down, lower,* place,** <SUBJ> Y. Is 30$_{32}$ Is 63$_{14}$ (unless §1) Ezk 40$_{2}$ (or em. וַתַּנְחֵנִי *and it led me*, i.e. נחה hi.) Ps 139$_{10}$ (if em. תַּנְחֵנִי *it will lead me* to תְּנִיחֵנִי *you will cause to rest upon me*),* Moses Ex 17$_{11}$, כֹּהֵן *priest* Ezk 44$_{30}$, יצא ptc. *one who goes out* Zc 6$_{8?}$, מִי *who?* Ps 60$_{11}$=108$_{11}$ (if em. נָחֵנִי who *will lead me?* to יְנִיחֵנִי who *will place me?*).

<OBJ> 1. that which is set down, Ezekiel Ezk 40$_{2}$ (or em.; see Subj.), worshipper Ps 60$_{11}$=108$_{11}$ (if em.; see Subj.), יָד *hand* Ex 17$_{11}$ Ps 139$_{10}$ (if em.; see Subj.), רוּחַ *spirit* Is 63$_{14}$ (unless §1) Zc 6$_{8}$, מַטֶּה *staff* Is 30$_{32}$, בְּרָכָה *blessing* Ezk 44$_{30}$. 2. set down upon, Moses Is 63$_{14}$ (unless §1), worshipper Ps 139$_{10}$ (if em.; see Subj.).

<PREP> בְּ of place, *in*, + אֶרֶץ *land*; אֶל *upon*, + בַּיִת *house* Ezk 44$_{30}$, הַר *mountain* Ezk 40$_{2}$ (or em.; see Subj.); עַל *upon*, + Assyrians Is 30$_{32}$; נוח hi. + noun without preposition, עַד *(upon the) throne* Ps 60$_{11}$=108$_{11}$ (if em.; see Subj.). <COLL> נוח hi. :: רום hi. *raise* Ex 17$_{11}$.

<ANT> §5 רום hi. *raise*.

Hi. B. 71.5.8 Pf. הִנִּיחַ (הִנַּח), Si הנחתי, הִנִּיחוּ; impf. יַנִּיחַ, 2ms תַּנַּח (תַּנְחֵנִי, תַּנִּיחֵנִי), אַנִּיחֶנּוּ, יַנִּיחוּ (יַנִּיחֻהוּ); + waw וְהִנִּיחַ (וְהִנִּיחוֹ, וְהִנִּיחָם, וְהִנַּחְתָּם), Si והניחתך, וְהִנַּחְתָּ (וְהִנַּחְתּוֹ), וַיַּנִּיחֵהוּ (וַיַּנַּח; וְהִנַּחְתֶּם, וְהִנִּיחוּךָ) וְהִנִּיחוּ, (וְהִנַּחְתִּיו) וְהִנַּחְתִּי, וַיַּנִּיחוּם, וַיַּנִּחֻהוּ, וַיַּנִּיחֻהוּ (וַיַּנִּיחוּ), 3fs וַתַּנַּח, וַיַּנִּיחֵם, וַיַּנִּחֵהוּ, (וַיַּנִּחוּם); impv. הַנַּח, הַנִּיחָה, הַנִּיחוּ (הַנִּחוּ); ptc. מַנִּיחַ, Q מניחים; inf. הַנִּיחוֹ (הַנִּיחָם).

1. place, set down, set aside; cause to rest, lower,* <SUBJ> Y. Gn 2$_{15}$ Is 14$_{1}$ Ezk 22$_{20}$ (or em. וְנָפַחְתִּי *and I will blow* or וְהִפַּחְתִּי *and I will cause to blow*) 37$_{1.14}$ Ps 61$_{3}$ (if em. תַּנְחֵנִי *may you lead me* [i.e. נחה hi.] to תַּנִּחֵנִי *may you place me*) Si 5$_{6(C)}$ (A ינוח *it will rest*) 16$_{11}$ (if em. יגיה *he will cause to blaze*, i.e. נגה hi.), Israel(ites) Lv 7$_{15}$ 24$_{12}$ Dt 14$_{28}$ 26$_{10}$ 4QOrd^{a} 1.2$_{5}$, גּוֹי *nation* 2 K 17$_{29}$, עֵדָה *assembly* Nm 15$_{34}$, בַּיִת *house* of Israel Am 5$_{7}$, Aaron Ex 16$_{33.34}$ Lv 16$_{23}$ Nm 15$_{34}$, Gideon Jg 6$_{18.20}$, Moses Nm 15$_{34}$ 17$_{19.22}$ 1 K 8$_{9}$, Samuel 1 S 10$_{25}$, Solomon 1 K 10$_{26}$ (if em. וַיַּנְחֵם *and he led them* to וַיַּנִּחֵם *and he placed them*) 2 C 1$_{14}$ 4$_{8}$ 9$_{25}$.

אִישׁ *man* Gn 19$_{16}$ Nm 19$_{9}$ Jos 4$_{3}$ 4QTohB^{b} 1$_{8}$ (... איש] והנ]יחוהו), אִשָּׁה *woman* Zc 5$_{11}$ (if em. וְהֻנִּיחָה *and it will be placed* [i.e. ho.] to וְהִנִּיחֻהָ *and they will place it*), *wife* Gn 39$_{16}$, בֵּן *son* 1 K 13$_{31}$ Ezk 44$_{19}$, of Israel Ex 16$_{23.24}$ Jos 4$_{8}$, אָח *brother* Gn 42$_{33}$, נַעַר *lad* Jos 6$_{23}$, מֶלֶךְ *king* 2 K 18$_{11}$ (if em. וַיַּנְחֵם to וַיַּנִּחֵם), כֹּהֵן *priest* Dt 26$_{4}$

Ezk 42$_{13.14}$ 44$_{19}$, לֵוִי *Levite* 1 S 6$_{18}$ Ezk 44$_{19}$, נָבִיא *prophet* 1 K 13$_{29.30}$, מְרַגֵּל *spy* Jos 6$_{23}$, חָזָק *strong one* Is 28$_{2}$, אַמִּיץ *mighty one* Is 28$_{2}$, זול ptc. *one who lavishes* Is 46$_{7}$; subj. not specified, Ezk 40$_{42}$ Ec 11$_{6}$ (unless §4).

<OBJ> אֱלֹהִים *god* 2 K 17$_{29}$, אֵל *god* Is 46$_{7}$, Israelites Is 14$_{1}$ 2 K 18$_{11}$ (if em.; see Subj.), עַם *people* Ezk 37$_{14}$, מִשְׁפָּחָה *clan* Jos 6$_{23}$, בַּיִת *house* of Israel Ezk 22$_{20}$ (or em.; see Subj.), Ezekiel Ezk 37$_{1}$, Lot Gn 19$_{16}$, אָדָם *human being* Gn 2$_{15}$, אִישׁ *man* Nm 15$_{34}$ 1 K 13$_{29}$, בֵּן *son* Lv 24$_{12}$, אָח *brother* Gn 42$_{33}$, פָּרָשׁ *cavalry* 1 K 10$_{26}$ (if em.; see Subj.) 2 C 1$_{14}$ 9$_{25}$, worshipper Ps 61$_{3}$ (if em.; see Subj.), יָד *hand* Ec 11$_{6}$ (unless §4), בָּשָׂר *flesh* Jg 6$_{20}$, עֶצֶם *bone* 1 K 13$_{31}$, נְבֵלָה *corpse* 1 K 13$_{30}$, מַצָּה *unleavened bread* Jg 6$_{20}$, מָן *manna* Ex 16$_{33.34}$, פְּרִי *fruit* Dt 26$_{10}$.

בֶּגֶד *garment* Gn 39$_{16}$ Lv 16$_{23}$ Ezk 42$_{14}$ 44$_{19}$ 11QT 32$_{10}$, מַטֶּה *rod* Nm 17$_{19.22}$, טֶנֶא *basket* Dt 26$_{4}$, כְּלִי *vessel* Ezk 40$_{42}$, אֲרוֹן *ark* 1 S 6$_{18}$, שׁוּלְחָן *table* 2 C 4$_{8}$, סֵפֶר *book* 1 S 10$_{25}$, רֶכֶב *chariot* 1 K 10$_{26}$ (if em.; see Subj.) 2 C 1$_{14}$, מֶרְכָּבָה *chariot* 2 C 9$_{25}$, אֵיפָה *ephah* Zc 5$_{11}$ (if em.; see Subj.), אֶבֶן *stone* Jos 4$_{3.8}$, לוּחַ *tablet* 1 K 8$_{9}$, אֵפֶר *ashes* Nm 19$_{9}$ 4QTohB[b] 1$_{8}$ ([והנ]יחוהו), קֹדֶשׁ *holy thing* Ezk 42$_{13}$, מַעֲשֵׂר *tithe* Dt 14$_{28}$, מִנְחָה *offering* Jg 6$_{18}$ Ezk 42$_{13}$, חַטָּאת *sin offering* Ezk 42$_{13}$, אָשָׁם *guilt offering* Ezk 42$_{13}$, צְדָקָה *righteousness* Am 5$_{7}$, רֹגֶז *anger* Si 5$_{6(C)}$ 16$_{11}$ (if em.; see Subj.), עֹדֶף *excess* Ex 16$_{23.24}$.

<PREP> לְ in ref. to subj. of נוח hi., + בֵּן *son* of Israel Ex 16$_{19}$; of direction, *to*, + אֶרֶץ *earth* Am 5$_{7}$; *for (the purpose of)*, + מִשְׁמֶרֶת *keeping* Ex 16$_{23.33.34}$ 4QTohB[b] 1$_{8}$ ([והנ]יחוהו); *at*, + עֶרֶב *evening* Ec 11$_{6}$ (unless §4).

בְּ of place, *in, onto, on (river)*, + Habor 2 K 18$_{11}$ (if em.; see Subj.), Halah 2 K 18$_{11}$ (if em.; see Subj.), Horeb 1 K 8$_{9}$, Jerusalem 1 K 10$_{26}$ (if em.; see Subj.) 2 C 1$_{14}$ 9$_{25}$, אֹהֶל *tent* Nm 17$_{19.22}$, בַּיִת *house* 2 K 17$_{29}$, מָלוֹן *lodging place* Jos 4$_{3}$, הֵיכָל *temple* 2 C 4$_{8}$, לִשְׁכָּה *chamber* Ezk 44$_{19}$, גַּן *garden* Gn 2$_{15}$, מִשְׁמָר *custody* Lv 24$_{12}$ Nm 15$_{34}$, עִיר *city* 1 K 10$_{26}$ (if em.; see Subj.) 2 C 1$_{14}$ 9$_{25}$, שַׁעַר *gate*, i.e. town Dt 14$_{28}$, מָקוֹם *place* Nm 19$_{9}$, קֶבֶר *grave* 1 K 13$_{30}$, צוּר *rock* Ps 61$_{3}$ (if em.; see Subj.), נָהָר *river* 2 K 18$_{11}$ (if em.; see Subj.); of instrument, *by (means of), with*, + יָד *hand*, i.e. force Is 28$_{2}$.

מִן partitive, *some of*, + בָּשָׂר *flesh* Lv 7$_{15}$.

אֶל *upon*, + חֲמוֹר *ass* 1 K 13$_{29}$, סֶלַע *rock* Jg 6$_{20}$, שׁוּלְחָן *table* Ezk 40$_{42}$.

עַל *upon, at*, + רָשָׁע *wicked one* Si 5$_{6(C)}$ 16$_{11}$ (if em.; see Subj.), אָבֵל הַגְּדוֹלָה *Abel-hagedolah* 1 S 6$_{18}$ (mss אֶבֶן great *stone*), אֲדָמָה *land* Is 14$_{1}$ Ezk 37$_{14}$, מְכוֹנָה *base* Zc 5$_{11}$ (if em.; see Subj.), בַּיִת *house*, i.e. niche 11QT 32$_{10}$ ([בתו]ים).

עִם *with*, + מֶלֶךְ *king* 1 K 10$_{26}$ (if em.; see Subj.) 2 C 1$_{14}$ 9$_{25}$.

אֵת *with*, + אִישׁ *man* Gn 42$_{33}$, אָדוֹן *lord* Gn 42$_{33}$.

מִחוּץ לְ *outside*, + עִיר *city* Gn 19$_{16}$, מַחֲנֶה *camp* Nm 19$_{9}$ Jos 6$_{23}$.

אֵצֶל *beside*, + אִשָּׁה *wife* Gn 39$_{16}$, עֶצֶם *bone* 1 K 13$_{31}$.

בְּתוֹךְ *within*, + בִּקְעָה *valley* Ezk 37$_{1}$.

עַד *until*, + בֹּקֶר *morning* Ex 16$_{23.24}$ Lv 7$_{15}$.

לִפְנֵי *before*, + Y. Ex 16$_{33}$ Nm 17$_{22}$ Dt 26$_{10}$ Jg 6$_{18}$ 1 S 10$_{25}$, עֵדוּת *testimony* Ex 16$_{34}$ Nm 17$_{19}$, מִזְבֵּחַ *altar* Dt 26$_{4}$.

תַּחַת *beneath*, i.e. in one's place, + אֵל *god* Is 46$_{7}$.

<COLL> נוח hi. + adverb, שָׁם *there* Lv 16$_{23}$ Jos 4$_{8}$ 1 K 8$_{9}$ Ezk 42$_{13.14}$ Zc 5$_{11}$ (if em.; see Subj.).

2. leave, leave behind, leave over, abandon, <SUBJ> Y. Nm 32$_{15}$ Jr 14$_{9}$ Ps 119$_{121}$ Jb 12$_{23}$ (if em. וַיַּנְחֵם *and he leads them* [i.e. נחה hi.] to וַיַּנִּחֵם *and he abandons them*), Israelites 11QT 58$_{15}$, גּוֹי *nation* 4QapJoseph[a] 1$_{3}$ ([הגוים]), Ben Sira Si 39$_{32}$, David 1 S 22$_{4}$ (if em. וַיַּנְחֵם *and he led them* [i.e. נחה hi.] to וַיַּנִּחֵם *and he left them*) 2 S 20$_{3}$, Elijah 1 K 19$_{3}$, Koheleth Ec 2$_{18}$, Nebuzaradan Jr 43$_{6}$, אִישׁ *man* Si 44$_{8}$, אָב *father* 2 S 16$_{21}$ Si 44$_{8}$, בֵּן *son* Ps 17$_{14}$, רַב *captain* of guards Jr 43$_{6}$, עזב ptc. *one who forsakes* Y. Is 65$_{15}$, מְאַהֵב *lover* Ezk 16$_{39}$, נֶפֶשׁ *soul* Si 6$_{3}$; subj. not specified, Ec 10$_{4}$.

<OBJ> Israel(ites) Nm 32$_{15}$ Jr 14$_{9}$, גּוֹי *nation* Jb 12$_{23}$ (if em.; see Subj.), אִשָּׁה *woman* 2 S 20$_{3}$ Jr 43$_{6}$, פִּלֶגֶשׁ *secondary wife* 2 S 16$_{21}$ 20$_{3}$, זוֹנָה *prostitute* Ezk 16$_{39}$, אָב *father* 1 S 22$_{4}$ (if em.; see Subj.), אֵם *mother* 1 S 22$_{4}$ (if em.; see Subj.), בֵּן *son* Si 6$_{3}$, אָח *brother* 11QT 58$_{15}$, נַעַר *lad* 1 K 19$_{3}$, worshipper Ps 119$_{121}$, נֶפֶשׁ *soul*, i.e. person Jr 43$_{6}$, שֵׁם *name* Is 65$_{15}$ Si 44$_{8}$, מָקוֹם *place* Ec 10$_{4}$, עָמָל *(product of) toil* Ec 2$_{18}$, עֹמֶדֶת *remnant* 4QapJoseph[a] 1$_{3}$ ([עומדת]), יֶתֶר *excess* Ps 17$_{14}$.

<PREP> לְ of benefit, *to, for*, + Israelites perh. 4Qap

Joseph^{a} 1_{3}, אָדָם *human being* Ec 2_{18}, עוֹלָל *child* Ps 17_{14}, עֹשֵׁק *oppressor* Ps 119_{121}; לְ *as*, + שְׁבוּעָה *curse* Is 65_{15}.

בְּ of place, *in*, + מִדְבָּר *steppe* Nm 32_{15}, עִיר *city* 11QT 58_{15}; *in (the form of), as*, + כְּתָב *writing* Si 39_{32}.

כְּ *as*, + עֵץ dry *tree* Si 6_{3}.

אֵת *with*, + Gedaliah Jr 43_{6}, בֵּן *son* Jr 43_{6}.

אֶת־פְּנֵי *in the presence of*, + מֶלֶךְ *king* 1 S 22_{4} (if em.; see Subj.).

<COLL> נוח hi. + adverb, שָׁם *there* 1 K 19_{3}; וְהִנִּיחוּךְ עֵירֹם וְעֶרְיָה *and I will leave you naked and bare* Ezk 16_{39}.

3. let alone, allow to remain, leave undisturbed, leave unweighed (1 K 7_{47}), <SUBJ> Y. Jg 2_{23} 3_{1} Jr 27_{11}, Israelites 11QT 43_{4} ([יני]חו), Abishai 2 S 16_{11}, Moses Ex 32_{10}, Solomon 1 K 7_{47}, אִישׁ *man* 2 K 23_{18}, מֶלֶךְ *king* Est 3_{8}; subj. not specified, Ho 4_{17} 4QMMT B_{10}.

<OBJ> עַם *people* Est 3_{8}, גּוֹי *nation* Jg 2_{23} 3_{1} Jr 27_{11}, מִנְחָה *grain offering* 4QMMT B_{10} ([מנחת]), כְּלִי *vessel* 1 K 7_{47}.

<PREP> לְ introducing object, + Y. Ex 32_{10}, Ephraim Ho 4_{17}, Benjaminite 2 S 16_{11}, אִישׁ *man* 2 K 23_{18}; of time, *to*, + יוֹם *day* 4QMMT B_{10}, שָׁנָה *year* 11QT 43_{4} ([יני]חו).

מִן of time, *from*, + יוֹם *day* 4QMMT B_{10}, שָׁנָה *year* 11QT 43_{4} ([יני]חו משנה); of cause, *on account of*, + רֹב *abundance* 1 K 7_{47}.

עַל *upon*, + אֲדָמָה *land* Jr 27_{11}.

4. let go of, <SUBJ> נַעַר *lad* Jg 16_{26}, עֶבֶד *servant* 2 S 16_{11}; subj. not specified, Ec 7_{18} 11_{6} (unless §1). <OBJ> Samson Jg 16_{26}, יָד *hand* Ec 7_{18} 11_{6} (unless §1). <PREP> לְ *at*, + עֶרֶב *evening* Ec 11_{6} (unless §1); מִן of direction, *from*, + זֶה *this* Ec 7_{18}. <COLL> נוח hi. :: אחז *hold* Ec 7_{18}.

5. allow, permit, <SUBJ> Y. Ps 105_{14}||1 C 16_{21} 4QpsEzek^{b} 1.24, שָׂבָע *satiety* Ec 5_{11}. <OBJ> אָדָם *human being* Ps 105_{14}, אִישׁ *man* 1 C 16_{21}, בֵּן *son* of Belial 4QpsEzek^{b} 1.24. <PREP> לְ introducing object, + עָשִׁיר *rich one* Ec 5_{11}. <COLL> לֹא־הִנִּיחַ אָדָם לְעָשְׁקָם *he allowed no human being to oppress them* Ps 105_{14}, var. 1 C 16_{21}, אֵינֶנּוּ מַנִּיחַ לוֹ לִישׁוֹן *it does not allow him to sleep* Ec 5_{11}.

Also Si 38_{28} 4QPrFêtes^{c} 189_{4} 11QT 33_{4} ([מני]חים).

<ANT> § 4 אחז *hold*.

Ho. A. 1 Pf. הוּנַח—**be given rest,** <SUBJ> impersonal Lm 5_{5}. <PREP> לְ of direction, *to*, + worshipper Lm 5_{5}.

Ho. B. 5 + waw הֻנִּיחָה; ptc. מֻנָּח—**1. be placed, deposited,** <SUBJ> אֵיפָה *ephah* Zc 5_{11} (or em. וְהִנִּיחֻהָ *and they will place it*, i.e. hi.), כֶּסֶף *silver* perh. 3QTr 9_{10} (כסף מנח הרב *much gold is deposited*; others כסף מן החרם *silver from the consecrated offerings* or כסף מנה חרם *a mina of silver, a consecrated offering*). <PREP> עַל *upon*, + מְכוֹנָה *base* Zc 5_{11} (or em.; see Subj.). <COLL> נוח ho. + adverb, שָׁם *there* Zc 5_{11} (or em.; see Subj.).

2a. be left free, <SUBJ> אֲשֶׁר *that which* Ezk 41_{9} (or em. אֲשֶׁר מֻנָּח to מֻנַּח *free space of* [see below]).

b. ptc. as noun, **free space, open space,** <CSTR> מֻנַּח בֵּית צְלָעוֹת *free space of the place of the side chambers* Ezk 41_{9} (if em.; see §2a Subj.); מְקוֹם הַמֻּנָּח *place of the free space* Ezk 41_{11}. <PREP> לְ of direction, *to(wards)* Ezk 41_{11}.*

⇒ נוֹחַ *rest*, נוּחָה *rest*, מָנוֹחַ I *resting place*, II *Manoah*, מְנוּחָה *resting place*, נִיחֹחַ *soothing*, נַחַת I *quietness*, II *Nahath*, הֲנָחָה *giving of rest*, יָנוֹחַ *Janoah*.

*נוח II 1 vb. **sigh** (unless נוח I *wait quietly for*)—**Qal** 1 Impf. אָנוּחַ—<SUBJ> Habakkuk Hb 3_{16}. <PREP> לְ of cause, *on account of*, + יוֹם *day* of trouble Hb 3_{16}.

⇒ מְנֻחָה *complaint*; cf. אנח *sigh*.

[נוֹחַ] 1.0.2 n.[m.] **rest**—sf. נוּחֶךָ—**1. resting place** of Y., <PREP> לְ of direction, *to(wards)*, + קוּם *arise* 2 C 6_{41} (= Ps 132_{8} מְנוּחָה *resting place*).

2. softness, low pitch, in ref. to trumpet signal to troops, <CSTR> קוֹל נוֹחַ *sound of softness*, i.e. soft sound 1QM $8_{7.14}$ (+ רדד pu. ptc. *subdued*; both + סמך pass. ptc. *sustained*).

⇒ נוח I *rest*.

*[נוּחָה] I n.f. **respite,** <PREP> מִן privative, *without*, + רדף hi. *pursue* Jg 20_{43} (if em. מְנוּחָה appar. *at the resting place* to מְנוּחָה; or em. מִנּוֹחָה *from Nohah* [נוֹחָה III]).

⇒ נוח I *rest*; cf. נוחה *rest*.

נֹוחָה II $_{1}$ pr.n.m. **Nohah,** fourth son of Benjamin, <NOM CL> נוֹחָה הָרְבִיעִי *Nohah was the fourth* 1 C 8$_{2}$.

[נוֹחָה] III pl.n. **Nohah,** town in Benjamin, <PREP> מִן of direction, *from,* + דרך hi. *tread down* Jg 20$_{43}$ (if em. מְנוּחָה *at the resting place* to מִנּוֹחָה *from Nohah*).

***[נוֹחָה]** $_{0.1}$ n.f. **rest**—cstr. Si נוחת—<NOM CL> ... טוב נוחת עולם מכאב נאמן *better is ... everlasting rest than continuous pain* Si 30$_{17}$. <CSTR> נוחת עולם *rest of everlastingness,* i.e. everlasting rest Si 30$_{17}$.

⇒ נוח I *rest*; cf. נוֹחָה I *respite*.

נוט $_{1}$ vb. **shake—Qal** $_{1}$ Impf. 3fs תָּנוּט—**shake, quake,** or **dangle, waver, sway,** <SUBJ> אֶרֶץ *earth* Ps 99$_{1}$ (|| רגז *tremble*), שָׁמַיִם *heavens* Jg 5$_{4}$ (if em. נָטְפוּ׃ הָרִים *they dropped. The mountains* to נָטוּ׃ פְּ־הָרִים *they shook. The mountains,* deleting גַּם־עָבִים נָטְפוּ מָיִם).*

<SYN> רגז *tremble*.

***[נָוִי]** $_{0.0.0.1}$ pr.n.m. **Navi,** father of Hoshaiah, <CSTR> בן נוי *son of Navi* Ḥorvat 'Uza ost. 1$_{3}$.

***[נוֹיָה]** $_{0.0.0.1}$ pr.n.f. **Noijah,** daughter of a king, <APP> בַּת *daughter* Bulla D14. <PREP> לְ of possession, *of, (belonging) to* Bulla D14.

נוית, see נָיוֹת *Naioth*.

נוֹכֵל *deceitful one,* see נכל *be deceitful*.

נוכרי, see נָכְרִי *foreign*.

***[נָוֶל]** n.m. **thread** (of life), <SUBJ> גזר ni. *be cut off* Ezk 37$_{11}$ (if em. נִגְזַרְנוּ לָנוּ *we have indeed been cut off* to נִגְזַר נָוְלֵנוּ *our thread has been cut off*).

נום I $_{6.1.4}$ vb. **be drowsy—Qal** $_{6.1.4}$ Pf. Q נמתי, נָמוּ; impf. יָנוּם; ptc. Q נם; inf. נוּם—**be drowsy, fall asleep, slumber,** <SUBJ> רֹעֶה *shepherd* Na 3$_{18}$, אַבִּיר *mighty one* Ps 76$_{6}$, צֹפֶה *sentry* Is 56$_{10}$, שֹׁמֵר *keeper* Ps 121$_{3.4}$, שֹׁעֶרֶת *doorkeeper* (fem.) 2 S 4$_{6}$ (if em. בָּאוּ עַד־תּוֹךְ הַבַּיִת לֹקְחֵי *those who took* wheat *came inside the house* to שֹׁעֶרֶת הַבַּיִת סֹקֶלֶת *the doorkeeper of the house was cleaning* and וַיַּכֻּהוּ *and they struck him* to וַתָּנָם וַתִּישַׁן *and she became drowsy and slept*), worshipper 11QPs^{a} 24$_{16}$; subj. not specified, Is 5$_{27}$ 4Q424 3$_{5}$. <OBJ> שֵׁנָה *sleep* Ps 76$_{6}$. <COLL> נום || ישן *sleep* Is 5$_{27}$ Ps 121$_{4}$, רדם ni. *be in a deep sleep* 4Q424 3$_{5}$, שׁכן *settle down* Na 3$_{18}$; + שׁכב *lie down* Is 56$_{10}$, חלם *dream* 11QPs^{a} 24$_{16}$; אֹהֲבֵי לָנוּם *they love to slumber* Is 56$_{10}$, [י]נום עד שלוש פעמים *he sleeps up to three times* 4QSD 1.2$_{2}$.

Also Si 40$_{7}$ 4QapJoshua^{a} 17$_{2}$.

<SYN> ישן *sleep,* רדם ni. *be in a deep sleep,* שׁכן *settle down*.

⇒ נוֹם *sleep,* נוּמָה *drowsiness,* תְּנוּמָה *slumber;* cf. נהם II *sleep*.

***נום** II vb. **speak—Qal,** <SUBJ> Y. Is 41$_{27}$ (if em. הִנֵּה הִנָּם *behold, behold them* to הִנְנִי נָם *behold, I am speaking*).

***[נוֹם]** n.[m.] **sleep,** לֹא־יֵאָמֵר עוֹד הַתֹּפֶת וְגֵיא בֶן־הִנֹּם כִּי אִם־גֵּיא הַהֲרֵגָה *it will not again be called Topheth or the Valley of the son of Hinnom, but the Valley of the Murder* Jr 7$_{32}$ (supposing a play on בֶן־הִנֹּם *son of Hinnom* and בֶּן־הַנֹּם *son of sleep,* i.e. child about to be sacrificed).

⇒ נום I *be drowsy*.

נוּמָה $_{1.4}$ n.f. **drowsiness, slumber,** <SUBJ> לבשׁ hi. *clothe* Pr 23$_{21}$. <OBJ> פרע hi. *disturb* Si 34$_{1(B).2(B)}$, פרג hi. *cause to be stunted* Si 34$_{1(Bmg).2(B).2(Bmg)}$, פרד hi. *divide,* i.e. disrupt Si 42$_{9(M, Yadin)}$ ([תפר]יד נומה).

⇒ נום I *be drowsy*.

נון, see נין *increase*.

נוּן $_{30.1.1}$ pr.n.m. **Nun**—נוֹן—father of Joshua, <NOM CL> נוֹן בְּנוֹ *Nun was his son* 1 C 17$_{27}$. <CSTR> בִּן־נוּן *son of Nun* Ex 33$_{11}$ Nm 11$_{28}$ 13$_{8.16}$ 14$_{6.30.38}$ 26$_{65}$ 27$_{18}$ 32$_{12.28}$

34$_{17}$ Dt 1$_{38.23}$ 32$_{44}$ 34$_{9}$ Jos 1$_{1}$ 2$_{1.23}$ 6$_{6}$ 14$_{1}$ 17$_{4}$ 19$_{49.51}$ 21$_{1}$ 24$_{29}$ Jg 2$_{8}$ 1 K 16$_{34}$ Ne 8$_{17}$ (lacking in ms) Si 46$_{1}$ 1QDM 1$_{12}$ ([בן נון]) 4QpsJub[b] 4$_{1}$ ([ב]ן).

נוס I $_{158.2.3}$ vb. **flee—Qal** $_{154.2.2}$ Pf. נָס, נָ֫סָה, נַ֫סְתִּי, נָסוּ, נַסְתֶּם, נָ֫סְנוּ; impf. יָנוּס, 2ms תָּנוּס, אָנ֫וּסָה, יָנ֫וּסוּ (יְנוּסוּן, יָנֻ֫סוּ), תָּנ֫וּסוּ (תְּנוּסוּן, תָּנֻ֫סוּ), נָנוּס (נָנ֫וּסָה); + waw וְנָס, וְנַסְתָּה, וְנָסוּ, וְנַסְתֶּם, וְנַ֫סְנוּ, וַיָּ֫נָס (וַיָּנֹס), 3fs וַתָּנֹס, וַיָּנֻ֫סוּ (וַיָּנ֫וּסוּ); impv. נֻ֫סוּ; ptc. נָס, נָסִים; inf. abs. נֹס, cstr. נוּס (נֻס, נֻסְךָ, נוּסָם, נֻסָם).

1. flee (away), escape, go away, flow away, <SUBJ> חַף *Apis,* Egyptian deity Jr 46$_{15}$ (if em. נִסְחַף *is swept away* to נָס חַף *Apis has fled*), Amorites Jos 10$_{11}$, Aramaeans 2 S 10$_{13.14.18}$||1 C 19$_{14.15.18}$ 1 K 20$_{20}$, Assyrians Is 31$_{8}$, Babylonians Jr 50$_{16}$ 51$_{6}$, Cushites 2 C 14$_{11}$, Egyptians Ex 14$_{25.27}$ Jr 46$_{5}$, Israelites Lv 26$_{17}$ Nm 16$_{34}$ Dt 28$_{25}$ 1 S 4$_{10.17}$ 2 S 18$_{17}$ 19$_{9}$ Is 30$_{16}$ (unless נוס IV *swing*) 30$_{16.17}$ Zc 2$_{10}$ 14$_{5}$ (mss וְנִסְתַּם *and it shall be stopped up,* from סתם) 15$_{5.5}$, Moabites 2 K 3$_{24}$ Jr 48$_{6}$, Philistines 1 S 14$_{22}$ 17$_{51}$ 19$_{8}$, עָם *people* Jos 8$_{5.6.6.15.20}$ 2 S 1$_{4}$ 17$_{2}$ 18$_{3.3}$ 19$_{4}$ 23$_{11}$||1 C 11$_{13}$ 2 K 8$_{21}$ Is 17$_{13}$ Na 3$_{13}$ (if em. נָשִׁים *women* to נָסִים *are fleeing*), מַחֲנֶה *camp,* i.e. army Jg 7$_{21(Qr).22}$ 2 K 7$_{7.7}$, Damascus Jr 49$_{24}$, Gibeah Is 10$_{29}$ (unless נוס II *flee*).

Adoni-bezek Jg 1$_{6}$, Ahaziah 2 K 9$_{27.27}$, Amaziah 2 K 14$_{19}$||2 C 25$_{27}$, Ben-hadad 1 K 20$_{30}$, David 1 S 19$_{10}$ 2 S 24$_{13}$||1 C 21$_{12}$ (1 C if em. נִסְפֶּה *being swept away* [i.e. ספה ni.] to נֻסְכָה *your fleeing*), Gaal Jg 9$_{40}$, Joab 1 K 2$_{28.29}$, Joram 2 K 9$_{23}$, Joseph Gn 39$_{12.13}$, Joshua Jos 8$_{5.6.6.15}$, Jotham Jg 9$_{21}$, Moses Ex 4$_{3}$, Rehoboam 1 K 12$_{18}$|| 2 C 10$_{18}$, Sisera Jg 4$_{15.17}$, Zalmunna Jg 8$_{12}$, Zebah Jg 8$_{12}$, אָדָם *human being* Pr 28$_{17}$, אִישׁ *man* Gn 39$_{15}$ Dt 19$_{11}$ Jos 7$_{4}$ 8$_{20}$ Jg 9$_{51}$ 20$_{45.47}$ 1 S 4$_{10.16}$ 17$_{24}$ 30$_{17}$ 31$_{1.7.7}$|| 1 C 10$_{1.7.7}$ 2 S 18$_{17}$ 19$_{9}$ 2 K 14$_{12}$||2 C 25$_{22}$ Is 13$_{14}$ Jr 50$_{16}$ Am 5$_{19}$, אִשָּׁה *woman* Jg 9$_{51}$, בֵּן *son* 2 S 13$_{29}$ Si 11$_{10(B)}$, of Ammon 2 S 10$_{14}$||1 C 19$_{15}$, of Israel Jg 20$_{32}$ 2 C 13$_{16}$, נַעַר *lad* 1 S 30$_{17}$ 2 K 9$_{10}$, מֶלֶךְ *king* Gn 14$_{10}$ Jos 10$_{16}$ 1 K 12$_{18}$||2 C 10$_{18}$ 2 K 9$_{27.27}$, בַּעַל *lord* Jg 9$_{51}$, עֶבֶד *servants* Gn 39$_{18}$, אֹמֶנֶת *(wet-)nurse* 2 S 4$_{4.4}$, נָבִיא *prophet* 2 K 9$_{10}$.

אֹיֵב *enemy* Dt 28$_{7}$, שׂנא pi. ptc. *one who hates* Nm 10$_{35}$ Ps 68$_{2}$, נכה hi. ptc. *one who strikes* Ex 21$_{13}$ Nm 35$_{11.15}$ Jos 20$_{9}$, רֹצֵחַ *killer* Nm 35$_{6.11.26.32}$ Dt 4$_{42.42}$ 19$_{3.4}$ Jos 20$_{3.4.6}$, רָשָׁע *wicked one* Pr 28$_{1}$, חקק ptc. *one who decrees* Is 10$_{3}$, קַל *swift one* Jr 46$_{6}$, אַמִּיץ *mighty one* Am 2$_{16}$, שָׂכִיר *hired one* Jr 46$_{21}$, עָתוּד *one prepared* for battle 1QM 15$_{9}$ ([ותנוס] ... [ע]תודי), נָס *fugitive* Am 9$_{1}$, יֹשֵׁב *inhabitant* Is 20$_{6}$ Jr 49$_{8.30}$, יתר ni. ptc. *one who remains* 1 K 20$_{30}$, שׁאר ni. ptc. *one who remains* Gn 14$_{10}$ Lv 26$_{36}$, לֵחַ *moisture* Dt 34$_{7}$ (unless נוס III *dry up*) Si 34$_{13}$ (unless both נסס *be dry*), מַיִם *water* Na 2$_{9}$ Ps 104$_{7}$, יָם *sea* Ps 114$_{3.5}$, אוֹר *light* Ps 4$_{7}$ (if em.; see Prep.), צֵל *shadow* Ca 2$_{17}$ 4$_{6}$, יָגוֹן *sighing* Is 35$_{10}$=51$_{11}$ 4QHod[a] 7.2$_{3}$, אֲנָחָה *sighing* Is 35$_{10}$=51$_{11}$, אֶחָד *one* of sons of prophets 2 K 9$_{3}$, אֲשֶׁר *one who* Dt 19$_{5}$; subj. not specified, Is 24$_{18}$ Jr 48$_{44(Qr)}$.

<OBJ> מָנוֹס *flight* Jr 46$_{5}$, מְנוּסָה *flight* Lv 26$_{36}$.

<PREP> לְ in ref. to subj. of נוס, + Assyrians Is 31$_{8}$; of direction, *to,* + אֹהֶל *tent* 1 S 4$_{10}$ 2 S 18$_{17}$ 19$_{9}$ 2 K 8$_{21}$ 14$_{12}$|| 2 C 25$_{22}$, אֶרֶץ *land* Jr 50$_{16}$; of cause, *on account of, at,* + קוֹל *sound* Nm 16$_{34}$; *for (the purpose of),* + עֶזְרָה *help* Is 10$_{3}$ 20$_{6}$.

בְּ of place, time, *in, during, at,* + דֶּרֶךְ *way* Dt 28$_{7.25}$, מִלְחָמָה *battle* 2 S 19$_{4}$, נֶשֶׁף *twilight* 2 K 7$_{7}$, יוֹם *day* Am 2$_{16}$ Zc 14$_{5}$, עֵת *time* 4QM[g] 4$_{3}$ ([וינוס]ו); of instrument, *by (means of), with,* + רֶגֶל *foot* Jg 4$_{15.17}$.

מִן of direction, *from,* + אֶרֶץ *land* Zc 2$_{10}$, מִלְחָמָה *battle* 2 S 1$_{4}$, שָׁם *there* Jos 20$_{6}$ 6QapSamKgs 33$_{3}$; *in (the direction of),* + מֶרְחָק *distance* Is 17$_{13}$; of cause, *on account of, at,* + קוֹל *sound* Is 24$_{18}$, גְּעָרָה *rebuke* Ps 104$_{7}$.

אֶל *to,* + מֶלֶךְ *king* 6QapSamKgs 33$_{3}$, סֶלַע *rock* Jg 20$_{45.47}$, אֹהֶל *tent* Jg 4$_{17}$ 1 K 2$_{28.29}$, אֶרֶץ *land* Is 13$_{14}$, עִיר *city* Nm 35$_{32}$ 1 K 20$_{30}$, אֶחָד *one* of the cities Dt 4$_{42}$ 19$_{5.11}$ Jos 20$_{4}$; *on account of, for the sake of,* + נֶפֶשׁ *soul,* i.e. life 2 K 7$_{7}$.

עַל *upon,* + סוּס *horse* Is 30$_{16}$ (unless נוס IV *swing*); *to,* + מִי *whom?* Is 10$_{3}$; *on account of,* + כֹּל *everything* Si 34$_{13(Bmg)}$.

מֵעַל *from (upon),* + רַב pl. *many* Ps 4$_{7}$ (if em. נְסָה־ *lift upon us* to נָסָה־עָלֵינוּ *he has taken from us* [נָסָה 3 ms pf.; עַל *from*]* or נָס מֵעָלֵינוּ *it has fled from us*.

עַד *as far as,* + Beth-shittah Jg 7$_{22}$, שָׂפָה *lip,* i.e. edge, of Abel-meholah Jg 7$_{22}$, בּוֹר *pit* Pr 28$_{17}$.

מִתּוֹךְ *from within,* + Babylon Jr 51$_{6}$.

לִפְנֵי *before*, + Israel(ites) Dt 28_{7}, Philistines 1 S 4_{17}, אִישׁ *man* Jos $8_{5.6.6}$, אֹיֵב *enemy* Dt 28_{25}, צַר *adversary* 2 S 24_{13}.

מִלִּפְנֵי *from before*, + Israel(ites) 1 C 19_{18}, כֹּל *everything* Si $34_{13(\text{Bmg})}$.

מִפְּנֵי *from before, on account of*, + Israelites Ex 14_{25} Jos 10_{11} 2 S 10_{18} 2 K 3_{24} 4QMg 4_{3} (וינוס[ו]), Judah 2 C 13_{16}, Philistines 1 S 31_{1}||1 C 10_{1} 2 S 23_{11}||1 C 11_{13}, חַיִל *army* 1QM 15_{9} ([תנוסו]), Abimelech Jg 9_{40}, Abishai 2 S 10_{14}||1 C 19_{15}, David 1 S 19_{8}, Joab 2 S 10_{13}||1 C 19_{14}, אִישׁ *man* Jos 7_{4} 1 S 17_{24}, אָח *brother* 1 C 19_{15}, צַר *adversary* 1 C 21_{12} (if em.; see Subj.), אֲרִי *lion* Am 5_{19}, נָחָשׁ *serpent* Ex 4_{3}, חֶרֶב *sword* Is 31_{8}, רַעַשׁ *earthquake* Zc 14_{5}, גְּעָרָה *rebuke* Is 30_{17}, פַּחַד *terror* Jr $48_{44(\text{Qr})}$, כֹּל *everything* Si $34_{13(\text{B})}$.

ה- of direction, *to(wards)*, + אֲפֵק *Aphek* 1 K 20_{30}, לָכִישׁ *Lachish* 2 K 14_{19}||2 C 25_{27}, הַר *mountain* Gn 14_{10}, מִדְבָּר *steppe* Jg $20_{45.47}$, חוּץ *outside* Gn $39_{13.18}$, שָׁם *there* Gn 19_{20} Ex 21_{13} Nm $35_{6.11.15.25.26}$ Dt 4_{42} $19_{3.4}$ Jos $20_{3.9}$.

נוס + noun without preposition or ה- of direction, יְרוּשָׁלַםִ *(to) Jerusalem* 1 K 12_{18}||2 C 10_{18}, מְגִדּוֹ *(to) Megiddo* 2 K 9_{27}, דֶּרֶךְ *(by) way of* Jos 8_{15} 2 K 9_{27}, גֵּיא *(to) the valley* Zc 14_{5} (mss וְנִסְתַּם *and it shall be stopped up*, from סתם), מִדְבָּר *(to the) steppe* Jos 8_{20}.

<COLL> נוס || ברח *flee* Jg 9_{21}, נוד *flee* Jr 49_{30}, חפז *hurry* Ps 104_{7}, מלט ni. *escape* Gn 19_{20} (+) 1 S 19_{10} Jr 46_{6} Am 9_{1}, פוץ *be scattered* Nm 10_{35} Ps 68_{2}, רכב *ride* Is 30_{16}; + יצא *go out* Gn $39_{13.15}$, רוץ *run* Jg $7_{21(\text{Qr})}$, סבב לְאָחוֹר *turn back* Ps $114_{3.5}$, מלט נֶפֶשׁ pi. *save one's life* Jr 48_{6} 51_{6}.

:: חכה pi. *wait* 2 K 9_{3}, עמד *stand* Jr 46_{21}, נשׂג hi. *arrive* Is 35_{10}=51_{11}.

+ adverb, יַחְדָּו *together* Jr 46_{21}, מַדּוּעַ *why?* Jr 46_{15} (if em.; see Subj.), עַל־כֵּן *therefore* Si $34_{13(\text{B})}$, הַיּוֹם *today* 1S 4_{16}, שָׁם *there* Is 20_{6}; with adj. as predicate, עָרוֹם יָנוּס *he shall flee away naked* Am 2_{16}.

Inf. abs. + finite form of נוס, 2 S 18_{3}.

מִבָּטֵנוּ אֲשֶׁר־נַסְנוּ שָׁם *our hope to which we fled* Is 20_{6}, הָעִיר הַזֹּאת קְרֹבָה לָנוּס שָׁמָּה *this city is near enough to flee to* Gn 19_{20}, מָקוֹם אֲשֶׁר יָנוּס שָׁמָּה *a place to which he shall flee* Ex 21_{13}, עָרִים ... לָנֻס שָׁמָּה *cities ... to which to flee* Dt 4_{42}, vars. Dt 19_{3} Jos 20_{9}, עָרֵי מִקְלָט ... לָנֻס שָׁמָּה *cities of refuge ... to flee there* Nm 35_{6} Jos 20_{3}, vars. Nm $35_{11.15.25.26}$, מִצְרַיִם נָסִים לִקְרָאתוֹ *the Egyptians fled at its approach* Ex 14_{27}, יָדַיִם לָנוּס *hands*, i.e. power, *to flee* Jos 8_{20}.

2. ptc. as noun, **fugitive, escaped one,** <SUBJ> נוס *flee* Am 9_{1}, עמד *stand* Jr 48_{45}. <NOM CL> קוֹל נָסִים ... מֵאֶרֶץ בָּבֶל *hark! (there are) fugitives ... from the land of Babylon* 50_{28} (unless *the sound of fugitives*). <OBJ> שׁאל *ask* Jr 48_{19}. <COLL> נוס ptc. || מלט ni. ptc. *escaped one* Jr 48_{19}, פָּלֵט *escaped one* Jr 50_{28}, פָּלִיט *escaped one* Am 9_{1}.

<SYN> §1 ברח *flee*, נוד *flee*, חפז *hurry*, מלט ni. *escape*, פוץ *be scattered*, רכב *ride*; §2 מלט ni. ptc. *escaped one*, פָּלֵט *escaped one*, פָּלִיט *escaped one*.

<ANT> §1 חכה pi. *wait*, עמד *stand*, נשׂג hi. *arrive*.

Polel 1 Pf. נֹסְסָה—**drive on** (unless נסס III *pass to and fro*), <SUBJ> רוּחַ *wind* Is 59_{19}. <PREP> בְּ introducing object, + נָהָר *river* Is 59_{19}.

Hi. 5.0.1 Pf. הֵנִיס; impf. יָנִיסוּ; + waw וַיָּנִיסוּ; inf. הָנִיס—**1. put to flight** (Dt 32_{20} 1QM 3_{5}), **cause to flee (for safety)** (Ex 9_{20}), **remove (to a safe place)** (Jg 6_{11}),* perh. **conceal** (Jg 6_{11}), <SUBJ> Gideon Jg 6_{11} (unless §2), בֵּן *son* Jg 6_{11}, פַּרְעֹה *Pharaoh* Ex 9_{20}, גְּבוּרָה *mighty deed* 1QM 3_{5}, שְׁנַיִם *two* Dt 32_{30}. <OBJ> עֶבֶד *servant* Ex 9_{20}, שׂנא pi. ptc. *one who hates* 1QM 3_{5}, מִקְנֶה *cattle* Ex 9_{20}, חִטָּה *wheat* Jg 6_{11}, רְבָבָה *ten thousand* Dt 32_{30}. <PREP> אֶל *to*, + בַּיִת *house* Ex 9_{20}; מִפְּנֵי *from before, on account of*, + Midianites Jg 6_{11} (unless §2). <COLL> נוס hi. || רדף *pursue* Dt 32_{30}, פוץ hi. *scatter* 1QM 3_{5}.

2. flee, <SUBJ> Moab Jr $48_{44(\text{Kt})}$ (unless הניס is from נִיס *fugitive*), Gideon perh. Jg 6_{11} (unless §1), מַחֲנֶה *camp*, i.e. army Jg $7_{21(\text{Kt})}$ (+ רוץ *run*). <PREP> מִפְּנֵי *from before, on account of*, + Midianites perh. Jg 6_{11} (unless §1), פַּחַד *terror* Jr $48_{44(\text{Kt})}$.

<SYN> §1 רדף *pursue*, פוץ hi. *scatter*.

Htpol. 1 Inf. הִתְנוֹסֵס—**flee (for safety),** unless נסס htpo. *rally to the banner*, <SUBJ> ירא ptc. *one who fears* Ps 60_{6}. <PREP> מִפְּנֵי *from before, on account of*, + קֶשֶׁט *bow* Ps 60_{6}. <COLL> מָנוֹס לְהִתְנוֹסֵס *a refuge to which to flee* Ps 60_{6} (if em. נֵס *banner* to מָנוֹס).*

⇒ מָנוֹס *flight*, מְנוּסָה *flight*.

*נוס II 1 vb. **tremble** (unless נוס I *flee*)—**Qal** 1 Pf. נָסָה—**tremble,** <SUBJ> Gibeah Is 10₂₉ (|| חרד *tremble*).

<SYN> חרד *tremble.*

*נוס III 1 **dry up** (unless נוס I *flee*)—**Qal** 1 Pf. נָס—**dry up,** <SUBJ> לֵחַ *moisture* Dt 34₇.

*נוס IV 1 **swing**—**Qal** 1 Impf. נָנוּס—**swing, dangle,** עַל־סוּס נָנוּס עַל־כֵּן תְּנוּסוּן *upon horse(s) we will swing; therefore you shall flee* (with play on נוס I *flee*) Is 30₁₆ (|| רכב *ride*).

נוע I 41.3.3 vb. **tremble**—**Qal** 25.1 Pf. נָעוּ; impf. 3fs תָּנוּעַ, Kt אנועך ,יְנוּעוּ; + waw וַיָּנַע ,וַיָּנֻעוּ ,וְנָעוּ; ptc. נָעוֹת ,נָע; inf. abs. נוֹעַ; cstr. נוּעַ—**1. tremble, quiver, sway, swing to and fro, stagger,** <SUBJ> אֱלִיל *idol* Is 19₁, Israelites Is 29₉, עָם *people* Ex 20₁₈, ירד ptc. *one who goes down* to the sea Ps 107₂₇, perh. miners Jb 28₄, שָׂפָה *lip* 1 S 1₁₃, לֵבָב *heart* Is 7₂, גֶּפֶן *vine* Jg 9₁₃ (unless נוע II *be rootless*), זַיִת *olive tree* Jg 9₉ (unless נוע II), תְּאֵנָה *fig tree* Jg 9₁₁ (unless נוע II), עֵץ *tree* Is 7₂, אַמָּה *doorpost* Is 6₄, מוֹסָד *foundation* 4QAdmon 1₃ (ו[י]נעו]), אֶרֶץ *earth* Is 9₂₀ (נֶעְתַּם *it is scorched* [עתם ni.] to נָעַת־ם *it trembles*)* 24₂₀.₂₀.

<PREP> כְּ *as,* + שִׁכּוֹר *drunkard* Is 24₂₀ Ps 107₂₇; מִן of cause, *on account of, at,* + קוֹל *voice* Is 6₄; עַל *over,* + עֵץ *tree* Jg 9₉.₁₁.₁₃ (unless all three נוע II *be rootless*); מִפְּנֵי *(from) before, on account of,* + Y. Is 19₁, רוּחַ *wind* Is 7₂.

<COLL> נוע || שכר *be drunk* Is 29₉; + נוד htpol. *sway* Is 24₂₀, דלל *hang down* Jb 28₄, חגג *reel* Ps 107₂₇, מסס ni. *melt* Is 19₁; inf. abs. + finite form of נוע Is 24₂₀; נָעוּ וְלֹא שֵׁכָר *they stagger but not (with) strong drink* Is 29₉.

2. wander, roam, <SUBJ> Israelites Am 8₁₂ Zc 10₂ (if em. נָסְעוּ *they journey* to נָעוּ) 10₂ (if em. יַעֲנוּ *they are afflicted* to יָנֻעוּ), עַם *people* Jr 14₁₀, בֵּן *son* Ps 109₁₀.₁₀, כֹּהֵן *priest* Lm 4₁₄.₁₅, נָבִיא *prophet* Lm 4₁₄.₁₅, שֹׁרֵר *watcher,* i.e. enemy Ps 59₁₆(Kt), עִיר *city* Am 4₈, מַעְגָּל *track* Pr 5₆.

<PREP> בְּ of place, + חוּץ *street* Lm 4₁₄; כְּמוֹ *as,* + צֹאן *sheep* Zc 10₂ (if em.; see Subj.); מִן of direction, *from,* + יָם *sea* Am 8₁₂, צָפוֹן *north* Am 8₁₂; אֶל *to,* + עִיר *city* Am 4₈; עַד *to,* + יָם *sea* Am 8₁₂, מִזְרָח *east* Am 8₁₂.

<COLL> נוע + שׁוט pol. *go to and fro* Am 8₁₂, נוץ *flee* Lm 4₁₅, שׁאל pi. *beg* Ps 109₁₀; + adverb, עִוֵּר *blindly* Lm 4₁₄, עַל־כֵּן *therefore* Zc 10₂ (if em.; see Subj.); + inf. of purpose, of אכל *eat* Ps 59₁₆(Kt), שׁתה *drink* Am 4₈; inf. abs. + finite form of נוע Ps 109₁₀.

3. perh. **beg** by going around as a suppliant, <SUBJ> Israelites Am 8₁₂, עִיר *city* Am 4₈. <PREP> אֶל *to,* + עִיר *city* Am 4₈; עַד *to,* + יָם *sea* Am 8₁₂, מִזְרָח *east* Am 8₁₂. <COLL> נוע + שׁוט pol. *go to and fro* Am 8₁₂; + inf. of purpose, of שׁתה *drink* Am 4₈.

4. ptc. as noun, **vagabond, wanderer,** <SUBJ> היה *be* Gn 4₁₂ (unless נוע II ptc. *rootless person*) 4₁₄. <NOM CL> באין אשה נע ונד *without a wife there is,* i.e. one without a wife is, *a vagabond and a wanderer* Si 36₃₀. <COLL> || נוד ptc. *wanderer* Gn 4₁₂ (unless נוע II ptc. *rootless person*) 4₁₄ (both נָע וָנָד) Si 36₃₀.

5. appar. **cause to wander,** 2 S 15₂₀(Kt) (prob. error for hi., as Qr; see Hi. §3).

<SYN> §1 שׁכר *be drunk;* §3 נוד ptc. *wanderer.*

Ni. 2 Impf. יִנּוֹעַ ,יִנּוֹעוּ—**be shaken,** <SUBJ> תְּאֵנָה *fig tree* Na 3₁₂; subj. not specified, Am 9₉. <PREP> בְּ of instrument, *by (means of), with,* + כְּבָרָה *sieve* Am 9₉.

Hi. 14.2.1 Pf. הֵנִיעָה; impf. יָנִיעַ (יָנַע), אֲנִיעָה (אֲנִיעֶךָ), יְנִיעוּן ,יָנִעוּ (יְנִיעוּן); + waw Q והניעכה ,וַהֲנִעוֹתִי ,וַיְנִעֵם, 3fs וַיָּנֻעוּ ,וַתְּנִיעֵנִי; impv. הֲנִיעֵמוֹ.

1. shake, <SUBJ> Y. Am 9₉, Job Jb 16₄, בַּת *daughter* 2 K 19₂₁||Is 37₂₂, עָשִׁיר *rich one* Si 13₇, אֹיֵב *enemy* Si 12₁₈, שָׂטָן *accuser* Ps 109₂₅, דבר ptc. *one who speaks* evil Ps 109₂₅, ראה ptc. *one who sees* Ps 22₈, עבר ptc. *one who passes by* Zp 2₁₅ Lm 2₁₅, יָד *hand* Dn 10₁₀. <OBJ> Daniel Dn 10₁₀, רֹאשׁ *head* (in scorn) 2 K 19₂₁||Is 37₂₂ Ps 22₈ 109₂₅ Lm 2₁₅ Si 12₁₈, יָד *hand* Zp 2₁₅, בַּיִת *house* of Israel Am 9₉. <PREP> בְּ of place, *in, among,* + גּוֹי *nation* Am 9₉; of instrument, *by (means of), with,* + ראשׁ *head* Si 13₇; בְּמוֹ *by (means of), with,* + רֹאשׁ *head* Jb 16₄; אֶל *to, at,* + בֵּן *son* Si 13₇; עַל *onto,* + בֶּרֶךְ *knee* Dn 10₁₀, כַּף *palm* of hand Dn 10₁₀; *to, at,* + בַּת *daughter* Lm 2₁₅, friends of Job Jb 16₄; אַחֲרֵי *after, behind,* + Sennacherib 2 K 19₂₁||Is 37₂₂, מֶלֶךְ *king* 2 K

19$_{21}$||Is 37$_{22}$. <COLL> נוע hi. || נוף hi. *wave* Si 12$_{18}$.

2. disturb, move, <SUBJ> אִישׁ *man* 2 K 23$_{18}$. <OBJ> עֶצֶם *bone* 2 K 23$_{18}$.

3. cause to wander, <SUBJ> Y. Nm 32$_{12}$ Ps 59$_{12}$, מֶלֶךְ *king* 2 S 15$_{20}$. <OBJ> Israel Nm 32$_{13}$, Gittite 2 S 15$_{20(Qr)}$, Ittai 2 S 15$_{20(Qr)}$, שֹׁרֵר *watcher*, i.e. enemy Ps 59$_{12}$. <PREP> בְּ of place, *in*, + מִדְבָּר *steppe* Nm 32$_{13}$; עִם *with*, + Israelites 2 S 15$_{20(Qr)}$; of instrument, *by (means of), with*, + חַיִל *power* Ps 59$_{12}$. <COLL> נוע hi. + noun used adverbially, הַיּוֹם *today* 2 S 15$_{20(Qr)}$, שָׁנָה *year* Nm 32$_{13}$.

4. wander, <SUBJ> שֹׁרֵר *watcher*, i.e. enemy Ps 59$_{16(Kt)}$ (+ לֶאֱכֹל *in order to eat;* Qr qal).

Also 4QapJoshua^a 3.1$_6$.

<SYN> §1 נוף hi. *wave.*

Htpol. 0.0.2 + waw ויתנועעו—**tremble,** <SUBJ> לֵב *heart* 4QDiscourse 2.2$_7$ (+ מוג htpol. *melt away*, מסס ni. *melt*); subj. not specified, 4QDiscourse 2.2$_9$ (ויתנ[ו]עעו; + מוג htpol.).

⇒ מְנַעַנְעִים *sistrum.*

***נוע** II 4 vb. **be rootless** (unless נוע I *tremble*)—**Qal** 3 Ptc. נָע; inf. נוּעַ—**1. be rootless, without support,** <SUBJ> גֶּפֶן *vine* Jg 9$_{13}$, זַיִת *olive tree* Jg 9$_9$, תְּאֵנָה *fig tree* Jg 9$_{11}$. <PREP> עַל *over*, + עֵץ *tree* Jg 9$_{9.11.13}$.

2. ptc. as noun, **rootless person,** <SUBJ> היה *be* Gn 4$_{12}$ (unless נוע I ptc. *wanderer*).

נוֹעַדְיָה 2 pr.n.m.&f. **Noadiah, 1.** Levite, son of Binnui, <NOM CL> עִמָּהֶם ... נוֹעַדְיָה *with them was ... Noadiah* Ezr 8$_{33}$. <APP> לֵוִי *Levite* Ezr 8$_{33}$.

2. female prophet, opponent of Nehemiah, <APP> נְבִיאָה *prophet* (fem.) Ne 6$_{14}$. <PREP> לְ introducing object, + זכר *remember* Ne 6$_{14}$.

⇒ יעד *appoint* + '' *Y.*

נוף I 35.7.6.1 vb. **wave—Polel** 1 Impf. יְנֹפֵף—**wave hand,** as hostile gesture, **shake fist,** יְנֹפֵף יָדוֹ הַר בַּת־צִיּוֹן *he* (the Assyrian) *will shake his fist at the mountain of the daughter of Zion* Is 10$_{32(Qr)}$.

Hi. 33.7.6.1 Pf. הֵנִיף, הֵנַפְתָּ, הֵנִיפוֹתִי; impf. Si יניף (יְנִיפֶנּוּ), 2ms תָּנִיף, Q יניפו; + waw וְהֵנִיף, וְהֵנַפְתָּ; וַיָּנֶף (וַיְנִיפֵהוּ); impv. Si הניף, הָנִיפוּ; ptc. מֵנִיף (מְנִיפוֹ), I מנפם; inf. הָנִיף (הֲנָפָה), Q הניפי, Si הניפו, הֲנִיפְכֶם).

1. wield, <SUBJ> Israelite(s) Ex 20$_{25}$ Dt 23$_{26}$ 27$_5$, Joshua Si 46$_2$, בֵּן *son* Si 46$_2$, חֹצֵב *stonemason* Siloam tunnel inscr.$_1$; subj. not specified, Jos 8$_{31}$ Is 10$_{15.15}$. <OBJ> חֶרֶב *sword*, i.e. tool Ex 20$_{25}$, מַשּׂוֹר *saw* Is 10$_{15}$, חֶרְמֵשׁ *sickle* Dt 23$_{26}$, בַּרְזֶל *iron (tool)* Dt 27$_5$ Jos 8$_{31}$, גַּרְזֶן *pickaxe* Siloam tunnel inscr.$_1$, שֵׁבֶט *rod* Is 10$_{15}$, כִּידוֹן *javelin* Si 46$_2$. <PREP> עַל *upon, over, against*, + אֶבֶן *stone* Dt 27$_5$ Jos 8$_{31}$, גָּזִית *hewn stone* Ex 20$_{25}$, קָמָה *standing grain* Dt 23$_{26}$, עִיר *city* Si 46$_2$.

2. wave the hand, in healing (2 K 5$_{11}$), in hostility (Is 11$_{15}$ 19$_{16}$ Zc 2$_{13}$ Jb 31$_{21}$ Si 12$_{18}$ 33$_3$), using a sling (Si 47$_4$), as signal (Is 13$_2$), to mark the end of trials (1QM 17$_9$), to show the way (Si 37$_{7[B]}$), **stretch out** the hand, to do something (1QH 16$_{22}$), <SUBJ> Y. Is 11$_{15}$ 19$_{16}$ Zc 2$_{13}$ 1QM 17$_9$, Elijah 2 K 5$_{11}$, Job Jb 31$_{21}$, יֹעֵץ *counsellor* Si 37$_{7(B)}$, worshipper 1QH 16$_{22.33}$, צַר *enemy* Si 12$_{18}$; subj. not specified, Is 13$_2$. <OBJ> יָד *hand* 2 K 5$_{11}$ Is 11$_{15}$ 13$_2$ 19$_{16}$ Zc 2$_{13}$ Jb 31$_{21}$ Si 12$_{18}$ 33$_3$ ([יד]) 37$_{7(B)}$ 47$_4$ 1QH 16$_{22.33}$ 1QM 17$_9$. <PREP> בְּ of accompaniment, *with, in*, + עְיָם perh. *heat* Is 11$_{15}$; אֶל *to(wards)*, + מָקוֹם *place* 2 K 5$_{11}$; עַל *over, against*, + Egyptians Is 19$_{16}$, עַם *people* Si 33$_3$, גּוֹי *nation* Zc 2$_{13}$, יָתוֹם *orphan* Jb 31$_{21}$, נָהָר *river* Is 11$_{15}$, קֶלַע *sling* Si 47$_4$. <COLL> נוף hi. || נוע hi. *shake* Si 12$_{18}$; + infinitive of purpose, of עזק *dig* 1QH 16$_{22}$.

3. wave an offering (unless נוף IV *treat as a special contribution*), in presenting it at the altar; of presenting contributions of gold objects for tabernacle (Ex 35$_{22}$), setting aside the Levites (Nm 8$_{11.13.15.21}$), <SUBJ> Aaron Lv 9$_{21}$ Nm 8$_{11.21}$, Moses Ex 29$_{24.26}$||Lv 8$_{27.29}$ Nm 8$_{13.15}$, אִישׁ *man* Ex 35$_{22}$, בֵּן *son* Lv 10$_{15}$, of Israel Lv 23$_{12}$, כֹּהֵן *priest* Lv 14$_{12.24}$ 23$_{11.11.20}$ Nm 5$_{25}$ 6$_{20}$, זָקֵן *elder* of priests 11QT 19$_4$ ([והניפ]ו זקני), קרב hi. ptc. *one who brings near*, i.e. offers Lv 7$_{30}$ 11QT 15$_{11}$ ([ויניפו] [המקריבים]); subj. not specified, 11QT 20$_{16}$.

<OBJ> 1. thing waved, לֵוִי *Levite* Nm 8$_{11.13.15}$, אַיִל *ram* 11QT 15$_{11}$ ([יניפו]), כֶּבֶשׂ *lamb* Lv 14$_{12}$ 23$_{20}$, שָׂעִיר *goat* Lv 23$_{20}$, חָזֶה *breast* Ex 29$_{26}$||Lv 8$_{29}$ Lv 7$_{30}$ 9$_{21}$ 10$_{15}$ 11QT 20$_{16}$, שׁוֹק *thigh* Ex 29$_{24}$||Lv 8$_{27}$ Lv 9$_{21}$ 10$_{15}$ 11QT 20$_{16}$, זְרוֹעַ *shoulder* Nm 6$_{20}$, אֶזְרוֹעַ *foreleg* 11QT 20$_{16}$,

לְחִי *cheek* 11QT 2016 ([הלחיים]), קֵבָה *stomach* 11QT 2016 ([הקבה]), חֵלֶב *fat* Ex 2924||Lv 827, אַלְיָה *fat tail* Ex 2924||Lv 827, יֹתֶרֶת *appendage* Ex 2924||Lv 827, כִּלְיָה *kidney* Ex 2924||Lv 827, חַלָּה *cake* Ex 2924||Lv 827 Nm 620, רָקִיק *wafer* Ex 2924||Lv 827 Nm 620, לֶחֶם *bread* 11QT 194 ([והניפו ... לחם]), כִּכָּר *loaf* Ex 2924, סַל *basket* of bread 11QT 1511 ([יניפו]), עֹמֶר *sheaf* Lv 2311.11.12, מִנְחָה *grain offering* Nm 525, לֹג *log* of oil Lv 1412.24.

2. waved as, תְּנוּפָה *wave offering* Ex 2924.26||Lv 827.29 Ex 3522 Lv 730 921 1015 1412.24 2320 Nm 620 811.13.15.21 11QT 1511 ([יניפו ... ת]נופה]) 194 ([והניפו ... תנופה]) 2016.

<PREP> לְ of benefit, *to, for,* + Y. Nm 813; *for (the purpose of),* + רָצוֹן *acceptance* Lv 2311; מִן *on,* + מָחֳרָת *morrow* Lv 2311; עַל *upon, with,* + כֶּבֶשׂ *lamb* Lv 2320, לֶחֶם *bread* Lv 2320; לִפְנֵי *before,* + Y. Ex 2924.26||Lv 827.29 Lv 730 921 1015 1412.24 2311.20 Nm 525 620 811.21 11QT 1511 ([יניפו ... לפני י']) 194 ([והניפו ... לפני י']).

<COLL> נוף hi. + קרב hi. *bring near,* i.e. offer Nm 525.

4. shake to and fro, sift, <SUBJ> Y. Is 3028 Si 4316(M) (B זעם hi. *make indignant*). <OBJ> גּוֹי *nation* Is 3028, הַר *mountain* Si 4316(M). <PREP> בְּ of instrument, *by (means of), with,* + נָפָה *sieve* Is 3028, כֹּחַ *strength* Si 4316(M).

<SYN> §2 נוע hi. *shake.*

Ho. 1 Pf. הוּנַף—**be waved,** of offering presented at altar, <SUBJ> חָזֶה *breast* Ex 2927 (+ רום ho. *be raised,* i.e. offered), שׁוֹק *thigh* Ex 2927.*

⇒ נָפָה I *sieve,* הֶנֶף *waving,* הֲנִיפָה *waving,* תְּנוּפָה *wave offering.*

*נוף II 2.1.4 vb. **sprinkle—Qal** 1.0.4 Pf. Q הניפותה, נַפְתִּי—**sprinkle, shed, make run,** <SUBJ> Y. 1QH 426 157 fr. 2.19.13, אִשָּׁה *woman* Pr 717, זוֹנָה *prostitute* Pr 717. <OBJ> 1. object sprinkled, רוּחַ *spirit* 1QH 426 157 fr. 2.19.13 ([רוח]), מִשְׁכָּב *bed* Pr 717. 2. sprinkled with, מֹר *myrrh* Pr 717, אֲהָל *aloe* Pr 717, קִנָּמוֹן *cinnamon* Pr 717. <PREP> בְּ *upon,* + worshipper 1QH 157; עַל *upon,* + עֶבֶד *servant* 1QH 426, עָפָר *dust* 1QH fr. 2.19. <COLL> נוף + infinitive of purpose, of כפר pi. *atone* 1QH fr. 2.113.

Hi. 1.1 Impf. Si יניף, 2ms תָּנִיף—**sprinkle, make to flow,** <SUBJ> Y. Ps 6810 (unless נוף IV *deliver in large measure*) Si 4317(B) (M יפרח *it flies*). <OBJ> גֶּשֶׁם *rain* Ps 6810 (unless נוף IV *deliver in large measure*), שֶׁלֶג *snow* Si 4317(B). <PREP> כְּ *as,* + רֶשֶׁף perh. *bird* Si 4317(Bmg).

⇒ נֹפֶת *flowing honey.*

*[נוף] III vb. **bow down—Qal,** <SUBJ> worshipper Ps 8816 (נָשָׂאתִי אֵמֶיךָ אָנוּפָה *I suffer your terrors, I bow down [beneath them];* if em. אָפוּנָה perh. *I am helpless*).

*נוף IV 20.0.1 vb. **declare superfluous** (unless נוף I, §3 *wave* an offering)—**Hi.** 20.0.1 Pf. הֵנִיף; impf. יְנִיפֶנּוּ, Q יניפו; + waw וְהֵנִיף, וְהֵנַפְתָּ; וַיָּנֶף (וַיְנִיפֵהוּ); inf. הָנִיף (הֲנִיפְכֶם)—**declare superfluous, treat as a special contribution** (denom. of תְּנוּפָה *special contribution, additional gift*), in presenting it at the altar; of presenting contributions of gold objects for tabernacle (Ex 3522), setting aside the Levites (Nm 811.13.15.21), <SUBJ> Aaron Lv 921 Nm 811.21, Moses Ex 2924.26||Lv 827.29 Nm 813.15, אִישׁ *man* Ex 3522, בֵּן *son* Lv 1015, of Israel Lv 2312, כֹּהֵן *priest* Lv 1412.24 2311.11.20 Nm 525 620, זָקֵן *elder* of priests 11QT 194 ([והניפו] זקני), קרב hi. ptc. *one who brings near,* i.e. offers Lv 730 11QT 1511 ([ויניפו המקריבים]); subj. not specified, 11QT 2016.

<OBJ> 1. thing waved, לֵוִי *Levite* Nm 811.13.15, אַיִל *ram* 11QT 1511 ([יניפו]), כֶּבֶשׂ *lamb* Lv 1412 2320, שָׂעִיר *goat* Lv 2320, חָזֶה *breast* Ex 2926||Lv 829 Lv 730 921 1015 11QT 2016, שׁוֹק *thigh* Ex 2924||Lv 827 Lv 921 1015 11QT 2016, זְרוֹעַ *shoulder* Nm 620, אֶזְרוֹעַ *foreleg* 11QT 2016, לְחִי *cheek* 11QT 2016 ([הלחיים]), קֵבָה *stomach* 11QT 2016 ([הקבה]), חֵלֶב *fat* Ex 2924||Lv 827, אַלְיָה *fat tail* Ex 2924||Lv 827, יֹתֶרֶת *appendage* Ex 2924||Lv 827, כִּלְיָה *kidney* Ex 2924||Lv 827, חַלָּה *cake* Ex 2924||Lv 827 Nm 620, רָקִיק *wafer* Ex 2924||Lv 827 Nm 620, לֶחֶם *bread* 194 ([והניפו ... לחם]), כִּכָּר *loaf* Ex 2924, סַל *basket* of bread 11QT 1511 ([יניפו]), עֹמֶר *sheaf* Lv 2311.11.12, מִנְחָה *grain offering* Nm 525, לֹג *log* of oil Lv 1412.24.

2. waved as, תְּנוּפָה *wave offering* Ex 2924.26||Lv 827.29 Ex 3522 Lv 730 921 1015 1412.24 2320 Nm 620 811.13.15.21 11QT 1511 ([יניפו ... ת]נופה]) 194 ([והניפו ... תנופה]) 2016.

<PREP> לְ of benefit, *to, for,* + Y. Nm 813; *for (the*

purpose of), + רָצוֹן *acceptance* Lv 23$_{11}$; מִן *on,* + מָחֳרָת *morrow* Lv 23$_{11}$; עַל *upon, with,* + כֶּבֶשׂ *lamb* Lv 23$_{20}$, לֶחֶם *bread* Lv 23$_{20}$; לִפְנֵי *before,* + Y. Ex 29$_{24.26}$||Lv 8$_{27.29}$ Lv 7$_{30}$ 9$_{21}$ 10$_{15}$ 14$_{12.24}$ 23$_{11.20}$ Nm 5$_{25}$ 6$_{20}$ 8$_{11.21}$ 11QT 15$_{11}$ ([יניפו] ... [לפני י']) 19$_4$ (והניפו ... לפני י']).

<COLL> נוף hi. + קרב hi. *bring near,* i.e. offer Nm 5$_{25}$.

*נוף V$_{35.7.6.1}$ vb. **raise—Polel** $_1$ Impf. יְנֹפֵף—**raise hand,** as hostile gesture, יְנֹפֵף יָדוֹ הַר בַּת־צִיּוֹן *he* (the Assyrian) *will raise his hand at the mountain of the daughter of Zion* Is 10$_{32(Qr)}$.

Hi. $_{33.7.6.1}$ Pf. הֵנִיף, הֵנַפְתָּ, הֲנִיפוֹתִי; impf. Si יניף, Q יניפו, יְנִיפֶנּוּ, 2ms תָּנִיף; + waw וַיָּנֶף, וְהֵנַפְתָּ, וְהֵנִיף (וַיְנִיפֵהוּ); impv. Si הניף, הָנִיפוּ; ptc. מֵנִיף (מְנִיפוֹ), I מנפם; inf. הָנִיף (הֲנִיפְכֶם, Si הניפו, Q הניפי, הֲנָפָה).

1. raise, wield a tool, <SUBJ> Israelite(s) Ex 20$_{25}$ Dt 23$_{26}$ 27$_5$, Joshua Si 46$_2$, בֵּן *son* Si 46$_2$, חֹצֵב *stonemason* Siloam tunnel inscr.$_1$; subj. not specified, Jos 8$_{31}$ Is 10$_{15.15}$. <OBJ> חֶרֶב *sword,* i.e. tool Ex 20$_{25}$, מַשּׂוֹר *saw* Is 10$_{15}$, חֶרְמֵשׁ *sickle* Dt 23$_{26}$, בַּרְזֶל *iron (tool)* Dt 27$_5$ Jos 8$_{31}$, גַּרְזֶן *pickaxe* Siloam tunnel inscr.$_1$, שֵׁבֶט *rod* Is 10$_{15}$, כִּידוֹן *javelin* Si 46$_2$. <PREP> עַל *upon, over, against,* + אֶבֶן *stone* Dt 27$_5$ Jos 8$_{31}$, גָּזִית *hewn stone* Ex 20$_{25}$, קָמָה *standing grain* Dt 23$_{26}$, עִיר *city* Si 46$_2$.

2. raise the hand, in healing (2 K 5$_{11}$), in hostility (Is 11$_{15}$ 19$_{16}$ Zc 2$_{13}$ Jb 31$_{21}$ Si 12$_{18}$ 33$_3$), using a sling (Si 47$_4$), as signal (Is 13$_2$), to mark the end of trials (1QM 17$_9$), to show the way (Si 37$_{7[B]}$), **stretch out** the hand, to do something (1QH 16$_{22}$), <SUBJ> Y. Is 11$_{15}$ 19$_{16}$ Zc 2$_{13}$ 1QM 17$_9$, Elijah 2 K 5$_{11}$, Job Jb 31$_{21}$, יֹעֵץ *counsellor* Si 37$_{7(B)}$, worshipper 1QH 16$_{22.33}$, צַר *enemy* Si 12$_{18}$; subj. not specified, Is 13$_2$. <OBJ> יָד *hand* 2 K 5$_{11}$ Is 11$_{15}$ 13$_2$ 19$_{16}$ Zc 2$_{13}$ Jb 31$_{21}$ Si 12$_{18}$ 33$_3$ ([יד]) 37$_{7(B)}$ 47$_4$ 1QH 16$_{22.33}$ 1QM 17$_9$. <PREP> בְּ of accompaniment, *with, in,* + עְיָם perh. *heat* Is 11$_{15}$; אֶל *to(wards),* + מָקוֹם *place* 2 K 5$_{11}$; עַל *over, against,* + Egyptians Is 19$_{16}$, עַם *people* Si 33$_3$, גּוֹי *nation* Zc 2$_{13}$, יָתוֹם *orphan* Jb 31$_{21}$, נָהָר *river* Is 11$_{15}$, קֶלַע *sling* Si 47$_4$. <COLL> נוף hi. || נוע hi. *shake* Si 12$_{18}$; + infinitive of purpose, of עזק *dig* 1QH 16$_{22}$.

3. raise, present an offering, of contributions of gold objects for tabernacle (Ex 35$_{22}$), setting aside the Levites (Nm 8$_{11.13.15.21}$), <SUBJ> Aaron Lv 9$_{21}$ Nm 8$_{11.21}$, Moses Ex 29$_{24.26}$||Lv 8$_{27.29}$ Nm 8$_{13.15}$, אִישׁ *man* Ex 35$_{22}$, בֵּן *son* Lv 10$_{15}$, of Israel Lv 23$_{12}$, כֹּהֵן *priest* Lv 14$_{12.24}$ 23$_{11.11.20}$ Nm 5$_{25}$ 6$_{20}$, זָקֵן *elder* of priests 11QT 19$_4$ ([והניפו זקני]), קרב hi. ptc. *one who brings near,* i.e. offers Lv 7$_{30}$ 11QT 15$_{11}$ ([ויניפו המקריבים]); subj. not specified, 11QT 20$_{16}$.

<OBJ> 1. thing presented, לֵוִי *Levite* Nm 8$_{11.13.15}$, אַיִל *ram* 11QT 15$_{11}$ ([יניפו]), כֶּבֶשׂ *lamb* Lv 14$_{12}$ 23$_{20}$, שָׂעִיר *goat* Lv 23$_{20}$, חָזֶה *breast* Ex 29$_{26}$||Lv 8$_{29}$ Lv 7$_{30}$ 9$_{21}$ 10$_{15}$ 11QT 20$_{16}$, שׁוֹק *thigh* Ex 29$_{24}$||Lv 8$_{27}$ Lv 9$_{21}$ 10$_{15}$ 11QT 20$_{16}$, זְרוֹעַ *shoulder* Nm 6$_{20}$, אֶזְרוֹעַ *foreleg* 11QT 20$_{16}$, לְחִי *cheek* 11QT 20$_{16}$ ([הלחיים]), קֵבָה *stomach* 11QT 20$_{16}$ ([הקבה]), חֵלֶב *fat* Ex 29$_{24}$||Lv 8$_{27}$, אַלְיָה *fat tail* Ex 29$_{24}$||Lv 8$_{27}$, יֹתֶרֶת *appendage* Ex 29$_{24}$||Lv 8$_{27}$, כִּלְיָה *kidney* Ex 29$_{24}$||Lv 8$_{27}$, חַלָּה *cake* Ex 29$_{24}$||Lv 8$_{27}$ Nm 6$_{20}$, רָקִיק *wafer* Ex 29$_{24}$||Lv 8$_{27}$ Nm 6$_{20}$, לֶחֶם *bread* 19$_4$ ([והניפו ... לחם]), כִּכָּר *loaf* Ex 29$_{24}$, סַל *basket* of bread 11QT 15$_{11}$ ([יניפו]), עֹמֶר *sheaf* Lv 23$_{11.11.12}$, מִנְחָה *grain offering* Nm 5$_{25}$, לֹג *log* of oil Lv 14$_{12.24}$.

2. presented as, תְּנוּפָה *offering* Ex 29$_{24.26}$||Lv 8$_{27.29}$ Ex 35$_{22}$ Lv 7$_{30}$ 9$_{21}$ 10$_{15}$ 14$_{12.24}$ 23$_{20}$ Nm 6$_{20}$ 8$_{11.13.15.21}$ 11QT 15$_{11}$ ([יניפו] ... ת]נופה]) 19$_4$ ([והניפו ... תנופה]) 20$_{16}$.

<PREP> לְ of benefit, *to, for,* + Y. Nm 8$_{13}$; *for (the purpose of),* + רָצוֹן *acceptance* Lv 23$_{11}$; מִן *on,* + מָחֳרָת *morrow* Lv 23$_{11}$; עַל *upon, with,* + כֶּבֶשׂ *lamb* Lv 23$_{20}$, לֶחֶם *bread* Lv 23$_{20}$; לִפְנֵי *before,* + Y. Ex 29$_{24.26}$||Lv 8$_{27.29}$ Lv 7$_{30}$ 9$_{21}$ 10$_{15}$ 14$_{12.24}$ 23$_{11.20}$ Nm 5$_{25}$ 6$_{20}$ 8$_{11.21}$ 11QT 15$_{11}$ ([יניפו] ... [לפני י']) 19$_4$ (והניפו ... לפני י']).

<COLL> נוף hi. + קרב hi. *bring near,* i.e. offer Nm 5$_{25}$.

<SYN> §2 נוע hi. *shake.*

Ho. $_1$ Pf. הוּנַף—**be presented,** of offering at altar, <SUBJ> חָזֶה *breast* Ex 29$_{27}$ (+ רום ho. *be raised,* i.e. offered), שׁוֹק *thigh* Ex 29$_{27}$.

⇨ הֶנֶף *presentation,* הֲנִיפָה *presentation,* תְּנוּפָה *offering.*

*נוף VI $_1$ vb. **deliver in large measure** (unless נוף II *sprinkle*)—**Hi.** $_1$ Impf. 2ms תָּנִיף—**deliver in large measure,** <SUBJ> Y. Ps 68$_{10}$. <OBJ> גֶּשֶׁם *rain* Ps 68$_{10}$.

נוּף I 1 n.[m.] **height,** <CSTR> יְפֵה נוֹף *fair of height* Ps 48₃ (unless נוֹף II *Memphis*).

***נוֹף** II pl.n. **Memphis,** Egyptian capital city, 20 km S of Cairo, ident. with נֹף at Is 19₁₃ Jr 2₁₆ 44₁ 46₁₄ 49₁₉ Ezk 30₁₃.₁₆, and מֹף at Ho 9₆ 4QpsEzekb 1.2₆, <CSTR> יְפֵה נוֹף *fair one of Memphis* (as a epithet for Zion) Ps 48₃ (unless נוֹף I *height*).

***נוּץ** I 1 vb. **flee** (unless נצה III *fly* or IV *hasten*)—**Qal** 1 Pf. נָצוּ—perh. **flee, go away,** <SUBJ> כֹּהֵן *priest* Lm 4₁₅ (or em. נָדוּ *they fled*, from נוד), נָבִיא *prophet* Lm 4₁₅ (or em.; see above).

***נוּץ** II vb. **sparkle** (unless נצץ *sparkle*)—**Pol.** 1 Ptc. נֹצְצִים—**sparkle,** <SUBJ> חַיָּה *living being* Ezk 1₇, שָׁמַיִם *heaven* perh. 1QM 12₅ ([נוצ]צים; others [נוצ]חים *shining*). <PREP> כְּ *as*, + עַיִן *eye*, i.e. sparkle, of burnished bronze Ezk 1₇.

נוֹצָה 4 n.f. **plumage**—נֹצָה; sf. נֹצָתָהּ—**plumage, feathers,** <NOM CL> אִם־אֶבְרָה חֲסִידָה וְנֹצָה appar. *is it (the) wing (of) the stork and (her) plumage?*, i.e. is it like these? Jb 39₁₃ (unless נֹצָה II *hawk*). <CSTR> רַב־נוֹצָה *great of plumage* Ezk 17₇, מְלֵא הַנּוֹצָה *full of plumage* Ezk 17₃ (if em.; see Coll.). <PREP> בְּ of accompaniment, *with*, + סור hi. *remove* Lv 1₁₆. <COLL> נוֹצָה + אֵבֶר *wing* Ezk 17₃, אֶבְרָה *wing* Jb 39₁₃, כָּנָף *wing* Ezk 17₃.₇, מֻרְאָה *crop* Lv 1₁₆; מְלֵא הַנּוֹצָה *full of plumage* Ezk 17₃ (or em. מְלֵא *full of*).

***[נוֹר]** 0.1 n.[m.] **fire**—sf. Si נורה—of the sun, <PREP> מִן of cause, *on account of*, + כוה ni. *be scorched* Si 43₄.

נוּשׁ I 1 vb. **be sick** (unless נוש II *tremble*)—**Qal** 1 + waw וָאָנוּשָׁה—**be sick,** <SUBJ> worshipper Ps 69₂₁ (or em. וַאֲנוּשָׁה *and it is incurable* [i.e. אנשׁ pass.], and transfer בָּשְׁתִּי וּכְלִמָּתִי *my shame and my disgrace* from previous verse, as subj.).

***נוּשׁ** II vb. **tremble** (unless נוש I *be sick*)—**Qal** 1 + waw וָאָנוּשָׁה—**tremble,** <SUBJ> worshipper Ps 69₂₁.

***[נוֹתוֹס]** 0.0.1 pr.n.m. **Nothos,** surname of Hananiah, <OBJ> יכח hi. *reprove* 4QRebukes 1.2₅.

נזה I 24.0.17 vb. **sprinkle**—**Qal** 4 Impf. יִזֶּה (יֵז); + waw וַיִּז—intrans., **spurt, spatter,** <SUBJ> נֵצַח *juice*, i.e. blood Is 63₃ (see also Prep. מִן partitive). <PREP> מִן partitive, *some of* (as subj. of נזה), + דָּם *blood* Lv 6₂₀.₂₀ 2 K 9₃₃; עַל *upon*, + בֶּגֶד *garment* Lv 6₂₀ Is 63₃, אֲשֶׁר *that which* Lv 6₂₀; אֶל *upon*, + סוּס *horse* 2 K 9₃₃, קִיר *wall* 2 K 9₃₃.

Hi. 20.0.16 Impf. יַזֶּה (Q יז), Q יזו; + waw וַיַּז, וְהִזֵּיתָ, וְהִזָּה; impv. הַזֵּה; ptc. מַזֶּה; inf. Q הזות—**1. sprinkle, spatter (something upon),** sometimes object not expressed but implied by context (Ex 29₂₁||Lv 8₃₀ Lv 4₁₇ 14₇.₅₁ 16₁₄.₁₄ 19₁₈.₁₉), <SUBJ> Y. 1QS 4₂₁, Aaron Lv 16₁₄.₁₄.₁₅.₁₉, Eleazar Nm 19₄, Moses Ex 29₂₁||Lv 8₃₀ Lv 8₁₁ Nm 8₇, אִישׁ *man* Nm 19₁₈ 4QSD 7.2₃ 4QNidd 1.1₆ (להזו[ת] [אי]ש), כֹּהֵן *priest* Lv 4₆.₁₇ 5₉ 14₇.₁₆.₂₇.₅₁ Nm 19₄, זָקֵן *elder* of priests 11QT 16₃, טָהוֹר *pure one* Nm 19₁₉ 4QMMT B₁₆, עַלוֹל *wrongdoer* 4QTohBc 1₇, נגע ptc. *one who touches* 11QT 50₁₄.₁₅; subj. not specified, Nm 19₂₁ 4QMMT B₁₄ 11QT 49₁₈.₂₀.

<OBJ> דָּם *blood* Lv 4₁₇ 14₅₁ 16₁₅, מַיִם *water* Lv 14₅₁ Nm 8₇ 19₁₈.₁₉.₂₁ 4QSD 7.2₃ ([מ]ן) 4QNidd 1.1₆ ([להזו]ת) 4QMMT B₁₄ ([מ]ים) 11QT 49₁₈, רוּחַ *spirit* 1QS 4₂₁ (see also Prep. מִן partitive).

<PREP> בְּ of time, *on*, + יוֹם *day* Nm 19₁₉ 4QSD 7.2₃ ([ב]יום) 11QT 49₁₈.₂₀ 50₃.₁₄.₁₅ 4QTohA 1.2₂; of instrument, *by (means of), with*, + אֶצְבַּע *finger* Lv 14₁₆.₂₇ 16₁₄.₁₉ 4QTohBb 1₄.

כְּ *as*, + מַיִם *water* 1QS 4₂₁.

מִן partitive, *some of* (as obj. of נזה hi.), + דָּם *blood* Ex 29₂₁||Lv 8₃₀ Lv 4₆ 5₉ 16₁₄.₁₄.₁₉ Nm 19₄ 4QTohBb 1₄ 11QT 16₃ ([מן הדם]), שֶׁמֶן *oil* Ex 29₂₁||Lv 8₃₀ Lv 8₁₁ 14₁₆.₂₇.

אֶל *upon*, + בַּיִת *house* Lv 14₅₁.

עַל *upon* 4QTohA 1.2₁, + Aaron Ex 29₂₁||Lv 8₃₀, גֶּבֶר *man* 1QS 4₂₁, בֵּן *son* Ex 29₂₁||Lv 8₃₀, כֹּהֵן *priest* 11QT 16₃, לֵוִי *Levite* Nm 8₇, טהר htp. ptc. *one who is being purified* Lv 14₇, נגע ptc. *one who touches* Nm 19₁₈, טָמֵא *impure one* Nm 19₁₉ 4QTohBc 1₇ 4QMMT B₁₆, נֶפֶשׁ *soul*, i.e. person Nm 19₁₈, פָּנִים *face*, i.e. front, of mercy seat Lv 16₁₄, כַּפֹּרֶת *mercy seat* Lv 16₁₅, מִזְבֵּחַ

altar Lv 8$_{11}$ 16$_{19}$, קִיר *wall*, i.e. side, of altar Lv 5$_{9}$, אֹהֶל *tent* Nm 19$_{18}$, כְּלִי *vessel* Nm 19$_{18}$, בֶּגֶד *garment* Ex 29$_{21}$||Lv 8$_{30}$, כֹּל *everyone* 11QT 49$_{18}$.

לִפְנֵי *before*, + Y. Lv 4$_{6.17}$ 14$_{16.27}$, כַּפֹּרֶת *mercy seat* Lv 16$_{14.15}$.

אֶת־פְּנֵי *in front of*, + פָּרֹכֶת *veil* Lv 4$_{6.17}$.

אֶל־נֹכַח פְּנֵי *towards the front of*, + אֹהֶל *tent* of meeting Nm 19$_{4}$.

ה- of direction, *towards*, + קֶדֶם *east* Lv 16$_{14}$.

<COLL> נזה hi. + adverb or adj. used as adverb, רִאשֹׁנָה *the first time* 4QTohA 1.2$_{1}$ (יזו עליו את הרישונה *they sprinkle upon him for the first time*), שֵׁנִית *a second time* 11QT 49$_{20}$ 50$_{3}$ ([השׁ]נית) 50$_{15}$; וְהִזָּה שֶׁבַע פְּעָמִים *and he shall sprinkle seven times* Lv 4$_{17}$, vars. Lv 4$_{6}$ 8$_{11}$ 14$_{7.16.27.51}$ 16$_{14.19}$ Nm 19$_{4}$.

2. sprinkle (something [with]), <SUBJ> עֶבֶד *servant* Is 52$_{15}$ (or em. יַזֶּה to יִרְגְּזוּ *they shall tremble* or יִבְזָהוּ *they shall despise him*; unless נזה II *leap*); subj. not specified, 1QS 3$_{9}$. <OBJ> גּוֹי *nation* Is 52$_{15}$ (or em.; see Subj.; unless נזה II *leap*), בָּשָׂר *flesh* 1QS 3$_{9}$ (יטהר בשרו להזות *his flesh shall be purified by sprinkling [it]*). <PREP> בְּ of instrument, *by (means of), with*, + מַיִם *water* 1QS 3$_{9}$. <COLL> נזה hi. + קדשׁ htp. *sanctify oneself* 1QS 3$_{9}$; + adverb, כֵּן *thus* Is 52$_{15}$ (or em.; see Subj.; unless נזה II *leap*).

Also 4QBapt 12$_{5}$.

Ho. 0.0.1 Pf. Q הוזו—**be sprinkled,** <SUBJ> עוֹר *skin* 4QD^{d} 2$_{11}$, בֶּגֶד *garment* 4QD^{d} 2$_{11}$, כְּלִי *vessel* 4QD^{d} 2$_{11}$ (כל[י]). <PREP> כְּ *according to*, + מִשְׁפָּט *ordinance* 4QD^{d} 2$_{11}$. <COLL> אחו[ר ה]וזותו את מימ[י הזיה] *after he has been sprinkled with the waters of sprinkling* 4QRitPur 1.12$_{7}$.

נזה II 1 vb. **leap—Qal, leap to one's feet,** in respect, <SUBJ> גּוֹי *nation* Is 52$_{15}$ (if em.; see Hi. Subj.). <COLL> נזה + adverb, כֵּן *thus* Is 52$_{15}$ (if em.).

Hi. 1 Impf. יַזֶּה—**cause to leap, startle,** unless נזה I *sprinkle*, <SUBJ> עֶבֶד *servant* Is 52$_{15}$ (or em. יַזּוּ *they will leap*, i.e. qal). <OBJ> גּוֹי *nation* Is 52$_{15}$ (or em.; see Subj.). <COLL> נזה hi. + adverb, כֵּן *thus* Is 52$_{15}$ (or em.; see Subj.).

נָזִיד 6 n.[m.] **pottage**—cstr. נְזִיד—**pottage, stew,** <OBJ> בשׁל pi. *boil* 2 K 4$_{38}$, זיד hi. *boil* Gn 25$_{29}$, נתן *give* Gn 25$_{34}$. <CSTR> נְזִיד עֲדָשִׁים *pottage of lentils* Gn 25$_{34}$; סִיר הַנָּזִיד *pot of the pottage* 2 K 4$_{39}$. <PREP> מִן partitive, *(some) of*, + אכל *eat* 2 K 4$_{40}$; אֶל introducing object, + נגע *touch* Hg 2$_{12}$. <COLL> נָזִיד || לֶחֶם *bread* Gn 25$_{34}$ Hg 2$_{12}$, יַיִן *wine* Hg 2$_{12}$, שֶׁמֶן *oil* Hg 2$_{12}$; + מַאֲכָל *food* Hg 2$_{12}$.

<SYN> לֶחֶם *bread*, יַיִן *wine*, שֶׁמֶן *oil*.

⇒ (?) זיד *be presumptuous*.

נָזִיר I 16.1 n.m. **consecrated one**—cstr. נְזִיר; sf. נְזִירֶךָ; pl. נְזִרִים; נְזִירֶיהָ (נְזִרֶיהָ)—**1. consecrated one, prince,** in ref. to Joseph (Gn 49$_{26}$ Dt 33$_{16}$), rulers of Zion (Lm 4$_{7}$), <SUBJ> זכך *be pure* Lm 4$_{7}$ (or em. נְעָרֶיהָ *her lads*), צחח *be dazzling*, i.e. white Lm 4$_{7}$ (or em.). <CSTR> קָדְקֹד נְזִיר אֶחָיו *crown of the prince of his brothers* Gn 49$_{26}$ Dt 33$_{16}$ (unless נָזִיר II *cursed one*).

2. Nazirite, one dedicated to Y. by vow that prescribes growing hair, avoiding contact with corpse, and abstaining from wine and other grape products, <SUBJ> היה *be* Jg 13$_{5.7}$, נדר *vow* Nm 6$_{21}$, שׁתה *drink* Nm 6$_{20}$, בוא *come* Nm 6$_{13}$ (if em.; see Obj.), קרב hi. *bring near*, i.e. offer Nm 6$_{13}$, לקח *take* Nm 6$_{18}$, נתן *give*, i.e. place Nm 6$_{18}$, גלח pi. *shave* Nm 6$_{18}$, htp. *shave oneself* Nm 6$_{19}$, עשׂה *do* Nm 6$_{21}$. <NOM CL> נזיר י׳ בנבואה שמואל *Samuel was a Nazirite of Y. in prophecy* Si 46$_{13}$ נְזִיר אֱלֹהִים אֲנִי *I am a Nazirite of God* Jg 16$_{17}$. <OBJ> שׁקה hi. *cause to drink* Am 2$_{12}$ (+ נָבִיא *prophet*), בוא hi. *bring* Nm 6$_{13}$ (or em. יָבִיא to יָבוֹא *he shall come*, and del. אֹתוֹ). <CSTR> נזיר י׳ *Nazirite of Y.* Si 46$_{13}$, נְזִיר אֱלֹהִים *Nazirite of God* Jg 13$_{5.7}$ 16$_{17}$; כַּפֵּי הַנָּזִיר *hands of the Nazirite* Nm 6$_{19}$, תּוֹרַת *law of* Nm 6$_{13.21}$, נֶדֶר נָזִיר *vow of a Nazirite* Nm 6$_{2}$. <APP> יהוסף נזר *Joseph the Nazirite* Frey 1285$_{4}$ (others יוסי בן דרן [ ] *Jose son of ...*; others יהויעמד *Jehojaamod*). <PREP> לְ *as*, + קום hi. *raise up* Am 2$_{11}$ (|| נָבִיא *prophet*).

3. untrimmed vine, <OBJ> בצר *harvest* Lv 25$_{11}$. <CSTR> עִנְּבֵי נְזִירֶךָ *grapes of your untrimmed vine* Lv 25$_{5}$.

<SYN> §2 נָבִיא *prophet*.

⇒ נזר *consecrate.*

*[נָזִיר] II $_2$ n.[m.] **accursed one** (unless נָזִיר I *prince*)—cstr. נְזִיר—in ref. to Joseph, <CSTR> קָדְקֹד נְזִיר אֶחָיו *crown of the one accursed of,* i.e. by, *his brothers* Gn 49$_{26}$ Dt 33$_{16}$.

נזל $_{16.1.1}$ vb. **flow—Qal** $_{15.1.1}$ Pf. נָזְלוּ (נָזֹלּוּ); impf. יִזַּל, 3fs תִּזַּל, יִזְּלוּ; ptc. נוֹזְלִים (נֹזְלִים, נֹזְלֵיהֶם)—**1. flow, trickle, distil** (Dt 32$_2$; Sam אזל ni. *go out*); of perfume, **waft** (Ca 4$_{16}$), <SUBJ> מַיִם *water* Nm 24$_7$ (or em.; see Prep.) Jr 18$_{14}$ Ps 147$_8$, אִמְרָה *word* Dt 32$_2$, הַר *mountain* Jg 5$_5$ (or em. נָזֹלּוּ *they quaked,* i.e. זלל III ni.), בֹּשֶׂם *perfume* Ca 4$_{16}$. <PREP> כְּ *as,* + טַל *dew* Dt 32$_2$, שְׂעִירִים *rain* Dt 32$_2$; מִן of direction, *from,* + דְּלִי *bucket* Nm 24$_7$ (or em. יִזַּל־מַיִם מִדָּלְיָו *water shall flow from his buckets* to מִדָּלְיו *from his clouds/thunderbolts* or יִזְּלוּ לְאֻמִּים מֵחֵילוֹ *the nations shall shake* [i.e. זלל III ni.] *because of his might*); מִפְּנֵי *from before,* + Y. Jg 5$_5$ (or em.; see Subj.). <COLL> נזל || ערף *drip* Dt 32$_2$.

2. trans., **flow with, pour out, rain down,** <SUBJ> עַפְעַף *eyelid* Jr 9$_{17}$, שַׁחַק *cloud* Is 45$_8$ Jb 36$_{28}$, מִדָּל I *cloud* or II *thunderbolt* Nm 24$_7$ (if em.; see §1 Prep.), מַעְיָן *spring* Si 14$_{10}$. <OBJ> מַיִם *water* Jr 9$_{17}$ Si 14$_{10}$, מָטָר *rain* Jb 36$_{28}$, צֶדֶק *righteousness* Is 45$_8$. <PREP> עַל *upon,* + שֻׁלְחָן *table* Si 14$_{10}$. <COLL> נזל || ירד *flow down with* Jr 9$_{17}$; + רעף *drip* Jb 36$_{28}$, hi. Is 45$_8$.

3. ptc. as noun, **a. stream, flood,** <SUBJ> נצב ni. *stand* Ex 15$_8$ (+ מַיִם *water,* תְּהוֹם *deep*). <OBJ> יצא hi. *bring out* Ps 78$_{16}$, יצק *pour* Is 44$_3$, שׁתה *drink* Ps 78$_{44}$ Pr 5$_{15}$. <CSTR> מקור נוזלים *source of streams* 1QH 16$_4$. <COLL> נזל ptc. || מַיִם *water* Is 44$_3$ Pr 5$_{15}$ 1QH 16$_4$; + מַיִם Ex 15$_8$ Ps 78$_{16}$ Ca 4$_{15}$, יְאֹר *(Nile-)stream* Ps 78$_{44}$, נָהָר *river* Ps 78$_{16}$, תְּהוֹם *deep* Ex 15$_8$; נֹזְלִים מִן־לְבָנוֹן *streams from Lebanon* Ca 4$_{15}$.

b. irrigator,* <CSTR> נֵד נֹזְלִים *dike(s) of irrigators* Ex 15$_8$.

<SYN> §1 ערף *drip;* §2 ירד *flow down with;* §3 מַיִם *water.*

Hi. $_1$ Pf. הִזִּיל—**cause to flow,** <SUBJ> Y. Is 48$_{21}$. <OBJ> מַיִם *water* Is 48$_{21}$. <PREP> מִן of direction, *from,* + צוּר *rock* Is 48$_{21}$.

נֹזֵל *stream,* see נזל *flow,* §3.

נֶזֶם $_{17}$ n.m. **ring**—cstr. נֶזֶם; sf. נִזְמָהּ; pl. נְזָמִים; cstr. נִזְמֵי—for nose (e.g. Gn 24$_{47}$ Is 3$_{21}$ Ezk 16$_{12}$), for ears (e.g. Ex 32$_{2.3}$), perh. of divine image (Gn 35$_4$),* distinctive Ishmaelite dress (Jg 8$_{24}$), <NOM CL> נֶזֶם זָהָב בְּאַף חֲזִיר אִשָּׁה יָפָה *a beautiful woman* without discretion *is a ring of gold in a swine's nose* Pr 11$_{22}$, נֶזֶם זָהָב ... מוֹכִיחַ חָכָם *a wise reprover is ... a ring of gold* Pr 25$_{12}$, נִזְמֵי זָהָב לָהֶם *rings of gold were theirs* Jg 8$_{24}$, הַנְּזָמִים אֲשֶׁר בְּאָזְנֵיהֶם *the rings that were in their ears* Gn 35$_4$, var. Ex 32$_{2.3}$.

<OBJ> ראה *see* Gn 24$_{30}$, שׁאל *ask for* Jg 8$_{26}$, עדה *deck oneself with* Ho 2$_{15}$, בוא hi. *bring* Ex 32$_{3.22}$, לקח *take* Gn 24$_{22}$, נתן *give* Gn 35$_4$ Jg 8$_{24}$ Jb 42$_{11}$, i.e. place Ezk 16$_{12}$, שׂים *place* Gn 24$_{47}$, שׁלך hi. *cast* Jg 8$_{25}$, פרק pi. *tear off* Ex 32$_2$, htp. Ex 32$_3$, סור hi. *remove* Is 3$_{21}$, טמן *hide* Gn 35$_4$.

<CSTR> נִזְמֵי הָאַף *rings of the nose,* i.e. nose rings Is 3$_{21}$, נֶזֶם זָהָב *ring of gold* Gn 24$_{22}$ Jb 42$_{11}$ Pr 11$_{22}$ 25$_{12}$, נִזְמֵי הַזָּהָב *the rings of gold* Ex 32$_{2.3}$ Jg 8$_{24}$ (זָהָב) Jg 8$_{26}$, נֶזֶם שְׁלָלוֹ *ring of his spoil* Jg 8$_{24.25}$; מִשְׁקַל נִזְמֵי *weight of the rings of* Jg 8$_{26}$.

<ADJ> אֶחָד *one* Jb 42$_{11}$.

<APP> כְּלִי *jewellery* Ex 35$_{22}$.

<COLL> נֶזֶם || טַבַּעַת *ring* Ex 35$_{22}$ Is 3$_{21}$, עָגִיל *(ear)ring* Ezk 16$_{12}$, צָמִיד *bracelet* Gn 24$_{22.30.47}$, חָח *brooch* Ex 35$_{22}$, כּוּמָז *ornament* Ex 35$_{22}$, עֲטֶרֶת *crown* Ezk 16$_{12}$, חֶלְיָה *jewellery* Ho 2$_{15}$; + נְטִיפָה *pendant* Jg 8$_{26}$, שַׂהֲרֹן *crescent* Jg 8$_{26}$, קְשִׂיטָה *weight* Jb 42$_{11}$.

<SYN> טַבַּעַת *ring,* עָגִיל *(ear)ring,* צָמִיד *bracelet,* חָח *brooch,* כּוּמָז *ornament,* עֲטֶרֶת *crown,* חֶלְיָה *jewellery.*

*[נְזָמָה] pr.n.[f.] **Nezamah,** <NOM CL> [בדרום] נזמ[ה] *in the south was Nezamah* XḤev/Se 8c.

*נזף $_{0.1}$ vb. **reprove—Hi.** $_{0.1}$ Impf. Si 2ms תַּזִּיף—**reprove, rebuke,** <SUBJ> בֵּן *son* Si 11$_7$ (+ סלף pi. *find fault*). <COLL> נזף hi. + adverb, אַחַר *afterwards* Si 11$_7$.

[נֶזֶק] n.[m.] **injury**—cstr. נֵזֶק—**injury** or perh. **trouble,*** <CSTR> נֵזֶק הַמֶּלֶךְ *injury of,* i.e. to, *the king,* or *trouble to the king* Est 7$_4$. <PREP> שׁוה בְּ *be equivalent* to Est 74.

נזר I 10.0.7 vb. **consecrate**—**Ni.** 4.0.6 Pf. Q נזרו; impf. יִנָּזֵר; impv. Q הנזר; + waw וַיִּנָּזְרוּ; inf. abs. הִנָּזֵר; cstr. Q הנזר—**1. consecrate oneself,** <SUBJ> אָב *father* Ho 910. <PREP> לְ of benefit, *to, for,* + בֹּשֶׁת *shame,* i.e. Baal Ho 910.

2. separate oneself from, abstain from, <SUBJ> אִישׁ *man* Ezk 147 CD 88(A)=1920(B), בֵּן *son* 4QDa 11 (ב[ני]), כֹּל *everyone* brought into covenant CD 615; subj. not specified, 4Q418 812. <PREP> מִן of direction, *from* 4Q RitPur 692, + עַם *people* CD 88(A)=1920(B), הוֹן *wealth* CD 615, דֶּרֶךְ *way* 4Q183 1.25 ([מדרו]ך) 4QDa 11 ([מדר]כי), תּוֹעֵבָה *abomination* 4Q418 812; מֵאַחֲרֵי *from (following),* + Y. Ezk 147. <COLL> נזר ni. || בדל ni. *separate oneself* CD 615 4Q418 812.

3. keep oneself away from, i.e. **respect as sacred,** <SUBJ> Aaron Lv 222, בֵּן *son* of Israel Lv 222. <PREP> מִן of direction, *from,* + קֹדֶשׁ *holiness,* i.e. holy thing Lv 222.

4. fast, <SUBJ> Bethel (or Bethel-sharezer and Regem-melech) Zc 72.

<SYN> §2 בדל ni. *separate oneself.*

Hi. 6.0.1 Impf. יַזִּיר; + waw וְהִזַּרְתֶּם, וְהִזִּיר; inf. הַזִּיר (הַזִּירוֹ)—**1. consecrate oneself, be a Nazirite,** <SUBJ> אִישׁ *man* Nm 62.5.6, אִשָּׁה *woman* Nm 62.5.6. <PREP> לְ of benefit, *to, for,* + Y. Nm 62.5.6. <COLL> הַיָּמִם אֲשֶׁר יַזִּיר *the days for which he separates himself* Nm 65.

2. separate oneself from, abstain from, <SUBJ> אִישׁ *man* Nm 63 CD 71, אִשָּׁה *woman* Nm 63. <PREP> כְּ *according to,* + מִשְׁפָּט *ordinance* CD 71; מִן of direction, *from,* + יַיִן *wine* Nm 63, שֵׁכָר *strong drink* Nm 63, זונות *fornication* CD 71.

3. consecrate, separate, <SUBJ> Aaron Lv 1531 (unless §4; Sam זהר hi. *warn*), Moses Lv 1531 (unless §4), אִישׁ *man* Nm 612, אִשָּׁה *woman* Nm 612. <OBJ> בֵּן *son* of Israel Lv 1531 (unless §4), יוֹם *day* Nm 612. <PREP> לְ of benefit, *to, for,* + Y. Nm 612; מִן of direction, *from,* + טֻמְאָה *uncleanness* Lv 1531 (unless §4).*

⇒ נָזִיר *consecrated one,* נֵזֶר *consecration.*

*__נזר__ II vb. 1 **guard against** (unless נזר I *separate from*)—**Hi.** 1 + waw וְהִזַּרְתֶּם—**guard against, warn against,** <SUBJ> Aaron Lv 1531, Moses Lv 1531. <OBJ> בֵּן *son* of Israel Lv 1531. <PREP> מִן of direction, *against,* + טֻמְאָה *uncleanness* Lv 1531.

נֵ֫זֶר I 25.0.3 n.m. **consecration**—cstr. נֵזֶר; sf. נִזְרוֹ, נִזְרֵךְ—**1. consecration, separation, Naziriteship,** <NOM CL> טָמֵא נִזְרוֹ *his consecration is impure* Nm 612, נֵזֶר אֱלֹהָיו עַל־רֹאשׁוֹ *the consecration of his God is upon his head* Nm 67, נֵזֶר שֶׁמֶן מִשְׁחַת אֱלֹהָיו עָלָיו *the consecration of the anointing oil of his God is upon him* Lv 2112. <OBJ> שׂים *place,* i.e. make 1QSb 428 ([ישימכה] נזר *may he make you consecration,* i.e. establish you as consecrated). <CSTR> נֵזֶר אֱלֹהָיו *consecration of,* i.e. to, *his God* Nm 67, נֵזֶר שֶׁמֶן *consecration of the oil of* Lv 2112; רֹאשׁ נִזְרוֹ *head of his consecration,* i.e. his consecrated head Nm 69.18.18, יְמֵי *days of* Nm 64.8.12.13, נֶדֶר *vow of* Nm 65, תּוֹרַת *law of* Nm 621. <PREP> עַל *according to* Nm 621.

2. hair (of consecration), of Nazirite (Nm 619), of woman, grown long (Jr 729), <OBJ> גזז *shave* Jr 729, גלח htp. *shave oneself of* Nm 619, שׁלך hi. *cast* Jr 729.

3. crown, diadem, usu. of a royal personage, as a sign of consecration (unless נֵזֶר II *flower*), <SUBJ> ציץ *shine* Ps 13218. <NOM CL> הַנֵּזֶר אֲשֶׁר עַל־רֹאשׁוֹ *the crown which was on his head* 2 S 110, אִם־נֵזֶר לְדוֹר וָדוֹר *is a crown,* i.e. does it endure, *to all generations?* Pr 2724(Qr) (or em. אוֹצָר *treasure*). <OBJ> בוא hi. *bring* 2 S 110, לקח *take* 2 S 110, נתן *give,* i.e. place Ex 296 2 K 1112||2 C 2311, שׂים *place* Lv 89, חלל pi. *profane* Ps 8940. <CSTR> נֵזֶר הַקֹּדֶשׁ *the crown of holiness,* i.e. the holy crown Ex 296||Lv 89 Ex 3930 4QIsaa 819 (ק[ודש]); אַבְנֵי נֵזֶר *(precious) stones of a crown* Zc 916, צִיץ נֵזֶר *plate of the crown of* Ex 3930. <APP> צִיץ *plate* Lv 89. <COLL> נֵזֶר || אֶצְעָדָה *bracelet* 2 S 110, עֵדוּת *testimony* 2 K 1112||2 C 2311; + חֹסֶן *wealth* Pr 2724.

Also 4QPrFêtesc 97.23.

<SYN> אֶצְעָדָה *bracelet,* עֵדוּת *testimony.*

⇒ נזר I *consecrate.*

*__נֵ֫זֶר__ II 9.0.1 n.m. **flower** (unless נֵזֶר I, §3 *crown*)—cstr.

נֵזֶר; sf. נִזְרוֹ—<SUBJ> צִיץ *shine* Ps 132$_{18}$. <NOM CL> הַנֵּזֶר אֲשֶׁר עַל־רֹאשׁוֹ *the flower that was on his head* 2 S 1$_{10}$, אִם־נֵזֶר לְדוֹר וָדוֹר *is a flower*, i.e. does it endure, *to all generations?* Pr 27$_{24(Qr)}$ (or em. אוֹצָר *treasure*). <OBJ> בוא hi. *bring* 2 S 1$_{10}$, לקח *take* 2 S 1$_{10}$, נתן *give*, i.e. place Ex 29$_6$ 2 K 11$_{12}$||2 C 23$_{11}$, שׂים *place* Lv 8$_9$, חלל pi. *profane* Ps 89$_{40}$. <CSTR> נֵזֶר הַקֹּדֶשׁ *the flower of holiness*, i.e. the holy flower Ex 29$_6$||Lv 8$_9$ Ex 39$_{30}$ 4QIsa^a 8$_{19}$ ([ק]ודש); אַבְנֵי נֵזֶר *(precious) stones of a flower* Zc 9$_{16}$, צִיץ נֵזֶר *plate of the flower of* Ex 39$_{30}$. <APP> צִיץ *plate* Lv 8$_9$. <COLL> אֶצְעָדָה || נֵזֶר *bracelet* 2 S 1$_{10}$, עֵדוּת *testimony* 2 K 11$_{12}$||2 C 23$_{11}$; + חֹסֶן *wealth* Pr 27$_{24}$.

<SYN> אֶצְעָדָה *bracelet*, עֵדוּת *testimony*.

נֹחַ 46.1.14 pr.n.m. **Noah**—Si, Q נוח—son of Lemech and father of Ham, Shem and Japheth, <SUBJ> היה *be* Gn 5$_{32}$ 6$_9$ Ezk 14$_{14}$, חיה *live* Gn 9$_{28}$, pi. *keep alive* Gn 7$_1$, hi. Gn 6$_{13}$, שׁאר ni. *remain* Gn 7$_{23}$, ילד hi. *beget* Gn 5$_{32}$ 6$_{10}$, פרה *be fruitful* Gn 9$_1$, רבה *increase* intrans. Gn 9$_1$, שׁרץ *be abundant* Gn 9$_1$, אמר *say* Gn 9$_{24}$ 4QCommGenA 2$_5$, ראה *see* Gn 7$_1$ 8$_{6.13}$ 4QCommGenA 1$_{13.21}$, ידע *know* Gn 8$_{11}$ 9$_{24}$ 4QCommGenA 2$_5$, יקץ *awake* Gn 9$_{24}$ 4QCommGenA 2$_5$, אכל *eat* Gn 9$_1$, שׁתה *drink* Gn 9$_{20}$, שׁכר *be drunk* Gn 9$_{20}$.

הלך htp. *walk* Gn 6$_9$, בוא *come* Gn 7$_{1.7.13}$, hi. *bring* Gn 6$_{13}$ 8$_6$, יצא *go out* Gn 8$_{15.18}$ 4QCommGenA 2$_2$ 4QCommGenD 3$_2$, hi. *bring out* Gn 8$_{15}$, עלה hi. *cause to go up*, i.e. offer Gn 8$_{20}$, שׁלח *send*, i.e. stretch, hand Gn 8$_6$, pi. *send* Gn 8$_{6.11}$ 4QCommGenA 1$_{13}$, סור hi. *remove* Gn 8$_{13}$ 4QCommGenA 1$_{21}$, מצא *find* favour Gn 6$_8$, ni. *be found* Si 44$_{17}$, חיל *wait* Gn 8$_{6.12}$ (or em. וַיָּחֶל in both to וַיְיַחֵל *and he waited*, i.e. יחל pi.) 4QCommGenA 1$_{13}$.

שׂים *place* Gn 6$_{13}$, לקח *take* Gn 6$_{13}$ 7$_1$ 8$_{6.20}$, כפר *cover over* Gn 6$_{13}$, גלה htp. *expose oneself* Gn 9$_{20}$, פתח *open* Gn 8$_6$ 4QCommGenA 1$_{13}$ (ויפ[תח]), נצל pi. *deliver* Ezk 14$_{14}$, hi. Ezk 14$_{20}$, עשׂה *make, do* Gn 6$_{13.22}$ 7$_5$ 8$_6$, יסף hi. *do again* Gn 8$_6$ 4QCommGenA 1$_{13}$, כלה pi. *complete* Gn 6$_{13}$, בנה *build* Gn 8$_{20}$, נטע *plant* Gn 9$_{20}$, חלל hi. *begin* Gn 9$_{20}$, מות *die* Gn 9$_{29}$.

<NOM CL> נֹחַ אִישׁ צַדִּיק *Noah was a righteous man* Gn 6$_9$, נֹחַ בֶּן־שֵׁשׁ מֵאוֹת שָׁנָה *Noah was a son of six hundred years*, i.e. was six hundred years old Gn 7$_6$, ... נֹחַ בְּתוֹכָהּ *(if) Noah ... was within it* Ezk 14$_{20}$.

<OBJ> קרא *call* name Gn 5$_{29}$, צוה pi. *command* Gn 6$_{22}$ 7$_{5.9.15}$, ברך pi. *bless* Gn 9$_1$, זכר *remember* Gn 8$_1$, ילד hi. *beget* Gn 5$_{30}$.

<CSTR> אֵשֶׁת נֹחַ *wife of Noah* Gn 7$_{13}$, בְּנֵי־ *sons of* Gn 7$_{13}$ 9$_{18.19}$ 10$_{1.32}$ 4QCommGenA 2$_7$ CD 3$_1$, תּוֹלְדֹת *generations of* Gn 6$_9$, חַיֵּי־ *life of* Gn 7$_{11}$ 4QCommGenA 1$_{1.4}$ 2$_1$ (all three נוח), יְמֵי־ *days of* Gn 9$_{29}$ Is 54$_{9(1QIsa^a)}$ (כימי; MT כִּי־מֵי *for the waters of*), מֵי *waters of* Is 54$_{9.9}$ (or del.).

<APP> אִישׁ *man* Ezk 14$_{14}$, צַדִּיק *righteous one* Si 44$_{17}$.

<PREP> לְ of direction, *to*, + אמר *say* Gn 6$_{13}$ 7$_1$ 9$_1$, ידע hi. *make known* 4QCommGenB 1$_4$ (לנו[ח]), בוא *come* 4QCommGenA 1$_1$, נתן *give* Gn 9$_1$; of possession, benefit, *(belonging) to, for*, + היה *be* Gn 6$_{13}$, עשׂה *do* Gn 9$_{24}$ 4QCommGenA 2$_5$, קום hi. *establish* 4QPrFêtes^b 3$_2$; *for (oneself)*, + לקח *take* Gn 6$_{13}$ 7$_1$, עשׂה *make* Gn 6$_{13}$.

בְּ introducing object, + רצה *favour* 5QRègle 1$_7$.

אֶל *to*, + אמר *say* Gn 9$_{8.17}$, דבר pi. *speak* Gn 8$_{15}$, בוא *come* Gn 6$_{13}$ 7$_{9.15}$ 8$_6$ 4QCommGenA 1$_{13}$, hi. *bring* Gn 8$_6$, שׁוב *go back* Gn 8$_{6.11}$, אסף *gather* Gn 6$_{13}$.

עִם *with*, + כרת ni. *be cut*, i.e. made Si 44$_{17(B)}$ (Bmg כרת *cut*, i.e. make).

אֵת *with* Gn 7$_{7.23}$ 8$_{1.15.18}$ 9$_8$, + בוא *come* Gn 7$_{13}$, יצא hi. *bring out* Gn 8$_{15}$, קום hi. *establish* covenant Gn 6$_{13}$, חיה hi. *keep alive* Gn 6$_{13}$.

מֵאֵת *from (with)*, + שׁלח pi. *send* Gn 8$_6$.

בַּעַד *behind*, + סגר *close* Gn 7$_{15}$.

בַּעֲבוּר *on account of*, + היה *be* Si 44$_{17}$.

בֵּין *between*, + נתן *give*, i.e. make, covenant Gn 9$_8$.

<COLL> נֹחַ שֵׁם חָם וָיָפֶת *Noah, Shem, Ham and Japheth* 1 C 1$_4$.

Also 4QCommGenA 2$_4$.

⇒ נוח *rest*.

*[נחב] vb. **be lean—Ni. be lean, dry up**, <SUBJ> קוֹל *voice* Jb 29$_{10}$ (if em. נֶחְבָּאוּ *they were hidden* [חבא ni.] to נָחֵב *it was dried up*).

נַחְבִּי 1 pr.n.m. **Nahbi**, Naphtalite, son of Vophsi, one of twelve spies sent by Moses, <NOM CL> לְמַטֵּה נַפְתָּלִי

נַחְבִּי *(belonging) to the tribe of Naphtali was Nahbi* Nm 13$_{14}$. <APP> בֵּן *son* Nm 13$_{14}$.

נחה I $_{39.0.1}$ vb. **lead—Qal** $_{11}$ Pf. נָחִיתָ, (נָחָם) נָחַנִי; + waw וְנָחֲךָ; impv. נְחֵה (נְחֵנִי)—**1. lead, guide,** perh. occasionally to otherworldly destination (Ps 5$_{9}$ 23$_{3}$ 73$_{24}$ 139$_{24}$ 143$_{10}$),* <SUBJ> Y. Gn 24$_{27}$ Ex 13$_{17}$ 15$_{13}$ Is 58$_{11}$ Ps 5$_{9}$ 27$_{11}$ 77$_{21}$ 139$_{24}$, Moses Ex 32$_{34}$, מִי *who?* Ps 60$_{11}$=108$_{11}$ (unless §2; or em. יַנְחֵנִי, i.e. hi. in same sense, or יְנִיחֵנִי who *will place me*, i.e. נוח hi.).

<OBJ> Israelites Is 58$_{11}$, עַם *people* Ex 13$_{17}$ 15$_{13}$ 32$_{34}$ Ps 77$_{21}$, עֶבֶד *servant* Gn 24$_{27}$, worshipper Ps 5$_{9}$ 27$_{11}$ 60$_{11}$=108$_{11}$ (unless §2; or em.; see Subj.) 139$_{24}$.

<PREP> בְּ of place, *in,* + אֹרַח *path* Ps 27$_{11}$, דֶּרֶךְ *way* Gn 24$_{27}$ Ps 139$_{24}$; of instrument, *by (means of), with,* + יָד *hand* Ps 77$_{21}$; of accompaniment, *with, in,* + חֶסֶד *loyalty* Ex 15$_{13}$, צְדָקָה *righteousness* Ps 5$_{9}$; כְּ *as,* + צֹאן *flock* Ps 77$_{21}$; אֶל *to,* + אֲשֶׁר *(the place) which,* Ex 32$_{34}$; עַד *unto,* + Edom Ps 60$_{11}$=108$_{11}$ (unless §2; or em.; see Subj.).

נחה + noun without preposition, בַּיִת *(to the) house* Gn 24$_{27}$, דֶּרֶךְ *(by) way (of)* Ex 13$_{17}$.

<COLL> נחה ‖ יבל hi. *bring* Ps 60$_{11}$=108$_{11}$; + נהל pi. *lead* Ex 15$_{13}$; + adverb, תָּמִיד *continually* Is 58$_{11}$.

2. perh. **offer** (unless §1), <SUBJ> מִי *who?* Ps 60$_{11}$=108$_{11}$ (‖ יבל hi. *bring* as tribute). <OBJ> 1. worshipper Ps 60$_{11}$=108$_{11}$. 2. עַד *throne* Ps 60$_{11}$=108$_{11}$.*

<SYN> יבל hi. *bring.*

Hi. $_{28.0.1}$ Pf. הִנְחַנִי ,הִנְחִיתָם; impf. יַנְחֵנִי (יַנְחֵנוּ ,יַנְחֵם), 3fs (אַנְחֶנָּה) אַנְחֵהוּ, 2ms (תַּנְחֵם) תַּנְחֵנִי (תַּנְחֵם ,תַּנְחֵנִי) תַּנְחֶה, יַנְחוּנִי; + waw וַיַּנְחֵם; inf. לְהַנְחֹתָם (Q לַנְחֹתָם ,להנחותם).

1. lead, guide, bring, <SUBJ> Y. Gn 24$_{48}$ Ex 13$_{21}$ Dt 32$_{12}$ Is 57$_{18}$ (or em. וַאֲנִחֵהוּ *and I will give him rest,* i.e. נוח hi.) Ps 23$_{3}$ 31$_{4}$ 61$_{3}$ (or em. תַּנִּיחֵנִי *may you place me,* i.e. נוח hi.) 67$_{5}$ 73$_{24}$ 78$_{14.53}$ 106$_{45}$ (if em. וַיִּנָּחֵם *and he relented* [נחם ni.] to וַיַּנְחֵם *and he led them*) 107$_{30}$ Jb 12$_{23}$ (or em. וַיַּנִּחֵם *and he abandons them,* i.e. נוח hi.) Ne 9$_{12}$, Balak Nm 23$_{7}$, David 1 S 22$_{4}$ (or em. וַיַּנִּחֵם *and he left them,* i.e. נוח hi.) Ps 78$_{72}$, Job Jb 31$_{18}$ 38$_{32}$, Solomon 1 K 10$_{26}$ (or em. וַיַּנִּחֵם *and he placed them*), מֶלֶךְ *king* Nm 23$_{7}$ 2 K 18$_{11}$ (or em. וַיַּנִּחֵם), מַשְׂכִּיל *instructor* 1QS 9$_{18}$, יָד *hand* Ps 139$_{10}$ (or em. תְּנִיחֵנִי *you will make it rest* [נוח hi.] or תִּקָּחֵנִי *it will take me*), רוּחַ *spirit* Ps 143$_{10}$, אוֹר *light* Ps 43$_{3}$, אֱמֶת *truth* Ps 43$_{3}$, תּוֹרָה *law* Pr 6$_{22}$, מִצְוָה *commandment* Pr 6$_{22}$, תֻּמָּה *integrity* Pr 11$_{3}$, מַתָּן *gift* Pr 18$_{16}$, עַמּוּד *pillar* of cloud Ne 9$_{19}$, שֵׁבֶט *rod* Ps 23$_{4}$ (if em. יְנַחֲמֻנִי *they will comfort me* to יַנְחֻנִי), מִשְׁעֶנֶת *staff* Ps 23$_{4}$ (if em.; see above), מִי *who?* Ps 60$_{11}$=108$_{11}$ (if em. נָחַנִי [qal] to יַנְחֵנִי).

<OBJ> Israelites 2 K 18$_{11}$ (or em.; see Subj.) Is 57$_{18}$ (or em.; see Subj.) Ps 78$_{14.53.72}$, Jacob (i.e. Israelites) Dt 32$_{12}$ Ps 78$_{72}$, עַם *people* Dt 32$_{12}$ Ps 78$_{72}$ 106$_{45}$ (if em.; see Subj.), גּוֹי *nation* Jb 12$_{23}$ (or em.; see Subj.), לְאֹם *nation* Ps 67$_{5}$, Balaam Nm 23$_{7}$, אָדָם *human being* Pr 18$_{16}$, אָב *father* 1 S 22$_{4}$ (or em.; see Subj.) Ne 9$_{12.19}$, אֵם *mother* 1 S 22$_{4}$ (or em.; see Subj.), בֵּן *son* Pr 6$_{22}$, of Israel Ex 13$_{21}$, עֶבֶד *servant* Gn 24$_{48}$, אַלְמָנָה *widow* Jb 31$_{18}$ (or em. אַנְחֶנָּה *I led her* to אַנְחֶנּוּ *I led him*), יָתוֹם *orphan* Jb 31$_{18}$ (if em.; see above), פָּרָשׁ *cavalry* 1 K 10$_{26}$ (or em.; see Subj.), יָשָׁר *upright one* Pr 11$_{3}$, worshipper Ps 23$_{3.4}$ (if em.; see Subj.) 31$_{4}$ 43$_{3}$ 61$_{3}$ (or em.; see Subj.) 73$_{24}$ 60$_{11}$=108$_{11}$ (if em.; see Subj.) 139$_{10}$ (or em.; see Subj.) 143$_{10}$, בָּחִיר *chosen one* 1QS 9$_{18}$, ירד ptc. *one who goes down* to the sea Ps 107$_{30}$, עַיִשׁ *Great Bear* Jb 38$_{32}$, נַחֲלָה *inheritance* Ps 78$_{72}$.

<PREP> לְ of accompaniment, *in, with,* + בֶּטַח *safety* Ps 78$_{14}$.

בְּ of place, *in, onto, on (river),* + Habor 2 K 18$_{11}$ (or em.; see Subj.), Halah 2 K 18$_{11}$ (or em.; see Subj.), Jerusalem 1 K 10$_{26}$ (or em.; see Subj.), אֶרֶץ *land* Ps 143$_{10}$, דֶּרֶךְ *way* Gn 24$_{48}$ Ps 143$_{10(mss)}$ Ne 9$_{19}$, אֹרַח *path* Ps 143$_{10(mss)}$, מַעְגָּל *path* Ps 23$_{3}$, צוּר *rock* Ps 61$_{3}$ (or em.; see Subj.), נָהָר *river* 2 K 18$_{11}$ (or em.; see Subj.).

בְּ of instrument, *by (means of), with,* + עֵצָה *counsel* Ps 73$_{24}$, דַּעַת *knowledge* 1QS 9$_{18}$, עָנָן *cloud* Ps 78$_{14}$, עַמּוּד *pillar* of cloud and fire Ne 9$_{12}$, אוֹר *light* Ps 78$_{14}$, תְּבוּנָה *understanding,* i.e. skill Ps 78$_{72}$.

כְּ *according to,* + רֹב *abundance* Ps 106$_{45}$ (if em.; see Subj.).

מִן of direction, *from,* + הַר *mountain* Nm 23$_{7}$; *from (the time of being in),* + בֶּטֶן *womb* Jb 31$_{18}$.

אֶל *to,* + מָחוֹז *harbour* Ps 107$_{30}$.

עַל *upon,* i.e. with, + בֵּן *son* Jb 38$_{32}$.

עַד *unto,* + Edom Ps 60$_{11}$=108$_{11}$ (if em.; see Subj.).

לִפְנֵי *before*, + גָּדוֹל *great one* Pr 18$_{16}$.

אֶת־פְּנֵי *in the presence of*, + מֶלֶךְ *king* 1 S 22$_4$ (or em.; see Subj.).

נחה hi. + noun without preposition, דֶּרֶךְ *(in the) way* Ex 13$_{21}$.

<COLL> נחה hi. || נהל pi. *lead* Ps 31$_4$, שׂכל hi. *instruct* 1QS 9$_{18}$; + בוא hi. *bring* Ps 43$_3$, יצא hi. *bring out* Jb 38$_{32}$, אחז *hold* Ps 139$_{10}$, שׁמר *keep* Pr 6$_{22}$; + adverb or noun used as adverb, בָּדָד *alone* Dt 32$_{12}$, שָׁם *there* Ps 139$_{10}$ (or em.; see Subj.), יוֹמָם *by day* Ps 78$_{14}$ Ne 9$_{12}$, לַיְלָה *by night* Ps 78$_{14}$ Ne 9$_{12}$.

2. perh. **free,** וְאֵין לָהֶם מְנַחֵם *and they have none who frees them* Ec 4$_1$ (if em. מְנַחֵם *comforter*).

<SYN> נהל pi. *lead*, שׂכל hi. *instruct*.

***נחה II** 1 vb. **support** (unless III *aim at* or IV *ally oneself* or from נוח *rest*)—**Qal** 1 Pf. נָחָה—**support, stand by,** <SUBJ> Aram Is 7$_2$. <PREP> עַל *beside, by*, + Ephraim Is 7$_2$.

***נחה III** 2 vb. **aim at** (unless נחה II *support* or IV *ally oneself*)—**Qal** 1 Pf. נָחָה—**incline towards,** <SUBJ> Aram Is 7$_2$. <PREP> עַל *to(wards)*, + Ephraim Is 7$_2$.

Ni. 1 + waw וַיִּנָּהוּ—**follow after,** <SUBJ> בֵּית *house* of Israel 1 S 7$_2$. <PREP> אַחֲרֵי *after*, + Y. 1 S 7$_2$.

Pi. aim, <SUBJ> Y. Ps 38$_3$ (if em. נִחֲתוּ *they sink* to נִחֲתָה *you aim*), זְרוֹעַ *arm* 2 S 22$_{35}$||Ps 18$_{35}$ (if em. וְנִחַת/וְנִחֲתָה to וְנִחַת). <OBJ> קֶשֶׁת *bow* 2 S 22$_{35}$||Ps 18$_{35}$ (if em.; see Subj.), חֵץ *arrow* Ps 38$_3$ (if em.; see Subj.). <PREP> בְּ *at*, + worshipper Ps 38$_3$ (if em.; see Subj.).

***נחה IV** 1 vb. **ally oneself** (unless נחה II *support* or III *aim at* or from נוח *rest*)—**Qal** 1 Pf. נָחָה—**ally oneself,** <SUBJ> Aram Is 7$_2$. <PREP> עַל *with*, + Ephraim Is 7$_2$.

נַחוּם 1.0.0.27 pr.n.m. **Nahum**—I נחם—**1.** prophet, Elkoshite, <CSTR> חֲזוֹן נַחוּם *vision of Nahum* Na 1$_1$. <APP> אֶלְקֹשִׁי *Elkoshite* Na 1$_1$.

2. one sent to deliver oil, <SUBJ> בוא *come* Arad ost. 17$_1$, שׁלח *send* Arad ost. 17$_1$, לקח *take* Arad ost. 17$_1$, נתן *give* Arad ost. 17$_8$, חתם *seal* Arad ost. 17$_1$. <OBJ> שׁלח *send* Arad ost. 16$_{10}$. <PREP> אֶל *to* Arad ost. 17$_1$.

3. father of Azariah, Seal 175 (6th cent.).

4. appar. son of Hizziliah, Seals 186 (Gibeon) 474 (Lachish) 900 (Jerusalem; all three 8th cent.) Jar Stamps 948 (הצלי[הו]) 955 (ה[צליהו]; both T. Beit Mirsim?, 8th cent.).

5. son of Hammon, Seal 202 (7th cent.).

6. appar. son of Elishama, Seal 244 (7th/6th cent.).

7. son of Annaniah, Seal 254 (Lachish, 7th cent.).

8. appar. son of Abdi, Seals 291 (T. el-Judeideh, 8th cent.) 470 (Lachish, 8th cent.) 743 (נ[ח]ם; Naḥal ʿArugot, 8th cent.) Jar Stamps 944 945 (נח[ם]) 946 (נח[ם]) 947 ([נ]חם; all four T. Beit Mirsim?, 8th cent.).

9. father of Eleazar, Seal 310 (6th/5th cent.).

10. father of Saul, Seal 311 (6th/5th cent.).

11. father of Shallum, Seal 373 (8th/7th cent.).

12. Seal 489 (Lachish).

13. father of Jekamiah, Seal 577 (T. Beit Mirsim?, 7th/6th cent.).

14. son of Rephaiah, Seal 621 (נ[ח]ם בן רפא[יהו]; T. Beit Mirsim?, 7th/6th cent.).

15. father of Pathah, Seal 653 (T. Beit Mirsim?, 7th/6th cent.).

16. Seal 676 (T. Beit Mirsim?, 7th/6th cent.).

17. appar. son of Sheba, Seal 702 ([נ]חם [ש]בע; T. Beit Mirsim?, 7th/6th cent.).

18. son of Sheelah, Seal 851 (City of David, 7th/6th cent.).

19. son of Mekimiah, Bulla D64.

20. appar. father of Hizda, Bulla DH54.

<CSTR> בן נחם *son of Nahum* Seals 175 (6th cent.) 310 311 (both 6th/5th cent.) 373 (8th/7th cent.) 577 653 676 (all three T. Beit Mirsim?, 7th/6th cent.). <APP> בֵּן *son* Seals 202 (7th cent.) 254 (Lachish, 7th cent.) 621 (נ[ח]ם; T. Beit Mirsim?, 7th/6th cent.) 851 (City of David, 7th/6th cent.) Bulla D64. <PREP> לְ of possession, *of, (belonging) to* Seals 186 (Gibeon, 8th cent.) 202 (7th cent.) 244 (7th/6th cent.) 254 (Lachish, 7th cent.) 291 (T. el-Judeideh, 8th cent.) 470 474 (both Lachish, 8th cent.) 621 (לנ[ח]ם; T. Beit Mirsim?, 7th/6th cent.) 743 (לנ[ח]ם; Naḥal ʿArugot, 8th cent.) 851 (ל[נ]חם; City of David, 7th/6th cent.) 900 (Jerusalem,

8th cent.) Jar Stamps 944 945 ([לנח[ם) 946 ([ל]נחם) 947 (ל[נ]חם) 948 955 (all six T. Beit Mirsim?, 8th cent.) Bulla D64.
⇒ נחם *comfort.*

נְחוּם 1 pr.n.m. **Nehum,** exile returning with Zerubbabel, <SUBJ> בוא *come* Ne 7_7 (||Ezr 2_2 רְחוּם *Rehum*).
⇒ נחם *be sorry.*

* **[נִחוּמִים]** I 1 n.[m.]pl. **inward parts**—נִחוּמַי—<SUBJ> כמר ni. *be kindled* Ho 11_8 (unless נִחֻמִים *compassion*).

[נִחוּמִים] II, see נִחֻמִים *comfort.*

נָחוֹר 18 pr.n.m. **Nahor, 1.** son of Serug and father of Terah, <SUBJ> חיה *live* Gn $11_{24.25}$, ילד hi. *beget* Gn $11_{24.25}$. <OBJ> ילד hi. *beget* Gn $11_{22.23}$. <COLL> שְׂרוּג נָחוֹר תָּרַח *Serug, Nahor, Terah* 1 C 1_{26}.

2. son of Terah and brother of Abram, <SUBJ> לקח *take* Gn 11_{29}. <OBJ> ילד hi. *beget* Gn $11_{26.27}$. <CSTR> אֱלֹהֵי נָחוֹר *God of Nahor* Gn 31_{53}, אֲבִי *father of* Jos 24_2, בֶּן־ *son of* Gn 24_{47} 29_5, אֵשֶׁת *wife of* Gn 11_{29} 24_{15}, עִיר *city of* Gn 24_{10}. <APP> אָח *brother* Gn $22_{20.23}$ 24_{15}. <PREP> לְ *for (oneself),* + לקח *take* Gn 11_{29}; of benefit, *for,* + ילד *bear* Gn $22_{20.23}$ $24_{24.47}$.

נָחוּשׁ 1 n.[m.] **bronze,** <NOM CL> אִם־בְּשָׂרִי נָחוּשׁ *is my flesh bronze?* Jb 6_{12} (+ אֶבֶן *stone*).
⇒ cf. נְחוּשָׁה *copper, bronze,* נְחֹשֶׁת *copper.*

נְחוּשָׁה I 10.0.3 n.f. **copper**—נְחֻשָׁה—**1. copper,** <COLL> אֶבֶן יָצוּק נְחוּשָׁה *one melts ore into copper* Jb 28_2 (+ בַּרְזֶל *iron*).

2. bronze, an alloy of copper and tin, <NOM CL> מִצְחֵךְ נְחוּשָׁה *your forehead is bronze* Is 48_4, מה[ר]יה נחושה *from its mountains there is bronze* 4QapJoshua[a] 11_7. <OBJ> שׂים *place,* i.e. make, hoofs into Mc 4_{13}=4QSb 5_{26} 4QapPs[b] 46_7, חשׁב *reckon* Jb 41_{19}. <CSTR> קֶשֶׁת־נְחוּשָׁה *bow of bronze* 2 S 22_{35}||Ps 18_{35} (unless נְחוּשָׁה II *enchantment*) Jb 20_{24}, דַּלְתוֹת *doors of* Is 45_2, אֲפִיקֵי *tubes of* Jb 40_{18}. <PREP> כְּ *as,* + נתן *give,* i.e. make Lv 26_{19}. <COLL> בַּרְזֶל || נְחוּשָׁה *iron* Lv 26_{19} Is 45_2 48_4 (+) Mc 4_{13}=4QSb 5_{26} Jb 20_{24} 40_{18} (both +) 41_{19} 4QapJoshua[a] 11_7 (+).
<SYN> בַּרְזֶל *iron.*
⇒ cf. נָחוּשׁ *bronze,* נְחֹשֶׁת *copper.*

נְחוּשָׁה II 1 n.f. **enchantment** (unless נְחוּשָׁה I *bronze*), <CSTR> קֶשֶׁת־נְחוּשָׁה *bow of enchantment,* i.e. enchanted bow 2 S 22_{35}||Ps 18_{35}.
⇒ נחשׁ *practise divination.*

[נְחוֹשֶׁת], see נְחֹשֶׁת *copper.*

נְחִילוֹת I 1 n.f.pl. perh. **flutes** (as name of a melody), technical term in psalm title, <PREP> אֶל־הַנְּחִילוֹת perh. *to (the accompaniment of) the flutes* Ps 5_1 (mss עַל *to*).
⇒ cf. חָלִיל *flute.*

* **נְחִילוֹת** II 1 n.f.pl. perh. **sickness,** term in psalm title, <PREP> אֶל־הַנְּחִילוֹת perh. *against sickness* Ps 5_1 (mss עַל *to*).
⇒ חלה *be sick.*

* **נְחִילוֹת** III 1 n.f.pl. perh. **inheritances,** term in psalm title, <PREP> אֶל־הַנְּחִילוֹת perh. *to (the melody of) inheritances* Ps 5_1 (mss עַל *to*).
⇒ נחל *inherit.*

[נָחִיר] 1 n.[m.] **nostril**—du. sf. נְחִירָיו—of Leviathan (Jb 41_{12}), Pharaoh as dragon (Ezk 32_2; if em.; see Prep.), <PREP> בְּ of instrument, *by (means of), with,* + גיח *burst out* Ezk 32_2 (if em. בְּנַהֲרוֹתֶיךָ *in your rivers* to בִּנְחִירֶיךָ *with your nostrils*); מִן of direction, *from (out of),* + יצא *go out* Jb 41_{12}.
⇒ נחר *snort.*

נחל I 59.7.34 vb. **inherit—Qal** 30.4.17 Pf. נָחַלְתִּי, נָחֲלוּ; impf. יִנְחַל, 2ms תִּנְחַל (תִּנְחָל), יִנְחֲלוּ (יִנְחָלוּ), יִנְחָלוּהָ, יִנְחָלוּם), נִנְחַל; + waw וְנָחַל, וְנָחַלְתָּ (וּנְחַלְתָּנוּ), וְנָחֲלוּ, וּנְחַלְתֶּם; וַיִּנְחֲלוּ; ptc. Si נוחל (Q נוחליכה, Q נוחליה); inf. נְחֹל (Q נחול)—**1. inherit, take possession of, hold as a**

possession; without obj., **have an inheritance** (Nm 18_{20} 26_{55} 32_{19} Jos 16_4 19_9 Jg 11_2).

<SUBJ> Y. Ex 34_9 Zc 2_{16} Ps 82_8 (unless נחל II *sift*), Aaron Nm 18_{20} Si 45_{22}, Jephthah Jg 11_2, Israel(ites) Ex 23_{30} Nm 26_{55} Dt 19_{14} Ezk 47_{14}, Ephraim Jos 16_4, Manasseh Jos 16_4, צָבָא *host* 1QS 4_{15}, אָדָם *human being* Si 10_{11}, אִישׁ *man*, i.e. each Nm 35_8 Ezk 47_{14}, אָב *father* Jr 16_{19}, בֵּן *son* Nm 32_{19} Jos 16_4 19_9, of Israel Jos 14_1, בַּת *daughter* Jos 17_6, זֶרַע *offspring* Ex 32_{13} Ps 69_{37}, לֵוִי *Levite* Nm $18_{23.24}$, חסה ptc. *one who takes refuge* Is 57_{13}, תָּמִים *blameless one* Pr 28_{10}, חָכָם *wise one* Pr 3_{35} Si 37_{26}, worshipper Ps 119_{111} (or em.; see Obj.), אֹהֵב *friend* Si $37_{5(Bmg)}$ (נוחל; B, D נלחם *fights*), פֶּתִי *simple one* Pr 14_{18}, עכר ptc. *one who troubles* Pr 11_{29}, יֶתֶר *remainder* Zp 2_9, מִי *who?* 4Q417 1.1_{11}; subj. not specified, 4QWiles $1_{8.11}$ 4Q416 2.3_7 4Q418 55_6 81_{14}.

<OBJ> Israel(ites) Ex 34_9, Judah Zc 2_{16}, Moab(ites) Zp 2_9, Zion Ps 69_{37}, בֵּן *son* of Ammon Zp 2_9, זוֹנָה *prostitute* 4QWiles $1_{8.11}$ (both [זונ]ה), רִמָּה *worm* Si 10_{11}, אֶרֶץ *land* Ex 23_{30} Is 57_{13} Ezk 47_{14} 4Q418 81_{14}, נַחֲלָה *inheritance* Nm $18_{23.24}$ 35_8 Dt 19_{14} Jos 17_6, אֲחֻזָּה *possession* 4Q418 55_{12}, רוּחַ *wind* Pr 11_{29}, הֶבֶל *vanity* Jr 16_{19}, שֶׁקֶר *falsehood* Jr 16_{19}, עָוֶל *injustice* 4Q417 1.1_{11} (ע[ו]ל), אִוֶּלֶת *folly* Pr 14_{18}, גַּאֲוָה *pride* 4QBéat 13_4, עֵדָה *testimony* Ps 119_{111} (or em. נַחֲלָתִי your testimonies are *my inheritance*), כָּבוֹד *glory* Pr 3_{35} Si 37_{26} 4Q417 1.1_{11} 4QBéat 14.2_{14}, טוֹב *good* Pr 28_{10}, שִׂמְחָה *joy* 4Q416 2.3_7, אֱמֶת *truth* 4Q418 55_6, אֵלֶּה *these* Jos 14_1.

<PREP> לְ of direction, *to*, + עוֹלָם *eternity* Ex 32_{13} Ps 119_{111}; *according to*, + שֵׁם *name* Nm 26_{55}.

בְּ of place, *in*, + אֶרֶץ *land* Nm 18_{20} Dt 19_{14} Jos 14_1, בַּיִת *house* Jg 11_2; introducing object, + גּוֹי *nation* Ps 82_8 (unless נחל II *sift*); partitive, *(some) of*, + מִפְלָג *division* 1QS 4_{16}.

כְּ *as, according to*, + אָח *brother* Ezk 47_{14} (אִישׁ כְּאָחִיו *each as his brother*, i.e. equally).

עִם *with*, + זָר *stranger* Si $37_{5(Bmg)}$.

אֵת *with*, + בֵּן *son* of Israel Nm 32_{19}.

בְּתוֹךְ *among*, + בֵּן *son* Jos 17_6, of Israel Nm $18_{23.24}$, נַחֲלָה *inheritance* Jos 19_9.

מֵעֵבֶר לְ *on the other side of, beyond*, + יַרְדֵּן *Jordan* Nm 32_{19}.

<COLL> נחל ‖ ירשׁ *possess* Is 57_{13} Ps 69_{37} (+), רום hi. *take up* Pr 3_{35}; + חלק נַחֲלָה *share inheritance* Si 45_{22}; + adverb, אַךְ *only* Jr 16_{19}; וְנָחַל י׳ אֶת־יְהוּדָה חֶלְקוֹ *and Y. shall inherit Judah (as) his portion* Zc 2_{16}.

2. divide as an inheritance, distribute, <SUBJ> אִישׁ *man* Nm 34_{17}, בֵּן *son* of Israel Jos 19_{49}, נָשִׂיא *prince* Nm 34_{18}. <OBJ> אֶרֶץ *land* Nm $34_{17.18}$ 19_{49}. <PREP> לְ of benefit, *for*, + בֵּן *son* of Israel Nm 34_{17}; *according to*, + גְּבוּל *border* Jos 19_{49}.

Also 1QH 6_6 perh. 4QapPs^a 6_1 4Q418 126.2_{16} 185_4 4QapMes 11_3 4QBéat 13_2 ([תנ]חל) 13_5 14.2_{14} ([ינחלו[ה)
33_1.

<SYN> §1 ירשׁ *possess*, רום hi. *take up*.

Pi. $_4$ Pf. נִחֲלוּ, נִחַל; inf. נַחֵל—**allocate portions to, distribute,** <SUBJ> Eleazar Jos $14_{1.2}$ (if em.; see Prep.) 19_{51}, Joshua Jos $14_{1.2}$ (if em.; see Prep.) 19_{51}, Moses Jos 13_{32}, בֵּן *son* Jos $14_{1.2}$ (if em.; see Prep.) 19_{51}, כֹּהֵן *priest* Jos $14_{1.2}$ (if em.; see Prep.) 19_{51}, ראשׁ *head* Jos 19_{51}, אֵלֶּה *these* Nm 34_{29}. <OBJ> 1. recipient, בֵּן *son* of Israel Nm 34_{29} Jos $14_{1.2}$ (if em.; see Prep.). 2. thing allocated, נַחֲלָה *inheritance* Jos 19_{51}, אֵלֶּה *these* Jos 13_{32} 14_1. <PREP> בְּ of place, *in, at*, + Shiloh Jos 19_{51}, אֶרֶץ *land* Nm 34_{29}, עֲרָבָה *plain* Jos 13_{32}; of instrument, *by (means of), with*, + גּוֹרָל *lot* Jos 14_2 (if em. בְּגוֹרַל נַחֲלָתָם *by the lot of their inheritance* to בַּגּוֹרָל נִחֲלוּ אוֹתָם *by lot they allocated portions to them*) 19_{51}; מֵעֵבֶר לְ *on the other side of, beyond*, + יַרְדֵּן *Jordan* Jos 13_{32}; לִפְנֵי *before*, + Y. Jos 19_{51}; נחל pi. + noun without preposition, פֶּתַח *(at the) entrance* Jos 19_{51}.

Hi. $_{17.2.16}$ Pf. הִנְחַלְתִּי, Q הנחלתו (הינחלתו); impf. יַנְחִיל (ינחילן Q), יַנְחִלֵם, יַנְחִלֶנָּה, ינחילכה Q, יַנְחִילְךָ, יַנְחִל), 2ms תַּנְחִיל (תַּנְחִילֶנָּה); + waw וְהִנְחַלְתֶּם, וְהִנְחַלְתִּי; Q וינחילם (Q וינחילנו, וינחילה); ptc. מַנְחִיל, Q מנחילי; inf. הַנְחִיל (הַנְחִילוֹ, הַנְחֵל, Si, Q הנחילם).

Cause to inherit, leave an inheritance to, give as an inheritance, allot, <SUBJ> Y. Dt 12_{10} 19_3 1 S 2_8 Jr 3_{18} 12_{14} Zc 8_{12} Si 44_{21} 1QH 4_{15} 1QS 4_{26} 11_7 1QSb 3_{28} 1QLitPr 3.2_3 4QMyst^a $3a.2_{14}$ 4Q417 2.1_{16} GnzPs 1_{19}, עֶלְיוֹן *the Most High* Dt 32_8 (unless נחל II *sift*), עַם *people* 1 C 28_8, Joshua Dt 1_{38} 3_{28} 31_7 Jos 1_6 Si 46_1, אִישׁ *man* Dt 21_{16}, בֵּן *son* Dt 1_{38} Jos 1_6 Si 30_{32} ([הנחו[ל) 46_1, אָח *brother* 1 C 28_8, נָשִׂיא *prince* Ezk 46_{18}, עֶבֶד *servant*

Is 49$_8$, מְשָׁרֵת *minister* Jos 1$_6$ Si 46$_1$, טוֹב *good one* Pr 13$_{22}$, חָכְמָה *wisdom* Pr 8$_{21}$.

<OBJ> 1. one who inherits, Israel(ites) Dt 13$_8$ 12$_{10}$ 19$_3$ Jr 12$_{14}$ Si 46$_1$ 1QSb 3$_{28}$, עַם *people* Dt 3$_{28}$ 31$_7$ Jos 1$_6$ 12$_{14}$ 4QapJoshua[a] 3.2$_{10}$ ([העם]), גּוֹי *nation* Dt 32$_8$ (unless נחל II *sift*), שְׁאֵרִית *remnant* of people Zc 8$_{12}$, David GnzPs 1$_{19}$, אָב *father* Jr 3$_{18}$, בֵּן *son* Dt 21$_{16}$ Ezk 46$_{18}$ Pr 13$_{22}$, זֶרַע *offspring* Si 44$_{21}$ perh. 1QH 4$_{15}$ 1QLitPr 3.2$_3$, עֶבֶד *servant* GnzPs 1$_{19}$, דַּל *poor one* 1 S 2$_8$, אֶבְיוֹן *needy one* 1 S 2$_8$, אהב ptc. *one who loves* Pr 8$_{21}$, שֹׁרֶשׁ *root* of Jesse GnzPs 1$_{19}$, אֲשֶׁר *one who* 1QS 11$_7$.

2. thing inherited, רוּחַ *spirit* 1QS 4$_{26}$, רֵאשִׁית *firstfruits* 1QSb 3$_{28}$, אֶרֶץ *land* Dt 13$_8$ 3$_{28}$ 12$_{10}$ 19$_3$ 31$_7$ Jos 1$_6$ Jr 3$_{18}$, כִּסֵּא *throne* 1 S 2$_8$, עֲטֶרֶת *crown* GnzPs 1$_{19}$, פְּאֵר *turban* GnzPs 1$_{19}$, נַחֲלָה *inheritance* Is 49$_8$ Jr 12$_{14}$, יֵשׁ *property* Pr 8$_{21}$, רֹב *abundance* 1QH 4$_{15}$, עֹשֶׁר *wealth* perh 4Q sapDidA 4$_1$, רִשְׁעָה *wickedness* 4QAges[a] 1$_9$, אַשְׁמָה *guilt* 4QAges[b] 2$_4$, אֲשֶׁר *that which* Dt 21$_{16}$, כֹּל *all* 1QLitPr 3.2$_3$, אֵלֶּה *these* Zc 8$_{12}$.

<PREP> לְ of direction, *to* or introducing object, + Enosh 4Q417 2.1$_{16}$, בֵּן *son* 1 C 28$_8$ 1QS 4$_{26}$; *before*, + עַיִן *eye* 4QapMos[c] 1.1$_4$.

בְּ of time, *in, on*, + יוֹם *day* Si 30$_{32}$ (הנח[ל]); partitive, *(some) of* or introducing object, + גּוֹרָל *lot* 1QS 11$_7$, כָּבוֹד *glory* 1QH 4$_{15}$; of accompaniment, *with*, + רִנָּה *joyful shout* GnzPs 1$_{19}$.

מִן of direction, *from*, + יָם *sea* Si 44$_{21}$, נָהָר *river* Si 44$_{21}$; partitive, *(some) of*, + אֲחֻזָּה *possession* Ezk 46$_{18}$.

עִם *with*, + עַם *people* 4Q417 2.1$_{16}$.

עַד *unto*, + יָם *sea* Si 44$_{21}$, אֶפֶס *end* of earth Si 44$_{21}$, עוֹלָם *eternity* 1 C 28$_8$.

Also 4QMidrEschat[b] 10$_{12}$ (וינח[יל]) 4QCitJub 1.1$_{12}$ 4Q 417 9$_2$ 4QSap[b] 16$_3$ 4QRitMar 314$_1$ (הנ[חילנו]).

Ho. $_1$ Pf. הָנְחַלְתִּי—**be allotted, be made to inherit**, <SUBJ> Job Jb 7$_3$ (+ מנה pi. *assign*). <OBJ> יֶרַח *month* of emptiness Jb 7$_3$. <PREP> לְ *for oneself*, + Job Jb 7$_3$.

Htp. $_{7.1.1}$ Impf. 2ms תִּתְנַחֲלוּ (תִּתְנֶחָלוּ); + waw וְהִתְנַחֲלוּם, וְהִתְנַחַלְתֶּם (L וְהִתְנַחַלְתֶּם)—**1. inherit, take as a possession for oneself**; without obj., **have an inheritance** (Si 36$_{16}$), <SUBJ> אִישׁ *man*, i.e. each Nm 32$_{18}$, בֵּן *son* of Israel Nm 32$_{18}$ 33$_{54.54}$ 34$_{13}$, בַּיִת *house* of Israel Is 14$_2$; subj. not specified, Si 36$_{16}$. <OBJ> עַם *people* Is 14$_2$, אֶרֶץ *land* Nm 33$_{54}$ 34$_{13}$, נַחֲלָה *inheritance* Nm 32$_{18}$. <PREP> לְ *according to*, + מִשְׁפָּחָה *clan* Nm 33$_{54}$, מַטֶּה *tribe* Nm 33$_{54}$; *as*, + עֶבֶד *slave* Is 14$_2$, שִׁפְחָה *female slave* Is 14$_2$; בְּ of instrument, *by (means of), with*, + גּוֹרָל *lot* Nm 33$_{54}$ 34$_{13}$; כְּ *as in*, + יוֹם *day* Si 36$_{16}$; עַל *upon*, + אֲדָמָה *land* Is 14$_2$.

2. divide as an inheritance, distribute, <SUBJ> Israelites Ezk 47$_{13}$. <OBJ> אֶרֶץ *land* Ezk 47$_{13}$. <PREP> לְ of direction, *to*, + שֵׁבֶט *tribe* Ezk 47$_{13}$. <COLL> גְּבוּל אֲשֶׁר תִּתְנַחֲלוּ אֶת־הָאָרֶץ *the border(s) by which you shall distribute the land* Ezk 47$_{13}$.

3. pass on as an inheritance, <SUBJ> בֵּן *son* of Israel Lv 25$_{46}$. <OBJ> עֶבֶד *slave* Lv 25$_{46}$, אָמָה *female slave* Lv 25$_{46}$. <PREP> לְ of direction, *to*, + בֵּן *son* Lv 25$_{46}$.

Also 6QDeut 1$_7$ (והתנחל[תם]).

⇨ נַחֲלָה I *inheritance*.

*נחל II $_4$ vb. **sift—Qal** $_1$ Impf. 2ms תְּנַחֵל—**sift** (unless נחל I *inherit*), <SUBJ> Y. Ps 82$_8$. <PREP> בְּ introducing object, + גּוֹי *nation* Ps 82$_8$.

Ni. $_1$ + waw וְנִחַלְתְּ—**be sifted** (unless חלל I ni. *be profaned*), <SUBJ> Jerusalem Ezk 22$_{16}$. <PREP> בְּ *because of* Ezk 22$_{16}$; לְעֵינֵי *in the presence of*, + גּוֹי *nation* Ezk 22$_{16}$.

Pi. $_1$ Pf. נֻחֲלוּ—**sift** (unless חלה I ni. *be made weak*), <SUBJ> Israel(ites) Jr 12$_{13}$.

Hi. $_1$ Inf. הַנְחֵל—**sift, sprinkle (as through a sieve)** (unless נחל I hi. *cause to inherit*), <SUBJ> עֶלְיוֹן *Most High* Dt 32$_8$. <OBJ> גּוֹי *nation* Dt 32$_8$.

נַחַל I $_{139.3.17}$ n.m. **wadi**—נָחַל; + ה- of direction נַחְלָה; cstr. נַחַל (נַחְלָה); du. נַחֲלַיִם; pl. נְחָלִים; cstr. נַחֲלֵי; sf. נְחָלֶיהָ—**1. wadi, river valley**, usu. with water only at certain seasons, <SUBJ> נטה ni. *stretch out* Nm 24$_6$ (unless נַחַל II *date palm*), עבד ni. *be ploughed* Dt 21$_4$ =11QT 63$_2$, זרע ni. *be sown* Dt 21$_4$=11QT 63$_2$, מלא ni. *be filled* with water 2 K 3$_{17}$.

<NOM CL> הַנַּחַל אֲשֶׁר עַל־פְּנֵי יָקְנְעָם *the wadi that is against the face*, i.e. to the east, *of Jokneam* Jos 19$_{11}$, sim. 1 K 17$_{3.5}$.

<OBJ> קרא *call*, i.e. name Nm 13$_{24}$, עבר *cross* Dt

$2_{13.13.14.24}$ 1 S 30_{10} 1 K 2_{37}, עשׂה *make*, i.e. turn into, pools 2 K 3_{16}, שׁקה hi. *water* Jl 4_{18}.

<CSTR> נַחַל אַרְנוֹן *wadi of Arnon* Dt $2_{24.36}$ $3_{8.12.16}$ 4_{48} Jos $12_{1.12}$ $13_{9.16}$ 2 K 10_{33}, אֶשְׁכֹּל *of Eshcol* Nm $13_{23.24}$ 32_{9} Dt 1_{24}, הַבְּשׂוֹר *of Besor* 1 S $30_{9.10.21}$, ־גְּרָר *of Gerar* Gn 26_{17}, זֶרֶד *of Zered* Nm 21_{12} (זָרֶד) Dt 2_{13} (זָרֶד) 2_{13} (זָרֶד) 2_{14}, יַבֹּק *of Jabbok* Dt 2_{37}, הכפא *of Kippa* 3QTr 5_{12}, כְּרִית *of Cherith* 1 K $17_{3.5}$, מִצְרַיִם *of Egypt* Nm 34_{5} (נַחְלָה) Jos $15_{4.47}$ (מִצְרָיִם) 1 K 8_{65}||2 C 7_{8} 2 K 24_{7} Is 27_{12}, הָעֲרָבָה *of the Arabah* Am 6_{14}, קִדְרוֹן *of Kidron* 2 S 15_{23} 1 K 2_{37} 15_{13}||2 C 15_{16} 2 K $23_{6.6.12}$ Jr 31_{40} 2 C 29_{16} 30_{14}, קִישׁוֹן *of Kishon* Jg $4_{7.13}$ (see also §2, Cstr.) 1 K 18_{40} Ps 83_{10}, קָנָה *of Kanah* Jos 16_{8} 17_{9}, שֹׂרֵק *of Sorek* Jg 16_{4}, הַשִּׁטִּים *of Shittim* Jl 4_{18}, נַחֲלֵי גָעַשׁ *wadis of Gaash* 2 S 23_{30}||1 C 11_{32}, הַבַּתּוֹת *of the precipices* Is 7_{19}, נַחַל הָעֲרָבִים *wadi of the willows* Is 15_{7}, נַחַל אֵיתָן perh. *wadi of continuity*, i.e. with a continuous stream (unless אֵיתָן is adj. *continuous*) Dt 21_{4}=11QT 63_{2} (see also §2, Cstr.).

שְׂפַת־נַחַל *lip*, i.e. edge, *of the wadi of* Dt 2_{36} 4_{48} Jos 12_{2} $13_{9.16}$ (see also §2, Cstr.), יַד *hand*, i.e. side, *of* Dt 2_{37}, תּוֹךְ הַנַּחַל *middle of the wadi* Dt 3_{16} Jos 12_{2} $13_{9.16}$ 2 S 24_{5}, סוֹף *end of* 2 C 20_{16}, עֹרְבֵי־נַחַל *ravens of the wadi* Pr 30_{17}, אִבֵּי הַנָּחַל *blossoms of the wadi* Ca 6_{11} (unless *of the date palm*, i.e. נַחַל II), עַרְבֵי־נָחַל *willows of the wadi* Lv 23_{40} Jb 40_{22} (נָחַל) Si 50_{12}, רִגְבֵי *clods of* Jb 21_{33} (נָחַל; unless נַחַל V *dust*), חַלְּקֵי־נַחַל *smooth stones of the wadi* Is 57_{6} (unless נַחַל III *tomb*), צוּר נְחָלִים *rock(s) of the wadis* Jb 22_{24}, אֶשֶׁד הַנְּחָלִים *slope of the wadis* Nm 21_{15} (Sam אֲשֶׁר הִנְחִלָם *which he apportioned*), עֲרוּץ *gully of* Jb 30_{6}, כָּל־הַנְּחָלִים *all the wadis* 1 K 18_{5}.

<APP> אַרְנוֹן *Arnon* Nm 21_{14}, יַבֹּק *Jabbok* Dt 3_{16} Jos 12_{2}, גְּבוּל *border* Dt 3_{16} Jos 12_{2}.

<ADJ> גָּדוֹל *great* 3QTr 10_{3}, אֵיתָן *continuous* or *devastating** perh. Dt 21_{4}=11QT 63_{2} (unless נַחַל אֵיתָן = *wadi of continuity*), זֶה *this* 2 K 3_{16}, הוּא *that* 2 K 3_{17}.

<PREP> לְ of direction, *(in)to*, + יצא hi. *bring out* 2 C 29_{16}, שׁלך hi. *cast* 2 C 30_{14}, נכה hi. *strike* river *into* Is 11_{15}; *(in relation) to, (in respect) of*, Jos 15_{7} (מִנֶּגֶב לְ *to the south of*) 17_{9} (נֶגְבָּה לְ *to the south of*) 17_{9} (מִצְּפוֹן לְ *to the north of*).

בְּ of place, *in* Dt 2_{36} Jg 16_{4} Ps 83_{10} 3QTr 5_{12}, + עלה *go up* Ne 2_{15}, שׁלח pi. *send* springs Ps 104_{10}, ישׁב *dwell* 1 K 17_{5}, hi. *leave* 1 S 30_{21}, חנה *encamp* Gn 26_{17} Nm 21_{12}, נוּחַ *rest* Is 7_{19}, ארב *lie in wait* 1 S 15_{5}, סתר ni. *hide oneself* 1 K 17_{3}, חפר *dig* Gn 26_{19}, בנה *build* 2 C 33_{14}, שׁחט *slay* Is 57_{5} (unless נַחַל III *tomb*), ערף *break neck* Dt 21_{4} 4QHalakhah[a] 13_{4} (וערפו ... בנח[ל]), pass. *have one's neck broken* Dt 21_{6}=11QT 63_{5}, שׂרף *burn* 1 K 15_{13}||2 C 15_{16} 2 K 23_{6}; introducing object, + עבר *cross* 2 S 15_{23}.

כְּ *as* Nm 24_{6} (unless נַחַל II *date palm*).

כְּמוֹ *as*, + בגד *be treacherous* Jb 6_{15}.

מִן of direction, *from* Dt 3_{8} Jos 12_{1} 1 S 17_{40} 2 K 24_{7}, + רוה pi. *draw water* 3QTr 10_{3}; *(originating) from, of* 2 S 23_{30}||1 C 11_{32}.

אֶל *to*, + זעק hi. *summon* Jg 4_{13}, הלך *go* 1 K 18_{5}, יצא hi. *bring out* 2 K 23_{6}, ירד hi. *bring down* Dt 21_{4}=11QT 63_{2} ([והורידו]) 1 K 18_{40}, שׁלך hi. *cast* 2 K 23_{12}, פגע *reach* Jos 19_{11}, משׁך *draw out* Jg 4_{7}.

עַל *upon, beside, over* Dt 3_{12} 2 K 10_{33}, + נשׂא *carry* Is 15_{7}.

עַד *unto, as far as* Dt $3_{16.16}$ Jos 12_{2} 15_{47} 1 K 8_{65}||2 C 7_{8} Jr 31_{40}, + בוא *come* Nm 13_{23} Dt 1_{24} 1 S 30_{9}, עלה *go up* Nm 32_{9}, סחב *drag* 2 S 17_{13}, חבט *beat out* Is 27_{12}, לחץ *oppress* Am 6_{14}.

ה- of direction, *to(wards)* Ezk 47_{19} (if em. נַחֲלָה *[to] Nahalah* to נַחְלָה), + היה *be* Ezk 48_{28} (if em. נַחֲלָה), סבב ni. *turn* Nm 34_{5}.

נַחַל without preposition or ה- of direction, *(at) the wadi, (to) the wadi*, + הלך *go* Jos 16_{8}, יצא *go out* Jos 15_{4}, ירד *go down* Jos 17_{9}.

<COLL> נַחַל || נָקִיק *cleft* of rock Is 7_{19}; + גַּנָּה *garden* Nm 24_{6}, מַעְיָן *spring* 1 K 18_{5}; שִׁבְעָה נְחָלִים *seven wadis* Is 11_{15}.

2. stream, river, torrent, <SUBJ> הלך *go* Ec $1_{7.7}$ 1QH 11_{29}, בוא *come* Ezk $47_{9.9}$, ירד *go down* Dt 9_{21}, עבר *pass* Ps 124_{4} (נַחְלָה, perh. accus. of manner)* Jb 6_{15}, ni. *be crossed* Ezk 47_{5}, שׁוב *go back* Ec 1_{7}, בקע ni. *break out* Is 35_{6} 1QH 11_{32}, גרף *sweep away* Jg 5_{21}, קדם pi. *precede*, i.e. overwhelm Jg 5_{21} (if em.; see Cstr.), שׁטף *overflow* Is 30_{28} 66_{12} Jr 47_{2} Ps 78_{20} 2 C 32_{24} 1QH 16_{17}, בעת pi. *overwhelm* 2 S 22_{5}||Ps 18_{5}, נבע *gush* Pr

184, חצה *reach to* Is 3028, יבשׁ *dry up* 1 K 177, הפך ni. *be turned* into pitch Is 349.

<NOM CL> נַחַל נֹבֵעַ מְקוֹר חָכְמָה *the fountain of wisdom is a gushing stream* Pr 184.

<OBJ> עבר *cross* Ezk 475, hi. *cause to cross* Gn 3224, בקע *split open* Ps 7415, שׁקה hi. *give to drink* Ps 369, סתם *stop up* 2 C 3224.

<CSTR> נַחֲלֵי מָיִם *streams of water* Dt 87 107 (מָיִם) Jr 319 1QH 175 4QapJoshuaª 114 4QHymnSap 22 ([מ]ים) 6QDeut 13 ([נחל]י מים), שֶׁמֶן *of oil* Mc 67, דְּבַשׁ וְחֶמְאָה *of honey and curds* Jb 2017, בְּלִיַּעַל *of Belial* 2 S 225||Ps 185 1QH 1129.32 1338 ([נחלי ב[ל]י]על), נַחַל קִישׁוֹן *stream of Kishon* 521.21 (see also §1, Cstr.), קְדוּמִים appar. *of ancient ones* Jg 521 (or em. קְדוּמִים to קִדְּמָם *it preceded them*), גָּפְרִית *of brimstone* Is 3033, נחלי זפת *streams of pitch* 1QH 1131 4QpsHodᶜ 310, נַחַל עֲדָנֶיךָ *stream of your delights* Ps 369, אֵיתָן *of continuity*, i.e. continuous stream (unless אֵיתָן is adj. *continuous*) Am 524 Si 4013 (see also §1, Cstr.).

שְׂפַת הַנַּחַל *lip*, i.e. edge, *of the stream* Ezk 476 (הַנָּחַל) 477 (see also §1, Cstr.), גפת נחל *bank of a stream* Si 4016(B) (M גפות *banks of*), אֲפִיק נְחָלִים *channel of streams* Jb 615, נַהֲרֵי נַחֲלֵי *rivers of streams of* Jb 2017 (or em. נַהֲרֵי to יִצְהָר *of oil*), אֶרֶץ נַחֲלֵי *land of streams of* Dt 87 107 4QapJoshuaª 114 6QDeut 13 ([נחל]י), כָּל־הַנְּחָלִים *all the streams* Ec 17 4QBerª 510 (כול נחלים).

<APP> מַיִם *water* Ezk 475, יְאֹר *river* 4QBerª 510.

<ADJ> אֵיתָן *continuous* or *devastating** (unless נַחַל אֵיתָן = *stream of continuity*) Am 524 Si 4013.

<PREP> לְ *as* or introducing predicate 1QH 1131, + היה *be* Jr 472 1QH 1617.

בְּ of place, *in* Lv 119.10; introducing object, + רצה *be pleased with* Mc 67.

כְּ *as* Is 3028.33 6612 Lm 218 Si 4013 1QH 175.

מִן *from (out of)*, + שׁתה *drink* 1 K 174.6 Ps 1107.

אֶל *(in)to*, + הלך hi. *lead* Jr 319, שׁלך hi. *cast* Dt 921.

עַל *upon, beside*, + עלה *go up*, i.e. grow Ezk 4712.

ה- of direction appar. *into*, + עבר *pass* Ps 1244 (but prob. עבר is subj. of נַחְלָה).

<COLL> נַחַל || מַיִם *water* Lv 119 Is 356 Am 524 Ps 7820 1244 Pr 184 (both +), נָהָר *river* Is 6612 Ps 7415 (+), יָם *sea* Lv 119.10, מִשְׁבָּר *breaker* 2 S 225||Ps 185, מַעְיָן *spring* Ps 7415 (מַעְיָן וָנָחַל) 2 C 3224, עָפָר *dust* Is 349; + עַיִן *spring* Dt 87, תְּהוֹם *deep*, i.e. fountain Dt 87, מִקְוֶה *collection* of waters 4QapMes 5.23, דֶּשֶׁן *fat* Ps 369.

3. grave trench, tunnel, mine shaft (unless נַחַל III *tomb* or IV *(mine) shaft* or VI *excavation, shaft*), <OBJ> פרץ *break open* mine shaft Jb 284. <CSTR> רִגְבֵי נַחַל *clods of the grave trench* Jb 2133. <PREP> בְּ of instrument, *by means of*, + עלה go up Ne 215 (וָאֱהִי עֹלֶה בַנַּחַל *and I went up by the tunnel*).

<SYN> §1 נָקִיק *cleft*; §2 מַיִם *water*, נָהָר *river*, יָם *sea*, מִשְׁבָּר *breaker*, מַעְיָן *spring*, עָפָר *dust*.

Also 4QOrdª 1.21 5QSela 9.117.*

⇒ (?) נַחֲלִיאֵל *Nahaliel*.

[נַ֫חַל] II 2 n.[m.] **date palm** (unless נַחַל I *wadi*)—נָ֫חַל; pl. נְחָלִים—<SUBJ> נטה ni. *stretch out* Nm 246. <CSTR> אִבֵּי הַנָּחַל *blossoms of the date palm* Ca 611. <PREP> כְּ *as* Nm 246.

⇒ (?) נַחֲלִיאֵל *Nahaliel*.

*נַ֫חַל III 2 n.[m.] **tomb** (unless נַחַל I *wadi* or *grave trench*)—pl. נְחָלִים—cut in rocks, <CSTR> חַלְּקֵי־נַחַל *smooth stones of the tomb* Is 576. <PREP> בְּ of place, *in*, + שׁחט *slay* children Is 575.

*נַ֫חַל IV 1 n.[m.] **(mine) shaft** (unless נַחַל I *grave trench* or VI *excavation, shaft*), <OBJ> פרץ *break open* Jb 284.

*נַ֫חַל V 1 n.[m.] **dust** 3 (unless נַחַל I *wadi* or *grave trench*), <CSTR> רִגְבֵי נָחַל *clods of dust* Jb 213.

*נַ֫חַל VI 1 n.[m.] **excavation, shaft** (unless I *tunnel* or נַחַל IV *[mine] shaft*), <OBJ> פרץ *break open* Jb 284.

נַחֲלָה I 222.12.77 n.f. **inheritance**—נַחֲלָת (Ps 166); cstr. נַחֲלַת; sf. נַחֲלָתִי, נַחֲלָתְךָ (נַחֲלָתֶךָ), Q נחלתכה, נַחֲלָתוֹ, Q נחלתה, נַחֲלָתֵנוּ, נַחֲלַתְכֶם, נַחֲלָתָם, נַחֲלָתָן; pl. נְחָלוֹת (נְחָלֹת).

1. inheritance, possession, inalienable hereditary **property,** of individuals (e.g. Nm 367 Dt 1914 Jos 3430 1 K 213 Mc 22), of daughter (e.g. Gn 3114 Nm 277 363 Jos 174.6 Jb 4215).

2. land as inheritance of (tribes and families of) Israel (e.g. Nm 26$_{53}$ 32$_{19}$ 33$_{54}$ 34$_{14}$ Dt 4$_{21}$ 29$_{7}$ Jos 11$_{23}$ 13$_{6}$ Jg 20$_{6}$ Ezk 47$_{14}$ 48$_{29}$ Ps 105$_{11}$||1 C 16$_{18}$ Si 46$_{8}$), of Esau (Ml 1$_{3}$), given to Israel by Y. (e.g. Dt 12$_{9}$ 15$_{4}$ 24$_{4}$ Jr 12$_{14}$ 17$_{4}$); as inheritance of Y. (Ex 15$_{17}$ Jr 2$_{7}$).

3. nations as inheritance of king (Ps 2$_{7}$), of people of Y. (Ps 111$_{6}$).

4. Y. as inheritance of priests and Levites (e.g. Nm 18$_{20}$ Dt 10$_{9}$ Jos 13$_{33}$ Ezk 44$_{28}$).

5. tithes and offerings as inheritance of Levites (e.g. Nm 18$_{21}$ Jos 13$_{14}$), priesthood as inheritance of Levites (Jos 18$_{7}$).

6. Israel as inheritance of Y. (e.g. Dt 4$_{20}$ 9$_{26}$ 1 S 10$_{1}$ 1 K 8$_{51}$ 2 K 21$_{14}$ Is 19$_{25}$ 63$_{17}$ Jr 10$_{16}$ Jl 2$_{17}$ Mc 7$_{14}$ Ps 28$_{9}$ 74$_{2}$).

7. inheritance as one's portion, share of righteousness, truth, etc. (e.g. 1QH 18$_{28}$ 1QS 4$_{24}$ 4QdivProv 1$_{2}$), the lot of light (CD 13$_{12}$), one's lot from Y. (Jb 20$_{29}$ 27$_{13}$ 31$_{2}$).

8. kingdom chosen by Y. for himself (Ps 47$_{5}$; if em. לָנוּ *for us* to לְנֵהוּ *for him*).*

<SUBJ> היה *be* Nm 27$_{11}$ 36$_{12}$ Dt 10$_{9}$ 18$_{1.2}$ Jos 19$_{1}$ Jr 12$_{8}$ Ezk 46$_{16.17}$ Ps 37$_{18}$ 4QapLam[a] 1.1$_{12}$ 4QT 6$_{4}$ (נחל[ה] [לו]א יהיה), בוא *come* Nm 32$_{19}$, סבב *turn*, i.e. be transferred Nm 36$_{7.9}$, הפך ni. *be turned over* Lm 5$_{2}$, ברך pass. *be blessed* Is 19$_{25}$, חלק ni. *be divided* Nm 26$_{56}$, נתן *give*, i.e. raise, voice Jr 12$_{8}$, pass. *be given* Nm 26$_{54}$, ni. *be given* Nm 26$_{62}$, מלא ni. *be filled* 4Q418 88$_{8}$ (נ[ח]לתכה), יסף ni. *be added* Nm 36$_{4}$, גרע ni. *be diminished* Nm 36$_{3.4}$, נפל *fall* Jg 18$_{1}$, בחל pu. *be gained by greed* Pr 20$_{21(Kt)}$ (or em. מְבַחֶלֶת *produces unripe fruit*, i.e. בחל I pi. ptc., with נַחֲלָה = *ill [tree]* as subj.), בהל pu. *be gained in haste* Pr 20$_{21(Qr)}$, שׁמם *be desolate* Is 49$_{8}$, לאה ni. *languish* Ps 68$_{10}$, שׁפר *be beautiful* Ps 16$_{6}$.

<NOM CL> י׳ הוּא נַחֲלָתוֹ *Y. is his inheritance* Dt 10$_{9}$ 18$_{2}$, var. Jos 13$_{33}$, אִשֵּׁי י׳ ... הוּא נַחֲלָתוֹ *the fire offerings of Y. ... are his inheritance* Jos 13$_{14}$, כְּהֻנַּת י׳ נַחֲלָתוֹ *the priesthood of Y. is his inheritance* Jos 18$_{7}$, אֲנִי ... נַחֲלָתְךָ *I am your ... your inheritance* Nm 18$_{20}$, var. Ezk 44$_{28}$, הוא ... נחלתכה *he is ... your inheritance* 4Q418 81$_{3}$, ה]ואה נחלותם] *it is their inheritances* 4QT 6$_{5}$, הֵם ... נַחֲלָתְךָ *they are ... your inheritance* Dt 9$_{29}$, var. 1 K 8$_{51}$, המה נחל[ת מלכי צ]דק *they are the inheritance of Melchizedek* 11QMelch 2$_{5}$, זֶה ... נַחֲלַת אִמְרוֹ *this is ... the inheritance of his word* Jb 20$_{29}$ (or em. אִמְרוֹ *his word* to מֹרֶא *rebellious one* or מַמְרֶה *rebellion*), var. Jb 27$_{13}$, זֹאת נַחֲלַת בְּנֵי־רְאוּבֵן *this is the inheritance of the sons of Reuben* Jos 13$_{23}$, vars. Jos 13$_{28}$ 15$_{20}$ 16$_{8}$ 18$_{20.28}$ 19$_{8+7t}$ Is 54$_{17}$, אֵלֶּה הַנְּחָלֹת *these are the inheritances* Jos 19$_{51}$, מֶה ... נַחֲלַת שַׁדַּי *what would be ... the inheritance of*, i.e. from, *the Almighty?* Jb 31$_{2}$.

נַחֲלַת י׳ בָּנִים *sons are an inheritance of*, i.e. from, *Y.* Ps 127$_{3}$, בַּיִת וָהוֹן נַחֲלַת אָבוֹת *house and wealth are the inheritance of*, i.e. from, *fathers* Pr 19$_{14}$, נַחֲלָתִי עֵדוֹתֶיךָ *your testimonies are my inheritance* Ps 119$_{11}$ (if em. נָחַלְתִּי *I have inherited*), חיים עולם נחלתם *their inheritance is life forever* 4Q418 69.2$_{13}$, הַעַיִט צָבוּעַ נַחֲלָתִי לִי *is my inheritance to me a coloured bird of prey?* Jr 12$_{9}$.

נח]לתם לבני בניהם] *their inheritance is to their sons' sons* Si 44$_{11(M\ [Yadin])}$, נחלת אהרן לכל זרעו *the inheritance of Aaron is to all his descendants* Si 45$_{25}$, הַעוֹד לָנוּ ... נַחֲלָה *is there still to us ... an inheritance?* Gn 31$_{14}$, אֵין לוֹ ... נַחֲלָה *there is to him no ... inheritance* Dt 12$_{12}$ 14$_{27.29}$, לֹא נַחֲלָה־לָנוּ *there is not to us an inheritance* 2 S 20$_{1}$, var. 1 K 12$_{16}$||2 C 10$_{16}$, אין נחלתה בתוך כול מאזרי נוגה *her inheritance is not among all who gird themselves with light* 4QWiles 1$_{7}$, להם כול נחלת אדם ולזרעם *to them is all the inheritance of Adam and to their descendants* 4QpPs[a] 1.3$_{1}$, מֵחֶבֶל בְּנֵי יְהוּדָה נַחֲלַת בְּנֵי שִׁמְעוֹן *from (part of) the territory of the sons of Judah was the inheritance of the sons of Simeon* Jos 19$_{9}$, מאתו נחלת כל חי *from him is the inheritance of every living being* 4Q416 3$_{2}$, נחלת אש לפני כבודו *the inheritance of fire was before his glory* Si 45$_{25}$.

<OBJ> ברך pi. *bless* 2 S 21$_{3}$ Ps 28$_{9}$, ידע *know* 4Q416 2.3$_{10}$ 4Q418 9$_{10(erased)}$ ([תדע] נח[ל]תו), יצא hi. *bring out* Dt 9$_{29}$ 1 K 8$_{51}$, עבר hi. *cause to pass* Nm 27$_{7.8}$, סבב *turn away* Si 9$_{6}$, בקשׁ pi. *seek* Jg 18$_{1}$, בחר *choose* Ps 47$_{5}$, עזב *forsake* Ps 94$_{14}$ 4QConfess 2$_{3.4}$ (ותע[זו]ב), נטשׁ *forsake* Jr 12$_{7}$.

נתן *give* Nm 16$_{14}$ 27$_{9.10.11}$ 36$_{2}$ Dt 4$_{21.38}$ 12$_{9}$ 15$_{4}$ 19$_{10}$ 20$_{16}$||11QT 62$_{13}$ Dt 21$_{23}$||11QT 64$_{13}$ Dt 24$_{4}$ 25$_{19}$ 26$_{1}$ Jos 13$_{8.14.33}$ 14$_{3.3}$ 17$_{4.4.14}$ 19$_{49}$ 1 K 21$_{3.4}$ Jr 3$_{19}$ 17$_{4}$ Ezk 47$_{23}$ Jl

2$_{17}$ Ml 1$_{3}$ (if em. לְתַנּוֹת *to jackals* to נָתַתִּי *I have given*, i.e. made) Ps 111$_{6}$ 135$_{12.12}$ 136$_{22}$ Jb 42$_{15}$ Si 44$_{23}$ 45$_{20}$ 4QapLam^{b} 1$_{1}$, i.e. make (into) Ps 2$_{8}$, חלק *share* Jos 18$_{2}$ Pr 17$_{2}$ Si 45$_{22}$, פלג pi. *divide* 4QPrEnosh 1.2$_{1}$ 4Q418 81$_{20}$ 4Q423 5$_{4}$ ([נ]חלת), נחל *inherit* Nm 18$_{23.24}$ 35$_{8}$ Dt 19$_{14}$ Jos 17$_{6}$, pi. *distribute* Jos 19$_{51}$, hi. *cause to inherit* Is 49$_{8}$ Jr 12$_{14}$, htp. *inherit* Nm 32$_{18}$, ירשׁ *possess* Nm 27$_{11}$ 36$_{8.8}$ Si 46$_{9}$ 4QpPs^{b} 1$_{7}$ ([י]ורשי), hi. *cause to possess* 4Q418 81$_{3}$ GnzPs 3$_{21}$, נפל hi. *cause to fall*, i.e. allot Ps 78$_{55}$, שׂים *place*, i.e. make Jr 2$_{7}$ Ml 1$_{3}$ (unless em.; see above), לקח *take* Nm 34$_{14.15}$ Jos 13$_{8}$ 18$_{7}$ Jb 27$_{13}$ 4Q417 1.1$_{18}$ 4Q418 81$_{11}$, רבה hi. *increase* Nm 26$_{54}$ 33$_{54}$ 1QH 18$_{28}$ 4QdivProv 1$_{2}$, מעט hi. *diminish* Nm 26$_{54}$ 33$_{54}$.

שׁחת hi. *destroy* Dt 9$_{26}$ Ru 4$_{6}$, בלע pi. *swallow* 2 S 20$_{19}$, עשׁק *oppress* Mc 2$_{2}$, ענה pi. *afflict* Ps 94$_{5}$, בוס pol. *trample* Jr 12$_{10(mss)}$ (L חֶלְקָתִי *my portion*), חלל pi. *profane* Is 47$_{6}$, מלא *fill* Jr 16$_{18}$ 1QM 12$_{12}$ 19$_{4}$, פדה *redeem* Dt 9$_{26}$, כון pol. *establish* Ps 68$_{10}$ (or em. נַחְלָה *weak one*, i.e. חלה ni. ptc.), אכל *eat* Dt 18$_{1}$ 4QT 6$_{4}$, hi. *feed with* Is 58$_{14}$, שׂנא *hate* Jr 12$_{8}$, תעב pi. *abhor* Ps 106$_{40}$.

<CSTR> נַחֲלַת י׳ *inheritance of Y.* 1 S 26$_{19}$ 2 S 20$_{19}$ 21$_{3}$ Ps 127$_{3}$, אֱלֹהִים *of God* 2 S 14$_{16}$ 4QShir^{b} 2.1$_{5}$ (אל[והי]ם), שַׁדַּי *of*, i.e. from, *the Almighty* Jb 31$_{2}$, יַעֲקֹב *of Jacob* Is 58$_{14}$, יִשְׂרָאֵל *of Israel* Jg 20$_{6}$, בֵּית *of the house* of Israel Ezk 35$_{15}$, הָעָם *of the people* Ezk 46$_{18}$ 4QConfess 2$_{9}$ (עם), גּוֹיִם *of the nations* Ps 111$_{6}$, הַמַּטֶּה *of the tribe* Nm 36$_{3.4}$, מַטֵּה *of the tribe of* Nm 36$_{4.7}$ Jos 15$_{20}$ 16$_{8}$ 19$_{8.23.31.39.48}$, שְׁנֵי הַמַּטּוֹת וַחֲצִי הַמַּטֶּה *of the two tribes and the half tribe* Jos 14$_{3}$.

נחלת אדם *inheritance of Adam* 4QpPs^{a} 1.3$_{1}$ 4Q418 256$_{1}$ ([נח]לת), אהרן *of Aaron* Si 45$_{25}$, מלכי צדק *of Melchizedek* 11QMelch 2$_{5.5}$ (נחל[ת מלכי צ]דק), נַחֲלַת צְלָפְחָד *inheritance of Zelophehad* Nm 36$_{2}$.

נחלת איש *inheritance of a man* 1QS 4$_{16.24}$ 4Q418 172$_{5}$, אב *of a father* 4Q418 138$_{1}$, נַחֲלַת אָבוֹת *inheritance of*, i.e. from, *fathers* Pr 19$_{14}$, אָבִיךָ *of your father* Is 58$_{14}$ (נַחֲלַת ...), אֲבֹתַי *of my fathers* 1 K 21$_{3.4}$ (אֲבוֹתַי), אֲבֹתָיו *of his fathers* Nm 36$_{8}$, אֲבֹתֵינוּ *of our fathers* Nm 36$_{3}$, אֲבִיהֶן *of their father* Nm 27$_{7}$, בְּנֵי *of the sons of* Jos 13$_{23.28}$ 16$_{9}$ 18$_{20.28}$ 19$_{1.9.16}$, בָּנָיו *of his sons* Ezk 46$_{17}$ (if em. נַחֲלָתוֹ *his inheritance*), עַבְדֵי *of the servants of* Is 54$_{17}$, עָרִיצִים *of the ruthless* Jb 27$_{13}$, נחלת רשׁע *inheritance of a wicked one* Si 8$_{10}$ (but prob. error for גחלת *coals of*), [חכמ]ים *of the wise ones* 4QMyst^{c} 2a$_{1}$, ידו *of his hand* 4QTanḥ 18$_{1}$, ארצות *of the lands* 1QM 10$_{15}$.

נַחֲלַת שָׂדֶה וָכֶרֶם *inheritance of field(s) and vineyard(s)* Nm 16$_{14}$, אֲחֻזָּתָם *of their possession* Nm 35$_{2}$, צְבִי צִבְאוֹת גּוֹיִם *of the beauty of beauties*, i.e. the most beautiful inheritance, *of the nations* Jr 3$_{19}$, אִמְרוֹ *of his word* Jb 20$_{29}$, נחלת אשׁ *inheritance of fire* Si 45$_{25}$ (unless אִשׁ *of a* single *man*), אמת *of truth* 4QpPs^{a} 1.4$_{12}$ 4Q416 4$_{3}$, כבוד *of glory* 4Q416 2.3$_{11}$, כול *of all* 4QpPs^{a} 1.3$_{10}$, כל חי *of every living being* 4Q416 3$_{2}$ 4Q417 2.1$_{19}$ ([נחל]ת כול) 4Q418 81$_{20}$ ([כו]ל), כל מושלים *of all who have dominion* 4Q423 5$_{4}$ ([נ]חלת).

עַם נַחֲלָה *people of an inheritance* Dt 4$_{20}$, שֵׁבֶט נַחֲלָתוֹ *tribe of his inheritance* Jr 10$_{16}$=51$_{19}$, נַחֲלָתֶךָ *of your inheritance* Ps 74$_{2}$, שִׁבְטֵי נַחֲלָתֶךָ *tribes of your inheritance* Is 63$_{17}$, צֹאן נַחֲלָתֶךָ *flock of your inheritance* Mc 7$_{14}$, עזובי נחלתכה *forsaken ones of your inheritance* 4QapLam^{b} 1$_{2}$, [י]ורשי הנחלה *those who possess the inheritance* 4QpPs^{b} 1$_{7}$, שֹׁסֵי נַחֲלָתִי *plunderers of my inheritance* Jr 50$_{11}$.

אֲחֻזַּת נַחֲלָה *possession of an inheritance* Nm 27$_{7}$, נַחֲלָתֵנוּ *of our inheritance* Nm 32$_{32}$, הַר נַחֲלָתְךָ *mountain of your inheritance* Ex 15$_{17}$, גְּבוּל נַחֲלָתוֹ *border of his inheritance* Jos 34$_{30}$ Jg 2$_{9}$, נַחֲלָתָם *of their inheritance* Jos 16$_{5}$ 19$_{10.41}$, שְׂדֵה נַחֲלַת *country of the inheritance of* Jg 20$_{6}$, גּוֹרַל נַחֲלָתֵנוּ *lot of our inheritance* Nm 36$_{3}$, נַחֲלָתָם *of their inheritance* Jos 14$_{2}$ (גּוֹרָל; or em. בְּגוֹרַל נַחֲלָתָם *by the lot of their inheritance* to בְּגוֹרָל נִחֲלוּ אוֹתָם *by lot they allocated portions to them*), חֶבֶל נַחֲלָתוֹ *allotted portion of his inheritance* Dt 32$_{9}$, נַחֲלַתְכֶם *of your inheritance* Ps 105$_{11}$||1 C 16$_{18}$, מחלקת נחלה *allotment of inheritance* Si 42$_{3(M)}$ (B מחלקות).

שברי נחלתך *fractures of your inheritance* GnzPs 2$_{9}$, ריב נחלת perh. *strife of*, i.e. for, *the inheritance of* 4Q418 172$_{5}$, שְׁאֵרִית נַחֲלָתִי *remnant of my inheritance* 2 K 21$_{14}$, נַחֲלָתוֹ *of his inheritance* Mc 7$_{18}$, רוב נחלתו *abundance of his inheritance* 1QH 6$_{19}$, כול נחלת *all the inheritance of* 4QpPs^{a} 1.3$_{1}$.

<APP> יִשְׂרָאֵל *Israel* Is 19$_{25}$ Jl 4$_{2}$ Ps 78$_{71}$, גָּאוֹן *pride* of Jacob Ps 47$_{5}$, אֶרֶץ *land* Dt 4$_{21.38}$ 15$_{4}$ 19$_{10}$ 24$_{4}$ 25$_{19}$ 26$_{1}$ Jr

3$_{19}$ Ps 135$_{12}$ Si 46$_{8}$, אֲדָמָה *land* Dt 21$_{23}$||11QT 64$_{13}$, עִיר *city* Dt 20$_{16}$||11QT 62$_{13}$ Jos 13$_{23.28}$ 16$_{9}$ 19$_{16.23.31.39.48}$, חָצֵר *village* Jos 13$_{23.28}$ 16$_{9}$ 19$_{16.23.31.39.48}$, גּוֹרָל *lot* Jos 17$_{14}$.

<PREP> לְ of direction, *to*, + הלך *go* Jg 2$_{6}$, יצא *go out* Jg 21$_{24}$, שׁוב hi. *bring back* Jr 12$_{15}$, שׁלח *send* Jos 24$_{28}$.

לְ *as* or introducing predicate perh. 4QBark^{f} 1.1$_{3}$, + היה *be* Jos 14$_{9.14}$ 24$_{32}$ Ezk 36$_{12}$ 44$_{28}$, נתן *give* Nm 18$_{21.24}$ Dt 29$_{7}$ Jos 11$_{23}$ 14$_{13}$ 1 K 8$_{36}$||2 C 6$_{27}$ Ps 136$_{21.22}$ 4QRP^{c} 23$_{5}$ 4QNarrC 1$_{7}$, בדל hi. *separate* 1 K 8$_{51}$, בחר *choose* Ps 33$_{12}$; *on account of, concerning* Ezk 35$_{15}$.

בְּ of place, *in(to), within, among* Ne 11$_{20}$ 4QPrayers^{b} 2$_{2}$ 4QShirShabb^{a} 1.1$_{13}$ 4Q416 2.4$_{11}$ (בנח[ל]תכה) 2.4$_{12}$ 3$_{1}$ 4Q423 8$_{2}$, + בוא *come* Ps 79$_{1}$, צלח *rush* appar. Si 8$_{10}$ (but prob. אל תצלח בנחלת is error for אל תצת גחלת *do not kindle the coals of*), רום hi. *raise up* 1QH 14$_{8}$, קרא ni. *be called* Gn 48$_{6}$, שׁעה htp. *tell* Si 44$_{8(Bmg)}$ (להשתעות; B להשענות *for support*), גבל *set boundary* CD 1$_{16}$, סוג hi. *remove* boundary Dt 19$_{14}$, רבה hi. *make great* 1QH fr. 2.2$_{16}$ ([ה]רבות).

בְּ *as, for* Ezk 46$_{16}$, + היה *be* Jos 19$_{2}$, נתן *give* Nm 18$_{26}$ 36$_{2}$, חלק ni. *be divided* Nm 26$_{53}$, pi. *divide* Jos 13$_{7}$, נפל *fall* Nm 34$_{2}$ Jg 18$_{1}$ Ezk 47$_{14.22}$, hi. *cause to fall*, i.e. allot Jos 13$_{6}$ 23$_{4}$ Ezk 45$_{1}$ 47$_{22}$ 48$_{29}$ (if em.; see below), ערב *give in pledge* 4Q416 2.2$_{18}$.

בְּ introducing object, + ידע *know* 4Q417 2.1$_{19}$ (בנחל[ת]), ירשׁ *possess* 4QTohB^{a} 2$_{2}$ (ו[י]רשו), נגע *touch* Jr 12$_{14}$ 4QapJoseph^{b} 3$_{10}$ (בנחל[ה]), רעה *pasture* Ps 78$_{71}$, עבר htp. *be angry with* Ps 78$_{62}$; *to*, + דבק *cling* Nm 36$_{7.9}$, ספח htp. *join oneself* 1 S 26$_{19}$; *over*, + משׁל hi. *give dominion* 4Q416 2.3$_{11}$ 4Q418 81$_{3}$ (בנ[חלתו]).

בְּ of cause, *on account of*, + שׂמח *rejoice* 4QpPs^{a} 1.4$_{12}$, בין hi. *understand* joy 4Q416 4$_{3}$; of accompaniment, *with, in*, + חוב *be guilty* 4Q418 138$_{1}$.

מִן of direction, *from* perh. 4Q415 1.2$_{4}$ perh. 11QMelch 2$_{5}$, + שׁמט *let drop* Jr 17$_{4}$; *from (being among)* perh. 4QTohB^{a} 3$_{5}$, + שׁמד hi. *destroy* 2 S 14$_{16}$; partitive, *(some) of, from (out of)*, + נתן *give* Nm 35$_{2}$ Jos 21$_{3}$ Ezk 46$_{17}$ 4QConfess 2$_{9}$, לקח *take* Ezk 46$_{18}$, גרע ni. *be diminished* Nm 36$_{3.4}$; *as*, + נפל hi. *cause to fall*, i.e. allot Ezk 48$_{29}$ (or em. בְּנַחֲלָה *as an inheritance*).

אֶל *to*, + בוא *come* Dt 12$_{9}$, hi. *bring* Si 46$_{8}$, שׁוב *go back* Jg 21$_{23}$.

עַל *to*, + יסף hi. *add* 4Q418 162$_{3}$ ([או]סיף), ni. *be added* Nm 36$_{3.4}$; *upon, over*, + קום hi. *raise up* name Ru 4$_{5.10}$; *over*, i.e. in charge of, + משׁח *anoint* 1 S 10$_{1}$; *against* Jr 12$_{9}$; *on account of*, + שׁפט ni. *enter into judgment* Jl 4$_{2}$.

עִם *with* Ec 7$_{11}$, + הלל htp. *glory* Ps 106$_{5}$.

כְּפִי *in accordance with*, + נתן *give* Nm 35$_{8}$, כתב *write* CD 13$_{12}$, שׂנא *hate* 1QS 4$_{24}$.

לְפִי *in accordance with* 1QS 4$_{16}$, + כתב *write* Jos 18$_{4}$.

בְּתוֹךְ *within* Jos 16$_{9}$, + היה *be* Jos 19$_{1}$, נחל *inherit* Jos 19$_{9}$.

זוּלַת *apart from*, + אוה htp. *desire* 4Q416 2.3$_{8}$.

<COLL> נַחֲלָה || חֵלֶק *portion* Gn 31$_{14}$ Nm 18$_{20}$ Dt 10$_{9}$ 12$_{12}$ 14$_{27.29}$ 18$_{1}$ 32$_{9}$ Jos 18$_{7}$ (both +) 2 S 20$_{1}$ 1 K 12$_{16}$||2 C 10$_{16}$ Jb 20$_{29}$ 27$_{13}$ 4Q418 81$_{3}$, אֲחֻזָּה *possession* Ezk 44$_{28}$ 46$_{16.18}$ (all three +) Ps 2$_{8}$, אֶרֶץ *land* Jr 2$_{7}$ 12$_{15}$ 16$_{18}$ (+) 1QM 12$_{12}$ 19$_{4}$, מְנוּחָה *resting place* Dt 12$_{9}$, בַּיִת *house* Jr 12$_{7}$ Mc 2$_{2}$ Lm 5$_{2}$, עַם *people* Dt 9$_{26.29}$ 1 K 8$_{51}$ Is 47$_{6}$ Jl 2$_{17}$ (both +) 4$_{2}$ Mc 7$_{14}$ (+) Ps 28$_{9}$ 78$_{62}$ (+) 78$_{71}$ 94$_{5.14}$ 106$_{40}$ (+) 1QH 14$_{8}$ 4QConfess 2$_{3.4}$; + חֶבֶל *allotted portion* Jos 17$_{14}$, גְּבוּל *border*, i.e. territory 4QShirShabb^{a} 1.1$_{13}$, שָׂכָר *reward* Ps 127$_{3}$.

נַחֲלָה לִבְנֵי יִשְׂרָאֵל *the inheritance of the sons of Israel* Nm 36$_{7}$, vars. Ps 135$_{12}$ 136$_{22}$, נַחֲלָה לָשֶׁבֶת *an inheritance in which to dwell* Jg 18$_{1}$, נחלתו בגורל האור *his inheritance in the lot of light* CD 13$_{12}$, נחלת איש באמת וצדק *the inheritance of a man in truth and righteousness* 1QS 4$_{24}$, נחלתו בדעת אמתכה *his inheritance in the knowledge of your truth* 1QH 18$_{28}$, נחלה בדעת אמתו *inheritance in the knowledge of his truth* 4QdivProv 1$_{2}$.

Also 4Q415 15$_{1}$ ([נ]חלתכה) 4Q417 2.1$_{24}$ 4Q418 185$_{2}$ 234$_{1}$ 4Q423 12$_{2}$ ([נ]חלתו) 4QsapHymnA 1.2$_{6}$ 11$_{1}$ 4QSap^{b} 23$_{3}$ 4QRitMar 21$_{5}$ 4QPrFêtes^{c} 10.4$_{6}$ 4QShir^{b} 38$_{1}$ 43$_{3}$ 4QOrd^{b} 32$_{1}$ 4QBéat 14.1$_{26}$ ([נח]לתכה) 14.2$_{1}$ ([נ]חלתכה) 5QRègle 23$_{5}$.

<SYN> חֵלֶק *portion*, אֲחֻזָּה *possession*, אֶרֶץ *land*, מְנוּחָה *resting place*, בַּיִת *house*, עַם *people*.*

⇒ נחל *inherit*.

*נַחֲלָה II $_{1}$ n.f. **wasting disease** (unless נַחֲלָה III destruction or חלה I ni. *be made weak*), <CSTR> יוֹם נַחֲלָה *day of destruction* Is 1711 (+ כְּאֵב *pain*).

*נַחֲלָה III 1 n.f. **destruction** (unless נַחֲלָה IV *wasting disease* or חלה I ni. *be made weak*), <CSTR> יוֹם נַחֲלָה *day of destruction* Is 1711 (+ כְּאֵב *pain*).

נַחֲלָה IV 2 pl.n. **Nahalah,** on southern border of land given to tribes of Israel, Ezk 4719 4828 (or em. both נַחְלָה *to the wadi [of Egypt],* i.e. נַחַל + ה- of direction).

נַחֲלָה V *one who is weak,* see חלה I, Ni.

נַחֲלִיאֵל 2 pl.n. **Nahaliel**—Sam נחלאל—station of Israelites E of Dead Sea, perh. a wadi, Wadi Wala or Wadi Zerqa Ma'in, <PREP> מִן of direction, *from* Nm 2119; נַחֲלִיאֵל without preposition, *to Nahaliel* Nm 2119. ⇒ (?) נַחַל II *date palm* + אֵל *God.*

נֶחֱלָמִי 3 gent. **Nehelamite,** belonging to Nehelam, as sing. noun, an individual **Nehelamite** (unless חלם ni. ptc. *the dreamer*), <SUBJ> דבר pi. *speak* Jr 2932, ראה *see* Jr 2932, שׁלח *send* Jr 2924. <APP> Shemaiah Jr 2924.31.42. <PREP> לְ of possession, *of, (belonging) to,* + היה *be* Jr 2932; אֶל *to,* + אמר *say* Jr 2924; *concerning,* + אמר *say* Jr 2931; עַל introducing object, + פקד *visit,* i.e. punish Jr 2932.

נַחֲלַת, see נַחֲלָה I *inheritance.*

נחם 108.3.18 vb. **regret—Ni.** 48.2.4 Pf. נִחַמְתִּי ,(נִחָם) נִחַם, (נִחָמְתִּי); impf. יִנָּחֵם ,אֶנָּחֵם (Q אנחמה); + waw וְנִחַם (וְנִחָם), וְנִחַמְתִּי ,וְנִחַמְתֶּם ,וַיִּנָּחֵם (וַיִּנָּחֶם) ,וַיִּנָּחֲמוּ; impv. הִנָּחֵם; ptc. נִחָם; inf. הִנָּחֵם.

1. regret, be sorry, repent (of), relent (Gn 66.7 Nm 2319 1 S 1529 Jr 428 Ps 773 1104),* <SUBJ> Y. Gn 66.7 3212.14 1 S 1511.35 2 S 2416||1 C 2115 Is 576 Jr 428 156 188.10 2016 263.13.19 4210 Ezk 2414 Jl 213.14 Am 73.6 Jon 39.10 42 Zc 814 Ps 10645 (or em. וַיִּנָּחֵם to וַיַּנְחֵם *and he led them,* i.e. נחה hi.) 1104, Ephraim Jr 3119, Job Jb 426, עַם *people* Ex 1317, אִישׁ *man* Jr 86, נֵצַח *glory* 1 S 1529.29. <PREP> כְּ *according to,* + רֹב *abundance* Ps 10645 (or em.; see Subj.); אֶל *concerning* or introducing object, + רָעָה *evil* 2 S 2416 Jr 263.13.19 4210; עַל *upon, in,* + עָפָר *dust* Jb 426, אֵפֶר *ashes* Jb 426; *concerning* or introducing object, + רָעָה *evil* Ex 3212.14 2 S 2416(mss)||1 C 2115 Jr 86 188 263(mss).13(mss) Jl 213 Jon 310 42, טוֹבָה *good* Jr 1810, זֹאת *this* Am 73.6, אֵלֶּה *these* Is 576.

<COLL> נחם ni. || חוס *pity* Ezk 2414, פרע *let go* Ezk 2414, שׁוּב *go back* Ex 3212 Jr 428 (both +) Jl 214 Jon 39; + זמם *plan* Jr 428, שׁקר pi. *deal falsely* 1 S 1529; followed by כִּי *that* Gn 66.7 1 S 1511.35; נִלְאֵיתִי הִנָּחֵם *I am too weary to relent* Jr 156.

2. be moved to pity, have compassion, <SUBJ> Y. Jg 218 Ps 9013, עַם *people* Jg 2115, בֵּן *son* of Israel Jg 216. <PREP> לְ *for, upon,* + Benjamin Jg 2115; אֶל *for, upon,* + Benjamin Jg 216, אָח *brother* Jg 216; עַל *for, upon* 1QH 826, + עֶבֶד *servant* Ps 9013; מִן of cause, *on account of,* + נְאָקָה *groaning* Jg 218.

3. comfort oneself, be comforted, be consoled, <SUBJ> בַּיִת *house* of Israel Ezk 1422, David 2 S 1339, Isaac Gn 2467, Judah Gn 3812, Rachel Jr 3115, בֵּן *son* Si 3817.23, מֶלֶךְ *king* 2 S 1339, פַּרְעֹה *Pharaoh* Ezk 3231, worshipper 1QH 147 1713, שׁתה ptc. *one who drinks* Ezk 3116, מִבְחָר *choice one* Ezk 3116, טוֹב *good one* Ezk 3116, עָנִי *poor one* perh. 4QBarka 1.11, נֶפֶשׁ *soul* Ps 773, עֵץ *tree* Ezk 3116.

<PREP> בְּ of place, *in,* + אֶרֶץ *land* Ezk 3116; עַל *concerning, for,* + Amnon 2 S 1339, בֵּן *son* Jr 3115, הָמוֹן *multitude* Ezk 3231 1QH 147, שָׁאוֹן *uproar* 1QH 147, חַיִל *army* Ezk 3231, חָלָל *slain one* Ezk 3231, רָעָה *evil* Ezk 1422, פֶּשַׁע *transgression* 1QH 1713, אֵבֶל *mourning* 4QBarka 1.11; אַחֲרֵי *after,* + אֵם *mother* Gn 2467; בַּעֲבוּר *on account of, for the sake of,* + עָוֹן *iniquity* Si 3817 (or em. עון to דון *grief*).

<COLL> מֵאֲנָה לְהִנָּחֵם *she refused to be comforted* Jr 3115, var. Ps 773, וְנִחַמְתֶּם עַל־הָרָעָה אֲשֶׁר הֵבֵאתִי ... אֵת כָּל־ אֲשֶׁר הֵבֵאתִי *and you shall be comforted concerning the misfortune I have brought ..., everything that I have brought* Ezk 1422 (or em. אֵת to אֶל־ *concerning*), הנחם עם צאת נפשו *be comforted when his soul departs* Si 3823.

4. gain satisfaction (for oneself), avenge oneself, <SUBJ> Y. Is 124, שְׁאָר *remainder* of Jews Est 916 (if em. נֹוחַ having rest to נִחוּם avenging themselves).* <PREP> מִן *from, upon,* + אֹיֵב *enemy* Est 9_{16} (if em.; see Subj.), צַר *enemy* Is 1_{24}. <COLL> נחם ni. || נקם ni. *avenge oneself* Is 1_{24}.

<SYN> §1 חוס *pity,* פרע *let go,* שׁוּב *go back;* §4 נקם ni. *avenge oneself.*

Pi. 51.1.12 Pf. נִחַם, נִחַמְתָּנִי; impf. יְנַחֵם (יְנַחֲמֵנִי, Q ינחמם), 3fs תְּנַחֲמֵנִי (תְּנַחֲמֵנוּ), 2ms תְּנַחֲמֵנִי, Q אנחם (אֲנַחֶמְךָ, אֲנַחֶמְכֶם), יְנַחֲמוּן (יְנַחֲמֻנִי), תְּנַחֲמוּנִי; + waw וָנִחַם, וַיְנַחֲמוּ, וַיְנַחֵם, וְנִחַמְתִּים; ptc. מְנַחֵם (מְנַחֶמְכֶם), מְנַחֲמִים, מְנַחֲמַי; impv. נַחֲמוּ; inf. נַחֵם (נַחֲמֵנִי, נַחֶמְךָ, נַחֲמוֹ).

1. comfort, console, <SUBJ> Y. Is 12_1 49_{13} $51_{3.3}$ 52_9 66_{13} Jr 31_{13} Zc 1_{17} Ps 71_{21} 86_{17} 119_{82} 1QH 13_3 (נחמ[תני]) 17_{13} 19_{32} fr. 21_3 4QBark[a] $1.1_{4.6}$ 4QBark[c] 2.1_{12}, Jerusalem Ezk 16_{54}, Naamathite Jb 2_{11}, Shuhite Jb 2_{11}, Temanite Jb 2_{11}, Boaz Ru 2_{13}, David 2 S 10_2 12_{14}, Bildad Jb 2_{11}, Eliphaz Jb 2_{11}, Hezekiah Si 48_{24}, Joseph Gn 50_{21}, Zophar Jb 2_{11}, אִישׁ *man,* i.e. each Jb 2_{11}, אֵם *mother* Is 66_{13} 4QBark[a] 1.1_6, בֵּן *son* Gn 37_{35}, בַּת *daughter* Gn 37_{35}, אָח *brother* Jb 42_{11} 1 C 7_{22}, אָחוֹת *sister* Jb 42_{11}, אָדוֹן *lord* Ru 2_{13}, עֶבֶד *servant* 1 C 19_2, רֵעַ *friend* Jb 2_{11} 21_{34}, מַלְאָךְ *messenger* 1 C 19_2, prophet Is 61_2=11QMelch 2_{20} (לנח[ם]), קֹסֵם *diviner* Zc 10_2, מַשְׂכִּיל *instructor* 1QS 10_{21}, ידע ptc. *one who knows* Jb 42_{11}, worshipper Lm 2_{13}, שֵׁבֶט *rod* Ps 23_4 (unless §2; or em. יַנְחֻנִי *they will lead me,* i.e. נחה hi., or יְנַהֲגֻנִי *they will lead me,* i.e. נהג pi.), מִשְׁעֶנֶת *staff* Ps 23_4 (unless §2; or em.; see above), עֶרֶשׂ *couch* Jb 7_{13}, חֶסֶד *loyalty* Ps 119_{76}, אֲשֶׁר *one who* Jb 29_{25}, מִי *who?* Is 51_{19} (unless אֲנַחֲמֵךְ is aph.), זֶה *this* Gn 5_{29} (or em. יְנִיחֵנוּ *he will give us rest,* i.e. נוח hi.); subj. not specified, Is 22_4 $40_{1.1}$ Jr 16_7 Ezk 14_{23}.

<OBJ> Israelites Is 12_1 66_{13}, עַם *people* Is 40_1 49_{13} 52_9, בַּיִת *house* of Israel Ezk 14_{23}, Jerusalem Is 51_{19} (unless אֲנַחֲמֵךְ is aph.), Samaria Ezk 16_{54}, Sodom Ezk 16_{54}, Zion Is 51_3 Zc 1_{17}, Bathsheba 2 S 12_{14}, Ephraim 1 C 7_{22}, Hanun 2 S 10_2||1 C 19_2 1 C 19_2, Isaiah Is 22_4, Jacob Gn 37_{35}, Job Jb 2_{11} 7_{13} 21_{34} 42_{11}, Lamech and family Gn 5_{29}, Ruth Ru 2_{13}, אִישׁ *man* Is 66_{13} 4QBark[a] 1.1_6, אִשָּׁה *wife* 2 S 12_{14}, אָב *father* 1 C 7_{22}, בַּת *daughter* Ezk 16_{54}, אָח *brother* Gn 50_{21}, בָּחוּר *young man* Jr 31_{13}, בְּתוּלָה *young woman* Jr 31_{13} Lm 2_{13}, זָקֵן *aged one* Jr 31_{13}, אָבֵל *mourner* Is 61_2=11QMelch 2_{20} (לנח[ם] [ה]אבלים) Jr 16_7 (if em. אֵבֶל *mourning* to אָבֵל) Jb 29_{25} Si 48_{24} 1QH fr. 21_3, worshipper Ps 23_4 (unless §2; or em.; see Subj.) 71_{21} 86_{17} $119_{76.82}$ 1QH 13_3 (נחמ[תני]) 17_{13} 19_{32} 4QBark[c] 2.1_{12}, דַּל *poor one* 4QBark[c] 1.1_1, כשל ni. ptc. *one who stumbles* in transgressions 4QPrFêtes[c] 12.1_5, חָרְבָּה *waste* Is 51_3.

<PREP> בְּ of place, time, *in, during,* + יְרוּשָׁלַםִ *Jerusalem* 4QBark[a] 1.1_6 (בירושל[ים]), עֵת *time* of distress 4QBark[c] 1.1_1, צוּקָה *distress* 1QH 17_{13}, יָגוֹן *grief* 1QH 19_{32}; of instrument, *by (means of), with,* + יֶלֶד *child* of righteousness 4QBark[c] 2.1_{12}; introducing object, + נָכֵא *stricken one* 1QS 10_{21} (בנכאים; =4QS[f] 5_1 בנכוחים *the straightforward*).

כְּ *according to,* + אִמְרָה *word* Ps 119_{76}.

מִן *from,* + מַעֲשֶׂה *work* Gn 5_{29}, עִצָּבוֹן *toil* Gn 5_{29}.

אֶל *concerning, for,* + אָב *father* 2 S 10_2.

עַל *concerning, for,* + אָב *father* 1 C 19_2, מֵת *dead one* Jr 16_7, שֹׁד *destruction* Is 22_4 רָעָה *evil* Jb 42_{11}; *on account of,* + אֵבֶל *mourning* Jr 16_7 (or em.; see Obj.).

<COLL> נחם pi. || רחם pi. *have compassion upon* Is 49_{13} 1QS 10_{21}, גאל *redeem* Is 52_9, עזר *help* Ps 86_{17}; + נוד *shake the head,* i.e. show grief Is 51_{19} Jb 2_{11} 42_{11}, שׂמח pi. *make glad* Jr 31_{13}, בחר *choose* Zc 1_{17}, דבר עַל־לֵב pi. *speak to the heart,* i.e. kindly or with encouragement Gn 50_{21} Is 40_1 Ru 2_{13}; + adverb or noun used adverbially, כֵּן *so* Is 66_{13} 4QBark[a] 1.1_6, עוֹד *again* Zc 1_{17}, מָתַי *when?* Ps 119_{82}, אֵיךְ *how?* Jb 21_{34}, הֶבֶל *in vain* Zc 10_2.

2. perh. **vindicate*** (unless §1), <SUBJ> שֵׁבֶט *rod* Ps 23_4, מִשְׁעֶנֶת *staff* Ps 23_4. <OBJ> worshipper Ps 23_4.

3. ptc. as noun, **comforter,** <SUBJ> רחק *be far* Lm 1_{16}, שׁוב hi. *bring back* Lm 1_{16}. <NOM CL> אָנֹכִי הוּא מְנַחֶמְכֶם *I am your comforter* Is 51_{12}, מְנַחֲמֵי עָמָל כֻּלְּכֶם *you are all troublesome comforters* Jb 16_2, אֵין לָהֶם מְנַחֵם *there is not to them a comforter* Ec $4_{1.1}$ (or em. מְנַקֵּם *one who takes vengeance* or מְנַחֵם *one who frees them,* i.e. נחה hi.), vars. Lm $1_{2.9.17.21}$. <OBJ> שׁלח *send* 2 S 10_3||1 C 19_3, בקשׁ pi. *seek* Na 3_7. <CSTR> מְנַחֲמֵי עָמָל *comforters of trouble,* i.e. troublesome comforters Jb 16_2. <PREP> לְ *for,* + קוה pi. *wait* Ps 69_{21}.

Also 4QHod[f] 3_3.

<SYN> §1 רחם pi. *have compassion upon*, גאל *redeem*, עזר *help*.

Pu. 2 Pf. נֻחָמָה; impf. תְּנֻחָמוּ—**be comforted,** <SUBJ> Israelites Is 66$_{13}$ (1QIsa^{a} htp.), עָנִי *afflicted one* Is 54$_{11}$. <PREP> בְּ of place, *in*, + Jerusalem Is 66$_{13}$.

Aph. 1 Impf. אֲנַחֲמֵךְ (unless pi.)—**comfort,** <SUBJ> מִי *who?* Is 51$_{19}$. <OBJ> Jerusalem Is 51$_{19}$.*

Htp. 7.0.2 Impf. יִתְנֶחָם, תתנחמו; + waw וְהִנֶּחָמְתִּי; וָאֶתְנֶחָם; ptc. מִתְנַחֵם; inf. הִתְנַחֵם—**1. (allow oneself to) be comforted,** <SUBJ> Israelites Is 66$_{13(1QIsa^a)}$ (MT pu.), Jacob Gn 37$_{35}$, worshipper Ps 119$_{52}$. <PREP> בְּ of place, *in*, + Jerusalem Is 66$_{13(1QIsa^a)}$. <COLL> וַיְמָאֵן לְהִתְנַחֵם *and he refused to be comforted* Gn 37$_{35}$.

2. comfort oneself, by plotting vengeance (Gn 27$_{42}$), taking vengeance (Ezk 5$_{13}$), <SUBJ> Y. Ezk 5$_{13}$, Esau Gn 27$_{42}$, אָח *brother* Gn 27$_{42}$. <PREP> לְ *with respect to*, + Jacob Gn 27$_{42}$, בֵּן *son* Gn 27$_{42}$. <COLL> מִתְנַחֵם ... לְהָרְגֶךָ *he comforts himself ... (by plotting) to kill you* Gn 27$_{42}$.

3. repent, <SUBJ> Y. Nm 23$_{19}$.

4. have compassion, <SUBJ> Y. Dt 23$_{36}$=Ps 135$_{14}$. <PREP> עַל *upon*, + עֶבֶד *servant* Dt 23$_{36}$=Ps 135$_{14}$.

Also 4QAdmonPar 3c$_{1}$.*

⇒ נֶחָמָה *comfort*, נִחֻמִים *comfort*, נֹחַם *compassion*, תַּנְחוּם *consolation*, נַחַם *Naham*, נַחוּם *Nahum*, נְחוּם *Nehum*, נְחֶמְיָה *Nehemiah*, נַחֲמָנִי *Nahamani*, מְנַחֵם *Menahem*, תַּנְחֻמֶת *Tanhumeth*.

נַחַם 1 pr.n.m. **Naham,** Judaean, brother-in-law of Hodiah, <CSTR> אֲחוֹת נַחַם *sister of Naham* 1 C 4$_{14}$.

⇒ נחם *comfort*.

נֹחַם 1 n.m. **compassion** or perh. **revenge,*** <SUBJ> סתר ni. *be hidden* Ho 13$_{14}$.*

⇒ נחם *regret*.

[נֶחָמָה] 2 n.f. **comfort**—sf. נֶחָמָתִי—**comfort, consolation,** <SUBJ> היה *be* Jb 6$_{10}$. <NOM CL> זֹאת נֶחָמָתִי בְעָנְיִי *this is my comfort in my affliction* Ps 119$_{50}$. <PREP> בְּלֹא *without*, + הלך pi. *go about* Jb 30$_{28}$ (if em. חַמָּה *sun*).

⇒ נחם *comfort*.

נְחֶמְיָה 8.1.0.14 pr.n.m. **Nehemiah**—I נחמיהו—**1.** governor of Judah, son of Hacaliah, <SUBJ> היה *be* Ne 1$_{1.4.11}$ 2$_{1.11.13.15}$ 13$_{6}$, הוה *be* Ne 6$_{6}$, יכל *be able* Ne 6$_{3}$, אמר *say* Ne 1$_{5}$ 2$_{3.7.17.20}$ 4$_{8.13.16}$ 5$_{7.8.13}$ 6$_{11}$ 7$_{3}$ 8$_{9}$ 13$_{9.11.17.19.19.21.22}$, נגד hi. *tell* Ne 2$_{12.16.18}$, בקשׁ pi. *seek* Ne 5$_{18}$, שׁאל *ask* Ne 1$_{2}$, ni. *ask leave* Ne 13$_{6}$, פלל htp. *pray* Ne 1$_{4.6}$ 2$_{4}$, ידה htp. *confess* Ne 1$_{6}$, קרא *call* Ne 5$_{12}$, שׁבע hi. *cause to swear* Ne 5$_{12}$ 13$_{25}$, ריב *argue* Ne 5$_{7}$ 13$_{11.17.25}$, קלל pi. *curse* Ne 13$_{25}$, עוד hi. *warn* Ne 13$_{15.21}$, שׁמע *hear* Ne 1$_{4}$ 5$_{6}$, ראה *see* Ne 4$_{8}$ 13$_{15.23}$, שׂבר *examine* Ne 2$_{13.15}$, ידע *know* Ne 13$_{10}$, נכר hi. *realize* Ne 6$_{12}$, בין *realize* Ne 13$_{7}$, ירא *be afraid* Ne 2$_{2}$ 6$_{13}$, אכל *eat* Ne 5$_{14}$, צום *fast* Ne 1$_{4}$, בכה *weep* Ne 1$_{4}$, אבל htp. *mourn* Ne 1$_{4}$.

הלך *go* Ne 2$_{16}$, בוא *come* Ne 2$_{7.8.9.11.15}$ 6$_{10}$ 13$_{6.7}$, יצא *go out* Ne 2$_{13}$, עלה *go up* Ne 2$_{15}$, hi. *bring up* Ne 12$_{31}$, ירד *go down* Ne 6$_{3}$, עבר *cross over* Ne 2$_{14}$, שׁוב *return* Ne 2$_{6.15.15.20}$; hi. *bring back* 13$_{9}$, *reply* Ne 6$_{4}$, קום *arise* Ne 2$_{12}$ 4$_{8}$, hi. *raise up* Si 49$_{13}$, ברח hi. *put to flight* Ne 13$_{28}$, רכב *ride* Ne 2$_{12}$, נשׂא *lift up* Ne 2$_{1}$, שׁלח *send* Ne 6$_{3.8}$, i.e. stretch out, hand Ne 13$_{21}$, קבץ *gather* Ne 7$_{5}$ 13$_{11}$, מצא *find* Ne 7$_{5}$, שׁלך hi. *throw* Ne 13$_{8}$, נער *shake* Ne 5$_{13}$, ישׁב *sit* Ne 1$_{4}$, עמד hi. *set up* Ne 4$_{7.7}$ 6$_{1.7}$ 7$_{1}$ 13$_{11.13.19.30}$, i.e. appoint Ne 12$_{31}$, נצב hi. *set up* Si 49$_{13}$, צוה pi. *put in charge* Ne 7$_{2}$, אצר hi. *appoint as treasurer* Ne 13$_{13}$.

עשׂה *do* Ne 2$_{16}$ 5$_{8.15.19}$ 6$_{3.13.14}$, בנה *build* Ne 2$_{5.20}$ 3$_{33}$ 6$_{1.6}$, רפא pi. *repair* Si 49$_{13}$, נתן *give* Ne 2$_{1.9}$, i.e. set Ne 2$_{6}$ 5$_{7}$, קנה *buy* Ne 5$_{8}$, נשׁה *lend* Ne 5$_{10}$, חזק hi. *hold* Ne 5$_{16}$, רפה hi. *leave alone* Ne 6$_{3}$, פשׁט *undress* Ne 4$_{17}$, טהר pi. *purify* Ne 13$_{30}$, חטא *commit sin* Ne 6$_{13}$, פרד ni. *be separate* Ne 4$_{13}$, מרט *pull hair out* Ne 13$_{25}$, נכה hi. *strike* Ne 13$_{25}$.

<NOM CL> עַל הַחֲתוּמִים נְחֶמְיָה *upon the sealed ones was Nehemiah* Ne 10$_{2}$ (or em. עַל הַחֲתוּמִים to הַחוֹתְמִים *those whc seal were* or אֵלֶּה הַחוֹתְמִים *these are those who seal*).

<OBJ> עבר hi. *cause to pass* Ne 2$_{7}$, שׁלח *send* Ne 2$_{6}$, צוה pi. *appoint* Ne 5$_{14}$, חרף pi. *taunt* Ne 6$_{13}$, ירא pi. *make afraid* Ne 6$_{9.14.19}$.

<CSTR> דִּבְרֵי נְחֶמְיָה *words of Nehemiah* Ne 1$_{1}$, יְמֵי *days of* Ne 12$_{26.47}$.

<APP> בֵּן *son* Ne 1$_{1}$ 10$_{2}$, פֶּחָה *governor* Ne 12$_{26}$, תִּרְשָׁתָא *governor* Ne 10$_{2}$.

<PREP> לְ of direction, *to*, + אמר *say* Ne 1$_{3}$ 2$_{2.4.6.18}$, נתן *give* Ne 2$_{7.8.8}$; of benefit, *for*, + עשׂה *do* Ne 5$_{18}$; introducing object, + זכר *remember* Ne 5$_{19}$ 13$_{14.22.31}$; *on the part of*, + חרה *be angry* Ne 5$_{6}$.

כְּמוֹ *as* Ne 6$_{11}$.

אֶל *to*, + שׁלח *send* Ne 2$_{5}$ 6$_{2}$.

עַל *upon* Ne 2$_{8.18}$, + חוס *have pity* Ne 13$_{22}$; *against*, + דבר pi. *speak* Ne 6$_{12}$; *with*, + מלך ni. *take counsel* Ne 5$_{7}$.

עִם *with* Ne 2$_{12.12}$ 12$_{40}$, + שׁלח *send* Ne 2$_{9}$.

אֵת, + היה *be* Ne 6$_{14}$.

לִפְנֵי *before* Ne 5$_{15}$, + אמר *say* Ne 6$_{19}$.

תַּחַת *under*, + עבר *pass* Ne 2$_{14}$.

אֵצֶל *beside* Ne 4$_{12}$.

אַחֲרֵי *behind* Ne 4$_{17}$.

<COLL> נחמיה יאדר זכרו *as for Nehemiah, his memory is exalted* Si 49$_{13}$.

2. ruler of half the district of Beth-zur, son of Azbuk, <SUBJ> חזק hi. *repair* Ne 3$_{16}$. <APP> בֵּן *son* Ne 3$_{16}$, שַׂר *ruler* Ne 3$_{16}$. <PREP> אַחֲרֵי *after*, + חזק hi. *repair* Ne 3$_{16}$.

3. exile returning with Zerubbabel, <SUBJ> בוא *come* Ezr 2$_{2}$||Ne 7$_{7}$.

4. Arad ost. 11$_{5}$, <PREP> מִן of direction, *from* Arad ost. 11$_{5}$ (מ[נ]חמיהו).

5. son of Jehoaz, <APP> בֵּן *son* Arad ost. 31$_{3}$.

6. Arad ost. 36$_{2}$, <CSTR> בן נחמיה[ו] *son of Nehemiah* Arad ost. 36$_{2}$.

7. official at Arad, <SUBJ> שׁלח Arad ost. 40$_{1}$.

8. Arad ost. 59$_{3}$, <APP> בֵּן *son* Arad ost. 59$_{3}$.

9. son of Micaiah, <APP> בֵּן *son* Seal 30 (Es-soda, 8th cent.). <PREP> לְ of possession, *of, (belonging) to* Seal 30 (Es-soda, 8th cent.).

10. appar. father of Hananiah, Seal 561 (נחמי[הו]; T. Beit Mirsim?, 7th/6th cent.).

11. Ḥorvat ʿUza jar inscr. 1$_{2}$ (נחמי[הו]).

12. Ḥorvat ʿUza jar inscr. 1$_{4}$, <PREP> לְ of possession, *of, (belonging) to* Ḥorvat ʿUza jar inscr. 1$_{4}$.

13. father of Shabtai, <CSTR> בן נחמיה *son of Nehemiah* Jerusalem ossuary inscr. 14.

14. father of Adaiah, <CSTR> בן נחמיה *son of Nehemiah* Seal 905 (7th cent.).

15. appar. father of Ephroah, Bulla D36.

16. appar. father of Maliah, Bulla D38.

17. appar. son of Jehoab, <PREP> לְ of possession, *of, (belonging) to* Bulla D65.

⇒ נחם *regret*.

נחמיהו, see נְחֶמְיָה *Nehemiah*.

נִחֻמִים 3.0.1 n.[m.]pl. **comfort**—pl. Q נחומים; sf. נִחוּמַי—

1. comfort, <OBJ> ענה *answer with* Zc 1$_{13}$, שׁלם pi. *requite with* Is 57$_{18}$ (1QIsa[a] תנחומים *consolations*). <APP> דְּבָרִים נִחֻמִים *words, comfort*, i.e. comforting words Zc 1$_{13}$ (+ דְּבָרִים טוֹבִים *kind words*).

2. compassion, <SUBJ> כמר ni. *be agitated* Ho 11$_{8}$ (unless נִחוּמִים *inward parts*; or em. נִחוּמַי to רַחֲמַי *my compassion*).

Also 4Q417 2.2$_{4}$.

⇒ נחם *regret*.

נַחֲמָנִי 1 pr.n.m. **Nahamani,** exile returning with Zerubbabel, <SUBJ> בוא *come* Ne 7$_{7}$.

⇒ נחם *comfort*.

***נחן** 1 vb. **groan** (unless חנן ni. *be pitied*)—**Pi.** 1 נֶחַנְתְּ—<SUBJ> יֹשֵׁב *inhabitant* of Lebanon Jr 22$_{23}$ (מַה־נֶּחַנְתְּ *how you will groan!*).

נַחְנוּ 6.0.0.1 pronoun **we**—נַחְנוּ—shorter form of אֲנַחְנוּ, <SUBJ> שׁמר *watch* Lachish ost. 4$_{10}$, עבר *pass* Nm 32$_{32}$, פשׁע *transgress* Lm 3$_{42}$, מרה *be rebellious* Lm 3$_{42}$.

<NOM CL> כֻּלָּנוּ בְּנֵי אִישׁ־אֶחָד נָחְנוּ *we are all the sons of one man* Gn 42$_{11}$ (+ אֲנַחְנוּ *we*), נַחְנוּ מָה *what are we?* Ex 16$_{7.8}$, נַחְנוּ עָלָיו *we shall be upon him* 2 S 17$_{12}$.

⇒ cf. אָנוּ *we*, אֲנַחְנוּ *we*.

נחץ I 1 vb. **urge—Qal** 1 Ptc. pass. נָחוּץ—pass. perh. **be urgent,** <SUBJ> דָּבָר *matter* of king 1 S 21$_{9}$.

***נחץ** II 1 vb. **be private—Qal** 1 Ptc. pass. נָחוּץ—pass. **be private,** <SUBJ> דָּבָר *matter* of king 1 S 21$_{9}$.

*נחר I 2 vb. **snort—Qal** 1 Pf. נָחַר—**snort,** <SUBJ> מַפֻּחַ *bellows* Jr 6$_{29}$ (unless חרר ni. *be set aglow*), כֹּל *everyone* Is 41$_{11}$ 45$_{24}$ (both if em. הַנֶּחֱרִים *those incensed* [חרה ni.] to הַנֹּחֲרִים *those who snort*).* <PREP> בְּ *against, at,* + Y. Is 41$_{11}$ 45$_{24}$ (both if em.; see Prep.).

Pi. 1 Pf. נִחֲרוּ—**be angry,** unless חרה I ni. *be angry,* <SUBJ> בֵּן *son* Ca 1$_{6}$. <PREP> בְּ *against,* + female lover Ca 1$_{6}$.

⇒ נַחַר *snorting,* נַחֲרָה *snorting,* נָחִיר *nostril.*

*נחר II 1 vb. **be parched** (unless חרר ni. *be scorched*)—**Ni.** 1 Pf. נִחַר—**be parched, be hoarse,** <SUBJ> גָּרוֹן *throat* Ps 69$_{4}$ (|| כלה *be dim*).

<SYN> כלה *be dim.*

[נַחַר] 1 n.[m.] **snorting**—sf. נַחְרוֹ—of horse, <CSTR> הוֹד נַחְרוֹ *splendour of his snorting* Jb 39$_{20}$.

Also perh. 4QpIsa[c] 56$_{1}$.

⇒ נחר *snort.*

[נַחֲרָה] 1 n.f. **snorting**—cstr. נַחֲרַת—of horses (Jr 8$_{16}$), Pharaoh as dragon (Ezk 32$_{2}$; if em.; see Prep.), <SUBJ> שׁמע ni. *be heard* Jr 8$_{16}$ (+ מִצְהָלָה *neighing*). <CSTR> נַחֲרַת סוּסָיו *snorting of his horses* Jr 8$_{16}$. <PREP> בְּ of accompaniment, *with,* + גיח hi. *burst out* Ezk 32$_{2}$ (if em. בְּנַהֲרוֹתֶיךָ *in your rivers* to בְּנַחֲרָתְךָ).

⇒ נחר *snort.*

נַחֲרַי 2 pr.n.m. **Naharai,** Beerothite, armour-bearer of Joab, <SUBJ> נשׂא *bear* arms 2 S 23$_{37}$||1 C 11$_{39}$. <APP> בְּאֵרֹתִי *Beerothite* 2 S 23$_{37}$||1 C 11$_{39}$.

נחשׁ I 11.0.1 vb. **practise divination—Pi.** 11 Pf. נִחֵשׁ, נִחַשְׁתִּי; impf. תְּנַחֲשׁוּ, יְנַחֲשׁוּ, יְנַחֵשׁ; + waw וַיְנַחֲשׁוּ; ptc. מְנַחֵשׁ, inf. abs. נַחֵשׁ—**1. practise divination, practice augury,** esp. through observation of natural phenomena (as distinct from קסם *divine by means of an oracle*)*; **learn by divination, observe omens** (Gn 30$_{27}$ [unless נחשׁ II *become rich*] 1 K 20$_{33}$), <SUBJ> Israelites Lv 19$_{26}$ 2 K 17$_{17}$, Laban Gn 30$_{27}$ (unless נחשׁ II *become rich*), Manasseh 2 K 21$_{6}$||2 C 33$_{6}$, אִישׁ *man* Gn 55$_{15}$ 1 K 20$_{33}$, אָדוֹן *lord* Gn 44$_{5.5}$. <PREP> בְּ of instrument, *by (means of), with,* + גָּבִיעַ *cup* Gn 44$_{5}$. <COLL> נחשׁ pi. || ענן po. *practise soothsaying* Lv 19$_{26}$ 2 K 21$_{6}$|| 2 C 33$_{6}$, כשׁף pi. *practise sorcery* 2 C 33$_{6}$; + קסם *practise divination* 2 K 17$_{17}$, עשׂה *appoint* mediums and necromancers 2 K 21$_{6}$||2 C 33$_{6}$, עבר hi. *make* child *pass* into fire 2 K 21$_{6}$||2 C 33$_{6}$; נַחֵשׁ יְנַחֵשׁ *he indeed practises divination* Gn 44$_{5.15}$.

2. ptc. as noun, **diviner,** <SUBJ> מצא ni. *be found* Dt 18$_{10}$=11QT 60$_{18}$ (|| מְעוֹנֵן *soothsayer,* מְכַשֵּׁף *sorcerer,* + קסם *practise divination,* שׁאל *inquire* of ghost, דרשׁ *inquire* of dead, חבר *cast* spell, עבר hi. *make* child *pass* into fire).

<SYN> §1 ענן po. *practise soothsaying,* כשׁף pi. *practise sorcery;* §2 מְעוֹנֵן *soothsayer,* מְכַשֵּׁף *sorcerer.*

⇒ נַחַשׁ *divination.*

*נחשׁ II 1 vb. **become rich** (unless נחשׁ I *practise divination*)—**Pi** 1 Pf. נִחַשְׁתִּי—**become rich,** <SUBJ> Laban Gn 30$_{27}$ (|| ברך pi. *bless*).

<SYN> ברך pi. *bless.*

נַחַשׁ 2 n.[m.] **divination**—pl. נְחָשִׁים—**divination, augury, omen,** <OBJ> קרא *call (for)* Nm 24$_{1}$. <NOM CL> לֹא־נַחַשׁ בְּיַעֲקֹב *there is no augury in Jacob* Nm 23$_{23}$ (|| קֶסֶם *divination*).

<SYN> קֶסֶם *divination.*

⇒ נחשׁ *practise divination.*

נָחָשׁ I 31 n.m. **serpent**—cstr. נְחַשׁ; pl. נְחָשִׁים—<SUBJ> היה *be* Gn 3$_{1}$ 49$_{17}$=4QCommGenC 5$_{4}$ ([נח]שׁ), אמר *say* Gn 3$_{1.4}$, אכל *eat* dust Gn 3$_{14}$, הלך *go* Gn 3$_{14}$ Jr 46$_{22}$, נשׁא hi. *beguile* Gn 3$_{13}$, עשׂה *do* Gn 3$_{14}$, שׁוף *bruise* Gn 3$_{14}$, נשׁך *bite* Nm 21$_{9}$ Am 5$_{19}$ 9$_{3}$ Ec 10$_{8.11}$, pi. Nm 21$_{6}$ Jr 8$_{17}$, שׁנן *sharpen* tongue Ps 140$_{4}$.

<OBJ> צוה pi. *command* Am 9$_{3}$, שׁלח *send* Nm 21$_{6}$ Jr 8$_{17}$, סור hi. *remove* Nm 21$_{7}$, שׂים *place* Nm 21$_{9}$, עשׂה *make* Nm 21$_{9}$ 2 K 18$_{4}$, כתת pi. *hammer into pieces* 2 K 18$_{4}$, חלל po. *pierce* Jb 26$_{13}$.

<CSTR> נְחַשׁ נְחֹשֶׁת *serpent of bronze* Nm 21$_{9.9}$ 2 K 18$_{4}$; שֹׁרֶשׁ נָחָשׁ *root of the serpent* Is 14$_{29}$, חֲמַת־ *venom of* Ps 58$_{5}$, דֶּרֶךְ *way of* Pr 30$_{29}$.

<APP> שָׂרָף *fiery serpent* Nm 21$_{6}$ Dt 8$_{15}$, צִפְעוֹנִי *ad-*

der Jr 8$_{17}$, לִוְיָתָן *Leviathan* Is 27$_{1.1}$.

<ADJ> בָּרִיחַ *fleeing* or *evil* or *dangerous* or *primaeval* Is 27$_1$ Jb 26$_{13}$, עֲקַלָּתוֹן *twisting* Is 27$_1$.

<PREP> לְ introducing predicate, + היה *be* Ex 4$_3$; *into*, + הפך ni. *be turned* Ex 7$_{15}$; of possession, *of*, *(belonging) to* Jr 8$_{17}$ (נְחָשִׁים ... אֲשֶׁר אֵין־לָהֶם לָחַשׁ *serpents ... of which there is no charming*, i.e. that cannot be charmed) 4QJub^h 37$_{18}$ ([לנ]חשים); כְּ *as* Jr 46$_{22}$, לחך pi. *lick* Mc 7$_{17}$, נשך *bite* Pr 23$_{32}$; אֶל *to, at*, + אמר *say* Gn 3$_{2.14}$, נבט hi. *look* Nm 21$_9$; עַל introducing object, + פקד *visit*, i.e. punish Is 27$_{1.1}$; מִפְּנֵי *from before*, + נוס *flee* Ex 4$_3$.

<COLL> נָחָשׁ || שְׁפִיפֹן *viper* Gn 49$_{17}$, צִפְעוֹנִי *adder* Pr 23$_{32}$, נֶשֶׁר *eagle* Pr 30$_{19}$, גֶּבֶר *man* Pr 30$_{19}$, אֳנִיָּה *ship* Pr 30$_{19}$; + צֶפַע *adder* Is 14$_{29}$, פֶּתֶן *adder* Ps 58$_4$, עַכְשׁוּב *asp* Ps 140$_4$, שָׂרָף *fiery serpent* Is 14$_{29}$, תַּנִּין *sea monster* Is 27$_1$, זֹחֵל *crawling thing* Mc 7$_{17}$.

נָחָשׁ עָפָר לַחְמוֹ *as for the serpent, dust shall be his food* Is 65$_{25}$, נָחָשׁ עֲלֵי־דֶרֶךְ *a serpent upon the way* Gn 49$_{17}$, נָחָשׁ עֲלֵי צוּר *a serpent upon the rock* Pr 30$_{19}$.*

<SYN> שְׁפִיפֹן *viper*, צִפְעוֹנִי *adder*, נֶשֶׁר *eagle*, גֶּבֶר *man*, אֳנִיָּה *ship*.

נָחָשׁ II 9 pr.n.m. **Nahash, 1.** king of Ammon, <SUBJ> אמר *say* 1 S 11$_2$, בוא *come* 1 S 12$_{12}$, עלה *go up* 1 S 11$_1$, חנה *encamp* 1 S 11$_1$, שׂים *place* 1 S 11$_2$, כרת *cut*, i.e. make, covenant 1 S 11$_{1.2}$, רפה hi. *leave alone* 1 S 11$_2$, מות *die* 1 C 19$_1$. <OBJ> עבד *serve* 1 S 11$_1$. <CSTR> בֶּן־נָחָשׁ *son of Nahash* 2 S 10$_2$||1 C 19$_2$. <APP> עַמּוֹנִי *Ammonite* 1 S 11$_{1.2}$, מֶלֶךְ *king* 1 S 12$_{12}$ 1 C 19$_1$. <PREP> אֶל *to*, + אמר *say* 1 S 11$_{1.2}$, יצא *go out* 1 S 11$_2$; תַּחַת *instead of*, + מלך *reign* 1 C 19$_1$.

2. father of Abigal and Zeruiah, <CSTR> בַּת־נָחָשׁ *daughter of Nahash* 2 S 17$_{25}$.

3. father of Shobi, perh. ident. with §1, <CSTR> בֶּן־נָחָשׁ *son of Nahash* 2 S 17$_{27}$.

נָחָשׁ III, see עִיר נָחָשׁ *Irnahash*.

*[נַחְשׁוֹל] 0.0.1 n.[m.] **gale**—pl. cstr. Q נחשולי—<CSTR> נחשולי ימים *gales of the seas* 1QH 10$_{12}$. <PREP> כְּ *as*, + המה *roar* 1QH 10$_{12}$.

נַחְשׁוֹן 10 pr.n.m. **Nahshon,** chief of Judah, son of Amminadab and brother-in-law of Aaron, <SUBJ> היה *be* Nm 7$_{12}$, ילד hi. *beget* Ru 4$_{20}$ 1 C 2$_{11}$, קרב hi. *bring near*, i.e. offer Nm 7$_{12}$. <NOM CL> לִיהוּדָה נַחְשׁוֹן *(belonging) to Judah was Nahshon* Nm 1$_7$, נָשִׂיא לִבְנֵי יְהוּדָה נַחְשׁוֹן *the prince of the sons of Judah was Nahshon* Nm 2$_3$, עַל־צְבָאוֹ נַחְשׁוֹן *over its army was Nahshon* Nm 10$_{14}$. <OBJ> ילד hi. *beget* Ru 4$_{20}$ 1 C 2$_{10}$. <CSTR> אֲחוֹת נַחְשׁוֹן *sister of Nahshon* Ex 6$_{23}$, קָרְבַּן *offering of* Nm 7$_{17}$. <APP> בֵּן *son* Nm 1$_7$ 2$_3$ 7$_{12.17}$ 10$_{14}$, נָשִׂיא *prince* 1 C 2$_{10}$. <COLL> נַחְשׁוֹן ... לְמַטֵּה יְהוּדָה *Nahshon ... of the tribe of Judah* Nm 7$_{12}$.

*[נַחְשִׁיר] I 0.0.3 n.m. **carnage,** <NOM CL> נחשיר חזק לפני אל ישראל *(there shall be) severe carnage before the God of Israel* 1QM 1$_9$ (unless נַחְשִׁיר II *hunting* or III *terror*). <ADJ> חָזָק *strong*, i.e. severe 1QM 1$_9$ (unless נַחְשִׁיר II *hunting*), גָּדוֹל *great* 1QM 1$_{10}$. <PREP> לְ of direction, *to*, + יצא *go out* 1QM 1$_{13}$ ([יצ]או); *resulting in*, + קרב htp. *draw near (for battle)* 1QM 1$_{10}$.

*[נַחְשִׁיר] II 0.0.1 n.m. **hunting** (unless נַחְשִׁיר I *carnage* or III *fear*), <NOM CL> נחשיר חזק לפני אל ישראל *(there shall be) strong hunting before the God of Israel* 1QM 1$_9$. <ADJ> חָזָק *strong* 1QM 1$_9$.

*[נַחְשִׁיר] III 0.0.1 n.m. **fear, terror** (unless נַחְשִׁיר I *carnage* or II *hunting*), <NOM CL> נחשיר חזק לפני אל ישראל *(there shall be) great fear before the God of Israel* 1QM 1$_9$. <ADJ> חָזָק *strong*, i.e. great 1QM 1$_9$.

נְחֹשֶׁת I 140.2.10 n.m.&f. **copper, bronze**—Q נחושת; cstr. נְחֹשֶׁת; sf. נְחֻשְׁתִּי, נְחָשְׁתָּהּ, נְחֻשְׁתָּם; du. נְחֻשְׁתַּיִם—**copper,** as ore (Dt 8$_9$ Si 48$_{17}$), **copper, bronze** (alloy of copper and tin), usu. as material; as spoil (2 S 8$_8$ 2 K 25$_{13}$||Jer 52$_{17}$), **bronze fetters** (sometimes archaizing*; du. Jg 16$_{21}$ 2 S 3$_{34}$ 2 K 25$_7$||Jr 52$_{11}$ Jr 39$_7$ 2 C 33$_{11}$ 36$_6$; sing. Lm 3$_7$), perh. **money** (Ezk 16$_{36}$; but prob. נְחֹשֶׁת II *indecency*), <SUBJ> היה *be* Dt 28$_{23}$ 11QT 3$_{15}$ ([יהיו נחו]שת), בוא *come* Nm 31$_{22}$, מרט pu. *be polished* 1 K 7$_{45}$, מרק pass. *be polished* 2 C 4$_{16}$ 1QM 5$_4$, צהב ho. *gleam* Ezr 8$_{27}$ (perh. נְחֹשֶׁת מֻצְהָב *orichalc*, a copper alloy),* ברר pass. *be purified* 11QT 3$_{17}$ ([נחו]שת ברור), חרר *burn* Ezk 24$_{11}$, מזז pu. *be joined together* 1QM 5$_{5.8}$, perh. שׁפך ni. *be poured out*, i.e. lavished Ezk 16$_{36}$ (but prob. נְחֹשֶׁת II *indecency*).

<NOM CL> נְחֹשֶׁת מִנְעָלֶיךָ *your bolts are (of) bronze* Dt 33$_{25}$ (mss מִנְעָלְךָ *your bolt* is), אַדְנֵיהֶם ... נְחֹשֶׁת, and vars. *their bases shall be ... (of) bronze* Ex 27$_{10.11.17}$||38$_{10.11.19}$ 27$_{18}$ 38$_{17.38}$, כָּל־יְתֵדֹתָיו ... נְחֹשֶׁת *all its pegs shall be ... (of) bronze* Ex 27$_{19}$, var. 38$_{20}$, המגן ... נחושת *the shield shall be (of) ... bronze* 1QM 5$_{5}$, [הכיר וכנו והר]שת נחושת *the laver and its stand and the network shall be (of) bronze* 11QT 3$_{16}$, כֻּלָּם נְחֹשֶׁת *they are all bronze* Ezk 22$_{18}$, var. Jr 6$_{28}$, הַכֹּל נְחֹשֶׁת *everything was bronze* 2 K 25$_{17}$||Jr 52$_{22}$.

<OBJ> בוא hi. *bring* Ex 35$_{5}$ Is 60$_{17}$, עבר hi. *cause to pass* through fire Nm 31$_{22}$, קרב hi. *bring near*, i.e. remove 2 K 16$_{14}$ (or del. נְחֹשֶׁת), נשׂא *carry* 2 K 25$_{13}$||Jer 52$_{17}$, לקח *take* Ex 25$_{3}$ 2 S 8$_{8}$||1 C 18$_{8}$, חצב *hew out* Dt 8$_{9}$, כון hi. *prepare* 1 C 22$_{3}$ 29$_{2}$ 4QSela 9.2$_{5}$ ([נחושת ... יכין]), נתן *give* 1 C 29$_{7}$, צפה pi. *overlay with* Ex 27$_{2.6}$||38$_{2.6}$ 2 C 4$_{9}$, עשׂה *make of* Ex 27$_{3}$||38$_{3}$ 30$_{18.18}$ 38$_{8.8}$ 1 K 7$_{27.45}$||2 C 4$_{16}$ 4QD^{d} 18.2$_{2}$, צור *form with* 1 K 7$_{15}$, רעע *break* Jr 15$_{12}$ (mss ידע *know*), כבד hi. *make heavy* Lm 3$_{7}$.

<CSTR> נְחֹשֶׁת הַתְּנוּפָה *bronze of the offering* Ex 38$_{29}$, כָּל־הַכֵּלִים *of all the vessels* 2 K 25$_{16}$.

חָרֵשׁ נְחֹשֶׁת *artisan of*, i.e. in, *bronze* Gn 4$_{22}$ 1 K 7$_{14}$, חָרָשֵׁי ... *artisans of ...*, i.e. in 2 C 24$_{12}$, נְחַשׁ *serpent of* Nm 21$_{9.9}$ 2 K 18$_{14}$ (both הַנְּחֹשֶׁת), עֵין *eye*, i.e. sparkle of Ezk 1$_{7}$ Dn 10$_{6}$, מַרְאֵה *appearance of* Ezk 40$_{3}$, הָרֵי *mountains of* Zc 6$_{1}$, יָם *sea of* 2 K 25$_{13}$||Jer 52$_{17}$ 1 C 18$_{8}$ (both הַנְּחֹשֶׁת).

כּוֹבַע נְחֹשֶׁת *helmet of bronze* 1 S 17$_{5}$, קוֹבַע *helmet of* 1 S 17$_{38}$, מִצְחַת *greaves of* 1 S 17$_{6}$, כִּידוֹן *javelin of* 1 S 17$_{6}$, מָגִנֵּי *shields of* 1 K 14$_{27}$||2 C 12$_{10}$ 1QM 5$_{4}$ (נחושת), חוֹמַת *wall of* Jr 15$_{20}$, חֹמוֹת *walls of* Jr 1$_{18}$, עַמּוּדֵי *pillars of* 2 K 25$_{13}$||Jr 52$_{17}$ (הַנְּחֹשֶׁת), בְּרִיחַ *bar of* 1 K 4$_{13}$, דַּלְתוֹת *doors of* Ps 107$_{16}$ 11QPsAp^{a} 5$_{9}$ (דל[תי נחושת]).

אוֹפַנֵּי נְחֹשֶׁת *wheels of bronze* 1 K 7$_{30}$, סַרְנֵי *axles of* 1 K 7$_{30}$, קַרְסֵי *clasps of* Ex 26$_{11}$||36$_{18}$, אַדְנֵי *bases of* Ex 26$_{37}$, רֶשֶׁת *network of* Ex 27$_{4}$||38$_{4}$, מִכְבַּר *grating of* Ex 35$_{16}$ 38$_{5.30}$ 39$_{39}$ (all four הַנְּחֹשֶׁת), מִזְבַּח *altar of* Ex 38$_{30}$ 39$_{39}$ 1 K 8$_{64}$||2 C 7$_{7}$ 2 K 16$_{15}$ Ezk 9$_{2}$ 2 C 1$_{5.6}$ (all eight הַנְּחֹשֶׁת) 4$_{1}$ 11QT 3$_{17}$ ([מזב]ח נחו[שת]), מַחְתּוֹת *censers of* Nm 17$_{4}$ (הַנְּחֹשֶׁת), כִּיּוֹר *platform of* 2 C 6$_{13}$, כִּיֹּרוֹת *basins of* 1 K 7$_{38}$, כְּלִי *vessel of* Lv 6$_{21}$, כְּלֵי *vessels of* Jos 6$_{19.24}$ (הַנְּחֹשֶׁת) 2 S 8$_{10}$||1 C 18$_{10}$ (כְּלֵי ...) 2 K 25$_{14}$||Jr 52$_{18}$ (הַנְּחֹשֶׁת) Ezk 27$_{13}$ Ezr 8$_{27}$ 1 C 18$_{8}$ (הַנְּחֹשֶׁת) 11QT 49$_{15}$.

לוח נחו[שת] *tablet of bronze* 11QT 34$_{1}$, מֻצַק *casting of* 1 K 7$_{16}$, קְבֻצַת ... נְחֹשֶׁת *gathering of ... bronze* Ezk 22$_{20}$, תְּרוּמַת ... *offering of ...* Ex 35$_{24}$, מִשְׁקַל הַנְּחֹשֶׁת *weight of the bronze* 1 K 7$_{74}$||2 C 4$_{18}$, כול ... הנחשת *any of ... the bronze* 4QD^{d} 18.2$_{2}$.

<APP> בָּקָר *oxen* 2 K 16$_{17}$ Jr 52$_{20}$, כֹּתֶרֶת *capital* 2 K 25$_{17}$||Jr 52$_{22}$, מְצִלְתַּיִם *cymbals* 1 C 15$_{19}$, תְּרוּמָה *offering* Ex 25$_{3}$||35$_{5}$, מִזְבַּח *altar* 2 K 16$_{14}$ (or del. נְחֹשֶׁת), שֶׁקֶל *shekel* 1 S 17$_{5}$ 2 S 21$_{16}$, כִּכָּר *talent* 1 C 29$_{7}$, דָּבָר *thing* Nm 31$_{22}$, מַעֲשֶׂה *work* 1QM 5$_{5}$.

<ADJ> קָלָל *burnished* Ezk 1$_{7}$ Dn 10$_{6}$, טָהוֹר *pure* 11QT 3$_{15}$ (נחו[שת]), טוֹב *good* Ezr 8$_{27}$, רַב *much* 1 C 18$_{8}$.

<PREP> לְ of direction, *to*, + נגשׁ ho. *be brought near* 2 S 3$_{34}$; of benefit, *for*, + כון hi. *establish* 1 C 29$_{2}$; of possession, *of, (belonging) to* 1 C 22$_{14.16}$ 11QT^{b} 12$_{14}$, + היה *be* 2 K 25$_{16}$||Jr 52$_{20}$.

בְּ of instrument, *by (means of), with*, + עשׂה *make* Ex 31$_{4}$||35$_{32}$ 1 K 7$_{14}$ 2 C 2$_{6.13}$, אסר *bind* Jg 16$_{21}$ 2 K 25$_{7}$||Jr 52$_{11}$ Jr 39$_{7}$ 2 C 33$_{11}$ 36$_{6}$; of accompaniment, *with*, + שׁוב *go back* Jos 22$_{8}$; of essence, *in, (consisting) of* 1QM 5$_{8}$.

כְּ *as* Si 48$_{17}$, + חלא hi. *show rust* Si 12$_{10}$.

מִן partitive, *(some) of*, + בוא hi. *bring* 4QD^{d} 18.2$_{2}$ ([יבא]).

מֵעַל *from upon*, + ירד hi. *take down* 2 K 16$_{17}$.

עַל *upon*, + נפח *blow* fire Ezk 22$_{20}$.

תַּחַת *instead of*, + בוא hi. *bring* Is 60$_{17}$.

<COLL> נְחֹשֶׁת || בַּרְזֶל *iron* Gn 4$_{22}$ Nm 31$_{22}$ Dt 28$_{23}$ 33$_{25}$ Jos 6$_{19.24}$ 22$_{8}$ Is 60$_{17.17}$ Jr 1$_{18}$ 6$_{28}$ 15$_{12}$ Ezk 22$_{18.20}$ Ps 107$_{16}$ 1 C 22$_{14.16}$ 29$_{2.7}$ 2 C 2$_{6.13}$ 24$_{12}$ 11QT 49$_{15}$; + בַּרְזֶל Dt 8$_{9}$ 1 C 22$_{3}$.

|| זָהָב *gold* Ex 25$_{3}$||35$_{5}$ 31$_{4}$||35$_{32}$ Nm 31$_{22}$ Jos 22$_{8}$ 2 S 8$_{10}$||1 C 18$_{10}$ 1 C 22$_{16}$ 29$_{2.7}$ 2 C 2$_{6.13}$ 1QM 5$_{5.8}$; + זָהָב Jos 6$_{19.24}$ 1 C 22$_{14}$; :: זָהָב Is 60$_{17}$.

|| כֶּסֶף *silver* Ex 25$_{3}$||35$_{5}$ 31$_{4}$||35$_{32}$ 35$_{24}$ Nm 31$_{22}$ Jos 22$_{8}$ 2 S 8$_{10}$||1 C 18$_{10}$ Ezk 22$_{20}$ 1 C 22$_{16}$ 29$_{2.7}$ 2 C 2$_{6.13}$ 1QM

5$_{5.8}$ 4QD[d] 18.2$_{2}$; + כֶּסֶף Ex 27$_{10.11.17}$||38$_{10.11.19}$ 27$_{18}$ 38$_{17}$ Jos 6$_{19.24}$ Ezk 22$_{18}$ 1 C 22$_{14}$.

|| בְּדִיל *tin* Nm 31$_{22}$ Ezk 22$_{18.20}$.

|| עֹפֶרֶת *lead* Nm 31$_{22}$ Ezk 22$_{18.20}$.

|| עֵץ *wood* 1 C 29$_{2}$ 2 C 2$_{13}$ 11QT 49$_{15}$; :: עֵץ Is 60$_{17}$.

|| אֶבֶן *stone* 2 C 2$_{6}$; + אֶבֶן 1 C 29$_{2}$.

|| אַרְגָּמָן *purple (material)* 2 C 2$_{6.13}$, תְּכֵלֶת *blue (material)* 2 C 2$_{13}$, כַּרְמִיל *crimson (material)* 2 C 2$_{6.13}$, בּוּץ *linen* 2 C 2$_{13}$, שַׂלְמָה *garment* Jos 22$_{8}$, מִקְנֶה *cattle* Jos 22$_{8}$.

נְחֹשֶׁת הַרְבֵּה מְאֹד *very much bronze* 2 S 8$_{8}$ (||1 C 18$_{8}$ רַבָּה מְאֹד), נְחֹשֶׁת לָרֹב אֵין מִשְׁקָל *much bronze (for which) there was no weight,* i.e. it could not be weighed 1 C 22$_{3}$, vars. 1 C 22$_{14.16}$.

Also 4Q415 7$_{2}$ ([נחושׁ]) 11QT 3$_{7}$ (נחו[שת]) 11QT[b] 31$_{1}$.

<SYN> בַּרְזֶל *iron,* זָהָב *gold,* כֶּסֶף *silver,* בְּדִיל *tin,* עֹפֶרֶת *lead,* עֵץ *wood,* אֶבֶן *stone,* אַרְגָּמָן *purple (material),* תְּכֵלֶת *blue (material),* כַּרְמִיל *crimson (material),* בּוּץ *linen,* שַׂלְמָה *garment,* מִקְנֶה *cattle.*

<ANT> זָהָב *gold,* עֵץ *wood.**

⇒ נְחֻשְׁתָּן *Nehushtan.*

[נְחֹשֶׁת] II 1 n.[f.] **indecency** (unless נְחֹשֶׁת I *copper,* i.e. money)—נְחֻשְׁתֵּךְ—**indecency, lust** or **menstrual blood** of woman, <SUBJ> שׁפך ni. *be poured out* Ezk 16$_{36}$ (+ עֶרְוָה *nakedness;* or em. הִשָּׁפֵךְ to חָשְׂפֵּךְ *your making bare*). <OBJ> חשׂף *make bare* Ezk 16$_{36}$ (if em.; see Subj.).

נְחֻשְׁתָּא 1 pr.n.f. **Nehushta,** mother of King Jehoiachin, daughter of Elnathan, <NOM CL> שֵׁם אִמּוֹ נְחֻשְׁתָּא *the name of his mother was Nehushta* 2 K 24$_{8}$. <APP> בַּת *daughter* 2 K 24$_{8}$.

נְחֻשְׁתָּן 1 pr.n.m. **Nehushtan,** name given to bronze serpent, <OBJ> קרא *call,* i.e. name 2 K 18$_{4}$.*

⇒ נְחֹשֶׁת cf. *copper, bronze,* נָחוּשׁ *bronze,* נְחוּשָׁה *copper.*

נחת I 8 vb. **go down—Qal** 3 Impf. יֵחַת, 3fs תֵּחַת (תִּחַת); + waw 3fs וַתִּנְחַת—**go down, descend, march against** (Jr 21$_{13}$ 2 K 6$_{8.9}$ [both if em.]), **sink deep** (Pr 17$_{10}$), perh. **go away** (Is 24$_{11}$ 51$_{6}$),* <SUBJ> Y. Jb 33$_{16}$ (if em. יַחְתֹּם *he seals* to יֵחָתֵם *he descends to them*), Aramaeans 2 K 6$_{9}$ (if em. נְחִתִּים *descending* [נָחֵת adj.] to נְחִתִּים), רָשָׁע *wicked one* Jb 21$_{13}$ (if em. יֵחָתּוּ *they are shattered* [i.e. חתת ni.] to יֵחָתּוּ), עֶבֶד *servant* 2 K 6$_{8}$ (if em. תַּחֲנֹתִי *my encamping* to תִּנְחָתוּ *you shall go down*), יָד *hand* Ps 38$_{3}$ (or em. וַתָּנַח *and it rested,* from נוח), גְּעָרָה *rebuke* Pr 17$_{10}$ (or em. תֵּחַת *will shatter* [חתת hi.]),* צְדָקָה *righteousness,* i.e. salvation Is 51$_{6}$ (unless חתת ni. *be shattered*), מִי *who?* Jr 21$_{13}$ (or em. יָחֵת *will shatter* [חתת hi.]*; + בוא *enter*); subj. not specified, Jb 17$_{16}$ (if em. נַחַת *rest* to נֵחַת *we shall descend*).

<PREP> בְּ of place, *into,* + בין hi. ptc. *understanding one* Pr 17$_{10}$ (or em.; see Subj.); of accompaniment, *with, in,* + רֶגַע *peace* Jb 21$_{13}$ (if em.; see Subj.); of cause, *on account of, for,* + מוּסָר *instruction* Jb 33$_{16}$ (if em.; see Subj.); מִן of comparison, *(more) than,* + נכה hi. inf. *striking* a fool a hundred times Pr 17$_{10}$; אֶל *to,* + מָקוֹם *place* 2 K 6$_{8}$ (if em.; see Subj.); עַל *upon, into,* + worshipper Ps 38$_{3}$ (or em.; see Subj.), עָפָר *dust* Jb 17$_{16}$ (if em.; see Subj.); *against,* + יֹשֶׁבֶת *inhabitant(s)* Jr 21$_{13}$ (or em.; see Subj.), צוּר *rock* Jr 21$_{13}$ (or em.; see Subj.); נחת + noun without preposition, שְׁאוֹל *(to) Sheol* Jb 21$_{13}$.

<COLL> נחת + adverb, יַחַד *together* Jb 17$_{16}$ (if em.; see Subj.), שָׁם *there* 2 K 6$_{9}$ (if em.; see Subj.).

Ni. 1 Pf. נִחֲתוּ—**sink, penetrate,** <SUBJ> חֵץ *arrow* Ps 38$_{3}$ (or em. נָחֲתָה *you aim* [נחה IV pi.]). <PREP> בְּ of place, *into,* + worshipper Ps 38$_{3}$ (or em.; see Subj.).

Pi. 3 + waw וְנִחֲתָה, וְנִחַת; inf. abs. נַחֵת—**1. bend, stretch** a bow (unless §3 or נחת II *be strong* or IV *fashion*), <SUBJ> זְרוֹעַ *arm* 2 S 22$_{35}$||Ps 18$_{35}$. <OBJ> קֶשֶׁת *bow* of bronze 2 S 22$_{35}$||Ps 18$_{35}$.

2. cause to sink, make smooth, <SUBJ> Y. Ps 65$_{11}$. <OBJ> גְּדוּד *furrow* Ps 65$_{11}$.

3. perh. **lower** (unless §1 or נחת IV *fashion*), <SUBJ> Y. 2 S 22$_{35}$||Ps 18$_{35}$ (or em. וְנִחַת *and it aims,* from נחה IV). <OBJ> קֶשֶׁת *bow* of bronze or enchantment 2 S 22$_{35}$||Ps 18$_{35}$ (or em.; see Subj.). <COLL> וְנִחַת ... זְרוֹעֹתָי *and he lowered ... (into) my arms* 2 S 22$_{35}$||Ps 18$_{35}$ (וְנִחֲתָה; or em.; see Subj.).

Pi. with infixed *t,* **lower,** <SUBJ> Y. Dt 22$_{27}$ (if em.

מִתַּחַת *underneath* to מְנַחֵת *one who lowers*). <OBJ> זְרוֹעַ *arm* Dt 33$_{27}$ (if em.; see Subj.).*

Hi. 1 Impv. הַנְחַת—**bring down, launch into battle*** (unless נחת III *deport*), <SUBJ> Y. Jl 4$_{11}$. <OBJ> גִּבּוֹר *warrior* Jl 4$_{11}$.

⇒ נָחֵת *descending*, נַחַת I *descent*.

***נחת II** 2 vb. **be strong** (unless נחת I pi. *bend, lower* or IV *fashion*)—**Pi.** 2 + waw וְנִחֲתָה, וְנִחַת—**make strong,** <SUBJ> זְרוֹעַ *arm* 2 S 22$_{35}$||Ps 18$_{35}$ (וְנִחַת קֶשֶׁת־נְחוּשָׁה זְרֹעֹתָי *and he makes strong my arms for a bronze bow*).

***נחת III** 1 vb. **deport** (unless נחת I hi. *bring down*)—**Hi.** 1 Impv. הַנְחַת—**deport,** <SUBJ> Y. Jl 4$_{11}$ (הַנְחַת י׳ גִּבּוֹרֶיךָ *deport your warriors, O Y.!*). <OBJ> גִּבּוֹר *warrior* Jl 4$_{11}$.

***נחת IV** 2 vb. **fashion** (unless נחת I pi. *bend, lower* or II *be strong*)—**Pi.** 2 + waw וְנִחֲתָה, וְנִחַת—**fashion, hew,** <SUBJ> Y. 2 S 22$_{35}$||Ps 18$_{35}$. <OBJ> 1. thing fashioned, זְרוֹעַ *arm* 2 S 22$_{35}$||Ps 18$_{35}$. 2. fashioned into, קֶשֶׁת *bow of* bronze 2 S 22$_{35}$||Ps 18$_{35}$ (וְנִחַת קֶשֶׁת־נְחוּשָׁה זְרֹעֹתָי *and he fashions my arms into a bow of bronze*).

[נָחֵת] 1 adj. **descending**—pl. נְחִתִּים—<NOM CL> שָׁם אֲרָם נְחִתִּים *there the Aramaeans are going down* 2 K 6$_{9}$ (or em. נֹחֲתִים *going down*, i.e. נחת ptc., or נֶחְבָּאִים *hiding themselves*, i.e. חבא ni. ptc.).

⇒ נחת *go down*.

[נַחַת] I 1 n.[m.] **descent** (unless נַחַת III *strength*)—cstr. נַחַת—of arm of Y., <OBJ> ראה hi. *cause to be seen* Is 30$_{30}$. <CSTR> נַחַת זְרוֹעוֹ *descent of his arm* Is 30$_{30}$ (|| הוֹד *majesty* of voice).

<SYN> הוֹד *majesty*.

⇒ נחת *go down*.

***נַחַת II** 7.4 n.[f.] **quietness**—נָחַת; cstr. נַחַת—**1. quietness, rest, calm, patience, peace,** <NOM CL> אֵין נַחַת *there is no quietness* Pr 29$_{9}$, נַחַת לָזֶה מִזֶּה *rest is to this one more than to that* Ec 6$_{5}$, עַל־עָפָר נָחַת *upon the dust there is rest* Jb 17$_{16}$ (or em. נֵחָת *we shall descend*).

<OBJ> מצא *find* Si 11$_{19}$ 34$_{21}$, בקשׁ pi. *seek* Si 30$_{34}$, ידע *know* Ec 6$_{5}$ (if transfer athnach).

<CSTR> מְלֹא כַף נָחַת *handful of peace* Ec 4$_{6}$.

<PREP> בְּ of instrument, accompaniment, *by (means of), with, in*, + הלך *go* Si 12$_{11}$, ישׁע ni. *be saved* Is 30$_{15}$, שׁמע ni. *be heard* Ec 9$_{17}$.

<COLL> נַחַת || שׁוּבָה *withdrawal* Is 30$_{15}$ (שׁוּבָה וָנַחַת); + שׁקט hi. inf. *quietness*, בִּטְחָה *confidence* Is 30$_{15}$; :: עָמָל *toil* Ec 4$_{6}$, רְעוּת *striving* Ec 4$_{6}$.

2. that which rests (on table), spread (of table), perh. **comfort,** <SUBJ> מלא *be full* Jb 36$_{16}$ (נַחַת שֻׁלְחָנְךָ מָלֵא דָשֶׁן *the spread of your table was full of fatness;* unless *the comfort of your table [which was] full of fatness*). <CSTR> נַחַת שֻׁלְחָנְךָ *the spread of your table* Jb 36$_{16}$.

<SYN> §1 שׁוּבָה *withdrawal*.

<ANT> עָמָל *toil*, רְעוּת *striving*.

⇒ נוח I *rest*.

***[נַחַת] III** 1 n.[m.] **strength** (unless נַחַת I *descent*)—cstr. נַחַת—of arm of Y., <OBJ> ראה hi. *cause to be seen* Is 30$_{30}$. <CSTR> נַחַת זְרוֹעוֹ *strength of his arm* Is 30$_{30}$ (|| הוֹד *majesty* of voice).

<SYN> הוֹד *majesty*.

נַחַת IV 5 pr.n.m. **Nahath, 1.** son of Reuel and grandson of Esau, <NOM CL> בְּנֵי רְעוּאֵל נַחַת *the sons of Reuel were Nahath …* 1 C 1$_{37}$, אֵלֶּה בְּנֵי רְעוּאֵל נַחַת *these are the sons of Reuel: Nahath …* Gn 36$_{13}$, sim. 36$_{17}$. <APP> אַלּוּף *chief* Gn 36$_{17}$.

2. Levite, son of Zophai and grandson of Elkanah, appar. ident. with Toah at 1 C 6$_{19}$ and Tohu at 1 S 1$_{1}$, <NOM CL> נַחַת בְּנוֹ *Nahath was his son* 1 C 6$_{11}$.

3. Levite, temple official at time of Hezekiah, <NOM CL> עֲזַרְיָהוּ וְנַחַת … פְּקִידִים *Azariah and Nahath … were overseers* 2 C 31$_{13}$.

***נטב** 1 vb. **drop**—**Qal** 1 Inf. מְטוֹב—**drop (word), speak,** <SUBJ> worshipper Ps 39$_{3}$ (הֶחֱשֵׁיתִי מְטוֹב *I was silent,* i.e. refrained, *from speaking;* unless מִטּוֹב *from good*).

Hi. drip, i.e. dispense, <SUBJ> לָשׁוֹן *tongue* Pr 15$_{2}$ (if em. תֵּיטִיב *it makes good* [יטב hi.] to תַּטִּיב). <OBJ> דַּעַת *knowledge* Pr 15$_{2}$ (if em.; see Subj.).

⇒ cf. נטף *drip*.

נטה 216.16.20.1 vb. **stretch out—Qal** 137.8.6 Pf. נָטָה, נָטְתָה, נָטִיתָ (Q נטיתה), נָטִיתִי, נָטוּ (Qr נָטָיו); impf. יִטֶּה (יֵט), 3fs תִּטֶּה, 2ms תֵּט, נִטֶּה; + waw וְנָטָה, וְנָטִיתִי, וַיֵּט (וַיֶּט־), 3fs וַתֵּט, וַיִּטּוּ; impv. נְטֵה; ptc. נֹטֶה (נוֹטֶה), נוֹטֵיהֶם; ptc. pass. נָטוּי, נְטוּיָה, Qr נְטוּיֹת (Kt נטוות); inf. נְטוֹת (נְטֹת, נְטֹתִי, נְטוֹתוֹ).

1. stretch out, hold out, extend, <SUBJ> Y. Gn 39$_{21}$ Ex 7$_{5}$ 15$_{12}$ 2 K 21$_{13}$ Is 5$_{25}$ 23$_{11}$ 34$_{11}$ 66$_{12}$ Jr 51$_{25}$ Ezk 6$_{14}$ 14$_{9.13}$ 16$_{27}$ 25$_{7.13.16}$ 35$_{3}$ Zp 1$_{4}$ 2$_{13}$ Lm 2$_{8}$ 1 C 21$_{10}$, Aaron Ex 7$_{19}$ 8$_{1.2.12.13}$, Joshua Jos 8$_{18.18.19.26}$ Si 46$_{2}$, Moses Ex 9$_{22.23}$ 10$_{12.13.21.22}$ 14$_{16.21.26.27}$, Sennacherib Si 48$_{18}$, בֵּן *son* Si 46$_{2}$, מֶלֶךְ *king* Ezk 30$_{25}$, חָרָשׁ *artisan* Is 44$_{13}$, רָשָׁע *wicked one* Jb 15$_{25}$, עָרִיץ *ruthless one* Jb 15$_{25}$, אֹיֵב *enemy* Ps 21$_{12}$, שׂנא ptc. *one who hates* Ps 21$_{12}$, ראשׁ *head*, i.e. column, of troops 1QM 8$_{8}$, חָכְמוֹת *wisdom* Pr 1$_{24}$, מִי *who?* Jb 38$_{5}$.

<OBJ> יָד *hand* Ex 7$_{5.19}$ 8$_{1.2.12(Sam).13}$ 9$_{22}$ 10$_{12.21.22}$ 14$_{16.21.26.27}$ Jos 8$_{19.26}$ Is 5$_{25}$ 23$_{11}$ Jr 51$_{25}$ Ezk 6$_{14}$ 14$_{9.13}$ 16$_{27}$ 25$_{7.13.16}$ 35$_{3}$ Zp 1$_{4}$ 2$_{13}$ Jb 15$_{25}$ Pr 1$_{24}$ Si 46$_{2}$ 48$_{18}$ 1QM 8$_{8}$, יָמִין *right hand* Ex 15$_{12}$, חֶרֶב *sword* Ezk 30$_{25}$, מַטֶּה *rod* Ex 8$_{12}$ 9$_{23}$ 10$_{13}$, קָו *line* 2 K 21$_{13}$ 34$_{11}$ Is 44$_{13}$ Jb 38$_{5}$ Lm 2$_{8}$, מִשְׁקֹלֶת *levelling instrument* 2 K 21$_{13}$, חֶסֶד *loyalty* Gn 39$_{21}$, שָׁלוֹם *peace* Is 66$_{12}$, כָּבוֹד *glory*, i.e. wealth Is 66$_{12}$, רָעָה *evil* Ps 21$_{12}$, שָׁלוֹשׁ *three (things)* 1 C 15$_{1}$.

<PREP> בְּ of accompaniment, *with*, + מַטֶּה *rod* Ex 8$_{1.12(Sam).13}$, כִּידוֹן *javelin* Jos 8$_{26}$; introducing object, + כִּידוֹן *javelin* Jos 8$_{18.18}$; *to*, + כְּלִי *weapon* 1QM 8$_{8}$; *for*, + אַרְבֶּה *locust* Ex 10$_{12}$.

כְּ *as* Is 66$_{12}$.

אֶל *to, against*, + Y. Jb 15$_{25}$, Ai Jos 8$_{18}$, Joseph Gn 39$_{21}$, אֶרֶץ *land* Ezk 30$_{25}$.

עַל *over, against*, + Ammonites Ezk 25$_{7}$, Edom Is 34$_{11}$ Ezk 25$_{13}$, Egypt Ex 7$_{5}$, Jerusalem 2 K 21$_{13}$ Ezk 16$_{27}$, Judah Zp 1$_{4}$, Philistines Ezk 25$_{16}$, Zion Si 48$_{18}$, עַם *people* Is 5$_{25}$, בַּיִת *house* of Israel Ezk 6$_{14}$, David 1 C 15$_{1}$, מֶלֶךְ *king* Ps 21$_{12}$, יֹשֵׁב *inhabitant* Zp 1$_{4}$, נָבִיא *prophet* Ezk 14$_{9}$, צָפוֹן *north* Zp 2$_{13}$, אֶרֶץ *land* Ex 10$_{12.13}$ Ezk 14$_{13}$ Jb 38$_{5}$, הַר *mountain* Jr 51$_{25}$ Ezk 35$_{3}$, יָם *sea* Ex 14$_{16.21.26.27}$ Is 23$_{11}$, נָהָר *river* Ex 7$_{19}$ 8$_{1}$, יְאֹר *(Nile-)stream* Ex 7$_{19}$ 8$_{1}$, אֲגַם *pool* Ex 7$_{19}$ 8$_{1}$, מִקְוֶה *collection* of water Ex 7$_{19}$, מַיִם *water* Ex 7$_{19}$ 8$_{2}$.

עַל *to*, + שָׁמַיִם *heaven* Ex 9$_{22.23}$ 10$_{21.22}$.

<COLL> נטה + גבר htp. *display might* Jb 15$_{25}$, חשׁב *devise* Ps 21$_{12}$, נוף hi. *wield* javelin Si 46$_{2}$.

2. spread out, pitch tent, <SUBJ> Y. Is 40$_{22}$ 42$_{5}$ 44$_{24}$ 51$_{13.16}$ (if em. לִנְטֹעַ *to plant* to לִנְטֹת) Jr 10$_{12}$ 51$_{15}$ Zc 12$_{1}$ Ps 104$_{2}$ Jb 9$_{8}$ 26$_{7}$ Si 43$_{23}$ 1QH 9$_{9}$ 11QPs^{a} 26$_{14}$, Abram Gn 12$_{8}$, David 2 S 6$_{17}$||1 C 16$_{1}$ 1 C 15$_{1}$ 2 C 1$_{4}$, Heber Jg 4$_{11}$, Isaac Gn 26$_{25}$, Jacob/Israel Gn 33$_{19}$ 35$_{21}$, Moses Ex 33$_{7}$, Nebuchadrezzar Jr 43$_{10}$, קֵינִי *Kenite* Jg 4$_{11}$, אֱנוֹשׁ *person* Si 14$_{25}$, מֶלֶךְ *king* Jr 43$_{10}$ Dn 11$_{45}$ (if em. יִטַּע *he shall pitch*, from נטע, to יִטֶּה), עֶבֶד *servant* Jr 43$_{10}$, יָד *hand* of Y. Is 45$_{12}$ Si 43$_{12}$; subj. not specified, Jr 10$_{20}$.

<OBJ> אֹהֶל *tent* Gn 12$_{8}$ 26$_{25}$ 33$_{19}$ 35$_{21}$ Jg 4$_{11}$ 2 S 6$_{17}$|| 1 C 16$_{1}$ Jr 10$_{20}$ 1 C 15$_{1}$ 2 C 1$_{4}$ Si 14$_{25}$ Dn 11$_{45}$ (if em.; see Subj.), שַׁפְרִיר *canopy* Jr 43$_{10}$, שָׁמַיִם *heavens* Is 40$_{22}$ 42$_{5}$ 44$_{24}$ 51$_{13.16}$ (if em.; see Subj.) Jr 10$_{12}$ 51$_{15}$ Zc 12$_{1}$ Ps 104$_{2}$ Jb 9$_{8}$ 1QH 9$_{9}$ 11QPs^{a} 26$_{14}$, צָפוֹן *north* Jb 26$_{7}$, קֶשֶׁת *rainbow* Si 43$_{12}$, אִי *island* Si 43$_{23(B)}$, אוֹצָר *storehouse* Si 43$_{23(Bmg)}$.

<PREP> לְ of benefit, *for*, + אֲרוֹן *ark* 2 S 6$_{17}$||1 C 16$_{1}$ 1 C 15$_{1}$ 2 C 1$_{4}$, כָּבוֹד *glory* 1QH 9$_{9}$; introducing object, + אֹהֶל *tent* Ex 33$_{3}$.

בְּ of place, *in*, + Jerusalem 2 C 1$_{4}$, תְּהוֹם *deep* 43$_{23}$; of instrument, accompaniment, *by (means of), with, in*, + תְּבוּנָה *understanding* Jr 51$_{15}$ 11QPs^{a} 26$_{14}$, גְּבוּרָה *might* Si 43$_{12(M)}$ (בגב[ורה]).

כְּ *as* Is 40$_{22}$ Ps 104$_{2}$.

עַל *over*, + אֶבֶן *stone* Jr 43$_{10}$, תֹּהוּ *void* Jb 26$_{7}$.

עַל יַד *beside*, + חָכְמָה *wisdom* Si 14$_{25}$.

עַד *as far as, by*, + אֵלוֹן *terebinth* Jg 4$_{11}$.

מֵהָלְאָה לְ *beyond*, + Migdal-eder Gn 35$_{21}$.

<COLL> נטה || מתח *spread out* Is 40$_{22}$, רקע *spread out* Is 42$_{5}$ (+) 44$_{24}$, יסד *found* Is 51$_{13}$ Zc 12$_{1}$, קום hi. *raise up* Jr 10$_{20}$, תלה *hang* Jb 26$_{7}$; + ברא *create* Is 42$_{5}$ 45$_{12}$, עשׂה *make* Is 44$_{24}$ 45$_{12}$ 51$_{13}$ Jr 10$_{12}$ 51$_{15}$, יצר *form* Zc 12$_{1}$, כון hi. *establish* Jr 51$_{15}$; + adverb, שָׁם *there* Gn 26$_{25}$ 33$_{19}$, לְבַד *alone* Is 44$_{24}$ Jb 9$_{8}$.

3. intrans., **spread out, extend,** <SUBJ> אֶשֶׁד *slope* Nm 21$_{15}$, מְנָלָה *acquisition* Jb 15$_{29}$ (or em. hi. *bring down* [§9], and em. מִנְלָם to מִנְלָם *their possessions*). <PREP> לְ of direction, *to, through,* + שֶׁבֶת *dwelling* of Ar Nm 21$_{15}$, אֶרֶץ *earth* Jb 15$_{29}$. <COLL> נטה + שׁען ni. *lean* Nm 21$_{15}$.

4a. bend, bow (Gn 49$_{15}$ 4QCommGenC 5$_1$ 2 S 22$_{10}$||Ps 18$_{10}$). **b. incline** (Ps 119$_{112}$); **c. thrust down** (Ps 17$_{11}$; or em.; see Subj.), <SUBJ> Y. 2 S 22$_{10}$||Ps 18$_{10}$, Issachar Gn 49$_{15}$ 4QCommGenC 5$_1$, worshipper Ps 119$_{112}$, רָשָׁע *wicked one* Ps 17$_{11}$ (or em. לְהַטּוֹת, i.e. hi.), אֹיֵב *enemy* Ps 17$_{11}$ (or em.; see above). <OBJ> שְׁכֶם *shoulder* Gn 49$_{15}$ 4QCommGenC 5$_1$ ([שכמו]), לֵב *heart* Ps 119$_{112}$, שָׁמַיִם *heaven* 2 S 22$_{10}$||Ps 18$_{10}$. <PREP> בְּ of place, *onto,* + אֶרֶץ *ground* Ps 17$_{11}$ (or em.; see Subj.). <COLL> וַיֵּט שִׁכְמוֹ לִסְבֹּל *and he bowed his shoulder to bear* Gn 49$_{15}$ 4QCommGenC 5$_1$ ([שכמו לסבול]), נָטִיתִי לִבִּי לַעֲשׂוֹת חֻקֶּיךָ *I have inclined my heart to perform your statutes* Ps 119$_{112}$.

5. intrans., **bend, bow,** <SUBJ> Y. Ho 11$_4$ (if em. וְאַט *and I used to bend down* [hi.] to וְאֵט), Samson Jg 16$_{30}$, שָׁמַיִם *heavens* Ps 68$_9$ (if em. נָטְפוּ *they dripped* to נָטָיו). <PREP> בְּ of accompaniment, *with, in,* + כֹּחַ *strength* Jg 16$_{30}$; אֶל *to,* + Ephraim Ho 11$_4$ (if em.; see Subj.); מִפְּנֵי *from before, at the presence of,* + Y. Ps 68$_9$ (if em.; see Subj.).

6. intrans., **turn, incline** (Jg 9$_3$ 1 S 14$_7$ 1 K 2$_{28.28}$, Ps 40$_2$), **decline** (Jg 19$_8$ 2 K 20$_{10}$ Ps 109$_{23}$ Si 9$_9$), perh. **go down** (Jb 15$_{29}$),* <SUBJ> Y. Ps 40$_2$, Joab 1 K 2$_{28.28}$, Jonathan 1 S 14$_7$, בֵּן *son* Si 9$_9$, לֵב *heart* Jg 9$_3$, צֵל *shadow* 2 K 20$_{10}$ Ps 109$_{23}$ (כְּצֵל כִּי־נְטוֹתִי *like a shadow I have indeed* [emphatic כִּי] *declined*),* יוֹם *day* Jg 19$_8$, מִלְחָמָה *battle* 1 S 4$_2$ (if em. וַתִּטֹּשׁ *and it spread out,* from נטשׁ, to וַתֵּט *and it inclined,* i.e. its outcome was decided), שָׁמַיִם Ps 68$_9$ (if em. נָטְפוּ *they dropped* to נָטוּ).

<PREP> לְ in ref. to subject of נטה, + Jonathan 1 S 14$_7$; בְּ of accompaniment, *with, in,* + דָּם *blood* Si 9$_9$; אֶל *to,* + worshipper Ps 40$_2$, שַׁחַת *pit* Si 9$_9$; אַחֲרֵי *after, in support of,* + Abimelech Jg 9$_3$, Absalom 1 K 2$_{28}$, Adonijah 1 K 2$_{28}$.

<COLL> לִנְטוֹת עֶשֶׂר מַעֲלוֹת *to decline ten steps* 2 K 20$_{10}$.

7. turn aside, deviate, <SUBJ> Israel(ites) Ex 23$_2$ Nm 20$_{17.21}$ 21$_{22}$, Asahel 2 S 2$_{19.21}$, Ben Sira Si 51$_{20}$, Jacob 1QJub[a] 27$_{19}$ ([יעקב]), Judah Gn 38$_{1.16}$, בֵּן *son* 1 S 8$_3$ Pr 4$_5$, אֹרֵחַ *wayfarer* Jr 14$_8$, worshipper Ps 119$_{51.157}$, אָתוֹן *she-ass* Nm 22$_{23.33.33}$, לֵבָב *heart* 1 K 11$_9$, אָשֻׁר *step* Ps 44$_{19}$ Jb 31$_7$, עָוֹן *iniquity* Si 7$_2$; subj. not specified, Nm 22$_{26}$ 4QD[a] 11$_{17}$.

<PREP> לְ in ref. to subject of נטה, + Asahel 2 S 2$_{21}$; of direction, *to,* + יָם *west* ([לימ]ה) 1QJub[a] 27$_{19}$, נֵצַח *everlastingness* Si 51$_{20}$.

בְּ of place, *in(to),* + שָׂדֶה *field* Nm 21$_{22}$, כֶּרֶם *vineyard* Nm 21$_{22}$; of time, *in, during,* + לַיְלָה *night* 1QJub[a] 27$_{19}$ ([בלילה]).

מִן of direction, *from,* + בֵּן *son* Si 7$_2$, דֶּרֶךְ *way* Nm 22$_{23}$ Jb 31$_7$ 1QJub[a] 27$_{19}$, אֹרַח *way* Ps 44$_{19}$, תּוֹרָה *law* Ps 119$_{51}$ 4QD[a] 11$_{17}$ ([מן ה]תורה), עֵדָה *testimony* Ps 119$_{157}$, אֹמֶר *word* Pr 4$_5$, wisdom Si 51$_{20}$.

אֶל *to,* + Tamar Gn 38$_{16}$, דֶּרֶךְ *way* Gn 38$_{16}$.

עַל *to,* + יָמִין *right* 2 S 2$_{21}$, שְׂמֹאל *left* 2 S 2$_{21}$.

מֵעַל *from,* + Edom Nm 20$_{21}$.

מֵעִם *from (being with),* + Y. 1 K 11$_9$.

עַד *to,* + אִישׁ *man* Gn 38$_1$.

לִפְנֵי *before,* + מַלְאָךְ *angel* Nm 22$_{33}$.

מִפְּנֵי *from before,* + מַלְאָךְ *angel* Nm 22$_{33}$.

אַחֲרֵי *after, in support of,* + רַב pl. *many, mighty* Ex 23$_2$, בֶּצַע *gain* 1 S 8$_3$.

נטה + noun without preposition, יָמִין *(to the) right* Nm 20$_{17}$ 22$_{26}$ 4QD[a] 11$_{17}$, שְׂמֹאל *(to the) left* Nm 20$_{17}$ 22$_{26}$ 4QD[a] 11$_{17}$ ([ושמאול]).

<COLL> נטה + סור *turn aside* 2 S 2$_{21}$, סוג ni. *turn back* Ps 44$_{19}$; + infinitive of purpose, הלך *go* 2 S 2$_{19}$, לין *lodge* Jr 14$_8$.

אֵין־דֶּרֶךְ לִנְטוֹת *there was no way to turn* Nm 22$_{26}$, וַתֵּט ... זֶה שָׁלֹשׁ רְגָלִים *and she turned aside ... these three times* Nm 22$_{33}$.

8. pass. **a.** (1) **be stretched out,** <SUBJ> יָד *hand* Is 5$_{25}$ 9$_{11.16.20}$ 10$_4$ 14$_{26.27}$ 4QM[a] 15$_6$ ([יד]), חֶרֶב *sword* 1 C 21$_{16}$. <PREP> עַל *over,* + Jerusalem 1 C 21$_{16}$, גּוֹי *nation* Is 14$_{26}$ 4QM[a] 15$_6$. <COLL> נטה pass. + שׁלף pass. *be drawn* 1 C 21$_{16}$; + adverb, עוֹד *still* Is 5$_{25}$ 9$_{11.16.20}$ 10$_4$; וַתֵּלַכְנָה נְטוּיוֹת גָּרוֹן *and they have walked outstretched of neck* Is 3$_{16(Qr)}$.

(2) pass. ptc. as attributive adj., **outstretched,** of זְרוֹעַ *arm* Ex 6_{6} Dt 4_{34} 5_{15} 7_{19} 9_{29} 11_{2} 26_{8} 1 K 8_{42} 2 K 17_{36} Jr 27_{5} 32_{17} Ezk $20_{33.34}$ Ps 136_{12} 2 C 6_{32}, אֶזְרוֹעַ *arm* Jr 32_{21}, יָד *hand* Jr 21_{5}.

<COLL> נטה pass. ptc. || חָזָק *strong* Dt 4_{34} 5_{15} 7_{19} 11_{2} 26_{8} 1 K 8_{42} Jr 21_{5} 32_{21} Ezk $20_{33.34}$ Ps 136_{12} 2 C 6_{32}, גָּדוֹל *great* Dt 9_{29} 2 K 17_{36} Jr 27_{5} $32_{17.21}$ 2 C 6_{32}, שׁפך pass. ptc. *poured out* Ezk $20_{33.34}$.

b. pass. **be spread out,** <SUBJ> יוֹם *day* Ps 102_{12}, רָקִיעַ *firmament* Ezk 1_{22}. <PREP> כְּ *as*, + צֵל *shadow* Ps 102_{12}, עַל *over*, + רֹאשׁ *head* Ezk 1_{22}.

c. be turned, <SUBJ> worshipper Ps 73_{2}. <COLL> אֲנִי נָטוּי רַגְלָי *I was turned with regard to my feet*, i.e. I stumbled Ps 73_{2}.

d. pass. ptc. as attributive adj., **leaning,** of קִיר *wall* Ps 62_{4}. <COLL> נטה pass. ptc. || דחה pass. ptc. *pushed*, i.e. tottering Ps 62_{4}.

<SYN> §2 מתח *spread out*, רקע *spread out*, יסד *found*, קום hi. *raise up*, תלה *hang*; §8a חָזָק *strong*, גָּדוֹל *great*, שׁפך pass. ptc. *poured out*.

Ni. 3 Pf. נָטָיו; impf. יִנָּטֶה, יִנָּטוּ—**1. stretch oneself out, extend, lengthen,** <SUBJ> נַחַל *wadi* Nm 24_{6}, צֵל *shadow* of evening Jr 6_{4}.

2. be stretched out, <SUBJ> קָו *line* Zc 1_{16}(Qr). <PREP> עַל *over*, + Jerusalem Zc 1_{16}.

Hi. 76.8.14.1 Pf. הִטָּה (הִטָּהוּ), הִטַּתּוּ, הִטֵּיתִי, הִטּוּ, הִטִּיתֶם; impf. יַטֶּה (יַטֶּךָ, Q יטכה, יַטֵּנוּ), 2ms תַּטֶּה (תַּט), אַטֶּה (אֵט), יַטּוּ; + waw וַיֵּט (וַיַּטֵּהוּ), 3fs וַתַּטֵּהוּ, וָאֵט, וַיַּטּוּ; impv. הַטֵּה (הַט), הַטִּי, הַטּוּ; ptc. מַטֶּה, מַטִּים, מַטֵּי; inf. הַטּוֹת (הַטֹּת, הַטֹּתָה).

1. stretch out, hold out, extend, <SUBJ> Y. Is 31_{3} Jr 6_{12} 15_{6} Ezr 7_{28} 9_{9}, בֵּן *son* Si 41_{19}, נַעֲרָה *young woman* Gn 24_{14}(Qr). <OBJ> יָד *hand* Y. Is 31_{3} Jr 6_{12} 15_{6}, אַצִּיל *elbow* Si 41_{19}, כַּד *jar* Gn 24_{14}, חֶסֶד *loyalty* Ezr 7_{28} 9_{9}. <PREP> עַל *against*, + Jerusalem Jr 15_{6}, יֹשֵׁב *inhabitant* Jr 6_{12}; *to*, + Israelites Ezr 9_{9}; *at*, + לֶחֶם *meal* Si 41_{19}; לִפְנֵי *before*, + מֶלֶךְ *king* Ezr 7_{28} 9_{9}, שַׂר *prince* Ezr 7_{28}, יֹעֵץ *counsellor* Ezr 7_{28}.

2. spread out, pitch tent, <SUBJ> Rizpah 2 S 21_{10}, אִשָּׁה *woman* Pr 7_{16} (if em. אֵטוּן מִצְרָיִם *thread of Egypt* to אֵטַנְּ מִצּוֹר *I have spread out* with multicoloured cloth *from Tyre*), בַּת *daughter* 2 S 21_{10}; subj. not specified, 2 S 16_{22} Is 54_{2}. <OBJ> אֹהֶל *tent* 2 S 16_{22}, יְרִיעָה *curtain* Is 54_{2}, שַׂק *sackcloth* 2 S 21_{10}, חֲטֻבוֹת *multicoloured cloth, canopy* Pr 7_{16} (if em.; see Subj.). <PREP> לְ of benefit, *for*, + Absalom 2 S 16_{22}, Rizpah 2 S 21_{10}; מִן of time, *from*, + תְּחִלָּה *beginning* of harvest 2 S 21_{10}; אֶל *upon*, + צוּר *rock* 2 S 21_{10}; עַל *upon*, + גַּג *roof* 2 S 16_{22}.

3. turn, direct, take aside, <SUBJ> Y. Pr 21_{1}, Balaam Nm 22_{23}, David 2 S 6_{10}||1 C 13_{13}, Hezekiah Si 48_{17}, Joab 2 S 3_{27}. <OBJ> Abner 2 S 3_{27}, אָתוֹן *she-ass* Nm 22_{23}, לֵב *heart* of king Pr 21_{1}, אֲרוֹן *ark* 2 S 6_{10}||1 C 13_{13}, מַיִם *water* Si 48_{17}. <PREP> עַל *to*, + כָּל־אֲשֶׁר *wherever* he wishes Pr 21_{1}; אֶל *to*, + בַּיִת *house* 1 C 13_{13}; אֶל־תּוֹךְ *inside*, + שַׁעַר *gate* 2 S 3_{27}, עִיר *city* Si 48_{17}; נטה + noun without preposition, דֶּרֶךְ *(to the) way* Nm 22_{23}, בַּיִת *(to the) house* 2 S 6_{10}.

4. thrust away, turn away, thrust down, <SUBJ> Y. Ps 27_{9}, Israel(ites) Am 2_{7}, בַּיִת *house* of Israel Am 5_{12}, אִישׁ *man* Si 35_{17}, זוֹנָה *prostitute* 4QWiles $1_{14.16}$ (both [הזונ]ה), חקק ptc. *one who decrees* Is 10_{2}, כתב pi. ptc. *one who writes* Is 10_{2}, עָרִיץ *ruthless one* Is 29_{21}, רָשָׁע *wicked one* Ps 17_{11} (if em. לִנְטוֹת *to thrust down* [qal] to לְהַטּוֹת), אֹיֵב *enemy* Ps 17_{11} (or em.; see above), לֵץ *scorner* Is 29_{21}, הלך ptc. *one who goes* 4QBéat 5_{11}, שׁקד ptc. *one who watches* Is 29_{21}, עָוֹן *iniquity* Jr 5_{25}; subj. not specified, Ml 3_{5} Jb 24_{4} Pr 18_{5} Lm 3_{35}.

<OBJ> עֶבֶד *servant* Ps 27_{9}, אֶבְיוֹן *poor one* Am 5_{12} Jb 24_{4}, דַּל *poor one* Is 10_{2}, גֵּר *sojourner* Ml 3_{5}, צַדִּיק *righteous one* Is 29_{21} Pr 18_{5}, פַּעַם *footstep* 4QWiles 1_{16}, מִשְׁפָּט *right* of man Lm 3_{35}, תּוֹכֵחָה *reproof* Si 35_{17}, עַוְלָה *injustice* 4QBéat 5_{11}, דֶּרֶךְ *way* Am 2_{7}, 4QWiles 1_{14}, אֵלֶּה *these* Jr 5_{25}.

<PREP> בְּ of place, *in*, + שַׁעַר *gate* Am 5_{12}; *onto*, + אֶרֶץ *ground* Ps 17_{11} (if em.; see Subj.); *in (the process of)*, + מִשְׁפָּט *judgment* Pr 18_{5}; of instrument, *by (means of), with*, + תֹּהוּ *emptiness* Is 29_{21}; of accompaniment, *with, in*, + אַף *anger* Ps 27_{9}.

מִן of direction, *from*, + דֶּרֶךְ *way* Jb 24_{4} 4QWiles 1_{16}, דִּין *justice* Is 10_{2}.

נֶגֶד *in front of*, + פָּנִים *face*, i.e. presence, of Most High Lm 3_{35}.

<COLL> נטה hi. + לקח כֹּפֶר *take bribe* Am 5_{12}, עשׁק

oppress Ml 35, נשׂא פָּנִים *lift face*, i.e. show partiality Pr 185, צרר *show hostility* Am 512.

5. pervert justice, <SUBJ> Israel(ites) Ex 232.6 Dt 1619 2417, אִישׁ *man* 11QT 5117, בֵּן *son* 1 S 83, מֶלֶךְ *king* 11QT 5719.20, שֹׁפֵט *judge* 11QT 5113, שֹׁטֵר *official* 11QT 5113, רָשָׁע *wicked one* Pr 1723, שֹׁחַד *bribe* 11QT 5113; subj. not specified, Dt 2719.

<OBJ> מִשְׁפָּט *justice* Ex 236 Dt 1619 2417 2719 1 S 83 11QT 5113.13.17 5719.20, אֹרַח *path* of justice Pr 1723.

<COLL> נטה hi. || סלף pi. *subvert* 11QT 5113; + נכר פָּנִים hi. *recognize face*, i.e. show partiality Dt 1619, לקח שֹׁחַד *take bribe* Dt 1619 1 S 83 Pr 1723 11QT 5113.17 5719, נטה אַחֲרֵי בֶּצַע *turn aside after gain* 1 S 83.

6. incline one's ear, heart, <SUBJ> Y. 1 K 858 2 K 1916||Is 3717 Ps 176 313 712 861 883 1023 1162 11936 1414 Dn 918 4QBarka 1.22 11QPsa 244, Israelites Jr 724.26, עַם *people* Jos 2423 Jr 254 Ps 781, Jerusalem Jr 445, עִיר *city* Jr 445, Ben Sira Si 5116, אִישׁ *man* Jr 3515, אָב *father* Jr 118 3414 3515, בֵּן *son* Pr 22 420 51.13 Si 48 633 99, בַּת *daughter* Ps 4511, מֶלֶךְ *king* Jr 1723, עֶבֶד *servant* Arad ost. 404 (ע[בדך]), יֹשֵׁב *inhabitant* Jr 1723 254 3515, worshipper Ps 495, צָמֵא *thirsty one* Is 553, אֲשֶׁר *one who* Is 553; subj. not specified, Pr 2217.

<OBJ> אֹזֶן *ear* 2 K 1916||Is 3717 Is 553 Jr 724.26 118 1723 254 3414 3515 Ps 176 313 4511 495 712 781 861 883 1023 1162 Pr 420 51.13 Dn 918 Si 48 633 5116 4QBarka 1.22 11QPsa 244, לֵב *heart* Ps 11936 1414 Pr 22 Si 99 Arad ost. 404 (ל[בה]), לֵבָב *heart* Jos 2423 1 K 858.

<PREP> לְ of direction, *to*, + מְלַמֵּד *teacher* Pr 513, עָנִי *poor one* Si 48, worshipper Ps 176 1162, דָּבָר *matter* Ps 1414, אֹמֶר *word* Ps 781 Pr 420, מָשָׁל *proverb* Ps 495, תְּבוּנָה *understanding* Pr 22 51, רִנָּה *cry* Ps 883.

כְּ *as*, + מְעַט *a little*, i.e. in a short time Si 5116.

אֶל *to*, + Y. Jos 2423 1 K 858, אִשָּׁה *wife* Si 99 (ליה[א]), worshipper Ps 313 712 1023, עֵדָה *testimony* Ps 11936, בֶּצַע *gain* Ps 11936, אֲשֶׁר *that which* Arad ost. 404.

<COLL> נטה hi. || פקח *open eyes* 2 K 1916||Is 3717 Dn 918 4QBarka 1.22, קשׁב hi. *make attentive* Pr 22 420 51; + שׁית *place*, i.e. apply, mind Pr 2217, אזן hi. *hear* Ps 781, שׁמע *hear* 2 K 1916||Is 3717 Is 553 Jr 724.26 118 1723 254 3414 3515 445 Ps 176 4511 Pr 513 2217 Dn 918 Si 633 4QBarka 1.22; + adverb, עַתָּה *now* Arad ost. 404; + infinitive of purpose, of שׁמע *hear* Jr 254, שׁוב *turn* Jr 445, עלל htp. *busy oneself* Ps 1414.

7. persuade (2 S 1915 Pr 721), **lead astray, cause to deviate,** <SUBJ> גּוֹי *nation* 1 K 112, Amasa 2 S 1915, אִישׁ *man* 4Q416 2.27 (א[י]ש), אִשָּׁה *woman, wife* 1 K 113.4 Pr 721, לֵב *heart* Is 4420, רֹב *greatness* of ransom Jb 3618.

<OBJ> נַעַר *lad* Pr 721, חָרָשׁ *artisan* Is 4420, Job Jb 3618, לֵב *heart* 1 K 113, לֵבָב *heart* 2 S 1915 1 K 112.4; obj. not specified, 4Q416 2.27.

<PREP> בְּ of instrument, *by (means of), with*, + רֹב *abundance* of persuasiveness Pr 721; כְּ *as* 2 S 1915; אַחֲרֵי *after*, + אֱלֹהִים *gods* 1 K 112.4.

<COLL> נטה hi. || נדח hi. *lead astray* Pr 721.

8. intrans., **turn aside, deviate,** <SUBJ> Job Jb 2311, בֵּן *son* Pr 427, חֹזֶה *seer* Is 3011, רֹאֶה *seer* Is 3011; subj. not specified, Ps 1255.

<PREP> מִן of direction, *from*, + אֹרַח *path* Is 3011.

<COLL> נטה hi. || סור *turn aside* Is 3011; הַמַּטִּים עֲקַלְקַלּוֹתָם *those who turn aside (to) their crookedness* Ps 1255 אַל־תֵּט־יָמִין וּשְׂמֹאול *do not turn aside (to) the right or the left* Pr 427.

9. bend, bow, bring down, <SUBJ> Y. Ps 1445, בֵּן *son* Si 625, רָשָׁע *wicked one* Jb 1529 (if em.; see Obj.). <OBJ> שְׁכֶם *shoulder* Si 625 4QBarke 63, שָׁמַיִם *heavens* Ps 1445, מִנוֹל *possessions* Jb 1529 (if em. מִנְלָם *their acquisition* to מִנְלָם *their possessions*, and em. יִטֶּה *it shall* not *spread out* to יַטֶּה *he shall* not *bring down*). <PREP> לְ of direction, *to*, + אֶרֶץ *earth* Jb 1529 (if em.; see Obj.).

10. intrans., **bend down** (Ho 114); **stretch out,** with ellipsis of נַפְשׁוֹתָם *themselves** (Am 28), <SUBJ> Y. Ho 114 (or em. וָאֵט, i.e. qal, in same sense), Israel(ites) Am 28. <PREP> אֶל *to*, + Ephraim Hos 114 (or em.; see Subj.); עַל *upon*, + בֶּגֶד *garment* Am 28; אֵצֶל *beside*, + מִזְבֵּחַ *altar* Am 28.

Also 4QMysta 183.

<SYN> §6 פקח *open eyes*, קשׁב hi. *make attentive*; §7 נדח hi. *lead astray*; §8 סור *turn aside*.*

⇒ מַטָּה *downwards*, מַטֶּה *staff, tribe*, מִטָּה *bed*, מֻטָּה *outspreading*, מֻטֶּה *injustice, perversity*.

נָטוּעַ *thing planted*, see נטע *plant*.

נְטוֹפָתִי, see נְטֹפָתִי *Netophathite.*

[נָטִיל] 1 adj. **laden**—pl. cstr. נְטִילֵי—as noun, **one laden,** <SUBJ> כרת ni. *be cut off* Zp 1_{11}. <CSTR> כָּל־ נְטִילֵי כֶסֶף *all the ones laden of,* i.e. with, *silver* Zp 1_{11}.
⇒ נטל *lift.*

[נָטִיעַ] 1 n.[m.] **plant**—pl. נְטִעִים—<SUBJ> perh. גדל pu. *be grown* Ps 144_{12} (+ זָוִית *cornerstone*). <PREP> כְּ *as* Ps 144_{12}.*
⇒ נטע *plant.*

[נְטִיפָה] 2 n.f. **pendant**—pl. נְטִיפוֹת (נְטִפוֹת)—in list of women's ornaments (Is 3_{19}), <OBJ> סור hi. *remove* Is 3_{19} (|| שֵׁרָה *bracelet,* + שַׂהֲרֹון *crescent,* רְעָלָה *veil,* עֶכֶס *anklet*). <PREP> לְבַד מִן *besides, apart from,* + היה *be* Jg 8_{26} (|| שַׂהֲרֹון *crescent,* + בֶּגֶד *garment*).
<SYN> שֵׁרָה *bracelet,* שַׂהֲרֹון *crescent.**
⇒ נטף *drip.*

[נְטִישָׁה] 3 n.f. **tendril**—pl. נְטִישׁוֹת; sf. נְטִישֹׁתַיִךְ, נְטִישׁוֹתֶיהָ—of vine, <SUBJ> עבר *pass* Jr 48_{32}, נגע *reach* Jr 48_{32}. <OBJ> סור hi. *remove* Is 18_5 (|| זַלְזַל *shoot*) Jr 5_{10}, תזז hi. *tear away* Is 18_5.
<SYN> זַלְזַל *shoot.**
⇒ נטשׁ *leave.*

נטל 4.1.2.1 vb. **lift—Qal** 3.1.2.1 Pf. נָטַל, I נטלתי; impf. יִטּוֹל, Q יטלון; ptc. נֹטֵל—**1. lift up** (Is 40_{15} [or em.; see §6 Subj.] CD 11_{10}).
2. lay upon (Lm 3_{28}), i.e. offer (2 S 24_{12}).
3. take away (MurEpBarC^{b}$_{10}$).
4. take counsel (Si $43_{8[B]}$).
5. perh. **weigh** (Arad ost. 60_1).
<SUBJ> Y. 2 S 24_{12} Is 40_{15} (or em.; see §6 Subj.) Lm 3_{28} (+ נשׂא *bear*), אִישׁ *man* CD 11_{10} (+ נשׂא); subj. not specified, Si $42_{8(B)}$ (נוטל; Bmg M כושל *one who stumbles*) MurEpBarC^{b}$_{10}$. <OBJ> חִטָּה *wheat* MurEpBarC^{b}$_{10}$, אִי *island* Is 40_{15} (or em.; see §6 Subj.), סֶלַע *rock* CD 11_{10}, עָפָר *dust,* i.e. soil CD 11_{10}, עֹל *yoke* Lm 3_{28}, עֵצָה *counsel* Si $42_{8(B)}$, שָׁלֹשׁ *three (things)* 2 S 24_{12}, 2 + 25 hekaths (measures of grain) Arad ost. 60_1. <PREP> בְּ of place, *in,* + בַּיִת *house* CD 11_{10}; of accompaniment, *with,* + זְנוּת *prostitution* Si $42_{8(B)}$; כְּ *as* Is 40_{15} (or em.; see §6 Subj.); עַל *over, upon,* + David 2 S 24_{12}, גֶּבֶר *man* Lm 3_{28}; אַחַר *after,* + שַׁבָּת *sabbath* MurEpBarC^{b}$_{10}$.
6. intrans., **be lifted up,** <SUBJ> אִי *island* Is 40_{15} (if em. יִטּוֹל *he lifts up* to יִטְּלוּ *they are lifted up*).* <PREP> כְּ *as,* + דַּק *fine one,* i.e. dust Is 40_{15} (if em.; see Subj.).
Pi. 1 + waw וַיְנַטְּלֵם—**lift up,** <SUBJ> Y. Is 63_9 (|| נשׂא *bear*). <OBJ> בַּיִת *house* of Israel Is 63_9.
<SYN> נשׂא *bear.**
⇒ נָטִיל *laden,* נֵטֶל *weight.*

[נֵטֶל] 1 n.[m.] **weight**—cstr. נֵטֶל—<CSTR> נֵטֶל הַחוֹל *weight of the sand* Pr 27_3 (|| כֹּבֶד *heaviness*).
<SYN> כֹּבֶד *heaviness.*
⇒ נטל *lift.*

נטע 58.2.8 vb. **plant—Qal** 57.1.7 Pf. נָטַע (נָטָע), נָטְעָה, נָטָעְתָּ, (נְטַעְתִּיךְ) נְטַעְתִּי, (נְטַעְתָּם, Q תעתה [GnzPs 1_7], Q נטעתה), נְטַעְתֶּם, נָטְעוּ; impf. יִטַּע, 2ms תִּטַּע (תִּטָּעֵמוֹ), תִּטְּעִי, יִטְּעוּ, תִּטָּעוּ; + waw וְנָטַעְתִּי (וּנְטַעְתִּיו, וּנְטַעְתִּיהוּ, וּנְטַעְתִּים), וְנָטְעוּ, וּנְטַעְתֶּם; וַיִּטַּע (וַיִּטָּעֵהוּ), 3ms וַתִּטָּעֶהָ (וַתִּטָּעֵם), וַיִּטְּעוּ; impv. נִטְעוּ; ptc. נֹטֵעַ (נוֹטֵעַ), נֹטְעִים; ptc. pass. נָטוּעַ, נְטוּעִים; inf. לִנְטוֹעַ (לִנְטֹעַ, לָטַעַת).
1. plant, also **transplant** (e.g. Ex 15_{17} Ps 80_9), **replant** (Ezk 36_{36}); with two objects, **plant with** (Is 5_2 Jr 2_{21}), <SUBJ> Y. Gn 2_8 Ex 15_{17} Nm 24_6 2 S 7_{10}||1 C 17_9 Is 51_{16} (or em. לִנְטֹת *to spread out*) Jr 2_{21} 11_{17} 12_2 24_6 31_{28} 32_{41} 42_{10} 45_4 Ezk 36_{36} Am 9_{15} Ps 44_3 80_9 104_{16} 1QH 16_5 (נ[טעת]ה) 4QDibHam^{a} 8_6 4QDiscourse 2.2_5 GnzPs 1_7, Israel(ites) Dt 6_{11} 16_{21} $28_{30.39}$ 2 K 19_{29}||Is 37_{30} Is 17_{10} $65_{21.22}$ Am 9_{14} Ps 107_{37} 11QT 52_1, עַם *people* Jos 24_{13} Am 9_{14}, גּוֹי *nation* 11QT 51_{20}, גּוֹלָה *exiles* Jr $29_{5.28}$, בַּיִת *house* of Israel Ezk 28_{26} Am 5_{11}, Abraham Gn 21_{33}, Jeremiah Jr 1_{10} Si 49_7, Koheleth Ec $2_{4.5}$, Noah Gn 9_{20}, אִישׁ *man* Dt 20_6 Zp 1_{13} 4QD^{a} 6.4_4 (טע[ ]), אִשָּׁה *wife* Pr 31_{16}, בֵּן *son* Jr 35_7, of Israel Lv 19_{23}, בְּתוּלָה *young woman* Jr 31_5, יָדִיד *beloved one* Is 5_2, חָרָשׁ *artisan* Is 44_{14}, נטע ptc. *one who plants* Jr 31_5, יָמִין *right hand* Ps 80_{16}; subj. not specified, Jr 18_9 31_5 Ps 94_9 Ec 3_2.
<OBJ> Israel(ites) 2 S 7_{10}||1 C 17_9 Jr 2_{21} 11_{17} 42_{10} Am 9_{15}, עַם *people* Ex 15_{17} 2 S 7_{10}||1 C 17_9 Am 9_{15}, גּוֹי *na-*

tion Jr 18$_{9}$, מַמְלָכָה *kingdom* Jr 18$_{9}$, עִיר *city* Jr 32$_{41}$, גָּלוּת *exiles* Jr 24$_{6}$, אָב *father* Ps 44$_{3}$, רָשָׁע *wicked one* Jr 12$_{2}$, בגד ptc. *disloyal one* Jr 12$_{2}$, אֹזֶן *ear* Ps 94$_{9}$.

אֲהָל *aloe* Nm 24$_{6}$, אֶרֶז *cedar* Ps 104$_{16}$, אֹרֶן *laurel* Is 44$_{14}$, אֶשֶׁל *tamarisk* Gn 21$_{33}$, זַיִת *olive* Dt 6$_{11}$ Jos 24$_{13}$, גֶּפֶן *vine* Ps 80$_{9}$, שֹׂרֵק *red grapes* Is 5$_{2}$ Jr 2$_{21}$, עֵץ *tree* Lv 19$_{23}$ Dt 16$_{21}$ Ec 2$_{5}$ 11QT 52$_{1}$ ([עץ]), כַּנָּה *stock* Ps 80$_{16}$ (or em. וְכַנָּה *and a stock* to וְכַנָּהּ *and its stock*, i.e. כֵּן IV, or וְגַנָּה *and a garden* or וְכוֹנְנָהּ *and restore it*), אֲשֵׁרָה *Asherah* Dt 16$_{21}$ 11QT 51$_{20}$ 52$_{1}$ ([אשרה]), תּוֹרָה *law* 4QDibHam^{a} 1.2$_{13}$, צְדָקָה *righteousness* GnzPs 1$_{7}$.

נֶטַע *plant(ation)* Is 17$_{10}$ Jr 31$_{5}$ (if em. נָטְעוּ נֹטְעִים *those who plant shall plant* to נֹטְעֵי נְטָעִים *those who plant plantations*), מַטָּע *plantation* 1QH 16$_{5}$ ([נט]עתה]), גַּן *garden* Gn 2$_{8}$ Jr 29$_{5.28}$ Ps 80$_{16}$ (if em.; see above) 4QDibHam^{a} 8$_{6}$ ([ג]ן), כֶּרֶם *vineyard* Gn 9$_{20}$ Dt 6$_{11}$ 20$_{6}$ 28$_{30.39}$ Jos 24$_{13}$ 2 K 19$_{29}$||Is 37$_{30}$ Is 5$_{2}$ 65$_{21}$ Jr 31$_{5}$ 35$_{7}$ Ezk 28$_{26}$ Am 5$_{11}$ 9$_{14}$ Zp 1$_{13}$ Ps 107$_{37}$ Pr 31$_{16}$ Ec 2$_{4}$, שׁמם ni. ptc. *desolated place* Ezk 36$_{36}$, שָׁמַיִם *heavens* Is 51$_{16}$ (or em.; see Subj.).

<PREP> לְ of benefit, *for*, + בָּחִיר *elect* 4QDiscourse 2.2$_{5}$ (ל[נ]ו); *for oneself*, + Israelites Dt 16$_{21}$ 11QT 52$_{1}$ ([לכה]), גּוֹי *nation* 11QT 51$_{20}$, Koheleth Ec 2$_{4}$.

בְּ of place, *in*, + לֵב *heart* 4QDibHam^{a} 1.2$_{13}$, Beer-sheba Gn 21$_{33}$, Eden Gn 2$_{8}$, אֶרֶץ *land* Jr 32$_{41}$ 4QDiscourse 2.2$_{5}$ GnzPs 1$_{7}$, הַר *mountain* Ex 15$_{17}$ Jr 31$_{5}$, גַּן *garden* Ec 2$_{5}$, פַּרְדֵּס *park* Ec 2$_{5}$, מָכוֹן *place* Ex 15$_{17}$; of time, *in*, + שָׁנָה *year* 2 K 19$_{29}$||Is 37$_{30}$; of accompaniment, *with, in*, + אֱמֶת *faithfulness* Jr 32$_{41}$.

מִן of instrument, *by (means of), with*, + פְּרִי *fruit* Pr 31$_{16}$.

עַל *upon*, + אֲדָמָה *land* Am 9$_{15}$.

<COLL> נטע || זרע *sow* Is 17$_{10}$ Jr 35$_{7}$ Ps 107$_{37}$, בנה *build* Dt 28$_{30}$ Is 65$_{21.22}$ Jr 1$_{10}$ 18$_{9}$ 24$_{6}$ 29$_{5.28}$ 31$_{28}$ 35$_{7}$ 42$_{10}$ 45$_{4}$ Ezk 28$_{26}$ 36$_{36}$ Am 5$_{11}$ 9$_{14}$ Zp 1$_{13}$ Ec 2$_{4}$ Si 49$_{7}$, יסד *found* Is 51$_{16}$, עשׂה *make* Am 9$_{14}$ Ec 2$_{4}$, יצר *form* Ps 94$_{9}$, שׁוב hi. *restore* Si 49$_{7}$, רבה hi. *increase* GnzPs 1$_{7}$, עזק pi. *dig* Is 5$_{2}$, סקל pi. *clear of stones* Is 5$_{2}$.

:: הרס *tear down* Jr 1$_{10}$ 24$_{6}$ 31$_{28}$ 42$_{10}$ 45$_{4}$ Si 49$_{7}$, נתץ *break down* Jr 1$_{10}$ 31$_{28}$ Si 49$_{7}$, נתשׁ *pluck up* Jr 1$_{10}$ 24$_{6}$ 31$_{28}$ 42$_{10}$ 45$_{4}$ Am 9$_{15}$ Si 49$_{7}$, אבד hi. *destroy* Jr 1$_{10}$ 31$_{28}$, רעע hi. *do harm* Jr 31$_{28}$.

+ adverb, עַל־כֵּן *therefore* Is 17$_{10}$, עוֹד *again* Jr 31$_{5}$. עֵת לָטַעַת *a time to plant* Ec 3$_{2}$.

2. pitch tent, <SUBJ> מֶלֶךְ *king* Dn 11$_{45}$ (or em. יֵטֶּה *he shall pitch*, from נטה). <OBJ> אֹהֶל *tent* Dn 11$_{45}$ (or em.; see Subj.).

3a. pass. **be planted, fixed,** <SUBJ> מַסְמֵר *nail* Ec 12$_{11}$.

b. pass. ptc. as noun, **planted thing,** <OBJ> עקר *uproot* Ec 3$_{2}$.

Also 11QT^{b} 33$_{2}$.

<SYN> §1 זרע *sow*, בנה *build*, יסד *found*, עשׂה *make*, יצר *form*, שׁוב hi. *restore*, רבה hi. *increase*, עזק pi. *dig*, סקל pi. *clear of stones*.

<ANT> §1 הרס *tear down*, נתץ *break down*, נתשׁ *pluck up*, אבד hi. *destroy*, רעע hi. *do harm*.

Ni. 1.1.1 Pf. נִטָּעוּ; impf. Si 3fs תנטע; ptc. Q נטעת—**be planted,** <SUBJ> רֹזֵן *ruler* Is 40$_{24}$ (|| זרע pu. *be sown*, + שׁרשׁ *take root*), שֹׁפֵט *judge* Is 40$_{24}$, גֶּפֶן *vine* 6QAllegory 1$_{6}$, צְדָקָה *righteousness*, i.e. kindness Si 3$_{14(A)}$ (corrected from תנתע appar. *it will be broken*).

<SYN> זרע pu. *be sown*.*

⇒ נטע I *plant*, נָטִיעַ *plant*, מַטָּע *planting*, מַטַּעַת *planting*, נְטָעִים *Netaim*.

[נֶ֫טַע] I 4.4.3 n.[m.] **plant**—נֶטַע; cstr. נְטַע; sf. נִטְעֵךְ, Si נטעו; pl. cstr. נִטְעֵי—**1. plant, shoot, progeny,** <SUBJ> היה *be* 4QD^{a} 6.4$_{2}$ ([יהיו]), פרח hi. *cause to flourish* Si 40$_{19(B)}$. <OBJ> נטע *plant* Is 17$_{10}$, נתשׁ *pluck up* Si 3$_{9}$ (+ שֹׁרֶשׁ *root*). <NOM CL> מנטע רע נטעו *his shoot is from an evil plant* Si 3$_{28}$. <CSTR> נטעי הכר[ם] *plants of the vineyard* 4QD^{a} 6.4$_{2}$, נִטְעֵי נַעֲמָנִים *plants of pleasantness*, i.e. pleasant plants Is 17$_{10}$, נטע שעשועים *plant of delight*, i.e. delightful plant 4QpsHod^{c} 2$_{3}$. <ADJ> רַע *evil* Si 3$_{28}$. <PREP> כְּמוֹ *as*, + עשׂה *make*, i.e. put out, branches Jb 14$_{9}$; מִן of direction, *from* Si 3$_{28}$; of comparison, *(more) than* Si 40$_{19(B)}$. <COLL> נֶטַע || שֶׁגֶר *offspring of cattle* Si 40$_{19(B)}$; + עֵץ *tree* 4QD^{a} 6.4$_{2}$, זְמוֹרָה *branch* Is 17$_{10}$; נטע בגנ[ת]ו ובכרמו *a plant in his garden and in his vineyard* 4QpsHod^{c} 2$_{3}$.

2. plantation, <NOM CL> אִישׁ יְהוּדָה נְטַע שַׁעֲשׁוּעָיו *the men of Judah are the plantation of his delight* Is 5$_{7}$. <OBJ> נטע *plant* Jr 31$_{5}$ (if em.; see Cstr.). <CSTR> נֹטְעֵי

נָטְעוּ נֹטְעִים *those who plant plantations* Jr 31$_{5}$ (if em. נָטְעוּ נֹטְעִים *those who plant shall plant*), נֶטַע שַׁעֲשׁוּעָיו *plantation of his delight*, i.e. his delightful plantation Is 5$_{7}$. <COLL> כֶּרֶם + נֶטַע *vineyard* Is 5$_{7}$.

3. planting, <CSTR> יוֹם נִטְעֵךְ *day of your planting* Is 17$_{11}$.

<SYN> §1 שֶׁגֶר *offspring of cattle.*

⇒ נטע *plant.*

*[נֶטַע] II n.[m.] **pavilion,** <APP> מִגְדָּל *tower* Ps 144$_{12}$ (if em. אֲשֶׁר בָּנֵינוּ כִּנְטִעִים מְגֻדָּלִים *may our sons be like plants full grown* to אַשְׁרֵי בָנֵינוּ כִּנְטָעִים מִגְדָּלִים *happy are our sons who are like pavilions [and like] towers*). <PREP> כְּ *as* Ps 144$_{12}$ (+ זָוִית *cornerstone*).

נְטָעִים 1 pl.n. **Netaim,** town in Judah, perh. in lowland, <CSTR> יֹשְׁבֵי נְטָעִים *inhabitants of Netaim* 1 C 4$_{23}$.

⇒ נטע *plant.*

נטף 18.0.8 vb. **drip—Qal** 9 Pf. נָטְפוּ (נָטָפוּ); impf. 3fs תִּטֹּף, יִטְּפוּ, 3fpl תִּטֹּפְנָה; ptc. נֹטְפוֹת—**drip, drop,** intransitively at Jb 29$_{22}$, <SUBJ> שָׂפָה *lip* Pr 5$_{3}$ Ca 4$_{11}$ 5$_{13}$, יָד *hand* Ca 5$_{5}$, הַר *mountain* Jl 4$_{18}$, שָׁמַיִם *heavens* Jg 5$_{4}$ (or em. נָטְיוּ *they inclined*, from נטה, or נָטְפוּ: הָרִים *they dropped. The mountains* to נָטוּ: פַּ־הָרִים *they shook. The mountains*, deleting (גַּם־עָבִים נָטְפוּ מָיִם)* Ps 68$_{9}$ (or em. נָטְיוּ *they bent*, from נטה), עָב *cloud* Jg 5$_{4}$, מִלָּה *word* Jb 29$_{22}$. <OBJ> מַיִם *water* Jg 5$_{4}$, עָסִיס *sweet wine* Jl 4$_{18}$, נֹפֶת *flowing honey* Pr 5$_{3}$ Ca 4$_{11}$, מֹר *myrrh* Ca 5$_{5.13}$. <PREP> בְּ of time, *in*, + יוֹם *day* Jl 4$_{18}$; עַל *upon* Jb 29$_{22}$; מִפְּנֵי *from before, at the presence of*, + Y. Ps 68$_{9}$ (or em.; see Subj.). <COLL> נטף || הלך *flow with* Jl 4$_{18}$.

<SYN> הלך *flow with.*

Hi. 9.0.8 Pf. Q הטיף; impf. 2ms תַּטִּיף, אַטִּף, יַטִּפוּ (יַטִּיפוּן), תַּטִּפוּ; + waw וְהִטִּיפוּ; impv. הַטֵּף; ptc. מַטִּיף; inf. abs. הטף—**1. drip,** <SUBJ> אִישׁ *man* CD 1$_{14}$, הַר *mountain* Am 9$_{13}$ (+ מוג htpol. *melt away*). <OBJ> מַיִם *water* of lies CD 1$_{14}$, עָסִיס *sweet wine* Am 9$_{13}$. <PREP> לְ of direction, *onto*, + Israel CD 1$_{14}$.

2a. preach, teach, prophesy, <SUBJ> Amos Am 7$_{16}$, אִישׁ *man* Mc 2$_{11}$, בֵּן *son* of man Ezk 21$_{2.7}$, מַטִּיף *preacher* CD 8$_{13}$, חשׁב ptc. *one who plans* iniquity Mc 2$_{6}$, פעל ptc. *one who does* evil Mc 2$_{6}$, לָשׁוֹן *tongue* Pr 15$_{2}$ (if em. תֵּיטִיב *it makes good* to תַּטִּיף); subj. not specified, Mc 2$_{6.6}$ CD 4$_{20.20}$ 19$_{25(B)}$ (=8$_{13[A]}$, §2b). <OBJ> אָדָם *human being* CD 19$_{25}$, דַּעַת *knowledge* Pr 15$_{2}$ (if em.; see Subj.). <PREP> לְ of direction, *to* Mc 2$_{11}$ CD 8$_{13}$; *concerning*, + יַיִן *wine* Mc 2$_{1}$, שֵׁכָר *strong drink* Mc 2$_{1}$, כָּזָב *lie* CD 19$_{25}$ (unless לכזב = *to lie*), אֵלֶּה *these (things)* Mc 2$_{6}$; אֶל *against*, + דָּרוֹם *south* Ezk 21$_{2}$, מִקְדָּשׁ *sanctuary* Ezk 21$_{7}$; עַל *against*, + בַּיִת *house* of Isaac Am 7$_{16}$. <COLL> נטף hi. || נבא ni. *prophesy* Ezk 21$_{2.7}$ Am 7$_{16}$.

2b. ptc. as noun, **preacher, teacher,** <SUBJ> היה *be* Mc 2$_{11}$, קום hi. *raise up* 1QpHab 10$_{9}$, תעה hi. *lead astray* 1QpHab 10$_{9}$ 1QpMic 10$_{4}$ ([יתעה]), יגע hi. *cause to toil* 1QpHab 10$_{9}$, נטף hi. *preach* CD 8$_{13}$, בנה *build* 1QpHab 10$_{9}$, perh. רוה hi. *saturate* 1QpHab 10$_{9}$. <NOM CL> צו הוא מטיף *Precept is a preacher* CD 4$_{19}$. <CSTR> מַטִּיף הָעָם *preacher of*, i.e. to, *the people* Mc 2$_{11}$, מטיף הכזב *preacher of lies* 1QpHab 10$_{9}$ 11$_{1}$ ([מטיף]) 1QpMic 10$_{4}$ CD 8$_{13}$ (כזב). <PREP> עַל *concerning* 1QpHab 10$_{9}$ 1QpMic 10$_{4}$.

Also 4QD^{d} 3$_{1}$.

<SYN> §2a נבא ni. *prophesy.**

⇒ נָטָף *stacte*, נֶטֶף *drop*, נְטִיפָה *pendant*, נְטֹפָה *Natoph*, נְטֹפָה *Netophah*; cf. נטב *drop.*

נָטָף 1 n.[m.] **incense** from the aromatic plant Commiphora opobalsami (also known as בֹּשֶׂם, בֶּשֶׂם, צְרִי, צֳרִי),* or perh. the incense **stacte,** oil of myrrh, <OBJ> לקח *take* Ex 30$_{34}$ (|| חֶלְבְּנָה *galbanum*, שְׁחֵלֶת *onycha*, + לְבוֹנָה *frankincense*). <APP> סַם *spice* Ex 30$_{34}$.

<SYN> חֶלְבְּנָה *galbanum*, שְׁחֵלֶת *onycha.**

⇒ נטף *drip.*

*[נְטֹף] 0.0.1 pl.n. **Natoph,** perh. ident. with נְטֹפָה *Netophah* at Ezr 2$_{22}$||Ne 7$_{26}$, <CSTR> שולי הנטף *edge of Natoph* 3QTr 9$_{1}$.

⇒ נטף *drip.*

[נֶטֶף] 1 n.[m.] **drop**—pl. cstr. נִטְפֵי—<OBJ> גרע pi. *distil* Jb 36$_{27}$. <CSTR> נִטְפֵי־מַיִם *drops of water* Jb 36$_{27}$ (or em. נְטָפִים מִיָּם *drops from the sea*; + מָטָר *rain*).*

⇒ נטף *drip*.

נְטִפָה, see נְטִיפָה *pendant*.

נְטֹפָה 2 pl.n. **Netophah,** town in Judah, perh. Kh. Bedd Fālūḥ, 4 km NE of Bethlehem, perh. ident. with נְטֹף *Natoph* at 3QTr 9₁, <CSTR> אַנְשֵׁי נְטֹפָה *men of Netophah* Ezr 2₂₂||Ne 7₂₆ (בֵּית־לֶחֶם וּנְטֹפָה *of Bethlehem and Netophah*).*

⇒ נטף *drip*, נְטֹפָתִי *Netophathite*.

נְטֹפָתִי 11 gent. **Netophathite**—נְטוֹפָתִי—belonging to Netophah, **1.** as noun, an individual **Netophathite,** <SUBJ> בוא *come* 2 K 25₂₃||Jr 40₈. <NOM CL> הָעֲשִׂירִי ... הַנְּטוֹפָתִי *... the tenth was ... the Netophathite* 1 C 27₁₃, var. 1 C 27₁₅. <APP> Ephai Jr 40₈, Heleb 2 S 23₂₉, Heldai 1 C 27₁₅, Heled 1 C 11₃₀, Maharai 2 S 23₂₈||1 C 11₃₀ 1 C 27₁₃, Seraiah 2 K 25₂₃.

2. as collective sing. noun, **Netophathites,** <NOM CL> בְּנֵי שַׂלְמָא בֵּית לֶחֶם וּנְטוֹפָתִי *the sons of Salma were Bethlehem and the Netophathites* 1 C 2₅₄ (or ins. אֲבִי *the father* of Bethlehem). <CSTR> אֲבִי ... נְטוֹפָתִי *father of ... the Netophathites* 1 C 2₅₄ (if em.; see Nom. Cl.), חַצְרֵי נְטֹפָתִי *villages of the Netophathites* Ne 12₂₈ 1 C 9₁₆ (נְטוֹפָתִי).*

⇒ נטף *drip*, נְטֹפָה *Netophah*.

נטר I 4.0.1 vb. **keep—Qal** 4.0.1 Pf. נָטַרְתִּי; + waw 2ms Q ותטר; ptc. נֹטֵרָה, נֹטְרִים—**keep, guard,** <SUBJ> female lover Ca 1₆.₆; subj. not specified, Ca 8₁₁.₁₂. <OBJ> פְּרִי *fruit* Ca 8₁₂, כֶּרֶם *vineyard* Ca 1₆.₆. <PREP> לְ *as*, + שָׁלָל *spoil* 4QTobit^e 9₂.

Also 4QBer^a 13₂ ([ר]יטו) 4QMyst^a 7₅.*

⇒ cf. נצר *keep*.

***נטר** II 5.0.15 vb. **be angry—Qal** 5.0.14 Impf. יִטּוֹר (יִנְטֹר), 2ms תִּטֹּר (Q תטור), אֶטּוֹר, Q יטורו; ptc. נוֹטֵר; inf. Q נטור—**be angry,** <SUBJ> Y. Jr 3₅.₁₂ Na 1₂=CD 9₅ Ps 103₉, Edom Am 1₁₁ (if em. וַיִּטְרֹף *and it tore* to וַיִּטֹּר), Israel(ites) Lv 19₁₈=CD 9₂, אִישׁ *man* 4QD^a 7.1₃ CD 7₂ 9₄ 19₁₈(B) (=8₅[A] ניטור appar. ni.), מַשְׂכִּיל *instructor* 1QS 10₂₀, אֲשֶׁר *one who* 1QS 7₈.

<PREP> לְ *against* 4QMidrEschat^a 2₁₃ ([נ]וטרים), CD 13₁₈, + אָח *brother* CD 19₁₈(B), רֵעַ *neighbour* 1QS 7₈ CD 14₂₂ ([יטור לרעהו]), אֹיֵב *enemy* Na 1₂=CD 9₅, שׁוּב ptc. *one who repents* 1QS 10₂₀; of direction, *to*, + עוֹלָם *eternity*, i.e. for ever Jr 3₅.₁₂, עַד *eternity*, i.e. for ever Am 1₁₁ (if em.; see Subj.).

בְּ of accompaniment, *with*, + אַף *anger* 1QS 10₂₀ 4QD^a 9.3₈, עֶבְרָה *wrath* 4QD^a 9.3₈ ([ע]ברה]), קִנְאָה *zeal* 4QMidrEschat^a 2₁₃ ([נ]וטרים), מִשְׁפָּט *justice* 4QMyst^b 7₂ ([בלוא [משפט] *without justice*); *in, concerning*, + דָּבָר *matter* of, i.e. punishable by, death 4QD^a 10.2₁.

מִן *from*, + יוֹם *day* CD 7₂ (מיום ליום *from day to day*).

אֵת *with*, i.e. against, + בֵּן *son* Lv 19₁₈=CD 9₂.

<COLL> נטר || שׁמר *keep* (without obj.) Jr 3₅, נקם *take vengeance* Lv 19₁₈=CD 9₂ Na 1₂=CD 9₅ 4QMyst^b 7₂ (+) CD 9₄ 19₁₈[B], רִיב *strive* Ps 103₉, שׂנא *hate* CD 19₁₈; :: אהב *love* Lv 19₁₈, רחם pi. *have compassion* 1QS 10₂₀; יטורו דם לשפוך *they will be angry so as to shed blood* 4QBéat 13₃.

<SYN> שׁמר *keep*, נקם *take vengeance*, רִיב *strive*, שׂנא *hate*.

<ANT> אהב *love*, רחם pi. *have compassion*.

Ni 0.0.1 Inf. abs. Q ניטור—**bear a grudge,** <SUBJ> אִישׁ *man* CD 8₅(A) (=19₁₈[B] נטור prob. qal; || נקם *take vengeance*, שׂנא *hate*). <PREP> לְ *against*, + אָח *brother* CD 8₅(A).

<SYN> נקם *take vengeance*, שׂנא *hate*.

נטשׁ I 40.4.3 vb. **leave—Qal** 33.4.2 Pf. נָטַשׁ (נְטָשָׁנוּ), נָטַשְׁתָּ, נָטַשְׁתִּי, נָטַשְׁתְּ, (נְטַשְׁתַּנִי); impf. יִטֹּשׁ (יִטְּשֵׁנִי, יִטּוֹשׁ, Q יטושנה), 2ms תִּטֹּשׁ (תִּטְּשֵׁנִי, Q תטושנו), נִטֹּשׁ; + waw וְנָטַשְׁתִּי, וּנְטַשְׁתִּהָ, וַיִּטֹּשׁ (וּנְטַשְׁתִּיךָ); וַיִּטְּשֵׁהוּ, וַתִּטֹּשׁ, 3fs; impv. נְטוֹשׁ; ptc. pass. נְטֻשִׁים, נְטוּשָׁה.

1. leave, <SUBJ> Y. Ho 12₁₅, David 1 S 17₂₀.₂₂.₂₈, רוּחַ *wind* Nm 11₃₁ (or em. וַיִּטֹּשׁ to וַיָּטָשׁ *and it hovered*, from טושׁ). <OBJ> שְׂלָו *quail* Nm 11₃₁, צֹאן *sheep* 1 S 17₂₀.₂₈ (מְעַט הַצֹּאן *the few sheep*), דָּם *blood(guilt)* Ho 12₁₅, כְּלִי *vessel* 1 S 17₂₂. <PREP> בְּ of place, *in*, + מִדְבָּר *steppe* 1 S 17₂₈; עַל *upon, beside*, + Ephraim Ho 12₁₅, מַחֲנֶה *camp* Nm 11₃₁; *with, in the charge of*, + שֹׁמֵר *keeper* 1 S 17₂₀, יָד *hand* 1 S 17₂₂, מִי *who?* 1 S 17₂₈.

2. forsake, abandon, cast away, <SUBJ> Y. Jg 6₁₃

1 S 12$_{22}$ 1 K 8$_{57}$ 2 K 21$_{14}$ Is 2$_{6}$ Jr 7$_{29}$ 12$_{7}$ 23$_{33.39}$ Ezk 29$_{5}$ 32$_{4}$ Ps 27$_{9}$ 78$_{60}$ 94$_{14}$ Si 47$_{22}$, Israel Is 44$_{21}$ (if em. תִּנָּשֵׁנִי *you shall* not *be forgotten by me* [i.e. נשׁה ni.] to תִּטְּשֵׁנִי *you shall* not *forsake me*), Jerusalem Jr 15$_{6}$, Jeshurun Dt 32$_{15}$, עַם *people* Ezk 31$_{12}$ (unless נטשׁ II *dash to the ground*), אָדָם *human being* 4QBéat 2.2$_{5}$, אָב *father* 1 S 10$_{2}$, בֵּן *son* Pr 1$_{8}$ 6$_{20}$ Si 8$_{8}$ 9$_{10}$, זָר *stranger* Ezk 31$_{12}$, עָרִיץ *terrible one* Ezk 31$_{12}$ (unless נטשׁ II); subj. not specified, Pr 17$_{14}$.

<OBJ> Y. Dt 32$_{15}$ Jr 15$_{6}$ Is 44$_{21}$ (if em.; see Subj.), Israel(ites) Jg 6$_{13}$ 1 K 8$_{57}$ Jr 23$_{33.39}$, עַם *people* 1 S 12$_{22}$ Is 2$_{6}$ Ps 94$_{14}$, בַּיִת *house* of Jacob Is 2$_{6}$, עִיר *city* Jr 23$_{39}$, דּוֹר *generation* Jr 7$_{29}$, שְׁאֵרִית *remnant* 2 K 21$_{14}$, נַחֲלָה *inheritance* Jr 12$_{7}$, מֶלֶךְ *king* Ezk 29$_{5}$ 32$_{4}$, פַּרְעֹה *Pharaoh* Ezk 29$_{5}$ 32$_{4}$, worshipper Ps 27$_{9}$, אֹהֵב *friend* Si 9$_{10}$, דָּגָה *fish* Ezk 29$_{5}$, אֶרֶז *cedar* Ezk 31$_{12.12}$ (unless both נטשׁ II *dash to the ground*), מִשְׁכָּן *dwelling place* Ps 78$_{60}$, אֹהֶל *tent* Ps 78$_{60}$, תּוֹרָה *teaching* Pr 1$_{8}$ 6$_{20}$, שִׂיחָה *musing* Si 8$_{8}$, חָכְמָה *wisdom* 4QBéat 2.2$_{5}$, חֶסֶד *loyalty* Si 47$_{22}$, דָּבָר *matter* 1 S 10$_{2}$, רִיב *strife* Pr 17$_{14}$.

<PREP> בְּ of place, time, *on, in, during*, + אֶרֶץ *ground* Ezk 32$_{4}$, עֳנִי *affliction* 4QBéat 2.2$_{5}$; מֵעַל־פְּנֵי *from the presence of*, + Y. Jr 23$_{39}$; בַּעֲבוּר *for the sake of*, + שֵׁם *name* 1 S 12$_{22}$; ה- of direction, *into*, + מִדְבָּר *steppe* Ezk 29$_{5}$.

<COLL> נטשׁ ‖ עזב *leave* 1 K 8$_{57}$ Jr 12$_{7}$ Ps 27$_{9}$ 94$_{14}$ 4QBéat 2.2$_{5}$, מאס *reject* Jr 7$_{29}$, טול hi. *throw* Ezk 32$_{4}$; + נתן *give*, i.e. deliver up Jg 6$_{13}$ 2 K 21$_{14}$ Jr 12$_{7}$, נבל pi. *spurn* Dt 32$_{15}$; :: שׁמע *hear* Pr 1$_{8}$, נצר *keep* Pr 6$_{20}$, רטשׁ htp. *abandon*, i.e. occupy, *oneself* Si 8$_{8}$.

3. leave fallow, <SUBJ> Israel(ites) Ex 23$_{11}$ (‖ שׁמט *let drop*). <OBJ> אֶרֶץ *land* Ex 23$_{11}$.

4. forego, relinquish, <SUBJ> Israel(ites) Ex 23$_{11}$. <OBJ> שָׁנָה *(crops of the) year* Ne 10$_{32}$, מַשָּׁא *interest* Ne 10$_{32}$.

5. disregard, <SUBJ> Y. Si 32$_{17}$. <OBJ> אַלְמָנָה *widow* Si 32$_{17}$, צְעָקָה *cry* Si 32$_{17(B)}$, אֲנָקָה *groaning* Si 32$_{17(Bmg)}$.

6. permit, <SUBJ> Jacob Gn 31$_{28}$. <OBJ> Laban Gn 31$_{28}$. <COLL> לֹא נְטַשְׁתַּנִי לְנַשֵּׁק *you did not permit me to kiss* Gn 31$_{28}$.

7. perh. **spread out,** <SUBJ> מִלְחָמָה *battle* 1 S 4$_{2}$ (unless נטשׁ II *clash* or III *be sharp*; or em. וַתֵּט *and it inclined*, i.e. its outcome was decided [from נטה] or וַתִּקֶשׁ *and it was hard* [from קשׁה]).

8. pass. **a. be spread out,** <SUBJ> Amalekites 1 S 30$_{16}$. <PREP> עַל־פְּנֵי *over (the face of)*, + אֶרֶץ *land* 1 S 30$_{16}$.

b. be drawn, <SUBJ> חֶרֶב *sword* Is 21$_{15}$ (or em. לְטוּשָׁה *sharpened*; ‖ דרך pass. *be trodden*, i.e. bent).
Also 4QDibHam[a] 7$_{10}$.

<SYN> §2 עזב *leave*, מאס *reject*, טול hi. *throw*; §3 שׁמט *let drop*; §8b דרך pass. *be trodden*.

<ANT> §2 שׁמע *hear*, נצר *keep*, רטשׁ htp. *abandon oneself*.

Ni. 6 Pf. נִטְּשָׁה, נִטְּשׁוּ; + waw וַיִּנָּטְשׁוּ—**1. be forsaken,** <SUBJ> בְּתוּלָה *young woman* of Israel Am 5$_{2}$. <PREP> עַל *upon*, + אֲדָמָה *ground* Am 5$_{2}$.

2. spread oneself out, be spread out, <SUBJ> Philistines Jg 15$_{9}$ 2 S 5$_{18.22}$, שְׁלוּחָה *shoot* Is 16$_{8}$ (+ עבר *pass*). <PREP> בְּ of place, *in*, + Lehi Jg 15$_{9}$, עֵמֶק *valley* of Rephaim 2 S 5$_{18.22}$.

3. hang loose, <SUBJ> חֶבֶל *rope* Is 33$_{23}$.

Pu. 1 Pf. נֻטָּשׁ—**be forsaken,** <SUBJ> אַרְמוֹן *fortress* Is 32$_{14}$ (‖ עזב pu. *be abandoned*).

<SYN> עזב pu. *be abandoned*.

Hi. 0.0.1 Ptc. מטישׁ—**leave,** <OBJ> שָׁלוֹם *peace* 4Q Nidd 2.2$_{6}$ ([שלו]מו). <PREP> לְ of benefit, *to, for*, + אֻמְלָל *languishing one* 4QNidd 2.2$_{6}$ ([לאומל]לי).*

⇒ נְטִישָׁה *tendril*.

***נטשׁ** II 3 vb. **dash to the ground, clash—Qal** 3 + waw וַיִּטְּשֵׁהוּ, 3fs וַתִּטֹּשׁ—**1. dash to the ground** (unless נטשׁ I *forsake*), <SUBJ> עַם *people* Ezk 31$_{12}$, עָרִיץ *terrible one* Ezk 31$_{12}$. <OBJ> אֶרֶז *cedar* Ezk 31$_{12.12}$.

2. clash, <SUBJ> מִלְחָמָה *battle* 1 S 4$_{2}$ (unless נטשׁ I *spread out* or III *sharpen*).

***נטשׁ** III 2 vb. **sharpen** (unless נטשׁ I *leave*)—**Qal** 2 + waw 3fs וַתִּטֹּשׁ; ptc. pass. נְטוּשָׁה—**1. be sharp,** <SUBJ> מִלְחָמָה *battle* 1 S 4$_{2}$.

2. pass. **be sharpened,** <SUBJ> חֶרֶב *sword* Is 21$_{15}$.

⇒ cf. לטשׁ *sharpen*.

[נִי] 1 n.[m.] **wailing**—sf. נִיהֶם—<PREP> בְּ of accompaniment, *with, in,* + נשׂא *raise* lamentation Ezk 27$_{32}$ (mss בְּנֵיהֶם *their sons;* or em. בְּנֵיהֶם = פְּנֵיהֶם *their faces,** or del.).*
⇨ נהה I *lament.*

[נִיב] I 2.1 n.[m.] **fruit**—cstr. Qr, Si נִיב; sf. נִיבוֹ—in ref. to praise (Is 57$_{19[Qr]}$), item of jewellery (Si 35$_{5[B]}$), <SUBJ> בזה ni. *be contemptible* Ml 1$_{12}$ (or del.). <OBJ> ברא *create* Is 57$_{19(Qr)}$. <CSTR> נִיב שְׂפָתָיִם *fruit of lips* Is 57$_{19(Qr)}$ (Kt נוב *fruit of*), ניב זהב *fruit of gold* Si 35$_{5(B)}$ (Bmg נוב זיר perh. *fruit [consisting] of a setting*). <APP> אֹכֶל *food* Ml 1$_{12}$ (or del. נִיבוֹ and em. אָכְלוֹ to כֻּלּוֹ *all of it*). <PREP> עַל *upon* Si 35$_{5(B)}$.
⇨ נוב *bear fruit.*

*[נִיב] II 1 **speech**—cstr. Qr נִיב—**speech, utterance,** <OBJ> ברא *create* Is 57$_{19(Qr)}$. <CSTR> נִיב זָרָה *speech of a strange woman* Pr 5$_{20}$ (if em. בְּנִי בְזָרָה *my son, by a strange woman* to בְּנִיב זָרָה *by the speech of a strange woman*), נִיב שְׂפָתָיִם *speech of lips* Is 57$_{19(Qr)}$ (Kt נוב). <PREP> בְּ of instrument, *by (means of), with,* + שׁגה *go astray* Pr 5$_{20}$ (if em.; see Cstr.), חצב *hew* Ho 6$_{5}$ (if em. בַּנְּבִיאִים *by the prophets* to בְּנִיבִי אִים *with my dreadful utterance*).
⇨ נוב II *flow.*

נֵיבָי 1 pr.n.m. **Nebai,** leader and co-signatory with Nehemiah, <NOM CL> רָאשֵׁי הָעָם ... נֵיבָי *the chiefs of the people were ... Nebai* Ne 10$_{20(Qr)}$ (Kt נובי *Nobai*).

[נִיד] 1 n.m. **shaking**—cstr. נִיד—of lips, as gesture of sympathy, <SUBJ> חשׂך *hold back* Jb 16$_{5}$. <CSTR> נִיד שְׂפָתַי *shaking,* i.e. consolation, *of my lips* Jb 16$_{5}$.
⇨ נוד I *move to and fro.*

נִידָה I 1 n.f. **impurity,** i.e. impure thing (unless נִידָה II *shaking of head*), <PREP> לְ introducing predicate, + היה *be* Lm 1$_{8}$.*
⇨ נדד *flee* or נדה *cast.*

*נִידָה II 1 n.f. **shaking of head,** in derision (unless נִידָה I *impurity*), <PREP> לְ introducing predicate, + היה *be* Lm 1$_{8}$.
⇨ נוד I *move to and fro.*

נָיוֹת 6 pl.n. **Naioth**—נָוֹת, Kt נוית—place to which David fled from Saul, in Ramah, unless *encampments,* <PREP> בְּ of place, *in(to)* 1 S 19$_{19.22}$, + בוא *come* 1 S 19$_{23}$, ישׁב *dwell* 1 S 19$_{18}$; מִן of direction, *from,* + ברח *flee* 1 S 20$_{1}$; אֶל *to,* + הלך *go* 1 S 19$_{23}$.
⇨ (?) נוה I *dwell.*

נִיחֹחַ 43.1.20 n.[m.] **soothing**—נִיחוֹחַ; cstr. Q ניחוח; sf. נִיחֹחִי, נִיחֹחֲכֶם; pl. sf. נִיחוֹחֵיהֶם—**1. soothing, pleasing, appeasement,** usu. of odour of sacrifices to Y., of sacrifices to idols (Ezk 6$_{13}$ 16$_{19}$ 20$_{28}$), of atonement (1QS 3$_{11}$). **2. pleasing odour** (4QapLam[a] 1.1$_{6}$ 4QS[e] 2$_{17}$ 4Q419 1$_{6}$), of righteousness (1QS 9$_{5}$).

<NOM CL> ניחוח אין בו *there is no pleasing odour in it* 4QapLam[a] 1.1$_{6}$.

<OBJ> קרב hi. *bring near,* i.e. offer 1Q8$_{9}$ (corrected to ריח ניחוח)=4QS[e] 2$_{17}$ (ל[ק]ר[יב]), נגשׁ hi. *bring near,* i.e. offer 4Q419 1$_{6}$.

<CSTR> ניחוח צדק *pleasing odour of righteousness* 1QS 9$_{5}$, רצונכה *of your acceptance* 4QRitPur 29.7$_{11}$ ([ני]חו[ח]); רֵיחַ נִיחֹחַ *odour of soothing,* i.e. soothing odour Gn 8$_{21}$ (הַנִּיחֹחַ) Ex 29$_{18.26}$ (both נִיחוֹחַ) 29$_{41}$ Lv 1$_{9}$ (נִיחוֹחַ) 1$_{13.17}$ 2$_{2.9.12}$ 3$_{5.16}$ 4$_{31}$ 6$_{8.14}$ 8$_{21.28}$ 17$_{6}$ 23$_{13.18}$ Nm 15$_{3.7.10.13.14.24}$ 18$_{17}$ 28$_{6.8.13.24.27}$ 29$_{2.6.8.13.36}$ Ezk 6$_{13}$ 16$_{19}$ 20$_{41}$ Si 45$_{16}$ 1QS 8$_{9(correction)}$ (ניחוח) 1QSb 3$_{1}$ ([ני]חוח) 4QJub[e] 21$_{7.9}$ ([ניח]וח) 4QSD 7.2$_{9}$ 4QMyst[a] 79$_{7}$ (רי[ח] [נ]יחוח) 11QT 13$_{12}$ ([ריח ניחוח]) 13$_{15}$ ([ר]י[ח] [ניחוח]) 14$_{7}$ ([ריח] ניחוח) 14$_{14.16}$ (both [ריח ניחוח]) 15$_{13}$ 16$_{10}$ (both ניחוח) 20$_{05}$ ([ריח ניחוח]) 20$_{8}$ ([ני]ח[ו]ח) 22$_{05}$ ([ריח ניחוח]) 22$_{8}$ ([ריח]) 23$_{6}$ ([ריח ניחוח]) 23$_{17}$ (ניחוח) 24$_{6}$ ([ניחוח]) 25$_{4.6}$ (both [ריח ניחוח]) 28$_{02}$ ([ניחו]ח) 28$_{2}$ (ר[יח ניחוח]) 28$_{6}$ (ניחוח) 29$_{011}$ ([ריח ניחוח]) 34$_{14}$ (ניחוח), נִיחֹחִי *of my soothing,* i.e. my soothing odour Nm 28$_{2}$, נִיחֹחֲכֶם *of your soothing,* i.e. your soothing odour Lv 26$_{31}$ 4QD[a] 11$_{4}$ (ניחוחכם), נִיחוֹחֵיהֶם *of their soothing,* i.e. their soothing odour Ezk 20$_{28}$, מקטרת ניחוח *incense of soothing,* i.e. soothing incense 1QM 2$_{5}$, קטורת *incense of* 11QPs[a] 18$_{9}$, זכרון *memorial of* 4QRitPur 29.7$_{10}$ ([ניחו]ח), כפורי

ניחוח *atonement of pleasing,* i.e. pleasing atonement 1QS 3_{11}.

<PREP> כְּ *as* 1QS 9_5 6QBen 1_1.

<COLL> קטורת ניחוח מיד צדיקים *soothing incense from the hand of the righteous* 11QPs^a 18_9.

Also 4QPrQuot 77.1_4.*

⇒ נוח I *rest.*

***[ניל]** vb. **acquire—Qal,** <SUBJ> דְּרוֹר *swallow* Ps 84_4 (if em. לָהּ *to her* to נָלָה *she has acquired*). <OBJ> קֵן *nest* Ps 84_4 (if em.; see Subj.).

⇒ מָנוֹל *possession.*

נין 1 vb. **increase—Qal** 1 Impf. Kt ינין (Qr ni. יִנּוֹן)—**increase, have descendants,** <SUBJ> שֵׁם *name* Ps 72_{17}(Kt) (or vocalize יְנַיֵּן pi. *he shall bear offspring;* ms כון ni. *be established*).

Ni. 1 Impf. Qr יִנּוֹן—**increase, have descendants,** <SUBJ> שֵׁם *name* Ps 72_{17}(Qr) (or em. יְנַיֵּן pi. *he shall bear offspring;* ms כון ni. *be established*).

Pi. bear offspring,* <SUBJ> מֶלֶךְ *king* Ps 72_{17} (if vocalize ינין *he shall increase* [Kt qal] to יְנַיֵּן *he shall bear offspring*). <PREP> לִפְנֵי *before,* + שֶׁמֶשׁ *sun,* i.e. as long as the sun lasts Ps 72_{17}.*

⇒ נִין *offspring.*

נִין 3.2 n.m. **offspring**—sf. נִינִי—**offspring, posterity,** <SUBJ> מאס ni. *be despised* Si 41_5(B, M), אבד *perish* Nm 21_{30} (if em. וַנִּירָם *and we became exalted* [from ירם] to נִינָם *their offspring*), שׂרף pass. qal *be burned* Ps 74_8 (if em. נִינָם יָחַד שָׂרְפוּ *let us utterly oppress* [from ינה] *them; they burned* to נִינָם יַחַד שֹׂרָפוּ *let their offspring be burned together*).* <NOM CL> נין נמאס דבר רעים *the word of evil persons is a despised offspring* Si 41_5(B), נין נמאס ת[ולד]ות רעים *the generations of the evil are a despised offspring* Si 41_5(M), לֹא נִין לוֹ *there is no offspring to him* Jb 18_{19}. <OBJ> כרת hi. *cut off* Is 14_{22} Si 47_{22}(Segal) ([יכרית]). <PREP> לְ *with,* + שׁקר *deal falsely* Gn 21_{23}. <COLL> נִין || נֶכֶד *progeny* Gn 21_{23} Is 14_{22} (נִין וָנֶכֶד) Jb 18_{19} Si 41_5 (+) 47_{22}; + שְׁאָר *remnant* Is 14_{22}, שָׂרִיד *survivor* Jb 18_{19}, שֵׁם *name* Is 14_{22}.

<SYN> נֶכֶד *progeny.**

⇒ נִין *increase.*

נִינָם, see ינה *oppress.*

נִינְוֵה 17 pl.n. **Nineveh,** capital of Assyria, on E bank of Tigris, <SUBJ> היה *be* Jon 3_3, הפך ni. *be overthrown* Jon 3_4, שׁדד pu. *be devastated* Na 3_7. <NOM CL> נִינְוֵה כִּבְרֵכַת־מַיִם *Nineveh is like a pool of water* Na 2_9. <OBJ> בנה *build* Gn 10_{11}, שׂים *place,* i.e. make, a desolation Zp 2_{13}.

<CSTR> אַנְשֵׁי נִינְוֵה *men of Nineveh* Jon 3_5, מֶלֶךְ *king of* Jon 3_6, מַשָּׂא *oracle of,* i.e. concerning Na 1_1.

<APP> הָעִיר הַגְּדוֹלָה *the great city* Jon 1_2 3_2 4_{11}.

<PREP> לְ of benefit, *for,* + בקשׁ pi. *seek* comforters Na 3_7; *for, on account of,* נוד *shake the head,* i.e. show sympathy Na 3_7; בְּ of place, *in, throughout* Jon 4_{11}, + ישׁב *dwell* 2 K 19_{36}||Is 37_{37}, אמר *say* Jon 3_7; אֶל *to,* + קרא *proclaim* Jon 3_2, הלך *go* Jon 1_2 $3_{2.3}$; עַל *upon,* + חוס *have pity* Jon 4_{11}; *against* perh. 2Q33 2_1 ([נינו[ה]), + קרא *cry* Jon 1_2; בֵּין *between* Gn 10_{12} (+ כֶּלַח *Calah*).

***[נִיס]** 1 n.m. **fugitive,** <SUBJ> נפל *fall* Jr 48_{44}(Kt) (unless הניס is hi. pf. of נוס *flee;* Qr הַנָּס *the one who flees,* i.e. נוס qal ptc.). <COLL> הניס מִפְּנֵי הַפַּחַד *the fugitive from the terror* Jr 48_{44}(Kt).

⇒ נוס *flee.*

נִיסָן 2 pr.n.[m.] **Nisan,** first month of postexilic Jewish calendar, previously called Abib, March/April, <NOM CL> הוּא נִיסָן *that is Nisan* Ezr 7_9 (if ins. נִיסָן). <CSTR> חֹדֶשׁ נִיסָן *month of Nisan* Est 3_7 Ne 2_1.

נִיצוֹץ 1.2 n.[m.] **spark**—Si נצוץ—<PREP> לְ introducing predicate, + היה *be* Is 1_{31} (+ נְעֹרֶת *tow*); מִן *from,* + רבה hi. *increase* live coal Si 11_{32}; עַד *unto* Si 42_{22}(M) (+ חָזוּת *[fleeting] glimpse*).

⇒ נצץ *shine.*

ניר I 3 vb. **break up—Qal** 3 Impv. נִירוּ; ptc. נֵר—**break up, till,** <SUBJ> Y. Pr 20_{27} (unless נֵר *lamp*), Israelites Ho 10_{12}, Jerusalem Jr 4_3, אִישׁ *man* of Judah Jr 4_3. <OBJ>

נִיר *untilled ground* Jr 43, נְשָׁמָה *soul* Pr 2027 (unless נֵר *lamp*). <PREP> לְ *for oneself,* + Israelites Ho 1012, Jerusalem Jr 43, אִישׁ *man* of Judah Jr 43.*

⇒ נִיר II *untilled ground.*

***נִיר** II vb. **shine—Qal shine with,** <SUBJ> ראשׁ *head* Ps 1415 (if em. יָנִי *let it* not *refuse* to יָנִיר *let it* not *shine*). <COLL> שֶׁמֶן ראשׁ אַל־יָנִיר ראשִׁי *with oil of essence,* i.e. fine oil, *do not let my head shine* Ps 1415 (if em.; see Subj.).

⇒ נִיר I *lamp*; cf. נֵר I *lamp.*

נִיר I 5 n.[m.] **lamp**—cstr. נִר—<SUBJ> היה *be* 1 K 1136 (unless נִיר II *untilled ground* or III *sign of power* or V *dominion*). <NOM CL> נִר רְשָׁעִים חַטָּאת *the lamp of the wicked is sin* Pr 214 (unless נִיר IV *mark*). <OBJ> נתן *give* 1 K 154 (unless נִיר II *untilled ground* or V *dominion*) 2 K 819||2 C 217 (unless נִיר II or V or VI *new break*). <CSTR> נִר רְשָׁעִים *lamp of the wicked* Pr 214 (mss נֵר *lamp of*).*

⇒ נִיר II *shine.*

נִיר II 7 n.[m.] **untilled ground**—cstr. נִיר—**untilled ground** (Jr 43 Ho 1012), **tillage** (Pr 1323), <OBJ> ניר *break up* Jr 43 Ho 1012. <NOM CL> רָב־אֹכֶל נִיר רָאשִׁים *the tillage of the poor is,* i.e. yields, *much food* Pr 1323. <CSTR> נִיר רָאשִׁים *tillage of the poor* Pr 1323.

2. perh. **field,** thus **dominion,*** <SUBJ> היה *be* 1 K 1136 (לְמַעַן הֱיוֹת־נִיר לְדָוִיד *so that there should be dominion for David;* unless נִיר I *lamp* or V *dominion*). <OBJ> נתן *give* 1 K 154 (unless נִיר I *lamp* or V *dominion*) 2 K 819||2 C 217 (unless נִיר I or V or VI *new break*).*

⇒ ניר I *break up.*

***נִיר** III 1 n.[m.] **sign of power** (unless נִיר I *lamp*), <SUBJ> היה *be* 1 K 1136.

*[**נִיר**] IV n.[m.] 1 **mark** (unless נִיר I *lamp*)—cstr. נֵר—<NOM CL> נֵר רְשָׁעִים חַטָּאת *the mark of the wicked is sin* Pr 214. <APP> רוּם־עֵינַיִם וּרְחַב־לֵב נֵר רְשָׁעִים *a high look and a proud heart, the mark of the wicked* Pr 214.

***נִיר** V 3 n.[m.] **dominion,** <SUBJ> היה *be* 1 K 1136 (unless נִיר I *lamp*), אבד *perish* Nm 2130 (if em. וַנִּירָם *and we shot them* [from ירה I] to וְנִירָם *and their dominion*). <OBJ> נתן *give* 1 K 154 2 K 819||2 C 217 (unless all three נִיר I *lamp* or II *untilled ground*).

***נִיר** VI 1 n.[m.] **new break, new beginning** (unless נִיר I *lamp* or II *untilled ground* or V *dominion*), <OBJ> נתן *give* 2 K 819||2 C 217.

[**נֵיר**], see נֵר *lamp.*

נִירָם, see ירם *be high.*

נכא I 1.0.1 vb. **strike—Qal** 0.0.1 + waw ויכא—**strike,** ויכא אותם *and he struck them* 4QpsJub[a] 13.

Ni. 1 Pf. נִכְּאוּ—**be struck, scourged out** (unless נכא II *be low* or III *be put to flight*), <SUBJ> בֵּן *son* Jb 308. <PREP> מִן of direction, *from,* + אֶרֶץ *land* Jb 308.*

⇒ נָכָא *stricken,* נָכֵא *stricken*; cf. נכה *strike.*

***נכא** II 1 vb. **be low** (unless נכא I *strike*)—**Ni.** 1 Pf. נִכְּאוּ—**be low,** <SUBJ> בֵּן *son* Jb 308. <PREP> מִן of comparison, *(more) than,* + אֶרֶץ *ground* Jb 308.

***נכא** III 1 vb. **put to flight** (unless נכא I *strike* or II *be low*)—**Ni.** 1 Pf. נִכְּאוּ—**be put to flight,** <SUBJ> בֵּן *son* Jb 308. <PREP> מִן of direction, *from,* + אֶרֶץ *land* Jb 308.

[**נָכָא**] 1 adj. **stricken**—pl. נְכָאִים—<COLL> תֶּהְגּוּ אַךְ־נְכָאִים *you shall moan, utterly stricken* Is 167.

⇒ נכא *strike.*

[**נָכֵא**] 3.0.3 adj. **stricken**—m. cstr. Q נכאה (Q נכאי), f. abs. נְכֵאָה, m.pl. Q נכאים, cstr. Q נכאי—**stricken, downcast, 1.** used attributively of רוּחַ *spirit* Pr 1722 (:: שָׂמֵחַ *glad*) 1814.

2. in nom. cl., used predicatively of רוּחַ *spirit* Pr 1513 (:: שָׂמֵחַ *glad*).

3. as noun, **stricken one, contrite one, downcast one,** <OBJ> בער hi. *kindle* 1QM 1110 (unless כאה

ni. ptc. *downcast one*), רדף *persecute* Ps 109_{16} (if em.; see Cstr.), מוּת pol. *kill* Ps 109_{16} (if em.; see Cstr.). <CSTR> נכאה רגלים או ידים *one stricken of*, i.e. lame in, *the legs or hands* 1QSa 2_5 (+ נגע pu. ptc. *one who is afflicted*, פִּסֵּחַ *lame*, עִוֵּר *blind*, חֵרֵשׁ *deaf*, אִלֵּם *dumb*), נכאי רוח *downcast one(s) of spirit* Is 66_2(1QIsa[a]) (MT נְכֵה *contrite one of*) 1QM 11_{10} (unless both כאה ni. ptc. *downcast one*), נְכֵא לֵבָב *stricken one of heart* Ps 10_{16} (if em. נִכְאֶה *discouraged one of*, i.e. כאה ni. ptc.). <PREP> בְּ introducing object, + נחם pi. *comfort* 1QS 10_{21} (unless כאה ni. ptc. *downcast one*; =4QS[f] 5_1 בנכוחים *the straightforward*)

<ANT> שָׂמֵחַ *glad*.

⇒ נכא *strike*.

נְכֹאת 2 n.f. **ladanum,** a spice, from resin of the cistus rose, <OBJ> ירד hi. *bring down* Gn 37_{25} (|| לֹט *myrrh*, בָּטְנָה *balm*) 43_{11} (|| לֹט *myrrh*, + צֳרִי, דְּבַשׁ *honey*, בָּטְנָה *pistachio*, שָׁקֵד *almond*), נשׂא *bear* Gn 37_{25}. <APP> מִנְחָה *present* Gn 43_{11}. <COLL> נְכֹאת וָלֹט *ladanum and myrrh* Gn 43_{11}, צְרִי וָלֹט *balm and myrrh* Gn 37_{25}.*

<SYN> לֹט *myrrh*, צֳרִי *balm*.

נִכְבָּד *weighty*, see כבד Ni. *be heavy*

נֶכֶד 3.2 n.m. **progeny**—sf. נֶכְדִּי—**progeny, posterity,** <NOM CL> לֹא נִין לוֹ וְלֹא־נֶכֶד בְּעַמּוֹ *there is no offspring to him or progeny among his people* Jb 18_{19}, נכד אויל [במדור רשע] *a foolish progeny is in the dwelling place of the wicked* Si 41_5(B, Segal). <OBJ> כרת hi. *cut off* Is 14_{22} Si 47_{22}(Segal) ([יכרית]). <ADJ> אֱוִיל *foolish* Si 41_5. <PREP> לְ *with*, + שׁקר *deal falsely* Gn 21_{23}. <COLL> נִין || נֶכֶד *offspring* Gn 21_{23} Is 14_{22} (נִין וָנֶכֶד) Jb 18_{19} Si 41_5 (+) 47_{22}; + שְׁאָר *remnant* Is 14_{22}, שָׂרִיד *survivor* Jb 18_{19}, שֵׁם *name* Is 14_{22}.

<SYN> נִין *offspring*.

נכה 502.3.23.1 vb. **strike—Ni.** 1 + waw וְנִכָּה—**be struck,** <SUBJ> Uriah 2 S 11_{15} (+ מוּת *die*).

Pu. 2 Pf. נֻכָּתָה, נֻכּוּ—**be beaten down,** by hail, <SUBJ> פִּשְׁתָּה *flax* Ex 9_{31}, שְׂעֹרָה *barley* Ex 9_{31}, חִטָּה *wheat* Ex 9_{32}, כֻּסֶּמֶת *spelt* Ex 9_{32}.

Hi. 483.3.22.1 Pf. הִכָּה (הִכָּהוּ, הִכָּם), הִכִּיתָ (הִכִּיתָה),
הִכִּיתִי (הִכִּיתִיךָ), הִכִּיתַנִי, הִכִּיתוֹ, הִכִּיתָנוּ, הִכּוּ (הִכּוּנִי, הִכֻּהוּ),
הִכִּיתֶם (הִכּוּם); impf. יַכֶּה (יַךְ, יַכְּכָה, Q יכנו, יַכֶּכָּה, יַכֵּם),
יַכּוּ (יַכּוּךָ), אַכֶּה (אַכֶּכָּה, אַכֶּנּוּ, אַכֵּהוּ), 2ms תַּכֶּה (תַּכֶּנּוּ),
נַכֶּה (נַכֶּנּוּ, נַכֵּהוּ), יַכֵּהוּ; + waw וְהִכָּה (וְהִכַּנִי, וְהִכָּנִי), וְהִכְּךָ,
וְהִכִּיתָ (וְהִכִּיתָ, וְהִכִּיתָה, וְהִכִּיתָם), וְהִכָּם, וְהִכָּהוּ, וְהִכֵּיתִי,
וְהִכֵּיתִי), וְהִכִּיתְךָ, וְהִכִּיתִיו, וְהִכְתִיו), וְהִכּוּנִי, וְהִכִּיתֶם; וַיַּכֶּה
וַיַּךְ, וַיַּכּוֹ, וַיַּכֵּהוּ, וַיַּכֶּהָ, וַיַּכֵּם), 3fs וַתַּךְ, וָאַכֶּה (וָאַךְ), וַיַּכּוּ
(וַיַּכֵּהוּ, וַיַּכּוּהָ, וַיַּכּוּם, וַיַּכֵּם), וַנַּךְ (וַנַּכֵּהוּ, וַנַּכֵּם; impv. הַכֵּה
(הַךְ, הַכֵּינִי), הַכּוּ (הַכֻּהוּ, הַכּוּם); ptc. מַכֶּה (מַכֵּךְ, מַכֵּהוּ), מַכֵּה,
מַכִּים, מַכּוֹת; inf. abs. הַכֵּה; cstr. הַכּוֹת (הַכֹּתִי, הַכּוֹתִי,
הַכֹּתְךָ, הַכּוֹתֶךָ, הַכֹּתוֹ, הַכּוֹתוֹ, הַכֹּתָהּ (Q הכותה), הַכֹּתָם
(הַכּוֹתָם).

1. strike, beat, beat down, a. as act of violence (Ex $2_{11.13}$ $21_{15.18.19.26}$ Dt 25_{11} 1 K $20_{35.35.37.37}$ 22_{24}||2 C 18_{23} Is 50_6 58_4 Jr 20_2 37_{15} Mc 4_{14} Ps 3_8 Jb 16_{10} Pr 23_{35} Ca 5_7 Lm 3_{30} Ne 13_{25}).

b. in punishment, chastisement (Dt $25_{2.2}$ Pr $17_{10.26}$ 19_{25} $23_{13.14}$).

c. with arrow shot from bow (1 K 22_{34}||2 C 18_{33} 2 K 9_{24}; perh. also 2 K $8_{28.29}$||2 C $22_{5.6}$ 2 K $9_{15.27}$), with tongue (Jr 18_{18}), with rod, for oppression (Is 10_{24} $14_{6.29}$), correction (Is 11_4).

d. water, with cloak (2 K $2_{8.14}$), the ground, with arrow (2 K $13_{18.18.19}$), rock, with pickaxe (Siloam tunnel inscr.4), hair, with sword (Ezk 5_2).

e. of striking a beast (Nm $22_{23.25.27.28.32}$ CD 11_6), capitals of sanctuary (Am 9_1), water, dust, rock, with rod (Ex $7_{17.20}$ $8_{12.13}$ $17_{5.6}$ Nm 20_{11}), water, with cloak (2 K $2_{8.14}$), the ground, with arrow (2 K $13_{18.18.19}$), rock, with pickaxe (Siloam tunnel inscr.4), hair, with sword (Ezk 5_2), bow out of hand (Ezk 39_3).

f. of barley cake striking tent (Jg 7_{13}); Y. striking river (Is 11_{15}), rock (Ps 78_{20}), vines and fig trees (Ps 105_{33}); goat striking ram (Dn 8_7); hail striking crops, people and animals (Ex $9_{25.25}$); sun, moon striking people (Is 49_{10} Jon 4_8 Ps 121_6); one's conscience striking one (1 S 24_5 2 S 24_{10}).

g. thrust fork into pot (1 S 2_{14}).

h. pin someone to wall with spear (1 S 18_{11} 19_{10}), to the ground (1 S 26_8).

i. clap hands, in anger or distress (2 K 11_{12} Ezk 6_{11}

21$_{14.22}$ 22$_{13}$).*

j. play harp (4QS^{d} 9$_{8}$).

k. of plant, **strike roots** (Ho 14$_{6}$ [or em.; see Cstr.] Si 40$_{15[Bmg]}$).

l. of roots, **penetrate** (1QH 16$_{23}$).

2. strike fatally, kill, in manslaughter, murder, assassination (Gn 37$_{21}$ Ex 2$_{12}$ 21$_{12.20}$ Lv 24$_{17}$ Nm 35$_{11.15.16.17.18.21.21.24.30}$ Dt 19$_{4.6.11}$ 21$_{1}$ 27$_{24.25}$ Jos 20$_{3.5.9}$ 1 S 20$_{33}$ 2 S 2$_{22.23}$ 4$_{6.7}$ 12$_{9}$ 13$_{28.30}$ 17$_{2}$ 18$_{11.15}$ 20$_{10}$ 1 K 15$_{27.29}$ 16$_{7.10.11.16}$ 2 K 10$_{9.11.17.25.25}$ 12$_{21.22}$ 14$_{5}$||2 C 25$_{3}$ 2 K 14$_{6}$ 15$_{10.14.25.30}$ 19$_{37}$||Is 37$_{38}$ 2 K 25$_{25}$ Is 66$_{3}$ Jr 26$_{23}$ 40$_{14.15.15}$ 41$_{2.3.9.16.18}$ 4QHalakhah^{a} 3.1$_{3}$ [[וה]כה]), as vengeance, retaliation, punishment (e.g. Gn 4$_{15}$ Jg 15$_{8}$ 2 S 1$_{15}$ 3$_{27}$ 2 K 9$_{7}$ 14$_{5}$ 2 K 21$_{24}$||2 C 33$_{25}$ 25$_{21}$||Jr 52$_{27}$ 2 C 25$_{16}$), in warfare, conquest (Dt 13$_{16.16}$=11QT 55$_{6.6}$ Dt 20$_{13}$=11QT 62$_{9}$ Jos 7$_{5.5}$ 10$_{26}$ 11$_{10.11.14.17}$ Jg 3$_{29.31}$ 9$_{43}$ 14$_{19}$ 15$_{15.16}$ 20$_{31.39.45}$ 21$_{10}$ 1 S 4$_{2}$ 14$_{14}$ 18$_{7.7.27}$ 21$_{12}$ 29$_{5}$ 31$_{2}$ 2 S 23$_{1}$ 8$_{5.13}$||1 C 18$_{5.12}$ 2 S 10$_{18}$ 11$_{21}$ 21$_{2.12.16.17.18.19.21}$||1 C 20$_{4.5.7}$ 2 S 23$_{20.21}$||1 C 11$_{22.23}$ 1 K 11$_{15}$ 20$_{20.21.29}$ 2 K 3$_{23}$ 6$_{21.21.22.22}$ Jr 20$_{4}$ Jr 21$_{7}$ 29$_{21}$ Ps 60$_{2}$ Jb 1$_{15.17}$ 2 C 13$_{17}$ 25$_{13}$; distinction form §3 not alw. clear), combat (1 S 17$_{9.9.25.26.27.46.49.50.57}$ 18$_{6}$ 19$_{5}$ 21$_{10}$ 2 S 14$_{6.7}$ Si 47$_{4}$); as punishment of Y. (Gn 8$_{21}$ 1 S 6$_{19.19}$ 2 S 6$_{7}$||1 C 13$_{10}$ 1 K 14$_{15}$ Jr 21$_{6}$ 33$_{5}$ Ezk 7$_{9}$ 9$_{5.7.8}$ Zc 13$_{7}$=CD 19$_{8}$; distinction from §5 not alw. clear), specif. firstborn of Egyptians (Ex 12$_{12.29}$ Nm 3$_{13}$ 8$_{17}$ 33$_{4}$ Ps 78$_{51}$ 105$_{36}$ 135$_{8}$ 136$_{10}$); killing of beasts (Lv 24$_{18.21}$ 1 S 17$_{35.36}$ 11QT 52$_{6}$ 55$_{8}$); beasts killing humans (1 K 20$_{36.36}$ Jr 5$_{6}$ 1QH 13$_{15}$ [ה[כו]תה]), worm killing plant (Jon 4$_{7}$).

3. attack, defeat, rout, destroy, subdue (Gn 14$_{5.7.15.17}$ 32$_{9.12}$ 34$_{30}$ 36$_{35}$||1 C 1$_{46}$ Nm 14$_{45}$ 21$_{24}$ 22$_{6}$ 25$_{17}$ 32$_{4}$ Dt 1$_{4}$ 2$_{33}$ 4$_{46}$ 29$_{6}$ Jos 7$_{3}$ 8$_{21}$ 9$_{18}$ 10$_{4.10.10.41}$ 11$_{8}$ 12$_{1.6.7}$ 13$_{12.21}$ 15$_{16}$ 19$_{47}$ Jg 1$_{4.5.8.10.12.17.25}$ 3$_{13}$ 6$_{16}$ 8$_{11}$ 9$_{44}$ 11$_{21.33}$ 12$_{4}$ 18$_{27}$ 20$_{37}$ 1 S 7$_{11}$ 11$_{11}$ 13$_{3.4}$ 14$_{31.48}$ 15$_{3.7}$ 19$_{8}$ 23$_{2.2.5}$ 30$_{1.17}$ 2 S 1$_{1}$ 5$_{8.20.24.25}$||1 C 14$_{11.15.16}$ 2 S 8$_{1.2.3.9.10}$||1 C 18$_{1.2.3.9.10}$ 2 S 15$_{14}$ 23$_{10.12}$ 1 K 15$_{20}$||2 C 16$_{4}$ 1 K 20$_{21}$ 2 K 3$_{19.24.25}$ 8$_{21}$||2 C 21$_{9}$ 2 K 10$_{32}$ 13$_{17.19.19.25}$ 14$_{7}$||2 C 25$_{11}$ 2 K 14$_{10.10}$||2 C 25$_{19}$ 2 K 15$_{16}$ 18$_{8}$ Is 10$_{20}$ 27$_{7}$ Jr 37$_{10}$ 43$_{11}$ 46$_{2.13}$ 47$_{1}$ 49$_{28}$ perh. Zc 9$_{4}$ Ps 78$_{66}$ 135$_{10}$ 136$_{17}$ Est 9$_{5}$ 1 C 4$_{43}$ 11$_{6.14}$ 20$_{1}$ 2 C 14$_{13.14}$ 25$_{14}$ 28$_{5.5.17.23}$ 1QpHab 3$_{1}$ 1QSb 1$_{7}$ [[יכה]] 4QpHos^{b} 2$_{3}$ 4QpNah 3.1$_{5}$ 4QComm GenA 4$_{1}$ [[ה]כה] 4QpsEzek^{a} 16.1$_{4}$ 4QSela 8$_{2}$ 9.1$_{4}$ 11QT 58$_{12}$); often involving complete slaughter (e.g. Nm 21$_{35}$ Dt 3$_{3}$ 7$_{2}$ Jos 8$_{22.24}$ 10$_{20.28.30.32.33.35.37.39.40}$ 11$_{8.12}$ 20$_{48}$ 1 S 22$_{19}$ 27$_{9}$ 1 C 4$_{41}$); subduing waves of sea (Zc 10$_{11}$).

4. strike with plague, etc. (Ex 3$_{20}$ 7$_{25}$ 9$_{15}$ 12$_{13}$ Nm 11$_{33}$ 14$_{12}$ Dt 28$_{22.27.35}$ 1 S 4$_{8}$ 5$_{6}$ 2 S 24$_{17}$ 2 K 19$_{35}$||Is 37$_{36}$ Am 4$_{9}$ Hg 2$_{17}$ Jb 2$_{7}$), blindness (Gn 19$_{11}$ Dt 28$_{28}$ 2 K 6$_{18}$ Zc 12$_{4}$), madness, confusion (Dt 28$_{28}$ Zc 12$_{4}$), hunger, nakedness (4QpHos^{a} 2$_{12}$), ban of destruction (Ml 3$_{24}$), **strike** someone, causing outbreak of tumours (1 S 5$_{9}$).

5. (of Y.) **strike in punishment, strike for correction** (Lv 26$_{24}$ Is 5$_{25}$ 9$_{12}$ 27$_{7}$ 30$_{31}$ 57$_{17}$ 60$_{10}$ Jr 2$_{30}$ 5$_{3}$ 14$_{19}$ 30$_{14}$ Ezk 32$_{15}$ Ho 6$_{1}$ Am 3$_{15}$ 6$_{11}$ Mc 6$_{13}$ Ps 69$_{27}$ 1 C 21$_{7}$ Si 10$_{13}$ 1QSb 1$_{7}$ [[יכה]] 1QDM 1$_{9}$ [[להכו]ת] 11QPs Ap^{a} 4$_{4}$) .

<SUBJ> Y. Gn 8$_{21}$ Ex 3$_{20}$ 7$_{25}$ 9$_{15}$ 12$_{12.13.29}$ Lv 26$_{24}$ Nm 3$_{13}$ 8$_{17}$ 11$_{33}$ 14$_{12}$ 32$_{4}$ 33$_{4}$ Dt 28$_{22.27.28.35}$ 1 S 5$_{6.9}$ 6$_{19.19}$ 2 S 5$_{24}$||1 C 14$_{15}$ 2 S 6$_{7}$||1 C 13$_{10}$ 1 K 14$_{15}$ 2 K 6$_{18}$ Is 5$_{25}$ 9$_{12}$ 11$_{15}$ 27$_{7}$ 30$_{31}$ 57$_{17}$ 60$_{10}$ Jr 2$_{30}$ 5$_{3}$ 14$_{19}$ 21$_{6}$ 30$_{14}$ 33$_{5}$ Ezk 7$_{9}$ 21$_{22}$ 22$_{13}$ 32$_{15}$ 39$_{3}$ Ho 6$_{1}$ Am 3$_{15}$ 4$_{9}$ 6$_{11}$ Mc 6$_{13}$ Hg 2$_{17}$ Zc 9$_{4}$ 12$_{4.4}$ Ml 3$_{24}$ Ps 3$_{8}$ 69$_{27}$ 78$_{20.51.66}$ 105$_{33.36}$ 135$_{8.10}$ 136$_{10.17}$ 1 C 21$_{7}$ Si 10$_{13}$ 1QDM 1$_{9}$ ([להכו]ת) 4QpHos^{a} 2$_{12}$ 11QPsAp^{a} 4$_{4}$, אֱלֹהִים *god* 1 S 4$_{8}$ 2 C 28$_{23}$, מַלְאָךְ *angel* Gn 19$_{11}$ 2 S 24$_{17}$ 2 K 19$_{35}$||Is 37$_{36}$, שָׂטָן *Satan* Jb 2$_{7}$.

Ahohite 1 C 11$_{14}$, Amalekites Nm 14$_{45}$ 1 S 30$_{1}$, Aramaeans 2 K 8$_{28.29}$||2 C 22$_{5.6}$ 2 K 9$_{15}$ (or em. all three הָרֹמִים *the archers*) 2 C 28$_{5}$, Assyrians Is 10$_{24}$, Benjamin(ites) Jg 20$_{39}$, Bethlehemite 2 S 21$_{19}$, Canaanites Gn 34$_{30}$ Nm 14$_{45}$, Chaldaeans Jb 1$_{17}$, Dan 4QSela 8$_{2}$, Edomites 2 C 28$_{17}$, Hushathite 2 S 21$_{18}$||1 C 20$_{4}$, Israel(ites) Nm 21$_{24.35}$ 25$_{17}$ Dt 1$_{4}$ 2$_{33}$ 3$_{3}$ 7$_{2}$ 13$_{16.16}$=11QT 55$_{6.6.8}$ Dt 20$_{13}$=11QT 62$_{9}$ Dt 29$_{6}$ Jos 8$_{21.22.24}$ 10$_{10.10.30.32.35.37}$ 11$_{8.8.11}$ Jg 11$_{21}$ 2 K 3$_{24.25}$ Jr 18$_{18}$ 37$_{10}$ perh. Zc 10$_{11}$ 11QT 52$_{6}$ 55$_{8}$ 58$_{12}$, Jews Est 9$_{5}$, Judah Jg 1$_{4.5.10.17}$, Kittim 1QpHab 3$_{1}$ ([הכתיאים]) Perizzites Gn 34$_{30}$, Philistines 1 S 4$_{2}$ 31$_{2}$ 2 S 21$_{12}$, Rephaim Jos 13$_{12}$, Sabaeans Jb 1$_{15}$, Simeon(ites) Jg 1$_{17}$, עַם *people* 1 S 14$_{31}$ 2 K 21$_{24}$||2 C 33$_{25}$ Is 58$_{4}$ 2 C 13$_{17}$ 14$_{13.14}$, גּוֹי *nation* Mc 4$_{14}$, בַּיִת *house* Jg 1$_{25}$ Is 58$_{4}$.

Aaron Ex 8$_{12.13}$, Abijah 2 C 13$_{17}$, Abimelech Jg 9$_{43}$, Abishai 1 S 26$_{8}$ 2 S 1 C 18$_{13}$, Abner 2 S 2$_{22.23}$, Abram Gn 14$_{15.17}$, Absalom 2 S 13$_{30}$ 15$_{14}$, Adoni-zedek Jos 10$_{4}$,

Adrammelech 2 K 19_{37}||Is 37_{38}, Ahithophel 2 S 17_{2}, Amaziah 2 K $14_{5.7}$||2 C 25_{11} 2 K $14_{10.10}$||2 C 25_{19} 2 C 25_{14}, Amos Am 9_{1}, Asa 2 C $14_{13.14}$, Baasha 1 K $15_{27.29}$ 16_{7}, Balaam Nm $22_{23.25.27.28.32}$, Balak Nm 22_{6}, Benaiah 2 S $23_{20.21}$||1 C $11_{22.23}$, Ben-hadad 1 K 15_{20}, David 1 S $17_{35.46.49.50.57}$ $18_{6.7.27}$ $19_{5.8}$ $21_{10.12}$ $23_{2.2.5}$ 27_{9} 29_{5} 30_{17} 2 S 1_{1} $5_{20.25}$||1 C $14_{11.16}$ 2 S $8_{1.2.3.5.9.10}$||1 C $18_{1.2.3.5.9.10}$ 2 S 8_{13} 10_{18} 12_{9} Si 47_{4}, Debir Jos 10_{4}, Eglon Jg 3_{13}, Eleazar 2 S 23_{10} 1 C 11_{14}, Elhanan 2 S 21_{19}||2 C 20_{5}, Elijah 2 K 2_{8}, Elisha 2 K 2_{14}, Esau Gn $32_{9.12}$, Chedorlaomer Gn $14_{5.7}$, Gideon Jg 6_{16} 8_{11}, Goliath 1 S 17_{9}, Hadad Gn 36_{35}||1 C 1_{46}, Hazael 2 K 10_{32}, Hezekiah 2 K 18_{8}, Hoham Jos 10_{4}, Hoshea 2 K 15_{30}.

Ishbi-benob 2 S 21_{16}, Ishmael 2 K 25_{25} Jr $40_{14.15}$ $41_{2.3.9.16.18}$, Japhia Jos 10_{4}, Jehoiakim Jr 26_{23}, J(eh)oram 2 K 8_{21}||2 C 21_{9}, Jehozabad 2 K 12_{22}, Jehu 2 K $9_{7.24}$ $10_{11.17}$, Jephthah Jg 11_{33}, Joab 2 S 3_{27} 20_{10} 1 K 11_{15} Ps 60_{2} 1 C 20_{1}, Joash 2 K $13_{17.28.18.19.19.19.25}$, Johanan Jr 40_{15}, Jonathan (son of Saul) 1 S 13_{3} 14_{14}, Jonathan (son of Shimei) 2 S 21_{21}||1 C 20_{7}, Joshua Jos $8_{21.22}$ 10_{20+8t} $11_{10.12.17}$ 12_{7}, Jozacar 2 K 12_{22}, Menahem 2 K $15_{14.16}$, Moses Ex $7_{17.20}$ $17_{5.6}$ Nm 20_{11} Dt 4_{46} 29_{6} Jos 12_{6} $13_{12.21}$, Nebuchadrezzar Jr 21_{7} 29_{21} 43_{11} $46_{2.13}$ 49_{28}, Nebuzaradan 4QpsEzek[a] 16.1$_{4}$, Nehemiah Ne 13_{25}, Passhur Jr 20_{2}, Pekah 2 K 15_{25}, Piram Jos 10_{4}, Samson Jg 14_{19} $15_{8.15.16}$, Saul 1 S 13_{4} 14_{48} $15_{3.7}$ $18_{7.11}$ 19_{10} 20_{33} 21_{12} 29_{5} 2 S 21_{2} 4QCommGenA 4_{1} (הכ[ה]), Shallum 2 K 15_{10}, Shamgar Jg 3_{31}, Shammah 2 S 23_{12}, Sharezer 2 K 19_{37}||Is 37_{38}, Sibbecai 2 S 21_{18}||1 C 20_{4}, Zedekiah 1 K 22_{24}||2 C 18_{23}, Zimri 1 K $16_{10.11.16}$.

אִישׁ *man* Ex 2_{11} $21_{18.20.26}$ Dt 19_{11} Jos $7_{3.5.5}$ Jg 12_{4} $20_{45.48}$ 1 S 7_{11} $17_{9.25.26.27}$ 18_{27} 2 S 18_{11} 1 K $20_{20.35.37.37}$ 22_{34}||2 C 18_{33} 2 K 3_{23} 25_{25} Jr $41_{2.9}$ 4QHalakhah[a] 3.1$_{3}$ ([וה]כה [איש]) CD 11_{6} Siloam tunnel inscr.$_{4}$, בֵּן *son* Gn 36_{35}||1 C 1_{46} Nm 22_{6} Jos 19_{47} Jg $1_{25(mss)}$ 3_{31} 18_{27} 20_{31} 2 S $4_{6.7}$ $21_{17.19}$||2 C 20_{5} 2 S 21_{21}||1 C 20_{7} 2 S $23_{10.12.20.21}$||1 C $11_{22.23}$ 1 K 15_{27} 22_{24}||2 C 18_{23} 2 K 12_{22} $14_{5.7}$ $15_{10.14.25.30}$ 18_{8} $19_{37(Qr)}$||Is 37_{38} 2 K 25_{25} Jr $40_{14.15.15}$ $41_{2.16.18}$ 1 C 4_{43} 11_{14} 18_{13} 2 C 25_{13}, of Israel Dt 4_{46} Jos 9_{18} 10_{20} 11_{14} $12_{1.6.7}$ Jg 3_{29} 21_{10} 1 K 20_{29}, of Judah Jg 1_{8}, of man (in ref. to Ezekiel) Ezk 5_{2} 6_{11} 21_{14}, אָח *brother* Gn 32_{12} 37_{21} Jg 1_{17} 2 S 21_{21}.

מֶלֶךְ *king* Gn $14_{5.7}$ Jos 10_{4} Jg 3_{13} 1 S 22_{19} 1 K 20_{21} (or em. וַיִּקַּח *and he took*) 20_{21} 2 K 3_{19} $6_{21.21.22.22}$ $13_{17.18.18.19.19.19}$ 14_{7} 25_{21}||Jr 52_{27} Jr 20_{4} 21_{7} 26_{23} 29_{21} $46_{2.13}$ 2 C 28_{5}, פַּרְעֹה *Pharaoh* Jr 47_{1}, שַׂר *commander* 1 K 11_{15} 15_{20} Jr 37_{15}, שָׁלִישׁ *officer* 2 K $10_{25.25}$ 15_{25}, רַב *chief* of bodyguards 4QpsEzek[a] 16.1$_{4}$, רָץ *guard* 2 K $10_{25.25}$ 11_{12}, נַעַר *lad* 1 S 2_{14} 2 S 1_{15} 18_{15}, עֶבֶד *servant* Jos 12_{6} 1 S 17_{36} 19_{5} 2 S 2_{31} 13_{28} 2 K $12_{21.22}$ 14_{5}||2 C 25_{3} Jr 43_{11}, כֹּהֵן *priest* 4QpHos[b] 2_{3}, מַשְׂכִּיל *instructor* 4QS[d] 9_{8}, רֵעַ *neighbour* 1 K 20_{35}, יֹשֵׁב *inhabitant* Gn 34_{30}, מצא ptc. *one who finds* Gn 4_{15}, שֹׁמֵר *sentry* Ca 5_{7}, נשׂא ptc. *one who bears* armour 1 S 14_{14} 2 S 18_{15}.

רָשָׁע *wicked one* Ex 2_{13}, רֹצֵחַ *slayer* Nm 35_{11} Dt 19_{4} Jos $20_{3.5}$, נכה hi. ptc. *one who strikes* Nm $35_{16.17.18.21}$, גֹּאֵל *avenger* Dt 19_{6}, אֹרֵב *ambush* Jg 20_{37}, לקח ptc. *one who takes* bribe Dt 27_{25}, חֹצֵב *stonemason* Siloam tunnel inscr.$_{4}$, רֹאשׁ *head*, i.e. column Jg 9_{44} 1 S 11_{11}, לֵב *heart*, i.e. conscience 1 S 24_{6} 2 S 24_{10}.

אַרְיֵה *lion* 1 K $20_{36.36}$ Jr 5_{6}, כְּפִיר *young lion* 4QpNah 3.1$_{5}$, צָפִיר *he-goat* Dn 8_{7}, תּוֹלַעַת *worm* Jon 4_{7}, שׁוֹשַׁנָּה *lily* Ho 14_{6} (or em.; see Prep.), שֹׁרֶשׁ *root* 1QH 16_{23}, חֹטֶר *shoot* Is 11_{4}, נֵצֶר *branch* Is 11_{4} Si $40_{15(Bmg)}$ (B נקה ni. *be held innocent*), מַטֶּה *rod* Is 14_{6}, שֵׁבֶט *rod* Is 14_{6}, חֶרֶב *sword* Zc 13_{7} 1QH 13_{15} (ה[כו]תה), בָּרָד *hail* Ex $9_{25.25}$, שָׁרָב *scorching wind* Is 49_{10}, שֶׁמֶשׁ *sun* Is 49_{10} Jon 4_{8} Ps 121_{6}, יָרֵחַ *moon* Ps 121_{6}, צְלִיל *cake* Jg $7_{13(Qr)}$, אֶחָד *one* 2 S 14_{6}, מִי *who?* Dt 21_{1} 2 S 11_{21} 2 K 10_{9}, אֵלֶּה *these* Ezk $9_{5.7.8}$ 1 C 4_{41}, אֲשֶׁר *one who* Jos 15_{16} Jg 1_{12}.

Subj. not specified, Ex $21_{12.15.19}$ Lv $24_{18.21}$ Nm $35_{15.21.24.30}$ Dt $25_{2.2.3.3.11}$ 27_{24} Jos 20_{9} 2 S 5_{8} 14_{7} 2 K 9_{27} 14_{6} Is 10_{20} 14_{29} 27_{7} 50_{6} 66_{3} Jb 16_{10} Pr $17_{10.26}$ 19_{25} $23_{13.14.35}$ Lm 3_{30} 1 C 11_{6} 2 C 25_{16}.

<OBJ> Abel-beth-maacah 1 K 15_{20}, Abel-maim 2 C 16_{4}, Ai Jos 7_{3} 8_{24}, Ashdod 1 S 5_{6}, Chinneroth 1 K 15_{20}, Dan 1 K 15_{20}||2 C 16_{4}, Debir Jos 10_{39}, Eglon Jos 10_{35}, Gaza Jr 47_{1}, Ijon 1 K 15_{20}||2 C 16_{4}, Gibeon Jos 10_{4}, Hebron Jos 10_{37}, Jerusalem/Zion Jg 1_{8} Jr 14_{19}, Kir-hareseth 2 K 3_{25}, Kiriath-sepher Jos 15_{16} Jg 1_{12}, Lachish Jos 10_{32}, Leshem Jos 19_{47}, Libnah Jos 10_{30}, Makkedah Jos 10_{28}, Nob 1 S 22_{19}, Rabbah 1 C 20_{1}, Tappuah 2 K 15_{16}, Ziklag 1 S 30_{1}, עִיר *city* Jos $10_{37.39}$ 11_{12} Jg 1_{25} 11_{33} 20_{37} 1 S 22_{19} 15_{14} 2 K 3_{19} 2 C 14_{13}

1QpHab 3$_{1}$.

Amalek(ites) 1 S 14$_{48}$ 15$_{3.7}$ 30$_{17}$ 2 S 1$_{1}$ 4QCommGenA 4$_{1}$ (הכ[ה]), Ammon(ites) 1 S 11$_{11}$, Amorites Gn 14$_{7}$ Dt 7$_{2}$, Aram(aeans) 1 K 20$_{29}$ 2 K 13$_{17.19.19}$, Ashdodites 1 S 5$_{6}$, Canaanites Dt 7$_{2}$ Jg 1$_{4.5.17}$, Chaldaeans Jr 41$_{3}$, Edom(ites) 2 K 8$_{21}$||2 C 21$_{9}$ 2 K 14$_{7.10}$||2 C 25$_{19}$ Ps 60$_{2}$, Egypt(ians) Ex 2$_{12}$ 3$_{20}$ 1 S 4$_{8}$ Ps 136$_{10}$, Emim Gn 14$_{5}$, Ephraim(ites) Jg 12$_{4}$, Gibeonites 2 S 21$_{2}$, Girgashites Dt 7$_{2}$, Gittite 2 S 21$_{19}$, Hittite(s) Dt 7$_{2}$ 2 S 12$_{9}$, Hivites Dt 7$_{2}$, Israel(ites) Lv 26$_{24}$ Dt 28$_{22.27.28.35}$ Jg 3$_{13}$ 1 K 14$_{15}$ 2 K 10$_{32}$ Is 27$_{7.7}$ 57$_{17}$ 60$_{10}$ Jr 5$_{3.6}$ 14$_{19}$ 20$_{4}$ 30$_{14}$ Am 4$_{9}$ Hg 2$_{17}$ Ps 121$_{6}$ 1 C 21$_{7}$ 4QpHos^{a} 2$_{12}$, Jebusites Dt 7$_{2}$ 2 S 5$_{8}$ 1 C 11$_{6}$, Jews Jr 41$_{3}$, Judah 2 C 28$_{17}$, Kedar Jr 49$_{28}$, Meunim 1 C 4$_{41(Qr)}$ (Kt Meinim), Midian(ites) Gn 36$_{35}$||1 C 1$_{46}$ Nm 25$_{17}$ Jg 6$_{16}$, Moab(ites) Jg 3$_{29}$ 2 S 8$_{2}$||1 C 18$_{2}$ 2 K 3$_{24}$, Perizzites Dt 7$_{2}$ Jg 1$_{4.5}$, Philistia/Philistine(s) Jg 3$_{31}$ 15$_{8}$ 1 S 7$_{11}$ 17$_{26.27.46.49.50.57}$ 18$_{6}$ 19$_{5}$ 21$_{10}$ 2 S 5$_{20}$||1 C 14$_{11}$ 2 S 5$_{25}$ 8$_{1}$||1 C 18$_{1}$ 2 S 21$_{17}$ 23$_{12}$ 2 K 18$_{8}$ Is 14$_{29}$ 1 C 11$_{14}$, Rephaim Gn 14$_{5}$, Zuzim Gn 14$_{5}$, עַם *people* Ex 9$_{15}$ Nm 14$_{12.45}$ 21$_{35}$ Dt 2$_{33}$ Jos 10$_{33}$ Jg 9$_{43}$ 11$_{21}$ 18$_{27}$ Is 5$_{25}$ 9$_{12}$ 10$_{24}$ 14$_{6}$ Jr 21$_{7}$ Mc 6$_{13}$, גּוֹי *nation* Dt 7$_{2}$ 2 K 6$_{18}$ Ps 135$_{10}$, בַּיִת *house* 1 K 15$_{29}$ 16$_{7.11}$ 2 K 9$_{7}$ Am 3$_{15}$ 6$_{11}$, מַמְלָכָה *kingdom* Jr 49$_{28}$.

Abimelech 2 S 11$_{21}$, Abinadab 1 S 31$_{2}$, Abner 2 S 3$_{27}$, Absalom 2 S 18$_{11.15}$, Ahab Jr 29$_{21}$, Ahaziah 2 K 9$_{27}$, Ahiman Jg 1$_{10}$, Amasa 2 S 20$_{10}$, Amnon 2 S 13$_{28}$, Asahel 2 S 2$_{22.23}$, Ben-hadad 2 K 13$_{25}$, Cain Gn 4$_{15}$, Chedorlaomer Gn 14$_{17}$, David 1 S 24$_{6}$ 2 S 21$_{16}$, Elah 1 K 16$_{10}$, Evi Jos 13$_{21}$, Gedaliah 2 K 25$_{25}$ 40$_{14.15}$ 41$_{2.16.18}$, Goliath 1 S 17$_{9}$ 21$_{10}$ 2 S 21$_{19}$ 24$_{10}$, Hadadezer 2 S 8$_{3.10}$||1 C 18$_{3.10}$, Horam Jos 10$_{33}$, Hur Jos 13$_{21}$, Ish-bosheth 2 S 4$_{6.7}$, Ishmael Jr 40$_{15}$, Jacob Gn 34$_{30}$, J(eh)oram 2 K 8$_{28.29}$||2 C 22$_{5.6}$ 2 K 9$_{15.24}$, Jeremiah Jr 18$_{18}$ 20$_{2}$, Joash 2 K 12$_{21.22}$ Jr 37$_{15}$, Job Jb 2$_{7}$, Jonathan 1 S 20$_{33}$ 31$_{2}$, Joseph Gn 37$_{21}$, Lahmi 2 C 20$_{5}$, Malchishua 1 S 31$_{2}$, Micaiah 1 K 22$_{24}$||2 C 18$_{23}$, Nadab 1 K 15$_{27}$, Og Nm 21$_{35}$ Dt 1$_{4}$ 3$_{3}$ 29$_{6}$ Jos 12$_{6}$, Pekah 2 K 15$_{30}$, Pekahiah 2 K 15$_{25}$, Reba Jos 13$_{21}$, Rekem Jos 13$_{21}$, Seraiah 2 K 25$_{21}$||Jr 52$_{27}$, Shallum 2 K 15$_{14}$, Saph 2 S 21$_{18}$, Saul 2 S 21$_{12}$, Sennacherib 2 K 19$_{37}$||Is 37$_{38}$, Sheshai Jg 1$_{10}$, Shobach 2 S 10$_{18}$, Sihon Dt 1$_{4}$ 2$_{33}$ 4$_{46}$ 29$_{6}$ Jos 12$_{6}$ 13$_{21}$ Jg 11$_{21}$, Sippai 1 C 20$_{4}$, Talmai Jg 1$_{10}$, Uriah (Hittite) 2 S 12$_{9}$, Uriah (prophet) Jr 26$_{23}$, Uzzah 2 S 6$_{7}$||1 C 13$_{10}$, Zechariah 2 K 15$_{10}$, Zedekiah (king) Jr 21$_{7}$, Zedekiah (prophet) Jr 29$_{21}$, Zephaniah 2 K 25$_{21}$||Jr 52$_{27}$, Zur Jos 13$_{21}$.

אָדָם *human being* Jos 11$_{14}$ Jr 21$_{6}$ Si 10$_{13}$, אִישׁ *man* Gn 19$_{11}$ Ex 2$_{11}$ 21$_{12}$ Dt 25$_{11}$ Jos 7$_{5.5}$ 8$_{21}$ Jg 1$_{4}$ 14$_{19}$ 15$_{15.16}$ 20$_{45}$ 1 S 5$_{9}$ 6$_{19}$ 17$_{9.25}$ 2 S 8$_{5}$||1 C 18$_{5}$ 2 S 21$_{21}$||1 C 20$_{7}$ 2 S 23$_{21}$||1 C 11$_{23}$ 1 K 20$_{20+7t}$ 2 K 10$_{25.25}$ 25$_{21}$||Jr 52$_{27}$ Is 66$_{3}$ Jr 33$_{5}$ Ne 13$_{25}$, גֶּבֶר *man* Lm 3$_{30}$ Si 47$_{4}$, אִשָּׁה *woman* Jg 21$_{10}$, אָב *father* Ex 21$_{15}$ 2 K 14$_{5}$||2 C 25$_{3}$, אֵם *mother* Gn 32$_{12}$ Ex 21$_{15}$ 11QT 52$_{6}$, בֵּן *son* Nm 21$_{35}$ Dt 2$_{33}$ Jg 11$_{33}$ 20$_{48}$ 1 S 31$_{2}$ 2 S 8$_{3}$ 11$_{21}$ 13$_{30}$ 1 K 16$_{10}$ 2 K 13$_{25}$ 15$_{10.14.25.30}$ Jr 2$_{30}$ 29$_{21}$ 40$_{15.15}$ 41$_{2.16.18}$ Pr 23$_{35}$ 2 C 25$_{11}$, of Israel 1QDM 1$_{9}$ ([להכו]ת), אָח *brother* 2 S 14$_{7}$ 2 C 20$_{5}$.

מֶלֶךְ *king* Gn 14$_{15.17}$ Nm 21$_{35}$ Dt 1$_{4}$ 3$_{3}$ 4$_{46}$ 29$_{6}$ Jos 10$_{10+7t}$ 11$_{8.8.10.12.17}$ 12$_{1.6.7}$ 13$_{21}$ 2 S 8$_{3}$||1 C 18$_{3}$ 2 S 17$_{2}$ 1 K 16$_{16}$ 22$_{34}$||2 C 18$_{33}$ 2 K 8$_{29}$ 9$_{27}$ 14$_{5}$||2 C 25$_{3}$ 2 K 19$_{37}$||Is 37$_{38}$ Ps 136$_{17}$, פַּרְעֹה *Pharaoh* Ex 9$_{15}$, שַׂר *commander* 2 S 10$_{18}$ 2 K 8$_{21}$||2 C 21$_{9}$ 2 K 25$_{21}$||Jr 52$_{27}$, נָשִׂיא *chief* Jos 13$_{21}$, נָסִיךְ *prince* Jos 13$_{21}$, נָדִיב *noble* Pr 17$_{26}$, שֹׁפֵט *judge* Mc 4$_{14}$, אֲרִאֵל *hero* 2 S 23$_{20}$||1 C 11$_{22}$ (if em. אֲרִ[י]אֵל perh. *[sons of] Ariel*), עֶבֶד *servant* Ex 21$_{20}$ 2 K 14$_{5}$ Jr 21$_{7}$, אָמָה *female servant* Ex 21$_{20}$, נַעַר *lad* 2 S 1$_{15}$ Jb 1$_{15.17}$ Pr 23$_{13.14}$, בְּכוֹר *firstborn* Ex 12$_{12.29}$ Nm 3$_{13}$ 8$_{17}$ 33$_{4}$ Ps 78$_{51}$ 105$_{36}$ 135$_{8}$, טַף *infant* Jg 21$_{10}$, זָכוּר *male* Dt 20$_{13}$=11QT 62$_{9}$, זָכָר *male* 1 K 11$_{15}$, סָרִיס *eunuch* 2 K 25$_{21}$||Jr 52$_{27}$, כֹּהֵן *priest* 2 K 25$_{21}$||Jr 52$_{27}$, נָבִיא *prophet* Jr 20$_{2}$ 2 C 25$_{16}$, שֹׁמֵר *keeper* of threshold 2 K 25$_{21}$||Jr 52$_{27}$, סֹפֵר *secretary* 2 K 25$_{21}$||Jr 52$_{27}$, רֵעַ *neighbour* Ex 2$_{13}$ 21$_{18}$ Dt 19$_{4.11}$ 27$_{24}$ Jos 20$_{5}$ 2 K 3$_{23}$, יֹשֵׁב *inhabitant* Dt 13$_{16}$=11QT 55$_{6}$ Jos 9$_{18}$ Jg 21$_{10}$ Is 10$_{24}$ Jr 21$_{6}$ Ezk 32$_{15}$.

כְּסִיל *fool* Pr 17$_{10}$, לֵץ *scorner* Pr 19$_{25}$, רֹצֵחַ *murderer* Dt 19$_{6}$, אֹיֵב *enemy* Jos 10$_{20}$ 1 S 26$_{8}$ Ps 3$_{8}$ 11QT 58$_{12}$, צַר *adversary* Ps 78$_{66}$, חַי *living being* Gn 8$_{12}$, חָלָל *slain one* Dt 21$_{1}$ Jg 20$_{31.39}$, רָשָׁע *wicked*, i.e. guilty, *one* Dt 25$_{2.3}$, קשׁר ptc. *one who conspires* 2 K 21$_{24}$||2 C 33$_{25}$, חַיִל *army* 2 S 8$_{9}$||1 C 18$_{9}$ Jr 37$_{10}$ 46$_{2}$ Zc 9$_{4}$, מַחֲנֶה *company* Gn 32$_{9}$ Jg 8$_{11}$ 1 C 14$_{15.16}$, נְצִיב *garrison* 1 S 13$_{3.4}$, רֹכֵב *rider* Zc 12$_{4}$, רֶכֶב *chariotry* 1 K 20$_{21}$ (or em.; see Subj.), רַגְלִי *infantry* 1 K 20$_{29}$, רֹעֶה *shepherd* Zc 13$_{7}$=CD 19$_{8}$, female lover Ca 5$_{7}$, שׁאר ni. ptc. *one who remains* 2 K 10$_{11.17}$ Jr 21$_{7}$, שְׁאָר *remnant* Is 10$_{20}$, שְׁאֵרִית *remnant* 1 C 4$_{43}$, פְּלֵיטָה *escaped ones* Is 10$_{20}$.

כַּף *hand* 2 K 11$_{12}$ Ezk 21$_{14.22}$ 22$_{13}$, עַיִן *eye* Ex 21$_{26}$, לְחִי *cheek* Ps 3$_{8}$ Jb 16$_{10}$, נֶפֶשׁ *soul*, i.e. life, person Lv 24$_{17.18}$ Nm 35$_{11.15.30}$ Dt 27$_{25}$ Jos 10$_{30.32.37}$ 11$_{11}$ 20$_{3.9}$ 1QH 13$_{15}$ (ה[כו]תה).

אֲרִי *lion* 1 S 17$_{35}$, דֹּב *bear* 1 S 17$_{35}$, סוּס 1 K 20$_{21}$ (or em.; see Subj.) Zc 12$_{4,4}$, אָתוֹן *she-ass* Nm 22$_{23.25.27.28.32}$, אַיִל *ram* Dn 8$_{7}$, בְּהֵמָה *beast* Lv 24$_{21}$ Jr 21$_{6}$ 11QT 55$_{8}$ CD 11$_{6}$, עֵשֶׂב *plant* Ex 9$_{25}$, קִיקָיוֹן *castor oil plant* Jon 4$_{7}$, גֶּפֶן *vine* Ps 105$_{33}$, תְּאֵנָה *fig tree* Ps 105$_{33}$, עֵץ *tree* 4QpsEzek^{a} 2$_{10}$ 4QNarrA 1$_{9}$, שֹׁרֶשׁ *root* Ho 14$_{6}$ (or em.; see Prep.).

שָׂדֶה *field*, i.e. country Gn 14$_{7}$, אֶרֶץ *land* Nm 32$_{4}$ Jos 10$_{40.41}$ 1 S 27$_{9}$ Is 11$_{4}$ Jr 43$_{11}$ 46$_{13}$ Ml 3$_{24}$, גְּבוּל *border*, i.e. territory 1 S 5$_{6}$ 2 K 15$_{16}$ 18$_{8}$, הַר *hill country* Jos 10$_{40}$, שְׁפֵלָה *lowland* Jos 10$_{40}$, בִּקְעָה *valley* 4QSela 9.14 ([ו]יכו), אֶשֶׁד *slope* Jos 10$_{40}$, נֶגֶב *Negeb* Jos 10$_{40}$, יְאֹר *Nile* Ex 7$_{25}$ 17$_{5}$, נָהָר *river* Is 11$_{15}$, מַיִם *water* Ex 7$_{20}$ 2 K 2$_{8.14}$, גַּל *wave* Zc 10$_{11}$, עָפָר *dust* Ex 8$_{12.13}$, סֶלַע *rock* Nm 20$_{11}$, צוּר *rock* Ps 78$_{20}$.

אֹהֶל *tent* Jg 7$_{13}$ 1 C 4$_{41}$ 2 C 14$_{14}$, כַּפְתּוֹר *capital* Am 9$_{1}$, קֶשֶׁת *bow* Ezk 39$_{3}$, נֵבֶל *harp* 4QS^{d} 9$_{8}$, גַּרְזֶן *pickaxe* Siloam tunnel inscr.$_{4}$, מִסְכְּנוֹת *stores* 2 C 16$_{4}$, מַעֲשֶׂה *work* Hg 2$_{17}$, רֵאשִׁית *first* of strength, i.e. firstborn Ps 78$_{51}$ 105$_{36}$, שְׁלִישִׁית *third part* Ezk 5$_{2}$, אֶחָד *one* 2 S 14$_{6}$, שְׁלֹשֶׁת אֲלָפִים *three thousand* 2 C 25$_{13}$, שְׁמוֹנָה עָשָׂר אֶלֶף *eighteen thousand* 2 S 8$_{13}$||1 C 18$_{12}$, מֵאָה שְׁמוֹנִים וַחֲמִשָּׁה אֶלֶף *a hundred and eighty-five thousand* 2 K 19$_{35}$||Is 37$_{36}$, אֲשֶׁר *one who* 2 K 6$_{22}$ 69$_{27}$ 1QSb 1$_{7}$ ([יכה את אשר]), אֵלֶּה *these* Jos 8$_{22}$ 2 K 10$_{9}$, כֹּל *all* Ex 9$_{25}$ Jg 9$_{44}$ 2 K 15$_{16}$; obj. not specified, Nm 35$_{16.17.18.21.21}$.

Obj. with which struck, מַכָּה *stroke* Nm 11$_{33}$ Dt 25$_{3}$ Jos 10$_{10.20}$ Jg 11$_{33}$ 15$_{8}$ 1 S 6$_{19}$ 14$_{14}$ 19$_{8}$ 23$_{5}$ 1 K 20$_{21}$ 2 K 8$_{29}$||2 C 22$_{6}$ 2 K 9$_{15}$ Is 14$_{6}$ 27$_{7}$ Jr 30$_{14}$ Est 9$_{5}$ 2 C 13$_{17}$ 28$_{5}$ 1QDM 1$_{9}$ ([להכו]ת ... [מכה]) 11QPsAp^{a} 4$_{4}$ (מ[כה]), הֶרֶג *slaughter* Est 9$_{5}$, אַבְדָן *destruction* Est 9$_{5}$, חֵרֶם *ban* Ml 3$_{24}$.

<PREP> לְ of instrument, *by (means of), with*, + פֶּה *mouth*, i.e. edge, of sword Nm 21$_{24}$ Dt 13$_{16}$=11QT 55$_{6}$ Dt 20$_{13}$=11QT 62$_{9}$ Jos 8$_{24}$ 10$_{28.30.32.35.37.39}$ 11$_{10.11.12.14}$ 19$_{47}$ Jg 1$_{8.25}$ 18$_{27}$ 20$_{37.48}$ 21$_{10}$ 1 S 22$_{19}$ 2 S 15$_{14}$ 2 K 10$_{25}$ Jr 21$_{7}$ Jb 1$_{15.17}$ 11QT 55$_{8}$ 58$_{12}$.

לְ *into*, + נַחַל *wadi* Is 11$_{15}$; of accompaniment, *with, in*, + שָׁוְא *vanity* Jr 2$_{30}$.

בְּ of place, *in(to)*, + Aphek 2 K 13$_{17}$, Ashteroth-karnaim Gn 14$_{5}$, Bezek Jg 1$_{4}$, Edom 1 K 11$_{15}$, Egypt Ps 78$_{51}$, Ge-melah 2 S 8$_{13}$||1 C 18$_{12}$ 2 K 14$_{7}$||2 C 25$_{11}$ Ps 60$_{2}$, Gibbethon 1 K 15$_{27}$, Gibeon Jos 10$_{10}$, Gilboa 2 S 21$_{12}$, Ibleam 2 K 15$_{10}$ (if em.; see below), Ham Gn 14$_{5}$, Ramah 2 K 8$_{29}$||2 C 22$_{6}$, Samaria 2 K 15$_{14.25}$, Shaveh-kiriathaim Gn 14$_{5}$, עִיר *city* Ezk 9$_{7}$, מַעֲלֶה *ascent* 2 K 9$_{27}$, מוֹרָד *descent* Jos 7$_{5}$, עֵמֶק *valley* 1 S 21$_{10}$, מִדְבָּר *steppe* 1 S 4$_{8}$, שָׂדֶה *field*, i.e. country Gn 36$_{35}$||1 C 1$_{46}$ 1 S 4$_{2}$, אֶרֶץ *land* Ex 12$_{29}$ Nm 3$_{13}$ 8$_{17}$ Ps 105$_{36}$, *ground* 1 S 26$_{8}$, צוּר *rock* 1QH 16$_{23}$, קִיר *wall* 1 S 18$_{11}$ 19$_{10}$, מְסִלָּה *highway* Jg 20$_{31}$, אָפִיק *channel* Si 40$_{15(Bmg)}$, יָם *sea* Zc 9$_{4}$ 10$_{11}$, מַעֲרָכָה *battle-line* 1 S 4$_{2}$, מַחֲנֶה *camp* 2 K 19$_{35}$||Is 37$_{36}$, אֹהֶל *tent* Ps 78$_{51}$, אַרְמוֹן *fortress* 2 K 15$_{25}$, דּוּד *pot* 1 S 2$_{14}$, כִּיֹּר *pot* 1 S 2$_{14}$, פָּרוּר *pot* 1 S 2$_{14}$, קַלַּחַת *cauldron* 1 S 2$_{14}$.

בְּ of time, *in, on*, + יוֹם *day* 1 S 14$_{31}$ 1 K 20$_{29}$, לַיְלָה *night* Ps 121$_{6}$, שָׁנָה *year* Jr 46$_{2}$, נְעוּרִים *youth* Si 47$_{4}$.

בְּ partitive, *(from) among*, + Aram(aeans) 2 S 8$_{5}$||1 C 18$_{5}$, Egypt(ians) Nm 33$_{4}$, Philistines 1 S 18$_{27}$, עַם *people* 1 S 6$_{19.19}$, אִישׁ *man* Jg 20$_{39}$.

בְּ of instrument, *by (means of), with*, + אִישׁ *man* 4QpNah 3.1$_{5}$, גָּדוֹל *great one* 4QpNah 3.1$_{5}$, יָד *hand* Nm 35$_{21}$, כַּף *hand* Ezk 6$_{11}$, אֶגְרֹף *fist* Ex 21$_{18}$ Is 58$_{4}$ CD 11$_{6}$, לְחִי *jawbone* Jg 15$_{15.16}$, לָשׁוֹן *tongue* Jr 18$_{18}$, מַקֵּל *rod* Nm 22$_{27}$, מַטֶּה *rod* Ex 7$_{17}$ 17$_{5}$ Nm 20$_{11}$, שֵׁבֶט *rod* Ex 21$_{20}$ Is 10$_{24}$ 11$_{4}$ 30$_{31}$ Pr 23$_{13.14}$ 4Q417 1.1$_{27}$, מַלְמָד *goad* Jg 3$_{31}$, חֶרֶב *sword* Dt 28$_{22}$ 2 S 12$_{9}$ 20$_{10}$ 2 K 19$_{37}$||Is 37$_{38}$ Jr 20$_{4}$ 26$_{23}$ 41$_{2}$ Ezk 5$_{2}$, חֲנִית *spear* 1 S 19$_{10}$ 26$_{8}$, אַחֲרֵי *back* of spear 2 S 2$_{23}$, אֶבֶן *stone* Ex 21$_{18}$ Nm 35$_{17}$, כְּלִי *instrument* Nm 35$_{16.18}$, בָּרָד *hail* Hg 2$_{17}$, עִוָּרוֹן *blindness* Dt 28$_{28}$ Zc 12$_{4}$, סַנְוֵרִים *blindness* Gn 19$_{11}$ 2 K 6$_{18}$, שַׁחֶפֶת *consumption* Dt 28$_{22}$, קַדַּחַת *fever* Dt 28$_{22}$, חַרְחֻר *violent heat* Dt 28$_{22}$, דַּלֶּקֶת *inflammation* Dt 28$_{22}$, שְׁחִין *boil* Dt 28$_{27.35}$ Jb 2$_{7}$, גָּרָב *eczema* Dt 28$_{27}$, טְחֹר *haemorrhoid* Dt 28$_{27(Qr)}$ 1 S 5$_{6(Qr)}$, עֹפֶל *haemorrhoid* Dt 28$_{27(Kt)}$ 1 S 5$_{6(Kt)}$, חֶרֶס *itch* Dt 28$_{27}$, שִׁגָּעוֹן *madness* Dt 28$_{28}$ Zc 12$_{4}$, תִּמְהוֹן *confusion* Dt 28$_{28}$ Zc 12$_{4}$, שִׁדָּפוֹן *blight* Dt 28$_{22}$ Am 4$_{9}$ Hg 2$_{17}$, יֵרָקוֹן *mildew* Dt 28$_{22}$ Am 4$_{9}$ Hg 2$_{17}$, דֶּבֶר *pestilence* Ex 9$_{15}$ Nm 14$_{12}$, מַכָּה *plague* 1 S 4$_{8}$, רָעָב *hunger* 4QpHos^{a} 2$_{12}$, עֵרֹם *nakedness* 4QpHos^{a} 2$_{12}$, פלא ni. ptc. *wonder* Ex 3$_{20}$.

בְּ of accompaniment, *with, in,* + שְׁגָגָה *inadvertence* Nm $35_{11.15}$ Jos $20_{3.9}$, אֵיבָה *enmity* Nm 35_{21}, סֵתֶר *secrecy* Dt 27_{24}, אַף *anger* Jr 33_5, קֶצֶף *anger* Is 60_{10}, חֵמָה *wrath* Jr 33_5, עֶבְרָה *wrath* Is 14_6.

בְּ introducing object, + Aram(aeans) 1 K 20_{21}, Ephraim 4QpHos[b] 2_3, Philistines 1 S 14_{31} 19_8 $23_{2.2.5}$ 2 S 23_{10}, עַם *people* Nm 11_{33} 22_6 2 S 24_{17}, מַחֲנֶה *camp*, i.e. army 2 S 5_{24}, Ahaz 2 C $28_{5.5.23}$, David 1 S 18_{11} 19_{10}, בֵּן *son* of Israel 2 C 13_{17}, מֶלֶךְ *king* 2 C 28_{23}, אֹיֵב *enemy* Est 9_5, אֶרֶץ *land* Ex 12_{13}, צוּר *rock* Ex 17_6, אֶלֶף *thousand* 1 S 18_7 21_{12} 29_5, רְבָבָה *ten thousand* 1 S 18_7 21_{12} 29_5.

בְּ *in respect of,* + בְּכוֹר *firstborn* Ps 136_{10}; *as,* + רִאשׁוֹן (fem.) *first (of all)* 1 C 11_6.

בִּבְלִי *without,* + דַּעַת *knowledge*, i.e. unintentionally Dt 19_4 Jos $20_{3.5}$.

כְּ *as* Jg 6_{16}, + לְבָנוֹן *Lebanon* Ho 14_6 (or em. לְבָנוֹן to לִבְנֶה *poplar*, and em. נכה hi. to נטה hi. *extend* or ירה hi. *throw*); *as at,* + פַּעַם *time* Jg 20_{31} (כְּפַעַם בְּפַעַם *as at other times*); *according to,* + דָּבָר *word* 2 K 6_{18}, כֹּל *everything* Jos 10_{32}; *about* (a specified number of), + אִישׁ *man* Jg $3_{29.31}$ 20_{31} 1 S 4_2.

מִן partitive, *(some) of, from (among),* + Ashekelon Jg 14_{19}, Benjamin(ites) Jg 20_{45} 2 S 2_{31}, Jews Ne 13_{25}, עַם *people* Jg 20_{31}, עִיר *city* 2 C 25_{13}, אִישׁ *man* Jos 7_5.

מִן of direction, time, *from,* + יָד *hand* Ezk 39_3, Havilah 1 S 15_7, Michmash 1 S 14_{31}, Tirzah 2 K 15_{16}, נֶשֶׁף *twilight* 1 S 30_{17}, עֶרֶב *evening* 1 S 30_{17}.

מִן ... עַד *from ... to,* i.e. both ... and, + אָדָם ... בְּהֵמָה *human being ... beast* Ex 9_{25} 12_{12} Ps 135_8, אִישׁ ... אִשָּׁה *man ... woman* 1 S 22_{19}, עִיר מְתֹם ... בְּהֵמָה *entire city ... beast* Jg 20_{48} (+ עַד כָּל־הַנִּמְצָא *and all that was found*), קָטֹן ... גָּדוֹל *small ... great* Gn 19_{11} 1 S 1 S 5_9, בְּכוֹר ... בְּכוֹר *firstborn ... firstborn* Ex 12_{29}, עוֹלֵל ... יוֹנֵק *child ... suckling* 1 S 22_{19} (+ וְשׁוֹר וַחֲמוֹר וָשֶׂה *and ox and ass and sheep*), מִגְדַּל נוֹצְרִים ... עִיר מִבְצָר *watch tower ... fortified city* 2 K 18_8.

מִן ... עַד *from ... as far as,* + Kadesh-barnea ... Gaza Jos 10_{41}, Baal-gad ... Mount Halak Jos 12_7, Aroer ... Minnith, Abel-keramim Jg 11_{33}, Geba ... Gezer 2 S 5_{24}||1 C 14_{16}, כַּף ... קָדְקֹד *sole* of foot ... *crown* of head Jb 2_7.

עַד *as far as,* + Azekah Jos 10_{10}, Gaza 2 K 18_8, Gibeon Jos 10_{41}, Makkedah Jos 10_{10}.

עַד־מִתַּחַת לְ *as far as below,* + Beth-car 1 S 7_{11}.

אֶל *to,* + כַּף *hand* Ezk $21_{14.22}$; *in,* + חֹמֶשׁ *abdomen* 2 S 2_{23} 4_6 20_{10}, מֶרְכָּבָה *chariot* 2 K 9_{27}; *on account of,* + דָּם *blood(shed)* Ezk 22_{13}, בֶּצַע *gain* Ezk 22_{13}.

עַל *upon, against* or introducing object, + לְחִי *cheek* 1 K 22_{24}||2 C 18_{23} Mc 4_{14}, רֹאשׁ *head* Jon 4_8, מַיִם *water* Ex 7_{17}, גַּרְזֶן *pickaxe* Siloam tunnel inscr.4 ([ג]רזן).

עַל *on account of, for,* + חַטָּאת *sin* Lv 26_{24}, שַׁל perh. *impudence* 2 S 6_7, יֹשֶׁר *uprightness* Pr 17_{26}.

עַל *together with, in addition to, more than with,* + בֵּן *son* 11QT 52_6, בַּיִת *house* Am 3_{15}, אֶרֶץ *land* of Naphtali 1 K 15_{20}, אֵלֶּה *these (lashes)* Dt 25_3.

כְּדֵי *according to, in proportion to,* + רִשְׁעָה *wickedness* Dt 25_2.

בְּקֶרֶב *within,* + אֶרֶץ *land* 1QDM 1_9 (להכו[ת]).

בֵּין *between,* + זְרוֹעַ *shoulder* 2 K 9_{24}, דֶּבֶק *appendage* 1 K 22_{34}||2 C 18_{33}, שִׁרְיָן *breastplate* 1 K 22_{34}||2 C 18_{33}.

בְּעֵבֶר *beyond,* + יַרְדֵּן *Jordan* Jos 12_7.

סְבִיבוֹת *around,* + עִיר *city* Ezk 5_2.

לִפְנֵי *before,* + עֵדָה *assembly* Nm 32_4, שֹׁפֵט *judge* Dt 25_2.

לְעֵינֵי *in the sight of, in the presence of,* + Israelites Jr 29_{21}, פַּרְעֹה *Pharaoh* Ex 7_{17}, עֶבֶד *servant* Ex 7_{17}.

קֳבָל *before,* + עָם *people* 2 K 15_{10} (or em. קָבָל־עָם to בְּיִבְלְעָם *in Ibleam*).

ה- of direction, *to(wards),* + Aijalon 1 S 14_{31}, Hamath 1 C 18_3, יָם *west* Jos 12_7, אֶרֶץ *ground* 2 S 2_{22} 18_{11} 2 K 13_{18}.

נכה hi. + noun without preposition or ה- of direction, חֹמֶשׁ *(in the) abdomen* 2 S 3_{27}, בַּיִת *(in the) house* 2 K 12_{21}.

<COLL> נכה || הלם *beat* Pr 23_{35}, רקע *stamp* Ezk 6_{11}, שׁבר pi. *break* Ex 9_{25} Ps 3_8 (+) 105_{33} Dn 8_7 (+) 11QT 58_{12}, טרף *tear* Ho 6_1, פצע *wound* Ca 5_7, מרט *pull out hair* Is 50_6 Ne 13_{25} (+), נפל hi. *cause to fall* 2 K 3_{19} (+) Ezk 39_3.

|| מות hi. *put to death* Jos 10_{26} 11_{17} 1 S $17_{35.50}$ 2 S 4_7 6_7||1 C 13_{10} 13_{28} 14_6 18_{15} 21_{17} 1 K 16_{10} 2 K 15_{30} 25_{21} Is 11_4; + מות *die* Ex $21_{12.20}$ Nm $35_{16.17.18}$ Dt 19_{11} 2 S 1_{15} 3_{27}

6_{7} 10_{18} 2 K 12_{22} $15_{10.14.25}$ 25_{25} Jr 21_{6} 41_{2}.

|| הרג *kill* Gn 4_{15} (+) Ps 135_{10}, pu. *be killed* Is 27_{7} (+), שׁחט *slaughter* Is 66_{3} (+), זבח *sacrifice* Is 66_{3} (+), ערף *break neck* Is 66_{3} (+).

|| כנע hi. *subdue* 2 S 8_{1}||1 C 18_{1}, נצח pi. *defeat* 11QT 58_{12}, שׁדד *despoil* Jr 5_{6}, בזז *plunder* 1QpHab 3_{1}, הרס *tear down* 1 C 20_{1}, נתשׁ *pluck up* 1 K 14_{15} (+).

+ חרם hi. *devote to ban of destruction* Dt 7_{2} 13_{16}=11QT 55_{6} Jos $10_{28.35.37.39.40}$ $11_{11.12}$ Jg 1_{17} 1 S 15_{3} 1 C 4_{41}, שׁחת pi. *destroy* Ex 21_{26}, כלה pi. *destroy* Jr 5_{3}, שׁמד hi. *destroy* Jos 11_{14} 2 K 10_{17}, שׁמד ni. *be destroyed* Gn 34_{30}, כחד ni. *be destroyed* Ex 9_{15}, שׁמם hi. *make desolate* Mc 6_{13}.

+ לחם ni. *fight* Jos 19_{47} Jg $1_{5.8}$ 12_{4} 1 S 17_{9} 19_{8} 23_{5} 2 S 8_{10}||1 C 18_{10}, לכד *capture* Jos $10_{28.32.35.37.39}$ $11_{12.17}$ 15_{16} 19_{47} Jg $1_{8.12}$, ירשׁ hi. *dispossess* Jos 13_{12} 19_{47}, ענשׁ *punish* Pr 17_{26}, יכח hi. *reprove* Pr 19_{25}.

:: רחם pi. *have compassion on* Is 60_{10}, חמל *spare* Ezk 9_{5}, חוס *pity* Ezk 9_{5}.

+ adverb or noun used adverbially, אַחֲרֵי־כֵן *afterwards* Jos 10_{26}, אָחוֹר *(so as to make fall) backwards* Ps 78_{66}, לָמָּה *why?* Ex 2_{13} 2 S 2_{22} Jr 40_{15} 2 C 25_{16}, יוֹמָם *by day* Ps 121_{6}, פַּעַם אַחַת *once* 1 S 26_{8}, פַּעֲמַיִם *twice* Nm 20_{11}, פְּעָמִים (specified number of) *times* 2 K $13_{18.19.25}$, זֶה שָׁלֹשׁ רְגָלִים *these three times* Nm $22_{28.32}$, אַרְבָּעִים *(with) forty (lashes)* Dt 25_{3}, מֵאָה *a hundred (times)* Pr 17_{10}, לְבַד *alone* 2 S 17_{2}, שָׁם *there* 2 S 3_{27} 5_{20}||1 C 14_{11} 2 S 6_{7} 18_{11}.

Inf. abs. + finite form of נכה hi., Dt 13_{16} 1 K 20_{37} (וַיַּכֵּהוּ הָאִישׁ הַכֵּה וּפָצֹעַ *and the man struck him, striking and wounding him*) 2 K 14_{10}.

בִּן הַכּוֹת *son of beating*, i.e. one who deserves to be beaten Dt 25_{2}, לֹא־אֹסִף עוֹד לְהַכּוֹת *I will never again strike* Gn 8_{21}, וְהִכַּנִי אֵם עַל־בָּנִים *and he shall destroy me, mother with children* Gn 32_{12}, לֹא נַכֶּנּוּ נָפֶשׁ *let us not strike him with respect to his soul*, i.e. fatally Gn 37_{21}, sim. Dt $19_{6.11}$ Jr $40_{14.15}$, לְהַכּוֹת נֶפֶשׁ דָּם נָקִי *to strike someone fatally, (shedding) innocent blood* Dt 27_{25}, וַיַּךְ אוֹתָם שׁוֹק עַל־יָרֵךְ *and he struck them hip upon thigh* Jg 15_{8}, וַנַּכֵּהוּ עַד־בִּלְתִּי הִשְׁאִיר־לוֹ שָׂרִיד *and we defeated him until no survivor was left to him* Dt 3_{3}, vars. Nm 21_{35} Jos 8_{22} $10_{28.30.33.37.39.40}$ 11_{8} 2 K 10_{11}, לְהַכּוֹתָם מַכָּה גְדֹלָה־מְאֹד עַד־תֻּמָּם *to destroy them with a very great slaughter until they were wiped out* Jos 10_{20}, וְהִכִּיתָ אֶת־אֲרָם עַד־כַּלֵּה *and you shall defeat the Aramaeans until you have made and end of them* 2 K 13_{19}, vars. 2 K 13_{17} Si 10_{13}, וְהִכָּה הַבַּיִת הַגָּדוֹל רְסִיסִים וְהַבַּיִת הַקָּטֹן בְּקִעִים *and he will strike the great house into fragments and the small house into bits* Am 6_{11}.

Also 4QCat 2_{2} 4QHalakhah[a] $3_{.14}$ (ה[מ]כה]) 4QD[h] 6_{2} perh. 4Q418 64_{1}.

<SYN> הלם *beat*, רקע *stamp*, שׁבר pi. *break*, טרף *tear*, פצע *wound*, מרט *pull out hair*, נפל hi. *cause to fall*, מות hi. *put to death*, הרג *kill*, הרס *tear down*, כנע hi. *subdue*, נצח pi. *defeat*, שׁדד *despoil*, בזז *plunder*.

<ANT> רחם pi. *have compassion on*, חמל *spare*, חוס *pity* .

Ho. 16.0.1 Pf. הֻכָּה (הוּכָּה), הֻכְּתָה, הֻכֵּיתִי, הֻכּוּ; impf. תֻּכּוּ; + waw וַיֻּכּוּ; וְהֻכָּה; ptc. מֻכֶּה, מֻכָּה, מֻכִּים, מֻכֵּי—

1. be beaten (Zc 13_{6} 1QM 14_{7}), as punishment (Ex $5_{14.16}$).

2. be struck fatally, be killed, of thief breaking in (Ex 22_{1}); as punishment (Nm $25_{14.14.15.18}$), in battle (Jr 18_{21}).

3. be defeated (Ezk 33_{21} 40_{1}).

4. be struck with plague, etc. (1 S 5_{12}); of plant, **be struck, blighted,** causing withering (Ho 9_{16} Ps 102_{4}).

5. be struck as punishment, by Y. (Is 1_{5} 53_{4}).

<SUBJ> Ephraim Ho 9_{16}, עַם *people* Is 1_{5}, גּוֹי *nation* Is 1_{5}, עִיר *city* Ezk 33_{21} 40_{1}, Cozbi Nm 25_{18}, אִישׁ *man* Nm $25_{14.14}$ 1 S 5_{12}, אִשָּׁה *woman* Nm 25_{15}, בֵּן *son* Is 1_{5}, בַּת *daughter* Nm 25_{18}, אָחוֹת *sister* Nm 25_{18}, זֶרַע *offspring* Is 1_{5}, בָּחוּר *youth* Jr 18_{21}, עֶבֶד *servant* Ex 5_{16} Is 53_{4}, שֹׁטֵר *officer* Ex 5_{14}, נָבִיא *servant* Zc 13_{6}, גַּנָּב *thief* Ex 22_{1}, לֵב *heart* Ps 102_{4}; subj. not specified, 1QM 14_{7}.

<PREP> לְ of direction, *to*, + שְׁכֶם *shoulder* 1QM 14_{7}; בְּ of time, *on*, + יוֹם *day* Nm 25_{18}; of instrument, *by (means of), with*, + עֹפֶל *haemorrhoid* 1 S $5_{12(Kt)}$, טְחֹר *haemorrhoid* 1 S $5_{12(Qr)}$; עַל *on account of*, + דָּבָר *matter* Nm 25_{18}; אֵת *with*, + Midianite (fem.) Nm 25_{14}.

נכה ho. + noun without preposition, בַּיִת *(in the) house* Zc 13_{6}, מָתְנַיִם *(from the) loins* 1QM 14_{7}.

<COLL> נכה ho. || הרג pass. *be killed* Jr 18_{21}; + נגע

pass. *be stricken* Is 53$_4$, ענה pu. *be afflicted* Is 53$_4$, מות *die* Ex 22$_1$, יָבֵשׁ *wither* Ho 9$_{16}$ Ps 102$_4$; + adverb, עַל־מֶה *why?* Is 1$_5$.

מֻכֵּה אֱלֹהִים *struck of,* i.e. by, *God* Is 53$_4$, מֻכֵּי־חֶרֶב *killed of,* i.e. by, *the sword* Jr 18$_{21}$.

<SYN> הרג pass. *be killed.**

⇨ נָכֶה *stricken,* נֵכֶה *stricken,* נָכוֹן *blow,* מַכָּה *stroke.*

[נָכֶה] 3.0.1 adj. **stricken**—cstr. נְכֵה (Q נכי)—**1. lame,** used attributively of בֵּן *son* 2 S 4$_4$ 9$_3$. <CSTR> נְכֵה רַגְלַיִם *lame of,* i.e. in, *the feet* 2 S 4$_4$ 9$_3$ (רַגְלָיִם).

2. contrite, meek, a. used attributively of אִישׁ 4QWays^a 1a.24 ([איש]). <CSTR> נכי שכלו *meek of,* i.e. in, *his mind* 4QWays^a 1a.24 (+ עָנָו *humble one*).

b. as noun, **contrite one,** <CSTR> נְכֵה־רוּחַ *contrite one of,* i.e. in, *spirit* Is 66$_2$ (1QIsa^a נכאי *downcast one[s] of;* + עָנִי *poor one,* חָרֵד *trembling one*). <PREP> אֶל *to,* + נבט hi. *look* Is 66$_2$.*

⇨ נכה hi. *strike.*

[נֵכֶה] 1 adj. **stricken**—pl. נֵכִים—as noun, **stricken one,** <SUBJ> אסף ni. *gather* intrans. Ps 35$_{15}$ (or em. כְּנָכְרִים *as strangers*), קרע *tear* Ps 35$_{15}$, דמם *cease* Ps 35$_{15}$.

⇨ נכה hi. *strike.*

נְכֹה 8 pr.n.m. **Neco**—נְכוֹ—king of Egypt at time of Josiah, <SUBJ> ראה *see* 2 K 23$_{29}$, בוא *bring* 2 C 36$_4$, עלה *go up* 2 K 23$_{29}$||2 C 35$_{20}$, שׁלח *send* 2 C 35$_{20}$, אסר *bind* 2 K 23$_{33}$, נתן *give,* i.e. impose 2 K 23$_{33}$, לקח *take* 2 K 23$_{34}$||2 C 36$_4$, מלך hi. *make king* 2 K 23$_{34}$, סבב hi. *turn,* i.e. change, name 2 K 23$_{34}$, לחם ni. *fight* 2 C 35$_{20}$, מות hi. *kill* 2 K 23$_{29}$. <OBJ> קרא *meet* 2 K 23$_{29}$||2 C 35$_{20}$, בהל pi. *hasten* 2 C 35$_{20}$. <CSTR> חֵיל ... נְכוֹ *army of ... Neco* Jr 46$_2$, דִּבְרֵי *words of* 2 C 35$_{22}$. <APP> פַּרְעֹה *Pharaoh* 2 K 23$_{29.33.34.35}$ Jr 46$_2$, מֶלֶךְ *king* 2 K 23$_{29}$||2 C 35$_{20}$ Jr 46$_2$. <PREP> לְ of direction, *to* 2 C 35$_{20}$, + נתן *give* 2 K 23$_{35}$; בְּ *against,* + לחם ni. *fight* 2 C 35$_{20}$.*

נְכוֹ, see נְכֹה *Neco.*

נָכוֹן I 1 n.[m.] **blow,** or **push, thrust,** <NOM CL> נָכוֹן לְמוֹעֲדֵי רָגֶל *a blow is to those whose steps are faltering* Jb 12$_5$ (unless נָכוֹן III *ready*).*

⇨ נכה hi. *strike.*

נָכוֹן II 1 pr.n.m. **Nacon,** owner of threshing floor where oxen stumbled when carrying ark, appar. ident. with Chidon at 1 C 13$_9$, <CSTR> גֹּרֶן נָכוֹן *threshing floor of Nacon* 1 C 13$_9$.

נָכוֹן III *certainty,* see כון *be upright,* Ni.

נכח, see נגח *gore,* Pi.

נֹכַח 25.5.3 n.[m.] **front**—Si, Q נוכח; sf. נִכְחוֹ—**1.** נֹכַח **a.** noun, **thing in front,** אכל כאיש נכח *eat like a man the thing in front (of you)* Si 34$_{16}$(Bmg).

b. prep. **in front of, before, opposite (to),** followed by noun or suffix in ref. to noun, Y. Jg 18$_6$, Aramaeans 1 K 22$_{35}$||2 C 18$_{34}$, Baal-zephon Ex 14$_2$, אִישׁ *man* Si 36$_{14}$, בוא ptc. *one who comes* Ezk 46$_9$, פָּנִים *face* Jr 17$_{16}$ Ezk 14$_{3.4.7}$ Lm 2$_{19}$ Si 8$_{15}$, עַיִן *eye* Pr 5$_{21}$, חַיִּים *life* Si 36$_{14}$, מַעֲלֶה *ascent* Jos 18$_{17}$, בַּיִת *house* Est 5$_1$, פֶּתַח *entrance* Est 5$_1$, שֻׁלְחָן *table* Ex 26$_{35}$||40$_{24}$ 11QT 9$_{13}$ ([נוכח השולח]ן), אוֹר *light* Si 36$_{14}$, אֵלֶּה *these* 1 K 20$_{29}$, זֶה *this* 11QT 33$_{10}$.

With verb, היה *be* Jr 17$_{16}$, הלך *go* Si 8$_{15}$, יצא *go out* Ezk 46$_9$ (נִכְחוֹ יֵצֵא *he shall go out in front of himself,* i.e. straight ahead), עמד *stand* Est 5$_1$, hi. *prop oneself up* 2 C 18$_{34}$, ho. *be propped up* 1 K 22$_{35}$, ישׁב *sit* Est 5$_1$, חנה *encamp* Ex 14$_2$ 1 K 20$_{29}$, שׂים *place* Ex 26$_{35}$||40$_{24}$ Ezk 14$_{4.7}$, נתן *give,* i.e. place Ezk 14$_3$ 11QT 9$_{13}$ ([נוכח]), שׁפך *pour* Lm 2$_{19}$.

2. נֹכַח לְ **in front of, opposite,** followed by noun, מַעֲלֵה *ascent* Jos 15$_7$.

3. לְנֹכַח **a. in front of,** followed by noun, צֹאן *flock* Gn 30$_{38}$; with verb, יצג hi. *place* Gn 30$_{38}$.

b. for, on behalf of, followed by noun, אִשָּׁה *wife* Gn 25$_{21}$; with verb, עתר *entreat* Gn 25$_{21}$.

c. as adverb, **forward, straight ahead,** of נבט hi. *look* Pr 4$_{25}$ (+ נֶגֶד *in front of*).

4. אֶל־נֹכַח פְּנֵי **towards the front of,** followed by noun, אֹהֶל *tent* Nm 19$_4$; with verb, נזה hi. *sprinkle* Nm

194.

5. אֶל־נֹכַח **to(wards) the front of,** followed by noun or suffix in ref. to noun, David 1 S 264 (if em. אֶל־נָכוֹן *of a certainty* to נִכְחוֹ), אֹהֶל 4QTohBb 15 ([א]ל[נוכח א]ון]הל); with verb, בוא *come* 1 S 264 (if em.), נזה hi. *sprinkle* 4QTohBb 15.

6. עַד־נֹכַח **as far as opposite,** followed by noun, Gibeah Jg 2043, Jebus Jg 1910, Lebo-hamath Ezk 4720; with verb, בוא *come* Jg 1910, דרך hi. *tread* Jg 2043.

Also 11QT 82.

⇒ cf. נָכֹחַ *straight.*

[נָכֹחַ] 8.2.2 adj. **straight**—sf. נְכֹחוֹ; fem. sing. נְכֹחָה (Si נְכוֹחָה); masc. plur. נְכֹחִים (Q נכוחים); fem. נְכֹחוֹת (Q נכוחות)—**straight, straightforward, right, 1.** used attributively of דָּבָר *word* Pr 2426.

2. in nom. cl., used predicatively of דָּבָר *matter* 2 S 153 (|| טוֹב *good*), הִיא *she* (wisdom) Si 622, כֹּל *all* Pr 89 (|| יָשָׁר *upright*); נכח בעיני י׳ *it is straightforward,* i.e. easy, *in the sight of Y.* Si 1121.

3. as noun, **a. straightforward one, upright one,** <PREP> בְּ introducing object, + נחם pi. *console* 4QSf 51 (בנכוחים; =1QS בנכאים *the stricken*).

b. straightness, uprightness, rectitude, (1) masc. sing., <COLL> הֹלֵךְ נְכֹחוֹ *one who walks in his uprightness* Is 572.

(2) fem. sing., <SUBJ> יכל *be able* Is 5914, בוא *come* Is 5914. <OBJ> עשׂה *do* Am 310.

(3) fem. plur., <OBJ> חזה *see* Is 3010 1QH 1015. <CSTR> אֶרֶץ נְכֹחוֹת *land of uprightness* Is 2610, חוזי נכוחות *ones who see uprightness* 1QH 1015.*

<SYN> §2 יָשָׁר *upright,* טוֹב *good.*

⇒ cf. נֹכַח *front.*

נכל 4 vb. **be deceitful—Qal** 1 Ptc. נוֹכֵל—ptc. as noun, **deceitful one, cheat,** <SUBJ> נדר *vow* Ml 114, זבח *sacrifice* Ml 114. <NOM CL> אָרוּר נוֹכֵל *cursed is the cheat* Ml 114.

Pi. 1 Pf. נִכְּלוּ—**deceive,** <SUBJ> Midianites Nm 2518. <PREP> לְ introducing object, + Israelites Nm 2518. <COLL> נִכְלֵיהֶם אֲשֶׁר־נִכְּלוּ לָכֶם *their deceitfulness with which they deceived you* Nm 2518.

Htp. 2 + waw וַיִּתְנַכְּלוּ; inf. הִתְנַכֵּל—**act deceitfully against, deal craftily with,** <SUBJ> אָח *brother* Gn 3718 (+ לַהֲמִיתוֹ *to kill him*), צַר *adversary* Ps 10525. <OBJ> Joseph Gn 3718. <PREP> בְּ introducing object, + עֶבֶד *servant* Ps 10525.

⇒ נֵכֶל *deceitfulness.*

[נֵכֶל] 1.0.1 n.[m.] **deceitfulness**—pl. sf. נִכְלֵיהֶם—**deceitfulness, craft,** <OBJ> נתן *give* Pr 1315 (if em. אֵיתָן *continuous* to אֵת נֵכֶל).* <PREP> בְּ of instrument, *by (means of), with,* + צרר *show hostility* Nm 2518; of accompaniment, *with, in,* + הלך *walk* 1QpHab 35 (|| מִרְמָה *deceit*). <COLL> נִכְלֵיהֶם אֲשֶׁר־נִכְּלוּ לָכֶם *their deceitfulness with which they deceived you* Nm 2518.

<SYN> מִרְמָה *deceit.*

⇒ נכל *be deceitful.*

*[נְכָנְיָהוּ] 0.0.0.1 pr.n.[m.] **Neconiah,** Arad ost. 721.

⇒ כון *be upright* + י׳ *Y.*

[נֶכֶס] 5.1.2 n.m. **wealth**—sf. Q נכסו; pl. נְכָסִים; cstr. Si נכסי; sf. Q נכסי—**wealth, riches,** <NOM CL> נכסו לכול קד[ושי] *his wealth is to all the holy ones of* 4QSh A1. <OBJ> נתן *give* Ec 518 62 2 C 112, שׁאל *ask for* 2 C 111. <CSTR> נכסי שקר *wealth of falsehood,* i.e. dishonestly obtained Si 58. <ADJ> רַב *much* Jos 228. <PREP> בְּ of accompaniment, *with,* + שׁוב *go back* Jos 228; מִן *from* XḤev/Se 4911; עַל introducing object, + בטח *trust in* Si 58. <COLL> נְכָסִים || עֹשֶׁר *riches* Ec 518 62 2 C 111.12, מִקְנֶה *cattle* Jos 228, זָהָב *gold* Jos 228, כֶּסֶף *silver* Jos 228, נְחֹשֶׁת *bronze* Jos 228, בַּרְזֶל *iron* Jos 228, שַׂלְמָה *garment* Jos 228, בַּיִת *house* XḤev/Se 4911, כָּבוֹד *glory* Ec 62 2 C 111.12.

<SYN> עֹשֶׁר *riches,* מִקְנֶה *cattle,* זָהָב *gold,* כֶּסֶף *silver,* נְחֹשֶׁת *bronze,* בַּרְזֶל *iron,* שַׂלְמָה *garment,* בַּיִת *house,* כָּבוֹד *glory.*

נכר I 40.4.16 vb. **recognize—Ni.** 1.1 Pf. נִכְּרוּ; impf. Si ינכר—**be recognized,** <SUBJ> אִישׁ *man* Si 1128, נָזִיר *prince* Lm 48. <PREP> בְּ of place, time, *in, at,* + חוּץ *street* Lm 48, אַחֲרִית *end* Si 1128.

Pi. 2 Pf. נִכַּר; impf. תְּנַכֵּרוּ—**recognize, have regard**

for, <SUBJ> Y. Jb 34$_{19}$ (+ נשׂא פָּנִים *lift face*, i.e. show partiality), friends of Job Jb 21$_{29}$. <OBJ> שׁוֹעַ *noble* Jb 34$_{19}$, אוֹת *sign* Jb 21$_{29}$. <PREP> לִפְנֵי *before*, + דַּל *poor one* Jb 34$_{19}$.

Hi. $_{38.3.16}$ Pf. הִכִּיר (הִכִּירוֹ), הכרתה Q, הכרתי Q, הִכִּירוּ, הכירום Q, הִכִּרֻהוּ, הִכִּירֻהוּ); impf. יַכִּיר (יַכִּירֶנּוּ, יַכִּירָנוּ), 2ms תַּכִּיר, אַכִּיר, יַכִּירוּם, תַּכִּירוּ; + waw וַיַּכֵּר (וַיַּכִּרֵהוּ), וַיַּכִּירָהּ, וַיַּכִּרֵם, (וָאַכִּירָה); impv. הַכֶּר־; ptc. מַכִּיר (מַכִּירֵךְ), מַכִּירִים; inf. abs. הַכֵּר; cstr. Si הכר (הַכִּירֵנִי)—**recognize** person or thing known (Gn 27$_{23}$ 37$_{33}$ 38$_{26}$ 42$_{7.8.8}$ Jg 18$_{3}$ 1 S 26$_{17}$ 1 K 18$_{7}$ 20$_{41}$ Jb 2$_{12}$ Ru 3$_{14}$), face, i.e. show partiality (Dt 1$_{17}$ 16$_{19}$ Pr 24$_{23}$ 28$_{21}$ Si 38$_{10}$ 11QT 51$_{12}$), **be acquainted with, know** (Ps 103$_{16}$ Jb 7$_{10}$ 24$_{13.17}$ 34$_{25}$ Si 15$_{19}$ 4QapPs[b] 45a$_{2}$ 4QHod[a] 1$_{3}$), **acknowledge*** (Dt 21$_{17}$ [or em.; see Subj.] 33$_{9}$ Is 61$_{9}$ 63$_{16}$ Jr 24$_{5}$ Jb 1$_{12}$ Dn 11$_{39}$ 1QH 6$_{19}$ 27$_{9}$ [[הכר]נו]), **pay attention (to)** (2 S 3$_{36}$ Jr 24$_{5}$ Ps 142$_{5}$ Ru 2$_{10.19}$ Si 38$_{20[Bmg]}$ 1QH 13$_{13}$ 15$_{13}$), **discern, understand, realize** (Jb 4$_{16}$ Ne 6$_{12}$ 13$_{24}$ 1QH 16$_{13}$ 4QapPs[b] 13$_{2}$ 4QMMT C$_{20}$), **distinguish** (Ezr 3$_{13}$), **observe, examine (in order to recognize)** (Gn 31$_{32}$ 37$_{32}$ 38$_{25}$).

<SUBJ> Y. Jr 24$_{5}$ Jb 34$_{25}$ (unless נכר IV *repudiate* or V *disapprove*), Israel(ites) Dt 1$_{17}$ 16$_{19}$ Si 15$_{19}$ 1QH 13$_{13}$ 15$_{13}$, Naamathite Jb 2$_{12}$, Shuhite Jb 2$_{12}$, Temanite Jb 2$_{12}$ 4$_{16}$, עַם *people* 2 S 3$_{36}$ Ezr 3$_{13}$, Bildad Jb 2$_{12}$, Boaz Ru 2$_{10}$, Eliphaz Jb 2$_{12}$ 4$_{16}$, Isaac Gn 27$_{23}$, Israel (Jacob) Is 63$_{16}$, Joseph Gn 42$_{7.8}$, Judah 38$_{25.26}$, Laban Gn 31$_{32}$, Nehemiah Ne 6$_{12}$, Obadiah 1 K 18$_{7}$, Saul 1 S 26$_{17}$, Zophar Jb 2$_{12}$, אָדָם *human being* 4QRitMar 1$_{1}$ (א[דם]), אִישׁ *man* Dt 21$_{17}$ (or em. יְבַכֵּר *he shall regard as firstborn*) 33$_{9}$ Jg 18$_{3}$ Jb 2$_{12}$ Ru 3$_{14}$, אָב *father* Gn 37$_{32.33}$, בֵּן *son* Ne 13$_{24}$ Si 38$_{10.20(Bmg)}$ (B זכר *remember*), אָח *brother* Gn 42$_{8}$, מֶלֶךְ *king* 1 K 20$_{41}$, שֹׁפֵט *judge* 11QT 51$_{12}$, שֹׁטֵר *officer* 11QT 51$_{12}$, רֵעַ *friend* Jb 2$_{12}$, נֹאֵף *adulterer* Jb 24$_{17}$, ראה ptc. *one who sees* Is 61$_{9}$, worshipper 1QH 6$_{19}$ 27$_{9}$ ([הכר]נו) 4QapPs[b] 45a$_{2}$ 4QHod[a] 1$_{3}$, מָקוֹם *place* Ps 103$_{16}$ Jb 7$_{10}$, אֲשֶׁר *one who* Dn 11$_{39}$; subj. not specified, Ps 142$_{5}$ Jb 24$_{13}$ Pr 24$_{23}$ 28$_{21}$ Ru 2$_{19}$ 1QH 16$_{13}$ 4QapPs[b] 13$_{2}$ 4QMMT C$_{20}$.

<OBJ> Israelites Is 63$_{16}$, גָּלוּת *exiles* Jr 24$_{5}$, Elijah 1 K 18$_{7}$, Jacob Gn 27$_{23}$, Job Jb 2$_{12}$, Joseph Gn 42$_{8}$, Ruth Ru 2$_{10.19}$, אִישׁ *man* 1 K 20$_{41}$, בֵּן *son* Dt 21$_{17}$ (or em.; see Subj.), אָח *brother* Gn 42$_{7.8}$ Dt 33$_{9}$, בְּכוֹר *firstborn* Dt 21$_{17}$ (or em.; see Subj.), מֶלֶךְ *king* Dn 11$_{39}$, רֵעַ *neighbour* Ru 3$_{14}$, זֶרַע *seed*, i.e. offspring Is 61$_{9}$, צֶאֱצָא *offspring* Is 61$_{9}$, ירד ptc. *one who goes down* to Sheol Jb 7$_{10}$, פָּנִים *face* Dt 1$_{17}$ 16$_{19}$ Pr 24$_{23}$ 28$_{21}$ Si 38$_{10}$ 11QT 51$_{12}$, קוֹל *voice* Jg 18$_{3}$ 1 S 26$_{17}$ Ezr 3$_{13}$, רִנָּה *cry* 1QH 13$_{13}$, צִיץ *flower* Ps 103$_{16}$, כְּתֹנֶת *tunic* Gn 37$_{33}$, מַרְאֶה *appearance* Jb 4$_{16}$, דֶּרֶךְ *way* Jb 24$_{13}$, מַעְבָּד *deed* Jb 34$_{25}$ (unless נכר IV *repudiate* or V *disapprove*), מִפְעָל *deed* Si 15$_{19}$, מַעֲנֶה *answer* 1QH 15$_{13}$, מִשְׁפָּט *judgment* 1QH 27$_{9}$ ([הכרנו משפטיכה]), בַּלָּהָה *terror* Jb 24$_{17}$, תּוֹעֵבָה *abomination* 4QapPs[b] 45a$_{2}$, שֹׁחַד *bribe* 1QH 6$_{19}$ (ש[וח]ד), אַחֲרִית *end* Si 38$_{20(Bmg)}$.

<PREP> לְ *for (the purpose of)*, + טוֹבָה *good* Jr 24$_{5}$; (distinguish) *in relation to, from*, + קוֹל *sound* Ezr 3$_{13}$; introducing object, + חַטָּאת *sin* 4QHod[a] 1$_{3}$ (ל[חטאת]), יָגוֹן *grief* 4QHod[a] 1$_{3}$ ([יגון]); בְּ of accompaniment, *in*, + מִשְׁפָּט *judgment* Dt 1$_{17}$ Pr 24$_{23}$ 11QT 51$_{12}$; מִן of direction, *from*, + מָקוֹר *source* 1QSb 3$_{19}$ (להכי[ן]רכה).

<COLL> נכר hi. || ידע *know* Dt 33$_{9}$ Is 63$_{16}$ 1QH 15$_{13}$ 4QapPs[b] 13$_{2}$, ראה *see* Dt 33$_{9}$ 1QH 16$_{13}$ (+), חשׁב *consider* 1QH 16$_{13}$; + לקח שֹׁחַד *take a bribe* Dt 16$_{19}$ 11QT 51$_{12}$, נטה מִשְׁפָּט hi. *pervert justice* Dt 16$_{19}$ 11QT 51$_{12}$; + adverb, כֵּן *so* Jr 24$_{5}$, עוֹד *still* Ps 103$_{16}$ Jb 7$_{10}$, לָכֵן *therefore* Jb 34$_{25}$ (unless נכר IV *repudiate* or V *disapprove*).

הַכֶּר־נָא לְךָ מָה עִמָּדִי *observe what there is of yours with me* Gn 31$_{32}$, הַכֶּר־נָא הַכְּתֹנֶת בִּנְךָ הִיא אִם־לֹא *examine whether it is the tunic of your son or not* Gn 37$_{32(Qr)}$, הַכֶּר־נָא לְמִי הַחֹתֶמֶת וְהַפְּתִילִים וְהַמַּטֶּה הָאֵלֶּה *examine whose these are, the signet and the cord and the staff* Gn 38$_{25}$, וַיַּכֵּר אֹתוֹ ... כִּי מֵהַנְּבִיאִים הוּא *and he recognized him ... that he was one of the prophets* 1 K 20$_{41}$, יַכִּירוּם כִּי הֵם זֶרַע בֵּרַךְ י׳ *they will acknowledge them, that they are offspring whom Y. has blessed* Is 61$_{9}$, הַכֵּר־פָּנִים לֹא־טוֹב *to show partiality is not good* Pr 28$_{21}$, var. Pr 24$_{23}$, אֵינָם מַכִּירִים לְדַבֵּר יְהוּדִית *they did not understand how to speak Judaean* Ne 13$_{24}$, אנחנו מכירים שבאוו *we realize that* some of the blessings and curses *have come* 4QMMT C$_{20}$, יַכִּיר לָתֶת לוֹ פִּי שְׁנַיִם *he shall acknowledge* the firstborn, *by giving him a double portion* Dt 21$_{17}$ (or em.; see Subj.).

Also 1QH fr. 8$_{6}$ 1QpPs 3$_{2}$ 4QapJoshua[a] 6.2$_{6}$ 4QShir[b]

127$_2$.

<SYN> ידע *know*, ראה *see*, חשב *consider*.

Ho. be known, הַמֻּכֶּרֶת גּוֹיִם בִּזְנוּנֶיהָ *the one known of*, i.e. by, *nations for her harlotry* Na 3$_4$ (if em. הַמֹּכֶרֶת *the one who sells*). <PREP> בְּ of instrument, *by (means of)*, + זְנוּנִים *harlotry* Na 3$_4$.

Htp. 1 Impf. יִתְנַכֶּר־—**make oneself known,** <SUBJ> נַעַר *lad* Pr 20$_{11}$. <PREP> בְּ of instrument, *by (means of), with*, + מַעֲלָל *deed* Pr 20$_{11}$.*

⇒ הַכָּרָה *recognition*, (?) מַכָּר *acquaintance*.

נכר II 7.2.1 vb. **be foreign—Ni.** 1.0.1 Impf. יִנָּכֵר; inf. Q הנכר—**act as a stranger, disguise oneself,** <SUBJ> Israelites 4QapPs[b] 69$_8$, שׂנא ptc. *one who hates* Pr 26$_{24}$. <PREP> בְּ of instrument, *by (means of), with*, + שָׂפָה *lip* Pr 26$_{24}$.

Pi. 3.1 Pf. נִכַּר; impf. יְנַכְּרוּ; + waw וַיְנַכְּרוּ—**1. misconstrue,** <SUBJ> צַר *adversary* Dt 32$_{27}$.

2. treat as a stranger, alienate, reject, <SUBJ> Y. 1 S 23$_7$ (unless נכר III pi. *sell*; or em. מכר *he has sold*), Israelites Jr 19$_4$, זָר *stranger* Si 11$_{34}$ (וינכר[י]ך). <OBJ> David 1 S 23$_7$ (unless נכר III pi. *sell*; or em.; see Subj.), מָקוֹם *place* Jr 19$_4$. <PREP> בְּ of place *in(to), among*, + יָד *hand* 1 S 23$_7$ (unless נכר III pi. *sell*; or em.; see Subj.), מַחְמָד *desirable thing* Si 11$_{34}$ (וינכר[י]ך).

Htp. 3.1 + waw וַיִּתְנַכֵּר; ptc. מִתְנַכֵּרָה; inf. Si התנכר—**act as a stranger, disguise oneself, pretend to be someone else,** <SUBJ> Joseph Gn 42$_7$, אִשָּׁה *wife* 1 K 14$_{5.6}$, חָכְמוֹת *wisdom* Si 4$_{17}$. <PREP> אֶל *towards*, + אָח *brother* Gn 42$_7$. <COLL> נכר htp. + adverb, לָמָּה זֶּה *why?* 1 K 14$_6$; בהתנכר אלך עמו *while disguising myself I will walk with him* Si 4$_{17}$.*

⇒ נֵכָר *foreignness*, נֵכֶר *misfortune*, נֹכֶר *misfortune*, נָכְרִי *foreign*.

***נכר III** 2 vb. **acquire** (unless from כרה II *purchase*)—**Qal** 1 + waw וָאֶכְּרֶהָ—**acquire, take legal possession of, purchase,** <SUBJ> Hosea Ho 3$_2$. <OBJ> אִשָּׁה *woman* Ho 3$_2$. <PREP> לְ of benefit, *to, for*, + Hosea Ho 3$_2$; בְּ of price, *(in exchange) for*, + כֶּסֶף fifteen pieces of *silver* Ho 3$_2$, חֹמֶר *homer* of barley Ho 3$_2$, לֶתֶךְ *lethech* of barley Ho 3$_2$.

Pi. 1 Pf. נִכַּר—perh. **sell*** (unless נכר II pi. *alienate*), <SUBJ> Y. 1 S 23$_7$. <OBJ> David 1 S 23$_7$. <PREP> בְּ of place *in(to)*, + יָד *hand* 1 S 23$_7$.*

***נכר IV** 2 vb. **remove, repudiate—Pi.** 1 Pf. נִכַּר—**remove** (unless נכר II *treat as a stranger* or IV *sell*), <SUBJ> Y. 1 S 23$_7$. <OBJ> David 1 S 23$_7$. <PREP> בְּ *into*, + יָד *hand* 1 S 23$_7$.

Hi. 1 Impf. יַכִּיר—**repudiate** (unless נכר I *recognize* or VI *disapprove of*), <SUBJ> Y. Jb 34$_{25}$. <OBJ> מַעְבָּד *way of life* Jb 34$_{25}$. <COLL> נכיר hi. + adverb, לָכֵן *therefore* Jb 34$_{25}$.

***נכר V** 1 vb. **disapprove of** (unless נכר I *recognize* or V *repudiate*)—**Hi.** 1 Impf. יַכִּיר—**disapprove of,** <SUBJ> Y. Jb 34$_{25}$. <OBJ> מַעְבָּד *deed* Jb 34$_{25}$. <COLL> נכיר hi. + adverb, לָכֵן *therefore* Jb 34$_{25}$.

נֵכָר 36.1.12 n.[m.] **foreignness**—Q נאכר; cstr. נֵכַר—**foreignness, strangeness,** i.e. belonging to another clan, tribe or nation, <CSTR> נֵכַר־הָאָרֶץ *foreignness*, i.e. foreign gods, *of the land* Dt 31$_{16}$; אֵל נֵכָר *god of foreignness*, i.e. foreign god Dt 32$_{12}$ Ml 2$_{11}$ Ps 81$_{10}$ (+ זָר *strange*) 4QDibHam[a] 1.5$_3$, אֱלוֹהַּ *god of* Dn 11$_{39}$, אֱלֹהֵי נֵכָר *gods of* Gn 35$_{2.4}$ (both הַנֵּכָר) Jos 24$_{20}$ 24$_{23}$ Jg 10$_{16}$ 1 S 7$_3$ (all three הַנֵּכָר) Jr 5$_{19}$ (+ זָר *stranger*) 2 C 33$_{15}$ (הַנֵּכָר), אֱלֹהֵי נֵכַר־הָאָרֶץ *gods of foreignness*, i.e. foreign gods, *of the land* Dt 31$_{16}$, הַבְלֵי נֵכָר *images of foreignness*, i.e. foreign images Jr 8$_{19}$.

עם נכר *people of foreignness*, i.e. foreign people Si 33$_3$, גוי *nation of* 4QapJoseph[a] 1$_9$ (=4QapJoseph[b] 1$_{11}$ נאכר) 11QT 57$_{11}$ 64$_7$ CD 14$_{15}$, בֶּן־נֵכָר *son of foreignness*, i.e. foreigner Gn 17$_{12.27}$ Ex 12$_{43}$ Lv 22$_{25}$ Is 56$_3$ (הַנֵּכָר) Ezk 44$_{9.9}$ CD 11$_2$ (הנכר) 4QMidrEschat[a] 3$_4$, בְּנֵי *sons of* 2 S 22$_{45.46}$ ||Ps 18$_{45.46}$ Is 56$_6$ (הַנֵּכָר) 60$_{10}$ 61$_5$ (+ זָר *stranger*) 62$_8$ Ezk 44$_7$ Ps 144$_{7.11}$ Ne 9$_2$ 4QapJoseph[b] 1$_{15}$ (נאכר) 4QpsMose[e] 2.1$_{10}$ (בני [נכר]) 4QapLam[b] 2 4QOrd[b] 2.2$_2$ (הנכר) 4QBéat 5$_7$, עבדי נאכר *servants of foreignness* 4QpsEzek[c] 2$_6$.

אַדְמַת נֵכָר *land of foreignness*, i.e. foreign land Ps 137$_4$, מִזְבְּחוֹת *altars of*, i.e. foreign altars 2 C 14$_2$ (הַנֵּכָר), כָּל־נֵכָר *all foreignness* Ne 13$_{30}$.

<PREP> מִן *from*, + טהר pi. *purify* Ne 13$_{30}$.
⇒ נכר II *be foreign.*

נֵכֶר 1 n.[m.] **misfortune,** <NOM CL> הֲלֹא ... נֵכֶר לְפֹעֲלֵי אָוֶן *is there not ... misfortune to the workers of iniquity?* Jb 31$_3$ (|| אֵיד *calamity*).
<SYN> אֵיד *calamity.*
⇒ נכר II *be foreign.*

[נֹכֶר] 1 n.[m.] **misfortune**—sf. נָכְרוֹ—<CSTR> יוֹם נָכְרוֹ *day of his misfortune* Ob$_{12}$ (+ אבד inf. *perishing,* צָרָה *distress*).
⇒ נכר II *be foreign.*

נָכְרִי 45.2.4 adj. **foreign**—Q נוכרי; fem. sing. נָכְרִיָּה; masc. pl. נָכְרִים; fem. pl. נָכְרִיּוֹת—**foreign, alien, strange, 1.** attributively of עַם *people* Ex 21$_8$, גּוֹי *nation* Si 49$_5$ (+ נָבָל *foolish* or *outcast*), אִישׁ *man* Dt 17$_{15}$=11QT 56$_{15}$ (:: אָח *brother*) Ec 6$_2$, אִשָּׁה *woman* 1 K 11$_{1.8}$ Ezr 10$_{2+6t}$ Ne 13$_{26.27}$, לָשׁוֹן *tongue,* i.e. speech Pr 6$_{24}$ (or em. לְשׁוֹן נָכְרִיָּה *alien speech* to לְשׁוֹן נָכְרִיָּה *speech of the alien* [fem.]), גֶּפֶן *vine* Jr 2$_{21}$, מַלְבּוּשׁ *clothing* Zp 1$_8$, אֶרֶץ *land* Ex 2$_{22}$ 18$_3$.

2. in nom. cl. used predicatively of עֲבֹדָה *work* Is 28$_{21}$ (|| זָר *strange*).

3. as noun, **foreigner, alien, stranger;** also collectively, **foreigners** (Jg 19$_{12}$), **a.** masc., <SUBJ> היה *be* Ps 69$_9$ (|| מוּזָר *stranger*) Jb 19$_{15}$ (+ זָר *stranger*), אמר *say* Dt 29$_{21}$, קרא *call* 1 K 8$_{43}$||2 C 6$_{33}$, הלל pi. *praise* Pr 27$_2$ (|| זָר), ראה *see* Dt 29$_{21}$, בוא *come* Dt 29$_{21}$ Ob$_{11}$ (|| זָר), ידה pi. *cast* lots Ob$_{11}$. <NOM CL> נָכְרִי אַתָּה *you are a foreigner* 2 S 15$_{19}$ (+ גֹּלֶה *exile*), נָכְרִי אֲשֶׁר לֹא־מִבְּנֵי יִשְׂרָאֵל הֵנָּה *foreigners who are not of the Israelites* Jg 19$_{12}$ (mss הֵם/הֵמָּה *they* [masc.]), הַנָּכְרִי אֲשֶׁר לֹא־מֵעַמְּךָ יִשְׂרָאֵל הוּא *the foreigner who is not of your people Israel* 1 K 8$_{41}$||2 C 6$_{32}$. <OBJ> נגשׂ *exact of* Dt 15$_3$ (:: אָח *brother*) 1QDM 3$_6$ (הנ[וכרי יגוש]). <CSTR> יַלְדֵי נָכְרִים *children of foreigners* Is 2$_6$, בֵּית נָכְרִי *house of a foreigner* Pr 5$_{10}$ (+ זָר *stranger*), עִיר נָכְרִי *city of foreigners* Jg 19$_{12}$ (or em. נָכְרִים *of foreigners*), כו[ל נכ]רי *any foreigner* 4QLeqet 1$_7$. <APP> דּוֹר *generation* Dt 29$_{21}$.

<PREP> לְ of direction, *to* 4QHalakhah[a] 7$_5$, + הפך ni. *be turned over* Lm 5$_2$ (|| זָר *stranger*), מכר *deliver (over)* Dt 14$_{21}$ 11QT 48$_6$, נשׁך hi. *lend on interest* Dt 23$_{21}$ (:: אָח *brother*); בְּ *from,* + גאל *redeem* 4QLeqet 1$_7$ (נכ[רי]); כְּ *as,* + אסף ni. *gather* intrans. Ps 35$_{15}$ (if em. נֵכִים *stricken ones* to כְּנָכְרִים); אֶל *concerning* 1 K 8$_{41}$||2 C 6$_{32}$; בַּעַד *on behalf of, for the sake of,* + חבל *hold liable for pledge given* Pr 20$_{16(Kt)}$ (|| זָר *stranger*). <COLL> גר זר נכרי ורש תפארתם יראת י׳ *(whether) sojourner, stranger, foreigner or pauper, their glory is the fear of Y.* Si 6$_{22(B)}$.

b. fem., <NOM CL> בְּאֵר צָרָה נָכְרִיָּה *a foreigner* (fem.) *is a narrow pit* Pr 23$_{27}$ (|| זוֹנָה *prostitute*), אָנֹכִי נָכְרִיָּה *I am a foreigner* Ru 2$_{10}$. <CSTR> חֵק נָכְרִיָּה *bosom of a foreigner* (fem.) Pr 5$_{20}$ (+ זָרָה *stranger* [fem.]), לְשׁוֹן *speech of* Pr 6$_{24}$ (if em.; see §1). <PREP> מִן *from,* + נצל hi. *deliver* Pr 2$_{16}$ (+ אִשָּׁה זָרָה *strange woman*), שׁמר Pr 7$_5$ (+ אִשָּׁה זָרָה); בַּעַד *on behalf of, for the sake of,* + חבל *hold liable for pledge given* Pr 20$_{16(Qr)}$ 27$_{13}$ (both || זָר *stranger*). <COLL> הֲלוֹא נָכְרִיּוֹת נֶחְשַׁבְנוּ לוֹ *are not we regarded by him as foreigners?* Gn 31$_{15}$.

Also 4QPrayer[c] 4.2$_2$.
<SYN> §2 זָר *strange;* §3a זָר *stranger,* מוּזָר *stranger;* §3b זוֹנָה *prostitute,* זָר *stranger.**
⇒ נכר II *be foreign.*

[נְכֹת] 2 n.[f.] **treasure**—sf. נְכֹתֹה (Q נכתיו)—<CSTR> בֵּית נְכֹת *house of treasure* Ps 68$_{13}$ (if em. נְוַת בַּיִת *inhabitant of the house*), נְכֹתֹה *of his treasure* 2 K 20$_{13}$ ||Is 39$_2$ (1QIsa[a] נכתיו).*

נלה I 1 vb. **finish—Hi.** 1 Inf. כַּנְּלֹתְךָ—**finish,** <SUBJ> שֹׁדֵד *destroyer* Is 33$_1$ (כַּנְּלֹתְךָ *when you have finished;* or em. with 1QIsa[a] כְּכַלֹּתְךָ *when you have finished,* i.e. כלה pi.). <COLL> כַּנְּלֹתְךָ לִבְגֹּד *when you have finished being treacherous* Is 33$_1$ (or em.; see Subj.).*

***נלה II** 1 vb. **obtain—Hi.** 1 Inf. כַּנְּלֹתְךָ—**obtain, attain to,** <SUBJ> שֹׁדֵד *destroyer* Is 33$_1$ (or em. with 1QIsa[a] כְּכַלֹּתְךָ *when you have finished,* i.e. כלה pi.). <COLL> כַּנְּלֹתְךָ לִבְגֹּד *when you have fully attained being treacherous* Is 33$_1$ (or em.; see Subj.).

⇒ מָנוֹל *possession.*

[נָלָשׁ] pr.n.m. **Nalash,** son of Abariah (or of Reebiah), <APP> בֵּן *son* Seal 910 (others מלשׁ *Malash*; 7th cent.). <PREP> לְ of possession, *of, (belonging) to* Seal 910 (others מלשׁ *Malash*; 7th cent.).

נִמְבְּזָה, see בזה *despise*, Ni.

***[נמה]** vb. **bring tidings—Qal bring tidings,** רִאשׁוֹן לְצִיּוֹן הִנֵּה הַנּוֹמֶה *behold I first am declaring it to Zion* Is 41$_{27}$ (if em. הִנָּם *behold them* to הַנּוֹמֶה, as 1QIsa[a] הנומה).

נִמְהָר *hasty one*, see מהר I *act quickly*, Ni.

נְמוּאֵל 3 pr.n.m. **Nemuel, 1.** Reubenite, son of Eliab and brother of Dathan and Abiram, <NOM CL> בְּנֵי אֱלִיאָב נְמוּאֵל *the sons of Eliab were Nemuel* Nm 26$_{9}$.

2. son of Simeon, appar. ident. with Jemuel at Gn 46$_{10}$ Ex 6$_{15}$, <NOM CL> בְּנֵי שִׁמְעוֹן נְמוּאֵל *the sons of Shimeon were Nemuel* 1 C 4$_{24}$. <PREP> לְ of possession, *of, (belonging) to* Nm 26$_{12}$.

⇒ נְמוּאֵלִי *Nemuelite.*

נְמוּאֵלִי 1 gent. **Nemuelite,** as collective sing. noun, **Nemuelites,** <CSTR> מִשְׁפַּחַת הַנְּמוּאֵלִי *clan of the Nemuelites* Nm 26$_{12}$.

⇒ נְמוּאֵל *Nemuel.*

[נָמוֹג] I *trembling one*, see מוג I *melt away*, Ni.

[נָמוֹג] II *wavering one*, see מוג II *waver*, Ni.

***[נִמְטָר]** 0.0.0.1 pr.n.[m.] **Nimtar,** appar. son of Hoshea, papMurPalimp$^{b}_{1}$.

נְמָלָה 2 n.f. **ant**—pl. נְמָלִים—<SUBJ> כון hi. *prepare* Pr 6$_{6}$ 30$_{25}$, אגר *gather* Pr 6$_{6}$. <NOM CL> הַנְּמָלִים עַם לֹא־עָז *the ants are a people not strong* Pr 30$_{25}$. <PREP> לְ of possession, *of, (belonging) to* Pr 6$_{6}$; אֶל *to*, + הלך *go* Pr 6$_{6}$.

נִמְצָא *survivor(s), refugee(s)*, see מצא I *find*, Ni. §10.

נָמֵר 6 n.m. **leopard**—pl. נְמֵרִים—<SUBJ> הפך *change spots* Jr 13$_{23}$, שׁקד *watch* Jr 5$_{6}$, רבץ *lie down* Is 11$_{6}$. <CSTR> הַרְרֵי נְמֵרִים *mountains of leopards* Ca 4$_{8}$. <PREP> כְּ *as*, + שׁוּר *watch* Hos 13$_{7}$; מִן of comparison, *(more) than*, + קלל *be swift* Hb 1$_{8}$. <COLL> נָמֵר || זְאֵב *wolf* Is 11$_{6}$ Jr 5$_{6}$ Hb 1$_{8}$, אֲרִי *lion* Ca 4$_{8}$, אַרְיֵה *lion* Jr 5$_{6}$, שַׁחַל *lion* Hos 13$_{7}$; + כּוּשִׁי *Cushite* Jr 13$_{23}$.*

⇒ זְאֵב *wolf*, אֲרִי *lion*, אַרְיֵה *lion*, שַׁחַל *lion.*

נִמְרֹד 4 pr.n.m. **Nimrod**—נִמְרוֹד—son of Cush and king of Babel, Erech and Accad; builder of Nineveh, Rehoboth-Ir, Calah and Resen, variously identified with the Assyrian deity Ninurta, with a Mesopotamian hero, Gilgamesh or Lugalbanda, or with the Assyrian king Tukulti-Ninurta,* <SUBJ> היה *be* Gn 10$_{8}$||1 C 1$_{10}$, חלל hi. *begin* Gn 10$_{8}$||1 C 1$_{10}$, יצא *go out* Gn 10$_{9}$, בנה *build* Gn 10$_{9}$. <OBJ> ילד *beget* Gn 10$_{8}$||1 C 1$_{10}$. <CSTR> אֶרֶץ נִמְרֹד *land of Nimrod* Mc 5$_{5}$ (+ אַשּׁוּר *Assyria*). <APP> גִּבּוֹר *mighty one* of hunting Gn 10$_{9}$. <PREP> כְּ *as* Gn 10$_{9}$.*

נִמְרָה 1 pl.n. **Nimrah,** town in Moab occupied by Gad, appar. ident. with Beth-nimrah at Nm 32$_{36}$ Josh 13$_{27}$, <APP> אֶרֶץ *land* Nm 32$_{3}$.

נִמְרִים 2 pl.n. **Nimrim,** in Moab, perh. Wādi Numēra, 12 km N of southern end of Dead Sea, <CSTR> מֵי נִמְרִים *waters of Nimrim* Is 15$_{6}$ Jr 48$_{34}$.

***[נֶמֶשׁ]** 0.0.0.3 pr.n.m. **Nemesh, 1.** T. 'Amal jar handle inscr. **2.** Kh. Tannin ost. (others שמן *oil*). **3.** son of Neriah, Seal 622 (T. Beit Mirsim?, 7th/6th cent.). **4.** son of Micaiah, Seal 852 (7th cent.).

<APP> בֵּן *son* Seals 622 ([ב]ן; T. Beit Mirsim?, 7th/6th cent.) 852 (7th cent.). <PREP> לְ of possession, *of, (belonging) to* T. 'Amal jar handle inscr. Seals 622 (T. Beit Mirsim?, 7th/6th cent.) 852 (7th cent.).

נִמְשִׁי 5 pr.n.m. **Nimshi, 1.** father of Jehu (1 K 19$_{16}$ 2 K 9$_{20}$ 2 C 22$_{7}$) or father of Jehoshaphat and grandfather of Jehu (2 K $9_{2.14}$; unless in both del. בֶּן־יְהוֹשָׁפָט *son of Jehoshaphat*), <CSTR> בֶּן־נִמְשִׁי *son of Nimshi* 1 K 19_{16} 2 K $9_{2.14.20}$ 2 C 22_7.

2. Samaria ost. 56, <PREP> לְ of possession, *of, (belonging) to* Samaria ost. 56 ([לנמשן]).

*[נִמְשָׁר] 0.0.0.3 pr.n.m. **Nimshar, 1.** son of Shual, Seal 623 (T. Beit Mirsim?, 7th/6th cent.). **2.** son of Shebaniah, Seal 624 (T. Beit Mirsim?, 7th/6th cent.). **3.** father of Menahem, ost. DH79_6 ([נמשר]). **4.** father of Ashiah, ost. DH79_7.

<CSTR> בן נמשר *son of Nimshar* ost. DH79_6 ([נמשר]) 79_7. <APP> בֵּן *son* Seals 623 624 (both T. Beit Mirsim?, 7th/6th cent.). <PREP> לְ of possession, *of, (belonging) to* Seals 623 624 (both T. Beit Mirsim?, 7th/6th cent.).

נָס *fugitive*, see נוס I *flee*.

נֵס I 21.0.3 n.[m.] **standard**—cstr. נֵס; sf. נִסִּי—**1. standard, banner, flag, ensign,** esp. as a mark of royal dignity,* as signal or rallying point (Is 5_{26} $11_{10.12}$ 13_2 18_3 31_9 49_{22} 62_{10} Jr $4_{6.21}$ 50_2 $51_{12.27}$ Ps 60_6 1QH 14_{34} 1QM 3_{15}), flag pole on hill (Is 30_{17}), pole supporting bronze serpent (Nm $21_{8.9}$), 'Y. is my standard' as name of altar (Ex 17_{15}), worshipper as a banner to the elect (1QH 10_{13}).

2. sail of ship (Is 33_{23} perh. Ezk 27_7).

3. sign, warning, in ref. to fate of Korah and his company (Nm 26_{10}).

<NOM CL> י׳ נִסִּי *Y. is my standard* Ex 17_{15}.

<OBJ> ראה *see* Jr 4_{21}, כתב *write* 1QM 3_{15}, נשׂא *raise* Is 5_{26} 11_{12} 13_2 18_3 Jr 4_6 50_2 $51_{12.27}$ 1QH 14_{34}, רום hi. *raise* Is 49_{22} 62_{10}, פרשׂ *spread out* Is 33_{23}, נתן *give* Ps 60_6 (unless נֵס III *[means of] flight*), שׂים *place*, i.e. make 1QH 10_{13}.

<CSTR> נס אל *banner of God* 1QM 3_{15}, נֵס עַמִּים *standard of the peoples* Is 11_{10}.

<PREP> לְ introducing predicate, + היה *be* Nm 26_{10} Ezk 27_7; *as*, + עמד *stand* Is 11_{10}; כְּ *as*, + יתר ni. *remain* Is 30_{17}; מִן of cause, *on account of*, + חתת *be terrified* Is 31_9 (unless נֵס II *trembling*); עַל *upon*, + שׂים *place* Nm $21_{8.9}$.

<COLL> נֵס || יָד *hand* Is 13_2 49_{22}, קוֹל *voice* Is 13_2 Jr 4_{21}, תֹּרֶן *mast* Is 30_{17} 33_{23} 1QH 14_{34}; + מִפְרָשׂ *sail* Ezk 27_7; נֵס לְהִתְנוֹסֵס *a banner to which to rally* Ps 60_6 (or em. מָנוֹס *a refuge* to which to flee), נס לבחירי צדק *a banner for the elect ones of righteousness* 1QH 10_{13}.

<SYN> יָד *hand*, קוֹל *voice*, תֹּרֶן *mast*.*

⇒ נסס V *rally to the banner*.

*נֵס II 1 n.[m.] **trembling** (unless נֵס I *standard*), <PREP> מִן of cause, instrument, *on account of, by (means of)*, + חתת *be terrified* Is 31_9.

⇒ נסס III *sway*.

*נֵס III 1 n.[m.] **(means of) flight** (unless נֵס I *standard*), <OBJ> נתן *give* Ps 60_6.

⇒ נוס I *flee*.

נסא, see נשׂא *lift*, Hi.

נְסִבָּה 1 n.f. **turn of affairs,** <SUBJ> היה 2 C 10_{15} (||1 K 12_{15} סִבָּה *turn of affairs*). <COLL> נְסִבָּה מֵעִם אֱלֹהִים *a turn of affairs from*, i.e. brought about by, *God* 2 C 10_{15}.

סבב *turn*.

*נסג 1 vb. **forge** (unless סוג ni. *depart*)—**Qal** 1 Impf. יַסַּג—**forge,** <SUBJ> subj. not specified, Mc 2_6. <OBJ> כְּלִמָּה II *speech* Mc 2_6.

נסה I 36.1.4.1 vb. **test—Pi.** 36.1.3.1 Pf. נִסָּה (Q ניסה, נִסָּהוּ), נִסִּיתֶם, נִסּוּנִי, נִסִּיתִי, נִסִּיתוֹ, נִסְּתָה; impf. אֲנַסֶּה (אֲנַסְּכָה), (תְּנַסּוּן) תְּנַסּוּ, (אֲנַסֶּנּוּ); + waw וַיְנַסּוּ, וַיְנַסֵּם; impv. נַס (נַסֵּנִי); ptc. מְנַסֶּה (Q מנשה); inf. נַסּוֹת (נַסֹּתְךָ, נַסֹּתֶךָ, נַסֹּתוֹ, נַסּוֹתוֹ, נַסֹּתָם)—**1. test, try, prove;** without object, **make a test** (Jg 6_{39}).

<SUBJ> Y. Gn 22_1 Ex 15_{25} (unless §3) 16_4 20_{20} Dt $8_{2.16}$ 13_4=11QT 54_{12} (מנשה) Dt 33_8 (unless §3) Jg 2_{22} 3_1 (unless both §3) 3_4 Ps 26_2 2 C 32_{31} 1QH 10_{14} 14_{26} (לנ[ס]ות) perh. 4QNarrF 1_5, Israelites Dt $6_{16.16}$ Ps $78_{18.41.56}$, עַם *people* Ex 17_2, Ahaz Is 7_{12}, Gideon Jg 6_{39}, Koheleth Ec 2_1 7_{23}, אִישׁ *man* Nm 14_{22}, אָב *father* Ps 95_9 106_{14}, בֵּן *son* Si 37_{27}, of Israel Ex 17_7, מַלְכָּה *queen* 1 K

10$_1$||2 C 9$_1$, מֶלְצַר *guardian* Dn 1$_{12.14}$.

<OBJ> Y. Ex 17$_{2.7}$ Nm 14$_{22}$ Dt 6$_{16}$ Is 7$_{12}$ Ps 78$_{18.41.56}$ 95$_9$ 106$_{14}$, Israel(ites) Ex 15$_{25}$ (unless §3) Dt 8$_{2.16}$ 13$_4$= 11QT 54$_{12}$ (מנשה) Jg 2$_{22}$ 3$_1$ (unless §3) 3$_4$, עַם *people* Ex 16$_4$ 20$_{20}$, Abraham Gn 22$_1$, Hezekiah 2 C 32$_{31}$, Koheleth Ec 2$_1$ (or em.; see below), Solomon 1 K 10$_1$||2 C 9$_1$, אִישׁ *man* Dt 33$_8$ (unless §3), עֶבֶד *servant* Dn 1$_{12.14}$, worshipper Ps 26$_2$, אהב ptc. *one who loves* discipline 1QH 10$_{14}$, נֶפֶשׁ *soul*, i.e. appetite Si 37$_{27}$, אֶבֶן *stone* 1QH 14$_{26}$ (לנ[סות]), שִׂמְחָה *joy* Ec 2$_1$ (if em. אֲנַסְּכָה *I will test you* to אֲנַסֶּנָּה *I will test it*, i.e. joy), זֹה *this* Ec 7$_{23}$.

<PREP> בְּ of place, time, *in, at, during*, + Massah Dt 6$_{16}$ 33$_8$ (unless §3), יְשִׁימוֹן *desert* Ps 106$_{14}$, לֵב *heart* Ps 78$_{18}$, חַיִּים *life* Si 37$_{27(B)}$, עָוֹן *iniquity* 4QConfess 1.2$_3$; of instrument, *by (means of), with*, + גּוֹי *nation* Jg 2$_{22}$ 3$_1$ (unless §3) 3$_4$, גִּזָּה *fleece* Jg 6$_{39}$, חֶמֶר *wine* Si 37$_{27(Bmg, D)}$, חִידָה *riddle* 1 K 10$_1$||2 C 9$_1$, שִׂמְחָה *joy* Ec 2$_1$ (or בְּ *namely*, if em.; see Obj.), חָכְמָה *wisdom* Ec 7$_{23}$.

<COLL> נסה pi. || בחן *test* Ps 26$_2$ 95$_9$ 1QH 10$_{14}$; + צרף *test* Ps 26$_2$, ריב *strive* Dt 33$_8$, תוה hi. *pain* Ps 78$_{41}$, מרה hi. *provoke* Ps 78$_{56}$.

נסה pi. + adverb or adverbial phrase, שָׁם *there* Ex 15$_{25}$ (unless §3), מָה *why?* Ex 17$_2$, יָמִים עֲשָׂרָה *for ten days* Dn 1$_{12.14}$, הַפַּעַם *this once* Jg 6$_{39}$, זֶה עֶשֶׂר פְּעָמִים *these ten times* Nm 14$_{22}$.

נסה pi. followed by (1) interrogative, לְמַעַן אֲנַסֶּנּוּ הֲיֵלֵךְ בְּתוֹרָתִי אִם־לֹא *so that I may test him (to ascertain) whether he will walk in my law or not* Ex 16$_4$, sim. Jg 2$_{22}$.

(2) לֵאמֹר *saying*, עַל נַסֹּתָם אֶת־י׳ לֵאמֹר הֲיֵשׁ י׳ בְּקִרְבֵּנוּ אִם־אָיִן *because they tested Y., saying, Is Y. among us or not?* Ex 17$_7$.

(3) infinitive of ידע *know* Dt 8$_2$ 13$_4$=11QT 54$_{12}$ (מנשה) Jg 3$_4$ 2 C 32$_{31}$, יטב hi. *do good* Dt 8$_{16}$, שׁאל *ask* Ps 78$_{18}$.

2a. attempt to do something, perh. ni., <SUBJ> אֱלֹהִים *god* Dt 4$_{34}$, אִישׁ *man* Lachish ost. 3$_9$, רַךְ *tender one* Dt 28$_{56}$, עָנֹג *delicate one* Dt 28$_{56}$. <PREP> לְ of direction, *to*, + נֵצַח *everlastingness*, i.e. ever (before) Lachish ost. 3$_9$.

<COLL> נסה pi. + infinitive of קרא *read* Lachish ost. 3$_9$, בוא *come* Dt 4$_{34}$, יצג hi. *place* Dt 28$_{56}$.

b. venture, perh. ni., <SUBJ> subj. not specified, Jb 4$_2$. <OBJ> דָּבָר *word* Jb 4$_2$. <PREP> אֶל *to*, + Job Jb 4$_2$.

3. train for military action, **give experience** of war,* unless §1, <SUBJ> Y. Ex 15$_{25}$ Dt 33$_8$ Jg 3$_1$. <OBJ> Israel Jg 3$_1$, עַם *people* Ex 15$_{25}$, אִישׁ *man* Dt 33$_8$. <PREP> בְּ of place, *in*, + Massah Dt 33$_8$; of agent, *by (means of), with*, + גּוֹי *nation* Jg 3$_1$. <COLL> נסה pi. + adverb, שָׁם *there* Ex 15$_{25}$.

<SYN> §1 בחן *test*.

Ni. 2 Pf. נִסִּיתִי, נִסָּה (see also §§2a, 2b)—**be trained,** to wear armour, <SUBJ> David 1 S 17$_{39.39}$.*

⇒ נִסּוּי *trial*, נִסָּיוֹן *test*.

נסה II *lift*, see נשׂא *lift*.

*[נִסּוּי] 0.2.4 n.[m.] **trial**—Si ניסוי; sf. Q נסויה; cstr. Q נסוי; pl. Q נסויים; sf. Q נסוייכה—**trial(s),** <PREP> נסוי שחת *trial of the pit* 4QTime 1.2$_2$. <PREP> בְּ of place, time, *in(to), during*, + בוא *come* 4QDibHam^a 1.5$_{18}$, שׁוב *go back*, i.e. repeat Si 37$_{1(E)}$ (בנסוי ישוב ונמלט *during trial[s] he is repeatedly delivered*), מצא ni. *be found* faithful Si 44$_{20}$; introducing object, + מאס *reject* 4QDibHam^a 1.6$_7$. <COLL> נִסּוּי *trial* || נֶגַע *affliction* 4QDibHam^a 1.6$_7$, צָרָה *distress* 4QDibHam^a 1.5$_{18}$.

Also 4QBéat 5$_3$.

⇒ נסה I *test*.

נסח

4.2.0.1 vb. **tear away—Qal** 3.1 Impf. יִסַּח (יִסָּחֵךְ, Si יסחם), יִסְּחוּ—**tear away, tear down,** <SUBJ> Y. Ps 52$_7$ (|| שׁרשׁ pi. *uproot*, + חתה *take*, נתץ *pull down*) Pr 15$_{25}$ (:: נצב hi. *establish*) Si 10$_{17}$ (יסחם corrected to וסחם *and he clears them away*, i.e. סחה pi.; + נתשׁ *pluck up*); subj. not specified, Pr 2$_{22}$ (or em. יִנָּסְחוּ [ni.] or יֻסְּחוּ [pass. qal or ho.] *they shall be plucked*; unless from סחה *sweep away;** + כרת ni. *be cut off*). <OBJ> גּוֹי *nations* Si 10$_{17}$, גִּבּוֹר *mighty one* Ps 52$_7$, בֹּגֵד *traitor* Pr 2$_{22}$ (or em.; see Subj.), בַּיִת *house* Pr 15$_{25}$. <PREP> מִן of direction, *from*, + אֹהֶל *tent* Ps 52$_7$, אֶרֶץ *land* Pr 2$_{22}$ (or em.; see Subj.) Si 10$_{17}$.

<SYN> שׁרשׁ pi. *uproot*.

<ANT> נצב hi. *establish*.

Ni. 1.1.0.1 Pf. I נסחה, Si נסחו; + waw וְנִסַּחְתֶּם—**be torn away,** <SUBJ> Israelites Dt 28$_{63}$ (or em. וְנִסְחַתֶּם, i.e.

pass. qal in same sense),* עַם *people* Si 48$_{15}$, בֹּגֵד *traitor* Pr 22$_{22}$ (if em.; see Qal Subj.). <PREP> מִן of direction, *from,* + אֶרֶץ *land* Pr 22$_{22}$ (if em.; see Qal Subj.) Si 48$_{15}$ (unless pass. qal;* + פוץ *be scattered*); מֵעַל *from (upon),* + אֲדָמָה *land* Dt 28$_{63}$ (or em.; see Subj.).

Also Ophel monumental inscr.4.

Ho. be torn away, <SUBJ> בֹּגֵד *traitor* Pr 22$_{22}$ (if em.; see Qal Subj.). <PREP> מִן of direction, *from,* + אֶרֶץ *land* Pr 22$_{22}$ (if em.; see Qal Subj.).*

⇒ מַסָּח *alternating.*

[נָסִיא], see נָשִׂיא I *prince.*

*\[**נִסָּיוֹן**\] 0.3 n.[m.] **test**—Si נסיונות—**test, trial,** <NOM CL> מן[ה]רבות שיחו נסיון *from the greatness of his talk there is a test,* i.e. he will test [you] with much talk Si 13$_{11}$. <PREP> בְּ of instrument, *by (means of), with,* + בחר *test* Si 4$_{17}$, קנה *acquire* Si 6$_{7}$.

⇒ נסה I *test.*

[נָסִיךְ] I 1 n.[m.] **libation**—sf. נְסִיכָם—**libation, drink offering,** <CSTR> יֵין נְסִיכָם *wine of their libation* Dt 32$_{38}$ (|| זֶבַח *sacrifice*).

<SYN> זֶבַח *sacrifice.**

⇒ נסך *pour out.*

*\[**נָסִיךְ**\] II 1 n.[m.] **molten image**—pl. sf. נְסִכֵיהֶם—<PREP> עִם *with,* + בוא *bring* Dn 11$_{8}$.

⇒ נסך *pour out.*

[נָסִיךְ] III 4.1 n.m. **prince**—pl. cstr. נְסִיכֵי; sf. נְסִיכֵמוֹ—**prince, leader,** <SUBJ> מרד *rebel* Si 16$_{7(B)}$, מרה *be rebellious* Si 16$_{7(A)}$. <NOM CL> שָׁמָּה נְסִיכֵי צָפוֹן *the princes of the north are there* Ezk 32$_{30}$. <OBJ> קום hi. *raise up* Mc 5$_{4}$, נכה hi. *strike* Jos 13$_{21}$, שׁית *place,* i.e. make Ps 83$_{12}$. <CSTR> נְסִיכֵי סִיחוֹן *princes of Sihon* Jos 13$_{21}$, צָפוֹן *of the north* Ezk 32$_{30}$, אָדָם *of human beings* Mc 5$_{4}$, נסיכי קדם *princes of old* Si 16$_{7}$, כָּל־נְסִיכֵמוֹ *all their princes* Ps 83$_{12}$. <APP> Evi Jos 13$_{21}$, Rekem Jos 13$_{21}$, Zur Jos 13$_{21}$, Hur Jos 13$_{21}$, Reba Jos 13$_{21}$, נָשִׂיא *prince* Jos 13$_{21}$, יֹשֵׁב *inhabitant* Jos 13$_{21}$. <PREP> לְ introducing object, + נשׂא *forgive* Si 16$_{7}$. <COLL> נָסִיךְ || רֹעֶה *shepherd* Mc 5$_{4}$, נָדִיב *noble* Ps 83$_{12}$; + נָשִׂיא *prince* Ezk 32$_{29}$; שְׁמֹנָה נְסִיכֵי *eight princes of* Mc 5$_{4}$.

<SYN> רֹעֶה *shepherd* Mc 5$_{4}$, נָדִיב *noble.**

⇒ נסך I *consecrate (with a libation).*

נסך I 26.0.2 vb. **pour out—Qal** 9.0.1 Pf. נָסַךְ (נָסֶךְ), נָסַכְתִּי; impf. תִּסְּכוּ, יִסְּכוּ; impv. נְסָה;* inf. לִנְסֹךְ—**1. pour out,** <SUBJ> Y. Is 29$_{10}$ Ps 4$_{7}$ (נְסָה, an anomalous spelling before the following guttural;* unless from נשׂא *lift*), Israelites Ex 30$_{9}$ Ho 9$_{4}$, בֵּן *son* Is 30$_{1}$ (unless §3), of Israel 11QT 21$_{10}$. <OBJ> רוּחַ *spirit* of deep sleep Is 29$_{10}$, יַיִן *wine* Ho 9$_{4}$ 11QT 11$_{12}$ ([לנסך יין]) 21$_{10}$, שֵׁכָר *strong drink* 11QT 21$_{10}$, נֶסֶךְ *libation* Ex 30$_{9}$, מַסֵּכָה *libation* Is 30$_{1}$ (unless §3), אוֹר *light* Ps 4$_{7}$ (נְסָה; unless from נשׂא *lift*). <PREP> לְ of direction, *to,* + Y. Ho 9$_{4}$; בְּ of time, *in, at,* + מוֹעֵד *appointed time* 11QT 11$_{12}$ ([במועד ... לנסך]); עַל *upon,* + Israelites Is 29$_{10}$, worshipper Ps 4$_{7}$ (נְסָה; unless from נשׂא *lift*), מִזְבֵּחַ *altar* Ex 30$_{9}$ 11QT 21$_{10}$. <COLL> לִנְסֹךְ מַסֵּכָה וְלֹא רוּחִי *pouring out a libation, but not (by) my spirit* Is 30$_{1}$, לנסך ... שנה בשנ[ה] *to pour out ... year by year* 11QT 21$_{10}$.

2. consecrate (with a libation), install, <SUBJ> Y. Ps 2$_{6}$ (or em.; see Ni. Coll.). <OBJ> מֶלֶךְ *king* Ps 2$_{6}$ (or em.). <PREP> עַל *upon,* + Zion Ps 2$_{6}$ (or em.), הַר *mountain* Ps 2$_{6}$ (or em.).

3. cast, or perh. **forge,** <SUBJ> בֵּן *son* Is 30$_{1}$ (unless §1), חָרָשׁ *artisan* Is 40$_{19}$, מִי *who?* Is 44$_{10}$ (+ יצר *form*). <OBJ> פֶּסֶל *image* Is 40$_{19}$ 44$_{10}$, מַסֵּכָה *image* Is 30$_{1}$ (unless §1).

Ni. 1 Pf. נִסַּכְתִּי—**1. be poured out,** i.e. emanate (or em. נְסַכְתִּי, i.e. pass. qal in same sense; unless נסך II *be woven*), <SUBJ> חָכְמָה *wisdom* Pr 8$_{23}$. <PREP> מִן of time, *from, since,* + עוֹלָם *everlastingness* Pr 8$_{23}$, קֶדֶם *ancient time* Pr 8$_{23}$, רֹאשׁ *head,* i.e. Eternal Pr 8$_{23}$.*

2. be consecrated (with a libation), <SUBJ> worshipper Ps 2$_{6}$ (if em.; see Coll.). <PREP> עַל *upon,* + Zion Ps 2$_{6}$ (if em.), הַר *mountain* Ps 2$_{6}$ (if em.). <COLL> נִסַּכְתִּי מַלְכּוֹ *I have been consecrated as his king* Ps 2$_{6}$ (if em. נָסַכְתִּי מַלְכִּי *I have consecrated my king*).

Pi. 1 + waw וַיְנַסֵּךְ, Q וינסכוה—**pour out as a libation,** <SUBJ> David 1 C 11$_{18}$ (||2 S 23$_{16}$ hi.). <OBJ> מַיִם *water* 1 C 11$_{18}$. <PREP> לְ of direction, *to,* + Y. 1 C 11$_{18}$.

Also 4QDibHam[a] 7$_{15}$.

Hi. $_{14}$ Pf. הִסִּכוּ; impf. אַסִּיךְ; + waw וַיַּסֵּךְ, וַיַּסִּיכוּ; impv. הַסֵּךְ; inf. abs. הַסֵּךְ (הַסִּיךְ); cstr. הַסֵּךְ—**pour out,** <SUBJ> עַם *people* Jr 7$_{18}$ 44$_{17.18.25}$, קָהָל *assembly* Jr 44$_{17}$, David 2 S 23$_{16}$ (|| 1 C 11$_{18}$ pi.), Jacob Gn 35$_{14}$, אִישׁ *man* Jr 44$_{17.18}$, אִשָּׁה *woman* Jr 44$_{17.18.19.19.25}$, אָב *father* Ezk 20$_{28}$, בֵּן *son* of Israel Nm 28$_{7}$, מֶלֶךְ *king* 2 K 16$_{13}$, worshipper Ps 16$_{4}$; subj. not specified, Jr 19$_{13}$ 32$_{29}$. <OBJ> נֶסֶךְ *libation* Gn 35$_{14}$ Nm 28$_{7}$ 2 K 16$_{13}$ Jr 7$_{18}$ 19$_{13}$ 32$_{29}$ 44$_{17.18.19.25}$ Ezk 20$_{28}$ Ps 16$_{4}$, מַיִם *water* 2 S 23$_{16}$. <PREP> לְ of direction, *to*, + Y. Nm 28$_{7}$ 2 S 23$_{16}$, אֱלֹהִים *god* Jr 7$_{18}$ 19$_{13}$ 32$_{29}$, מְלֶכֶת *queen* of heaven Jr 44$_{17.18.19.25}$; בְּ of place, *in*, + קֹדֶשׁ *sanctuary* Nm 28$_{7}$; עַל *upon*, + מַצֵּבָה *pillar* Gn 35$_{14}$. <COLL> נסך hi. || יצק *pour* Gn 35$_{14}$; + adverb, שָׁם *there* Ezk 20$_{28}$.

<SYN> יצק *pour*.

Ho. $_{2}$ Impf. יֻסַּךְ—**be poured out,** <SUBJ> subj. not specified, Ex 25$_{29}$||37$_{16}$. <PREP> בְּ of place, *in*, + קַשְׂוָה *jar* Ex 25$_{29}$||37$_{16}$.*

⇒ נֶסֶךְ I *libation*, II *molten image*, נָסִיךְ I *libation*, II *molten image*, III *prince*.

נסך II $_{2}$ vb. **weave—Qal** $_{1}$ Ptc. pass. נְסוּכָה—pass. **be woven,** <SUBJ> מַסֵּכָה *covering* Is 25$_{7}$ (+ לוט *cover*). <PREP> עַל *over*, + גּוֹי *nation* Is 25$_{7}$.

Ni. $_{1}$ Pf. נִסַּכְתִּי—**be woven, fashioned** (unless נסך I *be poured out*, i.e. emanate), <SUBJ> חָכְמָה *wisdom* Pr 8$_{23}$. <PREP> מִן of time, *from, since*, + עוֹלָם *everlastingness* Pr 8$_{23}$, קֶדֶם *ancient time* Pr 8$_{23}$, רֹאשׁ *head*, i.e. beginning Pr 8$_{23}$.*

⇒ מַסֵּכָה *covering*, מַסֶּכֶת *web*, perh. מוּסָךְ III *bench, divan*.

נֶ֫סֶךְ I $_{58.0.29.1}$ n.m. **libation**—נֶסֶךְ (נֶסֶךְ); cstr. נֶסֶךְ; sf. נִסְכּוֹ (נִסְכֹּה, Q נסכוה), נִסְכָּהּ, Q נסכם (Q נסכמה); pl. נְסָכִים; sf. נְסָכֶיהָ, נִסְכֵּיכֶם (נסכיכמה), נִסְכֵּיהֶם (Q נסכיהמה)—**libation, drink offering,** <SUBJ> היה *be* Nm 28$_{14}$ Ezk 45$_{17}$, קרב *draw near*, i.e. be offered 11QT 20$_{9}$, כרת ho. *be cut off* Jl 1$_{9}$, מנע ni. *be withheld* Jl 1$_{13}$.

<NOM CL> נִסְכֹּה יַיִן רְבִיעִת הַהִין *its libation shall be wine, a quarter of a hin* Lv 23$_{13}$, vars. Nm 28$_{7}$ 11QT 13$_{12}$, בְּיוֹם הַשַּׁבָּת ... נִסְכּוֹ *on the sabbath day shall be (offered) ... its libation* Nm 28$_{9}$, sim. 11QT 28$_{4}$ ([נסכ]מה) 28$_{8}$, נסכו עליה *its libation shall be upon it* 11QT 24$_{8.11}$ 29$_{03.05.08}$ (all three [נסכמה]), למתניהו ... נסך *to Mattaniah is ... a libation* Decanter inscr. (7th cent.).

<OBJ> נסך *pour out* Ex 30$_{9}$ 11QT 21$_{10}$, hi. Gn 35$_{14}$ Nm 28$_{7}$ 2 K 16$_{13}$ Jr 7$_{18}$ 19$_{13}$ 32$_{29}$ 44$_{17.18.19.19.25}$ Ezk 20$_{28}$ Ps 16$_{4}$, שׁפך *pour* Is 57$_{6}$, עשׂה *make*, i.e. offer Ex 29$_{40}$ Nm 6$_{17}$ 15$_{24}$, קרב hi. *bring near*, i.e. offer Lv 23$_{18.37}$ Nm 6$_{15}$ 29$_{21.24.27.30.33.37}$ 11QT 14$_{01}$ ([תקריבו ... נסכו]) 15$_{2}$ ([ויקריבו ... [נסכיהמה]) 15$_{9}$ ([מקריבים]) 17$_{14}$ 22$_{05}$ ([והקריבו ... נסכו]) 25$_{6}$ ([והק]רבתמה]) 25$_{14}$ 28$_{06.09}$ (both [והקרב]תם ... נס]ך]) 28$_{010}$ ([והקרב]תם ... [נסך]) 29$_{1}$ ([והקרבתמה ... נסכ]מה]) 11QT[b] 3$_{22}$ ([יקרי]בו]) 4$_{11}$, עלה hi. *cause to go up*, i.e. offer 1 C 29$_{21}$, קטר hi. *burn* 2 K 16$_{15}$ 11QT 16$_{9}$ ([נס]כו) 16$_{18}$ (נ]סכ]ו יקט]י]ר) 22$_{7}$, שׁאר hi. *leave* Jl 2$_{14}$, נתן *give*, i.e. place 11QT 24$_{5}$ ([ונתנו]).

<CSTR> נֶסֶךְ שֵׁכָר *libation of strong drink* Nm 28$_{7}$ 11QT 21$_{10}$, נסך [יינו] *libation of its wine* 11QT 24$_{5}$; קְשׂוֹת הַנָּסֶךְ *jugs of*, i.e. for, *the libation* Nm 4$_{7}$, ר[י]ח נסכיהם *aroma of their libations* 11QShirShabb 9$_{4}$, יין נסכו *wine of its libation* 11QT 34$_{13}$, מנחת *grain offering of* 11QT 26$_{8}$, כול נסכיהמה *all their libations* 11QT 29$_{6}$.

<APP> הִין *hin* Ex 29$_{40}$, יַיִן *wine* Ex 29$_{40}$ 11QT 28$_{06}$ ([נסך יי]ן) 28$_{09}$ ([נסך ... יי]ן) 28$_{010}$ ([נס]ך ... [יין]) Decanter inscr. (7th cent.), אִשֶּׁה *fire offering* Lv 23$_{37}$, בְּרָכָה *blessing* Jl 2$_{14}$.

<PREP> לְ *as, for (the purpose of)* 11QT 18$_{6}$, + עשׂה *make*, i.e. offer Nm 15$_{5}$ 11QT 14$_{14}$ ([ועשיתמה]) 14$_{15}$ ([ועשיתמה ... לנסך]) 29$_{3}$ ([תעשו]), קרב hi. *bring near*, i.e. offer Nm 15$_{7.10}$ 11QT 14$_{2.4.17}$ (all three ... תקריבו] [לנסך]) 19$_{14}$ (והקרבת]מה] [לנסך]); *concerning* 11QT 29$_{6}$; *namely, consisting of* Nm 29$_{39}$.

בְּ of accompaniment, *with* 2 C 29$_{35}$.

כְּ *as*, + עשׂה *make*, i.e. offer Ex 29$_{41}$ Nm 28$_{8}$ 11QT 13$_{15}$ ([כנסכה תעשה]).

עַל *in addition to* Nm 28$_{10}$, + עשׂה ni. *be made*, i.e. offered Nm 28$_{15.24}$, קרב hi. *bring near*, i.e. offer 11QT[b] 4$_{6}$ ([ויקריבו]).

עִם *with*, + קטר hi. *burn* 4QJub[d] 21$_{9}$ ([והקטרת]ה]) 11QT 20$_{8}$ ([ויק]טירו]) 23$_{17}$.

מִלְּבַד *besides, apart from* 11QT 28$_{1}$ ([מלבד ...)

[נסכה]), + קרב hi. *bring near*, i.e. offer Nm 29$_{11+9t}$, עשׂה *make*, i.e. offer Nm 28$_{31}$ 29$_{6}$.

אַחַר *after*, + קרב hi. *bring near*, i.e. offer 11QT 23$_{8}$ ([והקריבום] ... [נסכה]).

<COLL> שֶׁמֶן || נֶסֶךְ *oil* Gn 35$_{14}$, מִנְחָה *grain offering* Ex 29$_{41}$ 30$_{9}$ (both +) Lv 23$_{18.37}$ Nm 6$_{15.17}$ 15$_{24}$ 28$_{8.9.31}$ (all three +) 29$_{6+17t}$ 2 K 16$_{13}$ (+) 16$_{15}$ Is 57$_{6}$ Jl 1$_{9.13}$ 2$_{14}$ (all three מִנְחָה וָנֶסֶךְ) 4QJub^{e} 21$_{9}$ 11QT 15$_{9}$ 17$_{14}$ 20$_{8}$ 22$_{3}$ 23$_{16}$ 24$_{5.8}$ 25$_{6.14}$ 28$_{8.11}$ 34$_{13}$ (+), עֹלָה *burnt offering* Lv 23$_{37}$ Nm 15$_{24}$ 28$_{10.15.24.31}$ 29$_{6+9t}$ (all fifteen +) 29$_{39}$ 2 K 16$_{13}$ (+) 16$_{15}$ Ezk 45$_{17}$ 1 C 29$_{21}$ 2 C 29$_{35}$ (both +), זֶבַח *sacrifice* Lv 23$_{37}$ 1 C 29$_{21}$ (+).

נִסְכֵּיהֶם מִדָּם *their libations of blood* Ps 16$_{4}$.

Also 11QT 18$_{5}$ ([נ]סכו) 23$_{5}$ 11QT^{b} 4$_{9}$ 5$_{24}$.

<SYN> שֶׁמֶן *oil*, מִנְחָה *grain offering*, עֹלָה *burnt offering*, זֶבַח *sacrifice*.*

⇨ נסך I *pour out*.

[נֶ֫סֶךְ] II 4 n.m. **molten image**—sf. נִסְכּוֹ, נִסְכִּי; pl. sf. נִסְכֵּיהֶם—<SUBJ> צוה pi. *command* Is 48$_{5}$ (|| עֹצֶב *idol*, פֶּסֶל *image*). <NOM CL> רוּחַ וָתֹהוּ נִסְכֵּיהֶם *their molten images are wind and emptiness* Is 41$_{29}$, שֶׁקֶר נִסְכּוֹ *his molten images are falsehood* Jr 10$_{14}$=51$_{17}$ (+ פֶּסֶל *image*). <PREP> בְּ of place, *in* Jr 10$_{14}$=51$_{17}$.

<SYN> עֹצֶב *idol*, פֶּסֶל *image*.

⇨ נסך *pour out*.

נסס I 1 vb. **be sick** (unless נסס III *sway* or IV *suffer convulsions*)—**Qal** 1 Ptc. נֹסֵס—**be sick,** כִּמְסֹס נֹסֵס *as when one who is sick faints* Is 10$_{18}$.*

***נסס II** 1 **sparkle** (unless נסס III *sway*)—**Htpol.** 1 Ptc. מִתְנוֹסְסוֹת—perh. **sparkle,** <SUBJ> אֶבֶן *stone* of crown Zc 9$_{16}$ (or em. מִתְנוֹצְצוֹת *they sparkle* [i.e. נצץ htpo.], or del.). <PREP> עַל *upon*, + אֲדָמָה *land* Zc 9$_{16}$ (or em.; see Subj.).

⇨ cf. נצץ I *sparkle*.

***נסס III** 4 vb. **sway**—**Qal** 2 Ptc. נֹסֵס, נֹסְסָה—**pass to and fro** (Is 59$_{19}$; unless נוס I pol. *drive on*), **stagger** (Is 10$_{18}$; unless נסס I *be sick* or IV *suffer convulsions*), <SUBJ> רוּחַ *spirit* of Y. Is 59$_{19}$; subj. not specified, Is 10$_{18}$. <PREP> בְּ of place, *upon*, + נָהָר *river* Is 59$_{19}$.

Htpol. 2 Ptc. מִתְנוֹסְסוֹת; inf. הִתְנוֹסֵס—**sway, wave to and fro,** <SUBJ> נֵס *standard* Ps 60$_{6}$ (unless נסס V *rally to the banner*), אֶבֶן *stone* of crown Zc 9$_{16}$ (unless נסס II *sparkle*). <PREP> עַל *upon, over*, + אֲדָמָה *land* Zc 9$_{16}$ (unless נסס II *sparkle*).

⇨ cf. נוס II *tremble*, IV *swing*.

***נסס IV** 1 vb. **suffer convulsions** (unless נסס I *be sick* or III *sway*)—**Qal** 1 Ptc. נֹסֵס—**suffer convulsions,** כִּמְסֹס נֹסֵס *as when one suffering convulsions collapses* Is 10$_{18}$.

***נסס V** 1 **rally to the banner** (unless נוס htpol. *flee [for safety]*)—**Htpol.** 1 Inf. הִתְנוֹסֵס—**rally to the banner,** <SUBJ> ירא ptc. *one who fears* Ps 60$_{6}$. <PREP> מִפְּנֵי *from before, on account of*, + קֹשֶׁט *bow* Ps 60$_{6}$. <COLL> נֵס לְהִתְנוֹסֵס *a banner to which to rally* Ps 60$_{6}$ (or em. נֵס to מָנוֹס *a refuge* to which to flee).

⇨ נֵס *standard*.

***נסס VI** vb. **dry up** (unless נוס *flee*)—**dry up,** <SUBJ> לֵחַ *moisture* Dt 34$_{7}$ (if em. נָס appar. *fled* to נַס).

נסע I 5 vb. **pull up**—**Qal** 3 + waw וַיִּסַּע (וַיִּסָּעֵם)—**pull up, pull out,** <SUBJ> Samson Jg 16$_{3.14}$; subj. not specified, Is 33$_{20}$. <OBJ> דֶּלֶת *door* Jg 16$_{3}$, מְזוּזָה *doorpost* Jg 16$_{3}$, יָתֵד *peg* Jg 16$_{14}$ Is 33$_{20}$, אֶרֶג *loom* Jg 16$_{14}$, מַסֶּכֶת *web* Jg 16$_{14}$. <PREP> לְ of direction, *to*, + נֵצַח *everlastingness* Is 33$_{20}$; עִם *with*, + בְּרִיחַ *bar* Jg 16$_{3}$.

Ni. 2 Pf. נִסַּע—**be pulled up, removed,** <SUBJ> דּוֹר *dwelling* Is 38$_{12}$ (+ גלה ni. *be removed*), יֶתֶר *cord* Jb 4$_{21}$. <PREP> בְּ of accompaniment, *with* (unless בְּ = מִן *from*), + שׁכן ptc. *one who dwells* Jb 4$_{21}$.*

⇨ (?) מַסָּע *quarry*.

נסע II** 141.0.2 vb. **travel**—**Qal** 133 Pf. נָסַע, נָסְעוּ (נָסָֽעוּ); impf. יִסַּע, יִסְעוּ (יִסָּֽעוּ), תִּסְעוּ, נִסְעָה; + waw וְנָסַע (וְנָסָֽעוּ), וַיִּסַּע, וַיִּסְעוּ (וַיִּסָּֽעוּ) וַנִּסַּע (וַנִּסְעָה); impv. סְעוּ; ptc. נֹסֵעַ, נֹסְעִים; inf. abs. נָסוֹעַ; cstr. נְסֹעַ (נָסְעָם)—**travel, journey, move, go about, <SUBJ> מַלְאָךְ *angel* Ex 14$_{19}$, Egypt(ians) Ex 14$_{10}$, Israel(ites) 2 K 3$_{27}$ Zc 10$_{2}$ (or em. תָּעוּ or נָתְעוּ *they wander*) Ezr 8$_{31}$, Kohathites Nm 10$_{21}$, עַם *people* Nm 11$_{35}$ 12$_{15.16}$ Jos 3$_{3.14}$, עֵדָה *congregation* Ex 16$_1$ 17$_1$, בַּיִת *house(hold)* Gn 35$_{5.16}$, מַחֲנֶה *camp* Nm 4$_{5.15}$ 10$_{5.6}$, Abra(ha)m Gn 12$_{9.9}$ 20$_1$, Esau Gn 33$_{12}$, Ezra Ezr 8$_{31}$, Jacob/Israel Gn 33$_{12.17}$ 35$_{5.16.21}$ 46$_1$, Joshua Jos 3$_1$, Moses Dt 1$_{19}$ 2$_1$, Sennacherib 2 K 19$_{36}$||Is 37$_{37}$.

אִישׁ *man* Jg 18$_{11}$, i.e. each Nm 2$_{17.34}$, בֵּן *son* Nm 10$_{17}$, of Israel Ex 12$_{37}$ 13$_{20}$ 14$_{15}$ 19$_2$ 40$_{36.37}$ Nm 2$_{34}$ 9$_{17+8t}$ 10$_{12+5t}$ 14$_{25}$ 20$_{22}$ 21$_{4.10.11.12.13}$ 22$_1$ 33$_{3+41t}$ Dt 1$_{7.19.40}$ 2$_{1.24}$ 10$_{6.7}$ Jos 3$_1$ 9$_{17}$, אָח *brother* Gn 37$_{17}$, מֶלֶךְ *king* 2 K 19$_{8.36}$ ||Is 37$_{8.37}$, פקד pass. ptc. *numbered one* Nm 2$_{9.16.24.31}$, מַשְׁחִית *destroyer* Jr 4$_7$, רוּחַ *wind* Nm 11$_{31}$, עַמּוּד *pillar* of cloud Ex 14$_{19}$, אֹהֶל *tent* Nm 2$_{17}$, מִשְׁכָּן *tabernacle* Nm 1$_{51}$, אָרוֹן *ark* Nm 10$_{33.35}$, דֶּגֶל *standard* Nm 10$_{14.18.22.25}$, כֹּל *all* Gn 46$_1$; subj. not specified, Gn 11$_2$ Jr 31$_{24}$ (אִכָּרִים וְנָסְעוּ בַּעֵדֶר appar. *farmers and those who move with flocks*; or em. נֹסְעֵי).

<PREP> לְ in ref. to subj. of נסע, + Israelites Nm 14$_{25}$ Dt 1$_7$; *according to, by*, + מִשְׁפָּחָה *clan* Nm 2$_{34}$, צָבָא *host* Nm 10$_{14.18.22.25}$, דֶּגֶל *standard* Nm 2$_{17.31}$, מַסָּע *stage (of journey)* Ex 17$_1$ Nm 10$_{12}$.

בְּ of time, *in, at, during, throughout*, + חֹדֶשׁ *month* Nm 33$_3$, יוֹם *day* Nm 33$_3$ appar. Ezr 8$_{31}$ (בִּשְׁנֵים עָשָׂר לַחֹדֶשׁ הָרִאשׁוֹן *on the twelfth [day] of the first month*), רִאשׁוֹן fem. *first*, i.e. first of all Nm 10$_{13.14}$, מַסָּע *journey* Ex 40$_{36}$; of accompaniment, *with*, + עֵדֶר *flock* Jr 31$_{24}$.

כְּמוֹ *as*, + צֹאן *flock* Zc 10$_2$ (or em.; see Subj.).

מִן of direction, *from, in the direction of*, + Abronah Nm 33$_{35}$, Almon-diblathaim Nm 33$_{47}$, Alush Nm 33$_{14}$, Bene-jaakan Nm 33$_{32}$ Dt 10$_6$, Bethel Gn 35$_{16}$, Dibon-gad Nm 33$_{46}$, Dophkah Nm 33$_{13}$, Elim Ex 16$_1$ Nm 33$_{10}$, Eshtaol Jg 18$_{11}$, Etham Nm 33$_7$, Ezion-geber Nm 33$_{36}$, Gudgodah Dt 10$_7$, Haradah Nm 33$_{25}$, Hashmonah Nm 33$_{30}$, Hazzeroth Nm 12$_{16}$ Nm 33$_{18}$, Hor Nm 21$_4$ 33$_{41}$, Horeb Dt 1$_{19}$, Hor-haggidgad Nm 33$_{33}$, Iyim Nm 33$_{45}$, Jotbathah Nm 33$_{34}$, Kadesh Nm 20$_{22}$ 33$_{37}$, Kehelathah Nm 33$_{23}$, Kibroth-hattaavah Nm 11$_{35}$ 33$_{17}$, Lachish 2 K 19$_8$||Is 37$_8$, Libnah Nm 33$_{21}$, Makheloth Nm 33$_{26}$, Marah Nm 33$_9$, Mithkah Nm 33$_{29}$, Moseroth Nm 33$_{31}$, Oboth Nm 21$_{11}$ 33$_{44}$, Punon Nm 33$_{43}$, Rameses Ex 12$_{37}$ Nm 33$_{3.5}$, Rephidim Ex 19$_2$ Nm 33$_{15}$, Rimmon-perez Nm 33$_{20}$, Rissah Nm 33$_{22}$, Rithmah Nm 33$_{19}$, Shittim Jos 3$_1$, Succoth Ex 13$_{20}$ Nm 33$_6$, Tahath Nm 33$_{27}$, Terah Nm 33$_{28}$, Zalmonah Nm 33$_{42}$, Zorah Jg 18$_{11}$, מַחֲנֶה *camp* Nm 10$_{34}$, אֹהֶל *tent* Jos 3$_{14}$, קֶדֶם *east* Gn 11$_2$ 13$_{11}$, הַר *mountain* Nm 10$_{33}$ 21$_4$ 33$_{24.41.48}$, מִדְבָּר *steppe* Ex 17$_1$ Nm 33$_{12.16}$, יָם *sea* Nm 33$_{11}$, נָהָר *river* Ezr 8$_{31}$, מָקוֹם *place* Jos 3$_3$, שָׁם *there* Gn 20$_1$ Nm 21$_{12.13}$ Dt 10$_7$ Jg 18$_{11}$, זֶה *this (place)* Gn 37$_{17}$.

אֶל *to*, + מָקוֹם *place* Nm 10$_{29}$.

עַל *at*, + יָד *hand*, i.e. in position Nm 2$_{17}$; *according to*, + פֶּה *mouth*, i.e. command Nm 9$_{18.23}$ 10$_{13}$, בַּיִת *house* of fathers Nm 2$_{34}$.

מֵאֵת *from*, + Y. Nm 11$_{31}$.

מֵעַל *from*, + מֶלֶךְ *king* 2 K 3$_{27}$.

לִפְנֵי *before*, + בֵּן *son* of Israel Nm 10$_{33}$.

מִפְּנֵי *from before*, + Hahiroth Nm 33$_8$, מַחֲנֶה *host* Ex 14$_{19}$.

אַחֲרֵי *after, behind*, + בֵּן *son* of Israel Ex 14$_{10}$.

ה- of direction, *(to)wards*, + Succoth Gn 33$_{17}$ Ex 12$_{37}$, נֶגֶב *Negeb* Gn 12$_9$, מִדְבָּר *steppe* Dt 1$_{40}$ 2$_1$, אֶרֶץ *land* Gn 20$_1$.

נסע + noun without preposition or ה- of direction, גֻּדְגֹּדָה *(to) Gudgodah* Dt 10$_7$, חֲצֵרוֹת *(to) Hazeroth*, יָטְבָתָה *Jotbathah* Dt 10$_7$, מוֹסֵרָה *(to) Moserah* Dt 10$_6$, מִדְבָּר *(to the) steppe* Nm 14$_{25}$, דֶּרֶךְ *(on a) journey* Nm 10$_{33}$, *(by) way (of)* Nm 14$_{25}$ 21$_4$ Dt 1$_{40}$ 2$_1$, אֶרֶץ *(to a) land* Dt 10$_7$.

<COLL> נסע + הלך *go* Gn 33$_{12}$ Ex 14$_{19}$ Nm 33$_8$ Dt 1$_{19}$ Jos 3$_3$ 2 K 19$_{36}$||Is 37$_{37}$, בוא *come* Gn 46$_1$ Ex 16$_1$ 19$_2$ Nm 20$_{22}$ 33$_9$ Dt 1$_7$ Jos 3$_1$, יצא *go out* Nm 33$_3$ Jr 4$_7$, עלה *go up* Jr 4$_7$, עבר *pass* Nm 33$_8$ Dt 2$_{24}$, פנה *turn* Nm 14$_{25}$ Dt 1$_{7.40}$ 2$_1$, שׁוב *go back* Nm 33$_7$ 2 K 3$_{27}$ 19$_{36}$||Is 37$_{37}$, קום *arise* Dt 2$_{24}$, חנה *encamp* Ex 13$_{20}$ 17$_1$ 19$_2$ Nm 1$_{51}$ 2$_{34}$ 9$_{17.18.20.22.23}$ 12$_{16}$ 21$_{10.11.12.13}$ 22$_1$ 33$_{5+39t}$.

+ adverb, רִאשֹׁנָה *first* Nm 2$_9$, שְׁנִיִּם *second* Nm 2$_{16}$, שְׁלִשִׁים *third* Nm 2$_{24}$, לָאַחֲרֹנָה *last* Nm 2$_{31}$, כֵּן *so* Nm 2$_{34}$, אַחַר *afterwards* Nm 12$_{16}$.

+ infinitive of purpose of עבר *pass* Jos 3$_3$, סבב *go around* Nm 21$_4$.

וַיִּסַּע אַבְרָם הָלוֹךְ וְנָסוֹעַ *and Abram continued to journey on* Gn 12$_9$.

Also 4QRedInk 1.2$_1$.

Hi. 8.0.1 Impf. יַסַּע, 2ms תַּסִּיעַ, תַּסִּיעִי; + waw וַיַּסַּע, וַיַּסִּעוּ; ptc. מַסִּיעַ; inf. Q לסיע (Q להסיע)—**1. lead out, bring out,** <SUBJ> Y. Ps 78$_{26.52}$ (both + נהג pi. *lead*) 80$_{9}$, Moses Ex 15$_{22}$, עַיִן *eye* perh. Si 34$_{13(Bmg)}$ (תסיע, or תזיע *it sheds*, i.e. זוע hi.; B תדמע *it weeps*). <OBJ> Israel Ex 15$_{22}$, עַם *people* Ps 78$_{52}$, גֶּפֶן *vine* Ps 80$_{9}$, קָדִים *east wind* Ps 78$_{26}$, דִּמְעָה *tears* Si 34$_{13(Bmg)}$. <PREP> בְּ of place, *in*, + שָׁמַיִם *heavens* Ps 78$_{26}$; כְּ *as*, + צֹאן *flock* Ps 78$_{52}$; מִן of direction, *from*, + Egypt Ps 80$_{9}$, יָם *sea* Ex 15$_{22}$, פָּנִים *face* Si 34$_{13(Bmg)}$.

2. remove, move, <SUBJ> Y. Jb 19$_{10}$, אִישׁ *man* CD 1$_{16}$, אִשָּׁה *wife* 2 K 4$_{4}$. <OBJ> כְּלִי *vessel* 2 K 4$_{4}$, גְּבוּל *boundary* CD 1$_{16}$, תִּקְוָה *hope* Jb 19$_{10}$, בְּכִית *weeping* Ḥorvat ʿUza bowl inscr.$_{7}$ (Cross) (7th cent.). <PREP> כְּ *as* Jb 19$_{10}$.

3. quarry, <SUBJ> עַם *people* 1 K 5$_{31}$; subj. not specified, Ec 10$_{9}$ (|| בקע *split*). <OBJ> אֶבֶן *stone* 1 K 5$_{31}$. <SYN> §3 בקע *split*.

Also Ḥorvat ʿUza bowl inscr.$_{8}$ (Cross) (7th cent.).*

⇒ מַסָּע *journey*, (?) מַסָּע *quarrying*.

נסק, see שׂלק *burn*.

נִסְרֹךְ 2 pr.n.m. **Nisroch,** name of an otherwise unattested Assyrian god, prob. error for Nusku or Marduk,* or perh. conflation of the names Assur and Marduk,* in whose temple Sennacherib was assassinated, <CSTR> בֵּית נִסְרֹךְ *house of Nisroch* 2 K 19$_{37}$||Is 37$_{38}$. <APP> אֱלֹהִים *god* 2 K 19$_{37}$||Is 37$_{38}$.*

נָע I *vagabond, wanderer*, see נוע I *tremble*.

נָע II *rootless person*, see נוע III *be rootless*.

נֵעָה 1 pl.n. **Neah,** in Zebulun, <COLL> הַמְּתֹאָר הַנֵּעָה appar. *it* (boundary) *is inclined towards Neah* Jos 19$_{13}$ (or em. הַמְּתֹאָר [pu.] to וְתָאַר *and it inclines*, i.e. qal).

נֹעָה I 4 pr.n.f. **Noah,** daughter of Zelophehad, <SUBJ> היה *be* Nm 36$_{11}$. <NOM CL> אֵלֶּה שְׁמוֹת בְּנֹתָיו ... נֹעָה *these are the names of his daughters ... Noah* Nm 27$_{1}$ Jos 17$_{3}$, var. Nm 26$_{33}$.

*[**נֹעָה**] II 0.0.0.2 pl.n. **Noah,** <PREP> מִן of direction, *from* Samaria ost. 50$_{1}$ 52$_{1}$ (מנע[ה]; others תבע) 64$_{1}$.

[**נַעֲוָה**], see עוה *twist*, Ni.

*[**נַעֲוָיָה**] 0.0.5 n.f. **perversity**—cstr. Q נעוית; Q sf. נעויתי, Q נעויתכה, Q נעויתו—<CSTR> נעוית לבבי *the perversity of my heart* 1QH 4$_{19}$ 1QS 11$_{9}$, כול נעויתכה *all your perversity* 4Q417 1.1$_{13}$. <PREP> לְ perh. introducing object 4Q417 1.1$_{13}$; כְּ *according to*, + אחר pi. *detain* 1QS 5$_{24}$, יכח hi. *acknowledge (as just)* 1QS 10$_{11}$; עַל *for, on account of*, + חנן htp. *make supplication* 1QH 4$_{19}$; עִם *with* 1QS 11$_{9}$. <COLL> פֶּשַׁע + נַעֲוָיָה *transgression* 1QS 10$_{11}$ 11$_{9}$, חַטָּאת *sin* 1QS 11$_{9}$, עָוֹן *iniquity* 1QS 11$_{9}$.

⇒ עוה *twist*.

נְעוּרִים 46.7.6 n.f.pl. **youth**—pl. sf. נְעוּרַי (נְעֻרַי, נְעוּרָי), נְעוּרַיִךְ (נְעוּרַיְכִי, נְעוּרַיִךְ), נְעוּרֶיךָ (נְעוּרֶךָ, נְעֻרֶיךָ), (נְעֻרָי) נְעוּרָיו (נְעֻרָיו), נְעוּרֶיהָ (נְעֻרֶיהָ), נְעוּרֵינוּ, נְעוּרֵיהֶם, נְעוּרֵיהֶן—**(time of) youth,** <SUBJ> חדשׁ htp. *renew oneself* Ps 103$_{5}$.

<CSTR> בַּעַל נְעוּרֶיהָ *husband of her youth* Jl 1$_{8}$, אֵשֶׁת נְעוּרִים *wife of youth* Is 54$_{6}$ Si 15$_{2}$, נְעוּרֶיךָ *of your youth* Ml 2$_{14.15}$ Pr 5$_{18}$ (נְעוּרֶךָ), בְּנֵי הַנְּעוּרִים *the sons of youth* Ps 127$_{4}$, אַלּוּף נְעֻרָי *friend of my youth* Jr 3$_{4}$, נְעוּרֶיהָ *of her youth* Pr 2$_{17}$, שְׁדֵי נְעוּרָיִךְ *breasts of your youth* Ezk 23$_{21}$, חֶסֶד נְעוּרַיִךְ *loyalty of your youth* Jr 2$_{2}$ (|| כְּלוּלֹת *betrothal*), חֶרְפַּת נְעוּרָי *disgrace of my youth* Jr 31$_{19}$, זִמַּת נְעוּרָיִךְ *wickedness of your youth* Ezk 23$_{21}$, חַטֹּאות נְעוּרַי *sins of my youth* Ps 25$_{7}$ 11QPs^{a} 24$_{11}$ (חטאת), עֲוֹנוֹת נְעוּרָי *iniquities of my youth* Jb 13$_{26}$, יְמֵי נְעוּרַיִךְ *days of your youth* Ezk 16$_{22}$ (נְעוּרָיִךְ) 16$_{43.60}$ (נְעוּרָיִךְ), נְעוּרֶיהָ *of her youth* Ezk 23$_{19}$ Ho 2$_{17}$.

<PREP> בְּ of time, *in, during* Nm 30$_{17}$ Ps 144$_{12}$ (or em. בַּעֲרוּגֹתָם *in their garden beds*), + חכם *be wise* Si 47$_{14}$, אסר *bind oneself*, i.e. vow Nm 30$_{4}$ 11QT 53$_{17}$, זנה *prostitute oneself* Ezk 23$_{3}$, גור *prostitute oneself* Si 42$_{9(B)}$, שׁכב *lie down* Ezk 23$_{8}$, מאס ni. *be rejected* Si 42$_{9(M)}$ ([ת]מאס), נשׂא *bear* Lm 3$_{27}$, *take in marriage* Si 7$_{23}$, משׁל *allow to rule* Si 30$_{11}$, נכה hi. *strike* Si 47$_{4}$.

כְּ *as in* Lv 22$_{13}$.

מִן of time, *from, since* Gn 8$_{21}$ 1 S 17$_{33}$ Jr 22$_{21}$ Ps 71$_{5}$ 1QH[b] 1$_{10}$ 4QJub[h] 35$_{9}$ 4QPrayer[c] 1$_{4}$ ((מנעור[ ])), + היה *be* Gn 46$_{34}$, הלך htp. *go about* 1 S 12$_{2}$, בוא *come* 2 S 19$_{8}$, ירא *fear* 1 K 18$_{12}$, ידע *know* Si 51$_{15(11QPs^a)}$, למד *learn* Si 51$_{15(B)}$, pi. *teach* Ps 71$_{17}$ 1QSa 1$_{6}$ (מן נעו]ריו יל[מדהו), גדל *rear* Jb 31$_{18}$, יגע *toil* Is 47$_{12.15}$, יפע hi. *shine forth* 1QH 17$_{31}$, אכל *eat* Jr 3$_{24}$ Ezk 4$_{14}$, חטא *sin* Jr 3$_{25}$, שׁאן palel *be at ease* Jr 48$_{11}$, קנה hi. *cause to purchase*, i.e. enslave Zc 13$_{5}$ (or em. אָדָם הִקְנַנִי *a human being has enslaved me* to אֲדָמָה קִנְיָנִי *the land is my possession*), צרר *harass* Ps 129$_{1.2}$.

<SYN> כְּלוּלֹת *betrothal* Jr 2$_{2}$.*

⇒ נַעַר *youth*.

נְעִיאֵל 1 pl.n. **Neiel,** in Asher, perh. Kh. Ya'nīn, 15 km ESE of Akko, on the plain of Akko, <PREP> בְּ introducing object, + פגע *touch* Jos 19$_{27}$.

נָעִים I 13.0.1 adj. **pleasant**—cstr. נְעִים; m.pl. נְעִימִים (נְעִמִים, נְעִמִם); f.pl. נְעִמוֹת—**pleasant, delightful, lovely, 1.** used attributively of עֵץ *tree* 4Q423 2$_{1}$ (+ חמד ni. ptc. *desirable*), כִּנּוֹר *lyre* Ps 81$_{3}$ (unless נָעִים II *musical*), דָּבָר *word* Pr 23$_{8}$, הוֹן *wealth* Pr 24$_{4}$ (|| יָקָר *precious*).

2. in nom cl. used predicatively, מַה־נָּעִים שֶׁבֶת אַחִים גַּם־יָחַד *how pleasant is it when brothers dwell together* Ps 133$_{1}$ (|| טוֹב *good*), הִנְּךָ ... נָעִים *behold, you are ... lovely* Ca 1$_{16}$ (|| יָפֶה *beautiful*), כִּי נָעִים *for it/he is pleasant* Ps 135$_{3}$ 147$_{1}$ (+ נָאוֶה *fitting*; both || טוֹב) Pr 22$_{18}$, יש אוכל ... [נעי]ם *there is food that is ... pleasant* Si 36$_{23(B)}$.

3. as noun, **a. pleasant one,** <SUBJ> גבר *be strong* 2 S 1$_{23}$ (|| אהב ni. ptc. *beloved one*), קלל *be swift* 2 S 1$_{23}$, פרד ni. *be divided* 2 S 1$_{23}$. <CSTR> נְעִים זְמִרוֹת *pleasant one of the songs of* Israel 2 S 23$_{1}$ (unless §3d); נְאֻם ... נְעִים *utterance of ... the pleasant one of* Israel 2 S 23$_{1}$. <APP> Jonathan 2 S 1$_{23}$, Saul 2 S 1$_{23}$.

b. pleasant place, delightful place, <PREP> בְּ of place, *in*, + נפל *fall* Ps 16$_{6}$ (unless §3d; + שׁפר *be beautiful*).

c. pleasure, delight, <NOM CL> נְעִמוֹת בִּימִינְךָ *pleasures are in your right hand* Ps 16$_{11}$ (unless §3d; + שִׂמְחָה *joy*). <PREP> בְּ of accompaniment, *with, in,* + כלה pi. *spend* years Jb 36$_{11}$ (|| טוֹב *good*).

d. favourable omen or **person receiving a favourable omen,*** <NOM CL> נְעִמוֹת בִּימִינְךָ נֶצַח *in your right hand are always favourable omens* Ps 16$_{11}$ (unless §3c). <CSTR> נְאֻם ... נְעִים זְמִרַת *utterance of ... the favoured one, the guardian of* Israel 2 S 23$_{1}$ (if em. זְמִרוֹת *songs of* to זִמְרַת from זִמְרָה III *refuge*; unless §3a). <PREP> בְּ of place, *among*, + נפל *fall* Ps 16$_{6}$ (unless §3c).

<SYN> §1 יָקָר *precious*; §2 טוֹב *good*, יָפֶה *beautiful*, §3a אהב ni. ptc. *beloved one*, טוֹב *good*.*

⇒ נעם I *be pleasant*.

נָעִים II 2 adj. **musical** (unless נָעִים I *pleasant*)—cstr. נְעִים—**musical, sweet sounding, 1.** used attributively of כִּנּוֹר *lyre* Ps 81$_{3}$.

2. as noun, **sweet sounding one, singer,** <CSTR> נְעִים זְמִרוֹת *singer of the songs of* Israel 2 S 23$_{1}$; נְאֻם ... נְעִים *utterance of ... the singer of* Israel 2 S 23$_{1}$.

*****[נְעִימָה]** 0.1 n.f. **melody,** or perh. **pleasant sound,** given by bells on Aaron's robe, <OBJ> נתן *give* Si 45$_{9}$ (+ קוֹל *sound*).

⇒ נעם II *sing*, or נעם I *be pleasant*.

נעל I 6 vb. **lock—Qal** 6 Pf. נָעַל (נָעֶל); impv. נְעֹל; ptc. pass. נְעֻלוֹת, נָעוּל—**1. lock, bolt,** <SUBJ> Ehud Jg 3$_{23}$ (+ סגר *close*), נַעַר *lad* 2 S 13$_{17}$, מְשָׁרֵת *servant* 2 S 13$_{17.18}$. <OBJ> דֶּלֶת *door* Jg 3$_{23}$ 2 S 13$_{17.18}$. <SUBJ> אַחֲרֵי *after, behind,* + Tamar 2 S 13$_{18}$, זֹאת *this one* (i.e. Tamar) 2 S 13$_{17}$.

2. pass. **be locked, bolted, sealed,** <SUBJ> דֶּלֶת *door* Jg 3$_{24}$, גַּן *garden* Ca 4$_{12}$ (|| חתם pass. *be sealed*), גַּל *spring* Ca 4$_{12}$ (mss גַּן *garden*).

<SYN> §2 חתם pass. *be sealed*.

⇒ מַנְעוּל *bolt*, מִנְעָל *bolt*.

נעל II 2 vb. **provide with sandals—Qal** 1 + waw וָאֶנְעָלֵךְ—**provide with sandals,** with accus. of person and of material of sandals, <SUBJ> Y. Ezk 16$_{10}$ (|| לבשׁ hi. *dress with*, חבשׁ *bind*, כסה pi. *cover*). <OBJ> 1.

person shod, Jerusalem Ezk 16$_{10}$. 2. shod with, תַּחַשׁ *leather* Ezk 16$_{10}$.

<SYN> לבשׁ hi. *dress with*, חבשׁ *bind*, כסה pi. *cover*.

Hi. 1 + waw וַיַּנְעִלוּם—**provide with sandals,** <SUBJ> אִישׁ *man* 2 C 28$_{15}$ (|| לבשׁ hi. *dress with*, אכל hi. *feed*, שׁקה hi. *give to drink*, סוך *anoint*). <OBJ> מַעֲרֹם *nakedness*, i.e. naked one 2 C 28$_{15}$.

<SYN> לבשׁ hi. *dress with*, אכל hi. *feed*, שׁקה hi. *give to drink*, סוך *anoint*.

⇒ נַעַל *sandal*.

נַעַל 22 n.f. **sandal**—נַעַל; sf. נַעֲלִי, נַעַלְךָ, נַעֲלוֹ; du. נַעֲלַיִם; pl. נְעָלִים, נְעָלוֹת; sf. נְעָלֶיךָ, נְעָלָיו, נְעָלֵינוּ, נַעֲלֵיכֶם—**sandal,** removed on holy ground (Ex 3$_5$ Jos 5$_{15}$), when refusing to contract levirate marriage (Dt 25$_{9.10}$ Ru 4$_{7.8}$); as of little value (Am 2$_6$ 8$_6$).

<SUBJ> בלה *wear out* Dt 29$_4$ Jos 9$_{13}$. <NOM CL> נַעֲלֵיכֶם בְּרַגְלֵיכֶם *your sandals shall be on your feet* Ex 12$_{11}$ Ezk 24$_{23}$, vars. Jos 9$_5$ 1 K 2$_5$. <OBJ> נשׁל *remove* Ex 3$_5$ Jos 5$_{15}$, חלץ *remove* Dt 25$_9$ Is 20$_2$, שׁלף *remove* Ru 4$_{7.8}$, שׁלך hi. *cast* Ps 60$_{10}$||108$_{10}$, שׂים *place* on feet Ezk 24$_{17}$. <CSTR> שְׂרוֹךְ־נַעַל *thong of a sandal* Gn 14$_{23}$, נְעָלָיו *of his sandals* Is 5$_{27}$, חֲלוּץ הַנָּעַל *removed one of sandal*, i.e. whose sandal has been removed Dt 25$_{10}$. <ADJ> בָּלֶה *worn out* Jos 9$_5$, טלא pu. ptc. *patched* Jos 9$_5$. <PREP> בְּ of place, *in, upon*, + יפה *be beautiful* Ca 7$_2$, נתן *give*, i.e. place 1 K 2$_5$; of instrument, *by (means of), with*, + דרך hi. *tread* Is 11$_{15}$; בַּעֲבוּר *for the price of*, + מכר *deliver (over)* Am 2$_6$ (or em. נַעְלָם *bribe*), קנה *purchase* Am 8$_6$. <COLL> נַעַל || שִׂמְלָה *garment* Dt 29$_4$ Jos 9$_{5.13}$, חֲגוֹרָה *belt* 1 K 2$_5$, שַׂק *sackcloth* Is 20$_2$, פְּאֵר *turban* Ezk 24$_{17.23}$, כֶּסֶף *silver* Am 2$_6$ 8$_6$.

<SYN> שִׂמְלָה *garment*, חֲגוֹרָה *belt*, שַׂק *sackcloth*, פְּאֵר *turban*, כֶּסֶף *silver*.*

⇒ נעל II *provide with sandals*.

*[נַעֲלָם] 1.1.1 n.[m.] **bribe**—pl. נַעֲלָמִים—**bribe** (Am 2$_6$ [if em.; see Prep.]), in ref. to those who take bribes Ps 26$_4$ 1QH 12$_{13}$ [unless both עלם ni. ptc. *ones who conceal themselves*]), <NOM CL> המה נעלמים *they are (ones who take) bribes* 1QH 12$_{13}$. <OBJ> לקח *take* 1 S 12$_3$ (if em. וְאַעְלִים *that I should hide* to וְנַעֲלָם *or a bribe*) Si 46$_{19(Segal)}$ (לקח[תי]; unless עלם ni. ptc. *hidden thing*; || כֹּפֶר *ransom*). <PREP> בַּעֲבוּר *for the price of*, + מכר *deliver (over)* Am 2$_6$ (if em. נַעֲלַיִם appar. *a pair of sandals* to נַעְלָם), קנה *purchase* Am 8$_6$ (if em. נַעֲלָיִם); עִם *with*, + בוא *go in* Ps 26$_4$.

<SYN> כֹּפֶר *ransom*.

⇒ עלם *conceal*.

נעם I 8.4 vb. **be pleasant**—**Qal** 8.3 Pf. נָעֵמָה, נָעַמְתָּ (נָעֵמְתָּ), נָעֵמוּ, נָעַמְתְּ; impf. יִנְעַם, 3fs Si תנעם—**be pleasant, delightful, lovely,** perh. specifically **be sweet,*** <SUBJ> Jonathan 2 S 1$_{26}$, אָח *brother* 2 S 1$_{26}$, הָמוֹן *multitude* of Egypt Ezk 32$_{19}$, אַהֲבָה *love*, i.e. beloved one Ca 7$_7$ (or em. אַהֲבָה to אֲהֻבָה *beloved one*), תִּקְוָה *hope*, i.e. outcome Si 7$_{13}$, אֹמֶר *word* Ps 141$_6$, דַּעַת *knowledge* Pr 2$_{10}$ (or em. וְדַעַת לְנַפְשְׁךָ יִנְעָם *and knowledge will be pleasant to your soul* to לָדַעַת נַפְשְׁךָ מָעוֹן *that your soul may know a habitation*), מַכָּה *stroke* Si 36$_{23(B)}$, לֶחֶם *bread* Pr 9$_{17}$, מַאֲכָל *food* appar. Si 36$_{23(Bmg)}$, אֶרֶץ *land* Gn 49$_{15}$ (|| טוב *be good*), impersonal Pr 24$_{25}$.

<PREP> לְ of benefit, *to, for*, + David 2 S 1$_{26}$, יכח hi. ptc. *one who reproves* Pr 24$_{25}$, נֶפֶשׁ *soul* Pr 2$_{10}$ (or em.; see Subj.); מִן of comparison, *(more) than*, + מִי *whom?* Ezk 32$_{19}$, מַכָּה *stroke* Si 36$_{23(B)}$, מַאֲכָל *food* Si 36$_{23(Bmg)}$.

<COLL> נעם || טוב *be good* Gn 49$_{15}$, יפה *be beautiful* Ca 7$_7$, מתק *be sweet* Pr 9$_{17}$; + פלא ni. *be wonderful* 2 S 1$_{26}$; + adverb, מְאֹד *very* 2 S 1$_{26}$, מָה *how!* Ca 7$_7$.

Hi. 0.1 Pf. Si הנעים—**make pleasant** (unless נעם II *sing*), <SUBJ> David Si 47$_{9(Bmg)}$. <OBJ> קוֹל *sound* of song Si 47$_{9(Bmg)}$.*

⇒ נָעִים *pleasant*, נֹעַם *pleasantness*, נַעֲמָנִים *pleasantness*, מַנְעַמִּים *delicacies*, נְעִימָה *pleasant sound*, נַעַם *Naam*, נְעַמְאֵל *Neamel*, נָעֳמִי *Naomi*, נַעֲמָן *Naaman*, נַעֲמָה I, II *Naamah*, נַעֲמִי *Naamite*, נַעֲמָתִי *Naamathite*, אֲבִינֹעַם *Abinoam*, אֲחִינֹעַם *Ahinoam*.

*__נעם__ II 0.1 vb. **sing** (unless נעם I *be pleasant*)—**Hi.** 0.1 Pf. Si הנעים—**sing (with), make melodious,** <SUBJ> David Si 47$_{9(Bmg)}$. <OBJ> קוֹל *sound* of song Si 47$_{9(Bmg)}$.

⇒ (?) נְעִימָה *melody*.

[נַעַם] 1 pr.n.m. **Naam**—נַעַם—son of Caleb, <NOM

<CL> בְּנֵי כָּלֵב ... עִירוּ אֵלָה וָנָעַם *the sons of Caleb were ... Iru, Elah and Naam* 1 C 4$_{15}$.

⇒ נעם I *be pleasant.*

נֹעַם 7.1 n.m. **pleasantness**—cstr. נֹעַם (Si נועם)—**1. pleasantness, kindness, loveliness,** as name given to staff (Zc 11$_{7.10}$), <SUBJ> היה *be* Ps 90$_{17}$ (unless §2). <OBJ> חזה *see* Ps 27$_4$, קרא *call,* i.e. name Zc 11$_7$, לקח *take* Zc 11$_{10}$, גדע *hew down* Zc 11$_{10}$. <CSTR> נֹעַם־י׳ *pleasantness of Y.* Ps 27$_4$ (unless §2), אֲדֹנָי *of my Lord* Ps 90$_{17}$ (unless §2), נועם תירוש *pleasantness of new wine* Si 32$_6$. <APP> מַקֵּל *staff* Zc 11$_{10}$; דַּרְכֵי־נֹעַם *ways of pleasantness* Pr 3$_{17}$ (+ שָׁלוֹם *peace*), ־אִמְרֵי *words of* Pr 15$_{26}$ 16$_{24}$. <PREP> בְּ introducing object, + חזה *see* Ps 27$_4$ (unless §2); עַל *in addition to, with* Si 32$_6$.

2. apparition, affirmative response to an augury* (unless §1), <SUBJ> היה *be* Ps 90$_{17}$. <CSTR> נֹעַם־י׳ *apparition of Y.* Ps 27$_4$, אֲדֹנָי *of my Lord* Ps 90$_{17}$. <PREP> בְּ introducing object, + חזה *see* Ps 27$_4$.*

⇒ נעם I *be pleasant.*

*[נְעַמְאֵל] 0.0.0.1 pr.n.[m.] **Neamel,** perh. son of Peoreth, <PREP> לְ of possession, *of, (belonging) to* Seal 95 (Cadiz, 8th/7th cent.).

⇒ נעם I *be pleasant* + אֵל *God.*

נַעֲמָה I 4 pr.n.f. **Naamah, 1.** sister of Tubal-cain, <NOM CL> אֲחוֹת תּוּבַל־קַיִן נַעֲמָה *the sister of Tubal-cain was Naamah* Gn 4$_{22}$.

2. Ammonite, mother of Rehoboam, <NOM CL> שֵׁם אִמּוֹ נַעֲמָה *the name of his mother was Naamah* 1 K 14$_{21}$||2 C 12$_{13}$ 1 K 14$_{31}$. <APP> עַמּוֹנִי *Ammonite* 1 K 14$_{21}$|| 2 C 12$_{13}$ 1 K 14$_{31}$.*

⇒ נעם I *be pleasant.*

נַעֲמָה II 1 pl.n. **Naamah,** town in lowland of Judah, in the region of Lachish, <NOM CL> בַּשְּׁפֵלָה ... נַעֲמָה *in the lowland were ... Naamah* Jos 15$_{41}$. <APP> עִיר *city* Jos 15$_{41}$.

⇒ נעם I *be pleasant.*

נַעֲמִי 1 gent. **Naamite,** as collective noun, of descendants of Naaman, <CSTR> מִשְׁפַּחַת הַנַּעֲמָתִי *clan of the Naamites* Nm 26$_{40}$.

⇒ נעם I *be pleasant,* נַעֲמָן *Naaman.*

נָעֳמִי 21 pr.n.f. **Naomi,** wife of Elimelech, mother-in-law of Ruth, <SUBJ> היה *be* Ru 1$_{11}$ 4$_{16}$, זקן *be old* Ru 1$_{11}$, שׁאר ni. *remain* Ru 1$_3$, אמר *say* Ru 1$_{8.11.19.20}$ 2$_{2.20.20.22}$ 3$_1$, ילד *bear* Ru 1$_{11}$, הלך *go* Ru 1$_{20}$, בוא *come* Ru 1$_{22}$, שׁוב *go back* Ru 1$_{22}$ 4$_3$, בקשׁ pi. *seek* Ru 3$_1$, נשׁק *kiss* Ru 1$_8$, מכר *deliver (over)* Ru 4$_3$, לקח *take* Ru 4$_{16}$, שׂים *place* Ru 4$_{16}$.

<NOM CL> שֵׁם אִשְׁתּוֹ נָעֳמִי *the name of his wife was Naomi* Ru 1$_2$, הֲזֹאת נָעֳמִי *is this Naomi?* Ru 1$_{19}$.

<OBJ> שׁוב hi. *bring back* Ru 1$_{20}$, אהב *love* Ru 4$_{14}$.

<CSTR> אִישׁ נָעֳמִי *husband of Naomi* Ru 1$_3$, יַד *hand of* Ru 4$_{5.9}$.

<APP> חָמוֹת *mother-in-law* Ru 3$_1$.

<PREP> לְ of direction, *to* Ru 2$_2$, + אמר *say* Ru 1$_8$; of possession, benefit *(belonging) to, for* Ru 2$_1$, + היה *be* Ru 4$_{14}$, ילד pu. *be born* Ru 4$_{17}$, שׁבת hi. *cease* Ru 4$_{14}$; introducing object, + קרא *call,* i.e. name Ru 1$_{20.21}$, מרר hi. *make bitter* Ru 1$_{20}$, רעע hi. *harm* Ru 1$_{21}$; בְּ *against,* + ענה *testify* Ru 1$_{21}$; אֶל *to,* + אמר *say* Ru 2$_2$ 3$_1$ 4$_{14}$; עִם *with* Ru 1$_{22}$, + הלך *to* Ru 1$_{11}$, שׁוב *go back* Ru 2$_6$, עשׂה *do,* i.e. deal Ru 1$_8$; אֵת *with,* + שׁוב *go back* Ru 1$_8$.

⇒ נעם I *be pleasant.*

נַעֲמָן 16 pr.n.m. **Naaman, 1.** son of Benjamin (Gn 46$_{21}$), or son of Bela and grandson of Benjamin (Nm 26$_{40}$ 1 C 8$_4$), <SUBJ> היה *be* Nm 26$_{40}$ 1 C 8$_4$. <NOM CL> בְּנֵי בִנְיָמִן ... נַעֲמָן *the sons of Benjamin were ... Naaman* Gn 46$_{21}$. <PREP> לְ of possession, *of, (belonging) to* Nm 26$_{40}$.

2. Benjaminite, appar. son of Ehud, but prob. ident. with §1, <NOM CL> אֵלֶּה בְּנֵי אֵחוּד ... נַעֲמָן *these are the sons of Ehud ... Naaman* 1 C 8$_7$. <OBJ> גלה hi. *exile* 1 C 8$_7$.

3. army commander of king of Aram, <SUBJ> היה *be* 2 K 5$_1$, אמר *say* 2 K 5$_{11.17.21.23}$, פצר *urge* 2 K 5$_{11.23}$ (if em. ־וַיִּפְרָץ *and he broke out*), ראה *see* 2 K 5$_{21}$, ידע *know* 2 K 5$_{11}$, הלך *go* 2 K 5$_{9.11.17}$, בוא *come* 2 K 5$_{9.11}$, hi. *bring* 2 K 5$_{20}$, ירד *go down* 2 K 5$_{11}$, פנה *turn* 2 K 5$_{11}$,

שׁוּב *go back* 2 K 5_{11}, נפל *fall,* i.e. alight 2 K 5_{21}, עמד *stand* 2 K $5_{9.11}$, קרא *meet* 2 K 5_{21}, שׁחה htpal. *bow* 2 K 5_{17}, נשׂא pass. *be lifted,* i.e. favoured 2 K 5_1, טבל *dip* 2 K 5_{11}, רחץ *wash* 2 K $5_{9.11}$, טהר *be clean* 2 K $5_{9.11}$, קצף *be angry* 2 K 5_{11}, נתן *give* 2 K $5_{21.23}$, צור *bind* 2 K 5_{23}.

<OBJ> שׁלח *send* 2 K 5_6, אסף *gather,* i.e. remove, from leprosy 2 K 5_6, חשׂך *spare* 2 K 5_{20}.

<CSTR> אֵשֶׁת נַעֲמָן *wife of Naaman* 2 K 5_2, צָרַעַת *leprosy of* 2 K 5_{27}.

<APP> אֲרַמִּי *Aramaean* 2 K 5_{20}, שַׂר *commander* 1 K 5_1, עֶבֶד *servant* 2 K 5_6.

<PREP> לְ of direction, *to,* + שׁוּב *go back* 2 K 5_9; בְּ of agent, *by, through,* + נתן *give* 2 K 5_1; אֶל *to,* + דבר pi. *speak* 2 K 5_{11}, יצא *go out* 2 K 5_{11}, שׁלח *send* 2 K 5_9; מֵאֵת *from,* + לקח *take* 2 K 5_{20}; אַחֲרֵי *after,* + רוץ *run* 2 K $5_{20.21}$, רדף *pursue* 2 K 5_{21}.

⇒ נעם I *be pleasant,* נַעֲמִי *Naamite.*

נַעֲמָנִים 1 n.[m.]pl. **pleasantness,** <CSTR> נִטְעֵי נַעֲמָנִים *plants of pleasantness,* i.e. pleasant plants Is 17_{10}.*

⇒ נעם I *be pleasant.*

נַעֲמָתִי 4 gent. **Naamathite,** belonging to Naamah perh. in Arabia; as noun, an individual **Naamathite,** <SUBJ> אמר *say* Jb 11_1 20_1, ענה *answer* Jb 11_1 20_1, שׁמע *hear* Jb 2_{11} 20_1, הלך *go* Jb 42_9, בוא *come* Jb 2_{11}, יעד hi. *make an appointment* Jb 2_{11}, נוד *show grief* Jb 2_{11}, נחם pi. *comfort* Jb 2_{11}, עשׂה *do* Jb 42_9. <OBJ> ענה *answer* Jb 20_1, שׁוב hi. *answer* Jb 20_1. <APP> Zophar Jb 2_{11} 11_1 20_1 42_9, אִישׁ *man,* i.e. each one Jb 2_{11}, רֵעַ *friend* Jb 2_{11}. <PREP> בְּ of place, *(with)in* Jb 20_1; אֶל *to,* + דבר pi. *speak* Jb 42_9.

נַעֲצוּץ 2 n.[m.] **thornbush**—נַעֲצוּצִים—<CSTR> כֹּל הַנַּעֲצוּצִים *all the thornbushes* Is 7_{19} (|| נַהֲלֹל *watering place*). <PREP> בְּ of place, *on,* + נוח *rest* Is 7_{19}; תַּחַת *instead of,* + עלה *go up* Is 55_{13} (|| סִרְפָּד *nettle;* :: בְּרוֹשׁ *juniper*).

<SYN> סִרְפָּד *nettle,* נַהֲלֹל *watering place.*

<ANT> בְּרוֹשׁ *juniper.**

נער I 1 vb. **growl—Qal** 1 Pf. נָעֲרוּ—**1. growl,** <SUBJ> יֹשֵׁב *inhabitant* of Chaldaea Jr 51_{38}. <PREP> כְּ *as,* + כְּפִיר *young lion* Jr 51_{38}. <COLL> נער || שׁאג *roar* Jr 51_{38}; + adverb, יַחְדָּו *together* Jr 51_{38}.

2. groan, <SUBJ> worshipper Ps 88_{16} (if em. גֹּוֵעַ מִנֹּעַר *dying from [my] youth* to גֹּעֵ־ם נֹעֵר *groaning I die*).*

<SYN> שׁאג *roar.*

נער II 11.1 vb. **shake—Qal** 4 Pf. נָעַרְתִּי; ptc. נֹעֵר; ptc. pass. נָעוּר—**1. shake** (Is 33_{15}), **shake out** (Ne 5_{13}), **shake off (leaves)** (Is 33_9; unless נער III *strip* or V *be parched*), <SUBJ> Bashan Is 33_9, Carmel Is 33_9, Nehemiah Ne 5_{13}; subj. not specified, Is 33_{15}. <OBJ> כַּף *hand* Is 33_{15} (|| אטם *block* ear, עצם *shut* eyes), חֹצֶן *fold of garment* Ne 5_{13}. <COLL> נֹעֵר כַּפָּיו מִתְּמֹךְ בַּשֹּׁחַד *one who shakes his hands so as not to hold a bribe* Is 33_{15}.

2. pass. **be shaken out,** <SUBJ> אִישׁ *man* Ne 5_{13}. <COLL> כָּכָה יִהְיֶה נָעוּר וָרֵק *so may he be shaken out and (made) empty* Ne 5_{13}.

Also perh. 1QH 4_{10}.

<SYN> §1 אטם *block,* עצם *shut.*

Ni. 3 Pf. נִנְעַרְתִּי; impf. אִנָּעֵר, יִנָּעֲרוּ—**1. shake oneself free,** <SUBJ> Samson Jg 16_{20}.

2. be shaken off, <SUBJ> רָשָׁע *wicked one* Jb 38_{13}, worshipper Ps 109_{23}. <PREP> כְּ *as,* + אַרְבֶּה *locust* Ps 109_{23}; מִן of direction, *from,* + אֶרֶץ *earth* Jb 38_{13}.

Pi. 3.1 Pf. נִעֵר; impf. יְנַעֵר; + waw וַיְנַעֵר (Si וינעריהו)—**1. shake off, shake out,** <SUBJ> Y. Ex 14_{27} Ps 136_{15} Ne 5_{13}. <OBJ> Egyptians Ex 14_{27}, אִישׁ *man* Ne 5_{13}, פַּרְעֹה *Pharaoh* Ps 136_{15}, חַיִל *army* Ps 136_{15}. <PREP> בְּ of place, *in,* + יָם *sea* Ps 136_{15}; בְּתוֹךְ *in(to) the middle of,* + יָם *sea* Ex 14_{27}. <COLL> נער pi. + adverb, כָּכָה *thus* Ne 5_{13}.

2. shake free, <SUBJ> Y. Si 11_{12}. <OBJ> רֹשׁ *poor one* Si 11_{12}. <PREP> מִן of direction, *from,* + עָפָר *dust* Si 11_{12}.

Htp. 1 Impv. הִתְנַעֲרִי—**shake oneself free,** <SUBJ> Jerusalem Is 52_2, שְׁבִיָּה *captive* fem. Is 52_2 (if em. שְׁבִי *sit* to שְׁבִיָּה). <PREP> מִן of direction, *from,* + עָפָר *dust* Is 52_2.*

*נער III 11.1 vb. **strip—Qal** 4 Pf. נָעַרְתִּי; ptc. נֹעֵר; ptc. pass. נָעוּר—**1. strip, uncover, bare,** <SUBJ> Bashan Is 33$_{9}$ (unless נער II *shake* or V *be parched*), Carmel Is 33$_{9}$ (unless נער II or V), Nehemiah Ne 5$_{13}$; subj. not specified, Is 33$_{15}$. <OBJ> כַּף *hand* Is 33$_{15}$ (|| אטם *block* ear, עצם *shut* eyes), חֹצֶן *fold of garment* Ne 5$_{13}$. <COLL> נֹעֵר כַּפָּיו מִתְּמֹךְ בַּשֹּׁחַד *one who bares his hands so as not to hold a bribe* Is 33$_{15}$.

2. pass. **be shaken out,** <SUBJ> אִישׁ *man* Ne 5$_{13}$. <COLL> כָּכָה יִהְיֶה נָעוּר וָרֵק *so may he be stripped bare and (made) empty* Ne 5$_{13}$.

Also perh. 1QH 4$_{10}$.

<SYN> §1 אטם *block*, עצם *shut*.

Ni. 3 Pf. נִנְעַרְתִּי; impf. אִנָּעֵר, יִנָּעֲרוּ—**1. be rid of,** <SUBJ> Samson Jg 16$_{20}$.

2. be stripped bare, <SUBJ> רָשָׁע *wicked one* Jb 38$_{13}$, worshipper Ps 109$_{23}$ (unless נער VII ni. *lose one's youth*). <PREP> כְּ *as*, + אַרְבֶּה *locust* Ps 109$_{23}$ (unless נער VII ni. *lose one's youth*); מִן of direction, *from*, + אֶרֶץ *earth* Jb 38$_{13}$.

Pi. 3.1 Pf. נִעֵר; impf. יְנַעֵר; + waw וַיְנַעֵר (Si וינעריהו)—**strip, uncover, bare,** <SUBJ> Y. Ex 14$_{27}$ Ps 136$_{15}$ Ne 5$_{13}$ Si 11$_{12}$. <OBJ> Egyptians Ex 14$_{27}$, אִישׁ *man* Ne 5$_{13}$, פַּרְעֹה *Pharaoh* Ps 136$_{15}$, חַיִל *army* Ps 136$_{15}$ רשש ptc. *poor one* Si 11$_{12}$. <PREP> בְּ of place, *in*, + יָם *sea* Ps 136$_{15}$; מִן of direction, *from*, + עָפָר *dust* Si 11$_{12}$; בְּתוֹךְ *in(to) the middle of*, + יָם *sea* Ex 14$_{27}$. <COLL> נער pi. + adverb, כָּכָה *thus* Ne 5$_{13}$.

Htp. 1 Impv. הִתְנַעֲרִי—**bare oneself,** <SUBJ> Jerusalem Is 52$_{2}$, שְׁבִיָּה *captive* fem. Is 52$_{2}$ (if em. שְׁבִי *sit* to שְׁבִיָּה). <PREP> מִן of direction, *from*, + עָפָר *dust* Is 52$_{2}$.

⇒ נְעֹרֶת *tow*; cf. עור *be bare*.

*[נער] IV vb. **wander—Qal,** הַנֹּעֵר לֹא־יְבַקֵּשׁ *the wandering he will not seek* Zc 11$_{16}$ (if em. הַנַּעַר *the lad*).

*[נער] V 1 vb. **be parched** (unless נער II *shake* or III *strip*)—**Qal** 1 Ptc. נֹעֵר—**be parched, be dry,** <SUBJ> Bashan Is 33$_{9}$, Carmel Is 33$_{9}$.

*[נער] VI vb. **vacillate—Qal,** הַנֹּעֵר לֹא־יְבַקֵּשׁ *the vacillating he will not seek* Zc 11$_{16}$ (if em. הַנַּעַר *the lad*).

*[נער] VII 1 vb. **be a youth** (unless נער II *shake* or III *strip*)—**Ni.** 1 Pf. נִנְעַרְתִּי—**lose one's youth,** <SUBJ> worshipper Ps 109$_{23}$ (נִנְעַרְתִּי כִּי אֶרְבֶּה *I have lost my youth, truly I have aged*; if em. כָּאַרְבֶּה *as a locust*).

⇒ נַעַר *youth*, נַעֲרָה *young woman*, נֹעַר *(time of) youth*, נַעֲרוּת *youth*, נַעֲרוֹת *youth*, נְעַרְיָה *Neariah*.

נַעַר 240.4.11.9 n.m. **lad**—נָעַר; cstr. נַעַר; sf. נַעַרְךָ, נַעֲרוֹ, נַעֲרָהּ; pl. נְעָרִים; cstr. נַעֲרֵי; sf. נְעָרַי (נְעָרָי), נְעָרֶיךָ, נְעָרָיו, נְעָרֶיהָ, נְעָרֵינוּ, נַעֲרֵיהֶם—**1. boy, lad, youth** (e.g. Gn 21$_{12}$ 22$_{12}$ 43$_{8}$ 48$_{16}$ Jg 13$_{24}$ 1 S 17$_{33}$ 1 K 14$_{3}$ 2 K 2$_{23}$ Is 7$_{16}$), newborn (1 S 4$_{21}$), from birth (Jg 13$_{5.7}$), infant of three months (Ex 2$_{6}$), unable to speak (Is 8$_{4}$), not yet weaned (1 S 1$_{22}$), just weaned (1 S 1$_{24}$).

2. young man (e.g. Gn 34$_{19}$ Ex 24$_{5}$ 33$_{11}$ Jos 6$_{23}$ Jg 17$_{7}$ 1 S 2$_{17}$ 21$_{3}$ 25$_{5}$ 30$_{2}$ 2 S 1$_{5}$ 4$_{12}$ 14$_{21}$ 18$_{5}$ 20$_{11}$ 1 K 11$_{28}$ Is 3$_{4}$ Zc 2$_{8}$ 1 C 12$_{29}$), of marriageable age (Gn 34$_{19}$), aged seventeen (Gn 37$_{2}$).

3. servant, attendant (e.g. Gn 18$_{7}$ 22$_{3}$ 41$_{12}$ Nm 22$_{22}$ Jg 7$_{10}$ 19$_{3}$ 1 S 9$_{3}$ 2 S 13$_{28}$ 16$_{1}$ 2 K 4$_{19}$ Jb 1$_{15}$ Ru 2$_{5}$ Ne 4$_{10}$ 5$_{10}$ 6$_{5}$ 13$_{19}$ Arad ost. 110$_{1.2}$ Seals 406 933 [both 7th cent.]), **squire*** of king (e.g. 2 S 9$_{9}$ 2 K 19$_{6}$||Is 37$_{6}$ Est 2$_{2}$ 6$_{3}$), of provincial governor (1 K 20$_{14}$), of priest (1 S 2$_{13}$), of prophet (e.g. 1 K 18$_{43}$ 19$_{3}$ 2 K 4$_{12.38}$ 5$_{20}$ 6$_{15}$ 8$_{4}$ 9$_{4[mss]}$ CD 8$_{21}$), as armour-bearer (Jg 9$_{54}$ 1 S 14$_{1}$ 2 S 18$_{15}$ 19$_{18}$).

4. perh. **slave*** (Ho 11$_{1}$).

<SUBJ> היה *be* Gn 21$_{20}$ Jg 13$_{5.7}$ 17$_{7.11.12}$ 18$_{3}$ 1 S 2$_{11}$ 17$_{42}$ 25$_{14}$ 2 S 13$_{28}$ 1 K 20$_{15}$ Ps 37$_{25}$ Ne 4$_{16}$ 2 C 13$_{7}$ Si 51$_{13(B)}$, ילד pu. *be born* Jg 13$_{8}$, גמל ni. *be weaned* 1 S 1$_{22}$, גדל *become great*, i.e. grow up Gn 21$_{20}$ 25$_{27}$ Jg 13$_{24}$ 1 S 2$_{21.26}$, דגה *increase* Gn 48$_{16}$, חזק *be strong* 2 S 13$_{28}$, htp. *show oneself strong* 2 C 13$_{7}$, רבה hi. *do much* Si 35$_{7}$, יסף *add*, i.e. do again 1 S 9$_{8}$, זקן hi. *grow old* Pr 22$_{6}$, דמה *be like* Si 35$_{7}$.

אמר *say* Nm 11$_{27}$ Jg 18$_{3}$ 19$_{11}$ 1 S 2$_{15}$ 9$_{5.8.10}$ 25$_{5.14}$ 2 S 1$_{6}$ 1 K 18$_{43}$ 2 K 2$_{23}$ 4$_{12.25}$ 5$_{20}$ 6$_{15}$ 9$_{4}$ Ru 2$_{6}$ Est 2$_{2}$ 6$_{3.5}$ Si 35$_{7}$, דבר pi. *speak* 1 S 25$_{9}$ Si 35$_{7}$, נגד hi. *tell* Nm 11$_{27}$ 1 S 25$_{8.12.14}$ 2 S 1$_{5.6.13}$ 17$_{18}$, ספר pi. *tell* 2 K 8$_{4}$, קרא *call* 2 K 4$_{12}$ Is 8$_{4}$, ענה *answer* 1 S 9$_{8}$ Ru 2$_{6}$, שׁאל *ask* Jg 18$_{3}$ 1 S 25$_{5}$, pass. *be lent* 1 S 1$_{27}$, בכה *cry* Ex 2$_{6}$, זרר po. *sneeze*

2 K 4_{35}, פתר *interpret* Gn 41_{12}, קלס htp. *mock* 2 K 2_{23}, תעע pilp. *mock* 4QPrFêtes[c] 16_5, שׂחק *play* 2 S 2_{14}, גער *rebuke* Ru 2_{15}, גדף pi. *revile* 2 K 19_6||Is 37_6, ברך pi. *bless* Si 35_7, חרשׁ hi. *be silent* Si 35_7, ראה *see* 1 S 10_{14} 25_{25} 2 S $13_{28.34}$ 17_{18} 2 K 6_{17} Jb 29_8, ni. *appear* 1 S 1_{22}, נבט hi. *look* 1 K 18_{43}, ירא *fear* Jg 8_{20} 2 S 1_{13} 13_{28} 2 K 6_{15}, ידע *know* 1 S 20_{39} 2 S $1_{5.6}$ Is 7_{16} 8_4, נכר htp. *make oneself known* Pr 20_{11}, כתב *write* Jg 8_{14} Is 10_{19}, אכל *eat* Gn 14_{24} 2 S 16_2 4QSD 4_3.

הלך *go* Gn $22_{5.19}$ 43_8 Jg $19_{9.13}$ 1 S 2_{26} $9_{5.7.10.27}$ $14_{1.6}$ 20_{21}, htp. *go* 1 S $25_{14.27}$ 2 K 4_{24} $9_{4.4}$, בוא *come* Jos 6_{23} 19_{13} 1 S $2_{13.15}$ 9_{10} 10_{14} $20_{37.38.41}$ $25_{5.9.12}$ 2 K 5_{22} 9_4 1QM 7_3 CD 15_{16}, hi. *bring* 1 S 9_7 20_{40} 2 S 1_6 9_{10} 2 K 4_{19}, יצא *go out* 1 K $20_{17.19}$ 2 K 2_{23}, hi. *bring out* Jos 6_{23}, עלה *go up* Gn 44_{33} 1 S 9_{10} 25_5 1 K 18_{43}, hi. *cause to go up*, i.e. offer Ex 24_5, ירד *go down* Jg $7_{10.11}$, קרב *draw near* Jg 19_{13}, שׁוב *go back* Gn 22_5 1 S 9_5 25_{12} 1 K 18_{43}, סור *turn aside* Jg $19_{11.13}$ Pr 22_6, הפך *turn* 1 S 25_{12}, מושׁ I *depart* Ex 33_{11}, מושׁ II hi. *let feel* Jg 16_{26}, עזב *leave* Gn 44_{22} Ru 2_{15}, עבר *pass* Jg $19_{11.13}$ 1 S 9_{27} $14_{1.6}$ 25_{19}, חושׁ *hasten* 1 S 20_{38}, מהר pi. *hasten* Gn 18_7, צלח *rush* 2 S 19_{18}, רוץ *run* Nm 11_{27} 1 S $20_{36.36}$ 2 K 4_{25} 5_{20}, נוס *flee* 1 S 30_{17} 2 K 9_4, סבב *go round* 2 S 18_{15}, רגל pi. *spy* Jos 6_{23}, רכב *ride* 1 S 30_{17} 2 K 4_{24}, נהג *lead* 2 K 4_{24} Is 11_6, שׁלח *send* 2 S 1_{13} 13_{17}, pu. *be let loose* Pr 29_{15}, קרא *meet* 2 S 16_1 2 K 4_{25}, קרה ni. *chance to be present* 2 S 1_6, מצא *find* 1 S 9_{10} $20_{21.36}$ 25_8, לקט pi. *gather* 1 S 20_{38}, קבץ pass. *be gathered* Ne 5_{16}, פטר *remove oneself* Si 35_7, כשׁל *stumble* Lm 5_{13}.

קום *rise* Gn 22_{19} 43_8 Jg 19_9 2 S 2_{14}, pol. *raise oneself* Si 35_7, עמד *stand* 1 S 20_{38} 2 S 1_6, נצב ni. *stand* Ru $2_{5.6}$, ישׁב *dwell* Gn 21_{20} 1 S 1_{22}, *remain* Gn 22_5, גור *sojourn* Jg 17_7, לין *lodge* Jg $19_{11.13}$ Ne 4_{16}, שׁכב *lie down* Lm 2_{21}, ho. *be laid down* 2 K 4_{32}, אחר pi. *delay* Gn 34_{19}, htp. Si 35_7, נוח *cease* speaking 1 S 25_9, hi. *place* Jos 6_{23}, *let go of* Jg 16_{26}, עצר *restrain* 2 K 4_{24}, מאס *reject* Is 7_{16}, מעט pi. *make small*, i.e. brief Si 35_7, חבא ni. *hide oneself* Jb 29_8, נגע *touch* Ru 2_9, חזק hi. *hold* Jg 16_{26}, חגר *be girded* 1 S 2_{18}, נשׂא *carry* Jg 9_{54} 1 S $14_{1.6}$ 2 S 13_{34} 18_{15} 2 K 4_{19} 5_{23}, לקח *take* 1 S 2_{15} 20_{21} 2 S 1_6 4_{12} 2 K 5_{20}, נתן *give* 1 S 9_8, נשׁה *lend* Ne 5_{10}, שׁלם pi. *pay* Si 35_7.

שׁחה htpal. *worship* Gn 22_5, שׁרת pi. *serve* 1 S 2_{11} 3_1 13_{17} Est 2_2 6_3, עבד *till* 2 S 9_9, עשׂה *do* Gn 18_7 34_{19} Jg 18_3 2 S 13_{29} 1 K 11_{28} 2 K 6_{15}, שׁאב *draw (water)* Ru 2_9, שׁלל *draw out* Ru 2_{15}, שׁפת *set (on the fire)* 2 K 4_{38}, בשׁל pi. *boil* 2 K 4_{38}, יצק *pour* 2 K 9_4, זבח *sacrifice* Ex 24_5, קצץ pi. *cut* 2 S 4_{12}, חפץ *delight* Gn 34_{19}, בחר *choose* Is 7_{16}, כבד ni. *be honoured* Gn 34_{19}, נעל *lock* 2 S 13_{17}, פתח *open* 2 K 9_4, פקח *open* eyes 2 K 4_{35}, פשׁט *strip* Ne 4_{17}, יכל *be able* Gn 44_{22}, יעף *be weary* Is 40_{30}, יגע *be tired* Is 40_{30}, קיץ hi. *awake* 2 K 4_{31}, טרד *be persistent* Si 35_7, שׁלט *lord it over* Ne 5_{15}, ישׁע hi. *save* Jg 13_5.

שׁמר ni. *keep oneself* 1 S 21_5, צפה *watch* 2 S 13_{34}, רעה *pasture* sheep 1 S 25_{14}, פקד *miss* 1 S 25_{14}, זכה pi. *purify* Ps 119_9, תמם *be complete* 1 S 16_{11}, כלה pi. *finish* Ru 2_{21}, חלל hi. *begin* Jg 13_5, רהב *act stormily* Is 3_5, בושׁ hi. *put to shame* Pr 29_{15}, כלם hi. *humiliate* Ru 2_{15}, ho. *suffer harm* 1 S 25_{14}, תלה *hang* 2 S 4_{12}, רבה *shoot* Gn 21_{20}, שׁלף *draw* sword Jg 8_{20} 9_5, דקר *thrust through* Jg 9_{54}, נכה hi. *strike* 1 S 2_{13} 2 S 13_{28} 18_{15}, שׁחת pi. *destroy* 2 S 1_{13}, מות *die* Jg 13_7 2 S 1_{15} 1 K 14_{17} 2 K 4_{32} Is 65_{20} Jg 1_{19} Pr 23_{13}, pol. *kill* Jg 9_{54} 2 S 1_6, hi. *kill* 2 S 13_{28} 18_{15}, הרג *kill* 2 S 4_{12}, קבר *bury* 2 S 4_{12}.

<NOM CL> נַעַר יִשְׂרָאֵל *Israel was a lad* (or *slave*) Ho 11_1, הֲדַד נַעַר *Hadad was a lad* 1 K 11_{17}, שְׁלֹמֹה בְנִי נַעַר *Solomon my son is a lad* 1 C 22_5, מַלְכֵּךְ נָעַר *your king is a lad* Ec 10_{16}, הַנַּעַר נָעַר *the lad was a lad*, i.e. was young 1 S 1_{24} (or em. נָעַר to נָזִיר *a Nazirite*), בֶּן־מִי־זֶה הַנַּעַר *whose son is this lad?* 1 S 17_{55}, var. 17_{58}, הוּא נַעַר *he was a lad* Gn 37_2, עוֹדֶנּוּ נַעַר *he was still a lad* Jg 8_{20} 2 C 34_3 Si 30_{12}, נַעַר אַתָּה *you are a lad* 1 S 17_{33}, אָנֹכִי נַעַר *I am a lad* 1 K 3_7, vars. 1 S 30_{13} Jr $1_{6.7}$, אני נער *I was a lad* Si $51_{13(11QPs^a)}$, הַנַּעַר אֲשֶׁר־לוֹ *the lad who was his* 1 S 20_{40}, var. Ru 2_{21}, נַעֲרוֹ עִמּוֹ *his servant was with him* Jg 19_3, vars. Nm 22_{22} 1 S 9_5 20_{35}, שָׁם אִתָּנוּ נַעַר *a lad was with us there* Gn 41_{12}, הַנַּעַר אֵינֶנּוּ אִתָּנוּ *the lad is not with us* Gn 44_{30}, vars. Gn $44_{31.34}$, סְבִיבוֹתַי נְעָרָי *my lads were around me* Jb 29_5.

<OBJ> גמל *wean* 1 S 1_{22}, שׁאל *ask* Jg 8_{14} 1 S 25_8 Si $35_{7(B)}$, hi. *lend* 1 S 1_{27}, קרא *call* 2 S 13_{17}, ענה *answer* 1 S 9_{10}, צוה pi. *command* 2 S 4_{12} 13_{28} Ru $2_{9.15}$, ברך pi. *bless* Gn 48_{16} Jg 13_{24}, קלל pi. *curse* 2 K 2_{23}, ראה *see* 2 S 1_6 1 K 11_{28} 2 K 2_{23} Pr 7_7, בין *discern* Pr 7_7, ידע po. *cause to know* 1 S 21_3 (or em. ידע to יעד ni. *make*

appointment with), בוא hi. *bring* Gn 44_{32} Jg 18_3 1 S $1_{22.25}$ 9_{22}, שׁוב hi. *bring back* 2 S 14_{21}, עבר hi. *cause to pass* 1 S 20_{36}, שׁלח *send* Gn 43_8 Ex 24_5 1 S 20_{21} $25_{5.25}$ Ne 6_5, אסף *gather*, i.e. take in Jg 19_{13}, בקשׁ pi. *seek* Zc 11_{16} (or em. הַנַּעַר to הַנֶּעְדֶּרֶת *the missing* [עדר ni. ptc.] or הַנֹּעֵר *the wandering* [נער IV] or *the vacillating* [נער VI]), נהג *lead* Is 20_4, נשׂא *lift* Gn 21_{18}.

שׂים *place*, i.e. make Gn 21_{18}, נוח hi. *leave* 1 K 19_3, פקד *muster* 1 K 20_{15}, hi. *place in charge* 1 K 11_{28}, לקח *take* Gn 22_3 1 S 9_{22}, לכד *capture* Jg 8_{14}, שׂכר *hire* Jg 18_3, נתן *give*, i.e. make Is 3_4, שׁקה hi. *give a drink* Gn 21_{19}, ערב *stand surety for* Gn 44_{32}, חנן *show favour* Dt 28_{50}, פעם pi. *stir* Jg 13_{24}, אכל *consume* Jb 1_{16}, נכה hi. *strike* 2 S 1_{15} Jb $1_{15.17}$ Pr 23_{13}, רטשׁ pi. *dash in pieces* Is 13_{18}, נפץ pi. *shatter* Jr 51_{22}, אבד pi. *destroy* 1QpHab 6_{11}, מות hi. *kill* 2 S 13_{32}.

<CSTR> נַעַר אֱלִישָׁע *lad/servant of Elisha* 2 K 5_{20}, אשיהו *of Ashiah* ost. DH79$_7$, [אלנתן] *of Elnathan* Arad ost. 110_1, גדליה *of Gedaliah* Arad ost. 110_2, חגי *of Haggai* Seal 407 (7th cent.), יְהוֹנָתָן *of Jonathan* 1 S 20_{38}, יוכן *of Jochin* Seals 108 ([נע]ר; Beth-shemesh) 277 (נע[ר]; Ramat Raḥel) 486 (T. Beit Mirsim; all three 8th cent.), מתן *Mattan* Seal 783 (7th cent.), מְפִי־בֹשֶׁת *of Mephibosheth* 2 S 16_1, פרעשׁ *of Parosh* Seal 933 (7th cent.), שָׁאוּל *of Saul* 2 S 9_9, שׁפט *of Shaphat* Seal 406 (7th cent.).

נַעֲרֵי אַבְשָׁלוֹם *lads/servants of Absalom* 2 S 13_{29}, דָּוִד *of David* 1 S $25_{9.12}$, יוֹאָב *of Joab* 2 S 20_{11}, אֲדֹנִי *of my lord* 1 S 25_{25}, בְּנֵי יִשְׂרָאֵל *of the sons of Israel* Ex 24_5, מֶלֶךְ *of the king of* 2 K 19_6||Is 37_6 Est 2_2 $6_{3.5}$, שָׂרֵי *of the governors of* province 1 K $20_{14.15.17.19}$.

נַעַר אִישׁ *servant of the man of* God 2 K 5_{20} (... נַעַר) 8_4, נער ... בן *servant of ... the son of* ost. DH79$_7$, נַעַר הַנָּבִיא *servant of the prophet* 2 K $9_{4(mss)}$, הַכֹּהֵן *of the priest* 1 S $2_{13.15}$, בֵּית *of the house of* Saul 2 S 19_{18}, נערי שׁוא *lads of worthlessness*, i.e. worthless lads Si 16_1.

אֵם הַנַּעַר *mother of the lad* 2 K 4_{30}, עֵינֵי *eyes of* 2 K 6_{17}, בְּשַׂר *flesh of* 2 K 5_{14} (נַעַר), לֶב־ *heart of* Pr 22_{15} (נַעַר), פְּנֵי *face of* 2 K $4_{29.31}$, קוֹל *voice of* Gn $21_{17.17}$ Jg 18_3, מִשְׁפַּט־ *manner of* Jg 13_{12}, בֵּית־ *house of* Jg 18_{15}, חַטַּאת הַנְּעָרִים *sin of the lads* 1 S 2_{17}, כְּלֵי *vessels of* 1 S 21_6, תואר נערי *appearance of lads of* Si 16_1, חֲצִי נְעָרַי *half of my servants* Ne 4_{10}, כָּל־הַנְּעָרִים *all the lads* 2 S 13_{32}, כָּל־נְעָרַי *all my servants* Ne 5_{16}.

<APP> גָּלוּת *exiles* Is 20_4, יְהוּדִי *Jew* Est 3_{13}, Absalom 2 S 14_{21} $18_{5.12.29.32}$, Adoni-melech Seal 933 (7th cent.), Benaiah Seal 407 (7th cent.), Eliakim Seals 108 ([נע]ר; Beth-shemesh) 277 (נע[ר]; Ramat Raḥel) 486 (T. Beit Mirsim; all three 8th cent.), Gehazi 2 K $4_{12.25}$ 5_{20} 8_4 CD 8_{21}, Joshua Ex 33_{11}, Machi Arad ost. 110_2, Malchijah Seal 406 (7th cent.), Nethibiah Seal 783 (7th cent.), Purah Jg $7_{10.11}$, Samuel 1 S $2_{18.21.26}$ 3_1, Shemiah Arad ost. 110_1, Solomon 1 C 29_1, Zadok 1 C 12_{29}, Ziba 2 S 9_9 16_1 19_{18}.

אִישׁ *man* 1 S 30_{17}, בֵּן *son* Ex 33_{11} 2 S 13_{32} Is 65_{20} 1 C 29_1, זַעֲטוּט *lad* 1QM 7_3 4QSD 4_3 CD 15_{16} (ז[עטו]ט), עֶבֶד *servant* Gn 41_{12} 1 S 30_{13}, מְשָׁרֵת *servant* Ex 33_{11}, לֵוִי *Levite* Jg $18_{3.15}$, נָבִיא *prophet* 2 K 9_4 (הַנַּעַר הַנַּעַר הַנָּבִיא *the young man, the servant, the prophet*; mss הַנַּעַר נַעַר הַנָּבִיא *the young man, the servant of the prophet*), גִּבּוֹר *mighty one* 1 C 12_{29}, חֲסַר *one lacking* sense Pr 7_7, רַב pl. *many* 1QpHab 6_{11}, אֵלֶּה *these* 1 K 20_{19}.

<ADJ> מִצְרִי *Egyptian* 1 S 30_{13}, עִבְרִי *Hebrew* Gn 41_{12}, קָטֹן *small* 1 S 20_{35} 1 K 3_7 2 K 5_{14} Is 11_6, קָטָן *small* 1 K 11_{17} 2 K 2_{23}, אֶחָד *one* 1 S 25_{14}, זֶה *this* 1 S 1_{27}, הַלָּז *that* Zc 2_8.

<PREP> לְ of benefit, *to, for* Jg 19_{19} 1 S 25_{14} Jb 24_5, + היה *be* 1 K 14_3, לקח *take* Gn 21_{20}, עשׂה *do* Jg 18_3 1 S 14_6; לְאַט ... לַנַּעַר *(deal) gently ... with the lad* 2 S 18_5.

לְ of direction, *to* 4QPatr 6_3, + אמר *say* Jg 9_{54} 18_3 19_{13} 1 S $9_{5.7.10.27}$ 10_{14} $20_{21.36.40}$ $25_{5.19}$ 2 S 1_6 2 K $4_{12.24.38}$ Ru 2_5 CD 8_{21}, נגד hi. *tell* 1 S $9_{5.8}$ 10_{14}, ספר pi. *tell* Gn 41_{12}, קרא *call* 1 S 3_8, i.e. name 1 S 4_{21}, נתן *give* 1 S 9_{22} 2 K 5_{22} Pr 1_4, ni. *be given* 1 S 25_{27}, עשׂה *do* Gn 22_{12} Jg 13_8 4Q Patr 6_3 ([תעש לו]); *on*, + בוא (of sun) *go in*, i.e. set Jg 19_{13}.

לְ introducing object, + שׁאל *ask* Jg 18_{15}, חנך *train* Pr 22_6, נשׂא *lift*, i.e. urge Si $35_{7(Bmg)}$, חזק hi. *strengthen* CD 14_{16}; referring to subject of verb, + ישׁב *remain* Gn 22_5; *concerning*, + דאג *be anxious* 1 S 9_5.

לְ of possession, *of, (belonging) to* 2 S $18_{29.32}$ 2 K 9_4 4QJub^{i} 23_{23} ([לנער]) CD 14_{16} Seals 108 ([נע]ר; Beth-shemesh) 277 (נע[ר]; Ramat Raḥel; both 8th cent.) 406 (7th cent.) 407 (7th cent.) 486 (T. Beit Mirsim (8th cent.) 783 933 (both 7th cent.).

בְּ introducing object, + חזק hi. *hold* Gn 21$_{18}$, שׁמר *keep* 2 S 18$_{12}$, בחר *choose* 1 C 29$_{1}$, בער *burn* Jb 1$_{16}$; of accompaniment, *with*, + הלך *go* Ex 10$_{9}$; of agent, instrument, *by (means of), through*, + קרא ni. *let name be called* Gn 48$_{16}$, נתן *give* 1 K 20$_{14}$.

כְּ *as*, + היה *be* 2 S 18$_{32}$.

מִן of direction, *(away) from, to the side of* 1 S 20$_{21.37}$, + רחק hi. *make distant* Pr 22$_{15}$, מנע *withhold* Pr 23$_{13}$; *from*, i.e. both, young men and ... Gn 19$_{4}$ Jos 6$_{21}$ Est 3$_{13}$.

מִן partitive, *from among, (some) of* 1 S 16$_{18}$ 25$_{14}$ 26$_{22}$ 2 S 1$_{15}$ 20$_{11}$, + עמד hi. *cause to stand* Ne 13$_{19}$, שׁלח *send* 2 K 4$_{22}$, לקח *take* 1 S 9$_{3}$, אחז *seize* 2 S 2$_{21}$, בקע pi. *tear* 2 K 2$_{23}$.

אֶל *to*, + אמר *say* Gn 22$_{5}$ Jg 16$_{26}$ 19$_{11}$ 1 S 2$_{15}$ 10$_{14}$ 14$_{1.6}$ 2 S 1$_{5.13}$ 9$_{9}$ 13$_{28}$ 1 K 18$_{43}$ 2 K 4$_{12.24.25}$, דבר pi. *speak* 2 K 6$_{17}$ Zc 2$_{8}$, קרא *call* Jg 9$_{54}$ 2 S 1$_{6}$ 9$_{9}$, שׁוב *go back* Gn 22$_{5.19}$, שׁלח *send*, i.e. stretch, hand Gn 22$_{12}$, נתן *give* Gn 18$_{7}$ 1 S 20$_{40}$ 2 K 5$_{23}$; *for*, + פלל htp. *pray* 1 S 1$_{27}$.

עַל *upon*, + נפל *fall* Jb 1$_{19}$, חמל *have pity* Ex 2$_{6}$; *for*, + היה *be* 1 S 25$_{14}$; *on account of*, + רעע *be bad*, i.e. displeasing Gn 21$_{12}$.

בַּעַד *for the sake of*, + בקשׁ pi. *seek* Y. 2 S 12$_{16}$.

עִם *with* Ps 148$_{12}$; *to* + דבק *cling* Ru 2$_{21}$.

אֵת *with* 1 S 8$_{7}$ 2 K 6$_{15}$, + היה *be* Gn 21$_{20}$, יעד ni. *make appointment* 1 S 21$_{3}$ (if em.; see Obj.).

אַחֲרֵי *after* 1 K 20$_{19}$, + קרא *call* 1 S 20$_{37.38}$, פקד *muster* 1 K 20$_{15}$, בוא *come* 1 S 25$_{19}$.

תַּחַת *instead of*, + ישׁב *remain* Gn 44$_{33}$.

<COLL> נַעַר || בָּחוּר *youth* Is 40$_{30}$ Lm 2$_{21}$ (+) 5$_{13}$, בֵּן *son* Is 13$_{18}$ Ho 11$_{1}$ (both +) Si 16$_{1}$, קָטָן *small one* Si 30$_{12}$, פֶּתִי *simple one* Pr 1$_{4}$.

+ יֶלֶד *child* Ex 2$_{6}$, טַף *infant* Est 3$_{13}$ 1QpHab 6$_{11}$, תַּעֲלוּל perh. *infant* Is 3$_{4}$, פְּרִי־בֶטֶן *fruit of the womb* Is 13$_{18}$ 1QpHab 6$_{11}$, עֶבֶד *servant* Jg 19$_{13}$, אָמָה *female servant* Jg 19$_{19}$, אִישׁ *man* Gn 14$_{24}$, אִשָּׁה *woman* Est 3$_{13}$ 1QM 7$_{3}$ 1QpHab 6$_{11}$ 4QSD 4$_{3}$, פִּלֶגֶשׁ *secondary wife* Jg 19$_{9}$, בְּתוּלָה *young woman* Lm 2$_{21}$ 4QRitMar 19$_{3}$.

:: זָקֵן *old man* Gn 19$_{4}$ Ex 10$_{9}$ Dt 28$_{50}$ Jos 6$_{21}$ Is 3$_{5}$ (+) 20$_{4}$ Jr 51$_{22}$ Ps 148$_{12}$ Lm 2$_{21}$ Est 3$_{13}$ 1QpHab 6$_{11}$, יָשִׁישׁ *aged one* Jb 29$_{8}$, אָשִׁישׁ *adult* 1QpHab 6$_{11}$ 4QRitMar 7$_{4}$.

נַעַר as vocative 1 S 17$_{58}$ Si 35$_{7}$.

נַעַר אֶחָד *one lad* 1 S 25$_{14}$, שְׁנֵי נְעָרִים *two lads* 2 K 5$_{22}$, var. Gn 22$_{3}$ Nm 22$_{22}$ 2 K 5$_{23}$, עֲשָׂרָה נְעָרִים *ten lads* 1 S 25$_{5}$ 2 S 18$_{15}$, אַרְבַּע מֵאוֹת ... נַעַר *four hundred ... lads* 1 S 30$_{17}$.

נַעַר וָרָךְ *a lad and tender*, i.e. a tender lad 1 C 22$_{5}$ 29$_{1}$, נַעַר וְרַךְ־לֵבָב *a lad, and one tender of heart* 2 C 13$_{7}$, הַנַּעַר שְׁמוּאֵל הֹלֵךְ וְגָדֵל וָטוֹב *the lad Samuel continued to become great and favoured* 1 S 2$_{26}$.

Also 6QapSamKgs 60$_{2}$ Arad ost. 15$_{4}$.

<SYN> בָּחוּר *youth*, בֵּן *son*, קָטָן *small one*, פֶּתִי *simple one*.

<ANT> זָקֵן *old man*, יָשִׁישׁ *aged one*, אָשִׁישׁ *adult*.*

⇒ נער VII *be a youth*.

*[נֹעַר] n.m. **sparrow**, <PREP> כְּ *as (with)*, + קשׁר *bind*, i.e. play with Jb 40$_{29}$ (if em. לְנַעֲרוֹתֶיךָ *for your young women* to כְּנֹעַר).

נֹעַר 4 n.[m.] **(time of) youth**, <PREP> בְּ of time, *in*, + מות *die* Jb 36$_{14}$; מִן of time, *since*, + פנק pi. *pamper* Pr 29$_{21}$, גוע *expire* Ps 88$_{16}$ (or em. גֹּוֵעַ מִנֹּעַר *dying from [my] youth* to גֹּעֵ־ם נֹעַר *groaning I die*); of comparison, *(more) than in*, + רטפשׁ *be fresh* Jb 33$_{25}$ (+ עֲלוּמִים *youth*).*

⇒ נַעַר VII *be a youth*.

נַעֲרָה I 63.1.11 n.f. **young woman**—Kt נער;* pl. נְעָרוֹת; cstr. נַעֲרוֹת; sf. נַעֲרֹתַי (נַעֲרֹתָי), נַעֲרוֹתֶיךָ, נַעֲרוֹתָיו, נַעֲרֹתֶיהָ (נַעֲרוֹתֶיהָ)—**1. young woman, girl,** unmarried (e.g. Gn 24$_{14}$ 34$_{3}$ Jg 21$_{12}$ 1 K 1$_{2}$ Est 2$_{2}$), betrothed (e.g. Dt 22$_{23}$ 11QT 66$_{8}$), newly married (e.g. Dt 22$_{15}$), secondary wife (Jg 19$_{3+5t}$), widow (Ru 2$_{5}$).

2. maid, attendant, servant, in service of woman (e.g. Gn 24$_{61}$ Ex 2$_{5}$ 1 S 25$_{42}$ Pr 31$_{15}$ Est 2$_{9}$ 4$_{4}$), wisdom (Pr 9$_{3}$); gathering harvest (Ru 2$_{8.22.23.24}$).

<SUBJ> היה *be* Dt 22$_{19.23.29}$ 1 K 1$_{2.4}$ 2 K 5$_{2}$, אמר *say* Gn 24$_{14.16}$ 1 S 9$_{11}$ 2 K 5$_{2}$ Ru 2$_{6}$ Est 2$_{2.13}$, דבר pi. *speak* 2 K 5$_{4}$, ענה *answer* 1 S 9$_{11}$, נגד hi. *tell* Gn 24$_{16.28}$ Est 4$_{4}$, קרא ni. *be called* Est 2$_{13}$, זעק *cry out* 11QT 66$_{8}$, צעק *cry out* Dt 22$_{24}$=11QT 66$_{2}$ Dt 22$_{27}$, ראה pass. *be looked out* Est 2$_{9}$ 11QT 66$_{8}$, ידע *know (sexually)* Jg 21$_{12}$, הלך

go Gn 24$_{55.61}$ Ex 2$_{5}$ 1 S 25$_{42}$, בוא *come* Ru 2$_{6}$ Est 2$_{12.13}$ 4$_{4}$, יצא *go out* 1 S 9$_{11}$, ירד *go down* Gn 24$_{16}$, hi. *let down* Gn 24$_{16}$, עלה *go up* Gn 24$_{16}$, שׁוב *go back* Ru 2$_{6}$ Est 2$_{13}$, רוץ *run* Gn 24$_{16.28}$, מהר pi. *hasten* Gn 24$_{16}$, רכב *ride* Gn 24$_{61}$, קום *arise* Gn 24$_{61}$, עמד *stand* 1 K 1$_{2}$ Ru 2$_{6}$, ישׁב *sit* Ru 2$_{6}$, שׁכב *lie down* 1 K 1$_{2}$, מצא ni. *be found* Dt 22$_{28}$, נטה hi. *stretch out* Gn 24$_{14}$, שׁאב *draw (water)* Gn 24$_{16}$ 1 S 9$_{11}$, שׁקה hi. *give to drink* Gn 24$_{14.16}$, גמא hi. *allow to swallow* Gn 24$_{16}$.

ישׁב *remain* Gn 24$_{55}$, מלא pi. *fill* Gn 24$_{16}$, ערה pi. *empty* Gn 24$_{16}$, קבץ ni. *be gathered* Est 2$_{8}$, אסף *gather* Ru 2$_{6}$, לקט pi. *glean* Ru 2$_{6}$, עשׂה *do* Dt 22$_{21}$, שׁרת pi. *serve* 1 K 1$_{4}$, כלה pi. *finish* Gn 24$_{16}$, זנה *prostitute oneself* Dt 22$_{21}$, ארשׂ pu. *be betrothed* Dt 22$_{23.25.27.28}$ 11QT 66$_{8}$, יטב *be good*, i.e. pleasing Est 2$_{4.9}$, נשׂא *raise*, i.e. win, favour Est 2$_{9}$, מלך *be queen* Est 2$_{4}$, צום *fast* Est 4$_{16}$, מות *die* Dt 22$_{21.24}$, ho. *be put to death* 11QT 66$_{2}$.

<NOM CL> נַעֲרָה מוֹאֲבִיָּה הִיא *she is a young Moabite woman* Ru 2$_{6}$, הַנַּעֲרָה טֹבַת מַרְאֶה בְּתוּלָה *the young woman was good of appearance, ready for marriage* Gn 24$_{16(Qr)}$, sim. Est 2$_{7}$, הַנַּעֲרָה יָפָה *the young woman was beautiful* 1 K 1$_{4}$, הַנַּעֲרָה אֲשֶׁר מֵאֶרֶץ יִשְׂרָאֵל *the young woman who is from the land of Israel* 2 K 5$_{4}$, לְמִי הַנַּעֲרָה הַזֹּאת *whose is this young woman?* Ru 2$_{5}$.

<OBJ> ידע *know (sexually)* Gn 24$_{16}$ 1 K 1$_{4}$, אהב *love* Gn 34$_{3}$, בוא hi. *bring* Jg 21$_{12}$, יצא hi. *bring out* Dt 22$_{21}$, שׁלח *send* Pr 9$_{3}$, pi. *send away*, i.e. divorce Dt 22$_{19.29}$, בקשׁ pi. *seek* 1 K 1$_{2.3}$ Est 2$_{2}$, מצא *find* Dt 22$_{23.25.27.28}$ Jg 21$_{12}$ 1 S 9$_{11}$ 11QT 66$_{8}$, קרא *meet* Gn 24$_{16}$, קבץ *gather* Est 2$_{3}$, פתה pi. *seduce* 11QT 66$_{8}$, לקח *take* Est 2$_{7}$ 4QHalakhah^{a} 12$_{7}$ ([נ]ערה]), שׁבה *capture* 2 K 5$_{2}$, תפשׂ *seize* Dt 22$_{28}$, ענה pi. *violate* Dt 22$_{29}$, חבק pi. *embrace* Si 30$_{20}$, יכח hi. *appoint* Gn 24$_{14}$, נתן *give* Gn 34$_{12}$, שׁנה pi. *change* Est 2$_{9}$, סקל *stone* Dt 22$_{21.24}$=11QT 66$_{2}$.

<CSTR> נַעֲרוֹת אֶסְתֵּר *maids of Esther* Est 4$_{4}$, נַעֲרוֹת בֹּעַז *young women of Boaz* Ru 2$_{23}$; אֲבִי הַנַּעֲרָה *father of the young woman* Dt 22$_{15(Qr).16(Qr).19(Qr)}$=11QT 65$_{9.10.15}$ Dt 22$_{29(Qr)}$=11QT 66$_{10}$ Jg 19$_{3.4.5.6.8.9}$ 4QRitMar 108$_{3}$ (אב[י]), לֵב *heart of* Gn 34$_{3(Qr)}$, בְּתוּלֵי *(tokens of) virginity of* Dt 22$_{15(Qr)}$=11QT 65$_{10}$, תֹּר נַעֲרָה וְנַעֲרָה *turn of each young woman* Est 2$_{12}$, כָּל־נַעֲרָה *every young woman* Est 2$_{3}$.

<APP> בַּת *daughter* 4QHalakhah^{a} 12$_{7}$ ([נ]ערה]), בְּתוּלָה *young woman* Dt 22$_{23.28}$ Jg 21$_{12}$ 1 K 1$_{2}$ Est 2$_{2.3}$ 11QT 66$_{8}$, מוֹאֲבִי *Moabite* Ru 2$_{6}$.

<ADJ> יָפֶה *beautiful* 1 K 1$_{3}$, טוֹב *good* of appearance Est 2$_{2.3}$, קָטָן *small* 2 K 5$_{2}$, רַב pl. *many* Est 2$_{8}$, זֹאת *this* Ru 2$_{5}$ 4$_{12}$.

<PREP> לְ of direction, *to*, + אמר *say* 1 S 9$_{11}$, קרא *call* Gn 24$_{57}$, נתן *give* Pr 31$_{15}$ Est 2$_{9.9}$, ni. *be given* Est 2$_{13}$, עשׂה *do* Dt 22$_{26}$=11QT 66$_{6}$; of benefit, *for* Pr 27$_{27}$, + קשׁר *bind* Jb 40$_{29}$ (unless נַעֲרָה IV *sparrow*; or em. כְּנֹעַר or כְּנַעֲרָה *as [with] a sparrow* or כְּנַעֲרוֹת *as [with] the sparrows*); of possession, *of, (belonging) to* Dt 22$_{20.26.27}$=11QT 66$_{6.8}$, + היה *be* Est 2$_{12}$.

בְּ introducing object, + חזק hi. *take hold of* Dt 22$_{25}$, חפץ *delight in* Est 2$_{13}$; *to*, + דבק *cling* Ru 2$_{23}$.

מִן of agent, *by, through*, + נתן *give* Ru 4$_{12}$.

אֶל *to*, + אמר *say* Gn 24$_{14}$, הלך *go* Am 2$_{7}$.

עִם *with*, + בוא *come* Est 2$_{13}$, יצא *go out* Ru 2$_{22}$, שׁכב *lie down* Dt 22$_{23.25.28}$ 11QT 66$_{8}$; *to*, + דבק *cling* Ru 2$_{8}$.

אֵת *with*, + היה *be* Ru 3$_{2}$.

<COLL> בַּיִת || נַעֲרָה *household* Pr 31$_{15}$; + סָרִיס *eunuch* Est 4$_{4}$.

Qr, Sam נַעֲרָה Kt נער Gn 24$_{14.16.28.55.57}$ 34$_{3.3.12}$ Dt 22$_{15+12t}$.

חָמֵשׁ נַעֲרֹתֶיהָ *her five maids* 1 S 25$_{42}$, שֶׁבַע הַנְּעָרוֹת *the seven maids* Est 2$_{9}$, אַרְבַּע מֵאוֹת נַעֲרָה *four hundred young women* Jg 21$_{12}$.

Also 4QRitMar 19$_{3}$ ([נע]רות]).

<SYN> בַּיִת *household*.*

⇒ נַעַר VII *be a youth*.

*[נַעֲרָה] II 1 n.f. **sparrow** (unless נַעֲרָה I *young woman*)—pl. sf. נַעֲרוֹתֶיךָ—<PREP> לְ *as (with)*, + קשׁר *bind*, i.e. play Jb 40$_{29}$ (|| צִפּוֹר *bird*).

<SYN> צִפּוֹר *bird*.

נַעֲרָה III 3 pr.n.f. **Naarah,** one of the wives of Asshur, <SUBJ> היה *be* 1 C 4$_{5}$, ילד *bear* 1 C 4$_{6}$. <CSTR> בְּנֵי נַעֲרָה *sons of Naarah* 1 C 4$_{6}$. <APP> אִשָּׁה *wife* 1 C 4$_{5}$.

[נַעֲרָה] IV 1 pl.n. **Naarah**—+ ה- of direction נַעֲרָתָה—

in Ephraim, on border with Manasseh, appar. ident. with Naaran at 1 C 7$_{28}$, perh. T. el-Jisr, 5 km NNW of Jericho, <PREP> ה- of direction, *to*, + ירד *go down* Jos 16$_{7}$.

*[נֹעָרָה] n.f. **sparrow,** <PREP> כְּ *as (with)*, + קשׁר *bind*, i.e. play Jb 40$_{29}$ (if em. לְנַעֲרוֹתֶיךָ *for your young women* to כְּנֹעָרוֹת *as [with] the sparrows*).

*[נְעֻרוּת] 0.3 n.f. **youth**—sf. Si נערותי, Si נערותו—**(time of) youth,** <PREP> בְּ of time, *in*, + שׁמע *hear* teaching Si 51$_{28}$, פלל htp. *pray* Si 51$_{14(B)}$, כאף pi. *bend* head Si 30$_{12}$ (+ כשהוא קטן *while he is small*).
⇒ נַעַר VII *be a youth*.

[נְעֻרוֹת] 1 n.f.pl. **youth**—pl. sf. נְעֻרֹתֵיהֶם—**(time of) youth,** <PREP> מִן of time, *from, since*, + עשׂה *do* evil Jr 32$_{30}$.*
⇒ נַעַר VII *be a youth*.

נַעֲרַי 1 pr.n.m. **Naarai,** one of David's warriors, son of Ezbai, appar. ident. with Paarai at 2 S 23$_{35}$, <NOM CL> גִּבּוֹרֵי הַחֲיָלִים ... נַעֲרַי *the warriors of the armies were ... Naarai* 1 C 11$_{37}$.

נְעַרְיָה 3 pr.n.m. **Neariah, 1.** son of Shemaiah (or of Shecaniah, if em.) and descendant of Zerubbabel, <NOM CL> בְּנֵי שְׁמַעְיָה ... נְעַרְיָה *the sons of Shemaiah were ... Neariah* 1 C 3$_{22}$ (or del. בְּנֵי שְׁמַעְיָה to read בְּנֵי שְׁכַנְיָה ... נְעַרְיָה *the sons of Shecaniah were ... Neariah*). <CSTR> בֶּן־נְעַרְיָה *son of Neariah* 1 C 3$_{23}$ (or em. בְּנֵי *sons of*).

2. son of Ishi and Simeonite chief at time of Hezekiah, <NOM CL> נְעַרְיָה ... בְּרֹאשָׁם *Neariah ... was at their head* 1 C 4$_{42}$. <APP> בֵּן *son* 1 C 4$_{42}$.
⇒ נַעַר *lad* + יְ Y.

נַעֲרָן 1 pl.n. **Naaran,** in Ephraim, appar. ident. with Naarah at Jos 16$_{7}$, <NOM CL> אֲחֻזָּתָם וּמֹשְׁבֹתָם ... נַעֲרָן *their properties and dwelling places were ... Naaran* 1 C 7$_{28}$.

נְעֹרֶת 2 n.f. **tow,** coarse, flammable fibres of flax after removal from the woody part by pounding or stripping, <CSTR> פְּתִיל־הַנְּעֹרֶת *cord of tow* Jg 16$_{9}$. <PREP> לְ introducing predicate, + היה *be* Is 1$_{31}$.
⇒ נער III *strip*.

נֹף 7 pl.n. **Memphis,** Egyptian capital city, 20 km S of Cairo, ident. with מֹף at Ho 9$_{6}$ 4QpsEzek[b] 1.2$_{6}$, and perh. with נוֹף at Ps 48$_{3}$,* <SUBJ> היה *be* Jr 46$_{19}$, + נצה ni. *be ruined* Jr 46$_{19}$ (unless נִצְּתָה is יצת ni. *be burned*). <NOM CL> נֹף צָרֵי יוֹמָם appar. *Memphis shall be*, i.e. have, *adversaries by day* Ezk 30$_{16}$. <CSTR> בְּנֵי־נֹף *sons of Memphis* Jr 2$_{16}$, שָׂרֵי *princes of* Is 19$_{13}$, הֲמוֹן *multitude of* Ezk 30$_{15}$ (if em. נֹא *of No*, i.e. Thebes). <PREP> בְּ of place, *in, at*, + שׁמע hi. *proclaim* Jr 46$_{14}$, ישׁב *dwell* Jr 44$_{1}$; מִן *from*, + שׁבת hi. *cause* images *to cease* Ezk 30$_{13}$.*

נֶפֶג 4 pr.n.m. **Nepheg, 1.** Levite, son of Izhar, <NOM CL> בְּנֵי יִצְהָר קֹרַח וָנֶפֶג *the sons of Izhar were Korah and Nepheg* Ex 6$_{21}$.

2. son of David, <SUBJ> ילד ni. *be born* 1 C 3$_{7}$. <NOM CL> אֵלֶּה שְׁמוֹת הַיִּלֹּדִים לוֹ בִּירוּשָׁלָם ... נֶפֶג *these are the names of those born to him in Jerusalem ... Nepheg* 2 S 5$_{15}$, var. 1 C 14$_{6}$.

[נָפָה] I 1 n.f. **sieve** (unless נָפָה III *bridle*)—cstr. נָפַת—<CSTR> נָפַת שָׁוְא *sieve of worthlessness*, i.e. perh. to test worthlessness* Is 30$_{28}$. <PREP> בְּ of instrument, *by (means of), with*, + נוף hi. *sift* nations Is 30$_{28}$.*
⇒ נוף I *wave*.

[נָפָה] II 3 n.f. **height** (unless נָפָה III *district*)—cstr. נָפַת; pl. cstr. נָפוֹת—**height, hill-country,** <CSTR> נָפַת דֹּאר *height of Dor* (unless *Naphath-dor*) Jos 12$_{23}$ 1 K 4$_{11}$, נָפוֹת דּוֹר *heights of Dor* (unless *Naphoth-dor*) Jos 11$_{2}$ 12$_{23(mss)}$; כָּל־נָפַת *all the height of* 1 K 4$_{11}$. <PREP> לְ of possession, *of, (belonging to)* Jos 12$_{23}$; בְּ of place, *in* Jos 11$_{2}$; כָּל־נָפַת דֹּאר without preposition, *in all the height of Dor* 1 K 4$_{11}$.*
⇒ cf. נוֹף *elevation*.

*[נָפָה] III 4 n.f. **yoke, bridle; district**—cstr. נָפַת; pl. cstr. נָפוֹת—**1. yoke, bridle** (unless נָפָה I *sieve*), <CSTR> נָפַת שָׁוְא *bridle of worthlessness* Is 30$_{28}$. <PREP> בְּ of instrument, *by (means of), with*, + נוף hi. *sift* nations Is 30$_{28}$.

2. district (unless נָפָה II *height*), <CSTR> נָפַת דּאר *district of Dor* (unless *Naphath-dor*) Jos 12$_{23}$ 1 K 4$_{11}$, נָפוֹת דּוֹר *districts of Dor* (unless *Naphoth-dor*) Jos 11$_2$ 12$_{23(mss)}$; כָּל־נָפַת *all the district of* 1 K 4$_{11}$. <PREP> לְ of possession, *of, (belonging to)* Jos 12$_{23}$; בְּ of place, *in* Jos 11$_2$; כָּל־נָפַת דּאר without preposition, *in all the district of Dor* 1 K 4$_{11}$.

[נְפוּסִים], see נְפִיסִים *Nephisim.*

[נָפוּץ] *dispersed one,* see נפץ II *scatter.*

[נְפוּשְׂסִים] 1 pr.n.m. **Nephushesim** —Qr נְפִישְׁסִים—ancestor of family of temple servants, ident. with Nephisim in || at Ezr 2$_{50}$, perh. descended from the Ishmaelite tribe of Naphish, <CSTR> בְּנֵי נפושסים *sons of Nephushesim* Ne 7$_{52(Kt)}$ (Qr נְפִישְׁסִים *Nephishesim*).
⇒ (?) נָפִישׁ *Naphish.*

נפח I 13.1.5 vb. **blow—Qal** 9.1.3 נָפַחְתִּי, נָפְחָה; + waw וַיִּפַּח, וְנָפַחְתִּי; Q ויפחו; impv. פְּחִי; ptc. נֹפֵחַ; ptc. Q נופחים; ptc. pass. נָפוּחַ; inf. לָפַּחַת—**1. breathe, blow, fan,** <SUBJ> Y. Gn 2$_7$ Ezk 22$_{21}$ Hg 1$_9$ 4QDibHam^a 8$_5$ ([נ]פחתה), חָרָשׁ *artisan* Is 54$_{16}$, ילד ptc. *one who gives birth* Jr 15$_9$, רוּחַ *breath* Ezk 37$_9$ 4QpsEzek^a 2$_7$; subj. not specified, Ezk 22$_{20}$. <OBJ> נֶפֶשׁ *soul*, i.e. sigh or (last) breath Jr 15$_9$, נְשָׁמָה *breath* of life Gn 2$_7$ 4QDibHam^a 8$_5$ (נשמת ... נ]פחתה]), רוּחַ *breath* 4QpsEzek^a 2$_7$, אֵשׁ *fire* Ezk 22$_{20}$. <PREP> בְּ of place, *in(to), upon*, + הרג pass. ptc. *slain one* Ezk 37$_9$ 4QpsEzek^a 2$_7$ ([בהרוגים]), אַף *nostril* Gn 2$_7$ 4QDibHam^a 8$_5$ ([נ]פחתה), מְעַט *a little* Hg 1$_9$; introducing object, + אֵשׁ *fire* Is 54$_{16}$ Ezk 22$_{21}$; עַל *upon*, + בַּיִת *house* of Israel Ezk 22$_{21}$, כֶּסֶף *silver*, Ezk 22$_{20}$, נְחֹשֶׁת *bronze* Ezk 22$_{20}$, בַּרְזֶל *iron* Ezk 22$_{20}$, עֹפֶרֶת *lead* Ezk 22$_{20}$, בְּדִיל *tin* Ezk 22$_{20}$.

2. ptc. as noun, **smith,** <CSTR> כור נופחים *furnace of the smiths* 1QH 13$_{16}$.

3. pass. **be blown, be fanned,** of pot placed on fire, thus made to boil (Jr 1$_{13}$ Jb 41$_{12}$), <SUBJ> דּוּד *pot* Jb 41$_{12}$, סִיר *pot* Jr 1$_{13}$, כּוּר *furnace* Si 43$_4$.

Also 4QpsHod^c 3$_4$ ([נ]ופחים).

Ni. 1.0.1 Impf. ינפח; inf. Sam הנפח—**be blown, be fanned,** <SUBJ> כּוּר *furnace* 4Q416 4$_2$, אֵשׁ *fire* Nm 21$_{30(Sam)}$ (הנפח אש; MT נֹפַח אֲשֶׁר *Nophah which is*). <PREP> עַד *as far as*, + Medeba Nm 21$_{30(Sam)}$.

Pu. 1.0.1 Pf. נֻפָּח; ptc. Q מנפח—**be blown, be fanned,** <SUBJ> אֵשׁ *fire* Jb 20$_{26}$.

Also 4QNarrA 4$_2$.

Hi. 2 Pf. הִפַּחְתִּי, הִפַּחְתֶּם—**cause to breathe** (Jb 31$_{39}$; unless נפח II *beat, afflict*), **sniff at,** in contempt (Ml 1$_{13}$), <SUBJ> Job Jb 31$_{39}$, כֹּהֵן *priest* Ml 1$_{13}$. <OBJ> Y. Ml 1$_{13(TiqSoph)}$, נֶפֶשׁ *soul*, i.e. sigh or (last) breath Jb 31$_{39}$, שֵׁם *name* of Y. Ml 1$_{13}$.
⇒ מַפָּח *expiring*, מַפֻּחַ *bellows*, תַּפּוּחַ *apple.*

*נפח II 1 **beat, afflict** (unless נפח I *blow*)—**Hi.** 1 Pf. הִפַּחְתִּי—**beat, afflict,** <SUBJ> Job Jb 31$_{39}$. <OBJ> נֶפֶשׁ *soul* Jb 31$_{39}$.

נֹפַח 1 pl.n. **Nophah,** in Moab, <NOM CL> נֹפַח אֲשֶׁר עַד־מֵידְבָא *Nophah which is as far as Medeba* Nm 21$_{30}$ (for נֹפַח אֲשֶׁר Sam reads הנפח אש *a fire is fanned*, i.e. נפח ni.). <PREP> עַד *unto*, + שׁמם hi. *devastate* Nm 21$_{30}$.

נֹפֵחַ *smith*, see נפח I *blow.*

נְפִילִים, see נְפִלִים *giants.*

[נְפִישְׁסִים], see נְפוּשְׂסִים *Nephushesim.*

[נְפִיסִים] 1 pr.n.m. **Nephisim**—Qr נְפוּסִים—ancestor of family of temple servants, ident. with Nephushesim in || at Ne 7$_{52}$, perh. descended from the Ishmaelite tribe of Naphish, <CSTR> בְּנֵי נפיסים *sons of Nephisim* Ezr 2$_{50(Kt)}$ (Qr נְפוּסִים *Nephusim*).*
⇒ (?) נָפִישׁ *Naphish.*

נָפִישׁ 3 pr.n.m. **Naphish, 1.** eleventh son of Ishmael,

<NOM CL> אֵלֶּה שְׁמוֹת בְּנֵי יִשְׁמָעֵאל ... נָפִישׁ *these are the names of the sons of Ishmael ... Naphish* Gn 25_{15}, sim. 1 C 1_{31}.

2. tribe descended from §1, <PREP> עִם *with*, + עשׂה *make* war 1 C 5_{19}.

⇒ נפשׁ *breathe*; cf. (?) נְפוּשְׁסִים *Nephushesim*, נְפִיסִים *Nephisim*.

נֹפֶךְ $_{4.1}$ n.[m.] **turquoise, garnet,** or other (semi-) precious stone, in Aaron's breastplate (Ex 28_{18}||39_{11}), assoc. with wealth of Tyre (Ezk 27_{16} 28_{13} 28_{13}), <NOM CL> הַטּוּר הַשֵּׁנִי נֹפֶךְ *the second row is turquoise* Ex 28_{18}||39_{11}, כָּל־אֶבֶן יְקָרָה מְסֻכָתֶךָ אֹדֶם פִּטְדָה ... נֹפֶךְ *every precious stone was your covering—ruby, topaz ... turquoise* Ezk 28_{13}, בו נפך *in it* (gold necklace) *is turquoise* Si $35_{5(B)}$. <APP> אֶבֶן *stone* Ezk 28_{13}, perh. אַרְגָּמָן *purple,* i.e. deep-red Ezk 27_{16}. <PREP> בְּ partitive, *(some) of,* + נתן *give* Ezk 27_{16}.

נפל I $_{434.13.73}$ vb. **fall.**

Qal, p. 715a
1-20, senses of נפל as verb, p. 715b
Subjects, p. 716b
Prepositions, p. 718b
Collocations, p. 720a
21. ptc. as noun, **a. fallen one,** p. 720b
b. deserter, p. 720b
Pilel, p. 720b
Hi., p. 720b
1-13, senses of נפל hi., p. 721a
Subjects, p. 721b
Objects, p. 721b
Prepositions, p. 722a
Collocations, p. 722b
Ho., p. 723a
Htp., p. 723a

Qal $_{367.11.52}$ Pf. נָפַל (נָפֵל), נָפְלָה (נָפֵלָה), נָפַלְתָּ (נָפֵלְתָּ), נָפַלְתִּי, נָפְלוּ (נָפֵלוּ); impf. יִפֹּל (יִפּוֹל, יִפָּל־), 3fs תִּפֹּל (תִּפּוֹל, תִּפָּל־), 2ms תִּפֹּל (תִּפּוֹל), אֶפֹּל (אֶפֹּלָה, אֶפְּלָה), יִפְּלוּ (יִפֹּלוּ, Q יפולו), 3fpl תִּפֹּלְנָה, תִּפְּלוּ, 2fpl תִּפֹּלְנָה, נִפְּלָה; + waw וְנָפַל, וְנָפְלָה, וְנָפַלְתָּ (וְנָפַלְתָּה), וְנָפַלְתִּי, וְנָפְלוּ, וּנְפַלְתֶּם; וַיִּפֹּל (וַיִּפָּל־), 3fs וַתִּפֹּל, וָאֶפֹּל (וָאֶפְּלָה), וַיִּפְּלוּ; impv. נִפְלוּ; ptc. נֹפֵל (נוֹפֵל), נֹפֶלֶת, נֹפְלִים (Q נופלים, Q נופליהמה); inf. abs. נָפוֹל; cstr. נְפֹל (נְפוֹל, נָפְלוֹ, נִפְלוֹ, נִפְלָם).

1a. fall, of persons, oft. by accident (Gn 14_{10} 49_{17} Ex 21_{33} Lv $11_{32.33.35.37.38}$ Dt $22_{8.8}$=11QT $65_{6.6}$ 1 S 4_{18} 2 S 4_{4} 2 K 1_{2} $6_{5.6}$ Is 24_{18} Jr 8_{4} 23_{12} 46_{16} 48_{44} Ps 7_{16} 35_{8} 37_{24} [unless §13] 57_{7} 141_{10} Pr 22_{14} 26_{27} 28_{10} Ec $4_{10.10}$ 10_{8} Si 9_{3} 1QH 10_{29} 4QSD 7.1_{7} CD 11_{16}), through violence (1 S 17_{49} 2 S $2_{16.23.23}$); of beasts (4QSD 7.1_{6} CD 11_{13}); of objects (1 S 26_{20} 2 S 20_{8} 2 K $2_{13.14}$ Am 9_{9} Lm 5_{16}).

b. fall (down), descend, of dew (2 S 17_{12}), hailstones (Ezk 13_{11}), fire of Y. (1 K 18_{38} Jb 1_{16}), hair from head (1 S 14_{45} 2 S 14_{11} 1 K 1_{52}), shoulder blade from shoulder (Jb 31_{22}), bird into trap (Am 3_{5}), fruit from tree (Na 3_{12}), star (Is 14_{12}), wealth and people of Tyre into sea (Ezk $27_{27.34}$).

c. fall down, collapse, give way, of wall (Jos $6_{5.20}$ 1 K 20_{30} Is 30_{13} Jr 51_{44} Ezk $13_{11.12}$ 30_{20}), Jerusalem as wall (Ezk 13_{14}), bricks (Is 9_{9}), tent (Jg $7_{13.13}$), house (Jg 16_{30} Jb 1_{19}), tower (Is 30_{25} Jr 50_{15} Ezk 38_{20} [if em.; see Subj.]), steep places (Ezk 38_{20}), mountains, hills (Ho 10_{8} Jb 14_{18}), peg (Is 22_{25}), trees (Is 10_{34}=4QM[g] 5_{2} [[י]פול]) Zc 11_{2} Ec $11_{3.3}$), branches of tree (Ezk 31_{12}), horns of altar (Am 3_{14}), the earth (Is 24_{20}).

d. fall, drop, of countenance (Gn $4_{5.6}$).

2. fall, i.e. **a.** die (Ex 19_{21} 32_{28} Jg $5_{27.27.27}$ 2 S $3_{29.34.34.38}$ 21_{9} Is 31_{8}=1QM 11_{11} Ps 82_{7} Si 10_{10} [unless §2b] CD $2_{18.19}$ 4QHalakhah[a] 1_{3}), in warfare, conquest (Lv $26_{7.8}$ Nm $14_{3.43}$ Jos $8_{24.25}$ Jg 4_{16} 8_{10} 9_{40} 12_{6} 20_{44} 1 S 4_{10} 14_{13} 17_{52} 31_{1}||1 C 10_{1} 2 S $1_{4.12.19.25.27}$ 11_{17} 17_{9} 21_{22}||1 C 20_{8} 2 S 22_{39}||Ps 18_{39} 1 K 20_{25} 22_{30}||2 C 18_{19} Is 3_{25} 10_{4} 13_{15} Jr 20_{4} $25_{27.34}$ 39_{18} 44_{12} 49_{26}=50_{30} $51_{4.47.49.49}$ Ezk 5_{12} $6_{7.11.12}$ 11_{10} 17_{21} 23_{25} 24_{21} 25_{13} $30_{4.5.6.6.7}$ $32_{20.22.23.24.27}$ [or em.; see Subj.] 33_{27} $39_{4.23}$ Ho $7_{16.16}$ 14_{1} Am 7_{17} Ps 45_{6} [or em.; see Prep] 78_{64} Lm 2_{21} Dn 11_{26} 1 C $5_{10.22}$ 2 C 13_{17} 29_{9} 1QM 9_{7} 14_{3} 16_{11} 19_{10} [[נפלו]] 19_{11} 4QpNah 3.2_{6} 4QM[a] 10.2_{11} 4QM[b] 1_{9}), in flight (Lv 26_{36} Jr 46_{6} 2 C 14_{12}), through famine (Ezk 6_{11}), pestilence (Ezk 6_{11} Ps 91_{7} 1 C 21_{14}).

b. come to ruin, experience calamity (2 K 14_{10}||2 C 25_{19} Is 3_{8} 8_{15} $21_{9.9}$ 31_{3} 54_{15} Jr $6_{15.15}$=$8_{12.12}$ 46_{12} 49_{21} 50_{32} 51_{8} Ho 7_{7} Am 8_{14} Mc 7_{8} Ps 5_{11} 20_{9} 27_{2} Pr $11_{5.14.28}$

[or em.; see Subj.] 13$_{17}$ [or em.; see Subj.] 17$_{20}$ 24$_{16.17}$ 28$_{14.18}$ Est 6$_{13.13.13}$ Dn 11$_{19}$ Si 10$_{10}$ [unless §2a] 12$_{15}$ 25$_{21[Segal]}$ 1QM 16$_{.9}$ 18$_{2}$ 4QpNah 3.2$_{10}$).

c. perh. specifically **fall (into Sheol)** Jr 23$_{12}$ Ps 5$_{11}$ 36$_{13}$ 82$_{7}$ 118$_{13}$ Pr 7$_{26}$ 28$_{10}$.*

3. fall (in exhaustion), collapse (through lack of strength), of persons (2 S 1$_{10}$ Ps 10$_{10}$ 118$_{13}$ 145$_{14}$), arms of Pharaoh (Ezk 30$_{25}$), **fail,** of courage (1 S 17$_{32}$ Ps 45$_{6}$ [if em.; see Prep.]), understanding (4QSD 1.2$_{4}$).

4. fall away, waste away, of thigh (Nm 5$_{21.22}$ [if em.; see Subj.] 5$_{27}$), corpse (Nm 14$_{29.32}$).

6. be void, i.e. not reckoned (Nm 6$_{12}$), **fail (to be accomplished)** (Jos 21$_{45}$ 23$_{14.14}$ 1 K 8$_{56}$ 2 K 10$_{10}$).

7. be born (Is 26$_{18}$).

8. settle camp (Gn 25$_{18}$).*

9a. of lot, **fall** (Ezk 24$_{6}$ Jon 1$_{7}$ 1 C 26$_{14}$ Si 25$_{19}$ 1QH 11$_{27}$ [§11] CD 20$_{4}$). **b. fall (by lot), be allocated** (Nm 34$_{2}$ Jos 17$_{5}$ Jg 18$_{1}$ Ezk 47$_{14}$ Ps 16$_{6}$ 5/6ḤevBA 44$_{10.13}$). **c. receive by lot** (Ezk 47$_{22}$ [or em. hi.])

10. fall out, turn out, happen (Ru 3$_{18}$ Si 37$_{8}$).

11. fall upon, come upon, of sleep (Gn 15$_{12}$ 1 S 26$_{12}$ Jb 4$_{13}$ 33$_{15}$), terror, dread (Gn 15$_{12}$ Ex 15$_{16}$ [or em.; see Subj.] Jos 2$_{9}$ 1 S 11$_{7}$ Ps 55$_{5}$ [unless §13] 105$_{38}$ Jb 13$_{11}$ Est 8$_{17}$ 9$_{2.3}$), trembling (Dn 10$_{7}$), darkness (Gn 15$_{12}$), disaster (Is 47$_{11}$), reproach (Ps 69$_{10}$), word from Y. (Is 9$_{7}$), hand of Y. (Ezk 8$_{1}$), spirit of Y. (Ezk 11$_{5}$), battle shout (Is 16$_{9}$), evil time (Ec 9$_{12}$), time of anger (1QH 11$_{27}$), outpouring of wrath (1QH 11$_{27}$).

12. come before, be accepted, of supplication (Jr 36$_{7}$ 37$_{20}$ 42$_{2}$).

13. fall upon, i.e. attack (Jos 11$_{7}$ Jr 48$_{32}$ Ps 37$_{24}$ [unless §1a] 55$_{5}$ [unless §11] Jb 1$_{15}$).

14. fall into the hands of (Jg 15$_{18}$ 2 S 24$_{14.14}$||1 C 21$_{13.13}$ Lm 1$_{7}$ Si 6$_{2}$ 8$_{1}$ 4QJub^{a} 1$_{10}$).

15. fall away, desert (1 S 29$_{3}$ [unless §16] 2 K 7$_{4}$ 25$_{11}$||Jr 52$_{15}$ Jr 21$_{9}$ 37$_{13.14}$ 38$_{19}$ 39$_{9}$ 1 C 12$_{20.20.21}$ 2 C 15$_{9}$).

16. arrive (in camp) (1 S 29$_{3}$ [unless §15]).*

17. fall down (deliberately), prostrate oneself, throw oneself down, upon sword (1 S 31$_{4.5}$||1 C 10$_{4.5}$), in laughter (Gn 17$_{17}$), affection (Gn 33$_{4}$ 45$_{14}$ 46$_{29}$ 50$_{1}$ 1 S 20$_{41}$), respect for humans (Gn 44$_{14}$ 50$_{18}$ 1 S 25$_{23.24}$ 2 S 1$_{2}$ 9$_{6}$ 14$_{4.22}$ 19$_{19}$ 1 K 18$_{7}$ 2 K 4$_{37}$ Ru 2$_{10}$ Est 8$_{3}$), reverence for Y. or angel (Gn 17$_{3}$ Lv 9$_{24}$ Nm 16$_{22}$ 17$_{10}$ 20$_{6}$ Jos 5$_{14}$ Jg 13$_{20}$ 1 K 18$_{39}$ Ezk 1$_{28}$ 3$_{23}$ 9$_{8}$ 11$_{13}$ 43$_{3}$ 44$_{4}$ Jb 1$_{20}$ Dn 8$_{17}$ 1 C 21$_{16}$ 2 C 20$_{18}$ Si 50$_{17.21}$ 4QShirShabb^{f} 20.2$_{7}$), alarm (Nm 14$_{5}$ 16$_{4}$ 1 S 28$_{20}$), **bend down** (Si 12$_{15}$), **thrust oneself forward** (Jl 2$_{8}$).

18. alight, dismount, from camel (Gn 24$_{64}$), chariot (2 K 5$_{21}$).

19. be prostrate, lying down, fallen down, of persons, before ark (Jos 7$_{6.10}$), seeing vision (Nm 24$_{4.16}$), prophesying (1 S 19$_{24}$), on bed, couch (Ex 21$_{18}$ Est 7$_{8}$), collapsed on ground (Jg 19$_{26.27}$ 1 S 5$_{3.4}$ Am 5$_{2}$ Ps 36$_{13}$), dead on ground (Dt 21$_{1}$ Jg 3$_{25}$ 4$_{22}$ 1 S 31$_{8}$||1 C 10$_{8}$ Jr 9$_{21}$ Ezk 29$_{5}$ 35$_{8}$ 39$_{5}$ 2 C 20$_{24}$); of animals (Dt 22$_{4}$), booth (Am 9$_{11}$=CD 7$_{16}$=4QMidrEschat$_{4}$ 3$_{13}$); **be spread throughout** (Jg 7$_{12}$).

20. be inferior (Jb 12$_{3}$ 13$_{2}$), **be low** (Ne 6$_{16}$).

<SUBJ> אֱלֹהִים *god* Ps 82$_{7}$, Dagon 1 S 5$_{3.4}$, כְּרוּב *cherub* 4QShirShabb^{f} 20.2$_{7}$ (יפול[ו] ... ה[כרו]בים), עִיר *watcher,* i.e. angel CD 2$_{18}$ (appar. עידי is error for עירי), הֵילֵל *shining one* Is 14$_{12}$ (or em. הֵילָל *morning-star, crescent moon*).

Assyria Is 31$_{8}$=1QM 11$_{11}$ Ezk 32$_{22}$ 1QM 1$_{6}$, Babylon Is 21$_{9.9}$ Jr 51$_{8}$, Cub Ezk 30$_{5}$ (or em. כּוּב to לוּב *Libya*), Cush(ites) Jr 39$_{18}$ Ezk 30$_{5}$ 4QpsEzek^{a} 1$_{4}$ ([י]פול), Edom(ites) Jr 49$_{21}$ Ezk 25$_{13}$, Egyptians (Ezk 32$_{20}$), Hagrites 1 C 5$_{10}$, Israel(ites) Ho 14$_{1}$ Mc 7$_{8}$, Jerusalem Ezk 13$_{14}$, Jews Jr 38$_{19}$, Judah (nation) 2 K 14$_{10}$||2 C 25$_{19}$ Is 3$_{8}$ 2 C 20$_{18}$, Kittim 1QM 1$_{9}$, Lebanon Is 10$_{34}$=4QM^{g} 5$_{2}$ ([י]פול), Libya Ezk 30$_{5}$ (if em.; see above), Lud Ezk 30$_{5}$, Philistine(s) 1 S 14$_{13}$ 17$_{49}$, Put Ezk 30$_{5}$, Sabaeans Jb 1$_{15}$, Shunammite 2 K 4$_{37}$, עַם *people* Lv 9$_{24}$ Jos 11$_{7}$ 2 S 1$_{12}$ 1 K 18$_{39}$ Ezk 39$_{4}$ Jl 2$_{8}$ Ps 45$_{6}$ (or em.; see Prep.) Pr 11$_{14}$ Lm 1$_{7}$, גּוֹי *nation* Ne 6$_{16}$, אַחֲרִית *remnant* Ezk 23$_{25}$, שְׁאֵרִית *remnant* Jr 44$_{12}$, הָמוֹן *multitude* 1QM 19$_{10}$ ([נפלו]), קָהָל *company* Ezk 27$_{34}$ 32$_{22}$ Si 50$_{21}$, עֶרֶב *mixed company* Ezk 30$_{5}$, אֲגַף *troop* Ezk 39$_{4}$, חַיִל *army* 1 K 20$_{25}$ 1QM 19$_{10}$ ([נפלו]), מַחֲנֶה *camp,* i.e. army Jg 4$_{16}$.

Aaron Nm 14$_{5}$ 16$_{22}$ 17$_{10}$ 20$_{6}$, Abigail 1 S 25$_{23.24}$, Abner 2 S 3$_{34}$, Abram Gn 17$_{3.17}$, Adnah 1 C 12$_{21}$, Ahab 1 K 22$_{30}$||2 C 18$_{19}$, Ahaziah 2 K 1$_{2}$, Amaziah 2 K 14$_{10}$, Armoni 2 S 21$_{9}$, Asahel 2 S 2$_{23.23}$, Daniel Dn 8$_{17}$, David 1 S 20$_{41}$ 29$_{3}$ 2 S 24$_{14.14}$||1 C 21$_{13.13}$ 1 C 12$_{20}$ 21$_{16}$,

Ebed-melech Jr 39_{18}, Eli 1 S 4_{18}, Elihu 1 C 12_{21}, Esau Gn 33_4, Esther Est 8_3, Ezekiel Ezk 1_{28} 3_{23} 9_8 11_{13} 43_3 44_4, Gog Ezk $39_{4.5}$, Haman Est $6_{13.13.13}$ 7_8, Ishmael Gn 25_{18}, Jediael 1 C 12_{21}, Jeremiah Jr $37_{13.14}$, Joab 2 S 14_{22}, Job Jb 1_{20} 12_3 13_2, Jonathan 2 S 1_{12}, Joseph Gn 45_{14} 46_{29} 50_1, Joshua Jos 5_{14} $7_{6.10}$ 11_7, Jozabad 1 C 12_{21}, Judah Gn 44_{14}||2 C 25_{19}, Manoah Jg 13_{20}, Mephibosheth (son of Jonathan) 2 S 9_6, Mephibosheth (son of Saul) 2 S 21_9, Michael 1 C 12_{21}, Jozacar 1 C 12_{21} (if em. 2nd יוֹזָבָד to יוֹזָכָר), Moses Nm 14_5 $16_{4.22}$ 17_{10} 20_6, Naaman 2 K 5_{21}, Obadiah 1 K 18_7, Rebekah Gn 24_{64}, Ruth Ru 2_{10}, Samson Jg 15_{18}, Saul 1 S 19_{24} 28_{20} $31_{4.8}$||1 C $10_{4.8}$ 2 S $1_{10.12}$, Shimei 2 S 19_{19}, Sisera Jg 4_{22} $5_{27.27.27}$, Zillethai 1 C 12_{21}.

אִישׁ *man* Jos 8_{25} Jg 8_{10} $20_{44.46}$ 2 S 1_2 2_{16} 14_4 2 K 7_4 Jr 46_{16} Ezk 27_{27} 1 C 21_{14} 2 C 13_{17}, גֶּבֶר *man* Ps 37_{24}, מַת *man* Is 3_{25}, אִשָּׁה *woman, wife* Jg 13_{20} 19_{26}, פִּלֶגֶשׁ *secondary wife* Jg 19_{27}, אָב *father* 2 C 29_9, בֵּן *son* Jg 7_{12} 1 S 31_8||1 C 10_8 2 S 1_{12} 4_4 9_6 19_{19} 21_9 Is 14_{12} Ezk 24_{21} 30_5 Am 7_{17} Si 6_2 8_1 9_3 12_{15} 25_{21} 1QM 18_2, of Israel Nm $14_{3.43}$, בַּת *daughter* Ezk 24_{21} 32_{20} Am 7_{17}, אָח *brother* Gn 44_{14} 50_{18}, בָּחוּר *young man* Jr 49_{26}=50_{30} Ezk 30_{17} Lm 2_{21}, בְּתוּלָה *young woman* Am 5_2 Lm 2_{21}, עֶבֶד *servant* 1 S 29_3, מַלְאָךְ *messenger* Pr 13_{17} (or em. יַפִּל hi. *he causes to fall*).

מֶלֶךְ *king* Gn 14_{10} 2 K 14_{10} Jr 25_{27} Ezk 29_5 Ho 7_7 Dn 11_{19}, פַּרְעֹה *Pharaoh* Ezk 29_5, אָדוֹן *lord* Jg 3_{25}, נָשִׂיא *prince* Ezk $39_{4.5}$, שַׂר *prince* 2 S 3_{38} Ho 7_{16}, מֹשֵׁל *ruler* 4QpNah 3.2_{10} (מוש[לים]), כֹּהֵן *priest* Jr 6_{15}=8_{12} Ps 78_{64}, נָבִיא *prophet* Jr 6_{15}=8_{12} 23_{12} 37_{13}, worshipper Ps 118_{13}, זָקֵן *elder* Jos 7_6 1 C 21_{16}, אהב ptc. *one who loves* Jr 20_4, חבר ptc. *one who joins with* Si 12_{15}, רֵעַ *neighbour* Ex 21_{18} 2 S 2_{16}, יֹשֵׁב *inhabitant* Is 26_{18} Jr 49_{21} 2 C 20_{18}, גֵּר *sojourner* Ezk 47_{22} (or em. יַפִּילוּ hi. *they shall allocate*), רֹעֶה *shepherd* Jr 25_{34}.

אֹיֵב *enemy* Lv $26_{7.8.36}$ 2 S 22_{39}||Ps 18_{39} Ps 27_2 Pr 24_{17} Ne 6_{16}, שׁוֹרֵר *watcher*, i.e. enemy Ps 5_{11}, צַר *adversary* Ps 27_2, שׁבע ni. ptc. *one who swears* Am 8_{14}, זָעוּם *accursed one* Pr 22_{14}, חשׁב ptc. *one who devises* evil Ps 35_8, רָשָׁע *wicked one* Ps 7_{16} 141_{10} Pr 11_5, הפך ni. ptc. *one who is perverse* Pr 17_{20}, עשׁק ni. ptc. *one who is perverse* Pr 28_{18}, פעל ptc. *one who does* evil Ps 36_{13}, קשׁה pi. *one who hardens* his heart Pr 28_{14}, חפר ptc. *one who digs* Ec 10_8, כרה ptc. *one who digs* Pr 26_{27}, שׁגה pi. ptc. *one who leads astray* Pr 28_{10}.

רַגְלִי *foot soldier* 1 S 4_{10}, נשׂא ptc. *one who bears* armour 1 S 31_5||1 C 10_5, גִּבּוֹר *mighty one* 2 S $1_{19.25.27}$ Jr $46_{6.12}$ Ezk 32_{27} (or em. נְפִלִים *giants*) 1QH 10_{29} 4QM[b] 1_9, שֹׁדֵד *destroyer* Jr 48_{32}, חֹבֵל *sailor* Ezk 27_{27}, מַלָּח *mariner* Ezk 27_{27}, מַחֲזִיק *caulker* Ezk 27_{27}, עֹרֵב *merchant* Ezk 27_{27}, רֹכֵב *rider* Gn 49_{17}, יצא ptc. *one who goes out* Jr 21_9, קַל *swift one* Jr 46_6, נוס ptc. *one who flees* Is 24_{18} Jr 48_{44}, מִבְרָח *fugitive* Ezk 17_{21}, נפל ptc. *one who falls* Dt 22_8=11QT 65_6, *deserter* 2 K 25_{11}||Jr 52_{15} 39_9, ספה ni. ptc. *one who is caught* Is 13_{15}, חֵלְכָה *wretched one* Ps 10_{10}.

מִבְחָר *choice one* Ezk $17_{21(\text{mss})}$, נִכְבָּד *honourable one* 4QpNah 3.2_{10} ([נ]כבדים), צַדִּיק *righteous one* Pr 24_{16}, קָרוֹב *near one* Ezk 6_{12}, סמך ptc. *one who supports* Ezk $30_{6.6}$, עזר ptc. pass. *one who is helped* Is 31_3, בטח ptc. *one who trusts* Pr 11_{28} (unless נפל II *wither*; or em. יִבֹּל *he will wither*, i.e. נבל I), בקשׁ pi. ptc. *one who seeks* Ps 35_8.

פָּנִים *face*, i.e. countenance Gn $4_{5.6}$, יָד *hand* , Ezk 8_1, זְרוֹעַ *arm* Ezk 30_{25}, כָּתֵף *shoulder blade* Jb 31_{22}, יָרֵךְ *thigh* Nm $5_{21.22}$ (if em. לַנְפִּל hi. *to cause to fall away* to לִנְפֹּל *to fall away*) 5_{27}, רֹאשׁ *head*, i.e. chief 1 C 12_{21}, לֵב *heart*, i.e. courage 1 S 17_{32}, דָּם *blood* 1 S 26_{20}, קֶרֶן *horn* Am 3_{14}, בָּשָׂר *flesh* Si 50_{17} CD 2_{19}, רוּחַ *spirit* Ezk 11_5, נֶפֶשׁ *soul*, i.e. person 4QSD 7.1_7 CD 11_{16}, שֵׂכֶל *understanding* 4QSD 1.2_4 ([ש]לכו), נְבֵלָה *corpse* Jr 9_{21}, פֶּגֶר *corpse* Nm $14_{29.32}$ 2 C 20_{24}, חָלָל *slain one* Dt 21_1 Jg 9_{40} 1 S 17_{52} 31_1||1 C 10_1 Jr $51_{4.47.49.49}$ Ezk 6_7 30_4 $28_{23(\text{mss})}$ (L pilel) $32_{23.24}$ 35_8 Dn 11_{26} 1 C 5_{22} 2 C 13_{17} 1QM 9_7 14_3 16_{11} 17_{16} (ל[נפ]ול) 4QHalakhah[a] 13_3 4QM[a] 10.2_{11}.

בְּהֵמָה *beast* 4QSD 7.1_6 perh. 4QapJoseph[b] 4_6 CD 11_{13} (appar. תפיל is error for תפול, as at 4QD[f] 5.1_8), חֲמוֹר *ass* Ex 21_{33} Dt 22_4, שׁוֹר *ox* Ex 21_{33} Dt 22_4, צִפּוֹר *bird* Am 3_5.

אֶרֶז *cedar* Zc 11_2, עֵץ *tree* Ec $11_{3.3}$, דָּלִית *branch* Ezk 31_{12}, בִּכּוּרִים *first fruits* Na 3_{12}.

אֹהֶל *tent* Jg $7_{13.13}$, סֻכָּה *tent* Am 9_{11}=CD 7_{16}=4QMidr Eschat$_4$ 3_{13} (הנופל[ת]), בַּיִת *house* Jg 16_{30} Jb 1_{19}, of

Israel Ezk 611 1110 3823, חוֹמָה *wall* Jos 65.20 1 K 2030 Jr 5144, חַיִץ *wall* Ezk 1311, קִיר *wall* Ezk 1312, פֶּרֶץ *breach* in wall Is 3013, אָשְׁיָה *tower* Jr 5015, מִגְדָּל *tower* Is 3025 Ezk 3820 (if em. הַמַּדְרֵגוֹת *the steep places* to הַמִּגְדָּלוֹת *the towers*), לְבֵנָה *brick* Is 99, מַדְרֵגָה *steep place* Ezk 3820 (or em.; see above), הַר *mountain* Jb 1418, גִּבְעָה *hill* Ho 108, אֶרֶץ *land* Nm 342 Is 2420 Ezk 4714, מָקוֹם *place* 5/6ḤevBA 4410.13.

זָדוֹן *presumptuousness* Jr 5032, תַּרְדֵּמָה *deep sleep* Gn 1512 1 S 2612 Jb 413 3315, אֵימָה *terror* Gn 1512 Ex 1516 [or em. וַתַּפֵּל hi. *and you caused to fall*] Jos 29 Ps 555, פַּחַד *dread* Ex 1516 [or em.; see above] 1 S 117 Ps 10538 Jb 1311 Est 817 92.3, חֲרָדָה *trembling* Dn 107, הֹוָה *disaster* Is 4711, חֲשֵׁכָה *darkness* Gn 1512, מַתָּךְ *outpouring* of wrath 1QH 1127, יוֹם *day* Nm 612, עֵת *time* Ec 912, קֵץ *time* 1QH 1127.

טַל *dew* 2 S 1712, אֶבֶן hail *stone* Ezk 1311, צְרוֹר *pebble* Am 99, אֵשׁ *fire* 1 K 1838 Jb 116, חֶבֶל *measuring line* Ps 166, *(allotted) portion* Jos 175, קָו *line* 1QH 1127, נַחֲלָה *inheritance* Jg 181, גּוֹרָל *lot* Ezk 246 Jon 17 1 C 2614 Si 2519 CD 204, הוֹן *wealth* Ezk 2727, עִזָּבוֹן pl. *wares* Ezk 2727, מַעֲרָב *merchandise* Ezk 2727.34, אַדֶּרֶת *cloak* 2 K 213.14.

חֶרֶב *sword* 2 S 208, בַּרְזֶל *iron (axe head)* 2 K 65.6, יָתֵד *peg* Is 2225, עֲטָרָה *crown* Lm 516, דָּבָר *word* Is 97, *thing* Jos 2145 2314.14 1 K 856 Ru 318, תְּחִנָּה *supplication* Jr 367 3720 422, הֵידָד *shout* Is 169, חֶרְפָּה *reproach* Ps 6910.

מִי *whoever* Is 5415, שְׁלִישִׁית *third* Ezk 512, אֶחָד *one* Ec 410, שְׁנַיִם *two* Ec 410, אֶלֶף *thousand* Jg 126 Ps 917, רְבָבָה *ten thousand* Ps 917, רַב pl. *many* Ex 1921 Is 815 4QJuba 110 (ר[בי]ם), רֹב *multitude* 4QpNah 3.26, כֹּל *all* Jos 824, מִי *whoever* Is 5415, אֲשֶׁר *one who* Ezk 3327 1QM 1911, אֵלֶּה *these* 2 S 2122||1 C 208, הֵמָּה *they* Ps 209; subj. not specified, Nm 244.16 Dt 228=11QT 656 2 S 329.34 Jr 615=812 84 Ps 577 14514 2 C 159 Si 1010 378.

<PREP> לְ of place, *on, in,* + מִשְׁכָּב *bed* Ex 2118; of direction, benefit, *to, for,* + Israelites Ezk 4714, שֵׁבֶט *tribe* Jg 181, Almah 5/6ḤevBA 4413, Shelemiah 1 C 2614, Tehinnah 5/6ḤevBA 4413, אִישׁ *man* 4QSD 1.24 (א[י]ש), בֵּן *son* 5/6ḤevBA 4413, of Israel Nm 342, אַף *face* 1 S 2041, אֶרֶץ *ground* Ezk 3820 Am 314; of instrument, *by (means of),* + פֶּה *mouth,* i.e. edge, of sword Jos 824 Jg 416, חֶרֶב *sword* Lv 267.8; of cause, *on account of,* + Babylon Jr 5149; *as,* + רֹב *multitude* 2 C 159.

בְּ of place, direction, *in(to), at, upon, throughout* perh. 5Q14 13, + Israel 2 S 338 Is 97, Egypt Ezk 304.6, Ramoth-gilead 1 K 2230||2 C 1819, יָד *hand* Jg 1518 2 S 2414.14||1 C 2113.13 Lm 17 Si 62 81 4QJuba 110 ([ביד]), עַיִן *eye,* i.e. sight Ne 616, לֵב *heart* of seas Ezk 2727, אֶרֶץ *land* Jr 4412 514, שָׂדֶה *field* Dt 211 4QHalakhaha 133 (בו[שדה]), חֵלֶק *portion* 5/6ḤevBA 4410, מִדְבָּר *steppe* Nm 1429.32, הַר *mountain* 1 S 311.8||1 C 101.8, גִּבְעָה *hill* Ezk 358, גַּיְא *valley* Ezk 358, עֵמֶק *valley* Jg 712, אָפִיק *channel* Ezk 358, דֶּרֶךְ *way* Dt 224 1 S 1752, גּוּמָּץ *pit* Ec 108, שַׁחַת *pit* Ps 716 Pr 2627 2818 (if em.; see below), שְׁחוּת *pit* Pr 2810, מִכְמֹר *net* Ps 14110, רֶשֶׁת *net* Ps 358, מְצוֹדָה *net* Si 93, פַּח *trap* 1QH 1029, רְחוֹב *square* Jr 4926=5030, אֲפֵלָה *darkness* Jr 2312, שׁוֹאָה *ruin* Ps 358, רַע *evil* Pr 1317 (or em.; see Subj.), רָעָה *evil* Pr 1720 2814, נָעִים *pleasant place* Ps 166, דָּרוֹם *south* Ec 113, צָפוֹן *north* Ec 113, כְּלִי *vessel* perh. 4QTohA 2.210 ([י]פול [בו]), אֲשֶׁר *(the place) where* Jg 527.

בְּ of time, *in, on, at, during,* + יוֹם *day* Ex 3228 Jos 825 Jg 2046 Ezk 2727 1QM 19 4QpNah 3.26 4QSD 7.16.7 ([ביום]), עֵת *time* Jg 126, תְּחִלָּה *beginning* 2 S 179, מִלְחָמָה *battle* Is 325, אַחַת *one (time),* i.e. all at once Pr 2818 (or em. בְּאַחַת to בְּשַׁחַת *into a pit*).

בְּ of instrument, agent, *by (means of),* + יָד *hand* 2 S 2122||1 C 208 1 C 510, חֶרֶב *sword* Nm 143.43 2 S 112 329 Is 325 1315 318=1QM 1111 Jr 204 3918 Ezk 512 611.12 1110 1721 2325 2421 2513 2823(mss) (L pilel) 305.6.17 3222.23.24 3327 3923 Ho 716 141 Am 717 Ps 7864 Lm 221 2 C 299 1QM 1911, רָעָב *famine* Ezk 611, דֶּבֶר *pestilence* Ezk 611.

בְּ of cause, *on account of,* + עָצוּם *mighty one* Ps 1010, רִשְׁעָה *wickedness* Pr 115, יֳפִי *beauty* Si 2521(Segal) ([ביפי]); of accompaniment, *with,* + אַדִּיר *majestic one* Is 1034=4QM8 52 (באדיר י]פול]), נפל ptc. *one who falls* Jr 615=812; partitive, *(some) of,* as subj. of נפל, + עַם *people* 2 S 179; *upon, against,* + מֶלֶךְ *king* Jos 117; *as, for,* + נַחֲלָה *inheritance* Nm 342 Jg 181 Ezk 4714; *according to,* + רָז *mystery* 1QM 1611 4QMa 10.211 (ב[רזי]); introducing object, + נַחֲלָה *inheritance* Ezk 4722 (or em.; see Subj.).

כְּ *as,* + שַׂר *prince* Ps 827, אַרְבֶּה *locust* Jg 712, דֹּמֶן

dung Jr 9$_{21}$, כְּלִי *vessel* Jr 25$_{34}$ (or em. כִּכְלִי חֶמְדָּה *like a precious vessel* to בִּבְלִי חֶמְלָה *without compassion*); *about (specified number of)*, + אִישׁ *man* Ex 32$_{28}$.

מִן of direction, *from, at*, + שְׁכֶם *shoulder* Jb 31$_{22}$, יָמִין *right hand* Ps 91$_{7}$, צַד *side* Ps 91$_{7}$, גָּג *roof* Dt 22$_{8}$=11QT 65$_{6}$, שָׁמַיִם *heaven* Is 14$_{12}$ Jb 1$_{16}$, גְּבוּרָה *might* perh. 4QHod^{b} 1$_{1}$ (מגבור[תם]).

מִן partitive, 1. *(some) of, (any) of*, as subj. of נפל, + Cushites 2 C 14$_{12}$, Manasseh 1 C 12$_{20}$, עַם *people* Ex 32$_{28}$ 2 S 1$_{4}$ 11$_{17}$, עֶבֶד *servant* 2 S 11$_{17}$, שֶׁרֶץ *swarming thing* Lv 11$_{32.33}$, שַׂעֲרָה *hair* 1 S 14$_{45}$ 2 S 14$_{11}$ 1 K 1$_{52}$, נְבֵלָה *carcass* Lv 11$_{35.37.38}$.

2. *from (among)*, + Benjamin Jg 20$_{44.46}$, Ephraim Jg 12$_{6}$, Israel 1 S 4$_{10}$ 1 C 21$_{14}$ 2 C 13$_{17}$ 15$_{9}$, עַם *people* Ex 19$_{21}$, עָרֵל *uncircumcised one* Ezk 32$_{27}$ (or em.; see Subj.), דָּבָר *thing* Jos 21$_{45}$ 23$_{14.14}$ 1 K 8$_{56}$ 2 K 10$_{10}$.

מִן of cause, *on account of*, + מוֹעֵצָה *counsel* Ps 5$_{11}$; of comparison, *(more) than, (with respect) to*, + רֵעַ *friend* of Job Jb 12$_{3}$ 13$_{2}$.

לְבַד מִן *apart from*, + אֶרֶץ *land* Jos 17$_{5}$.

אֶל *to*, + Chaldaeans Jr 37$_{13}$ 38$_{19}$, Saul 1 C 12$_{20}$, מֶלֶךְ *king* 2 K 25$_{11}$||Jr 52$_{15}$ (2 K if em. עַל *to*), אָדוֹן *lord* 1 C 12$_{20}$, יֹעֵץ *counsellor* Si 37$_{8}$; *on(to), (in)to*, + פָּנִים *face* 2 S 14$_{22}$ Ezk 43$_{3}$ 44$_{4}$, מַיִם *water* 2 K 6$_{5}$, מַחֲנֶה *camp* 2 K 7$_{4}$, בּוֹר *pit* CD 11$_{13}$, פַּחַת *pit* Is 24$_{18}$ Jr 48$_{44}$ CD 11$_{13}$, מַיִם *water* 4QSD 7.1$_{6}$, מָקוֹם *place* CD 11$_{16}$; *upon, against*, + רֵעַ *neighbour* Jr 46$_{16}$.

אֶל־תּוֹךְ *inside, into the middle of*, + כְּלִי *vessel* Lv 11$_{32}$.

עַל *upon, at* Jos 2$_{9}$, + Egyptians Ps 105$_{38}$, Israelites Ho 10$_{8}$, עַם *people* Jg 16$_{30}$ 1 S 11$_{7}$ 26$_{12}$ Est 8$_{17}$ 9$_{2}$, עִיר *city* Ezk 24$_{6}$, Abram Gn 15$_{12.12}$, Ezekiel Ezk 8$_{1}$ 11$_{5}$, Jonah Jon 1$_{7}$, אִישׁ *man* 1 K 20$_{30}$ Jb 4$_{13}$ 33$_{15}$ Dn 10$_{7}$, אִשָּׁה *woman* Si 25$_{19}$, בֵּן *son* Ec 9$_{12}$, בַּת *daughter* of Chaldaeans Is 47$_{11}$, נַעַר *lad* Jb 1$_{19}$, שַׂר *prince* Est 9$_{3}$, סֶרֶן *lord* Jg 16$_{30}$, אֲחַשְׁדַּרְפָּן *satrap* Est 9$_{3}$, פֶּחָה *governor* Est 9$_{3}$, רֵעַ *friend* of Job Jb 13$_{11}$, יֹשֵׁב *inhabitant* Ex 15$_{16}$ (or em.; see Subj.), worshipper Ps 55$_{5}$ 69$_{10}$, עשׂה ptc. *one who does* Est 9$_{3}$, עזב ni. ptc. *abandoned one* 1QH 11$_{27}$, עלם ni. ptc. *concealed one* 1QH 11$_{27}$, פָּנִים *face* Gn 17$_{3.17}$ 50$_{1}$ Lv 9$_{24}$ Nm 14$_{5}$ 16$_{4.22}$ 17$_{10}$ 20$_{6}$ Jos 5$_{14}$ 7$_{6.10}$ Jg 13$_{20}$ 1 S 17$_{49}$ 25$_{23}$ 2 S 9$_{6}$ 14$_{4}$ 1 K 18$_{7.39}$ Ezk 1$_{28}$ 3$_{23}$ 9$_{8}$ 11$_{13}$ Ru 2$_{10}$ Dn 8$_{17}$ 1 C 21$_{16}$ Si 50$_{17}$, פֶּה *mouth* Na 3$_{12}$, צַוָּאר *neck* Gn 33$_{4}$ 45$_{14}$ 46$_{29}$, רֶגֶל *foot* 1 S 25$_{24}$ 2 K 4$_{37}$, זֶרַע *seed* Lv 11$_{37.38}$, קָצִיר *harvest* Is 16$_{9}$, בָּצִיר *grape harvest* Jr 48$_{32}$, קַיִץ *summer fruit* Is 16$_{9}$, חֶרֶב *sword* 1 S 31$_{4.5}$|| 1 C 10$_{4.5}$, פַּח *snare* Am 3$_{5}$, אֲדָמָה *ground* 2 S 17$_{12}$, הַר *mountain* Ezk 39$_{4}$, מִטָּה *couch* Est 7$_{8}$, מִשְׁפָּט *judgment* 1QH 11$_{27}$, כֹּל *anything* Lv 11$_{32.35}$.

עַל *to*, + Chaldaeans Jr 21$_{9}$ 37$_{14}$, David 1 C 12$_{20.21}$, Nebuzaradan Jr 39$_{9}$, מֶלֶךְ *king* 2 K 25$_{11}$ (or em. אֶל *to*, with ||Jr 52$_{15}$), רַב *captain* of (body)guards Jr 39$_{9}$; *on account of*, + Goliath 1 S 17$_{32}$, עָנִי *afflicted one* Is 54$_{15}$.

מֵעַל *from (upon)* 5Q14 1$_{2}$, + Elijah 2 K 2$_{13.14}$, גָּמָל *camel* Gn 24$_{64}$, מֶרְכָּבָה *chariot* 2 K 5$_{21}$, כִּסֵּא *seat* 1 S 4$_{18}$.

מֵעִם appar. *on account of*, + לָשׁוֹן *tongue*, i.e. speech 4QpNah 3.2$_{10}$ (מ[עם]).

מֵאֵת *from*, + מֶלֶךְ *king* 1 K 20$_{25}$.

אֵת *with*, + Israelites Ezk 47$_{22}$ (or em.; see Subj.).

בְּאֵין *without, for lack of*, + תַּחְבֻּלָה *guidance* Pr 11$_{14}$.

בְּעַד *through*, + יָד *hand*, i.e. side, of gate 1 S 4$_{18}$, שְׂבָכָה *lattice* 2 K 1$_{2}$, שֶׁלַח *weapons* Jl 2$_{8}$.

בְּתוֹךְ *among, within, in the middle of*, + Babylon Jr 51$_{47}$, Sidon Ezk 28$_{23(mss)}$ (L pilel), שֵׁבֶט *tribe* Jg 18$_{1}$ Ezk 47$_{22}$ (or em.; see Subj.), לִמֵּד *pupil* CD 20$_{4}$, חָלָל *slain one* Ezk 32$_{20}$, הַר *mountain* Ezk 6$_{7}$, שִׁיחָה *pit* Ps 57$_{7}$, מִלְחָמָה *battle* 2 S 1$_{25}$.

בְּקֶרֶב *among, in the middle of* 4QpsEzek^{e} 25$_{1}$.

עַל־פְּנֵי *over against, beside*, + אָח *brother* Gn 25$_{18}$; *upon*, + שָׂדֶה *field* Jr 9$_{21}$ Ezk 39$_{5}$.

לִפְנֵי *before*, + Y. Jr 36$_{7}$ 2 C 20$_{18}$ 4QShirShabb^{f} 20.2$_{7}$ (יפול[ו]), Israelites Lv 26$_{7.8}$, קָהָל *assembly* Nm 14$_{5}$, Jeremiah Jr 42$_{2}$, Jonathan 1 S 14$_{13}$, Joseph Gn 44$_{14}$ 50$_{18}$, Mordecai Est 6$_{13.13}$, בֵּן *son* 2 S 3$_{34}$, מֶלֶךְ *king* 2 S 19$_{19}$ Jr 37$_{20}$, אָדוֹן *lord* Jr 37$_{20}$, רֶגֶל *foot* Est 8$_{3}$, אֲרוֹן *ark* Jos 7$_{6}$ 1 S 5$_{3.4}$ (unless לְפָנָיו = *before him*, i.e. he fell forward); *before oneself*, i.e. face downward, + Dagon 1 S 5$_{3}$.

לְאַפֵּי *before*, + David 1 S 25$_{23}$.

מִנֶּגֶד פְּנֵי *away from (the presence of)*, + Y. 1 S 26$_{20}$.

עַד *as far as*, + Ekron 1 S 17$_{52}$, Gaza 1 S 17$_{52}$, פֶּתַח *entrance* Jg 9$_{40}$; *until*, + יוֹם *day* Jg 18$_{1}$, עֶרֶב *evening* Jos 7$_{6}$, אוֹר *light*, i.e. dawn Jg 19$_{26}$.

סָבִיב *round about,* + Jerusalem Ezk 5$_{12}$.

מֵאַחֲרֵי *behind, after,* + קֹצֵר *reaper* Jr 9$_{21}$.

תַּחַת *beneath,* + מֶלֶךְ *king* Ps 45$_6$ (or em. תַּחְתֶּיךָ יִפְּלוּ בְּלֵב *beneath you they will fall; in the heart of* to תַּחְתֶּיךָ יִפּוֹל לֵב *beneath you; the heart of* the king's enemies *will fail*), הָרוּג *slain one* Is 10$_4$, רֶגֶל *foot* 2 S 22$_{39}$||Ps 18$_{39}$; *beneath oneself, in one's place,* + חוֹמָה *wall* Jos 6$_{5.20}$.

ה- of direction, *to(wards), upon,* + אֶרֶץ *ground* Gn 44$_{14}$ Jos 5$_{14}$ 7$_6$ Jg 3$_{25}$ 13$_{20}$ 1 S 5$_{3.4}$ 14$_{45}$ 17$_{49}$ 20$_{41}$ 26$_{20}$ 28$_{20}$ 2 S 1$_2$ 14$_{4.11.22}$ 1 K 1$_{52}$ 2 K 10$_{10}$ Jb 1$_{20}$ 2 C 20$_{24}$ Si 50$_{17}$, מִזְרָח *east* 1 C 26$_{14}$, שָׁם *there* Gn 14$_{10}$ Ex 21$_{33}$.

נפל + noun without preposition or ה- of direction, פֶּתַח *(at the) entrance* Jg 19$_{26.27}$, מָקוֹם *(in the) place* Ec 11$_3$, אֶרֶץ *(to the) earth* Am 9$_9$.

<COLL> נפל || כשל *stumble* Is 3$_8$ 8$_{15}$ (+) 31$_3$ Jr 46$_{6.12.16}$ (all three +) 50$_{32}$ Ps 27$_2$ Pr 24$_{17}$, ni. Jr 6$_{15}$ Pr 24$_{16}$ (both +) Dn 11$_{19}$, שׁבר ni. *be broken* Is 8$_{15}$ Jr 51$_8$ Ezk 31$_{12}$ Jb 31$_{22}$ 2 C 14$_{12}$ (+), גדע ni. *be cut down* Is 22$_{25}$, pu. Is 9$_9$, הרס ni. *be torn down* Jr 50$_{15}$, כתת ho. *be crushed* 1QM 18$_2$, כרע *bow down* Jg 5$_{27}$ Is 10$_4$ Ps 20$_9$, כפף pass. *be bowed down* Ps 145$_{14}$, שׁכב *lie down* Jg 5$_{27}$, מות *die* 2 S 1$_4$ 2$_{23.23}$ 11$_{17}$ Jr 44$_{12}$ (all five +) Ezk 5$_{12}$ 6$_{12}$ Ps 82$_7$, כלה *come to an end* Is 31$_3$ (+) Ezk 5$_{12}$ 6$_{12}$, בוא *come* Is 47$_{11}$, צבה *swell* Nm 5$_{27}$.

+ שׁחה htpal. *bow down* Jos 5$_{14}$ 1 S 20$_{41}$ 25$_{23}$ 2 S 1$_2$ 9$_6$ 14$_{4.22}$ 2 K 4$_{37}$ Jb 1$_{20}$ Ru 2$_{10}$ 2 C 20$_{18}$ Si 50$_{17}$, דחה ni. *be thrust down* Jr 23$_{12}$, טול ho. *be thrown down* Ps 37$_{24}$, דקר ni. *be thrust through* Is 13$_{15}$, אבד *perish* 2 S 1$_{27}$, נבל *crumble away* Jb 14$_{18}$, גוע *expire* CD 2$_{19}$, דמם ni. *be destroyed* Jr 49$_{26}$=50$_{30}$, תמם *come to an end* Jr 44$_{12}$, חרה *be angry* Gn 4$_{5.6}$, כסה pi. *cover* Ho 10$_8$.

:: קום *rise* Is 24$_{20}$ Jr 8$_4$ 25$_{27}$ Am 5$_2$ 8$_{14}$ Mc 7$_8$ Ps 20$_9$ 36$_{13}$ Pr 24$_{16}$ 1QM 18$_2$, עוד htpol. *be restored* Ps 20$_9$, פרח *flourish* Pr 11$_{28}$ (unless נפל II *wither*).

+ adverb or noun used adverbially, אָחוֹר *backwards* Gn 49$_{17}$, אֲחֹרַנִּית *backwards* 1 S 4$_{18}$, פִּתְאֹם *suddenly* Jr 51$_8$ Ec 9$_{12}$, מְאֹד *greatly* Ne 6$_{16}$, שָׁם *there* Jg 5$_{27}$ 2 S 2$_{23.23}$ Ezk 8$_1$ Ps 36$_{13}$ Pr 22$_{14}$ 1QM 19$_{11}$ 4QM^{b} 1$_9$, יַחַד *together* 2 S 21$_9$, יַחְדָּו *together* 2 S 2$_{16}$ Jr 46$_{12}$, לָכֵן *therefore* Jr 49$_{26}$, לָמָּה *why?* Gn 4$_6$ Jos 7$_{10}$ (לָמָּה זֶּה) Si 8$_1$ 37$_8$ (למה זה), אָנָה *where?* 2 K 6$_6$, אֵיךְ *how!* 2 S 1$_{19.25.27}$ Is 14$_{12}$ Ru 3$_{18}$, יוֹם *day* 1 S 19$_{24}$ 2 S 3$_{38}$, לַיְלָה *night* 1 S 19$_{24}$, מָחָר *tomorrow* Si 10$_{10}$, שֵׁנִית *a second time* Si 50$_{21}$, שֶׁבַע *seven (times)* Pr 24$_{16}$.

נָפוֹל תִּפּוֹל *you will surely fall* Est 6$_{13}$, וַיִּפֹּל מְלֹא־קוֹמָתוֹ אַרְצָה *and he fell with his full height to the ground* 1 S 28$_{20}$, בְּתֵת י׳ אֶת־יְרֵכֵךְ נֹפֶלֶת *when Y. makes your thigh fall away* Nm 5$_{21}$, אֲדֹנֵיהֶם נֹפֵל אַרְצָה מֵת *their lord was lying dead upon the ground* Jg 3$_{25}$, sim. Jg 4$_{22}$, נָפַל שָׁדוּד *he fell down destroyed* Jg 5$_{27}$, וַיִּפֹּל עָרֹם *and he lay naked* 1 S 19$_{24}$, יוֹם נָפְלוֹ *the day when he deserted* 1 S 29$_3$, בָּבֶל לִנְפֹּל חַלְלֵי יִשְׂרָאֵל perh. *Babylon was the cause of the slain ones of Israel falling* Jr 51$_{49}$, לא יפול להצילך *he does not bend down to deliver you* Si 12$_{15}$, וישנו לנפל *and they again prostrated themselves* Si 50$_{21}$, יחלו לנפול *they begin to fall* 1QM 16$_{11}$.

21. ptc. as noun, **a. fallen one,** <OBJ> קום hi. *raise* 1QM 14$_{11}$ (:: רָם *high one*), רום hi. *raise* 4QHod^{a} 7.1$_{17}$ (+ כשל ptc. *one who stumbles*). <CSTR> ידי נופלי[ם] *hands of the fallen* 4QBark^{c} 1.1$_1$.

b. deserter, <SUBJ> נפל *desert* 2 K 25$_{11}$||Jr 52$_{15}$ Jr 39$_9$. <OBJ> גלה hi. *exile* 2 K 25$_{11}$||Jr 52$_{15}$ 39$_9$.

Also 4QTobit^{e} 8$_2$ 4QCommGenC 3$_2$ 4QapPs^{b} 36$_1$ 4QparaKings 111$_6$ (נפל[תי]) 133$_1$ 4QpsEzek^{e} 55$_3$ 4Q418 8$_{11}$ 4QM^{a} 23$_3$ ([נופל]ים) 4QPrFêtes^{c} 12.1$_2$ 6QapSam Kgs 30$_2$ 6QHymn 4$_3$.

<SYN> §1-19 כשל *stumble,* שׁבר ni. *be broken,* גדע ni., pu. *be cut down,* הרס ni. *be torn down,* כתת ho. *be crushed,* כרע *bow down,* כפף pass. *be bowed down,* שׁכב *lie down,* מות *die,* כלה *come to an end,* בוא *come,* צבה *swell.*

<ANT> §1-19 קום *rise,* עוד htpol. *be restored,* פרח *flourish;* §20 רָם *high one.*

Pilel 1 + waw וְנִפְלַל—**fall,** by sword, <SUBJ> חָלָל *slain one* Ezk 28$_{23}$ (mss ni.). <SUBJ> בְּ of instrument, *by (means of),* + חֶרֶב *sword* Ezk 28$_{23}$ (mss ni.); בְּתוֹךְ *within,* + Sidon Ezk 28$_{23}$ (mss ni.).

Hi. 61.2.18 Pf. הִפִּיל (הִפִּל), הִפִּילָה, Q הפלתה (הִפַּלְתָּם, הִפַּלְנוּ, (הִפִּילֻהוּ) הִפִּילוּ, הִפַּלְתִּי, (הפלתנו Q; impf. יַפִּיל יַפִּילוּ, אַפִּיל, (תפילך Si, תַּפֵּל) תַּפִּיל 2ms, תַּפִּיל 3fs, (יַפִּלֵם), נַפִּילָה, (תַּפִּלוּ) תַּפִּילוּ, (יַפִּילוּן); + waw וְהִפִּילוֹ, וְהִפַּלְתִּי, (וְהִפַּלְתִּים, וְהִפַּלְתִּיו) וְהִפִּילוּ; וַיַּפֵּל (וַיַּפִּלֵם), 3fs וַתַּפֵּל, 2ms וַתַּפֵּל Q ,וַיַּפִּילוּ (וַיַּפִּלוּ); impv. הַפִּלֶהָ, הַפִּילוּ; ptc. מַפִּיל,

מַפִּילִים; inf. לְהַפִּיל (לַנְפֵּל, Q לפיל, הַפִּילְכֶם).

1a. cause to fall, cause to drop, of persons (Ps 140$_{11}$), things (Ezk 30$_{22}$ 39$_{3}$); **place** among nations (Ps 106$_{27}$ [or em.; see Subj.]).

b. cause to fall down, cause to descend, of birds (Ps 78$_{28}$), stars (Dn 8$_{10}$).

c. cause to fall down, cause to collapse, demolish,* of wall (2 S 20$_{15}$), **fell** tree (2 K 3$_{19.25}$ 6$_{5}$), **knock out** tooth (Ex 21$_{27}$).

d. let fall, let drop, of countenance, i.e. look in anger (Jr 3$_{12}$), light of countenance (Jb 29$_{24}$).

2. cause to fall, bring down, i.e. **a.** cause to die (1 S 18$_{25}$ 2 K 19$_{7}$||Is 37$_{7}$ Jr 19$_{7}$ Ezk 6$_{4}$ 32$_{12}$ Ps 106$_{26}$ Pr 7$_{26}$ Dn 11$_{12}$ 2 C 32$_{21}$ 1QM 3$_{8}$ 6$_{3.5}$ 8$_{11}$ 9$_{1.18}$ [[יפי[לו]]] 11$_{8}$ 16$_{8}$ 17$_{14}$ 4QM^{a} 1$_{13}$ [[להפי]ל]]). **b.** bring to ruin (Ps 37$_{14}$ 73$_{18}$ Pr 13$_{17}$ [if em.; see Subj.]). **c.** perh. bring down, i.e. slaughter (Ps 37$_{14}$). **d.** cause to depart (4QD^{a} 5.2$_{10}$; corrected to ho.).

3. cause to fall away, cause to waste away, of thigh (Nm 5$_{22}$; or em.; see Subj.).

4. let fall (to the ground), let fail, of words (1 S 3$_{19}$ Est 6$_{10}$ Si 47$_{22}$).

5. drop, abandon (Jg 2$_{19}$).

6. give birth to, cause to be born (Is 26$_{19}$).

7. cast stone (Nm 35$_{23}$), cedars into fire (Jr 22$_{7}$).

8a. cast (lot) (1 S 14$_{42}$ Is 34$_{17}$ Jon 1$_{7.7}$ Ps 22$_{19}$ Jb 6$_{27}$ Est 3$_{7}$ 9$_{24}$ Ne 10$_{35}$ 11$_{1}$ 1 C 24$_{31}$ 25$_{8}$ 26$_{13.14}$ 1QH 15$_{34}$ 1QS 4$_{26}$ [[לה]פיל]] 1QSb 4$_{26}$ 4QTanḥ 16$_{2}$ 4QAges^{b} 1.2$_{5}$ [הפ]י[ל] 4Q418 81$_{5}$). **b. throw in one's lot among,** i.e. join together with (Pr 1$_{14}$). **c. cause to fall (by lot), allocate** (Jos 13$_{6}$ Ezk 45$_{1}$ 47$_{22.22}$ [if em.; see Subj.] 48$_{29}$ Ps 78$_{55}$ 1QH 11$_{22}$ 1QM 13$_{9}$).

9. cause to fall upon, cause to come upon, of sleep (Gn 2$_{21}$ Pr 19$_{15}$), terror, dread (Ex 15$_{16}$ [if em.; see Subj.] Jr 15$_{8}$).

10. cause to fall before, present, of supplication (Jr 38$_{26}$ 42$_{9}$ Dn 9$_{18.20}$)

11. cause to lie down (Dt 25$_{2}$).

12a. make inferior, reduce, rank (4QTohA 1.1$_{1}$).

b. debase (oneself), disgrace (oneself), with object the same as subject of verb (Si 7$_{7}$).

13. appar. **fall,** but prob. error for qal (CD 11$_{13}$; see Qal).

<SUBJ> Y. Gn 2$_{21}$ Ex 15$_{16}$ (if em. תִּפֹּל *it fell* [qal] to וַתַּפֵּל *and you caused to fall*) 2 K 19$_{7}$||Is 37$_{7}$ Is 34$_{17}$ Jr 3$_{12}$ 15$_{8}$ 19$_{7}$ Ezk 6$_{4}$ 30$_{22}$ 32$_{12}$ 39$_{3}$ Ps 73$_{18}$ 78$_{28.55}$ 106$_{26.27}$ (or em. וּלְהָפִיץ *and to scatter,* i.e. פוץ hi.) 140$_{11}$ Si 47$_{22}$ 1QH 11$_{22}$ 15$_{34}$ 1QM 11$_{8}$ 13$_{9}$ 1QS 4$_{26}$ ([לה]פיל]) 4Q418 81$_{5}$.

Israel(ites) 1 S 14$_{42}$ 2 K 3$_{19.25}$ Ezk 45$_{1}$ 47$_{22}$ 48$_{29}$ Dn 9$_{18}$, עַם *people* 2 S 20$_{15}$ Ne 10$_{35}$, עֵדָה *congregation* of evildoers Ps 22$_{19}$, שְׁאָר *remainder* Ne 11$_{1}$, דֶּגֶל *battalion* 1QM 6$_{3}$, Daniel Dn 9$_{20}$, Haman Est 6$_{10}$ 9$_{24}$, Jeremiah Jr 38$_{26}$ 42$_{9}$, Joshua Jos 13$_{6}$ 23$_{4}$ 1 S 3$_{19}$, Saul 1 S 18$_{25}$, אִישׁ *man* Ex 21$_{27}$ 1QM 17$_{14}$ 4QD^{a} 5.2$_{10}$ ([איש]; hi. corrected to ho.) 4QM^{a} 1$_{13}$ ([להפי]ל]), i.e. each one Jon 1$_{7.7}$ 4QAges^{b} 1.2$_{5}$ (הפ]י[ל), אִשָּׁה *woman* Pr 7$_{26}$, בֵּן *son* Pr 1$_{14}$ 1 C 24$_{31}$ 25$_{8}$ Si 7$_{7}$, of Israel Jg 2$_{19}$, יָצִיא *one who comes out,* i.e. son 2 C 32$_{21}$, רֵעַ *friend* of Job Jb 6$_{27}$, מֶלֶךְ *king* Dn 11$_{12}$, שֹׁפֵט *judge* Dt 25$_{2}$, כֹּהֵן *priest* Ne 10$_{35}$, לֵוִי *Levite* Ne 10$_{35}$, ירא ptc. *one who fears* Y. 1QSb 4$_{26}$, שֹׁעֵר *gatekeeper* 1 C 26$_{13.14}$, מַלְאָךְ *messenger* Pr 13$_{17}$ (if em. יִפֹּל *he falls* [qal] to יַפֵּל), מַלָּח *mariner* Jon 1$_{7.7}$, נכה hi. ptc. *one who strikes* Nm 35$_{23}$, מַשְׁחִית *destroyer* Jr 22$_{7}$, רָשָׁע *wicked one* Ps 37$_{14}$.

יָד *hand* 1QM 3$_{8}$ 9$_{1}$ 16$_{8}$, קֶרֶן *horn* Dn 8$_{10}$, זִק *flaming arrow* 1QM 6$_{3}$, זֶרֶק *javelin* 1QM 8$_{11}$, אֶרֶץ *earth* Is 26$_{19}$, מַיִם *water* Nm 5$_{22}$ (or em. לַנְפֵּל *to cause to fall away* to לִנְפֹּל *to fall away,* i.e. qal), גּוֹרָל *lot* Is 34$_{17}$, עַצְלָה *laziness* Pr 19$_{15}$, אֶחָד *one* 2 K 6$_{5}$; subj. not specified, Ezk 47$_{22}$ (if em. יִפְּלוּ *they shall receive by lot* [qal] to יַפִּילוּ) Jb 29$_{24}$ Est 3$_{7}$.

<OBJ> Israel 1QM 13$_{9}$, Jerusalem Jr 19$_{7}$, Judah Jr 19$_{7}$, גּוֹי *nation* Jos 23$_{4}$ Ps 78$_{55}$ 1QM 11$_{8}$, הָמוֹן *multitude* Ezk 32$_{12}$, גְּדוּד *troop* 1QM 11$_{8}$, David 1 S 18$_{25}$, אָב *father* Ps 106$_{26}$, בֵּן *son* Si 7$_{7}$, מֶלֶךְ *king* 2 K 19$_{7}$||Is 37$_{7}$ 2 C 32$_{21}$, עָנִי *poor one* Ps 37$_{14}$, אֶבְיוֹן *needy one* Ps 37$_{14}$, רָשָׁע *wicked one* Dt 25$_{2}$ Ps 73$_{18}$, הלל ptc. *one who acts foolishly* Ps 73$_{18}$, סבב hi. ptc. *one who surrounds* Ps 140$_{11}$, גֵּר *sojourner* Ezk 47$_{22}$ (if em.; see Subj.), חָלָל *slain one* Ezk 6$_{4}$ Pr 7$_{26}$ 1QM 3$_{8}$ 6$_{3.5}$ 8$_{11}$, רְפָאִים *shades* Is 26$_{19}$, זֶרַע *seed,* i.e. offspring Ps 106$_{27}$, שֵׁן *tooth* Ex 21$_{27}$, יָרֵךְ *thigh* Nm 5$_{22}$ (or em.; see Subj.), פָּנִים *face,* i.e. countenance Jr 3$_{12}$, שֵׁם *name* 4QD^{a} 5.2$_{10}$ (corrected to ho.), עוֹף

birds Ps 78$_{28}$, עֵץ *tree* 2 K 3$_{19.25}$, אֶרֶז *cedar* Jr 22$_{7}$, קוֹרָה *beam* 2 K 6$_{5}$, חוֹמָה *wall* 2 S 20$_{15}$, אֶבֶן *stone* Nm 35$_{23}$, חֶרֶב *sword* Ezk 30$_{22}$, חֵץ *arrow* Ezk 39$_{3}$, כְּלִי *object* Nm 35$_{23}$.

גּוֹרָל *lot* Jon 1$_{7.7}$ Ps 22$_{19}$ Pr 1$_{14}$ Ne 10$_{35}$ 11$_{1}$ 1 C 24$_{31}$ 25$_{8}$ 26$_{13.14}$ 1QH 11$_{22}$ 15$_{34}$ 1QS 4$_{26}$ (לה[פיל]) 1QSb 4$_{26}$ 4QTanḥ 16$_{2}$ 4QAges^b 1.2$_{5}$ (הפ[י]ל) 4Q418 81$_{5}$, פּוּר *Pur*, i.e. lot Est 3$_{7}$ 9$_{24}$, נַחֲלָה *inheritance* Ps 78$_{55}$, אֶרֶץ *land* Jos 13$_{6}$ Ezk 45$_{1}$ 47$_{22}$ 48$_{29}$, דָּבָר *thing* Est 6$_{10}$, תְּחִנָּה *supplication* Jr 38$_{26}$ 42$_{9}$ Dn 9$_{20}$, תַּחֲנוּן *supplication* Dn 9$_{18}$, אוֹר *light* of countenance Jb 29$_{24}$, תַּרְדֵּמָה *deep sleep* Gn 2$_{21}$, אֵימָה *terror* Ex 15$_{16}$ (if em.; see Subj.), בֶּהָלָה *dismay* Jr 15$_{8}$, פַּחַד *dread* Ex 15$_{16}$ (if em.; see Subj.), עִיר *excitement*, i.e. terror Jr 15$_{8}$, תֹּכֶן *rank* 4QTohA 1.1$_{1}$, רִבּוֹא *ten thousand* Dn 11$_{12}$.

<PREP> לְ of direction, benefit, *to, for*, + Israel(ites) Jos 13$_{6}$ 23$_{4}$ Ezk 47$_{22}$, שֵׁבֶט *tribe* Ezk 48$_{29}$, זָקֵן *elder* Jos 23$_{4}$, שֹׁפֵט *judge* Jos 23$_{4}$, שֹׁטֵר *officer* Jos 23$_{4}$, גֵּר *sojourner* Ezk 47$_{22}$, רֹאשׁ *head*, i.e. chief Jos 23$_{4}$, חַי *living thing* 1QS 4$_{26}$ (לה[פיל]), wild beasts Is 34$_{17}$; of instrument, *by (means of)*, + מַשּׁוּאוֹת *deceptions* Ps 73$_{18}$; *according to*, + אֱמֶת *truth* 1QM 13$_{9}$.

בְּ of place, *in(to), among*, + קְהִלָּה *assembly* Si 7$_{7}$, עֵדָה *assembly* 1QH 15$_{34}$, גּוֹי *nation* Ps 106$_{27}$, אֶרֶץ *land* 2 K 19$_{7}$||Is 37$_{7}$, מִדְבָּר *steppe* Ps 106$_{26}$, מַהֲמֹרָה *pit* Ps 140$_{11}$, רַע *evil* Pr 13$_{17}$ (if em.; see Subj.), גּוֹרָל *lot* 1QM 13$_{9}$.

בְּ of instrument, agent, *by (means of)*, + יָד *hand* 1 S 18$_{25}$ Jr 19$_{7}$ 1QM 11$_{8}$, חֶרֶב *sword* 2 K 19$_{7}$||Is 37$_{7}$ Jr 19$_{7}$ Ezk 32$_{12}$ 2 C 32$_{21}$, חֶבֶל *measuring line* Ps 78$_{55}$, אַף *anger* 1QM 6$_{3}$, מִשְׁפָּט *judgment* 1QM 6$_{3}$.

בְּ *as*, + נַחֲלָה *inheritance* Jos 13$_{6}$ 23$_{4}$ Ezk 45$_{1}$ 47$_{22}$ 48$_{29}$(mss); *at, against*, + Israel Jr 3$_{12}$, מְשׁוּבָה *apostate one* Jr 3$_{12}$; introducing object, + חָלָל *slain one* 1QM 9$_{1.18}$ ([יפי]ל[ו] בח[ללים]) 16$_{8}$ 17$_{14}$ 4QM^a 1$_{13}$ 18$_{4}$ (both ל[הפי]ל), נַחֲלָה *inheritance* Ezk 47$_{22}$ (if em.; see Subj.).

כְּ ... כְּ *as ... as*, i.e. both alike, + קָטֹן ... גָּדוֹל *small ... great* 1 C 26$_{13}$.

מִן of direction, *from*, + יָד *hand* Ezk 30$_{22}$ 39$_{3}$, אֱמֶת *truth* 4QD^a 5.2$_{10}$ (הפיל שמו מן האמת *he causes his name to fall from the truth* corrected to הופל שמו מן האמות *his name is cast down from the nations*); of time, *from*, מִיּוֹם לְיוֹם וּמֵחֹדֶשׁ לְחֹדֶשׁ *from day to day and from month to month* Est 3$_{7}$.

מִן partitive, 1. *(some) of, (any) of*, as obj. of נפל hi., + צָבָא *host* Dn 8$_{10}$, כּוֹכָב *star* Dn 8$_{10}$, מַעֲלָל *deed* Jg 2$_{19}$, דֶּרֶךְ *way* Jg 2$_{19}$, דָּבָר *word* 1 S 3$_{19}$ Si 47$_{22}$; 2. *from among*, + כֹּל *everything* Est 6$_{10}$.

מִן appar. *as*, + נַחֲלָה *inheritance* Ezk 48$_{29}$ (mss בְּ *as*).

עַל *upon*, + Jerusalem Jr 15$_{8}$, אָדָם *human being* Gn 2$_{21}$, יָתוֹם *orphan* Jb 6$_{27}$, יֹשֵׁב *inhabitant* Ex 15$_{16}$ (if em.; see Subj.), נֶפֶשׁ *soul*, i.e. person Nm 35$_{23}$; *(in)to*, + אֵשׁ *fire* Jr 22$_{7}$; *for*, + לְבוּשׁ *garment* Ps 22$_{19}$, קָרְבָּן *offering* Ne 10$_{35}$.

עִם *with*, + מַלְאָךְ *angel* 1QSb 4$_{26}$.

אֵת *with*, + Israelites Ezk 47$_{22}$ (if em.; see Subj.).

לְפִי *according to*, + רוּחַ *spirit* 1QS 4$_{26}$ (לה[פיל]).

לְעֻמַּת *corresponding to*, + אָח *brother* 1 C 24$_{31}$, בֵּן *son* 1 C 24$_{31}$; וַיַּפִּילוּ גּוֹרָלוֹת ... לְעֻמַּת כַּקָּטֹן כַּגָּדוֹל מֵבִין עִם־תַּלְמִיד *and they cast lots ... according to (this principle), as the small, so the great, teacher together with scholar* 1 C 25$_{8}$.

בְּתוֹךְ *among*, + חַטָּא *sinner* Pr 1$_{14}$.

בְּקֶרֶב *within*, + מַחֲנֶה *camp* Ps 78$_{28}$.

סָבִיב לְ *around*, + מִשְׁכָּן *dwelling* Ps 78$_{28}$.

בֵּין *between*, + Jonathan 1 S 14$_{42}$, Saul 1 S 14$_{42}$, בֵּן *son* 1 S 14$_{42}$.

לִפְנֵי *before*, + Y. Jr 42$_{9}$ Dn 9$_{18.20}$, גִּלּוּל *idol* Ezk 6$_{4}$, Ahimelech 1 C 24$_{31}$, David 1 C 24$_{31}$, Haman Est 3$_{7}$, Zadok 1 C 24$_{31}$, מֶלֶךְ *king* Jr 38$_{26}$, אֹיֵב *enemy* Jr 19$_{7}$, רֹאשׁ *head*, i.e. chief 1 C 24$_{31}$.

ה- of direction, *to*, + אֶרֶץ *ground* 1 S 3$_{19}$ Dn 8$_{10}$ Si 47$_{22}$.

<COLL> נפל hi. || נכה hi. *strike* 2 K 3$_{19}$ (+) Ezk 39$_{3}$, רשׁע hi. *condemn as guilty* Si 7$_{7}$, שׂים *place* 1QH 15$_{34}$; + זרה pi. *scatter* Ps 106$_{27}$, טבח *slay* Ps 37$_{14}$, כנע hi. *subdue* 1QM 6$_{3}$; + adverb, פִּתְאֹם *suddenly* Jr 15$_{8}$.

גּוֹרָלוֹת הִפַּלְנוּ עַל־קָרְבַּן ... לְהָבִיא *we have cast lots for the offering ... to bring (it)* Ne 10$_{35}$, sim. Ne 11$_{1}$, וַיַּפִּילוּ גּוֹרָלוֹת מִשְׁמֶרֶת *and they cast lots (for their) service* 1 C 25$_{8}$, יחלו להפיל *they shall begin to bring down* 1QM 17$_{14}$, vars. 1QM 16$_{8}$ 4QTohA 1.1$_{1}$.

Also 4Q392 2$_{3}$.

<SYN> נכה hi. *strike*, רשׁע hi. *condemn as guilty*,

שִׂים *place*.

Ho. $_{0.0.1}$ Pf. הופל—**be caused to fall, be cast down,** הופל שמו מן האמות *his name is cast down from the nations* 4QD^{a} 5.2$_{10}$ (corrected from הפיל שמו מן האמת *he causes his name to fall from the truth*).

Htp. $_{5.0.2}$ Pf. הִתְנַפַּלְתִּי; + waw וָאֶתְנַפַּל; ptc. מִתְנַפֵּל; inf. הִתְנַפֵּל—**1. throw oneself upon,** <SUBJ> Joseph Gn 43$_{18}$ (|| גלל htpo. *roll oneself upon*). <PREP> עַל *against*, + אִישׁ *man* Gn 43$_{18}$.

2. prostrate oneself, lie prostrate, <SUBJ> Ezra Ezr 10$_{1}$, Moses Dt 9$_{18.25.25}$ 2QapMoses 1$_{4}$ ([ויתנפ]ל), worshipper 1QH 8$_{15}$ 12$_{4}$ (+ חנן htp. *make supplication*). <PREP> כְּ *as at*, + רִאשׁוֹן fem. *first (time)* Dt 9$_{18}$; לִפְנֵי *before* 2QapMoses 1$_{4}$ ([ויתנפל]ל לפני]), + Y. Dt 9$_{18.25}$, בַּיִת *house* of Y. Ezr 10$_{1}$.

<COLL> וָאֶתְנַפַּל ... אַרְבָּעִים יוֹם וְאַרְבָּעִים לַיְלָה *and I lay prostrate ... forty days and forty nights* Dt 9$_{18}$, var. Dt 9$_{25}$.

<SYN> §1 גלל htpo. *roll oneself upon*.*

⇒ נְפִלִים *giants*, נֵפֶל *miscarriage*, מַפָּל *refuse*, מַפָּלָה *ruin*, מַפֶּלֶת *downfall*.

נפל* II $_{1}$ vb. **wither** (unless נפל I *fall*)—**Qal** $_{1}$ Impf. יִפֹּל—**wither,** <SUBJ> בטח ptc. *one who trusts* in riches Pr 11$_{28}$ (פרח *flourish*).

<ANT> פרח *flourish* Pr 11$_{28}$.

⇒ cf. נבל *wither*.

נֹפֵל *fallen one*, see נפל I *fall*.

נֵ֫פֶל $_{3}$ n.m. **miscarriage**—נֵפֶל; cstr. נֵ֫פֶל—<SUBJ> חזה *see* Ps 58$_{9}$, טמן pass. *be concealed* Jb 3$_{16}$ (+ עוֹלֵל *child*), תעב ni. *be abhorred* Is 14$_{19}$ (if em.; see Prep.). <NOM CL> טוֹב מִמֶּנּוּ הַנָּפֶל *a miscarriage is better off than he* Ec 6$_{3}$. <CSTR> נֵפֶל אֵשֶׁת appar. *miscarriage of a woman* Ps 58$_{9}$ (or em. אֵשֶׁת to אִשָּׁה, or נֵפֶל אֵשֶׁת בַּל־חָזוּ שָׁמֶשׁ *[as] the miscarriage of a woman, they have not seen [the] sun* to וְאֵשֶׁת בַּל־חָזָה שָׁמֶשׁ *and [as] a mole [that] has not seen [the] sun*). <PREP> כְּ *as* Ps 58$_{9}$ (if ins. כְּ), + היה *be* Jb 3$_{16}$, שׁלך ho. *be cast out* Is 14$_{19}$ (if em. כְּנֵצֶר *as a branch*); כְּמוֹ *as* Ps 58$_{9}$ (unless em. נֵפֶל to כְּנֵפֶל).*

⇒ נפל *fall*.

נִפְלָאוֹת, see פלא *be wonderful*, Ni.

נְפִלִים $_{3.0.1}$ n.m.pl. **giants**—נְפִלִים; cstr. Q נפילי—**giants, Nephilim,** perh. **fallen ones,** i.e. **dead,*** antediluvians (Gn 6$_{4}$), early inhabitants of Canaan (Nm 13$_{33.33}$), <SUBJ> היה *be* Gn 6$_{4}$ (+ גִּבֹּרִים *mighty ones*, אַנְשֵׁי הַשֵּׁם *men of renown*), גִּבּוֹר *mighty one* Ezk 32$_{27}$ (if em. נֹפְלִים *fallen*). <NOM CL> [אלה הנ]פ[יל]ים *these are the giants* 11QJub 5$_{1}$. <OBJ> ראה *see* Nm 13$_{33}$. <APP> בֵּן *son* of Anak Nm 13$_{33}$. <PREP> מִן *(originating) from* Nm 13$_{33}$; אֵת *with*, + שׁכב *lie down* Ezk 32$_{27}$ (if em.; see Subj.).

Also 1Q36 16$_{3}$.*

⇒ נפל *fall*.

נפף* $_{1.1}$ vb. **sprinkle—Qal,** with spices, <SUBJ> woman Pr 7$_{17}$ (if em. נַפְתִּי appar. *I have waved [?]* to נַפֹּתִי *I have sprinkled*). <OBJ> 1. thing sprinkled, מִשְׁכָּב *bed* Pr 7$_{17}$ (if em.; see Subj.). 2. thing sprinkled with, מֹר *myrrh* Pr 7$_{17}$ (if em.; see Subj.), אֲהָלִים *aloes* Pr 7$_{17}$ (if em.; see Subj.), קִנָּמוֹן *cinnamon* Pr 7$_{17}$ (if em.; see Subj.).

Hi. $_{1.1}$ **sprinkle,** <OBJ> thing sprinkled with, גֶּשֶׁם *rain* Ps 68$_{10}$ (unless נוף IV *deliver in large measure*), שֶׁלֶג *snow* Si 43$_{17(B)}$.

⇒ cf. נוף II *sprinkle*, נוב *be full of sap*.

נפץ I $_{18}$ vb. **shatter—Qal** $_{2}$ Ptc. pass. נָפוּץ; inf. abs. נָפוֹץ—**1. shatter, smash,** <SUBJ> Gideon Jg 7$_{19}$, אִישׁ *man* Jg 7$_{19}$; subj. not specified, Dn 12$_{7}$ (if em. נַפֵּץ יַד *shattering the hand*, i.e. power, *of* to יַד נֹפֵץ *the hand of the one who shatters*). <OBJ> עַם *people* Dn 12$_{7}$ (if em.; see Subj.), כַּד *jar* Jg 7$_{19}$.

2. pass. **be shattered,** <SUBJ> עֶצֶב *vessel* Jr 22$_{28}$ (+ בזה ni. *be despised*).

Pi. $_{15}$ Impf. 2ms תְּנַפְּצֵם, יְנַפֵּצוּ; + waw וְנִפֵּץ, וְנִפַּצְתִּי (וְנִפַּצְתִּים); inf. נַפֵּץ—**break up, shatter, smash to pieces,** <SUBJ> Y. Jr 13$_{14}$ 51$_{20+8t}$, Hiram 1 K 5$_{23}$, מֶלֶךְ *king* Ps 2$_{9}$, צעה ptc. *one who tilts* Jr 48$_{12}$, -שֶׁ *one who* Ps 137$_{9}$; subj. not specified, Dn 12$_{7}$ (or em. נֹפֵץ, i.e. qal).

<OBJ> גּוֹי *nation* Jr 51$_{20}$ Ps 2$_{9}$, אִישׁ *man* Jr 51$_{22}$, i.e. each one Jr 13$_{14}$, אִשָּׁה *woman* Jr 51$_{22}$, אָב *father* Jr 13$_{14}$,

בֵּן *son* Jr 13₁₄, מֶלֶךְ *king* Jr 13₁₄, פֶּחָה *governor* Jr 51₂₃, סָגָן *official* Jr 51₂₃, כֹּהֵן *priest* Jr 13₁₄, נָבִיא *prophet* Jr 13₁₄, רֹעֶה *shepherd* Jr 51₂₃, אִכָּר *farmer* Jr 51₂₃, זָקֵן *elderly one* Jr 51₂₂, נַעַר *lad* Jr 51₂₂, בָּחוּר *young man* Jr 51₂₂, בְּתוּלָה *young woman* Jr 51₂₂, עוֹלֵל *child* Ps 137₉, יֹשֵׁב *inhabitant* Jr 13₁₄, רֹכֵב *rider* Jr 51₂₁.₂₁, יָד *hand*, i.e. power Dn 12₇ (or em.; see Subj.), סוּס *horse* Jr 51₂₁, עֵדֶר *flock* Jr 51₂₃, צֶמֶד *pair (of oxen)* Jr 51₂₃, רֶכֶב *chariot* Jr 51₂₁, דֹּבְרָה *raft* 1 K 5₂₃, נֵבֶל *jar* Jr 48₁₂.

<PREP> בְּ of agent, instrument, *by (means of), with* Jr 51₂₀₊₈ₜ.

כְּ *as*, + כְּלִי *vessel* Ps 2₉.

אֶל *against*, + סֶלַע *rock* Ps 137₉.

<COLL> נפץ pi. ‖ שׁחת hi. *destroy* Jr 51₂₀, רעע *break* Ps 2₉; + adverb, שָׁם *there* 1 K 5₂₃.

<SYN> שׁחת hi. *destroy*, רעע *break*.

Pu. ₁ Ptc. מְנֻפָּצוֹת—**be smashed to pieces,** <SUBJ> אֶבֶן chalk *stone* Is 27₉.*

⇒ נֶפֶץ *cloudburst*, מַפָּץ *shattering*, מַפֵּץ *club*.

נפץ II ₄.₀.₁ vb. **scatter—Qal** ₄.₀.₁ Pf. נָפַץ, נָפְצָה, נָפְצוּ; ptc. pass. נְפֻצוֹת; inf. abs. Q נפוץ—**1. scatter, disperse,** <SUBJ> עַם *people* 1 S 13₁₁, גּוֹי *nation* Is 33₃ (‖ נדד *flee*), אֶרֶץ *earth* Gn 9₁₉. <PREP> בְּ of place, *on*, + עַיִן *eye* 4QTobit[e] 5₂ ([בעיניו]); מִן *from*, + אֵלֶּה *these* Gn 9₁₉; of cause, *on account of*, + רוֹמְמוּת *uplifting* Is 33₃; מֵעַל *from*, + Saul 1 S 13₁₁.

2. pass. ptc. as noun, **dispersed one,** <OBJ> קבץ pi. *gather* Is 11₁₂ (‖ נדח ni. ptc. *banished one*). <CSTR> נְפֻצוֹת יְהוּדָה *dispersed ones of Judah* Is 11₁₂.

<SYN> §1 נדד *flee*; §2 נדח ni. ptc. *banished one*.*

⇒ cf. פוץ *be scattered*.

נֶ֫פֶץ ₁.₀.₁ n.[m.] **cloudburst,** or **pattering of rain,** <SUBJ> שׁחת hi. *destroy* 1QH 10₂₇ (‖ זֶרֶם *downpour*, + הָמוֹן *roar* of mighty waters). <PREP> בְּ of instrument, *by (means of), through*, + ראה hi. *show* majesty Is 30₃₀ (‖ זֶרֶם *downpour*, + אֶבֶן hail *stone*, זַעַף *raging*, לַהַב *flame* of fire); כְּ *as* 1QH 10₂₇. <COLL> נֶפֶץ וָזֶרֶם *cloudburst and downpour* Is 30₃₀ 1QH 10₂₇ 4QpIsa[c] 25₃ ([נפץ ו]זרם).

<SYN> זֶרֶם *downpour*.*

⇒ נפץ I *shatter*.

נפשׁ ₃ vb. **breathe—Ni.** ₃ Impf. יִנָּפֵשׁ; + waw וַיִּנָּפֵשׁ—**be refreshed, refresh oneself,** <SUBJ> Y. Ex 31₁₇, עַם *people* 2 S 16₁₄, בֵּן *son* of female slave Ex 23₁₂, מֶלֶךְ *king* 2 S 16₁₄, גֵּר *sojourner* Ex 23₁₂. <COLL> נפשׁ ‖ שׁבת *rest* Ex 31₁₇, נוח *rest* Ex 23₁₂; + adverb, שָׁם *there* 2 S 16₁₄.

<SYN> שׁבת *rest*, נוח *rest*.

⇒ נֶפֶשׁ *soul*, נָפִישׁ *Naphish*.

נֶ֫פֶשׁ I ₇₅₄.₆₄.₁₉₇.₂ n.f. **soul**—נֶפֶשׁ; cstr. נֶפֶשׁ; sf. נַפְשִׁי, נַפְשְׁךָ, נַפְשָׁהּ, (נפשה Q) נַפְשׁוֹ, נַפְשֵׁךְ, (נפשכה Q), נפשיך Si, נַפְשֵׁךְ), נַפְשֵׁנוּ, נַפְשְׁכֶם, (נבשכם I, נפשכמה Q) נַפְשָׁם (נפשמה Q); pl. נְפָשׁוֹת (נְפָשֹׁת), נְפָשִׁים; cstr. נַפְשׁוֹת (נַפְשֹׁת); sf. נַפְשֹׁתֵינוּ (נַפְשׁוֹתֵינוּ), נַפְשֹׁתֵיכֶם (נַפְשׁוֹתֵיכֶם, נפשותיכמה Q), נַפְשֹׁתָם (נַפְשׁוֹתָם, נפשותמה Q).

1. palate, throat, gullet, p. 724b

2. neck, p. 725a

3. appetite, hunger, desire, wish, p. 725a

4. soul, heart, mind, p. 725b

5. breath, last breath, soul, p. 728a

6. life, lives; soul; eternal life, p. 728b

7. being, creature(s), p. 730a

8a. person, individual, p. 730b

8b. collectively, **persons, people,** p. 731a

8c. perh. **deceased person, (dead) body,** p. 731b

8d. perh. specif. **slave,** p. 732a

9a. נֶפֶשׁ with pronominal suffix, as personal pronoun, p. 732a

9b. as reflexive pronoun, **oneself,** p. 732b

9c. as possessive pronoun, p. 733b

10. sustenance, p. 733b

11. perfume, p. 733b

12. sepulchre, (funerary) monument, p. 733b

1. palate, throat,* gullet, <SUBJ> היה *be* Jr 31₁₂, קוץ *loathe* Nm 21₅, עשׁשׁ *be worn out* Ps 31₁₀ (unless §4), שׁקק *rush about*, i.e. long for drink Is 29₈ Ps 107₉ (unless §4), נגע *touch* Jb 6₇ (unless §3 or §9a), ענג htp. *delight oneself* Is 55₂ (unless §4), שׂבע *be satisfied* Ps 63₆ (unless §3) 123₄ (unless §4), מלא ni. *have one's fill*

Ec 6$_7$ (unless §3), תעב pi. *abhor* Ps 107$_{18}$ (unless §4), מוג htpol. *melt away* Ps 107$_{26}$ (unless §4), מלט ni. *escape* Ps 124$_7$ (unless §9a).

<NOM CL> נַפְשֵׁנוּ יְבֵשָׁה *our throat is dry* Nm 11$_6$, רֵיקָה נַפְשׁוֹ *his throat is empty* Is 29$_8$, הֶאָח נַפְשֵׁנוּ *aha, (this is) our throat!* Ps 35$_{25}$ (unless §3), נַפְשִׁי כְּאֶרֶץ־עֲיֵפָה לְךָ *my throat is like a weary,* i.e. thirsty, *land for you* Ps 143$_6$ (unless §4).

<OBJ> רחב hi. *make wide* Is 5$_{14}$ Hb 2$_5$, ריק hi. *keep empty* Is 32$_6$, שׂבע hi. *satisfy* Is 58$_{11}$ (unless §3) Ps 107$_9$ (unless §4), מלא pi. *fill* Jr 31$_{25}$ Ps 107$_9$, רוה hi. *make drink* Jr 31$_{25}$, דמם po. *quieten* Ps 131$_2$ (unless §4).

<CSTR> נֶפֶשׁ רָעֵב *throat of the hungry* Is 32$_6$, צָרַי *of my adversaries* perh. Ps 27$_{12}$ (unless §3); דַּאֲבוֹן נֶפֶשׁ *dryness of throat* Dt 28$_{65}$ (unless *languishing of soul,* i.e. §4).

<ADJ> עָיֵף *weary* Jr 31$_{25}$, i.e. thirsty Pr 25$_{25}$, רָעֵב *hungry* Ps 107$_9$ (unless §4).

<PREP> לְ of benefit, *to, for* Pr 16$_{24}$; בְּ of direction, *to,* + נתן *give* perh. Ps 27$_{12}$ (unless §3), שׁלח *send* Ps 106$_{15}$ (unless §9a or §10); כְּ *like,* + גַּן רָוֶה *watered garden* Jr 31$_{12}$; עַל *upon* Pr 25$_{25}$; *over,* + עבר *pass* Ps 124$_{4.5}$ (unless both §2); עַד *as far as,* + בוא *come* Ps 69$_2$ (unless §2), אפף *surround* Jon 2$_6$ (unless §2).

<COLL> פֶּה || נֶפֶשׁ *mouth* Is 5$_{14}$, עַיִן *eye* Dt 28$_{65}$ (unless §4), עֶצֶם *bone* Pr 16$_{24}$.

2. neck,* <SUBJ> בוא *come* Ps 105$_{18}$, דבק *cling* Ps 119$_{25}$ (unless §4), מלט ni. *escape* Ps 124$_7$ (unless §1 or §9a). <OBJ> טרף *tear* Ps 7$_3$ (unless §9a), נצל hi. *deliver* Pr 22$_{21}$ (unless §6), בחר *choose* Jb 7$_{15}$ (unless §9a), כפף *be bowed down* Ps 57$_7$ (unless §4). <CSTR> בָּתֵּי הַנֶּפֶשׁ perh. *houses of the neck,* i.e. collars* Is 3$_{20}$ (unless *of breath,* i.e. perfume containers [§5] or נֶפֶשׁ III *perfume*). <PREP> מִן *from,* + כלה pi. *destroy* Is 10$_{18}$ (מִנֶּפֶשׁ וְעַד־בָּשָׂר *from the neck to the male organ;* unless §5); עַל *over,* + עבר *pass* Ps 124$_{4.5}$ (unless both §1); עַד *as far as,* + בוא *come* Ps 69$_2$ (unless §1), נגע *reach* Jr 4$_{10}$, אפף *surround* Jon 2$_6$ (unless §1). <COLL> רֶגֶל + נֶפֶשׁ *foot* Ps 105$_{18}$.

3. appetite,* hunger, desire, wish, distinction from §§1, 4, not alw. clear, <SUBJ> הלך *go,* i.e. wander Ec 6$_9$ (or em. הֲלֹךְ to מֵהֲלֹךְ *wandering of*), מלא ni. *have one's fill* Ec 6$_7$ (unless §1), htp. Ex 15$_9$, שׂבע *be satisfied* Jr 50$_{19}$ Ps 63$_6$ (unless §1), רעה *feed upon* Pr 15$_{14}$ (if em.; see Cstr.), נגע *touch* Jb 6$_7$ (unless §1 or §9a), בחר *choose* Si 37$_{28}$, מאן pi. *refuse* Jb 6$_7$, זהם pi. *abhor* Jb 6$_7$ (if em. הֵמָּה כִּדְוֵי *they are as the sickness of* to זָהֲמָה כְדֵי my soul *abhors as often as* I eat) 33$_{20}$, עמל *toil* Pr 16$_{26}$, שׁחת hi. *destroy* Si 6$_4$ 19$_3$ (ת[שחית]).

<NOM CL> הֶאָח נַפְשֵׁנוּ *aha, (this is) our wish!* Ps 35$_{25}$ (unless §1), נֶפֶשׁ בֹּגְדִים חָמָס *the desire of the treacherous is (for) violence* Pr 13$_2$.

<OBJ> שׂבע pi. *satisfy* Ezk 7$_{19}$ Pr 6$_{30}$, hi. Is 58$_{11}$ (unless §1 or §2), רעב hi. *allow to hunger* Pr 10$_3$, נסה pi. *prove* Si 37$_{27}$, חרה *kindle* Si 51$_{19(11QPs^a)}$, טרד *continually arouse* Si 51$_{20(11QPs^a)}$, חסר pi. *cause to lack* Ec 4$_8$ (unless §9b).

<CSTR> נֶפֶשׁ צַדִּיק *appetite/desire of the righteous* Pr 10$_3$, עָמֵל *of a labourer* Pr 16$_{26}$, כְּסִילִים *of fools* Pr 15$_{14}$ (if em. פִּי *mouth of* [Qr; Kt פני *face of*]), בֹּגְדִים *of the treacherous* Pr 13$_2$, אֹיְבָיו *of his enemies* Ps 41$_3$, צָרַי *of my adversaries* Ps 27$_{12}$, שֹׂנְאוֹתַיִךְ *of those who hate you* Ezk 16$_{27}$, בְּהֶמְתּוֹ *of his beast* Pr 12$_{10}$ (unless §6).

בַּעַל נֶפֶשׁ *possessor of an appetite* Pr 23$_2$, רְחַב־ *one wide of* Pr 28$_{25}$, עז נפש *strong one of appetite,* i.e. with a strong appetite Si 40$_{30(M)}$ (B עוז *strength of;* Bmg עז נפשות *strong of appetites*), עַזֵּי־נֶפֶשׁ *strong ones of appetite* Is 56$_{11}$, יד נפש *hand,* i.e. power, *of desire* Si 6$_2$, שְׂבַע נַפְשׁוֹ *satisfaction of his appetite* Pr 13$_{25}$, הֲלָךְ־נֶפֶשׁ *wandering of desire* Ec 6$_9$ (if em.; see Subj.), רחוב נפש *breadth of desire* 1QS 4$_9$, כל נפש *every appetite* Si 37$_{28}$.

<ADJ> עַז *strong* Si 6$_4$ 19$_3$.

<PREP> לְ of benefit, *to, for* Ho 9$_5$ Si 37$_{27}$, שׁאל *ask for* food Ps 78$_{18}$ (unless §10), ערב *be sweet* Pr 13$_{19}$, חסר *lack* Ec 6$_2$ (unless §4); *according to,* + שׁלח pi. *let go* Dt 21$_{14}$ Jr 34$_{16}$; בְּ of direction, *to,* + נתן *give* Ezk 16$_{27}$ Ps 27$_{12}$ Si 37$_{27}$; *according to,* + אסר *bind* Ps 105$_{22}$, שׁער *reckon* Pr 23$_7$ (unless §4); כְּ *according to,* + אכל *eat* Dt 23$_{25}$.

<COLL> הַוָּה || נֶפֶשׁ *desire* Pr 10$_3$, מֵעֶה *stomach* Ezk 7$_{19}$, חַיָּה *life* Jb 33$_{20}$; + פֶּה *mouth* Pr 16$_{26}$.

4. soul, heart, mind, as seat of desire, will, feelings and emotions, also of intellect (e.g. Jos 23$_{14}$ Ps

13$_{3}$ 139$_{14}$ Pr 2$_{10}$ 24$_{14}$ Si 47$_{15}$ [נפ[שך]] 51$_{26}$ 1QH 17$_{7}$); soul of Y. (Lv 26$_{11.30}$ Jg 10$_{16}$ 1 S 2$_{35}$ Is 1$_{14}$ 42$_{1}$ Jr 6$_{8}$ 14$_{19}$ Ezk 23$_{18.18}$ Ps 11$_{5}$ Jb 23$_{13}$ Pr 6$_{16}$); distinction from §§ 3, 9, not alw. clear.

<SUBJ> היה *be* Jr 31$_{12}$, נגד hi. *tell* 11QPs^{a} 19$_{8}$, ידה hi. *praise* 11QPs^{a} 19$_{8}$, הלל pi. *praise* Ps 146$_{1}$11QPs^{a} 19$_{8}$, htp. *boast* Ps 34$_{3}$, ברך pi. *bless* Ps 103$_{1.2.22}$ 104$_{1.35}$ 4QBark^{a} 1.2$_{1}$, שׁוה pi. *cry for help* Jb 24$_{12}$, שׁאג *roar* 11QPs^{a} 19$_{8}$, זכר *remember* Lm 3$_{20}$, שׁכח *forget* Ps 103$_{2}$, ידע *know* Ps 139$_{14}$, שׂיח pol. *meditate* 1QH 17$_{7}$, דמה *be silent* Ps 62$_{2}$ (if em.; see Nom. Cl.), דמם *be silent* Ps 62$_{6}$ (mss דּוּמִיָּה is *silence*), חכה pi. *wait* Ps 33$_{20}$, קוה pi. *wait* Ps 130$_{5}$, יחל hi. *hope* Ps 42$_{6.12}$ 43$_{5}$.

שׁאל *ask* Dt 14$_{26}$, אוה pi. *desire* Dt 12$_{20}$ 14$_{26}$ 1 S 2$_{16}$ 2 S 3$_{21}$ 1 K 11$_{37}$ Mc 7$_{1}$ Jb 23$_{13}$ Pr 21$_{10}$ 1QS 10$_{19}$ 4Q418 127$_{2}$ 11QT 53$_{2}$ ([א]ותה), htp. Pr 13$_{4}$, חשׁק *desire* Gn 34$_{8}$ Si 51$_{19(B)}$, כסף ni. *long for* Ps 84$_{3}$, ערג *long for* Ps 42$_{2}$, אהב *love* Ca 1$_{7}$ 3$_{1.2.3.4}$, גיל *rejoice* Is 61$_{10}$ Ps 35$_{9}$, שׂמח *rejoice* Si 51$_{29}$ 4QAdmon 1.2$_{8}$ (נפ[שכם]) 11QPs^{a} 22$_{15}$, שׂישׂ *exult* Ps 35$_{9}$, רנן *shout for joy* Ps 71$_{23}$, רצה *be pleased with* Is 42$_{1}$, חפץ *delight in* Is 66$_{3}$, *be willing* 1 C 28$_{9}$ perh. 4QAdmonPar 3.2$_{5}$, ענג htp. *delight oneself* Is 55$_{2}$ (unless §1), שׁעע pilp. *delight* 1QH 17$_{8}$ (תשת[ע]שע) 19$_{7}$, נחם ni. *be comforted* Ps 77$_{3}$, רחב *be wide* 1QH 20$_{1}$, חזק *be strong* 1QH 10$_{28}$, שׂבע *be sated* Ps 88$_{4}$ 123$_{4}$ (unless §1) Ec 6$_{3}$, דשׁן pu. *be saturated* Pr 13$_{4}$.

יצא *go out*, i.e. faint Ca 5$_{6}$, שׁוב *go back* Ps 116$_{7}$, נשׂא *lift* Si 51$_{26}$, דרך *march* with strength Jg 5$_{21}$, שׁקק *rush about* Ps 107$_{9}$ (unless §1), בוס *trample* Pr 27$_{7}$, דבק *cling* Gn 34$_{3}$ Ps 63$_{9}$ 119$_{25}$ (unless §2) 4QPrEnosh 1.2$_{11}$ 4Q392 1$_{3}$ 4QBark^{d} 10$_{1}$ ([ד]בקה נפש[י]) 4QHymnPr 47$_{1}$, קשׁר ni. *be bound* 1 S 18$_{1}$, קצר *be short*, i.e. impatient, vexed Nm 21$_{4}$ Jg 10$_{16}$ 16$_{16}$ Zc 11$_{8}$, בהל ni. *be dismayed* Ps 6$_{4}$, שׁחח htpo. *be cast down* Ps 42$_{6.7.12}$ 43$_{5}$ 1QH 16$_{32}$, שׁוח *sink down* Ps 44$_{25}$ Lm 3$_{20(Qr)}$ (Kt hi. in same sense), כפף *be bowed down* Ps 57$_{7}$ (unless §2), בכה *weep* Jr 13$_{17}$, עגם *be grieved* Jb 30$_{25}$, שׁפך htp. *be poured out* Jb 30$_{16}$, אבל *mourn* Jb 14$_{22}$, דלף *be sleepless* Ps 119$_{28}$ (unless דלף II *shed tears* or III *collapse* or IV *be oppressed*), המה *moan* Ps 42$_{6.12}$ 43$_{5}$.

כנע ni. *be humbled* 4QapPs^{b} 45$_{2}$, ירע *tremble* Is 15$_{4}$, מוג htpol. *melt away* Ps 107$_{26}$ (unless §1), כלה *be weak*, i.e. long for Ps 84$_{3}$, עיף *be faint* Jr 4$_{31}$, עטף htp. *faint* Jon 2$_{8}$ Ps 107$_{5}$ 1QH 16$_{29}$, דאב *languish* Jr 31$_{25}$ (or em.; see Adj.) 4Q418 127$_{1}$, עשׁשׁ *be worn out* Ps 31$_{10}$ (unless §1) 1QH 13$_{34}$, צמא *be thirsty* Ps 42$_{3}$ 63$_{2}$ Si 51$_{24}$, גרס *be crushed* Ps 119$_{20}$, ישׁר *be upright* Hb 2$_{4}$, שׂים *place* Ca 6$_{12}$.

שׂנא *hate* 2 S 5$_{8(4QSam^{a})}$ Is 1$_{14}$ Ps 11$_{5}$, בחל *reject* Zc 11$_{8}$ (or em. בָּחֲלָה to גָּעֲלָה *it abhorred*), געל *abhor* Lv 26$_{11.15.30.43}$ Jr 14$_{19}$ Zc 11$_{8}$ (if em.; see above) 1QS 3$_{1}$ 4QD^{a} 11$_{7}$ 4QpsMos^{d} 1.1$_{4}$ 4QDibHam^{a} 1.6$_{7}$ 11QT 59$_{9}$, תעב pi. *abhor* Ps 107$_{18}$ (unless §1) 1QH 7$_{18}$ 8$_{19}$ (ת[עב]ה) 18$_{29}$ CD 1$_{21}$, קוט *loathe* Jb 10$_{1}$, קוץ *loathe* Si 50$_{25}$, זנח *reject* Lm 3$_{17}$ (or em. ni. *be rejected*), יקע *be alienated* Jr 6$_{8}$ Ezk 23$_{17.18.18.22.28}$, חסר pi. *dishonour* Si 14$_{2}$ (or em. חסד pi. *reproach*).

<NOM CL> דּוּמִיָּה נַפְשִׁי *my soul is silence*, i.e. waits silently Ps 62$_{2}$ (or em. דּוֹמִיָּה *is silent*, from דמה) 62$_{6(mss)}$ (L דֹּמִּי *be silent*, from דמם), מעגל נפש מטעמו *his delicacy is a pollution of the soul* Si 40$_{29(B)}$ (Bmg מעגל נפשו מטעמי זבד *delicacies given as a gift are the pollution of his soul*), אִם־יֵשׁ נַפְשְׁכֶם *if there is your soul*, i.e. if you are so disposed 2 K 9$_{15}$, אֵין נַפְשִׁי אֶל־הָעָם הַזֶּה *my soul would not be*, i.e. I would not be favourably disposed, *to this people* Jr 15$_{1}$, מָרָה נֶפֶשׁ כָּל־הָעָם *the soul of all the people was bitter* 1 S 30$_{6}$, var. 2 K 4$_{27}$, נַפְשִׁי לַאדֹנָי *my soul is to*, i.e. waits for, *my Lord* Ps 130$_{6}$, [לך נפש[י *my soul is to*, i.e. waits for, *you* 4QBark^{d} 10$_{1}$, כְּגָמֻל עָלַי נַפְשִׁי *my soul is upon me like a weaned child* Ps 131$_{2}$, נַפְשִׁי כְּאֶרֶץ־עֲיֵפָה לְךָ *my soul is like a weary*, i.e. thirsty, *land for you* Ps 143$_{6}$ (unless §1), נפשו אתו *his mind is with him* Si 34$_{20}$, var. 34$_{20}$, נֶפֶשׁ רְעֵבָה כָּל־מַר מָתוֹק *(to) the hungry soul everything bitter is sweet* Pr 27$_{7}$.

<OBJ> שׁוב pol. *restore* Ps 23$_{3}$, hi. Ps 19$_{8}$ Pr 25$_{13}$ Ru 4$_{15}$ Lm 1$_{11.16.19}$ 1QH 13$_{18}$ (נפשי corrected to סערה *tempest*) 14$_{23}$, דמם po. *quieten* Ps 131$_{2}$ (unless §1), ידע *know* Ex 23$_{9}$, נצר *watch* Pr 24$_{12}$, שׂמח pi. *make glad* Ps 86$_{4}$ 1QH 19$_{30}$, שׁעע pilp. *delight* Ps 94$_{19}$ 1QH 18$_{31}$, רוה pi. *saturate* Jr 31$_{14}$, hi. Jr 31$_{25}$, מלא pi. *fill* Jr 31$_{25}$ Ps 107$_{9}$ (unless §1), שׂבע hi. *satisfy* Ps 107$_{9}$ (unless §1), נשׂא *lift*, i.e. direct one's desire toward, long for Dt 24$_{15}$ Jr 22$_{27}$

44_{14} (both pi.) Ho 4_8 Ps 24_4 Pr 19_{18}, perh. *lift*, i.e. flee for protection to* Ps 25_1 86_4 143_8, נתן *give*, i.e. set 1 C 22_{19} Si $51_{20(B).26}$ 4QapPs[b] 45_2, חבר pi. *join* 11QPs[a] 18_1 ([חברו]), ארך hi. *hold back* Jb 6_{11}, פדה *redeem* Ps 71_{23}, נצל hi. *deliver* GnzPs 3_{25}.

בכה *bewail* Ps 69_{11} (or em. בכה to hi. *make* soul *weep* or דכה hi. *crush* soul or ענה pi. *afflict* soul or מכך hi. *make* soul *low*), דכא pi. *crush* 1QH 13_{17}, שׁפך *pour out* 1 S 1_{15} Ps 43_5, ערה hi. *pour out* to death Is 53_{12}, אדב hi. *sicken* 1 S 2_{33} (or em. לַאֲדִיב to לְהָדִיב *to cause to pine away*, i.e. דוב hi.), דאב hi. *cause to languish* Si 4_1, יגה hi. *grieve* Jb 19_2, מרר hi. *embitter* Jb 27_2.

<CSTR> נֶפֶשׁ־הָעָם *soul of the people* Nm 21_4, כָּל־הָעָם *of all the people* 1 S 30_6, דָּוִד *of David* 1 S 18_1 2 S 5_8, יְהוֹנָתָן *of Jonathan* 1 S 18_1, אֲדֹנָיו *of his masters* Pr 25_{13}, הַגֵּר *of the sojourner* Ex 23_9, הַכֹּהֲנִים *of the priests* Jr 31_{14}, עַבְדֶּךָ *of your servant* Ps 86_4 1QH 18_{29} 19_{30} (both עבדכה), חָרֻצִים *of the diligent* Pr 13_4, עָצֵל *of the sluggard* Pr 13_4 (if em.; see App.), רָשָׁע *of a wicked one* Pr 21_{10}, ־חֲלָלִים *of the pierced ones* Jb 24_{12}, נפש עני *soul of an afflicted one* Si 4_1, אוהביו *of those who love him* GnzPs 3_{25} (corrected to אוהבו *of him who loves him*).

יְדִדוּת נַפְשִׁי *loved one of my soul* Jr 12_7, שְׂנֻאֵי נֶפֶשׁ *(ones) hated of*, i.e. by, *the soul of* 2 S $5_{8(mss, Qr)}$, [א]רורי הנפשו[ת] *ones cursed of (their) souls* 4QMishC[a] 1_6, מַר נֶפֶשׁ *bitter (one) of soul* 1 S 22_2 Si 4_1, *bitterness of* Ezk 27_{31}, מַר נַפְשִׁי *bitterness of my soul* Is 38_{15} Jb 7_{11} 10_1, מָרַת נֶפֶשׁ *bitter (one)* (fem.) *of soul* 1 S 1_{10} (נָפֶשׁ), מָרֵי *bitter (ones) of* Jg 18_{25} 1 S 17_8 Jb 3_{20} Pr 31_{36} (both נָפֶשׁ), אַגְמֵי *distressed (ones) of* Is 19_{10} (נָפֶשׁ), מרורי נפש *bitterness of soul* 1QH 5_{12} 1QpHab 9_{11}, נפשי *of my soul* 1QH 13_{12}.

צָרַת נַפְשׁוֹ *distress of his soul* Gn 42_{21} 1QH 7_{16}, צרת נפשי *distress of my soul* 1QH 13_{12} 17_{28} (נפש[י]) 4QBark[d] 2.1_6 (נפש[י]), נפישנו *of our soul* 4QDibHam[a] 1.6_8 (corrected from נישנו), צָרוֹת נַפְשִׁי *troubles of my soul* Ps 31_8, עֲמַל נַפְשׁוֹ *trouble of his soul* Is 53_{11}, כאב נפשו *pain of his soul* Si 4_6, דַּאֲבוֹן נֶפֶשׁ *languishing of soul* Dt 38_{65} (unless *dryness of throat*, i.e. §1), ענות נפשו *humbling of his soul* 1QS 3_8 4QBéat 2.2_6.

שְׁאָט נֶפֶשׁ *contempt of the soul*, i.e. utter contempt Ezk 36_5, תעבות נפש *abominations of the soul* 4Q418 81_2, תּוֹעֲבַת נַפְשׁוֹ *abomination of his soul* Pr $6_{16(Qr)}$ (Kt תועבות *abominations of*), מעגל נפש *pollution of the soul* Si $40_{29(B)}$ (Bmg נפשו *of his soul*).

תַּאֲוַת־נֶפֶשׁ *desire of the soul* Is 26_8, נַפְשׁוֹ *of his soul* Ps 10_3, תאות נפשך *desire of your soul* Si 5_1, אַוַּת נַפְשְׁךָ *desire of your soul* Dt $12_{15.20.21}$ (נַפְשֶׁךָ) 1 S 23_{20} 11QT 53_2 ([אות נפשכה]), נַפְשׁוֹ *of his soul* Dt 18_6=11QT 60_{13} Jr $2_{24(Kt)}$, נַפְשָׁהּ *of her soul* Jr $2_{24(Qr)}$, הַוַּת נַפְשׁוֹ *desire of his soul* Mc 7_3, חשק נפשי perh. *desire of my soul* 4QBark[e] 6_2, מַחְמַל נַפְשְׁכֶם *compassion of your soul* Ezk 24_{21} (or em. מַחְמַל to מַחְמַד *desirable thing of*), מַשָּׂא נַפְשָׁם *lifting up*, i.e. desire, *of their soul* Ezk 24_{25}, מְשִׁיבַת נָפֶשׁ *restoring the soul* Ps 19_8, עֲצַת־נָפֶשׁ *counsel of the soul* Pr 27_9 (unless §11), חזון נפשו *vision of his mind* Si 40_6.

כָּל־נֶפֶשׁ *all the soul* 2 K 23_3 Jr 31_{25} 1QH 7_{10} 1QS 1_2 ([כול נפש]) 5_9 (כול) 4QS[d] 1_6 4QDibHam[a] 1.2_{13} CD 15_{10} ([כ]ל) 15_{12}, כָּל־נַפְשְׁךָ *all your soul* Dt 4_{29} (נַפְשֶׁךָ) 6_5 10_{12} 26_{16} 30_2 (all three נַפְשֶׁךָ) $30_{6.10}$ (נַפְשֶׁךָ) 4QapMos[a] 1.1_3 (כו]ל נפשכה]) 4QMMT C_{16} (כו]ל]) 4QBéat 14.2_{12} ([כול] נפשכה), כל־נַפְשׁוֹ *all his soul* 2 K 23_{25} 2 C 34_{31}, כָּל־נַפְשְׁכֶם *all your* (pl.) *soul* Dt 11_{13} 13_4=11QT 54_{13} (כול נפשכמה) Jos 22_5 23_{14}, כָּל־נַפְשָׁם *all their soul* 1 K 2_4 8_{48}|| 2 C 6_{38} 4QErr 1_{12} 11QT 59_{10} (כול נפשמה).

<APP> נַפְשׁוֹ עָצֵל *his soul, the sluggard* Pr 13_4 (or em. נֶפֶשׁ *soul of*, or del. נַפְשׁוֹ).

<ADJ> עָיֵף *weary* Jr 31_{25}, דָּאֵב *languishing* Jr 31_{25} (if em. דָּאֲבָה every soul *[that is] languishing*), רָעֵב *hungry* Ps 107_9 (unless §1) Pr 27_7, מַר *bitter* Jb 21_{25}, שְׂבֵעָ *sated* Pr 27_7.

<PREP> לְ of benefit, *to, for*, + ידע *know* Pr 24_{14} (or em. דְּעֶה *know* to דֵּעָה *knowledge* is ... for), נעם *be pleasant* Pr 2_{10}, חסר *lack* Ec 6_2 (unless §3); of direction, *to* perh. 4QBark[d] 5_3, + נתן *give* Pr 29_{17}, נוח hi. *give rest* 4Q417 1.1_{22}.

בְּ of instrument, accompaniment, *by (means of), with* perh. 4QAdmonPar 3.2_5 4QErr 1_{12} perh. 4QBark[e] 12_3 4QDibHam[a] 1.2_{13}, + ידע *know* Jos 23_{14}, הלך *walk* 1 K 2_4, שׁוב *go back* Dt $30_{2.10}$ 1 K 8_{48}||2 C 6_{38} 2 K 23_{25} 1QS 5_9 4QS[d] 1_6 (ל[שוב]) 4QapMos[a] 1.1_3 ([בכו]ל נפשכה) 4QMMT C_{16} (ב[כו]ל) 11QT 59_{10} CD 15_{10} (... לש[וב]

[ב]כ[ל] נפש) 15$_{10}$, דרשׁ *seek* Dt 4$_{29}$ 2 C 15$_{12}$ 1QS 1$_{2}$ ([ב]כול נפש]), אהב *love* Dt 6$_{5}$ 13$_{4}$=11QT 54$_{13}$ Dt 30$_{6}$ 4Q Béat 14.2$_{12}$ ([תאהוב ... בכול] נפשכה), עבד *serve* Dt 10$_{12}$ 11$_{13}$ Jos 22$_{5}$ 1 C 28$_{9}$, עשׂה *do* Dt 26$_{16}$, שׁמר *keep* 2 K 23$_{3}$||2 C 34$_{31}$, כסה pi. *fill* Si 47$_{15}$ (ב[נפ]שך), ברר *cleanse* 1QH 7$_{10}$, מות *die* Jb 21$_{25}$.

בְּ of place, *in* Ezk 25$_{6.15}$ perh. 1QH fr. 11$_{9}$ perh. 4Q DibHam[a] 5.2$_{7}$ (בנפש[כה]; unless מנפש[כה] *from your soul*), + שׂית *place* Ps 13$_{3}$, רהב hi. perh. *make proud* Ps 138$_{3}$ (or em. רהב hi. to רבה hi. *increase*), אמר *say* 11Q Ps[a] 28$_{5}$, שׂיח *meditate* 4QMidrEschat[b] 9$_{9}$, שׁער *reckon* Pr 23$_{7}$ (unless §3).

בְּ *to*, + קשׁר ni. *be bound* 1 S 18$_{1}$; *according to*, + עשׂה *do* 1 S 2$_{35}$.

כְּ *as* Dt 13$_{7}$=11QT 54$_{20}$.

עַל *upon*, + שׂים *place* Dt 11$_{18}$; *with*, + גמל *deal generously* Ps 116$_{7}$.

אֵת *with* Gn 23$_{8}$ (אִם־יֵשׁ אֶת־נַפְשְׁכֶם לִקְבֹּר *if it is with*, i.e. agreeable, *to your soul to bury*), המה *moan* 4Qps Ezek[a] 3$_{2}$.

<COLL> נֶפֶשׁ || לֵבָב *heart* Dt 4$_{29}$ 6$_{5}$ 10$_{12}$ 11$_{13.18}$ 13$_{4}$=11QT 54$_{13}$ Dt 26$_{16}$ 30$_{2.6.10}$ Jos 22$_{5}$ 23$_{14}$ 1 S 2$_{35}$ 1 K 2$_{4}$ 8$_{48}$ 2 K 23$_{25}$ Ezk 36$_{5}$ Ps 13$_{3}$ 1 C 22$_{19}$ 2 C 15$_{12}$ 34$_{31}$ 4QMMT C$_{16}$ 11QT 59$_{10}$, לֵב *heart* 2 K 23$_{3}$ Pr 2$_{10}$ (+) 24$_{12}$ 27$_{9}$ (+) 1 C 28$_{9}$ 2 C 6$_{38}$ 1QS 5$_{9}$ 4QS[d] 1$_{6}$ 4QDibHam[a] 1.2$_{13}$ CD 15$_{10.12}$, רוּחַ *spirit* Is 26$_{9}$ Jb 7$_{11}$ 1QS 3$_{8}$ (+), בָּשָׂר *flesh* Ps 63$_{2}$, עַיִן *eye* Dt 28$_{65}$ (unless §1) 1 S 2$_{33}$ Jr 13$_{17}$ (+) Ezk 24$_{21.25}$ Ps 31$_{10}$ 1QH 13$_{34}$ (+), בֶּטֶן *abdomen* Ps 31$_{10}$ 44$_{26}$, קֶרֶב *inward part* Ps 94$_{19}$ (+) 103$_{2}$, מְאֹד *might* Dt 6$_{5}$ 2 K 23$_{25}$.

+ חַיִּים *life* Ps 88$_{4}$, שֵׂיבָה *old age* Ru 4$_{15}$.

נַפְשִׁי *my soul*, as vocative Jg 5$_{21}$ Ps 42$_{6.12}$ 43$_{5}$ 62$_{6}$ 103$_{1.2.22}$ 104$_{1.35}$ 116$_{7}$ 146$_{1}$ 4QBark[a] 1.2$_{1}$.

נַפְשִׁי אִוִּיתִיךָ *I yearn for you with my soul* Is 26$_{9}$, הֵם מְנַשְּׂאִים נַפְשָׁם לָשׁוּב *they set their heart to return* Jr 22$_{27}$ 44$_{14}$, מְדֻכְדַּךְ נפש *one crushed with respect to soul* Si 4$_{4}$.

5. breath, last breath, soul, as inner being, <SUBJ> יצא *go out* Gn 35$_{18}$ Si 38$_{23}$, שׁוב *go back* 1 K 17$_{21.22}$, להט pi. *set ablaze* Jb 41$_{13}$.

<NOM CL> בּוֹ נֶפֶשׁ חַיָּה *in it was the breath of life* Gn 1$_{30}$, כל אשר לא נפש עליו *everyone in whom there is no breath* 4QHalakhah[a] 13$_{6}$

<OBJ> נפח *breathe* Jr 15$_{9}$, hi. *cause to breathe* Jb 31$_{39}$.

<CSTR> נֶפֶשׁ בְּעָלֶיהָ *last breath of its owners* Jb 31$_{39}$, נֶפֶשׁ חַיָּה *breath of life* Gn 1$_{30}$; מַפַּח־נָפֶשׁ *expiring of the soul* Jb 11$_{20}$ Si 30$_{20}$, בָּתֵּי הַנֶּפֶשׁ perh. *houses of breath*, i.e. perfume containers Is 3$_{20}$ (unless *of the neck*, i.e. collars [§2] or נֶפֶשׁ III *perfume*).

<PREP> לְ of benefit, *to, for*, + היה *be* Pr 3$_{22}$; מִן *from*, i.e. both ... and, + כלה pi. *destroy* Is 10$_{18}$ (unless §2).

<COLL> נֶפֶשׁ || גַּרְגֶּרֶת *throat* Pr 3$_{22}$; :: בָּשָׂר *flesh* Is 10$_{18}$.

6. life, lives; soul, as the vital self, distinction from §9 not alw. clear; pl. perh. **eternal life** (Pr 11$_{30}$),* <SUBJ> היה *be* 1 S 25$_{29}$ 1 K 20$_{39.42}$ Jr 21$_{9}$ 38$_{2}$ 39$_{18}$, יקר *be precious* 1 S 26$_{21}$ 2 K 1$_{13.13.14}$, גדל *be great*, i.e. precious 1 S 26$_{24.24}$, נגע *draw near* Si 51$_{6}$ 1QH 14$_{24}$ (נפ[שי תגיע]), קרב *draw near* Jb 33$_{22}$, גור *sojourn* 1QH 11$_{25}$, נוח *rest* Antinoopolis inscr.$_{3}$, נצל ni. *be delivered* Gn 32$_{31}$, קשׁר pass. *be bound* Gn 44$_{30}$, צרר pass. *be bound* 1 S 25$_{29}$, שׁפך htp. *be poured out* Lm 2$_{12}$, נתן ni. *be given* Est 7$_{3}$.

<NOM CL> הַדָּם הוּא הַנָּפֶשׁ *the blood is the life* Dt 12$_{23}$=11QT 53$_{6}$ 4QJub[d] 21$_{18}$ ([הנפש]), נֶפֶשׁ כָּל־בָּשָׂר דָּמוֹ הִיא *the life of all flesh is its blood* Lv 17$_{14 (Qr)}$, נֶפֶשׁ הַבָּשָׂר בַּדָּם הִיא *the life of the flesh is in the blood* Lv 17$_{11 (Qr)}$, עוֹד נַפְשִׁי בִּי *my life is still within me* 2 S 1$_{9}$, בְּיָדוֹ נֶפֶשׁ כָּל־חָי *in his hand is the life of every living thing* Jb 12$_{10}$ GnzPs 3$_{22}$, var. 11QPs[a] 19$_{3}$, נַפְשִׁי בְכַפִּי תָמִיד *my life is in my hand continually* Ps 110$_{109}$, כָּל־הַנְּפָשׁוֹת לִי *all lives are mine* Ezk 18$_{4}$, נֶפֶשׁ תַּחַת נָפֶשׁ *a life shall be for a life* Lv 24$_{18}$, var. 2 K 10$_{24}$, sim. Dt 19$_{21}$=11QT 61$_{12}$ (בְּנֶפֶשׁ), נַפְשֵׁנוּ תַחְתֵּיכֶם *our life shall be in place of you*, i.e. of your life Jos 2$_{14}$.

<OBJ> בקשׁ pi. *seek* Ex 4$_{19}$ 1 S 20$_{1}$ 22$_{23.23}$ 23$_{15}$ 25$_{29}$ 2 S 4$_{8}$ 16$_{11}$ 1 K 19$_{10.14}$ Jr 4$_{30}$ 11$_{21}$ 19$_{7.9}$ 21$_{7}$ 22$_{25}$ 34$_{20.21}$ 38$_{16}$ 44$_{30}$ 46$_{26}$ 49$_{37}$ Ps 35$_{4}$ 38$_{13}$ 40$_{15}$ 54$_{5}$ 63$_{10}$ 70$_{3}$ 86$_{14}$ Pr 29$_{10}$ Si 51$_{3}$ 1QH 10$_{21}$ 11QT 59$_{19}$, דרשׁ *require* Gn 9$_{5}$, שׁאל *ask for* 1 K 19$_{4}$ Jon 4$_{8}$ (both + לָמוּת *to die*) Jb 31$_{30}$, קוה pi. *wait for* Ps 56$_{7}$, ארב *lie in wait for* Ps 59$_{4}$, צדה *lie in wait for* 1 S 24$_{12}$, צוד *hunt* Pr 6$_{26}$ (unless נֶפֶשׁ II *abundance*), pol. Ezk 13$_{18.18.20}$, אפף *surround* 1QH 13$_{39}$.

נתן *give* Ex 21_{23} Jr 45_5 Ps 74_{19} 4QpsEzek^a 13.2_3, שׂים *place* in hand Jg 12_3 1 S 19_5 28_{21} Jb 13_{14}, *make* 1 K 19_2 Is 53_{10} 1QH 11_6 ([נפשן]), לקח *take* 1 S 24_{12} 1 K $19_{4.10.14}$ Ezk 33_6 Jon 4_3 Ps 31_{14} Pr 1_{19} 11_{30}, נשׂא *take* 2 S 14_{14}, חבל *take in pledge* Dt 24_6, שׁלה *draw out* Jb 27_8, שׁלך hi. *cast*, i.e. risk Jg 9_{17}, אסף *gather*, i.e. take away Jg $18_{25.25}$ Ps 26_9, ספה *snatch away* Ps 40_{15}, קלע pi. *sling out* 1 S 25_{29}, מגר *throw down* 11QPs^a 24_5, חשׁק *cling to* Is 38_{17} (or em. חָשַׁקְתָּ to חָשַׂכְתָּ *you have withheld*).

חטא *sin against*, i.e. endanger or forfeit Hb 2_{10} Pr 20_2, דוב hi. *cause to pine away* Lv 26_{16}, חרף pi. *reproach* Jg 5_{18}, נכה hi. *strike*, i.e. kill Lv $24_{17.18}$ 1QH 13_{15} (ה[כו]תה), כרת hi. *cut off* Ezk 17_{17}, אבד pi. *destroy* Ezk 22_{27}, טרף *tear* 1QH 13_{14}, אכל *eat* Dt 12_{23}=11QT 53_6, קבע *rob of* Pr 22_{23}, חשׂך *withhold* Is 38_{17} (if em.; see above) Ps 78_{50} (unless §8d) Jb 33_{18}.

ידע *be concerned for* Pr 12_{10}, סמך *support* 1QH 10_7, עזר *help* 1QH 10_{34} 15_{23}, עשׂה *make* Jr 38_{16}, בנה *build*, i.e. edify 11QPs^a 24, שׁמר *preserve* Ps 25_{20} 86_2 97_{10} 121_7 Jb 2_6 Pr 13_3 16_{17} 19_{16} 22_5 4QBark^d 2.1_5 1QM 14_{10}, *watch for* Ps 71_{10}, שׁוב hi. *bring back* Ps 35_{17} Jb 33_{30}, חיה pi. *keep alive* Ezk 13_{18} 18_{27}, חלץ pi. *deliver* Ps 6_5 1QS 11_{13}, נצל hi. *deliver* Jos 2_{13} Jr 20_{13} Ezk $3_{19.21}$ $14_{14.20}$ 33_9 Ps 22_{21} (unless §2) 33_{19} 56_{14} 86_{13} 116_8 Pr 14_{25} 23_{14} 1QH 13_{13} 4QBark^a 1.2_1 11QPs^a 18_{15} ([נפש]ם), ישׁע hi. *save* Ps 72_{13} 1QH 10_{23}, מלט pi. *save* 1 S 19_{11} 2 S $19_{6.6.6.6}$ 1 K $1_{12.12}$ Jr 48_6 $51_{6.45}$ Ezk 33_5 Am $2_{14.15}$ Ps 89_{49} 116_4 1QMyst 1.1_4, פלט pi. *save* Ps 17_{13} 1QH 13_{18} 17_{33}, גאל *redeem* Ps 72_{14}, פדה *redeem* 2 S 4_9 1 K 1_{29} Ps 34_{23} 49_{16} 55_{19} Jb 33_{28} Si 51_2 1QH $10_{32.35}$ 11_{19}.

<CSTR> נֶפֶשׁ ... שְׁלֹמֹה *life of ... Solomon* 1 K 1_{12}, נֶפֶשׁ הָאָדָם *life of a human being* Gn 9_5 Lv 24_{17} (אָדָם), אִישׁ *of a man* Jon 1_{14} (הָאִישׁ) Pr 13_8, נָשֶׁיךָ *of your wives* 2 S 19_6, פִּלַגְשֶׁיךָ *of your secondary wives* 2 S 19_6, הָאָב *of the father* Ezk 18_4, הַבֵּן *of the son* Ezk 18_4, בִּנְךָ *of your son* 1 K 1_{12}, בָּנֶיךָ *of your sons* 2 S 19_6, נפשות בניכם *lives of your sons* 4QpsEzek^e 55_4, נֶפֶשׁ אָחִיו *life of his brother* 2 S 14_7, עוֹלָלַיִךְ *of your infants* Lm 2_{19}, אֲדֹנִי *of my lord* 1 S 25_{29}, בְּעָלָיו *of its possessors* Pr 1_{19}, עבדכה *of your servant* 1QH 13_{15}, עֲבָדֶיךָ *of your servants* 2 K 1_{13}, עֲבָדָיו *of his servants* Ps 34_{23}, בֵּיתֶךָ *of your house(hold)* Jg 18_{25}, בֵּית *of the house(hold) of* 1 S 22_{22}, אֹיְבֶיךָ *of your enemies* 1 S 25_{29} 1 K 3_{11}, נפש איביו *life of his enemies* 4QpsEzek^a 13.2_3, נֶפֶשׁ שֹׂנְאֶיךָ *life of your enemies* 2 C 1_{11}, רֹצֵחַ *of a murderer* Nm 35_{31}.

נֶפֶשׁ אֶבְיוֹן *life of a poor one* Jr 20_{13} 1QH 10_{32} 11_{24} 13_{18} 4QBark^a 1.2_1, נפש עני *life of an afflicted one* 1QH 13_{13}, עני ורש *of an afflicted and poor one* 1QH 10_{34} 13_{14}, נַפְשׁוֹת אֶבְיוֹנִים *the lives of the poor* Jr 2_{34} (or em. אֶבְיוֹנִים to נְבִיאִים *the prophets*) Ps 72_{13}, צַדִּיק *of a righteous one* Ps 94_{21} CD 1_{20}, נַפְשׁוֹת חֲסִידָיו *lives of his loyal ones* Ps 97_{10}, נפש פדותכה *lives of your ransom*, i.e. ransomed ones 1QM 14_{10}.

נֶפֶשׁ בְּהֵמָה *life of a beast* Lv 24_{18}, בְּהֶמְתּוֹ *of his beast* Pr 12_{10} (unless §3), תּוֹרֶךָ *of your turtle dove* Ps 74_{19}, הַבָּשָׂר *of the flesh* Lv 17_{11}, כָּל־בָּשָׂר *of all flesh* Lv 17_{14}, אַחַד מֵהֶם *of one of them* 1 K 19_2, כָּל־חָי *of every living thing* Jb 12_{10} 11QPs^a 19_3 (כול חי) GnzPs 3_{22}, נפש רבים *life of many* Si 13_{12}.

מְבַקְשֵׁי נַפְשָׁם *those who seek their life* Jr $19_{7.9}$ 21_7 $34_{20.21}$ 46_{26} 49_{37}, נַפְשִׁי *my life* Ps 35_4 38_{13} 40_{15} 70_3 Si 51_3, נַפְשְׁךָ *your life* Jr 22_{25}, נַפְשׁוֹ *his life* Jr 44_{30} 11QT 59_{19}, שֹׁמְרֵי נַפְשִׁי *those who watch for my life* Ps 71_{10}, מַכֵּה נֶפֶשׁ *one who strikes the life of*, i.e. kills Lv 24_{18}, סֹמְכֵי נַפְשִׁי *upholders of my life* Ps 54_6, דַּם נַפְשׁוֹת *blood of the lives of* Jr 2_{34}, פִּדְיֹן נַפְשׁוֹ *ransom of his life* Ex 21_{30}, נַפְשָׁם *of their life* Ps 49_9 (פִּדְיוֹן), פדוי נפשם *ransom of their life* 4QD^e 2.2_9, פד[ו]ת נפשו *ransom of his life* 4Q Halakhah^a 9_3, כֹּפֶר נֶפֶשׁ *ransom of the life of* Pr 13_8, גֹּעַל נַפְשֵׁךְ *abhorrence of your life* Ezk 16_5, מוֹקֵשׁ נַפְשׁוֹ *snare of*, i.e. for, *his life* Pr 18_7, כָּל־נֶפֶשׁ *any life of* Lv 24_{17}, *all the lives of* 1 S 22_{22}, כָּל־הַנְּפָשׁוֹת *all lives* Ezk 18_4.

<APP> דָּם *blood* Gn 9_4.

<ADJ> יָקָר *precious* Pr 6_{26} (נֶפֶשׁ יְקָרָה perh. *weighty person*;* unless נֶפֶשׁ II *abundance*), רַב pl. *many* Ezk 17_{17}, זֹאת *this* Jr 38_{16}.

<PREP> לְ of benefit, *to, for*, + לקח *take* Pr 22_{25}; *(in exchange) for*, + לקח *take* ransom Nm 35_{31}; *for (the sake of)*, + ירא *fear* Jos 9_{24}, חרד *tremble* Ezk 32_{10}; of purpose, *for*, + צפן *lie hid* Pr 1_{18}, טמן *hide* snare 1QH 10_{29}; *against*, + איב *be an enemy* 4Q415 2.2_5; *namely, that is to say* Gn 9_5 (+ דָּם *blood*).

בְּ of price, *(in exchange) for, at the cost of, at the*

risk of Nm 17$_{3}$ Dt 19$_{21}$=11QT 61$_{12}$ Pr 7$_{23}$ Arad ost. 24$_{18}$, + דבר pi. *speak* 1 K 2$_{23}$, הלך *go* 2 S 23$_{17}$, בוא hi. *bring* Lm 5$_{9}$ 1 C 11$_{19}$, תעה hi. *lead astray* Jr 42$_{20}$, שׁתה *drink* 1 C 11$_{19}$, מות hi. *kill* 2 S 14$_{7}$.

בְּ of instrument, *by (means of)*, + כפר pi. *make atonement* Lv 17$_{11}$; of accompaniment, *with* Lv 17$_{14}$, + אכל *eat* Gn 9$_{4}$, קשׁר pass. *be bound* Gn 44$_{30}$; of cause, *on account of*, + אבד *perish* Jon 1$_{14}$; of purpose, *for*, + נקשׁ htp. *lay a snare* 1 S 28$_{9}$; *against*, + עשׂה *do* 2 S 18$_{13}$.

בְּ *in (respect of), as regards* Ps 17$_{9}$ (אֹיְבַי בְּנֶפֶשׁ *my enemies as regards life*, i.e. my mortal enemies), + סבב perh. *cause [harm]* 1 S 22$_{22}$ (or em. סַבֹּתִי to חַבְתִּי *I am guilty*, from חוב).

כְּ *as* 1 K 19$_{2}$ Ezk 18$_{4.4}$.

אֶל *for*, + הלך *go* 1 K 19$_{3}$, נוס *flee* 2 K 7$_{7}$.

עַל *against*, + גדד *band together* Ps 94$_{21}$ (or em. יָגוֹדּוּ to יָגוּרוּ *they show hostility*) CD 1$_{20}$, קשׁר *conspire* Si 13$_{12}$, גור *show hostility* Ps 94$_{21}$ (if em.; see above) 1QH 10$_{24}$; *for (the sake of)*, + מלט ni. *escape* Gn 19$_{17}$, נשׂא *lift* hands Lm 2$_{19}$, עמד *stand up* Est 8$_{11}$ 9$_{16}$ 4Q Rebukes 1.1$_{2}$ (לעמוד עול[), בקשׁ pi. *plead* Est 7$_{7}$, דבק *cling* perh. 4QBark^{e} 3$_{1}$; *concerning* 5QOrd^{a} 2$_{5}$.

בַּעַד *for the sake of*, + נתן *give* Jb 2$_{4}$.

חֵלֶף *in return for* 4QHalakhah^{a} 13$_{4}$.

תַּחַת *in place of, (in exchange) for* Lv 24$_{18}$ 2 K 10$_{24}$, + היה *be* 1 K 20$_{39.42}$, נתן *give* Ex 21$_{23}$.

<COLL> נֶפֶשׁ || חַיִּים *life* Ps 26$_{9}$, חַיָּה *life* Ps 74$_{19}$ 78$_{50}$ Jb 33$_{18.22.28}$ (+) Si 51$_{6}$, רוּחַ *breath* Jb 12$_{10}$ GnzPs 3$_{22}$, בָּשָׂר *flesh* Dt 12$_{23}$=11QT 53$_{6}$ (+) Jb 13$_{14}$ Si 51$_{2}$ 11QPs^{a} 19$_{3}$, דָּם *blood* Ps 72$_{14}$ 94$_{21}$ (both +) Pr 1$_{18}$, עַיִן *eye* Dt 19$_{21}$=11QT 61$_{12}$ Lv 26$_{16}$ Ps 116$_{8}$, שֵׁן *tooth* Dt 19$_{21}$=11QT 61$_{12}$, רֶגֶל *foot* Ps 56$_{14}$ 116$_{8}$ Si 51$_{2}$, עַם *people* Est 7$_{3}$, יָחִיד *only one* fem. Ps 22$_{21}$ 35$_{17}$.

+ עָקֵב *footstep* Ps 56$_{7}$.

נְפָשׁוֹת ... לְעַמִּי *lives ... belonging to my people* Ezk 13$_{18}$, נְפָשׁוֹת לָכֶנָה *your own lives* Ezk 13$_{18}$, לֹא נַכֶּנּוּ נָפֶשׁ *let us not strike him with respect to (his) life*, i.e. fatally Gn 37$_{21}$, sim. Dt 19$_{6.11}$ Jr 40$_{14.15}$, וּרְצָחוֹ נֶפֶשׁ *and he murders him with respect to (his) life* Dt 22$_{26}$=11QT 66$_{7}$.

7. being, creature(s), <SUBJ> היה *be* Ezk 47$_{9}$, רמשׂ *creep* Gn 1$_{21}$ Lv 11$_{46}$, שׁרץ *swarm* Lv 11$_{46}$. <NOM CL> נֶפֶשׁ הַחַיָּה אֲשֶׁר בַּמָּיִם *the living creatures that are in the water* Lv 11$_{10}$, כָּל־נֶפֶשׁ חַיָּה אֲשֶׁר אִתְּכֶם *every living creature that is with you* Gn 9$_{12}$, var. Gn 9$_{10}$. <OBJ> קרא *call*, i.e. name Gn 2$_{19}$ (or del.), יצא hi. *bring out* Gn 1$_{24}$, שׁרץ *swarm with* Gn 1$_{21}$.

<CSTR> שֶׁרֶץ נֶפֶשׁ *swarms of creatures* Gn 1$_{20}$; כָּל־נֶפֶשׁ *every creature* Gn 1$_{21}$ 9$_{10.12}$ Lv 11$_{10.46.46}$ Ezk 47$_{9}$ 4QParGenEx 1$_{8}$ (]כול הנפ[ש) CD 12$_{12}$. <APP> בְּהֵמָה *beast* Gn 1$_{24}$, חַיָּה *(wild) beast* Gn 1$_{24}$, רֶמֶשׂ *creeping thing* Gn 1$_{24}$. <ADJ> חַי *living* Gn 1$_{20.21.24}$ 2$_{7.19}$ (or del. נֶפֶשׁ חַיָּה) 9$_{10.12.15.16}$ Lv 11$_{10.46}$ Ezk 47$_{9}$ 4QParGenEx 1$_{8}$ (]לרדות בכול הנפ[ש) CD 12$_{12}$.

<PREP> לְ introducing predicate, + היה *be* Gn 2$_{7}$; *concerning* Lv 11$_{46}$; בְּ *over*, + רדה *have dominion* 4Q ParGenEx 1$_{8}$ (]הנפ[ש); מִן partitive, *from among* Lv 11$_{10}$; אֵת *with*, + קום hi. *establish* covenant Gn 9$_{10}$; עַד *unto* CD 12$_{12}$; בֵּין *between* Gn 9$_{15.16}$, + נתן *give*, i.e. make, covenant Gn 9$_{12}$.

<COLL> נֶפֶשׁ followed by בְּ *among, including*, + בְּהֵמָה *beasts* Gn 9$_{10}$, חַיָּה *(wild) beasts* Gn 9$_{10}$, עוֹף *birds* Gn 9$_{10}$, בָּשָׂר *flesh* Gn 9$_{15.16}$.

8a. person, individual, of either sex (like אָדָם *human being*), <SUBJ> היה *be* Nm 19$_{18}$, היה *live* Ezk 13$_{19}$, שׁבע ni. *swear* Lv 5$_{4}$, שׁמע *hear* Lv 5$_{1}$, דרשׁ *seek* Lm 3$_{25}$, אכל *eat* Lv 7$_{18.20.25.27}$ 17$_{10.12.15}$, קרב hi. *bring near*, i.e. offer Lv 2$_{1}$ Nm 15$_{27}$, פנה *turn* Lv 20$_{6}$, נפל *fall* 4QSD 7.1$_{7}$ CD 11$_{16}$, נגע *touch* Lv 5$_{2}$ 7$_{21}$ 22$_{6}$ Nm 10$_{22}$, נשׂא *bear* Lv 7$_{18}$, לקט *glean* 4QD^{b} 6$_{7}$, גנב *steal* Dt 24$_{7}$, טמא *be impure* Lv 22$_{6}$ Nm 19$_{22}$, אשׁם *be guilty* Nm 5$_{6}$, שׁגג *commit error* Nm 15$_{28}$, חטא *sin* Lv 4$_{2.27}$ 5$_{1.15.17}$ Nm 15$_{27}$ Ezk 18$_{4.20}$ 4QD^{a} 11$_{2}$, מעל *commit unfaithful act* Lv 5$_{15.21}$, עשׂה *do* Lv 4$_{27}$ 5$_{17.21}$ 18$_{29}$ 23$_{30}$ Nm 15$_{30}$, רעב *be hungry* Pr 19$_{15}$, ענה ni. *be afflicted* Is 58$_{10}$, pu. Lv 23$_{29}$, htp. *afflict oneself* 11QT 25$_{11}$, כרת ni. *be cut off* Gn 17$_{14}$ Ex 12$_{15.19}$ 31$_{14}$ Lv 7$_{20.21.25.27}$ 18$_{29}$ 19$_{8}$ 22$_{3}$ 23$_{29}$ Nm 9$_{13}$ 15$_{30.31.31}$ 19$_{13.20}$ 4QpsJub^{a} 2.1$_{1}$ (הנ[פש]) 11QT 25$_{11}$, מות *die* Nm 35$_{30}$ Ezk 13$_{19}$ 18$_{4.20}$.

<NOM CL> בְּלֹא־דַעַת נֶפֶשׁ לֹא־טוֹב *a person without knowledge is not good* Pr 19$_{2}$, בְּעֶרְכְּךָ נְפָשֹׁת לַי׳ *the persons shall be to Y. according to your valuation* Lv 27$_{2}$.

<OBJ> חיה pi. *keep alive* Ezk 13$_{19}$, שׁלח pi. *let go* Ezk 13$_{20}$, לקח *take* Gn 36$_{6}$, קנה *acquire* Lv 22$_{11}$, שׁבע hi.

satisfy Is 58$_{10}$ 4QAdmon 1.1$_1$, פוח *dishearten* Si 4$_2$, נכה hi. *strike* Nm 35$_{11.15.30}$ Dt 27$_{25}$, כרת hi. *cut off* Lv 17$_{10}$, אבד hi. *destroy* Lv 23$_{30}$, הרג *kill* Nm 31$_{19}$ 11QPsAp^a 3$_9$, מות hi. *kill* Ezk 13$_{19}$.

<CSTR> נפש אדם *person (consisting) of a human being* 4QSD 7.1$_7$ CD 11$_{16}$, נֶפֶשׁ רְמִיָּה *person of laxness* Pr 19$_{15}$, נַפְשׁוֹת בֵּיתוֹ *the persons of his household* Gn 36$_6$, מִכְסַת נְפָשֹׁת *number of persons* Ex 12$_4$ (Sam מִכְסוֹת *numbers of*), מִסְפַּר נַפְשֹׁתֵיכֶם *number of your persons* Ex 16$_{16}$.

מַכֵּה נֶפֶשׁ *one who strikes a person (fatally)* Nm 35$_{11.15.30}$ Jos 20$_{3.9}$, דַּם־נָפֶשׁ *blood of a person* Pr 28$_{17}$, כֶּסֶף נַפְשׁוֹת *money (in payment) of persons of* 2 K 12$_5$, כָּל־נֶפֶשׁ *each person* Ex 12$_{16}$ Lv 7$_{27}$ 17$_{12.15}$ 23$_{29.30}$ (both הַנֶּפֶשׁ) 4QAdmon 1.1$_1$ 11QT 25$_{11}$ (כול הנפש), כָּל־נַפְשׁוֹת *all the persons of* Gn 36$_6$ (unless §8d).

<APP> קִנְיָן *acquisition* Lv 22$_{11}$, מֶכֶס *tribute* Nm 31$_{28}$ (or del.), דָּוֶה *weak one* Si 4$_2$ (דווה).

<ADJ> חָסֵר *needy* Si 4$_2$, אֶחָד *one* Lv 4$_{27}$ Nm 15$_{27}$ 31$_{28}$ (אֶחָד נֶפֶשׁ; Sam אַחַת; or del. נֶפֶשׁ) 4QD^b 6$_7$, שֵׁנִי *second* perh. 6QapSamKgs 57$_3$, הַהִיא *that* Gn 17$_{14}$ Ex 12$_{15.19}$ 31$_{14}$ Lv 7$_{20.21.27}$ 19$_8$ 20$_6$ 22$_3$ Nm 5$_6$ 9$_{13}$ 15$_{30.31}$ 19$_{13.20}$ (all sixteen Qr הַהִיא; Kt ההוא) 4QpsJub^a 2.1$_1$ ([הנ]פש).

<PREP> לְ of benefit, *for*, + עשׂה ni. *be done* perh. 11QT^b 7$_{25}$; of agent, *by*, + אכל ni. *be eaten* Ex 12$_{16}$; *as*, + שׁוב hi. *restore* perh. 4Q417 1.1$_{22}$.

בְּ *upon* Nm 15$_{31}$; *against*, + נתן *give*, i.e. set, face Lv 17$_{10}$ 20$_6$, עוד hi. *testify* Nm 35$_{30}$.

עַל *upon*, + נזה hi. *sprinkle* Nm 19$_{18}$; *for, on behalf of*, + כפר pi. *make atonement* Nm 15$_{28}$; *concerning*, + אמר *say* 4QD^a 11$_2$.

<COLL> לְהַכּוֹת נֶפֶשׁ דָּם נָקִי *to strike a person fatally, (shedding) innocent blood* Dt 27$_{25}$.

8b. collectively, **persons, people,** <SUBJ> היה *be* Ex 1$_{5.5}$, בוא *come* Gn 46$_{26.27}$, בזה *despise* Is 49$_7$ (or em. בְּזֹה to בְּזוּי *one despised of*, i.e. by, persons; or em. לִבְזֹה נַפְשׁוֹ to לִבְזֹה נֶפֶשׁ *to one who despises himself**).

<NOM CL> מִכְסָם לַי׳ שְׁנַיִם וּשְׁלֹשִׁים נָפֶשׁ *their tribute for Y. was thirty-two persons* Nm 31$_{40}$, בְּנֵי יוֹסֵף ... נֶפֶשׁ שְׁנָיִם *the sons of Joseph were ... two persons* Gn 46$_{27}$, כָּל־נֶפֶשׁ אַרְבָּעָה עָשָׂר *all the persons were*, i.e. numbered, *fourteen* Gn 46$_{22}$, sim. Gn 46$_{15.25.26.27}$ Nm 31$_{35.40.46}$ Jr 52$_{30}$, כָּל־הַנֶּפֶשׁ אֲשֶׁר־בָּהּ *all the persons that were in it* Jos 10$_{28+6t}$ 11$_{11}$.

<OBJ> ילד *bear* Gn 46$_{18}$, לקח *take* Gn 12$_5$ (unless §8d) Jr 43$_6$, גלה hi. *exile* Jr 52$_{29.30}$, נתן *give* Gn 14$_{21}$, עשׂה *make*, i.e. acquire Gn 12$_5$ (unless §8d), נוח hi. *leave* Jr 43$_6$, חרם hi. *utterly destroy* Jos 10$_{28.35.37.39}$ 11$_{11}$, נכה hi. *strike* Jos 10$_{30.32.37}$ 11$_{11}$, אכל *devour* Ezk 22$_{25}$.

<CSTR> נֶפֶשׁ אָדָם *persons (consisting) of humans* Nm 31$_{35.40.46}$ Ezk 27$_{13}$ 1 C 5$_{21}$, בָּנָיו וּבְנוֹתָיו *of his sons and daughters* Gn 46$_{15}$; בְּזוּי נֶפֶשׁ *one despised of*, i.e. by, *persons* Is 49$_7$ (if em.; see Subj.), כָּל־נֶפֶשׁ *all the persons* Gn 46$_{22.25.26}$ (הַנֶּפֶשׁ) 46$_{26.27}$ (הַנֶּפֶשׁ) Nm 31$_{35}$ Jos 10$_{28.30.32.35.37.37}$ (all five הַנֶּפֶשׁ) 10$_{39}$ 11$_{11}$ Jr 43$_6$ (both הַנֶּפֶשׁ) 52$_{30}$, *all the persons of* Gn 46$_{15}$.

<APP> יצא ptc. *one who goes out* of thigh, i.e. offspring Gn 46$_{26}$ Ex 1$_5$, אֵלֶּה *these* Gn 46$_{18}$.

<PREP> בְּ of essence, *as, consisting of*, + ירד *go down* Dt 10$_{22}$.

בְּ of price, *(in exchange) for*, + נתן *give* Ezk 27$_{13}$.

<COLL> רְכוּשׁ || נֶפֶשׁ *possessions* Gn 12$_5$ 14$_{21}$, גּוֹי *nation* Is 49$_7$.

שֵׁשׁ עֶשְׂרֵה נָפֶשׁ *sixteen persons* Gn 46$_{18}$, שְׁנַיִם וּשְׁלֹשִׁים נָפֶשׁ *thirty-two persons* Nm 31$_{40}$, שִׁבְעִים נֶפֶשׁ seventy persons Ex 1$_5$ (נָפֶשׁ) Dt 10$_{22}$, נֶפֶשׁ שֶׁבַע מֵאוֹת אַרְבָּעִים וַחֲמִשָּׁה *seven hundred and forty-five persons* Jr 52$_{30}$, נֶפֶשׁ שְׁמֹנֶה מֵאוֹת וּשְׁלֹשִׁים וּשְׁנָיִם *eight hundred and thirty-two persons* Jr 52$_{29}$, נֶפֶשׁ אָדָם מֵאָה אָלֶף *a hundred thousand persons* 1 C 5$_{21}$.

8c. perh. **deceased person, (dead) body,*** <CSTR> נֶפֶשׁ אָדָם *dead body of a human being* Nm 9$_{6.7}$ 19$_{11.13}$ (הָאָדָם) 4QD^d 8.2$_4$ 4QNidd 4$_5$, נֶפֶשׁ מֵת *body of the dead* Nm 6$_6$, נַפְשׁוֹת *bodies of* Lv 21$_{11}$ 11QT 16$_4$ (נפשות [מת]); טְמֵא־נֶפֶשׁ *impure one of*, i.e. made unclean by, *a body* Lv 22$_4$ Hb 2$_{13}$, טמאת הנפש *impurity of the body* 4QTohB^c 1$_8$, כָּל־נֶפֶשׁ *any body of* Nm 19$_{11}$, כָּל־נַפְשׁוֹת *all the bodies of* Lv 21$_{11}$ 11QT 16$_4$ ([כול נפשות]).

<APP> מֵת *dead one* Nm 19$_{13}$.

<PREP> לְ *for (the sake of), on account of* Nm 5$_2$, + נתן *give*, i.e. place, cuttings in flesh Lv 19$_{28}$, טמא *be impure* Nm 9$_{6.7.10}$ 4QD^d 8.2$_4$ (יטמאו ל[נפש]) 4QTohA 1.1$_9$ 11QT 45$_{17}$, htp. *defile oneself* Lv 21$_1$; *concerning* 4QNidd 4$_5$; *namely, that is to say* Nm 19$_{11}$.

בְּ introducing object, + נגע *touch* Nm 19$_{13}$.

עַל *to*, + בוא *come* Lv 21$_{11}$ Nm 6$_6$ 11QT 16$_4$ ([על כול] [נפשות ... יבוא]); *on account of, for (the sake of)*, + חטא *sin* Nm 6$_{11}$, נתן *give*, i.e. place, incision 11QT 48$_9$.

8d. perh. specif. **slave,*** <OBJ> לקח *take* Gn 12$_5$ (unless §8b) 36$_6$ (unless §8b), עשׂה *make*, i.e. acquire Gn 12$_5$ (unless §8b), חשׂך *withhold* Ps 78$_{50}$ (unless §6). <CSTR> כָּל־נַפְשׁוֹת *all the persons of* Gn 36$_6$ (unless §8a).

9a. נֶפֶשׁ with pronominal suffix, as personal pronoun, (1) נַפְשִׁי **I, me** (Gn 12$_{13}$ 19$_{20}$ 27$_{4.25}$ 19$_{19}$ Nm 23$_{10}$ Jg 16$_{30}$ 1 K 20$_{32}$ Jr 4$_{19}$ 9$_8$ 18$_{20}$ Ezk 4$_{14}$ Ps 3$_3$ 7$_{3.6}$ 11$_1$ 16$_{10}$ 30$_4$ 35$_{3.7.12}$ 41$_5$ 57$_{2.5}$ 66$_{16}$ 69$_{18}$ 88$_{15}$ 94$_{17}$ 109$_{20}$ 119$_{129.167.175}$ 120$_{2.6}$ 141$_8$ 142$_{5.8}$ 143$_{3.11}$ perh. Jb 6$_7$ 7$_{15}$ 16$_4$ Ec 7$_{28}$ Lm 3$_{24.51}$ Si 16$_{17}$ 1QH 10$_{20.31}$ 4QapPs^b 33$_{10}$ GnzPs 2$_1$), in ref. to Y. (Jr 5$_{9.29}$), (2) נַפְשְׁךָ, etc., **you** (Gn 27$_{19.31}$ 1 S 1$_{26}$ 17$_{55}$ 20$_{3.4}$ 25$_{26}$ 2 S 11$_{11}$ 14$_{19}$ 1 K 20$_{31}$ 2 K 2$_{2.4.6}$ 4$_{30}$ Is 43$_4$ Jr 38$_{17.20}$ Si 34$_{15}$ 4QparaKings 9$_7$ [נפש[כה]]), in ref. to Y. (1QH 12$_{21}$), (3) נַפְשֵׁךְ **you** fem. (Is 51$_{23}$), (4) נַפְשׁוֹ **he** (Ps 25$_{13}$ Si 20$_{13}$), (5) נַפְשֵׁנוּ **we, us** (Ps 66$_9$ 124$_7$), (6) נַפְשְׁכֶם **you** masc. pl. (Jb 16$_4$ Is 55$_3$), (8) נַפְשָׁם **they, them** (Is 3$_9$ 46$_2$ Ps 105$_{15}$ Jb 36$_{14}$ 1Q37 1$_2$).

<SUBJ> חיה *live* Gn 12$_{13}$ 19$_{20}$ 1 K 20$_{32}$ Is 55$_3$ Jr 38$_{17.20}$ Ps 119$_{175}$, ראה *see* 4QapPs^b 33$_{10}$, אמר *say* 1 S 20$_4$ Lm 3$_{24}$, ברך pi. *bless* Gn 27$_{4.19.25.31}$, הלל pi. *praise* Ps 119$_{175}$, שׁמע *hear* Jr 4$_{19}$, בחר *choose* Jb 7$_{15}$ (unless §2), בטח *trust* GnzPs 2$_1$, בקשׁ pi. *seek* Ec 7$_{28}$, נגע *touch* Jb 6$_7$ (unless §1 or §3), הלך *go* Is 46$_2$, בוא *come* Gn 49$_6$, מלט ni. *escape* Ps 124$_7$ (unless §1 or §2), חסה *seek refuge* Ps 57$_2$, לין *lodge* Ps 25$_{13}$, שׁכן *dwell* Ps 94$_{17}$ 120$_6$, נצר *keep* Ps 119$_{129}$, שׁמר *keep* 119$_{167}$, טמא pu. *be defiled* Ezk 4$_{14}$, מות *die* Nm 23$_{10}$ Jg 16$_{30}$ Jb 36$_{14}$, נקם htp. *avenge oneself* Jr 5$_{9.29}$ 9$_8$.

<NOM CL> לוּ־יֵשׁ נַפְשְׁכֶם *if you were* Jb 16$_4$, חֵי נַפְשְׁךָ *(as) you are alive* 1 S 1$_{26}$ 17$_{55}$ 20$_3$ 25$_{26}$ 2 S 11$_{11}$ 14$_{19}$ 2 K 2$_{2.4.6}$ 4$_{30}$ 4QparaKings 9$_7$ ([חי נפש[כה]), מה נפשי *what am I?* Si 16$_{17}$, חכם במעט דבר נפשו *(as for) a wise person, he is with smallness of speech*, i.e. few words Si 20$_{13}$.

<OBJ> חיה hi. *let live* Gn 19$_{19}$ 1 K 20$_{31}$, רפא *heal* Ps 41$_5$, יצא hi. *bring out* Ps 142$_8$ 143$_{11}$, רדף *pursue* Ps 7$_6$ 143$_3$, נצל hi. *deliver* Ps 120$_2$, עלה hi. *bring up* Ps 30$_4$, טרף *tear* Ps 7$_3$ (unless §2), עזב *abandon* Ps 16$_{10}$, זנח *reject* Ps 88$_{15}$, ערה pi. *lay bare* Ps 141$_8$, שׂים *place* Ps 66$_9$ 1QH 10$_{20}$.

<PREP> לְ of direction, *to*, + אמר *say* Is 51$_{23}$ Ps 11$_1$ 35$_3$, גמל *repay* 1Q37 1$_2$; of benefit, *to, for* Is 3$_9$ (אוֹי לְנַפְשָׁם *woe to them*), + חפר *dig* Ps 35$_7$, כרה *dig* pit Jr 18$_{20}$, עשׂה *do* Ps 66$_{16}$; reflexive, *for (oneself)*, + שׂבע *be sated* Ps 123$_4$; of possession, *of, (belonging) to* Ps 35$_{12}$; *concerning*, + אמר *say* Ps 3$_3$; introducing object, + דרשׁ *care for* Ps 142$_5$, עלל po. *deal severely with* Lm 3$_{51}$.

בְּ *against*, + שׁלח pi. *send* Ps 106$_{15}$ (unless §1 or §10).

כְּ *as* Si 34$_{15}$ 1QH 12$_{21}$.

אֶל *to*, + קרב *draw near* Ps 69$_{18}$.

עַל *over*, + עמד *stand* 1QH 10$_{31}$ ([עמ]דה); *against*, + דבר pi. *speak* Ps 109$_{20}$.

תַּחַת *in place of* Jb 16$_4$, + נתן *give* Is 43$_4$.

<COLL> נֶפֶשׁ || כָּבוֹד *soul* Gn 49$_6$, חַיָּה *life* Ps 143$_3$ (+) Jb 36$_{14}$; + רֶגֶל *foot* Ps 66$_9$.

נַפְשִׁי בְּתוֹךְ לְבָאִם אֶשְׁכְּבָה *as for me, I lie down among lions* Ps 57$_5$.

9b. as reflexive pronoun, **oneself,** without pronominal suffix (Nm 30$_{14}$ Si 7$_{21}$ 10$_{25}$ 34$_2$ 11QT 54$_2$ [[נפש]]); with pronominal suffixes, (1) נַפְשִׁי **myself** (Ps 35$_{13}$ Jb 9$_{21}$ Ec 4$_8$ 1QH 6$_{17}$ 4QHymnSap 1.1$_1$), (2) נַפְשְׁךָ, etc., **yourself** (Dt 4$_9$ Is 58$_{10}$ Si 3$_{18}$ 4$_{7.20.22.27}$ 9$_{2.6}$ 10$_{28}$ 14$_{11.16}$ 30$_{21.23}$ 35$_{23}$ 37$_{2.8}$ 4Q416 2.2$_{15.17}$), (3) נַפְשֵׁךְ **yourself** (Est 4$_{13}$), (4) נַפְשׁוֹ, etc., **himself** (Ex 30$_{12}$ Nm 30$_3$ 1 S 18$_{1.3}$ Is 44$_{20}$ 49$_7$ [if em.; see §8b Subj.] 58$_5$ Ps 22$_{30}$ 49$_{19}$ Jb 18$_4$ 32$_2$ Pr 6$_{32}$ 8$_{36}$ 11$_{17}$ 15$_{32}$ 19$_8$ 21$_{23}$ [unless §10] Ec 2$_{24}$ Si 7$_{20}$ 10$_{29.29}$ 14$_{4.5.6}$ 20$_{22}$ 35$_{24}$ 37$_{8.19.22}$ 1QS 5$_{8.10}$ 7$_{3.9}$ 4QOrd^a 1.2$_6$ 4QS^d 1$_6$ 4QBer^c 1$_{4.5}$ [[נ]פשו]] 11QT 39$_8$ 53$_{15}$ Mur 24 C$_{19}$ D$_{20}$ MurEpBeth-Mashiko$_{10}$ 5/6ḤevBA 44$_{27.28.29.30}$ CD 12$_{11}$ 16$_1$ [appar. error for נפשו *himself* = 4QD^f 4.2$_4$] 16$_{4.7.9}$), in ref. to Y. (Jr 51$_{14}$ Am 6$_8$). (5) נַפְשָׁהּ **herself** (Nm 30$_{5+8t}$ Jr 3$_{11}$ 11QT 53$_{16.18.19.21}$ 54$_4$ Mur 29 verso$_3$), (6) נַפְשֵׁינוּ, etc., **ourselves** (Nm 31$_{50}$ Is 58$_3$ Jr 26$_{19}$ 1QLitPr 1$_2$ [[נפ[שותינו]]), (7) נַפְשְׁכֶם, etc., **yourselves** (Ex 30$_{15.16}$ Lv 11$_{43.44}$ 16$_{29.31}$ 17$_{11}$ 20$_{25}$ 23$_{27.32}$ Nm 29$_7$ Dt 4$_{15}$ Jos 23$_{11}$ Jr 6$_{16}$ 17$_{21}$ 37$_9$ 44$_7$ 1QDM 2$_9$), (8) נַפְשָׁם, etc., **themselves** (Is 47$_{14}$ Est 9$_{31}$ 11QT 15$_{14}$ 51$_9$).

<OBJ> חיה pi. *keep alive* Ps 22$_{30}$, שׁמר *keep* Dt 4$_9$ Pr

21$_{23}$ (unless §10) Si 35$_{23.23.24}$ 37$_{8}$, מנע *hold back* Si 14$_{4}$, נצל hi. *deliver* Is 44$_{20}$ 47$_{14}$, פוק hi. *bring out* Is 58$_{10}$ (unless §10), ראה hi. *show* Ec 2$_{24}$, ברך pi. *bless* Ps 49$_{19}$, פתה pi. *persuade* Si 30$_{23}$, חשב *think about* Si 37$_{8(Bmg)}$, ידע *be concerned about* Jb 9$_{21}$, אהב *love* Pr 19$_{8}$, כבד pi. *honour* Si 10$_{28}$, שׁרת pi. *serve* Si 14$_{11}$, צדק pi. *justify* Jr 3$_{11}$ Jb 32$_{2}$, רבה hi. *make great* 4Q416 2.2$_{17}$ ([תר]בה), יצע hi. *extend* Si 4$_{27}$, נתן *give* Si 7$_{20}$ 9$_{6}$ 30$_{21}$, קנא hi. *sell* Si 9$_{2}$, גמל *deal generously with* Pr 11$_{17}$, פנק pi. *pamper* Si 14$_{16}$.

חסר pi. *cause to lack* Ec 4$_{8}$ (unless §3), ירשׁ hi. *dispossess* Si 20$_{22}$, מעט pi. *make small* Si 3$_{18(A)}$, שׁפל hi. *abase* Si 3$_{18(C)}$ 4Q416 2.2$_{15}$, נשׁא hi. *deceive* Jr 37$_{9}$, מאס *despise* Pr 15$_{32}$, קלה hi. *dishonour* Si 10$_{29}$, בזה *despise* Is 49$_{7}$ (if em.; see §8b Subj.), רשׁע hi. *condemn* Si 10$_{29}$, טמא pi. *make impure* Lv 11$_{44}$, שׁקץ pi. *make abominable* Lv 11$_{43}$ 20$_{25}$ 11QT 51$_{9}$ CD 12$_{11}$, ענה pi. *afflict* Lv 16$_{29.31}$ 23$_{27.32}$ Nm 29$_{7}$ 30$_{14}$ Is 58$_{3.5}$ Ps 35$_{13}$ 1QLitPr 1$_{2}$ (ענינו נפ[שותינו]) 11QT 25$_{11}$ 54$_{2}$ ([לענות נפש]), חמס *treat violently* Pr 8$_{36}$, טרף *tear* Jb 18$_{4}$, אבד pi. *destroy* Si 20$_{22}$, שׁחת hi. *destroy* Pr 6$_{32}$.

<CSTR> כֹּפֶר נַפְשׁוֹ *ransom of*, i.e. for, *himself* Ex 30$_{12}$ 4QOrd^{a} 1.2$_{6}$ 11QT 39$_{8}$ ([כופר]), אִסַּר נַפְשָׁהּ *vow of herself* Nm 30$_{13}$, אַהֲבַת נַפְשׁוֹ *love of himself*, i.e. as he loved himself 1 S 20$_{17}$.

<PREP> לְ of direction, *to(wards)*, + יאל ni. *foolish* Si 37$_{19(Bmg, D)}$; of benefit, *to, for* Si 14$_{5.6}$ 37$_{24}$, + מצא *find* Jr 6$_{16}$, שׁמר ni. *take heed* Dt 4$_{15}$ Jos 23$_{11}$ 1QDM 2$_{9}$ ([השׁ]מרו), חכם ni. *show oneself to be wise* Si 37$_{22}$, נקם *take vengeance* 1QS 7$_{9}$ 4QBer^{c} 1$_{4}$ (יקום ל[נפשו]); *concerning*, + חשׁב *think* Si 37$_{8(B)}$; *against*, + נשׂא *lift* face, i.e. show partiality Si 4$_{22(C)}$; introducing object, + אהב hi. *endear* Si 4$_{7}$, גאל *redeem* Si 37$_{19(B, C)}$, ישׁע hi. *save*, i.e. disregard the law 4QBer^{c} 1$_{5}$ ([לנ]פשו]).

בְּ of place, *within*, + דמה pi. *think* Est 4$_{13}$; of instrument, *by (means of) through*, + שׁבע ni. *swear* Jr 51$_{14}$ Am 6$_{8}$; *in respect of, for (the sake of)*, + שׁמר ni. *take heed* Jr 17$_{21}$.

כְּ *as* Si 37$_{2}$, + אהב *love* 1 S 18$_{1.3}$ Si 7$_{21(C)}$ 34$_{2}$, חבב pi. *love* Si 7$_{21(A)}$ 10$_{25(B)}$ 4QHymnSap 1.1$_{1}$ (חו[בב]).

אֶל *to, against*, + עשׂה *do* Jr 44$_{7}$; *(because) of*, + בושׁ *be ashamed* Si 4$_{20}$.

עַל *upon*, + אסר *bind* oath, vow Nm 30$_{3+9t}$ 11QT 53$_{15.16.18.19.21}$ 54$_{4}$, קום pi. *impose (an obligation)* Est 9$_{31}$, hi. 1QH 6$_{17}$ 1QS 5$_{8.10}$ 4QS^{d} 1$_{6}$ (יק[י]ם) CD 16$_{1.4.7}$ (all three יָקוּם; appar. error for יקים) 16$_{9}$ (יק[י]ם).

עַל *for, on behalf of*, + כפר pi. *make atonement* Ex 30$_{15.16}$ Lv 17$_{11}$ Nm 31$_{50}$, מלא pi. *complete* 11QT 15$_{14}$; in legal documents, *on behalf of* oneself, i.e. in person Mur 24 C$_{19}$ D$_{20}$ ([ע]ל) Mur 29 verso$_{3}$ MurEpBeth-Mashiko$_{10}$ 5/6ḤevBA 44$_{27.28.29.30}$.

עַל *against*, + עשׂה *do* Jr 26$_{19}$, נשׂא *lift* face, i.e. show partiality Si 4$_{22(A)}$; *to*, + בדל ho. *be separated*, i.e. placed in solitary confinement 1QS 7$_{3}$.

<COLL> נֶפֶשׁ ‖ שְׁאֵר *flesh*, i.e. self Pr 11$_{17}$, זֶרַע *offspring* Est 9$_{31}$, לֵב *heart* Si 30$_{23}$; + חַיִּים *life* Jb 9$_{21}$.

9c. as possessive pronoun, (1) נַפְשִׁי **my**, <CSTR> שֹׂטְנֵי נַפְשִׁי *my accusers* Ps 71$_{13}$, שנאי נפשי *my enemies* 4QapPs^{b} 31$_{5}$, צֹרְרֵי נַפְשִׁי *my adversaries* Ps 143$_{12}$, חַטַּאת נַפְשִׁי *my (own) sin* Mc 6$_{7}$, רִיבֵי נַפְשִׁי *my causes* Lm 3$_{58}$ (+ חַיִּים *life*).

(2) נַפְשׁוֹ **his**, <CSTR> שֹׁפְטֵי נַפְשׁוֹ *his judges*, i.e. those who condemn him Ps 109$_{31}$, שׂוֹנֵא נַפְשׁוֹ *his (own) enemy* Pr 29$_{24}$, שונאי נפשו *his enemies* GnzPs 1$_{24}$, מָרַּת נַפְשׁוֹ *its (own) bitterness* Pr 14$_{10}$, משפט נפשו *his judgment* 4QMyst^{b} 7$_{3}$.

10. sustenance,* <OBJ> פוק hi. *bring out* Is 58$_{10}$ (unless §9b or נֶפֶשׁ II *abundance*), שׁמר *keep* Pr 21$_{23}$ (unless §9b). <PREP> לְ of benefit, *for* Ho 9$_{4}$, + שׁאל *ask for* food Ps 78$_{18}$ (unless §3); בְּ *against*, + שׁלח pi. *send* Ps 106$_{15}$ (unless §9a).

11. perfume,* <CSTR> עֲצַת־נֶפֶשׁ *forest of perfume* Pr 27$_{9}$ (unless §4 or נֶפֶשׁ III *odour*).

12. sepulchre, (funerary) monument, <CSTR> נפש בן רבה *sepulchre of Ben Rabbah* 3QTr 1$_{5}$. <PREP> בְּ of place, *in* 3QTr 1$_{5}$.

Also 1QH 11$_{6}$ 1QDM 4$_{7}$ 6QapSamKgs 29$_{1}$ 4QpIsa^{c} 4.1$_{12}$ 14$_{7}$ 4QWiles 2$_{1}$ 4Q185 1.2$_{1}$ ([נ]פשכם) 4QHalakhah^{a} 8$_{3}$ (נפש[ו]) 4QMyst^{a} 23$_{4}$ 4QparaKings 144$_{2}$ 4QpsEzek^{a} 10.1$_{6}$ 4QapJerB 6$_{1}$ 4QpsEzek^{e} 9$_{2}$ 4QBapt 10$_{1}$ ([נ]פ[ש]) 4Q418 12$_{2}$ ([נ]פשכה) 55$_{1}$ 237$_{2}$ 4Q423 8$_{1}$ 4QsapHymnA 11$_{4}$ ([נ]פשו) 4QBark^{d} 11$_{1}$ ([נפ]שי) 4QPrayer^{e} 1$_{6}$ 4QSap^{b} 5$_{6}$ 4QDibHam^{b} 120$_{1}$ 4QRitPur 1.12$_{3}$ 76$_{3}$ 4QBéat 14.1$_{10}$ ([נפ]שכה) 14.1$_{13}$ 6QfrProph 1$_{1}$.

<SYN> §1 פֶּה *mouth*, עַיִן *eye*, עֶצֶם *bone*; §3 הַוָּה *desire*, מֵעֶה *stomach*, חַיָּה *life*; §4 לֵבָב *heart*, לֵב *heart*, רוּחַ *spirit*, בָּשָׂר *flesh*, עַיִן *eye*, בֶּטֶן *abdomen*, קֶרֶב *inward part*, מְאֹד *might*; §5 גַּרְגֶּרֶת *throat* Pr 3$_{22}$; §6 חַיִּים *life*, חַיָּה *life*, רוּחַ *breath*, בָּשָׂר *flesh*, דָּם *blood*, עַיִן *eye*, שֵׁן *tooth*, רֶגֶל *foot*, עַם *people*, יָחִיד *only one*; §8b רְכוּשׁ *possessions*, גּוֹי *nation*; §9a כָּבוֹד *soul*, חַיָּה *life*; §9b שְׁאֵר *flesh*, זֶרַע *offspring*, לֵב *heart*.

<ANT> §5 בָּשָׂר *flesh*.*

⇒ נפשׁ *breathe*.

*נֶפֶשׁ II 2 n.f. **abundance** (unless נֶפֶשׁ I *soul*), <OBJ> פוק hi. *bring out* Is 58$_{10}$, צוד *hunt*, i.e. seek Pr 6$_{26}$. <ADJ> יָקָר *precious* Pr 6$_{26}$.

*נֶפֶשׁ III 2 n.[m.] **perfume** (unless נֶפֶשׁ I *soul*)—נֶפֶשׁ—**perfume, odour,** <CSTR> עֲצַת־נֶפֶשׁ *tree of perfume*, i.e. odoriferous tree Pr 27$_9$, בָּתֵּי הַנֶּפֶשׁ *houses*, i.e. boxes, *of perfume* Is 3$_{20}$.

[נֶפֶת] 1 n.f. **height**—נֶפֶת—perh. in ref. to the height of Dor, <NOM CL> שְׁלֹשֶׁת הַנָּפֶת perh. *the third is the height* Jos 17$_{11}$.

⇒ נוף V *raise*.

נֹפֶת 6.0.1 n.m. **flowing honey**—cstr. נֹפֶת—<NOM CL> נֹפֶת מָתוֹק עַל־חִכֶּךָ *flowing honey is sweet upon your palate* Pr 24$_{13}$. <OBJ> נטף *drip* Pr 5$_3$ Ca 4$_{11}$, בוס *trample* Pr 27$_7$. <CSTR> נֹפֶת צוּפִים *flowing honey of*, i.e. from, *the comb* Ps 19$_{11}$; פלגי נפת *streams of flowing honey* Ps 119$_{129}$(11QPs^a) (MT פְּלָאוֹת *wonderful*). <PREP> מִן of comparison, *(more) than* Ps 19$_{11}$, + מתק *be sweet* 4QapJoseph^b 3$_5$ ([מת]קו). <COLL> דְּבַשׁ || נֹפֶת *honey* Ps 19$_{11}$; + דְּבַשׁ Pr 24$_{13}$ Ca 4$_{11}$, חָלָב *milk* Ca 4$_{11}$, יַיִן *wine* 4QapJoseph^b 3$_5$.

<SYN> דְּבַשׁ *honey*.*

⇒ נוף II *sparkle*.

נֶפְתּוֹחַ 2 pl.n. **Nephtoah,** on border of Judah and Benjamin, perh. ʿĒn Lifta, 4 km NW of Jerusalem, <CSTR> מֵי נֶפְתּוֹחַ *waters of Nephtoah* (unless *spring of Merneptah*) Jos 15$_9$ 18$_{15}$.*

[נַפְתּוּלִים] 1 n.[m.]pl. **wrestlings**—pl. cstr. נַפְתּוּלֵי—<CSTR> נַפְתּוּלֵי אֱלֹהִים *wrestlings of God*, i.e. mighty wrestlings Gn 30$_8$. <COLL> נַפְתּוּלֵי אֱלֹהִים נִפְתַּלְתִּי *I have wrestled with wrestlings of God* Gn 30$_8$.

⇒ פתל *twist*.

[נַפְתֻּחִי] 2 gent. **Naphtuhite**—pl. נַפְתֻּחִים—perh. **belonging to Ptah,** deity of the Egyptian city Memphis,* <OBJ> ילד *beget* Gn 10$_{13}$||1 C 1$_{11}$.*

נַפְתָּלִי 51.0.7 pr.n.m. **Naphtali, 1.** second son of Jacob and Bilhah, <SUBJ> יצא *go out* 4QJub^h 3$_5$ ([ויצא]). <NOM CL> בְּנֵי בִלְהָה ... נַפְתָּלִי *the sons of Bilhah were ... Naphtali* Gn 35$_{25}$, אֵלֶּה שְׁמוֹת בְּנֵי יִשְׂרָאֵל ... נַפְתָּלִי *these are the names of the sons of Israel: ... Naphtali* Ex 1$_4$, sim. 1 C 2$_2$. <OBJ> קרא *call* Gn 30$_8$. <CSTR> בְּנֵי נַפְתָּלִי *sons of Naphtali* Gn 46$_{24}$.

2. usu. tribe with §1 as eponymous ancestor, with its assoc. territory, <SUBJ> היה *be* 11QT^b 6$_{15}$ ([והיו]), עמד *stand* Dt 27$_{13}$, ישׁב *dwell* Jg 1$_{33}$, ירשׁ *possess* Dt 33$_{23}$, hi. *dispossess* Jg 1$_{33}$, קרב hi. *bring near*, i.e. offer 11QT^b 6$_{15}$ ([המקריבים]).

<NOM CL> נַפְתָּלִי אַיָּלָה *Naphtali is a hind* Gn 49$_{21}$ (or em. אֵילָה *terebinth*), זְבֻלוּן עַם ... וְנַפְתָּלִי *Zebulun is a people ... Naphtali too* Jg 5$_{18}$, נפתלי ... לצפון *Naphtali shall be ... to the north* 11QT 39$_{13}$, עַל גְּבוּל אָשֵׁר ... נַפְתָּלִי *on the border of Asher was ... Naphtali* Ezk 48$_3$.

<OBJ> ראה hi. *show* Dt 33$_{23}$, זעק hi. *call together* Jg 4$_{10}$.

<CSTR> מַטֵּה נַפְתָּלִי *tribe of Naphtali* Nm 1$_{43}$ 2$_{29}$ 13$_{14}$ Jos 21$_{6.32}$ 1 K 7$_{14}$ 1 C 6$_{47.61}$, מִשְׁפְּחֹת *clans of* Nm 26$_{50}$, בְּנֵי *sons of* Nm 1$_{42}$ 2$_{29}$ 7$_{78}$ 10$_{27}$ 26$_{48}$ 34$_{28}$ Jos 19$_{32.32}$ Jg 4$_6$ 1 C 7$_{13}$ 11QT 45$_{04}$ ([בני נפתלי]), שָׂרֵי *princes of* Ps 68$_{28}$, שַׁעַר *gate of* Ezk 48$_{34}$ 4Q365a 2.2$_{3.3}$ 11QT 41$_{9.9}$ 45$_{03.04}$ (both [שער נפתלי]), עָרֵי *cities of* 2 C 16$_4$, גְּבוּל *border of* Ezk 48$_4$, הַר *hill-country of* Jos 20$_7$, אֶרֶץ *land of* Dt 34$_{2(ms)}$ 1 K 15$_{20}$ 2 K 15$_{29}$ Is 8$_{23}$ (אַרְצָה), [עולת נפתלי] *burnt offering of Naphtali* 11QT 25$_{01}$, כָּל־נַפְתָּלִי *all Naphtali* Dt 34$_2$.

<APP> אֶרֶץ *land* Dt 33$_{23}$, אֶחָד *one (tribe)* Ezk 48$_3$.

<ADJ> שְׂבַע *satisfied* Dt 33$_{23}$, מָלֵא *full* Dt 33$_{23}$.

<PREP> לְ of possession, *of, (belonging) to* Nm 1$_{15}$

1 C 27$_{19}$; *concerning*, + אמר *say* Dt 33$_{23}$; בְּ of place, *in(to), through* 1 K 4$_{15}$, + שׁלח *send* Jg 6$_{35}$; מִן of direction, *from*, + זעק ni. *be called together* Jg 7$_{23}$; partitive, *(some of), from among* 1 C 12$_{35}$; עַד *as far as* 1 C 12$_{41}$ 2 C 34$_{6}$.

<COLL> קֶדֶשׁ נַפְתָּלִי *Kedesh (in) Naphtali* Jg 4$_{6}$.

⇒ (?) פתל *twist*.

[נֵץ] I $_{1.2.1}$ n.f. **blossom** —sf. נִצָּהּ—of vine, <SUBJ> עלה *go up* Gn 40$_{10}$ (or em. נִצָּה *blossom* or נִצָּתָהּ *its blossom*), גרע *diminish* Si 51$_{15(11QPs^a)}$. <PREP> כְּ *as* Si 50$_{8}$ (appar. כנצפענפי is an error for כנץ בענפים *as blossom on the branches*), + נבל *wither* 1QH 18$_{32}$.

⇒ נצץ *sparkle*; cf. נִצָּה *blossom*, נִצָּץ *blossom*.

נֵץ II $_{3}$ n.m. **hawk**, bird of prey prohibited as food, <SUBJ> אכל ni. *be eaten* Lv 11$_{16}$, אבר hi. *fly* Jb 39$_{26}$, פרשׂ *spread* wings to the south, in migration Jb 39$_{26}$. <OBJ> אכל *eat* Dt 14$_{15}$, שׁקץ pi. *despise* Lv 11$_{14}$. <COLL> נֵץ לְמִינָהּ *the hawk of any kind* Lv 11$_{16}$||Dt 14$_{15}$.*

⇒ cf. נִצָּה II *hawk*.

נצא $_{1}$ vb. **fly—Qal** $_{1}$ Inf. abs. נָצֹא—**fly away,** <SUBJ> Moab Jr 48$_{9}$ (נָצֹא תֵּצֵא *flying away, it shall go out*; or em. נָצֹה תִּצֶּה *it shall go to utter ruin*).

⇒ cf. נצה III *fly*.

נצב I $_{75.0.7}$ vb. **stand—Qal** $_{0.0.1}$ Ptc. pass. Q נצובים—pass. **be stood, positioned,** 4QapJerB 20$_{4}$.

Ni. $_{51.0.2}$ Pf. נִצְּבָה (נִצָּבָה), נִצְּבוּ; + waw וְנִצַּבְתָּ, וְנִצְּבוּ; ptc. נִצָּב, נִצָּבָה (נִצֶּבֶת), נִצָּבִים, נִצָּבוֹת—**1. stand, position oneself, stand upright** (Gn 37$_{7}$ Ex 15$_{8}$), for warfare (1 S 17$_{16}$ perh. Am 7$_{7}$),* **present oneself** (Ex 34$_{2}$), **be set over,** i.e. in charge of (Ru 2$_{5.6}$), **be set, stand firm** (Ps 119$_{89}$ Lm 2$_{4}$ [or em.; see Subj.]); perh. **be healthy** (Zc 11$_{16}$; but prob. נצב II); perh. נִצָּב **in a standing position,** as a choral direction,* or del. as vertical dittograph* (Ps 39$_{6}$).

<SUBJ> Y. Gn 28$_{13}$ Is 3$_{13}$ Am 7$_{7}$ 9$_{1}$ Ps 82$_{1}$=11QMelch 2$_{10}$ ([נ]צב), מַלְאָךְ *angel* Nm 22$_{23.31.34}$, Edomite 1 S 22$_{9}$, Israelites Dt 29$_{9}$, עַם *people* Ex 18$_{14}$ 33$_{8}$, שֵׁבֶט *tribe* Dt 29$_{9}$ (or em. רָאשֵׁיכֶם שִׁבְטֵיכֶם *your heads, your tribes* to רָאשֵׁי שִׁבְטֵיכֶם *the heads of your tribes*), Aaron Ex 5$_{20}$, Abiram Nm 16$_{27}$, Balak Nm 23$_{6.17}$, Dathan Nm 16$_{27}$, Doeg 1 S 22$_{9}$, Moses Ex 5$_{20}$ 7$_{15}$ 17$_{9}$ 33$_{21}$ 34$_{2}$, אָדָם *human being* Ps 39$_{6}$ (unless נצב III *vanish* or נְצָב II *image*), אִישׁ *man* Gn 18$_{2}$ Ex 33$_{8}$ Dt 29$_{9}$ Jg 18$_{16}$, אִשָּׁה *woman, wife* Nm 16$_{27}$ 1 S 1$_{26}$, בֵּן *son* Nm 16$_{27}$, טַף *infant* Nm 16$_{27}$, נַעַר *lad* Ru 2$_{5.6}$, עֶבֶד *servant* Gn 24$_{13.43}$ 1 S 22$_{6.7}$ 2 S 13$_{31}$, כֹּהֵן *priest* Jg 18$_{16}$.

שַׂר *prince* Nm 23$_{6}$, שֵׁגָל *(queen-)consort* Ps 45$_{10}$, שֹׁטֵר *officer* Dt 29$_{9}$, רָץ *guard* 1 S 22$_{17}$, זָקֵן *elder* Dt 29$_{9}$, ראשׁ *head* Dt 29$_{9}$, appar. יָמִין *right hand* Lm 2$_{4}$ (or em. נִצָּב יְמִינוֹ *his right hand is set* to חֵץ בִּימִינוֹ *an arrow is in his right hand*), אַרְיֵה (of warrior) *lion* Is 21$_{8}$ (or em. with 1QIsa^{a} הָרֹאֶה *the lookout*), אֲלֻמָּה *sheaf* Gn 37$_{7}$, נֹזְלִים *floods* Ex 15$_{8}$ (or em. נִצְּבוּ *they swelled up*, i.e. צבה I ni.*), מַעֲרָכָה *battle-line* 4QM^{a} 1$_{11}$, דָּבָר *word* Ps 119$_{89}$, חָכְמָה *wisdom* Pr 8$_{2}$, תְּבוּנָה *understanding* Pr 8$_{2}$; subj. not specified, Gn 45$_{1}$ 1 S 4$_{20}$ perh. Zc 11$_{16}$ (but prob. נצב II).

<PREP> לְ of direction, *to*, + Y. Ex 34$_{2}$, עוֹלָם *everlastingness*, i.e. for ever Ps 119$_{89}$; of place, *at*, + יָמִין *right hand* Ps 45$_{10}$.

בְּ of place, *in*, + עֵדָה *assembly* Ps 82$_{1}$=11QMelch 2$_{10}$ ([נ]צב בע[דת])), דֶּרֶךְ *way* Nm 22$_{23.31.34}$, ראשׁ *top* Pr 8$_{2}$, שָׁמַיִם *heaven* Ps 119$_{89}$ (unless בְּ of comparison דְּבָרְךָ נִצָּב בַּשָּׁמָיִם *your word is more fixed than the heavens*),* זֶה *this (place)* 1 S 22$_{26}$; of accompaniment, *with, in*, + כֶּתֶם *gold* Ps 45$_{10}$.

כְּ *as*, + צַר *enemy* Lm 2$_{4}$ (or em.; see Subj.), הֶבֶל *breath* Ps 39$_{6}$ (if em.; see Coll.; unless נצב III *vanish* or נְצָב II *image*).

כְּמוֹ *as in*, + נֵד *heap* Ex 15$_{8}$.

מִן of time, *from*, + בֹּקֶר *morning* Ex 18$_{14}$.

עַל *beside*, + Abraham Gn 18$_{2}$, Jacob perh. Gn 28$_{13}$ (unless *above* ladder), Joseph Gn 45$_{1}$, Moses Ex 18$_{14}$, Saul 1 S 22$_{6.7}$, אִשָּׁה *wife* 1 S 4$_{20}$, כַּלָּה *daughter-in-law* 1 S 4$_{20}$, עֶבֶד *servant* 1 S 22$_{9}$, מֶלֶךְ *king* 1 S 22$_{17}$, עַיִן *spring* Gn 24$_{13.43}$, דֶּרֶךְ *way* Pr 8$_{2}$, חוֹמָה *wall* Am 7$_{7}$ (unless *upon*), מִזְבֵּחַ *altar* Am 9$_{1}$, עֹלָה *burnt offering* Nm 23$_{6.17}$.

עַל *upon, above*, + ראשׁ *top* of hill Ex 17$_{9}$ 34$_{2}$, צוּר *rock* Ex 33$_{21}$, סֻלָּם *ladder* perh. Gn 28$_{13}$ (unless *beside* Jacob), חוֹמָה *wall* Am 7$_{7}$ (unless *beside*); *over*, i.e. in charge of, + קֹצֵר *reaper* Ru 2$_{5.6}$; *at*, + מִשְׁמֶרֶת *watch* Is 21$_{8}$.

עִם *with, beside*, + Eli 1 S 1$_{26}$

לִפְנֵי *before*, + Y. Dt 29$_{9}$.

עַד *until*, + עֶרֶב *evening* Ex 18$_{14}$.

בֵּית *between, among*, + נְתִיבָה *path* Pr 8$_{2}$.

נצב ni. + noun without preposition, פֶּתַח *(at) the entrance* Ex 33$_{8}$ Nm 16$_{27}$ Jg 18$_{16}$.

<COLL> נצב ni. || עמד *stand* Is 3$_{13}$ 21$_{8}$; + קום *arise* Gn 37$_{7}$ Ex 33$_{8}$, ערם ni. *be piled up* Ex 15$_{8}$, קפא *congeal* Ex 15$_{8}$; + adverb or noun used adverbially, שָׁם *there* Ex 34$_{2}$, הַיּוֹם *today* Dt 29$_{9}$, לַיְלָה *night* Is 21$_{8}$; + infinitive of purpose, קרא *meet* Ex 5$_{20}$ 7$_{15}$ Nm 22$_{34}$, פלל htp. *pray* 1 S 1$_{26}$, ריב *contend* Is 3$_{13}$.

נִצָּבִים קְרֻעֵי בְגָדִים *standing by with their garments rent* 2 S 13$_{31}$, יָצְאוּ נִצָּבִים *they went out (and) were standing* Nm 16$_{27}$, כָּל־הֶבֶל כָּל־אָדָם נִצָּב *every human stands as (only) any breath* Ps 39$_{6}$ (or em. כְּהֶבֶל *as a breath*; mss lack כָּל־ *any*).

2. ptc. as noun, **a. head,** <COLL> שְׁמוּאֵל עֹמֵד נִצָּב עֲלֵיהֶם *Samuel was standing as head over them* 1 S 19$_{20}$.

b. governor, deputy, officer, <SUBJ> כול pilp. *provide for* 1 K 5$_{7}$, עדר pi. *let lack* 1 K 5$_{7}$. <NOM CL> נִצָּב מֶלֶךְ *a deputy was king* 1 K 22$_{48}$ (mss נְצִיב *deputy*), לִשְׁלֹמֹה ... נִצָּבִים *to Solomon were ... governors* 1 K 4$_{7}$. <CSTR> שָׂרֵי הַנִּצָּבִים *chiefs of the officers* 1 K 5$_{30}$ 9$_{23}$|| 2 C 8$_{10(Qr)}$ (Kt הנציבים *the officers*). <PREP> עַל *over*, i.e. in charge of 1 K 4$_{5}$. <APP> אִישׁ *man*, i.e. each 1 K 5$_{7}$. <ADJ> אֵלֶּה *these* 1 K 5$_{7}$. <COLL> שְׁנֵים־עָשָׂר נִצָּבִים עַל־כָּל־יִשְׂרָאֵל *twelve governors over all Israel* 1 K 4$_{5}$.

<SYN> §1 עמד *stand*.

Hi. 21.0.4 Pf. הִצִּיבוּ ,הִצַּבְתָּ ,הִצִּיב; impf. יַצִּיב (יַצֵּב); + waw וַיַּצֵּב (וַיַּצֶּב־ ,וַיַּצִּיבֵנִי), 2ms וַתַּצִּיבֵנִי ,וַיַּצִּבוּ; impv. הַצִּיבִי; ptc. מַצִּיב; inf. הַצִּיב—**1. set up, erect, cause to stand,** <SUBJ> Y. Ps 78$_{13}$, Bethelite 1 K 16$_{34}$, Absalom 2 S 18$_{18}$, Hadadezer 1 C 18$_{3}$, Hiel 1 K 16$_{34}$, Jacob Gn 33$_{20}$ 35$_{14.20}$, Saul 1 S 15$_{12}$, אִישׁ *man* Jos 6$_{26}$=4Q Testim$_{23}$, בֵּן *son* of Israel 2 K 17$_{10}$, בְּתוּלָה *young woman* of Israel Jr 31$_{21}$, מֶלֶךְ *king* 1 C 18$_{3}$, חָכְמוֹת *wisdom* Pr 9$_{1}$ (if em. חָצְבָה *she has hewn out* to הִצִּיבָה *she has set up*); subj. not specified, 2 S 18$_{17}$ 4QTestim$_{26}$ (ויצ[יבו]).

<OBJ> יָד *monument* 1 S 15$_{12}$ 1 C 18$_{3}$, גַּל *heap* of stones 2 S 18$_{17}$, מִזְבֵּחַ *altar* Gn 33$_{20}$, מַצֵּבָה *pillar* Gn 35$_{14.20}$ 2 S 18$_{18}$ 2 K 17$_{10}$, עַמּוּד *pillar* Pr 9$_{1}$ (if em.; see Subj.), אֲשֵׁרָה *Asherah* 2 K 17$_{10}$, צִיּוּן *sign-post* Jr 31$_{21}$, דֶּלֶת *door* Jos 6$_{26}$=4QTestim$_{23}$ 1 K 16$_{34}$, חוֹמָה *wall* 4Q Testim$_{26}$ (ויצ[יבו]), מִגְדָּל *tower* 4QTestim$_{26}$ (ויצ[יבו]), מַיִם *water* Ps 78$_{13}$.

<PREP> לְ reflexive, *for oneself*, + Absalom 2 S 18$_{18}$, Saul 1 S 15$_{12}$, בֵּן *son* of Israel 2 K 17$_{10}$, בְּתוּלָה *young woman* of Israel Jr 31$_{21}$; of benefit, *for*, + עִיר *city* 4QTestim$_{26}$ (ויצ[יבו]).

בְּ of place, *in, at*, + מָקוֹם *place* Gn 35$_{14}$, נָהָר *river* 1 C 18$_{3}$; of time, *in, during*, + חַיִּים *life* 2 S 18$_{18}$; of price, *at the cost of*, + Segub 1 K 16$_{34(Qr)}$ (Kt Segib), צָעִיר *young one* Jos 6$_{26}$=4QTestim$_{23}$ 1 K 16$_{34}$.

כְּ *according to*, + דָּבָר *word* 1 K 16$_{34}$.

כְּמוֹ *as*, + נֵד *heap* Ps 78$_{13}$.

עַל *upon, over, beside*, + Absalom 2 S 18$_{17}$, קְבוּרָה *grave* Gn 35$_{20}$, גִּבְעָה *hill* 2 K 17$_{10}$.

תַּחַת *under*, + עֵץ *tree* 2 K 17$_{10}$.

<COLL> נצב hi. || יסד pi. *found* Jos 6$_{26}$=4QTestim$_{23}$ 1 K 16$_{34}$, שׂים *place* Jr 31$_{21}$; + adverb, שָׁם *there* Gn 33$_{20}$.

2. set, place, <SUBJ> Y. Ps 41$_{13}$ Lm 3$_{12}$ CD 2$_{3}$, Abraham Gn 21$_{28.29}$, רָשָׁע *wicked one* Jr 5$_{26}$. <OBJ> worshipper Ps 41$_{13}$ Lm 3$_{12}$, כִּבְשָׂה *ewe-lamb* Gn 21$_{28.29}$, מַשְׁחִית *snare* Jr 5$_{26}$, חָכְמָה *wisdom* CD 2$_{3}$, תּוּשִׁיָּה *sound wisdom* CD 2$_{3}$. <PREP> לְ of direction, *to*, + עוֹלָם *everlastingness*, i.e. for ever Ps 41$_{13}$; כְּ *as*, + מַטָּרָה *target* Lm 3$_{12}$; לִפְנֵי *before*, + Y. Ps 41$_{13}$ CD 2$_{3}$. <COLL> נצב hi. + adverb, לְבַד *alone* Gn 21$_{28.29}$.

3. fix, establish, <SUBJ> Y. Dt 32$_{8}$ Ps 74$_{17}$ Pr 15$_{25}$. <OBJ> גְּבוּל *boundary* Dt 32$_{8}$ Ps 74$_{17}$ Pr 15$_{25}$. <PREP> לְ *according to*, + מִסְפָּר *number* Dt 32$_{8}$. <COLL> נצב hi. + יצר *form* Ps 74$_{17}$; :: נסח *tear down* Pr 15$_{25}$.

4. perh. **set straight,* sharpen,** <SUBJ> subj. not specified, 1 S 13$_{21}$. <OBJ> דָּרְבָן *goad* 1 S 13$_{21}$.

Also 4QM^{h} 2$_{8}$.

<SYN> §1 יסד pi. *found*, שׂים *place*.

<ANT> §3 :: נסח *tear down*.

Ho. 3 Pf. הֻצַּב; ptc. מֻצָּב—**be set up, established;** perh. **be propped up** (Jg 9$_{6}$),* <SUBJ> סֻלָּם *ladder* Gn 28$_{12}$, אֵלוֹן *terebinth* Jg 9$_{6}$ (or em. הַמַּצֵּבָה terebinth of *the pillar*); subj. not specified, Na 2$_{8}$ (וְהֻצַּב גֻּלְּתָה הֹעֲלָתָה *while he was established she was exiled, was taken up*; unless הֻצַּב *is poured out* [from צבב *pour*] or pr.n. *Huzzab* or from צַב *train of captives*; or em. וְהֻצְאָה גָּלְתָה בַעֲלָתָה *and his lady was taken out, exiled* or הוּצְאָה בְּגָלוּת הַבַּעֲלָה *the lady was taken out into exile*). <PREP> ־ָה of direction, *to(wards), upon*, + אֶרֶץ *earth* Gn 28$_{12}$.*

⇒ נִצָּב I *hilt*, נְצִיב I *pillar*, II *Nezib*, מַצָּב *standing place*, מֻצָּב *siege mound*, מַצָּבָה *guard*, מַצֵּבָה *pillar*.

*נצב II $_{1}$ vb. **be weak** (unless נצב I *stand*)—**Ni.** $_{1}$ Ptc. נִצָּבָה—**be weak, exhausted,** <SUBJ> subj. not specified, Zc 11$_{16}$ (לֹא יְרַפֵּא הַנִּצָּבָה a shepherd who *does not heal the weak*; || שׁבר ni. *be broken*).

<SYN> שׁבר ni. *be broken*.

*נצב III $_{1}$ vb. **vanish** (unless נצב I *stand* or נְצָב II *image*)—**Ni.** $_{1}$ Ptc. נִצָּב—**vanish, die,** <SUBJ> אָדָם *human being* Ps 39$_{6}$. <PREP> כְּ *as*, + הֶבֶל *breath* Ps 39$_{6}$ (if em. כְּהֶבֶל to כָּל־הֶבֶל).

נִצָּב I $_{1}$ n.m. **hilt** of sword, <SUBJ> בוא *go in* Jg 3$_{11}$ (+ לַהַב *blade*).*

⇒ נצב I *stand*.

*נְצָב II $_{1}$ n.[m.] **image, semblance** (unless נצב I ni. *stand* or III ni. *vanish*), <NOM CL> כָּל־אָדָם נְצָב *every human is (but) a mere semblance* Ps 39$_{6}$.

⇒ נצב I *stand*.

נְצָב III *head, governor*, see נצב I *stand*, Ni. §2.

נְצִבֵי, see נְצִיב I *pillar*.

נצה I $_{8.2}$ vb. **fight**—**Ni.** $_{5.1}$ Impf. 2ms Si תינץ, יִנָּצוּ; + waw וַיִּנָּצוּ; ptc. נִצִּים—**fight, quarrel,** <SUBJ> עִבְרִי *Hebrew* Ex 2$_{13}$, אִישׁ *man* Ex 2$_{13}$ 21$_{22}$ Lv 24$_{10}$ Dt 25$_{11}$, בֵּן *son* Lv 24$_{10}$ Si 8$_{3}$, אָח *brother* Dt 25$_{11}$, שְׁנַיִם *two (sons)* 2 S 14$_{6}$. <PREP> בְּ of place, *in*, + מַחֲנֶה *camp* Lv 24$_{10}$, שָׂדֶה *field* 2 S 14$_{6}$; עִם *with*, + אִישׁ *man* Si 8$_{3}$. <COLL> נצה ni. + adverb, יַחְדָּו *together* Dt 25$_{11}$.

Pi. $_{0.1}$ Impf. Si. ינצה—perh. **set in motion,** <SUBJ> Y. Si 43$_{5(Bmg)}$ (B נצח pi. *cause to shine*). <OBJ> אַבִּיר *mighty one* Si 43$_{5(Bmg)}$. <COLL> דבריו ינצה *(by) his words he sets in motion* Si 43$_{5(Bmg)}$.

Hi. $_{3}$ Pf. הִצּוּ; inf. הַצּוֹתוֹ (הַצּוֹתָם)—**fight, strive,** <SUBJ> עֵדָה *assembly* Nm 26$_{9}$, Abiram Nm 26$_{9}$, Dathan Nm 26$_{9}$, David Ps 60$_{2}$, קְרִיא *summoned one* Nm 26$_{9(Qr)}$ (Kt קרא pass. ptc. in same sense). <PREP> בְּ of place, *in, among*, + עֵדָה *assembly* Nm 26$_{9}$; עַל *against*, + Y. Nm 26$_{9}$, Aaron Nm 26$_{9}$, Moses Nm 26$_{9}$; אֶת *with* (unless object marker), + Aram-naharaim Ps 60$_{2}$, Aram-zobah Ps 60$_{2}$.

⇒ מַצָּה *strife*, מַצּוּת *strife*.

*נצה II $_{5}$ vb. **go to ruin**—**Qal** $_{1}$ Impf. תִּצֶּינָה—**go to ruin,** <SUBJ> Moab Jr 48$_{9}$ (if em. נָצֹא תֵּצֵא *flying away, it shall go out* to נָצֹה תִּצֶּה *it shall go to utter ruin*), עִיר *city* Jr 4$_{7}$ (+ לָשׂוּם אַרְצֵךְ לְשַׁמָּה *to make your land a desolation*).

Ni. $_{4}$ Pf. נִצְּתָה; ptc. נִצִּים—**be in ruins, be ruined, be laid waste,** <SUBJ> נֹף *Memphis* Jr 46$_{19}$ (unless נִצְּתָה is יצת ni. *be burned*; + לְשַׁמָּה תִהְיֶה *it shall be a desolation*), עִיר *city* Jr 2$_{15(Kt)}$ (Qr יצת ni.; + וַיָּשִׁיתוּ אַרְצוֹ לְשַׁמָּה *and they made his land a desolation*), אֶרֶץ *land* Jr 9$_{11}$ (unless נִצְּתָה is יצת ni.; + אבד *be destroyed*), נָוֶה *pasture* Jr 9$_{9}$ (if em. נִצְּתוּ *they are burned* to נִצּוּ), גַּל *heap* 2 K 19$_{25}$||Is 37$_{26}$ (גַּלִּים נִצִּים *ruined heaps*, i.e. heaps of ruin). <PREP> כְּ *as*, + מִדְבָּר *steppe* Jr 9$_{11}$; מִבְּלִי *without*, + אִישׁ *man* Jr 9$_{9}$ (if em.; see Subj.), יֹשֵׁב *inhabitant* Jr 2$_{15(Kt)}$, עבר ptc. *one who passes* Jr 9$_{11}$.

נצה III $_{1}$ vb. **fly** (unless נצה IV *hasten* or נוץ I *flee*)—**Qal** $_{1}$ Pf. נָצוּ—**fly,** <SUBJ> כֹּהֵן *priest* Lm 4$_{15}$ (or em. נָדוּ *they fled*, from נוד), נָבִיא *prophet* Lm 4$_{15}$ (or em.; see above).

⇒ cf. נצא *fly*.

*נצה IV $_{1}$ vb. **hasten** (unless נצה III *fly* or נוץ I *flee*)—**Qal** $_{1}$ Pf. נָצוּ—**hasten,** <SUBJ> כֹּהֵן *priest* Lm 4$_{15}$, נָבִיא *prophet* Lm 4$_{15}$.

*נצה V $_{1}$ vb. **be joined** (unless נצה III *fly* or IV *hasten* or נוץ I *flee*)—**Qal** $_{1}$ Pf. נָצוּ—**be joined,** <SUBJ> exiles Lm 4$_{15}$.

נִצָּה $_{2}$ n.f. **blossom**—sf. נִצָּתוֹ—of vine (Gn 40$_{10}$ [if em.; see Subj.] Is 18$_{5}$), olive (Jb 15$_{33}$), <SUBJ> היה *be* Is 18$_{5}$ (+ בֹּסֶר *unripe grape*), עלה *go up* Gn 40$_{10}$ (if em. נִצָּהּ *its blossom* [from נֵץ] to נִצָּה *blossom* or נִצָּתָהּ *its blossom*). <OBJ> שׁלך hi. *cast off* Jb 15$_{33}$ (|| בֹּסֶר *unripe grape*).

<SYN> בֹּסֶר *unripe grape*.

⇒ נצץ I *sparkle*; cf. נֵץ I *blossom*, נִצָּץ *blossom*.

נֹצָה I, see נוֹצָה *plumage*.

נֹצָה II $_{1}$ n.f. **hawk,** <NOM CL> אִם־אֶבְרָה חֲסִידָה וְנֹצָה appar. *is it (the) wing (of) the stork or hawk?*, i.e. is it like these? Jb 39$_{13}$ (unless נֹצָה *[her] plumage*, from נוֹצָה).

⇒ cf. נֵץ II *hawk*.

*[**נָצוּר**] I $_{1}$ n.[m.] **secret place** or perh. **watch-hut** (unless נָצוּר II *mountain* or נצר ptc. pass. *secret places*)—pl. נְצוּרִים—<PREP> בְּ of place, *in*, + לין *lodge* Is 65$_{4}$.

⇒ נצר *keep*.

*[**נָצוּר**] II $_{1}$ n.[m.] **mountain** (unless נצר ptc. pass. *secret places*)—pl. נְצוּרִים—<PREP> בְּ of place, *in*, + לין *lodge* Is 65$_{4}$.

נָצוּר *preserved one*, נצר I *keep*.

נְצוּרָה *murmuring throng*, see נצר II *murmur*.

נְצוּרִים *secret places*, see נצר *keep*, Qal §3c (2).

***נצח** I $_{64.0.8}$ vb. **oversee**—**Pi.** $_{64.0.8}$ Ptc. מְנַצֵּחַ, מְנַצְּחִים; inf. נַצֵּחַ—**1. oversee, supervise** work assoc. with temple (Ezr 3$_{8.9}$ 1 C 23$_{4}$ 2 C 2$_{1}$ 34$_{12.13}$), **lead** music of temple (1 C 15$_{21}$), **direct** military operations (1QM 8$_{1.9.12.16}$ 9$_{2}$ 16$_{7}$), <SUBJ> Azaziah 1 C 15$_{21}$, Eliphelehu 1 C 15$_{21}$, Jahath 2 C 34$_{12}$, Jeiel 1 C 15$_{21}$, Jeshua Ezr 3$_{9}$, Kadmiel Ezr 3$_{9}$, Mattithiah 1 C 15$_{21}$, Meshullam 2 C 34$_{12}$, Mikneiah 1 C 15$_{21}$, Obadiah 2 C 34$_{12}$, Obed-edom 1 C 15$_{21}$, Zechariah 2 C 34$_{12}$, כֹּהֵן *priest* 1QM 8$_{9.12}$ 9$_{2.2}$ 16$_{7}$, לֵוִי *Levite* Ezr 3$_{8.9}$ 2 C 34$_{12.13}$, בֵּן *son* Ezr 3$_{9}$, אָח *brother* Ezr 3$_{9}$, שְׁלֹשֶׁת אֲלָפִים וְשֵׁשׁ מֵאוֹת *three thousand six hundred* 2 C 2$_{1}$, עֶשְׂרִים וְאַרְבָּעָה אֶלֶף *twenty-four thousand* 1 C 23$_{4}$; subj. not specified, 1QM 8$_{1}$.

<OBJ> אִישׁ *man* 1QM 8$_{1}$, יָד *hand*, i.e. signal, of battle 1QM 8$_{12}$, מִלְחָמָה *battle* 1QM 8$_{9.16}$ ([מל[חמה) 9$_{2.2}$ 16$_{7}$.

<PREP> לְ introducing object, + עשׂה ptc. *one who does* work 2 C 34$_{13}$.

עַל *upon*, + שְׁמִינִית *eight-stringed instrument* 1 C 15$_{21}$ (unless *on the octave* or *according to the eighth key*); introducing object, + אִישׁ *man* 2 C 2$_{1}$, סַבָּל *burden-bearer* 2 C 2$_{1}$, חֹצֵב *stonemason* 2 C 2$_{1}$, עשׂה ptc. *one who does* work Ezr 3$_{9}$, מְלָאכָה *work* Ezr 3$_{8}$ 1 C 23$_{4}$.

2. ptc. as noun, **a. overseer, supervisor,** <SUBJ> עבד hi. *put to work* 2 C 2$_{17}$. <OBJ> עשׂה *make*, i.e. appoint 2 C 2$_{17}$. <COLL> שְׁלֹשֶׁת אֲלָפִים וְשֵׁשׁ מֵאוֹת מְנַצְּחִים *three thousand six hundred supervisors* 2 C 2$_{17}$.

b. perh. **director of music,** or **the famous one*** (with לְ of possession), <PREP> לְ of benefit, *to*, *for* Hb 3$_{19}$ Ps 4$_{1}$ 5$_{1}$ 6$_{1}$ 8$_{1}$ 9$_{1}$ 11$_{1}$ 12$_{1}$ 13$_{1}$ 14$_{1}$ 18$_{1}$ 19$_{1}$ 20$_{1}$ 21$_{1}$ 22$_{1}$ 31$_{1}$ 36$_{1}$ 39$_{1}$ 40$_{1}$ 41$_{1}$ 42$_{1}$ 44$_{1}$ 45$_{1}$ 46$_{1}$ 47$_{1}$ 49$_{1}$ 51$_{1}$ 52$_{1}$ 53$_{1}$ 54$_{1}$ 55$_{1}$ 56$_{1}$ 57$_{1}$ 58$_{1}$ 59$_{1}$ 60$_{1}$ 61$_{1}$ 62$_{1}$ 64$_{1}$ 65$_{1}$ 66$_{1}$ 67$_{1}$ 68$_{1}$ 69$_{1}$ 70$_{1}$ 75$_{1}$ 76$_{1}$ 77$_{1}$ 80$_{1}$ 81$_{1}$ 84$_{1}$ 85$_{1}$ 88$_{1}$ 109$_{1}$ 139$_{1}$ 140$_{1}$ 4QparaKings 15$_{5}$.

***נצח** II $_{0.3.3}$ vb. **shine**—**Qal** $_{0.3.1}$ (unless pi.) Pf. Si נצח; impf. Si ינצח—**shine, flash,** <SUBJ> בָּרָק *lightning* Si 35$_{10.10}$, שָׁמַיִם *heaven* perh. 1QM 12$_{5}$ ([נוצ[חים); others [נוצ[צים *sparkling*; unless נצח IV *conquer*), חֵן *favour* Si 35$_{10}$. <PREP> לִפְנֵי *before*, + דַּכָּא *contrite one* Si 35$_{10}$, בושׁ ptc. *one who is ashamed* Si 35$_{10}$, בָּרָד *hail* Si 35$_{10.10}$.

Pi. $_{0.2}$ Impf. Si ינצח, 3fs Si תנצח—**cause to shine, make brilliant,** <SUBJ> Y. Si 43$_{5(B)}$ (Bmg נצה pi. perh. *set in motion*), גְּבוּרָה *might* Si 43$_{13(B)}$, גְּעָרָה *rebuke* Si 43$_{13(M)}$. <OBJ> אַבִּיר *mighty one* Si 43$_{5(B)}$, זִיקָה *flaming arrow* Si 43$_{13(B, M)}$ (Bmg זִק *flaming arrow*). <COLL> דבריו ינצח *(by) his words he causes* his mighty ones

to shine Si 43$_{5(B)}$.
⇒ נֵצַח II *glory*.

נצח III $_{1}$ vb. **endure—Ni.** $_{1}$ Ptc. נִצַּחַת—ptc. as adj., **enduring, persistent,** used attributively of מְשׁוּבָה *apostasy* Jr 8$_{5}$.*
⇒ נֵצַח I *endurance.*

***נצח** IV $_{0.0.2}$ vb. **conquer—Qal** $_{0.0.1}$ Pf. Q נצחו—**1. be victorious, prevail,** <SUBJ> עַם *people* of the elect ones 1QM 12$_{5}$ ([נוצ]חים; unless עם *with* the elect ones; or unless נצח II *shine*).

2. conquer, defeat, <SUBJ> Israelites 11QT 58$_{11}$ (+ שׁבר *break,* נכה hi. *strike*). <OBJ> אֹיֵב *enemy* 11QT 58$_{11}$.

Pi. $_{0.0.1}$ Inf. Q נצח—**be victorious over,** 4QBark^{c} 1.1$_{1}$ (unless לנצח is *for ever,* i.e. נֵצַח I), <SUBJ> subj. not specified, 4QBark^{c} 1.1$_{1}$. <PREP> לְ introducing object, + רוּחַ *spirit* perh. 4QBark^{c} 1.1$_{1}$; בְּ perh. of instrument, *by (means of),* + בִּינָה *understanding* 4QBark^{c} 1.1$_{1}$.

Htp. $_{0.0.1}$ Ptc. מתנצחת—**be directed,** perh. **prevail,** <SUBJ> מִלְחָמָה *battle* 1QM 16$_{9}$ 17$_{15}$ (המל[חמ]ה) (מ]תנצח[ת). <PREP> בְּ *against,* + Kittim 1QM 16$_{9}$ 17$_{15}$ ([מ]תנצח]ת בכ]תיים]).
⇒ נֵצַח III *victory.*

נֶ֫צַח I $_{41.3.39.1}$ n.m. **endurance**—נֶ֫צַח; cstr. נֵצַח; pl. נְצָחִים—**1. endurance, everlastingness, endlessness,** <SUBJ> היה *be* Jr 15$_{18}$ (לָמָּה הָיָה כְאֵבִי נֶצַח *why is my pain endlessness?,* i.e. endless).

<CSTR> נֵצַח נְצָחִים *everlastingness of everlastingness* Is 34$_{10}$ Si 51$_{20(B)}$ 1QH 15$_{31-32}$ GnzPs 1$_{11}$ 3$_{27}$, נצח לב *endurance of the heart of* 4QMidrEschat ^{b} 9$_{9}$ (unless נֵצַח II *purification*); מַשֻּׁאוֹת נֶצַח *ruins of everlastingness,* i.e. everlasting ruins Ps 74$_{3}$ (or נֵצַח II, *of preeminence,* i.e. of the utmost ruin), דורות נצח *generations of everlastingness,* i.e. everlasting generations 1QH 9$_{16}$ fr. 5$_{7}$ (דורי) 4QBer^{a} 1/2$_{12}$ (רורי perh. error for דורי), חיי *life of* 1QS 4$_{7}$ 4QCitJub 1.1$_{9}$ (ח[י]י) 4QShir^{b} 2.14 6QHymn 2$_{2}$ CD 3$_{20}$, כבוד *glory of* 4QHod^{a} 7.2$_{9}$, זעות *terror of* 1QS 4$_{12}$, ארורות *curses of* 4QBer^{d} 1$_{2}$ (נצ[ח]) 4QBéat 15$_{4}$ 5Q16 1$_{3}$, שׁני *years of* 1QH 9$_{19}$, קצי *times of* 1QH 9$_{24}$ 1QSb 4$_{26}$.

<PREP> לְ of direction, *to,* **a.** לָנֶצַח *to everlastingness,* i.e. (1) *for ever* 4QpsHod^{a} 1$_{4}$, + חיה *live* Ps 49$_{10}$, ראה *see* Ps 10$_{11}$, זכר *remember* GnzPs 4$_{13}$, שׁכח *forget* Am 8$_{7}$ Ps 74$_{19}$ Lm 5$_{20}$, ni. *be forgotten* Ps 9$_{19}$, נאץ pi. *revile* Ps 74$_{10}$ (unless לָנֶצַח *utterly* or from נֵצַח II *glory*), שׂנא *hate* 1QS 4$_{1}$, יצא *go out* Hb 1$_{4}$ 1QS 4$_{19}$, hi. *cause to go out* 1QH 4$_{25}$, ישׁב *be inhabited* Is 13$_{20}$ Jr 50$_{39}$, hi. *cause to sit* Jb 36$_{7}$, שׁכן *dwell* Ps 68$_{17}$, סתר ni. *hide oneself* Ps 89$_{47}$ (unless לָנֶצַח *utterly*), עמד *stand,* i.e. remain GnzPs 4$_{26}$, אכל *devour* 2 S 2$_{26}$, בלע pi. *swallow* Is 25$_{8}$, דושׁ *thresh* Is 28$_{28}$, נתץ *break down* Ps 52$_{7}$ (unless לָנֶצַח *utterly*), נתשׁ *uproot* Ps 9$_{7}$ (if em.; see below), נסע *pull out* Is 33$_{20}$, תקף *prevail against* Jb 14$_{20}$ (unless לָנֶצַח *utterly*), אנף *be angry* Ps 79$_{5}$ (unless לָנֶצַח *utterly*), קצף *be angry* Is 57$_{16}$, זנח *reject* Ps 44$_{24}$ (unless נֵצַח II) 74$_{1}$ (unless לָנֶצַח *utterly*), ריב *strive* Ps 103$_{9}$, שׁמר *keep* Jr 3$_{5}$ Am 1$_{11}$ (if em.; see below).

כון ni. *be established* 1QH 12$_{13.22}$, hi. *establish* 1QH 15$_{25}$ ([לנצח]), נתן *give,* i.e. make, king GnzPs 1$_{23}$ ([נתתו לנצח]), עשׂה *make* 4QMyst^{a} 6.1$_{4}$, אבד *perish* Jb 4$_{20}$ 20$_{7}$ GnzPs 2$_{21}$, רוח pi. *make wide* i.e. give relief 4QBark^{c} 1.1$_{1}$ (unless לנצח is נצח IV *conquer*), אפס *cease* Ps 77$_{9}$, שׁבת hi. *cease* 1QH 15$_{15}$, תמם *come to an end* Ps 9$_{7}$ (תַּמּוּ חֳרָבוֹת לָנֶצַח *they have come to an end [so as to be] ruins for ever;* or transfer לָנֶצַח to following clause and em. וְעָרִים *and cities* to עָרֵיהֶם *their cities* you have uprooted for ever) Si 40$_{14}$.

(2) *ever (before),* + נסה pi. *attempt* to read Lachish ost. 3$_{10}$.

(3) *successfully,** *so as to endure,* + דבר pi. *speak* Pr 21$_{28}$, פלט pi. appar. *escape* Jb 23$_{7}$.

(4) as superlative, *utterly** (unless לָנֶצַח *for ever*), + נתץ *break down* Ps 52$_{7}$, זנח *reject* Ps 74$_{1}$, נאץ pi. *revile* Ps 74$_{10}$, אנף *be angry* Ps 79$_{5}$, סתר ni. *hide oneself* Ps 89$_{47}$, תקף *prevail against* Jb 14$_{20}$.

b. לָנֶצַח נְצָחִים *to everlastingness of everlastingness,* i.e. for ever and ever Is 34$_{10}$, + נגד hi. *tell* GnzPs 3$_{27}$, נטה *turn aside* Si 51$_{20(B)}$, כון ni. *be established* 1QH 15$_{31-32}$.

c. לנצחים *to everlastingness,* i.e. for ever, + עמד

stand 1QS 11$_{12}$.

מִן of direction, *from* 4QPrayer^{c} 2$_{3}$ (מנצח לעד *from everlastingness to perpetuity*).

עַל *concerning* 4QMidrEschat^{b} 9$_{9}$ (עַ[ל]; unless נֵצַח II *purification*).

עַד *unto*, i.e. (1) *for ever* 1QH 21$_{14}$, + ראה *see* Ps 49$_{20}$; (2) *to the utmost limit* Jb 34$_{36}$.

נֵצַח without preposition, (1) *(to) everlastingness*, i.e. for ever Ps 16$_{11}$, + שׁמר *keep* wrath Am 1$_{11}$ (or em. שְׁמָרָה נֶצַח *he kept it for ever* to שָׁמַר לָנֶצַח *he kept for ever*), שׁכח *forget* Ps 13$_{2}$ (unless נֵצַח *utterly*).

(2) *utterly*,* + שׁכח *forget* Ps 13$_{2}$ (unless נֵצַח *for ever*).

<COLL> נֵצַח || עוֹלָם *eternity* 1QH 9$_{16.24}$ (+) 1QS 4$_{7.12}$ (+) 4QHod^{a} 7.2$_{9}$, עַד *perpetuity* 1QS 4$_{7.12}$.

לָנֶצַח + לְעוֹלָם *for ever* Is 57$_{16}$ Jr 3$_{5}$ Ps 103$_{9}$, לָעַד *for ever* Am 1$_{11}$ Ps 9$_{19}$ 1QS 4$_{1.19}$ GnzPs 3$_{27}$, לְדוֹר וָדוֹר *throughout all generations* Ps 77$_{9}$, עַד־דּוֹר וָדוֹר *unto all generations* Is 13$_{20}$ Jr 50$_{39}$, מִדּוֹר לָדוֹר *from generation to generation* Is 34$_{10}$.

לנצח נצחים + לעולם לעולם *for ever and ever* GnzPs 1$_{11}$.

2. faithful one* (unless נֵצַח II *glory*), <SUBJ> שׁקר pi. *deal falsely* 1 S 15$_{29}$. <CSTR> נֵצַח יִשְׂרָאֵל *faithful one of Israel* 1 S 15$_{29}$.

Also 1QH 17$_{25}$ 4QShirShabb^{d} 1.1$_{25}$ 4Q418 238$_{4}$.

<SYN> §1 עוֹלָם *eternity*, עַד *perpetuity*.*

⇒ נצח III *endure*.

*נֵ֫צַח II 5.0.1 n.m. **glory**—cstr. נֵצַח; sf. נִצְחִי—**1. glory, eminence**, perh. as divine title, **Glory** (1 S 15$_{29}$ perh. Ps 44$_{24}$ 74$_{10}$ [if לְ־ is emph. lamed in both]*). <SUBJ> שׁקר pi. *deal falsely* 1 S 15$_{29}$ (unless נֵצַח I *faithful one*), נחם ni. *repent* 1 S 15$_{29}$, אבד *perish* Lm 3$_{18}$ (unless נֵצַח IV *juice*, i.e. blood; or em. רַחְצִי *my confidence*; || תּוֹחֶלֶת *hope*). <NOM CL> לְךָ ... הַנֵּצַח *to you is ... the glory* 1 C 29$_{11}$ (|| גְּדֻלָּה *greatness*, גְּבוּרָה *might*, תִּפְאֶרֶת *beauty*, הוֹד *splendour*). <CSTR> נֵצַח יִשְׂרָאֵל *glory of Israel* 1 S 15$_{29}$ (unless נֵצַח I *faithful one*). <COLL> לְ emphatic, + נאץ pi. *revile* Ps 74$_{10}$ (unless נֵצַח I *everlastingness*), זנח *reject* Ps 44$_{24}$ (unless נֵצַח I).

2. perh. **purification** (unless נֵצַח I *endurance*), <CSTR> נצח לב *purification of the heart of* 4QMidrEschat^{b} 9$_{9}$. <PREP> עַל *concerning* 4QMidrEschat^{b} 9$_{9}$ (עַ[ל]).

<SYN> §1 גְּדֻלָּה *greatness*, גְּבוּרָה *might*, תִּפְאֶרֶת *beauty*, הוֹד *splendour*, תּוֹחֶלֶת *hope*.

⇒ נצח II *shine*.

*נֵ֫צַח III 0.0.2 n.[m.] **victory**, <OBJ> כתב *write* 1QM 4$_{13}$. <CSTR> נצח אל *victory of God* 1QM 4$_{13}$ (|| יְשׁוּעָה *salvation*); לשון נצח perh. *tongue of victory* 4QHod^{a} 7.1$_{14}$.

<SYN> יְשׁוּעָה *salvation*.

⇒ נצח IV *conquer*.

[נֵ֫צַח] IV 3 n.m. **juice**—sf. נִצְחִי, נִצְחָם—of grape, in ref. to blood, <SUBJ> נזה *spatter* Is 63$_{3}$, אבד *perish* Lm 3$_{18}$ (unless נֵצַח II *glory*). <OBJ> ירד hi. *bring down*, i.e. pour Is 63$_{6}$.

נְצִיב I 14.1.1 n.m. **pillar**—cstr. נְצִיב; pl. נְצִיבִים (נְצִבִים); cstr. נְצִבֵי (Si נציבי)—**1. pillar**, <SUBJ> היה *be* Gn 19$_{26}$. <CSTR> נְצִיב מֶלַח *pillar of salt* Gn 19$_{26}$; אדר נציב perh. *majesty of a pillar* 4QapPs^{b} 31$_{7}$.

2. governor, deputy, <NOM CL> נְצִיב מֶלֶךְ *a deputy was king* 1 K 22$_{48(mss)}$ (L נִצָּב *deputy*), נְצִיב אֶחָד אֲשֶׁר בָּאָרֶץ *there was one governor who was over the land* 1 K 4$_{19}$.

3. garrison, שָׁם נְצִבֵי פְלִשְׁתִּים *garrisons of the Philistines are there* 1 S 10$_{5}$, נְצִיב פְּלִשְׁתִּים אָז בֵּית לָחֶם *the garrison of the Philistines was then at Bethlehem* 1 C 11$_{16}$, נְצִיב פְּלִשְׁתִּים אֲשֶׁר בְּגֶבַע *the garrison of the Philistines which was at Geba* 1 S 13$_{3}$. <OBJ> נכה hi. *strike* 1 S 13$_{3.4}$, כנע hi. *subdue* Si 46$_{18}$, שׂים *place* 2 S 8$_{6}$||1 C 18$_{6(ms)}$ 2 S $_{14.14}$ 1 C 18$_{13}$, נתן *give*, i.e. place 2 C 17$_{2}$. <CSTR> נְצִיב פְּלִשְׁתִּים *garrison of the Philistines* 1 S 13$_{3.4}$ 1 C 11$_{16}$, נְצִבֵי פְּלִשְׁתִּים *garrisons of the Philistines* 1S 10$_{5}$, נציבי צר *garrisons of the enemy* Si 46$_{18}$ (|| סֶרֶן *lord*); שָׂרֵי הנציבים *chiefs of the officers* 2 C 8$_{10(Kt)}$ (Qr הַנִּצָּבִים *the officers*, as ||1 K 9$_{23}$).

<ADJ> אֶחָד *one* 1 K 4$_{19}$.

<SYN> §2 סֶרֶן *lord*.*

⇒ נצב I *stand*.

נְצִיב II 1.0.0.2 pl.n. **Nezib,** town in lowlands of Judah, perh. Kh. Bēt Neṣīb, 30 km SW of Jerusalem, <NOM CL> בַּשְּׁפֵלָה ... נְצִיב *in the lowland was ... Nezib* Jos 15$_{43}$. <APP> עִיר *city* Jos 15$_{43}$. <COLL> נצב למלך *(from the city of) Nezib, to the king* Fiscal Bulla 2* Bulla D98 (נצב .. למלך).

⇒ נצב I *stand*.

נציות uncertain word, 4QCrypt 1.2$_{4}$ (נצי[ו]ת).

נְצִיחַ $_{2}$ pr.n.m. **Neziah,** head of family of postexilic temple servants (Nethinim), <CSTR> בְּנֵי נְצִיחַ *sons of Neziah* Ezr 2$_{54}$||Ne 7$_{56}$.

⇒ נצח *endure*.

[נָצִיר] I $_{1}$ adj. **preserved**—pl. cstr. Kt נצירי—used as noun, **preserved one,** <OBJ> שׁוב hi. *bring back* Is 49$_{6}$ (|| שֵׁבֶט *tribe*). <CSTR> נצירי יִשְׂרָאֵל *preserved ones of Israel* Is 49$_{6(Kt)}$ (Qr נְצוּרֵי *preserved ones of,* i.e. ptc. pass. נצר).

<SYN> שֵׁבֶט *tribe*.

⇒ נצר *keep*.

[נָצִיר] II pr.n.m. **Nazir,** <CSTR> בן נציר *son of Nazir* Frey 1285$_{1}$ (others הציר *the painter* or הציד *the hunter*).

נצל $_{213.7.34}$ vb. **deliver—Ni.** $_{15.1.5}$ Pf. נִצַּלְנוּ; impf. יִנָּצֵל, 2ms תִּנָּצֵל, תִּנָּצְלִי, אִנָּצְלָה, יִנָּצְלוּ (יִנָּצֵלוּ); + waw וַתִּנָּצֵל; Q ונצלו; impv. הִנָּצֵל; ptc. Q ניצל; inf. הִנָּצֵל—**be delivered, deliver oneself, escape,** <SUBJ> Israelites Jr 7$_{10}$, David 4QMMT C$_{26}$ (נ[נ]צל), Hezekiah 2 K 19$_{11}$||Is 37$_{11}$, אִישׁ *man* Ezk 14$_{16.18}$, בֵּן *son* Pr 6$_{3.5}$, of Israel Am 3$_{12}$, בַּת *daughter* of Zion Mc 4$_{10}$, עֶבֶד *servant* Dt 23$_{16}$, אֶבְיוֹן *poor one* 4QpPs^{a} 1.2$_{9}$, מֶלֶךְ *king* 2 K 19$_{11}$||Is 37$_{11}$ Ps 33$_{16}$, יֹשֵׁב *inhabitant* Is 20$_{6}$, בצע ptc. *one who makes unjust gain* Hb 2$_{9}$, בָּחִיר *elect one* 1QpMic 8$_{8}$ (ינצל[ו]), worshipper Ps 69$_{15}$, נֶפֶשׁ *soul* Gn 32$_{31}$, רַב pl. *many* Si 34$_{6}$; subj. not specified, CD 4$_{18}$.

<PREP> בְּ of time, *in, on,* + יוֹם *day* Si 34$_{6(Bmg)}$; of instrument, *by (means of), with,* + רֹב *greatness* of strength Ps 33$_{16}$; of accompaniment, *with,* + פֵּאָה *corner* of bed Am 3$_{12}$, דְּמֶשֶׁק *damask* of couch Am 3$_{12}$.

כְּ *as,* + צְבִי *gazelle* Pr 6$_{5}$, צִפּוֹר *bird* Pr 6$_{5}$.

מִן of direction, *from,* + שֹׂנֵא *enemy* Ps 6$_{3}$, מַעֲמַקִּים *depths* Ps 69$_{15}$, יָד *hand* Pr 6$_{5}$ (or em. מִיָּד to מִמָּצוֹד *from the net* or מִצַּיָּד *from the hunter*), כַּף *hand* Hb 2$_{9}$, פַּח *snare* Pr 6$_{5(mss)}$ 4QpPs^{a} 1.2$_{9}$, רָעָה *evil* Si 34$_{6(B)}$, צָרָה *trouble* 4QMMT C$_{26}$ (נ[נ]צל), יוֹם *day* 1QpMic 8$_{8}$, זֶה *this* CD 4$_{18}$.

אֶל *to,* + Israelite Dt 23$_{16}$.

עַל *upon,* + אֶרֶץ *earth* 4QParGenEx 2$_{3}$ (על [הארץ]).

מֵעִם *from,* + אָדוֹן *master* Dt 23$_{16}$.

מִפְּנֵי *from,* + מֶלֶךְ *king* Is 20$_{6}$.

<COLL> נצל ni. || ישׁע ni. *be saved* Ps 33$_{16}$ Si 34$_{6}$, עלה *go up* CD 4$_{18}$; + מלט ni. *escape* Is 20$_{6}$, גאל *redeem* Mc 4$_{10}$; + adverb, לְבַד *alone* Ezk 14$_{16.18}$, כֵּן *so* Am 3$_{12}$, שָׁם *there* Mc 4$_{10}$.

<SYN> ישׁע ni. *be saved,* עלה *go up*.

Pi. $_{4}$ Impf. יְנַצְּלוּ; + waw וַיְנַצְּלוּ, וְנִצַּלְתֶּם—**1. strip, plunder, take spoil,** <SUBJ> עַם *people* Ex 12$_{36}$ 2 C 20$_{25}$, Jehoshaphat 2 C 20$_{25}$, בֵּן *son* of Israel Ex 3$_{22}$. <OBJ> Egyptians Ex 3$_{22}$ 12$_{36}$. <PREP> לְ reflexive, *for oneself,* + עַם *people* 2 C 20$_{25}$, Jehoshaphat 2 C 20$_{25}$. <COLL> וַיְנַצְּלוּ לָהֶם לְאֵין מַשָּׂא *they took spoil for themselves so that there was no carrying,* i.e. more than could be carried 2 C 20$_{25}$ (+ בזז *plunder*).

2. deliver, <SUBJ> Daniel Ezk 14$_{14}$, Job Ezk 14$_{14}$, Noah Ezk 14$_{14}$, אִישׁ *man* Ezk 14$_{14}$. <OBJ> נֶפֶשׁ *soul,* i.e. life, self Ezk 14$_{14}$. <PREP> בְּ of instrument, *by (means of), with,* + צְדָקָה *righteousness* Ezk 14$_{14}$.

Pu. be delivered, <SUBJ> רַע *wicked* Jb 21$_{30}$ (if em. יוּבָלוּ *are brought* to יֻצְּלוּ *are delivered*).

Hi. $_{191.6.28}$ Pf. הִצִּיל (Q היציל, הִצַּלְנִי, הִצִּלָנִי, הִצִּילוֹ, הִצִּילָנוּ, הִצִּילָם), הִצַּלְתָּ (Q הצלתני), הִצַּלְתִּיךָ, הִצִּילוּ, הִצַּלְתֶּם, הִצַּלְנוּ; impf. יַצִּיל (יַצֵּל, יַצִּילֵנִי, יַצִּילְךָ, יַצִּלֵךְ, Q יצילכה, יַצִּילֵנוּ, יַצִּילֵהוּ, יַצִּילֶנָּה, יַצִּילֵנוּ, יַצִּילֵם), 3fs תַּצִּיל (תַּצִּילֵנוּ, תַּצִּילֵם), 2ms תַּצִּיל (תַּצֵּל, תַּצִּילֵנִי, תַּצִּילֵם), אַצִּיל (אַצִּילְךָ), יַצִּילוּ (יַצִּילֵךְ, Q יצילום); + waw וְהִצִּיל, Q והצלתנו, וְהִצַּלְתִּי (וְהִצַּלְתִּי, וְהִצַּלְתִּיךָ, וְהִצַּלְתִּים), וְהִצִּילוּ, וְהִצַּלְתֶּם; וַיַּצֵּל (וַיַּצִּלֵנִי, וַיַּצִּילֵהוּ, וַיַּצִּילֶהָ, וַיַּצִּילֵנוּ, וַיַּצִּלֵם), 2ms Q ותצל (Q ותצילני, Q ותצילם), וָאַצִּיל (וָאַצִּל), וַיַּצִּילוּהָ; impv. הַצֵּל (הַצִּילָה, הַצִּילֵנִי, הַצִּילֵנוּ), הַצִּילוּ; ptc. מַצִּיל, Si מצלת; inf. abs. הַצֵּל; cstr. הַצִּיל (הַצִּילֵנִי, הַצִּילְךָ, הַצִּילֵךְ, הַצִּלֵךְ, הַצִּילוֹ, הַצִּילָם).

1. **take away, snatch away,** <SUBJ> Y. Gn 31$_{9.16}$ Ho 2$_{11}$ Ps 119$_{43}$, Sheba 2 S 20$_{6}$, בֵּן *son* 2 S 20$_{6}$. <OBJ> מִקְנֶה *cattle* Gn 31$_{9}$, עֹשֶׁר *riches* Gn 31$_{16}$, צֶמֶר *wool* Ho 2$_{11}$, פֵּשֶׁת *flax* Ho 2$_{11}$, עַיִן *eye*, i.e. cause harm or perh. elude 2 S 20$_{6}$, דָּבָר *word* Ps 119$_{43}$. <PREP> מִן of direction, *from*, + אָב *father* Gn 31$_{16}$, פֶּה *mouth* Ps 119$_{43}$.

2. **deliver, save, rescue; recover** cities (Jg 11$_{26}$), territory (1 S 7$_{14}$), property (1 S 30$_{18.22}$), <SUBJ> Y. Gn 32$_{12}$ Ex 3$_{8}$ 5$_{23.23}$ 6$_{6}$ 12$_{27}$ 18$_{4.8.9.10.10}$ Dt 23$_{15}$ Jos 24$_{10}$ Jg 6$_{9}$ 8$_{34}$ 10$_{15}$ 1 S 7$_{3}$ 10$_{18}$ 12$_{10.11}$ 17$_{37.37}$ 26$_{24}$ 2 S 12$_{7}$ 22$_{1.18.49}$||Ps 18$_{1.18.49}$ 2 K 17$_{39}$ 18$_{30.30.32.35}$||Is 36$_{15.15.18.20}$ 2 K 20$_{6}$||Is 38$_{6}$ Is 31$_{5}$ 50$_{2}$ Jr 1$_{8.19}$ 15$_{20.21}$ 20$_{13}$ 39$_{17}$ 42$_{11}$ Ezk 13$_{21.23}$ 34$_{10.12.27}$ Zc 11$_{6}$ Ps 7$_{2}$ 22$_{9.21}$ 25$_{20}$ 31$_{3.16}$ 33$_{19}$ 34$_{5.18.20}$ 35$_{10}$ 39$_{9}$ 40$_{14}$ 51$_{16}$ 54$_{9}$ 56$_{14}$ 59$_{2.3}$ 69$_{15}$ 70$_{2}$ 71$_{2}$ 79$_{9}$ 86$_{13}$ 91$_{3}$ 97$_{10}$ 106$_{43}$ 107$_{6}$ 109$_{21}$ 119$_{170}$ 120$_{2}$ 142$_{7}$ 143$_{9}$ 144$_{7.11}$ Jb 5$_{19}$ Ezr 8$_{31}$ Ne 9$_{28}$ 1 C 16$_{35}$ 2 C 32$_{11.14.15.17}$ Si 4$_{10}$ 51$_{2.8}$ 1QH 10$_{31}$ 11$_{5.38}$ ([ותצילני]) 13$_{13}$ 1QpHab 8$_{2}$ 4QBibPar 1$_{8}$ 4QpPs[a] 3.4$_{21}$ ([ו]י[צילם]) 4Q185 1.2$_{3}$ 4QJub[d] 21$_{20}$ ([להצ]י[לך]) 4QapPs[b] 33$_{6}$ perh. 44$_{3}$ 4QBark[a] 1.2$_{1.4.8}$ 1.3$_{1}$ (ה[נצל]תם) 1.3$_{2}$ 4QBark[d] 2.1$_{4.10}$ 4QDibHam[a] 1.2$_{16}$ 1.6$_{12}$ 1.7$_{2}$ 11QPs[a] 18$_{15.16}$ ([מ]צי[ל]) 19$_{10}$ GnzPs 3$_{25}$, אֱלֹהִים *god* 2 K 18$_{33.34}$||Is 36$_{18.19}$ 2 K 19$_{12}$||Is 37$_{12}$ Is 44$_{17}$ Ps 82$_{4}$ 2 C 25$_{15}$ 32$_{13.14.15.17}$, פֶּסֶל *image* Is 44$_{17}$ 1QpHab 12$_{14}$, Melchizedek 11QMelch 2$_{13.25}$ (both [יצי]ל[מה]).

Ammonites Jg 11$_{26}$, Hararite 2 S 23$_{12}$, Israel 1 S 7$_{14}$, עַם *people* Jr 22$_{3}$, עֵדָה *assembly* Nm 35$_{25}$, בַּיִת *house* Jr 21$_{12}$, Daniel Ezk 14$_{20.20}$, David 1 S 17$_{35}$ 30$_{8.8.18.18}$, Eleazar 1 C 11$_{14}$, Hezekiah 2 K 18$_{29}$||Is 36$_{14}$, Job Ezk 14$_{20.20}$, Joshua Jos 9$_{26}$, Noah Ezk 14$_{20.20}$, Reuben Gn 37$_{21.22}$, Saul 1 S 14$_{48}$, Shammah 2 S 23$_{12}$, אִישׁ *man* Ex 2$_{19}$ Jos 2$_{13}$ 1 S 30$_{22}$ Ezk 14$_{16.18}$ Ho 2$_{12}$, i.e. each one 2 K 18$_{33}$||Is 36$_{18}$, אִשָּׁה *wife* Dt 25$_{11}$, אָב *father* Jg 9$_{17}$, בֵּן *son* Jos 22$_{31}$ 2 S 23$_{12}$ Ps 72$_{12}$ Pr 24$_{11}$ 1 C 11$_{14}$ of man, in ref. to Ezekiel Ezk 3$_{19.21}$ 33$_{9}$, עֶבֶד *servant* Jr 22$_{3}$, מֶלֶךְ *king* 2 S 14$_{16}$ 19$_{10}$ Jr 22$_{3}$ Ps 72$_{12}$, נָסִיךְ *prince* Mc 5$_{5}$, מוֹשִׁיעַ *saviour* Is 19$_{20}$, רָב *defender* Is 19$_{20}$, רֹעֶה *shepherd* Am 3$_{12}$ Mc 5$_{5}$, חָרָשׁ *artisan* Is 44$_{20}$, הבר ptc. *one who divides* heavens Is 47$_{14(Qr)}$, חזה ptc. *one who sees* stars Is 47$_{14}$, ידע hi. ptc. *one who makes known* Is 47$_{14}$, חבר ptc. *one who joins* Si 12$_{15}$, גלל htpo. ptc. *one who rolls about* in iniquity Si 12$_{15}$, עֵד *witness* Pr 14$_{25}$, פֶּה *mouth* Pr 12$_{6}$.

קִיקָיוֹן *castor oil plant* Jon 4$_{6}$, זָהָב *gold* Ezk 7$_{19}$ Zp 1$_{18}$, כֶּסֶף *silver* Ezk 7$_{19}$ Zp 1$_{18}$, קִבּוּץ *collection (of idols)* Is 57$_{13}$, תֹּהוּ *emptiness*, i.e. idols 1 S 12$_{21}$, צְדָקָה *righteousness* Ezk 33$_{12}$ Pr 10$_{2}$ 11$_{4.16}$, i.e. almsgiving Si 40$_{24(Bmg)}$ (B צדק *righteousness*), תְּבוּנָה *understanding* Pr 2$_{12.16}$, מְזִמָּה *discretion* Pr 2$_{12.16}$, בְּרִית *covenant* CD 14$_{2}$, מִי *who?* 1 S 4$_{8}$ 2 K 18$_{35}$||Is 36$_{20}$; subj. not specified, Dt 32$_{39}$ Jg 18$_{28}$ 2 S 14$_{6}$ Is 5$_{29}$ 42$_{22}$ 43$_{13}$ Ho 5$_{14}$ Mc 5$_{7}$ Ps 7$_{3}$ 50$_{22}$ 71$_{11}$ Jb 5$_{4}$ 10$_{7}$ Pr 19$_{19}$ 23$_{14}$ Dn 8$_{4.7}$ Si 8$_{16}$ 1QM 14$_{11}$.

<OBJ> Cushite Jr 39$_{17}$, Egyptians Is 19$_{20}$, Israel(ites) Ex 18$_{8.9.10}$ Dt 23$_{15}$ 1 S 14$_{48}$ 2 K 17$_{39}$ 18$_{29.30.32}$||Is 36$_{14.15.18}$ Is 57$_{13}$ Ezk 7$_{19}$ Ezr 8$_{31}$ 2 C 32$_{11.14.15}$ 4QDibHam[a] 1.6$_{12}$ ([ישר]אל), Philistines 1 S 4$_{8}$, עַם *people* Ex 3$_{8}$ 5$_{23}$ 18$_{10}$ Jos 24$_{10}$ 1 S 12$_{11}$ 2 S 19$_{10}$ Jr 42$_{11}$ Ezk 13$_{21.23}$ Ps 106$_{43}$ 2 C 25$_{15}$ 32$_{14.15.17.17}$ 4QDibHam[a] 1.6$_{12}$, גּוֹי *nation* 2 K 19$_{12}$||Is 37$_{12}$ 1QpHab 12$_{14}$, בַּיִת *house* Ex 12$_{27}$, of Israel 1 S 7$_{3}$, David 1 S 17$_{37.37}$ 26$_{24}$ 2 S 12$_{7}$ 22$_{1.18.49}$||Ps 18$_{1.18.49}$, Ebed-melech 39$_{17}$, Hezekiah 2 K 20$_{6}$||Is 38$_{6}$, Isaac 4QJub[d] 21$_{20}$ ([להצ]י[לך]), Jacob Gn 32$_{12}$ 4QBibPar 1$_{8}$, Jeremiah Jr 1$_{8.19}$ 15$_{20.21}$, Job Jb 5$_{19}$, Johanan Jr 42$_{11}$, Joseph Gn 37$_{21.22}$, Moses Ex 18$_{4}$.

אָדָם *human being* Zp 1$_{18}$, אִישׁ *husband* Dt 25$_{11}$, אִשָּׁה *wife* 1 S 30$_{18}$, אָב *father* 1 S 12$_{10}$ Ne 9$_{28}$, אֵם *mother* Ho 2$_{12}$, בֵּן *son* Jr 42$_{11}$ Ezk 14$_{16.18.20}$ Pr 2$_{12.16}$ Si 4$_{10}$ 12$_{15}$ 11QMelch 2$_{25}$ ([בני] ... [יצי]ל[מה]), of Israel Ex 6$_{6}$ Jos 22$_{31}$ Jg 6$_{9}$ 8$_{34}$ 10$_{15}$ 1 S 10$_{18}$, בַּת *daughter* Ex 2$_{19}$ Ezk 14$_{16.18.20}$, i.e. village Jg 11$_{26}$, אָמָה *female servant* 2 S 14$_{16}$, בַּעַל *lord* Jg 9$_{17}$, שַׂר *commander* Jr 42$_{11}$, יֹשֵׁב *inhabitant* Jos 9$_{26}$ Ps 91$_{3}$, חָרָשׁ *artisan* Is 44$_{17}$, עשה ptc. *one who does* 1QpHab 8$_{2}$.

Worshipper Ps 7$_{2}$ 22$_{9}$ 25$_{20}$ 31$_{3.16}$ 34$_{5}$ 39$_{9}$ 40$_{14}$ 51$_{16}$ 54$_{9}$ 59$_{2.3}$ 69$_{15}$ 70$_{2}$ 71$_{2}$ 79$_{9}$ 109$_{21}$ 119$_{170}$ 142$_{7}$ 143$_{9}$ 144$_{7.11}$ 1 C 16$_{35}$ 1QH 10$_{31}$ 11$_{5.38}$ ([ותצילני]) 4QBark[d] 2.1$_{4.10}$ 4QDibHam[a] 1.7$_{2}$ 11QPs[a] 19$_{10}$, חָסִיד *loyal one* Ps 97$_{10}$, גאל ptc. *redeemed one* Ps 107$_{6}$, לקח pass. ptc. *one taken* Pr 24$_{11}$, רֹצֵחַ *killer* Nm 35$_{25}$, גזל pass. ptc. *one who has been robbed* Jr 21$_{12}$ 22$_{3}$, חסה ptc. *one who seeks refuge* Si 51$_{8}$, הלך htp. ptc. *one who walks* CD 14$_{2}$, צַדִּיק *righteous one* Ezk 33$_{12}$ Ps 34$_{18.20}$ 4QpPs[a] 3.4$_{21}$ ([צדיקים] ... [ו]י[צילם]), יָשָׁר *upright one* Pr 11$_{6}$ 12$_{6}$, תָּמִים *blameless one* 11QPs[a] 18$_{16}$ ([מצי]ל [תמימים]), אֶבְיוֹן,

poor one Ps 35_{10} Ps 72_{12} 82_{4}, דַּל *poor one* Ps 82_{4}, עָנִי *afflicted one* Ps 35_{10} Ps 72_{12}, עָנָו *humble one* 4QBark^a $1.2_{4.8}$.

שֶׂה *sheep* 1 S 17_{35}, צֹאן *flock* Ezk $34_{10.12.27}$, כֶּרַע *leg* Am 3_{12}, רֶגֶל *foot* Ps 56_{14} Si 51_{2}, נֶפֶשׁ *soul*, i.e. life, self Jos 2_{13} Is 44_{20} 47_{14} Jr 20_{13} Ezk $3_{19.21}$ $14_{14.20}$ 33_{9} Ps 22_{21} 33_{19} 56_{14} 86_{13} 116_{8} 120_{2} Pr 14_{25} 23_{14} 1QH 13_{13} 4QBark^a 1.2_{1} 11QPs^a 18_{15} ([נפש]ם) GnzPs 3_{25}, רוּחַ *spirit* GnzPs 3_{25}, יָחִיד *only one* fem. Ps 22_{21}, נַחֲלָה *inheritance* Ps 106_{43}, בְּדָל *piece* of ear Am 3_{12}, Aroer Jg 11_{26}, Heshbon Jg 11_{26}, Jerusalem 2 K 18_{35}||Is 36_{20}, Samaria 2 K 18_{34}||Is 36_{19}, עִיר *city* Jg 11_{26} 2 K 20_{6}||Is 38_{6}, אֶרֶץ *land* 2 K $18_{33.35}$||Is $36_{18.20}$ 2 C 32_{13}, גְּבוּל *border*, i.e. territory 1 S 7_{14}, חֶלְקָה *plot of land* 2 S 23_{12}||1 C 11_{14}, שָׁלָל *spoil* 1 S 30_{22}, כֹּל *everything* 1 S 30_{18}.

<PREP> לְ introducing object, + Jonah Jon 4_{6}, בטח pass. *one who trusts* perh. 4QapPs^b 44_{3}, אַיִל *ram* Dn 8_{7}.

בְּ of time, *in, at*, + יוֹם *day* Jr 39_{17} Ezk 7_{19} 33_{12} Zp 1_{18} 1QpHab 12_{14} 11QMelch 2_{13} ([ביום ההואה יצי]ל[מה]), עֵת *time* Jg 11_{26}; of instrument, *by (means of), with*, + צְדָקָה *righteousness* Ezk 14_{20}; of cause, *on account of*, + צְדָקָה *righteousness* Ps 71_{2}; *from*, + צָרָה *trouble* Jb 5_{19}, מָעוֹן *den* of lions 1QH 13_{13}.

כְּ *according to*, + אִמְרָה *word* Ps 119_{170}, רַחֲמִים *compassion* Ne 9_{28}, טוּב *goodness* Ps 109_{21} (if em. כִּי־טוֹב *for good* to כְּטוּב *according to the goodness of*), רֹב *greatness* of compassion and righteousness 11QPs^a 19_{10}.

מִן of direction, *from*, + Assyrians Mc 5_{5}, גּוֹי *nation* 1 C 16_{35}, עֵדָה *assembly* 1QH 10_{31}, אִישׁ *man* 2 S 22_{49}||Ps 18_{49} Pr 2_{12}, אִשָּׁה *woman* Pr 2_{16}, אֹיֵב *enemy* 2 S 22_{18}||Ps 18_{18} Ps 59_{2} 143_{9}, שׂנא ptc. *one who hates* 2 S 22_{18}||Ps 18_{18}, רֹדֵף *pursuer* Ps 31_{16} 142_{7}, חָזָק *strong one* Ps 35_{10}, גזל ptc. *one who robs* Ps 35_{10}, פעל ptc. *one who does* evil Ps 59_{3}, נָכְרִי fem. *foreigner* Pr 2_{16}.

יָד *hand, power* (מִיַּד sometimes perh. as compound prep. *from*) Gn 32_{12} $37_{21.22}$ Ex 2_{19} 3_{8} $18_{9.10}$ Nm 35_{25} Dt 25_{11} 32_{39} Jos 9_{26} 22_{31} 24_{10} Jg 6_{9} 8_{34} 9_{17} 1 S 4_{8} $7_{3.14}$ 10_{18} $12_{10.11}$ 14_{48} $17_{37.37}$ 2 S 12_{7} 2 K 17_{39} $18_{29.33.34.35.35}$||Is $36_{18.19.20.20}$ Is 43_{13} 47_{14} Jr 15_{21} 20_{13} 21_{12} 22_{3} 42_{11} Ezk $13_{21.23}$ 34_{27} Ho 2_{12} Zc 11_{6} Ps $18_{1.1}$ 22_{21} 31_{16} 82_{4} 97_{10} $144_{7.11}$ Jb 10_{7} Dn $8_{4.7}$ 2 C 25_{15} 32_{13+6t} Si 51_{2} 4QpPs^a 3.4_{21} (ו[י]צילם) 4QJonathan 1_{9} ([מציל ... מיד]) 11QPs^a 18_{16} ([מצי]ל ... [מיד]) 11Q Melch 2_{13} ([יצי]ל[מה מיד]) 2_{25} ([יצי]ל[מה מי]ד) GnzPs 3_{25}, כַּף *hand* 2 S 14_{16} 19_{10} 22_{1}||Ps 18_{1} 2 K 20_{6}||Is 38_{6} Ezr 8_{31} 2 C 32_{11}, פֶּה *mouth* 1 S 17_{35} Ezk 34_{10} Am 3_{12}, שָׂפָה *lip* Ps 120_{2}, לָשׁוֹן *tongue* Ps 120_{2}, דָּם *blood(guilt)* Ps 51_{16} (or em. מִדָּמִים to מִדּוּמָם *from the stillness*).

עֲבֹדָה *labour* Ex 6_{6}, חֶרֶב *sword* Ex 18_{4} Ps 22_{21}, מוֹקֵשׁ *snare* CD 14_{2}, פַּח *snare* Ps 91_{3}, קוֹשׁ *snare* 4QBark^d 2.1_{4}, צָרָה *distress* 1 S 26_{24} Ps 34_{18} 54_{9} 4QBark^a 1.3_{1} ([מ]כול צרה ה[צל]תם) 4QDibHam^a 1.7_{2}, מְצוּקָה *distress* Ps 107_{6}, רָעָה *misery* Jon 4_{6} Ps 34_{20}, מְגוֹרָה *fear* Ps 34_{5}, פֶּשַׁע *transgression* Ps 39_{9}, דְּחִי *stumbling* Ps 56_{14}, חָמָס *violence* 4QBibPar 1_{8}, דֶּבֶר *pestilence* Ps 91_{3}, רֶשֶׁף *pestilence* 4QJub^d 21_{20} ([להצי]ילך [מ]כול רשף), מָוֶת *death* Jos 2_{13} Ps 33_{19} 56_{14} Pr 10_{2} 11_{4}, שְׁאוֹל *Sheol* Ps 86_{13} Pr 23_{14}, שַׁחַת *destruction* Si 4_{10}, מַשְׁחִית *destroyer* 1QH 11_{38} ([ותצילני מכו]ל משחיתים), קִנְאָה *jealousy* 1QH 10_{31}, טִיט *mud* Ps 69_{15} 4QBark^d 2.1_{10} ([מטיט]), מַיִם *water* Ps 144_{7}, דֶּרֶךְ *way* Pr 2_{12}, בַּיִת *house* of judgment 1QpHab 8_{2}, מָקוֹם *place* Ezk 34_{12}, אֶרֶץ *land* 4QDibHam^a 1.6_{12} ([מכול]), עֵת *time* 11QPs^a 18_{15}.

מִן of comparison, *(more) than*, + שְׁנַיִם *two* Si 40_{24}.

מִתַּחַת *from under*, + יָד *hand* Ex 18_{10}.

בַּעֲבוּר *on account of, for the sake of*, + Y. 4QBark^a 1.3_{2}, עָמָל *toil* 1QpHab 8_{2}, אֱמוּנָה *faithfulness* 1QpHab 8_{2}, חֶסֶד *loyalty* 4QBark^a 1.2_{4}.

<COLL> נצל hi. || ישׁע hi. *save* Jr 15_{20} 42_{11} Ps 7_{2} (+) 59_{3} 71_{2} (+), מלט pi. *deliver* 2 S 19_{10}, hi. Is 31_{5} (+), פלט pi. *deliver* Ps 22_{9} 71_{2} 82_{4}, פדה *redeem* Jr 15_{21} Si 51_{2}, שׂגב pi. *set on high*, i.e. protect Ps 59_{2}, פצה *snatch away* Ps $144_{7.11}$ Si 51_{2} (+), קבץ pi. *gather* 1 C 16_{35}, יעל hi. *profit* 1 S 12_{21} Pr 10_{2} 11_{4} (both +), חשׂך *hold back* Pr 24_{11} (+) Si 51_{2}.

+ גאל *redeem* Ex 6_{6} Si 51_{8}, גנן *protect* Is 31_{5}, פסח *pass over* Is 31_{5}, שׁמר *keep* Ps 25_{20}, חיה pi. *keep alive* Ps 33_{19}.

+ adverb or noun used adverbially, מְהֵרָה *quickly* Ps 31_{3}, מַדּוּעַ *why?* Jg 11_{26}, הַיּוֹם *today* Jg 10_{15}, פְּעָמִים רַבּוֹת *many times* Ps 106_{43}, רַבּוֹת עִתִּים *many times* Ne 9_{28}.

inf. abs. + finite form of נצל hi. Ex 5_{23} 30_{8} 2 K 18_{30}||Is

36$_{15}$ 2 K 18$_{33}$.

בְּיוֹם הִצִּיל י׳ *in the day when Y. delivered* 2 S 22$_{1}$||Ps 18$_{1}$, והצלתנו מחטוא לכה *and you will deliver us from sinning against you* 4QDibHam[a] 1.2$_{16}$.

Also 4QMidrEschat[a] 2$_{6}$ 4QparaKings 143$_{1}$ 4QBéat 32$_{2}$ (ותצילנ[ ]).

<SYN> §2 ישׁע hi. *save,* מלט pi. *deliver,* פלט pi. *deliver,* פדה *redeem,* שׂגב pi. *set on high,* i.e. protect, פצה *snatch away,* קבץ pi. *gather,* יעל hi. *profit,* חשׂך *hold back.*

Ho. $_{2}$ Ptc. מֻצָּל—**be snatched, be rescued,** <SUBJ> רָשָׁע *wicked one* Jb 21$_{30}$ (if em. יוּבָלוּ *they are brought* to יֻצָּל *he is rescued*), אוּר *fire-brand* Am 4$_{11}$ Zc 3$_{2}$. <PREP> לְ *in, during,* + יוֹם *day* Jb 21$_{30}$ (if em.; see Subj.); מִן of direction, + אֵשׁ *fire* Zc 3$_{2}$, שְׂרֵפָה *burning* Am 4$_{11}$.

Also perh. 1Q38 4$_{5}$ (מוצל[ין]).

Htp. $_{1}$ + waw וַיִּתְנַצְּלוּ—**strip oneself of,** <SUBJ> בֵּן *son* of Israel Ex 33$_{6}$. <OBJ> עֲדִי *ornaments* Ex 33$_{6}$. <PREP> מִן *from (the time at),* + הַר *mountain* Ex 33$_{6}$.

Maphul $_{0.0.1}$ Ptc. Q מצול—**be delivered,** <SUBJ> מִי *who?* 4QMMT C$_{24}$. <PREP> מִן of direction, + צָרָה *trouble* 4QMMT C$_{24}$.*

⇒ הַצָּלָה *deliverance.*

[נִצָּן] $_{1.0.1}$ n.[m.] **blossom**—pl. נִצָּנִים; cstr. Q נצני—<SUBJ> ראה ni. *appear* Ca 2$_{12}$. <CSTR> נצני ארגמון *flowers of purple* 4QBéat 2.3$_{5}$.

⇒ נצץ *sparkle;* cf. נֵץ *blossom,* נִצָּה *blossom.*

***[נֶ֫צֶף]** $_{0.0.0.2}$ n.[m.] **nezeph,** weight of c. 10 grams, Weight 31, <CSTR> רבע נצף *quarter of a nezeph* Weight 33.

***[נִצְפָּה]** $_{0.0.1}$ n.f. **caper bush,** perh. **vine,** as source of new wine, <PREP> מִן of direction, *from,* + היה *be* 4QpsEzek[b] 1.2$_{5}$.

נצץ I $_{4.0.2}$ vb. **sparkle—Qal** $_{1}$ Ptc. נֹצְצִים—**sparkle** (unless נוץ II pol. *sparkle*), <SUBJ> חַיָּה *living being* Ezk 1$_{7}$, שָׁמַיִם *heaven* 1QM 12$_{5}$ (נוצ[צים]; others נוצ[חים] *shining,* from נצח II *shine*). <PREP> כְּ *as,* + עַיִן *eye,* i.e. sparkle, of burnished bronze Ezk 1$_{7}$.

Hi. $_{3.0.2}$ Pf. הֵנֵ֫צוּ; impf. יָנֵאץ, Q ינצו—**blossom, flourish,** <SUBJ> רִמּוֹן *pomegranate* Ca 6$_{11}$ 7$_{13}$ (|| פתח pi. *open;* both || פרח *bud*), שָׁקֵד *almond tree* Ec 12$_{5}$ (unless נצץ II *become dry*), בָּכָא *balsam tree* 4QBen 1$_{3}$ (בכ[איכה]), עָלֶה *leaf* 11QPs[a] 24$_{13}$ (ע[ל]יו).

<SYN> פרח *bud,* פתח pi. *open.*

Htpol. sparkle, <SUBJ> אֶבֶן *stone* of crown Zc 9$_{16}$ (if em. מִתְנוֹסְסוֹת *they sparkle* [i.e. נסס htpo.] to מִתְנוֹצְצוֹת). <PREP> עַל *upon,* + אֲדָמָה *land* Zc 9$_{16}$ (if em.; see Subj.).*

⇒ נֵץ I *blossom,* נִצָּה *blossom,* נִצָּן *blossom;* cf. נוץ II *sparkle.*

***נצץ** II $_{1}$ vb. **become dry** (unless נצץ I hi. *blossom*)—**Hi.** $_{1}$ Impf. יָנֵאץ—**become dry,** <SUBJ> שָׁקֵד *almond tree* Ec 12$_{5}$.

נצר I $_{63.2.5}$ vb. **keep—Qal** $_{63.2.5}$ Pf. נָצְרוּ, נָצַ֫רְתִּי, נְצַרְתֶּם; impf. יִצֹּר (יִצְּרֶ֫נְהוּ), 3fs תִּצֹּר (תִּצְּרֶ֫ךָּ, תִּנְצְּרֶ֫כָּה), 2ms תִּצֹּר (Q תנצור, תִּצְּרֵ֫נִי, תִּנְצְּרֵ֫נִי, תִּצְּרֶ֫נּוּ), אֶצֹּר (אֶצְּרָה, אֶצְרָה), יִצְּרוּ (יִנְצֹרוּ, Q יצורו, יִצְּרוּנִי), אֶצָּרְךָ, אֶצְּרֶ֫נָּה (אֶצְּרֶ֫נָּה, יִנְצְּרֻ֫הוּ), 3fpl תִּצֹּ֫רְנָה; impv. נְצֹר (Si נצור, נִצְרָה, נִצְּרֶ֫הָ); ptc. נֹצֵר (נוֹצֵר, נֹצְרָהּ), נֹצְרִים (נוֹצְרִים), נֹצְרֵי, Q נוצרת; ptc. pass. נָצוּר, נְצוּרָה, נְצֻרַת, נְצוּרֵי, נְצֻרוֹת; inf. abs. נָצוֹר; cstr. לִנְצֹר (Q נצור).

1a. keep (safely), preserve, protect (Dt 32$_{10}$ Is 26$_{3}$ 42$_{6}$ 49$_{8}$ Ps 12$_{8}$ 31$_{24}$ 32$_{7}$ 40$_{12}$ 61$_{8}$ 64$_{2}$ 140$_{2.5}$ Pr 2$_{8.11}$ 4$_{6}$ 13$_{6}$ 20$_{28}$ Si 7$_{24}$ 4QBark[c] 1.1$_{4}$).

b. watch, guard vineyard (Is 27$_{3.3}$), fig tree (Pr 27$_{18}$), fortification (Na 2$_{2}$), knowledge (Pr 22$_{12}$), soul (Pr 24$_{12}$), spirit (Pr 20$_{27}$; if em.; see Subj.), way (Pr 16$_{17}$ 23$_{26[Qr]}$), perh. specif. **keep from indiscretion,*** speech (Ps 34$_{14}$ 141$_{3}$ Pr 13$_{3}$), heart (Pr 4$_{23}$).

c. keep, observe commandments, law, covenant, etc. (Dt 33$_{9}$ Ps 25$_{10}$ 78$_{7}$ 105$_{45}$ 119$_{2+9t}$ Pr 3$_{1}$ 6$_{20}$ 28$_{7}$ Si 35$_{24}$ 4QWiles 1$_{15}$ 4QsapHymnA 1.1$_{5}$ 4QBéat 5$_{9}$), wisdom, knowledge, etc. (Pr 3$_{21}$ 4$_{13}$ 5$_{2}$), loyalty (Ex 34$_{7}$).

<SUBJ> Y. Ex 34$_{7}$ Dt 32$_{10}$ Is 26$_{3}$ 27$_{3}$ 42$_{6}$ 49$_{8}$ Ps 12$_{8}$ 31$_{24}$ 32$_{7}$ 64$_{2}$ 140$_{2.5}$ 141$_{3}$ Pr 2$_{8}$ 20$_{27}$ (if em. נֵר *lamp* to נֹצֵר *watches*) 4QBark[c] 1.1$_{4}$, Israel(ites) Na 2$_{2}$ Ps 105$_{45}$, אִישׁ *man* Ps 34$_{14}$, אָב *father* Dt 33$_{9}$, אֵם *mother* Dt 33$_{9}$, בֵּן

son Dt 33$_9$ Ps 78$_7$ Pr 3$_{21}$ 4$_{23}$ 6$_{20}$ Si 7$_{24}$, אָח *brother* Dt 33$_9$, דּוֹר *generation* Ps 78$_7$, worshipper Ps 119$_{22+6t}$, ירא ptc. *one who fears* God 4QBéat 5$_9$, בָּחוּר *chosen one* 4QWiles 1$_{15}$, עַיִן *eye* Pr 22$_{12}$ 23$_{26(Qr)}$ (Kt רצה *delight in*), שָׂפָה *lip* Pr 5$_2$ (or em. יִנָּצֵרוּ *they shall be safeguarded*, i.e. ni.), לֵב *heart* Pr 3$_1$, נֶפֶשׁ *soul* Ps 119$_{129}$, חֶסֶד *loyalty* Ps 40$_{12}$ 61$_8$ Pr 20$_{28}$, אֱמֶת *faithfulness* Ps 40$_{12}$ 61$_8$ Pr 20$_{28}$, צְדָקָה *righteousness* Pr 13$_6$, חָכְמָה *wisdom* Pr 4$_6$, בִּינָה *understanding* Pr 4$_6$, תְּבוּנָה *understanding* Pr 2$_{11}$; subj. not specified, Ps 25$_{10}$ 119$_2$ Pr 13$_3$ 16$_{17}$ 24$_{12}$ 27$_{18}$ 28$_7$ Si 35$_{24}$ 4QsapHymnA 1.1$_5$ (נוצר[ין]).

<OBJ> עַם *people* Dt 32$_{10}$, Jacob Dt 32$_{10}$, בֵּן *son* Pr 2$_{11}$ 4$_6$, עֶבֶד *servant* Is 42$_6$ 49$_8$, מֶלֶךְ *king* Ps 61$_8$ Pr 20$_{28}$, worshipper Ps 12$_8$ 32$_7$ 40$_{12}$ 140$_{2.5}$, אֱמֻן *faithful one* Ps 31$_{24}$, פֶּה *mouth* Pr 13$_3$, לָשׁוֹן *tongue* Ps 34$_{14}$, לֵב *heart* Pr 4$_{23}$, שְׁאֵר *flesh* Si 7$_{24}$, נֶפֶשׁ *soul* Pr 24$_{12}$, נְשָׁמָה *spirit* Pr 20$_{27}$ (if em.; see Subj.), יֵצֶר *imagination* Is 26$_3$, חַיִּים *life* Ps 64$_2$, תְּאֵנָה *fig-tree* Pr 27$_{18}$, כֶּרֶם *vineyard* Is 27$_3$, מְצוּרָה *fortification* Na 2$_2$, בְּרִית *covenant* Dt 33$_9$ Ps 25$_{10}$, חֶסֶד *loyalty* Ex 34$_7$, אֱמֶת *truth* 4QsapHymnA 1.1$_5$ (נוצר[י] אמ[ת), תֹּם *blamelessness*, i.e. blameless one Pr 13$_6$, דַּעַת *knowledge* Pr 5$_2$ (or em.; see Subj.) 22$_{12}$, חָכְמָה *wisdom* Pr 4$_{13}$, תּוּשִׁיָּה *sound wisdom* Pr 3$_{21}$, מְזִמָּה *discretion* Pr 3$_{21}$, מִצְוָה *commandment* Ps 78$_7$ 119$_{15}$ Pr 2$_{11}$ 6$_{20}$ 4QWiles 1$_{15}$, פִּקּוּד *precept* Ps 119$_{56.69.100}$, עֵדָה *testimony* Ps 25$_{10}$ 119$_{2.22.129}$, תּוֹרָה *law* Ps 105$_{45}$ 119$_{34}$ Pr 28$_7$ Si 35$_{24}$ 4QBark^c 1.1$_4$, חֹק *statute* Ps 119$_{145}$, אֹרַח *path* Pr 2$_8$, דֶּרֶךְ *way* Ps 119$_{33}$ Pr 16$_{17}$ 23$_{26(Qr)}$ 4QBéat 5$_9$.

<PREP> לְ of benefit, *for*, + אֶלֶף *thousand* Ex 34$_7$; *at*, + רֶגַע *moment*, i.e. every moment Is 27$_3$; בְּ of instrument, *by (means of), with*, + לֵב *heart* Ps 119$_{69}$; כְּ *as*, + אִישׁוֹן *pupil* of eye Dt 32$_{10}$; מִן *from*, + אִישׁ *man* of violence Ps 140$_{2.5}$, דּוֹר *generation* Ps 12$_8$, פַּחַד *dread* Ps 64$_2$, צַר *distress* Ps 32$_7$, רַע *evil* Ps 34$_{14}$; of comparison, *(more) than*, + מִשְׁמָר *guard* Pr 4$_{23}$; עַל *over*, + דַּל *door* of lips Ps 141$_3$; לִפְנֵי *before*, + worshipper 4QBark^c 1.1$_4$.

<COLL> נצר ‖ שׁמר *keep* Dt 33$_9$ Ps 12$_8$ (+) 105$_{45}$ 119$_{34}$ 140$_5$ 141$_3$ Pr 2$_{8.11}$ 5$_2$ 13$_3$ 16$_{17}$ 27$_{18}$ Si 35$_{24}$, צפה *watch* Na 2$_2$, תכן *examine* Pr 24$_{12}$, חלץ pi. *deliver* Ps 140$_2$; + עזר *help* Is 49$_8$.

:: נטשׁ *forsake* Pr 6$_{20}$, סלף pi. *subvert* Pr 13$_6$ 22$_{12}$.

+ adverb or noun used adverbially, תָּמִיד *continually* Ps 40$_{12}$, עֵקֶב *(to the) end* Ps 119$_{33}$, יוֹם *(by) day* Is 27$_3$, לַיְלָה *(by) night* Is 27$_3$, שָׁלוֹם *(in) peace, safely* Is 26$_3$.

נְצֹר ... שְׂפָתֶיךָ מִדַּבֵּר מִרְמָה *guard ... your lips from speaking deceit* Ps 34$_{14}$.

2. ptc. as noun, a. watcher, sentry, guardian, in ref. to Y. (Jb 7$_{20}$), <SUBJ> קרא *call* Jr 31$_6$ (unless נצר II ptc. *murmuring throng*), עלה *go up* Jr 31$_6$, עשׂה *make* booth Jb 27$_{18}$. <NOM CL> נֹצֵר מַטָּעוֹ י׳ *the guardian of his plantation is Y.* Is 60$_{21}$ (if em. נֵצֶר מטעו *shoot of my planting* [Kt] and add י׳ with 1QIsa^a). <OBJ> שׂים *place* Jb 7$_{20}$. <CSTR> נֹצֵר הָאָדָם *watcher of humans* Jb 7$_{20}$, נֹצֵר מַטָּעוֹ *the guardian of his plantation* Is 60$_{21}$ (if em.; see Nom. Cl.); מִגְדַּל נוֹצְרִים *tower of the watchers*, i.e. watchtower 2 K 17$_9$ 18$_8$. <PREP> לְ of benefit, *to, for*, + פעל *do* Jb 7$_{20}$. <COLL> נֹצֵר as vocative Jb 7$_{20}$.

b. blockaders, besiegers, <SUBJ> היה *be* Jr 4$_{16}$ (unless נצר II ptc. *murmuring throng*; or em. צָרִים *besiegers*, from צור, or *banded together*, from צרר),* בוא *come* Jr 4$_{16}$, נתן *give* voice Jr 4$_{16}$.

3. pass. a. be secretive, be wily (unless נצר II *murmur*), <SUBJ> אִשָּׁה *woman* Pr 7$_{10}$ (נְצֻרַת לֵב *wily of heart*, i.e. with a wily heart), זוֹנָה *prostitute* Pr 7$_{10}$.

b. be blockaded, be besieged (unless נצר II *murmur*), <SUBJ> עִיר *city* Is 1$_8$.

c. pass. ptc. as noun, (1) **preserved one,** <SUBJ> מות *die* Ezk 6$_{12}$. <OBJ> שׁוב hi. *bring back* Is 49$_6$ (‖ שֵׁבֶט *tribe*). <CSTR> נְצוּרֵי יִשְׂרָאֵל *preserved ones of Israel* Is 49$_{6(Qr)}$ (Kt נצירי *preserved ones of*).

(2) masc. pl. נְצוּרִים **secret places,** <PREP> בְּ of place, *in*, + לין *lodge* Is 65$_4$ (unless from נָצוּר I *secret place* or II *mountain*; or em. בֵּין צוּרִים *among the rocks*; ‖ קֶבֶר *tomb*).

(3) fem. pl. נְצֻרוֹת **secret things, hidden things,** <OBJ> שׁמע hi. *cause to hear* Is 48$_6$ (‖ חָדָשׁ pl. *new things*), ידע *know* Is 48$_6$.

Also 4QBéat 8$_1$ (unless נוצרת is יצר ni. *be formed*).

<SYN> §1 שׁמר *keep*, צפה *watch*, תכן *examine*, חלץ pi. *deliver*; §3b שֵׁבֶט *tribe*; §3c קֶבֶר *tomb*.

<ANT> §1 נטשׁ *forsake*, סלף pi. *subvert*.

Qal Pass., be preserved, <SUBJ> עַל־חֹק *injustice* Ps 94$_{20}$ (if em. יֹצֵר עָמָל עֲלֵי־חֹק *the one who forms trouble according to statute* to יֹצֵר עַל־חֹק יֻצַּר *the ar-*

*chitect of injustice is preserved).**

Ni. be safeguarded, <SUBJ> שָׂפָה *lip* Pr 5$_{2}$ (if em. יִנָּצְרוּ qal *they shall keep* to יִנְצֹרוּ).

⇨ נָצוּר *secret place,* נָצִיר I *preserved.*

*נצר II $_{4}$ vb. **murmur** (unless נצר I *keep*)—**Qal** $_{4}$ Ptc. נֹצְרִים; ptc. pass. נְצֻרָה, נְצֻרַת—**1.** ptc. as noun, **murmuring throng,** <SUBJ> קרא *call* Jr 31$_{6}$, בוא *come* Jr 4$_{16}$.

2. pass. **a. be tumultuous,** <SUBJ> אִשָּׁה *woman* Pr 7$_{10}$ (נְצֻרַת לֵב *tumultuous of heart,* i.e. with a tumultuous heart), זוֹנָה *prostitute* Pr 7$_{10}$.

b. hum, <SUBJ> עִיר *city* Is 1$_{8}$.

נֵצֶר I $_{4.1.6}$ n.m. **shoot**—cstr. נֵצֶר; sf. Si נצרו—**shoot, branch(es),** <SUBJ> פרה *sprout* Is 11$_{1}$ (|| חֹטֶר *shoot*), עמד *stand,* i.e. arise Dn 11$_{7}$ (if em.; see Prep.), ידע ni. *be known* 1QH 16$_{10}$, חשׁב ni. *be esteemed* 1QH 16$_{10}$, תעב ni. *be abhorred* Is 14$_{19}$ (unless נֵצֶר II *putrefying matter*), נכה hi. *strike roots* Si 40$_{15(Bmg)}$.

<OBJ> גדל pi. *make great,* i.e. cause to grow 1QH 14$_{15}$ (+ לעופי מטעת עולם *into branches of an everlasting planting*) 15$_{19}$ (|| מַטָּע *plant*), פרח hi. *cause to sprout* (unless intrans. *sprout,* with נֵצֶר as subj.) 1QH 16$_{6}$ (+ למטעת עולם *into an everlasting planting*) 16$_{10}$ (+ למטעת אמת *into a planting of truth*).

<CSTR> נֵצֶר מַטָּעַי *shoot of my planting* Is 60$_{21(Qr)}$ (Kt מטעו, 1QIsa^{b} מטעיו *of his planting;* or em. מטע י׳ *of the planting of Y.*), נֵצֶר שָׁרָשֶׁיהָ appar. *shoot of her roots* Dn 11$_{7}$ (or em.; see Prep.), נצר עליו *branches of its leaves* 1QH 16$_{8}$, נצר חמס *shoot of violence* Si 40$_{15}$ (Bmg, M) (B נוצר מחמס *that which is formed from violence,* i.e. יצר ni.), ק[ו]דשׁ *of holiness* 1QH 16$_{10}$.

<APP> מַעֲשֵׂה יָדַי *work of my hands* Is 60$_{21}$.

<PREP> בְּ introducing object, + רעה *feed on* 1QH 16$_{8}$; כְּ *as,* + שׁלך ho. *be cast out* Is 14$_{19}$ (or em. כְּנֵפֶל *as a miscarriage*); מִן partitive, *(one) from (among)* Dn 11$_{7}$ (or em. מִנֵּצֶר שָׁרָשֶׁיהָ *one from the shoot of her roots* to נֵצֶר מִשָּׁרָשֶׁיהָ *a shoot from her roots*) perh. 4QAdmon Par 2.2$_{8}$.*

*נֵצֶר II $_{1}$ n.m. **putrefying matter**—<PREP> כְּ *like,* + שׁלך ho. *be cast out* Is 14$_{19}$ (וְאַתָּה הָשְׁלַכְתָּ ... כְּנֵצֶר נִתְעָב *and you are cast out ... like loathed putrefying matter;* unless נֵצֶר I *branch;* or em. כְּנֵפֶל *as a miscarriage*).

נֹצֵר *watcher, sentry, guardian,* see נצר I *keep.*

*נְצֻרָה $_{1}$ n.f. **seal,** <OBJ> שׁית *set* Ps 141$_{3}$ (|| שָׁמְרָה *guard* or *muzzle*).

<SYN> שָׁמְרָה *guard* or *muzzle.*

⇨ נצר *keep.*

נְצֻרוֹת *secret things, hidden things,* see נצר *keep,* §3c (3).

נֹצְרִים *murmuring throng,* see נצר II *murmur.*

*נצת $_{29.2}$ vb. **kindle** (unless יצת *kindle*)—**Qal** $_{4}$ Impf. תִּצַּתְנָה, יִצַּתּוּ; + waw וַתִּצַּת—**be kindled with fire, kindle, burn up,** <SUBJ> רִשְׁעָה *guilt* Is 9$_{17}$, קוֹץ *thorn-bush* Is 33$_{12}$, שַׁעַר *gate* of Babylon Jr 51$_{58}$, בַּת *daughter,* i.e. village Jr 49$_{2}$.

<PREP> בְּ *in, with,* + אֵשׁ *fire* Is 33$_{12}$ Jr 49$_{2}$ 51$_{58}$; introducing object, + סְבַךְ *thicket* Is 9$_{17}$.

Ni. $_{8.1}$ Pf. נִצְּתוּ, נִצְּתָה; + waw וְנִצְּתָה—**become inflamed, be burned up, break out,** <SUBJ> חֵמָה *anger* of Y. 2 K 22$_{13.17}$ Si 16$_{6}$, אֶרֶץ *land* Jr 9$_{11}$, הַר *mountain* Jr 9$_{9}$, Memphis Jr 46$_{19}$, עִיר *city* Jr 2$_{15(Qr)}$ (Kt נצה ni. *be destroyed*), שַׁעַר *gate* Ne 1$_{3}$ 2$_{17}$, נָוֶה *pasturage* Jr 9$_{9}$.

<PREP> בְּ of instrument, *by (means of), with,* + אֵשׁ *fire* Ne 1$_{3}$ 2$_{17}$; בְּ *against,* + עַם *people* 2 K 22$_{13}$, Judah 2 K 22$_{13}$, Josiah 2 K 22$_{13}$, גּוֹי *nation* Si 16$_{6}$, מָקוֹם *place* 2 K 22$_{17}$; כְּ *as,* + מִדְבָּר *steppe* Jr 9$_{11}$; מֵאֵין *without,* + יֹשֵׁב *inhabitant* Jr 46$_{19}$; מִבְּלִי *without,* + יֹשֵׁב *inhabitant* Jr 2$_{15}$, אִישׁ *man* Jr 9$_{9}$, עבר ptc. *one who passes by* Jr 9$_{11}$.

Hi. $_{17.1}$ Pf. הִצִּית, הִצַּתִּי, הִצִּיתוּ; impf. תַּצִּיתוּ; + waw וַיַּצֶּת־, וַיַּצִּיתוּ (וַיַּצִּתוּ); impv. הַצִּיתוּהָ (Kt הוציתיה); ptc. מַצִּית—**set on fire, set fire to,** <SUBJ> י׳ *Y.* Jr 11$_{16}$ 17$_{27}$ 21$_{14}$ 43$_{12}$ 49$_{27}$ 50$_{32}$ Ezk 21$_{3}$ Am 1$_{14}$ Lm 4$_{11}$, עַם *people* Jg 9$_{49}$, Chaldaean Jr 32$_{29}$, גִּבּוֹר *warrior* Jos 8$_{8.19}$ Jr 51$_{30}$, עֶבֶד *servant* 2 S 14$_{30.30.31}$; subj. not specified, Si 49$_{6}$.

<OBJ> עִיר *city* Jos 8$_{8.19}$ Jr 32$_{29}$, קִרְיָה *city* Si 49$_{6}$, מִשְׁכָּן *dwelling place* Jr 51$_{30}$, צְרִיחַ *vault* Jg 9$_{49}$, חֶלְקָה *common field* 2 S 14$_{30.30.31}$, אֵשׁ *fire* Jr 11$_{16}$ 17$_{27}$ 21$_{14}$ 43$_{12}$ 49$_{27}$ 50$_{32}$ Ezk 21$_{3}$ Am 1$_{14}$ Lm 4$_{11}$.

<PREP> לְ of agent, *by (means of)*, + קוֹל *voice* Jr 11$_{16}$; בְּ of place, *in, at*, + Zion Lm 4$_{11}$, עִיר *city* Jr 50$_{32}$, בַּיִת *house*, i.e. temple Jr 43$_{12}$, חוֹמָה *wall* Jr 49$_{27}$ Am 1$_{14}$, שַׁעַר *gate* Jr 11$_{16}$, יַעַר *forest* Jr 21$_{14}$ Ezk 21$_{3}$; of instrument, *by (means of)*, + אֵשׁ *fire* Jos 8$_{8.19}$ 2 S 14$_{30.30.31}$ Jr 32$_{29}$; עַל *upon*, + עַם *people* Jg 9$_{49}$; *against*, + זַיִת *olive tree* Jr 11$_{16}$.

⇨ (?) יָצִת *Jazith*; cf. יצת *kindle*.

נקב I $_{20}$ vb. **pierce—Qal** $_{14}$ Pf. נָקַבְתָּ, נָקְבָה; impf. יִקֹּב־ (יִקֳּבֶנּוּ), 2ms תִּקּוֹב, יִקֳּבֵהוּ; + waw וַיִּקֹּב; impv. נָקְבָה; ptc. נֹקֵב; pass. נָקוּב, נְקֻבֵי; inf. נָקְבוֹ—**1. pierce, bore,** <SUBJ> Y. Hb 3$_{14}$, Jehoiada 2 K 12$_{10}$, Job Jb 40$_{26}$, כֹּהֵן *priest* 2 K 12$_{10}$, קָנֶה *reed* 2 K 18$_{21}$||Is 36$_{6}$, אוֹר *light* Jb 3$_{8}$ (יִקְּבֻהוּ אֹרְרֵי־יוֹם *let the light-rays of day pierce it;** unless *let those who curse the day curse it*, i.e. יִקְּבֻהוּ is from קבב); subj. not specified, Jb 40$_{24}$. <OBJ> כַּף *hand* 2 K 18$_{21}$||Is 36$_{6}$, אַף *nose* Jb 40$_{24}$, לְחִי *cheek* Jb 40$_{26}$, ראשׁ *head* Hb 3$_{14}$, חֹר *hole* 2 K 12$_{10}$, לַיְלָה *night* Jb 3$_{8}$ (unless יִקְּבֻהוּ is from קבב *curse*). <PREP> בְּ of place, *in*, + דֶּלֶת *lid* of chest 2 K 12$_{10}$; of instrument, *by (means of), with*, + חוֹחַ *hook* Jb 40$_{26}$, מוֹקֵשׁ *snare* Jb 40$_{24}$, מַטֶּה *rod* Hb 3$_{14}$.

2. designate, <SUBJ> Jacob Gn 30$_{28}$, פֶּה *mouth* of Y. Is 62$_{2}$. <OBJ> שֵׁם *name* Is 62$_{2}$, שָׂכָר *wages* Gn 30$_{28}$.

3. blaspheme (unless נקב II *slander*), <SUBJ> בֵּן *son* of Israelite woman Lv 24$_{11}$ (+ קלל pi. *curse*); subj. not specified, Lv 24$_{16.16}$. <OBJ> שֵׁם *name*, i.e. Y. Lv 24$_{11.16.16}$.

4. pass. **a. be pierced,** i.e. have holes, <SUBJ> צְרוֹר *bag*, perh. as specially marked for taxation* Hb 1$_{6}$.

b. pass. ptc. as noun, **distinguished one,** <CSTR> נְקֻבֵי רֵאשִׁית הַגּוֹיִם *distinguished ones of the first of the nations* Am 6$_{1}$ (+ שַׁאֲנָן *secure one*, בטח ptc. *one who trusts*). <PREP> לְ of direction, *to*, + בוא *come* Am 6$_{1}$.

Ni. $_{6}$ Pf. נִקְּבוּ—**1. be bored, cut through,** <SUBJ> אַמָּה *cubit* Siloam tunnel inscr.$_{2}$ ([להנק]ב), tunnel Siloam tunnel inscr.$_{4}$ (if rd. להנקבה, i.e. לְהִנָּקְבָה *its boring through*).*

2. be designated, <SUBJ> אִישׁ *man* Nm 1$_{17}$ 2 C 28$_{15}$ 31$_{19}$, שְׁאָר *rest* of chosen ones 1 C 16$_{41}$, כֹּל *all* Ezr 8$_{20}$, שְׁמֹנָה עָשָׂר אֶלֶף *eighteen thousand* 1 C 23$_{2}$. <PREP> בְּ of instrument, *by (means of)*, + שֵׁם *name* Nm 1$_{17}$ Ezr 8$_{20}$ 1 C 23$_{2}$ 16$_{41}$ 2 C 28$_{15}$ 31$_{19}$. <COLL> נִקְּבוּ בְּשֵׁמוֹת לְהֹדוֹת לַי׳ *they were designated by name to give thanks to Y.* 1 C 16$_{41}$; sim. with infinitive of בוא *come* 1 C 23$_{2}$, מלך hi. *make king* 1 C 23$_{2}$, נתן *give* portions 2 C 31$_{19}$.

⇨ נֶקֶב I *engraving*, II *pipe*, III *passage, mine*, נְקֻבָה *boring through*, נְקֵבָה *female*, מַקֶּבֶת *hammer*.

*נקב II $_{3}$ vb. **slander—Qal** $_{14}$ + waw וַיִּקֹּב; ptc. נֹקֵב; inf. נָקְבוֹ—**slander, blaspheme** (unless נקב I *pierce*), <SUBJ> בֵּן *son* of Israelite woman Lv 24$_{11}$ (+ קלל pi. *curse*); subj. not specified, Lv 24$_{16.16}$. <OBJ> שֵׁם *name*, i.e. Y. Lv 24$_{11.16.16}$.

⇨ cf. קבב *curse, slander*.

[**נֶקֶב**] I $_{1}$ n.[m.] **engraving** (unless נֶקֶב II *pipe* or III *mine*)—pl. sf. נְקָבֶיךָ—appar. feature or item of jewellery, **engraving, socket, spangle,** perh. specif. **plaque** of metal inset with precious stones or **bead** pierced for threading,* <SUBJ> כון pol. *be prepared* Ezk 28$_{13}$. <CSTR> מְלֶאכֶת תֻּפֶּיךָ וּנְקָבֶיךָ *work of your settings and your engravings* Ezk 28$_{13}$.

⇨ נקב *pierce*.

*[**נֶקֶב**] II $_{1}$ n.[m.] **pipe** (unless נֶקֶב I *engraving* or III *mine*)—pl. sf. נְקָבֶיךָ—**pipe, flute,** musical instrument that is hollowed out, <SUBJ> כון pol. *be prepared* Ezk 28$_{13}$. <CSTR> מְלֶאכֶת תֻּפֶּיךָ וּנְקָבֶיךָ *work of your timbrels and your pipes* Ezk 28$_{13}$.*

⇨ נקב *pierce*.

*נֶקֶב III $_{2}$ n.[m.] **mine**—pl. sf. נְקָבֶיךָ—**passage, mine,** <SUBJ> כון pol. *be prepared* Ezk 28$_{13}$ (unless נֶקֶב I *engraving* or II *pipe*). <APP> וַאֲדָמִי הַנֶּקֶב *and Adami the mine* Jos 19$_{33}$ (unless pl.n. *Adami-nekeb*).

*[**נֶקֶב**] IV $_{1}$ n.[m.] **orifice** (unless נֶקֶב I *engraving* or III *mine*)—pl. sf. נְקָבֶיךָ—orifice of female or her-

maphrodite body, <SUBJ> כון pol. *be prepared* Ezk 28$_{13}$. <CSTR> וְזָהָב מְלֶאכֶת תֻּפֶּיךָ וּנְקָבֶיךָ *and gold was the work of your (?) and your orifices* Ezk 28$_{13}$.
⇒ נקב *pierce.*

נֶ֫קֶב V, see אֲדָמִי הַנֶּקֶב *Adami-nekeb.*

*[**נִקְבָּה**] 0.0.0.3 n.f. **boring through, tunnelling,** <SUBJ> תמם *be complete* Siloam tunnel inscr.$_1$ ([תמת]; others [זאת] *this is*). <CSTR> דבר הנקבה *manner of the boring through* Siloam tunnel inscr.$_1$, ים *day of* Siloam tunnel inscr.$_4$ (unless = הִנָּקְבֹה, i.e. נקב ni. inf. *its boring through*).
⇒ נקב *pierce.*

נְקֵבָה 22.0.7 n.f. **female,** of humans (Gn 1$_{27}$ 5$_5$ Lv 12$_{5.7}$ 15$_{33}$ 27$_{4.5.6.7}$ Nm 5$_3$ 31$_{15}$ Jr 31$_{22}$ 4QJub^a 2$_{14}$ [[נק]בה] 4QSD 7.2$_{16}$ 4QTohA 1.1$_7$ CD 4$_{21}$), animals (Gn 6$_{19}$ 7$_{3.9.16}$ Lv 3$_{1.6}$ 4$_{28.32}$ 5$_6$), image (Dt 4$_{16}$), <SUBJ> היה *be* Gn 6$_{19}$, בוא *come* Gn 7$_{9.16}$, סבב po. *encompass,* i.e. protect Jr 31$_{22}$.

<NOM CL> אִם־נְקֵבָה *if it is a female* Lv 3$_1$ 4QTohA 1.1$_7$ perh. 4Q418 236$_2$, sim. Lv 27$_4$, זָכָר אוֹ נְקֵבָה *whether it is male or female* Lv 3$_6$.

<OBJ> חיה pi. *let live* Nm 31$_{15}$, ברא *create* Gn 1$_{27}$ 5$_2$ CD 4$_{21}$, עשׂה *make* 4QJub^a 2$_{14}$ ([נק]בה עשה), ילד *bear* Lv 12$_5$ 4QSD 7.2$_{16}$, בוא hi. *bring* Lv 4$_{28.32}$ 5$_6$, לקח *take* Gn 7$_3$.

<CSTR> תַּבְנִית ... נְקֵבָה *image of ... a female* Dt 4$_{16}$, כָּל־נְקֵבָה *every female* Nm 31$_{15}$.

<APP> קָרְבָּן *offering* Lv 4$_{28}$, אָשָׁם *guilt offering* Lv 5$_6$, שְׂעִירָה *she-goat* Lv 4$_{28}$ 5$_6$, כִּשְׂבָּה *ewe* Lv 5$_6$; שִׁבְעָה שִׁבְעָה זָכָר וּנְקֵבָה *seven pairs, male and female* Gn 7$_3$, שְׁנַיִם שְׁנַיִם ... זָכָר וּנְקֵבָה *two of each ... male and female* Gn 7$_9$.

<ADJ> תְּמִימָה *without blemish* Lv 4$_{32}$.

<PREP> לְ introducing object, + ילד *bear* Lv 12$_7$; of price, *(in exchange) for,* + היה *be* Lv 27$_{5.6.7}$; appar. *among,* + זוב *flow,* i.e. have discharge Lv 15$_{33}$; עַד *unto,* i.e. (both ...) and, + שׁלח pi. *send away* Nm 5$_4$.

<COLL> נְקֵבָה :: זָכָר *male* Gn 1$_{27}$ 5$_2$ 6$_{19}$ 7$_{3.9.16}$ Lv 3$_{1.6}$ 12$_7$ 15$_{33}$ 27$_{4.5.6.7}$ Nm 5$_3$ Dt 4$_{16}$ 4QJub^a 2$_{14}$ ([נק]בה) 4QTohA 1.1$_7$ CD 4$_{21}$, גֶּבֶר *man* Jr 31$_{22}$.

זָכָר וּנְקֵבָה מִכָּל־בָּשָׂר *male and female of all flesh* Gn 7$_{16}$, נְקֵבָה מִן־הַצֹּאן *a female from the flock* Lv 5$_6$.

Also 4QBapt 10$_{11}$ 4Q415 9$_{12}$ 4QRitPur 14.9$_1$.

<ANT> זָכָר *male,* גֶּבֶר *man.**
⇒ נקב *pierce.*

נָקֹד 9 adj. **speckled**—m.pl. נְקֻדִּים, f.pl. נְקֻדּוֹת—**1.** used attributively of שֶׂה *sheep* Gn 30$_{32}$ (|| טָלוּא *spotted* [or del. נָקֹד and טָלוּא]) 30$_{32}$ (|| טָלוּא; + חום *brown*), עֵז *she-goat* Gn 30$_{35}$ (|| טָלוּא; + חום).

2. in nom. cl. used predicatively of עַתּוּד *he-goat* Gn 31$_{10.12}$ (both || עָקֹד *striped,* בָּרֹד *mottled*), כֹּל *all* Gn 30$_{33}$ (|| טָלוּא *speckled;* + חום *brown*).

3. as noun, **speckled (kid),** <SUBJ> היה *be* Gn 31$_8$ (|| עָקֹד *striped*). <OBJ> ילד *bear* Gn 30$_{39}$ (|| טָלוּא *spotted,* עָקֹד *striped*) 31$_8$ (|| עָקֹד).

<SYN> טָלוּא *spotted,* עָקֹד *striped,* בָּרֹד *mottled.*
⇒ cf. נְקוֹד *spot,* נְקֻדָּה *bead.*

נֹקֵד I 2 n.m. **sheep breeder** (unless נֹקֵד II *soothsayer* or III *cultic official*)—pl. נֹקְדִים—**sheep breeder, shepherd,** of Mesha, king of Moab (2 K 3$_4$), of Amos (Am 1$_1$), <SUBJ> היה *be* 2 K 3$_4$. <NOM CL> נוֹקֵד אָנֹכִי *I am a shepherd* Am 7$_{14}$ (if em. בוֹקֵר *herdsman*). <PREP> בְּ *(one) of, from (among),* + היה *be* Am 1$_1$ (+ מִתְּקוֹעַ *from Tekoa*).*

***נֹקֵד II** 2 n.m. **soothsayer** (unless נֹקֵד I *sheep breeder* or III *cultic official*)—pl. נֹקְדִים—**soothsayer, hepatoscoper,** of Mesha, king of Moab (2 K 3$_4$), of Amos (Am 1$_1$), <SUBJ> היה *be* 2 K 3$_4$. <PREP> בְּ *(one) of, from (among),* + היה *be* Am 1$_1$ (+ מִתְּקוֹעַ *from Tekoa*).

***נֹקֵד III** 2 n.m. **cultic official** (unless נֹקֵד I *sheep breeder* or II *soothsayer*)—pl. נֹקְדִים—of Mesha, king of Moab (2 K 3$_4$), of Amos (Am 1$_1$), <SUBJ> היה *be* 2 K 3$_4$. <PREP> בְּ *(one) of, from (among),* + היה *be* Am 1$_1$ (+ מִתְּקוֹעַ *from Tekoa*).

[**נְקֻדָּה**] 1 n.f. **bead**—pl. cstr. נְקֻדּוֹת—**bead,** perh. of glass, globular or drop-shaped, <CSTR> נְקֻדּוֹת הַכֶּסֶף

beads of silver Ca 1_{11} (+ תּוֹרֵי זָהָב perh. *pendants of gold*). <PREP> עִם *with* Ca 1_{11}.*

⇒ cf. נָקֹד *speckled*, נִקּוּד *spot*.

נִקֻּדִים, see נִקּוּד *crumb*.

נקה I $_{44.6.8.1}$ vb. **be clean—Qal** $_1$ Inf. abs. נָקֹה—**1. be clear, be exempt from punishment,** <SUBJ> Edom Jr 49_{12}. <COLL> אַתָּה הוּא נָקֹה תִּנָּקֶה *will you indeed be exempt from punishment?* Jr 49_{12}.

2. trans. **exempt from punishment,** <SUBJ> Y. Ps 99_8 (if em. נֹקֵם *one who avenges* to נֹקָם *one who exempts them from punishment*, i.e. ptc. with sf.). <OBJ> קרא ptc. *one who calls* on name of Y. Ps 99_8 (if em.; see Subj.). <PREP> עַל *for*, + עֲלִילָה *misdeed* Ps 99_8 (if em.; see Subj.).

3. perh. **cleanse,*** <SUBJ> Y. Ps 99_8 (if em. נֹקֵם *one who avenges* to נֹקָם *one who cleanses them*). <OBJ> קרא ptc. *one who calls* on name of Y. Ps 99_8 (if em.; see Subj.). <PREP> עַל *concerning*, i.e. from, + עֲלִילָה *misdeed* Ps 99_8 (if em.; see Subj.).

Ni. $_{25.6.5.1}$ Pf. נִקָּה, נִקֵּיתָ, נִקֵּיתִי (נקתי I); impf. יִנָּקֶה, 2ms תִּנָּקֶה, תִּנָּקוּ; + waw וְנִקְּתָה (וְנִקָּתָה), וְנִקָּה, וְנִקֵּיתָ, וְנִקֵּיתִי; impv. הִנָּקִי; inf. abs. הִנָּקֵה—**1. be cleaned out, emptied, banished,** <SUBJ> Zion Is 3_{26}, גנב ptc. *one who steals* Zc 5_3, שׁבע ni. ptc. *one who swears* Zc 5_3. <PREP> כָּמוֹ *according to*, + אָלָה *curse* Zc $5_{3.3}$.

2. empty oneself, i.e. ejaculate, <SUBJ> יָד *penis* Is $65_{3(1QIsa^a)}$ (וינקו ידים על האבנים *and penises empty themselves into vaginas;* MT וּמְקַטְּרִים *and burning incense*). <PREP> עַל *into*, + אֶבֶן *vagina* Is $65_{3(1QIsa^a)}$ (על האבנים; MT עַל־הַלְּבֵנִים *on tiles*).

3. be free (from guilt), be blameless, <SUBJ> Jerusalem Jr 2_{35}, Samson Jg 15_3, אִישׁ *man* Nm 5_{31}, עֶבֶד *servant* Meṣad Ḥashavyahu ost. 1_{11}, i.e. worshipper Ps 19_{14}, קָרוֹב *one who is near*, i.e. approaches CD 5_{15}; subj. not specified, 4Q416 2.3_5. <PREP> מִן *from, of*, + אָשָׁם *guilt* Meṣad Ḥashavyahu ost. 1_{11} ([מא]שם), עָוֹן *(guilt of) iniquity* Nm 5_{31}, פֶּשַׁע *transgression* Ps 19_{14}; *from*, i.e. in respect of 4Q416 2.3_5, + Philistines Jg 15_3. <COLL> נקה ni. :: אשם *be guilty* CD 5_{15}, נשׂא *bear* guilt Nm 5_{31}; + noun used as adverb, הַפַּעַם *this time* Jg 15_3.

4. be clear, be exempt from punishment, distinction from §2 not alw. clear, <SUBJ> Edom Jr $49_{12.12}$, אִישׁ *man* 4QD[f] 2_5, בֵּן *son* Si 7_8, מֶלֶךְ *king* Jr $25_{29.29.29}$, עֵד false *witness* Pr $19_{5.9}$, נכה hi. ptc. *one who strikes* Ex 21_{19}, נגע ptc. *one who touches* Pr 6_{29}, אוץ ptc. *one who hastens* Pr 28_{20} Si 11_{10}, רדף ptc. *one who pursues* gold Si 34_5, קשׁה hi. ptc. *one who stiffens* the neck Si 16_{11}, גָּבֹהַּ *exalted one* Pr 16_5, שָׂמֵחַ *one who is glad* at calamity Pr 17_5, רַע *evil one* Pr 11_2, זָדוֹן *presumptuousness*, i.e. presumptuous one Si 9_{12}, יצר ni. ptc. *that which is formed* from violence Si $40_{15(B)}$ (Bmg יכה *strike root*, i.e. נכה hi.), מִי *who?* 1 S 26_9.

<PREP> בְּ *in respect of, on account of*, + אֶחָד *one (sin)* Si 7_8; עַד *until*, + מִשְׁפָּט *judgment* 4QRitPur 29.7_{20}.

<COLL> נקה ni. || מלט ni. *be delivered* Pr 11_{21} (+) 19_5; + אבד *perish* Pr 19_9; + adverb, אָז *then* 4QD[f] 2_5, עֵת *(to the) time (of)* death Si 9_{12}; inf. abs. + finite form of נקה ni. Jr 25_{29}; inf. abs. qal + finite form of נקה ni. Jr 49_{12}.

5. be free, exempt (from obligation), <SUBJ> עֶבֶד *servant* Gn $24_{8.41}$. <PREP> מִן *from*, + אָלָה *oath* Gn 24_{41}, שְׁבוּעָה *oath* Gn 24_8.

6. be free (from harm), <SUBJ> אִשָּׁה *woman* Nm $5_{19.28}$. <PREP> מִן *from*, + מַיִם *water* of bitterness Nm 5_{19}.

7. be cleared, settled, <SUBJ> עִנְיָן *matter* MurEp Jonathan$_9$ ([וינ]קה ענ[י]ן).

<SYN> §4 מלט ni. *be delivered*.

<ANT> §3 אשׁם *be guilty* CD 5_{15}, נשׂא *bear* guilt.

Also 4QD[a] 5.1_1 (תנק[ה]א) 4Q408 10_{25}.

Pi. $_{18.0.3}$ Pf. נִקֵּיתִי; impf. יְנַקֶּה, 2ms תְּנַקֵּנִי (תְּנַקֵּהוּ), אֲנַקֶּךָ; impv. נַקֵּנִי; inf. abs. נַקֵּה—**1. leave unpunished;** without object, **remit punishment** (Ex 34_7 Nm 14_{18} Na 1_3), <SUBJ> Y. Ex 20_7||Dt 5_{11} Ex $34_{7.7}$ Nm $14_{18.18}$ Jr $30_{11.11}$ $46_{28.28}$ Jl $4_{21.21}$ (unless נקה II *pour out*; or em. וְנִקַּמְתִּי *and I will avenge*) 4_{21} (unless both §4) Na $1_{3.3}$, Solomon 1 K 2_9, בֵּן *son* 1 K 2_9.

<OBJ> Benjaminite 1 K 2_9, Israel Jr 30_{11}, Jacob Jr 30_{11} 46_{28}, Shimei 1 K 2_9, בֵּן *son* 1 K 2_9, עֶבֶד *servant* Jr 30_{11} 46_{28}, דָּם *blood* Jl $4_{21.21}$ (unless both §4), אֲשֶׁר *one who* Ex 20_7||Dt 5_{11}.

<COLL> inf. abs. + finite form of נקה pi. Ex 34_7 Nm

14$_{18}$ Jr 30$_{11}$ 46$_{28}$ Na 1$_{3}$ 4QDibHam^{a} 6$_{14 (correction)}$ (תנק[ה]).

2. declare as innocent, acquit, <SUBJ> Y. Ps 19$_{13}$ Jb 9$_{28}$ 10$_{14}$ Kh. Beit Lei graf. 6$_{1}$ (נקה יה; others פקד יה *Yah has visited;* others המוריה *Moriah*) 6$_{2}$ (נקה יה; others נוה יה *habitation of Yah*). <OBJ> Job Jb 9$_{28}$ 10$_{14}$, עֶבֶד *servant,* i.e. worshipper Ps 19$_{13}$. <PREP> מִן *from, of,* + עָוֹן *iniquity* Jb 10$_{14}$, סתר ni. ptc. fem. *hidden fault* Ps 19$_{13}$.

3. cleanse, empty, <OBJ> כַּף *hand* 4Q417 2.1$_{24}$. Also 5Q19 2$_{2}$ (ת[נ]קו).

4. pour out* (unless §1), <SUBJ> Y. Jl 4$_{21.21}$ (וְנִקֵּיתִי דָּמָם לֹא־נִקֵּיתִי *and I will pour out the blood of those I have not (hitherto) poured out,* or *and I will pour out the blood of those I have not found pure,* i.e. §1). <OBJ> דָּם *blood* Jl 4$_{21.21}$.

⇒ נָקִי *clean,* נִקָּיוֹן *cleanness,* (?) מְנַקִּית *bowl.*

***נקה II** $_{3}$ vb. **pour out** (unless נקה I *be clean*)—Ni. $_{1}$ + waw וְנִקָּתָה—<SUBJ> Zion Is 3$_{26}$ (וְנִקָּתָה לָאָרֶץ תֵּשֵׁב *and poured out,* i.e. empty, *she sits on the ground*).

Pi. $_{2}$ Pf. נִקֵּיתִי—<SUBJ> Y. Jl 4$_{21.21}$ (unless נקה II pi. *leave unpunished;* or em. וְנִקַּמְתִּי *and I will avenge*). <OBJ> דָּם *blood* Jl 4$_{21.21}$ (וְנִקֵּיתִי דָמָם לֹא־נִקֵּיתִי *and I will pour out their blood, [which] I have not [hitherto] poured out*).

[נָקוֹב] *distinguished one,* see נקב *pierce,* §4b.

[נִקּוֹד] $_{3}$ n.[m.] **crumb**—pl. נִקֻּדִים—**1. crumb,** of stale bread (unless §2), <SUBJ> היה *be* Jos 9$_{5.12}$ (both + יבשׁ *be dry*).

2. spot, mould,* in bread (unless §1), <SUBJ> היה *be* Jos 9$_{5.12}$ (both + יבשׁ *be dry*).

3. biscuit, or **small pastry,** perh. with hole in the centre or topped with seeds,* given as present, <OBJ> לקח *take* 1 K 14$_{3}$ (|| לֶחֶם *bread;* + דְּבַשׁ *honey*).

<SYN> §3 לֶחֶם *bread.**

⇒ cf. נָקֹד *speckled,* נְקֻדָּה *bead.*

נְקוֹדָא $_{4}$ pr.n.m. **Nekoda, 1.** head of family of post-exilic temple servants (Nethinim) (Ezr 2$_{48}$||Ne 7$_{50}$). **2.** head of postexilic Judaean family that could not prove its genealogy (Ezr 2$_{60}$||Ne 7$_{62}$).

<CSTR> בְּנֵי נְקוֹדָא *sons of Nekoda* Ezr 2$_{48.60}$||Ne 7$_{50.62}$.

***[נִקּוּף]** $_{0.0.1}$ n.[m.] **gleaning**—cstr. Q נקוף—**gleaning, striking off (of olives),** <CSTR> נקוף זית *gleaning of olives* 4QD^{e} 3.2$_{15}$. <PREP> בְּ *concerning* 4QD^{e} 3.2$_{15}$ ([ב]נקוף).

⇒ נקף *strike off.*

נְקֻטָה, see קוט *feel loathing.*

נָקִי $_{43.0.7}$ adj. **clean**—נָקִיא; cstr. נְקִי; m.pl. נְקִיִּם (נְקִיִּים, Q נקיאים), f.pl. Q נקיות—**1. clean, pure,** used attributively of חִטָּה *wheat* Mur 24 B$_{17}$ C$_{15}$ (נקי[ות]) D$_{16}$ (all three || יָפֶה *fair*).

2. free, exempt (from obligation), used predicatively, (1) with היה *be,* <SUBJ> אִישׁ *man* Dt 24$_{5}$ Jos 2$_{20}$, בֵּן *son* of Gad and Reuben Nm 32$_{22}$, עֶבֶד *servant* Gn 24$_{41}$.

(2) in nom. cl., with אֲנַחְנוּ *we* Jos 2$_{17}$; אֵין נָקִי *no one was exempt* 1 K 15$_{22}$.

<COLL> נָקִי מֵאָלָתִי *free from my oath* Gn 24$_{41}$, נְקִיִּם מִי׳ *free from,* i.e. in respect of, *Y.* Nm 32$_{22}$, נְקִיִּם מִשְּׁבֻעָתֵךְ *free from,* i.e. in respect of, *your oath* Jos 2$_{17.20}$, נָקִי ... לְבֵיתוֹ שָׁנָה אֶחָת *free ... for the sake of his household for one year* Dt 24$_{5}$.

3. innocent, blameless, guiltless, a. used attributively of עַם *people* Ps 94$_{21}$ (if em.; see below), אָדָם *human being* Ps 94$_{21}$ (if em.; see below), אִישׁ *man* Jb 22$_{30}$ (if em. אִי *not*), אֶבְיוֹן *poor one* Jr 2$_{34}$, דָּם *blood* Dt 19$_{10.13 (ms, Sam)}$ 21$_{8.9}$=11QT 63$_{7.8}$ Dt 27$_{25}$ 1 S 19$_{5}$ 2 K 21$_{16}$ 24$_{4}$ Is 59$_{7}$ Jr 7$_{6}$ 22$_{3}$ 26$_{15}$ Jl 4$_{19}$ Jon 1$_{14}$ Ps 94$_{21}$ (or em. וְדָם *and blood* to וְעַם *and a people* or אָדָם *a human being* or תָּם *the blameless one* and the innocent) 106$_{38}$ Pr 6$_{17}$ 4QDibHam^{a} 8$_{14}$ ([דם נקי]). <COLL> צַדִּיק + נָקִי *righteous one* Ps 94$_{21}$.

b. used predicatively, (1) with היה *be,* <SUBJ> אַתֶּם *you* Gn 44$_{10}$.

(2) in nom. cl., with מֶלֶךְ *king* 2 S 14$_{9}$ Lachish ost. 6$_{11}$ (ונק[י] שלמה המלך) perh. *and the king is wholly inno-*

cent; others [וביר]שלם הנ[נ]ה למלך *and in Jerusalem, behold to the king*), בַּעַל *owner* Ex 21$_{28}$, אָנֹכִי *I* 2 S 3$_{28}$, אֲנַחְנוּ *we* Jos 2$_{19}$, הֵם *they* 4QD^a 8.1$_3$ (=CD 15$_{13}$ [נק]יאים), כִּסֵּא *throne* 2 S 14$_9$, מַמְלָכָה *kingdom* 2 S 3$_{28}$.

<COLL> נָקִי ... מֵעִם י׳ עַד־עוֹלָם מִדְּמֵי אַבְנֵר *innocent ... before Y. for ever of (shedding) the blood of Abner* 2 S 3$_{28}$.

c. used as noun, **clean one, innocent one, blameless one,** <SUBJ> עור htpol. *stir oneself* Jb 17$_8$, לעג *mock* Jb 22$_{19}$, נשׂא *lift* Ps 24$_4$, חלק *divide* Jb 27$_{17}$, מלט ni. *be delivered* Jb 22$_{30}$ (אִי־נָקִי *[one that is not] innocent*; or em. see Coll.), אבד *perish* Jb 4$_7$.

<NOM CL> מִי הוּא נָקִי *who is the innocent one?* Jb 4$_7$.

<OBJ> מלט pi. *deliver* Jb 22$_{30}$ (אִי־נָקִי *[one that is not] innocent*; or em.; see Coll.), רשׁע hi. *condemn* Ps 94$_{21}$ (if em. וְדָם נָקִי *and innocent blood* to תָּם וְנָקִי *the blameless and the innocent one*), הרג *kill* Ex 23$_7$ Ps 10$_8$.

<CSTR> נְקִי כַפַּיִם *one clean of hands* Ps 24$_4$; דַּם־הַנָּקִי *blood of the innocent one* Dt 19$_{13}$ (ms, Sam הַדָּם) 2 K 24$_4$ Jr 22$_{17}$, נְקִיִּם *of innocent ones* Jr 19$_4$, מַסַּת נְקִיִּם *calamity of the innocent ones* Jb 9$_{23}$.

<PREP> לְ *for*, + צפן ni. *hide oneself (in ambush)* Pr 1$_{11}$; עַל *against*, + לקח *take* bribe Ps 15$_5$ (unless §4).

<COLL> נָקִי || בַּר *pure one* Ps 24$_4$, צַדִּיק *righteous one* Ex 23$_7$ Jb 22$_{19}$ (+) 27$_{17}$, יָשָׁר *upright one* Jb 4$_7$ 17$_8$ (+), דָּם *blood* Pr 1$_{11}$; + חֵלְכָה *hapless one* Ps 10$_8$.

אִי־נָקִי *(one who is) not innocent* Jb 22$_{30}$ (or em. אִי to אֶת־ object-marker or אִישׁ־ innocent *man* or אֱלֹהִים *God* delivers an innocent one).

4. hungry,* used as noun, **hungry one,** <PREP> עַל *upon*, i.e. from + לקח *take* compensation Ps 15$_5$ (unless §3c).

Also 4QLeqet 2$_6$.

<SYN> §1 יָפֶה *fair*; §3 בַּר *pure one*, צַדִּיק *righteous one*, יָשָׁר *upright one*, דָּם *blood*.*

⇒ נקה *be clean.*

נָקִיא, see נָקִי *clean.*

נִקָּיוֹן 5 n.[m.] **cleanness**—נִקָּיֹן; cstr. נִקְיוֹן—**1. cleanness** (unless §3), <OBJ> נתן *give* Am 4$_6$. <CSTR> נִקְיוֹן שִׁנַּיִם *cleanness of teeth* Am 4$_6$ (+ חֹסֶר לֶחֶם *lack of bread*).

2. innocence, purity, <OBJ> יכל *attain* Ho 8$_5$. <CSTR> נִקְיֹן כַּפַּי *innocence of my hands* Gn 20$_5$ (|| תֹּם *integrity*). <PREP> בְּ of accompaniment, *with, in*, + עשׂה *do* Gn 20$_5$, רחץ *wash* hands Ps 26$_6$ 73$_{13}$ (+ זִכִּיתִי לְבָבִי *I have kept my heart pure*).

3. hunger* (unless §1), <OBJ> נתן *give* Am 4$_6$. <CSTR> נִקְיוֹן שִׁנַּיִם *hunger of teeth*, i.e. hungry mouths Am 4$_6$ (+ חֹסֶר לֶחֶם *lack of bread*).*

⇒ נקה *be clean.*

[נָקִיק] 3 n.[m.] **cleft**—cstr. נְקִיק; pl. cstr. נְקִיקֵי—of rock, <CSTR> נְקִיק הַסֶּלַע *a cleft of the rock* Jr 13$_4$, נְקִיקֵי הַסְּלָעִים *clefts of the rocks* Is 7$_{19}$ (|| נַחַל *wadi*). <PREP> בְּ of place, *in*, + טמן *hide* Jr 13$_4$, נוח *rest* Is 7$_{19}$; מִן of direction, *from*, + צוד *hunt* Jr 16$_{16}$ (+ הַר *mountain*, גִּבְעָה *hill*).

<SYN> נַחַל *wadi.*

*[**נִקְלָה**] 0.0.1 pr.n.m. **Niklah,** one who drafted tenancy agreement, son of Jehonathan, <SUBJ> כתב *write* Mur 24 D$_{20}$. <APP> בֵּן *son* Mur 24 D$_{20}$.

נקם 35.1.18 vb. **avenge—Qal** 13.0.18 Impf. יִקֹּם (יִקּוֹם), 2ms תִּקֹּם (Q תקום); + waw וּנְקָמַּנִי; impv. נְקֹם; ptc. נֹקֵם (Q נוקם), נֹקֶמֶת (Q נוקמת), Q נוקמי; inf. abs. נָקֹם (Q נקום); cstr. נְקֹם—**avenge, take vengeance,** perh. sometimes **champion, save,*** <SUBJ> Y. Dt 32$_{43}$ 1 S 24$_{24}$ Is 35$_4$ (if em. נָקָם *vengeance* to נֹקֵם *taking vengeance*) Ezk 24$_8$ Na 1$_{2.2.2}$=CD 9$_5$ Ps 99$_8$ (or em. נֹקֵם to נֹקָם *one who exempts them from punishment*, i.e. נקה ptc.) perh. 4QMyst^a 53$_7$ 4QAdmonPar 3.2$_6$, Melchizedek 11QMelch 2$_{13}$, Edom Ezk 25$_{12}$, Israel(ites) Lv 19$_{18}$=CD 9$_2$, גּוֹי *nation* Jos 10$_{13}$, Joab 1 K 2$_5$ (if em. וַיָּשֶׂם *and he placed* to וַיִּקֹּם *and he avenged*), Moses Nm 31$_2$, אִישׁ *man* 1QS 5$_{12}$ CD 9$_4$, i.e. each CD 8$_5$, נטר ptc. *one who is angry* 4QMyst^a 7$_5$ ([ל]נ[ק]ו[ם]), ראשׁ *head* CD 19$_{24}$, חֶרֶב *sword* Lv 26$_{25}$ CD 1$_{17}$ 19$_{13}$, עֶבְרָה *wrath* 1QS 4$_{12}$, כֹּל *all* CD 8$_5$; subj. not specified, 1QS 2$_6$ 7$_9$ 4QBer^f 1$_3$ 4QMyst^b 7$_2$.

<OBJ> 1. person on whom vengeance is taken, אֹיֵב *enemy* Jos 10_{13}. 2. person or thing for whom vengeance is taken, David 1 S 24_{13}, דָּם *blood* Dt 32_{43} 1 K 2_5 (if em.; see Subj.). 3. נָקָם *vengeance* Lv 26_{25} Ezk 24_8 25_{12} 1QS 2_6 5_{12} 4QBer[f] 1_3 4QMyst[a] 53_7 11QMelch 2_{13} CD 1_{17} 19_{13}, נְקָמָה *vengeance* Nm 31_2 CD 19_{24}.

<PREP> לְ of benefit, *for*, + נֶפֶשׁ *soul*, i.e. self 1QS 7_9; *against, upon*, + צַר *adversary* Na 1_2=CD 9_5, בַּיִת *house* of Judah Ezk 25_{12}.

בְּ of time, *in, during*, + שָׁלוֹם *peace* 1 K 2_5 (if em.; see Subj.); of instrument, *by (means of), with*, + אָלָה *curse* 1QS 5_{12}; of cause, *on account of*, + מַעַל *treachery* 4QAdmonPar 3.2_6.

מִן *from*, i.e. upon, + David 1 S 24_{13}.

מִיַּד *from (the hand of)*, i.e. upon 4QAdmonPar 3.2_6.

מֵאֵת *from*, i.e. upon, + Midianites Nm 31_2.

עַל *upon*, + עֲלִילָה *misdeed* Ps 99_8 (or em.; see Subj.).

<COLL> נקם || נטר *be angry* Lv 19_{18}=CD 19_{18} Na 1_2=CD 9_5 4QMyst[b] 7_2 (+) CD 9_4, ni. CD 8_5; + שׁוב נָקָם hi. *take vengeance* Dt 32_{43}, עלה חֵמָה hi. *bring up wrath* Ezk 24_8; נָקֹם יִנָּקֵם *he shall surely be avenged* Ex 21_{20}, נוקם לנטור בלוא [משפט] *one who takes vengeance by being angry unjustly* 4QMyst[b] 7_2.

Also 4QpsJub[a] 1_8 4QDibHam[b] 122_2 perh. Kenyon jar handle.

<SYN> נטר *bear a grudge*.

Ni. 12.1 Pf. נִקְמוּ, נִקַּמְתִּי; impf. אִנָּקְמָה, יִנָּקֵם; + waw וַיִּנָּקְמוּ; וְנִקַּמְתִּי; impv. הִנָּקְמוּ, הִנָּקֵם; inf. הִנָּקֵם—**1. avenge oneself, take revenge,** <SUBJ> Y. Is 1_{24} Jr 15_{15} 46_{10}, Edom(ites) Ezk 25_{12}, Jews Est 8_{13}, Joshua Si 46_1, Philistines Ezk 25_{15}, גּוֹי *nation* Jr 50_{15}, Samson Jg 15_7 16_{28}, Saul 1 S 14_{24}, בֵּן *son* Si 46_1, מֶלֶךְ *king* 1 S 18_{25}, אָדוֹן *lord* Is 1_{24}, אָבִיר *mighty one* Is 1_{24}, מְשָׁרֵת *minister* Si 46_1, שְׁאָר *rest* of the Jews Est 9_{16} (if em. נוֹחַ *resting* to נִקּוֹם *avenging oneself*).

<OBJ> נָקָם *vengeance* Jg 16_{28} Ezk 25_{15} Si 46_1.

<PREP> לְ of benefit, *for*, + Jeremiah Jr 15_{15}; בְּ *upon*, + Babylon Jr 50_{15}, Philistines Jg 15_7, בַּיִת *house* of Judah Ezk 25_{12}, אֹיֵב *enemy* 1 S 18_{25}; of accompaniment, *with, in*, + שְׁאָט *contempt* Ezk 25_{15}; מִן *from*, i.e. upon, + אֹיֵב *enemy* 1 S 14_{24} Is 1_{24} Est 8_{13} 9_{16} (if em.; see Subj.), צַר *adversary* Jr 46_{10}, רֹדֵף *persecutor* Jr 15_{15}.

<COLL> נקם ni. || נחם ni. *gain satisfaction for oneself* Is 1_{24}; אִנָּקְמָה נְקַם־אַחַת מִשְּׁתֵי עֵינַי *I will avenge myself the vengeance of*, i.e. for, *my two eyes* Jg 16_{28}, להנקם נקמי אויב *to take revenge of*, i.e. upon, *the enemy* Si 46_1, יוֹם נְקָמָה לְהִנָּקֵם *a day of vengeance to avenge himself* Jr 46_{10}.

2. be avenged, <SUBJ> עֶבֶד *slave* Ex 21_{20}, אָמָה *female slave* Ex 21_{20}. <COLL> נָקֹם יִנָּקֵם *he shall surely be avenged* Ex 21_{20}.

<SYN> §1 נחם ni. *gain satisfaction for oneself.*

Pi. 2 + waw וְנִקַּמְתִּי—**avenge,** <SUBJ> Y. 2 K 9_7 Jr 51_{36} (|| ריב *plead* cause) Jl 4_{21} (if em. וְנִקֵּיתִי *and I will leave unpunished* to וְנִקַּמְתִּי *and I will avenge*). <OBJ> דָּם *blood* 2 K 9_7 Jl 4_{21} (if em.; see Subj.), נְקָמָה *vengeance* Jr 51_{36}.

<SYN> ריב *plead.*

Ho. 3 Impf. יֻקַּם (יֻקָּם)—**be avenged,** <SUBJ> Cain Gn 4_{15} (unless נקם ho. = *suffer vengeance*, with הֹרֵג *one who kills* as subj.) 4_{24}, עֶבֶד *slave* Ex 21_{21}. <COLL> שִׁבְעָתַיִם יֻקַּם *he shall be avenged sevenfold* Gn $4_{15.24}$.

Htp. 5 Impf. 3fs תִּתְנַקֵּם; ptc. מִתְנַקֵּם—**1. avenge oneself,** <SUBJ> נֶפֶשׁ *soul*, i.e. self Jr $5_{9.29}$ 9_8. <PREP> בְּ *upon*, + גּוֹי *nation* Jr $5_{9.29}$ 9_8.

2. ptc. as noun, **avenger,** <OBJ> שׁבת hi. *destroy* Ps 8_3. <PREP> מִפְּנֵי *in the presence of, on account of* Ps 44_{17}. <COLL> אֹיֵב || מִתְנַקֵּם *enemy* Ps 8_3 44_{17}.

<SYN> §2 אֹיֵב *enemy.**

⇒ נָקָם *vengeance*, נְקָמָה *vengeance.*

נָקָם 17.5.16 n.m. **vengeance**—cstr. נְקַם; pl. cstr. Si נקמי—(ident. in meaning to נְקָמָה *vengeanace*) **1. vengeance,** usu. of Y.; of humans (Jg 16_{28} Ezk $25_{12.15}$ Pr 6_{34}). **2.** perh. **victory*** (Ps 58_{11}).

<NOM CL> לִי נָקָם *vengeance is mine* Dt 32_{35} (Sam לְיוֹם *for the day of* vengeance).

<OBJ> נקם *take vengeance* Lv 26_{25} Ezk 24_8 25_{12} 1QS 2_6 5_{12} 4QBer[f] 1_3 4QMyst[a] 53_7 11QMelch 2_{13} CD 1_{17} 19_{13}, ni. *avenge oneself* Jg 16_{28} Ezk 25_{15} Si 46_1, שׁוב hi. *bring* Dt $32_{41.43}$ Si 12_6 32_{23} 4Q418 126.2_6, לקח *take* Is 47_3, עשׂה *do* Mc 5_{14}, חזה *see* Ps 58_{11}.

<CSTR> נקמי אויב *vengeance of*, i.e. upon, *the ene-*

my Si 46_{1}, נְקַם־בְּרִית *vengeance of,* i.e. for, *the covenant* Lv 26_{25} CD 1_{17} 19_{13}, אַחַת מִשְּׁתֵּי עֵינַי *of,* i.e. for, *one of my two eyes* Jg 16_{28}, נקם משפטי *vengeance of the judgments of* God 11QMelch 2_{13}; בִּגְדֵי נָקָם *garments of vengeance* Is 59_{17}, יוֹם *day of* Dt $32_{35(Sam)}$ Is 34_{8} 61_{2} 63_{4} Pr 6_{34} Si $5_{7(A)}$ 1QM 7_{5} $15_{3.6}$ (both [נקם]) 1QS 9_{23} 10_{19} (שבי appar. *ones who turn to* corrected to יום), עת נקם *time of vengeance* Si $5_{7(C)}$, מועד *appointed time of* 1QM 15_{6}, משפטי *judgments of* Si 48_{7}, עברת *wrath of* 4QM^{h} 2_{10}, זכרון *memorial of* 1QM 3_{7}.

<COLL> גְּמוּל || נָקָם *recompense* Is 35_{4}, שִׁלּוּם *recompense* Is 34_{8}, רָצוֹן *favour* Is 61_{2}, גְּאוּלִים *redemption* Is 63_{4}, חֵמָה *wrath* Ezk 24_{8}; + שִׁלֵּם Dt 32_{35}.

הִנֵּה אֱלֹהֵיכֶם נָקָם יָבוֹא *behold, your God will come with vengeance* Is 35_{4} (unless *behold your God! Vengeance will come;* or em. נֹקֵם *taking vengeance*), נְקַם לֵאלֹהֵינוּ *the vengeance of our God* Is 61_{2}.

Also 4Q418 159.2_{1} 4QM^{a} 10.2_{15}.

<SYN> גְּמוּל *recompense,* שִׁלּוּם *recompense,* רָצוֹן *favour,* גְּאוּלִים *redemption,* חֵמָה *wrath.**

⇒ נקם *avenge;* cf. נְקָמָה *vengeance.*

נְקָמָה 27.1.10 n.f. **vengeance**—cstr. נִקְמַת; sf. נִקְמָתִי, נִקְמָתְךָ (Q נקמתכה), נִקְמָתֵךְ, נִקְמָתֵנוּ, נִקְמָתָם; pl. נְקָמוֹת (נְקָמֹת)—(ident. in meaning to נָקָם *vengeance*) **1. vengeance,** usu. of Y.; of humans (Nm 31_{2} Ezk 25_{15} Lm 3_{60} CD $8_{12[A]}$=$19_{24[B]}$); sometimes plural (Jg 11_{36} 2 S 4_{8} 22_{48}||Ps 18_{48} Ps $94_{1.1}$ Si 39_{30} 4QShir^{b} 35_{1}); pronominal suffixes alw. subjective, except 1QS 2_{9}. **2.** perh. **victory*** (2 S 22_{48}||Ps 18_{48}).

<SUBJ> ידע ni. *be known* Ps 79_{10}.

<NOM CL> נִקְמַת י׳ הִיא *it is the vengeance of Y.* Jr 50_{15} 51_{11}.

<OBJ> נקם *take vengeance* Nm 31_{2} CD $19_{24(B)}$, pi. Jr 51_{36}, נתן *give, place* Nm 31_{3} 2 S 4_{8} 22_{48}||Ps 18_{48} Ezk $25_{14.17}$, לקח *take* Jr 20_{10}, עשׂה *do* Jg 11_{36} Ezk 25_{17} Ps 149_{7} 1QpHab 9_{2} 4QapLam^{b} 1_{8} CD $8_{12(A)}$, נגד hi. *declare* Jr $50_{28.28}$, ראה *see* Jr 11_{20} 20_{12} Lm 3_{60}, ידע *know* Ezk 25_{14}, כתב *write* 1QM 4_{12}.

<CSTR> נִקְמַת י׳ *vengeance of Y.* Nm 31_{3} Jr $50_{15.28}$ 51_{11}, נקמת אל *vengeance of God* 1QM 4_{12} 1QS 1_{11}, נִקְמַת בְּנֵי *vengeance of,* i.e. for, *the sons of* Israel Nm 31_{2}, נִקְמַת דַּם־ *vengeance of,* i.e. for, *the blood of* Ps 79_{10}, הֵיכָלוֹ *of his temple* Jr 50_{28} 51_{11}, נקמת אפו *vengeance of his anger* 1QM 3_{6}, קנאתו *of his jealousy* 4QShir Shabb^{a} 1.1_{18}; אֵל נְקָמוֹת *God of vengeance* Ps $94_{1.1}$, חרב נקמות *sword of vengeance* Si 39_{30}, משפט *judgment of* 4QShir^{b} 35_{1}, יוֹם נְקָמָה *day of vengeance* Jr 46_{10}, עֵת *time of* Jr 51_{6}.

<ADJ> גָּדוֹל *great* Ezk 25_{17}.

<PREP> לְ *for (the purpose of)* 1QM 3_{6}, + נשׂא *lift* face 1QS 2_{9}; בְּ of instrument, *by (means of), with,* + עשׂה *act* Ezk 25_{15}; of place, time, *in, at, during* 1QS 1_{11} 4QShirShabb^{a} 1.1_{18}.

<COLL> רִיב || נְקָמָה *strife* Jr 51_{36} 1QM 4_{12}, תּוֹכֵחָה *correction* Ps 149_{7}, מִלְחָמָה *battle* 1QM 4_{12}, גְּמוּל *recompense* 1QM 4_{12}, שִׁלּוּם *recompense* 1QM 4_{12}, גְּבוּרָה *might* 1QM 4_{12}, כֹּחַ *strength* 1QM 4_{12}; + מַחֲשָׁבָה *scheme* Lm 3_{60}.

נִקְמָתְךָ מֵהֶם *your vengeance upon them* Jr 11_{20} 20_{12}, var. Jr 20_{10}, [נק]מות בדורשי החלקות *vengeance upon the seekers of smooth things* 4QpNah 3.1_{7}.

Also 4QPrayer^{e} 1_{4}.

<SYN> רִיב *strife,* תּוֹכֵחָה *correction,* מִלְחָמָה *battle,* גְּמוּל *recompense,* שִׁלּוּם *recompense,* גְּבוּרָה *might,* כֹּחַ *strength.*

⇒ נקם *avenge;* cf. נָקָם *vengeance.*

*[נִקָנֹר] 0.0.0.1 pr.n.m. **Nicanor,** <APP> נקנר אלכסא perh. *Nicanor the Alexandrian* Jerusalem add. inscr. 2.

נקע 3 vb. **recoil—Qal** 3 Pf. נָקְעָה—**recoil, be alienated,** <SUBJ> נֶפֶשׁ *soul,* i.e. self Ezk $23_{18.22.28}$. <PREP> מִן of direction, *from,* + אהב pi. ptc. *one who loves* Ezk 23_{22}, אֲשֶׁר *one who* Ezk 23_{28}; מֵעַל *from (upon),* + אָחוֹת *sister* Ezk 23_{18}.

⇒ cf. יקע *be dislocated.*

נקף I 2.0.1 vb. **strike off—Ni. be stripped off,** <SUBJ> עוֹר *skin* Jb 19_{26} (if em.; see Pi. Coll.). <PREP> כְּ *like,* + זֹאת *this* Jb 19_{26} (if em.; see Pi. Coll.).

Pi. 2 Pf. נִקְּפוּ; + waw וְנִקַּף—**strip off, cut down,** <SUBJ> Y. Is 10_{34} (=4QM^{g} 5_{1} pu.); subj. not specified,

Jb 19$_{26}$ (unless נקף II pi. *mark off;* or em.; see Coll.). <OBJ> עוֹר *skin* Jb 19$_{26}$ (or em.; see Coll.), סְבַךְ *thicket* Is 10$_{34}$. <PREP> בְּ of instrument, *by (means of), with,* + בַּרְזֶל *iron (axe)* Is 10$_{34}$. <COLL> נקף + adverb, זֹאת *thus* Jb 19$_{26}$ (unless נקף II pi. *mark off;* or em. נִקְּפוּ־זֹאת *they have thus stripped off* to נִקַּף כְּזֹאת *it has been stripped off like this,* i.e. ni.).

Pu. 0.0.1 **be cut down,** <SUBJ> סְבַךְ *thicket* 4QMg 5$_{1}$ (ונוקפו] סבכי]; =Is 10$_{34}$ pi.). <PREP> בְּ of instrument, *by (means of), with,* + בַּרְזֶל *iron (axe)* 4QMg 5$_{1}$ (ונוקפו ... בברזול]).

⇒ נֹקֶף *striking (off),* נִקּוּף *gleaning.*

נקף II 18.3.1 vb. **go around—Qal** 1 Impf. יִנְקֹפוּ—**go around,** i.e. be celebrated in yearly cycle, <SUBJ> חַג *feast* Is 29$_{1}$.

Pi. 1 Pf. נִקְּפוּ—perh. **mark off*** (unless נקף I pi. *strip off*), <SUBJ> subj. not specified, Jb 19$_{26}$. <COLL> נקף + adverb, זֹאת *thus* Jb 19$_{26}$.

Hi. 17.3.1 Pf. הִקִּיף, הִקִּיפָה, הִקִּיפוּ (הִקִּיפוּנִי); impf. יַקִּיפוּ (Q יקיפום), תַּקִּפוּ; + waw וַיַּקֵּף, וְהִקַּפְתֶּם, וְהִקִּיפוּ (Si וַיַּקִּפוּ ,(ויקיפהו (Si ויקיפוהו); impv. הַקִּיפוּהָ; ptc. מַקִּיפִים (מַקִּפִים); inf. abs. הַקֵּף (הַקִּיף).

1. go around, a. transitive, <SUBJ> אִישׁ *man* Jos 6$_{3}$, אֲרוֹן *ark* Jos 6$_{11}$, זְעָקָה *cry* Is 15$_{8}$; subj. not specified, Ps 48$_{13}$. <OBJ> Zion Ps 48$_{13}$, עִיר *city* Jos 6$_{3.11}$, גְּבוּל *border* Is 15$_{8}$. <COLL> נקף hi. ‖ סבב *go around* Ps 48$_{13}$; + סבב Jos 6$_{3}$, hi. *cause to go round* Jos 6$_{11}$; + noun used adverbially, פַּעַם אֶחָת *once* Jos 6$_{3.11}$.

b. intransitive, **complete a circle, come to a full end,** <SUBJ> יוֹם *day* of feast Jb 1$_{5}$.

2. encircle, encompass, surround, <SUBJ> Y. Jb 19$_{6}$ Lm 3$_{5}$ Si 45$_{9}$, עֵדָה *company* Ps 22$_{17}$, חַיִל *army* 2 K 6$_{14}$, אִישׁ *man,* i.e. each 2 C 23$_{7}$, בֵּן *son* Si 50$_{12}$, שַׂר *commander* 2 K 11$_{8}$, מֹשֵׁל *ruler* of Kittim 1QpHab 4$_{7}$, לֵוִי *Levite* 2 C 23$_{7}$, אֹיֵב *enemy* Ps 17$_{9}$, סוּס *horse* 2 K 6$_{14}$, רֶכֶב *chariot* 2 K 6$_{14}$, פְּקָעִים *gourds* 1 K 7$_{24}$, קֶשֶׁת *(rain)-bow* Si 43$_{12}$, דְּמוּת *likeness* of oxen 2 C 4$_{3}$, בְּעוּת *terror* Ps 88$_{18}$.

<OBJ> Aaron Si 45$_{9}$, Simon Si 50$_{12}$, בֵּן *son* Si 50$_{12}$, מֶלֶךְ *king* 2 C 23$_{7}$, כֹּהֵן *priest* Si 50$_{12}$, worshipper Ps 22$_{17}$, יָם *sea (of bronze)* 1 K 7$_{24}$‖2 C 4$_{3}$, חוּק *circle,* i.e. vault of heaven Si 43$_{12(B)}$ (unless חֹק *statute,* i.e. boundary; Bmg הוד *splendour*), מִבְצָר *fortification* 1QpHab 4$_{7}$.

<PREP> בְּ of instrument, *by (means of) with,* + כָּבוֹד *glory* Si 43$_{12}$; כְּ *as,* + עֲרָבָה *poplar* Si 50$_{12}$; עַל introducing object, + Job Jb 19$_{6}$, מֶלֶךְ *king* 2 K 11$_{8}$, worshipper Ps 17$_{9}$ 88$_{18}$, עִיר *city* 2 K 6$_{14}$.

<COLL> נקף hi. ‖ סבב *go around* Ps 22$_{17}$; + סבב 1 K 7$_{24}$‖2 C 4$_{3}$ Ps 88$_{18}$, שׁדד *despoil* Ps 17$_{9}$.

+ adverb, סָבִיב *round about* 1 K 7$_{24}$‖2 C 4$_{3}$ 2 K 11$_{8}$‖ 2 C 23$_{7}$ Si 45$_{9}$, יַחַד *altogether* Ps 88$_{18}$.

מְצוּדוֹ עָלַי הִקִּיף *he has surrounded me with his net* or *siegeworks* Jb 19$_{6}$, וַיַּקֵּף רֹאשׁ וּתְלָאָה *and he has surrounded (me) with bitterness and hardship* Lm 3$_{5}$, ויקיפהו פעמונים ורמונים המון *and he surrounded him with bells and pomegranates, a multitude* Si 45$_{9}$, יקיפום לתופשם *they surround them to capture them* 1QpHab 4$_{7}$.

3. round off, trim, <SUBJ> Israelites Lv 19$_{27}$ (‖ שׁחת hi. *trim*). <OBJ> פֵּאָה *corner* of head Lv 19$_{27}$.

<SYN> §§1, 2 סבב *go around;* §3 שׁחת hi. *trim.**

⇒ נִקְפָּה *rope.*

[נֹקֶף] 2.0.1 n.[m.] **striking (off)**—cstr. נֹקֶף; sf. Q נקפה—**striking** of olive trees to harvest olives (Is 17$_{6}$ 24$_{13}$), **gleaning** of olives (4QD^{e} 3.2$_{15}$), <NOM CL> נקפה [אחד משלו]שים *its gleaning is one out of thirty* 4QD^{e} 3.2$_{15}$. <CSTR> נֹקֶף זַיִת *striking of olive trees* Is 17$_{6}$ 24$_{13}$. <PREP> כְּ *as at* Is 17$_{6}$ 24$_{13}$.

⇒ נקף I *strike off.*

נִקְפָּה 1 n.f. **rope,** <NOM CL> תַּחַת חֲגוֹרָה נִקְפָּה *instead of a belt there will be a rope* Is 3$_{24}$.

⇒ נקף II *go round.*

נקר 6 vb. **bore—Qal** 2 Impf. יִקְּרוּהָ; inf. נָקוֹר—**gouge out** (1 S 11$_{2}$), **peck out** (Pr 30$_{17}$), <SUBJ> Ammonite 1 S 11$_{2}$, Nahash 1 S 11$_{2}$, עֹרֵב *raven* Pr 30$_{17}$ (‖ אכל *eat*). <OBJ> עַיִן *eye* 1 S 11$_{2}$ Pr 30$_{17}$.

<SYN> אכל *eat.*

Pi. 3 Pf. נִקַּר; impf. 2ms תְּנַקֵּר; + waw וַיְנַקְּרוּ—**gouge out** eyes (Nm 16$_{14}$ Jg 16$_{21}$), **bore away** bones (Jb 30$_{17}$), <SUBJ> Philistines Jg 16$_{21}$, Moses Nm 16$_{14}$, לַיְלָה

night Jb 30_{17} (unless Y. is subj.; or em.; see Prep.; + ערק *gnaw*). <OBJ> עַיִן *eye* Nm 16_{14} Jg 16_{21}, עֶצֶם *bone* Jb 30_{17} (or em.; see Prep.). <PREP> מֵעַל *from (upon)*, + Job Jb 30_{17} (or em. נִקַּר מֵעָלַי *bores [them] from me* to נִקְדוּ מֵעָלַי *they are inflamed* [יקד ni.] *more than a cauldron*).*

Pu. 1 Pf. נֻקַּרְתֶּם—**be dug,** <SUBJ> רדף ptc. *one who pursues* Is 51_{1} (|| חצב pu. *be hewn out*), בקשׁ pi. ptc. *one who seeks* Is 51_{1}. <COLL> מַקֶּבֶת בּוֹר נֻקַּרְתֶּם *the quarry from which you were dug* Is 51_{1}.

<SYN> חצב pu. *be hewn out*.*

⇒ נְקָרָה *crevice*.

[נְקָרָה] 2.0.1 n.f. **crevice**—cstr. נִקְרַת (Q ניקרת); pl. cstr. נִקְרוֹת—**crevice, cleft** of rock, **cave,** <CSTR> נִקְרַת הַצּוּר *crevice of the rock* Ex 33_{22}, נִקְרוֹת הַצֻּרִים *crevices of the rocks* Is 2_{21}, ניקרת הטבילה *cave of immersion* 3QTr 1_{12}. <PREP> בְּ of place, *in(to)*, + בוא *come* Is 2_{21}, שִׂים *place* Ex 33_{22}; עַד *unto* 3QTr 1_{12}.*

⇒ נקר *bore*.

נקשׁ I 1.1 vb. **strike—Qal** 1.1 Ptc. נוֹקֵשׁ—**1. strike,** <SUBJ> סִיר *(metal) pot* Si 13_{2}. <PREP> בְּ introducing object, + פָּרוּר *(earthenware) pot* Si 13_{2}.

Pi. 2 Impf. + waw וַיְנַקְּשׁוּ—**harass** or **revile,*** <SUBJ> בקשׁ pi. ptc. *one who seeks* life Ps 38_{13}.

נקשׁ II 5.1 vb. **ensnare—Qal** 1.1 Ptc. נוֹקֵשׁ—<SUBJ> Y. Ps 9_{17} (or em. נוֹקַשׁ *he is trapped*, i.e. יקשׁ ni.). <OBJ> רָשָׁע *wicked one* Ps 9_{17} (or em.; see Subj.). <PREP> בְּ of instrument, *by (means of), with*, + פֹּעַל *work* of own hands Ps 9_{17} (or em.; see Subj.).

Also perh. 4QSap^{b} 14_{2} (קוש[י]).

Ni. 1. Impf. Si ינקש, 2ms תִּנָּקֵשׁ—**be ensnared, be lured,** <SUBJ> Israelites Dt 12_{20}, אִישׁ *man* Si $41_{2(B)}$ (Bmg נוקש *he is trapped*, i.e. יקשׁ ni.). <PREP> בְּ of instrument, *by (means of), with*, + כֹּל *everything* Si $41_{2(B)}$; אַחֲרֵי *after*, + גּוֹי *nation* Dt 12_{30}.

Pi. 2 Impf. יְנַקֵּשׁ; + waw וַיְנַקְּשׁוּ—**1. ensnare,** i.e. seize, <SUBJ> נוֹשֶׁה *creditor* Ps 109_{11} (or em. חפשׂ pi. *search for* or בקשׁ pi. *seek*; + בזז *plunder*). <PREP> לְ introducing object, + כֹּל *everything* Ps 109_{11} (or em.; see Subj.).

2. lay snares, <SUBJ> בקשׁ pi. ptc. *one who seeks* life Ps 38_{13}.

Htp. 1 Ptc. מִתְנַקֵּשׁ—**lay snare,** <SUBJ> Saul 1 S 28_{9}. <PREP> בְּ of purpose, *for*, + נֶפֶשׁ *soul*, i.e. life 1 S 28_{9}. <COLL> לָמָה אַתָּה מִתְנַקֵּשׁ בְּנַפְשִׁי לַהֲמִיתֵנִי *why are you laying a snare for my life to kill me?* 1 S 28_{9}.

Also perh. 4QRitPur 64_{7} (התקש[ ]).*

⇒ cf. יקשׁ *trap*, קושׁ *lay snare*.

נֵר I 44.3.2 n.m. **lamp**—cstr. נֵר; sf. נֵרוֹ ,נֵרָהּ; pl. נֵרֹת (נֵרוֹת); sf. נֵרֹתֶיהָ (Q נרותיה), נֵרֹתֵיהֶם—in tabernacle (Ex 25_{37}|| 37_{23} 27_{20} $30_{7.8}$ 35_{14} $39_{37.37}$ $40_{4.25}$ Lv $24_{2.4}$ Nm 4_{9} $8_{2.2.3}$), temple (1 K 7_{49}||2 C 4_{21} 2 C 4_{20} 13_{11} 29_{7} 11QT 9_{12} 11QT^{b} 5_{22}), shrine at Shiloh (1 S 3_{3}), prophetic vision (Zc 4_{2}), tent (Jb 18_{6}); for work at home (Pr 31_{18}), for searching (Zp 1_{12}), prepared by Y. for anointed one (Ps 132_{17}); lamp of Y. (Jb 29_{3} Pr 20_{27} [or em.; see Cstr.]), the wicked (Jb 21_{17} Pr 13_{9} $21_{4[mss]}$ 24_{20}), one who curses parents (Pr 20_{20}); word of Y. as a lamp (Ps 119_{105}), commandment as a lamp (Pr 6_{23}); lamp, in ref. to Y. (2 S 22_{29}), David (2 S 21_{17}), sun (Si 39_{17}).

<SUBJ> אור hi. *give light* Nm 8_{2}, הלל hi. *shine* Jb 29_{3}, דעך *be extinguished* Jb 18_{6} 21_{17} Pr 13_{9} 20_{20} 24_{20}, כבה *be extinguished* 1 S 3_{3} Pr 31_{18}, חפשׂ *search* Pr 20_{27}.

<NOM CL> נֵר מִצְוָה *the commandment is a lamp* Pr 6_{23}, נֵר־לְרַגְלִי דְבָרֶךָ *your word is a lamp to my foot* Ps 119_{105}, אַתָּה נֵירִי *you are my lamp* 2 S 22_{29}||Ps 18_{29} (Ps if em.; see Obj.), נֵר י׳ נִשְׁמַת אָדָם *the spirit of a human being is a lamp of Y.* Pr 20_{27} (unless נֵר is from נִיר *till*; or em.; see Cstr.), נֵר רְשָׁעִים חַטָּאת *the lamp of the wicked is sin* Pr $21_{4(mss)}$ (L נִר *lamp of*; unless נֵר II *mark*), שִׁבְעָה נֵרֹתֶיהָ עָלֶיהָ *its seven lamps are upon it* Zc 4_{2}, לַנֵּרוֹת אֲשֶׁר עַל־רֹאשָׁהּ *to the lamps that are upon the top of it* Zc 4_{2}.

<OBJ> עשׂה *make* Ex 25_{37}||37_{23} 35_{14} 1 K 7_{49}||2 C 4_{21} 2 C 4_{20} 11QT 9_{11} ([ועשיתה ... נרותיה]), בוא hi. *bring* Ex $39_{37.37}$, עלה hi. *cause to go up*, i.e. light or set up Ex 25_{37} 30_{8} $40_{4.25}$ Lv 24_{2} Nm $8_{2.3}$, יטב hi. *make good*, i.e. dress Ex 30_{7}, ערך *arrange* Lv 24_{4} Ps 132_{17} 11QT 9_{14} ([וערכו ... הנרות]), hi. Si 39_{17} 50_{18}, כסה pi. *cover* Nm 4_{9},

אור hi. *light* 2 S 22$_{29(mss)}$||Ps 18$_{29}$ (or del. תָּאִיר) 11QT 9$_{12}$ ([י]אירו), בער pi. *kindle* 2 C 4$_{20}$ 13$_{11}$, כבה pi. *extinguish* 2 S 21$_{17}$ 2 C 29$_{7}$.

<CSTR> נֵר י׳ *lamp of Y.* Pr 20$_{27}$ (or em. נֵר to נֹצֵר Y. *watches*), אֱלֹהִים *of God* 1 S 3$_{3}$, יִשְׂרָאֵל *of Israel* 2 S 21$_{17}$, רְשָׁעִים־ *of the wicked* Jb 21$_{17}$ Pr 13$_{9}$ 21$_{4(mss)}$ (L נִר *lamp of*; unless נֵר II *mark*) 24$_{20}$, נֵרֹת הַמַּעֲרָכָה *lamps of the row* Ex 39$_{37}$; אוֹר נֵר *light of the lamp* Jr 25$_{10}$, כול נרותיה *all its lamps* 11QT 9$_{12}$.

<PREP> לְ of possession, *of, (belonging) to* Zc 4$_{2}$ 1 C 28$_{15.15.15}$; בְּ of place, *in*, + בער hi. *burn* 11QT^b 5$_{22}$; of instrument, *by (means of), with*, + חפשׂ *search* Zp 1$_{12}$.

<COLL> נֵר || אוֹר *light* Ps 119$_{105}$ Jb 18$_{6}$ 29$_{3}$ (+) Pr 6$_{23}$, מֶלְקָחַיִם *tongs* Ex 37$_{23}$ Nm 4$_{9}$ 1 K 7$_{49}$||2 C 4$_{21}$, מַחְתָּה *snuff-dish* Ex 37$_{23}$ Nm 4$_{9}$, קֶרֶן *horn* Ps 132$_{17}$; + מְנוֹרָה *lampstand* Ex 35$_{14}$ Nm 4$_{9}$ 1 C 28$_{15.15.15}$ 2 C 4$_{20}$ 13$_{11}$, כְּלִי *utensil* Nm 4$_{9}$.

שִׁבְעַת הַנֵּרוֹת *the seven lamps* Nm 8$_{2}$, נֵרֹתֶיהָ שִׁבְעָה *its seven lamps* Ex 25$_{37}$||37$_{23}$ 11QT 9$_{11.12}$ (both [נרותיה [שבעה), var. Zc 4$_{2}$.

Also Si 26$_{17}$.

<SYN> אוֹר *light*, מֶלְקָחַיִם *tongs*, מַחְתָּה *snuff-dish*, קֶרֶן *horn*.*

⇨ cf. נִיר *lamp*; נֵרִיָּה *Neriah*.

*[נֵר] II $_{1}$ n.[m.] **mark** (unless נֵר I *lamp*)—cstr. נֵר—<NOM CL> נֵר רְשָׁעִים חַטָּאת *the lamp of the wicked is sin* Pr 21$_{4(mss)}$ (L נִר *mark of*). <CSTR> נֵר רְשָׁעִים *lamp of the wicked* Pr 21$_{4(mss)}$ (L נִר *mark of*).

נֵר III $_{16}$ pr.n.m. **Ner, 1.** son of Abiel and father of Abner, <SUBJ> ילד hi. *beget* 1 C 8$_{33}$||9$_{39}$. <NOM CL> נֵר אֲבִי־אַבְנֵר *Ner was the father of Abner* 1 S 14$_{51}$. <CSTR> בֶּן־נֵר *son of Ner* 1 S 14$_{50}$ 26$_{5.14}$ 2 S 2$_{8.12}$ 3$_{23.25.28.37}$ 1 K 2$_{5.32}$ 1 C 26$_{28}$. <APP> דּוֹד *uncle* of Saul 1 S 14$_{50}$.

2. Benjaminite, son of Jeiel and Maacah, 1 C 8$_{30}$ (if ins.) ||9$_{36}$.

נִר, see נִיר I *lamp*.

נרא, see נֵרִיָּה *Neriah*.

נֵרְגַל $_{1}$ pr.n.m. **Nergal,** Sumerian netherworld deity, whose image and cult was brought to Samaria by the people of Cuth(a), <OBJ> עשׂה *make* 2 K 17$_{30}$.

⇨ נֵרְגַל שַׂר־אֶצֶר *Nergal-sharezer*.

נֵרְגַל שַׂר־אֶצֶר $_{2}$ pr.n.m. **Nergal-sharezer,** Babylonian officer (Rab-mag) involved in the fall of Jerusalem, perh. ident. with the Assyrian king Neriglissar, <SUBJ> בוא *come* Jr 39$_{3}$, ישׁב *sit* Jr 39$_{3}$, שׁלח *send* Jr 39$_{13}$, לקח *take* Jr 39$_{13}$, נתן *give*, i.e. place Jr 39$_{13}$. <OBJ> ראה *see* Jr 39$_{3}$. <APP> שַׂר *commander* Jr 39$_{3}$, רַב־מָג *Rab-mag* Jr 39$_{3.13}$.

נֵרְדְּ $_{3}$ n.m. **nard**—sf. נִרְדִּי; pl. נְרָדִים—**nard,** aromatic plant and the ointment perfume and incense perfume made from it, <SUBJ> נתן *give* fragrance Ca 1$_{12}$. <APP> פְּרִי *fruit* Ca 4$_{14}$ (|| כַּרְכֹּם *saffron*; + אֲהָל *aloe*, לְבוֹנָה *frankincense*, קִנָּמוֹן *cinnamon*, קָנֶה aromatic *cane*). <PREP> עִם *with* Ca 4$_{13}$ (or em. נְרָדִים to וְרָדִים *roses* [i.e. וֶרֶד pl.]; + כֹּפֶר *henna*).

<SYN> כַּרְכֹּם *saffron*.*

נרי, see נֵרִיָּה *Neriah*.

נֵרִיָּה $_{10.0.1.51}$ pr.n.m. **Neriah**—נֵרִיָּהוּ (Q נריה, I נרי, I נריו, I נרא)—**1.** son of Mahseiah and father of Baruch and Seraiah, <CSTR> בֶּן־נֵרִיָּה *son of Neriah* Jr 32$_{12.16}$ 36$_{4.8.14.32}$ (both נֵרִיָּהוּ) 43$_{3.6}$ (נֵרִיָּהוּ) 45$_{1}$ 51$_{59}$ CD 8$_{20}$. <APP> בֵּן *son* Jr 32$_{12}$ 51$_{59}$.

2. father of Mattaniah, <CSTR> בן נריהו *son of Neriah* Lachish ost. 1$_{5}$.

3. Lachish inscr. 26, <PREP> לְ of possession, *of, (belonging) to* Lachish inscr. 26 (ל[נריהו]).

4. Lachish inscr. 28, <APP> בֵּן *son* Lachish inscr. 28 (לנ]ריהו בן]; others לי]הובנה] *to Jehobanah*). <PREP> לְ of possession, *of, (belonging) to* Lachish inscr. 28 (לנ]ריהו בן] *to Neriah the son of*; others לי]הובנה] *to Jehobanah*).

5. son of Seariah (others Sedariah), <APP> בֵּן *son* Arad ost. 31$_{4}$.

6. Beersheba graf. 2, <PREP> לְ of possession, *of, (belonging) to* Beersheba graf. 2.

7. appar. father of Hananiah, Gibeon jar handle inscr. 22 24 32 33 ([נרא]) 37 38 40 42 (both [נ]רא) 45 46 47 48 49 (נ[ר]א) 50 57 62.

8. father of Domliah (others Remaliah), <CSTR> בן נריהו *son of Neriah* Seal 19 (Jerusalem, 7th cent.).

9. appar. father of Hananiah, Seal 50 (Jerusalem, 7th cent.).

10. appar. son of Meshullam, <PREP> לְ of possession, *of, (belonging) to* Seal 56.

11. Seal 127 (Palestine?, 8th cent.), <PREP> לְ of possession, *of, (belonging) to* Seal 127 (Palestine?, 8th cent.).

12. appar. son of Shebna, <PREP> לְ of possession, *of, (belonging) to* Seals 196 (Ramat Raḥel, 8th cent.) 789 (Jerusalem, 8th cent.) Jar Stamps 920 (8th cent.) 964 (Lachish, 8th cent).

13. Seal 208 (En-Gedi, 6th cent.; others נרת *Narath;* others מרא *Mara*), <PREP> לְ of possession, *of, (belonging) to* Seal 208 (En-Gedi, 6th cent.).

14. son of Parosh, <APP> בֵּן *son* Seal 255 ([בן]; Lachish, 7th cent.). <PREP> לְ of possession, *of, (belonging) to* Seal 255 ([ל]נריהו; Lachish, 7th cent.).

15. appar. father of Obadiah, Seal 281 (Beer-sheba, 8th cent.).

16. appar. son of Zaphan, PREP> לְ of possession, *of, (belonging) to* Seal 360 (7th cent.).

17. father of Uzziah, <CSTR> בן נריהו *son of Neriah* Seal 422 (7th cent.).

18. son of the king, <APP> בֵּן *son* Seals 507 (נרי[הו] ב[ן; T. Beit Mirsim?, 7th/6th cent.) 719 (Judaea, 7th cent.). <PREP> לְ of possession, *of, (belonging) to* Seals 507 (לנרי[הו]; T. Beit Mirsim?, 7th/6th cent.) 719 (Judaea, 7th cent.).

19. father of Berechiah, <CSTR> בן נריהו *son of Neriah* Seal 509 (T. Beit Mirsim?, 7th/6th cent.) Bulla 922 (7th/6th cent.).

20. appar. father of Ahikam, Seal 515 (T. Beit Mirsim?, 7th/6th cent.).

21. father of Zaccur, <APP> בֵּן *son* Seal 550 (T. Beit Mirsim?, 7th/6th cent.). <CSTR> בן נריהו *son of Neriah* Seal 550 (T. Beit Mirsim?, 7th/6th cent.).

22. father of Nemesh, <CSTR> ב[ן] נריהו *son of Neriah* Seal 662 (T. Beit Mirsim?, 7th/6th cent.).

23. appar. son of Adonijah (אדני[הו]), <PREP> לְ of possession, *of, (belonging) to* Seal 625 (T. Beit Mirsim?, 7th/6th cent.).

24. appar. son of Asherahi, <PREP> לְ of possession, *of, (belonging) to* Seal 626 (T. Beit Mirsim?, 7th/6th cent.).

25. appar. son of Asheriahath ([א]שריחת), <PREP> לְ of possession, *of, (belonging) to* Seal 627 (T. Beit Mirsim?, 7th/6th cent.).

26. son of Hizziliah, <APP> בֵּן *son* Seal 628 (T. Beit Mirsim?, 7th/6th cent.). <PREP> לְ of possession, *of, (belonging) to* Seal 628 (T. Beit Mirsim?, 7th/6th cent.).

27. appar. son of Gashmi, <PREP> לְ of possession, *of, (belonging) to* Seal 727 (7th cent.).

28. appar. son of Ahimelech, <PREP> לְ of possession, *of, (belonging) to* Seal 739 (7th cent.).

29. appar. son of Mattan, <PREP> לְ of possession, *of, (belonging) to* Seal 745 (c. 700).

30. appar. father of Seraiah, Seal 780 (7th cent.).

31. son of Shebaniah, <APP> בֵּן *son* Seal 787 (Jerusalem, 8th cent.). <PREP> לְ of possession, *of, (belonging) to* Seal 787 (Jerusalem, 8th cent.).

32. appar. son of Domliah, <PREP> לְ of possession, *of, (belonging) to* Seal 836 (City of David, 7th/6th cent.).

33. appar. son of Nahal, <PREP> לְ of possession, *of, (belonging) to* Seal 934 (7th cent.).

34. father of Benaiah, <CSTR> בן נריהו *son of Neriah* Bulla D39. <APP> בֵּן *son* Bulla D39 (ב[ן]).

35. appar. father of Joram, Bulla D54.

36. son of Malchijah, <PREP> לְ of possession, *of, (belonging) to* Bulla D66.

37. son of Meshullam, <PREP> לְ of possession, *of, (belonging) to* Bulla D67. <APP> בֵּן *son* Bulla D67.

⇒ נֵר I *lamp* + יְ׳ *Y.*

נֵרִיָּהוּ, see נֵרִיָּה *Neriah.*

נריו, see נֵרִיָּה *Neriah.*

[נָרָת] pr.n. **Narath,** Seal 208 (En-Gedi, 6th cent.; others מרא *Mara*; others נרא *Neriah*), <PREP> לְ of possession, *of, (belonging) to* Seal 208 (En-Gedi, 6th cent.).

נשׂא I 659.27.68 vb. **lift**—

Qal

1a. lift up, take up, raise, erect, p. 759a

1b. lift face, p. 760a

1c. lift head, number, p. 760b

1d. lift hand, p. 761a

1e. lift foot, p. 761b

1f. lift eyes, p. 761b

1g. lift soul, heart, p. 762a

1h. lift voice, p. 762a

1i. lift, take up, i.e. **utter,** p. 763a

2. carry, bear, transport, etc., p. 763b

3a. bear, suffer, endure, p. 765a

3b. suffer punishment for, p. 766a

4. forgive, pardon, p. 766a

5. support, sustain, p. 766a

6. bear a capacity of, contain, hold, p. 766b

7. take, receive, accept, take away, carry away, p. 766b

8. obtain favour, kindness, p. 767a

9. take (woman) in marriage, p. 767b

10. bring, present, p. 767b

11. place, set, p. 767b

12. bear fruit, produce, yield, p. 768a

13. perh. **raise up, rear,** p. 768a

14. carry out, perform, p768a

15. of heart, **a. stir, impel,** p. 768a

15b. make presumptuous, or perh. **carry away,** p. 768a

16. withdraw money from bank, p. 768a

17. intrans. **a. rise up, heave,** p. 768a

17b. rise up against, lift oneself up, exalt oneself, be exalted, p. 768b

17c. arise, occur, p. 768b

18. pass. **a. be lifted up,** i.e. **uttered,** p. 768b

18b. נְשָׂא פָנִים,

(1) **be lifted of face,** i.e. **be favoured, be respected,** p. 768b

(2) as noun, **honoured one, high-ranking one,** p. 768b

18c. be carried, p. 768b

18d. be forgiven,

(1) נְשָׂא עָוֹן **be forgiven of,** i.e. for, **iniquity,** p. 769a

(2) נְשׂוּי־פֶּשַׁע **be forgiven of,** i.e. for, **transgression,** p. 769a

Niphal, p. 769a

1a. be lifted up, be raised up, be exalted, lift oneself up, rise, p. 769a

1b. ptc. as adj., **lifted up, exalted,** p. 769b

(1) used attributively, p. 769b

(2) as noun, **that which is lifted up, lofty one, exalted one,** p. 769b

2. be carried, p. 769b

3. be taken away, be carried away, p. 769b

4. be beguiled, be enticed, p. 769b

Piel, p. 770a

1a. lift up, p. 770a

1b. exalt, p. 770a

1c. lift up one's soul, i.e. **desire,** p. 770a

2. bear, carry, p. 770a

3. support, sustain, help, p. 770a

Hiphil, p. 770b

1. cause to bear, p. 770b

2. bring, p. 770b

Hithpael, lift oneself up, exalt oneself, be exalted, p. 770b

Qal 601.25.58 Pf. נָשָׂא (נְשָׂאֲךָ, נְשָׂאוֹ), נָשְׂאָה (נְשָׂאַתְנִי), נָשָׂאתָ (נָשָׂאתָה, נְשָׂאתַנִי), נְשָׂאתִים, נָשָׂאתִי, נָשְׂאוּ (נָשׂוּא, נָשָׂאוּ), (נְשָׂאוּם), נְשָׂאתֶם; impf. יִשָּׂא (יִשָּׂאֵנִי, יִשָּׂאֲךָ, יִשָּׂאֵהוּ, יִשָּׂאֶנָּה), 3fs תִּשָּׂא (תִּשָּׂאֵם), 2ms תִּשָּׂא (תִּשָּׂאֵנִי, Q תשה), תִּשְׂאִי, אֶשָּׂא (אֶשָּׂאֶנּוּ, Q אשה), יִשְׂאוּ (יִשָּׂאוּ, יִשָּׂאוּנְךָ, יִשָּׂאֻהוּ, יִשָּׂאֻנוּ, יִשָּׂאוּם), 3fpl תִּשֶּׂנָה, תִּשְׂאוּ (תִּשָּׂאוּ, תִּשָּׂאוּן), 2fpl תִּשֶּׂאינָה, נִשָּׂא (נִסָּה); + waw וְנָשָׂא (וּנְשָׂאוֹ), וְנָשָׂאתָ (וּנְשָׂאתַנִי), וְנָשָׂאתִי (mss וְנָשִׂיתִי), וְנָשְׂאוּ (וְנָשׂוּ, וְנָשָׂאוּ), וּנְשָׂאתֶם; וַיִּשָּׂא (וַיִּשָּׂאֵהוּ, וַיִּשָּׂאֶהָ, וַיִּשָּׂאֵם), 3fs וַתִּשָּׂא (וַתִּשָּׂאֵנִי, וַתִּשָּׂאֵהוּ), 2ms וַתִּשָּׂא, וָאֶשָּׂא, וַיִּשְׂאוּ

(וַיִּשָּׂאֶהוּ, וַיִּשָּׂאוּם, וַיִּשָּׂאֵם), 3fpl וַתִּשֶּׂאנָה (וַתִּשֶּׂנָה); impv. נְשָׂא (נְסָה, שָׂא, Si שאה, שָׂאֶהוּ), שְׂאִי, שְׂאוּ (שָׂאוּנִי); ptc. נֹשֵׂא (נוֹשֵׂא, Q נושה), נֹשֵׂאת, נֹשְׂאִים, נֹשְׂאֵי, נֹשְׂאֹת (נֹשְׂאוֹת); ptc. pass. cstr. נְשׂוּא (נְשֵׂא, נְשׂוּי), נְשֻׂאִים; inf. abs. נָשׂא (נָשׂוֹא); cstr. נְשֹׂא (נְשׂוֹא, שְׂאֵת, לָשֵׂאת, שׂוֹא, מַשְּׂאוֹת, שְׂאֵתִי, נָשְׂאִי, שְׂאֵתוֹ, Q שאתה).

1a. lift up, take up, raise, erect (11QMelch 3_{10}), <SUBJ> Y. Is 5_{26} 10_{26} 11_{12} Jr $23_{39(mss)}$ (unless §1h; L נשׁה *forget*) Ps 4_{7} (נְסָה *lift up* [ms נְשָׂא]; unless from נסך *pour out*, as an anomalous spelling before the following guttural;*or em. נָס *it has fled* or נָסְעָה *it has departed* or נְטֵה *stretch out*) 102_{11} Jb 30_{22} 1QSb 3_{3} 5_{23} (ה[אכ]ש[י]), כְּרוּב *cherub* Ezk $10_{16.19}$ 11_{22}, Assyrians Is 10_{24}, Israelites Jr 4_{6} Ho 8_{10} (if em. מִנְּשֹׂא *from appointing*) Am 5_{26}, Shunammite 2 K $4_{36.37}$, Zion Mur 6 1_{4}, גּוֹי *nation* Is 2_{4}||Mc 4_{3} Zc 2_{4}, Abimelech Jg 9_{48}, Bidkar 2 K $9_{25.26}$, Esau Gn 33_{5}, Hagar Gn 21_{18}, Jacob Gn 31_{17}, Job Jb 13_{14}.

אִישׁ *man* Jos 4_{3} Jon $1_{12.15}$ Ne $5_{7(mss)}$, אִשָּׁה *woman* Zc 5_{9}, בֵּן *son* Jr 6_{1} Si 13_{2}, of Israel Jos 4_{8}, אָח *brother* Gn 42_{26}, דּוֹד *uncle* Am 6_{10} (or em. וּנְשָׂאוֹ דּוֹדוֹ וּמְסָרְפוֹ *and his uncle and he who burns him shall take him up* to וְנִשְׁאֲרוּ מְתֵי מִסְפָּר *and a few men shall remain*), עֶבֶד *servant* 2 S 2_{32}, מֶלֶךְ *king* Jr 51_{12}, חֹר *noble* Ne $5_{7(mss)}$, שָׁלִישׁ *officer* 2 K $9_{25.26}$, סָגָן *official* Ne $5_{7(mss)}$, כֹּהֵן *priest* Jos $6_{6.12}$, נָבִיא *prophet* 1 K 13_{29}, worshipper Ps 116_{13}, אֹמֶנֶת *nurse* 2 S 4_{4}, רָץ *guard* 1 K 14_{28}||2 C 12_{11}, שׂרף pi. ptc. *one who burns* Am 6_{10} (or em.; see above).

תּוֹלַעַת *worm* 1QH 14_{34}, שַׁעַר *gate* Ps $24_{7.9}$, פֶּתַח *door* Ps 24_{9} (or em. הִנָּשְׂאוּ *be lifted up*, i.e. ni.), רוּחַ *wind* Ex 10_{19}, *spirit* 2 K 2_{16} Ezk $3_{12.14}$ 8_{3} $11_{1.24}$ 43_{5}, קָדִים *east wind* Jb 27_{21}, מַיִם *water* Gn 7_{17}, דַּבֶּרֶת *word* Dt 33_{3} (if em. יִשָּׂא מִדַּבְּרֹתֶיךָ *he receives some of your words* to יִשָּׂאוּם דַּבְּרֹתֶיךָ *your words shall lift them up*); subj. not specified, Is 13_{2} 18_{3} Jr 50_{2} 51_{27} Ezk 17_{9} (or em. לְמַשְּׂאוֹת *to destroy*, i.e. משׁא inf.).

<OBJ> כִּיּוּן *Kivvun* Am 5_{26}, סִכּוּת *Sakkuth* Am 5_{26}, צֶלֶם *image* Am 5_{26}, כּוֹכָב *star* of god Am 5_{26}, עַם *people* Jr $23_{39(mss)}$, Asahel 2 S 2_{32}, Ezekiel Ezk $3_{12.14}$ 8_{3} $11_{1.24}$ 43_{5}, Job Jb 30_{22}, Jonah Jon $1_{12.15}$, Joram 2 K $9_{25.26}$, אָדָם *human being* Jb 27_{21}, אִשָּׁה *wife* Gn 31_{17}, בֵּן *son* Gn 31_{17} 2 S 4_{4} 2 K $4_{36.37}$, נַעַר *lad* Gn 21_{18}, מֶלֶךְ *king* Am 5_{26}, אָדוֹן *lord* 2 K 2_{16}, קָדוֹשׁ *holy one* Dt 33_{3} (if em.; see Subj.), worshipper Ps 102_{11}, נָבִיא *prophet* Jr $23_{39(mss)}$, עָרִיץ *ruthless one* Jb 27_{21}, נְבֵלָה *corpse* 1 K 13_{29}, רֹאשׁ *head*, perh. = widen gate* Ps $24_{7.9}$, כָּנָף *wing* Ezk $10_{16.19}$ 11_{22}, קֶרֶן *horn* Zc 2_{4}, בָּשָׂר *flesh* Jb 13_{14}, אַרְבֶּה *locust* Ex 10_{19}, גֶּפֶן *vine* Ezk 17_{9} (or em.; see Subj.), שׂוֹכָה *branch* Jg 9_{48}, שֶׁבֶר *grain* Gn 42_{26}.

תֵּבָה *ark* Gn 7_{17}, אֲרוֹן *ark* Jos $6_{6.12}$, חֶרֶב *sword* Is 2_{4}||Mc 4_{3}, מָגֵן *shield* 1 K 14_{28}||2 C 12_{11}, נֵס *standard* Is 5_{26} 11_{12} 13_{2} 18_{3} Jr 50_{2} $51_{12.27}$ 1QH 14_{34}, מַשְׂאֵת *beacon* Jr 6_{1}, עַמּוּד *column* 11QMelch 3_{10}, כּוֹס *cup* Ps 116_{13}, מַטֶּה *staff* Is $10_{24.26}$, מַשָּׂא *burden* Ne $5_{7(mss)}$ (L נשׁא ... מַשָּׁא *lend ... a debt*, i.e. cause to be indebted), כָּבֵד *that which is heavy* Si 13_{2}, אֵיפָה *ephah* Zc 5_{9}, אֶבֶן *stone* Jos $4_{3.8}$, עֲטָרָה *crown* 1QSb 3_{3} ([עטרת]), אוֹר *light* of countenance Ps 4_{7} (נְסָה; unless from נסך *pour out*, as an anomalous spelling before the following guttural;* or em.; see Subj.).

<PREP> לְ in ref. to subj., + אִישׁ *man* Jos 4_{3}; of direction, *to*, + גּוֹי *nation* Is 5_{26} 11_{12}, רוּם *height* 1QSb 5_{23} (ה[אכ]ש[י]); *according to*, + מִסְפָּר *number* Jos 4_{8}.

בְּ of place, *in, on(to), upon*, + אָח *brother* Ne $5_{7(mss)}$, רֹאשׁ *head* 1QSb 3_{3}, שֵׁן *tooth* Jb 13_{14}, דֶּרֶךְ *way*, i.e. manner Is $10_{24.26}$, אֶרֶץ *earth* Jr 51_{27}.

מִן of direction, *from*, + שֹׁרֶשׁ *root* Ezk 17_{9} (or em.; see Subj.), זֶה *this (place)* Jos 4_{3}, מַצָּב *standing place* Jos 4_{3}.

אֶל *towards, upon, onto, against*, + גּוֹי *nation* Is 2_{4}||Mc 4_{3}, Joseph Gn 39_{7}, חוֹמָה *wall* Jr 51_{12}, אֶרֶץ *land* Zc 2_{4}, רוּחַ *wind* Jb 30_{22}.

עַל *upon*, + Beth-haccherem Jr 6_{1}, עַל *upon*, + worshipper Ps 4_{7} (נְסָה; unless from נסך *pour out*, as an anomalous spelling before the following guttural;* or em.; see Subj.), גָּמָל *camel* Gn 31_{17}, חֲמוֹר *ass* Gn 42_{26}, הַר *mountain* Is 13_{2}; *against*, + עַם *people* Is 10_{24}; *on account of*, + מָה *what?* Jb 13_{14}.

מִתּוֹךְ *from (the middle of)*, + Jordan Jos $4_{3.8}$.

בֵּין *between*, + אֶרֶץ *earth* Ezk 8_{3} Zc 5_{9}, שָׁמַיִם *heaven* Ezk 8_{3} Zc 5_{9}.

ה- of direction, *towards*, + צִיּוֹן *Zion* Jr 4_{6}.

נשׂא + noun without preposition or ה- of direction, הַר *(to) mountain* Is 18_{3}.

<COLL> נשׂא || לקח *take* Ezk 3_{14}, שׂים *place* Jb 13_{14}; +

רכב hi. *cause to ride* Jb 30_{22}, שִׂים עַל־שְׁכֶם *place on shoulder* Jg 9_{48}; + adverb, מָה *why?* Si 13_2 ([מה]); וְנָשִׁיתִי אֶתְכֶם נָשֹׁא *and I will utterly lift you up* Jr $23_{39(mss)}$ (L נשה *forget*).

1b. lift face,* (1) of someone else, i.e. **show partiality to, grant favour to, respect, accept** (Gn 19_{21} 32_{21} Lv 19_{15} Dt 10_{17} 28_{50} 1 S 25_{35} 2 K 3_{14} Ml $1_{8.9}$ 2_9 Ps 82_2=11QMelch 2_{11} [[תשׂ]או] Jb $13_{8.10}$ 32_{21} 34_{19} $42_{8.9}$ Pr 6_{35} 18_5 Lm 4_{16} Si 42_1 1QH 6_{19} 4QJub¹ 23_{23} [[י]שאו]; with ellipsis of פָּנִים *face*, Gn 4_7). (2) one's own face, i.e. **look upwards** (2 K 9_{32} 4QJub^g 25_{11}), without fault (2 S 2_{22} Jb 11_{15} 22_{26} 2QapMoses 1_5), **show partiality, show favour** to someone (Nm 6_{26} Si 4_{22} 32_{16} 1QS 2_4 1QSb $2_{2.3}$ [[ישׂ]א] $3_{1.2}$ [[ישׂ]א] 3_4 [[ישׂ]א]), **enter into judgment** with someone (1QS 2_9).

<SUBJ> Y. Nm 6_{26} Dt 10_{17} Ml 1_9 Jb $42_{8.9}$ Si 32_{16} 1QS $2_{4.9}$ 1QSb $2_{2.3}$ ([ישׂ]א) $3_{1.2}$ (ישׂ[א]) 3_4 ([ישׂ]א), אֱלֹהִים *god* Ps 82_2=11QMelch 2_{11} ([תשׂ]או), מַלְאָךְ *angel* Gn 19_{21}, Buzite Jb 32_{21}, Israelite Lv 19_{15}, גּוֹי *nation* Dt 28_{50} perh. Lm 4_{16}, Abner 2 S 2_{22}, David 1 S 25_{35}, Elihu Jb 32_{21}, Elisha 2 K 3_{14}, Esau Gn 32_{21}, Jehu 2 K 9_{32}, Job Jb 11_{15} 22_{26}, Moses 2QapMoses 1_5 ([א]שא), Rebekah 4QJub^g 25_{11}, גֶּבֶר *man* Jb 6_{35}, בֵּן *son* Jb 32_{21} Si 4_{22} 42_1, פֶּחָה *governor* Ml 1_8, רֵעַ *friend* Jb $13_{8.10}$, כֹּהֵן *priest* Ml 2_9, צַדִּיק *righteous one* Jb 34_{19}, worshipper 1QH 6_{19}, רָשָׁע *wicked one* 4QJub¹ 23_{23} ([רשע]י ... [י]שאו); subj. not specified, Gn 4_7 Pr 18_5.

<OBJ> פָּנִים *face* Gn 19_{21} 32_{21} Lv 19_{15} Nm 6_{26} Dt 10_{17} 28_{50} 1 S 25_{35} 2 S 2_{22} 2 K 3_{14} 9_{32} Ml $1_{8.9}$ Jb 11_{15} $13_{8.10}$ 22_{26} 32_{21} 34_{19} $42_{8.9}$ Ps 82_2=11QMelch 2_{11} ([תשׂ]או) Pr 18_5 Lm 4_{16} Si 4_{22} 32_{16} 42_1 1QH 6_{19} 1QS 2_4 1QSb 2_2 ([פניו]) 2_3 ([ישׂ]א ... פניו) $3_{1.2}$ (ישׂ[א]) 3_4 (ישׂ[א] פניו) 2QapMoses 1_5 ([א]שא) 4QJub^g 25_{11} ([פ]ניה) 4QJub¹ 23_{23} (... [פנ]י [י]שאו).

<PREP> לְ *in respect of, concerning,* + דָּבָר *matter* Gn 19_{21}; *against,* + נֶפֶשׁ *soul*, i.e. self Si $4_{22(C)}$; *for (the purpose of),* + שָׁלוֹם *peace* 1QS 2_4, נְקָמָה *vengeance* 1QS 2_9.

בְּ of place, *in,* + סֵתֶר *secret place* Jb 13_{10}; *in (the matter of), concerning,* + תּוֹרָה *instruction* Ml 2_9.

מִן privative, *without,* + מוּם *blemish* Jb 11_{15}.

אֶל *to* 1QSb $3_{1.4}$ ([ישׂ]א ... אל), + Y. Jb 22_{26} 2QapMoses 1_5 ([אליך] ... [א]שא), עֵדָה *assembly* 1QSb 3_2 ([ישׂ]א), Joab 2 S 2_{22}, אִישׁ *man* 1QS 2_4, בֵּן *son* of Israel Nm 6_{26}, אָח *brother* 2 S 2_{22}, דַּל *poor one* Si 32_{16}, חַלּוֹן *window* 2 K 9_{32}.

עַל *against,* + נֶפֶשׁ *soul*, i.e. self Si $4_{22(A)}$.

ה- of direction, *to(wards),* + שָׁמַיִם *heaven* 4QJub^g 25_{11} ([השמימה]).

<COLL> נשׂא פָּנִים ‖ הדר *honour* Lv 19_{15}, רצה *accept favourably* Ml 1_8; + חנן *be gracious to* Dt 28_{50} Lm 4_{16}, נכר pi. *have regard for* Jb 34_{19}, שׁפט *judge* unjustly Ps 82_2, ריב *plead* Jb 13_8, לקח שֹׁחַד *take bribe* Dt 10_{17}, כנה pi. *grant title* Jb 32_{21}, חטא *sin* Si 42_1; + adverb, אָז *then* Jb 11_{15}, אֵיךְ *how?* 2QapMoses 1_5 ([א]שא).

אִם־תֵּיטִיב שְׂאֵת perh. *if you do well, is there not acceptance?* Gn 4_7, שְׂאֵת פְּנֵי־רָשָׁע לֹא־טוֹב *to show partiality to a wicked one is not good* Pr 18_5.

1c. (1) **lift (one's own) head,** i.e. **show independence, defiance** (Jg 8_{28} Zc 2_4 Ps 83_3 Jb 10_{15} Si 30_{34}); with ellipsis of ראשׁ *head*, **presume*** (Jb 34_{31} [unless §3a]). (2) **lift head of someone else,** i.e. **grant favour to, exalt** (Gn 40_{13} Si $11_{1.13}$ perh. 1QSb 4_{23}), **take note of*** (Gn $40_{13.19.20}$), **pardon** (2 K 25_{27} [if add וַיּוֹצֵא אֹתוֹ *and he brought him out*] ‖Jr 52_{31} or **free** from prison (2 K 25_{27}), **take census of, count** (Ex 30_{12} Nm $1_{2.49}$ 4_{22} 26_2 $31_{26.49}$). (3) **lift number of,** i.e. **count, list** (Nm 3_{40} 1 C 27_{23}).

<SUBJ> Y. Si 11_{13} perh. 1QSb 4_{23}, Midian(ites) Jg 8_{28}, Aaron Nm 4_2, David 1 C 27_{23}, Eleazar Nm 26_2 31_{26}, Evil-merodach 2 K 25_{27}‖Jr 52_{31}, Job Jb 10_{15}, Moses Ex 30_{12} Nm $1_{2.49}$ 3_{40} $4_{2.22}$ 26_2 31_{26}, אִישׁ *man* Zc 2_4, בֵּן *son* Nm 26_2, פַּרְעֹה *Pharaoh* Gn 40_{13} 40_{19} 40_{20}, מֶלֶךְ *king* 2 K 25_{27}‖Jr 52_{31}, עֶבֶד *servant* Nm 31_{49} Si 30_{34}, כֹּהֵן *priest* Nm 26_2 31_{26}, ראשׁ *head*, i.e. chief Nm 31_{26}, שׂנא pi. ptc. *one who hates* Ps 83_3, חָכְמָה *wisdom* Si 11_1; subj. not specified, Jb 34_{31} (unless §3a).

<OBJ> ראשׁ *head, sum* Gn $40_{13.19.20}$ Ex 30_{12} Nm $1_{2.49}$ $4_{2.22}$ 26_2 $31_{26.49}$ Jg 8_{28} 2 K 25_{27}‖Jr 52_{31} Zc 2_4 Ps 83_3 Jb 10_{15} Si 11_1 30_{34}, מִסְפָּר *number* Nm 3_{40} 1 C 27_{23}.

<PREP> לְ *according to, by,* + פקד pass. ptc. *numbered one* Ex 30_{12}, מִשְׁפָּחָה *clan* Nm 1_2 4_{22}, בַּיִת *house* of father Nm 1_2 4_{22}.

בְּ *according to, by,* + מִסְפָּר *number* Nm 1_2; introducing object, + ראשׁ *head* Si 11$_{13}$ 1QSb 4$_{23}$.

מִן of direction, *from*, + בַּיִת *house* of imprisonment 2 K 25$_{27}$||Jr 52$_{31}$.

מֵעַל *from (upon)*, + שַׂר *chief* baker Gn 40$_{19}$.

בְּתוֹךְ *among*, + בֵּן *son* of Israel Nm 1$_{49}$, עֶבֶד *servant* Gn 40$_{20}$.

<COLL> נשׂא ראשׁ + פקד *visit*, i.e. number Nm 1$_{49}$ 3$_{40}$, שׁוב hi. *restore* to office Gn 40$_{13}$, רום pol. *exalt* Si 11$_{13}$, תלה *hang* Gn 40$_{19}$, המה *be in tumult* Ps 83$_3$.

לֹא יָסְפוּ לָשֵׂאת רֹאשָׁם *they did not again lift their head* Jg 8$_{28}$.

1d. lift hand, to bless people (Lv 9$_{22}$ Si 50$_{20}$), to swear oath (Ex 6$_8$ Nm 14$_{30}$ Dt 32$_{20}$ Ezk 20$_{5+6t}$ 36$_7$ 44$_{12}$ 47$_{14}$ Ps 106$_{26}$ Ne 9$_{15}$), to show power (Ps 10$_{12}$), in hostility (2 S 18$_{28}$ 20$_{21}$), awe, reverence (Hb 3$_{10}$ Ps 119$_{48}$), prayer (Ps 28$_2$ 63$_5$ 134$_2$ Lm 2$_{19}$ appar. Si 40$_{14}$), as signal (Is 49$_{22}$).

<SUBJ> Y. Ex 6$_8$ Nm 14$_{30}$ Dt 32$_{40}$ Is 49$_{22}$ Ezk 20$_{5+6t}$ 36$_7$ 44$_{12}$ Ps 10$_{12}$ Ne 9$_{15}$, Aaron Lv 9$_{22}$, Sheba 2 S 20$_{21}$, Simon Si 50$_{20}$, אִישׁ *man* 2 S 18$_{28}$, בֵּן *son* 2 S 20$_{21}$ Si 50$_{20}$, בַּת *daughter* of Zion Lm 2$_{19}$, עֶבֶד *servant* Ps 134$_2$, כֹּהֵן *priest* Si 50$_{20}$, worshipper Ps 28$_2$ 63$_5$ 119$_{48}$, wicked one appar. Si 40$_{14}$, תְּהוֹם *deep* Hb 3$_{10}$ (or em. רוֹם יָדֵיהוּ נָשָׂא: שֶׁמֶשׁ *it lifted its hand on high. The sun* to מוֹעֲדָיו נָשָׂא שֶׁמֶשׁ *the sun forgot its seasons* or מְדוֹרֵיהוּ נָשָׂא שֶׁמֶשׁ *the sun forgot its turning points* or מִזְרָחֹה נָשָׂא שֶׁמֶשׁ *the sun forgot its rising*).

<OBJ> יָד *hand* Ex 6$_8$ Lv 9$_{22}$ Nm 14$_{30}$ Dt 32$_{40}$ 2 S 18$_{28}$ 20$_{21}$ Is 49$_{22}$ Ezk 20$_{5+6t}$ 36$_7$ 44$_{12}$ 47$_{14}$ Hb 3$_{10}$ (or em.; see Subj.) Ps 10$_{12}$ 106$_{26}$ 134$_2$ Ne 9$_{15}$ Si 50$_{20}$, כַּף *hand* Ps 63$_5$ 119$_{48}$ Lm 2$_{19}$ appar. Si 40$_{14}$ (but perh. כֵּף *rock*).

<PREP> לְ of direction, *to*, + זֶרַע *seed*, i.e. offspring Ezk 20$_{5.5.6}$, בַּיִת *house* of Israel Ezk 20$_{15}$, אָב *father* Ps 106$_{26}$, בֵּן *son* Ezk 20$_{23.28}$.

בְּ of place, *in*, + מִדְבָּר *steppe* Ezk 20$_{15.23}$; of accompaniment, *with (the invocation of), in*, + שֵׁם *name* Ps 63$_5$; *against*, + David 2 S 20$_{21}$, מֶלֶךְ *king* 2 S 18$_{28}$ 20$_{21}$, אָדוֹן *lord* 2 S 18$_{28}$.

אֶל *to(wards)*, + Y. Lm 2$_{19}$ (if em.; see below), עַם *people* Lv 9$_{22}$, גּוֹי *nation* Is 49$_{22}$, שָׁמַיִם *heaven* Dt 32$_{40}$, דְּבִיר *inner sanctuary* Ps 28$_2$, מִצְוָה *commandment* Ps 119$_{48}$ (or em. אֵלֶיךָ *to you*).

עַל *over*, + קָהָל *congregation* Si 50$_{20}$; *concerning*, + לֵוִי *Levite* Ezk 44$_{12}$; *for, on behalf of*, + נֶפֶשׁ *soul*, i.e. life Lm 2$_{19}$.

נשׂא יָד + noun without preposition, קֹדֶשׁ *(towards the) sanctuary* Ps 134$_2$.

<COLL> נשׂא יָד/כַּף || רום hi. *raise* standard Is 49$_{11}$; + נתן *give* voice Hb 3$_{10}$, ברך pi. *bless* Ps 63$_5$ 134$_2$, אמר *say* Ezk 20$_5$; followed by infinitive of נתן *give* Ex 6$_8$ Ezk 20$_{28.42}$ 47$_{14}$ Ne 9$_{15}$, בוא hi. *bring* Ezk 20$_{15}$ (לְבִלְתִּי הָבִיא *not to bring*), יצא hi. *bring out* Ezk 20$_6$, נפל hi. *cause to fall* Ps 106$_{26}$, שׁכן pi. *cause to dwell* Nm 14$_{30}$, פוץ hi. *disperse* Ezk 20$_{23}$, זרה pi. *scatter* Ezk 20$_{23}$; followed by oath introduced by אִם־לֹא Ezk 36$_7$; + noun used adverbially, רוֹם *on high* Hb 3$_{10}$.

1e. lift foot, i.e. **set out, get away,*** <SUBJ> David (unless §7), Jacob Gn 29$_1$, worshipper Ps 55$_{13}$ (if em.; see Obj.). <OBJ> רֶגֶל *foot* Gn 29$_1$; with ellipsis of רֶגֶל, 1 S 17$_{20}$ (unless §7) Ps 55$_{13}$ (or ins. רֶגֶל).

1f. lift eyes, i.e. **look up,** with ellipsis of עַיִן *eye* Ps 139$_{20}$* (unless §18a) 4QpsJub^a 2.1$_5$, <SUBJ> Israel(ites) Dt 4$_{19}$ Is 40$_{26}$ Jr 13$_{20}$, Beth-shemesh 1 S 6$_{13}$, Jerusalem/Zion Is 49$_{18}$ 60$_4$ Jr 3$_2$, עַם *people* Is 51$_6$, לְאֹם *nation* Is 51$_6$, Abra(ha)m Gn 13$_{14}$ 18$_2$ 22$_{4.13}$ 4QpsJub^a 2.1$_5$ (א[ב]רהם) perh. 2.1$_{14}$ ([אב]רהם), Balaam Nm 24$_2$, Daniel Dn 8$_3$ 10$_5$, David 1 C 21$_{16}$, Ezekiel Ezk 8$_5$, Isaac Gn 24$_{63}$, Jacob 31$_{10.12}$ 33$_1$, Joseph Gn 43$_{29}$, Joshua Jos 5$_{13}$, Lot Gn 13$_{10}$, Moses Dt 3$_{27}$, Oholibah Ezk 23$_{27}$, Rebekah Gn 24$_{64}$, Sennacherib 2 K 19$_{22}$||Is 37$_{23}$, Zechariah Zc 2$_{1.5}$ 5$_{1.5.9}$ 6$_1$.

אִישׁ *man* Jg 19$_{17}$ Ezk 18$_6$ Ps 139$_{20}$ (unless 18a), אִשָּׁה *wife* Gn 39$_7$, בֵּן *son* Ezk 18$_{12.15}$, of Israel Ex 14$_{10}$, of man, in ref. to Ezekiel Ezk 8$_5$, אָח *brother* Gn 37$_{25}$, נַעַר *lad* 2 S 13$_{24}$, מֶלֶךְ *king* 2 K 19$_{22}$||Is 37$_{23}$, רֵעַ *friend* Jb 2$_{12}$, worshipper Ps 121$_1$ 123$_1$, צֹפֶה *sentry* 2 S 18$_{24}$, רָשָׁע *wicked one* Ps 139$_{20}$ (unless 18a), פָּרִיץ *violent one* Ezk 18$_{12}$, יֹשֵׁב *inhabitant* Ezk 33$_{25}$.

<OBJ> עַיִן *eye* Gn 13$_{10.14}$ 18$_2$ 22$_{4.13}$ 24$_{63.64}$ 31$_{10.12}$ 33$_{1.5}$ 37$_{27}$ 39$_7$ 43$_{29}$ Ex 14$_{10}$ Nm 24$_2$ Dt 3$_{27}$ 4$_{19}$ Jos 5$_{13}$ Jg 19$_{17}$ 1 S 6$_{13}$ 2 S 13$_{24}$ 18$_{24}$ 2 K 19$_{22}$||Is 37$_{23}$ Is 40$_{26}$ 49$_{11}$ 51$_6$ 60$_4$ Jr 3$_2$ 13$_{20}$ Ezk 8$_{5.5}$ 18$_{6.12.15}$ 23$_{27}$ 33$_{25}$ Zc 2$_{1.5}$ 5$_{1.5.9}$ 6$_1$ Ps 121$_1$ 123$_1$ Jb 2$_{12}$ Dn 8$_3$ 10$_5$ 1 C 21$_{16}$.

<PREP> לְ of direction, *to*, + שָׁמַיִם *heaven* Is 51$_6$, שָׁוְא

vanity Ps 139$_{20}$ (unless 18a).

בְּ of time, *on*, + יוֹם *day* Gn 22$_{4}$.

מִן of direction, + רָחוֹק *distance* Jb 2$_{12}$.

אֶל *to(wards)*, + Y. Ps 123$_{1}$, Egyptians Ezk 23$_{27}$, גִּלּוּל *idol* Ezk 18$_{6.12.15}$ 33$_{25}$, הַר *mountain* Ps 121$_{1}$.

עַל *to*, + שְׁפִי *bare height* Jr 3$_{2}$.

ה- of direction, *towards*, + יָם *west* Dt 3$_{27}$, צָפוֹן Dt 3$_{27}$, תֵּימָן *south* Dt 3$_{27}$, מִזְרָח Dt 3$_{27}$, שָׁמַיִם *heavens* Dt 4$_{19}$.

נשׂא + noun without preposition or ה- of direction, מָרוֹם *(to the) height*, i.e. on high 2 K 19$_{22}$||Is 37$_{23}$ Is 40$_{26}$, דֶּרֶךְ *(towards the) way (of)* Ezk 8$_{5.5}$.

<COLL> נשׂא עַיִן + ראה *see* Gn 13$_{10.14}$ 18$_{2}$ 22$_{4.13}$ 24$_{63.64}$ 31$_{10.12}$ 33$_{1.5}$ 37$_{27}$ 43$_{29}$ Nm 24$_{2}$ Dt 3$_{27}$ 4$_{19}$ Jos 5$_{13}$ Jg 19$_{17}$ 1 S 6$_{13}$ 2 S 13$_{24}$ 18$_{24}$ Is 40$_{26}$ 49$_{18}$ 60$_{4}$ Jr 3$_{2}$ 13$_{20}$ Zc 2$_{1.5}$ 5$_{1.5.9}$ 6$_{1}$ Dn 8$_{3}$ 10$_{5}$ 1 C 21$_{16}$, נבט hi. *look* Is 51$_{6}$, רום hi. *raise* voice 2 K 19$_{22}$||Is 37$_{23}$; + adverb, סָבִיב *round about* Is 49$_{18}$ 60$_{4}$.

1g. lift soul, heart, i.e. **set heart, desire,** perh. **flee for protection** to Y.* (Ps 25$_{1}$ 86$_{4}$ 143$_{8}$); **turn heart away from, forget about** (Si 7$_{35}$), <SUBJ> בֵּן *son* Si 7$_{35}$, שָׂכִיר *hired worker* Dt 24$_{15}$, כֹּהֵן *priest* Ho 4$_{8}$, worshipper Ps 25$_{1}$ 86$_{4}$ 143$_{8}$ Lm 3$_{41}$, נְקִי *clean one* Ps 24$_{4}$, בַּר *pure one* Ps 24$_{4}$, חָנֵף *profane one* Jb 27$_{8}$ (if em. יֵשֶׁל אֱלוֹהַּ *God draws out* to יִשָּׂא לֶאֱלוֹהַּ *he lifts to God*); subj. not specified, Pr 19$_{18}$.

<OBJ> נֶפֶשׁ *soul* Dt 24$_{14}$ Ho 4$_{8}$ Ps 24$_{4}$ 25$_{1}$ 86$_{4}$ 143$_{8}$ Jb 27$_{8}$ (if em.; see Subj.) Pr 19$_{18}$, לֵבָב *heart* Lm 3$_{41}$, לֵב *heart* Si 7$_{35}$.

<PREP> לְ of direction, *to(wards)*, + Y. Jb 27$_{8}$ (if em.; see Subj.), שָׁוְא *vanity* Ps 24$_{4}$; מִן of direction, *(away) from*, + אֹהֵב *friend* Si 7$_{35}$ (or em. מאוהב to מאודב *from one that is sick*); אֶל *to(wards), upon*, + Y. Ps 25$_{1}$ 86$_{4}$ 143$_{8}$ Lm 3$_{41}$, שָׂכָר *wages* Dt 24$_{15}$, עָוֹן *iniquity* Ho 4$_{8}$; *with*, + כַּף *hand* Lm 3$_{41}$ (or em. עַל *with*).

1h. lift voice, in weeping, lamentation (Gn 21$_{16}$ 27$_{38}$ 29$_{11}$ Jg 2$_{4}$ 21$_{2}$ 1 S 11$_{4}$ 24$_{17}$ 30$_{4}$ 2 S 3$_{32}$ 13$_{26}$ Jb 2$_{12}$ Ru 1$_{9.14}$ 1QH 17$_{4}$), exultation (Is 24$_{14}$ 52$_{8}$), to speak aloud (Jg 9$_{7}$ Si 46$_{20}$); of roar of waters (Ps 93$_{3.3.3}$); with ellipsis of קוֹל *voice*, **speak out, cry out** (Nm 14$_{1}$ Is 3$_{7}$ 42$_{2.11}$ Jr 23$_{39[mss]}$ [unless §1a] Ho 13$_{1}$ [unless §17b] Na 1$_{5}$ [unless §17a] Hb 1$_{7}$ [unless שְׂאֵתוֹ *his dignity*] Ps 89$_{10}$* [unless §17a] 93$_{3}$* 139$_{20}$ [if em.; see Subj.] Jb 41$_{17}$ [unless שֵׂתוֹ *his uprising*] Si 13$_{22}$), **sing** (Jb 21$_{12}$), **speak to** (Si 35$_{7[Bmg]}$), **play** flute of lips (1QS 10$_{9}$).

<SUBJ> Y. Jr 23$_{39(mss)}$ (unless §1a), Chaldaeans Hb 1$_{7}$ (unless שְׂאֵתוֹ *his dignity*), Ephraim Ho 13$_{1}$ (unless §17b), Israelites Is 24$_{14}$, עַם *people* Jg 2$_{4}$ 21$_{2}$ 1 S 11$_{4}$ 30$_{4}$, עֵדָה *assembly* Nm 14$_{1}$, David 1 S 30$_{4}$, Esau Gn 27$_{38}$, Hagar Gn 21$_{16}$, Jacob Gn 29$_{11}$, Jotham Jg 9$_{7}$, Samuel Si 46$_{20}$, Saul 1 S 24$_{17}$ 30$_{4}$, בֵּן *son* 2 S 13$_{26}$, כַּלָּה *daughter-in-law* Ru 1$_{9.14}$, אָח *brother* Is 3$_{7}$, רֵעַ *friend* Jb 2$_{12}$, יֹשֵׁב *inhabitant* Na 1$_{5}$ (unless §17a), צֹפֶה *sentry* Is 52$_{8}$, מֶלֶךְ *king* 2 S 3$_{32}$, עֶבֶד *servant* Is 42$_{2}$, מַשְׂכִּיל *instructor* 1QS 10$_{9}$, רָשָׁע *wicked one* Jb 21$_{12}$, עָר *adversary* Ps 139$_{20}$ (if em. נָשָׂא perh. *it is uttered* to נָשְׂאוּ *they cry out*), לִוְיָתָן *Leviathan* Jb 41$_{17}$ (unless שֵׂתוֹ *his uprising*), אֶרֶץ *earth* Na 1$_{5}$ (unless §17a), תֵּבֵל *world* Na 1$_{5}$ (unless §17a), מִדְבָּר *steppe* Is 42$_{11}$, עִיר *city* Is 42$_{11}$, גַּל *wave* Ps 89$_{10}$ (unless §17a), נָהָר *flood* Ps 93$_{3.3.3}$, מִטָּה *bed* 1QH 17$_{4}$ ([מטתי]); subj. not specified, Si 13$_{22}$ 35$_{7(Bmg)}$.

<OBJ> קוֹל *voice* Gn 21$_{16}$ 27$_{38}$ 29$_{11}$ Jg 2$_{4}$ 9$_{7}$ 21$_{2}$ 1 S 11$_{4}$ 24$_{17}$ 30$_{4}$ 2 S 3$_{32}$ 13$_{26}$ Is 24$_{14}$ 52$_{8}$ Ps 93$_{3}$ Jb 2$_{12}$ Ru 1$_{9.14}$ Si 46$_{20}$ 4QapMos^{c} 2.1$_{8}$, דֳּכִי *(sound of) pounding* Ps 93$_{3}$, חָלִיל *(sound of) flute* of lips 1QS 10$_{9}$.

<PREP> לְ of direction, *to*, + בֵּן *son* Si 35$_{7(Bmg)}$ (ישא לך; B ישאלך if *one asks you*); *for (the purpose of)*, + שָׁוְא *vanity*, i.e. in vain Ps 139$_{30}$ (if em.; see Subj.).

בְּ of time, *in, on*, + יוֹם *day* Is 3$_{7}$; *in (the giving of)*, + נְבוּאָה *prophecy* Si 46$_{20}$ ([בנבוא[ה]); of accompaniment, + קַו *line*, i.e. tune 1QS 10$_{9}$; introducing object, + קוֹל *sound* 1QH 17$_{4}$.

כְּ *according to*, + תֹּף *tambourine* Jb 21$_{12}$, כִּנּוֹר *lyre* Jb 21$_{12}$.

מִן of direction, *from*, + אֶרֶץ *ground* Si 46$_{20}$.

מִפְּנֵי *in the presence of, on account of* Na 1$_{5}$ (unless §17a).

<COLL> נשׂא || צעק *cry out* Is 42$_{2}$; + בכה *weep* Gn 21$_{16}$ 27$_{38}$ 29$_{11}$ Jg 2$_{4}$ 21$_{2}$ 1 S 11$_{4}$ 24$_{17}$ 30$_{4}$ 2 S 3$_{32}$ 13$_{26}$ Jb 2$_{12}$ Ru 1$_{9.14}$, קרא *cry* Jg 9$_{7}$, רנן *shout for joy* Is 24$_{14}$ 42$_{11}$, pi. Is 52$_{8}$, צוח *cry aloud* Is 42$_{11}$, שׂמח *rejoice* Jb 21$_{12}$, שׁמע קוֹל hi. *make voice heard* Is 42$_{2}$, מוג htpol. *melt away* Na 1$_{5}$ (unless §17a), רעשׁ *shake* Na 1$_{5}$ (unless §17a).

וַתִּשָּׂא כָּל־הָעֵדָה וַיִּתְּנוּ אֶת־קוֹלָם *and all the assembly lifted and gave out their voice*, i.e. gave out a loud cry

Nm 14_{1} (+ בכה *weep*).

1i. lift, take up, i.e. **utter; compose** (Si 44_{5}), <SUBJ> Y. 2 K 9_{25} Jr 9_{9}, Israelites Ex $20_{7.7}$||Dt $5_{11.11}$ Ex 23_{1} Is 14_{4} Ps 81_{3}, Jerusalem/Zion Jr 7_{29}, Amos Am 5_{1}, Balaam Nm $23_{7.18}$ $24_{3.15.20.21.23}$, Ezekiel Ezk 19_{1}, Isaiah 2 K 19_{4}||Is 37_{4}, Jeremiah Jr 7_{16} 11_{14}, Job Jb 27_{1} 29_{1}, אִישׁ *man* 1 K $8_{31(mss)}$||2 C $6_{22(mss)}$ (L נשה *lend*, i.e. exact), בֵּן *son* 2 K 19_{4}||Is 37_{4}, of man, in ref. to Ezekiel Ezk 27_{2} 28_{12} 32_{2}, נָשִׂיא *prince* Ezk 26_{17}, נָבִיא *prophet* 2 K 19_{4}||Is 37_{4}, worshipper Ps 16_{4}, חֹבֵל *sailor* Ezk 27_{32}, מַלָּח *mariner* Ezk 27_{32}, קין pol. ptc. *one who laments* Jr 9_{17}, רֵעַ *friend* of Job Jb 4_{2}, רָשָׁע *wicked one* Ps 50_{16}, עֶרֶשׂ *couch* 1QH 17_{4}, אֵלֶּה *these* Hb 2_{6}; subj. not specified, Mc 2_{4} Ps 15_{3} Si 44_{5}.

<OBJ> שֵׁם *name* Ex $20_{7.7}$||Dt $5_{11.11}$ Ps 16_{4}, שֵׁמַע false *report* Ex 23_{1}, דָּבָר *word* Am 5_{1} Jb 4_{10}, מַשָּׂא *oracle* 2 K 9_{25}, מָשָׁל *discourse* Nm $23_{7.18}$ $24_{3.15.20.21.23}$ Is 14_{4} Mc 2_{4} Hb 2_{6} Jb 27_{1} 29_{1} Si 44_{5}, מְלִיצָה *mocking poem* Hb 2_{6}, חֶרְפָּה *reproach* Ps 15_{3}, חִידָה *riddle* Hb 2_{6}, אָלָה *oath* 1 K $8_{31(mss)}$||2 C $6_{22(mss)}$ (L נשה *lend*, i.e. exact), רִנָּה *cry* Jr 7_{16} 11_{14}, תְּפִלָּה *prayer* 2 K 19_{4}||Is 37_{4} Jr 7_{16} 11_{14}, זִמְרָה *song* Ps 81_{3}, קִינָה *lamentation* Jr 7_{29} 9_{9} Ezk 19_{1} 26_{17} $27_{2.32}$ 28_{12} 32_{2} Am 5_{1}, נְהִי *lamentation* Jr $9_{9.17}$, בְּכִי *weeping* Jr 9_{9}, בְּרִית *covenant* Ps 50_{16}.

<PREP> לְ *for (the purpose of)*, + שָׁוְא *vanity* Ex $20_{7.7}$|| Dt $5_{11.11}$.

בְּ of time, *in, on*, + יוֹם *day* Mc 2_{4}; of instrument, accompaniment, *by (means of), with, in*, + כְּתָב *writing* Si 44_{5}, נִי *wailing* Ezk 27_{32}; *upon, from*, + רֵעַ *neighbour* 1 K $8_{31(mss)}$||2 C $6_{22(mss)}$ (L נשה *lend*, i.e. exact); introducing object, + קִינָה *lamentation* 1QH 17_{4}.

אֶל *to*, + Job Jb 4_{2}; *over, concerning*, + Tyre Ezk 27_{32}, מֶלֶךְ *king* Ezk 32_{2}, פַּרְעֹה *Pharaoh* Ezk 32_{2}, נָשִׂיא *prince* Ezk 19_{1}.

עַל *upon*, + פֶּה *mouth* Ps 50_{16}, שָׂפָה *lip* Ps 16_{4}, שְׁפִי *bare height* Jr 7_{29}; *over, concerning, against* Hb 2_{6}, + Israelites Jr 9_{17}, Tyre Ezk 26_{17} 27_{2}, בַּיִת *house* of Israel Am 5_{1}, מִשְׁפָּחָה *clan* Mc 2_{4}, Ahab 2 K 9_{25}, אָב *father* 2 K 9_{25}, מֶלֶךְ *king* Is 14_{4} Ezk 28_{12}, קָרֹב *near one*, i.e. neighbour Ps 15_{3}, הַר *mountain* Jr 9_{9}, נָוָה *pasture* Jr 9_{9}.

בַּעַד *for the sake of, on behalf of*, + עַם *people* Jr 7_{16} 11_{14}, שְׁאֵרִית *remnant* 2 K 19_{4}||Is 37_{4}.

<COLL> נשׂא + פלל htp. *pray* Jr 7_{16} 11_{14}, פגע *intercede* Jr 7_{16}, נתן *give*, i.e. sound, musical instruments Ps 81_{3}, קין pol. *lament* Ezk 27_{32}, נהה *lament* Mc 2_{4}, אלה hi. *invoke a curse* 1 K $8_{31(mss)}$||2 C $6_{22(mss)}$ (L נשה *lend*, i.e. exact), אמר *say* Nm $23_{7.18}$ $24_{3.15.20.21.23}$ Ezk 26_{17} 28_{12} 32_{2} Jb 27_{1} 29_{1}.

2. carry, bear, transport a load, burden, **share a burden** (Ex 18_{22}), **help carry,** i.e. **ease** complaint (Jb 7_{13}); perh. **wear** garment (4QapLam[a] 1.2_{11}), ephod (1 S 2_{28} 14_{3} 22_{18}).

<SUBJ> Y. Ex 19_{4} Dt 1_{31} Is 1_{14} 40_{11} 46_{4} 4QDibHam[a] 6_{6}, images Jr 10_{5}, מַלְאָךְ *angel* Ps 91_{12}, Beerothite 2 S 23_{37}||1 C 11_{39}, Chaldaeans 2 K 25_{13}||Jr 52_{17}, Elam Is 22_{6}, Ephraim perh. Ho 8_{10} (if מַשָּׂא is inf.), Israel(ites) Dt 14_{26}, Judah Jr $17_{21.27}$, Kohathites Nm 10_{21}, Moab(ites) Is 15_{7}, עַם *people* 2 S $6_{3.4}$, מִשְׁפָּחָה *clan* Nm 4_{25}, שֵׁבֶט *tribe* Dt 10_{8}, חַיִל *army* 2 C $14_{7.7}$, Aaron Ex $28_{12.29}$, Abiathar 1 K 2_{26}, Ahijah 1 S 14_{3}, David 1 S 16_{21} 2 S $6_{3.4}$, Elzaphan Lv $10_{4.5}$, Hezekiah 2 K 18_{14}, Job Jb 31_{36}, Joseph Gn 47_{30}, Mishael Lv $10_{4.5}$, Moses Nm $11_{12.14.17}$ Dt $1_{9.12}$ 1QDM 2_{7} ([אשא]), Naharai 23_{37}||1 C 11_{39}, אִישׁ *man* Gn 44_{1} Ex 18_{22} Nm 11_{17} 13_{23} Dt 1_{31} 1 S 17_{41} 22_{18} Hg 2_{12} Zc 6_{13} 1 C 5_{18} CD 11_{9}, גֶּבֶר *man* Lm 3_{27}, אָב *father* 1 S 2_{28}, בֵּן *son* Gn 46_{5} 47_{30} 50_{13} Lv $10_{4.5}$ Nm 4_{15} 7_{9} 10_{17} Dt 31_{9} 1 S 14_{3} Is 30_{6} 1 C 12_{25} 15_{15} Si 6_{25}, of man, in ref. to Ezekiel Ezk 12_{6}, בָּחוּר *youth* Lm 5_{13}, נַעַר *lad* 1 S $14_{1.6}$ 2 S 18_{15} 2 K $4_{19.20}$ 5_{23}.

מֶלֶךְ *king* 2 K 18_{14} 23_{4} Jr $17_{21.27}$, נָשִׂיא *prince* Ezk 12_{12}, גִּבּוֹר *mighty one* 2 S 23_{16}, סֹפֵר *secretary* 2 C 24_{11}, פָּקִיד *officer* 2 C 24_{11}, כֹּהֵן *priest* Dt 31_{9} Jos 3_{3+7t} $4_{9.10.16.18}$ Jos $6_{4.6.8.13}$ 8_{33} 1 K 2_{26} 8_{3}, לֵוִי *Levite* Nm 1_{50} Dt 31_{25} Jos 3_{3} 8_{33} 2 S 15_{24} 1 C $15_{2.2.26.27}$ 23_{26} 2 C 5_{4}, אֹמֵן *nurse* Nm 11_{12} CD 11_{11}, זול ptc. *one who spends* Is 46_{7}, זרע ptc. *one who sows* Ps 126_{6} (or del. נשׂא) 126_{6}, סַבָּל *burden bearer* appar. 1 K 5_{29} (or em.; see Obj.), יֹשֵׁב *inhabitant* Jr $17_{21.27}$ 11QT 43_{14}, גָּמָל *camel* Gn 37_{25} 1 K 10_{2}||2 C 9_{1} Is 60_{6}, בֶּכֶר *young camel* Is 60_{6}, חֲמוֹר *ass* Gn 45_{23}, אָתוֹן *she-ass* Gn 45_{23}, נֶשֶׁר *eagle* Dt 32_{11} 4QDibHam[a] 6_{8}, עֲגָלָה *cart* Gn 45_{27} 46_{5}, אֳנִי *fleet* 1 K $10_{11.22}$, אֳנִיָּה *ship* 2 C 9_{21}, מִשְׁכָּב *bed* Jb 7_{13}, כְּלִי *vessel* 4QTohA 1.2_{5}, רוּחַ *wind* Ex 10_{13}, חָכְמָה *wisdom* Si 6_{25}, אֶחָד *one* 1 S $10_{3.3.3}$, שָׁלוֹשׁ *three* 1 C 11_{18}.

Subj. not specified, Gn 43$_{34}$ Ex 25$_{14.27}$||37$_{5.14}$ 27$_{7}$||38$_{7}$ 30$_{4}$||37$_{27}$ 37$_{15}$ Lv 11$_{25.28.40}$ 15$_{10}$ Jos 3$_{15}$ Jg 9$_{54}$ 1 S 4$_{4}$ 14$_{7+6t}$ 17$_{7}$ 31$_{4.4.5}$||1 C 10$_{4.4.5}$ 1 S 31$_{6}$ 2 S 6$_{13}$ 2 K 14$_{20}$||2 C 25$_{28}$ Is 45$_{20}$ 52$_{11}$ Jb 24$_{10}$ Ne 4$_{11}$ 4QapLam^{a} 1.2$_{11}$ 4QSD 7.1$_{8}$ 4QTohA 1.2$_{4}$ 4QTohB^{c} 1$_{5}$ ([הנוש]א) 1$_{13}$ 4QMMT B$_{23}$ 11QT 51$_{4}$.

<OBJ> אֵל *god* Is 46$_{7}$, Israel(ites) Dt 1$_{9.31}$, עַם *people* Nm 11$_{12.14}$ 4QDibHam^{a} 6$_{6}$, בַּיִת *house* of Jacob Ex 19$_{4}$, Amaziah 2 K 14$_{20}$||2 C 25$_{28}$, Ezekiel Ezk 12$_{7}$, Jacob Gn 45$_{27}$ 46$_{5.5}$ 47$_{30}$ 50$_{13}$, אִשָּׁה *wife* Gn 46$_{5}$, אָב *father* Gn 45$_{27}$ 46$_{5.5}$, בֵּן *son* Ex 28$_{43}$ Dt 1$_{31}$, of Israel Ex 19$_{4}$, אָח *brother* Lv 10$_{4.5}$, יֶלֶד *child* 2 K 4$_{19.20}$, טַף *infants* Gn 46$_{5}$, יֹנֵק *suckling child* Nm 11$_{12}$ CD 11$_{11}$, ישׁב ptc. *one who dwells* Ps 91$_{12}$, שׁוֹפָר *ram's horn* Jos 6$_{4.6.8.13}$, שֵׁם *name* Ex 28$_{12.29}$, נְבֵלָה *carcass* Lv 11$_{28.40}$ 4QMMT B$_{23}$, בָּשָׂר *flesh* Hb 2$_{12}$ 11QT 51$_{4}$, עוֹר *skin* 11QT 51$_{4}$, צִפֹּרֶן *nail* 11QT 51$_{4}$, גְּדִי *kid* 1 S 10$_{3}$, טָלֶה *suckling ewe* Is 40$_{11}$, קוֹף *ape* 1 K 10$_{22}$||2 C 9$_{21}$, אַרְבֶּה *locust* Ex 10$_{13}$, גּוֹזָל *fledgling* Dt 32$_{11}$, תֻּכִּיִּים *peacocks* 1 K 10$_{22}$||2 C 9$_{21}$.

נְכֹאת *ladanum* Gn 37$_{25}$, לֹט *myrrh* Gn 37$_{25}$, צֳרִי *balm* Gn 37$_{25}$, לְבוֹנָה *frankincense*, בֹּשֶׂם *spice* 1 K 10$_{2}$||2 C 9$_{1}$, סַמָּן *spice* CD 11$_{9}$, אֶשְׁכּוֹל *cluster* of grapes Nm 13$_{23}$, אֲלֻמָּה *sheaf* Ps 126$_{6}$, עֹמֶר *sheaf* Jb 24$_{10}$, בַּר *grain* Gn 45$_{23}$, לֶחֶם *bread* Gn 45$_{23}$, כִּכָּר *loaf* 1 S 10$_{3}$, *talent* of silver 2 K 5$_{23}$, מָזוֹן *food* Gn 45$_{23}$, אֹכֶל *food* Gn 44$_{1}$, מַעֲשֵׂר *tithe* Dt 14$_{24}$, מַשְׂאֵת *portion* Gn 43$_{34}$, חֲלִיפָה *change* of garments 2 K 5$_{23}$, מַיִם *water* 2 S 23$_{16}$||1 C 11$_{18}$, עֵץ *wood* Is 45$_{20}$, אֶבֶן precious *stone* 1 K 10$_{2}$||2 C 9$_{1}$, זָהָב *gold* 1 K 10$_{2.22}$||2 C 9$_{1.21}$ 1 K 10$_{11}$ Is 60$_{6}$, כֶּסֶף *silver* 1 K 10$_{22}$||2 C 9$_{21}$, נְחֹשֶׁת *bronze* 2 K 25$_{13}$||Jr 52$_{17}$, שֶׁנְהַבִּים *ivory* 1 K 10$_{22}$||2 C 9$_{21}$, עָפָר *dust* 2 K 23$_{4}$.

קֹדֶשׁ *holiness*, i.e. holy things Nm 7$_{9}$, מִקְדָּשׁ *sanctuary* Nm 10$_{21}$, מִשְׁכָּן *tabernacle* Nm 1$_{50}$ 10$_{17}$ 1 C 23$_{26}$, אֹהֶל *tent* Nm 4$_{25}$, יְרִיעָה *curtain* Nm 4$_{25}$, קֶלַע *hanging* Nm 4$_{25}$, מִכְסֶה *cover* Nm 4$_{25}$, מָסָךְ *screen* Nm 4$_{25}$, מֵיתָר *cord* Nm 4$_{25}$, אֲרוֹן *ark* Ex 25$_{14}$||37$_{5}$ Dt 10$_{8}$ 31$_{9.25}$ Jos 3$_{3+8t}$ 4$_{9.10.16.18}$ 8$_{33}$ 1 S 4$_{4}$ 2 S 6$_{3.4.13}$ 2 S 15$_{24}$ 1 K 2$_{26}$ 8$_{3}$||2 C 5$_{4}$ 1 C 15$_{2.2.15.26.27}$, *chest* for money 2 C 24$_{11}$, בְּרִית *covenant* Jos 3$_{17}$ (mss אֲרוֹן בְּרִית *ark of the covenant of*), שֻׁלְחָן *table* Ex 25$_{27}$||37$_{14}$ 37$_{15}$, מִזְבֵּחַ *altar* Ex 27$_{7}$||38$_{7}$ 30$_{4}$||37$_{27}$, אֵפוֹד *ephod* 1 S 2$_{28}$ 14$_{3}$ 22$_{18}$, נֵבֶל *jar* 1 S 10$_{3}$, לְבוּשׁ *garment* 4QapLam^{a} 1.2$_{11}$ ([הלבו]שים), קַלַּחַת *pot* 4QTohB^{c} 1$_{5}$ (הנוש]א ק]לחת), כְּלִי *vessel, implement* Nm 1$_{50}$ 4$_{26}$ Is 52$_{11}$ 1 C 23$_{26}$ 4QSD 7.1$_{8}$ 4QTohA 1.2$_{4}$, *baggage* Ezk 12$_{6.7.12}$, *weapon* (alw. נֹשֵׂא כֵלִים and vars., *one who carries weapons, armour-bearer*) Jg 9$_{54}$ 1 S 14$_{1+8t}$ 16$_{21}$ 31$_{4.4.5}$||1 C 10$_{4.4.5}$ 1 S 31$_{6}$ 2 S 18$_{15}$ 23$_{37}$||1 C 11$_{39}$, מָגֵן *shield* 1 C 5$_{18}$ 2 C 14$_{7}$, צִנָּה *shield* 1 S 17$_{7.41}$ 1 C 12$_{25}$ 2 C 14$_{7}$, חֶרֶב *sword* 1 C 5$_{18}$, רֹמַח *spear* 1 C 12$_{25}$ 2 C 14$_{7}$, אַשְׁפָּה *quiver* Is 22$_{6}$, מֶשֶׁךְ *trail* Ps 126$_{6}$ (or del. נשׂא).

טֹרַח *burden* Dt 1$_{12}$ Is 1$_{14}$ 1QDM 2$_{7}$ ([אשא]), סֵבֶל *burden* 1 K 5$_{29}$ (if em. סַבָּל *burden bearer*), מַשָּׂא *burden* Dt 1$_{12}$ 2 K 7$_{8}$ (6QKgs משואם; MT מִשָּׁם *from there*) Jr 17$_{21.27}$, עֹל *yoke* Lm 3$_{27}$ 4QWays^{b} 1.2$_{9}$, טְחוֹן *millstone* Lm 5$_{13}$, יִתְרָה *abundance* Is 15$_{7}$, פְּקֻדָּה *store* Is 15$_{7}$, אוֹצָר *treasure* Is 30$_{6}$, חַיִל *wealth* Is 30$_{6}$, הוֹד *honour* Zc 6$_{13}$, רִיב *strife* Dt 1$_{12}$, שְׁכָבָה *lying down* of seed, i.e. ejaculate 4QTohA 1.2$_{5}$, סֵפֶר *book* Jb 31$_{36}$, אֲשֶׁר *that which* 2 K 18$_{14}$, כֹּל *anything* Lv 15$_{10}$ 11QT 43$_{14}$.

<PREP> לְ *as*, + זִכָּרוֹן *memorial* Ex 28$_{12}$; *before*, + עַיִן *eye* Ezk 12$_{6.7}$.

בְּ of place, time, *in, on, among, during*, + כָּתֵף *shoulder* Nm 7$_{9}$, חֵיק *bosom* Nm 11$_{12}$ Is 40$_{11}$, חֹשֶׁן *breastpiece* Ex 28$_{29}$, כֻּתֹּנֶת *tunic* Lv 10$_{5}$, כָּנָף *skirt* of garment Hg 2$_{12}$, עֲגָלָה *cart* Gn 46$_{5}$, רֶכֶב *chariot* Is 22$_{6}$, דֶּרֶךְ *way* Dt 1$_{31}$, יוֹם *day* Jr 17$_{21}$, עֲלָטָה *darkness* Ezk 12$_{12}$, נְעוּרִים *youth* Lm 3$_{27}$; of instrument, *by (means of), with*, + בַּד *pole* Ex 25$_{14}$||38$_{7}$ 30$_{4}$||37$_{27}$, מוֹט *pole* Nm 13$_{23}$; introducing object, + מַשָּׂא *burden* Nm 11$_{17}$, סֵבֶל *burden* Ne 4$_{11}$, שִׂיחַ *complaint* Jb 7$_{13}$.

מִן of direction, *from*, + Egypt Gn 47$_{30}$, Ophir 1 K 10$_{11}$, בַּיִת *house* 2 S 6$_{3.4}$, שָׁם *there* 1 S 4$_{4}$; partitive, *some of* (as object of נשׂא), + נְבֵלָה *carcass* Lv 11$_{25}$ 11QT 51$_{4}$, עֶצֶם *bone* 11QT 51$_{4}$, טוּב *goodness*, i.e. produce Gn 45$_{23}$, תְּאֵנָה *fig* Nm 13$_{23}$, רִמּוֹן *pomegranate* Nm 13$_{23}$.

אֶל *to*, + אֵם *mother* 2 K 4$_{19}$, מָקוֹם *place* 2 C 24$_{11}$; *upon*, + כָּתֵף *shoulder* Ezk 12$_{12}$.

עַל *upon*, + אִישׁ *man* CD 11$_{9}$, סוּס *horse* 2 K 14$_{20}$||2 C 25$_{28}$, אֶבְרָה *wing* Dt 32$_{11}$ 4QDibHam^{a} 6$_{8}$ ([אברתו]), כָּנָף *wing* Ex 19$_{4}$ Ps 91$_{12}$ 4QDibHam^{a} 6$_{6}$ ([על כנפי]), כָּתֵף *shoulder* Ex 28$_{12}$ Is 30$_{6}$ 46$_{7}$ Ezk 12$_{6.7}$, שְׁכֶם *shoulder* Jb 31$_{36}$, דַּבֶּשֶׁת *hump (of camel)* Is 30$_{6}$, לֵב *heart* Ex 28$_{29.30}$; *over*, + נַחַל *wadi* Is 15$_{7}$; *to*, + עַם *people* Is 30$_{6}$, אֲדָמָה *land* Nm 11$_{12}$.

אֵת *with*, + Moses Ex 18$_{22}$ Nm 11$_{17}$.

מֵאֵת פְּנֵי *from before*, + קֹדֶשׁ *sanctuary* Lv 10$_{4}$.

לִפְנֵי *before*, + Y. Ex 28$_{12.30}$ Jos 6$_{8}$ 1 S 2$_{28}$, David 1 K 2$_{26}$, Gehazi 2 K 5$_{23}$, אָב *father* 1 K 2$_{26}$, אֲרוֹן *ark* Jos 6$_{4.6.8(mss).13}$.

אֶל־מִחוּץ לְ *(to) outside*, + מַחֲנֶה *camp* Lv 10$_{4.5}$.

ה- of direction, *to*, + בָּבֶל *Babylon* 2 K 25$_{13}$||Jr 52$_{17}$, אֶרֶץ *land* Gn 50$_{13}$.

נשׂא + noun without preposition or ה- of direction, בֵּית־אֵל *(to) Bethel* 2 K 23$_{4}$.

<COLL> נשׂא || סבל *bear* Is 46$_{4.7}$, דרך *tread* bow 1 C 5$_{18}$ 2 C 14$_{7}$; + עמס *carry* Ne 4$_{11}$, נחם pi. *comfort* Jb 7$_{13}$; + adverb or noun used adverbially, לְבַד *alone* Nm 11$_{14.17}$ Dt 1$_{9.12}$ 1QDM 2$_{7}$ ([אשא לבדי]), אֵיכָה *how?* Dt 1$_{12}$ 1QDM 2$_{7}$ ([אי]כה [אשא]), פֶּלֶא *wonderfully* 4QDibHam^{a} 6$_{6}$ (פלא[י]ם).

כַּאֲשֶׁר יוּכְלוּן שְׂאֵת *as (much as) they are able to carry* Gn 44$_{1}$, לֹא־אוּכַל ... לָשֵׂאת *I am not able ... to carry* Nm 11$_{14}$ Dt 1$_{9}$, var. Dt 14$_{24}$, נִלְאֵיתִי נְשֹׂא *I am weary of bearing (it)* Is 1$_{14}$, לֹא לָשֵׂאת אֶת־אֲרוֹן הָאֱלֹהִים *no one is to carry the ark of God* except the Levites 1 C 15$_{2}$, נָשׂוֹא יִנָּשׂוּא *they have to be carried*, lit. 'carrying they are carried' Jr 10$_{5}$ (mss יִנָּשְׂאוּ), רְעֵבִים נָשְׂאוּ עֹמֶר *the hungry carry sheaves* Jb 24$_{10}$.

3a. bear, suffer, endure guilt, punishment, affliction, etc., **bear with** someone (Jb 21$_{3}$), <SUBJ> Y. Jr 44$_{22}$, Elam Ezk 32$_{24.25}$, Ephraim Jr 31$_{19}$, Israelite(ites) Lv 19$_{17}$=CD 9$_{8}$ Ezk 34$_{29}$ Mc 6$_{16}$, Jacob Ezk 39$_{26}$ (or em. וְנָשׁוּ *and they shall forget*, from נשׁה), Jerusalem/Zion Jr 10$_{19}$ Ezk 16$_{52.54}$ perh. Ezk 36$_{15}$, Sidonians Ezk 32$_{30}$, גּוֹי *nation* Ezk 36$_{7}$, עִיר *city* Mc 7$_{9}$, בַּיִת *house* of father Nm 18$_{1}$, of Israel Ezk 39$_{26}$ (or em.; see above), הָמוֹן *multitude* Ezk 32$_{24.25}$, Aaron Ex 28$_{30.38.43}$ Lv 22$_{9}$ Nm 18$_{1.1}$, Cain Gn 4$_{13}$, Eleazar Lv 10$_{17}$, Ithamar Lv 10$_{17}$, Jeremiah Jr 15$_{15}$.

אִישׁ *man, husband* Lv 20$_{17.19.20}$ 24$_{15}$ Nm 9$_{13}$ 30$_{16}$ 1QS 6$_{1}$ 11QT 35$_{7}$ 54$_{1}$ ([ונשא] ... א[ישה]), אִשָּׁה *woman* Nm 5$_{31}$, אָב *father* Ezk 18$_{20}$, בֵּן *son* Lv 22$_{9}$ Nm 18$_{1.1}$ Ezk 18$_{19.20}$ Pr 9$_{12}$ Si 11$_{33}$, of Israel Nm 14$_{34}$ 18$_{22}$, of man, in ref. to Ezekiel Ezk 4$_{4.5.6}$, אָחוֹת *sister* Lv 20$_{19}$, דּוֹדָה *aunt* Lv 20$_{20}$, נָסִיךְ *prince* Ezk 32$_{30}$, רֵעַ *friend* Jb 21$_{3}$, עֶבֶד *servant* Is 53$_{4.12}$, לֵוִי *Levite* Nm 18$_{23.32}$ Ezk 44$_{10.12.13}$, כֹּהֵן *priest* 11QT 35$_{14}$, נָבִיא *prophet* Ezk 14$_{10}$, דרשׁ ptc. *one who inquires* Ezk 14$_{10}$, worshipper Ps 55$_{13}$ (or §1e, if ins. רֶגֶל *foot* as obj.) 69$_{8}$ Ps 88$_{16}$ 89$_{51}$, אכל ptc. *one who eats* Lv 19$_{8}$, גָּדוֹל *great one* Pr 19$_{19(Qr)}$ (Kt גרל *lot*), נֶפֶשׁ *soul*, i.e. person Lv 7$_{18}$ 17$_{16}$.

שָׂעִיר *goat* Lv 16$_{22}$ 11QT 26$_{13}$, אֶרֶץ *earth* Pr 30$_{21}$, הַר *mountain* Ezk 36$_{6}$, גִּבְעָה *hill* Ezk 36$_{6}$, גַּיְא *valley* Ezk 36$_{6}$, אָפִיק *channel* Ezk 36$_{6}$, מִי *who?* Pr 18$_{14}$; subj. not specified, Lv 5$_{1.17}$ Jb 34$_{31}$ (unless §1c; or em. נִשֵּׁאתִי *I was beguiled*, i.e. נשׁא ni.) 4Q417 1.1$_{23}$ CD 15$_{4}$.

<OBJ> עַם *people*, i.e. reproaches from them Ps 89$_{51}$ (or em. כָּל־רַבִּים *all the many* peoples to כְּלִמַּת *insult of* or כָּל דִּבַּת *all the defamation of*), Job Jb 21$_{3}$, רוּחַ downcast *spirit* Pr 18$_{14}$, עֹנֶשׁ *penalty* Pr 19$_{19}$.

עָוֹן *punishment, guilt* Gn 4$_{13}$ Ex 28$_{38.43}$ Lv 5$_{1.17}$ 7$_{18}$ 10$_{17}$ 16$_{22}$ 17$_{16}$ 19$_{8}$ 20$_{17.19.20}$ Nm 5$_{31}$ 14$_{34}$ 18$_{1.1.23}$ 30$_{16}$ Ezk 4$_{4.5.6}$ 14$_{10}$ 44$_{10.12}$ 1QS 6$_{1}$ 4QD^{a} 7.1$_{4}$ (עוו[ן]) 4Q417 1.1$_{23}$ 4QPrayer^{c} 1$_{15}$ ([נ]שא) 4QOrd^{b} 2.2$_{5}$ 11QT 26$_{13}$ 35$_{7}$ 54$_{1}$ ([ונשא]), חֵטְא *sin* Lv 19$_{17}$=CD 9$_{8}$ Lv 22$_{9}$ 24$_{15}$ Nm 9$_{13}$ 18$_{22.32}$ Is 53$_{12}$ 11QT 35$_{14}$, חַטָּאָה *sin* CD 15$_{4}$, מַעַל *sin* Ezk 39$_{26}$ (or em.; see Subj.), מִשְׁפָּט *judgment* Ex 28$_{30}$.

חֳלִי *sickness*, i.e. affliction Is 53$_{4}$ Jr 10$_{19}$, מוּם *blemish* Si 11$_{33}$, חֶרְפָּה *reproach* Jr 15$_{15}$ 31$_{19}$ Ezk 36$_{15}$ Mc 6$_{16}$ 69$_{8}$, כְּלִמָּה *disgrace, insult* Ezk 16$_{52.54}$ 32$_{24.25.30}$ 34$_{29}$ 36$_{6.7}$ 39$_{26}$ (or em.; see Subj.) 44$_{13}$, תּוֹעֵבָה *abomination* Ezk 44$_{13}$, זַעַף *anger* Mc 7$_{9}$, אֵימָה *terror* Ps 88$_{16}$.

<PREP> בְּ of place, *in*, + חֵיק *bosom* Ps 89$_{51}$; partitive, *some of*, + עָוֹן *guilt* Ezk 18$_{19.20.20}$.

אֶל *to*, + אֶרֶץ *land* Lv 16$_{22}$.

עַל *upon*, + שָׂעִיר *goat* Lv 16$_{22}$; *on account of, for (the sake of)* Lv 22$_{9}$ Nm 18$_{32}$, + Y. Jr 15$_{15}$ Ps 69$_{8}$, רֵעַ *neighbour* 1QS 6$_{1}$ CD 9$_{8}$, עָמִית *neighbour* Lv 19$_{17}$.

עִם *with*, + ירד ptc. *one who goes down* Ezk 32$_{24.25}$.

אֵת *with*, + ירד ptc. *one who goes down* Ezk 32$_{30}$.

מִפְּנֵי *on account of*, + רֹעַ *evil* Jr 44$_{22}$, תּוֹעֵבָה *abomination* Jr 44$_{22}$.

תַּחַת *under*, + אַרְבַּע *four (things)* Pr 30$_{21}$.

<COLL> נשׂא || סבל *bear* Is 53$_{4}$; + כפר pi. *make atonement* Lv 10$_{17}$; :: נקה ni. *be free (from guilt)* Nm 5$_{3}$; + adverb or noun used adverbially, תָּמִיד *continually* Ex 28$_{30}$, עוֹד *again* Ezk 34$_{29}$ 36$_{15}$, יוֹם *day* Nm 14$_{34}$, לְבַד *alone* Jb 91$_{12}$, לָמָּה *why?* Si 11$_{33}$ 4Q417 1.1$_{23}$; גָּדוֹל עֲוֹנִי

מִנְּשֹׂא *my punishment is too great to bear* Gn 4$_{13}$.

3b. suffer punishment for, <SUBJ> Jerusalem/Zion Ezk 16$_{58}$, Oholah Ezk 23$_{49}$, Oholibah Ezk 23$_{35.49}$, בֵּן *son* Nm 14$_{33}$. <OBJ> זְנוּת *prostitution* Nm 14$_{33}$, תַּזְנוּת *prostitution* Ezk 23$_{35}$, חֵטְא *sin* Ezk 23$_{49}$, זִמָּה *wickedness* Ezk 16$_{58}$ 23$_{35}$, תּוֹעֵבָה *abomination* Ezk 16$_{58}$.

4. forgive, pardon, <SUBJ> Y. Gn 18$_{24.26}$ Ex 32$_{32}$ 34$_7$ Nm 14$_{18.19}$ Jos 24$_{19}$ Is 2$_9$ Ho 1$_{6.6}$ (or em. both; see Coll.) 14$_3$ Mc 7$_{18}$ Ps 25$_{18}$ 32$_5$ 85$_3$ 99$_8$ Jb 7$_{21}$ Jb 11$_6$ (if em. יַשֶּׁה *he forgets* [נשה hi.] to יִשָּׂא) Si 16$_{7.11}$ 1QH 4$_{12}$ (ל[שאת]) 4$_{15}$ (ל[שאת]) 8$_{25}$ 4QDibHam^a 1.2$_7$ ([נ]שאת[ה]) CD 3$_{18}$, בֵּן *son* Si 30$_{11}$, מַלְאָךְ *angel* Ex 23$_{21}$, Aaron Ex 10$_{17}$, David 1 S 25$_{28}$, Joseph Gn 50$_{17.17}$, Moses Ex 10$_{17}$, Samuel 1 S 15$_{25}$.

<OBJ> פֶּשַׁע *transgression* Gn 50$_{17}$ Ex 34$_7$ Jb 7$_{21}$, חַטָּאת *sin* Gn 50$_{17}$ Ex 10$_{17}$ 32$_{32}$ 34$_7$ Nm 14$_{18}$ 1 S 15$_{25}$, עָוֺן *iniquity, guilt* (unless נשׂא עָוֺן *bear iniquity*, i.e. §3a)* Ex 34$_7$ Nm 14$_{18}$ Ho 14$_3$ (or em. תִּשָּׂא to מַשָּׂא *burden* of guilt) Mc 7$_{18}$ Ps 32$_5$ 85$_3$.

<PREP> לְ of benefit, *for*, + Job (if em.; see Subj.); introducing object, + עַם *people* Nm 14$_{19}$ Is 2$_9$, בַּיִת *house* Is 2$_9$ Ho 1$_6$, אָב *father* 4QDibHam^a 1.2$_7$ ([נ]שאת[ה]), נָסִיךְ *prince* Si 16$_7$, פֶּשַׁע *transgression* Gn 50$_{17}$ Ex 23$_{21}$ Jos 24$_{19}$ 1 S 25$_{28}$ 1QH 4$_{12}$ (ל[שאת פשע]) 4$_{15}$ (ל[שאת]) 8$_{25}$ CD 3$_{18}$, חַטָּאָה *sin* 1QH 4$_{12}$ (ל[שאת]), חַטָּאת *sin* Jos 24$_{19}$ Ps 25$_{18}$, עָוֺן *iniquity* 1QH 4$_{12}$ (ל[שאת]), שְׁחִיתָה *fault* Si 30$_{11}$, מָקוֹם *place* Gn 18$_{24}$.

מִן *from, since (being in)*, + Egypt Nm 14$_{19}$; partitive, *some of*, + עָוֺן *guilt* Jb 11$_6$ (if em.; see Subj.).

עַד *unto*, + הֵנָּה *here*, i.e. until now Nm 14$_{19}$.

בַּעֲבוּר *on account of, for the sake of*, + צַדִּיק *righteous one* Gn 18$_{26}$.

<COLL> נשׂא || סלח *pardon* Si 13$_{22}$, כסה pi. *cover* Ps 85$_3$; + עבר *pass over* transgression Mc 7$_{18}$, hi. *cause* iniquity *to pass* Jb 7$_{21}$; :: ספה *sweep away* Gn 18$_{24}$.

עַתָּה שָׂא נָא חַטָּאתִי אַךְ הַפַּעַם *pray now, forgive my sin only this once* Ex 10$_{17}$, לֹא אוֹסִיף עוֹד אֲרַחֵם ... כִּי־נָשֹׂא אֶשָּׂא *I will no more have compassion ... that I should at all forgive* Ho 1$_6$ (or em. שָׂנֹא אֶשְׂנָא because *I utterly hate* or לֹא אֶשָּׂא because *I will not forgive*).

5. support, sustain, <SUBJ> אֶרֶץ *land* Gn 13$_6$ 36$_7$. <OBJ> Abram Gn 13$_6$, Esau Gn 36$_7$, Jacob Gn 36$_7$, Lot Gn 13$_6$. <PREP> מִפְּנֵי *on account of*, + מִקְנֶה *cattle* Gn 36$_7$. <COLL> לֹא־נָשָׂא אֹתָם הָאָרֶץ לָשֶׁבֶת יַחְדָּו *the land could not support them dwelling together* Gn 13$_6$.

6. bear a capacity of, contain, hold, <SUBJ> בַּת *bath* Ezk 45$_{11}$, אֵיפָה *ephah* Ezk 45$_{11}$. <OBJ> מַעֲשֵׂר *tenth* of homer Ezk 45$_{11}$, עֲשִׂירִית *tenth* of homer Ezk 45$_{11}$.

7. take, receive, accept, take away, carry away, distinction from §§1-2 not alw. clear, <SUBJ> Y. 2 S 14$_{14}$ Ho 5$_{14}$ Ml 2$_3$ (if em.; see below), כְּרוּב *cherub* Ezk 10$_7$, Israel(ites) Dt 12$_{26}$ 11QT 53$_9$ 58$_{12}$, Judah 1 K 15$_{22}$|| 2 C 16$_6$, Philistines 1 C 10$_9$, עַם *people* Ex 12$_{34}$ 2 C 14$_{12}$, קָהָל *assembly* Ezk 38$_{13}$, Asa 2 C 14$_{12}$, David 1 S 17$_{20}$ (unless §1e) 2 S 5$_{21}$ 1 C 18$_{11}$ 21$_{24}$, Esau Gn 27$_3$, Jehoseph XḤev/Se 49$_9$, Moses Nm 16$_{15}$, Nebuchadrezzar Ezk 29$_{19}$, Nehemiah Ne 2$_1$, Ruth Ru 2$_{18}$, Solomon 1 K 5$_{23}$.

אָדָם *human being* Ec 5$_{18}$, אִישׁ *man* 2 S 5$_{21}$ 1 C 10$_{12}$ CD 12$_7$ 13$_{14}$, בֵּן *son* Gn 27$_3$ Jg 21$_{23}$ XḤev/Se 49$_9$, אָח *brother* Gn 45$_{19}$ Jg 16$_{31}$, מֶלֶךְ *king* Ezk 29$_{19}$ 1 C 18$_{11}$, בַּעַל *owner* Ec 5$_{14}$ (unless §16), מֶלְצַר *guardian* Dn 1$_{16}$, worshipper Ps 139$_9$, קָדוֹשׁ *holy one* Dt 33$_3$ (or em.; see Prep.), נָקִי *clean one* Ps 24$_5$, בַּר *pure one* Ps 24$_5$, מְצֹרָע *leper* 2 K 7$_8$, רֹפֵא *physician* Si 38$_2$, יֹשֵׁב *inhabitant* Ezk 39$_{10}$, בקשׁ pi. ptc. *one who seeks* 11QT 59$_{19}$, דרשׁ ptc. *one who seeks* Si 35$_{14(Bmg)}$ (B יקח *he will receive*), חשׁב ptc. *one who devises* Mc 2$_2$, פעל ptc. *one who does* Mc 2$_2$, עשׂה ptc. *one who makes* Jb 32$_{22}$, שֹׁמֵר *sentry* Ca 5$_7$.

יָד *hand* Si 4$_{31(C)}$ (A לקחת *to receive*), רוּחַ *wind* Is 41$_{16}$ 57$_{13}$ 4Q185 1.1$_{11}$, *spirit* 1 K 18$_{12}$, נֶפֶשׁ *soul* Si 51$_{26}$, אֲרִי *lion* 1 S 17$_{34}$, דֹּב *bear* 1 S 17$_{34}$, סְעָרָה *tempest* Is 40$_{24}$, עָוֺן *iniquity* Is 64$_5$; subj. not specified, Is 8$_4$ 38$_{21}$ Jr 49$_{29}$ Ml 2$_3$ (or em. וְנָשָׂא אֶתְכֶם אֵלָיו *and he shall take you to it* to וְנָשָׂאתִי אֶתְכֶם מֵעָלַי *and I* [Y.] *will take you away from my presence*).

<OBJ> עָצָב *image* 2 S 5$_{21}$, קִבּוּץ *collection (of images)* Is 57$_{13}$, Buzite Jb 32$_{22}$, Israelites Is 64$_5$, Elihu Jb 32$_{22}$, Elijah 1 K 18$_{12}$, Samson Jg 16$_{31}$, אִשָּׁה *wife* Jg 21$_{23}$, בֵּן *son* Jb 32$_{22}$, אָב *father* Gn 45$_{19}$, רֹזֵן *ruler* Is 40$_{24}$, שֹׁפֵט *judge* Is 40$_{24}$, כֹּהֵן *priest* Ml 2$_3$, גּוּפָה *body* 1 C 10$_{12}$, רֹאשׁ *head* 1 C 10$_9$, כָּנָף *wing* Ps 139$_9$, נֶפֶשׁ *soul*, i.e. life 2 S 14$_{14}$ 11QT 59$_{19}$, חֲמוֹר *ass* Nm 16$_{15}$, שֶׂה *sheep* 1 S 17$_{34}$, גָּמָל *camel* Jr 49$_{29}$, שְׂעֹרָה *barley* Ru 2$_{18}$, בָּצֵק *dough* Ex

12$_{34}$, דְּבֵלָה *fig-cake* Is 38$_{21}$, פַּתְבַּג *delicacy* Dn 1$_{16}$, יַיִן *wine* Dn 1$_{16}$ Ne 2$_{1}$.

עֵץ *tree, wood* 1 K 5$_{22}$ 15$_{22}$||2 C 16$_{6}$ Ezk 39$_{10}$, אֶבֶן *stone* 1 K 15$_{22}$||2 C 16$_{6}$, זָהָב *gold* 2 K 7$_{8}$ Ezk 38$_{13}$ 1 C 18$_{11}$, כֶּסֶף *silver* 2 K 7$_{8}$ Ezk 38$_{13}$ 1 C 18$_{11}$, בֶּגֶד *garment* 2 K 7$_{8}$, רְדִיד *mantle* Ca 5$_{7}$, יְרִיעָה *curtain* Jr 49$_{29}$, קֶשֶׁת *bow* Gn 27$_{3}$, תְּלִי *quiver* Gn 27$_{3}$, כְּלִי *weapon* Gn 27$_{3}$, חַיִל *wealth* Is 8$_{4}$, הָמוֹן *wealth* Ezk 29$_{19}$, שָׁלָל *spoil* Is 8$_{4}$ 2 C 14$_{12}$ 11QT 58$_{12}$, חֵלֶק *portion* Ec 5$_{18}$, מַשְׂאֵת *gift* Si 38$_{2}$, כְּלִי *vessel* Jr 49$_{29}$, *weapon* 1 C 10$_{9}$, בַּיִת *house* Mc 2$_{2}$, גִּבְעָה *hill* Is 41$_{16}$, הַר *mountain* Is 41$_{16}$, אֵשׁ *fire* Ezk 10$_{7}$, קֹדֶשׁ *holy thing* Dt 12$_{26}$ 11QT 53$_{9}$, נֶדֶר *freewill offering* Dt 12$_{26}$ 11QT 53$_{9}$, בְּרָכָה *blessing* Ps 24$_{5}$, צְדָקָה *righteousness* Ps 24$_{5}$, לֶקַח *teaching* Si 35$_{14(Bmg)}$, מַשָּׂא *load*, i.e. instruction Si 51$_{26}$, שְׁטָר *document* XḤev/Se 49$_{9}$, מְאוּמָה *anything* Ec 5$_{14}$ (unless §16), אֲשֶׁר *that which* 1 C 21$_{24}$.

<PREP> לְ *for (oneself)* Jr 49$_{29}$; *according to*, + מִסְפָּר *number* Jg 21$_{23}$.

בְּ of place, + Judah perh. 4QapElsée 3$_{5}$ (נ]שׂא]); of price, *(in exchange) for*, + עָמָל *toil* Ec 5$_{14}$ (unless §16).

כְּ *as* Is 40$_{24}$, + רוּחַ *wind* Is 64$_{5}$, מְעַט *a little*, i.e. soon Jb 32$_{22}$.

מִן of direction, *from*, + Amalek 1 C 18$_{11}$, Ammonites 1 C 18$_{11}$, Edom 1 C 18$_{11}$, Moab 1 C 18$_{11}$, גּוֹי *nation* 1 C 18$_{11}$, עֵדָה *assembly* Nm 16$_{15}$, Korah Nm 16$_{15}$, שָׂדֶה *field* Ezk 39$_{10}$, שָׁם *there* 2 K 7$_{8}$.

מִן partitive, (1) *some of* (as obj. of נשׂא), + דַּבֶּרֶת *word* Dt 33$_{3}$ (or em. יִשָּׂא מִדַּבְּרֹתֶיךָ *he receives some of your words* to יְשָׂאוּם דַּבְּרֹתֶיךָ *your words shall lift them up*), הוֹן *wealth* CD 12$_{7}$; (2) *from (among)*, + מְחֹלְלָה *dancer* Jg 21$_{23}$, עֵדֶר *flock* 1 S 17$_{34}$.

אֶל *to* Ml 2$_{3}$ (or em.; see Subj.).

עַל *to*, + אֲשֶׁר *(place) where* 1 K 18$_{12}$.

מֵעַל *from (upon), from the presence of*, + Y. Ml 2$_{3}$ (if em.; see Subj.), female lover Ca 5$_{7}$.

מֵאֵת *from*, + Y. Ps 24$_{5}$, מֶלֶךְ *king* Si 38$_{2}$.

לִפְנֵי *before*, + מֶלֶךְ *king* Is 8$_{4}$.

<COLL> נשׂא || לקח *take* Is 57$_{13}$ Jr 49$_{29}$ Ezk 38$_{13}$, בזז *plunder* Ezk 29$_{19}$, שׁלל *despoil* Ezk 29$_{19}$ 38$_{13}$, פוץ hi. *scatter* Is 41$_{16}$; + פשׁט hi. *strip* 1 C 10$_{9}$; :: נתן *give* Dn 1$_{16}$ CD 13$_{14}$ (יתו[ן]); + נתן Ne 2$_{1}$.

8. obtain favour, kindness, <SUBJ> Esther Est 2$_{15.17}$ 5$_{2}$, בֵּן *son* Si 35$_{2}$, נַעֲרָה *young woman* Est 2$_{9}$, מַלְכָּה *queen* Est 5$_{2}$. <OBJ> חֵן *favour* Est 2$_{15.17}$ 5$_{2}$, שֵׂכֶל appar. *favour* Si 35$_{2}$, חֶסֶד *kindness* Est 2$_{9.17}$. <PREP> בְּ of place, *in*, + עַיִן *eye*, i.e. sight Est 2$_{15}$ 5$_{2}$; מִן of comparison, *(more) than*, + בְּתוּלָה *young woman* Est 2$_{17}$; עַל *on account of, (in exchange) for*, + מוּסָר *discipline* Si 35$_{2}$; לִפְנֵי *before, in the presence of*, + מֶלֶךְ *king* Est 2$_{9.17}$. <COLL> נשׂא חֶסֶד + יטב בְּעֵינֵי *be good in the eyes of*, i.e. pleasing to Est 2$_{9}$.

9. take (woman) in marriage, either for oneself or for one's sons, <SUBJ> Israel Ezr 9$_{2}$, Jews Ne 13$_{25}$, עַם *people* Ezr 9$_{2}$, Abijah 2 C 13$_{21}$, Jehoiada 2 C 24$_{3}$, Rehoboam 2 C 11$_{21}$, בֵּן *son* Ru 1$_{4}$ 1 C 23$_{22}$ Si 7$_{23}$, אָח *brother* 1 C 23$_{22}$, מֶלֶךְ *king* 11QT 57$_{15.18}$, כֹּהֵן *priest* Ezr 9$_{2}$, לֵוִי *Levite* Ezr 9$_{2}$, אֵלֶּה *these* Ezr 10$_{44}$. <OBJ> אִשָּׁה *wife* Ru 1$_{4}$ Ezr 10$_{44}$ 2 C 11$_{21}$ 13$_{21}$ 24$_{3}$ Si 7$_{23(A)}$ 11QT 57$_{15}$, פִּלֶגֶשׁ *secondary wife* 2 C 11$_{21}$, בַּת *daughter* Ezr 9$_{12}$ 1 C 23$_{22}$, אַחֵר fem. *another one* 11QT 57$_{18}$. <PREP> לְ in ref. to subj., *to, for (oneself)*, + Israel Ezr 9$_{2}$, Jews Ne 13$_{25}$, עַם *people* Ezr 9$_{2}$, Abijah 2 C 13$_{21}$, Jehoiada 2 C 24$_{3}$, בֵּן *son* Ru 1$_{4}$, מֶלֶךְ *king* 11QT 57$_{18}$, כֹּהֵן *priest* Ezr 9$_{2}$, לֵוִי *Levite* Ezr 9$_{2}$; of benefit, *for (someone else)*, + בֵּן *son* Ezr 9$_{2.12}$ Ne 13$_{25}$ Si 7$_{23}$; בְּ of time, *in, during*, + נְעוּרִים *youth* Si 7$_{23}$; מִן partitive, (1) *some of* (as obj.), + בַּת *daughter* Ezr 9$_{2}$ Ne 13$_{25}$; (2) *from among*, + בַּת *daughter* 11QT 57$_{15}$, בַּיִת *house* of father 11QT 57$_{18}$. <COLL> נשׂא :: נתן *give* Ezr 9$_{12}$; + לקח *take in marriage* 11QT 57$_{15}$.

10. bring, present, <SUBJ> Y. Dt 28$_{49}$, Aram(aeans) 2 S 8$_{6}$||1 C 18$_{6}$, Moab(ites) 2 S 8$_{2}$||1 C 18$_{2}$, עַם *people* Jg 3$_{18}$, בַּיִת *house* of Israel Ezk 20$_{31}$, מִשְׁפָּחָה *clan* Ps 96$_{8}$|| 1 C 16$_{29}$, Elihu Jb 36$_{3}$, עֶבֶד *servant* 2 S 8$_{2.6}$||1 C 18$_{2.6}$, הַר *mountain* Ps 72$_{3}$ (unless §12), גִּבְעָה *hill* Ps 72$_{3}$ (unless §12).

<OBJ> גּוֹי *nation* Dt 28$_{49}$, מִנְחָה *tribute, offering* Jg 3$_{18}$ 2 S 8$_{2.6}$||1 C 18$_{2.6}$ Ps 96$_{8}$||1 C 16$_{29}$, מַתָּנָה *gift* Ezk 20$_{31}$, דֵּעַ *knowledge* Jb 36$_{3}$, שָׁלוֹם *peace* Ps 72$_{3}$ (unless §12).

<PREP> בְּ introducing object, + צְדָקָה *peace* Ps 72$_{3}$ (unless §12); מִן of direction, *from*, + רָחוֹק *distance* Dt 28$_{49}$ Jb 36$_{3}$ (לְמִן *from*), קָצֶה *end* of earth Dt 28$_{49}$; עַל *against*, + Israel(ites) Dt 28$_{49}$.

11. place, set, <SUBJ> כֹּהֵן *priest* 4QTohB^{b} 1$_{3}$

(ונ[ו]שא ... [הכוהן]); subj. not specified, Jb 6$_2$. <OBJ> דָּם *blood* 4QTohB^b 1$_3$ (ו[נ]שא), הַוָּה *ruin* Jb 6$_2$. <PREP> בְּ of place, *in*, + מֹאזְנַיִם *balances* Jb 6$_2$, כְּלִי *vessel* 4QTohB^b 1$_3$ (ו[נ]שא). <COLL> נשׂא + adverb, יַחַד *together* Jb 6$_2$.

12. bear fruit, produce, yield, <SUBJ> עֵץ *tree* Jl 2$_{22}$ Hg 2$_{19}$ 1QH 18$_{25}$ ([ע]ץ), תְּאֵנָה *fig tree* Hg 2$_{19}$, גֶּפֶן *vine* Ezk 17$_8$ Hg 2$_{19}$, רִמּוֹן *pomegranate* Hg 2$_{19}$, יֹנֶקֶת *shoot* Ezk 17$_{23}$, הַר *mountain* Ezk 36$_8$ Ps 72$_3$ (unless §10) Jb 40$_{20}$, גִּבְעָה *hill* Ps 72$_3$ (unless §10). <OBJ> פְּרִי *fruit* Ezk 17$_8$ 36$_8$ Jl 2$_{22}$, בּוּל *produce* Jb 40$_{20}$, עָלֶה *leaf* 1QH 18$_{25}$, עָנָף *bough* Ezk 17$_{23}$, שָׁלוֹם *peace* Ps 72$_3$ (unless §10). <PREP> לְ of direction, benefit, *to, for*, + Israel Ezk 36$_8$, עַם *people* Ezk 36$_8$ Ps 72$_3$, בְּהֵמוֹת *Behemoth* Jb 40$_{20}$; בְּ introducing object, + צְדָקָה *peace* Ps 72$_3$ (unless §10). <COLL> נשׂא || עשׂה *make* Ezk 17$_{8.23}$, נתן *give* Ezk 36$_8$ Jl 2$_{22}$.

13. perh. **raise up, rear,** <OBJ> בֵּן *son* 4QpsEzek^e 7$_4$. <PREP> לְ *as, for (the purpose of)* perh. 4QpsEzek^e 7$_4$ (ל[ ]).

14. carry out, perform, <SUBJ> אִישׁ *man* 1QSa 1$_{20}$. <OBJ> מַשָּׂא *business* 1QSa 1$_{20}$.

15. of heart, **a. stir, impel,** <SUBJ> לֵב *heart* Ex 35$_{21.26}$ 36$_2$. <OBJ> אִישׁ *man* Ex 35$_{21}$, אִשָּׁה *woman* Ex 35$_{26}$, כֹּל *everyone* Ex 36$_2$. <PREP> בְּ of instrument, *by (means of), with*, + חָכְמָה *wisdom* Ex 35$_{26}$. <COLL> נשׂא || נדב *impel* Ex 35$_{21}$; נְשָׂאוֹ לִבּוֹ לְקָרְבָה *his heart stirred him to draw near* Ex 36$_2$.

15b. make presumptuous, or perh. **carry away,*** <SUBJ> לֵב *heart* 2 K 14$_{10}$||2 C 25$_{19}$. <OBJ> Amaziah 2 K 14$_{10}$||2 C 25$_{19}$, מֶלֶךְ *king* 2 K 14$_{10}$||2 C 25$_{19}$. <COLL> נְשָׂאֲךָ לִבְּךָ לְהַכְבִּיד *your heart has made you presumptuous so as to glorify yourself* 2 C 25$_{19}$ (or em. לְהַכְבִּיד to הִכָּבֵד *be honoured*).

16. withdraw money from bank* (unless §7), <SUBJ> בַּעַל *owner* Ec 5$_{14}$. <OBJ> מְאוּמָה *anything* Ec 5$_{14}$. <PREP> בְּ partitive, *(some) of, from among*, + עָמָל *toil*, i.e. savings Ec 5$_{14}$.

17. intrans. **a. rise up, heave** (unless §1h), <SUBJ> אֶרֶץ *earth* Na 1$_5$ (or em. וַתִּשָּׁא *and it is devastated*, i.e. שׁאה ni.), תֵּבֵל *world* Na 1$_5$ (or em.), יֹשֵׁב *inhabitant* Na 1$_5$ (or em.), גַּל *wave* Ps 89$_{10}$ (or em. בִּשְׁאוֹן *at the roar of* its waves). <PREP> מִפְּנֵי *in the presence of, on account of* Na 1$_5$ (or em.; see Subj.). <COLL> נשׂא + מוג htpol. *melt away* Na 1$_5$, רעשׁ *shake* Na 1$_5$.

17b. rise up against, lift oneself up, exalt oneself, be exalted, <SUBJ> Ephraim Ho 13$_1$ (unless §1h; or em. נִשָּׂא *he was exalted* [ni.] or נָשִׂיא he was *a prince*), אִישׁ *man* Ps 139$_{20}$ (if em. נָשֻׂא לַשָּׁוְא עָרֶיךָ perh. *it is uttered in vain [by] your adversaries* to וְנָשְׂאוּ לַשָּׁוְא עָלֶיךָ *and they lift themselves up against you for vanity*), אֹיֵב *enemy* Ps 89$_{23}$ (if em. יַשִּׁא *he will* not *deceive* [נשׁא hi.] to יִשָּׂא), רָשָׁע *wicked one* Ps 139$_{20}$ (if em.; see above). <PREP> לְ *for (the purpose of)*, + שָׁוְא *vanity*, i.e. in vain Ps 139$_{30}$ (if em.; see Subj.); בְּ of place, *in, among*, + Israel Ho 13$_1$ (or em.; see Subj.); *against* David Ps 89$_{23}$ (if em.; see Subj.), עֶבֶד *servant* Ps 89$_{23}$ (if em.; see Subj.); עַל *against*, + Y. Ps 139$_{20}$ (if em.; see Subj.).

17c. arise, occur, <SUBJ> רִיב *strife* Hb 1$_3$, מָדוֹן *contention* Hb 1$_3$.

18. pass. **a. be lifted up,** i.e. **uttered,** <SUBJ> subj. unspecified, perh. name of Y., נָשֻׂא לַשָּׁוְא עָרֶיךָ perh. *it is uttered in vain (by) your adversaries* Ps 139$_{20}$ (unless *they lift up [their eyes]* [i.e. §1f]; or em. נָשֻׂא to נָשְׂאוּ *they cry out* [i.e. §1h]; וְנָשְׂאוּ לַשָּׁוְא עָלֶיךָ *and they lift themselves up against you for vanity*). <PREP> לְ *for (the purpose of)*, + שָׁוְא *vanity*, i.e. in vain Ps 139$_{30}$ (unless §1f); עַד *unto*, + Y. Ps 139$_{20(mss)}$ (L עָרֶיךָ perh. *your adversaries*).

18b. נְשֻׂא פָנִים (1) **be lifted of face,** i.e. **be favoured, be respected,** <SUBJ> Naaman 2 K 5$_1$, שַׂר *commander* 2 K 5$_1$.

(2) as noun, **honoured one, high-ranking one,** <SUBJ> ישׁב *dwell* Jb 22$_8$, <NOM CL> נְשׂוּא פָנִים הוּא הָרֹאשׁ *the honoured one is the head* Is 9$_{14}$. <OBJ> סור hi. *remove* Is 3$_3$. <COLL> נְשׂוּא פָנִים || שַׂר *commander* Is 3$_3$, זָקֵן *elder* Is 9$_{14}$; + נָבִיא *prophet* Is 9$_{14}$, אִישׁ זְרוֹעַ *man of arm*, i.e. powerful man Jb 22$_8$.

18c. be carried, <SUBJ> בַּיִת *house* of Jacob Is 46$_3$, שְׁאֵרִית *remnant* Is 46$_3$, מַעֲמָסָה *burden* Is 46$_1$ (if em. נְשֻׂאֹתֵיכֶם עֲמוּסוֹת מַשָּׂא לַעֲיֵפָה *your carried things are borne, a burden for a weary [beast]* to כְּמַעֲמָסוֹת נְשֻׂאוֹת לִבְהֵמָה עֲיֵפָה *as burdens carried by a weary beast*). <PREP> לְ of agent, *by*, + בְּהֵמָה *beast* Is 46$_1$ (if em.; see

Subj.); מִן *from, since (the time of being in)*, + רַחַם *womb* Is 46$_3$. <COLL> נשׂא pass. || עמס pass. *be borne* Is 46$_3$.

18d. be forgiven, (1) נְשֻׂא עָוֹן **be forgiven of,** i.e. for, **iniquity,** <SUBJ> עַם *people* Is 33$_{24}$.

(2) נְשׂוּי־פֶּשַׁע **be forgiven of,** i.e. for, **transgression,** <SUBJ> subj. not specified, Ps 32$_1$. <COLL> נשׂא pass. || כסה pass. *be covered* Ps 32$_1$.

Also 4Q185 1.2$_{11}$ 4QDibHam[a] 2.7$_8$ 4QPrFêtes[c] 53$_2$, perh. 4QOrd[b] 9.14 (שאת[ ]) 11QMelch 7$_9$ (שאנו[י]).

<SYN> §1a לקח *take*, שׂים *place*; §1b הדר *honour*, רצה *accept favourably*; §1d רום hi. *raise* standard; §1h צעק *cry out*; §2 סבל *bear*, דרך *tread* bow; §4 סלח *pardon*, כסה pi. *cover*; §7 לקח *take*, בזז *plunder*, שׁלל *despoil*, פוץ hi. *scatter*; §12 עשׂה *make*, נתן *give*; §15a נדב *impel*; §17b שַׂר *commander*, זָקֵן *elder*; §17c עמס pass. *be borne*; §17d כסה pass. *be covered*.

<ANT> §3a נקה ni. *be free (from guilt)*; §4 ספה *sweep away*; §7 נתן *give*; §9 נתן *give*.

Ni. 34.2.4 Pf. נִשָּׂא, נִשֵּׂאת; impv. יִנָּשֵׂא, אֶנָּשֵׂא, יִנָּשְׂאוּ (יִנָּשֵׂאוּ, יִנָּשׂוּא), 3fpl תִּנָּשֶׂאנָה, תִּנָּשֶׂאוּ; + waw וְנִשָּׂא; impv. הִנָּשֵׂא, הִנָּשְׂאוּ; ptc. נִשָּׂא, נִשָּׂאָה (נִשֵּׂאת); inf. abs. נִשֵּׂאת; cstr. הִנָּשֵׂא (הִנָּשְׂאָם), נִשָּׂאִים, נִשָּׂאוֹת.

1a. be lifted up, be raised up, be exalted, lift oneself up, rise, <SUBJ> Y. Is 33$_{10}$ Ps 7$_7$ 1QM 14$_{16}$, אִישׁ *man* Ps 139$_{20}$ (if em. נָשֻׂא לַשָּׁוְא עָרֶיךָ perh. *it is uttered in vain [by] your adversaries* to וְנִשְּׂאוּ לַשָּׁוְא עָלֶיךָ *and they lift themselves up against you for vanity*), עֶבֶד *servant* Is 52$_{13}$, שֹׁפֵט *judge* Ps 94$_2$, רַב pl. *many* Si 11$_6$, חַיָּה *living being* Ezk 1$_{19.20}$, יָד *hand* 1QM 18$_1$ (בהו[נ]שא), עַפְעַף *eyelid* Pr 30$_{13}$, הַר *mountain* Is 2$_2$||Mc 4$_1$, גַּיְא *valley* Is 40$_4$, אוֹפַן *wheel* Ezk 1$_{19.20.21}$, כִּכָּר *talent*, i.e. lead cover Zc 5$_7$, פֶּתַח *door* Ps 24$_{7.9}$ (if em. שְׂאוּ *lift up* to הִנָּשְׂאוּ *be lifted up*), מַלְכוּת *kingdom* 1 C 14$_2$, מִשְׁפָּט *judgment* Jr 51$_9$, אוֹר *light* Jb 36$_{32}$ (if em. כִּסָּה *he has covered* to נִסָּה [= נִשָּׂא] *it is lifted up*).

<PREP> לְ *for (the purpose of)*, + שָׁוְא *vanity*, i.e. in vain Ps 139$_{30}$ (if em.; see Subj.).

בְּ of accompaniment, *with, in*, + מַגֵּפָה *slaughter* 1QM 18$_1$ (בהו[נ]שא), הָדָר *splendour* 1QNoah 13$_2$ (נשא[י]); *against*, + עֶבְרָה *fury* Ps 7$_7$.

מִן of comparison, *(more) than*, + גִּבְעָה *hill* Is 2$_2$||Mc 4$_1$.

מֵעַל *from (upon)*, + אֶרֶץ *earth* Ezk 1$_{19.21}$.

עַל *upon*, + כַּף *hand* Jb 36$_{32}$ (if em.; see Subj.); *against*, + Y. Ps 139$_{20}$ (if em.; see Subj.), בְּלִיַּעַל *Belial* 1QM 18$_1$ (בהו[נ]שא), חַיִל *army* 1QM 18$_1$ (בהו[נ]שא ... חו[י]ל).

עַד *unto*, + שַׁחַק *sky* Jr 51$_9$.

לְעֻמַּת *alongside*, + חַיָּה *living being* Ezk 1$_{20.21}$.

<COLL> נשׂא ni. || גבה *be high* Is 52$_{13}$, רום *be high* Is 52$_{13}$ Pr 30$_{13}$ 1QM 14$_{16}$, רמם ni. *be exalted* Is 33$_{10}$; + קום *arise* Ps 7$_7$, נגע *reach* Jr 51$_9$; :: שׁפל *be low* Is 40$_4$; + adverb, עַתָּה *now* Is 33$_{10}$, לְמַעְלָה *on high* 1 C 14$_2$.

1b. ptc. as adj., **lifted up, exalted,** (1) used attributively of אֶרֶז *cedar* Is 2$_{13}$, הַר *mountain* Is 57$_7$, גִּבְעָה *hill* Is 2$_{14}$ 30$_{25}$, כִּסֵּא *throne* Is 6$_1$. <COLL> נשׂא ni. ptc. || גָּבֹהַּ *high* Is 30$_{25}$ 57$_7$, רום ptc. *high* Is 2$_{13.14}$ 6$_1$.

(2) as noun, **that which is lifted up, lofty one, exalted one,** <SUBJ> אמר *say* Is 57$_{15}$, שׁפל *be low* Is 2$_{12}$. <CSTR> כָּל־נִשָּׂא *all that is lifted up* Is 2$_{12}$. <PREP> עַל *against* Is 2$_{12}$. <COLL> נשׂא ni. ptc. || רום ptc. *high one* Is 2$_{12}$ (+) 57$_{15}$; + גֵּאֶה *proud one* Is 2$_{12}$.

2. be carried, <SUBJ> בַּת *daughter* Is 49$_{22}$, אהב ptc. *one who loves* Is 66$_{12}$, אבל htp. ptc. *one who mourns* Is 66$_{12}$, שֻׁלְחָן *table* Ex 25$_{28}$, הֵמָּה *they*, in ref. to images Jr 10$_{5.5}$.

<PREP> בְּ of instrument, *by (means of), with*, + בַּד *pole* Ex 25$_{28}$; עַל *upon*, + כָּתֵף *shoulder* Is 49$_{22}$, צַד *side*, perh. hip Is 66$_{12}$.

<COLL> נשׂא ni. || שׁעע polp. *be fondled* Is 66$_{12}$.

נָשׂוֹא יִנָּשׂוּא *they must surely be carried* Jr 10$_5$.

3. be taken away, be carried away, <SUBJ> הָמוֹן *multitude* Dn 11$_{12}$, כֹּל 2 K 20$_{17}$||Is 39$_6$; subj. not specified, 2 S 19$_{43.43}$.

<PREP> לְ of agent, *by*, + אִישׁ *man* 2 S 19$_{43}$.

ה- of direction, *to*, + בָּבֶל *Babylon* 2 K 20$_{17}$.

נשׂא ni. + noun without preposition or ה- of direction, בָּבֶל *(to) Babylon* Is 39$_6$.

<COLL> נִשֵּׂאת נִשָּׂא לָנוּ *has anything been carried away by us?* 2 S 19$_{43}$.

4. be beguiled, be enticed, <SUBJ> לֵב *heart* Si 46$_{11}$.

Also 4QMyst[a] 33$_3$.

<SYN> §1a גבה *be high,* רום *be high,* רמם ni. *be exalted;* §1b גָּבֹהַּ *high,* רום ptc. *high (one);* §2 שׁעע polp. *be fondled.*

<ANT> §1a שׁפל *be low.*

Pi. 13 Pf. נִשֵּׂא (נִשְּׂאוּ ,נִשָּׂא, נִשְּׂאוּ); impf. יְנַשְּׂאוּהוּ; + waw וְנִשָּׂא ;(וַיְנַשְּׂאֵם) וַיְנַשְּׂאֵהוּ; impv. נַשְּׂאֵם; ptc. מְנַשְּׂאִים—**1a. lift up,** perh. **carry away** (Am 4$_2$), <SUBJ> Y. Ps 69$_{15}$ (or em.; see Prep.); subj. not specified, Am 4$_2$. <OBJ> appar. פָּרָה *cow* Am 4$_2$ (or em. אֶתְכֶם *you* to אַפְּכֶם *your nose*), אַחֲרִית *end,* i.e. remnant Am 4$_2$. <PREP> בְּ of instrument, *by (means of), with,* + צִנָּה *hook* Am 4$_2$, סִירָה *hook* Am 4$_2$; מִן of direction, *from,* + מַעֲמָק *depth* Ps 69$_{15}$ (if em. מִשֹּׂנְאַי וּמִמַּעֲמַקֵּי *from those who hate me and from the depths of* to מְנַשְּׂאַי מִמַּעֲמַקֵּי *who lift me up from the depths of*).

1b. exalt, <SUBJ> Y. 2 S 5$_{12}$, Ahasuerus Est 3$_1$, מֶלֶךְ *king* Est 3$_1$ 5$_{11}$. <OBJ> Agagite Est 3$_1$, Haman Est 3$_1$ 5$_{11}$, בֵּן *son* Est 3$_1$, מַמְלָכָה *kingdom* 2 S 5$_{12}$. <PREP> בַּעֲבוּר *for the sake of,* + Israel 2 S 5$_{12}$, עַם *people* 2 S 5$_{12}$. <PREP> עַל *above,* + שַׂר *prince* Est 5$_{11}$, עֶבֶד *servant* Est 5$_{11}$. <COLL> נשׂא pi. || גדל pi. *promote* Est 3$_1$ 5$_{11}$.

1c. lift up one's soul, i.e. desire, <SUBJ> שְׁאֵרִית *remnant* of Judah Jr 44$_{14}$, Coniah Jr 22$_{27}$, אֵם *mother* Jr 22$_{27}$, בֵּן *son* Jr 22$_{27}$, מֶלֶךְ *king* Jr 22$_{27}$. <OBJ> נֶפֶשׁ *soul* Jr 22$_{27}$ 44$_{14}$. <COLL> נשׂא pi. + infinitive of purpose of שׁוב *go back* Jr 22$_{27}$ 44$_{14}$.

2. bear, carry, <SUBJ> Y. Is 63$_9$. <OBJ> בַּיִת *house* of Israel Is 63$_9$. <COLL> נשׂא pi. || נטל *lift up* Is 63$_9$; + noun used adverbially, יוֹם *day* Is 63$_9$.

3. support, sustain, help, supply with, <SUBJ> Y. Ps 28$_9$, Hiram 1 K 9$_{11}$, אִישׁ *man* Ezr 1$_4$, מֶלֶךְ *king* 1 K 9$_{11}$, שַׂר *prince* Est 9$_3$, אֲחַשְׁדַּרְפָּן *satrap* Est 9$_3$ Ezr 8$_{36}$, פֶּחָה *governor* Est 9$_3$, עשׂה ptc. *one who does* work Est 9$_3$. <OBJ> Jews Est 9$_3$, עַם *people* Ps 28$_9$ Ezr 8$_{36}$, בַּיִת *house* of Y. Ezr 8$_{36}$, Solomon 1 K 9$_{11}$, שׁאר ni. ptc. *one who remains* Ezr 1$_4$. <PREP> לְ *according to,* + חֵפֶץ *desire* 1 K 9$_{11}$; בְּ of instrument, *by (means of), with,* + בְּהֵמָה *beast* Ezr 1$_4$, עֵץ *tree* 1 K 9$_{11}$, זָהָב *gold* 1 K 9$_{11}$ Ezr 1$_4$, כֶּסֶף *silver* Ezr 1$_4$, רְכוּשׁ *goods* Ezr 1$_4$; עַד *unto,* + עוֹלָם *everlastingness* Ps 28$_9$. <COLL> נשׂא pi. || רעה *tend* Ps 28$_9$.

<SYN> §1b גדל pi. *promote;* §2 נטל *lift up;* §3 רעה *tend.*

Hi. 2.0.3 Impf. Q ישיאנו; + waw וְהִשִּׂיאוּ—**1. cause to bear,** <SUBJ> כֹּהֵן *priest* Lv 22$_{16}$, בֵּן *son* of priest 4QMMT B$_{13}$ ([בני] ... מסיא[י]ם) B$_{27}$ ([בני]); subj. not specified, 1QS 5$_{14}$. <OBJ> 1. person, עַם *people* 4QMMT B$_{13}$ (מסיא[י]ם) B$_{27}$, אִישׁ *man* 1QS 5$_{14}$, בֵּן *son* of Israel Lv 22$_{16}$. 2. thing borne, עָוֹן *iniquity* Lv 22$_{16}$ 1QS 5$_{14}$ 4QMMT B$_{13}$ (מסיא[י]ם) B$_{27}$.

2. bring, <SUBJ> Israel 2 S 17$_{13}$ (or em. יָשִׂימוּ *they shall place*). <OBJ> חֶבֶל *rope* 2 S 17$_{13}$ (or em.; see Subj.). <PREP> אֶל *to,* + עִיר *city* 2 S 17$_{13}$ (or em.; see Subj.).

Htp. 10.0.3 Impf. יִתְנַשָּׂא, 3fs תִּתְנַשֵּׂא (תִּנַּשֵּׂא), יִנַּשְּׂאוּ, תִּתְנַשְּׂאוּ (Q תתנסו); + waw Q והנשא; וַיִּנַּשֵּׂא; ptc. מִתְנַשֵּׂא; inf. הִתְנַשֵּׂא—**lift oneself up, exalt oneself, be exalted,** <SUBJ> Y. 1 C 29$_{11}$, Egypt Ezk 29$_{15}$, עַם *people* Nm 23$_{24}$, Aaron Nm 16$_3$, Adonijah 1 K 1$_5$, Hezekiah 2 C 32$_{23}$, Ithiel Pr 30$_{32}$, Moses Nm 16$_3$, Ucal Pr 30$_{32}$, בֵּן *son* 1 K 1$_5$ Dn 11$_{14}$ (or em. יִנָּשְׁאוּ *they shall be deluded,* i.e. נשׁא II ni.), זַרְזִיר *strong one,* i.e. cockerel Pr 30$_{31}$ (if em. מָתְנַיִם *loins* to מִתְנַשֵּׂא *exalted,* i.e. strutting), מַמְלָכָה *kingdom* Ezk 17$_{14}$, מַלְכוּת *kingdom* Nm 24$_7$ 4QBer[a] 7.1$_5$ 4QBer[b] 5$_{10}$ ([בהנשׂ]א מלכותכה). <PREP> לְ *in relation to,* + כֹּל *all* 1 C 29$_{11}$; *before,* + עַיִן *eye* 2 C 32$_{23}$; *as,* + ראשׁ *head* 1 C 29$_{11}$; כְּ *as,* + אֲרִי *lion* Nm 23$_{24}$; עַל *over, above,* + גּוֹי *nation* Ezk 29$_{15}$, קָהָל *assembly* of Y. Nm 16$_3$; בְּתוֹךְ *among,* + עַם *people* 4QBer[a] 7.1$_5$ (עמ[י]ם). <COLL> נשׂא htp. || קום *arise* Nm 23$_{24}$; + רום *be high* Nm 24$_7$; + adverb, עוֹד *again* Ezk 29$_{15}$, מַדּוּעַ *why?* Nm 16$_3$; + infinitive of purpose of עמד hi. *cause* vision *to stand* Dn 11$_{14}$.

Also 4QParGenEx A$_1$ 4QM[h] 1$_7$.

<SYN> קום *arise.**

⇒ נְשׂוּאָה *carried thing,* נָשִׂיא I *prince,* (?) II *mist,* III *one brought,* מַשָּׂא I *burden,* (?) II *utterance,* III *tribute,* IV *Massa,* מַשָּׂאָה *burden,* מַשְׂאֵת I *gift,* II *utterance,* III *beacon,* שְׂאֵת *exaltation,* שִׂיא *loftiness,* שִׂיאֹן *Sion.*

*[נשׂא] II vb. **smoke—Hi. smoke, fume,** <SUBJ> כָּבֵד *liver* Is 30$_{27}$ (if em. כֹּבֶד מַשָּׂאָה *heaviness of burden* to כָּבֵד מַשִּׂיאָה *his liver is fuming*).

נשׂג I $_{49.10.16}$ vb. **reach—Hi.** $_{49.10.16}$ Pf. הִשִּׂיגוּ, הִשִּׂיגָה (הִשִּׂיגוּנִי, Q השיגוהו, הִשִּׂיגוּהָ, Q השיגום); impf. יַשִּׂיג (יַשֵּׂג, תַּשִּׂיגֵנוּ, תַּשִּׂיגֵהוּ, תשיגך Si) תַּשִּׂיג 3fs ,(יַשִּׂיגֵם, ישיגך Si יַשִּׂיגוּ, (אַשִּׂיגֵם, אַשִּׂגֶנּוּ) אַשִּׂיג, תשיגי Q, תַּשִּׂיג 2ms ,(תַּשִּׂיגֵם (וְהִשַּׂגְנוּ, וְהִשִּׂיגוּ) וְהִשִּׂיג waw + ;תַּשִּׂיגוּם ,(ישיגוך Si ,יַשִּׂיגוּן), וַיַּשֵּׂג (והשיגום Q, וְהִשִּׂיגֶךָ) וְהִשִּׂיגוּךָ, וְהִשַּׂגְתֶּם, וְהִשִּׂיגָה (מַשִּׂיגֵהוּ) מַשִּׂיג .ptc ;(וישיגוני Q ,וַיַּשִּׂגוּ) וַיַּשִּׂיגוּ ,(וַיַּשִּׂגֵם), מַשֶּׂגֶת; inf. abs. הַשֵּׂג.

1. reach, overtake, come upon, <SUBJ> Egyptians Ex 14_{9}, חַיִל *army* 2 K 25_{5}||Jr 52_{8} Jr 39_{5}, Absalom 2 S 15_{14}, David 1 S $30_{8.8.8}$, Laban Gn 31_{25}, אֵם *mother* Ho 2_{9}, מֶלֶךְ *king*, etc. Jos 2_{5}, אֹיֵב *enemy* Ps 7_{6}, גֹּאֵל *avenger* of blood Dt 19_{6}, רֹדֵף *pursuer* Lm 1_{3}, worshipper Ps 18_{38}, יָד *hand* 4QTohA 1.2_{6}, רֶגֶל *foot* 4QTohA 1.2_{6} ([רג]לו), דַּיִשׁ *threshing* Lv 26_{5}, בָּצִיר *grape harvest* Lv 26_{5}, שִׂמְחָה *gladness* Si 6_{4}, טוֹב *good* Pr 13_{21} (if em. יְשַׁלֶּם־ *it shall repay* to יַשִּׂגֵם *it shall overtake them*), צְדָקָה *righteousness* Is 59_{9}, בְּרָכָה *blessing* Dt 28_{2} Si 3_{8}, קְלָלָה *curse* Dt $28_{15.45}$ 1QDM 1_{10} ([הקללו]ת), רָעָה *evil* Si 6_{12} 7_{1}, עָוֹן *iniquity* Ps 40_{13}, חָרוֹן *burning* of anger Ps 69_{25}, כְּלִמָּה *reproach* Mc 2_{6} (if em. יִסַּג *it shall* not *depart* [i.e. סוג ni.] to יַשִּׂגֵנוּ *it shall* not *overtake us*), בַּלָּהָה *terror* Jb 27_{20}, מִלְחָמָה *war* Ho 10_{9}, חֶרֶב *sword* Jr 42_{16} Jb 41_{18} (unless §7) 1 C 21_{12}, יוֹם *day* Gn 47_{9}, דָּבָר *word* Zc 1_{6}, חֹק *statute* Zc 1_{6}, אֲשֶׁר *one who* Gn $44_{4.6}$; subj. not specified, 1QH 13_{29}.

<OBJ> Israel(ites) Dt $28_{2.15.45}$ Is 59_{9} Ho 10_{9}, Judah Lm 1_{3}, עַם *people* Ex 14_{9} Jr 42_{16}, David 2 S 15_{14}, Jacob Gn 31_{25}, Johanan Jr 42_{16}, Zedekiah Jr 39_{5} 52_{8}, גְּדוּד *troop* 1 S 30_{8}, אָדָם *human being* Jb 27_{20}, אִישׁ *man* Gn $44_{4.6}$ Jos 2_{5}, אָב *father* Zc 1_{6}, בֵּן *son* Jr 42_{16} Si 3_{8} 6_{12} 7_{1}, of Israel 1QDM 1_{10}, מֶלֶךְ *king* 2 K 25_{5}, שַׂר *commander* Jr 42_{16}, עֶבֶד *servant* 2 S 15_{14}, worshipper Ps 40_{13} 1QH 13_{29}, מְאַהֵב *lover* Ho 2_{9}, צַדִּיק *righteous one* Pr 13_{21} (if em.; see Subj.), עָרִיץ *terrible one* Jb 27_{20}, שׂנא ptc. *one who hates* Si 6_{4}, אֹיֵב *enemy* Ex 15_{9} Ps 18_{38} 69_{25}, רֹצֵחַ *killer* Dt 19_{6}, נֶפֶשׁ *soul*, i.e. self Ps 7_{6}, לִוְיָתָן *Leviathan* Jb 41_{18} (unless §7), זֶרַע *seed time* Lv 26_{5}, בָּצִיר *grape harvest* Lv 26_{5}, יוֹם *day* Gn 47_{9}.

<PREP> בְּ of place, *in*, + Gibeah Ho 10_{9}, עֲרָבָה *plain* 2 K 25_{5}||Jr 52_{8} Jr 39_{5}, אֶרֶץ *land* Jr 42_{16}, מֵצַר *narrow place* 1QH 13_{29}.

כְּ *as*, + מַיִם *water* Jb 27_{20}.

בֵּין *within*, + מֵצַר *distress* Lm 1_{3}.

<COLL> נשׂג hi. + דבק *keep close* Jr 42_{16}, אפף *surround* Ps 40_{13}, רדף *pursue* Gn 44_{4} Ex 14_{9} 15_{9} Dt 19_{6} 28_{45} Jos 2_{5} 1 S $30_{8.8}$ 2 K 25_{5}||Jr 52_{8} Jr 39_{5} Hos 2_{9} Ps 7_{6} 18_{38} Lm 1_{3}; :: רחק *be distant* Is 59_{9}; + adverb, שָׁם *there* Jr 42_{16}; הַשֵּׂג תַּשִּׂיג *you shall surely overtake* 1 S 30_{8}, פי שנים רעה תשיג *you will come upon evil twofold* Si 12_{5}.

2. reach, i.e. **be able to afford, have sufficient, be sufficient,** <SUBJ> יָד *hand* Lv 5_{11} $14_{21.22.30.31.32}$ 25_{26} (+ מצא כְּדֵי *find sufficient for*) $25_{47.49}$ 27_{8} Nm 6_{21} Ezk 46_{7} 1QS 7_{8} 4QDa 6.2_{12} (י[ד]ו]) 4QDf 3_{2} (ידו לוא] ה[שיגה) 4Q418 126.2_{13}.

<OBJ> בֵּן *son*, i.e. young, of dove Lv 14_{22}, תֹּר *turtledove* Lv 14_{22}, דַּי *sufficiency* 4QDa 6.2_{12} ([די]) 4QDf 3_{2} ([ה]שיגה), אֲשֶׁר *that which* Lv $14_{22.30.31}$ 27_{8} Nm 6_{21} Ezk 46_{7}.

<PREP> לְ of direction, *to*, i.e. for + מַחְסוֹר *need* 4Q418 126.2_{13}; introducing object, + בֵּן *son*, i.e. young, of dove Lv 5_{11}, תֹּר *turtledove* Lv 5_{11}; בְּ introducing object, or *for (the cost of)*, + טָהֳרָה *purification* Lv 14_{32}.

<COLL> אם לוא תשיג ידו לשלמו *if he cannot afford to repay it* 1QS 7_{8}.

3. attain to, gain, obtain, <SUBJ> Zion 11QPsa 22_{13}, אָדָם *human being* 4QBéat 2.2_{3}, בֵּן *son* Si 6_{18} 12_{5}, ירא ptc. *one who fears* Si 6_{16}, שׁחר pi. ptc. *one who seeks* Y. Si 35_{14}, בוא ptc. *one who comes* Pr 2_{19} CD 6_{10}, פדה pass. ptc. *ransomed one* Is 35_{10}=51_{11} (unless §5).

<OBJ> אֹהֵב *friend* Si 6_{16}, אֹרַח *path* Pr 2_{19} 4QBéat 15_{8}, מְחֹקְקָה *statute* CD 6_{10}, חָכְמָה *wisdom* Si 6_{18} 4QBéat 2.2_{3}, צֶדֶק *righteousness* 11QPsa 22_{13}, רָעָה *evil* Si 12_{5}, צְרוֹר *bundle* of life Si 6_{16}, מַעֲנֶה *answer* Si 35_{14}, שָׂשׂוֹן *joy* Is 35_{10}=51_{11} (unless §5), שִׂמְחָה *gladness* Is 35_{10}=51_{11} (unless §5).

<PREP> בְּ of time, *in*, + עֵת *time* Si 12_{5}; of price, *(in exchange) for*, + טוֹבָה *good* Si 12_{5}; זוּלַת *apart from*, + מְחֹקְקָה *statute* CD 6_{10}.

<COLL> נשׂג hi. || לקח *take* Si 35_{14}, קבל pi. *receive* 11QPsa 22_{13}.

4. appreciate, understand, accept, <SUBJ> אִישׁ *man* 1QS 6_{14}, בֵּן *son* Si 12_{12} 34_{22}. <OBJ> אֹמֶר *word* Si 12_{12} 34_{22}, מוּסָר *discipline* 1QS 6_{14}. <PREP> בְּ of time, *in, at,* + אַחֲרִית *end* Si 34_{22}; לְ *in, at,* + אָחוֹר *future* Si 12_{12}.

5. perh. **arrive, come about,** unless §3, <SUBJ> שָׂשׂוֹן *joy* Is 35_{10}=51_{11} (:: נוס *flee*), שִׂמְחָה *gladness* Is 35_{10}=51_{11}.

6. cause to reach, put, <SUBJ> subj. not specified, 1 S 14_{26} (or em. מֵשִׁיב *turned*, i.e. שׁוב hi.). <OBJ> יָד *hand* 1 S 14_{26} (or em.; see Subj.). <PREP> אֶל *to,* + פֶּה *mouth* 1 S 14_{26} (or em.; see Subj.).

7. perh. **hunt*** (unless §1), <SUBJ> subj. not specified, Jb 41_{18}. <OBJ> לִוְיָתָן *Leviathan* Jb 41_{18}. <COLL> נשׂג hi. + noun used adverbially, חֶרֶב *(with a) sword* Jb 41_{18}.

Also 1QH 4_{9} 4QMyst[b] 9_{1} 4QsapHymnA 4_{3} 4Q418 188_{7}.

<SYN> §3 לקח *take,* קבל pi. *receive.*

<ANT> §1 רחק *be distant,* נוס *flee.*

⇒ הַשָּׂגָה *reaching,* הַשִּׂיגָה *reaching.*

*[נשׂג] II 1 vb. **hunt—Hi.** Ptc. מַשִּׂיגֵהוּ—<SUBJ> hunter, Jb 41_{18} (מַשִּׂיגֵהוּ חֶרֶב בְּלִי תָקוּם *though one hunt him (with) a sword you will not succeed*). <OBJ> Leviathan Jb 41_{18}. <PREP> בְּ of instrument, *with,* + חֶרֶב *sword* Jb 41_{18}.

נשׁה I, see נסה I *test.*

נשׁה II, see נשׂא *lift.*

[נְשׂוּאָה] 1 n.f. **carried thing**—pl. sf. נְשֻׂאֹתֵיכֶם—in ref. to images of Bel and Nebo, <SUBJ> עמס pass. *be borne* Is 46_{1} (or em.; see Nom. Cl.). <NOM CL> נְשֻׂאֹתֵיכֶם עֲמוּסוֹת מַשָּׂא לַעֲיֵפָה *your carried things are borne, a burden for a weary (beast)* Is 46_{1} (or move מַשָּׂא to earlier clause and em. to כְּמַעֲמָסוֹת נְשֻׂאוֹת לִבְהֵמָה עֲיֵפָה *as burdens carried by a weary beast*).

⇒ נשׂא I *lift.*

נָשִׂיא I 130.1.45.1 n.m. **prince**—Q נשי; cstr. נְשִׂיא (Q נשי, Q נסיא, Q נסי); pl. נְשִׂיאִים (נְשִׂאִם, נְשִׂאִים); cstr. נְשִׂיאֵי (Q נשיי); sf. נְשִׂיאֶהָ, נְשִׂיאֵיהֶם (נְשִׂאֵהֶם)—**prince, chief, leader, a.** of or from Edom (Ezk 32_{29}), Egypt (Ezk 30_{13}), Hivites (Gn 34_{2}), Kedar (Ezk 27_{21}), Meshech and Tubal (Ezk $38_{2.3}$ 39_{1}), Midian (Nm 25_{18} Jos 13_{21}), the sea (Ezk 26_{16}), the earth (Ezk 39_{18}).

b. in ref. to Abraham (Gn 23_{6}; unless נָשִׂיא II *one brought*), descendants of Ishmael (Gn 17_{20} 25_{16}).

c. leaders of (the congregation of) Israel (e.g. Ex 16_{22} 34_{31} 35_{27} Nm 1_{44} 4_{34} 7_{2} 16_{2} 31_{13} 32_{2} Jos 9_{15} Ezk 19_{1} 21_{17} 22_{6} 45_{9}), tribes of Israel (e.g. Nm 1_{16} 2_{3+11t} 7_{2+15t} 1 C 2_{10} 1QM 3_{15}), father's house (Nm $3_{24.30.35}$ 17_{17} 25_{14} Jos 22_{14} 1 K 8_{1}||2 C 5_{2} 2 C 1_{2}), family (1 C 4_{38}).

d. specif. prince of the congregation, i.e. ruler (1QSb 5_{20} 4QM[g] 5_{4} 4QapMos[b] 1.3_{1} CD 7_{20}), leader of sons of light (1QM 5_{1}).

e. particular rulers, Simeon bar Cosiba (e.g. Mur 24 B_{3} $E_{2.7}$ XḤev/Se 30_{1} 5/6ḤevBA $44_{2.7}$ XḤev/Se 49_{3} Bar-Kochba Revolt Year 2 Coin 193), Solomon (1 K 11_{34}), Zedekiah (e.g. Ezk 12_{10}).

f. future king (e.g. Ezk 44_{3} 45_{7} 46_{2} 48_{21}), ident. with David (Ezk 34_{24} 37_{25}).

g. angelic figures, including the high priest of the angels* (e.g. 4QShirShabb[d] $1.1_{1.21.23}$).

<SUBJ> היה *be* Ezk 21_{17} 22_{6} 30_{13} 38_{3} 4QapMos[b] 1.3_{1}, חיה hi. *let live* Jos 9_{19}, רבה hi. *multiply* CD 5_{1}, אמר *say* Jos $9_{19.21}$ 22_{14} Ezk 26_{16} 38_{3}, דבר pi. *speak* Jos 9_{21} 22_{14}, נגד hi. *tell* Ex 16_{22}, ברך pi. *bless* 4QShirShabb[d] 1.1_{26} (יברכו), שׁבע ni. *swear* Jos $9_{15.18.19}$, שׁמע *hear* Jos 22_{30}, חשׁב *devise* Ezk 38_{3}, אכל *eat* Ezk 44_{3}.

בוא *come* Ex 16_{22} Jos 22_{14} Ezk 38_{3} 44_{3} $46_{2.8.10}$, hi. *bring* Ex 35_{27} Lv 4_{22} Nm 7_{2}, יצא *go out* Nm 31_{13} Ezk 44_{3} $46_{2.8.10(mss).12}$, עלה *go up* Ezk 38_{3}, hi. *bring up* 1 K 8_{1}||2 C 5_{2}, ירד *go down* Ezk 22_{16}, קרב *draw near* Nm $7_{2(Sam^{mss})}$, hi. *bring near,* i.e. offer Nm 7_{2+6t} (if ins. נָשִׂיא at Nm 7_{12}) Ezk 46_{4}, יעד ni. *gather oneself* Nm 10_{4}, קהל hi. *assemble* Ezk 38_{3}, קרא *meet* Nm 31_{13}, שׁוב *go back* Ex 34_{31} Jos 22_{32}, hi. *bring back* Jos 22_{32} Ezk 38_{3}, קום *rise* Nm 16_{2}, נשׂא *lift* Ezk 12_{12} 26_{16}, רום hi. *raise,* i.e. remove Ezk 45_{9}, סור hi. *remove* Ezk 26_{16} 45_{9}, נפל *fall* Ezk 39_{1}, עמד *stand* Ezk 46_{2}, ישׁב *sit, dwell* Ezk 26_{16} 44_{3} Si $41_{17(B)}$ Mur 24 B_{3} ([יושב]) C_{3} (יו[שב]) D_{3} ([יו]שב[א]) E_{2} F_{3} I_{3} (both [יושב]), שׁכב *lie down* Ezk 32_{29}, נגע *touch* Jos 9_{19}, פשׁט *strip* Ezk 26_{16}, לבשׁ *dress oneself in* Ezk 7_{27} 26_{16}, חטא *sin* Lv 4_{22}, אשׁם *be guilty* Lv 4_{22}.

עשׂה *do* Lv 4_{22} Jos 9_{19} Ezk $45_{9.17.22}$ $46_{4.12}$, כון ni. *be ready* Ezk 38_{3}, hi. *prepare* Ezk 38_{3}, יכל *be able* Jos 9_{19}, נתן *give* Nm 17_{21} Ezk 45_{8} 46_{16}, ni. *be given*, i.e. placed Ezk 32_{29}, נחל hi. *cause to inherit* Ezk 46_{18}, לקח *take* Ezk 46_{18}, סמך *lay* Lv 4_{22}, פקד *number* Nm 1_{44} $4_{34.46}$, ni. *be mustered* Ezk 38_{3}, חרד *tremble* Ezk 26_{16}, שׁמם *be appalled* Ezk 26_{16}, שׁחט *slaughter* Lv 4_{22}, מות hi. *put to death* 4QMg 5_{4}, מגר pass. *be delivered up* Ezk 21_{17}, שׁלל *despoil* Ezk 38_{3}, בזז *plunder* Ezk 38_{3}, ינה hi. *oppress* Ezk 45_{8} 46_{18}.

‹NOM CL› המלך הוא נשיא הקהל *the king is the prince of the assembly* CD 7_{17} (if ins. נשיא), השבט הוא נשיא כל העדה *the staff is the prince of all the congregation* CD 7_{20}, עַבְדִּי דָוִד נָשִׂיא בְתוֹכָם *my servant David shall be prince among them* Ezk 34_{24}, sim. 37_{25}, נָשִׂיא ... נַחְשׁוֹן בֶּן־עַמִּינָדָב *the prince was ... Nahshon the son of Amminadab* Nm 2_{3}, vars. Nm 2_{5+10t} $3_{24.30.32.35}$, בַּיּוֹם הַשְּׁלִישִׁי נָשִׂיא לִבְנֵי זְבוּלֻן *on the third day it was the prince of the sons of Zebulun* Nm 7_{24}, vars. Nm 7_{30+8t}, שָׁמָּה ... כָּל־נְשִׂיאֶיהָ *there are ... all its princes* Ezk 32_{29}, הַנָּשִׂיא הַמַּשָּׂא הַזֶּה *this oracle is*, i.e. concerns, *the prince* Ezk 12_{10} (or ins. ־עַל this oracle is *about* the prince).

הוּא נָשִׂיא *he was a prince* 1 C 5_{6}, נְשִׂיא אֱלֹהִים אַתָּה *you are a prince of God*, i.e. a mighty prince Gn 23_{6} (unless נָשִׂיא II *one brought*), הֵם נְשִׂיאֵי הַמַּטֹּת *they were the princes of the tribes* Nm 7_{2}, אֵלֶּה ... נְשִׂיאִם *these are ... princes* Gn 25_{16} 1 C 4_{48}, var. Nm 1_{16}, [הנ]שי אשר ברוש *the prince who is at the head* 4QMf 10_{3a}, כֹּל נָשִׂיא בָהֶם *everyone shall be a leader among them* Nm 13_{2}, נשיאי הדגלים ברנ[י]שונ[ה] *princes of the battalions shall be first* 11QT 21_{5}, עֲשָׂרָה נְשִׂאִים עִמּוֹ *ten princes were with him* Jos 22_{14}, נשיי עמו עמו *princes of his people shall be with him* 11QT 57_{12}, הַנָּשִׂיא אֲשֶׁר בְּתוֹכָם *the prince who is among them* Ezk 12_{12}, var. Ezk 46_{10}, הנשיא אשר לכול העדה *the prince who is of all the congregation* 4QapMosb 1.3_{1}.

‹OBJ› ילד hi. *beget* Gn 17_{20} 1 C 2_{10}, ברך pi. *bless* 1QSb 5_{20}, ארר *curse* Ex 22_{27}, כתב *write* 1QM 3_{3}, בוא hi. *bring* Ezk 39_{1}, יצא *bring out* Ezk 38_{3}, עלה hi. *bring up* Ezk 39_{1}, שׁשׁא pi. perh. *lead on* Ezk 39_{1} (or em. שׁשׁא pi. to נשׁא hi. *deceive*), לקח *take* Nm $34_{18.18}$, קהל hi. *assemble* 1 K 8_{1}||2 C 5_{2}, שׁוב pol. *turn* Ezk 38_{3} 39_{1}, נכה hi. *strike* Jos 13_{21}, נתן *give* Ezk 39_{1}, שׁית *place*, i.e. make 1 K 11_{34}, בחר *choose* 1QSb 5_{20} ([בחר]).

‹CSTR› נשיאי אל *princes of God* 1QM 3_{3}, נְשִׂיא אֱלֹהִים *prince of God*, i.e. mighty prince Gn 23_{6} (unless נָשִׂיא II *one brought*), הָאָרֶץ *of the land* Gn 34_{2}, נְשִׂיאֵי הָאָרֶץ *princes of the earth* Ezk 39_{18}, הַיָּם *of the sea* Ezk 26_{16}.

נְשִׂיא יִשְׂרָאֵל *prince of Israel* Ezk 21_{30} Mur 24 B_{3} (נסיא [י]שרא[ל]) B_{9} ([נ]סיא [ישר]אל) C_{3} (נסיא [ישראל]) D_{3} (נסיא [ישרא]ל) E_{2} ([ישרא]ל) F_{3} ([נ]ש[י]א [י]שר[אל]) D_{18} ([יש]ראל) E_{7} (נסיא) G_{3} ([נש]יא ישראל]) I_{3} (נסיא [יש]ראל) 5/6ḤevBA $44_{2.7}$ XḤev/Se 30_{1} (נסי) XḤev/Se 49_{3} Bar-Kochba Revolt Year 2 Coin 193, נְשִׂיאֵי יִשְׂרָאֵל *princes of Israel* Nm 1_{44} 4_{46} $7_{2.84}$ Ezk 19_{1} 21_{17} 22_{6} 45_{9}, נְשִׂיא בְּנֵי *prince of the sons of* Judah 1 C 2_{10}.

נְשִׂיא מִדְיָן *prince of Midian* Nm 25_{18}, נְשִׂיאֵי מִדְיָן *princes of Midian* Jos 13_{21}, ־קֵדָר *of Kedar* Ezk 27_{21}.

נשיא עמכה *prince of your people* 4Q423 5_{3}, נשיי עמו *princes of his people* 11QT 57_{12}, נְשִׂיאֵי הָעֵדָה *princes of the congregation* Ex 16_{22} Nm 4_{34} 16_{2} (עֵדָה) 31_{13} 32_{2} Jos $9_{15.18}$ 22_{30}, נשיא העדה *prince of the congregation* 1QM 5_{1} (כול העדה *of all the congregation*) 1QSb 5_{20} 4QpIsaa 5_{3} 4QMg 4_{2} ([נ]שיא) 4_{6} ([העדה]) 5_{4} 6_{2} ([נשי]א) CD 7_{20} (כל העדה), הקהל *of the assembly* CD 7_{17} (if ins. נשיא), [השׁ]בט *of the tribe* 1QM 3_{15} (נשי), נְשִׂיאֵי הַמַּטֹּת *princes of the tribes* Nm 7_{2} 11QT 22_{2} ([נשיאי] [המטות]), מַטּוֹת *of the tribes of* Nm 1_{16}, הַלֵּוִי *of the Levites* Nm 3_{32}, נשי מררי *prince of Merari* 1QM 4_{1}, נְשִׂיא יִשָּׂשכָר *prince of Issachar* Nm 7_{18}, נְשִׂיא בֵית *prince of the house of* Nm $3_{24.30.35}$ 25_{14}, נְשִׂיאֵי הָאָבוֹת *princes of the fathers' (houses)* 1 K 8_{1}||2 C 5_{2}.

נְשִׂיא נְשִׂיאֵי *chief of the princes of* Nm 3_{32}, נְשִׂיא רֹאשׁ *prince of the head*, i.e. chief prince, *of* Ezk $38_{2.3}$ 39_{1}, נשיאי רוש *princes of the head*, i.e. chief princes 4QShirShabbd $1.1_{1.6}$ ([נש]יאי רוש]) 1.1_{10} ([ר]וש]) 1.1_{17} (נש]יאי) [רו]ש) 1.1_{19} ([נש]יאי רוש]) $1.1_{21.23.26}$ ([רוש]) 4QShirShabbf 3.1_{12a} 4QShirShabbf 3.2_{6}.

נשיאי משנה *princes of the second order* 4QShirShabba 3.2_{2}, נשיאי משני *princes of the second order of* 4QShirShabbf 13_{2} ([נש]יאי משני]) 13_{7} ([משׁ]ני]), נשיא קו[דש] *prince of holiness* 4QShirShabbb 23_{1}, [נשי]אי פלא *princes of wonder* 4QShirShabbf 13_{5}, נשיאי כוה[נות] *princes of the priesthoods of* 4QShirShabbd 1.2_{21}, [נשיא

[מ]לחמה[ה] *prince of battle* 1QM 19$_{12}$, נשיאי הדגלים *princes of the battalions* 11QT 21$_{5}$.

מלך נשיאי *king of the princes of* 4QShirShabb^{a} 1.2$_{14}$, רָאשֵׁי נְשִׂיא נְשִׂיאֵי *chief of the princes of* Nm 3$_{32}$, הַנְּשִׂיאִים *chiefs of the princes* 1 C 7$_{40}$ 4QShirShabb^{d} 1.2$_{20}$ (נשיאים), ראשי נשיאי *chiefs of the princes of* 4Q ShirShabb^{d} 1.2$_{21}$, בַּת־נְשִׂיא *daughter of the prince of* Nm 25$_{18}$, יד ... נשיא *hand of ... the prince of* Mur 24 B$_{3}$ (נסיא) C$_{3}$ ([יד] ... נסיא) D$_{3}$ ([יד] ... [נ]ש[י]א) E$_{2}$ (נסיא) F$_{3}$ (י[ד]) G$_{3}$ ([יד] ... נש[יא]) I$_{3}$ ([יד] ... נסיא), ידי ... נשיאי *hands of ... the princes of* XḤev/Se 49$_{3}$, דַּם־נְשִׂיאֵי *blood of the princes of* Ezk 39$_{18}$, שם הנשיא *name of the prince* 1QM 3$_{15}$ 4QM^{f} 10$_{4a}$ ([שם]), שם נשי *name of the prince of* 1QM 3$_{15}$ 4$_{1}$,

מ[ג]ן נשיא *shield of the prince of* 1QM 5$_{1}$, [אוצר] נסיא *treasury of the prince of* Mur 24 D$_{18}$, משני [נשי]אי *second order of the princes of* 4QShirShabb^{f} 13$_{5}$.

שְׁנֵי הַנְּשִׂאִים *two of the princes* Nm 7$_{3}$.

כֹּל נָשִׂיא *every prince* 2 C 1$_{2}$, כָּל־הַנְּשִׂאִים *all the princes* Ex 34$_{31}$ (הַנְּשִׂאִים) Jos 9$_{19}$ 4QM^{a} 1$_{5}$ ([כו]ל הנשיא[ים]), כָּל־נְשִׂיאֵי *all the princes of* Ex 16$_{22}$ Nm 31$_{13}$ Ezk 21$_{17}$ 26$_{16}$ (כֹּל) 27$_{21}$ 4QShirShabb^{d} 1.1$_{26}$ (כול) 4QM^{a} 1$_{4}$ (כול [נש]יאי), כָּל־נְשִׂיאֶיהָ *all its princes* Ezk 32$_{29}$, נְשִׂיאֵהֶם *all their princes* Nm 17$_{17}$ (נְשִׂיאֵהֶם) 17$_{21}$.

<APP> חִוִּי *Hivite* Gn 34$_{2}$, Abidan Nm 7$_{60}$, Ahiezer Nm 7$_{66}$, Ahihud Nm 34$_{27}$, Ahira Nm 7$_{78}$, Bukki Nm 34$_{22}$, Eliab Nm 7$_{24}$, Eliasaph Nm 7$_{42}$, Elishama Nm 7$_{48}$, Elizaphan Nm 34$_{25}$, Elizur Nm 7$_{30}$, Evi Jos 13$_{21}$, Gamaliel Nm 7$_{54}$, Gog Ezk 38$_{2.3}$ 39$_{1}$, Hamor Gn 34$_{2}$, Hanniel Nm 34$_{23}$, Hur Jos 13$_{21}$, Kemuel Nm 34$_{24}$, Nahshon Nm 7$_{12}$ (if ins. נָשִׂיא) 1 C 2$_{10}$, Nethanel Nm 7$_{18}$, Pagiel Nm 7$_{72}$, Paltiel Nm 34$_{26}$, Pedahel Nm 34$_{28}$, Reba Jos 13$_{21}$, Rekem Jos 13$_{21}$, Shelumiel Nm 7$_{36}$, Sheshbazzar Ezr 1$_{8}$, Simeon (bar Cosiba) Mur 24 B$_{3.9}$ ([ש]מעון [נ]סיא) C$_{3}$ ([שמעון]) D$_{3}$ ([שמעון] ... [נ]ש[י]א) F$_{3}$ ([שמעון]) E$_{2.7}$ G$_{3}$ ([שמעון] ... נש[יא]) I$_{3}$ ([שמעו]ן) 5/6ḤevBA 44$_{2.7}$ XḤev/Se 30$_{1}$ XḤev/Se 49$_{3}$ Bar-Kochba Revolt Year 2 Coin 193, Zimri Nm 25$_{14}$, Zur Jos 13$_{21}$.

אִישׁ *man* Nm 16$_{2}$, בֵּן *son* Gn 25$_{16}$ Nm 7$_{18+10t}$ 25$_{14}$ 34$_{22+6t}$ Mur 24 B$_{3}$ C$_{3}$ D$_{3}$ ([בן] ... [נ]ש[י]א) E$_{2}$ F$_{3}$ ([בן]) G$_{3}$ ([בן] ... נש[יא]) I$_{3}$ ([בן]) 5/6ḤevBA 44$_{2.7}$ XḤev/Se 30$_{1}$ XḤev/Se 49$_{3}$, קָרִיא *one called* Nm 1$_{16}$ 16$_{2}$, ראשׁ *head* Nm 1$_{16}$ 7$_{2}$ 10$_{4}$ 36$_{1}$ 1 K 8$_{1}$||2 C 5$_{2}$ 2 C 1$_{2}$, נָסִיךְ *prince* Jos 13$_{21}$, חָלָל *profane one* Ezk 21$_{30}$, רָשָׁע *wicked one* Ezk 21$_{30}$ (or em. חֲלַל רֶשַׁע *profane one of wickedness*), appar. רִבּוֹא *ten thousand* 1QM 3$_{16}$.

<ADJ> אֶחָד *one* Nm 7$_{11.11.21.21}$ 34$_{18.18}$ Jos 22$_{14.14}$.

<PREP> לְ of benefit, *to, for* Ezk 45$_{16}$ XḤev/Se 30$_{1}$, + פתח *open* Ezk 46$_{12}$, גבר *be mighty* 4QShirShabb^{b} 3$_{3}$ ([תג]בר ... לנביא[י]), סלח ni. *be pardoned* Lv 4$_{22}$, עשׂה ni. *be made* 11QT 42$_{14}$; reflexive, *for (oneself)*, + כון hi. *prepare* Ezk 38$_{3}$.

לְ of possession, *of, (belonging) to* Nm 17$_{21.21}$ Ezk 45$_{7}$ 48$_{21.21.22}$ perh. 4QapMos^{b} 1.3$_{3}$ perh. 4QShirShabb^{a} 3.2$_{2}$ 4QShirShabb^{d} 1.1$_{1.6}$ (לנש[יאי]) 1.1$_{10}$ 4QShirShabb^{f} 3.1$_{12a}$ 5/6ḤevBA 44$_{2.7}$, + היה *be* Ezk 48$_{22}$.

לְ of direction, *to*, + אמר *say* Ezk 38$_{3}$ 2 C 1$_{2}$, ספר *count* Ezr 1$_{8}$, שׁוב *go back* Ezk 46$_{17}$.

בְּ partitive, *from among* 4QShirShabb^{d} 1.1$_{17.19}$ (both [בנש]יאי) 1.1$_{21.23}$ 4QShirShabb^{f} 3.2$_{6}$ 13$_{2}$ ([בנש]יאי) 13$_{7}$ ([ב]נשיאי); *against*, + היה *be* Ezk 21$_{17}$.

מִן of direction, *from*, + חכר *rent* Mur 24 B$_{9}$ ([חכרתי] [מן] ... [נ]ס[יא]) E$_{7}$; of cause, *on account of*, + בושׁ *be ashamed* Si 41$_{17}$.

אֶל *to(wards)*, + אמר *say* Nm 32$_{2}$, דבר pi. *speak* Ex 34$_{31}$, ידע hi. *make known* Lv 4$_{22}$, שׂים *place* face Ezk 38$_{2}$; *over, concerning*, + נשׂא *lift* Ezk 19$_{1}$; *against* Ezk 38$_{3}$ 39$_{1}$.

עַל *upon, against*, + היה *be* Jos 9$_{19}$, לון ni. *murmur* Jos 9$_{18}$, נבא ni. *prophesy* Ezk 38$_{2}$; (of duty) *upon*, + היה *be* Ezk 45$_{17}$; *for, on behalf of* Nm 7$_{3}$, + כפר pi. *make atonement* Lv 4$_{22}$; *concerning* Ezk 12$_{10}$ (if em.; see Nom. Cl.), + כתב pass. *be written* CD 5$_{1}$.

עִם *with* 11QT 22$_{2}$ ([עם נשיא]) 11QT^{b} 5$_{23}$, + נגשׁ *draw near* 1QM 19$_{12}$ ([עם נשיא]).

מֵאֵת *from* Nm 7$_{84}$, + לקח *take* Nm 17$_{17}$.

לִפְנֵי *before*, + דבר pi. *speak* Nm 36$_{1}$, בוא hi. *bring* 4QM^{g} 4$_{6}$, קרב *draw near* Jos 17$_{4}$, עמד *stand* Nm 27$_{2}$.

<COLL> נָשִׂיא || מֶלֶךְ *king* Ezk 7$_{27}$ 32$_{29}$; + נָסִיךְ *prince* Ezk 32$_{29}$, שַׂר *commander* 2 C 1$_{2}$ Si 41$_{17(Bmg, M)}$ 1QM 4$_{1}$ 11QT 42$_{14}$, שֹׁפֵט *judge* 2 C 1$_{2}$, זָקֵן *elder* 1 K 8$_{1}$||2 C 5$_{2}$ 11QT 42$_{14}$, ראשׁ *head* 11QT 42$_{14}$.

נָשִׂיא as vocative, Ezk 21$_{30}$ 38$_{3}$ 39$_{1}$ 45$_{9}$.

שְׁנֵים־עָשָׂר נְשִׂאִם עֲשָׂרָה נְשִׂאִים *ten princes* Jos 22$_{14}$, *twelve princes* Gn 17$_{20}$ 25$_{16}$, var. 11QT 57$_{12}$, חֲמִשִּׁים וּמָאתַיִם נְשִׂיאֵי עֵדָה *two hundred and fifty princes of the congregation* Nm 16$_{2}$.

נָשִׂיא בְעַמְּךָ *a prince among your people* Ex 22$_{27}$, נָשִׂיא לִבְנֵי יְהוּדָה *the prince of the sons of Judah* Nm 2$_{3}$, vars. Nm 2$_{5+10t}$ 7$_{24+9t}$, הַנָּשִׂיא לִיהוּדָה *the prince of Judah* Ezr 1$_{8}$, נָשִׂיא לָראוּבֵנִי *a prince of the Reubenites* 1 C 5$_{6}$.

Also 4QShirShabb^{b} 14.2$_{6}$.

<SYN> מֶלֶךְ *king*.*

⇒ נשׂא I *lift*.

*[נָשִׂיא] II $_{4.0.1}$ n.[m.] **mist**—pl. נְשִׂאִים (נְשִׂיאִים)—**mist, vapour, cloud,** <NOM CL> נְשִׂאִים וְרוּחַ וְגֶשֶׁם אָיִן *(as when) there are clouds and wind but no rain* Pr 25$_{14}$. <OBJ> עלה hi. *cause to rise* Jr 10$_{13}$=51$_{16}$ Ps 135$_{7}$ 11QPs^{a} 26$_{15}$ ([נשיא]ים). <COLL> נָשִׂיא + בָּרָק *lightning* Jr 10$_{13}$=51$_{16}$ Ps 135$_{7}$, רוּחַ *wind* Jr 10$_{13}$=51$_{16}$ Ps 135$_{7}$ Pr 25$_{14}$.

⇒ נשׂא (?) *lift*.

*[נָשִׂיא] III $_{1}$ n.[m.] **one brought** (unless נָשִׂיא I *prince*)—cstr. נְשִׂיא—<NOM CL> נְשִׂיא אֱלֹהִים אַתָּה *you are one brought of*, i.e. by, *God* Gn 23$_{6}$. <CSTR> נְשִׂיא אֱלֹהִים *one brought of*, i.e. by, *God* Gn 23$_{6}$.

⇒ נשׂא *lift*.

נשׂק, see שׂלק *burn*.

נשׁא I $_{5.0.1}$ vb. **lend—Qal** $_{5}$ + waw וְנָשָׁא; ptc. נֹשֶׁא, נֹשְׁאִים—**1. lend, cause to be indebted with,** <SUBJ> Israelite Dt 24$_{10(ms, Sam)}$ (L נשׁה hi. *lend*), חֹר *noble* Ne 5$_{7}$, סָגָן *official* Ne 5$_{7}$, אִישׁ *man*, i.e. each Ne 5$_{7}$. <OBJ> מַשָּׁא *debt* Ne 5$_{7}$ (mss מַשָּׂא ... נשׂא *impose ... a burden*), מַשָּׁאָה *debt* Dt 24$_{10(ms, Sam)}$. <PREP> בְּ *to* or introducing object, + אָח *brother* Ne 5$_{7}$, רֵעַ *neighbour* Dt 24$_{10(ms, Sam)}$.

2. borrow, <SUBJ> אֲשֶׁר *one who* Is 24$_{2}$. <PREP> בְּ *from*, + נֹשֶׁה *creditor* Is 24$_{4}$ (|| לוה *borrow*).

3. exact an oath from, impose an oath upon (mss נשׂא *lift*), <SUBJ> אִישׁ *man* 1 K 8$_{31}$||2 C 6$_{22}$ (+ אלה hi. *invoke a curse*). <OBJ> אָלָה *oath* 1 K 8$_{31}$||2 C 6$_{22}$. <PREP> בְּ *upon, from*, + רֵעַ *neighbour* 1 K 8$_{31}$||2 C 6$_{22}$.

4. ptc. as noun, **lender, creditor,** <NOM CL> לוֹ נֹשֶׁא *there was to him a creditor* 1 S 22$_{2}$.

<SYN> §2 לוה *borrow*.

Hi. $_{0.0.1}$ Pf. Q השאתה—perh. **lend, be a creditor,** <PREP> בְּ *to* or introducing object perh. 4QparaKings 109$_{1}$.*

⇒ מַשָּׁא *debt*, מַשָּׁאָה *debt*; cf. נשׁה *lend*.

נשׁא II $_{11.1}$ vb. **deceive—Ni.** $_{1.1}$ Pf. נִשְּׁאוּ; impf. 3fs Si תנשה—**1. be deluded,** <SUBJ> בֵּן *son* Dn 11$_{14}$ (if em. יִנָּשְׂאוּ *they shall lift themselves up* [נשׂא htp.] to יִנָּשְׁאוּ), שַׂר *prince* of Memphis Is 19$_{13}$ (|| יאל ni. *be foolish*).

2. be deceived, be beguiled, be enticed, <SUBJ> בַּת *daughter* Si 42$_{10(Bmg)}$ (+ פתה htp. *be seduced*); subj. not specified, Jb 34$_{31}$ (if em.; נָשָׂאתִי *I have borne* to נִשֵּׁאתִי *I was beguiled*). <PREP> בְּ of place, *in*, + בַּיִת *house* Si 42$_{10(Bmg)}$.

<SYN> יאל ni. *be foolish*.

Hi. $_{15}$ Pf. הִשִּׁיא (הִשִּׁיאַנִי, הִשִּׁיאֶךָ), הִשֵּׁאתָ, הִשִּׁיאוּךָ; impf. יַשִּׁיא (יַשִּׁא, Qr יַשִּׁי, יַשִּׁאֶךָ), יַשִּׁיאוּ, תַּשִּׁאוּ; inf. abs. הַשֵּׁא—**1. deceive, beguile,** <SUBJ> Y. 2 K 19$_{10}$||Is 37$_{10}$ Jr 4$_{10.10}$ Ezk 39$_{2}$ (if em. וְשִׁשֵּׁאתִיךָ *and I will lead you on* [שׁשׁא pi.] to וְהִשֵּׁאתִיךָ), Israelites Jr 37$_{9}$, Hezekiah 2 K 18$_{29}$||Is 36$_{14}$||2 C 32$_{15}$, אִישׁ *man* Ob$_{7}$, כֹּהֵן *priest* Lm 1$_{19}$ (if em. וְיָשִׁיבוּ *that they might restore* [שׁוב hi.] to וַיַּשִּׁיאוּ), נָבִיא *prophet* Jr 29$_{8}$, קֹסֵם *diviner* Jr 29$_{8}$, זָקֵן *elder* Lm 1$_{19}$ (if em.; see above), אֹיֵב *enemy* Ps 89$_{23}$ (or em. יִשָּׂא *he will* not *rise up*, from נשׂא), נָחָשׁ *serpent* Gn 3$_{13}$, זָדוֹן *presumptuousness* Jr 49$_{16}$||Ob$_{3}$, תִּפְלֶצֶת *horror* Jr 49$_{16}$.

<OBJ> Edom Ob$_{7}$, Israelites 2 C 32$_{15}$, Gog Ezk 39$_{2}$ (if em.; see Subj.), Hezekiah 2 K 19$_{10}$||Is 37$_{10}$, אִשָּׁה *woman* Gn 3$_{13}$, נָשִׂיא *prince* Ezk 39$_{2}$ (if em.; see Subj.), שׁכן ptc. *one who dwells* Jr 49$_{16}$||Ob$_{3}$, נֶפֶשׁ *soul*, i.e. self Jr 37$_{9}$ Lm 1$_{19}$ (if em.; see Subj.).

<PREP> לְ introducing object, + Israelites 2 K 18$_{29}$||Is 36$_{14}$, גֹּלָה *exiles* Jr 29$_{8}$, Jerusalem Jr 4$_{10}$, עַם *people* Jr 4$_{10}$; בְּ introducing object, + David Ps 89$_{23}$ (or em.; see Subj.), עֶבֶד *servant* Ps 89$_{23}$ (or em.; see Subj.).

<COLL> נשׁא hi. || סות hi. *mislead* 2 C 32$_{15}$.

הַשֵּׁא הִשֵּׁאתָ *you have utterly deceived* Jr 4$_{10}$.

2. intrans., **be deceitful,** <SUBJ> מָוֶת *death* Ps 55$_{16}$ (Qr) (יַשִּׁי מָוֶת *may death be deceitful*; Kt ישימות appar.

may *desolations* be upon). <PREP> עַל *against*, + אֱנוֹשׁ *person* Ps 55$_{16(Qr)}$, אַלּוּף *companion* Ps 55$_{16(Qr)}$, מְיֻדָּע *intimate friend* Ps 55$_{16(Qr)}$.

<SYN> §1 סות hi. *mislead*.

⇒ מַשָּׁאָה *deception*, מַשָּׁאוֹן *deception*.

נשׁא III, see נשׁה II *forget*.*

נֹשֶׁא *lender, creditor*, see נשׁא *lend*.

נשׁב 3.1.1 vb. **blow—Qal** 1.1.1 Pf. נָשְׁבָה; impf. Si ישוב—**blow,** <SUBJ> רוּחַ *breath* of Y. Is 40$_{17}$ 4Q185 1.1$_{10}$ ([נשב[ה). <PREP> בְּ of place, *upon*, + חָצִיר *grass* Is 40$_{17}$, צִיץ *flower* Is 40$_{17}$.

Also Si 43$_{20(M)}$.

Hi. 2.1 Impf. יַשֵּׁב (Si ישיב); + waw וַיַּשֵּׁב—**1. cause to blow,** <SUBJ> Y. Ps 147$_{18}$ Si 43$_{20(B)}$ (M qal). <OBJ> רוּחַ *wind* Ps 147$_{18}$, צִנָּה *coolness* of north wind Si 43$_{20}$.

2. frighten away, <SUBJ> Abram Gn 15$_{11}$. <OBJ> עַיִט *birds of prey* Gn 15$_{11}$.

3. perh. privative, **stifle,*** <SUBJ> Y. Ps 68$_{23}$ (if em.; see Obj.), חָכָם *wise one* Pr 29$_{8}$ (if em. יָשִׁיבוּ *they turn away* [שׁוב hi.] to יַשִּׁיבוּ), מַעֲנֶה *answer* Pr 15$_{1}$ (if em. יָשִׁיב *it turns away* [שׁוב hi.] to יַשִּׁיב). <OBJ> אַף *anger* Pr 29$_{8}$ (if em.; see Subj.), חֵמָה *wrath* Pr 15$_{1}$ (if em.; see Subj.), בָּשָׁן *serpent* Ps 68$_{23}$ (if em. אֲדֹנָי מִבָּשָׁן אָשִׁיב *the Lord* said, *I will bring him back* [שׁוב hi.] *from the snake* to אֲדֹנָ־ים בָּשָׁן אַשִּׁיב *the Lord* said, *I stifled the snake*).*

⇒ cf. נשׁף *blow*.

נשׁה I 13.0.5 vb. **lend —Qal** 10.0.3 Pf. נָשׁוּ, נָשִׁיתִי; ptc. נֹשֶׁה (נוֹשֶׁה), נֹשִׁים (Q נושים), נוֹשֵׁי—**1. lend, be a creditor,** <SUBJ> Israelite Dt 24$_{11}$, Jeremiah Jr 15$_{10}$, Nehemiah Ne 5$_{10}$, אָח *brother* Ne 5$_{10}$, נַעַר *lad* Ne 5$_{10}$, חֹר *noble* Ne 5$_{10.11}$, סָגָן *official* Ne 5$_{10.11}$; subj. not specified, Jr 15$_{10}$ 4Q417 1.2$_{7}$. <OBJ> דָּגָן *grain* Ne 5$_{10.11}$, יִצְהָר *fresh oil* Ne 5$_{11}$, תִּירוֹשׁ *new wine* Ne 5$_{11}$, כֶּסֶף *money* Ne 5$_{10.11}$. <PREP> בְּ *to* 4Q417 1.2$_{7}$, + Jeremiah Jr 15$_{10}$, אִישׁ *man* Dt 24$_{11}$, אָח *brother* Ne 5$_{10.11}$; בַּעַד *on behalf of, for the sake of*, + רֵעַ *neighbour* 4Q417 1.2$_{7}$.

2. ptc. as noun, **creditor,** <SUBJ> בוא *come* 2 K 4$_{1}$, לקח *take* 2 K 4$_{1}$, נקשׁ pi. *ensnare* Ps 109$_{11}$ (or em. נקשׁ pi. to חפשׂ pi. *search for* or בקשׁ pi. *seek*), שׁלם pi. *pay* 2 K 4$_{7}$ (if em. נִשְׁיֵךְ [Qr; Kt נשיכי] *your debt* to נֹשַׁיִךְ), משׁל *rule* Is 3$_{12}$ (if em. נָשִׁים *women* to נֹשִׁים *creditors*). <CSTR> רום נושים *haughtiness of creditors* 4QSh A$_{2}$. <PREP> לְ reflexive, *for oneself*, + לקח *take* 2 K 4$_{1}$; of direction, *to*, + מכר *sell* Is 50$_{1}$; כְּ *as* Is 24$_{2}$, + היה *be* Ex 22$_{24}$; מִן partitive, *from among* Is 50$_{1}$. <COLL> נשׁה ptc. || לוה ptc. *lender* Is 24$_{2}$; + שׂים נֶשֶׁךְ *place*, i.e. exact, *interest* Ex 22$_{24}$.

<SYN> §2 לוה ptc. *lender*.

Also 4Q417 1.2$_{6}$.

Hi. 3.0.2 Pf. הִשָּׁה; impf. יַשֶּׁה, 2ms תַּשֶּׁה—**lend, cause to be indebted with,** <SUBJ> Y. Jb 11$_{6}$* (unless נשׁה II hi. *cause to be forgotten*) 39$_{17}$ (unless נשׁה II hi. *cause to forget*), Israelite Dt 24$_{10}$ (ms, Sam נשׁא *lend*), אִישׁ *man* CD 10$_{18}$, בַּעַל *possessor* of debt, i.e. creditor Dt 15$_{2}$=11QMelch 2$_{3}$. <OBJ> 1. one who lends, רְנָנִים appar. *ostrich* Jb 39$_{17}$ (unless נשׁה II hi. *cause to forget*). 2. thing lent, חָכְמָה *wisdom* Jb 39$_{17}$ (unless נשׁה II hi. *cause to forget*), מַשָּׁאָה *debt* Dt 24$_{10}$, כֹּל *anything* CD 10$_{18}$. <PREP> לְ of benefit, *for*, + Job Jb 11$_{6}$ (unless נשׁה II hi. *cause to be forgotten*); בְּ *to* or introducing object, + רֵעַ *neighbour* Dt 15$_{2}$=11QMelch 2$_{3}$ ([ברעהו]) Dt 24$_{10}$ CD 10$_{18}$; מִן of comparison, *(less) than*, + עָוֺן *guilt* Jb 11$_{6}$ (unless נשׁה II hi. *cause to be forgotten*).*

⇒ נְשִׁי *debt*, מַשֶּׁה *debt*.

נשׁה II 7.0.1 vb. **forget—Qal** 3 Pf. נָשִׁיתִי; + waw וְנָשִׁיתִי; inf. abs. נָשֹׁא—**forget,** <SUBJ> Y. Jr 23$_{39.39}$ (mss both נשׁא I *lift*), Israel Dt 32$_{18}$ (if em. תֶּשִׁי [perh. שׁיה *neglect*] to תַּשֶּׁה) Is 44$_{21}$ (if em. תִּנָּשֵׁנִי *you shall* not *be forgotten by me* [ni.] to תַּשֵּׁנִי or תִּנְשֵׁנִי *you shall* not *forget me*), מֶלֶךְ *king* Ps 2$_{12}$ (if em. נַשְּׁקוּ־בַר appar. *kiss the son* to נֹשֵׁי קֶבֶר *ones who forget the grave* or נֹשֵׁי קֹבֵר *ones who forget him who buries*),* worshipper Lm 3$_{17}$, שֶׁמֶשׁ *sun* Hb 3$_{10}$ (if em. רוֹם יָדֵיהוּ נָשָׂא: שֶׁמֶשׁ *it lifted its hand on high. The sun* to מוֹעָדָיו נָשָׁא שֶׁמֶשׁ *the sun forgot its seasons* or מְדוֹרֵיהוּ נָשָׁא שֶׁמֶשׁ *the sun forgot its turning points* or מִזְרָחָה נָשָׁא שֶׁמֶשׁ *the sun forgot its rising*).

<OBJ> Y. Is 44$_{21}$ (if em.; see Subj.), עַם *people* Jr 23$_{39}$ (mss נשׁא I *lift*), כֹּהֵן *priest* Jr 23$_{39}$ (mss נשׁא I), נָבִיא *prophet* Jr 23$_{39}$ (mss נשׁא I), קֹבֵר *one who buries* Ps 2$_{12}$

(if em.; see Subj.), קֶבֶר *grave* Ps 2$_{12}$ (if em.; see Subj.), צוּר *rock* Dt 32$_{18}$ (if em.; see Subj.), טוֹבָה *good* Lm 3$_{17}$, מוֹעֵד *season* Hb 3$_{10}$ (if em.; see Subj.), מִזְרָח *rising* Hb 3$_{10}$ (if em.; see Subj.).

<COLL> וְנָשִׁיתִי אֶתְכֶם נָשֹׁא *and I will utterly forget you* Jr 23$_{39}$ (mss וְנָשִׂיתִי אֶתְכֶם נָשֹׂא *and I will utterly lift you up*).

Ni. $_{1}$ Pf. 2ms תִּנָּשֵׁנִי—**be forgotten** (unless נשה III ni. *be given up*), <SUBJ> Israel Is 44$_{21}$ (or em.; see Coll.). <COLL> לֹא תִנָּשֵׁנִי *you shall not be forgotten by me* Is 44$_{21}$ (or em. תִּשֵּׁנִי or תִּנְשֵׁנִי *you shall* not *forget me*).

Pi. $_{1}$ Pf. נַשַּׁנִי—**cause to forget,** <SUBJ> Y. Gn 41$_{51}$. <OBJ> 1. one who forgets, Joseph Gn 41$_{51}$. 2. thing forgotten, עָמָל *trouble* Gn 41$_{51}$, בַּיִת *house* Gn 41$_{51}$.

Hi. $_{2}$ Pf. הִשָּׁה; impf. יַשֶּׁה—**cause to forget** (unless נשה I hi. *lend*), <SUBJ> Y. Jb 39$_{17}$. <OBJ> 1. one who forgets, רְנָנִים appar. *ostrich* Jb 39$_{17}$. 2. thing forgotten, חָכְמָה *wisdom* Jb 39$_{17}$.

2. cause to be forgotten, overlook (unless נשה I hi. *cause to be indebted*), <SUBJ> Y. Jb 11$_{6}$ (or em.; see Prep.). <PREP> לְ of benefit, *for*, + Job Jb 11$_{6}$ (or em. יַשֶּׁה לְךָ to יִשְׁאָלְךָ *he requires of you*; or em. יַשֶּׁה to יִשָּׂא *he forgives*); מִן partitive, *some of*, + עָוֹן *guilt* Jb 11$_{6}$ (or em.).

Htp. $_{0.0.1}$ Pf. התנשיתה—**forget, overlook,** <SUBJ> Y. 4QBark^{a} 1.2$_{3}$. <OBJ> רום *haughtiness* of eyes 4QBark^{a} 1.2$_{3}$. <PREP> מִן *from* or *on account of*, + worshipper 4QBark^{a} 1.2$_{3}$.

Niphtal, forget, <SUBJ> צוּר *rock* Jr 18$_{14}$ (if em. יִנָּתְשׁוּ *they shall be plucked up* to יִנָּתְשׁוּ *they shall forget*), לְבָנוֹן *Lebanon* Jr 18$_{14}$ (if em.). מַיִם flowing *water* Jr 18$_{14}$ (if em; see Subj.).*

⇒ נְשִׁיָּה *forgetfulness*, יִשִּׁיָּה *Isshiah*, יִשִּׁיָּהוּ *Isshiah*, מְנַשֶּׁה *Manasseh*.

*נשה III $_{1}$ vb. **give up—Ni.** $_{1}$ Impf. 2ms תִּנָּשֵׁנִי—**be given up** (unless נשה II *be forgotten*), <SUBJ> Israel Is 44$_{21}$ (or em.; see Coll.). <COLL> לֹא תִנָּשֵׁנִי *you shall not be given up by me* Is 44$_{21}$.

נשה IV, see נשא II *deceive*.

נָשֶׁה $_{1}$ n.[m.] **sciatic nerve,** <NOM CL> הַנָּשֶׁה אֲשֶׁר עַל־כַּף הַיָּרֵךְ *the sciatic nerve that is in the socket of the hip* Gn 32$_{33}$. <OBJ> אכל *eat* Gn 32$_{33}$.

נֹשֶׁה *creditor*, see נשה I *lend*.

[נְשִׁי] $_{1}$ n.[m.] **debt**—sf. Qr נִשְׁיֵךְ (Kt נשיכי)—<OBJ> שלם pi. *pay* 2 K 4$_{7}$ (or em.; נֹשַׁיִךְ *your creditors*, i.e. נשה ptc.).

⇒ נשה I *lend*.

נְשִׁיָּה $_{1}$ n.f. **forgetfulness,** <CSTR> אֶרֶץ נְשִׁיָּה *land of forgetfulness* Ps 88$_{13}$ (+ חֹשֶׁךְ *darkness*).

⇒ נשה II *forget*.

*[נָשִׁים] I n.m.pl. **men,** byform of אֲנָשִׁים as pl. of אִישׁ *man*, <SUBJ> גיל II *live* Ps 2$_{12}$ (if em. נַשְּׁקוּ־בַר appar. *kiss the son* to נְשֵׁי קֶבֶר *men of the grave*, i.e. mortal men).

⇒ אִישׁ *man*.

נָשִׁים II, see אִשָּׁה *woman*.

[נְשִׁיקָה] $_{2}$ n.f. **kiss**—pl. cstr. נְשִׁיקוֹת—<SUBJ> עתר ni. *be abundant* Pr 27$_{6}$ (+ פֶּצַע *wound*). <CSTR> נְשִׁיקוֹת שׂוֹנֵא *kisses of an enemy* Pr 27$_{6}$, פִּיהוּ *of his mouth* Ca 1$_{2}$. <PREP> מִן of instrument, *by (means of), with* or partitive, *(some) of* (as obj.), + נשק *kiss* Ca 1$_{2}$.

⇒ נשק *kiss*.

נשך I $_{11.1}$ vb. **bite—Qal** $_{9}$ Pf. נָשַׁךְ; impf. יִשֹּׁךְ (יִשָּׁךְ, יִשְּׁכֶנּוּ); + waw וּנְשָׁכוֹ (וּנְשָׁכָם); ptc. נֹשֵׁךְ, נֹשְׁכִים; ptc. pass. נָשׁוּךְ—**1. bite,** <SUBJ> נָבִיא *prophet* Mc 3$_{5}$, נָחָשׁ *serpent* Nm 21$_{9}$ Am 5$_{19}$ 9$_{3}$ Ec 10$_{8.11}$, שְׁפִיפֹן *viper* Gn 49$_{17}$, יַיִן *wine* Pr 23$_{32}$. <OBJ> Israelites Am 9$_{3}$, אִישׁ *man* Nm 21$_{9}$, עָקֵב *heel* Gn 49$_{17}$, פרץ ptc. *one who breaks through* a wall Ec 10$_{8}$. <PREP> בְּ of instrument, *by (means of), with*, + שֵׁן *tooth* Mc 3$_{5}$; בְּלֹא *without*, + לַחַשׁ *charming* Ec 10$_{11}$; כְּ *as*, + נָחָשׁ *serpent* Pr 23$_{32}$. <COLL> נשך ‖ פרש hi. *sting* Pr 23$_{32}$; + noun used adverbially, אַחֲרִית *(at the) end* Pr 23$_{32}$.

2. pass., be bitten, <SUBJ> חֹבֵר *charmer* Si 12$_{13}$;

subj. not specified, Nm 21$_{8}$.

<SYN> §1 פרשׁ hi. *sting*.

Pi. 2 + waw וַיְנַשְּׁכוּ; וְנִשְּׁכוּ—**bite,** <SUBJ> נָחָשׁ *serpent* Nm 21$_{6}$ Jr 8$_{17}$, שָׂרָף *fiery serpent* Nm 21$_{6}$, צִפְעֹנִי *adder* Jr 8$_{17}$. <OBJ> Israelites Jr 8$_{17}$, עַם *people* Nm 21$_{6}$.

נשׁך II 5 vb. **pay interest—Qal** 2 Impf. יַשִּׁךְ; ptc. נֹשְׁכֶיךָ—**1. pay interest,** perh. specif. on a money loan, <SUBJ> subj. not specified, Dt 23$_{20}$.

2. ptc. as noun, **creditor,** or perh. **debtor,** <SUBJ> קום *arise* Hb 2$_{7}$ (+ זוע pilp. ptc. *one who terrifies*).

Hi. 3 Impf. 2ms תַּשִּׁיךְ—**cause to pay interest, lend on interest,** <SUBJ> Israelite(s) Dt 23$_{20.21.21}$. <OBJ> נֶשֶׁךְ *interest* Dt 23$_{20}$. <PREP> לְ of direction, *to*, + אָח *brother* Dt 23$_{20.21}$, נָכְרִי *foreigner* Dt 23$_{21}$.

⇒ נֶשֶׁךְ *interest.*

נֶ֫שֶׁךְ 12 n.[m.] **interest**—cstr. נֶ֫שֶׁךְ—**interest, usury,** perh. specif. on a money loan (as distinct from תַּרְבִּית and מַרְבִּית *interest*, specif. on a loan of food),* <OBJ> שׂים *place*, i.e. exact Ex 22$_{24}$, לקח *take* Lv 25$_{36}$ Ezk 18$_{17}$ 22$_{12}$, נשׁך hi. *cause to pay interest* Dt 23$_{20.20.20}$. <CSTR> נֶשֶׁךְ אֹכֶל *interest of*, i.e. on, *food* Dt 23$_{20}$, כֶּסֶף *of*, i.e. on, *money* Dt 23$_{20}$, כָּל־דָּבָר *of*, i.e. on, *anything* Dt 23$_{20}$. <PREP> בְּ of price, *(in exchange) for*, + נתן *give* Lv 25$_{37}$ Ezk 18$_{8.13}$ Ps 15$_{5}$ 4QD^{b} 4$_{10}$ ([יתן] ... בנש[ך]); of instrument, *by (means of), with*, + רבה hi. *increase* wealth Pr 28$_{8}$. <COLL> נֶשֶׁךְ || תַּרְבִּית *increase* Lv 25$_{36.37}$ Ezk 18$_{8.13}$ (both +) 18$_{17}$ 22$_{12}$ Pr 28$_{8}$.

<SYN> תַּרְבִּית *increase.**

⇒ נשׁך II *pay interest.*

[נֹשֵׁךְ] *creditor*, see נשׁך II *pay interest.*

נִשְׁכָּה 3.0.11 n.f. **chamber**—sf. נִשְׁכָּתוֹ; pl. נְשָׁכוֹת; sf. Q נשכותמה—**chamber, room,** alw. (except perh. Ne 3$_{30}$) in temple area; for storage (Ne 12$_{44}$), <SUBJ> היה *be* 11QT 45$_{1}$ ([והיו כול הנשכות]), בנה pass. *be built* 11QT 42$_{9}$. <NOM CL> לחוצה מזה הנשכה *on the outside of it is the chamber* 4Q365a 2.2$_{9}$, var. 11QT 42$_{05}$ ([לחוצה מזה] [הנשכות]), לבני שמעון ... נשכותמה *to the sons of Simeon shall be ... their chambers* 11QT 44$_{10}$, vars. 11QT 44$_{8.12}$. <OBJ> עשׂה *make* Ne 13$_{7}$ 11QT 41$_{17}$ 42$_{5}$ ([תעשה]), חלק pi. *apportion* 11QT 44$_{3}$ ([הנשכות]) 44$_{6}$ ([תח]לק), טהר pi. *purify* 11QT 45$_{6}$. <CSTR> [רוחב הנשכה] *breadth of a chamber* 11QT 42$_{05}$, כול הנשכות *all the chambers* 11QT 42$_{3}$ 45$_{1}$ ([כול הנשכות]). <PREP> לְ of benefit, *to, for*, + עשׂה *do* 11QT 42$_{3}$ ([תעשה]); בְּ of place, *in(to)*, + כנס *gather* Ne 12$_{44}$; עַל *over*, + פקד ni. *be appointed* Ne 12$_{44}$, נֶגֶד *opposite*, + חזק hi. *repair* Ne 3$_{30}$.

<COLL> חֶדֶר + נִשְׁכָּה *room* 11QT 42$_{4.9}$ 44$_{6.8.10.12}$, פַּרְוָר *portico* 11QT 42$_{9}$.

[שמונה] עשרה נשכה *eighteen chambers* 11QT 42$_{5}$, שתים וחמשים נשכות *fifty-two chambers* 11QT 44$_{12}$, ארבע וחמשים נשכה *fifty-four chambers* 11QT 44$_{8}$, שמונה ומאה נשכה *a hundred and eight chambers* 11QT 44$_{6}$, שבעים [ומאתים נשכה] *two hundred and seventy chambers* 11QT 45$_{2}$, [שש ושמונים וחמש מאות נשכה] *five hundred and eighty-six chambers* 11QT 45$_{2}$; הַנְּשָׁכוֹת לָאוֹצָרוֹת לַתְּרוּמוֹת לָרֵאשִׁית וְלַמַּעַשְׂרוֹת *the chambers for the stores, the contributions, the firstfruits and the tithes* Ne 12$_{44}$.

Also 11QT^{b} 11$_{22}$.

⇒ cf. לִשְׁכָּה *chamber.*

נשׁל 7 vb. **slip off—Qal** 6 Impf. יִשַּׁל; + waw ונשל; impv. שַׁל—**1. slip off, drop off,** <SUBJ> זַיִת *olive* Dt 28$_{40}$, בַּרְזֶל *iron (axehead)* Dt 19$_{5}$. <PREP> מִן of direction, *from*, + עֵץ *wood (handle)* Dt 19$_{5}$.

2. remove, take off, <SUBJ> Joshua Jo 5$_{15}$, Moses Ex 3$_{5}$. <OBJ> נַעַל *sandal* Ex 3$_{5}$ Jos 5$_{15}$. <PREP> מֵעַל *from (upon)*, + רֶגֶל *foot* Ex 3$_{5}$ Jos 5$_{15}$.

3. clear away, drive away, <SUBJ> Y. Dt 7$_{1.22}$. <OBJ> Amorites Dt 7$_{1}$, Canaanites Dt 7$_{1}$, Girgashites Dt 7$_{1}$, Hittites Dt 7$_{1}$, Hivites Dt 7$_{1}$, Jebusites Dt 7$_{1}$, Perizzites Dt 7$_{1}$, גּוֹי *nation* Dt 7$_{1.22}$. <PREP> מִפְּנֵי *from before*, + Israel(ites) Dt 7$_{1.22}$. <COLL> וְנָשַׁל ... אֶת־הַגּוֹיִם הָאֵל ... מְעַט מְעָט *and he will clear away ... these nations ... little by little* Dt 7$_{22}$.

Also 1Q29 2$_{4}$ ([ונש]ל).

Pi. 1 + waw וַיְנַשֵּׁל—**clear away, drive away,** <SUBJ> מֶלֶךְ *king* of Edom 2 K 16$_{6}$. <OBJ> Jews 2 K 16$_{6}$. <PREP> מִן of direction, *from*, + Elath 2 K 16$_{6}$.

נשם 1 vb. **pant—Qal** 1 Impf. אֶשֹּׁם (1QIsa^{a} אשמה)—**1. pant, gasp** (unless from שׁמם *be desolate*),* <SUBJ> Y. Is 42_{14}. <PREP> כְּ *as*, + ילד ptc. fem. *one who gives birth* Is 42_{14}. <COLL> אֶפְעֶה אֶשֹּׁם וְאֶשְׁאַף יָחַד *I will groan, I will pant and gasp at the same time* Is 42_{14}.

2. pant after, desire,* <SUBJ> Gad Dt 33_{21} (if em. שָׁם *there* to יִשֹּׁם *he pants after*).* <OBJ> חֶלְקָה *plot of land* Dt 33_{21} (if em.; see Subj.).

Hi. cause to breathe, <SUBJ> לִוְיָתָן *Leviathan* Jb 41_{23} (if em. יָשִׂים *he places* to יַשִּׁים *he causes to breath*, i.e. froth). <OBJ> יָם *sea* Jb 41_{23} (if em.; see Subj.). <PREP> כְּ *as*, + מֶרְקָחָה *pot* Jb 41_{23} (if em.; see Subj.).*

⇒ נְשָׁמָה *breath*, תִּנְשֶׁמֶת *chameleon, owl.*

נְשָׁמָה 24.2.5.1 n.f. **breath**—נִשְׁמַת; sf. נִשְׁמָתִי, Si נשמתך, נִשְׁמָתוֹ, I נשמתה; pl. נְשָׁמוֹת—**1. breath** of humans and animals, as evidence of life (e.g. Gn 7_{22} 1K 17_{17} Is 2_{22} Dn 10_{17} Si 9_{13}), perh. breath as facilitating speech (e.g. Jb 26_{4} Dn 10_{17}).*

2. breath of God, as a blast (2 S 22_{16}||Ps 18_{16} Jb 4_{9} 4QapPs^{b} 29_{3} [מנש[מת]]), as imparted to humans (e.g. Gn 2_{7} Jb 32_{8} 33_{4}).

3. person, soul (e.g. Dt 20_{16} Jos $11_{11.14}$ perh. 4Qps Ezek^{a} 4_{8}* Frey 1536_{3}).

<SUBJ> היה *be* 4QpsEzek^{a} 4_{8}, יתר ni. *remain* Jos 11_{11} 1 K 17_{17}, שׁאר ni. *remain* Dn 10_{17}, יצא *go out* Jb 26_{4}, בער *burn* Is 30_{33}, עשׂה *make* Is 57_{16}, בין hi. *cause to understand* Jb 32_{8}, הלל pi. *praise* Ps 150_{16}.

<NOM CL> נֵר י׳ נִשְׁמַת אָדָם *the spirit of a human being is a lamp of Y.* Pr 20_{27} (or em. נֵר to נֹצֵר Y. *watches*), נִשְׁמָתִי בִי *my breath is within me* Jb 27_{3} (unless נִשְׁמָתִי *his breath*),* var. Si 30_{29}, נְשָׁמָה בְּאַפּוֹ *breath is in his nostrils* Is 2_{22}=1QS 5_{17}, נִשְׁמַת רוּחַ חַיִּים בְּאַפָּיו *the breath of the spirit of life was in its nostrils* Gn 7_{22}, נשמתה לחיי עולם *may her soul be to*, i.e. have, *eternal life!* Frey 1536_{3}.

<OBJ> חיה pi. *keep alive* Dt 20_{16} 11QT 62_{14}, שׁאר hi. *leave* Jos 11_{14} 1 K 15_{29}, נפח *breathe* Gn 2_{7}, נצר *watch* Pr 20_{27} (if em.; see Nom. Cl.), נתן *give* Is 42_{5} 11QPs^{a} 19_{4}, לקח *take* Si 9_{13}, אסף *gather* Jb 34_{14}, חרם hi. *devote to destruction* Jos 10_{40}.

<CSTR> נִשְׁמַת י׳ *breath of Y.* Is 30_{33}, אֵל *of God* Jb 37_{10}, אֱלוֹהַ *of God* Jb 4_{9}, שַׁדַּי *of the Almighty* Jb 32_{8} 33_{4}, אָדָם (spirit) *of a human being* Pr 20_{27}, חַיִּים *of life* Gn 2_{7}, רוּחַ *of the spirit* of life Gn 7_{22}, (blast) *of the breath of* Y.'s nostrils 2 S 22_{16}||Ps 18_{16} 4QapPs^{b} 29_{3} (נש[מת]), נשמת כול בשר *breath of all flesh* 11QPs^{a} 19_{4}, נִשְׁמַת־מִי *whose breath?* Jb 26_{4}; כָּל־נְשָׁמָה *every breathing thing* Dt 20_{16} Jos 10_{40} (הַנְּשָׁמָה) $11_{11.14}$ 1 K 15_{29} Ps 150_{6} (כֹּל הַנְּשָׁמָה) 11QT 62_{14} (כול).

<PREP> מִן of cause, *on account of*, + גלה ni. *be uncovered* 2 S 22_{16}||Ps 18_{16}, אבד *perish* Jb 4_{9} 4QapPs^{b} 29_{3} (מנש[מת]); of instrument, *by (means of), with*, + נתן *give* ice Jb 37_{10}.

<COLL> רוּחַ || נְשָׁמָה *spirit* Is 42_{5} 57_{16} (+) Jb 4_{9} 27_{3} 32_{8} (+) 33_{4} 34_{14}; + נֶפֶשׁ *soul* 11QPs^{a} 19_{4}, אָדָם *human being* Jos 11_{14}, שָׂרִיד *survivor* Jos 10_{40}, נֶפֶשׁ *soul*, i.e. person Jos 11_{11}.

Also 4QShirShabb^{b} 3_{1}.

<SYN> רוּחַ *spirit.**

⇒ נשם *breathe.*

נשׁף 2 vb. **blow—Qal** 2 Pf. נָשַׁפְתָּ, נָשַׁף—**blow,** <SUBJ> Y. Ex 15_{10} Is 40_{24}. <PREP> בְּ *upon*, + רֹזֵן *ruler* Is 40_{24}, שֹׁפֵט *judge* Is 40_{24}; of instrument, *by (means of), with*, + רוּחַ *wind* Ex 15_{10}.

⇒ נֶשֶׁף I *twilight*, יַנְשׁוּף *screech owl*; cf. נשׁב *blow.*

נֶשֶׁף I 12.1.1 n.[m.] **twilight**—נָשֶׁף; cstr. נֶשֶׁף; sf. נִשְׁפּוֹ—**1.** usu. **twilight** of evening. **2. twilight** of morning (Ps 119_{147} Jb 7_{4}). **3. darkness** in general (Jr 13_{16} Jb 3_{9} Si 35_{16}). <OBJ> שׁמר *watch* Jb 24_{15}, שׂים *place*, i.e. turn, into trembling Is 21_{4} (unless נֶשֶׁף II *trace*). <CSTR> נֶשֶׁף חִשְׁקִי *twilight of my desire*, i.e. that I desired Is 21_{4} (unless נֶשֶׁף II *trace*); הָרֵי נֶשֶׁף *mountains of*, i.e. in the, *twilight* Jr 13_{16}, כּוֹכְבֵי נִשְׁפּוֹ *stars of its twilight* Jb 3_{9}, אפלות נשף *shades of twilight* 4QWiles 1_{5}.

<PREP> בְּ of time, *in, at*, + קום *arise* 2 K 7_{5}, נוס *flee* 2 K 7_{7}, צעד *step* Pr 7_{9} (+ עֶרֶב יוֹם *evening of the day*), אחר pi. *stay behind* Is 5_{11} (|| בֹּקֶר *morning*); introducing object, + קדם pi. *precede*, i.e. rise before Ps 119_{147}; כְּ *as at*, + כשׁל *stumble* Is 59_{10} (:: צָהֳרַיִם *noon*); מִן of direction, *from*, + יצא hi. *bring out* guidance Si 35_{16}; of time, *from*, + נכה hi. *strike* 1 S 30_{17} (+ וְעַד־הָעֶרֶב לְמָחֳרָתָם

and until the evening of the next day); עַד *until*, + שׂבע *be sated with* tossings Jb 7_{4}.

<SYN> בֹּקֶר *morning*.

<ANT> צָהֳרַיִם *noon*.

⇒ נשׁף *blow*.

*[נֶשֶׁף] II $_{1}$ n.[m.] **trace** (unless נֶשֶׁף I *twilight*)—cstr. נֶשֶׁף—**trace, faint suspicion,** <OBJ> שׂים *place*, i.e. turn, into trembling Is 21_{4}. <CSTR> נֶשֶׁף חִשְׁקִי *trace of my desire* Is 21_{4}.

נשׁק I $_{31}$ vb. **kiss—Qal** $_{25}$ Pf. נָשַׁק, נָשְׁקוּ; impf. יִשַּׁק (יִשָּׁקֵנִי), אֶשְׁקָה (אֶשְׁקְךָ), יִשָּׁקוּן; + waw וַיִּשַּׁק, וָאֶשָּׁק, וַנִּשְׁקָה, 3fs וַתִּשַּׁק, וַיִּשְּׁקוּ (וַיִּשָּׁקֵהוּ); impv. שְׁקָה; inf. לִנְשֹׁק־—**kiss, kiss one another** (Ps 85_{11} [or em. ni.]), <SUBJ> Israelites Ho 13_{2}, Aaron Ex 4_{27}, Absalom 2 S 15_{5}, Elisha 1 K 19_{20}, Esau Gn 33_{4}, Israel/Jacob Gn 29_{11} 48_{10}, Joab 2 S 20_{9}, Joseph Gn 50_{1}, Moses Ex 18_{7}, Naomi Ru 1_{9}, Orpah Ru 1_{14}, Samuel 1 S 10_{1}, אִישׁ *man*, i.e. each 1 S 20_{41}, אִשָּׁה *man* Pr 7_{13}, בֵּן *son* Gn $27_{26.27}$ 1 K 19_{20}, מֶלֶךְ *king* 2 S 14_{33} 19_{40}, שׁוב hi. ptc. *one who replies* Pr 24_{26} (unless נשׁק IV *seal*), male lover Ca 1_{2}, female lover Ca 8_{1}, פֶּה *mouth* 1 K 19_{18}, יָד *hand* Jb 31_{27} (unless נשׁק IV), צֶדֶק *righteousness* Ps 85_{11} (unless נשׁק III *be in order*; or em. נָשָׁקוּ *they have kissed oneanother* [ni.] or נָשֹׁקוּ *they have rushed together* [from שׁקק]), שָׁלוֹם *peace* Ps 85_{11} (unless נשׁק III *be in order*; or em.; see above).

<OBJ> Jacob Gn 33_{4}, Saul 1 S 10_{1}, רֵעַ *neighbour* 1 S 20_{41}, female lover Ca 1_{21}, male lover Ca 8_{1}, עֵגֶל *calf* Ho 13_{2}, שָׂפָה *lip* Pr 24_{26} (unless נשׁק IV *seal*).

<PREP> לְ introducing object, + בַּעַל *Baal* 1 K 19_{18}, Absalom 2 S 14_{33}, Amasa 2 S 20_{9}, Barzillai 2 S 19_{40}, Isaac Gn $27_{26.17}$, Moses Ex 4_{27}, Rachel Gn 29_{11}, אִישׁ *man* 2 S 15_{5}, אָב *father* Gn $27_{26.27}$ 50_{1} 1 K 19_{20}, חֹתֵן *father-in-law* Ex 18_{7}, אֵם *mother* 1 K 19_{20}, חָמוֹת *mother-in-law* Ru 1_{14}, בֵּן *son* Gn 48_{10}, כַּלָּה *daughter-in-law* Ru 1_{9}, נַעַר *young man* Pr 17_{13}, פֶּה *mouth* Jb 31_{27} (unless נשׁק IV *seal*), שָׂפָה *lip* Pr 24_{26}.

מִן of instrument, *by (means of), with* or partitive, *(some) of* (as obj.), + נְשִׁיקָה *kiss* Ca 1_{2}.

<COLL> נשׁק ‖ חבק pi. *embrace* Gn 33_{4} (+) 48_{10}, כרע *bow* 1 K 19_{18}; + שׁחה htpal. *bow down* Ex 18_{7} 1 S 20_{41}.

<SYN> חבק pi. *embrace*, כרע *bow*.

Ni. kiss one another, <SUBJ> צֶדֶק *righteousness* Ps 85_{11} (if em. נָשָׁקוּ [qal] to נִשָּׁקוּ), שָׁלוֹם *peace* Ps 85_{111} (or em.).

Pi. $_{5}$ + waw וַיְנַשֵּׁק (וַיְנַשֶּׁק־); impv. נַשְּׁקוּ; inf. נַשֵּׁק—**kiss,** <SUBJ> Joseph Gn 45_{15}, Laban Gn 29_{13} 31_{28} 32_{1}, מֶלֶךְ *king* Ps 2_{12} (or em.; see Obj.), שֹׁפֵט *judge* Ps 2_{12} (or em.; see Obj.). <OBJ> בַּר *son* Ps 2_{12} (or em. נַשְּׁקוּ־בַר *kiss the son* to נֹשֵׁי קֶבֶר *ones who forget the grave* or נֹשֵׁי קֹבֵר *ones who forget him who buries* or נְשֵׁי קֶבֶר *men of the grave* or del. נַשְּׁקוּ־בַר or em. בַּר to בְּרַגְלָיו *his feet*).* <PREP> לְ introducing object, + Jacob Gn 29_{13}, בֵּן *son* Gn 31_{28} 32_{1}, בַּת *daughter* Gn 31_{28} 32_{1}, אָח *brother* Gn 45_{15}; בְּ introducing object, + רֶגֶל *foot* Ps 2_{12} (if em.; see Obj.). <COLL> נשׁק pi. ‖ חבק pi. *embrace* Gn 29_{13}; לֹא נְטַשְׁתַּנִי לְנַשֵּׁק *you did not permit me to kiss* Gn 31_{28}.

<SYN> חבק pi. *embrace*.

Hi. $_{1}$ Ptc. מַשִּׁיקוֹת—**touch,** <SUBJ> אִשָּׁה *woman*, i.e. each Ezk 1_{23} (if em. יְשָׁרוֹת *straight* to מַשִּׁיקוֹת *touching*) 3_{13}, כָּנָף *wing* of living being Ezk 3_{13} (if em.). <PREP> אֶל *against* or introducing object, + אָחוֹת *sister*, i.e. the other Ezk 1_{23} (if em.; see Subj.) 3_{13}.*

⇒ נְשִׁיקָה *kiss*.

נשׁק II $_{3}$ vb. **be equipped (with)—Qal** $_{3}$ Ptc. נֹשְׁקֵי (נוֹשְׁקֵי)—**equipped (with), be armed (with),** <SUBJ> בֵּן *son* of Ephraim Ps 78_{9} (נוֹשְׁקֵי רוֹמֵי־קֶשֶׁת *armed, shooting the bow*), גִּבּוֹר *mighty one* 1 C 12_{2}; subj. not specified, 2 C 17_{17}. <OBJ> קֶשֶׁת *bow* 1 C 2_{12} 2 C 17_{17} (both נֹשְׁקֵי קֶשֶׁת *armed of*, i.e. with, *the bow*), מָגֵן *shield* 2 C 17_{17} (נֹשְׁקֵי ... מָגֵן *armed of*, i.e. with, *... a shield*).

⇒ נֶשֶׁק I *weapons*.

*נשׁק III $_{2.0.1}$ vb. **be in order—Qal** $_{1.0.1}$ Impf. יִשַּׁק, Q ישקו—**be in order, stand side by side, submit oneself,** <SUBJ> עַם *people* Gn 41_{40} (unless נשׁק IV *seal [the lips]* or V *acquiesce*; or em. יָשֹׁק *they shall rush about* [from שׁקק] or יִקְשַׁב *they shall pay attention*), צֶדֶק *righteousness* Ps 85_{11} (unless נשׁק I *kiss*), שָׁלוֹם *peace* Ps 85_{11} (unless נשׁק I *kiss*), כֹּל *all* CD 13_{3}. <PREP> עַל *according to*, + פֶּה *mouth*, i.e. command

Gn 41$_{40}$ CD 13$_{3}$.

Hi. 1 Ptc. מַשִּׁיקוֹת—**keep in line,** <SUBJ> אִשָּׁה *woman*, i.e. each Ezk 1$_{23}$ (if em. יְשָׁרוֹת *straight* to מַשִּׁיקוֹת *touching*) 3$_{13}$, כָּנָף *wing* of living being Ezk 3$_{13}$ (if em.). <PREP> אֶל *against* or introducing object, + אָחוֹת *sister*, i.e. the other Ezk 1$_{23}$ (if em.; see Subj.) 3$_{13}$.

*נשׁק IV 3 vb. **seal**—**Qal** 3 Impf. יַשֵּׁק (יִשַּׁק); + waw 3fs וַתִּשַּׁק—**seal (the lips),** i.e. be silent, <SUBJ> עַם *people* Gn 41$_{40}$ (unless נשׁק III *be in order*), שׁוּב hi. ptc. *one who replies* Pr 24$_{26}$ (unless נשׁק I *kiss*), יָד *hand* Jb 31$_{27}$ (unless נשׁק I). <OBJ> שָׂפָה *lip* Pr 24$_{26}$ (unless נשׁק I *kiss*). <PREP> לְ introducing object, + פֶּה *mouth* Jb 31$_{27}$ (unless נשׁק I *kiss*); עַל *according to*, + פֶּה *mouth*, i.e. command Gn 41$_{40}$ (unless נשׁק III *be in order*).

*נשׁק V 1 vb. **acquiesce** (unless נשׁק III *be in order* or IV *seal [the lips]*)—**Qal** 1 Impf. יִשַּׁק—**acquiesce, yield,** <SUBJ> עַם *people* Gn 41$_{40}$. <PREP> עַל *according to*, + פֶּה *mouth*, i.e. command Gn 41$_{40}$.

נֶשֶׁק 10 n.[m.] **weapons**—נֶשֶׁק (נֵשֶׁק); cstr. נֶשֶׁק (נֵשֶׁק)—**1. weapons, military equipment,** <NOM CL> ... אִתְּכֶם הַנָּשֶׁק *with you are ... the weapons* 2 K 10$_{2}$. <OBJ> בוא *bring* 1 K 10$_{25}$||2 C 9$_{24}$ (unless נֵשֶׁק *perfume*), קרא *meet* Jb 39$_{21}$ (unless §3). <CSTR> נֵשֶׁק בַּרְזֶל *weapons of iron* Jb 20$_{24}$, נֵשֶׁק בֵּית *weapons of the house of* the forest Is 22$_{8}$. <APP> מִנְחָה *present* 1 K 10$_{25}$||2 C 9$_{24}$ (unless נֵשֶׁק *perfume*). <PREP> בְּ of instrument, *by (means of), with*, + בער pi. *kindle* fire Ezk 39$_{9.10}$; introducing object, + שׂלק hi. *set fire to* Ezk 39$_{9}$; מִן of direction, *from*, + ברח *flee* Jb 20$_{24}$; אֶל *to*, + נבט hi. *look* Is 22$_{8}$.

<COLL> נֶשֶׁק || מָגֵן *shield* Ezk 39$_{9}$, צִנָּה *(large) shield* Ezk 39$_{9}$, קֶשֶׁת *bow* Ezk 39$_{9}$ Jb 20$_{24}$ (+), חֵץ *arrow* Ezk 39$_{9}$, מַקֵּל *staff* Ezk 39$_{9}$, רֹמַח *spear* Ezk 39$_{9}$; + כְּלִי *vessel* 1 K 10$_{25}$||2 C 9$_{24}$, שַׂלְמָה *garment* 1 K 10$_{25}$||2 C 9$_{24}$, בֹּשֶׂם *spice* 1 K 10$_{25}$||2 C 9$_{24}$, סוּס *horse* 1 K 10$_{25}$||2 C 9$_{24}$ 2 K 10$_{2}$, פֶּרֶד *mule* 1 K 10$_{25}$||2 C 9$_{24}$, רֶכֶב *chariot* 2 K 10$_{2}$, עִיר מִבְצָר *fortified city* 2 K 10$_{2}$.

2. armoury, <CSTR> עֲלֹת הַנֶּשֶׁק *ascent of*, i.e. to, *the armoury* Ne 3$_{19}$.

3. battle, <OBJ> קרא *meet* Jb 39$_{21}$ (unless §1), <CSTR> יוֹם נֶשֶׁק *day of battle* Ps 140$_{8}$.

<SYN> §1 מָגֵן *shield*, צִנָּה *(large) shield*, קֶשֶׁת *bow*, חֵץ *arrow*, מַקֵּל *staff*, רֹמַח *spear*.

⇒ נשׁק II *be in order*.

נֵשֶׁק I 2 n.[m.] **perfume,** unless = נֶשֶׁק *weapons*, <OBJ> בוא *bring* 1 K 10$_{25}$||2 C 9$_{24}$ (+ בֹּשֶׂם *spice*, שַׂלְמָה *garment*, כְּלִי *vessel*, סוּס *horse*, פֶּרֶד *mule*). <APP> מִנְחָה *present* 1 K 10$_{25}$||2 C 9$_{24}$.

נֵשֶׁק II, see נֶשֶׁק *weapons*.

*[נַשָּׁר] n.[m.] **herald,** <CSTR> רַעַם נַשָּׁרִים *thunder*, i.e. shouting, *of heralds* Jb 39$_{25}$ (if em. שָׂרִים *princes*). <PREP> כְּ *as* Ho 8$_{1}$ (אֶל־חִכְּךָ שֹׁפָר כַּנַּשָּׁר *set a trumpet to your lips like a herald*; if em. כַּנֶּשֶׁר *as an eagle* to כַּנַּשָּׁר).

נֶשֶׁר 26.0.4 n.m. **eagle**—נֶשֶׁר; pl. נְשָׁרִים; cstr. נִשְׁרֵי—bird of prey, whether **eagle** (e.g. Ex 19$_{4}$ Dt 32$_{14}$ 38$_{49}$ 2 S 1$_{23}$ Jr 4$_{13}$ Hb 1$_{8}$ Pr 23$_{5}$ La 4$_{9}$) or **vulture** (e.g. Jr 44$_{16}$ Ezk 17$_{3}$ Mc 1$_{16}$ Pr 30$_{17}$ Jb 39$_{27}$);* prohibited as food (Lv 11$_{13}$ Dt 14$_{12}$), <SUBJ> היה *be* Ezk 17$_{7}$, בוא *come* Ezk 17$_{3}$, hi. *bring* Ezk 17$_{3}$, גבה hi. *raise oneself* Jb 39$_{27}$, רום hi. *make high* nest Jb 39$_{27}$, חושׁ *hasten* Hb 1$_{8}$, טושׂ *rush* Jb 9$_{26}$, דאה *fly* Dt 28$_{49}$, רחף pi. *hover* Dt 32$_{11}$=4QDibHam^{a} 6$_{7}$, פרשׂ *spread wings* Dt 32$_{11}$=4QDibHam^{a} 6$_{7}$, עור hi. *stir* Dt 32$_{11}$=4QDibHam^{a} 6$_{7}$, נשׂא *carry* Dt 32$_{11}$=4QDibHam^{a} 6$_{7}$, לקח *take* Dt 32$_{11}$=4QDibHam^{a} 6$_{7}$ Ezk 17$_{3}$, קטף *pluck off* Ezk 17$_{3}$, נתק *pull out* Ezk 17$_{7}$, נתן *give*, i.e. place Ezk 17$_{3}$, שׁכן *dwell* Jb 39$_{27}$, לין htpol. *abide* Jb 39$_{27}$, חפר *search* Jb 39$_{27}$, נבט hi. *look* Jb 39$_{27}$, אכל *eat* Hb 1$_{8}$, ni. *be eaten* Lv 11$_{13}$, שׁקה hi. *water* Ezk 17$_{7}$.

<NOM CL> [אח]ד נשר *one (face) was (that of) an eagle* 4QpsEzek^{a} 4$_{9}$.

<OBJ> שׁקץ pi. *abominate* Lv 11$_{13}$, אכל *eat* Dt 14$_{12}$.

<CSTR> נִשְׁרֵי שָׁמַיִם *eagles of the heavens* Lm 4$_{19}$; בְּנֵי־נֶשֶׁר *sons of the eagle* Pr 30$_{17}$, פְּנֵי־נֶשֶׁר *face of an eagle* Ezk 1$_{10}$ 10$_{14}$ (נָשֶׁר), כַּנְפֵי נְשָׁרִים *wings of eagles* Ex 19$_{4}$ 4QDibHam^{a} 6$_{7}$ ([כנפי]), דֶּרֶךְ הַנֶּשֶׁר *way of the eagle*

Pr 30_{19}.

<APP> אֵלֶּה *these* Lv 11_{13}.

<ADJ> גָּדוֹל *great* of wings Ezk $17_{3.7}$, אֶרֶךְ *long* of pinions Ezk 17_{3}, רַב *great* of plumage Ezk 17_{7}, מָלֵא *full* of plumage Ezk 17_{3}, אֶחָד *one* Ezk 17_{7} (or em. אֶחָד to אַחֵר *another*).

<PREP> לְ of direction, *to*, + שׁלח pi. *send*, i.e. shoot out, branches Ezk 17_{7}.

כְּ *as* Ho 8_{1} (or em. כַּנֹּצֵר or כַּשֹּׁמֵר *as a sentry* or כַּנֹּשֵׂר *as a herald*), + עלה *go up* Jr 49_{22}, hi. *cause to go up*, i.e. grow, wings Is 40_{31}, גבה hi. *make* nest *high* Jr 49_{16}, *raise oneself* Ob_{4}, דאה *fly* Jr 48_{40} 49_{22}, עוף *fly* Hb 1_{8}, חלף *pass* Jb 9_{26}, פרשׂ *spread* wings Jr 48_{40} 49_{22}, רחב hi. *make wide* baldness Mc 1_{16}, חדשׁ htp. (of youth) *be renewed* Ps 103_{5}, אכל *eat* 1QpHab 3_{11}.

מִן of comparison, *(more) than*, + קלל *be swift* 2 S 1_{23} Jr 4_{13} Lm 4_{19}.

עַל *to*, + כפן perh. *stretch out hungrily* Ezk 17_{7} (mss כנף perh. *thrust*).

<COLL> נֶשֶׁר || אֲרִי *lion* 2 S 1_{23}, אַרְיֵה *lion* Ezk 1_{10} 10_{14}, שׁוֹר *ox* Ezk 1_{10}, עֵגֶל *calf* 4QpsEzek[a] 4_{9}, נָחָשׁ *serpent* Pr 30_{19}, אָדָם *human being* Ezk 1_{10} 10_{14} 4QpsEzek[a] 4_{9}, גֶּבֶר *man* Pr 30_{19}, כְּרוּב *cherub* Ezk 10_{14}, אֳנִיָּה *ship* Pr 30_{19}; + עֹרֵב *raven* Pr 30_{17}.*

<SYN> אֲרִי *lion*, אַרְיֵה *lion*, שׁוֹר *ox*, עֵגֶל *calf*, נָחָשׁ *serpent*, אָדָם *human being*, גֶּבֶר *man*, כְּרוּב *cherub*, אֳנִיָּה *ship*.

נשׁת 3 vb. **be dry—Qal** 2 Pf. נָשְׁתָה (נָשֵׁתָּה)—**be dry, be parched, be exhausted,** <SUBJ> לָשׁוֹן *tongue* Is 41_{17}, גְּבוּרָה *might* Jr 51_{30}. <PREP> בְּ of cause, *on account of*, + צָמָא *thirst* Is 41_{17}.

Ni. 1 + waw וְנִשְּׁתוּ—**be dried up,** <SUBJ> מַיִם *water* Is 19_{5} (+ יבשׁ *be dry*, חרב *be dry*) Jr 18_{14} (if em. יִנָּתְשׁוּ *they will be rooted up* to יִנָּשְׁתוּ). <PREP> מִן of direction, *from*, + יָם *sea* Is 19_{5}.

נִשְׁתְּוָן 2 n.[m.] **letter,** <CSTR> כְּתָב הַנִּשְׁתְּוָן *writing of the letter* Ezr 4_{7}, פַּרְשֶׁגֶן *copy of* Ezr 7_{11}.

[נָתוּק] *animal that is torn*, see נתק *tear*.

[נָתוּשׁ] *uprooted one*, see נתשׁ *pluck up*.

נתח 9.0.1 vb. **cut into pieces—Pi.** 9.0.1 Pf. נִתַּח; impf. 2ms וַיְנַתְּחֶהָ ,וַיְנַתְּחֵהוּ) וַיְנַתֵּחַ ;וַיְנַתְּחֵהוּ ,תְּנַתֵּחַ + waw וְנִתַּח), וַאֲנַתְּחֶהָ; ptc. Q מנתחים—**cut into pieces,** <SUBJ> Elijah 1 K 18_{33}, Moses Ex 29_{17} Lv 8_{20}, Saul 1 S 11_{7}, אָדָם *human being* Lv $1_{6.12}$, אִישׁ *husband* Jg 20_{6}, אָדוֹן *master* Jg 19_{29}, לֵוִי *Levite* Jg 20_{6}, נָבִיא *prophet* 1 K 18_{23}. <OBJ> פִּלֶגֶשׁ *secondary wife* Jg 19_{29}, אַיִל *ram* Ex 29_{17} Lv 8_{20}, פַּר *bull* 1 K $18_{23.33}$ 11QT 34_{9}, זָכָר *male* sheep or goat Lv 1_{12}, עֹלָה *burnt offering* Lv 1_{6}, צֶמֶד *yoke* of oxen 1 S 11_{7}. <PREP> לְ *into*, + נֵתַח *piece* Ex 29_{17} Lv $1_{6.12}$ 8_{20} Jg 19_{29} 11QT 34_{9}; *according to*, + עֶצֶם *bone* Jg 19_{29}.

⇒ נֵתַח *piece*.

נֵתַח 14.1.3 n.m. **piece**—pl. נְתָחִים; sf. נְתָחָיו ,נְתָחֶיהָ, Q נתחיהמה—**piece** of meat, <NOM CL> נתחיו אצלו *its pieces shall be beside it* 11QT 34_{12}. <OBJ> קטר hi. *burn* Lv 8_{20}, ערך *arrange* Lv 1_{8}, אסף *gather* Ezk $24_{4.4}$, קבל pi. *receive* Si 50_{12}, מלח *salt* 11QT 34_{10}, רתח pi. *boil* Ezk $24_{5(ms)}$ (L רְתָח *boiling*). <CSTR> כָּל־נֵתַח *every piece* Ezk 24_{4}. <APP> כָּתֵף *shoulder* Ezk 24_{4}, יָרֵךְ *thigh* Ezk 24_{4}. <ADJ> טוֹב *good* Ezk 24_{4}. <PREP> לְ *into*, + נתח *cut* Ex 29_{17} Lv $1_{6.12}$ 8_{20} Jg 19_{29} 11QT 34_{10}; *according to*, i.e. piece by piece, + יצא hi. *bring out* Ezk $24_{6.6}$, מצא hi. *bring* Lv 9_{13}; עַל *upon, beside*, + נתן *give*, i.e. place Ex 29_{17}.

<COLL> נֵתַח || ראשׁ *head* Ex 29_{17} Lv 1_{8} 8_{20} 9_{13} (+), פֶּדֶר *suet* Lv 1_{8} 8_{20}; + קֶרֶב *inner parts* 11QT 34_{10}, כֶּרַע *leg* 11QT 34_{10}; שְׁנֵים עָשָׂר נְתָחִים *twelve pieces* Jg 19_{29}.

<SYN> ראשׁ *head*, פֶּדֶר *suet*.

⇒ נתח *cut into pieces*.

נָתִיב 5.0.1 n.m. **path**—cstr. נְתִיב; pl. cstr. Q נתיבי—<SUBJ> שׁוח *sink* Pr 2_{18} (if em. בֵּיתָהּ *her house* to נְתִיבָהּ *her path*). <OBJ> שׁזף *see* Jb 28_{7}, ידע *know* Jb 28_{7} GnzPs 3_{5}, דרך hi. *tread* Jb 28_{7}, פלס pi. *clear* Ps 78_{50}, אור hi. *cause to shine* Jb 41_{24}. <CSTR> נְתִיב מִצְוֹתֶיךָ *path of your commandments* Ps 119_{35}, נתיבי צדקך *paths of your righteousness* GnzPs 3_{5}; דֶּרֶךְ נְתִיבָהּ *way of her path* Pr 12_{28} (if em. נְתִיבָה *of the path*),* כל נתיבי *all the paths of* GnzPs 3_{5}. <PREP> בְּ *in*, + חפץ *delight* Ps

119_{35}; עַל *upon*, + טמן pass. *be concealed* Jb 18_{10}, עדה *pass* Jb 28_7.*

⇒ נְתַבְיָהוּ *Nethibiah*; cf. נָתִיב *path*.

נְתִיבָה I $_{21.0.10}$ n.f. **path**—sf. נְתִיבָתִי, נְתִיבָתָם; pl. נְתִיבוֹת (Q נתיבת); cstr. נְתִיבוֹת (נְתִבוֹת); sf. נְתִיבוֹתַי (נְתִיבֹתַי), נְתִיבֹתָיו, נְתִיבוֹתֶיהָ, נְתִיבוֹתֵיהֶם—**path, pathway,** of stars (1QH 9_{12}), <NOM CL> כָּל־נְתִיבוֹתֶיהָ שָׁלוֹם *all her paths are peace* Pr 3_{17}, נתיבו[תי]ה אשמות פשע *her paths are the guilt of transgression* 4QWiles 1_{10}, נְתִיבָתִי זַכָּה *my path is pure* Jb 16_{17} (if em. תְּפִלָּתִי *my prayer*), אין נתיבת *there are no paths* 1QH 14_{24}.

<OBJ> ידע *know* Is 42_6 Ps 142_4, בין *understand* Jb 38_{20}, בחר *choose* 1QH 12_4, הלך *walk in* Jg 5_6 Jr 18_{15}, נתן *give*, i.e. *place* Is 43_{16}, שׂים *place* Is 43_{19} (if em. נְהָרוֹת *rivers* to נְתִיבוֹת), מצא *find* Ho 2_8, פתח *open* 4QD[e] 2.2_{20}, עקשׁ pi. *make crooked* Is 59_8, עוה pi. *twist* Lm 3_9, נתס *break up* Jb 30_{13}.

<CSTR> נְתִיבוֹת בֵּיתוֹ *paths of*, i.e. to, *its house* Jb 38_{20}, עוֹלָם *of ancient time*, i.e. ancient paths Jr 6_{16} (נְתִבוֹת), מִשְׁפָּט *of justice* Pr 8_{20}, נתיבות צדק *paths of righteousness* CD 1_{16}, צדקה *of righteousness* 1QH 15_{14}, שלום *of peace* 1QH fr. 3_3, שחת *of*, i.e. to, *the pit* 4QD[e] 2.2_{20}.

דֶּרֶךְ נְתִיבָה *way of the path* Pr 12_{28} (or em. נְתִיבָהּ *of her path* or מְשׁוּבָה *of apostasy* or תּוֹעֵבָה *of abomination*), הֹלְכֵי נְתִיבוֹת *those who walk in the paths* Jg 5_6, מְשֹׁבֵב נְתִיבוֹת *restorer of paths* Is 58_{12} (unless נְתִיבָה II *ruin*; or em. נְתִיצוֹת *of ruins*; 1QIsa[b] משיב *restorer of*), כָּל־נְתִיבוֹתֶיהָ *all her paths* Pr 3_{17}.

<APP> דֶּרֶךְ *way* Jr 6_{16}.

<PREP> לְ of benefit, *to, for* Ps 119_{105} perh. 4QShir Shabb[a] 1.2_{10} (לנתיבו[ת]); *concerning*, + שׁאל *ask* Jr 6_{16}; *according to* 1QH 9_{12} (לנתיבות[ם]), + ישׁר pi. *direct* 1QH 15_{14}.

בְּ of place, *in* 1QH 12_4, + דרך hi. *lead* Is 42_{16}, תעה *stray* Pr 7_{25}, ישׁב *remain* Jb 24_{13}.

מִן of direction, *from*, + סור *turn aside* CD 1_{16}, מנע *withhold* foot Pr 1_{15}.

עַל *upon*, + שׂים *place* Jb 19_8.

בְּתוֹךְ *among*, + הלך pi. *walk* Pr 8_{20}.

בֵּית *between, among*, + נצב ni. *stand* Pr 8_2 (or em. בֵּית to בֵּין *among*).

<COLL> דֶּרֶךְ ‖ נְתִיבָה *way* Is 42_{16} 43_{16} 59_8 Jr 6_{16} (both +) 18_{15} Ho 2_8 Jb 24_{13} Pr 1_{15} (all three +) 3_{17} 7_{25} (+) 8_2 12_{28} Lm 3_9 1QH 12_4 14_{24} (all four +) 4QWiles 1_{10} 4QD[e] 2.2_{20}, אֹרַח *path* Jg 5_6 Ps 142_4 Jb 19_8 (all three +) Pr 8_{20} 4QWiles 1_{10}, מַעְגָּל *way* 4QWiles 1_{10} Is 59_8 (+), רֶגֶל *foot* Ps 119_{105}; + שְׁבִיל *way* Jr 18_{15} 4QWiles 1_{10}, פֶּרֶץ *breach* Is 58_{12}.

שבע נתיבו[ת] *seven paths* 4QShirShabb[a] 1.2_{10}, נְתִיבוֹת לָשָׁבֶת *paths in which to dwell* Is 58_{12} (or em.; see Cstr.).

Also 4QpHos[a] 1_7.

<SYN> דֶּרֶךְ *way*, אֹרַח *path*, מַעְגָּל *way*, רֶגֶל *foot*.

⇒ cf. נָתִיב *path*.

*[**נְתִיבָה**] II $_1$ n.f. **ruin** (unless נְתִיבָה I *path*)—pl. נְתִיבוֹת—<CSTR> מְשֹׁבֵב נְתִיבוֹת *restorer of paths* Is 58_{12} (+ פֶּרֶץ *breach*). <COLL> נְתִיבוֹת לָשָׁבֶת *ruins in which to dwell* Is 58_{12}.

[**נְתַבְיָהוּ**] $_{0.0.0.1}$ pr.n.m. **Nethibiah**, servant of Mattan, <APP> נַעַר *servant* Seal 783 (7th cent.). <PREP> לְ of possession, *of, (belonging) to* Seal 783 (7th cent.).

⇒ נָתִיב *path* + ׳י *Y*.

[**נָתִין**] $_{17.0.1}$ n.m. **temple servant**—pl. נְתִינִים—alw. pl. **temple servants, Nethinim,** a group of postexilic cultic functionaries, <SUBJ> היה *be* Ne 3_{26}, בוא hi. *bring* Ezr $8_{17(Qr)}$ (Kt הנתונים *those assigned*, i.e. נתן ptc. pass.), ישׁב *dwell* Ezr 2_{70}‖Ne 7_{72} Ne 3_{26} 9_2‖1 C 9_2 Ne 11_{21}, חזק hi. *take hold of*, i.e. join with Ne 10_{29}.

<NOM CL> כָּל־הַנְּתִינִים וּבְנֵי עַבְדֵי שְׁלֹמֹה שְׁלֹשׁ מֵאוֹת תִּשְׁעִים וּשְׁנָיִם *all the Nethinim and the sons of the servants of Solomon were three hundred and ninety-two* Ezr 2_{58}‖Ne 7_{60}, אלה הנתינ[נים] *these are the Nethinim* 4QNetin 1_1.

<OBJ> נתן *give*, i.e. appoint Ezr 8_{20}.

<CSTR> בֵּית הַנְּתִינִים וְהָרֹכְלִים *house of the Nethinim and the merchants* Ne 3_{31}, כָּל־הַנְּתִינִים *all the Nethinim* Ezr 2_{58}‖Ne 7_{60}.

<APP> Iddo Ezr $8_{17(Qr)}$, אִישׁ *man*, i.e. each Ne 11_3, בֵּן *son* Ezr 2_{43}‖Ne 7_{46}, אָח Ezr $8_{17(Qr)}$.

<PREP> מִן partitive, *some of* (as subj.) Ezr 8_{20}, + עלה *go up* Ezr 7_{7}; אֶל *to*, + דבר pi. *speak* Ezr $8_{17(Qr)}$ (Kt הנתונים *those assigned*, i.e. נתן ptc. pass.); עַל *over*, i.e. in charge of Ne 11_{21}.

<COLL> כֹּהֵן || נָתִין *priest* Ezr 2_{70}||Ne 7_{72} Ezr 7_{7} Ne 10_{29} 11_{3}||1 C 9_{2}, לֵוִי *Levite* Ezr 2_{70}||Ne 7_{72} Ezr 7_{7} 8_{20} (+) 10_{29} 11_{3}||1 C 9_{2}, שֹׁעֵר *porter* Ezr 2_{70}||Ne 7_{72} Ezr 7_{7} Ne 10_{29}, מְשֹׁרֵר *singer* Ezr 2_{70}||Ne 7_{72} Ezr 7_{7} Ne 10_{29}; + עַם *people* Ezr 2_{70}||Ne 7_{72} Ne 10_{29}, יִשְׂרָאֵל *Israel* Ezr 2_{70}|| Ne 7_{72}, בֵּן *son* of Israel Ezr 7_{7}, of servants of Solomon Ezr 2_{58}||Ne 7_{60} Ne 11_{3}.

נְתִינִים מָאתַיִם וְעֶשְׂרִים *two hundred and twenty Nethinim* Ezr 8_{20}.

Also perh. 4Q523 1_{7} (נתו/ינים).

<SYN> כֹּהֵן *priest*, לֵוִי *Levite*, שֹׁעֵר *porter*, מְשֹׁרֵר *singer*.*

⇒ (?) נתן *give*.

*[נְתִיצָה] n.f. **ruin**, <CSTR> מְשֹׁבֵב נְתִיצוֹת *restorer of ruins* Is 58_{12} (if em. נְתִיבוֹת *of paths*; + גֹּדֵר פֶּרֶץ *repairer of the breach*). <COLL> נְתִיצוֹת לָשֶׁבֶת *ruins in which to dwell* Is 58_{12} (if em.; see Cstr.).

נתך 21.0.3 vb. **pour out—Qal** 7 Impf. 3fs תִּתַּךְ; + waw 3fs וַתִּתַּךְ—**pour out** (intrans.), **be poured out**, <SUBJ> אַף *anger* Jr 44_{6}, חֵמָה *wrath* Jr 42_{18} 44_{6} 2 C 12_{7} 34_{25}, אָלָה *curse* Dn 9_{11}, שְׁבוּעָה *oath* Dn 9_{11}, שְׁאָגָה *roaring* Jb 3_{24}, חרץ ni. ptc. *that which is determined* Dn 9_{27}.

<PREP> בְּ *upon*, + Jerusalem 2 C 12_{7}, מָקוֹם *place* 2 C 34_{25}; of instrument, *by (means of), with*, + יָד *hand* 2 C 12_{7}; כְּ *as*, + מַיִם *water* Jb 3_{24}; עַל *upon*, + Israelites Dn 9_{11}, שְׁאֵרִית *remnant* Jr 42_{18}, שׁמם ptc. *one who makes desolate* Dn 9_{27}.

<COLL> נתך + בער *burn* Jr 44_{6}; + adverb, כֵּן *so* Jr 42_{18}.

Ni. 8.0.3 Pf. נִתַּךְ, נִתְּכָה; impf. Q ינתך; + waw וְנִתְּכָה, וְנִתַּכְתֶּם; ptc. נִתֶּכֶת—**1. pour out** (intrans.), **be poured out**, <SUBJ> מָטָר *rain* Ex 9_{33}, מַיִם *water* 2 S 21_{10}, הָמוֹן *tumult* of water Jr 10_{13}=51_{16} (if em. לְקוֹל תִּתּוֹ *when he utters his voice* to לְקוֹלוֹ נִתַּךְ *at his voice there is poured out*), אַף *anger* Jr 7_{20} 42_{18}, חֵמָה *wrath* Jr 7_{20} 42_{18} Na 1_{6} 2 C 34_{21}. <PREP> לְ *at, on account of*, + קוֹל *voice* Jr 10_{13}=51_{16} (if em.; see Subj.); בְּ *upon*, + Israelites 2 C 34_{21}; כְּ *as*, + אֵשׁ *fire* Na 1_{6}; אֶל *upon*, + מָקוֹם *place* Jr 7_{20}; עַל *upon*, + אָדָם *human being* Jr 7_{20}, בֵּן *son* 2 S 21_{7}, יֹשֵׁב *inhabitant* Jr 42_{18}, בְּהֵמָה *beast* Jr 7_{20}, עֵץ *tree* Jr 7_{20}, פְּרִי *fruit* Jr 7_{20}; ה- of direction, *onto*, + אֶרֶץ *earth* Ex 9_{33}.

2. be melted, <SUBJ> בַּיִת *house* of Israel Ezk 22_{21}, אִישׁ *man* CD 20_{3}, מוט htpol. ptc. *capricious one* 4Q424 1_{5} (מתמ[ו]טט), טֻמְאָה *impurity* Ezk 24_{11} (+ תמם *be consumed*). <PREP> בְּתוֹךְ *in the middle of*, + Jerusalem Ezk 22_{21}, עִיר *city* Ezk 24_{11}, כּוּר *furnace* CD 20_{3}. <COLL> נתך ni. + adverb, כֵּן *so* 4Q424 1_{5}.

Also 4QUnidF 1_{1}.

Hi. 5 Pf. הִתִּיכוּ; impf. 2ms תַּתִּיכֵנִי; + waw וְהִתַּכְתִּי; וַיַּתִּיכוּ; inf. הַנְתִּיךְ—**1. pour out** (trans.), <SUBJ> Y. Jb 10_{10} (|| קפא hi. *congeal*), Hilkiah 2 K 22_{4} (if em. יַתֵּם *let him sum up* [תמם hi.] to יַתֵּךְ), Joah 2 C 34_{9} (if em. וַיִּתְּנוּ *and they gave* [from נתן] to וַיַּתִּכוּ), Maaseiah 2 C 34_{9} (if em.; see above), Shaphan 2 C 34_{9} (if em.; see above), בֵּן *son* 2 C 34_{9} (if em.; see above), שַׂר *commander* 2 C 34_{9} (if em.; see above), מַזְכִּיר *recorder* 2 C 34_{9} (if em.; see above), עֶבֶד *servant* 2 K 22_{9}||2 C 34_{17}, כֹּהֵן *priest* 2 K 22_{4} (if em.; see above). <OBJ> Job Jb 10_{10}, כֶּסֶף *money* 2 K 22_{4} (if em.; see Subj.) 22_{9}||2 C 34_{17} 2 C 34_{9} (if em.; see Subj.). <PREP> כְּ *as*, + חָלָב *milk* Jb 10_{10}.

2. melt, <SUBJ> Y. Ezk 22_{20}; subj. not specified, Ezk 22_{20}. <OBJ> בַּיִת *house* of Israel Ezk 22_{20}, כֶּסֶף *silver* Ezk 22_{20}, נְחֹשֶׁת *bronze* Ezk 22_{20}, בַּרְזֶל *iron* Ezk 22_{20}, עֹפֶרֶת *lead* Ezk 22_{20}, בְּדִיל *tin* Ezk 22_{20}.

<SYN> §1 קפא hi. *congeal*.

Ho. 1 Impf. תֻּתְּכוּ—**be melted**, <SUBJ> בַּיִת *house* of Israel Ezk 22_{22}. <PREP> בְּתוֹךְ *in the middle of*, + Jerusalem Ezk 22_{22}. <COLL> התך ho. + adverb, כֵּן *so* Ezk 22_{22}.

⇒ הִתּוּךְ *melting*.

נתן 2015.62.228.26 vb. **give**—

Qal, morphology, p. 785b

1. give, a. give (to), grant, bestow (upon), pay, in various senses, p. 786a

Subjects, p. 787a

Objects, p. 789b

Prepositions, p. 794b

Collocations, p. 800a

2a. מִי יִתֵּן **who will grant?,** i.e. **would that!, if only!, oh that it were!,** p. 800b

2b. מִי־יִתֶּן לִי **who will grant me?,** i.e. **oh that I had!,** p. 801a

3. give out, sound out, utter voice, send, p. 801a

4. place, p. 801b

a. place, put, set, p. 801b

b. turn shoulder, **stretch out** hand, **shoot out** branches, p. 801b

c. cast lots, p. 801b

d. fasten, set up, build, p. 802a

e. spread, p. 802a

f. pour out, p. 802a

g. impose, lay obligation, p. 802a

h. afflict with, send against; (of punishment, guilt, blemish etc.) **bring upon,** p. 802a

i. appoint, assign, designate; call an assembly, p. 802a

j. make, establish, p. 802a

k. appar. **place one's self,** p. 802a

Subjects, p. 802a

Objects, p. 803a

Prepositions, p. 805a

Collocations, p. 807b

5a. make (into), cause to be, make as, appoint as, place as, p. 807b

(1) with two objects, p. 807b

(2) with object + לְ *into, as,* p. 808a

(3) with object + בְּ *as,* p. 808a

(4) with object + כְּ *as,* p. 808a

Subjects, p. 808a

Objects, 1. p. 808a

Objects, 2. p. 808b

Prepositions, p. 809a

Collocations, p. 810a

5b. make out as, take as, p. 810b

6. cause, make happen, p. 810b

7. allow, permit, enable, p. 810b

8. be placed, p. 811a

9. pass. **a. be given, be assigned, be appointed,** p. 811a

9b. be placed, be stationed, p. 811a

Qal Passive, p. 811b

1. be given, be granted, p. 811b

2. be placed, p. 811b

3. be spread, i.e. suspended, p. 811b

4. be poured out, p. 812a

Niphal, p. 812a

1. be given, be granted, be bestowed (upon), p. 812a

Subjects, p. 812a

Prepositions, p. 812b

Collocations, p. 813a

2. מִי יִנָּתֵן **who will let it be granted?,** i.e. **would that it were granted!, if only!,** p. 813a

3. be given out, be uttered, p. 813a

4. be placed, set, p. 813a

5. be made into, be made like, p. 813b

6. be allowed, permitted, p. 813b

Hophal, p. 813b

Qal 1924.58.214.26 Pf. נָתַן (נָתֶן, נְתָנַנִי, נְתָנֵנִי, נְתָנְךָ, נְתָנוֹ, נְתָנָהּ, נָתַתִּי, נָתַתְּ, (נְתַתָּנִי, תַּתָּה, נָתַתָּה) נָתַתָּ, (נָתֲנָה) נָתְנָה, (נְתָנָם, נְתָנָנוּ (נָתֲנוּ) נָתְנוּ, (נְתַתִּים, נְתַתִּיהָ, נְתַתִּיו, נְתַתִּיךָ, נְתַתִּיךְ, נָתֲתִי), Q נתנוהו, נְתָנוּךָ) נְתַנּוּ, נְתַתֶּם; impf. יִתֵּן (יִתֶּן־, יִתְּנֵנִי, יִתֶּנְךָ, Q יתנכה, יִתְּנֶנּוּ, יִתְּנֶנָּה, Q יתנהה, יִתְּנֵם), 3fs תִּתֵּן, 2ms תִּתֵּן (תִּתֶּן־, תִּתְּנֵנִי, תִּתְּנוֹ, תִּתְּנֵהוּ, תִּתְּנֶנּוּ, תִּתְּנֶנָּה, תִּתְּנֵם), תִּתְּנִי, אֶתֵּן (אֶתֶּן־, אֶתְּנָה, אֶתְּנֶהָ, אֶתֶּנְךָ, אֶתְּנֵךְ, אֶתְּנֵהוּ, אֶתְּנֶנּוּ, אֶתְּנֶנָּה), יִתְּנוּ (יִתְּנוּ, יִתְּנֻהוּ), תִּתְּנוּ (תִּתְּנוּ, תִּתְּנֻהוּ, תִּתְּנוּם), נִתֵּן (נִתְּנָה).

+ waw וְנָתַן (וּנְתָנְךָ, Q ונתנכה, וּנְתָנוֹ, וּנְתָנָהּ, וּנְתָנָם, Q ונתנמה), וְנָתַתָּה, וְנָתַתָּ (וְנָתַתָּה, וּנְתַתָּם), 2fs וּנְתַתִּיהוּ, וְנָתַתִּי (וְנָתַתִּי, וּנְתַתִּיךָ, וּנְתַתִּיו, וּנְתַתִּיהוּ, וּנְתַתִּיהָ, וּנְתַתִּים), וְנָתְנוּ, וּנְתַתֶּם, וּנְתַנּוּ (וּנְתָנוּךָ); וַיִּתֵּן (וַיִּתֶּן־, וַיִּתֶּנְךָ, וַיִּתְּנֵהוּ, וַיִּתְּנָהּ, וַיִּתְּנֶנּוּ, וַיִּתְּנֵם, Q וינתם), 3fs וַתִּתֵּן (וַתִּתֶּן־, וַתִּתְּנֵהוּ), 2ms וַתִּתֵּן (וַתִּתֶּן־, וַתִּתְּנָה, וַתִּתְּנֵם), וַתִּתְּנִים, וָאֶתֵּן (וָאֶתֶּן־, וָאֶתְּנָה, וָאֶתֶּנְךָ, וָאֶתְּנֵךְ, וָאֶתְּנֶנָּה, וָאֶתְּנֶהָ, וָאֶתְּנֵם), וַיִּתְּנוּ (וַיִּתְּנֻהוּ, וַיִּתְּנוּהוּ, וַיִּתְּנוּם, וַיִּתְּנֵם), וַנִּתְּנָה.

impv. תֵּן (תֶּן־, Si תֶּין, תְּנָה, תְּנֵהוּ, תְּנֶנָּה, תְּנֵם), תְּנִי (תֵּנִי), תְּנוּ; ptc. נֹתֵן (נוֹתֵן, נֹתְנֵךְ, נֹתְנָךְ, נֹתְנוֹ), נֹתְנִים (Q נותנים), נֹתְנֵי; ptc. pass. נָתוּן, נְתֻנִים (נְתוּנִם, נְתוּנִים), נְתֻנוֹת; inf. abs. נָתוֹן (נָתֹן); cstr. נְתֹן (נְתָן־, תֵּת, לָתֵת, לָתֶת־, לְתִתֵּן, בְּתֵת, תִּתִּי, תִּתְּךָ, תִּתֵּךְ, תִּתּוֹ, תִּתָּהּ, תִּתֵּנוּ, תִּתָּם, תְּנָה).

1. give, a. give (to), grant, bestow (upon), pay, in various senses including (examples only in each category) **a.** hand over, deliver up, of items (e.g. Gn 3$_{6}$ 18$_{7}$ 21$_{14}$ 27$_{17}$ 35$_{4}$ Ex 22$_{6}$ 24$_{12}$ 31$_{18}$ Nm 7$_{5}$ Dt 5$_{22}$ 31$_{9}$ 1 S 20$_{40}$ 1 K 15$_{18}$ 2 K 11$_{10}$||2 C 23$_{9}$ 2 K 22$_{5}$||2 C 34$_{10}$ Jr 32$_{12}$ 36$_{32}$ Ezk 3$_{3}$ 7$_{21}$ Pr 31$_{24}$ Ezr 8$_{36}$ Ne 2$_{9}$), kingdom (1 S 15$_{28}$ 28$_{17}$ 2 S 16$_{8}$ 1 K 11$_{11.35.38}$ 14$_{8}$), power, authority (Is 22$_{21}$ Si 49$_{5}$), people (Is 43$_{6}$), especially enemies, opponents, persons sought, etc. (e.g. Ex 23$_{31}$ Nm 21$_{2}$ Dt 1$_{27}$ 2$_{24}$ 3$_{2}$ 7$_{16}$ 19$_{12}$ 20$_{13}$=11QT 62$_{9}$ Dt 21$_{10}$=11QT 63$_{10}$ Jos 2$_{24}$ 6$_{2}$ 7$_{7}$ 8$_{1.7.18}$ 10$_{8.30.32}$ 11$_{8}$ 21$_{44}$ Jg 1$_{2.4}$ 2$_{14}$ 2$_{23}$ 3$_{10.28}$ 4$_{7.14}$ 6$_{1.13}$ 7$_{2.7.9.14.15}$ 8$_{3.7}$ 11$_{21.30.32}$ 13$_{1}$ 15$_{12.13}$ 16$_{23.24}$ 18$_{10}$ 20$_{13.28}$ 1 S 11$_{12}$ 14$_{10.12.37}$ 17$_{47}$ 23$_{4.14}$ 24$_{5.11}$ 26$_{23}$ 28$_{19.19}$ 30$_{23}$ 2 S 5$_{19.19}$||1 C 14$_{10.10}$ 2 S 14$_{7}$ 20$_{21}$ 21$_{6.9}$ 1 K 18$_{9}$ 20$_{13.28}$ 22$_{6.12}$||2 C 18$_{5.11}$ 1 K 22$_{15}$ 2 K 3$_{10.13.18}$ 13$_{3}$ 17$_{20}$ 21$_{14}$ Is 34$_{2}$ 42$_{24}$ 47$_{5}$ Jr 12$_{7}$ 15$_{9}$ 20$_{4}$ 21$_{7}$ 22$_{25}$ 26$_{24}$ 27$_{6.6}$ 29$_{21}$ 32$_{3.28}$ 34$_{2.20.21}$ 38$_{16.19.20}$ 43$_{3}$ 44$_{30.30}$ 46$_{26}$ Ezk 11$_{9}$ 16$_{27.39}$ 21$_{36}$ 23$_{9.28}$ 25$_{4.10}$ 29$_{19}$ 31$_{11}$ 39$_{23}$ Mc 6$_{14}$ Ps 27$_{12}$ 41$_{3}$ 78$_{61}$ 106$_{41}$ 118$_{18}$ 124$_{6}$ Lm 1$_{14}$ Dn 1$_{2}$ Ne 9$_{24.27.30}$ 1 C 22$_{18}$ 2 C 13$_{16}$ 16$_{8}$ 24$_{24}$ 25$_{20}$ 28$_{5.9}$ 36$_{17}$ 1QpHab 9$_{10}$ 4QpPs^{a} 3.4$_{9}$ 4QapJoseph^{b} 1$_{4}$ 2$_{8}$ 4QpsMos^{e} 1$_{8}$ 2.1$_{5}$ 4QBark^{a} 1.2$_{5}$ CD 1$_{4.6}$; distinction from §4 not alw. clear); to famine (Jr 18$_{21}$ 2 C 32$_{11}$), sword (Jr 15$_{9}$ 25$_{31}$ Mc 6$_{14}$ 4QpsEzek^{d} 1.2$_{5}$ CD 1$_{4}$), power of one's own inclination (Si 15$_{14}$); of Y. giving up Israel (1 K 14$_{16}$ Ho 11$_{8}$ Mc 5$_{2}$); give over feet to slipping, i.e. allow to slip (Ps 66$_{9}$ 121$_{3}$ [or §7; if em.; see Obj.]); hold out, surrender one's back, cheeks (Is 50$_{6}$ Lm 3$_{30}$), one's hand (Jr 50$_{15}$), give one's hand, i.e. make pledge (Ezr 10$_{19}$), pledge one's allegiance (1 C 29$_{24}$ 2 C 30$_{8}$).

b. bestow graciously (e.g. Gn 24$_{35}$ 27$_{28}$ Ex 16$_{29}$ 32$_{29}$ Lv 6$_{10}$ 7$_{32}$ 26$_{4}$ Dt 11$_{14}$ 12$_{15}$ 28$_{23}$ 1 K 8$_{36}$||2 C 6$_{27}$ Jr 5$_{24}$ Ho 2$_{10}$ Zc 10$_{1}$ Ps 84$_{12}$ 85$_{13}$ 1 C 29$_{25}$).

c. supply, provide with (e.g. Gn 24$_{32}$ 28$_{20}$ 43$_{24}$ 45$_{21}$ Ex 5$_{7}$ 10$_{25}$ 16$_{8}$ Dt 10$_{18}$ 1 K 5$_{23.24}$ Ps 104$_{27}$ 111$_{5}$ 136$_{25}$ 145$_{15}$ Ne 2$_{8}$ 1 C 21$_{23}$).

d. serve, distribute, food (1 K 19$_{21}$ 2 K 4$_{42}$ Ezk 18$_{7}$), apportion offerings (2 C 31$_{14.15.19}$), feed animal (Gn 42$_{27}$).

e. show favour (Jr 16$_{13}$ Mc 7$_{20}$ Pr 3$_{34}$), grant mercy (Gn 43$_{14}$ Dt 13$_{18}$ Jr 42$_{12}$), victory (Jg 15$_{18}$ 2 K 5$_{1}$), vengeance (2 S 4$_{8}$ 22$_{48}$||Ps 18$_{48}$).

f. grant a request (1 S 1$_{17.27}$ Ps 37$_{4}$ 106$_{15}$ Est 5$_{8}$ 11Q Ps^{a} 24$_{4}$), desire, wish (Ps 21$_{3}$ 140$_{9}$ Jb 6$_{8}$ Ru 1$_{9}$).

g. sell (Gn 47$_{16.17}$ Pr 31$_{24}$ CD 13$_{14}$), allow to purchase (Gn 23$_{4.9.9}$ 1 K 21$_{2.4.6.6.15}$ 1 C 21$_{22}$).

h. lend (Lv 25$_{37}$ Ezk 18$_{8.13}$ Ps 15$_{5}$), give in pledge (Gn 38$_{18}$).

i. render amount due (Ex 5$_{18}$ Lv 27$_{23}$), in payment of debt (4Q416 2.2$_{5}$), as purchase price, payment for property or goods (Gn 23$_{13}$ Nm 20$_{19}$ Dt 2$_{28}$ 14$_{26}$ 1 K 9$_{11}$ 21$_{2.2.6}$ Ezk 27$_{12+6t}$ Ca 8$_{7}$ Lm 1$_{11}$ 1 C 21$_{25}$ 2 C 2$_{9}$), bride-gift (Gn 34$_{11.12}$ 1 K 9$_{16}$), as ransom (Ps 49$_{8}$ 4Q Ord^{a} 1.2$_{6}$), wages, payment for service (Gn 30$_{28.31}$ 38$_{16}$ Ex 2$_{9}$ Dt 24$_{15}$ Jg 17$_{10}$ 1 S 9$_{8}$ 1 K 5$_{20}$ 2 K 12$_{8}$ Jr 22$_{13}$ Ezk 16$_{33}$ Ho 2$_{7}$ Jon 1$_{3}$ Ezr 3$_{7}$), allowance for living (1 K 11$_{18}$ Jr 37$_{21}$ 40$_{5}$), compensation or penalty (Ex 21$_{19.22.23.30.32}$ Nm 5$_{7}$ Dt 22$_{29}$=11QT 66$_{10}$ 4QHalakhah^{a} 4$_{2}$), tax, tribute (Gn 47$_{25}$ 2 K 15$_{19.20}$ 18$_{15.16}$ 23$_{35.35.35}$ 2 C 17$_{5}$ 26$_{8}$ 27$_{5}$ 28$_{21}$ 11QT 58$_{12}$).

j. as reward, prize (Jg 14$_{12.13.19}$ 16$_{5}$ 2 S 4$_{10}$ 18$_{11}$ 1 K 8$_{32.39}$||2 C 6$_{23.30}$ Pr 13$_{15}$), spoil, booty (Jr 15$_{13}$ 17$_{3}$ 20$_{5}$ 45$_{5}$), recompense for deeds (Jr 17$_{10}$ 32$_{19}$ Ezk 7$_{9}$ Ps 28$_{4.4}$ GnzPs 4$_{21}$).

k. as gift (Gn 20$_{14}$ 21$_{27}$ 24$_{53}$ 25$_{6}$ 45$_{22}$ 1 K 10$_{10}$||2 C 9$_{9}$ Ezk 46$_{16}$ Mc 1$_{14}$ Jb 42$_{11}$ Est 2$_{18}$).

l. as offering, to Y. or his priests (Gn 14$_{20}$ Ex 22$_{28.29}$ Ex 30$_{12.13.14.15}$ Lv 7$_{32}$ 15$_{14}$ 22$_{22}$ 23$_{38}$ 27$_{9}$ Nm 15$_{21}$ 18$_{12}$ Dt 18$_{3}$ Ezk 44$_{30}$ Mc 6$_{7}$ Ps 51$_{18}$ Ec 4$_{17}$ 2 C 31$_{4}$ 35$_{8}$ Si 7$_{31}$), Molech (Lv 18$_{21}$ 20$_{2.3.4}$), idols (Ezk 6$_{13}$ 16$_{21}$); as contribution to building or service of temple (Ne 7$_{69}$ 12$_{47}$ 1 C 29$_{3}$).

m. as inheritance, of family property (Gn 25$_{5}$ Dt 21$_{17}$ 2 S 9$_{9}$ Jb 42$_{15}$), of land for Israelite tribes (e.g. Gn 12$_{7}$ 17$_{8}$ 24$_{7}$ 26$_{3}$ 28$_{13}$ 35$_{12}$ 48$_{4}$ Ex 6$_{4}$ 12$_{25}$ 20$_{12}$||Dt 5$_{16}$ Ex 32$_{13}$ Lv 14$_{34}$ 20$_{24}$ 25$_{2}$ Nm 13$_{2}$ 15$_{2}$ 27$_{12}$ Dt 1$_{8}$ 8$_{10}$ 12$_{9}$ 21$_{23}$ 26$_{1}$ Jos 1$_{6}$ 5$_{6}$ 11$_{23}$ 13$_{8}$ 14$_{3}$ 1 K 8$_{34}$||2 C 6$_{25}$ 2 K 21$_{8}$ Jr 7$_{7}$ Ezk 36$_{28}$ Ps 135$_{12}$ Ne 9$_{8}$ 2 C 20$_{7}$).

n. in marriage or for the purpose of sex; of daughter or other female member of family (Gn 24$_{41}$ 29$_{19.19.26.27.28}$ 34$_{8.9.14.16.20}$ 38$_{26}$ 41$_{45}$ Ex 2$_{21}$ 22$_{16}$ Dt 7$_{3}$ 22$_{16}$=11QT 65$_{11}$ Jos 15$_{16.17}$||Jg 1$_{12.13}$ Jg 3$_{6}$ 21$_{1.18.18}$ 1 S 17$_{25}$ 18$_{17.19.21.27}$ 1 K 11$_{19}$ Jr 29$_{6}$ Ezr 9$_{12}$ Ne 2$_{1}$ 10$_{31}$ 13$_{25}$ 1 C 2$_{35}$ 4Q TNaph 1$_{2.10}$ 4QD^{f} 3$_{9}$); of father giving daughter to someone other than her husband (Jg 15$_{2.6}$ 1 S 25$_{44}$), wife giving female servant to husband (Gn 16$_{3}$ 30$_{4.9.18}$), Y. giving one's wife to someone else (2 S 12$_{11}$), Solomon giving Abishag to Adonijah (1 K 2$_{17}$), master giving a wife to his slave (Ex 21$_{4}$); to Benjaminites, from women spared from Jabesh-gilead (Jg 21$_{14}$), captured from daughters of Shiloh (Jg 21$_{22}$); of trees in parable (2 K 14$_{9}$||2 C 25$_{18}$).

o. give one's lying down, i.e. have sex (Lv 18$_{20.23}$ 20$_{15}$ Nm 5$_{20}$).

p. cause hurt (Pr 10$_{10}$ Si 36$_{25}$), strife (Pr 13$_{10}$).

q. assign (Ex 30$_{16}$ Nm 3$_{9}$ 2 K 8$_{6}$ Ezk 4$_{5}$ 15$_{6}$ 45$_{6}$ 47$_{23}$ 1QSa 1$_{19}$).

r. entrust* (Gn 30$_{35}$ 39$_{4}$ Ex 22$_{6}$ Ps 115$_{16}$ Jr 39$_{14}$ Ca 8$_{17}$ 1QpHab 5$_{4}$).

s. ascribe, attribute (1 S 18$_{8.8}$ Ps 68$_{35}$ Jb 1$_{22}$ 36$_{3}$ Si 10$_{28}$), allege (Ps 50$_{20}$ Si 11$_{31}$).

t. reveal, display* (Ezk 27$_{10}$ Ps 115$_{1}$ Pr 23$_{31}$ Si 42$_{12[B]}$), show sign, produce miracle (Ex 7$_{9}$ Dt 6$_{22}$ 13$_{2}$=Dt 5$_{48}$ Jos 2$_{12}$ 1 K 13$_{3.5}$ Is 7$_{14}$ Ne 9$_{10}$ 2 C 32$_{24}$), inform of (2 S 24$_{9}$||1 C 21$_{5}$), specify (Ne 2$_{6}$).

u. pay attention (Lachish ost. 3$_{12}$).

v. institute (Lv 25$_{24}$ Ezk 20$_{12}$), implement (Si 13$_{12}$).

w. yield, bear, produce (Gn 4$_{12}$ 49$_{20.21}$ Lv 25$_{19}$ 26$_{4.4.20.20}$ Dt 11$_{17}$ Ezk 34$_{27.27}$ Jl 2$_{22}$ Zc 8$_{12.12.12}$ Ps 1$_{3}$ 67$_{7}$ 85$_{13}$ perh. Pr 12$_{12}$ [or em.; see Subj.]) 4Q423 2$_{3}$; of rock producing water (Nm 20$_{8}$).

<SUBJ> Y. Gn 1$_{29}$ 9$_{3}$ 12$_{7}$ 13$_{15.17}$ 15$_{2.3.7.18}$ 17$_{8.16}$ 24$_{7.35}$ 26$_{3.4}$ 27$_{28}$ 28$_{4.4.13.20.22}$ 29$_{33}$ 30$_{6.18}$ 31$_{9}$ 35$_{12.12}$ 43$_{14.23}$ 48$_{4.9}$ Ex 6$_{4.8.8}$ 12$_{25}$ 13$_{5.11}$ 16$_{8.15.29}$ 20$_{12}$||Dt 5$_{16}$ Ex 23$_{31}$ 24$_{12}$ 25$_{16.21}$ 31$_{18}$ 32$_{13.29}$ 33$_{1}$ Lv 6$_{10}$ 7$_{32}$ 10$_{17}$ 14$_{34}$ 17$_{11}$ 20$_{24}$ 23$_{10}$ 25$_{2.38}$ 26$_{4.6}$ Nm 8$_{19}$ 10$_{29}$ 11$_{18.21}$ 13$_{2}$ 14$_{8}$ 15$_{2}$ 18$_{7+8t}$ 20$_{12.24}$ 21$_{2.2.3.16.34}$ 25$_{12}$ 27$_{12}$ 32$_{7.9}$ 33$_{53}$ 34$_{13}$ Dt 1$_{8+6t}$ 2$_{5+9t}$ 3$_{2.3.18.19.20}$ 4$_{1.21.38.40}$ 5$_{22.31}$ 6$_{10.22.23}$ 7$_{13.16.24}$ 8$_{10.18}$ 9$_{6.10.11.23}$ 10$_{4.11.18}$ 11$_{9+5t}$ 12$_{1.9.15.21}$ 13$_{13.18}$=11QT 55$_{2.11}$ Dt 15$_{4.7}$ 16$_{5.17.18.20}$ 17$_{2}$=11QT 55$_{16}$ Dt 17$_{14}$=11QT 56$_{12}$ Dt 18$_{9}$= 11QT 60$_{16}$ Dt 19$_{1.2.8.8.10.14}$ 20$_{13.14.16}$=11QT 62$_{9.11.13}$ Dt 21$_{1.10}$=11QT 63$_{10}$ Dt 21$_{23}$=11QT 64$_{13}$ Dt 24$_{4}$ 25$_{15.19}$ 26$_{1+6t}$ 27$_{2.3}$ 28$_{7.11.12.52.53.65}$ 29$_{3}$ 30$_{20}$ 31$_{7}$ 32$_{49.52}$ 34$_{4}$ Jos 1$_{2.3.6.11.13.15}$ 2$_{9.14}$ 2$_{24}$ 5$_{6}$ 6$_{2.16}$ 7$_{7}$ 8$_{1.7.18}$ 10$_{8.30.32}$ 11$_{8}$ 18$_{3}$ 21$_{43.43.44}$ 23$_{13.15.16}$ 24$_{3.4.4.8.11.13}$ Jg 1$_{2.4}$ 2$_{14.23}$ 3$_{10.28}$ 4$_{7.14}$ 6$_{1.9.13}$ 7$_{2.7.9.14.15}$ 8$_{3.7}$ 11$_{21.30.30.32}$ 12$_{3}$ 13$_{1}$ 15$_{18}$ 18$_{10}$ 20$_{28}$ 1 S 1$_{11.17.27}$ 2$_{10}$ 14$_{10.12.37}$ 15$_{28}$ 17$_{47}$ 23$_{4.14}$ 24$_{5.11}$ 26$_{23}$ 28$_{17.19.19}$ 30$_{23.23}$ 2 S 4$_{8}$ 5$_{19.19}$||1 C 14$_{10.10}$ 2 S 5$_{19}$ 12$_{8.8.11}$ 16$_{8}$ 22$_{36.48}$||Ps 18$_{36.48}$ 1 K 1$_{48}$ 3$_{5.6.9.12.13}$||2 C 1$_{12}$ 1 K 5$_{9.21}$||2 C 2$_{11}$ 1 K 5$_{26}$ 8$_{32+6t}$||2 C 6$_{23+6t}$ 1 K 8$_{56}$ 9$_{7}$||2 C 7$_{20}$ 1 K 11$_{11+5t}$ 13$_{26}$ 14$_{8.15.16}$ 15$_{4}$ 17$_{14}$ 18$_{1}$ 20$_{13.28}$ 22$_{6.12}$||2 C 18$_{5.11}$ 1 K 22$_{15}$ 2 K 3$_{5.9}$||2 C 1$_{7.10}$ 2 K 3$_{12.13.18}$ 5$_{1}$ 8$_{19}$||2 C 21$_{7}$ 2 K 13$_{3.5}$ 17$_{20}$ 21$_{8.14}$ 22$_{8}$ Is 7$_{14}$ 8$_{18}$ 22$_{21}$ 30$_{20.23}$ 34$_{2}$ 40$_{29}$ 41$_{27}$ 42$_{5.8}$ 43$_{3.4.20}$ 45$_{3}$ 47$_{6}$ 48$_{11}$ 50$_{4}$ 56$_{5.5}$ 61$_{8}$ 62$_{8}$ Jr 3$_{8.15.19}$ 5$_{24}$ 7$_{7.14}$ 8$_{10.13}$ 11$_{5}$ 12$_{7}$ 14$_{13}$ 15$_{9.13}$ 16$_{13.15}$ 17$_{3.4.10}$ 18$_{21}$ 19$_{7}$ 20$_{4.5.5}$ 21$_{7}$ 22$_{25}$ 23$_{39}$ 24$_{7.10}$ 25$_{5.31}$ 27$_{5.6.6}$ 28$_{14}$ 29$_{11.21}$ 30$_{3}$ 31$_{35}$ 32$_{3+5t}$ 34$_{2.20.21}$ 35$_{15}$ 42$_{12}$ 44$_{30.30}$ 45$_{5}$ 46$_{26}$ Ezk 2$_{8}$ 3$_{3}$ 4$_{5.6.15}$ 7$_{9.21}$ 11$_{9.17.19.19}$ 15$_{6.6}$ 16$_{17.19.27.39.61}$ 20$_{11+5t}$ 21$_{32.36}$ 23$_{9.28}$ 25$_{4.10}$ 28$_{25}$ 29$_{5.19.20.21}$ 31$_{11}$ 33$_{27}$ 36$_{26.26.28}$ 37$_{25}$ 39$_{4.11.23}$ 47$_{14}$ Ho 2$_{10.17}$ 9$_{14.14.14}$ 11$_{8}$ 13$_{10.11}$ Jl 2$_{23}$ Am 4$_{6}$ 9$_{15}$ Mc 5$_{2}$ 7$_{20}$ Zp 3$_{5}$ Hg 2$_{9}$ Zc 3$_{7}$ 10$_{1}$ Ml 2$_{5}$ Ps 20$_{5}$ 21$_{3.5}$ 27$_{12}$ 28$_{4.4}$ 29$_{11}$ 41$_{3}$ 55$_{23}$ 60$_{6}$ 61$_{6}$ 66$_{9}$ 68$_{12.36}$ 72$_{1}$ 74$_{14.19}$ 78$_{20.24.46.61.66}$ 84$_{12}$ 85$_{8.13}$ 86$_{16}$ 99$_{7}$ 104$_{27.28}$ 105$_{11}$|| 1 C 16$_{18}$ Ps 105$_{44}$ 106$_{15.41}$ 111$_{5.6}$ 115$_{1.16}$ 118$_{18}$ 124$_{6}$ 127$_{2}$ 135$_{12}$ 136$_{21.26}$ 140$_{9}$ 144$_{10}$ 145$_{15}$ 146$_{7}$ 147$_{9}$ 148$_{6}$ Jb 1$_{21}$ Jb 3$_{20}$ 5$_{10}$ 6$_{8}$ 35$_{10}$ 36$_{6.31}$ 37$_{10}$ (or em.; see Obj.) Pr 2$_{6}$ 3$_{34}$ perh. 10$_{24}$ (or em. יֻתַּן *it will be granted*, i.e. qal pass.) Ru 1$_{6.9}$ 4$_{12.13}$ Ec 2$_{26.26}$ 3$_{10}$ 5$_{17.18}$ 6$_{2}$ 8$_{15}$ 9$_{9}$ 12$_{7}$ Lm 3$_{65}$ Dn 1$_{2.17}$ Ezr 1$_{2}$ 7$_{6}$ 9$_{8.9.9.13}$ Ne 9$_{8+14t}$ 1 C 22$_{9.12.18}$ 25$_{5}$ 28$_{5}$ 29$_{19.25}$ 2 C 1$_{27}$ 13$_{5.16}$ 16$_{8}$ 20$_{7}$ 24$_{24}$ 25$_{9.20}$ 28$_{5.9.21}$ 30$_{12}$ 32$_{24.29}$ 36$_{17.23}$ Si 15$_{14.17(B)}$ (unless qal pass.) 38$_{6}$ 44$_{22.23}$ 45$_{7.17.20.20.26}$ 46$_{9}$ 47$_{5.11}$ 49$_{5}$ 50$_{23}$ 51$_{22.30}$ 1QH 9$_{15}$ ([ותתנם]) 10$_{7}$ 18$_{27}$ 19$_{27}$ 1QM 14$_{6}$ 1QpHab 5$_{4}$ 9$_{10}$ 10$_{3}$ 1QS 11$_{7}$ 1QDM 2$_{2}$ ([לת]תה) 1QSb 3$_{5.26}$ 5$_{18}$ ([י]תן) 5$_{25}$ 4QpPs^{a} 3.4$_{9}$ 4QJub^{i} 23$_{22}$ ([ו]יתן) 4QJub^{a} 1$_{13}$ ([ונת]תי) 4QJub^{d} 21$_{22}$ 4QJub^{g} 25$_{12}$ 4QJub^{h} 40$_{5}$ 4QCommGenA 2$_{8}$ 4QD^{a} 11$_{11}$ 4QRP^{c} 23$_{5}$ 4QapPent 9$_{4}$ 4QapJoseph^{b} 1$_{4}$ 3$_{8}$ 4QapPs^{b} 69$_{4}$ 4QapJoshua^{a} 11$_{3}$ 12$_{3}$ 4QparaKings 104$_{7}$ 4QpsEzek^{a} 2$_{1}$ 4QpsMos^{e} 1$_{8}$ 2.1$_{5}$ 4QConfess 2$_{7}$ 4Q417 2.1$_{17}$ 4QBark^{a} 1.2$_{5.10}$ 4QBark^{c} 1.1$_{2}$ 4QapLam^{b} 1$_{1}$ 4QBéat 1$_{1}$ 11QPs^{a} 19$_{4}$ 24$_{4}$ 27$_{3}$ 11QM 1.2$_{9}$ 11QT 51$_{16}$ 53$_{3}$ 61$_{02}$ ([נתת]י) CD 14$_{5.6}$ GnzPs 1$_{6}$ 3$_{15.21}$ 4$_{21}$ Kuntillet ʿAjrud add. inscr. 2, אֱלֹהִים *god* Jg 16$_{23.24}$.

Ammonites 2 C 26$_{8}$, Aram(aeans) Ezk 27$_{16}$, Babylon Jr 50$_{15}$, Edom(ites) Ezk 27$_{16(mss)}$ 36$_{5}$, Egypt(ians) Ezk 17$_{15}$ 2QJub^{b} 46$_{2}$ ([מצרים]), Hittite Gn 23$_{11.11.11}$, Israel(ites) Ex 21$_{23}$ 22$_{28.29}$ Lv 5$_{16.24}$ Lv 7$_{32.36}$ Dt 7$_{3}$ 14$_{21.25.26}$ 15$_{9.10.10.10.14}$ 16$_{10}$ 18$_{4}$ 24$_{15}$ 26$_{12.13.14}$ 29$_{7}$ Jg 1$_{20}$ 1 S 17$_{10}$ 2 K 15$_{20}$ Jr 13$_{16}$ Ezk 44$_{28.30}$ 45$_{6}$ 47$_{23}$ Mc 6$_{7}$ Ezr 9$_{12}$ Ne 10$_{31}$ 12$_{47}$ 1 C 6$_{40.41.42.50.52}$ 1QM 12$_{7}$ (נ[ת]נו]) 11QT 58$_{12}$, Javan Ezk 27$_{13.19}$, Jerusalem Ezk 16$_{21.33.34.36.41}$, Jews Jr 38$_{19.20}$ Ne 13$_{25}$, Jezreelite 1 K 21$_{4.6.6,15}$, Judah Ezk 17$_{17}$ 2 C 17$_{5}$, Lud Ezk 27$_{10}$, Meshech Ezk 27$_{13}$, Persia Ezk 27$_{10}$, Philistine(s) 1 S 6$_{5}$ 17$_{44}$, Put Ezk 27$_{10}$, Tarshish Ezk 27$_{12}$, Timnite Jg 15$_{6}$, Tubal Ezk 27$_{13}$, Vedan Ezk 27$_{19}$.

עַם *people* Gn 47$_{24}$ Ex 32$_{24}$ Dt 18$_{3}$ Lm 1$_{11}$ Ezr 3$_{7}$ 10$_{11}$ 1 C 29$_{14}$ 2 C 31$_{4}$, גּוֹי *nation* Is 43$_{9}$ Jl 4$_{3}$ Ps 79$_{2}$ perh. 4QapJoseph^{b} 1$_{7}$, לְאֹם *nation* Is 42$_{9}$, מַמְלָכָה *kingdom* Ps 68$_{35}$, מִשְׁפָּחָה *clan* Gn 24$_{41}$, שֵׁבֶט *tribe* Jg 20$_{13}$, *rod* Pr 29$_{15}$, בַּיִת *house* Gn 35$_{4}$, of Israel Ezk 6$_{13}$, עֵדָה *assembly* Jg 21$_{14}$, גּוֹלָה *exiles* Jr 29$_{6}$, שְׁאֵרִית *remainder* Ezk 36$_{5}$ Ne 7$_{71}$, רַב pl. *many* CD 14$_{13}$.

Aaron Ex 7$_{9}$, Abimelech Gn 20$_{14.16}$, Abra(ha)m Gn 14$_{20.21}$ 18$_{7}$ 21$_{14.27}$ 23$_{13}$ 25$_{5.6}$ 4QpsJub^{a} 2.2$_{1}$ (ו[י]תן), Achish 1 S 27$_{6}$, Ahab 1 K 20$_{5}$ 21$_{2.2.6}$, Ahasuerus Est 8$_{1.7}$, Ahaz 2 C 28$_{21}$, Ahimelech 1 S 21$_{4}$ 22$_{10.10}$, Amariah 2 C 31$_{15}$, Amaziah 2 C 25$_{9}$, Araunah 2 S 24$_{23}$, Artaxerxes Ezr 7$_{11}$, Asa 1 K 15$_{18}$, Asaph Ne 2$_{8}$, Asher Gn 49$_{20}$, Balak Nm 22$_{18}$ 24$_{13}$, Ben Sira Si 51$_{17}$, Caleb Jos 15$_{16.17}$||Jg 1$_{12.13}$ Jos 15$_{19.19.19}$||Jg 1$_{15.15}$, David 1 S 17$_{46}$ 2 S 4$_{10}$ 9$_{9}$ 1 K 5$_{23}$ Ps 132$_{4}$ 1 C 21$_{25}$ 28$_{11}$ 29$_{3.14}$ Si 47$_{8}$, Eden 2 C 31$_{15}$, Eleazar Nm 32$_{29}$, Eliashib Arad ost. 1$_{2.10}$ 2$_{1.7}$ 3$_{2}$ 4$_{1.3}$ 7$_{2}$ 8$_{1}$ 10$_{2}$ ([נתן] ... [אל[י]שב]) 11$_{2}$ 12$_{2.5}$ (both [אל[י]שב]) 14$_{2}$ ([נתן] ... [אל[יש]ב]) Arad ost. 18$_{4.6}$, Eliezer Ezr 10$_{19}$, Elihu Jb 36$_{3}$, Elijah 1 K 17$_{23}$ 18$_{9.26}$, Elisha 1 K 19$_{21}$, Elkanah 1 S 1$_{4.5}$, Ephron Gn 23$_{9.9.11.11.11}$, Esau 4QJub^{h} 36$_{14}$ ([ואתן]).

Gedaliah Ezr 10$_{19}$, Gemariah Arad ost. 40$_{10}$ ([גמר]יהו]) 40$_{12}$ ([נתת]י] ... [גמר]יהו]), Hamor Gn 34$_{21}$, Hannah 1 S 1$_{11}$, Hegai Est 2$_{9.9}$, Hezekiah 2 K 18$_{15.16}$ 2 C 32$_{11}$, Hilkiah 2 K 22$_{5(Kt).8.10}$||2 C 34$_{15.18}$ 2 C 35$_{8}$, Hiram 1 K 5$_{24}$, Hoshaiah Lachish ost. 3$_{12}$ (others אתננהו *I can repeat it*), Huram 2 C 8$_{2}$, Isaac Gn 27$_{37}$, Ish-bosheth 2 S 3$_{14}$, Ithiel Pr 30$_{8}$, Jacob/Israel Gn 25$_{34}$ 48$_{22}$, Jael Jg 5$_{25}$, Jarib Ezr 10$_{19}$, Jehiel 2 C 35$_{8}$, Jehoiada 2 K 11$_{10}$|| 2 C 23$_{9}$ 2 K 12$_{8}$ 2 C 24$_{12}$, Jehoiakim 2 K 23$_{35.35}$, Jeremiah Jr 32$_{12.16}$ 36$_{32}$ 43$_{3}$, Jeroboam Si 47$_{23}$, Jeshua 2 C 31$_{15}$, Jezebel 1 K 21$_{7}$, Joab 2 S 18$_{11}$ 24$_{9}$||1 C 21$_{5}$, Joah 2 C 34$_{9.10}$, Job Jb 1$_{22}$ 35$_{7}$ 39$_{19}$, Jonah Jon 1$_{3}$, Jonathan 1 S 18$_{4}$ 20$_{40}$, Jose MurEpJonathan 1$_{3}$, Joseph Gn 45$_{21.21.22.22}$ 47$_{11.16.17.19}$, Joshua Nm 32$_{29}$ 11$_{23}$ 12$_{7}$ 14$_{12.13}$ 15$_{13}$ 17$_{4.14}$ 22$_{7}$, Judah Gn 38$_{16.17.18.18.26}$.

Kore 2 C 31$_{14}$, Laban Gn 29$_{19.19.24.27.28.29}$ 30$_{26.28.31.31}$ 46$_{18.25}$ 4QTNaph 1$_{2}$, Leah Gn 30$_{9.14.18}$, Maaseiah 2 C 34$_{9.10}$ Ezr 10$_{19}$, Menahem 2 K 15$_{19}$, Micah Jg 17$_{10}$, Miniamin 2 C 31$_{15}$, Mordecai Est 4$_{8}$, Moses Ex 7$_{9}$ 17$_{2}$ 30$_{16}$ Nm 3$_{9.48.51}$ 7$_{5.6.7.8.9}$ 11$_{13.13}$ 16$_{14}$ 19$_{3}$ 27$_{4.7.7}$ 31$_{29.30.41.47}$ 32$_{33.40}$ Dt 3$_{12.13.15.16.20}$ 31$_{9}$ Jos 1$_{14.15}$ 9$_{24}$ 12$_{6}$ 13$_{8+6t}$ 14$_{3.3}$ 17$_{4}$ 18$_{7}$ 22$_{4.7}$, Naaman 2 K 5$_{22.23}$, Nabal 1 S 25$_{8.11}$, Naboth 1 K 21$_{2.3.4.6.6.15}$, Nahum Arad ost 17$_{8}$, Nebuzaradan Jr 39$_{10.14}$, Nebushazban Jr 39$_{14}$, Nehemiah Ne 2$_{1.6.9}$ Arad ost. 40$_{10.12}$ ([נתת]י), Nergal-sharezer Jr 39$_{14}$.

Oholah Ezk 23$_{7}$, Onan Gn 38$_{9}$, Ornan 1 C 21$_{22.22.23.23}$, Rachel Gn 30$_{4}$, Rehoboam 2 C 11$_{23}$, Ruth Ru 2$_{18}$. Samson Jg 14$_{9.12.19}$, Samuel 1 S 8$_{6}$ 9$_{22.23}$, Sarai Gn 16$_{3}$, Saul 1 S 18$_{17.21.27}$ 25$_{44}$, Shaphan 2 C 34$_{9.10}$, Shecaniah 2 C 31$_{15}$, Shechem Gn 34$_{11.12.21}$, Shemaiah 2 C 31$_{15}$, Sheshan 1 C 2$_{35}$, Sihon Dt 2$_{28}$, Solomon 1 K 2$_{17}$ 5$_{20.25.25}$ 9$_{11.12}$ 10$_{13}$||2 C 9$_{12}$ 1 K 10$_{13}$ Ca 8$_{11}$ 2 C 2$_{9}$ Si 47$_{19}$, Ucal Pr 39$_{8}$, Zechariah 2 C 35$_{8}$, Zedekiah Jr 38$_{16}$.

אָדָם *human being* Ec 2$_{21}$, אִישׁ *man* Gn 24$_{32}$ 34$_{21}$ 42$_{34}$ 43$_{24.24}$ Ex 2$_{21}$ 21$_{19.22}$ 22$_{6.9}$ Lv 20$_{2.3.4.15}$ 22$_{14.22}$ Lv 27$_{9.23}$ Nm 5$_{7.10.20}$ Dt 21$_{17}$ 22$_{29}$=11QT 66$_{10}$ Dt 28$_{55}$ Jos 2$_{12}$ Jg 8$_{5.15.24.25.25}$ 15$_{12.13}$ 21$_{1}$ 1 S 2$_{15.16}$ 10$_{4}$ 30$_{11,12.22}$ 1 K 13$_{3.5}$ Ezk 18$_{7.8.16}$ 27$_{10}$ Ps 49$_{8}$ Jb 2$_{4}$ Ru 3$_{17}$ 4$_{7}$ Ca 8$_{7}$ 2 C 31$_{19}$ 4QOrd^{a} 1.2$_{6.7}$ 4QD^{e} 4$_{9}$ 5$_{14}$ (י[ת]ן) 4QD^{f} 3$_{9}$ CD 13$_{14}$ Arad ost. 40$_{8}$ ([נתן]), i.e. each Ex 30$_{12}$ Jg 8$_{24}$ 16$_{5}$ 20$_{36}$ Jb 42$_{11}$, גֶּבֶר *man* Lm 3$_{30}$, אִשָּׁה *woman, wife* Gn 3$_{6.12}$ 16$_{3}$ Nm 5$_{7}$ 1 S 18$_{8.8}$ 2 S 14$_{7}$ 1 K 17$_{19}$ 21$_{7}$ 2 K 6$_{28.29}$ Pr 31$_{15.24}$ Est 1$_{20}$.

אָב *father* Ex 22$_{16}$ Dt 22$_{16}$=11QT 65$_{11}$ Jg 15$_{2}$ 21$_{22}$ Jb 42$_{15}$ 2 C 21$_{3}$, אֵם *mother* Jg 17$_{4}$, בֵּן *son* Gn 23$_{9.9}$ 34$_{8.9.14.16.21}$ Nm 32$_{29}$ Jos 7$_{19}$ 1 S 22$_{7.10.10.13}$ 2 S 3$_{14}$ 1 K 19$_{21}$ Ezk 18$_{13}$ Pr 3$_{28}$ 5$_{9}$ 6$_{4}$ 23$_{26}$ 29$_{17}$ Ezr 8$_{36}$ 1 C 29$_{24}$ 2 C 27$_{5}$ 31$_{14}$ 34$_{9.10}$ Si 4$_{5}$ 7$_{31}$ (ת[ן]) 7$_{33}$ 9$_{6}$ 10$_{28(B)}$ 12$_{4.5.5}$ 14$_{13.16.16}$

30$_{21.28}$ 32$_{12}$ 36$_{20.21}$ 37$_{27}$ 41$_{19}$ 47$_{23}$ MurEpJonathan 1$_{3}$, of Israel Ex 5$_{18}$ Lv 18$_{20.21.23}$ 23$_{38}$ 25$_{24.37.37}$ Nm 15$_{21}$ 18$_{12}$ 19$_{3}$ 20$_{19}$ 27$_{9.10.11}$ 35$_{2+11t}$ Jos 19$_{49.50}$ 21$_{3+6t}$ Jg 3$_{6}$ 21$_{7}$ 1 C 6$_{49}$ 2 C 30$_{8}$ 11QT 22$_{11}$, בַּר *son* Pr 31$_{3.6}$, בַּת *daughter* Ex 2$_{9}$ Si 42$_{12(B)}$, of Zion Mc 1$_{14}$ Lm 2$_{18}$, אָח *brother* Jg 21$_{22}$ 1 K 9$_{13}$ Jb 42$_{11}$, אָחוֹת *sister* Jb 42$_{11}$, יֶלֶד *child* 11QT 39$_{8}$ ([ונתן]) 39$_{10}$ ([ונתנו]).

מֶלֶךְ *king* Dt 2$_{28}$ 1 S 8$_{14.15}$ 17$_{25}$ 2 S 21$_{6.9}$ 1 K 2$_{17}$ 9$_{11.16}$ 10$_{13}$||2 C 9$_{12}$ 1 K 10$_{13}$ 11$_{18.18}$ 13$_{7.8}$ 20$_{5}$ 2 K 8$_{6}$ Jr 38$_{16}$ 40$_{11}$ Est 1$_{19}$ 2$_{18}$ 3$_{10}$ 5$_{8}$ 8$_{1.2.7}$ Dn 11$_{17}$ Ezr 7$_{6.11}$ Ne 2$_{8}$ 2 C 24$_{12}$, מַלְכָּה *queen* 1 K 10$_{10.10}$||2 C 9$_{9.9}$, פַּרְעֹה *Pharaoh* Gn 41$_{45}$ 45$_{18}$ 47$_{22}$ Ex 5$_{10}$ 10$_{25}$ 1 K 9$_{16}$ 11$_{18.18.19}$, אָדוֹן *lord* Gn 24$_{36}$ 42$_{34}$ Ex 21$_{4}$ Nm 36$_{2.2}$ Lachish ost. 4$_{11}$ 9$_{3}$ Arad ost. 18$_{4.6}$ Meṣad Ḥashavyahu ost. 1$_{13}$ ([ותת]ן), בַּעַל *owner, lord* Ex 21$_{30.32}$ Jg 9$_{4}$, סֶרֶן *lord* of Philistines Jg 16$_{5}$, נָשִׂיא *prince* Nm 17$_{21}$ Ezk 45$_{8}$ 46$_{16.17}$, שַׂר *commander* Jg 8$_{6}$ 1 C 29$_{7.24}$ 2 C 34$_{9.10}$ 11QT 21$_{06}$ ([ונתנו שרי]) Meṣad Ḥashavyahu ost. 1$_{13}$ ([ותת]ן), רַב *chief* Jr 39$_{10.14}$ 40$_{5}$, גִּבּוֹר *mighty one* 2 K 15$_{20}$ 1 C 29$_{24}$, נָגִיד *leader* 2 C 35$_{8}$, מְבַקֵּר *overseer* CD 14$_{14}$, שֹׁטֵר *officer* Ex 5$_{7}$, שֹׁפֵט *judge* CD 14$_{14}$, רַב־מָג *Rabmag* Jr 39$_{14}$, רַב־סָרִיס *Rabsaris* Jr 39$_{14}$, רַב־שָׁקֵה *Rabshakeh* 2 K 18$_{23}$||Is 36$_{8}$, מַזְכִּיר *recorder* 2 C 34$_{9.10}$, מֶלְצַר *guardian* Dn 1$_{16}$, תִּרְשָׁתָא *governor* Ne 7$_{69}$, זָקֵן *elder* Dt 19$_{12}$ 22$_{19}$=11QT 65$_{15}$ Jos 20$_{4}$ 21$_{18}$, נֹגֵשׂ *taskmaster* Ex 5$_{7}$, סֹפֵר *secretary* 2 K 12$_{12.15.16}$.

נַעַר *lad* 1 S 9$_{8}$, עֶבֶד *servant* Gn 24$_{53.53}$ Jos 1$_{15}$ 9$_{24}$ 12$_{6}$ 13$_{8}$ 18$_{7}$ 22$_{4}$ 2 K 22$_{9}$||2 C 34$_{17}$, מְשָׁרֵת *attendant* 2 K 4$_{42.43}$, טַבָּח *cook* 1 S 9$_{23}$, כֹּהֵן *priest* Nm 32$_{29}$ 1 S 21$_{4.7.10}$ 2 K 11$_{10}$||2 C 23$_{9}$ 2 K 12$_{8.12.15.16}$ 22$_{5(Kt).10}$||2 C 34$_{18}$ Ml 2$_{2}$ 4QpNah 3.1$_{12}$ ([כוה]ני ...]יתנוהו), לֵוִי *Levite* Nm 18$_{28}$ 2 C 31$_{14}$ 35$_{12}$, נָבִיא *prophet* Dt 13$_{2}$=Dt 54$_{8}$, חֹלֵם *dreamer* Dt 13$_{2}$=Dt 54$_{8}$, worshipper Ps 51$_{18}$ 1QH 4$_{20}$, שֹׁעֵר *gate keeper* 2 C 31$_{14}$, female lover Ca 7$_{13}$, מְאַהֵב *lover* Ho 2$_{7.14}$, מֵרֵעַ *friend* Jg 14$_{13}$, ידע *one who knows* Jb 42$_{11}$, בין hi. ptc. *one who understands* 4QBéat 14$_{2.20}$, זכר hi. ptc. *one who mentions* Is 62$_{7}$, שמר ptc. *one who keeps* Est 2$_{9.9}$ Ne 2$_{9}$.

יֹשֵׁב *inhabitant* 2 C 31$_{4}$, בוא ptc. *one who comes* Ezr 8$_{36}$, עבר ptc. *one who passes* Ex 30$_{13.14}$, רֹכֵל *trader* Ezk 27$_{22}$, עֹשֶׂה *maker* Jb 35$_{10}$, *worker* 2 K 22$_{5}$||2 C 34$_{10}$ 2 C 34$_{11}$, זוב ptc. *one who has a discharge* Lv 15$_{14}$, עָשִׁיר *rich one* Ex 30$_{15}$, דַּל *poor one* Ex 30$_{15}$, צַדִּיק *righteous one* Ps 37$_{21}$ 112$_{9}$ Pr 21$_{26}$, טוֹב *good one* Pr 22$_{9}$, פֶּתִי *simple one* perh. 4Q185 1.2$_{2}$, חֹטֵא *sinner* Ec 2$_{26}$, רָשָׁע *wicked one* Ps 50$_{20}$, רַע *evil one* Pr 13$_{10}$ (if em.; see below), בְּלִיַּעַל *worthless one* 1 S 30$_{22}$, רֵיק *empty one* Pr 13$_{10}$ (if em.; see below), צֹרֵר *adversary* Ps 69$_{22}$, נִרְגָּן *slanderer* Si 11$_{31}$, כְּסִיל *fool* Ec 4$_{17}$, גַּנָּב *thief* Pr 6$_{31}$, קרץ ptc. *one who winks* Pr 10$_{10}$, אַכְזָרִי *cruel one* Si 13$_{12}$ (or em.; see Obj.), ראשׁ *head*, i.e. chief Nm 32$_{29}$ Ezr 2$_{69}$||Ne 7$_{70}$ Ne 7$_{69}$, לֵב *heart* Si 36$_{25}$, זֶרַע *offspring* Ezk 17$_{18}$.

אַיָּלָה *hind* Gn 49$_{21}$, עֵץ *tree* Lv 26$_{4.20}$ Ezk 34$_{27}$ Ps 1$_{3}$, אֶרֶז *cedar* 2 K 14$_{9}$, תְּאֵנָה *fig tree* Jl 2$_{22}$, גֶּפֶן *vine* Jl 2$_{22}$ Zc 8$_{12}$ Ca 2$_{13}$, דּוּדָאִים *mandrakes* Ca 7$_{14}$, שֹׁרֶשׁ *root* Pr 12$_{12}$ (or em. יִתֵּן *it produces* to בְּאֵיתָן is *with continuity*, i.e. continues, or יִתַּן *it will be constant* [i.e. יתן II], or יִכֹּן *it shall be firm* [i.e. כון ni.]), נֵרְדְּ *nard* Ca 1$_{12}$, יַיִן *wine* Pr 23$_{31}$, אֶרֶץ *land* Lv 25$_{19}$ 26$_{4.20}$ 2 K 23$_{35}$ Ezk 27$_{17}$ 34$_{27}$ Zc 8$_{12}$ Ps 67$_{7}$ 85$_{13}$, אֲדָמָה *ground* Gn 4$_{12}$ Dt 11$_{17}$, סֶלַע *rock* Nm 20$_{8}$, שָׁמַיִם *heaven* Jr 14$_{22}$ Zc 8$_{12}$, גֶּשֶׁם *rain* Is 55$_{10}$, שֶׁלֶג *snow* Is 55$_{10}$, מַיִם *water* 1QDM 2$_{10}$ ([ל]תת ... [ה]מים), שֶׂכֶל *sense* Pr 13$_{15}$, תּוֹכַחַת *reproof* Pr 29$_{15}$, אֲשֶׁר *one who* Mc 3$_{5}$, מִי *who?* Is 42$_{24}$ Jb 38$_{36}$ 11QPs^{a} 24$_{14}$ MurEpBarC^{b} 1$_{9}$, אֶחָד *one* Gn 42$_{27}$.

Subj. not specified, Gn 29$_{26}$ 42$_{25}$ Jos 14$_{4}$ 21$_{2}$ Jg 21$_{18}$ 1 S 11$_{12}$ 18$_{19}$ 27$_{5}$ 2 S 20$_{21}$ 1 K 3$_{25.26.27}$ 18$_{23}$ 2 K 22$_{5(Qr)}$||2 C 34$_{10}$ Is 29$_{11}$ 50$_{6}$ 61$_{3}$ Jr 22$_{13}$ 26$_{24}$ 37$_{21}$ 48$_{9}$ Ezk 16$_{33}$ 21$_{16}$ 30$_{21}$ 43$_{19}$ Ps 15$_{5}$ 72$_{15}$ (or em. יֻתַּן *may there be given*, i.e. qal pass.) 120$_{3}$ Pr 1$_{4}$ 4$_{2}$ 9$_{9}$ 13$_{10}$ (or em. רַק *only* to רֵק *empty one* or רַע *evil one*, as subj.; or em. יִתֵּן to יֻתַּן, i.e. qal pass.) 22$_{16}$ 26$_{8}$ 28$_{27}$ 31$_{31}$ Ec 11$_{2}$ Est 2$_{3}$ 6$_{9}$ Dn 1$_{12}$ 11$_{21}$ Ne 2$_{7}$ 1 C 29$_{8}$ Si 3$_{17(A)}$ 10$_{28(A)}$ 32$_{13(Bmg)}$ 1QSa 1$_{19}$ 4Q416 2.2$_{5}$ 2.3$_{10}$ 4Q418 81$_{6}$.

<OBJ> Amon of Thebes Jr 46$_{26}$, אֱלֹהִים *god* Gn 35$_{4}$ Jr 46$_{26}$, Ammonites Jg 11$_{30.32}$ 12$_{3}$ Ezk 21$_{36}$ 25$_{4}$, Amorites Jos 24$_{8.11}$, Canaanites Nm 21$_{3}$ Jos 24$_{11}$ Jg 1$_{4}$ Ne 9$_{24}$, Cush(ites) Is 43$_{3}$ 2 C 16$_{8}$, Egypt(ians) Gn 16$_{3}$ Is 43$_{3}$ Jr 46$_{26}$, Ephraim Ho 11$_{8}$, Girgashites Jos 24$_{11}$, Hittites Gn 23$_{4}$ Jos 24$_{11}$, Israel(ites) Dt 1$_{27}$ Jg 2$_{14}$ 1 S 28$_{19}$ 1 K 11$_{38}$ 14$_{16}$ 2 K 13$_{3}$ Is 42$_{24}$ Mc 5$_{2}$ 4QpsMos^{e} 1$_{8}$ 2.1$_{5}$ CD 1$_{4.5.6}$, Jebusites Jos 24$_{11}$, Judah Jr 20$_{4}$ 2 C 25$_{20}$ 28$_{9}$ 32$_{11}$, Libyans 2 C 16$_{8}$, Midian(ites) Jg 7$_{2.7.14}$, Moab(ites) Jg 3$_{28}$ 2 K 3$_{18}$ Ezk 25$_{10}$, Perizzites Jos 24$_{11}$ Jg 1$_{4}$, Philistines 1 S 14$_{10.37}$ 17$_{47}$ 23$_{4}$ 2 S 5$_{19.19}$||1 C 14$_{10.10}$, Seba Is 43$_{3}$,

Shunammite 1 K 217.

עַם *people* Nm 212.34 Dt 32.3 716 Jos 77 81 Jg 1121 Is 476 Jr 217 3420 Ezk 1715 Ps 10641 Ne 922.24, גּוֹי *nation* Jg 223 Is 342, לְאֹם *nation* Is 434, מַמְלָכָה *kingdom* Ezr 12 Ne 922 2 C 135 2 C 3623, שֵׁבֶט *tribe* 1 K 1113.31.35.36, בַּיִת *house* 2 S 128.8 1 K 1118 Est 81.7 4QConfess 28, of Israel Ezk 119 3923, צָבָא *army* Is 342, גְּדוּד *band* 1 S 3023, מַחֲנֶה *camp* Jg 79.14.15 1 S 2819, הָמוֹן *multitude* 1 K 2013.28.

Abishag 1 K 217, Achsah Jos 1516.17||Jg 112.13, Ahab Jr 2921, Ahaz 2 C 285, Armoni 2 S 219, Asenath Gn 4145, Azariah Jr 433, Bilhah Gn 2929 304 4625 4QTNaph 110, Cushan-rishathaim Jg 310, David 1 S 2314, Gog Ezk 394, Hagar Gn 163, Hannah 4QTNaph 12, Hophra Jr 4430, Isaac Jos 243, Jacob Jos 244 4QJubf 2512 ([י]קו[ב]), Jehoiakim Dn 12, Jeremiah Jr 2624 3816 3919, Johanan Jr 433, Mephibosheth 2 S 219, Merab 1 S 1817.19, Michal 1 S 1821.27 2544 2 S 314, Og Nm 2134 Dt 32.3, Oholah Ezk 239, Oholibah Ezk 2328, Oreb Jg 83, Rachel Gn 2919.19.28, Rebekah Gn 2717, Samson Jg 1512.13 1623, Saul 1 S 2411 2623, Seba 2 S 2021, Sihon Dt 224.30 Jg 1121, Sisera Jg 47.14, Tamar Gn 3826, Zalmunna Jg 87, Zebah Jg 87, Zedekiah (king) Jr 217 3421 3819 4430, Zedekiah (prophet) Jr 2921, Zeeb Jg 83, Zilpah Gn 2924 309 4618.

אָדָם *human beings* Is 434 Si 1514, אִישׁ *man* Dt 1912 Jg 2013 1 S 1112 1412 1 K 1326 Jr 3420 433, אִשָּׁה *woman, wife* Gn 2441 3026 Ex 214 Jg 152.6 Jg 2114.18.18 1 S 1710 2544 2 S 314 1211 2021 1 K 1119 205 Jr 810, אָב *father* Ne 927.30, אֵם *mother* 4QTNaph 110, בֵּן *son* Gn 187 1716 306 489 Lv 1514 Dt 2853 Jg 2013.28 2 S 2021 216.9 1 K 36 521||2 C 211 1 K 1719 205 2 K 628.29 Jr 1821 2921 Ezk 1621 4319 1 C 255 285 4QJubd 2122 ([בני]) 4QJubg 2512 ([בן]), of Israel Jg 61 131 2 C 1316, בַּת *daughter* Gn 2919.19.28 348.9.16.21 4145 Ex 221 Dt 73 2216=11QT 6511 Dt 2853 Jos 1516.17||Jg 112.13 Jg 36 211 1 S 1725 1817.19.21.27 2544 2 K 149||2 C 2518 Jr 296 Dn 1117 Ezr 912 Ne 1031 1325 1 C 235 255 4QDe 514 ([בתו ית]ן) 4QDf 39, אָח *brother* Gn 2737 4234, אָחוֹת *sister* Gn 3414 1 K 1119 Ezk 1661, יֶלֶד *child* Gn 3026 1 K 1723 Is 818 Jl 43, יָלוּד *child* 1 K 326.27, בְּתוּלָה *young woman* Ex 2216, נַעֲרָה *young woman* Est 29, צָעִיר *small one*, i.e. younger (daughter) Gn 2926.

מֶלֶךְ *king* Nm 2134 Dt 224.30 32.3 724 Jos 62 81 108.30 118 Jg 310 1 S 86 2 K 310.13 Jr 217 3421 3819 4430.30 4626 Ezk 295 Ho 1310.11 Ne 924 4QpsMosd 42, פַּרְעֹה *Pharaoh* Jr 4430 4626 Ezk 295, בַּעַל *lord* Jos 2411, נָשִׂיא *prince* Ezk 394, שַׂר *prince* Jg 47 83 Jr 3420.21 Ho 1310, עֶבֶד *servant* Gn 2014 2435 1 K 189 Jr 217, שִׁפְחָה *female servant* Gn 163 2014 2435 2924 2929 304.9.18, סָרִיס *eunuch* 2 K 86 Jr 3420, בְּכוֹר *firstborn* Ex 2228 Dt 1425 Mc 675, כֹּהֵן *priest* Jr 3420 1QpHab 910 4QpPsa 3.49 ([הכו]הן), לֵוִי *Levite* Nm 39 819, נָבִיא *prophet* 4QapPsb 694 11QT 6102 (נתתי ... [נביא]), worshipper Ps 2712 11818 1246 Lm 114, מוֹשִׁיעַ *saviour* 2 K 135 Ne 927, מְבַשֵּׂר *messenger* Is 4127, עֵד *witness* Is 439, רֹעֶה *shepherd* Jr 315, שׂכל hi. ptc. *one who considers* Ps 413, אֹיֵב *enemy* Dt 2110=11QT 6310 Dt 2144 Jg 328 1623.24 1 S 245, חרב hi. ptc. *one who lays waste* Jg 1624, נכה hi. ptc. *one who strikes* 2 S 147, רָשָׁע *wicked one* Jr 2531.

יֹשֵׁב *inhabitant* Ex 2331 Ezk 156 Ne 924 1 C 2218, *one sitting* on throne 1 K 148, יְדִדוּת *loved one* Jr 127, עָנִי *needy one* 4QBarka 1.2, נְבֵלָה *corpse* Dt 1421 Jr 197 Ps 792, פֶּגֶר *corpse* 1 S 1746, טִבְחָה *slaughter*, i.e. meat 1 S 2511, זֶרַע *seed* Gn 4719 1 S 815 Is 5510, *offspring* Gn 153 389 1 S 111.11 2 K 1720 Ru 412, הֵרָיוֹן *conception* Ru 413.

יָד *hand* Jr 5015 Ezk 1718 Ezr 1019 1 C 2924 2 C 308, i.e. monument Is 565, צִיץ perh. *wing* Jr 489, עַיִן *eye* Dt 293, i.e. sparkle Pr 2331, אֹזֶן *ear* Dt 293, זְרוֹעַ *shoulder* Dt 183, שְׁכֶם *shoulder*, i.e. slope Gn 4822, פֶּה *mouth*, i.e. portion Dt 2117, לְחִי *cheek* Dt 183 Is 506 Lm 330, לָשׁוֹן *tongue* Is 504, קֶרֶן *horn*, i.e. power Si 495, חָזֶה *breast* Lv 734, שַׁד *breast* Ho 914, קֵבָה *stomach* Dt 183, רֶחֶם *womb* Ho 914, גֵּו *back* Is 506, כֶּסֶל *loins* Si 4719, שׁוֹק *thigh* Lv 732.34, דָּם *blood* Lv 1711 Ezk 1636.

לֵב *heart* Dt 2865 293 1 K 39.12 Jr 247 3239 Ezk 1119.19 3626.26 Pr 2326 2 C 3012 4Q183 1.24 4QBarka 1.210 4Q DibHama 182 ([נ]תתה), לֵבָב *heart* 1 C 2919, נֶפֶשׁ *soul*, i.e. self Si 96 3021, i.e. persons Gn 1421 Ezk 2713 (if em. נֶפֶשׁ to בְּנֶפֶשׁ), i.e. life Ex 2123 Jr 455 Ps 7419 perh. 4Qps Ezeka 13.23, בָּשָׂר *flesh* Ex 168 Nm 1113.13.18.21 1 S 215 1744 1 K 1921 Ps 792, רוּחַ *spirit* Is 425 Ec 127 Ne 920 1QSb 525 ([רוח]) 11QPsa 273, נְשָׁמָה *breath* Is 425 11QPsa 194, רֵיחַ *odour* Ezk 613 Ca 112 213 714, שֵׁם *name* Is 565, צְפִיעַ *dung* Ezk 415(Qr) (Kt צפוע).

מִקְנֶה *cattle* Gn 319, בָּקָר *cattle* Gn 2014 2114 2435 Nm 75.6.7.8 Dt 1221 1 C 2123 2 C 358, פַּר *bull* 1 K 1823.26 Ezk

43$_{20}$, פָּרָה *heifer* Nm 19$_{3}$, שׁוֹר *ox* Ex 22$_{9.29}$ Nm 7$_{5}$, צֹאן *sheep* Gn 20$_{14}$ 21$_{14}$ 24$_{35}$ Ex 22$_{29}$ Dt 12$_{21}$, שֶׂה *sheep* Ex 22$_{9}$, כֶּבֶשׂ *sheep* 11QT 22$_{11}$, אַיִל *ram* Lv 5$_{16}$ 11QT 22$_{11}$, סוּס *horse* 2 K 18$_{23}$||Is 36$_{8}$ Ezk 17$_{15}$ Est 6$_{9}$, חֲמוֹר *ass* Gn 24$_{35}$ Ex 22$_{9}$, גָּמָל *camel* Gn 24$_{35}$, תַּנִּין *sea monster* Ezk 29$_{5}$, לִוְיָתָן *Leviathan* Ps 74$_{14}$, בְּהֵמָה *beast* Ex 22$_{9}$, חַיָּה *beast* Jr 27$_{6}$ 28$_{14}$, תֹּר *turtledove* Lv 15$_{14}$.

עֵץ *wood* 1 K 5$_{24}$ Ezk 15$_{6}$ Ne 2$_{8}$ 4QpsJub^{a} 2.2$_{1}$ (ו[י]תן [את העצים]), פְּרִי *fruit* Lv 25$_{19}$ 26$_{4.20}$ Ezk 34$_{27}$ Mc 6$_{7}$ Zc 8$_{12}$ Ps 1$_{3}$ 11QM 1.2$_{9}$ ([פר]י), אֶרֶז *cedar* Ezk 31$_{11}$, רֹאשׁ *poison* Ps 69$_{22}$, זֵרָעֹן *vegetable* Dn 1$_{16}$, רֵאשִׁית *firstfruits* Nm 18$_{12}$ Dt 18$_{4}$ Ezk 44$_{30}$, יְבוּל *produce* Lv 26$_{4.20}$ Dt 11$_{17}$ Ezk 34$_{27}$ Zc 8$_{12}$ Ps 67$_{7}$ 78$_{46}$ 85$_{13}$, תְּבוּאָה *produce* Is 30$_{23}$ 1QDM 2$_{10}$ ([ל]תת ... [התבו]אה), תְּנוּבָה *produce* 11QM 1.2$_{9}$, עֵשֶׂב *plant* Gn 1$_{29}$ Dt 11$_{15}$ Zc 10$_{1}$, חִטָּה *wheat* Ezk 27$_{17}$ (if del. בְּ *in exchange for*) 1 C 21$_{23}$ 2 C 2$_{9}$ 27$_{5}$ MurEpBarC^{b} 1$_{9}$, שְׂעֹרָה *barley* Ru 3$_{17}$ 2 C 2$_{9}$ 27$_{5}$ perh. T. 'Ira ost. 2 (unless שמ is an abbreviation for שמן *oil*), דָּגָן *grain* Is 62$_{8}$ Ho 2$_{10}$ Ps 78$_{24}$ 11QM 1.2$_{9}$, תֶּבֶן *straw* Gn 24$_{32}$ Ex 5$_{7.10}$, מִסְפּוֹא *provender* Gn 24$_{32}$ 42$_{27}$ 43$_{24}$.

אֹכֶל *food* Lv 25$_{37}$ Ps 104$_{27}$ 145$_{15}$ Jb 36$_{31}$, מַאֲכָל *food* Ezr 3$_{7}$, מַכֹּלֶת *food* 1 K 5$_{25}$, טֶרֶף *food* Ps 111$_{5}$ Pr 31$_{15}$ 4Q417 1.2$_{3}$, מָזוֹן *food* 2 C 11$_{23}$, לֶחֶם *bread* Gn 21$_{14}$ 25$_{34}$ 27$_{17}$ 28$_{20}$ 47$_{16.17}$ Ex 16$_{8.15}$ Dt 10$_{18}$ Jg 8$_{6.15}$ 1 S 10$_{4}$ 21$_{4}$ 22$_{13}$ 25$_{11}$ 30$_{11}$ 1 K 5$_{23}$ 2 K 4$_{42}$ Is 30$_{20}$ Is 55$_{10}$ Ezk 16$_{19}$ 18$_{7.16}$ Ho 2$_{7}$ Ps 78$_{20}$ 136$_{25}$ 146$_{7}$ 147$_{9}$ Ru 1$_{6}$ Ne 9$_{15}$ Lachish ost. 9$_{3}$ Arad ost. 2$_{1}$ 10$_{2}$ ([נתן] ... [לח]ם), כִּכָּר *loaf* Jg 8$_{5}$, קֶמַח *flour* Arad ost. 8$_{1}$ 12$_{2}$, מַטְעַם *delicacy* Gn 27$_{17}$, מַעֲדָן *delicacy* Gn 49$_{20}$ 4QCommGenA 6$_{1}$, דְּבַשׁ *honey* Jg 14$_{9}$ Ezk 27$_{17}$ (if del. בְּ *in exchange for*), צִמּוּק *cluster of raisins* 1 S 30$_{12}$, פֶּלַח *slice* of fig-cake 1 S 30$_{12}$, נָזִיד *pottage* Gn 25$_{34}$, צֵידָה *provisions* Gn 42$_{25}$ 45$_{21}$ 1 S 22$_{10}$, אֲרֻחָה *ration of food* Jr 40$_{5}$.

חֵלֶב *fat*, i.e. best Nm 18$_{12.12}$, חָלָב *milk* Jg 5$_{25}$, שֶׁמֶן *oil* Is 61$_{3}$ Ezk 27$_{17}$ (if del. בְּ *in exchange for*) Ezr 3$_{7}$ 2 C 2$_{9}$ Arad ost. 4$_{1}$ 12$_{2}$ 17$_{8}$ perh. T. 'Ira ost. 2 (unless שמ is an abbreviation from שערים *barley*), יִצְהָר *fresh oil* Ho 2$_{10}$ 11QM 1.2$_{9}$, יַיִן *wine* Pr 31$_{6}$ Ne 2$_{1}$ 2 C 2$_{9}$ Lachish ost. 9$_{3}$ ([יין]) Arad ost. 1$_{2}$ 2$_{1}$ 4$_{4}$ 8$_{1}$ 10$_{2}$ ([נתן]) 11$_{2}$, תִּירוֹשׁ *new wine* Ho 2$_{10}$ 11QM 1.2$_{9}$, שֵׁכָר *strong drink* Pr 31$_{6}$, חֹמֶץ *vinegar* Arad ost. 2$_{7}$, מִשְׁתֶּה *drink* Ezr 3$_{7}$.

מַיִם *water* Gn 24$_{32}$ 43$_{24}$ Ex 17$_{2}$ Nm 20$_{8}$ 21$_{16}$ Dt 2$_{28}$ 1 S 25$_{11}$ Is 30$_{20}$ 43$_{20}$ Ne 9$_{20}$, נָהָר *river* Is 43$_{20}$, גֶּשֶׁם *rain* Lv 26$_{4}$ 1 K 17$_{14}$ Jr 5$_{24}$, מָטָר *rain* Dt 11$_{14}$ 28$_{12}$ 1 K 8$_{36}$||2 C 6$_{27}$ 1 K 18$_{1}$ Is 30$_{23}$ Jb 5$_{10}$, יוֹרֶה *early rain* Dt 11$_{4}$ Jr 5$_{24}$, מוֹרֶה *early rain* Jl 2$_{23}$, מַלְקוֹשׁ *latter rain* Dt 11$_{14}$ Jr 5$_{24}$, רְבִיבִים *showers* Jr 14$_{22}$, טַל *dew* Zc 8$_{12}$, קֶרַח *frost* Jb 37$_{10}$ (or em. יֻתַּן frost *is given*, i.e. qal pass.).

זָהָב *gold* Gn 24$_{35}$ Ex 32$_{24}$ Nm 22$_{18}$ 24$_{13}$ 1 K 15$_{18}$ 20$_{5}$ 2 K 23$_{35.35}$ Ezk 7$_{21}$ Ezr 2$_{69}$||Ne 7$_{70}$ Ne 7$_{69.71}$ 1 C 29$_{3.7}$, כֶּסֶף *silver, money* Gn 20$_{16}$ 23$_{13}$ 24$_{35}$ 45$_{22}$ Ex 21$_{32}$ 22$_{6}$ 30$_{16}$ Lv 25$_{37}$ Nm 3$_{48.51}$ 22$_{18}$ 24$_{13}$ Dt 14$_{26}$ 22$_{19}$=11QT 65$_{15}$ Dt 22$_{29}$=11QT 66$_{10}$ Jg 9$_{4}$ 16$_{5}$ 17$_{4.10}$ 2 S 18$_{11}$ 1 K 15$_{18}$ 20$_{5}$ 21$_{2}$ 2 K 12$_{8.12.15.16}$ 15$_{20}$ 2 K 22$_{5.5.9}$||2 C 34$_{10.10.17}$ 2 K 23$_{35.35.35}$ Ezk 7$_{21}$ Ps 15$_{5}$ Ezr 2$_{69}$||Ne 7$_{70}$ Ezr 3$_{7}$ Ne 7$_{71}$ 1 C 29$_{3.7}$ 2 C 24$_{12}$ 34$_{9.11}$ 4QOrd^{a} 1.2$_{6.7}$, נְחֹשֶׁת *bronze* 1 C 29$_{7}$, בַּרְזֶל *iron* 1 C 29$_{7}$, כְּלִי *jewellery* Gn 24$_{53}$ Ezk 16$_{17}$, *goods* Ex 22$_{6}$, *weapon* 1 S 20$_{40}$ Si 12$_{5}$, טַבַּעַת *ring* Est 3$_{10}$ 8$_{2}$, נֶזֶם *ring* Gn 35$_{4}$ Jg 8$_{24.25}$ Jb 42$_{11}$, חוֹתָם *seal* Gn 38$_{18}$, רָאמֹת *coral* Ezk 27$_{16}$, נֹפֶךְ *emerald* Ezk 27$_{16}$, כַּדְכֹּד *agate* Ezk 27$_{16}$, אֶבֶן precious *stone* 1 K 10$_{10}$||2 C 9$_{9}$ 1 C 29$_{8}$, בֹּשֶׂם *spice* 1 K 10$_{10.10}$||2 C 9$_{9.9}$, צֳרִי *balm* Ezk 27$_{17}$ (if del. בְּ *in exchange for*), תַּמְרוּקִים *cosmetic treatment* Est 2$_{3.9}$, יְקָר *precious things* Jr 20$_{5}$, *honour* Est 1$_{20}$, מִגְדָּנוֹת *precious things* Gn 24$_{53}$, מַחְמָד *precious thing* Lm 1$_{11(Qr)}$, מַחְמֹד *precious thing* Lm 1$_{11(Kt)}$.

אוֹצָר *treasure* 1 K 15$_{18}$ (or em. וְאֶת־אוֹצְרוֹת *and the treasures of* to וּבְאוֹצְרוֹת *and in the treasures of*) Is 45$_{3}$ Jr 15$_{13}$ 17$_{3}$ Jr 20$_{5}$ GnzPs 3$_{15}$, מַטְמוֹן *treasure* Gn 43$_{23}$ Is 45$_{3}$, סְגֻלָּה *treasure* 1 C 29$_{3}$, הוֹן *wealth* Pr 6$_{31}$ Ca 8$_{7}$ 4QpNah 3.1$_{12}$ ([י]תנוהו) 4QapJoshua^{a} 20.2$_{5}$, חַיִל *wealth* Jr 15$_{13}$ 17$_{3}$ Jl 2$_{22}$ Pr 31$_{3}$ 4QBer^{b} 5$_{8}$ ([חיל] ... לת[ת]) GnzPs 3$_{15}$, *army* 2 C 24$_{24}$, חֹסֶן *wealth* Jr 20$_{5}$, נְכָסִים *wealth* Ec 5$_{18}$ 6$_{2}$ 2 C 1$_{12}$, עֹשֶׁר *wealth* 1 K 3$_{13}$||2 C 1$_{12}$ Pr 30$_{8}$ Ec 5$_{18}$ 6$_{2}$ 2 C 1$_{12}$, יְגִיעַ *property* Jr 20$_{5}$ Ps 78$_{46}$, רְכוּשׁ *property* 2 C 32$_{29}$, שָׁלָל *spoil* Dt 20$_{14}$=11QT 62$_{11}$.

בֶּגֶד *garment* Gn 24$_{53}$ 28$_{20}$, לְבוּשׁ *garment* Est 6$_{9}$, מַעֲטֶה *garment* Is 61$_{3}$, שִׂמְלָה *garment* Dt 10$_{18}$, מְעִיל *robe* 1 S 18$_{4}$, כֻּתֹּנֶת *tunic* Ne 7$_{69.71}$, סָדִין *linen wrapper* Jg 14$_{12.13}$, חֲגוֹר *girdle* Pr 31$_{24}$, חֲגוֹרָה *girdle* 2 S 18$_{11}$, פְּאֵר *turban* Is 61$_{3}$, בּוּץ *fine linen* Ezk 27$_{16}$, נַעַל *sandal* Ru 4$_{7}$, אַרְגָּמָן *purple* Ezk 27$_{16}$, מְאוּזָּל *woven material* Ezk 27$_{19}$ (or em. מֵאוּזָל *from Uzal*), רִקְמָה *embroidery* Ezk 27$_{16}$, מַד *armour* 1 S 18$_{4}$, חֲלִיפָה *change* of clothing Gn

45$_{22.22}$ Jg 14$_{12.13.19}$ 2 K 5$_{22.23}$, פָּתִיל *cord* Gn 38$_{18}$, חֵמֶת *skin bottle* Gn 21$_{14}$.

מַטֶּה *staff* Gn 38$_{18}$ Nm 17$_{21}$, חֶרֶב *sword* 1 S 21$_{10}$ 22$_{10.13}$ Ezk 21$_{16}$, חֲנִית *spear* 2 K 11$_{10}$||2 C 23$_{9}$, מָגֵן *shield* 2 S 22$_{36}$||Ps 18$_{36}$, שֶׁלֶט *shield* 2 K 11$_{10}$||2 C 23$_{9}$, מוֹרַג *threshing sledge* 1 C 21$_{23}$, נֵס *standard* Ps 60$_{6}$, גָּדֵר *wall* Ezr 9$_{9}$, דֶּלֶת *door* 2 K 18$_{16}$, אֹמְנָה *doorpost* 2 K 18$_{16}$, נִיר *lamp* 1 K 15$_{4}$ 2 K 8$_{19}$||2 C 21$_{7}$, מִזְרָק *basin* Ne 7$_{69}$, יָתֵד *peg* Ezr 9$_{8}$, לוּחַ *tablet* of stone Ex 24$_{12}$ 31$_{18}$ Dt 5$_{22}$ 9$_{10.11}$ 10$_{2}$, עֲגָלָה *waggon* Gn 45$_{21}$ Nm 7$_{5.6.7.8}$, תַּבְנִית *pattern* 1 C 28$_{5}$.

חֹזֶק *strength* 1QM 14$_{6}$, כֹּחַ *strength* Gn 4$_{12}$ Dt 8$_{18}$ Is 40$_{29}$ 4Q423 2$_{3}$, עֹז *strength* 1 S 2$_{10}$ Ps 29$_{11}$ 68$_{35.36}$ 78$_{61}$ 86$_{16}$ Si 47$_{5}$ 4QapJoseph^{b} 2$_{7}$, אֹמֶץ *might* 1QM 14$_{6}$, גְּבוּרָה *might* Jb 39$_{19}$, עָצְמָה *might* Si 46$_{9}$, תַּעֲצֻמָה *might* Ps 68$_{36}$, מֹשֶׁל *rule* Si 13$_{12}$ (or em. אכזרי יתן מושל *a cruel one implements rule* to מושל אכזרי לא יחן *a cruel ruler has no pity*), מִמְשָׁל *dominion* 4QMyst^{a} 6.1$_{15}$, מֶמְשָׁלָה *authority* Is 22$_{21}$, מְלוּכָה *kingdom* 2 S 16$_{8}$ 1 K 11$_{35}$, מַמְלָכָה *kingdom* Nm 32$_{33}$ 1 S 28$_{17}$ 1 K 11$_{11}$ 14$_{8}$, מַמְלְכוּת *kingdom* 1 S 15$_{28}$, מַלְכוּת *royal status* Est 1$_{19}$.

אֱמֶת *faithfulness* Mc 7$_{20}$, חֶסֶד *loyalty* Mc 7$_{20}$ 4QJub^{h} 40$_{5}$ ([חסד]), טוּב *good* Dt 26$_{11}$ Ps 85$_{13}$, טוּב *goodness* Gn 45$_{18}$ Ne 9$_{35}$, טוֹבָה *goodness* 4Q418 81$_{6}$, בְּרָכָה *blessing* Gn 28$_{4}$ 32$_{29}$ Dt 12$_{15}$ 16$_{17}$ Jos 15$_{19}$||Jg 1$_{15}$ 11QT 53$_{3}$, רַחֲמִים *mercy* Gn 43$_{14}$ Dt 13$_{18}$=11QT 55$_{11}$ Jr 42$_{12}$ Meṣad Ḥashavyahu ost. 1$_{13}$ ([ותתן] ... רח[מם]), חֵן *favour* Ps 84$_{12}$ Pr 3$_{34}$ 13$_{15}$ 4QJub^{h} 40$_{5}$ ([חן]), חֲנִינָה *favour* Jr 16$_{13}$, דּוֹד *love* Ca 7$_{13}$, קֹדֶשׁ *holiness*, i.e. holy thing Lv 22$_{14}$ Dt 26$_{13}$ 1 S 21$_{7}$ 2 C 31$_{14}$ Si 45$_{20}$, צֶדֶק *righteousness* Jb 36$_{3}$, צְדָקָה *righteousness* Ps 72$_{1}$, שָׁלוֹם *peace* Lv 26$_{6}$ Nm 25$_{12}$ Jr 14$_{13}$ Hg 2$_{9}$ Ml 2$_{5}$ 1 C 22$_{9}$ 1QSb 3$_{5}$ ([שלו]ם), שֶׁקֶט *quiet* 1 C 22$_{9}$, דֳּמִי *silence* Is 62$_{7}$, מְנוּחָה *(place of) rest* Dt 12$_{9}$ 1 K 8$_{56}$, פוּגַת *respite* Lm 2$_{18}$, שַׁבָּת *sabbath* Ex 16$_{29}$ Ezk 20$_{12}$, שֶׁבֶת *cessation* 4QHalakhah^{a} 4$_{2}$ (שב[תו]), נִקָּיוֹן *cleanness* Am 4$_{6}$.

כָּבוֹד *glory* 1 S 6$_{5}$ 1 K 3$_{13}$||2 C 1$_{12}$ Is 42$_{8}$ 48$_{11}$ Jr 13$_{16}$ Ml 2$_{2}$ Ps 84$_{12}$ 115$_{1}$ Pr 26$_{8}$ Ec 6$_{2}$ Si 49$_{5}$ 1QSb 5$_{18}$ ([ית]ן) 2QJub^{b} 46$_{2}$ (כב[ודם]), תִּפְאֶרֶת *glory* Ps 78$_{61}$, יְקָר *honour* 4QMishC^{a} 2$_{1}$ (ל[תת]), הָדָר *honour* Ezk 27$_{10}$ 4Q416 2.3$_{10}$, הוֹד *splendour* Pr 5$_{9}$ Dn 11$_{21}$ 1 C 29$_{25}$ Si 45$_{7}$ 51$_{17(11QPs^{a})}$, אוֹר *light* Jb 3$_{20}$, תֹּאַר *form*, i.e. beauty Si 42$_{12(B)}$.

חָכְמָה *wisdom* 1 K 5$_{9.26}$ Pr 2$_{6}$ 29$_{15}$ Ec 2$_{26}$ 2 C 1$_{10}$ Si 45$_{26}$ 50$_{23}$ 4QBéat 1$_{1}$ GnzPs 1$_{6}$, תּוּשִׁיָּה *sound wisdom* 1QS 11$_{7}$, בִּינָה *understanding* Jb 38$_{36}$ 1 C 22$_{12}$ Si 38$_{6}$, תְּבוּנָה *understanding* 1 K 5$_{9}$, שֶׂכֶל *understanding* 1 C 22$_{12}$ 1QH 18$_{27}$ 19$_{27}$ 4QapJoseph^{b} 2$_{5}$ ([נ]תן) 4Q418 149$_{6}$, שׂכל hi. inf. abs. *insight* Dn 1$_{17}$, עָרְמָה *prudence* Pr 1$_{4}$, דֵּעָה *knowledge* 1QS 11$_{7}$ 4QBark^{c} 1.1$_{2}$, דַּעַת *knowledge* Pr 1$_{4}$ Ec 2$_{26}$ 4QCreatC 2$_{2}$ ([דע]ת), מַדָּע *knowledge* Dn 1$_{17}$, טַעַם *discernment* Si 10$_{28}$, מְזִמָּה *discretion* Pr 1$_{4}$ 1QS 11$_{7}$.

לֶקַח *teaching* Pr 4$_{2}$, תּוֹרָה *law* Ex 24$_{12}$ Dt 31$_{9}$ Ezr 7$_{6}$ Ne 9$_{13}$ 4QparaKings 104$_{7}$ ([התורה]), מִצְוָה *commandment* Ex 24$_{12}$ Si 45$_{17}$, חֹק *statute* Ezk 20$_{25}$ Ps 99$_{7}$ Ne 9$_{13}$ Si 47$_{11}$ 4QD^{a} 11$_{11}$ 4QapJoseph^{b} 3$_{8}$, i.e. fixed allowance Gn 47$_{22}$ Pr 31$_{15}$, fixed order Ps 148$_{6}$, חֻקָּה *statute* Ezk 20$_{11}$, i.e. fixed order Jr 31$_{35}$, מִשְׁפָּט *justice, statute* Ezk 20$_{25}$ 21$_{32}$ Zp 3$_{5}$ Ps 72$_{1}$ Jb 36$_{6}$ Ne 9$_{13}$ 1QpHab 5$_{4}$ 10$_{3}$ 4QD^{a} 11$_{11}$, דָּת *decree* Ezr 8$_{36}$, בְּרִית *covenant* Nm 25$_{12}$ Si 44$_{22}$ 4QpsEzek^{a} 2$_{1}$, אוֹת *sign* Dt 6$_{22}$ 13$_{2}$=Dt 54$_{8}$ Jos 21$_{2}$ Is 7$_{14}$ Ne 9$_{10}$ 4QpsJub^{b} 1$_{4}$ ([נ]תתי) Lachish ost. 4$_{11}$, מוֹפֵת *wonder* Ex 7$_{9}$ Dt 6$_{22}$ 13$_{2}$=Dt 54$_{8}$ 1 K 13$_{3.5}$ Ne 9$_{10}$ 2 C 34$_{24}$.

תּוֹדָה *praise* Jos 7$_{19}$, *confession* Ezr 10$_{11}$, תְּהִלָּה *praise* Is 42$_{8}$, הוֹדָאָה *thanksgiving* Si 51$_{17(B)}$, הוֹדָה *thanksgiving* Si 47$_{8}$ 4QsapDidA 1$_{8}$ (הדות), זָמִיר *song* Jb 35$_{10}$, שִׁירָה *song* 4QpsHod^{c} 1$_{4}$ ([וי]תן), עֵדוּת *testimony* Ex 25$_{16.21}$ Si 36$_{20}$, יֶשַׁע *salvation* Ps 85$_{8}$, תְּשׁוּעָה *victory* Jg 15$_{18}$ 2 K 5$_{1}$ Ps 144$_{10}$, תִּקְוָה *hope* Jr 29$_{11}$, אַחֲרִית *future* Jr 29$_{11}$, רְפָאָה *remedy* Ezk 30$_{21}$, מִחְיָה *reviving* Ezr 9$_{9}$, חַיִּים *life* Ml 2$_{5}$ Jb 3$_{20}$ Ec 9$_{9}$ 4QBark^{d} 2.1$_{11}$, שֵׁנָה *sleep* Ps 127$_{2}$ 132$_{4}$ Pr 6$_{4}$, תְּנוּמָה *slumber* Ps 132$_{4}$ Pr 6$_{4}$.

שִׂמְחָה *joy* Ec 2$_{26}$, מַעֲדָן *delight* Pr 29$_{17}$, חֶמְדָּה *desire* GnzPs 3$_{15}$, חֵפֶץ *desire* 1 K 5$_{24}$ 10$_{13}$||2 C 9$_{12}$, מַאֲוַי *desire* Ps 140$_{9}$, תַּאֲוָה *desire* Ps 21$_{3}$ Pr 10$_{24}$ (or em.; see Subj.), שְׁאֵלָה *request* 1 S 1$_{17.27}$ Ps 106$_{15}$ Est 5$_{8}$ Si 41$_{19}$ 11QPs^{a} 24$_{4}$, מִשְׁאָלָה *request* Ps 37$_{4}$, תִּקְוָה *hope* Jb 6$_{8}$, מַשָּׂא *task* 1QSa 1$_{19}$, עִנְיָן *task* Ec 2$_{36}$ 3$_{10}$, הַשִּׂיגָה *attainment* Si 14$_{13}$, הֲקִימָה *fulfilment (of promise)* 4QConfess 2$_{7}$, בְּכֹרָה *firstborn's privilege* 4QJub^{h} 36$_{14}$ ([ואתן את בכורתי]), כְּהֻנָּה *priesthood* Nm 18$_{7}$, מִשְׁמֶרֶת *charge* Nm 18$_{8}$, מַהֲלָךְ *(right of) access* Zc 3$_{7}$.

נְקָמָה *vengeance* 2 S 4_{8} 22_{48}||Ps 18_{48}, עַצֶּבֶת *hurt* Pr 10_{10} Si 36_{25}, חֶרְפָּה *reproach* Ps 78_{66}, בּוּז *contempt* 1QM 12_{7} ([נ]תנו), לַעַג *derision* 1QM 12_{7} ([נ]תנו), קֶלֶס *derision* 1QM 12_{7} ([נ]תנו), תִּפְלָה *unseemliness* Jb 1_{22}, מְגִנָּה *insolence* of heart Lm 3_{65}, מַצָּה *strife* Pr 13_{10} (or em.; see Subj.), קֶשֶׁר *conspiracy* Si 11_{31}, תַּזְנוּת *prostitution* Ezk 23_{7}, שְׁכֹבֶת *lying down* Lv $18_{20.23}$ 20_{15} Nm 5_{20}, דֳּפִי *blemish* Ps 50_{20}, מִכְשׁוֹל *stumbling block* Si 47_{23}, כִּלָּיוֹן *failure* of eyes Dt 28_{65}, דַּאֲבוֹן *languishing* of soul Dt 28_{65}, מוֹט *slipping* Ps 55_{23} 66_{9} 121_{3} (or §7; if em. both לָמוּט *to slip*).

אֶרֶץ *land* Gn 12_{7} $13_{15.17}$ $15_{7.18}$ 17_{8} 24_{7} $26_{3.4}$ $28_{4.13}$ $35_{12.12}$ 48_{4} Ex $6_{4.8.8}$ 12_{25} $13_{5.11}$ 32_{13} 33_{1} Lv 14_{34} 23_{10} $25_{2.38}$ Nm 13_{2} 14_{8} 15_{2} $20_{12.24}$ 21_{34} 27_{12} $32_{7.9.29.33}$ 33_{53} 34_{13} 36_{2} Dt $1_{8.25.35.36.39}$ $2_{12.19.24.29}$ $3_{2.18.20}$ $4_{1.21.38}$ 5_{31} $6_{10.23}$ 8_{10} $9_{6.23}$ 10_{11} $11_{9.17.31}$ 12_{1} $15_{4.7}$ 16_{20} 17_{14}=11QT 56_{12} Dt 18_{9}=11QT 60_{16} Dt 19_{1+5t} 24_{4} 25_{19} $26_{1.2.3.9.15}$ $27_{2.3}$ $28_{7.52}$ 29_{7} 31_{7} $32_{49.52}$ 34_{4} Jos 1_{2+6t} $2_{9.14.24}$ 5_{6} $8_{1.7}$ 9_{24} 11_{23} $12_{6.7}$ 18_{3} $21_{43.43}$ 22_{4} 23_{16} Jos 24_{13} Jg 1_{2} 6_{9} 18_{10} 1 K $8_{36.48}$||2 C $6_{27.38}$ 1 K 11_{18} Jr 3_{19} 7_{7} Jr 11_{5} $27_{5.6.6}$ 30_{3} $32_{22.22}$ Ezk $20_{15.28.42}$ $29_{19.20}$ $36_{5.28}$ 37_{25} 45_{8} 47_{14} Ps 105_{11}||1 C 16_{18} Ps 105_{44} 115_{16} 135_{12} 136_{21} Ne $9_{8.15.36}$ 2 C 20_{7} 1QH 9_{15} ([ותתנם]) 4QCommGenA 1_{8} 4QRP^{c} 23_{5} perh. 4Qap Joshua^{a} 11_{3} 4QPatr 7_{3} ([הארץ]) 11QT 51_{16}, אֲדָמָה *land* Ex 20_{12}||Dt 5_{16} Lv 20_{24} Dt 4_{40} 7_{13} $11_{9.21}$ $21_{1.23}$=11QT 64_{13} Dt 25_{15} $26_{10.15}$ 28_{11} 30_{20} Jos $23_{13.15}$ 1 K $8_{34.40}$||2 C $6_{25.31}$ 1 K 9_{7}||2 C 7_{20} 1 K 14_{15} 2 K 21_{8} Jr 16_{15} 24_{10} 25_{5} 35_{15} Ezk 11_{17} 28_{25}.

עִיר *city* Nm 32_{33} 35_{2+8t} Dt $3_{12.19}$ 13_{13}=11QT 55_{2} (עריכה) Dt $20_{13.16}$=11QT $62_{9.13}$ Jos 1_{16} 8_{1} 19_{50} $21_{2.3.8.9}$||1 C $6_{49.50}$ Jos $21_{13.21}$||1 C $6_{42.52}$ 1 K $9_{11.12.13.16}$ Jr 23_{39} $32_{3.28}$ 34_{2} 2 C 8_{2} 1QDM 2_{2} (ל[תת] ... [ער]ים), שַׁעַר *gate*, i.e. city Dt $16_{5.18}$ 17_{2}=11QT 55_{16}, חָצֵר *village* Jos 21_{12}||1 C 6_{41}, צָפוֹן *north* Is 43_{6}.

Abdon Jos 21_{21}||1 C 6_{52}, Ai Jos 8_{18}, Aijalon Jos 21_{21}||1 C 6_{52}, Ain Jos 21_{13}, Alemeth 1 C 6_{42}, Almon Jos 21_{13}, Anathoth Jos 21_{13}||1 C 6_{42}, Anem 1 C 6_{52}, Aner 1 C 6_{52}, Ar Dt 2_{9} 3_{13}, Ashan 1 C 6_{42}, Ashtaroth 1 C 6_{52}, Bashan Dt 3_{13}, Beeshterah Jos 21_{21}, Beth-horon Jos 21_{21}||1 C 6_{52}, Beth-shemesh Jos 21_{13}||1 C 6_{42}, Bezer Jos 21_{21}||1 C 6_{52}, Bileam 1 C 6_{52}, Daberath Jos 21_{21}||1 C 6_{52}, Debir Jos 21_{13}||1 C 6_{42}, Dimnah Jos 21_{21}, Elteke Jos 21_{21}, En-gannim Jos 21_{21}, Eshtemoa Jos 21_{13} 1 C 6_{42}, Gath-rimmon Jos 21_{21}||1 C 6_{52}, Geba Jos 21_{13}||1 C 6_{42}, Gezer Jos 21_{21}||1 C 6_{52} 1 K 9_{16}, Gibbethon Jos 21_{21}, Gibeon Jos 21_{13}, Gilead Nm 32_{40} Dt 3_{15}, Golan Jos 21_{21}||1 C 6_{52}, Hammon 1 C 6_{52}, Hammoth-dor Jos 21_{21}, Hebron Jos 14_{13} 21_{13}||1 C 6_{42} Jg 1_{20} 1 C 6_{40}, Helkath Jos 21_{21}, Heshbon Jos 21_{21}||1 C 6_{52}, Hilez 1 C 6_{42} (mss Hilen), Holon Jos 21_{13}, Hukok 1 C 6_{52}.

Jahaz Jos 21_{21}||1 C 6_{52}, Jarmuth Jos 21_{21}, Jattir Jos 21_{13} 1 C 6_{42}, Jazer Jos 21_{21}||1 C 6_{52}, Jericho Jos 6_{2}, Jerusalem/Zion Jr 22_{25} Ezk $16_{27.39}$, Jokmeam 1 C 6_{52}, Juttah Jos 21_{13}, Kartah Jos 21_{21}, Kartan Jos 21_{21}, Kedemoth Jos 21_{21}||1 C 6_{52}, Kedesh Jos 21_{21}||1 C 6_{52}, Kibzaim Jos 21_{21}, Kiriathaim 1 C 6_{52}, Kiriath-arba Jos 15_{13} 21_{11}, Kishion Jos 21_{21}, Lachish Jos 10_{32}, Libnah Jos 10_{30} 21_{13} 1 C 6_{42}, Mahanaim Jos 21_{21}||1 C 6_{52}, Mashal 1 C 6_{52}, Mephaath Jos 21_{21}||1 C 6_{52}, Mishal Jos 21_{21}, Nahalal Jos 21_{21}, Ramoth Jos 21_{21}||1 C 6_{52}, Ramoth-gilead 1 K $22_{6.12}$||2 C $18_{5.11}$ 1 K 22_{15}, Rehob Jos 21_{21}||1 C 6_{52}, Rimmono 1 C 6_{52}, Shechem Jos 21_{21}||1 C 6_{52}, Taanach Jos 21_{21}, Tabor 1 C 6_{52}, Timnath-serah Jos 19_{50}, Ziklag 1 S 27_{6}.

הַר *hill country* Dt 1_{20} 2_{5} Jos 14_{12} 24_{4} Am 9_{15}, גַּיְא *valley* Ezk 39_{11}, שָׂדֶה *field* Gn 23_{11} Jos 21_{12}||1 C 6_{41} 1 S 8_{14} 22_{7} Jr 8_{10}, יָגֵב *field* Jr 39_{10}, מִגְרָשׁ *land outside city walls* Nm $35_{2.4.7}$ Jos $21_{2.3.8}$||1 C 6_{49} Jos $21_{11.13.21}$||1 C $6_{42.52}$ 1 C 6_{40}, כֶּרֶם *vineyard* 1 S $8_{14.15}$ 22_{7} 1 K 21_{2+6t} Jr 39_{10} Ho 2_{17} Ca 8_{11} 4QConfess 2_{8}, זַיִת *olive grove* 1 S 8_{14} 4QConfess 2_{8}, מְעָרָה *cave* Gn $23_{9.9.11.11.11}$, קֶבֶר *grave* Ezk 39_{11}, בָּמָה *high place* 4QpsEzek^{d} 1.2_{5} ([במותי]), מָקוֹם *place* Nm 10_{29} Jos 1_{3} 20_{4} Jg 20_{36} 1 S 9_{22} 27_{5} Jr 7_{14} Ezk 39_{11} 1 C $21_{22.22}$ Si 4_{5} 1QSb 3_{26}, יָם *sea* 1QH 9_{15} ([ותתנם]), תהום *deep* 1QH 9_{15} ([ותתנם]), בּוֹר *cistern* 4QConfess 2_{8} (בורות), מִקְוֶה *pool* 4QConfess 2_{8} (מקו[ה]), גֻּלָּה *spring* Jos $15_{19.19}$||Jg $1_{15.15}$, דֶּרֶךְ *way* Jr 32_{39} Pr 31_{3}.

נַחֲלָה *inheritance* Nm 16_{14} $27_{9.10.11}$ 36_{2} Dt 12_{9} Jos $13_{8.14.33}$ $14_{3.3}$ $17_{4.4}$ 18_{7} 19_{49} 1 K $21_{3.4}$ Is 47_{6} Jr 3_{19} 17_{4} Ezk 44_{28} 47_{23} Ps 106_{41} 111_{6} Jb 42_{15} Si 44_{23} 45_{20} 4QapLam^{b} 1_{1}, אֲחֻזָּה *possession* Gn 23_{4} 47_{11} Nm $27_{4.7}$ Ezk 44_{28} 45_{6}, יְרֻשָּׁה *possession* Dt 3_{20} Ps 61_{6}, חֶבֶל *territory* Jos 17_{14}, חֵלֶק *portion* Jos 14_{4} 15_{13} Ec 2_{21} 11_{2} Si 7_{31} (תן חלקם), מָנָה *portion* 1 S $1_{4.5}$ $9_{23.23}$ Est 2_{9} 2 C 31_{19}, מְנָת *portion*

Ne 12$_{47}$ 2 C 31$_{4}$, גּוֹרָל *lot* Jos 17$_{14}$, מַתָּן *gift* Gn 34$_{12}$ Si 7$_{33}$, מַתָּנָה *gift* Gn 25$_{6}$ Ezk 46$_{16.17}$ 2 C 21$_{3}$ Si 3$_{17(A)}$, מַתַּת *gift* 1 K 13$_{7}$, מַשְׂאֵת *gift* Jr 40$_{5}$ Est 2$_{18}$, נֵדֶה *gift* Ezk 16$_{33}$, נָדָן *gift* Exk 16$_{33}$, שִׁלּוּחִים *parting gift* Mc 1$_{14}$, מֶכֶס *tribute* Nm 31$_{41}$.

מֹהַר *bride-gift* Gn 34$_{12}$, מֶכֶר *price* Nm 20$_{19}$, כֹּפֶר *ransom* Ex 30$_{12}$ Ps 48$_{8}$ 11QT 39$_{8}$ ([ונתן כופר]), פְּדוּת *ransom* 4QRP^{c} 6a.2$_{6}$ ([פ]דות), פִּדְיוֹן *ransom* Ex 21$_{30}$, גְּאֻלָּה *redemption* Lv 25$_{24}$, עֵרָבוֹן *pledge* Gn 38$_{17.18}$, עֵרֶךְ *(amount of) valuation* Lv 27$_{23}$ Jg 17$_{10}$, אֶתְנַן *fee* Ezk 16$_{34.41}$ Ho 2$_{14}$, מִחְיָה *livelihood* Jg 17$_{10}$, שָׂכָר *hire, reward* Gn 30$_{18.28}$ Ex 2$_{9}$ Dt 24$_{15}$ 1 K 5$_{20}$ Jon 1$_{3}$ Si 51$_{22.30}$ CD 14$_{13}$, פֹּעַל *wages* Jr 22$_{13}$, פְּעֻלָּה *recompense* Is 61$_{8}$ Si 36$_{21}$, יְגִיעַ *product of labour* 4QapLam^{b} 1$_{1}$, עִזָּבוֹן *wares* Ezk 27$_{12.14}$ (or em. בְּעִזְבוֹנַיִךְ *in exchange for your wares*) 27$_{22}$, מַעֲרָב *merchandise* Ezk 27$_{13.17}$ (or em. both to בְּמַעֲרָבֵךְ *in exchange for your merchandise*).

תְּרוּמָה *offering* Ex 30$_{13.14.15}$ Nm 18$_{8.11.19.24.28}$ 2 C 31$_{14}$, קָרְבָּן *offering* Nm 7$_{5}$, זֶבַח *sacrifice* Ex 10$_{25}$ Ps 51$_{18}$ Ec 4$_{17}$, עֹלָה *burnt offering* Ex 10$_{25}$ 2 C 35$_{12}$, אָשָׁם *guilt offering* Lv 5$_{16}$, חַטָּאת *sin offering* Lv 10$_{17}$, נְדָבָה *freewill offering* Lv 23$_{38}$, מִנְחָה *grain offering* Lv 6$_{10}$, *tribute* 2 C 17$_{5}$ 26$_{8}$, אִשֶּׁה *fire offering* Lv 22$_{22}$, מִשְׁחָה *consecrated portion* Lv 7$_{36}$.

אֹמֶר *word* Gn 49$_{21}$ (or em אִמְרֵי־ *words of* to אֲמִרֵי־ *branches of* or *antlers of* beauty) Ps 68$_{12}$, דָּבָר *word* 4QapPent 9$_{4}$, מִלָּה *word* 4QTanḥ 16$_{3}$, הָגוּ *meditation* 4Q417 2.1$_{17}$, סֵפֶר *document* 2 K 22$_{8.10}$||2 C 34$_{15.18}$ Is 29$_{11}$ Jr 3$_{8}$ 32$_{12.16}$, מְגִלָּה *scroll* Jr 36$_{32}$ Ezk 3$_{3}$, פַּרְשֶׁגֶן *copy* Ezr 7$_{11}$, פַּתְשֶׁגֶן *copy* Est 4$_{8}$, אִגֶּרֶת *letter* Ne 2$_{7.9}$, מִכְתָּב *letter* Arad ost. 40$_{10}$ ([המכתבים]) 40$_{12}$, מַעֲנֶה *reply* 1QH 10$_{7}$, שֶׁמֶשׁ *sun* Jr 31$_{35}$, פִּתְחוֹן *opening* of mouth Ezk 29$_{21}$, כּוֹכָב *star* Jr 31$_{35}$, יוֹם *day* Ezk 4$_{6}$ Ec 8$_{15}$, שָׁנָה *year* Ezk 4$_{5}$ Pr 5$_{9}$, זְמָן *time* Ne 2$_{6}$.

מִשְׁקָל *weight* 1 C 21$_{25}$, שֶׁקֶל *shekel* 2 K 15$_{20}$ 1 C 21$_{25}$, דַּרְכְּמֹן *daric* Ezr 2$_{69}$||Ne 7$_{70}$ Ne 7$_{69.71}$ 1 C 29$_{7}$, כִּכָּר *talent* 1 K 10$_{10}$||2 C 9$_{9}$ 2 K 5$_{22.23}$ 15$_{19}$ 1 C 29$_{7}$ 2 C 25$_{9}$ 27$_{5}$, *loaf* Jr 37$_{21}$, מָנֶה *mina* Ezr 2$_{69}$||Ne 7$_{70}$ Ne 7$_{71}$, כֹּר *cor* 1 K 5$_{25}$ 2 C 2$_{9}$ 27$_{5}$, בַּת *bath* 2 C 2$_{9}$ Arad ost. 1$_{2}$ 2$_{1}$ 3$_{2}$ 4$_{3}$ 7$_{2}$ 10$_{2}$ ([נתן]) 11$_{2}$ (all seven abbreviated ב), קְשִׂיטָה *kesitah* Jb 42$_{11}$.

רֹב *abundance* Gn 27$_{28}$, מִסָּה *sufficiency* Dt 16$_{10}$, מְלֹא *fullness* Nm 22$_{18}$ 24$_{13}$, רֹחַב *broadness* 1 K 5$_{9}$, אֹרֶךְ *length* of days Ps 21$_{5}$, תָּוֶךְ *middle* Dt 3$_{16}$, חֲצִי *half* Dt 3$_{12}$ 1 K 3$_{25}$ 13$_{8}$, מַחֲצִית *half* Ex 30$_{13.15}$ 11QT 39$_{10}$ ([ונתנו מחצית]), רֶבַע *quarter* of shekel 1 S 9$_{8}$, חֲמִישִׁית *fifth* Gn 47$_{24}$ Nm 5$_{7}$, מַעֲשֵׂר *tithe* Gn 14$_{20}$ Nm 18$_{21.26}$ Dt 14$_{25}$ 26$_{12}$ 11QT 58$_{12}$, אֶחָד *one* Nm 31$_{30.47}$ 11QT 58$_{12}$ 4QTNaph 1$_{2}$, אֶלֶף *thousand* 1 S 18$_{8}$, רְבָבָה *ten thousand* 1 S 18$_{8}$, תֹּכֶן *quota* Ex 5$_{18}$, מִסְפָּר *number* 2 S 24$_{9}$||1 C 21$_{5}$ Ec 5$_{17}$, עֹמֶדֶת perh. *one standing*, i.e. remnant 4QapJoseph^{b} 1$_{7}$, יֶתֶר *remainder* Dt 3$_{13}$, שׁאר ni. ptc. *one who remains* Jr 21$_{7}$, שְׁאֵרִית *remnant* 2 K 21$_{14}$ Jr 15$_{9}$ 40$_{11}$, פְּלֵיטָה *remnant* Ezr 9$_{13}$, מצא ni. ptc. *that which is found* 1 S 21$_{4}$, אָחֻז *selection* Nm 31$_{30.47}$ (or del. אָחֻז in both), חֹסֶר *lack* Am 4$_{6}$, רֵישׁ *poverty* Pr 30$_{8}$.

כֹּל *all* Gn 9$_{3}$ 24$_{36}$ 25$_{5}$ 28$_{22}$ Lv 5$_{24}$ 2 S 9$_{9}$ 24$_{23}$ Jb 2$_{4}$ 1 C 21$_{23}$ 2 C 36$_{17}$ Si 15$_{17(B)}$ (unless qal pass.) 4QParGenEx 2$_{13}$ ([הכו]ל) Arad ost. 40$_{8}$ ([כל] ... [נתן]), מְאוּמָה *anything* Gn 30$_{31}$ Lachish ost. 3$_{12}$ ([ל]א אתן בה וכל מאומ[ה]) *I will not pay any attention to it at all*; others אתננהו אל מאומ[ה] *I can repeat it [with respect] to anything*, i.e. in the smallest detail), אֲשֶׁר *that which, one who* Gn 34$_{11}$ Nm 5$_{10}$ Dt 15$_{14}$ Jg 16$_{24}$ 1 S 25$_{8}$ 30$_{23}$ 2 S 4$_{10}$ 1 K 3$_{13}$ 10$_{13}$||2 C 9$_{12}$ Ezk 2$_{8}$ 33$_{27}$ Mc 6$_{14}$ Ru 2$_{18}$, -שֶׁ *that which* Si 30$_{28}$, זֶה *this* Gn 29$_{33}$ Ex 30$_{13}$, זֹאת *this* (fem.) Gn 29$_{27}$, מָה *what?* Gn 15$_{2}$ 30$_{31}$ 38$_{16}$ 1 K 3$_{5}$||2 C 1$_{7}$ Ho 9$_{14}$ Ps 120$_{3}$ Jb 35$_{7}$ Si 37$_{27}$.

With second object, give something (1) *(as a)* שִׁפְחָה *female servant* Gn 29$_{24}$, מַאֲכָל *food* Is 62$_{8}$ Ps 74$_{14}$ 79$_{2}$, טֶרֶף *prey* Ps 124$_{6}$, מַתָּנָה *gift* Nm 18$_{7}$, נַחֲלָה *inheritance* Dt 4$_{21.38}$ 15$_{4}$ 19$_{10}$ 20$_{16}$=11QT 62$_{13}$ Dt 21$_{23}$=11QT 64$_{13}$ Dt 24$_{4}$ 25$_{19}$ 26$_{1}$ 11$_{23}$ Jos 17$_{14}$ Ps 135$_{12}$, אֲחֻזָּה *possession* Gn 48$_{4}$, יְרֻשָּׁה *possession* Dt 2$_{5.9.9.19.19}$ Jos 12$_{6.7}$, מוֹרָשָׁה *possession* Ex 6$_{8}$, חֶבֶל *allotted portion* Ps 105$_{11}$||1 C 16$_{18}$, חֵלֶק *portion* Lv 6$_{10}$, שִׁלֻּחִים *dowry* 1 K 9$_{16}$, תְּרוּמָה *offering* Lv 7$_{32}$ Nm 15$_{21}$, פְּעֻלָּה *recompense* Ezk 29$_{20}$, כֹּפֶר *ransom* Is 43$_{3}$ 4QOrd^{a} 1.2$_{6}$, פְּדוּיִם perh. *ransom* Nm 3$_{48}$, קֹדֶשׁ *holiness*, i.e. holy thing Lv 27$_{23}$, מוֹרָא *fear* Ml 2$_{5}$.

(2) *for* פֶּשַׁע *transgression* Mc 6$_{7}$, חַטָּאת *sin* Mc 6$_{7}$.

<PREP> לְ in ref. to subj., + Aaron Ex 7$_{9}$, Moses Ex 7$_{9}$, בַּת *daughter* of Zion Lm 2$_{18}$.

לְ of direction, *to* Is 50$_{4}$ Pr 23$_{26}$ Ec 5$_{17}$ 9$_{9}$ Si 45$_{26}$ 51$_{30}$

1QSb 3_5 5_{25} ([לכה]) 4Q183 1.2_4 4QTNaph $1_{2.10}$ 4QpsJub^{b} 1_4 ([נ]תתי) 4_3 ([נת]תי) 4QTohB^{a} 1_6 ([לת]ת) 4QMishC^{a} 2_1 ([ל]תת) 4QapPent 9_4 (ל[כמ]ה) 4QapJoseph^{b} 2_5 ([נ]תן) 2_7 4QapPs^{b} 69_4 4QpsMos^{d} 4_2 4Q418 81_6 4Q423 2_3 4QBark^{a} 1.2_{10} 4QBark^{c} 1.2_4 4QPatr 7_3 4Q474 1_7 4QSap^{b} 8_2 4QDibHam^{a} 18_2 4QDibHam^{c} 131_5 (both [נ]תתה) 131_8 ([נת]תה) 4QPrFêtes^{b} 40_1 4QBéat 1_1 13_2 (לה[ם]) Arad ost. 40_8 ([נתן ל]הם) Kuntillet ʿAjrud add. inscr. 2.

+ Y. Ex $22_{28.29}$ $30_{12.13}$ Lv 22_{22} 23_{38} 27_9 Nm 15_{21} 18_{12} Jos 7_{19} 1 S 1_{11} 6_5 Is 62_7 Jr 13_{16} Ps 49_8 68_{35} Jb 35_7 Ezr 10_{11} 1 C 29_{14} 2 C 30_8 Si 32_{12} 47_8 1QH 4_{20} 11QT 39_8 ([ונתן]) 39_{10} ([ונתנו]), Molech Lv $20_{2.3.4}$, גִּלּוּל *idol* Ezk 6_{13} 16_{36}, פֶּסֶל *image* Is 42_8, מַלְאָךְ *angel* 4QPseud^{a} 1_3.

Agagite Est 3_{10}, Aram 2 K 5_1, Benjamin(ites) Jg 20_{36} $21_{1.14.18.18.22}$ 1 S 22_7, Edom(ites) Ezk 36_5, Egyptians Gn $47_{16.17}$, Gad(ites) Dt $3_{12.16.18.19.20}$ 29_7 Jos $1_{13.14.15}$ 12_6 $13_{8.8}$ 18_7 22_4, Ephraim Ho $9_{14.14}$ Si 47_{23}, Hebrew Dt 15_{14}, Israel(ites) Ex 6_4 12_{25} 20_{12}||Dt 5_{16} Dt $1_{20.25}$ $2_{5.12.19.29}$ 3_{20} $4_{1.21.38.40}$ 5_{31} $6_{10.23}$ $7_{13.16}$ $8_{10.18}$ $9_{6.23}$ $11_{17.31}$ $12_{1.9.15.21}$ 13_2=Dt 5_{48} Dt $13_{13.18}$=11QT $55_{2.11}$ Dt $15_{4.7}$ $16_{5.17.18.20}$ 17_2=11QT 55_{16} Dt 17_{14}=11QT 56_{12} Dt 18_9=11QT 60_{16} Dt $19_{1.2.8.10.14}$ $20_{14.16}$=11QT $62_{11.13}$ Dt $21_{1.23}$=11QT 64_{13} Dt 24_4 $25_{15.19}$ 26_{1+6t} $27_{2.3}$ $28_{7.11.52.53.65}$ 29_3 Jos 1_3 $2_{9.14}$ 5_6 9_{24} 11_{23} 21_{43} $23_{13.15.16}$ 24_{13} Jg 6_{13} 1 S 8_6 1 K 8_{56} 9_7||2 C 7_{20} 2 K 13_5 Jr 3_{15} 7_{14} 8_{13} 17_4 $32_{22.39}$ Ezk $20_{11.12}$ Ho $13_{10.11}$ Am 9_{15} Ps 78_{24} 105_{11}||1 C 16_{18} Ps 135_{12} Ezr $9_{9.9}$ Si 50_{23} 1QDM 2_2 ([ל]תת) 2_{10} ([ל]תת) 4QJub^{a} 1_{13} ([ונת]תי) 4QRP^{c} 23_5 4QConfess $2_{7.8}$ 11QM 1.2_9 11QT 51_{16} 53_3 61_{02} ([נתתי לכה]), Jerusalem Is 41_{27} Ezk $16_{17.19.61}$, Jezreelite 1 K 21_6, Judah Jr 40_{11}, Kenizzite Jos 14_{12}, Kittim Arad ost. 1_2 $2_{1.7}$ $4_{1.3}$ 7_2 8_1 (לכת[י]ם) 10_2 ([נתן לכת]ים) 11_2 14_2 ([נתן ל]כתים), Kerosite Arad ost. 18_6, Moab Jr 48_9, Philistine 1 S 17_{10}, Reuben(ites) Dt $3_{12.16.18.19.20}$ 29_7 Jos $1_{13.14.15}$ 12_6 $13_{8.8}$ 18_7 22_4, Sidonians Ezr 3_7, Tyrians Ezr 3_7.

עַם *people* Ex $5_{7.10}$ $13_{5.11}$ 17_2 Nm $11_{13.13.18.21}$ 21_{16} Dt 10_{11} 31_7 Jos $1_{2.11}$ 6_{16} Jg 8_5 1 K 8_{36}||2 C 6_{27} 1 K 8_{56} 18_{23} 19_{21} 2 K $4_{42.43}$ Is 30_{20} 42_5 Jr 7_7 14_{13} 16_{13} 25_5 32_{22} 39_{10} 42_{12} Am 9_{15} Ps 29_{11} 68_{36} 74_{14} (or em. לְעָם לְצִיִּים *to the people to the desert dwellers* to לְעַמְלְצֵי יָם *to the sharks of the sea*) 111_6 135_{12} Ru 1_6 Ne 10_{31} 2 C 6_{25} 4QpsEzek^{a} 2_1, גּוֹי *nation* Si 49_5 4QapJoseph^{b} 3_8, מַטֶּה *tribe* Nm 34_{13} Jos $13_{15.24}$, שֵׁבֶט *tribe* Jos 12_7 $13_{14.33}$, מִשְׁפָּחָה *clan* Jos 21_{21}||1 C 6_{52}, בַּיִת *house* Dt 26_{11} Is 7_{14} Jr 3_{19} Ezk $11_{17.19.19}$ $20_{15.28}$ $36_{26.26}$ 45_8 Pr 31_{15} 1 C 29_3 2 C 35_{12}, עֵדָה *assembly* Nm 14_8 16_{14}, גּוֹלָה *exiles* Jr 29_{11}, גָּלוּת *exiles* Jr 24_7, צָבָא *army* Jg 8_6, גְּדוּד *troop* 2 C 25_9, שְׁאֵרִית *remnant* Jr 24_{10} Ezk 36_5, יתר ni. ptc. *one remaining* Jg 21_7.

Aaron Lv $7_{34.36}$ Nm $3_{9.48.51}$ $18_{8.8.11.12.19.28}$ Ps 99_7 Si $45_{7(Bmg).17.20.20}$, Abimelech Gn 21_{27}, Abra(ha)m Gn $13_{15.17}$ $15_{2.3.7}$ 16_3 $17_{8.16}$ 20_{14} 23_{4+5t} 28_4 35_{12} Ex 6_8 Dt 1_8 30_{20} Jos 24_3 Mc 7_{20} Ps 105_{11} 4QCommGenA 2_8, Achsah Jos $15_{19.19.19}$||Jg $1_{15.15}$, Adonijah 1 K 2_{17}, Ahab 1 K $21_{2.3.6.6.7.15}$, Amaziah 2 C 25_9, Azariah Dn 1_{16}, Balaam Nm 22_{18} 24_{13}, Ben-hadad 1 K 20_5, Ben Sira Si 51_{22}, Boaz Ru 4_{12}, Cain Gn 4_{12}, Caleb Dt 1_{36} Jos $14_{12.13}$ 21_{12}||1 C 6_{41} Jg 1_{20} Si 46_9, Cyrus Is 45_3 Ezr 1_2 2 C 36_{23}, Daniel Dn 1_{16}, David 1 S 18_{4+5t} $21_{7.10}$ 25_8 $27_{5.6}$ 28_{17} 30_{23} 2 S $12_{8.8}$ $22_{36.48}$||Ps $18_{36.48}$ 1 K 3_6 5_{21}||2 C 2_{11} 1 K 15_4 2 K 8_{19}||2 C 21_7 1 C $21_{22.22}$ 28_5 2 C 13_5 Si 47_{11} 11QPs^{a} 27_3, Eleazar Lv 10_{17} Nm 31_{41}, Elijah 1 K 17_{19} 18_{23}, Esau Gn 25_{34} Dt 2_5 Jos 24_4, Esther Est $8_{1.7}$, Ezekiel Ezk 4_{15}, Ezra Ezr $7_{6.11}$, Gabriah Arad ost. 60_4 ([לגב]ריהו), Gideon Jg 8_{24}, Gog Ezk 39_{11}.

Hadad 1 K $11_{18.19}$, Haman Est 3_{10}, Hamor, *et al.* Gn $34_{9.16}$, Hannah 1 S 1_5, Hananiah Dn 1_{16}, Hathach Est 4_8, Heman 1 C 25_5, Hezekiah 2 K 18_{23}||Is 36_8 2 C $32_{24.29}$, Hiram 1 K $5_{20.25.25}$ $9_{11.12.13}$, Isaac Gn 25_5 26_3 35_{12} Ex 6_8 Dt 1_8 30_{20} Jos 24_4 Ps 105_{11}, Isaiah Is 8_{18}, Ithamar Lv 10_{17}, Jacob/Israel Gn 27_{37} $28_{4.13.20.22}$ $29_{19.27.28}$ $30_{4.9.31.31}$ 31_9 35_{12} Ex 6_8 Dt 1_8 30_{20} Ezk 28_{25} 37_{25} Mc 7_{20} Ps 105_{11} Si 44_{23} 4QJub^{h} 36_{14} ([ואתן ... ליעקוב]), Jarha 1 C 2_{35}, Jehoshaphat 2 C 17_5, Jeremiah Jr 37_{21} 40_5, Jeroboam 1 K $11_{31.35.38}$ 14_8, Jeshua (son of Galgula) Mur EpBarC^{b} 1_9, Johanan Jr 42_{12}, Joseph Gn 41_{45} $48_{9.22}$ 4QJub^{h} 40_5 ([ליוסף]), Joshua (son of Nun) Jos $19_{49.50}$, Joshua (priest) Zc 3_7, Jotham 2 C 27_5.

Kusanal ([לקו]סענל), Leah Gn $29_{24.33}$ 46_{18}, Levi Ml 2_5, Machir Nm 32_{40} Dt 3_{15}, Melchizedek Gn 14_{20}, Mishael Dn 1_{16}, Mordecai Est 8_2, Moses Ex 2_{21} 32_{24} Ps 99_7, Naboth 1 K $21_{2.2.6}$, Nebuchadnezzar/Nebuchadrezzer Jr 27_6 28_{14} Ezk $29_{19.20}$, Neco 2 K 23_{35}, Nehemiah Ne $2_{7.8.8}$, Noah Gn 9_3, Ornan 1 C 21_{25}, Othniel Jos 15_{17}||Jg 1_{13}, Palti 1 S 25_{44}, Peninnah 1 S 1_4,

Phinehas Nm 25$_{12}$, Pul 2 K 15$_{19}$, Rachel Gn 29$_{29}$ 30$_{6.9}$ 46$_{25}$, Rahab Jos 2$_{12}$, Rebekah 4QJub^{g} 25$_{12}$, Ruth Ru 3$_{17}$ 4$_{13}$, Samson Jg 14$_{13}$, Samuel Ps 99$_{7}$, Saul 1 S 9$_{22}$ 10$_{4}$ 18$_{8}$, Shaphan 2 K 22$_{10}$||2 C 34$_{18}$, Shechem Gn 34$_{8.16}$, Shelah Gn 38$_{26}$, Shemariah Arad st. 18$_{4}$, Solomon 1 K 3$_{5}$||2 C 1$_{7}$ 1 K 3$_{12.13}$ 5$_{9.24.26}$ 1 K 10$_{10}$||2 C 9$_{9}$ 1 C 28$_{11}$ 29$_{19}$ 2 C 1$_{10}$ 8$_{2}$, Tamar Gn 38$_{16.18.18}$, Uzziah 2 C 26$_{8}$.

אָדָם *human being* Gn 1$_{29}$ 3$_{12}$ Ec 2$_{21.26}$ 5$_{18}$ 8$_{15}$ Si 15$_{17(B)}$ (unless qal pass.) 4QCreatC 2$_{2}$ GnzPs 4$_{21}$, אֱנוֹשׁ *person* Si 38$_{6}$, אִישׁ *man, husband* Gn 3$_{6}$ 16$_{3}$ 29$_{19}$ 30$_{18}$ 34$_{14.21}$ 43$_{23}$ Ex 22$_{16}$ Dt 22$_{16}$=11QT 65$_{11}$ Jg 8$_{15}$ 17$_{10}$ 1 S 9$_{8}$ 17$_{25}$ 25$_{11}$ 30$_{11.12.22}$ 2 S 18$_{11}$ 1 K 8$_{39}$||2 C 6$_{30}$ 1 K 13$_{7.7}$ Jr 17$_{10}$ 29$_{6}$ 32$_{19}$ 35$_{15}$ Ezk 46$_{16}$ Zc 10$_{1}$ Ec 6$_{2}$ 4QD^{e} 5$_{14}$ (]יתן[), i.e. each Gn 45$_{22}$ Jr 35$_{15}$ Ezk 11$_{17.19}$, בַּעַל *husband* Est 1$_{20}$, זָכָר *male* Si 42$_{12(B)}$, אִשָּׁה *woman, wife* Jg 16$_{5}$ 1 S 1$_{4}$ 1 K 9$_{16}$ 2 K 8$_{6}$ Pr 31$_{3.31}$ Si 37$_{19}$, i.e. each Ru 1$_{9}$, לְחֵנָה *secondary wife* Pr 31$_{3}$ (if em. לְמְחוֹת *to wipe out* to לְלְחֵנוֹת *to the secondary wives of*).

אָב *father* Gn 34$_{16}$ 47$_{11}$ Dt 1$_{8.35}$ 11$_{9,21}$ 19$_{8}$ 22$_{19}$=11QT 65$_{15}$ Dt 22$_{29}$=11QT 66$_{10}$ Dt 30$_{20}$ Jos 1$_{6}$ 21$_{43}$ 24$_{3}$ Jg 14$_{9}$ 1 K 3$_{6.26.27}$ 8$_{34.40.48}$||2 C 6$_{25.31.38}$ 1 K 14$_{15}$ 2 K 21$_{8}$ Jr 7$_{14}$ 11$_{5}$ 16$_{15}$ 23$_{39}$ 24$_{10}$ 25$_{5}$ 30$_{3}$ 32$_{22}$ 35$_{15}$ Ezk 20$_{42}$ 36$_{28}$ 47$_{14}$ Ps 105$_{44}$ Ne 9$_{13.15.15.20.22.27.35.36}$, אֵם *mother* Gn 24$_{53}$ Jg 14$_{9}$ 1 K 17$_{23}$ Ho 2$_{10.14.17}$, חָמוֹת *mother-in-law* Ru 2$_{18}$, בֵּן *son* Gn 9$_{3}$ 24$_{36}$ 25$_{6}$ 27$_{28}$ 34$_{8}$ 38$_{26}$ 45$_{21.21}$ Lv 7$_{34.36}$ 10$_{17}$ Nm 3$_{9.48.51}$ 7$_{7.8.9}$ 18$_{8.11.19.21}$ 25$_{12}$ 32$_{29.33.40}$ Dt 1$_{36.39}$ 2$_{9.19}$ 7$_{3}$ 21$_{17}$ Jos 13$_{24}$ 14$_{12.13}$ 15$_{17}$||Jg 1$_{13}$ Jos 17$_{14}$ 19$_{49.50}$ 21$_{12.13}$|| 1 C 6$_{41.42}$ Jg 3$_{6}$ 1 S 1$_{4}$ 22$_{10.10.13}$ 25$_{8.44}$ 2 S 9$_{9}$ 1 K 2$_{17}$ 11$_{13.36}$ 2 K 14$_{9}$||2 C 25$_{18}$ Jr 42$_{12}$ Ezk 20$_{25}$ 25$_{4.10}$ 44$_{28}$ Ps 72$_{1}$ 115$_{16}$ 147$_{9}$ Pr 4$_{2}$ Ec 3$_{10}$ Est 3$_{10}$ Ezr 9$_{12}$ Ne 13$_{25}$ 1 C 6$_{40}$ 22$_{12}$ 28$_{11}$ 29$_{19}$ 2 C 11$_{23}$ 13$_{5}$ 21$_{3}$ Si 10$_{28(A)}$ 1QH 18$_{27}$ CD 13$_{14}$ 4QapLam^{b} 1$_{1}$ MurEpBarC^{b} 1$_{9}$ MurEpJonathan 1$_{3}$, of man, in ref. to Ezekiel Ezk 4$_{5.6}$ 29$_{21}$, of Israel Ex 6$_{8}$ 16$_{8.15.29}$ Lv 17$_{11}$ 20$_{24}$ 23$_{10}$ 25$_{2.38}$ Nm 10$_{29}$ 13$_{2}$ 15$_{2}$ 20$_{12.24}$ 27$_{12}$ 32$_{7.9}$ 33$_{53}$ 36$_{2}$ Dt 32$_{49.52}$ Jos 1$_{2}$ 18$_{3}$ Jg 6$_{9}$ 2QJub^{b} 46$_{2}$ ([לבני]), בַּת *daughter* Gn 29$_{24.29}$ 46$_{22.25}$ Nm 18$_{11.19}$ 27$_{4.7}$ 36$_{2}$ Jos 15$_{19.19.19}$||Jg 1$_{15.15}$ Jos 17$_{4.4}$ 1 S 1$_{4}$ 1 K 9$_{16}$, כַּלָּה *daughter-in-law* Ru 1$_{9}$, אָח *brother* Gn 20$_{16}$ 24$_{53}$ 38$_{9}$ 42$_{25.33}$ 43$_{14}$ 45$_{18}$ 47$_{11}$ Nm 27$_{9.10}$ Dt 3$_{20}$ 15$_{9.10.10.14}$ Jos 1$_{15}$ 15$_{14}$ 1 S 30$_{23}$ Ezk 11$_{17.19}$ 2 C 31$_{15}$ Si 7$_{16}$.

טַף *infant* Dt 1$_{39}$, יֶלֶד *child* Dn 1$_{17}$, בְּכוֹר *firstborn* Dt 21$_{17}$, נַעַר *lad* 1 S 9$_{22}$ 2 K 5$_{22}$ Pr 1$_{4}$, נַעֲרָה *young woman* Pr 31$_{15}$ Est 2$_{9.9}$, עֶבֶד *servant* Gn 24$_{41}$ Ex 21$_{4}$ 1 S 8$_{14.15}$ 25$_{8}$ 1 K 3$_{6.9}$ 11$_{11}$ 2 K 8$_{19}$ Jr 27$_{6}$ Ezk 28$_{25}$ 37$_{25}$ Ps 86$_{16}$ Dn 1$_{12}$ 1 C 2$_{35}$ 2 C 2$_{9}$ 1QH 19$_{27}$ GnzPs 1$_{6}$, אָמָה *female servant* 1 S 1$_{11}$, סָרִיס *eunuch* 1 S 8$_{15}$ Is 56$_{5.5}$, טַבָּח *cook* 1 S 9$_{23}$.

מֶלֶךְ *king* Gn 14$_{20.21}$ 1 S 2$_{10}$ 2 S 24$_{23}$ 1 K 10$_{10.10}$||2 C 9$_{9.9}$ 2 K 15$_{20}$ 18$_{16}$ Jr 27$_{6}$ 28$_{14}$ 29$_{19.20}$ Ps 21$_{3.5}$ 72$_{1.15}$ (or em. qal pass.) 144$_{10}$ Dn 11$_{17}$ Ezr 1$_{2}$ Ne 2$_{1.6}$ 2 C 2$_{11}$ 12$_{7}$ 28$_{21}$ 1QM 12$_{7}$ ([נ]תנו) 11QT 58$_{12}$, מַלְכָּה *queen* 1 K 10$_{13}$|| 2 C 9$_{12}$ Est 8$_{1}$, פַּרְעֹה *Pharaoh* Gn 47$_{24}$ 2 K 23$_{35.35}$, אָדוֹן *lord* Gn 24$_{35}$ Ex 21$_{32}$ Arad ost. 40$_{12}$, שַׂר *commander* 2 K 11$_{10}$||2 C 23$_{9}$ Jr 42$_{12}$ 2 C 12$_{7}$, אֲחַשְׁדַּרְפַּן *satrap* Ezr 8$_{36}$, פֶּחָה *governor* Ezr 8$_{36}$ Ne 2$_{9}$, גִּבּוֹר *mighty one* 1QM 12$_{7}$ ([נ]תנו), חָזָק *strong one* 4QMyst^{a} 6.1$_{15}$, סֹפֵר *secretary* 2 K 22$_{10}$ Ezr 7$_{11}$.

כֹּהֵן *priest* Gn 47$_{22}$ Lv 5$_{16}$ 7$_{34}$ 22$_{14}$ Nm 5$_{10}$ 18$_{28}$ 31$_{41}$ Dt 18$_{3.4}$ Ezk 44$_{28.30}$ Ezr 7$_{11}$ 2 C 35$_{8}$ 11QT 22$_{11}$ 58$_{12}$, לֵוִי *Levite* Nm 18$_{21.26}$ 31$_{30.47}$ 35$_{2.2.4.6.7.8.14}$ Dt 26$_{12.13}$ Jos 14$_{3.4}$ 21$_{2.3.8}$||1 C 6$_{49}$ Jos 21$_{11}$ Ezk 44$_{28}$ 11QT 22$_{11}$ 58$_{12}$, נָבִיא *prophet* 1 K 18$_{26}$, worshipper Ps 20$_{5}$ 85$_{8}$ 115$_{1}$ 4QapPs^{b} 19.1$_{4}$ 11QPs^{a} 24$_{4.14}$, ירא ptc. *one who fears* Ps 60$_{6}$ 111$_{5}$, מְלַמֵּד *teacher* Si 51$_{17}$, חָכָם *wise one* Pr 9$_{9}$ 4QBark^{c} 1.1$_{2}$, כבד pi. ptc. *one who glorifies* 4Q416 2.3$_{10}$, צַדִּיק *righteous one* 1 K 8$_{32}$||2 C 6$_{23}$ Ps 55$_{23}$, טוֹב *good one* Ec 2$_{26}$ Si 12$_{4}$.

יֹשֵׁב *inhabitant* Jr 24$_{10}$ 35$_{15}$, גֵּר *sojourner* Dt 10$_{18}$ 14$_{21}$ 26$_{12.13}$, רֵעַ *neighbour* 1 S 15$_{28}$ 28$_{17}$ 2 S 12$_{11}$ Jr 22$_{13}$ Ru 4$_{7}$, רְעוּת *fellow* (fem.) Est 1$_{19}$, מֵרֵעַ *friend* Jg 14$_{12}$ 15$_{2.6}$, אֹהֵב *friend* Si 14$_{13}$ 4QCommGenA 2$_{8}$, מְאַהֵב *lover* Ezk 16$_{33}$, male lover Ca 7$_{13}$, יָדִיד *beloved one* Ps 127$_{2}$, הרה ptc. *one who conceives* Ho 2$_{10.14.17}$, דבר ptc. *one who speaks* Ps 28$_{4.4}$, נגד hi. ptc. *one who tells* Jg 14$_{19}$ 2 S 4$_{10}$, נטר ptc. *one who keeps* Ca 8$_{11}$, הלך ptc. *one who walks* Is 42$_{5}$, עשׂה ptc. *one who does* 2 K 12$_{15}$ 22$_{5}$ 2 C 24$_{12}$, פעל ptc. *one who does* Ps 28$_{4.4}$, *maker* Jb 36$_{3}$, בֹּנֶה *builder* 2 C 34$_{11}$, צֹרֵף *smith* Jg 17$_{4}$, חָרָשׁ *artisan* 2 C 34$_{11}$, חֹטֵב *hewer* 2 C 2$_{9}$, כרת ptc. *one who cuts* 2 C 2$_{9}$, עָשִׁיר *rich one* Pr 22$_{16}$, כְּנַעֲנִי *merchant* Pr 31$_{24}$, זֹרֵעַ *sower* Is 55$_{10}$.

זָר *stranger* 4QapLam^{b} 1$_{1}$, אַלְמָנָה *widow* Dt 26$_{12.13}$, יָתוֹם *orphan* Dt 26$_{12.13}$, אֶבְיוֹן *poor one* Dt 15$_{9.10.10}$ Ps 112$_{9}$ Si 32$_{13(Bmg)}$, דַּל *poor one* Pr 22$_{9}$ Si 4$_{5}$ GnzPs 3$_{15}$,

רָשׁ *poor one* Pr 28$_{27}$, עָנִי *needy one* Pr 3$_{34(Kt)}$, עָנָו *humble one* Pr 3$_{34(Qr)}$, רָעֵב *hungry one* Ezk 18$_{7.16}$ Ps 146$_{7}$, מְדֻכְדָּךְ *crushed one* Si 4$_{5}$, עָמֵל *sufferer* Jb 3$_{20}$, מַר *bitter one* Jb 3$_{20}$, אָבֵל *mourner* Is 61$_{3}$, מַר *bitter one* Pr 31$_{6}$, אכל ptc. *one who eats* Is 55$_{10}$, נָמוֹג *trembling one* 1QM 14$_{6}$, יָעֵף *weary one* Is 40$_{29}$, אבד ptc. *one who perishes* Pr 31$_{6}$, מֵת *dead one* Dt 26$_{14}$.

אֹיֵב *enemy* Is 62$_{8}$, צֹרֵר *adversary* Est 3$_{10}$, קום ptc. *one who rises up* Lm 3$_{65}$, בזז ptc. *one who plunders* Is 42$_{24}$, שׁסה po. ptc. *one who despoils* Is 42$_{24(Kt)}$, יוֹרֵשׁ *conqueror* Jr 8$_{10}$, נכה hi. ptc. *one who strikes* Is 50$_{6}$ Lm 3$_{30}$, אַכְזָרִי *cruel one* Pr 5$_{9}$, מחה ptc. *one who wipes out* Pr 31$_{3}$ (if em. לַמְחוֹת *to wipe out* [מחה hi.] to לְמֹחוֹת *to those who wipe out* [qal ptc.]), מרט ptc. *one who pulls out hair* Is 50$_{6}$, רֹצֵחַ *killer* Jos 20$_{4}$, זֹנָה *prostitute* Ezk 16$_{33}$ Si 9$_{6}$, חֹטֵא *sinner* Ec 2$_{26}$, רָשָׁע *wicked one* Ezk 7$_{21}$ Ps 28$_{4.4}$, זֵד *presumptuous one* Si 12$_{5.5}$, פֶּתִי *simple one* Pr 1$_{4}$, כְּסִיל *fool* Pr 26$_{8}$.

עַיִן *eye* Ps 132$_{4}$ Pr 6$_{4}$, עַפְעַף *eyelid* Ps 132$_{4}$ Pr 6$_{4}$, לָשׁוֹן *tongue* Ps 120$_{3}$, שֵׁן *teeth* Ps 124$_{6}$, שְׁכֶם *shoulder* 1QM 14$_{6}$, זֶרַע *offspring* Gn 12$_{7}$ 13$_{15}$ 15$_{18}$ 17$_{8}$ 24$_{7}$ 26$_{3.4}$ 28$_{4.13}$ 35$_{12}$ 48$_{4}$ Ex 32$_{13}$ 33$_{1}$ Dt 1$_{8}$ 11$_{9}$ 34$_{4}$ Ezk 17$_{15}$ Ne 9$_{8}$ 2 C 20$_{7}$ 4QD^{a} 11$_{11}$, בָּשָׂר *flesh* Ps 136$_{25}$, שְׁאֵר *flesh*, i.e. relative Nm 27$_{11}$, נֶפֶשׁ *soul* Pr 29$_{17}$ Si 10$_{28(B)}$ 37$_{27}$, רוּחַ *spirit* 1QH 9$_{15}$ ([ותתנם]) 4Q417 2.1$_{17}$, שֵׁם *name* Ml 2$_{2}$ Ps 115$_{1}$ 4QsapDidA 1$_{8}$, זָכָר *male* 2 C 31$_{19}$.

סוּס *horse* Jb 39$_{19}$, חֲמוֹר *ass* Gn 42$_{27}$ 43$_{24}$, אַרְיֵה *lion* 1 K 13$_{26}$, בְּהֵמָה *beast* 1 S 17$_{44}$ Jr 19$_{7}$ Ps 147$_{9}$, חַיָּה *beast* 1 S 17$_{46}$ Ezk 29$_{5}$ 33$_{27}$ 39$_{4}$ Ps 74$_{19}$ 79$_{2}$, עוֹף *bird* 1 S 17$_{44,46}$ Jr 19$_{7}$ Ezk 29$_{5}$ 79$_{2}$, עַיִט *birds of prey* Ezk 39$_{4}$, שֶׂכְוִי perh. *cock* Jb 38$_{36}$, אַרְבֶּה *locust* Ps 78$_{46}$, חָסִיל *locust* Ps 78$_{46}$, חַי *living thing* 4Q417 1.2$_{3}$ ([לכו]ל חי).

חֶרֶב *sword* Jr 15$_{9}$ 25$_{31}$ Mc 6$_{14}$ 4QpsEzek^{d} 1.2$_{5}$ CD 1$_{4}$, רָעָב *famine* Jr 18$_{21}$, טֶבַח *slaughter* Is 34$_{2}$, כָּלָה *destruction* CD 1$_{5}$, שְׁבִי *captivity* Ps 78$_{61}$, אוֹצָר *treasury* Ezr 2$_{69}$||Ne 7$_{70}$ Ne 7$_{69}$ 1 C 29$_{8}$, אֵשׁ *fire* Ezk 15$_{6}$, מָוֶת *death* Ps 118$_{18}$, דִּין *judgment* Si 30$_{21}$, מִשְׁפָּט *judgment* 2QapDavid 2$_{4}$ 4QJub^{i} 23$_{22}$ ([ויתן]), שִׁבְיָה *captivity* 4QJub^{i} 23$_{22}$ ([ויתן ... לשביה]), שִׁלֻּמָה *retribution* perh. 4QNarrB 1$_{4}$, שָׁוְא *vanity* perh. 4Q185 1.2$_{2}$ (לשא), עֹרֶל *uncircumcision* of lips 1QH 10$_{7}$ ([לער]ול).

אַחֵר *another* Is 42$_{8}$ 48$_{11}$ Jr 8$_{10}$ Ezk 46$_{17}$ Pr 5$_{9}$ Si 30$_{28}$ 51$_{8}$ ([ויתן לאחר]), אָחוֹר *another* Si 49$_{5}$, חֲצִי *half* tribe Nm 32$_{33}$ 34$_{13}$ Dt 3$_{13}$ 29$_{7}$ Jos 1$_{13.14.15}$ 12$_{6}$ 13$_{29}$ 18$_{7}$ 22$_{4}$, אֶחָד *one* Dt 28$_{55}$ 1 K 3$_{25}$, שֶׁבַע *seven* Ec 11$_{2}$, שְׁמֹנָה *eight* Ec 11$_{2}$, כֹּל *all* Gn 45$_{22}$ Ps 104$_{28}$ 145$_{15}$ 2 C 31$_{19}$ 4QPseud^{b} 2$_{2}$ ([כו]ל), אֲשֶׁר *one who* Lv 5$_{24}$ Nm 5$_{7}$ Jos 15$_{16}$||Jg 1$_{12}$ Jr 27$_{5}$ 1QS 11$_{7}$ 4QD^{f} 3$_{9}$ GnzPs 3$_{21}$.

לְ of benefit, *to, for,* + בַּיִת *household* 1 K 5$_{25}$, כֹּהֵן *priest* 1 S 2$_{15}$, גָּמָל *camel* Gn 24$_{32}$, בְּהֵמָה *beast* Dt 11$_{15}$, זֶרַע *seed, offspring* Lv 18$_{20}$, אֶרֶץ *land* Lv 25$_{24}$, מְלָאכָה *work* Ne 7$_{69}$, עֲבֹדָה *service* 1 C 29$_{7}$, פֶּסַח *passover* 2 C 35$_{8}$, יוֹם *day* Arad ost. 2$_{1}$, עֲשִׂירִי *tenth (month)* Arad ost. 7$_{2}$.

לְ *for (a period of),* + יוֹם *day* Jr 37$_{21}$; *to, throughout,* + דּוֹר *generation* Nm 15$_{21}$, עוֹלָם *everlastingness*, i.e. for ever 2 C 13$_{5}$ 20$_{7}$.

לְ *as, for (the purpose of)* (distinction from §5a not alw. clear), + אִשָּׁה *wife* Gn 16$_{3}$ 29$_{28}$ 30$_{4.9}$ 34$_{8}$ 41$_{45}$ Dt 22$_{16}$ Jos 15$_{16.17}$||Jg 1$_{12.13}$ Jg 21$_{1.7}$ 1 S 18$_{17.27}$ 1 K 2$_{17}$ 2 K 14$_{9}$|| 2 C 25$_{18}$ 1 C 2$_{35}$, בַּת *daughter* Ezk 16$_{61}$, עֶבֶד *servant* Gn 27$_{37}$, שִׁפְחָה *female servant* Gn 29$_{29}$, עֹלָה *burnt offering* 1 C 21$_{23}$, מִנְחָה *grain offering* 1 C 21$_{23}$, חַטָּאת *sin offering* Ezk 43$_{19}$, אָכְלָה *food, fuel* Ezk 15$_{6}$ 29$_{5}$ 39$_{4}$ 4QJub^{i} 23$_{22}$ ([ויתן]), מַאֲכָל *food* Jr 19$_{7}$, עֵץ *wood* 1 C 21$_{23}$, חֹק *statute* Lv 7$_{34}$ Nm 18$_{8.11.19}$, נַחֲלָה *inheritance* Nm 18$_{21.24}$ Dt 29$_{7}$ Jos 14$_{13}$ 1 K 8$_{36}$||2 C 6$_{27}$ Ps 136$_{21}$ 4QRP^{c} 23$_{5}$, אֲחֻזָּה *possession* Gn 17$_{8}$ 23$_{9}$ Lv 14$_{34}$ Nm 32$_{29}$ Dt 32$_{49}$ 1QS 11$_{7}$, מוֹרָשָׁה *possession* Ezk 25$_{4.10}$ 36$_{5}$, חֹק *statute*, i.e. fixed allowance Si 45$_{20}$, בַּז *plunder* Jr 15$_{13}$ 17$_{3}$ Ezk 7$_{21}$ 4QJub^{i} 23$_{22}$ ([ויתן]), שָׁלָל *spoil* Jr 45$_{5}$ Ezk 7$_{21}$, בֶּדֶק *(repair of) breach* 2 K 12$_{8}$, מֶמְשָׁלָה *rule* 1QH 9$_{15}$ ([ותתנם לממשלה]), אוֹר *light* Jr 31$_{35}$, שָׁנָה *year* Ezk 4$_{6}$, צְדָקָה *righteousness* Jl 2$_{23}$.

לְ *according to,* + שֵׁבֶט *tribe* Ezk 45$_{8}$, מִשְׁפָּחָה *clan* Jos 13$_{15.24}$, מִסְפָּר *number* Ezk 4$_{5}$, מִפְלַגָּה *division* 2 C 35$_{12}$, מַכְבִּיר *abundance* Jb 36$_{31}$, רֹב *abundance* 11QM 1.2$_{9}$.

לְ *in respect of,* + אִישׁ *man* 2 K 15$_{20}$.

לְ *concerning,* + מַעֲשֶׂה *deed* Si 36$_{20}$ (למראש מעשיך appar. *concerning, from of old, your deeds*).

לְ introducing object, + פְּלֵיטָה *deliverance* 2 C 12$_{7}$.

בְּ of place, *in, at, throughout, among,* + Bashan Jos 22$_{7}$, Israel Ezk 39$_{11}$ 44$_{28}$, Jerusalem 1 K 15$_{4}$ Ezr 9$_{9}$, Judah Ezr 9$_{9}$, Egypt Dt 6$_{22}$, יָמִין *right hand* Si 47$_{5}$, רֹאשׁ *head*

1 S 9_{22}, אַמְתַּחַת *sack* Gn 43_{23}, אֶרֶץ *land* Lv 26_6 Nm 35_{14} Jos 14_4, גְּבוּל *border*, i.e. territory Jr 15_{13}, שָׂדֶה *field* Dt 11_{15} Zc 10_1, מִדְבָּר *steppe* Is 43_{20}, יְשִׁימוֹן *desert* Is 43_{20}, גַּיְא *valley* 4QapJoseph^b 1_7, מְעָרָה *cave* 1 S 24_{11}, עִיר *city* 1 S 27_5 Am 4_6, שַׁעַר *gate*, i.e. city Dt 12_{15}, בַּיִת *house* Is 56_5, מָעוֹן *dwelling place* 1QSb 3_{26} ([במעון]), חוֹמָה *wall* Is 56_5, מָקוֹם *place* Jr 14_{13} Am 4_6 Ezr 9_8, זֶה *this (place)* Gn 48_9.

בְּ *into, onto* (distinction from §4 not alw. clear), + יָד *hand* Gn 27_{17} Ex 10_{25} 23_{31} Nm $21_{2.34}$ Dt 1_{27} $2_{24.30}$ $3_{2.3}$ 7_{24} 19_{12} 20_{13}=11QT 62_9 Dt 21_{10}=11QT 63_{10} Jos 2_{24} 6_2 7_7 $8_{1.7.18}$ $10_{8.30.32}$ 11_8 21_{44} Jos $24_{8.11}$ Jg $1_{2.4}$ $2_{14.23}$ $3_{10.28}$ $4_{7.14}$ 6_1 $7_{2.7.14.15}$ $8_{3.7}$ $11_{21.30.32}$ 12_3 13_1 $15_{12.13}$ $16_{23.24}$ 18_{10} 20_{28} 1 S $14_{10.12.37}$ 17_{47} 1 S 21_4 $23_{4.14}$ $24_{5.11}$ 26_{23} $28_{19.19}$ 30_{23} 2 S $5_{19.19}$||1 C $14_{10.10}$ 2 S 16_8 21_9 1 K 15_{18} 18_9 $20_{13.28}$ $22_{6.12}$||2 C $18_{5.11}$ 1 K 22_{15} 2 K $3_{10.13}$ 13_3 17_{20} 21_{14} Is 22_{21} 47_6 Jr $20_{4.5}$ 21_7 22_{25} 26_{24} 27_6 29_{21} $32_{3.28}$ $34_{2.20.21}$ $38_{16.19}$ 43_3 $44_{30.30}$ 46_{26} Ezk 7_{21} 11_9 16_{39} 21_{36} $23_{9.28}$ 31_{11} 39_{23} Ps 78_{61} 106_{41} Lm 1_{14} Dn 1_2 Ne $9_{24.27.30}$ 1 C 22_{18} 2 C 13_{16} 16_8 24_{24} 25_{20} $28_{5.9}$ 36_{17} Si 15_{14} 1QpHab 5_4 9_{10} 4QJub^a 1_{13} ([ונת]תי ... ביד]) 4QJub^d 21_{22} 4QpPs^a 3.4_9 4QapJoseph^b 1_4 2_8 4QparaKings 31_2 4QpsMos^e 1_8 2.1_5 ([ביד]) 4QBark^a 1.2_5 4QPrayer^g 1_2 4QNarrB 1_2 CD 1_6 Arad ost. 17_8, כַּף *hand* Jg 6_{13} Jr 12_7, חֵיק *bosom* 2 S 12_8, נֶפֶשׁ *soul*, i.e. desire Ezk 16_{27} Ps 27_{12} 41_3, אִשָּׁה *woman* Nm 5_{20}, בְּהֵמָה *beast* Lv 18_{23} 20_{15}.

בְּ of time, *in, on*, + בֹּקֶר *morning* Ex 16_8 Zp 3_5, עֶרֶב *evening* Ex 16_8, יוֹם *day* Ex 22_{29} Lv 5_{24} 27_{23} Dt 24_{15} 1 S 27_6 1 K 13_3 Ezk 39_{11} Ne 12_{47} 1 C 22_9, לַיְלָה *night* Jb 35_{10}, שָׁנָה *year* 2 C 27_5, עֵת *time* Dt 11_{14} 28_{12} Jr 5_{24} Ps 1_3 104_{27} 145_{15} Si 51_{30}; followed by date Arad ost. 17_8.

בְּ of price, *(in exchange) for*, + זוֹנָה *prostitute* Jl 4_3, רֹאשׁ *head*, i.e. chief Ezk 28_{22}, נֶפֶשׁ *soul*, i.e. person Ezk 27_{13} (or del. בְּ), מִקְנֶה *cattle* Gn $47_{16.17}$, סוּס *horse* Gn 47_{17}, חֲמוֹר *ass* Gn 47_{17}, חִטָּה *wheat* Ezk 27_{17} (or del. בְּ), דְּבַשׁ *honey* Ezk 27_{17} (or del. בְּ), שֶׁמֶן *oil* Ezk 27_{17} (or del. בְּ), אֹכֶל *food* Lm 1_{11}, צְרִי *balm* Ezk 27_{17} (or del. בְּ), כְּלִי *vessel* Ezk 27_{13}, מַעֲרָב *merchandise* Ezk $27_{13.17}$ (both if ins. בְּ), עִזָּבוֹן *wares* Ezk 27_{14} (if ins. בְּ) $27_{16.19}$, אֶבֶן precious *stone* Ezk 27_{22}, זָהָב *gold* Ezk 27_{22}, כֶּסֶף *silver, money* Gn 23_9 Dt 2_{28} 14_{25} 1 K $21_{6.15}$ Ezk 27_{12} 1 C 21_{22}, בְּדִיל *tin* Ezk 27_{12}, עֹפֶרֶת *lead* Ezk 27_{12}, מָקוֹם *place* 1 C 21_{25}, מְחִיר *price* Jr 15_{13} 17_3, נֶשֶׁךְ *interest* Lv 25_{37} Ezk $18_{8.13}$ Ps 15_5, תַּרְבִּית *increase* Lv 25_{37} 4QD^b 4_{10} ([יתן]), עֲבֹדָה *service* Gn 29_{27}, אַהֲבָה *love* Ca 8_7, כֹּל *all* Dt 14_{26}.

בְּ of instrument, *by (means of)*, + Naaman 2 K 5_1, שַׂר *commander* 2 K 5_1, יָד *hand* Jg 15_{18} 4QparaKings 104_7, רוּחַ *spirit* 4QapPs^b 69_4, גּוֹרָל *lot* Nm 36_2.

בְּ of accompaniment, *with, in*, + אֱמֶת *truth* Is 61_8, טוּב *good* 4QDibHam^c 131_8 ([נת]תה), עָרְמָה *prudence* 4QMishC^a 2_1 ([ל]תת ... בערמ[ה]), שִׂמְחָה *joy* Ezk 36_5, עֶבְרָה *wrath* Ho 13_{11}, זָדוֹן *presumptuousness* Pr 13_{10} (or em.; see Subj.), רַע *evil* of eye 4QBéat 13_2, מַעֲשֶׂה *deed* Si 47_8, עֲבֹדָה *service* 1QSa 1_{19} (ב[עבו]דת).

בְּ *according to*, + פְּלִיל *(decision of) judge* Ex 21_{22}, מַחֲלֹקֶת *division* Jos $11_{23(mss)}$ $12_{7(mss)}$ 2 C 31_{15}, דָּבָר *word* 1 K 13_5.

בְּ *concerning, (with respect) to*, + סֵפֶר *letter* Lachish ost. 3_{12} ([ל]א אתן בה וכל מאומ[ה] *I will not pay any attention to it at all*; others אתננהו אל מאומ[ה] *I can repeat it [with respect] to anything*, i.e. in the smallest detail).

בְּ *as, for (the purpose of)*, + בָּרוּת *food* Ps 69_{22}, נַחֲלָה *inheritance* Nm 18_{26} 36_2, אֲחֻזָּה *possession* Jos 21_{12}, עֲרֻבָּה *pledge* 4QD^b 4_9 ([יתן] ... [בע]רובות).

בְּ *against*, + עַם *people* Ne 9_{10}, בַּיִת *house(hold)* Dt 6_{22}, בֵּן *son* Ps 50_{20}, פַּרְעֹה *Pharaoh* Dt 6_{22} Ne 9_{10}, עֶבֶד *servant* Ne 9_{10}, מַחְמָד *desirable thing* Si 11_{31}.

בְּ of cause, *on account of*, + חַטָּאת *sin* Jr 15_{13} 17_3, בָּמָה *high place* Jr 17_3.

כְּ *as* Gn 9_3 2 C 31_{15}; *as at*, + יוֹם *day* Dt 2_{30} 4_{38}; *as though it were (for)*, + מְעַט *few* 2 C 12_{17} (unless כִּמְעַט = cause to be *hardly*, i.e. §5a).

כְּ *according to*, + יָד *hand* Est 2_{18} 7_6 Ne 2_8, לֵבָב *heart* Ps 20_5 Kuntillet ʿAjrud add. inscr. 2, פְּרִי *fruit* of deeds Jr 17_{10} 32_{19}, פֹּעַל *deed* Ps 28_4, מַעֲשֶׂה *deed* Ps 28_4, מַתָּנָה *gift* Si $33_{12(B)}$ ([כ]מתנתו), מַתַּת *gift* Si $32_{12(Bmg)}$, מִצְוָה *commandment* Dt 26_{13}, מַחֲלֹקֶת *division* Jos 11_{23} 12_7, צְדָקָה *righteousness* 1 K 8_{32}||2 C 6_{23}, רַחֲמִים *compassion* Ne 9_{27}, דֶּרֶךְ *way* 1 K 8_{39}||2 C 6_{30} Jr 17_{10} 32_{19} Ezk 7_9 GnzPs 4_{21}, כֹּל *everything* Ex 21_{30} 1 K 5_{20} 8_{56}.

מִן *(the territory) from*, i.e. beginning at (as obj.), + Aroer Dt 3_{12}, Gilead Dt 3_{16}.

מִן partitive, (1) *(some) of* (as obj.), + בַּת *daughter* Jg 21$_{7}$, זֶרַע *offspring* Lv 18$_{21}$ 20$_{2.3.4}$, בָּשָׂר *flesh* Dt 28$_{55}$, אַיִל *ram* 11QT 21$_{06}$ ([ונתנו ... מן הכבשים]), כֶּבֶשׂ *sheep* 11QT 21$_{06}$ ([ונתנו ... מן האילים]), עֵץ *(fruit of) tree* Gn 3$_{12}$, פְּרִי *fruit* Pr 31$_{31}$, דוּדָאִים *mandrakes* Gn 30$_{14}$, זֵרֹעַ *vegetable* Dn 1$_{12}$, יַיִן *wine* Arad ost. 1$_{10}$, טַל *dew* Gn 27$_{28}$, רֵאשִׁית *first* of coarse meal Nm 15$_{21}$, לֶחֶם *bread* Pr 22$_{9}$, שָׁמֵן *fertile place* Gn 27$_{28}$, זָהָב *gold* Ps 72$_{15}$ (or em. qal pass.), שָׁלָל *spoil* 1 S 30$_{22}$, אֶרֶץ *land* Dt 2$_{5.9.19}$, עִיר *city* Nm 35$_{8}$, קֹדֶשׁ *holiness*, i.e. holy thing Dt 26$_{14}$, שָׂכָר *wages* CD 14$_{14}$, כֹּל *anything* Lv 27$_{9}$.

(2) *from among, out of*, + Beth-togarmah Ezk 27$_{14}$, מַטֶּה *tribe* Jos 21$_{9}$||1 C 6$_{50}$ Jos 21$_{13.21}$, בַּיִת *house* Jg 9$_{4}$, בַּת *daughter* Jg 21$_{18}$, אָמָה *female servant* 4QTNaph 1$_{2}$, יָד *hand* 1 C 29$_{14}$, אִשֶּׁה *fire offering* Lv 6$_{10}$, זֶבַח *sacrifice* Lv 7$_{32}$, תְּרוּמָה *offering* Nm 18$_{28}$, יַיִן *wine* Arad ost. 3$_{2}$, שָׁלָל *spoil* 11QT 58$_{12}$, נַחֲלָה *inheritance* Nm 35$_{2}$ Ezk 46$_{17}$, אֲחֻזָּה *possession* Nm 35$_{8}$.

מִן of instrument, agent, *by (means of), with, through*, + Sarai Gn 17$_{16}$, אִשָּׁה *wife* Gn 17$_{16}$, נַעֲרָה *young woman* Ru 4$_{12}$, נְשָׁמָה *breath* Jb 37$_{10}$ (or em.; see Obj.).

מִן of comparison, *more than*, + זֶה *this* 2 C 25$_{9}$.

מִן *upon, against*, + Saul 2 S 4$_{8}$.

אֶל *to*, + Israel(ites) Dt 13$_{2}$ Jr 3$_{8}$, Baruch Jr 32$_{12.16}$ 36$_{32}$, David 1 C 21$_{5}$, Eleazar Nm 19$_{3}$, Gedaliah Jr 39$_{14}$, Hagar Gn 21$_{14}$, Jacob Gn 35$_{4}$, Moses Ex 25$_{16.21}$ 31$_{18}$ Nm 17$_{21}$ Dt 5$_{22}$ 9$_{10.11}$ 10$_{4}$, Shaphan 2 K 22$_{8}$||2 C 34$_{15}$, אִישׁ *man*, i.e. each Nm 7$_{5}$, בֵּן *son* Dt 31$_{9}$ Jr 32$_{12.16}$ 36$_{32}$ 39$_{14}$, of man, in ref. to Ezekiel Ezk 2$_{8}$ 3$_{3}$, מֶלֶךְ *king* 2 S 24$_{9}$, נַעַר *lad* Gn 18$_{7}$ 1 S 20$_{40}$ 2 K 5$_{23}$, עֶבֶד *servant* Meṣad Ḥashavyahu ost. 1$_{13}$ (ותתן [עב]דך), רֵעַ *neighbour* Ex 22$_{6.9}$, כֹּהֵן *priest* Lv 15$_{14}$ Nm 19$_{3}$ Dt 31$_{9}$ Ezk 43$_{19}$, לֵוִי *Levite* Nm 7$_{5.6}$ Ezk 43$_{19}$, סֹפֵר *scribe* Jr 36$_{32}$, ידע ptc. *one who knows* Is 29$_{11}$, מְשֻׁבָה *apostate* Jr 3$_{8}$.

אֶל *according to*, + פֶּה *mouth*, i.e. word Jos 15$_{13}$ 17$_{4}$.

עַל *upon, in, to*, + Assyrians Ezk 23$_{7}$, Israel 1 C 22$_{9}$, Moresheth-gath Mc 1$_{14}$, Aaron Si 45$_{7(B)}$, Isaac 4QpsJub^{a} 2.2$_{1}$ ([ו]יתן ... [על ישחק]), Solomon 1 C 29$_{25}$, בֵּן *son* Ex 32$_{29}$ 4QpsJub^{a} 2.2$_{1}$ ([ו]יתן ... [על ... בנו]), מִבְחָר *choice one* Ezk 23$_{7}$, בזה ni. ptc. *despised one* Dn 11$_{21}$, יָד *hand* 2 K 12$_{12.16}$ 22$_{5.9}$||2 C 34$_{10.17}$ Est 6$_{9}$ CD 14$_{13}$, i.e. charge 1 C 29$_{8}$, פֶּה *mouth* Mc 3$_{5}$, מִזְבֵּחַ *altar* Lv 22$_{22}$, אֶרֶץ *land* 1 K 8$_{36}$||2 C 6$_{27}$, מָקוֹם *place* Jr 45$_{5}$.

עַל *over*, i.e. in charge of, + עַם *people* 1 K 5$_{21}$.

עַל *besides, in addition to*, + עִיר *city* Nm 35$_{6}$.

עַל *for (the purpose of)*, + עֲבֹדָה *service* Ex 30$_{16}$.

עַל *according to*, + פֶּה *mouth*, i.e. word Nm 3$_{51}$ Jos 19$_{50}$ 2 K 23$_{35}$.

עַל *on account of, for the sake of*, + אֱמֶת *truth* Ps 115$_{1}$, חֶסֶד *loyalty* Ps 115$_{1}$.

עַל־פְּנֵי *upon*, + אֶרֶץ *earth* Jb 5$_{10}$, אֲדָמָה *earth* 1 K 17$_{14}$ 18$_{1}$.

לְמִן *from*, + עוֹלָם *everlastingness*, i.e. from of old Jr 25$_{5}$.

עַד *until, unto*, + יוֹם *day* Dt 29$_{3}$, עֵת *time* Mc 5$_{2}$, עוֹלָם *everlastingness*, i.e. for ever Gn 13$_{15}$ Jr 25$_{5}$; *(the territory) as far as* (as obj.), + Jabbok Dt 3$_{16}$, נַחַל *wadi* Dt 3$_{16}$, גְּבוּל *border* Dt 3$_{16}$; *even as far as*, i.e. together with, + חֶרֶב *sword* 1 S 18$_{4}$, קֶשֶׁת *bow* 1 S 18$_{4}$, חֲגוֹר *girdle* 1 S 18$_{4}$; *as much as*, + מִדְרָךְ *treading place* Dt 2$_{5}$.

כְּפִי *according to*, + עֲבֹדָה *service* Nm 7$_{5.7.8}$, נַחֲלָה *inheritance* Nm 35$_{8}$.

חֵלֶף *in return for*, + עֲבֹדָה *service* Nm 18$_{21}$.

בַּעַד *for the sake of*, + נֶפֶשׁ *soul*, i.e. life Jb 2$_{4}$.

מֵאֵת *from*, + בֵּן *son* of Israel Nm 18$_{26}$.

מִקֶּרֶב *from among*, + אָח *brother* 11QT 61$_{02}$ ([נתתי ... מקרב אחיכה]).

מִקְצָת *some of* (as obj.), + כְּלִי *vessel* Dn 1$_{2}$.

מִלְּבַד *besides*, + אֲשֶׁר *that which* 1 K 10$_{13}$||2 C 9$_{12}$.

לְעֻמַּת *alongside*, + תְּרוּמָה *contribution* Ezk 45$_{6}$.

בְּעַד *for the sake of*, + פצע pass ptc. *wounded one* CD 14$_{14}$ ([פ]צעם).

לְמַעַן *for the sake of*, + David 1 K 11$_{13}$, עֶבֶד *servant* 1 K 11$_{13}$.

בִּגְלַל *on account of*, + חַטָּאת *sin* 1 K 14$_{16}$.

בְּתוֹךְ *among*, + Hittites Gn 23$_{9}$, עַם *people* 1QpHab 10$_{3}$, בַּיִת *house* of Israel Ezk 29$_{21}$, בֵּן *son* of Israel Jos 14$_{3}$ 15$_{13}$ 19$_{49}$, אָח *brother* Nm 27$_{4.7}$ Jos 17$_{4.4}$ Jb 42$_{15}$.

בְּעֵבֶר *beyond*, + Jordan Dt 3$_{20}$ Jos 1$_{14.15}$ Jos 13$_{8}$ 22$_{4.7(Kt)}$.

מֵעֵבֶר *beyond*, + Jordan Jos 22$_{7(Qr)}$.

מֵעֵבֶר לְ *on the other side of, beyond*, + Jordan Nm 35$_{14}$ Jos 14$_{3}$.

לִפְנֵי *before*, + אִישׁ *man* Gn 43$_{14}$, בְּכִירָה *firstborn daughter* Gn 29$_{26}$, פַּרְעֹה *Pharaoh* 4QJub^{h} 40$_{5}$, אֹיֵב *enemy* Jr 15$_{9}$, חַי *living one* Si 7$_{33}$.

לְעֵינֵי *in the sight of*, + Israelites Dt 6$_{22}$, Jews Jr 32$_{12}$, Hanamel Jr 32$_{12}$, בֵּן *son* Gn 23$_{11}$, דּוֹד *uncle* Jr 32$_{12}$.

תַּחַת *under*, + שֶׁמֶשׁ *sun* Ec 8$_{15}$ 9$_{9}$; *under (the authority of)*, + David 1 C 29$_{24}$.

תַּחַת *in place of, (in exchange) for*, + Israel(ites) Is 43$_{3.4}$, נֶפֶשׁ *soul*, i.e. life Ex 21$_{23}$ Is 43$_{4}$, רוּחַ *spirit* Is 61$_{3}$, כֶּרֶם *vineyard* 1 K 21$_{2.2}$, אֵפֶר *ashes* Is 61$_{3}$, גֵּל *dung* Ezk 4$_{15}$, אֵבֶל *mourning* Is 61$_{3}$.

נתן + noun without preposition, בְּרִית *(by means of a) covenant* 2 C 13$_{5}$.

<COLL> נתן || שׁלח *send* Jb 5$_{10}$, נשׂא *bear* Ezk 36$_{8}$ Jl 2$_{22}$, מכר *deliver (over)* Jl 4$_{3}$, שׁבר hi. *sell* Dt 2$_{28}$, שׁוב hi. *repay* GnzPs 4$_{21}$, מגן pi. *deliver up* Ho 11$_{8}$, נגר hi. *deliver up* Jr 18$_{21}$, רבה hi. *increase* Is 40$_{29}$ Ho 2$_{10}$, יסף hi. *add* Ps 120$_{3}$, חנן *be gracious* Ps 37$_{21}$, ידע hi. *make known* Pr 9$_{9}$, עשׂה *do* Est 5$_{8}$.

:: חשׂך *withhold* Pr 21$_{26}$, כלא *withhold* Is 43$_{6}$, מנע *withhold* Ne 9$_{20}$ Si 7$_{33}$ (+) 12$_{4}$ 11QPs^{a} 24$_{4}$, נשׂא *take* Dn 1$_{16}$ Ezr 9$_{12}$ Ne 13$_{25}$ CD 13$_{14}$, לקח *take* Gn 14$_{21}$ 34$_{9.16.21}$ Dt 7$_{3}$ Jg 3$_{6}$ Jr 29$_{6}$ Ho 13$_{11}$ Jb 1$_{21}$ Ne 10$_{31}$.

+ לקח *take* Gn 3$_{6}$ 18$_{7}$ 20$_{14}$ 21$_{14.27}$ 23$_{13}$ 30$_{9}$ 38$_{28}$ 48$_{22}$ Ex 30$_{16}$ Lv 7$_{34}$ 15$_{14}$ Nm 7$_{5.6}$ 18$_{28}$ 31$_{29.30.47}$ Dt 19$_{12}$ 29$_{7}$ Jos 11$_{23}$ Jg 14$_{19}$ 15$_{6}$ 17$_{4}$ 1 S 2$_{15.16}$ 8$_{14}$ 10$_{4}$ 25$_{11}$ 2 S 12$_{11}$ 20$_{3}$ 21$_{9}$ 1 K 11$_{35}$ 15$_{18}$ 17$_{19.23}$ 18$_{26}$ 19$_{21}$ Jr 36$_{32}$ 39$_{14}$ Ezk 16$_{61}$ 18$_{8.13}$ Ps 15$_{5}$ Jb 35$_{7}$.

+ יהב *give* Gn 47$_{16}$, שׁקה hi. *give to drink* Ps 69$_{22}$, ראה hi. *show* Ps 85$_{8}$, שׁלם pi. *pay* Pr 6$_{31}$, פדה *ransom* Ps 49$_{8}$, פזר pi. *scatter* Ps 112$_{9}$, מטר hi. *rain* Ps 78$_{24}$, כון hi. *prepare* Ps 78$_{20}$, מלא pi. *fulfil* Ps 20$_{5}$, אמר לְ *say*, i.e. assign, *to* 1 K 11$_{18}$.

+ adverb or noun used adverbially, כֵּן *thus* Ps 127$_{2}$, מַהֵר *quickly* 4Q416 2.2$_{5}$, מְהֵרָה *quickly* Arad ost. 12$_{2}$, טוֹב *good*, i.e. better Gn 29$_{19}$, לְבַד *alone* 2 S 20$_{21}$, אֵיךְ *how?* Ho 11$_{6}$, שָׁם *there* Ezk 6$_{13}$ 39$_{11}$ 47$_{23}$, רַק *only* Pr 13$_{10}$ (or em. רַק to רֵק *empty one* or רַע *evil one*), עוֹד *again* Is 62$_{8}$ Ezk 16$_{41}$ 4Q417 2.1$_{17}$, אָז *then* 1 K 9$_{11}$, עַתָּה *now* 1 S 2$_{16}$ Arad ost. 1$_{2}$ 2$_{1}$ 3$_{2}$ 7$_{2}$ 8$_{1}$ 11$_{2}$ 14$_{2}$ ([עת נתן]), מָחָר *tomorrow* Jg 20$_{28}$ Pr 3$_{28}$, יוֹמָם *by day* Jr 31$_{35}$, לַיְלָה *by night* Jr 31$_{35}$, הַיּוֹם *today* Ex 32$_{29}$ 1 S 24$_{11}$ 26$_{23}$ 1 K 14$_{8}$ 20$_{13}$, הַיּוֹם הַזֶּה *this day* 1 S 17$_{46}$ 2 S 4$_{8}$, כָּל־הַיָּמִים *all the days*, i.e. for ever Dt 4$_{40}$ 2 K 8$_{19}$||2 C 21$_{7}$, [כול ימי] *all the days of* 2QJub^{b} 46$_{2}$, כול ימיו *all his days* 4QOrd^{a} 1.2$_{7}$, דְּבַר־יוֹם בְּיוֹמוֹ *thing of a day in its day*, i.e. as was required each day Ne 12$_{47}$, שָׁנָה בְשָׁנָה *year by year* 1 K 5$_{25}$, שֶׁבַע שָׁנִים *(for) seven years* Jg 6$_{1}$, עוֹלָם וָעֶד *for ever and ever* Ps 21$_{6}$, רק [פ]עם אחת *only once* 4QOrd^{a} 1.2$_{7}$.

Inf. abs. + finite form of נתן, Nm 21$_{2}$ 27$_{7}$ Dt 15$_{10}$ Jg 8$_{25.25}$ 11$_{30}$ 2 S 5$_{19}$.

לֹא תֹסֵף תֵּת *it shall no longer yield* Gn 4$_{12}$, שִׁבְתּוֹ יִתֵּן *he shall give*, i.e. pay for, *his sitting* (being unable to work) Ex 21$_{19}$, אֲשֶׁר לְתִתִּי־לוֹ בְּשֹׂרָה perh. *that which was for me to give him (for his) tidings* 2 S 4$_{10}$, מִזַּרְעֲךָ לֹא־תִתֵּן לְהַעֲבִיר לַמֹּלֶךְ *you shall not give any of your offspring to cause them to pass*, i.e. offer them, *to Molech* Lv 18$_{21}$, רַב הָעָם ... מִתִּתִּי אֶת־מִדְיָן בְּיָדָם *the people are too many ... for me to give the Midianites into their hand* Jg 7$_{2}$, חָלִילָה לִּי מֵי׳ מִתִּתִי *may Y. prevent me from giving* 1 K 21$_{3}$, וָאֶתֵּן לָהֶם יַעַבְרוּם *and that which I gave them has passed from them* Jr 8$_{13}$, וּנְתַתִּיו perh. *and I will give it (to him)* Ezk 21$_{32}$, יִתֵּן י׳ לָכֶם וּמְצֶאןָ מְנוּחָה *may Y. grant that you find a place of rest* Ru 1$_{9}$, וַיִּתְּנוּ יָדָם לְהוֹצִיא נְשֵׁיהֶם *and they gave their hand*, i.e. pledged, *to expel their wives* Ezr 10$_{19}$, לָתֵת אֶתְכֶם לָמוּת *to give you over to die* 2 C 32$_{11}$, ברית כל ראשון נתנו appar. *he gave to him the covenant of every forbear* Si 44$_{22}$, יתנכה ... מקומכה appar. *may he give (to) you ... your place* 1QSb 3$_{26}$.

2a. מִי יִתֵּן **who will grant?**, i.e. **would that!, if only!, oh that it were!**, often a forlorn wish, followed by (1) inf. with pronominal suffix, of מות *die* Ex 16$_{3}$ 2 S 19$_{1}$.

(2) verbal clause(s), beginning הַחֲרֵשׁ תַּחֲרִישׁוּן *that you would be utterly silent* Jb 13$_{5}$, בִּשְׁאוֹל תַּצְפִּנֵנִי *that you would hide me in Sheol* Jb 14$_{13}$, אֱלוֹהַּ דַּבֵּר *that God would speak* Jb 11$_{5}$, יָדַעְתִּי וְאֶמְצָאֵהוּ *that I knew so that*, i.e. how, *I might find him* Jb 23$_{3}$, וְהָיָה לְבָבָם *that there was their heart*, i.e. that they were so minded Dt 5$_{29}$, וְיִכָּתְבוּן מִלָּי *that my words were written* Jb 19$_{23}$, בַּסֵּפֶר וְיֻחָקוּ *that they were inscribed in a book* Jb 19$_{23}$, תָּבוֹא שֶׁאֱלָתִי *that my request would come*, i.e. that I would have it Jb 6$_{8}$.

(3) noun, בֹּקֶר *morning* Dt 28_{67}, עֶרֶב *evening* Dt 28_{67}.

(4) noun, as subj. of nom. cl., כָּל־עַם י׳ נְבִיאִים כִּי־נָתַן י׳ *that all the people of Y. were prophets, that Y. would place* Nm 11_{29}, רֹאשִׁי מַיִם וְעֵינִי מְקוֹר דִּמְעָה *my head were waters and my eyes a fountain of tears* Jr 8_{23}, אֶת־הָעָם בְּיָדִי *this people (that it were) in my hand* Jg 9_{29}, מִצִּיּוֹן יְשׁוּעַת יִשְׂרָאֵל *the salvation of Israel was from Zion* Ps 14_{7}||53_{7} (יְשֻׁעוֹת), טָהוֹר מִטָּמֵא *that a pure thing would be from an impure one* Jb 14_{4}, מִבְּשָׂרוֹ לֹא נִשְׂבָּע *that there was one not satisfied with his meat* Jb 31_{13}.

(5) pronominal suffix as subj. of nom. cl., מִי יִתֶּנְךָ כְּאָח לִי *oh that you were as a brother to me* Ca 8_{1}, מִי־יִתְּנֵנִי כְיַרְחֵי־קֶדֶם *oh that I were as in the months of old* Jb 29_{2}.

(6) objective pronominal suffix, appar. as equivalent of לְ *to* with suffix, מִי־יִתְּנֵנִי שָׁמִיר שַׁיִת בַּמִּלְחָמָה *would that I had thorns (and) briars in the battle* Is 27_{4}, מִי־יִתְּנֵנִי בַמִּדְבָּר מְלוֹן אֹרְחִים *would that I had a traveller's lodging place in the steppe* Jr 9_{1}.

b. מִי־יִתֶּן לִי **who will grant me?**, i.e. **oh that I had!**, + אֵבֶר כַּיּוֹנָה *wings like a dove* Ps 55_{7}, שֹׁמֵעַ לִי *one who listened to me* Jb 31_{35}.

3. give out, sound out, utter voice, send, i.e. make proclamation (2 C 24_{9}), <SUBJ> Y. Ex 9_{23} 1 S $12_{17.18}$ 2 S 22_{14}||Ps 18_{13} Jr 10_{13}=51_{16} 25_{30} Jl 2_{11} 4_{16} Am 1_{2} Ps 46_{7} 68_{34}, Jerusalem/Zion Jr 22_{20}, Moabites Jr 48_{34}, עֵדָה *assembly* Nm 14_{1}, צָבָא *host* of heaven 1QH 11_{35}, Joseph Gn 45_{2}, בֵּן *son* Pr 2_{3}, אֹיֵב *enemy* perh. Lm 2_{7}, נֹצֵר *besieger* Jr 4_{16} (or em. נֹצְרִים to צָרִים *besiegers*), רכב pt. *one who rides* Ps 68_{34}, כְּפִיר *young lion* Jr 2_{15} Am 3_{4}, עוֹף *birds* Ps 104_{12}, נַחֲלָה *inheritance* Jr 12_{8}, שַׁחַק *sky* Ps 77_{18}, תְּהוֹם *deep* Hb 3_{10}, חָכְמוֹת *wisdom* Pr 1_{20}, תְּבוּנָה *understanding* Pr 8_{1}, שִׁיר *song* Si 50_{18}, פַּעֲמֹן *bell* Si 45_{9}; subj. not specified, Ps 81_{3} 2 C 24_{9}.

<OBJ> קוֹל *voice, thunder* Gn 45_{2} Ex 9_{23} Nm 14_{1} 1 S $12_{17.18}$ 2 S 22_{14}||Ps 18_{14} Jr 2_{15} 4_{16} 10_{13}=51_{16} 22_{20} 25_{30} 48_{34} Jl 2_{11} 4_{16} Am 1_{2} 3_{4} Hb 3_{10} Ps 77_{18} 104_{12} Pr 1_{20} 2_{3} 8_{1} Lm 2_{7} Si 50_{18}, i.e. proclamation 2 C 24_{9}, בָּרָד *hail* Ex 9_{23}, מָטָר *rain* 1 S $12_{17.18}$, תֹּף *timbrel* Ps 81_{3}, כִּנּוֹר *lyre* Ps 81_{3}, נְעִימָה *melody* Si 45_{9}.

<PREP> לְ of direction, *to*, or of purpose, *for*, + תְּבוּנָה *understanding* Pr 2_{3}.

בְּ of place, *in, throughout*, + Judah 2 C 24_{9}, Jerusalem 2 C 24_{9}, בַּיִת *house* Lm 2_{7}, רְחוֹב *broad place* Pr 1_{20}; of time, *on*, + יוֹם *day* 1 S 12_{18}; of accompaniment, *with, in*, + בְּכִי *weeping* Gn 45_{2}, צַעַד *step* Si 45_{9}; introducing object, + קוֹל *voice* Jr 12_{8} Ps 46_{7} 68_{34} 1QH 11_{35}.

כְּ *as on*, + יוֹם *day* Lm 2_{7}.

מִן of direction, *from*, + Zoar Jr 48_{34}, מָעוֹן *dwelling place* Jr 25_{30}, מְעוֹנָה *dwelling place* Am 3_{4}.

עַל *against*, + Y. Jr 12_{8}, עִיר *city* Jr 4_{16}.

עִם *with*, + נֵבֶל *harp* Ps 81_{3}.

עַד *unto, as far as*, + Horonaim Jr 48_{34}, Eglath-shelishiyah Jr 48_{34}.

מִבֵּין *from among*, + עֳפִי *foliage* Ps 104_{12}.

לִפְנֵי *before*, + חַיִל *army* Jl 2_{11}.

<COLL> נתן קול + בכה *weep* Nm 14_{1}, קרא *call* Pr 2_{3} 8_{1}, צעק *cry out* Jr 22_{20}, רנן *cry aloud* Pr 1_{20}, שׁאג *roar* Jr 2_{15} 25_{30} Jl 4_{16} Am 1_{2} 3_{4}, רעם hi. *thunder* 2 S 22_{14}||Ps 18_{14}, זרם po. *pour* water Ps 77_{18}, נשׂא *lift* hand Hb 3_{10}.

לְקוֹל תִּתּוֹ *when he utters his voice* Jr 10_{13}=51_{16} (or em. לְתִתּוֹ קוֹל *when he utters [his] voice* or לְקוֹלוֹ נִתַּךְ *at his voice there is poured out*), וַיִּתְּנוּ־קוֹל ... לְהָבִיא *and they made a proclamation ... to bring* 2 C 24_{9}.

4. place, in various senses, including (examples only in each category), **a. place, put, set** somewhere (e.g. Gn 1_{17} 9_{13} 15_{10} 18_{9} 39_{20} 40_{3} 41_{42} 43_{23} Ex 5_{21} 12_{7} 25_{12} 29_{3} 31_{6} 34_{33} 40_{5} Lv 1_{7} 4_{7} 8_{7} 10_{1} Nm 4_{6} 5_{17} 15_{38} Dt 18_{18} Jos 15_{19}||Jg 1_{15} Jg 7_{16} 1 S 6_{8} 17_{38} 1 K 2_{5} 6_{19} 12_{29} 2 K 12_{10} 16_{14} Is 41_{19} Jr 1_{9} 27_{2} 32_{14} Ezk 3_{20} 29_{4} Ps 40_{4} Ezr 1_{7}), over, i.e in charge of (Gn 41_{41} 1 K $2_{35.35}$ 10_{17}||2 C 9_{16}), into someone's charge (Gn 30_{35} 32_{17} $39_{4.8.22}$ 42_{37} 2 S 10_{10}|| 1 C 19_{11} 2 C 3_{16}), person into someone's bosom (Gn 16_{5} 17_{2}), one's mind to do something (Ec $1_{13.17}$ 7_{21} $8_{9.16}$ Dn 10_{12} 1 C 22_{19} 2 C 11_{16} Si 12_{11}), one's soul (Si 7_{20} $51_{20(B).26}$), one's face (2 C 20_{3}); one's favour in the sight of (Gn 39_{21} Ex 3_{21} 11_{3} 12_{36}), dread upon someone (Dt 2_{25} 11_{25}), fire against, i.e. set fire to (Ezk $30_{8.12.16}$).

b. turn shoulder (Zc 7_{11} Ne 9_{29}), face (Dn 9_{3} 10_{15} CD 4_{16}), neck (2 C 29_{6}), **stretch out** hand (Gn 38_{28} Ex 7_{4} 2 K $10_{15.15}$), i.e. make terms with (Lm 5_{6}), **shoot out** branches (Ezk 36_{8}).

c. cast lots (Lv 16_{8} 1QS 2_{17}).

d. **fasten** (Ex 25$_{26}$ 28$_{25.27}$||39$_{18.20}$ 39$_{31}$), **set up** (Ex 40$_{8.33}$ Dn 11$_{31}$ 12$_{11}$), **build** (Si 47$_7$).

e. **spread*** (Dt 11$_{25}$ Ezk 30$_{13}$ 32$_{23.24.26.32}$).

f. **pour out*** (Nm 19$_{17}$ 1 K 2$_5$ Jr 23$_{40}$ Ezk 23$_{25}$ 24$_8$ 25$_{17}$ 30$_{14}$ 36$_{27}$ 37$_{14}$ 39$_{21}$; perh. also Ex 9$_{23}$ Jr 10$_{13}$=51$_{16}$ [all three §3] Ps 78$_{66}$ 85$_{13}$ [both §1] 105$_{32}$ [§5a] Jb 5$_{10}$ [§1]).

g. **impose** (Dt 26$_6$ 1 K 12$_{4.9}$||2 C 10$_{4.9}$ 2 K 18$_{14}$ 23$_{33}$ Ezk 26$_{17}$), **lay obligation** upon oneself (Ne 10$_{33}$).

h. **afflict with, send against** (Dt 7$_{15.17}$ 2 S 24$_{15}$||1 C 21$_{14}$); (of punishment, guilt, blemish etc.) **bring upon, bring over** (1 K 8$_{32}$||2 C 6$_{23}$ Jr 26$_{15}$ Ezk 7$_{3.4.5.8}$ 9$_{10}$ 11$_{21}$ 16$_{43}$ 17$_{19}$ 22$_{31}$ 23$_{49}$ 25$_{14.17}$ Jon 1$_{14}$ Si 30$_{31}$ 47$_{20}$).

i. **write down (as an accusation)*** (Ps 69$_{28}$).

j. **appoint, assign, designate** (e.g. Ex 31$_6$ Nm 14$_4$ Dt 16$_{18}$ 17$_{15}$ Jos 20$_{2.8}$ 1 S 2$_{28}$ 12$_{13}$ 2 S 11$_{16}$ 2 K 23$_{5.11}$ Ezr 8$_{20}$ Ne 9$_{17}$ 2 C 32$_6$ 11QT 48$_{14}$ 51$_{11}$), **call** an assembly (Ne 5$_7$).

k. **make** covenant (Gn 9$_{12}$ 17$_2$), **establish** laws (Lv 26$_{46}$), people in land (Ezk 37$_{26}$), the practice of thanksgiving (1 C 16$_7$).

l. appar. **place one's self** (Ezk 19$_8$; or em.; see Obj.).

<SUBJ> Y. Gn 1$_{17}$ 9$_{12.13}$ 17$_2$ 39$_{21}$ Ex 3$_{21}$ 7$_4$ 11$_3$ 12$_{36}$ 31$_{6.6}$ 35$_{34}$ 36$_{1.2}$ Lv 14$_{34}$ 17$_{10}$ 20$_{3.6}$ 26$_{11.17.30.46}$ Nm 11$_{25.29}$ Dt 1$_{8.21}$ 2$_{25.31.33.36}$ 4$_8$ 7$_{2.15.23}$ 11$_{25.26.32}$ 18$_{18}$=11QT 61$_{05}$ ([ונתתי]) Dt 21$_8$=11QT 63$_7$ Dt 23$_{15}$ 26$_{19}$ 28$_{1.48}$ 30$_7$ 31$_5$ Jos 10$_{12}$ Jg 11$_9$ 1 S 2$_{28}$ 12$_{13}$ 2 S 24$_{15}$||1 C 21$_{14}$ 1 K 5$_{17.19}$ 8$_{32.46}$||2 C 6$_{23.36}$ 1 K 9$_6$||2 C 7$_{19}$ 1 K 10$_{9.24}$||2 C 9$_{8.23}$ 1 K 22$_{23}$||2 C 18$_{22}$ 2 K 19$_7$||Is 37$_7$ Is 22$_{22}$ 41$_{19}$ 42$_1$ 43$_{16}$ 46$_{13}$ Jr 1$_9$ 6$_{21}$ 9$_{12}$ 21$_8$ 23$_{40}$ 26$_4$ 28$_{14}$ 31$_{33}$ 32$_{40}$ 44$_{10}$ Ezk 3$_{20}$ 4$_8$ 6$_5$ 7$_{3.4.8}$ 9$_{10}$ 11$_{19.21}$ 14$_8$ 15$_7$ 16$_{11.12.43}$ 17$_{19.22}$ 21$_{20}$ 22$_{31}$ 23$_{24.25.21}$ 24$_8$ 25$_{14.17}$ 26$_{20}$ 28$_{14.17}$ 29$_4$ 30$_{8+5t}$ 32$_{5.8.32}$ (or em. נָתַתִּי *I have placed* to נָתַן *he* [Pharaoh] *has placed*) 36$_{26.27.29}$ 37$_{6+5t}$ 38$_4$ 39$_{21}$ Jl 3$_3$ Jon 1$_{14}$ Zc 3$_9$ Ps 4$_8$ 10$_{14}$ 33$_7$ 40$_4$ 69$_{28}$ Ec 3$_{11}$ Dn 9$_{10}$ Ezr 7$_{27}$ Ne 2$_{12}$ 7$_5$ 9$_{35.37}$ 1 C 14$_{17}$ 2 C 20$_{22}$ Si 45$_{5(Bmg)}$ (B שִׂים *place*) 1QH 4$_{17}$ 5$_{25}$ 6$_8$ 8$_{20}$ 12$_{26}$ 13$_6$ 16$_4$ ([נ]תתני) 17$_{10}$ 18$_{22}$ 19$_4$ 20$_{12}$ 21$_{12}$ ([נ]תתה) fr. 3$_{14}$ fr. 2.1$_5$ 1QpHab 2$_8$ 1QS 4$_{17.18}$ 1QLitPr 3.2$_6$ (ות[תנ]ם) 4QAdmon 1$_7$ 4QapPs^b 45a$_4$ 4QsapHymnA 1.1$_4$ 4QShir^b 48$_1$ 11QT 59$_{19.20}$, כְּרוּב *cherub* Ezk 10$_7$, בְּלִיַּעַל *Belial* CD 4$_{16}$.

Assyria Ezk 32$_{23}$, Egyptian(s) Dt 26$_6$ 4QJub^f 39$_4$ 4QJub^h 39$_{11}$ (both [המצרי]), Elam Ezk 32$_{24}$, Israel(ites) Lv 2$_{1.15}$ 5$_{11}$ Dt 11$_{29}$ 15$_{17.18}$ 17$_{15}$=11QT 56$_{15}$ Dt 23$_{25}$ Jos 6$_{24}$ Zc 7$_{11}$ Ne 10$_{33}$ 13$_5$ 11QT 48$_{9.14}$ 51$_{11}$, Jerusalem Ezk 16$_{18.19}$, Meshech Ezk 32$_{26}$, Philistines 1 S 6$_8$, Tubal Ezk 32$_{26}$, עַם *people* Jr 26$_{15}$ 29$_{26}$, גּוֹי *nation* Jr 27$_8$ Ezk 19$_{8.9}$ 11QT 51$_{21}$, מַמְלָכָה *kingdom* Jr 27$_8$, עֵדָה *assembly* Ex 12$_7$ Nm 14$_4$ 16$_7$, קָהָל *assembly* Ezk 23$_{49}$, הָמוֹן *multitude* Ezk 32$_{23.24.36}$, מִשְׁפָּחָה *clan* Jr 1$_{15}$, בַּיִת *house* of Israel Ezk 43$_8$, עִיר *city* Ezk 26$_{17}$.

Aaron Ex 5$_{21}$ 16$_{33}$ Lv 9$_9$ 16$_{8.13.18.21}$ Nm 4$_{6.7.10.10.14}$ 17$_{11.12}$, Abihu Lv 10$_1$, Abra(ha)m Gn 18$_8$, Ahaz 2 K 16$_{17}$, Asa 2 C 16$_{10}$, Ben Sira Si 51$_{20(B)}$, Bezalel, *et al.* Ex 37$_{13}$ 39$_{16.17.18.20.25.31}$, Caleb Jos 15$_{19}$||Jg 1$_{15}$, Daniel Dn 9$_3$ 10$_{12.15}$, David 2 S 20$_3$ Ezr 8$_{20}$ 1 C 16$_7$ Si 47$_7$, Elijah 1 K 18$_{23}$, Evil-merodach 2 K 25$_{28}$||Jr 52$_{32}$, Gideon Jg 7$_{16}$, Hezekiah 2 K 18$_{23}$||Is 36$_8$ 2 C 32$_6$, Jacob Gn 30$_{40}$ 32$_{17}$, Jehoiada 2 K 12$_{10}$ 2 C 23$_{11}$, Jehonadab 2 K 10$_{15.15}$, Jehoshabeath 2 C 22$_{11}$, Jehoshaphat 2 C 17$_{2.2}$ 20$_3$, Jeremiah Jr 27$_2$ 32$_{14}$ 35$_5$, Jeroboam 1 K 12$_{29}$, Joab 2 S 10$_{10}$||1 C 19$_{11}$ 2 S 11$_{16}$ 1 K 2$_5$, Joseph Gn 41$_{48.48}$, Koheleth Ec 1$_{13.17}$ 8$_{9.16}$ 9$_1$, Korah Nm 16$_7$, Laban Gn 30$_{35}$, Moses Ex 5$_{21}$ 25$_{12+5t}$ 26$_{32.33.34.35}$ 27$_5$ 28$_{14+6t}$ 29$_{3.6.12.17.20}$ 30$_{6.18.18.36}$ 34$_{33}$ 40$_{5+11t}$ Lv 8$_{7+6t}$ 24$_7$ Nm 27$_{20}$ Dt 30$_{1.15.19}$ 2 C 5$_{10}$, Nadab Lv 10$_1$, Neco 2 K 23$_{33}$, Nebuchadnezzar/Nebuchadrezzar Ezk 26$_{8.9}$ Ezr 1$_7$ 2 C 36$_7$, Nehemiah Ne 5$_7$, Pashhur Jr 20$_2$, Rehoboam 2 C 11$_{11}$, Sarai Gn 16$_5$, Saul 1 S 17$_{38}$, Simeon (Bar Cosiba) MurEp BarC^a 1$_5$, Solomon 1 K 6$_{6.19.27}$ 7$_{16.39.39}$||2 C 4$_{10}$ 1 K 7$_{51}$||2 C 5$_1$ 2 C 3$_{16.16}$ 4$_{6.7}$ 6$_{13}$ Si 47$_{20}$ (ו[ת]תן), Zedekiah Jr 37$_{18}$, Zephaniah Jr 29$_{26}$.

אִישׁ *man* Ex 30$_{33}$ Lv 24$_{19.20}$ Nm 5$_{15}$ 31$_3$ Dt 24$_{1.3}$ Ezk 14$_3$ 23$_{42}$ 1QS 2$_{17}$, i.e. each Gn 15$_{10}$ Lv 10$_1$ Nm 14$_{4.17.18}$ Jr 1$_{15}$, גֶּבֶר *man* Lm 3$_{29}$, אָב *father* Gn 42$_{37}$ 1 K 12$_{4.9}$||2 C 10$_{4.9}$ Ne 9$_{17.29}$ 2 C 29$_6$, בֵּן *son* Lv 1$_7$ 10$_1$ Nm 4$_{6.7.10.10.14}$ 1 K 2$_5$ 2 K 10$_{15.15}$ Jr 29$_{26}$ Ezk 25$_4$ 2 C 17$_{2.2}$ Si 8$_3$ 12$_{11}$ 30$_{31}$ MurEpBarC^a 1$_5$, of man, in ref. to Ezekiel Ezk 4$_{1.2.2.9}$, of Israel Lv 19$_{14.28.28}$ 26$_1$ Nm 15$_{38}$ Jos 20$_{2.8}$ 2 C 31$_6$, בַּת *daughter* 2 C 22$_{11}$, אָח *brother*, i.e. other Nm 14$_4$, תְּאוֹם *twin* Gn 38$_{28}$.

מֶלֶךְ *king* 1 K 2$_{35.35}$ 6$_6$ 10$_{17}$||2 C 9$_{16}$ 2 K 16$_{14.17}$ 18$_{14}$

19$_{18}$||Is 37$_{19}$ 2 K 23$_{5.11}$ Jr 37$_{18}$ 52$_{11}$ Ezk 26$_{8.9}$ 2 C 17$_{19}$, פַּרְעֹה *Pharaoh* Gn 40$_{3}$ 41$_{10.41.42.43}$ 2 K 23$_{33}$ Ezk 32$_{32}$ (if em.; see above) 4QJub[h] 40$_{7}$, שַׂר *chief* Gn 39$_{22}$ 40$_{11.13.21}$ Jr 26$_{15}$ 37$_{15}$ Ezr 8$_{20}$ 1 C 22$_{19}$, אָדוֹן *master* Gn 39$_{4.8.20}$, גִּבּוֹר *mighty one* 1QM 12$_{11}$=19$_{3}$, עֶבֶד *servant* Jr 37$_{18}$, שָׂכִיר *hired servant* Si 7$_{20(C)}$ (A שוכך appar. error), מְשָׁרֵת *attendant* 2 K 4$_{43.44}$, כֹּהֵן *priest* Lv 4$_{7.18.25.30.34}$ 14$_{14+5t}$ Nm 5$_{17.18}$ 6$_{19}$ 2 K 11$_{12}$||2 C 23$_{11}$ 2 K 12$_{10.10}$ Ezk 45$_{19}$ 11QT 16$_{16}$ 23$_{12}$ ([ונת]ן) 26$_{3}$ ([ונתן הכו]הן) 26$_{12}$ 11QT[b] 1$_{25}$ ([הכוהנ]ים ... ונת]ו]), לֵוִי *Levite* 2 C 35$_{3}$, worshipper Lm 5$_{6}$, נָזִיר *Nazirite* Nm 6$_{18}$, זָקֵן *elder* 11QT 16$_{02}$ ([זקני ... ונתנו]) 16$_{2}$, יֹשֵׁב *inhabitant* Ezk 26$_{17}$, חַי *living one* Ec 7$_{2}$, רָשָׁע *wicked one* Ps 119$_{110}$, זְרוֹעַ *arm*, i.e. army Dn 11$_{31}$.

נֶשֶׁר *eagle* Ezk 17$_{5}$, אֶרֶז *cedar* Ezk 31$_{10}$, עֵץ *tree* Ezk 31$_{14}$, הַר *mountain* Ezk 36$_{8}$, חָכְמָה *wisdom* Pr 4$_{9}$, חֲרָדָה *fear* Pr 29$_{25}$, מִי *who?* Is 41$_{2}$; subj. not specified, Nm 19$_{17}$ Is 53$_{9}$ (or em. וַיֻּתַּן *and it was placed*, i.e. qal pass.) Jr 37$_{4}$ 38$_{7}$ Ezk 3$_{25}$ 21$_{34}$ 32$_{25.27}$ 43$_{20}$ Ps 8$_{2}$ Ec 7$_{21}$ Dn 12$_{11}$ 2 C 11$_{16}$ 24$_{8}$ Si 50$_{28}$ 51$_{26}$ 4QMMT C$_{9}$.

<OBJ> אֱלֹהִים *god* 2 K 18$_{14}$ 19$_{18}$||Is 37$_{19}$, Ammonites Jg 11$_{9}$ Ezk 21$_{34}$, Amorites Dt 7$_{2}$ Jos 10$_{12}$, Canaanites Dt 7$_{2}$, Girgashites Dt 7$_{2}$, Hittites Dt 7$_{2}$, Hivites Dt 7$_{2}$, Israel(ites) Dt 26$_{19}$ 28$_{1}$ Ezk 37$_{26}$ CD 4$_{16}$, Jebusites Dt 7$_{2}$, Perizzites Dt 7$_{2}$, עַם *people* 1 K 8$_{46}$||2 C 6$_{36}$ 1QLitPr 3.2$_{6}$ ([ותת]נם), גּוֹי *nation* Dt 7$_{2.23}$ 31$_{5}$ Is 41$_{2}$, מַחֲנֶה *camp* Ezk 4$_{2}$, חַיִל *army* 2 C 17$_{2}$, נְצִיב *garrison* 2 C 17$_{2}$, קְהִלָּה *assembly* Ne 5$_{7}$.

Achsah Jos 15$_{19}$||Jg 1$_{15}$, Benaiah 1 K 2$_{35}$, Benjamin Gn 42$_{37}$, Jeremiah Jr 20$_{2}$ 37$_{4.15.18}$ 38$_{6}$, Joash 2 C 22$_{11}$, Joseph Gn 39$_{20}$ 41$_{41.43}$ 4QJub[h] 39$_{11}$ ([יוסף]), Oholiab Ex 31$_{6}$, Sihon Dt 2$_{31.33}$, Uriah 2 S 11$_{16}$, Zadok 1 K 2$_{35}$, Zedekiah Jr 52$_{11}$.

אִישׁ *man* Dt 17$_{15}$=11QT 56$_{15}$ Jr 29$_{26}$, אִשָּׁה *woman* 2 S 20$_{3}$, פִּלֶגֶשׁ *secondary wife* 2 S 20$_{3}$, בֵּן *son* Ex 31$_{6}$ 1 K 2$_{35}$ 5$_{19}$ 2 C 22$_{11}$, of herd Gn 18$_{8}$, בַּת *daughter* Jos 15$_{19}$, מֶלֶךְ *king* 1 S 12$_{13}$ 1 K 10$_{9}$||2 C 9$_{8}$ Ezk 28$_{11.17}$ Ne 9$_{37}$ 11QT 59$_{20}$, שַׂר *chief* Gn 40$_{3}$ 41$_{10}$ 2 C 32$_{6}$, שֹׁפֵט *judge* Dt 16$_{18}$ 11QT 51$_{11}$, נָגִיד *leader* 2 C 11$_{11}$, שֹׁטֵר *officer* Dt 16$_{18}$ 11QT 51$_{11}$, סָרִיס *eunuch* Gn 40$_{3}$, שִׁפְחָה *female servant* Gn 16$_{5}$, כֹּהֵן *priest* 1 K 2$_{35}$, כֹּמֶר *priest* 2 K 23$_{5}$, נָבִיא *prophet* Jr 20$_{2}$, רֹאֶה *seer* 2 C 16$_{10}$, נָתִין *temple servant* Ezr 8$_{20}$, worshipper 1QH 16$_{4}$ ([נ]תתני) 4QapPs[b] 45a$_{4}$, מֵינֶקֶת *nurse* 2 C 22$_{11}$, רֹכֵב *rider* 2 K 18$_{23}$||Is 36$_{8}$, אָסִיר *prisoner* Gn 39$_{22}$, אֹיֵב *enemy* Dt 23$_{15}$ perh. 1 K 5$_{17}$ 11QT 59$_{19}$, פֶּגֶר *corpse* Lv 26$_{30}$ Ezk 6$_{5}$.

יָד *hand* Gn 38$_{28}$ Ex 7$_{4}$ 2 K 10$_{15.15}$ Lm 5$_{6}$ 1QM 1$_{17}$ 12$_{11}$=19$_{3}$, זְרוֹעַ *shoulder* Nm 6$_{19}$, כָּתֵף *shoulder (piece)* Ex 28$_{25}$||39$_{18}$ Zc 7$_{11}$, צַוָּאר *neck* Jr 27$_{8}$ 2 C 29$_{6}$, כֶּרַע *leg* Ex 29$_{17}$, רֶגֶל *foot* 1QM 12$_{11}$=19$_{3}$ (רג[ל]ך), פֶּה *mouth* Lm 3$_{29}$, פָּנִים *face* Gn 30$_{40}$ Lv 17$_{10}$ 20$_{3.6}$ 26$_{17}$ Ezk 14$_{8}$ 15$_{7}$ Dn 9$_{3}$ 10$_{15}$ 2 C 20$_{3}$ CD 4$_{16}$, רֹאשׁ *head*, i.e. chief Nm 14$_{4}$ Ne 9$_{17}$, שֵׂעָר *hair* Nm 6$_{18}$, דָּם *blood* Ex 12$_{7}$ 29$_{12.20}$ Lv 4$_{25.30.34}$ 8$_{15.23}$ 9$_{9}$ 14$_{14.25}$ 16$_{18}$ Dt 21$_{8}$=11QT 63$_{7}$ 1 K 2$_{5}$ Jr 26$_{15}$ Ezk 24$_{8}$ 43$_{20}$ 45$_{19}$ Jl 3$_{3}$ Jon 1$_{14}$ 11QT 16$_{02}$ ([ונתנו]) 11QT[b] 1$_{25}$ (ונת[ו]), קֶרֶב *inner parts* Ex 29$_{17}$, גִּיד *sinew* Ezk 37$_{6}$.

לֵב *heart*, i.e. mind Ec 1$_{13.17}$ 7$_{21}$ 8$_{9.16}$ Dn 10$_{12}$ Si 12$_{11}$ 4QMMT C$_{9}$ ([לבנו]), לֵבָב *heart*, i.e. mind 1 C 22$_{19}$ 2 C 11$_{16}$, בָּשָׂר *flesh* Ezk 32$_{5}$, נֶפֶשׁ *soul* Si 7$_{20}$ 51$_{20(B).26}$, רוּחַ *spirit* Nm 11$_{25.29}$ 1 K 22$_{23}$||2 C 18$_{22}$ 2 K 19$_{7}$||Is 37$_{7}$ Is 42$_{1}$ Ezk 11$_{19}$ 36$_{26.27}$ 37$_{6.14}$ 1QH 4$_{17}$ 5$_{25}$ 8$_{20}$ 20$_{12}$ fr. 3$_{14}$.

פַּר *bull* 1 K 18$_{23}$, עֵדֶר *drove* Gn 32$_{17}$, תַּיִשׁ *he-goat* Gn 30$_{35}$, עֵז *she-goat* Gn 30$_{35}$, סוּס *horse* 2 K 23$_{11}$, כְּפִיר *young lion* Ezk 19$_{9}$.

אֶרֶז *cedar* Is 41$_{19}$, שִׁטָּה *acacia* Is 41$_{19}$, הֲדַס *myrtle* Is 41$_{19}$, עֵץ *tree, wood* Is 41$_{19}$ Ezk 37$_{19}$ Si 8$_{3}$, צַמֶּרֶת *tree-top* Ezk 17$_{22}$ 31$_{10.14}$, עָנָף *branches* Ezk 36$_{8}$, חִטָּה *wheat* Ezk 4$_{9}$, שְׂעֹרָה *barley* Ezk 4$_{9}$, דֹּחַן *millet* Ezk 4$_{9}$, פּוֹל *beans* Ezk 4$_{9}$, עֲדָשָׁה *lentil* Ezk 4$_{9}$, כֻּסֶּמֶת *spelt* Ezk 4$_{9}$, זֶרַע *seed* Ezk 17$_{5}$, רִמּוֹן *pomegranate* 2 C 3$_{16}$, עֵנָב *grape* Dt 23$_{25}$, חֶמְאָה *curd* Gn 18$_{8}$, חָלָב *milk* Gn 18$_{8}$, שֶׁמֶן *oil* Lv 2$_{15}$ Ezk 16$_{18}$, לֶחֶם *bread* Ex 25$_{30}$ 29$_{3}$ Ezk 16$_{19}$, חַלָּה *cake* Ex 29$_{3}$ Nm 6$_{19}$, רָקִיק *wafer* Nm 6$_{19}$, מֶלַח *salt* 11QT 20$_{13}$, אֹכֶל *food* Gn 41$_{48.48}$, מַיִם *water* Ex 30$_{18}$ 40$_{7.30}$ Nm 19$_{17}$.

קְטֹרֶת *incense* Lv 16$_{13}$ Nm 16$_{17.18}$ 17$_{12}$ Ezk 16$_{18}$, לְבֹנָה *frankincense* Lv 2$_{1}$ 5$_{11}$ 24$_{7}$ Nm 5$_{15}$ Ne 13$_{5}$ 11QT 8$_{9}$ ([ונתת]ה ... [לבונה]) 8$_{12}$, מִנְחָה *grain offering* Nm 5$_{18}$ Ne 13$_{5}$ 11QT 24$_{5}$ ([ויתנו ... מנ]חת), אִשֶּׁה *fire offering* 1 S 2$_{28}$.

מָאוֹר *luminary* Gn 1$_{17}$, אֵשׁ *fire* Lv 10$_{1}$ Nm 16$_{7}$ 17$_{11}$ Ezk 10$_{7}$ 30$_{8.14.16}$ Jl 3$_{3}$, תִּימָרָה *column* of smoke Jl 3$_{3}$, חֹשֶׁךְ *darkness* Ezk 32$_{8}$, אֶבֶן *stone* Lv 26$_{1}$ Zc 3$_{9}$ 11QT 51$_{21}$, עָפָר *dust* Nm 5$_{17}$, זָהָב *gold* Jos 6$_{24}$ 1 K 7$_{51}$||2 C 5$_{1}$, כֶּסֶף *silver, money* Jos 6$_{24}$ 1 K 7$_{51}$||2 C 5$_{1}$ 2 K 12$_{10}$.

קֶשֶׁת *bow* Gn 9$_{13}$ 4QAdmon 1$_{7}$, חֶרֶב *sword* Ex 5$_{21}$ Ezk

30$_{24.25}$ 32$_{27}$, מָגֵן *shield* 1 K 10$_{17}$||2 C 9$_{16}$, מַרְצֵעַ *awl* Dt 15$_{17}$, מַפְתֵּחַ *key* Is 22$_{22}$, חח *hook* Ezk 29$_4$ 38$_4$, פַּח *trap* Ps 119$_{110}$, מוֹקֵשׁ *snare* Pr 29$_{25}$, כֶּבֶל *fetter* MurEpBarC^a 1$_5$, מוֹסֵרָה *bond* Jr 27$_2$, עֹל *yoke* Dt 28$_{48}$ 1 K 12$_{4.9}$||2 C 10$_{4.9}$ Jr 28$_{14}$, מוֹטָה *bar* Jr 27$_2$, לְבֵנָה *brick* Ezk 4$_1$, לוּחַ *tablet* 2 C 5$_{10}$, כּוֹס *cup* Gn 40$_{11.13.21}$, נֵזֶר *crown* Ex 29$_6$ 2 K 11$_{12}$|| 2 C 23$_{11}$, עֲטֶרֶת *crown* Ezk 16$_{12}$ 23$_{42}$ 11QT 17$_1$ ([עט]רות), לִוְיָה *garland* Pr 4$_9$, קוֹבַע *helmet* 1 S 17$_{38}$, טַבַּעַת *ring* Gn 41$_{42}$ Ex 25$_{12.26}$||37$_{13}$ 28$_{23.27}$||39$_{16.20}$ 4QJub^h 40$_7$ ([הטבעת]), נֶזֶם *ring* Ezk 16$_{12}$, עָגִיל *(ear)ring* Ezk 16$_{12}$, צָמִיד *bracelet* Ezk 16$_{11}$ 23$_{42}$, פַּעֲמֹן *bell* Ex 39$_{25}$, שׁוֹפָר *trumpet* Jg 7$_{16}$, רֶשֶׁת *net* Ex 27$_5$, מְצוּדָה *net* Ezk 19$_8$ (if em. מִמְּדִינוֹת *from the provinces* to מְצוּדוֹת *nets*), שַׁרְשְׁרָה *chain* Ex 28$_{14}$ 2 C 3$_{16}$, עֲבֹת *cord* Ex 28$_{24}$||39$_{17}$ Ezk 3$_{25}$ 4$_8$, פְּתִיל *cord* Ex 39$_{31}$ Nm 15$_{38}$, אֵפֹד *ephod* Lv 8$_7$, כְּתֹנֶת *tunic* Lv 8$_7$, כְּסוּי *covering* Nm 4$_6$, מִשְׁכָּב *bed* Ezk 32$_{25}$.

מְנוֹרָה *lampstand* Nm 4$_{10.10}$ 2 C 4$_7$ 11QT 9$_{12}$ ([המנורה]), לַפִּיד *torch* Jg 7$_{16}$, כַּפֹּרֶת *mercy seat* Ex 25$_{21}$ 26$_{34}$ 40$_{20}$, מִזְבֵּחַ *altar* Ex 30$_6$ 40$_{5.6}$ 2 K 16$_{14}$, שֻׁלְחָן *table* Ex 26$_{35}$ 40$_{22}$, אֲרוֹן *ark* 1 S 6$_8$ 1 K 6$_{19}$ 2 K 12$_{10}$ 2 C 24$_8$ 35$_3$, יָם *sea* 1 K 7$_{39}$||2 C 4$_{10}$ 2 K 16$_{17}$, כִּיּוֹר *laver* Ex 30$_{18}$ 40$_7$ 2 C 4$_6$, *platform* 2 C 6$_{13}$, מְנַקִּית *bowl* Nm 4$_7$, קְעָרָה *dish* Nm 4$_7$, כַּד *jar* Jg 7$_{16}$, קַשְׂוָה *jar* Nm 4$_7$, יָע *shovel* Nm 4$_{14}$, מִזְרָק *basin* Nm 4$_{14}$, גָּבִיעַ *cup* Jr 35$_5$, כּוֹס *cup* Jr 35$_5$ Ezk 23$_{31}$, מַחְתָּה *firepan* Nm 4$_{14}$, מִזְלָגָה *fork* Nm 4$_{14}$, כַּף *ladle* Nm 4$_7$, כְּלִי *vessel* Nm 4$_{10.10.14}$ Jos 6$_{24}$ 1 K 7$_{51}$||2 C 5$_1$ Ezr 1$_7$ Ne 13$_5$ 2 C 36$_7$, פָּרֹכֶת *veil* Ex 26$_{32.33}$, מַסְוֶה *veil* Ex 34$_{33}$, מָסָךְ *screen* Ex 40$_{8.33}$, אוּרִים *Urim* Ex 28$_{30}$ Lv 8$_8$, תֻּמִּים *Thummim* Ex 28$_{30}$ Lv 8$_8$, בְּרִיחַ *bar* Ex 40$_{18}$, סַף *threshold* Ezk 43$_8$, מְזוּזָה *doorpost* Ezk 43$_8$, אֶדֶן *base* Ex 40$_{18}$, מְכוֹנָה *base* 1 K 7$_{39}$, כֹּתֶרֶת *capital* 1 K 7$_{16}$, כְּרוּב *cherub* 1 K 6$_{27}$, כִּסֵּא *throne* 2 K 25$_{28}$||Jr 52$_{32}$ Jr 1$_{15}$, מִגְרָעָה *recess* 1 K 6$_6$, דָּיֵק *siege wall* Ezk 26$_8$.

חָכְמָה *wisdom* Ex 31$_6$ 36$_{1.2}$ 10$_{24}$||2 C 9$_{23}$, בִּינָה *understanding* 1QH 6$_8$ 1QpHab 2$_8$ (ב[ינ]ה) 4QsapHymnA 1.1$_4$ 4QShir^b 48$_1$, תְּבוּנָה *understanding* Si 45$_{5(Bmg)}$, דֵּעָה *knowledge* 4QsapHymnA 1.1$_4$, בְּרָכָה *blessing* Dt 11$_{26.29}$ 30$_{1.19}$, קֹדֶשׁ *holiness*, i.e. holy thing 1 K 7$_{51}$||2 C 5$_1$, טוֹב *good* Dt 30$_{15}$, חֵן *favour* Gn 39$_{21}$ Ex 3$_{21}$ 11$_3$ 12$_{36}$, תְּשׁוּעָה *salvation* Is 46$_{13}$, כָּבוֹד *glory* Ezk 39$_{21}$, צְבִי *glory* Ezk 26$_{20}$, הוֹד *splendour* Ps 8$_2$, חַיִּים *life* Dt 30$_{15.19}$ 4QTwoWays 2$_2$ ([החיים]), שִׂמְחָה *joy* Ps 4$_8$, הוֹדָה *thanksgiving* 1QH 19$_4$, שִׁיר *song* Ps 40$_4$, תְּהִלָּה *praise* Ps 40$_4$ 1QH 19$_4$ ([תהל]ה).

תְּחִנָּה *supplication* 1QH 17$_{10}$, דָּבָר *word, thing* Dt 18$_{18}$=11QT 61$_{05}$ ([ונתתי דברי]) 30$_1$ Jr 1$_0$, סֵפֶר *document* Dt 24$_{1.3}$ Jr 32$_{14}$, חתם pass. ptc. *sealed thing* Jr 32$_{14}$, בְּרִית *covenant* Gn 9$_{12}$ 17$_2$ Ezk 17$_{19}$, עֵדוּת *testimony* Ex 25$_{16.21}$ 40$_{20}$ 2 K 11$_{10}$||2 C 23$_9$, תּוֹרָה *law* Lv 26$_{46}$ Dt 4$_8$ Jr 9$_{12}$ 26$_4$ 31$_{33}$ Jr 44$_{10}$ Dn 9$_{10}$ Si 45$_{5(Bmg)}$, חֹק *statute* Lv 26$_{46}$ Dt 11$_{32}$, חֻקָּה *statute* 1 K 9$_6$||2 C 7$_{19}$ Jr 44$_{10}$, מִשְׁפָּט *judgment* Ezk 23$_{24}$, *ordinance* Lv 26$_{46}$ Dt 11$_{32}$, מִצְוָה *commandment* 1 K 9$_6$||2 C 7$_{19}$ Si 45$_{5(Bmg)}$, עֲבֹדָה *labour* Dt 26$_6$, מִשְׁמָר *guard* 1QH fr. 2.1$_5$, מוֹפֵת *portent* Jl 3$_3$.

יִרְאָה *fear* Dt 2$_{25}$ Jr 32$_{40}$ Ezk 30$_{13}$, מוֹרָא *fear* Dt 11$_{25}$ 1QH 12$_{26}$, פַּחַד *dread* Dt 2$_{25}$ 11$_{25}$ 1 C 14$_{17}$, חִתִּית *terror* Ezk 26$_{17}$ 32$_{23.24.26.32}$, אָלָה *oath, curse* Dt 30$_7$ Ezk 17$_{19}$, קְלָלָה *curse* Dt 11$_{26.29}$ 30$_{1.19}$, רַע *evil* Dt 30$_{15}$, עָוֹן *iniquity* Lv 16$_{21}$ 11QT 26$_{12}$, *punishment* Ps 69$_{28}$, פֶּשַׁע *transgression* Lv 16$_{21}$, חַטָּאת *sin* Lv 16$_{21}$ 11QT 26$_{12}$, אַשְׁמָה *guilt* 11QT 26$_{12}$, זִמָּה *wickedness* Ezk 23$_{49}$, מָוֶת *death* Dt 30$_{15.19}$ 4QTwoWays 2$_2$ ([המות]), שִׁקּוּץ *detested thing* Dn 11$_{31}$ 12$_{11}$, תּוֹעֵבָה *abomination* Ezk 7$_{3.8}$, חֶרְפָּה *reproach* Jr 23$_{40}$, כְּלִמָּה *insult* Jr 23$_{40}$, נְקָמָה *vengeance* Nm 31$_3$ Ezk 25$_{14.17}$, קִנְאָה *jealousy* Ezk 23$_{25}$, אֵיבָה *enmity* 1QS 4$_{17}$, מִכְשׁוֹל *stumbling block* Lv 19$_{14}$ Jr 6$_{21}$ Ezk 3$_{20}$ 14$_3$.

מְחִי *stroke* of battering ram Ezk 26$_9$, שֶׂרֶט *incision* Lv 19$_{28}$, שָׂרֶטֶת *incision* 11QT 48$_9$, קַעֲקַע *tattoo* Lv 19$_{28}$, מוּם *disfigurement* Lv 24$_{19.20}$ Si 30$_{31}$ 47$_{20}$ (ות[תן]), נֶגַע *plague* Lv 14$_{34}$, חֳלִי *sickness* Dt 7$_{15}$, מַדְוֶה *disease* Dt 7$_{17}$, דֶּבֶר *pestilence* 2 S 24$_{15}$||1 C 21$_{14}$, רָעָב *famine* Ezk 36$_{29}$, אִבְחָה *slaughter* Ezk 21$_{20}$ (or em. אִבְחַת to טֶבַח or טִבְחַת in same sense), מָצוֹר *siege* Ezk 4$_2$, מַאֲרָב *ambush* 2 C 20$_{22}$, מַפָּץ *shattering* 4QpsHod^c 3$_4$ ([ל]תת; unless מַפֵּץ *club*).

מִקְדָּשׁ *sanctuary* Ezk 37$_{26}$, מִשְׁכָּן *dwelling* Lv 26$_{11}$ Ezk 25$_4$, קֶבֶר *grave* Is 53$_9$ (or em.; see Subj.), אֶרֶץ *land* Dt 1$_{8.21}$ 2$_{31}$ Ne 9$_{35}$, עִיר *city* Jos 20$_2$ Si 47$_7$, Bezer Jos 20$_8$, Golan Jos 20$_8$, Ramoth Jos 20$_8$, מָקוֹם *place* 11QT 48$_{14}$, דֶּרֶךְ *way* 1 K 8$_{32}$||2 C 6$_{23}$ Is 43$_{16}$ Jr 21$_8$ Ezk 7$_4$ 9$_{10}$ 11$_{21}$ 16$_{43}$ 22$_{31}$, נְתִיבָה *path* Is 43$_{16}$, תְּהוֹם *deep* Ps 33$_7$, קֵץ *end* 1QS 4$_{18}$, קָצָה *end* Ex 28$_{25}$, עוֹלָם *eternity* Ec 3$_{11}$, מִשְׁעָן *support* 1QH 18$_{22}$, חוּם *brown one* Gn 30$_{35}$.

גּוֹרָל *lot* Lv 16$_{8}$ 1QS 2$_{17}$ 11QT 26$_{3}$ ([ונתן]), עֹנֶשׁ *fine* 2 K 23$_{33}$, כִּכָּר *talent* 2 K 23$_{33}$, בֶּתֶר *part* Gn 15$_{10}$, מְלֹא *fullness* of omer of manna Ex 16$_{33}$, שְׁלִישִׁית *third* of shekel Ne 10$_{33}$, מַעֲשֵׂר *tithe* Ne 13$_{5}$, מְנָת *portion* Ne 13$_{5}$ (if em. מִצְוֹת *commandment of* to מְנָיוֹת), יתר ni. ptc. *remainder* Lv 14$_{18.29}$, יֶתֶר *remainder* 2 S 10$_{10}$||1 C 19$_{11}$, מָה *what?* Ne 2$_{12}$, אֲשֶׁר *that which, one who* 2 K 18$_{14}$ 2 C 17$_{19}$, אֶחָד *one* 1 K 12$_{29}$, זֶה *this* 2 K 4$_{43}$ Ec 9$_{1}$, אֵלֶּה Si 50$_{28}$, כֹּל *everything* Gn 30$_{35}$ 39$_{4.8}$ Lv 8$_{27}$ Dt 2$_{36}$ 4QJub^{f} 39$_{4}$ ([הכול]).

<PREP> לְ in ref. to subj., + Israelites Dt 16$_{18}$ 11QT 51$_{11}$, בֵּן *son* of Israel Jos 20$_{2}$.

לְ of direction, *to(wards), onto,* + רֹאשׁ *head* Pr 4$_{9}$, דָּבָר *thing* Ec 7$_{21}$, מַעֲשֶׂה *deed* Ec 8$_{9}$, מִין *kind* CD 4$_{16}$.

לְ *at,* + רֹאשׁ *head* 11QT 59$_{20}$, זָנָב *tail* 11QT 59$_{20}$.

לְ of benefit, *to, for,* + Y. Lv 16$_{8}$ 2 C 9$_{8}$ 11QT 26$_{3}$ ([ונתן ... לי']), Azazel Lv 16$_{8}$ 11QT 26$_{3}$ ([ונתן ... לעזאזל]), Elam Ezk 32$_{25}$, שֵׁבֶט *tribe* Dt 16$_{18}$, בַּיִת *house* 1 S 2$_{28}$, שֶׁמֶשׁ *sun* 2 K 23$_{11}$, עֲבֹדָה *service* Ezr 8$_{20}$ Ne 10$_{33}$.

לְ *as, for (the purpose of),* + רֵיחַ *odour* Ezk 16$_{19}$.

לְ *for (the sake of), on account of,* + worshipper Ps 119$_{110}$, נֶפֶשׁ *soul,* i.e. deceased person Lv 19$_{28}$.

לְ *upon, against,* + יֹשֵׁב *inhabitant* Ezk 26$_{17}$.

בְּ of place, *in(to), over, on, among, beside,* + Ammonites Ezk 25$_{4}$, Philistines Si 47$_{7}$, עַם *people* Ezk 37$_{14}$, גּוֹי *nation* Ezk 39$_{21}$, הָמוֹן *multitude* Ezk 32$_{25}$, Bezalel Ex 36$_{1}$, Oholiab Ex 36$_{1}$, Oholibah Ezk 23$_{25}$, אָדָם *human being* Lv 24$_{20}$, אִישׁ *man* Ex 36$_{1}$, בֵּן *son* of Israel Lv 19$_{28}$, מֶלֶךְ *king* 2 K 19$_{7}$||Is 37$_{7}$, עָמִית *neighbour* Lv 24$_{19}$, worshipper 1QH 4$_{17}$ 5$_{25}$ 8$_{20}$ ([בי]) 20$_{12}$ fr. 3$_{14}$, יָד *hand* Gn 40$_{13}$ Ex 5$_{21}$ Dt 24$_{1.3}$ Jg 7$_{16}$ Ezk 23$_{31}$ 30$_{24.25}$ Ps 10$_{14}$ Si 45$_{5(Bmg)}$ 4QJub^{h} 40$_{7}$ ([ביד]), i.e. charge Gn 30$_{35}$ 32$_{17}$ 39$_{4.8.22}$ 2 S 10$_{10}$||1 C 19$_{11}$, רֶגֶל *foot* MurEpBarC^{a} 1$_{5}$, אֹזֶן *ear* Dt 15$_{17}$ 1QH 21$_{12}$ ([נ]תתה), פֶּה *mouth* Dt 18$_{18}$=11QT 61$_{05}$ ([ונתתי ... בפיהו]) 1 K 22$_{23}$||2 C 18$_{22}$ Jr 1$_{9}$ Ps 40$_{4}$ 1QH 17$_{10}$ 19$_{4}$, לָשׁוֹן *tongue* 1QH 19$_{4}$, לְחִי *jaw* Ezk 29$_{4}$ 38$_{4}$, עֹרֶף *neck* 1QM 12$_{11}$=19$_{3}$, רֹאשׁ *head* Ezk 16$_{12}$, i.e. first 1 C 16$_{7}$, חֵיק *bosom* Gn 16$_{5}$, לֵב *heart* Ex 31$_{6}$ 35$_{34}$ 36$_{2}$ 1 K 10$_{24}$||2 C 9$_{23}$ Ps 4$_{8}$ Ec 3$_{11}$ Ezr 7$_{27}$ 1QH 6$_{8}$ 1QpHab 2$_{8}$ ([ב]לבו), לֵבָב *heart* Jr 32$_{40}$ 4QsapHymnA 1.1$_{4}$ 4QShir^{b} 48$_{1}$ ([ב]לב[בי]), עֶצֶם *bone* Ezk 37$_{6}$, בָּשָׂר *flesh* Lv 19$_{28}$ 11QT 48$_{9}$, חֲגוֹרָה *girdle* 1 K 2$_{5}$, נַעַל *sandal* 1 K 2$_{5}$, דֶּלֶת *door* Dt 15$_{17}$, שַׁעַר *gate* 2 C 24$_{8}$, מַחְתָּה *censer* Lv 10$_{1}$ Nm 16$_{7}$, כְּלִי *vessel* Jr 32$_{14}$ Ezk 4$_{9}$, *weapon* 1QM 1$_{17}$ ([בכל[י]), עֹל *yoke* Jr 27$_{8}$, שַׁרְשְׁרָה *chain* 2 C 3$_{16}$, מִשְׁמָר *custody* Gn 40$_{3}$ 41$_{10}$, שָׁמַיִם *heaven* Jl 3$_{3}$, רָקִיעַ *firmament* Gn 1$_{17}$, עָנָן *cloud* Gn 9$_{13}$ 4QAdmon 1$_{7}$ ([בקשת]), אֵשׁ *fire* Lv 1$_{7}$ 18$_{14}$ 19$_{18}$||Is 37$_{19}$, Dan 1 K 12$_{29}$, Zion Is 46$_{13}$, עִיר *city* Gn 41$_{48}$ 2 C 17$_{2.2.19}$, שַׁעַר *gate,* i.e. city Dt 16$_{18}$ 11QT 51$_{11}$, קֹדֶשׁ *holy place* Ex 26$_{34}$, הֵיכָל *temple* 2 C 4$_{7}$ 36$_{7}$, אֹהֶל *tent* Ex 30$_{36}$ 40$_{22}$, בַּיִת *house* Lv 14$_{34}$ 2 C 9$_{16}$ Jr 52$_{11}$ Ezr 1$_{7}$ 2 C 35$_{3}$, חֶדֶר *chamber* 2 C 22$_{11}$, אוֹצָר *treasury* 1 K 7$_{51}$||2 C 5$_{1}$ Ps 33$_{7}$, Horeb 2 C 5$_{10}$, מְצוּרָה *fortress* 2 C 11$_{11}$, אֶרֶץ *land* Lv 26$_{1}$ Ezk 26$_{20}$ 30$_{13}$ 32$_{15.24.26.32}$ Jl 3$_{3}$ 2 C 17$_{2}$ perh. 4QpsHistA 1$_{3}$, שָׂדֶה *field* Ezk 17$_{5}$, מִדְבָּר *steppe* Is 41$_{19}$, הַר *mountain* Lv 26$_{46}$, עָפָר *dust* Lm 3$_{29}$, יָם *sea* Is 43$_{16}$, מַיִם *water* Is 43$_{16}$, מָקוֹר *spring* 16$_{4}$ ([נ]תתני), יָמִין *right* 2 K 12$_{10(Kt)}$, כָּבוֹד *honour* S47$_{20}$ (ו[ת]תן), מִשְׁפָּט *judgment* 4QapPs^{b} 45a$_{4}$.

בְּ *against, upon,* + Edom Ezk 25$_{14}$, Egypt Ex 7$_{4}$ 30$_{8.16}$, Israel 2 S 24$_{15}$||1 C 21$_{14}$, Midian Nm 31$_{3}$, Zoan Ezk 30$_{14}$, Philistines Ezk 25$_{17}$, אִישׁ *man* Lv 20$_{3}$ Ezk 14$_{8}$ perh. 4Q 417 3$_{1}$, בֵּן *son* of Israel Lv 26$_{17}$, שׂנא ptc. *one who hates* Dt 7$_{15}$, יֹשֵׁב *inhabitant* Ezk 15$_{7}$, רֹאשׁ *head* 1 K 8$_{32}$||2 C 6$_{23}$ Ezk 9$_{10}$ 11$_{21}$ 16$_{43}$ 17$_{19}$ 22$_{31}$, נֶפֶשׁ *soul,* i.e. person Lv 17$_{10}$ 20$_{6}$, חוֹמָה *wall* Ezk 26$_{9}$.

בְּ of time, *in, at,* + עֵת *time* 2 C 20$_{22}$.

בְּ of instrument, *by (means of), with,* + אֶצְבַּע *finger* Ex 29$_{12}$ Lv 8$_{15}$ 11QT 16$_{16}$ 23$_{12}$ ((ונתן[ן])) 11QT^{b} 1$_{25}$ ([ונתן ... באצבעם]), יָד *hand* Lv 26$_{46}$ Ezk 25$_{14}$ Dn 9$_{10}$, חַח *hook* Ezk 19$_{9}$.

בְּ of cause, *on account of,* + חַטָּאת *sin* Ne 9$_{37}$.

כְּ *something like,* + זֹאת *this* Ezr 3$_{27}$.

כְּ *according to,* + מִשְׁפָּט *manner* Gn 40$_{13}$.

מִן of direction, *from,* + מִשְׁכָּן *dwelling place* 2 C 29$_{6}$.

מִן *(positioned away) from, on, at,* + כָּתֵף *shoulder,* i.e. side 1 K 7$_{39}$||2 C 4$_{10}$, יָמִין *right* 2 K 12$_{10(Qr)}$ 2 C 4$_{6.7}$, שְׂמֹאול *left* 2 C 4$_{6.7}$, רֹאשׁ *head,* i.e. top Ezk 17$_{22}$.

מִן partitive, *(some) of* (as obj.), + דָּם *blood* Lv 4$_{7.18}$ 8$_{24}$ 11QT 16$_{2}$ ([ונ]תנו) 16$_{16}$ 23$_{12}$ ((ונתן מ]דמו)), שֶׁמֶן *oil* Ex 30$_{33}$ Lv 14$_{28}$, קְטֹרֶת *incense* Ex 30$_{36}$, הוֹד *splendour* Nm 27$_{20}$, יֶתֶר *remainder* Lv 14$_{17}$.

אֶל *to(wards), (in)to, onto,* + Y. Dn 9$_{3}$, יֹשֵׁב *inhabitant*

Jr 26_{15}, יָד *hand* Ezk 23_{43}, צַוָּאר *neck* Ezk 21_{34}, חֹפֶן *hollow of hand* Ezk 10_{7}, חֹשֶׁן *breastpiece* Lv 8_{8}, לֵב *heart*, i.e. mind Ec 7_{2} 9_{1} Ne 2_{12} 7_{5}, פִּנָּה *corner* Ezk 43_{20} 45_{19}, מִכְסֶה *cover* Nm 4_{10}, מַיִם *water* Nm 5_{17}, אֲרוֹן *ark* Ex $25_{16.21}$ 40_{20}, כְּלִי *vessel* Dt 23_{25}, עֲגָלָה *cart* 1 S 6_{8}, מַהְפֶּכֶת *stocks* Jr 29_{26}, צִינֹק *iron collar* Jr 29_{26}, מְזוּזָה *doorpost* Ezk 45_{19}, בַּיִת prison *house* Gn 39_{20} 40_{3} 37_{18}, בּוֹר *pit* Jr 38_{7}, עִיר *city* Jr 26_{15}, מָקוֹם *place* Gn 39_{20} 40_{3} 2 S 11_{16}, גְּבוּל *border* Ezk 43_{20}, עָקֹד *striped one* Gn 30_{40}, חוּם *brown one* Gn 30_{40}.

אֶל *before*, + עַם *people* Jr 6_{21}.

עַל *upon, at, beside, against* 4QParGenEx 2_{5} perh. 4QNarrB 1_{3} 11QT 8_{12} 24_{5} ([ויתנו עליו]), + Israel(ites) Dt 26_{6} 1 K 12_{4}||2 C 10_{4} Ne 10_{33}, Tyre Ezk 26_{8}, עַם *people* Nm 11_{29} 1 K 12_{9}||2 C 10_{9} Jr 26_{15} 1QH 12_{26}, גּוֹי *nation* 1 C 14_{17}, בַּיִת *house* of Israel Ezk 36_{26}, Aaron Lv $8_{7.7}$, Hezekiah 2 K 18_{14}, Joshua Nm 27_{20}, Oholah Ezk 23_{49}, Oholibah Ezk 23_{49}, אִישׁ *man* Nm 11_{25} 27_{20} Jon 1_{14}, בֵּן *son* Nm 27_{20} 2 K 11_{12}||2 C 23_{11} 2 C 20_{22}, of man, in ref. to Ezekiel Ezk 3_{25} 4_{8}, מֶלֶךְ *king* 2 K 18_{14}, שַׂר *prince* Jr 26_{15}, חֹר *noble* Ne 5_{7}, זָקֵן *elder* Nm 11_{25}, סָגָן *official* Ne 5_{7}, עֶבֶד *servant* Is 42_{1}, בָּחִיר *elect one* Is 42_{1}, נָבִיא *prophet* Jr 23_{40}, זָר *stranger*, i.e. lay Israelite Ex 30_{33}, אֹיֵב *enemy* Dt 30_{7}, שׂנא ptc. *one who hates* Dt 30_{7}, פֶּגֶר *corpse* Lv 26_{30}.

יָד *hand* Gn 41_{42} Ezk 16_{11}, בֹּהֶן *thumb, big toe* Ex 29_{20} Lv $8_{23.24}$ $14_{14.17.25.28}$, פַּעַם *foot* Ex 25_{12}, אֹזֶן *ear* Ezk 16_{12}, תְּנוּךְ *lobe* of ear Ex 29_{20} Lv $8_{23.24}$ $14_{14.17.25.28}$ 11QT 16_{2} ([ונ]תנו ... [על תנוך]), אַף *nose* Ezk 16_{12}, קֶרֶן *horn* of altar Ex 29_{12} Lv $4_{7.18.25.30.34}$ 8_{15} 9_{9} 16_{18} Ezk 43_{20} 11QT 16_{02} ([ונתנו על קרנות]) 16_{16} 23_{12} ([ונת]ן) 11QT[b] 1_{25} (ונת]ו על [קרנות]), צַוָּאר *neck* Dt 28_{48} Jr 27_{2} 28_{14}, שְׁכֶם *shoulder* Is 22_{22}, כָּתֵף *shoulder-piece* Ex 28_{27}||29_{20}, חֹשֶׁן *breastpiece* Ex 28_{30}, רֹאשׁ *head* Ex 29_{17} Lv $14_{18.29}$ 16_{21} 1 S 17_{38} Ezk 23_{42} 11QT 26_{12}, i.e. top 1 K 7_{16} 2 C 3_{16}, פָּנִים *face* Ex 34_{33}, לֵב *heart* Si 50_{28}, דָּם *blood* Lv 14_{17}, עֶצֶם *bone* Ezk 37_{6}, כָּתֵף *shoulder*, i.e. side 1 K 7_{39}, יָרֵךְ *side* Ex 40_{22} 2 K 16_{14}, צֵלָע *side* Ex 25_{12} 26_{35}, פֵּאָה *corner* Ex 25_{26}||37_{13}, פִּנָּה *corner* 11QT 23_{12} ([ונת]ן), קָצָה *end* Ex 28_{23}||39_{16}, מַעֲרָכָה *row* Lv 24_{7} 11QT 8_{9} (ונתת]ה על שתי] המערכות), נֵתַח *piece* Ex 29_{17}.

סוּס *horse* 2 K 18_{23}||Is 36_{8}, שָׂעִיר *goat* Lv 16_{8} 11QT 26_{3} ([ונתן]), עֵץ *wood* 1 K 18_{23} Ezk 37_{19}, קֶמַח *flour* Nm 5_{15}, סֹלֶת *fine flour* Lv 2_{1}, קָרְבָּן *offering* Nm 5_{15} 11QT 20_{13}, מִנְחָה *grain offering* Lv 2_{15}, חַטָּאת *sin offering* Lv 5_{11}, עָוֹן *punishment* Ps 69_{28}, בֶּגֶד *cloth* Nm 4_{7}, מִצְנֶפֶת *turban* Ex 39_{6}, צִיצִת *tassel* Nm 15_{38}, חוֹמָה *wall* Jr 1_{15}, מְזוּזָה *doorpost* Ex 12_{7} Ezk 45_{19}, מַשְׁקוֹף *lintel* Ex 12_{7}, שַׁעַר *gate* Ezk 21_{20}, עַמּוּד *pillar* Ex 26_{32}, מוֹט *pole* Nm 4_{10}, אֲרוֹן *ark* Ex 25_{21} 26_{34} 40_{20} Nm 4_{6}, מִזְבֵּחַ *altar* Lv 1_{7} Nm 4_{14}, שֻׁלְחָן *table* Ex 25_{30}, מַחְתָּה *censer* Nm $16_{17.18}$ 17_{11}, מִשְׁבְּצָה *setting* Ex $28_{14.25}$, כִּסֵּא *throne* 1 K 5_{19} 10_{9}||2 C 9_{8}, מַרְצֶפֶת *pavement* 2 K 16_{17}, בָּמָה *high place*, i.e. pile, of slain 1QM 12_{11}=19_{3} ([על במותי]), אֶרֶץ *land* 2 K 23_{33} Ezk 32_{8}, אֲדָמָה *land* Ezk $7_{3.4.8}$, הַר *mountain* Dt 11_{29} Ezk 32_{5}, צְחִיחַ *surface* Ezk 24_{8}, Jerusalem Ezk $4_{2.2}$, עִיר *city* Jr 1_{15} Ezk $4_{2.2}$, מָקוֹם *place* Lv 14_{28}, עָפָר *dust* Nm 19_{17}, אֵשׁ *fire* Lv 16_{13} Nm 6_{18} Si 8_{3}, בֶּצַע *unjust gain* 1QH 18_{22}, אֵלֶּה *these* 4QMMT C_{9} ([אלה]).

עַל *above*, + גּוֹי *nation* Dt 26_{19} 28_{1}, שָׁמַיִם *heavens* Ps 8_{2}.

עַל *(in)to*, + יָד *hand*, i.e. charge Gn 42_{37}, כַּף *hand* Gn $40_{11.21}$ Lv 8_{27} Nm 5_{18} 6_{19}, טַבַּעַת *ring* Ex 28_{24}||39_{17}, צִיץ *plate* Ex 39_{31}, סַל *basket* Ex 29_{3}, מַהְפֶּכֶת *stocks* Jr 20_{2}.

עַל *over*, i.e. in charge of, + Israel(ites) Dt 17_{15}=11QT 56_{15} Ne 9_{37}, עַם *people* 1 S 12_{13} 2 C 32_{6}, צָבָא *army* 1 K 2_{35}, אֶרֶץ *land* Gn $41_{41.43}$.

עַל *on account of, for (the sake of)*, + נֶפֶשׁ *soul*, i.e. deceased person 11QT 48_{9}.

עַל־פְּנֵי *upon*, + עַם *people* Dt 2_{25}, אֶרֶץ *land* Dt 11_{25}.

מֵעַל *above*, + כִּסֵּא *throne* 2 K 25_{28}.

מִמַּעַל לְ *above*, + כִּסֵּא *throne* Jr 52_{32}.

בֵּין *among*, + עִיר *city* 11QT 48_{14}.

בְּתוֹךְ *within, among*, + בֵּן *son* of Israel Lv 26_{11}, ארר pass. ptc. *accursed one* 1QS 2_{17}, לָבִיא *lion* 1QH 13_{6}, רִמּוֹן *pomegranate* Ex 39_{25}, עִיר *city* Gn 41_{48}, בַּיִת *house* 1 K 6_{27}, עֲזָרָה *court* 2 C 6_{13}.

בְּקֶרֶב *within, among*, + Israel Dt 21_{8}=11QT 63_{7}, עַם *people* Dt 21_{8}=11QT 63_{7}, בַּיִת *house* of Israel Jr 31_{33} Ezk 11_{19} $36_{26.27}$, אִישׁ *man* Ezk 11_{19}, אָח *brother* Ezk 11_{19}.

בְּעֵינֵי *in the sight of*, + Egyptians Ex 3_{21} 11_{3} 12_{36}, שַׂר *chief* Gn 39_{21}.

עִם *with*, + Y. 4QapPs[b] 45_{a4}.

אֵת *with*, + כְּרוּב *cherub* Ezk 28_{14} (if em. ־אַתְּ *you* to

אֶת־), Bezalel Ex 31$_{6}$, בֵּן *son* Ex 31$_{6}$, עָשִׁיר *rich one* Is 53$_{9}$, רָשָׁע *wicked one* Is 53$_{9}$, סַף *threshold* Ezk 43$_{8}$.

עַד *until*, + יוֹם *day* Jr 52$_{11}$.

בֵּין *between, among*, + Y. Gn 9$_{12}$ 17$_{2}$ Lv 26$_{46}$, Abram Gn 17$_{2}$, Noah Gn 9$_{12}$, בֵּן *son* Gn 9$_{12}$, of Israel Lv 26$_{46}$, נֶפֶשׁ *soul* Gn 9$_{12}$, אֹהֶל *tent* Ex 30$_{18}$ 40$_{7}$, מִזְבֵּחַ *altar* Ex 30$_{18}$ 40$_{7}$, מִפְלַגָּה *division* 1QS 4$_{17}$.

אֶל־בֵּין *among*, + עֲבֹת *foliage* Ezk 31$_{10.14}$ (or in both em. עֲבוֹתִים to עָבוֹת *clouds*).

אֵצֶל *beside*, + מִזְבֵּחַ *altar* 2 K 12$_{10}$, מְזוּזָה *doorpost* Ezk 43$_{8}$.

לְעֻמַּת *close by*, + מַחְבֶּרֶת *joining* Ex 28$_{27}$ ||39$_{20}$.

מִחוּץ לְ *outside*, + פָּרֹכֶת *veil* Ex 40$_{22}$.

לִקְרַאת *opposite*, + רֵעַ *neighbour*, i.e. other one Gn 15$_{10}$.

אֶל־מוּל פְּנֵי *in front of*, + אֵפֹד *ephod* Ex 28$_{25}$||39$_{18}$.

מִמּוּל *from the front of*, + נֶגֶב *south* 1 K 7$_{39}$||2 C 4$_{10}$.

מִמּוּל פְּנֵי *from the front of*, + אֵפֹד *ephod* Ex 28$_{27}$||39$_{20}$.

לִפְנֵי *before* (distinction from §1 not alw. clear) Is 41$_{2}$ perh. 1Q30 2$_{1}$, + Y. Ex 25$_{30}$ Lv 4$_{7}$ 16$_{13}$, צֶלֶם *image* Ezk 16$_{18.19}$, גִּלּוּל *idol* Ezk 6$_{5}$, Chaldaeans Ezk 23$_{24}$, Israel(ites) Dt 1$_{8.21}$ 2$_{31.33.36}$ 4$_{8}$ 7$_{2.23}$ 11$_{26.32}$ 23$_{15}$ 30$_{1.15.19}$ 31$_{5}$ 1 K 9$_{6}$||2 C 7$_{19}$ Jr 9$_{12}$ Dn 9$_{10}$ 4QTwoWays 2$_{2}$ ([לפניכה]), Jews Jr 44$_{10}$, עַם *people* 2 K 4$_{44}$ Jr 21$_{8}$, עִיר *city* Jr 26$_{4}$, Jephthah Jg 11$_{9}$, Joseph 4QJub^{f} 39$_{4}$ ([לפנו]), Joshua Zc 3$_{9}$, Koa Ezk 23$_{24}$, Pekod Ezk 23$_{24}$, Shoa Ezk 23$_{24}$, אִישׁ *man* Gn 18$_{8}$ 2 K 4$_{43}$, אָב *father* Jr 44$_{10}$ Ne 9$_{35}$, בֵּן *son* Jr 35$_{5}$ Ezk 23$_{24}$, of man. in ref. to Ezekiel Ezk 4$_{1}$, of Israel Jos 10$_{12}$, מֶלֶךְ *king* Ezk 28$_{17}$ 11QT 59$_{19}$, פֶּחָה *governor* Ezk 23$_{24}$, סָגָן *officer* Ezk 23$_{24}$, בָּחוּר *youth* Ezk 23$_{24}$, אֹיֵב *enemy* 1 K 8$_{46}$||2 C 6$_{36}$, עִוֵּר *blind one* Lv 19$_{14}$, צַדִּיק *righteous one* Ezk 3$_{20}$, מְאַהֵב *lover* Ezk 23$_{24}$, פָּרֹכֶת *veil* Ex 30$_{6}$, דְּבִיר *inner sanctuary* 11QT 9$_{12}$ ([לפני הדביר]), פֶּתַח *entrance* Ex 40$_{6}$, עֵדוּת *testimony* Ex 30$_{36}$, אֲרוֹן *ark* Ex 40$_{5}$.

נֹכַח *in front of*, + פָּנִים *face* Ezk 14$_{3}$, שֻׁלְחָן *table* 11QT 9$_{12}$ ([נוכח השולח]ן).

תַּחַת *under*, + רֹאשׁ *head* Ezk 32$_{27}$, כַּף *sole* of foot 1 K 5$_{17}$, כַּרְכֹּב *edge* Ex 27$_{5}$, קֶרֶס *hook* Ex 26$_{33}$.

תַּחַת *in place of*, + Abiathar 1 K 2$_{35}$, David 1 K 5$_{19}$, Joab 1 K 2$_{35}$, אָב *father* 1 K 5$_{19}$.

אַחֲרֵי *after*, + חָכְמָה *wisdom* Si 51$_{20(B)}$.

ה- of direction, *into*, + שָׁם *there* Ex 16$_{33}$ 30$_{18}$ 40$_{30}$ 2 K 12$_{10}$, חוּץ *outside* 2 C 24$_{8}$, צָפוֹן *north* 2 K 16$_{14}$, אֶרֶץ *ground* Dn 10$_{15}$.

נתן + noun without preposition or ה- of direction, אַשּׁוּר *(to) Assyria* Lm 5$_{6}$, מִצְרַיִם *(to) Egypt* Lm 5$_{6}$, בַּיִת *(in a/the) house* 2 S 20$_{3}$ 10$_{17}$ Jr 37$_{4.15}$ 2 C 16$_{10}$ 4QJub^{h} 39$_{11}$ ([בית]), מָקוֹם *(in the) place* 4QJub^{h} 39$_{11}$ ([מקום]), פֶּתַח *(at the) entrance* Jr 1$_{15}$, אוֹצָר *(into the) treasury* Jos 6$_{24}$, אֶרֶץ *(in the) land* Jos 15$_{15}$||Jg 1$_{15}$, עֲרֵמָה *(in a) heap* 2 C 31$_{6}$, מִצְוָה *(according to the) commandment* Ne 13$_{5}$ (or em. מִצְוַת to מְנָיוֹת *portions of*).

<COLL> נתן || שִׂים *place* Ex 40$_{20}$ Lv 2$_{15}$ 5$_{11}$ Nm 16$_{7}$ 17$_{11}$ Dt 7$_{15}$ 17$_{15}$=11QT 56$_{15}$ 1 K 2$_{5}$ 12$_{29}$ Is 41$_{19}$ Ezk 4$_{2}$; + שִׂים *place* Ex 29$_{6}$ 40$_{8.18.30}$ Lv 8$_{8}$ 1 K 18$_{23}$ Ezk 15$_{7}$ 17$_{5}$.

|| ישׁב pi. *establish* Ezk 25$_{4}$, יצק *pour* Nm 5$_{15}$, שׁפך *pour* Ezk 26$_{8}$, מגן pi. *bestow upon* Pr 4$_{9}$; קום hi. *raise up* Ezk 26$_{8}$; + קום hi. Ex 40$_{18.33}$ Lv 26$_{1}$.

+ פרשׂ *spread* Nm 4$_{6.7.14}$, עשׂה *make* Lv 26$_{1}$, כנס *gather* Ps 33$_{7}$, סור hi. *remove* Ezk 36$_{26}$, לקח *take* Gn 15$_{10}$ 18$_{8}$ 39$_{20}$ Ex 12$_{7}$ 16$_{33}$ 29$_{12.20}$ 40$_{20}$ Lv 4$_{25.30.34}$ 8$_{15.23}$ 14$_{14.25}$ 16$_{18}$ Nm 4$_{12}$ 5$_{17}$ 6$_{18.19}$ Dt 1 S 6$_{8}$ 2 K 12$_{10}$ Jr 32$_{14}$ Ezk 4$_{1.3.9}$ 10$_{7}$ 17$_{5.22}$ 43$_{20}$ 45$_{19}$.

+ adverb or noun used adverbially, שָׁם *there* Ex 40$_{7}$ 1 K 6$_{19}$, סָבִיב *round about* Lv 8$_{15}$ 16$_{18}$ 1 K 6$_{6}$ Jr 1$_{15}$ Ezk 43$_{20}$, לְמַעְלָה *upwards* 11QT 59$_{20}$, לְמַטָּה *downwards* 11QT 59$_{20}$, עֶלְיוֹן *high* Dt 26$_{19}$ 28$_{1}$, הַיּוֹם *today* Dt 11$_{26.32}$.

לְהוֹרֹת נָתַן בְּלִבּוֹ *he has put (it) in his heart to teach* Ex 35$_{34}$, נָתַתִּי אֶת־לִבִּי לִדְרוֹשׁ *I set my mind to seek* Ec 1$_{13}$, sim. Ec 1$_{17}$ 8$_{16}$ Dn 10$_{12}$ 1 C 22$_{19}$ 2 C 11$_{16}$ Si 12$_{11}$, וַיִּתֵּן יְהוֹשָׁפָט אֶת־פָּנָיו לִדְרוֹשׁ *and Jehoshaphat set his face to seek* 2 C 20$_{3}$.

5a. make (into), cause to be, make as, appoint as, place as (1) with two objects (Gn 17$_{5}$ Ex 18$_{25}$ 23$_{27}$ Lv 26$_{31}$ Nm 21$_{29}$ Dt 1$_{15}$ 28$_{24}$ Jos 9$_{27}$ 11$_{6}$ 22$_{25}$ 2 S 22$_{41}$||Ps 18$_{41}$ 1 K 14$_{7}$ 16$_{2}$ Is 3$_{4}$ 55$_{4}$ Jr 1$_{5}$ 6$_{27}$ 9$_{10}$ 29$_{26}$ 34$_{18}$ [or em.; see Obj. 2] 34$_{22}$ Ezk 3$_{17}$ 4$_{3}$ 6$_{14}$ 12$_{6}$ 15$_{8}$ 16$_{7.38}$ 22$_{4}$ 25$_{13}$ 26$_{19.21}$ 29$_{12}$ 30$_{12}$ 32$_{15}$ 33$_{7.28.29}$ 34$_{26}$ 35$_{3,7.9}$ 44$_{14}$ Jl 2$_{19}$ Ps 2$_{8}$ 39$_{6}$ 69$_{12}$ 89$_{28}$ 105$_{32}$ Dn 8$_{13}$ Ezr 9$_{8}$ Ne 13$_{26}$ 2 C 2$_{10}$ 1QS 2$_{5}$ 1QLitPr 3.1$_{5}$ 4QTNaph 1$_{3}$ 4QDiscourse 2.2$_{6}$ 4QPrFêtes^{b} 1$_{1}$ [[נתת]ה] 4QSela 9.2$_{11}$ GnzPs 1$_{23}$ [[נת]תו]), first of which is indicated by מִן partitive (1 K 9$_{22}$ 1 C 16$_{4}$); with noun and adjective as objects (Ps 18$_{33}$ Jr 49$_{15}$||Ob 2 Ezk 3$_{8}$

Ml 29 Lm 113 Ne 111).

(2) with object + לְ *into, as* (Gn 176.20 484 Ex 71 Nm 521 Dt 2813 Jos 1713 1 K 850 Is 4023 426.24(Qr) 4328 496.8 Jr 118 514 910 1210 154.20 204 249 2518 266 2918 3016 3417 5125 Ezk 514 720 2346 255.7 264.14 2818 2910 332 Jl 217 Mc 616 Zp 320 Ps 10646 Dn 19 Ne 336 1 C 1722 2 C 720 89 98 2 C 2516 298 307 3525 1QH 1510 4QDiscourse 2.26 4QBarka 1.29 GnzPs 210).

(3) with object + בְּ *as* (Nm 2129 1 C 1219).

(4) with object + כְּ *as* (Lv 2619 1 K 1027.27||2 C 927.27 1 K 163 2122 2 K 99 Is 412 Jr 1912 248 266 2917 3418 [if em.; see Obj. 2]) Ezk 167 282.6 Ho 116 Ps 4412 14716 Ru 411 2 C 115.15.

<SUBJ> Y. Gn 175.6.20 484 Ex 71 2327 2619.31 Nm 521 Dt 2813.24 Jos 116 2225.41||Ps 1841 1 K 850 147 162.3 2122 2 K 99 Is 34 4023 426 4328 496.8 554 Jr 15.18 514 627 910.10 154.20 1912 204 248.9 266.6 2917.18.26 3016 3417.18.22 4915|| Ob2 Jr 5125 Ezk 38.9.17 514 614 720 126 158 167.38 224 255.7.13 264.14.19.21 2818 2910.12 3012 3215 337.28.29 3426 353.7.9 4414 Ho 116 Jl 217.19 Mc 616 Zp 320 Ml 29 Ps 28 1833 396 4412 8928 10532 10646 14716 Ru 411 Lm 113 Dn 19 Ezr 98 Ne 111 336 1326 1 C 1722 2 C 210 720 98 298 307 1QH 1510 1QS 25 1QLitPr 3.15 4QDiscourse 2.26 4Q Barka 1.29.4QPrFêtesb 11 ([נתת]ה) 4QSela 9.211 GnzPs 123 ([נת]תו) 210, Chemosh Nm 2129.

עַם *people* Ezk 332, Amaziah 2 C 2516, David 1 C 1219 164, Jeremiah Jr 2518, Joshua Jos 927, Moses Ex 1825 Dt 115, Solomon 1 K 922||2 C 89, בֵּן *son* of man, in ref. to Ezekiel Ezk 43, of Israel Jos 1713, מֶלֶךְ *king* 1 K 1027.27|| 2 C 927.27 2 C 115.15, נָגִיד *prince* Ezk 282.6, רֹעֶה *shepherd* Jr 1210, worshipper Ps 6912, מִי *who?* Is 412.24; subj. not specified, Ezk 2346 Dn 813 2 C 3525.

<OBJ> 1. Ammonite Ne 336, Shilonite(s) 4QSela 9.211, Israel(ites) Dt 2813 Is 4224(Qr) 4328 3417 Ho 116 Zp 320 Ezr 98 1 C 1722, Canaanites Jos 1713, Edom Jr 4915||Ob2 Ezk 2513, Jerusalem Ezk 1638 224, Judah 2 C 298, Rabbah Ezk 255.7, Tyre Ezk 264.14.19.21, עַם *people* 1 K 850 Jr 154 2917.18 Jl 219 Ps 10646 1 C 1722, גּוֹי *nation* Jr 2518 Ps 13, בַּיִת *house* 1 K 163 2122 2 K 99 Jr 266, שְׁאֵרִית *remnant* Jr 248.9, צָבָא *army* Dn 813, Abra(ham) Gn 175.6, Baasha 1 K 162, Daniel Dn 19, David Is 554 Ps 8928 GnzPs 123 ([נת]תו), Ishmael Gn 1720, Jacob Gn 484, Jeremiah Jr 15.18 627 1520, Jeroboam 1 K 147, Moses Ex 71 perh. 4QDiscourse 2.26, Oholah Ezk 2346, Oholibah Ezk 2346, Pashhur Jr 204, Sanballat Ne 336, Solomon Ne 1326 2 C 210 98, Tobiah Ne 336, Zedekiah Jr 248.9, Zephaniah Jr 2926.

אִישׁ *man* Ex 1825 Dt 115 Jr 3418 Ezk 332 1QS 25, אִשָּׁה *woman* Nm 521 Ru 411, אָב *father* 2 C 307, בֵּן *son* Nm 2129 Jr 2926 1 C 1219, of man, in ref. to Ezekiel Ezk 317 514 126 337, בַּת *daughter* Nm 2129, אָח *brother* Jr 2917.18 2 C 307, נַעַר *lad* Is 34, עֶבֶד *servant* Is 426 496.8 Ps 8928, בָּחִיר *elect one* Is 426, מֶלֶךְ *king* Jr 248.9 2917.18 Ezk 2818, רֹזֵן *ruler* Is 4023, שַׂר *prince* Jr 248, כֹּהֵן *priest* Ml 29, לֵוִי *Levite* Ezk 4414, נָבִיא *prophet* 2 C 2516, worshipper Ps 4412 Lm 113 1QH 1510 GnzPs 210, אֹיֵב *enemy* Ex 2327 2 S 2241||Ps 1841, בזז ptc. *one who plunders* Jr 3016, רָשָׁע *wicked one* 1QLitPr 3.15 4QPrFêtesb 11 ([נתת]ה רשעים), יֹשֵׁב *inhabitant* Jos 927 Jr 248.9 Mc 616.

אֹזֶן *ear* Ne 111, רֹאשׁ *head*, i.e. chief Dt 115, מֵצַח *forehead* Ezk 39, פָּנִים *face* Ezk 38, לֵב *heart* Ezk 282, לֵבָב *heart* Ezk 286, שֵׁם *name* 4QTNaph 13, שֶׂה *sheep* Ezk 3426, אֶרֶז *cedar* 1 K 1027||2 C 927 2 C 115, גֶּשֶׁם *rain* Ps 10532, מָטָר *rain* Dt 2824, שֶׁלֶג *snow* Ps 14716, זָהָב *gold* Ezk 720 2 C 115, כֶּסֶף *silver* 1 K 1027||2 C 927 Ezk 720 2 C 115, חֶרֶב *sword* Is 412, קֶשֶׁת *bow* Is 412, מַחֲבַת *plate* Ezk 43, שַׂק *sackcloth* Ps 6912, דָּבָר *word* Jr 514.

שָׁמַיִם *heavens* Lv 2619, אֶרֶץ *land* Lv 2619 Ezk 614 158 2910.12 3215 3328.29, חֶלְקָה *plot of land* Jr 1210, נַחֲלָה *inheritance* Jl 217 Ps 10646, עִיר *city* Lv 2631 Jr 910 1912 266 3422 Ezk 2619 Mc 616, Jerusalem Jr 910 Ezk 167, Jordan Jos 2225, יְאֹר *Nile-streams* Ezk 3012, הַר *mountain* Jr 5125 Ezk 353.7.9, אֶפֶס *end* of earth Ps 28, דֶּרֶךְ *way* Ps 1833, מַחְשָׁךְ *dark place* 4QBarka 1.29, מַעְקָשׁ *crooked place* 4QBarka 1.29, בַּיִת *house* 2 C 720, סָבִיב pl. *surroundings* Ezk 3426, קִינָה *lamentation* 2 C 3525, יוֹם *day* Ps 396, כֹּל *all* the kings Jos 116.

2. made into, placed as, Zilpah 4QTNaph 13, אָב *father* Gn 175, נָגִיד *leader* 1 K 147 162 Is 554, בְּכוֹר *first born* Ps 8928, רֹאשׁ *head*, i.e. chief Ex 1825, עֹרֶף *back of neck*, i.e. cause to turn back of neck Ex 2327 2 S 2241||Ps 1841, מֶלֶךְ *king* Ne 1326 2 C 210 GnzPs 123 ([נת]תו), מְצַוֶּה *commander* Is 554, שַׂר *commander* Ex 1825 Dt 115 Is 34, שֹׁטֵר *officer* Dt 115, כֹּהֵן *priest* Jr 2926,

נָבִיא *prophet* Jr 1$_{5}$, מְשָׁרֵת *minister* 1 C 16$_{4}$, עֵד *witness* Is 55$_{4}$, פָּלִיט *fugitive* Nm 21$_{29}$, עֶבֶד *slave* 1 K 9$_{22}$ 4QSela 9.2$_{11}$, חֹטֵב *hewer* Jos 9$_{27}$, שֹׁאֵב *drawer* Jos 9$_{27}$, בָּחוֹן *assayer* Jr 6$_{27}$, מִבְצָר *fortification* Jr 6$_{27}$ (or em. מִבְצָר to מְבַצֵּר *assayer* or del.), צֹפֶה *sentry* Ezk 3$_{17}$ 33$_{7}$, שׁמר ptc. *one who keeps* charge Ezk 44$_{14}$, חָלָל *slain one* Jos 11$_{6}$, עֶלְיוֹן *most high* Ps 89$_{28}$.

ראשׁ *head*, i.e. chief Dt 1$_{15}$, דָּם *blood* Ezk 16$_{38}$, עֵגֶל *calf* Jr 34$_{18}$ (or em. כָּעֵגֶל *as the calf*), לְבוּשׁ *clothing* Ps 69$_{12}$, קִיר *wall* Ezk 4$_{3}$, בָּרָד *hail* Ps 105$_{32}$, אָבָק *powder* Dt 28$_{24}$, עָפָר *powder* Dt 28$_{24}$, חָרָבָה *dry land* Ezk 30$_{12}$, חָרְבָּה *waste* Lv 26$_{31}$ Ezk 25$_{13}$, מְשַׁמָּה *waste* Ezk 6$_{14}$ 33$_{28.29}$ 35$_{3}$, שְׁמָמָה *desolation* Jr 9$_{10}$ 34$_{22}$ Ezk 6$_{14}$ 15$_{8}$ 29$_{12}$ 32$_{15}$ 33$_{28.29}$ 35$_{3.9}$, מְשִׁסָּה *spoil* Is 42$_{24(Qr)}$, מִרְמָס *trampled ground* Dn 8$_{13}$, מוֹפֵת *portent* Ezk 12$_{6}$, חֶרְפָּה *reproach* Ezk 22$_{4}$ Jl 2$_{19}$, קַלָּסָה *derision* Ezk 22$_{4}$, בַּלָּהָה *terror* Ezk 26$_{21}$, זַעֲוָה *trembling* 1QS 2$_{5}$, מְחִיגָה *cause of reeling* 4QDiscourse 2.2$_{6}$, גְּבוּל *border* Jos 22$_{25}$, בְּרָכָה *blessing* Ezk 34$_{26}$, מִחְיָה *reviving* Ezr 9$_{8}$, נַחֲלָה *inheritance* Ps 2$_{8}$, אֲחֻזָּה *possession* Ps 2$_{8}$, כֹּפֶר *ransom* 1QLitPr 3.1$_{5}$ ([כ]ופרינו) 4QPrFêtes^{b} 1$_{1}$ ([נתתן]ה כופרנו), טֶפַח *handbreadth* Ps 39$_{6}$, רְבָבָה *ten thousand* Ezk 16$_{7}$ (or em. רְבָבָה to וּרְבִי *and multiply* or וְרָבִית *and you shall multiply*).

Made to be, תָּמִים *safe* Ps 18$_{33}$, קָטֹן *small* Jr 49$_{15}$||Ob$_{2}$, שָׁפָל *low* Ml 2$_{9}$, בזה pass. ptc. *despised* Jr 49$_{15}$, ni. ptc. Ml 2$_{9}$, שׁמם ptc. *desolated* Lm 1$_{13}$, דָּוֶה *faint* Lm 1$_{13}$, חָזָק *hard* Ezk 3$_{8}$, קַשָּׁב *attentive* Ne 1$_{11}$.

<PREP> לְ *into, as,* or introducing object, + אֱלֹהִים *God* Ex 7$_{1}$ 4QDiscourse 2.2$_{6}$, עַם *people* 1 C 17$_{22}$, גּוֹי *nation* Gn 17$_{6.20}$, קְהַל *company* of peoples Gn 48$_{4}$, ראשׁ *head* Dt 28$_{13}$, זָנָב *tail* Dt 28$_{13}$, שֵׁם *name* Zp 3$_{20}$, מֶלֶךְ *king* 2 C 9$_{8}$, עֶבֶד *slave* 2 C 8$_{9}$, מַס *forced labour* Jos 17$_{13}$, צֹפֶה *sentry* Ezk 33$_{2}$, יֹעֵץ *counsellor* 2 C 25$_{16}$, עֵצָה *counsel* 1QH 15$_{10}$, בְּרִית *covenant* Is 42$_{6}$ 49$_{8}$, חֹק *statute* 2 C 35$_{25}$, רַחֲמִים *compassion* 1 K 8$_{50}$ Ps 106$_{46}$ Dn 1$_{9}$, חֶסֶד *kindness* Dn 1$_{9}$, תְּהִלָּה *praise* Zp 3$_{20}$, מָשָׁל *proverb* Jr 24$_{9}$ 2 C 7$_{20}$, שְׁנִינָה *taunt* Jr 24$_{9}$ 2 C 7$_{20}$, גִּדּוּף *reproach* Is 43$_{28}$, חֶרְפָּה *reproach* Jr 29$_{18}$ Ezk 5$_{14}$ Jl 2$_{17}$, שְׁרֵקָה *hissing* Jr 25$_{18}$ 29$_{18}$ Mc 6$_{16}$ 2 C 29$_{8}$, זְוָעָה *trembling* Jr 15$_{4(Kt)}$ 24$_{9(Kt)}$ 29$_{18(Kt)}$ 34$_{17(Kt)}$ 2 C 29$_{8(Kt)}$, זַעֲוָה *trembling* Jr 15$_{4(Qr)}$ 24$_{9(Qr)}$ 29$_{18(Qr)}$ 34$_{17(Qr)}$ Ezk 23$_{46}$ 2 C 29$_{8(Qr)}$, מָגוֹר *terror* Jr 20$_{4}$, אָלָה *curse* Nm 5$_{21}$ Jr 29$_{18}$, קְלָלָה *curse* Jr 24$_{9}$ 25$_{18}$ 26$_{6}$, שְׁבוּעָה *oath* Nm 5$_{21}$, נִדָּה *impurity* Ezk 7$_{20}$.

גַּל *heap* Jr 9$_{10}$, חָרְבָּה *waste* Jr 25$_{18}$ Ezk 5$_{14}$ 29$_{10}$, מְשַׁמָּה *waste* Ezk 35$_{7(mss)}$, שַׁמָּה *desolation* Jr 25$_{18}$ 29$_{18}$ Mc 6$_{16}$ 2 C 29$_{8}$ 30$_{7}$, שְׁמָמָה *desolation* Ezk 29$_{10}$ 35$_{7}$, שִׁמְמָה *desolation* Ezk 35$_{7}$, חֵרֶם *devoted object* Is 43$_{28}$, בַּז *plunder* Jr 30$_{16}$ Ezk 23$_{46}$ 25$_{7(Qr)}$, בִּזָּה *plunder* Ne 3$_{36}$, עִיר *city* Jr 1$_{18}$, עַמּוּד *pillar* Jr 1$_{18}$, חוֹמָה *wall* Jr 1$_{18}$ 15$_{20}$, מָעוֹן *dwelling place* Jr 9$_{10}$, מִדְבָּר *steppe* Jr 12$_{10}$, מִישׁוֹר *level ground* 4QBark^{a} 1.2$_{9}$, נָוֶה *pasture* Ezk 25$_{5}$, מַרְבֵּץ *resting place* Ezk 25$_{5}$, הַר *mountain* Jr 51$_{25}$, צְחִיחַ *surface* of rock Ezk 26$_{4.14}$, אוֹר *light* Is 42$_{6}$ 49$_{6}$ 4QBark^{a} 1.2$_{9}$ GnzPs 2$_{10}$, אֵשׁ *fire* Jr 5$_{14}$, אֵפֶר *ashes* Ezk 28$_{18}$, בַּג *share* Ezk 25$_{7(Kt)}$, אַיִן *nothing* Is 40$_{23}$.

לְ of direction, benefit, *to, for,* + Y. 1 C 17$_{22}$, עַם *people* Jr 15$_{20}$ Ezk 33$_{2}$, גּוֹי *nation* Jr 1$_{5}$ 26$_{6}$ Ezk 22$_{4}$ 25$_{7}$, מַמְלָכָה *kingdom* Jr 24$_{9}$ 29$_{18}$ 34$_{17}$, שֵׁבֶט *tribe* Dt 1$_{15}$, בַּיִת *house* of Israel Ezk 3$_{17}$ 12$_{6}$ 33$_{7}$, David 2 S 22$_{41}$||Ps 18$_{41}$, Pashhur Jr 20$_{4}$, מֶלֶךְ *king* Jr 15$_{4}$, פַּרְעֹה *Pharaoh* Ex 7$_{1}$, אֹהֵב *friend* Jr 20$_{4}$, יֹשֵׁב *inhabitant* Ezk 7$_{20}$, עָיֵף *weary one* 1QH 15$_{10}$ (לעפים), אֶרֶץ *land* Ezk 22$_{4}$, מְלָאכָה *work* 2 C 8$_{9}$, עֲבֹדָה *service* Ezk 44$_{14}$, אֲשֶׁר *that which* Ezk 44$_{14}$, נֵצַח *everlastingness*, i.e. for ever GnzPs 1$_{23}$ (נת[תו] [לנצח]).

לְ *against*, + עַם *people* Jr 1$_{18}$, מֶלֶךְ *king* Jr 1$_{18}$, שַׂר *prince* Jr 1$_{18}$, כֹּהֵן *priest* Jr 1$_{18}$.

לְ *before*, + עַם *people* Ml 2$_{9}$.

בְּ of place, *in, among,* + עַם *people* Jr 6$_{27}$ Zp 3$_{20}$ 2 C 7$_{20}$, גּוֹי *nation* Jr 29$_{18}$ 49$_{15}$||Ob$_{2}$ Ezk 5$_{14}$ Jl 2$_{19}$, אָדָם *human beings* Jr 49$_{15}$, מוֹשָׁב *dwelling place* Ezk 6$_{14}$, אֶרֶץ *land* Ne 3$_{36}$, עַבְדוּת *bondage* Ezr 9$_{8}$.

בְּ of time, *in, on,* + יוֹם *day* Jos 9$_{27}$.

בְּ *as,* or introducing object, + שְׁבִית *captives* Nm 21$_{29}$ (unless given *into captivity*, i.e. §1), ראשׁ *head*, i.e. chief 1 C 12$_{19}$.

בְּ of instrument, *by (means of), through,* + עֹז *strength* GnzPs 2$_{10}$.

בְּיַד *by means of, through,* + נקם ptc. *one who takes vengeance* 1QS 2$_{5}$.

כְּ *as,* + בַּיִת *house* 1 K 16$_{3}$ 21$_{22}$ 2 K 9$_{9}$, Admah Ho 11$_{6}$, Shiloh Jr 26$_{6}$, Topheth Jr 19$_{12}$, Leah Ru 4$_{11}$, Rachel Ru 4$_{11}$, לֵב *heart* Ezk 28$_{2.6}$, עֵגֶל *calf* Jr 34$_{18}$ (if em.; see

Obj. 2), צֹאן *sheep* Ps 44$_{12}$, שִׁקְמָה *sycamore* 1 K 10$_{27}$|| 2 C 9$_{27}$ 2 C 1$_{15}$, תְּאֵנָה *fig* Jr 24$_{8}$ 29$_{17}$, צֶמַח *plant* Ezk 16$_{7}$, בַּרְזֶל *iron* Lv 26$_{19}$, נְחֻשָׁה *bronze* Lv 26$_{19}$, אֶבֶן *stone* 1 K 10$_{27}$||2 C 9$_{27}$ 2 C 1$_{15}$, שָׁמִיר *adamant* Ezk 3$_{9}$, עָפָר *dust* Is 41$_{2}$, קַשׁ *stubble* Is 41$_{2}$, צֶמֶר *wool* Ps 147$_{16}$.

כְּ *as at*, + יוֹם *day* Jr 25$_{18}$.

כְּ *at*, + עֵת *time* Jos 11$_{6}$.

מִן of direction, *from*, + מִדְבָּר *steppe* Ezk 6$_{14}$.

מִן partitive, *some of* (as first obj.), + בֵּן *son* of Israel 1 K 9$_{22}$||2 C 8$_{9}$, לֵוִי *Levite* 1 C 16$_{4}$.

אֶל *to*, + Israel(ites) Ex 23$_{27}$.

עַל *over, in charge of*, + Israel(ites) Dt 1$_{15}$ 1 K 14$_{7}$ 16$_{2}$ Ne 13$_{26}$ 2 C 9$_{8}$, עַם *people* 1 K 14$_{7}$ 16$_{2}$ 2 C 2$_{10}$, אַדִּיר *mighty one* 4QDiscourse 2.2$_{6}$.

עַל *to, for*, + Israel 2 C 35$_{25}$.

עַל *against*, + אֶרֶץ *land* Jr 1$_{18}$.

עַל *on account of*, + תּוֹעֵבָה *abomination* Ezk 33$_{29}$.

בִּגְלַל *on account of*, + Manasseh Jr 15$_{4}$, בֵּן *son* Jr 15$_{4}$, מֶלֶךְ *king* Jr 15$_{4}$.

עַד *until*, + עוֹלָם *everlastingness*, i.e. for ever 1 C 17$_{22}$.

בְּתוֹךְ *among*, + עַם *people* Nm 5$_{21}$, אֶרֶץ *land* Ezk 29$_{12}$.

בֵּין *between*, + Ezekiel Ezk 4$_{3}$, עִיר *city* Ezk 4$_{3}$.

לְעֵינֵי *in the sight of*, + ראה ptc. *one who sees* Ezk 28$_{18}$, עבר ptc. *one who passes* Ezk 5$_{14}$.

לִפְנֵי *before*, + Israel Jos 11$_{6}$, שַׂר *commander* Dn 1$_{9}$, שׁבה ptc. *one who takes captive* 1 K 8$_{50}$ Ps 106$_{46}$, אֲרוֹן *ark* 1 C 16$_{4}$.

תַּחַת *in place of*, + Jehoiada Jr 29$_{26}$, כֹּהֵן *priest* Jr 29$_{26}$.

ה- of direction, *to(wards)*, + Diblah Ezk 6$_{14}$.

<COLL> נתן || שׂים *place*, i.e. make, as Ho 11$_{6}$.

+ עשׂה *make* Is 40$_{23}$, עמד hi. *cause to stand* GnzPs 2$_{10}$, לקח *take* Ezk 4$_{3}$ 33$_{2}$.

+ adverb or adverbial phrase, עוֹד *again* Jl 2$_{19}$, אֵיךְ *how?* Ho 11$_{6}$, מָחָר *tomorrow* Jos 11$_{6}$, כָּל־הַיּוֹם *all the day* Lm 1$_{13}$.

וּנְתַתָּם לְרַחֲמִים *and you shall make them into compassion*, i.e. give them compassion 1 K 8$_{50}$, vars. Ps 106$_{46}$ Dn 1$_{9}$, לְתִתֵּנוּ מִחְיָה *to make us into reviving*, i.e. give us reviving Ezr 9$_{8}$, וַיִּתֵּן ... מְשָׁרְתִים וּלְהַזְכִּיר וּלְהוֹדוֹת וּלְהַלֵּל *and he appointed ... as ministers and to invoke and give thanks and praise* 1 C 16$_{4}$.

5b. make out as, take as, <SUBJ> אִישׁ *man* Gn 42$_{30}$, Eli 1 S 1$_{16}$. <OBJ> brothers of Joseph Gn 42$_{30}$, אָמָה *female servant* 1 S 1$_{16}$. <PREP> כְּ *as*, + מְרַגֵּל *spy* Gn 42$_{30}$; לִפְנֵי *before*, i.e. as, בַּת *daughter* of worthlessness 1 S 1$_{16}$.

6. cause, make happen, <SUBJ> Y. Nm 5$_{21}$ Dt 28$_{7.25}$. <OBJ> אֹיֵב *enemy* Dt 28$_{7}$, יָרֵךְ *thigh* Nm 5$_{21}$, בֶּטֶן *abdomen* Nm 5$_{21}$. <COLL> בְּתֵת י׳ ... נֹפֶלֶת *when Y. causes ... to fall away* Nm 5$_{21}$, יִתֶּנְךָ י׳ נִגָּף *Y. will cause you to be defeated* Dt 28$_{25}$, var. Dt 28$_{7}$.

7. allow, permit, enable (5QRègle 2$_{7}$) to do something, to be, to have, <SUBJ> Y. Gn 20$_{6}$ 31$_{7}$ Ex 12$_{23}$ Nm 22$_{13}$ Dt 18$_{14}$ Ps 16$_{10}$ 66$_{9}$ 121$_{3}$ (both, if em.; see Coll.) Jb 9$_{18}$ 24$_{23}$ 2 C 20$_{10}$, Amorites Jg 1$_{34}$, Edom Nm 20$_{21}$, Israelites Jos 10$_{19}$, Baasha 1 K 15$_{17}$||2 C 16$_{1}$, David 1 S 24$_{8}$, Job Jb 31$_{30}$, Rizpah 2 S 21$_{10}$, Saul 1 S 18$_{2}$, Sihon Nm 21$_{23}$, מֶלֶךְ *king* Ex 3$_{19}$ 1 K 15$_{17}$||2 C 16$_{1}$ Est 8$_{11}$, אָב *father* Jg 15$_{1}$, בֵּן *son* of Israel Jg 3$_{28}$, בַּת *daughter* 2 S 21$_{10}$, worshipper 4QapPs^{b} 45a$_{2}$, מַעֲלָל *deed* Ho 5$_{4}$; subj. not specified, Ec 5$_{5}$.

<OBJ> Israel(ites) Ex 3$_{19}$ Nm 20$_{21}$ 21$_{23}$ Ho 5$_{4}$, Abimelech Gn 20$_{6}$, Balaam Nm 22$_{13}$, David 1 S 18$_{2}$, Job Jb 9$_{18}$, Samson Jg 15$_{1}$, אִישׁ *man* Jg 3$_{28}$ 1 S 24$_{8}$, אָב *father* Gn 31$_{7}$, בֵּן *son* of Dan Jg 1$_{34}$, חָסִיד *loyal one* Ps 16$_{10}$, אֹיֵב *enemy* Jos 10$_{19}$, מַשְׁחִית *destroyer* Ex 12$_{23}$, פֶּה *mouth* Ec 5$_{5}$, חֵךְ *palate* Jb 31$_{30}$, רֶגֶל *foot* Ps 66$_{9}$ 121$_{3}$ (both, if em.; see Coll.), נֶפֶשׁ *soul*, i.e. self 4QapPs^{b} 45a$_{2}$, חַיָּה *beast* 2 S 21$_{10}$, עוֹף *birds* 2 S 21$_{10}$.

<PREP> לְ introducing object, + Israel(ites) Dt 18$_{14}$ 2 C 20$_{10}$, Jews Est 8$_{11}$, Levi 5QRègle 2$_{7}$, אַבִּיר *mighty one* Jb 24$_{23}$.

מִלִּפְנֵי *(from) before*, + Y. 4QapPs^{b} 45a$_{2}$ (מלפנ[יך]).

<COLL> נתן + inf. of ראה *see* Ps 16$_{10}$, הלך *go* Ex 3$_{19}$ Nm 22$_{13}$, בוא *come* Ex 12$_{23}$ Jos 10$_{19}$ Jg 15$_{1}$ 2 C 20$_{10}$, ירד *go down* Jg 1$_{34}$, עבר *pass* Nm 20$_{21}$ 21$_{23}$ Jg 3$_{28}$, שׁוב *go back* 1 S 18$_{2}$ Ho 5$_{4}$, hi. *bring back*, i.e. regain, breath Jb 9$_{18}$, קום *rise up* 1 S 24$_{8}$, קהל ni. *assemble* Est 8$_{11}$, עמד *stand* Est 8$_{11}$, נגע *touch* Gn 20$_{6}$, נוח *rest* 2 S 21$_{10}$, כנע ni. *be humbled* 4QapPs^{b} 45a$_{2}$, חטא *sin* Jb 31$_{30}$, hi. *cause to sin* Ec 5$_{5}$, רעע hi. *harm* Gn 31$_{7}$, אבד pi. *destroy* Est 8$_{11}$, שׁמד hi. *destroy* Est 8$_{11}$, הרג *kill* Est 8$_{11}$, בזז *plunder*

Est 8$_{11}$, מוט *slip* Ps 66$_{9}$ 121$_{3}$ (both, if em. לָמוֹט *to slipping* to לָמוּט), אגד *bind* 5QRègle 2$_{7}$.

+ adverb, עַל־כֵּן *therefore* Gn 20$_{6}$.

אַתָּה לֹא כֵן נָתַן לְךָ י׳ *as for you, Y. has not allowed you (to do) so* Dt 18$_{14}$, יִתֶּן־לוֹ לָבֶטַח *he allows them to be in security* Jb 24$_{23}$, לְבִלְתִּי תֵּת יֹצֵא וָבָא *to permit no one to go out or come in* 1 K 15$_{17}$||2 C 16$_{1}$.

8. be placed,* <SUBJ> הוֹד *splendour* Ps 8$_{2}$. <PREP> עַל *upon, above,* + שָׁמַיִם *heaven* Ps 8$_{2}$.

9. pass. **a. be given, be assigned, be appointed,** <SUBJ> Eliashib Ne 13$_{4}$, בֵּן *son* Dt 28$_{32}$, בַּת *daughter* Dt 28$_{32}$, אָח *brother* 1 C 6$_{33}$, כֹּהֵן *priest* Ne 13$_{4}$, לֵוִי *Levite* Nm 3$_{9.9}$ 8$_{16.16.19}$ 18$_{6}$ 1 C 6$_{33}$, צֹאן *sheep* Dt 28$_{31}$, כֶּסֶף *money* Est 3$_{11}$, בֶּצַע *extortion* Si 7$_{6}$, חָכְמָה *wisdom* 2 C 1$_{12}$, מַדָּע *knowledge* 2 C 1$_{12}$. <PREP> לְ of direction, benefit, *to, for,* + Y. Nm 8$_{16}$ 18$_{6}$, עַם *people* Dt 28$_{32}$, Aaron Nm 3$_{9}$ 8$_{19}$, Haman Est 3$_{11}$, Solomon 2 C 1$_{12}$, בֵּן *son* Nm 3$_{9}$ 8$_{19}$, אֹיֵב *enemy* Dt 28$_{31}$, עֲבֹדָה *service* 1 C 6$_{33}$; בְּ *over,* + לִשְׁכָּה *chamber* Ne 13$_{4}$; בְּ of price, *(in exchange) for,* + תָּמִים *integrity* Si 7$_{6}$; מֵאֵת *from,* + בֵּן *son* of Israel Nm 3$_{9}$; מִתּוֹךְ *from among,* + בֵּן *son* of Israel Nm 8$_{16.19}$. <COLL> נְתֻנִים לַי׳ לַעֲבֹד *given to Y. to serve* Nm 18$_{6}$.

b. be placed, be stationed, <SUBJ> שַׂר *commander* 11QT 58$_{4}$. <PREP> בְּ of place, *in, on,* + עִיר *city* 11QT 58$_{4}$, לוּחַ *tablet* 11QT 34$_{1}$ (נתו[נים]).

Also Si 47$_{22}$ 1QH 16$_{14}$ 4QCommGenA 5$_{7}$ perh. 4QCommGenC 14$_{2}$ ([נתן]) 4QD[f] 3$_{6}$ 4QCryptA 3.14 4Q Myst[a] 6.1$_{6}$ 66$_{4}$ 4QapJoseph[b] 1$_{22}$ 4QapJoshua[a] 6.2$_{1}$ (ויתננ[ו]) 4QparaKings 81$_{2}$ ([נו]תן) 4QpsEzek[a] 25$_{2}$ 4Qps Ezek[e] 26$_{1}$ 4Q415 30$_{2}$ 4Q417 32$_{3}$ 4Q418 19$_{1}$ 4Q419 1$_{7}$ 4Q423 6$_{1}$ 4QsapDidB 4.2$_{1a}$ 4QZedek 2$_{2}$ 4QPrFêtes[c] 78$_{2}$ ([נ]תתה) 4QShir[b] 144$_{2}$ 4QRitPur 21.8$_{1}$ 4QOrd[b] 28$_{3}$ 4Q520 39$_{1}$ 4QapMes 12$_{1}$ 4QSela 9.2$_{1}$ (נתתנ[ו]) perh. 4Q 523 1$_{7}$ (נתו/ינים) 6QapSamKgs 33$_{2}$ Arad ost. 28$_{2}$ 71$_{1}$ 111$_{3}$ Kuntillet ʿAjrud inscr. D2$_{2}$.

<SYN> §1 שׁלח *send,* נשׂא *bear,* מכר *deliver (over),* שׁבר hi. *sell,* שׁוב hi. *repay,* מגן pi. *deliver up,* נגר hi. *deliver up,* רבה hi. *increase,* יסף hi. *add,* חנן *be gracious,* ידע hi. *make known,* עשׂה *do;* §4 שׂים *place,* ישׁב pi. *establish,* יצק *pour,* שׁפך *pour,* קום hi. *raise up,* מגן pi. *bestow upon;* §5 שׂים *place,* i.e. make.

<ANT> §1 חשׂך *withhold,* כלא *withhold,* מנע *withhold,* לקח *take,* נשׂא *take.*

Qal Pass. (unless **Ho.**) 8.1.1 Impf. יֻתַּן, 3fs Q תתן; + waw וַיֻּתַּן—**1. be given, be granted,** <SUBJ> Shunammite 1 K 2$_{21}$, Abishag 1 K 2$_{21}$, אִישׁ *man* 2 S 21$_{6(Qr)}$, סְגוֹר *fine gold* Jb 28$_{15}$, קֶרַח *frost* Jb 37$_{10}$ (if em. יִתֶּן־ *he* [Y.] *gives* to יֻתַּן), חָכְמָה *wisdom* perh. 4Q185 1.2$_{14}$, תַּאֲוָה *desire* Pr 10$_{24}$ (if em. יִתֵּן *he will give* to יֻתַּן *it will be granted*), מַצָּה *strife* Pr 13$_{10}$ (if em. יִתֵּן *one gives* to יֻתַּן), אֶרֶץ *land* Nm 32$_{5}$, נַחֲלָה *inheritance* Nm 26$_{54}$, מַשָּׂא *burden* 2 K 5$_{17}$, כֹּל *everything* Si 15$_{17(B)}$ (unless qal).

<PREP> לְ of direction, *to,* + Gibeonites 1 S 21$_{6(Qr)}$, Adonijah 1 K 2$_{21}$, אָב *father* 4Q185 1.2$_{14}$, אָח *brother* 1 K 2$_{21}$, אָדָם *human being* Si 15$_{17(B)}$ (unless qal), מֶלֶךְ *king* Ps 72$_{15}$ (if em.; see below), עֶבֶד *servant* Nm 32$_{5}$ 2 K 5$_{17}$.

לְ *as, for (the purpose of),* + אִשָּׁה *wife* 1 K 2$_{21}$, אֲחֻזָּה *possession* Nm 32$_{5}$.

מִן partitive, (1) *(some) of* (as subj.), + זָהָב *gold* Ps 72$_{15}$ (if em. יִתֶּן־ *may he give* to יֻתַּן).

(2) *from among,* + בֵּן *son* 2 S 21$_{6(Qr)}$.

מִן of instrument, *by (means of),* + נְשָׁמָה *breath* Jb 37$_{10}$ (if em.; see Subj.).

לְפִי *according to,* + פקד pass. ptc. *numbered one* Nm 26$_{54}$.

תַּחַת *in exchange for,* + חָכְמָה *wisdom* Jb 28$_{15}$, בִּינָה *understanding* Jb 28$_{15}$.

<COLL> נתן qal pass. + adverb, כֵּן *so* 4Q185 1.2$_{14}$; אִישׁ לְפִי פְקֻדָיו יֻתַּן נַחֲלָתוֹ *(as for) each, according to his numbered ones shall his inheritance be given* Nm 26$_{54}$.

2. be placed, <SUBJ> Absalom 2 S 18$_{9}$ (unless §3; 4QSam[a] ויתל *and he hung,* from תלה), מַיִם *water* Lv 11$_{38}$ (unless §4), קֶבֶר *grave* Is 53$_{9}$ (if em. וַיִּתֵּן *and he placed* to וַיֻּתַּן *and it was placed*). <PREP> עַל *upon,* + זֶרַע *seed* Lv 11$_{38}$ (unless §4); אֶת *with,* + רָשָׁע *wicked one* Is 53$_{9}$ (if em.; see Subj.); בֵּין *between,* + שָׁמַיִם *heaven* 2 S 18$_{9}$ (unless §3), אֶרֶץ *earth* 2 S 18$_{9}$ (unless §3).

3. be spread, i.e. suspended* (unless §2), Absalom 2 S 18$_{9}$. <PREP> בֵּין *between,* + שָׁמַיִם *heaven* 2 S 18$_{9}$, אֶרֶץ *earth* 2 S 18$_{9}$.

4. be poured out* (unless §2), <SUBJ> מַיִם *water* Lv 11$_{38}$. <PREP> עַל *upon*, + זֶרַע *seed* Lv 11$_{38}$.

Ni. 83.5.14 Pf. נִתַּן (נִתָּן), נִתְּנָה (נִתָּנָה), נִתְּנוּ (נִתָּנוּ), נִתְּנוּ (Si נִתָּנוּ, Q נתנתו); impf. יִנָּתֵן (יִנָּתֶן, יִנָּתֶן־), 3fs תִּנָּתֵן (תִּנָּתֶן־), 2ms תִּנָּתֵן, יִנָּתְנוּ; + waw וְנִתַּן, וְנִתְּנָה, וְנִתַּתֶּם; 3fs וַתִּנָּתֵן, וַיִּנָּתְנוּ; ptc. נִתָּן; inf. abs. הִנָּתֹן; cstr. הִנָּתֵן—**be given, be granted, be bestowed (upon),** i.e. (examples only) be handed over, be delivered up, be surrendered, of item (2 K 22$_{7}$ Is 29$_{12}$), of people (Gn 9$_{2}$ Lv 26$_{25}$ 2 S 21$_{6[Kt]}$ 2 K 18$_{30}$||Is 36$_{15}$ 2 K 19$_{10}$||Is 37$_{10}$ Jr 21$_{10}$ 32$_{4.24.36.43}$ 34$_{3}$ 37$_{17}$ 38$_{3.18}$ 39$_{17}$ 46$_{24}$ Dn 11$_{6.11}$ Ezr 9$_{7}$ 1 C 5$_{20}$ 2 C 18$_{14}$ 28$_{5}$ Si 11$_{6[B].6}$ 1QpHab 4$_{8}$ 9$_{6}$ 4QpPs[a] 1.2$_{19}$ 4QJub[h] 35$_{15}$ 4Q NarrC 1$_{13}$), be entrusted, committed (2 K 22$_{7}$ 2 C 34$_{16}$), be assigned (Ezk 47$_{11}$ 1 C 2$_{13}$), (of decree) be issued, proclaimed (Est 3$_{15}$ 4$_{8}$ 8$_{13.14}$ 9$_{14}$), (of moral blemish) be displayed, found (Si 44$_{19}$); be given in marriage (Gn 38$_{14}$ 1 S 18$_{19}$), as payment for service (Ezk 16$_{34}$), to priests as due (Lv 10$_{14}$).

<SUBJ> Aramaeans 2 C 18$_{14}$, Cushite Jr 39$_{17}$, Hagrites 1 C 5$_{20}$, Israel(ites) Lv 26$_{25}$ Ezr 9$_{7}$ 4QpNah 3.1$_{12}$, עַם *people* Est 7$_{3}$ 4QNarrC 1$_{13}$, הָמוֹן *multitude* Dn 11$_{11}$, Ahaz 2 C 28$_{5}$, Ebed-melech Jr 39$_{17}$, Esau 4QJub[h] 35$_{16}$, Merab 1 S 18$_{19}$, Tamar Gn 38$_{14}$, Zedekiah Jr 32$_{4.4}$ 34$_{3}$ 37$_{17}$, אִישׁ *man* 2 S 21$_{6(Kt)}$, אִשָּׁה *wife* Si 26$_{3}$, בֵּן *son* Is 9$_{5}$, בַּת *daughter* 1 S 18$_{19}$ Dn 11$_{6}$, of Egypt Jr 46$_{24}$, מֶלֶךְ *king* Jr 32$_{4.4}$ 34$_{3}$ 37$_{17}$ Ezr 9$_{7}$, כבד ni. *honoured one* Si 11$_{6(B).6}$, כֹּהֵן *priest* Ezr 9$_{7}$, בוא hi. ptc *one who brings* Dn 11$_{6}$, ילד ptc. *one who begets* Dn 11$_{6}$ (or em. וְהַיֹּלְדָהּ *and the one who begat her* to וִילָדֶיהָ *and her children*), חזק hi. ptc. *one who takes hold* Dn 11$_{6}$, רָשָׁע *wicked one* 4QpPs[a] 1.2$_{19}$, קֶרֶן *horn* 4QapPs[b] 46b$_{2}$, נֶפֶשׁ *soul*, i.e. life Est 7$_{3}$, חָזֶה *breast* Lv 10$_{14}$, שׁוֹק *thigh* Lv 10$_{14}$.

עֵדֶר *flock* Jr 13$_{20}$, צֹאן *flock* Jr 13$_{20}$, חַיָּה *beast* Gn 9$_{2}$, עוֹף *birds* Gn 9$_{2}$, דָּג *fish* Gn 9$_{2}$, עֵץ *wood* Ezk 15$_{4}$, לֶחֶם *bread* Is 33$_{16}$, אֲרֻחָה *ration of food* 2 K 25$_{30}$||Jr 52$_{34}$, תֶּבֶן *straw* Ex 5$_{16.18}$, כֶּסֶף *money* 2 K 22$_{7}$, חֶרֶב *sword* Ezk 32$_{20}$ (or em. נִתָּנָה to אִתּוֹ a sword is *with him*), מִבְצָר *fortification* 1QpHab 4$_{8}$, סֵפֶר *book* Is 29$_{12}$, אֲסֻפָּה *collection (of proverbs)* Ec 12$_{11}$, נְבוּאָה *prophecy* 11QPs[a] 27$_{11}$, דָּת *decree* Est 3$_{15}$ 4$_{8}$ 8$_{14}$ 9$_{14}$, פַּתְשֶׁגֶן *copy* of document Est 3$_{14}$ 8$_{13}$, תּוֹרָה *law* Ne 10$_{20}$.

Jerusalem 2 K 19$_{10}$||Is 37$_{10}$, עִיר *city* 2 K 18$_{30}$||Is 36$_{15}$ Jr 21$_{10}$ 32$_{24.25.36}$ 38$_{3.3.18}$, הַר *mountain* Ezk 35$_{12}$, גִּבְעָה *hill* Jos 24$_{33}$, בִּצָּה *marsh* Ezk 47$_{11}$, גֶּבֶא *swamp* Ezk 47$_{11}$, אֶרֶץ *land* Jr 32$_{43}$ Ezk 11$_{15}$ 33$_{24}$ Jb 9$_{24}$ 15$_{19}$, נַחֲלָה *inheritance* Nm 26$_{62}$, בְּכֹרָה *firstborn's privilege* 1 C 5$_{1}$ 4QJub[h] 36$_{14}$, בְּרָכָה *blessing*, i.e. present 1 S 25$_{27}$, כָּבוֹד *glory* Is 35$_{2}$, הָדָר *splendour* Is 35$_{2}$, הוֹן *wealth* 1QpHab 9$_{6}$, אֶתְנַן *fee* Ezk 16$_{34}$, חָכְמָה *wisdom* perh. 4Q185 1.2$_{8}$ 11QPs[a] 18$_{3}$, מַחֲשָׁבָה *design* 2 C 2$_{13}$, חֻפְשָׁה *freedom* Lv 19$_{20}$, שְׁאֵלָה *request* Est 7$_{2}$, תְּעוּדָה *testimony* 1QH 10$_{37}$, בְּרִית *covenant* 4QCommGenA 5$_{4}$, מוּם *blemish* Si 44$_{19}$, מְנָת *portion* Ne 13$_{10}$, אֲשֶׁר *that which* Si 15$_{17(A)}$, כֹּל *all* Gn 9$_{2}$ Ezk 31$_{14}$ Est 2$_{13}$ 2 C 34$_{16}$, impersonal Est 5$_{3.6}$ 9$_{12}$.

<PREP> לְ of direction, *to* 4QpNah 3.1$_{12}$, + Gibeonites 1 S 21$_{6(Kt)}$, Meholathite 1 S 18$_{19}$, עַם *people* Is 9$_{5}$, Adriel 1 S 18$_{19}$, David 4QCommGenA 5$_{4}$ 11QPs[a] 27$_{11}$, Esther Est 5$_{3.6}$ 7$_{2.3}$ 9$_{12}$, Huram-abi 2 C 2$_{13}$, Jacob 4QJub[h] 36$_{14}$ ([לו]), Jehoiachin 2 K 25$_{30}$||Jr 52$_{34}$, Phinehas Jos 24$_{33}$, Shelah Gn 38$_{14}$, אָדָם *human being* Si 15$_{17(A)}$ 4Q185 1.2$_{8}$, אִשָּׁה *woman* Lv 19$_{20}$, בֵּן *son* Jos 24$_{33}$ 1 C 5$_{1}$ 11QPs[a] 27$_{11}$, of Israel Ex 5$_{18}$, עֶבֶד *servant* Ex 5$_{16}$, נַעַר *lad* 1 S 25$_{27}$, נַעֲרָה *young woman* Est 2$_{13}$, מֶלֶךְ *king* Jr 13$_{20}$, מַלְכָּה *queen* Est 5$_{3}$ 7$_{2.3}$ 9$_{12}$, גְּבִירָה *queen mother* Jr 13$_{20}$, לֵוִי *Levite* Nm 26$_{62}$, חָכָם *wise one* Jb 15$_{19}$, worshipper 4QapPs[b] 46b$_{1}$, יֹשֵׁב *inhabitant* Ezk 33$_{24}$, אֹזֶן *ear* 1QH 10$_{37}$, זֶרַע *offspring* 4QCommGenA 5$_{4}$, Jerusalem Ezk 16$_{34}$, עֲרָבָה *desert* Is 35$_{2}$, הַר *mountain* of Seir Ezk 35$_{12}$, מֶלַח *salt* Ezk 47$_{11}$, אֵשׁ *fire* Ezk 15$_{4}$, מָוֶת *death* Ezk 31$_{14}$.

לְ *as, for (the purpose of)*, + אִשָּׁה *wife* Gn 38$_{14}$ 1 S 18$_{19}$, מוֹרָשָׁה *possession* Ezk 11$_{15}$ 33$_{24}$, אָכְלָה *fuel* Ezk 15$_{4}$ 35$_{12}$, מִשְׁפָּט *judgment* 4QpPs[a] 1.2$_{19}$.

לְ *at*, + אַחֲרִית *end* 1QpHab 9$_{6}$.

בְּ of place, *in*, + Egypt 4QNarrC 1$_{13}$, Susa Est 3$_{15}$ 4$_{8}$ 8$_{14}$ 9$_{14}$, הַר *hill country* Jos 24$_{33}$, מְדִינָה *province* Est 3$_{14}$ 8$_{13}$, בִּירָה *fortress* Est 3$_{15}$ 8$_{14}$.

בְּ *into*, + יָד *hand* Gn 9$_{2}$ Lv 26$_{25}$ 2 K 18$_{30}$||Is 36$_{15}$ 19$_{10}$||Is 37$_{10}$ Jr 21$_{10}$ 32$_{4.24.25.36.43}$ 34$_{3}$ 37$_{17}$ 38$_{3.18}$ 39$_{17}$ 46$_{24}$ Jb 9$_{24}$ Dn 11$_{11}$ Ezr 9$_{7}$ 1 C 5$_{20}$ 2 C 18$_{14}$ 28$_{5}$ 34$_{16}$ Si 11$_{6(B).6}$ 1Qp Hab 4$_{8}$ 9$_{6}$ 4QpPs[a] 1.2$_{19}$ 4QJub[h] 35$_{16}$.

בְּ of time, *in*, + קֵץ *period* 4QNarrC 1$_{13}$.

בְּ *as*, + חֵלֶק *portion* Si 26$_{3}$ (unless בְּ of accompaniment).

בְּ of accompaniment, *in, with,* + כָּבוֹד *glory* Si 44$_{19}$.

בְּ of instrument, *by (means of), with,* + חֶרֶב *sword* Jr 32$_{36}$, רָעָב *famine* Jr 32$_{36}$, דֶּבֶר *pestilence* Jr 32$_{36}$.

בְּ of cause, *on account of,* + עָוֹן *iniquity* Ezr 9$_7$, שְׁאֵלָה *request* Est 7$_3$, בַּקָּשָׁה *request* Est 7$_3$.

בְּיַד *by (means of), with,* + Moses Ne 10$_{30}$, עֶבֶד *servant* Ne 10$_{30}$.

מִן *from (among),* + זֶבַח *sacrifice* Lv 10$_{14}$.

מִן of agent, *by,* + רֹעֶה *shepherd* Ec 12$_{11}$.

מֵאֵת *from,* + מֶלֶךְ *king* 2 K 25$_{30}$||Jr 52$_{34}$.

אֶל *to,* + אֶרֶץ *land* Ezk 31$_{14}$.

עַל *to,* + אֲשֶׁר *one who* Is 29$_{12}$.

עַל *into,* + יָד *hand* 2 K 22$_7$.

בְּתוֹךְ *among,* + בֵּן *son* of Israel Nm 26$_{62}$.

עִם *with,* + חָכָם *skilful one* 2 C 2$_{13}$, שָׁלָל *spoil* 1QpHab 9$_6$.

עַד *until, unto,* + דּוֹר *generation* 4QCommGenA 5$_4$, יוֹם *day* Jr 52$_{34}$.

מִפְּנֵי *on account of,* + חֶרֶב *sword* Jr 32$_{24}$, רָעָב *famine* Jr 32$_{24}$, דֶּבֶר *pestilence* Jr 32$_{24}$.

מִלִּפְנֵי *from before,* + עֶלְיוֹן *the Most High* 11QPs[a] 27$_{11}$.

<COLL> נתן ni. || ילד pu. *be born* Is 9$_5$, מלט ni. *escape* Jr 32$_4$ 34$_3$, עשׂה ni. *be done* Est 5$_6$ 7$_2$ 9$_{12}$.

+ adverb or noun used adverbially, שֵׁנִית *a second time* 4QNarrC 1$_{13}$, חֹק *(as a) statute,* i.e. allocation Lv 10$_{14}$, יוֹם *day* Jr 52$_{34}$, דְּבַר־יוֹם בְּיוֹמוֹ *thing of a day in its day,* i.e. as was required each day 2 K 25$_{30}$||Jr 52$_{34}$.

Inf. abs. + finite form of נתן ni. Jr 32$_4$ 38$_3$.

פַּתְשֶׁגֶן הַכְּתָב לְהִנָּתֵן דָּת *a copy of the document to be issued as a decree* Est 8$_{13}$.

2. מִי יִנָּתֵן **who will let it be granted?,** i.e. **would that it were granted!, if only!,** followed by verbal clause beginning מי ינתן ויהיה לבבם *would that they had a heart,* i.e. that they were so minded 4QTestim$_3$ (=Dt 5$_{29}$ qal).

3. of sound, **be given out, be uttered,** <SUBJ> שָׁאוֹן *noise* Jr 51$_{55}$.

4. be placed, set, <SUBJ> Edom Ezk 32$_{29}$, Elam Ezk 32$_{25}$, Israel Ho 8$_{10}$ (if em. יִתְנוּ *they shall hire* [from תנה] to נִתְּנוּ *they are placed*), צָבָא *army* Dn 8$_{12}$, מֶלֶךְ *king* Ezk 32$_{29}$, נָשִׂיא *prince* Ezk 32$_{29}$, כֶּתֶר *crown* Est 6$_8$, קֶבֶר *grave* Ezk 32$_{23}$, מוּם *blemish* Lv 24$_{20}$, סֶכֶל *folly* Ec 10$_6$, חִתִּית *terror* Ezk 32$_{25}$.

<PREP> בְּ of place, *in, on, among,* + גּוֹי *nation* Ho 8$_{10}$ (if em.; see Subj.), אִישׁ *man* Lv 24$_{20}$, ראשׁ *head* Est 6$_8$, יַרְכָּה *distant part* Ezk 32$_{23}$, מָרוֹם *height* Ec 10$_6$, אֶרֶץ *land* Ezk 32$_{25}$.

בְּ of accompaniment, *with, in,* + פֶּשַׁע *transgression* Dn 8$_{12}$, גְּבוּרָה *might* Ezk 32$_{29}$ (or בְּ *despite*).

עַל *against,* + תָּמִיד *continual offering* Dn 8$_{12}$.

אֵת *with,* + חָלָל *slain one* Ezk 32$_{29}$.

בְּתוֹךְ *among,* + חָלָל *slain one* Ezk 32$_{25}$.

5. be made into, be made like, <SUBJ> בֵּן *son* Is 51$_{12}$. <COLL> חָצִיר יִנָּתֵן *he is made like grass* Is 51$_{12}$.

6. be allowed, permitted, ... יִנָּתֵן גַּם־מָחָר לַיְּהוּדִים לַעֲשׂוֹת *also tomorrow may it be permitted to the Jews,* i.e. may they be permitted, ... *to do* Est 9$_{13}$.

<SYN> §1 ילד pu. *be born.*

Ho. see Qal Pass.; perh. also 4QOrd[b] 10.1$_9$ (הותנה).*

⇒ (?) נָתִין *temple servant,* אֶתְנַן *fee,* מַתָּן I *gift,* II *Mattan,* מַתָּנָה I *gift,* II *Mattanah,* מַתַּת *gift,* נָתָן *Nathan,* אֶלְנָתָן *Elnathan,* יְהוֹנָתָן *J(eh)onathan,* יוֹנָתָן *Jonathan,* מַתְּנַי *Mattenai,* מַתַּנְיָה *Mattaniah,* מַתַּנְיָהוּ *Mattaniah,* מַתִּתְיָה *Mattithiah,* מַתִּתְיָהוּ *Mattithiah,* מַתַּתָּה *Mattattah,* נְתַנְאֵל *Nethanel,* נְתַנְיָה *Nethaniah,* נְתַנְיָהוּ *Nethaniah,* נְתַן־מֶלֶךְ *Nathan-melech.*

נָתָן 42.1.0.6 pr.n.m. **Nathan, 1.** prophet at time of David, <SUBJ> היה *be* 1 K 1$_8$, אמר *say* 2 S 7$_{3.4}$||1 C 17$_{2.3}$ 2 S 12$_{1.7.13}$ 1 K 1$_{11.24.34}$, דבר pi. *speak* 2 S 7$_{17}$||1 C 17$_{15}$, ראה *see* 2 S 7$_2$, הלך *go* 2 S 7$_4$||1 C 17$_3$ 2 S 12$_{15}$, hi. *lead* 1 K 1$_{38}$, בוא *come* 2 S 12$_1$ 1 K 1$_{11.22.23.32}$ Ps 51$_2$, עלה *go up* 1 K 1$_{34.45}$, ירד *go down* 1 K 1$_{38}$, hi. *bring down* 1 K 1$_{32}$, רכב hi. *cause to ride* 1 K 1$_{32.38.44}$, עמד *stand* Si 47$_1$, יצב htp. *stand* Si 47$_1$, מלא pi. *confirm* 1 K 1$_{11}$, שׁחה htpal. *bow down* 1 K 1$_{23}$, לקח *take* 1 K 1$_{32}$, משׁח *anoint* 1 K 1$_{34.45}$, תקע *sound trumpet* 1 K 1$_{34}$. <NOM CL> הִנֵּה נָתָן *here is Nathan* 1 K 1$_{23}$. <OBJ> קרא *call* 1 K 1$_{10}$, שׁלח *send* 2 S 12$_1$ 1 K 1$_{44}$. <CSTR> יַד נָתָן *hand of Nathan* 2 S 12$_{25}$ (or בְּיַד *by means of*), דִּבְרֵי *words of* 1 C 29$_{29}$ 2 C 9$_{29}$, ... מִצְוַת *commandment of ...* 2 C 29$_{25}$. <APP> נָבִיא *prophet* 2 S 7$_2$||1 C 17$_1$ 2 S 12$_{25}$ 1 K 1$_{8+8t}$ Ps 51$_2$ 1 C

29$_{29}$ 2 C 9$_{29}$ 29$_{25}$. <PREP> לְ of direction, *to*, + אמר *say* 1 K 1$_{32}$; introducing object, + קרא *call* 1 K 1$_{24.32}$; אֶל *to*, + היה *be* 2 S 7$_{4}$||1 C 17$_{3}$, אמר *say* 2 S 7$_{2}$||1 C 17$_{1}$ 2 S 12$_{5.13}$.

2. son of David, <SUBJ> ילד nu. *be born* 1 C 3$_{5}$. <NOM CL> אֵלֶּה שְׁמוֹת הַיִּלֹּדִים לוֹ בִּירוּשָׁלָ͏ִם ... נָתָן *these are the names of those born to him in Jerusalem ... Nathan* 2 S 5$_{14}$||1 C 14$_{4}$ (הַיִּלּוֹדִים).

3. father of David's warrior Igal (2 S 23$_{36}$), or brother of David's warrior Joel (1 C 11$_{38}$), <CSTR> בֶּן־נָתָן *son of Nathan* 2 S 23$_{36}$, אֲחִי *brother of* 1 C 11$_{38}$.

4. father of Solomon's officials Azariah and Zabud, <CSTR> בֶּן־נָתָן *son of Nathan* 1 K 4$_{5.5}$.

5. head of family, perh. ident. with §1 or 2, <CSTR> בֵּית־נָתָן *house of Nathan* Zc 12$_{12}$.

6. envoy from Ezra, <SUBJ> בוא hi. *bring* Ezr 8$_{16}$, דבר pi. *speak* Ezr 8$_{16}$. <OBJ> צוה pi. *command* Ezr 8$_{16}$. <APP> ראשׁ *head* Ezr 8$_{16}$ (or em. אִישׁ *man*). <PREP> לְ of direction, *to*, + שׁלח *send* Ezr 8$_{16}$.

7. husband of non-Jewish wife, <NOM CL> בְּנֵי בִנּוּי ... נָתָן *the sons of Binnui were ... Nathan* Ezr 10$_{39}$.

8. son of Attai and father of Zabad, descendant of Judah, <SUBJ> ילד hi. *beget* 1 C 2$_{36}$. <OBJ> ילד hi. *beget* 1 C 2$_{36}$.

9. Samaria ost. 45$_{3}$, <COLL> [ ]יו נתן מיצ[ת] *Nathan from Jazith* Samaria ost. 45$_{3}$ (others יונתן *Jonathan*).

10. Seal 503 (T. Beit Mirsim?, 7th/6th cent.).

11. appar. son of Ahimelech, Seal 629 (T. Beit Mirsim?, 7th/6th cent.).

12. appar. son of Pedaiah, Seal 630 (T. Beit Mirsim?, 7th/6th cent.).

13. appar. son of Elijah, Seal 747 (c. 700).

14. appar. son of Maas, Seal 765 (7th cent.).

15. Ḥorvat 'Uza jar inscr. 1$_{2}$, <CSTR> ידי נתן *hands of Natthan* Ḥorvat 'Uza jar inscr. 1$_{2}$.

<NOM CL> נתן אשר [ע]ל בית *Nathan who is over the house* Seal 503 (T. Beit Mirsim?, 7th/6th cent.). <PREP> לְ of possession, *of, (belonging) to* Seals 503 629 630 (all three T. Beit Mirsim?, 7th/6th cent.) 747 (c. 700) 765 (7th cent.).

⇨ נתן *give*.

נְתַנְאֵל 14 pr.n.m. **Nethanel, 1.** chief of Issachar, son of Zuar, <SUBJ> קרב hi. *bring near*, i.e. offer Nm 7$_{18}$. <NOM CL> נָשִׂיא לִבְנֵי יִשָּׂשכָר נְתַנְאֵל *the prince of the sons of Issachar was Nethanel* Nm 2$_{5}$, לְיִשָּׂשכָר נְתַנְאֵל *(belonging) to Issachar was Nethanel* Nm 1$_{8}$, עַל צְבָא מַטֵּה לִבְנֵי יִשָּׂשכָר נְתַנְאֵל *over the army of the tribe of the sons of Issachar was Nethanel* Nm 10$_{15}$. <CSTR> קָרְבַּן נְתַנְאֵל *offering of Nethanel* Nm 7$_{23}$. <APP> בֵּן *son* Nm 1$_{8}$ 2$_{5}$ 7$_{18.23}$ 10$_{15}$, נָשִׂיא *prince* Nm 7$_{18}$.

2. fourth son of Jesse, <NOM CL> נְתַנְאֵל הָרְבִיעִי *Nethanel was the fourth* 1 C 2$_{14}$.

3. priest at time of David, <SUBJ> חצצר hi. *sound trumpet* 1 C 15$_{24}$. <APP> כֹּהֵן *priest* 1 C 15$_{24}$.

4. Levite, father of Shemaiah, <CSTR> בֶּן־נְתַנְאֵל *son of Nethanel* 1 C 24$_{6}$.

5. fifth son of Obed-edom, <NOM CL> נְתַנְאֵל הַחֲמִישִׁי *Nethanel was the fifth* 1 C 26$_{4}$.

6. prince sent by Jehoshaphat to teach in cities of Judah, <SUBJ> למד pi. *teach* 2 C 17$_{7}$. <APP> שַׂר *prince* 2 C 17$_{7}$. <PREP> לְ introducing object, + שׁלח *send* 2 C 17$_{7}$.

7. Levite at time of Josiah, <SUBJ> רום hi. *raise*, i.e. contribute 2 C 35$_{9}$. <APP> אָח *brother* 2 C 35$_{9}$.

8. priest, son of Pashhur, husband of non-Jewish wife, <NOM CL> מִבְּנֵי פַּשְׁחוּר ... נְתַנְאֵל *of the sons of Pashhur was ... Nethanel* Ezr 10$_{22}$.

9. head of family of priests, <NOM CL> לִידַעְיָה נְתַנְאֵל *(belonging) to Jedaiah was Nethanel* Ne 12$_{21}$.

10. priest's son and musician at dedication of walls of Jerusalem, <NOM CL> נְתַנְאֵל ... בִּכְלֵי שִׁיר דָּוִיד *Nethanel ... was with David's instruments of song* Ne. 12$_{36}$. <APP> אָח *brother* Ne 12$_{36}$.

11. Seal 720, <PREP> לְ of possession, *of, (belonging) to* Seal 720 (with correction).

⇨ נתן *give* + אֵל *God*.

נְתַנְיָה 20.0.0.7 pr.n.m. **Nethaniah**—נְתַנְיָהוּ—**1.** son of Elishama and father of Gedaliah's murderer Ishmael, <CSTR> בֶּן־נְתַנְיָה *son of Nethaniah* 2 K 25$_{23}$||Jr 40$_{8}$ (נְתַנְיָהוּ) 2 K 25$_{25}$||Jr 41$_{1}$ Jr 40$_{14.15}$ 41$_{2+9t}$ (נְתַנְיָהוּ at 41$_{9}$). <APP> בֵּן *son* 2 K 25$_{25}$||Jr 41$_{1}$.

2. son of Shelemiah and father of Jehudi, <CSTR>

בֶּן־נְתַנְיָהוּ *son of Nethaniah* Jr 36$_{14}$. <APP> בֵּן *son* Jr 36$_{14}$.

3. Asaphite temple musician, <NOM CL> לִבְנֵי אָסָף ... נְתַנְיָה *of the sons of Asaph were ... Nethaniah* 1 C 25$_2$, הַחֲמִישִׁי נְתַנְיָהוּ *the fifth (lot) was (for) Nethaniah* 1 C 25$_{12}$.

4. Levite sent by Jehoshaphat to teach in cities of Judah, <NOM CL> עִמָּהֶם ... נְתַנְיָהוּ *with them was ... Nethaniah* 2 C 17$_8$. <APP> לֵוִי *Levite* 2 C 17$_8$.

5. father of Ezer, Arad ost. 23$_8$ (נתני[הו]).

6. Arad ost. 56.

7. father of Ophai, Kh. el-Qom tomb inscr. 1$_2$ 2.

8. son of Buzi, Seal 31 (7th cent.).

9. son of Obadiah, Seal 32 (Es-Soda, 8th cent.).

10. father of Jedoniah, Seal 870 (7th cent.).

11. T. en-Naṣbeh inscr. 2 (לנת[ניו]),

<CSTR> בן נתניהו *son of Nethaniah* Arad ost. 23$_8$ (נתני[הו]) 56 Kh. el-Qom tomb inscr. 1$_2$ 2 Seal 870 (7th cent.). <APP> בֵּן *son* Seals 31 (7th cent.) 32 (Es-Soda, 8th cent.). <PREP> לְ of possession, *of, (belonging) to* Seals 31 (7th cent.) 32 (Es-Soda, 8th cent.) T. en-Naṣbeh inscr. 2 (לנת[ניו]).

⇒ נתן *give* + '' *Y.*

נְתַנְיָהוּ, see נְתַנְיָה *Nethaniah*.

נְתַן־מֶלֶךְ $_{1.0.0.1}$ pr.n.m. **Nathan-melech, 1.** official at time of Josiah, <CSTR> לִשְׁכַּת נְתַן־מֶלֶךְ *chamber of Nathan-melech* 2 K 23$_{11}$. <APP> סָרִיס *eunuch* 2 K 23$_{11}$.

2. servant of the king, prob. ident. with §1, <APP> עֶבֶד *servant* Bulla D9. <PREP> לְ of possession, *of, (belonging) to* Bulla D9.

⇒ נתן *give* + מֶלֶךְ *king*.

נתס I $_1$ vb. **break up—Qal** $_1$ Pf. נָתְסוּ—**break up,** <SUBJ> פִּרְחַח *brood* Jb 30$_{13}$. <OBJ> נְתִיבָה *path* Jb 30$_{13}$.

⇒ cf. נתע I *break*, נתץ *pull down*, נתק *tear away*, נתשׁ *pluck up*.

*נתס II $_1$ vb. **place thorns (in)—Qal** $_1$ Pf. נָתְסוּ—**place thorns (in),** <SUBJ> פִּרְחַח *brood* Jb 30$_{13}$. <OBJ> נְתִיבָה *path* Jb 30$_{13}$.

נתע I $_{1.1}$ vb. **break—Ni.** $_{1.1}$ Pf. Si תנתע, נִתָּעוּ—**be broken,** <SUBJ> שֵׁן *tooth* of young lion Jb 4$_{10}$ (unless נתע II *cease*; or em. נִתָּצוּ *they are broken*, i.e. נתץ ni.), צְדָקָה *righteousness* appar. Si 3$_{14}$ (prob. error for תנטע *it shall be planted*; so corrected in ms A). <PREP> תַּחַת *instead of, in exchange for*, + עֲנָוָה *humility* Si 3$_{14}$(C); תְּמוּר *instead of, in exchange for*, + חַטָּאת *sin* Si 3$_{14}$(A).*

⇒ (?) מַלְתָּעוֹת *jawbone*; cf. נתס *break up*, נתץ *pull down*, נתק *tear away*, נתשׁ *pluck up*.

*נתע II $_1$ vb. **cease** (unless נתע I *break* or III *be pulled out*)—**Ni.** $_1$ נִתָּעוּ—**cease,** <SUBJ> שֵׁן *tooth* of young lion Jb 4$_{10}$, קוֹל *voice* of fierce lion Jb 4$_{10}$, שְׁאָגָה *roaring* Jb 4$_{10}$.

*נתע III $_1$ **pull out** (unless נתע I *break* or II *cease*)—**Ni.** $_1$ נִתָּעוּ—**be pulled out, be knocked out,** <SUBJ> שֵׁן *tooth* of young lion Jb 4$_{10}$.

נתץ $_{42.1.1}$ vb. **pull down—Qal** $_{31.1.1}$ Pf. נָתַץ (נָתָץ), נָתְצוּ (נָתָצוּ); impf. יִתֹּץ (יִתְּצֵנִי), יִתְּצוּ, אֶתֹּץ, (יִתָּצֵךְ), תִּתְּצוּן, תִּתֹּצוּ (תתוצו Q); + waw וַיִּתֹּץ, וַיִּתְּצוּ (וַיִּתְּצֻהוּ), וְנָתַץ, וְתִתְּצוּ; impv. נְתֹץ; ptc. pass. נְתֻצִים; inf. לִנְתוֹץ—**1. pull down, break down; break** teeth (Ps 58$_7$), <SUBJ> Y. Jr 18$_7$ 31$_{28}$ Ps 9$_7$ (if em. נָתַשְׁתָּ *you have plucked up*) 52$_7$ 58$_7$ Jb 19$_{10}$, Chaldaeans Jr 39$_8$ Ezk 26$_{12}$, Israelites Ex 34$_{13}$ Dt 7$_5$ Jg 2$_2$ Is 22$_{10}$ 11QT 2$_6$, עַם *people* 2 K 11$_{18}$||2 C 23$_{17}$, חַיִל *army* 2 K 25$_{10}$||Jr 52$_{14}$, Abimelech Jg 9$_{45}$, Gideon/Jerubbaal Jg 6$_{32}$ 8$_{9.13}$, Jeremiah Jr 1$_{10}$ Si 49$_7$, Nebuchadrezzar Ezk 26$_9$, בֵּן *son* Jg 6$_{30.31}$ 8$_{13}$, מֶלֶךְ *king* 2 K 23$_{7.8.12.15}$ Ezk 26$_9$, רָץ *guard* 2 K 10$_{27.27}$, שָׁלִישׁ *officer* 2 K 10$_{27.27}$; subj. not specified, Lv 14$_{45}$.

<OBJ> מַמְלָכָה *kingdom* Jr 1$_{10}$ 18$_7$, גּוֹי *nation* Jr 18$_7$, גִּבּוֹר *mighty one* Ps 52$_7$, Job Jb 19$_{10}$, מַלְתָּעוֹת *fangs* Ps 58$_7$, מִזְבֵּחַ *altar* Ex 34$_{13}$ Dt 7$_5$ Jg 2$_2$ 6$_{30.31.32}$ 2 K 23$_{12.15}$ 11QT 2$_6$ ([מזבחות]יהמה), מַצֵּבָה *pillar* 2 K 10$_{27}$, בַּיִת *house* Lv 14$_{45}$ 2 K 10$_{27}$ 11$_{18}$||2 C 23$_{17}$ 2 K 23$_7$ Is 22$_{10}$ Jr 31$_{28}$ Ezk 26$_{12}$, בָּמָה *high place* 2 K 23$_{8.15}$, מִגְדָּל *tower* Jg 8$_{9.17}$ Ezk 26$_9$, עִיר *city* Jg 9$_{45}$ Ps 9$_7$ (if em.; see Subj.), חוֹמָה *wall* 2 K 25$_{10}$||Jr 52$_{14}$ Jr 39$_8$, אֶבֶן *stone* Lv 14$_{45}$, עֵץ *wood* Lv

14_{45}, עָפָר *dust*, i.e. plaster Lv 14_{45}.

<PREP> לְ of direction, *to*, + נֵצַח *everlastingness*, i.e. for ever Ps 52_7; בְּ of instrument, *by (means of), with*, + חֶרֶב *sword* Ezk 26_9.

<COLL> נתץ || נתשׁ *pluck up* Jr 1_{10} 18_7 31_{28} Si 49_7, הרס *tear down* Jr 1_{10} 31_{28} Ezk 26_{12} Ps 58_7 Si 49_7, גדע pi. *hew down* Dt 7_5, כרת *cut down* Ex 34_{13} Jg 6_{30}, שׁבר pi. *break* Ex 34_{13} Dt 7_5 2 K 11_{18}||2 C 23_{17}, שׂרף *burn* Dt 7_5 2 K 23_{15} (+) Jr 39_8, אבד hi. *destroy* Jr 1_{10} 18_7 31_{28} Si 49_7, רעע hi. *harm* Jr 31_{28}.

+ נסח *tear away* Ps 52_7, שׁרשׁ pi. *uproot* Ps 52_7, חתה *take* Ps 52_7.

:: בנה *build* Jr 1_{10} 31_{28} Si 49_7, נטע *plant* Jr 1_{10} 31_{28} Si 49_7, שׁוב hi. *restore* Si 49_7.

+ adverb, סָבִיב *round about*, i.e. on every side Jb 19_{10}.

2. pass. **be pulled down,** in order to make a defence, <SUBJ> בַּיִת *house* Jr 33_4. <PREP> אֶל *against*, + סֹלְלָה *siege mound* Jr 33_4, חֶרֶב *sword* Jr 33_4.

<SYN> §1 נתשׁ *pluck up*, הרס *tear down*, גדע pi. *hew down*, כרת *cut down*, שׁבר pi. *break*, שׂרף *burn*, אבד hi. *destroy*, רעע hi. *harm*.

<ANT> §1 בנה *build*, נטע *plant*, שׁוב hi. *restore*.

Ni. 2 Pf. נִתְּצוּ—**1. be pulled down, be ruined,** <SUBJ> עִיר *city* Jr 4_{26} (mss יצת ni. *be burned up*) $9_{15(mss)}$ (L יצת ni.), צוּר *rock* Na 1_6 (ms יצת ni.). <PREP> מִן of cause, *on account of* or of agent, *by*, + Y. Na 1_6; מִבְּלִי *without*, + יֹשֵׁב *inhabitant* Jr $9_{15(mss)}$ (L יצת ni.); מִפְּנֵי *on account of*, + Y. Jr 4_{26}, חָרוֹן *wrath* Jr 4_{26}.

2. be broken, <SUBJ> שֵׁן *tooth* of young lion Jb 4_{10} (if em. נִתָּעוּ *they are broken* [נתע ni.] to נִתָּצוּ).

Pi. 7 Pf. נִתַּץ; + waw וְנִתַּצְתֶּם, וְנִתְּצוּ; וַיְנַתֵּץ, וַיְנַתְּצוּ—**tear down,** <SUBJ> Chaldaeans 2 C 36_{19}, Israel(ites) Dt 12_3 2 C 31_1 34_4, Hezekiah 2 C 33_3, Josiah 2 C 34_7, אָב *father* 2 C 33_3, מְאַהֵב *lover* Ezk 16_{39}, רָמָה *height* Ezk 16_{39}. <OBJ> מִזְבֵּחַ *altar* Dt 12_3 2 C 31_1 $34_{4.7}$, בָּמָה *high place* 2 C 31_1 33_3, חוֹמָה *wall* 2 C 36_{19}. <PREP> בְּ of place, *in*, + Ephraim 2 C 31_1, Manasseh 2 C 31_1; מִן *from*, + Benjamin 2 C 31_1, Judah 2 C 31_1; לִפְנֵי *before*, + Josiah 2 C 34_4. <COLL> נתץ pi. || הרס *tear down* Ezk 16_{39}, גדע pi. *hew down* Dt 12_3 2 C 31_1 34_4 (+), שׁבר pi. *break* Dt 12_3 2 C 31_1 34_4 (+), כתת pi. *beat* 2 C 34_7, שׂרף *burn* Dt 12_3 2 C 36_{19}.

<SYN> הרס *tear down*, גדע pi. *hew down*, שׁבר pi. *break*, כתת pi. *beat*, שׂרף *burn*.

Pu. 1 Pf. נֻתַּץ—**be torn down,** <SUBJ> מִזְבֵּחַ *altar* Jg 6_{28}. <COLL> נתץ pu. || כרת pu. *be cut down* Jg 6_{28}.

<SYN> כרת pu. *be cut down*.

Ho. (unless **Qal Pass.**) 1 יֻתַּץ—**be broken up,** <SUBJ> תַּנּוּר *oven* Lv 11_{35}, כִּיר *cooking furnace* Lv 11_{35}.

⇨ cf. נתס I *break up*, נתע I *break*, נתק *tear away*, נתשׁ *pluck up*.

[נְתַצְבַּעַל] pr.n.m. **Nethazbaal,** Meṣad Ḥashavyahu ost. 6_1 ([נ]תצבעל; others עניבעל *Anibaal*).

נתק 27.0.3 vb. **tear away**—**Qal** 3.0.1 Impf. Q יתקו; אֶתְּקֶנְךָּ; + waw וּנְתַקְּנֻהוּ; ptc. pass. נָתוּק—**1. tear away, pull off,** <SUBJ> Y. Jr 22_{24}. <OBJ> Coniah (as signet ring) Jr 22_{24}, בֵּן *son* Jr 22_{24}, מֶלֶךְ *king* Jr 22_{24}. <PREP> בְּ of instrument, *by (means of), with*, + זִק *fetter* 1QH 16_{35}; מִן of direction, *from*, + שָׁם *there* Jr 22_{24}.

2. draw away, lure away, <SUBJ> בֵּן *son* of Israel Jg 20_{32}. <OBJ> בֵּן *son* of Benjamin Jg 20_{32}. <PREP> מִן of direction, *from*, + עִיר *city* Jg 20_{32}; אֶל *to*, + מְסִלָּה *highway* Jg 20_{32}.

3. pass. ptc. as noun, **animal that is torn,** <OBJ> קרב hi. *bring near*, i.e. offer Lv 22_{24} (|| מעך pass. *be pressed*, כתת pass. *be crushed*, כרת pass. *be cut*), perh. עשׂה *do*, i.e. prepare (for sacrifice) Lv 22_{24}.

<SYN> §3 מעך pass. *be pressed*, כתת pass. *be crushed*, כרת pass. *be cut*.

Ni. 10.0.1 Pf. נִתַּק, נִתְּקוּ (נִתָּקוּ); impf. יִנָּתֵק, יִנָּתֵקוּ; + waw וַיִּנָּתְקוּ—**1. be torn apart, be snapped, be torn away,** <SUBJ> רָשָׁע *wicked one* Jb 18_{14}, חֶבֶל *cord* Is 33_{20} Ec 12_6 (if em. יֵרָחֵק *it is* not *removed* to יִנָּתֵק), מֵיתָר *cord* Jr 10_{20}, מְשֻׁלָּשׁ *threefold cord* Ec 4_{12}, פְּתִיל *string* of tow Jg 16_9, שְׂרוֹךְ *thong* of sandal Is 5_{27}, זִמָּה *plan* Jb 17_{11} (or em. זִמֹּתַי *my plans* to זַמֹּתַי appar. *I planned* my days that have passed), מוֹרָשׁ *desire* Jb 17_{11}. <PREP> בְּ of accompaniment, *with, in*, + מְהֵרָה *speed* Ec 4_{12}; מִן of direction, *from*, + אֹהֶל *tent* Jb 18_{14}. <COLL> נתק ni. || פתח ni. *be loosened* Is 5_{27}; + נסע *pull* out Is 33$_{20}$, שׁדד pu. *be destroyed* Jr 10$_{20}$.

2. be torn out, be pulled up, <PREP> מִן of direction, *from*, + שֹׁרֶשׁ *root* 4QpsHod^c 2$_9$.

3. be separated, be removed, in metal smelting, <SUBJ> רַע *dross* Jr 6$_{29}$.

4. be drawn away, be lured away (Jos 8$_{16}$), **be lifted out** (Jos 4$_{18}$), <SUBJ> עַם *people* Jos 8$_{16}$, כַּף *sole* of foot Jos 4$_{18}$. <PREP> מִן of direction, *from*, + עִיר *city* Jos 8$_{16}$; אֶל *onto*, + חָרָבָה *dry ground* Jos 4$_{18}$.

<SYN> §1 פתח ni. *be loosened* Is 5$_{27}$.

Pi. 11.0.1 Pf. נִתַּקְתִּי, נִתְּקוּ; impf. יְנַתֵּק, תְּנַתְּקִי, אֲנַתֵּק, תְּנַתְּקוּ (perh. 2ms*), נְנַתְּקָה; + waw וַיְנַתֵּק (וַיְנַתְּקֵם); inf. Q נתק—**1. tear apart, snap, break,** <SUBJ> Y. Jr 30$_8$ Na 1$_{13}$ Ps 107$_{14}$, Israel Jr 2$_{20}$, Samson Jg 16$_{9.12}$, מֶלֶךְ *king* Ps 2$_3$, רֹזֵן *ruler* Ps 2$_3$, גָּדוֹל *great one* Jr 5$_5$; subj. not specified, Is 58$_6$ 1QH 5$_{37}$.

<OBJ> יֶתֶר *bow-string* Jg 16$_9$, עֲבֹת *cord* Jg 16$_{12}$ 1QH 5$_{37}$, מוֹטָה *bar (of yoke)* Is 58$_6$, מוֹסֵרָה *bond* Jr 2$_{20}$ 5$_5$ 30$_8$ Na 1$_{13}$ Ps 2$_3$ 107$_{14}$.

<PREP> כְּ *as*, + (as obj.) חוּט *thread* Jg 16$_{21}$.

מֵעַל *from upon*, + זְרוֹעַ *arm* Jg 16$_{12}$.

<COLL> נתק pi. || שׁבר *break* Jr 2$_{20}$ 5$_5$ 30$_8$ Na 1$_{13}$; + שׁלך hi. *cast* Ps 2$_3$; עבותים לאין נתק *cords that one cannot snap* 1QH 5$_{37}$.

2. tear out, pull out, <SUBJ> Oholibah Ezk 23$_{24}$, נֶשֶׁר *eagle* Ezk 17$_9$. <OBJ> שַׁד *breast* Ezk 23$_{24}$, שֹׁרֶשׁ *root* Ezk 17$_9$. <COLL> נתק pi. || קסס po. *strip off* Ezk 17$_9$; + גרם pi. *gnaw* Ezk 23$_{24}$.

<SYN> §1 שׁבר *break*.

Hi. 2 Impv. הַתִּקֵם; inf. הַתִּיקֵנוּ—**draw out, lure away,** <SUBJ> Y. Jr 12$_3$, עַם *people* Jos 8$_6$, Joshua Jos 8$_6$. <OBJ> רָשָׁע *wicked one* Jr 12$_3$, בֹּגֵד *treacherous one* Jr 12$_3$, inhabitants of Ai Jos 8$_6$. <PREP> כְּ *as*, + (as obj.) צֹאן *sheep* Jr 12$_3$; מִן of direction, *from*, + עִיר *city* Jos 8$_6$.

Ho. 1 Pf. הָנְתְּקוּ—**be drawn away, be lured away,** <SUBJ> בֵּן *son* of Benjamin Jg 20$_{31}$. <PREP> מִן of direction, *from*, + עִיר *city* Jg 20$_{31}$.*

⇨ נֶתֶק *scall*; cf. נתס *break up*, נתע I *break*, נתץ *pull down*, נתשׁ *pluck up*.

נֶתֶק 14.0.4 n.m. **scall**—נֶתֶק—**scall,** itching disease of the scalp; in ref. to person with the disease (Lv 13$_{33}$), <SUBJ> פשׂה *spread* Lv 13$_{32.34.35.36}$, עמד *stand*, i.e. stop spreading Lv 13$_{37}$, רפא ni. *be healed* Lv 13$_{37}$. <NOM CL> נֶתֶק הוּא *it is a scall* Lv 13$_{30}$, בו ... נתק *in him is ... scall* 11QT 48$_{17}$. <OBJ> ראה *see* Lv 13$_{34}$, גלח pi. *shave* Lv 13$_{33}$ 4QD^a 6.1$_9$, סגר hi. *shut up* Lv 13$_{33}$. <CSTR> נתק הרוש והזו[קן] *scall of the head and the beard* 4QD^a 6.1$_5$; נֶגַע הַנֶּתֶק *disease of scall* Lv 13$_{31.31}$, מַרְאֵה *appearance of* Lv 13$_{32}$, משפט נתק *ordinance of*, i.e. concerning, *the scall of* 4QD^a 6.1$_5$, [צרעת נתק] *leprosy of scall* 11QT 46$_{01}$. <PREP> לְ *concerning* Lv 14$_{54}$; בְּ of instrument, *by (means of), with*, + נגע pu. *be afflicted* 11QT 48$_{15}$; עַל *upon* Pr 25$_{20}$ (if ins. עַל־נֶתֶק וּמַיִם *upon scall and water* upon natron). <COLL> נֶגַע || נֶתֶק *disease* 11QT 48$_{15}$, צָרַעַת *leprosy* 11QT 48$_{15.17}$; + צָרַעַת Lv 13$_{30}$ 14$_{54}$.

<SYN> נֶגַע *disease* 11QT 48$_{15}$, צָרַעַת *leprosy*.*

⇨ נתק *tear away*.

נתר I 5.0.4 vb. **be loose—Ni.** 0.0.1 Impf. [י]נתר—**be released,** <PREP> מִפְּנֵי *(from) before*, + זֶרֶם *downpour* 4Q424 1$_4$ ([י]נתר).

Hi. 5.0.3 Impf. יַתֵּר; + waw וַיַּתֵּר (וַיַּתִּירֵהוּ), Q ואתר; ptc. מַתִּיר; inf. abs. הַתֵּר—**loosen, release, allow to break bonds, set free,** <SUBJ> Y. 2 S 22$_{33}$ Ps 79$_{11}$ (if em. הוֹתֵר *leave over* [יתר hi.] to הַתֵּר *release*) 146$_6$ Jb 6$_9$ 4QapMes 2.2$_8$, מֶלֶךְ *king* Ps 105$_{20}$, מְבַקֵּר *overseer* CD 13$_{10}$; subj. not specified, Is 58$_6$.

<OBJ> Joseph Ps 105$_{20}$, אָסוּר *prisoner* Ps 146$_7$ 4QapMes 2.2$_8$, בֵּן *son* of death Ps 79$_{11}$ (if em.; see Subj.), יָד *hand* Jb 6$_9$, אֲגֻדָּה *bond* Is 58$_6$, חַרְצֻבָּה *fetter* CD 13$_{10}$, דֶּרֶךְ *way* 2 S 22$_{33}$.

<COLL> נתר hi. || פתח pi. *loosen* Is 58$_6$ Ps 105$_{20}$.

וַיַּתֵּר תָּמִים דַּרְכִּי perh. *and he has loosened my way safely*, i.e. made it safe 2 S 22$_{33}$(Qr) (or em. וָאַתֵּר *and I leap* safely on my way, i.e. נתר I; ||Ps 18$_{33}$ וַיִּתֵּן *and he has given*, i.e. made, my way safe).

Ho. <SUBJ> צַדִּיק *righteous* Pr 12$_{26}$ (if em. יֻתַּר).*

Also 4QapMes 2.3$_1$.

<SYN> פתח pi. *loosen*.

*__נתר__ II 3.0.1 vb. **spring—Qal** 1.0.1 Impf. יִתַּר; inf. Q לנתור—**spring, start up, leap,** <SUBJ> David 2 S 22$_{33}$

(if em.; see Coll.), לֵב *heart* Jb 37_{1}, עוֹף *winged insects* 11QT 48_{5}. <PREP> בְּ of instrument, *be (means of), with*, + כֶּרַע *leg* 11QT 48_{5}; מִן of direction, *from*, + מָקוֹם *place* Jb 37_{1}; עַל *upon*, + אֶרֶץ *earth* 11QT 48_{5}. <COLL> נתר + חרד *tremble* Jb 37_{1}; וְאֶתַּר תָּמִים דַּרְכִּי *and I leap safely on my way* 2 S 22_{33} (if em. וַיַּתֵּר *and he has loosened*, i.e. נתר II hi.).

Pi. $_{1}$ Inf. נַתֵּר—**leap,** <SUBJ> עוֹף *winged insects* Lv 11_{21}. <PREP> בְּ of instrument, *be (means of), with*, + כֶּרַע *leg* Lv 11_{21}; עַל *upon*, + אֶרֶץ *earth* Lv 11_{21}.

Hi. $_{1}$ + waw וַיַּתֵּר—**cause to leap, cause to start** (unless נתר III *tear*), <SUBJ> Y. Hb 3_{6}. <OBJ> גּוֹי *nation* Hb 3_{6}.*

*נתר III $_{2}$ vb. **tear** (unless נתר I *release* or II *spring*) —**Hi.** $_{2}$ + waw וַיַּתֵּר; inf. הַתֵּר—**tear asunder,** <SUBJ> Y. Hb 3_{6}; subj. not specified, Is 58_{6}. <OBJ> גּוֹי *nation* Hb 3_{6}, <OBJ> גּוֹי *nation* Hb 3_{6}, אֲגֻדָּה *bond* Is 58_{6}. <COLL> נתר hi. || פתח pi. *loosen* Is 58_{6}.

*[נתר] IV $_{2}$ vb. **snatch away—Qal** $_{1}$ Impf. יִתַּר—**fall away,** <SUBJ> צַדִּיק *righteous one* Pr 12_{26} (if em.; see Prep.), לֵב *heart* Jb 37_{1} (יֶחֱרַד לִבִּי וְיִתַּר מִמְּקוֹמוֹ *my heart trembles and falls from its place*, or *sinks*). <PREP> מִן of direction, *from*, + מָקוֹם *place* Jb 37_{1}, רָעָה *harm* Pr 12_{26} (if em. יָתֵר מֵרֵעֵהוּ *he searches out his neighbour* to יִתַּר מֵרָעָה *he snatches himself away from harm*). <COLL> נתר + חרד *tremble* Jb 37_{1}.

Hi. $_{1}$ Impf. יַתֵּר—**snatch away**, Y. Jb 6_{9} (יַתֵּר יָדוֹ וִיבַצְּעֵנִי *would that he would snatch me away [with] his hand and cut me off*). <OBJ> 1. person snatched, Job Jb 6_{9}. 2. means of snatching, יָד *hand* Jb 6_{9}.

Ho. be snatched away, be delivered, <SUBJ> צַדִּיק *righteous one* Pr 12_{26} (if em.; see Prep.). <PREP> מִן *from*, + רָעָה *harm* Pr 12_{26} (if em. יָתֵר מֵרֵעֵהוּ *he searches out his neighbour* to יֻתַּר מֵרָעָה *he is delivered from harm*).

*[נתר] V $_{1}$ vb. **hop—Pi.** $_{1}$ Inf. נַתֵּר—**leap,** <SUBJ> עוֹף *winged insects* Lv 11_{21} (כְּרָעַיִם מִמַּעַל לְרַגְלָיו לְנַתֵּר בָּהֵן עַל־הָאָרֶץ they have *legs above their feet with which to hop on the ground*).

נֶ֫תֶר I $_{2}$ n.[m.] **natron**—נֶתֶר—a form of sodium carbonate, used in making soap, <PREP> בְּ of instrument, *by (means of), with*, + כבס pi. *wash* Jr 2_{22} (+ בֹּרִית *soap*); עַל *upon* Pr 25_{20} (חֹמֶץ עַל־נָתֶר *vinegar upon natron*; unless נֶתֶר II *wound*).*

*[נֹ֫תֶר] II $_{1}$ n.[m.] **wound**—נֶתֶר—<PREP> עַל *upon* Pr 25_{20} (חֹמֶץ עַל־נָתֶר *vinegar upon a wound*).

נתשׁ $_{21.3.1}$ vb. **pluck up—Qal** $_{16.3.1}$ Pf. נָתַשְׁתָּ; impf. 3fs Si תנתש (unless pi.), אֶתּוֹשׁ; + waw וְנָתַשְׁתִּי, וְנָתַשׁ (ונתשתים); וַיִּתְּשֵׁם; ptc. נֹתֵשׁ (נֹתְשָׁם), pass. Q נתושים; inf. abs. נָתוֹשׁ; cstr. לִנְתוֹשׁ (נְתֹשׁ)—**1. pluck up, uproot,** <SUBJ> Y. Dt 29_{27} 1 K 14_{15} Jr $12_{14.14.15.17.17}$ 18_{7} 24_{6} 31_{28} 42_{10} 45_{4} Mc 5_{13} Ps 9_{7} (or em. נָתַצְתָּ *you have broken down*) 2 C 7_{20} Si 10_{17}, Jeremiah Jr 1_{10} Si 49_{7}, קְלָלָה *curse* Si 3_{9} (unless pi.).

<OBJ> Israel(ites) Dt 29_{27} 1 K 14_{15} Jr 42_{10} 2 C 7_{20}, גּוֹי *nation* Jr 12_{17} 18_{7} Si 10_{17}, מַמְלָכָה *kingdom* Jr 1_{10} 18_{7}, בַּיִת *house* Jr $12_{14.15}$ 31_{28}, גָּלוּת *exiles* Jr 24_{6}, שָׁכֵן *neighbour* Jr 12_{14}, אֶרֶץ *land* Jr 45_{4}, עִיר *city* Ps 9_{7} (or em.; see Subj.), נֶטַע *plant* Si 3_{9} (unless pi.), אֲשֵׁרָה *Asherah* Mc 5_{13}, אֲשֶׁר *that which* Jr 45_{4}.

<PREP> בְּ of accompaniment, *with, in*, + אַף *anger* Dt 29_{27}, קֶצֶף *anger* Dt 29_{27}, חֵמָה *wrath* Dt 29_{27}.

מֵעַל *from (upon)*, + אֲדָמָה *land* Dt 29_{27} 1 K 14_{15} Jr 12_{14} 2 C 7_{20}.

מִתּוֹךְ *from among*, + שָׁכֵן *neighbour* Jr 12_{14}.

מִקֶּרֶב *from among*, + Israelites Mc 5_{13}.

<COLL> נתשׁ || נתץ *pluck up* Jr 1_{10} 18_{7} 31_{28} Si 49_{7}, הרס *tear down* Jr 1_{10} 24_{6} 31_{28} 42_{10} 45_{4} Si 49_{7}, אבד hi. *destroy* Jr 1_{10} 12_{17} 18_{7} 31_{28} Si 49_{7}, רעע hi. *harm* Jr 31_{28}; + נסח *tear away* Si 10_{17}, שׁמד hi. *destroy* Mc 5_{13}.

:: בנה *build* Jr 1_{10} 24_{6} (+) 31_{28} 42_{10} 45_{4} (both +) Si 49_{7}, נטע *plant* Jr 1_{10} 24_{6} 31_{28} 42_{10} 45_{4} Si 49_{7}, שׁוב hi. *restore* Si 49_{7}, יסד pi. *establish* Si 3_{9}.

Inf. abs. + finite form of נתשׁ, Jr 12_{17}.

2. pass. ptc. as noun, **uprooted one, expelled one,** <OBJ> נהל pi. *lead* 4QapMes 2.2_{13} (+ רָעֵב *hungry one*).

<SYN> §1 נתץ *pluck up*, הרס *tear down*, אבד hi. *destroy*, רעע hi. *harm*.

<ANT> §1 בנה *build*, נטע *plant*, שׁוב hi. *restore*, יסד pi. *establish*.

Ni. 4 Impf. יִנָּתֵשׁ, 3fs תִּנָּתֵשׁ, יִנָּתְשׁוּ—**be plucked up, uprooted,** <SUBJ> Israelites Am 9$_{15}$, מַלְכוּת *kingdom* Dn 11$_{4}$, עֵמֶק *valley* Jr 31$_{40}$, מַיִם *water* appar. Jr 18$_{14}$ (or em. יִנָּשְׁתוּ *they shall be dried up* [נשׁת ni.] or יִנְּשׁוּ *they shall forget* [נשׁה II niphtal]). <PREP> מֵעַל *from (upon)*, + אֲדָמָה *land* Am 9$_{15}$. <COLL> נתשׁ ni. || הרס ni. *be torn down* Jr 31$_{40}$; + נטע *plant* Am 9$_{15}$; + adverb, עוֹד *again* Am 9$_{15}$.

<SYN> הרס ni. *be torn down*.

Pi. See Qal.

Ho. 1 + waw וַתֻּתַּשׁ—**be plucked up, be uprooted,** <SUBJ> גֶּפֶן *vine* Ezk 19$_{12}$. <PREP> בְּ of accompaniment, *with, in*, + חֵמָה *wrath* Ezk 19$_{12}$.

⇒ cf. נתס I *break up*, נתע I *break*, נתץ *pull down*.

Bibliography

AASOR Annual of the American Schools of Oriental Research

AB Anchor Bible

ABD David Noel Freedman (ed.), *The Anchor Bible Dictionary* (New York: Doubleday, 1992), 6 vols.

AbrN *Abr-Nahrain*

ADPV Abhandlungen des Deutschen Palästinavereins

Aeg *Aegyptus*

AfO *Archiv für Orientforschung*

AION *Annali dell'istituto orientale di Napoli*

AION-Ling *Annali dell'istituto orientale di Napoli. Sezione linguistica*

AJSL *American Journal of Semitic Languages and Literatures*

ALUOS *The Annual of Leeds University Oriental Society*

AnOr Analecta orientalia

AOAT Alter Orient und Altes Testament

ArOr *Archiv orientální*

ASTI *Annual of the Swedish Theological Institute*

ATD Das Alte Testament Deutsch

AusBR *Australian Biblical Review*

AUSS *Andrews University Seminary Studies*

BA *Biblical Archaeologist*

BAR *Biblical Archaeology Review*

BASOR *Bulletin of the American Schools of Oriental Research*

BBB Bonner biblische Beiträge

BBET Beiträge zur biblischen Exegese und Theologie

BEATAJ Beiträge zur Erforschung des Alten Testaments und des antiken Judentums

BeO *Bibbia e oriente*

BethM *Beth Mikra*

BETL Bibliotheca ephemeridum theologicarum lovaniensium

*BH*3 *Biblia hebraica* (ed. Rudolf Kittel; Stuttgart: Priviligierte Württembergische Bibelanstalt, Stuttgart, 3rd edn, 1937)

BHS *Biblia hebraica stuttgartensia* (ed. K. Elliger and W. Rudolph; Stuttgart: Deutsche Bibelgesellschaft, 1968)

Bib *Biblica*

BibOr Biblica et Orientalia

BIFAO *Bulletin de l'Institut français d'archéologie orientale*

BiOr *Bibliotheca orientalis*

BiTrans *The Bible Translator*

BK(AT) Biblischer Kommentar: Altes Testament

BN *Biblische Notizen*

BSOAS *Bulletin of the School of Oriental and African Studies*

BWANT Beiträge zur Wissenschaft vom Alten und Neuen Testament

BZ *Biblische Zeitschrift*

BZAW Beihefte zur *Zeitschrift für die alttestamentliche Wissenschaft*

CBOTS Coniectanea Biblica. Old Testament Series

CBQ *Catholic Biblical Quarterly*

CdE *Chronique d'Egypte*

Dalman, *Arbeit* Gustaf Dalman, *Arbeit und Sitte in Palästina* (Schriften des Deutschen Palästina-Instituts; Gütersloh: C.

Bertelsmann, 1928), 8 vols.

DCH — *The Dictionary of Classical Hebrew* (ed. David J.A. Clines; Sheffield: Sheffield Academic Press, 1993–)

DJD — Discoveries in the Judaean Desert

DSD — *Dead Sea Discoveries*

EI — *Eretz Israel*

EncJud — *Encyclopaedia Judaica* (ed. C. Roth; Jerusalem: Encyclopaedia Judaica, 1971–72)

EstBíb — *Estudios Bíblicos*

ETL — *Ephemerides theologicae lovanienses*

ExpT — *Expository Times*

FolOr — *Folia Orientalia*

FRLANT — Forschungen zur Religion und Literatur des Alten und Neuen Testaments

Gesenius–Buhl — *Wilhelm Gesenius' Hebräisches und aramäisches Handwörterbuch über das Alte Testament* (ed. Frants Buhl; Leipzig: F.C.W. Vogel, 1915)

GKC — A.E. Cowley (ed.), *Gesenius' Hebrew Grammar, as Edited and Enlarged by the Late E. Kautzsch* (Oxford: Clarendon Press, 1910)

GLECS — *Comptes rendus du Groupe linguistique d'études chamito-sémitiques*

Greg — *Gregorianum*

HALAT — Ludwig Koehler and Walter Baumgartner, *Hebräisches und aramäisches Lexikon zum Alten Testament* (Leiden: E.J. Brill, 1967–95), 5 vols.

HALOT — Ludwig Koehler and Walter Baumgartner, *The Hebrew and Aramaic Lexicon of the Old Testament* (trans. M.E.J. Richardson; Leiden: E.J. Brill, 1994–), 5 vols.

HAR — *Hebrew Annual Review*

HAT — Handbuch zum Alten Testament

HSM — Harvard Semitic Monographs

HSS — Harvard Semitic Studies

HTR — *Harvard Theological Review*

HUCA — *Hebrew Union College Annual*

IB — George Arthur Buttrick (ed.), *The Interpreter's Bible* (Nashville: Abingdon Press, 1956)

IDB — George Arthur Buttrick (ed.), *The Interpreter's Dictionary of the Bible* (4 vols.; Nashville: Abingdon Press, 1962)

IDBS — Keith Crim (ed.), *The Interpreter's Dictionary of the Bible. Supplementary Volume* (Nashville: Abingdon Press, 1976)

IEJ — *Israel Exploration Journal*

IOS — *Israel Oriental Studies*

JANESCU — *Journal of the Ancient Near Eastern Society of Columbia University*

JAOS — *Journal of the American Oriental Society*

Jastrow — Marcus Jastrow, *A Dictionary of the Targumim, the Talmud Babli and Yerushalmi, and the Midrashic Literature* (London: Luzac, 1903)

JBL — *Journal of Biblical Literature*

JCS — *Journal of Cuneiform Studies*

JEOL — *Jaarbericht ... ex oriente lux*

JJS — *Journal of Jewish Studies*

JNES — *Journal of Near Eastern Studies*

JNWSL — *Journal of Northwest Semitic Languages*

JPOS — *Journal of the Palestine Oriental Society*

JPS — Jewish Publication Society Version

JQR — *Jewish Quarterly Review*

JRAS — *Journal of the Royal Asiatic Society*

JSOR — *Journal of the Society of Oriental Research*

JSOT — *Journal for the Study of the Old Testament*

JSOTSup — *Journal for the Study of the Old Testament*, Supplement Series

JSS — *Journal of Semitic Studies*

JSSEA — *Journal of the Society for the Study of Egyptian Antiquities*

JTS — *Journal of Theological Studies*

KAT — Kommentar zum Alten Testament

KB — Ludwig Koehler and Walter Baumgartner (eds.), *Lexicon in Veteris Testamenti libros* (Leiden: E.J. Brill, 1953)

LB — *Linguistica Biblica*

Lesh — *Lešonénu*

MEstArabH — Miscelanea de estudios arabes y hebraicos

Mus — *Le Muséon*

MUSJ — Université Saint-Joseph, Beyrouth (Syrie).

Mélanges de la Faculté Orientale
NEB New English Bible
NICOT New International Commentary on the Old Testament
NIV New International Version
NJB New Jerusalem Bible
OBL Orientalia et Biblica Lovaniensia
OBO Orbis biblicus et orientalis
OLZ *Orientalistische Literaturzeitung*
Or *Orientalia*
OrAnt *Oriens Antiquus*
OrSuec *Orientalia Suecana*
OTL Old Testament Library
OTS *Oudtestamentische Studiën*
PAAJR Proceedings of the American Academy for Jewish Research
PEQ *Palestine Exploration Quarterly*
RB *Revue biblique*
RHPR *Revue d'histoire et de philosophie religieuses*
RHR *Revue de l'histoire des religions*
RicLing *Ricerche linguistiche*
RivBib *Rivista Biblica*
RQ *Revue de Qumran*
RScRel *Recherches de science religieuse*
RSO *Rivista degli studi orientali*
RSV Revised Standard Version
SBFLA *Studii biblici franciscani liber annuus*
SBLDS Society of Biblical Literature Dissertation Series
SBLMS Society of Biblical Literature Monograph Series
SchwThUmschau *Schweizerische Theologische Umschau*
ScrHieros Scripta Hierosolymitana
SEÅ *Svensk exegetisk årsskrift*
Sem *Semitica*
SJOT *Scandinavian Journal of the Old Testament*
SR *Studies in Religion/Sciences religieuses*
STDJ Studies on the Texts of the Desert of Judah
StTh *Studia theologica*
SUNT Studien zum Umwelt des Neuen Testaments
Syr *Syria*
Tarb *Tarbiẓ*
TB Theologische Bücherei
TDOT G. Johannes Botterweck and Helmer Ringgren, *Theological Dictionary of the Old Testament* (Grand Rapids: William B. Eerdmans, 1974–) [original: *Theologisches Wörterbuch zum Alten Testament* (Stuttgart: W. Kohlhammer), 1970–]
Thomas, *Lexicon* D. Winton Thomas, *A Hebrew and English Lexicon of the Old Testament* (1970; unpublished)
TLOT Ernst Jenni and Claus Westermann (eds.), *Theological Lexicon of the Old Testament* Peabody, MA: Hendrickson, 1997) [original: *Theologisches Handwörterbuch zum Alten Testament* (München: Chr. Kaiser), 1971–76]
TLZ *Theologische Literaturzeitung*
TS *Theological Studies*
TTS Trierer Theologische Studien
TynB *Tyndale Bulletin*
TZ *Theologische Zeitschrift*
UF *Ugarit-Forschungen*
VD *Verbum domini*
VT *Vetus Testamentum*
VTSup *Vetus Testamentum*, Supplements
WBC Word Biblical Commentary
WD *Wort und Dienst*
WMANT Wissenschaftliche Monographien zum Alten und Neuen Testament
WO *Die Welt des Orients*
WZKM *Wiener Zeitschrift für die Kunde des Morgenlandes*
ZA *Zeitschrift für Assyriologie*
ZAH *Zeitschrift für Althebraistik*
ZÄS *Zeitschrft für ägyptische Sprache*
ZAW *Zeitschrift für die alttestamentliche Wissenschaft*
ZDMG *Zeitschrift der deutschen morgenländischen Gesellschaft*
ZDPV *Zeitschrift des deutschen Palästina-Vereins*
Zorell Franz Zorell, *Lexicon Hebraicum veteris testamenti* (Rome: Pontificium Institutum Biblicum, 1963)

מ

ם־ (enclitic mem)—[1] H.L. Ginsberg, כתבי אוגרית/ *The Ugarit Texts* (Jerusalem: Bialik, 1936), pp. 129-31; [2] H.L. Ginsberg, 'The Ugaritic Texts and Textual Criticism', *JBL* 62 (1943), pp. 109-15 (115); [3] W.F Albright, 'The Oracles of Balaam', *JBL* 63 (1944), pp. 207-33 (a: 215 n. 45; b: 219 n. 83; c: 221 n. 93; d: 213); [4] John Hastings Patton, *Canaanite Parallels in the Book of Psalms* (Baltimore: Johns Hopkins Press, 1944), pp. 12-13; [5] William Foxwell Albright, 'The Old Testament and Canaanite Language', *CBQ* 7 (1945), pp. 5-31 (23-24); [6] Theodor H. Gaster, 'Psalm 29', *JQR* 37 (1946–47), pp. 55-65 (64-65 n. 32); [7] Frank M. Cross and David Noel Freedman, 'The Blessing of Moses', *JBL* 67 (1948), pp. 191-210 (193); [8] H.L. Ginsberg, 'Some Emendations in Isaiah', *JBL* 69 (1950), pp. 51-60 (54); [9] W.F. Albright, 'The Psalm of Habakkuk', in *Studies in Old Testament Prophecy Presented to Professor Theodore H. Robinson* (ed. H.H. Rowley; Edinburgh: T. & T. Clark, 1950), pp. 1-18 (15 n. y); [10] William L. Moran, 'The Putative Root *'tm* in Is. 9:18', *CBQ* 12 (1950), pp. 153-54; [11] W.F. Albright, 'A Catalogue of Early Hebrew Lyric Poems (Psalm lxviii)', *HUCA* 23 (1950–51), pp. 1-39 (24); [12] David Noel Freedman, 'Notes on Genesis', *ZAW* 64 (1952), pp. 190-94; [13] Mitchell J. Dahood, 'Canaanite-Phoenician Influence in Qoheleth', *Bib* 33 (1952), pp. 30-52, 191-22 (194-95); [14] Frank Moore Cross and David Noel Freedman, 'A Royal Song of Thanksgiving: II Sam 22 = Psalm 18', *JBL* 72 (1953), pp. 15-34 (a: 17 n. n; b: 26 n. 41; c: 28 n. 63); [15] Roger T. O'Callaghan, 'Echoes of Canaanite Literature in the Psalms', *VT 4* (1954), pp. 164-76 (170-71); [16] Frank M. Cross and David Noel Freedman, 'The Song of Miriam', *JNES* 14 (1955), pp. 237-50 (246 n. 25); [17] Nahum M. Sarna, 'Some Instances of the Enclitic *-m* in Job', *JJS* 6 (1955), pp. 108-10; [18] W.F. Albright, 'Some Canaanite-Phoenician Sources of Hebrew Wisdom', in *Wisdom in Israel and in the Ancient Near East, Presented to Professor Harold Henry Rowley ... in Celebration of his Sixty-Fifth Birthday* (ed. M. Noth and D. Winton Thomas; VTSup, 3; Leiden: E.J. Brill, 1955), pp. 1-15 (11 n. 3); [19] M. Dahood, 'Enclitic Mem and Emphatic Lamedh in Psalm 85', *Bib* 37 (1956), pp. 338-40; [20] M. Dahood, 'Some Northwest Semitic Words in Job', *Bib* 38 (1957), pp. 306-20 (315-17); [21] Horace D. Hummel, 'Enclitic *Mêm* in Early Northwest Semitic, Especially Hebrew', *JBL* 76 (1957), pp. 85-107; [22] A. Jirku, 'Weitere Fälle von afformativem *-ma* im Hebräischen', *VT* 7 (1957), pp. 391-92; [23] William F. Albright, 'The Refrain «and God saw ki tôb»', in *Mélanges bibliques redigés en l'honneur de André Robert* (Travaux de l'Institut catholique de Paris, 4; Paris: Bloud & Gay, 1957), pp. 22-26 (24); [24] M. Dahood, 'The Value of Ugaritic for Textual Criticism', *Bib* 40 (1959), pp. 160-70 (168-69); [25] David N. Freedman, 'Archaic Forms in Early Hebrew Poetry, *ZAW* 72 (1960), pp. 101-107; [26] Mitchell Dahood, review of Hans-Joachim Kraus, *Psalmen* (1958–60), *Bib* 42 (1961), pp. 383-85 (385); [27] William L. Moran, 'The Hebrew Language in its Northwest Semitic Background', in *The Bible and the Ancient Near East: Essays in Honour of William Foxwell Albright* (ed. G. Ernest Wright; London: Routledge & Kegan Paul, 1961), pp. 54-72 (60); [28] P.J. Calderone, 'The Rivers of "Maṣor"', *Bib* 42 (1961), pp. 423-32; [29] M. Dahood, '*Nādâ* "To Hurl" in Ex 15,16' *Bib* 43 (1962), pp. 248-49 (248); [30] Mitchell Dahood, 'Philological Notes on Jer 18,14-15', *ZAW* 74 (1962), pp. 207-209 (207); [31] Mitchell Dahood, 'Ugaritic Studies and the Bible', *Greg* 43 (1962), pp. 55-79 (65-66); [32] Otto Rössler, 'Die Präfixkonjugation Qal der

Verba Iae Nûn im Althebräischen und das Problem der sogenannten Tempora', *ZAW* 74 (1962), pp. 125-41 (128); [33] Mitchell Dahood, 'Qoheleth and Northwest Semitic Philology', *Bib* 43 (1962), pp. 349-65 (365); [34] M. Dahood, review of C. Rabin (ed.), *Studies in the Bible* (1961), *Bib* 43 (1962), pp. 544-46 (545); [35] Mitchell Dahood, 'Northwest Semitic Philology and Job', in *The Bible in Current Catholic Thought: Gruenthaner Memorial Volume* (ed. J.L. McKenzie; St Mary's Theological Studies, 1; New York, Herder & Herder, 1962), pp. 55-74; [36] Mitchell Dahood, *Proverbs and Northwest Semitic Philology* (Scripta Pontificii Instituti Biblici, 113; Rome: Pontificium Institutum Biblicum, 1963), p. 12; [37] M. Dahood, review of J. Carmignac and P. Guilbert, *Les textes de Qumran traduits et annotés* (1961), *Bib* 44 (1963), pp. 231-33 (232); [38] M. Dahood, review of *The Torah: The Five Books of Moses* (1962), *Bib* 45 (1964), pp. 281-83 (283); [39] M. Dahood, 'Ugaritic Lexicography', in *Mélanges Eugène Tisserant. I. Ecriture sainte—Ancien orient* (Studi e testi, 231; Città del Vaticano: Bibliotheca Apostolica Vaticana, 1964), pp. 81-104; [40] Mitchell Dahood, *Ugaritic–Hebrew Philology: Marginal Notes on Recent Publications* (BibOr, 17; Rome: Pontifical Biblical Institute, 1965), pp. 27, 34, 50; [41] M. Dahood, review of William Hugh Brownlee, *The Meaning of the Qumran Scrolls of the Bible* (1964), *Bib* 46 (1965), pp. 388-89 (389); [42] Mitchell Dahood, 'Punic *hkkbm 'l* and Isa 14,13', *Or* 34 (1965), pp. 170-72 (171); [43] M. Dahood, 'Hebrew–Ugaritic Lexicography III', *Bib* 46 (1965), pp. 311-32; [44] M.H. Pope, *Job* (AB, 15; Garden City, NY: Doubleday, 1965); [45] M. Dahood, 'Hebrew–Ugaritic Lexicography IV', *Bib* 47 (1966), pp. 403-19 (412-13, 417); [46] Mitchell Dahood, *Psalms I: 1–50* (AB, 16; Garden City, NY: Doubleday, 1966); [47] M. Dahood, 'Hebrew–Ugaritic Lexicography V', *Bib* 48 (1967), pp. 421-38; [48] Mitchell Dahood, *Psalms II: 51–100* (AB, 17; Garden City, NY: Doubleday, 1968; 3rd edn, 1979); [49] Mitchell Dahood, 'The Phoenician Contribution to Biblical Wisdom Literature', in *The Role of the Phoenicians in the Interaction of Mediterranean Civilizations* (ed. William A. Ward; Beirut: American University in Beirut, 1968), pp. 123-52; [50] Thomas F. McDaniel, 'Philological Studies in Lamentations. II', *Bib* 49 (1968), pp. 199-220 (201-202); [51] James Barr, *Comparative Philology and the Text of the Old Testament* (Oxford: Oxford University Press, 1968), pp. 31-34; [52] H.J. van Dijk, *Ezekiel's Prophecy on Tyre (Ez. 26,1–28,19): A New Approach* (BibOr, 20; Rome: Pontifical Biblical Institute, 1968); [53] Donald Watson Goodwin, *Text-Restoration Methods in Contemporary U.S.A. Biblical Scholarship* (Istituto orientale di Napoli. Pubblicazioni del Seminario di semitistica. Ricerche, 5; Naples: Istituto orientale, 1969), pp. 53-64; [54] Anton C.M. Blommerde, *Northwest Semitic Grammar and Job* (BibOr, 22; Rome: Pontifical Biblical Institute, 1969); [55] Francis I. Andersen, *The Hebrew Verbless Clause in the Pentateuch* (JBLMS, 14; Nashville: Abingdon Press, 1970), pp. 48, 124 n. 13; [56] Francis I. Andersen, 'Biconsonantal Byforms of Weak Hebrew Roots', *ZAW* 82 (1970), pp. 270-75; [57] W.A. van der Weiden, *Le livre des Proverbes: Notes philologiques* (BibOr, 23; Rome: Biblical Institute Press, 1970); [58] Mitchell Dahood, *Psalms III: 101–150* (AB, 17A; Garden City, NY: Doubleday, 1970); [59] Liudger Sabottka, *Zephanja: Versuch einer Neuübersetzung mit philologischer Kommentar* (BibOr, 25; Rome: Biblical Institute Press, 1972); [60] Ludwig Koehler and Walter Baumgartner *et al.* (eds.), *Hebräisches und aramäisches Lexikon zum Alten Testament*, II (Leiden: E.J. Brill, 1974); [61] Willibald Kuhnigk, *Nordwestsemitische Studien zum Hoseabuch* (BibOr, 27; Rome: Biblical Institute Press, 1974); [62] E.F. Campbell, *Ruth* (AB; Garden City, NY: Doubleday, 1975), p. 146; [63] Mitchell Dahood, 'Hebrew Lexicography: A Review of W. Baumgartner's *Lexikon*, Volume II', *Or* 45 (1976), pp. 327-65 (345-46); [64] J.C.L. Gibson, *Canaanite Myths and Legends* (Edinburgh: T. & T. Clark, 2nd edn, 1978), p. 150b; [65] Anthony R. Ceresko, *Job 29–31 in the Light of Northwest Semitic* (BibOr, 36; Rome: Biblical Institute Press, 1980); [66] Francis I. Andersen and David Noel Freedman, *Hosea: A New Translation with Introduction and Commentary* (AB, 24; New York: Doubleday, 1980); [67] Cyrus H. Gordon, *Forgotten Scripts: Their*

Ongoing Discovery and Decipherment (New York: Basic Books, rev. edn, 1982), pp. 169-71; [68] Cyrus H. Gordon, 'The "Waw Conversive": From Eblaite to Hebrew', *PAAJR* 50 (1983), pp. 87-90; [69] Walter D. Michel, *Job in the Light of Northwest Semitic*, I (BibOr, 42; Rome: Biblical Institute Press, 1987); [70] Gary A. Rendsburg, 'Eblaite *Ù-MA* and Hebrew *WM-*', in *Eblaitica: Essays on the Ebla Archives and Eblaite Language*, I (ed. Cyrus H. Gordon, Gary A. Rendsburg and Nathan H. Winter; Winona Lake, IN: Eisenbrauns, 1987), pp. 34-41; [71] Cyrus H. Gordon, '*WM*- "and" in Eblaite and Hebrew', in *Eblaitica: Essays on the Ebla Archives and Eblaite Language*, I (ed. Cyrus H. Gordon, Gary A. Rendsburg and Nathan H. Winter; Winona Lake, IN: Eisenbrauns, 1987), pp. 29-30; [72] Constance Wallace, '*WM-* in Nehemiah 5:11', in *Eblaitica: Essays on the Ebla Archives and Eblaite Language*, I (ed. Cyrus H. Gordon, Gary A. Rendsburg and Nathan H. Winter; Winona Lake, IN: Eisenbrauns, 1987), p. 31; [73] John A. Emerton, 'Are There Examples of Enclitic *mem* in the Hebrew Bible?', in *Texts, Temples, and Traditions: A Tribute to Menahem Haran* (ed. Michael V. Fox, Victor Avigdor Hurowitz, Avi Hurvitz *et al.*; Winona Lake, IN: Eisenbrauns, 1996), pp. 321-38.

following conjunctive waw—Francis I. Andersen, *The Hebrew Verbless Clause in the Pentateuch* (JBLMS, 14; Nashville: Abingdon Press, 1970), pp. 48, 124 n. 13; E.F. Campbell, *Ruth* (AB; Garden City, NY: Doubleday, 1975), p. 146; Cyrus H. Gordon, *Forgotten Scripts: Their Ongoing Discovery and Decipherment* (New York: Basic Books, rev. edn, 1982), pp. 169-71; Cyrus H. Gordon, 'The "Waw Conversive": From Eblaite to Hebrew', *PAAJR* 50 (1983), p. 90; Gary A. Rendsburg, 'Eblaite *Ù-MA* and Hebrew *WM*', in *Eblaitica: Essays on the Ebla Archives and Eblaite Language*, I (ed. Cyrus H. Gordon, Gary A. Rendsburg and Nathan H. Winter; Winona Lake, IN: Eisenbrauns, 1987), pp. 34-41.

internal enclitic mem—Mitchell Dahood, 'Ugaritic Studies and the Bible', *Greg* 43 (1962), pp. 55-79 (66); Mitchell Dahood, *Psalms I: 1–50* (AB, 16; Garden City, NY: Doubleday, 1966), p. 147.

no enclitic mem—G.R. Driver, *Canaanite Myths and Legends* (Edinburgh: T. & T. Clark, 1956), p. 130 n. 2; G.R. Driver, review of Mitchell Dahood, *Proverbs and Northwest Semitic Philology* (1963), *JSS* 10 (1965), pp. 112-17 (116); John A. Emerton, 'Are There Examples of Enclitic *mem* in the Hebrew Bible?', in *Texts, Temples, and Traditions: A Tribute to Menahem Haran* (ed. Michael V. Fox, Victor Avigdor Hurowitz, Avi Hurvitz *et al.*; Winona Lake, IN: Eisenbrauns, 1996), pp. 321-38.

מַאֲבוּס *cattle-pen*—Thomas, *Lexicon*, I (1970), p. 77.

Jr 50_{26}—Horace D. Hummel, 'Enclitic *Mêm* in Early Northwest Semitic, Especially Hebrew', *JBL* 76 (1957), pp. 85-107.

מְאֹד I (orthography)—Hartmut Stegemann, 'Zu Textbestand und Grundgedanken von *1QS* III, 13—IV, 26', *RQ* 13 (1988), pp. 95-131 (104); Johann Cook, 'Orthographic Peculiarities in the Dead Sea Biblical Scrolls', *RQ* 14 (1989–90), pp. 293-305 (296); P. Wernberg-Møller, 'Two Biblical Hebrew Adverbs in the Dialect of the Dead Sea Scrolls', in *A Tribute to Geza Vermes: Essays on Jewish and Christian Literature and History* (ed. Philip R. Davies and Richard T. White; JSOTSup, 100; Sheffield: JSOT Press, 1990), pp. 21-35 (21-26, 32-33).

very—B. Kedar-Kopfstein, 'מְאֹד *meʾoḏ*', *TDOT*, VIII (1997; orig. 1983–84), pp. 39-41.

מָאֵד I *Grand One, Almighty* (divine name)—Mitchell Dahood, *Psalms II: 51–100* (AB, 17; Garden City, NY: Doubleday, 1968; 3rd edn, 1979), p. 360; M. Dahood, 'Comparative Philology Yesterday and Today', *Bib* 50 (1969), pp. 70-79 (79); Mitchell Dahood, *Psalms III: 101–150* (AB, 17A; Garden City, NY: Doubleday, 1970), pp. xxvi, xxviii, 59, 109, 174, 184, 189, 190, 318, 336; David Noel Freedman, 'God Almighty in Ps 78,59', *Bib* 54 (1973), p. 268; M. Dahood, 'Northwest Semitic Notes on Genesis', *Bib* 55 (1974), pp. 76-82; L. Viganò, *Nomi e titoli di YHWH alla luce del semitico del Nord-ovest* (BibOr, 31; Rome: Biblical Institute Press, 1976), pp. 78-80, 84; Mitchell Dahood, 'Hebrew Lexicography: A Review of W. Baumgartner's *Lexikon*, Volume II', *Or* 45 (1976), pp. 327-65 (346); M. Dahood,

'Ebla, Ugarit and the Old Testament', in *Congress Volume: Göttingen 1977* (VTSup, 29; Leiden: E.J. Brill, 1978), pp. 81-112 (101-102); Walter D. Michel, *Job in the Light of Northwest Semitic*, I (BibOr, 42; Rome: Biblical Institute Press, 1987), p. 185.

very (מְאֹד), not *Grand One*—Oswald Loretz, '*d m'd* "Everlasting Grand One" in den Psalmen', *BZ* 16 (1972), pp. 245-48; David Marcus, 'Ugaritic Evidence for "The Almighty/The Grand One"?', *Bib* 55 (1974), pp. 404-407.

מָאֵד II *calamity*, perh. as name for Sheol (cf. אֵיד *distress*)—Mitchell Dahood, *Psalms III: 101–150* (AB, 17A; Garden City, NY: Doubleday, 1970), pp. 148, 185; Mitchell Dahood, 'Hebrew–Ugaritic Lexicography X', *Bib* 53 (1972), pp. 386-403 (400-401).

מָאֹד I *burden, distress* (cf. אֵיד *distress*, Arab. ma'âwidu *misfortunes*)—G.R. Driver, 'Studies in the Vocabulary of the Old Testament. II', *JTS* 32 (1930–31), pp. 250-57 (256); G.R. Driver, 'Problems in the Hebrew Text of Proverbs', *Bib* 32 (1951), pp. 173-97 (182); Thomas, *Lexicon*, I (1970), p. 176; A.A. Anderson, *The Book of Psalms; Vol. 1: Psalms 1-72* (NCB; Grand Rapids: Wm B. Eerdmans, 1972), p. 251.

מָאֹד II *nightfall* (cf. Arab. 'âda *press down, incline, come on [of evening]*)—A. Guillaume, 'מְאֹד in I. Samuel xx, 19', *PEQ* 86 (1954), pp. 83-86; G.R. Driver, 'Old Problems Re-examined', *ZAW* 80 (1968), pp. 174-83 (177); Thomas, *Lexicon*, I (1970), p. 176.

מאה pi. *repeat a hundred times*—M. Dahood, *Ugaritic–Hebrew Philology: Marginal Notes on Recent Publications* (BibOr, 17: Rome: Pontifical Biblical Institute, 1965), p. 13; M. Dahood, 'Hebrew–Ugaritic Lexicography IV', *Bib* 47 (1966), pp. 403-19 (413); Mitchell Dahood, *Psalms I: 1–50* (AB, 16; Garden City, NY: Doubleday, 1966), p. 142; Mitchell Dahood, review of John M. Allegro, *Discoveries in the Judaean Desert of Jordan*, V (1968), *Bib* 50 (1969), pp. 270-72 (271-72); Mitchell Dahood, *Psalms III: 101–150* (AB, 17A; Garden City, NY: Doubleday, 1970), p. 107; J; cf. *HALOT*, II, p. 539a.

מֵאָה *century, company*—Mitchell Dahood, 'Hebrew Lexicography: A Review of W. Baumgartner's *Lexikon*, Volume II', *Or* 45 (1976), pp. 327-65 (346).

morphology—Elisha Qimron, *The Hebrew of the Dead Sea Scrolls* (HSS, 29; Atlanta, GA: Scholars Press, 1986), p. 26; Elisha Qimron and John Strugnell, *Qumran Cave 4; V: Miqṣat ma'aśe ha-Torah* (DJD, 10; Oxford: Clarendon Press, 1994), p. 45.

רָ ע מְאַת—Ec 8_{12}—*a hundred evils*—Robert Gordis, *Koheleth—The Man and His World: A Study of Ecclesiastes* (New York: Schocken, 1951), p. 287.

רַע מְאַת—Ec 8_{12}—*the evil of hundreds*—C.L. Seow, *Ecclesiastes: A New Translation with Introduction and Commentary* (AB, 18C; New York: Doubleday, 1997), pp. 287-88.

מְאוּמָה *anything*—Alice Faber, 'Indefinite Pronouns in Early Semitic', in *Fucus: A Semitic/Afrasian Gathering in Remembrance of Albert Ehrman* (ed. Yoël L. Arbeitman; Amsterdam Studies in the Theory and History of Linguistic Science, IV/58; Amsterdam: J. Benjamin, 1988), pp. 221-38.

מָאוֹר *luminary*—Sverre Aalen, *Die Begriffe 'Licht' und 'Finsternis' im AT, im Spätjudentum und in Rabbinismus* (Skrifter det Norske videnskaps-akademi, II, Hist.-filos. klasse; 1951.1; Oslo: J. Dybwad, 1951).

moon—Mitchell Dahood, *Psalms II: 51–100* (AB, 17; Garden City, NY: Doubleday, 1968; 3rd edn, 1979), p. 207.

Ps 90_8—Mitchell Dahood, *Ugaritic–Hebrew Philology: Marginal Notes on Recent Publications* (BibOr, 17: Rome: Pontifical Biblical Institute, 1965), p. 27; Thomas, *Lexicon*, I, (1970), p. 243.

מְאוּרָה I *light-hole* (cf. אוֹר *light*)—BDB, p. 22b; Gesenius–Buhl, p. 393a; Zorell, p. 404.

מְאוּרָה II *den*—RSV, JPS.

lair—NJB.

nest—NIV.

מְאוּרָה III *fiery coals (?)*—*HALOT*, II, p. 539b.

מְאוּרָה IV *eye* (cf. אוֹר *light*)—cf. Gesenius–Buhl, p. 393a.

מְאוּרָה V *young* (cf. Akk. mūru)—KB, p. 489b.

מֹאזְנַיִם *balances*—R. North, 'מֹאזְנַיִם *mō'zᵉnayim*', *TDOT*, VIII (1997; orig. 1983–84), pp. 41-44.

מַאֲכָל *food*—Ludwig Koehler, 'Problems in the Study of the Language of the Old Testament', *JSS* 1 (1956), pp. 3-24 (20-22).

Na 1_4—G.R. Driver, 'Linguistic and Textual Problems:

Minor Prophets. II', *JTS* 39 (1938), pp. 260-73 (271).

מַאֲכֶלֶת *fuel*—BDB, p. 38b; Ludwig Koehler, 'Problems in the Study of the Language of the Old Testament', *JSS* 1 (1956), pp. 3-24 (20-22); Thomas, *Lexicon*, I (1970), p. 443.

food—*HALOT*, II, p. 540a.

מַאֲמָץ *efforts*—KB, p. 490a.

exertion—*HALOT*, II, p. 540a.

power—BDB, p. 55b.

wealth, expense—Gustav Hölscher, *Das Buch Hiob* (HAT, I/17; Tübingen: J.C.B. Mohr, 2nd edn, 1952), p. 84; N.H. Tur-Sinai, *The Book of Job* (Jerusalem: Kiryath Sepher, revised edn, 1967), p. 500.

מאן *refuse*—H. Ringgren, 'מאן *m'n*', *TDOT*, VIII (1997; orig. 1983–84), pp. 44-46.

מאס I *reject*—H. Wildberger, 'מאס *m's*' , *TLOT*, II (1997; orig. 1976), pp. 651-60; S. Wagner and H.-J. Fabry, 'מָאַס *mā'as*', *TDOT*, VIII (1997; orig. 1983–84), pp. 47-60; Lester J. Kuyper, 'The Repentance of Job', *VT* 9 (1959), pp. 91-94; Norbert Lohfink, 'Zu Text und Form von Os 4,4-6', *Bib* 42 (1961), pp. 303-32 (320-23).

without object, *feel loathing, contempt, revulsion*—Dale Patrick, 'The Translation of Job xlii 6', *VT* 26 (1976), p. 370; Walter D. Michel, *Job in the Light of Northwest Semitic*, I (BibOr, 42; Rome: Biblical Institute Press, 1987), p. 174; John Briggs Curtis, 'On Job's Response to Yahweh', *JBL* 98 (1979), pp. 497-511 (503).

pi. *accept* (privative pi'el)—M. Dahood, 'Hebrew–Ugaritic Lexicography XII', *Bib* 55 (1974), pp. 381-93 (382).

מאס II *flow* (byform of מסס *melt*)—BDB, p. 549b.

melt, i.e. *cower*—David A. Diewert, 'Job xxxvi 5 and the Root *m's* II', *VT* 39 (1989), pp. 71-77.

melt, i.e. *submit*—William Morrow, 'Consolation, Rejection, and Repentance in Job 42:6', *JBL* 105 (1986), pp. 211-25 (214-15).

מאס III *discharge pus, suppurate* (byform of מסס *melt*)—G.R. Driver, 'Problems in the Hebrew Text of Job', in *Wisdom in Israel and in the Ancient Near East, Presented to Professor Harold Henry Rowley ... in Celebration of his Sixty-Fifth Birthday* (VTSup, 3; Leiden: E.J. Brill, 1955), pp. 72-93 (75).

מאס IV *gape open* (cf. Arab. ma'asa)—G.R. Driver, 'Problems in the Hebrew Text of Job', in *Wisdom in Israel and in the Ancient Near East, Presented to Professor Harold Henry Rowley ... in Celebration of his Sixty-Fifth Birthday* (VTSup, 3; Leiden: E.J. Brill, 1955), pp. 72-93 (75-76).

מאס V *err, transgress* (byform of מסס *melt*)—*HALOT*, II, p. 541a.

מְאַסֵּף *gathering*—J. Carmignac, 'Précisions apportées au vocabulaire de l'hébreu biblique par la Guerre des Fils de Lumière contre les Fils de Ténèbres', *VT* 5 (1955), pp. 345-65 (364).

withdrawal (cf. אסף §2 *remove*)—G.R. Driver, review of J. van der Ploeg, *Le Rouleau de la guerre. Traduit et annoté avec une Introduction* (1959), *JTS* ns 11 (1960), pp. 366-69 (368); Thomas, *Lexicon*, I (1970), p. 737.

מַאְפִּלָה (a land) *late* in bearing produce (cf. MH השנים מאפילות *the years in which the crops ripen late*)—J. Levy, *Chaldäisches Wörterbuch über die Targumim und einen grossen Theil des rabbinischen Schriftthums*, I (Leipzig: Baumgartner, 1881), p. 54b.

waterless, becoming parched late in the season—G.R. Driver, 'Hebrew Notes on Prophets and Psalms', *JTS* 41 (1940), pp. 162-75 (165-66); Thomas, *Lexicon*, I (1970), p. 781.

מַאְפֵלָה *darkness* (cf. אֹפֶל *darkness*)—J. VanderKam and J.T. Milik, 'Jubilees', in *DJD*, XIII (1994), pp. 1-185 (16).

מַאְפֵּלְיָה *deep darkness* (with ־יָה as a superlative)—William McKane, *A Critical and Exegetical Commentary on Jeremiah*, I (ICC; Edinburgh: T. & T. Clark, 1986), p. 52.

מְאַפֵּס *Meappes* (cf. אפס *cease*)—G.R. Driver, 'Old and New Semitic Texts', *PEQ* 70 (1938), pp. 188-92 (191-92).

מאר *feel hatred*—Ps 4_5 71_{10}—G.R. Driver, 'Notes on the Psalms. I. 1–72', *JTS* 43 (1942), pp. 149-60 (150, 160).

מְאָרֵב *ambush*—2 C 20_{22}—G.R. Driver, in Thomas, *Lexicon*, I (1970), p. 828.

מְאֵרָה II *starvation* (cf. Arab. 'arra IV *be weak*)—Thomas, *Lexicon*, I (1970), p. 897.

מְאֵרָה III *twitching (of limbs)* (cf. Akk. arāru *fear*, arurtu *twitching of limbs*)—Thomas, *Lexicon*, I (1970), p. 897.

מְאַשֵּׁר *evergreen tree, cedar* (byform of תְּאַשּׁוּר *box-tree*)—M. Dahood, 'Hebrew–Ugaritic Lexicography IV', *Bib* 47 (1966), pp. 403-19 (413-14).

מַאֲשֶׁר *that which*—M. Dahood, 'Hebrew–Ugaritic Lexicography IV', *Bib* 47 (1966), pp. 403-19 (414).

מֵאָת *a hundred times*—M. Dahood, 'Qoheleth and Recent Discoveries', *Bib* 39 (1958), pp. 302-18 (306); M. Dahood, *Ugaritic–Hebrew Philology: Marginal Notes on Recent Publications* (BibOr, 17: Rome: Pontifical Biblical Institute, 1965), p. 14.

מַבּוּל *flood, water above the firmament*—Joachim Begrich, 'Mabbūl. Eine exegetisch-lexikalische Studie', *Zeitschrift für Semitistik und verwandte Gebiete* 6 (1928), pp. 135-33 (= *Gesammelte Studien zum Alten Testament* [ed. Walther Zimmerli; TB, 21; München: Chr. Kaiser, 1964], pp. 39-54); David Neiman, 'The Supercaelian Sea', *JNES* 28 (1969), pp. 243-49; P. Stenmans, 'מַבּוּל *mabbûl*'', *TDOT*, VIII (1997; orig. 1983–84), pp. 60-65; Roger W. Cowley, 'Technical Terms in Biblical Hebrew?', *TynB* 37 (1986), pp. 21-28 (27-28); O. Loretz, 'KTU 1.101:1-3a und 1.2 IV 10 als Parallelen zu Ps 29,10', *ZAW* 88 (1987), pp. 415-21; Chaim Cohen, 'ה' למבול ישב (תה' כט, י) — פירוש חדש [ה' למבול ישב (Ps 29:10): A New Interpretation]', *Lesh* 53 (1989), pp. 193-201, I-III.

flood of fire—Robert Gordis, *The Book of Job* (New York: Jewish Theological Seminary, 1978), p. 193.

לְמַבּוּל *from before the Flood*—D.T. Tsumura, '"The Deluge" (*mabbūl*) in Psalm 29:10', *UF* 20 (1988), pp. 351-55.

מַבּוּעַ *public fountain*—J.T. Milik, 'Le rouleau de cuivre provenant de la grotte 3Q (3Q15)', in *DJD*, III (1962), pp. 199-302 (242.56).

מַבָּט *hope*—F. Nötscher, 'Entbehrliche Hapaxlegomena in Jesaia', *VT* 1 (1951), pp. 299-302 (301).

מַבָּךְ *fountain, water-source*—H. Louis Ginsberg, כתבי אוגרית / *The Ugarit Texts* (Jerusalem: Bialik, 1936), p. 28; H.L. Ginsberg, 'The Ugaritic Texts and Textual Criticism', *JBL* 62 (1943), pp. 109-15 (111); George M. Landes, 'The Fountain at Jazer', *BASOR* 144 (1956), pp. 30-37 (32); *HALOT*, II, p. 542b.

מַבֵּל *fire* (cf. Akk. nablu, Ug. nblat *fires*)—M. Dahood, 'Some Northwest-Semitic Words in Job', *Bib* 38 (1957), pp. 306-20 (312-13, 314); Lester L. Grabbe, *Comparative Philology and the Text of the Old Testament: A Study in Methodology* (SBLDS, 34; Missoula, MT, 1977), pp. 76-77; David J.A. Clines, *Job 1–20* (WBC, 17; Dallas: Word Books, 1989), p. 407.

מַבְלֵל *mixed herbs* (cf. בלל *mix*, Akk. riqqū ballutu *mixed spices*)—G.R. Driver, 'Problems in the Hebrew Text of Job', in *Wisdom in Israel and in the Ancient Near East, Presented to Professor Harold Henry Rowley ... in Celebration of his Sixty-Fifth Birthday* (VTSup, 3; Leiden: E.J. Brill, 1955), pp. 72-93 (79); Thomas, *Lexicon*, II (1970), p. 206 (s.v. מַבְלוּלָה).

מִבְנֶה *structure*—Yigael Yadin, 'A Note on DSD IV 20', JBL 74 (1955), pp. 40-42.

מַבְנִית I *construction, frame*—Mitchell Dahood, 'Northwest Semitic Philology and Job', in *The Bible in Current Catholic Thought: Gruenthaner Memorial Volume* (ed. J.L. McKenzie; St Mary's Theological Studies, 1; New York, Herder & Herder, 1962), pp. 55-74 (63-64); M. Dahood, review of Johann Maier, *Die Texte vom Toten Meer* (1960), *Bib* 44 (1963), pp. 228-29; M.H. Pope, *Job* (AB, 15; Garden City, NY: Doubleday, 1965), p. 139; M. Dahood, 'Hebrew–Ugaritic Lexicography IV', *Bib* 47 (1966), pp. 403-19 (414); *HALOT*, II, p. 542b; James Barr, review of L. Koehler and W. Baumagrtner, *Hebräisches und aramäisches Lexicon zum Alten Testament*, Lieferung II (3rd edn, 1974), *JSS* 20 (1975), pp. 236-41 (239).

edifice—Thomas, *Lexicon*, II (1970), p. 253.

structure—Carol Newsom, *Songs of the Sabbath Sacrifice: A Critical Edition* (HSM, 27; Atlanta: Scholars Press, 1985), pp. 40, 221.

מַבְנִית II *likeness* (cf. Akk. nabnītu *image*)—G.R. Driver, 'Linguistic and Textual Problems: Minor Prophets. I', *JTS* 39 (1938), pp. 154-66 (164).

מַבְעֵרָה *burning* (cf. בער *burn*)—G.R. Driver, in Thomas, *Lexicon*, II (1970), p. 290.

מִבְצָר *fortification*—H. Haag, 'מִבְצָר *mibṣār*', *TDOT*, VIII (1997; orig. 1983–84), pp. 65-68.

Jr 6:27—G.R. Driver, 'Two Misunderstood Passages of the Old Testament', *JTS* ns 6 (1955), pp. 82-87 (85).

מְבַצֵּר *Vendemiator, the Vintager, a star* (cf. בצר *cut, glean*)—Georg Hoffmann, 'Versuche zu Amos', *ZAW* 3 (1883), pp. 87-126 (111); G.R. Driver, 'Two Astronomical Passages in the Old Testament', *JTS* ns 4 (1953), pp. 208-12 (208-10).

מְבַקֵּר *inspector*—John F. Priest, 'Mebaqqer, Paqid and the Messiah', *JBL* 81 (1962), pp. 55-61; Peter van der Osten-Sacken, 'Bemerkungen zu Stellung des Mebaqqer in der Sektenschrift', *ZNW* 55 (1964), pp. 18-26.

מִבְרָח I *flight, fugitive*—Zorell, p. 406b.

fugitive—BDB, p. 138a; Gesenius–Buhl, p. 394b; JPS, NIV.

מִבְרָח II *commander*—NEB.

court, staff—Thomas, *Lexicon*, II (1970), p. 368.

hero (cf. Syr. barḥa *leader*)—Godfrey Rolles Driver, 'Problems of the Hebrew Text and Language', in *Alttestamentliche Studien Friedrich Nötscher zum sechzigsten Geburtstage 19. Juli 1950 gewidmet* (BBB, 1; ed. Hubert Junker and Johannes Botterweck; Bonn: Hanstein, 1950), pp. 46-61 (50).

מִבְרָח III *picked men* (cf. Arab. burḥa *best of anything*)—Joseph Reider, 'Contributions to the Scriptural Text', *HUCA* 24 (1952–53), pp. 85-106 (90); RSV, NJB.

מְבַשֵּׂר *refuter* (cf. בשׂר II *refute*)—cf. James Barr, *Comparative Philology and the Text of the Old Testament* (Oxford: Oxford University Press, 1968), p. 324.

מַגְבִּישׁ *Magbish* (place name)—Gary A. Herion, *ABD*, IV, p. 463.

מִגְבָּל *kneading, shaping* (cf. גבל II *forge*)—Thomas, *Lexicon*, III (1970), p. 24.

מִגְבָּעָה I *headband*—Manfred Görg, 'Die Kopfbedeckung des Hohenpriesters', *BN* 3 (1977), pp. 24-26 (24 n. 6).

מִגְבָּעָה II *hilly place*—G.R. Driver, 'Linguistic and Textual Problems: Jeremiah', *JQR* 28 (1937–38), pp. 97-129 (99).

מגד II pi. *make excellent, abundant* (cf. מֶגֶד *excellence*)—G.R. Driver, 'Hebrew Notes on Prophets and Psalms', *JTS* 41 (1940), pp. 162-75 (171).

מֶגֶד *excellence*—BDB, p. 550b.

harvest of fruits; precious gifts—*HALOT*, II, p. 543a.

מִגְדָּל I *chest, box*—Arnold E. Ehrlich, *Randglossen zur hebräischen Bibel*, VII (r.p. Hildesheim: Georg Olms, 1968 [original 1908–14]), pp. 13-14; Jastrow, I, p. 726a; G.R. Driver, 'Isaiah i–xxxix: Textual and Linguistic Problems', *JSS* 13 (1968), pp. 36-57 (53).

heap, pile—Thomas, *Lexicon*, III (1970), p. 68.

raised bed—BDB, p. 153b.

tower—Lawrence A. Sinclair, *An Archaeological Study of Gibeah (Tell el-Ful)* (AASOR, 34-35; New Haven: American Schools of Oriental Research, 1960), p. 7 n. 7; D. Kellermann, 'מִגְדָּל *migdāl*'', *TDOT*, VIII (1997; orig. 1983–84), pp. 69-73.

tower as defensive shield (*testudo*)—Yigael Yadin, *The Scroll of the War of the Sons of Light against the Sons of Darkness* (Oxford: Oxford University Press, 1962), pp. 187-90.

tower as military formation, G.R. Driver, review of Yigael Yadin, *The Scroll of the War of the Sons of Light against the Sons of Darkness* (1962), *Hibbert Journal* 60 (1961–62), pp. 351-53 (353).

treasures—NEB.

מִגְדַּל־עֹז *towered fortress* (composite noun)—Mitchell Dahood, *Psalms II: 51–100* (AB, 17; Garden City, NY: Doubleday, 1968; 3rd edn, 1979), p. 85.

Ps 144_{12}—G.R. Driver, 'Notes on the Psalms. II. 73–150', *JTS* 44 (1943), pp. 12-23 (23).

מִגְדֹּל *Migdol*—William L. Holladay, *Jeremiah 2: A Commentary on the Book of the Prophet Jeremiah, Chapters 26–52* (Hermeneia; Minneapolis: Fortress Press, 1989), p. 303.

מְגַדֵּפָה *blasphemy* (cf. גדף *revile*)—Thomas, *Lexicon*, III (1970), p. 75.

מָגוֹר III *storage pit*, i.e. *heart, mind* (cf. מְגוּרָה *grain pit*, מַמְּגוּרָה *granary*, Arab. mujawwar *pit*)—*HALOT*, II, p. 544b.

מָגוֹר IV *throat* (cf. גָּרוֹן *neck, throat*)—Mitchell Dahood, *Psalms II: 51–100* (AB, 17; Garden City, NY: Doubleday, 1968; 3rd edn, 1979), p. 35.

מְגוּרָה I *barn, bin*—Thomas, *Lexicon*, I (1970), p. 93.

granary, grain pit—Paul Haupt, 'Greek *sīrôs*, silo, and *sōros*, stack', *JBL* 40 (1921), pp. 170-72 (172); *HALOT*, II, p. 544b.

מְגוּרָה II *furrow*—Klaus Koch, 'Haggais unreines Volk', *ZAW* 79 (1967), pp. 52-66 (60 n. 20).

מְגוּרָה III *pool* (cf. Arab. mājā' *cistern, basin, pond*)—M. Sprengling, 'Joel 1, 17a', *JBL* 38 (1919), pp. 129-41

(136-38).

מְגָזָה *ford* (cf. Aram. מְגָזְתָא)—J.T. Milik, 'Le rouleau de cuivre provenant de la grotte 3Q (3Q15)', in *DJD*, III (1962), pp. 199-302 (240.29); Thomas, *Lexicon*, III (1970), p. 109.

מַגָּל *sickle* (cf. Ug. gml *hooked, curved staff*)—Mitchell Dahood, 'The Linguistic Position of Ugaritic in the Light of Recent Discoveries', in *Sacra Pagina: Miscellanea Biblica Congressus Internationalis Catholici de Re Biblica*, I (ed. J. Coppens, A. Descamps and E. Massaux; BETL, 12-13; Gembloux: J. Duculot, 1959), pp. 267-79 (273); J. Feliks, 'Agricultural Methods and Implements in Ancient Eretz Israel', *EncJud*, II (1971), cols. 374-81 (377).

מְגַמָּה *multitude, totality* (cf. Arab. djamma *be abundant*)—Paul Humbert, *Problèmes du livre d'Habacuc* (Mémoires de l'Université de Neuchâtel, 18; Neuchâtel: Secrétariat de l'Université, 1944), pp. 36-37; *HALOT*, II, p. 545a.

מגן I *bestow* and *shield*—Michael V. Fox, *Proverbs 1–9* (AB, 18A; New York: Doubleday, 2000), p. 176.

deliver (cf. MH מַגָּן *gift*, Phoen. mgn *present*)—*HALOT*, II, p. 545a.

give—M. O'Connor, 'Semitic **mgn* and its Supposed Sanskrit Origin', *JAOS* 109 (1989), pp. 25-32.

present with a gift—Johannes Friedrich, *Phonizisch-punische Grammatik* (AnOr, 32; Rome: Pontificium Institutum Biblicum, 1951), p. 121; *HALOT*, II, p. 545a.

מגן II *beseech* (cf. Ug. mgn)—Harold R. (Chaim) Cohen, *Biblical Hapax Legomena in the Light of Akkadian and Ugaritic* (SBLDS, 37; Missoula, MT: Scholars Press, 1978), pp. 138-39.

מָגֵן *benefactor, suzerain* (cf. Ug. mgn *bestow*)—M. Dahood, 'The Divine Name *'Ēlî* in the Psalms', *TS* 14 (1963), pp. 452-57 (456); M. Dahood, 'Hebrew–Ugaritic Lexicography I', *Bib* 44 (1963), pp. 289-303 (298); Mitchell J. Dahood, 'Ugaritic Lexicography' [review of Joseph Aistleitner, *Wörterbuch der ugaritischen Sprache* (1963)], in *Mélanges Eugène Tisserant. I. Ecriture sainte—Ancien orient* (Studi e testi, 231; Città del Vaticano; Bibliotheca Apostolica Vaticana, 1964), pp. 81-104 (94); M. Dahood, review of *The Torah: The Five Books of Moses* (1962), *Bib* 45 (1964), pp. 281-83 (282); M. Dahood, 'Hebrew–Ugaritic Lexicography III', *Bib* 46 (1965), pp. 311-32 (325); M. Dahood, 'Hebrew–Ugaritic Lexicography IV', *Bib* 47 (1966), pp. 403-19 (414); Mitchell Dahood, *Psalms I: 1–50* (AB, 16; Garden City, NY: Doubleday, 1966), pp. 16-17, 45-46, 114; Mitchell Dahood, *Psalms II: 51–100* (AB, 17; Garden City, NY: Doubleday, 1968; 3rd edn, 1979), pp. 72, 282, 283, 286-87; Mitchell Dahood, *Psalms III: 101–150* (AB, 17A; Garden City, NY: Doubleday, 1970), pp. xxi, xxxviii, 141, 186, 282, 329; D.N. Freedman, 'The Refrain in David's Lament over Saul and Jonathan', in *Ex orbe religionum: Studia Geo Widengren XXIV mense apr. MCMLXXII quo die lustra tredecim feliciter explevit oblata ab collegis, discipulis, amicis, collegae magistro amico congratulantibus*, I (ed. J. Bergman, K. Drynjeff and H. Ringgren; Numen Supplements, 21; Leiden: E.J. Brill, 1972), pp. 115-26 (122-23); Mitchell Dahood, 'Northwest Semitic Notes on Genesis' [review of D.N. Freedman, 'Genesis', in *The New American Bible* (1970)], *Bib* 55 (1974), pp. 76-82 (78); D.N. Freedman, M.P. O'Connor and H. Ringgren, 'מָגֵן *māgēn*; גָּנַן *gānan*; צִנָּה *ṣinnâ*; שֶׁלֶט *šeleṭ*', *TDOT*, VIII (1997; orig. 1983–84), pp. 74-87 (85-87).

benefactor and *shield* (מָגֵן)—Gary A. Rendsburg, 'Notes on Genesis xv', *VT* 42 (1992), pp. 266-72 (267-68); Gary A. Rendsburg, 'Word Play in Biblical Hebrew: An Eclectic Collection', in *Puns and Pundits: Word Play in the Bible and Near Eastern Literature* (ed. Scott B. Noegel; Bethesda, MD: CDL Press, 2000), pp. 137-62 (139).

not *suzerain* but *shield*—James Barr, 'Philology and Exegesis: Some General Remarks, with Illustrations from Job', in *Questions disputées d'Ancien Testament* (ed. C. Brekelmans; BETL, 33; Leuven, 1974), pp. 39-61 (= *Comparative Philology and the Text of the Old Testament, with Additions and Corrections* (Winona Lake, IN: Eisenbrauns, 1987), pp. 362-87 [369-72]).

מִגֵּן *beggar* (cf. Ug. mgn *beg, entreat*)—W.F. Albright, 'Some Canaanite-Phoenician Sources of Hebrew Wisdom', in *Wisdom in Israel and in the Ancient Near East, Presented to Professor Harold Henry Rowley ... in Celebra-*

tion of his Sixty-Fifth Birthday (ed. M. Noth and D. Winton Thomas; VTSup, 3; Leiden: E.J. Brill, 1955), pp. 1-15 (9-10).

מָגֵן I *shield*—D.N. Freedman, M.P. O'Connor and H. Ringgren, 'מָגֵן *māgēn*; גָּנַן *gānan*; צִנָּה *ṣinnâ*; שֶׁלֶט *šeleṭ*, *TDOT*, VIII (1997; orig. 1983–84), pp. 74-87.

מָגֵן II *protection* (cf. גנן *cover*, מָגֵן *shield*)—Menahem Mansoor, *The Thanksgiving Hymns* (STDJ, 3; Leiden: E.J. Brill, 1961), p. 146.

מָגֵן III *bold, powerful, insolent* (cf. Arab. mājin *bold*)—G.R. Driver, 'Studies in the Vocabulary of the Old Testament. IV', *JTS* 33 (1931–32), pp. 38-47 (44); G.R. Driver, 'Studies in the Vocabulary of the Old Testament. VI', *JTS* 34 (1933), pp. 375-85 (383-84); G.R. Driver, 'Nachtrag, hauptsächlich nach Mitteilungen G.R. Drivers, Oxford, vom 7.2 und 23.3.1962', in Berend Gemser, *Sprüche Salomos* (HAT, I/16; Tübingen: J.C.B. Mohr [Paul Siebeck], 2nd edn, 1963), pp. 111-14 (111); James Barr, *Comparative Philology and the Text of the Old Testament* (Oxford: Oxford University Press, 1968), pp. 241-42; M. O'Connor, 'Semitic *mgn and its Supposed Sanskrit Origin', *JAOS* 109 (1989), pp. 25-32 (29).

shameless—*HALOT*, II, p. 545b.

מָגֵן IV *benefactor, suzerain*—M. Dahood, review of *Semitica. Cahiers publiés par l'Institut d'études sémitiques de l'Université de Paris*, *Bib* 45 (1964), pp. 129-30 (129); see also מָגָן *benefactor, suzerain*.

donor—M. O'Connor, 'Yahweh the Donor', *Aula Orientalis* 6 (1988), pp. 47-60.

מֶגֶן *gift* (or מָגָן)—Wilhelm Rudolph, *Hosea* (KAT, 13/1; Gütersloh: Gerd Mohn, 1966), p. 108; *HALOT*, II, p. 545b; O. Loretz, '*mgn*—"Geschenk" in Gen 15,1', *UF* 6 (1974), p. 492.

אִישׁ מֶגֶן *man of gifts*, i.e. beggar—M. O'Connor, 'Semitic *mgn and its Supposed Sanskrit Origin', *JAOS* 109 (1989), pp. 25-32 (28).

מְגִנָּה II *shamelessness* (cf. Arab. majāna)—G.R. Driver, 'Studies in the Vocabulary of the Old Testament. VI', *JTS* 34 (1933), pp. 375-85 (383-84); *HALOT*, II, p. 546a.

מִגְעֶרֶת II *dysentery* (cf. Arab. ǧa'ra *void, dung*)—Thomas, *Lexicon*, III (1970), p. 196.

מַגֵּפָה *plague*—H.D. Preuss, 'נָגַף *nāgap*; נֶגֶף *negep*; מַגֵּפָה *maggēpâ*', *TDOT*, IX (1998; orig. 1984–86), pp. 210-13.

מִגְרוֹן I *Migron*—BDB, p. 550b; *HALOT*, II, p. 546a; Andrés Fernández, '*Geographica*: Ḥefer; Migron; el gran Bamah de Gabaón', in *Miscellanea Biblica B. Ubach* (ed. Romualdo M.ª Díaz; Scripta et documenta, 1; Montserrat: Montisserrati, 1953), pp. 137-45 (138-42).

Migron = Wadi es-Swenit—Patrick M. Arnold, 'Migron', *ABD*, IV, pp. 822-23.

מִגְרוֹן II *threshing floor* (cf. גֹּרֶן)—M. Dahood, review of Lawrence A. Sinclair, *An Archaeological Study of Gibeah (Tell el-Ful)*, and Ray E. Cleveland, *The Excavation of the Conway High Place (Petra) and the Soundings at Khirbet Ader* (AASOR, 34-35; New Haven: American Schools of Oriental Research, 1960), *Bib* 44 (1963), pp. 110-11 (111).

מֶגְרָפָה I *shovel* (cf. גרף *sweep away*)—BDB, p. 175b; *HALOT*, II, p. 546b [s.v. מִגְרָף]; J. Feliks, 'Agricultural Methods and Implements in Ancient Eretz Israel', *EncJud*, II (1971), cols. 374-81 (377).

מֶגְרָפָה II *floodwater, alluvial soil*—Thomas, *Lexicon*, III (1970), p. 221.

מֶגְרָפָה III *dyke*—NEB.

מִגְרָשׁ I *common, common-land, open land*—BDB, p. 177a.

land outside city walls—L. Delekat, 'Zum hebräischen Wörterbuch', *VT* 14 (1964), pp. 7-66 (13-23); James Barr, '*Migraš* in the Old Testament', *JSS* 29 (1984), pp. 15-31.

pasture land—*HALOT*, II, p. 546b.

מִגְרָשׁ II *driven wave*—G.R. Driver, 'Ezekiel: Linguistic and Textual Problems', *Bib* 35 (1954), pp. 145-59 (147); Thomas, *Lexicon*, III (1970), p. 230.

מַגָּשׁ *offering* (cf. נגשׁ *approach*)—Helmut Utzschneider, *Künder oder Schreiber? Eine These zum Problem des »Schriftprophetie« auf Grund von Maleachi 1,6–2,9* (BEATAJ, 19; Frankfurt a.M.: Peter Lang, 1989), p. 25 n.7.

מַד I *garment*—G.R. Driver, 'Problems in the Hebrew Text of Proverbs', *Bib* 32 (1951), pp. 173-97 (177); A. Dupont-Sommer, 'L'instruction sur les deux esprits dans le «Manuel de Discipline»', *RHR* 142 (1952), pp. 5-35 (27).

undergarment—B. Margalit, 'Ugaritic Lexicography II', *RB* 90 (1983), pp. 556-62; Meir Malul, 'Some Comments on B. Margalit's "Ugaritic Lexicography II"', *RB* 93 (1986), pp. 415-18 (416).

morphology—Mitchell Dahood, *Psalms III: 101–150* (AB, 17A; Garden City, NY: Doubleday, 1970), p. 252; Alan D. Corré, 'Hebrew—Some Modest Proposals', in *Semitic Studies in Honor of Wolf Leslau on the Occasion of his Eighty-Fifth Birthday*, I (ed. Alan S. Kaye; Wiesbaden: Harrassowitz, 1991), pp. 245-51 (246-47).

מַד II *measure*—H.-J. Fabry, 'מָדַד *mādad*; מִדָּה *middâ*; מַד *mad*; מֵמַד *memad*', *TDOT*, VIII (1997; orig. 1983–84), pp. 118-34.

מִדְבָּר I *steppe*—Robert W. Funk, 'The Wilderness', *JBL* 78 (1959), pp. 205-14 (205-209); Hans-Harald Mallau, *Die theologische Bedeutung des Wüste im Alten Testament* (Diss. Kiel, 1963); S. Talmon, 'מִדְבָּר *midbār*; עֲרָבָה *ʿarābâ*', *TDOT*, VIII (1997; orig. 1983–84), pp. 87-118.

underworld—Hartmut Schmökel, 'Zur kultischen Deutung des Hohenliedes', *ZAW* 64 (1952), pp. 148-55 (153-54).

as superlative—Mitchell Dahood, *Psalms II: 51–100* (AB, 17; Garden City, NY: Doubleday, 1968; 3rd edn, 1979), pp. 116-17.

Ps 105$_{27}$—M. Dahood, 'Hebrew–Ugaritic Lexicography IV', *Bib* 47 (1966), pp. 403-19 (414); Mitchell Dahood, *Psalms III: 101–150* (AB, 17A; Garden City, NY: Doubleday, 1970), p. 59.

מִדְבָּר II *mouth; oasis*—B.J. Segal, 'Double Meanings in the Song of Songs', *Dor Le Dor* 16 (1987), pp. 250-51 [Heb].

מדד I *measure*—H.-J. Fabry, 'מָדַד *mādad*; מִדָּה *middâ*; מַד *mad*; מֵמַד *memad*', *TDOT*, VIII (1997; orig. 1983–84), pp. 118-34.

Jb 7$_4$—Joseph Reider, 'מִדַּד in Job 7 4', *JBL* 39 (1920), pp. 60-65.

מִדָּה I *(act of) measurement*—B.W. Dombrowski, 'The Meaning of the Qumran Terms «T'WDH» and «MDH»', *RQ* 7 (1969–71), pp. 567-74 (572-74); H.-J. Fabry, 'מָדַד *mādad*; מִדָּה *middâ*; מַד *mad*; מֵמַד *memad*', *TDOT*, VIII (1997; orig. 1983–84), pp. 118-34.

מִדָּה II *garment*—A. Dupont-Sommer, 'L'instruction sur les deux esprits dans le «Manuel de Discipline»', *RHR* 142 (1952), pp. 5-35 (27); A.R.C. Leaney, *The Rule of Qumran and its Meaning* (London: SCM Press, 1966), pp. 144, 152; cf. BDB, p. 551b.

מִדָּה III *tribute* (cf. Akk. ma(n)dattu)—Maximilian Ellenbogen, *Foreign Words in the Old Testament: Their Origin and Etymology* (London: Luzac & Co. 1962), p. 98.

מַדְהֹב II *driven out persons*—Thomas, *Lexicon*, IV (1970), p. 64.

מַדְהֵבָה I *might, power, oppression*—Harry M. Orlinsky, '*Madhebah* in Isaiah xiv 4', *VT* 7 (1957), pp. 202-203.

מַדְהֵבָה II *rout, defeat* (cf. Arab. dahbu *rout*)—G.R. Driver, review of E.L. Sukenik, *The Dead Sea Scrolls of the Hebrew University* (1955), *JTS* ns 8 (1957), pp. 141-43 (142); G.R. Driver, review of Svend Holm-Nielsen, *Hodayoth: Psalms from Qumran* (1960), *JTS* ns 13 (1962), pp. 371-78 (375-76); Thomas, *Lexicon*, IV (1970), p. 64.

מָדו *garment*—morphology—Alan D. Corré, 'Hebrew—Some Modest Proposals', in *Semitic Studies in Honor of Wolf Leslau on the Occasion of his Eighty-Fifth Birthday*, I (ed. Alan S. Kaye; Wiesbaden: Harrassowitz, 1991), pp. 245-51 (246-47).

מַדּוּחִים I (cf. נדח I *thrust, banish*)—*driving out, exile*—T. Kronholm, 'נָדַח *nādaḥ*; מַדּוּחִים *maddûḥîm*', *TDOT*, IX (1998; orig. 1984–86), pp. 235-41.

enticement—BDB, p. 623a.

transgression—*HALOT*, II, p. 548a.

מַדּוּחִים II (cf. נדח II *impel, wield*)—*false claims*—Godfrey Rolles Driver, 'Hebrew Roots and Words', *WO* 1 (1947–52), pp. 406-15 (409 n. 22).

מַדּוּחִים III *folly* (cf. Arab. 'andaghun *fool*)—Alfred Guillaume, *Hebrew and Arabic Lexicography: A Comparative Study*, IV (Leiden: E.J. Brill, 1965; = *AbrN* 4 [1964–65]), p. 9.

מָדוֹן II *contempt* (cf. Arab. dāna *be mean, weak, despised*)—H.P. Chajes, 'Notes de lexicographie hébraïque', *REJ* 44 (1902), pp. 223-29 (226-27); cf. Thomas, *Lexicon*, IV (1970), p. 110; Mitchell Dahood, *Psalms II: 51–100* (AB, 17; Garden City, NY: Doubleday, 1968; 3rd edn, 1979), p. 257.

מַדּוּעַ *why*—not distinct semantically from לָמָּה *why?*—J. Barr, '"Why?" in Biblical Hebrew', *JTS* ns 36 (1985), pp. 1-33.

with ref. to factual matters—Alfred Jepsen, 'Warum?', in *Das Ferne und nahe Wort: Festschrift Leonhard Rost zur Vollendung seines 70. Lebensjahres am 30. November 1966 gewidmet* (BZAW, 105; Berlin: A. Topelmann, 1967), pp. 106-13.

with ref. to past and present—D. Michel, '"Warum? und wozu?": Eine bisher übersehene Eigentümlichkeit des Hebräischen und ihre Konsequenzen für das alttestamentliche Geschichtsverständnis', in *'Mitten im Tod, vom Leben umfangen': Gedenkschrift für Werner Kohler* (ed. Jochanan Hesse; Studien zur interkulturellen Geschichte des Christentums, 48; Frankfurt am Main: P. Lang, 1988), pp. 191-210.

מְדוֹר *dwelling place, station, turning point* of sun at solstice (cf. Aram. מְדוֹרָא *dwelling place*)—G.R. Driver, 'Linguistic and Textual Problems: Minor Prophets. III', *JTS* 39 (1938), pp. 393-405 (396).

מַדְחֶפָה *blow* (cf. דחף *drive, hasten*)—*HALOT*, II, p. 548b.

exile, as a name for the underworld—Mitchell Dahood, *Psalms III: 101–150* (AB, 17A; Garden City, NY: Doubleday, 1970), p. 306.

sudden fall—Zorell, p. 412a.

thrust—BDB, p. 191a; Gesenius–Buhl, p. 399b.

מָדַי *Media*—I.M. Diakanoff, 'עָרי מדי. The Cities of the Medes', in *Ah, Assyria ... Studies in Assyrian History and Ancient Near Eastern Historiography Presented to Hayim Tadmor* (ed. Mordechai Cogan and Israel Eph'al; ScrHieros, 33; Jerusalem: Magnes Press, 1991), pp. 13-20.

מְדִינָה I *town, region, state*—Meir Fraenkel, '*Medina* (מדינה) = Stadt, Bezirk, Staat', *ZAW* 70 (1958), pp. 253-54; M. Dahood, 'The Phoenician Background of Qoheleth', *Bib* 47 (1966), pp. 264-82 (267).

מְדִינָה II *place of judgment*—James L. Kugel, 'Qohelet and Money', *CBQ* 51 (1989), pp. 32-49 (37).

מְדִינָה III *prefect*—Mitchell Dahood, 'The Phoenician Background of Qoheleth', *Bib* 47 (1966), pp. 264-82 (267-68).

מדל I *cloud*—Mitchell J. Dahood, 'Ugaritic Lexicography' [review of Joseph Aistleitner, *Wörterbuch der ugaritischen Sprache* (1963)], in *Mélanges Eugène Tisserant. I. Ecriture sainte—Ancien orient* (Studi e testi, 231; Città del Vaticano; Bibliotheca Apostolica Vaticana, 1964), pp. 81-104 (87); M. Dahood, 'Hebrew–Ugaritic Lexicography IV', *Bib* 47 (1966), pp. 403-19 (414-16); Svi Rin and Shifra Rin, 'Ugaritic–Old Testament Affinities II', *BZ* 11 (1967), pp. 174-92 (184).

מדל II *thunderbolt* (cf. מְטִיל *iron rod*, Akk. mudulu *rod*)—Johannes C. de Moor, 'Der *mdl* Baals im Ugaritischen', *ZAW* 78 (1966), pp. 69-71.

מְדְלִי *scales* (cf. Eth. dalawa *weigh*)—D. Winton Thomas, '»A Drop of a Bucket«? Some Observations on the Hebrew Text of Isaiah 40 15', in *In Memoriam Paul Kahle* (ed. Matthew Black and Georg Fohrer; BZAW, 103; Berlin: A. Töpelmann, 1968), pp. 214-21 (220).

מַדָּע I *(carnal) knowledge*—Mitchell Dahood, 'Hebrew Lexicography: A Review of W. Baumgartner's *Lexikon*, Volume II', *Or* 45 (1976), pp. 327-65 (347).

mind—G.R. Driver, 'Three Difficult Words in *Discipline* (iii. 3-4, vii. 5-6, 11)', *JSS* 2 (1957), pp. 247-50 (248).

מַדָּע II *repose* (cf. Arab. maudūʿ *repose, rest*)—D. Winton Thomas, 'A Note on Eccles. x. 20', *JTS* 50 (1949), p. 177; G.R. Driver, 'Problems and Solutions', *VT* 4 (1954), pp. 225-45 (233); Thomas, *Lexicon*, X (1970), p. 150.

מַדָּע III *friend* (cf. Ug. mdʿ, Akk. mūdū)—M. Dahood, *Ugaritic–Hebrew Philology: Marginal Notes on Recent Publications* (BibOr, 17: Rome: Pontifical Biblical Institute, 1965), p. 61; Mitchell Dahood, 'Canaanite Words in Qoheleth 10,20', *Bib* 46 (1965), pp. 210-12; Mitchell Dahood, 'Hebrew–Ugaritic Lexicography III', *Bib* 46 (1965), pp. 311-32; M. Dahood, 'Hebrew–Ugaritic Lexicography IV', *Bib* 47 (1966), pp. 403-19 (416).

מַדָּע IV *kinsman* (cf. מֹדַע)—cf. Zorell, p. 412b.

מַדָּע V *messenger* (cf. Ug. mndʿ)—M. Dahood, 'Qoheleth and Recent Discoveries', *Bib* 39 (1958), pp. 302-18 (312); cf. James Barr, *Comparative Philology and the Text of the Old Testament* (Oxford: Oxford University Press, 1968), pp. 23, 328.

מַדֵּף I *trap, stone sealing a tomb*—J.T. Milik, 'Le rouleau de cuivre provenant de la grotte 3Q (3Q15)', in *DJD*, III (1962), pp. 199-302 (246.82).

מֶדֶר *wet clay* (MH; cf. Arab. madr *mud brick*, Eth. mədr *earth*)—N.H. Tur-Sinai, *The Book of Job* (Jerusalem:

Kiryath Sepher, revised edn, 1967), p. 515; James Barr, *Comparative Philology and the Text of the Old Testament* (Oxford: Oxford University Press, 1968), p. 190.

מִדְרוֹךְ *treading place*—J. VanderKam and J.T. Milik, 'Jubilees', in *DJD*, XIII (1994), pp. 1-185 (101).

מִדְרָס *floor, treading place*—Carol Newsom, *Songs of the Sabbath Sacrifice: A Critical Edition* (HSM, 27; Atlanta: Scholars Press, 1985), p. 297.

מִדְרָשׁ *explanation, development* of existing data—Giovanni Rinaldi, 'Alcuni termini ebraici relativi alla letteratura', *Bib* 40 (1959), pp. 267-89 (277).

מָה I *what?*—morphology—מָה before non-laryngeal consonants—Gary A. Rendsburg, *Linguistic Evidence for the Northern Origin of Selected Psalms* (SBLMS, 43; Atlanta: Scholars Press, 1990), pp. 25-26; Gary A. Rendsburg, 'Morphological Evidence for Regional Dialects in Ancient Hebrew', in *Linguistics and Biblical Hebrew* (ed. Walter R. Bodine; Winona Lake, IN: Eisenbrauns, 1992), pp. 65-88 (71-72).

מָה M. Dahood, 'Canaanite-Phoenician Influence in Qoheleth', *Bib* 33 (1952), pp. 30-52, 191-221 (195); M. Dahood, 'The Language of Qoheleth', *CBQ* 14 (1952), pp. 227-32; M. Dahood, 'Hebrew–Ugaritic Lexicography IV', *Bib* 47 (1966), pp. 403-19 (416).

how (much)?—M. Dahood, 'Hebrew–Ugaritic Lexicography IV', *Bib* 47 (1966), pp. 403-19 (416); Mitchell Dahood, *Psalms III: 101–150* (AB, 17A; Garden City, NY: Doubleday, 1970), p. 184.

what? (Jb 15_2)—M. Dahood, 'Comparative Philology Today and Yesterday' [review of James Barr, *Comparative Philology and the Text of the Old Testament* (Oxford: Oxford University Press, 1968)], *Bib* 50 (1969), pp. 70-79 (73).

what, of what nature? (Ex 3_{13})—Yehuda T. Radday, '"Wie ist sein Name?" (Ex 3:13)', *LB* 58 (1986), pp. 87-104.

what? (1 K 14_{14})—John Gray, *I & II Kings: A Commentary* (OTL; London: SCM Press, 3rd revised edn, 1977), p. 335.

what ails? what need is there?—Mitchell Dahood, *Proverbs and Northwest Semitic Philology* (Scripta Pontificii Instituti Biblici, 113; Rome: Pontificium Institutum Biblicum, 1963), p. 60.

what is wrong with?—William F. Albright, 'Archaic Survivals in the Text of Canticles', in *Hebrew and Semitic Studies Presented to Godfrey Rolles Driver* (ed. D. Winton Thomas and W.D. McHardy; Oxford: Clarendon Press, 1963), pp. 1-7 (4-5).

whatever (indefinite relative pronoun)—Mitchell J. Dahood, 'Canaanite-Phoenician Influence in Qoheleth', *Bib* 33 (1952), pp. 30-52, 191-221 (195-96).

מָה אַתֶּם *how have you fared?*—G.R. Driver, 'Problems in Judges Newly Discussed', *ALUOS* 4 (1962–63), pp. 6-25 (18).

מָה שֶׁ־ *that which*—M. Dahood, 'Canaanite-Phoenician Influence in Qoheleth', *Bib* 33 (1952), pp. 30-52, 191-221 (45).

מָה שֶׁ־ *whatever*—M. Dahood, 'Canaanite-Phoenician Influence in Qoheleth', *Bib* 33 (1952), pp. 30-52, 191-221 (45).

בְּלִי־מָה *not anything*—Markus Witte, *Philologische Notizen zu Hiob 21–27* (BZAW, 234; Berlin: Walter de Gruyter, 1995), p. 136.

מָה II *not* (cf. Arab. ma)—E. Dhorme, *A Commentary on the Book of Job* (London: Thomas Nelson, 1984), p. 23; Benedikt Hartman, 'Es gibt keinen Gott ausser Jahwe: Zur generellen Verneinung im Hebräischen', *ZDMG* 110 (1961), pp. 229-35 (232-33); Marvin H. Pope, *Job: Introduction, Translation and Notes* (AB, 15; Garden City, NY: Doubleday, 1965), p. 116 (2nd edn, p. 123); Mitchell Dahood, 'Hebrew Lexicography: A Review of W. Baumgartner's *Lexikon*, Volume II', *Or* 45 (1976), pp. 327-65 (347); cf. BDB, p. 553b §2a; *HALOT*, II, p. 551b §C.

in compound double negatives—Mitchell Dahood, 'The Emphatic Double Negative *m'yn* in Jer 10:6-7', *CBQ* 37 (1975), pp. 458-59; Mitchell Dahood, 'Hebrew Lexicography: A Review of W. Baumgartner's *Lexikon*, Volume II', *Or* 45 (1976), pp. 327-65 (347).

מהה *delay*—H.-J. Fabry, 'מהה *mhh*; אחר *'ḥr*', *TDOT*, VIII (1997; orig. 1983–84), pp. 134-37.

מָהִיר I *quick*—E. Vogt, 'Einige hebräische Wortbedeutungen', *Bib* 48 (1967), pp. 57-74; H. Ringgren, 'מהר *mhr*; מְהֵרָה *mᵉhērâ*; מָהִיר *māhîr*', *TDOT*, VIII (1997; orig. 1983–84), pp. 138-42.

מָהִיר II *skilled* (cf. Eth. mähärä *teach*)—Zorell, p. 414b; Edward Ullendorff, 'The Contribution of South Semitics to Hebrew Lexicography', *VT* 6 (1956), pp. 190-98 (195); A.F. Rainey, 'The Soldier-Scribe in *Papyrus Anastasi I*', *JNES* 26 (1967), pp. 58-60; James Barr, *Comparative Philology and the Text of the Old Testament* (Oxford: Oxford University Press, 1968), p. 295; H. Ringgren, 'מהר *mhr*; מְהֵרָה *mᵉhērâ*; מָהִיר *māhîr*', *TDOT*, VIII (1997; orig. 1983–84), pp. 138-42; G.A. Rendsburg, *Linguistic Evidence for the Northern Origin of Selected Psalms* (SBLMS, 43; Atlanta: Scholars Press, 1990), pp. 46-47.

scribe, as divine title—Mitchell Dahood, *Psalms II: 51–100* (AB, 17; Garden City, NY: Doubleday, 1968; 3rd edn, 1979), p. 252.

מהל I *dilute* (cf. MH, Aram. מהל *cut*, MH מוֹהַל *broth*)—*HALOT*, II, p. 552b; Mitchell Dahood, '"Weaker than Water": Comparative *beth* in Isaiah 1,22', *Bib* 59 (1978), pp. 91-92 (91).

מהל II *circumcise, weaken* (cf. MH, Aram. מהל *circumcise*)—BDB, p. 554b.

מהל III *weaken* (cf. Arab. mahuna *be weak*)—Zorell, p. 414b.

מהל IV *weaken* (cf. אמל *be weak*)—Mitchell Dahood, '"Weaker than Water": Comparative *beth* in Isaiah 1,22', *Bib* 59 (1978), pp. 91-92 (92).

מַהֲלָךְ *processional way*—Is 35₈—G.R. Driver, 'Glosses in the Hebrew Text of the Old Testament', in *L'Ancien Testament et l'orient. Etudes présentées aux VIes Journées Bibliques de Louvain (11-13 septembre 1954)* (OBL, 1; Louvain-Leuven: Publications Universitaires / Instituut voor Orientalisme, 1957), pp. 123-61 (126 n. 8).

מַהֲלֻכָה *gait*—Thomas, *Lexicon*, V (1970), p. 155.

מהמ I *melt*—G.R. Driver, 'Hebrew Notes on the "Wisdom of Jesus ben Sirach"', *JBL* 53 (1934), pp. 273-90 (284).

מהמ II *be pleasant* (cf. Arab. mahiha)—G.R. Driver, 'Problems in Aramaic and Hebrew Texts', in *Miscellanea orientalia dedicata Antonio Deimel annos 70 complenti* (AnOr, 12; Rome: Pontificio Istituto Biblico, 1935), pp. 46-70 (67).

מַהֲמֹרָה *bottomless pit* (cf. Ug. mhmrt *chasm*)—*HALOT*, II, p. 553a.

effusion (cf. Arab. hammâr *raining*)—L. Delekat, 'Zum hebräischen Wörterbuch', *VT* 14 (1964), pp. 7-66 (25-26).

deep pit—G.A. Rendsburg, *Linguistic Evidence for the Northern Origin of Selected Psalms* (SBLMS, 43; Atlanta: Scholars Press, 1990), p. 96.

flood, watery pit—BDB, p. 243a.

whirlpool—Zorell, p. 415a.

pits filled with rain—KB (1958), p. 500a.

underworld pit (cf. Mot's city Hmry)—M. Dahood, *Ugaritic–Hebrew Philology: Marginal Notes on Recent Publications* (BibOr, 17: Rome: Pontifical Biblical Institute, 1965), p. 56; M. Held, 'Pits and Pitfalls in Akkadian and Biblical Hebrew', *JANESCU* 5 (1973) 188-90; Harold R. (Chaim) Cohen, *Biblical Hapax Legomena in the Light of Akkadian and Ugaritic* (SBLDS, 37; Missoula, MT: Scholars Press, 1978), pp. 121-22.

watery depths—Thomas, *Lexicon*, V (1970), p. 186.

מהר I *hasten*—E. Vogt, 'Einige hebräische Wortbedeutungen', *Bib* 48 (1967), pp. 57-74 ('II. "Eilig tun" als adverbielles Verb und der Name des Sohnes Isaias' in Is 8,1", pp. 63-69); H. Ringgren, 'מהר *mhr*; מְהֵרָה *mᵉhērâ*; מָהִיר māhîr', *TDOT*, VIII (1997; orig. 1983–84), pp. 138-42; Jean Carmignac, 'L'infinitif absolu chez Ben Sira et à Qumran', *RQ* 12 (1986), pp. 251-61 (259).

מהר IV *sell, betray* (denominative of מֹהַר *gift*)—Robert Gordis, *The Book of Job* (New York: Jewish Theological Seminary, 1978), p. 57.

מהר *warrior* (cf. Ug. mhr)—A. Jirku, 'Zu "Eilebeute' in Jes. 8, 1.3', *TLZ* 75 (1950), col. 118.

מֹהַר *bride gift*—Angelo Tosato, 'Il trasferimento dei beni nel matrimonio israelitico', *BeO* 27 (1985), pp. 129-48; E. Lipiński, 'מֹהַר *mōhar*', *TDOT*, VIII (1997; orig. 1983–84), pp. 142-49; E. Lipiński, 'La donation matrimoniale dans l'ancien droit hébraïque', in *Šulmu. Papers on the Ancient Near East Presented at [the] International Conference of Socialist Countries (Prague, Sept. 30–Oct. 3, 1986)* (ed. Petr Vavroušek and Vladimír Souček; Prague: Charles University, 1988), pp. 173-93.

מַהֵר שָׁלָל חָשׁ בַּז *Mahar-shalal-hash-baz*—S. Morenz, '"Eilebeute"', *TLZ* 74 (1949), cols. 697-99; A. Jirku, 'Zu "Eilebeute' in Jes. 8, 1.3', *TLZ* 75 (1950), col. 118.

מְהֵרָה *haste*—H. Ringgren, 'מהר *mhr*; מְהֵרָה *mᵉhērâ*; מָהִיר

māhîr', *TDOT*, VIII (1997; orig. 1983–84), pp. 138-42.

מַהֲתַלָּה *deception*—F. Nötscher, 'Entbehrliche Hapaxlegomena in Jesaia', *VT* 1 (1951), pp. 299-302 (302).

מוֹ *water* (cf. Eblaite ma-wu *water*)—Mitchell Dahood, '"A Sea of Troubles": Notes on Psalms 55:3-4 and 140:10-11', *CBQ* 41 (1979), pp. 604-607 (605-606); M. Dahood, 'Love and Death and their Biblical Reflection', in *Love and Death in the Ancient Near East: Essays in Honor of Marvin H. Pope* (ed. John H. Marks and Robert M. Good; Guilford, CT: Four Quarters Publishing, 1987), pp. 93-99 (98); Walter D. Michel, *Job in the Light of Northwest Semitic*, I (BibOr, 42; Rome: Biblical Institute Press, 1987), pp. 143, 147, 148, 216, 228, 265.

מוג I *melt* (cf. Arab. māja *surge* [of the sea])—BDB, p. 556a; A. Baumann, 'מוּג *mûg*', *TDOT*, VIII (1997; orig. 1983–84), pp. 149-52.

Jr 49₂₃—G.R. Driver, 'Linguistic and Textual Problems: Jeremiah', *JQR* 28 (1937–38), pp. 97-129 (126).

מוג II *wave, waver* (cf. Arab. mwj *billow*)—*HALOT*, II, p. 555a; Mitchell Dahood, 'Hebrew Lexicography: A Review of W. Baumgartner's *Lexikon*, Volume II', *Or* 45 (1976), pp. 327-65 (347-48); A. Baumann, 'מוּג *mûg*', *TDOT*, VIII (1997; orig. 1983–84), pp. 149-52.

מוֹגֵן *beggar* (cf. Ug. mgn *beg, entreat*)—W.F. Albright, 'Some Canaanite-Phoenician Sources of Hebrew Wisdom', in *Wisdom in Israel and in the Ancient Near East, Presented to Professor Harold Henry Rowley ... in Celebration of his Sixty-Fifth Birthday* (ed. M. Noth and D. Winton Thomas; VTSup, 3; Leiden: E.J. Brill, 1955), pp. 1-15 (9-10).

מוד *shake, convulse*, see מיד.

מוד II *love* (cf. ידד *love*)—M. Dahood, review of J.A. Sanders, *Discoveries in the Judaean Desert of Jordan.* IV. *The Psalms Scroll of Qumrân Cave 11* (1965), *Bib* 47 (1966), pp. 141-44 (143).

מוֹדָה *measure* (noun) (cf. מדד *measure*)—Robert Deutsch and Michael Heltzer, *New Epigraphic Evidence from the Biblical Period* (Tel Aviv–Jaffa: Archaeological Center Publication, 1995), pp. 81-83.

מוט *dislodge*—G.R. Driver, 'Notes on the Psalms. I. 1–72', *JTS* 43 (1942), pp. 149-60 (156).

stumble, i.e. *die*—Mitchell Dahood, *Psalms I: 1–50* (AB, 16; Garden City, NY: Doubleday, 1966), pp. 78-79; Mitchell Dahood, *Psalms II: 51–100* (AB, 17; Garden City, NY: Doubleday, 1968; 3rd edn, 1979), pp. 38-39.

totter—A. Baumann, 'מוט *mwṭ*; מוֹט *môṭ*; מוֹטָה *môṭâ*', *TDOT*, VIII (1997; orig. 1983–84), pp. 152-58.

מוֹט II *pole*—A. Baumann, 'מוט *mwṭ*; מוֹט *môṭ*; מוֹטָה *môṭâ*', *TDOT*, VIII (1997; orig. 1983–84), pp. 152-58.

מוֹט III *quagmire*, name for the underworld (cf. מוט *stumble*)—Mitchell Dahood, *Psalms II: 51–100* (AB, 17; Garden City, NY: Doubleday, 1968; 3rd edn, 1979), p. 122; Mitchell Dahood, *Psalms III: 101–150* (AB, 17A; Garden City, NY: Doubleday, 1970), p. 200.

מוֹטָה *pole joining yoke and plough or cart*—Wolfgang Zwickel, '*mōṭāh* = "Jochhaken"', *BN* 57 (1991), pp. 37-40.

yoke—A. Baumann, 'מוט *mwṭ*; מוֹט *môṭ*; מוֹטָה *môṭâ*', *TDOT*, VIII (1997; orig. 1983–84), pp. 152-58.

yoke-pegs—William L. Holladay, *Jeremiah 2: A Commentary on the Book of the Prophet Jeremiah, Chapters 26–52* (Hermeneia; Minneapolis: Fortress Press, 1989), pp. 119-20.

מוֹטָח *club* (cf. תּוֹתָח *club*, Arab. mîtaḫatu *club, mace*)—Mitchell Dahood, 'New Readings in Lamentations', *Bib* 59 (1978), pp. 174-97 (189).

מוֹכִיחַ *umpire*—William A. Irwin, 'Job's Redeemer', *JBL* 81 (1962), pp. 217-29.

מול *circumcise*—Jack M. Sasson, 'Circumcision in the Ancient Near East', *JBL* 85 (1966), pp. 473-76; Michael V. Fox, 'The Sign of the Covenant: Circumcision in the Light of the Priestly *'ot* Etiologies', *RB* 81 (1974), pp. 557-96; Robert Althann, '*mwl* "circumcise" with the *lamedh* of Agency', *Bib* 62 (1981), pp. 239-40; G. Mayer, 'מוּל *mûl*; מוּלָה *mûlâ*', *TDOT*, VIII (1997; orig. 1983–84), pp. 158-62.

Jos 5₅—G.R. Driver, 'Notes on Joshua', in *The Seventy-Fifth Anniversary Volume of the JQR* (Philadelphia, 1967), pp. 149-65 (155).

מוּל *in front of*—Joseph Reider, 'The Etymology of Hebrew *mūl* or *mōl* and its Bearing on *tmōl* and *'etmōl*', *HUCA* 12–13 (1937–38), pp. 89-101.

מוֹלָד *birth* (cf. ילד *give birth*)—Menahem Mansoor, *The Thanksgiving Hymns* (STDJ, 3; Leiden: E.J. Brill, 1961),

p. 114 n. 3.
מוֹלֶדֶת *birthplace*—Paul Joüon, 'Notes de lexicographie hébraïque', *Bib* 7 (1926), pp. 162-70 (168-69); H. Haag, 'מוֹלֶדֶת *môledeṯ*', *TDOT*, VIII (1997; orig. 1983–84), pp. 162-67.
מוּלָה *circumcision*—G. Mayer, 'מוּל *mûl*; מוּלָה *mûlâ*', *TDOT*, VIII (1997; orig. 1983–84), pp. 158-62.
מוּם *blemish, injury*—Michael V. Fox, *Proverbs 1–9* (AB, 18A; New York: Doubleday, 2000), p. 307.
מוֹסָד I *foundation*—מוֹסְדֵי אֶרֶץ *laws of nature*—V.A. Hurowitz, 'Nursling, Advisor, Architect? 'amôn and the Role of Wisdom in Proverbs 8,22-31', *Bib* 80 (1999), pp. 391-400 (394 n. 9).
remains—Wolfgang Lau, *Schriftgelehrte Prophetie in Jes 56–66: Eine Untersuchung zu den literarischen Bezügen in den letzten elf Kapiteln des Jesajabuches* (BZAW, 225; Berlin: Walter de Gruyter, 1994), pp. 255-56.
מוֹסָד II *council* (byform of סוֹד *council*)—Carol Newsom, *Songs of the Sabbath Sacrifice: A Critical Edition* (HSM, 27; Atlanta: Scholars Press, 1985), pp. 113-14.
מוּסָךְ II *fence, rampart*—Wolfgang Zwickel, 'Die Kultreform des Ahas (2 Kön 16,10-18)', *SJOT* 7 (1993), pp. 250-62 (259).
מוּסָךְ III *bench, divan* (cf. נסך II *fashion*)—A.M. Honeyman, review of Ludwig Koehler and Walter Baumgartner, *Lexicon in Veteris Testamenti Libros* (1953), *VT* 5 (1955), pp. 214-23 (220-21); M.J. Mulder, 'Was war die am Tempel gebaute "Sabbathalle" in II Kön. 16,18?', in *Von Kanaan bis Kerala: Festschrift für Prof. Mag. Dr. Dr. J.P.M. van der Ploeg O.P. zur Vollendung des siebzigsten Lebensjahres am 4. Juli 1979* (ed. W.C. Delsman, J.T. Nelis, J.R.T.M. Peters *et al.*; AOAT, 211; Kevelaer: Butzon & Bercker, 1982), pp. 161-72.
מוּסָר *instruction*—Jb 20₃—M. Dahood, 'Some Northwest-Semitic Words in Job', *Bib* 38 (1957), pp. 306-20 (315).
Pr 13₁—G.R. Driver, 'Problems in "Proverbs"', *ZAW* 50 (1932), pp. 141-48 (144).
מוֹסָר I *bond* (cf. מוֹסֵר, אסר *bind*)—M. Dahood, 'Some Northwest-Semitic Words in Job', *Bib* 38 (1957), pp. 306-20 (311).
מוֹסָר II *heart, basis, essence* (cf. Ug. srr, Arab. sirru *choice part, secret*)—Mitchell Dahood, *Proverbs and Northwest Semitic Philology* (Scripta Pontificii Instituti Biblici, 113; Rome: Pontificium Institutum Biblicum, 1963), pp. 34-35.
מוֹסֵר I *conjunction*—A. Dupont-Sommer, 'Contribution à l'exégèse du *Manuel de discipline* x 1-8', *VT* 2 (1952), pp. 229-43 (237).
מוֹעֵד II *horde*—*HALOT*, II, p. 558b (? *multitude*); M. Dahood, 'Northwest Semitic Texts and Textual Criticism of the Hebrew Bible', in *Questions disputées d'Ancien Testament* (ed. C. Brekelmans; BETL, 33; Leuven, 1974), pp. 11-37 (34).
מוֹעֵד I *appointment, meeting*—K. Koch, 'מוֹעֵד *mô'ēḏ*', *TDOT*, VIII (1997; orig. 1983–84), pp. 167-73.
season of the year—A. Dupont-Sommer, 'Contribution à l'exégèse du *Manuel de discipline* x 1-8', *VT* 2 (1952), pp. 229-43 (236).
time—J. Carmignac, 'Précisions apportées au vocabulaire de l'hébreu biblique par la Guerre des Fils de Lumière contre les Fils de Ténèbres', *VT* 5 (1955), pp. 345-65 (354).
אֹהֶל מוֹעֵד *tent of meeting*—Menahem Haran, 'The Nature of the "'Ohel Mo'edh" in Pentateuchal Sources', *JSS* 5 (1960), pp. 50-65.
מוֹעֵד II *early fruit* (cf. Arab. m'd *fresh, tender [fruit]*)—G.R. Driver, 'Hebrew Notes on the "Wisdom of Jesus ben Sirach"', *JBL* 53 (1934), pp. 273-90 (288).
מוּעָז *arrogance* (cf. יעז *be insolent*)—Tadeusz Penar, *Northwest Semitic Philology and the Hebrew Fragments of Ben Sira* (BibOr, 28; Rome: Biblical Institute Press, 1975), p. 34.
מוּעָף I *darkness* (cf. עוף II *be dark*)—BDB, p. 734a.
מוּעָף II *glimmering, gleam, lustre* (cf. עיף III *glitter*)—H.L. Ginsberg, 'An Unrecognized Allusion to Kings Pekah and Hoshea of Israel (Isa 8:23', *EI* 5 (1958), pp. 61*-65* (62a*, 64a*); J. Schirmann, 'דפים נוספים מתוך "בן־סירא" (Some Additional Leaves from Ecclesiasticus in Hebrew)', *Tarb* 29 (1959–60), pp. 125-34 (130).
מוּעָף III *flight, escape* (cf. עוף *fly*)—Is 8₂₃—NEB.
מוֹעֵצָה II *disobedience* (cf. עֵצָה II *hard struggle, disobedience*)—Godfrey Rolles Driver, 'Hebrew Roots and Words', *WO* 1 (1947–52), pp. 406-15 (411).
מוּעָקָה II *ulcer* (cf. [?] Ug. 'qq *consume*)—Mitchell Dahood,

Psalms II: 51–100 (AB, 17; Garden City, NY: Doubleday, 1968; 3rd edn, 1979), pp. 122-23.

מוֹפֵת *sign*—S. Wagner, 'מוֹפֵת *môpēṯ*', *TDOT*, VIII (1997; orig. 1983–84), pp. 174-81.

target—Mitchell Dahood, *Psalms II: 51–100* (AB, 17; Garden City, NY: Doubleday, 1968; 3rd edn, 1979), p. 173.

מוֹצָא I *canal* (not *source*)—J.T. Milik, 'Le rouleau de cuivre provenant de la grotte 3Q (3Q15)', in *DJD*, III (1962), pp. 199-302 (242.57).

מוֹצָא II *star, sparkler*—Mitchell Dahood, 'Northwest Semitic Philology and Job', in *The Bible in Current Catholic Thought: Gruenthaner Memorial Volume* (ed. J.L. McKenzie; St Mary's Theological Studies, 1; New York, Herder & Herder, 1962), pp. 55-74 (67); M. Dahood, 'Hebrew–Ugaritic Lexicography III', *Bib* 46 (1965), pp. 311-32 (321); M. Dahood, 'Hebrew–Ugaritic Lexicography IV', *Bib* 47 (1966), pp. 403-19 (416); Mitchell Dahood, *Psalms I: 1–50* (AB, 16; Garden City, NY: Doubleday, 1966), pp. 93-94.

מוֹצָא III *smelter*—Mitchell Dahood, *Proverbs and Northwest Semitic Philology* (Scripta Pontificii Instituti Biblici, 113; Rome: Pontificium Institutum Biblicum, 1963), p. 52.

מוֹצָא *stream, channel*—J.T. Milik, 'Le rouleau de cuivre provenant de la grotte 3Q (3Q15)', in *DJD*, III (1962), pp. 199-302 (242).

מוּצָק III *outpouring* (cf. יצק *pour out*)—M. Dahood, 'Hebrew–Ugaritic Lexicography VII', *Bib* 50 (1969), pp. 337-56 (339-40).

מוּצֶקֶת I *spout*—Carol L. Meyers and Eric M. Meyers, *Haggai, Zechariah 1–8: A New Translation with Introduction and Commentary* (AB, 25B; Garden City, NY: Doubleday, 1987), pp. 236-37.

(cf. צוק *be narrow*)—K. Möhlenbrink, 'Die Leuchter im fünften Nachtgesicht des Propheten Sacharja: eine archäologische Untersuchung', *ZDPV* 52 (1929), pp. 257-86 (285).

מוּצֶקֶת II *cast metal*—Heinz-Günther Schöttler, *Gott inmitten seines Volkes: Die Neuordnung des Gottesvolkes nach Sacharja 1–6* (TTS, 43; Trier: Paulinus-Verlag, 1987), pp. 109-11.

reed—*HALOT*, II, p. 559a.

מוֹקֵד *hearth*—Ps 102_4—Godfrey Rolles Driver, 'Problems of the Hebrew Text and Language', in *Alttestamentliche Studien Friedrich Nötscher zum sechzigsten Geburtstage 19. Juli 1950 gewidmet* (BBB, 1; ed. Hubert Junker and Johannes Botterweck; Bonn: Hanstein, 1950), pp. 46-61 (53).

מוֹקֵשׁ *bait, decoy*—G.R. Driver, 'Reflections on Recent Articles', *JBL* 73 (1954), pp. 131-46 (131-36); Hayyim Heller, 'חדושים במקרא (New Biblical Interpretations)', in *Zvi Karl Memorial Volume* (ed. A. Weiser and B.Z. Luria; Jerusalem: Kiryath Sepher, 1960), pp. 48-53 (51); E. Vogt, '«Ihr Tisch werde zur Falle» (Ps 69,23', *Bib* 43 (1962), pp. 79-82; S.M. Paul, *Amos—A Commentary on the Book of Amos* (Hermeneia; Minneapolis: Fortress Press, 1991), p. 111.

clap net—G. Gerleman, 'Contributions to the Old Testament Terminology of the Chase', *Bulletin de la Société Royale des Lettres de Lund* (Lund: Gleerup, 1946), p. 82.

snare (cf. Arab. wiṯâqun [by metathesis] *fetter*)—L. Kopf, 'Arabische Etymologien und Parallelen zum Bibelwörterbuch', *VT* 8 (1958), pp. 161-215 (178-79); Hartmut N. Rösel, 'Kleine Studien zur Auslegung des Amosbuches', *BZ* NF 42 (1998), pp. 2-18 (11-12).

striker—G.R. Driver, 'Reflections on Recent Articles', *JBL* 73 (1954), pp. 125-36 (131-36).

Ps 109_{16}—Mitchell Dahood, *Psalms III: 101–150* (AB, 17A; Garden City, NY: Doubleday, 1970), p. 106.

Ps 141_9—Mitchell Dahood, *Psalms III: 101–150* (AB, 17A; Garden City, NY: Doubleday, 1970), p. 314.

Jb 40_{24}—G.R. Driver, 'Difficult Words in the Hebrew Prophets', in *Studies in Old Testament Prophecy Presented to Professor Theodore H. Robinson* (ed. H.H. Rowley; Edinburgh: T. & T. Clark, 1950), pp. 52-72 (60-61).

Pr 21_6—Godfrey Rolles Driver, 'Problems of the Hebrew Text and Language', in *Alttestamentliche Studien Friedrich Nötscher zum sechzigsten Geburtstage 19. Juli 1950 gewidmet* (BBB, 1; ed. Hubert Junker and Johannes Botterweck; Bonn: Hanstein, 1950), pp. 46-61 (56-57); Thomas, *Lexicon*, II (1970), p. 337.

מוֹקֵשׁ II *boomerang*—G.R. Driver, 'Linguistic and Textual Problems: Minor Prophets. II', *JTS* 39 (1938), pp. 260-

73 (262); G.R. Driver, 'Reflections on Recent Articles', *JBL* 73 (1954), pp. 125-36 (133).

מוּר I *acquire* (qal)—Robert Gordis, 'On Methodology in Biblical Exegesis', *JQR* 61 (1970), pp. 93-118 (102-103) [= Gordis, *The Word and the Book: Studies in Biblical Language and Literature* (New York: Ktav, 1976), pp. 1-26].

change, exchange—H. Ringgren, 'מוּר *mwr*', *TDOT*, VIII (1997; orig. 1983–84), pp. 182-84.

obtain—Mitchell Dahood, 'Hebrew Lexicography: A Review of W. Baumgartner's *Lexikon*, Volume II', *Or* 45 (1976), pp. 327-65 (348).

מוּר II *quake* (cf. Arab. *mâra*)—Ps 46₃—Godfrey Rolles Driver, 'Problems of the Hebrew Text and Language', in *Alttestamentliche Studien Friedrich Nötscher zum sechzigsten Geburtstage 19. Juli 1950 gewidmet* (BBB, 1; ed. Hubert Junker and Johannes Botterweck; Bonn: Hanstein, 1950), pp. 46-61 (51); M. Dahood, 'The Value of Ugaritic for Textual Criticism', *Bib* 40 (1959), pp. 160-70 (167-68); *HALOT*, II, p. 560a.

מוֹרָא I *Fear*, as name for God—Talia Thorion-Vardi, 'MWR' in Pešer Habaquq VI, 5', *RQ* 46 (1986), p. 282.

מוֹרַג *threshing sledge*—J. Feliks, 'Agricultural Methods and Implements in Ancient Eretz Israel', *EncJud*, II (1971), cols. 374-81 (378).

מוֹרָד I *descent, slope*—BDB, p. 434a.

mountainside, precipice—A. Schwarzenbach, *Die geographische Terminologie im Hebräischen des Alten Testaments* (Leiden: E.J. Brill, 1954), p. 29; *HALOT*, II, p. 560b.

2 K 7₂₉—John Gray, *I & II Kings: A Commentary* (OTL; London: SCM Press, 3rd revised edn, 1977), p. 195.

מוֹרָד II *rivulet, watering place* (cf. Arab. *maurid*)—R. Köbert, '*môrād* (Mi. 1,4) «Tränke»', *Bib* 39 (1958), pp. 82-83.

מוֹרָה III *muzzle* (cf. ירה *guide, instruct*)—Mitchell Dahood, *Psalms I: 1–50* (AB, 16; Garden City, NY: Doubleday, 1966), p. 59.

מוֹרָה III *teacher*—Ps 9₂₁—Mitchell Dahood, 'New Readings in Lamentations', *Bib* 59 (1978), pp. 174-97 (183).

leader—Ps 84₇—Godfrey Driver, 'Water in the Mountains!', *PEQ* 102 (1970), pp. 83-91 (88).

מוֹרֶה צֶדֶק *true lawgiver*—Gert Jeremias, *Der Lehrer der Gerechtigkeit* (SUNT, 2; Göttingen: Vandenhoeck &

Ruprecht, 1963); J. Weingreen, 'The Title Môrēh Ṣedeḳ', *JSS* 6 (1961), pp. 162-64; Rudolph Meyer, 'Melchizedek von Jerusalem und Moresedek von Qumran', in *Volume du Congrès: Genève 1965* (VTSup, 15; Leiden: E.J. Brill, 1966), pp. 228-39 (232-34); A.M. Honeyman, 'Notes on a Teacher and a Book. I. Moreh Haṣṣedeq', *JJS* 4 (1953), pp. 131-32 (131); John C. Reeves, 'The Meaning of *Moreh Ṣedeq* in the Light of 11QTorah', *RQ* 13 (1988), pp. 287-98.

מוֹרֵה שֶׁקֶר *teacher of lies*—Stanislav Segert, 'Zur Habakuk-Rolle aus dem Funde vom Toten Meer III', *ArOr* 22 (1954), pp. 444-59 (457-58).

מוֹרָשׁ II *desire*—E. Dhorme, *A Commentary on the Book of Job* (London: Thomas Nelson, 1984), p. 251; Zorell, p. 421a; *HALOT*, II, p. 561a.

מוֹרָשׁ III *string* (cf. Aram. *marša rope*)—N.H. Tur-Sinai, *The Book of Job: A New Commentary* (Jerusalem: Kiryath-Sepher, 1957), pp. 281-82.

מוּשׁ I *depart*—morphology—hi. Mitchell Dahood, 'Hebrew Lexicography: A Review of W. Baumgartner's *Lexikon*, Volume II', *Or* 45 (1976), pp. 327-65 (349).

depart—H. Ringgren, 'מִישׁ/מוּשׁ *mûš/mîš*', *TDOT*, VIII (1997; orig. 1983–84), pp. 184-85.

מוּשׁ II *feel*—H. Ringgren, 'מִישׁ/מוּשׁ *mûš/mîš*', *TDOT*, VIII (1997; orig. 1983–84), pp. 184-85.

מוֹשָׁב I *office*—Tadeusz Penar, *Northwest Semitic Philology and the Hebrew Fragments of Ben Sira* (BibOr, 28; Rome: Biblical Institute Press, 1975), p. 31.

seat, throne—M. Dahood, *Ugaritic–Hebrew Philology: Marginal Notes on Recent Publications* (BibOr, 17; Rome: Pontifical Biblical Institute, 1965), p. 63.

מוֹשָׁבָה *settlement, transportation*—G.R. Driver, 'Hebrew Notes on "Song of Songs" and "Lamentations"', in *Festschrift Alfred Bertholet zum 80. Geburtstag gewidmet von Kollegen und Freunden* (ed. Walter Baumgartner [*et al.*]; Tübingen: J.C.B. Mohr, 1950), pp. 134-46 (136).

מוֹשִׁיעַ *advocate*—John Sawyer, 'What Was a Mošia'?', *VT* 15 (1965), pp. 475-86.

מוּת *become mortal*—Julian Morgenstern, 'The Mythological Background of Psalm 82', *HUCA* 14 (1939), pp. 29-126 (72-73).

die—G. Gerleman, 'מות *mût*', *TLOT*, II (1997; orig. 1976), pp. 660-64; H. Ringgren, K.-J. Illman and H.-J. Fabry, 'מוּת *mûṯ*; מָוֶת *māweṯ*; תְּמוּתָה *t^{e}mûṯâ*; מְמוֹתִים *m^{e}môṯîm*', *TDOT*, VIII (1997; orig. 1983–84), pp. 185-209.

מֵתִים *the dead, place of the dead*—Mitchell Dahood, *Psalms II: 51–100* (AB, 17; Garden City, NY: Doubleday, 1968; 3rd edn, 1979), p. 303.

as superlative—D. Winton Thomas, 'A Consideration of Some Unusual Ways of Expressing the Superlative in Hebrew', *VT* 3 (1953), pp. 209-24 (219-22).

Hb 1_{12}—Mitchell Dahood, 'Hebrew–Ugaritic Lexicography IX', *Bib* 52 (1971), pp. 337-56 (346 n. 2).

Jb 33_{22}—G.R. Driver, 'Once Again Abbreviations', *Textus* 4 (1965), pp. 76-94 (91); Mitchell Dahood, 'Hebrew–Ugaritic Lexicography XI', *Bib* 54 (1973), pp. 351-66 (356).

Pr 14_{33} La 1_{20}—Mitchell Dahood, 'Hebrew Lexicography: A Review of W. Baumgartner's *Lexikon*, Volume II', *Or* 45 (1976), pp. 327-65 (349).

מָוֶת *death*—Nicholas J. Tromp, *Primitive Conceptions of Death and the Nether World in the Old Testament* (BibOr, 21; Rome: Pontifical Biblical Institute, 1969); H. Ringgren, K.-J. Illman and H.-J. Fabry, 'מוּת *mûṯ*; מָוֶת *māweṯ*; תְּמוּתָה *t^{e}mûṯâ*; מְמוֹתִים *m^{e}môṯîm*', *TDOT*, VIII (1997; orig. 1983–84), pp. 185-209.

personified as deity Death or Mot—Umberto Cassuto, 'Il palazzo di Ba'al nella tavola II AB di ras Shamra', *Or* ns 7 (1938), pp. 265-90 (267); A. Pohl, 'Miszellen. 3) Jeremias 9, 20', *Bib* 22 (1941), pp. 36-37; H.L. Ginsberg, 'The Ugaritic Texts and Textual Criticism', *JBL* 62 (1943), pp. 109-15 (113-14); Svi Rin, 'The מות of Grandeur', *VT* 9 (1959), pp. 324-25; G.R. Driver, review of A.S. Kapelrud, *The Ras Shamra Discoveries and the Old Testament* (1963), *JSS* 10 (1965), pp. 120-21 (120); Geo Widengren, *Sakrales Königtum im Alten Testament und im Judentum* (Stuttgart: W. Kohlhammer, 1955), p. 70; G. Rinaldi, ''az kammāwet', *BeO* 5 (1963), p. 212; G.R. Driver, '"Another Little Drink"—Isaiah 28:1-22', in *Words and Meanings: Essays Presented to David Winton Thomas* (ed. Peter R. Ackroyd and Barnabas Lindars; Cambridge: Cambridge University Press, 1968), pp. 47-67 (58).

as superlative—Charles Cutler Torrey, *The Second Isaiah: A New Interpretation* (Edinburgh: T. & T. Clark, 1928), p. 423; D. Winton Thomas, 'A Consideration of Some Unusual Ways of Expressing the Superlative in Hebrew', *VT* 3 (1953), pp. 209-24 (219-22); P.P. Saydon, 'Some Unusual Ways of Expressing the Superlative in Hebrew and Maltese', *VT* 4 (1954), pp. 432-33; D. Winton Thomas, 'Textual and Philological Notes on Some Passages in the Book of Proverbs', in *Wisdom in Israel and in the Ancient Near East, Presented to Professor Harold Henry Rowley ... in Celebration of his Sixty-Fifth Birthday* (ed. M. Noth and D. Winton Thomas; VTSup, 3; Leiden: E.J. Brill, 1955), pp. 280-92 (288-89); Svi Rin, 'The מות of Grandeur', *VT* 9 (1959), pp. 324-25; A. Phillips, 'The Interpretation of 2 Samuel xii 5-6', *VT* 16 (1966), pp. 242-44; G.R. Driver, 'Isaiah 52_{13}–53_{12}: The Servant of the Lord', in *In Memoriam Paul Kahle* (ed. Matthew Black and Georg Fohrer; BZAW, 103; Berlin: A. Töpelmann, 1968), pp. 90-105 (102-103).

אַל־מָוֶת *immortality*—BDB, p. 39a; Zorell, p. 50a; M. Dahood, 'Immmortality in Proverbs 12,28', *Bib* 41 (1960), pp. 176-81; G.R. Driver, review of M. Dahood, *Proverbs and Northwest Semitic Philology* (1963), *JSS* 10 (1965), pp. 112-17 (112).

בֶּן מָוֶת *arch villain*, lit. son of death—A. Phillips, 'The Interpretation of 2 Samuel xii 5-6', *VT* 16 (1966), pp. 242-44.

Is 44_{14}—Mitchell Dahood, 'Hebrew–Ugaritic Lexicography XII', *Bib* 55 (1974), pp. 381-93 (386).

Is 53_{9}—W.F. Albright, 'The High Place in Ancient Palestine', in *Volume du Congrès. Strasbourg 1956* (VTSup, 4; Leiden: E.J. Brill, 1956), pp. 242-58 (244-26); Joseph Reider, 'Etymological Studies in Biblical Hebrew', *VT* 2 (1952), pp. 113-30 (118).

Ps 88_{6} Jb 33_{22}—M. Dahood, 'Hebrew–Ugaritic Lexicography V', *Bib* 48 (1967), pp. 421-38 (435-36).

מִזְבֵּחַ *altar*—C. Dohmen, 'מִזְבֵּחַ *mizbēaḥ*', *TDOT*, VIII (1997; orig. 1983–84), pp. 209-25.

מָזֶה I *sucked out, emaciated* (cf. Arab. mazza *suck*)—BDB, p. 561a; Zorell, p. 423b; *HALOT*, II, p. 564b.

מָזֶה II *thin, weak, emaciated* (cf. Arab. raziya *be thin, weak*, as *badal* of *maziya)—Alfred Guillaume, *Hebrew and Arabic Lexicography: A Comparative Study*, IV (Leiden:

E.J. Brill, 1965; = *AbrN* 4 [1964–65]), pp. 17-18.

מְזֶה III *storeplace* (cf. מְזוּ *storehouse*)—Meir Wallenstein, 'The Palaeography of the *Zayin* in the Hymns Scroll with Special Reference to the Interpretation of Related Obscure Passges', *VT* 9 (1959), pp. 101-107 (105-106).

מִזֶּה *spurt* (cf. נזה *spurt*)—E. Wiesenberg, 'A Note on מזה in Psalm lxxv 9', *VT* 4 (1954), pp. 434-39; *HALOT*, II, p. 565a.

מְזוּזָה *doorpost*—J. van der Ploeg, 'La Règle de la Guerre: Traduction et notes', *VT* 5 (1955), pp. 372-420 (403); Maximilian Ellenbogen, *Foreign Words in the Old Testament: Their Origin and Etymology* (London: Luzac & Co. 1962), p. 99; J. Milgrom, 'מְזוּזָה *mezûzâ*', *TDOT*, VIII (1997; orig. 1983–84), pp. 225-27.

מָזוֹר I *wound* (cf. זור *press down*)—BDB, p. 267a.

מָזוֹר II *sore, ulcer, boil* (cf. MH מזר *decay*, Arab. maḏira)—*HALOT*, II, p. 565a.

מָזוֹר III *running sore* (cf. זור *flow*)—Mitchell Dahood, 'Philological Notes on Jer 18,14-15', *ZAW* 74 (1962), pp. 207-209 (208); Mitchell Dahood, *Proverbs and Northwest Semitic Philology* (Scripta Pontificii Instituti Biblici, 113; Rome: Pontificium Institutum Biblicum, 1963), p. 33.

מָזוֹר IV *net, noose* (cf. זור *draw tight*)—G.R. Driver, 'Problems in the Hebrew Text of Proverbs', *Bib* 32 (1951), pp. 173-97 (173-74); *HALOT*, II, p. 565a.

מזורות I *rotten eggs* (cf. Syr. maḏūrāṭā)—Preben Wernberg-Møller, 'A Note on זור "to stink"', *VT* 4 (1954), pp. 322-25 (325); G.R. Driver, review of Svend Holm-Nielsen, *Hodayoth: Psalms from Qumran* (1960), *JTS* ns 13 (1962), pp. 371-78 (374).

מַזּוֹרוֹ III *planets*—Menahem Mansoor, *The Thanksgiving Hymns* (STDJ, 3; Leiden: E.J. Brill, 1961), p. 109 n. 7.

מז *weld together* (cf. MH מזמז *soften*)—Yigael Yadin, *The Scroll of the War of the Sons of Light against the Sons of Darkness* (Oxford: Oxford University Press, 1962), p. 280.

melt, refine (byform of מסס *melt*)—J. Carmignac, 'Précisions apportées au vocabulaire de l'hébreu biblique par la Guerre des Fils de Lumière contre les Fils de Ténèbres', *VT* 5 (1955), pp. 345-65 (347).

מֵזַ I *shipyard* (? cf. Eg. mdḥ *construct framework of wooden ship*)—*HALOT*, II, p. 565b; Hans Wildberger, *Isaiah 13–27: A Continental Commentary* (Minneapolis: Fortress Press, 1997), p. 409.

Is 23_{10}—Wilhelm Rudolph, 'Jesaja 23, 1-14', in *Festschrift Friedrich Baumgärtel zum 70. Geburtstag, 14. Januar 1958, gewidmet von den Mitarbeitern am Kommentar zum Alten Testament (KAT)* (ed. Johannes Herrmann and Leonhard Rost; Erlanger Forschungen, 10; Erlangen: Universitätsbund Erlangen, 1959), pp. 166-74 (169).

מֵזַח II *girdle* (cf. Eg. mğḥ)—Dalman, *Arbeit* V, pp. 232-40; J.J. Hess, 'Beduinisches zum Alten und Neuen Testament', *ZAW* 35 (1915), pp. 120-31 (131); Thomas O. Lambdin, 'Egyptian Loanwords in the Old Testament', *JAOS* 73 (1953), pp. 145-55 (152).

מֵזַח III *impudence* (cf. מֵצַח *brow*)—Paul Joüon, 'Notes philologiques sur le texte hébreu de Job: 1, 5; 9, 35; 12, 21; 28, 1; 28, 27; 29, 14', *Bib* 11 (1930), pp. 322-24 (323).

מַזְכִּיר *recorder*—N. Avigad, 'Hebrew Seals and Sealings and their Significance for Biblical Research', in *Congress Volume: Jerusalem, 1986* (ed. J.A. Emerton; VTSup, 40; Leiden: E.J. Brill, 1988), pp. 7-16 (9-10).

royal herald—R. de Vaux, *Ancient Israel: Its Life and Institutions* (London: Darton, Longman & Todd, 1961), p. 132.

vizier (not *herald*)—K.A. Kitchen, 'Egypt and Israel during the First Millennium B.C.', *Congress Volume: Jerusalem, 1986* (ed. J.A. Emerton; VTSup, 40; Leiden: E.J. Brill, 1988), pp. 107-23 (113-14).

מַזָּל *flow, utterance* (cf. נזל *flow*)—Meir Wallenstein, 'The Palaeography of the *Zayin* in the Hymns Scroll with Special Reference to the Interpretation of Related Obscure Passges', *VT* 9 (1959), pp. 101-107 (102-103); Mitchell Dahood, 'Ugaritic Studies and the Bible', *Greg* 43 (1962), pp. 55-79 (78 n. 58); M. Dahood, review of Johann Maier, *Die Texte vom Toten Meer* (1960), *Bib* 44 (1963), pp. 228-29 (229); Mitchell Dahood, *Proverbs and Northwest Semitic Philology* (Scripta Pontificii Instituti Biblici, 113; Rome: Pontificium Institutum Biblicum, 1963), p. 20; Mitchell Dahood, *Psalms I: 1–50* (AB, 16; Garden City, NY: Doubleday, 1966), p. 75.

no such word—J.A. Emerton, 'The Meaning of the Root

mzl in Ugaritic', *JSS* 14 (1969), pp. 22-33 (29-30).

מַזָּלָה *pit* (cf. מַזָּל *flow*)—Mitchell Dahood, 'Ugaritic Studies and the Bible', *Greg* 43 (1962), pp. 55-79 (78); Mitchell Dahood, *Psalms I: 1–50* (AB, 16; Garden City, NY: Doubleday, 1966), p. 75.

מַזָּלוֹת *constellations of the zodiac*—BDB, p. 561a; *HALOT*, II, p. 565b.

planets—G.R. Driver, 'Two Astronomical Passages in the Old Testament', *JTS* ns 7 (1956), pp. 7-8; B. Landsberger and J.V. Kinnier-Wilson, 'The Fifth Tablet of *Enuma Eliš*', *JNES* 20 (1961), pp. 154-79 (170-72).

(cf. Akk. mazzaltu)—Maximilian Ellenbogen, *Foreign Words in the Old Testament: Their Origin and Etymology* (London: Luzac & Co. 1962), p. 100.

מְזִמָּה *private thoughts, caginess*—Michael V. Fox, 'Words for Wisdom: תבונה and בינה; ערמה and מזמה; עצה and תושיה', *ZAH* 6 (1993), pp. 149-65 (159-60).

מִזְמוֹר *psalm*—Lienhard Delekat, 'Probleme der Psalmenüberschriften', *ZAW* 76 (1964), pp. 280-97 (282-83).

מַזְמֵרָה *pruning knife*—Samuel Yeivin, 'הערות בלשניות, ט (Philological Notes, IX)', *Lesh* 27 (1963–65), pp. 1-9.

מְזַמֶּרֶת II *musical instrument*—Victor Avigdor Hurowitz, 'Solomon's Golden Vessels (1 Kings 7:48-50) and the Cult of the First Temple', in *Pomegranates and Golden Bells: Studies in Biblical, Jewish, and Near Eastern Ritual, Law, and Literature in Honor of Jacob Milgrom* (ed. David P. Wright, David Noel Freedman and Avi Hurvitz; Winona Lake, IN: Eisenbrauns, 1995), pp. 151-64 (155-56).

מְזָנִים *clouds* (cf. Arab. muzn)—H. Torczyner (Tur-Sinai), 'The Firmament and the Clouds: Rāqîaʿ and Sheḥāqîm', *StTh* 1 (1948), pp. 188-96 (196); H. Torczyner, 'Additional Note', *StTh* 2 (1948), p. 98; cf. D. Winton Thomas, 'A Drop of a Bucket? Some Observations on the Hebrew Text of Isaiah 40_{15}', in *In Memoriam Paul Kahle* (ed. Matthew Black and Georg Fohrer; BZAW, 103; Berlin: A. Töpelmann, 1968), pp. 214-21 (217); Thomas, *Lexicon*, I (1970), p. 286.

מְזַעְזֵעַ I *reminding* (cf. Aram. *call to mind*)—*Tanakh: A New Translation of the Holy Scriptures according to the Traditional Hebrew Text* (Philadelphia: Jewish Publication Society, 1985), p. 1065.

מְזַעְזֵעַ II *shaking* (pilp. ptc. of זוע *shake*)—BDB, p. 266a; *HALOT*, I, p. 267a.

מְזַעְזֵעַ III *barking* (pilp. ptc. of זעה)—M. Dahood, 'Hebrew–Ugaritic Lexicography II', *Bib* 45 (1964), pp. 393-412 (405); Mitchell J. Dahood, 'Ugaritic Lexicography' [review of Joseph Aistleitner, *Wörterbuch der ugaritischen Sprache* (1963)], in *Mélanges Eugène Tisserant. I. Ecriture sainte—Ancien orient* (Studi e testi, 231; Città del Vaticano; Bibliotheca Apostolica Vaticana, 1964), pp. 81-104 (88).

מְזִקָּה *canal, conduit*—J.T. Milik, 'Le rouleau de cuivre provenant de la grotte 3Q (3Q15)', in *DJD*, III (1962), pp. 199-302 (244.72).

מזר *stretch out* (cf. Syr. mzar *bind, tie, stretch oneself*)—Gemser; *HALOT*, II, p. 566a.

מַזָּרוֹת *boat of Arcturus*—S. Mowinckel, *Die Sternnamen im Alten Testament* (Oslo: Groondahl, 1928), pp. 27-29.

Hyades—Gustav Hölscher, *Das Buch Hiob* (HAT, I/17; Tübingen: J.C.B. Mohr, 2nd edn, 1952), p. 90; N.H. Tur-Sinai, *The Book of Job* (Jerusalem: Kiryath Sepher, revised edn, 1967), pp. 530-32; (cf. זור *flow*) Mitchell Dahood, 'Philological Notes on Jer 18,14-15', *ZAW* 74 (1962), pp. 207-209 (208); Mitchell Dahood, *Proverbs and Northwest Semitic Philology* (Scripta Pontificii Instituti Biblici, 113; Rome: Pontificium Institutum Biblicum, 1963), p. 33.

Hyades, Venus, or southern Zodiac—Rudolf Meyer, review of A. Dupont-Sommer, *Le Livre des Hymnes découvert près de la Mer Morte (1QH)* (1957), *TLZ* 84 (1959), cols. 659-661 (660-61).

planets—Menahem Mansoor, *The Thanksgiving Hymns* (STDJ, 3; Leiden: E.J. Brill, 1961), p. 109; *HALOT*, II, p. 566b.

Venus in its two phases—G. Schiaparelli, *Astronomy in the Old Testament* (Oxford: Clarendon Press, 1904), pp. 74-89.

Zodiac—G.R. Driver, 'Two Astronomical Passages in the Old Testament', *JTS* ns 7 (1956), pp. 1-22 (4-8); Thomas, *Lexicon*, I (1970), p. 272.

Zodiac of the southern hemisphere—J.J. Hess apud KB, p. 510b; Georg Fohrer, *Das Buch Hiob* (KAT, 16; Gütersloh: Gerd Mohn, 1963), p. 492.

מְזָרִים II *press* (cf. זור II *squeeze*)—N.H. Tur-Sinai, *The Book of Job* (Jerusalem: Kiryath Sepher, revised edn, 1967), pp. 510-11.

מִזְרָחִי *eastern*—J.T. Milik, 'Le rouleau de cuivre provenant de la grotte 3Q (3Q15)', in *DJD*, III (1962), pp. 199-302 (286-87).

מִזְרָע *place of sowing*—P. Sacchi, 'Nota a Is 19, 7', *RivBib* 13 (1965), pp. 169-70.

מִזְרָק *basin*—A.M. Honeyman, 'The Pottery Vessels of the Old Testament', *PEQ* (1939), pp. 76-90 (83-84); J.T. Milik, 'Le rouleau de cuivre provenant de la grotte 3Q (3Q15)', in *DJD*, III (1962), pp. 199-302 (253,141); Victor Avigdor Hurowitz, 'Solomon's Golden Vessels (1 Kings 7:48-50) and the Cult of the First Temple', in *Pomegranates and Golden Bells: Studies in Biblical, Jewish, and Near Eastern Ritual, Law, and Literature in Honor of Jacob Milgrom* (ed. David P. Wright, David Noel Freedman and Avi Hurvitz; Winona Lake, IN: Eisenbrauns, 1995), pp. 151-64 (156-57).

מחא I *clap*—Nili S. Fox, 'Clapping Hands as a Gesture of Anguish and Anger in Mesopotamia and Israel', *JANESCU* 23 (1995), pp. 49-60.

מחא III *destroy* (cf. Aram.)—Joseph Reider, 'Etymological Studies in Biblical Hebrew', *VT* 4 (1954), pp. 276-95 (287-88).

מחא IV, see מחה III, *be full of marrow*.

מַחֲבָן *fertile* (perhaps *rotten*) *place* (cf. Arab. ḥibnun *burning sore*)—L. Delekat, 'Zum hebräischen Wörterbuch', *VT* 14 (1964), pp. 7-66 (26-27).

מְחַבְּרָה *brace, truss*—*HALOT*, II, p. 567b.

(wooden) beam (not *clamp*)—Piet Dirksen, 'What Are the *mᵉḥabbᵉrôt* in 1 Chron. 22:3?', *BN* 80 (1995), pp. 23-24.

מַחְבֶּרֶת *embellishment*—Karl Georg Kuhn, 'Der gegenwärtige Stand der Erforschung der in Palästina neu gefundenen hebräischen Handschriften', *TLZ* 81 (1956), cols. 25-29 (28).

מַחֲבַת *griddle*—A.M. Honeyman, 'The Pottery Vessels of the Old Testament', *PEQ* (1939), pp. 76-90 (84).

מחה *wipe*—L. Alonso-Schökel, 'מָחָה *māḥâ*', *TDOT*, VIII (1997; orig. 1983–84), pp. 227-31.

wipe out—Is 5_{17}—G.R. Driver, 'Linguistic and Textual Problems: Isaiah i–xxxix', *JTS* 38 (1937), pp. 36-50 (38).

מָחָה *prophet* (fem.) (cf. Akk. maḫḫūtu)—Edouard Lipiński, 'Emprunts suméro-akkadiens en hébreu biblique', *ZAH* 1 (1988), pp. 61-73 (68-69).

מְחוּגָה *lathe*—Karl Elliger, *Deuterojesaja. I* (BK XI/1; Neukirchen: Neukirchener Verlag, 1978), pp. 407, 428.

compass—Silvia Schroer, *In Israel gab es Bilder: Nachrichten von darstellender Kunst im Alten Testament* (OBO, 74; Freiburg, Switzerland: Universitätsverlag, 1987), p. 218.

מָחוֹז *city*—BDB, p. 562b.

harbour—Yehezkel Kutscher, 'לשאלתו מלוניות', *Lesh* 8 (1937), pp. 136-45 (140-45); Israel Eitan, 'A Contribution to Isaiah Exegesis (Notes and Short Studies in Biblical Philology)', *HUCA* 12–13 (1937–38), pp. 55-88 (70); Thomas, *Lexicon*, VIII (1970), p. 66; *HALOT*, II, p. 568a; R. Borger, 'Weitere ugaritologische Kleinigkeiten. III. Hebäisch *mḥwz* (Psalm 107,30), *UF* 1 (1969), pp. 1-4; Mitchell Dahood, *Psalms III: 101–150* (AB, 17A; Garden City, NY: Doubleday, 1970), p. 88.

מָחוֹל I *dance* (from חלל III, as 1 Kings 1_{40})—Benno Landsberger, 'Einige unerkannt gebliebene oder verkannte Nomina des Akkadischen', *WZKM* 56 (1960), pp. 109-29 (119 n. 30).

מְחוֹת *full measure* (cf. Phoen. למחת *in full measure*)—Mitchell J. Dahood, 'Ugaritic *DRKT* and Biblical *DEREK*', *TS* 15 (1954), pp. 627-31 (629).

מֶחֱזָה *aperture for light, spy-hole*—*HALOT*, II, p. 568b.

light, place of seeing, window—BDB, p. 303b.

light space, storey—Thomas, *Lexicon*, VIII (1970), p. 109.

window—Georg Richter, 'Der salomonische Königspalast: Eine exegetische Studie', *ZDPV* 40 (1917), pp. 171-225 (183-85); Gesenius–Buhl, p. 413b; Zorell, p. 426a.

מִחְיָה *formation of new flesh*—*HALOT*, II, p. 568b.

materials for repair (cf. חיה pi. *repair, rebuild*)—Godfrey Rolles Driver, 'Problems of the Hebrew Text and Language', in *Alttestamentliche Studien Friedrich Nötscher zum sechzigsten Geburtstage 19. Juli 1950 gewidmet* (BBB, 1; ed. Hubert Junker and Johannes Botterweck; Bonn: Hanstein, 1950), pp. 46-61 (52).

patch of flesh—Jacob Milgrom, *Leviticus 1–16: A New Translation with Introduction and Commentary* (AB, 3; New York: Doubleday, 1991), p. 784.

מְחִיר *value*—E. Lipiński, 'מְחִיר *mᵉḥîr*', *TDOT*, VIII (1997; orig. 1983–84), pp. 231-34.

מְחַלֵּב *Mehalleb*—Rafael Frankel, 'Mahalab', *ABD*, IV, pp. 472-73.

מְחֹלָה *dance* (from חלל III, as in 1 Kings 1_{40})—Benno Landsberger, 'Einige unerkannt gebliebene oder verkannte Nomina des Akkadischen', *WZKM* 56 (1960), pp. 109-29 (119 n. 30).

dance in a ring—Gesenius–Buhl, p. 414a; *HALOT*, II, p. 569a.

dance with singing—W.F. Albright, 'Archaic Survivals in the Text of Canticles', in *Hebrew and Semitic Studies Presented to Godfrey Rolles Driver* (ed. D. Winton Thomas and W.D. McHardy; Oxford: Clarendon Press, 1963), pp. 1-7 (5 n. 4).

מַחֲלֻיִים *sickness, suffering*—Josef Scharbert, *Der Schmerz im Alten Testament* (BBB, 8; Bonn: Peter Hanstein, 1955), pp. 37-38.

מַחֲלָף I *knife* (cf. MH חֲלִיפָה)—BDB, p. 322b; M. Dahood, 'Hebrew–Ugaritic Lexicography IV', *Bib* 47 (1966), pp. 403-19 (416).

מַחֲלָף II *censer*—RSV.

מַחֲלָף III *repaired* (cf. חלף hi. *replace, renew*)—NJB.

מַחֲלָף IV *changed, to be changed* (rd. מְחֻלָּף from חלף hi. *replace, renew*)—Wilhelm Rudolph, *Esra und Nehemia samt 3. Esra* (HAT, I/20; Tübingen: J.C.B. Mohr [Paul Siebeck], 1949), p. 5.

מַחְלָפָה I *plait*—Dalman, *Arbeit*, V, p. 268.

plait as hanging down—G.R. Driver, 'Studies in the Vocabulary of the Old Testament. VI', *JTS* 34 (1933), pp. 375-85 (381 n. 3).

מַחְלָפָה II *copious hair* (cf. חלף II *pierce*, Ug. ḫlp *be sharp, cut*)—Nic. J. Tromp, 'De radice *ḥlp* in lingua hebraica', *VD* 41 (1963), pp. 299-304.

מַחֲלָצָה II *white garments* (cf. Arab. ḫalaṣa *be pure, white*)—D. Winton Thomas, 'A Note on מחלצות in Zechariah iii 4', *JTS* 33 (1931–32), pp. 279-80; cf. D. Winton Thomas, 'A Note on חליצותם in Judges xiv 19', *JTS* 34 (1933), p. 165; *HALOT*, II, p. 569b.

מַחֲלְקוֹת *distribution* (cf. חלק *divide*)—Zorell, p. 426b.

מַחֲלֹקֶת I *tribal division*—Joel P. Weinberg, 'Die soziale Gruppe im Weltbild des Chronisten', *ZAW* 98 (1986), pp. 72-95 (77).

מַחֲלֹקֶת II *smoothness* (cf. חלק II *be smooth*)—BDB, p. 325b; (?) *HALOT*, II, p. 570.

מָחֲלַת I *Mahalath*—E. Werner, 'Music', *IDB*, III, pp. 457-69 (459).

melancholic air—cf. Gesenius–Buhl, p. 414a; Zorell, p. 426b.

song (cf. Eth. māḥlēt *song*)—Gesenius–Buhl, p. 414a.

מַחְמָד *Machomades, Syrtes*—Melville Scott, *The Message of Hosea* (London: SPCK, 1921), pp. 138-40; G.R. Driver, review of J.L. Palache, *Semantic Notes on the Hebrew Lexicon* (1959), *JSS* 5 (1960), pp. 423-25 (424); Thomas, *Lexicon*, VIII (1970), p. 233.

מַחְמָל *compassion* (cf. Arab. ḥamala *bear*)—L. Kopf, 'Arabische Etymologien und Parallelen zum Bibelwörterbuch', *VT* 8 (1958), pp. 161-215 (172).

desire—Thomas, *Lexicon*, VIII (1970), p. 243.

longing—*HALOT*, II, p. 570a.

thing pitied, object of compassion—BDB, p. 328b; Zorell, p. 427a.

מַחְמֶצֶת *sour-tasting*—*HALOT*, II, p. 570b; William H.C. Propp, *Exodus 1–18: A New Translation with Introduction and Commentary* (AB, 2; New York: Doubleday, 1998), p. 406.

מַחֲנֶה *camp*—gender—GKC, §122l, n. 1.

camp—morphology—GKC, §93ss.

mantlet (cf. MH כָּנוּת *shop*)—Seton Lloyd, *Foundations in the Dust: The Story of Mesopotamian Exploration* (London: Oxford University Press, 1947; London: Thames & Hudson, revd edn, 1980), p. 154; G.R. Driver, 'Ezekiel: Linguistic and Textual Problems', *Bib* 35 (1954), pp. 145-59 (147-48); cf. James Barr, *Comparative Philology and the Text of the Old Testament* (Oxford: Oxford University Press, 1968), p. 327.

מַחֲנֵה־דָן *Mahaneh-dan*—Brian P. Irwin, 'Mahaneh-dan', *ABD*, IV, pp. 472-73.

מַחֲנַיִם *Mahanaim*—Diana V. Edelman, 'Mahanaim', *ABD*, IV, pp. 472-73.

מַחֲנָק *the Strangler*, i.e. Mot, the god of death—Francis I. Andersen, *Job: An Introduction and Commentary* (London: Inter-Varsity Press, 1976), p. 137.

מַחְסֶה *(place of) refuge*—*HALOT*, p. 571a.

refuge, shelter—BDB, p. 340a.

shelter (not *refuge*)—Paul Joüon, 'Racine חסה', *Bib* 6 (1925), pp. 421-22.

מְחַפֵּשׂ *investigator*, as divine appellative (cf. חפשׂ *search*)—Mitchell Dahood, *Psalms II: 51–100* (AB, 17; Garden City, NY: Doubleday, 1968; 3rd edn, 1979), p. 106.

מחץ I *immerse violently, plunge into*—Johannes C. de Moor, 'Ugaritic Lexicography', in *Studies on Semitic Lexicography* (ed. Pelio Fronzaroli; Quaderni di semitistica; Florence: Istituto di linguistica e di lingue orientali, Università di Firenze, 1973), pp. 61-102 (89 n. 1).

strike—L. Alonso Schökel, 'מָחַץ *māḥaṣ*', *TDOT*, VIII (1997; orig. 1983–84), pp. 235-37.

strike (not *pierce*)—G.R. Driver, 'Problems in Judges Newly Discussed', *ALUOS* 4 (1962–63), pp. 6-25 (11).

strike, slay—Moshe Held, '*mḫṣ*/**mḫš* in Ugaritic and Other Semitic Languages (A Study in Comparative Lexicography)', *JAOS* 79 (1958), pp. 169-76 (171-72).

Ps 68_{24}—Mitchell Dahood, 'Hebrew Lexicography: A Review of W. Baumgartner's *Lexikon*, Volume II', *Or* 45 (1976), pp. 327-65 (350-51).

מחץ II *dip* (cf. Akk. maḫāṣu *dip*)—F. Delitzsch, *Prolegomena eines neuen hebräisch-aramäischen Wörterbuches zum Alten Testament* (Leipzig: J.C. Hinrichs, 1888), pp. 69-71; James Barr, *Comparative Philology and the Text of the Old Testament* (Oxford: Oxford University Press, 1968), p. 192.

מחץ III *run* (cf. Arab. maḥaṣa)—Zorell, p. 428a.

מחצב *smite*—Mitchell Dahood, 'Northwest Semitic Philology and Job', in *The Bible in Current Catholic Thought: Gruenthaner Memorial Volume* (ed. J.L. McKenzie; St Mary's Theological Studies, 1; New York, Herder & Herder, 1962), pp. 55-74 (56); Mitchell Dahood, *Psalms II: 51–100* (AB, 17; Garden City, NY: Doubleday, 1968; 3rd edn, 1979), p. 307.

מַחְצֵב *hewing*—Paul Joüon, 'Notes de lexicographie hébraïque', *MUSJ* 10 (1925), pp. 3-47 (17-18).

מְחֹקֵק *sceptre*—Sofia Cavalletti, 'La terminologia biblica per «bastone»', *Antonianum* 28 (1953), pp. 411-24 (422-23).

מֶחְקָר *recess*—Mitchell Dahood, *Psalms II: 51–100* (AB, 17; Garden City, NY: Doubleday, 1968; 3rd edn, 1979), p. 353.

מחר *appraise, value* (cf. מְחִיר *price*)—Mitchell Dahood, *Psalms III: 101–150* (AB, 17A; Garden City, NY: Doubleday, 1970), p. 103.

מָחָר *tomorrow*—Simon J. de Vries, 'The Time Word *maḥar* as a Key to Tradition Development', *ZAW* 87 (1975), pp. 65-79; G. André, 'מָחָר *māḥār*; מָחֳרָת *moḥºrāṯ*', *TDOT*, VIII (1997; orig. 1983–84), pp. 237-41.

מַחֲרֵב *laying waste*—G.R. Driver, 'Linguistic and Textual Problems: Jeremiah', *JQR* 28 (1937–38), pp. 97-129 (113).

מַחֲרֵשָׁה *ploughshare*—BDB, p. 361a (s.v. מַחֲרֵשָׁה); *HALOT*, II, p. 572a (s.v. מַחֲרֵשָׁה).

מַחֲרֵשָׁה *goad* (cf. חרשׁ *engrave, devise*, thus מַחֲרֵשָׁה *crafted, forged tool*)—Stephen L. Cook, 'The Text and Philology of I Samuel xiii 20-21', *VT* 44 (1994), pp. 250-54 (251-52).

מָחֳרָת *morrow*—G. André, 'מָחָר *māḥār*; מָחֳרָת *moḥºrāṯ*', *TDOT*, VIII (1997; orig. 1983–84), pp. 237-41; Nina L. Collins, 'The Start of the Pre-exilic Calendar Day of David and the Amalekites: A Note on 1 Samuel xxx 17', *VT* 41 (1991), pp. 203-10.

מַחֲשָׁב I *design, devising*—G.R. Driver, review of A. Dupont-Sommer, *Le Livre des Hymnes découvert près de la mer mort (1QH). Traduction intégrale avec introduction et notes* (1957), *JTS* ns 10 (1959), pp. 124-26 (125); Menahem Mansoor, *The Thanksgiving Hymns* (STDJ, 3; Leiden: E.J. Brill, 1961), p. 120 n. 12.

מַחְשָׁב II *fissure, network* (cf. חשׁב *weave*)—Emile Puech, 'Note de lexicographie hébraïque qumrânienne (*mṣw* /*yrwq*, *mḥšbym*, *śwṭ*)', in *Solving Riddles and Untying Knots: Biblical, Epigraphic, and Semitic Studies in Honor of Jonas C. Greenfield* (ed. Ziony Zevit, Seymour Gitin and Michael Sokoloff; Winona Lake, IN: Eisenbrauns, 1995), pp. 181-89 (181-84).

מַחְשָׁךְ *dark thoughts*—G.R. Driver, 'Notes on the Psalms. II. 73–150', *JTS* 44 (1943), pp. 12-23 (13).

מַחְתָּה *firepan*—Menaḥem Haran, 'The Uses of Incense in the Ancient Israelite Ritual', *VT* 10 (1960), pp. 113-29 (121); Victor Avigdor Hurowitz, 'Solomon's Golden Vessels (1 Kings 7:48-50) and the Cult of the First Temple', in *Pomegranates and Golden Bells: Studies in Biblical, Jewish, and Near Eastern Ritual, Law, and Litera-*

ture in Honor of Jacob Milgrom (ed. David P. Wright, David Noel Freedman and Avi Hurvitz; Winona Lake, IN: Eisenbrauns, 1995), pp. 151-64 (158).

מַטְאֲטֵא II *means of destruction*, perh. *implement for pounding, crushing* (cf. Arab. waṭi'a *tread upon, trample*, waṭ'a *violence, force*)—L. Kopf, 'Arabische Etymologien und Parallelen zum Bibelwörterbuch', *VT* 8 (1958), pp. 161-215 (174-75); Thomas, *Lexicon*, IX (1970), p. 3.

מַטְבֵּחַ *bloodbath, defeat*—Gesenius–Buhl, p. 417a.

means of slaughter—Zorell, p. 429b.

place of slaughter—BDB, p. 371a; *HALOT*, II, p. 573a.

מָטֶה *reaching* (cf. Aram. מטא *reach*)—G.R. Driver, 'Problems in "Proverbs"', *ZAW* 50 (1932), pp. 141-48 (146).

מַטֶּה I *rod*—morphology—J. Carmignac, 'Précisions apportées au vocabulaire de l'hébreu biblique par la Guerre des Fils de Lumière contre les Fils de Ténèbres', *VT* 5 (1955), pp. 345-65 (347).

Pr 24$_{11}$—Mitchell Dahood, *Proverbs and Northwest Semitic Philology* (Scripta Pontificii Instituti Biblici, 113; Rome: Pontificium Institutum Biblicum, 1963), p. 51.

tribe—Athalya Brenner, 'על מַטֶּה וּשֵׁבֶט וסיווגן הסמנטי (On *Maṭṭeh* and *Šēbeṭ* and Their Semantic Classification)', *Lesh* 44 (1980), pp. 100-108 [Heb]; H. Simian-Yofre and H.-J. Fabry, 'מַטֶּה *maṭṭeh*', *TDOT*, VIII (1997; orig. 1983–84), pp. 241-49; Rainer Neu, '"Israel" vor der Entstehung des Königtums', *BZ* 30 (1986), pp. 204-21; A. Ososti Mojola, 'Translating the Term "Tribe" in the Bible—with Special Reference to African Languages', *BiTrans* 40 (1989), pp. 208-11.

tribe in process of settling—William Johnstone, 'Old Testament Technical Expressions in Property Holding: Contributions from Ugarit', *Ugaritica* 6 (1969), pp. 309-17 (311-13).

מַטֶּה II *mace* (cf. Akk. miṭṭu *mace*)—Sofia Cavalletti, 'La terminologia biblica per «bastone»', *Antonianum* 28 (1953), pp. 411-24 (413-17); David Toshio Tsumura, 'Ugaritic Poetry and Habakkuk 3', *TynB* 40 (1989), pp. 24-48 (36-37).

מִטָּה *bed*—Alfred Guillaume, 'Isaiah's Oracle against Assyria (Isaiah 30, 27-33) in the Light of Archaeology', *BSOAS* 17 (1955), pp. 413-15.

מְטֹהָר *splendour, lustre* (cf. טהר *be pure, clean*, Ug. ṭhr *(pure) gem*)—M. Dahood, 'Is *Eben Yiśrā'ēl* a Divine Title?', *Bib* 40 (1959), pp. 1002-1007 (1004-1005); M. Dahood, 'Hebrew–Ugaritic Lexicography IV', *Bib* 47 (1966), pp. 403-19 (417); Mitchell Dahood, *Psalms II: 51–100* (AB, 17; Garden City, NY: Doubleday, 1968; 3rd edn, 1979), p. 319.

purity—*HALOT*, II, p. 573b.

מָטוּ *war, company* (cf. ESA mṭw)—W.F. Albright, 'The Psalm of Habakkuk', in *Studies in Old Testament Prophecy Presented to Professor Theodore H. Robinson* (ed. H.H. Rowley; Edinburgh: T. & T. Clark, 1950), pp. 1-18 (15).

מְטִיל I *rod*—BDB, p. 564b; *HALOT*, II, p. 574a (s.v. מָטִיל).

Is 40$_{18}$—Joh. Hempel, 'Zu Jes 50 $_6$', *ZAW* 76 (1964), p. 327.

מְטִיל II *strong* (cf. Hitt. muwat(t)alli- *strong*, Akk. mutallu *noble, proud*)—Chaim Rabin, 'Hittite Words in Hebrew', *Or* 32 (1963), pp. 113-39 (131-32).

מְטִיל III *destroyer* (cf. Ug. ṭll *fall*)—Joh. Hempel, 'Zu Jes 50 $_6$', *ZAW* 76 (1964), p. 327.

מֵטֵל *trap (?), Fäller* (cf. Ug. ṭll *fall*)—Joh. Hempel, 'Zu Jes 50 $_6$', *ZAW* 76 (1964), p. 327.

מִטָּל *dew* (cf. טַל)—I. Ben-David, 'Additions to Biblical Hebrew Lexicography', *Lesh* 62 (1992), pp. 293-99, I.

מַטְמוֹן I *provisions* stored in silo—Paul Haupt, 'Greek *sīrôs*, silo, and *sōros*, stack', *JBL* 40 (1921), pp. 170-72 (172).

מַטְמוֹן II *crypt* (cf. טמן *hide*)—M. Dahood, 'Northwest Semitic Texts and Textual Criticism of the Hebrew Bible', in *Questions disputées d'Ancien Testament* (ed. C. Brekelmans; BETL, 33; Leuven, 1974), pp. 11-37 (30).

מַטְמֹנֶת *treasure*—Zorell, p. 430a.

מַטָּע *plantation*—I.F.M. Brayley, '"Yahweh is the Guardian of His Plantation": A Note on Is. 60,21', *Bib* 41 (1960), pp. 275-86 (277); J. Reindl and H. Ringgren, 'נָטַע *nāṭa'*; מַטָּע *maṭṭā'*; נֶטַע *neṭa'*, נְטִעִים *neṭi'îm*; שָׁתַל *šāṭal*', *TDOT*, IX (1998; orig. 1984–86), pp. 387-94.

מָטָר *rain*—H.-J. Zobel, 'מָטָר *māṭār*; גֶּשֶׁם *gešem*; זֶרֶם *zerem*', *TDOT*, VIII (1997; orig. 1983–84), pp. 250-65.

מַטָּרָה *target, guard*—H. Madl, 'נָטַר *nāṭar*; מַטָּרָה *m aṭṭārâ*', *TDOT*, IX (1998; orig. 1984–86), pp. 402-406.

מִי *who?*—M. Dahood, 'Canaanite-Phoenician Influence in

Qoheleth', *Bib* 33 (1952), pp. 30-52, 191-221 (195); M. Dahood, 'The Language of Qoheleth', *CBQ* 14 (1952), pp. 227-32 (231).

in what state—G. Rinaldi, *'mj (mî)'*, *BeO* 9 (1967), p. 118.

what?—G.R. Driver, 'Problems in Judges Newly Discussed', *ALUOS* 4 (1962–63), pp. 6-25 (18-19); G.R. Driver, 'Colloquialisms in the Old Testament', in *Mélanges Marcel Cohen: Etudes de linguistique, ethnographie et sciences connexes offertes par ses amis et ses élèves à l'occasion de son 80ème anniversaire* (The Hague: Mouton, 1970), pp. 232-39.

what, of what nature? (Ex 3:13)—YehudaT. Radday, '"Wie ist sein Name?" (Ex 3:13)', *LB* 58 (1986), pp. 87-104.

whoever (indefinite relative pronoun)—Mitchell J. Dahood, 'Canaanite-Phoenician Influence in Qoheleth', *Bib* 33 (1952), pp. 30-52, 191-221 (195-96).

מִי יוֹדֵעַ *who knows?*—J.L. Crenshaw, 'The Expression *mî yôdēa'* in the Hebrew Bible', *VT* 36 (1986), pp. 274-88.

מִי יִתֵּן *would that!*—B. Jongeling, 'L'expression *my ytn* dans l'Ancien Testament', *VT* 24 (1974), pp. 32-40.

מיאמן *Miamun*—Manfred Görg, 'Zum judäischen Personennamen *MY'MN*', *BN* 38–39 (1987), pp. 33-35; Robert Deutsch and Michael Heltzer, *New Epigraphic Evidence from the Biblical Period* (Tel Aviv–Jaffa: Archaeological Center Publication, 1995), p. 56.

מיד *shake, convulse* (cf. Arab. māda)—G.R. Driver, 'Hebrew Notes', *ZAW* 52 (1934), pp. 51-56 (54-55); James Barr, *Comparative Philology and the Text of the Old Testament* (Oxford: Oxford University Press, 1968), p. 252; *HALOT*, II, p. 555a.

מֵיטָב *best*—J.J. Rabinowitz, 'Exodus xxii 4 and the Septuagint Version Thereof', *VT* 9 (1959), pp. 40-46 (43-44).

מִיכָל II *collection, container, hoard* (cf. כול *contain*)—A.M. Honeyman, review of Ludwig Koehler and Walter Baumgartner, *Lexicon in Veteris Testamenti Libros* (1953), *VT* 5 (1955), pp. 214-23 (220); *HALOT*, II, p. 576b.

מיל *ward off* (cf. Arab. m'l *attack; avert*)—G.R. Driver, 'Hebrew Notes', *ZAW* 52 (1934), pp. 51-56 (54).

מַיִם *water*—Philippe Reymond, *L'eau, sa vie, et sa signification dans l'Ancien Testament* (VTSup, 6; Leiden: E.J. Brill, 1958); H.-J. Fabry and R.E. Clements, 'מַיִם *mayim*', *TDOT*, VIII (1997; orig. 1983–84), pp. 265-88.

bodily fluids, humours—G.R. Driver, 'Theological and Philological Problems in the Old Testament', *JTS* 47 (1946), pp. 156-66 (160).

menstrual discharge—G.R. Driver, 'Theological and Philological Problems in the Old Testament', *JTS* 47 (1946), pp. 156-66 (160).

semen—G.R. Driver, 'Theological and Philological Problems in the Old Testament', *JTS* 47 (1946), pp. 156-66 (160); Preben Wernberg-Møller, 'Notes on the Manual of Discipline (DSD) i 18, ii 9, ii 1-4, 9, vii 10-12, and xi 21-22', *VT* 3 (1953), pp. 195-202 (201).

אַמַּת מַיִם *canal*, lit. mother of waters—G.R. Driver, 'Geographical Problems', *EI* 5 (1958), pp. 16*-20* (17*-18*); J.T. Milik, 'Le rouleau de cuivre provenant de la grotte 3Q (3Q15)', in *DJD*, III (1962), pp. 199-302 (242.58).

יְצִיאַת מַיִם *canal* (not *source*)—J.T. Milik, 'Le rouleau de cuivre provenant de la grotte 3Q (3Q15)', in *DJD*, III (1962), pp. 199-302 (242.57).

מַיִם זָרִים *running waters*—M. Dahood, 'Philological Notes on Jer 18,14-15', *ZAW* 74 (1962), pp. 207-209 (207, 208); Mitchell Dahood, *Proverbs and Northwest Semitic Philology* (Scripta Pontificii Instituti Biblici, 113; Rome: Pontificium Institutum Biblicum, 1963), p. 33; M. Dahood, 'Hebrew–Ugaritic Lexicography IV', *Bib* 47 (1966), pp. 403-19.

מַיִם חַיִּים *living water*, i.e. spring water—Jacob Milgrom, *Leviticus 1–16: A New Translation with Introduction and Commentary* (AB, 3; New York: Doubleday, 1991), pp. 836-38, 923-25.

מַיִם לַחַץ *water of oppression*—L. Kopf, 'Arabische Etymologien und Parallelen zum Bibelwörterbuch', *VT* 9 (1959), pp. 247-87 (261); M. Dahood, 'Hebrew–Ugaritic Lexicography IV', *Bib* 47 (1966), pp. 403-19 (417-18).

מַיִם רַבִּים *great waters* of underworld—Herbert G. May, 'Some Cosmic Connotations of *Mayim Rabbîm* "Many Waters"', *JBL* 74 (1955), pp. 9-21; Mitchell Dahood, *Psalms I: 1–50* (AB, 16; Garden City, NY: Doubleday, 1966), p. 110.

מֵי פָנִים *waters of the face*, i.e. *feeling of shame*—L. Kopf,

'Arabische Etymologien und Parallelen zum Bibelwörterbuch', *VT* 9 (1959), pp. 247-87 (260-61).

קוֹל מַיִם *voice of water*, i.e. waterfall—J.T. Milik, 'Le rouleau de cuivre provenant de la grotte 3Q (3Q15)', in *DJD*, III, 1962, pp. 199-302 (242.54).

רחץ בַּמַּיִם *wash in water*—J.F. Elwolde, 'Distinguishing the Linguistic from the Exegetical—The Case of Numbers in MT and 11QT[a]', in *The Scrolls and the Scriptures: Qumran Fifty Years After* (ed. Stanley E. Porter and Craig A. Evans; Roehampton Institute London Papers, 3/JSPSup, 26; Sheffield: Sheffield Academic Press, 1997), pp. 129-41.

מִין *kind*—Ed. König, 'Die Bedeutung des hebräischen מין', *ZAW* 31 (1911), pp. 133-46; P. Beauchamp and H.-J. Fabry, 'מִין *mîn*', *TDOT*, VIII (1997; orig. 1983–84), pp. 288-91.

likeness, resemblance (cf. Arab. myn *create; fruitfulness, procreation of living beings of the same species*—H. Cazelles, 'MYN—espèce, race ou ressemblance', in *Ecole des langues orientales anciennes de l'Institut catholique de Paris: Mémorial du cinquantenaire, 1914–1964* (ed. Eugène Tisserant; Travaux de l'Institut Catholique de Paris, 10; Paris: Bloud & Gay, 1964), pp. 105-108.

no such word in BH—Chaim Rabin, 'Etymological Miscellanea', in *Studies in the Bible* (ed. Chaim Rabin; ScrHieros, 8; Jerusalem: Magnes Press, 1961), pp. 384-400 (392-93).

מיץ I *press, oppress*—F. Nötscher, 'Entbehrliche Hapaxlegomena in Jesaia', *VT* 1 (1951), pp. 299-302 (301).

מיץ II *churn (milk), press, stir up* (cf. Akk. mâṣu, Arab. maḫadu *churn milk*)—Moshe Held, '*mḫṣ/*mḫš* in Ugaritic and Other Semitic Languages (A Study in Comparative Lexicography', *JAOS* 79 (1958), pp. 169-76 (171); Moshe Held, 'Marginal Notes to the Biblical Lexicon', in *Biblical and Related Studies Presented to Samuel Iwry* (ed. Ann Kort and Scott Morschauser; Winona Lake, IN: Eisenbrauns, 1985), pp. 93-103 (97-103).

מיר *procure* (cf. Arab. m'r)—Joseph Reider, 'Etymological Studies in Biblical Hebrew', *VT* 2 (1952), pp. 113-30 (123-24).

מֵירָשׁ *new wine* (cf. Ug. mrṯ, Aram. מֵירַת *must, juice*)—Theodor H. Gaster, 'Canticles i. 4', *ExpT* 72 (1960–61), p. 195.

מֵישַׁע *Mesha* (cf. Moabite משע *Mesha*, perh. pronounced môša')—S. Morag, 'Meša (A Study of Certain Features of Old Hebrew Dialect)', *EI* 5 (1958), pp. 138-44; Mordechai Cogan and Hayim Tadmor, *II Kings: A New Translation with Introduction and Commentary* (AB, 11; New York: Doubleday, 1988), p. 43.

מֵישָׁרִים II (type of) *wine* (perh. metathesis of מֵירָשׁ)—cf. Michael V. Fox, *The Song of Songs and Ancient Egyptian Love Songs* (Madison, WI: University of Wisconsin Press, 1985), p. 99.

מֵישָׁרִים III *smoothness*—Michael V. Fox, *The Song of Songs and Ancient Egyptian Love Songs* (Madison, WI: University of Wisconsin Press, 1985), pp. 99-100.

מֵישָׁרִים IV *gullet*—Mitchell Dahood, *Psalms I: 1–50* (AB, 16; Garden City, NY: Doubleday, 1966), p. 300.

מֵיתָר *cord*—M. Dahood, 'Some Aphel Causatives in Ugaritic', *Bib* 38 (1957), pp. 62-73 (64-65).

מַכְאֹב *torture*—G.R. Driver, 'Problems and Solutions', *VT* 4 (1954), pp. 225-45 (239).

מַכְבֵּנָה *Machbenah*—David Salter Williams, 'Machbenah', *ABD*, IV, p. 458.

מַכְבֵּר *cover, mat*—*HALOT*, II, p. 579a.

grating (cf. Eg. mk *covering* and bj3 rwḏ)—Manfred Görg, 'Methodological Renarks on Comparative Studies of Egyptian and Biblical Words and Phrases', in *Pharaonic Egypt: The Bible and Christianity* (ed. Sarah Israelit Groll; Jerusalem: Magnes Press, 1985), pp. 57-64, 353-55 (61).

netted cloth, coverlet—BDB, p. 460b.

rug, blanket—Thomas, *Lexicon*, XI (1970), p. 79.

מַכָּה *blow*—J. Conrad, 'נכה *nkh*; מַכָּה *makkâ*; נָכֶה *nāḵeh*; נכא *nk*'', *TDOT*, IX (1998; orig. 1984–86), pp. 415-23.

מִכְוָה *burn*—Pr 20₃₀—Wolfram von Soden, 'Die Nominalform *taqtûl* im Hebräischen und Aramäischen', *ZAH* 2 (1989), pp. 77-85 (82); Wolfram von Soden, 'Kränkung, nicht Schläge in Sprüche 20,30', *ZAW* 102 (1990), pp. 120-21.

מָכוֹן *foundation* of throne—Hellmut Brunner, 'Gerechtigkeit als Fundament des Thrones', *VT* 8 (1958), pp. 426-28.

מְכוֹנָה *property, estate*—Tadeusz Penar, *Northwest Semitic*

Philology and the Hebrew Fragments of Ben Sira (BibOr, 28; Rome: Biblical Institute Press, 1975), pp. 68-69.

מַכְלֻבֹת *tongs* (cf. Arab. kullāb)—Arnold E. Ehrlich, *Randglossen zur hebräischen Bibel*, VII (r.p. Hildesheim: Georg Olms, 1968 [original 1908–14]), p. 357.

מִכְמָס *Michmas*—Patrick M. Arnold, 'Michmash', *ABD*, IV, pp. 814-15.

מִכְמָר *fishing net*—*HALOT*, II, p. 580b.

מִכְמֶרֶת *fishing-net*—BDB, p. 485b; Zorell, p. 434b; *HALOT*, II, p. 580b.

(cf. Akk. nakmaru)—Maximilian Ellenbogen, *Foreign Words in the Old Testament: Their Origin and Etymology* (London: Luzac & Co. 1962), p. 101.

מֶכֶס *excise, levy, toll*—Abraham Malamat, 'The Ban in Mari and in the Bible', in *Biblical Essays: Proceedings of the Ninth Meeting of "Die Ou-Testamentiese Werkgemeenskap in Suid-Afrika"* (Potchefstroom: Pro Rege-Pers Beperk, 1967), pp. 40-49 (48 n. 23).

(cf. Akk. makāsu *collect taxes*)—Maximilian Ellenbogen, *Foreign Words in the Old Testament: Their Origin and Etymology* (London: Luzac & Co. 1962), p. 102.

מכר *deliver, transfer*—Z.W. Falk, 'Hebrew Legal Terms', *JSS* 12 (1967), pp. 241-44; E. Lipiński, 'Le mariage de Ruth', *VT* 26 (1976), pp. 124-27; Edward Lipiński, 'Sale, Transfer, and Delivery in Ancient Semitic Terminology', in *Gesellschaft und Kultur im alten Vorderasien* (ed. Horst Klengel; Schriften zur Geschichte und Kultur des alten Orients, 15; Berlin: Akademie-Verlag, 1982), pp. 173-85 (173-78); E. Lipiński, 'מכר *mkr*', *TDOT*, VIII (1997; orig. 1983–84), pp. 291-96.

Na 3_4—Mitchell Dahood, 'Causal Beth and the Root *NKR* in Nahum 3,4', *Bib* 52 (1971), pp. 395-96.

מכר II htp. *practise deceit, guile* (cf. Arab. makara)—D. Winton Thomas, 'The Root מכר in Hebrew', *JTS* 37 (1936), pp. 388-89; D. Winton Thomas, 'A Further Note on the Root מכר in Hebrew', *JTS* ns 3 (1952), p. 214; cf. *HALOT*, II, p. 582a.

מַכָּר I *benefactor*—NJPS.

business assessor—John Gray, *I & II Kings: A Commentary* (OTL; London: SCM Press, 3rd revised edn, 1977), p. 586; E. Lipiński, 'מכר *mkr*', *TDOT*, VIII (1997; orig. 1983–84), pp. 291-96 (294).

client—NAB.

merchant—W.F. Albright, review of James A. Montgomery, *A Critical and Exegetical Commentary on the Books of Kings* (1951), *JBL* 71 (1952), pp. 245-53 (251); *HALOT*, II, p. 582a.

temple-teller—James A. Montgomery and Henry Snyder Gehman, *A Critical and Exegetical Commentary on the Books of Kings* (ICC; Edinburgh: T. & T. Clark, 1951), pp. 429, 432.

מַכָּר II *acquaintance* (cf. נכר *recognize*)—BDB, p. 648b; Gesenius–Buhl, p. 423a; Zorell, p. 435b.

מַכָּר III *sale* (cf. מכר *sell*)—Logan S. Wright, '*Mkr* in 2 Kings xii 5-17 and Deuteronomy xviii 8', *VT* 39 (1989), pp. 438-48.

מֶכֶר *value*—מֶכֶר עַל־הָאָבוֹת *patrimony*—G.R. Driver, 'Two Problems in the Old Testament Examined in the Light of Assyriology', *Syr* 33 (1956), pp. 70-78 (77-78).

מִכְרֶה I *pit* (cf. כרה *dig*)—BDB, p. 500a; Zorell, p. 435b.

(salt-)mine—*HALOT*, II, p. 582a.

מִכְרֶה II *heap* (cf. Aram. כְּרִי, Akk. karū *heap*)—G.R. Driver, 'Hebrew Notes on Prophets and Psalms', *JTS* 41 (1940), pp. 162-75 (173); Gillis Gerleman, *Zephanja textkritisch und literarisch untersucht* (Lund: C.W.K. Gleerup, 1942), p. 37.

מְכֵרָה I *counsel* (cf. Eth. 'amkärä *advise*)—Edward Ullendorff, 'The Contribution of South Semitics to Hebrew Lexicography', *VT* 6 (1956), pp. 190-98 (194); James Barr, *Comparative Philology and the Text of the Old Testament* (Oxford: Oxford University Press, 1968), pp. 57, 270; *HALOT*, II, p. 582b.

Gn 49_5—Bruce Vawter, 'The Canaanite Background of Genesis 49', *CBQ* 17 (1955), pp. 1-18 (3-4).

מְכֵרָה II *weapon* (cf. כור II *bore, dig [?]*)—BDB, p. 468b; J.A. Emerton, 'Some Difficult Words in Genesis 49', in *Words and Meanings: Essays Presented to David Winton Thomas* (ed. Peter R. Ackroyd and Barnabas Lindars; Cambridge: Cambridge University Press, 1968), pp. 81-83.

מְכֵרָה III *goad, staff* (cf. Akk. makkaru)—G.R. Driver, 'Some Hebrew Roots and their Meanings', *JTS* 23 (1921–22), pp. 69-73 (70).

מְכֵרָה IV *beguilement* (cf. Arab. makara *beguile*)—A. Ben-

Shemesh, 'In Arabia They Call', *AusBR* 10 (1962), pp. 10-14 (13-14).

מְכֵרָת *circumcision blade* (cf. כרת *cut*)—Mitchell J. Dahood, '*Mkrtyhm* in Genesis 49,5', *CBQ* 23 (1961), pp. 54-56; Paul Beauchamp, review of Roland de Vaux, *La Genèse (La Sainte Bible)* (2nd edn, 1962), *Bib* 44 (1963), pp. 373-74 (373); M. Dahood, review of *The Torah: The Five Books of Moses* (1962), *Bib* 45 (1964), pp. 281-83; M. Dahood, 'Hebrew–Ugaritic Lexicography IV', *Bib* 47 (1966), pp. 403-19 (418); G.R. Cardona, 'Armeno *mkrtel* "battezzare" ed un hapax biblico', *AION-Ling* 7 (1966), pp. 89-100.

Gn 49$_5$ *covenanter*—Francis I. Andersen, 'Moabite Syntax', *Or* 35 (1966), pp. 81-120 (106-107).

מִכְשׁוֹל *stumbling block*—J. Schirmann, 'דפים נוספים מתוך "בן־סירא" (Some Additional Leaves from Ecclesiasticus in Hebrew)', *Tarb* 29 (1959–60), pp. 125-34 (132, line 21).

מכשל *bring down to destruction* (blend of מוך/מכך *sink* and כשל *stumble*)—Liudger Sabottka, *Zephanja: Versuch einer Neuübersetzung mit philologischer Kommentar* (BibOr, 25; Rome: Biblical Institute Press, 1972), pp. 8-10; Mitchell Dahood, 'Hebrew Lexicography: A Review of W. Baumgartner's *Lexikon*, Volume II', *Or* 45 (1976), pp. 327-65 (351-52).

מִכְתָּב *writing, especially on papyrus*—Carleton T. Hodge, 'Miktam', in *Semitic Studies in Honor of Wolf Leslau on the Occasion of his Eighty-Fifth Birthday, November 14th, 1991* (ed. Alan S. Kaye; Wiesbaden: Harrassowitz, 1991), pp. 634-44.

inscription—Elias J. Bickerman, 'The Edict of Cyrus in Ezra 1', *JBL* 65 (1946), pp. 249-75 (272-73).

Is 10$_1$—H.L. Ginsberg, 'The Ugaritic Texts and Textual Criticism', *JBL* 62 (1943), pp. 109-15 (115); Horace D. Hummel, 'Enclitic *Mêm* in Early Northwest Semitic, Especially Hebrew', *JBL* 76 (1957), pp. 85-107 (94); Mitchell Dahood, 'Hebrew Lexicography: A Review of W. Baumgartner's *Lexikon*, Volume II', *Or* 45 (1976), pp. 327-65 (352).

מִכְתָּם I *writing on clay tablet*—C.T. Hodge, 'Miktam', in *Semitic Studies in Honor of Wolf Leslau on the Occasion of his Eighty-Fifth Birthday, November 14th, 1991* , I (ed. Alan S. Kaye; Wiesbaden: Harrassowitz, 1991), pp. 634-44.

מִכְתָּם II *secret prayer*—Raymond Tournay, 'Sur quelques rubriques des Psaumes', in *Mélanges bibliques redigés en l'honneur de André Robert* (Travaux de l'Institut catholique de Paris, 4; Paris: Bloud & Gay, 1957), pp. 197-204 (201-204).

whispered prayer (cf. Akk. katâmu *cover, shut*)—B.D. Eerdmans, *The Hebrew Book of Psalms* (OTS, 4; Leiden: E.J. Brill, 1947), pp. 75-76.

מִכְתָּם III *inscription on stone slab* (cf. כתם *inscribe*)—Mitchell Dahood, *Psalms I: 1–50* (AB, 16; Garden City, NY: Doubleday, 1966), p. 87; Mitchell Dahood, *Psalms II: 51–100* (AB, 17; Garden City, NY: Doubleday, 1968; 3rd edn, 1979), p. 41.

inscription, epigram (cf. LXX στηλογραφία)—H.L. Ginsberg, 'Psalms and Inscriptions of Petition and Acknowledgment', in *Louis Ginzberg: Jubilee Volume on the Occasion of his Seventieth Birthday. English Section,* I (New York: The American Academy for Jewish Research, 1945) pp. 159-71 (169-70); L. Delekat, 'Zum hebräischen Wörterbuch', *VT* 14 (1964), pp. 7-66 (31-32); *HALOT*, II, p. 582b.

psalm for a particular occasion—Giovanni Rinaldi, 'Alcuni termini ebraici relativi alla letteratura', *Bib* 40 (1959), pp. 267-89 (277).

מִכְתָּם IV *gold-lettered inscription* (cf. כֶּתֶם *gold*)—Mitchell Dahood, *Psalms I: 1–50* (AB, 16; Garden City, NY: Doubleday, 1966), p. 87.

מִכְתָּם V *song sung to the capped reed pipe* (cf. Akk. kitmu *flute*)—Thomas, *Lexicon*, XI (1970), p. 522.

מַכְתֵּשׁ *molar*—L. Dürr, review of Otto Eissfeldt, *Die Quellen des Richterbuches* (1925), *OLZ* 29 (1926), cols. 643-46 (646).

מַל *hair*—D. Winton Thomas, 'Liber Jesaiae', *BHS*, p. 764 (on Is 57$_9$).

מלא *do fully*—G.R. Driver, 'Linguistic and Textual Problems: Jeremiah', *JQR* 28 (1937–38), pp. 97-129 (99-100).

empty—Francis I. Andersen, *Job: An Introduction and Commentary* (London: Inter-Varsity Press, 1976), p. 175.

fill—M. Dahood, 'The Phoenician Background of

Qoheleth', *Bib* 47 (1966), pp. 264-82 (277); M. Dahood, 'Karatepe Notes', *Bib* 44 (1963), pp. 70-73 (72); M. Delcor, 'מלא *ml'* , *TLOT*, II (1997; orig. 1976), pp. 664-66; L.A. Snijders and H.-J. Fabry, 'מָלֵא *mālē'*; מְלֹא *melō'*; מְלֵאָה *millu'â*; מִלֻּאִים *millu'îm*; מִלּוֹא *millô'*, *TDOT*, VIII (1997; orig. 1983–84), pp. 297-308.

fulfil—M. Dahood, 'Hebrew–Ugaritic Lexicography IV', *Bib* 47 (1966), pp. 403-19 (418-19).

pi. htp. *mass, proclaim mobilization*—D. Winton Thomas, 'מלאו in Jeremiah IV. 5', *JJS* 3 (1952), pp. 47-52.

pi. *heap high*—Mitchell Dahood, *Psalms III: 101–150* (AB, 17A; Garden City, NY: Doubleday, 1970), p. 118.

pi. *make fully ready*—G.R. Driver, 'Linguistic and Textual Problems: Jeremiah', *JQR* 28 (1937–38), pp. 97-129 (127).

all together, help, every one!—G.R. Driver, 'Jeremiah, XII, 6', *JJS* 5 (1954), pp. 177-78.

מָלֵא *full one,* i.e. sea—Mitchell Dahood, *Psalms II: 51–100* (AB, 17; Garden City, NY: Doubleday, 1968; 3rd edn, 1979), p. 190.

מלא יָד *fill the hand*—Abraham Malamat, "The Ban in Mari and in the Bible', in *Biblical Essays: Proceedings of the Ninth Meeting of "Die Ou-Testamentiese Werkgemeenskap in Suid-Afrika"* (Potchefstroom: Pro Rege-Pers Beperk, 1967), pp. 40-49 (48 n. 20); Mathias Delcor, 'Réflexions sur l'investiture sacerdotale sans onction à la fête du nouvel an d'après *Le Rouleau du Temple* de Qumrân', in *Hellenica et Judaica: Hommage à Valentin Nikiprowetzky* (ed. A. Caquot, M. Hadas-Lebel and J. Riaud; Leuven: Peeters, 1986), pp. 155-64 (155-56); Jacob Milgrom, *Leviticus 1–16: A New Translation with Introduction and Commentary* (AB, 3; New York: Doubleday, 1991), pp. 538-40.

Ps 73_{10}—Georgio R. Castellino, 'Salmo 73,10', *Studi orientalistici in onore di Giorgio Levi della Vida*, I (Pubblicazioni dell'Istituto per l'Oriente, 52; Rome: Istituto per l'Oriente, 1956), pp. 141-50.

Ps 110_6—G.R. Driver, 'Psalm cx: Its Form, Meaning and Purpose', in ספר סגל. *Studies in the Bible Presented to Professor M.H. Segal by his Colleagues and Students* (ed. J.M. Grintz and J. Liver; Publications of the Israel Society for Biblical Research, 17; Jerusalem, 1964), pp. 17*-31* (25*).

מִלֹּא *ordination offering*—L.A. Snijders and H.-J. Fabry, 'מָלֵא *mālē'*; מְלֹא *melō'*; מְלֵאָה *millu'â*; מִלֻּאִים *millu'îm*; מִלּוֹא *millô'*, *TDOT*, VIII (1997; orig. 1983–84), pp. 297-308; Jacob Milgrom, *Leviticus 1-16: A New Translation with Introduction and Commentary* (AB, 3; New York: Doubleday, 1991), pp. 436-37.

מְלֹא *fullness*—L.A. Snijders and H.-J. Fabry, 'מָלֵא *mālē'*; מְלֹא *melō'*; מְלֵאָה *millu'â*; מִלֻּאִים *millu'îm*; מִלּוֹא *millô'*, *TDOT*, VIII (1997; orig. 1983–84), pp. 297-308.

מִלֻּאָה *setting*—L.A. Snijders and H.-J. Fabry, 'מָלֵא *mālē'*; מְלֹא *melō'*; מְלֵאָה *millu'â*; מִלֻּאִים *millu'îm*; מִלּוֹא *millô'*, *TDOT*, VIII (1997; orig. 1983–84), pp. 297-308.

מַלְאָךְ *angel*—Robert North, 'Separated Spiritual Substances in the Old Testament', *CBQ* 29 (1967), pp. 419-43.

angel, messenger—R. Ficker, 'מַלְאָךְ *mal'āk*', *TLOT*, II (1997; orig. 1976), pp. 666-72; D.N. Freedman, B.E. Willoughby, H. Ringgren and H.-J. Fabry, 'מַלְאָךְ *mal'āḵ*', *TDOT*, VIII (1997; orig. 1983–84), pp. 308-25; Edmond Jacob, 'Variations et constantes dans la figure de l'ange de YHWH', *RHPR* 68 (1988), pp. 405-14.

delegate (of high priest) concerning vows—Mitchell J. Dahood, 'Canaanite-Phoenician Influence in Qoheleth', *Bib* 33 (1952), pp. 30-52, 191-221 (207).

salesman—Mitchell Dahood, 'Textual Problems in Isaia', *CBQ* 22 (1960), pp. 400-409 (403-404).

workman—R. North, 'Centrifugal and Centripetal Tendencies in the Judaic Cradle of Christinaity', in *Populus Dei: Studi in onore Alfredo Ottaviani per il cinquantesimo di sacerdozio*, I (ed. H. Cazelles, R. de Vaux, P. Grelot *et al.*; Rome: Communio, 1966), pp. 615-51 (621).

with play on מֶלֶךְ *king*—Gary A. Rendsburg, 'Word Play in Biblical Hebrew: An Eclectic Collection', in *Puns and Pundits: Word Play in the Bible and Near Eastern Literature* (ed. Scott B. Noegel; Bethesda, MD: CDL Press, 2000), pp. 137-62 (157-58).

Is 23_2—M. Dahood, 'Textual Problems in Isaia', *CBQ* 22 (1960), pp. 400-409 (403).

Na 1_4—G.R. Driver, 'Linguistic and Textual Problems: Minor Prophets. II', *JTS* 39 (1938), pp. 260-73 (271).

Ec 5_5—M. Dahood, 'Hebrew–Ugaritic Lexicography IV',

Bib 47 (1966), pp. 403-19 (418-19); Mitchell Dahood, 'The Phoenician Background of Qoheleth', *Bib* 47 (1966), pp. 264-82 (282).

מְלָאכָה *work*—Edward L. Greenstein, 'Trans-Semitic Idiomatic Equivalency and the Derivation of Hebrew *ml'kh*', *UF* 11 (1979), pp. 329-36; H.-J. Fabry, J. Milgrom and D.P. Wright, 'מְלָאכָה *melā'kâ*', *TDOT*, VIII (1997; orig. 1983–84), pp. 325-31.

trade, trading mission—W.F. Albright, 'Specimens of Late Ugaritic Prose', *BASOR* 150 (1958), pp. 36-38 (38 n. 14); Mitchell Dahood, *Psalms III: 101–150* (AB, 17A; Garden City, NY: Doubleday, 1970), p. 86.

מַלְאָכוּת *messenger*—Zorell, p. 439b.

מִלֵּאת I *inclusion within a border*—Zorell, p. 439b.

setting, border, rim—BDB, p. 571.

setting of the teeth—Augustinus Bea, *Canticum Canticorum: novam interpretationem latinam cum textu masoretico et notis exegeticis* (Rome: Pontifical Biblical Institute, 1953), p. 48; Wilhelm Rudolph, *Das Buch Ruth. Das Hohe Lied. Die Klagelieder* (KAT, XVII/1-3; Gütersloh: Gerd Mohn, 1962), pp. 158-59.

מִלֵּאת II *waterhole, pond* (cf. MH מליתא)—E.Y. Kutscher, 'Mittelhebräisch und jüdisch-aramäisch im neuen Köhler–Baumgartner', in *Hebräische Wortforschung: Festschrift zum 80. Geburtstag von Walter Baumgartner* (VTSup, 16; Leiden: E.J. Brill, 1967), pp. 158-75 (170).

מִלֵּאת III *stream* (cf. Syr. melê'ā *flood, stream*)—cf. Wilhelm Rudolph, *Das Buch Ruth. Das Hohe Lied. Die Klagelieder* (KAT, XVII/1-3; Gütersloh: Gerd Mohn, 1962), p. 159.

מִלֵּאת IV *pool* (cf. Akk. milū *flood*)—Theophile J. Meek, 'The Song of Songs', *IB*, V, pp. 89-148 (129).

מִלֵּאת V *fullness* (cf. מְלֹא *fullness*)—Gillis Gerleman, *Ruth. Das Hohelied* (BKAT, 18; Neukirchen–Vluyn: Neukirchener Verlag, 1965), pp. 171, 174.

מַלְבֵּן *brickmould; brick-terrace, clay floor*—*HALOT*, II, p. 587a.

brickmould; quadrangle—BDB, p. 527b.

foundation, brick terrace (cf. Akk. nalbanu *brickwork*, nalbantu *bricked foundation*)—G.R. Driver, 'Linguistic and Textual Problems: Jeremiah', *JQR* 28 (1937–38), pp. 97-129 (122).

מלה *be full* (byform of מלא)—G.R. Driver, 'Studies in the Vocabulary of the Old Testament. III', *JTS* 32 (1930–31), pp. 361-66 (366).

filled place—J.T. Milik, 'Le rouleau de cuivre provenant de la grotte 3Q (3Q15)', in *DJD*, III (1962), pp. 199-302 (248.97).

מִלָּה *word*—Gary A. Rendsburg, 'The Northern Origin of "The Last Words of David" (2 Sam 23,1-7)', *Bib* 69 (1988), pp. 113-21 (117-18).

מִלּוֹא *citadel*—W. Harold Mark, 'Millo', *ABD*, IV (1992), pp. 834-35.

esplanade—J.T. Milik, 'Le rouleau de cuivre provenant de la grotte 3Q (3Q15)', in *DJD*, III (1962), pp. 199-302 (248.97).

filling up—L.A. Snijders and H.-J. Fabry, 'מָלֵא *mālē*'; מְלֹא *melō*'; מְלֵאָה *millu'â*; מִלֻּאִים *millu'îm*; מִלּוֹא *millô*', *TDOT*, VIII (1997; orig. 1983–84), pp. 297-308.

mound of earth between city and wall—Richard C. Steiner, 'New Light on the Biblical *Millo* from Hatran Inscriptions', *BASOR* 276 (1989), pp. 15-23.

מִלּוֹא II *location of palace of Pharaoh's daughter* (cf. Eg. m3rw *court-garden*)—Manfred Görg, 'Methodological Remarks on Comparative Studies of Egyptian and Biblical Words and Phrases', in *Pharaonic Egypt: The Bible and Christianity* (ed. Sarah Israelit Groll; Jerusalem: Magnes Press, 1985), pp. 57-64, 353-55 (60, 353-34).

מַלּוּחַ *orache*—E. Dhorme, *A Commentary on the Book of Job* (trans. Harold Knight; Nashville: Thomas Nelson, 1984), pp. 432-33.

saltwort, mallow—Zorell, p. 440a.

מְלוּכָה *king*—M. Dahood, 'Hebrew–Ugaritic Lexicography IV', *Bib* 47 (1966), pp. 403-19 (419); Mitchell Dahood, *Psalms I: 1–50* (AB, 16; Garden City, NY: Doubleday, 1966), p. 143.

kingship—H. Ringgren, K. Seybold and H.-J. Fabry, 'מֶלֶךְ *melek*; מָלַךְ *mālak*; מְלוּכָה *melûkâ*; מַלְכוּת *malkût*; מַמְלָכָה *mamlākâ*; מַמְלָכוּת *mamlākût*', *TDOT*, VIII (1997; orig. 1983–84), pp. 346-75.

מלח I *salt*—V.A. Hurowitz, 'Salted Incense—Exodus 30,35; Maqlu VI 111-113; IX 118-120', *Bib* 68 (1967) pp. 178-94; H. Eising, 'מֶלַח *melaḥ*', *TDOT*, VIII (1997; orig. 1983–84), pp. 331-33.

be grey, dark (cf. Arab. malaḥa *become salt, be grey*)—G.R. Driver, 'Linguistic and Textual Problems: Isaiah xl–

lxvi', *JTS* 36 (1935), pp. 396-406 (402); G.R. Driver, 'L'interprétation du texte masorétique à la lumière de la lexicographie hébraïque', *ETL* 26 (1950), pp. 337-53 (349-50).

mixed with salt—Menaḥem Haran, 'The Uses of Incense in the Ancient Israelite Ritual', *VT* 10 (1960), pp. 113-29 (125 n. 3).

rub in salt water—*HALOT*, II, p. 588a.

מלח II *dissociate, disaggregate, dissipate*—J. Carmignac, 'Le sens de la racine מלח dans la Bible et à Qumrân', in *Studi sull'Oriente e la Bibbia offerti al P. Giovanni Rinaldi nel 60 compleanno da allievi, colleghi, amici* (Genoa: Studio e vita, 1967), pp. 77-81.

tear to pieces (? cf. Arab. malaḫa *dismember; draw a sword*)—BDB, p. 571b; *HALOT*, II, p. 588a.

מלח III *be dark* (cf. Arab. maliḥa *be grey*)—G.R. Driver, 'L'interprétation du texte masorétique à la lumière de la lexicographie hébraïque', *ETL* 26 (1950), pp. 337-53 (349-50); G.R. Driver, review of E.L. Sukenik, *The Dead Sea Scrolls of the Hebrew University* (1955), *JTS* ns 8 (1957), pp. 141-43 (142).

מַלָּח *mariner* (cf. Akk. malāḫu)—Maximilian Ellenbogen, *Foreign Words in the Old Testament: Their Origin and Etymology* (London: Luzac & Co. 1962), p. 103; Eva Strömberg Krantz, *Des Schiffes Weg mitten im Meer: Beiträge zur Erforschung der nautischen Terminologie des Alten Testaments* (CBOT, 19; Lund: C.W.K. Gleerup, 1982), pp. 182-84.

מֶלַח I *salt*—A.M. Honeyman, 'The Salting of Shechem', *VT* 3 (1953), pp. 192-94; Edward Ullendorff, 'Ugaritic Marginalia II', *JSS* 7 (1962), pp. 339-51 (345-46); F. Charles Fensham, 'Salt as Curse in the Old Testament and the Ancient Near East', *BA* 25 (1962), pp. 48-50.

מֶלַח II *frayed clothing*—J. Carmignac, 'Le sens de la racine מלח dans la Bible et à Qumrân', in *Studi sull'Oriente e la Bibbia offerti al P. Giovanni Rinaldi nel 60 compleanno da allievi, colleghi, amici* (Genoa: Studio e vita, 1967), pp. 77-81.

מְלֵחָה *salty place*—M. Dietrich and O. Loretz, 'Der Vertrag zwischen Šuppiluliuma und Niqmandu', *WO* 3 (1964–66), pp. 206-45 (221 n. 60).

Jb 30$_4$—N.H. Tur-Sinai, *The Book of Job* (Jerusalem: Kiryath Sepher, revised edn, 1967), p. 421.

מְלָחִים *cleverness* (cf. Ug. mlḥ *sharp*)—Mitchell J. Dahood, 'Canaanite-Phoenician Influence in Qoheleth', *Bib* 33 (1952), pp. 30-52, 191-221 (211).

מִלְחָמָה I *troops*—M. Dahood, 'Canaanite-Phoenician Influence in Qoheleth', *Bib* 33 (1952), pp. 30-52, 191-221 (211); M. Dahood, 'The Phoenician Background of Qoheleth', *Bib* 47 (1966), pp. 264-82 (277); M. Dahood, 'Hebrew–Ugaritic Lexicography IV', *Bib* 47 (1966), pp. 403-19 (419); G.R. Driver, 'Notes on Joshua', in *The Seventy-Fifth Anniversary Volume of the JQR* (Philadelphia, 1967), pp. 149-65 (156).

war—H.D. Preuss, 'מִלְחָמָה *milḥāmâ*; לָחַם *lāḥam*', *TDOT*, VIII (1997; orig. 1983–84), pp. 334-45.

weapon of war—M.Th. Houtsma, 'לֶחֶם—לָחוּם—מִלְחָמָה', *ZAW* 22 (1902), pp. 329-31 (329-30); Paul Joüon, 'Notes de lexicographie hébraïque', *MUSJ* 4 (1911), pp. 1-18 (2-3); G.R. Driver, 'On תפשי המלחמה (Num. 31.27)', *JQR* 37 (1946-47), p. 85; G.R. Driver, 'Hebrew Notes on "Song of Songs" and "Lamentations"', in *Festschrift Alfred Bertholet zum 80. Geburtstag gewidmet von Kollegen und Freunden* (ed. Walter Baumgartner [*et al.*]; Tübingen: J.C.B. Mohr, 1950), pp. 134-46 (146 n. 1); Zorell, p. 441a; G.R. Driver, 'Notes on Joshua', in *The Seventy-Fifth Anniversary Volume of the JQR* (Philadelphia, 1967), pp. 149-65 (156); Mitchell Dahood, *Psalms II: 51–100* (AB, 17; Garden City, NY: Doubleday, 1968; 3rd edn, 1979), p. 218; Francis I. Andersen and David Noel Freedman, *Hosea: A New Translation with Introduction and Commentary* (AB, 24; Garden City, NY: Doubleday, 1980), p. 195.

מִלְחָמָה II *adaptation, harmony, sistrum* (cf. Syr. lḥm *adapt music*)—G.R. Driver, 'Isaiah i–xxxix: Textual and Linguistic Problems', *JSS* 13 (1968), pp. 36-57 (51).

מלט I pi. *deliver*—Ec 9$_{15}$—M. Dahood, 'Canaanite-Phoenician Influence in Qoheleth', *Bib* 33 (1952), pp. 30-52, 191-221 (50); M. Dahood, 'The Language of Qoheleth', *CBQ* 14 (1952), pp. 227-32 (230).

מלט II *be bald* (cf. מרט, Arab. malaṭa)—*HALOT*, II, p. 589b.

מלט III *rub, bite* (cf. Akk. marāṭu *rub*, Arab. maraṭa *pluck out hair, scrape smooth*, Eth. malaṭa *pluck out hair*)—G.R. Driver, 'Problems in the Hebrew Text of Job', in *Wis-*

dom in Israel and in the Ancient Near East, Presented to Professor Harold Henry Rowley ... in Celebration of his Sixty-Fifth Birthday (VTSup, 3; Leiden: E.J. Brill, 1955), pp. 72-93 (80-81); Godfrey R. Driver, 'Ugaritic and Hebrew Words', *Ugaritica* 6 (1969), pp. 181-86 (185).

מלט IV *cleave, stick* (cf. מֶלֶט *mortar, cement*, Arab. malaṭa *join [with cement]*)—N.H. Tur-Sinai, *The Book of Job* (Jerusalem: Kiryath Sepher, revised edn, 1967), p. 301.

מֶלֶט *clay floor*—*HALOT*, II, p. 590a.

mortar, cement—BDB, p. 572b; Zorell, p. 441b.

מְלִילָה *ear of corn*—Dalman, *Arbeit*, I, p. 456.

מֵלִיץ I *interpreter, intermediary* (cf. Phoen. מלץ; not from ליץ *scorn*, as in *DCH*, IV, p. 544b)—Maurice A. Canney, 'The Hebrew מֵלִיץ', *AJSL* 40 (1923–24), pp. 135-37; Zorell, p. 394b; *HALOT*, II, p. 590a.

official—Tadeusz Penar, *Northwest Semitic Philology and the Hebrew Fragments of Ben Sira* (BibOr, 28; Rome: Biblical Institute Press, 1975), p. 30.

מֵלִיץ II *one who speaks freely* (cf. ליץ *talk freely*)—H. Neil Richardson, 'Some Notes on ליץ and its Derivatives', *VT* 5 (1955), pp. 163-79.

מְלִיצָה I *mocking poem*(cf. ליץ *scorn*)—BDB, p. 539b.

allusive expression, proverb—*HALOT*, II, p. 590a.

מְלִיצָה II *allusive saying* (cf. מלץ *slip*)—H. Neil Richardson, 'Some Notes on ליץ and its Derivatives', *VT* 5 (1955), pp. 163-79 (78).

epigram—Michael V. Fox, *Proverbs 1–9* (AB, 18A; New York: Doubleday, 2000), pp. 63-64.

(cf. ליץ *interpret*)—Giovanni Rinaldi, 'Alcuni termini ebraici relativi alla letteratura', *Bib* 40 (1959), pp. 267-89 (277-78); KB, p. 529b; *HALOT*, II, p. 590a.

מְלִיצָה III *sharp* or *obscure saying* (cf. לוץ *turn astray*, Arab. lâṣa *turn astray*)—Zorell, p. 441b.

מְלִיצָה IV *sweet saying* (cf. מלץ *be sweet*)—N.H. Tur-Sinai, פשוטו של מקרא, IV/1 (Jerusalem: Kiryath Sepher, 1967), p. 261; cf. Zorell, p. 441b.

מְלִיצָה V *trope, saying that puts things in different words* (cf. מֵלִיץ *interpreter*)—cf. Michael V. Fox, *Proverbs 1–9* (AB, 18A; New York: Doubleday, 2000), p. 64.

מלך I *be king*—H. Ringgren, K. Seybold and H.-J. Fabry, 'מֶלֶךְ *meleḵ*; מָלַךְ *mālaḵ*; מְלוּכָה *melûḵâ*; מַלְכוּת *malḵûṯ*; מַמְלָכָה *mamlāḵâ*; מַמְלָכוּת *mamlāḵûṯ*', *TDOT*, VIII (1997; orig. 1983–84), pp. 346-75.

מלך II *counsel* (cf. Aram.)—Godfrey Rolles Driver, 'Problems of the Hebrew Text and Language', in *Alttestamentliche Studien Friedrich Nötscher zum sechzigsten Geburtstage 19. Juli 1950 gewidmet* (BBB, 1; ed. Hubert Junker and Johannes Botterweck; Bonn: Hanstein, 1950), pp. 46-61 (50); James Barr, *Comparative Philology and the Text of the Old Testament* (Oxford: Oxford University Press, 1968), pp. 188-89.

מלך III *tear away, take possession* (cf. Aram.)—L. Kopf, 'Arabische Etymologien und Parallelen zum Bibelwörterbuch', *VT* 9 (1959), pp. 247-87 (261-62); James Barr, *Comparative Philology and the Text of the Old Testament* (Oxford: Oxford University Press, 1968), p. 188.

מלך IV *own* (cf. Arab. malaka)—H. Louis Ginsberg, *Studies in Koheleth* (New York: Jewish Theological Seminary of America, 1950), pp. 9-10, 13-14.

מֶלֶךְ *counsel* (cf. Aram.)—Joseph Reider, 'Etymological Studies in Biblical Hebrew', *VT* 4 (1954), pp. 276-95 (287-88).

מַלָּךְ *counsellor* (cf. Akk. mâlik)—W.F. Albright, 'Some Canaanite-Phoenician Sources of Hebrew Wisdom', in *Wisdom in Israel and in the Ancient Near East, Presented to Professor Harold Henry Rowley ... in Celebration of his Sixty-Fifth Birthday* (ed. M. Noth and D. Winton Thomas; VTSup, 3; Leiden: E.J. Brill, 1955), pp. 1-15 (15).

מֶלֶךְ *king*—Werner Vycichl, 'Le titre de roi des rois (*neguša nagašt*). Etude historique et comparative sur la monarchie en Ethiopie', *Annales d'Ethiope* 2 (1957), pp. 193-203; J.A. Soggin, 'מֶלֶךְ *melek*', *TLOT*, II (1997; orig. 1976), pp. 672-80; H. Ringgren, K. Seybold and H.-J. Fabry, 'מֶלֶךְ *meleḵ*; מָלַךְ *mālaḵ*; מְלוּכָה *melûḵâ*; מַלְכוּת *malḵûṯ*; מַמְלָכָה *mamlāḵâ*; מַמְלָכוּת *mamlāḵûṯ*', *TDOT*, VIII (1997; orig. 1983–84), pp. 346-75; Jean Carmignac, 'Roi, royauté et royaume, dans la liturgie angélique', *RQ* 12 (1986), pp. 177-86 (178-81); Anna Maria Schwemer, 'Gott als König und seine Königsherrschaft in den Sabbatliedern aus Qumran', in *Königsherrschaft Gottes und himmlischer Kult im Judentum, Urchristentum und in der hellenistischen Welt* (ed.

Martin Hengel and Anna Maria Schwemer; WUNT, 55; Tübingen: J.C.B. Mohr, 1991), pp. 45-118.

as a divine name—Marvin H. Pope, *El in the Ugaritic Texts* (VTSup, 2; Leiden: E.J. Brill, 1955), pp. 25-27; G. Rinaldi, 'Melek come nome proprio di divinità', *BeO* 6 (1964), p. 77; Tadeusz Penar, *Northwest Semitic Philology and the Hebrew Fragments of Ben Sira* (BibOr, 28; Rome: Biblical Institute Press, 1975), p. 63; Mitchell Dahood, 'Hebrew Lexicography: A Review of W. Baumgartner's *Lexikon*, Volume II', *Or* 45 (1976), pp. 327-65 (353); Jerzy Woniak, 'Ugaritic Parallel of Jahwe *melek 'ōlâm* ', *FolOr* 20 (1979), pp. 171-73.

מֶלֶךְ שָׂרִים *king of kings*—Shalom M. Paul, 'משא מלך שרים. Hosea 8:8-10 and Ancient Near Eastern Royal Epithets', in *Studies in Bible* (ed. Sara Japhet; Scr Hieros, 31; Jerusalem, 1986), pp. 193-204 (199-200).

בֶּן הַמֶּלֶךְ *king's son*—Manfred Görg, 'Zum Titel *BN HMLK* ("Königssohn")', *BN* 29 (1985), pp. 7-11.

Ps 45_2—Mitchell Dahood, 'Vocative *Lamedh* in the Psalter', *VT* 16 (1966), pp. 299-311 (306).

Ps 138_4—Mitchell J. Dahood, 'Ugaritic *DRKT* and Biblical *DEREK*', *TS* 15 (1954), pp. 627-31 (630).

Ec 1_{12}—*counsellor*—W.F. Albright, 'Some Canaanite-Phoenician Sources of Hebrew Wisdom', in *Wisdom in Israel and in the Ancient Near East, Presented to Professor Harold Henry Rowley ... in Celebration of his Sixty-Fifth Birthday* (ed. M. Noth and D. Winton Thomas; VTSup, 3; Leiden: E.J. Brill, 1955), pp. 1-15 (15).

מֹלֶךְ I H. Cazelles, 'Encore un texte sur mālik', *Bib* 88 (1957), pp. 485-87; H.-P. Müller, 'מֹלֶךְ *mōlek*', *TDOT*, VIII (1997; orig. 1983–84), pp. 375-88; G.C. Heider, *The Cult of Molek: A Reassessment* (JSOTSup 43; Sheffield: JSOT Press, 1985); John Day, *Molech: A God of Human Sacrifice in the Old Testament* (University of Cambridge Oriental Publications, 41; Cambridge: Cambridge University Press, 1989); George C. Heider, 'Molech', *ABD*, IV (1992), pp. 895-98; K.A.D. Smelik, 'Moloch, Molekh or Molk-Sacrifice? A Reassessment of the Evidence Concerning the Hebrew Term Molekh', *SJOT* 9 (1995), pp. 133-42 (141-42).

Molek, a deity to whom children were dedicated—M. Weinfeld, 'The Worship of Molech and of the Queen of Heaven and its Background', *UF* 4 (1972), pp. 135-54; M. Weinfeld, 'Moloch, Cult of', *EncJud*, XII, cols. 230-33.

molk, a type of sacrifice—Otto Eissfeldt, *Molk als Opferbegriff im Punischen und Hebräisch und das Ende des Gottes Moloch* (Beiträge der Religionsgeschichte des Altertums, 3; Halle: Niemeyer, 1935).

מֹלֶךְ II *kingdom* (cf. מלך *reign*)—W.F. Albright, 'The Oracles of Balaam', *JBL* 63 (1944), pp. 207-33 (218 n. 70); Mitchell Dahood, *Psalms III: 101–150* (AB, 17A; Garden City, NY: Doubleday, 1970), p. 267.

מֹלֶךְ III *counsellor* (cf. Akk. mâlik)—W.F. Albright, 'Some Canaanite-Phoenician Sources of Hebrew Wisdom', in *Wisdom in Israel and in the Ancient Near East, Presented to Professor Harold Henry Rowley ... in Celebration of his Sixty-Fifth Birthday* (ed. M. Noth and D. Winton Thomas; VTSup, 3; Leiden: E.J. Brill, 1955), pp. 1-15 (15).

מַלְכָּה *queen*—compared with גְּבִירָה *queen-mother*—C.H. Gordon, 'Ugaritic RBT/RAABÎTU', in *Ascribe to the Lord: Biblical and Other Studies in Memory of Peter C. Craigie* (ed. Lyle Eslinger and Glen Taylor; JSOT Sup, 67; Sheffield: JSOT Press, 1988), pp. 127-32.

מַלְכוּת *kingship*—Victor Maag, 'Malkūt Jhwh', *Congress Volume: Oxford, 1959* (VTSup, 7; Leiden: E.J. Brill, 1960), pp. 129-53; E. Lipiński, *La royauté de Jahwé dans la poésie et le culte de l'ancien Israël* (Brussels: Paleis der Academiën, 1965); H. Ringgren, K. Seybold and H.-J. Fabry, 'מֶלֶךְ *melek*; מָלַךְ *mālak*; מְלוּכָה *melûkâ*; מַלְכוּת *malkût*; מַמְלָכָה *mamlākâ*; מַמְלָכוּת *mamlākût*', *TDOT*, VIII (1997; orig. 1983–84), pp. 346-75; Jean Carmignac, 'Roi, royauté et royaume, dans la liturgie angélique', *RQ* 12 (1986), pp. 177-86 (181-82).

מַלְכִּי־צֶדֶק *Melchizedek*—H.E. Del Medico, 'Melchisédech', *ZAW* 69 (1957), pp. 160-70; Joseph A. Fitzmyer, '"Now This Melchizedek ..." (Heb 7,1)', *CBQ* 25 (1963), pp. 305-21 Rudolph Meyer, 'Melchizedek von Jerusalem und Moresedek von Qumran', in *Volume du Congrès: Genève 1965* (VT Sup, 15; Leiden: E.J. Brill, 1966), pp. 228-39; A.S. van der Woude, 'Melchisedek als himmlische Erlösergestalt in den neugefundenen eschatologischen Midraschim aus Qumran Höhle XI',

OTS 14 (1965), pp. 354-73.

מֹלֶכֶת *Hammolecheth*—BDB, p. 574b.

sister who rules—*HALOT*, II, p. 593b.

מלל II *speak*—G.R. Driver, 'Hebrew Poetic Diction', in *Congress Volume: Copenhagen 1953* (VTSup, 1; Leiden: E.J. Brill, 1953), pp. 26-39 (30).

מַלְמָד *goad*—Dalman, *Arbeit*, II, pp. 117-18.

מַלְקֵט *gleaning* (noun) (cf. לקט *glean*)—G.R. Driver, 'Hebrew Notes on Prophets and Psalms', *JTS* 41 (1940), pp. 162-75 (163).

מַלְקוֹשׁ *late rain*—Dalman, *Arbeit*, I, pp. 302-304; R.B.Y. Scott, 'Meteorological Phenomena and Terminology in the Old Testament', *ZAW* 64 (1952), pp. 11-25 (14-15, 23).

מֶלְתָּחָה *clothes store*—Chaim Rabin, 'Etymological Miscellanea', in *Studies in the Bible* (ed. Chaim Rabin; ScrHieros, 8; Jerusalem: Magnes Press, 1961), pp. 384-400 (391-92).

cloakroom (cf. Ug. m'lḫ)—Otto Eissfeldt, 'The Alphabetical Cuneiform Texts from Ras Shamra Published in "Le Palais royal d'Ugarit", Vol. II, 1957', *JSS* 6 (1960), pp. 1-49 (46); John Gray, *I & II Kings: A Commentary* (OTL; London: SCM Press, 3rd revised edn, 1977), p. 561.

מַלְתָּעוֹת *jawbone* (cf. Akk. latû *lacerate*)—G.R. Driver, 'Notes on Hebrew Lexicography', *JTS* 23 (1922), pp. 405-10 (407).

fangs, jaws—M. Dahood, 'The Etymology of *Malta'ot* (Ps 58,7)', *CBQ* 17 (1955), pp. 300-303; W.F. Albright, review of *Studia Orientalia Ioanni Pedersen Septuagenario ... Dicata* (1953), *JAOS* 76 (1956), pp. 233-36 (234); M. Dahood, 'Hebrew–Ugaritic Lexicography IV', *Bib* 47 (1966), pp. 403-19 (419); Mitchell Dahood, *Psalms II: 51–100* (AB, 17; Garden City, NY: Doubleday, 1968; 3rd edn, 1979), p. 61.

מַמְּגוּרָה *granary*—H.N. Richardson, 'Granary', *IDB*, II (1962), p. 469.

silo—Paul Haupt, 'Greek *sīrôs*, silo, and *sōros*, stack', *JBL* 40 (1921), pp. 170-72 (172).

Jl 1_{17}—Wilhelm Rudolph, 'Ein Beitrag zum hebräischen Lexikon aus dem Joelbuch', in *Hebräische Wortforschung: Festschrift zum 80. Geburtstag von Walter Baumgartner* (VTSup, 16; Leiden: E.J. Brill, 1967), pp. 244-50 (246-47).

מֵמַד *measurement*—H.-J. Fabry, 'מָדַד *māḏaḏ*; מִדָּה *middâ*; מַד *maḏ*; מֵמַד *memaḏ*', *TDOT*, VIII (1997; orig. 1983–84), pp. 118-34.

מָמוֹן *wealth*—Ps 2_8—Mitchell Dahood, *Psalms I: 1–50* (AB, 16; Garden City, NY: Doubleday, 1966), p. 12.

מָמוֹת *death, manner of death*—H. Ringgren, K.-J. Illman and H.-J. Fabry, 'מוּת *mûṯ*; מָוֶת *māweṯ*; תְּמוּתָה *temûṯâ*; מְמוֹתִים *memôṯîm*', *TDOT*, VIII (1997; orig. 1983–84), pp. 185-209.

מַמְזֵר *Ashdodite*—E. Nestle, 'Miscellen. 2. Der Mamzer aus Ashdod', *ZAW* 20 (1900), pp. 164-72 (166-67); Henri Cazelles, 'La mission d'Esdras', *VT* 4 (1954), pp. 113-40 (121).

half-caste—E. Neufeld, *Ancient Hebrew Marriage Laws, with Special Reference to General Semitic Laws and Customs* (London: Longmans, Green & Co. 1944), pp. 224-46; Karl Elliger, 'Ein Zeugnis aus der jüdischen Gemeinde im Alexanderjahr 332 v. Chr. Eine territorialgeschichtliche Studie zu Sach 9 1-8', *ZAW* 62 (1949–50), pp. 63-115 (81-82).

non-Judaean—Christoph Bultmann, *Der Fremde im antiken Juda: Eine Untersuchung zum sozialen Typenbegriff* »ger« *und seinem Bedeutungswandel in der alttestamentlichen Gesetzgebung* (FRLANT, 153; Göttingen: Vandenhoeck & Ruprecht, 1992), pp. 110-17.

מְמָךְ *sinkhole*, a name for Sheol (cf. Ug. mk *sink*)—M. Dahood, 'Hebrew–Ugaritic Lexicography V', *Bib* 48 (1967), pp. 421-38 (425-26).

מִמְכָּר *mortgaged property*—E. Lipiński, 'מכר *mkr*', *TDOT*, VIII (1997; orig. 1983–84), pp. 291-96 (296).

sale of sacrificial animals—Logan S. Wright, '*Mkr* in 2 Kings xii 5-17 and Deuteronomy xviii 8', *VT* 39 (1989), pp. 438-48.

מִמְכֶּרֶת *sale, transfer of possession*—E. Lipiński, 'מכר *mkr*', *TDOT*, VIII (1997; orig. 1983–84), pp. 291-96 (296).

מַמְלָכָה *kingdom*—H. Ringgren, K. Seybold and H.-J. Fabry, 'מֶלֶךְ *meleḵ*; מָלַךְ *mālaḵ*; מְלוּכָה *melûḵâ*; מַלְכוּת *malḵûṯ*; מַמְלָכָה *mamlāḵâ*; מַמְלָכוּת *mamlāḵûṯ*', *TDOT*, VIII (1997; orig. 1983–84), pp. 346-75; Jean Carmignac, 'Roi, royauté et royaume, dans la liturgie angélique', *RQ* 12

(1986), pp. 177-86 (182-83).

king—Zorell, p. 455a; W.F. Albright, 'A Catalogue of Early Hebrew Lyric Poems (Psalm lxviii)', *HUCA* 23:1 (1950–51), pp. 1-39 (34); O. Loretz, 'Neues Verständnis einiger Schriftstellen mit Hilfe des Ugaritischen', *BZ* 2 (1958), pp. 287-91 (290-91); M. Dahood, review of Bertil Albrektson, *Studies in the Text and Theology of the Book of Lamentations* (1963), *Bib* 44 (1963), pp. 547-49 (548); W.L. Moran, in *The Bible in Current Catholic Thought: Gruenthaner Memorial Volume* (ed. J.L. McKenzie; St Mary's Theological Studies, 1; New York, Herder & Herder, 1962), pp. 10-17 (12); M. Dahood, 'The Phoenician Background of Qoheleth', *Bib* 47 (1966), pp. 264-82 (268); M. Dahood, 'Hebrew–Ugaritic Lexicography IV', *Bib* 47 (1966), pp. 403-19 (419); Mitchell Dahood, 'Vocative *Lamedh* in the Psalter', *VT* 16 (1966), pp. 299-311 (306); Mitchell Dahood, *Psalms III: 101–150* (AB, 17A; Garden City, NY: Doubleday, 1970), pp. 20, 262.

מַמְלֶכֶת—H. Cazelles, '*Mamleket* et ses compléments en hébreu', *GLECS* 8 (1959), p. 57.

Lm 2_2—Mitchell Dahood, 'New Readings in Lamentations', *Bib* 59 (1978), pp. 174-97 (179).

מַמְלָכוּת *kingdom*—H. Ringgren, K. Seybold and H.-J. Fabry, 'מֶלֶךְ *meleḵ*; מָלַךְ *mālaḵ*; מְלוּכָה *m^{e}lûḵâ*; מַלְכוּת *malḵûṯ*; מַמְלָכָה *mamlāḵâ*; מַמְלָכוּת *mamlāḵûṯ*', *TDOT*, VIII (1997; orig. 1983–84), pp. 346-75.

מִמְסָךְ I *mixed wine* (cf. מסך *mix*)—E. Vogt, 'Einige hebräische Wortbedeutungen', *Bib* 48 (1967), pp. 57-74 ('III. Der Mischkrug im A.T. und der Vergleich in Hl 7,3', pp. 69-72); John Pairman Brown, 'The Mediterranean Vocabulary of the Vine', *VT* 19 (1969), pp. 146-70 (153-55); G.A. Rendsburg, *Linguistic Evidence for the Northern Origin of Selected Psalms* (SBLMS, 43; Atlanta: Scholars Press, 1990), pp. 77-78; Carey Ellen Walsh, *The Fruit of the Vine: Viticulture in Ancient Israel* (HSM, 60; Winona Lake, IN: Eisenbrauns, 2000), pp. 204-205.

מִמְסָךְ II *bowl, amphora* (cf. Ug. mmskn)—Paul Joüon, 'Notes de lexicographie hébraïque', *MUSJ* 4 (1911), pp. 1-18 (3); Zorell, p. 445a; Mitchell Dahood, *Proverbs and Northwest Semitic Philology* (Scripta Pontificii Instituti Biblici, 113; Rome: Pontificium Institutum Biblicum, 1963), p. 49; R.B.Y. Scott, *Proverbs. Ecclesiastes: A New Translation with Introduction and Commentary* (AB, 18; Garden City, NY: Doubleday, 1965), p. 142; M. Dahood, 'Ugaritic ušn, Job 12,10 and 11 Psa Plea 3-4', *Bib* 47 (1966), pp. 107-108; M. Dahood, 'The Phoenician Background of Qoheleth', *Bib* 47 (1966), pp. 264-82 (282); M. Dahood, 'Hebrew–Ugaritic Lexicography V', *Bib* 48 (1967), pp. 421-38 (426-27).

jug of mixed wine—*HALOT*, p. 595b.

מֶמֶר *bitterness*—H. Ringgren and H.-J. Fabry, 'מרר *mrr*; מַר *mar*; מֹרָה *mōrâ*; מָרוֹר *mārôr*; מְרִירוּת *m^{e}rîrûṯ*; מְרֵרָה *m^{e}rērâ*; מְרוֹרָה *m^{e}rôrâ*; מֶמֶר *memer*; מַמְרֹרִים *mamrōrîm*; תַּמְרוּרִים *tamrûrîm*', *TDOT*, IX (1998; orig. 1984–86), pp. 15-19.

מַמְרֹרִים *bitterness*—H. Ringgren and H.-J. Fabry, 'מרר *mrr*; מַר *mar*; מֹרָה *mōrâ*; מָרוֹר *mārôr*; מְרִירוּת *m^{e}rîrûṯ*; מְרֵרָה *m^{e}rērâ*; מְרוֹרָה *m^{e}rôrâ*; מֶמֶר *memer*; מַמְרֹרִים *mamrōrîm*; תַּמְרוּרִים *tamrûrîm*', *TDOT*, IX (1998; orig. 1984–86), pp. 15-19.

מִמְשַׁח I *anointing*—Knud Jeppesen, 'You Are a Cherub, but No God!', *SJOT* 5 (1991), pp. 83-94.

מִמְשַׁח II *extension* (cf. משח III *measure*)—Mitchell J. Dahood, 'Ugaritic Lexicography' [review of Joseph Aistleitner, *Wörterbuch der ugaritischen Sprache* (1963)], in *Mélanges Eugène Tisserant. I. Ecriture sainte—Ancien orient* (Studi e testi, 231; Città del Vaticano; Bibliotheca Apostolica Vaticana, 1964), pp. 81-104 (95); cf. BDB, p. 603b; *HALOT*, II, p. 596a.

מִמְשַׁח III *sparkling* (cf. mašāḫu *shine*)—H. Torczyner, 'Presidential Address', *JPOS* 16 (1935), pp. 1-8 (5); cf. *HALOT*, II, p. 596a.

מִמְשָׁל *dominion*—H. Gross, 'מָשַׁל *māšal* II; מֹשֶׁל *mōšel*; מִמְשָׁל *mimšāl*; מֶמְשָׁלָה *memšālâ*', *TDOT*, IX (1998; orig. 1984–86), pp. 68-71.

מֶמְשָׁלָה *dominion*—H. Gross, 'מָשַׁל *māšal* II; מֹשֶׁל *mōšel*; מִמְשָׁל *mimšāl*; מֶמְשָׁלָה *memšālâ*', *TDOT*, IX (1998; orig. 1984–86), pp. 68-71.

מִמְשָׁק II *place of possession* (cf. Arab. wasaqa *contain*)—Alfred Guillaume, *Hebrew and Arabic Lexicography: A Comparative Study*, IV (Leiden: E.J. Brill, 1965; = *AbrN* 4 [1963–64]), p. 9.

מָן *manna*—Alfred Kaiser, 'Neue Naturwissenschaftliche

Forschungen auf der Sinai-Halbinsel (besonders zur Mannafrage)', *ZDPV* 53 (1930), pp. 63-75; F.S. Bodenheimer, 'The Manna of Sinai', *BA* 10 (1947), pp. 2-6; P. Maiberger, 'מָן *mān*', *TDOT*, VIII (1997; orig. 1983–84), pp. 389-95.

with play on מָן *what?*—Gary A. Rendsburg, 'Word Play in Biblical Hebrew: An Eclectic Collection', in *Puns and Pundits: Word Play in the Bible and Near Eastern Literature* (ed. Scott B. Noegel; Bethesda, MD: CDL Press, 2000), pp. 137-62 (142-43).

as bread of the gods—Wolfram Herrmann, 'Götterspeise und Göttertrank in Ugarit und Israel', *ZAW* 72 (1960), pp. 205-16 (215-16).

מַן *how many?*—Mitchell Dahood, *Psalms I: 1–50* (AB, 16; Garden City, NY: Doubleday, 1966), p. 274.

מַן *whoever*—W.F. Albright, 'A Catalogue of Early Hebrew Lyric Poems (Psalm lxviii)', *HUCA* 23:1 (1950–51), pp. 1-39 (29, 38).

Ps 61_8—G.R. Driver, 'Abbreviations in the Massoretic Text', *Textus* 1 (1960), pp. 112-31 (125).

מֵן *string*—Ps 45_9—A. Caquot, 'Cinq observations sur le Psaume 45', in *Ascribe to the Lord: Biblical and Other Studies in Memory of Peter C. Craigie* (ed. Lyle Eslinger and Glen Taylor; JSOTSup, 67; Sheffield: JSOT Press, 1988), pp. 253-64 (257-58).

מִן *from*—Nahum M. Sarna, 'The Interchange of the Prepositions *Beth* and *Min* in Biblical Hebrew', *JBL* 78 (1959), pp. 310-16; Mitchell Dahood, *Psalms I: 1–50* (AB, 16; Garden City, NY: Doubleday, 1966), p. 106; M. Dahood, 'Hebrew–Ugaritic Lexicography V', *Bib* 48 (1967), pp. 421-38 (427); Georg Schmuttermayr, 'Ambivalenz und Aspektdifferenz: Bemerkungen zu den hebräischen Präpositionen ב, ל und מן', *BZ* 15 (1971), pp. 29-51; J.H. Hospers, 'Das Problem der sogenannten semantischen Polarität im Althebräischen', *ZAH* 1 (1988), pp. 32-39 (36-37).

away from—R.B Salters, 'Lamentations 1.3: Light from the History of Exegesis', in *A Word in Season: Essays in Honour of William McKane* (ed. James D. Martin and Philip R. Davies; JSOTSup, 42; Sheffield: JSOT Press, 1986), pp. 73-89 (77-79).

before—Massimo Baldacci, 'Osservazioni su un possibile valore di *min* nell'ebraico biblico', *BeO* 27 (1985), pp. 105-12.

from—Mitchell Dahood, *Psalms III: 101–150* (AB, 17A; Garden City, NY: Doubleday, 1970), pp. 395-96.

from and *without* in the same clause—G.R. Driver, 'Notes on the Psalms. II. 73–150', *JTS* 44 (1943), pp. 12-23 (20).

immediately after—David J.A. Clines, *Job 1–20* (WBC, 17; Dallas: Word Books, 1989), p. 72.

in—Mitchell Dahood, *Psalms I: 1–50* (AB, 16; Garden City, NY: Doubleday, 1966), p. 106; Mitchell Dahood, *Psalms II: 51–100* (AB, 17; Garden City, NY: Doubleday, 1968; 3rd edn, 1979), p. 148.

in from outside—Michael V. Fox, *The Song of Songs and the Ancient Egyptian Love Songs* (Madison, WI: University of Wisconsin Press, 1985), pp. 112, 144.

originating from—Ps 4_8—M. Mannati, 'Sur le sens de *min* en Ps iv 8', *VT* 20 (1970), pp. 361-66.

starting from—G.R. Driver, 'Problems in Judges Newly Discussed', *ALUOS* 4 (1962–63), pp. 6-25 (15-16).

without—Mitchell Dahood, 'New Readings in Lamentations', *Bib* 59 (1978), pp. 174-97 (182 n. 21); Mitchell Dahood, 'New Readings in Lamentations', *Bib* 59 (1978), pp. 174-97 (192-93); Mitchell Dahood, 'Northwest Semitic Notes on Genesis' [review of D.N. Freedman, 'Genesis', in *The New American Bible* (1970)], *Bib* 55 (1974), pp. 76-82 (79).

partitive really מִן of source or origin—Takamitsu Muraoka, 'Biblical Hebrew Philological Notes (2)', in *Studies in Semitic Linguistics in Honor of Joshua Blau* (= Jerusalem Studies in Arabic and Islam, 15 [1992]), pp. 43-54 (47-50).

מִמְּךָ *your offspring*—Mitchell Dahood, 'Hebrew Lexicography: A Review of W. Baumgartner's *Lexikon*, Volume II', *Or* 45 (1976), pp. 327-65 (353).

וָמָעְלָה *and upward*—Gershon Brin, 'The Formula "From ... and onward/upward" (מ... והלאה/ומעלה)', *JBL* 99 (1980), pp. 161-71.

מַנְגִּינָה *mocking song*—Giovanni Rinaldi, 'Alcuni termini ebraici relativi alla letteratura', *Bib* 40 (1959), pp. 267-89 (281-82).

Lm 3_{63}—Otto Rössler, 'Die Präfixkonjugation Qal der

Verba I^ae Nûn im Althebräischen und das Problem der sogenannten Tempora', *ZAW* 74 (1962), pp. 125-41 (128).

מְנָדָּה II *widespread* (cf. Arab. nada'a *widen, male spacious*)—A. Guillaume, 'Paronomasia in the Old Testament', *JSS* 9 (1964), pp. 282-90 (289-90).

מנה *count*—M. Dahood, 'Stichometry and Destiny in Ps 23,4', *Bib* 60 (1979), pp. 417-19; J. Conrad, 'מָנָה *mānâ*; מְנָת *m^e nāṯ*; מְנִי *m^e nî*', *TDOT*, VIII (1997; orig. 1983–84), pp. 396-401.

count money, be a merchant—Mitchell Dahood, *Psalms II: 51–100* (AB, 17; Garden City, NY: Doubleday, 1968; 3rd edn, 1979), p. 150.

pi. *apportion, ration*—S. Gevirtz, 'Asher in the Blessing of Jacob (Genesis xlix 20)', *VT* 37 (1987), pp. 154-63 (158-59).

Ps 61₈—Mitchell Dahood, *Psalms II: 51–100* (AB, 17; Garden City, NY: Doubleday, 1968; 3rd edn, 1979), p. 88.

מָנָה II *fate* (cf. Arab. manan)—J. Schirmann, 'דפים נוספים מתוך "בן־סירא" (Some Additional Leaves from Ecclesiasticus in Hebrew)', *Tarb* 29 (1959–60), pp. 125-34 (133); cf. *HALOT*, II, p. 599b.

מָנֶה *mina*—Maximilian Ellenbogen, *Foreign Words in the Old Testament: Their Origin and Etymology* (London: Luzac & Co. 1962), pp. 104-105.

מִנְהָרָה II *signal station* (cf. נהר II *shine*)—cf. George F. Moore, *A Critical and Exetical Commentary on Judges* (ICC; Edinburgh: T. & T. Clark, 1895, pp. 178, 180; J. Gray, *Joshua, Judges and Ruth* (NCB; London: Nelson, 1967), p. 295.

מָנוֹחַ II *Manoah*—Hermann Michael Niemann, *Die Daniten: Studien zur Geschichte eines altisraelitischen Stammes* (FRLANT, 135; Göttingen: Vandenhoeck & Ruprecht, 1985), pp. 152-75, 246 n. 120.

מְנוּחָה *resting place, home*—Jürgen Ebach, 'Über »Freiheit« und »Heimat«. Aspekte und Tendenzen der מְנוּחָה', in *Ernten, was man sät: Festschrift für Klaus Koch zu seinem 65. Geburtstag* (ed. Dwight R. Daniels, Uwe Glessmer and Martin Rösel; Neukirchen–Vluyn: Neukirchener Verlag, 1991), pp. 495-518.

royal seat—M. Metzger, 'Himmlische und irdische Wohnstatt Jahwes', *UF* 2 (1970), pp. 139-58 (157).

Gn 49₁₅—M. Dahood, 'Hebrew–Ugaritic Lexicography V', *Bib* 48 (1967), pp. 421-38 (427-28).

מָנוֹל *possession, property* (cf. Phoen. ינל, Arab. nāla *give*)—Mitchell Dahood, 'Northwest Semitic Philology and Job', in *The Bible in Current Catholic Thought: Gruenthaner Memorial Volume* (ed. J.L. McKenzie; St Mary's Theological Studies, 1; New York, Herder & Herder, 1962), pp. 55-74 (60-61); Zorell, p. 450a; *HALOT*, II, p. 600b; Lester L. Grabbe, *Comparative Philology and the Text of the Old Testament: A Study in Methodology* (SBLDS, 34; Missoula, MT, 1977), pp. 67-69; Mitchell Dahood, review of Lester L. Grabbe, *Comparative Philology and the Text of Job: A Study in Methodology* (1977), *Bib* 59 (1978), pp. 429-32 (429-30).

מָנוֹן I *arrogant, insolent*—*HALOT*, II, p. 600b.

disdainful (cf. Arab. mnn *recall* [a gift], *reproach* [a person for a gift])—G.R. Driver, 'Linguistic and Textual Problems: Ezekiel', *Bib* 19 (1938), pp. 60-69 (61); cf. BDB, p. 584b (dub.).

מָנוֹן II *weak, weakling* (cf. Ug. mnn *be weakened*)—Joseph Reider, 'Etymological Studies in Biblical Hebrew', *VT* 4 (1954), pp. 276-95 (285-86); Mitchell Dahood, *Ugaritic–Hebrew Philology: Marginal Notes on Recent Publications* (BibOr, 17: Rome: Pontifical Biblical Institute, 1965), p. 64.

מָנוֹן III *pained* (cf. אנן *complain*)—Alfred Guillaume, *Hebrew and Arabic Lexicography: A Comparative Study*, II (Leiden: E.J. Brill, 1965; = *AbrN* 2 [1960–61]), p. 22.

מָנוֹן *weak, weakling* (cf. Arab. mnn *be weak, make weak*)—Joseph Reider, 'Etymological Studies in Bilical Hebrew', *VT* 4 (1954), pp. 276-95 (285-86); D. Winton Thomas, in Derek Kidner, *The Proverbs: An Introduction and Commentary* (London: Tyndale Press, 1964), p. 176.

מָנוֹס *flight, refuge*—L. Delekat, 'Zum hebräischen Wörterbuch', *VT* 14 (1964), pp. 7-66 (28-31); J. Reindl, 'נוּס *nûs*; מָנוֹס *mānôs*; מְנוּסָה *m^e nûsâ*', *TDOT*, IX (1998; orig. 1984–86), pp. 286-93.

מְנוּסָה *flight*—J. Reindl, 'נוּס *nûs*; מָנוֹס *mānôs*; מְנוּסָה *m^e nûsâ*', *TDOT*, IX (1998; orig. 1984–86), pp. 286-93.

מָנוֹר *beam* of weaver—Dalman, *Arbeit*, V, pp. 112-13.

heddle-rod—Yigael Yadin, 'Goliath's Javelin and the מנור ארגים', *PEQ* 87 (1955), pp. 58-69; Kurt Galling, 'Goliath und seine Rüstung', in *Volume du Congrès: Genève 1965* (VTSup, 15; Leiden: E.J. Brill, 1966), pp. 150-69 (158-61).

מְנוֹרָה *lampstand*—Carol L. Meyers, *The Tabernacle Menorah: A Synthetic Study of a Symbol from the Biblical Cult* (ASOR Dissertation Series, 2; Missoula, MT: Scholars Press, 1976); C.L. Meyers and H.-J. Fabry, 'מְנוֹרָה *menôrâ*', *TDOT*, VIII (1997; orig. 1983–84), pp. 401-407; G. Rinaldi, '*menôrâ*, Ex 25,31', *BeO* 26 (1984), p. 204.

מִנְזָר I *consecrated one, prince* (cf. נזר *dedicate*)—BDB, p. 634a.

מִנְזָר II *guard* (cf. Akk. maṣṣāru)—Zorell, p. 449a.

מִנְזָר III *courtier* (cf. Akk. manzazu)—James Kennedy, *An Aid to the Textual Amendment of the Old Testament* (Edinburgh: T. & T. Clark, 1928), p. 72; H. Torczyner, 'A Hebrew Incantation against Night Demons from Biblical Times', *JNES* 6 (1947), pp. 18-29; *HALOT*, II, p. 601a; Kevin J. Cathcart, 'Micah 2:4 and Nahum 3:16-17 in the Light of Akkadian', in *Fucus: A Semitic/Afrasian Gathering in Remembrance of Albert Ehrman* (ed. Yoël L. Arbeitman; Amsterdam Studies in the Theory and History of Linguistic Science, IV/58; Amsterdam: J. Benjamin, 1988), pp. 191-200; Ann Jeffers, *Magic and Divination in Ancient Palestine and Syria* (Studies in the History and Culture of the Ancient Near East, 8; Leiden: E.J. Brill, 1996), pp. 110-11.

מִנְזָר IV *exorcist, conjuror* (cf. Akk. nazāru)—Paul Haupt, 'The Book of Nahum', *JBL* 26 (1907), p. 34.

מִנְחָה *offering*—M. Weinfeld and H.-J. Fabry, 'מִנְחָה *minḥâ*', *TDOT*, VIII (1997; orig. 1983–84), pp. 407-21; Gary A. Anderson, *Sacrifices and Offerings in Ancient Israel: Studies in their Social and Political Importance* (HSM, 41; Atlanta: Scholars Press, 1987), esp. pp. 27-34; Alfred Marx, *Les offrandes végétales dans l'Ancien Testament: Du tribut d'hommage au repas eschatologique* (VTSup, 57; Leiden: E.J. Brill, 1994), pp. 1-27; Jacob Milgrom, *Leviticus 1–16: A New Translation with Introduction and Commentary* (AB, 3; New York: Doubleday, 1991), pp. 196-201.

מִנְחָה *complaint* (cf. נוח II *sigh, wail*)—G.R. Driver, 'Studies in the Vocabulary of the Old Testament. VIII', *JTS* 36 (1935), pp. 293-301 (300).

מְנִי *Meni, Destiny*—BDB, p. 584b; *HALOT*, II, p. 602a; Mitchell Dahood, 'Stichometry and Destiny in Psalm 23,4', *Bib* 60 (1979), pp. 417-19 (418); J. Conrad, 'מָנָה *mānâ*; מְנָת *menāṭ*; מְנִי *menî*', *TDOT*, VIII (1997; orig. 1983–84), pp. 396-401.

מִנִּית II *rice* (cf. Tamil unṭi)—C. Rabin, 'Rice in the Bible', *JSS* 11 (1966), pp. 2-9; *HALOT*, II, p. 602b.

מנן hi. *be disdainful, ungrateful* (cf. מָנוֹן *disdainful*, Arab. mnn *recall* (a gift), *reproach* (a person for a gift)—G.R. Driver, 'Linguistic and Textual Problems: Ezekiel', *Bib* 19 (1938), pp. 60-69 (61).

מנע *withhold*—Menahem Zvi Kaddari, 'בלשון המקרא "מצא" תיאות תחבירי־סמאנטי של' (Syn–tac–tic Presentation of a Biblical Hebrew Verb *(mṣ')*', in *Studies in Hebrew and Semitic Languages Dedicated to the Memory of Prof. Eduard Yechezkel Kutscher* (ed. Gad B. Sarfatti, Pinḥas Artzi, Jonas C. Greenfield *et al.*; Ramat-Gan: Bar-Ilan University Press, 1980), pp. 18-25 [Heb]; H.-J. Fabry, 'מָנַע *māna*'', *TDOT*, VIII (1997; orig. 1983–84), pp. 421-27; Eliezer Rubinstein, 'עיון סמנטי בפעלי מניעה בלשון המקרא' (Verbs of Prevention: A Semantic Study in Biblical Hebrew)', in *Proceedings of the Tenth World Congress of Jewish Studies, Jerusalem, August 16-24, 1989*. Division D, Volume 1: *The Hebrew Language; Jewish Languages* (Jerusalem: World Union of Jewish Studies, 1990), pp. 1-6 [Heb].

מַנְעַמִּים *delicacies*—T. Kronholm, 'נעם נָעַם *nā'am*; נָעִים *nā'îm*; נֹעַם *nō'am*; מַנְעַמִּים *man'ammîm*; נַעֲמָנִים *na'ₐmānîm*', *TDOT*, IX (1998; orig. 1984–86), pp. 467-74; G.A. Rendsburg, *Linguistic Evidence for the Northern Origin of Selected Psalms* (SBLMS, 43; Atlanta: Scholars Press, 1990), p. 100.

מְנַעַנְעִים *sounding rattle*—Hans Seidel, *Musik im Altisrael: Untersuchungen zur Musikgeschichte und Musikpraxis Altisraels anhand biblischer und ausserbiblischer Texte* (BEATAJ, 12; Frankfurt a.M.: P. Lang, 1989), p. 76.

מְנַצֵּחַ *overseer*—G.W. Anderson, 'נֵצַח *neṣaḥ*; לַמְנַצֵּחַ *lamenaṣṣēaḥ*', *TDOT*, IX (1998; orig. 1984–86), pp. 529-33 (532-33).

מְנַקִּית *bowl*—BDB, p. 667b (s.v. מְנַקִּיָּה); Victor Avigdor

Hurowitz, 'Solomon's Golden Vessels (1 Kings 7:48-50) and the Cult of the First Temple', in *Pomegranates and Golden Bells: Studies in Biblical, Jewish, and Near Eastern Ritual, Law, and Literature in Honor of Jacob Milgrom* (ed. David P. Wright, David Noel Freedman and Avi Hurvitz; Winona Lake, IN: Eisenbrauns, 1995), pp. 151-64 (162-63).

vessel for libation—J.T. Milik, 'Le rouleau de cuivre provenant de la grotte 3Q (3Q15)', in *DJD*, III (1962), pp. 199-302 (253.143); *HALOT*, II, p. 603a.

מְנָת *portion*—J. Conrad, 'מָנָה *mānâ*; מְנָת *m^e nāṯ*; מְנִי *m^e nî*', *TDOT*, VIII (1997; orig. 1983–84), pp. 396-401.

מַס *levy, corvée*—A. Biram, 'מס עובד', *Tarb* 23 (1952), pp. 137-42; I. Mendelsohn, 'State Slavery in Ancient Palestine', *BASOR* 85 (1942), pp. 16-17; I. Mendelsohn, 'On Corvée Labor in Ancient Canaan and Israel', *BASOR* 167 (1962), pp. 31-35; A.F. Rainey, 'Compulsory Labour Gangs in Ancient Israel', *IEJ* 20 (1970), pp. 191-202; R. North, 'מַס *mas*; סֵבֶל *sēḇel*', *TDOT*, VIII (1997; orig. 1983–84), pp. 427-30.

מַס עֹבֵד *state slavery*—I. Mendelsohn, 'State Slavery in Ancient Palestine', *BASOR* 85 (1942), pp. 16-17; Menahem Haran, 'The Gibeonites, the Nethinim and the Sons of Solomon's Servants', *VT* 11 (1961), pp. 158-69 (163).

מַס עֹבֵד not *state slavery*—A. Biram, 'מס עבד', *Tarb* 23 (1952), p. 17; A.F. Rainey, 'Compulsory Labour Gangs in Ancient Israel', *IEJ* 20 (1970), pp. 191-202 (191).

subject to tribute—David Künstlinger, 'I. עֲדֵי עֹבֵד. II. לְמַס עֹבֵד', *OLZ* 34 (1931), cols. 611-12.

מֵסַב *round cushion*—M. Dahood, 'Love and Death at Ebla and their Biblical Reflections', in *Love and Death in the Ancient Near East: Essays in Honor of Marvin H. Pope* (ed. John H. Marks and Robert M. Good; Guilford, CT: Four Quarters Publishing, 1987), pp. 93-99 (96).

מְסִבָּה *staircase*—Johann Maier, *The Temple Scroll: An Introduction, Translation and Commentary* (JSOTSup, 34; Sheffield: JSOT Press, 1985), p. 87.

מַסְגֵּר I *smith, metalworker* (cf. סגר II *smelt*, Arab. sajara *roast*)—BDB, p. 689b (as = מַסְגֵּר II *prison*); *HALOT*, II, p. 604b.

מַסְגֵּר II *prison* (cf. סגר *shut*)—BDB, p. 689b (as = מַסְגֵּר I *smith*); *HALOT*, II, p. 604a.

as name for Sheol—M. Dahood, 'Hebrew–Ugaritic Lexicography V', *Bib* 48 (1967), pp. 421-38 (428); Mitchell Dahood, *Psalms III: 101–150* (AB, 17A; Garden City, NY: Doubleday, 1970), pp. 317, 319.

מַסְגֵּר III *women of the harem* (cf. Akk. sigrīte)—G.R. Driver, 'Linguistic and Textual Problems: Jeremiah', *JQR* 28 (1937–38), pp. 97-129 (116-18).

מִסְגֶּרֶת I *panel, rim; stronghold*—BDB, p. 689b; Zorell, p. 451b.

מִסְגֶּרֶת II *stronghold, prison*—cf. *HALOT*, II, p. 604: 'separate root (?)'.

מִסְדְּרוֹן *air-shaft* (cf. פַּרְשְׁדוֹן)—Fr. Delitzsch, apud L. Dürr, review of Otto Eissfeldt, *Die Quellen des Richterbuches* (1925), *OLZ* 29 (1926), cols. 643-46 (645).

armoury, equipping room (cf. Akk. sadāru, Arab. tašaḏḏara *(be) draw(n) up in military order*)—Chaim Rabin, 'Etymological Miscellanea', in *Studies in the Bible* (ed. Chaim Rabin; ScrHieros, 8; Jerusalem: Magnes Press, 1961), pp. 384-400 (393-94).

lavatory—O. Glaser, 'Zur Erzählung von Ehud und Eglon (Ri. 3, 14-26)', *ZDPV* 55 (1932), pp. 81-82.

porch, colonnade—BBD, p. 690b; Zorell, p. 451b; cf. *HALOT*, II, p. 604b.

מסה *melt*—H. Ringgren, 'מסס *mss*; מסה *msh*', *TDOT*, VIII (1997; orig. 1983–84), pp. 437-39.

with לֵב *heart*—B. Kedar-Kopfstein, 'Synästhesien im biblischen Althebräisch in Übersetzung und Auslegung', *ZAH* 1 (1988), pp. 47-60, 147-85 (156).

מַסָּה I *trial, testing*—F.J. Helfmeyer, 'נִסָּה *nissâ*; מַסּוֹת *massôṯ*; מַסָּה *massâ*', *TDOT*, IX (1998; orig. 1984–86), pp. 443-55.

מַסָּה II *Massa*—F.J. Helfmeyer, 'נִסָּה *nissâ*; מַסּוֹת *massôṯ*; מַסָּה *massâ*', *TDOT*, IX (1998; orig. 1984–86), pp. 443-55.

מִסָּה *measure*—*HALOT*, II, p. 604b.

proportion—Zorell, p. 451b.

sufficiency—BDB, p. 588a [s.v. מִסַּת].

מַסְוֶה *veil*—Fritz Dumermuth, 'Moses strahlendes Gesicht', *TZ* 17 (1961), pp. 241-48; Hugo Gressmann, *Mose und seine Zeit: Ein Kommentar zu den Mose-Sagen* (FRLANT, 18; Göttingen: Vandenhoek & Ruprecht, 1913), pp. 246-51; Georg Hoffmann and Hugo Gressmann,

'Teraphim. Masken und Winkorakel in Ägypten und Vorderasien', *ZAW* 40 (1922), pp. 75-137 (76-97); A. Jirku, 'Das Gesichtsmaske des Mose', *ZDPV* 67 (1944–45), pp. 43-45.

מַסָּה I *by turns*—*HALOT*, II, p. 605a.

מַסָּה II *detachment, relief body of troops* (cf. nisiḫtu *extract*, Arab. nasagha *substitute, replace*)—G.R. Driver, 'Studies in the Vocabulary of the Old Testament. VI', *JTS* 34 (1933), pp. 375-85 (376).

מסך I *mix (wine)*—Dalman, *Arbeit*, VI, p. 129; E. Vogt, 'Einige hebräische Wortbedeutungen', *Bib* 48 (1967), pp. 57-74 ('III. Der Mischkrug im A.T. und der Vergleich in Hl 7,3', pp. 69-72); John Pairman Brown, 'The Mediterranean Vocabulary of the Vine', *VT* 19 (1969), pp. 146-70 (153-55); G.A. Rendsburg, *Linguistic Evidence for the Northern Origin of Selected Psalms* (SBLMS, 43; Atlanta: Scholars Press, 1990), pp. 77-78; Carey Ellen Walsh, *The Fruit of the Vine: Viticulture in Ancient Israel* (HSM, 60; Winona Lake, IN: Eisenbrauns, 2000), pp. 204-205.

מסך II *draw, pour* (cf. Ug. msk)—Zorell, p. 452a; M. Dahood, 'Hebrew–Ugaritic Lexicography II', *Bib* 45 (1964), pp. 393-412 (408); M. Dahood, *Ugaritic–Hebrew Philology: Marginal Notes on Recent Publications* (BibOr, 17: Rome: Pontifical Biblical Institute, 1965), p. 64; M. Dahood, 'Hebrew–Ugaritic Lexicography V', *Bib* 48 (1967), pp. 421-38 (428); Mitchell Dahood, *Psalms II: 51–100* (AB, 17; Garden City, NY: Doubleday, 1968; 3rd edn, 1979), p. 214.

מֶסֶךְ I *mixed wine*—G.A. Rendsburg, *Linguistic Evidence for the Northern Origin of Selected Psalms* (SBLMS, 43; Atlanta: Scholars Press, 1990), pp. 77-78.

מֶסֶךְ II *bowl*—Mitchell J. Dahood, 'Ugaritic Lexicography' [review of Joseph Aistleitner, *Wörterbuch der ugaritischen Sprache* (1963)], in *Mélanges Eugène Tisserant. I. Ecriture sainte—Ancien orient* (Studi e testi, 231; Città del Vaticano; Bibliotheca Apostolica Vaticana, 1964), pp. 81-104 (95).

מַסֵּכָה I *forged metal* (cf. נסך *forge, cast metal*)—Oswald Loretz and Ingo Kottsieper, *Colometry in Ugaritic and Biblical Poetry: Introduction, Illustrations and Topical Bibliography* (Ugaritisch-Biblische Literatur, 5; Altenberge: CIS-Verlag, 1987), pp. 61-63.

image—C. Dohmen, 'מַסֵּכָה *massēḵâ*', *TDOT*, VIII (1997; orig. 1983–84), pp. 431-37; C. Dohmen, 'נָסַךְ *nāsak*; נֶסֶךְ *nesek*; נָסִיךְ *nāsîk*; מַסֵּכָה *massēḵâ*; מַסֶּכֶת *masseket*; סוּךְ II *sûk*; אָסוּךְ *'āsûk*', *TDOT*, IX (1998; orig. 1984–86), pp. 455-60.

image (as forged, not cast)—Christoph Dohmen, *Das Bilderverbot: Seine Entstehung und seine Entwicklung im Alten Testament* (BBB, 62; Bonn: Peter Hanstein, 1985), pp. 49-54.

image (as forged, perh. previously cast)—Silvia Schroer, *In Israel gab es Bilder: Nachrichten von darstellender Kunst im Alten Testament* (OBO, 74; Freiburg, Switzerland: Universitätsverlag, 1987), pp. 310-14.

מַסֵּכָה III *libation* (cf. נסך *pour*)—cf. BDB, p. 651a; *HALOT*, II, p. 605b [both conflate מַסֵּכָה I *image* and III *libation*].

libation to make an alliance—KB, p. 542a.

מִסְכֵּן *poor*—BDB, p. 587b.

(cf. Akk. muškênum)—E.A. Speiser, 'The *muškênum*', *Or* 27 (1958), pp. 19-28 (27); Maximilian Ellenbogen, *Foreign Words in the Old Testament: Their Origin and Etymology* (London: Luzac & Co. 1962), p. 108.

מְסַכֵּן I *steward, keeper* (cf. סכן *be of service*)—Joseph Reider, 'Etymological Studies in Biblical Hebrew', *VT* 2 (1952), pp. 113-30 (117-18).

מְסַכֵּן II *one who sets up* (cf. Ug. skn)—John Gray, *The Legacy of Canaan: The Ras Shamra Texts and their Relevance to the Old Testament* (VTSup, 5; Leiden: E.J. Brill, 1957), p. 192 (2nd edn, 1965, pp. 262-63).

מְסֻכָּן I *poor* (סכן III pu. ptc.)—BDB, p. 698b; Zorell, p. 554a; cf. *HALOT*, II, p. 606a.

Is 40_{20}—G.R. Driver, 'Linguistic and Textual Problems: Isaiah xl–lxvi', *JTS* 36 (1935), pp. 396-406 (396-98); Andrew Wilson, *The Nations in Deutero-Isaiah: A Study on Composition and Structure* (Lewiston, NY: Edwin Mellen Press, 1986), pp. 149-50.

Is 40_{20}—*connoisseur*—Paul Trudinger, '"To whom then will you liken God?" (A Note on the Interpretation of Isaiah xl 18-20)', *VT* 17 (1967), pp. 220-25.

מְסֻכָּן II *mulberry tree* or *wood* (cf. Akk. musukkānu)—Heinrich Zimmern, *Akkadische Fremdwörter als Beweis für babylonischen Kultureinfluss* (Leipzig: J.C. Hinrichs,

1915), p. 53; Wolfram von Soden, *Akkadisches Handwörterbuch*, II (Wisebaden: Otto Harrassowitz, 1972), p. 678a; G.R. Driver, 'Glosses in the Hebrew Text of the Old Testament', in *L'Ancien Testament et l'orient. Etudes présentées aux VIes Journées Bibliques de Louvain (11-13 septembre 1954)* (OBL, 1; Louvain-Leuven: Publications Universitaires / Instituut voor Orientalisme, 1957), pp. 123-61 (129); D. Winton Thomas, in *BHS*, p. 735; Maximilian Ellenbogen, *Foreign Words in the Old Testament: Their Origin and Etymology* (London: Luzac & Co., 1962), pp. 106-107.

palm—H. Zimmern, '*mesukkân* Jes. 40,20 = ass. *musukkânu* "Palme"', *ZA* 9 (1894), pp. 111-12.

מְסֻכָּן III *sisu tree* or *wood*, a costly Indian wood (cf. Hindi sīsū)—Ilya Gershevitch, 'Sissoo at Susa (OPers. *yakā-* = *Dalbergia sissoo* Roxb.)', *BSOAS* 19 (1957), pp. 317-20; A.R. Millard and I.R. Snook, 'Isaiah 40:20, Towards a Solution', *TyndB* 14 (1964), pp. 12-13; Harold R. (Chaim) Cohen, *Biblical Hapax Legomena in the Light of Akkadian and Ugaritic* (SBLDS, 37; Missoula, MT: Scholars Press, 1978), p. 133; Manfred Hutter, 'Jes 40,20—kulturgeschichtliche Notizen zu einer Crux', *BN* 36 (1987), pp. 31-36; H.G.M. Williamson, 'Isaiah 40,20—A Case of Not Seeing the Wood for the Trees', *Bib* 67 (1987), pp. 1-20.

מְסֻכָּן IV *thing formed* (cf. Ug. skn *make a statue, form*)—Tryggve N.D. Mettinger, 'The Elimination of a *Crux*? A Syntactic and Semantic Study of Isaiah xl 18-20', in *Studies on Prophecy* (VTSup, 26; Leiden: E.J. Brill, 1974), pp. 77-83.

מִסְכְּנוֹת II *forced labour* (cf. Akk. muškênum *state dependant*)—E.A. Speiser, 'The *muškênum*', *Or* 27 (1958), pp. 19-28 (27).

מִסְכְּנוֹת III *threshing places* (cf. Akk. maškānum)—E.A. Speiser, 'The *muškênum*', *Or* 27 (1958), pp. 19-28 (27 n. 3).

מַסֶּכֶת *warp*—Dalman, *Arbeit*, V, p. 101; L. Bellinger, 'Cloth', *IDB*, I (1962), pp. 650-55; C. Dohmen, 'נָסַךְ *nāsak*; נֶסֶךְ *nesek*; נָסִיךְ *nāsîk*; מַסֵּכָה *massēkâ*; מַסֶּכֶת *masseket*; סוּךְ II *sûk*; אָסוּךְ *'āsûk*', *TDOT*, IX (1998; orig. 1984–86), pp. 455-60.

מְסִלָּה II *high praise* (cf. סלל *cast up* causeway; *raise* a song; pilp. *extol*)—G.R. Driver, 'Textual and Linguistic Problems of the Book of Psalms', *HTR* 29 (1936), pp. 171-95 (187-88); Mitchell Dahood, *Psalms II: 51–100* (AB, 17; Garden City, NY: Doubleday, 1968; 3rd edn, 1979), p. 281; Godfrey Driver, 'Water in the Mountains!', *PEQ* 102 (1970), pp. 83-91 (87).

מְסִלָּה III *gatehouse, gateway* (cf. Akk. mušlālu)—David A. Dorsey, 'Another Peculiar Term in the Book of Chronicles: מְסִלָּה "Highway"?', *JQR* 75 (1984–85), pp. 385-91.

מַסְלוּל *causeway*—cf. Louis Keimer, 'Notes de lecture (suite)', *BIFAO* 56 (1957), pp. 97-120 (116-17).

מְסָמָא *sealingstone*—J.T. Milik, 'Le rouleau de cuivre provenant de la grotte 3Q (3Q15)', in *DJD*, III (1962), pp. 199-302 (243.63).

מַסְמֵר *nail*—Hans Wilhelm Hertzberg, 'Palästinische Bezüge im Buche Kohelet', in *Festschrift Friedrich Baumgärtel zum 70. Geburtstag, 14. Januar 1958, gewidmet von den Mitarbeitern am Kommentar zum Alten Testament (KAT)* (ed. Johannes Herrmann and Leonhard Rost; Erlanger Forschungen, 10; Erlangen: Universitätsbund Erlangen, 1959), pp. 63-73 (71).

sceptre—Kurt Galling, 'The Scepter of Wisdom: A Note on the Gold Sheath of Zendjirli and Ecclesiastes 12:11', *BASOR* 119 (1950), pp. 15-18 (17-18).

מסס *collapse*—G.R. Driver, 'Isaiah i–xxxix: Textual and Linguistic Problems', *JSS* 13 (1968), pp. 36-57 (41-42).

melt—H. Ringgren, 'מסס *mss; msh*', *TDOT*, VIII (1997; orig. 1983–84), pp. 437-39.

refine—J. Carmignac, 'Précisions apportées au vocabulaire de l'hébreu biblique par la Guerre des Fils de Lumière contre les Fils de Ténèbres', *VT* 5 (1955), pp. 345-65 (347).

with לֵב *heart*—B. Kedar-Kopfstein, 'Synästhesien im biblischen Althebräisch in Übersetzung und Auslegung', *ZAH* 1 (1988), pp. 47-60, 147-85 (156).

מַסַּע I *quarry, quarrying*—BDB, p. 652b; M.Z. Kaddari and H. Ringgren, 'נָסַע *nāsa'*; מַסַּע *massa'*; מַסָּע *massā'*', *TDOT*, IX (1998; orig. 1984–86), pp. 461-64.

quarried, i.e. undressed stones—KB, p. 543a; cf. *HALOT*, II, p. 607a;

מַסָּע II *missile, dart*—BDB, p. 652b; M.Z. Kaddari and H.

Ringgren, 'נָסַע *nāsa'*; מַסַּע *massa'*; מַסָּע *massā*'', *TDOT*, IX (1998; orig. 1984–86), pp. 461-64.

spear—Zorell, p. 453a.

weapon—*HALOT*, II, p. 607a.

Jb 40_{18}—N.H. Tur-Sinai, *The Book of Job* (Jerusalem: Kiryath Sepher, 1967), p. 573.

מַסַּע I *journey* (cf. נסע II *travel*)—cf. G.R. Driver, 'Supposed Arabisms in the Old Testament', *JBL* 55 (1936), pp. 101-20 (115); cf. Alfred Guillaume, *Hebrew and Arabic Lexicography: A Comparative Study*, I (Leiden: E.J. Brill, 1965; = *AbrN* 1 [1959–60]), pp. 11, 28-29.

journey; travel—BDB, p. 652b; Zorell, p. 453a; *HALOT*, II, p. 607a [all three conflate I and II]; M.Z. Kaddari and H. Ringgren, 'נָסַע *nāsa'*; מַסַּע *massa'*; מַסָּע *massā*'', *TDOT*, IX (1998; orig. 1984–86), pp. 461-64.

מַסַּע II *breaking* of camp (cf. נסע I *pull up, out*)—cf. Alfred Guillaume, *Hebrew and Arabic Lexicography: A Comparative Study*, I (Leiden: E.J. Brill, 1965; = *AbrN* 1 [1959–60]), pp. 28-29.

מִסְעָד I *bannister*—Zorell, p. 453a.

parapet—*HALOT*, II, p. 607a.

support—BDB, p. 708b.

unknown—Raphael Weiss, 'Textual Notes', *Textus* 6 (1968), pp. 127-31 (130).

מִסְעָד II *step* (cf. Arab. ṣa'ida *go up*)—Alfred Guillaume, *Hebrew and Arabic Lexicography: A Comparative Study*, III (Leiden: E.J. Brill, 1965; = *AbrN* 3 [1962–63]), pp. 5-6.

מִסְעָר *storm* (cf. סער *storm*)—Zorell, p. 453a.

מִסְפֵּד *mourning ritual*—Giovanni Rinaldi, 'Alcuni termini ebraici relativi alla letteratura', *Bib* 40 (1959), pp. 267-89 (278).

place of mourning—G.R. Driver, 'Linguistic and Textual Problems: Minor Prophets. II', *JTS* 39 (1938), pp. 260-73 (265).

מִסְפָּחָה *head covering*—*HALOT*, II, p. 607b,

veil, shawl—BDB, p. 705b; G.R. Driver, 'Linguistic and Textual Problems: Ezekiel', *Bib* 19 (1938), pp. 60-69 (63-64); KB, p. 543a.

מִסְפַּחַת *scab*—Jacob Milgrom, *Leviticus 1–16: A New Translation with Introduction and Commentary* (AB, 3; New York: Doubleday, 1991), p. 782.

מִסְפָּר I *number*—em. מִסַּפֵּר (inf.) *without numbering* or מִסֵּפֶר *without number* (סֵפֶר II *number*)—Pope, Job, 126; Mitchell Dahood, 'Hebrew Lexicography: A Review of W. Baumgartner's *Lexikon*, Volume II', *Or* 45 (1976), pp. 327-65 (354).

number; account—BDB, p. 708b; Zorell, p. 453b; *HALOT*, II, p. 607b [all conflate מִסְפָּר I and II].

Ps 147_5—Mitchell Dahood, *Psalms III: 101–150* (AB, 17A; Garden City, NY: Doubleday, 1970), p. 345.

מִסְפָּר II *account, narrative*—L. Kopf, 'Arabische Etymologien und Parallelen zum Bibelwörterbuch', *VT* 9 (1959), pp. 247-87 (268-69).

מִסְפָּר III *border* (cf. Aram סְפָר)—James Barr, *Comparative Philology and the Text of the Old Testament* (Oxford: Oxford University Press, 1968), p. 331.

מִסְפֶּרֶת *scholarship, learning*—*HALOT*, II, p. 608a.

מסר I *count*—Z. Ben-Ḥayyim, 'Traditions in the Hebrew Language, with Special Reference to the Dead Sea Scrolls', in *Aspects of the Dead Sea Scrolls* (ed. Chaim Rabin and Yigael Yadin; Scripta Hierosolymitana, 4; Jerusalem: Magnes Press, 1965), pp. 200-14 (211-13).

מסר IV *select*—*HALOT*, II, p. 608a.

מֹסָר *discipline*—BDB, p. 416 (s.v. מוּסָר); Zorell, p. 454a.

מִסְרָב *obstinacy* (cf. סָרַב *rebel*)—Wilhelm Rudolph, *Jeremia* (HAT, I/12; Tübingen: J.C.B. Mohr [Paul Siebeck], 1958), p. 84.

מְסָרֵף I *maternal uncle* (cf. association with דּוֹד *paternal uncle* in Am 6_{10})—G.R. Driver, 'Linguistic and Textual Problems: Minor Prophets. II', *JTS* 39 (1938), pp. 260-73 (263); G.R. Driver, 'A Hebrew Burial Custom', *ZAW* 66 (1955), pp. 314-15 (314).

מְסָרֵף II *one who burns incense* (cf. שׂרף *burn*)—BDB, p. 977a [s.v. שׂרף Pi.].

מְסָרֵף III *one who anoints the dead with spices* (cf. MH סְרָף *resin, aromatic spices*)—G.R. Driver, 'A Hebrew Burial Custom', *ZAW* 66 (1955), pp. 314-15; Eduard Yechezkel Kutscher, 'למילון המקראי' (Notes to the Biblcal Lexicon)', in *Hebrew and Aramaic Studies* (ed. Zeev Ben-Hayyim, Aharon Dotan and Gad Sarfatti; Jerusalem: Magnes Press, 1977), pp. 338-45 (342-46); S.M. Paul, *Amos: A Commentary on the Book of Amos* (Hermeneia; Minneapolis: Fortress Press, 1991), pp. 215-

16.

מַסֹּרֶת *collecting point* (= מַאֲסֹרֶת, from אסר *gather*)—G.R. Driver, review of A. Dupont-Sommer, *The Essene Writings from Qumran* (1961), *JTS* ns 13 (1962), pp. 367-71 (368).

מָסֹרֶת II *rule, tradition*—J. Carmignac, 'Précisions apportées au vocabulaire de l'hébreu biblique par la Guerre des Fils de Lumière contre les Fils de Ténèbres', *VT* 5 (1955), pp. 345-65 (350-51).

number, bond, tradition—Z. Ben-Ḥayyim, 'Traditions in the Hebrew Language, with Special Reference to the Dead Sea Scrolls', in *Aspects of the Dead Sea Scrolls* (ed. Chaim Rabin and Yigael Yadin; Scr Hieros, 4; Jerusalem: Magnes Press, 1965), pp. 200-14 (212).

מָסֹרֶת III *muster-roll*—Thomas, *Lexicon*, I (1970), p. 748.

מָסֹרֶת IV *division*—Yigael Yadin, *The Scroll of the War of the Sons of Light against the Sons of Darkness* (Oxford: Oxford University Press, 1962), pp. 40-41.

מָסֹרֶת V *command-post*—Thomas, *Lexicon*, I (1970), p. 749.

מֹסֵרֹת *Moseroth*—Yehuda T. Radday, 'Vom Humor in biblischen Ortsnamen', in *»Wünschet Jerusalem Frieden«. Collected Communications to the XIIth Congress of the International Organization for the Study of the Old Testament, Jerusalem 1986* (ed. Matthias Augustin and Klaus-Dietrich Schunck; BEATAJ, 13; Frankfurt a.M.: Peter Lang, 1988), pp. 431-46 (440).

מֹסֶרֶת *chastisement* (cf. יסר *discipline*)—G.R. Driver, 'Studies in the Vocabulary of the Old Testament. VIII', *JTS* 36 (1935), pp. 293-301 (297).

מַעֲבָד II *way* (cf. Arab. mu'abbadun *well-trodden path*)—Alfred Guillaume, *Studies in the Book of Job, with a New Translation* (Leiden: E.J. Brill, 1968), p. 120.

מַעֲבֶה *foundry*—J.T. Milik, 'Le rouleau de cuivre provenant de la grotte 3Q (3Q15)', in *DJD*, III (1962), pp. 199-302 (259.209); *HALOT*, II, p. 608b.

thickness, compactness—BDB, p. 716a.

thickness, depth of soil—John Gray, *I & II Kings: A Commentary* (OTL; London: SCM Press, 3rd revised edn, 1977), p. 199.

מַעֲבוֹ II *burning*—Alfred Guillaume, 'Isaiah's Oracle against Assyria (Isaiah 30, 27-33) in the Light of Archaeology', *BSOAS* 17 (1955), pp. 413-15.

מַעְגָּל I *track* (cf. עֲגָלָה *cart*, MH עגל pi. *roll*)—BDB, p. 722b; *HALOT*, II, p. 609; Moshe Held, 'Hebrew ma'gāl: A Study in Lexical Parallelism', *JANESCU* 6 (1974), pp. 107-16.

מַעְגָּל II *entrenchment*—BDB, p. 722b (s.v. מַעְגָּל I).

ring of waggons—*HALOT*, II, p. 609.

מַעְגָּל III *pasture*—Mitchell Dahood, *Psalms I: 1–50* (AB, 16; Garden City, NY: Doubleday, 1966), p. 146; M. Dahood, 'Hebrew–Ugaritic Lexicography V', *Bib* 48 (1967), pp. 421-38 (429); Mitchell Dahood, *Psalms II: 51–100* (AB, 17; Garden City, NY: Doubleday, 1968; 3rd edn, 1979), p. 116.

מעד *shake*—H. Ringgren, 'מָעַד *mā'aḏ*', *TDOT*, VIII (1997; orig. 1983–84), pp. 440-41.

מַעֲדָן I *delicacy*—S. Talmon, 'I Sam xv 32b—A Case of Conflated Readings?', *VT* 11 (1961), pp. 456-57.

מַעֲדָן II *bond*—BDB, p. 588b; Zorell, p. 454b; *HALOT*, II, p. 609b.

מַעֲדָן III *faltering*—S. Talmon, 'I Sam xv 32b—A Case of Conflated Readings?', *VT* 11 (1961), pp. 456-57.

מַעֲדָן IV *reluctant* (cf. Arab. 'anada *be resistant*)—KB, p. 544b; Alfred Guillaume, *Hebrew and Arabic Lexicography: A Comparative Study*, II (Leiden: E.J. Brill, 1965; = *AbrN* 2 [1960–61]), pp. 22-23.

מְעֻדָּנָה *Meuddanah*—Nahman Avigad, 'The King's Daughter and the Lyre', *IEJ* 28 (1978), pp. 146-51 (146-47); J.J. Stamm, 'Hebräische Frauennamen', in *Hebräische Wortforschung: Festschrift zum 80. Geburtstag von Walter Baumgartner* (VTSup, 16; Leiden: E.J. Brill, 1967), pp. 301-39 (313).

מַעֲדֶנֶת *company, chorus* of Pleiades (cf. Ug. 'dn *host*, Arab. 'adānatun *company*)—G.R. Driver, 'Two Astronomical Passages in the Old Testament', *JTS* ns 7 (1956), pp. 1-22 (2-4).

מַעְדֵּר *hoe*—BDB, p. 727b; KB 545a; Zorell, p. 454b; *HALAT*, II, p. 576b (not *plough*, as *HALOT*, II, p. 609b); J. Feliks, 'Agricultural Methods and Implements in Ancient Eretz Israel', *EncJud*, II (1971), col. 377.

מֵעֶה *gut, belly*—Frithiof Rundgren, 'Semitische Wortstudien', *OrSuec* 11 (1961), pp. 99-136 (121-27); H. Ringgren, 'מֵעִים *mē'îm*', *TDOT*, VIII (1997; orig. 1983–84), pp. 458-60.

Jb 3_{10}—Francis I. Andersen, *Job: An Introduction and Commentary* (London: Inter-Varsity Press, 1976), p. 105.

Lm 1_{20}—G.R. Driver, 'Hebrew Notes on "Song of Songs" and "Lamentations"', in *Festschrift Alfred Bertholet zum 80. Geburtstag gewidmet von Kollegen und Freunden* (ed. Walter Baumgartner [*et al.*]; Tübingen: J.C.B. Mohr, 1950), pp. 134-46 (137).

מָעָה I *coin*—A. Wolters, 'The Copper Scroll and the Vocabulary of Mishnaic Hebrew', *RQ* 14 (1990), pp. 483-95 (492).

מעה II *multitude* (cf. Arab. may'iyya company)—J. Gray, *The Legacy of Canaan* (VTSup 5; Leiden: E.J. Brill, 1957), p. 192 (2nd edn, 1965, p. 263).

מָעוֹג I *cake*—BDB, p. 728a.

circle—Ps 35_{16}—J.T. Milik, 'Deux documents inédits du désert de Juda', *Bib* 38 (1957), pp. 245-68 (255).

Ps 35_{16}—D. Winton Thomas, 'Psalm xxxv. 15f.', *JTS* ns 12 (1961), pp. 50-51.

מָעוֹג II *provisions*—*HALOT*, II, p. 610a.

מָעוֹג III *round silo*, thus provisions kept in a silo—J.T. Milik, 'Deux documents inédits du désert de Juda', *Bib* 38 (1957), pp. 245-68 (255 n. 2).

מָעוֹג IV *place to which one turns for provisions* (cf. Arab. ma'aj)—Ludwig Koehler, 'Alttestamentliche Wortforschung. Mā'ōg 1. Könige 17,12', *TZ* 6 (1950), pp. 472-73; KB, p. 545a; cf. *HALOT*, II, p. 610a.

מָעוֹג V *lame person* (cf. Arab. 'a'waj)—G.R. Driver, 'On Psalm 35:16', *TZ* 9 (1953), pp. 468-69.

מָעוֹז I *fortress* and *refuge*—H.-J. Zobel, 'מָעוֹז *mā'ôz*', *TDOT*, VIII (1997; orig. 1983–84), pp. 441-48.

refuge—Na 1.7—M. Dahood, review of Gillis Gerleman, *Das Hohelied* (1963), *Bib* 45 (1964), pp. 287-88 (288).

מָעוֹז II *stronghold, strength* (cf. עזז *be strong*).

מָעוֹזֵן *refuge* (cf. מָעוֹז)—*HALOT*, II, p. 610b.

מִעוּט *diminution*—Zorell, p. 455a.

מָעוֹן I *dwelling place*—H.D. Preuss, 'מָעוֹן *mā'ôn*; מְעֹנָה *m^{e}'ōnâ*', *TDOT*, VIII (1997; orig. 1983–84), pp. 449-52.

heavenly dwelling place—Mitchell Dahood, *Psalms II: 51–100* (AB, 17; Garden City, NY: Doubleday, 1968; 3rd edn, 1979), pp. 136-37.

Jr 7_{21}—Mitchell Dahood, 'Emphatic *Lamedh* in Jer 14:21 and Ezek 34:29', *CBQ* 37 (1975), pp. 341-42 (341).

Ps 8_{3}—Mitchell Dahood, *Psalms I: 1–50* (AB, 16; Garden City, NY: Doubleday, 1966), p. 50.

Ps 69_{19}—Mitchell Dahood, *Psalms II: 51–100* (AB, 17; Garden City, NY: Doubleday, 1968; 3rd edn, 1979), p. 161.

Ps 107_{41}—Mitchell Dahood, *Psalms III: 101–150* (AB, 17A; Garden City, NY: Doubleday, 1970), p. 90.

מָעוֹן II *help* (cf. Arab. 'âna *help*)—G.R. Driver, 'Supposed Arabisms in the Old Testament', *JBL* 55 (1936), pp. 101-20 (114-15); Zorell, p. 455a; L. Kopf, 'Arabische Etymologien und Parallelen zum Bibelwörterbuch', *VT* 8 (1958), pp. 161-215 (187-88); Mitchell Dahood, *Psalms II: 51–100* (AB, 17; Garden City, NY: Doubleday, 1968; 3rd edn, 1979), p. 172.

מָעוֹן III *reminder, occasion* of sin (cf. עָוֹן *sin*)—S.D. Goitein, 'Mā'ōn—A Reminder of Sin', *JSS* 10 (1965), pp. 52-53.

מְעוֹנָה *dwelling place*—H.D. Preuss, 'מָעוֹן *m ā'ôn*; מְעֹנָה *m^{e}'ōnâ*', *TDOT*, VIII (1997; orig. 1983–84), pp. 449-52.

מְעוֹנֵן *diviner by brontomancy* (cf. עָנָן *cloud*)—Victor Avigdor Hurowitz, review of Frederick H. Cryer, *Divination in Israel and its Near Estern Environment: A Socio-Historical Investigation* (1994), *JQR* 87 (1997), pp. 416-20 (418).

מַעֲזֵן *mart* (cf. Arab. 'az'ana *share, distribute*)—G.R. Driver, 'Isaiah i–xxxix: Textual and Linguistic Problems', *JSS* 13 (1968), pp. 36-57 (49).

מעט I *be few, small*—H.-J. Zobel, 'מָעַט *mā'aṭ*; מְעַט *m^{e}'aṭ*', *TDOT*, VIII (1997; orig. 1983–84), pp. 452-58.

מעט II *draw, stretch* (cf. Arab. m'ṭ *pluck, draw*)—G.R. Driver, 'Linguistic and Textual Problems: Ezekiel', *Bib* 19 (1938), pp. 60-69 (68).

מְעַט *a little*—מעט I *be few, small*—H.-J. Zobel, 'מָעַט *mā'aṭ*; מְעַט *m^{e}'aṭ*', *TDOT*, VIII (1997; orig. 1983–84), pp. 452-58; Gottfried Vanoni, 'Volkssprichwort und YHWH-Ethos: Beobachtungen zu Spr 15,16', *BN* 35 (1986), pp. 73-108 (81-82); Josef Wehrle, 'Zur syntaktisch-semantischen Funktion der PV [Präpositionalverbindung] *k·=m'aṭ* in Ijob 32,22', *BN* 55 (1990), pp. 77-95.

כִּמְעַט (rd. כִּי מְעַט *little indeed*, with emphatic כִּי)—Mitchell Dahood, 'Hebrew Lexicography: A Review of W. Baumgartner's *Lexikon*, Volume II', *Or* 45 (1976), pp. 327-65 (354).

מַעֲטֶפֶת *garment*—J. Schirmann, 'דפים נוספים מתוך "בן־סירא" (Some Additional Leaves from Ecclesiasticus in Hebrew)', *Tarb* 29 (1959–60), pp. 125-34 (130).

מְעִי *ruin*—Mitchell Dahood, 'Hebrew Lexicography: A Review of W. Baumgartner's *Lexikon*, Volume II', *Or* 45 (1976), pp. 327-65 (354-55).

מְעִיל *robe*—Dalman, *Arbeit*, V, pp. 228-31.

מַעְיָן *spring*—J.A. Emerton, '"Spring and Torrent" in Psalm lxxiv 15', in *Volume du Congrès: Genève 1965* (VTSup, 15; Leiden: E.J. Brill, 1966), pp. 122-33 (125-27).

מְעִינִי *Minaean*—Ernst Axel Knauf, 'Mu'näer und Mëuniter', *WO* 16 (1985), pp. 114-22.

מעל *be unfaithful*—R. Knierim, 'מעל *m'l* ', *TLOT*, II (1997; orig. 1976), pp. 680-82; H. Ringgren, 'מָעַל *mā'al*; מַעַל *ma'al*', *TDOT*, VIII (1997; orig. 1983–84), pp. 460-63.

commit sacrilege—Jacob Milgrom, *Leviticus 1–16: A New Translation with Introduction and Commentary* (AB, 3; New York: Doubleday, 1991), p. 320.

מַעַל *unfaithfulness*—H. Ringgren, 'מָעַל *mā'al*; מַעַל *ma'al*', *TDOT*, VIII (1997; orig. 1983–84), pp. 460-463.

sacrilege—Jacob Milgrom, *Leviticus 1–16: A New Translation with Introduction and Commentary* (AB, 3; New York: Doubleday, 1991), p. 320.

מַעֲלָה I *staircase*—J.T. Milik, 'Le rouleau de cuivre provenant de la grotte 3Q (3Q15)', in *DJD*, III (1962), pp. 199-302 (247.93).

step in a sun-clock—Is 38:8—James Barr, *Biblical Words for Time* (SBT, 33; London: SCM Press, 1962), p. 103 n. 3 (2nd edn, 1969, p. 108 n. 1).

מַעֲלָה II *extolment* (cf. עלה *go up*)—M. Dahood, review of J.A. Sanders, *Discoveries in the Judaean Desert of Jordan. IV. The Psalms Scroll of Qumrân Cave 11* (1965), *Bib* 47 (1966), pp. 141-44 (143); M. Dahood, 'Hebrew–Ugaritic Lexicography V', *Bib* 48 (1967), pp. 421-38 (429); Mitchell Dahood, *Psalms III: 101–150* (AB, 17A; Garden City, NY: Doubleday, 1970), p. 195.

מַעֲבָּה *stagnant pool*—G.R. Driver, 'Hebrew Notes on the "Wisdom of Jesus ben Sirach"', *JBL* 53 (1934), pp. 273-90 (284).

מַעֲמָסָה *stone weight used in sport*—Zorell, p. 458b; *HALOT*, II, p. 614a.

stone used as barricade—G.R. Driver, 'Old Problems Re-examined', *ZAW* 80 (1968), pp. 174-83 (180).

מַעֲנָה *furrow*—G.R. Driver, 'Old Problems Re-examined', *ZAW* 80 (1968), pp. 174-83 (174).

place for task (?), field for ploughing—BDB, p. 776a.

plough furrow, where plough is turned—Dalman, *Arbeit*, II, pp. 171-72; L. Delekat, 'Zum hebräischen Wörterbuch', *VT* 14 (1964), pp. 7-66 (38-39); *HALOT*, II, p. 615a.

מַעֲנֶה II *purpose* (cf. ענה III *be troubled*)—G.R. Driver, review of Mitchell Dahood, *Proverbs and Northwest Semitic Philology* (Scripta Pontificii Instituti Biblici, 113; Rome: Pontificium Institutum Biblicum, 1963), *JSS* 10 (1965), pp. 112-17 (113); KB, p. 549b; *HALOT*, II, p. 614b.

מַעֲצָד *axe* (cf. MH מַעֲצָד *small axe*, Ug. m'ṣd)—BDB, p. 781a; Gesenius–Buhl, p. 447b.

billhook—KB, p. 550a.

blacksmith's tool—*HALOT*, II, p. 615a.

מַעֲצָה *disobedience*—Godfrey Rolles Driver, 'Problems of the Hebrew Text and Language', in *Alttestamentliche Studien Friedrich Nötscher zum sechzigsten Geburtstage 19. Juli 1950 gewidmet* (BBB, 1; ed. Hubert Junker and Johannes Botterweck; Bonn: Hanstein, 1950), pp. 46-61 (54).

מַעֲקֶה *parapet*—Dalman, *Arbeit*, VII, pp. 82-83; Hans-Peter Müller, 'Die Wurzeln עיק, יעק und עוק', *VT* 21 (1971), pp. 556-64 (561-62).

מַעֲרָב II *merchandise* (cf. ערב IV *offer, deliver*)—G.R. Driver, 'Difficult Words in the Hebrew Prophets', in *Studies in Old Testament Prophecy Presented to Professor Theodore H. Robinson* (ed. H.H. Rowley; Edinburgh: T. & T. Clark, 1950), pp. 52-72 (64-65).

מַעֲרָבָה *west*—Zorell, p. 460a.

מַעֲרֶה I *bare place*—BDB, p. 789a.

glade, clearing—*HALOT*, II, p. 615b.

waste land (cf. Arab. ma'ir *bare soil*)—G.R. Driver, 'Isaiah i–xxxix: Textual and Linguistic Problems', *JSS* 13 (1968), pp. 36-57 (52); KB, p. 550b; *HALOT*, II, p. 616a.

מַעֲרֶה II *approaches, vicinity* (cf. Arab. 'rr *go back to*)—Godfrey Rolles Driver, 'Mistranslations in the Old Testament', *WO* 1 (1947–52), pp. 39-31 (30).

מְעָרָה II *cleared field* (cf. Arab. ma'ir)—*HALOT*, II, p. 616a.

מַעֲרָף *drop (of rain)*—Zorell, p. 460.

מַעֲשֶׂה I *deed*—Jb 33_{17}—Joseph Reider, 'Etymological Studies in Biblical Hebrew', *VT* 4 (1954), pp. 276-95 (291-93).

מַעֲשֶׂה II *covering; clouds* (cf. Arab. ghašiya *hide*)—G.R. Driver, review of Svend Holm-Nielsen, *Hodayoth: Psalms from Qumran* (1960), *JTS* ns 13 (1962), pp. 371-78 (374); G.R. Driver, 'Three Difficult Words in *Discipline* (iii. 3-4, vii. 5-6, 11)', *JSS* 2 (1957), pp. 247-50 (249).

covering—Is 59_{6}—Israel Eitan, 'A Contribution to Isaiah Exegesis (Notes and Short Studies in Biblical Philology)', *HUCA* 12–13 (1937–38), pp. 55-88 (83).

clouds—Joseph Reider, 'Etymological Studies in Biblical Hebrew', *VT* 4 (1954), pp. 276-95 (284).

מַעֲשֶׂה III *evening, evening feast* (cf. Arab. 'aša *sup*, 'ašîyu *evening*)—G.R. Driver, 'Old Problems Re-examined', *ZAW* 80 (1968), pp. 174-83 (177).

מַעֲשֶׂה IV *storehouse* (cf. עשׂה *gather, harvest*)—Mitchell Dahood, *Psalms III: 101–150* (AB, 17A; Garden City, NY: Doubleday, 1970), p. 39.

מַעֲשֵׂר *cultic offering* (cf. Ug. 'šr *prepare banquet, invite to banquet*)—Norberto Airoldi, 'La cosidetta "decima" israelitica antica', *Bib* 55 (1974), pp. 179-210.

libation (cf. Ug. 'šrt)—H. Cazelles, 'La dîme israélite et les textes de Ras Shamra', *VT* 1 (1951), pp. 131-34; James Barr, *Comparative Philology and the Text of the Old Testament* (Oxford: Oxford University Press, 1968), p. 333.

tithe—Gary A. Anderson, *Sacrifices and Offerings in Ancient Israel: Studies in their Social and Political Importance* (HSM, 41; Atlanta: Scholars Press, 1987), pp. 77-90.

not necessarily a tenth—Norberto Airoldi, 'La cosidetta "decima" israelitica antica', *Bib* 55 (1974) 179-210; H. Jagersma, 'The Tithes in the Old Testament', in *Remembering All the Way* (OTS, 21 Leiden: E.J. Brill, 1981), pp. 116-28; Joseph M. Baumgarten, 'The First and Second Tithes in the *Temple Scroll*', in *Biblical and Related Studies Presented to Samuel Iwry* (ed. Ann Kort and Scott Morschauser; Winona Lake, IN: Eisenbrauns, 1985), pp. 5-15; Joseph M. Baumgarten, 'On the Non-Literal Use of *ma'ăšēr/dekatē*', *JBL* 103 (1984), pp. 245-51.

מִפְאָר *glory* (cf. תִּפְאֶרֶת *beauty. glory*)—M. Dahood, review of J.A. Sanders, *Discoveries in the Judaean Desert of Jordan. IV. The Psalms Scroll of Qumrân Cave 11* (1965), *Bib* 47 (1966), pp. 141-44 (143); M. Dahood, 'Hebrew–Ugaritic Lexicography V', *Bib* 48 (1967), pp. 421-38 (430).

מִפְגָּע *target*—Jb 36_{32}—G.R. Driver, 'Problems in the Hebrew Text of Job', in *Wisdom in Israel and in the Ancient Near East, Presented to Professor Harold Henry Rowley ... in Celebration of his Sixty-Fifth Birthday* (VTSup, 3; Leiden: E.J. Brill, 1955), pp. 72-93 (90).

מַפָּח *breathing out*, i.e. *expiring*—BDB, p. 656a.

disappointment—Zorell, p. 461b.

heartache—*HALOT*, II, p. 617b.

מַפֻּחַ *bellows*—Dalman, *Arbeit*, IV, p. 24.

(cf. Sab. mnfḫt)—Edward Ullendorff, 'South Arabian Etymological Marginalia', *BSOAS* 15 (1953), pp. 157-59 (158).

Jr 6_{29}—G.R. Driver, 'Two Misunderstood Passages of the Old Testament', *JTS* ns 6 (1955), pp. 82-87 (85).

מֻפִּים II *defects* (in the scribe's archetype) (cf. Syr. maupyān *deficient*)—G.R. Driver, 'Glosses in the Hebrew Text of the Old Testament', in *L'Ancien Testament et l'orient. Etudes présentées aux VIes Journées Bibliques de Louvain (11-13 septembre 1954)* (OBL, 1; Louvain-Leuven: Publications Universitaires / Instituut voor Orientalisme, 1957), pp. 123-61 (156).

מֵפִיץ II *club, hammer* (cf. מַפֵּץ *hammer*)—Zorell, p. 462a.

מִפְלָג *course* of wood between stone in a wall—G.R. Driver, review of Svend Holm-Nielsen, *Hodayoth: Psalms from Qumran* (1960), *JTS* ns 13 (1962), pp. 371-78 (376-77).

separation—J. Carmignac, 'Précisions apportées au vocabulaire de l'hébreu biblique par la Guerre des Fils de Lumière contre les Fils de Ténèbres', *VT* 5 (1955), pp. 345-65 (364).

מִפְלַגָּה *division, family group*—Joel P. Weinberg, 'Die soziale Gruppe im Weltbild des Chronisten', *ZAW* 98 (1986), pp. 72-95 (77).

מִפְלָט *place of refuge*—L. Delekat, 'Zum hebräischen Wörterbuch', *VT* 14 (1964), pp. 7-66 (13-23).

Ps 55_{9}—Mitchell Dahood, *Psalms II: 51–100* (AB, 17;

Garden City, NY: Doubleday, 1968; 3rd edn, 1979), p. 33.

Ps 144$_2$—Mitchell Dahood, *Psalms III: 101–150* (AB, 17A; Garden City, NY: Doubleday, 1970), p. 329.

מִפְלֶצֶת *dreadful thing*—Silvia Schroer, *In Israel gab es Bilder: Nachrichten von darstellender Kunst im Alten Testament* (OBO, 74; Freiburg, Switzerland: Universitätsverlag, 1987), p. 38.

מִפְלָשׂ *floating, hovering* of a cloud—*HALOT*, II, p. 618a.

swaying, poising—BDB, p. 814a.

מִפְקָד *guard*—Joseph Garfinkel, 'הוראת המלה ׳מפקד׳ באוסטרקון תל עירא (The Meaning of the Word MPQD in the Tel 'Ira Ostracon)', *Lesh* 52 (1987), pp. 68-74.

farewell (cf. Akk. ana ili paqādu *commit to God*)—G.R. Driver, 'Hebrew Notes on the "Wisdom of Jesus ben Sirach"', *JBL* 53 (1934), pp. 273-90 (279).

roll-call, census—Itzhaq Beit-Arieh, 'A First Temple Period Census Document', *PEQ* 115 (1983), pp. 105-108.

מִפְרָץ II *wadi*—E. Täubler, *Biblische Studien: Die Epoche der Richter* (Tübingen: J.C.B. Mohr, 1958), pp. 117-19.

מִפְשָׂעָה *buttocks, place requiring a covering* (cf. Arab. fašagha *cover*)—Ludwig Koehler, 'Hebräische Vokabeln III', *ZAW* 58 (1940–41), pp. 228-34 (228).

stepping region of body, hip, buttocks (cf. פשׂע *step, march*)—BDB, p. 832b.

מַפְתֵּחַ *key*—Dalman, *Arbeit*, VII, pp. 53-54, 71-73; Victor Avigdor Hurowitz, 'Solomon's Golden Vessels (1 Kings 7:48-50) and the Cult of the First Temple', in *Pomegranates and Golden Bells: Studies in Biblical, Jewish, and Near Eastern Ritual, Law, and Literature in Honor of Jacob Milgrom* (ed. David P. Wright, David Noel Freedman and Avi Hurvitz; Winona Lake, IN: Eisenbrauns, 1995), pp. 151-64 (160).

מִפְתָּן *inner side of threshold*—Herbert Donner, 'Die Schwellenhüpfer: Beobachtungen zu Zephanja 1, 8f.', *JSS* 15 (1970), pp. 42-55; Wolfgang Zwickel, 'סף II und מפתן', *BN* 70 (1993), pp. 25-27.

podium for the image of a deity—Gillis Gerleman, *Zephanja textkritisch und literarisch untersucht* (Lund: C.W.K. Gleerup, 1942), pp. 7-9; KB, p. 210.

מֹץ *chaff*—Dalman, *Arbeit*, III, pp. 137-38; H. Ringgren, 'מֹץ *mōṣ*', *TDOT*, VIII (1997; orig. 1983–84), pp. 464-65.

מצא I *arrive*—Joshua Blau, 'Marginalia Semitica II', *IOS* 2 (1972), pp. 57-82 (67-72).

find—morphology—qal passive—David Noel Freedman, 'Notes on Genesis', *ZAW* 64 (1952), pp. 190-94 (191); M. Dahood, 'Qoheleth and Recent Discoveries', *Bib* 39 (1958), pp. 302-18 (314); Mitchell Dahood, 'The Phoenician Background of Qoheleth', *Bib* 47 (1966), pp. 264-82 (278); W. von Soden, 'Kleine Beiträge zum Ugaritischen und Hebräischen', in *Hebräische Wortforschung: Festschrift zum 80. Geburtstag von Walter Baumgartner* (VTSup, 16; Leiden: E.J. Brill, 1967), pp. 290-300.

find—G. Gerleman, 'מצא *mṣ*'', *TLOT*, II (1997; orig. 1976), pp. 682-84.; Anthony R. Ceresko, 'The Function of Antanaclasis (mṣ' "to find" || mṣ' "to reach, overtake, grasp"), in Hebrew Poetry, Especially in the Book of Qoheleth', *CBQ* 44 (1982), pp. 551-59; S. Wagner and H.-J. Fabry, 'מָצָא *māṣā*'', *TDOT*, VIII (1997; orig. 1983–84), pp. 465-83; Yitzhaq Tzadka, 'מצא אשה מצא טוב: A Semantic-Syntactic Analysis of מצא', *Lesh* 56 (1991–92), 353-60, V [Heb].

reach, overtake, seize—Mitchell Dahood, 'Northwest Semitic Philology and Job', in *The Bible in Current Catholic Thought: Gruenthaner Memorial Volume* (ed. J.L. McKenzie; St Mary's Theological Studies, 1; New York, Herder & Herder, 1962), pp. 55-74 (57); Mitchell Dahood, *Psalms I: 1–50* (AB, 16; Garden City, NY: Doubleday, 1966), p. 195; Mitchell Dahood, 'The Phoenician Background of Qoheleth', *Bib* 47 (1966), pp. 264-82 (277); Mitchell Dahood, *Psalms III: 101–150* (AB, 17A; Garden City, NY: Doubleday, 1970), p. 146; Dahood, "Northwest Semitic Texts', pp. 20, 22, 30.

ni. *be captured, seized*—Samuel Iwry, 'והנמצא—A Striking Reading in 1QIs[a]', *Textus* 5 (1966), pp. 35-43.

ni. ptc. *survivor, refugee*—Samuel Iwry, 'והנמצא—A Striking Reading in 1QIs[a]', *Textus* 5 (1966), pp. 35-43 (42).

מצא אַחֲרֵי *find fault with*—G.R. Driver, 'Problems and Solutions', *VT* 4 (1954), pp. 225-45 (230).

מָצוּא (qal pass. ptc.) *found*, i.e. *present* (cf. MH מָצוּי)—

G.R. Driver, 'Problems and Solutions', *VT* 4 (1954), pp. 225-45 (231).

Jr 15_{16}—G.R. Driver, 'Linguistic and Textual Problems: Jeremiah', *JQR* 28 (1937–38), pp. 97-129 (114).

Pr 19_{8}—Mitchell Dahood, 'Hebrew Lexicography: A Review of W. Baumgartner's *Lexikon*, Volume II', *Or* 45 (1976), pp. 327-65 (355).

מצא II *suffice* (cf. Akk. maṣu *be wide*, perh. Syr. mṣā *be able*)—G.R. Driver, 'Some Hebrew Roots and their Meanings', *JTS* 23 (1921–22), pp. 69-73 (72); C.F. Burney, [Note], *JTS* 23 (1921–22), p. 73.

מצא III *drain* (cf. מצה)—G.R. Driver, 'Linguistic and Textual Problems: Jeremiah', *JQR* 28 (1937–38), pp. 97-129 (107).

מַצָּב I *mound*—Zorell, p. 464a.

palisade, entrenchment—BDB, p. 663a.

post—J. Reindl, 'יצב/נצב *nṣb/yṣb*; נִצָּב *niṣṣāḇ*; נְצִיב *neṣîḇ*; מַצָּב *maṣṣāḇ*; מִ/מַצָּבָה *mi/maṣṣāḇâ*; מֻצָּב *muṣṣāḇ*', *TDOT*, IX (1998; orig. 1984–86), pp. 519-29 (525-26).

post, outpost (?)—KB, p. 554b.

מַצָּבָה *standing place*—J. Reindl, 'יצב/נצב *nṣb/yṣb*; נִצָּב *niṣṣāḇ*; נְצִיב *neṣîḇ*; מַצָּב *maṣṣāḇ*; מִ/מַצָּבָה *mi/maṣṣāḇâ*; מֻצָּב *muṣṣāḇ*', *TDOT*, IX (1998; orig. 1984–86), pp. 519-29 (526-27).

מַצֵּבָה *standing stone*—Carl F. Graesser, 'Standing Stones in Ancient Palestine', *BA* 35 (1972), pp. 34-63; Samuel Iwry, 'Maṣṣēbāh and bāmāh in 1Q Isaiah[A] 6 13', JBL 76 (1957), pp. 225-32; J. Gamberoni, 'מַצֵּבָה *maṣṣēḇâ*', *TDOT*, VIII (1997; orig. 1983–84), pp. 483-94.

in relation to בָּמָה—W.F. Albright, 'The High Place in Ancient Palestine', in *Volume du Congrès. Strasbourg 1956* (VTSup, 4; Leiden: E.J. Brill, 1956), pp. 242-58 (248, 251).

Is 6_{13}—G.R. Driver, 'Isaiah i–xxxix: Textual and Linguistic Problems', *JSS* 13 (1968), pp. 36-57 (38).

מְצָד *Masada*—*HALOT*, II, p. 621b.

stronghold—BDB, p. 844b; KB, p. 55a; K.-D. Schunck, 'מְצוּדָה *meṣûḏâ*; *מָצוֹד *māṣôḏ*; מְצוֹדָה *meṣôḏâ*; מְצָד *meṣāḏ*', *TDOT*, VIII (1997; orig. 1983–84), pp. 501-505.

Pr 12_{12}—G.R. Driver, 'Nachtrag, hauptsächlich nach Mitteilungen G.R. Drivers, Oxford, vom 7.2 und 23.3.1962', in Berend Gemser, *Sprüche Salomos* (HAT, I/16; Tübingen: J.C.B. Mohr [Paul Siebeck], 2nd edn, 1963), pp. 111-14 (112).

מצה *drain*—G.R. Driver, 'Linguistic and Textual Problems: Jeremiah', *JQR* 28 (1937–38), pp. 97-129 (107).

מַצָּה I *(festival of) Unleavened Bread*—Herbert Haag, 'Das Mazzenfest des Hiskia', in *Wort und Geschichte: Festschrift für Karl Elliger zum 70. Geburtstag* (ed. Hartmut Gese and Hans Peter Rüger; AOAT, 18; Kevelaer: Butzon & Bercker, 1973), pp. 87-94; Jörn Halbe, 'Erwägungen zu Ursprung und Wesen des Massotfestes', *ZAW* 87 (1975), pp. 324-46; Hans-Joachim Kraus, *Worship in Ancient Israel: A Cultic History of the Old Testament* (Oxford: Basil Blackwell, 1966), pp. 47-55; Eckhart Otto, *Das Mazzotfest im Gilgal* (BWANT, 107; Stuttgart: W. Kohlhammer, 1975); B.N. Wambacq, 'Les Maṣṣôt', *Bib* 61 (1980), pp. 31-54; D. Kellermann, 'מַצָּה *maṣṣâ*; מַצּוֹת *maṣṣôṯ*', *TDOT*, VIII (1997; orig. 1983–84), pp. 494-501.

נְחֹשֶׁת מֻצְהָב—מֻצְהָב *orichalc*—G.R. Driver, 'Babylonian and Hebrew Notes', *WO* 2 (1954–59), pp. 19-26 (24-25).

מָצוֹד I *net*—K.-D. Schunck, 'מְצוּדָה *meṣûḏâ*; *מָצוֹד *māṣôḏ*; מְצוֹדָה *meṣôḏâ*; מְצָד *meṣāḏ*', *TDOT*, VIII (1997; orig. 1983–84), pp. 501-505.

מָצוֹד II *stronghold*—Pr 12_{12}—G.R. Driver, 'Nachtrag, hauptsächlich nach Mitteilungen G.R. Drivers, Oxford, vom 7.2 und 23.3.1962', in Berend Gemser, *Sprüche Salomos* (HAT, I/16; Tübingen: J.C.B. Mohr [Paul Siebeck], 2nd edn, 1963), pp. 111-14 (112).

מָצוֹד *game* (cf. צַיִד)—Mitchell Dahood, 'Hebrew Lexicography: A Review of W. Baumgartner's *Lexikon*, Volume II', *Or* 45 (1976), pp. 327-65 (355).

מְצוֹדָה *net*—K.-D. Schunck, 'מְצוּדָה *meṣûḏâ*; *מָצוֹד *māṣôḏ*; מְצוֹדָה *meṣôḏâ*; מְצָד *meṣāḏ*', *TDOT*, VIII (1997; orig. 1983–84), pp. 501-505.

מְצוּדָה I *eyrie*—G.R. Driver, 'Job 39: 27-28: The *ky*-bird', *PEQ* 104 (1972), pp. 64-66 (66).

hiding place—K.-D. Schunck, 'מְצוּדָה *meṣûḏâ*; *מָצוֹד *māṣôḏ*; מְצוֹדָה *meṣôḏâ*; מְצָד *meṣāḏ*', *TDOT*, VIII (1997; orig. 1983–84), pp. 501-505.

מְצוּדָה III *steppe, place of wandering* (cf. צוד III *wander*, Ug. ṣd)—Mitchell Dahood, 'Ugaritic Studies and the Bible', *Greg* 43 (1962), pp. 55-79 (72); M. Dahood,

'Hebrew–Ugaritic Lexicography V', *Bib* 48 (1967), pp. 421-38 (430); Mitchell Dahood, *Psalms II: 51–100* (AB, 17; Garden City, NY: Doubleday, 1968; 3rd edn, 1979), p. 122.

מִצְוָה *commandment*—H. Ringgren and B. Levine, 'מִצְוָה *miṣwâ*', *TDOT*, VIII (1997; orig. 1983–84), pp. 505-14; Michael V. Fox, *Proverbs 1–9* (AB, 18A; New York: Doubleday, 2000), p. 108.

מְצוּלָה *depth*—H.-J. Fabry, 'מְצוּלָה *meṣûlâ*; מְצוֹלָה *meṣôlâ*; צוּלָה *ṣûlâ* II; צָלַל *ṣālal* II', *TDOT*, VIII (1997; orig. 1983–84), pp. 514-19.

depth, as term for underworld—Mitchell Dahood, *Psalms II: 51–100* (AB, 17; Garden City, NY: Doubleday, 1968; 3rd edn, 1979), p. 160.

מָצוֹר II *watchtower*—Giovanni Rinaldi, 'Note ebraiche', *Aeg* 34 (1954), pp. 35-62 (45-46).

מָצוֹר III *creature* (cf. צור *fashion*)—G.R. Driver, review of A. Dupont-Sommer, *The Essene Writings from Qumran* (1961), *JTS* ns 13 (1962), pp. 367-71 (368).

מָצוֹר IV *Egypt* (cf. מִצְרַיִם *Egypt*)—BDB, p. 596a; *HALOT*, II, p. 623b; P.J. Calderone, 'The Rivers of "Maṣor"', *Bib* 42 (1961), pp. 423-32; Charles Fontinoy, 'Les noms l'Egypte en hébreu et leur étymologie', *CdE* 64 (1989), pp. 90-97 (93).

מָצוֹר IV *Egypt*—BDB, p. 596a; KB, p. 557.

מָצוֹר VIII *whey*, i.e. glacier rivulets (cf. Arab. muḏāratu-llabani *whey*)—Harry Torczyner, *Die Bundeslade und die Anfänge der Religion Israels* (Berlin: Philo, 2nd edn, 1930), p. 67.

מְצוּרָה II *distress*—*HALOT*, II, p. 623b.

מצח *tread* (cf. Ug. mṣḫ)—Joseph Reider, 'Contributions to the Scriptural Text', *HUCA* 24 (1952–53), pp. 85-106 (101); James Barr, *Comparative Philology and the Text of the Old Testament* (Oxford: Oxford University Press, 1968), p. 330.

מִצְחָה *greaves*—Kurt Galling, 'Goliath und seine Rüstung', *Volume du Congrès: Genève 1965* (VTSup, 15; Leiden: E.J. Brill, 1966), pp. 150-69 (163-64).

מִצִּירוֹק I *spittle*—1QS 11_{21} =4QS^{j} 1_{9} 4QShir^{b} 28_{3}—Emile Puech, 'Note de lexicographie hébraïque qumrânienne (*m-ṣw/yrwq, mḥšbym, śwṭ*)', in *Solving Riddles and Untying Knots: Biblical, Epigraphic, and Semitic Studies in Honor of Jonas C. Greenfield* (ed. Ziony Zevit, Seymour Gitin and Michael Sokoloff; Winona Lake, IN: Eisenbrauns, 1995), pp. 181-89 (181).

מַצְלַחַת *success*—Zorell, p. 466a.

מְצָן *thicket, place of thorns, thornbrake* (cf. צֵן *thorn*)—Walter D. Michel, *Job in the Light of Northwest Semitic*, I (BibOr, 42; Rome: Biblical Institute Press, 1987), p. 111 (following M. Dahood).

מִצְפָּה *Mizpah*—Patrick M. Arnold, 'Mizpah', *ABD*, IV (1992), pp. 879-81.

מַצְפּוֹן *hiding place*—E. Dhorme, *A Commentary on the Book of Job* (trans. Harold Knight; Nashville: Thomas Nelson, 1984), p. 60.

מצץ *suck*—Ernst Würthwein, 'Erwägungen zu Psalm 73', in *Festschrift Alfred Bertholet zum 80. Geburtstag gewidmet von Kollegen und Freunden* (ed. Walter Baumgartner [*et al.*]; Tübingen: J.C.B. Mohr, 1950), pp. 532-49 (543 n. 3) (= *Wort und Existenz: Studien zum Alten Testament* [Göttingen: Vandenhoeck & Ruprecht, 1970], pp. 161-96 [172 n. 3]); Harold R. (Chaim) Cohen, *Biblical Hapax Legomena in the Light of Akkadian and Ugaritic* (SBLDS, 37; Missoula, MT: Scholars Press, 1978), pp. 87-89; Moshe Held, 'Marginal Notes to the Biblical Lexicon', in *Biblical and Related Studies Presented to Samuel Iwry* (ed. Ann Kort and Scott Morschauser; Winona Lake, IN: Eisenbrauns, 1985), pp. 93-103 (99-100).

מֵצַר *confinement*, as name for the underworld—Mitchell Dahood, *Psalms III: 101–150* (AB, 17A; Garden City, NY: Doubleday, 1970), p. 156.

מַצָּרָה I *watch*—*HALOT*, II, p. 624b.

מַצָּרָה II *guard-house* (cf. Akk. maṣṣartu)—G.R. Driver, 'Ezekiel: Linguistic and Textual Problems', *Bib* 35 (1954), pp. 145-59 (154).

מִצְרִי pr.n.m. *Mizri*—Robert Deutsch and Michael Heltzer, *New Epigraphic Evidence from the Biblical Period* (Tel Aviv–Jaffa: Archaeological Center Publication, 1995), pp. 92, 95.

מִצְרַיִם I*Egypt*—H. Ringgren and H.-J. Fabry, 'מִצְרַיִם *miṣrayim*', *TDOT*, VIII (1997; orig. 1983–84), pp. 519-30; Charles Fontinoy, 'Les noms l'Egypte en hébreu et leur étymologie', *CdE* 64 (1989), pp. 90-97 (93-97).

מִצְרַיִם II *Mizraim, Musri*—H. Winckler, *Alttestamentliche*

Untersuchungen (Leipzig: Pfeiffer, 1892), pp. 168-74; A.S. Kapelrud, 'Mizraim', IDB, III, p. 409.

not *Musri* but *Egypt*—H. Tadmor, 'Que and Muṣri', *IEJ* 11 (1961), pp. 143-50; Paul Garelli, 'Nouveau coup d'œil sur Muṣur', in *Hommages à André Dupont-Sommer* (ed. A. Caquot and M. Philonenko; Paris: Adrien-Maisonneuve, 1971), pp. 37-48; Nadav Na'aman, 'Looking for *KTK*', *WO* 9 (1977–78), pp. 220-39 (225 n. c); Mordechai Cogan and Hayim Tadmor, *II Kings: A New Translation with Introduction and Commentary* (AB, 11; New York: Doubleday, 1988), p. 82.

מִצְרִי *Musri*, see מִצְרַיִם II *Mizraim*.

מַק *musty smell*—KB, p. 558b.

rottenness—BDB, p. 597a; Zorell, p. 467b.

stench—*HALOT*, II, p. 625b; Alfred Guillaume, *Hebrew and Arabic Lexicography: A Comparative Study*, II (Leiden: E.J. Brill, 1965; = *AbrN* 2 [1960–61]), p. 23.

מַקֶּבֶת I *hammer*—BDB, p. 666b; KB, p. 558b; A.S. Kapelrud, 'מַקֶּבֶת *maqqeḇeṯ*; פַּטִּישׁ *paṭṭîš*; מַפֵּץ *mappēṣ*', *TDOT*, VIII (1997; orig. 1983–84), pp. 531-32; J. Scharbert, 'נָקַב *nāqaḇ*; נֶקֶב *neqeḇ*; נְקֵבָה *neqēḇâ*; מַקֶּבֶת *maqqeḇeṯ*', *TDOT*, IX (1998; orig. 1984–86), pp. 551-53.

hammer; excavation—Zorell, p. 467b; *HALOT*, II, p. 625b.

מַקֶּבֶת II *excavation*—BDB, p. 666b.

fissure—J.Gerald Janzen, 'Rivers in the Desert of Abraham and Sarah and Zion (Isaiah 51:1-3)', *HAR* 10 (1986), pp. 139-55 (145).

hole, mouth of cistern—KB, p. 559a.

hollow—A.S. Kapelrud, 'מַקֶּבֶת *maqqeḇeṯ*; פַּטִּישׁ *paṭṭîš*; מַפֵּץ *mappēṣ*', *TDOT*, VIII (1997; orig. 1983–84), pp. 531-32.

מִקְדָּה *immigrant trader* (cf. Syr. qaddī *traded profitably*)—Is 2_{6}—G.R. Driver, 'Isaiah i–xxxix: Textual and Linguistic Problems', *JSS* 13 (1968), pp. 36-57 (37).

מִקְדָּשׁ *sanctuary* (not *temple building*)—Jacob Milgrom, *Leviticus 1–16: A New Translation with Introduction and Commentary* (AB, 3; New York: Doubleday, 1991), pp. 754-55.

(heavenly) sanctuary—Mitchell Dahood, *Psalms II: 51–100* (AB, 17; Garden City, NY: Doubleday, 1968; 3rd edn, 1979), p. 152.

מקדש אדם *temple of humans*—Devorah Dimant, '*4Q Florilegium* and the Idea of the Community as Temple', in *Hellenica et Judaica: Hommage à Valentin Nikiprowetzky* (ed. A. Caquot, M. Hadas-Lebel and J. Riaud; Leuven : Peeters, 1986), pp. 165-89 (176-80).

מִקְדָּשׁ *holiest part*—Jacob Milgrom, *Leviticus 1–16: A New Translation with Introduction and Commentary* (AB, 3; New York: Doubleday, 1991), p. 1058.

מַקְהֵל *assembly, convocation*—Mitchell Dahood, *Psalms II: 51–100* (AB, 17; Garden City, NY: Doubleday, 1968; 3rd edn, 1979), p. 148.

Ps 68_{27}—W.F. Albright, 'A Catalogue of Early Hebrew Lyric Poems (Psalm lxviii)', *HUCA* 23:1 (1950–51), pp. 1-39 (30); Mitchell Dahood, *Ugaritic–Hebrew Philology: Marginal Notes on Recent Publications* (BibOr, 17: Rome: Pontifical Biblical Institute, 1965), p. 27; Thomas, *Lexicon*, I (1970), p. 243.

מַקְהֵלֹת *Makhelot* as play on קָהָל *tumult, rebellious assembly*)—Yehuda T. Radday, 'Vom Humor in biblischen Ortsnamen', in *»Wünschet Jerusalem Frieden«. Collected Communications to the XIIth Congress of the International Organization for the Study of the Old Testament, Jerusalem 1986* (ed. Matthias Augustin and Klaus-Dietrich Schunck; BEATAJ, 13; Frankfurt a.M.: Peter Lang, 1988), pp. 431-46 (437, 440).

מִקְוֶה I *hope*—BDB, p. 876a; *HALOT*, II, p. 626a; P.A.H. de Boer, 'Etude sur le sens de la racine *qwh*', *OTS* 10 (1954), pp. 225-46 (241).

מִקְוֶה II *collection, collected mass*—BDB, p. 876b; David Noel Freedman, 'Notes on Genesis', *ZAW* 64 (1952), pp. 190-94 (193); P.A.H. de Boer, 'Etude sur le sens de la racine *qwh*', *OTS* 10 (1954), pp. 225-46 (241).

collecting place—*HALOT*, II, p. 626b.

pool, as appellative for God—M. Dahood, 'Hebrew–Ugaritic Lexicography V', *Bib* 48 (1967), pp. 421-38 (430); Mitchell Dahood, 'Congruity of Metaphors', in *Hebräische Wortforschung: Festschrift zum 80. Geburtstag von Walter Baumgartner* (VTSup, 16; Leiden: E.J. Brill, 1967), pp. 40-49 (46); Mitchell Dahood, 'The Metaphor in Jeremiah 17,13', *Bib* 48 (1967), pp. 109-10.

Gn 1_{9}—William F. Albright, 'The Refrain «and God saw ki tôb»', in *Mélanges bibliques redigés en l'honneur de André Robert* (Travaux de l'Institut catholique de Paris, 4; Paris: Bloud & Gay, 1957), pp. 22-26 (24);

Mitchell Dahood, 'The Metaphor in Jeremiah 17,13', *Bib* 48 (1967), pp. 109-10 (109).

מִקְוֶה III *abode* (cf. Syr. qwā *remain*)—M. Wallenstein, 'Some Lexical Material in the Judean Scrolls', *VT* 4 (1954), pp. 211-24 (214); Zorell, p. 468a.

מָקוֹם *burial place, tomb* (Phoen. mqm)—M. Dahood, 'Northwest Semitic Philology and Job', in *The Bible in Current Catholic Thought: Gruenthaner Memorial Volume* (ed. J.L. McKenzie; St Mary's Theological Studies, 1; New York, Herder & Herder, 1962), pp. 55-74 (61-62); M. Dahood, review of J. Carmignac and P. Guilbert, *Les textes de Qumran traduits et annotés* (1961), *Bib* 44 (1963), pp. 231-33 (231); Marvin H. Pope, *Job: Introduction, Translation and Notes* (AB, 15; Garden City, NY: Doubleday, 3rd edn, 1973, pp. 117, 124; E. Lipiński, *La royauté de Yahvé dans la poésie et le culte de l'ancien Israël* (Brussels: Paleis der Academiën, 1965), p. 118 n. 2; Lester L. Grabbe, *Comparative Philology and the Text of the Old Testament: A Study in Methodology* (SBLDS, 34; Missoula, MT: Scholars Press, 1977), pp. 69-72; cf. James Barr, *Comparative Philology and the Text of the Old Testament* (Oxford: Oxford University Press, 1968), pp. 292, 334; Roger W. Cowley, 'Technical Terms in Biblical Hebrew?', *TynB* 37 (1986), pp. 21-28 (26-27).

estate, property, fief—William Johnstone, 'Old Testament Technical Expressions in Property Holding: Contributions from Ugarit', *Ugaritica* 6 (1969), pp. 309-17 (314-15).

home, abode—M. Dahood, 'Hebrew–Ugaritic Lexicography V', *Bib* 48 (1957), pp. 421-38 (431); Mitchell Dahood, *Psalms I: 1–50* (AB, 16; Garden City, NY: Doubleday, 1966), pp. 162, 228; Mitchell Dahood, *Psalms III: 101–150* (AB, 17A; Garden City, NY: Doubleday, 1970), p. 29.

place—J. Gamberoni and H. Ringgren, 'מָקוֹם *māqôm*', *TDOT*, VIII (1997; orig. 1983–84), pp. 532-44.

place (euphemism for Y.)—cf. Peter R. Ackroyd, 'Two Hebrew Notes', *ASTI* 5 (1966–67), pp. 82-86 (82-84).

plot of land—D.N. Premnath, 'Latifundialization and Isaiah 5.8-10', *JSOT* 40 (1988), pp. 49-60 (55).

sanctuary—A. Cowley, 'On The Meaning of מָקוֹם in Hebrew', *JTS* 17 (1916), pp. 174-76; Laurence E. Browne, 'A Jewish Sanctuary in Babylonia', *JTS* 17 (1916), pp. 400-401; E. Lipiński, *La royauté de Yahvé dans la poésie et le culte de l'ancien Israël* (Brussels: Paleis der Academiën, 1965), p. 118 n. 2; cf. Roger W. Cowley, 'Technical Terms in Biblical Hebrew?', *TynB* 37 (1986), pp. 21-28.

מָקוֹם *(in) place of, instead of*—G.R. Driver, 'Isaiah i–xxxix: Textual and Linguistic Problems', *JSS* 13 (1968), pp. 36-57 (53-54).

מָקוֹם אֶחָד *one place*, i.e. Sheol—Peter R. Ackroyd, 'Two Hebrew Notes', *ASTI* 5 (1966–67), pp. 82-86 (82-85).

מקום היד *latrine (?)*—G.R. Driver, review of E.L. Sukenik, *The Dead Sea Scrolls of the Hebrew University* (1955), *JTS* ns 8 (1957), pp. 141-43 (142).

מָקוֹם קָדוֹשׁ *tomb, burial place*—Mitchell Dahood, 'Qoheleth and Northwest Semitic Philology', *Bib* 43 (1962), pp. 349-65 (360).

Gn 1_{9}—David Noel Freedman, 'Notes on Genesis', *ZAW* 64 (1952), pp. 190-94 (193).

Jb 33_{22}—G.R. Driver, 'Once Again Abbreviations', *Textus* 4 (1965), pp. 76-94 (91).

מְקוֹמָה *opposition* (cf. Arab. maqāmat *resistance*)—G.R. Driver, 'Studies in the Vocabulary of the Old Testament. VIII', *JTS* 36 (1935), pp. 293-301 (300-301); G.R. Driver, 'Linguistic and Textual Problems: Minor Prophets. II', *JTS* 39 (1938), pp. 260-73 (269); cf. James Barr, *Comparative Philology and the Text of the Old Testament* (Oxford: Oxford University Press, 1968), p. 334.

מָקוֹר I *fountain*—H. Ringgren, 'מָקוֹר *māqôr*', *TDOT*, VIII (1997; orig. 1983–84), pp. 545-48.

Jr 18_{14}—W.F. Albright, 'A Catalogue of Early Hebrew Lyric Poems (Psalm lxviii)', *HUCA* 23:1 (1950–51), pp. 1-39 (23).

as appellative for God—M. Dahood, 'Hebrew–Ugaritic Lexicography V', *Bib* 48 (1967), pp. 421-38 (430).

מָקוֹר II *convocation* (cf. קור *call, invoke*, Ug. qr)—M. Dahood, 'Hebrew–Ugaritic Lexicography V', *Bib* 48 (1967), pp. 421-38 (431).

מִקְטָר *incense altar*—J. Brinktrine, 'Existierte im alttestamentlichen Schrifttum das Wort מִקְטָר?', *Bib* 33

(1952), pp. 90-94.

מִקְטָר *frankincense*—*HALOT*, II, p. 627b.

incense—Wolfgang Zwickel, *Räucherkult und Räuchergeräte: Exegetische und archäologische Studien zum Räucheropfer im Alten Testament* (OBO, 97; Freiburg, Switzerland: Universitätsverlag, 1990), pp. 310-11.

ho. ptc. of קטר *make sacrifice smoke*—Zorell, p. 721b; KB, p. 836b.

מִקְטֶרֶת *censer, cup, casket*—Wolfgang Zwickel, *Räucherkult und Räuchergeräte: Exegetische und archäologische Studien zum Räucheropfer im Alten Testament* (OBO, 97; Freiburg, Switzerland: Universitätsverlag, 1990), pp. 243-44.

offering of incense—J. Carmignac, 'Précisions apportées au vocabulaire de l'hébreu biblique par la Guerre des Fils de Lumière contre les Fils de Ténèbres', *VT* 5 (1955), pp. 345-65 (364).

מְקַטֶּרֶת *utensils for smoke-cult*—Wolfgang Zwickel, *Räucherkult und Räuchergeräte: Exegetische und archäologische Studien zum Räucheropfer im Alten Testament* (OBO, 97; Freiburg, Switzerland: Universitätsverlag, 1990), pp. 328-29.

מַקֵּל *penis*—H.L. Ginsberg, 'Lexicographical Notes', in *Hebräische Wortforschung: Festschrift zum 80. Geburtstag von Walter Baumgartner* (VTSup, 16; Leiden: E.J. Brill, 1967), pp. 71-82 (74-75).

rod—Sofia Cavalletti, 'La terminologia biblica per «bastone»', *Antonianum* 28 (1953), pp. 411-24 (411-13); G. André, 'מַקֵּל *maqqēl*', *TDOT*, VIII (1997; orig. 1983–84), pp. 548-51.

rod for divination—Friedrich Küchler, 'Das priesterliche Orakel in Israel und Juda', in *Wolf Wilhelm Grafen von Baudissin zum 26. September 1917 überreicht von Freunden und Schülern* (ed. Wilh. Frankenberg and Friedr. Küchler; Abhandlungen zur semitischen Religionskunde und Sprachwissenschaft; Giessen: A. Töpelmann, 1918), pp. 285-301 (292-93); Ann Jeffers, *Magic and Divination in Ancient Palestine and Syria* (Studies in the History and Culture of the Ancient Near East, 8; Leiden: E.J. Brill, 1996), pp. 188-89.

מִקְלָט *refuge*—H.H. Schmid, 'מִקְלָט *miqlāṭ*', *TDOT*, VIII (1997; orig. 1983–84), pp. 552-56.

מִקְמָשׁ *heap* (cf. קִמּוֹשׁ *thistles, nettles*)—G.R. Driver, 'Hebrew Notes on Prophets and Psalms', *JTS* 41 (1940), pp. 162-75 (173).

מִקְנֶה *goods* (not necessarily *cattle*)—G. Rinaldi, '*mqnh* (*miqneh*)', *BeO* 20 (1978), p. 60; John F.A. Sawyer, 'Cain and Hephaestus: Possible Relics of Metal-Working Traditions in Genesis 4', *AbrN* 24 (1986), pp. 155-66 (160).

מִקְצֹעַ *corner*, seen from inside—J.T. Milik, 'Le rouleau de cuivre provenant de la grotte 3Q (3Q15)', in *DJD*, III (1962), pp. 199-302 (239.11).

מַקְצֻעָה I *knife* for carving wood (cf. קצע I *scrape*)—*HALOT*, II, p. 628b.

scraping tool—BDB, p. 893a; Zorell, p. 469b; KB, p. 561b.

מַקְצֻעָה II *square* for working wood (cf. קצע II *make a corner*)—Silvia Schroer, *In Israel gab es Bilder: Nachrichten von darstellender Kunst im Alten Testament* (OBO, 74; Freiburg, Switzerland: Universitätsverlag, 1987), p. 218.

מקק *rot*—haphtil—Mitchell Dahood, 'Hebrew Lexicography: A Review of W. Baumgartner's *Lexikon*, Volume II', *Or* 45 (1976), pp. 327-65 (356).

Ps 44_{20}—Mitchell Dahood, *Psalms I: 1–50* (AB, 16; Garden City, NY: Doubleday, 1966), p. 267.

Ps 102_{6}—Mitchell Dahood, *Psalms III: 101–150* (AB, 17A; Garden City, NY: Doubleday, 1970), p. 12.

מִקְרָא *festival day*—Ernst Kutsch, 'מִקְרָא', *ZAW* 65 (1953), pp. 247-53.

מְקָרָה *living room* (cf. Arab. maqarrun)—L. Kopf, 'Arabische Etymologien und Parallelen zum Bibelwörterbuch', *VT* 8 (1958), pp. 161-215 (201).

מְקֵרָה *cool place, summer palace*—G.R. Driver, 'Problems in Judges Newly Discussed', *ALUOS* 4 (1962–63), pp. 6-25 (6).

מְקַרְקַר *echoing shout* (cf. Aram. קרקר *low*, Arab. qarqara *roar*)—G.R. Driver, 'Isaiah i–xxxix: Textual and Linguistic Problems', *JSS* 13 (1968), pp. 36-57 (47-48).

מִקְרָשׁ *frame* of a bed, perh. *chip* from its leg (cf. קֶרֶשׁ *board*)—G.R. Driver, 'Difficult Words in the Hebrew Prophets', in *Studies in Old Testament Prophecy Presented to Professor Theodore H. Robinson* (ed. H.H. Rowley; Edinburgh: T. & T. Clark, 1950), pp. 52-72

(69).

מִקְשֶׁה *locks of hair*—Dalman, *Arbeit*, V, p. 337.

מַר I *bitter*—H. Ringgren and H.-J. Fabry, 'מרר *mrr*; מַר *mar*; מֹרָה *mōrâ*; מָרוֹר *mārôr*; מְרִירוּת *m^{e}rîrûṯ*; מְרֵרָה *m^{e}rērâ*; מְרוֹרָה *m^{e}rôrâ*; מֶמֶר *memer*; מַמְרֹרִים *mamrōrîm*; תַּמְרוּרִים *tamrûrîm*', *TDOT*, IX (1998; orig. 1984–86), pp. 15-19; B. Kedar-Kopfstein, 'Synästhesien im biblischen Althebräisch in Übersetzung und Auslegung', *ZAH* 1 (1988), pp. 47-60, 147-85 (147, 154).

bitter (not *strong*)—Dennis Pardee, 'The Semitic Root *mrr* and the Etymology of Ugaritic *mr(r) // brk**', *UF* 10 (1978), pp. 249-88; Tikva Frymer-Kensky, 'The Strange Case of the Suspected Sotah (Numbers v 11-31)', *VT* 34 (1984), pp. 11-26 (25-26); Dennis Pardee, '*mārîm* in Numbers v', *VT* 35 (1985), pp. 112-15.

illness—Dennis Pardee, '*mārîm* in Numbers v', *VT* 35 (1985), pp. 112-15.

poisonous—Mitchell Dahood, *Psalms II: 51–100* (AB, 17; Garden City, NY: Doubleday, 1968; 3rd edn, 1979), p. 104.

מַר II *strong* (cf. Aram. מרר, Ug. Arab. mrr *be strong*)—Mitchell Dahood, 'Northwest Semitic Philology and Job', in *The Bible in Current Catholic Thought: Gruenthaner Memorial Volume* (ed. J.L. McKenzie; St Mary's Theological Studies, 1; New York, Herder & Herder, 1962), pp. 55-74 (59); Oswald Loretz, 'Weitere ugaritisch-hebräische Parallelen', *BZ* NF 3 (1959), pp. 290-94 (293); Walter D. Michel, *Job in the Light of Northwest Semitic*, I (BibOr, 42; Rome: Biblical Institute Press, 1987), p. 317; Svi Rin and Shifra Rin, 'Ugaritic–Old Testament Affinities II', *BZ* 10 (1957), pp. 174-92 (189); M. Dahood, 'Qoheleth and Recent Discoveries', *Bib* 39 (1958), pp. 302-18 (308-10); G.R. Driver, 'Ugaritic Problems', in *Studia Semitica Philologica necnon Philosophica Iohanni Bakoš Dicata* (ed. Stanislaus Segert; Bratislava, 1965), pp. 95-110 (102); Mitchell Dahood, 'The Phoenician Background of Qoheleth', *Bib* 47 (1966), pp. 264-82 (276); Mitchell Dahood, *Psalms III: 101–150* (AB, 17A; Garden City, NY: Doubleday, 1970), p. 21; Laurence Kutler, 'A "Strong" Case for Hebrew *mar*', *UF* 16 (1984), pp. 111-18.

מַר III *drop* (cf. Arab. marr *pass by, flow*)—BDB, p. 601b.

מַר IV *dust* (cf. Arab. mūr dust moving in the air)—D. Winton Thomas, 'A Drop of a Bucket? Some Observations on the Hebrew Text of Isaiah 40 $_{15}$', in *In Memoriam Paul Kahle* (ed. Matthew Black and Georg Fohrer; BZAW, 103; Berlin: A. Töpelmann, 1968), pp. 214-21 (219-21).

Pr 31$_{6}$—Mitchell Dahood, 'The Archaic Genitive Ending in Proverbs 31,6', *Bib* 56 (1975), p. 241.

מֹר I *myrrh*—G.R. Driver, 'Technical Terms in the Pentateuch', *WO* 2 (1954–59), pp. 254-63 (259-61); Gus W. van Beek, 'Frankincense and Myrrh', *BA* 23 (1960), pp. 69-95; J. Hausmann, 'מֹר *mōr*', *TDOT*, VIII (1997; orig. 1983–84), pp. 556-60; Kjeld Nielsen, *Incense in Ancient Israel* (VTSup, 38; Leiden: E.J. Brill, 1986), p. 61.

מָר־דְּרוֹר *myrrh of pearls*—G.R. Driver, 'Technical Terms in the Pentateuch', *WO* 2 (1954–59), pp. 254-63 (260).

מֹר II *foam* (cf. Arab. mwr *tossing of waves, dust raised by the wind*)—Joseph Reider, 'Etymological Studies in Biblical Hebrew', *VT* 2 (1952), pp. 113-30 (121).

מרא II *strike, beat* (cf. Arab. mry *be rebellious*)—*beat* the air with the wings—BDB, p. 597a; Gustav Hölscher, *Das Buch Hiob* (HAT, I/17; Tübingen: J.C.B. Mohr, 2nd edn, 1952), p. 92.

מרא III *graze, feed* (cf. Ug, mr' *become fat*, Akk. marū *fatten*)—Rudolf Kittel, 'Liber Isaiae', in *BH*^{3}, p. 624; D. Barthélemy, 'Le grand rouleau d'Isaïe trouvé près de la Mer Morte', *RB* 57 (150), pp. 530-49 (542); *HALOT*, II, p. 630a.

מרא IV *act the man* (cf. Arab. maru'a *be manly, affect manliness*)—G.R. Driver, 'Birds in the Old Testament. II. Birds in Life', *PEQ* 87 (1955), pp. 129-40 (138).

מַרְאָה *mirror*—J. Carmignac, 'Précisions apportées au vocabulaire de l'hébreu biblique par la Guerre des Fils de Lumière contre les Fils de Ténèbres', *VT* 5 (1955), pp. 345-65 (350); *HALOT*, II, p. 631a.

מַרְאָה *edict* (cf. Aram. מרא *command*, Ug. mr' *command*)—Mitchell Dahood, *Psalms I: 1–50* (AB, 16; Garden City, NY: Doubleday, 1966), pp. 123-24.

מֻרְאָה *crissum* (cf. MH רְאִי *excrement*)—Jacob Milgrom, *Leviticus 1–16: A New Translation with Introduction and Commentary* (AB, 3; New York: Doubleday, 1991), pp.

169-70.

crop, craw (cf. MH רֵאִי *crop)*—BDB, p. 597b; *HALOT*, II, p. 631a.

מְרַאֲשׁוֹת *head support*—*HALOT*, II, p. 631a.

מֵרַב *Merab*—Scott C. Layton, 'The Hebrew Personal Name Merab: Its Etymology and Meaning', *JSS* 38 (1993), pp. 193-207.

מַרְבֶּה *abundance*—Godfrey Rolles Driver, 'Problems of the Hebrew Text and Language', in *Alttestamentliche Studien Friedrich Nötscher zum sechzigsten Geburtstage 19. Juli 1950 gewidmet* (BBB, 1; ed. Hubert Junker and Johannes Botterweck; Bonn: Hanstein, 1950), pp. 46-61 (49).

מַרְבִּית *interest*, specifically on a loan of food—Samuel E. Loewenstamm, 'נשך and מ/תרברת', *JBL* 88 (1969), pp. 78-80.

מַרְגֵּמָה II *heap of stones*—J. de Fraine, 'מַרְגֵּמָה (Prov 26, 8)', in *Fourth World Congress of Jewish Studies*, I (Jerusalem: World Union of Jewish Studies, 1967), pp. 131-35.

מרד *rebel*—R. Knierim, 'מרד *mrd* ', *TLOT*, II (1997; orig. 1976), pp. 684-86; L. Schwienhorst, 'מָרַד *mārad*; מֶרֶד *mered*; מַרְדּוּת *mardût*', *TDOT*, IX (1998; orig. 1984–86), pp. 1-5.

מֶרֶד *rebellion*—L. Schwienhorst, 'מָרַד *mārad*; מֶרֶד *mered*; מַרְדּוּת *mardût*', *TDOT*, IX (1998; orig. 1984–86), pp. 1-5.

מַרְדּוּת I *rebelliousness*—L. Schwienhorst, 'מָרַד *mārad*; מֶרֶד *mered*; מַרְדּוּת *mardût*', *TDOT*, IX (1998; orig. 1984–86), pp. 1-5.

מַרְדּוּת II *discipline, education*—Zorell, p. 471b.

מִרְדָּף *pursuit*—J. Carmignac, 'Précisions apportées au vocabulaire de l'hébreu biblique par la Guerre des Fils de Lumière contre les Fils de Ténèbres', *VT* 5 (1955), pp. 345-65 (351); M. Dahood, 'Hebrew–Ugaritic Lexicography V', *Bib* 48 (1967), pp. 421-38 (432).

מרה I *be obstinate*—R. Knierim, 'מרה *mrh*', *TLOT*, II (1997; orig. 1976), pp. 687-88; L. Schwienhorst, 'מָרָה *mārâ*; מְרִי *merî*', *TDOT*, IX (1998; orig. 1984–86), pp. 5-10.

rebel—Ps 105_{28}—Mitchell Dahood, *Psalms II: 51–100* (AB, 17; Garden City, NY: Doubleday, 1968; 3rd edn, 1979), p. 60.

מרה III *feed, graze*—K. Koenen, 'Textkritische Anmerkungen zu schwierigen Stellen im Tritojesaja', *Bib* 69 (1988), pp. 564-73 (568-70).

מרה IV *be strong* (byform of מרר V *be strong*)—Mitchell Dahood, 'Proverbs 8,22-31: Translation and a Commentary', *CBQ* 30 (1958), pp. 512-21 (519); Mitchell Dahood, *Psalms III: 101–150* (AB, 17A; Garden City, NY: Doubleday, 1970), pp. 21-22.

מָרָה II *instruction, revelation* (cf. ירה *teach*)—Herbert Chanan Brichto, 'The Case of the *Śōṭā* and a Reconsideration of Biblical "Law"', *HUCA* 46 1975), pp. 55-70 (59).

מָרָה *disputed matter* (cf. מרר *rebel*, Arab. marā III *dispute*, miryatun *doubt*)—G.R. Driver, 'Two Problems in the Old Testament Examined in the Light of Assyriology', *Syr* 33 (1956), pp. 70-78 (73-74).

מֹרָה *bitterness*—H. Ringgren and H.-J. Fabry, 'מרר *mrr*; מַר *mar*; מֹרָה *mōrâ*; מָרוֹר *mārôr*; מְרִירוּת *merîrût*; מְרֵרָה *merērâ*; מְרוֹרָה *merôrâ*; מֶמֶר *memer*; מַמְרֹרִים *mamrōrîm*; תַּמְרוּרִים *tamrûrîm*', *TDOT*, IX (1998; orig. 1984–86), pp. 15-19.

מַרְהֵבָה *boisterous, raging behaviour*—BDB, p. 923b.

onslaught—P. Wernberg-Møller, 'The Contribution of the Hadayot to Biblical Textual Criticism', *Textus* 4 (1964), pp. 133-75 (146); *HALOT*, II p. 633a.

overbearingness—M. Dahood, 'Hebrew–Ugaritic Lexicography V', *Bib* 48 (1967), pp. 421-38 (432).

trouble—F. Nötscher, 'Entbehrliche Hapaxlegomena in Jesaia', *VT* 1 (1951), pp. 299-302 (300).

Is 14_4—Harry M. Orlinsky, '*Madhebah* in Isaiah xiv 4', *VT* 7 (1957), pp. 202-203.

מְרוֹ *violent man, oppressor* (with prosthetic aleph אֱמְרוֹ; cf. Arab. amr *man*)—Israel Eitan, *A Contribution to Biblical Lexicography* (Contributions to Oriental History and Philology, 10; New York: Columbia University Press, 1924), pp. 53-55.

מְרוֹגֶלֶת *clothing for legs*—J. Carmignac, 'Précisions apportées au vocabulaire de l'hébreu biblique par la Guerre des Fils de Lumière contre les Fils de Ténèbres', *VT* 5 (1955), pp. 345-65 (364).

מָרוֹם *height*, as divine title, *Exalted One*—Mitchell Dahood, *Psalms I: 1–50* (AB, 16; Garden City, NY: Doubleday,

1966), pp. xxxviii, 44-45, 63, 177; M. Dahood, 'Hebrew–Ugaritic Lexicography V', *Bib* 48 (1967), pp. 421-38 (432); L. Vigano, 'Il titolo divino *mrom: L'Eccelso*', *SBFLA* 24 (1974), pp. 186-201.

Jr 51$_{53}$—Mitchell Dahood, 'Hebrew Lexicography: A Review of W. Baumgartner's *Lexikon*, Volume II', *Or* 45 (1976), pp. 327-65 (357).

מַרְזֵחַ *feasting (?)*—O. Eissfeldt, 'Etymologische und archäologische Erklärung alttestamentlichen Wörter', *OrAnt* 5 (1966), pp. 165-76 (166-70) (= *Kleine Schriften*, IV [Tübingen: J.C.B. Mohr, 1968], pp. 285-96); O. Loretz, 'Ugaritisch-biblisch *mrzḥ* »Kultmahl, Kultverein« in Jer 16,5 und Am 6,7: Bemerkungen zur Geschichte des Totenkultes in Israel', in *Künder des Wortes: Beiträge zur Theologie der Propheten. Josef Schreiner zum 60. Geburtstag* (ed. Lothar Ruppert, Peter Weimar and Erich Zenger; Würzburg: Echter Verlag, 1982), pp. 87-94; H.-J. Fabry, 'מַרְזֵחַ *marzēaḥ*', *TDOT*, XI (1998; orig. 1984–86), pp. 10-15; Alessandro Catastini, 'Una nuova iscrizione fenicia e la "coppa di Yahweh"', in *Studi i onore di Edda Bresciani* (ed. S.F. Bondì, S. Pernigotti, F. Serra *et al.*; Pisa: Giardini, 1985), pp. 111-18; Philip J. King, 'The Marzeah Amos Denounces—Using Archaeology to Interpret a Biblical Text', *BAR* 14/4 (1988), pp. 34-44; Susan Ackerman, 'A *Marzēaḥ* in Ezekiel 8:7-13?", *HTR* 82 (1989), pp. 267-81; Philip J. King, 'The *marzēaḥ*: Textual and Archaeological Evidence', *EI* (1989) (Yigael Yadin Memorial Volume), pp. 98*-106*; Eleanor Ferris Beach, 'The Samaria Ivories, *Marzeaḥ*, and Biblical Text', *BA* 56 (1993), pp. 94-104; Frédéric Gangloff and Jean-Claude Haelewyck, 'Osée 4,17-19. Un marzeah en l'honneur de la déesse Anat?', *ETL* 71 (1995), pp. 370-82.

מרח *rub, spread on ointment* (cf. Eg. mrḫ.t *ointment*)—W.F. Albright, 'In Reply to Dr. Gaster's Observations', *BASOR* 93 (1944), pp. 23-25 (24); Thomas O. Lambdin, 'Egyptian Loanwords in the Old Testament', *JAOS* 73 (1953), pp. 145-55 (152).

מֶרְחָב *broad place*, as term for Sheol—Willibald Kuhnigk, *Nordwestsemitische Studien zum Hoseabuch* (BibOr, 27; Rome: Biblical Institute Press, 1974), pp. 50-53; Mitchell Dahood, *Psalms I: 1–50* (AB, 16; Garden City, NY: Doubleday, 1966), pp. 111, 189.

broad place, as term for Yahweh's heavenly dwelling—Mitchell Dahood, *Psalms III: 101–150* (AB, 17A; Garden City, NY: Doubleday, 1970), p. 156.

מַרְחֶשֶׁת *pan with lid*—A.M. Honeyman, 'The Pottery Vessels of the Old Testament', *PEQ* (1939), pp. 76-90 (84); Jacob Milgrom, *Leviticus 1–16: A New Translation with Introduction and Commentary* (AB, 3; New York: Doubleday, 1991), p. 185.

מָרִים *blessing* (cf. Ug. mrr *bless*)—J.M. Sasson, 'Numbers 5 and the "Waters of Judgement"', *BZ* NF 16 (1972), pp. 249-51.

מַרְיָם *desire* (cf. רום *desire*)—G.R. Driver, apud D. Winton Thomas, 'Notes on Some Passages in the Book of Proverbs', *JTS* 38 (1937), pp. 400-403 (403).

מְרֵרָה *act of violence* (cf. מרר *be strong*)—Mitchell Dahood, 'Northwest Semitic Philology and Job', in *The Bible in Current Catholic Thought: Gruenthaner Memorial Volume* (ed. J.L. McKenzie; St Mary's Theological Studies, 1; New York, Herder & Herder, 1962), pp. 55-74 (59-60); Anton C.M. Blommerde, *Northwest Semitic Grammar and Job* (BibOr, 22; Rome: Pontifical Biblical Institute, 1969), p. 69.

מְרִירוּת *bitterness*—H. Ringgren and H.-J. Fabry, 'מרר *mrr*; מַר *mar*; מֹרָה *mōrâ*; מָרוֹר *mārôr*; מְרִירוּת *m^{e}rîrûṯ*; מְרֵרָה *m^{e}rērâ*; מְרוֹרָה *m^{e}rôrâ*; מֶמֶר *memer*; מַמְרֹרִים *mamrōrîm*; תַּמְרוּרִים *tamrûrîm*', *TDOT*, IX (1998; orig. 1984–86), pp. 15-19.

מְרִירִי I *poisonous*—Walter D. Michel, *Job in the Light of Northwest Semitic*, I (BibOr, 42; Rome: Biblical Institute Press, 1987), pp. 47-50.

מְרִירִי II *demon* (cf. Arab. mara *pass by*)—Robert Gordis, 'The Asseverative Kaph in Ugaritic and Hebrew', *JAOS* 63 (1943), pp. 176-78 (177-78); Robert Gordis, *The Book of Job* (New York: Jewish Theological Seminary, 1978), p. 33.

מְרִירִי III *mighty* (cf. מרר IV *be strong*)—Laurence Kutler, 'A "Strong" Case for Hebrew *mar*', *UF* 16 (1984), pp. 111-18.

מֶרְכָּב *means for riding*—Jacob Milgrom, *Leviticus 1–16: A New Translation with Introduction and Commentary* (AB,

3; New York: Doubleday, 1991), p. 916.

war-chariot depot—*HALOT*, II, p. 636a.

מֶרְכָּבָה *chariot*—Ca 6₁₂—Michael V. Fox, *The Song of Songs and the Ancient Egyptian Love Songs* (Madison, WI: University of Wisconsin Press, 1985), pp. 154, 156.

מַרְכֹּלֶת *market-place*—BDB, p. 940b.

trading—*HALOT*, II, p. 636b.

מִרְמָה I *disillusionment*—*HALOT*, II, p. 636b.

image, figurine—Mitchell Dahood, *Psalms I: 1–50* (AB, 16; Garden City, NY: Doubleday, 1966), pp. 32, 151; M. Dahood, 'Hebrew–Ugaritic Lexicography V', *Bib* 48 (1967), pp. 421-38 (433); Mitchell Dahood, *Psalms II: 51–100* (AB, 17; Garden City, NY: Doubleday, 1968; 3rd edn, 1979), p. 39.

slander—Alfred Guillaume, 'Magical Terms in the Old Testament', *JRAS* 69 (1942), pp. 111-31 (120); G.R. Driver, 'Three Difficult Words in *Discipline* (iii. 3-4, vii. 5-6, 11)', *JSS* 2 (1957), pp. 247-50 (248-49).

מַרְעֶה *pasturage supervisor* (cf. מִרְעֶה *pasture*, Akk. merḫum *pasturage supervisor*)—Jonathan D. Safran, 'Ahuzzath and the Pact of Beer-Sheba', *ZAW* 101 (1989), pp. 184-98 (191-98).

מַרְפֵּה *relaxation, remission*—G.R. Driver, review of Svend Holm-Nielsen, *Hodayoth: Psalms from Qumran* (1960), *JTS* ns 13 (1962), pp. 371-78 (373).

מרץ II *be forceful, difficult* (cf. Akk. marāṣu *be difficult, inaccessible*)—N.S. Doniach, 'Job vi 25. √ מרץ', *JTS* 31 (1929–30), p. 291.

be bitter (cf. Akk. marāṣu *be ill, displeasing*)—G.R. Driver, 'Some Hebrew Words', *JTS* 29 (1927–28), pp. 390-96 (394-95).

be strong, force, compel (by *addad*)—Robert Gordis, *The Book of Job* (New York: Jewish Theological Seminary, 1978), p. 76.

מרץ III *be victorious* (cf. Arab. maraḍa *be in the right*)—W. Emery Barnes, 'Job vi 25. √ מרץ', *JTS* 31 (1929–30), pp. 291-92.

מַרְצֵעַ *awl*—Dalman, *Arbeit*, V, pp. 197, 286.

מַרְצֶפֶת *pavement*—BDB, p. 954a; Zorell, p. 475b; KB, p. 568b.

plastered stone, plastered floor—*HALOT*, II, p. 638a.

מֶרְקַחַת *bowl for ointment, perfume or mixed wine*—A.M. Honeyman, 'The Pottery Vessels of the Old Testament', *PEQ* (1939), pp. 76-90 (84).

מרר I *be bitter*—H. Ringgren and H.-J. Fabry, 'מרר *mrr*; מַר *mar*; מֹרָה *mōrâ*; מָרוֹר *mārôr*; מְרִירוּת *merîrûṯ*; מְרֵרָה *merērâ*; מְרוֹרָה *merôrâ*; מֶמֶר *memer*; מַמְרֹרִים *mamrōrîm*; תַּמְרוּרִים *tamrûrîm*', *TDOT*, IX (1998; orig. 1984–86), pp. 15-19.

מרר II *flow* (cf. Arab. marra *pass by, go, flow*; marmara *make flow*)—J.Gerald Janzen, 'Rivers in the Desert of Abraham and Sarah and Zion (Isaiah 51:1-3)', *HAR* 10 (1986), pp. 139-55 (150 n. 16).

מרר III *be strong, harden* (cf. Ug. mrr)—Svi Rin and Shifra Rin, 'Ugaritic–Old Testament Affinities II', *BZ* 10 (1957), pp. 174-92 (189); William A. Ward, 'Comparative Studies in Egyptian and Ugaritic', *JNES* 20 (1961), pp. 31-40 (36); Mitchell Dahood, *Psalms III: 101–150* (AB, 17A; Garden City, NY: Doubleday, 1970), pp. 21, 75; Laurence Kutler, 'A "Strong" Case for Hebrew *mar*', *UF* 16 (1984), pp. 111-18; cf. Dennis Pardee, 'The Semitic Root *mrr* and the Etymology of Ugaritic *mr(r) // brk**', *UF* 10 (1978), pp. 249-88.

מָרֹר *bitter thing*—H. Ringgren and H.-J. Fabry, 'מרר *mrr*; מַר *mar*; מֹרָה *mōrâ*; מָרוֹר *mārôr*; מְרִירוּת *merîrûṯ*; מְרֵרָה *merērâ*; מְרוֹרָה *merôrâ*; מֶמֶר *memer*; מַמְרֹרִים *mamrōrîm*; תַּמְרוּרִים *tamrûrîm*', *TDOT*, IX (1998; orig. 1984–86), pp. 15-19.

מְרֵרָה *gall*—H. Ringgren and H.-J. Fabry, 'מרר *mrr*; מַר *mar*; מֹרָה *mōrâ*; מָרוֹר *mārôr*; מְרִירוּת *merîrûṯ*; מְרֵרָה *merērâ*; מְרוֹרָה *merôrâ*; מֶמֶר *memer*; מַמְרֹרִים *mamrōrîm*; תַּמְרוּרִים *tamrûrîm*', *TDOT*, IX (1998; orig. 1984–86), pp. 15-19.

מְרֹרָה I *bitter thing, poison*—M. Dahood, 'Qoheleth and Recent Discoveries', *Bib* 39 (1958), pp. 302-18 (308-10); J.M. Sasson, 'Numbers 5 and the Waters of Judgment', *BZ* 16 (1972), pp. 249-51; H. Ringgren and H.-J. Fabry, 'מרר *mrr*; מַר *mar*; מֹרָה *mōrâ*; מָרוֹר *mārôr*; מְרִירוּת *merîrûṯ*; מְרֵרָה *merērâ*; מְרוֹרָה *merôrâ*; מֶמֶר *memer*; מַמְרֹרִים *mamrōrîm*; תַּמְרוּרִים *tamrûrîm*', *TDOT*, IX (1998; orig. 1984–86), pp. 15-19.

venom—Dennis Pardee, '*merôrât-petanîm* »Venom« in Job 20 ₁₄', *ZAW* 91 (1979), pp. 401-16.

מְרֹרָה II *strong thing*—William A. Ward, 'Comparative Studies in Egyptian and Ugaritic', *JNES* 20 (1961), pp.

31-40 (36).

מַשָּׂא I *burden*—F. Stolz, 'נשׂא *nś'* "to lift, bear', *TLOT*, II (1997), pp. 769-74; H.-P. Müller, 'מַשָּׂא *maśśā'*; מַשֹּׂא *maśśō'*; מַשָּׂאָה *maśśā'â*; מַשְׂאוֹת *maś'ôṯ*; מַשְׂאֵת *maś'ēṯ*; *מִשֵּׂאת *miśśē'ṯ*; שְׂאֵת *śe'ēṯ*; *שִׂיא *śî''*, *TDOT*, IX (1998; orig. 1984–86), pp. 20-24; D.N. Freedman, B.E. Willoughby, H.-J. Fabry and H. Ringgren, 'נָשָׂא *nāśā'*; מַשְׂאֵת *maś'ēṯ*; מַשֹּׂא *maśśō'*; מַשָּׂאָה *maśśā'â*; נָשִׂיא II *nāśî'* II; שְׂאֵת *śe'ēṯ*; שִׂיא *śî'*; מַשָּׂא *maśśā''*, *TDOT*, X (1999; orig. 1986), pp. 24-40.

not different from מַשָּׂא II *utterance*—P.A.H. de Boer, 'An Enquiry into the Meaning of the Term משׂא', *OTS* 5 (1948), pp. 197-214.

Ho 8₁₀—G.R. Driver, 'Linguistic and Textual Problems: Minor Prophets. I', *JTS* 39 (1938), pp. 154-66 (158).

Ho 14₃—Wolfram von Soden, '"Die Sündenlast in Hosea 14,3', *ZAH* 2 (1989), pp. 91-92.

מַשָּׂא II *utterance*—G.R. Driver, 'Hebrew Notes on Prophets and Psalms', *JTS* 41 (1940), pp. 162-75 (167); W. McKane, 'משׂא in Jeremiah 23 33-40', in *Prophecy: Essays Presented to Georg Fohrer on his Sixty-Fifth Birthday, 6 September 1980* (BZAW, 150; Berlin: A. Töpelmann, 1980), pp. 35-54; H.-P. Müller, 'מַשָּׂא *maśśā'*; מַשֹּׂא *maśśō'*; מַשָּׂאָה *maśśā'â*; מַשְׂאוֹת *maś'ôṯ*; מַשְׂאֵת *maś'ēṯ*; *מִשֵּׂאת *miśśē'ṯ*; שְׂאֵת *śe'ēṯ*; *שִׂיא *śî''*, *TDOT*, IX (1998; orig. 1984–86), pp. 20-24; D.N. Freedman, B.E. Willoughby, H.-J. Fabry and H. Ringgren, 'נָשָׂא *nāśā'*; מַשְׂאֵת *maś'ēṯ*; מַשֹּׂא *maśśō'*; מַשָּׂאָה *maśśā'â*; נָשִׂיא II *nāśî'* II; שְׂאֵת *śe'ēṯ*; שִׂיא *śî'*; מַשָּׂא *maśśā''*, *TDOT*, X (1999; orig. 1986), pp. 24-40.

utterance of praise—Carol Newsom, *Songs of the Sabbath Sacrifice: A Critical Edition* (HSM, 27; Atlanta: Scholars Press, 1985), p. 369.

not different from מַשָּׂא I *burden*—P.A.H. de Boer, 'An Enquiry into the Meaning of the Term משׂא', *OTS* 5 (1948), pp. 197-214.

Si 38₂—Tadeusz Penar, *Northwest Semitic Philology and the Hebrew Fragments of Ben Sira* (BibOr, 28; Rome: Biblical Institute Press, 1975), pp. 63-64.

מַשָּׂא III *tribute*—Shalom M. Paul, 'משא מלך שרים. Hosea 8:8-10 and Ancient Near Eastern Royal Epithets', in *Studies in Bible* (ed. Sara Japhet; ScrHieros, 31; Jerusalem, 1986), pp. 193-204 (197).

מַשָּׂא IV *Massa*—W.F. Albright, 'The Biblical Tribe of Massa' and Some Congeners', in *Studi orientalistici in onore di Giorgio Levi della Vida*, I (Pubblicazioni dell'Istituto per l'Oriente, 52; Rome: Istituto per l'Oriente, 1956), pp. 1-14; (6-10); Ernst Axel Knauf, *Ismael: Untersuchungen zur Geschichte Palästinas und Nordarabiens im 1. Jahrtausend v.Chr.* (ADPV; Wiesbaden: O. Harrassowitz, 2nd edn, 1989), p. 73.

מַשָּׂאָה *burden*—H.-P. Müller, 'מַשָּׂא *maśśā'*; מַשֹּׂא *maśśō'*; מַשָּׂאָה *maśśā'â*; מַשְׂאוֹת *maś'ôṯ*; מַשְׂאֵת *maś'ēṯ*; *מִשֵּׂאת *miśśē'ṯ*; שְׂאֵת *śe'ēṯ*; *שִׂיא *śî''*, *TDOT*, IX (1998; orig. 1984–86), pp. 20-24; D.N. Freedman, B.E. Willoughby, H.-J. Fabry and H. Ringgren, 'נָשָׂא *nāśā'*; מַשְׂאֵת *maś'ēṯ*; מַשֹּׂא *maśśō'*; מַשָּׂאָה *maśśā'â*; נָשִׂיא II *nāśî'* II; שְׂאֵת *śe'ēṯ*; שִׂיא *śî'*; מַשָּׂא *maśśā''*, *TDOT*, X (1999; orig. 1986), pp. 24-40.

מַשָּׂאָה *smoke-signal* (cf. נשׂא *lift up*, מַשְׂאֵת *beacon, fire-signal*)—V. Sasson, 'An Unrecognized "Smoke-Signal" in Isaiah xxx 27', *VT* 33 (1983), pp. 90-95.

מַשְׂאֵת I *gift, offering*—H.-P. Müller, 'מַשָּׂא *maśśā'*; מַשֹּׂא *maśśō'*; מַשָּׂאָה *maśśā'â*; מַשְׂאוֹת *maś'ôṯ*; מַשְׂאֵת *maś'ēṯ*; *מִשֵּׂאת *miśśē'ṯ*; שְׂאֵת *śe'ēṯ*; *שִׂיא *śî''*, *TDOT*, IX (1998; orig. 1984–86), pp. 20-24; D.N. Freedman, B.E. Willoughby, H.-J. Fabry and H. Ringgren, 'נָשָׂא *nāśā'*; מַשְׂאֵת *maś'ēṯ*; מַשֹּׂא *maśśō'*; מַשָּׂאָה *maśśā'â*; נָשִׂיא II *nāśî'* II; שְׂאֵת *śe'ēṯ*; שִׂיא *śî'*; מַשָּׂא *maśśā''*, *TDOT*, X (1999; orig. 1986), pp. 24-40.

מַשְׂאֵת III *beacon, fire-signal*—M. Dahood, 'Northwest Semitic Texts and Textual Criticism of the Hebrew Bible', in *Questions disputées d'Ancien Testament* (ed. C. Brekelmans; BETL, 33; Leuven, 1974), pp. 11-37 (35).

מְשֵׂה *place where a sheep can be eaten*—Chaim Rabin, 'Etymological Miscellanea', in *Studies in the Bible* (ed. Chaim Rabin; ScrHieros, 8; Jerusalem: Magnes Press, 1961), pp. 384-400 (394).

מְשׂוּכָה *hedge* (cf. שׂוך *close*)—BDB, p. 962a [*HALOT*, II, p. 640b, conflates מְשׂוּכָה and מְשׂוּכָה].

מְשׂוּכָה *hedge* (cf. שׂכך *cover*)—BDB, p. 968a.

מְשׂוֹרָה *dominion*—F. Nötscher, 'Entbehrliche Hapaxlegomena in Jesaia', *VT* 1 (1951), pp. 299-302 (302); G.R. Driver, 'Three Notes', *VT* 2 (1952), pp. 356-57 (357).

מְשׂוּרָה *hollow measure* (cf. Arab. mašār, mišwārah *bee-*

hive)—Chaim Rabin, 'Etymological Miscellanea', in *Studies in the Bible* (ed. Chaim Rabin; ScrHieros, 8; Jerusalem: Magnes Press, 1961), pp. 384-400 (394-95).

מָשׁוֹשׁ II *rottenness* (cf. סוס *be rotten*)—E. Dhorme, *A Commentary on the Book of Job* (London: Thomas Nelson, 1984), p. 124.

what is rotten—*HALOT*, II, p. 640b.

מַשְׂטֵמָה I *animosity*—BDB, p. 966a.

hostility—J. Carmignac, 'Précisions apportées au vocabulaire de l'hébreu biblique par la Guerre des Fils de Lumière contre les Fils de Ténèbres', *VT* 5 (1955), pp. 345-65 (353-54).

persecution—*HALOT*, II, p. 640b.

מַשְׂטֵמָה II *cord, noose, fetter* (cf. Syr. sṭam *bind*)—G.R. Driver, 'Linguistic and Textual Problems: Minor Prophets. I', *JTS* 39 (1938), pp. 154-66 (159); cf. Gesenius–Buhl, p. 465a.

מֵשִׂים *attention* (ellipsis for מֵשִׂים לֵב *setting to heart*)—Friedrich Horst, *Hiob I. 1-19* (BKAT, XVI/1; Neukirchen–Vluyn: Neukirchener Verlag, 1968), p. 61; cf. Gillis Gerleman, *BHS*, p. 1231.

מַשְׂכִּיל I (psalm of) *success* (cf. שׂכל hi. *prosper*)—G.W. Ahlström, *Psalm 89: Eine Liturgie aus dem Ritual des leidenden Königs* (Lund: C.W.K. Gleerup, 1959), pp. 21-26; Lienhard Delekat, 'Probleme der Psalmenüberschriften', *ZAW* 76 (1964), pp. 280-97 (282-83).

מַשְׂכִּיל II *responsive song* (cf. שׂכל II *lay crosswise*)—Klaus Koenen, '*Maśkîl*—»Wechselgesang«. Eine neue Deutung zu einem Begriff der Psalmenüberschriften', *ZAW* 103 (1991), pp. 109-12.

מַשְׂכִּיל III *instructive song, sense-giving harmony* (cf. שׂכל *be wise*)—M. Gertner, 'Terms of Scriptural Interpretation: A Study in Hebrew Semantics', *BSOAS* 25 (1962), pp. 11-27 (23).

skilful song—Mitchell Dahood, *Psalms I: 1-50* (AB, 16; Garden City, NY: Doubleday, 1966), p. 286.

מַשְׂכִּיל IV *instructor, monitor* (cf. שׂכל hi. *be intelligent*)—A. Dupont-Sommer, 'L'instruction sur les deux esprits dans le «Manuel de Discipline»', *RHR* 142 (1952), pp. 5-35 (12).

מַשְׂכִּית I *relief*—Silvia Schroer, *In Israel gab es Bilder: Nachrichten von darstellender Kunst im Alten Testament* (OBO, 74; Freiburg, Switzerland: Universitätsverlag, 1987), pp. 337-41.

image; imagination—*HALOT*, II, p. 641a.

showpiece, figure, imagination—BDB, p. 967b.

אֶבֶן מַשְׂכִּית *wishing stone*—Victor Avigdor Hurowitz, 'אבן משכית—A New Interpretation', *JBL* 118 (1999), pp. 201-208.

מַשְׂכִּית II *desire*—Victor Avigdor Hurowitz, 'אבן משכית—A New Interpretation', *JBL* 118 (1999), pp. 201-208.

מִשְׂפָּח I *outpouring of blood, bloodshed*—BDB, p. 705b (s.v. ספח; cf. סָפִיחַ *outpouring*); J. Carmignac, 'Précisions apportées au vocabulaire de l'hébreu biblique par la Guerre des Fils de Lumière contre les Fils de Ténèbres', *VT* 5 (1955), pp. 345-65 (351).

מִשְׂפָּח II *legal infringement*(cf. Arab. fašagha *deviate*, fasḥ, fasḫ *nullification*)—KB, p. 571a; *HALOT*, II, p. 641a.

מַשְׂרֵת *pan*—A.M. Honeyman, 'The Pottery Vessels of the Old Testament', *PEQ* (1939), pp. 76-90 (84); J. Carmignac, 'Précisions apportées au vocabulaire de l'hébreu biblique par la Guerre des Fils de Lumière contre les Fils de Ténèbres', *VT* 5 (1955), pp. 345-65 (364).

משׁשׁ *melt, trickle* (byform of מסס)—F.C. Burkitt, 'The Waters of Shiloah that Go Softly: A Note on Isaiah viii 6', *JTS* 12 (1911), pp. 294-95; G.R. Driver, 'Glosses in the Hebrew Text of the Old Testament', in *L'Ancien Testament et l'orient. Etudes présentées aux VIes Journées Bibliques de Louvain (11-13 septembre 1954)* (OBL, 1; Louvain-Leuven: Publications Universitaires / Instituut voor Orientalisme, 1957), pp. 123-61 (145).

מַשׁ I *Mash*—W.F. Albright, 'The Biblical Tribe of Massa' and Some Congeners', in *Studi orientalistici in onore di Giorgio Levi della Vida*, I (Pubblicazioni dell'Istituto per l'Oriente, 52; Rome: Istituto per l'Oriente, 1956), pp. 1-14 (2-3).

מַשׁ II *swamp* (cf. Ug. mšmš)—Anthony R. Ceresko, *Job 29–31 in the Light of Northwest Semitic* (BibOr, 36; Rome: Biblical Institute Press, 1980), p. 49.

מַשׁ III *statue* (vocalization unknown) (cf. Phoen. מש)—Mitchell Dahood, 'Chiasmus in Job: A Text-Critical and Philological Criterion', in *A Light unto My Path: Old Testament Studied in Honor of Jacob M. Myers* (ed.

Howard N. Bream, Ralph D. Heim and Carey A. Moore; Gettysburg Theological Studies, 4; Philadelphia: Temple University Press, 1974), pp. 119-30 (124).

משׁא *sweep away, destroy* (cf. Akk. mašû *be ruined*, Syr. mšā' *remove*)—G.R. Driver, 'Linguistic and Textual Problems: Ezekiel', *Bib* 19 (1938), pp. 60-69 (66).

מַשָּׁא *debt, interest*—*HALOT*, II, p. 641b; F.L. Hossfeld and E. Reuter, 'נָשָׁא *nāšā'* II; נשׁה *nšh*; מַשָּׁא *m aššā'*; מַשָּׁאוֹת *maššā'ôṯ*; נְשִׁי *nešî'*, *TDOT*, X (1999; orig. 1986), pp. 55-59.

נשׁא מַשָּׁא בְּ *take over a creditor's debt against someone*—*HALOT*, II, p. 641b.

מַשָּׁאָה *debt*—F.L. Hossfeld and E. Reuter, 'נָשָׁא *nāšā'* II; נשׁה *nšh*; מַשָּׁא *maššā'*; מַשָּׁאוֹת *maššā'ôṯ*; נְשִׁי *nešî'*, *TDOT*, X (1999; orig. 1986), pp. 55-59.

מַשְׁאָב *drawing-place of water*—BDB, p. 980b.

trough, drinking pipe—Dalman, *Arbeit*, VI, pp. 269-70; Philippe Reymond, *L'eau, sa vie, et sa signification dans l'Ancien Testament* (VTSup, 6; Leiden: E.J. Brill, 1958), p. 143; *HALOT*, II, p. 642a.

מְשֹׁאָה *devastation* (cf. שׁוֹאָה *devastation*)—BDB, p. 996a.

wasteland—*HALOT*, II, p. 642a (s.v. מְשׁ(וֹ)אָה).

מַשְּׁאָה *deception* (cf. נשׁא II *deceive*)—BDB, p. 674a; *HALOT*, II, p. 643a (s.v. מַשּׁוּאָה).

ruins—Ps 74_{3}—*HALOT*, II, p. 642a (s.v. מַשֻּׁאוֹת).

as name for the underworld—Mitchell Dahood, *Psalms II: 51–100* (AB, 17; Garden City, NY: Doubleday, 1968; 3rd edn, 1979), p. 192.

מִשְׁאָל *Mishal*—David W. Baker, 'Mishal', *ABD*, IV, p. 871.

מִשְׁאֶרֶת *kneading trough, tray*—Dalman, *Arbeit*, IV, pp. 54-55; A.M. Honeyman, 'The Pottery Vessels of the Old Testament', *PEQ* (1939), pp. 76-90 (84).

מִשְׁבָּר *breaker*—B. Kedar-Kopfstein, 'מִשְׁבָּרִים *mišbārîm*', *TDOT*, IX (1998; orig. 1984–86), pp. 25-27.

rage—Mitchell Dahood, *Psalms II: 51–100* (AB, 17; Garden City, NY: Doubleday, 1968; 3rd edn, 1979), pp. 304-305.

מִשְׁבֶּת II *shattering* (cf. שׁבב, Ug. ṯbb *shatter*)—M. Dahood, 'Is *Eben Yiśrā'ēl* a Divine Title?', *Bib* 40 (1959), pp. 1002-1007 (1003-1004).

מִשְׁגֶּה *error* (cf. שׁגג *err*)—Menahem Mansoor, *The Thanksgiving Hymns* (STDJ, 3; Leiden: E.J. Brill, 1961), p. 107 n. 7.

מַשֶּׁה *part of patrimony*—H. Cazelles, review of C. Schaeffer (ed.), *Le palais royal d'Ugarit* (1955), *VT* 6 (1956), pp. 218-22 (220).

מֹשֶׁה *Moses*—H. Cazelles and H.-J. Fabry, 'מֹשֶׁה *mōšeh*', *TDOT*, IX (1998; orig. 1984–86), pp. 28-43.

Moses (cf. Eg. mose *child*)—J. Gwyn Griffiths, 'The Egyptian Derivation of the Name Moses', *JNES* 12 (1953), pp. 225-31.

זֶה מֹשֶׁה *the One of Moses*—Mitchell Dahood, 'Hebrew Lexicography: A Review of W. Baumgartner's *Lexikon*, Volume II', *Or* 45 (1976), pp. 327-65 (357-58).

מְשׁוּבָה *idleness* (cf. שׁוב II *sit*, byform of ישׁב *sit*)—Mitchell Dahood, *Proverbs and Northwest Semitic Philology* (Scripta Pontificii Instituti Biblici, 113; Rome: Pontificium Institutum Biblicum, 1963), pp. 6-7; J.C. Greenfield, 'Stylistic Aspects of the Sfire Trreaty Inscriptions', *AcOr* 29 (1965), p. 4 n. 9a; Mitchell Dahood, *Psalms I: 1–50* (AB, 16; Garden City, NY: Doubleday, 1966), pp. 44, 148; M. Dahood, 'Hebrew–Ugaritic Lexicography V', *Bib* 48 (1967), pp. 421-38 (433).

משׁח I *anoint*—Ernst Kutsch, *Salbung als Rechtsakt im Alten Testament und im Alten Orient* (BZAW, 87; Berlin: A. Töpelmann, 1963); K.R. Veenhof, review of E. Kutsch, *Salbung als Rechtsakt im Alten Testament und im Alten Orient* (1963), *BiOr* 23 (1966), pp. 308-13; K. Seybold, 'מָשַׁח *māšaḥ* I; מָשִׁיחַ *māšîaḥ*', *TDOT*, IX (1998; orig. 1984–86), pp. 43-54; T.N.D. Mettinger, *King and Messiah* (CBOTS, 8; Lund: LiberLeromedel), pp. 185-232; Jacob Milgrom, *Leviticus 1–16: A New Translation with Introduction and Commentary* (AB, 3; New York: Doubleday, 1991), pp. 517-19, 533-35.

anoint, properly *smear with the finger*—Ruth Amiran, 'The "Arm-Shaped" Vessel and its Family', *JNES* 21 (1962), pp. 161-74 (174).

משׁח II *mar* (cf. Arab. masaḫa *gall* the back of a camel and *exhaust it, fray* thread, masīḫ *ugly*)—Alfred Guillaume, 'Some Readings in the Dead Sea Scroll of Isaiah', *JBL* 76 (1957), pp. 40-43 (41-42); G.R. Driver, 'Isaiah 52_{13}–53_{12}: The Servant of the Lord', in *In Memoriam Paul Kahle* (ed. Matthew Black and Georg Fohrer; BZAW, 103; Berlin: A. Töpelmann, 1968), pp. 90-105 (92);

James Barr, *Comparative Philology and the Text of the Old Testament* (Oxford: Oxford University Press, 1968), p. 285.

משׁח III *measure* (cf. MH, Akk. mašāḫu)—G.R. Driver, 'Hebrew Notes on Prophets and Psalms', *JTS* 41 (1940), pp. 162-75 (169-70); J.T. Milik, 'Le rouleau de cuivre provenant de la grotte 3Q (3Q15)', in *DJD*, III (1962), pp. 199-302 (254.153-54); K. Seybold, 'מָשַׁח *māšaḥ* I; מָשִׁיחַ *māšîaḥ*', *TDOT*, IX (1998; orig. 1984–86), pp. 43-54 (44); cf. *HALOT*, II, p. 644a.

stretch out, extend (cf. Ug. mšḫ, Akk. mašāḫu)—Mitchell J. Dahood, 'Ugaritic Lexicography' [review of Joseph Aistleitner, *Wörterbuch der ugaritischen Sprache* (1963)], in *Mélanges Eugène Tisserant. I. Ecriture sainte—Ancien orient* (Studi e testi, 231; Città del Vaticano; Bibliotheca Apostolica Vaticana, 1964), pp. 81-104 (95); B. Couroyer, 'Corne et arc', *RB* 73 (1966), pp. 510-21 (517-21); Mitchell Dahood, *Psalms I: 1–50* (AB, 16; Garden City, NY: Doubleday, 1966), p. 107.

מֶשַׁח *distance*—cf. J.T. Milik, 'Le rouleau de cuivre provenant de la grotte 3Q (3Q15)', in *DJD*, III (1962), pp. 199-302 (254.153-54).

מִשְׁחָה I *anointing*—J. Carmignac, 'Précisions apportées au vocabulaire de l'hébreu biblique par la Guerre des Fils de Lumière contre les Fils de Ténèbres', *VT* 5 (1955), pp. 345-65 (348).

anointing oil—A. Wolters, 'The *Copper Scroll* and the Vocabulary of Mishnaic Hebrew', *RQ* 14 (1990), pp. 483-95 (492).

ointment, consecrated portion—BDB, p. 603b [conflating מִשְׁחָה I and II].

מִשְׁחָה II *portion* (cf. משׁח *measure*)—J. Milgrom, *Leviticus 1–16: A New Translation with Introduction and Commentary* (AB, 1991), pp. 433-34.

share, allotment—*HALOT*, II, p. 644a.

מִשְׁחָה III *consecrated portion* (cf. משׁח *anoint*)—BDB, p. 603b.

מָשְׁחָה I *anointing* (cf. משׁח *anoint*)—KB, p. 573b; *HALOT*, II, p. 644a.

anointing; portion—Zorell, p. 479b [conflating מָשְׁחָה I and II].

מָשְׁחָה II *portion*—BDB, p. 603b; KB, p. 573b; *HALOT*, II, p. 644a.

מִשְׁחוֹר *darkness* (cf. שׁחר *be black*)—Menahem Mansoor, *The Thanksgiving Hymns* (STDJ, 3; Leiden: E.J. Brill, 1961), p. 139 n. 14.

מַשְׁחִית I *destruction*—Michael V. Fox, *Proverbs 1–9* (AB, 18A; New York: Doubleday, 2000), p. 235.

מִשְׁחָר I *dawn*—Ps 110$_3$—Hans Joachim Stoebe, 'Erwägungen zum Psalm 110 auf dem Hintergrund von 1. Sam. 21', in *Festschrift Friedrich Baumgärtel zum 70. Geburtstag, 14. Januar 1958, gewidmet von den Mitarbeitern am Kommentar zum Alten Testament (KAT)* (ed. Johannes Herrmann and Leonhard Rost; Erlanger Forschungen, 10; Erlangen: Universitätsbund Erlangen, 1959), pp. 175-91 (188); William P. Brown, 'A Royal Performance: Critical Notes on Psalm 110:3aγ-b', *JBL* 117 (1998), pp. 93-96.

מִשְׁחָר II *radiance* (cf. Akk. mašraḫu)—G.R. Driver, 'Studies in the Vocabulary of the Old Testament. IV', *JTS* 33 (1931–32), pp. 38-47 (46); G.R. Driver, 'Psalm cx: Its Form, Meaning and Purpose', in ספר סגל. *Studies in the Bible Presented to Professor M.H. Segal by his Colleagues and Students* (ed. J.M. Grintz and J. Liver; Publications of the Israel Society for Biblical Research, 17; Jerusalem, 1964), pp. 17*-31* (23*).

מִשְׁטָר *rule, authority*—BDB, p. 1009b.

inscription, writing—N.H. Tur-Sinai (Torczyner), 'Šiṭir šamê, die Himmelsschrift', *ArOr* 17/2 (1949), pp. 419-33; J. van der Ploeg, 'Les *šōṭᵉrim* d'Israël', *OTS* 10 (1954), pp. 185-96 (189); Georg Fohrer, *Das Buch Hiob* (KAT, 16; Gütersloh: Gerd Mohn, 1963), p. 508; *HALOT*, II, p. 645a.

law, inscribed decree—Robert Gordis, *The Book of Job* (New York: Jewish Theological Seminary, 1978), pp. 451-52.

מֶשִׁי *costly material for garments*—BDB, p. 603b; Maximilian Ellenbogen, *Foreign Words in the Old Testament: Their Origin and Etymology* (London: Luzac & Co. 1962), p. 109.

fine cloth—*HALOT*, II, p. 645a.

shawl—Chaim Rabin, 'Hittite Words in Hebrew', *Or* 32 (1963), pp. 113-39 (130).

silk (cf. Arab. wašy)—Alfred Guillaume, *Hebrew and Arabic Lexicography: A Comparative Study*, IV (Leiden: E.J. Brill, 1965; = *AbrN* 4 [1964–65]), p. 9.

Bibliography to Mem

מָשִׁיחַ *anointed one*—K. Seybold, 'מָשַׁח *māšaḥ* I; מָשִׁיחַ *māšîaḥ*', *TDOT*, IX (1998; orig. 1984–86), pp. 43-54.

מָשִׁיר *song* (cf. שִׁיר *song*)—Mitchell Dahood, 'Hebrew Lexicography: A Review of W. Baumgartner's *Lexikon*, Volume II', *Or* 45 (1976), pp. 327-65 (358); Mitchell Dahood, 'Ugaritic *mšr*, "song", in Psalms 28,7 and 137,3', *Bib* 58 (1977), pp. 216-17.

משך I *draw*—H. Ringgren, 'מָשַׁךְ *māšak*', *TDOT*, IX (1998; orig. 1984–86), pp. 55-58.

lay out for burial—G.R. Driver, 'Hebrew Notes on Prophets and Psalms', *JTS* 41 (1940), pp. 162-75 (170).

sustain—G.R. Driver, 'Problems and Solutions', *VT* 4 (1954), pp. 225-45 (225-26).

משך יָד *make common cause with*—G.R. Driver, 'Linguistic and Textual Problems: Minor Prophets. I', *JTS* 39 (1938), pp. 154-66 (157).

משך II *seize* (cf. Ug. mtk, Arab. masaka)—Harry Torczyner, 'Dunkle Bibelstellen', in *Vom Alten Testament: Karl Marti zum siebzigsten Geburtstage gewidmet* (ed. Karl Budde; BZAW, 41; Giessen: A. Töpelmann, 1925), pp. 274-80 (280); G.R. Driver, 'Two Astronomical Passages in the Old Testament', *JTS* ns 7 (1956), pp. 1-22 (3); N.H. Tur-Sinai, *The Book of Job* (Jerusalem: Kiryath Sepher, 1967), p. 335; E. Dhorme, *A Commentary on the Book of Job* (London: Thomas Nelson, 1984), p. 391; cf. Alfred Guillaume, *Hebrew and Arabic Lexicography: A Comparative Study*, II (Leiden: E.J. Brill, 1965; = *AbrN* 2 [1960–61]), pp. 23-24.

משך III *scent* (cf. Arab. maššaka *scent with musk*)—Alfred Guillaume, *Hebrew and Arabic Lexicography: A Comparative Study*, II (Leiden: E.J. Brill, 1965; = *AbrN* 2 [1960–61]), pp. 23-24.

מֶשֶׁךְ II *bag* (cf. משך *pull*)—Dalman, *Arbeit*, III, pp. 304-305; Ludwig Koehler, 'Hebräische Vokabelnn II', *ZAW* 55 (1937), pp. 161-74 (161-62).

bag (cf. משך II *seize*)—Robert Gordis, 'Psalm 9–10—A Textual and Exeegetical Study', *JQR* 48 (1957–58), pp. 104-221(116-17).

leather bag, pouch—Zorell, p. 481a; *HALOT*, II, p. 646a; Georg Schmuttermayr, *Psalm 9–10: Studien zur Textkritik und Ubersetzung* (St Ottilien: EOS Verlag, 1985), pp. 187-89.

מֶשֶׁךְ III *price*—Robert Gordis, 'Psalm 9–10—A Textual and Exeegetical Study', *JQR* 48 (1957–58), pp. 104-221 (117).

מִשְׁכָּב *bed*—Ps 88_6—M. Dahood, 'Hebrew–Ugaritic Lexicography V', *Bib* 48 (1967), pp. 421-38 (434).

bedding—Jacob Milgrom, *Leviticus 1–16: A New Translation with Introduction and Commentary* (AB, 3; New York: Doubleday, 1991), p. 909.

place of lying down in ecstasy or prayer—Godfrey Rolles Driver, 'Problems of the Hebrew Text and Language', in *Alttestamentliche Studien Friedrich Nötscher zum sechzigsten Geburtstage 19. Juli 1950 gewidmet* (BBB, 1; ed. Hubert Junker and Johannes Botterweck; Bonn: Hanstein, 1950), pp. 46-61 (49).

place of sitting at ritual meals, triclinium—J.T. Milik, 'Le rouleau de cuivre provenant de la grotte 3Q (3Q15)', in *DJD*, III (1962), pp. 199-302 (248.108).

tomb—A. Wolters, 'The *Copper Scroll* and the Vocabulary of Mishnaic Hebrew', *RQ* 14 (1990), pp. 483-95 (489).

בֵּית מִשְׁכָּב *dining couch, place for sitting at meals, triclinium*—J.T. Milik, 'Le rouleau de cuivre provenant de la grotte 3Q (3Q15)', in *DJD*, III (1962), pp. 199-302 (248.108).

מִשְׁכָּן *dwelling*—Werner Schmidt, 'מִשְׁכָּן als Ausdruck jerusalemer Kultsprache', *ZAW* 75 (1963), pp. 91-92; D. Kellermann, 'מִשְׁכָּן *miškān*', *TDOT*, IX (1998; orig. 1984–86), pp. 58-64.

tabernacle (within the Tabernacle)—Jacob Milgrom, *Leviticus 1–16: A New Translation with Introduction and Commentary* (AB, 3; New York: Doubleday, 1991), p. 516.

Tabernacle—Richard Elliott Friedman, 'Tabernacle', *ABD*, VI, pp. 292-300.

tomb—J.T. Milik, 'Le rouleau de cuivre provenant de la grotte 3Q (3Q15)', in *DJD*, III (1962), pp. 199-302 (249.100); Mitchell Dahood, *Psalms I: 1–50* (AB, 16; Garden City, NY: Doubleday, 1966), p. 299; Mitchell Dahood, *Psalms II: 51–100* (AB, 17; Garden City, NY: Doubleday, 1968; 3rd edn, 1979), p. 138.

מִשְׁכַּן עֵדוּת *tabernacle of the testimony*—L. Rost, 'Die Wohnstätte des Zeugnisses', in *Festschrift Friedrich Baumgärtel zum 70. Geburtstag, 14. Januar 1958, gewid-*

met von den Mitarbeitern am Kommentar zum Alten Testament (KAT) (ed. Leonhard Rost and Johannes Herrmann; Erlangen: Universitätsbund Erlangen, 1959), pp. 158-65.

מִשְׁכְּנוֹת *dwelling(s)*—plural in ref. to one dwelling—Mitchell Dahood, *Psalms III: 101–150* (AB, 17A; Garden City, NY: Doubleday, 1970), p. 384; *HALOT*, II, p. 647a.

מֹשֶׁכֶת *belt* of Orion (cf. Arab. masakatun *bracelet, fetter*)—G.R. Driver, 'Two Astronomical Passages in the Old Testament', *JTS* ns 7 (1956), pp. 1-22 (3-4).

bracelet, fetter—*HALOT*, II, p. 646b.

cord (cf. משך *drag, grasp*)—BDB, p. 604b.

משל I *rule*—J.A. Soggin, 'משל *mšl*', *TLOT*, II (1997; orig. 1976), pp. 689-91; H. Gross, 'מָשַׁל *māšal* II; מֹשֶׁל *mōšel*; מִמְשָׁל *mimšāl*; מֶמְשָׁלָה *memšālâ*', *TDOT*, IX (1998; orig. 1984–86), pp. 68-71.

משל II *be like*—K.-M. Beyse, 'מָשַׁל *māšal* I; מָשָׁל *māšāl*', *TDOT*, IX (1998; orig. 1984–86), pp. 64-67; Hedwige Rouillard, *La pericope de Balaam (*Nombres *22–24): La prose et les «oracles»* (Etudes bibliques, ns 4; Paris: Gabalda, 1985), pp. 246-54.

Gn 3₁₆—J.J. Schmitt, 'Like Eve, like Adam', *Bib* 72 (1991), pp. 1-22.

מָשָׁל I *parable*—L. Pirot, 'Le mašal dans l'A.T.', *RSR* 37 (1950), pp. 565-80; A.S. Herbert, 'The Parable (*Māšāl*) in the Old Testament', *SJT* 7 (1954), pp. 180-96; A.R. Johnson, 'מָשָׁל', in *Wisdom in Israel and in the Ancient Near East, Presented to Professor Harold Henry Rowley ... in Celebration of his Sixty-Fifth Birthday* (ed. M. Noth and D. Winton Thomas; VTSup, 3; Leiden: E.J. Brill, 1955), pp. 162-69; Giovanni Rinaldi, 'Alcuni termini ebraici relativi alla letteratura', *Bib* 40 (1959), pp. 267-89 (279-81); William McKane, *Proverbs: A New Approach* (OTL; London: SCM Press, 1970), pp. 23-33; David Winston Suter, '*Māšāl* in the Similitudes of Enoch', *JBL* 100 (1981), pp. 193-212; Timothy Polk, 'Paradigms, Parables, and *Mĕšālîm*: On Reading the *Māšāl* in Scripture', *CBQ* 45 (1983), pp. 564-83; K.-M. Beyse, 'מָשַׁל *māšal* I; מָשָׁל *māšāl*', *TDOT*, IX (1998; orig. 1984–86), pp. 64-67.

מֶשֶׁל I *rule*—H. Gross, 'מָשַׁל *māšal* II; מֹשֶׁל *mōšel*; מִמְשָׁל *mimšāl*; מֶמְשָׁלָה *memšālâ*', *TDOT*, IX (1998; orig. 1984–86), pp. 68-71.

מְשֻׁלֶּמֶת *Meshullemeth*—Robert Deutsch and Michael Heltzer, *New Epigraphic Evidence from the Biblical Period* (Tel Aviv–Jaffa: Archaeological Center Publication, 1995), pp. 86-88.

מְשַׁמָּה I *devastated region; amazement*—Zorell, p. 483a.

devastation; horror—BDB, p. 1031b.

horror, dread—*HALOT*, II, p. 649a.

מְשַׁמָּה II *Meshammah*—G.R. Driver, 'Linguistic and Textual Problems: Minor Prophets. I', *JTS* 39 (1938), pp. 154-66 (155).

מִשְׁמָר I *guard, surveillance*—David A. Diewert, 'Job 7:12: Yah, Tannin and the Surveillance of Job', *JBL* 106 (1987), pp. 203-15 (209-10).

guarding (not *thing guarded*)—Michael V. Fox, *Proverbs 1–9* (AB, 18A; New York: Doubleday, 2000), p. 185.

siege guard—J. Gerald Janzen, 'Another Look at God's Watch over Job (7:12)', *JBL* 108 (1989), pp. 109-14.

מִשְׁמָר II *muzzle* (cf. Ug. šbm)—Mitchell Dahood, 'mišmār "muzzle" in Job 7 12', *JBL* 80 (1961), pp. 270-71; M. Dahood, review of Friedrich Horst, *Hiob* (1960), *Bib* 43 (1962), pp. 225-26 (226); James Barr, 'Hebrew and Ugaritic *šbm*?', *JSS* 18 (1973), pp. 17-39 (23-24); Lester L. Grabbe, *Comparative Philology and the Text of the Old Testament: A Study in Methodology* (SBLDS, 34; Missoula, MT: Scholars Press, 1977), pp. 55-58.

מִשְׁמָר III *wakefulness* (cf. שִׁמֻּר *vigil*, Arab. samara *be awake*)—Arnold E. Ehrlich, *Randglossen zur hebräischen Bibel*, VI (r.p. Hildesheim: Georg Olms, 1968 [original 1908–14]), p. 210.

מִשְׁמָרָה *guardhouse*—J.T. Milik, 'Le rouleau de cuivre provenant de la grotte 3Q (3Q15)', in *DJD*, III (1962), pp. 199-302 (249.111).

מִשְׁמֶרֶת *guard duty*—J. Milgrom, L. Harper and H.-J. Fabry, 'מִשְׁמֶרֶת *mišmereṯ*', *TDOT*, IX (1998; orig. 1984–86), pp. 72-78; Jacob Milgrom, *Leviticus 1–16: A New Translation with Introduction and Commentary* (AB, 3; New York: Doubleday, 1991), p. 7.

מִשְׁנָה *bladder* (cf. Arab. mš'nt)—N.H. Tur-Sinai, 'Unverstandene Bibelworte', *VT* 1 (1951), pp. 307-309 (309).

מִשְׁנֶה I *duplicate* of document—J.T. Milik, 'Le rouleau de cuivre provenant de la grotte 3Q (3Q15)', in *DJD*, III (1962), pp. 199-302 (252.135).

Second Quarter of Jerusalem—Benjamin Mazar, 'Jerusalem: From Isaiah to Jeremiah', in *Congress Volume: Jerusalem 1986* (ed. J.A. Emerton; VTSup, 40; Leiden: E.J. Brill, 1988), pp. VTS 40 (1988), pp. 1-6 (3-4); Gary A. Herion, 'Second Quarter', *ABD*, VI, p. 1065.

מִשְׁנֶה II *equivalent*—M. Tsevat, 'Alalakhiana', *HUCA* 29 (1958), pp. 109-43 (125-26); Gerhard von Rad, 'כִּפְלַיִם in Jes 40 2 = Äquivalent', *ZAW* 79 (1967), pp. 80-82; cf. James Barr, *Comparative Philology and the Text of the Old Testament* (Oxford: Oxford University Press, 1968), p. 337.

not *equivalent* but *double*—James M. Lindenberger, 'How Much for a Hebrew Slave? The Meaning of *Mišneh* in Deut 15:18', *JBL* 110 (1991), pp. 479-82 (479).

מִשְׁנֶה III *the best* (cf. Eth. mašney)—Israel Eitan, 'A Contribution to Isaiah Exegesis (Notes and Short Studies in Biblical Philology)', *HUCA* 12–13 (1937–38), pp. 55-88 (86-87).

מִשְׁעִי II *rubbing* (from שׁעה *smear*, byform of שׁעע)—G.R. Driver, 'Difficult Words in the Hebrew Prophets', in *Studies in Old Testament Prophecy Presented to Professor Theodore H. Robinson* (ed. H.H. Rowley; Edinburgh: T. & T. Clark, 1950), pp. 52-72 (64).

מִשְׁעִי III *midwife* (cf. Eg. ms-'3)—Manfred Görg, 'Ein verkanntes Wort für die "Hebamme" in Ez 16,4', *BN* 58 (1991), pp. 13-16 (15).

מִשְׁעִי IV *smoothness* (cf. Aram. שׁעי, Arab. ša'a *anoint*)—Angel Saenz-Badillos, 'Un hapax biblique: *lĕ-miš'y* en Ez 16,4', in *Mélanges bibliques et orientaux en l'honneur de M. Mathias Delcor* (ed. A. Caquot, S. Légasse and M. Tardieu; AOAT, 215; Kevelaer: Butzon & Bercker, 1985), pp. 349-57.

מַשְׁעֵנָה *support*—John Elwolde, 'Distinguishing the Linguistic and the Exegetical: The Biblical Book of Numbers in the Damascus Document', *DSD* 7 (2000), pp. 1-25 (4-5).

מִשְׁפָּחָה *clan*—William Johnstone, 'Old Testament Technical Expressions in Property Holding: Contributions from Ugarit', *Ugaritica* 6 (1969), pp. 309-17 (313-14); C.B. Taber, 'Kinship and Family', *IDBS* (1976), pp. 519-24; H.-J. Zobel, 'מִשְׁפָּחָה *mišpāḥâ*', *TDOT*, IX (1998; orig. 1984–86), pp. 79-85; C.J.H. Wright, 'Family', *ABD*, II, pp. 761-69.

phratry—Francis I. Andersen, 'Israelite Kinship Terminology and Social Structure', *BiTrans* 20 (1969), pp. 29-39.

protective assocation of families—Norman K. Gottwald, *The Tribes of Israel: A Sociologyof the Religion of Liberated Israel, 1250–1050* BCE (Maryknoll: Orbis Books, 1979; r.p. Sheffield: Sheffield Academic Press, 1999), pp. 257-84, 301-18.

מִשְׁפָּט *court, place of judgment*—Mitchell Dahood, *Psalms I: 1–50* (AB, 16; Garden City, NY: Doubleday, 1966), p. 4; Mitchell Dahood, *Psalms III: 101–150* (AB, 17A; Garden City, NY: Doubleday, 1970), p. 323.

destiny—M. Dahood, 'Hebrew–Ugaritic Lexicography V', *Bib* 48 (1967), pp. 421-38 (435).

justice—B. Johnson, 'מִשְׁפָּט *mišpāṭ*; שֶׁפֶט *šepeṭ*; שְׁפוֹט *šᵉpôṭ*', *TDOT*, IX (1998; orig. 1984–86), pp. 86-98; M. Weinfeld, שפט וצדקה בישראל ובעמים (*Justice and Righteousness in Israel and the Nations: Equality and Freedom in Ancient Israel in Light of Social Justice in the Ancient Near East*) (Jerusalem: Magnes Press, 1985) [Heb]; Herbert Niehr, *Herrschen und Richten: Die Wurzel* špṭ *im Alten Orient und im Alten Testament* (Forschung zur Bibel, 54; Würzburg: Echter, 1986); H. Cazelles, 'Mishpat (*mṯpṭ*) à Ugarit', in *Autour de l'Exode (Etudes)* (Sources bibliques; Paris: Gabalda, 1987), pp. 167-74.

just one—Mitchell Dahood, *Psalms I: 1–50* (AB, 16; Garden City, NY: Doubleday, 1966), p. 231.

moderation. measure—Mitchell Dahood, 'Qoheleth and Northwest Semitic Philology', *Bib* 43 (1962), pp. 349-65 (359-60).

rank—Tadeusz Penar, *Northwest Semitic Philology and the Hebrew Fragments of Ben Sira* (BibOr, 28; Rome: Biblical Institute Press, 1975), p. 65.

restraint, discretion—Mitchell Dahood, *Proverbs and Northwest Semitic Philology* (Scripta Pontificii Instituti Biblici, 113; Rome: Pontificium Institutum Biblicum, 1963), p. 56.

בַּעַל מִשְׁפָּט *legal opponent* (cf. Akk. bēl dîni)—Yitzhaq Avishur, 'מי בעל משפטי יגש אלי (יש׳ נ, ח) בין דפוסי'

מי בעל) סגנון מקראי לתרגום — בבואה מאכדית משפטי יגש אלי (Is. 50:8)—A Stylistic Feature of Biblical Hebrew or a Translated Akkadian Phrase?)', *Lesh* 52 (1987), pp. 18-25, II.

מֵעֹצֶר וּמִמִּשְׁפָּט—Is. 53_{8}—*from a just position of power*—G.W. Ahlström, 'Notes to Isaiah 53:8f', *BZ* 13 (1969), pp. 95-98 (96-97).

מִשְׁפְּתַיִם I *fire-places, ash-heaps* (cf. שׁפת *set on the fire*)—BDB, p. 1046a.

hearth—Paul Haupt, 'Der achtundsechzigste Psalm', *AJSL* 23 (1907), pp. 220-40 (236 n. 57); W.F. Albright, 'A Catalogue of Early Hebrew Lyric Poems (Psalm lxviii)', *HUCA* 23:1 (1950–51), pp. 1-39 (22, 37).

מִשְׁפְּתַיִם II *saddle-bags of a mule* (cf. Ug. mṯpdm, Arab. maṯāfid)—KB, p. 580b; *HALOT*, II, p. 652a.

מִשְׁפְּתַיִם III *divided sheepfold*—Hans-Jürgen Zobel, *Stammesspruch und Geschichte: Die Angaben der Stammessprüche von Gen 49, Dtn 33 und Jdc 5 über die politischen und kultischen Zustände im damaligen 'Israel'* (BZAW, 95; Berlin: A. Töpelmann, 1965), p. 16.

sheepfolds—Gesenius–Buhl, p. 473a.

מִשְׁפְּתַיִם IV *double wall*—Zorell, p. 486a.

מִשְׁפְּתַיִם V *grazing places* (cf. שׁפה [?] *graze*)—Haim Gil'adi, 'מִשְׁפְּתַיִם', *BethM* 76 (1978), pp. 33-44, 119.

מֶשֶׁק I *possession* (cf. מִמְשָׁק *possession*, perh. מֶשֶׁךְ *drawing up, trail*)—BDB, p. 606b; Zorell, p. 486b.

מֶשֶׁק II *libation*—Francesco Vattioni, 'Ancora su *ben-mešeq* di *Gen.* 15,2', *RSO* 40 (1965), pp. 9-12.

בן משק ביתי *one who pours libations on my grave*—M. Dahood, *Ugaritic–Hebrew Philology. Marginal Notes on Recent Publications* (BibOr, 17; Rome: Pontifical Biblical Institute, 1965), p. 65.

מֶשֶׁק III *Meshek*—Horst Seebass, 'Gen 15 2b', *ZAW* 75 (1963), pp. 317-19.

מַשָּׁק I *infestation* (cf. שׁקק *run about*)—*HALOT*, II, p. 652a.

running, rushing—BDB, p. 1055a; Gesenius–Buhl, p. 473b; Zorell, p. 486b.

rushing, assault—KB, p. 580b.

מַשָּׁק II *swarm, host* of locusts (from נשׁק *arrange*)—L. Kopf, 'Arabische Etymologien und Parallelen zum Bibelwörterbuch', *VT* 9 (1959), pp. 247-87 (267).

מִשְׁקֶלֶת *level*—BDB, p. 1054a.

level or *plumbline*—Zorell, p. 486b.

(mason's level)—*HALOT*, II, p. 652b.

plumbline—Gesenius–Buhl, p. 473b.

משׁשׁ II *arrive* (cf. MH ממשמש ובא *approach*, Arab. massa *meet*)—Hans Peter Rüger, 'Zum Text von Sir 40 $_{10}$ und Ex 10 $_{21}$', *ZAW* 82 (1970), pp. 102-109.

מַשְׁתִּין בְּקִיר—מַשְׁתִּין *those capable of participating in the cult*—M. Bič, 'Maštîn BeQîr', *VT* 4 (1954), pp. 413-15; R. Borger, 'Mubaqqir Qarbâtim', *VT* 5 (1955), p. 434.

מַת I *man*—K.-M. Beyse and H.-J. Fabry, 'מת *mt*', *TDOT*, IX (1998; orig. 1984–86), pp. 98-101.

mortal—J.J. Gluck, '*mat–'nš* = Mortal', in *Proceedings of the Sixth World Congress of Jewish Studies*, I (Jerusalem: World Union of Jewish Studies, 1973), pp. 121-26.

soldier—M. Dahood, 'Northwest Semitic Texts and Textual Criticism of the Hebrew Bible', in *Questions disputées d'Ancien Testament* (ed. C. Brekelmans; BETL, 33; Leuven, 1974), pp. 11-37 (36).

Ps 17_{14}—Mitchell Dahood, *Psalms I: 1–50* (AB, 16; Garden City, NY: Doubleday, 1966), pp. 98-99.

Ps 143_{3}—Mitchell Dahood, *Psalms III: 101–150* (AB, 17A; Garden City, NY: Doubleday, 1970), p. 323.

Ne 4_{7}—Wilhelm Rudolph, *Esra und Nehemia samt 3. Esra* (HAT, I/20; Tübingen: J.C.B. Mohr [Paul Siebeck], 1949), p. 126.

מַת II *truly*—Mitchell Dahood, 'Amos 6,8 *metā'ēb*', *Bib* 59 (1978), pp. 265-66 (263).

מֹת *louse* (cf. Akk. mutu)—G.R. Driver, 'Linguistic and Textual Problems: Isaiah xl–lxvi', *JTS* 36 (1935), pp. 396-406 (399).

מֶתֶג *muzzle*—Mitchell Dahood, *Psalms I: 1–50* (AB, 16; Garden City, NY: Doubleday, 1966), pp. 196-97; M. Dahood, 'Hebrew–Ugaritic Lexicography V', *Bib* 48 (1967), pp. 421-38 (435).

מְתוּשָׁאֵל *Methushael* (cf. מַת *man*, שְׁאוֹל *Sheol*, i.e. man, worshipper, of the god Sheol)—Matitiahu Tsevat, 'The Canaanite God Šälaḥ', *VT* 4 (1954), pp. 41-49 (45).

מתח *spread out*—Norman C. Habel, '"He who stretches out the heavens"', *CBQ* 34 (1972) 417-30.

מִתְחָה *spreading out* of hands—Robert Gordis, 'Critical Notes on the Blessing of Moses', *JTS* 34 (1933), pp. 390-92 (392); KB, p. 582a; *HALOT*, II, p. 654a.

מָתַי *when?*—E. Jenni, 'מָתַי *matay* ', *TLOT*, II (1997; orig. 1976), pp. 691-92; H. Ringgren, 'מָתַי *māṯay*', *TDOT*, IX (1998; orig. 1984–86), pp. 101-103.

מְהַתְּלָה *deception* (cf. תלל *deceive*)—F. Nötscher, 'Entbehrliche Hapaxlegomena in Jesaia', *VT* 1 (1951), pp. 299-302 (302).

מְתַלְּעָה *jawbone* (metathesis of מַלְתָּעָה)—G.R. Driver, 'Notes on Hebrew Lexicography', *JTS* 23 (1922), pp. 405-10.

jawbone—*HALOT*, II, p. 654b.

jaws—Ha 3_{14}—G.R. Driver, 'Linguistic and Textual Problems: Minor Prophets. III', *JTS* 39 (1938), pp. 393-405 (397).

teeth, fangs—BDB, p. 1069a; M. Dahood, 'The Etymology of *Malta'ot* (Ps 58,7)', *CBQ* 17 (1955), pp. 180-83; M. Dahood, 'Hebrew Lexicography: A Review of W. Baumgartner's *Lexikon*, Volume II', *Or* 45 (1976) 359.

מְתֹם *healthy part of the body*—*HALOT*, II, p. 654b.

soundness—BDB, p. 1071a.

well-being—Ps 38_4—Mitchell Dahood, *Psalms I: 1–50* (AB, 16; Garden City, NY: Doubleday, 1966), p. 235.

מַתָּן *gift*—E. Lipiński and H.-J. Fabry, 'נָתַן *nāṯan*; מַתָּן *mattān*; מַתָּנָה *mattānâ*; מַתַּת *mattaṯ*; אֶתְנָה *'eṯnâ*; אֶתְנַן/אֶתְנָן *'eṯnān/'eṯnan'*, *TDOT*, X (1999; orig. 1986), pp. 90-108.

מַתָּנָה I *gift*—E. Lipiński and H.-J. Fabry, 'נָתַן *nāṯan*; מַתָּן *mattān* ; מַתָּנָה *mattānâ*; מַתַּת *mattaṯ*; אֶתְנָה *'eṯnâ*; אֶתְנַן/אֶתְנָן *'eṯnān/'eṯnan'*, *TDOT*, X (1999; orig. 1986), pp. 90-108.

dedication—E.A. Speiser, 'Unrecognized Dedication', *IEJ* 13 (1963), pp. 69-73 (73).

Nm 21_{18}—G.R. Driver, 'Geographical Problems', *EI* 5 (1958), pp. 16*-20* (17*).

מַתָּנָה II *violence* (cf. ינה *be violent, oppress*)—Mitchell Dahood, 'Hebrew Lexicography: A Review of W. Baumgartner's *Lexikon*, Volume II', *Or* 45 (1976), pp. 327-65 (359); R. Gelio, 'Osservazioni critiche sul *māšāl* d i Qoh. 7,5-7', *Lateranum* 54 (1988), pp. 1-15.

מֹתֶן *strength* (cf. MH, Arab. matuna *be stout, steady*)—G.R. Driver, 'Problems and Solutions', *VT* 4 (1954), pp. 225-45 (229-30); James Barr, *Comparative Philology and the Text of the Old Testament* (Oxford: Oxford University Press, 1968), pp. 91-92.

מְתָנָה *strength* (cf. MH מְתָנָה *strength*, Arab. matuna *be stout, steady*)—G.R. Driver, 'Problems and Solutions', *VT* 4 (1954), pp. 225-45 (229-30); James Barr, *Comparative Philology and the Text of the Old Testament* (Oxford: Oxford University Press, 1968), pp. 91-92.

מתניה *Mattaniah*—Stefan Timm, 'Anmerkungen zu vier neuen hebräischen Namen', *ZAH* 2 (1989), pp. 188-98 (189).

מָתְנַיִם *musculature linking upper part of body with lower* (not *loins*)—Moshe Held, 'Studies in Comparative-Semitic Lexicography', in *Studies in Honor of Benno Landsberger on his Seventy-Fifth Birthday, April 21, 1965* (ed. Hans G. Güterbock and Thorkild Jacobsen; Oriental Institute of the University of Chicago, Assyriological Studies, 10; Chicago: Chicago University Press, 1965), pp. 395-406 (405-406).

פתח מָתְנַיִם *open the loins*, i.e. *cause to run*—M. Dahood, 'Hebrew and Ugaritic Equivalents of Accadian *pitū purīdā*', *Bib* 39 (1958), pp. 67-69 (68).

מתק *be sweet* (cf. Luwian mitgaimi *sweet*)—Chaim Rabin, 'Hittite Words in Hebrew', *Or* 32 (1963), pp. 113-39 (130); B. Kedar-Kopfstein, 'מָתַק *māṯaq*; מָתוֹק *māṯôq*; מֹתֶק *mōṯeq*; מֶתֶק *meṯeq*; מַמְתַקִּים *mameṯaqqîm*', *TDOT*, IX (1998; orig. 1984–86), pp. 103-107.

of אוֹר *light*—B. Kedar-Kopfstein, 'Synästhesien im biblischen Althebräisch in Übersetzung und Auslegung', *ZAH* 1 (1988), pp. 47-60, 147-85 (53-54).

מתק II *suck* (cf. Syr. mtaq *suck*)—cf. BDB, p. 608b.

suckle—N.H. Tur-Sinai, *The Book of Job* (Jerusalem: Kiryath Sepher, revised edn, 1967), pp. 334-35.

מָתָק *sweetness, lover*—S. Terrien, *Job* (Commentaire de l'Ancien Testament, 13; Neuchâtel: Delachaux & Niestlé, 1963), pp. 178-79.

מָתָק II *intoxicating drink, wine* (cf. Arab. takka *overcome* [of wine])—Joseph Reider, 'Etymological Studies in Biblical Hebrew', *VT* 4 (1954), pp. 276-95 (282-83).

מָתֵק *sweetness*—*HALOT*, II, p. 655b.

מֶתֶק *sweetness*—BDB, p. 608b; Mitchell Dahood, *Proverbs and Northwest Semitic Philology* (Scripta Pontificii Instituti Biblici, 113; Rome: Pontificium Institutum Biblicum, 1963), pp. 36-37.

מִתְקָה *Mithkah*, i.e. *sweetening, forgiving*—Yehuda T. Radday, 'Vom Humor in biblischen Ortsnamen', in

»Wünschet Jerusalem Frieden«. Collected Communications to the XIIth Congress of the International Organization for the Study of the Old Testament, Jerusalem 1986 (ed. Matthias Augustin and Klaus-Dietrich Schunck; BEATAJ, 13; Frankfurt a.M.: Peter Lang, 1988), pp. 431-46 (440).

מַתַּת *gift*—E. Lipiński and H.-J. Fabry, 'נָתַן *nāṯan;* מַתָּן *mattān* ; מַתָּנָה *mattānâ;* מַתַּת *mattaṯ;* אֶתְנָה *'eṯnâ;* אֶתְנַן/אֶתְנָן *'eṯnān/'eṯnan'*, *TDOT*, X (1999; orig. 1986), pp. 90-108.

נ

נָא I *please,* for politeness or as entreaty—Gesenius-Kautzsch-Cowley, §§105*b* n. 1, 110*d;* P. Joüon, *Grammaire de l'hébreu biblique* (Rome, 2nd edn, 1947, §105*c-d;* Paul Joüon, *A Grammar of Biblical Hebrew, Translated and Revised by T. Muraoka* (2 vols.; Rome: Pontificio Istituto Biblico, 1991), §105c; Timothy Wilt, 'A Sociolinguistic Analysis of *nā''*, *VT* 56 (1996), pp. 237-55; Ahouva Shulman, 'The Particle נָא in Biblical Hebrew Prose', *HAR* 40 (1999), pp. 57-82.

as notation of logical consequence—Thomas O. Lambdin, *Introduction to Biblical Hebrew* (London: New York: Scribner, 1973), p. 170; Bruce K. Waltke and M. O'Connor, *An Introduction to Biblical Hebrew Syntax* (Winona Lake, IN: Eisenbrauns, 1990), pp. 578, 684.

for emphasis—Choon Leong Seow, *A Grammar for Biblical Hebrew* (Nashville: Abingdon Press, 1987), p. 173.

נֹאד *parchment*—Mitchell Dahood, *Psalms II: 51–100* (AB, 17; Garden City, NY: Doubleday, 1968; 3rd edn, 1979), p. 46.

skin bottle—Dalman, *Arbeit*, IV, p. 254.

Ex 15_8—A. Wolters, 'Not Rescue but Destruction: Rereading Exodus 15:8', *CBQ* 52 (1990), pp. 223-40.

נאה *be fitting*—K.-M. Beyse, 'נאה *n'h;* נָאוֶה *nā'weh'*, *TDOT*, IX (1998; orig. 1984–86), pp. 108-109.

נָאָה *comely place, oasis* (cf. נאה *be comely*)—John H. Hayes, *Amos: The Eighth-Century Prophet: His Times and his Preaching* (Nashville: Abingdon Press, 1988), pp. 64-65.

נָאֶה *fitting*—Zorell, p. 490a.

נאו *praise* (verb) (cf. נוה II *glorify*)—Mitchell Dahood, 'Vocative *Lamedh* in the Psalter', *VT* 16 (1966), pp. 299-311 (305); Mitchell Dahood, *Psalms I: 1–50* (AB, 16; Garden City, NY: Doubleday, 1966), p. 200; Mitchell Dahood, *Psalms II: 51–100* (AB, 17; Garden City, NY: Doubleday, 1968; 3rd edn, 1979), p. 343.

נָאוֶה *beautiful*—K.-M. Beyse, 'נאה *n'h;* נָאוֶה *nā'weh'*, *TDOT*, IX (1998; orig. 1984–86), pp. 108-109.

as gloss on נָעִים *pleasant* (to distinguish it from נָעִים *tuneful* [cf. Arab. nghm])—G.R. Driver, 'Glosses in the Hebrew Text of the Old Testament', in *L'Ancien Testament et l'orient. Etudes présentées aux VIes Journées Bibliques de Louvain (11-13 septembre 1954)* (OBL, 1; Louvain-Leuven: Publications Universitaires / Instituut voor Orientalisme, 1957), pp. 123-61 (136).

נִאוּפִים *adultery*—Ho 7_6—Mitchell Dahood, 'Hebrew Lexicography: A Review of W. Baumgartner's *Lexikon*, Volume II', *Or* 45 (1976), pp. 327-65 (359).

urge to commit adultery—KB, p. 585b; *HALOT*, II, p. 657b.

נָאוֹר *the Shining One* (cf. Akk. nannāru)—G. Rinaldi, 'Salmo 76', *BeO* 2 (1960), p. 92. [Ps 76.5]

נְאֻם *oracle*—D. Vetter, 'נְאֻם *ne'um'* , *TLOT*, II (1997; orig. 1976), pp. 692-94; H. Eising, 'נְאֻם *ne'um'*, *TDOT*, IX (1998; orig. 1984–86), pp. 109-13; Gary A. Rendsburg, 'The Northern Origin of "The Last Words of David" (2 Sam 23,1-7)', *Bib* 69 (1988), pp. 113-21 (115-16); Gary A. Rendsburg, 'Hebrew Philological Notes (I)', *Hebrew Studies* 40 (1999), pp. 27-32 (29-30).

נאף *commit adultery*—Michael Fishbane, 'Accusations of Adultery: A Study of Law and Scribal Practice in Numbers 5:11-31', *HUCA* 45 (1974), pp. 25-45; Henry

McKeating, 'Sanctions against Adultery in Israelite Society, with Some Reflections on Methodology in the Study of Old Testament Ethics', *JSOT* 11 (1979), pp. 57-72; Anthony Phillips, 'Another Look at Adultery', *JSOT* 20 (1981), pp. 3-25; D.N. Freedman, B.E. Willoughby and H.-J. Fabry, 'נָאַף *nā'ap*', *TDOT*, IX (1998; orig. 1984–86), pp. 113-18; J.H. Tigay and H.H. Cohn, 'Adultery', *EncJud*, II, cols. 313-16.

נַאֲפוּפִים *tokens of adultery*—Francis I. Andersen and David Noel Freedman, *Hosea: A New Translation with Introduction and Commentary* (AB, 24; Garden City, NY: Doubleday, 1980), pp. 224-25.

נאץ *disdain*—H. Wildberger, 'נאץ *n'ṣ*', *TLOT*, II (1997; orig. 1976), pp. 694-96; L. Ruppert, 'נָאַץ *nā'aṣ*; נְאָצָה *ne'āṣâ*; נֶאָצָה *ne'āṣâ*; *TDOT*, IX (1998; orig. 1984–86), pp. 118-25.

נְאָצָה *reviling*—L. Ruppert, 'נָאַץ *nā'aṣ*; נְאָצָה *ne'āṣâ*; נֶאָצָה *ne'āṣâ*; *TDOT*, IX (1998; orig. 1984–86), pp. 118-25.

נֶאָצָה *disgrace*—L. Ruppert, 'נָאַץ *nā'aṣ*; נְאָצָה *ne'āṣâ*; נֶאָצָה *ne'āṣâ*; *TDOT*, IX (1998; orig. 1984–86), pp. 118-25.

נאר II *curse* (byform of ארר)—G.R. Driver, 'Hebrew Notes on "Song of Songs" and "Lamentations"', in *Festschrift Alfred Bertholet zum 80. Geburtstag gewidmet von Kollegen und Freunden* (ed. Walter Baumgartner [*et al.*]; Tübingen: J.C.B. Mohr, 1950), pp. 134-46 (138).

נבא *prophesy*—H.-P. Müller, 'נָבִיא *nāḇî'*; נבא *nb'* niphal and hithpael; נְבִיאָה *neḇî'â*; נְבוּאָה *neḇû'â'*, *TDOT*, IX (1998; orig. 1984–86), pp. 129-50.

נבו I *Nebo*—Michele Piccirillo, 'Nebo, Mount', *ABD*, IV, pp. 1056-58.

נְבוּאָה *prophecy*—H.-P. Müller, 'נָבִיא *nāḇî'*; נבא *nb'* niphal and hithpael; נְבִיאָה *neḇî'â*; נְבוּאָה *neḇû'â'*, *TDOT*, IX (1998; orig. 1984–86), pp. 129-50.

נִבוֹ *offspring* (cf. נוב *bear fruit*)—N.H. Tur-Sinai, *The Book of Job* (Jerusalem: Kiryath Sepher, revised edn, 1967), p. 196.

נְבוּזַרְאֲדָן *Nebuzaradan* (cf. Akk. Nabû-zēr-iddina *Nabu has given me offspring*)—K.L. Tallqvist, *Assyrian Personal Names* (Acta Societatis Scientiarum Fennicae, 53.1; Helsinki, 1914), p. 164a; Mordechai Cogan and Hayim Tadmor, *II Kings: A New Translation with Introduction and Commentary* (AB, 11; New York: Doubleday, 1988), pp. 318-19.

נִבְחַז *Nibhaz*—F. Hommel, 'Die Götter Nibḫaz und Tartaḳ. 2. Kön. 17, 31', *OLZ* 15 (1912), col. 118; W.F. Albright, review of James A. Montgomery, *A Critical and Exegetical Commentary on the Books of Kings* (1951), *JBL* 71 (1952), pp. 245-53 (252); William J. Fulco, 'Nibhaz', *ABD*, IV, p. 1104.

נבט hi. *accept graciously*—Pieter A. Verhoef, *The Books of Haggai and Malachi* (NICOT, 13; Grand Rapids: William B. Eerdmans, 1988), p. 66.

hi. *look*—H. Ringgren, 'נבט *nbṭ*', *TDOT*, IX (1998; orig. 1984–86), pp. 126-28.

נָבִיא *prophet*—Herrmann Kees, 'Der berichtende Gottesdiener', *ZÄS* 85 (1960), pp. 138-43; G. Rinaldi, '*Nābî'*', *BeO* 11 (1969), p. 86; J. Jeremias, 'נָבִיא *nābî'*', *TLOT*, II (1997; orig. 1976), pp. 697-710; Manfred Görg, 'Der *Nābî'*—"Berufener" oder "Seher"?', *BN* 17 (1982), pp. 23-25; Manfred Görg, 'Weiteres zur Etymologie von *nâbī'*', *BN* 22 (1983), pp. 9-11; H.-P. Müller, 'נָבִיא *nāḇî'*; נבא *nb'* niphal and hithpael; נְבִיאָה *neḇî'â*; נְבוּאָה *neḇû'â'*, *TDOT*, IX (1998; orig. 1984–86), pp. 129-50; H.-P. Müller, 'Zur Herleitung von *nābî'*', *BZ* 29 (1985), pp. 22-27; M. Görg, 'Addenda zur Diskussion von *nābî'*', *BZ* 11 (1986), pp. 25-36; Walter W. Müller, 'Sudsemitische Marginalien zur Etymologie von *nābī'*', *BN* 32 (1986), pp. 31-37; Manfred Görg, 'Randbemerkungen zum jüngsten Lexikonartikel zu *nābī'*', *BN* 26 (1985), pp. 7-16; Peter Michaelsen, 'Ecstasy and Possession in Ancient Israel: A Review of Some Recent Contributions', *SJOT* 2 (1989), pp. 28-54; Daniel E. Fleming, 'The Etymological Origins of the Hebrew *nābî'*: The One Who Invokes God', *CBQ* 55 (1993), pp. 217-24; Ann Jeffers, *Magic and Divination in Ancient Palestine and Syria* (Studies in the History and Culture of the Ancient Near East, 8; Leiden: E.J. Brill, 1996), pp. 81-95; Terry L. Fenton, 'Deuteronomistic Advocacy of the *nābî'*: 1 Samuel ix 9 and Questions of Israelite Prophecy', *VT* 47 (1997), pp. 23-42 (33-35).

(cf. בוא hi. *bring*)—John Briggs Curtis, 'A Folk Etymology of nābî'', *VT* 29 (1979), pp. 491-93.

נְבִיאָה *prophet* (fem.)—H.-P. Müller, 'נָבִיא *nāḇî'*; נבא *nb'* niphal and hithpael; נְבִיאָה *nᵉḇî'â*; נְבוּאָה *nᵉḇû'â'*, *TDOT*, IX (1998; orig. 1984–86), pp. 129-50.

נבך *pour out* (cf. Ug. nbk)—George M. Landes, 'The Fountain at Jazer', *BASOR* 144 (1956), pp. 30-37 (31-34); M. Dahood, *Ugaritic–Hebrew Philology: Marginal Notes on Recent Publications* (BibOr, 17: Rome: Pontifical Biblical Institute, 1965), pp. 65-66; Mitchell Dahood, *Psalms II: 51–100* (AB, 17; Garden City, NY: Doubleday, 1968; 3rd edn, 1979), pp. 158, 281.

נֵבֶךְ I *spring*—George M. Landes, 'The Fountain at Jazer', *BASOR* 144 (1956), pp. 30-37 (31); M. Dahood, 'Hebrew–Ugaritic Lexicography V', *Bib* 48 (1957), pp. 421-38 (436).

נֵבֶךְ II *sandy depths* (cf. Arab. nabkun *shifting sands*)—G.R. Driver, 'Studies in the Vocabulary of the Old Testament. VI', *JTS* 34 (1933), pp. 375-85 (379).

נבל I *wither*—H.-J. Fabry, 'נָבֵל *nāḇēl*; נְבֵלָה *nᵉḇēlâ*; נֹבֶלֶת *nōḇeleṯ*', *TDOT*, IX (1998; orig. 1984–86), pp. 151-57.

Is 28₄—G.R. Driver, '"Another Little Drink"—Isaiah 28:1-22', in *Words and Meanings: Essays Presented to David Winton Thomas* (ed. Peter R. Ackroyd and Barnabas Lindars; Cambridge: Cambridge University Press, 1968), pp. 47-67 (50).

נבל II *be foolish*—H.-J. Fabry, 'נָבֵל *nāḇēl*; נְבֵלָה *nᵉḇēlâ*; נֹבֶלֶת *nōḇeleṯ*', *TDOT*, IX (1998; orig. 1984–86), pp. 151-57.

pi. *declare void, consider invalid*—Gillis Gerleman, "Der Nicht-Mensch: Erwägungen zur hebräischer Wurzel *nbl*", *VT* 24 (1974), pp. 147-58.

נבל III *be sacrilegious; treat with contempt* (cf. Akk. nabālu *separate from*)—Wolfgang M.W. Roth, 'Nbl', *VT* 10 (1960), pp. 394-409.

נבל IV *treat ignominiously*—Paul Joüon, 'Racine נבל au sens de *bas, vil, ignoble*', *Bib* 5 (1924), pp. 357-61.

נָבָל I *foolish*—André Caquot, 'Sur une désignation vétérotestamentaire de «l'insensé»', *RHR* 155 (1959), pp. 1-16; Trevor Donald, 'The Semantic Field of "Folly" in Proverbs, Job, Psalms, and Ecclesiates', *VT* 13 (1963), pp. 285-92; M. Sæbø , 'נָבָל *nābāl*' , *TLOT*, II (1997; orig. 1976), pp. 710-14; J. Marböck, 'נָבָל *nāḇāl*; נְבָלָה *nᵉḇālâ*', *TDOT*, IX (1998; orig. 1984–86), pp. 157-71.

of no account—Gillis Gerleman, "Der Nicht-Mensch: Erwägungen zur hebräischer Wurzel *nbl*", *VT* 24 (1974), pp. 147-58.

נָבָל II *outcast, sacrilegious* (cf. נבל III *be sacrilegious*, Akk. nabālu *separate from*)—Wolfgang M.W. Roth, 'Nbl', *VT* 10 (1960), pp. 394-409.

נָבָל III *noble* (cf. Arab. nabala)—Alfred Guillaume, *Hebrew and Arabic Lexicography: A Comparative Study*, II (Leiden: E.J. Brill, 1965; = *AbrN* 2 [1960–61]), p. 24.

נָבָל IV *low-class, ignominious* (cf. נבל IV *treat ignominiously*)—Paul Joüon, 'Racine נבל au sens de *bas, vil, ignoble*', *Bib* 5 (1924), pp. 357-61; Robert Gordis, *The Book of Job* (New York: Jewish Theological Seminary, 1978), p. 332; David J.A. Clines, *Job 1–20* (WBC, 17; Dallas: Word Books, 1989), p. 54.

נָבָל V *Nabal*—Y. Devir, 'Nabal the Carmelite: A Study on the Nature of a Biblical Personal Name', *Lesh* 20 (1956), pp. 97-104 [Heb]; Yehuda T. Radday, 'Humour in Names', in *On Humour and the Comic in the Hebrew Bible* (ed. Yehuda T. Radday and Athalya Brenner; JSOTSup, 92; Bible and Literature Series, 23; Sheffield: Almond Press, 1990), pp. 59-97 (62-63).

נֵבֶל I *jug*—A.M. Honeyman, 'The Pottery Vessels of the Old Testament', *PEQ* (1939), pp. 76-90 (84-85); K. Seybold, 'נֵבֶל *nēḇel*', *TDOT*, IX (1998; orig. 1984–86), pp. 172-74.

leather bottle; earthen jar—BDB, p. 614a; Zorell, p. 494a.

not *leather bottle*—*HALOT*, II, p. 664a.

נֵבֶל II *harp, lute. guitar*—BDB, p. 614a.

harp—E. Werner, 'Musical Instruments', *IBD*, III, pp. 469-76 (475).

(?) harp—*HALOT*, II, p. 664a.

lute, lyre—Zorell, p. 494b; Ivor H. Jones, 'Music and Musical Instruments', *ABD*, IV, pp. 930-39 (937).

נֵבֶל III *young shoot, sprig* (vocalization uncertain; cf. Aram. נִבְלָא, Akk. niblu, niplu, Arab. nabula IV *yield ripe dates*)—G.R. Driver, '"Another Little Drink"—Isaiah 28:1-22', in *Words and Meanings: Essays Presented to David Winton Thomas* (ed. Peter R. Ackroyd and Barnabas Lindars; Cambridge: Cambridge University Press, 1968), pp. 47-67.

נְבָלָה *folly; godlessness, wickedness*—Gesenius–Buhl, p. 481a; J. Marböck, 'נָבָל *nāḇāl*; נְבָלָה *nᵉḇālâ*', *TDOT*, IX (1998; orig. 1984–86), pp. 157-71.

sacrilege—Wolfgang M.W. Roth, 'Nbl', *VT* 10 (1960), pp.

394-409.

senselessness; disgrace—BDB, p. 615a.

serious disorderly conduct—Anthony Phillips, '*Nebalah*—A Term for Serious Disorderly and Unruly Conduct', *VT* 25 (1975), pp. 237-42.

stupidity, wilful sin—*HALOT*, II, p. 664b.

vileness—Zorell, p. 494b.

נְבֵלָה *carcass*—H.-J. Fabry, 'נָבֵל *nāḇēl*; נְבָלָה *nᵉḇēlâ*; נֹבֶלֶת *nōḇeleṯ*', *TDOT*, IX (1998; orig. 1984–86), pp. 151-57; Jacob Milgrom, *Leviticus 1–16: A New Translation with Introduction and Commentary* (AB, 3; New York: Doubleday, 1991), pp. 653-54, 702-703.

corpse as sacrilegious—Wolfgang M.W. Roth, 'Nbl', *VT* 10 (1960), pp. 394-409.

נַבְלוּת II *ruin, degeneration, withering away* (cf. נבל I *wither*)—Saul M. Olyan, '"In the Sight of her Lovers": On the Interpretation of *nablūt* in Hos 2,12', *BZ* 36 (1992), pp. 255-61 (261).

נְבֶלֶת I *unripe fig(s)* (cf. MH, Aram. נִבְלָא *fallen figs*)—G.R. Driver, 'Isaiah i–xxxix: Textual and Linguistic Problems', *JSS* 13 (1968), pp. 36-57 (54).

withered fruit—*HALOT*, II, p. 664b; H.-J. Fabry, 'נָבֵל *nāḇēl*; נְבָלָה *nᵉḇēlâ*; נֹבֶלֶת *nōḇeleṯ*', *TDOT*, IX (1998; orig. 1984–86), pp. 151-57.

נבע I *belch*—Mitchell Dahood, *Psalms II: 51–100* (AB, 17; Garden City, NY: Doubleday, 1968; 3rd edn, 1979), p. 69.

pour out—F. Vattioni, 'La III iscrizione di Sfiré A 2 e Proverbi I, 23', *AION* ns 13 (1963) 279-86.

נבע II *ferment* (cf. Arab. nabagha)—G.R. Driver, 'Problems and Solutions', *VT* 4 (1954), pp. 225-45 (231-32).

נבך *pour, flow* (cf. Ug. nbk)—Mitchell Dahood, 'Ezekiel 19,10 and Relative *kî*', *Bib* 56 (1975), pp. 96-99 (97 n. 1); Mitchell Dahood, *Psalms II: 51–100* (AB, 17; Garden City, NY: Doubleday, 1968; 3rd edn, 1979), p. 158.

נֶבֶשׁ *soul* (byform of נֶפֶשׁ)—Mitchell Dahood, 'Comparative Philology Yesterday and Today' [review of James Barr, *Comparative Philology and the Text of the Old Testament* (1968)], *Bib* 50 (1969), pp. 70-79 (74-75).

נֶגֶב I *south country, Negeb*—Steven A. Rosen, Itzhaq Beit-Arieh and Avraham Negev, 'Negeb', *ABD*, IV, pp. 1061-68.

נֶגֶב II *provision* (cf. Ug. ngb *supply [an army with food]*)—M. Dahood, *Ugaritic–Hebrew Philology. Marginal Notes on Recent Publications* (BibOr, 17; Rome: Pontifical Biblical Institute, 1965), p. 66.

נגד *communicate*—C. Westerman, 'נגד *ngd*', *TLOT*, II (1997; orig. 1976), pp. 714-18; F. Garcia-López, 'נגד *ngd*', *TDOT*, IX (1998; orig. 1984–86), pp. 174-86.

tell—Mats Eshkult, 'Über einige hebräische Verben des Sprechens—Etymologie und Metapher', *OrSuec* 38–39 (1989–90), pp. 31-35.

נֶגֶד I *over against*—A. Vaccari, 'Una particella avversativa in tre salmi', *BeO* 6 (1964), pp. 73-77.

toward—Mitchell Dahood, *Psalms II: 51–100* (AB, 17; Garden City, NY: Doubleday, 1968; 3rd edn, 1979), pp. 17, 302.

נֶגֶד II *blow* (cf. Aram. נִגְדָּא)—N.H. Tur-Sinai, *The Book of Job* (Jerusalem: Kiryath Sepher, revised edn, 1967), pp. 181-82.

נֶגֶד III *honest, forthright, candid things* (cf. נֶגֶד *[directly] before*)—Luc Grollenberg, 'A propos de Prov. vii, 6 et xvii, 27', *RB* 59 (1952), pp. 40-43; Michael V. Fox, *Proverbs 1–9* (AB, 18A; New York: Doubleday, 2000), p. 269.

נִגְדָּל *fortified city* (cf. דגל IV *be brave* [not in *DCH*, II)—M. Dahood, 'Love and Death at Ebla and their Biblical Reflections', in *Love and Death in the Ancient Near East: Essays in Honor of Marvin H. Pope* (ed. John H. Marks and Robert M. Good; Guilford, CT: Four Quarters Publishing, 1987), pp. 93-99 (96).

נגה *shine*—H. Eising and H.-J. Fabry, 'נָגַהּ *nāgah*; נֹגַהּ *nōgah*; נְגֹהוֹת *nᵉgōhôṯ*', *TDOT*, IX (1998; orig. 1984–86), pp. 186-87.

נֹגַהּ *brightness*—H. Eising and H.-J. Fabry, 'נָגַהּ *nāgah*; נֹגַהּ *nōgah*; נְגֹהוֹת *nᵉgōhôṯ*', *TDOT*, IX (1998; orig. 1984–86), pp. 186-87.

4QpsEzek[a] 4_6—D. Dimant and J. Strugnell, 'The Merkabah Vision in *Second Ezekiel* (*4Q385* 4)', *RQ* 14 (1990), pp. 331-48 (338).

נְגֹהָה *brightness*—H. Eising and H.-J. Fabry, 'נָגַהּ *nāgah*; נֹגַהּ *nōgah*; נְגֹהוֹת *nᵉgōhôṯ*', *TDOT*, IX (1998; orig. 1984–86), pp. 186-87.

נָגִיד *commander*—Frank Moore Cross, *Canaanite and Hebrew Epic: Essays in the History of the Religion of Israel* (Cambridge, MA: Harvard University Press, 1973), p. 220.

leader—J. van der Ploeg, 'Les chefs du peuple d'Israël et leurs titres', *RB* 57 (1950), pp. 40-61 (45-47); J.J. Glück, 'Nagid—Shepherd', *VT* 13 (1963), pp. 144-50; J.R. Bartlett, 'Zadok and his Successors at Jerusalem', *JTS* ns 19 (1968), pp. 1-18 (13); E. Lipiński, 'Nagid, der Kronprinz', *VT* 24 (1974), pp. 497-99; G.F. Hasel, 'נָגִיד *nāgîḏ*', *TDOT*, IX (1998; orig. 1984–86), pp. 187-202; U. Rüterswörden, *Die Beamten in der israelitischen Königsszeit: Eine Studie zu* sr *und vergleichbaren Begriffen* (BWANT, 117; Stuttgart: W. Kohlhammer, 1985), pp. 101-103.

as divine appellative—M. Dahood, 'Hebrew–Ugaritic Lexicography V', *Bib* 48 (1967), pp. 421-38 (436); Mitchell Dahood, *Psalms II: 51–100* (AB, 17; Garden City, NY: Doubleday, 1968; 3rd edn, 1979), pp. 24-25; Mitchell Dahood, *Psalms III: 101–150* (AB, 17A; Garden City, NY: Doubleday, 1970), p. 105.

derivation—M. Brettler, *God is King: Understanding an Israelite Metaphor* (JSOTSup, 76; Sheffield: JSOT Press, 1989), pp. 33-35.

נְגִינָה *mocking song*—Giovanni Rinaldi, 'Alcuni termini ebraici relativi alla letteratura', *Bib* 40 (1959), pp. 267-89 (281-82).

song—Mitchell Dahood, 'New Readings in Lamentations', *Bib* 59 (1978), pp. 174-97 (195).

נגן *play (stringed instrument)*—Giovanni Rinaldi, 'Alcuni termini ebraici relativi alla letteratura', *Bib* 40 (1959), pp. 267-89 (281-82).

Ps 77_7—Mitchell Dahood, *Psalms II: 51–100* (AB, 17; Garden City, NY: Doubleday, 1968; 3rd edn, 1979), pp. 227-28.

נגע I *touch*—M. Delcor, 'נגע *ng*'', *TLOT*, II (1997; orig. 1976), pp. 718-19; L. Schwienhorst, 'נָגַע *nāga*'; נֶגַע *nega*'', *TDOT*, IX (1998; orig. 1984–86), pp. 203-209; B. Kedar-Kopfstein, 'Synästhesien im biblischen Althebräisch in Übersetzung und Auslegung', *ZAH* 1 (1988), pp. 47-60, 147-85 (155).

נגע II *rest* (cf. Arab. naja'a *be at ease*)—Israel Eitan, *A Contribution to Biblical Lexicography* (Contributions to Oriental History and Philology, 10; New York: Columbia University Press, 1924), p. 12 n. 24.

נגע III *sit* (cf. Syr. ng')—G.R. Driver, 'Notes on the Psalms. I. 1–72', *JTS* 43 (1942), pp. 149-60 (154).

נֶגַע *affection*—Jacob Milgrom, *Leviticus 1–16: A New Translation with Introduction and Commentary* (AB, 3; New York: Doubleday, 1991), p. 776.

blow, affliction—Klaus Seybold, *Das Gebet des Kranken im Alten Testament: Untersuchungen zur Bestimmung und Zuordnung der Krankheits- und Heilungspsalmen* (WMANT, 99; Stuttgart: W. Kohlhammer, 1973), pp. 25-26; L. Schwienhorst, 'נָגַע *nāga*'; נֶגַע *nega*'', *TDOT*, IX (1998; orig. 1984–86), pp. 203-209.

skin disease—J.M. Baumgarten, 'The 4Q Zadokite Fragments on Skin Disease', *JJS* 41 (1990), pp. 153-65 (158-59, 162-64); E. Qimron, 'Notes on the 4Q Zadokite Fragment on Skin Disease', *JJS* 42 (1991), pp. 256-59 (258).

נגף *strike*—H.D. Preuss, 'נָגַף *nāgap*; נֶגֶף *negep*; מַגֵּפָה *maggēpâ*', *TDOT*, IX (1998; orig. 1984–86), pp. 210-13.

נֶגֶף *plague*—H.D. Preuss, 'נָגַף *nāgap*; נֶגֶף *negep*; מַגֵּפָה *maggēpâ*', *TDOT*, IX (1998; orig. 1984–86), pp. 210-13.

נגר I not *pour* but נגר *d r a g*—Israel Ben-David, 'למילון המקרא (Additions to Biblical Hebrew Lexicography)', *Lesh* 56 (1991-92), pp. 293-99 (293-98), I [Heb, Eng abstract].

נגר II *smite*—Mitchell Dahood, *Psalms I: 1–50* (AB, 16; Garden City, NY: Doubleday, 1966), p. 241-42; Mitchell Dahood, *Psalms II: 51–100* (AB, 17; Garden City, NY: Doubleday, 1968; 3rd edn, 1979), p. 100.

נִגֶּרֶת *torrent* (cf. נגר *pour*)—*HALOT*, II, p. 670a.

נגשׂ *be a creditor*—G.R. Driver, 'Linguistic and Textual Problems: Isaiah i–xxxix', *JTS* 38 (1937), pp. 36-50 (38).

oppress—M. Dahood, A. Magnante and L. Provera, 'Instrumental lamedh in II Samuel 3,34', *Bib* 61 (1980), p. 261.

seize—E. Lipiński, 'נָגַשׂ *nāgaś*', *TDOT*, IX (1998; orig. 1984–86), pp. 213-15.

נגשׁ *approach*—H. Ringgren, 'נָגַשׁ *nāgaš*', *TDOT*, IX (1998), pp. 215-19.

divine, make contact with the divinity—Samuel Iwry, 'New Evidence for Belomancy in Ancient Palestine and

Phoenicia', *JAOS* 81 (1961), pp. 27-34 (33-35).

meet—M. Dahood, 'Hebrew–Ugaritic Lexicography V', *Bib* 48 (1967), pp. 421-38 (436).

נֵד I *dam*—KB, p. 595b; *HALOT*, II, p. 671a.

dike—W.F. Albright, 'From the Patriarchs to Moses. II. Moses out of Egypt', *BA* 36 (1973), pp. 448-76 (61-62).

heap—BDB, p. 622b.

hill, mountain, wall—Frank M. Cross and David Noel Freedman, 'The Song of Miriam', *JNES* 14 (1955), pp. 237-50 (241, 246).

wall—James Muilenburg, 'A Liturgy on the Triumphs of Yahweh', in *Studia Biblica et Semitica Theodoro Christiano Vriezen ... dedicata* (Wageningen: H. Veenman & Zonen, 1966), pp. 233-51 (242).

Ex 15_{8}—Al Wolters, 'Not Rescue but Destruction: Rereading Exodus 15:8', *CBQ* 52 (1990), pp. 223-40 (228).

נֵד II *mist, fog* (cf. Arab. nada(y) *mist*)—A. Ben-Shemesh, 'In Arabia They Call', *AusBR* 10 (1962), pp. 10-14 (13).

נֵד III *mud-bank* (cf. Akk. nīdu)—G.R. Driver, 'Notes on Joshua', in *The Seventy-Fifth Anniversary Volume of the JQR* (Philadelphia, 1967), pp. 149-65 (154).

נֹד I *changeable circumstances*—*HALOT*, II, p. 671a.

life of a fugitive—Zorell, p. 504a.

wandering—BDB, p. 627a.

נֹד II *grief, lament*—Mitchell Dahood, *Psalms II: 51–100* (AB, 17; Garden City, NY: Doubleday, 1968; 3rd edn, 1979), p. 45.

נֹד III *wineskin*—Al Wolters, 'Not Rescue but Destruction: Rereading Exodus 15:8', *CBQ* 52 (1990), pp. 223-40 (235).

נדב *be freely willing*—J. Conrad, 'נדב *ndb*; נְדָבָה *n^{e}d̲āb̲â*; נָדִיב *nād̲îb̲*; נְדִיבָה *n^{e}d̲îb̲â*', *TDOT*, IX (1998; orig. 1984–86), pp. 219-26.

impel—J.P. Weinberg, 'The Word *ndb* in the Bible: A Study in Historical Semantics and Biblical Thought', in *Solving Riddles and Untying Knots: Biblical, Epigraphic, and Semitic Studies in Honor of Jonas C. Greenfield* (ed. Ziony Zevit, Seymour Gitin and Michael Sokoloff; Winona Lake, IN: Eisenbrauns, 1995), pp. 365-75.

volunteer—Simon Légasse, 'Les pauvres en esprit et les "volontaires" de Qumran', *NTS* 8 (1961–62), pp. 336-45.

נְדָבָה *freewill*—J. Conrad, 'נדב *ndb*; נְדָבָה *n^{e}d̲āb̲â*; נָדִיב *nād̲îb̲*; נְדִיבָה *n^{e}d̲îb̲â*', *TDOT*, IX (1998; orig. 1984–86), pp. 219-26.

freewill offering—Jacob Milgrom, *Leviticus 1–16: A New Translation with Introduction and Commentary* (AB, 3; New York: Doubleday, 1991), pp. 218-19, 419-20.

nobility, generosity—Mitchell Dahood, *Psalms II: 51–100* (AB, 17; Garden City, NY: Doubleday, 1968; 3rd edn, 1979), pp. 26-27.

noble utterance—Mitchell Dahood, *Psalms III: 101–150* (AB, 17A; Garden City, NY: Doubleday, 1970), p. 185.

voluntary act—J.P. Weinberg, 'The Word *ndb* in the Bible: A Study in Historical Semantics and Biblical Thought', in *Solving Riddles and Untying Knots: Biblical, Epigraphic, and Semitic Studies in Honor of Jonas C. Greenfield* (ed. Ziony Zevit, Seymour Gitin and Michael Sokoloff; Winona Lake, IN: Eisenbrauns, 1995), pp. 365-75 (371).

Dt 23_{24} Ps 54_{8}—M. Dahood, 'Hebrew–Ugaritic Lexicography V', *Bib* 48 (1967), pp. 421-38 (435).

נִדְגָּלוֹת I *admirable sights*—*DCH*, II (1995), p. 414b (s.v. דגל II *look*).

aurora borealis or *comets*—Steven T. Byington, 'Brief Communications', *JBL* 39 (1920), pp. 77-82 (82).

celestial phenomena (cf. דָּגוּל *remarkable*)—G.R. Driver, 'Problems and Solutions', *VT* 4 (1954), pp. 225-45 (231 n. 2).

conspicuous stars—S.D. Goitein, '*Ayumma kannidgalot* (Song of Songs vi. 10): "Splendid like the brilliant stars"', *JSS* 10 (1965), pp. 220-21.

great sights—Robert Gordis, *The Song of Songs and Lamentations: A Study, Modern Translation and Commentary* (New York: Ktav, revised edn, 1974), p. 90.

pre-eminence—Samuel Krauss, 'The Archaeological Background of Some Passages in the Song of Songs', *JQR* 32 (1941–42), pp. 115-37 (136-37).

signs of the Zodiac—Wilhelm Rudolph, *Das Buch Ruth. Das Hohe Lied. Die Klagelieder* (KAT, XVII/1-3; Gütersloh: Gerd Mohn, 1962), p. 162.

נִדְגָּלוֹת II *bannered, supplied with standards*—BDB, p. 186a;

Gesenius–Buhl, p. 156a; Zorell, p. 167a.

bannered troops—DCH, II (1995), p. 414b (s.v. דגל I *raise standard*).

troop with banners—HALOT, I, p. 213a.

נדד I *flee*—derivation—M.L. Greenberg, 'The Etymology of niddāh "(Menstrual) Impurity"', in *Solving Riddles and Untying Knots: Biblical, Epigraphic, and Semitic Studies in Honor of Jonas C. Greenfield* (ed. Ziony Zevit, Seymour Gitin and Michael Sokoloff; Winona Lake, IN: Eisenbrauns, 1995), pp. 69-77.

flee—W. Gross, 'נָדַד *nāḏaḏ*', *TDOT*, IX (1998), pp. 227-32.

ho. *thrust away*—2 S 23₆—H. Neil Richardson, 'The Last Words of David: Some Notes on II Samuel 23:1-7', JBL 90 (1971), pp. 257-66 (264-65).

Is 38₁₅—G.R. Driver, 'Isaiah i–xxxix: Textual and Linguistic Problems', *JSS* 13 (1968), pp. 36-57 (56).

נדד II *be burned up* (cf. Eth. näddä *be burnt up*)—G.R. Driver, 'Studies in the Vocabulary of the Old Testament. VI', *JTS* 34 (1933), pp. 375-85 (379-80); Israel Eitan, 'A Contribution to Isaiah Exegesis (Notes and Short Studies in Biblical Philology)', *HUCA* 12–13 (1937–38), pp. 55-88 (65).

נדד III *bow down* (cf. Ug.)—Mitchell Dahood, *Psalms I: 1–50* (AB, 16; Garden City, NY: Doubleday, 1966), p. 257; Mitchell Dahood, *Psalms II: 51–100* (AB, 17; Garden City, NY: Doubleday, 1968; 3rd edn, 1979), pp. 107, 141.

נדה II *throw* (cf. Ug. ndy, Akk. nadû)—M. Dahood, '*Nādâ* "To Hurl" in Ex 15,16' *Bib* 43 (1962), pp. 248-49 (248); Mitchell Dahood, *Psalms I: 1-50* (AB, 16; Garden City, NY: Doubleday, 1966), pp. 190, 224.

pi. *escape*—M. Dahood, '*Nādâ* "To Hurl" in Ex 15,16' *Bib* 43 (1962), pp. 248-49 (249 n. 2).

נדה III pi. *make* or *declare impure* (denominative of נִדָּה *impurity*)—M.L. Greenberg, 'The Etymology of niddāh "(Menstrual) Impurity"', in *Solving Riddles and Untying Knots: Biblical, Epigraphic, and Semitic Studies in Honor of Jonas C. Greenfield* (ed. Ziony Zevit, Seymour Gitin and Michael Sokoloff; Winona Lake, IN: Eisenbrauns, 1995), pp. 69-77 (76-77).

נִדָּה I *expulsion, exclusion*—J. Milgrom, D.P. Wright and H.-J. Fabry, 'נִדָּה *niddâ*', *TDOT*, IX (1998; orig. 1984–86), pp. 232-35.

impurity (cf. נדד *flee*)—as requiring distance—Moshe Greenberg, 'The Etymology of נִדָּה "(Menstrual) Impurity"', in *Solving Riddles and Untying Knots: Biblical, Epigraphic, and Semitic Studies in Honor of Jonas C. Greenfield* (ed. Ziony Zevit, Seymour Gitin and Michael Sokoloff; Winona Lake, IN: Eisenbrauns, 1995), pp. 69-77 (181-84); Jacob Milgrom, *Leviticus 1–16: A New Translation with Introduction and Commentary* (AB, 3; New York: Doubleday, 1991), pp. 744-45.

נִדָּה II *bleeding, menstruation—HALOT*, II, p. 673a.

flow of blood (cf. נדה I *cast, throw*)—Baruch A. Levine, *Numbers 1–20: A New Translation with Introduction and Commentary* (AB, 4A; New York: Doubleday, 1993), pp. 465-66.

separation, abomination, defilement—HALOT, II, p. 673a.

נדח I *expel, thrust* (cf. Arab. nadaḥa)—BDB, p. 623a (cf. Arab. nadagha *push*); Godfrey Rolles Driver, 'Hebrew Roots and Words', *WO* 1 (1947–1952), pp. 406-15 (408-409); T. Kronholm, 'נָדַח *nāḏaḥ*; מַדּוּחִים *maddûḥîm*', *TDOT*, IX (1998; orig. 1984–86), pp. 235-41.

נדח II *wield, impel* (cf. Arab. nadagha *push*)—Godfrey Rolles Driver, 'Hebrew Roots and Words', *WO* 1 (1947–1952), pp. 406-15 (408-409); *HALOT, II*, p. 673b; T. Kronholm, 'נָדַח *nāḏaḥ*; מַדּוּחִים *maddûḥîm*', *TDOT*, IX (1998; orig. 1984–86), pp. 235-41.

נדח III *widen* (cf. Arab. nada'a *widen, make spacious*)—A. Guillaume, 'Paronomasia in the Old Testament', *JSS* 9 (1964), pp. 282-90 (289-90).

נָדִיב *military leader*—David J.A. Clines, *Job 1–20* (WBC, 17; Dallas: Word Books, 1989), p. 301.

noble, of people—J. Conrad, 'נדב *ndb*; נְדָבָה *neḏāḇâ*; נָדִיב *nāḏîḇ*; נְדִיבָה *neḏîḇâ*', *TDOT*, IX (1998; orig. 1984–86), pp. 219-26; G. Barbiero, 'Die "Wagen meines edlen Volkes" (Hld 6,12): eine strukturelle Analyse', *Bib* 78 (1997), pp. 174-89; J.P. Weinberg, 'The Word *ndb* in the Bible: A Study in Historical Semantics and Biblical Thought', in *Solving Riddles and Untying Knots: Biblical, Epigraphic, and Semitic Studies in Honor of Jonas C. Greenfield* (ed. Ziony Zevit, Seymour Gitin and Michael Sokoloff; Winona Lake, IN: Eisenbrauns, 1995), pp. 365-75 (369-70).

prince—J. van der Ploeg, 'Les chefs du peuple d'Israël et leurs titres', *RB* 57 (1950), pp. 40-61 (53-57).

opposite to נָבָל *of no account*—Gillis Gerleman, "Der Nicht-Mensch: Erwägungen zur hebräischer Wurzel *nbl*", *VT* 24 (1974), pp. 147-58 (156-58).

נְבִיבָה *nobility*—J. Conrad, 'נדב *ndb;* נְדָבָה *nedābâ;* נָדִיב *nādîb;* נְדִיבָה *nedîbâ*', *TDOT*, IX (1998; orig. 1984–86), pp. 219-26; J.P. Weinberg, 'The Word *ndb* in the Bible: A Study in Historical Semantics and Biblical Thought', in *Solving Riddles and Untying Knots: Biblical, Epigraphic, and Semitic Studies in Honor of Jonas C. Greenfield* (ed. Ziony Zevit, Seymour Gitin and Michael Sokoloff; Winona Lake, IN: Eisenbrauns, 1995), pp. 365-75 (369).

noble deed—G.R. Driver, 'Studies in the Vocabulary of the Old Testament. IV', *JTS* 33 (1931–32), pp. 38-47 (46); G.R. Driver, 'Psalm cx: Its Form, Meaning and Purpose', in ספר סגל. *Studies in the Bible Presented to Professor M.H. Segal by his Colleagues and Students* (ed. J.M. Grintz and J. Liver; Publications of the Israel Society for Biblical Research, 17; Jerusalem, 1964), pp. 17*-31* (23*).

נדף I *blow away*—Ps 68₃—A. Jirku, 'Zu Psalm lxviii 3a', *VT* 5 (1955), pp. 203-204.

Pr 21₆—Godfrey Rolles Driver, 'Problems of the Hebrew Text and Language', in *Alttestamentliche Studien Friedrich Nötscher zum sechzigsten Geburtstage 19. Juli 1950 gewidmet* (BBB, 1; ed. Hubert Junker and Johannes Botterweck; Bonn: Hanstein, 1950), pp. 46-61 (56-57).

נדף II *dry up* (cf. Arab. nadifa *was dried up*)—A. Guillaume, 'A Note on Isaiah xix. 7', *JTS* ns 14 (1963), pp. 382-83.

נדר *vow*—Jesse L. Boyd, 'The Etymological Relationship between *NDR* and *NZR* Reconsidered', *UF* 17 (1986), pp. 61-75.

נדר *vow*—C.A. Keller, 'נדר *ndr*' , *TLOT*, II (1997; orig. 1976), pp. 719-22; O. Kaiser, 'נָדַר *nādar;* נֶדֶר *neder*', *TDOT*, IX (1998; orig. 1984–86), pp. 242-55; Tony W. Cartledge, *Vows in the Hebrew Bible and the Ancient Near East* (JSOTSup, 147; Sheffield: JSOT Press, 1992); Jacques Berlinerblau, 'The Israelite Vow: Distress or Daily Life?', *Bib* 72 (1991), pp. 548-55.

נֶדֶר *vow*—O. Kaiser, 'נָדַר *nādar;* נֶדֶר *neder*', *TDOT*, IX (1998; orig. 1984–86), pp. 242-55; Adrian Schenker, 'Gelübde im Alten Testament: unbeachtete Aspekte', *VT* 39 (1989), pp. 87-91.

נֹהַּ *eminency, distinction*—BDB, p. 627a.

unexplained—*HALOT*, II, p. 675a.

נהג I *drive*—W. Gross, 'נָהַג *nāhag*', *TDOT*, IX (1998; orig. 1984–86), pp. 255-59.

be led (to Sheol)—Tadeusz Penar, *Northwest Semitic Philology and the Hebrew Fragments of Ben Sira* (BibOr, 28; Rome: Biblical Institute Press, 1975), pp. 9-10.

נהג II *lament*—W. Gross, 'נָהַג *nāhag*', *TDOT*, IX (1998; orig. 1984–86), pp. 255-59.

נהה II *follow, be devoted to* (cf. MH נהי *follow eagerly*)—James Barr, *Comparative Philology and the Text of the Old Testament* (Oxford: Oxford University Press, 1968), pp. 231-32, 264-65.

follow (cf. Arab. nahā(y) *came to*)—G.R. Driver, 'Studies in the Vocabulary of the Old Testament. VI', *JTS* 34 (1933), pp. 375-85 (377).

hold to, stick to—KB, p. 599a; *HALOT*, II, p. 675b.

נהה III *turn* (cf. Akk. nê'u *turn*)—M. Weinfeld, 'Jeremiah and the Spiritual Metamorphosis of Israel', *ZAW* 88 (1976), pp. 17-56 (20 n. 12).

נְהִיָה I *lamentation*—J. Carmignac, 'Précisions apportées au vocabulaire de l'hébreu biblique par la Guerre des Fils de Lumière contre les Fils de Ténèbres', *VT* 5 (1955), pp. 345-65 (351).

נהל I *lead, care for*—Gesenius–Buhl, p. 489a.

lead, give rest—BDB, p. 624b; Zorell, p. 502a.

escort, transport—*HALOT*, II, p. 675b.

נהל II *give rest* (cf. Akk. nālu *lie down, rest*)—P. Haupt, 'The Hebrew Stem *nahal*, to Rest', *AJSL* 22 (1905), pp. 195-206; A.S. Kapelrud, 'נָהַל *nāhal*', *TDOT*, IX (1998; orig. 1984–86), pp. 260-61.

נַהֲלָל *Nahalal*—John L. Peterson, 'Nahalal', *ABD*, IV, pp. 994-95.

נַהֲלֹל I *pasture*—BDB, p. 625a.

watering place—*HALOT*, II, p. 676a.

נַהֲלֹל II *shrub, thorny bush*—Dalman, *Arbeit*, II, p. 323.

נהם I *growl with hunger, be hungry* (cf. Arab. nahama, nahima *roar with hunger*)—G.R. Driver, 'Studies in the

Vocabulary of the Old Testament. VII', *JTS* 35 (1934), pp. 380-93 (386); G.R. Driver, 'Nachtrag, hauptsächlich nach Mitteilungen G. R. Drivers, Oxford, vom 7.2 und 23.3.1962', in Berend Gemser, *Sprüche Salomos* (HAT, I/16; Tübingen: J.C.B. Mohr [Paul Siebeck], 2nd edn, 1963), pp. 111-14 (111).

נחם II *sleep* (cf. Ug. nhm *sleep*)—Walter D. Michel, *Job in the Light of Northwest Semitic*, I (BibOr, 42; Rome: Biblical Institute Press, 1987), p. 268 (following M. Dahood).

נְהָמָה II *yearning* (cf. נחם I *growl, be hungry*)—G.R. Driver, 'Studies in the Vocabulary of the Old Testament. VII', *JTS* 35 (1934), pp. 380-93 (386).

נהר I *flow* (cf. נָהָר *river*)—BDB, p. 625b; *HALOT*, II, p. 676b; H. Ringgren, L.A. Snijders and H.-J. Fabry, 'נָהָר *nāhār*; נְהַר *nahar*', *TDOT*, IX (1998; orig. 1984–86), pp. 261-70.

נהר II *shine* (cf. Aram.)—BDB, p. 626a; *HALOT*, II, p. 676b; H. Ringgren, L.A. Snijders and H.-J. Fabry, 'נָהָר *nāhār*; נְהַר *nahar*', *TDOT*, IX (1998; orig. 1984–86), pp. 261-70.

נהר III *be noisily excited, come in noisy excitement* (cf. Syr. har *bark*, Arab. harr *howl*)—G.R. Driver, 'Notes on the Psalms. II. 73–150', *JTS* 44 (1943), pp. 12-23 (14-15).

נָהָר I *river*—H. Ringgren, L.A. Snijders and H.-J. Fabry, 'נָהָר *nāhār*; נְהַר *nahar*', *TDOT*, IX (1998; orig. 1984–86), pp. 261-70.

stream—Is 59_{19}—G.R. Driver, 'Difficult Words in the Hebrew Prophets', in *Studies in Old Testament Prophecy Presented to Professor Theodore H. Robinson* (ed. H.H. Rowley; Edinburgh: T. & T. Clark, 1950), pp. 52-72 (55).

ocean current—Aubrey R. Johnson, *Sacral Kingship in Ancient Israel* (Cardiff: University of Wales Press, 2nd edn, 1967), p. 67 n. 1; Mitchell Dahood, *Psalms I: 1–50* (AB, 16; Garden City, NY: Doubleday, 1966), p. 151; M. Dahood, 'Hebrew–Ugaritic Lexicography V', *Bib* 48 (1967), pp. 421-38 (437); G.M. Landes, 'The Kerygma of the Book of Jonah', *Interpretation* 21 (1967), pp. 3-31 (6 n. 14).

Ps 89_{26}—Mitchell Dahood, *Psalms II: 51–100* (AB, 17; Garden City, NY: Doubleday, 1968; 3rd edn, 1979), p. 317.

נָהָר II *oil* (cf. נהר *shine*, Arab. tanwîr *lighting, oil*)—H.P. Chajes, 'Note lessicali a proposito della nuova edizione del Gesenius–Buhl', *Giornale della Società Asiatica Italiana* 19 (1906), pp. 175-86 (181-82); N.H. Tur-Sinai, *The Book of Job* (Jerusalem: Kiryath Sepher, revised edn, 1967), p. 314; M. Dahood, 'Hebrew–Ugaritic Lexicography V', *Bib* 48 (1967), pp. 421-38 (437).

נוב *bear fruit*—BDB, p. 626a.

be full of sap (cf. Arab. nūb *abundant rain*)—Godfrey Rolles Driver, 'Hebrew Roots and Words', *WO* 1 (1947–52), pp. 406-15 (406-407).

flow—Mitchell Dahood, *Proverbs and Northwest Semitic Philology* (Scripta Pontificii Instituti Biblici, 113; Rome: Pontificium Institutum Biblicum, 1963), p. 20; Mitchell Dahood, *Psalms II: 51–100* (AB, 17; Garden City, NY: Doubleday, 1968; 3rd edn, 1979), p. 93.

prosper—*HALOT*, II, p. 677b.

נוד I *shake, show pity*—H. Ringgren, 'נוּד *nûḏ*', *TDOT*, IX (1998; orig. 1984–86), pp. 271-72.

נוד II *grieve, lament*—Mitchell Dahood, *Psalms II: 51–100* (AB, 17; Garden City, NY: Doubleday, 1968; 3rd edn, 1979), p. 162.

Ps 119_{83}-–Mitchell Dahood, *Psalms III: 101–150* (AB, 17A; Garden City, NY: Doubleday, 1970), p. 183.

נוֹד *Nod*—Yehuda T. Radday, 'Vom Humor in biblischen Ortsnamen', in *»Wünschet Jerusalem Frieden«. Collected Communications to the XIIth Congress of the International Organization for the Study of the Old Testament, Jerusalem 1986* (ed. Matthias Augustin and Klaus-Dietrich Schunck; BEATAJ, 13; Frankfurt a.M.: Peter Lang, 1988), pp. 431-46 (442-43); Manfred Görg, 'Kain und das "Land Nod"', *BN* 71 (1994), pp. 5-12 (8-9).

נוה II *beautify*—BDB, p. 627a.

glorify—*HALOT*, II, p. 678b.

נוה III *aim at* (cf. Arab. nwy I *aim at*, II *carry out*)—G.R. Driver, 'Linguistic and Textual Problems: Minor Prophets. III', *JTS* 39 (1938), pp. 393-405 (395); cf. Gesenius–Buhl, p. 491a.

reach an objective—*HALOT*, II, p. 678a

reach, settle—W.F. Albright apud Frank M. Cross and David Noel Freedman, 'The Song of Miriam', *JNES* 14 (1955), pp. 237-50 (243 n. e).

qal *aim at;* hi. *admire*—Frank M. Cross and David Noel

Freedman, 'The Song of Miriam', *JNES* 14 (1955), pp. 237-50 (243-44).

נָוֶה *abode of shepherd or flocks; habitation*—BDB, p. 627b.

camp, settlement (of prophets)—P. Kyle McCarter, *I Samuel: A New Translation with Introduction and Commentary* (AB, 8; Garden City, NY: Doubleday, 1980), p. 328.

encampment, pasturage—W.F. Albright, 'A Catalogue of Early Hebrew Lyric Poems (Psalm lxviii)', *HUCA* 23:1 (1950–51), pp. 1-39 (22); A. Malamat, 'Mari and the Bible: Some Patterns of Tribal Organization and Institutions', *JAOS* 82 (1962), pp. 143-50 (146); Abraham Malamat, 'Pre-Monarchical Social Institutions in Israel in the Light of Mari', in *Congress Volume: Jerusalem 1986* (ed. J.A. Emerton; VTSup, 40; Leiden: E.J. Brill, 1988), pp. 165-76 (168-72).

grazing place, stopping place; settlement—*HALOT*, II, p. 678b.

pasture, dwelling place—H. Ringgren, 'נָוֶה *nāweh*', *TDOT*, IX (1998; orig. 1984–86), pp. 273-77.

נָוָה *grazing place; settlement*—*HALOT*, II, p. 678b.

pasture, meadow—BDB, p. 627b.

pasture—F.D. Coggan, 'The Meaning of חטא in Job v.24', *Journal of the Manchester Egyptian and Oriental Society* 17 (1932), pp. 53-56.

Ps 83_{13}—M. Dahood, review of Hans-Joachim Kraus, *Psalmen* (1958–60), *Bib* 42 (1961), pp. 383-85 (384).

נוח I *rest*—Antonio García del Moral, 'Sobre el significado del verbo «nû^{a}ḥ» en Is 11^{2}', *MEstArabH* 10,2 (Granada 1961), pp. 33-63; F. Stolz, 'נוח *nûaḥ*', *TLOT*, II (1997; orig. 1976), pp. 722-24; H.D. Preuss, 'נוּחַ *nûaḥ*; מְנוּחָה *m^{e}nûḥâ*', *TDOT*, IX (1998; orig. 1984–86), pp. 277-86.

hi. *place, versetzen*—Eliezer Rubinstein, 'עיון סמנטי בפעלי מניעה בלשון המקרא (Verbs of Prevention: A Semantic Study in Biblical Hebrew)', in *Proceedings of the Tenth World Congress of Jewish Studies, Jerusalem, August 16-24, 1989*. Division D, Volume 1: *The Hebrew Language; Jewish Languages* (Jerusalem: World Union of Jewish Studies, 1990), pp. 1-6 [Heb].

hi. *cause to rest, lower*—Mitchell Dahood, *Psalms III: 101–150* (AB, 17A; Garden City, NY: Doubleday, 1970), p. 290.

Ps 60_{11} 139_{10}—M. Bogaert, 'Les suffixes verbaux non accusatifs dans le sémitique nord-occidental et particulièrement en hébreu', *Bib* 45 (1964), pp. 220-47 (236-37); Mitchell Dahood, *Psalms II: 51–100* (AB, 17; Garden City, NY: Doubleday, 1968; 3rd edn, 1979), p. 81; M. Dahood, 'Hebrew–Ugaritic Lexicography V', *Bib* 48 (1967), pp. 421-38 (438).

נוח II *sigh* (byform of אנח *sigh*)—G.R. Driver, 'Studies in the Vocabulary of the Old Testament. VI', *JTS* 34 (1933), pp. 375-85 (377); KB, p. 602b; *HALOT*, II, p. 680a.

נוֹחָה I *respite, rest* (cf. נוח *rest*)—G.R. Driver, 'Problems in Judges Newly Discussed', *ALUOS* 4 (1962–63), pp. 6-25 (20-21); Zorell, p. 505a.

נוט *dangle, waver*—BDB, p. 630a; G.R. Driver, 'Notes on the Psalms. II. 73–150', *JTS* 44 (1943), pp. 12-23 (19).

shake—Ruth Scoralick, *Trishagion und Gottesherrschaft: Psalm 99 als Neuinterpretation von Tora und Propheten* (SBS, 138; Stuttgart: Verlag Katholisches Bibelwerk, 1989), pp. 18-22.

tremble—*HALOT*, II, p. 680b.

Ps 99_{1}—Edouard Lipiński, 'Juges 5,4-5 et Psaume 68,8-11', *Bib* 48 (1967), pp. 185-206 (185-95).

נֶוֶל *thread (of life)* (cf. Aram. נול *weave*, נַוְלָא *loom*)—J. Begrich, *Der Psalm des Hiskia: Ein Beitrag zum Verständnis von Jesaja 38,10-20* (FRLANT, NF, 25; Göttingen: Vandenhoeck & Ruprecht, 1926), pp. 31-32; *HALOT*, II, p. 680b.

נום II *speak* (cf. MH נום)—Christof Hardmeier, '"Geschwiegen habe ich seit langem ... wie die Gebärende schreie ich jetzt." Zur Komposition und Geschichtstheologie von Jes 42,14–44,23', *WD* 20 (1989), pp. 155-79 (160 n. 19).

נוֹם *sleep* (noun) (cf. נום *sleep*)—William L. Holladay, *Jeremiah 1: A Commentary on the Book of the Prophet Jeremiah* (Hermeneia; Philadelphia: Fortress Press, 1986), p. 269.

נוס I *flee*—S. Schwertner, 'נוס *nûs*', *TLOT*, II (1997; orig. 1976), pp. 725-27; J. Reindl, 'נוּס *nûs*; מָנוֹס *mānôs*; מְנוּסָה *m^{e}nûsâ*', *TDOT*, IX (1998; orig. 1984–86), pp. 286-93.

hi. *flee*—Mitchell J. Dahood, 'Ugaritic Lexicography' [review of Joseph Aistleitner, *Wörterbuch der ugari-*

tischen Sprache (1963)], in *Mélanges Eugène Tisserant. I. Ecriture sainte—Ancien orient* (Studi e testi, 231; Città del Vaticano; Bibliotheca Apostolica Vaticana, 1964), pp. 81-104 (87).

hi. *move quickly away*—G.R. Driver, 'Problems in Judges Newly Discussed', *ALUOS* 4 (1962–63), pp. 6-25 (12).

Ps 47—M. Dahood, review of Hans-Joachim Kraus, *Psalmen* (1958–60), *Bib* 42 (1961), pp. 383-85 (384).

נוס II *tremble* (cf. Syr. nas *tremble*)—G.R. Driver, 'Linguistic and Textual Problems: Isaiah i–xxxix', *JTS* 38 (1937), pp. 36-50 (39).

נוס III *dry up* (cf. Arab. nassa *become dry*)—Alfred Guillaume, *Hebrew and Arabic Lexicography: A Comparative Study*, II (Leiden: E.J. Brill, 1965; = *AbrN* 2 [1960–61]), p. 25.

נוס IV *swing, dangle* (cf. Arab. nāsa)—Israel Eitan, 'A Contribution to Isaiah Exegesis (Notes and Short Studies in Biblical Philology)', *HUCA* 12–13 (1937–38), pp. 55-88 (72).

נוע I *beg*—Arnold E. Ehrlich, *Randglossen zur hebräischen Bibel*, III (r.p. Hildesheim: Georg Olms, 1968 [original 1908–14]), pp. 110-11.

shake—H. Ringgren, 'נוּעַ *nûa*'', *TDOT*, IX (1998; orig. 1984–86), pp. 293-95; Ernst Jenni, 'Verba gesticulationis im Hebräischen', in *Text, Methode und Grammatik: Wolfgang Richter zum 65. Geburtstag* (ed. Walter Gross, Hubert Irsigler and Theodor Seidl; St Ottilien: EOS Verlag, 1991), pp. 191-203.

Is 9_{18}—William L. Moran, 'The Putative Root *'tm* in Is. 9, 18', *CBQ* 12 (1950), pp. 153-54; M. Dahood, review of C. Rabin (ed.), *Studies in the Bible* (1961), *Bib* 43 (1962), pp. 544-46 (545); M. Dahood, review of E.Y. Kutscher, *The Land and Linguistic Background of the Isaiah-Scroll (IQIsa[a])* (1974), *Bib* 56 (1975), pp. 260-64 (263).

נוע II *be rootless, without support*—J. Ebach and U. Rüterswörden, 'Pointen in der Jothamfabel', *BN* 31 (1986), pp. 11-18.

נוף I *move to and fro, wave, besprinkle*—BDB, p. 631b.

shake sieve—Edouard Lipiński, 'Juges 5,4-5 et Psaume 68,8-11', *Bib* 48 (1967), pp. 185-206 (202-203).

swing—H. Ringgren, 'נוף *nwp*; תְּנוּפָה *tenûpâ*', *TDOT*, IX (1998; orig. 1984–86), pp. 296-99.

נוף II *sprinkle* (cf. Arab. naffa *sow* the earth, *blow* the nose)—G.R. Driver, 'Problems in "Proverbs"', *ZAW* 50 (1932), pp. 141-48 (142-43); *HALOT*, II, p. 682b.

flow, distil (cf. נוב)—Godfrey Rolles Driver, 'Hebrew Roots and Words', *WO* 1 (1947–52), pp. 406-15 (407 n. 7); Mitchell Dahood, *Proverbs and Northwest Semitic Philology* (Scripta Pontificii Instituti Biblici, 113; Rome: Pontificium Institutum Biblicum, 1963), p. 20.

נוף III *bow down* (cf. Syr. nāf)—G.R. Driver, 'Notes on the Psalms. II. 73–150', *JTS* 44 (1943), pp. 12-23 (17).

נוף IV *declare superfluous, treat as a special contribution* (denom. of תְּנוּפָה *special contribution, additional gift*; cf. Akk. nūptu *additional payment*)—G.R. Driver, 'Three Technical Terms in the Pentateuch', *JSS* 1 (1956), pp. 97-103 (102-103); W.F. Albright, 'A Catalogue of Early Hebrew Lyric Poems (Psalm lxviii)', *HUCA* 23:1 (1950–51), pp. 1-39 (20); H. Ringgren, 'נוף *nwp*; תְּנוּפָה *tenûpâ*', *TDOT*, IX (1998; orig. 1984–86), pp. 296-99.

נוף V *raise* (cf. Arab. nāfa *be high*)—L. Kopf, 'Arabische Etymologien und Parallelen zum Bibelwörterbuch', *VT* 9 (1959), pp. 247-87 (262-65); J. Milgrom, 'The Alleged Wave-Offering in Israel and in the Ancient Near East', *IEJ* 22 (1972), pp. 33-38 (34); H. Ringgren, 'נוף *nwp*; תְּנוּפָה *tenûpâ*', *TDOT*, IX (1998; orig. 1984–86), pp. 296-99; Jacob Milgrom, *Leviticus 1–16: A New Translation with Introduction and Commentary* (AB, 3; New York: Doubleday, 1991), pp. 461-73 (469).

נוף VI *deliver in large measure* (cf. נוֹף *height*, Arab. nauf *surplus*, Akk. nūptu *exeptional payment*, nāpu *give as surplus*)—Edouard Lipiński, 'Juges 5,4-5 et Psaume 68,8-11', *Bib* 48 (1967), pp. 185-206 (202-203).

נוֹף II *Memphis* (= נֹף)—Michael L. Barré, 'The Seven Epithets of Zion in Ps 48,2-3', *Bib* 69 (1988), pp. 557-63 (560-63).

נוץ I *flee* (cf. Arab. n'ṣ)—G.R. Driver, 'Studies in the Vocabulary of the Old Testament. VI', *JTS* 34 (1933), pp. 375-85 (378); G.R. Driver, 'Hebrew Notes on "Song of Songs" and "Lamentations"', in *Festschrift Alfred Bertholet zum 80. Geburtstag gewidmet von Kollegen und Freunden* (ed. Walter Baumgartner [*et al.*]; Tübingen: J.C.B. Mohr, 1950), pp. 134-46 (142); *HALOT*, II, p. 682b.

נוץ II *sparkle* (cf. Arab. nâḍa *shine, be in movement*)—Zorell,

p. 506a; J. Carmignac, 'Précisions apportées au vocabulaire de l'hébreu biblique par la Guerre des Fils de Lumière contre les Fils de Ténèbres', *VT* 5 (1955), pp. 345-65 (351-52).

נושׁ II *tremble* (cf. Ug. 'anš)—Maurice Sznycer, 'Sur un passage du poème ougaritique de Ba'al et Yam (III AB)', *Sem* 17 (1967), pp. 23-27 (27).

נזה I *sprinkle*—J. Milgrom, D.F. Wright and H.-J. Fabry, 'נָזָה *nāzâ*', *TDOT*, IX (1998; orig. 1984–86), pp. 300-304.

נזה II *make to leap*—Zorell, p. 507a.

spring, leap (dub.)—BDB, p. 633b.

startle—G.R. Driver, 'Isaiah 52_{13}–53_{12}: The Servant of the Lord', in *In Memoriam Paul Kahle* (ed. Matthew Black and Georg Fohrer; BZAW, 103; Berlin: A. Töpelmann, 1968), pp. 90-105 (92).

נָזִיר I *Nazirite*—J. Kühlewein, 'נָזִיר *nāzîr*' , *TLOT*, II (1997; orig. 1976), pp. 727-29; G. Mayer, 'נזר *nzr*; נֵזֶר *nēzer*; נָזִיר *nāzîr*', *TDOT*, IX (1998; orig. 1984–86), pp. 306-11.

נָזִיר II *cursed* (cf. Akk. nazāru *curse*)—G.R. Driver, 'Some Hebrew Roots and their Meanings', *JTS* 23 (1921–22), pp. 69-73 (69-70).

נזל *flow down*—P. Maiberger, 'נָזַל *nāzal*', *TDOT*, IX (1998; orig. 1984–86), pp. 304-306.

irrigate—W.F. Albright, 'From the Patriarchs to Moses. II. Moses out of Egypt', *BA* 36 (1973), pp. 448-76 (61-62).

נֶזֶם *earring* of divine image—Victor Avigdor Hurowitz, 'Who Lost an Earring? Genesis 35:4 Reconsidered', *CBQ* 62 (2000), pp. 28-32.

נזף *accuse, reject*—Zorell, p. 507b.

נֶזֶק *trouble, bother* (cf. Akk. nazāqu *bother*)—H.L. Ginsberg, 'Lexicographical Notes', in *Hebräische Wortforschung: Festschrift zum 80. Geburtstag von Walter Baumgartner* (VTSup, 16; Leiden: E.J. Brill, 1967), pp. 71-82 (81).

נזר I *consecrate*—G. Mayer, 'נזר *nzr*; נֵזֶר *nēzer*; נָזִיר *nāzîr*', *TDOT*, IX (1998; orig. 1984–86), pp. 306-11.

dedicate—Jesse L. Boyd, 'The Etymological Relationship between *NDR* and *NZR* Reconsidered', *UF* 17 (1986), pp. 61-75.

נזר II *guard against, warn* (cf. Arab. naḏara)—G.R. Driver, 'Studies in the Vocabulary of the Old Testament. VI', *JTS* 34 (1933), pp. 375-85 (380); L. Kopf, 'Arabische Etymologien und Parallelen zum Bibelwörterbuch', *VT* 8 (1958), pp. 161-215 (183); G. Rinaldi, '*nzr*', *BeO* 9 (1967), p. 95.

נֵזֶר I *consecration, diadem*—G. Mayer, 'נזר *nzr*; נֵזֶר *nēzer*; נָזִיר *nāzîr*', *TDOT*, IX (1998; orig. 1984–86), pp. 306-11.

diadem—Jacob Milgrom, *Leviticus 1–16: A New Translation with Introduction and Commentary* (AB, 3; New York: Doubleday, 1991), pp. 512-23.

נֵזֶר II *flower* (cf. Eg. nzr.t *snake goddess* or nśr.t *flame*)—Manfred Görg, 'Die Kopfbedeckung des Hohenpriesters', *BN* 3 (1977), pp. 24-26; Manfred Görg, 'Weiteres zu *nzr* ("Diadem")', *BN* 4 (1977), pp. 7-8.

נֹחַ *Noah* (*long-lived*; cf. נוח *be stretched out, rest*)—G.R. Driver, 'L'interprétation du texte masorétique à la lumière de la lexicographie hébraïque', *ETL* 26 (1950), pp. 337-53 (350); Martin Noth, 'Noah, Daniel und Hiob in Ezechiel xiv', *VT* 1 (1951), pp. 251-60 (254-57).

נחב *be lean, dry up* (cf. Aram.)—N.H. Tur-Sinai, *The Book of Job* (Jerusalem: Kiryath Sepher, revised edn, 1967), p. 412.

נחה I *lead*—E. Jenni, 'נחה *nḥh*', *TLOT*, II (1997; orig. 1976), pp. 729-30; C. Barth, 'נָחָה *nāḥâ*', *TDOT*, IX (1998; orig. 1984–86), 311-18; Hedwige Rouillard, *La pericope de Balaam* (Nombres *22–24): La prose et les «oracles»* (Etudes bibliques, ns 4; Paris: Gabalda, 1985), pp. 215-16.

lead to otherworldly destination—Mitchell Dahood, *Psalms I: 1–50* (AB, 16; Garden City, NY: Doubleday, 1966), pp. 33, 147; Mitchell Dahood, *Psalms II: 51–100* (AB, 17; Garden City, NY: Doubleday, 1968; 3rd edn, 1979), pp. 85, 129, 195; Mitchell Dahood, *Psalms III: 101–150* (AB, 17A; Garden City, NY: Doubleday, 1970), pp. 299, 326.

offer—M. Dahood, 'Hebrew–Ugaritic Lexicography VI', *Bib* 49 (1968), pp. 355-69 (357).

hi. *free*—Ec 4_1—M. Dahood, 'The Phoenician Background of Qoheleth', *Bib* 47 (1966), pp. 264-82 (272).

Ps 106_{45}—Mitchell Dahood, *Psalms III: 101–150* (AB, 17A; Garden City, NY: Doubleday, 1970), p. 76.

נחה II *stand by, support* (cf. Ug. nḥw *proceed to*, Arab. nḥw *turn towards*)—*HALOT*, II, p. 685b; O. Loretz, 'Ugaritisch *nḥw* und hebräisch *nḥh* im Kontext der Legende vom syrisch-ephraemitischen Krieg', *UF* 29 (1997), pp. 511-28.

נחה III *aim at, incline towards* (cf. Arab. naḥa *direct oneself*)—G.R. Driver, 'Studies in the Vocabulary of the Old Testament. VI', *JTS* 34 (1933), pp. 375-85 (377); G.R. Driver, 'Textual and Linguistic Problems of the Book of Psalms', *HTR* 29 (1936), pp. 171-95 (173); Godfrey Rolles Driver, 'Hebrew Roots and Words', *WO* 1 (1947–1952), pp. 406-15 (410); G.R. Driver, 'Babylonian and Hebrew Notes', *WO* 2 (1954–59), pp. 19-26 (26); G.R. Driver, 'Hebrew Notes', *VT* 1 (1951), pp. 241-50 (248); J.D. Michaelis apud J.A. Emerton, 'Notes on Jeremiah 12 9 and on Some Suggestions of J.D. Michaelis about the Hebrew Words naḥā, 'æbrā, and jadă'', *ZAW* 81 (1969), pp. 182-91 (188-89).

נחה IV *ally oneself* (cf. Akk. nâḫu)—Otto Eissfeldt, 'nûaḥ "sich vertragen"', *SchwThUmschau* 20 (1950), pp. 71-74 (= *Festschrift für Ludwig Koehler zu dessen 70. Geburtstag*, pp. 23-26); = Otto Eissfeldt, *Kleine Schriften*, III [ed. Rudolf Sellheim and Fritz Maass; Tübingen: J.C.B. Mohr (Paul Siebeck), 1966], pp. 124-28).

נְחוּמִים *inward parts*—M. Dahood, 'Hebrew–Ugaritic Lexicography VI', *Bib* 49 (1968), pp. 355-69 (358).

נְחוּשָׁה I *copper, bronze*—H.-J. Fabry, 'נְחֹשֶׁת *neḥōšet*; נְחוּשָׁה *neḥûšâ*; נְחֻשְׁתָּן *neḥuštān*', *TDOT*, IX (1998; orig. 1984–86), pp. 370-80.

נְחוּשָׁה II *enchantment* (cf. נחשׁ II *practise divination*)—M. Dahood, review of Sigmund Mowinckel, *The Psalms in Israel's Worship* (1962), *Bib* 45 (1964), pp. 109-11 (110).

נְחִילוֹת I *played on the flute* (cf. חָלִיל *flute*)—cf. BDB, p. 636a; *HALOT*, II, p. 686a.

unexplained—BDB, p. 636a; *HALOT*, II, p. 686a.

נְחִילוֹת II *against sickness* (cf. חלה *be sick*)—cf. *HALOT*, II, p. 686a.

נְחִילוֹת III *inheritances* (cf. נַחֲלָה *inheritance*)—Zorell, p. 508b.

נחל *assign property, apportion*—A. Malamat, 'Mari and the Bible: Some Patterns of Tribal Organization and Institutions', *JAOS* 82 (1962), pp. 143-50 (147-50); A. Malamat, ''מארי והמקרא: לדפוסי המשמר השבטי' (Mari and the Bible: Patterns of Tribal Organization', in ספר סגל. *Studies in the Bible Presented to Professor M.H. Segal by his Colleagues and Students* (ed. J.M. Grintz and J. Liver; Jerusalem: Kiryat Sepher, 1964), pp. 19-32 (29-31) [Heb].

inherit—E. Lipiński, 'נָחַל *nāḥal*; נַחֲלָה *naḥalâ*', *TDOT*, IX (1998; orig. 1984–86), pp. 319-35.

נחל II *sift* (cf. Arab. naḥala, Akk. naḫālu, Syr. neḥal)—G.R. Driver, 'Textual and Linguistic Problems of the Book of Psalms', *HTR* 29 (1936), pp. 171-95 (187); G.R. Driver, 'Linguistic and Textual Problems: Jeremiah', *JQR* 28 (1937–38), pp. 97-129 (112); G.R. Driver, 'Three Notes', *VT* 2 (1952), pp. 356-57.

נַחַל I *grave trench, tunnel, mine shaft*—Manfred Weise, 'Jesaja 57 5f.', ZAW 72 (1960), pp. 25-32 (29-31); *HALOT*, II, p. 687a.

ravine (perh. with perennial stream)—J.T. Milik, 'Le rouleau de cuivre provenant de la grotte 3Q (3Q15)', in *DJD*, III (1962), pp. 199-302 (240.28).

wadi—L.A. Snijders and H.-J. Fabry, 'נַחַל *naḥal*; אֵיתָן *'êṯān*', *TDOT*, IX (1998; orig. 1984–86), pp. 335-40.

נַחַל אֵיתָן *devastating* (not *perennial*) *torrent*—L.A. Snijders and H.-J. Fabry, 'נַחַל *naḥal*; אֵיתָן *'êṯān*', *TDOT*, IX (1998; orig. 1984–86), pp. 335-40 (336-38).

Ps 1244—Mitchell Dahood, *Psalms III: 101–150* (AB, 17A; Garden City, NY: Doubleday, 1970), p. 212.

נַחַל II *date-palm*—*HALOT*, II, p. 687b.

palm-tree—BDB, p. 636b.

נַחַל III *tomb*—Charles A. Kennedy, 'Isaiah 57:3-6: Tombs in the Rocks', *BASOR* 275 (1989), pp. 47-52 (48-49); cf. *HALOT*, II, p. 687a.

נַחַל IV *(mine) shaft* (cf. Arab. khalalun *gap*, khallatun *hole*)—Alfred Guillaume, *Hebrew and Arabic Lexicography: A Comparative Study*, IV (Leiden: E.J. Brill, 1965; = *AbrN* 3 [1964–65]), p. 10.

נַחַל V *dust*—B. Jacob, 'Das hebräische Sprachgut im Christlich-Palästinischen', *ZAW* 22 (1902), pp. 83-113 (102) = B. Jacob, 'Christlich-Palästinisches', *ZDMG* 55 (1901), pp. 135-45 (141).

נַחַל VI *excavation, shaft* (cf. Akk. niḫlu)—G.R. Driver, 'Problems in Job', *AJSL* 52 (1936), pp. 160-70 (162).

נַחֲלָה I *inheritance*—A. Malamat, 'Mari and the Bible: Some Patterns of Tribal Organization and Institutions', *JAOS* 82 (1962), pp. 143-50 (147-50); H. Langhammer,

'Die Verheissung vom Erbe. Ein Beitrag zur biblischen Sprache', *BiLeb* 8 (1967), pp. 157-65; G. Wanke, 'נַחֲלָה *naḥ^a^lâ*', *TLOT*, II (1997; orig. 1976), pp. 731-34; E. Lipiński, 'נָחַל *nāḥal*; נַחֲלָה *naḥ^a^lâ*', *TDOT*, IX (1998; orig. 1984–86), pp. 319-35; Abraham Malamat, 'Pre-Monarchical Social Institutions in Israel in the Light of Mari', in *Congress Volume: Jerusalem 1986* (ed. J.A. Emerton; VTSup, 40; Leiden: E.J. Brill, 1988), pp. 165-76 (172-75).

kingdom—Mitchell Dahood, *Psalms I: 1–50* (AB, 16; Garden City, NY: Doubleday, 1966), p. 285.

נַחֲלָה II *destruction* (cf. Eth. nehlä *collapse*)—Israel Eitan, 'A Contribution to Isaiah Exegesis (Notes and Short Studies in Biblical Philology)', *HUCA* 12–13 (1937–38), pp. 55-88 (65).

נַחֲלָה III *wasting disease* (cf. Arab. naḥila *was wasted, worn out with emaciation*)—G.R. Driver, 'Isaiah i–xxxix: Textual and Linguistic Problems', *JSS* 13 (1968), pp. 36-57 (45).

chronic illness—*HALOT*, II, p. 688a.

נחם morphology—aphel—Mitchell Dahood, 'Some Aphel Causatives in Ugaritic', *Bib* 38 (1957), pp. 62-73 (70 n. 1).

avenge—G.R. Driver, 'Problems and Solutions', *VT* 4 (1954), pp. 225-45 (237).

be sorry (not *repent*)—John Briggs Curtis, 'On Job's Response to Yahweh', *JBL* 98 (1979), pp. 497-511 (499-500).

comfort—H.J. Stoebe, 'נחם *nḥm*', *TLOT*, II (1997; orig. 1976), pp. 734-39; H. Simian-Yofre and H.-J. Fabry, 'נחם *nḥm*', *TDOT*, IX (1998; orig. 1984–86), pp. 340-55.

change one's mind—Thorir Thordensen, 'Notes on the Semiotic Context of the Verb *niḥam* in the Book of Jonah', *SEÅ* 54 (1989), pp. 226-35.

have bad, unpleasant, feelings—K. Jongeling, 'Joab and the Tekoite Woman', *JEOL* 30 (1987–88), pp. 116-22 (118-20).

relent—John Bright, *Jeremiah: A New Translation with Introduction and Commentary* (AB, 21; Garden City, NY: Doubleday, 1965), p. 31; Mitchell Dahood, *Psalms II: 51–100* (AB, 17; Garden City, NY: Doubleday, 1968; 3rd edn, 1979), pp. 226-27.

repent—Raphael Loewe, 'Jerome's Treatment of an Anthropopathism', *VT* 2 (1952), pp. 261-72.

vindicate—David Noel Freedman, 'The Twenty-Third Psalm', in *Michigan Oriental Studies in Honor of George C. Cameron* (ed. Louis L. Orlin; Ann Arbor: Department of Near Eastern Studies, The University of Michigan, 1976), pp. 139-66 (157-59).

נֹחַם *revenge, vengefulness*—H.L. Ginsberg, 'Lexicographical Notes', in *Hebräische Wortforschung: Festschrift zum 80. Geburtstag von Walter Baumgartner* (VTSup, 16; Leiden: E.J. Brill, 1967), pp. 71-82 (78-79).

נחן *groan*—Mitchell Dahood, 'Ugaritic Studies and the Bible', *Greg* 43 (1962), pp. 55-79 (70); Mitchell Dahood, *Ugaritic–Hebrew Philology: Marginal Notes on Recent Publications* (BibOr, 17: Rome: Pontifical Biblical Institute, 1965), p. 66; M. Dahood, 'Hebrew–Ugaritic Lexicography VI', *Bib* 49 (1968), pp. 355-69 (358-59).

נחץ I *be urgent (?)*—BDB, p. 637b, Gesenius–Buhl, p. 498b; Zorell, p. 511a; *HALOT*, II, p. 690a.

נחץ II *be private* (cf. Arab. khaṣṣ *be private*)—Alfred Guillaume, *Hebrew and Arabic Lexicography: A Comparative Study*, I (Leiden: E.J. Brill, 1965; = *AbrN* 1 [1959–60]), pp. 11, 27-28.

נחר I *snort in rage* (cf. Aram. נחר, Akk. naḫāru *snort*)—G.R. Driver, 'Studies in the Vocabulary of the Old Testament. VI', *JTS* 34 (1933), pp. 375-85 (381); G.R. Driver, 'Studies in the Vocabulary of the Old Testament. VII', *JTS* 35 (1934), pp. 380-93 (393); G.R. Driver, 'Linguistic and Textual Problems: Isaiah xl–lxvi', *JTS* 36 (1935), pp. 396-406 (398-99); G.R. Driver, 'Two Misunderstood Passages of the Old Testament', *JTS* ns 6 (1955), pp. 82-87 (85).

נחר II *be hoarse* (cf. Syr. ḥar, Arab. kharr *snore*)—G.R. Driver, 'Notes on the Psalms. II. 73–150', *JTS* 44 (1943), pp. 12-23 (14 n. 4).

נחשׁ *divine*—Otto Sauermann, *Untersuchungen zu der Wortgruppe* נחשׁ (Vienna: Mayer, 1952); cf. W. von Soden, review of Otto Sauermann, *Untersuchungen zu der Wortgruppe* נחשׁ (1952), *WZKM* 53 (1956), pp. 157-60; H.-J. Fabry, 'נָחָשׁ *nāḥāš*; נחשׁ *nḥš*; אֶפְעֶה *'ep'eh*; זָחַל *zāḥal*; עַכְשׁוּב *'akšûḇ*; פֶּתֶן *peṯen*; צֶפַע *ṣepa'*; צִפְעוֹנִי

ṣip'ônî; קִפֹּז *qippōz*; שְׁפִיפֹן *šᵉpîpōn'*, *TDOT*, IX (1998; orig. 1984–86), pp. 356-69; Frederick H. Cryer, *Divination in Ancient Israel and its Near Eastern Environment: A Socio-Historical Investigation* (JSOTSup, 142; Sheffield: JSOT Press, 1994); Herbert B. Huffmon, 'Priestly Divination in Israel', in *The Word of the Lord Shall Go Forth: Esssays in Honor of David Noel Freedman in Celebrationof His Sixtieth Birthday* (ed. Carol L. Meyers and M. O'Connor; Winona Lake, IN: Eisenbrauns, 1983), pp. 355-59; Ann Jeffers, *Magic and Divination in Ancient Palestine and Syria* (Studies in the History and Culture of the Ancient Near East, 8; Leiden: E.J. Brill, 1996).

divine by observation of natural phenomena—Hedwige Rouillard, *La pericope de Balaam (*Nombres *22–24): La prose et les «oracles»* (Etudes bibliques, ns 4; Paris: Gabalda, 1985), pp. 301-309 (304).

נחשׁ II *become rich* (cf. Akk. naḫāšu)—N.M. Waldman, *JQR* 55 (1964), pp. 164-65.

נַחַשׁ *divination, enchantment*—BDB, p. 638b.

magic curse, omen—*HALOT*, II, p. 690b.

spell—KB, p. 610a.

נָחָשׁ *snake*—Karen Randolph Joines, *Serpent Symbolism in the Old Testament: A Linguistic, Archaeological, and Literary Study* (Haddonfield, NJ: Haddonfield House, 1974); Maria Luisa Mayer Modena, 'Il tabù linguistico e alcune denominazioni del serpente in semitico', *Acme* 35 (1982), pp. 173-90; H.-J. Fabry, 'נָחָשׁ *nāḥāš*; נחשׁ *n ḥš*; אֶפְעֶה *'ep'eh*; זָחַל *zāḥal*; עַכְשׁוּב *' akšûḇ*; פֶּתֶן *peṯen*; צֶפַע *ṣepa'*; צִפְעוֹנִי *ṣip'ônî*; קִפֹּז *qippōz*; שְׁפִיפֹן *šᵉpîpōn'*, *TDOT*, IX (1998; orig. 1984–86), pp. 356-69; Giovanni Garbini, 'Le Serpent d'Airain et Moïse', *ZAW* 100 (1988), pp. 264-67.

נַחְשׁוֹל *gale* (cf. MH)—Jastrow, p. 897a.

נַחְשִׁיר I *carnage* (cf. Pers. nakhčīr hunt, fight, carnage)—J.P. Asmussen, 'Das iranische Lehnwort nashir in der Kriegsrolle von Qumrân (1QM),' *AcOr* 26 (1961), pp. 3-20; Yigael Yadin, *The Scroll of the War of the Sons of Light against the Sons of Darkness* (Oxford: Oxford University Press, 1962), p. 260.

נחשׁיר II *hunting*(cf. Pers. naḥjîr, Syr. naḥšîr)—G.R. Driver, review of E.L. Sukenik, *The Dead Sea Scrolls of the Hebrew University* (1955), *JTS* ns 8 (1957), pp. 141-43 (142).

נחשׁיר III *fear, terror*—Chaim Rabin, 'Hittite Words in Hebrew', *Or* 32 (1963), pp. 113-39 (132-33).

נְחֹשֶׁת I *bronze, copper*—H.-J. Fabry, 'נְחֹשֶׁת *nᵉḥōšeṯ*; נְחוּשָׁה *nᵉḥûšâ*; נְחֻשְׁתָּן *nᵉḥuštān'*, *TDOT*, IX (1998; orig. 1984–86), pp. 370-80.

copper-ore—Godfrey Driver, 'Water in the Mountains!', *PEQ* 102 (1970), pp. 83-91 (86).

bronze fetters (as an archaizing idiom)—Mordechai Cogan and Hayim Tadmor, *II Kings: A New Translation with Introduction and Commentary* (AB, 11; New York: Doubleday, 1988), p. 318.

נְחֹשֶׁת מֻצְהָב *orichalc*, yellow copper alloy—G.R. Driver, 'Babylonian and Hebrew Notes', *WO* 2 (1954–59), pp. 19-26 (24-25).

נְחֹשֶׁת I *lust, harlotry*—BDB, p. 639a.

menstruation—KB, p. 610b; *HALOT*, II, p. 691b.

נְחֻשְׁתָּן *Nehushtan*—H.-J. Fabry, 'נְחֹשֶׁת *nᵉḥōšeṯ*; נְחוּשָׁה *nᵉḥûšâ*; נְחֻשְׁתָּן *nᵉḥuštān'*, *TDOT*, IX (1998; orig. 1984–86), pp. 370-80.

נחת I *bend* bow—B. Couroyer, '*nḥt*: «Encorder un arc» (?)', *RB* 88 (1981), pp. 13-18.

go away—G.R. Driver, 'Linguistic and Textual Problems: Isaiah xl–lxvi', *JTS* 36 (1935), pp. 396-406 (402); G.R. Driver, 'Linguistic and Textual Problems: Isaiah i–xxxix', *JTS* 38 (1937), pp. 36-50 (42).

go down—BDB, p. 639a.

pi. *lower*—M. Dahood, review of Sigmund Mowinckel, *The Psalms in Israel's Worship* (1962), *Bib* 45 (1964), pp. 109-101 (110).

pi. with infixed *t*—Mitchell Dahood, *Proverbs and Northwest Semitic Philology* (Scripta Pontificii Instituti Biblici, 113; Rome: Pontificium Institutum Biblicum, 1963), pp. 45-46.

hi. *bring down* army to battle—James A. Montgomery and Henry Snyder Gehman, *A Critical and Exegetical Commentary on the Books of Kings* (ICC; Edinburgh: T. & T. Clark, 1951), p. 382; Mordechai Cogan and Hayim Tadmor, *II Kings: A New Translation with Introduction and Commentary* (AB, 11; New York: Doubleday, 1988), p. 72.

hi. *launch into battle*—Theodor H. Gaster, 'The Battle of

the Rain and the Sea', *Iraq* 4 (1937), pp. 21-32 (28 n. 13).

נחת II *be strong*—Robert M. Good, 'Hebrew and Ugaritic *NḤT*', UF 17 (1986), pp. 153-56; Manfred Görg, 'Marginalien zur Basis *nḥt*', *BN* 32 (1986), 20-21.

נחת III hi. *deport*—*HALOT*, II, p. 692b.

נחת IV *hew, fashion* (cf. Arab. ḥt, naḥata)—Joseph Reider, 'Etymological Studies in Biblical Hebrew', *VT* 2 (1952), pp. 113-30 (114-15); Julian Obermann, 'How Baal Destroyed a Rival', *JAOS* 67 (1947), pp. 195-208 (199); P. Kyle McCarter, *I Samuel: A New Translation with Introduction and Commentary* (AB, 9; Garden City, NY: Doubleday, 1984), pp. 454, 459-60, 470-71.

נַחַת II *calm, patience*—James Muilenburg, 'A Qoheleth Scroll from Qumran', *BASOR* 135 (1954), pp. 20-28 (25); cf. M. Metzger, 'Himmlische und irdische Wohnstatt Jahwes', *UF* 2 (1970), pp. 139-58 (157-58); *HALOT*, II, p. 692b.

peace—Mitchell J. Dahood, 'Canaanite-Phoenician Influence in Qoheleth', *Bib* 33 (1952), pp. 30-52, 191-221 (46-47); Mitchell Dahood, 'Qoheleth and Northwest Semitic Philology', *Bib* 43 (1962), pp. 349-65 (355).

נַחַר III *strength*—Maximilian Ellenbogen, *Foreign Words in the Old Testament: Their Origin and Etymology* (London: Luzac & Co., 1962), p. 112; Robert M. Good, 'Hebrew and Ugaritic *NḤT*', *UF* 17 (1986), pp. 153-56; Manfred Görg, 'Marginalien zur Basis *nḥt*', *BN* 32 (1986), pp. 20-21.

נטו *drop* (byform of נטף *drip*)—Mitchell Dahood, *Psalms I: 1–50* (AB, 16; Garden City, NY: Doubleday, 1966), p. 240.

נט I *go down*—Ps 68_9—Ernst Vogt, '«Die Himmel troffen» (Ps 68,9)?', *Bib* 46 (1965), pp. 207-209.

stretch out—H. Ringgren, 'נָטָה *nāṭâ*', *TDOT*, IX (1998; orig. 1984–86), pp. 381-87; Hedwige Rouillard, *La pericope de Balaam (*Nombres *22–24): La prose et les «oracles»* (Etudes bibliques, ns 4; Paris: Gabalda, 1985), pp. 356-58.

stretch out—hi. intrans., with ellipsis of נַפְשׁוֹתָם *themselves*—G.R. Driver, 'Linguistic and Textual Problems: Minor Prophets. II', *JTS* 39 (1938), pp. 260-73 (261).

spread out—Norman C. Habel, '"He who stretches out the heavens"', *CBQ* 34 (1972), pp. 417-30.

Ps 109_{23}—Mitchell Dahood, *Psalms III: 101–150* (AB, 17A; Garden City, NY: Doubleday, 1970), p. 107.

נטִיַע I *plant*—J. Reindl and H. Ringgren, *'נָטַע nāṭa'; מַטָּע maṭṭā'; נֶטַע neṭa', נְטִעִים neṭi'îm; שָׁתַל šāṯal'*, *TDOT*, IX (1998; orig. 1984–86), pp. 387-94.

נְטִיפָה *pendant*—H. Madl, *'נָטַף nāṭap; נָטָף nāṭāp; נֶטֶף neṭep; נְטִ(י)פוֹת neṭîpôṯ; נְטֹפָה neṭōpâ; נְטֹפָתִי neṭōpāṯî'*, *TDOT*, IX (1998; orig. 1984–86), pp. 395-406.

נְטִישָׁה *tendril*—J. Lundbom and H.-J. Fabry, *'נָטַשׁ nāṭaš; נְטִישָׁה neṭîšâ'*, *TDOT*, IX (1998; orig. 1984–86), pp. 407-12.

נטל *weigh heavily*—G.R. Driver, 'Hebrew Notes on "Song of Songs" and "Lamentations"', in *Festschrift Alfred Bertholet zum 80. Geburtstag gewidmet von Kollegen und Freunden* (ed. Walter Baumgartner [*et al.*]; Tübingen: J.C.B. Mohr, 1950), pp. 134-46 (140).

Is 40_{15}—D. Winton Thomas, '»A Drop of a Bucket«? Some Observations on the Hebrew Text of Isaiah 40 $_{15}$', in *In Memoriam Paul Kahle* (ed. Matthew Black and Georg Fohrer; BZAW, 103; Berlin: A. Töpelmann, 1968), pp. 214-21 (218-19).

נטע *plant*—J. Reindl and H. Ringgren, *'נָטַע nāṭa'; מַטָּע maṭṭā'; נֶטַע neṭa', נְטִעִים neṭi'îm; שָׁתַל šāṯal'*, *TDOT*, IX (1998; orig. 1984–86), pp. 387-94; Hedwige Rouillard, *La pericope de Balaam (*Nombres *22–24): La prose et les «oracles»* (Etudes bibliques, ns 4; Paris: Gabalda, 1985), pp. 356-58.

נֶטַע I *plant*—J. Reindl and H. Ringgren, *'נָטַע nāṭa'; מַטָּע maṭṭā'; נֶטַע neṭa', נְטִעִים neṭi'îm; שָׁתַל šāṯal'*, *TDOT*, IX (1998; orig. 1984–86), pp. 387-94.

progeny—Tadeusz Penar, *Northwest Semitic Philology and the Hebrew Fragments of Ben Sira* (BibOr, 28; Rome: Biblical Institute Press, 1975), p. 5.

נֶטַע II *pavilion* (cf. Sab. nṭ't *kiosk, caravanserai*)—G.R. Driver, 'Notes on the Psalms. II. 73–150', *JTS* 44 (1943), pp. 12-23 (23).

נטף *drip, drop*—H. Madl, *'נָטַף nāṭap; נָטָף nāṭāp; נֶטֶף neṭep; נְטִ(י)פוֹת neṭîpôṯ; נְטֹפָה neṭōpâ; נְטֹפָתִי neṭōpāṯî'*, *TDOT*, IX (1998; orig. 1984–86), pp. 395-406.

drip, pour forth (cf. Eg. dj *drip, overflow*)—William A.

Ward, 'Notes on Some Egypto-Semitic Roots', *ZÄS* 95 (1968), pp. 65-72 (70-72).

Ps 68₉—Ernst Vogt, '«Die Himmel troffen» (Ps 68,9)?', *Bib* 46 (1965), pp. 207-209.

Ps 99₁—Edouard Lipiński, 'Juges 5,4-5 et Psaume 68,8-11', *Bib* 48 (1967), pp. 185-206 (185-95).

נָטָף *incense*—H. Madl, 'נָטַף *nāṭap;* נָטָף *nāṭāp;* נֶטֶף *neṭep;* נְטִ(י)פוֹת *neṭîpôṯ;* נְטֹפָה *neṭōpâ;* נְטֹפָתִי *neṭōpāṯî*', *TDOT*, IX (1998; orig. 1984–86), pp. 395-406; Kjeld Nielsen, *Incense in Ancient Israel* (VTSup, 38; Leiden: E.J. Brill, 1986), p. 65 n. 423; Yehuda Feliks, 'The Incense of the Tabernacle', in *Pomegranates and Golden Bells: Studies in Biblical, Jewish, and Near Eastern Ritual, Law, and Literature in Honor of Jacob Milgrom* (ed. David P. Wright, David Noel Freedman and Avi Hurvitz; Winona Lake, IN: Eisenbrauns, 1995), pp. 125-49 (125).

נֶטֶף *drop*—H. Madl, 'נָטַף *nāṭap;* נָטָף *nāṭāp;* נֶטֶף *neṭep;* נְטִ(י)פוֹת *neṭîpôṯ;* נְטֹפָה *neṭōpâ;* נְטֹפָתִי *neṭōpāṯî*', *TDOT*, IX (1998; orig. 1984–86), pp. 395-406.

נְטֹפָה *Netophah*—H. Madl, 'נָטַף *nāṭap;* נָטָף *nāṭāp;* נֶטֶף *neṭep;* נְטִ(י)פוֹת *neṭîpôṯ;* נְטֹפָה *neṭōpâ;* נְטֹפָתִי *neṭōpāṯî*', *TDOT*, IX (1998; orig. 1984–86), pp. 395-406.

נְטֹפָתִי *Netophathite*—H. Madl, 'נָטַף *nāṭap;* נָטָף *nāṭāp;* נֶטֶף *neṭep;* נְטִ(י)פוֹת *neṭîpôṯ;* נְטֹפָה *neṭōpâ;* נְטֹפָתִי *neṭōpāṯî*', *TDOT*, IX (1998; orig. 1984–86), pp. 395-406.

נטר I *keep* (byform of נצר *keep*)—Moshe Held, 'Studies in Biblical Homonyms in the Light of Akkadian', *JANESCU* 3 (1970–71), pp. 46-55; H. Madl, 'נָטַר *nāṭar;* מַטָּרָה *maṭṭārâ*', *TDOT*, IX (1998; orig. 1984–86), pp. 402-406; Wolfram von Soden, 'Hebräisch *nāṭar* I und II', *UF* 17 (1986), pp. 412-14.

keep; keep anger—BDB, p. 643a; *HALOT*, II, p. 695a [both conflating נטר I and II].

נטר II *be angry* (cf. Akk. nadāru)—G.R. Driver, 'Studies in the Vocabulary of the Old Testament. III', *JTS* 32 (1930–31), pp. 361-66 (361-63); Zorell, p. 514b; KB, p. 613b; H. Madl, 'נָטַר *nāṭar;* מַטָּרָה *maṭṭārâ*', *TDOT*, IX (1998; orig. 1984–86), pp. 402-406.

נטשׁ I *abandon, spread out*—J. Lundbom and H.-J. Fabry, 'נָטַשׁ *nāṭaš;* נְטִישָׁה *neṭîšâ*', *TDOT*, IX (1998; orig. 1984–86), pp. 407-12.

נטשׁ II *dash to ground, clash in battle* (cf. Arab. waṭasa *struck violently*)—G.R. Driver, 'Problems in the Hebrew Text of Proverbs', *Bib* 32 (1951), pp. 173-97 (182); James Barr, *Comparative Philology and the Text of the Old Testament* (Oxford: Oxford University Press, 1968), p. 257.

נטשׁ III *sharpen* (byform of לטשׁ)—M. Dahood, 'Hebrew–Ugaritic Lexicography VI', *Bib* 49 (1968), pp. 355-69 (361-62).

נִי *wailing*—Ezk 27₃₂—Mitchell Dahood, 'Hebrew–Ugaritic Lexicography IX', *Bib* 52 (1971), pp. 337-56 (339-40).

נִיב II *speech, utterance*—Zorell, p. 515a; M. Dahood, 'Hebrew–Ugaritic Lexicography VI', *Bib* 49 (1968), pp. 355-69 (362).

נִידָה I *impurity* (cf. נִדָּה)—BDB, p. 622b.

נִידָה II *shaking of the head* (cf. ניד)—*HALOT*, II, p. 696a.

נִיחֹחַ *appeasement*—*HALOT*, II, p. 696a.

comforting aroma—P.A.H. de Boer, 'God's Fragrance', in *Studies in the Religion of Ancient Israel* (VTSup, 23; Leiden: E.J. Brill, 1972), pp. 37-47; K. Koch, 'נִיחוֹחַ *nîḥôaḥ*', *TDOT*, IX (1998; orig. 1984–86), pp. 412-15.

quieting, soothing, tranquillizing—BDB, p. 629a; Zorell, p. 515a.

smell of appeasement—KB, p. 614b.

ניל *acquire* (cf. מִנְלִים *possessions*)—Mitchell Dahood, *Psalms II: 51–100* (AB, 17; Garden City, NY: Doubleday, 1968; 3rd edn, 1979), p. 280.

נִין *get descendants*—*HALOT*, II, p. 696b.

increase—BDB, p. 630 (s.v. נון); Zorell, p. 515b.

sprout forth—KB, p. 614b

pi. *bear offspring*—Mitchell Dahood, *Psalms II: 51–100* (AB, 17; Garden City, NY: Doubleday, 1968; 3rd edn, 1979), p. 184; M. Dahood, 'Hebrew–Ugaritic Lexicography VI', *Bib* 49 (1968), pp. 355-69; *HALOT*, II, p. 696b.

נִין *offspring*—Ps 74₈—M. Dahood, 'Hebrew–Ugaritic Lexicography VI', *Bib* 49 (1968), pp. 355-69 (362).

נִיס *fugitive* (cf. נוס *flee*)—KB, p. 615a; Zorell, p. 515b.

flight—*HALOT*, II, p. 696b (s.v. נָיִס).

נִיסָן *Nisan*—G. Battista Bruzzone, 'I mesi nella bibbia: Nisan', *BeO* 27 (1985), pp. 223-27.

(cf. Akk. nisānu)—Maximilian Ellenbogen, *Foreign Words in the Old Testament: Their Origin and Etymology*

(London: Luzac & Co., 1962), p. 113.

נִיר I *break up, till*—Pr 20₂₇—Samuel E. Loewenstamm, 'Remarks on Proverbs xvii 12 and xx 27', *VT* 37 (1987), pp. 221-24 (223).

freshly till—BDB, p. 644b.

plough for the first time—*HALOT*, II, p. 697a.

נִיר II *shine* (cf. נִיר *light*)—Mitchell Dahood, *Psalms III: 101–150* (AB, 17A; Garden City, NY: Doubleday, 1970), p. 312.

נִיר I *lamp*—BDB, p. 633a; *HALOT*, II, p. 697a; Martin Noth, *Könige*, I (BKAT, IX/1; Neukirchen: Neukirchener Verlag, 1968), p. 243; D. Kellermann, 'נֵר *nēr*; נִיר *nîr*', *TDOT*, X (1999; orig. 1986), pp. 14-24.

נִיר II *field, dominion*—Ehud Ben Zvi, 'Once the Lamp Has Been Kindled ... A Reconsideration of the Meaning of the MT *Nîr* in 1 Kgs 11:36; 15:4; 2 Kgs 8:19 and 2 Chr 21:7', *AusBR* 39 (1991), pp. 19-30 (23).

prepared virgin soil—*HALOT*, II, p. 697a.

untilled ground—BDB, p. 644b; Dalman, *Arbeit*, II, p. 137.

נִיר III *sign of power*—Manfred Görg, 'Ein "Machtzeichen" Davids 1 Könige xi 36', *VT* 35 (1985), pp. 363-67.

נִיר IV *mark* (cf. Arab. nûratu *branded mark*)—G.R. Driver, 'Problems in the Hebrew Text of Proverbs', *Bib* 32 (1951), pp. 173-97 (185).

נִיר V *dominion* (cf. Aram. נִיר *yoke*, Akk. nīrum *yoke*, Arab. nīr *yoke*)—Paul D. Hanson, 'The Song of Heshbon and David's NÎR', *HTR* 61 (1968), pp. 297-320 (310-13); Mordechai Cogan and Hayim Tadmor, *II Kings: A New Translation with Introduction and Commentary* (AB, 11; New York: Doubleday, 1988), p. 95; D. Kellermann, 'נֵר *nēr*; נִיר *nîr*', *TDOT*, X (1999; orig. 1986), pp. 14-24 (18).

נִיר VI *new break, new beginning* (cf. נִיר II *break up* ground—Martin Noth, 'Jerusalem und die israelitische Tradition', *OTS* 8 (1950), pp. 28-46 (36-37) = 'Jerusalem and the Israelite Tradition', in *The Laws in the Pentateuch and Other Studies* (trans. D.R. Ap-Thomas; Edinburgh: Oliver & Boyd, 1966), pp. 132-44 (137-38); cf. Martin Noth, *Könige*, I (BKAT, IX/1; Neukirchen: Neukirchener Verlag, 1968), p. 243.

נכ I *strike*—J. Conrad, 'נכה *nkh*; מַכָּה *makkâ*; נָכֶה *nāḵeh*; נכא *nk*'', *TDOT*, IX (1998; orig. 1984–86), pp. 415-23.

נכא II *be low*—Robert Gordis, *The Book of Job* (New York: Jewish Theological Seminary, 1978), p. 332.

נכא III *put to flight* (cf. Arab. nakā)—Alfred Guillaume, *Studies in the Book of Job, with a New Translation* (Leiden: E.J. Brill, 1968), p. 114.

נְכֹאת *ladanum*—Ludwig Koehler, 'Hebräische Vokabeln III', *ZAW* 58 (1940–41), pp. 228-34 (232-34); Kjeld Nielsen, *Incense in Ancient Israel* (VTSup, 38; Leiden: E.J. Brill, 1986), p. 63.

נִכְבָּד *weighty*—J. van der Ploeg, 'Les «nobles» israélites', *OTS* 9 (1951), pp. 49-64 (54-55).

נכה hi. *strike*—J. Conrad, 'נכה *nkh*; מַכָּה *makkâ*; נָכֶה *nāḵeh*; נכא *nk*'', *TDOT*, IX (1998; orig. 1984–86), pp. 415-23.

נכה יָד *strike hand (in anger or distress)*—Nili S. Fox, 'Clapping Hands as a Gesture of Anguish and Anger in Mesopotamia and Israel', *JANESCU* 23 (1995), pp. 49-60.

נָכֶה *stricken*—J. Conrad, 'נכה *nkh*; מַכָּה *makkâ*; נָכֶה *nāḵeh*; נכא *nk*'', *TDOT*, IX (1998; orig. 1984–86), pp. 415-23.

נְכֹה *Neco*—T.R. Hobbs, 'Neco', *ABD*, IV, pp. 1060-61.

נָכוֹן I *blow*—BDB, p. 646b.

thrust—KB, p. 616b; *HALOT*, II, p. 698b.

נֹכַח *straight*—Menahem Kister, 'מוקדם ומאוחר בעיות—לקסי קוגר אפיות (Lexical Problems—Early and Late)', *Tarb* 61 (1991-92), pp. 45-59, III-IV [Heb].

נֵכֶל *deceitfulness*—Pr 13₁₅—M. Dahood, 'Hebrew–Ugaritic Lexicography VI', *Bib* 49 (1968), pp. 355-69 (363-64); Mitchell Dahood, 'Congruity of Metaphors', in *Hebräische Wortforschung: Festschrift zum 80. Geburtstag von Walter Baumgartner* (VTSup, 16; Leiden: E.J. Brill, 1967), pp. 40-49 (42-43).

נכר I *recognize*—M. Dahood, 'Qoheleth and Northwest Semitic Philology', *Bib* 43 (1962), pp. 349-65 (351); Mitchell Dahood, 'Causal Beth and the Root NKR in Nahum 3,4', *Bib* 52 (1971), pp. 395-96; B. Lang and H. Ringgren, 'נכר *nkr*; נֵכָר *nēḵār*; נָכְרִי *noḵrî*', *TDOT*, IX (1998; orig. 1984–86), pp. 423-32; Maria Patrizia Sciumbata, 'I lessemi a radicale *nkr* del campo lessicale dei verbi della conoscenza nella bibbia ebraica', *RivBib* 44 (1996), pp. 3-29.

acknowledge—David J.A. Clines, *Job 1–20* (WBC, 17; Dallas: Word Books, 1989), pp. 60-61.

acknowledge, thus *acquire legal possession*—A. Douglas Tushingham, 'A Reconsideration of Hosea, Chapters 1–3', *JNES* 12 (1953), pp. 150-59 (153-54); Leroy Waterman, 'Hosea, Chapters 1–3, in Retrospect and Prospect', *JNES* 14 (1955), pp. 100-109 (105).

נכר II *be foreign*—B. Lang and H. Ringgren, 'נכר *nkr*; נֵכָר *nēkār*; נָכְרִי *nokrî*', *TDOT*, IX (1998; orig. 1984–86), pp. 423-32.

falsify—N.H. Tur-Sinai, *The Book of Job* (Jerusalem: Kiryath Sepher, revised edn, 1967), pp. 332-33.

treat as strange—Marvin H. Pope, *Job: Introduction, Translation and Notes* (AB, 15; Garden City, NY: Doubleday, 3rd edn, 1973, p. 156.

pi. *alienate*—G.R. Driver, 'Some Hebrew Words', *JTS* 29 (1928), pp. 390-96 (395-96).

נכר III *acquire* (cf. Ug. nkr)—J. Gray, *The Legacy of Canaan* (VTSup, 5; Leiden: E.J. Brill, 1957), p. 190 (2nd edn, 1965, p. 141 n.1); James Barr, *Comparative Philology and the Text of the Old Testament* (Oxford: Oxford University Press, 1968), p. 267 n. 1.

acquire formal legal possession—Walter Vogels, 'Hosea's Gift to Gomer (Hos 3,2)', *Bib* 69 (1988), pp. 412-21 (418).

buy (byform of כרה *buy*)—*HALOT*, II, p. 700a.

purchase—Robert Gordis, 'Hosea's Marriage and Message: A New Approach', *HUCA* 25 (1954), pp. 9-35 (25-26 n. 37); Wilhelm Rudolph, *Hosea* (KAT, 13/1; Gütersloh: Gerd Mohn, 1966), pp. 84-85; *HALOT*, II, p. 700a.

pi. *sell*—Robert Gordis, 'Hosea's Marriage and Message: A New Approach', *HUCA* 25 (1954), pp. 9-35 (25-26 n. 37).

נכר IV hi. *repudiate* (cf. Arab *nakara*, Syr.)—Frank Zimmerman, 'Notes on Some Difficult Old Testament Passages', *JBL* 55 [1936], pp. 303-308 (306-307).

discriminate against, repudiate, remove—A.M. Honeyman, review of Ludwig Koehler and Walter Baumgartner, *Lexicon in Veteris Testamenti Libros* (1953), *VT* 5 (1955), pp. 214-23 (222).

נכר V *disapprove of* (cf. Arab *ankara*)—Alfred Guillaume, *Studies in the Book of Job, with a New Translation* (Leiden: E.J. Brill, 1968), p. 120.

נֵכָר *stranger*—R. Martin-Achard, 'נֵכָר *nēkār*', *TLOT*, II (1997; orig. 1976), pp. 739-41; B. Lang and H. Ringgren, 'נכר *nkr*; נֵכָר *nēkār*; נָכְרִי *nokrî*', *TDOT*, IX (1998; orig. 1984–86), pp. 423-32.

נָכְרִי *alien*—Michael V. Fox, *Proverbs 1–9* (AB, 18A; New York: Doubleday, 2000), pp. 134-41.

outsider—J. Hoftijzer, 'Ex. xxi 8', *VT* 7 (1957), pp. 388-91 (390).

stranger—Francesco Vattioni, 'La "straniera" nel libro dei Proverbi', *Augustinianum* 7 (1967), pp. 352-57; B. Lang and H. Ringgren, 'נכר *nkr*; נֵכָר *nēkār*; נָכְרִי *nokrî*', *TDOT*, IX (1998; orig. 1984–86), pp. 423-32; Christoph Bultmann, *Der Fremde im antiken Juda: Eine Untersuchung zum sozialen Typenbegriff »ger« und seinem Bedeutungswandel in der alttestamentlichen Gesetzgebung* (FRLANT, 153; Göttingen: Vandenhoeck & Ruprecht, 1992).

נְכֹת *treasure*—בֵּית נְכֹת *treasure-house* (cf. Akk. bīt nakkamti)—Maximilian Ellenbogen, *Foreign Words in the Old Testament: Their Origin and Etymology* (London: Luzac & Co., 1962), p. 114; Harold R. (Chaim) Cohen, *Biblical Hapax Legomena in the Light of Akkadian and Ugaritic* (SBLDS, 37; Missoula, MT: Scholars Press, 1978), pp. 40, 67 nn. 110-12.

נלה I *finish*—cf. BDB, p. 649a.

emend to כלה—Zorell, p. 518b; *HALOT*, II, p. 701a.

נלה II *obtain* (cf. מָנוֹל *acquisition*, Arab. nāl *obtain*)—Gesenius–Buhl, p. 506b; cf. BDB, p. 649a.

נמה *bring tidings* (cf. Arab. namā)—Alfred Guillaume, 'Some Readings in the Dead Sea Scroll of Isaiah', *JBL* 76 (1957), pp. 40-43 (40-41); G.R. Driver, *The Judaean Scrolls: The Problem and a Solution* (Oxford: Basil Blackwell, 1965), pp. 435, 444; James Barr, *Comparative Philology and the Text of the Old Testament* (Oxford: Oxford University Press, 1968), pp. 182, 193.

נָמֵר *leopard*—M.J. Mulder, 'נָמֵר *nāmēr*', *TDOT*, IX (1998; orig. 1984–86), pp. 432-37.

נִמְרֹד *Nimrod*—Peter Machinist, 'Nimrod', *ABD*, IV, pp. 1116-18.

נֵס I *standard*—H.-J. Fabry, 'נֵס *nēs*; נסס *nss* II', *TDOT*, IX (1998; orig. 1984–86), pp. 437-42.

standard as mark of royal dignity—Manfred Görg, *'nes–*

ein Herrschaftsemblem?', *BN* 14 (1981), pp. 11-17.

signal, not *sail*—G.R. Driver, 'Isaiah i–xxxix: Textual and Linguistic Problems', *JSS* 13 (1968), pp. 36-57 (54).

נֵס II *trembling* (cf. נוס II *tremble*)—G.R. Driver, 'Linguistic and Textual Problems: Isaiah i–xxxix', *JTS* 38 (1937), pp. 36-50 (45).

נֵס III *flight, means of flight* (cf. נוס I *flee*)—G.R. Driver, 'Textual and Linguistic Problems of the Book of Psalms', *HTR* 29 (1936), pp. 171-95; G.R. Driver, 'Linguistic and Textual Problems: Isaiah i–xxxix', *JTS* 38 (1937), pp. 36-50 (45).

נסג *forge* (cf. Arab. nasaja)—Joseph Reider, 'Etymological Studies in Biblical Hebrew', *VT* 4 (1954), pp. 276-95 (280); James Barr, *Comparative Philology and the Text of the Old Testament* (Oxford: Oxford University Press, 1968), p. 15.

נסה *test*—G. Gerleman, 'נסה *nsh*', *TLOT*, II (1997; orig. 1976), pp. 741-42; F.J. Helfmeyer, 'נִסָּה *nissâ*; מַסּוֹת *massôt*; מַסָּה *massâ*', *TDOT*, IX (1998; orig. 1984–86), pp. 443-55).

pi. *give experience of*—Moshe Greenberg, 'נסה in Exodus 20 20 and the Purpose of the Sinai Theophany', *JBL* 79 (1960), pp. 273-76.

train—Otto Eissfeldt, 'Zwei verkannte militär-technische Termini im Alten Testament', *VT* 5 (1955), pp. 232-38 (235-38).

נִסּו *trial*—Zorell, p. 519b.

נס *pluck* (cf. Aram. נסך *remove*)—Zorell, p. 519b; Mitchell Dahood, *Proverbs and Northwest Semitic Philology* (Scripta Pontificii Instituti Biblici, 113; Rome: Pontificium Institutum Biblicum, 1963), p. 8; R.B.Y. Scott, *Proverbs. Ecclesiastes: A New Translation with Introduction and Commentary* (AB, 18; Garden City, NY: Doubleday, 1965), p. 42; M. Dahood, 'Hebrew–Ugaritic Lexicography VI', *Bib* 49 (1968), pp. 355-69 (365); Mitchell Dahood, *Psalms II: 51–100* (AB, 17; Garden City, NY: Doubleday, 1968; 3rd edn, 1979), p. 15.

Pr 2_{22}—*HALOT*, II, p. 749b (from סחה *sweep away*).

נִסָּי *test*—Zorell, p. 519b.

נָסִ I *libation; molten image*—BDB, p. 651a; Zorell, p. 519b; KB, p. 619b; *HALOT*, II, p. 702b [all conflating נָסִיךְ I and II].

נָסִיךְ II *molten image* (cf. נסך *pour out*).

נָסִיךְ III *prince*—J. van der Ploeg, 'Les chefs du peuple d'Israël et leurs titres', *RB* 57 (1950), pp. 40-61 (57).

נסך I *pour*—C. Dohmen, 'נָסַךְ *nāsak̲*; נֶסֶךְ *nesek̲*; נָסִיךְ *nāsîk̲*; מַסֵּכָה *massēk̲â*; מַסֶּכֶת *massek̲et̲*; סוּךְ II *sûk̲*; אָסוּךְ *'āsûk̲*', *TDOT*, IX (1998; orig. 1984–86), pp. 455-60.

pour (water), cast (metal)—W.A. Ward, 'Some Egyto-Semitic Roots', *Or* 31 (1962), pp. 397-412 (406).

forge (not *cast*)—Christoph Dohmen, *Das Bilderverbot: Seine Entstehung und seine Entwicklung im Alten Testament* (BBB, 62; Bonn: Peter Hanstein, 1985), pp. 49-54.

with obj. אֱלֹהִים אֲחֵרִים *other gods*—Ambrogio Alghisi, 'L'espressione «altri dei» nella fraseologia deuteronomistica (*Deut.–2 Reg.; Ier*)', *RivBib* 33 (1985), pp. 135-63, 263-90 (159).

Ps 4_7—Jacques Meysing, 'Note d'exégèse: une nouvelle conjecture à propos du psaume 4, verset 7 b', *RScRel* 40 (1966), pp. 154-57.

Pr 8_{23}—Mitchell Dahood, 'Proverbs 8,22-31: Translation and Commentary', *CBQ* 30 (1968), pp. 512-21 (515).

נסך II *weave*—C. Dohmen, 'נָסַךְ *nāsak̲*; נֶסֶךְ *nesek̲*; נָסִיךְ *nāsîk̲*; מַסֵּכָה *massēk̲â*; מַסֶּכֶת *massek̲et̲*; סוּךְ II *sûk̲*; אָסוּךְ *'āsûk̲*', *TDOT*, IX (1998; orig. 1984–86), pp. 455-60.

נֶסֶךְ *libation*—C. Dohmen, 'נָסַךְ *nāsak̲*; נֶסֶךְ *nesek̲*; נָסִיךְ *nāsîk̲*; מַסֵּכָה *massēk̲â*; מַסֶּכֶת *massek̲et̲*; סוּךְ II *sûk̲*; אָסוּךְ *'āsûk̲*', *TDOT*, IX (1998; orig. 1984–86), pp. 455-60.

נסס II *sparkle*—Wilhelm Rudolph, *Haggai—Sacharja 9–14—Sacharja 9–14—Maleachi* (KAT, XIII/4; Gütersloh: Gerd Mohn, 1976), p. 185; NEB (Zc 9.16); cf. Zorell, p. 520b.

נסס III *sway, stagger, wave to and fro* (cf. Akk. nussusu *shake*, Arab. naznaza *shake the head*)—G.R. Driver, 'Some Hebrew Roots and their Meanings', *JTS* 23 (1921–22), pp. 69-73 (71); G.R. Driver, 'Studies in the Vocabulary of the Old Testament. VI', *JTS* 34 (1933), pp. 375-85 (375); G.R. Driver, 'Linguistic and Textual Problems: Isaiah i–xxxix', *JTS* 38 (1937), pp. 36-50 (45); *HALOT*, II, p. 703b.

נסס IV *suffer convulsions* (cf. Akk. nasāsu *sway to and fro, be convulsed*)—G.R. Driver, 'Isaiah i–xxxix: Textual and Linguistic Problems', *JSS* 13 (1968), pp. 36-57 (42).

נסס V *rally to the banner, assemble around the standard* (cf. נֵס

standard)—Julius Lewy, 'The Assyrian Calendar', *ArOr* 11 (1939–40), pp. 35-46 (39); *HALOT*, II, p. 704a; H.-J. Fabry, 'נֵס *nēs*; נסס *nss* II', *TDOT*, IX (1998; orig. 1984–86), pp. 437-42.

נסס VI *dry up* (cf. Arab. nassa)—Jeffrey H. Tigay, 'לא נס לחה "He Had Not Become Wrinkled" (Deuteronomy 34:7)', in *Solving Riddles and Untying Knots: Biblical, Epigraphic, and Semitic Studies in Honor of Jonas C. Greenfield* (ed. Ziony Zevit, Seymour Gitin and Michael Sokoloff; Winona Lake, IN: Eisenbrauns, 1995), pp. 345-50.

נסע I *pull up, out* (cf. Arab. naza'a)—Alfred Guillaume, *Hebrew and Arabic Lexicography: A Comparative Study*, I (Leiden: E.J. Brill, 1965; = *AbrN* 1 [1959–60]), pp. 28-29.

pull up; travel BDB, p. 652a; Zorell, p. 520b; *HALOT*, p. 704a; M.Z. Kaddari and H. Ringgren, 'נָסַע *nāsa'*; מַסַּע *massa'*; מַסָּע *massā*", *TDOT*, IX (1998; orig. 1984–86), pp. 461-64 [all conflating נסע I and II].

נסע II *travel, go about* (cf. Arab. nasa'a *journey*)—G.R. Driver, 'Supposed Arabisms in the Old Testament', *JBL* 55 (1936), pp. 101-20 (115); Alfred Guillaume, *Hebrew and Arabic Lexicography: A Comparative Study*, I (Leiden: E.J. Brill, 1965; = *AbrN* 1 [1959–60]), pp. 11, 28-29; M. Delcor, 'Quelques cas de survivances du vocabulaire nomade en hébreu biblique', *VT* 25 (1975), pp. 307-22.

נִסְרֹךְ *Nisroch*—Emil G. Kraeling, 'The Death of Sennacherib', *JAOS* 53 (1933), pp. 335-46 (335-38); J.P. Lettinga, 'A Note on 2 Kings xix 37', *VT* 7 (1957), pp. 105-106.

נעורים *youth*—H.F. Fuhs, 'נַעַר *na'ar*; נַעֲרָה *na'ᵃrâ*; נְעוּרִים *nᵉ'ûrîm*; נְעֻרוֹת *nᵉ'urôṯ*; נֹעַר *nō'ar*', *TDOT*, IX (1998; orig. 1984–86), pp. 474-85.

נָעִים I *favourable omen* or *person receiving a favourable omen*—J.D. Levenson, 'A Technical Meaning for *n'm* in the Hebrew Bible', *VT* 35 (1985), pp. 61-67 (65-67).

pleasant—T. Kronholm, 'נָעֵם *nā'am*; נָעִים *nā'îm*; נֹעַם *nō'am*; מַנְעַמִּים *man'ammîm*; נַעֲמָנִים *na'ᵃmānîm*', *TDOT*, IX (1998; orig. 1984–86), pp. 467-74.

נָעִים II *musical* (cf. Arab. naghama *speak in a low voice*)—BDB, p. 654a.

נְעִימָה *melody*—cf. Zorell, p. 521b [as fem. of נָעִים *pleasant*].

נעל I *lock; provide with sandals*—KB, p. 621b; *HALOT*, II, p. 705a [conflating נעל I and II].

lock—BDB, p. 653a; Zorell, p. 521b.

נעל II *provide with sandals*—BDB, p. 653a; Zorell, p. 521b.

נַעַל *sandal*—H. Ringgren, 'נַעַל *na'al*', *TDOT*, IX (1998; orig. 1984–86), pp. 465-67.

נַעֲלָם *bribe*—Robert Gordis, '"Na'ᵃlam" and Other Observations on the Ain Feshka Scrolls', *JNES* 9 (1950), pp. 44-47 (44-46); N.H. Tur-Sinai, פשוטו של מקרא (Jerusalem: Bialik, 1967), III/2, pp. 454-55; Gordis, 'Studies in the Book of Amos', in *American Academy for Jewish Research Jubilee Volume 1928–29/1978–79* (ed. S.A. Baron and J.L. Barzilay; PAAJR 46-47; New York: American Academy for Jewish Research, 1980), pp. 201-64 (213-15); S.M. Paul, *Amos: A Commentary on the Book of Amos* (Hermeneia; Minneapolis: Fortress Press, 1991), pp. 78-79.

נעם I *be pleasant*—T. Kronholm, 'נָעֵם *nā'am*; נָעִים *nā'îm*; נֹעַם *nō'am*; מַנְעַמִּים *man'ammîm*; נַעֲמָנִים *na'ᵃmānîm*', *TDOT*, IX (1998; orig. 1984–86), pp. 467-74; Gary A. Rendsburg, *Linguistic Evidence for the Northern Origin of Selected Psalms* (SBLMS, 43; Atlanta: Scholars Press, 1990), pp. 30-31; G.A. Rendsburg, 'Additional Notes on "The Last Words of David" (2 Sam 23, 1-7)', *Bib* 70 (1989), pp. 403-408.

be sweet—Baruch Margalit, *The Ugaritic Poem of AQHT: Text, Translation, Commentary* (BZAW, 182; Berlin: de Gruyter, 1989), p. 379 n. 51.

נעם II *sing* (cf. MH נעם hi. *sing*)—cf. BDB, p. 654; cf. Gesenius–Buhl, p. 509b.

נֹעַם *apparition*—J.D. Levenson, 'A Technical Meaning for *n'm* in the Hebrew Bible', *VT* 35 (1985), pp. 61-67.

pleasantness—T. Kronholm, 'נָעֵם *nā'am*; נָעִים *nā'îm*; נֹעַם *nō'am*; מַנְעַמִּים *man'ammîm*; נַעֲמָנִים *na'ᵃmānîm*', *TDOT*, IX (1998; orig. 1984–86), pp. 467-74.

נַעֲמָה—J.J. Stamm, 'Hebräische Frauennamen', in *Hebräische Wortforschung: Festschrift zum 80. Geburtstag von Walter Baumgartner* (VTSup, 16; Leiden: E.J. Brill, 1967), pp. 301-39 (323).

נַעֲמָנִים *pleasantness*—T. Kronholm, 'נָעֵם *nā'am*; נָעִים *nā'îm*; נֹעַם *nō'am*; מַנְעַמִּים *man'ammîm*; נַעֲמָנִים *na'ᵃmānîm*',

TDOT, IX (1998; orig. 1984–86), pp. 467-74.

נַעֲצוּץ *camel-thorn*—KB, p. 622b; *HALOT*, II, p. 706b.

thornbush (cf. Arab. nu'ḍ)—BDB, p. 654b; Zorell, p. 522a; L. Kopf, 'Arabische Etymologien und Parallelen zum Bibelwörterbuch', *VT* 8 (1958), pp. 161-215 (183).

נער I *growl, groan* (cf. Arab. na'ara *snore, roar*)—BDB, p. 654a; Mitchell Dahood, *Psalms II: 51–100* (AB, 17; Garden City, NY: Doubleday, 1968; 3rd edn, 1979), p. 306; *HALOT*, II, p. 706a.

נער II *shake* (cf. Arab. naghara *boil, be angry*)—BDB, p. 654b; *HALOT*, II, p. 707a.

נער III *strip, uncover* (cf. עור *be bare*)—D. Wolfers, 'The Verb *n'r* in the Bible', *Jewish Bible Quarterly* 18 (1989–90), pp. 27-31; David Wolfers, *Deep Things out of Darkness: The Book of Job: Essays and a New English Translation* (Kampen: Kok Pharos, 1995), pp. 510-13.

נער IV *wander* (cf. Arab. na'irun *restless*)—Alfred Guillaume, *Hebrew and Arabic Lexicography: A Comparative Study*, II (Leiden: E.J. Brill, 1965; = *AbrN* 2 [1960–61]), p. 25.

נער V *be dry* (cf. Arab. gharina)—Alfred Guillaume, *Hebrew and Arabic Lexicography: A Comparative Study*, III (Leiden: E.J. Brill, 1965; = *AbrN* 3 [1962–63]), p. 5.

נער VI *vacillate* (cf. Arab. na'ara *be in tumult*)—G.R. Driver, 'Studies in the Vocabulary of the Old Testament. VI', *JTS* 34 (1933), pp. 375-85 (378); G.R. Driver, 'Studies in the Vocabulary of the Old Testament. VII', *JTS* 35 (1934), pp. 380-93 (393).

נער VII *be a youth*—ni. privative—Mitchell Dahood, *Psalms III: 101–150* (AB, 17A; Garden City, NY: Doubleday, 1970), p. 108.

נַעַר *youth*—Hans-Peter Stähli, *Knabe–Jüngling–Knecht: Untersuchungen zum Begriff* נער *im Alten Testament* (BBET, 7; Frankfurt a.M.: Peter Lang, 1978); H.F. Fuhs, 'נַעַר *na'ar;* נַעֲרָה *na'ărâ;* נְעוּרִים *ne'ûrîm;* נְעֻרוֹת *ne'urôt;* נֹעַר *nō'ar*', *TDOT*, IX (1998; orig. 1984–86), pp. 474-85.

high-born servant—John MacDonald, 'The Status and Role of the Na'ar in Israelite Society', *JNES* 35 (1976), pp. 147-70; John MacDonald, 'The Role and Status of the ṣuḫārū in the Mari Correspondence', *JAOS* 96 (1976), pp. 57-68.

knightly squire—B. Cutler and MacDonald, 'Identification of the na'ar in the Ugaritic Texts', *UF* 8 (1976), pp. 27-35.

slave—M. Dahood, 'Northwest Semitic Texts and Textual Criticism of the Hebrew Bible', in *Questions disputées d'Ancien Testament* (ed. C. Brekelmans; BETL, 33; Leuven, 1974), pp. 11-37 (17); Carlos Alonso Fontela, 'La esclavitud a través de la Biblia', *EstBíb* 43 (1985), pp. 89-124, 237-74 (95-96).

servant or *official* (the na'ar seals)—Anson F. Rainey, 'Private Seal-Impressions: A Note on Semantics', *IEJ* 16 (1966), pp. 187-90; Nachman Avigad, 'New Light on the Na'ar Seals', in *Magnalia Dei: The Mighty Acts of God: Essays on the Bible and Archaeology in Memory of G. Ernest Wright* (ed. Frank Moore Cross, Werner E. Lemke and Patrick D. Miller, Jr; Garden City, NY: Doubleday, 1976), pp. 294-300; N. Avigad, 'The Contribution of Hebrew Seals to an Understanding of Israelite Religion and Society', in *Ancient Israelite Religion: Essays in Honor of Frank Moore Cross* (ed. Patrick D. Miller, Paul D. Hanson and S. Dean McBride; Philadelphia: Fortress Press, 1987), pp. 195-208 (205); Yosef Garfinkel, 'The Eliakim Na'ar Yokan Seal Impressions: Sixty Years of Confusion in Biblical Archaeological Research', *BA* 53 (1990), pp. 74-79 (77-78); Anson Rainey, 'A Rejoinder to the Eliakim Na'ar Yokan Seal Impressions', *BA* 54 (1991), p. 61.

נֹעָר *sparrow* (cf. Arab. nughar)—D. Winton Thomas, 'Job xl 29*b*: Text and Translation', *VT* 14 (1964), pp. 114-16; Robert Gordis, 'Job xl 29—An Additional Note', *VT* 14 (1964), pp. 491-94.

נֹעַר *(time of) youth*—H.F. Fuhs, 'נַעַר *na'ar;* נַעֲרָה *na'ărâ;* נְעוּרִים *ne'ûrîm;* נְעֻרוֹת *ne'urôt;* נֹעַר *nō'ar*', *TDOT*, IX (1998; orig. 1984–86), pp. 474-85.

נַעֲרָה I *young woman*—Kt נער—Bernard J. Bamberger, 'Qetanah, Na'arah, Bogereth', *HUCA* 32 (1961), pp. 281-94; H.F. Fuhs, 'נַעַר *na'ar;* נַעֲרָה *na'ărâ;* נְעוּרִים *ne'ûrîm;* נְעֻרוֹת *ne'urôt;* נֹעַר *nō'ar*', *TDOT*, IX (1998; orig. 1984–86), pp. 474-85.

נַעֲרָה II *sparrow*—Robert Gordis, 'Job xl 29—An Additional Note', *VT* 14 (1964), pp. 491-94.

נֹעָרָה *sparrow* (cf. Arab. nugharat)—D. Winton Thomas, 'Job xl 29*b*: Text and Translation', *VT* 14 (1964), pp. 114-16; Robert Gordis, 'Job xl 29—An Additional Note', *VT* 14 (1964), pp. 491-94.

נְעֻרוֹת *youth*—Zorell, p. 523a.

נְעֻרוֹת *youth*—H.F. Fuhs, 'נַעַר *na'ar*; נַעֲרָה *na'arâ*; נְעוּרִים *ne'ûrîm*; נְעֻרוֹת *ne'urôt*; נֹעַר *nō'ar*', *TDOT*, IX (1998; orig. 1984–86), pp. 474-85.

נֹף *Memphis*—Donald B. Redford, 'Memphis', *ABD*, IV, pp. 689-71.

נָפָה I *sieve* (cf. נוף *swing to and fro*, or Arab. nafâ *sweep away* refuse, *raise* dust; MH נָפָה *flour sieve*)—BDB, p. 632a; G.R. Driver, 'Problems in "Proverbs"', *ZAW* 50 (1932), pp. 141-48 (143); G.R. Driver, 'Linguistic and Textual Problems: Isaiah i–xxxix', *JTS* 38 (1937), pp. 36-50 (44); *HALOT*, II, p. 708b.

נָפָה II *height* (cf. נוֹף *elevation*, Arab. nāfa *be tall*))—BDB, p. 632b; cf. Zorell, p. 523a.

נָפָה III *yoke, bridle* (cf. Arab. nāf *yoke*)—H.L. Ginsberg, 'An Obscure Hebrew Word', *JQR* 22 (1931–32), pp. 143-45; *HALOT*, II, p. 708b.

district (as area ploughed)—G.R. Driver, 'Three Technical Terms in the Pentateuch', *JSS* 1 (1956), pp. 97-103 (103 n. 1).

נפח I *blow*—P. Maiberger, 'נָפַח *nāpaḥ*', *TDOT*, IX (1998; orig. 1984–86), pp. 485-88.

נפח II *beat, afflict* (cf. Arab. nafaḥa *beat*)—Alfred Guillaume, *Hebrew and Arabic Lexicography: A Comparative Study*, III (Leiden: E.J. Brill, 1965; = *AbrN* 3 [1962–63]), p. 5.

נְפִילִים *Nephilim*—Anne Draffkorn Kilmer, 'The Mesopotamian Counterparts of the Biblical *Nĕpīlîm*', in *Perspectives on Language and Text: Essays and Poems in Honor of Francis I. Andersen's Sixtieth Birthday* (Winona Lake, IL: Eisenbrauns, 1987), pp. 39-43.

Nephilim, fallen ones (in death)—Ronald S. Hendel, 'Of Demigods and the Deluge: Toward an Interpretation of Genesis 6:1-4', *JBL* 106 (1987), pp. 13-26 (22).

נֹפֶךְ *green semi-precious stone*—*HALOT*, II, p. 709b.

moonstone—J.S. Harris, 'The Stones of the High Priest's Breastplate', *ALUOS* 5 (1963–65), pp. 40-62 (50-52).

precious stone, perh. *ruby* or *carbuncle*—BDB, p. 656b.

turquoise, malachite (cf. Eg. mfk3t)—Thomas O. Lambdin, 'Egyptian Loanwords in the Old Testament', *JAOS* 73 (1953), pp. 145-55 (152).

נֹפֶךְ אַרְגָּמָן *deep-red garnet*—G.R. Driver, 'Ezekiel: Linguistic and Textual Problems', *Bib* 35 (1954), pp. 145-59 (156).

נְפִיסִים *Nephisim*—Ran Zadok, 'Remarks on Ezra and Nehemiah', *ZAW* 94 (19982), pp. 296-98; Ernst Axel Knauf, *Ismael: Untersuchungen zur Geschichte Palästinas und Nordarabiens im 1. Jahrtausend v.Chr.* (ADPV; Wiesbaden: O. Harrassowitz, 2nd edn, 1989), p. 152.

נפל I *alight* from mount—M. Delcor, 'Quelques cas de survivances du vocabulaire nomade en hébreu biblique', *VT* 25 (1975), pp. 307-22 (313-14).

arrive (in camp)—M. Delcor, 'Quelques cas de survivances du vocabulaire nomade en hébreu biblique', *VT* 25 (1975), pp. 307-22 (314).

fall—H. Seebass, 'נָפַל *nāpal*; נֵפֶל *nēpel*; נְפִילִים *nepîlîm*', *TDOT*, IX (1998; orig. 1984–86), pp. 488-97.

fall (into Sheol)—Mitchell Dahood, *Psalms I: 1–50* (AB, 16; Garden City, NY: Doubleday, 1966), p. 36; M. Dahood, 'Hebrew–Ugaritic Lexicography VI', *Bib* 49 (1968), pp. 355-69 (367); Mitchell Dahood, *Psalms II: 51–100* (AB, 17; Garden City, NY: Doubleday, 1968; 3rd edn, 1979), pp. 270; Mitchell Dahood, *Psalms III: 101–150* (AB, 17A; Garden City, NY: Doubleday, 1970), p. 158.

fall upon, attack—Mitchell Dahood, *Psalms I: 1–50* (AB, 16; Garden City, NY: Doubleday, 1966), p. 231; Mitchell Dahood, *Psalms II: 51–100* (AB, 17; Garden City, NY: Doubleday, 1968; 3rd edn, 1979), p. 32.

settle, camp—M. Delcor, 'Quelques cas de survivances du vocabulaire nomade en hébreu biblique', *VT* 25 (1975), pp. 307-22 (314).

waste away—C.F. Whitley, 'The Positive Force of the Hebrew Particle בל', *ZAW* 84 (1972), pp. 213-19 (215-16).

נפל לְפָנָיו *fall forward*—G.R. Driver, 'Linguistic and Textual Problems: Isaiah i–xxxix', *JTS* 38 (1937), pp. 36-50 (48).

hi. *bring down*, i.e. slaughter—Mitchell Dahood, *Psalms I: 1–50* (AB, 16; Garden City, NY: Doubleday, 1966), p. 229.

hi. *bring down (walls), demolish, maim*—Jonas C. Greenfield, 'Lexicographical Notes I', *HUCA* 29 (1958), pp. 203-28 (215-17).

hi. *let* (the face) *fall*, i.e. *show a downcast look*—G.R. Driver, 'Problems in the Hebrew Text of Job', in *Wisdom in Israel and in the Ancient Near East, Presented to Professor Harold Henry Rowley ... in Celebration of his Sixty-Fifth Birthday* (VTSup, 3; Leiden: E.J. Brill, 1955), pp. 72-93 (87-88).

נפל II *wither* (byform of נבל *wither*)—Mitchell Dahood, *Proverbs and Northwest Semitic Philology* (Scripta Pontificii Instituti Biblici, 113; Rome: Pontificium Institutum Biblicum, 1963), p. 24; Mitchell Dahood, 'Congruity of Metaphors', in *Hebräische Wortforschung: Festschrift zum 80. Geburtstag von Walter Baumgartner* (VTSup, 16; Leiden: E.J. Brill, 1967), pp. 40-49 (49); R.B.Y. Scott, *Proverbs. Ecclesiastes: A New Translation with Introduction and Commentary* (AB, 18; Garden City, NY: Doubleday, 1965), p. 87.

נֵפֶל *miscarriage*—H. Seebass, 'נָפַל *nāpal*; נֵפֶל *nēpel*; נְפִילִים *nᵉpîlîm*', *TDOT*, IX (1998; orig. 1984–86), pp. 488-97 (497).

נְפִלִים *giants*—H. Seebass, 'נָפַל *nāpal*; נֵפֶל *nēpel*; נְפִילִים *nᵉpîlîm*', *TDOT*, IX (1998; orig. 1984–86), pp. 488-97 (497); L. Perlitt, *Riesen im Alten Testament* (Nachrichten der Akademie der Wissenschaften zu Göttingen, phil.-hist. Klasse 1990, 1; Göttingen: Vandenhoeck & Ruprecht, 1990).

נפף *sprinkle* (cf. נוף II *sprinkle*, נוב *be full of sap*)—G.R. Driver, 'Problems in "Proverbs"', *ZAW* 50 (1932), pp. 141-48 (142-43); Godfrey Rolles Driver, 'Hebrew Roots and Words', *WO* 1 (1947–52), pp. 406-15 (407 n. 7).

נפי I *shatter* (cf. Arab. faḍḍa)—Alfred Guillaume, *Hebrew and Arabic Lexicography: A Comparative Study*, I (Leiden: E.J. Brill, 1965; = *AbrN* 1 [1959–60]), pp. 11, 29; cf. *HALOT*, II, p. 711a (Arab. nafaḍa, Akk. napāṣu); cf. BDB, p. 658b.

נפ II *disperse* (cf. Arab. faṣa)—Alfred Guillaume, *Hebrew and Arabic Lexicography: A Comparative Study*, I (Leiden: E.J. Brill, 1965; = *AbrN* 1 [1959–60]), pp. 11, 29; cf. BDB, p. 659a; cf. *HALOT*, II, p. 711a (Arab. faḍā).

נֶפֶ *driving storm*—BDB, p. 658a; Zorell, p. 525b. *pattering of rain*—*HALOT*, II, p. 711b.

נֶפֶשׁ I *soul, life*—Daniel Lys, *Nephesh: Histoire de l'âme dans la révélation d'Israël au sein des religions proche-orientales* (Etudes d'histoire et de philosophie religieuses, 50; Paris: Presses Universitaires de France, 1959); A. Murtonen, *The Living Soul: A Study of the Meaning of the Word næfæš in the Old Testament Hebrew Language* (Studia Orientalia, 23.1; Helsinki: Societas Orientalis Fennica, 1958); H.A. Brongers, 'Das Wort "NPŠ" in den Qumranschriften', *RQ* 4 (1963), pp. 407-15; C. Westerman, 'נֶפֶשׁ *nepeš*', *TLOT*, II (1997; orig. 1976), pp. 743-59; Risto Lauha, *Psychophysischer Sprachgebrauch im AT: Eine strukturalsemantische Analyse von* לב, נפש *und* רוח. I. *Emotionen* (Annales Academiae Scientiarum Fennicae, Dissertationes Humanarum Litterarum, 35; Helsinki: Suomalainen Tiedeakatemia, 1983); H. Seebass, 'נֶפֶשׁ *nepeš*', *TDOT*, IX (1998; orig. 1984–86), pp. 497-519.

appetite—L. Kopf, 'Arabische Etymologien und Parallelen zum Bibelwörterbuch', *VT* 8 (1958), pp. 161-215 (183); Mitchell Dahood, 'Qoheleth and Northwest Semitic Philology', *Bib* 43 (1962), pp. 349-65 (357-58); Mitchell Dahood, *Proverbs and Northwest Semitic Philology* (Scripta Pontificii Instituti Biblici, 113; Rome: Pontificium Institutum Biblicum, 1963), pp. 18, 26-27, 47.

emotions—Ziony Zevit, 'Phoenician *nbš/npš* and its Hebrew Semantic equivalents', in *Sopher Mahir: Northwest Semitic Studies Presented to Stanislav Segert* (ed. Edward M. Cook; Winona Lake, IN: Eisenbrauns, 1990), pp. 337-44.

life and *abundance* (נֶפֶשׁ II) in the same sentence (Is 58$_{10}$)—G.R. Driver, 'Problems and Solutions', *VT* 4 (1954), pp. 225-45 (242).

neck—Lor. Dürr, 'Hebr. נֶפֶשׁ = akk. napištu = Gurgel, Kehle', *ZAW* 43 (1925), pp. 262-69; G.R. Driver, 'Misreadings in the Old Testament', *WO* 1 (1948), pp. 234-38 (238); Mitchell Dahood, *Psalms I: 1–50* (AB, 16; Garden City, NY: Doubleday, 1966), pp. 41-42, 141; G.R. Driver, 'Isaiah i–xxxix: Textual and Linguistic Problems', *JSS* 13 (1968), pp. 36-57 (41); Mitchell Dahood, *Psalms II: 51–100* (AB, 17; Garden City, NY:

Doubleday, 1968; 3rd edn, 1979), pp. 53, 156; Mitchell Dahood, *Psalms III: 101–150* (AB, 17A; Garden City, NY: Doubleday, 1970), p. 56, 176-77, 213.

perfume—Mitchell Dahood, *Proverbs and Northwest Semitic Philology* (Scripta Pontificii Instituti Biblici, 113; Rome: Pontificium Institutum Biblicum, 1963), p. 54.

sepulchre, funerary monument—J.T. Milik, 'Le rouleau de cuivre provenant de la grotte 3Q (3Q15)', in *DJD*, III (1962), pp. 199-302 (247.85).

slave—G.R. Driver, 'Hebrew Mothers', *ZAW* 67 (1956), pp. 246-48 (249).

sustenance (cf. Akk. napištu *(sustenance of) life*—Victor Avigdor Hurowitz, 'A Forgotten Meaning of *Nepeš* in Isaiah lviii 10', *VT* 47 (1997), pp. 43-52.

throat—Lor. Dürr, 'Hebr. נֶפֶשׁ = akk. napištu = Gurgel, Kehle', *ZAW* 43 (1925), pp. 262-69; Julien Weill, 'Le sens de נֶפֶשׁ dans Prov 23 7a', *ZAW* 44 (1926), pp. 62-63; M. Dahood, review of Hans-Joachim Kraus, *Psalmen* (1958–60), *Bib* 42 (1961), pp. 383-85 (384); M. Dahood, review of R. de Langhe (ed.), *Le Psautier. Ses origines. Ses problèmes littéraires. Son influence* (1961), *Bib* 44 (1963), pp. 104-106 (105); Mitchell Dahood, 'Qoheleth and Northwest Semitic Philology', *Bib* 43 (1962), pp. 349-65 (358); Mitchell Dahood, *Psalms I: 1–50* (AB, 16; Garden City, NY: Doubleday, 1966), pp. 168, 189, 215; J.A. Emerton, 'The Textual Problems of Isaiah v 14', *VT* 17 (1967), pp. 135-42 (135 n. 1); M. Dahood, 'Hebrew–Ugaritic Lexicography VI', *Bib* 49 (1968), pp. 355-69 (368); Mitchell Dahood, *Psalms III: 101–150* (AB, 17A; Garden City, NY: Doubleday, 1970), pp. 71, 83, 85, 87, 209, 324; Jacob Milgrom, *Leviticus 1–16: A New Translation with Introduction and Commentary* (AB, 3; New York: Doubleday, 1991), p. 684.

not *corpse*—Diethelm Michel, '*næpæš* als Leichnam?', *ZAH* 7 (1994), pp. 81-84.

Michael Barré, 'Mesopotamian Light on the Idiom *nāśâ' nepeš* ', *CBQ* 52 (1990), pp. 46-54.

בֵּית נֶפֶשׁ *collar* (cf. נֶפֶשׁ *neck*)—Israel Eitan, 'A Contribution to Isaiah Exegesis (Notes and Short Studies in Biblical Philology)', *HUCA* 12–13 (1937–38), pp. 55-88 (57).

נְפָשׁוֹת (plur.) *eternal life*—Mitchell Dahood, *Proverbs and Northwest Semitic Philology* (Scripta Pontificii Instituti Biblici, 113; Rome: Pontificium Institutum Biblicum, 1963), pp. 24-25.

נֶפֶשׁ יְקָרָה *weighty person*—D. Winton Thomas, 'Textual and Philological Notes on Some Passages in the Book of Proverbs', in *Wisdom in Israel and in the Ancient Near East, Presented to Professor Harold Henry Rowley ... in Celebration of his Sixty-Fifth Birthday* (ed. M. Noth and D. Winton Thomas; VTSup, 3; Leiden: E.J. Brill, 1955), pp. 280-92 (283-84).

נֶפֶשׁ מֵת *demon of disease*—Miriam Seligson, *The Meaning of* נפש מת *in the Old Testament* (Studia Orientalia, 16.2; Helsinki: Societas Orientalis Fennica, 1951).

נשׂא נֶפֶשׁ אֶל *flee for protection to*—Michael L. Barré, 'Mesopotamian Light on the Idiom *nāśā' nepeš*', *CBQ* 52 (1990), pp. 46-54.

Is 49₇—G.R. Driver, 'Linguistic and Textual Problems: Isaiah xl–lxvi', *JTS* 36 (1935), pp. 396-406 (401).

נֶפֶשׁ II *abundance* (cf. Akk. napāšu *be plentiful*, napšu *plentiful)*—G.R. Driver, 'Hebrew Notes', *ZAW* 52 (1934), pp. 51-56 (53-54); W. von Soden, 'Zu ZAW 52, 53f.', *ZAW* 53 (1935), pp. 291-92; G.R. Driver, 'Suggestions and Objections', *ZAW* 55 (1937), pp. 68-71 (68-69); W. von Soden, 'Nachwort zu G.R. Drivers "Objections"', *ZAW* 55 (1937), pp. 71-72; G.R. Driver, 'Problems and Solutions', *VT* 4 (1954), pp. 225-45 (243-44); G.R. Driver, 'Nachtrag, hauptsächlich nach Mitteilungen G.R. Drivers, Oxford, vom 7.2 und 23.3.1962', in Berend Gemser, *Sprüche Salomos* (HAT, I/16; Tübingen: J.C.B. Mohr [Paul Siebeck], 2nd edn, 1963), pp. 111-14 (111).

abundance and *life* (נֶפֶשׁ I) in the same sentence (Is 58₁₀)—G.R. Driver, 'Problems and Solutions', *VT* 4 (1954), pp. 225-45 (242).

נֶפֶשׁ III *odour, perfume* (cf. Akk. nipšu *scent)*—G.R. Driver, 'Hebrew Notes on the "Wisdom of Jesus ben Sirach"', *JBL* 53 (1934), pp. 273-90 (54); G.R. Driver, 'Suggestions and Objections', *ZAW* 55 (1937), pp. 68-71 (69-70); W. von Soden, 'Nachwort zu G.R. Drivers "Objections"', *ZAW* 55 (1937), pp. 71-72.

נֹפֶת *honey*—Dalman, *Arbeit*, I, p. 548.

(cf. נוף II *sprinkle*)—G.R. Driver, 'Problems in "Proverbs"', *ZAW* 50 (1932), pp. 141-48 (142-43).

מֵי נֶפְתּוֹחַ *spring of Merneptah*—Gary Rendsburg, 'Merneptah in Canaan', *JSSEA* 11 (1981), pp. 171-172 (corrigenda, *JSSEA* 12 [1982]).

נַפְתְּחִי *belonging to Ptah* (cf. Eg. n3 pṯḥ)—G.A. Rendsburg, 'Gen 10:13-14: An Authentic Hebrew Tradition Concerning the Origin of the Philistines', *JNWSL* 13 (1987), pp. 89-96 (91).

נֵץ II *falcon*—*HALOT*, II, p. 714b.

hawk—G.R. Driver, 'Birds in the Old Testament. I. Birds in Law', *PEQ* 87 (1955), pp. 5-20 (13-14); J. Milgrom, *Leviticus 1–16: A New Translation with Introduction and Commentary* (AB, 3; New York: Doubleday, 1991), p. 663.

hawk—John Tamulénas, 'Översättningen av fågellistorna i Lev 11:13-19 och Deut 14:11-18', *SEÅ* 57 (1992), pp. 28-59 (46).

hawk, falcon—BDB, p. 665b.

נצב I *stand*—J. Reindl, 'נצב/יצב *nṣb/yṣb*; נִצָּב *niṣṣāḇ*; נְצִיב *n^{e}ṣîḇ*; מַצָּב *maṣṣāḇ*; מ/מַצֵּבָה *mi/maṣṣāḇâ*; מֻצָּב muṣṣāḇ', *TDOT*, IX (1998; orig. 1984–86), pp. 519-29.

stand in prayer—D.R. Ap-Thomas, 'Notes on Some Terms Relating to Prayer', *VT* 6 (1956), pp. 225-41 (227-28).

stand, take up position for controversy—Victor Sasson, 'The Language of Rebellion in Psalm 2 and in the Plaster Texts from Deir 'Alla', *AUSS* 24 (1986), pp. 147-54 (152-53).

stand, take up position for warfare—Christoph Uehlinger, 'Der Herr auf der Zinnmauer: Zur dritten Amos-Vision (Am vii 7-8)', *BN* 48 (1989), pp. 89-104 (96).

ni. ptc. *in a standing position*—Joseph Reider, 'Contributions to the Scriptural Text', *HUCA* 24 (1952–53), pp. 85-106 (100).

hi. *set straight* oxgoad—William Foxwell Albright, *The Excavation of Tell Beit Mirsim*. Vol III. *The Iron Age* (AASOR 21-23 [1941–43]; New Haven: American Schools of Oriental Research, 1943), p. 33.

ho. *be propped up*—G.R. Driver, 'Studies in the Vocabulary of the Old Testament. VII', *JTS* 35 (1934), pp. 380-93 (390).

Ex 15_8—A. Wolters, 'Not Rescue but Destruction: Rereading Exodus 15:8', *CBQ* 52 (1990), pp. 223-40 (228).

Na 2_8—G.R. Driver, 'Farewell to Queen Huzzab', *JTS* ns 15 (1964), pp. 296-98; Carl A. Keller, 'Die theologische Bewältigung der geschichtlichen Wirklichkeit in der Prophetie Nahums', *VT* 22 (1972), pp. 399-419 (411 n. 1).

Ps 39_6—D. Winton Thomas, 'נִצָּב in Psalm xxxix, 6', in ספר סגל. *Studies in the Bible Presented to Professor M.H. Segal by his Colleagues and Students* (ed. J.M. Grintz and J. Liver; Jerusalem: Kiryat Sepher, 1964), pp. 10*-16*.

Ps 119_{89}—M. Dahood, review of Stanley Gevirtz, *Patterns in the Early Poetry of Israel* (1963), *Bib* 45 (1964), pp. 280-81 (281).

נצב II *be weak* (cf. Arab. naṣiba *be tired*)—J. Barth, 'הַנִּצָּבָה Sach 11 16', *ZAW* 36 (1916), pp. 117-19; G.R. Driver, 'Studies in the Vocabulary of the Old Testament. VI', *JTS* 34 (1933), pp. 375-85 (378); Alfred Guillaume, *Hebrew and Arabic Lexicography: A Comparative Study*, II (Leiden: E.J. Brill, 1965; = *AbrN* 2 [1960–61]), p. 25; *HALOT*, II, p. 715a.

נצב III *vanish, die* (cf. Arab. naḍaba *ooze away, dry up, vanish*)—L. Kopf, 'Arabische Etymologien und Parallelen zum Bibelwörterbuch', *VT* 9 (1959), pp. 247-87 (265).

נִצָּב I *hilt*—J. Reindl, 'נצב/יצב *nṣb/yṣb*; נִצָּב *niṣṣāḇ*; נְצִיב *n^{e}ṣîḇ*; מַצָּב *maṣṣāḇ*; מ/מַצֵּבָה *mi/maṣṣāḇâ*; מֻצָּב *muṣṣāḇ*', *TDOT*, IX (1998; orig. 1984–86), pp. 519-29 (525).

נְצָב II *image* (cf. Nab., Punic נצב *image, stela*)—Mitchell Dahood, *Psalms I: 1–50* (AB, 16; Garden City, NY: Doubleday, 1966), p. 241.

נצה II *go to ruin* (cf. OSA nḍw, Arab. ndw *destroy*)—*HALOT*, II, p. 715b.

נצה IV *hasten* (cf. Arab. nḍ' *cross quickly*)—G.R. Driver, 'Hebrew Notes on "Song of Songs" and "Lamentations"', in *Festschrift Alfred Bertholet zum 80. Geburtstag gewidmet von Kollegen und Freunden* (ed. Walter Baumgartner [*et al.*]; Tübingen: J.C.B. Mohr, 1950), pp. 134-46 (141).

נצה V *be joined* (cf. Arab. naṣā)—G.R. Driver, 'Notes on the

Text of "Lamentations"', *ZAW* 52 (1934), pp. 308-309 (308); D. Winton Thomas, 'The Language of the Old Testament', in *Record and Revelation: Essays on the Old Testament by Members of the Society for Old Testament Study* (ed. H. Wheeler Robinson; Oxford: Clarendon Press, 1939), pp. 374-402 (396); James Barr, *Comparative Philology and the Text of the Old Testament* (Oxford: Oxford University Press, 1968), pp. 262-63.

נָצוּר I *secret place* (cf. נצר *keep*)—*HALOT*, II, p. 716a; cf. BDB, p. 666a.

watch-hut (?)—KB, p. 629b.

נָצוּר II *mountain*—Mitchell Dahood, 'Textual Problems in Isaia', *CBQ* 22 (1960), pp. 400-409 (408-409); John J. Scullion, 'Some Difficult Texts in Isaiah cc. 56–66 in the Light of Modern Scholarship', *UF* 4 (1972), pp. 105-28 (127).

נצח I *conquer*—Maurice Sznycer, '"J'ai remporté la victoire sur tous nos ennemis ...": brèves remarques sur le verbe *nṣḥ*', *Sem* 41–42 (1991–92), pp. 89-100.

oversee, inspect—*HALOT*, II, p. 716a.

pi. ptc. מְנַצֵּחַ *famous*—Lienhard Delekat, 'Probleme der Psalmenüberschriften', *ZAW* 76 (1964), pp. 280-97 (287-90).

נצח II *shine* (cf. Aram., Syr. *shine*, Arab. naṣaha, Eth. naṣaḥa *be clear, pure*)—Zorell, p. 528a [conflated with נצח I *oversee*]; cf. BDB, p. 663b.

be splendid—מְנַצֵּחַ *with splendour, solemnity*—Jesús Enciso Viana, 'Indicaciones musicales en los títulos de los Salmos', in *Miscellanea Biblica B. Ubach* (ed. Romualdo M.ª Díaz; Scripta et documenta, 1; Montserrat: Montisserrati, 1953), pp. 185-91.

נצח III *be pre-eminent, enduring*—BDB, p. 663b.

נצח IV *conquer* (cf. MH, Aram.)—cf. Maurice Sznycer, '"J'ai remporté la victoire sur tous nos ennemis ...": brèves remarques sur le verbe *nṣḥ*', *Sem* 41–42 (1991–92), pp. 89-100.

נֵצַח I *eminence, endurance*—BDB, p. 664a.

endurance (cf. OSin nṣḥ *duration*)—W.F. Albright, 'The Early Alphabetic Inscriptions from Sinai and their Decipherment', *BASOR* 110 (1948), pp. 6-25 (18 n. 63).

faithful one—L. Kopf, 'Arabische Etymologien und Parallelen zum Bibelwörterbuch', *VT* 8 (1958), pp. 161-215 (184).

glory—G.W. Anderson, 'נֵצַח *neṣaḥ*; לַמְנַצֵּחַ *lamenaṣṣēaḥ*', *TDOT*, IX (1998; orig. 1984–86), pp. 529-33.

Glory, as divine title—BDB, p. 664a; Mitchell Dahood, *Psalms II: 51–100* (AB, 17; Garden City, NY: Doubleday, 1968; 3rd edn, 1979), p. 203.

לָנֶצַח *successfully*—G.R. Driver, 'Problems in "Proverbs"', *ZAW* 50 (1932), pp. 141-48 (144-45).

לָנֶצַח *utterly*—D. Winton Thomas, 'The Use of נֵצַח as a Superlative in Hebrew', *JSS* 1 (1956), pp. 106-109; Peter R. Ackroyd, 'נצח—εἰς τέλος', *ExpT* 80 (1968–69), p. 126; L. Kopf, 'Arabische Etymologien und Parallelen zum Bibelwörterbuch', *VT* 8 (1958), pp. 161-215 (186); P.P. Saydon, 'Some Unusual Ways of Expressing the Superlative in Hebrew and Maltese', *VT* 4 (1954), pp. 432-33; J.A. Emerton, 'The Interpretation of Proverbs 21,28', *ZAW* 100 Supplement (1988), pp. 161-70.

לָנֶצַח *forever* (not *utterly*)—Paul Joüon, 'Notes de lexicographie hébraïque', *Bib* 7 (1926), pp. 162-70 (162-63).

נֵצַח III *victory* (cf. נצח IV *conquer*, MH נִצָּחוֹן *might*)—cf. W.F. Albright, 'The Early Alphabetic Inscriptions from Sinai and their Decipherment', *BASOR* 110 (1948), pp. 6-25 (18 n. 63) (*vigour, vitality, endurance*; cf. OSin nṣḥ *duration*).

נֵצַח IV *juice, blood*—BDB, p. 664b; André Caquot, Maurice Sznycer and Andrée Herdner, *Textes ougaritiques. I. Mythes et légendes*, I (Paris: Cerf, 1974), p. 260 n. m.

juice, life-blood—Lm 3_{18}—Mitchell Dahood, 'New Readings in Lamentations', *Bib* 59 (1978), pp. 174-97 (184); John J. Scullion, 'Some Difficult Texts in Isaiah cc. 56–66 in the Light of Modern Scholarship', *UF* 4 (1972), pp. 105-28 (122).

in play on נצח II *glory*—Is $63_{3.6}$—G.R. Driver, '"Another Little Drink"—Isaiah 28:1-22', in *Words and Meanings: Essays Presented to David Winton Thomas* (ed. Peter R. Ackroyd and Barnabas Lindars; Cambridge: Cambridge University Press, 1968), pp. 47-67 (57).

נְצִיב I *governor*—Udo Rüterswörden, *Die Beamten der israelitischen Königszeit: Eine Studie zu śr und vergleichbaren Begriffen* (BWANT, 117; Stuttgart: W. Kohlhammer,

1985), pp. 107-109.

pillar—J. Reindl, 'נצב/יצב *nṣb/yṣb*; נִצָּב *niṣṣāḇ*; נְצִיב *neṣîḇ*; מַצָּב *maṣṣāḇ*; מִ/מַצָּבָה *mi/maṣṣāḇâ*; מֻצָּב *muṣṣāḇ*', *TDOT*, IX (1998; orig. 1984–86), pp. 519-29 (526-27).

stela, pillar, column—Gonzague Ryckmans, 'Notes Epigraphiques. Cinquième série. VIII. Le sens de quelques termes usités comme titres de stèles', *Mus* 71 (1958), pp. 125-39 (130-32).

נצל *deliver*—F.L.Hossfeld and B. Kalthoff, 'נצל *nṣl*; הַצָּלָה *haṣṣālâ*', *TDOT*, IX (1998; orig. 1984–86), pp. 533-40.

rescue—U. Bergmann, 'נצל *nṣl*' , *TLOT*, II (1997; orig. 1976), pp. 760-62.

נצץ I *sparkle*—J. Carmignac, 'Précisions apportées au vocabulaire de l'hébreu biblique par la Guerre des Fils de Lumière contre les Fils de Ténèbres', *VT* 5 (1955), pp. 345-65 (351-52).

נצץ II *become dry* (cf. Arab. naṣṣa)—Alfred Guillaume, *Hebrew and Arabic Lexicography: A Comparative Study*, II (Leiden: E.J. Brill, 1965; = *AbrN* 2 [1960–61]), p. 26.

נצר *guard*—G. Sauer, 'נצר *nṣr*' , *TLOT*, II (1997; orig. 1976), pp. 762-63; S. Wagner, 'נָצַר *nāṣar*', *TDOT*, IX (1998; orig. 1984–86), pp. 541-49.

keep—Moshe Held, 'Studies in Biblical Homonyms in the Light of Akkadian', *JANESCU* 3 (1970–71), pp. 46-55.

keep from indiscretion—Michael V. Fox, *Proverbs 1–9* (AB, 18A; New York: Doubleday, 2000), pp. 185-86.

Jr 4$_{16}$—G.R. Driver, 'Linguistic and Textual Problems: Jeremiah', *JQR* 28 (1937–38), pp. 97-129 (100).

Ps 94$_{20}$—Mitchell Dahood, *Psalms II: 51–100* (AB, 17; Garden City, NY: Doubleday, 1968; 3rd edn, 1979), p. 350.

נצר II *murmur* (cf. Aram. נצר *chirp* [of a cricket], Syr. neṣar *chirp, murmur*, Ug. nṣr *shriek [?]*)—Chaim Rabin, 'Noṣerim', *Textus* 5 (1966), pp. 44-52.

נֵצֶר I *shoot*—S. Wagner, 'נֵצֶר *nēṣer*', *TDOT*, IX (1998; orig. 1984–86), pp. 549-51.

נֵצֶר II *putrefying matter* (cf. MH נֵצֶל *decayed matter*)—G.R. Driver, 'Glosses in the Hebrew Text of the Old Testament', in *L'Ancien Testament et l'orient. Etudes présentées aux VIes Journées Bibliques de Louvain (11-13 septembre 1954)* (OBL, 1; Louvain-Leuven: Publications Universitaires / Instituut voor Orientalisme, 1957), pp. 123-61 (138).

נְצָרָה *seal*—Mitchell Dahood, 'mišmār "muzzle" in Job 7 12', *JBL* 80 (1961), pp. 270-71.

נצת *kindle* (cf. יצת)—Francis I. Andersen and David Noel Freedman, *Amos: A New Translation with Introduction and Commentary* (AB, 24A; New York: Doubleday, 1989), pp. 281-82.

נקב I *pierce*—J. Scharbert, 'נָקַב *nāqaḇ*; נֶקֶב *neqeḇ*; נְקֵבָה *neqēḇâ*; מַקֶּבֶת *maqqeḇeṯ*', *TDOT*, IX (1998; orig. 1984–86), pp. 551-53.

Hb 1$_6$—Lutz Bauer, *Zeit des Zweiten Tempels—Zeit der Gerechigkeit. Zur sozio-ökonomischen Konzeption im Haggai–Sacharja–Maleachi-Korpus* (BEATAJ, 31; Frankfurt a.M.: P. Lang, 1992), p. 159.

Jb 3$_8$—Edward Ullendorff, 'Job iii 8', *VT* 11 (1961), pp. 350-51.

Siloam—W.F. Albright, review of Alexander Heidel, *The Babylonian Genesis: The Story of Creation* (1942), *JBL* 62 (1943), pp. 366-70 (370).

נקב II *slander, blaspheme* (cf. קבב *curse*)—Zorell, p. 530a.

נֶקֶב I *engraving, socket*—BDB, p. 666a

plaque, bead—G.R. Driver, 'Uncertain Hebrew Words', *JTS* 45 (1944), pp. 13-14 (14).

נֶקֶב II *pipe, flute*—M.C. Astour, 'Remarks on KTU 1.96', in *Cananea Selecta: Festschrift fur Oswald Loretz zum 60. Geburtstag* (Studi epigraphici e linguistici sul Vicino Oriente Antico, 5; Verona: Essedue Edizioni, 1988), pp. 13-24 (18).

נֶקֶב III *passage, mine*—*HALOT*, II, p. 719a.

mine—W.F. Albright, 'The Early Alphabetic Inscriptions from Sinai and their Decipherment', *BASOR* 110 (1948), pp. 6-22 (13); KB, p. 631b.

pass—KB, p. 631b.

נֶקֶב IV *orifice* of the female body—Edward Lipiński, 'Les conceptions et couches merveilleuses de 'Anath', *Syr* 42 (1965), pp. 45-73 (49-52); cf. J. Scharbert, 'נָקַב *nāqaḇ*; נֶקֶב *neqeḇ*; נְקֵבָה *neqēḇâ*; מַקֶּבֶת *maqqeḇeṯ*', *TDOT*, IX (1998; orig. 1984–86), pp. 551-53 (552).

נְקֵבָה *female*—J. Scharbert, 'נָקַב *nāqaḇ* ; נֶקֶב *neqeḇ*; נְקֵבָה *neqēḇâ*; מַקֶּבֶת *maqqeḇeṯ*', *TDOT*, IX (1998; orig. 1984–86), pp. 551-53; J. Gerald Janzen, 'Rivers in the Desert of Abraham and Sarah and Zion (Isaiah 51:1-3)', *HAR* 10 (1986), pp. 139-55 (148).

נֹקֵד I *manager of sheep herds*—P.C. Craigie, 'Amos the *nōqēd* in the Light of Ugaritic', *SR* 11 (1982), pp. 29-33.

sheep breeder—A. Jeffers, *Magic and Divination in Ancient Palestine and Syria* (Studies in the History and Culture of the Ancient Near East, 8; Leiden: E.J. Brill, 1996), pp. 111-16.

shepherd—Hans Joachim Stoebe, 'Der Prophet Amos under sein bürgerliche Beruf', *WD* 5 (1957), pp. 160-81; S. Segert, 'Zur Bedeutung des Wortes *Nōqēd*', in *Hebräische Wortforschung: Festschrift zum 80. Geburtstag von Walter Baumgartner* (VTSup, 16; Leiden: E.J. Brill, 1967), pp. 279-83; John Wright, 'Did Amos Inspect Livers?', *AusBR* 23 (1975), pp. 3-11.

(cf. Ug. nqd)—Maximilian Ellenbogen, *Foreign Words in the Old Testament: Their Origin and Etymology* (London: Luzac & Co., 1962), p. 115.

נֹקֵד II *soothsayer, hepatoscoper* (cf. Akk. naqādu *probe* liver in augury)—Milos Bič, 'Der Prophet Amos—Ein Haepatoskopos', *VT* 1 (1951), pp. 293-96; A. Murtonen, 'The Prophet Amos—A Hepatoscoper?', *VT* 2 (1952), pp. 170-71; M. Bič, 'Maštîn BeQîr', *VT* 4 (1954), pp. 413-15; H.J. Stoebe, 'Der Prophet Amos under sein bürgerliche Beruf', *WD* 5 (1957), pp. 160-81; S. Segert, 'Zur Bedeutung des Wortes *Nōqēd*', in *Hebräische Wortforschung: Festschrift zum 80. Geburtstag von Walter Baumgartner* (VTSup, 16; Leiden: E.J. Brill, 1967), pp. 279-83; John Gray, *I and II Kings: A Commentary* (OTL; Philadelphia: Westminster Press, 2nd edn, 1970), p. 484; John Wright, 'Did Amos Inspect Livers?', *AusBR* 23 (1975), pp. 3-11.

נֹקֵד III *cultic official*—I. Engnell, *Studies in Divine Kingship in the Ancient Near East* (Uppsala: Almqvist & Wiksell, 1943), p. 8; Tadanori Yamashita, 'Noqed', in *Ras Shamra Parallels: The Texts from Ugarit and the Hebrew Bible* (ed. Loren R. Fisher; AnOr, 50; Rome: Pontifical Biblical Institute, 1975), II, pp. 63-64; M. Dietrich and O. Loretz, 'Die ugaritische Berufsgruppe der *nqdm* und das Amt des *rb nqdm*', *UF* 9 (1977), pp. 336-37.

נְקֻדָּה *bead*—Tryggve N.D. Mettinger, 'The Nominal Pattern *qᵉtullā* in Biblical Hebrew', *JSS* 16 (1971), pp. 2-14 (6).

glass bead—KB, p. 632a.

glass bead, circular or drop-shaped pendant—*HALOT*, II, p. 720a.

point, drop—BDB, p. 667a.

נקה I qal *cleanse*—C.F. Whitley, 'Psalm 99 5', *ZAW* 85 (1973), pp. 227-30; Mitchell Dahood, *Psalms II: 51–100* (AB, 17; Garden City, NY: Doubleday, 1968; 3rd edn, 1979), p. 370.

ni. *be innocent*—C. van Leeuwen, 'נקה *nqh*', *TLOT*, II (1997; orig. 1976), pp. 763-67; G. Warmuth, 'נָקָה *nāqâ*; נָקִי *nāqî*; נִקָּיוֹן *niqqāyôn*', *TDOT*, IX (1998; orig. 1984–86), pp. 553-63.

ni. *be poured out, emptied*—Matitiahu Tsevat, 'Some Biblical Notes', *HUCA* 24 (1952–53), pp. 107-14 (109-10).

נקה II *pour out* (cf. Akk. naqû)—G.R. Driver, 'Linguistic and Textual Problems: Minor Prophets. III', *JTS* 39 (1938), pp. 393-405 (401-402); Matitiahu Tsevat, 'Some Biblical Notes', *HUCA* 24 (1952–53), pp. 107-14 (109-10).

pour out, empty—G. Warmuth, 'נָקָה *nāqâ*; נָקִי *nāqî*; נִקָּיוֹן *niqqāyôn*', *TDOT*, IX (1998; orig. 1984–86), pp. 553-63.

נִקּוּד *cake strewn with something*—KB, p. 632a.

small pastry—*HALOT*, II, p. 720a.

spot, mould—G.R. Driver, 'Notes on Joshua', in *The Seventy-Fifth Anniversary Volume of the JQR* (Philadelphia, 1967), pp. 149-65 (157-58).

sweet bread garnished with seeds—John Gray, *I and II Kings: A Commentary* (OTL; Philadelphia: Westminster Press, 2nd edn, 1970), p. 336.

נָקִי *clean*—G. Warmuth, 'נָקָה *nāqâ*; נָקִי *nāqî*; נִקָּיוֹן *niqqāyôn*', *TDOT*, IX (1998; orig. 1984–86), pp. 553-63.

hungry—Mitchell Dahood, 'The Phoenician Background of Qoheleth', *Bib* 47 (1966), pp. 264-82 (265 n. 1); Mitchell Dahood, *Psalms I: 1–50* (AB, 16; Garden City, NY: Doubleday, 1966), p. 85.

נִקָּיוֹן *hunger*—Mitchell Dahood, 'The Phoenician Background of Qoheleth', *Bib* 47 (1966), pp. 264-82 (265 n.1).

innocence—G. Warmuth, 'נָקָה *nāqâ*; נָקִי *nāqî*; נִקָּיוֹן *niqqāyôn*', *TDOT*, IX (1998; orig. 1984–86), pp. 553-63.

נקם *avenge*—G. Sauer, 'נקם *nqm*', *TLOT*, II (1997; orig. 1976), pp. 767-69; E. Lipiński, 'נָקַם *nāqam*; נָקָם *nāqām*; נְקָמָה *nᵉqāmâ*', *TDOT*, X (1999; orig. 1986), pp. 1-9; K.

Lawson Younger, *Ancient Conquest Accounts: A Study in Ancient Near Eastern and Biblical History Writing* (JSOTSup, 98; Sheffield: JSOT Press, 1990), pp. 234-36; H.G.L. Peels, *The Vengeance of God: The Meaning of the Root NQM and the Function of the NQM-Texts in the Context of Divine Revelation in the Old Testament* (OTS, 31; Leiden: E.J. Brill, 1995).

champion, save—William Foxwell Albright, *History, Archaeology and Christian Humanism* (London: Adam & Charles Black, 1965), p. 96 n. 24.

make a payment in compensation—Moshe Greenberg, 'More Reflections on Biblical Criminal Law', *Studies in Bible* (ed. Sara Japhet; ScrHieros, 31; Jerusalem, 1986), pp. 1-19 (11-14).

נָקָם *victory*—Mitchell Dahood, *Psalms II: 51–100* (AB, 17; Garden City, NY: Doubleday, 1968; 3rd edn, 1979), p. 63.

נקף *go around*—F.V. Reiterer, 'נָקַף *nāqap*', *TDOT*, X (1999; orig. 1986), pp. 10-14.

go around—in reference to 'circular time'—N.H. Snaith, 'Time in the Old Testament', in *Promise and Fulfilment: Essays Presented to Professor S.H. Hooke in Celebration of his Ninetieth Birthday* (ed. F.F. Bruce; Edinburgh: T. & T. Clark, 1963), pp. 175-86.

mark off—Robert Gordis, *The Book of Job* (New York: Jewish Theological Seminary, 1978), p. 206.

נקר *bore*—Jb 30_{17}—John Gray, 'The Massoretic Text of the Book of Job, the Targum and the Septuagint Version in the Light of the Qumran Targum (11QtargJob)', *ZAW* 86 (1974), pp. 331-50 (345).

נְקָרָה *crevice*—J.T. Milik, 'Le rouleau de cuivre provenant de la grotte 3Q (3Q15)', in *DJD*, III (1962), pp. 199-302 (241.35).

נקשׁ I *knock, strike*—BDB, p. 669a; Zorell, p. 532b.

harass, revile (cf. Arab. naqasa)—G.R. Driver, 'Textual and Linguistic Problems of the Book of Psalms', *HTR* 29 (1936), pp. 171-95 (180-81).

נקשׁ II *ensnare* (cf. יקשׁ *trap*, קושׁ *lay snare*)—Zorell, p. 532b; *HALOT*, II, p. 723a.

נֵר I *lamp*—D. Kellermann, 'נֵר *nēr*; נִיר *nîr*', *TDOT*, X (1999; orig. 1986), pp. 14-24.

נֵר II *mark* (cf. Arab. nûratu *branded mark*)—G.R. Driver, 'Problems in the Hebrew Text of Proverbs', *Bib* 32 (1951), pp. 173-97 (185).

נֵרְדְּ *nard*—Wilfred H. Schoff, 'Nard', *JAOS* 43 (1923), pp. 216-28; John Pairman Brown, 'The Mediterranean Vocabulary of the Vine', *VT* 19 (1969), pp. 146-70 (160-64); Kjeld Nielsen, *Incense in Ancient Israel* (VTSup, 38; Leiden: E.J. Brill, 1986), p. 64.

נשׂא I *bear*—morphology (Ho 8_{10})—G.R. Driver, 'Linguistic and Textual Problems: Minor Prophets. I', *JTS* 39 (1938), pp. 154-66 (158).

bear (not *forgive*) *sin*—Baruch J. Schwartz, 'The Bearing of Sin in the Priestly Literature', in *Pomegranates and Golden Bells: Studies in Biblical, Jewish, and Near Eastern Ritual, Law, and Literature in Honor of Jacob Milgrom* (ed. David P. Wright, David Noel Freedman and Avi Hurvitz; Winona Lake, IN: Eisenbrauns, 1995), pp. 3-21.

lift, bear—F. Stolz, 'נשׂא *nś*'' , *TLOT*, II (1997; orig. 1976), pp. 769-74.

lift up—Menahem Moreshet, 'בעקבות לשׂאת ולתת (Tracing לשׂאת and לתת)', *Lesh* 43 (1979), pp. 295-30; D.N. Freedman, B.E. Willoughby, H.-J. Fabry and H. Ringgren, 'נָשָׂא *nāśā*'; מַשְׂאֵת *maś'ēṯ*; מַשּׂא *maśśō*'; מַשָּׂאָה *maśśā'â*; נָשִׂיא II *nāśî*' II; שְׂאֵת *śe'ēṯ*; שִׂיא *śî*'; מַשָּׂא *maśśā*'', *TDOT*, X (1999; orig. 1986), pp. 24-40.

raise up (to kingship)—G.R. Driver, 'Linguistic and Textual Problems: Minor Prophets. I', *JTS* 39 (1938), pp. 154-66 (158).

rise up (intrans.)—Mitchell Dahood, *Psalms II: 51–100* (AB, 17; Garden City, NY: Doubleday, 1968; 3rd edn, 1979), p. 317.

start—J.T. Milik, 'Deux documents inédits du désert de Juda', *Bib* 38 (1957), pp. 245-68 (252 n. 3).

withdraw money from bank—Norbert Lohfink, 'Kohelet und die Banken: Zur Übersetzung von Kohelet v 12-16', *VT* 39 (1989), pp. 488-95 (491).

נשׂא (with לֵב *heart* as subj.) *carry away*—Mordechai Cogan and Hayim Tadmor, *II Kings: A New Translation with Introduction and Commentary* (AB, 11; New York: Doubleday, 1988), p. 156.

נשׂא *lift up* (the foot), i.e. *start, get away*—G.R. Driver, 'Studies in the Vocabulary of the Old Testament. IV',

JTS 33 (1931–32), pp. 38-47 (41-42); G.R. Driver, 'Babylonian and Hebrew Notes', *WO* 2 (1954–59), pp. 19-26 (19); J.T. Milik, 'Deux documents inédits du désert de Juda', *Bib* 38 (1957), pp. 245-68 (252).

נשׂא יָדַיִם *lift up the hands* (in prayer)—Jacob Milgrom, *Leviticus 1–16: A New Translation with Introduction and Commentary* (AB, 3; New York: Doubleday, 1991), pp. 586-87.

נשׂא נֶפֶשׁ אֶל *flee for protection to (a person)*—Michael L. Barré, 'Mesopotamian Light on the Idiom *nāśā' nepeš* ', *CBQ* 52 (1990), pp. 46-54.

נשׂא נֶפֶשׁ אֶל *direct one's desire toward, long for (a thing)*—BDB, p. 670b; *HALOT*, II, p. 725b; Hans Walter Wolff, *Anthropology of the Old Testament* (Philadelphia: Fortress Press, 1979), p. 16; Michael L. Barré, 'Mesopotamian Light on the Idiom *nāśā' nepeš* ', *CBQ* 52 (1990), pp. 46-54.

נשׂא עַיִן *cast the eyes* (not *raise the eyes*)—S. C. Reif, 'A Root to Look Up: A Study of the Hebrew *ns' 'yn*', in *Congress Volume: Salamanca, 1983* (ed. J.A. Emerton; VTSup, 36; Leiden: E.J. Brill, 1985), pp. 230-44.

נשׂא עַיִן *lift up the eyes* (with ellipsis of עין)—Mitchell Dahood, *Psalms III: 101–150* (AB, 17A; Garden City, NY: Doubleday, 1970), p. 297.

bear punishment—Jacob Milgrom, *Leviticus 1–16: A New Translation with Introduction and Commentary* (AB, 3; New York: Doubleday, 1991), p. 295.

נשׂא פָּנִים *lift up the face*, i.e. show favour—Mayer I. Gruber, 'The Many Faces of Hebrew נשׂא פָּנִים »lift up the face«', *ZAW* 95 (1983), pp. 252-60.

נשׂא קוֹל *lift up the voice* (with ellipsis of קוֹל)—G.R. Driver, 'Studies in the Vocabulary of the Old Testament. VI', *JTS* 34 (1933), pp. 375-85 (384); G.R. Driver, 'Linguistic and Textual Problems: Minor Prophets. I', *JTS* 39 (1938), pp. 154-66 (163); G.R. Driver, 'Linguistic and Textual Problems: Minor Prophets. III', *JTS* 39 (1938), pp. 393-405 (394); G.R. Driver, 'Hebrew Notes on Prophets and Psalms', *JTS* 41 (1940), pp. 162-75 (167); G.R. Driver, 'Notes on the Psalms. II. 73–150', *JTS* 44 (1943), pp. 12-23 (18); Matitiahu Tsevat, 'Alalakhiana', *HUCA* 29 (1958), pp. 109-36 (119).

נשׂא ראשׁ *lift up the head, presume*—G.R. Driver, 'Hebrew Poetic Diction', in *Congress Volume, Copenhagen 1953* (VTSup, 1; Leiden: E. J. Brill, 1953), pp. 26-39 (39-40).

נשׂא ראשׁ *lift up the head*, i.e. *take note of*—E.A. Speiser, 'Census and Ritual Expiation in Mari and Israel', *BASOR* 149 (1958), pp. 17-25 (21) (= *Oriental and Biblical Studies*, pp. 171-86); E.A. Speiser, *Genesis: Introduction, Translation, and Notes* (AB, 1; Garden City, NY: Doubleday, 1964), p. 308.

נשׂא ראשׁ *lift up the head* in joy—Mayer I. Gruber, *Aspects of Nonverbal Communication in the Ancient Near East* (Studia Pohl, 12; Rome: Biblical Institute Press, 1980), pp. 598-613.

נשׂא ראשׁ (שַׁעַר) *lift up the head of a gate*, i.e. widen—Oswald Loretz, *Ugarit-Texte und Thronbesteigungspsalmen: Die Metamorphose des Regenspenders Baal-Jahwe (Ps 24, 7-10; 29; 47; 93; 95-100 sowie Ps 77, 17-20; 114). Erweiterte Neuauflage von 'Psalm 29. Kanaanäische El- und Baaltraditionen in jüdischer Sicht'* (Ugaritisch-Biblische Literatur, 7; Münster: Ugarit-Verlag, 1988), pp. 259-63 (262-63).

נשׂא רֶגֶל *lift up the foot*, i.e. *start, get away*—G.R. Driver, 'Studies in the Vocabulary of the Old Testament. IV', *JTS* 33 (1931–32), pp. 38-47 (41-42).

נשׂא II *smoke, fume* (cf. מַשְׂאֵת II *smoke-signal*)—M. Dahood, 'Northwest Semitic Texts and Textual Criticism of the Hebrew Bible', in *Questions disputées d'Ancien Testament* (ed. C. Brekelmans; BETL, 33; Leuven, 1974), pp. 11-37 (35). (For כָּבֵד *liver* as fem., cf. M. Dahood, 'Ugaritic–Hebrew Syntax and Style', *UF* 1 (1969), pp. 15-36 [23].)

נשׂג I *reach*—J. Hausmann, 'נָשַׂג *nāśag*' *TDOT*, X (1999; orig. 1986), pp. 40-44.

נשׂג II *hunt* (cf. Arab. našaja *hunt*)—Alfred Guillaume, *Hebrew and Arabic Lexicography: A Comparative Study*, II (Leiden: E.J. Brill, 1965; = *AbrN* 2 [1960–61]), p. 26.

נשׂה III *give up* (cf. Arab. nāsa *give up* a work)—Israel Eitan, 'A Contribution to Isaiah Exegesis (Notes and Short Studies in Biblical Philology)', *HUCA* 12–13 (1937–38), pp. 55-88 (79).

נָשִׂיא I *chieftain*—J. van der Ploeg, 'Les chefs du peuple d'Israël et leurs titres', *RB* 57 (1950), pp. 40-61 (47-51);

H. Niehr, 'נָשִׂיא *nāśî*'', *TDOT*, X (1999; orig. 1986), pp. 44-53; Jacob Milgrom, *Leviticus 1–16: A New Translation with Introduction and Commentary* (AB, 3; New York: Doubleday, 1991), pp. 246-47.

president, leader, chieftain (not *prince*)—E.A. Speiser, 'Background and Function of the Biblical nāśī'', *CBQ* 25 (1963), pp. 111-17.

prince of angels—Carol Newsom, *Songs of the Sabbath Sacrifice: A Critical Edition* (HSM, 27; Atlanta: Scholars Press, 1985), pp. 26-27.

royal prince—Michael A. Knibb, 'The Interpretation of *Damascus Document* VII, 9*b*–VIII, 2*a* and XIX, 5*b*-14', *RQ* 15 (1991–92), pp. 243-51 (250).

compared with מֶלֶךְ *king*—Iain W. Provan, *Hezekiah and the Books of Kings: A Contribution to the Debate about the Composition of the Deuteronomistic History* (BZAW, 172; Berlin: de Gruyter, 1988), p. 103.

נָשִׂי II *mist*—D.N. Freedman, B.E. Willoughby, H.-J. Fabry and H. Ringgren, 'נָשָׂא *nāśā*'; מַשְׂאֵת *maś'ēt*; מַשֹּׂא *maśśō*'; מַשָּׂאָה *maśśā'â*; נָשִׂיא II *nāśî*' II; שְׂאֵת *śe'ēt*; שִׂיא *śî*'; מַשָּׂא *maśśā*'', *TDOT*, X (1999; orig. 1986), pp. 24-40.

נָשִׂיא III *one brought* (cf. נשׂא *bear, bring*)—M.H. Gottstein, 'נשיא אלהים (Gen. xxiii 6)', *VT* 3 (1953), pp. 298-99.

נשא I *lend*—F.L. Hossfeld and E. Reuter, 'נָשָׁא *nāšā*' II; נשה *nšh*; מַשָּׁא *maššā*'; מַשָּׁאוֹת *maššā'ôṯ*; נְשִׁי *ne**šî*', *TDOT*, X (1999; orig. 1986), pp. 55-59; Rainer Kessler, 'Das hebräische Schuldenwesen: Terminologie und Metapher', *WD* 20 (1989), pp. 181-96 (182-83).

נשׁא II *deceive*—H. Ringgren, 'נשׁא *nš*' I', *TDOT*, X (1999; orig. 1986), pp. 53-55.

נשׁא III *forget* (byform of נשׁה)—Ha 3_{10}—G.R. Driver, 'Linguistic and Textual Problems: Minor Prophets. III', *JTS* 39 (1938), pp. 393-405 (396).

נשׁב hi. privative *stifle*—Mitchell Dahood, 'Hebrew–Ugaritic Lexicography IX', *Bib* 52 (1971), pp. 337-56 (349-50); Mitchell Dahood, *Psalms II: 51–100* (AB, 17; Garden City, NY: Doubleday, 1968; 3rd edn, 1979), p. 145.

נשׂג *reach*—J. Hausmann, 'נָשַׂג *nāśag*', *TDOT*, X (1999; orig. 1986), pp. 40-44.

נשׁד I *lend*—Jb 39_{17}—M. Dahood, 'Hebrew–Ugaritic Lexicography VII', *Bib* 50 (1969), pp. 337-56 (337); F.L. Hossfeld and E. Reuter, 'נָשָׁא *nāšā*' II; נשה *nšh*; מַשָּׁא *maššā*'; מַשָּׁאוֹת *maššā'ôṯ*; נְשִׁי *nešî*', *TDOT*, X (1999; orig. 1986), pp. 55-59.

נשׁה II *forget*—G.R. Driver, 'Linguistic and Textual Problems: Minor Prophets. III', *JTS* 39 (1938), pp. 393-405 (396); M. Dahood, 'Hebrew–Ugaritic Lexicography VII', *Bib* 50 (1969), pp. 337-56; G. Rinaldi, '*nšh* (*nšy*)', *BeO* 13 (1971), p. 26; H. Ringgren, 'נָשָׁה *nāšâ*; נְשִׁיָּה *nešîyyâ*', *TDOT*, X (1999; orig. 1986), pp. 60-61.

infixed -t conjugation—Mitchell Dahood, 'Philological Notes on Jer 18,14-15', *ZAW* 74 (1962), pp. 207-209 (207); Mitchell Dahood, 'Hebrew–Ugaritic Lexicography XI', *Bib* 54 (1973), pp. 351-66 (356).

Ps 2_{12}—William L. Holladay, 'A New Proposal for the Crux in Ps ii 12', *VT* 28 (1979) 110-12; Mitchell Dahood, 'The Composite Divine Name in Psalms 89,16-17 and 140,9', *Bib* 61 (1980), pp. 277-78 (277 n. 2).

נְשִׁי *debt*—F.L. Hossfeld and E. Reuter, 'נָשָׁא *nāšā*' II; נשה *nšh*; מַשָּׁא *maššā*'; מַשָּׁאוֹת *maššā'ôṯ*; נְשִׁי *nešî*', *TDOT*, X (1999; orig. 1986), pp. 55-59.

נְשִׁיָּה *forgetfulness*—H. Ringgren, 'נָשָׁה *nāšâ*; נְשִׁיָּה *nešîyyâ*', *TDOT*, X (1999; orig. 1986), pp. 60-61.

נָשִׁים *men* (cf. Ug. nšm)—Mitchell Dahood, *Psalms I: 1–50* (AB, 16; Garden City, NY: Doubleday, 1966), p. 13.

נְשִׁיקָה *kiss*—K.-M. Beyse, 'נָשַׁק *nāšaq*; נְשִׁיקָה *nešîqâ*', *TDOT*, X (1999; orig. 1986), pp. 72-76.

נשׁך I *bite*—A.S. Kapelrud, 'נָשַׁךְ *nāšaḵ*; נֶשֶׁךְ *nešeḵ*', *TDOT*, X (1999; orig. 1986), pp. 61-65.

נשׁך II *pay interest*—Samuel E. Loewenstamm, 'נשך and מ/תרבית', *JBL* 88 (1969), pp. 78-80.

נֶשֶׁךְ *interest*—A.S. Kapelrud, 'נָשַׁךְ *nāšaḵ*; נֶשֶׁךְ *nešeḵ*', *TDOT*, X (1999; orig. 1986), pp. 61-65.

interest (on a money loan)—Samuel E. Loewenstamm, 'נשך and מ/תרבית', *JBL* 88 (1969), pp. 78-80.

נשׁם *yearn*—Frank M. Cross and David Noel Freedman, 'The Blessing of Moses', *JBL* 67 (1948), pp. 191-210 (208 n. 71).

Is 42_{14}—P. Wernberg-Møller, 'Defective Spellings in the Isaiah-Scroll of St Mark's Monastery', *JSS* 3 (1958), pp. 244-64 (263).

נְשָׁמָה *breath*—T.C. Mitchell, 'The Old Testament Usage of nešâmâ', *VT* 11 (1961), pp. 177-87; H. Lamberty-Zielinski, 'נְשָׁמָה *nešāmâ*', *TDOT*, X (1999; orig. 1986), pp. 65-70.

breath as facilitating speech—Klaus Koch, 'Der Güter Gefährlichstes, die Sprache, dem Menschen gegeben ... Überlegungen zu Gen 2,7', *BN* 48 (1989), pp. 50-60.

soul—D. Dimant and J. Strugnell, 'The Merkabah Vision in *Second Ezekiel* (*4Q385* 4)', *RQ* 14 (1990), pp. 331-48 (338).

God's breath (Jb 27$_3$)—M. Dahood, 'Hebrew–Ugaritic Lexicography VII', *Bib* 50 (1969), pp. 337-56 (339).

נֶשֶׁף I *twilight*—B. Kedar-Kopfstein, 'נֶשֶׁף *nešep*', *TDOT*, X (1999; orig. 1986), pp. 70-72.

נֶשֶׁף II *trace, faint suspicion* (cf. Arab. nasafa VIII *whisper* words, nasîfu *trace, secret conversation*)—G.R. Driver, 'Notes on Isaiah', in *Von Ugarit nach Qumran: Beiträge zur alttestamentlichen und altorientalischen Forschung, Otto Eissfeldt zum 1. September 1957 dargebracht von Freunden und Schülern* (ed. J. Hempel and L. Rost; BZAW, 77; Berlin: A. Töpelmann, 1961), pp. 42-48 (44).

נשק I *kiss* (cf. Akk. našāku, Arab. našiqa *smell*,—Immanuel Löw, 'Der Kuss', MGWJ 65 [1921], pp. 253-76, 323-49) (=Wissenschaftliche Abhandlungen des Leo Baecks Instituts, 16; Tübingen, 1967, pp. 641-76); K.-M. Beyse, 'נָשַׁק *nāšaq*; נְשִׁיקָה *nešîqâ*', *TDOT*, X (1999; orig. 1986), pp. 72-76; John Ellington, 'Kissing in the Bible: Form and Meaning', *BiTrans* 41 (1990), pp. 409-16.

Ps 2$_{12}$—W.L. Holladay, 'A New Proposal for the Crux in Ps ii 12', *VT* 28 (1979) 110-12; Mitchell Dahood, 'The Composite Divine Name in Psalms 89,16-17 and 140,9', *Bib* 61 (1980), pp. 277-78 (277 n. 2).

Ps 85$_{11}$—G.R. Driver, 'Textual and Linguistic Problems of the Book of Psalms', *HTR* 29 (1936), pp. 171-95 (188).

נשק III *be in order* (cf. Arab. nâsaqa baina *follow in file*, Eth. nesūq *arrange in order*)—G.R. Driver, 'Ezekiel: Linguistic and Textual Problems', *Bib* 35 (1954), pp. 145-59 (147); L. Kopf, 'Arabische Etymologien und Parallelen zum Bibelwörterbuch', *VT* 9 (1959), pp. 247-87 (266-67); A.A. Macintosh, 'A Consideration of the Problems Presented by Psalm ii. 11 and 12', *JTS* ns 27 (1976), pp. 1-14.

נשק IV *seal* (cf. Arab. nasaqa *seal, fasten together*)—Jeffrey M. Cohen, 'An Unrecognized Connotation of *nšq peh* with Special Reference to Three Biblical Occurrences', *VT* 32 (1982), pp. 416-24.

נשק V *acquiesce, yield*—*HALOT*, II, p. 731a (as נשק II).

נַשָּׁר *herald* (cf. Arab. naššār)—Harry Torczyner, 'Dunkle Bibelstellen', in *Vom Alten Testament: Karl Marti zum siebzigsten Geburtstage gewidmet* (ed. Karl Budde; BZAW, 41; Giessen: A. Töpelmann, 1925), pp. 274-80 (277-78); N.H. Tur-Sinai, *The Book of Job* (Jerusalem: Kiryath Sepher, revised edn, 1967), p. 551; James Barr, *Comparative Philology and the Text of the Old Testament* (Oxford: Oxford University Press, 1968), pp. 26-28; Grace I. Emmerson, 'The Structure and Meaning of Hosea viii 1-3', *VT* 25 (1975), pp. 700-10 (702-704).

נֶשֶׁר *eagle and vulture*—Othmar Keel, *Jahwes Entgegnung an Ijob: Eine Deutung von Ijob 38–41 vor dem Hintergrund der zeitgenössischen Bildkunst* (FRLANT, 121; Göttingen: Vandenhoeck & Ruprecht, 1978), p. 69 n. 234; T. Kronholm, 'נֶשֶׁר *nešer*', *TDOT*, X (1999; orig. 1986), pp. 77-85; Hans-Peter Müller, 'Die Funktion divinatorischen Redens und die Tierbezeichnungen der Inschrift von Tell Deir 'Allā', in *The Balaam Text from Deir 'Alla Re-Evaluated* (ed. J. Hoftijzer and G. van der Kooij; Leiden: E.J. Brill, 1991), pp. 185-205 (195-96); Meindert Dijkstra, 'Response to H.-P. Müller and M. Weippert', in *The Balaam Text*, pp. 206-17 (211).

griffon-vulture (Gyps fulvus)—G.R. Driver, 'Birds in the Old Testament. I. Birds in Law', *PEQ* 87 (1955), pp. 5-20 (8-9); J. Milgrom, *Leviticus 1–16: A New Translation with Introduction and Commentary* (AB, 3; New York: Doubleday, 1991), pp. 662; ohn Tamulénas, 'Översättningen av fågellistorna i Lev 11:13-19 och Deut 14:11-18', *SEÅ* 57 (1992), pp. 28-59 (36-37).

(golden) eagle—G.R. Driver, 'Birds in the Old Testament. I. Birds in Law', *PEQ* 87 (1955), pp. 5-20 (8-9); G.R. Driver, 'Once Again: Birds in the Bible', *PEQ* 90 (1958), pp. 56-58 (56-57).

נְתִיב *path*—Pr 12$_{28}$—M. Dahood, 'Hebrew–Ugaritic Lexicography VII', *Bib* 50 (1969), pp. 337-56 (340).

נְתִיבָה II *ruin, what has been cut down* (cf. Akk. natābu *cut off*)—G.R. Driver, 'Notes on Isaiah', in *Von Ugarit nach*

Qumran: Beiträge zur alttestamentlichen und altorientalischen Forschung, Otto Eissfeldt zum 1. September 1957 dargebracht von Freunden und Schülern (ed. J. Hempel and L. Rost; BZAW, 77; Berlin: A. Töpelmann, 1961), pp. 42-48 (48).

נָתִין *temple servant*—Menahem Haran, 'The Gibeonites, the Nethinim and the Sons of Solomon's Servants', *VT* 11 (1961), pp. 158-69; Joel P. Weinberg, 'Netînîm und »Söhne der Sklaven Salomos« im 6.–4. Jh. v.u.Z.', *ZAW* 87 (1975), pp. 355-71; Magen Broshi and Asa Yardeni, 'On netinim and False Prophets', in *Solving Riddles and Untying Knots: Biblical, Epigraphic, and Semitic Studies in Honor of Jonas C. Greenfield* (ed. Ziony Zevit, Seymour Gitin and Michael Sokoloff; Winona Lake, IN: Eisenbrauns, 1995), pp. 29-37.

נְתִיצָה *ruin* (cf. נתץ *pull down)*—*HALOT*, II, p. 732b.

נתך *pour out*—A. Stiglmair, 'נָתַךְ *nāṯaḵ*', *TDOT*, X (1999; orig. 1986), pp. 85-89.

נתן *give*—morphology—qal pass.—W.F. Albright, 'The High Place in Ancient Palestine', in *Volume du Congrès, Strasbourg 1956* (VTSup, 4; Leiden: E.J. Brill, 1957), pp. 242-58 (244-26); Mitchell Dahood, 'Phoenician Elements in Isaiah 52:13–53:12', in *Near Eastern Studies in Honor of William Foxwell Albright* (ed. Hans Goedicke; Baltimore: The Johns Hopkins Press, 1971), pp. 63-73 (70); D.W. Young, 'Notes on the Root ˆtn in Biblical Hebrew', *VT* 10 (1960), pp. 457-59; Menahem Moreshet, 'בעקבות לשאת ולתת (Tracing לשאת and לתת)', *Lesh* 43 (1979), pp. 295-301.

bring over—H.J. van Dyck, 'A Neglected Connotation of Three Hebrew Verbs', *VT* 18 (1968), pp. 16-30; S.C. Reif, 'A Note on a Neglected Connotation of *ntn*', *VT* 20 (1970), pp. 114-16.

display—Mitchell Dahood, *Psalms III: 101–150* (AB, 17A; Garden City, NY: Doubleday, 1970), p. 140.

entrust—Mitchell Dahood, *Psalms III: 101–150* (AB, 17A; Garden City, NY: Doubleday, 1970), p. 142.

give—C.J. Labuschagne, 'נתן *ntn*' , *TLOT*, II (1997; orig. 1976), pp. 774-91; E. Lipiński and H.-J. Fabry, 'נָתַן *nāṯan*; מַתָּן *mattān*; מַתָּנָה *mattānâ*; מַתַּת *mattaṯ*; אֶתְנָה *'eṯnâ*; אֶתְנַן/אֶתְנָן *'eṯnān/'eṯnan*', *TDOT*, X (1999; orig. 1986), pp. 90-108.

pour out—H.J. van Dyck, 'A Neglected Connotation of Three Hebrew Verbs', *VT* 18 (1968), pp. 16-30 S.C. Reif, 'A Note on a Neglected Connotation of *ntn*', *VT* 20 (1970), pp. 114-16.

sell—Mitchell Dahood, *Proverbs and Northwest Semitic Philology* (Scripta Pontificii Instituti Biblici, 113; Rome: Pontificium Institutum Biblicum, 1963), p. 61.

spread—H.J. van Dyck, 'A Neglected Connotation of Three Hebrew Verbs', *VT* 18 (1968), pp. 16-30.

write down as accusation—Mitchell Dahood, *Psalms II: 51–100* (AB, 17; Garden City, NY: Doubleday, 1968; 3rd edn, 1979), p. 163.

מִי יִתֵּן *would that!*—B. Jongeling, 'L'expression *my ytn* dans l'Ancien Testament', *VT* 24 (1974), pp. 32-40.

נתן אֵשׁ *stoke fire* (not kindle)—Jacob Milgrom, *Leviticus 1–16: A New Translation with Introduction and Commentary* (AB, 3; New York: Doubleday, 1991), pp. 157-58.

נתן יָד *make terms with*—G.R. Driver, 'Hebrew Notes on "Song of Songs" and "Lamentations"', in *Festschrift Alfred Bertholet zum 80. Geburtstag gewidmet von Kollegen und Freunden* (ed. Walter Baumgartner [*et al.*]; Tübingen: J.C.B. Mohr, 1950), pp. 134-46 (142-43).

Ps 8_2—D.W. Young, 'Notes on the Root נתן inBiblical Hebrew', *VT* 10 (1960), pp. 457-99.

נתס II *place thorns* (cf. Arab. natsun *thorns*)—Robert Gordis, *The Book of Job* (New York: Jewish Theological Seminary, 1978), pp. 333-34.

נתע I *break* (byform of נתץ *break*)—M. Dahood, 'The Etymology of Malta'ot (Ps 58,7)', *CBQ* 17 (1955), pp. 180-83; *HALOT*, II, p. 735b.

נתע II *cease* (cf. Eth. nat'a *flee*)—Israel Eitan, *A Contribution to Biblical Lexicography* (Contributions to Oriental History and Philology, 10; New York: Columbia University Press, 1924), pp. 9-10.

נתע III *pull out* (cf. Arab. na'ṯa'a *pull out* a tooth)—Alfred Guillaume, *Hebrew and Arabic Lexicography: A Comparative Study*, III (Leiden: E.J. Brill, 1965; = *AbrN* 3 [1962–63]), p. 5; cf. Mitchell Dahood, *Psalms II: 51–100* (AB, 17; Garden City, NY: Doubleday, 1968; 3rd edn, 1979), p. 61.

נתע *plant*—Hedwige Rouillard, *La pericope de Balaam* (Nombres 22–24)*: La prose et les «oracles»* (Etudes bibliques, ns 4; Paris: Gabalda, 1985), pp. 356-58.

נתץ *pull down*—C. Barth, 'נָתַץ *nāṯaṣ*', *TDOT*, X (1999; orig. 1986), pp. 108-14.

נתק *break*—T. Kronholm, 'נָתַק *nāṯaq*; נֶתֶק *neṯeq*', *TDOT*, X (1999; orig. 1986), pp. 115-19.

pi. *break*—Is 58$_6$—M. Dahood, 'Hebrew–Ugaritic Lexicography VII', *Bib* 50 (1969), pp. 337-56 (340-41).

נֶתֶק *scall*—T. Kronholm, 'נָתַק *nāṯaq*; נֶתֶק *neṯeq*', *TDOT*, X (1999; orig. 1986), pp. 115-19; J. Milgrom, *Leviticus 1–16: A New Translation with Introduction and Commentary* (AB, 3; New York: Doubleday, 1991), p. 793.

נתר I *be loose* (cf. perh. Arab. natara *tear* garment)—BDB, p. 684 (s.v. נתר I); G. Rinaldi, '*ntr*', *BeO* 8 (1966), p. 79; P. Maiberger, 'נָתַר *nāṯar*; נֶתֶר *neṯer*', *TDOT*, X (1999; orig. 1986), pp. 119-22.

(cf. Arab. naṭara *fall down*)—*HALOT*, II, p. 736a (s.v. נתר I).

Pr 12$_{26}$—J.A. Emerton, 'A Note on Proverbs xii. 26', *ZAW* 76 (1964), pp. 191-93.

נתר II *spring, start up*—BDB, p. 684a (s.v. נתר II).

leap (cf. Arab. natala *spring up silently*)—*HALOT*, II, p. 736b (s.v. נתר II); P. Maiberger, 'נָתַר *nāṯar*; נֶתֶר *neṯer*', *TDOT*, X (1999; orig. 1986), pp. 119-22.

נתר III *tear apart* (cf. Akk. nutturu)—G.R. Driver, 'Difficult Words in the Hebrew Prophets', in *Studies in Old Testament Prophecy Presented to Professor Theodore H. Robinson* (ed. H.H. Rowley; Edinburgh: T. & T. Clark, 1950), pp. 52-72 (70); *HALOT*, II, p. 737a (s.v. נתר III).

נתר IV *snatch away;* intrans. *fall away* (cf. Arab. natara *drag violently, tear*)—G.R. Driver, 'Difficult Words in the Hebrew Prophets', in *Studies in Old Testament Prophecy Presented to Professor Theodore H. Robinson* (ed. H.H. Rowley; Edinburgh: T. & T. Clark, 1950), pp. 52-72 (71-72).

נתר V *hop, leap, start up* (cf. Akk. tarāru *quiver, tremble*, Arab. tarrun *trotting rapidly, prancing*)—G.R. Driver, 'Difficult Words in the Hebrew Prophets', in *Studies in Old Testament Prophecy Presented to Professor Theodore H. Robinson* (ed. H.H. Rowley; Edinburgh: T. & T. Clark, 1950), pp. 52-72 (71-72); G.R. Driver, 'Some Hebrew Medical Expressions', *ZAW* 65 (1953), pp. 255-62 (257 n. 7); James Barr, *Comparative Philology and the Text of the Old Testament* (Oxford: Oxford University Press, 1968), p. 290.

נֶתֶר I *natron* (cf. Aram. נִתְרָא, Akk. nitiru)—G.R. Driver, 'Problems and Solutions', *VT* 4 (1954), pp. 225-45 (240-41); P. Maiberger, 'נָתַר *nāṯar*; נֶתֶר *neṯer*', *TDOT*, X (1999; orig. 1986), pp. 119-22.

niter, natron (cf. Eg. nčry, ntry)—Thomas O. Lambdin, 'Egyptian Loanwords in the Old Testament', *JAOS* 73 (1953), pp. 145-55 (152-53); Maximilian Ellenbogen, *Foreign Words in the Old Testament: Their Origin and Etymology* (London: Luzac & Co., 1962), p. 117.

נֶתֶר II *wound* (cf. Arab. natrutun *deep wound*)—G.R. Driver, 'Problems and Solutions', *VT* 4 (1954), pp. 225-45 (240-41).

נתשׁ *pluck up*—J. Hausmann, 'נָתַשׁ *nāṯaš*', *TDOT*, X (1999; orig. 1986), pp. 123-26.

ENGLISH–HEBREW INDEX

abandon 639, 679, 721
abiding 460
ability to turn back 515
ability to utter proverbs 539
abode 387, 390, 460, 636
abomination 622
abortion 473
above 402
abstain from 651
abundance 477, 734
abundant, make 130
accept 121, 586, 758, 771
accepted, be 716
access, (right of) 164
accident 471
accompany with a stringed instrument 607
accomplish 280
accomplished, be 277
account 375
accursed one 650
achieve 435
achieve, 635
achievement 416
acknowledge 693
acquaintance 149, 273
acquainted with, be 693
acquiesce 781
acquire 167, 186, 682, 694
acquire with bride-gift 167
acquisition 565
acquisition(s) 354
acquit 750
act as a stranger 694
act deceitfully against 692
act foolishly 593
act ignominiously 593
act of apostasy 514
act of judgment 556
act of mortgaging 330
act of rebellion 514
act quickly 165
act sacrilegiously 593
act the man 474
action 416
activity 416, 540
adaptation 297
adhere (to) 629
admirable sights 620
admire 636
adorn 578
adulterer 580
adultery 579, 581
advantage 202
advice 322
afar 485
affirmative response to an augury 706
afflict (with) 609
afflict with 785
afflicted, be 609
afflict 714
affliction 182, 449, 457, 604, 611
afford 435
afford, be able to 771
after 337, 339
against 337, 343, 359, 603
against what? 160
agony 492
agreement 182
aim 654
aim at 635, 654
air-shaft 360
alien 695
alienate 694
alienated, be 753
alight 716
all around 361
all over 359
allocate 721
allocate portions to 656
allocated, be 716
allot 656
allotment 219
allotted, be 657
allow 640, 785
allow to break bonds 817
allow to remain 640
allusive saying 301
alluvial soil 138
ally oneself 654
Almighty 103
almost 395
aloof from 604
altar 202
alter 187
ambush 123
ambush, (people waiting in) 123
ambush, (place of) 123
amount 270, 370
amount that fills 283
amphora 333, 594
and older 404
angel 285
angle 470
Angle, the 470
angry, be 667, 679
anguish 449
animal that is pressed 398
animal that is torn 816
annihilate 214
annihilated one 215
annihilated, be 215

announce 599
announced, be 602
annul 634
anoint 515
anointed 517
anointed one 517, 520
anointing 333, 517, 518, 522
answer 409
ant 696
anything 115, 116, 151
apostasy 514
apostate 515
apparatus 416
apparition 706
appearance 474
appeasement 681
appetite 724, 725
appoint 345, 346, 785
appoint as 785
appointed feast, (time of) 181
appointed place 179, 433
appointed signal 182
appointed time 179
appointed, be 345, 346, 785
appointment 176, 179, 182, 433
apportion 346
apportioned, be 346
appraise 229
appraiser 229
appreciate 771
approach 614
approaches 412
arise 758
ark 260
arm oneself with 279
armed (with), be 780
armed troop 222
armour 139
armoury 360, 781
army 222, 413
Arnon 263
arrange payment (to oneself) 346
arrangement 413
array 413, 415
arrival 124
arrive 567, 608, 772
arrive (at) 608
arrive (in camp) 716
arrogance 386
arrow 368
as a freewill offering, given be 618
as a special contribution, treat 646
as far as opposite 604, 692
as though it were 427
ascent 404, 405, 406
ash-heaps 564
aside, take 674
assault 565, 611
assemble en masse 281
assembling 471
assembly 459, 470
assembly, (meeting of) 191
assembly, place of 178, 471
assign 345, 346, 785
assigned duty 495
assigned, be 785
assume authority 531
assurance 580
asylum 467
at 337, 342
at (the end of) 337, 339
at a distance 604
at all 116
at the front of 174
at work (with an axe), be 625
attack 685
attain to 610, 771
attempt to do something 698
attendant 708, 711
attention 503
attention (to), pay 693
attractive, make 524
augury 667
augury; practise 667
authority 334
authority, assume 531
avenge 751, 752
avenge oneself 663, 752
avenged, be 752
avenger 752
aversion 514
away from 337, 341
away from (the presence of) 604
awl 492
axe 134, 410
bagful 525
bait 186
baked food 122
baking tray 214
balances 118
balancing 432
bald, be 299
ballista 103
banish 624, 625
banished one 624
banished one(s) 624
banished, be 749
bank 131
banner 697
bannister 369
bar 172
bard 537
bare 708
bare oneself 708
bare place 410
bargaining 330
bark 585
base 267, 268
basis 177
bastard 330
battle 294, 413, 781
battle-line 413
be (found to be) sufficient 439
be (found) 439
be (too) few 391
be (too) small 391
be a creditor 614, 775, 776
be a youth 708
be able to afford 771
be accepted 716
be accomplished 277
be acquainted with 693
be afflicted 609
be alienated 753
be allocated 716
be allotted 657
be allowed 785

be angry 667, 679
be annihilated 215
be announced 602
be anointed, anointed, be 517
be appointed 345, 346, 785
be apportioned 346
be armed (with) 780
be assigned 785
be at work (with an axe) 625
be avenged 752
be bald 299
be banished 624, 749
be beaten 690
be beaten down 684
be beautiful 578
be beguiled 758, 775
be besieged 745
be betrayed 167
be bitten .i.bitten, be 777
be bitter 493
be blameless 749
be blighted 690
be blockaded 745
be blown 714
be blown away 626
be bolted 704
be bored 747
be born 716
be broken 815, 816
be broken up 816
be brought low 269, 621
be brought near 617
be burned up 621, 746
be captured 439
be carried 758
be carried away 758
be cast down 137, 723
be caught 439
be caused to die 199
be caused to fall 723
be changed 187
be chased away 620, 625
be circumcised 173, 328
be clean 749
be cleaned out 749
be clear 749
be comely 578
be comforted 663, 665
be comparable 537
be completed 277
be conscripted 376
be consecrated (with a
libation) 699
be consoled 663
be counted 346, 376
be counted as 346
be cut down 754
be cut off 328
be cut through 747
be dark 293
be dead 192
be deceitful 692, 775
be deceived 775
be defeated 613, 690
be delayed 524
be delightful 705
be delivered 297, 741, 744, 818
be delivered of 299
be delivered over 272
be delivered up 137, 376, 614
be deluded 775
be designated 747
be despised 121
be detected 439
be determined 276
be difficult 492
be diluted 164
be diminished 391
be directed 739
be discarded 620
be discouraged 367
be discovered 439
be disdainful 354
be dissipated 293
be distressed 614
be dominated 536
be drained dry 442
be drained out 442
be drained out 443
be drawn (out) 393
be drawn .i.drawn, be 680
be drawn away 817
be dried up 627, 782
be driven about 626
be driven away 624, 626
be drowsy 641
be dry 708, 782
be dug 755
be emptied 749
be encountered 439
be enraged 494
be ensnared 755
be enticed 758, 775
be equipped (with) 780
be established 736
be exalted 758
be excellent 130
be exchanged 187
be excluded 621
be exempt (from obligation)
749
be exempt from punishment
749
be exhausted 737, 782
be fallen down 716
be fanned 714
be fashioned 700
be few 391
be filled with 277, 291
be fitting 578
be fixed 677
be foolish 593
be forceful 492
be foreign 694
be forgiven 758
be forgiven of 758
be forgotten 777
be forsaken 680
be found 439
be found (as) 442
be found (out) 439
be found (to be so) 439
be found in someone's
possession 439
be found out (as guilty) 439
be found to be correct 439
be free (from guilt) 749
be free (from harm) 749
be freely devoted 618
be frightened 367
be fulfilled 277

be full 276
be full in number 279
be full of 277
be full of marrow 215
be full of sap 634
be full of water 277
be full of 291
be fully set 276
be fully with 279
be full 291
be gained 439
be given 785
be given as a freewill offering 618
be given out 785
be given rest 640
be granted 785
be grey 293
be grievous 492
be handed over 376
be handed over (as) 442
be hard pressed 614
be healthy 735
be hoarse 667
be humiliated 269
be hurled 621
be hurried (to destruction) 165
be impure 621
be in danger of death 192
be in order 780
be in ruins 737
be inferior 716
be joined 737
be joined together 208
be killed 199, 690
be kindled with fire 746
be king 301
be knocked out 815
be lacking 189
be lean 652
be led 629
be led away 629
be led in procession 629
be left free 640
be lifted of face 758
be lifted out 817
be lifted up 676, 758
be like 537
be like(ned) 537
be locked 704
be loose 817
be lovely 705
be low 173, 683, 716
be lured 755
be lured away 817
be lying down 716
be made into 785
be made king 304
be made like 785
be made to drop 171
be made to inherit 657
be made to slip 171
be malignant 122
be measured 142
be melted 784
be met 439
be moved 171
be moved to pity 663
be noisily excited 632
be numbered 346
be obliterated 215
be offered 376, 617
be oppressed 614
be out of joint 380
be paid in full 279
be painful 122, 492
be parched 667, 708, 782
be patient 524
be permitted 785
be pierced 747
be placed 640, 785
be placed .i.placed, be 785
be plagued 609
be planted 677
be pleasant 165, 328, 705
be plucked up 819
be polished 485, 493
be positioned 735
be poured out 613, 699, 700, 784, 785
be present 439
be presented 647
be preserved 745
be pressed 398
be private 666
be prolonged 524
be propped up 736
be prostrate 716
be provided 376
be pulled away 525
be pulled down 816
be pulled out 815
be pulled up 701
be pulled up 817
be put to death 199
be put to flight 683
be queen 301
be radiant (with joy) 632
be rained down 240
be rained upon 240
be raised up 758
be rebellious 474, 480
be rebellious (against) 480
be reckoned as 346
be recognized 692
be reduced 391
be refreshed 724
be rejected 121
be released 817
be removed 701, 817
be reported 602
be reprobate 121
be rescued 744
be respected 758
be reviled 581
be rid of 708
be rootless 645
be rubbed raw 485
be rubbed with salt water 293
be ruined 816
be sacrilegious 593
be safeguarded 746
be sated with 277
be satisfied 277
be scented 525
be scoured 493
be sealed 704
be secretive 745
be seized 439
be selected 376
be separated 817

be set 735
be set in 282
be set over 735
be set up 736
be set with 282
be settled 749
be shaken 171, 644
be shaken off 707
be shaken out 707, 708
be sharp 680
be sharpened 680
be shattered 723
be sick 492, 648, 701
be sickening 492
be sifted 657
be sinful 400
be smashed to pieces 724
be smeared 517
be smitten 614
be smooth 328
be smooth-skinned 485
be snapped 816
be snatched 305, 744
be snatched away 818
be sorry 663
be spilt 613
be sprained 380
be spread 785
be spread out 211, 674, 680
be spread throughout 716
be sprinkled 649
be stationed 785
be stood 735
be stretched out 613, 673
be stricken 609, 613
be stripped bare 708
be stripped off 753
be strong 481, 494, 671
be struck 683
be struck fatally 690
be struck with plague 690
be sufficient 442, 771
be sweet 573, 705
be taken away 758
be tall 525
be thrown 137
be thrust 624
be thrust out 624
be told 602
be torn apart 816
be torn away 305, 698, 816
be torn down 816
be torn out 817
be tossed about 172
be trained 698
be treated with contempt 581
be turned 674
be turned into 235
be ungrateful 354
be uprooted 819
be urgent 666
be uttered 758, 785
be victorious 492, 739
be victorious over 739
be void 716
be waved 646
be weak 737
be weakened 164
be wily 745
be wiped out 215
be withheld 355
be without support 645
be worthless 368
be woven 700
be, cause to 785
be,routed 613
beacon 500
bead 747, 748
beam-work 471
beam 214
bear 524, 758
bear a capacity of 758
bear a grudge 679
bear fruit 758
bear offspring 682
bear, cause to 758
beat 474, 684, 714
beat down 684
beaten down, be 684
beaten track 365
beaten, be 690
beatings 165
beautiful 578
beautiful, be 578
beautify 635
beauty 430
because of 337, 342
become dry 744
become few 392
become inflamed 746
become king 301
become mortal 192
become poor 173
become rich 667
become sweet 573
bed 237, 526
bedding 526
befall 435, 610
befall, cause to 441
befit 578
before 174, 241, 337, 343, 603, 691
beggar 134
beguile 775
beguiled, be 758, 775
beguilement 274
behaviour 365, 416
behold 586
behold, please 577
being 724, 730
being anointed 517
belch 597
bell 451
bellows 431
belly 382
below 234
below) 263
belt 531
bench 176, 369
bend 670, 673
bend down 716
beneath 234
benefactor 134
Benjaminite 242
beseech 134
besieged, be 745
besiegers 745
best 251, 544
best part 251
bestow (upon) 784
bestow upon 134

betray 167
betrayed, be 167
beyond 337, 339
bier 237, 526
bile 494
billhook 410
birth 174
birthplace 174
biscuit 750
bite 299, 777
bite oneself 299
bitter 472, 487
bitter grief, show 493
bitter herb 494
bitter one 472, 487
bitter plague 494
bitter thing 472, 494
bitter, be 493
bitter, make 493
bitterly 472
bitterness 333, 472, 482, 487, 494
bitterness, cause 494
bitterness, show 493
bladder 549
blameless 750
blameless one 751
blameless, be 749
blanket 363
blaspheme 747
blasphemy 132, 581
blemish 175
blended 208
blessing 487
blighted, be 690
blockaded, be 745
blockaders 745
bloodshed 505
blossom 735, 738, 744
blotted out, cause to be 215
blow 146, 216, 266, 604, 611, 691, 714, 776, 779
blow away 626
blow, cause to 776
blown away, be 626
blown, be 714
boast 635
bodily fluids 255
bodyguard 545
boil 207
bold one 136
bolt 355, 704
bolted, be 704
bond 177, 178, 377, 381, 408
boomerang 186
booty 328
border 376
border defence 363
bore 747, 754
bore away 754
bored, be 747
boring through 748
born, be 716
born, cause to be 721
borrow 775
bounty 130
bow 673
bow down 621, 646
bowel(s) 382
bowl 212, 333, 356, 363
box 132
brace 214
branch(es) 746
bray 631
bread, slice of 383
break 815, 817
break down 815
break out 746
break up 682, 723, 815
breaker 508
breaking 369
breaking in 234
breaking of law 505
breath 724, 728, 779
breath of God 779
breathe 714, 724
breathe, cause to 714, 779
breathing out 430
breeches 270
bribe 571, 705
brick pavement 290
brickmould 290
bride-gift 167
bridle 568, 714
brighten 605
brightness 605
brilliant, make 738
bring 441, 524, 616, 653, 758
bring down 671
bring down, cause to 721
bring near 610, 616
bring out 703
bring tidings 696
bring together 610
bring upon 785
broad place 484
broken, be 815, 816
bronze 655, 668
bronze fetters 668
broom 234
broth 493
brought low, be 269, 621
brought near, be 617
brow 451
buckler 135
build 785
building 127
bulwark 363
burden 103, 107, 408, 495, 499
burglary 234
burn up 746
burned up, be 621, 746
burning 128, 185, 379, 505
burning, place of 466
burst out 597
business 288, 416
business assessor 273
buttocks 433
buying 466
by 337
by (means of) 337, 343
by turns 361
by what (means)? 160
byway 365
byword 291
caginess 209
cake baked on griddle 214
cake, slice of 383
cakes 444
calamity 103, 144, 361
calamity, experience 715

call 785
calm 671
calmness 492
camp 222, 716
canal 184, 211
capacity 501
caper bush 744
capricious one 172
captured, be 439
carcass 432, 596
carnage 668
carnal knowledge, place of 149
carried away, be 758
carried thing 772
carried, be 758
carry 524, 758
carry away 758
carry out 758
carrying 496
cart 380
carving 467
case to be judged 558
cast 621, 699, 721
cast (lot) 721
cast away 679
cast down 610
cast down, be 723
cast lots 785
cast metal 185
casting 185
catapult 103
catapults 208
catch (hold of) 435
cattle 468
cattle-pen 102
caught, be 439
cause 558, 785
cause bitterness 494
cause death 197
cause of reeling 216
cause of ruin 234
cause pain 122
cause sweetness 573
cause to be 785
cause to be blotted out 215
cause to be born 721
cause to be forgotten 777
cause to be indebted with 775, 776
cause to be seen 587
cause to be wiped out 215
cause to bear 758
cause to befall 441
cause to blow 776
cause to breathe 714, 779
cause to bring down 721
cause to cease 638
cause to collapse 721
cause to come 441
cause to come upon 721
cause to descend 721
cause to deviate 675
cause to disintegrate 360
cause to drive 629
cause to drop 721
cause to fall 721
cause to fall (by lot) 721
cause to fall away 721
cause to fall before 721
cause to fall down 721
cause to ferment 597
cause to flee 635
cause to flee (for safety) 643
cause to flow 592, 650
cause to follow 524
cause to forget 777
cause to have contempt 581
cause to leap 649, 818
cause to lie down 721
cause to meet 441
cause to melt 360
cause to overtake 441
cause to pay interest 778
cause to prosper 634
cause to reach 610, 772
cause to reign 303
cause to rest 637
cause to rest upon 638
cause to rot 470
cause to rule (over) 536
cause to shine 605, 738
cause to sink 670
cause to stand 736
cause to start 818
cause to touch 610
cause to wander 635, 644, 645
cause to waste away 721
cause wrath to blaze 605
caused to die, be 199
caused to fall, be 723
cave 412, 755
cave country 412
cease 189, 637, 815
cedar 123
celebration 505
censer 219, 234, 466
census 433
cessation 509
chaff 434
chain 381, 408
chamber 778
champion 751
chance 471
change 186, 187, 481
changed, be 187
channel 431
charge, have 531
chariot 380, 488
chariot depot 488
chariotry 487, 488
chase away 620, 625
chased away, be 620
chastisement 177, 378, 479
cheat 692
cheerfulness 127
chequerwork 508
chest 132
chief 772
chief officer 606
choice 125
choice produce 130, 544
choicest (one) 125
choicest (one[s]) 125
chorus 381
churn (milk) 262
churning 262
circle 359, 383
circumcise 164, 173, 328
circumcised one 173
circumcised, be 173, 328
circumcision 173, 175

circumcision blade 274
citadel 291
clamp 214
clan 554
clap 213, 684
clash 680
clay floor 299
clean 750
clean one 751
clean, be 749, 750
cleaned out, be 749
cleanness 751
cleanse 749, 750
cleanse away 493
cleansing 551
clear away 778
clear, be 749
cleavage 129
cleave 299
cleft 751, 755
cleverness 294
cliff 150
cloak 240
cloth 139
clothes store 329
clothing 139, 290
clothing for legs 482
cloud 148, 427, 775
cloudburst 724
clouds 210
club 173, 431, 433
coat 396
collapse 269, 367, 715
collapse (through lack of strength) 716
collapse, cause to 721
collect less 392
collecting point 378
collection 254, 459
collection of waters 459
come 610
come about 772
come across 435
come before 716
come in noisy excitement 632
come quickly 166
come to a full end 754
come to ruin 715
come upon 716, 771
come upon, cause to 721
come, cause to 441
comely 578
comely one 579
comely, be 578
comfort 664, 665, 666
comfort oneself 663, 665
comforted, (allow oneself to) be 665
comforted, be 663, 665
comforter 664
coming 124
coming (together) 124
coming back 514
coming in 124, 170
coming to rest 347
command 119
command post 378
command(ment) 446
commander 129, 606
commandment 446
commit (sin) 400
commit adultery 580
commit sacrilege 400
common cause, make 524
compactness 379
company 223, 238, 381, 460, 541
comparable to 604
comparable, be 537
compass 215
compassion 222, 665, 666
compassion, (object of) 222
compassion, have 663
complaint 353
complete 280, 493
complete (a transaction) 493
complete a circle 754
complete, be 279
completed, be 277
completely 103
composition 416
conceal 643
conduct 365
conduct oneself 628
conduit 211
confidence 126
Confinement 453
confirm 281
conflict 294
confusion 124
conjunction 377
conjuror 350
conquer 739
conscripted, be 376
consecrate 278, 281, 651
consecrate (with a libation) 699
consecrate as priest 281
consecrate oneself 651
consecrated one 350, 649
consecrated part 458
consecrated portion 518
consecration 283, 651
consecration (to the priesthood) 283
consecration offering 283
consider 586
consignment 495
consolation 665
console 664
consoled, be 663
conspicuous sights 620
constellations 208
constraint 185
construction 416
contact 137
contact, one who has 137
contain 758
container 254
contempt (for), have 581
contempt have, cause to 581
contempt treated with, be 581
contempt, (object of) 145
contempt, have 581
contempt, treat with 593
contention 145, 147, 444, 482, 486
contents 284
continue 142
continue on 630
contrary to 604
contrite 691

contrite one 683, 691
control, (have) 531
convocation 466, 470
convulse 251
convulsions, suffer 701
cool place 471
coolness 471
copious hair 219
copper 655, 668
copy 549
cord 265, 503, 531
corner 469
corner (piece) 469
corner rooms 165
corpse 596
corpses 596
correct (building) procedure 415
correction 177
corresponding to 604
cosmetic treatment 484
cost 217
couch 237, 359, 452
council 176, 240
counsel 182, 274, 304, 322
counsel, seek 304
counsel, take 304
counsellor 322
count 345, 376
counted as, be 346
counted, be 346, 376
countenance 474
counterpane 363
counting 375, 433
coupling 214
course 219, 365, 379, 432, 484
court 545, 558
courtier 350
cover 266, 477
covered way 176
covering 136, 271, 361, 363, 365, 427
cower 122
craft 288, 692
crafting 233
crafting, 230
created being 416
creature 416, 450
creature(s) 450, 724, 730
creditor 775, 776, 778
creditor, be a 775, 776
crevice 755
crissum 476
crop 185
crown 651
crucible 457
crumb 750
crumble away 592
crush 227, 228, 399
crushing 234, 482
crypt 239
cucumber field 472
cultic official 748
cunning simile 127
cup-bearer 565
cup-bearer, office of 565
curd-like things 221
current 632
curse 123, 582
curtain 362
custody 545, 547
custom 347, 563
cut down 753
cut down, be 754
cut into pieces 782
cut off 328
cut off, be 328
cut through, be 747
cymbals 451
dam 617
dance 216, 218
dancing 216, 218
dangle 641, 644
dark place 233
dark thoughts 233
dark, be 293
darkness 122, 182, 233, 390, 519, 779
dart 368
dash to the ground 680
date palm 659
dawn 519
day of assembly 471
dead 196
dead, be 192
deal craftily with 692
dearly 103
death 199, 200, 330
death, (manner of) 330
death, put to 197
deathbed 526
debase (oneself) 721
debt 506, 507, 509, 777
debtor 778
decay 470, 592
deceased person 724, 731
deceit 401, 489
deceitful one 692
deceitful, be 692, 775
deceitfulness 692
deceive 692, 775
deceived, be 775
deception 168, 507, 570
decision 557
declare 328, 599
declare as innocent 750
declare impure 621
declare superfluous 646
decline 673
decoration 361
decoration, 230
decoy 186
decree 228
deed 288, 378, 406, 416, 432
deep darkness 122
deep, the 449
defeat 137, 144, 267, 612, 626, 685, 739
defeated, be 613, 690
defect 175
defects 431
defiance 485
defy 480
degeneration 596
degree 404
delay 163
delayed, be 524
delicacies 355
delicacy 240, 381, 544
delicateness 381
delicious food 381

delight 221, 381, 704
delightful 704
delightful place 704
delightful, be 705
deliver 298, 741, 742
deliver (over) 271
deliver oneself 273, 741
deliver oneself from 299
deliver up 134, 376, 441, 613
deliver up oneself 273
delivered of, be 299
delivered over, be 272
delivered up, be 137, 376
delivered, be 297, 741, 744, 818
deluded, be 775
demolish 721
demon 487
den 117
denounce 602
depart 171, 189, 620
departure 184
departure, point of 184
deport 671
deposited 640
depth 228, 408, 448
depth, of earth 230
deputation 541
deputy 736, 740
descend 670, 715
descend, cause to 721
descendants, have 682
descending 671
descent 188, 671
desert 139, 716
deserter 715, 720
design 230, 416
designate 747, 785
designated, be 747
desirable thing 221
desire 115, 189, 487, 724, 725, 758, 779
desire, (object of) 221
desolation 543
despair 361, 487
despise 120, 581
despised, be 121
destiny 353, 354, 563
destroy 213, 685
destroyer 239
destruction 138, 519, 663
detachment 362
detect 435
detected, be 439
determined, be 276
devastation 125, 507, 543
development 150
deviate 673
deviate, cause to 675
device 233
devising 229
dew 239
diadem 651
didactic 537
die 171, 192, 737
difficult, be 492
dike 617
dilute 164
diluted, be 164
diminish 392
diminished, be 391
diminution 387
dining couch 526
dip 227
direct 674, 738
directed, be 739
direction 461
director of music 738
disappear 367, 525
disappointment 431
disapprove of 694
discarded, be 620
discern 693
discharge pus 122
discharging 541
discipline 177, 376, 479
discomfiture 163
discourage 368, 634
discouraged, be 367
discourse 537
discourse, (written) 150
discover 435
discovered, be 439
discretion 209, 564
disdain 581
disdainful one 349
disdainful, be 354
disease 144, 218, 611
disfigurement 175, 519
disgrace 581, 595
disgrace (oneself) 721
disguise oneself 694
dishonour 593
disillusionment 489
disintegrate, cause to 360
dislodge 172
dismay, (cause of) 234
dismiss 190
dismount 716
disobedience 182, 410
disorderly conduct 595
dispatching 541
disperse 724
dispersed one 724
disperser 431
display 587
disposition 413
disputed matter 481
disregard 680
dissipate 170
dissipated, be 293
dissolve 170, 360, 367
distance 485, 518
distance oneself 621
distant place 485
distil 650
distinguish 693
distinguished one 747
distress 144, 182, 185, 449, 450, 453
distressed, be 614
distribute 656
district 147, 714
disturb 645
disturbance 163
divan 177
divide as an inheritance 656
divided sheepfolds 565
divination 469, 667
divination, practise 667
divine 617
diviner 667

division 219, 377, 431, 432, 545, 547
do fully 281
do not 577
document 275
dominate 531
dominated, be 536
dominion 334, 505, 539, 540, 683
dominion, (sphere of) 335
doorpost 206
double (share) 549
double wall 565
downcast 683
downcast one 683
downfall 146, 432
downtrodden one 173
downwards 234
drag (along, off, away) 522
drain 442, 443
drained dry, be 442
drained out, be 442
draw 362, 393, 524, 616
draw away 816
draw bow 281
draw milk 453
draw near 610, 614
draw out 817
draw up 524
drawing (of water) 522
drawn away (allow oneself to), be 624
drawn away, be 817
dread 133, 187
dried up, be 627, 782
drink 565, 568
drink offering 699, 700
drip 672, 678
drive 626, 628
drive about 626
drive away 173, 618, 625, 778
drive on 629, 643
drive, cause to 629
driven about, be 626
driven away, be 624, 626
driven out person 144
driven wave 139
driving 347
drop 172, 473, 592, 671, 678, 715, 721
drop (of rain) 415
drop (word) 671
drop off 778
drop, be made to 171
drop, cause to 721
droves (of horses) 460
drowsiness 641
drowsy, be 641
dry up 627, 644, 652, 701
dry, be 708, 782
dry, become 744
due 446
due season 179
dug, be 755
dung-pit 148
duplicate 549
dust 473, 659
duty 547
dwell 635
dwelling 133, 191, 267, 528
dwelling place 133, 146, 190, 268, 387, 390, 460
dwelling-place 528
dyke 138
dysentery 137
e. creation 416
eagle 781
ear of corn 300
early rain 188
easily 103
east 211
eastern 212
eastern side 211
echo sound 471
echoing shout 471
edict 476
effusion 165
Egypt 450, 454
Egyptian 453
Egyptians 453, 454
elevated place 482
elevation 405, 499
emaciated 206
eminence 740
emission of spittle 451
emptied, be 749
empty 281, 750
empty oneself 749
empty space 410, 412, 413
enable 785
encampment 222, 380
encampment, (place of) 222
enchantment 655
encircle 754
enclave 123
enclosure 175, 269, 501
encompass 754
encounter 434
encountered, be 439
endlessness 739
endurance 739
endure 739, 758
enduring 739
engraving 747
enigma 301
enraged, be 494
ensign 697
ensnare 755
ensnared, be 755
enter, (those who) 124
entering 124
enterprise 540
enticed, be 758, 775
enticement 144
entirety 570
entitlement 564
entrails 382
entrance 123, 170
entrust (to) 536
entry (act of) 124
entryway 123
environs 359
envoy 300
episode 416
equipped (with), be 780
equivalen 549
equivalent 551
erect 736, 758
err 122
error 509
escape 182, 297, 349, 620, 621,

642, 741
escape from 299
escaped one 643
esplanade 291
essence 177
establish 736, 785
established, be 736
estate 268, 460
eternal life 728
evaporate 367
evening 427
evening feast 427
event 416
evergreen tree 123
everlastingness 739
everywhere 359
evidence 182
exact (payment) of 614
exact an oath from 775
exactor (of tribute) 614
exalt 758
exalt oneself 758
exaltation 483, 496
exalted 758
Exalted One 483, 758
exalted, be 758
examine (in order to recognize) 693
excavation 457, 659
exceedingly 402
excellence 130
excellent, be 130
excellent, make 130
exchange 187, 481
exchanged, be 187
exclude 621
excluded, be 621
excrement 476
execution of judgment 558
exempt (from obligation) 750
exempt (from obligation), be 749
exempt from punishment, be 749
exertion 119
exhausted, be 737, 782
exile 146, 624
exist 439
exit 183
exorcist 350
expanse 433, 484
expectation 126
expel 620
expelled one 818
expense 119
experience calamity 715
experience, give 698
expert 164
expiring 430
explain 599
explanation 150
export 184
expound 599
extend 142, 524, 672
extend to 610
extending 540
extension 333
extent 143
extol 610
extolment 405
extortion 430, 484
extortioner 262
extract 202
eye 117
eyrie 445
fade 327, 592
fade away 367
fail (to be accomplished) 716
faint 170
faint suspicion 780
faintness 487
fall 432, 720
fall (by lot) 716
fall (by lot), cause to 721
fall (down) 715
fall (in exhaustion) 716
fall (into Sheol) 716
fall asleep 641
fall away 716
fall away, cause to 721
fall before, cause to 721
fall down (deliberately) 716
fall down, cause to 721
fall into the hands of 716
fall out 716
fall upon 716
fall, cause to 721
fall. 715
fallen down, be 716
fallen one 715, 720
false claims 144
falter 380
faltering 381
faltering (step) 381
fan 714
fangs 329
fanned, be 714
farewell 433
fashion 671
fashioned, be 700
fasten 785
fat 544
fate 346, 471
fatling 213, 486, 544
fattening 477
fattest, healthiest, part 544
favourable omen 704
favoured, be 758
fear 133, 187, 668
fear, (object of) 133, 187
fearful thing 187
feast 567
feasting 484
feathers 648
feed 481
feed on the fat of the land 474
feel 190, 567
feel contempt 120
feel hatred 122
feel loathing 120
feel revulsion 120
feeling of shame 260
feet 478
fell 721
felled tree trunk 432
female 748
female prophet 215
fence 176
fend off 173
ferment 597
ferment, cause to 597

fertile land 214
fertile place 214
fester 122, 470
festival 181
festive robe 219
fetter 177, 178, 503
few 393, 395
few(er) 392
few, be 391
few, become 392
few, make 392
fief 460
field 683
fiery coals 117
fight 737
figure 301, 474
filled place 291
filled with, be 277, 291
file 365
fill 277
fill in 281
fill with 278
final number 370
find 434
find (from one's resources) 435
find (one's way to) 435
find (out) 435
find (possible to do) 435
find (to be so) 435
find (written) 435
find fault with 435
find sufficient 435
find to be sound 435
fine cloth 520
finish 695
fire, be kindled with 746
fire, set on 746
fire, set to 746
fire 127, 648
fire-places 564
fire-signal 500
firepan 233
firm place 408
fish 259
fishing net 270
fishing-net 270
fissure 230
fissure 457
fit for 604
fitting, be 578
fitting 578
fixed, be 677
fix 736
flag 697
flap 474
flash 738
flavoured with marrow 215
flee 297, 620, 634, 642, 648
flee (away) 642
flee away 621
flee, cause to 635
flight of steps 404
flight, (means of) 697
flight, put to 643
flight 182, 349, 452
fling 621
flock 491
flood 124, 632, 650
floodwater 138
floor 150
flourish 744
flow (away) 122
flow away 642
flow with 650
flow, cause to 592, 650
flow, make 646
flow 121, 128, 208, 494, 597, 613, 632, 634, 650
flow (with) 634
flower 651
flowing honey 734
flowing lock 219
fluctuate 170
flute 747
flutes 655
flutter 620
fly 735, 737
fly away 620, 735
fly out 299
foam 473
fodder 370
fold 269
fold (of flesh) 431
follow 524, 629
follow after 654
follow, cause to 524
follow, wholly 281
following after 569
folly 145, 595
food 118, 119, 207, 269
fool, treat as a 593
foolish 593
foolish, be 593
foolish, make 593
footstep 452
for 691
for (rea-son of) 337
for (reason of) 337, 342
for lack of 337, 341
for when 570
for, on behalf of 237
force(s) 222
forced labour 365
forceful, be 492
ford 133, 379
forego 680
forehead 450
foreign 695
foreign, be 694
foreigner 695
foreigners 695
foreignness 694
forge 697, 699
forged work 130
forget 776
forget, cause to 777
forgetfulness 777
forgive 218, 758
forgiven, be 758
forgotten, be 777
forgotten, cause to be 777
fork 208
formation 450
formation of new flesh 217
forsake 679
forsaken, be 680
forthright things 604
fortification 128, 450
fortified city 604
fortress 128, 450
fortune 471

forward 691
found (as), be 442
found (to be so), be 439
found (written), be 439
found out (as guilty), be 439
found to be correct, be 439
found, be 439
foundation 175, 176, 267, 268, 360
foundation, laying of 176
founding 176
foundry 379
fountain 127, 459, 465
fragment 276
frame 172, 472
framework 360
frayed clothing 294
free 654
free (from guilt), be 749
free (from harm), be 749
free space 640
freely 619
freely devoted, be 618
freewill 619
freewill offering 619
fresh 182
fresh figs 182
friend 149, 490
friendship 264
frighten 368
frighten away 776
frightened, be 367
from 337, 339
from (among) 337, 340
from (being) 337, 342
from (doing) 337, 342
from (out of) 337, 338
from above 402
from before 174, 604
from opposite 604
from the face of 260
from the front of 174
from then on 404
from ... and above/and over 404
front 173, 691
fruit 634, 681
frustrate 634
fuel 119
fugitive 129, 620, 643, 682
fulfilled, be 277
fulfil 280
fulfilment 277
full 282, 283
full in number, be 279
full measure 216
full of 282
full of marrow, be 215
full of sap, be 634
full of water, be 277
full of, be 277, 291
full one 282, 283
full produce 284
full weight 566
full, be 276, 291
fullness 283, 290
fully 283
fully set, be 276
fully trust 279
fully with, be 279
fume 770
funeral meal 484
furnishing, (skilfully crafted) 230
furrow 133, 409
future 229
gain 435, 771
gain satisfaction (for oneself) 663
gait 164
gale 668
gall 494
game 445
gape open 122
garment 139, 144, 290, 396
garnet 715
garrison 442, 740
gasp 779
gate 365
gatehouse 366
gatepost 206
gateway 366
gathering 122
general 134
generosity 619
generous (one) 626
generously 619
genitalia 391
genitals 125, 382
gentleness 492
giants 723
gift 136, 346, 350, 499, 570, 571, 574, 621, 626
gifts 570
girdle 208
girl 711
give 130, 784
give (to) 784
give as an inheritance 656
give birth to 299, 721
give control (over) 536
give dominion 536
give experience 698
give guidance 628
give in full 281
give light to 605
give out 785
give responsibility (for) 536
give rest 630
give rest to 637
give up 777
give way 380, 715
given out, be 785
given, be 785
giving 540
gleam 182
gleaning 329, 750, 754
glorify 635
glory 430, 740
gnaw oneself 299
go 239
go about 701
go around 754
go astray 624
go away 642, 648, 670
go down 670, 673
go quickly 166
go to ruin 737
goad 229, 328
going back 514
going out 183

going out, place of 183
gold-lettered inscription 276
goods 362, 495
gore 605
gore, prone to 606
gouge out 754
government 501, 505, 539
governor 736, 740
grain 382
grain bin 133
grain offering 351
grain pit 133
granary 102, 133, 206, 329
Grand One 103
grant 784
granted, be 785
grating 266
grave 526, 528
grave trench 659
graze 474, 481
grazing ground 540
grazing land 491, 636
grazing places 565
greatly 103
greatness 477
greaves 451
grey, be 293
grief 618
grief, (cause of) 347
grief, show 635
grieve 635
grievous, be 492
groan 581, 582, 631, 666, 707
groaning 582, 631
grope 190, 567
ground 336
group of people 223
group of those feasting 484
growing-place 184
growl 631, 707
growl with hunger 631
growling 631
growth 184
grudge, bear a 679
guard 242, 350, 433, 442, 545, 547, 679, 744
guard against 651
guard(ing) 545
guard-duty 547
guard-house 453
guardhouse 547
guardian 328, 745
guardianship 547
guidance, give (Ec 23). 628
guide 630, 653
guiltless 750
gullet 264, 724
gush 596
gut(s) 382
habitation 191, 636
hair 276
hair (of consecration) 651
hair, locks of 472
half 228
hammer 431, 433, 457
hammered work 472
hand down 376
hand over 376
handed over (as), be 442
handed over, be 376
handing over 377
handiwork 288
hang loose 680
hanging 188
happen 610, 716
happen, make 785
hard pressed, be 614
harden 494
hardly 396
hardship 457
harmony 297
harp 595
haste 146, 167
haste, make 167
hasten 165, 737
hastily 166, 167
hasty one 165
hatred, feel 122
haughtily 484
haul (along, off, away) 522
have an inheritance 656, 657
have charge 531
have compassion 663
have contempt 581
have contempt (for) 581
have descendants 682
have one's fill of 277
have regard 692
have repose 637
have rest 637
have sufficient 771
hawk 735, 738
he 732
head 736
head support 477
headband 130
headcovering 370
headdress 130
healing 491
health 491
healthy 544
healthy, be 735
heap 131, 274, 460, 617
heap of stones 478
heap of stones (unless heap of straw 568
heap up 281
hearing 544, 545
heart 177, 724, 725
heartache 431
hearth 185, 186
hearths 129
heave 758
heaven 483
heavenly messenger 285
heavenly phenomena 620
heddle-rod 349
hedge 361, 501
heel 452
height 402, 404, 482, 648, 713, 734
height (of heaven) 483
help 389, 552, 758
hepatoscoper 748
herald 781
hero 129
herself 732
hesitantly 381
hew 671
hewing 228
bring down to destruction 275

hidden place 378
hidden store 239
hidden things 745
hidden treasure 453
hiding 378
hiding place 213, 214, 238, 378, 453
high praise 366
high(er) 403
high-ranking officer 132
high-ranking one 758
highway 365
hill 405, 617
hill-country 713
hilly place 130
hilt 737
himself 732
hinder 634
hire 217
his 733
hit 435
hoard 254
hoarse, be 667
hoe 382
hold 524, 758
hold as a 655
hold back 354
hold on 525
hold oneself back 355
hold out 672
holding up 495
hole 218
holiest part 459
hollow 276, 449
hollow out 583
hollow place 347
holy things 458
home 387, 460
homeless one 482
homelessness 482
honest 604
honest things 604
honour 626
honoured one 758
hop 818
hope 126, 459
hope, (object of) 126
horde 179
horrible image 432
horror 543
horror, (cause of) 234
host 222
hostility 502
how (much)! 151
how is it possible to? 151
how long until? 161
how long? 161
how long?, 569
how many? 336
how much longer? 570
how much? 151
how often! 161
how often? 161
how? 150, 151
humiliated, be 269
humours 255
hundred 107
hunger 724, 725, 751
hungry 751
hungry one 751
hunt 772
hunting 668
hurl down 613
hurled, be 621
hut 293
I 732
idleness 515
idol 363
if now 577
if only! 785
if you now 577
ignominious 594
illness 473, 514
image 363, 504, 737
imagination 504
immediately 396
immediately after 337, 339
impediment 410
impel 618, 625, 758
impetuous utterance 126
implement (rule) 531
implement for pounding 234
impose 785
impose an oath upon 775
imprisonment 545
impudence 208
impure thing 622
impure, be 621
impure, declare 621
impure, make 621
impurity 681
impurity (unless hD
nI II flow of blood) 621
in 337
in (the direction of) 337
in (the direction of), to(wards) 338
in confidence 264
in a standing position 735
in abundance 477
in any measure 143
in anything 116
in bitterness 472
in contrast with 604
in danger of death, be 192
in from the outside 337, 339
in front of 174, 603, 691
in front of oneself 603
in line, keep 781
in no way 143
in noisy excitement, come 632
in order, be 780
in procession led, be 629
in ruins, be, .i.be ruined 737
in someone's possession found, be 439
in the estimation of 337, 343
in the future 229, 402
in the presence of 603
in what (part)? 160
in which way? 151
inactivity 509
inadvertent sin 515
incense 466, 678
incense altar 466
incline 673
incline towards 654
increase 477, 682
indebted with, cause to be 775, 776
indecency 670

indecisiveness 514
individual 724, 730
ineffectual, make 634
inferior, be 716
inferior, make 721
infestation 565
inflamed, become 746
inform 599
inform against 602
inhabited place 191
inherit 655
inherit, cause to 656
inheritance 659
inheritance from father 274
inheritance, give as 656
inheritance, have 656, 657
inheritance, leave to 656
inheritance, pass on as 657
inheritances 655
injury 650
injustice 238
inner person 382
innocence 751
innocent 750
innocent one 751
innocent, declare as 750
inquiry 150
inscription 275, 276
inset 360
insolent 136, 349
insolent one 136
instead of 461
instruction 177, 481
instructive or skilful song 504
intelligence 149
interest 477, 778
interest, cause to pay 778
internal organs 382
interpretation 150
interpreter 300
intoxicating drink 570
investigator 227
invite 602
inward parts 655
irrigated land 565
irrigator 650
item for sale 330
jar 594
jaw 570
jawbone 329, 570
jaws 329
jewel 478
join 208, 214, 610
join in combat 606
joined together, be 208
joining, place of 214
journey 164, 368, 701
journey, stage of 368
journey, start of 368
joy 501
joyful place 501
joyful sound 501
Judan 263
judgement, place of 148
judgment 556
judgment, act of 556
judgment, execution of 558
juice 567, 740
just 396
just measure 564
just one 559
justice 559
justice, pervert 675
keen 167
keep 679, 744
keep (safely) 744
keep from indiscretion 744
keep in line 781
keep oneself away from 651
key 434
kill 197, 685
killed, be 199, 690
kind 262
kindle 746
kindled with fire, be 746
kindness 706
kindred 174
king 292, 305, 331, 520
king, be 301
king, made be 304
king, make 303
kingdom 292, 322, 323, 331, 333, 660
kingship 292, 323, 332, 333
kinsman 149
kiss 777, 780
kiss one another 780
kneaded, thing 129
kneading 129
kneading tray 507
kneading trough 293, 507
knife 119, 210, 219, 470
knock out 721
knocked out, be 815
know 693
knowledge 149
known, make 599
lack 226
lacking, be 189
lad 708
ladanum 684
laden 676
laid waste, be 737
lair 390
lame 691
lame person 384
lament 618, 629, 635
lament (with) 629
lamentation 629, 630
lamenter 635
lamp 683, 755
lampstand 349
lance 294
land outside city walls 138
land sold 274
landing place 433
last breath 724, 728
late in bearing produce 122
lathe 215
latrine 185, 229
latter rain 329
lattice-work 266
laud 578
laughter, (object of) 502
launch into battle 671
lavatory 360
lay eggs 299
lay obligation 785
lay out for burial 524
lay snares 755
lay upon 676

laying down 541
laying of foundation 176
lead 629, 630, 653, 738
lead (away) 628
lead astray 624, 675
lead away 629
lead on 630
lead one's life 628
lead out 703
leader 606, 699, 772
lean, be 652
leaning 674
leap 649, 818
leap to one's feet 649
leap, cause to 649, 818
learn 435
learn by divination 667
leash 349
least 392
leave 639, 679
leave an inheritance to 656
leave behind 639
leave fallow 680
leave over 639
leave undisturbed 299, 640
leave unpunished 749
leave unweighed 640
leavened thing 222
leaving 259
led astray 624
led away, be 629
left free, be 640
legal infringement 505
legal possession of, take 694
legal right 564
lend 775, 776
lend on interest 778
lender 775
lengthen 674
leopard 696
less than 235
lest 151
let alone 640
let child have its own way 536
let drop 721
let escape 299
let fail 721
let fall 172, 721
let fall (to the ground) 721
let feel 190
let go of 640
let touch 190, 610
letter 782
level 567
level ground 415
levelling implement 567
levy 358
lewdness 596
libation 364, 565, 699, 700
lie down, cause to 721
lie prostrate 723
life 217, 724, 728
life, (preservation of) 217
lift 676, 758
lift eyes 758
lift face 758
lift foot 758
lift hand 758
lift head 758
lift heart 758
lift oneself up 758
lift soul 758
lift up 676, 758
lift up one's soul 758
lift voice 758
lift?number 758
lifted out, be 817
lifted up 758
lifted up, be 676, 758
lifting up 495
light 117, 605, 629, 633
light-hole 117
like (the construction of) 427
like(ned), be 537
like(ness) 539
like, be 537
likeness 128, 539
limit 370
line 223
linger 163
lintel 566
litter 237
little 395
little by little 395
little thing 395
livelihood 217
lives 724, 728
livestock 288, 468
living beings 217
living room 471
load 495
loaf 383
location 460
lock 219, 704
locked, be 704
locks of hair 472
locust 173
lodging place 292
lofty one 758
loins 573
longing, (object of) 222
look 586
lookout 545
looped pattern 214
loose, be 817
loosen 817
lose hair 485
lose heart 367, 592
lose one's youth 708
loudly 283
louse 568
love 171, 264
loveliness 706
lovely 704
lovely, be 705
lover 574
low pitch 640
low, be 173, 683, 716
low-class 594
lower 234, 638, 670
luminary 116
lure away 816, 817
lured away, be 817
lured, be 755
lust 670
lustre 182, 238
lying (down) 527
lying down 526
lying down, be 716
lying in wait 123
Maabadiah 379

Maacah 399
Maacath 399
Maacathite 399
Maacathites 400
Maadai 381
Maadiah 381
maah 382
Maai 396
Maaleh 406
Maarath 416
Maas 122
Maasai 427
Maaseiah 427, 428
Maaseio 429
Maash 123
Maaz 409
Maaziah 391
Maban 127
mace 237, 294
Machbannai 266
Machbaram 266
Machbenah 265
Machi 268
Machir 268
Machirite 269
Machnadebai 270
Machomades 222
Machpelah 271
Machtesh 276
Madach 148
Madai 146
Madar 149
made into, be 785
made like, be 785
Madmannah 148
Madmen 148
Madmenah 148
Madon 145
Magbish 129
Magdiel 131
Magen 136
magnification 132
Magnus 137
Magog 132
Magpiash 137
Mahalalel 164
Mahalath 220, 221
Mahaleb 218
Mahanaim 225
Mahanaimite 225
Mahanite 225
Maharai 167
Mahath 233
Mahavite 216
Mahazioth 216
Maher-shalal-hash-baz 168
Mahlah 218
Mahli 218
Mahlite 219
Mahmam 222
Mahol 216
Mahseiah 227
Mahtosh 234
maid 711
majority 477
Makaz 469
make 785
make (into) 785
make (oneself) sweet 573
make a freewill offering 618
make a test 697
make a vow 627
make abundant 130
make as 785
make attractive 524
make bitter 493
make brilliant 738
make common cause 524
make excellent 130
make few 392
make flourish 634
make foolish 593
make full ready 281
make happen 785
make haste 167
make impure 621
make ineffectual, 634
make inferior 721
make known 599
make melodious 705
make oneself known 694
make oneself pleasant 165
make out as 785
make pleasant 705
make presumptuous 758
make queen 303
make run 646
make smooth 485, 670
make to flow 646
make-up 416
Makheloth 459
making 416
Makka 265
Makkedah 457
Makliah 467
Malachi 290
Malash 329
Malcam 327
Malchi 325
Malchi(j)ah 325
Malchiel 325
Malchielite 325
Malchiner 327
Malchiram 327
Malchishua 327
Maliah 299
malignant, be 122
Mallothi 293
mallow 291
Malluch 292
Malluchi 292
Mamre 333
man 568
Manahath 353
Manahathite 353
Manahathites 353
Manasseh 356
Manassite 357
Manassites 357
Manes 354
manna 336
manner 563
Mano 347
Manoah 348
Manor 356
Manos 354
mantlet 222
manufacture 416
Maoch 387
Maon 390
Maonite 390

mar 518
Mara 474
Marah 481
Maralah 491
march 524
march against 670
Marcheshvan 485
marching 433
Mareshah 495
mariner 293
marital bed 526
mark 683, 756
mark off 754
market place 489
Maroth 484
marrow 213
Marsarzeruchin 490
Marsena 490
mart 391
Masbala 359
Mash 506
Mashal 539
maskil 503
Masrekah 506
mass 281
mass oneself 282
Massa 499
Massah 361
Massaite 499
massing 134
master 531
mastery 539
maternal uncle 377
Matred 241
Matrite 242
Mattan 570
Mattanah 572
Mattaniah 572
Mattathah 574
Mattenai 572
Mattithiah 574
Mauzzijah 387
maxim 537
Mazdaeus 206
Mazzaroth 211
me 732
meadow 636
meal 415
means of destruction 234
means of slaughter 234
Mearah 413
measure 139, 141, 143, 171, 361, 501, 518
measure out (recompense) deeds 141
measure(ment) 139
measured, be 142
measurement 143, 330, 518, 570
measuring 143
Mebunnai 127
Mecherathite 275
Meconah 270
Medad 251
Medan 149
Mede 146
Medeba 251
Medes 146
Media 146
mediator 300
meet 215, 434, 615
meet, cause to 441
meeting 179
meeting place 179
meeting, tent of 179
Megiddo 130
Mehalleb 218
Mehetabel 163
Mehida 216
Mehir 217
Meholathite 221
Mehujael 216
Mehuman 163
Meken 467
Mekimiah 467
Melatiah 299
Melchiresha 327
Melchizedek 326
Melech 322
melodious, make 705
melody 704
melt 165, 170, 208, 360, 367, 368, 506, 784
melt away 170
melt, (cause to) 170
melt, cause to 360
melted, be 784
melting 358, 359
memorial stone 442
Memphis 430, 648, 713
Memshath 336
Memucan 330
men 777
Menahem 353
Meni 354
menstrual blood 670
menstrual discharge 255
Meonothai 390
Mephaath 262
Mephibosheth 431
Merab 477
Meraiah 486
Meraioth 486
Meraniah 490
Merari 495
Merarite 495
Merarites 495
Merathaim 495
merchandise 274, 330, 411
merchant 167, 345
Mered 479
Meremoth 489
Meres 490
Merib-baal 486
Meribah 486
Meriri 487
Merodach 479
Merodach-baladan 479
Merom 484
Meronothite 490
Meroz 482
Mesha 263, 506
Meshach 263
Meshammah 544
Meshammesh 549
Meshech 525
Meshek 565
Meshelemiah 543
Meshezabel 520
Meshillemith 543
Meshillemoth 543

Meshobab 514
Meshuchim 515
Meshullam 541
Meshullemeth 515, 543
message 290
messenger 284, 290, 602
messiah 517
met, be 439
metalworker 359
Metheg-ammah 569
Methuselah 569
Methushael 569
Meuddanah 381
Mezer 453
Mezobaite 443
Miamun 250
Mibhar 126
Mibsam 129
Mibtahiah 126
Mibzar 128
Mica 251
Micah 252, 253
Micaiah 253
Michael 252
Michal 254
Michmas 269
Michmash 269
Michmethath 270
Michri 274
Middin 146
middle 228
Midian 146
Midianites 147
midrash 150
midwife 552
Migdal-eder 132
Migdal-el 132
Migdal-gad 132
Migdol 132
mighty 487
mighty one 136
Migron 138
Mijamin 261
Mikloth 467
Mikneiah 469
Miknemelech 469
Miktam 276
Milalai 328
Milcah 323
Milcom 327
military equipment 781
military might 336
military post 442
military staff 129
milk, draw 453
Millo 291
mina 347
Minaean 398
mind 149, 724, 725
mine 184, 274, 747
mine shaft 659
Miniamin 354
Minni 354
Minnith 354
miracle 183
Miriam 487
Mirmah 489
mirror 474
miscarriage 723
misconstrue 694
misery 618
misfortune 695
Misgab 501
Mishael 263
Mishal 507
Misham 552
Mishan 553
Mishma 545
Mishmannah 544
Mishneh 549
Mishraite 567
Mishraites 567
mislead 524
Mispar 376
Mispereth 376
Misrephoth-maim 506
missile 368
mission 541
mist 617, 775
mistake 509, 515
Mithkah 574
Mithnite 572
Mithredath 574
mix (wine) 362
mixed herbs 127
mixed wine 363
mixed with salt 293
Mizar 452
Mizpah 452
Mizpeh 453
Mizraim 457
Mizri 454
Mizzah 206
Moab 168
Moabite 169
Moabites 168
Moadiah 182
mock 185
mocking poem 301
mocking song 345
moderation 564
Mokir 186
Moladah 174
Molech 322
Molid 175
molten image 699, 701
money 217, 668
moral verse 537
Morashtite 189
Mordecai 479
Moreh 188
Moresheth-gath 189
Moriah 189
morrow 230
mortar 276, 299
mortgaged land 274
mortgaged property 330
mortgaging, act of 330
Moserah 178
Moseroth 378
Moses 510
most exalted one(s) 483
most fertile, area 544
Mot 200
mould 750
mound 291
mountain 617, 738
mountain fastness 443, 445
mourning 369
mourning, place of 369
mouth 141

mouth of cervix 508
move 172, 645, 701
move away 615
move to and fro 634
moved to pity, be 663
moved, be 171
moving 540
Moza 185, 444
much 477
mud-bank 618
muddied waterhole 492
mulberry tree 364
mulberry wood 364
multitude 134, 284, 382, 477
Muppim 431
Mushi 192
Mushite 192
music 210, 496
music (of stringed instruments) 607
musical 704
musical instrument 210
musician 607
Musri 457
muster 345, 433
Muster Gate 433
muster-roll 377
mustering place 433
muzzle 188, 226, 546, 568
my 733
myrrh 473
myself 732
Naam 705
Naamah 706
Naaman 706
Naamathite 707
Naamite 706
Naarah 712
Naarai 713
Naaran 713
Nabal 594
Nabi 587
Naboth 585
Nacon 691
Nadab 618
Nahabath 578
Nahal 631
Nahalah 663
Nahalal 631
Nahaliel 663
Nahalol 631
Naham 665
Nahamani 666
Naharai 667
Nahash 668
Nahath 671
Nahbi 652
Nahor 655
Nahshon 668
Nahum 654
nail 367
Naioth 681
naked person 415
nakedness 391, 410, 415
Nalash 696
Naomi 706
Naphish 714
Naphtali 734
Naphtuhite 734
Narath 757
nard 756
narrative 375
narrow place 453
Nathan 813
Nathan-melech 815
Natoph 678
natron 818
Naveh 637
Navi 641
Nazir 741
Nazirite 649
Naziriteship 651
Neah 703
Neamel 706
Neariah 713
nearly 395
Nebai 681
Nebaioth 592
Neballat 596
Nebat 587
Nebo 583, 584
Nebuchadrezzar 584
Nebushazban 585
Nebuzaradan 584
neck 433, 724, 725
Neco 691
Neconiah 692
Nedabiah 620
needed thing 226
Negbi 598
Negeb 597, 598
Nehelamite 663
Nehemiah 665
Nehum 655
Nehushta 670
Nehushtan 670
Neiel 704
neighing 444
Nekoda 750
Nemesh 696
Nemuel 696
Nemuelite 696
Nemuelites 696
Nepheg 713
Nephilim 723
Nephisim 714
Nephtoah 734
Nephushesim 714
Ner 756
Nergal 756
Nergal-sharezer 756
Neriah 756
net 207, 270, 444, 445
Netaim 678
Nethanel 814
Nethaniah 814
Nethazbaal 816
Nethibiah 783
Nethinim 783
Netophah 679
Netophathite 679
Netophathites 679
network 230
new beginning 683
new break 683
new wine 263
next day 230
Nezamah 650
nezeph 744
Neziah 741
Nezib 740

Nibhaz 586
Nibshan 597
Nicanor 753
nightfall 103
Niklah 751
Nimrah 696
Nimrim 696
Nimrod 696
Nimshar 697
Nimshi 696
Nimtar 696
Nineveh 682
Nisan 682
Nisroch 703
No 577
Noadiah 645
Noah 652, 703
Nob 582
Nobah 585, 586
nobility 626
noble 625
noble (one) 626
noble deed 626
noble thing 626
noble things 606
noble utterance 619
Nod 635
Nodab 635
Nogah 605
Nohah 641
Noijah 641
noisily excited, be 632
noose 207, 503
Nophah 714
nostril 655
not 162
not anything 159
not at all 143
nothing 115, 116
nothing(ness) 159
Nothos 648
nourishment 118
number 270, 345, 354, 370, 377
number, report of 370
numbered, be 346
numbering 375
Nun 641
oar 515
oasis 578
object 288
object of distress 107
object of joy 501
obligation 446
obliterate 214
obliterated, be 215
obscure saying 301
observe 693, 744
observe omens 667
obstacle 275, 613
obstinacy 377
obtain 186, 435, 695, 771
obtain favour 758
obtain kindness 758
occupation 416
occur 758
odour 734
of 339
of what value/importance is 151
offence 574
offer 376, 610, 653
offer oneself 618
offer oneself for sale 273
offer willingly 618
offered, be 376, 617
offering 139, 350, 499, 571
offering of incense 466
office of cup-bearer 565
office, (holding) 407
officer 736
official 350
office 191, 442, 460
official 300
offspring 174, 382, 682
Oh no! 577
oh that I had! 785
oh that it were! 785
oil 518, 633
ointment mixture 493
ointment, pot of 493
old clothing 294
omen 667
on 337
on account of 337, 342
on account of what? 161
on behalf of 691
on high 402, 482, 483
on the next day 230
on top 402
one approaching 235
one brought 775
one charged with burning incense 377
one full of 282
one grieving 635
one plagued 609
one reaching 235
one stricken 609
one who burns incense 377
one who controls 533
one who despairs 358
one who draws (bow) 524
one who fails 358
one who goes back 515
one who goes out 185
one who has contact 137
one who melts 358
one who speaks freely 300
one's own kind 262
ones born 174
oneself 724, 732
oneself known, make 694
onslaught 482
ooze 367
open space 640
opening 434
opening (up) 434
opportunity 461
oppose, 633
opposite 173, 603
opposite (to) 691
opposition 465
oppress 262, 614
oppressed, be 614
oppressor 482, 614
ordain 281
order 370
ordinance 561
ordinance(s) 520
orifice 747
origin 174, 185, 268

ornament 504
ornate robe 269
ourselves 732
out of joint, put 380
outcast 593
outcast(s) 624
outpouring 185, 570
outrage 595
outspreading 238
outstretched 674
over 604
overflow 277, 281
overlook 586, 777
oversee 738
overseer 738
overtake 435, 608, 771
overtake, cause to 441
overthrow 165
own 305
owner 305
pacify 638
paid in full, be 279
pain 265
pained 349
painful, be 122, 492
palate 724
pall 363
pampered woman 382
pan 485, 506
panel 360
panic 163
pant 779
pant after 779
parable 537
parapet 410
parched late in the season 122
parched, be 667, 708, 782
parchment 578
pardon 758
part 220
particle 382
pass 379
pass of the staff 236
pass on as an inheritance 657
pass to and fro 701
Pass. be thrown 621
passage 164, 747
passage, (winding) 359
passageway 379
passing 379
pasturage 491
pasturage supervisor 491
pasture 380, 491, 631, 636
pasturing 491
patch 217
path 379, 782, 783
pathway 783
patience 671
patient, be 524
patrimony 274
pattering of rain 724
pauper 364
paved way 365
pavement 492
pavilion 678
pay 784
pay attention (to) 693
pay interest 778
pay less 392
peace 264, 348, 671
peck out 754
pendant 676
penetrate 670, 685
penis 467
people 724, 731
perfection 269
perform 758
perfume 493, 724, 733, 734, 781
permit 640, 680, 785
persecution 480
persistent 739
person 724, 730, 779
person or thing purchased 467
person receiving a favourable omen 704
persons 724, 731
persuade 675
perversity 238, 703
pervert 524
pervert justice 675
pestilence 137
picked men 129
piece 782
pierce 747
pierced, be 747
pile 146, 467
pile (of coins) 131
pilgrimage 404
pillar 442, 449, 740
pin 684
pinch off 328
pine 367
pine away 470
pipe 185, 747
pit 165, 208, 274
pitch tent 672, 677
pitchfork 211
pity oneself 635
place 267, 407, 460, 638, 736, 758, 785
place as 785
place for slaughter 234
place of assembly 178, 471
place of burning 466
place of feasting 484
place of feet 478
place of going out 183
place of head 476
place of joining 214
place of judgment 148
place of lying down 526
place of mourning 369
place of possession 336
place of sitting 190
place of sowing 212
place of spreading 433
place of thorns 451
place of wandering 446
place of watching 547
place of, dwelling 133
place of, sojourning 133
place one's self 785
place thorns (in) 815
place to which one turns for provisions 383
place where sheep can be eaten 501
place/seat of judgment 558
placed, be 640, 785
placed, be, .i.be set 785
plague 137, 144, 200, 267, 611,

613
plagued, be 609
plain 263
plait 219
plaiting 508
plan 182, 209, 230, 274
planets 208
plant 239, 240, 676, 677
plant with 676
plantation 239, 240, 677
planted thing 677
planted, be 677
planting 239, 240, 678
planting, (act of) 239
planting, (object of) 239, 240
planting, (place of) 239, 240
plastered floor 492
plate 214
plateau 263
platform 406
play 685
play (a stringed instrument) 607
pleasant 704
pleasant one 704
pleasant place 578, 704
pleasant sound 704
pleasant, be 328
pleasant, make 705
pleasantness 706, 707
please 577
please let it not be so! 577
please let not 577
pleasing 681
pleasing odour 681
pleasure 221, 704
plot 209
plough furrow 409
ploughshare 229
pluck up 818
plucked up, be 819
plumage 648
plumbline 567
plunder 515, 551, 741
plunge into 227
point of departure 184
poising 432
poison 494
poisonous 472
poisonous one 487
pole 172
polish 485, 493
polished, be 485, 493
pool 133, 254, 290, 459
poor 364
poor one 173, 364
porch 360
portent 183
portion 143, 220, 337, 346, 347, 357
portions, allocate to 656
position 191, 407, 442, 460, 499
position on head 477
position oneself 735
positioned, be 735
possession 189, 540, 565, 659
possession (though purchase) 468
possession of, take 655
possession, hold as 656
possession, take 305
possessions 349, 354
possesssion for oneself, take as 657
post 460
posterity 682, 684
postpone 621
pot of ointment 493
pottage 649
pour 362, 597, 613
pour down 613
pour out 592, 596, 597, 650, 699, 700, 750, 784, 785
pour out as a libation 699
pour out.i.pour out 750
poured out, be 613, 699, 700, 784, 785
poverty 365
power 119, 473
power, sign of 683
practice augury 667
practise deceit 273
practise divination 667
practise guile 273
praise 163, 164, 578
prayer mat 526
pre-eminence 628
preach 678
preacher 678
precious thing 221, 222
precious things 132
prediction 537
prefect 148
prefer 121
pregnant 283
pregnant woman 283
prescribed portion 518
present 350, 441, 616, 647, 721, 758
present oneself 735
present, be 439
presented, be 647
preserve 744
preserved 741
preserved one 741, 745
preserved, be 745
press 212, 262, 398, 614
pressed, be 398
pressing 262
pressure 262
presume 531
pretend to be someone else 694
prevail 739
prey 445
price 217, 274, 525
prince 350, 606, 626, 649, 699, 772
prison 360
private thoughts 209
private, be 666
proclaim king 303
procure 263
produce 416, 758
produce (fruit) 634
product 416
production 416
production, (process of) 416
profit 202, 477
progeny 677, 684
prolong 523

prolonged, be 524
prone to gore 606
pronouncement 498
proper measure 564
property 103, 268, 288, 330, 460, 659
prophecy 537, 582, 584
prophesy 582, 678
prophet 587, 592
prophetic oracle 579
prophets 520
proportion 361
propped up, be 736
prosper 634
prosper, cause to 634
prostrate oneself 621, 716, 723
prostrate, be 716
protect 744
protection 136, 545
protection, (place of) 384
prove 697
proverb 537, 539
proverbial wisdom 539
proverbs 537
provide 435
provide with 630
provide with sandals 704
provided, be 376
province 147
provision 598
provisions 207, 239, 383
provoke 474, 480, 492
psalm 209
psalm of success 503
pudenda 410, 415
pull 509, 522, 523
pull (along, off, away) 522
pull away 524
pull down 815
pull off 816
pull out 509, 523, 701, 815, 817
pull out hair (of) 485
pull up 523, 701
pulled away, be 525
pulled down, be 816
pulled out, be 815
pulled up, be 701
pulpit 131
purchase 467, 694
purchase price 468
pure 750
purification 740
purity 238, 751
purpose 209, 230, 288, 409
pursuit 480
push 605, 691
put 772, 785
put out of joint 380
put to death 197
put to flight, be 683
put to flight 643, 683
put to sleep 631
putrefy 470
putrefying matter 746
pyre 146
quadrangle 290
Quagmire 172
quake 187, 641
quantity 370
quarrel 737
quarrelling 145, 147
quarry 703
queen 323, 327
queen, be 301
queen, make 303
quick 164
quick one 164
quickly 166, 167
quieten 638
quietness 671
quiver 644
race 484
radiance 519
radiant (with joy), be 632
rafter 471
rage 508
raging 482
rags 294
rain 240, 241
rain down 650
rain, (cause it to) 240
rain, drop of 415
rained down, be 240
rained upon, be 240
raise 647, 758
raise hand 647
raise up 758
raised bed 131
raised platform 131
raised up, be 758
raising 404, 495, 499
rally to the banner 701
ramp 365, 369
rampart 176
rash 370
ravine 379
raw 577
rawness 217
razor 188
reach 215, 435, 608, 771
reach (as far as) 610
reach one's goal 610
reach the age 610
reach, cause to 610, 772
reaching 235
reading 471
realize 693
realm 323, 331, 333, 335
rear 758
reason 460
rebatement 138
rebel 478, 515
rebel (against) 478
rebellion 333, 478, 485, 514
rebellious (against), be 480
rebellious one(s) 485
rebellious, be 474, 480
rebelliousness 479, 481, 485
rebuke 137, 650
receive 758
receive by lot 716
recess 138, 228
recite 537
reckon as 345
reckoned as, be 346
reckoning 270
recognize 692
recognized, be 692
recoil 753
recoil in horror 621
recompense 504

recover 742
recovery 217
rectitude 692
reduce 392, 721
reduce in size 392
reduce output 392
reduced, be 391
reeling, cause of 216
refine 208
refrain 355
refresh oneself 724
refreshed, be 724
refreshment 348
refuge 349, 384, 387, 432, 467
refuge, (place of) 384
refuse 116, 119, 354, 431, 634
refuse (to do something) 120
regard 586
regard favourably 586
regard for, have 693
regret 663
reign (over) 301
reign of, (period of) 333
reign, (period of) 325, 333
reign, cause to 303
reject 120, 694
rejected, be 121
relative 149
release 817
released, be 817
relent 663
relief 504
relief body of troops 362
relieve 638
relinquish 680
reluctant 381
remain 439, 635
remain, allow to 640
remedy 491
reminder of sin 389
remit punishment 749
remove 190, 694, 778
remove (to a safe place) 643
removed, be 701, 817
repeat a hundred times 107
repent 665
repent (of) 663
replant 676
replenish 281
report 599
report of number 370
repose 149
repose, have 637
repository 206
reprobate, be 121
reprove 650
reptile 490
repudiate 582, 694
reputation 164
request 507
rescue 742
rescued, be 744
reservoir 459
respect as sacred 651
respected, be 758
respite 640
responsibility 495
responsive song 503
rest 347, 348, 611, 637, 640, 641, 671
rest upon 637
rest upon, cause to 638
rest, (place of) 478
rest, cause to 637
rest, coming to 347
rest, give to 637
rest, have 637
resting place 347, 348, 477, 640
restlessness 621
restoration 514
restrain 354, 633
restraint 410, 564
retinue 545
return 404, 514
revelation 481
revenge 665
revenge, take 752
reverence 187
revile 581
reviling 581
reviving 217
revolt 478
reward 136, 141, 505
rice 354
rich food 544
rich, become 667
riches 692
rid of, be 708
rift 129
right 692
righteousness 264
rim 360
ring 650
ring of waggons 380
rise 758
rise up 758
rise up against 758
rising, (place of) 211
river 632, 658
river valley 657
rivulet 188
road 361, 365, 366
road, (main) 365
roam 644
roaring 631
robe 144, 214, 396
Rock of Divisions 220
rocky place 366
rod 235, 238, 466, 552
roof 404
room 460, 778
rootless person 645
rootless, be 645
rope 265, 754
rot 470
rot, cause to 470
rotten eggs 207
rotten land 214
rottenness 457
rough place 410
round off 754
round silo 383
rout 144, 612, 685
routed, be 613
row 413
row (of shewbread) 415
royal robes 325
royal seat 348
royal status 325
royalty 292, 325, 332
rub 299, 484, 492

rubbed raw, be 485
rubbed with salt water, be 293
rubbing 552
rubbish dump 229
rug 139
ruin 146, 234, 275, 396, 432, 519, 596, 783, 784
ruin(s) 432
ruin, cause of 234
ruined, be 737, 816
rule 323, 334, 520, 531, 539
rule (over), cause to 536
ruler 305, 533, 606, 614
rulers 334
run 122, 227
run, make 646
running 484
rushing about 565
sacred place 457
sacred site 460
sacreligious, be 593
sacreligiously, act 593
sacrilege 401, 595
sacrilege, commit 400
sacrilegious person 593
saddle 487, 488
saddle-bags of a mule 565
sadness 380
safeguarded, be 746
sag 269
sage 537
sail 433, 697
sailor 293
sale 273, 331
salesman 288
salt 293
salt land 294
salted 293
saltwort 291
salvation 192
sanctuary 457, 460
sandal 705
sandy depths 592
sated with, be 277
satisfaction (for oneself), gain 663
satisfied, be 277
satisfy 281, 638
save 298, 299, 742, 751
saw 137, 501
saying that puts things in different words 301
scab 370
scales 118, 148
scall 817
scatter 625, 724
scatterer 431
scent 525
scented, be 525
sceptre 235, 367
scheme 209, 230, 364
scholarship 376
sciatic nerve 777
scoured, be 493
scourged out 683
scrape 328
scraping tool 470
screen 362, 364
Scribe 164
script 275
scroll 134
seal 746, 781
seal (the lips) 781
sealed, be 704
sealing stone 366
search with hands 567
searching 228
searching out 228, 229
season 220, 293
seat 190, 488
second 549
second brood 549
second child 549
second quarter 549
secret 378
secret (place) 378
secret places 745
secret prayer 276
secret things 745
secretive, be 745
security 126
sedan 237
seeing 476
seek counsel 304
seen, cause to be 587
seize 525
seized, be 439
select 376
selected, be 376
self 382
self-deceit 489
sell 167, 271, 694
semblance 737
semen 255
send 346, 785
send against 785
send rain 240
sending 540, 541
sending (a replacement) 541
sentence 557
sentry 545, 745
separate 651
separate oneself from 651
separated, be 817
separation 432, 651
sepulchre 724, 733
serpent 667
servant 708, 711
serve 167
session 191
set 281, 736, 758, 785
set (arrow) 281
set aside 638
set down 638
set fire to 746
set free 817
set in motion 737
set in, be 282
set on fire 746
set over, be 735
set straight 736
set up 736, 785
set up, be 736
set with, be 282
set, be 735, 785
setting 283, 284, 290, 508
setting (of sun) 411
setting aside 541
setting out from 369
settle 635, 716
settle down 637

settled, be 749
settlement 192
several 161
sexual intercourse 416
sexual misconduct 596
shaft 235, 659
shake 171, 187, 251, 380, 641, 644, 707
shake fist 645
shake head 635
shake off (leaves) 707
shake oneself free 707
shake out 707
shake the head 635
shake to and fro 646
shaken off, be 707
shaken out, be 707, 708
shaken, be 644
shaking 172, 347, 681
shaking of head 681
shaking, (object of) 347
shamelessness 137, 596
share 220, 346, 357
sharp saying 301
sharp, be 680
sharpen 680, 736
sharpened, be 680
shatter 227, 723
shattered, be 723
shattering 433, 509
shattering blow 433
shawl 370, 396
sheath 626
shed 646
sheep breeder 748
sheet 363
shelter 214, 378
Sheol 460
shepherd 748
shepherding 491
shewbread, row of 415
shield 134, 135
shift 547
shine 605, 632, 683, 738
shine with 683
shine, cause to 605, 632, 738
shining 605
Shining One 579
shipyard 208
shoot 677, 746
shoot out 785
shovel 138
show bitter grief 493, 494
show bitterness 493
show bitterness (to) 493
show grief 635
shower of rain 241
sick, be 492, 648, 701
sickbed 526
sicken 492
sickening, be 492
sickle 134
sickness 218, 219, 655
siege 449
siege mound 442
siegeworks 445, 446, 450
sieve 713
sift 646, 657
sifted, be 657
sigh 640
sight 474, 476
sight, admirable 620
sign 183, 697
sign of power 683
silk 520
silo 329
sin 400
since 337, 339
sinew 265
sinful, be 400
sinfulness 401
sing 705
sing (with) 705
singer 704
sink 269, 670
sink deep 670
sink, cause to 670
sinkhole 330
sinning 401
sistrum 297, 355
sisu tree 364
sisu wood 364
sit 611
site 267, 460
Sithri 263
situation 191
size 143
skill 233
skilled 164
skin 578
skin bottle 577
skin disease 611
sky 483
slander 329, 489, 747
slander, blaspheme 747
slaughter 137, 234, 267
slaughter, means of 234
slaughter, place for 234
slave 708
slay 197
sleep 631
sleep, put to 631
slice (of bread) 383
slice of cake 383
sling 478
slip 171, 380
slip away 297
slip in 297
slip off 778
slip Si 3729(B) 240
slip, be made to 171
slippery saying 301
slipping 172
slope 188
slumber 641
small 393
small one 452
small pastry 750
small thing 387, 452
smash 723
smash to pieces 723
smashed to pieces, be 724
smelter 185
smite 614
smith 359, 714
smoke 770
smoke signal 499
smooth, be 328
smooth, make 485, 670
smooth-skinned, be 485
smoothness 552

snap 817
snapped, be 816
snare 270, 323, 444, 445, 503
snares, lay 755
snatch away 742, 818
snatched away, be 818
snatched, be 305, 744
sniff at 714
snort 667
snorting 667
snowfall 241
snuffdish 234
snuffer 210
so as not to be 337, 342
so as not to do 337, 342
so that not 337, 342
socket 747
soften 170
softness 640
sojourning 133
sojourning place 133
solid casting 449
solid mass 185
something 116, 159
something reduced 392
something reserved 547
something to keep watch over 547
song 210, 522
song sung to the capped reed pipe 276
soon 167, 396
soothing 681
soothsayer 748
sore 207
sororach 327
sorry, be 663
soul 597, 724, 725, 779
sound out 785
sounding rattle 355
source 174, 184, 459, 465
source (of water) 397
source (of waters) 127
south 598
south country 597
sovereignty 332, 333
sow 523
space 460
spade 138
spangle 747
spark 682
sparkle 648, 701, 744
sparkler 185
sparkling 334
sparrow 711, 712, 713
spatter 648
spatter (something upon) 648
speak 328, 641, 671
species 262, 554
specification 564, 570
specified number 570
speckled 748
speckled (kid) 748
spectacle 476
speech 291, 498, 681
speed 167
spice 493
spices 493
spilt, be 613
spittle emission of 451
splendour 238
spoil 328
spoil, take 741
spokesperson 300
spot 750
spout 597
sprained, be 380
spread 785
spread (of table) 671
spread by rubbing 484
spread out 569, 680
spread out, be 211, 674, 680
spread throughout, be 716
spread, be 785
spreading 433
spreading out 433
spreading place 519
spreading, place of 433
sprig 595
spring 125, 184, 397, 465, 584, 592, 817
sprinkle 646, 648, 723
sprinkle (as through a sieve) 657
sprinkle (something [with]) 649
sprinkled, be 649
spurn 120, 581, 582, 593
spurt 206, 648
square 470
squeeze 398
squeezing 262
squire 708
stab 149
stacte 678
staff 235, 274, 466, 552, 553
stage 404
stage of journey 368
stagger 172, 644, 701
staircase 404
staircase, (winding) 359
stalk 235
stall 477
stand 264, 268, 735
stand by 654
stand firm 735
stand side by side 780
stand upright 735
stand, cause to 736
standard 697
standing (up) 407
standing ground 408
standing place 442
star 185
stars 620
start of journey 368
start up 817
start, cause to 818
starting from 337, 339
startle 649
starvation 123
statement 370
station 146, 407
stationed, be 785
statue 506
steep place 150
stem 235
stench 457
step 369, 404, 452
steppe 139, 446
stew 649

stick 299, 552, 553
stifle 776
still 638
stimulate 524
stir 618, 758
stir up 262
stir- 262
stocks 165
stood, be 735
stopping 410
storage pit 133
storehouse 206, 427
storehouses 365
storeplace 206
storm 369
story 416
straight 692
straight ahead 691
straightforward 692
straightforward one 692
straightness 692
strange 695
strangeness 694
stranger 695
stranger, act as a 694
stranger, treat as a 694
strangler 225
strangling 225
straw, heap of 568
strayed one 624
stream 254, 290, 632, 650, 658
strength 103, 385, 473, 571, 572, 671
strengthen 494
strengthen oneself 494
strengthened 473
stretch 670
stretch oneself out 142, 674
stretch out 645, 647, 672, 785
stretched out, be 613, 673
stricken 683, 691
stricken one 683, 691
stricken, be 609, 613
strife 145, 147, 444, 450, 486
strife, (object of) 145
strike 215, 474, 609, 612, 683, 684
strike (against) 215
strike down 612
strike fatally 685
strike for correction 685
strike in punishment 685
strike off 753
strike roots 685
strike through 227
striker 186
striking 613, 754
striking (off) 754
striking off (of olives) 750
string 189, 265, 336
stringed instrument 336
strip 708, 741
strip off 753
strip oneself of 744
stripe 266
stripped bare, be 708
stripped off, be 753
stripping 230
strive 737
stroke 137, 266, 379, 611
strong 238, 473
strong thing 495
strong(est) 544
strong, be 671
strongest 544
stronghold 128, 360, 385, 443, 445, 500
struck 684
struck fatally, be 690
struck with plague, be 690
struck, be 683
structure 127, 416
stubbornness 377
study 150, 228, 229
stumble 171, 612
stumbling block 275
stumbling, (cause of) 275
stump 443
sturdy 544
subdue 685
subject 336
subjects 545
subjugate 531
subjugation 125
submit oneself 780
substance 416
substitution 541
success 451
suck 453, 573
suddenly 396
suffer 758
suffer convulsions 701
suffer punishment for 758
suffering 219, 265
sufficiency 361
sufficient, be 442, 771
sufficient, find 435
sufficient, have 771
suffice 442
suitable 578, 579
summer palace 471
summoning 471
sun, setting of 411
sunrise 211
superfluous, declare 646
supervise 738
supervisor 738
supplies 364
supply 630
supply with 758
support 369, 552, 553, 654, 758
surf 508
surrender 134
surround 754
surroundings 359
survive 297
survivors 217
sustain 524, 758
sustenance 217, 552, 553, 724, 733
suzerain 134
swamp 506
swarm 122, 565
sway 634, 641, 644, 701
sweep away 506
sweet 569
sweet drink 336
sweet saying 301
sweet sounding 704
sweet sounding one 704
sweet thing 569

sweet things 336
sweet, be 573, 705
sweet, become 573
sweetness 336, 569, 574
sweetness, cause 573
swift 167
swing 644
swing to and fro 644
sympathize 635
tabernacle 527
table 359
tableland 263
take 676, 758
take (woman) in marriage 758
take as 785
take as a possession for oneself 657
take aside 674
take away 676, 742, 758
take counsel 304
take legal possession of 694
take off 778
take possession 305
take possession of 655
take revenge 752
take spoil 741
take up 758
take vengeance 751
taken away, be 758
taking 466
tall, be 525
target 242, 430
task 288, 416, 495
taskmaster 614
tasty dish 240
tax 144, 359, 499
taxation 359
teach 678
teacher 678
tear 818
tear apart 817
tear asunder 818
tear away 305, 698, 816
tear down 698, 816
tear out 817
tears 255
tell 537, 599
teller of proverbs 537
temple servant 783
temple servants 783
tender 182
tendril 676
tent of meeting 179, 265
tenth 429
terms 446
terrace 290
terrible deed 187
terror 103, 133, 187, 234, 415, 668
test 697, 699
test, make a 697
testing 361
Thebes 577
them 732
theme 537
they 732
thicket 451
thin 206
thing in front 691
thing kneaded 129
thing needed 226
thing prophesied 582
thing seen 476
thong 178
thornbush 631, 707
thorns, place of 451
those who dwell 191
those who enter 124
thought 149, 230, 504
thread 641
threat 137
threshing 138, 150
threshing floor 138
threshing place 365
threshing sledge 188
threshold 434
throat 133, 724
through 337, 342
throughout 359
throw 137, 621
throw down 137
throw in one's lot among 721
throw oneself down 716
throw oneself upon 723
thrown, be 137, 621
thrust 146, 216, 624, 684, 691
thrust aside 621
thrust away 624, 674
thrust down 673, 674
thrust oneself forward 716
thrust out, be 624
thrust, be 624
thunderbolt 148
tidings, bring 696
till 682
tillage 683
time 347
time of dwelling, (length of) 191
tithe 429
to be so, find 435
to be sound, find 435
tokens of adultery 579
told, be 602
tomb 460, 659
tomorrow 229
tomorrow at this time 229
tongs 269, 329
too much for 337, 341
tooth 570
torment 453
torn apart, be 816
torn away, be 305, 698, 816
torn down, be 816
torn out, be 817
torrent 613, 632, 658
torture 265
tossed about, be 172
tossings 621
total (number) 370
totality 134
totter 171
totterer 172
touch 608, 780
touch with 610
touch, cause to 610
tow 713
toward 603
towards the front of 691
tower 130, 131
town 147, 215

trace 780
track 379
trade 288, 416
trader 272
trading 489
trading mission 288
tradition 377
trail behind 524
train 698
trained, be 698
training 177
trampled ground 490
trampling 125
trampling place 490
transfer of possession 331
transgress 122, 400
transgression 401
transmission 377
transmit 376
transplant 676
transport 758
transport(ing) 495
transportation 192
trap 149, 177, 207, 239
travel 368, 701
travel by 630
tray 506
treachery 489
tread 450
treading place 150
treasure 239, 269, 695
treat as a fool 593
treat as a special contribution 646
treat as a stranger 694
treat with contempt 593
tremble 170, 644, 645, 648
trembling 697
trembling one 170
triad 543
trial 361, 457, 698, 699
trial(s) 698
tribe 235
tribute 144, 270, 350, 496, 499
trickle 506, 650
trim 754
troops 294
troops, relief body of 362
trope 301
trouble 650
truly 568
truss 214
trust 126
trust fully 279
trustworthiness 580
try 697
tunnel 659
tunnelling 748
turban 130, 451
turn 629, 785
turn aside 673
turn away 171, 674
turn back, ability to 515
turn of affairs 697
turn out 716
turned, be 674
turning 165, 514
turning back 515
turning point 146
turquoise 715
twice as much 549
twilight 779
twitching (of limbs) 123
type 554
ulcer 182, 207
uncleanness 149
uncover 708
undergarment 139
understand 693, 771
understanding 126, 149
undertaking 541
unit 377
unleavened bread 444
unripe fig(s) 596
until what (time?) 161
untilled ground 683
untrimmed vine 649
upper room 404
upright one 692
uprightness 692
uproot 818
uprooted one 818
uprooted, be 819
upside down 402
upwards 234, 402, 484
urge 666
urge on 628
urgent, be 666
urine 255
us 732
use 288
usury 778
utter 328, 596, 758
utter a prophetic oracle 579
utter proverbs, ability to 539
utter voice 785
utterance 128, 184, 208, 498, 579, 681
utterance of praise 498
uttered, be 758, 785
uttering of proverbs 539
utterly 103
vacillate 708
vagabond 644
value 217, 229, 274, 566
value of mortgage 330
valuer 229
vanish 293, 737
vapour 775
variability 618
vassal (nation) 545
veil 361, 363, 370
Vendemiator 129
vengeance 752, 753
vengeance, take 751
venom 494
venture 698
very 103
very great 106
very much 103
very soon 396
vicinity 412
victorious over, be 739
victorious, be 492, 739
victory 740, 752, 753
vigil 547
vigour 473
vine 744
Vintager, the 129
violence 572
violent man 482

visible form 474
vision 216, 474, 476
void 125, 151
void, be 716
voluntarily 619
voluntariness 619
volunteer 618
votive offering 628
vow 627
vulture 781
wadi 433, 657
waft 650
wages 217, 505
waggons, ring of 380
wail (with) 629
wailing 369, 629, 681
wait 163
wait quietly for 637
wait, lying in 123
wakefulness 546
wall 617
wander 634, 644, 645, 708
wander about 620
wander, cause to 635, 644
wanderer 635, 644
wandering 482, 618
war 238, 294
ward off 255
wardrobe 329
ware 466
wares 330
warn against 651
warning 177, 697
warp 365
warrior 167
wash 260
wash away 360
waste 392
waste away 121, 214, 716
wasting disease 662
watch 242, 453, 545, 547, 744
watch(ing) 545
watcher 745
watching, place of 547
watchtower 445, 450, 452
water 168, 251, 255
watering hole 506
watering place 188, 631
waterless 122
waters, collection of 459
wave 170, 645
wave hand 645
wave to and fro 701
waved, be 646
waver 170, 641
waver, (cause to) 170
wavering one 171
way 365
way of life 484
way out 183
we 666, 732
weak 206, 349
weak one 349
weak, be 737
weaken 164
weakened 206
weakened, be 164
weakling 349
wealth 119, 330, 692
weapon 274, 368
weapons 781
weapons of war 294
wear oneself out 592
weave 700
weaver's beam 349
web 365
weigh 676
weight 495, 566, 676
well 103
well-being 570
west 410, 411
western 412
wet clay 149
what a weariness! 570
what ails? 151
what does A mean to B? 151
what flows 634
what happens? 151, 159
what if? 151
what is read 471
what is settled 567
what is taking place? 159
what is the significance of 151
what is there? 151
what is/are ... doing? 151
what is/are ... like? 151
what is/are? 151
what kind of? 151
what need is there? 151
what(ever) 151
what? 150, 242, 336
when? 161, 569
where now, please? 577
where? 160
which (is/are)? 151
which one(s)? 242
white garments 219
who will grant me? 785
who will grant? 785
who will let it be granted? 785
who? 242, 336
whoever 243, 250, 336
wholly follow 281
whom? 242
whose? 242, 249
why is/are ... here? 151
why? 145, 150
wicked plan 209
wickedness 495
wield 524, 625, 645, 647
wilderness 139
willing 625
willing (one) 626
wilt 327
wily, be 745
window 216
wine 363, 570
wineskin 618
wipe 214
wipe clean 214
wipe out 214
wiped out, be 215
wiped out, cause to be 215
wish 724, 725
with 337, 343
with (the 337
with (the sanction of) 339
with what 160
withdraw 392, 758
withdrawal 122, 514
wither 327, 592, 723

withered fruit 596
withering away 596
withheld, be 355
withhold 354
without 337, 341
without support, be 645
woe now! 577
womb 382
women of the harem 360
wonder 183
wondrous work 431
word 119, 291
work 288, 416, 432
work (giving the appearance) of 416
work achieved 416
work(ing) 416
work, (product of) 288
working 416
worthless, be 368
would that it were granted! 785
would that! 785
wound 207, 227, 266, 818
woven, be 700
wrath to blaze, cause 605
wrestlings 734
wring 328
wring out 443
write down (as an accusation) 802
writing 275, 520
writing, (piece of) 275
yarn 238
yearning 631
yield 758, 781
yoke 172, 714
you 732
young 118
young man 708
young shoot 595
young woman 711
younger brother 549
your offspring 337, 343
yourself 732
yourselves 732
youth 703, 708, 713
youth, (time of) 703, 711, 713
youth, be a 708
youth, lose one's 708